# A Parent's Guide to Childhood Cancer

*The Children's Hospital of Philadelphia Series:*

A Parent's Guide to Childhood Emergencies
A Parent's Guide to Allergies and Asthma
A Parent's Guide to Attention Deficit Disorders
A Parent's Guide to Childhood and Adolescent Depression
A Parent's Guide to Eating Disorders and Obesity
A Parent's Guide to Childhood Cancer

THE CHILDREN'S HOSPITAL OF PHILADELPHIA

# A PARENT'S GUIDE TO CHILDHOOD CANCER

Lisa J. Bain

A DELL TRADE PAPERBACK

A DELL TRADE PAPERBACK

Published by
Dell Publishing
a division of
Bantam Doubleday Dell Publishing Group, Inc.
1540 Broadway
New York, New York 10036



Library of Congress Cataloging-in-Publication Data

Bain, Lisa J.
A parent's guide to childhood cancer / Lisa J. Bain ; foreword by C. Everett Koop.
p. cm.
Includes bibliographical references and index.
ISBN 0-440-50692-1
1. Tumors in children—Popular works. I. Title.
RC281.C4B26 1995
618.92'994—dc20 94-40100
CIP

Printed in the United States of America

Published simultaneously in Canada

July 1995

10 9 8 7 6 5 4 3 2

BVG

# ◆ CONTENTS ◆

# ◆ FOREWORD ◆

Prior to the mid-1960s the diagnosis of cancer during childhood was almost tantamount to a death sentence within a fairly short period of time. Of course the prognosis depended on the type of cancer the child had. Most of the more than one hundred pediatric malignancies were and still are in the leukemia family. Today 70 percent of those children diagnosed with one of the diseases associated with blood or blood-forming tissues survive into adulthood. It has taken three decades of research and treatment to reach this point.

In my early days at The Children's Hospital of Philadelphia, I was deeply involved in the surgical management of children with solid tumors. As we added radiation and chemotherapy as postoperative modalities, it became clear that each patient with cancer needed an oncologist to coordinate his or her treatment. It was equally important to realize that scientific investigation was necessary if survival rates were to improve. Enter Dr. Audrey E. Evans.

I recruited her from Chicago to Children's Hospital in 1969. British-born, she had been trained in Boston. One of her first actions was to unify the oncology service. Her philosophy of having an oncology unit within the Hospital was put into effect immediately. No longer were these terribly sick children scattered throughout the Hospital, usually in a bed next to a child whose illness was not as serious. Two changes took place. The parents became supportive of one another because they were together, and the internal Hospital community became aware that the oncology program was a distinct service within the Hospital constellation. Dr. Evans worked in a national cooperative group, responsible in particular for improving the survival of children with Wilms' tumor. In those days two out of ten children survived; now eight out of ten live.

I had been convinced that the most common solid tumor of childhood, the neuroblastoma, behaved most unusually in small infants; in spite of widespread disease, they survived. After the arrival of Dr. Evans and Dr. Giulio D'Angio, we offered a classification and treatment protocol for this tumor, which provides the guidelines for neuroblastoma management.

The Children's Hospital of Philadelphia was named a Cancer Research and Treatment Center under the National Cancer Program of 1973.

Dr. Evans intensified the training program by taking on young physicians who wished to become oncologists. She established a scientific advisory board. Dr. Evans was joined in 1976 by Dr. D'Angio, who was appointed director of the Hospital's Cancer Research Center. The Children's Hospital pioneered in several areas of cancer research and treatment and in so doing became internationally renowned for that subspecialty. One such study concerned long-term survivors. Dr. Anna T. Meadows headed the project and took over the Oncology Division when Drs. Evans and D'Angio stepped down as directors.

Today, 1,500 children are seen annually by the Hospital's cancer specialists. Countrywide there are about nine thousand new cases of pediatric cancer diagnosed annually. Where to go for treatment? In most cases your child will be referred to a regional hospital that specializes in childhood cancer. You will find state-of-the-art treatment and, if it is a children's center, a focus on the child that is rarely attainable elsewhere.[1]

Parents whose children have been diagnosed with cancer should become as educated about the disease as possible. In addition to learning about the course of the disease, available treatments, and their reactions, parents should avail themselves of the services of the hospital's Social Work Department. In addition to the support social workers offer parents, they can help find financial aid through various community and government programs and coordinate a host of other services that may be helpful.

This book contains a bibliography and a list of resources that are useful as well.

*C. Everett Koop, M.D.*
Surgeon-in-Chief Emeritus
The Children's Hospital of Philadelphia

[1] Pediatric Oncology Group, "Progress Against Childhood Cancer: The Pediatric Oncology Group Experience" *Pediatrics* 89: (1992) 597–600.

# ◆ ACKNOWLEDGMENTS ◆

This book would not have been possible were it not for a remarkable group of health care professionals at The Children's Hospital of Philadelphia and its affiliated institutions, Children's Seashore House and The Philadelphia Child Guidance Center. For months I observed these doctors, nurses, psychologists, social workers, child life specialists, and others in action. I was constantly amazed by their dedication and compassion, a reflection of the ideals of Dr. Audrey E. Evans, who directed the Oncology Division in its early days nearly twenty-five years ago. The list below includes people I interviewed and/or people who reviewed my manuscripts:

David Beele, A.C.S.W., L.S.W.
Social Work Coordinator, Division of Oncology, The Children's Hospital of Philadelphia

Jean Belasco, M.D.
Medical Director, Home Care Service, Oncologist, The Children's Hospital of Philadelphia
Clinical Associate Professor of Pediatrics, University of Pennsylvania School of Medicine

Bret Boyer, Ph.D.
Psychologist, Division of Oncology, The Children's Hospital of Philadelphia

Patricia Brophy, R.N., M.S.N.
Clinical Nurse Specialist in Oncology, The Children's Hospital of Philadelphia

Nancy Bunin, M.D.
Director of the Bone Marrow Transplant Program, The Children's Hospital of Philadelphia
Assistant Professor of Pediatrics, University of Pennsylvania School of Medicine

Marie Burkhauser
Child Life Specialist in Oncology, The Children's Hospital of Philadelphia

Giulio J. D'Angio, M.D.
Professor of Radiation Oncology and Pediatric Oncology, University of Pennsylvania School of Medicine

Anne E. Kazak, Ph.D.
Director of Psychosocial Services in the Division of Oncology, The Children's Hospital of Philadelphia
Associate Professor of Psychology in Pediatrics and Psychiatry, University of Pennsylvania School of Medicine

Beverly Lange, M.D.
Associate Director for Clinical Affairs, Division of Oncology, The Children's Hospital of Philadelphia
Professor of Pediatrics, University of Pennsylvania School of Medicine

Anna T. Meadows, M.D.
Director, Oncology Division, The Children's Hospital of Philadelphia
Professor of Pediatrics, University of Pennsylvania School of Medicine

Mae L. Page, M.A., L.S.W.
Bereavement Coordinator, The Children's Hospital of Philadelphia

Patrick S. Pasquariello, Jr., M.D.
Director, Diagnostic Center, The Children's Hospital of Philadelphia
Professor of Pediatrics, University of Pennsylvania School of Medicine

Jerilynn Radcliffe, Ph.D.
Director, Cognitive Development Assessment Service, Pediatric Psychology, Children's Seashore House
Clinical Assistant Professor of Pediatrics, University of Pennsylvania School of Medicine

Luis Schut, M.D.
Neurosurgeon, The Children's Hospital of Philadelphia
Professor of Surgery, University of Pennsylvania School of Medicine

Alberto C. Serrano, M.D.
Medical Director, Philadelphia Child Guidance Center
Professor of Psychiatry, University of Pennsylvania School of Medicine

Barbara S. Shapiro, M.D.
Assistant Director of Pain Service, The Children's Hospital of Philadelphia
Assistant Professor of Pediatrics, University of Pennsylvania School of Medicine

Michael Silver, M.D.
Medical Director, Inpatient Services, Philadelphia Child Guidance Center
Clinical Assistant Professor of Psychiatry and Pediatrics, University of Pennsylvania School of Medicine

Leslie N. Sutton, M.D.
Neurosurgeon, The Children's Hospital of Philadelphia
Assistant Professor of Neurosurgery, University of Pennsylvania School of Medicine

Richard Womer, M.D.
Division of Oncology, The Children's Hospital of Philadelphia
Associate Professor of Pediatrics, University of Pennsylvania School of Medicine

There are, in addition, a large group of social workers, psychologists, nurses, residents, and attending physicians who allowed me to sit in on their meetings and gain from their expertise. I especially want to acknowledge social workers Lisa Gagen, Bernadette Foley, Stephanie Fooks, and Caren Lindner; psychologist Lauren Riordan; and nurses Marie Savacool and Paula Browning, who allowed me to tag along with them for full days.

The expertise of these professionals is reflected in this book, but would have been meaningless without the input of many parents and children who shared with me their thoughts and feelings throughout their ordeals. My special thanks go to Jack and Christy Federspiel and to Maryanne Schiller.

Writing this book was both an honor and a challenge. I am deeply grateful to Shirley Bonnem for giving me this opportunity and to her assistant Dorothy Barnes; my editor at Dell, Betsy Bundschuh; and my literary agent Nancy Love for their support and assistance. Finally, I wish to acknowledge my own children, Joshua and Noah Skaroff; they are my constant inspiration.

# ◆ INTRODUCTION ◆

One summer afternoon I sat on the beach with a woman I had known only briefly. We watched our children splashing in the surf, and I told her about my current writing project: a book about childhood cancer. She gestured knowingly toward her nine-year-old son out in the water—he had survived a brain tumor only two years earlier. She knew, better than I ever would, what a harrowing experience it was to learn that your child has cancer. She would be but one of many parents who would share their stories with me.

To my eye Sean[1] appeared normal. He was a big boy, cheerful, active, and pleasant. I would learn later, however, that Sean, like many children who survive cancer, bears lifelong reminders of his illness. The treatment he received for his brain tumor caused permanent damage to his nervous system that was only beginning to show up in his schoolwork. His mother, a teacher, keeps a watchful eye on his progress in school, knowing that learning difficulties are likely to arise as school becomes more challenging. Physically, too, he is likely to differ from his peers. Again because of treatment he received, his total growth is likely to be diminished, although at age nine he was somewhat bigger than average. That, combined with some visual impairment caused by the tumor, means that he may have difficulty keeping up with his peers on the playing fields.

[1] Not his real name. Like all the other children and parents mentioned in this book, his name was changed to protect the family's privacy.

Sean's family also bears reminders of his ordeal. The terror that accompanied his diagnosis is indelibly impressed into their memories. Like many families Sean's had been tested and had come out stronger, but nevertheless scarred.

Over the course of doing research for this book, I came to understand that Sean's experience is in many ways typical of children affected with cancer in the 1990s. Like so many others Sean survived his disease (for more on the issue of survival, see chapter 1). In fact over 70 percent of children diagnosed with cancer today will survive well into adulthood, making this one of the true medical success stories of our lifetime. Yet a statistic such as this does not tell the whole story. Childhood cancer is not an illness that is forgotten once cured. Its effects spread far and wide—both through a child's family and through time.

This book aims to address the many issues that families face, beginning with diagnosis, moving through treatment and its complications, and beyond treatment. Because of the complexity of a disease such as cancer, no book of this type could hope to provide all the information that families will need. However, it should help direct people to resources that can assist them in their search for answers. Throughout the book I alternate using the pronouns *he/she, him/her,* and *his/hers.* This is meant to reflect the fact that, except where indicated otherwise, cancer and its complications affect both boys and girls.

Despite the dramatic gains in the battle against childhood cancer, some children will not survive. The issues of death and dying are addressed in chapter 14, yet this is primarily a book about life—about fighting to stay alive and living fully, whether that life is short or long.

# CHAPTER 1

# What Is Cancer?

When her parents first told her she had cancer, Janine began to cry. Her doctor asked, "Do you know what cancer is?" and Janine tearfully shook her head no.

Janine was only eight years old at the time, but she had already captured the fear that most of us feel at the word *cancer*. Yet like many others, adults and children alike, Janine knew little more about the disease than that it was something terrible and scary.

Most people never need to learn the facts about cancer, but Janine was one of approximately nine thousand American children under the age of nineteen who each year are diagnosed with some form of cancer.[1] And

[1] Pediatric Oncology Group, "Progress Against Childhood Cancer: The Pediatric Oncology Group Experience," *Pediatrics* 89 (1992) 597–600.

so Janine and her parents had to learn, and had to learn fast.

When a child is newly diagnosed with cancer, parents often feel that they are being buried by an avalanche—new information comes fast and in huge quantities. Moreover they often must make decisions about their child's care immediately, even as the shock of the diagnosis is becoming a reality and before they have had a chance to process the new information.

In truth no one really expects parents to understand all that is thrown at them in those early days. Says oncologist Richard Womer, M.D., "From the time we say, 'Your child has cancer,' families absorb about 5 percent of everything that is said. So I try to keep the initial diagnostic conference very simple, with the big themes being: This is cancer. Kids die from it despite the best we can do. We're doing our best. Here's generally what we can expect. Here's what treatment will be all about in broad general terms. And most importantly, it's not your fault."

More general information about what cancer is and what causes it can come later, says Dr. Womer. But it is important. A broad understanding of what cancer is and also what it isn't can help parents understand the specifics of their child's illness and can clarify misconceptions. This will help parents evaluate the information they receive over the next few years and may also alleviate some concerns. Chapter 1 covers some of this general information.

## Cancer Describes a Group of Illnesses

Cancer sometimes seems as if it's everywhere. You probably know several people whose lives have been affected by cancer. In my life I can think of many: When I was in high school, my friend Tom died of cancer. My uncle Bob did too. My friend Ellen was recently diagnosed and is in the middle of treatment. Although these three people all were touched by cancer, in reality they had three different diseases: It was leukemia that felled Tom; my uncle had liver cancer; and Ellen, breast cancer. And these are just three of the more than one hundred known types of cancer.

The differences among these illnesses have dramatic implications for all cancer patients, but particularly for children with cancer. Because, as we shall see, the types of cancer that affect children are different from those that affect adults and because nearly 70 percent of children diagnosed with cancer today will survive their illness (terms such as *survive* are further discussed below).

What links these diseases is that all involve the uncontrolled growth of certain cells in the body. Most normal human cells grow and divide in order to replace other cells that have died. Normal cells have internal control mechanisms to ensure that the rate at which new cells are generated matches but does not exceed the rate at which old cells die. In cancer, however, this mechanism goes haywire. The cell becomes "transformed" and begins to grow in an unregulated manner. Scientists can visualize this property when they grow cells in the laboratory. Normal cells grow and divide to form an orderly, single-cell layer on the surface of a culture dish. The cells stop dividing when they contact another cell. In contrast, cancer cells grow haphazardly. They pile up on one another, divide unevenly, and keep on dividing. Says Dr. Womer, "Cancer cells don't respect each other's boundaries."

In the body the overproduction of cancer cells can result in normal cells being crowded out or in the production of a solid mass called a tumor. Cancer cells can invade normal tissue and they can be spread, via the bloodstream, to establish new tumors in sites distant from the original tumor. This is called *metastasis.* It is these two characteristics—invasion and metastasis—that define a *malignant* tumor. Not all tumors are malignant, however. Growths that are made up of cells that neither invade nor metastasize are called *benign.* Depending on where they grow, benign tumors can also be dangerous if they put pressure on or in some other way interfere with the normal function of certain organs, such as the brain or heart.

The type of cancer that develops depends on the cell type that becomes transformed. Any cell can be transformed. It happens when a mistake is made during cell division. The mistake, called a mutation, occurs deep within the cell, in the genetic material called *DNA* (deoxyribonucleic acid). "You just need one little mutation in one cell," says Anna Meadows, M.D., director of the Cancer Research Center and the Division of Oncology at The Children's Hospital of Philadelphia. "When you think of the many millions of cells in each of our bodies and the number of times each cell turns over, it is amazing that we have so few cancers."

## Cancer in Children Differs from Cancer in Adults

Most cancers take many years to develop—as much as twenty years or more! This explains why the incidence of cancer is much lower in children that in adults. About one out of every six people will develop cancer during their lifetime, but only one out of every six hundred children does so. Moreover children don't get the same types of cancer as adults do. Says Dr. Meadows, "Children's cancers are diseases of developing cells, what we call embryonal tissues—

the developing blood system, the developing nervous system, and the developing kidney, for example." In contrast the most common forms of adult cancers—lung, colon, and breast—develop in formed organs and are almost never seen in children.

## Treating and Curing Cancer in Children

The differences between adult and childhood cancers and between the different types of cancer have dramatic implications in terms of both prognosis and treatment. Children are more likely than adults to be cured. Overall nearly 70 percent of children with cancer, versus about 50 percent of adults with cancer, will survive five years after diagnosis.[2]

Treatment approaches vary as well. In general, children's cancers are more responsive to chemotherapy and children tolerate it better, while adults tolerate radiation therapy better. Chemotherapy, because it circulates throughout the body, is especially effective in treating cancers of the blood system (leukemias), while radiation therapy and surgery are more effective in treating discrete tumors. In addition different types of cancers are sensitive to radiation therapy or chemotherapy to differing degrees.

## The Meaning of "Cure"

When people talk about treating and curing cancer, they may use different terms depending on the type of cancer and the stage of treatment. The term *remission*, for example, im-

[2] Five-year relative survival rates 1981–87, from L.A.G. Ries, et al., *Cancer Statistics Review, 1973–1988*, National Cancer Institute. NIH Pub. No. 91-2789, 1991.

plies that the number of cancer cells present has been lessened or diminished to the point where they can no longer be detected by routine blood tests, physical exam, or X-ray studies. Remission does not necessarily mean that the cancer cells have been eliminated. In children with leukemia, for example, cancer cells circulate throughout the body, making it difficult if not impossible to tell whether all the wayward cells have been eliminated. Thus, the term remission is appropriately applied to a child with leukemia who has no signs of disease. If the leukemia returns, the disease is said to have *relapsed*.

For children with many kinds of solid tumors it may be possible to remove surgically the original, or primary, tumor. Sometimes the primary tumor may have grown and invaded other areas to the extent that it cannot be removed surgically. In addition almost always tumor cells will have metastasized, that is, escaped, from the primary tumor and spread to other parts of the body to seed new tumors. Finally, sometimes solid tumors appear to be completely eliminated, only to reappear months or years later. This is called *recurrence* or *relapse*.

Treatment regimens for various types of cancer differ greatly. They can last for anywhere from a few months for certain types of cancer to several years for others, such as leukemia. But at some point treatment stops and the child is said to be cancer-free. This doesn't mean, however, that the disease is cured, says Dr. Meadows. "There are known risks of relapse after treatment is stopped. For some diseases it can be less than a 5 percent risk, while for others it can be up to 15 percent. But we stop treatment because we believe that the child has had enough and we'd like to avoid long-term toxicity as much as we can. We pick a stopping point at which the majority of children will be cured. But we tell the parents that this doesn't mean the child is cured. Not yet." The stopping point may further be based on evidence that continuing treatment will not reduce the risk that the disease will return.

The point at which a child will be pronounced "cured" depends on the disease, continues Dr. Meadows. For some cancers, such as Wilms' tumors of the kidney and non-Hodgkin's lymphoma, if the child hasn't relapsed in two or three years, the chances are excellent, greater than 99 percent, that the cancer will not come back. With other forms of cancer a longer waiting period is needed. With acute lymphocytic leukemia, for example, a child is not considered cured until four years of relapse-free remission following discontinuation of therapy have passed.

## Better Outcomes in Treating Children's Cancer

The outlook for children with cancer has undergone a revolution in the past thirty years. The change has been most dramatic for acute lymphocytic leukemia (ALL), one of the most common cancers in children. During the early sixties fewer than 5 percent of children diagnosed with ALL survived five years; yet by the mid-eighties the survival rate had jumped to over 70 percent. Other types of cancer, which are discussed on the following pages, also have experienced improvements, some more dramatic than others. Overall the news is good: 28 percent of children diagnosed with cancer between 1960 and 1963 survived five years, compared with 66.8 percent of those diagnosed between 1981 and 1987.[3]

Dr. Womer cautions against putting too much importance

[3] These figures are based on relative survival rates for whites, ages 0–14, for the periods 1960–63 and 1981–87, from L.A.G. Ries, et al., *Cancer Statistics Review, 1973–1988*, National Cancer Institute. NIH Pub No. 91-2789, 1991.

on these statistics. "First of all, remember that five years from diagnosis you don't have a patient who is 75 percent alive and 25 percent dead; any individual patient has either made it or not. And secondly what we know about prognosis reflects what we were doing five years ago. We don't have crystal balls. But we hope that what we're doing now is better than what we were doing five years ago."

## Types of Cancer in Children

7-East. That's the wing of The Children's Hospital of Philadelphia that houses the hospital's pediatric oncology patients. Walk through the halls and you'll see children of all shapes, sizes, and colors. You quickly learn that cancer doesn't play favorites.

And just as the children are all different, so, too, are their diseases. From the top of the head to the tips of the toes, children's cancer can affect any part of the body. In fact at any one time as many as twenty different diseases or more may be represented among the thirty children on the floor. Some of these diseases occur frequently enough that the doctors, nurses, and other care providers develop a ready familiarity and an almost standard treatment approach. Others are so rare that an individual hospital may see only one or two cases per year.

What this means for parents is that more or less information may be available, depending on a child's individual diagnosis. However, many general principles apply to even the rarest forms of cancer. And while this general information may not tell you specifically what lies ahead for your child, it can provide you with a framework from which you can search for more specific answers to your questions.

Children's cancers fall into two major groups: leukemias and solid tumors. The leukemias are diseases of the blood and thus circulate throughout the body, while solid tumors are growths found at specific sites. The cancers that affect children most frequently are the various leukemias and tumors of the brain and central nervous system; together these two groups account for about half of all childhood cancers.

### *THE LEUKEMIAS*

Leukemia is a malignancy of the blood and blood-forming tissues. Several different types of leukemia may occur in a child depending on which type of blood cell is affected. In order to explain how leukemia develops, we must first describe the different cells of the blood and how they are formed. The blood cells are formed in the bone marrow, the soft, spongy material in the hollow centers of bones. This is where the most immature type of cell, the stem cell, differentiates to form all the different cell types that are needed in the blood: the red blood cells (also called *erythrocytes,* or *RBCs*), which carry oxygen to the tissues; the white blood cells *(leukocytes,* or *WBCs),* which make up the body's defense system; and the platelets *(thrombocytes),* which help control bleeding by helping the blood to clot.

A cell that takes the leukocyte pathway further differentiates into either a *granulocyte, monocyte,* or *lymphocyte.* Granulocytes may also be called neutrophils, polymorphs or polys, or segs; monocytes may also be called macrophages. Granulocytes and monocytes engulf and destroy foreign materials including bacteria. Lymphocytes are the effector cells of the immune system. There are two major types, called *T cells* and *B cells.* B cells produce antibodies—protein molecules that allow the body to recognize and eliminate foreign invaders, such as infectious agents (e.g., bacteria and viruses) and transplanted tissues. T cells perform a variety of immunologic functions including "helping" and "suppressing" the immune response. Lymphocytes are also responsible for the phenomenon called *immunologic memory,* which allows the body to remember agents to which it has previously been exposed and to mount a rapid defense.

Leukemia may affect any one of these three types of white blood cells (less frequently red blood cells and platelets may also be affected). Most commonly the immature lymphocyte is affected, causing the disease called acute lymphocytic leukemia, or ALL (see below). The immature cell type is called a *lymphoblast,* or more commonly, a *blast.* As leukemic blasts build up in the marrow, they crowd out normal blood cells that should be developing. Eventually the child with leukemia begins to suffer the consequences of having too few of these essential blood cells. When red blood cells are depleted, the child looks pale and feels tired because the blood is not supplying sufficient oxygen to the tissues. Bleeding problems, including bruising and the appearance of small red spots, or *petechiae,* may occur if platelets are depleted; and infections develop when normal white blood cells are lacking. The buildup of blasts in the bone marrow may also cause bone pain in children with leukemia.

If the child sees a doctor at this point, a simple blood test may detect an abnormality in the number of circulating white blood cells. Further testing will be needed, however, to confirm a diagnosis of leukemia and to determine which white blood cell type is affected. Treatments differ depending on the specific type of leukemia.

Leukemia may also spread beyond the blood to the brain and spinal cord or to the testicles. When this happens, the treatment regimen needs to include therapies specifically targeted to these sites.

**ALL** The most common type of childhood leukemia affects the lymphocytes. Acute lymphoblastic (or lymphocytic) leukemia, or ALL, occurs in about 80 percent of children diagnosed with leukemia. It is called *acute* because, without treatment, the disease is fatal within a few weeks or months. *Lymphoblastic* refers to the cell type that overproduces in the bone marrow. These immature lymphoblasts are unable to produce antibodies or carry out other functions of mature lymphocytes. ALL actually encompasses several subtypes of disease. ALL may involve pre-T, pre-B, T-, or B- lymphocytes. At the time of diagnosis, tests will be done to try to determine precisely which cell type is affected, as this will influence the child's prognosis and the course of treatment. Most childhood leukemia affects pre-B cells, or B-lymphocyte precursors.

In addition to determining the cell type affected, diagnostic studies will also involve other aspects of the disease, which will help determine the likelihood that the cancer will respond to treatment. If a child is determined to be in a high-risk category, that is, that the type of cancer may be more resistant to treatment, more aggressive therapy will be given. Factors that influence risk include patient-related features such as age and sex, the white blood cell and platelet counts at diagnosis, whether the liver, spleen, and lymph nodes are massively enlarged, whether there is a mass in the thymus (a gland in the chest), and characteristics of the chromosomes of the leukemic cells.

The cure of ALL is one of the major medical triumphs of the last twenty years. Before 1970 less than 10 percent of children survived five years. Today it is expected that 75 percent of children with ALL will be cured of their disease.

**AML.** When acute leukemia occurs in nonlymphoid blood cells, it is called *AML—acute myeloid (or myelocytic) leukemia.* About 15 to 20 percent of children diagnosed with leukemia will have AML. The symptoms of AML resemble those of ALL; blood testing is required to make the proper diagnosis.

AML is more common in adults; however, it sometimes occurs in teenagers and children. Usually AML involves immature granulocytes (myeloblasts) or monocytes (monoblasts). Less frequently immature platelets (megakaryoblasts) or red cells (erythroblasts) may be affected. Rarely the leukemic cell type is too immature to be classified as either lymphocytic, monocytic, or granulocytic; in these cases the leukemia may be classified as *undifferentiated leukemia (AUL)* or *acute stem cell leukemia.*

The progress in treating AML has been less marked than that achieved with ALL. Current statistics suggest that about 40 percent of children diagnosed with AML will survive four years after diagnosis. Indicators of a good prognosis include lower white blood cell count and more rapid induction of remission. Because of the relatively poor prognosis with standard therapy, doctors treat AML very aggressively. Treatment usually involves long hospitalization and may include relatively new approaches, including bone marrow transplantation (chapter 6) and immunotherapy (chapter 7).

**CML and Other Leukemias** Even less frequently a child may have *chronic myelogenous leukemia,* or *CML,* or a *preleukemia* or *myelodysplasia.* Myelodysplasia is a condition in which the blood cells mature and proliferate abnormally. Sometimes myelodysplasia evolves into leukemia. CML accounts for only about 2 percent of all cases of childhood leukemia. As implied by its name, CML may come on gradually and may not become life-threatening nearly as quickly as does ALL or AML. The symptoms may go on for many years. The same is true for preleukemias and myelodysplasia. Until recently CML was nearly always fatal. Today, however, children with CML have the option of bone marrow transplantation (chapter 6), which proves curative in as many as 65 percent of patients. However, bone marrow transplantation is not possible for all patients.

### *BRAIN TUMORS*

Brain and other central nervous system (CNS) tumors are the most common solid tumors of childhood, affecting some 3,000 to 3,500 children each year in the United States. They differ in several significant ways from other types of solid tumors and as a result have given rise to a separate branch of oncology called neurooncology. Like other areas of oncology, neurooncology has made some tremendous strides, according to neurosurgeon Luis Schut, M.D. For example, says Dr. Schut, "We have made enormous progress with one particular type of tumor called medulloblastoma. When I was a resident, telling a family that their child had medulloblastoma was like telling them their child would die in five years. Now 75 percent of children live more than five years, and 65 percent live more than ten years."

Brain tumors range from relatively benign or slow-growing masses to highly invasive cancers, but all have the potential for serious consequences because of their location in the brain. About half of all brain tumors are histologically benign, meaning that the cells do not appear malignant when studied in the laboratory. If those tumors can be surgically removed, the child will be cured, although sometimes these tumors are not removable via surgery. (In contrast other types of benign solid tumors rarely are not removable by surgery.) Nevertheless some children survive for many years with a stable, inactive tumor in their brain. Overall about 60 percent of children diagnosed with brain tumors will survive into adulthood.

Brain tumors also differ from other solid tumors because of their great potential for significant damage even if the cancer is cured. And unlike other types of solid tumors, brain tumors are unlikely to spread to other parts of the body, although they may come back in the same place after being removed.

Brain tumors may evade diagnosis for some time because the early symptoms can be vague: headaches, vomiting, nausea, and irritability. Sometimes symptoms can be picked up by an ophthalmologic exam. Only at later stages do more obvious symptoms appear. Once a brain tumor has been recognized, improved imaging techniques mean that the diagnosis can be made much more accurately than was previously possible.

Brain tumors are classified according to their location in the brain. This is an important characteristic because it may determine the treatment approach (for instance, whether surgery is feasible) and it may help predict the child's outcome, both in terms of survivability and potential for neurologic damage. Tumors are also classified by histopathology, that is, the cellular characteristics of the tumor cells. This information may give clues about the tumor's likelihood of metastasis and its sensitivity to different treatment approaches. For example some types of tumors are sensitive to radiation and chemotherapy, while others are not. The terms malignant and benign when applied to childhood brain tumors refer only to the histology and do not necessarily reflect the outcome for the patient. For example the pineal germinoma is a "malignant" tumor, but one that is almost always curable with radiation, whereas brainstem gliomas may be histologically "benign" but prove fatal because they often cannot be removed surgically.

The treatment for a brain tumor may include surgery, if possible, radiation therapy, and chemotherapy. Both the tumor and the treatment may damage brain tissue. Therefore current trials emphasize controlling the tumor without impairing function, especially intelligence.

Treatment for brain tumors goes far beyond that aimed at eradicating the cancer, however. Neurooncologist Beverly Lange, M.D., says that rehabilitation through a multidisciplinary team is critical. "Treating brain tumors tends to require many specialists: neurosurgeons, neurologist, psychologists, maybe ophthalmologists, and sometimes audiologists," she says.

### *OTHER SOLID TUMORS*

The names of the different types of solid tumors usually end with the suffix *-oma* (which means "growth" in Greek.) The beginning of the word describes the site of the tumor or the cell type from which the tumor arose. *Blast* in the name indicates that the cancer cell is an immature, precursor cell. The solid tumors that most commonly affect children include brain tumors, lymphomas, sarcomas, neuroblastoma, Wilms' tumor, retinoblastoma, and teratomas. These are all discussed below. Another family of solid tumors, called *carcinomas,* rarely affect children but account for most adult cancers.

Most of the solid tumors are staged according to the size of the primary tumor, the extent to which it can be removed by surgery, and the degree to which it has metastasized. Table I describes a general staging system. However, for each disease, staging criteria may vary. The stage of a tumor will help determine the treatment strategy used. In general the more advanced stages of disease will require more aggressive treatment.

**Sarcomas** Sarcomas arise from connective tissue, such as muscle or bone. This group of diseases is further broken down according to the specific cell type involved. The most common sarcomas seen in children are *rhabdomyosarcoma,* which originates in muscle; *osteogenic sarcoma* (also called *osteosarcoma),* which originates in bone; and Ewing's sarcoma, which also originates in bone. Less common types of sarcoma affect tendons, ligaments, and muscle sheaths *(fibrosarcoma);*

Table 1.1
**Staging of Solid Tumors**

|  |  |
|---|---|
| Stage I | Tumor is completely removed and has not spread to other tissues and lymph nodes |
| Stage II | Tumor is removed but has spread to surrounding tissues and lymph nodes |
| Stage III | Tumor cannot be completely removed |
| Stage IV | Tumor has spread throughout the body |

linings of joints and tendon sheaths *(synovial sarcoma);* nerve sheaths *(neurofibrosarcoma);* or cartilage *(chondrosarcoma).*

Sarcomas tend to be very invasive and frequently metastasize to the lung. They respond differently to chemotherapy depending on the specific cell type involved. Surgical removal of the tumor is usually the first line of treatment, followed by further treatment to prevent metastasis.

*Rhabdomyosarcoma* most often develops in the muscles of the head, neck, pelvis, and extremities of children between the ages of two and six and fifteen and nineteen. Signs may be obvious, such as a lump or swelling in the affected area. When diagnosed at Stage I, rhabdomyosarcoma has an excellent prognosis. But as with other solid tumors, the prognosis declines as the stage increases.

*Osteosarcoma* is the most commonly seen bone malignancy. It tends to affect the long bones of the arms and legs, occurring near the ends of the bones, especially at the knee. At the time of diagnosis metastases often are already visible in the lung, requiring aggressive therapy both for the tumor itself and for the renegade cells spreading throughout the body. Surgery may involve amputation of the limb, although more complex surgical procedures that spare the limb may be possible. With surgery plus multiagent chemotherapy, about 60 percent of patients will survive beyond five years with no signs of disease.

*Ewing's sarcoma* is the second most common type of bone cancer seen in children. It is usually seen in Caucasian teenagers. African-Americans are almost never affected by this type of cancer. Although thought of as a bone tumor, the cell of origin is really a precursor nerve cell. Thus it may arise in nonbony as well as bony sites. Tumors occur in the extremities about 50 percent of the time, usually in the shaft of the bones rather than in their ends. Other sites include the pelvis, chest wall, and in or around the spinal column.

**Lymphoma** Lymphomas are solid tumors of the lymphatic system. The lymph system is a network of vessels and organs that operate throughout the body to fight infections and other diseases. The tiny vessels carry a thin, colorless liquid called lymph, which contains the lymphocytes needed to fight infections. Along these vessels small bean-shaped organs called *lymph nodes* filter out particles and bacteria so that they can be destroyed and eliminated by the lymphocytes. During an infection the nodes that drain the infected area may become swollen with the large numbers of accumulating lymphocytes and infectious particles. Other organs that are part of the lymph system include the spleen, thymus gland, and tonsils. Lymphomas may occur in lymph glands as well as in *extranodal* sites (outside the lymph nodes). Like leukemia the cancerous cells are easily disseminated throughout the body. Therefore lymphomas usually require systemic treatment.

Lymphomas are classified as either Hodgkin's disease or non-Hodgkin's lymphoma, based on their cell type.

*Hodgkin's Disease* This type of lymphoma is named after the English physician who first described it. Hodgkin's disease usually strikes people in their twenties but rarely occurs in young children. Young children who are affected have a somewhat better prognosis in comparison to adults with Hodgkin's disease. Some three-fourths of children under the age of seventeen diagnosed with Hodgkin's disease will survive at least twenty years.

Hodgkin's disease usually first appears in the lymph nodes of the neck and chest, but can spread to other nodes and elsewhere in the body. As with other forms of cancer, staging of the disease directs therapy and helps predict outcome. The outlook is excellent in early-stage disease, with survival rates at ten years approaching 100 percent.

*Non-Hodgkin's Lymphoma.* The various non-Hodgkin's lymphomas constitute about 7 to 10 percent of pediatric malignancies and occur more frequently in boys than in girls, usually between the ages of five and twelve. These tumors include a number of cellular subtypes, which are classified as lymphoblastic or nonlymphoblastic. Nonlymphoblastic lymphomas are further divided into *large-cell lymphoma* and *Burkitt's* or *non-Burkitt's small-cell lymphoma.* Depending on the particular subtype, tumors may occur almost anywhere throughout the body, especially in the bowel and upper chest. Lymphomas tend to grow very rapidly but can be cured if caught early. In a book about their son's experience with Burkitt's lymphoma, Geralyn and Craig Gaes describe how the tumor grew from a golf-ball-sized lump to a growth ten inches in diameter in a little more than one day.[4]

Non-Hodgkin's lymphomas are staged according to how much the disease has spread. The staging system directs therapy and predicts outcome. Thus Stage I disease (a single tumor) has both a higher rate of cure and a less intensive

[4] *You Don't Have to Die: One Family's Guide to Surviving Childhood Cancer,* by Geralyn and Craig Gaes and Philip Bashe (New York: Villard Books, Random House, Inc., 1992).

therapy regimen than does Stage IV disease, in which the cancer has spread to the central nervous system or bone marrow. Even Stage IV disease is potentially curable, however, especially with new therapy regimens that are evolving. Today more than two-thirds of children diagnosed with non-Hodgkin's lymphoma can be expected to survive beyond five years.

**Neuroblastoma** Neuroblastoma is one of the most common forms of cancer in very young children and is rarely found in adults. It arises in immature cells of the sympathetic nervous system. The sympathetic nervous system stimulates involuntary actions, such as blushing or dilation of the pupils. All organs of the body are supplied with sympathetic nerves; thus neuroblastoma may arise virtually anywhere in the body. Most often it is found in the abdomen, either in one of the adrenal glands, which sit on top of the kidneys, or along the side of the spine. Other sites include the chest and neck. Neuroblastoma is highly malignant and often has spread to the lymph nodes, liver, bone marrow, or bone before diagnosis.

As with many other forms of cancer, diagnosis involves staging of the disease so that therapy plans can be designed appropriately. Stages are designated I through IV, with a special classification called IV-S. This indicates that although the disease is widely disseminated, no bone involvement is found. Patients with IV-S disease are usually babies. They may improve with no treatment other than surgery. Neuroblastoma often has already progressed to Stage IV by the time of diagnosis; the most aggressive therapy is required for such children. The likelihood of cure correlates with the patient's age and stage of disease at diagnosis, with younger children (less than one year old) who have early-stage disease faring best.

**Wilms' Tumor** Most kidney cancers in children are Wilms'

tumors, also known as *nephroblastoma.* The kidneys are essential organs that filter wastes from the body and make urine. Wilms' tumor arises from a kidney cell that becomes transformed during the earliest stages of development; thus it occurs primarily in young children between two and five years of age.

As with other forms of childhood cancer, many of the symptoms associated with Wilms' tumor are vague and nonspecific. Sometimes a parent will notice an abdominal lump or blood in the urine. Wilms' tumor may also be associated with a number of developmental abnormalities, including aniridia (the absence of the iris or colored part of the eye). Children with these disorders have a much greater than average incidence of Wilms' tumor.

The treatment plan and prognosis for a child with Wilms' tumor depends on the degree of metastases (stage) and the histology (cell type). Children with more advanced disease and "unfavorable" histology will require more aggressive treatment. According to oncologist Giulio D'Angio, M.D., parents should not be scared off by terms such as *unfavorable histology.*

"When we talk about favorable and unfavorable, it is in relationship to the treatments that are available [at the time]." Consequently as treatments change, a certain histology that is classified as "unfavorable" may become responsive to treatment. Thus early-stage Wilms' tumor with unfavorable histology is curable in the majority of patients.

Wilms' tumor may involve one or both kidneys. When both kidneys are involved, it is designated stage V. A kidney tumor usually necessitates removal of the kidney. If both kidneys are affected, the doctor will stage and treat the tumors in each kidney separately, and every attempt to save at least one kidney will be made, since a person can live normally with just one kidney.

**Retinoblastoma** This is a rare type of cancer of the eye that mainly affects children younger than five years of age. The affected cells are in the retina, a thin membrane on the back of the eye where images are captured. In about 40 percent of cases, retinoblastoma is inherited. Your doctor will be able to tell you if your child's retinoblastoma is of the heritable type. If one child in your family has heritable retinoblastoma, other children should also have regular eye exams as they have a somewhat greater risk than the average child of also developing the disease. One or both eyes may be affected. When tumors occur in both eyes, the disease is always of the heritable type.

Staging of your child's disease will determine therapy, which may include surgery to remove the eye. Should this be necessary, the eye can be replaced with an artificial eye. Although sight will be lost in that eye, modern artificial eyes look quite realistic. More important, sight in the remaining eye should not be affected. Usually if both eyes are involved and surgery is indicated, only the eye with the larger tumor will be removed. The remaining eye may be treated with radiation therapy, photocoagulation, or cryotherapy to preserve vision if at all possible.

Retinoblastoma is a highly curable form of cancer. With early diagnosis over 90 percent of children are cured.

**Germ-Cell Tumors** Germ-cell tumors account for about 3 percent of all pediatric cancers. They are most commonly found in the lower back and pelvis (ovary) and the testes. Other sites include the mediastinum (chest) and brain. Girls are affected more often than boys up until the age of fourteen, when the rate of testicular cancer begins to rise sharply in boys.

The major types of germ-cell tumors are *teratomas, germi-*

*nomas,* and *endodermal sinus tumors* (yolk sac carcinoma). Teratomas are the most common and are usually benign. Treatment varies with the cell type and site affected and may include surgery, radiation, and/or chemotherapy.

## CHAPTER 2

# Why My Child?

Of all the questions asked by friends and family, the one that bothers Francie the most is when people ask, "Why did your child get cancer?" The question Francie hears is "What did you do that caused this?" or "How can I keep this from happening to my child?"

As the parent of a child with cancer Francie has of course asked herself similar questions: "What did I do wrong?" and "What could I have done to prevent it?" Although her doctor had emphasized over and over that she was not at fault,

Francie's questions and nagging guilt feelings never completely went away. And until scientists are able to answer definitely the question "Why does a child get cancer?" worry, guilt, and suspicion are likely to remain.

There is no shortage of suspected culprits. Diet, environmental agents, viruses, and heredity have all been cited as potential causes of childhood cancer. Many parents believe that they know what caused their child's cancer. But according to John J. Mulvihill, in one of the leading pediatric oncology textbooks, "Parents' perceptions echo popular scientific beliefs that 80% of cancers are due to the environment, including factors grouped as lifestyle, such as diet. . . . [However] impressive as this evidence may be for adult tumors, it is nearly absent with regard to childhood cancer."[1]

Thus while adult cancers are often preventable through behavioral changes such as quitting smoking (a step that would drastically reduce the incidence of lung cancer) and protecting oneself from sun exposure (to avoid skin cancer), prevention of childhood cancer is a much more elusive goal. The nature of childhood cancer partially explains this difference. Most adult cancers occur in cells that line various organs and thereby are exposed to the environment. But children's cancers occur primarily in rapidly developing tissues that have no such environmental exposure.

This does not mean that environmental agents play *no* role in the development of childhood cancer. However, cancer specialists believe that environment alone is not enough, that a "collision" of factors is required for cancer to develop in a child. "There is not *one* cause," says Dr. Richard Womer. "Cancer is caused by a number of events interacting by chance in a particular cell." These factors *may* include hered-

[1] John J. Mulvihill, in Phillip A. Pizzo and David G. Poplack, eds., *Principles and Practice of Pediatric Oncology*, 2nd ed. (Philadelphia: J.B. Lippincott, 1993).

ity, predisposing conditions (such as a disease that depresses the immune response), viruses, chemicals, emotions, radiation, and finally "just plain bad luck."

Dr. Womer draws an analogy to a traffic accident: Suppose you are involved in a crash two blocks from your house one morning when another motorist runs a stop sign. If you ask, "What caused the crash?" your first answer might be, "The other motorist." Or you might come up with some other factors. You might say that the crash wouldn't have happened if you had left the house five minutes earlier, if you had taken a different route, if the other motorist hadn't been distracted by a bicyclist coming in the other direction, or if he hadn't been driving too fast because he was late for work because his alarm clock had malfunctioned. Are you at fault? Is it the bicyclist? The alarm clock? In fact a number of factors converged at a particular moment in time to cause the accident. It was just your bad luck to be there at that time.

Similarly with cancer, multiple factors converge. Gradually scientists are beginning to understand the relative importance of many of these factors, with the hope that eventually some cancers may be prevented. However, it's important to remember that the risks imposed by many of the factors discussed below are relatively small. Thus even if some environmental agent was shown to double the incidence of acute lymphocytic leukemia (ALL), for example, the risk would only increase from about 1 in 25,000 to 1 in 12,500 per year.[2] Remember this when you're wondering if you could have prevented your child's illness. We all do our best to reduce our children's risk of injury or illness, but our lives will never be totally risk-free.

[2] Incidence of childhood ALL in the United States is approximately 4 per 100,000 children younger than fifteen years, according to David G. Poplack, in Pizzo and Poplack, eds., *Principles and Practice of Pediatric Oncology*.

## Heredity and Genetics

When people talk about genetic diseases, they are usually referring to diseases that are passed from one generation to the next, in much the same way that traits such as blue eyes are passed. The classic example of a genetic disease is hemophilia, a disease that usually occurs only in boys but that is passed to a boy from his mother's side of the family. If the child gets the gene from his mother, he gets the disease.

Most cancers are not thought to be hereditary in this sense. No one single gene determines whether a person will get a certain type of cancer. However, genetics does appear to play a role in some forms of cancer in much the same way that genetics plays a role in the development of many other diseases, such as diabetes. A gene or genes interact with some other known or unknown factors in a particular cell that transforms into a cancer cell.

Scientists can determine the relative influence of genetics on the development of cancer by studying the extended families of cancer patients and by studying pairs of twins in which one or both siblings have cancer. These family studies reveal clues about the inheritance patterns of certain diseases and can yield useful information about the likelihood that another child in the family will get cancer. For most types of cancer, when one child in a family is affected, siblings are not at high risk of also being affected, although their risk may be higher than that faced by the general population. For example siblings of a child with leukemia have about a two- to four-fold greater-than-average risk of developing the disease.[3] For a few types of childhood cancer, however, genetics plays a bigger role. If your child is thought to have a heritable

[3] Poplack, ibid.

type of cancer, a geneticist or genetics counselor can advise you about the risks facing your other children.

Much of what is known about the genetics of cancer has come from studies of *retinoblastoma*. This is one of the few cancers for which genetics may play a predominant role. A retinoblastoma gene has been identified and children who inherit this gene have a 95 percent chance of developing eye cancer by the age of five. Still, most cases of retinoblastoma are of a nonheritable type.

In 1976 Dr. Alfred G. Knudson proposed a model for how retinoblastoma develops. This model has since been confirmed. Dr. Knudson said that two genetic events are required. Susceptible individuals, he proposed, inherit one of these genetic errors and will develop tumors in reaction to only one additional event or "hit." Nonsusceptible individuals require two independent hits and thus are much less likely to develop these tumors. If they do develop retinoblastoma, it affects one eye only.

Only about 10 percent of children with retinoblastoma have a family history of the disease, yet about 40 percent of tumors are of the heritable type. This is because in most cases the mutation in the retinoblastoma gene occurred spontaneously in the reproductive cells of the parent. Once this happens, the child has a 50 percent chance of passing the gene on to his or her offspring. This is the first "hit." Once the mutation has occurred, however, only one other "hit" is required for retinoblastoma to develop.

Retinoblastoma may occur either unilaterally (in one eye only) or bilaterally (in both eyes, either simultaneously or at different times). Bilateral retinoblastoma is always of the heritable type; unilateral tumors may be nonheritable.

Among the other cancers for which genetics plays an important role are Wilms' tumor and neuroblastoma. However, the genetic basis of these types of cancer is less clear than that for retinoblastoma. Multiple genes may be involved.

Genetics plays an important role in the development of cancer in another group of children who inherit diseases that make them more likely to develop cancer. These can be immunodeficiency diseases, such as ataxia telangiectasia, Wiskott-Aldrich syndrome, or severe combined immunodeficiency disease (SCID); or diseases that interfere with the cells' ability to repair mutations in the DNA, such as xeroderma pigmentosum, Bloom's syndrome, and Fanconi's anemia. Other genetic diseases that predispose a child to develop cancer include von Recklinghausen's neurofibromatosis and the Li-Fraumeni syndrome.

For most cancers the role of genetics is much less clear. Cancer starts at the level of the gene, where errors cause cell differentiation and proliferation to go awry. In a sense, then, all cancer is genetically based. Exactly how the genetic makeup affects a child's likelihood of getting cancer, however, is extremely complex.

In order to understand the genetics of cancer, it may be helpful to consider how cells normally divide and differentiate. Each human cell (except sperm and egg cells) contains twenty-three pairs of chromosomes on which is written the blueprint for the entire organism. An organism grows by repeatedly doubling its number of cells. During this process the chromosomes replicate, split, and the cell divides. It is during the replication and division of chromosomes that mistakes may occur. These mistakes may occur if the chromosome doesn't replicate entirely accurately, if information on the chromosomes gets mixed up, or if the chromosomes do not split correctly. Sometimes these mistakes lead to cancer because they cause the cells to grow in an unregulated fashion.

Some types of cancer are associated with a particular type

of mistake. For example a certain form of chronic myelogenous leukemia occurs when specific portions of chromosome number 9 and chromosome number 22 switch places; this is known as translocation. Other types of cancer may occur when portions of chromosomes are deleted or replicated incorrectly. In some cases only one mistake is needed to transform a cell, and all the daughter cells will contain that same mistake. Scientists can then take the cells from a certain tumor, study the chromosomes and genes of that cell, and try to determine what kind of mistake caused the tumor to occur. This field of science—molecular genetics—is still relatively young but is moving quickly. As a result there are frequent new and exciting discoveries. For example, scientists in several groups around the world have shown that in many children with leukemia, the leukemic blasts show a characteristic chromosomal defect: a specific section of chromosome number 11 breaks and switches places with a section of chromosome number 4. This error causes the cells to become leukemic blasts. The scientists have even identified the specific gene produced as a consequence of this break, a so-called leukemia gene. This discovery may lead to better diagnostic tests and eventually to treatments specifically targeted to different types of leukemia.

But does it really tell us what caused the child's leukemia? No one knows yet, but it may be that the chromosomes of some people are more likely than others to break at this critical point when hit with a potential mutagen (for instance, a virus, toxin, or X ray). In other words there may be a genetic component in many types of childhood cancer, although genetics alone cannot explain the malignancy.

Thus when a newspaper headline heralds, GENETIC CAUSE OF COMMON LEUKEMIA FOUND,[4] the interpretation of that headline

[4] *Philadelphia Inquirer*, November 13, 1992, p. A1.

depends on your point of view. A scientist might say that the cause of leukemia is a break at this specific gene. But that doesn't tell us what caused the gene to break. From a parent's perspective, knowing the "cause" should answer the question "Why did my child get cancer?" But we are a long way from really knowing the answer to that question.

## The Search for Other Causes of Childhood Cancer

Many factors have been suggested as potential causes for childhood cancer, yet few have been proven culpable. Two different types of investigation may be conducted in these searches. The first approach is taken by scientists known as epidemiologists, who study communities of people with varying incidences of disease. These scientists gather extensive data about the environmental exposures and other characteristics of affected and nonaffected people living in these areas. From these data scientists hope they can determine whether certain environmental factors cause cancer. The second approach is taken by scientists who try to determine, in the laboratory, whether an agent or exposure causes mutations in cells. Many substances, both naturally occurring and man-made, have been shown to be mutagenic. However, in most cases, epidemiologists have been unable to show that exposures to these substances correlate with an increase in cancer.

Every few years we hear of a "cluster" of childhood cancer cases, and epidemiologists begin searching for a reason for the cluster. Perhaps the most notorious of these occurred in the early 1980s in the vicinity of the Sellafield nuclear reprocessing plant in England, where a tenfold increased incidence of childhood leukemia and non-Hodgkin's lymphoma was observed. Epidemiologists searching for clues that would explain this observation eventually concluded that fathers who worked at the plant and who had experienced high exposures to radiation before conception of their children were more likely to have children with cancer. These conclusions surprised many scientists, in part because studies of the offspring of atomic-bomb survivors had revealed no such increased incidence of cancer. Yet no other plausible explanation has yet been found.

Other clusters of childhood cancer have also been reported. As with the Sellafield incident, these observations prompted groups of epidemiologists to search for causes. Some of these studies are discussed on the following pages. One intriguing report, also from England, has suggested that children from affluent families are at higher risk of developing leukemia. More studies are under way to determine why this might be.

A number of factors have been implicated in various studies as increasing the risk for childhood cancer. In all but a few cases the data are too sparse to draw any firm conclusions, and the suggested increase in risk is quite small. Radiation is the most notable exception to this statement and is discussed further on the following pages. Other factors that have been implicated as increasing the risk of developing childhood cancer include prenatal exposure to antinausea medication, marijuana, or other drugs; ingestion of cured meat, tainted seafood, or other food additives; and exposure to environmental toxins in the air or water. Even those studies that have found a positive correlation between these exposures and the risk of childhood cancer show relatively modest increases in risk. More compelling evidence suggesting causes for childhood cancer falls into one of three major areas: viruses, ionizing radiation, and low-level electromagnetic radiation. These are discussed on the following pages.

## Radiation

Radiation is the most well understood cause of cancer. Much of what we know about radiation comes from the experiences of people who were exposed to radiation after atomic bombs were dropped on the cities of Hiroshima and Nagasaki at the end of World War II. In addition to the hundreds of thousands who were killed immediately or within a short period of time from radiation sickness, many thousands more developed leukemia or lymphoma over the next decade.

For most of us diagnostic X rays represent our biggest potential exposure to radiation. While the doses to which a person is exposed during a diagnostic procedure are considerably lower than those that have been shown definitively to be hazardous, some experts feel that diagnostic X rays may still be responsible for some cancers. With proper safety precautions and minimal use, however, diagnostic X rays are thought to be relatively safe. X rays used for therapeutic purposes are thought to present a greater risk because dosages are much higher—0.5 rads for a chest X ray versus 5,000 rads to treat certain solid tumors.

Exposure to X rays takes on a special meaning for children with cancer. High-dose radiation in many cases will be part of the treatment plan that saves a child's life. Unfortunately radiation given as cancer therapy can also lead to a second malignancy at some later date. Overall, children who are successfully treated for cancer develop a second cancer at a rate sevenfold higher than normal during the first five years after initial diagnosis. This does not appear to be treatment related. The risk then rises to tenfold more than normal, and about 75 percent of this increase can be attributed to radiation therapy; the remaining 25 percent is due to chemotherapy or other factors. Still the chance of getting another cancer is not very high—only about one in ten, compared with about one in one hundred twenty years later.

## Electromagnetic Fields

Since 1979 a debate has raged over whether electromagnetic fields (EMFs), such as those produced by high-power electrical lines and other electrical equipment, cause cancer. The debate was sparked by an epidemiologic study that found that children living near high-current electric power lines were at a risk of developing leukemia or lymphoma that was two to three times higher than normal. That study was criticized for methodologic problems, but it launched a number of other studies, including one reported in 1992 by a group of Swedish researchers that showed as much as a fourfold increased risk of leukemia among children living near power lines. In the intervening years a number of other studies were also done, some supporting and some refuting the original claims. One study linked a slight increased incidence of childhood cancer with electric-blanket use. Another suggested that the incidence of brain tumors also rose with increasing exposure to EMFs.

Currently scientists split over the issue of whether EMFs cause cancer. Some take the position that a relatively stable incidence of leukemia and lymphoma among children over the last twenty-five years despite huge increases in electric-power generation and electrical-appliance use argues against an association. Others dismiss the epidemiologic evidence because laboratory studies have failed to show that EMFs cause negative biologic effects. The only thing that these researchers can agree on is that in any case the risk of developing leukemia is very small, even in "high cancer" areas.

## Viruses

Viruses could conceivably play a role in the development of cancer either directly by causing changes in the DNA of the host or indirectly by suppressing the immune system, which would normally help eliminate any tumor cells that arise. Several types of animal and human adult cancers have been linked to certain viruses; however, the evidence for a viral cause of childhood cancer is far less convincing.

Ever since the 1960s the Epstein-Barr virus (EBV), which causes infectious mononucleosis, has been suggested as a cause of Burkitt's lymphoma. But while EBV can be found in cell cultures obtained from most Africans with the Burkitt's lymphoma, it is rarely found in cell cultures from people outside of Africa. Furthermore, while Burkitt's lymphoma is a rare form of cancer in the United States, EBV infection is widespread—occurring in nearly 100 percent of the population, often asymptomatically. Clearly EBV infection alone does not cause the American form of Burkitt's lymphoma. Whether it plays any role at all is still to be determined.

Despite the lack of clear evidence linking a virus to any form of childhood cancer, many scientists still believe that viruses play an important role. Their beliefs are bolstered by the fact that viruses have been strongly linked to the development of several adult human cancers. Evidence suggests that the hepatitis-B virus leads to the development of hepatocellular carcinoma (liver cancer) and that human T-cell lymphotropic virus (HTLV-I) plays a critical role in the development of adult T-cell leukemia, for example. In addition, immunosuppression brought on by the human immunodeficiency virus (HIV) leads to the development of some cancers, including B-cell lymphomas.

Some scientists have suggested that viruses might contribute to the development of cancer only if the infection occurs at a vulnerable time during development. If this is true, it might explain how viruses could cause cancer in some children but not in others, and it also might explain the occurrence of some clusters of childhood cancer.

## CHAPTER 3

# Where Do I Go?

Your child's preliminary diagnosis may have been made at a local hospital, but in most cases a child with cancer will be referred to a regional hospital that specializes in children's cancer. These centers have much to offer you, most important, state-of-the-art treatment approaches and facilities. The nearest center may be a good distance from your home. However, most cancer specialists and parents agree that the disruptions posed by obtaining care far from home may be a necessary part of saving your child's life.

## Why Go to a Children's Cancer Center?

Children's cancer centers offer optimal care for several reasons. First they have more experience in dealing with relatively rare diseases. Even the most common type of childhood cancer, ALL, affects only a few thousand children each year in the entire United States. Many community hospitals have little or no experience dealing with childhood cancer. Contrast that with a children's cancer center. The Children's Hospital of Philadelphia, for example, diagnoses about 250 cases of childhood cancer each year and cares for a total of about 1,500 children with various cancers. "And there's no question that if you do something a lot, you do it better than if you do it less often," says Dr. Anna Meadows.

A second reason for obtaining treatment from a children's cancer center relates to the differences between children and adults. Not only are their diseases different, but their general medical, social, and emotional needs are different too.

Francie recalls a time when she and her husband decided to get their six-year-old daughter, Libby, treated at their local community hospital rather than driving three hours to Philadelphia. What had become almost routine at The Children's Hospital—chemotherapy plus a blood transfusion when Libby's platelets were low—turned into an ordeal at the local hospital. First, says Francie, the atmosphere was different. "Adults moan and groan about getting chemotherapy much more than kids do," she says. But even more troubling, the medical staff was not accustomed to the medical needs of her daughter and they were not experienced in dealing with discomfort and anxiety in an eight-year-old.

The third reason for obtaining care at a children's cancer center is that this is where new treatments are tested. The importance of participating in trials of new therapies goes beyond finding what is best for your child, say pediatric oncologists. "This is how we acquire enough information to arrive at the best treatments of the future," says Dr. Meadows.

## Choosing a Children's Cancer Center

For many parents geography will determine their choice of a cancer center. Your family physician or the doctor who diagnosed your child will usually make arrangements for you to be seen at that hospital. If you are not satisfied with your physician's choice, ask for names of other institutions and physicians who treat the type of cancer your child has.

Sometimes your doctor will recommend that you consult or receive treatment from a physician or hospital that is very far away, even though another children's cancer center may be closer. This is particularly true for very rare cancers or for cancers that have been unresponsive to standard therapy but for which an investigational therapy is being tested only at certain locations. If this kind of specialized treatment is necessary, you may be able to get most of your treatment closer to home and only occasional treatments far away. Obtaining care at two different institutions can create some additional logistical problems for your family, but in many cases the problems will be outweighed by the benefits of being close to home at least part of the time.

Dr. Giulio D'Angio recalled such a case. A child from New York who had lost a kidney to cancer three years earlier had developed cancer in his remaining kidney. The Children's Hospital of Philadelphia had developed a novel technique for treating cases like this without removing the remaining kidney. The technique involved removing the tumor and inserting a radioactive source into the kidney to destroy any remaining tumor cells. Dr. D'Angio consulted with the child's physician and arranged everything that was necessary—including the urologic surgeon, radiation therapist, and oncologist—before the child came to Philadelphia. Then, once the child had recovered sufficiently, he was discharged back to his home to receive continuing care at the hospital where he was originally treated.

"Our goal is to try to keep the family and the referring physician together as a unit," says D'Angio. "We bring them here only when we believe there is something we can do very particularly or if parents insist on coming here for one reason or another. We try to discourage them from doing so, because it's costly and disruptive for a family to come long distances. We therefore work very closely with the referring physician for continuing care to be given in the community whenever possible."

If you decide to travel far from home to get treatment for your child, you will need to find out about support services that are available, both in your hometown and at the hospital you have chosen. The hospital will have social workers and/or psychologists who can help you identify and obtain the services you need. In your home community these services may include an array of social service and mental health agencies not associated with a hospital. You may have to leave other family members, including young children, at home. Refer to chapter 11 for more information about the special needs of siblings.

At some point in your diagnosis/treatment odyssey you may want to get a second opinion. Doctors today are accustomed to such requests from parents and will provide you with lists of other experts in the relevant field. However, you should be aware that specialists are not always unanimous in their opinions about the best treatments available. Thus if you call three or four different doctors, you may be confronted with three or four different opinions about the best plan. Each doctor's opinion may be valid, says Dr. D'Angio. "It may be that treatment A is very much better at one hospital while treatment B may be very much better at another." Furthermore, some doctors may be unfamiliar with new or experimental therapies that are offered at only a few institutions. Fundamentally, says Dr. D'Angio, your choice may come down to a question of trust. "Parents will have to make a decision based on how they feel about the institution and the people they have met."

## Participating in Clinical Trials

One of the first decisions you may be asked to make after admission to a children's cancer center is whether to participate in a trial of a new treatment approach. Some parents balk at the idea of participating in clinical studies. They say, "I just want the best treatment for my child and I don't want him to be a guinea pig."

Dr. Richard Womer has this response: "I tell them, 'We would love to give the best treatment if we knew what it was. But in my view, we're not going to have the best treatment until we can cure one hundred percent of the patients one hundred percent of the time with no side effects. And until then, we have an obligation to try to learn something from every patient we take care of.' "

Clinical research trials of new children's cancer therapies are carried out under the auspices of several collaborative research organizations, such as the Children's Cancer Group (CCG) in the United States. Doctors and scientists from over one hundred institutions participate in research protocols through the CCG. Another large American research group is the Pediatric Oncology Group (POG). By carrying out research through these organizations, large numbers of patients can be enrolled in a particular study, making it possible to obtain answers more quickly and with greater certainty than would be possible if individual researchers carried out separate trials. Most trials involve hundreds of children and take three to five years just to accumulate the necessary numbers to make statistics meaningful.

Over the past thirty years clinical research has made possible dramatic improvements in cure rates, but the changes have come gradually. Says Dr. Womer, "We make this slow leapfrogging progress. There very rarely are breakthroughs, just what often seem like little tiny baby steps. And after a whole lot of these steps, you've gotten somewhere."

For example, by 1960 several drugs had been discovered to treat ALL. By testing different combinations of them researchers had determined that certain drugs were useful in the early days of treatment while others were effective later on when only a few stray leukemic cells remained. Still most children with ALL died from the disease when it reappeared in the central nervous system. Then another step was tested which seemed to prevent CNS recurrence. This step was further refined and today is the basis for modern treatment of ALL—treatment that leads to cure in nearly 70 percent of affected children.

Clinical studies are divided into Phase I–, II–, or III–type investigations. Phase I and II trials are designed to gather preliminary information about new or unproven therapies. Therefore these trials are only offered to a limited number of patients for whom all proven alternatives have failed. Phase I studies try to determine the appropriate dosages and risks of new therapies. When doses and toxicity are determined, the drug moves into a Phase II study, which tests the effectiveness of the drug against specific tumors. It is only after a new therapy has passed these two phases that it can move into Phase III clinical trials, in which the treatment is compared to the existing standard treatment. When a child is offered a Phase I or II therapy, the parents are told that the treatment may be of no benefit to their child, but that the information gained will further knowledge about potential benefits of the therapy being tested.

Phase III clinical trials are usually designed with two "arms," with patients assigned randomly to one or the other. One arm consists of the standard treatment; the other arm is some variation of that standard. "It's something that we have reason to believe is better, based on preliminary data," says Dr. Womer. "Sometimes it is better, sometimes it isn't. And once in a while the investigational arm turns out to be worse, but that doesn't happen very often." Sometimes the investigational treatment turns out to have unexpected or undesirable side effects.

For some types of cancer for which the cure rates are already high, the test arm may call for a reduction in therapy, with the goal of reducing side effects. For example, in the third National Wilms' Tumor Study (NWTS) one of the proven antitumor drugs, doxorubicin, was eliminated in some groups of patients because of its potential for causing heart problems. No negative side effects had been seen in children receiving this drug as it was given in the NWTS, according to Dr. D'Angio. But there was evidence that the drug damaged a certain number of muscle cells in the heart.

"We weren't reassured by what we found five or ten years after treatment; we were concerned about what might happen when the patient was fifty or sixty years old," says Dr. D'Angio. Studies in England had suggested that another one of the chemotherapy agents—vincristine—could be intensified. Thus the trial was designed to see whether increasing vincristine and decreasing doxorubicin would maintain the overall cure rate. The results of the trial showed that for at least two categories of disease the elimination of doxorubicin had not worsened the outcome. For the third category the results were less clear, so the drug is still used for those children.

"It's really a tribute to the physicians looking after these children, and to the parents, that they were willing to do a study to see whether you could eliminate what was shown to be an effective drug," says Dr. D'Angio. "I think that's the spirit of clinical trials—that people are trying to find out what is better, not only in terms of cure, but better in every sense of the word."

Dr. Womer emphasizes that these trials simply provide guidelines for treatment. "No matter what a study says, the patient *always* comes first. We won't do something to a patient's detriment just because it says to do it in the protocol. We take kids off study all the time when they have unacceptable toxicity or if the study doesn't work for them for some other reason."

Choosing whether to participate in a clinical trial can be a difficult decision. Doctors who participate in these investigations are required to provide extensive information to parents about the potential risks and benefits of the treatment and about what parents can expect in terms of treatment schedules, diagnostic tests, side effects, and so on. They must also inform parents that the treatment is not known to be better than standard therapy. This process that doctors must go through is called *informed consent.* It can be a disconcerting experience for parents who feel ill equipped to understand the lengthy documents they are given. Dr. D'Angio, in fact, maintains that it is nearly impossible to obtain consent that is truly informed and understood, given the complex medical issues involved. "We go through the very complete consent form in detail and provide them with a copy to take home, to read and reread as necessary. We try to be sure they understand the broad outlines and the reasons for the study before asking that the form is signed."

Doctors are required by law to obtain written consent before they can use an experimental treatment. However, even when parents sign such a document, they are not bound to the treatment and can opt out at any time. The document simply certifies that the procedures have been fully explained.

## Coping with the Hospital

When your child is first diagnosed and then periodically throughout the course of treatment, you can expect to spend many hours, days, or even weeks at the hospital. Much will be expected of you, both in terms of helping your child and in terms of fitting yourself and your family into the hospital environment.

### *PARTICIPATING IN YOUR CHILD'S CARE*

You will probably be asked to become an active participant in your child's care. However, your degree of participation will depend on both your child's needs and your own willingness and ability to help with specific aspects of his care.

Says Oncology Clinical Nurse Specialist Patricia Brophy, "We invite parents to participate at any level that they want. I think most parents would be here all that they can, but they deal with things like looking after other children, jobs, paying the bills, and doing the wash, and so they tend not to spend all of their time here. And there is a healthy aspect to getting out of the hospital for a period of time."

Some parents, says Brophy, will take on many of the physical tasks involved in their child's care, such as bathing, brushing teeth, and so on. Other parents prefer not to get involved in this way but will entertain their child for hours on end. Both approaches are valuable for parents and children alike. Children want and need their care to be provided by parents, and parents want and need to care for their children. In either case, Brophy says, it is important for parents to encourage their child to develop trust in the nursing staff, "because sooner or later the child is going to need that trust."

One of the first things you may be asked to do is to keep a journal of all your child's medications, treatments, and reactions to those treatments. Zach says this is just what happened when his twelve-year-old son, Chad, was first diagnosed with leukemia. "Our first response was, 'We're never going to be able to keep track of all this. And besides, isn't it the hospital's job?' " recalled Zach. "But we learned that we do need to keep track and that it was good for us to do it."

### *HOSPITAL CHAOS*

There will probably be a large number of professionals involved in your child's care, not only oncologists, nurses, and psychosocial professionals but also a number of other specialists in areas such as radiology, anesthesiology, neurology, nephrology, nutrition, and others. Further, in large medical centers, most of which are teaching hospitals, a team of attending physicians, postdoctoral fellows, and residents may care for your child. The *attending physician* directs the care and coordinates the several activities entailed. *Fellows* are fully trained physicians who have chosen to specialize in oncology and are completing further training in that field. *Residents* are physicians in training to become pediatricians.

Attendings, fellows, and residents rotate among their duties in the hospital, clinic, and research laboratories. Thus the physician who is caring for your child when she is first admitted may not be the one caring for her later on. Likewise the nursing staff will change as shifts and schedules change.

Ideally this large retinue of care providers will make you feel supported. But whenever you have a large number of professionals interacting with you and your child, there are bound to be some breakdowns—miscommunications and overlaps—that lead you to feel that you are falling through the cracks. The professionals you will be dealing with know this about their institutions, and they will usually sympathize with you when things aren't going smoothly. More important, they can help you plug up the leaks and straighten out miscommunications. Your responsibility in this is to tell someone when your needs aren't being met.

The psychosocial and nursing staff can be particularly helpful in this regard. They can help explain medical facts presented to you by your child's doctors and they can help you remember exactly what the doctor said. In addition they can help you deal with stress and anxiety and can help resolve inconsistent messages you may receive from the many people involved in your child's care. As described in chapter 1, no one really expects you to remember everything you are told, particularly in the early days of your child's illness. The doctors and nurses expect you to have many questions, and it is their job to answer them.

Nurse Brophy cautions, however, that issues of medical care can rarely be seen in black and white. So, despite the efforts at teamwork, you may hear several different treatment plans discussed by different members of the team. "Families get extremely frustrated," she says. "Part of good care is straightening out our act so that we don't put families in that bind."

*RULES AND REGULATIONS*

Many children's hospitals, including The Children's Hospital of Philadelphia, will allow one parent to sleep in the child's room at night. This can allay anxiety in parent and child alike. However, it may also pose additional problems and exacerbate the intensity of the hospital experience. Hospital stays require close interaction with other families, who may have totally different backgrounds, values, and ways of dealing with stress. To some extent you will have little control over this aspect of hospital life, although the staff may make rooming adjustments if you ask. For example Sherry and Donna, two mothers in the hospital with their baby daughters who had cancer, requested a room together and developed a close friendship—finding that they were able to support each other through stressful times. At the other end of the spectrum, Francie requested and got a move away from the family with whom she was sharing a room. Their constant arguing, no doubt an expression of their own fear and distress, elevated Francie's own anxiety to a near breaking point. Luckily another room was available at that time, which made the move possible.

In order for hospitals to cope with cancer and other illnesses that involve entire families, rules are needed. Generally visitation by parents is allowed twenty-four hours a day. However, limits may be placed on other visitors, particularly children. At The Children's Hospital of Philadelphia, for example, siblings under the age of fourteen are not allowed unless prior permission is obtained. In implementing the rule Ms. Brophy says that the nursing staff tries to strike a balance between the emotional needs of the child-patient and his family and the medical needs of all the children on the floor.

"If a child is away from home for a long time, his brothers and sisters need to have some access to him," says Nurse Brophy. "But we need to balance that with the real hazards of having children on the floor. If kids are there and are not supervised, they can become an impediment to safe care. And the other real issue is infection. There is no possible way that we can adequately screen every child who comes into the environment. Measles on the floor could kill a couple of our kids, and chicken pox is a pain in the neck, as well as potentially life threatening."

## Getting Care Outside of the Hospital

Once a child's treatment program has been clearly established, many aspects of your child's care can be managed in a nonhospital setting—either in a clinic or at home. You will need to be educated in certain aspects of that care, such as how to recognize problems and what to do when they arise. You will also probably be taught to perform certain procedures so that your child can return home. These matters are discussed in the next section of this book.

CHAPTER 4

# Total Care—A Multimodal Approach to Treatment

The basic approach to treating children with cancer has not changed significantly over the last twenty years, says Dr. Anna T. Meadows. Today, as in the 1970s, chemotherapy, radiation therapy, and surgery form the basis of most therapeutic regimens. What has changed, however, is the precision with which treatment is delivered. "In the seventies we just wanted to cure as many kids as we could. In the last ten years we've been looking at how we can tailor our treatment to be more precise. We'd like to use pistols rather than shotguns," she says.

The pistols that oncologists have developed include a few new drugs. But even more important have been the realizations that different types of cancer vary in their responses to different anticancer agents and that combinations of drugs in many cases work better than single agents. In the area of radiation therapy new techniques have been developed that allow more precise delivery of radiation or that allow higher doses of radiation to be used safely.

Today most cancers are treated with multiple therapeutic modalities, with regimens tailored to take maximum advantage of the different approaches and the interactions between various methods. In some cases tailoring treatment means reducing or eliminating certain elements of the treatment program, while in other cases it means adding therapeutic options that were previously thought unnecessary. For example radiation therapy is known to be particularly damaging to children and therefore it is avoided whenever possible. With some types of cancer, such as Wilms' tumor, radiation was thought to be the most effective therapy available; however, through extensive research into the risks associated with various subtypes of Wilms', doctors can now identify the many patients who have a relatively good prognosis even when radiation therapy is not used. Conversely, doctors formerly thought that some forms of cancer could be totally eliminated with surgery, but more recently they have realized that it is necessary to add chemotherapy to the regimen to prevent later recurrences and metastases.

Along with these changes in the way traditional cancer treatments are delivered, there have been some new weapons in the oncologist's arsenal. Bone marrow transplantation, although developed back in the early sixties, has only in the last few years become standard therapy for some types of leukemia and is now also sometimes applied to other types of cancer as well. Meanwhile immunologists have been busy developing therapies that stimulate a patient's own immune system to eliminate cancer cells.

These are just a few examples of the developments over

the last two decades that have led to the significantly improved cure rates discussed in chapter 1. But of equal importance to these new treatments are ancillary methods of supporting patients through their various therapy regimens. These methods include aggressive antibiotic therapy, provision of blood products, treatment of pain, and nutritional supplementation.

Chapters 5 through 8 discuss these various aspects of treatment. But first some basic information about the care your child will receive.

## The Road Map

When you first receive your child's diagnosis, your doctor will most likely sketch out a broad outline of the therapeutic plan. Sometimes referred to as *road maps,* these plans vary significantly depending on the type of cancer a child has. Furthermore much of what you are told at this early stage will be somewhat tentative and may need revision depending on the side effects your child encounters and how your child responds to early treatment. If your child is enrolled in a clinical trial, her care will be guided by a very specific *protocol,* or plan. This protocol is written to ensure that all participants in the study follow the same treatment course so that legitimate conclusions can be drawn from the results. You will be required to sign an informed-consent form indicating that you understand the benefits and risks of the treatments proposed. However, as mentioned earlier, your child can be taken off the study at any time if he seems to be responding unfavorably or if he is experiencing serious side effects.

During treatment your child's medical status is continuously monitored, and the road map guides therapy accordingly. Sometimes the side effects of a treatment may alter the planned course. For example chemotherapy and radiation therapy may cause too drastic a drop in the level of circulating white blood cells. When this happens, extra measures must be taken to protect the child from infection, and further chemotherapy may be delayed until the child's white blood cells have a chance to recover. In other cases the definitive treatment may not even be determined until after response to initial treatment is evaluated. This is frequently the case with bone tumors, where the extent of surgery will not be known until chemotherapy has had a chance to shrink the tumor. In other words the road map you receive in the early days of your child's therapy will not necessarily show you your ultimate destination or all the stops along the way. But it may indicate the direction in which to turn when you reach certain crossroads.

## Where Your Child Will Receive Care

Your child's diagnosis and therapy program will play an important role in determining where your child will receive care—in the hospital, in the out-patient clinic, or at home. There is often a place for all three patient-care settings in your child's treatment program, says Dr. Richard Womer. "Inpatient, outpatient, and home chemotherapy are not tightly sealed compartments. Many patients move back and forth between them." For example some patients will have treatment started in the clinic and will then check into the hospital or go home for continuation of the treatment.

The initial diagnostic workup and beginning of therapy frequently but not always entails a hospital stay, which may vary from a few days to weeks or even months. At the time of diagnosis your doctor may be able to tell you generally what to expect in terms of hospitalization. However, no one can accurately predict how your child will respond to therapy.

According to Dr. Womer, some children never require hospitalization. For example, children with Hodgkin's disease frequently receive both their diagnosis and treatment on an outpatient basis. Other children, for example those with osteosarcoma, will almost certainly require some hospitalization. A hospital stay will be required if your child needs surgery or a very complicated chemotherapy regimen, if she becomes extremely immunosuppressed and needs isolation from her normal environment, or if she needs a great deal of supportive care.

Inpatient hospitalization offers a number of benefits. At the hospital your child will receive constant care and surveillance, and rapid response if she has any adverse reactions. It also gives you greater access to other specialists who can be of great support to you and your child: child life specialists, social workers, psychologists, nutritionists, and so on. And nurses and doctors will always be available to answer your questions.

On the downside, hospital stays can be very stressful for your entire family. Your child will probably want you to stay with her most of the time, and some institutions expect this from parents. Parents work this out in a number of ways. Sometimes one parent will take an extended leave of absence from work or quit a job completely in order to be at the hospital. In other families parents take turns staying with the child. In either case one or both parents may be pulled away from the rest of the family for an extended period of time. Other children, then, not only miss their sibling who is sick and away at the hospital but miss their parents too. And of course the parent's life is turned upside down as well.

Some chemotherapy regimens and most radiation therapy can be delivered in an outpatient setting. Outpatient clinics offer some of the same advantages as do hospitals—skilled nursing care and access to a variety of specialists and technologies. In addition the setting is often less stressful. However, to obtain care in an outpatient clinic requires frequent, sometimes daily, trips to the facility. For patients who live some distance from the clinic, this may cause great difficulty. Furthermore even when insurance will pay for outpatient care, it rarely pays out-of-pocket expenses, which can become daunting.

For many families home care can be a good alternative. It offers your child the most normal environment possible, which can alleviate his anxiety, stress, and fear. It offers you the opportunity to stay connected with other family members, friends, and neighbors.

Yet home care carries a tremendous responsibility. Even though you may have frequent visits from a home care nurse, you will be in large measure responsible for your child's basic physical and medical care, and it will be up to you to recognize potential problems. Further, with all the extra equipment and supplies needed, your home may come to resemble a hospital. Caring for a child at home almost always adds stress to a household. For some families the benefits may outweigh the added burden. However, other families may find the added burden simply too much to handle. Some hospitals, such as The Children's Hospital of Philadelphia, have a home care division through which home care can be coordinated. There are also independent home care companies that provide services. Your doctor, nurse, and/or the psychosocial staff at the hospital should be able to put you in contact with home care specialists who can help you determine if it is a realistic alternative.

If you are considering home care, here are some of the

factors you may want to consider: How much of the expense of home care will your insurance cover? How comfortable are you with attending to your child's medical and physical needs? Depending on your child's treatment program, you may be required to give injections or hook up an intravenous infusion of fluids or medications to the central venous catheter, draw blood, keep track of urine output, and give other medications that your child may resist. Do you have space and other necessary facilities to store medicines properly and to set up a "mini" laboratory? How much support can you expect from other family members and friends? Usually at least two adults who are capable of delivering care must be available.

The decision about where your child will receive care is usually made by your physician in consultation with the entire treatment team, including home care specialists. Remember that you are a part of this team! Also remember that as your child proceeds through treatment, you can reevaluate the situation and change it if it doesn't seem to be working.

Every family has its own set of strengths, weaknesses, resources, and capabilities. Moreover your choice may change at different stages of your child's treatment program. For example eight-year-old Diana received her initial treatment for Ewing's sarcoma in the hospital, but found the hospital routine almost unbearable, and she longed to sleep in her own bed. Her parents opted to provide care at home. Diana's mother, Alice, quickly learned all the skills she needed to care for her daughter at home but, after several months of home care, decided that for her the process was overwhelming. A better option for Alice and Diana was to drive nearly two hours in each direction for five days in a row, and then to spend the entire day at the clinic while Diana received her chemotherapy. Alice, who stopped working when her daughter got sick, feels that the clinic visits are worth the hassle because Diana sleeps better in her own bed and the family gets weekends together.

## Procedures, Procedures, and More Procedures

Twelve-year old Chad came to The Children's Hospital of Philadelphia after his pediatrician had detected abnormal blood counts. Chad had been feeling tired for a few weeks, but other than that had no obvious signs of illness; yet his doctor wanted to "rule out leukemia." When the doctor at Children's wanted to do a bone marrow aspirate, Chad's first reaction was, "Can you knock me out?" But the doctor told Chad the procedure would be over quickly, and it was. Unfortunately the results confirmed the pediatrician's suspicion, and Chad began a seemingly endless series of procedures. Over the next few weeks Chad endured more bone marrow aspirates as well as a painful bone marrow biopsy and several spinal taps.

Chad's experience was typical for a child with leukemia. Children with other types of cancer are faced with a variety of other procedures in addition to these. In fact it is these procedures that some children and parents find to be the most difficult part of having cancer. And it doesn't end when a firm diagnosis is reached. Throughout the treatment and follow-up phases of the illness, more procedures will be required as the health care team tries to monitor a child's response to treatment.

The procedures that your child will have to undergo will vary depending on the type of cancer he has. Children with leukemia require frequent bone marrow aspirates, bone marrow biopsies, and lumbar punctures (spinal taps). Children with solid tumors will need many of these same procedures as well as biopsies and various imaging studies, including X rays, CT (computed tomography) scans, MRI (magnetic resonance imaging), ultrasound, and bone scans. And nearly all children with cancer will be poked and prodded in numerous other ways. Strong pain medicines, such as morphine, and sedatives are often given to relieve the pain and anxiety associated with procedures. Sometimes general anesthesia may be necessary. Relaxation therapy and hypnosis may also be helpful. These measures are discussed more fully in chapter 8.

### *BLOOD TESTS*

Probably the first and most frequent procedure your child will face is a blood analysis. Nurses or specially trained blood-drawers (called *phlebotomists)* will draw blood through a needle inserted into a vein, or will obtain just a few drops of blood by puncturing the skin with a sharp lancet. Usually this is done on a finger (a *finger stick),* or in babies from the heel (a *heel stick).* The blood is sent to a laboratory for a *complete blood count,* a test that measures the various components of the blood. As your child goes through diagnosis and treatment, you will become familiar with the terms listed in Table 1 and with the expected results.

### *INTRAVENOUS LINES*

Many children with cancer will need frequent intravenous injections of chemotherapy, nutritional solutions, and/or blood transfusions. In order to avoid the need for the frequent placement of needles into a vein, a procedure that can be painful, difficult, and upsetting, many children receive *indwelling catheters.* These are thin tubes (catheters) that are placed into one of the major blood vessels leading to the heart and that exit the body at the skin surface, usually on the

TABLE 4.1
**Interpreting a Complete Blood Count**

| Blood Component | Meaning | Normal Range | Areas of Concern |
|---|---|---|---|
| Hemoglobin (Hgb) | Measures oxygen-carrying capacity of blood | 10–13 gm/100 ml | Low values (less than 8.5) may suggest need for transfusion of packed red blood cells. |
| Hematocrit (Hct) | Percentage of blood made up of red blood cells; also a measure of oxygen-carrying capacity | 35%–49% in children; 49%–54% in newborns | |
| White Blood Cells (total) | Indication of body's ability to fight infection | 5,000–10,000, but in child receiving chemotherapy: 2,000–5,000 | Low values indicate a high risk of infection. |
| Neutrophils (expressed as ANC—absolute neutrophil count) | Indication of body's ability to fight bacterial infection | Approx. 1,500–7,000; infants normally have lower counts than adults | ANC of less than 500 means child is at high risk of infection. |
| Platelets | Helps blood clot | 150,000–400,000 | If counts fall below 20,000, a platelet transfusion may be needed |

chest. The most commonly used types are called Broviac or Hickman catheters. These devices provide easy access to the bloodstream—doctors and nurses can both draw blood and give injections into the catheter without having to stick another needle into a vein. They are placed during a surgical procedure, usually under general anesthetic.

Indwelling catheters have proved very beneficial for children with cancer because they significantly reduce the pain and stress associated with getting frequent IV treatments. Yet they are not without problems. Because they pierce the body's protective covering (the skin), they can provide an entryway for infectious agents into the body. For this reason the access site on the child's body must be kept scrupulously clean, with frequent changes in the sterile dressing that covers it and flushing of the outer part of the line with a sterile solution. If an infection does develop, it can quickly spread throughout the body. Therefore any sign of infection in a child with an indwelling catheter must be given prompt attention and may require hospitalization. If your child gets an indwelling catheter, you will be instructed in its care and in how to recognize problems.

### *SPINAL TAP (LUMBAR PUNCTURE), BONE MARROW ASPIRATE, AND BONE MARROW BIOPSY*

A spinal tap is done to test the fluid that surrounds and bathes the brain and spinal cord. When cancer has spread to the central nervous system, abnormal cells can often be detected in this fluid. To obtain a sample of the fluid, a doctor or nurse inserts a needle between the bones of the spine and into the space around the spinal cord and then withdraws a small portion of the fluid.

Spinal taps can be somewhat painful and very anxiety-provoking. Usually the nurse or doctor will anesthetize the skin around the insertion site to help reduce the pain. The child must hold very still in a curled position while the needle is inserted.

The bone marrow aspirate and bone marrow biopsy can be even more painful and upsetting. Often a child will be sedated before undergoing a bone marrow aspirate or biopsy. These tests are done so that pathologists can examine the bone marrow directly for evidence of cancer.

Bone marrow can be found in the hollows of many large bones, but it is easiest to obtain from the hip bone. For a bone marrow aspirate the child lies facedown, sometimes with a pillow under the hips. Then a large needle is inserted through the skin and into the middle of the hipbone, and a small portion of the bone marrow is withdrawn. The procedure for a bone marrow biopsy is similar, except that the needle is larger and a small piece of bone is removed along with the marrow. Bone marrow aspirate results will be available within a few hours; biopsy results may take several days.

For any of these tests children often want their parents to be with them. However, in order for parents to be an asset rather than a hindrance for these procedures, they must stay calm and reassuring. For some parents this is no easy task, as the procedures often look as painful as they must feel. The treatment team can work with parents on learning to maintain their composure so that they can be a tremendous source of support to their children. They can, for instance, guide their children through behavioral methods of managing pain (see chapter 8).

### *IMAGING STUDIES*

Generally, imaging studies are not painful, although they may provoke significant anxiety in children (and adults!). Some of these studies will require injections of substances that enhance the images. If the study requires the child to stay still for a prolonged period of time, sedatives may be used.

**Plain film X rays** are the most familiar type of imaging tool and are widely used in children with cancer. In fact in many hospitals chest X rays are routine for any child being admitted. X rays are also used to look for evidence of abnormal growths or obstructions in many parts of the body. The pictures produced are two-dimensional, with relatively poor resolution when compared with the newer imaging techniques, CT and MRI (see below).

The type of radiation used for producing X rays can be hazardous, although at the doses used diagnostically it is relatively safe as long as precautions are followed. After a person has an X ray, he is not radioactive. For some types of X rays your child will need to drink or be injected with a solution that will increase contrast in the resulting pictures. These solutions do not themselves contain radioactive substances and are relatively safe, with infrequent side effects. Your radiologist will explain the risks of the procedure.

**Ultrasound** is an imaging technique that uses sound waves to produce pictures of internal structures, especially in the abdomen. The test is totally noninvasive and considered completely harmless. The person who is conducting the ultrasound scan will spread gel over the area of the body that is being imaged; then she will move a small electronic device called a transducer over the body. The transducer produces sound waves that penetrate the body and are then reflected back as "echoes" when they reach certain structures, such as tumors. Air, such as is found in the lungs or sometimes in the bowel, and bone interfere with the transmission of sound waves. This limits the usefulness of ultrasound as a diagnostic technique. In addition the quality of the pictures is poor when compared with CT or MRI, which are described below.

**Computed tomography (CT)** uses X rays to produce

three-dimensional pictures with great detail and resolution. The CT scanner is a huge machine that moves back and forth over your child while pictures are taken. A scan may take about thirty minutes, during which you will not be allowed to stay with your child because of the risk of exposing you unnecessarily to radiation. Sometimes young children are sedated for CT scans. In addition contrast agents such as those described for plain film X rays may be used in conjunction with CT.

**Magnetic resonance imaging (MRI)** is a newer technique that for many uses has proved superior to CT. In addition, the technique is considered safer because it does not use x-rays. A contrast agent is sometimes needed. MRI exposes the patient to powerful magnetic fields and radiofrequency energy, both of which appear to be safe.

If your child is having an MRI scan, he will first need to remove all jewelry, retainers, watches, or anything else metallic. Dental braces are not a problem. Then he will lie on a flat surface that can be pushed inside a huge cylindrical magnet. When he is properly positioned, the scan starts. Your child will hear a loud thumping noise, followed by other rhythmic beats. MRI requires the child to keep still for as long as thirty to ninety minutes. For this reason young children are sometimes sedated. Some people feel too confined or claustrophobic inside the magnet. If this is true for your child, behavioral techniques may help, or he may be given drugs that will help him relax.

**Bone scanning** is a test used to see whether cancer has spread to the bones. In this type of test a radioactive substance is injected into the patient's veins. This substance has an affinity for areas of bone in which active growth is taking place, such as a tumor. However, there are other reasons that bone can attract the substance; therefore any positive result on a bone scan must be further evaluated by other tests.

When your child comes in for a bone scan, she will be injected with the substance. After about three hours she will be placed on a table while a device called a scintillation camera takes pictures that will show where the radioactive compound has gone. This takes about thirty to sixty minutes, during which the child must lie very still. Sedation may be required. The scintillation camera does not use X rays, and the radioactivity of the test substance fades quickly with time. The levels of radioactivity are not hazardous to your child or to others nearby.

This is by no means a complete list of all the procedures your child will encounter. If you have any questions about procedures being performed on your child, your doctor or nurse will be able to explain. The more questions you ask and the more informed you become, the better able you will be to become an active participant in your child's treatment team.

## CHAPTER 5

# Chemotherapy, Radiation Therapy, and Surgery

Most children's cancers are treated with chemotherapy, radiation therapy, and/or surgery. Each of these therapies has specific benefits but may also have significant unpleasant side effects. Moreover, when the therapies are used in combination, both the benefits and the side effects may be intensified.

When your child's therapy program is mapped out, your doctor will provide you with information about the specific components of that program, including the side effects your child may experience. This chapter does not attempt to give you that kind of specific information. Rather we discuss these therapies in a general manner, which may help you interpret the information you receive and seek remedies for some of your child's difficulties.

## Chemotherapy

In 1948 Dr. Sidney Farber at Children's Medical Center in Boston described how a drug called aminopterin could induce temporary remission in children with leukemia. Thus began the modern age of chemotherapy for childhood cancer. Farber had shown that aminopterin resulted in an improvement in survival time, but eventually all the patients relapsed, and most died as their cancers became resistant to the drug. In addition many children experienced severe side effects. These two problems—resistance and toxicity—guided research over the next forty years.

Survival statistics gradually improved as new drugs with varying degrees of effectiveness were developed. More important, combinations of these drugs proved to be significantly better than drugs given alone, in terms of both avoiding resistance and minimizing toxicity. Another major improvement came in the 1960s when treatments were developed to attack stray leukemia cells that were hiding in the central nervous system (CNS), protected from drugs that circulated in the bloodstream.

These two major advances—multiagent chemotherapy and preventive (prophylactic) CNS treatment—were "giant steps" on the path to dramatically improved survival statistics for children with leukemia. And they were accompanied by many other significant advances. Even today new agents are being sought to increase survival and decrease toxic reactions.

Chemotherapy is the cornerstone of treatment for the various leukemias and for many other cancers. In addition chemotherapy is often used to supplement other treatments such as surgery or radiation therapy. For example a common therapy regimen for some solid tumors calls for an intense period of chemotherapy following surgery. The rationale for this form of chemotherapy—known as *adjuvant* chemotherapy—is that after the bulk of the tumor has been removed or destroyed through surgery or radiation, chemotherapy can seek out and destroy stray cancer cells that have escaped into the bloodstream. Thus spread of the tumor is prevented.

Adjuvant chemotherapy has led to dramatically improved survival statistics for many types of pediatric cancer, including Wilms' tumor, Ewing's sarcoma, osteosarcoma, rhabdomyosarcoma, lymphomas, and brain tumors.

Chemotherapy may also be used prior to surgery to shrink a tumor so that it can be more safely and effectively removed. This is called *neoadjuvant* chemotherapy. Sometimes this makes less radical surgical procedures possible. For example in some cases of osteosarcoma, neoadjuvant chemotherapy can sometimes shrink the tumor enough so that the affected bone can be removed and replaced with an artificial bone, thus avoiding the need for amputation of the limb.

For children with brain tumors chemotherapy can reduce or delay the need for radiation therapy, leading to a better long-term outcome. Later in this chapter the risks associated with radiation therapy are discussed.

### *HOW CHEMOTHERAPY WORKS AND WHY IT SOMETIMES DOESN'T WORK*

Different chemotherapeutic agents work through different mechanisms. Most anticancer drugs exert their effects by interfering with a cell's ability to reproduce. In order for a cell to grow and divide, it goes through a series of steps in which the genetic material (the DNA) in the nucleus is replicated, transcribed into a form that is readable by the cell's protein-making machinery, and then translated into the proteins needed for various cell functions. Some anticancer agents interfere with DNA replication, others with the transcription process, and others with translation. Still others interfere with the function of the proteins themselves.

The cellular machinery just described is extraordinarily resourceful when a drug interferes with one step in this process; the cell can often find a way to get around the problem. This is what happens when a tumor cell becomes resistant to a certain agent. The ability of cells to become resistant has several important ramifications when it comes to developing effective anticancer regimens. First, by using multiple drugs that interfere at different parts of the cell cycle, even if resistance to one drug develops, the cell is likely to remain sensitive to other drugs. This realization led to combination chemotherapy, which has proven to be superior to single-agent therapy. (Combination chemotherapy also benefits from the fact that sometimes multiple drugs interact so that their combined effectiveness is even better than their additive effects would be.) Second, if cells are hit very hard in the beginning of treatment, they may be destroyed before they have a chance to develop resistance. This explains why initial treatment is often very intense. Third, even if a cancer becomes resistant to one set of drugs, it may still be sensitive to another set. This is why chemotherapy regimens may change over the course of a child's treatment. Nevertheless it is true that the first try offers the best hope for eradicating cancer.

Since chemotherapeutic agents attack cells during division, it is only actively proliferating cells that are sensitive to the drugs. Tumor cells generally divide much more rapidly than normal cells; thus they are more sensitive to chemotherapy. But certain types of normal cells also divide rapidly and therefore are also damaged by chemotherapy. These include cells in the bone marrow, hair cells, and the cells of mucous membranes. As a result some of the most common side effects of chemotherapy include depletion of various types of blood cells, hair loss, and breakdown of the mucosal linings of the mouth and digestive tract.

### *HOW MUCH CHEMOTHERAPY IS NEEDED?*

In determining the dose of drug to be used, doctors refer to the *therapeutic index.* This term describes a ratio between the dose of drug that will achieve a satisfactory response and the dose at which significant side effects will occur.

In order to achieve the best results, many chemotherapy regimens will maximize the dose intensity, particularly in the beginning. This has become possible because of improvements in methods for supporting a child through the side effects. These improvements include new drugs and other techniques for dealing with nausea and vomiting and new agents that promote the replenishment of depleted bone marrow cells (supportive care is discussed in chapter 8). In addition, when cancer cells are found only in the central nervous system, drugs can be injected directly into the spinal column (this is called *intrathecal injection),* rather than into the entire body. This not only allows for delivery of the drug directly to where it's needed but also avoids the *blood-brain barrier,* a barrier in the central nervous system that prevents substances or organisms that are circulating in the blood from reaching the brain.

Chemotherapy regimens vary over time and depending on the disease being treated. For example chemotherapy for leukemia is typically divided into four treatment stages:

TABLE 5.1

| | |
|---|---|
| Induction of remission | Combinations of drugs given in high doses to eliminate most leukemia cells. |
| Consolidation | After remission is achieved, some leukemia cells still remain. More high-dose chemotherapy is given to eradicate these cells. |
| CNS preventive therapy | Intrathecal chemotherapy and/or cranial irradiation may be given to prevent central nervous system relapse of leukemia. |
| Maintenance | Lower dose, less toxic chemotherapy will be given for up to several years to prevent relapse. |

The doses of chemotherapy required to battle different types of cancer vary. Better diagnostic techniques, including molecular biologic analysis of specific genetic defects, now allow doctors in some cases to determine whether a particular cancer is at high or low risk of returning after initial remission is achieved. A cancer determined to be at *high risk,* then, might be treated with more aggressive therapy; while one at *low risk* might require less. As a result of the better classification of these different subtypes, today children with some high-risk cancers have the same likelihood of cure as children with low-risk subtypes. The difference, however, is in the treatments used.

### *HOW IS CHEMOTHERAPY GIVEN?*

Chemotherapy is usually given by mouth or intravenously. Some drugs may also be given by injection into a muscle (intramuscularly) or under the skin (subcutaneously) or by direct injection into the spinal canal (intrathecally). The mode of administration depends on the drug being given and the dose needed. Intravenous chemotherapy may require infusion of the drug over several hours or even days. This may mean that your child is hospitalized for the treatments, or that you must spend several hours at a time in the clinic, or that you supervise chemotherapy treatments at home. Your doctor should be able to tell you what you can expect in this regard.

### *SIDE EFFECTS OF CHEMOTHERAPY*

For many children the side effects of chemotherapy seem almost worse than the disease itself. Not only do therapeutic drugs damage normal tissues as well as cancer cells, but the drugs also have direct toxic effects on normal cells. Further, the chemotherapeutic drugs may interact with other drugs the child is taking. However, there are steps that can be taken to minimize your child's reactions.

Some drug reactions occur immediately or within several hours of administration of the drug. These are called *acute* reactions. Other side effects appear within weeks or months; these are referred to as *intermediate* or *delayed* reactions. *Late* reactions are those that occur many years after treatment. Less is known about late reactions because it is only relatively recently that large enough numbers of children were surviving long enough to develop late reactions. However, this is now an active area of research at many institutions, including The Children's Hospital of Philadelphia.

Most chemotherapeutic agents can cause nausea, vomiting, bone marrow depression (also called *myelosuppression),* and allergic reactions. Many also cause hair loss *(alopecia)* and mucositis. A more extensive list of possible side effects is provided in Table 5.2

TABLE 5.2

**Coping with the Common Side Effects of Chemotherapy**

| Body System | Side Effect | What May Help |
|---|---|---|
| Digestive tract | Nausea, vomiting | Antinausea drugs<br>Sedation to sleep through nausea<br>Eat lightly 3 to 4 hours before treatment<br>Eat slowly<br>Clear liquid diet<br>Rest after meals<br>Don't mix hot and cold foods<br>Avoid sweet or greasy foods |
| | Diarrhea | Avoid milk products<br>Give clear liquids (not fruit juice or sports drinks) |
| | Constipation | Increase fluids<br>Give high-fiber foods<br>Stool softeners if doctor recommends<br>Call doctor if more than 2 days go by without a bowel movement, or if child has diarrhea, abdominal pain, or hard stools |
| | Heartburn | Give $^{1}/_{2}$ glass of milk mixed with 1 or 2 tablespoons antacid<br>Avoid lying down flat immediately after eating |
| Mouth | Change in taste | Suck on sour candy ball |
| | Mouth sores | Use topical painkillers at least 1 hour before meals<br>Brush teeth with sponge toothbrush or cotton swab |

*table continues next page*

| Body System | Side Effect | What May Help |
| --- | --- | --- |
| | | Rinse mouth every 2 to 3 hours and after meals with salt water, bicarbonate (baking soda) solution, or water<br>Avoid very cold, hot, spicy, or acidic foods |
| Skin/hair | Hair loss | Use mild shampoo<br>Cut hair short<br>Avoid hair dryers, electric curlers, etc.<br>Use a satin pillow<br>Use a wide-tooth comb<br>Select a wig before all hair falls out<br>Keep head covered to prevent sunburn (in summer), heat loss (in winter)<br>Try a variety of hats, scarves, etc. |
| | Inflammation | Call doctor if redness, pain, or swelling occurs |
| | Dry, itching skin | Use mild soap and moisturizer. (If child is receiving radiation therapy, check with doctor before using moisturizer.) |
| | Moist skin | Wash 2 to 3 times each day; pat dry with clean towel or dry with a hair dryer set to coolest setting; lightly powder with cornstarch. |
| | Rashes | Doctor may prescribe medication |
| | Sun sensitivity | Avoid sun exposure; use a sunblock (at least SPF 15) |
| Bladder | Bladder irritation and infection | Force fluids on day of treatment and on days before and after treatment.<br>Avoid caffeinated beverages<br>Report to doctor increased frequency, decreased output, painful urination, or cloudy urine |

*table continues next page*

| Body System | Side Effect | What May Help |
|---|---|---|
| | Bloody or discolored urine | Drink plenty of fluids |
| Nervous system | Numbness<br>Difficulty walking<br>Hand tremors<br>Jaw pain<br>Drooping eyelids<br>Weakened hand grasp | Report symptoms to doctor |
| | Seizures | Move objects that may cause injury out of the way<br>Monitor child's breathing<br>Do not place anything in child's mouth<br>Stay calm and call for help |
| Systemic (involving the entire body) | Fever | Call doctor if temperature exceeds 100.5°F or 37.8°C<br>Do not give acetaminophen (Tylenol) unless told to do so by doctor |
| | Bone marrow depression (child has low WBCs, RBCs, platelets) | Doctor will follow closely and provide transfusions if necessary<br>Keep your child away from other children who are ill<br>Call doctor if child is exposed to known infectious illness (measles, chicken pox) or if child has increased bruising or bleeding or if child is pale, tired, and/or short of breath |
| | Allergic reaction—fever, fainting, rash, difficulty breathing | Call doctor immediately |

*table continues next page*

| Body System | Side Effect | What May Help |
|---|---|---|
| | Loss of appetite | Make eating more pleasant with soft lighting, music, friends<br>Avoid stress at mealtimes<br>Encourage child to exercise 5 to 10 minutes 1/2 hour before meals<br>Give frequent small meals and snacks<br>Encourage child to eat slowly<br>Encourage child to eat a large breakfast<br>Use foods high in protein and calories (milk shakes, peanut butter, etc.) |
| | Increased appetite, weight gain | Avoid salt and high-salt foods<br>Provide small, frequent meals<br>Use low-calorie foods |
| Other | Lung irritation—cough, shortness of breath, difficulty breathing | Report to doctor |
| | Hearing loss | Report to doctor |

Longer-term side effects include possible growth retardation and, with some drugs, possible effects on the heart, liver, and kidneys. Throughout your child's life your doctor should continue to monitor the function of these organs and your child's overall health. Long-term effects are discussed further in chapter 14.

## Radiation Therapy

Radiation therapy has proven to be a potent weapon in the fight against cancer. It combines two important attributes of surgery and chemotherapy: It aids in the local elimination of a tumor and it also kills stray cancer cells that may have spread from the primary tumor. In addition radiation treatments are painless, relatively quick, and often do not require hospitalization. However, radiation therapy presents significant risks, especially to children. Therefore it is always used with caution and may not be used at all in infants.

Radiation therapy utilizes a form of energy known as ionizing radiation. Diagnostic X rays that you or your child may have received also rely on ionizing radiation but in much lower doses. At the doses used for radiation therapy ionizing radiation has the ability to change the structure of the DNA (the genetic material) in a cell's nucleus. This does not usually lead directly to cell death, but it hampers the cell's ability to reproduce. Some cells are more sensitive than others to the damaging effects of radiation. Cells that are rapidly dividing are among the most sensitive. This includes tumor cells as well as normal cells in the bone marrow, hair follicles, and mucous membranes.

As with chemotherapy the effectiveness of radiation therapy depends on the therapeutic index, that is, a balance between the anticancer effects and the toxic side effects on normal tissue. Tumor cells are generally more sensitive to radiation than are normal cells because they divide at a faster rate. However, in growing children certain normal cells, such as those in the bones, also divide at a rapid rate. When the toxic effects on these normal cells exceeds the therapeutic benefits, radiation therapy is no longer an option. Normal cells are better able to repair radiation-induced damage to the DNA. There are also chemical differences in cells that can affect their sensitivity to radiation.

Ionizing radiation for radiation therapy may be delivered in one of two ways: either externally from a radiation-producing machine or internally by placing radiation-emitting materials into or near the tumor itself. This second form of radiation therapy, known as *brachytherapy,* is seldom used for childhood cancer.

In order to minimize the potential damage to normal tissue, radiation therapy programs use a variety of strategies. First and most important radiation is avoided or minimized as much as possible by using chemotherapy and surgery. Second, when radiation is needed, the therapy program is planned very carefully to avoid unnecessary exposure of sensitive tissue. Third, elaborate shields may be constructed to block radiation from reaching sensitive structures. And fourth, the regimen is designed to maximize the superior ability of normal tissue to repair itself. This involves dividing the necessary radiation dose into fractions and delivering those fractions at timed intervals, between which normal tissue healing can take place.

### *PREPARING FOR RADIATION THERAPY*

Although radiation treatments are not painful, they can provoke much anxiety in children and parents alike. To help allay some of your child's anxiety, your doctor may recommend a preparatory visit to the radiation therapy department. At this visit the doctor, nurse, or radiation therapist can show your child the various machines that will be used and can answer her questions. If your child wishes to do so, she may be able to climb up on the treatment table and explore the treatment room. The guide may be able to show your child that although she will be in the room alone, the doctors will always be able to see her on a monitor just outside the door. Taking the mystery out of the treatment process often allows a child to relax more during the treatment itself. This is especially important with radiation therapy because your child will need to cooperate and hold very still for as long as a few minutes during the treatment itself.

Before radiation therapy begins, your child's doctor will

plan the treatment very carefully. This process will usually involve several imaging studies, such as X rays or CT scans, which will help the doctor define precisely the area to be treated. The doctor will make tiny marks, or *tattoos,* on your child's skin to assure proper placement of the radiation beam. These marks will be practically invisible and are not painful to receive; the skin is only "pricked" as it would be if your child was receiving a TB tine test.

After the initial imaging studies, a trial run of the treatment will be done on a specially designed machine that allows the radiation therapist to "simulate" what will actually happen during radiation treatments. During this simulation your child is exposed to low doses of radiation, similar to those associated with diagnostic X rays. The simulation allows your child's doctors and other specialists to design custom-made shields and blocks that will protect sensitive tissues during treatment, and to calculate the exact dosages of radiation that will be needed.

### *THE TREATMENT ITSELF*

Radiation treatments may be scheduled every weekday for several weeks, depending on your child's cancer. They are usually done on an outpatient basis. In recent years some physicians have been delivering radiation at more frequent intervals. This strategy, called *hyperfractionation,* permits the delivery of a larger total dose but allows normal tissue repair between fractions. Hyperfractionated radiation therapy may require hospitalization. Throughout radiation therapy your child's blood counts will be monitored, and treatment may be delayed or the schedule changed if it appears that the radiation is destroying too many of the essential blood cells.

Radiation treatments are also used in conjunction with bone marrow transplantation (see chapter 6). In this case *total body irradiation (TBI)* is given in sufficiently high doses to totally destroy the patient's immune system so that the donated marrow is not rejected. Until the new marrow establishes itself, however, the patient is completely defenseless against infection. Therefore when TBI is used, the patient must be isolated in a protected environment for several weeks, and elaborate measures must be taken to protect the child from the outside world.

*SIDE EFFECTS OF RADIATION THERAPY*

The side effects of radiation therapy vary, depending on the dose, frequency of treatments, and area irradiated. The treatments themselves are painless, and your child will show no immediate visible changes. Within a few days, however, he may develop flulike symptoms including nausea, vomiting, drowsiness, irritability, and loss of appetite. Other side effects begin to appear after two or three weeks, as outlined in Table 5.3. Since the mucous membranes are extra sensitive to radiation damage, the linings of the mouth, rectum, and intestine are especially vulnerable. One of the most common and perplexing side effects of radiation to the head is something known as *somnolence syndrome.* This often appears one to two months after radiation therapy is completed, when a family might expect the side effects to be waning. Instead the child seems listless, fatigued, and sleepy; may lose his appetite; and may experience frequent headaches and low-grade fevers. This will usually disappear within a few weeks. Another symptom that may appear at this time is something called *Lhermitte's sign,* in which the child feels as if an electrical charge pulses through his body when he bends his head forward. Like somnolence syndrome, this will usually disappear on its own and is not usually associated with permanent neurologic damage.

TABLE 5.3

**Coping with the Side Effects of Radiation Therapy**
**Early reactions (occurring within days or weeks)**

| Body System | Side Effect | What May Help |
|---|---|---|
| Skin/hair | Redness, blistering<br>Hair loss (after about 2 to 3 weeks) | Leave skin open to air<br>Use ointments only if doctor-approved<br>Will regrow within 2 to 3 months<br>Use mild shampoo<br>Cut hair short<br>Avoid hair dryers, electric curlers, etc.<br>Use a satin pillow<br>Use a wide-tooth comb<br>Select a wig before all hair falls out<br>Keep head covered to prevent sunburn (in summer), heat loss (in winter)<br>Try a variety of hats, scarves, etc. |
| | Puffy ears | Will go away |
| Eyes | Redness | Will go away |
| Mouth | Soreness | Use topical painkillers at least 1 hour before meals<br>Brush teeth with sponge toothbrush or cotton swab<br>Rinse mouth every 2 to 3 hours and after meals with hydrogen peroxide diluted with equal parts mouthwash and water; make sure child does not swallow this solution<br>Avoid very cold, hot, spicy, or acidic foods |
| | Dry mouth | Drink plenty of water<br>Suck on ice chips or sugarless lozenges or chew gum<br>Rinse with a saline solution or mouthwash, as recommended by doctor; avoid alcohol-containing products |

*table continues next page*

| Body System | Side Effect | What May Help |
|---|---|---|
| | Thrush | Doctor will prescribe medication |
| Digestive tract | Nausea, vomiting | Antinausea drugs<br>Sedation to sleep through nausea<br>Eat lightly 3 to 4 hours before treatment<br>Eat slowly<br>Clear liquid diet<br>Rest after meals<br>Don't mix hot and cold foods<br>Avoid sweet or greasy foods |
| | Diarrhea | Avoid milk products<br>Give clear liquids (not fruit juice or sports drinks) |
| | Loss of appetite | Make eating more pleasant with soft lighting, music, friends<br>Avoid stress at mealtimes<br>Encourage child to exercise 5 to 10 minutes 1/2 hour before meals<br>Give frequent small meals and snacks<br>Encourage child to eat slowly<br>Encourage child to eat a large breakfast<br>Use foods high in protein and calories (milk shakes, peanut butter, etc.) |
| | Bowel urgency | Encourage regular bowel movements<br>Increase fluids<br>Give high-fiber foods<br>Call doctor if child has abdominal pain, hard stools, or diarrhea |
| Urinary tract | Bladder urgency | Report to doctor |
| Lungs | Dry cough | Report to doctor |
| Systemic (involving entire body) | Fatigue | Encourage rest and frequent naps |

*table continues next page*

| Body System | Side Effect | What May Help |
| --- | --- | --- |
| | Bone marrow failure (depletion of white and red blood cells, resulting in bleeding and loss of immunity) | Transfusions may be given<br>Protection from environment |

Radiation therapy can prevent bones from growing normally, resulting in stunted growth of the irradiated area as well as asymmetries and deformities. Depending on the dose, radiation can also have significant long-term effects on the hormones that control growth and reproduction; and like chemotherapy it may cause late-occurring damage to the lungs, heart, liver, kidney, and bowels. Finally, radiation itself is a carcinogen (cancer-causing agent). Therefore radiation therapy may predispose your child to developing a second type of cancer at some later time. Your doctor will discuss with you the follow-up tests your child will need to assess the health of these various body systems. Long-term consequences of radiation therapy are discussed further in chapter 14.

## Surgery

Most children with brain tumors and other solid tumors will require surgery as part of their treatment plans. For some benign tumors surgery alone will be all the treatment needed. But for most malignancies, radiation and/or chemotherapy will be used in combination with surgery as a means of eliminating not only the primary tumor but any metastases as well.

Prior to surgery a child with a solid tumor will usually have several imaging studies done so that the surgeon can visualize the location and size of the tumor and plan the surgical approach. However, the imaging studies do not reveal the type of tumor present. For this, tumor tissue needs to be examined under a microscope.

A *biopsy* involves removing a small piece of the tumor and sending it to the laboratory, where pathologists analyze the cellular makeup of the tumor. Usually this is a surgical procedure done under a general anesthetic (that is, the patient is unconscious during the procedure), although sometimes a doctor will use a less invasive method of obtaining the sample. Pathologists examine a quickly frozen slice of tissue to establish a preliminary diagnosis. Then more extensive testing will be done to confirm the initial findings. Some tumors are removed completely at the time of the initial surgical procedure. This would be considered, for example, if removal of the tumor would not damage surrounding vessels, nerves, or organs, or cause any serious cosmetic damage. It might also be considered if the doctor determines that cutting into the tumor would not release cancer cells into the bloodstream, which could spread elsewhere in the body.

For other types of solid tumors, however, the treatment plan will not be designed until the permanent diagnosis is confirmed, as much as five days later. Dr. Richard Womer says that it is risky to make major decisions about potentially disfiguring or disabling surgery on the basis of a frozen section. "For most of the tumors we deal with [sarcomas], we get the data, complete the staging, assemble the whole picture, and *then* start the treatment." An additional advantage of delaying major surgery for sarcomas is that pretreatment with chemotherapy may shrink the tumor sufficiently that less radical surgery will be needed. With osteosarcoma, for example, a patient may have six cycles of chemotherapy over a two- to three-month period prior to surgery.

With brain tumors, removal of the tumor may immediately follow the preliminary diagnosis, while the patient is still under anesthesia and the brain is exposed. Says neurosurgeon Leslie N. Sutton, M.D., "The biopsy tells us how aggressive we have to be. With some [brain] tumors you have to be very aggressive surgically because if you don't, they will come back and because no other treatment works. There are other tumors, however, for which we have other methods that are more effective and a lot safer than surgery. If you're dealing with that sort of tumor, you don't want to take a lot of risks doing a potentially dangerous operation. All you need to do is establish the diagnosis and then stop."

### *RISKS AND CONCERNS ASSOCIATED WITH GENERAL SURGERY*

Surgery for cancer carries with it all the same risks as those associated with other types of surgery. These risks are relatively low today because of overall improvements in anesthesia and supportive care; however, cancer and chemotherapy impose a few additional concerns, especially with regard to infections and wound healing. Thus your oncologist and surgeon will have to work closely in order to coordinate your child's care. Says Dr. Womer, "From a surgical point of view, once you do an operation, you would like the patient not to have chemotherapy for a month or six weeks. From an oncologist's point of view you'd like to start chemotherapy the next day. So we have to work together to decide the earliest time that we can resume chemotherapy without imposing an undue risk."

Your child's outcome after surgery depends on the type, stage, and site of the cancer and on your child's age. The impact of surgery on your child's life will depend not only on the physical consequences of the surgery but on your family's ability to adapt to the changes that come.

Sometimes removal of a tumor requires removal of the affected organ as well. For example, treatment for retinoblastoma often requires removal of the entire affected eye and replacement with an artificial eye. Although this will not restore sight in the eye, the cosmetic results can be quite good. Treatment for Wilms' tumor may require removal of the kidney. As long as one healthy kidney remains, the child should retain adequate kidney function. Other soft-tissue tumors may require removal of all or part of other essential organs.

Bone tumors may require amputation of a limb or other less radical surgery to spare the limb and preserve some function. At the time of diagnosis it may be unclear whether amputation will be needed. Only after chemotherapy and radiation therapy are complete will it be possible to determine accurately the extent of surgery that will be necessary. Dr. Womer says, however, that he often discusses amputation at the initial family meeting, even though it may not be needed. "Usually the first question a parent asks is 'Is my child going to die?' and the second question is, 'If my child lives, will he have his limb or not?' But even if a parent is too afraid to voice this question, it's always there and should be addressed."

Limb salvage procedures have been gaining in popularity over the past decade. According to Dr. Womer, limb salvage procedures are now possible for about two-thirds of osteosarcoma patients, compared with fewer than one-third who underwent limb-salvage procedures ten years ago. This procedure involves surgically removing the part of the bone affected by tumor as well as safety margins on each side of the tumor and then replacing that segment of bone with an artificial implant. Since the artificial implant will not grow, limb salvage is usually not available to young children, although some physicians are experimenting with implants that can be lengthened as needed to accommodate the growth of the child.

Dr. Womer says that parents need to understand that even when amputation is not needed, there is no way to treat a tumor in a limb without some disability. Radiation carries with it side effects, as discussed earlier, that may alter the growth of an irradiated bone, leading to some deformity. Amputation creates obvious disabilities, although artificial limbs are becoming better each year. With limb salvage, even though the outcome may be less obvious, the disability may be similar to that of amputation.

No matter what treatment decision is made, families often need some time to adjust their expectations. The delay before surgery, during which chemotherapy and radiation therapy are given, provides this opportunity. Some parents prefer to delay telling the child about the possibility of amputation or other disability until after the surgical decision is made. Others prefer to bring their children in on the discussions earlier. Dr. Womer says each approach has advantages and disadvantages. At The Children's Hospital of Philadelphia, psychosocial professionals are usually brought into the discussion whenever it takes place. They, along with the rest of the treatment team, help the family evaluate their options, make plans, and begin the adjustment process.

Child life specialist Marie Burkhauser is one such professional who is particularly skilled at communicating effectively with the child. Says Dr. Womer, "She's very inventive and is able to come up with activities for kids that help them understand the surgery better and even rehearse it to a certain degree. She's able to uncover a lot of anxieties, secrets, and issues that we—the children, the parents, and the doctors—may not have been aware of."

Another preparatory step that is usually taken is to introduce the family to another child who has had similar surgery. Such a patient can let the family know "what things are like on the other side," says Dr. Womer. When parents meet another parent who has been through a similar ordeal, they can often begin to accept their own predicament.

### *RISKS AND CONCERNS ASSOCIATED WITH BRAIN SURGERY*

The risks associated with brain surgery have also been dramatically lessened over the past decade. Neurosurgeon Luis Schut, M.D., attributes this to many factors: better diagnostic techniques, anesthesia, radiation therapy, and chemotherapy; newly developed specialties in neurooncology and intensive care; and new surgical techniques including the operating microscope, which provides better visualization of intricate details in the brain, and the ultrasonic aspirator, which allows surgeons to remove the tumor with less damage to surrounding tissue.

The delivery of neurosurgical services has also changed. At The Children's Hospital of Philadelphia and other large multidisciplinary medical centers, teams of specialists work together to deliver care in an efficient and expedient manner. As a result hospital stays have been shortened. For example Dr. Schut described a patient he had seen just that morning: "I saw her in the office today and now she's going home. She will come back the morning of the operation and will be admitted straight to the operating room. Then she'll go to the intensive care unit after surgery. The next morning she should be out of ICU, and four days later she probably will be home.

"While I'm working with the child, there are two nurses who will be instructing the parents outside of the operating room. The day after surgery the oncologist, social workers, and psychologists will all be there talking to the parents."

Dr. Schut says the shortened hospital stays have advantages for the children, who usually prefer to be at home. But it places additional demands on parents. One of the major concerns following brain surgery is swelling around the brain. Most children are given steroids to decrease this swelling. These steroids can have disturbing side effects: especially increased appetite and an artificial cheerfulness that culminates in an emotional "crash" when the steroids are withdrawn. Another problem is frequently seen in children who have operations on a certain part of the brain called the posterior fossa. About half of all brain tumors are found in this area. For some poorly understood reason, children with these operations frequently develop extraordinary psychological changes, including refusal to speak, extreme negativity, and refusal to do things for themselves.

The treatment team can help parents prepare for these sometimes bewildering psychological and behavioral changes. But sometimes, says Dr. Schut, parents are told to get tough. "Otherwise the child can become very dependent. I tell the parents before surgery that I don't want them to feel too sorry for the child. It sounds cruel, but otherwise they can prolong these problems forever."

After brain tumor surgery children may have a variety of disabilities, both physical and intellectual. However, Dr. Schut says this has more to do with the disease itself and is not usually a result of the surgery. Sometimes rehabilitative therapy can help restore lost abilities, but this will depend on the extent of neurologic damage. If brain tissue was destroyed by the tumor, the lost abilities may never come back, although other areas of the brain may compensate. If, however, brain tissue was pushed or compressed by the tumor but not destroyed, the function will come back. Dr. Schut says that at the time of surgery it's difficult to predict which functions and abilities will be restored. "We can guess, but we don't really know," he says.

### *CRYOTHERAPY AND PHOTOCOAGULATION THERAPY*

These are surgical procedures that may be used to remove some small tumors of the eye and skin. *Cryotherapy* destroys the tumor by freezing it at very low temperatures (–200° C), while *photocoagulation therapy* causes its destruction with laser beams.

# CHAPTER 6

# Bone Marrow Transplantation

Since the first bone marrow transplant was performed in 1968 on an infant with an immune disorder, its importance in treating blood diseases and cancer has grown. Today bone marrow transplantation is considered the treatment of choice for some forms of leukemia and is also used to treat a variety of solid tumors. However, it remains a technologically complex procedure with limited availability around the country. And its costs are high, both in the financial sense and in terms of its practical and emotional demands on a family.

Although bone marrow transplantation (BMT) is still a relatively young form of therapy, it has already yielded dramatic results in some areas. For example, prior to the use of bone marrow transplantation, a diagnosis of juvenile chronic myelogenous leukemia (CML) meant an almost-certain death sentence. With a transplant, however, the chance of cure is good—greater than 60 percent of transplanted patients reach the three-year mark with no signs of disease.

Like other forms of transplantation, a bone marrow transplant involves replacing a diseased organ—the bone marrow—with a healthy one. Bone marrow is the spongy tissue found in the hollow centers of bones. It contains primitive cells that will divide and differentiate to form all the different types of blood cells—red blood cells, white blood cells, and platelets. In leukemia it is the bone marrow itself that is diseased.

Unlike other forms of transplantation, however, a doctor can't just go in and remove the diseased tissue with a scalpel. Rather the host bone marrow must be destroyed with highly toxic chemotherapeutic agents, radiation, or both. Furthermore, after the new tissue is transplanted, it may not begin to function for several weeks. Thus during the period after the host marrow is destroyed and before the donor marrow takes hold, the patient is at great risk of infection, depleted of the red blood cells that would carry oxygen throughout the body, and depleted of platelets, which promote blood clotting. Therefore a child undergoing a bone marrow transplant is likely to require a great deal of supportive care for an extended period of time. The term *supportive care* used in this case indicates that medical support, such as blood products and antibiotics (see chapter 8) is needed to help the child weather various complications. The term is also used to describe the medical support given to children in the terminal phases of disease (chapter 14).

A procedure similar to the one described above may be used when a child's cancer does not itself affect the bone marrow but when a cure requires such massive doses of chemotherapy or radiation therapy that the child's bone marrow is destroyed. In this case the "transplant" is done to rescue the child's hematopoietic (blood-forming) system; thus you may hear the term *bone marrow rescue* used to describe your child's procedure. Bone marrow rescue is sometimes used in children who have neuroblastoma or other solid tumors.

## Types of Bone Marrow Transplants

Bone marrow transplants are usually divided into three different types, depending on the source of the donated marrow. The earliest bone marrow transplants were done in children who had an identical twin. This type of transplant, called *syngeneic (syn* = "same"; *geneic* = "genes") avoids the problems of incompatibility between different people's tissue types. Obviously, however, it severely limits the number of children who would be candidates for the procedure.

*Allogeneic (allo* = "other"; *geneic* = "genes") transplants are done between genetically dissimilar individuals. Until recently these were only possible when the affected child had a sibling or other close relative who had a similar, although not identical, genetic makeup, as determined by extensive testing. However, more recent advances in determining genetic compatibility of tissues has opened up the procedure to unrelated donors. In addition scientists have developed methods for pretreating the marrow so that problems with genetic incompatibility are reduced. As a result many more children are potential candidates for a bone marrow transplant.

The third type of bone marrow transplant, called an *autologous* transplant, is not really a transplant at all because the patient's own bone marrow is used for the procedure. For this type of procedure, the patient's marrow must be relatively free of cancer cells, or it must be treated to cleanse it of cancerous cells. After the marrow is collected, the patient goes through high-dose chemotherapy and/or total body irradiation to eradicate the cancer and destroy the remaining hematopoietic system. Then the collected marrow is reinfused. In children, autologous transplants are used primarily in children with acute myeloid leukemia (AML), neuroblastoma, and other solid tumors.

## Finding a Donor

The first, and sometimes most difficult, part of a bone marrow transplant is finding a suitable donor. In order for foreign tissue to transplant successfully into a person, the donor and host must share certain genetic traits. These traits are inherited from parents in the same way that some more obvious traits, such as eye color, are inherited. However, these traits are not visible. Rather they are molecules found on the surface of each cell in a person's body. In order to determine whether donor and host cells are compatible, scientists analyze these cell-surface molecules, which are called *HLA antigens* (human leukocyte antigens).

Because of the way HLA antigens are inherited, a child and his sibling have about a one-in-four chance of having inherited the same combination of antigens from their mother and father. Only 25 to 30 percent of patients will have an HLA-compatible sibling donor. For this reason a national registry of volunteer donors has been established. This registry, called the National Marrow Donor Program (NMDP), has recruited and tissue-typed over one million potential donors as of October 1993. From this large pool of donors a compatible match can often be found for a patient who needs

TABLE 6.1
**Childrens' Cancers Treated with Bone Marrow Transplants**

| Type of Cancer | Conditions That Call for BMT | Types of Transplants Done |
|---|---|---|
| Acute lymphocytic leukemia (ALL) | High-risk ALL in first remission or failure to achieve remission<br>Relapse on chemotherapy<br>Second or subsequent remission | Allogeneic with sibling matched or unrelated donor |
| Acute myelocytic leukemia (AML) | If HLA-matched sibling is available<br>If HLA-matched sibling is not available<br>Relapsed disease | Allogeneic<br>Autologous<br>Autologous or allogeneic |
| Chronic myelogenous leukemia (CML) | All cases—BMT is only curative therapy available | Allogeneic |
| Neuroblastoma | Disseminated disease—minimal residual disease prior to transplant | Autologous<br>Allogeneic |
| Non-Hodgkin's lymphoma | In relapse—responsive to chemotherapy | Autologous<br>Allogeneic |
| Hodgkin's disease | | Syngeneic (limited studies have been done) |
| Brain tumors, Ewing's sarcoma, germ cell tumor, Wilms' tumor | Advanced disease | Limited studies have been done |

a bone marrow transplant but does not have a compatible related donor.

In an attempt to find a compatible match, friends and family members may wish to be screened. To find out more about how this is done, ask your physician, psychosocial professional, or contact the NMDP (see "Resources").

According to Dr. Nancy Bunin, director of the Bone Marrow Transplant Program at The Children's Hospital of Philadelphia, a compatible donor can usually be found for a Caucasian child within four to six months. The outlook for African-American children or other racial minorities is worse, she says, because HLA types are ethnically determined and the percentage of minorities in the national registry is less than in the overall population. This is changing, however, as more minorities volunteer for the registry.

## Obtaining Marrow for Transplantation

For most healthy people the process of donating bone marrow presents few risks, although it may require a hospital admission. It has been done in children as young as two months old. Less than 10 percent of the donor's marrow is collected, an amount that should be fully replenished within a few weeks. During that period of time the donor still has plenty of bone marrow to produce all the necessary blood components.

Marrow collection ("harvest") is done under general anesthesia. A needle is inserted from the back into the donor's pelvic bone. Then the marrow is withdrawn (aspirated) with a syringe. After the bone marrow has been harvested, the donor may feel some discomfort and stiffness, but this will usually last no longer than a few days. The donor will usually be discharged from the hospital one day after the harvest and will be able to resume normal activities.

## Preparing for a Bone Marrow Transplant

Once your doctor has determined that a bone marrow transplant is the best available option for your child, your family will begin the long process of preparing psychologically, financially, and physically for the procedure. The health care team will want to make sure that you understand the risks and benefits of the medical procedure your child will undergo and that you are prepared to work actively for your child's recovery. If one of your other children is the donor, the health care team will want to ensure that the child understands the risks and benefits faced and that the marrow is being donated voluntarily.

The bone marrow transplant itself will not be scheduled until a donor is found. Then, about two weeks before the transplant, your child will be admitted to the hospital to begin preparations. If your child does not already have an indwelling catheter (see chapter 4), one will be inserted at this time.

Most hospitals that do bone marrow transplants have special facilities to protect the patient from the environment. These measures are taken because children receiving bone marrow transplants are severely immunosuppressed and are therefore extremely vulnerable to infections. At The Children's Hospital of Philadelphia, for example, the ten-bed Bone Marrow Transplant Unit houses four separate laminar airflow rooms and six HEPA-filtered rooms. These are rooms that are equipped with very efficient filtration systems. They prevent any nonfiltered air, which might carry potential hazards, from entering the room. In addition the Bone Marrow Unit uses other special procedures to isolate its patients from contaminants. This includes scrupulous cleaning practices and detailed rules about hand-washing procedures that must be followed by anyone entering the room.

Your child will be restricted to this facility until there are enough neutrophils in his blood to fight infection. This means that he will require a great deal of support and care to endure his isolation without becoming depressed or otherwise emotionally distraught. The nurses and psychosocial staff at the hospital should be available to help you care for your child in this way. They can offer suggestions about appropriate toys and books that can be brought into the unit and can help you through difficult periods by providing respite and assistance with your child. You may be allowed to bring in stereos, tape players, radios, TVs, or electronic games as long as they are adequately disinfected.

Conditioning for the transplant begins four to ten days before the transplant itself. Your child will receive high doses of chemotherapy and possibly total body irradiation (TBI), which will destroy the bone marrow. Although total body irradiation is thought to be the most effective way of destroying the marrow, long-term effects can be profound on a growing child (see chapter 14). Thus many centers are trying to use chemotherapy alone. As with other forms of therapy, researchers are attempting to find the appropriate balance between the risks and the benefits of these two approaches. It may not be possible to eliminate TBI for some transplants, according to Dr. Bunin.

When your child is ready, the new bone marrow will be infused through the indwelling catheter. The infusion may be done rapidly or over a few hours. The new bone marrow cells will migrate to the appropriate sites in the child's body and begin producing the different types of blood cells needed. However, it will take several weeks before one can detect the new cells on a blood test.

## Waiting for the Transplant to "Take"

Following a bone marrow transplant, a child will be depleted of all types of blood cells for about two to six weeks until the transplanted marrow engrafts and begins producing blood cells. During this period your child may need a great deal of supportive care, including nutritional supplementation. Table 6.2 lists some of the supportive care that is frequently needed by a child undergoing a transplant. These topics are discussed more fully in chapter 8.

TABLE 6.2
**Supportive Care for Bone Marrow Transplants**

| Problem | Supportive Care Provided |
|---|---|
| Pancytopenia (depletion of all types of blood cells) | Transfusion with irradiated blood products<br>• Platelets<br>• Red blood cells<br>Treatment with agents that stimulate proliferation of blood cells (G-CSF, GM-CSF) |
| Infections (generalized) | Intravenous antibiotics<br>Isolation from other people, especially people with infectious diseases |
| Gastrointestinal infections | Low-bacteria diet<br>Mouth care<br>Liquid antibiotics |
| Anorexia (inability to eat sufficient amounts) | Intravenous nutrition |

## Complications of Bone Marrow Transplants

Bone marrow transplant patients face complications on several fronts. First, they are exposed to massive doses of chemotherapy and radiation therapy, and so may experience intensely the sorts of reactions discussed in chapter 5. Their immune systems and their blood-forming systems are completely destroyed and may not be reconstituted for many months, making them particularly vulnerable to infections and related complications. In addition, allogeneic bone marrow transplant patients deal with foreign tissue that has been infused into their bodies. This sets them up for one of the most common and serious complications of bone marrow transplantation—*graft-versus-host disease (GVHD).*

**GVHD** is an immune reaction in which lymphocytes produced by the transplanted bone marrow recognize the cells of the host as "nonself" (or foreign) and mount an attack. This is in fact what lymphocytes are programmed to do. In a normal individual it is this ability to discern self from nonself that allows the immune system to attack and destroy invading microorganisms or other foreign substances. This capacity to recognize self and nonself is largely a function of the HLA antigens, which were discussed earlier. When the HLA antigens of the donor and host match, the likelihood of GVHD decreases. Thus syngeneic and autologous transplants are not complicated by GVHD.

GVHD may be mild or severe and occurs in about 30 to 70 percent of sibling-matched transplants. In its acute phase the symptoms may mimic the side effects of chemoradiotherapy —rash, diarrhea, and jaundice (yellowing of the skin and eyes) caused by liver dysfunction. For this reason a biopsy may be needed for the doctor to determine whether in fact GVHD is occurring.

*Chronic GVHD* refers to GVHD that appears later or persists long after the transplant. Symptoms may include changes in skin pigmentation, texture, and thickness; joint contractures; mouth dryness and ulcers, difficulty swallowing and malabsorption, which can lead to weight loss; chronic liver disease; and eye dryness, pain, and light sensitivity. Rare side effects include obstructive lung disease, vaginal inflammation and constriction, and a muscle disease called myasthenia gravis.

GVHD may be prevented or minimized by several techniques. Most centers use at least one medicine, such as cyclosporine or methotrexate, to help prevent GVHD or to decrease its severity. For an unrelated donor transplant, the donor marrow may be pretreated to remove the cells that are likely to cause GVHD. At this time different institutions are using different pretreatment regimens, trying to determine which is best. If GVHD develops, it is usually controlled by other medicines, such as steroids. It can, however, result in life-threatening complications.

**Infections** are also a common complication of bone marrow transplantation. The preparative regimen that a child receives before the transplant may leave the immune system suppressed for as long as a year. In the first few weeks following the transplant all the cell types are depleted including the granulocytes, which are important for fighting bacterial and fungal infections. Even after these cells begin to reappear in the blood, however, other white cells (lymphocytes) may not function normally, and viral illnesses become a major concern.

Bacterial and fungal infections are treated with antibiotics and antifungal agents, which may be given as a preventive measure after bone marrow transplant. There are few drugs available to protect a person or treat a viral infection; however, intravenous gamma globulin may provide some protection. Other preventive measures involve isolation of the child from other children with illnesses such as chicken pox, measles, and herpes. If exposed to one of these viruses, your child may be given a product called *hyperimmune globulin* or *varicella-zoster immune globulin.* This provides antibodies against the virus that your child is no longer able to produce.

Another treatment given to help children recover from immunosuppression are agents that promote the proliferation of the white blood cells that are needed to fight infection. These agents are discussed in chapter 8.

**Interstitial pneumonitis** is one of the most important causes of death following a bone marrow transplant. It can be caused by infection or possibly by radiation damage to the lung itself. The infectious agents that have been implicated include a very common virus called cytomegalovirus (CMV), which in healthy people may cause infection with few or no symptoms; herpes simplex virus (HSV); or pneumocystis carinii. Often no particular virus is found.

**Late-occurring effects** of bone marrow transplantation are often related to the total body irradiation undergone prior to the transplant. Total body irradiation almost always leaves a child permanently sterile, and it may also impair growth. Growth hormone and other hormone production may be decreased, leading to various endocrinologic problems that can sometimes be treated with hormone therapy. Cataracts may occur following TBI, but the incidence is reduced when irradiation is given over several days.

Both high-dose chemotherapy and radiation may have potential long-term effects on major organs such as the heart, kidneys, and lungs. Also, both chemotherapy and TBI may increase the chance of developing a second kind of cancer, and both may lead to learning problems. There is no definitive way to predict whether a child will experience these problems later in life. Chapter 15 discusses these long-term problems in more detail.

## CHAPTER 7

# New and Alternative Therapies

Although most children's cancers are treated with one or more of the approaches discussed in chapters 5 and 6, there may come a time when your doctor suggests an alternative approach either in addition to or instead of the more common methods. Or you may hear about some form of therapy that is being promoted. Suggestions may come from your doctor, from friends or family members, or through television, magazine, or newspaper articles. However the suggestion comes to you, you may have to make decisions based on limited evidence and possibly at times of very high stress. This chapter discusses some of the new approaches that have shown promise as well as some of the alternatives that are being promoted by people outside of the medical mainstream.

## Immunotherapy

One of the hottest areas in cancer research over the past few years has been immunotherapy—a form of therapy in which a person's own immune system is recruited to fight disease. Although immunotherapy has been around for nearly two hundred years—since Edward Jenner vaccinated the first person against small pox—it has been developed as a tool in the fight against cancer only relatively recently. So far it has shown promise primarily in adult cancers of the skin and kidney and has not been studied extensively in children's cancers. Nevertheless excitement about the potential of immunotherapy has grown as scientists have discovered more about how the immune system works.

The immune system is a complex network of interacting cells, proteins, and chemical messengers. It fights disease by recognizing and destroying foreign substances in the body, such as bacteria and viruses. It also recognizes as foreign cells from another individual (such as in a transplant) as well as cells that have undergone some kind of change, such as can happen when a cell becomes cancerous. It is this last property of the immune system that is exploited in immunotherapy against cancer. By stimulating certain aspects of the immune system, scientists believe they can facilitate a more effective attack on cancerous cells.

Immunotherapy against cancer takes many different forms. Of those types currently being investigated, three that hold particular promise are biologic response modifiers, monoclonal antibodies, and vaccines.

## *BIOLOGIC RESPONSE MODIFIERS*

*Biologic response modifiers* are chemicals that, in the intact immune system, allow cells to communicate with one another. These chemicals, called *cytokines,* serve a variety of functions. They may recruit other cells of the immune system, cause certain cell types to multiply, or suppress the activity of other cells. The types of cytokines that are used therapeutically in the fight against cancer are the interferons, interleukins, and tumor necrosis factor. In humans these substances are produced in minuscule quantities; however, they are now mass-produced in the laboratory through recombinant DNA technology.[1]

*Interferons* are substances that are produced by white blood cells or other cells in response to viruses, bacteria, and other stimuli. There are three types of interferons, known as alpha, beta, and gamma. These three substances work in a variety of ways, affecting the various cells of the immune system. Alpha and beta interferons have both antitumor and antiviral properties. In children with cancer these agents have been tested against leukemia, osteosarcoma, brain tumors, and neuroblastoma.

Interferon-alpha also suppresses proliferation of cells. It is this property that has been successfully exploited in the treatment of adult-type chronic myelogenous leukemia (CML). When given in the early stages of that disease, while it is still in its chronic phase, interferon-alpha has been shown to induce remission in up to three-fourths of patients. Although it's still too early to tell how long-lasting this remission can

[1] *Recombinant DNA technology* refers to the newest biotechnology or genetic engineering approaches being used in the medical and pharmacologic industry. Scientists working in these areas have learned how to manipulate genes in bacteria and other organisms so that they can produce large quantities of pure and biologically active substances.

be, in many cases it may prolong remission long enough that a bone marrow donor can be found for transplant.

*Interleukins* and *tumor necrosis factor (TNF)* play different roles in the coordinated immune attack on cancer cells. In laboratory research, for example, one of the interleukins, interleukin-2 (IL-2), has been shown to stimulate the proliferation of lymphokine-activated killer (LAK) cells and natural killer (NK) cells, so called because they attack and kill cancerous cells. Interleukins and TNF have been used with limited success in some adult cancers, but have not yet been widely studied in children.

TABLE 7.1
**Immunotherapy**

| **Agent** | **Action** | **Types of Cancer Investigated** | **Toxicities** |
|---|---|---|---|
| Interferon-alpha (IFN-α) | Antiviral<br>Antitumor<br>Inhibits proliferation<br>Interacts with other factors | ALL (acute lymphocytic leukemia)<br>Osteosarcoma<br>CML (chronic myelogenous leukemia) | Common: flulike symptoms (fever, chills, rigors, malaise, muscle aches)<br>Less common: depletion of white and red blood cells, headache, inability to concentrate, abnormal sensations |
| Interferon-beta (IFN-β) | Antiviral<br>Antitumor<br>Inhibits proliferation<br>Interacts with other factors | Brain tumors | Same as IFN-alpha<br>Rare: marrow suppression, seizures, stupor, coma |

*table continues next page*

| Agent | Action | Types of Cancer Investigated | Toxicities |
|---|---|---|---|
| Interferon-gamma (IFN-γ) | Modulates immune system by activating various cell types and stimulating antibody production<br>Antimicrobial | Neuroblastoma | Same as IFN-alpha |
| Interleukin-2 (IL-2) | Stimulates lymphocyte proliferation<br>Induces cells that kill tumors | | Nausea<br>Vomiting<br>Diarrhea<br>Rash<br>Red blood cell depletion<br>Neurologic (sleepiness, disorientation, coma)<br>Water retention<br>Weight gain |
| Tumor necrosis factor (TNF) | Inhibits proliferation of tumor cells<br>Directly attacks and kills tumor cells | | Fever<br>Rigor<br>Nausea<br>Vomiting<br>Slight depletion of platelets and granulocytes<br>Seizures<br>Confusion<br>Low blood pressure |

### *MONOCLONAL ANTIBODIES*

The second type of immunotherapy uses substances called monoclonal antibodies. *Antibodies* are substances that are produced by lymphocytes called B cells in response to foreign invaders such as microbes. Each B cell produces a single type of antibody molecule that recognizes a specific invader.

When a circulating B cell comes in contact with a germ against which it is directed, the B cell multiplies and pumps out millions of identical antibody molecules, which aid in the elimination of the germ.

The extraordinary specificity of antibodies is exploited in the production of monoclonal antibodies. Antibodies against a variety of antigens, including tumor antigens, are raised in the laboratory. Scientists have found a way of inducing a single cell to produce a large quantity of identical antibody molecules, thus the term *monoclonal* ("one-clone") antibodies. Monoclonal antibodies are like guided missiles—they can be directed specifically against a certain cell type. When attached to other substances, such as cell-killing agents, they theoretically could deliver the agent directly to the intended cell, bypassing all normal cells. This is the idea behind the use of monoclonal antibodies for cancer therapy. The hope is that monoclonal antibodies would make therapy much more specific and therefore reduce toxicity. At this time, the technology is still being developed and is used only on an investigational basis.

### *VACCINES*

Vaccines may also prove useful in the prevention of cancer recurrences, although research in this area is still at a very preliminary level. The idea behind cancer vaccines is that the immune system could be primed to patrol the body for tumor cells and to mount an immune attack if such cells arise. In order for this idea to become a reality, scientists must determine which parts of a tumor cell will elicit the most effective immune response and then find a way, possibly through genetic engineering, to produce the vaccine.

## Alternative Therapies

Most parents will do just about anything to ensure that their child with cancer gets the best care possible. So it's no wonder that many parents explore types of treatment that are offered outside of the medical mainstream. Some parents turn to these approaches because of their ethnic, cultural, or religious beliefs; the "alternatives" in these cases may actually be what could be called "traditional" forms of medicine. Others try alternative forms of therapy because they want to cover all the bases. Some people are distrustful of the medical establishment. Some believe that the alternative truly offers a better chance at cure. And still others resort to alternative treatments out of desperation when standard care doesn't seem to be working.

Oncologist Jean Belasco, M.D., says that shortly after the television show *60 Minutes* ran a story about ground-up shark cartilage as a treatment for cancer, she began getting calls from parents who wanted to try it. She recalled one father who sat crying and said to her, "I know that I'm probably going to get ripped off. I know it's not going to work. But if my son dies and he doesn't get this, I'll feel guilty."

This story illustrates the torment that parents face as they search for something that will save their child. Despite the many successes in treating childhood cancer, current therapy is less than ideal—it sometimes causes much suffering and it still doesn't always work. As a result scientists, doctors, and parents continue to look for better methods. Often, especially for parents, that search takes them outside of the usual health-care delivery system, into less familiar territory, where the accepted scientific guidelines for judging the effectiveness of a therapy may no longer apply.

The attraction of alternative forms of therapy is easy to

understand. Frequently proponents or practitioners of these approaches offer exactly what parents want: promises that the treatment will cure the child or at least minimize suffering and hope at a time when all seems hopeless. Doctors are less likely to give these promises or offer what they consider to be false hope. Schooled in the scientific method, doctors are more likely to speak in probabilities. And because of their ethical and legal obligation to obtain *informed* consent, doctors will be sure to present potential negative aspects of a treatment along with the possible benefits.

The term *alternative therapy* is used here to encompass a wide variety of approaches ranging from relatively simple steps that parents may take to improve their child's overall health when used in conjunction with conventional therapy to more radical steps that require a child to forgo conventional treatment altogether. Other authors have called these approaches "unproven," "unorthodox," "unconventional," or "controversial."

While some people and medical organizations scoff at the whole notion of alternative therapies, the National Institutes of Health is not among these nay-sayers. In 1993 the NIH established the Office of Alternative Therapies, which provides grants to scientists investigating a wide variety of alternative approaches.

Alternative therapies go in and out of fashion, and it is not the intention of this chapter to discuss them individually. They can be broadly classified into four groups:

**1.** Alternative agents, such as the recently touted shark cartilage, that will fight cancer or summon the body's natural defenses to fight cancer

**2.** Therapies that presume cancer to be the result of an imbalance or deficiency in the body and that suggest the cancer can be cured by correcting the imbalance. This group includes treatments that use massive doses of vitamins (megavitamin therapy), some dietary approaches ("macrobiotic" diets), and "metabolic" therapies that aim to detoxify the body

**3.** Spiritual or faith-healing approaches

**4.** "Mind-body" approaches that promote mental imagery or other methods of engaging your child's mind in the fight against cancer.

Although most alternative therapies have little medical evidence to back them up, some may prove useful, whereas others may be either useless or even harmful. Mind-body approaches, such as hypnosis, relaxation, and guided imagery (see chapter 8) are among the alternatives that are already widely accepted as helpful for some children.

*EVALUATING ALTERNATIVE THERAPIES*

Every alternative has both proponents and detractors, making it difficult for parents to evaluate the pros and cons of an approach they are considering. In general, scientific studies of these therapies have yet to prove any of them beneficial. Nevertheless alternative therapies can sometimes help parents feel more in control of what is happening to their child and they can help parents feel that they are doing everything that is possible. They can sometimes restore hope, which is thought to be an important ally in the fight against cancer. Further as adjuncts to conventional forms of therapy some methods, such as hypnosis, can help relieve pain and distress (see chapter 8 for more on nonpharmacologic methods of pain control).

But in evaluating the possible harmful effects of a treatment, parents must sometimes look beyond the obvious question of whether the treatment itself will cause harm. Even alternative treatments that, at worst, appear benign, may place added stress on both the child and the family. For example, for many children with cancer, eating can be a difficult and unpleasant experience. In order to get such a child to consume enough calories to meet basic nutritional requirements, high-calorie and sweet foods that the child likes, such as milk shakes, may be recommended. Forcing such a child to eat a certain type of restricted diet, such as a macrobiotic diet, may take away from the child one of her only sources of pleasure and may be harmful nutritionally. Further, it may set up serious confrontations between parents and child, which can damage this most important of relationships.

Some of these approaches may require distant travel. This can have a negative impact on the child's emotional state and quality of life. Many of these approaches are also quite expensive, which can add considerable stress to a family.

Dr. Belasco encourages parents to discuss the alternatives they are considering with their child's doctor, nurse, and/or psychosocial support professional. Although these people may know little about the specific alternative suggested, they may be able to direct parents to resource materials. Further, they often can help parents explore their concerns, hopes, and fears that may be complicating the decision-making process.

Many parents, however, are reluctant to raise these issues with their child's doctor. They may worry that doctors will automatically reject the alternative as "quackery" or that suggesting an alternative may offend the doctor and thus may have negative consequences on how the doctor treats their child. Most health professionals, however, are quite accustomed to hearing about these alternatives and understand the stress the parents are under. Further, Dr. Belasco says, a thorough discussion of these issues is important if parents are going to be able to trust their health care team.

"I encourage families to bring in whatever it is that they

see in the paper or hear about. Because if we can talk about it from the beginning and we can trust one another, we are better able to work together to take care of their child. If we can talk through it, we can help parents not to be so vulnerable and we will be in a better position to know what's right for them and their family."

While being open to discussing alternatives, however, Dr. Belasco warns parents to beware of approaches that make grandiose promises or that claim to be victims of a massive conspiracy by the medical establishment. Most troubling, she says, are those alternatives that suggest to parents or children that they are in some way responsible for the disease through something they did or did not do. "It's impossible for me to believe that any of these kids, or their parents for that matter, brought this on themselves. And the last thing we want is for parents to feel guilty because they didn't look hard enough or didn't do everything exactly right. Medicine is not that perfect."

# CHAPTER 8

# Supportive Care

According to Dr. Anna T. Meadows, improvements in supportive care are in large measure responsible for better results in the fight against cancer. Supportive care aims not to treat the cancer itself but rather to help children withstand the side effects of treatment or the secondary consequences of the disease, such as pain and susceptibility to infections. Better methods of providing nutrition, combatting infection, relieving pain, and promoting the recovery of depleted blood components have meant that more aggressive therapy can be used with greater safety and with less suffering.

## Nutrition

Maintaining good nutrition throughout a child's treatment for cancer can help the patient tolerate the difficult treatments discussed in chapters 5 and 6. Good nutrition will also help a child keep up with normal activities, combat infections, and grow as normally as is possible. At the same time, a child with cancer may have increased nutritional demands because the cancer interferes with the body's utilization of nutrients and/or because it may increase a child's energy needs.

Thus nutrition is often a major concern for children with cancer. Common treatments leave many children nauseated and unable to keep food down, and they can also alter the way foods taste. This can be further complicated by physical problems that affect a child's ability to eat or digest food. Tumors or surgical procedures that affect any part of the digestive system may create obvious problems. In addition chemotherapy and radiation therapy can cause inflammation at all levels of the digestive tract, from the mouth to the intestines, making eating and digesting painful and problematic. On top of these difficulties a child's emotional state may affect his desire for food and willingness to cooperate with a dietary plan. Parental emotions, too, may be important. Parents who feel helpless in the face of their child's disease may invest much effort into providing a high-quality diet; yet this intense effort can cause increased anxiety for parents and child alike.

The management of a child's nutritional needs will be dictated by the specific problems encountered and by their severity. Often a pediatric dietician will be called in to evaluate a child's nutritional needs and help the health care team devise an effective nutritional plan. For most children, during most of their treatment, nutrition can be maintained through dietary planning, nutritional supplementation, and sometimes antinausea medications such as Ondansetron (Zofran). Children with cancer need diets high in both calories and protein; thus a diet that might be considered adequate or healthful for other people may not meet the needs of a child with cancer. For example vegetarian diets can be deficient in absorbable iron; diets that include large quantities of fruits and vegetables will be high in bulk but low in protein and calories; and diets that restrict dairy products may provide insufficient quantities of calcium. Even the most healthful diet, however, will be inadequate if the child won't eat it. Therefore sometimes foods that might not otherwise be considered healthful, for example milk shakes or "junk" food, may be key to providing sufficient calories. High-protein supplements may also be needed.

When the gastrointestinal tract is capable of digesting food but intake is inadequate to meet nutritional requirements, tube feedings may be required. This requires the placement of a small soft tube, called a *nasogastric,* or *NG tube,* through the nose and into the stomach or intestine. Supplemental formulas can then be delivered directly to the gastrointestinal tract. Tube feedings may be used in addition to or instead of regular meals. Tube feedings are usually given only at night while the child is sleeping, although the tube may be left in place at other times. In this way the child should be able to continue with normal activities during the daytime.

When the gastrointestinal tract is damaged to the point that ingested food or formula cannot be tolerated, or when vomiting, nausea, or other complications have led to poor nutrition, nutrients can be delivered directly to the bloodstream. This form of nutrition, called *total parenteral nutrition*

*(TPN),* usually requires the placement of a central venous catheter (discussed in chapter 4). TPN can lead to metabolic abnormalities; therefore it requires close monitoring of blood levels of certain enzymes, sugars, fats, and electrolytes.

Both tube feedings and TPN may be delivered at home when a child is being treated on an outpatient basis. Before the child is discharged home, parents are taught to place the NG tube, to check to see that it is in the correct position, and to deliver the formula; or to care for the central catheter and administer TPN. Many parents and children find that placement of the NG tube is particularly difficult; however, with practice and relaxation most can master the procedure. Some older children can learn to insert the tubes themselves.

## Pain

Most children with cancer will experience pain at some time during their treatment. The pain may be caused by the disease itself, or it may be a consequence of the treatment or procedures. In fact, according to Barbara Shapiro, M.D., associate director of the Pain Service at The Children's Hospital of Philadelphia, "Children tell us again and again that the procedures are the worst part of having cancer."

Managing pain is important not only for children with cancer but for their parents as well. For parents the anguish comes in watching their child suffer. And for both children and their parents, feelings of helplessness aggravate the situation. Thus the management of cancer pain requires parents, children, and health care professionals to work together.

In order for pain control to be effective, it must be appropriate to the needs of the child. This means that the pain itself must be understood for all its complexity. Cancer-related pain, such as the bone pain associated with cancers that involve the bone marrow or pain inflicted by tumor invasion, will be treated differently from the intestinal pain that sometimes comes about as a consequence of chemotherapy or radiation therapy. Furthermore pain is not simply the sensation that results when the body has suffered some traumatic insult. Influencing the perception of pain are factors such as hope or hopelessness, anxiety, depression, fatigue, nausea, and memories of previous painful experiences. A child's developmental level also influences the perception of and ability to cope with pain. When procedures cause discomfort, for example, very young children may not be able to understand that the event will be short-lived or that they may gain some benefit from the painful procedure.

As a result of all these complicating factors pain management follows no clearly defined guidelines. "There's no blanket answer," says Dr. Shapiro. "There's an art to it."

Nevertheless there have been great advances in the management of pain. Some of this has come about simply through the recognition that even very young children experience pain in real and significant ways. Up until about the 1980s many physicians and scientists believed that the nervous systems of young children were too immature to allow for the perception of pain. This belief was bolstered by the inability of people to recognize when a child was in pain. Furthermore anesthetics and analgesics that were used for adults were considered too risky for young children. As a result pain in children was frequently undertreated. But advances in the understanding of children's pain and in the delivery of anesthetics and analgesics has led to significant changes in both the pharmacologic and nonpharmacologic treatment of pain in children.

### *PHARMACOLOGIC APPROACHES*

There are many drugs available to treat pain in children (see tables 8.1 and 8.2). The choice of which ones to use will depend on the cause, location, and severity of the child's pain and on complicating factors, such as those described earlier.

Medications may exert many different effects that contribute to their pain-management properties. Drugs that relieve pain are called *analgesics,* those that block the sensation of pain or touch are called *anesthetics,* and those that exert a soothing, tranquilizing effect are called *sedatives.* Anesthetics are further subdivided into *general, local, regional,* and *topical* anesthetics, depending on the extent of their anesthetic effect. Topical anesthetics, for example, anesthetize only the skin and are thus used to block the pain associated with injections.

General anesthetics anesthetize the entire body and are used during surgery. They are often given as inhalation agents. The specialist who administers a general anesthetic—called an *anesthesiologist*—carefully monitors the child's breathing and other vital signs throughout the period of administration, since these agents may cause respiratory depression. With appropriate monitoring, however, general anesthetics are usually safe, even in very young children.

In addition to analgesics, anesthetics, and sedatives, there are a number of other agents that produce effects that contribute to pain relief. Known as *adjuvant drugs* (table 8.2), these agents may lessen anxiety, cause amnesia (so that the child doesn't remember the pain or distress), or reduce inflammation, for example. Frequently they will be given in combination with analgesics. For example, for very distressing procedures in which a child's anxiety is contributing to the pain, an analgesic and an antianxiety agent may be given together.

**Concerns About Pain Medications** The undertreatment of children's pain continues to this day, in part because assessment of pain can be difficult and in part because children, parents, and health care professionals cling to long-held myths about pain and pain medications.

Recognizing when a child is in pain can be difficult in all age groups but for different reasons. Very young children may lack the verbal and nonverbal skills necessary to communicate to their parents that they are in pain. Babies may wriggle and cry, but show few specific signs of where or how much it hurts. Toddlers may show more easily recognizable signs—grimacing, gritting their teeth, crying, or clutching the painful area. However, sometimes when the pain is severe, young children and older children alike may be very quiet and still, because moving or crying increases the pain. Pain in children may also contribute to nonspecific symptoms, such as agitation and irritability. As children mature, their expressions of pain get further complicated by their fears and expectations about what the pain means. On the one hand expressions of pain may gain much-wanted attention for the child, and this may influence her experience of pain. This is not to say that the child doesn't feel the pain. Pediatric cancer specialists say that children rarely, if ever, fabricate pain.[1] On the other hand a child may avoid telling anyone about her pain out of fear that more painful treatments or procedures will be ordered.

While there is no sure way to quantify pain, health professionals have been trying to develop more objective measures of a child's pain. This might include assigning numerical values that "rate" the pain experience, or using pictures of facial expressions that correspond to how a child feels. No one other than the child will ever really know how severe the

[1] Angela W. Miser and James S. Miser, "The Treatment of Cancer Pain in Children," *Pediatric Clinics of North America* 36, no. 4 (August 1989): 979–99.

pain is; thus it is important for parents and health professionals to work *with* the child in any pain-management program.

Even when a child's discomfort is obvious, however, there are barriers to adequate relief. In our society many people harbor negative ideas about pain medication. They may think that it is a sign of inner strength to "tough it out" when it hurts. Or that pain medication should be taken only as a last resort, when other measures fail to bring relief or when pain is unbearable. In actuality taking pain medication earlier rather than later may prevent many of the associated problems that intensify painful experiences—anxiety, depression, fatigue, and so on.

Finally, the most dreaded fear associated with giving strong pain medication is that the child will become addicted to the drug. Children face constant messages in school and on TV that "drugs" are bad and that they should "say no" to drugs. So it may be hard to convince people that taking drugs to relieve pain is very different from taking them to get high, particularly when similar substances may be involved. However, years of research have shown that very few people get addicted to drugs taken for pain relief.

Much of the worry about addiction stems from confusion about the terms *tolerance, dependence,* and *addiction. Tolerance* refers to the situation in which a given dose of drug becomes no longer sufficient to produce the desired effects, and a higher dose is needed. *Dependence* refers to a physiologic state that may occur if a drug is given regularly for as little as a few weeks. Upon withdrawal of a drug to which a person is dependent, the person will experience physical withdrawal symptoms, such as restlessness, sleeplessness, irritability, and sweating. These symptoms can be avoided by withdrawing the drug gradually. Both dependence and tolerance disappear after a drug is withdrawn.

*Addiction,* however, refers to psychological dependence

characterized by overwhelming craving and obsession with obtaining the drug. Drugs with addictive potential include the strong analgesics derived from opium or its relatives (these are called *opioid analgesics)* that may be used to treat cancer pain. As stated earlier, addiction rarely occurs in children receiving these drugs for pain relief. Nevertheless these drugs are monitored carefully to prevent the rare instance of abuse.

Pain medications may be delivered in a variety of ways—orally; by injection into a vein; under the skin (subcutaneously); or into a muscle (intramuscularly). The method of administration will be determined by the choice of drug, by the severity of the child's pain, and by other aspects of the child's condition. Often combinations of drugs will be given. When pain is chronic or long lasting, drugs may be given continuously or on a regular schedule rather than on an as-needed basis. This has been shown to provide better and more even pain control because the child does not have to suffer through periods of waiting for the next dose to take effect. It can also help the child sleep better. One of the newer innovations in pain management allows the child to determine for himself when more medication is needed. This method, called *patient-controlled analgesia, or PCA,* uses a programmable pump that is connected to an intravenous line. When the child feels the need, he can push a button to self-administer a preset dose of drug. At some institutions PCA is used on children as young as seven years old. In addition to providing appropriate levels of pain medication it has the added advantage of giving back to the child a sense of control over the situation.

### *NONPHARMACOLOGIC APPROACHES*

Although the drugs described above are powerful, they may not adequately address the child's anxieties, fears, and

TABLE 8.1
**Commonly Used Pain Medications**

| Type of Drug | Name of Drug | Use | Action | Side Effects |
|---|---|---|---|---|
| Mild pain reliever | Acetaminophen (Tylenol) | Mild pain | Analgesia | Few; rare cases of sensitivity |
| NSAIDs (nonsteroidal antiinflammatory drugs) | Aspirin<br>Ibuprofen<br>(Pediaprofen, Advil) | Mild pain | Analgesia<br>Antiinflammatory | May mask fever, cause gastrointestinal upset, and bleeding problems |
| Weak opioids | Codeine (often given with paracetamol) | Mild to moderate pain | Analgesia | Dizziness, Nausea |
| Strong opioids—short-acting | Morphine<br><br>Hydromorphone (Dilaudid)<br>Meperidine (Demerol)<br><br>Fentanyl (more potent than morphine)<br>Alfentanil<br>Sulfentanil | Dull, continuous pain<br><br>Moderate to severe pain<br>*Not* for chronic pain<br>*Not* for chronic pain<br>Short procedures<br>Short procedures<br>Premedication for surgery | Sedation<br>Analgesia | Constipation<br>Nausea, Vomiting<br>Respiratory<br>Depression |
| Strong opioids—long acting | Methadone | Long-term analgesic therapy | Analgesia | Same as other strong opioids |

TABLE 8.2
**Adjuvant Drugs Used for Pain Relief**

| Type of Drug | Name of Drugs | Use | Action | Side Effects |
|---|---|---|---|---|
| Antihistamines | Benadryl | | Sedation<br>Antihistamine | Dry mouth<br>Dizziness<br>Upset stomach |
| Benzodiazepam | Diazepam (Valium)<br>Oxazepam<br>Lorazepam (Ativan) | | Relieves anxiety<br>Relieves pain from muscle spasms<br>Conscious sedation | Increases respiratory depression effects of opioids<br>May cause nausea, vomiting, hallucinations, pain on injection, tolerance, dependence |
| | Midazolam (Versed) | Premedication for painful procedures | Induces amnesia | |
| Barbiturates | Methohexital<br>Thiopental<br>Pentobarbital | Sedation for procedures<br>Maintenance of sleep | Sedation<br>Hypnosis | Lowers pain threshold<br>May cause pain on injection |
| Nonbarbiturate anesthetics | Ketamine | Procedures | Analgesia<br>Anesthesia | Elevated blood pressure<br>Respiratory depression<br>Hallucinations<br>Delirium |

| Antidepressants | Imipramine (Tofranil), amitriptyline, for example | Nerve pain<br>Helpful with sleep problems | Analgesia<br>Increases effects of opioids | Cardiac arrhythmias<br>Drowsiness |
|---|---|---|---|---|
| Anticonvulsants | Carbamazepine (Tegretol)<br>Phenytoin (Dilantin)<br>Clonazepam | Nerve pain, especially if shooting or stabbing | Analgesia | Blood abnormalities<br>Drowsiness<br>Dizziness |
| Stimulants | Dextroamphetamine<br>Methylphenidate (Ritalin) | | Decrease sleepiness<br>Decrease respiratory depression<br>Enhance analgesic effects of opioids | Loss of appetite<br>Stomach upset<br>Irritability |
| Neuroleptics | Methotrimeprazine<br>Chlorpromazine | Nausea<br>Confused or combative child | Antinausea<br>Controls agitation<br>Analgesia | Dystonia (muscle tone abnormalities) |
| Corticosteroids | Dexamethasone, for example | Relief of pain caused by inflammation or pressure | Antiinflammatory | Increased appetite |

depression—all of which contribute to the experience of pain. For this reason drugs alone may be insufficient. Behavioral (psychological) techniques have been used with much success as valuable aids for pain management in children with cancer.

Behavioral techniques include relaxation, guided imagery, and hypnosis. According to Dr. Shapiro, these methods are effective because they encourage behavior that is incompatible with agitation, and because they give the child a sense of control. They are especially effective in managing procedural pain, because procedures are predictable in terms of when they will occur, and behavioral strategies can be timed accordingly. Further, as noted earlier, procedures are among the most painful aspects of having cancer. Some of the less painful procedures, such as *venipuncture* (inserting a needle into a vein) can often be managed with behavior strategies alone, but most of the more distressing procedures will require a combination of drugs and behavioral techniques. Psychologist Bret Boyer, Ph.D., says that behavioral techniques can also help manage painful and difficult experiences not associated with procedures. "A nice side effect is that when kids or parents learn to do this stuff, it's adaptable for when the kid can't fall asleep or if he's afraid of the dark, has a stomachache, or whatever," says Dr. Boyer.

For dealing with procedural pain, Dr. Boyer says behavioral techniques are most effective if they are learned and practiced before a painful procedure is done. For example, he began working with Chad shortly after the twelve-year-old was diagnosed with ALL. In preparation for a seemingly endless series of spinal taps and bone marrow aspirations and biopsies, Dr. Boyer began teaching Chad to use visual imagery to distract his thoughts from the upcoming procedure. For Chad this meant focusing his mind on computer games. By verbally describing to Dr. Boyer all the details of a sophisticated game, Chad found that his mind would be fully occupied throughout the procedure. Sometimes children say they don't even feel the needle insertion, says Dr. Boyer. But even when this does not fully work, and the child does feel the needle, the child may be able to divert his attention quickly back to visual imagery immediately after the procedure begins.

For Chad guided imagery provided a means of distraction. For other children imagery may be used for relaxation or hypnosis. The key, according to Dr. Boyer, is to customize the approach according to the individual child's interests and developmental level. "A seven-year-old boy may not be interested in relaxing, which might be very pleasant for you or me, but he might be able to imagine fighting a dragon. That's not very relaxing, but certainly can be distracting, especially if we make it vivid with lots of detail," says Dr. Boyer. Hypnosis involves dissociating certain sensations, he continues. For example both parents and children may have had the experience of being so busy and intense with some activity that they don't notice they have cut themselves until they see the blood.

"A lot of people think of hypnosis, relaxation, and guided imagery as mysterious, new-age things," says Boyer. "What I try to do is to demystify these ideas and to make them understandable in terms of how they can be strategically used to serve certain purposes in order to achieve some goal."

Even children as young as three or four years old can benefit from this kind of intervention, although younger children sometimes need a more concrete type of distraction. For example, when three-year-old Ricky has bone marrow aspirates done as part of his treatment for AML, Dr. Boyer and Ricky's mother blow bubbles with him. Blowing bubbles is fun and engaging for young children, and adds a breathing aspect to the intervention, which aids in relaxation. Another mother reads her child a book throughout a procedure. Dr. Boyer says that while these interventions are useful before, during, and after procedures, sometimes a child breaks focus and begins to cry. "At this point it is important to reengage the child, to reduce his distress," says Dr. Boyer. "Parents need to learn not to give up if this happens."

Chad's father, Zachary, said that visual imagery helped Chad feel more in control and imbued him with a sense of self-confidence. "He learned that although he couldn't control *when* the procedures were done, he might be able to control *how*," said Zachary.

Dr. Shapiro says that for optimum pain management, attention should also be given to other aspects of the pain-management regimen. For example, she suggests the child's room and bed should be considered safe and private places, in which painful procedures will not be done.

## Blood Products

Radiation therapy and chemotherapy, as well as some cancers themselves, can deplete a child's blood system of necessary components—the red blood cells that deliver oxygen to tissues, the white blood cells that fight infections, and the platelets that help the blood to clot. In fact it is this side effect that can limit the amount of radiation or chemotherapy given. Blood transfusions can replace depleted cells, but transfusions can bring on a new set of potential problems including circulatory problems, immunologic reactions against the transfused cells, and transmission of infectious diseases, including AIDS and hepatitis. Fortunately, improved testing of blood products means that infectious-disease transmission is very rare.

Until the 1960s whole blood was used for transfusions. Since then, however, the blood has been separated into the various cell types, and transfusions are done using only the cells that are necessary:

**Packed red blood cells** are given to children who suffer from anemia, which can be a complication of leukemia or a side effect of intensive chemotherapy.

**Platelet** transfusions are given to prevent excessive bleeding. Platelet deficiency, known as *thrombocytopenia,* can cause visible bleeding under the skin or in the mouth, or internal bleeding of the membranes lining the gastrointestinal tract. Worse, thrombocytopenia can lead to brain hemorrhage. Some doctors will give platelet transfusions only if symptoms appear, while other doctors will monitor platelet counts and begin regular transfusions when levels fall below a certain predetermined level.

**Granulocytes** are white blood cells that are important in combatting infections. They are also called *neutrophils,* and their levels are expressed as the *ANC,* or *absolute neutrophil count.* A low ANC is referred to as *neutropenia.* In the 1970s granulocyte transfusions were common in neutropenic patients. Today, however, because of better infection-control procedures, granulocyte transfusions are less common.

Since the early 1990s two new agents have become available for supporting children with neutropenia. These two agents, *granulocyte colony-stimulating factor (G-CSF),* and *granulocyte macrophage colony-stimulating factor (GM-CSF),* are substances that stimulate the proliferation of granulocytes and/or macrophages. *Macrophages* (also known as *monocytes)* are cells that are important for fighting infections. G-CSF and GM-CSF are naturally occurring substances that are now produced in the laboratory using modern methods of recombinant DNA technology. Therefore they carry with them no risk of transmissible infection or transfusion reactions.

Though they sound like nearly identical products, they have different mechanisms of action and are used for different conditions. GM-CSF is used to stimulate recovery of the cells of the bone marrow in patients undergoing bone marrow transplants. G-CSF is used for chemotherapy-induced neutropenia. Table 8.3 outlines the various products that are used to replenish the blood in children with cancer.

## Infection Control

Infections are one of the greatest risks to children with cancer. To begin with, their immune systems may be seriously suppressed as a result of disease, especially in the case of the leukemias. On top of that, chemotherapy and radiation therapy can further deplete the cells that defend against infection. Thus a major part of supporting a child with cancer involves preventing infections and treating them when they do occur. Chapters 5 and 6 discuss many of the steps taken in this effort when a child is receiving chemotherapy or radiation therapy, or when the child is getting a bone marrow transplant.

### *PREVENTION*

Prevention of infection is the first line of defense. First every effort is made to avoid exposure. The single most important measure in this regard is hand washing. Everyone who comes into contact with the child should first wash his hands thoroughly. The child must also be protected from exposure to common childhood illnesses, such as chicken pox and measles, which can threaten the life of an immunosuppressed child. Since many of these infections are contagious even before they become apparent in a seemingly

TABLE 8.3
**Blood Products**

| Problem | Symptoms | Treatment | Side Effects |
|---|---|---|---|
| Anemia (depletion of red blood cells) | Tiredness<br>Fatigue<br>Decreased activity<br>Irritability | Transfusion with red blood cells | Rash<br>Itching<br>Fever<br>Transfusion reactions<br>Infectious-disease transmission |
| Thrombocytopenia (depletion of platelets) | Bruising<br>Red spots (petechiae)<br>Bleeding of mouth | Platelet transfusion | Rash<br>Itching<br>Fever<br>Transfusion reactions<br>Infectious-disease transmission |
| Neutropenia (depletion of white blood cells) | Infections<br>Fever | G-CSF | Most common: bone pain<br>Also reported: enlarged spleen, mild hair loss |
| | | GM-CSF | Most common: flulike symptoms (fever, muscle aches, lethargy)<br>Less common: low blood pressure |

healthy child, most pediatric cancer centers restrict visits by children, even siblings of the patients. In a hospital, where many infections arise, rigorous cleaning and disinfecting procedures will be followed. For children at especially high risk, such as those undergoing bone marrow transplants, efforts to keep the environment as germ-free as possible will include isolation in rooms with filtered air systems and strict limitations on who and what is allowed in the child's room.

Other steps aimed at preventing infections include the prophylactic administration of antibiotics and antifungal agents; blood component and cell-stimulating factor therapy, which are discussed earlier; and immunization. Immunization is a tricky issue for children with cancer. Vaccines may be ineffective when a child's immune system is suppressed. Further some vaccines are made with live viruses that have been altered to make them less dangerous, and these live virus vaccines can be dangerous in a child with cancer. Other vaccines are made with killed viruses or with only certain components of viruses. Many factors go into the decision of whether to immunize a child against infectious diseases. These factors include the child's risk of exposure, the age of the child, the type of therapy the child is receiving, and the child's diagnosis. Your doctor will weigh all the factors before deciding which course to take.

If your child is exposed to an illness such as chicken pox or measles, your doctor may choose to use what is called *passive immunization. Passive* refers to the fact that the child is not actively producing the immune response, but that immunity is being passed on from another source. This is possible in some cases because the substances that are necessary for fighting disease are proteins, called antibodies, which circulate in the blood. These antibodies can be obtained from healthy, immune individuals; pooled and concentrated into what is called *immune* or *hyperimmune* serum globulin, and injected into the immunosuppressed child to provide some protection against the disease.

### *TREATMENT*

Treatment of infections requires the administration of drugs that will kill the offending microorganisms. In the ideal situation your doctor would know exactly what microbe was causing the infection and thus could prescribe a drug that was specifically targeted against that germ. But frequently a child will show only nonspecific signs of infection, such as fever. In such a case the doctor will often begin treating the child for an infection even before a firm diagnosis is made. Since fever may occur for reasons other than infection, this sometimes means that antibiotics are given when not actually required. However, in certain situations the risk that a child could develop a life-threatening infection far outweighs the problems associated with antibiotic therapy. For example if an indwelling catheter becomes infected, the infection can quickly become a generalized blood infection (*septicemia*) with serious consequences. Thus any sign of fever in a child with an indwelling catheter should be treated immediately and aggressively. Usually this means that the child will be hospitalized and given intravenous antibiotics, and the catheter may be pulled out. Some other infections may be treated with oral or topical agents, depending on the site and type of infection.

CHAPTER 9

# Social and Emotional Needs of the Family

When a child is diagnosed with cancer, a whole cadre of health professionals spring into action, all with a common purpose of helping families fight the disease. At times, it may seem as if the only thing that is important is vanquishing the illness. But treating childhood cancer involves more than fighting the disease itself.

From the very first moment that a family enters a children's cancer center, there are health professionals available to address social and emotional needs. The services that are available will vary from institution to institution. The child's doctors and nurses provide specific information about the child's medical needs and will in most cases pay close attention to the emotional impact on parents. In addition many hospitals employ psychosocial professionals to address further the social and emotional issues confronting families and to help prepare them for the challenges they will face in the coming months. At The Children's Hospital of Philadelphia, for example, the psychosocial staff includes psychologists, social workers, and child life specialists, who work as a team to meet the varying needs of children and their families. Other hospitals use a different approach, but at a minimum every hospital will probably have a social work department.

Moreover the array of resources available to families who have a child with cancer extends far beyond the hospital building. Outside agencies such as those listed in the Resources section; church, synagogue, and community groups; friends; and family all are potential sources of care and support. The psychosocial staff at your institution, as well as the other members of your child's health care team, are there not only to provide you with support but to help you gain access to support from other resources.

## Getting Through the Early Days

Parents frequently walk around shell-shocked during the first few days or weeks after diagnosis. Although this is a time when they are being confronted with enormous amounts of information and when they are asked to make crucial decisions about their child's care, many parents describe the time as "a blur."

Penetrating the fog, however, are powerful emotions: grief, fear, and sometimes anger. It sometimes seems a wonder that parents are able to function during this time at all, but they do. How? Partly through their overriding concern about their child's well-being and partly with the help of others. These others may include doctors who go to great lengths to explain things simply yet in detail; nurses who help translate technical jargon into terms families can understand and who can function as a sort of "memory bank" for parents who don't really hear all of what they are being told; and psychosocial professionals who can assist with both emotional and concrete needs, whether this means calling people who need to be called, arranging for a bed for the night, or providing counselling or referral to counselors in the home community.

Says Social Work Coordinator David Beele, A.C.S.W., L.S.W., "Initially we want to see how we can help them that day, that hour, so that they can help their child. We join first with the parents because they know their child best, and they are the people to whom the child will be looking for support."

Psychologist Anne Kazak, Ph.D., says that her primary message to parents is that there are people available to help them and that one way or another they will get through this stressful period. "We tell them to take it one day at a time," says Dr. Kazak. "But parents come back to me and say it's really more like one hour at a time."

### *TELLING YOUR CHILD*

One of the first crises that parents face involves telling their child about the diagnosis and what it means. Precisely what, when, and how parents tell their child about cancer will vary depending on the child's developmental level and on their family's normal communication style. In years past, a diagnosis of cancer was often hidden from a child with the thought that "What he doesn't know can't hurt him." But most cancer specialists today recommend that children be told as much as they are able to understand. Children are quite perceptive and are likely to know that something is wrong despite attempts to deny it. Further, when a child senses that he is not being told the truth, his imagination can conjure up terrifying thoughts, but he is not given the opportunity to ask questions that might allay some of his fears and anxieties. Finally, when a child is not told the truth, he learns not to trust those who are caring for him. Psychologists John Spinetta and Patricia Deasy-Spinetta, who have written extensively on the subject, conclude, "We believe that it is best to address the issue of the seriousness of the child's illness from the time of diagnosis. In this way energy that would be wasted in maintaining deceit can be applied to the very real problem of helping the child live with a life-threatening illness."[1]

Although honesty and truthfulness are thought to be of paramount importance, hope is also a necessary ingredient. Some parents feel that if they tell the child themselves, their own fears and anguish will surface and overshadow their hopefulness. For this reason parents often need a chance to digest the diagnosis themselves before they feel prepared to tell their child. Thus the doctor often meets first with the parents before the child is told. This gives parents a chance to ask questions and express their anguish and fear in private, without raising undue alarm in their child.

No amount of delay, however, will truly prepare parents for the task in front of them. Again, the health care team can help. For example, nurses and psychosocial professionals can help parents decide how to tell a child about cancer in a way that will be understandable to him. Some parents ask the doctor to deliver the diagnosis; others want the doctor there to answer questions. In general, says oncologist Beverly

[1] John J. Spinetta and Patricia Deasy-Spinetta, "Talking with Children Who Have a Life-threatening Illness," in John J. Spinetta and Patricia Deasy-Spinetta, eds., *Living with Childhood Cancer* (St. Louis: Mosby, 1981).

Lange, M.D., "Kids have told us that they prefer to have their parents give them bad information, particularly in the beginning. But parents sometimes want us there because they feel they can't even get the words out, or that they'll show too much emotion."

Although children may not have many questions at first, as the diagnosis begins to sink in and the child begins to adjust to changes in her daily routine, more questions are likely to arise. Parents are also likely to think up more questions over the following days or weeks. Says Nurse Patricia Brophy, "I tell parents, 'You don't need to think of everything right here and now. Things will keep coming up, and there are a lot of people you can call. It's not a need that gets met in one day.' "

### *COPING WITH A CANCER DIAGNOSIS*

Everyone has a different way of coping with bad news. Some parents cope by seeking out a great deal of information, getting second opinions, and asking lots of questions. Other parents immediately reach for sources of emotional support. Some parents and children react fairly calmly and can quickly get to the business of treatment. Others are devastated by the news. There is no one "right" way of reacting to news as shocking as that of a cancer diagnosis. Moreover the early days may be so chaotic and confusing that "coping" has not yet truly begun. Gradually, however, the reality of the diagnosis will set in, and the days become somewhat more predictable. And despite parents' fears that they will never be able to meet the challenges they face, most do.

During this time the child's medical needs take center stage, as treatment begins in earnest. Parents may feel as if they are taking a crash course in pediatric oncology as gradually terms that previously sounded like a foreign language become incorporated into their daily speech. Meanwhile lives are turned upside down. For those who are lucky enough to have supportive family and friends close by, the adjustments may take place relatively smoothly. Others may have more difficulty juggling their conflicting responsibilities —to other family members, home, and job.

For those who are accustomed to being independent and in control, their first challenge may be to ask for help from extended family members, friends, and neighbors. Some parents find this particularly difficult. "You learn to be humble," said Alice, whose daughter, Diana, was being treated for Ewing's sarcoma. "It was hard at first to accept the help people offered, but friends made it possible to get through."

Dr. Kazak reminds parents that they won't need help forever and that they will be able to give it back at some point. "Most people agree that they would want to do the same thing if it was their neighbor [who needed help] rather than themselves," says Dr. Kazak.

Psychosocial staff members can help in a variety of ways at this time. They may be able to direct families to resources in the community that are available to help in these times of crisis. Such resources might include a nearby Ronald McDonald House, where family members can stay during a child's hospitalization.

Many parents find that active participation in their child's care helps them cope with the stress they feel. Participation can relieve feelings of powerlessness, uselessness, and guilt. At the same time, the child benefits because those who are most important to him are providing the hands-on care he needs. How parents participate varies from family to family, and some parents find active participation itself stressful. Further some parents attempt to take on too much at a time when what they really need is to give up some responsibilities and "just be a mom or dad."

Other strategies that parents may find useful in helping

them cope with the stress of their child's illness and hospitalization include exercise, relaxation, or some other activity that takes their mind off the situation for brief periods of time. For example, Sherry and Donna, two mothers who met while their children were hospitalized with cancer, occasionally took a break to go shopping.

Many parents agree that when they can maintain a positive outlook and good communication with their spouses and other family members, and can work cooperatively with the health care team, the stress of the situation becomes more manageable. This can be particularly difficult for single parents, however, who may feel isolated and overwhelmed by the burden they must shoulder alone. These parents may find their psychosocial team to be particularly helpful for both emotional and practical support.

## Getting Help

Even in families who appear to be adjusting smoothly to their new situation, powerful emotions may be boiling just under the surface. So it's no wonder when relatively minor frustrations or setbacks erupt into an angry outburst or emotional collapse. Psychologist Bret Boyer, Ph.D., says that one of his goals is to help parents understand the true source of their anxiety.

For example, when their son, Lenny, was in the hospital for a second bone marrow transplant, his parents exploded in anger about the hospital bureaucracy, directing their wrath at the nursing staff. Dr. Boyer validated their anger, noting that hospitals can be extremely frustrating, but he sensed that their real anxiety stemmed from understandable fears that the second transplant, like the first, was not going to cure Lenny's leukemia.

"Once someone says, 'I'm anxious and scared and I wish there was something I could do to relieve that,' then we can come up with ideas to address their needs directly," says Dr. Boyer. "It can be anything from giving an ear so they can talk about why they are frightened and anxious, all the way up through helping them develop something that decreases anxiety." Possibilities include exercise or other recreational activities, pursuing hobbies, relaxation, or self-hypnosis, for example. Says Dr. Boyer, "It makes sense for them to be frightened, and they don't have to pretend not to be."

Psychosocial professionals not only offer their services directly to children and their families, they can also serve as a bridge with the medical staff—informing them of families' social and emotional concerns and needs. For example, at the weekly psychosocial and nursing staff meeting, Social Worker Lisa Gagen spoke about Angie, an eleven-year-old girl who was newly diagnosed with osteosarcoma. Angie was refusing to cooperate with her doctors and nurses, especially when it came time to start intravenous lines. She also refused even to discuss pain management. Ms. Gagen learned that Angie was a tomboy, angry about the potential loss of her leg. She was also worried about the chemotherapy causing her hair to fall out, and she was feeling guilty, saying, "If I hadn't told them [her parents] that my leg hurt, I wouldn't be here."

Ms. Gagen shared with the team some of Angie's emotional needs. "I was concerned that she would be labeled difficult, when she was really scared and anxious," says Ms. Gagen. Together the team worked out strategies for addressing some of Angie's anxieties and giving her some control over the situation.

Although many children's cancer centers offer a wide array of psychological support services, parents may find it difficult to gain access to them. Some people simply don't know what services exist. Generally the longer a child is in the hospital, the more parents will learn about available services. But even if parents know that psychosocial services exist, they may feel reluctant to pursue them for a variety of reasons. Some parents think that their problems are not of sufficient severity to warrant professional help, while others find the thought of talking to a psychologist or social worker too scary and pathologizing.

However, Dr. Kazak encourages parents to maintain a connection with the psychosocial support team, even when things appear to be going smoothly. "People are afraid that if they see a therapist, it means they're crazy. But that's not the case. They are going through one of the hardest things that they could ever possibly go through, and we are trained to help. A major event like this can really shake up a person's sense of who they are and what they've been doing. There are bound to be a lot of repercussions."

Not all cancer treatment centers offer extensive psychosocial services. However, there are other support services available in the community. For a psychological counselling referral Dr. Kazak suggests that parents ask their oncologist and/or the hospital's social work department. Referrals may also be obtained from clergy, the family doctor, or friends. "Find out who is respected and appropriately credentialed, and feel free to ask questions, such as whether they've had experience working with people who are going through similar experiences," advises Dr. Kazak.

Psychiatrist Michael Silver, M.D., of the Philadelphia Child Guidance Center, adds, "It's perfectly legitimate to interview mental health professionals over the phone to get information about what sorts of experience they have."

## *OTHER SOURCES OF SUPPORT*

Whether or not the hospital offers extensive support services, families can also benefit from a number of other resources. To find out what is available, contact the local chapters of the American Cancer Society and the Candlelighters Childhood Cancer Foundation (CCCF). The Resources section at the end of this book lists information about these and a number of other organizations that can provide assistance. It also lists books that parents may find helpful.

These organizations, as well as your local hospital or cancer center, may offer support groups for children with cancer, their parents, and/or other family members. Parent support groups can be very therapeutic, says Dr. Kazak. "Parents talk, they meet each other, they befriend each other; they become very close friends. There's an incredible bonding that goes on. It's very powerful to be able to talk with other people who have gone through similar experiences." For groups to function optimally Dr. Kazak recommends that they have a strong facilitator or be supported by a solid organization, such as Candlelighters. "It makes a difference to have a good facilitator who can keep the momentum going or stop people from monopolizing the group. Otherwise these groups can become destructive or they can peter out."

Children's groups are helpful for somewhat different reasons. They give children with cancer the opportunity to be themselves—to not be afraid to show their bald heads or Broviac catheters. They also give children a chance to talk with other children about their fears and anxieties about having a life-threatening illness, issues that children may be afraid to discuss with their parents or their friends who are not ill. Many children with cancer have the opportunity to attend summer camps expressly designed for them. These camps give them the opportunity to escape briefly from the watchful eyes of overprotective parents and to relax with their peers. They have the added benefit of giving parents some time off for themselves or for the rest of the family.

Many families turn to religion for support. Hospital-based chaplains or private clergy can provide pastoral counselling as parents struggle with questions about why their child has gotten cancer. Many parents find comfort from their religious experience, their relationship with God, and faith in a higher power. In addition families who are affiliated with a particular church, synagogue, mosque, or other religious group may find that their congregation provides a caring community available to help in countless ways—providing meals, caring for children, and so on. For some people, however, a child getting cancer can cause a crisis of faith. They may even feel let down by God. Even so, clergy may help parents wrestle with their feelings, and the religious community may offer practical support and companionship.

Of course not all social and emotional support comes from formally structured organizations such as those listed above. Family and friends can be the greatest source of all for both practical help and emotional strength. Often friends simply need to be told what is needed and they will make themselves available to satisfy those needs. However, sometimes parents of children with cancer will find it necessary to place limits on the help provided by their friends and family. This places a burden on the child's parents to make their needs clear and to say no when it becomes necessary. At times parents may resist placing such limits, fearing that they will appear ungrateful. In the long run, however, most people want to be helpful and will appreciate the parents' honesty in setting limits.

For example, when Libby and her parents were in the hospital during the Christmas season, friends of the family wanted to decorate the house so that Libby's brothers wouldn't feel left out of the holiday spirit. Libby's mother felt that the gesture might create some additional problems and asked her friends not to decorate the house. She did, however, take them up on their offer to wrap the family's Christmas presents so that when the boys came to the hospital on Christmas Day, their presents were ready and waiting.

## Particular Times of Added Stress

Certain events during a child's treatment for cancer may precipitate especially stressful reactions. These are times when parents may need special attention from their friends, family, and health care team. Yet they are also times when asking for that help becomes particularly difficult.

### *WHEN COMPLICATIONS OCCUR*

Despite the many improvements in treatment and supportive care, unexpected complications will arise. These can be very disheartening for the entire family. Just when parents are beginning to feel adjusted to their child's illness, complications can upset that precarious balance once again.

### *RELAPSE*

Some parents say that a relapse is worse even than the initial diagnosis. When Libby relapsed after nearly a year on maintenance chemotherapy, her parents could no longer hold back their tears. "We just cried," says Francie. "We told her it was because we knew what she would be going through," including more procedures, chemotherapy, and radiation therapy. But there were other reasons for their tears, reasons they didn't share at first with their daughter. They knew that although a cure was still possible, Libby's chance of cure was now diminished. Even more distressing, their hopes had been dashed, just as those hopes were beginning to take hold.

*GOING OFF TREATMENT*

Surprisingly one of the most stressful times for a family may be when the child goes off treatment. "It's much more traumatic than people realize," says Dr. Kazak. "People have mixed feelings. It's not that they want to keep coming to the hospital or, God knows, that they want to keep having chemo. But their lives have become deeply connected to their team."

Oncologist Richard Womer, M.D., adds, "People tend to be more together on treatment than off because they feel as though they're doing something and the security blanket is there. Then, all of the sudden, they're not doing anything anymore. They're just waiting to see whether things are going to come back or not. Families tend to get somewhat unraveled then."

The stress of going off treatment may be hard for some people to understand. Family members and friends alike sometimes pressure parents to "get on with their lives" or to "put it behind them." People may say or think, "You're so lucky. Your child has survived." The parents, however, may not feel so lucky, and may not find it easy to leave the experience behind. In addition, going off treatment may also allow other concerns, which had been put on the back burner, to emerge. Parents faced with these confusing emotions may benefit from talking to other parents or to members of their health care team who understand that it takes time to recover from the trauma of cancer treatment. When that time stretches on and interferes with the family's ability to function, help from a mental health professional may be needed.

## Special Considerations for Teens

Being a teenager is hard enough for a healthy child. Having cancer, however, makes adolescence that much more difficult. Moreover, being the parent of a teenager becomes much more difficult when that child has cancer.

Like healthy adolescents, teenagers with cancer want more independence and more control over decisions that affect them. At the same time, peer relationships become increasingly important, and teens struggle with issues of identity and sexuality. But cancer throws a monkey wrench into the normal teenage passages. Rather than becoming more independent, teens with cancer may find themselves more needy than ever before. And while they still need and want nurturing, they may find parental attention to be stifling their personal growth. In other words being a teenager with cancer may be like trying to mix oil and water. Conflicts are bound to arise.

Prolonged hospitalization for a teenager may add to these difficulties. Children's cancer centers often employ child life specialists and provide playrooms to encourage children's socialization and activity; yet while these may be great for younger children, they may not meet the needs of adolescents. Children of this age often do well in less organized settings, where they can "hang out," play ball, or otherwise interact with peers. Some hospitals will establish teen groups to reduce their patients' sense of isolation, although oftentimes children of this age will seem withdrawn. According to Dr. Kazak, such behavior is developmentally appropriate for adolescents. Other hospitals will group their patients according to age rather than illness so that teens with cancer are mixed in with their peers who are experiencing other kinds of illnesses and injuries. For many teenagers, maintaining contact with non-ill friends can be very helpful. The psychosocial staff can work with parents to determine how best to meet the social and emotional needs of their adolescent children, both in and out of the hospital.

When adolescents are able to care for themselves, they may benefit from feeling more independent and in control. Sometimes, however, this can go too far. Randall, for example, learned to care for his Broviac catheter, start intravenous medications, and perform other simple tasks that parents are often asked to help with. But Randall's nurse sensed that the young man was feeling more and more isolated and anxious about his increasing responsibilities. Finally she said to him, "Give yourself a break. You don't have to do all this. There are a lot of people to support you."

Teenagers need and usually want to be involved in decisions about their care. Harold, for example, a fourteen-year-old with a rare type of testicular tumor, was the type of person who wanted to know everything about what was happening to him. He got angry when his mother told him that everything was okay; he felt that indicated that things were going on behind his back. His mother meanwhile was trying to keep his spirits up and minimize his fear and anxiety. But Harold felt he was being lied to and demanded more honesty.

Sometimes a teenager's wishes will conflict with those of his parents, but often with the help of other members of the health care team, both can have their needs met. For example, seventeen-year-old Leon had osteosarcoma in his right leg. When he and his parents met with the oncologist and orthopedic surgeon, Leon said, "Maybe we should just cut it off," a statement that greatly distressed his mother, who wanted to try to save the leg. But Dr. Womer explained to Leon's mother that Leon was old enough to have some say in his care. Leon, his mother, and the doctors finally agreed to try a limb salvage operation.

Compliance is another major problem with adolescents. Once they start feeling better, says Dr. Beverly Lange, teenagers will often stop taking prescribed medications. Since a cure may depend on faithful adherence to the treatment regimen, monitoring by parents may be needed. However, this may provoke anger in the young person, who feels the parent is being overprotective or overbearing. Psychosocial staff can often work with the family to find mutually acceptable forms of monitoring that will ensure both that the child retains his sense of control and that the medication is being taken.

## Marriage and Family

The extraordinary pressures on families can strain even those with strong, close-knit relationships. As a result some families break apart. But many others become closer as a result of their intense shared experience. Andrea, whose baby daughter, Wendy, was hospitalized with neuroblastoma, said, "I don't know how marriages survive this. My marriage is on hold, my career is on hold; everything is on hold." Yet Moira, whose son, Sean, was treated for a brain tumor, says the ordeal helped her marriage. "It made us rethink what is really important," she said.

Marital stress can arise from a number of sources in addition to those that affect any marriage. Andrea, for example, felt angry about being almost solely responsible for Wendy's care. Although she understood that her husband needed to keep working in order to pay Wendy's mounting medical bills, and she acknowledged her husband's contribution to the care of their other child, she nevertheless felt angry that her husband had never learned to care for Wendy's Broviac or to administer medications. She also resented having to give up her job while her husband kept his. Andrea tried to be exceedingly patient with Wendy, but she needed a way to vent her frustration and anxiety about Wendy's condition, and she did so by getting angry at her husband. Consequently Andrea and her husband became progressively more estranged.

Francie reported a similar experience during her daughter, Libby's, treatment for leukemia. Meanwhile Francie's husband, Carl, felt excluded from and jealous about the intense relationship between Francie and Libby. Such stories are repeated over and over again by parents of children with cancer. In the book *Childhood Cancer and the Family,* social scientists Mark Chesler and Oscar Barbarian presented the results of hundreds interviews with families of children with cancer.[2] They cited several issues that are especially important for couples coping with a child's cancer: making time for themselves when they can share feelings and information; accepting each other's differences; and including each other in the everyday care of their ill child and the rest of the family.

Many couples find ways to handle this stress. But if parents are experiencing any of these conflicts, they should feel free to contact the psychosocial professional on their team. If one is not available at your hospital, a referral for counselling or family therapy can be requested.

Many parents enter into this experience having already separated or divorced. To all the other challenges that must be faced, these parents must also try to put aside their differences or animosities in order to support their child. Parents

[2] Mark A. Chesler and Oscar A. Barbarian, *Childhood Cancer and the Family* (New York: Brunner/Mazel, 1987).

find different ways of handling this added difficulty. While Leeann was in the hospital getting a bone marrow transplant, her parents, who were in the midst of a bitter divorce, arranged to split their days at the hospital with no overlap. They made an exception, however, when Leeann was scheduled to have difficult procedures done. At those times Leeann wanted them both at her side, and they did their best to get along.

Single-parent families face other problems. Caring for a child with cancer is at times an awesome job, particularly when there are other children in the family who must be cared for. All parents feel torn by their conflicting responsibilities to their sick child and their other children if they have them. Single parents, however, often have fewer options if there is no other adult to help share child care and financial and emotional responsibilities. Extended family members, friends, and other resources in the community may be especially important in helping single parents cope with these burdens.

## Changing Family Roles

A child's illness almost always causes a major shift in the roles and expectations of family members. As with other stresses, people react to their new demands differently. Generally the earlier families are able to accept that their roles will change, the better able they are to shape those changes. They may be able to plan ahead rather than just reacting to difficult situations.

Alice made the transition with relative ease. She quit her job when Diana got sick and began a new "full-time" job caring for her daughter. Meanwhile Alice's husband, Tony, and her teenage son, Jeffrey, had to learn to take care of themselves to a greater degree. "This is a year out of our lives, and there is nothing else now," says Alice. "Everything else is on hold."

But transitions are more difficult for many families. The reasons are numerous. Employers may be unwilling to give parents time off from work, although the recently enacted Family Leave Act should help some families in this regard. The law requires many employers to allow up to twelve weeks' unpaid leave, with continuation of medical benefits, when a child or other family member is ill. Even if employers are willing to give parents the time, however, financial pressures may demand that both parents, or a single parent, keep working. In addition young children at home may place enormous demands on parents' energies. And finally, few parents are prepared, emotionally or practically, to accommodate their new roles. Psychosocial support is geared to help parents handle these and other difficulties.

CHAPTER 10

# Parenting the Child with Cancer

Parenting is a challenge even under the best of circumstances. When a child has cancer, it becomes still more complicated. Increased stress on all members of the family, uncertainty about what lies ahead, and upheavals in the family's daily routine all combine to make the job of parenting especially difficult. Further, parents may feel that they have failed in their primary parental duty—that of protecting their child from harm. Even though they may understand intellectually that their child's cancer is not their fault and that its occurrence was beyond their control, they may still harbor guilty feelings. As a result they may lose confidence in their ability to parent effectively. On top of all that the normal tasks of parenting, such as setting limits, providing discipline, and so forth, may at times seem unimportant in light of a child's pressing medical needs.

Nonetheless mental health professionals encourage parents to treat their ill child as normally as possible. From the earliest days after diagnosis it can be helpful to think of the child as a survivor and to prepare for an eventual cure. This means not putting off until later matters such as setting limits, imposing discipline, and helping their child through the normal developmental hurdles the child will face.

Of course everyone knows that there's nothing normal about a child having cancer. These are normal children facing a highly abnormal situation, which means that parents are challenged to maintain some normalcy in their children's lives yet at the same time make adaptations when they are needed.

## Behavior and Discipline

Disciplining a sick child is not easy, especially when the child has a life-threatening illness and may not have a chance to learn from her mistakes. But ask parents what happened when they didn't impose discipline: Francie, Libby's mother, says that by the end of the three-month period of induction therapy, the six-year-old was screaming for whatever she wanted. And she usually got it. Finally, when Libby claimed that she wanted to "get rid of" her little brother, Francie decided the time had come for professional help. She called the psychologist at The Children's Hospital of Philadelphia and began a series of counselling sessions, first with the entire family, then with Libby and her parents, and finally just Libby alone. "The psychologist told us that Libby had the whole family wrapped around her finger," says Francie.

With the psychologist's help the family learned to restructure their interactions and treat Libby more normally so that she would realize that she wasn't the only important person in the family.

"It's important for parents to maintain certain expectations [of their child with cancer]," says psychiatrist Michael Silver. "First because we don't know how the child will perceive being treated differently; second to avoid problems down the road; and third to avoid problems with siblings." A child might interpret different treatment as a sign that he hasn't long to live or that the parents have given up hope, for example. Further a child with cancer might perceive a loss of structure as additional evidence that his world is falling apart and is beyond control. Over and over again children with cancer say they want their lives to return to normal. Although they might be hesitant to admit that they want more discipline or structure, these are the normal conditions of childhood.

In order to provide appropriate and effective discipline, however, parents must first determine what they can legitimately expect from their child. Acceptable behavior for child with cancer may be different from that for a healthy child. Moreover expectations may change over the course of a child's treatment. A mental health professional in consultation with a child's oncologist can help parents determine which behaviors are appropriate at various times during treatment.

There are plenty of reasons for changes in a child's behavior when he has cancer. Anxiety, fear, and anger about the illness can lead to "acting out" behaviors, such as tantrums in a young person. Feeling sick all the time or being in pain may also produce an angry, unhappy, and/or uncooperative child. Medication given for cancer treatment, pain, or other problems may also result in behavior changes or in fatigue or weakness that may affect how a child acts. And sometimes the cancer itself influences a child's behavior, especially when cancer affects the central nervous system.

Behavioral, intellectual, and emotional changes may even be among the earliest signs of disease. For example, nine-year-old Roberto was diagnosed with a type of brain tumor called medulloblastoma, but only after several months of visits to a family doctor. The doctor had attributed his various symptoms, including personality changes, to a psychological ailment. When Roberto's symptoms worsened to the point that he couldn't walk a straight line or stand on one foot, a doctor ordered the diagnostic tests that indicated a brain tumor. By this time, says his mother, Theresa, the personality changes were extreme. "He was angry and irrational, screaming at me, 'I'm going to have you arrested!' "

Following the diagnosis, surgery, and radiation therapy for the tumor, Roberto's normally cheerful and engaging personality reemerged, said his mother, but he faced other difficulties. "He's a very, very determined kid and was always very active. Now he has to take a rest at school every day. As he feels better, he wants to do more, but his activity level is still restricted, so that's hard for him. Plus he wants his friends to come over and play, but they don't always come. I don't know if they're afraid or what."

Roberto's story illustrates how cancer itself may influence a child's behavior and also how treatment can affect a child's capabilities and emotions. Roberto's difficulties changed over time, as did the manner in which his mother dealt with him. Understanding the reasons for a child's behavior will help parents and mental health professionals devise appropriate strategies for dealing with problems that arise.

Roberto's mother was dealing with a child who sometimes wanted to do more than he was really capable of doing. Other parents, however, may deal with children who don't seem to do much of anything, and parents may wonder if the child is "using" his illness to gain special treatment even when special consideration is not needed. Again the health care team may be able to help determine what the child's true capabilities are. Psychosocial professionals may also help your child understand and put aside fears that are preventing him from returning to normal activities. Prolonged helplessness, such as that which may occur when a child is hospitalized for a long time, can make anyone assume that abilities have been lost. A child may need to be convinced that he really can do more.

Part of dealing with a child's behavioral changes often involves dealing with the reactions of siblings. Siblings may not understand why their brother or sister is given special consideration, especially after the initial treatment period has passed and the child with cancer appears to be "back to normal."

Libby's ten-year-old brother, Sam, for example, resented the fact that Libby only had to practice the piano for five minutes while he had to practice for fifteen minutes. Francie had assumed, but never explained to Sam, that Libby was experiencing bone pain that worsened when she sat at the piano for longer than a few minutes. Once Sam knew this, he became more understanding of Libby's special needs. But he still at times resented the special treatment his sister received. "Her brothers don't really understand," says Francie. "I thought they would after all this time, but they don't."

Special treatment not only made Libby's brothers resentful, says Francie, it also gave Libby a distorted view of her place within the family. "If I had to do it over again, I would spend more time with the boys so that Libby would have realized that she wasn't the only one who was important," says Francie. "I had to tell her, 'I love Sam, and I love [younger brother] Joey. I don't love you more just because you're sick.' " Other things that Francie says she would do differently include listening to Libby more in order to pinpoint patterns in her behavior, not giving in to everything she wanted, and not allowing people to give her so many presents. "I would stop and think, 'What would I do if she were a normal child?' " says Francie.

## Unexpected Parenting Tasks

Of course parenting involves much more than setting limits and providing discipline. As parents we must also provide our children guidance through life's twists and turns. But even the most skilled parents will probably be unprepared to deal with the tasks they face when their child has cancer. These include helping the child process his fears, including fears about death and dying; helping the child maintain hope in the face of a life-threatening disease; and helping the child confront changes in physical appearance and well-being, changes that may persist throughout life.

### *HELPING A CHILD PROCESS FEARS*

More than anything else, young children fear separation from their parents. As a result, hospitalization, even with mom or dad nearby, may increase a young child's fearfulness and anxiety. As the child grows older, other aspects of cancer also evoke fear—the pain, the prospect of not being able to do things as before, and, by the age of eight or ten, the possibility of dying. Even though a child may be relatively healthy, the possibility of dying may come to mind from time to time.

Parents naturally do not want their children to dwell on these fears. But oncology professionals encourage parents to be as open and honest as possible with their children, even when the subject is death. When fears are held inside or denied expression, say the experts, a child may become even more anxious and fearful. Helping a child process his fears doesn't always take place in conversations, however. Young children often express themselves through play. Using a doll as a surrogate, for example, a child may be able to explore concerns about painful procedures or other aspects of having cancer. Other children may express themselves through drawing.

Children sometimes hold their fear inside even when parents give plenty of opportunity for expression. One reason a child might do this is to protect her parents from distress. A child who will not share her deepest fears with a parent, however, may open up to a psychosocial professional, another member of the health care team, or a trusted friend. Child life specialists are particularly adept at getting young children to express themselves through play. Psychosocial professionals may also be called upon to help children process their fears and anxieties when the parents find that their own anxiety gets in the way.

### *HELPING A CHILD MAINTAIN HOPE*

With prolonged illnesses such as cancer it is sometimes difficult for children to maintain hope, even when progress is being made. Yet many people feel that a fighting spirit is a necessary ingredient in the treatment of cancer. When that ingredient is missing, when a child gives up hope, the prospects for cure seem to diminish as well. Thus one important task for parents of children with cancer is to help their child maintain hope. This does not mean denying the child's suffering or raising false hopes, but providing understanding, encouragement, and emotional support during the bleakest times.

There may be times when parents themselves feel discouraged, fatigued, or in some other way ill equipped to nurture hope in their child. Again, family members, friends, or members of the health care team may be able to help, either by providing emotional support to the parents or by giving them a brief respite from their parental responsibilities.

### *HELPING A CHILD DEAL WITH CHANGE*

For many children, especially adolescents, self-image is closely tied to physical appearance. So it's no wonder that one of the greatest concerns of teenagers is anxiety about being bald or in some other way looking different from their peers. Baldness is one of the most visible "symbols" that children with cancer carry with them even as they reenter the normal world. It sets them apart from the other children in their peer group.

Another major physical change that a child may face is that of amputation. Surprisingly parents often have more difficulty dealing with this than their children do, according to Dr. Richard Womer. "Kids and teenagers are extremely resilient. Usually within a few minutes or sometimes within a few days of finding out [that they are going to have an amputation], they have lots of questions and they're eager to get on with it. But parents go through hell. Adults are a lot less resilient than kids. We tell parents that they are going through a worse time than their child, that their child is going to be fine, and that their job is to be supportive and not restrictive."

Parental encouragement alone may be insufficient to alleviate a child's anxiety about these physical changes. What may help, however, is for the child to talk to other children who have gone through similar experiences. Children who are anticipating baldness will share stories about the best time and place to get a wig; and about crazy hats, scarves, or other head coverings that have been fun to wear instead of wigs. Children who are facing amputation will see how other children have managed with similar disabilities.

Says Dr. Womer, "We try to have someone of similar sex, similar age, and similar surgery come and speak to our patients and their families, to let them know what things are like on the other side."

*TAKING CARE OF YOURSELF*

Another task that parents of children with cancer face is that of taking care of themselves, and relieving their children of that responsibility. According to Dr. Silver, one of the biggest burdens for children with cancer is feeling that they must take care of their parents. Children who shoulder this burden hide their own feelings inside and may miss the opportunity to process their fears and anxieties.

## Protection and Overprotection

A major task of parenting is to prepare children for the future and then to let them live it themselves. This task doesn't disappear when a child has cancer; it only becomes more difficult to accomplish. It becomes more difficult when it seems to conflict with another parental duty: that of protecting children from harm. When a child experiences a trauma such as that of having cancer, the line between protection and overprotection often becomes blurred.

During the early phases of a child's illness parents often shower their children with attention and affection. Usually this is appropriate and comforting for the child. But after those early days, weeks, or months have passed and the child increasingly needs or wants to return to a more normal existence, the same amount of attention and affection can truly be smothering. This can deny children the opportunity to go through normal developmental tasks of separating from parents and becoming more independent. An older child might become rebellious. In addition, when a parent is overprotective, the child may become unreasonably fearful.

Margaret said that when her three-year-old daughter, Alison, came home after nine months in the hospital, "We just wanted to hold her and keep her at home. But our doctor kept telling us that we had to get her into school." Despite their reluctance, Margaret and her husband did send Alison to school, where the teachers discovered learning disabilities that received early attention.

Margaret's near-overprotectiveness stemmed from her desire to cherish the baby whom she felt had almost been taken away from her. Protectiveness may also cross the line into overprotectiveness when parents are unsure of what their children are truly capable of accomplishing and want to protect them from physical harm as well as from disappointment or failure.

Theresa, for example, straddled the line carefully. Her son, Roberto, longed to get back on the basketball court after treatment for a brain tumor. With rehabilitation therapy his condition continued to improve, yet he wanted to do more than his doctors would allow. Theresa supported his ambition, but worried. "Bending over to pick up a ball, he loses his balance. And if a ball came right at him, he could really be hurt. I need to know he's safe." In an attempt to meet Roberto's desire to do more yet still protect him as much as was necessary, Theresa stayed in close contact with his oncologist, neurosurgeons, and physical therapists, as well as his teachers and therapists at school. "I explained to Roberto that the physical therapist was preparing him for an adapted gym program at school," said Theresa. With Roberto's determination and the therapy, Theresa expects to see the day when Roberto will be back on the court. "I'm a shooter," said Roberto. "And I make most of my shots."

Issues of protectiveness and overprotectiveness become somewhat more complicated with adolescents. What might pass as a normal level of parental concern to other adults or to younger children may seem like overprotectiveness to a teenager. Meanwhile what seems like typical behavior to a teenager may be seen as unnecessarily risky by parents. Again, parents may want to consult with their child's doctors or with psychosocial professionals to determine whether certain behaviors are acceptable. Other parents of teenagers with cancer may also offer an illuminating perspective. Parent support groups or other types of parent-to-parent networks may help in this regard.

Doctors caution that while teenagers are old enough to be a part of the decision-making process regarding their care, they still usually need parental support and guidance. This is particularly important when a teenager needs long-term medications that are self-administered. As discussed earlier, adolescents often have a sense of invulnerability and may not take seriously the need to continue with medication when they are feeling better. Parents thus sometimes need to monitor their teenager's medication to be sure that treatment regimens are fully completed.

CHAPTER 11

# Siblings Are Special

With all a family's attention focused on their child with cancer, it's no wonder that the needs of siblings sometimes fade into the background. But in recent years professionals who work in the field of pediatric oncology have shifted the focus to some degree. Siblings, they say, are sometimes the family members who suffer the most when a child gets cancer.

Parents usually know that their other children have needs that aren't being met, but they often feel helpless to change the situation in light of their sick child's pressing needs. "I can't really parent my healthy children the way I used to," said one mother. "I don't have anything left. All of my energy is focused on Mindy."

Added another mother, "It makes me feel like my best is not good enough. But it *is* my best."

These parents were sharing their feelings at a workshop devoted to siblings that was held at The Children's Hospital of Philadelphia. While brothers and sisters of the cancer patients met in the oncology clinic for a day of learning, sharing, and fun, their parents met upstairs to talk among themselves and with psychosocial professionals from the Oncology Department.

Early in the workshop the children's comments were mostly about the extra attention and gifts that their ill siblings receive. Said ten-year-old Shari, whose brother, Randy, has a brain tumor: "Everybody goes up to Randy and says, 'Hi, how're you doing.' And they don't even remember my name. He gets tons of money for doing diddly squat, and I have to do laundry five times just to get five dollars."

Added eight-year-old Vicky, "People give Larry stuff he really wants, and they give me trolls. I hate trolls."

The children recognized the reasons that their brothers and sisters were getting special treatment and gifts, but they nevertheless felt normal pangs of jealousy. And worse, they often felt guilty about their jealousy. But the sibling workshop gave them a chance to express their feelings, a place where no one would say, "You shouldn't feel that way," or "You should be more understanding."

Moreover the children expressed other losses: "I can't fool around with my brother anymore the way I used to," said nine-year-old Jeff. Added Shari, "Randy used to be so much fun. Now he's afraid to run around. And the medicines he takes make him act really weird."

The parents at the workshop voiced other concerns about the effect of the illness on their well children. "Their lives are forever changed," said one father. "They've lost their innocence."

Well children suffer for a variety of reasons when a sibling has cancer. Babies may be deprived of parental attention and time to bond with their mother and father. Toddlers experience absences from their parents as signs of rejection. And older children, even though they may have some understanding that their brother or sister is sick and that mommy and daddy are taking care of him, are likely to feel rejected, angry, and resentful anyway. Their whole world is turned upside down, yet the people on whom they rely for support and guidance through such upheavals may be absent for long periods of time. They experience fear, grief, and confusion about their brother or sister's condition yet may have no one with whom to share their feelings. Parents at least often meet other parents at the hospital with whom they can share concerns, but well children may feel totally isolated. They may think that somehow they have caused their brother or sister to become ill and may thus feel guilty. Or they may fear that they, too, will get cancer. Older children sometimes feel burdened by their increasing responsibilities. Some suffer in silence, while others rebel and create more immediate problems at home. Some find that their buried anger surfaces many years later.

Surprisingly siblings may fare worst of all when their brother or sister's condition improves. This is a time when parents may feel for the first time that they can breathe a sigh of relief and tend to other matters. Meanwhile siblings may think that finally it is their chance for their parents' undivided attention, and when they don't get it, renewed anger and jealousy may erupt.

Research into the effects of cancer on well siblings, though sparse, supports the observations of parents and professionals who work with families. Psychologist John Spinetta assessed how well the emotional needs of various family members were met and concluded that siblings of children with cancer fared significantly worse than did their ill siblings or their parents.[1] Not only did siblings experience greater emotional distance from their parents, but they also suffered in other areas, such as self-image, adaptability, anxiety, and depression.

How children react to the stress of cancer in the family varies with age. Younger children tend to act out their fear and confusion by throwing tantrums, regressing to more babyish behavior, and showing more signs of sibling rivalry. Older children may exhibit psychosomatic symptoms, more oppositional behavior, poorer school grades, and sometimes alcohol and drug abuse.

## Help for Siblings

"So this is reality," said one mother at the sibling workshop. "What do you do?"

"First," answered the psychologist who led the group, "listen to your kids and validate their feelings." Though you may not be able to change the way they feel, you can at least give them an outlet for expression of their feelings, thereby reducing the likelihood that their fears and anxieties will surface in more destructive behaviors.

Other suggestions for helping your well children cope with their sister's or brother's illness include the following:

- Provide information as openly and honestly as possible. Reassure your children that they are not responsible for the illness nor are they in danger of "catching" it. The National Cancer Institute, the American Cancer Society,

[1] John J. Spinetta, "The Sibling of the Child with Cancer," in John J. Spinetta and Patricia Deasy-Spinetta, eds., *Living with Childhood Cancer* (St. Louis: Mosby, 1981).

and other organizations have produced several publications that can help you find the right words to use with children of different ages. Ask your oncologist, social worker, or other health care provider for these publications or contact these agencies directly (see "Resources").

- Share your own feelings and give your children permission and the opportunity to express their feelings of fear and sadness rather than keeping those feelings bottled up inside. Reassure your children, however, that they don't have to take care of you. Many children say they avoid talking to their parents about their feelings out of concern that they may be adding to their parents' grief. Don't assume that your children are not suffering just because they don't initiate conversations about their feelings. Watch for other signs of anxiety, fear, or anger in their play or conversations about unrelated topics.

- Take time to check in with your well children periodically to see how they are doing. While parents may find it difficult to stay on top of their well children's activities to the extent to which they are accustomed, periodic checks may at least help catch problems before they have a chance to escalate. Some parents choose to convene regular family meetings to discuss a variety of family issues other than the ill child's cancer. These meetings can provide a chance to shift the focus from the ill child and to place the other children's concerns at center stage.

- Let your child's school and teachers know what is happening, and ask them to alert you if your child begins behaving in an uncharacteristic way. School is often the place where a child's anxiety first becomes apparent.

Further many schools have professionals available to help children deal with sadness and anxiety. School personnel may, however, need to be educated about cancer and about the special needs of siblings. The American Cancer Society and the National Cancer Institute produce publications addressed specifically to educators. In addition it may be necessary to remind school personnel that although your well children may need special consideration at this time, they should be treated as normally as possible. Well children, like their ill brothers and sisters, usually don't want to be seen as different from their peers.

◆ Demystify your sick child's treatment by bringing siblings along on clinic and hospital visits. Ask your doctor or nurse to meet with the children and to answer questions. Children will respond to this approach with varying levels of interest. Francie says that when she brought Libby's brothers to the clinic, they weren't interested in seeing their sister get treatment, they just wanted to play Nintendo. While this visit may not have achieved the goal that Francie had in mind, that is, to make the children more sensitive to the distress that Libby was going through during her treatments, it did nevertheless normalize the situation and make the boys feel less distanced from Libby's ordeal.

Sometimes psychosocial professionals at the hospital or clinic will be available to meet with your well children while your ill child is receiving treatment. The child life specialist, for example, might work with siblings in the playroom, using toys or art to encourage them to express their feelings.

◆ Try to arrange to spend some special time with your well children. "Fun time" is usually the first thing that is eliminated when a family must deal with a traumatic event such as cancer. When Libby was away at a special camp for kids with cancer, Francie let her sons choose some special activities that they could do together. "Usually they have to do what Libby wants to do and they resent that," she said.

- Enlist other family members, friends, church members, and so on to help out by doing special things with your well children. This can mean taking a teenage girl shopping for a prom dress, going bowling with a ten-year-old, or taking a simple trip to the playground with a preschooler.

How your well children react to their sister's or brother's illness is as unpredictable as children themselves. Some children show obvious signs of distress, whereas others will go on with their lives as if little had happened. Even those who appear unfazed may be struggling inside, however; and psychosocial professionals warn that when well siblings' emotional needs aren't met, the damage can be long-lasting. Moreover, well siblings may be the family members who live the longest with memories of the cancer experience. Sometimes repressed anger, fear, and sadness may not reemerge until much later.

While the problems faced by siblings of children with cancer may be great, these same children can also be a tremendous source of strength and support for the entire family. They may, for example, maintain the ill child's social connections in the neighborhood and at school even when the child is absent for extended periods. In addition a sibling may be someone for an ill child to turn to with concerns he doesn't feel comfortable sharing with his mother and father. For example, when fourteen-year-old Harold was treated for a rare type of testicular tumor, his older brother was someone with whom he could share concerns about fertility and sexual function. Siblings may also help the ill child adjust to hospital procedures and treatments by talking about the situation from a child's point of view.

It's important for parents to acknowledge all that the well children do directly or indirectly to support the child with cancer—whether it means coming to visit, making a get-well card, or just being a good sport about the inconvenience and disruption of having a family member, as well as mom and dad, at the hospital for an extended period of time.

# CHAPTER 12

# Back to School

For most children with cancer, getting back to a normal life means going back to school. School is central to children's lives, not just because of the academic learning that goes on there but for the social interactions as well. Thus, although parents and tutors may be able to substitute for the book learning that children miss when they are sick, school is the best place for children to learn the other lessons of life that will be so important as they mature into adults.

For these reasons most pediatric cancer specialists recommend that children return to school as soon as possible. Generally children are eager to get back as well, although they may feel anxious and uncertain as the return date approaches. Parents are likely to experience their own anxiety.

Many parents fear that their child will be stigmatized, teased, or rejected by friends. But according to psychologist Robert Noll and his colleagues, this is not the case. Noll found that when children with cancer go back to school, they are accepted and liked by their classmates.[1] Noll's study varied from many others because he surveyed the children themselves rather than assessing parents' or teachers' perceptions of children's reactions.

This doesn't mean that an individual child will not have problems with peer relationships. Many children do, whether they are healthy or sick. For sick children their relationships with classmates may be complicated by fear, misplaced pity, or other feelings that they or their peers are experiencing. If a child seems to be experiencing problems with peers, it's important to address those problems with the help of a psychosocial professional, a school counselor, the child's teacher, and/or others who may be able to help. Otherwise the child's difficulties interacting with peers may lead to other kinds of social problems as he grows up.

Many children with cancer will not be able to return to school for some time, however, because of prolonged hospitalization, side effects of treatment, or symptoms of the cancer. Yet these children have educational and social needs similar to those of their peers who are in school, and these needs will need to be addressed in some other way.

Regardless of when a child with cancer returns to school, the social and educational impact of cancer may be with him for the remainder of his school days. Thus parents must continue to monitor their child's progress, help with difficulties that may arise, and advocate for their child when needs are not being met satisfactorily.

[1] Robert Noll, "Peer Relationships of Children with Cancer," *CCCF Quarterly Newsletter* 16, no. 3 (Fall 1992).

## Preparing for a Return to School

Preparation for a child's return to school should begin as soon as possible after diagnosis, even though it may be unclear when school reentry will be possible. The necessary preparations may be managed by a psychosocial professional at the hospital or clinic, by a professional designated by the child's school or school district, by the parents, or by a combination of all the above. Whoever manages the process, they must be attentive to a variety of issues, including (a) providing the ill child with educational materials and/or a tutor that will allow her to keep up with school work during an absence; (b) identifying special needs that the child has with regard to learning ability; (c) educating the child's teachers and other school personnel about cancer and about what can be expected of the child upon return; and (d) making sure that siblings of the ill child are getting their needs met at school.

Probably the single most important factor for successful school reentry is that all those involved in the child's care communicate openly. When parents are juggling all their other responsibilities, maintaining open communication with the school may be difficult. Friends, other family members (including siblings), or a child's teachers can be of tremendous help at this time.

The school and teachers need to be informed about medical information as it relates to the child's education and health at school. This includes issues affecting attendance; physical limitations that your child may experience; side effects of treatment that may otherwise affect a child's ability to function during the school day (fatigue, vision or hearing impairments, irritability, and so on); medications that will be given or taken at school; and the child's risk of catching infections from other kids.

## Preparing Your Child and Classmates

For many children the prospect of returning to school after a prolonged absence elicits conflicting feelings—both excitement *and* anxiety about getting back to normal and reestablishing friendships. Anxiety may be heightened if a child looks different, requires special treatment, or is unable to do things as well as before.

Parents, teachers, and others involved in a child's care may help ease the transition both by providing the child an opportunity to talk about his fears and anxieties and by preparing the child's classmates for the upcoming return. A visit to the classroom by the child's parent or a health care provider can help remove some of the mystery about cancer. It can also help explain to the other children why a child with cancer sometimes gets special treatment, for example being excused from physical education. The American Cancer Society, the Candlelighters Children's Cancer Foundation, the Leukemia Society of America, and many other organizations offer age-appropriate materials that may be helpful for classroom presentations. A psychosocial professional may help you obtain these materials, or you may contact these organizations directly.

Francie, for example, visited Libby's class at school before Libby returned. She took with her a book about leukemia written for children, and a "Charlie Brown" video about children facing serious illness. These "props" helped open up a discussion among the second-graders, in which they felt free to ask difficult questions: Could they "catch" leukemia from Libby? Would she still be able to play with them? During her visit to the classroom Francie told the children about some differences they would notice when Libby returned—she had lost her hair; she had a "Broviac," which meant she had to be extra careful on the playground; she might miss some more days of school; and she might be too tired to play sometimes.

Moira took a different approach to preparing Sean's classmates for his upcoming return after treatment for a brain tumor. She arranged for a social worker from The Children's Hospital of Philadelphia to visit Sean's class to teach them about what it meant to have a brain tumor and to prepare them for changes they would see in Sean when he returned. In addition the social worker inquired whether Sean's eleven-year-old sister, Brenda, wanted someone to speak to her class.

"I hadn't even thought of that," said Moira. "But Brenda said, 'Yes!' It turned out that she was embarrassed by the way Sean looked."

For some children with cancer the beginning of a new school year may elicit renewed anxiety as they anticipate a new group of classmates and teachers who are unfamiliar with their illness. Thus parents may find themselves returning to the classroom year after year to educate a new group of children. As the children grow older, their classmates' level of understanding will change as well, and the presentation may have to be modified for older children with different sorts of questions.

For some children, particularly teenagers, the desire not to be different may outweigh their need for special consideration. Sixteen-year-old Aaron, for example, said that at first his classmates gave him emotional support, especially when he had difficulty concentrating and keeping up with the rest of the class. But when his initial intensive chemotherapy was over, he wanted to be treated normally. As he proceeded through high school, he stopped telling teachers and classmates about his leukemia. "I want to earn friends on my own, so I try not to use my illness to get special treatment. I don't want cancer to interrupt my life constantly. And I don't want the teachers to label me."

For Aaron the decision to keep quiet about having cancer has both good and bad consequences. No matter how exciting the school day is, he says, he finds himself exhausted when he gets home. Sometimes his peers don't understand when he cannot join them in after-school activities; but with his good friends there are "no questions asked." He says that whereas he was "lackadaisical" about school before having cancer, he now pushes himself hard so that he won't get left behind. "I try not to take homebound learning; I try not to escape. The more you escape, the more depressed you get," he says.

## Special Needs

Cancer can have an impact on a child's education for a variety of reasons. Prolonged or frequent absences from school create obvious impediments. And even when a child is able to attend school regularly, side effects of treatment, such as fatigue, may hamper productivity. On top of all that, some forms of treatment may cause neurologic impairment that may affect short- and long-term memory, speed of information processing, and the ability to learn new information. Long-term consequences such as these are discussed further in chapter 15.

If your child cannot return to school for an extended period of time, or if she needs special educational intervention when she does return, the public school should provide whatever intervention is necessary. This may include a home- or hospital-based tutor. Or modifications may be needed in the classroom.

Schools approach the challenge of educating a child with cancer in a variety of ways. Some school districts have systems in place for such situations, whereas other schools will be inventing a system as they go along. No matter whether a school district is large or small, however, it is required by federal law to provide for a child with special needs. Public Law 94-142, the Federal Education for All Handicapped Children Act, applied mostly to handicapped children, also covers children with lesser learning disabilities and "other health impaired" children who have "limited strength, vitality, or alertness due to chronic or acute health problems."

Many children with cancer can function in a regular school program quite well, with few modifications. However, when any modifications are needed, PL 94-142 will be a parent's ally in ensuring those modifications are made. The vehicle used by PL 94-142 is the Individualized Education Plan (IEP). This written document, prepared by educators and parents together, outlines the child's level of functioning, short- and long-term goals, and the steps that will be taken to achieve those goals. Parents must approve the IEP. If parents do not feel that the IEP adequately addresses their child's needs, they have the right to refuse to sign and to appeal for a change in the plan.

Once the plan has been established, it will be important for teachers, parents, and children to remain flexible. Sharon, who was hired by the school district to tutor thirteen-year-old Kelly, described the educational program that has been developed to meet Kelly's needs: "When Kelly can, she comes to school for four periods a day, two of which are academic subjects. I pick up the slack. We've done math in the kitchen, drawn maps of Disneyworld (after a family trip), and done a lot of journal writing. Flexibility is the real key."

Some parents choose to have their children educated in private schools. While these schools are not required by law to provide special education if it is required, many will go to great lengths to meet a child's needs. Moreover some schools specialize in educating children with special needs. In addition some private schools are well equipped to provide other kinds of support that a child with cancer may need. For example Francie chose private school for her children because she felt that their social and emotional needs would be better met in the smaller, more intimate environment of the school she chose.

## Working with the School

Because school will be such an important part of your child's return to a normal life, it will be especially important for you to maintain good communication with teachers and other important people in the school. Many parents find that teachers are tremendously helpful and supportive during their child's illness, both with the ill child and with healthy siblings. Teachers may, for example, encourage the ill child's classmates to send notes and cards frequently, or to try in some way to include the child in special activities. For example on Halloween, when ten-year-old Sarah was too ill to attend the school's party and parade, her teachers arranged for the class to parade past Sarah's house. Sarah dressed up in costume and sat at the picture window, waving at her classmates. It was a special time for Sarah, said her father, and was greatly appreciated by the entire family.

Keeping in touch with a child's teacher may not be enough, however. Other members of the school staff as well as substitute teachers must also be informed about your child's special needs. Penny Kreinberg, past president of the Oregon chapter of Candlelighters Childhood Cancer Foundation and the mother of a child with a brain tumor, devised a form to facilitate better communication with all staff members who would interact with her child. She asked that the form be photocopied and distributed to all such staff members. The form provides space for parents to outline their child's medical and emotional concerns and to specify what steps should be taken should crises occur. Teachers and counselors have found the forms helpful, says Kreinberg, who has made them available to other parents in the Oregon area.[2]

Parents' experiences with schools vary widely and are highly dependent on the parents' ability to advocate for their child's needs. The bottom line, said Kathleen, mother of a ten-year-old with rhabdomyosarcoma, is "hope for the best, prepare for the worst, look ahead at educational opportunities, and utilize every source you can in your community." Kathleen says that her son's teachers provided emotional as well as educational support after his diagnosis. "His teacher came in and read to him when he was in the midst of treatment. I wasn't looking ahead, because I didn't have hope." But the teacher had the foresight to see beyond the illness.

[2] Penny Kreinberg, "Building Bridges," *Candlelighters Childhood Cancer Foundation Quarterly Newsletter* 16, no. 3 (Fall 1992).

CHAPTER 13

# Financial Concerns

As if having a child with a life-threatening disease weren't itself stressful enough, many parents face tremendous financial stress as well. There are few things that can be more devastating financially to a family than serious illness in a child. A family's finances are hit hard from two directions: first because of the astronomical expenses that may accumulate over the course of their child's treatment and second because the parents' earning power may be seriously disrupted.

How families cope with the financial stress of having a child with cancer varies depending on the family's resources; the nature of the child's illness and the medical care that is required; assistance that is available in the community, which may vary significantly from state to state and locale to locale; and how well the family is able to take advantage of resources that are available.

Some families are fortunate to have comprehensive health insurance that will cover most of their child's medical expenses. But even these families may be devastated by the tremendous nonmedical expenses that mount throughout a child's illness. For those families who have little or no health insurance, the financial burdens are even more complex and overwhelming. These families may find themselves seeking help from numerous agencies, both governmental and private, in an effort to make ends meet.

Whether a family has health insurance or not, the effort required to meet financial obligations may be intense. Hospitals, insurance companies, and other funding agencies may all create a bureaucratic jumble, generating countless bills and forms that need to be filled out. And these forms and bills may come when families are least prepared to cope with the frustration of paperwork. Parents naturally want to devote their energy to the pressing physical and emotional needs of their child and family. But those who have been through it say that parents should begin keeping track of expenses and payments right away, before they get out of hand. Members of the health care team, including social workers, financial counselors, and business office representatives may be able to advise parents regarding these matters.

## Medical Expenses

Medical expenses may be paid by a combination of private health insurance, public assistance, the parents' assets and income, and contributions from other sources, such as family members and friends. Medical bills can mount rapidly and sometimes will exceed parents' ability to pay. When this happens, a financial adviser from the hospital or clinic may step in to help make arrangements for payment. Sometimes the institution will absorb part of the debt; or they may spread payments out over a period of time. They may also help a family apply for financial aid from one or more state or federal agencies.

### *HEALTH INSURANCE*

As this book is being written, the topic of health care reform has taken center stage in our nation. How this will affect our children's access to quality medical care, particularly when faced with a chronic or life-threatening disease, has yet to be determined. Health care reform may significantly change the nature of and access to health insurance such that families will no longer have to worry that a life-threatening illness will lead to major financial difficulties. At the present time, however, access to health care remains a complex and confusing ordeal.

Health insurance plans vary in terms of what and how much they will cover, where care may be provided, what steps must be taken to obtain coverage, and the types of documentation that are required. As soon as possible after your child is diagnosed with cancer, you should obtain a complete and current copy of your insurance policy and go over it with a fine-toothed comb. In this way you may be able to avoid surprises later on, such as denied claims or steep charges for which you are responsible.

Some policies, for example, have a *lifetime cap.* This means that once the company has paid out a specified amount for your child, the insurance runs out. When you signed up for your policy, $100,000 may have seemed like a huge amount that would never be reached, but if your child has cancer and requires lengthy treatments and hospitalizations, you may find yourselves approaching that amount fairly rapidly.

Insurance policies may also require that you pay a significant portion of the charges. For example the insurance company may pay 80 percent, while you pay 20 percent. That might have sounded like a good deal when your family was relatively healthy, but 20 percent of the bill for a child's treatment for cancer can quickly deplete all your savings. Further when you read the fine print of the policy, you may discover that it covers only 80 percent of the "usual" or "reasonable" cost of various services. If that is the case and your institution charges more, you may be responsible for the difference. Again, a close reading of your policy may clarify some of these issues.

Health maintenance organizations (HMOs) present a different set of potential problems, although the coverage may be better overall. Generally HMOs "manage" care more rigorously. That means that they may refuse to cover certain procedures unless they can be proved necessary. HMOs often require that every procedure or treatment be preapproved by a primary-care provider; if it is not, the company may refuse to pay. This puts the burden on you to pay close attention to the treatments your child is receiving and to plan ahead when preapproval may be required.

Negotiating your way through the health insurance maze can be difficult and frustrating and will require that you be vigilant and persistent. "Don't take no from insurance companies," said one mother. "You may have to make several appeals, and you'll have to try not to be wishy-washy. Insurance companies have a human side, too, but you have to be aggressive."

## *FINANCIAL AID FOR MEDICAL EXPENSES*

Federal and state governments and private agencies may provide financial assistance if you do not have health insurance or to supplement any health insurance you do have. A social worker or other psychosocial professional or a financial adviser at the hospital or clinic may be able to help you obtain support from a variety of sources, including those listed below:[1]

- **Medicaid** is the federal and state government's program for providing medical assistance to people who are unemployed or have low income. All states have some sort of Medicaid program, but these programs vary from state to state in terms of eligibility requirements and what services are covered. Families who qualify for AFDC (Aid for Families with Dependent Children, commonly called welfare) are automatically eligible for Medicaid. To apply for Medicaid, contact the local Department of Human Services or Department of Public Assistance.

- **Supplemental Security Income (SSI)** is another federally funded program available to certain people with medical conditions that limit their ability to function normally. SSI comes as a cash grant and entitles a person to Medicaid. Eligibility for SSI is based on the parent's income, but is granted to the patient, not to the parents. Applications are filed with the Social Security Administration. Some hospitals have a representative from the Social Security Administration on site at spe-

[1] Taken in part from Shirley Bonnem and Judith Ross, "Financial Issues in Pediatric Cancer," in Philip A. Pizzo and David G. Poplack, eds., *Principles and Practice of Pediatric Oncology*, 2nd ed. (Philadelphia; J. B. Lippincott, 1993).

cific times. Even parents who have private insurance may qualify for SSI if certain income limits are met.

- **Crippled Children's Program** or **Special Child Health Services** (as it is known in some states) is available in some states to provide free health-related services to children with crippling or chronic diseases. Eligibility requirements vary from state to state. Apply at your county or state department of health.
- **National societies,** such as the Leukemia Society of America and the American Cancer Society, may provide funds to help cover certain medical and nonmedical expenses. They may also loan certain types of equipment for home care or other reasons.
- **Local foundations and charities** may provide assistance in the form of cash grants to help cover nonmedical expenses. To find out about these programs, ask your social worker and other members of your health care team, or call the local chapters of national organizations such as the American Cancer Society, Candlelighters Childhood Cancer Foundation, or the Leukemia Society of America.

## Nonmedical Expenses

Even when insurance covers most or all of a child's medical expenses, nonmedical expenses can be overwhelming. During Wendy's hospitalization and treatment for neuroblastoma, for example, her mother, Andrea, faced huge out-of-pocket expenses at the same time that her income ceased. Andrea slept at the hospital so that she could be nearby at all times, but needed money to buy food for herself, to park her car, to pay for the baby-sitter who stayed home with Wendy's brother, to make long-distance phone calls to concerned family and friends, and for countless other miscellaneous items. Meanwhile Alice traveled by car so that her daughter Diana could receive clinic treatments for Ewing's sarcoma. She accumulated large expenses for gas, parking, bridge tolls, food, and child care.

Families who must travel long distances to receive care are particularly hard hit by these nonmedical expenses. When lodging is needed for family members to stay overnight, some are able to find a warm, comfortable haven in one of the many Ronald McDonald Houses throughout the United States. Other sources of financial support may be available from agencies such as those listed above. To find out about these resources, parents should ask not only the professionals with whom they interact but other parents as well.

Many of the nonmedical expenses that parents incur as a result of their child's treatment are tax-deductible. This includes the cost of traveling to and from the hospital or clinic, parking, and bridge tolls. Keep close track of these tax-deductible expenses as well as other expenses that you incur. A tax specialist may help you discover other expenses that are deductible.

## Fund-raising

Even families with good insurance and stable incomes often find themselves in a difficult financial situation when their child has cancer. A variety of creative solutions can be employed at such times. For example Alice's neighbor organized a celebrity auction and carnival, which raised $15,000. Other families receive direct donations from people in the community who want to help. Parents who have received such assistance recommend placing the money in a trust fund and hiring a lawyer to help administer the fund. This can help protect a family from tax liability and other complications.

CHAPTER 14

# Death and Dying

When a child is diagnosed with cancer, treatment tends to be swift and sometimes aggressive. Severe side effects of treatment are endured with the hope that an all-out assault on the illness will bring about the desired consequence—elimination of the disease and a return to good health.

Sometimes, however, even the most aggressive treatment fails to halt the disease. A decision point is reached: Should treatment be continued, intensified, or stopped? Questions are asked about how much the child can endure and about whether the likelihood of success is so low that intense treatment seems cruel rather than curative.

Not all families face these questions. For some the death of their child comes quickly. For others it comes unexpectedly as a result of some unforeseen complication. No matter the circumstances, coping with the loss of a child is a searing experience for everyone close to the child, especially the parents. It will likely be the most significant event in the family's history, with long-term ramifications. Getting through it will require strength and stamina.

## Eva's Story

Eva was diagnosed with leukemia just after her sixth birthday. After intensive treatment with chemotherapy and radiation therapy, remission was achieved, and she began to receive maintenance chemotherapy. But within a few months she began experiencing headaches and burning eyes. Testing confirmed her parents' fears: The leukemia had relapsed into her central nervous system (CNS).

Another round of treatment began with even more intensity than the first round. Remission again was achieved, and she was able to start third grade in the fall.

Then came the bad news—another relapse, this time into the bone marrow. In late October Eva entered the hospital for more treatment.

Her doctor, Jean Belasco, M.D., says that when Eva was first diagnosed, and even with her first relapse, the chance that she would survive remained high. But as the disease progressed, the balance started to change. Dr. Belasco discussed the situation with Eva's parents.

"At the beginning they had lots of hope, but were also given the possibility that she could die. When she had the CNS relapse, there was a 30 to 50 percent chance that she would be cured. That gave her a fighting chance. But once she had a bone marrow relapse, the only hope was to get her into remission and get her a bone marrow donor. The chances were overwhelming that she might die, but there was still a small chance of survival."

The family continued to maintain hope, said Dr. Belasco. But when remission could not be achieved and no bone marrow donor was available, "We all knew there was absolutely no medical chance of her surviving the disease. Then our choices were, Do we continue to try to slow the disease with chemotherapy or do we just try to keep her comfortable?"

The health care team and family met as they had been meeting all along. Through the many months of Eva's illness they had come to know one another well. And more important they had come to trust one another. Eva's parents decided, with the guidance of their health care team and their God, that their daughter had been through enough.

Said her father, "Our job as parents had changed from taking care of her to helping her die. It's not something I ever thought I'd have to do."

Added her mother, "They didn't teach this in parenting class."

Decisions such as those that Eva's family made are extremely difficult and are highly individualized, says Dr. Belasco. "Each child and each family and each disease is different, and it's not for me to choose for them whether to accept their child's illness or to resign themselves to his death. It's a gradual journey. Some families say that continuing the fight will energize them—that it's what they need to do for their own survival or for fear that their child would otherwise feel abandoned. Other families say that the fight is deenergizing and that what they want to do is focus instead on quality of life. Eventually most families focus on quality of life, but we can't force somebody to that point."

## The Shift to Supportive Care

When a child's care shifts from a focus on curing the disease to one of supporting the child through the terminal phases of the disease, the medical needs of the child may increase as the disease, which was formerly held in check, begins to make the child sicker. At the same time, the amount of support the family needs may also increase. Because of uncertainty about the family's goals and expectations there may be a transition period during which a family's medical, nursing, and psychosocial support needs must be reevaluated.

In an effort to address the needs of families during this time, some hospitals have established special programs in supportive care. Dr. Belasco directs such a program at The Children's Hospital of Philadelphia.

"Supportive care is for any child who has cancer that has recurred or for a child who has some other severe chronic disease that is medically complicated and for which there is a significant chance that the child may die," says Dr. Belasco. "We try to improve continuity between the hospital and the family and prevent isolation of the family when hospitalization ends."

Adds hospital bereavement coordinator Mae L. Page, L.S.W., "The emphasis is on living and the quality of life that we can give to the child."

Supportive care may include a continuation of cancer treatment if that will improve pain control or a child's ability to continue with normal activities. Other services that may come under the category of supportive care are pain management, nutritional support, blood-product support, and infection control. These measures are all discussed in chapter 8.

Supportive care may be provided in the hospital or clinic

or at home. A supportive-care service can be especially valuable when care is being provided at home, says Dr. Belasco, because otherwise families tend to become very isolated. "The transition period from cure to incurable is a very isolated time. What home care does is provide more continuity, decrease the amount of isolation at home even as the medical problems are increasing, and just provide more services."

One of the most important aspects of supportive care, according to Dr. Belasco, is communication. "We continue to talk through all the problems—what they mean, what we can fix, what we can't fix, what can make the problem better. Sometimes we think that we scare parents by telling them too much, but the reality is that they are scared of the very worst things you can imagine."

During Eva's last few weeks Dr. Belasco says that most of her time with the family was spent talking. For example they talked about how Eva's parents could adjust the dose of morphine so that Eva would be as pain-free as possible. "I wanted her parents to know how to do it in case they were in a situation where they needed to do it themselves. They needed to know what to do and how to do it, and they needed to know it was okay for them to be their child's advocate." Adjusting morphine dose can be particularly difficult for families because they may fear that they are hastening the child's death. While this may be true to some extent, the increased morphine should also improve the quality of the child's life.

Continues Dr. Belasco, "We also need to talk to parents and kids about dying. Some people are uncomfortable talking about it, and that isolates parents and children."

Ms. Page concurs with Dr. Belasco. "Somewhere inside themselves children know that they are dying. Even if they aren't able to define death in adult terms, children often have a sense that the body is weary and is wearing out."

According to Ms. Page, young children's fears center primarily around the issue of separation. "To walk closely with the child into the darkness and the unknown can be very helpful," she says. "For example one three-and-a-half-year-old told her mother she saw a light but that she was resisting going toward it. Her mother tearfully said, 'It's okay to go to the light, God is there.' But the child said, 'I don't want to leave you.' Mom wisely said, 'I'm holding your hand and I'll walk with you.' Both mom and child had a peace-filled ending."

For older children, says Ms. Page, both their body and their spirits may tell them that the end is near. "They may be very weary of the restrictive and often painful life that treatment brings. It doesn't really give them joy or the freedom to live. When death comes, it may be a relief."

Ms. Page says that children will often not talk about their fears or perceptions about dying because they want to protect their parents. At the same time, mom and dad may be afraid that by talking about death they will destroy the child's hope. "Unfortunately what often happens in these cases is that children and their families are distanced from the close intimacy they've known throughout the illness, and both carry their fears in masked positive conversation.

"The word *death* does not have to be used, but it's important for parents to be open to hearing their child's fear and questions and to give truthful responses. It is a very difficult and sometimes impossible task for a parent. Parents do the best they can and also they do what they believe to be best for their child," says Ms. Page.

## To Die at Home or at the Hospital—An Individual Choice

For families who have the opportunity to choose, many prefer that their child die at home. According to Dr. Belasco, home was the choice for about 80 percent of the children who have died while receiving care from the supportive-care service.

Ten-year-old Sarah, for example, was adamant. She desperately wanted to be at home with her entire family nearby. She begged her parents not to take her back to the hospital, which for her was associated with unpleasant memories of treatment and isolation from her sisters. Her parents agreed, and even when Sarah reached the final stages of her disease and needed close medical attention, her mother and father found a way to provide that care at home.

While many families opt for their child to die at home, it is by no means a unanimous choice. Moreover it is a highly individual decision, says Dr. Belasco. "Individual families are different, and the diseases are different. Some diseases may be more amenable to giving therapy at home. In addition the child may feel happier and safer at home, while the parents may feel better able to take care of their other children and have more control over the situation."

When families choose to stay home, they take on a difficult task. Preparations must be made to deal with a wide range of medical crises that may arise, including hemorrhages, convulsions, and severe infections. In planning for end-stage home care, families should discuss with their health care team what should be done under different circumstances. In addition parents must make arrangements regarding what will be done at the time of death—who will pronounce death and what will be done with the body.

Sometimes a family will have chosen for the child to die at home, or will have promised the child that he will be allowed to die at home, but then find it too difficult to manage. "They may get right down to the wire and say, 'I can't do this at home,' " says social worker Ms. Page. "We really try to keep a family's options open so that they know they can come back to the hospital if they need to, even if they just come back for a while and then go home again."

But other families make a different decision. Eva's family felt safer delegating the nursing, doctoring, and social work care to the professionals at the hospital. Recalls Dr. Belasco, "They said they just wanted to be her parents. They knew she was going to change and they didn't want to be alone at home with that. For them it worked better to focus all their energy on getting Eva prepared to die and helping her get through it. And then, once she died, they felt they could put all their focus on their other children."

Eva's parents' decision was due in part to the fact that they lived several hours away from the hospital and wanted more immediate access to professional care if the need arose. But the decision also added strain to other parts of their family life. It would be more than two months before Eva died. For her brothers that meant a long period of time during which their parents were absent from home. And it also limited their access to their sister during her final weeks. Nevertheless Eva and her brothers were able to say the things that needed to be said before she died. Eva and her oldest brother communicated with each other through letters. It was through those letters that Eva's brother was able to ask her what it felt like to be dying and Eva was able to share some of her thoughts about dying with him.

Whether a family opts for their child to die at home or in the hospital, Mae Page advises families to make a nest.

"It just means making your place. The child needs to feel

the safety, the comfort, the sense of 'that's mine,' as well as some control over who comes in and out and what is said. It's especially important in the hospital. We try to make the setting theirs, and then we become guests in this place they've made home."

Eva's family settled into their nest for what would be a long time. They decorated the room to be as homelike as possible and made space for the dozens of gifts that Eva received. They asked the medical staff to write *Do Not Resuscitate (DNR)* orders, which instructed the staff not to go to extraordinary means to revive Eva if she suffered a cardiac arrest. They requested that the medical staff not work up problems that arose; for example if Eva developed a fever, they requested treatment only to relieve suffering but not to cure the underlying cause. They asked for minimal intervention from the staff.

Most important the family spent time taking care of Eva. According to Ms. Page, this can be the most difficult task of all. "Listening and staying present with someone who doesn't talk is one of the hardest things you can do. But it's very, very important."

The two staff members who increased their attention during this time were the child life specialists. Over the years of Eva's treatment they had become special friends and knew how to play with Eva despite her reduced capacity. At times they would come in just to talk, play, or see Eva's new toys. At other times they would introduce play or artistic activities that might help Eva process some of her feelings about dying.

The attention of the child life specialists not only provided an outlet for Eva, it also gave Eva's parents a few minutes of respite. "It's so hard," said Eva's father. "It's hard to accept that tomorrow isn't going to be any better than today."

When Eva died, her family was nearby. It would be the beginning of a new chapter in all their lives.

## Memorials

Some families choose to memorialize a child's life by planting a tree in the child's honor, or by asking that contributions be made to a favorite charity. The list of possibilities is endless. These memorials provide a means with which to celebrate a child's life rather than simply commemorating her death. Sarah's family, for example, established a memorial in Sarah's name, which provides toys for children at the hospital where Sarah was treated. Their many days and nights at the hospital had alerted them to the need for such items for children who face long hospitalizations. Friends of the family and Sarah's classmates used the memorial fund as a way of expressing their sorrow over her death in a way that was life-affirming.

Some families memorialize their child by asking that contributions be made to cancer research, with the hope that such research will someday prevent the deaths of other children. This allows some people to ascribe a greater meaning to their child's life.

## The Work of Bereavement

When Eva died, her family was ready to move on. But according to Mae Page, their work was not yet done. "It's a slow moving on. The grief of a child goes on for a very long time for most people," says Ms. Page.

Because of the work Eva's family had done in preparation

for her death—work that included saying good-bye and letting Eva know that it was okay for her to leave—Ms. Page said the family could move into the bereavement period without the possible burden of regret for things left unsaid. Nevertheless the family's bereavement would be a long healing process.

Ms. Page runs bereavement groups to help families through this difficult time. When families get together, she says, most of what they need to do is tell their stories. "They need to verbalize it, and there are not a lot of places to do that. Very shortly after a child dies, people are ready for you to get on with it. They can be nice and tolerant for a little while, but it's far too painful for them to stay present and listen, especially if they've never dealt with death themselves. Even family members and best friends will want to put it away. And that's so grievous for families."

The bereavement groups give families a chance to share their sorrow and also to validate their feelings. It's not unusual, says Ms. Page, for parents to think they've finished their grieving, only to be hit again by another wave of grief. In the groups parents learn that this experience, while painful, is completely normal. The groups also offer other family members, including siblings of the dead child, an opportunity to talk about their losses.

"Most children do not process grief in a way that families recognize," says Ms. Page. "Even very young children go through a grieving process—a sense of loss, of separation. Yet children for the most part have a great desire to try to bring some normalcy and safety back to their own world. So they are prone not to show their feelings. They don't want mom to cry anymore and they don't want dad working double shifts. A child will work very hard thinking there's some way he can bring normalcy back to their lives. But when we get them into groups with their peers, then they can let down and really say the things and do the things that they need to do."

Few bereavement programs exist that are geared specifically to families of children who have died, and those that are often focus on deaths from violence or suicide. These programs may not meet the needs of parents who have lost children to cancer. Some families set up their own, informal groups with families nearby. For example Eva's family got together with four other couples whose children had died of cancer. Connecting with this group reduced their isolation and helped them normalize their life.

CHAPTER 15

# Long-term Consequences of Childhood Cancer

Oncologist Anna T. Meadows, M.D., estimates that by the year 2000 at least one in every one thousand young adults will be a survivor of childhood cancer.

These survivors and their families bear reminders, both physical and mental, of the experience of having cancer. The very same treatments that may have saved these children's lives—radiation therapy, chemotherapy, and surgery—may produce less desired effects as well, including impaired or altered growth, damage to organs, impaired fertility, and even second cancers. In addition those treatments may produce less obvious scars, such as learning difficulties and emotional problems.

For many years pediatric oncologists devoted nearly all

their attention to the goal of survival. But with overall survival now approaching 70 percent, the attention of many experts has shifted toward a look at the future of these children. This movement has been led by Dr. Meadows, who recognized in the early 1970s the importance of looking at long-term consequences of childhood cancer treatment. At that time, says Dr. Meadows, there weren't many long-term survivors, "but we knew that would change."

As more is becoming known about the long-term consequences of cancer treatments, attempts are being made to minimize adverse outcomes by adjusting treatment regimens. For example in chapter 3 we discussed how, in the third National Wilms' Tumor Study, a drug with the potential for causing long-term heart problems was eliminated in favor of a higher dose of a different drug. The results of that trial proved that for certain categories of disease the latter approach was equally effective but probably less damaging over the long term.

This is but one example of how treatments have evolved with an eye toward long-term outcome. As a result some of the long-term complications being seen today may become nonexistent in the future. At the same time, however, limited experience with certain types of treatment means that complications may yet arise that have not been anticipated. This is why survivors of childhood cancer must remain especially vigilant about their overall health and well-being as they grow.

## Medical Consequences of Treatment for Childhood Cancer

The major areas of medical concern for survivors of childhood cancer are (a) that growth will be stunted or otherwise abnormal; (b) that organs will sustain long-term or late-occurring damage; (c) that fertility will be impaired; and (d) that the cancer will return or that a different type of cancer will occur. Table 15.1 summarizes the late effects that may occur subsequent to childhood cancer and the precautions that should be followed.

### *GROWTH*

Growth may be affected either because of direct radiation-induced damage to growing tissue or because of damage to the pituitary gland, which produces hormones necessary for normal growth. Growth impairment may result in stunting or, if radiation has been applied to only one side of the body, disfigurement from disproportional growth. Maintaining normal weight may help minimize the problems created by disproportional growth. In addition physical therapy or other adaptations may be useful.

When overall growth is stunted, administration of synthetic growth hormone may be helpful. This should be given before a child reaches puberty. After that time the growing parts of the bones will have fused and growth hormone will no longer be effective. Since synthetic growth hormone has been available only relatively recently, the long-term effects are not known and its use remains somewhat controversial.

### *ORGAN DAMAGE*

Although chemotherapeutic agents are known to be harsh poisons, only a few appear to cause long-term damage to organs. Drugs known as anthracyclines (doxorubicin or adriamycin and daunorubicin or daunomycin), for example, may cause cardiac problems many years after treatment. Thus, people who have been treated with these drugs should be followed closely by a cardiologist and should be careful

TABLE 15.1

**Late Effects of Treatment for Childhood Cancer[1]**

| Treatment | Risks | Follow-up Care | Other Precautions |
|---|---|---|---|
| Radiation: *Abdomen* | Liver and kidney problems<br><br>Malabsorption | Laboratory analyses of liver and kidney function<br>Metabolic studies | |
| *Chest* | Lung damage<br>Breast cancer | Lung-function tests<br>Routine mammograms after age 25 | DO NOT SMOKE.<br>Perform breast self-examination. |
| *Head or neck* | Thyroid abnormalities<br>Eye damage<br>Teeth damage<br>Growth abnormalities<br>Intellectual impairment | Thyroid exam<br>Eye exam<br>Dental exam<br>Growth hormone if pituitary damage led to growth abnormality<br>Educational intervention | |
| *Scrotum* | Delayed sexual maturation<br><br>Infertility<br>Testicular cancer | Hormone treatments if necessary<br>Infertility counseling<br>Perform testicular self-examination. | |
| *Spine* | Scoliosis<br>Growth abnormalities | Yearly exam to monitor growth | Keep weight down.<br>Physical therapy |

| | | | |
|---|---|---|---|
| Chemotherapy:<br>*Alkylating agents* | Infertility; also early menopause in women<br><br>Leukemia | Infertility counseling<br>Hormonal treatment | Women with regular periods should not delay childbearing. |
| *Anthracyclines* | Heart abnormalities | Cardiac monitoring | See a doctor before starting an exercise program.<br>Women should also see a doctor if planning to have children.<br>Cocaine is a cardiac toxin—don't take it! |
| *Cyclophosphamide*<br>*Ifosfamide* | Kidney, bladder damage | Urinalysis and tests for kidney function | |
| *Cisplatinum* | Hearing loss<br>Kidney damage | Hearing test<br>Urinalysis and tests for kidney function | |
| Surgery:<br>*Nephrectomy (removal of kidney)* | Damage to remaining kidney | Monitoring of kidney function<br>Monitoring of blood pressure | Maintain normal weight.<br>Reduce salt intake.<br>Exercise moderately.<br>Avoid contact sports. |

[1] Adapted from *Taking Charge of Your Health: A Guide to Medical Follow-up for Adults Who Had Cancer in Childhood*, by Anna T. Meadows, et al., The Children's Hospital of Philadelphia.

when engaging in strenuous physical activity. This includes the physical strain of childbirth.

Organ damage may also arise as a consequence of radiation therapy. For example radiation to the chest may result in long-term damage to the lungs, and radiation to the abdomen may lead to kidney damage and subsequent high blood pressure.

Surgery may produce obvious long-term organ complications. Treatment for kidney cancer, for example, may involve the removal of one kidney. While only one kidney is necessary to perform the vital functions of filtering the blood, people who have lost a kidney must remain especially careful about the health of their remaining organ. This means obtaining regular exams, including laboratory assessment of kidney function; and avoiding other situations that might put added stress on the kidney, such as being overweight, eating a high-salt diet, or engaging in high-risk contact sports.

### *FERTILITY*

Fertility may be affected by radiation therapy, chemotherapy, or surgery. Irradiation of the testes in boys or the ovaries in girls may lead to delayed sexual maturation and sometimes infertility. After testicular irradiation, treatment with the male hormone testosterone may allow secondary sexual characteristics (for example, deepening of the voice, growth of facial hair, and sexual function) to develop; however, the treatment will not restore fertility. Chemotherapy, particularly with alkylating agents such as cyclophosphamide or cytoxan, may also affect sexual maturation and subsequent fertility.

The loss of fertility can be a devastating blow to survivors of childhood cancer as well as to their parents. Counseling may be desirable, to help a person both cope with the loss and make plans for the future. Options such as adoption may be considered. In addition, teenagers should be counseled about the risk of contracting sexually transmitted diseases.

### *SECOND CANCERS*

About 3 to 12 percent of people who were treated for childhood cancer will experience a second cancer later in life. While this is still a minority of those who are treated for cancer, it represents a risk ten to twenty times greater than normal. The increased risk may be the result of an inherited predisposition to cancer (see chapter 2) or it may be a consequence of treatments the child received. Or it may be a combination of both factors.

Radiation is a well-known cancer-causing agent. Thus, radiation therapy may lead to second cancers. Depending on the site treated with radiation therapy, a person may be at higher risk for cancers of the breast, lung, colon, bone, and soft tissue.

Chemotherapy may also increase a person's risk of developing a second cancer. In particular, alkylating agents may increase the risk of developing leukemia.

Because of the increased risk of developing cancer, survivors of childhood cancer should be counseled about other risk factors and about preventative steps they can take. Steps such as avoiding overexposure to the sun, not smoking, and performing regular breast self-exams are important for everyone, but they take on an added meaning in a person who has already survived cancer once.

## Educational Consequences of Treatment for Childhood Cancer

In chapter 12 we discussed some of the difficulties that children may face as they prepare to return to school. In addition to these initial difficulties, many children who are treated for cancer experience long-term changes in their ability to learn. The most severe of these changes occur as a result of high-dose radiation to the brain, such as that given to treat certain types of brain tumors. Lower-dose radiation and chemotherapy may also produce less severe and sometimes quite subtle changes in learning ability.

Psychologist Jerilynn Radcliffe, Ph.D., evaluates learning and developmental problems in children who have been treated for brain tumors. In her studies, children who have been treated experienced significant I.Q. losses over two years.[1] The losses can be much greater for children younger than seven, and less for older children, she says. "Sometimes there isn't much in the way of I.Q. loss, but the kids go on to show learning problems. The most frequently reported problems are with memory. They just don't remember in the short term. This means that although they can remember things from the past, new information is much harder for them to acquire and hold on to."

The implications of Dr. Radcliffe's and others' research are twofold. First, radiation is avoided whenever possible. In leukemic patients, for example, high-dose radiation was at one time used to prevent relapse into the central nervous

[1] I.Q.2 (intelligence quotient) is determined using one of several types of standardized tests. These tests measure verbal ability as well as several nonverbal skills. The score is stated as the child's mental age (as determined by the test) divided by his chronological age and then multiplied by 100. Thus a child who is ten years old and scores at the predicted level of a nine-year-old, would have an I.Q. of 90: $^{9}/_{10} \times 100 = 90$.

system; but now chemotherapy is the treatment of choice. Unfortunately some children still require radiation to prevent relapse into the nervous system. Furthermore, because of the extreme vulnerability of younger children, treatment regimens for brain tumors are designed to avoid brain irradiation if at all possible in children younger than age three. This may mean delaying radiation therapy by treating with chemotherapy until the child is over three and then considering whether radiation therapy is still needed.

The second implication of this research is that when children do require brain irradiation (or other forms of irradiation), the treatment must be followed with close attention to their learning experiences, and with intervention when necessary. I.Q. declines usually do not become apparent for two or more years after brain irradiation, and no further decline in I.Q. may be seen after about five years. However, as learning demands become more complex in later years, subtle changes in learning ability may create problems for a child. A psychologist with expertise in this area should be able to advise parents about the potential impact that a specific treatment may have had on learning.

There is still much to be learned about the long-term implications of cranial and other types of irradiation. At The Children's Hospital of Philadelphia, for example, neuropsychological studies are being conducted on children with leukemia who relapse, children who receive total body irradiation before bone marrow transplantation, and other children who receive radiation therapy. As new information is gathered, treatment regimens are refined. But even with the accumulation of new research, there are few hard-and-fast rules about how an individual child's learning will be affected. Thus, continued vigilance will be needed.

Many treatment centers, including The Children's Hospital of Philadelphia, offer direct consultation with schools when patients are experiencing learning difficulties. These services can include helping parents obtain appropriate testing for their child, interpreting the tests and formulating the IEP, and consulting with teachers about appropriate learning methods and behavioral concerns.

For example, short-term memory deficits show up in the classroom primarily in math, spelling, and remembering facts, says Dr. Radcliffe. Reading and remembering concepts and ideas may be somewhat less affected. In addition, a child's learning may be affected by fatigue, hearing loss, inattentiveness or distractibility, and what Dr. Radcliffe calls a slow response rate. "They move slowly; they write slowly; they need extra time for tests to get everything written down from the board," she says.

With appropriate educational planning, however, these children can often adapt, says Dr. Radcliffe. After evaluating a child's cognitive functioning, she develops an educational plan and works with the child's school to implement it. She may suggest, for example, that a child be allowed extra time to complete tasks, or that the child be allowed to take tests without time pressure. For children with memory deficits, material may be better mastered if it is presented in smaller chunks. Memory aids and tutoring may also be beneficial. Some children who have received brain irradiation will function better if they are placed in special education classes for the learning disabled (see chapter 12).

Parents must continue to advocate for their children for many years after their treatment, says Dr. Radcliffe. "What I've found is that schools are usually very responsive to meeting the needs of these children initially, when their lives are being threatened. But two or three years down the road, when the children are well and it's all history, the child's current teacher may not even know about the cancer experience. That's when there may be problems. Schools often don't really appreciate the extent of the treatments and the effects on cognitive development."

## Psychological and Emotional Consequences of Treatment for Childhood Cancer

Less is known about the long-term psychological and emotional consequences of childhood cancer. According to psychologist Anne Kazak, Ph.D., most people live a fairly normal life after being cured of childhood cancer. But, she continues, "There has always been a group of kids who aren't very well adjusted, and it's sometimes hard to figure out why."

For some the reasons are fairly straightforward. Physical differences, such as amputations, may affect self-esteem and self-image, although some children use their physical limitations as an incentive to push themselves to high levels of achievement. Other children experience long-term anger, which may be held in check for some time only to erupt later in life. They may be angry because, after all they have been through, still more obstacles lie in their paths, for instance ongoing cardiac problems or the development of a new medical problem associated with the cancer treatment. While their parents and others may try to stress the positive—"At least you're alive"—children may feel less fortunate as they compare themselves to other, healthy peers.

Another group of people experience more puzzling and scary consequences of their illness. In talking to people as long as twelve years after they have completed their treatment, Dr. Kazak has found that many continue to have extremely bothersome memories about the entire treatment experience. "And it's true even more strongly for parents than for kids," she says. What these people are experiencing, according to Dr. Kazak, are "post-traumatic stress symptoms," not unlike the symptoms experienced by other people who have experienced other traumatic events. In addition, says Dr. Kazak, "A lot of people feel that they don't have the right to complain, because, after all, they're the lucky ones. But I don't think people are very lucky if they're having flashbacks and nightmares several times a week."

Dr. Kazak says that until more research is done in this area, it will be hard to know how common these problems are or how best to treat people. In the meantime, she suggests, people should consider receiving counseling from the psychosocial staff of their oncology center or from a private counselor. In addition, parent support groups or organizations such as Candlelighters may provide emotional support and practical suggestions.

## Follow-up Care for Cancer Survivors

Dr. Meadows established the first follow-up clinic at The Children's Hospital of Philadelphia, which today is a model for similar institutions. The clinic enrolls patients who have been free of disease for five years and have been off treatment for at least two years.

"We see patients once a year so that we can keep track of how they're developing, not because we expect to detect abnormalities then. We want to know what is going on with them so that in case they should develop symptoms or signs of something between visits, we would know their baseline."

When children are on their own as young adults, the follow-up clinic does not continue to provide their general care. Instead it attempts to set the person up with a provider in the community who will fulfill that role. That provider might be an internist or, if the person is at risk for cardiac problems, it might be a cardiologist. A woman at risk for fertility problems might be set up with a gynecologist, whereas someone who had lost a kidney might be set up with a nephrologist. Since many physicians in the community may have little experience with people who were treated for childhood cancer, Dr. Meadows and her staff also assist them in a consulting capacity.

The other primary function of the follow-up clinic, according to Dr. Meadows, is to educate childhood cancer survivors about steps they can take to reduce their risk of adverse consequences. "We talk to them about safe sex, wearing seat belts, and not smoking," says Dr. Meadows. "Later we might talk to them about their possibility of fertility or sterility; we might recommend replacement hormones if they need that, or even send them to psychiatrists if that's what they need."

The focus of the intervention varies according to individual needs, says Dr. Meadows. This is determined both by the individual's physical condition and by a thorough review of the treatments the person has received.

# • BIBLIOGRAPHY •

Ablin, Arthur R. *Supportive Care of Children with Cancer.* Baltimore: Johns Hopkins University Press, 1993.

Adams, David Walter, and Eleanor J. Deveau. *Coping with Childhood Cancer: Where Do We Go from Here.* Reston, Va.: Reston Publishing Co., 1984.

Bearison, David J. *They Never Want to Tell You: Children Talk About Cancer.* Cambridge, Mass.: Harvard University Press, 1991.

Bombeck, Erma. *I Want to Grow Hair, I Want to Grow Up, I Want to Go to Boise: Children Surviving Cancer.* New York: Harper & Row Publishers, 1989.

Bracken, Jeanne Munn. *Children with Cancer, A Comprehensive Reference Guide for Parents.* New York: Oxford University Press, 1986.

Chesler, Mark A., and Oscar A. Barbarian. *Childhood Cancer and the Family: Meeting the Challenge of Stress and Support.* New York: Brunner/Mazel, 1987.

D'Angio, Giulio; Davendralingam Sinniah; Anna T. Meadows; Audrey E. Evans; and Jon Pritchard, eds. *Practical Pediatric Oncology: The Practice of the Cancer Center, The Children's Hospital, Philadelphia.* Great Britain: Edward Arnold, 1992.

Gaes, Geralyn and Graig, and Philip Bashe. *You Don't Have to Die: One Family's Guide to Surviving Childhood Cancer.* New York: Villard Books, 1992.

Krementz, Jill. *How It Feels to Fight for Your Life.* New York: A Fireside Book, Simon & Schuster, 1989.

Kushner, Harold S. *When Bad Things Happen to Good People.* New York: Schocken Books, 1981.

Nessim, Susan, and Judith Ellis. *CANCERVIVE: The Challenge of Life After Cancer.* Boston: Houghton Mifflin Company, 1991.

Pizzo, Philip A., and David G. Poplack. *Principles and Practice of Pediatric Oncology,* 2nd edition. Philadelphia: J. B. Lippincott, 1993.

Rolsky, Joan Taska. *Your Child Has Cancer: A Guide to Coping.* Philadelphia: Committee to Benefit the Children, St. Christopher's Hospital for Children, 1992.

HERE Spinetta, John J. and Patricia Deasy-Spinetta, eds. *Living with Childhood Cancer.* St. Louis: Mosby, 1981.

Tomal, David R. and Annette. *Every Parent's Nightmare: A Young Family's Triumph Over Their Son's Critical Illness.* Grand Rapids, Mich.: Zondervan Publishing House, 1993.

# ◆ RESOURCES ◆

The following organizations can provide information and support, both emotional and practical:

**American Brain Tumor Association**
2720 River Road
Des Plaines, IL 60018
(708) 827-9910 or (800) 886-2282

Offers free services including patient education publications, referrals to brain tumor support groups and physicians around the country, a pen-pal program, and a newsletter. Publishes *A Primer of Brain Tumors.*

**American Cancer Society**
1599 Clifton Road, N.W.
Atlanta, GA 30329
(800) ACS-2345

Provides educational programs and other services for people with cancer and their families.

**Candlelighter's Childhood Cancer Foundation**
1901 Pennsylvania Avenue, N.W., Suite 1001
Washington, DC 20006
(202) 659-5136
Toll free hot line: (800) 366-2223

An international network of support groups for parents of children with cancer. Their mission is to educate, support, serve, and advocate for families of children with cancer, survivors of childhood cancer, and the professionals who work with them.

Publishes newsletters for parents and children as well as other informational brochures and handbooks. The national organization can direct parents to their local group.

**Children's Oncology Camps of America**
c/o Linda Wells, R.N.
7 Richland
Medical Park, SC 29203

Camps organized specifically for children with cancer and their families, to provide them with normal life experiences.

**Compassionate Friends**
P.O. Box 1347
Oak Brook, IL 60521
(312) 323-5010

A self-help organization that offers friendship and understanding to bereaved parents. Publishes newsletter and other informational materials.

**Leukemia Society of America**
600 Third Avenue
New York, NY 10016
(800) 955-4LSA

A volunteer health agency with local chapters dedicated to finding the cause and cure of leukemia and related disease. Provide support groups, educational materials, and financial assistance for outpatient chemotherapy drugs and therapy, transportation, and transfusions.

**Make-A-Wish Foundation of America**
2600 North Central Avenue
Suite 936
Phoenix, AZ 85004
(602) 240-6060
(800) 722-9474

A nonprofit organization that fulfills the wishes of children with life-threatening or terminal illnesses. Contact them directly or through a psychosocial professional.

**National Brain Tumor Foundation**
323 Geary Street, Suite 510
San Francisco, CA 94102
(800) 93-4-CURE
(415) 296-0404
fax: (415) 296-9303

Pursues two major goals: to improve the quality of life for brain tumor patients and to find a cure through research. Funds research, provides an educational guide for patients and families, publishes a newsletter, refers patients and family members to support groups, provides the "Support Line" to connect patients with professional caregivers and survivors of the disease.

**National Cancer Institute**
Building 31, Room 10A24
9000 Rockville Pike
Bethesda, MD 20892
(800) 4-CANCER to order publications
(301) 402-5874 to call the CancerFax computer

Provides a number of cancer information services to patients and family members. Call (800) 4-CANCER to order any of their numerous free publications or to get a list of publications available. Another service, CancerFax, provides quick access (via fax machine) to the latest cancer information available, twenty-four hours a day, seven days a week. You can call CancerFax from a fax machine telephone. Listen for the CancerFax voice prompt, and press "1" for a listing of all the information available. The listing provides six-digit codes for different types of information. Enter the code, then press the # key on your fax phone, then press the start/copy or receive key on the fax machine and hang up your fax phone.

**National Coalition for Cancer Survivorship**
1010 Wayne Avenue, 5th floor
Silver Spring, MD 20910
(301) 650-9127

Provides information (publications and newsletter) for living well after a diagnosis of cancer. Annual Assembly brings together survivors, caregivers, and cancer organizations/institutions. Will help people locate support within their community.

**National Marrow Donor Program**
3433 Broadway Street, NE, Suite 400
Minneapolis, MN 55413
(800) MARROW-2

Network maintains a computerized data bank of available donor volunteers nationwide.

**Ronald McDonald Houses**
Golin/Harris Communications, Inc.
500 North Michigan Avenue
Chicago, IL 60611
(312) 836-7384

Provides housing for families in a homelike environment—a "home away from home"—while their child is being hospitalized.

# ◆ INDEX ◆

# *The* EVERYDAY PARENTING TOOLKIT

ALSO BY ALAN E. KAZDIN, PH.D.

*The Kazdin Method for Parenting the Defiant Child*

# *The* Everyday Parenting Toolkit

---

THE KAZDIN METHOD FOR EASY, STEP-BY-STEP, LASTING CHANGE FOR YOU AND YOUR CHILD

---

Alan E. Kazdin, Ph.D.

WITH CARLO ROTELLA

MARINER BOOKS
HOUGHTON MIFFLIN HARCOURT
Boston • New York

First Mariner Books edition 2014



www.hmhco.com

*Library of Congress Cataloging-in-Publication Data*
Kazdin, Alan E.
Everyday parenting toolkit : the Kazdin method for easy, step-by-step, lasting change for you and your child / Alan E. Kazdin.
p. cm.
ISBN 978-0-547-98554-1 ISBN 978-0-544-22782-8 (pbk.)
1. Child rearing. 2. Parenting. I. Title.
HQ769 .K345 2013
649'.64—dc23
[B]
2012537349

Printed in the United States of America
DOC 10 9 8 7
4500797926

# *Contents*

# *Acknowledgments*

We would like to thank our children for all they have taught us, and we would like to thank the many parents we have encountered whose dedication to child rearing has been an inspiration and an example.

# *Introduction*

A lot of people associate the word *science* with cold, remote abstractions, the opposite of your relationship to your kids. But scientists who investigate parenting and child rearing are finding out all kinds of things that can make family life not only easier for parents and children but also warmer, closer, and happier. In psychology and related fields, researchers are studying everything from the most effective way to ask your child to do something (the way that's most likely to lead to the child doing it) to how and why parents punish so much even though it doesn't work very well. The body of good research produced by these scientists grows more robust and useful every day. Their findings confirm some instinctive parental habits. For instance, research on the effects of comforting touch is telling us more and more about how good for your kids it is, not just psychologically but biologically, to be hugged by you. When you follow the urge to hug your child frequently, the likely good effects include not only reducing stress and promoting bonding and attachment but also strengthening the child's immune system. The research also shows why other ingrained parental habits make life only more difficult for adults and children alike. Take nagging, for example. We (I say "we" because I'm a parent, too) tend to act as if repeatedly reminding a child to do something makes the child more likely to do it, but the science clearly shows that the opposite is true: more reminders equals less chance of compliance.

There's good science out there, and parents need it more than ever. They're pulled in more directions than ever before and get less help than ever from other adults. They have less time with their families because of the normalizing of the two-career couple (or, for that matter, the three-job or four-job couple) and the technology-assisted expansion of work to fill even the smallest gaps in the day, so that parents are never beyond the reach of e-mails or text messages that draw them away from family time and back to work. There are also more single parents than ever before: in the United States, 41 percent of births are to an unmarried parent, and many parents are raising kids largely alone because of divorce. More grandparents have primary responsibility for rearing children, and there are more blended families in which different approaches to raising children can come into conflict. And, crucially, parents are increasingly isolated, cut off from the support systems and sources of advice that have traditionally helped with child rearing, such as neighbors and grandparents.

That all translates into more and different kinds of stress on parents. You try mightily not to pass this stress on to your kids, but its effects can sneak up on you. Take, for example, that typical twenty-first-century mini-storm in which you get an emergency text message from the office and then your toddler melts down or your preteen goes into attitude overdrive. "Just my luck," you may think. "This is the last thing I need right now." It's natural to think of the simultaneous onset of work-related and family-related crises as a coincidence—bad parental luck—but they're often deeply connected. A number of studies show in detail how stressors on parents modify how they interact with their children, often in ways that increase noncompliance. When a parent is under stress, especially when stress is made worse by isolation, the effects can be measured by changes in tone of voice, the quality of prompts to children, patience, and the ability to pay attention to a child—all of which can make a child more difficult to manage. Just a little more edge in your voice, just a little more or less slack in reaction time can make the difference between a child doing what's asked of him and pitching a fit. And, of course, a difficult child is another stressor, which in turn stretches and isolates the parent even further, and the whole cycle goes around faster and faster.

Feeling on their own and in need of support, parents increasingly turn to our age's principal substitute for community and extended family: the Internet. Studies show (yes, somebody's studying this) that parents go online for advice more than they go to their own parents or to others who are raising children of the same age. And there is indeed some useful information to be had online if you know where to look. The problem is that much of it is not presented in a way to make it useful to nonscientists, and, more important, even the best advice is buried in an electronic infinity of bad advice, bad science or anti-science, and confident admonitions to do things that won't work and may well make your life worse: talking your child's tantrums to death, for instance, or whupping the badness out of your child, or using time out for hours until your child learns her lesson. It can be difficult to tell the good advice apart from the bad, especially when you're not an expert and in a hurry. And you probably *are* in a hurry, especially these days.

I direct the Yale Parenting Center, a service for families at Yale University that works with parents who want help with their children. Families in nearby cities and states come to the center for face-to-face sessions, and through our online setup we work with others from across the nation and in other countries. We see all kinds of kids and parents, all sorts of situations and problems, including some very extreme ones, but typically we focus on families that are dealing with the common challenges of child rearing. Sometimes these parents need a little help to get them through a rough patch, a child's particularly challenging developmental stage, or a sticky situation—of which we've seen all kinds, including a lot of out-of-control tantrums, teasing and fighting among siblings, children who won't do homework or practice an instrument, and every kind of teen attitude you can imagine. And sometimes they don't have a pressing problem at all, and they're just looking for assistance with normal day-to-day parenting, like managing multiple kids' schedules or preparing for a fast-approaching transition to adolescence.

We've seen thousands of children at the Yale Parenting Center, from toddlers to teens. But it's important to make clear that the methods I'm presenting to you in this book are not just the product of my own experience. They're drawn from the findings of science, which means that they're drawn from the experiences of a much larger pool—thousands of scientists and all the many, many people they have studied. These experiences have been systematically collected and analyzed, and that analysis is continuously tested and refined. Science does not have all the answers, of course, but it's our best means of accumulating information and improving knowledge over time. The scientific method has allowed us to make gradual progress to the point that we can control diseases that used to be incurable; it's why we can send a spaceship to Mars, which used to be a science-fiction fantasy; and it's why we can now effectively treat formerly intractable afflictions like anxiety and depression. This book is based on what scientists in psychology and allied fields—not just me, but a whole profession's worth of fellow investigators—have learned that can help you do everything from toilet training your child to dealing with typical teen issues like enforcing curfews and managing greater independence.

The parents I meet need a guide that bridges the gap to the best science and makes it immediately available to them in the most practical ways. So that's what I set out to do in this book. I've already written a book for parents that focuses on the particular challenges of dealing with defiant and oppositional children (*The Kazdin Method for Parenting the Defiant Child*); this book, by contrast, is intended for parents who are dealing with the kinds of everyday challenges that come up in most households. It brings the most useful results of the research on parenting and child development to you in the form of concrete tools and strategies for your home, illustrates their applicability with everyday examples, provides guidelines on how to use the tools to address fresh situations that may come up in your household, and focuses on routine everyday life behaviors that are challenges to most parents most of the time. This is a parenting handbook for daily life, in other words, at a time when many parents feel, for good reason, that they need more guidance than ever before.

Think of this book as a how-to manual that not only offers effective solutions to common parenting problems but also shows you how to break down and deal with the bewilderingly infinite variety of challenges that come up as you raise your children. It's a book you can turn to when dealing with typical concerns ranging from specific behavior problems to more general matters that transcend the label of behavior, like attitude or character. It will help you work on a concrete issue, such as toilet training or brushing teeth, teaching a child to accept "no" without a tantrum, or smoothing out a conflict-ridden after-school or curfew routine. It will show you how to help your child take more responsibility for doing homework, practicing an instrument, doing chores, or coming home on time. And it will offer ways to help a child develop interests and qualities like respect for others, honesty, good friendships, or altruism. Parents aren't concerned only with behavior, of course; they're urgently interested in their children's character and developing attitude toward the world. But those larger traits will inevitably be expressed as behavior—an honest child will tell the truth; a generous child will perform acts of generosity. By building those behaviors we also work on developing the broader qualities associated with them.

I'll offer plenty of examples, but I won't try to go through all imaginable possibilities case by case. I think it's vitally important to show you a few basic, flexible principles that you can adapt and apply on your own to the limitless variety of situations that come up in the course of regular family life. These basic principles aren't abstractions (of the unobjectionable-but-vague "be firm but fair" variety the parenting literature abounds in); rather, they're specific tools with specific uses, simple enough to master quickly but adaptable to deal with the most complex family situations.

Let's say, for instance, that your twelve-year-old is dragging her heels on weekday mornings and your five-year-old turns every trip to the supermarket into a tragic opera. You'd really like to fix these problems now, and you don't want to embark on some extended personal odyssey of discovery to get to the solutions. So, you check this book—not because it devotes a separate chapter each to morning routines and trips to the supermarket but because a quick look will allow you to review some basic and extremely handy principles. In each case, you know what you don't want the child to do, but have you translated your wishes into a clearly defined *behavior* you do want and can explain to your child? Now, how do you set up the behavior with effective *antecedents* to increase the chances of success? Do you have the *consequences* lined up to reinforce the right behavior, lock it in, and turn it into a habit?

The core of this book is the ABCs: A for antecedents, which is everything that happens before your child does (or doesn't do) what you want him to do; B for behaviors; and C for consequences, which is what happens after your child does (or doesn't do) what you want. The book brings together research in these three areas—how what happens before, during, and after affects the likelihood that a child will do what parents want her to do. I'll show you how to break down a problem into these three components, and I'll offer you tools to deal with each of them.

The first four chapters introduce you to the ABCs—antecedents, behaviors, and consequences—and how to use them. (It takes four chapters because I devote two to consequences, the most overused and widely misunderstood part of the equation.) Chapter five is about what's going on around the behavior, the more general climate of a household. Often, you can raise your overall chances of success in improving behavior by making a simple adjustment in the routines of family life: the context.

Finally, in chapter six I focus, with examples, on how to put the pieces together. Along the way, as I've said, I'll be sure to show you not only how to use the tools but how to decide which tool you'll reach for in a given situation.

It's important to underscore that the *how* really matters here. Many of the good-behavior techniques I present to you have many variations. That's what makes them adaptable to so many different circumstances. Time out and positive reinforcement, for instance, are used not only with children in household, baby-sitting, camp, preschool, and school settings, but also with adults in nursing homes, the military, sports training, and many other settings. Parents can take advantage of the great flexibility of these techniques, adapting them to their own needs, but they still have to use them properly. Success can often depend on relatively subtle nuances in how you use the technique. Time out, for example, is a very popular tool in the parental toolkit, but it's usually used improperly. Yes, variations are possible, but there are, in fact, more and less effective ways to use time out, and an understanding of the difference between them begins with an understanding of what time out really means: a brief break from any reinforcing events of any kind. And yet adults often do things that undermine the effectiveness of time out: dragging the child to a time-out spot and forcibly keeping her there (which is stimulation, and the wrong kind of stimulation at that); letting the time out go on too long (only the first minute is necessary for changing behavior; everything after that is either neutral in effect or, after about ten minutes, counterproductive); ordering the child to spend the time out contemplating and repenting his sins (when in fact the point of time out is to do nothing at all).

You may recognize some or many of the techniques I discuss. Often, a reader will be familiar with a particular tool, but that doesn't mean it's been used properly in the past. You may have said "Good job!" to your child until it makes you ill to hear yourself say it, but I can show you what the science says about how to praise more effectively—and, as a bonus, you can offer a lot less of it and still get better results.

In that connection, it's important to emphasize that this book isn't another version of a reward program. If you know the parenting literature or have searched online for help with parenting, you may be overly familiar with sticker charts and the like. You may even have tried such programs, with mixed success at best. A successful program requires all three components: As, Bs, and Cs. Point programs—also known as sticker charts—show up a few times in this book, but always as a minor part of a more comprehensive approach. As they're typically used, sticker charts concentrate all of a parent's effort on the Cs, the consequences, with little attention to antecedents or shaping the desired behavior as it develops. But that's like training a pilot only how to land a plane, not how to take off and fly in all kinds of weather. You have to build a behavior gradually and encourage it to occur in circumstances that make success more likely, and you can't do it all with consequences. That explains why consequence-only programs for improving children's behavior, including some very popular ones, don't work very well. For instance, some families, schools, and even fast-food chains offer incentives for children who get good grades, but that's throwing consequences at long-term outcomes, which is usually doomed to fail. If you want to teach someone to play the piano, you don't save up all rewards until the budding musician can play a Beethoven concerto; you shape interim processes like learning scales, practicing regularly, and so on.

So the *how* (how you use the tools) matters as much as the *what* (the tools themselves). You have to use the tools properly, especially when you're just starting to work on building up a new behavior, getting it to occur frequently, and locking it in with the most effective consequences. But you don't have to be perfect. Less-than-perfect applications of the techniques in this book will still be very likely to improve your child's behavior. (And, because human beings and not robots are involved, a much greater likelihood of success is all one can responsibly claim for these methods. The research shows that they work most of the time on most people, and at the Yale Parenting Center we see lots of families whose experience confirms that finding.)

And there's no need to change your life to use every single one of the techniques I offer you in every possible situation. I'm not proselytizing here. If you're satisfied with your child's behavior in a given area—he goes to bed on time and without any problem, she practices the piano without too much fuss—you don't need to consult this book about it. Sometimes you just don't need to use a tool; if you can open jars of food or remove screws and nails from the wall with your bare hands, leave the tools in the box. But sometimes you really need a tool. If you keep running into the same conflict at the same flash point—meals, screen time, clothing, manners, cell phone, attitude, whatever it is—and you're sick of lecturing, threatening, wheedling, and punishing, you can make life less stressful for all by reaching for one or more of the tools in the kit presented by this book, and using it properly.

*The*

# EVERYDAY PARENTING TOOLKIT

# 1

## Laying the Groundwork for Good Behavior

### *A for Antecedents*

Antecedents are everything that happens immediately before a behavior—how you address your child, what the child is doing at the time, even the look on your face. Want your child to go to bed on time? To take a bath or do a chore? To tell you where she's going after school? To listen better or be more physically active? What happens before each of these behaviors, or before the moment you want it to happen, greatly affects the likelihood that the behavior will occur. Temperaments and family situations do vary, and different children will be more or less oppositional or cooperative (as any parent with more than one child will tell you), but it's still true that the way you use antecedents can influence a child to do what you wish . . . or adamantly refuse to do it.

Antecedents influence all kinds of behavior in everyday life. A wave from a friend is an antecedent; when you walk over and say hello, that's the behavior cued by the wave; and the pleasure of human contact is the consequence. A warning not to eat spoiled food is an antecedent, too, and it's intended to lead to a certain behavior: eating only food that's safe to eat. If you ignore that antecedent and scarf down mold-covered lunchmeat, you're putting yourself in line for the memorably negative consequence of painful and messy stomach trouble.

When we set out to use antecedents consciously, we do it because we're confident that a certain antecedent has an influence on what happens next. So, one person invited out to a fancy dinner might starve himself all day to gear up to take maximum advantage of the opportunity, but another might eat a snack before the dinner to improve her chances of exercising moderation and not overeating when faced with all that fabulous food. In both cases, the dinner guest consciously does something before arriving that will have an effect on how he or she behaves at the meal.

But the effect of antecedents is not always so obvious. Often, in fact, that effect happens at a level well below our own conscious sense of what we're up to. For example, there's a fascinating area of research in psychology called "priming," which mostly consists of presenting cues to people and then having them engage in some seemingly unrelated activity, like solving a logic problem or arranging a list of words in alphabetical order. Participants in the experiments are not aware of the relationship between the priming cue and the activity they then do, and yet there's a measurable effect on their behavior. Showing test participants a briefcase—seemingly incidentally—before asking them to complete a task made them more competitive, but a glimpse of a backpack made them more cooperative with others. The smell of all-purpose cleaner made them neater. Participants who were given a warm cup of coffee to hold tended to see the personalities of people they encountered during the study as a little more "warm," emotionally, than did participants who didn't hold a cup of coffee. When asked what made them feel more competitive or neat-minded, or why they felt that the stranger they encountered had a warm personality, they couldn't identify the priming influence as a cue. The research on priming should remind us that we're often unaware of how antecedents have a strong effect on our thoughts, feelings, and actions. But the fact that we're often unaware of that effect doesn't detract from their power.

When it comes to parenting, the first thing to bear in mind is that most of us rely too heavily on consequences—punishments, especially, but also rewards—when we're trying to change a child's behavior or mindset. It's natural to fixate on the behaviors or attitudes we don't want and then react to them with reprimands or promises of big rewards to try to get rid of them, neither of which works very well. The human brain is actually hard-wired to respond to negative stimuli, so parents seeking to change their children's behavior have to push back against their own human tendency to be better at noticing and reacting to negative than to positive things.

You will have more success, and life will be easier for you and for your children, if you take more advantage of the power of antecedents. There's a great deal you can do in advance that will make it very likely that the behavior you want will happen when you want it to, whether what you're after is something very specific, like doing homework, or something more general, like listening to you more attentively or speaking respectfully or being more motivated to get off the couch.

This means that you have to know what behaviors you would like, and when you want them. When you have an idea of what you're looking for, it's easier to use antecedents to make it happen. That also gets you out of the habit of just noticing what you don't want, and unwittingly reinforcing it with your exasperated attention. I'll have more to say about all that in the next chapter, which concentrates on the behavior itself. For now, let's stick to antecedents.

## Your antecedents toolkit

Let's start with some common types of antecedents. I'll go through them one by one. What we're doing here is putting some equipment in your toolkit—ways to set up the behavior you want.

*Prompts* are antecedents that directly instruct a specific behavior, such as "Please pick up the clothes on your floor now." They can be verbal instructions, written or physical cues (a note on the refrigerator door, a list of things to do, colored strips of tape on the fingerboard of a child's violin to guide the placement of his fingers), gestures (waving to someone to come in or go out), physical guidance (putting a child's hands in the proper position on a musical instrument or a tool), or modeling (demonstrating how to hold a fork or jump rope). Each type of prompt can be used alone or in combination, and each is directed toward promoting a desired response by conveying what it is and, sometimes, how to do it.

It's natural to favor one type of prompt. Typical family life, for instance, seems to feature a great deal of verbal instruction in the form of shouting from room to room, which doesn't produce much in the way of desired behaviors. (The content of the shouted statement is equivalent to a prompt—"Come in here and clean up this mess you made!"—but the delivery in the form of a shout from a distance will undermine the request and is more likely to lead to noncompliance.) But combining different kinds of prompts is much more effective. If you tell your child to clean her room, that might work, but it will be more effective, especially when you're just beginning to try to establish the behavior as a habit, if you tell her what you want and then say, "Let's go start it together," and then go to her room with her and model the behavior (pick up one piece of clothing off the floor and put it in the laundry bag). Or you could try taking turns as a prompt: I do one, you do one.

Many parents have an almost instinctive resistance to "I do one, you do one" and other such strategies. Understandably, they want their child to be independent, and they fear that helping him do every little task will not teach him to do things on his own. But that's a misplaced worry. It's efficient and effective to be close by at first and to help a lot early in training, because initiating behavior and getting the early steps going are the most difficult part. Firming up the habit later on is relatively easy. As more of the behavior occurs (more cleaning up on her own, more homework time), it works well for a parent to stop offering prompts and back off.

*Fading* refers to the gradual removal of a prompt. If you abruptly remove a prompt too early in training, you may be interfering with the establishing of a habit. But if your child is consistently doing the behavior when you prompt her to, you can begin to reduce and finally omit the prompt. For example, teaching someone how to serve in tennis or how to play the piano may include reminders (prompts) regarding how to hold the racket or how to place fingers on the keys. As the beginner learns, the nature of the prompt may change—from "Hold your fingers like this" (with the teacher modeling the position) to just saying the word *fingers* without any other statement or modeling. Also, you can provide prompts less frequently. The correct behaviors are reinforced without reminders, and soon these behaviors do not need to be prompted at all, or only very rarely. Finally, the behavior is reinforced without prompts.

If you are going to use just a verbal prompt, it helps to remember that the more concrete and specific the statement, the better. "Please bring me the phone" is much better than "Could you bring me the phone?" (an open-ended question that naturally leads a child to think, "Yes, I am capable of bringing you the phone," but not necessarily to bring you the phone right now) or just "Bring me the phone," a command that eliminates all possibility of choice, with bad effects I will get to in a minute. Both the open-ended question and the imperious command are less effective than making a polite and specific request. Similarly, "Fix your shoes! You're nine years old!" is very unclear and open-ended; "Please tie your shoelaces" is much more likely to produce the results you want.

As you can probably tell, the "please" matters a great deal—both because it conveys a sense of choice to a child and because it serves to control your own tone. It's harder to yell and speak harshly when you begin with "please." Choice, a warm tone, and politeness all help to produce the results you want, as I'll explain when I tell you about other sorts of antecedents.

First, though, one story about the importance of tone and "please" as antecedents. One of the mothers who came to the Yale Parenting Center for help complained that her nine-year-old daughter, Rena, never listened to her when she asked her to start homework, practice her flute, or help with setting or clearing the table. I asked the mother to pretend I was the child to see how she asked Rena to do something. The mother made very clear statements about what to do: "Go to your room and start practicing your flute." The content of the prompt was perfect in clarity. But the tone was a little harsh and she made no effort to soften the request, which therefore felt more like an order. The mother's natural tone of voice sounded harsh to begin with, even when she was just talking about something with me or with the staff at the Parenting Center, and when she spoke to her daughter, it was even a bit harsher.

There is more to getting compliance from a child than tone of voice and presentation, but a harsh tone can all by itself lead to noncompliance. We had the mother practice putting "please" in front of her requests. We asked her to smile a little, too. The "please" and the smile helped make the request much less harsh—they at once controlled how the mother made the statement (more sweetly) and in the process raised the likelihood that the child would comply. (Try it yourself. Even if the content of a command is stern, it sounds gentler if you smile and say "please" while issuing it.) We also had the mother practice going over to her daughter and speaking more softly. So the full package was to say "please," smile, and go closer to the child so Rena's mother could speak more softly and still be heard. Rena almost instantly began to comply more often with her mother's requests and virtually stopped arguing and talking back, which had been a problem before.

Note that we didn't ask Rena's mother to be any more lenient or to change her policies at all. We just helped her make a couple of slight changes in the tone of her antecedents.

*Setting events* influence a behavior without offering a direct, narrowly focused prompt. They set the stage for a behavior. For instance, reading to a young child to help him wind down before bedtime will increase the chances of a smooth transition to sleep. Setting events can be broad in scope or very specific, and they're used throughout everyday life. The cinnamon cookie smell wafting through the house on display by a realtor or the soft music one hears when boarding an airplane are setting events for desired outcomes: making an offer on a house, taking your seat calmly. Parents arguing before school can be a setting event for their child being noncompliant at school and getting into trouble. We can break down setting events further into whether they make a behavior more or less likely to occur.

Dress codes in schools are a classic setting event intended to promote disciplined and orderly behavior. Dress codes in restaurants, similarly, don't just give the proprietors an excuse to exclude some people; they're also intended to increase the likelihood that dressed-up customers will behave courteously. Giving a child a good-natured challenge ("I bet you can't do this") is often an effective setting event, because it helps motivate the child to try a behavior, increasing the likelihood that it will happen. I know of no generally accepted scientific explanation for exactly why challenges work so well, but the research does suggest some possibilities. It shows us that competition is a terrific motivator, and it's possible that a challenge sets up an implied competition with some standard, like a runner testing himself against the clock, or with a peer group. That's why it can help if you add to the challenge something like "It's OK if you can't do it now, because it's really hard for a kid your age. But maybe when you're older . . ."

A setting event can also make a behavior *less* likely to happen. Eating a big meal before you go to the supermarket decreases the chances that you'll buy a lot of food there. Some convenience store owners pipe classical music out to the parking lot to decrease the likelihood that teenagers will choose to loiter near the store. And, as Rena's mother learned, ordering a child to do something with a drill sergeant tone makes it less likely that the child will do it. "You get over here right this second!" is a prompt, but the harsh tone and stern facial expression with which a parent delivers that prompt also constitute a setting event that makes it less likely that the child will, in fact, get over there right then.

If there's even a whiff of coercion in a command—and in this example there's much more than a whiff, since the child is given no glimmer of choice in the matter—the child is less likely to comply. One interpretation of why that's so is that being coerced even a little leads a child to anticipate consequences he's likely to regret. That is, the "or else" in the implied "do it, or else" is a consequence, and that shades the child's reaction to the "do it" part. People in general are risk-averse, and the child responds to someone trying to force him to do X with the conviction that X is not something the child would otherwise do and therefore might have some undesirable effects for him. A second interpretation is that being told to do something is mildly aversive and leads to escape behavior. One escape behavior is not to do what you're being told to do; another is leaving the situation. Force, or the threat of it, is aversive and invokes a reaction.

With almost any message, how it's delivered can dictate whether you increase or decrease the chances of a certain behavior. For example, hotels want guests to reuse their towels, which conserves energy and saves money. The usual request is something like "Help save the environment and reuse your towels." That purely rational approach, based on a belief that everyone would reuse towels if they just understood how important it is, doesn't work very well. Understanding is a pretty poor motivator to comply with a request: people who smoke understand that it's bad for them, but they do it anyway. But if the hotel adds to the message some statement about other guests reusing their towels, it creates the impression that reusing towels is a social norm, which is a stronger motivator for compliance and thereby makes conservation much more likely to occur. So the message should say something like "Three out of every four people who stay in this room have reused their towels" and *then* make the request. The information that others are doing it is a setting event that greatly increases the likelihood of the guest engaging in the desired behavior.

As a parent, saying to your four-year-old, "Hey, 75 percent of other four-year-olds brush their teeth" isn't going to work. But you *can* say something like "You don't have to brush your teeth now"—or, during toilet training, "You don't have to use the toilet now"—"because you'll be able to do it when you are a bigger boy." Invoking the "bigger boy" is a way of saying that all big boys brush their teeth, so you're offering a social norm by saying that many people do it, *and* phrasing it as a challenge, *and* you're offering choice, all of which increase the chances of success.

Here's a situation I encountered at the Parenting Center that could be addressed by concentrating on setting events. I was working with a family of four that included mother, father, a seven-year-old girl, and a three-year-old boy named Max. The daughter brushed her teeth with no problem, but Mom and Dad could not get Max to brush his teeth on a regular basis. Often the parents—almost always the mother—would take Max to the bathroom and stand there to watch him brush his teeth. There was usually a fight, and often the mother "won" by getting Max to put the toothpaste on the brush and brush for just a few seconds. Then the argument would shift, predictably, to whether or not a few seconds "counted" as tooth brushing. Mom, who was normally a pretty easygoing person, found herself saying things like "Your teeth are all going to rot in your head and people will say, 'Who's that pathetic old toothless man?' and I'll say, 'Oh, he's not an old man; that's my son, Max, and he never brushed his teeth properly.'" She also found herself comparing Max unfavorably to his sister: "Your sister brushed her teeth every night with no problem when she was your age. What's wrong with you?" Comparing a child to a sibling like this usually lowers, rather than raises, your chances of getting the behavior you want, because it compares him to only one other person, as opposed to social norming (as the hotel strategy is called), which implies that many, many people pretty much like him carry out the behavior. Also, the comparisons will build Max's resentment toward his sister, which could turn into a significant distraction and lead him to avoid his parents a little more. So the comparisons decreased the parents' chances of getting tooth brushing from Max on a regular basis.

Once in a while the mother would take the brush from Max and start brushing his teeth herself, but this required a little force and the situation deteriorated from there: Max cried, the frustrated mother often brushed vengefully, meltdowns ensued. As often as not Mom just let it go, not even bothering to tell Max to brush his teeth, since this drama over tooth brushing would interfere with a peaceful bedtime, and she wasn't willing to risk it. Better a well-rested child with bad oral hygiene, she figured, than a child who's both sleep-deprived *and* rotten-toothed.

We asked the mother to practice delivering antecedents in a different way. We asked her to walk Max to the bathroom and say, in a calm and even nonchalant way, "I would like you to brush your teeth. Most children who are four or five years old brush their teeth. If you don't want to or can't do it, that's OK. Maybe just rinse your mouth with a mouthful of water." So now she's using social norming by telling him that most children his age and older do it; she's offering an implicit but good-natured challenge by including "if you don't want to or can't do it"; she's offering a choice by telling him he doesn't have to do it; and she's getting rid of her own tone of desperation and of anticipating the brushing battle, both of which decreased the likelihood of getting any tooth brushing out of Max. (And, on the behavior side, which we'll get to in the next chapter, having Max rinse out his mouth is a good start toward shaping the full behavior she wants, and she's also using what's called "response priming" by taking Max to the bathroom, the first step toward brushing his teeth, without demanding the whole sequence every time.)

So they tried a few nights of the new approach. At first, Max washed out his mouth but didn't brush. The mother reported being able to stay low-key, nonchalant. The nights were pleasant—a little rinse of the mouth and then off to bed, with no scenes. On the fourth night, he said he would like to try brushing his teeth. The mother did not jump up and down (she understood that desperation could turn off the behavior) but said that was "nice" and asked if he wanted her to come in with him. He said no, brushed his teeth, and Mom walked him to bed. His breath smelled like fresh toothpaste and she commented how great that smelled and what a big boy he was to brush his own teeth—just like Mom and Dad did. She was impressed with the changes in the child; we were impressed with her careful practice of the antecedents with us and then her execution on the battlefield—which was, in fact, not a battlefield anymore.

*High- and low-probability requests.* People do some things more readily than others when requests are made of them. Requests likely to be complied with are referred to as high-probability requests:

“Please come here and hug me,” for instance, or “Pl ish this leftover apple pie.” Other requests made b low-probability requests, are less likely to be complied with. do your chores,” for instance, or “Please start your homework.” The likelihood of a child complying with a low-probability request can be greatly increased by preceding it with two or three high-probability requests—that is, embedding some requests in the context of others can increase compliance. If you want your child to do twenty minutes of homework and she tends to resist, you can begin to develop that behavior by first asking her to do something she’ll usually do with no problem, like feeding the fish or bringing you something. Or take her to the store and ask her to please go get a specific item that she likes and put it in the shopping cart. If you start with those high-probability requests and then go to the low-probability request, “Now please get started on your homework,” it’s more likely to succeed. You might expect that a child has a limited capacity for doing what she’s told, a capacity you don’t want to waste by piling up trivial requests to do things, but the research tells us the opposite: there’s a kind of behavioral momentum, a tendency for compliance to persist, and you can get it going with a series of high-probability requests.

Here’s a good practical example. A team of researchers describe a case in which the goal was to get a twenty-two-month-old child to cooperate with a complex medical procedure. The boy had a serious bowel condition that required multiple surgeries, and he had an intravenous line that had to be cared for by his parents. The little boy would not keep still. He kicked, he pulled at the sterile line, he made life difficult for himself and his parents. The low-probability request was to hold still so the medical procedure could be completed. Getting compliance was achieved by first going through some high-probability requests: “Touch your head,” “Say ‘Mom,’” “Blow Mom a kiss,” and *then* “Hold still.” The last request, a low-probability request, was much more likely to lead to compliance when preceded by the first three, all high-probability requests.

And of course, this technique works in the other direction. My advice to preteens and teens is to use high-probability requests liberally, and not to just start out with "Can I have a second cell phone? How about a car?" The teen who draws on the lessons of this body of research will begin with high-probability requests—"May I kiss your cheek again because you are the best parent ever? Could I set the dinner table and do all of the dishes by myself tonight? I would like another chore so I can do more to help maintain the house"—and *then* tack on the low-probability request here. And it will help to allow parents a feeling of choice (of which more below): "Could I have one of those Italian sports cars for my birthday? Either the bright yellow or red would be fine." OK, I offer the advice to teens with tongue in cheek, but the underlying principle in play is no joke.

And this isn't just about parents and children, of course. During a study of real-life situations in which hostages were taken during a robbery, audio transcripts from three robberies allowed a researcher to break down interactions between the hostage taker and law enforcement agents. Requests made of the hostage taker that were classified as high-probability—likely to be complied with—included "How can we contact your wife?" and "Please spell that name for me." The low-probability requests were the sticking points: "Give up a hostage"; "Go to the door with your hands up." The results showed that the hostage taker was much more likely to comply with a low-probability request if it was preceded by three or more high-probability requests.

*Choice.* As I mentioned before, choice is an antecedent. If a child feels that he has a choice about whether to do what's asked of him, he's more likely to do it. The choice can be empty or trivial to you, but it's not to him. "Put on a jacket; we're going outside" might be sufficient to get the behavior you want, but "Please put on your jacket or a sweater—it's your choice—and we'll go outside" is much more likely to work. Especially as your child gets older, you want to look for opportunities to give real choices between alternatives that are both acceptable to you. If you're trying to get a reluctant child interested in music lessons but you don't care as much about what specific instrument he plays, you might take him to a music store and let him play around with the instruments, an activity that implies a choice about which instrument to settle on. Once an instrument is chosen, you can offer choice where possible: "You can practice your violin before we eat or right after dinner." As a general rule, lowering the amount of coercion in your lives (the amount of "Because I said so," whether explicitly stated or just implied) will increase overall compliance.

Offering choice can have subtle and unexpected benefits. One of the moms at the Yale Parenting Center was very concerned about the whereabouts of her fourteen-year-old daughter after school, a well-placed concern under almost any circumstances, as unmonitored teens often get into much greater trouble—more sex, alcohol and other substance use, more risky behavior such as driving with older peers—than monitored peers. Added to the usual concerns, Maya was a sexually mature fourteen-year-old, and very attractive. Older boys were pursuing her, and the mother was concerned about sexual activity and alcohol. Maya usually came home from school one to two hours after dismissal. Her mother grilled her. "Where were you? Who were you with? What did you do?" All good questions but, especially if delivered rapid-fire as she came in the door, all setting events for Maya going straight to her room without talking much to her mom.

When the mother came to the Parenting Center and asked for help, we suggested she chat with Maya when they were both calm. We directed the mother to use one of these chats to explain her concern and suggest two ways they could handle her desire to know where Maya was and what she was doing: (1) Maya could use her cell phone to report where she was, or (2) Maya could come home to check in and then go out with her friends. The mother told Maya that either one of these would be fine, or Maya could suggest some other idea, as long as they could both agree on it. She also told Maya that if on any day she did not report in, the next day she would have to come home directly from school and stay there (a consequence). Constructive use of antecedents here included Mom's calm presentation at a time when no argument or nagging was likely to occur, and her presenting Maya with a choice of alternatives or even coming up with a new one.

Unexpectedly, Maya chose *both* of the alternatives her mother had offered. She wanted to call home by 3:15 (school got out at 2:45) or be home by 3:15—and she wanted to have the option each day. The mother agreed. Even more surprisingly, and it was a very pleasant surprise, on about half the school days over the next few months Maya came home and elected to stay in and chat with her mother rather than going out again.

## Which antecedents should you use?

I have covered a variety of antecedents. How to select among them in any given instance? One place to start: it is almost always useful to select both a prompt (a direct way of getting behavior) and a setting event (a more indirect way). These work together well.

On the prompt side, the usual is just to give instructions or make a request. That's fine, but if you have any difficulty in getting the behavior, there are more effective prompts such as doing the task (just a small part) with the child or modeling the task (doing it right before the child does to show what you mean or how it's done).

On the setting event side, think of what can be done to make it easier for the behavior to occur. I mentioned offering a choice if possible, because offering options makes compliance with the request more likely. The usual choice—"You either do this, or else"—isn't much of a choice. Instead, offer real options: "I can help you, or would you rather do it yourself?" or "You can do this now all at once or do a little now and a little later."

Also, think about any setting events that are currently interfering with getting the behaviors you want. Is there anything happening right before your request that may make the child less compliant or responsive? One example of this you may be familiar with: a very young child who is hungry, thirsty, or tired is not likely to be compliant or agreeable. For very young children—and many adults, too—hunger, thirst, and exhaustion are such powerful negative setting events that nothing else is likely to be accomplished until those are resolved. Be on the alert for influences that may be making it more difficult to get the behavior you want.

I also mentioned high-probability requests as a setting event. You may not use this tool very often, but it can be useful. If you think your next request will inevitably be met with resistance, get compliance on some easy ones first. You are building compliance, and that helps produce further compliance. This tool is also good to have in your kit because it conveys the role of momentum. That is, once you get one behavior, you can get onto a sort of behavioral roll. That doesn't mean you will definitely get what you want, but it does increase the likelihood.

Whatever you select, there are a couple of points to keep in mind. Antecedents are extremely useful, but they're the least-well-used tool in everyday parenting. As I have noted before, if all is going well and you are getting the behavior you want and in the way you want, you can keep your tools in the box for another day. But if you want to get some behavior you aren't getting, antecedents are strong aids.

## The how

Even if you've got the right tools, success depends heavily on how you use them. Tone of voice, use of the word *please,* subtle prompts (the research shows that how close you are to a child, physically, when you ask for a behavior can make a big difference), and timing can all matter a great deal. The "how" really matters when it comes to antecedents. As I've already discussed, the same words, delivered in different ways, can be more or less likely to lead to a desired behavior.

For example, in a group setting (when other students are present in a class, when there's a brother or sister in the room, and so on) both commands and reprimands are more effective if they are whispered or spoken softly from up close to the child, rather than called out from across the room. Nobody has proven exactly why this is so, but some things we have already talked about probably come to bear on it. Prompts called out from across a room tend to be perceived as harsher because a louder command is more likely to startle a child. Also, loud commands in general are associated more with "startle situations," like fire drills and urgent statements on the order of "Don't cross the street until I get there," all of which necessarily remove any illusion of choice. But a loud prompt isn't an obvious emergency situation like a fire drill, and the removal of choice now acts only to make it less likely that the child will comply. Also, a public request for a certain behavior feels more coercive because there's an implied possibility of shame, which feels like the threat of punishment. Not doing what you ask would then be public defiance on the child's part, which you would feel more obliged to meet with negative consequences. So public commands and reprimands put the child in a corner, so to speak, where she feels the lack of wiggle room. Going up close to her and whispering a prompt in a gentle tone is much more likely to succeed.

One of the most common misuses of antecedents is to up the coercion stakes from the outset with threats, ultimatums, power plays, and arguments from authority ("Because I said so"; "Do it or else"). These antecedents have been proven to promote noncompliance. Give anyone—not just your child but your spouse or coworker—the feeling that he or she must do something, that there is no choice, and you will decrease the chances that the person will comply with this and probably other requests.

Stress, too, has a powerful effect on compliance. It makes antecedents measurably less effective, for instance. If you find it hard to be calm and positive when you first get home from work, build in some unwinding time for yourself before you start asking your children for this behavior or that. Removing the stress from your voice and manner will make it more likely that you'll get somewhere with your requests.

Another common misuse of antecedents is to pour on the prompts at the wrong moment. Picture a tween or teen just returned from school, backpack still over her shoulder, engaging in one-handed texting. When she walks through the door, a parent comes on strong with caring questions: "How was your day? Anything going on at school? How's your homework for today? You forgot your lunch this morning, so what did you eat? What did you do after school?" Each question is fine, and they may all be delivered sweetly, but the barrage of questions before the child has fully transitioned from the peer world to home gives her a mental version of the bends, the affliction that divers suffer when they come up from the depths too quickly for their bodies to adjust to the change in pressure. The onslaught of questions is a setting event for *not* interacting with you. The individual questions are all nicely delivered antecedents for some pleasant parent-child interaction, but the timing is off. Give her some private time first, so that she can choose to make her reentry into the family scene.

A more dramatic version of this scenario can happen when a child of divorced parents comes back to one parent after spending time with the other. If you're on him when he walks in the door—"How was it at your dad's? Was his new girlfriend there? Was that weird for you? Is she nice? Just in rough general terms, what would you estimate as her body mass index?"—each successive question makes it less likely that the two of you will have the interaction you're hoping for. Give him some time to readjust.

Also, it pays to think about the antecedents offered by the general atmosphere of a household. For example, it's perfectly normal for parents to argue once in a while, but arguments and fights between parents, especially if they become routine, are antecedents for disruptive behavior by children. We'll get to this in depth in the chapter on context.

## A couple of examples

Let's look at a couple of examples in more detail to show how to pick and use the proper antecedents.

• • •

Getting a young child to bed can emphasize the crucial role of setting events. Bedtime is usually an occasion for lots and lots of prompts, most of them ineffective: each time you order your child to go to bed and stay in bed and he doesn't, the effectiveness of *any* bedtime-related prompt is degraded. And when the prompts don't work, we go, in desperation, straight from antecedents to an overemphasis on dire consequences: "If you don't stay in bed this time, I'm taking away your teddy bear *forever.*" In addition, of course, when you say such dire things your voice becomes agitated and you've removed all illusion of choice, and so you enter into the territory of what's technically called an "abolishing operation"—that is, the wrong kind of setting event, the wrong kind of antecedent.

Instead, look to the right kind of setting events, those conditions around bedtime that make it more likely that it will go smoothly. That means going back at least an hour in advance of bedtime and planning it like the landing of a jet—the wheels-down moment of the child between the covers is just the last of a series of well-rehearsed moves. The winding-down sequence often includes a bath, a story, and a quiet chat with a parent once the child is in bed, and it shouldn't include computer activities, video games, or TV programs that stimulate the child shortly before bedtime.

Controlling the setting events this way, you create a calmer pre-bedtime routine that consists of a series of things you do that increase the likelihood that the behavior will occur. Each winding-down activity increases the likelihood that the next activity will happen without a fuss, building to the desired outcome: the child gets into bed and goes to sleep without going to war over it. All of the sections of our toolkit are available, of course. Parents can praise a child for completing any of the activities in the pre-bed sequence, but consequences like praise take a back seat to antecedents in this example. Antecedents are where the most effective small changes can be made to the routine to get the result you want.

Let's say you want your teenager to tell you where she is and who she's with after school on days when she doesn't come straight home.

Start with the prompt you give her on her way out of the house in the morning: "Please give me a call after school to let me know where you are and that you're all right. I love you, and I feel better when I know you are safe." You're calm, you imply choice by saying "please," you offer affection—those are setting events that make it more likely that she'll do what you ask. And now strengthen the verbal prompt and setting events (calm, choice, affection) with a touch or a kiss, whatever your teen can stand, on the way out.

A prompt is most effective when it comes as close to the behavior as possible, so doing it right before she leaves for school is better than doing it the night before. The same rule applies to space as well as time: the closer you are to your child when you deliver a prompt, the better. In ideal conditions, you get close in both senses. Let's say Grandma comes over and gives your toddler a toy. He runs over to you, wildly excited, to show it to you. You crouch down to his level and say, quietly, "All right, now go say thank you to Grandma." You're close to the child, and you're prompting the behavior right when you want him to do it, while Grandma's standing right there across the living room, ready to be thanked. In less-than-ideal conditions—that is, in normal conditions—when offering a prompt you just try to get as close as you can to the child in space and to the behavior in time.

Or let's say you want your child to do his homework rather than the usual fooling around on Facebook. When he comes home, allow fifteen or twenty minutes of downtime. Ask him to come and keep you company, if he'd like that. You can have a snack together, or ask him to help you with something that he does easily—like, say, updating the operating system on your smartphone.

Allowing some downtime is a setting event for beginning the homework routine smoothly. Remember, as I've already mentioned, the traditional first-thing-through-the-door parental interrogation is a setting event for not interacting with you—and also for not doing any routine activity associated with you, like homework.

Inviting him to keep you company, share a snack, and answer

your questions about your smartphone are all high-probability requests, setting the stage for the moment of truth. Calmly, and with perhaps a slight smile, you say, "Please start your homework now. I will help you get started if you would like." That's a nice prompt—firm, clear, but gentle, and also offering a choice: "If you want me to help you, I will."

So far, these are all antecedents. You're setting up and framing what you want to happen in ways that make it more likely to happen.

## Combining

Antecedents can be very effective in their own right, but they also work in concert with tools drawn from the other categories we will discuss. I've spotlighted antecedents in this chapter, but they're also part of the bigger picture.

Let's say your twelve-year-old son and nine-year-old daughter are bickering and you want them to stop. Antecedents can be very useful here. You might take your son aside in a private moment and say, "Please stop all this arguing and name-calling. Let's get you and your sister apart for a while. Come with me to the kitchen and help me get lunch ready." And you can add more: "I know this is not all your fault, but I need you to help me put an end to the bickering. You're now like one of the grownups in this house, and I know you can control yourself better." This takes away implied blame, which is an antecedent for reacting negatively to you. You can apportion blame later, if you need to; for now, you just want to end the arguing in a constructive way. Treating a preteen like an adult is often a setting event for compliance.

Let's say it works. He stops arguing with his sister and starts to walk away with you. That's the behavior you want. So, it's time for the right consequences. You lean over to him and praise him quietly, being specific about what was good about what he did. "That was really great, and very mature of you. I asked you to stop bickering, and you did." A relaxed high-five might be good right here, to reinforce the verbal praise with touch, thereby increasing the likelihood of compliance with your requests in the future.

In the next chapter we'll focus on the second stage of this sequence, the behavior itself. First, though, let's wrap up the discussion of antecedents.

## Conclusion

Antecedents come before the behavior. Sometimes they come right before, as when you prompt a child to set the table or wash her hands. Sometimes they come well before, as when you start the winding-down sequence an hour before bedtime.

The most effective antecedents are delivered calmly, without harshness, with "please" and the promise of flexibility in one's request, which implies choice. If that strikes you as the kind of wimpy parenting advice that has led to moral decline in our formerly moral nation, think of it this way: a parent who pours on the harshness and coercion is broadcasting a signal that she's not confident that her commands will be obeyed; a parent who's confident of the outcome can afford to be relaxed about a prompt.

When you are stressed—when you're expecting a tough day at work and you're under a deadline to get out of the house and the zipper broke on your child's only clean pair of jeans—you will lose your cool. That's normal. But realize that your normal reaction will greatly influence your interactions with your child at that moment. You will talk with more desperation, your requests will be more like commands, and, if you're dealing with a small child, you will be just a little rougher in putting his arms through the sleeves of his jacket. You will get more resistance as a result; the change in antecedents will produce opposition. That's normal, too. Your own calm, confident, relaxed assertion of authority is one of the most important antecedents at your disposal—a setting event for success when you're seeking to change your child's behavior or mindset.

Now, some reminders about basic dos and don'ts when using the antecedents I've talked about in this chapter. These are fundamental matters of approach, no matter what kind of antecedent you employ.

**Dos**

- Be calm.
- Be clear and specific in prompting what you want.
- Bear in mind that tone of voice and facial expression can affect the likelihood of getting the behavior.
- Be near the child and speak softly if you can.
- Put "please" in front of any request because it helps increase the likelihood of compliance.
- Try to use prompts when they are most effective, by offering them right before the behavior you want.
- Give choices when possible because doing so increases the likelihood of compliance.
- Use a range of antecedents. If you usually concentrate on prompts, think a little about setting events. If you're stuck on a low-probability request that your child doesn't often fulfill, try stringing together some high-probability requests in front of it.

**Don'ts**

- Don't point dramatically or snap your fingers at your child while ordering him to do something.
- Don't use phrases like "because I said so" or "because I am your parent."
- Don't rattle off a given prompt several times within a brief time period. This is nagging, and a lot of good research has confirmed what people who have been nagged already know from experience: nagging doesn't work very well.
- Don't harp on the negative consequences to come if the child doesn't do what you want. This kind of threatening, whether of the "your teeth will all fall out before you're twenty-one if you don't brush them" variety or of the "I will give you such a smack" variety, is remarkably ineffective.
- Don't worry that all these antecedents are just babying the child, cajoling, or making the child dependent on you. Just the

opposite—antecedents are useful in getting exactly the behaviors you want and in getting them to occur consistently later, once the antecedents are a distant memory.

- Don't give in to the urge to go straight to consequences when you're not seeing the behavior you want. You can work wonders with antecedents.

# 2

## What You Want to Change

### *B for Behaviors*

Behavior consists of any action or response you can observe. Talking, walking, tantruming, fighting, helping, cooperating, complying—all are behaviors. Most of what parents want to change or develop in their children qualifies as behavior. Typically, they want to see one of three kinds of change: they want a child to do something she doesn't ordinarily do or has never done or does only once in a while; or they want more of a behavior the child already does (practice the piano longer, read more pages or more advanced books, do homework for more minutes); or they want to develop a sequence of separate tasks that go together but are actually a bunch of different behaviors—like taking care of a dog (food, water, a walk twice a day) or getting ready for school in the morning (getting out of bed, showering, getting dressed, coming downstairs on time to eat and pack a backpack).

But it's important to recognize that as parents we do not want just a pile of behaviors. We often have larger goals in view, like building character and developing personality traits. We want the child to have broad virtues such as honesty, independence, diligence, and kindness, and to be respectful and to express gratitude. We don't want just one honest act, one isolated act of kindness. No, we are hoping to raise a decent, strong person, which adds up to a lot more than just whatever specific behaviors we had time to focus on at home.

As it turns out, the way to develop any of those characteristics is to develop individual examples of it, which of course brings us back to changes in behavior. If you would like your child to be kind, start by helping her make a habit of kind gestures. You can begin with just a couple of them—in the home, say, toward her younger brother—and then extend them outward toward non-family members, strangers, and so on. If you're trying to develop kindness as a general set of behaviors, to raise a child who is kind in many ways and in many different situations, you don't have to develop each different way in which kindness is shown. Once a child learns to engage in kind actions in a few areas of life, other expressions of kindness that you didn't train will increase as well.

Even when we're concentrating on just behavior, we often want chunks of behavior rather than picky little bits of action. You want a child to do his regular chores, for instance. If that includes setting the table and your child is older, you may not have to separately train him where to put the fork, then the knife, then the spoon, then the napkin. Your child may well have seen you set the table many times (you already modeled the behavior for him, which is a strong way to teach it) and may have helped you do it. With other children, especially younger ones, you might indeed have to start by building one piece of behavior at a time—where the fork goes, and so on. We begin with what the child can do, and then build from there. Wherever we start, we're heading to the same place: setting the table as a cluster of behaviors within the larger cluster of doing one's chores. One strength of this approach is that it can be individualized to meet a child where he is, beginning with what the child can do and building from there.

Often, building the characteristics associated with the behavior is as important as or more important than the particular behavior itself. Consistency is a good example. A child might do her homework on Monday and Tuesday but then tail off as the week goes on. Another might practice an instrument for twenty minutes on one day, skip the next, and play for only five minutes on the following day. When consistency becomes a problem, we can focus on and alter consistency itself as if it were a separate behavior. I'll show you how in this chapter.

So while developing specific behaviors often does involve thinking about one concrete action at a time, it does *not* mean that we have to separately train a child to do every single thing we want her eventually to be able to do. We focus on concrete and specific behaviors not only because it's important to us that our child can do them but also because the training carries over to very similar behaviors that we don't have to train. Establishing a particular behavior can be the end in itself ("I just want her to do her homework every day") or a means to a broader end ("I want her to be a responsible and organized person").

## Your behaviors toolkit

Unlike in chapter one, when I filled the antecedents toolkit with a variety of antecedents for you to choose from (prompts, setting events, and so on), this time I'll walk you through a process: how to identify the behavior you want and how to work with your child to develop it. You will have some choices about which tools you use to build a behavior (shaping, simulations, jump-starting), but in this chapter we're going to concentrate more on how you work through the *process* of setting goals and then getting the behavior you want.

*Setting your goals.* To begin with, you need to *specify what you want your child to do.* As odd as it may seem, parents rarely specify to each other or to themselves, let alone to their children, the behaviors they want in their children. They're very clear on what they *don't* want to see. As soon as the child does something annoying, problematic, or disrespectful—lying, refusing to bathe, leaving new clothes strewn on the floor, teasing a sibling, swearing—parents are typically ready to pounce. But they rarely specify what exactly it is that they *do* want. This is the negativity bias, the hard-wired human tendency to respond to negative stimuli that I've already mentioned, in action.

Specifying sounds simple, and it can be. It's merely describing what the behavior you want would look like. Be concrete. "I want my child to be nice" describes a character trait, not a behavior. "I want my child to share toys with his sister and speak politely to her when they watch TV or we eat dinner together" is more useful because it describes behaviors you want and the circumstances in which you want them. At the Yale Parenting Center we help parents specify behaviors in concrete terms by asking them to pass "the stranger test"—that is, to describe the behavior they want to see as if they were speaking to a stranger who had no idea of what their child did or what the behavior would look like. Ask yourself, "What exactly would the behavior I want my child to do look like? What would she say and do, and how would she act?"

This initial step is a very important part of the process. A couple in their late thirties came to the Yale Parenting Center for help with their five-year-old son, Daryl, who was, they said, constantly bullying his seven-year-old sister, Ella. They wanted help in getting him to be nice to her. We always begin by hearing the story as the parents frame it, and Daryl's parents' desire to move from "constantly bullying" to "being nice" oriented us in a general way to the challenge at hand. But we needed details, especially specific behaviors that Daryl did that we could change. The father resisted my request for specifics. Understandably, he felt that Daryl did so many things wrong that we shouldn't limit our efforts to changing just one or two of them. He wanted to get Daryl to be nicer to his sister in all ways, whether or not we could specify them all at the outset.

I explained that we would in fact address the full range of his concerns and general goals, but to do that we needed to focus now on a few behaviors they found especially troublesome. We would specify those, change those, and work on others as needed. There was no need to focus on each and every possible behavior that Daryl would conceivably come up with. Rather, once we changed a handful of key behaviors, probably one to three of those, other behaviors would change along with them. It's like training a child to play the piano,

I told Daryl's father. The child learns to read music and play a song. Then we teach him to play another song. The behavior of reading music and playing can now extend to many other pieces without us having to focus on each piece as if it constituted a completely fresh and new skill. Similarly, we teach a child to be considerate in a few situations (for example, in play with the children next door, in sharing a dessert with a sibling), and then other, similar behaviors come up on their own. When a grandparent gives our child a present, we prompt the child with "What do you say to Grandma?" and the child dutifully says, "Thank you." But if we do our job as parents properly, the behavior carries over into many other situations that we didn't specifically prepare him for. Your child will one day be saying "thank you" to teachers, colleagues, and lots of other people who aren't his grandmother. Being specific allows us to change behavior, and that specific focus is the best way to achieve the general goals. I asked Daryl's parents to just try this approach.

After some chatting, we identified three of Daryl's worst offenses: he would go into his sister's room when she wasn't there and dump toys off her dresser; he would hit the back of her head, mostly to tease rather than hurt her, whenever he walked by close enough to reach her; he made mocking facial expressions at her at the dinner table. The task was to give me a picture of what happened, what things really looked like, what was said, how it sounded, and so on, and the parents did a fine job of specifying. Their imitation of Daryl's dinner-table faces, in particular, conveyed just how deeply annoying he could be.

The parents felt that dumping the toys and hitting caused the most trouble, so we concentrated on those two offenses. We developed a program for Daryl that focused on replacing these behaviors with positive interactions with his sister. Any time he played peacefully, spoke pleasantly, gave her something (handed her a toy, passed the salt at the dinner table), or had any other positive contact with her, the parents praised him for it and awarded him points toward a small prize he could earn (a consequence, which I'll deal with in depth in the next two chapters). We had a program in place for three weeks, and the parents felt there were great changes in the overall tenor of the interactions Daryl had with his sister. We worked on and changed the specific behaviors of dumping toys and hitting the back of his sister's head, but more general changes occurred, too. Daryl did indeed become nicer to his sister, and it began with specifying what his parents wanted him to do.

*Identify the positive opposite.* It's likely that many of the behaviors you want to change are behaviors you want to decrease and get rid of—like Daryl's assaults on his sister, or a child spending too much time on the computer or cell phone, or whining, or fighting, or sitting around in her room too much. These are all common concerns, and alterable, but in order to address them we have to begin by defining our objective in a different way. Any time you think of a behavior that you want to reduce or eliminate, the first thing to say to yourself (as a prompt to yourself about what you should do next) is "What's the positive opposite?" That is, what exactly is the behavior you want in its place? Describe what it would look like if you were a radio sports announcer describing exactly what a player was doing so that the listening audience would get a clear idea of what you saw.

Positive opposites are the behaviors you want, the ones you develop to take the place of the behaviors you don't want. So if you want less bickering and fighting between siblings, identify the positive opposite behavior: "I want my children to treat each other with respect when they play, ride in the car, or sit at the table together." If you want less whining, reframe your desire as a positive opposite: "I want her to ask me questions just once, in a big-girl voice." Tantrums, which many parents see as intimidatingly difficult to change, are actually often pretty easy to reduce and eliminate. But first you need to define the positive opposite of a tantrum: walking away from a provoking situation, calmly expressing disagreement without yelling or throwing things, and so on.

The case of Daryl and his sister illustrates the use and importance of positive opposites. Daryl's mother and father knew what behaviors were annoying and had to be eliminated to make home life tolerable for Daryl's sister, Ella. We also asked them to specify some concrete actions they would like Daryl to do that would count as interacting nicely with Ella. They came up with a list that included items such as saying anything nice to Ella; playing together in the same room, either cooperatively or separately, while talking nicely; giving something to her (handing her a toy, passing food at the dinner table). The most effective way to eliminate the undesirable or inappropriate behaviors would be to build up these others to replace them, which is what we did. But the first step was to look to positive opposites to properly set our goals.

If the behavior you want is really a cluster of behaviors, which is often the case, *break it down into clear, doable steps*. Sometimes we are working with one behavior that we simply want more of, or want to see more consistently (such as doing homework, playing quietly). But often we want to develop a set of separate behaviors that go together and follow one from another. Getting ready for school is a good example. This is not just one single behavior we want more of—rather, it's a set of behaviors, or even a set of separate clusters of behaviors, that begins with getting out of bed on time, picking out clothes to wear and getting dressed, coming to the breakfast table, getting school materials together, doing any morning chores, and being out the door, presentable and equipped, on time.

When there are several steps or behaviors along the way, it's important to specify each one. Breaking down the sequence, a practice called "task analysis," is a way of proceeding from the general goal (getting ready for school) to a number of small, trainable, and highly concrete behaviors. The purpose of task analysis is twofold: to identify specific behaviors or steps that are required, and to specify the sequence in which these component behaviors are performed. Task analysis can make it a lot easier to develop a complex set of behaviors.

One example of task analysis is training children how to respond if a fire breaks out in their home. Safely escaping from a fire is not one behavior—such as running like hell to the exit, an instinctive response that can be fatal. Rather, a proper evacuation is a complex set of behaviors, codified by firefighters and other experts after a lot of task analysis and testing in simulated and real situations, and the behaviors can vary depending on factors like how far along the fire is, its exact location, and whether smoke is pouring under include crawling on the floor to avoid smok door to check how hot it is, deciding whether or cover the crack under the door to stop the sm and so on. If escaping safely from a fire is the general go divided into trainable steps that encompass several differen scenarios. Using antecedents, behaviors, and consequences, and repeated practice, experts have come up with a reliable system to teach children how to escape from their home safely.

Daryl's parents did something similar when they broke down being nicer to his sister into a list of behaviors they wanted to see more of—positive opposites of his current bad treatment of his sister—and then picked a couple to begin to build up. "Being nicer" is an abstraction, but when they broke it down into its component elements, they were able to identify specific behaviors they could work on.

## How to get the behavior you want

There are three ways to work on building up the behavior you want: shaping and simulations, which are the two main ones, and jump-starting, which has more specialized uses. You choose the one that best fits where your child is right now. If you're seeing just bits and pieces of the behavior you want, you start with shaping. If you're not seeing the behavior in any form, even partial, or it happens so rarely that you wouldn't have enough opportunities to practice it, you start with simulations. If the child has done the behavior many times but doesn't do it often enough or consistently enough, or used to do it more and now does it less, you might go with jump-starting. Whichever approach you choose, you begin the same way: specify the behavior you want to change, identify the positive opposites of any behaviors you want to eliminate, and then choose which method to use in building up the behavior you want.

*Shaping* is one of the most potent—and typically underused or misused—tools for getting the behavior you want. You shape a behav-

adually developing it and locking it in, by providing rewarding sequences for small portions, components, or approximations of e behavior you want. For example, if we want a child to do an hour of homework, we begin with brief periods, maybe five or ten minutes. If we want the child to engage in a sequence of behaviors, like taking care of all of his daily chores without being reminded, we may begin by focusing on just the first or second behavior in the set. Shaping begins by asking where the child is right now: Does the child *ever* do the behavior you want? Sometimes the answer is "a little bit, once in a while." Sometimes the answer is "never." Does the child do anything now that even begins to approach the goal? If you want one hour of homework, say, then how much does the child do now, and how frequently? We begin where the child is, and we set out to develop a little more of the behavior, or a little more frequency, until we end up at the goal. Shaping is how we get there. There's an important element of consequences to it: you're arranging to see many repetitions of the action you want and provide positive consequences for it. I'll talk more about consequences in the next two chapters, but in this chapter I'll try to stick to the behavior aspect of shaping.

Parents sometimes use shaping without knowing it. For example, when you're trying to develop use of the word *mommy* or *daddy* in an infant, you will usually reinforce any approximation (*ma, da,* or anything close) by smiling, hugging, and praising effusively. At the same time, but usually without thinking about it, you will typically not give the same level of attention to sounds that aren't close to the words you're listening for. Over time, then, you will tend to reinforce sounds and syllables that come closer to the words *mommy* and *daddy.* (And as you sit close to your child and say over and over, "Can you say 'Mama'? Can you say 'Daddy'?" you're effectively using antecedents. Your modeling of the lip movements and repetition of the sounds are excellent prompts. Your enthusiastic smile and close presence are setting events that will keep your child focused, interested, and eager to please. The prompts and setting events will help your child pronounce the words you want to hear.)

Here's a typical example of shaping. A mom complained that her three-and-a-half-year-old son, Anton, absolutely refused to eat any vegetables as part of dinner, with the exception of French fries (if you count them as a vegetable, about which there's some debate). The dinner routine in that home was 100 percent predictable. The mom usually served salad, a meat or pasta dish, and a cooked vegetable. Anton wouldn't touch the salad or the cooked vegetable. Anton's parents lectured him about why he should eat vegetables, and he listened in dignified silence to their various dire predictions of illness and early death, but nothing they said affected his refusal to eat any vegetable other than French fries. Sometimes his mom made French fries separately for him, just to get something vegetable-like into him. She occasionally threatened to withhold dessert or TV if he didn't eat his vegetables, but she soon abandoned this hard-line approach. She also tried to meet him halfway by declaring that it would be fine if he had just a few forkfuls of vegetables, but that didn't work, either.

The bar-lowering move to the standard of "a few forkfuls" was on the right track because it decreased what was required of Anton in a way that was roughly analogous to shaping. But shaping is not merely lowering the bar; it begins with what the individual already does, then gradually steps up the required behavior. Of course, antecedents and consequences also need to be included as part of shaping.

Because Anton did not eat vegetables at all, you might think that this situation called for simulations rather than shaping; remember, I said earlier that simulations are especially useful when you're not seeing the target behavior at all. But in the case of Anton we went with shaping, for three reasons. First, Anton already had key components of the behavior down. Though he was turning up his nose at vegetables, he ate rapidly, using his fork with dexterity. We just had to change some of the foods he placed on that fork. Second, there were opportunities to work on changing behavior each day that a normally occurring, regular meal was served—that is, we had plenty of chances to work on developing the behavior without relying on simulations. Finally, we wanted to use mealtime directly, not a simulation of it, because we could tell that some of the antecedents and consequences routinely being used in the household were making eating vegetables more of a problem. The number of prompts, the tone employed in giving them, the threats, the dire predictions of what happens to people who don't eat their vegetables—it was all making eating vegetables less likely.

We suggested shaping and a point chart, with an adjustment of antecedents to help increase the chances of success. At the beginning of dinner, the mom told Anton that he could leave the vegetables on his plate without eating them (good antecedents: choice, and a reduction of parental desperation). There was a new point program for him based on dinner. He could earn two points that would be placed on his chart (on the refrigerator) if he put some vegetables on his fork and just touched his lips with it. He could then cash in points to get small rewards that mattered to him—ten minutes extra to stay up and play before bedtime, a glow-in-the-dark ball, a special outing to the park with his father, and so on. He did not have to eat the vegetables on his fork, and he could put them right down once they'd touched his lips. The mom, adopting a nonchalant manner that we coached her in, showed him what this would look like. She noted that she did not worry about Anton eating vegetables—he would probably do that when he was older, like most four-year-olds do (more good antecedents: social norming, and a challenge by implying he is not ready or able yet but will be at some future date). Anton practiced once, and the mom praised that and added, "Remember, you do not have to eat the vegetables." On the first night, he picked up some cooked carrots with his fork, brought them to his lips, and then put them down. His dad said, "That was really good!" and his mom said, "You just earned two points!" Then the mom and dad went on with their conversation. When Anton did it again, they gave him a lot of attention again: praise, points, enthusiasm. All the while, the mother and father were, as usual, modeling eating vegetables, a good positive influence, but now they had removed from the dinner routine many of the negatives—lecturing, pressure, cajoling, and moralizing—all setting events that could suppress the behavior they wanted.

After three dinners in which Anton got points by touching the forkful of vegetables to his lips, his parents informed him that now, to get points, he had to taste the vegetable (put a piece on his tongue), and if he swallowed it he would get double points, but of course he didn't have to swallow it. For the first five minutes of dinner, the whole family made a game to see who could get the smallest piece to stay on the fork to taste and swallow. They were laughing about this, and mock-argued about whose piece was really smaller. Anton ate the part on his tongue. The mother had helped this process along by compromising on her usual austere nutritional habits—using more frozen vegetables and seasoning them with some not-so-healthy ingredients that she knew Anton would like.

They then moved to requiring one full bite of vegetables for points. The next step would have been to move to two bites in order to get any points, but by then Anton would eat a few bites of vegetables and leave a little on his plate by the end of the meal, which was about the same as he did for meat, pasta, and other foods. The parents were satisfied. Also, by this time Anton had some vegetable preferences: he asked for more peas with a sauce and mixed vegetables, and he declared himself less fond of cauliflower and Brussels sprouts. The parents ended the program and dropped the topic of vegetables completely, and from that point on Anton reliably ate them—usually all or almost all of the portions of his favorites, and at least some when his mother served other vegetables.

A few key points about shaping are illustrated by this example. First, it's often difficult for parents to shape behavior. We are often distracted by the fact that the child knows the behavior we want and knows how to do it. Yet shaping is based on what the child *does* now—not on what he knows—and how to get him to a higher level of performance. What a child knows and does not do is not all that relevant—to contemplate it just demoralizes us as parents and tempts us to mislabel the child's behavior as manipulative. Second, we don't demand perfection. This is not a standard we hold for our own performance, and it's the enemy of shaping, which begins where the child is and moves forward from there. In the case of Anton, no demand was made that he eat all of the vegetables served or that he even eat vegetables every night. Shaping requires a flexibility that's not always easy to embrace. Parenting seems easier when we can have rules that never change and have no fluidity, but more effective parenting (that is, for building relationships and behaviors) includes choice, compromise, and tiny vacations from some rules (for example, what has to be eaten at dinner, but not safety-related rules).

*Simulation: practice under artificial conditions.* The main goal of our method is to get the desired behavior to occur and then to have rewarding consequences follow. Done properly, this repeated sequence locks in the behavior as a habit and carries over to new situations.

So the first goal is just to get the behavior to occur so it can be reinforced. Ideally, the behavior occurs in everyday situations. Shaping is one way to get the behavior to happen, but that requires some early steps or small portions of the behavior to be performed so they can be rewarded. Sometimes the behavior doesn't occur even in partial forms that can be used to begin shaping, and that's when simulation becomes most useful.

If the behavior never occurs, or occurs so rarely that training and repeated practice can't take place, we set up artificial conditions to get it to happen. For young children, it's usually a game or "pretend" session in which they can develop and repeat a behavior. For older children, the simulation can be presented as practice or role-playing.

Let's start with what to do if the behavior you want never occurs. At the Yale Parenting Center we encounter situations like this all the time. For example, in one case, a six-year-old girl named Lia had an explosive tantrum any time she didn't get her way or wasn't ready to do something when her parents asked her to. The tantrums were effective in getting her parents to stop making demands, but of course they couldn't stop making some requests and saying no to her at least once in a while. Lia's parents described her tantrums as "explosive," a combination of being wildly upset, hitting her parents, throwing things, throwing herself on the floor, and continuing to cry or scream inconsolably for long stretches. (Often, her parents would unwittingly prolong the tantrum by holding Lia to restrict her movements, or by yelling or threatening in response to her.)

We asked whether there was ever a nonexplosive tantrum. If there were milder tantrums, we could praise those, increase the likelihood of milder tantrums, and shape increasingly milder tantrums on the way to eliminating all tantrums. But no: the parents reported that every one of Lia's tantrums was explosive and way out of proportion to its apparent cause.

Simulations are perfect for this situation because they allow the child to practice the desired behavior under conditions when everyone is calm and when there is virtually no chance of a real tantrum. We went over how to do this with Lia's parents, and then they introduced the task to Lia when she was calm. Her mother said, "I have an idea for a new game I would like to play. This is called the Tantrum Game" (the exact name doesn't matter). "Here's how it works. First, you can earn points in this game." You can see that antecedents are already in play here as part of the simulation. We use the notion of *game* and make this *playful* because these are setting events that increase the likelihood of compliance and getting the exact behavior you have specified to the child. Similarly, the comment that points can be earned serves as a setting event for the child doing what you will request. Delivered calmly, with a smile, in a playful way, a reminder that your child can earn points is very different from parental pressure—desperation, authoritarian commands, no choice. Mentioning the points also puts the enticing cues of rewards right before the behavior and establishes the incentive front and center. This need be done only once or twice early on in the program; we will want to fade the prompts as we go along.

So Lia's mom went on to explain that "this game is just pretend" and that the goal was to see if Lia could have a "good" tantrum. "If you have a good tantrum, you earn tickets that I have here," said the mom, showing Lia a roll of carnival-like tickets, since Lia loved carnivals (but points on a chart posted on the refrigerator would also be fine), "and with these tickets you can earn some great rewards." These rewards were mostly privileges, minor ones that mattered a lot to Lia and weren't a big deal for her parents (staying up ten minutes later, choosing the menu for dinner), plus a very cheap hair ornament or two (Lia really liked arranging her own hair), that kind of thing. The whole apparatus of points and earned rewards is not absolutely necessary—praise works just fine as a reward when delivered correctly (see the next chapter)—but the points help structure the task for everyone and make it much easier for both the child and parent to follow through.

The mom then explained to Lia that in a "good" tantrum she could get upset but she couldn't scream or hit anyone. We had selected these two components of the tantrum to eliminate first, to initiate the process of gradually shaping milder and milder tantrums. For shaping, we do not need or even want a "perfect" tantrum, only a milder-than-usual tantrum. Remember, the key to shaping is to start out keeping the bar low. If the bar is lower than you think it should be, you are doing a good job of resisting the natural impulse to ask for too much behavior too soon.

After the mother had explained the game, she said, "In one minute I'm going to say no to you. This is just pretend, but I'm going to say, 'No, you can't watch TV tonight.' If you say back to me, 'Why not?' in a calm way and without crying or hitting me, you can earn a ticket. Remember, this is just a game: you really can watch TV tonight." (All of these prefatory comments are great antecedents. First, they state exactly what the parent wants [prompts]. Second, the tone of the interaction—calm, playful, in the context of a pretend game [setting events]—is completely altered from the usual one in which tantrums occur, all of which maximizes the likelihood that the child will do the behaviors, will actually enjoy doing them, and is likely to want to practice a couple of times to earn praise or points. Remember, the goal is to get behavior to occur, and to occur repeatedly.)

Then the mom leaned over to Lia, smiled, and whispered prompts to help Lia succeed: "OK, here we go. It's just pretend, and if you have a good tantrum you can get tickets," and she held the tickets up so Lia could see them. (When developing behavior, one wants to have prompts come immediately before the behaviors are to occur, at least initially.) Then she said, in a regular voice, but gently, "You can't watch TV tonight." With all this heavy use of good antecedents, Lia was unlikely to have a tantrum and very likely to earn the tickets plus praise. So they began, and she had a "good" tantrum, milder than usual and mostly play-acted, and the mother provided effusive praise: "I can't believe you had such a great tantrum. You were pretty calm, you kept your hands to yourself, and you didn't throw anything." Then she rubbed Lia's head affectionately and gave her a ticket.

They could have stopped there for the day, but practice opportunities are the key to this approach. We wanted the child to do it all again. The mother gave a new antecedent—a challenge, as I mentioned in the previous chapter. With a playful, mischievous smile on her face, she looked at Lia and said, "I'll bet you can't do two good tantrums in a row. No six-year-old on earth could do that!" As has been the case virtually every time we have used this technique, the child, in this case Lia, said while nodding vigorously, "No, I can do it. I can do two!" The mom replied with playful skepticism, "I don't know—but ohhh-kayyyy"—as if sighingly giving in against her better judgment—"let's try." They repeated the game with a different scenario—telling Lia that she couldn't go to a friend's house—and of course Lia, who had been nicely primed to succeed, won again. Effusive praise and a ticket followed. That could be the end of simulation for that day, with much accomplished.

The program would be repeated the next day, and the next; the child should have many opportunities within a fairly brief time. At the Parenting Center, we recommend at least a couple of such prompted trials per day, but there is no research to support any particular number and we have worked with parents whose schedules restricted them to just one per day. The general rule is: the more practice opportunities and trials in which behavior can occur and be reinforced, the better.

I mentioned that shaping may be part of simulations. We first want the child to have a milder tantrum than usual during the simulation. Shaping here may refer to beginning by omitting just one component—so a good tantrum might be no hitting, or no swearing, depending on the ingredients of the tantrum—and then gradually omitting more. Over the course of shaping, antecedents are used to help move forward: "I'll bet you can't have a tantrum this time with no hitting *and* no swearing, but if you don't hit and don't swear you can earn *two* tickets," and so on.

After the simulations begin, there are likely to be unprompted occasions when the child does not have a tantrum or has a low-magnitude tantrum (a little whining). That is, the simulations also affect behavior in nonsimulated conditions. You should enthusiastically praise these unprompted mild or milder-than-usual tantrums outside of the Tantrum Game the first few times they occur. The effect of this is to greatly increase the likelihood of milder real-life tantrums. Yet the key to getting this behavior is several practice trials in simulated circumstances. In Lia's case, the mom practiced the simulated tantrums for six days in the course of a week—she missed one of the days. Lia got the hang of it, and her pretend tantrums became milder even without shaping. To the mom's shock, Lia had two mild versions of a regular tantrum (nonsimulated), in a grocery store and about going to bed on time. We had practiced for this moment, so the mom was sure to be very effusive: "I can't believe it! We weren't even playing the Tantrum Game and you had such a big-girl tantrum!" (No points are really needed here and praise delivered well will do the trick.)

It took about two weeks to get tantrums in everyday situations down to a tolerable level and frequency, at which point the game ended because Lia's parents felt that tantrums were no longer a big problem. About a month later, Lia had a pretty explosive tantrum—not as bad as her old doozies, but worse than her recent mild ones. The mom suppressed the urge to panic about a relapse and just walked away, so as to not make things worse. The parents attributed the more severe tantrum to the fact that Lia was very tired after their return from an all-day drive. It turned out to be an isolated event, and Lia's parents dealt with it by ignoring it.

I should note that parents are often stunned when we suggest that they praise a tantrum in any form. They want to get rid of tantrums or make them minimal, and so they logically see praise for their child disagreeing with them or making a scene as exactly the wrong approach. It galls them to reward any kind of tantrum, even one that's notably milder than the usual meltdown. This is when I remind them that as parents they often do reward behaviors that are just little approximations of what they want. I've already mentioned the shaping of a very young child's use of the words *mommy* and *daddy*, and there are other common examples. When you're teaching your child how to swing a bat or catch a baseball, you are very tolerant of imperfections along the way and praise mediocre versions of the behavior as part of the process of getting to more skilled versions of it. Teaching your child to ice-skate or to ride a bike involves a lot of practice under fake conditions: holding the child's arms or holding the bike so it cannot possibly tip over. Yes, mild tantrums are different from these examples because no one is calm or having fun and the two parties have competing views about what should happen—so praising a mild tantrum can feel counterintuitive. But forget for a moment that the behavior in question is a tantrum and just think of it as behavior. We have two powerful tools, shaping and simulation, to get the behavior you want, and rewarding a milder tantrum makes perfect sense.

As I said before, simulations are really useful in two types of situations. I've discussed the first, in which the behavior one wants never seems to occur, which makes it hard to shape even faint approximations of it. The second situation is when the circumstances in which the behavior arises do not occur very often and yet you still want the child to be trained. To take a familiar example from well outside the sphere of child rearing, one major goal in training commercial airline pilots is teaching them how to handle emergency situations—many different kinds of emergencies based on all the things that can go wrong with various combinations of mechanical failure, weather, and so on. One cannot shape good pilot responses while passengers are traveling, not only for safety but because the varied types of situations that pilots ought to be trained in don't occur often enough. So a situation needs to be set up in which the pilot can practice the needed behaviors often and in many different situations so that when a real emergency does come up, the behaviors have been well developed and established. So airline pilots work in a machine called a simulator, a realistic version of the cockpit of a commercial airplane, that allows programming of diverse scenarios, even very exotic emergencies, to which the pilot can practice responding.

In child rearing, there are some situations in which the behavior doesn't occur often but you would like your child to have a well-honed, consistent response. Escaping from a home fire (as I mentioned earlier) and what to do in a medical emergency (call 911) are examples. In each situation, you can't wait for a real fire or health emergency to start developing the needed responses.

Another example is a project that was intended to train a dozen six- and seven-year-olds, six boys and six girls, to not play with handguns. A real but disabled handgun was used. The children were trained in simulated conditions in which a trainer practiced and role-played what to do when he encountered a gun. The safe behaviors that were practiced included not touching the gun, immediately leaving the vicinity of the gun, and telling an adult about it. Children practiced along with the trainer. In order to determine if simulation worked, the children were assessed in real situations at home and at school where they spontaneously encountered a gun (disabled) to see what they would do. Children showed the well-practiced safety behaviors without knowing they were being tested. The test was run again five months later and all children continued to show safe reactions to the situation.

You could do something similar to train young children in what to do when they encounter, for example, a bottle of medicine. You know what you don't want them to do: pick up the bottle, get it open, eat or drink the contents. Now, express that as a positive opposite: do not touch the bottle, get away from it, go and tell an adult right away. To build up that set of behaviors, you can create a simulation game in which you put some medicine bottles on the table and your child can earn rewards by responding properly to them. You can teach even a very small child not to touch the bottle and to go get a parent and say some simple alert phrase, like "Bottle, bottle." Have her practice that response, and reward her every time she gets it right. This is a good example for another reason. As parents we are prone to think that if we convey that medicines are dangerous and the children understand us, that will be enough. We all wish this were the case, but (I will repeat this more than once in this book, because it's important) understanding something is not a strong basis for getting behaviors one wants in ourselves or other people.

*Jump-starting* is less commonly used than shaping and simulation, but in some situations it's the ideal tool. Sometimes the child readily engages in some behavior and has often done so on recent occasions, but the parents want to see more of it, or to see it more consistently. This is a situation in which the child is more than just familiar with the idea of the behavior—the child has actually done it before, and more than once. In such instances, extensive shaping and simulations to get the behavior to occur may not be required. The response merely has to be primed in some way. Jump-starting, more technically known as "response priming," refers to getting the child into early steps in a sequence or chain of responses. Doing the early steps in a sequence increases the probability of performing the rest of the steps.

A father complained to us that his thirteen-year-old son, Oscar, was too sedentary. Oscar liked sports but mostly as something to watch on TV and to reduce to statistics online. The father was especially concerned because he himself was very active and athletic, and so was his wife. Every Sunday afternoon, the father's friends from work (at a software company) would play touch football for a few hours. Other fathers brought their kids, who often played in the games. The games were more fun than competitive, and there was probably as much break time for scarfing soda, beer, and potato products as for playing actual football. The father wanted to get Oscar to come play football with him on Sundays. He said it would be fun, it would be a favor to him, it would be quality time they could spend together. But Oscar always refused. It is fine to begin with reason and appeals, but they are not likely to work, so be prepared to quickly move on to more effective strategies. (Reason and appeals can clarify the behaviors that are wanted, though, so they can still be useful antecedents to a shaping program.)

Think of playing football with all of the guys as the end of a long series of behaviors. Jump-starting begins with the question "Are there early behaviors that can lead to this end behavior?" If so, we wanted to put Oscar in one of the early behaviors and not worry for now about getting all the way to the final one: playing football with the guys. If we could get one of the early behaviors, the likelihood was greatly increased that the later behaviors would follow. We asked how far away the football field was from home—about a five-minute drive. We wanted that information to see if one of our options for Oscar was feasible. We instructed the father before going to play football to ask Oscar to come with him but *not* to play football. We told him to say he just wanted to be with Oscar that day, just to spend the time. (There were other children there and not all played football, and even those who played didn't play all the time.) The father told Oscar that they would be there together at the field, but that there were lots of breaks during any of which he could drive Oscar back home if Oscar didn't like being there. (Choice of staying—great antecedent.) Oscar agreed to go as long as he was not forced to play—another good adjustment in antecedents, removing all hints of parental desperation and pressure, which might well have acted as a setting event for Oscar choosing not to go to the football field.

Oscar went to the field. His father told him to get a soda and burger if he wanted; the game would start up in about twenty minutes. Oscar's dad had asked a couple of his friends to say to Oscar how nice it was to see him, and they did, which made him feel welcome. Also, Oscar was interacting with some of the other children—tossing a football back and forth a little. Just getting Oscar to the field had put him in the early steps of the sequence—and as the early steps in a sequence occur, other behaviors closer to the goal are likely to increase. In this case, Oscar's dad was very obviously happy to have Oscar there, and it became a weekly event. For the first four or five Sundays, Oscar's dad asked nonchalantly (to get rid of any desperate hope that could promote not going), "Would you like to go today?" We asked the father to drop the question once it was clear that Oscar started to automatically get ready to go and that this was now part of the routine.

After a couple of Sundays, Oscar developed some acquaintances and routinely threw the ball around and ate some food. There was no longer a concern about Oscar playing football, but when one of the friends entered the game, Oscar joined in too so they could be on the same team. He began to play sporadically during the Sunday games—but, mainly, Oscar's dad was just glad that he came, got out of the house, and spent some time with him. Oscar played in the games about as much as the other children, and when he wasn't playing he was either tossing a football or horsing around with friends and getting physical activity as a bonus.

## The most common errors in developing behavior

Shaping sounds easy and not actually that difficult to do, but it is routinely done in such a way that it fails. There are two related errors that can make it fail. The first and more common is that parents move too quickly when trying to get the final behavior. Shaping requires providing consequences for steps along the way. But the steps—what the child can do, the partial and approximate versions of the desired behavior—ought to be pretty consistent before moving on. Parents often move in steps that are too big or move from one step to another too quickly.

If you want your child to play a musical instrument, she begins by learning how to hold the instrument, how it makes sound, how to read music. Shaping can be slow as the child practices individual notes, combinations, scales, chords, and then a song that draws on versions of these. This is a familiar sequence. If you do this with incorrect shaping, where the child practices notes just once or twice, then moves to combinations or chords, then the scales, each practiced only once or twice, you guarantee that the final behavior, playing the song, will sound bad, and you'll be tempted to conclude that shaping doesn't work.

You want your child to do an hour of homework after school each school day. You tell him he must do this because when you were a child that's what you did. The request and the comment about what you did will fail as a way of changing behavior. Now you add ineffective statements number two—"Other kids do their homework. What's your problem?"—and number three: "Don't expect to get into college without doing homework." All of these statements do a fine job of expressing frustration, but they won't succeed in changing behavior. In the homework example, there's no shaping. We jumped straight to sixty minutes and used only prompts (do it!) to get the behavior. First, shape the behavior by requiring just a few minutes (five or ten), and mix in some antecedents, such as you helping for the first few minutes ("Come on, let's do this together; I can help"), which can be faded later. When you've had a few or several days of consistency, move to a slightly longer time, and so on up to the full hour. Praise consistency as you require more and more time. If the teacher or the school is pressuring everyone to get the homework done and you feel that pressure, you may well be tempted to press for the full homework time right away. Chances are you'll get a fight each time, and at the end of two weeks you will have not made progress. Shaping slowly can get you there faster and better.

If the most common error that makes shaping ineffective is trying to move too quickly or via chunks of behavior that are too large, how do you know if you're going too fast or taking too-big steps? The child's behavior is the guide. If she did ten minutes of homework pretty consistently but didn't ever manage forty-five minutes at all when you moved right up to that longer stretch, backtrack to an intermediate stage like fifteen or twenty minutes. One excellent feature of shaping is that it's very forgiving. If you move forward too quickly and don't get the behavior you want, just backtrack to an intermediate step and move forward more gradually from there to where you want to go. Don't fall for the common parental myth about backtracking as giving in, being weak, or beginning a deadly slide down a slippery slope—misreadings of shaping that tie one hand behind your back as you try to effectively use the tools introduced in this chapter.

The second shaping error is a variant of the first one. Occasionally, parents provide incentives for outcomes rather than for progress along the way. A good example of this error comes from businesses such as fast-food restaurants that offer some special reward (money, food) for anyone who brings in a report card with all As. Such a long-delayed all-consequence "program" is guaranteed to fail. No kid who isn't already earning As will be induced to suddenly earn them by the promise of free super-size fries in the remote future. The approach of this book emphasizes reinforced practice and developing skills and habits. If those are solidly developed, outcomes are likely to be positive, but we rarely focus on some distant outcome. The process, rather than the outcome in isolation, builds the desired behaviors. One could make a similar argument about the increasingly widespread practice of pegging the pay of teachers to their students' test scores at the end of the term. This use of consequences encourages the teacher to get the outcome, no matter what. One way is to teach to the test with little regard for building students' study habits and intellectual range; another is to give students the answers to the tests, a kind of cheating we're likely to see more of as such policies become more common.

What should you take away from this brief survey of errors in developing behavior? Concentrate on providing reinforcement for processes (the specific desired behaviors) leading to outcomes (some longer-term goal, like a character trait). Provide reinforcers for studying, doing homework, and talking at the dinner table about something learned at school or read as homework. These will also be effective in improving outcomes, but providing reinforcement just for outcomes (getting mostly or all As) does not teach the requisite behaviors, doesn't develop habits, and can even encourage behaviors you are against, like cheating. I mention this in the context of shaping because going for outcomes over process—the end result without the steps to get there—amounts to a kind of negative opposite of shaping.

## The most important concept

The key concept of this chapter and of this book is *practice of the desired behavior.* We want the behavior to occur so that consequences can be applied. Do the behavior, get the consequences; do the behavior, get the consequences. In the next chapter I refer to this as *reinforced practice,* to emphasize both the behavior occurring and the positive consequences that follow. A key part of practice is specifying the goal that one has in mind. Once you've identified it, you can work toward it with shaping, simulation, and/or jump-starting.

## Conclusion

Behavior refers to what you want to change. The change may be an end in itself, like getting your child to do homework, or a path toward broad characteristics—like honesty or showing respect—that you wish your child to have. It is important to specify in concrete terms the behavior that you would like to change. More often than not, parents (and teachers, spouses—all of us) focus on the behavior we don't like and want to get rid of. The place to start is describing the positive opposite, that specific behavior you would like in place of the objectionable one. Sometimes the opposite is easy. I want my spouse to stop leaving the cap off the toothpaste! The positive opposite is, obviously, putting the cap on the toothpaste container. But for interpersonal behavior (stop teasing, stop shouting, stop picking on your angelic sister who can do no wrong), identifying the positive opposite requires a little more work. It's worthwhile to do it, though. We insist on this work because we can eliminate behaviors much more effectively when we focus on developing behaviors to replace them. Sometimes we just want to develop positive behavior when there's no negative one in its place to get rid of. Here, too, ask the same basic questions: What is the behavior you want? What would it look like? Answers to these questions greatly influence the effectiveness of the intervention.

When you draw on the important behavioral parts of the ABC approach, these reminders may help:

**Dos**

- Specify the positive behavior you want in concrete terms, even if your primary goal is to get rid of annoying or disturbing behavior.
- If there is a sequence or set of separate behaviors, specify each one and the order in which they occur; it will make the program much more effective.
- Use shaping to begin to develop the behavior you specified.
- Be patient with shaping (with both yourself and the child); we

are building habits, and moving slowly is usually the best way to do that so behavior takes the form you like and is locked in.

- If the behavior never occurs, set up simulations so you can use antecedents, shaping, and consequences to develop the behavior.
- If the child has the behavior well established but does not do it now, try jump-starting the behavior. Remember, "well established" means the child has done this behavior often in the past, not just that he "knows" (understands) what to do.
- Combine all the techniques in this chapter with antecedents as we discussed in the previous chapter—good antecedents (prompts, setting events) really speed up the process of developing behavior.
- Keep in mind the goal—we want the behavior to be practiced often, and ABCs are directed toward that intention.

**Don'ts**

- Don't identify general qualities like honesty or altruism as the starting point to change behavior. Start with specific behaviors and work toward them.
- Don't think that because a person knows how to do something that he or she will do it, will do it consistently, and will not need special help to develop the habit of doing it.
- Don't be frustrated because one child can do a behavior without a lot of effort on your part and another child requires shaping or other special techniques. There are enormous differences among all of us as people; this is the norm.

# 3

## Reinforcing Good Behavior
### *C for Consequences*

Consequences are what happen after a behavior: reward, punishment, or nothing at all. Each type of consequence can have a significant effect on whether a behavior continues or drops out—and that's true even when there's no consequence at all after the behavior, because even the lack of a consequence can influence behavior. I will take each type of consequence in turn over the course of two chapters. I'll start in this chapter with using rewards, the technical term for which is *positive reinforcement,* and then in the next chapter deal with punishment and also *extinction,* which is the technical name for purposeful ignoring of behavior.

First, let me say that consequences present a special challenge to us at the Yale Parenting Center because it's the section of the toolkit that parents who come to us for help typically have the most experience with. Antecedents might come as a new idea to them, and the notion of shaping and other such approaches to responding to a child's behavior might take some getting used to, but if they already have strong convictions about any aspect of parenting, it's likely to be in the area of consequences. After all, punishment is a consequence, and parents often have a lot of experience with punishment. But punishment is the least important and least effective kind of consequence.

The subject of consequences isn't as obvious as it might appear at first. The research offers us plenty of practical guidance and insight, some of which may well strike you as counterintuitive. At the center of this chapter is positive reinforcement, a powerful technique for building up the behaviors you want, and therefore for eliminating behaviors you don't want. You have a lot of options when you use positive reinforcement; I'll devote this chapter to putting them in your toolkit and showing you how to use them.

## Your consequences toolkit

*Positive reinforcement* refers to the practice of using reinforcing consequences to increase the chances that a behavior will be repeated in the future. In this chapter I freely use the term *reinforcer* rather than *reinforcing consequences,* just to keep it simpler. I would just say "reward," but there's a subtle difference between a reinforcer and a reward. A *reward* is something that a person likes and regards as valuable. If you ask a child to list rewards, she'll probably list toys, special food treats, a pony, whatever age-appropriate goodies strike her as desirable. A *reinforcer* is something that is shown to increase behavior if employed systematically as a consequence following behavior. Often, rewards—money for an adult, say, or toys for children—are reinforcers. That is, the recipient views them as valuable, *and* they can change behavior. Yet there are many reinforcers that your child might not identify as particularly rewarding—for instance, your child might very well not describe your attention and praise as valued rewards—but nevertheless function as strong reinforcers. There's a lesson that makes this distinction important: even if your child does not identify something as a reward, it can still change behavior; and, in a complementary way, just because a person says something is rewarding does not automatically mean that it can be used as a reinforcer and effectively change behavior.

There are several types of reinforcers to be used in positive reinforcement. We focus on two that are most useful.

*Praise and attention:* Paying attention to a specific behavior and delivering approval for it in the form of a positive statement, a smile, a touch. This is not as self-evident as it sounds. It often requires a conscious effort to get in the habit of paying positive attention to the behaviors you want, rather than the usual routine of reacting negatively to the behaviors you don't want.

Praise can be remarkably effective, but it has to be offered in a certain way to change behavior. Simply saying "Good job!" a hundred times a day won't help much. I'll have more to say later in this chapter about how to use praise. But first, here's why I strongly advocate the use of praise to change behavior:

- When delivered properly, it can be very effective.
- It's similar to the attention and approval that people often use in everyday interactions, so using praise doesn't require parents to make the kind of changes in their habits that other (more artificial, less natural) reinforcers like a points system might entail. Turning to notice something a child did, smile and touch approvingly, or show disapproval with a look—all of these are "attention in the rough," habits that parents already have. We will craft that attention and approval to make a huge difference in changing child behavior, but it's a refinement of what you already do.
- Unlike a system of points, you don't have to keep track of anything. We resort to points only if praise by itself is not working very well, if parents have trouble remembering to give praise, or if there are reasons to offer special incentives along with praise just to get the program going.
- Even if points are used, praise still is the reinforcer that gets the main emphasis.

Points, stars, stickers, and so on can be useful, as I've just mentioned, if praise alone needs a boost at first. These are tokens that can be used to buy rewards. For example, a child can earn points for doing homework or going to bed on time. The points are like money and can be used to buy items or special activities—privileges like choosing the family's dinner menu, a slightly later bedtime, or extra time on the computer—that have prices based on the number of points.

Setting up a point chart has several steps, which include specifying

1. The target behaviors
2. The number of points that can be earned for performing the behaviors
3. The rewards (what the points can buy)
4. The number of points the rewards cost

The program can be simple. You can start it with only one or two behaviors you wish to develop, awarding one or two points for each behavior. Then have a reward list, a few items or privileges to buy that have low point values (two, three, four points) and then maybe something big—say, a twenty-five-point special treat or privilege—that the child can save up points to earn. These extra rewards are called "backup rewards," just to make it clear that your child will see getting the points, and of course your attention and praise, as a strong reinforcer in its own right.

*Point chart* is the term used most frequently in parenting programs. The technical name for a point chart is a *token economy*, emphasizing that the tokens (points, stars, and so on) are just the medium of exchange. Token economies have been used effectively with many different types of people and in many different situations, including the home, schools, hospitals, daycare centers, nursing homes, the military, colleges (for example, to reduce alcohol consumption, to improve practice performances on athletic teams), and business and industry (for example, to improve workers' safety practices and punctuality). In short, such programs have been very effective in many different contexts—and yet the points and charts are not absolutely necessary. That is, there's no inherent magic in a point chart; the behavior could be changed with just improved prompts and shaping and praise. The tokens merely provide a good way to structure and prompt parent behavior, especially the systematic use of consequences.

• • •

Using reinforcers to build up a desired behavior seems straightforward enough, but, as with our other procedures, the *how*—exactly how the reinforcer is administered—determines whether it will effectively change behavior.

## Using positive reinforcement to reduce and eliminate unwanted behaviors

It's a rule of thumb that positive reinforcement is always related to increasing some behavior. But we have to reckon with the fact that much of what parents want to accomplish is to decrease or get rid of behavior—interrupting, playing with food, picking on a sibling, talking back, lying, stealing, . . . the list is endless. Can positive reinforcement help in getting rid of these behaviors? Yes. In fact, positive reinforcement is the *only* reliable way to eliminate these behaviors. So here I'll run through some reinforcement-based techniques for reducing or eliminating behaviors.

*1. Reinforcement of positive opposites.* In general, when you want to eliminate any behavior, whether it's a child's, spouse's, or colleague's, you begin with the very first step: Identify the positive opposite, the goal toward which you want to work. This means describing precisely what behaviors you do want to see in place of those you want to eliminate. Once you have that goal in view, you can use the ABCs—antecedents, behaviors, consequences—to reinforce the behavior you do want, always being careful not to accidentally attend to behavior you don't want. But it all flows from the first step: What is the behavior you want?

This first step is vitally important. At the Yale Parenting Center, at the end of our parent training, we present a set of common hypothetical situations in which we ask parents how they would get rid of some annoying behavior—rudeness at the dinner table, say, or acting up at the supermarket. We know we have been effective if in each case the parent begins by saying something like "Well, the positive opposite behavior we want would be . . ." When parents answer by skipping the first step and going straight to a consequence, like time out or ignoring the behavior, we know that we have been only mildly effective with them—that is, those strategies are OK, but they're not the first place to start and also not very effective as behavior-change procedures. You can't reinforce the positive opposite until you've identified it, and if you can't reinforce the positive opposite, it's very difficult to get rid of an unwanted behavior. You don't like the way your spouse squeezes the toothpaste from the middle of the tube? Go ahead, keep complaining about it, shake your head, endlessly repeat lines like "Why can't you just squeeze the @&%! toothpaste from the bottom of the tube? Is that too much to ask?" It will get you nowhere. But if after five or twenty-five years of this you switch to reinforcing positive opposites and using ABCs, you'll get somewhere. And the first step is identifying the behavior you want: in this case, squeezing the toothpaste tube from the bottom.

One father, Ray, conducted business from home, spending much of his workday dealing with suppliers whose goods he sold on his website. His "office" was actually in a corner of the dining room. He was on the phone often, and his business depended on it. His older child was six years old and at school most of the day; but his four-year-old daughter, Anna, developed the habit of talking to Daddy and asking for things when he was on the phone. She constantly interrupted him. "Can I go out to play? Is it OK to eat something now? When will you be off the phone? Can you play with me?" It was as if a phone call had become a cue for Anna to talk to her father. On the weekends, her brother joined her in interrupting Ray's calls.

Interrupting is a particularly interesting problem, from my point of view, because it's hard to ignore, and if it is ignored, the child will often just escalate until the interruption can no longer be ignored, at which point the adult either gives in to the request, shouts out a reprimand, or screams to his spouse to get in here and deal with the kids. The process is a good example of the power of attention to inappropriate behavior and the wrong kind of shaping, which in this case produced more and more intense interruptions. That's what was happening to Ray, the work-at-home dad. Business calls became occasions for a household upheaval, frequently culminating in a meltdown.

What to do? Well, you know where to begin: What exactly is the behavior you want? In this case, Ray wanted Anna to make no requests during a call and to make any request before or after the call. Now, put yourself in his place and think ABCs. Start with antecedents. What can you do before you get a call? When you're not on the phone, you can calmly tell the child to please not interrupt. You should explain exactly what counts as interrupting, and explain to her that your answer to anything she asks for during a call is automatically no, but if she waits until you're off the phone to ask, the answer could be yes or could be no, depending on the question, but you'll do your best to make it yes, if you can.

When a new behavior is developing, prompts right before the behavior are likely to be especially effective. But Ray couldn't know exactly when a call was about to come in, so he explained everything to his daughter as his workday began. When the first ring of a call came through and Anna was visibly nearby, he said to her, "OK, Anna, now's your chance to see if you can wait to talk until the phone call is done." (This was a nice, quick little challenge.)

We thought Ray could use shaping effectively in this situation, too—that a partial sample of a behavior should be praised as well. We decided that two minutes into the first couple of calls during a given day, Ray would put his hand over the receiver of the phone and go over to Anna and smile, give a big OK hand gesture with his arm outstretched above his head, quietly whisper praise for not interrupting, and give her a gentle touch if he could. A couple of these per day would be great. We wanted the praise for not interrupting at all to be immediate and really effusive. If Anna was interrupting every single call, giving Ray no chance to reinforce not-interrupting, it would be time to do some simulations to practice not-interrupting—he could call it the Phone Game and make sure she got plenty of praise, points, whatever it took, as a result of doing the right thing while he pretended to be on the phone.

Now, the consequences. We wanted Ray to reinforce the positive opposite, which was Anna making requests before or after the call, and that he would not attend to, turn around to face, or make eye contact with her if she made a request during the call. Requests made when Ray was not on the phone should be praised. "This is great! You're asking me for a snack when I'm not on the phone!" We reminded Ray to add a pat or a hug, and between calls to praise either no interrupting or less interrupting.

Ray and his wife really liked the idea for the program because it was concrete. Sometimes the mother would be nearby in the house and could praise Anna (or, on weekends, both children) for playing nicely and not talking to her father when he was on the phone.

Ray made or received at least twenty calls a day. We asked him to tally each call and put a check mark next to it if he was interrupted. Interruptions went down from about thirteen each day to five in the first two days of the program, and then to zero after five days. We needed two weekends to get rid of weekend call interruptions by the six-year-old—not very much practice could occur for the older child during the week. Eight days into the program, the mom and dad stopped the praise during the week. Interruptions were holding steady at zero, and they praised that, but it seemed that the need for a carefully executed praise program was over. After two weekends, interruptions seemed like a nonissue. Four and then eight weeks later, Ray reported one interruption, but he had ignored it, and interrupting stopped being an issue in that home.

This was a very typical household situation. Your child teases the pet, does not pick up his laundry, comes into your bedroom too early on a Sunday morning, spills food on the floor . . . just keep filling in the rest. Your first step, in response, should be to ask, "What's the positive opposite?"

Reinforcing positive opposites is your all-in-one tool, useful in almost all situations. But there are two more specialized variations of using reinforcement to reduce behaviors that you'll find useful to have in your kit.

2. *Reinforcing other behavior that isn't quite the positive opposite.* What if the child never seems to do *any* of the positive opposite be-

havior? Sometimes a child does something frequently that you want to get rid of. Positive opposites are easy to identify, and of course you do that. But if he never does anything like the positive opposite, how can you reinforce it? One option is to use simulations to practice the desired behavior—a B (of the ABCs) option we discussed in the previous chapter. Also, shaping was a B strategy we discussed in that chapter, but here it seems as if the child is not even close to showing crumbs of the desired behavior that we could build on to develop the final behaviors we want. So you need another way to address the problem, and there's a C (consequence) solution that you can turn to.

This solution consists of reinforcing everything or virtually everything the child does *other than* the undesired behavior. Essentially, we look at the child and say, for the moment, we are going to classify everything he does as either (1) what we want to eliminate or (2) everything else. Everything else is the "other" behavior. We adopt this when the behaviors we want to eliminate are so frequent that we need to get some control right away.

I had a memorable introduction to this approach when I worked with a ten-year-old child named Evan in a regular fifth-grade elementary school classroom. The teacher asked for my help because one of her students—Evan—was distressingly active. *Active* is really a pale word to describe this child. Evan walked on the desks during lessons, stepping from desk to desk, stomping on other students' work as he went. While he did this he talked out loud, saying things to the teacher as if nothing else was going on. She said he was never in his seat. I observed the class for a few periods on separate days and the teacher wasn't exaggerating: this child just never sat down.

What to reinforce? A positive opposite would be sitting quietly in his seat, doing the work, and paying attention. But this package of behavior never occurred, and in fact none of its components ever occurred, which meant that shaping did not seem possible, at least at first. So we decided to begin with praising Evan for any behavior other than walking on desks or talking out loud. Sometimes he was silent for a little while. True, he'd be standing next to his desk, and he wouldn't be working, but during these moments he wasn't doing either of the two behaviors the teacher wanted to reduce: walking across the desks and talking out loud. It wasn't quite the ideal positive opposite of his disruptive behavior, but it was better, so it was a place to start.

I stayed in the room for thirty minutes for two days to help prompt the teacher. I had a sheet of colored paper (two sheets stapled together, actually), one side red and the other side green. When Evan was engaging in anything other than the behaviors we wanted to eliminate, I immediately held up the green sheet. This was a prompt to the teacher to praise him and, if feasible (depending on where she was standing), to do this up close, quietly, and with a physical pat. If it wasn't feasible for her to get over to him, she just praised out loud from where she was. It was important to help the teacher because the usual thing we do, the instinctive thing for a species wired by evolution to overreact to negative stimulus, is to let things go unremarked upon when behavior is fine and therefore not threatening.

The teacher quickly mastered this approach, and in the thirty minutes I was there she went over to Evan three times—I prompted the first two; she did the third on her own. (I was fading my prompts to her, a technique you learned in chapter one.) On the second day, I went to class and she went over to him twice unprompted. She did not see her third opportunity to reinforce Evan's better-than-awful behavior, as she was turned facing the board, so I held up the green side of the sheet as soon as she turned around, and she reinforced the behavior then. We had agreed that we would do this program only in the morning, to see if we were having any effect, and then if it went well, we would extend it to the afternoon. The main reason for this was that administering reinforcement (praise) correctly and frequently is hard work, and she had other students to attend to.

After a few days, it was clear that this regimen greatly increased not walking on desks and not talking out loud. Now, occasionally, Evan was even sitting in his seat, a behavior that previously had never seemed to occur. Now we switched from praising any nondisruptive behavior to focusing on sitting in his seat, a component of the positive opposite we hoped to develop. Any time Evan was in his seat, even if he wasn't paying attention or doing his work, the teacher praised that behavior specifically. If he was also focusing on a classroom task, she added special praise for that. This was slow going (after all, the teacher did have a room full of other students to teach) and it took a few weeks, but we were able to get Evan to a point where he spent most of his time in his seat, and we completely eliminated walking on the desks, his most wildly disruptive behavior. As a bonus, his habit of talking out of turn in class dropped out on its own. Apparently, his talking was linked to walking on the desks, and when we eliminated desk walking the talking went with it.

The excellent effects of this approach, reinforcing other behavior short of the positive opposite, have been evident in many cases in which we've worked with parents in the home. For example, two brothers, four and five years old, were constantly arguing, teasing, and picking on each other. The parents found this surprising and annoying—surprising because they had expected that their sons would appreciate having a natural playmate in the household, and annoying because there was no letup in the conflict. The only times of peace came when one of the boys was not home (the five-year-old was in school). I first queried the parents on what exactly they wanted to see, the positive opposites. They wanted parallel play (in the same room without fighting) or cooperative play (both doing the same thing together, like playing with blocks or even just watching TV together) or peace during some activity other than play (for example, dinner, drives to church in the car, errands). The parents explained to me that there was no significant stretch of peace when the boys were together, and they asked if there was any way to get control of the constant teasing. From among our B (for behavior) options we could have chosen simulations, a Getting-Along game they could play. But we could also take the C (consequences) route and address the problem with reinforcement of other behavior.

We defined "other behavior" to mean any time the boys were in view of each other (in the same room, in the car) and there was a brief period without their annoying each other or bickering. The program had two parts. When the boys were together and not bickering, one of the parents would praise them. The boys were also told that if they could be together for two minutes without arguing, they would receive a point. So we weren't really reinforcing a positive opposite. Instead, we reinforced anything other than bickering, teasing, and being annoying. Another way to say "anything but" is "other behavior," and that's why this approach is called reinforcing other behavior.

The points were earned as a team. The boys earned or didn't earn the points together—so there was never a situation in which just one boy could earn points. And the rewards they could buy with the points went to both boys, never just one. So, for example, they could spend four points on staying up fifteen minutes longer before bedtime; both boys got to stay up. When they accumulated four points, they could cash them in for that reward, or they could agree to let the points "ride" for some other reward. The parents, who knew their sons well, asked what would happen if the boys argued over the reward and couldn't agree on one. We explained that the boys had to agree on the reward, and they had to get the same one. If they bickered and couldn't agree on one, no reward was given that night, but they could bank the points until the next day. (It's important that you choose rewards that your child really values, not just things you think he should value.) This worked out pretty well. Both boys placed high value on extending their bedtime and on playing certain backyard games that required their father's participation, so it wasn't hard to get them to agree on spending their points.

When they praised, the parents exclaimed over how big and grown-up the brothers were acting. They were sure to be effusive, and to be specific about what the boys were doing: "You're sitting together with no arguing." And they remembered to add a physical pat or touch when they could. After about three days of this, the boys were still bickering, but there were stretches of not-bickering and even moments when they actually spoke nicely to each other. The parents stepped up their praise at such moments and gave special bonus points (five). Over time the parents made a gradual move from reinforcing other behavior (anything but . . .) to reinforcing some of the positive opposites—like the boys speaking nicely to each other—they had identified at the beginning. In a week, the parents felt there were great changes and kept up the praise but stopped the point program. (They let the brothers trade in all leftover points for a major weekend outing.) The bickering did not stop completely, but it fell to a manageable level, and the parents felt that some amount of bickering was to be expected. They felt the program was successful, especially because the boys actually started to play more together, rather than merely tolerating each other's existence.

This was another case in which we started out with reinforcing any behavior other than the disruptive behavior, and then, as we began to see some of the positive opposites occur, we moved more specifically to reinforcing those.

*3. Reinforcing disruptive behaviors when they happen less often.* This one seems really counterintuitive, but stay with me. Let's say a behavior—shouting, swearing, saying something nasty, being aggressive—occurs ten times a day, or ten times before lunch. One way to eliminate the behavior is to shape fewer and fewer instances of the behavior. The child can be praised if he engages in the behavior only eight times. This seems distressingly wrong to many parents, and I often hear some version of "Let me get this straight: my child is saying nasty things and I'm praising him for it?" Yes, that's what's happening, and you're doing it because you're shaping the process of fewer and fewer of these nasty things being said until you can eliminate them entirely.

For example, I worked with a seven-year-old boy, Ted, who bullied other children in his classroom. Once I heard about this, of course, I asked the teacher to specify what she meant and what bullying meant for this boy. He teased others, pushed them, and messed up their work as they tried to write at their desks. Along with that, he said nasty things about them—how stupid they were, how funny they looked, and so on. As soon as the class settled in at the beginning of the school day, he started to pick on children seated near him, and he kept it up all day.

We wanted to reinforce the positive opposite, interacting with others nicely, but Ted seemed to have only two modes: bullying or silence. We told Ted he could earn a very special treat for himself and the entire class. If he could do what was asked, the class would get an extra recess or a special mystery story right before lunch break. Each day that Ted earned the privilege, he could choose which one it would be, recess or the story. To earn it, he had to not pick on other people for fifteen minutes after class started, at 8:30 a.m. (We of course specified exactly what picking on people consisted of.) If he did not bully anyone by 8:45, he would earn the reward. We told him this was hard to do and we were not sure he could do it (all great antecedents here; see chapter one), but we would give it a try.

With all of that buildup, on the first day Ted met the criterion and the teacher quietly went to him at 8:45 and told him, effusively, that because he hadn't said anything nasty to anyone, the class would earn a reward, no matter what he did for the rest of the morning. And now he could choose the reward! Ted was pretty mild for the rest of the morning; he engaged in a little bullying, but for him it was good. (We asked the teacher to protect any victims from being upset, intimidated, or hurt as soon as she saw any sign of bullying, by asking the victim to come over to her. We wanted her to try very temporarily to not attend to Ted—the risk was too great that she would accidentally reinforce bullying that way.) We continued this for three more days. One day he didn't earn the privilege, but after two days in a row on which he did, we said, "OK, now it gets really hard"—a good challenge antecedent. "Can you go for a whole half-hour?"

And so on. Over three and a half weeks we shaped the behavior so that he received the special reward at the end of the day, rather than before lunch, and if he made it through the whole day, there was an extended recess *and* a story. Then we praised him for making it for two and then three days in a row. His bullying and nasty comments were mostly eliminated. Added to this all along was reinforcing of any positive prosocial interaction—we tried to catch him when he engaged in positive opposite behavior once in a while. That part made the program much more likely to be effective. Ted didn't in fact have only two modes, bullying and silence. Like a lot of bullies, he actually did have some interactions with other children that were fine—chatting in line, talking about a TV show or something odd that had happened in a game, that kind of thing. We viewed these regular, neutral exchanges as prosocial and praised them whenever they occurred. We "caught him being socially functional," in other words, and reinforced it.

So in addition to systematically eliminating Ted's bullying, the undesired behavior, by shaping longer and longer periods without the behavior occurring, we also reinforced its positive opposite—prosocial interactions with other children. We needed to do both because merely increasing the non-bullying interactions might not have eliminated the bullying; there was enough time in the day for Ted to bully a little and get along a little. So we worked on decreasing the bullying *and* building up its positive opposite.

This example focuses on gradually decreasing the frequency of a behavior. One can also take a behavior that has many components—I previously mentioned a tantrum that might include hitting, swearing, shouting, and crying for a long time. Less intense versions can be shaped by concentrating on knocking out one of the components at a time, or reducing its intensity, until there's not much tantrum left, and then none at all. That means that for a short period you'll be praising "good" tantrums, which I hope no longer feels utterly insane to you.

## How to use reinforcers so they actually work

Positive reinforcement puts some extremely useful new tools in your toolkit. But, as we saw in previous chapters, outlining your options in using positive reinforcement is just part of the information you need to use this approach effectively. It's the *what,* and now I need to talk about the *how.* Reinforcers have to be provided in a special way, and that applies to whether praise or tokens or other rewards are used. If they aren't provided this way, they don't work very well. So, the *how:*

1. Provide the reinforcer (praise, for instance) immediately after the behavior whenever you can. Behavior and reinforcer need to be closely connected in time. If, one or two minutes after your child cleaned up her room, you say, "You picked up all the clothes in your room and you made your bed, too; that's really great," your praise can make that same behavior much more likely in the future. If you say the same thing to her one

day after she cleans up her room, it's not likely to change that behavior at all.

2. Convey exactly what the reinforcer is given for. What exactly are those behaviors you want to increase in the future? Specifying exactly what they are will really help. So "You picked up all the clothes in your room and you made your bed, too; that's really great" is much more effective than "Good job!" Of course, it's OK to say "Good job" (enthusiastically), if it's followed by statements of exactly what the job was and what made it good.
3. Use a high-quality reinforcer. This doesn't mean expensive rewards. It means, for instance, that when praising young children you need to be effusive and enthusiastic. Mediocre, nonchalant, and low-key praise for young children just does not work as well. Quality is also influenced by combining verbal praise with a touch or positive physical gesture—rubbing the child's shoulder, a high-five, a hug—whatever suits the parent-child style. The idea is to do something physical, approving, and affectionate. If points are being used, do not give one point for the behavior if the child needs at least twenty points to buy a reward. There's no advantage in being stingy. Make it worthwhile and relatively easy for your child to get enough points to buy the cheapest (in points) reward. Remember, you will drop all of the points soon enough, so this is just temporary. Also, when points are given, pair that with effusive praise, and be as enthusiastic as the market will bear: that is, with young children, extremely enthusiastic (think of a game-show host communicating hearty approval to a colleague on a neighboring mountaintop); with older children, less effusive; with teenagers, low-key but still clearly pleased.
4. As a behavior is developing, try to provide the reinforcer every time the behavior occurs. This is not always practical, but try. Performing the behavior will occur at a higher rate and the habit can be developed sooner if you can provide

the reward every time, or close to it, that the behavior is performed.

These requirements might seem at first blush as if they're not very special, but bear in mind that most programs for changing children's behavior fail because the reinforcer is delayed too long after the behavior or is given irregularly (not even close to almost every time), and/or the quality of reinforcers is really poor. For example, parents who come to the Yale Parenting Center routinely tell us that they already do praise their child often and well. Then we work individually with these parents to train them to maximize the effectiveness of praise, and they can see that praise to change behavior effectively is very different from the usual praise most parents give. It's a lesson that I, too, had to learn as a parent. Knowing what the research says and actually doing it are two different things.

Similarly, it's hard to find a parent in the developed world who has not used a point chart—and chances are that point chart has failed to help in any way. The key to success lies in the delivery, in the *how*.

One very common reason for the failure of a point program is that a parent is misled to see magic in the points themselves, not in the key principles of positive reinforcement that the points are designed to facilitate. Also, as we have noted, points are consequences—and consequences are just part of the ABCs that are needed for effective and long-lasting behavior change. When points are used, sometimes they distract parents from praising, but praise, the constant in any reward program, will be the main basis for changing behavior. Points are almost never a substitute or replacement for praise. Just the opposite, in fact: most of the time, praise alone will do the job and points aren't needed.

One mom who came to see me at the Yale Parenting Center wanted her eight-year-old daughter, Isabella, nicknamed Izzie, to practice the piano every day. She had gone through the usual parenting ploys that we have all used: complaining that lessons were expensive and would be a complete waste if Izzie did not practice, declaring that she was embarrassed and ashamed because the teacher said that Izzie clearly was not trying very hard, threatening to withhold TV and computer time if Izzie didn't practice, and so on. That's all standard parenting. The effects of the mom's ploys were predictable; they didn't help, and now the nightly drama of practicing the piano had become a parent-versus-child battleground.

The mom went on the Web for help and found point charts as an option. She thought that giving Izzie points on a chart for practicing would do the trick. The mom printed out a sheet to keep track of points and announced to Izzie that the old regime of taking away TV and computer time was over. Izzie could watch and indulge. If she practiced thirty to forty minutes of piano, as her teacher asked, she would get ten points each time. Any week when she earned forty or more points, they would do a special activity on the weekend—a movie of Izzie's choice, shopping for one small toy, going to a nearby amusement park.

This program had some benefits. For one thing, losing TV and computer time as punishment definitely would not have worked or made Izzie like or want to play the piano, so dumping that was a step in the right direction.

But the program didn't work. Or, rather, it worked on the first night, probably because the novelty of it all and Mom's enthusiasm for a new approach piqued Izzie's interest. But she rapidly lost interest in it, and now the nagging went like this: "Why aren't you practicing? Look at all the good things we can do if you practice."

The mother came to us for help, enormously frustrated and perplexed as to why the program she started had not worked. We explained to her that the program failed because:

- There was no shaping. Don't start by requiring the full thirty or forty minutes of practice time to qualify for points—that alone would make the program ineffective. We start where the child is—if practice is zero minutes, we begin with three to five minutes. As this becomes consistent, we can move to more.
- What exactly constituted "practice" wasn't specified very well. Izzie should know exactly what was expected of her. Just sitting on the bench plinking keys? Doing specific tasks that the music teacher prescribed?

- The reinforcer was very delayed—until the end of the week—and that alone would doom the program to failure. Early in developing behavior there should be no or minimal delay between the desired behavior and the consequence. As behavior develops, delays in the consequences are fine, but early delays mean early program failure.
- Praise was not a part of this program. That, too, all by itself, could readily explain why the program didn't work. Think of points as an addition to a praise program rather than the other way around. Basically, your praise and attention to your child are hugely influential, and a couple of trinkets or privileges are not anywhere near as effective. Also, using praise could help bridge the delay of the reinforcer until the weekend activity.
- The mom didn't take advantage of several kinds of A (antecedents) and B (behaviors) options that would have improved her chances of success. For instance, at the beginning, sitting with her child, taking turns, doing a simulated Practice the Piano game for a few minutes to get more points; having the child teach the mom one of her exercises; listening to piano versions of songs Izzie liked, to give her an extra incentive to learn to play the instrument; going to a music store to pick out the music for some songs Izzie liked and could play would be great. Alternatively, the mom could be in the room with Izzie for the first few minutes and then out of the room for a few more minutes (coming back in to praise when those minutes went well), and gradually remove herself from the scene of practice. We want children to like playing their instruments, and the parent can do a lot to help that happen, especially by using antecedents effectively—in this case, the mom could use her presence to help or join in, then gradually fade that presence.
- Points can be a distraction (to the parent) if the parent believes that the points themselves will improve behavior. The action is not where the points are; it's in repeated practice and use of As, Bs, and Cs to make that happen. And remember that when it

> comes to the Cs, we lead with our strength—parent praise delivered with the ingredients I've stressed: be effusive, state the exact behaviors being praised, add something nonverbal like an affectionate touch.

That seems like a lot of stuff to fix, but actually all Izzie's mother had to do was to make a few changes for the program to be effective.

First, we started with ten minutes of her sitting with Izzie as a way to begin practice—this was an antecedent: "Let's start *our* practice now"—and then walking to the room with the mom's arm around Izzie or holding her hand. (Use of "our" is a good setting event because it begins with sharing the task, working together, and not someone ordering someone else to do something.) The mom asked Izzie to start with one exercise the teacher had given her and to explain it to the mom to help her understand. Putting the child in this teaching position gave her more control over the situation. (Being in control has effects similar to those of choice—it increases the likelihood of engaging in the desired behaviors.) Izzie wasn't always being told what to do but could tell her mother how to do it. Then they played something from the lesson for that week for the rest of the ten minutes. When the ten minutes ended (the mom set up a kitchen timer in the room where Izzie practiced), they got up and stopped, or they could work on "Chopsticks" or some other simple piece just for fun; Izzie could choose. More often than not, she chose to do it. Among other things, she enjoyed being better at "Chopsticks" than her mother was.

After several days of this, the mother walked her daughter to the room and had her start without her: "You get started; I'll be back in a minute." The mother returned in a minute or two. Practice continued. We increased the amount of time in five- to ten-minute increments and trimmed the amount of time the mom was in the room. Soon she was coming in ten minutes and then twenty minutes after Izzie had begun, and finally only at the end of the practice to play "Chopsticks" or a Christmas carol they both liked and had added to their repertoire of duet practice. Many of these practice sessions ended in laughter as they practiced the fun piece and made little improvisations, as when Izzie introduced part of "Chopsticks" in the middle of a Christmas carol. The tone of the practice and parent-child exchanges about it had changed.

The mother praised Izzie at first for going to practice sessions with her, for starting on an exercise, for teaching her about her lesson so nicely, then for practicing while the mom was not even in the room, and eventually for doing the whole practice. I suggested she contact the teacher about the program and make sure the teacher noticed and commented on any improvements evident in the lessons themselves. That was a delayed reinforcer for more and better practice, since Izzie saw the teacher only once a week, but it helped.

We eventually ended with the mom providing intermittent praise for practice. Also, we wanted to give the child some options about practice. One day a week she could take a break from practicing if she wanted to. Izzie selected this option the first week and then irregularly in the following months. Also, during the week she began to show a behavior that made her mother very happy: Izzie would occasionally sit at the piano outside of her practice sessions and play an exercise or song from the lesson.

By fixing the program, it might seem at first as if we made it harder for the mom to get Izzie to practice. After all, there was more parent involvement in the early stage, and the mom had to do more prompting and then fade her presence. But really we just gave her a little more focus, a little more purpose. Effective programs are not more complex than ineffective ones. The difference usually lies in tinkering with the *how,* and in fact ineffective programs usually require more work because they don't produce progress, everyone is stressed, and after two days, two weeks, or two months everyone is still at square one because the program didn't work.

Perhaps the best example of constructive tinkering in this program was in the use of praise—hardly a rearrangement of anyone's life or routine. Usual parental praise ("That's good, Tommy") is not nearly as effective as the praise we have been talking about. So a critical part of Izzie's piano practice program was having the mother praise in a way that would be much more effective—that is, enthusiastically specifying exactly what the behaviors were that were being praised, and with some physical gesture. Learning to praise that way takes a little work at first, but in the long run praising effectively, in ways that produce results that allow you to fade and then discontinue such praise for a desired behavior, is far less work than saying "Good job!" ten thousand times with no effect.

## Putting it all together

You want your four-year-old boy to come over to you when you ask. He loves to run around, which is great, but he also likes to run away from you when you are at the park or walking to the park. He thinks it's loads of fun, but you are worried about his safety; you've even thought about one of those leashes for children. But you want to try a praise program first. The positive opposite is easily defined: coming to you when you ask, the first time. This never seems to occur, so—as we discussed in the last chapter—you set up a game to simulate walking to the park. You call this the Come-to-Me game. In the house you position yourself in different places—different corners of the living room, then in different rooms—and ask him to come to you. When he comes to you, you give him high-quality praise. That means you do it right away, and you do it every time he comes to you when you ask him to. Very effusively, you say, "That was GREAT! I asked you to come and you came right away!" and you lean over and give him a hug (the nonverbal component that, when added to your words, makes the reinforcer more effective). And you want to do this at least a couple of times a day for a week or so as your schedule allows. The key is to create repeated opportunities for your child to do the behavior and receive the reinforcers.

That sequence of reinforced practice—do the behavior, get the positive reinforcer, do it again—is the single most important idea in this book. There is no magic in the reinforcer all by itself, even if it's a ridiculously extravagant reward. Giving your child a pony as a reward won't help him get in the habit of coming to you when you ask him to. Only reinforced practice will get him there, even if the reinforcer is "nothing more" than your attention and praise. We use antecedents to get the behavior to occur, and we use consequences to help lock it in. But the key is the middle part—repetition of the behavior—and providing effective reinforcers greatly increases the likelihood that the behavior will continue in the future.

Another example: Let's say you're shaping your preteen to clean her room. You have forgotten whether there is a throw rug, wall-to-wall carpet, or a hardwood floor under the months-old layers of discarded food packaging, dirty and "clean" clothes, books and loose pages, shoeboxes, and plastic bags from a variety of stores. You are shaping having clean sections of the room. You start off with having her clear one three-square-foot corner (she gets to choose which corner—good use of choice here) so that the floor is perfectly visible. She can't just pile the stuff up on another part of the floor; she has to show you that she put the stuff away. She says she's done for that morning and wants you to check. She earns points for doing this correctly and of course you also use praise. You go in and see that the space is clear, she shows you where the clothes are hung up in her closet, and there's a plastic bag of trash in the doorway ready to go downstairs. You praise with just a slightly raised voice. Teens often do not respond as well to really effusive praise, which they regard as embarrassingly uncool.

Science isn't ready to grapple with uncoolness as a research topic, but I can offer a thumbnail explanation for why you need to tone down your praise with a teenager. There's a brief period in life, spanning preadolescence and early adolescence, in which it may appear that parents, their values, and their approval move from being very positive in a child's eyes to being neutral or even negative. Two reassuring points are in order here. First, this does not happen with all or even most adolescents. Second, this is not their real view; they have not abandoned all your values, they still value you and need your input, and they do not in fact want to be alienated from them while they are on a biological, psychological, and social roller coaster set in motion by massive hormonal and brain changes and corresponding emotional and cognitive changes—a complex of upheaval that also, of course, contributes to changes in behavior. That said, you may find that your approval becomes embarrassing or irritating to your adolescent child, especially when your approval takes the form of a loud public reminder that your child is in fact a child and under your control. With an adolescent, effusiveness and public displays may be received as attacks on the child's developing sense of dignity. This means that the effusive, excited, and wonderful praise that worked so well when your child was younger has to change. Now more reserved, more private, and less intrusive praise is more effective. It will still work very well—if it's specific, immediate, paired with a physical gesture . . . you know the drill—but it needs to scale down. If you're wondering, as many parents do, how you can tell when to tone down the praise, the guidelines are easy on this. If there are consistent signs that your praise is aversive—your child grimaces, shies away from you, tries to cut you off, shows the clearest look of disgust you have ever seen, and so on—take those signs as a cue to tone down effusiveness. But don't make the mistake of taking such reactions as cues to stop praise. Instead, move to a quieter, more intimate style of praise—to low-key comments of approval delivered up close and in a low voice, paired with a light touch on the shoulder or a mimed high-five from across the room.

In the case of the preteen with the messy room who has taken the first steps toward cleaning it up, you still tell her that she did well, being sure to specify what she did, and then you give her a high-five or thumbs-up—still curbing your uncoolness, of course. Then you say, "OK, you earned five points on the chart, and you can cash those in for more computer time or credit on your iTunes account."

So the program proceeds. When the designated corner is clear on most days (let's say four out of five), the program extends to another corner. Now, to earn the points both corners have to be cleared, and of course two corners equals more points. You praise if only one corner of the room has been cleared, but you give points (plus praise, of course) if both are cleared. You might say something like "This is great; you kept that corner clear. I can't give you points because this other corner is not so clear, but we'll have another chance at points tomorrow." When faced with half-good or otherwise partially successful results, try to resist the urge to "caboose," the unhelpful habit of tacking a criticism onto your praise (as in "This corner's clean but this one's a pigsty"). Caboosing negates the good effects of the praise it follows. Just praise what was good, and remind the child what she can do to get even more reinforcers, like points.

One family working with the Yale Parenting Center on such a clean-room program eventually got to the point of having all of the room clear except one corner. The daughter then asked her parents if she could leave that one corner without having to worry about keeping it perfectly clean. The parents asked us about that and we said this was a very reasonable request, it gave the child control over her own room, and saying yes would show the child that her parents could compromise—all excellent things to do in parenting. We asked the parents to work out the specific boundaries of the messy corner in the room—"one corner" meant an area bounded by the end of the bed on one side and the beginning of the rug on the other, and so on. Also, the parents insisted that food was off limits even in the messy corner because it could lead to unacceptable problems like bad smells, insects, or rodents.

In shaping, as this program reflects (one corner, then add the next, and then the next), perfection is never required. Not every day and not every corner had to be perfect. The cliché "Perfect is the enemy of the good" applies here. We can build strong habits, consistency, and enduring characteristics, none of which requires demanding perfection. One can get excellent behavior by shaping, but perfection is usually unfair to demand of humans. The natural worry is "If I don't demand perfection now, won't my daughter just learn to be mediocre in everything?" No, she will find many things in life that compel her heart and enthusiasm, and your demanding that she do little tasks around the house with perfection is not likely to influence that.

## Conclusion

"Consequences" refers to what follows behavior. This chapter focused on what should be the main type of consequences: positive reinforcement. This is a central component of virtually all behavior-change programs we are discussing because positive reinforcement is used to directly increase behaviors you wish to develop—and therefore, indirectly, to decrease and eliminate the behaviors you don't want. And when you reach into your toolkit for a consequence, be sure to grab praise first. This is the tool that will carry you very far as a reinforcer—if it's done right and contains the three critical ingredients: age-appropriate enthusiasm, a specific description of what you're praising, and a component of touch to go along with your words. With those ingredients, you can lock in the behaviors, habits, and broader characteristics you wish.

At the center of everything we're trying to accomplish is the concept of reinforced practice: we want the behavior to occur repeatedly (the practice part) and use consequences (reinforcement) to make that happen. This is important to mention because there is no magic in reinforcement (consequences) or in the antecedents either. Each is a critical means toward the end. We want the behavior to occur repeatedly so we can shape it, build consistency in the behavior (lock it in as a habit), and move on (fade and then stop the program as the behavior becomes a habit).

Positive reinforcement is all about building up the behaviors you want, but I realize that many of parents' most urgent goals have to do with decreasing and eliminating undesired behaviors. That's why I emphasize reinforcement of positive opposites. The importance of this will be even clearer in the next chapter when we get to punishment, the most used but often the least effective way of changing behavior.

When you use positive reinforcement, here are some things to keep in mind:

**Dos**

- Specify the behavior you want to develop in clear terms so you will be consistent in providing reinforcing consequences.
- Have a plan—what you want that behavior to look like when this program is over. Now identify steps along the way (shaping) that you will reinforce (for example, with praise). Without a plan, reinforcement is likely to be given unsystematically and will not change the child's behavior.

- Emphasize praise. Usually it works all by itself as the main consequence. If you include a point program, points are in addition to praise, not a replacement for it. For children age ten or eleven and under (but this is approximate), make sure your praise is effusive and followed by a very clear statement about exactly what behaviors you are praising, and then add something physical that is approving or affectionate (touch, pat, hug). For preteens and above (eleven to sixteen, depending on your judgment of the maturity of the child), the three ingredients (praise, statement, physical gesture) may need to change to accommodate the normal (but fortunately temporary) adolescent feeling that anything parents do, think, believe, or support is misguided and uncool. Praise quietly and not in a public way, but still do say exactly what you liked (no change on this) and add some physical gesture that is acceptable—it could be a high-five that just touches the child's hand, or a high-five in the air; it could be thumbs-up as a gesture indicating approval—something like that. If physical contact would be pushing it, a gesture will do.
- Deliver any reinforcer in the way that is required to change behavior, which means:
- Deliver it immediately after the behavior (rather than delaying it).
- Say exactly what you are praising—specify the behaviors.
- For young children, make that praise effusive—it makes a difference.
- Add nonverbal praise—touch, hug, affectionate pat on the shoulder, and so on.
- Try to reinforce often as the behavior is developing—every time or almost every time it occurs, as feasible.

**Don'ts**

- Don't improvise rewards or incentives for random behaviors that you want done around the house. Winging it will guarantee failure. Consequences are part of a systematic plan to develop particular behaviors or a set of behaviors. Repeated practice of a particular behavior or set of behaviors is the goal, and using reinforcers to get that target behavior to occur repeatedly is your aim.

- Don't confuse your ordinary nurturing and caring parenting with what we are focusing on in this book. Praise and hugs, for example, can be given in many ways and often. I am not saying that all praise, hugs, and touches should focus on changing behavior. If you are an affectionate parent, keep it up. If you are warm and loving with your child, do not change or stop. I am saying that when you have as a goal to increase or decrease a particular behavior, to develop habits, and to develop broad characteristics (honesty, consideration, respect), praise can now *also* be used strategically. When used in this strategic way, praise and hugs (consequences) have to be used systematically and in concert with other factors (antecedents, behaviors) to reach a goal.
- Don't make the mistake of thinking you need wildly attractive incentives to get the behavior you want. There's not much demonstrated correlation between the cost of rewards and their effectiveness as reinforcers. A trip to Disney World may be a whopper of a reward, but it could well turn out to be an ineffective reinforcer, while the privilege of picking what the family eats for dinner tonight may be an extremely effective reinforcer if it's properly used. And the whole notion of rewards, large or small, is secondary to the main point here. The crucial thing to bear in mind is that in the vast majority of instances, your attention and praise, used carefully in the ways I've suggested in this chapter, will be enough to develop the behaviors you desire.

# 4

## Decreasing Misbehavior

### *More on Consequences*

I devoted the entire previous chapter to positive reinforcement because it's the most effective way to use consequences to develop behavior. As I've explained, the key concept is reinforced practice—that is, getting the behavior to occur (the "practice" part) and following that with reinforcing consequences (the "reinforced" part) so the behavior will occur again. Arranging for many repetitions of this sequence allows for shaping and then developing the habit consistently.

But positive reinforcement is not the only kind of consequence. Reinforcers aren't the only response you can make to your child's behavior that influences whether it occurs again. Punishment is also a consequence, and it's part of everyday life, familiar to any parent—or, in fact, to any child or anyone who used to be a child. The same is true of another kind of consequence: not responding at all to a behavior, the technical term for which is *extinction*. There are, however, many nuances in how these kinds of consequences can be used to influence behavior, and each has more and less effective variations.

It's common for parents and other adults who have responsibility for children to rely heavily on punishment as a primary tool for changing behavior, but the best research says in no uncertain terms that if punishment has a useful role, it's as a secondary adjunct to positive reinforcement. If punishment worked best, I'd say so and urge you to rely on it, but it doesn't work best. Still, like not responding to behavior, punishment can indeed help change behavior, and I'll show you how to use both tools most effectively.

I'll consider punishment and not responding to behavior separately in this chapter, since each has its own unique qualities and effects. But they have one major trait in common. Both can change behavior, but not on their own. Whether they work depends completely on combining them with a program of positive reinforcement that develops behavior to replace the behavior you're trying to get rid of.

## Punishment

*Punishment* as psychologists in my field define it is very different from the term as used in everyday life, in both the what (definition) and the how (when and how it's delivered). As a technical term, *punishment refers solely to presentation or removal of events after a behavior that reduces the probability or likelihood of that behavior occurring in the future.* In our programs at the Yale Parenting Center, punishment is used to decrease some behavior, and that's it. But in everyday life, punishment has many other agendas. In child rearing, teaching, law enforcement, and other pursuits, we punish not only to change behavior but also to serve justice by trying to make the consequence fit the crime, inspire remorse, teach a moral lesson, or send a message. Many of these other motives are worthwhile and even admirable, but they can get in the way of improving behavior. It's often the case that parents (and teachers, and the legal system) end up pursuing multiple (and often vaguely defined) goals at cross-purposes when they try to use punishment to *both* change behavior *and* impart other lessons. I fully understand that you may want to use punishment to send a message, teach a lesson, and so on, but if you really want to change your child's behavior, make that your priority, which means conceiving of and using punishment in a different way. Sending messages, teaching lessons, teachable moments—these are all wonderful parenting clichés of our time, but not effective strategies for developing behavior.

It's a useful exercise to ask yourself at the moment before you punish, "What's my main goal here? Do I want to make a statement of some kind by showing that this behavior cannot be tolerated in this home, that people do not do this, and so on; or do I want to make this behavior not occur in the future?" These different goals usually call for different actions. The desire to make a statement tends to lead to stark dramatic punishment—shouting, stern reprimands, anger—followed with an explanation along the lines of "What if everybody acted like that?" or "If you do that, the world will think you are a complete jerk." If you want to change behavior, you will respond differently; think first of building up the positive opposite, and use very gentle punishment, if any.

I de-emphasize punishment in our programs for five reasons:

1. Punishment does not teach a child positive behaviors to engage in. Getting rid of what you do not want does not immediately put into the child's repertoire what you want (positive opposite), even if the child understands what to do. For example, either in a very admirable and measured way or after blowing up spectacularly, you may tell your child not to be so rough when playing with the baby because the baby is young and can easily get hurt. Your child may listen to this and even give you a reassuring nod to show that he understands, and he probably does understand. Unfortunately, that may not change his behavior at all. Instead, reinforce your child for being gentle with the baby.
2. Punishment is not very effective. Yes, it may well suppress behavior immediately—a shout, a slap, a loud reprimand is often temporarily effective right at the moment it occurs. But the science on this shows clearly that the rate of the problem behavior (the number of times it happens each day, each week, each month) does not change with punishment, even though you witnessed an immediate change at the moment you punished. So the behavior keeps happening and you

keep punishing—and, to make matters worse, the natural human tendency is for the punishment to escalate as the child adjusts to it. So now you have to punish a lot more to get that initial immediate pause in the behavior, and it's still going to come back as often as ever. Children adapt to that more intense punishment so that it has no stronger an effect than the less intense punishment.

3. Alternative procedures such as positive reinforcement can often be used to achieve the same goal as punishment—namely, to decrease or eliminate a behavior—and without punishment's side effects. So reinforcement of positive opposites is much more effective than any of the punishment options. For example, as your frequently misbehaving child walks down the aisle of the grocery store and does not touch items on the shelves, you say, "Great! You kept your hands to yourself and didn't touch anything on the shelves as we just walked down this aisle!" (Now do a quick touch.) That will work wonders, and you can pair that with occasional very mild reprimands when he does touch items on the shelves, as long as you praise the desired behavior more frequently than you punish the undesired behavior.
4. Punishment often is associated with undesirable side effects such as emotional reactions (crying), escape and avoidance (for example, staying away from a punitive parent), and aggression (such as hitting others, including you). Also, shouting at, reprimanding, or shaking the child can get the child very upset, but don't mistake that reaction for a sign that the child's behavior will improve. Some side effects go beyond just getting upset. For example, moderate to frequent spanking (a few times a month) helps make a child more aggressive. Parents often take these side effects (especially crying) as a sign that punishment must be working, but in fact these effects have almost nothing to do with getting the behavior to stop.
5. Punishment can inspire undesirable associations with various people (parents, teachers), situations (home, school), and

> behaviors (doing homework) that are important for a child. A vital objective in rearing a well-socialized child is to foster positive attitudes toward these important people, situations, and behaviors; their frequent association with punishment makes it harder to achieve that objective. For example, parents often think their adolescents can talk to them about anything, but teens often avoid parents because they fear reprimands and judgment, to which teens are especially sensitive. This is especially harmful when they avoid parents on important but touchy topics, like peer relations, sex, and substance use.

So why even talk about punishment? Well, it *is* used often in everyday life, frequently in ways that are ineffective and can actually do harm, principally via side effects. Also, there is a genuine role for punishment in an effective program for changing behavior, and clarifying that role can improve your effectiveness as a parent. In addition, I recognize that parents don't just respond to behavior. It's likely that you punish for all kinds of reasons that go well beyond changing behavior, so you might as well know how punishment affects behavior.

## Your punishment toolkit

There are three broad categories of punishment: things you present to the child, things you take away, and things you require your child to do.

*Things you present to the child,* the technical term for which is *aversive consequences:* shouting, reprimands, threats, and other responses that the child dislikes and would rather avoid (so, the negative opposite of a reward). This category embraces everything from a warning look (which, used properly, can work very well) to counting to three (less effective) to hauling off and belting a child (which won't do any good and which I would never endorse). They're all grouped together because if you're trying to improve behavior, the threat of such a punishment *is* a punishment. Parents do not need research to prove that this kind of punishment, when it's the primary means of trying to improve behavior, is not effective beyond the immediate moment. The reason parents find themselves saying things like "If I have told you once, I have told you a thousand times" is that scolding, threatening, raising a hand to warn of an impending blow, the blow itself, and all other aversive consequences are ineffective when it comes to permanently reducing or eliminating a behavior. In fact, frequent reprimands have been shown to actually make an undesirable behavior happen *more* frequently. So if this is your favored method for dealing with misbehavior, get used to doing it all the time, and be prepared for your child to adapt to the punishment faster than you can escalate it, a nasty household arms race that's both unnecessary and harmful to all.

*Things you take away,* or *withdrawal of positive events,* meaning time out, removing a point if a point chart is being used, and other methods of taking away something the child likes and wants. The most common version is time out, which psychologists call by its more precise name: *time out from reinforcement,* which refers to *withdrawal of a positive reinforcer for a certain period of time.* During the time-out interval, the child does not have access to the positive reinforcers that are normally available in the setting. For example, a child may be isolated from others in class for ten minutes. During that time she will not interact with peers or have access to activities, privileges, or the teacher's attention.

Time out can be very brief to be effective. Just the first minute or couple of minutes does the work of changing behavior. More time out does not make it more effective, and more than about ten minutes can begin to have negative side effects. The child can sit on a chair, go to his room, or sit in a special place where he can be supervised but doesn't receive attention. Time out has nothing to do with contemplating one's sins or considering what might have been done better. It works on pigeons, rats, and other animals incapable of moral reflection, and it works the same way on children—and adults, for that matter. (I am not saying that your child resembles even the cutest rat or pigeon in any way, but think about this: a ball, a shoe, and a feather don't resemble each other, but it's fair to say that gravity works on all of them. And so with your future Nobel laureate of a child, who responds to time out and gravity in the same ways that all sorts of living things do.)

The effectiveness of time out depends on a brief, temporary loss of access to the usual reinforcers, and that's all. The crucial ingredient is delineating a brief period during which reinforcement is unavailable. Ideally, during this period *all* sources of reinforcement are withdrawn. This ideal is not always attainable. For example, if a child is sent to her room as punishment, removal from the existing sources of reinforcement qualifies as time out. However, all reinforcement may not be withheld; she may engage in a number of reinforcing activities such as playing a computer game, listening to music, or sleeping. Despite these possibilities, sending her to her room will do if it's the only option. Better would be sitting on a chair or couch or in a corner for just a brief period.

Time out usually removes an individual from the situation. But sometimes, if the child can't be removed, reinforcers available in the setting can be stopped for a brief period. One variation of time out is called *planned ignoring,* a period of time in which the parent, teacher, or other person makes no reinforcing contact with the child. This would include no comments, eye contact, nonverbal pats, or praise. Here is a good use of planned ignoring: Say your three-year-old child occasionally hits you. After you are hit, you ignore the child for one or two minutes. Before, you would have attended to her, grabbed her hand, and said, "You do not hit Mommy!"—all behaviors that are likely not to work, at best, and, at worst, to increase hitting in the future. When you respond with planned ignoring, after the child hits you, you stay in the room, but for two minutes you make no eye contact and you don't talk to or interact with the child for this brief time period. This is "time out" because the child has no access to your attention. After the time elapses, you resume all of your usual activities with the child. This is one example where the child receives time out but is not isolated or excluded physically from the situation.

In a nutshell, time out should be

- Used sparingly, because the side effects of excessive punishment are more significant than any benefits the time out might have. If you're giving more than one or two per day for the same offense, that's too much.
- Brief, because the time out's positive effect on behavior is almost all concentrated in its first minute or two. Some parents feel obliged to add more time to satisfy their sense of justice, but the extra time has no value in terms of changing behavior. If you feel that you must go beyond one or two minutes, treat ten minutes as the extreme upper limit.
- Immediate, following as closely as possible upon the behavior that made it necessary. If you can, do it on the spot, not when you get home from the store or playground. Delayed time out is ineffective.
- Done in isolation from others, with the child in a separate room or sitting alone in a chair off to one side. Complete isolation is not needed if you feel it would be good to keep an eye on the child.
- Administered calmly, not in anger or as an act of vengeance, and without repeated warnings, which lose their effect if they are not regularly followed with consequences. Make clear to the child which behaviors led to time out, and then be consistent about declaring one when such behavior occurs. One warning is plenty. Later in this chapter I will say more about how to make time out effective, including the less familiar but vitally important concept of "time in."

Withdrawing privileges is another familiar punishment often used in the home. You temporarily take away something the child likes to do or is granted routinely—TV time, use of a cell phone or bicycle, time with friends, and so on. This approach can be effective, but only if you keep two important principles in mind when you use it.

First, the child should know ahead of time exactly what the penalty is, well before you invoke it. In the usual home situation, the parent wings it on the spot: "What did you just say to me? That's it, we're giving away your dog and I'm not paying for college!" Shooting from the hip like that, being arbitrary or appearing to be arbitrary, is a setting event for your child to have tantrums, get upset, and otherwise make a scene. And punishment improvised on the spot is not only likely to appear arbitrary and unfair but also to be more severe than punishment that was planned in advance, all of which leads to more side effects. So specify in advance what privileges will be taken away and for how long; then invoke the punishment, if necessary, calmly and without unnecessary drama.

Second, brevity is the key when withdrawing privileges. I know you're tempted to declare, "You can't use your bike for two weeks!" This is not necessary—one or two days maximum would have the same effect, since the behavior-changing power of the consequence lies in the initial moment of taking away a privilege, not in the long duration of its removal. I know that one or two days may not feel like a punishment that adequately fits the crime, and from the standpoint of justice you may well be right. But it's all that's necessary to change behavior. Also, a bicycle is often a source of contact with peers that usually we want to foster. Try to find another way to satisfy the demands of justice.

*Things you require your child to do:* work or activity that the child regards as unpleasant. If you use this consequence, the chore should be brief. Here, too, requiring more effort—more time weeding the garden, more time cleaning the garage—does not increase the effectiveness of punishment. The required work can be unrelated to the offense being punished, like having to stack firewood for using bad language, or related to the offense, like cleaning up and fixing vandalism done to a school building.

## Effects of punishment

*Immediacy of effects.* This is a tricky notion because it has two meanings. First, the punishment (shout, threat) may stop the behavior in the moment. Even a stark punishment with major negative side effects—like a slap in the face, which of course I would never condone—will interrupt the behavior. This immediate but short-lived effect causes a parent to fall into what is called the "punishment trap." The momentary success of the punishment unwittingly reinforces the person delivering punishment (you) and *develops the habit further in the parent.*

Here's how it works. The child is doing something annoying, the parent shouts or pounds the table, the child's inappropriate behavior stops. This is a type of reinforcement of the parent that locks in shouting or whatever the punishment was. That is, the immediate effectiveness locks in parent behavior; the delayed ineffectiveness of the punishment, which does nothing to decrease recurrences of the bad behavior, has no real impact on the parent's tendency to punish. For example, I have worked with many parents who abuse their children—I mean that their punishments rise above the line drawn by the law to define child abuse—and they know it's not working but they do it anyway. They've been seduced and trapped by the immediate but temporary cessation of the child's misbehavior that happens right at the moment they punish.

The second meaning of "immediacy of effects" is that if punishment is going to have any longer-term effect, more than just interrupting a behavior at that moment, this effect should start to be evident soon—like, in a couple of days. A punishment-centered behavior-change program usually won't work at all, but if it does work, you would see a slight decrease in the behavior in the first few days. Let me be clear about what this means: the behavior doesn't just temporarily stop at the moment you punish; it recurs less often. This doesn't have to be a large decrease, but it should be at least a discernible trend. If you don't see the improvement right away, you can conclude that punishment isn't going to work. I mention this because more than one parent has said to me something like "I'm going to keep punishing him"—in one case hitting, in another case holding the child by the shoulders and shaking—"until he gets the message and stops hitting other kids." Chances are that the child will get the message, which is "me hitting usually leads to my dad shaking me," but this punishment will not be more effective over time. Knowing, understanding, and grasping the message will not change behavior and certainly will not develop the positive (opposite) behavior you wish for your child.

Bottom line: Punishment is not likely to work, but if it is going to work, you will see an inkling of the effects right away. Even if you do see that improvement, bear in mind that the punishment is likely to get less rather than more effective over time in light of this next characteristic.

*Recovery from punishment.* Again, the most critical point is that punishment usually does not have the enduring effect of reducing and eliminating behavior. But sometimes it does have a very different enduring effect, one that's bad for both child and parent. What happens is that the child adapts to the punishment, the technical term for which is *recovery from punishment.* The punishment continues when the behavior occurs but loses its effects as the child adapts to the punishment, causing the unwanted behavior to go back to its pre-punishment rate. This adaptation to punishment often leads the parent to escalate: instead of shouting, much harsher shouting and a threat; instead of one blow, a few blows; instead of hitting with a hand, hitting with a belt. Most parents do not go to the highest level of escalation, but a surprising number escalate well beyond any level they intended to reach or feel comfortable reaching. They sink deeper into the punishment trap because more and more severe punishment continues to stop the behavior for the moment.

*Undesirable side effects*. Punishment can have many undesirable side effects. They're called side effects because they're not related to the goals of punishment or to whether punishment even is working. The irony of all of this is that even when punishment is not working, the side effects emerge. Medicines come to market because their therapeutic effects (how they help the problem) are worthwhile despite side effects (consequences that are annoying, painful, or even dangerous).

Punishment that doesn't work is like chemotherapy that makes your hair fall out and makes you nauseous but has no effect on cancer.

The side effects of punishment include the following:

*Emotional reactions:* being upset, crying, begging, and so on. Parents sometimes even say, "You *ought to* be upset!" Seeing the child's emotional upset also contributes to the punishment trap by suggesting to the parent that the punishment is working, that it fit the crime, or that a lesson is being learned. Yet whether the child is upset or not is unrelated to the effectiveness of punishment. Getting your child to cry, wail, plead for mercy while crying—none of this is related to behavior change.

*Escape and avoidance.* A child will seek to get away from a person (parent, teacher) or a situation (school, dinnertime at home) that is frequently associated with punishment. If a child wants to escape from or avoid parents or teachers, he'll be less likely to seek out these adults in time of need—when he has a problem, when he needs counsel or understanding. The opposite of avoidance is approach, and children are less likely to approach adults who punish relatively frequently—here, "relatively" means in relation to how much positive reinforcement that adult gives them. Also, we want to be sure the child does not wish to escape from situations (for example, home, classroom) that should be associated with comfort, learning, and other major positives. When something leads to escape, it has become aversive. Punishing a child for, say, not practicing an instrument can backfire on a parent because it can make an otherwise positive experience or activity truly aversive.

*Aggression.* Punishment sometimes results in aggressive behavior, usually against the person who is delivering punishment. If you hit or spank a child, the likelihood of being hit back is pretty high. Once that occurs (and no parent can take that calmly), punishment usually escalates. Even with a punishment as mild as time out, here is a common scenario: The parent tells the child to go to her room for a few minutes of time out. The child says no. Now the parent may forcibly take the child to time out—grabbing and lifting the child, forcibly walking the child to time out. This is almost a guarantee that the child will flail with her arms and hit the parent. The parent usually then increases the force of his grip, resulting in more aggressive behavior and a cascade of emotional effects to go along with an increase in the child's aggression.

So what should the parent do when the child refuses time out? Have a backup plan set in advance, such as taking away a privilege. So you say, "Go to your room for five minutes of time out." The child says, "No, I won't." You then give one—just one—warning: "Once more, I am asking you to go to time out." If the child still refuses, then no warnings, no lectures, no tirades on your part. You just say, "OK, you lose TV privileges tonight" or whatever else you had decided in advance would be the lost privilege. And you walk away—calmly, not in a hot or cold fury, not as if making a dramatic exit—to avoid the ensuing back-and-forth.

It's important that you work out in advance what the penalty will be, and that you tell your child in advance whenever possible. When you specify a punishment in advance, you can include punishment options you wish to retain: "If you don't go straight into time out when I tell you to, you will lose a privilege that will either be TV for the day or computer time for the day." But it's even better to name just one punishment and to be specific about it. The main reason is that if parents have worked out an explicit punishment ahead of time and have laid things out for their child in advance, they are less likely to wing it on the spot when the offense happens. In the heat of the moment, with everyone yelling and angry, winging it is risky because your reaction is likely to be more severe and arbitrary, as in "That's it, you just lost your favorite doll FOR THE REST OF YOUR LIFE!" The greater severity is likely to produce more side effects without any benefit in behavior change. The arbitrariness will be an antecedent for the child's negative reaction (not just side effects) because she feels she has no real say, control, or choice in anything in the home. As setting events go, "arbitrary" can be considered the opposite of choice. When you take away a predetermined, known, reasonably chosen privilege in a calm way, rather than reacting excitedly in the heat of the moment, your reasonableness and consistency in keeping to a plan will positively influence your child's behavior and compliance beyond this particular incident.

*Modeled punishment.* When you punish, you're modeling punishment for your child. We know from research that children "discipline" their peers in the same ways their parents discipline them. This is not a problem if you punish in moderation, but it can become one if you go overboard. That's one of the reasons that the most aggressive children are those whose parents hit them a lot. So when you punish, you are doing more than using a procedure that is likely to be ineffective—you're teaching a way of interacting with others. Moderation, restraint, and lots of positive reinforcement for positive opposite behavior mitigate all of this.

## How to use punishment so it actually works

1. The single most important factor in using punishment is that, whatever punishment is used, it must play a minor role in the behavior-change program. The effectiveness of punishment depends on whether and how often the positive opposite is reinforced. Punishment by itself is a losing battle. It just doesn't teach the behaviors you want, and without that, a strategy of suppressing little instances of the behavior here and there does not work beyond the moment. But punishment is not useless; the research shows that a strong reinforcement program can be enhanced by very occasional punishment when the child doesn't do the behavior you're trying to develop.

By way of illustration, take time out, a popular punishment that virtually everyone knows about. The effectiveness of time out depends on what you do during "time in," which refers to all the time that the child is not in time out. If the desirable behavior is consistently and frequently rewarded during time in, a well-used time out will help develop the behavior you want. As a guide, for every time the child is placed in time out, be sure the positive opposite behavior is reinforced four or five times more during time in. Reinforced practice of the desired behavior is the guiding concept of the approach; punishment on its own will not teach the child what to do.

Bottom line: There is no such thing in this book as a punishment program. There is a positive reinforcement program that includes occasional and mild punishment as a component. Also, positive reinforcement supplemented by punishment is much less likely to have the undesirable side effects associated with punishment alone. The positive reinforcement leads to all sorts of more positive side effects—good emotional reactions, more cooperative rather than aggressive behavior, a stronger bond between parent and child.

2. Keep punishment mild. Making the punishment fit the crime may well make sense from some perspectives (like a desire to instill an appreciation of justice), but not from the standpoint of changing behavior. So your child stays out past her curfew and you are thinking, "Do I take away her iPad and cell phone for a week or two, or just a day or two?" The offense seems to deserve a week or two, and a day or two feels to you as if she's getting off too lightly. Yet, the day or two will have the maximum effect on changing behavior. More is not better in punishment, because more is not more effective and it produces more bad side effects. Mild punishment can be effective when strong positive reinforcement is in place around it. What that means is that a disapproving look, a few minutes of time out, or saying, "No, don't do that" would virtually never work as a stand-alone punishment program, yet when built into a reinforcement program, these and other forms of mild punishment can help change behavior.

3. Do not use as punishing consequences any activities you want your child to like. Some traditional school punishments violate this principle. Common examples include doing extra homework, having to read more in an assigned book, staying after school, staying in class during recess, writing an essay about why the behavior was wrong, or writing "I will not . . ." over and over on the board à la Bart Simpson.

Short of corporal punishment, these are the worst possible punishing consequences. We want children to have a positive attitude toward homework, books, staying in school, and so on. Staying after school could easily be a reward if you set it up right; we want being in class to be desired; and we never want reading and writing to be associated with punishment. At home the same problem can emerge if a parent punishes a child by having him work on reading, practice an instrument, or sit with a parent (so he can be monitored and controlled better). Most parents do not want reading, practicing, or being with them to become negative—so if you use an activity as punishment, give some thought to choosing one that doesn't attach an aversive association to something you actually want your child to do or like.

At home, there are additional examples of punishments one ought to be cautious about using. For example, a commonly used punishment is taking away some privilege for a while: "You can't use your bike for two weeks"; "You're grounded and can't have activities with friends for a month"; and so on. This seems innocuous enough, but it's counterproductive. We want the child to socialize with peers, and bike riding and going out with friends (if safe and otherwise fine) are good for the child. Here is a case where taking away the privilege might be effective but the duration of the consequence is questionable. If your child rides her bike every day, two days of taking away the bike is plenty. There's no added benefit to piling on more days or weeks. A steeper penalty does not have a stronger impact on children's behavior.

Bottom line: Devote your principal energy to positively reinforcing the positive opposites; if you do punish, do it mildly and don't use a behavior you want as a punishment.

4. When punishment is used as part of a reinforcement program, it should be delivered immediately after the behavior. If the purpose is changing behavior, delayed punishment—"When we get home you're going to be sorry," or "Yesterday you teased the cat, so today you can't go out and play"—isn't worth the trouble.
5. Punish consistently and try to catch all or most instances of misbehavior with the punishment you selected. Punishing irregularly, catching the behavior a few times and letting other instances go, is doomed to failure. No matter how many times you punish behavior, be sure the positive opposite is reinforced for many more instances. Otherwise you basically have a punishment program, and be prepared for that to be ineffective and frustrating.
6. Behaviors you want to eliminate often have positive reinforcement associated with them. Ask yourself, when the child does this unwanted behavior, "Is there a response that makes it likely to happen again?" If that's the case, punishment is not likely to work. Here's why: the annoying behavior is immediately reinforced, and punishment after that sequence won't undo that chain. For example, in a class, if when a child shouts out even just one peer laughs or smiles or gives some attention, the child's shouting is being reinforced by his peers. The teacher might jump in immediately and say, "Two minutes of time out for you," but it's too late; the behavior has already been reinforced. Punishment will not work if reinforcement for the behavior is squeezed in first.

Delayed negative consequences do not overcome immediate reinforcing consequences. A child who takes another's lunch money, for instance, experiences immediate reinforcement of his act. He gets both the money and the frightened victim's submissiveness, a powerful cocktail of rewards. Any negative consequences will be delayed; eventually he may get caught and perhaps punished with detention or suspension, and his crimes may someday pull him into a long-term engagement with the legal system that impinges on his life chances in all sorts of ways. But those delayed consequences don't exert a strong influence for many reasons, key among which is that delayed punishment doesn't break the powerful behavior-building sequence of lunch-money theft followed by immediate reinforcement. In a different universe in which the consequences were reversed, as soon as the lunch-money thief said, "Gimme your lunch money," he would suffer all the consequences that normally take years and even decades to show up: horrible pangs of remorse, existential despair, instantaneous teleportation to lockup in juvie and then the adult penitentiary, and a terrible beating or two from the fellow criminals he will eventually encounter there. Then, weeks, months, years later, he'd get the delayed rewards: a couple of dollars and the pleasure of his victim's submissive response to him. In that universe, stealing lunch money would not be reinforced, and he'd stop doing it right away. But that's not the way it works.

Remember the punishment trap, when a parent's habit of punishing the child gets locked in? That's another case in which the immediate consequences (the child stops misbehaving the moment she's punished) control the parent's behavior, even though the delayed consequences (in the hours and days that follow) show that the behavior has not changed at all—it still happens just as often. The parents who come to the Yale Parenting Center often recognize the delayed consequences; they know their constant punishment isn't working. But their recognition that what they're doing is failing in the long run is not as strong an influence on their behavior as immediate reinforcement. That's what makes it a trap. The punishment continues or even increases even though no one (child, parent, teacher) believes it's working.

Bottom line: Ask yourself, "When the child does this disruptive behavior, what happens?" Is the "what happens" something that might help maintain the behavior? If so, try to break the connection. That can be hard to do; it's one of the reasons that reinforcing positive opposites is so important and so effective. You might not be able to stop others from attending to some disruptive behavior, but developing positive opposites will give them fewer opportunities to attend to it.

## Punishment as a secondary part of a reinforcement program

There are four interrelated reasons why reinforcement should be the primary element of a program that also uses punishment:

- Positive reinforcement for alternative behavior increases the effectiveness of punishment, making it more effective in quickly and thoroughly reducing unwanted behavior. You can compensate for many limitations of punishment by providing reinforcers for alternative or other positive behaviors.
- Reinforcement can develop appropriate behaviors to displace the inappropriate behaviors that are to be eliminated. This is important because, while punishment can help to eliminate behaviors, it's not effective in building new ones.
- When you're positively reinforcing alternative behavior, less severe punishments are likely to be more effective than would otherwise be the case. Mildly aversive events that normally would have little or no effect—a grimace, calmly saying no—are much more likely to be effective in a richly reinforcing environment.
- Finally, positive reinforcement combined with punishment can reduce or eliminate undesirable side effects that might result from the use of punishment alone. Milder and fewer punishments are likely to be needed with positive reinforcement in place for developing prosocial behavior.

One parent at the Yale Parenting Center had an eight-year-old who constantly resisted her instructions. He just said, "No, I won't" to all sorts of routine requests: Get dressed so we can go, get ready for bed, come down to breakfast, finish eating your vegetables, and so on. She thought she was not being consistent in handling these situations, so she began punishing each instance with a very loud shout; she never hit the child, but occasionally she would slap the table with a flat hand to accompany the shout with a loud noise and aggressive gesture.

A little background is relevant. The mother had been divorced for eight months when she came to us. She and her son lived alone, and the boy made weekly overnight visits to his father. The divorce had two likely effects. First, children (and parents, too) often show disturbances in behavior—more psychological problems, stress reactions, moodiness, and the like—during that period of adjustment after any shakeup like a loss, move, or divorce. Even positive events, like the birth of a sibling, can have such effects. They're likely to go away on their own, but it may take some time. The child's behavior, and perhaps the mother's behavior as well, might temporarily be different from what it was and will soon be. Second, the mother now had a much more stressful life. In addition to her high-powered job as a prosecuting attorney, she had sole responsibility for all of the tasks that had been partially shared—paying bills, handling daycare—and now some new ones, like negotiating custody arrangements with her ex. When her child was sick or when daycare arrangements after school collapsed for some reason, the mother was on her own to manage it all. All of this led her to feel very stressed, which she recognized. We already know from chapter one that stress on a parent can contribute to a child's noncompliance because it affects tone of voice, level of urgency, the parent's willingness to give a choice, and other factors that influence the likelihood that a request will get the desired response. This is not about fault; it's about how we can effectively mobilize ABCs to change behavior.

We began the program exactly the way I hope you are thinking we did—with positive opposites. What behavior did the mom want? She wanted her son to do what she asked "without any lip" (her term). We asked the mom to "catch" all instances in which he did comply with a request—she had indicated that there were some, but it was clear that she really attended to and responded to the instances when he refused. We conveyed that the instances when he did do what he was asked were the ones to care about, take notice of, and praise. We practiced the praise in two separate sessions. She still felt he should be punished when he didn't do what he was asked to do, so we included a brief, nonverbal, disapproving look. Specifically, the mom was to shake her head back and forth (as if saying no with body English) and then purse her lips as part of the disapproving grimace. This was to be very brief (left, right, left head turn, count to three and no more). The main program was, of course, reinforcement of the desired behavior. That program would probably work all by itself, but we were also shaping the mom to use milder punishment. Also, as the research shows, if you're pursuing a strong positive reinforcement program, introducing occasional mild punishment (a look, mild disapproval) can speed the process a little—not a lot, but just a little.

We asked the mom to praise as many instances of compliance as she could and not to give the disapproving look more than two or three times per day. We added some antecedents to take the tone and stress out of the instructions to the child: we practiced using "please" first and having the mother smile a bit more when giving instructions. Both of these were likely to take the edge off of the instructions and so help compliance.

Within nine days, the child complied with almost all requests. The mother was really surprised and credited us with the change. But of course all the changes were made by her. While her son did not comply every single time, there was no more battle of wills. We also conveyed that it would still be good to praise compliance once in a while with words and hugs, especially if it was something especially difficult for the child or a request that he had not complied with recently. Also, we reminded her that it is common, normative, and very human for children (and adults) not to comply 100 percent of the time, and it would be unrealistic and unfair to expect anything close to that. We checked on progress, and after a while the program (praise and disapproving looks) dropped out because it was no longer necessary: noncompliance was not an issue.

During one of our follow-up calls we asked her about her punishment practices more generally and what she was doing. She laughed over the phone and said, "It's all about positive opposites! Were you trying to trick me with that question?"

## To punish or not to punish?

The research shows us that punishment is wildly overrated and overused as a way of changing behavior, and not among the most useful tools in a parent's toolkit, but the science does not quite support being categorically opposed to it. When used properly, even just a mild look of disapproval can be punishment, and it can be a useful adjunct to change behavior.

Many of my fellow professionals *are* categorically against punishing children, but most of their concerns are in relation to spanking and hitting children and extend beyond the purely scientific into the moral and legal realms. For example, it's usually against the law for one adult to hit another. Violation of the law has penalties, like going to jail. Yet in most countries there is no parallel law that protects the child in this way.

Once one throws out spanking and other aggressive forms of punishment—threatening, shouting, and so forth—and moves to milder punishments like calm reprimands or briefly isolating a child in his room, many of the objections subside, and that's where I see an acceptable place for punishment as part of a larger program to change behavior. But let me underscore that the science doesn't show any value at all in hitting children, and it does show that physical punishment, even when moderate and not abusive, can have long-term negative consequences for physical health (it's associated with more illnesses, earlier than usual death in adulthood), mental health (higher rates of psychiatric disorder in adulthood), and academic problems (children do more poorly in school and drop out of high school at higher rates). And yet research on the United States shows that everyday methods of punishment still include spanking for most children.

I advise against severe punishment and any punishment program that isn't associated with a strong reinforcement program for positive opposites. Punishment by itself is not likely to work and has all sorts of side effects, including harming relationships. Also, as we've seen, there is a tendency to escalate ineffective punishment. And I want to caution you against wasting your efforts on any punishment that is ineffective, even if it is mild, because it displaces effective procedures you could be using to make the changes you would like in your child's behavior.

Yet, research supports the view that when there's a positive reinforcement program to develop behavior, very mild punishment can help. A brief time out, a mild reprimand, some corrective feedback, a brief loss of a privilege—these can help a program work, as long as the emphasis is on positive reinforcement and punishment is an adjunct to this program.

**Dos**

- Think of the positive opposite whenever there is some annoying, disturbing, or otherwise undesirable behavior you want to eliminate. That's always the first step. Specify that behavior as a starting point to develop a reinforcement program.
- Develop a plan for how to reinforce the behavior. Maybe shaping or a simulation (chapter two) is needed. But what behavior will be reinforced and what reinforcer will be used? Praise is the default reinforcer because it can be so effective when delivered correctly.
- Employ a mild form of punishment.
- Accept that effective punishment will probably not fit the crime.
- Keep in mind that punishment by itself, severe or mild, is not likely to work beyond the moment in changing behavior. Reinforcing positive opposites is always key.
- Bear in mind that punishment is secondary to a reinforcement program; once a reinforcement program is in place, mild punishment can be effective as an adjunct.
- Be sure that instances of reinforcing the positive far outnumber instances of administering the mild punishment on any given day.

**Don'ts**

- Don't waste your creativity on coming up with novel ways to punish misbehavior.
- Don't believe for a moment that you are teaching a lesson or sending a message by rapid punishment of some act. Punishment does not teach what to do, and without teaching that, the effects on what not to do are extremely short-lived.
- Don't believe that knowing and doing are necessarily related. A

lot of parents tell me something like "My child needs to know that such behavior will not be tolerated in this house." That is fine as a statement, and I expect that your child, if she's old enough to discuss it, knows the rule. But knowing and understanding the rule by itself will not lead to your child changing the behavior. Bottom line: To teach knowing and understanding, talk about the rules, especially when everyone is calm. Look for opportunities to point out examples of following the rules if you see something on TV, in a store, at the mall. Say to your child, "Look how that boy is playing so nicely with his baby sister." But bear in mind that none of the above will be sufficient to get the behavior you want. Don't confuse ways of imparting knowledge with ways of changing behavior. Imparting knowledge is a useful first step, but the first step by itself does not get up the stairs to the behaviors you want. You still need reinforced practice and positive opposites for that.

## Withholding reinforcement

Many unwanted behaviors are maintained by consequences that follow from them. For example, temper tantrums and interrupting others during conversations are often unwittingly reinforced by a parent's attention. When you're trying to reduce a behavior, not paying attention to it can help by eliminating the connection between the behavior and the consequences that follow.

Often, an unwanted behavior may have received some reinforcer—for instance, when a child talks back, she gets lots of attention from a parent in the form of lectures, yelling, and other engagement. Withholding reinforcement means that the behavior (talking back, in this case) no longer receives that reinforcer (parental attention in any form), and it eventually decreases in frequency.

For example, when you're trying to start your car, the behavior (turning the key, pressing a pedal) is usually followed by the reinforcing consequence (car starting). But when your car is not working, your behavior of repeatedly turning the key stops pretty quickly after several unsuccessful attempts. Similarly, you may warmly greet a particular stranger whom you pass each day. Your behavior (saying hello and smiling) may be followed by positive reinforcement (acknowledgment and a similar greeting by the other person). If the other person's responses were no longer forthcoming, your behavior would be likely to decrease and perhaps cease. When the reinforcement that followed your behavior is no longer forthcoming, you're likely to do less of that behavior.

A typical example from the Yale Parenting Center was Danica, a four-year-old girl who played with her food at the dinner table. She made shapes of things on her plate or picked up some food with a utensil, raised the utensil high, and dropped the food back on her plate, and she also spit out food while blurting out something she wanted to say. Invariably, her parents were right there with something corrective: "Don't play with your food; finish chewing and swallowing before you talk," and so on. This corrective action was intended as punishment, but it was also attention for behaviors the parents wanted to get rid of.

Yes, negative attention can be a positive reinforcer for behavior. This is one reason why we make a distinction between rewards (something the recipient subjectively values or likes) and reinforcers. Probably no one on the planet would say that a reprimand is a reward, but because it entails paying attention to the child, it can reinforce a behavior.

As part of a program to decrease Danica's annoying and messy behaviors at the table, we began to break the connection between her misbehavior and her parents' pattern of paying attention to her. We wanted to reorient their displays of purposeful attention to moments when she was behaving in ways they approved of, ways they wanted to reinforce. As I'll explain later, programs of withholding reinforcement are not very effective by themselves, so the program was also part of—you guessed it—reinforcing positive opposites: eating correctly, speaking with no food in her mouth, and so on.

## Your withholding reinforcement toolkit

Because many behaviors are maintained by attention, the most common variation of withholding reinforcement is no longer paying attention to the behavior. This means looking away from the child or not making eye contact when she engages in the behavior. The tricky part is that sometimes the child's behavior is maintained by a reinforcer that's different from the one you've identified.

For example, in the case of Danica, the four-year-old with terrible table manners, the mother and father provided attention, and we thought that might well be the unintended reinforcer. But the rest of the story was very relevant. Danica had twin older brothers, age six, who were raucously amused at Danica's food behavior. They laughed each time her food splatted back onto the plate. One liked to wipe his forehead, laughing, as if her food had hit him. This sibling attention could have been the reinforcer maintaining the behavior, by itself or along with parental attention. Withholding reinforcement means no longer providing the reinforcer that is maintaining the behavior, but you have to be sure about the reinforcer to target.

We needed a two-pronged program. First, of course, we wanted a reinforcement program of positive opposites. The parents praised Danica at least three times during a meal for appropriate use of food and utensils. We specified praising at least three times, rather than "when you see it or when you can," as a concrete guide to help them. (There's no research specifying that praising three times per meal is a magic number. We just wanted to make it clear that reinforcing the positive opposite should happen a lot more than punishing the unwanted behavior, and we specified a number of times to help them remember to praise and to redirect their attention away from looking out for misbehavior. Praising good behavior four or five times per meal would be even better.)

Second, we wanted to remove sibling attention and laughing. To address that, we had the parents institute a group dessert program. The children were told that at the end of dinner there would be a dessert they could choose from between two options. They would get the dessert if Danica did not play with her food *or* if Danica played with her food but the brothers did not laugh or react in any way. The mother had the idea of putting the dessert on the counter, conspicuously visible from the kitchen table. This was clever on her part because seeing the reinforcer that can be earned is an antecedent (setting event) that increases the likelihood of getting the behavior. A shaping nuance: we suggested that the dessert-earning program at first not be for the whole meal—that is, we suggested breaking the time period of the meal into halves, and shaping more and more time of sibling behavior. Thus, at first if Danica did not play with food for the second fifteen minutes (second half of dinner) or her brothers didn't laugh if she did, the dessert would be earned. We chose the second half because that would make dessert—the reinforcer—immediately follow the desired behavior, and immediacy makes the program much more effective. If we chose the first half, that might have worked, too, but there would be a delay between great first-half behavior and the reinforcer.

Once this partial program was succeeding regularly, the parents could move to making good first- and second-half periods a requirement for earning dessert. The mother thought it would be easier just to include the whole meal, so she started with that. No harm done. If the whole-meal plan failed, if it turned out that the children weren't ready to do the full set of good behaviors required for the dessert, it would be easy to switch to the shaping plan. It turned out the mother was right. The full-meal plan worked, dessert was regularly earned, and most importantly, sibling consequences that helped maintain playing with food were eliminated.

Withholding reinforcement was also used in one study to reduce awakening in the middle of the night among infants. Nighttime waking, evident in 20 to 50 percent of infants, can be a significant problem for parents. And yet parents may play a role in sustaining night waking by attending to the infant in ways that reinforce the behavior. In the study, waking up during the night was defined as a sustained noise (more than a minute) from the infant between onset of sleep and an agreed-upon waking time in the morning. After measuring wakings for each infant, parents were instructed to no longer give attention to night wakings. If the parent had any concern about the health or safety of the child, the parent was told to enter the room, check the child quietly and in silence with a minimum of light, and leave immediately if there was no problem. This practice of withholding reinforcement led to a dramatic decrease in night wakings. The program was ended, and evaluation three months and then two years later showed that wakings were no longer a problem.

## Characteristics of withholding reinforcement

Like punishment, withholding reinforcement is not very effective when used by itself, although it can be useful when combined with positive reinforcement. Here are four characteristics of withholding reinforcement that give you a more nuanced sense of how it works:

*Gradual reduction in behavior.* Although withholding reinforcement effectively decreases and often eliminates behavior, the process usually is very gradual, both initially and overall. It could take many days. Several unreinforced responses may occur before behavior begins to decline. When the undesirable behaviors are dangerous or severely disruptive, the delayed effects of withholding reinforcement can be unacceptable.

*The burst.* At the beginning of a program of withholding reinforcement, the frequency of the child's unwanted behavior may become greater than it was before the program began. Things really may get worse before they get better; that's the burst. Numerous examples of the burst pervade everyday experience. For example, turning on a radio (behavior) is usually followed by some sound (reinforcer). If the radio no longer works so that no reinforcement (sound) occurs, attempts to turn on the radio will eventually stop. However, before this occurs, the response may temporarily increase in frequency (several on/off turns) and in intensity or vigor. The same is likely to occur when you're trying to start your car. If the car won't start (the reinforcer is no longer forthcoming after turning the key—the behavior), you'll stop trying to start the car. But before you do stop, there's likely to be a rapid burst of several vigorous attempts to start the car.

In parenting, one place where you're likely to see the burst is in the going-to-bed ritual. Let's say that a child has a little tantrum and creates a scene before going to bed. The parents have been going into the room, reasoning and then shouting at the child—attention that could be maintaining the bedtime tantrums. The tantrums are not the parents' fault, but now that the tantrums are occurring, their attention could be the reinforcer maintaining the behavior. Say the parents read this book but skip the part about the burst, and they decide they're not going to attend to the tantrums anymore. That is, they're going to use withholding reinforcement. So on the first night the child goes to bed and has a tantrum, and the parents don't go into the room but just let it go. The tantrum lasts fifteen minutes before the child becomes quiet and apparently goes to sleep. So far, so good. On the second or perhaps third night, the parents are doing nothing different—still ignoring. But the child's tantrum goes to thirty minutes and is more intense, too—all worse than it was before the withholding reinforcement program started. The parents now say, "Hey, this withholding reinforcement business doesn't work." They may go into the room and provide attention and comfort or perhaps some reprimands. Such attention (parental reinforcement) will increase the probability of intense tantrums because it comes when the behavior is worse than usual, so from the child's point of view that's what's being reinforced: stepping up the tantrums to get attention. To the parents, of course, withholding reinforcement may appear to be failing because the behavior has become worse. However, the effects of the program are merely beginning; that is, the more intense tantrum means that it's working.

Parents, teachers, or other persons who may be involved in a withholding reinforcement program ought to be forewarned of the possibility of a burst so that they don't overreact to a temporary increase in the unwanted behavior. But my experience is that forewarning is not very helpful. In the midst of a burst and tantrum, the parents look at each other and say, "That psychologist knows nothing!" and desperately rush into the room to shout at the child, "You'd better get to sleep! Now stop fooling around, or we will take away your junior year in college once you get bigger."

Instead of or in addition to the forewarning, it's better to add positive reinforcement for positive opposites to the program, as I will explain in detail later. The combined program is much more likely to reduce the likelihood of the burst. All that said, an initial burst of responses does not always occur when withholding reinforcement is used on its own as the intervention. However, when it does occur, don't reinforce this more intense version of the unwanted behavior. The danger of falling into the trap of reinforcing that more intense behavior adds to the risk of relying on a withholding reinforcement program in the absence of other procedures.

*Spontaneous recovery.* So you have made it past the burst and apologized for those nasty things you said to your psychologist over the phone, and now the behavior (minutes of tantrum) may be declining. We are still not home free. After a program of withholding reinforcement has progressed, an unwanted behavior may temporarily reappear, even though it has not been reinforced. That's called *spontaneous recovery,* the temporary recurrence of a nonreinforced behavior. When a behavior comes back, it's usually not as bad (extreme, severe) as it was before the withholding reinforcement program started and not anywhere near as bad as the burst. For example, if a child's tantrums are ignored, the duration of tantrums will probably decrease over time, possibly after an initial burst of responses. Now let us say we are down to no tantrums on some nights and three or four minutes of light whimpering on other nights. Now out of the clear blue, there is spontaneous recovery in which one night the tantrum goes back up to ten minutes. This will probably drop out on the next night and the behavior will continue to decline.

But, as with the burst, a major concern raised by spontaneous recovery is that the response may be accidentally reinforced. When withholding reinforcement is proceeding well and then for no apparent reason the behavior increases rather than continues to decline, it's understandable that some parents will look at each other again and repeat, "Told you, that psychologist knows nothing!" and then run into the child's room and tell him to go to sleep or this time he will also lose his senior year of college. It's important to realize that the spontaneous recurrence of a response during a withholding reinforcement program doesn't necessarily reflect the ineffectiveness of the procedure. We don't know why this happens and can't predict when exactly it will happen, but we know it's a normal part of the process. You have to be disciplined and stick to your commitment to extinguish the behavior. Like the burst, the spontaneous recovery should pass quickly.

*Possible side effects.* Withdrawing reinforcement may result in the child having emotional responses such as agitation, frustration, rage, aggression, and feelings of failure. The transition from positive reinforcement to withholding reinforcement is aversive and leads to side effects similar to those evident with punishment. So, there are emotional effects, and sometimes aggression. This should be a familiar process. For example, what happens after you put money into a malfunctioning vending machine? Once it becomes clear that the machine won't reinforce your behavior with the usual soda or candy bar, you are likely to rage, curse, and physically attack it. When you're repeatedly trying to start your car (behavior) and the reinforcer (car starting) is not forthcoming (extinction), are you likely to be all smiles, or to shout and smack the steering wheel?

In other contexts, individuals who have experienced repeated reinforcement of certain responses respond to the cessation of such reinforcement as a failure. For example, when an athlete performs poorly, he may swear, consider himself a loser, and throw a tennis racket or baseball bat to the ground in disgust. The notion of a poor loser signifies a person who engages in emotional behavior when his or her responses are not reinforced in a contest—that is, when the crowd no longer roars approval and the pleasure of winning is denied. A silver lining: with a program of withholding reinforcement, when side effects occur, they are likely to be temporary and to diminish as the target response is extinguished. Consequently, the side effects are usually not as bad as those associated with punishment.

## The key challenge: controlling the source of reinforcement

Withholding reinforcement sounds easy enough, even if it's not very effective by itself. Identify the reinforcer after the behavior (often attention) and just stop giving it. Of course, it's not always that simple. First, you need to exercise very careful control over reinforcers. Any accidental reinforcement may rapidly bring back the behavior you are trying to get rid of and make the process of eliminating the behavior even longer. Second, there are many situations in which you can't easily control the reinforcer that follows the behavior. For example, reinforcement is particularly difficult to control when it's provided by siblings or peers. Playing with food at the dinner table among siblings or clowning in the classroom are examples where the other children are likely to be the main source of reinforcement. A common problem in schools is bullying, and among the many influences that maintain it are peer attention and peers joining in to abet the bully. In fact, as research on bullying shows, when peers do not provide supportive attention and actually try to intervene to stop the bullying, bullying usually stops within ten seconds.

It's virtually impossible to control reinforcement for some behaviors. Consider Willie Sutton, a famously colorful bank robber whose mastery of disguises became part of his renown. In his memoir he says, "Why did I rob banks? Because I enjoyed it. I loved it. I was more alive when I was inside a bank, robbing it, than at any other time in my life. I enjoyed everything about it so much that one or two weeks later I'd be out looking for the next job." For Willie, the more obvious reinforcers—free money, the submissiveness of people he robbed at gunpoint—actually didn't seem to matter very much. Many behaviors, including such confounding activities as self-harming (for example, cutting oneself) or head banging (among some children with autism), are reinforced by consequences associated with the behavior itself (reduction of anxiety, the stimulation and vibration of the hitting). You can see why identifying and controlling the reinforcer can be difficult. If we go back to the more common situation—attending to a behavior as the main reinforcer—even here it's not always easy to be consistent. Among the reasons is that a withholding reinforcement program can take a long time, and you have to be diligent about not attending to the behavior as the gradual change occurs.

As a parent, you may make requests of your child to stop doing something, but the behavior is maintained by reinforcers not readily under your control. You may tell your child to stop bullying a sibling or neighbor, but bullying brings immediate reinforcement in the form of the victim's submission, and that connection is hard to control with delayed consequences. Or you would like your child to play computer games much less than he does, but that's hard to control because of the reinforcing value, the jolt of stimulation he gets when he plays the games. Parents of a fourteen-year-old boy came to the Yale Parenting Center because they had just discovered pornography on his computer in his room. The parents insisted that he stop watching and promised to take his computer away if they caught him disobeying. That approach was doomed to fail because of the rewarding value to the boy of searching for, finding, and watching the pornography. Sometimes the reinforcer can be identified, but extraordinary measures are needed to obtain control. In this example of Internet pornography, we helped the parents come up with a more promising plan: they tried to control the behavior by moving the computer to the dining room and controlling their son's use of it so that he was never unsupervised while he was on it.

There are ways to change each of the behaviors just mentioned, and withholding reinforcement can play a role, but not the main role. For that we need positive reinforcement of positive opposites.

## How to use withholding reinforcement so it actually works

1. The single most important factor in using withholding reinforcement is exactly the same as for punishment: it is a secondary procedure best used as a complement to a positive

reinforcement program. The effectiveness of withholding reinforcement depends on whether and how often the positive opposite is reinforced. Withholding reinforcement is a very slow process that often includes a return of the unwanted behavior in the form of the burst and spontaneous recovery. If one pairs withholding reinforcement with a strong reinforcement program, the undesired behavior drops out much more quickly and is less likely to come back in bursts along the way.

2. Be as sure as you can that the behavior you are trying to extinguish is not maintained by some reinforcer other than your attention. If your attention is not the reinforcer maintaining the behavior (as in the case of Danica's brothers thinking her food antics were funny), your ignoring the behavior will completely fail. Ask yourself, "When my child does this behavior, is there any response that occurs to maintain it?" If that's the case, make sure you end those consequences if you can. If you can't, withholding reinforcement won't work, but don't give up hope. Reinforcement of positive opposites should do the trick.

**Dos**

- Identify any consequences that might be following and helping maintain the behavior you want to eliminate.
- Try to break that connection so the consequence (often it's attention, and remember that even a reprimand can reinforce) is not provided anymore.
- Immediately consider what a positive opposite would be and start a reinforcement program for that.

**Don'ts**

- Don't believe that merely ceasing to provide attention will work very effectively. Withholding reinforcement is slow and not very effective when used alone.
- Don't accidentally reinforce the unwanted behavior. The burst and spontaneous recovery will put you to the test!

- Don't forget about positive reinforcement. Withholding reinforcement does not work very well when used by itself, but it can work very well when it's part of a program that also reinforces positive opposites.

## Conclusion

Punishment and withholding reinforcement are consequences that can have a role in changing behavior as part of our ABCs. They share some important characteristics. First, by itself, neither punishment nor withholding reinforcement is likely to be very effective. The reason is that neither teaches or develops the behavior you want. Neither offers opportunities for reinforced practice, so punishment and withholding reinforcement must remain secondary procedures, part of a larger program that centers on positively reinforcing the behavior one wishes.

Punishment and withholding reinforcement can be useful adjuncts. Mild punishment in the form of a look, gesture, statement, brief time out, or brief loss of a privilege can be effective if a positive reinforcement program is in place. Withholding reinforcement is important, too, because it's often useful to ask whether the disruptive behavior might unwittingly be maintained by some reinforcer in the setting. Attention (from siblings, peers, adults) is a likely culprit, or the behavior itself (for example, fighting, shouting) may lead to its own reinforcement (for example, submission by others). We want to break connections between inappropriate behavior and unwitting consequences that might maintain that behavior. Often that's not easy to do. Happily, we do not have to break the connection to change behavior. Reinforcement of positive opposites can still help here. Even so, always check what could be maintaining that disruptive behavior and try to stop those consequences if feasible.

# 5

## The Routines of Family Life

### *Creating the Context for Success*

So far we've focused on filling your parenting kit with tools that can be used to alter specific behaviors and develop broader characteristics like cooperation, persistence, or generosity. But this chapter takes a step back from the nuts-and-bolts details of the ABCs to consider broader issues of parenting, the context or background of daily life. Psychologists call this context a "nurturing environment," and they devote effort to studying it because it makes a huge difference in how your child functions. The quality of a nurturing environment also directly affects your use of the ABCs, the tools in the toolkit, because it can have a strong effect on whether and how challenges emerge in your child's behavior, and on the ease or difficulty you encounter in addressing them.

A nurturing environment is to the psychological development of a child like exercise and physical activity are to her physical well-being. Exercise and activity—running around, playground visits, playing games outside, walking instead of going everywhere by car—are good for the body in the short and long run. They are a background set of activities that have broad effects on health, including decreasing the likelihood that a wide range of mental and physical problems will occur later in your child's life. Exercise in this general sense is not a specific treatment for some problem—as opposed to, say, particular leg-strengthening exercises used to treat a knee injury. Similarly, as parents you can create a nurturing environment in the home that can influence the general health and functioning of your child and make child rearing less challenging.

Providing a nurturing environment is discussed less in the media than exercise, but both are very well studied scientifically. And the bodies of research on both show that a nurturing environment and exercising share similarities in their benefits. Both are related to

- Mental health—better adjustment, fewer negative symptoms such as depression, greater ability to manage and reduce anxiety and stress
- Physical health—stronger immune system, less illness, a longer life span more likely
- Academic functioning—better performance in school, greater chance of graduating high school or college

Providing a nurturing home environment doesn't replace the tools I have described, and the tools don't substitute for a nurturing environment. Rather, they work together to bring out the best in your child and to put him on the best course that you as a parent can provide. Most children's lives eventually happen out of the home; the context you create for their lives in the home provides a sound preparation for that.

In this chapter I'll address several different aspects of providing a nurturing environment. They're all science-tested and valuable, and I urge you as you read to consider each in turn—even those that might already seem familiar to you—and how it might fit into your life. It may be difficult for you to imagine doing all of them all the time, but don't panic. Think about other recommendations you've seen that are based on sound research. Recommendations for how to eat in a healthy way, for instance, now often depend on the idea of a food plate as a guide. The plate has various portions of what we ought to eat as part of a healthy diet to control weight, slow aging, and reduce our risk for many diseases. Probably nobody can meet every single guideline and eat the recommended amounts of nuts, fruits, beans, whole grains, vegetables, and so on in a given day, but any effort you can make in that direction will help. It's worthwhile to do your level best to incorporate as many of these recommendations as you can into your habits.

As you read this chapter's survey of ways to foster a nurturing environment, think of it as a kind of psychological food plate for parenting and family life. I realize that it's unlikely that anyone can implement every recommendation on any given day, but your family will benefit from whatever part of it you can do. It's not an all-or-nothing proposition; try to do as much as you reasonably can. And, in addition to describing a number of basic features of family life that parents may be able to control for the good of the family, I'm also going to add a sort of No-No Plate of things you should limit or eliminate from your household, to the extent possible.

## 1. Promote good communication with your child as early as possible

Good communication refers to genuine exchanges in which you and your child talk to each other and, even more important, listen to each other. The specific topics under discussion matter less than developing and sustaining open lines of communication. Your child needs someone to help cope with and handle the stressors of her life, a person to turn to for sympathetic attention and advice as childhood blooms into adolescence. Anything you can do to enable communication is a significant investment in your child's well-being.

Most parents feel and say that their children can talk to them about anything. In principle and at some high level of abstraction they are absolutely right. Yet, while most children *want* to go to their parents about difficult topics, they often shy away from actually doing it because they expect that when they raise the touchy subject, the parent will respond with an opinion, directive, family ethical imperative ("We *never* . . ."), or dated story only vaguely related to the child's concerns. All of these typical parental reactions are aversive, leading to avoidance (as I described in chapter four) of even discussing such topics.

It's common for us as parents to feel that we have shown such deep and consistent commitment—think endless diapers, cleanups, sitting up with our sick child—that our children must know we're there for them. They do, in fact, know that, but knowing it is not the same as actually coming to you to talk about a difficult topic. The latter is a behavior, and, as I've explained earlier, when it comes to behavior, knowing and doing are pretty much unrelated. But if your child can come to you to discuss difficult situations with some confidence, based on experience, that you will listen and not preach or rant, this will greatly help his adjustment to stressors and traumas in everyday life. Also, open lines of communication will help you identify problems in their early stages and intervene long before they escalate. What makes this all especially interesting is that children actually prefer to talk to their parents about difficult topics—sex, drugs, you name it—rather than to their peers. So it pays to reduce the barriers that prevent them from doing so.

**What you can do**

First, get rid of saying to your child, or say no more than once per year, "You can talk to me about anything." Such a general reassurance about your approachability is what we call an "oblique antecedent," indirect and very far away from the behavior it encourages (it may be months before something comes up that the child feels he has to discuss with you) and is not likely to influence your child actually to come to you. Also, the proof is in what you model, not what you say. Ask yourself if it's really true that your child can come to you to talk about anything. Is the gate truly open, or, at least when it comes to certain touchy topics, does your child feel that there is actually a twelve-foot-thick wall she couldn't even try to blast through?

Second, listen to your child and her opinions, not only because it's good for her mental health and self-esteem but because of the exchange it represents. You listen because you want your child to share her views with you, and you expect the same level of attention from her. Think of negotiation not just as you talking and then your child talking but as you listening and then your child listening. That's the key. Your modeling of this behavior early in life will make later interactions with your child much easier. How do you know if you are really listening? Well, if you're waiting for your child to stop talking so you can correct her misconceptions, that's a pretty good definition of not listening. If you're thinking that something in what your child is saying might be new, deeply felt, and possibly disturbing, and that you need to respond by acknowledging that it's important, asking for clarification, or encouraging your child to give you more details about his experience, those are pretty good signs that you're listening.

Third and related, be an "askable" parent. This term is used to describe parents whose children feel comfortable coming to them to talk, especially about touchier subjects like intimacy, relationships, sexual orientation, substance use, confessions—in other words, about life. One key to being askable is how you respond during the conversation. After you've heard what your child has to say, do not begin by refuting it. Point out anything good in what your child said and praise your child for coming to you about it at all, to reinforce openness and exchange, even if you then propose a different way of thinking about it. And never use *dumb, stupid,* or other belittling words.

"Of course," you're thinking. "What kind of idiot would do that?" Well, lots of parents, even good and loving parents, do something like it. Again, and be honest with yourself: when your child talks, does he get the feeling that you're just impatiently waiting for him to finish so that you can state your opinion at length and in detail?

As an early teen, one of my daughters figured out how to get me to talk with her about an important topic that might ordinarily lead to my predictable judgmental reactions. Once in a while she would ask if we could talk "as friends" rather than father and daughter. A normal reaction would be for me to riff on how dads and friends are different, how I am not her friend in some ways and better than a friend in other ways, how *dad* spelled backwards is still *dad* but *friend* makes no sense when spelled backwards, and so on. But because she caught me off guard the first time, before I'd had a chance to rehearse my "not-friend" speech, I had no real choice but to agree. Asking me to talk as friends was a setting event, an effective antecedent that made me less likely to fall back on the usual parental judgments. (She had intuited a lesson from this book's first chapter, that getting behavior you want is as much about antecedents as about consequences.)

After all, when friends speak to each other about important or intimate topics, they don't usually hammer each other with statements like "That was terrible judgment! How many times have I told you not to do that?" My daughter wanted to talk with me about some relationship problem she was having—nothing shocking, but it mattered to her. She just wanted to lay it out and tell me what she thought, and she wanted me to listen nonjudgmentally and not weigh in with a solution. This was one of several requests she made during her teen years to suspend our usual roles for a moment in order to communicate better and differently. And I tried to let her modeling of this approach influence me; as she got a little older, I tried to tell her stories about my own experiences that would be of interest but did not have a moralizing message.

That brings up one more thing you can do: be a model for your child by talking about your own daily life. I don't mean baring your soul in an uncomfortable way ("I never truly loved your mother") or stressing your child with complaints or gossip about family or work ("I'm telling you, my supervisor is a total drunken SOB"). Rather, I mean that you can model talking about your life—stories about your own school days, stories about your workday, stories about minor frustrations and small pleasures and vivid memories. Modeling exchanges of this sort will do more to make you an askable parent than will declaring to your child, "You can talk to me about anything."

## 2. Build positive family connections

Promoting good communication between you and your child early will certainly be a plus to family life, but the parent-child bond and communication are part of a larger family network that's also important. Whether you've got a big family in your home or just a single parent and a child, the quality of interactions with relatives living in the home and beyond it can be of great help in promoting positive behavior by your child. Children with positive family lives do better in school and are less likely to show behavioral problems and symptoms of clinical dysfunction. That family life makes such a difference can hardly be news. But what you can do and its impact may come as news to you.

**What you can do**

First, the quality of family life is greatly influenced by rituals and routines that give structure to the week, the month, the year. The research suggests that the regularity of the activities is what's important, rather than the specific content of them. Having such rituals and routines helps reduce stress and anxiety among children and helps them avoid some risky behaviors as they turn into teens and young adults.

Rituals and routines can be extremely modest. Every Friday afternoon you might go food shopping, for instance, or on Saturdays you have a pancake breakfast, or you stop at a certain park when you come home from Grandma's house, and so on. A regular drive to ballet or swimming can double as both simple logistics and a week-ordering routine that gives you a regular time to talk about how things are going with friends, school, romance, and so on. Aim for regularity and frequency, but don't be so rigid that the routine becomes an additional source of pressure. You're trying here to build a reservoir of predictable experiences—which, in addition to all the other benefits, will become the basis of good memories. Good experiences founded in routines will build your relationship and make you more effective in everything you do as a parent, whether you are focusing on the usual ABCs with a younger child or on potentially serious issues with an older one. Small regular investments in your relationship are like regular deposits in your savings account. They accrue slowly, and the added amount at any given moment may look like nothing, but the compound interest, building on what was added before, is enormous.

Second, connect your child to other family members, including those of different generations. There are lots of benefits of such connections, including family routines that stabilize a child's life, and opportunities for the child to bond with and learn from adults who aren't his parents, a skill he's going to need to develop in life. Extended-family connections have not been widely studied in relation to children's behavior, but some recent research shows that children with connections to extended family have a reduced risk of problem behaviors.

Families tend to spread out, so it's not always easy to keep in touch, but try to build relationships that provide for continuity and roots with older generations but also for bonding with any of your child's closer-in-age relatives—cousins, for instance. If they live far away, it's worth bringing everyone together during the holidays, even if all parties have to travel to meet in the middle. If you're not around extended family, and especially if you're a single parent, perhaps try to make some time—a picnic or outing, say, or any kind of visit—in which you and your child can spend time with another single parent with a child. Often a church or other community connection is a good way to find such peers, and there's at least one international organization for single parents and their children. Also, you can establish routines for using social networking (Skype, Facebook) to keep in touch with a grandmother, uncle, or cousin.

Finally, don't buy into the myth of quality time; value quantity time, and provide as much of it as your life allows. Be around, be together, and maintain family routines linked to regular household business, like meals and errands. This kind of mundane quantity time is much more significant than that one memorable quality-time outing to a big event at which you spend a lot of money. Quality time is nice, but it's never a substitute for quantity time. Imagining that it might be was the rationale of a busy generation. A very special forty minutes of parent-and-child time per weekend is a good thing—and it's lovely if you don't spend that time arguing—but you need plenty of quantity time as well to help get the child to the place you might like him to be in life.

Think about quantity versus quality in reading to your child. It's better to read pretty good children's stories to her every day for twenty minutes than to go all week without reading to her and then on Sunday read the greatest children's book of all time to her for three hours. She's going to get a lot more out of a daily dose of reading, and it's far more likely to positively affect her reading skills and academic performance.

One appealing thing about quantity time is that you don't have to do anything special or have a scheduled activity; just arrange to be together, to be available to each other and interact normally.

## 3. Promote positive social behavior

*Positive social behavior* is a broad term covering the ability to interact with others in constructive ways. I'm talking here about the basics of getting along with others: cooperating, being sensitive or responsive to others, maintaining relationships, being able to engage with others. These behaviors vary markedly over the course of one's life as different types of relationships emerge, a sequence that begins with a child's relationship to parents and siblings and extends to playmates, friends, schoolmates, teachers, eventually a spouse or partner, and, in time, perhaps your child's own children. In childhood, the basis of such relationships throughout life takes form.

We know that children who engage in positive social behaviors do better in their schoolwork and also are less likely to engage in disruptive behavior, bullying, and substance use and abuse. Over the years, research has shown that these positive social behaviors are especially important early in life. To prepare children for entering school, for many years the emphasis was on giving them early exposure to academic activities, such as learning how to read as early as possible. To be sure, such activities are important, but current views focus more on social behavior, preparing children for school by developing their ability to interact with others, to cooperate, share, play nicely, and listen to adults. This is understandable. No child gets kicked out of daycare or even first grade for failing to master multiplication tables or the interpretation of *Curious George*, but children, including three-year-olds in daycare, do get suspended all the time for failures in social behavior—the negative opposite of those basic social skills I just mentioned. So positive social behaviors are important early in life, and their importance continues in the elementary through high school years, and of course into and throughout adulthood.

Some children come into the world ready to be in a receiving line, to smile, greet, and welcome every stranger on the planet. But most of us are not in that group, so it's good to know that there are ways to help our children develop positive social behaviors. We know all this from studies that actually develop social behavior and evaluate its benefits over time and across many areas of functioning. At the Yale Parenting Center, we have studied this for decades and have shown that when positive social behaviors are developed in children who are having difficulties, many other parts of their lives change, including improved school functioning, better peer relations at school, better family relations, and fewer symptoms of psychiatric disorders.

**What you can do**

Help your child develop good relations with others as opportunities arise, and, with reinforced practice in mind, look for ways to increase the number of opportunities for positive social behaviors, especially if they're not occurring often enough now to reinforce and build on. Children come into the world with different temperaments; there are biological propensities for being withdrawn, shy, flexible, gregarious, extroverted, and all shades in between. Any parent with one child understands this, but parents with two or more children are often stunned by how two children can be so different so early in life. Differences in temperament mean that different children will find it more or less natural or easy to do certain things, like being social.

If social relations come pretty easily to your child, it won't take much work for you to cultivate these skills. A play date, a sleepover, taking one of her friends with you on a family outing once in a while—that might be all that's needed. Also, if there are neighbors to play with casually or other play opportunities that require little arrangement, all the better. As your child engages in social interaction, monitor how he is doing. Especially with younger children, parents almost always monitor for safety, but I'm talking about a different kind of attention to your child at play. Do you see any problems with sharing, taking turns, being reasonable with the other person? If you're seeing a repeated negative social behavior that you want to address, go immediately to the next and all-important step: What are the positive opposites for you to develop?

The strategies outlined in prior chapters might be helpful if a particular area needs a little work. That is, think about antecedents to help promote a particular social behavior, shape to develop small activities that may help along the way, and use special praise for the right kind of interactions. You may need to help out a lot, especially in the early stages—for instance, by walking a younger child to the park and staying nearby (setting events to make it easier for positive social behavior to occur). Commands ("Just go over there and play with those kids like everyone else") are not very useful as prompts for many children. Better to accompany the child and look for slight social behavior to reinforce, like playing near someone or handing another child a toy. Let your child be your guide as to where shaping begins. Remember, when it comes to a particular aptitude or behavior, shaping begins with just a slight step up from what your child actually does now.

Even if your child is withdrawn and doesn't start up with others easily, you can still work on social relations. Start with small doses, not a full sleepover or four-hour play date. Shaping and a more gradual approach can really help. If that still seems like a stretch for your child, have him select a friend to accompany all of you on a family outing to the beach, an amusement park, whatever you enjoy. Your child and his friend will be together, but your child has the security of your presence as you begin the process of shaping that will eventually lead to more independent socialization without you so close by.

You can do plenty to help your child build social skills, and your efforts will pay off. As your child reaches school age and leaves the home more and more on her own, her adjustment will be much better if she is socially adept. That doesn't mean she has to be popular; research shows the benefits and protections of social support can stem from having even just one friend.

Another way to help build positive social relations is to develop one or more competencies in a child that involve or eventually will involve activities with other people. It's useful to help your child develop some skill, interest, or talent that can continue over many years and pay dividends in social engagement. In relation to social behavior, not all areas are equal. That is, some are more likely to promote interactions and connections with other people over time. So first-person-shooter video games don't hold much promise, but music lessons, for instance, not only build skill on an instrument, but they also bring the child into contact with other children at lessons, recitals, school orchestras, and perhaps loud jam sessions in your home. Music entails many solo hours of practice, of course, but they lead to engagement with others. Other arts (for example, theater, dance) and sports (such as gymnastics or baseball) may do the same in terms of building competence and fostering social behavior along the way.

You and your child will naturally select an activity according to your own preferences, but among the possible choices give special consideration to those activities that are likely to be more social over time and that are likely to be lifelong or nearly so. We want the child to be involved with others and to gain the mental and physical health benefits that socialization provides. We are talking about childhood, but the mental and physical benefits of positive social behaviors are lifelong.

## 4. Foster flexibility in your household

Flexibility refers to openness to change and compromise—and I'm talking about your own flexibility more than your child's. Flexibility can be difficult to accomplish when running a home because there's so much that cannot be flexible, such as getting out the door on time in the morning, ensuring that meals are on time, scheduling babysitting coverage, making sure that homework goes from the child's backpack to her desk to done and back into the backpack, and so on. In many contexts, *flexible* just sounds like another word for *loose,* and in many cases loose won't do.

But by "flexible" I mean trying to compromise when you can, and more and more as your child gets older and starts expressing preferences. The other extreme would be very clear and rigid statements delivered from authority: "Do it because I said so." You know now from your mastery of antecedents that such statements actually foster oppositional behavior and more noncompliance. And you also know that choice, real or in appearance, fosters compliance. In chapter one those lessons were related to specific strategies to change behavior, and here I bring up flexibility as a broader contextual influence, but the two kinds of flexibility are definitely related.

Flexibility and compromise represent a Goldilocks mean, a sweet spot, of parenting. It's difficult to be "just right." For example, we know that a child will have more behavior problems at home and at school when a parent is either too permissive (and is fairly unstructured and lays down few limits or guidelines) or too tight and restrictive (is authoritarian, controlling, with lots of rules and limits). Both extremes increase the risk for a negative outcome.

**What you can do**

There is much you can do to be flexible and set that as a tone for your family. You do need to set up consistent expectations for responsibilities at home and at school, and there's nothing wrong with maintaining high standards, but it's also useful to go out of your way to have discussions in which you listen to your child's view and make some decisions based on that.

Parents are often devoted to slippery-slope logic: "If I let this seemingly small thing go, I lose control, and my child will become a barbarian and will loot and burn our household, leaving no stone atop another." But that's typically the opposite of what happens. Go to war over every minor thing and you will lose both the battles and the war. You will also do some harm to your long-term relationship with your child, by making her more likely to see you as an unapproachable rather than an askable parent. And the metaphor of battles and war is misguided from the outset because it suggests that you are pitted against your child. A better metaphor: You are sailing a ship toward a goal of a well-adjusted, functioning, non-freeloading adulthood for your child. This requires tacking, which can look as if one is veering away from the goal, but tacking is often the best way to take advantage of the prevailing wind and make progress toward the goal.

Compromise when you can, and let some things go when you can. Consider bedtime, curfew, messy room, and weird personal appearance as areas in which you can give a little. When you give a little there, you can gain credibility, control, and reasonableness when the topics shift to rings through unlikely orifices, taking two years off high school to learn about the retro hippie network in the Southwest, and other subjects more likely to inspire a categorical *No!* from you.

At the Yale Parenting Center we find it helpful to discuss with parents whether they can bend or give in on some of their specific concerns. Parents and families differ, and it's important to find the flexible areas in each case. These areas of "give" can be little things for young children—loosening the rules around foods to eat on a given night, or what to wear on a given day—but for teens the process of negotiating can be more daunting and the stakes go up. One thing we suggest to parents is that they be less concerned about stage- or age-related events that are not likely to be harmful in themselves, are not likely to have permanent effects, and are part of the teen's age or culture. So torn jeans, orange hair, even a small nose stud—all stage-related, and maybe you can let them go. Or maybe not; each family is different, as I said, and flexibility differs in each case. But there are other situations—very provocative clothing, dating older men, using birth control at ages eleven and twelve (all issues that have come up at the Parenting Center)—that take the stakes up several notches and can lead in many directions to effects that last well beyond any temporary stage of development. In these cases you would be on sound ground not to compromise. When you're dealing with a matter somewhere in the middle—what time your child comes home from school, when and how often he checks in with you when he's out, using the computer, buying music files—can you reach an agreement that considers your child's views? Remember, if you're thinking slippery slope as the rationale for not wavering, you are likely to make yourself less effective as a parent and less likely to be a resource as someone to come to in time of need.

Flexibility and compromise are not primarily about the specific detail you may be negotiating. They're about your broader parenting style. In these negotiations you're also promoting positive communication, establishing yourself as askable, and modeling reasonableness.

## 5. Monitor the child and limit opportunities for behavioral problems

Monitoring means keeping track of where your child is, what he's doing, and whom he's with. Monitoring is most important for physical safety in the early years. Obviously, you don't want your toddler running into the street, getting onto playground equipment in ways that she's not ready for, or going off with strangers. But monitoring also plays a very large role in your child's adjustment, particularly in the preteen and teen years, and is an important contextual influence on development.

Whether children are monitored relates directly to the behavioral problems they experience. The teenage children of parents who monitor their whereabouts and activities are much less likely to engage in sexual activity and illicit drug use and other risky behavior. Also, more intense monitoring is associated with greater reduction in risk taking. This is referred to as a "dose-response relation": the higher the dose, the greater the impact. If you feel awkward and uncool about hounding your poor child, remember that there's a strong dose-response relation between monitoring and decreased risk. It's important to mention that risky behavior has important implications for physical health; we're still talking about basic safety, in a sense. Sexual activity in the young is usually unprotected, and the risk of sexually transmitted disease is a concern. Illicit drug use relates to overdose, more risky behavior, and death and serious injury, often car-related. All of this is documented, not merely scare tactics.

I want to make clear that monitoring is very compatible with giving your child freedom and responsibility. It doesn't mean keeping her at home, or driving her everywhere, or fearing the world. The witch knew where Rapunzel was—up in the tower, locked away from the world—but that didn't make her a model parent (and, by the way, it turns out that the witch didn't know who Rapunzel was spending time with in the tower, or what they were doing, a good illustration of the truth that lockdown isn't the same as monitoring). Knowing where your child is, who else is there, and who's in charge should go hand in hand with equipping and encouraging her self-confidently to explore her world, a goal incompatible with hovering-helicopter surveillance, obsessive check-ins every few minutes, and setting fearful, drastic limits on your child's movements.

One area where monitoring frequently comes up is after-school time, which can be difficult to keep track of if both parents are at work. It's even more difficult for a single parent. Yet you do need to know where your child is after school, whom he's with, and what he's doing. Not only are adolescents who are not monitored generally more likely to engage in all sorts of risky behavior, but lack of supervision after school is specifically associated with greater depression and poor grades.

In general, over the course of development, boys engage in more risky behavior than do girls. There can be many reasons for this, but one of them is thought to be the fact that parents monitor teenage girls more closely than they do boys. For example, girls have earlier curfews and more household chores to do. There's nothing fair or enlightened about this gender difference, but it has the effect of reducing girls' risk taking and improving their outcomes.

But there is more to monitoring than coplike surveillance, and quality matters as much as quantity. The members of families in which parents monitor their children have stronger ties, are more involved with one another, have warmer relationships, and are more cohesive and communicate better. A more approachable, askable parent with a warm relationship to a child will have more success in monitoring without turning into a warden. To that end, it helps to make monitoring normal and mutual in your household, which you can model by talking to your children about your day at the dinner table or during rides in the car. It also helps to begin early. Monitoring will not work if all of a sudden when your child hits age twelve you develop a new intense interest in her whereabouts that takes the form of verbal waterboarding. Also, making your home a place where your child can bring friends while you are there is a form of low-key monitoring that strikes a compromise with the adolescent brain's craving for contact with peers.

In the twenty-first century, monitoring your child's whereabouts to limit opportunities for problem behaviors is a commitment that extends into the virtual world. First, you have to set limits on access to computers, smartphones, tablets, and other such devices. Here, too, if you can't monitor how the computer is being used, all sorts of untoward things can happen: children and adolescents can readily get to sites that you would not approve of (pornography sites, for instance), engage in activities that can promote problem behaviors (video games and activities that focus on violence, stealing, and general hatefulness), and get caught up in online bullying.

**What you can do**

Establish early in the child's life that all family members routinely should know where everyone is. As your child is developing, make it natural to ask about activities at the dinner table. Make sure to establish a routine of monitoring and caring about where other family members are. The objective here is not a family police state; rather, it's a household in which everyone takes a supportive interest in the lives and well-being of others. Establishing that climate will save you, years later, from the chore of ineffectively interrogating your teen to determine where he was and what he was doing during the fifty-three extra minutes it took him to get home from school.

For older children and teens, you might try to develop the habit of calling in periodically (not every minute) to keep in touch. The cell phone has had plenty of bad effects on family life—distraction, separation, bad manners, and so on—but it does have the virtue of providing a handy way for older children to keep in touch.

Limiting the child's opportunity for problem behavior involves knowing whom she's with. Let's say your child is going to a friend's house after school. That sounds good and maybe especially good because you are fostering social relations, which we have already covered. But it could also be unwise. Will there be an adult at the house? Is that adult responsible or flaky? Perhaps give the parents over there a call before the event to confirm. Your child might say, "What, you don't trust me?" It's a fair question. The answer is yes, but your child is still a child, which means you need to know what's going on. We know already from piles of studies that the teenage years are a time when risky behavior increases; that's common. We know too that when teens are with each other and no adults are directly involved, risky behavior goes up a notch.

You are trying to get your child through a difficult period. That doesn't mean you'll cut out all risk—or would want to cut it all out, since adolescents who take no risks at all tend toward the same negative life outcomes (greater risk for poor physical and mental health in adulthood) as those who take too many—but it does mean that you want to channel that risk-taking impulse away from danger, especially by minimizing situations in which such dangerous risk taking is more likely to take place.

Another thing you can do is to build and model bonds to conventional values; working hard in school, time with family, and constructive extracurricular activities are still rewarded in the long run in our society. Developing these values early in childhood reduces the likelihood of aggressive behavior and risky activities later during adolescence, for instance. I have seen many parents loudly dismiss the value of classes their children are attending or comment freely on the incompetence of a specific teacher or schoolteachers in general. Yes, they're modeling candor, but at the price of undermining values that in the long run will greatly increase the likelihood of their child making it to adulthood ready for the next phases of life. (If it helps, remember that your child probably did not select his school; you probably did.)

Establishing routines and rituals within the family—special holidays, meals, weekly errands done together with a child, activities in the home that are a regular part of everyday life—can facilitate bonding to the family. Your evident valuing of reading and learning, of teachers and their mission, of doing well in school, and of other aspects of education will be helpful in a preventive way later. This doesn't mean expecting perfect or even necessarily high achievement, but it does mean explicitly valuing academic effort and an appreciation of school. And it also obliges you to model the behavior you want: not only respect for school but also moderation, reason, hard work, whatever you expect of your children. The research shows, for instance, that parents who talk about the riskiness of substance abuse and who don't engage in it themselves measurably reduce their children's risk.

### 6. Minimize negative social and psychological conditions for the child

I have been talking about making the most of positive contextual influences that will make child rearing a little easier and that will boost the likelihood that your child can function well in different ways: physical and mental health, school performance, relations with other people, and more. These contextual influences also increase the effectiveness of all of the strategies I have discussed in the other chapters. When the nurturing environment is strong, everything works better: antecedents, shaping, praise, even (brief, mild) punishment.

But then there's the other side: trying to minimize conditions that are harmful to development. Several household conditions can be toxic in the sense that they have negative short- and long-term effects on child development. At the extreme, I don't think I need to tell you that physical abuse of any kind puts a child at risk for a variety of serious negative outcomes and can greatly harm physical and mental health, but less extreme household conditions can also have very negative effects, and here I think I can pass along some advice derived from the research that may be of use to you.

Children living in stressful environments because of their interactions with others can suffer surprising negative effects. For instance, changes that have been identified in the brains of children under prolonged stress in the home appear to underlie not only the psychological symptoms you'd expect, such as depression and anxiety, but also deficits in verbal IQ. Even when a child isn't being physically abused, the damage is biological. For example, if a child is subjected to verbal or emotional abuse by parents on a regular basis or continually exposed to parental conflict in the home, the range of undesirable outcomes includes a weakening of the child's immune system, so that he's more likely to get sick. If the stress conditions continue—and we don't know exactly how long they must continue to have this effect—the weakening of the immune system endures and his system doesn't bounce back. This is why children who grow up in harsh and stressful environments do not live as long as they otherwise would be expected to and are more likely eventually to die of cancer, heart disease, and other serious diseases. And verbal abuse is only one producer of consistent stress. Others include a parent turning hot and cold emotionally or being wildly inconsistent in rules and enforcement, so that the child can't depend on her.

I talked about building routines and rituals and how important they are. The other side of that coin, a household without enough routines, falls into a state sometimes called "family chaos." Its main trait is not enough predictability in parents' behavior and family activities. It puts a lot of stress on a child when she doesn't know if or when dinner will happen on a given night, or whether she can count on her parents for a ride, when bedtime will be, or whether the rules have changed and how strictly they will be enforced. One father we saw at the Yale Parenting Center generally didn't care about chores but, when he'd had too much to drink, screamed at his child for not doing all of the dishes, and he pulled him out of bed at night to "finish the job" in the kitchen. The exact standard isn't what's important here; each home can set its own. But big swings in standards or in what's likely to happen when a standard isn't met can become a major stressor. Routines and rituals allay a child's anxiety and make for a much more harmonious home life; chaos in routines and wide fluctuations in parents' behavior increase the child's risk for many problems related to stress, anxiety, and behavior problems in school.

A word on punishment, specifically corporal punishment. Regular hitting of a child, even if it doesn't reach the legal definition of child abuse (which usually means leaving marks on the child and/or using an object other than one's hand to hit), can have exactly the effects we are talking about on physical well-being (depressing the function of the immune system), psychological well-being (increasing aggressive behavior, for example), and academic functioning (making strong academic achievement less likely and placement in special classes for behavioral problems more likely).

There is no reason to panic because you argue with your spouse or yell at your children now and then or have even swatted your child on a rare occasion. Most people with spouses or children do that. We're talking about sustained, ongoing stress, not the usual ups and downs of family life.

Among the challenges for us as parents is that often we do not know the sources of the child's stress. For example, bullying is one of the most stressful experiences schoolchildren report, and their parents usually are unaware of it. The challenge of helping with children's stressors increases because children experience their own stress but also the spillover of their parents' stress. Parental stress, whether it's caused by financial problems or difficulties at work or relationship woes, filters down to the child.

**What you can do**

Stress is part of normal life. You can start by making sure that your child isn't getting an overdose of it in the form of prolonged household conflict, relentless belittling and dismissive comments, harsh and frequent punishment, or unreasonable levels of family chaos.

In any life there will be crises, such as divorce, moving the child away from friends and a familiar school, bouncing back and forth in joint custody, and the like. These can be very stressful. Try to be as comforting and understanding as possible, and to keep activities and routines as consistent as possible with pre-crisis activities (especially if the crisis is a divorce). One of the lessons that authorities and researchers have learned from responses to natural disasters like hurricanes, earthquakes, and tsunamis is that they need to be ready in advance to get the schools open again as fast as possible after the disaster hits. Among the many positive effects of a return to school is the sense of returning families to a familiar routine and sense of purpose.

The specific tools and strategies I've outlined in the previous chapters can have a positive influence on the overall conditions of stress that are toxic to a child. Our own studies at Yale have shown that parents who carry out the strategies we teach (ABCs) to change a child's behavior are more consistent in their parenting, which lowers the stress on all members of the household. Not only does the child's behavior improve, but parents who are no longer winging it in angry desperation experience much less stress in their lives. That lowers the stress on both parents and children in a mutually reinforcing way, and family relationships improve.

This is a good place to make an important point about the mutually supporting relationship between the contextual influences I'm talking about in this chapter and the tools and skills (the ABCs) I've presented to you in the chapters that came before. When you use the ABCs, you not only change your child's behavior, you also change your household's psychological climate, the context. And the reverse is also true: when you work to improve the context, one major benefit is that it makes your use of the ABCs to change behavior more effective. Improving context by improving communication with your child or strengthening her bond to constructive values won't, all by itself, get her to complete her homework or not beat up her brother, but it makes it easier for you to use the ABCs successfully to address specific matters like homework or fighting.

Finally, in terms of what you can do, I have been emphasizing praise as a way to change behavior. The praise I've covered in this book is very strategic (you want to change something in the child) and has to be done in a special way to be effective (enthusiastic, state exactly what you are praising, end with a nonverbal pat, touch, high-five). In terms of stressors and helping your child, the other, not-so-strategic kind of praise and affection is also important. Hugs, expressions of love and support, and clear indications of the joy you take in your child all are important to build the secure attachment of your child to you. That secure attachment will improve your child's development and also provide a foundation to address the often daunting challenges of life once the child begins leaving the home. When we ask parents who come to the Yale Parenting Center if they praise their children, they invariably say yes, a lot, all the time. They're talking about the general nonstrategic praise that makes for a great context for a developing child. We end up focusing with them on strategic praise, as part of the ABCs to change child behavior, the kind of praise that virtually no parent does without special training (or reading this book). Both types are important, and one does not substitute for the other.

## 7. Minimize negative biological conditions

We know more and more about the intricate relationship between physical and psychological health. I've just gone over some ways in which psychological influences or experiences such as being stressed or feeling ostracized can affect physical health—by, for example, weakening the immune system. Also, we know that the reverse influence also occurs: research on adults shows, for example, that physiological or biological conditions such as a heart attack or taking medications for various disorders can influence psychological health—affecting the onset of depression or disturbances in thinking.

But biological factors that influence your child's psychological health are less well understood than many online sources would have us believe. On the Web, for example, there's unlimited advice about special diets and which foods to consume or avoid, and you will find assurances that various vitamins and hormones, spices, or suppositories will prevent and treat all sorts of conditions related to child development, especially psychological disorders like attention deficit hyperactivity disorder, autism, or depression. Most of the claims turned up by a Google search are just not supported by research. It is so difficult for us as citizens to tell what is promising and might be helpful and what is just an opinion with no strong basis. The difference is important because many ineffective elixirs stop people from seeking more effective interventions. Also, some have harmful side effects.

Yet we do know that some biological factors do promote or thwart child development, and we can highlight main influences. First, prenatal habits and nutrition are important beyond the obvious physical development of the child. Substance use in pregnancy such as cigarette smoking and moderate to heavy alcohol use is well known to relate to various physical conditions that can afflict a child (for example, defects in the heart and kidneys, facial abnormalities), but it also relates to behavioral and psychological problems such as hyperactivity, aggression, and learning disabilities. The relations are not one to one in the sense that all early exposures of the fetus to these substances invariably lead to these other outcomes. But substance use, along with poor diet during pregnancy and general poor health of the mother, increase the risk (that is, the likelihood) of behavioral problems emerging in the child. Yet it's also true, and this is an especially frustrating aspect of these relationships, that a parent can engage in the very best prenatal habits and things can still go wrong in the child's development.

A few toxins in the environment that can influence a child's behavior are known and ought to be controlled. Cigarette smoke is a primary example. Children who have secondary exposure to cigarette smoke in the home—that is, the children don't smoke, but their parents or others in the house do—are much more likely to have behavioral problems, including aggressive and hyperactive behaviors, as well as a variety of respiratory diseases, hay fever, ear diseases, eczema, heart disease, sudden infant death syndrome, cognitive deficits (impairment of thought processes), reduced math and reading skills, and premature death.

Are the behavior problems caused by the cigarette smoke and its residues? We aren't certain yet, but many other potential contributing factors have been isolated and evaluated, including parents' income and education levels, which are also related to child health, and they don't explain away the correlation between cigarette smoke and children's behavior problems. Again, we can't conclude that the smoke causes behavioral problems in all children, but it does make such problems more likely. National surveys in the United States as well as many other studies have shown that children in homes where at least one parent smokes are much more likely to show aggressive behavior and other behavior problems. A strong body of research details the dangers of secondary smoke for children and also adults, especially if they are in situations (home, work) where they are getting a regular dose of secondary exposure.

And then there's tertiary exposure, which means exposure to traces of smoke that for years remain on the walls and other surfaces in the home, in the car, on parents' hair, and so on. It's less well studied than secondary smoking, but tertiary smoke exposure is known to have harmful physical effects on infants and children, increasing the risk for asthma and other respiratory diseases. The impact on behavior and learning is not yet clear, but some evidence suggests that tertiary smoke may impair a child's cognitive development (thinking) and ability to concentrate and be related to a greater risk of hyperactivity. In general, children are more likely to have behavior problems in a home where there is cigarette smoking or the products of cigarette smoking. Child rearing might be a little easier if this contextual influence were removed from your family's environment.

Deposits of lead, a heavy metal, accumulate in the body, including in the brain, and lead to serious physical health problems and in heavy doses even death. Lead exposure has all sorts of psychological effects that have been well documented. Children exposed to relatively low levels of lead show lower IQ scores and do more poorly on tasks involving math or reading, or that require concentration. They are more likely to be hyperactive and to experience mental retardation. Lead has been controlled pretty well in the United States in recent years and is much less of a problem than it once was. Lead-based paint, lead-lined plumbing, leaded-gas fumes from gas in cars, and other such sources have been limited. Still, some cans of food from foreign countries use lead, some imported candies still have lead in the wrappers, and some ceramic containers, particularly from other countries, have lead that can leach into food or drink taken from them.

**What you can do**

Obviously, it's essential to do your best to keep your child away from cigarette smoke, lead, and other toxins. But is there anything positive to be said about biological factors that can help child rearing and relate to children's behavior? Yes. For instance, studies have shown that diets low in omega-3 fatty acids are related to psychological problems, including depression and aggression. These fatty acids are found in fish, such as salmon, tuna, and halibut; in other seafood, including algae and krill (granted, algae and krill omelets are hard to find in most restaurants); and in some plants and nut oils. They play a major role in brain functioning, heart health, and normal growth and development. In relation to behavior, evidence suggests that taking omega-3 supplements during pregnancy can increase a child's mental processing ability and reduce discipline problems four years after the child is born. The work is proceeding but it's still preliminary. Researchers are currently trying to determine the most effective dose and whether there are any short- or long-term negative effects, so we don't yet know enough about omega-3 fatty acids to advise parents to take some pills and expect fewer discipline problems. No one vitamin, mineral, or food trumps balance, moderation, and generally healthful eating.

## 8. Take care of yourself

Your need to take care of yourself isn't limited to a concern with your effectiveness as a parent. But I mention it here, and in fact end this chapter on context with it, because taking care of yourself is related to your child's functioning in the home and provides an important contextual influence.

It's easy to forget to keep yourself in good mental and physical shape for child rearing. Parenting, running a household, working, sustaining a relationship, and planning for multiple futures (your children's, your own, perhaps your parents') combine to put a lot of stress on you. The challenges keep coming at you—and coming back at you, because you can't ever settle any one of them for good and cross it off your list of things to do. You're in for a long haul, the proverbial marathon and not a sprint, and you're going to need to be in shape for it. Actually, it's more of a triathlon, with three potentially exhausting legs—childhood, adolescence, adulthood—and you have to be in shape for all three.

It's important that you see to your own needs, and not just your child's, by building in your own downtime, your own social interaction, your own special routines with your spouse or friends. This isn't "me generation" propaganda or "I come first" selfishness; it's what the research on parent-child interaction tells us about the best route to effective parenting. If you're flat-out all the time, you're going to break down, or at least show the negative effects of that stress in how you interact with your child. Invest a little of your energy in yourself; it will pay off for your family, and you'll also be modeling for your children the importance of taking care of oneself, a skill you want them to learn. As airplane safety instructions remind us, you'll be a lot more use to your loved ones if you put on your own oxygen mask before you help your children put on theirs.

**What you can do**

You are the best judge of what influences help you retain sanity in a complex world. One person may find sustenance and renewal in gardening, another in playing in a band, volunteering, or taking a long walk. You're a grownup; I won't presume to tell you how to take care of yourself. But, as a rough guide, think of each of the categories discussed in this chapter as applying to you, too. "Build positive social relations," for example, means that you should have at least one friend you can rely on, and if you don't, take the time to work on it a bit. Even from the narrow standpoint of equipping yourself for child rearing, it's time well invested. Quantity time with your child may be more important than quality time, but quantity time is not very useful if you are feeling isolated, depressed, stressed, impatient, or under the gun without an ally to turn to.

## Conclusion

Context refers to broad, general influences on child rearing and development. I have saved them for last because they are not as useful in changing behavior when you have specific goals in mind such as getting your child to eat vegetables, to speak respectfully, to stop driving the downstairs neighbors crazy by jumping up and down on the floor, or to play gently with the dog. These and endless other areas of interest are readily addressed by the ABCs and your skill in using them.

The bigger-picture topics grouped in this chapter under the heading of context all represent influences that can powerfully affect the level of effort you have to expend on child rearing, the level of problem behaviors you have to deal with, and therefore your effectiveness in using the ABCs to get the results you want. Some of these connections of context and behavior change are easily seen. For example, if you don't take care of yourself (one of our contextual influences), your voice may be a little more stressed when you talk to your child, an antecedent for your child to not comply with your request to set the table for dinner (a request that, when you're under more stress, is more likely to come off as a command). Or, if a household is lacking in routines and tends toward chaos, bedtimes can fluctuate wildly, which means children are likely to be less well rested and more irritable and therefore less compliant with a parent's request to set the table. It's not accurate or useful to regard that noncompliance as the child's fault or as your fault—this is not about fault. It is about aligning the two sets of influences, the ABCs and context, to make child rearing easier.

I haven't even attempted to cover every significant contextual influence, and just because I didn't mention a specific aspect of context here doesn't mean that it's unimportant or unstudied in the scientific literature. The logic I followed in taking an admittedly partial pass through this chapter's vast subject matter was to focus on some major contextual influences that set the tone of the home, have been well studied by scientists, and are most likely to support and make more effective your use of ABCs. Keeping squarely in view that this book is about putting tools in the toolkit and using them effectively, I've let that priority guide me in my treatment of context.

# 6

## The Kazdin Method

### *In Real Life*

Throughout this book I've shown you how to use the ABCs and how to think about context to change your child's behavior and habits of mind. Your parenting toolkit is filled. Now I want to take you step by step through some behavior-change programs that apply the tools to the kinds of challenges that come up in everyday real-life settings. If you are wondering how to begin, which tool to pick up first, and how to lay out and complete the task, this chapter will help by giving you some examples that will serve as models for developing programs in your own home. Don't worry if your exact situation or problem isn't covered here. I'll concentrate on process, and my aim is to use these examples to help you set up your own programs to address your specific concerns. Before I get to the examples, let's start with a Kazdin Method blueprint, a summary of all the tools you can adapt to your own purposes.

### The Kazdin Method blueprint

***Step 1. Start by specifying the goal behaviors. What do you want your child to do?***

Define what you want in specific terms. What is the behavior you want to occur, and when? What would the behavior look like if it were exactly the way you wanted it to be? If you're interested in decreasing or eliminating some behavior, remember to specify and focus on the positive opposite.

It's valuable to write out exactly in a sentence or two what you want to see in your child. It's not as obvious as it sounds. A parent said to me, "I know when my kid eats vegetables at dinner: like never!" Yes, but in specifying the behavior, what will be the goal? Eating at least three forkfuls of vegetables? Eating all of the vegetables you serve him every night? Do some vegetables—say, fried potatoes—not count? Being specific makes a difference once we get to shaping and consequences. Fuzzy behavioral goals in the beginning can lead to very inconsistent reinforcement, so it pays to be specific up front. You can't specify everything that will come up, but try to paint a clear verbal picture of what the behavior you want looks like.

***Step 2. Antecedents: How do you get the behavior going?***

Use verbal prompts—clear statements, usually preceded by "please," with a positive (rather than authoritarian) tone, that specify exactly what you would like. The effectiveness of prompts is not increased by mere repetition; in fact, repetition decreases your effectiveness by making your prompts aversive.

You can use physical prompts, too, like gestures and modeling. You can, for instance, help the child with early parts of the behavior: "Let's do this together," or "Let's take turns; I can go first," or "Let's take turns and toss this coin to see who gets to go first" (a good addition of a little game or competition here).

You can also use setting events, which help set the stage for a behavior in addition to your use of prompts to specifically guide or instruct it. What is going on right before the behavior you want and leading up to that? Is there something you can control to make the behavior more likely? Well before bedtime, for instance, start some winding-down routine that is calm, quiet, leading to getting into bed. More generally, plan transitions from one activity to the next so that you're not springing abrupt changes or demands on your child if you can avoid it. Ask yourself, "If I want my child to do X soon, is what he's doing now a good or seamless transition to that?" If not, schedule something that sets a little better tone or platform for going to the next behavior.

If you feel it's likely that your child will resist what you're asking her to do, set the stage with some high-probability requests. These are requests she's likely to follow, like doing something with you, helping you, having a snack with you, anything that will not be perceived as a chore. High-probability requests can increase compliance with low-probability requests.

Give choices when you can because choice is a setting event that increases the likelihood of getting the behavior you would like. Even when there's no real choice to make—for example, homework has to be done before school tomorrow—there can still be choices along the way. "Would you like me to start the homework with you, or do you want to start on your own?" "Do you want to do the homework tonight at the kitchen table, while I'm preparing dinner, or in your room as usual?"

Finally, a challenge is a great setting event. For young children, a playful "I'll bet you can't . . ." can be a very effective setting event that motivates behavior and increases the likelihood of getting the behavior you wish.

### *Step 3. Behaviors: What can you do to get to the final behaviors you want?*

Think of the final behavior you want. What would you like the behavior to look like, as specified in Step 1? Write it down at the bottom of a blank sheet of paper. Now describe exactly what your child usually does right now. Write that down at the top. Think of these two lines you've written as the first and last of a list of steps. The top of the list, the first line, is what your child is doing now—say, no homework, and she won't even sit at her desk. The last line, the bottom of the list, is the final behavior that you want—forty-five minutes of homework in which the child is sitting at her desk at home, without having to be told, doing schoolwork assigned by the teacher.

Now consider shaping as inserting into the list some intermediate steps between the top of the list (nada) and the bottom (the final behavior). We want to shape the child's behavior in such a way that we systematically move from what the child does now to the next step (say, sitting down with homework in front of her for a minute), and the next (doing a few minutes of homework), and so on to the final behavior. Shaping will develop the behavior systematically and consistently so that the program will not have to be in place forever.

Avoid the trap of saying to yourself, "My child already knows how to do this final behavior, even if she refuses to do it, so shaping isn't needed." Remember that knowing that something is true about a behavior—smoking is bad for you, donating to charity to help children is good, eating spinach and broccoli is really wise, being less sarcastic with my in-laws would be good—is only weakly related to one's actual behavior. The point of departure for shaping is beginning with what a person actually does now.

If the behavior you want never occurs or is very infrequent, set up simulations in which you can get the behavior you want under fake or pretend conditions. Make up a game (for example, the Tantrum Game) and use antecedents (prompts, modeling, setting events like playfulness and choice), shaping (ask for just a little at first), and consequences (spectacular praise). How do you decide whether to use shaping by itself or to set up simulations? As a rough guide, if the behavior does not occur once or twice a day in any form so it cannot be shaped, go to simulations for a week.

Sometimes the child has done a particular behavior (a chore, for instance, or a school assignment) in the past but has stopped or slacked off for some reason, and you just want him to start doing it again. Here is a case where the child really has done the behavior (rather than just knowing how to do it), so shaping is not needed—no need to develop the final behavior. Also, simulations aren't needed because the behavior does occur, if you could only get your child started on it again. This is where jump-starting can come in handy. You help the child with early steps, to just get started. If the behavior is doing homework and he can do that, go with him to start the first task—then you can leave or fade yourself out as he gets going on the homework. When you jump-start, you ask yourself, "What can I do positively just to prime the pump and get the behavior going?"

Helping with early steps can get the sequence of behavior going, and you can also use antecedents—a challenge, a choice—and then, of course, effusively praise starting without you.

Behavior is a key step because the goal of the program is to get the behavior to occur often, regularly, and consistently. Shaping, simulations, and jump-starting are valuable aids to getting the behavior to occur so that you can reinforce it—and reinforced practice is the key to success.

***Step 4. Positive consequences: What positive consequences will you use to follow the behavior?***

You want to provide a reinforcing consequence for the behavior you are developing. What are the consequences you can provide regularly when the behavior occurs? Praise is the default consequence to consider—your praise and attention are likely to be very powerful. Yet praise has to be delivered in a special way if it is to be used strategically to change behavior. You need to be enthusiastic, say what exactly you are praising, and then add something nonverbal like an affectionate touch or high-five.

Points and point charts can be used. Points are provided for behavior and are used to buy agreed-on rewards. To provide a point chart you need a medium of exchange (such as marks, stars, tallies), rewards that can be purchased by the points, and a list of what behaviors earn how many points and how many points are required to buy each reward. Points can be useful to help structure and organize your effort to change behavior, but they can be a distraction, too. The magic is not in the points at all. Even when you are awarding points, the praise and attention that come with them remain important. Keep in mind that your objective is reinforced practice, getting the behavior to occur and providing reinforcing consequences, and points are merely one of several types of consequences.

***Step 5. Punishment: Is there any punishment that can be a constructive part of the program?***

Punishment is not needed to change behavior in most settings. Also, remember that punishment does not teach a child what to do and only temporarily suppresses the behavior you're trying to eliminate. At the same time, I recognize that as a parent you will want to punish some behaviors that you just don't allow in your home. So, if you have to use it, make sure punishment is mild and brief. A few minutes of time out is just as effective as a longer period of time out; take away a privilege for the day or evening, not two weeks. Most critical of all, any time you punish a behavior, make sure you're reinforcing the positive opposite of that behavior more frequently. If you're not getting enough chances to reinforce the behavior you want, consider shaping or simulations.

Also, if you are going to use punishment, plan it in advance. How many minutes of time out do you give for talking back disrespectfully? Where? In your child's room? Somewhere else? And if your child does not go to time out right away, what privilege will you take away, and for how long? Also, what if you wish to use punishment while you're riding in the car or shopping, and time out is not possible? Choose a privilege in advance that you can withdraw in such situations. When they don't plan in advance, parents often select an unnecessarily harsh punishment in the heat of the moment, which greatly increases the likelihood of undesirable side effects.

There's also withholding reinforcement—not attending to misbehavior. To the extent possible, ignore and walk away from behaviors you don't like. Attention to behavior, even reprimands or other negative attention, can reinforce the very behaviors you wish to eliminate. It is important to make the point that not all reinforcers that maintain behavior are positive, lovely events. When you get mad, when you yell and scream and rage at your child, you're still providing more contact, giving more (negative) attention to a behavior—all of which could unwittingly be maintaining behavior because such attention works like positive reinforcement. No child would identify your angry reaction as a reward, but it's still a reinforcer (that's why psychologists distinguish between reinforcers and rewards; they're often but not always the same) because your negative response is still attention, which can sustain a behavior like oxygen feeds a fire.

*Step 6. Do a quick check of context*

The preceding steps address specific procedures to use in developing a behavior-change program. Yet the context, the more general background or atmosphere in which you use the tools in this book, is extremely important. Context can have a big effect on the behaviors you may want to change, and on your success in changing them. For example, if there is a major disruption in a child's routines and activities, or a stressful event such as a separation, move, change in schools or classrooms, or an illness in the family—any such event that disrupts a more stable context could easily lead to an increase in the child's misbehavior. In these cases the child's misbehaviors are a common part of adaptation and will come and go as the routine hits an unstable patch and then becomes more stable again. In these situations, focus on putting as many of the context pieces we have outlined back into place as you can. Often you can diminish behavioral problems by checking on context alone and doing what you can to reestablish a familiar routine. Remember that the list includes promoting good communication with your child; building positive family connections; promoting positive social behavior; fostering flexibility in your household; monitoring your child—knowing where he is, whom he's with, what he's doing; minimizing negative social, psychological, and biological conditions for your child; and taking care of yourself.

## Real-life applications

Let's apply the steps more concretely to real children and real programs from the Yale Parenting Center.

***Real life No. 1: Rory, a three-year-old who has mastered the word* no**

Rory is a three-year-old boy who lives at home with two older brothers who are in elementary school. The mother and father report that Rory never complies with what they ask. He doesn't come down to dinner when called, get ready for bed, get dressed to go to the store, take a nap, or do anything else they ask him to do. The parents have heard about the "terrible twos" but did not experience them with their other sons when they were Rory's age. (The "terrible twos" usually refers to not listening rather than to tantrums and other, more serious misbehavior like fighting or destroying things, and when the so-called terrible twos do emerge, it usually happens at about age three.) All of a sudden it seems as if Rory has a will of his own, and his parents don't know how to manage him. In many such cases, parents become more forceful, a little harsher, and a little more insistent on being listened to. They often feel it's important to set limits and make clear who's in charge. That's understandable, but the usual method employed by parents is a show of strength, and that's an antecedent for more resistance and less compliance.

We begin with the first step of asking what the parents would like to see—the goal behaviors of the program we are to develop. They don't just want Rory to stop saying no all the time; they want him actually to do what they ask. We decide together that the positive opposite of saying no and not doing what they ask is to comply with their requests. We're shooting for consistency here, not perfection. I point out just as background that even the best-behaved children comply only about 80 percent of the time when asked to do something. We don't have parallel research on adults, but probably spouses, partners, colleagues, friends, relatives, and others do not comply all the time either. And if that doesn't persuade you to lighten up a little, remember that we do not even comply with our own instructions to ourselves (think: New Year's resolutions). So, although we won't insist on perfection, we have the goal behavior down: doing what is asked—within a minute of being asked, in fact, just to keep it precise.

Further discussion with the parents reveals that Rory sometimes does comply with requests. That's important to know because if the behavior occurs a little, we can easily build on that. Remember, if the behavior never, ever occurs, we might have to do simulations just to get it going. But it turns out Rory goes to the bathroom and brushes his teeth with his parents before going to bed, then goes to bed, then asks for a story and listens to it. Also, after some meals with the family he is asked to clear his place, as his brothers do, and he does that, too. So we have some positive-opposite good behavior to work with.

Let's consider antecedents. We already know the behavior occurs, but we want to check if there are antecedents that could be used better. Are there some antecedents that are interfering with compliance? I ask the parents to pretend I'm Rory and to tell me to do something, especially something Rory is likely to refuse to do. The mother asks me to get my jacket because we're going to the store. She looks me in the eye and holds up one finger on her right hand about chest high and points not at me or straight up but somewhere in between and says, "Rory—get your jacket; we are going to the store." This is a reasonable prompt, but it's easy to tell the mom is battle-worn. She's ready for noncompliance and has, understandably, already loaded her next response ready to fire when needed. We can help here. The prompt is good in content, clearly directing a specific behavior, but it could be improved in the setting-event parts. I ask her not to make any gestures with her finger. The pointing could decrease the likelihood of compliance because it adds a little look of force or authority. Also, her matter-of-fact, neutral tone is not bad, but it could be better. I ask her to smile as she speaks (to help control the pleasantness of tone). Finally, I ask her to begin the prompt with "please." All of these accompaniments to the prompt make compliance more likely.

She asks, "I have to do all of this just to get him to comply?" I assure her that it's just for a little while. Then I pretend she is Rory and say, with a gentle tone, no pointing, a smile, and "please," "Rory, please put on your jacket; we're going to the store. I can help you if you would like." Doing something with the child to help the behavior along is a nonverbal prompt. Giving Rory a choice (help if he would like) increases the likelihood of compliance. Also, actually helping him would be a prompt that could easily be faded later.

Still on antecedents, I mention that once in a while she can precede her prompt with a comment like "Rory, this might be hard to do. It's something you will be able to do easily when you're a bigger boy, but let's try just for the heck of it," after which she can go into her regular prompt, as we've practiced. This big-boy comment, a gentle challenge (as I discussed in chapter one), is a very important setting event that increases the likelihood he will comply.

Now to consequences. Rory does in fact comply with many of his parents' requests. The parents, like the rest of us, they tend to let the good responses go unnoticed and focus on the noncompliance. For a little while, we need to change this.

We ask the parents to find at least three opportunities each day to praise an instance in which Rory did listen and did what they wanted. There is no magic in the number three, but we give this as a minimum. Reinforced practice (occurrence of the behavior followed by praise) is the central concept, and we want repeatedly to connect behavior to positive consequences for compliance.

The father asks the reasonable question "Why praise him for something he's already doing?" The answer is that we want to increase compliance in all situations, and so for a little while we want to praise all compliance. It will spill over and improve compliance in the situations where Rory may now say no.

In addition to an increase in praise for compliance, we want to single out those instances when Rory has been likely to say no. If Rory complies with one of those requests, the parent's praise should be ecstatic. "I cannot *believe* you did that just like a big boy!" Now, if your spouse or someone else is around, bring that person into the room and tell him all about the amazingly excellent behavior. As that other adult enters the room, say, "Wait until you hear this: 'big boy' Rory did . . . exactly as I asked and right away! Can you believe it?" and the other adult will no doubt jump in, grasping the letter and spirit of the exercise, and that praise will further help. If all of this feels over the top, too much, and unnecessary—remember, it's all temporary while we're developing behavior, and these early steps are important and will help. And remember, also, that Rory is three, which means that over-the-top enthusiasm when his parents praise him will greatly increase their chances of success.

What if a child does not comply with a request? This is very likely to occur as we are developing behavior; we will not jump from a little to complete compliance. And, as I noted, even angelic children (or adults) do not comply all the time. If the request isn't urgent (say, getting out of the house for a doctor's appointment) and you can walk away from him if he says no, that would be one option. More likely the parent can provide a mild form of punishment. "OK, if you won't get dressed, I will dress you, and you lose fifteen minutes of your TV show tonight"—or "you get no dessert," or something equivalent. Be calm and nonpunitive in your tone, and if you have to dress him, do not do it harshly as if you are mad. That will lead to side effects, among them your getting hit in the face.

More focused consequences (better praise for compliance) and better antecedents should reduce the frequency of "no" and increase Rory's compliance. But there could well be one or two important areas that are still not improved. There are further options, such as simulation of these two areas in a game that earns points. For example, if Rory is still very difficult about taking a nap, his parents can set up a game in which he can earn points by getting ready to take a nap in a simulated situation (that is, they play the game when it's not really nap time), then cash in those points for a small extra reward or privilege: a chance to reach in a grab bag of little prizes, ten minutes of extra time before going to bed, that kind of thing. Alternatively, they can tell Rory that there are Special Rory Challenges. These are the requests for him to do the tasks he still finds it more difficult to comply with, like getting ready to take a nap. Before they ask him to do one of these, they say, "OK, here comes a Special Rory Challenge," then prompt as usual. When he complies in these situations, they of course lavish praise on him, but also add a special reward. Usually this won't be needed, but the term Special Rory Challenge is an antecedent that will mark these situations nicely for Rory, and the extra or special consequence can bring these around if they have not otherwise led to compliance.

***Real life No. 2: Emma, a six-year-old who has perfected dawdling***

Emma is a six-year-old in the first grade. She lives at home with her mother, father, and four-year-old brother. Emma's mom really wants help with her child's dawdling. Emma has trouble getting ready for anything—for school, her dance lesson on Saturdays, appointments of any kind, and just going to the grocery store. The most important, frustrating, and frequent situation in which this occurs is getting ready for school each weekday morning. She has not mastered "getting ready," although her mother has explained several times that "*ready* means that in the morning you are down here at the table, sitting, ready to eat breakfast so you can get to school on time. What part of that don't you understand?" Understanding is not, of course, the issue. It's a behavior problem.

The first step is to select the behaviors we want to develop and define them clearly. We will work eventually with more than one of the situations, but we pick one to begin with. Doing that will allow us to focus and achieve some change, and to make sure the procedures are effective and implemented carefully. Also, if Emma improves her ability to get ready in one situation (say, school-day mornings), the effect will spread on its own to other situations (say, before ballet on Saturdays) and we will not have to focus on each one in turn.

So we focus on her getting down to breakfast on time on school days. Emma's mom wants her downstairs at about 7:25, ready to eat breakfast, which is usually waiting for her on the table. She wants Emma to eat and be ready for the school bus, which arrives between 7:50 and 8:00. Once the bus pulls up, the driver waits no more than a minute before driving off. (When Emma misses the bus, her mom has to drive her to school and then drive in the opposite direction to take her brother to daycare.)

I ask a little more about the behavior. What, exactly, happens now? I ask this for two reasons. First, I want to see "where Emma is," because knowing what she already does will be a starting point for selecting where to begin shaping. Second, I want to check on all the antecedents because it's likely we could do a lot there to help get the desired behavior. I learn that the mom wakes Emma up at about 6:50 and asks her to get dressed. Then the mom is back and forth from the kitchen to Emma's bedroom upstairs several times to push her along verbally with prompts: "Come on, get dressed, what are you doing now? Don't dawdle!" This continues, with everyone growing more tense and peeved, until Emma gets downstairs at about 7:35 or 7:40, backpack in hand, gobbles some cereal, and is semi-gently pushed out the door while her mom hands her a lunch bag pretty much the way relay sprinters pass the baton. If Emma eats breakfast, has all her stuff for school, and is out the door by the time the bus pulls up, that's a "good day" scenario, although even on a good day her mom is already drained from the struggle to keep Emma on schedule. And on bad days, of course, the baton gets dropped and the morning implodes.

So here is our program. The goal is for Emma to get ready without her mom coming into the room and directing her so much. Having her mom constantly going in and out of the room will at best get Emma out the door on time, but only for one day at a time; it will not teach her to do the behavior without heavy pressure, and the cost is too great: having to keep the pressure on really wears out her mother before the mother's day has even had a chance to begin. We want to decrease the antecedents (prompts) because there are way too many, and we want to change their tenor (the mom's voice is usually tense, full of urgency and hurry). We want the mom to be calm, say "please" before the prompt, and prompt less.

On the behavior side, shaping is definitely needed. We want Emma downstairs on time all ready to eat breakfast and then to go out the door. We can break down all of this into parts. We will focus on three. First, being dressed and downstairs on time. To shape that we will reinforce any approximations of being ready (for example, partially dressed) but provide special rewards if Emma does more than that and is ready on time. Second, we will focus on two component behaviors separately: having her backpack ready for school and having her clothes ready to put on in the morning. We can work on both of these behaviors by having Emma complete them the night before. So on Sunday night, for example, she can earn praise and another incentive if she has her backpack all packed and ready to go for Monday morning and also if she has her clothes picked out and ready to put on in her room. Emma working on these the night before serves as jump-starting, or priming, the behavior of getting ready the next morning. That is, we have her already engaging in getting-ready behaviors the night before, so when she wakes up, she's already a few steps into the morning routine.

On the consequences side, we'll use praise for any of the steps that are completed, but we'll add a point chart to help Emma's parents. The point chart will be a simple sheet of paper marked with horizontal and vertical lines. Under the heading for each behavior, the mom will put an X whenever Emma earns a point for doing it. Next to the chart is a list of what the Xs earn: 2 Xs = dessert at dinner or an extra story read by Mom or Dad before bedtime, or a Wii game with her brother before dinner; 3 Xs = play with Mom's iPad (which is entirely off limits now) under Mom's supervision, or stay up fifteen minutes later on Friday or Saturday night; 5 Xs = a toy grab bag (Emma closes her eyes, reaches into a brown paper bag, and picks one toy from those that are in there); 15 Xs = a weekend movie at a movie theater, a trip to a nearby amusement park, or going fishing at a nearby pier. Emma helped make this list. Her parents asked her what were some things she would like to do, so they're confident that these are rewards she's eager to get.

When the parents present the program to Emma, they tell her there's a way for her to earn some things she would like by getting ready on time. There are two ways to earn points. First, there's "night-before prep." She can earn one point on any school night (Sunday through Thursday) if she has her backpack downstairs before bedtime on the kitchen counter all ready to go to school. She can earn another point if she has the clothes she's going to wear (shoes, socks, the outfit) all laid out on or by her dresser in her room before bedtime. Her dad helps her do this for the first week, just to help her get the idea and into the routine. Also, getting ready partially in this way removes much of the tension. There is no time pressure at night, and there will be less the next morning. Time pressure is a setting event for oppositional behavior, so it's good to reduce or eliminate it.

In the morning Emma can earn two points if she's completely dressed by 7:25 *and* if her mom has to remind Emma to get dressed only once. If Emma is not dressed by 7:25, the mom finishes dressing her and Emma doesn't get any points. Mom will praise partial dressing or showing other progress toward getting dressed ("It's good you picked out your clothes and put them on your bed," for instance, or "I can see you are almost all dressed—very good!"), so it's not an all-or-nothing scenario, but Emma gets the points only if both criteria are met. This is absolutely critical. In developing behavior (via praise in this case) one reinforces any approximations or improvements in behavior. So here we are praising partial dressing and getting close, but we save points and even more effusive praise for when the final behavior is achieved. This is the best of all worlds—praise for improvement and a special incentive for actually doing the desired behavior completely.

On Sunday evening, the program officially starts. Emma's dad agrees to be in charge of the "night-before prep" phase. He goes to her right after dinner, way before bedtime, and says, "Let's earn some Emma points" and holds her hand as they walk to her room. (Hand holding on the way is a nice setting event to get the behavior requested.) Then he says, "You can get a point if you get your backpack all ready and we take it down to the kitchen so it's there to grab on your way to the school bus." (Mentioning the point is a setting event that will increase the likelihood of the behavior.) He asks her to show him exactly what she needs to do to get the backpack ready, since he doesn't know. Emma puts a few things in, describing each step out loud, and the dad thanks her for explaining—all great to keep the tone positive. He praises her for doing this so quickly. "Great, Emma—you got this all ready so fast! How did you do that?" he says with an expression of pride and amazement, and then rubs the back of her head gently. Then he says, "Let's go downstairs to put it on the counter for tomorrow morning." As soon as she does that, the dad takes her over to the point chart and marks an X—gives her some praise, a hug, and says, "You're pretty good at this for just the first time; did you practice when I wasn't looking?" If Emma smiles and is proud of herself, which she's likely to be, that's all to the good.

The dad says, "We can stop here, or if you want we can work on the clothes and get them ready for tomorrow. You'll get a point for that, but we don't have to do that now if you don't want to." Dad nicely uses choice here as a setting event to increase the likelihood of compliance. He could have said, "Emma, now we have to get your clothes ready." That wording is a little less desirable here because "have to" increases the likelihood of an "over my dead body or in your dreams" reaction on Emma's part. If Emma does the clothes, too, there's more praise and another trip to the refrigerator to add a point to her chart.

Why not do the backpack upstairs and while up there just do the clothes and save the extra trip up and down stairs? Because, at first, two trips are better. One behavior occurs (backpack) and then it gets its immediate reward (trip to the point chart), then the other behavior occurs (clothes) and gets its own immediate reward (trip to the point chart). Also, doing it this way circumvents the problem that would come up if Emma does only one of the two tasks and the dad then has to mix praise and points with a comment like "Well, maybe next time you can get a point for getting your clothes ready, too." In the beginning, take one behavior and its consequence at a time. When both behaviors are consistent, it then becomes efficient to award points for both with one trip to the point chart after both are done. In fact, to make that transition one could even use a challenge as a setting event. "All right, Emma, you've been doing the backpack and clothes really well, but here's the challenge. Can you do them both one right after the other before we go downstairs and do the points? You will still get all your points, but doing two things in a row—that's pretty hard" (said playfully). "You want to try"—choice—"or is it just too hard?"—challenge. Emma will probably move to two in a row, and Dad can praise that. "You really *are* good at this," and then he states exactly what the "this" is and touches her shoulder gently.

In the morning, the mom awakens Emma as usual and gives a calm reminder after an affectionate good morning. "OK, you can earn some more points if you like. Please get dressed and come to the kitchen by 7:25." There's a clock in Emma's room and Emma can tell time. "If you want any help, just call me. That's fine for this first week. If you come down completely dressed by 7:25 or I come up and see you are dressed, you get two points. If you are not dressed by then, I will dress you to make sure we get the school bus on time. If I dress you, you won't get any points."

For the first three or four days, Emma's dad helps her with the night-before prep. Then they try a challenge: "I'll bet you can't do this on your own. Let's see." Here Emma is being asked to go to her room and do both behaviors. Dad says to Emma, "Call me to come up when you're ready for me to see." When Emma has done both behaviors, the dad goes upstairs, praises, and they come down to get the points. He tells Emma she's so big and mature in doing this, she gets to mark the "prep" points on the chart herself. Throughout all of this, the parents put the emphasis on praising Emma each night for getting the backpack ready and getting her clothes together without any help.

In the first week Emma gets completely dressed by 7:25 on three days but not completely dressed on two days. On those two less successful days, the mom looks for reasons to praise Emma when she comes into Emma's room at 7:25: "Great, you're almost completely dressed! I can't give you points today, but you have another chance tomorrow. It's so great that you were almost all dressed. What a big girl!" Praise for approximations of the behavior is important for shaping. Praise for trying and for partial success is also good.

After doing the program for a while, Emma has getting ready in the morning down, and she's consistently doing the two behaviors the night before. Also, on most of the days she comes down dressed and on time, or a minute or two early. The mom and dad make a big deal of this with their praise. They already have faded themselves—that is, they don't have to be present in the moment as a setting event to get the behavior or as a prompt to help. Now it's time to get rid of the points.

They say, "You're such a big girl you don't even need points to help you do this. We're going to add something special on Friday or Saturday. At the end of any week when you have come down every morning on time ready to go to school, you can choose either a dinner and dessert you want at home on Friday or a family activity on Saturday." If she's not ready on one day, Mom still goes up and finishes dressing her. Emma still gets praise for doing things well, even partially well, but no more points—just praise, and that special activity when she has been ready on time every morning for a solid week. The special activity is very delayed as a reinforcer, which is fine after behavior is well established.

Pretty soon Emma has all of this down as a habit—she is getting ready on time, routinely, and not under the control of parents or points. The point program is dropped and the Friday or Saturday event is done only the first week, after which everyone kind of loses track of that loose program. That's all fine, too. You have to be very systematic in the beginning and then can be loose as a way of fading the program—just the way we are naturally loose as years go by in not reminding our child to say "thank you," to use a napkin rather than a sleeve, to say "I'm sorry" when an apology is needed.

***Real life No. 3: Logan's school behavior has the teacher on his parents' case***

Logan is a nine-year-old boy who is doing pretty well in the fourth grade. He's in middle reading and math groups and has some friends; overall, he's doing fine. He lives with his mom and younger sister; the mother and father were divorced two years ago, and Logan and his sister see their dad one day on the weekends, and they sometimes stay overnight. The mother has a mail-order business buying and selling merchandise through eBay and works at home.

It's mid-October when the mother comes to the Yale Parenting Center. After six weeks of the new school term, the teacher is starting to call or send e-mails two or three times a week. Apparently Logan is disrupting others and getting into trouble for talking during work or study time and not doing what he's supposed to do. The mother, in disbelief, tells us that he has been sent to a detention room three times already in a two-week period. That and the teacher's many calls mean the mother can't just let it go for now. She's under pressure to deal with the problem.

The teacher's calls include the reminder that she has twenty-three other students to attend to, that she can't do anything special for Logan because of that, and that the mom needs to take care of this. To make sure mother anxiety is high, the teacher says that if this keeps up, she will recommend Logan for special education class placement where someone else can deal with his disruptive behavior.

The mother feels that the pressure's on her, but that she's not in a good position to deal with the problem. "I'm not at school," she says. "What can *I* do to help?" She has told Logan to behave or else there will be more problems for him at school. It's understandable that she's been driven to making those statements, but predictably they have no real effect on changing Logan's behavior. (They are poor prompts—distant from the situation, not followed with reinforcement for engaging in the right behavior—and will have no effect on changing behavior. They also can increase Logan's anxiety, which will not motivate him to behave better. And even if they did motivate him, great motivation alone does not lead to behavior change if that behavior is not well developed in the child's repertoire.) We can adapt our tools to this situation, I tell her.

But first, to get the whole picture, what exactly is the behavior? We look at the teacher's list of disruptive behaviors and ask her (by e-mail) if there are other things to add to that. There's one: sometimes Logan blurts out things in class without raising his hand, and that's disruptive and unfair to others who do raise their hands. And with that addition we pretty much have the behavior down.

Because the consequences part of this program is a little novel, let's go to that and come back to antecedents and behaviors in a moment. I tell the mom that because the teacher has too many children to attend to and can't give Logan the one-on-one attention necessary to carry out a full behavior-change program in school, we are going to do a *home-based reinforcement program*. It has two main parts:

1. A token economy (point chart) set up at home. Logan can earn points each day based on his performance in class. We give points for behavior, which I'll come to in a moment. The points can be exchanged for things that Logan would like. The mom consults Logan and he lists these rewards: staying up half an hour later on a weeknight and one hour later on a weekend night, more computer time, cooler (colored) sneakers to replace his white ones (which no one else on the planet

supposedly wears), baseball cards, Pokémon cards, rental of a video game, and a cell phone. The mother agrees to all except the cell phone. Point values are calibrated so that some things can be earned easily: two to three points earns staying up late; three points for fifteen minutes more computer time (computer is restricted in the home and the computer is in the family room where it can be supervised); five points for a pack of baseball cards; and so on. There are also bigger items for which Logan has to save: ten points for a (nonviolent) video game; fifty points for cooler sneakers.

2. A way of measuring behavior to determine how many points Logan earns.

Each weekday, Logan takes a white 3-by-5-inch card to school. On the cards are three smiley-type faces, each next to a number: 2 has a very cheery smiley face and means that Logan had a really good day with very little or almost no disruptive behavior; 1 has a gently smiling face and means that Logan was a little disruptive and was not really great but not out of control or horrible; and 0 has a neutral flat-mouth face and means that Logan was pretty disruptive. (The mom bought sheets of smiley faces at a party store, but just drawing them would be fine, too.) There's a sheet at home and one e-mailed to the teacher to define what behaviors rate a 2, 1, or 0.

The mother asks the teacher to circle the 2, 1, or 0 on the 3-by-5 card, initial it, and send it home with Logan each day. The teacher feels that she can easily do that. If for some reason the card does not get scored, the teacher agrees to respond to an e-mail from Logan's mom.

The program is simple. Each day, Logan earns one point just for bringing home the card and handing it to his mom—for participating, in other words. He earns two more points if the teacher circled 2, one more point if 1, and no more points if the teacher circled 0. He loses a point if he starts arguing with his mom or the teacher about points earned that day, the way a baseball player can get kicked out of the game for arguing with the ump about a called strike. After his mom looks at the card (as soon as Logan comes home from school), marks (they could be stars, check marks, or some other symbol) are added to a chart on the wall that notes his points for the day and total points left in his account (total points minus any purchases). After the points are entered, Logan can cash in by identifying something he wants, or just let the points ride.

We are still on consequences. The mother asks the teacher to praise Logan any time he gets a 2 or a 1, but the real praise comes from the mother when Logan arrives home with a 2 or a 1 on his card. Yes, she praises a 1 (that's shaping), although she praises a 2 more strenuously. If Logan receives a 0, she gives him the point on the chart for bringing the card home and says in a calm, matter-of-fact tone, "Tomorrow is another chance, and you may earn more points then." (It's important to keep this brief, not to interrogate: "What did you do to make the teacher circle 0?" All such comments undermine the program; they're setting events that are inherently confrontational and will promote escape and avoidance, which could nix the program if Logan begins refusing to bring the card home.)

On her own, the mother adds something special when Logan receives a 2. She calls it a "2 treat licorice" because it's given for a 2 and the two of them eat it together. She keeps some licorice around for them to have whenever there's a 2 on the card. This is not needed in the program, but it's a nice addition to make a 2 extra special and to speed up shaping a little with an extra incentive for excellent behavior. Also, besides the licorice as reinforcer (and yes, I know, you can't use sweets as reinforcers too much and we do not advocate or rely on them at the Parenting Center), it's also parent-child time together to celebrate good behavior.

On the antecedents front, on the way to school the mother provides a gentle reminder as she hands Logan the card: "Good luck today in earning points; I'm thinking about you and I hope you can do it. It's hard to do, and don't feel too bad if you can't get all the points today." This is more of a setting event than a prompt (which would be more direct: "Remember, pay attention, do not blurt out . . ."), and it takes some of the pressure off, which increases the likelihood that Logan will do what's asked of him.

On the behavior front, shaping is key. After the first week, Logan is doing pretty well with mostly 1s and 2s. We ask the mother to add one extra bonus point any time Logan has two consecutive days of 2 on the card. So if on both Monday and Tuesday he has a 2, he gets the usual points for that and also a special bonus point. Then on Wednesday, he has a 2 again and so again receives a bonus point—because Tuesday and Wednesday were two 2 days in a row. This practice of adding a special incentive for consistency could be stretched out to three days in a row and so on, but it's best to proceed slowly to be sure the early steps are stable.

This sort of home-based reinforcement program is useful for school behavior problems. We have also used this kind of program for athletic practices, day camp, and other such situations where we can't ask the adult in charge to stick to a special program like administering praise for positive opposites on any regular basis that would have a significant effect. Asking a teacher or other supervising adult to fill out a card is reasonable and effective. In some recent cases, we've omitted the card and had teachers or others text the parent at the end of the day. But we prefer a physical card because it's tangible feedback that the child can touch and see.

*Real life No. 4: Olivia's jarring irritability and attitude*

Olivia, a twelve-year-old girl, is not especially physically or socially mature for her age. She still looks like a girl, while some of her peers are starting to be more shapely as they mature physically. This is what Olivia's parents mention when I see them. They kind of like her immaturity and late development; they are not in a rush to have an adolescent in the home. One girl in Olivia's class is already dating, and another has been caught by the teacher while sexting, which makes Olivia's parents shudder. They are waiting with dread for the first sign of adolescence in their daughter, the first shoe to drop, but they talk about it as if it's a guillotine, not a shoe, that will be dropping. They have come to the Yale Parenting Center because they think it's all just beginning, and in a way they didn't expect.

For starters, the family is close, engages in many family activities, has all sorts of good routines about meals, weekend activities, occasional field trips, and periodic vacations. So a lot of the contextual influences are already in place and positive. Olivia and her eight-year-old sister get along well; there's no real sibling rivalry, competition, or routine tension. But now, at age twelve, Olivia's showing a change in personality around the house. She's irritable much of the time and acts as if living at home with her parents is a prison sentence for a crime she did not commit. She does not go after her younger sister much, but she freely tells her parents that they are selfish and don't really love her; loses her temper and makes cutting remarks; and says that she doesn't want any of whatever is being served for dinner, even when her mother buys and prepares a favorite food—which, Olivia notes emphatically, she doesn't like anymore.

When offered a special treat that she's enjoyed before or invited to go someplace with her mother just to be together, where a light "No, thank you" would have done the job, now she replies with a stretched-out, sarcastic "Nooooooo," wagging her head and adopting a pained facial expression that conveys the ridiculous stupidity of the question. Acting lessons could never have perfected this level of irritability and dismissiveness, and the parents wonder where she got it and why. In addition, Olivia's obvious irritability casts a dark cloud over the dinner table. Conversation becomes stilted, and both Mom and Dad are tense and moody because of something nasty that Olivia just said or no doubt will soon say.

Before I address how to change this pattern of behavior, I tell the parents that irritability in adolescence is common. It's not inevitable, but it does occur. In young girls, other things can come on as well, like poor body self-image, lower self-esteem, more depression (which includes increased irritability), and, in more extreme cases, talk of self-harm and suicide. Small doses of each of these can occur; in their extreme they warrant seeing a professional. But this irritability is common and includes the mindset that "if my parents want this, do this, or think this, I don't want any part of it."

It would be nice merely to say to parents, "Sit tight; this will pass." But if you are in the home and a verbal mortar is aimed at you much of the day, you can't let it pass. You will have shell shock from all the bombardment, and some of the comments will be direct hits on your soul. And there's no need to put up with it.

A little praise program is not likely to do the trick. Praise will be included, but we want more powerful rewards that are not usually needed. We choose a point program here.

What behavior do we want? We want to focus on just one to begin with, but the parents insist that there's a whole suite of problem behaviors and any one of them could come up at any time. It will not be great for their morale to control eye rolling or sarcastic tone if in the next minute they're told to shut up or that no one really cares what they think, offenses that they will then feel obliged to punish severely. So we list all the behaviors of concern and take them all on in one program. How can we take on many behaviors and still use shaping? Hold on.

In terms of antecedents, what can we do to influence the likelihood that Olivia won't erupt in obnoxious behavior? The parents have already tried being kind and sweet, trying to show empathy or understanding, being harsh in return ("You'd better get control of your mouth and attitude"), and tiptoeing around Olivia in the hope that they won't set her off. We decide to try other antecedents.

The parents tell her, "It's fine to be upset and obnoxious around the house. Lots of teens go through that. There will be consequences when you cross the line into serious disrespect and meanness, but you can choose what to say or do." This antecedent does not feed the problem but removes all fighting and coercion, and that can decrease some of the irritability. The setting event disarms Olivia a bit by saying, in effect, "Your behavior is understandable, even normal, and we expect it." Also, such a disarming comment conveys that there are limits, so understanding and legitimizing her teen behavior is not a carte blanche to misbehave. It also decreases futile extended parent-child exchanges. (It is useful here to be disarming and matter-of-fact, without condescending with words or tone that might convey the equivalent of "You are just an immature brat and we are having as much trouble putting up with you as you are with us." Hold that thought for the parent support group that should be available for free to every parent raising an adolescent who is going through a bumpy period of development.) I tell the parents not to make the mistake of worrying that they're being weak or not setting limits. Actually, they're being quite strong by controlling the situation much better, and the program sets very effective limits.

Second, the parents draw up a list of annoying teen behaviors that they're concerned about and put it in a kitchen drawer where Olivia can see it any time she wants to. It's not posted on the refrigerator, which could embarrass the hyper-touchy Olivia, but everyone knows where it is and can get to it.

Now, as to the behavior itself, we definitely want to use shaping. We base shaping on time—that is, the amount of time Olivia goes without exhibiting one of these teen behaviors. If she can do that, she can earn points for all sorts of things she would like. The amount of time will change as she makes progress, of which more in a moment.

Consequences consist of a few things. She can earn points and exchange them for items like cosmetics, which she likes a great deal, and privileges like cell phone time, iTunes, TV time, and loosening of the parents' strict rules on makeup. This loosening is good for contextual reasons, too. The parents will need to start yielding more as Olivia's life will increasingly be outside her family and in the world. Tightening up and taking up slippery-slope thinking here can foster a lot more oppositional teen behavior, more time out of the home, and more time ignoring deeply ingrained but often hard-to-see household values. Loosening where you can (allowing more latitude in hairstyle and color of fingernails, for instance, or putting up with louder and perhaps coarser music than you'd normally want in the house) helps you to hold firm where you can't loosen up (for example, no tattoos, no music that includes foul language or promotes what you regard as terrible values).

Also, the parents offer low-key (rather than effusive) praise almost any time Olivia speaks decently to them. When she says something pleasant or at least minimally civil, the mom goes over to her and says something like "It's good to have another adult in the home—you! You are speaking so nicely," and then she gives her a thumbs-up and goes on about her business. The parent shouldn't linger in this situation, which could go downhill fast. One adolescent at the Parenting Center would say, "I don't need your f'in praise!" We can be pretty sure that means the praise was not rewarding (as subjectively valued by the recipient), but, still, it definitely was a positive reinforcer, and the adolescent's behavior changed in that case without any point program. A parent can barely resist responding to such provocative comments—so better to leave the exchange as soon as possible.

Finally, the parents use withholding reinforcement. The mother's reaction in particular often makes Olivia's teen behaviors have more monumental impact than they should. Yet there are times when her parents can't just ignore Olivia, so we practice a low-key reaction with the mother. She smiles slightly, a kind of Mona-Lisa-plus-just-a-little-expression that we practice with parents at the Parenting Center, and then walks away. The smile, which communicates a certain faint amusement at the daughter's fumbling efforts to get her mother's goat, as if to say, "Ah, yes, I was twelve once," is mildly aversive because it's a little dismissive, so it qualifies as a punishment. Mild punishment is all right as part of a program that strongly reinforces the positive opposites of the behavior that's being punished.

The program: The parents tell Olivia that she's growing up and so there are going to be changes in the home. They make a list of the various irritable things Olivia says and does in the home, and they put it where she can get it out and look at it, but she doesn't have to. They tell her that these irritable behaviors will go away as she becomes a young woman. It's OK for her to be irritable because she might not be able to control it, but if she can control her irritability and not do what's on the list, she can earn things like cosmetics, privileges, and other things she wants.

Here's how we'll do it. When Olivia comes home from school, she can be as irritable as she wants to be and do the behaviors on the list. But if she goes ten minutes without doing any of those things on the list, she earns five points. That can happen each day. Here's the catch: she has to say something to her parents, even if it's only "Hi," rather than just hiding in her room to let the ten minutes elapse. After the ten minutes, Olivia can do all the irritable "teen behaviors" she wants. (That antecedent of calling them "teen behaviors" and giving her free rein to do them is very likely to decrease the behaviors, too.) Over time the ten minutes is extended. Whenever Olivia has a lapse and does something on the list during the period when she can earn points for not doing it, the mom or dad just smiles and walks off slowly. If Olivia asks, "Well, did I get the damn points?" the parent replies, calmly, "Not today, but you have another chance tomorrow," and walks away.

One more feature: Saturday is a free day on which the program is suspended—no demands to act more grown-up, and no points can be earned. This is a smart addition because it gives freedom and takes pressure off. Also, this will help later, when Olivia's behavior has improved in long enough stretches that the family can make the transition from awarding points to just reinforcing good behavior with praise and attention. Olivia's parents tell her that she should feel free to do the "teen behaviors" on the free day if she wants to or can't help it. Legitimizing "teen behaviors" is an antecedent that takes some of the enjoyment (reward value) out of them; it also helps the parents to control their reactions, which can fuel continued obnoxious behavior.

## Summing up

The four real-life examples I've just gone through are different in the behaviors they focus on, the ages of the children, and the circumstances. Yet they outline programs that can be individualized to your child, preteen, or adolescent. We know this because similar applications have been successfully adapted to toddlers, college and professional athletes, soldiers in basic training, employees in business and industry, the elderly, and others. So if you are thinking that this approach will never work with your child or that it can't be applied to this or that behavior, chances are you are wrong. (I admit that telling a person that she or he is wrong is a bad antecedent and is quite likely to evoke opposition to what I have just said.)

Right or wrong, try your way first, and then try the toolkit this book offers, only if your first attempt did not work to your satisfaction. Consider the toolkit as your backup when you want to develop a new behavior or you see a problem—your child's throwing food, not eating vegetables, sitting and watching TV or playing with the computer all day—and you can't fix it using the methods you already use, or when it looks as if these usual methods are not quite getting your child where you would like her to be. Sometimes you can screw a bolt on or off by hand and really do not need a wrench. Sometimes you need a wrench, and it's good to have one as backup. And so our toolkit.

## An exercise (a quiz!)

In this chapter I provided a template for how to use the toolkit and what to do in what order. Then I applied the template to typical problems that come up at different ages. Now it's your turn. Here is a friendly set of quizlike prompts to help you design a behavior-change program. Fill in—write in—your answers to these as an exercise that will be a great start for you in developing effective programs to change behaviors you want to change. We will assume for this example that we are working with a young child, preschool through elementary-school age. Just fill in the blanks—if you have a real example, that's great (and my condolences), but making one up will still call on your newfound skills. (Heads up: I'm about to use some tried-and-true antecedents on you.) You can take the quiz or skip it, as you like (choice). I'm sure you'll do fine, but I don't expect any reader to get them all right (gentle challenge).

The behavior you want to change in your child is: (Give a brief statement here like "talking nicely to his sister more often.")

______________________________________________

If there's a behavior you want to decrease or eliminate, what is it, *and* what's the positive opposite you want to build up in its place? ______________________________________

______________________________________________

Now define in a little more detail what the good behavior would look like. (For example, if you could tell him what to say, what would he say to his sister?) ______________________

________________________________________________

________________________________________________

What would be a good prompt you could offer to increase the likelihood of the behavior? ______________________

________________________________________________

Are there any setting events that could be used to make it more likely that he would do the desired behavior? (For instance, is there a game or some other activity that he and his sister like or do well together that makes social interaction between them more cooperative?) ______________________

________________________________________________

________________________________________________

Does the behavior you want to see ever occur at all, or at the moment is it really zero and never? If the behavior occurs or if small pieces or approximations of the behavior occur, note here what they are and when they have occurred. Just one or two examples would be fine. ______________________

________________________________________________

________________________________________________

________________________________________________

If the child is only doing approximations of the desired behavior, we will want to use shaping. So here list some of the steps along the way from what the child does now (for example, says nice things once in a while) to what you would like him to do (say nice things almost all of the time). List steps along the way (such as saying nice things twice a day, then four times a day). ______________________

________________________________________________

________________________________________________

If the behavior never occurs or occurs rarely, what could you do? (If you need to go to a simulation game, what would the game be?) ________________________________

________________________________________

You will use praise as a main consequence to reinforce the behavior. Describe what that praise should be like. That is, for it to be effective, what three elements should it have?

- The tone of the praise should be ______________ .
- When you praise, you should state exactly ______________ .
- Then you should go over to the child and ______________ .

You will use some punishment to address behavior you want to decrease, so whenever the child does it (for example, says something nasty to his sister), what will you do?

________________________________________

________________________________________

## Keep in mind

***Avoid blame (especially self-blame)***

Be careful not to blame yourself for your child's undesirable behaviors. I mention this because I have seen many parents, especially mothers, who blame themselves for their children's serious problems (autism, for instance, or an eating disorder) and for the everyday challenges of the type we have been discussing (tantrums, nastiness, not listening, and so on). We know that human behavior is influenced by so many factors that it's usually impossible to isolate one as *the* cause. It's unlikely that you're the sole or even main cause of your child's misbehavior. Actually, in any given case you may have little or no role in the misbehavior at all. But behavior is malleable, which means that you can take the lead in changing your child's behavior for the better. So while you shouldn't waste energy on holding yourself responsible for undesirable behaviors you see in your child now, take heart in knowing that you *can* change those behaviors.

Model the behaviors you wish, provide the contextual influences we have discussed, and then apply the tools we illustrated. You'll be surprised by the results. Parents who work with us at the Yale Parenting Center are usually relieved to discover just how much they can change behavior, and they typically benefit from reduced stress in the home, better relationships among family members, and other such changes. But their strongest response is surprise that their children's behavior can be changed. In science, the ability of the brain to change is referred to as "plasticity." In developing new habits, new ways of responding in everyday situations, we can work directly on changing the brain, and this can happen over the entire life span. Remember the expression "You can't teach an old dog new tricks"? It's wrong. Just as your child can learn new behaviors and attitudes, you can learn how to change your child's behavior.

***Just get through a tantrum***

Let's say you have a program in place with your child to reduce or eliminate extreme tantrums. You're focusing on positive opposites and the program seems to be working. The extreme tantrums are down from two per day to two per week. Also, their length and severity are trending down. But the child still has the tantrums, and you've got a question: "What do I do when we're in the middle of the tantrum? There is no positive opposite to reinforce, no opportunity for praise. It's a total meltdown. Where and how do I use the ABCs?"

The program mostly happens when there *isn't* a tantrum going on, and we're confident that it will reduce and eventually eliminate extreme tantrums. There is much less one can do during a tantrum, but there are some things.

Perhaps the best analogy to a tantrum is a person who's drowning. You don't try to teach the person how to swim right then; you just do what you can to save her. Later, when she's not drowning, you can teach her how to swim, which is the positive opposite of drowning, and that will eventually decrease the likelihood of drowning.

So you are in the middle of a doozy of a tantrum. What to do?

First, make sure everyone is safe—from crashing into the furniture, from being hit by a flying elbow or thrown objects. Do what you can to ensure safety.

Second, don't argue with your child, don't reason with him, don't do anything physical—like drag him to a different room or restrain him physically—unless it's absolutely necessary. Do not drag him to time out or otherwise try to punish him in the middle of the tantrum. Each of these is likely to increase the tantrum's magnitude and duration, and anything physical is likely to lead to side effects, the most common of which is you being hit. I have seen this happen enough times to know that a parent who gets hit in such a situation usually becomes furious and escalates whatever punishment he was using or thinking of using. Once you start increasing your involvement—more lecturing, more shouting, more physical touching, holding, restraining—the emotional side effects of punishment, the child's disruptive behavior, your stress, and your escalation of punishment all move fast in the wrong direction.

Third, as soon as you can safely walk away, do so, even if the child follows you. We *want* ignoring because the likelihood of attending to the tantrum will unwittingly reinforce tantrum behavior.

Fourth, as the tantrum winds down, is there any positive feature you have seen? Did the child calm down more quickly than usual, did he not swear this time, did he not throw anything this time? If there is something that clearly is better than usual as his tantrums go, praise that softly and gently. Do not make something up, but praise any conspicuous improvement in the nature of this tantrum compared to a previous or usual one.

Fifth, do not return to the tantrum as a discussion topic later with some moralizing or reflective lesson. "You know, that big explosive tantrum yesterday was not fun for anyone." Forget it. It's much better to invest your time and effort in reinforcing calm behavior and being able to handle any frustration, however major or minor.

The same general approach applies to other blowups, like a teenager flying into a rage or two siblings getting into a serious fight. Make sure everyone is safe, don't engage, walk away as soon as you can, reinforce any feature of the event that was an improvement over the usual, and don't keep harping on it. Just get through it. Then, when things have calmed down, go back to reinforcing positive opposites.

*You can't punish the behavior away*

As a parent you have the unique role of teaching your child what to do in the home, at school, in life. Punishment will not do that. But so much of what we want to change in our children is about eliminating or reducing irritating behavior, and that tends to lead to punishment. No matter how much I have noted that punishment is not an effective procedure for changing behavior, it will be difficult to avoid.

There are strong forces that help maintain our use of ineffective punishment. First, there is the punishment trap I discussed in chapter four: the immediate cessation of the negative behavior after we shout, scream, or hit maintains our use of those punishment practices even though beyond that moment the actual frequency of the behavior we punished does not change. Second, researchers have learned recently that aggressive behavior activates and stimulates reward centers in the human brain, and punishing a child is aggressive behavior. The act of punishing looks as if it has effects in the brain similar to those caused by the use of an illicit drug. That surge of feeling qualifies as a reward—it feels good—which means that for many parents just punishing the child to get rid of behavior will be maintained by its own internal reward, even if it patently doesn't work. Third, there's another kind of reward, a sense of satisfaction, in feeling that you have done something about the problem of your child's misbehavior. And if you think it was the "right" thing to do, morally, that only increases your satisfaction.

I do not expect to overcome all of these attractions of punishment. And, as I have discussed, merely explaining the severe limitations of punishment will not do much to sway anyone. Even if you're convinced, understanding by itself is a weak influence on behavior. If you say to someone at a restaurant, "You know that the Double Chocolate Mud Mountain in front of you right now has enough calories to feed a family of sixteen for a day," that person is likely to say, "Yeah, I know," and then smile and eat it.

The way to overcome the pull of punishment is to use methods that work better. Use positive opposites to develop behavior and you'll see a lot more success. That doesn't mean that you should never punish. Mild, brief punishment doesn't do much harm, and it can help. But keep the proportions sound: a lot of positive reinforcement, a little punishment.

A check on yourself: if you are consistently punishing a given behavior, you need to begin a positive-opposite program instead. Now try to, and arrange to, catch the child being good—engaging in the positive opposite. How often? There is no scientifically tested answer, but make sure there are many more opportunities to reinforce positive opposites than to punish the undesired behavior.

***Age- and stage-related behaviors***

So many of the challenging behaviors children present are age- or stage-related. By that I mean they come on fairly predictably and also go away. Among these are thumb sucking, clumsiness (dropping glasses, spilling), interrupting, having toileting accidents after you thought the child was fully toilet trained, lying, disagreeing with you no matter what you say, showing off, not paying attention at school, talking too much or too little, teen attitude, and more.

In general, these behaviors have several characteristics in common. They are so intensely annoying that you want to sue the hospital for not telling you about them when you and your infant were discharged after your delivery. You did not do anything to deserve them and you shouldn't have to put up with them. And when these behaviors have a victim or target, you are the one wearing the bull's-eye T-shirt, and you're also the cleanup maintenance staff who has to deal with any messes they cause.

These behaviors vary markedly among children. If you have more than one child, they probably won't show the same behaviors. Some children show a lot of them, and others show none or almost none. This plays with your mind. You find yourself engaging in a depressing internal monologue. "Why is this child so high on the rotten scale? Is it because of something I did? Why does my own child hate me? I don't deserve this. This child is totally out of control. Can parents run away from home?"

Some of these behaviors are part of development, and here are a few things to keep in mind:

1. The behavior is likely to go away by itself or in the course of your usual parenting. This can be said confidently because there are very few teenagers who are still having toileting accidents or sucking their thumbs.
2. You need to make a decision as to whether the behavior is tolerable, whether you can wait it out or not. This is all a matter of degree and personal choice, affected by the level of intensity in the behavior of your child and by your own tolerance level.
3. Is the behavior interfering with functioning? If the child is in trouble at school, a sibling in the home is made very anxious or disturbed by the behavior, or family relations are significantly interfered with in some other way, these are good reasons to intervene. Start with the toolkit this book provides. If the behavior is very extreme, you may want to call on professional help.

## Conclusion

So now you've got a toolkit full of tools, and instructions about how to use them properly. You may well be excited to give it all a try, and you may also be worrying, like a person embarking on a new diet, that you'll find it hard to follow through. Bear a couple of things in mind as you go forward.

First, the programs do not require perfection, but the more carefully you carry out the procedures, the more likely you will see behavior change and the sooner you can stop a program completely.

Second, any particular program is likely to be fairly short-lived.

The typical period of a program to, say, eliminate tantrums or build better homework habits is a few weeks. So don't think of embarking on a program as a lifelong commitment to praising homework-doing every single time you see it. Yes, you'll want to be on it as much as possible for a couple of weeks, perhaps even as much as a month, but then you'll fade back to a regular level of parental interest and involvement. And, in fact, if the program has gone well, you'll be able to be a lot less involved in getting your child to do his homework because he'll be doing it on his own (one of the things you were reinforcing in the program), and you won't be nagging him about it and checking up on him all the time.

So you don't have to be perfect, and you won't be doing any program indefinitely. When you identify a behavior you want to see more or less of, you'll plan the appropriate program, do it as intensely as you can for a brief period, then fade it out and move on.

You have worked so hard to raise your child. The effort and commitment on your part began immediately at birth—probably well before birth, in fact. You have ambitions and goals for your child—and also some frustrations, because sometimes it seems that your child is the only person in the household who is not cooperating in the heroic effort to give him or her a better life. The tools you've been mastering in this book are not mere techniques to eliminate an annoying behavior here or there. That's never the goal of child rearing. We want to help our children develop as individuals who can function well in what they do and have skills and aptitudes that will make their lives more rewarding for themselves and for others. The toolkit can help you build behaviors and, through that, larger habits and traits of character you want your child to have. They're not just tools to fix a leak here and there; they're tools to help build a good life for your family, now and well into the future.

# *Notes*

## Introduction

vii *The body of good research:* In this book I draw on a great deal of research, in keeping with my intent to bring you the practical benefits of the best scientific work on parenting and child rearing. Occasionally I will identify the source when I make a specific claim based on a specific study, but if you wish to go more deeply into the research, much of it is cited in a more technical text: A. E. Kazdin, *Behavior Modification in Applied Settings,* 7th ed. (Long Grove, IL: Waveland Press, 2013).

viii *There are also more single parents:* Source: E. Wildsmith, N. R. Steward-Streng, and J. Manlove, "Childbearing Outside of Marriage: Estimates and Trends in the United States," *Child Research Brief* (November 2011), Publication #201129 4301, Washington, DC (http://www.childtrends.org/Files/Child_Trends-2011_11_01_RB_NonmaritalCB.pdf).

## 1. Laying the Groundwork for Good Behavior

11 *A team of researchers:* Source: J. J. McComas, D. P. Wacker, and L. J. Cooper, "Increasing Compliance with Medical Procedures: Application of the High-Probability Behavior Request Procedure to a Toddler," *Journal of Applied Behavior Analysis* 31 (1998): 287–90.

## 2. What You Want to Change

42 *Another example is a project:* Source: R. G. Miltenberger, C. Flessner, B. Gatheridge, B. Johnson, M. Satterlund, and K. Egemo, "Evaluation of

Behavioral Skills Training to Prevent Gun Play in Children," *Journal of Applied Behavior Analysis* 37 (2004): 513–16.

## 4. Decreasing Misbehavior

104 *Withholding reinforcement was also used:* Source: K. G. France and S. M. Hudson, "Behavior Management of Infant Sleep Disturbance," *Journal of Applied Behavior Analysis* 23 (1990): 91–98.

## 5. The Routines of Family Life

136 *Are the behavior problems caused:* Sources: S. C. J. Huijbregts, J. R. Séguin, M. Zoccolillo, M. Boivin, and R. E. Tremblay, "Maternal Prenatal Smoking, Parental Antisocial Behavior, and Early Childhood Physical Aggression," *Developmental Psychopathology* 20 (2008): 437–53. M. Weitzman, S. Gortmaker, and A. Sobol, "Maternal Smoking and Behavior Problems of Children," *Pediatrics* 90 (1992): 342–49.

# *Additional Resources*

Visit our websites

Yale Parenting Center: http://childconductclinic.yale.edu
Press and interviews: http://www.alankazdin.com

Additional readings by the authors on
parenting in everyday situations

"Tiny Tyrants: How to Really Change Your Kid's Behavior" http://www.slate.com/id/2188744/.

"Family Feuds: How to Make 'Timeouts' Less Like Bar Fights" http://www.slate.com/id/2194331/.

"Spare the Rod: Why You Shouldn't Hit Your Kids" http://www.slate.com/id/2200450/.

"Why Can't Johnny Jump Tall Buildings? Parents Expect Way Too Much From Their Kids" http://www.slate.com/id/2204113.

"Reading Isn't Fundamental: How to Help Your Child Learn to Read" http://www.slate.com/id/2206105/.

"Your Kids Will Imitate You: Use It as a Force for Good" http://www.slate.com/id/2209882/.

"No, You Shut Up! What to Do When Your Kid Provokes You Into an Inhuman Rage" http://www.slate.com/id/2210616/.

"The Messy Room Dilemma: When to Ignore Behavior, When to Change It" http://www.slate.com/id/2214678/.

"I Think I'm Worried About My Kid" http://www.slate.com/id/2218374/.

"Bullies: They Can Be Stopped, but It Takes a Village" http://www.slate.com/id/2223976/.

"Plan B: What to Do When All Else Has Failed to Change Your Kid's Behavior" http://www.slate.com/id/2228559/.

"Like a Rat: Animal Research and Your Child's Behavior" http://www.slate.com/id/2234707/.

"No Brakes! Part I: Risk and the Adolescent Brain" http://www.slate.com/id/2243435/.

"No Brakes! Part II: The Best Way to Guide Your Teenager Through the High-Risk Years" http://www.slate.com/id/2243436/.

"If You're Good, I'll Buy You a Toy: The Difference Between Bribing Your Child and Rewarding Your Child" http://www.slate.com/id/2248766.

"Get Off Facebook and Do Something! How to Motivate an Inert Child" http://www.slate.com/id/2254448/.

"Children and Stress: The New Science on Chronically Harsh and Conflict-Ridden Households" http://www.slate.com/id/2262309/.

# Index

# Making the GRADE

## Everything Your 5th Grader Needs to Know

by

Kathleen Ermitage

## About the Author

Kathleen Ermitage has spent more than 13 years creating educational products used in social studies, math, science, and reading classrooms nationwide. She holds an M.A. in literature from Northwestern University and is a published author of children's books.



*All inquiries should be addressed to:*
Barron's Educational Series, Inc.
250 Wireless Boulevard
Hauppauge, New York 11788
**http://www.barronseduc.com**

International Standard Book No. 0-7641-2481-1

*Library of Congress Catalog Card No.* 2002044063

**Library of Congress Cataloging-in-Publication Data**
Ermitage, Kathleen.
Making the grade: everything your fifth grader needs to know / by Kathleen Ermitage.
p. cm.
Includes bibliographical references (p. 362) and index.
ISBN 0-7641-2481-1
1. Fifth grade (Education)—Curricula. I. Title.

LB15715th .E76 2003
372.19—dc21 2002044063

Printed in Hong Kong
9 8 7 6 5 4 3 2 1

# Table of Contents

## MATH

# How to Use This Book

Welcome to the *Making the Grade* series! These seven books offer tools and strategies for hands-on, active learning at the kindergarten through sixth-grade levels. Each book presents real-world, engaging learning experiences in the core areas of language arts, math, science, and social studies at age-appropriate levels.

## Who should use this book?

Whether you're a stay-at-home or working parent with children in school, a homeschooler who's taking control of your children's education, or a teacher who's looking for additional ideas to supplement classroom learning experiences, this book is for you.

- If you have children in school, *Making the Grade* can be used in conjunction with your child's curriculum because it offers real-world, hands-on activities that exercise the concepts and topics he or she is being taught in school.
- If you're a homeschooler who's taking control of your children's education, this series presents you with easy-to-access, engaging ways to interact with your child.
- If you're a teacher, this book also can be a source for additional activities.

This book is your passport to a whole new world, one that gives you enough support to be a successful "teacher" while encouraging independent learning with one child or shared learning among your children.

## What is *Making the Grade*?

We're glad you asked! First, we'd like to tell you what it's not. It's not a textbook series. Rather, each book in the series delivers age-appropriate content in language arts, math, science, and social studies in an open-ended, flexible manner that incorporates the "real" world. You can use this book as a supplement to your core learning instruction or use it to get a jump-start on the fundamentals.

Each subject section presents lessons comprised of both "teaching" pages and "student" pages. And each book in the *Making the Grade* series is perforated for flexible learning so that both you and your child can tear out the pages that you're working on and use one book together.

## How do the lessons work?

The teaching and student pages work together. The lesson instruction and teaching ideas for each specific lesson appear first. Activities that offer opportunities for your child to practice the specific skills and review the concepts being taught follow. Creativity and imagination abound! Throughout each lesson, hands-on activities are incorporated using concepts that are meaningful and relevant to kids' daily lives. The activities account for all types of learning styles—visual, auditory, or kinesthetic learning. For more information on learning styles, see the Glossary on page 351.

### *Objective and Background*

Each lesson opens with an objective that tells you exactly what the lesson is about. The background of the lesson follows, giving you the rationale behind the importance of the material being addressed. Each lesson is broken down for you so that you and your student can see how the skills and concepts taught are useful in everyday situations.

### *Materials and Vocabulary*

Have you ever done a project and found out you're missing something when you get to the end? A list of materials is given up front so you'll know what you need before you begin. The lessons take into account that you have access to your local library, a computer and the Internet, writing instruments, a calculator, and a notebook and loose paper, so you won't find these listed. The materials are household items when possible so that even the most technical of science experiments can be done easily. The *Making the Grade* series paves the way for your learning experience whether you and your student are sitting side by side on the couch or in a classroom, at the library, or even on vacation!

Following the materials list, vocabulary words may be given offering clear, easy-to-understand definitions.

### *Let's Begin*

Let's Begin is just that, "Let's Begin!" The instructional portion of the lesson opens with easy, user-friendly, numbered steps that guide you through the teaching of a particular lesson. Here you'll find opportunities to interact with your student and engage in discussions about what he or she is learning. There also are opportunities for your student to practice his or her critical-thinking skills to make the learning experience richer.

In the margins are interesting facts about what you're studying, time-savers, or helpful ideas.

### *Ways to Extend the Lesson*

Every lesson concludes with ways to extend the lesson—teaching tips, such as hints, suggestions, or ideas, for you to use in teaching the lesson or a section of the lesson. Each lesson also ends with an opportunity for you to "check in" and assess how well your student has mastered the skill or grasped the concepts being taught in the lesson. The For Further Reading section lists books that you can use as additional references and support in teaching the lesson. It also offers your student more opportunities to practice a skill or a chance to take a deeper look into the content.

### *Student Learning Pages*

Student Learning Pages immediately follow the teaching pages in each lesson. These pages offer fun opportunities to practice the skills and concepts being taught. And there are places where your student gets to choose what to do next and take ownership of his or her learning!

### *Visual Aids*

Throughout the book you'll see references to the Venn Diagram, Comparison Chart, Web, Sequence Chain, and Grid found in the back of the book. Many lessons incorporate these graphic organizers, or visual methods of organizing information, into the learning. If one is used in a lesson, it will be listed in the materials so that prior to the lesson you or your student can make a photocopy of it from the back of the book or you can have your student copy it into his or her notebook. See the Glossary for more information on graphic organizers.

## What about field trips or learning outside the classroom?

Some unique features of the *Making the Grade* series are the In Your Community activities at the end of each subject section. These activities describe ways to explore your community, taking advantage of your local or regional culture, industry, and environment while incorporating the skills learned in the lessons. For example, you can have your student help out at a farmer's market or with a local environmental group. These unique activities can supplement your ability to provide support for subjects. The activities give your student life experiences upon which he or she can build and expand the canvas upon which he or she learns.

These pages are identified in the Table of Contents so that you can read them first as a way to frame your student's learning.

## How do I know if my student is learning the necessary skills?

Although each lesson offers an opportunity for on-the-spot assessment, a formalized assessment section is located in the back of this book. You'll find a combination of multiple-choice and open-ended questions testing your student on the skills, concepts, and topics covered.

Also, at the end of every subject section is a We Have Learned checklist. This checklist provides a way for you and your student to summarize what you've accomplished. It lists specific concepts, and there is additional space for you and your student to write in other topics you've covered.

## Does this book come with answers?

Yes. Answers are provided in the back of the book for both the lessons and assessment.

## What if this book uses a homeschooling or educational term with which I'm not familiar?

In addition to the vocabulary words listed in the lessons, a two-page Glossary is provided in the back of the book. Occasionally terms will surface that may need further explanation in order for the learning experience to flourish. In the Glossary you'll find terms explained simply to help you give your student a rewarding learning experience free from confusion.

## Will this book help me find resources within the schools for homeschoolers?

In Communicating Between Home and School, there are suggestions for how to take advantage of the opportunities and resources offered by your local schools and how these benefits can enhance your homeschooling learning experiences.

## I'm new to homeschooling. How can I find out about state regulations, curriculum, and other resources?

In For Homeschoolers at the beginning of the book, you'll find information about national and state legislation, resources for curriculum and materials, and other references. Also included is a comprehensive list of online resources for everything from homeschooling organizations to military homeschooling to homeschooling supplies.

## How can I use this book if my student attends a public or private school?

*Making the Grade* fits into any child's educational experience—whether he or she is being taught at home or in a traditional school setting.

# For Homeschoolers

Teaching children at home isn't a new phenomenon. But it's gaining in popularity as caregivers decide to take a more active role in the education of their children. And despite prejudices that still exist, homeschoolers regularly succeed in college, the workplace, and society.

Whether you're new to homeschooling or have been educating your children at home for quite some time, you've probably found that the homeschooling path can be riddled with detours and unhelpful information. This book hopes to minimize those detours by offering information on state regulations, homeschooling approaches and curriculum, and other resources to keep you on the path toward a rewarding learning experience.

## Regulations

There never has been a federal law prohibiting parents from homeschooling their children. A homeschooler isn't required to have a teaching degree nor is he or she required to teach children in a specific location. Nonetheless, each state has its own set of regulations, educational requirements, and guidelines for those who homeschool.

Some states and areas of the United States have stricter regulations than others. Alabama; Alaska; Arizona; California; Delaware; Guam; Idaho; Illinois; Indiana; Kansas; Kentucky; Michigan; Mississippi; Missouri; Montana; Nebraska; New Jersey; New Mexico; Oklahoma; Puerto Rico; Texas; Virgin Islands; Washington, D.C.; Wisconsin; and Wyoming are considered to have a low level of regulation. Maine, Massachusetts, Minnesota, Nevada, New York, North Dakota, Pennsylvania, Rhode Island, Utah, Vermont, Washington, and West Virginia are considered to have a high level of regulation. The remaining states and areas not mentioned are considered to have a moderate level of homeschooling regulation.

But what does low, moderate, and high regulation mean? These classifications indicate the level of regulation that a particular state can enforce upon someone who has chosen to teach a child at home. Within each of these levels there are also varying rules and laws.

These regulations begin with how to enter the world of homeschooling. Some states, such as New Jersey, don't require parents to notify the school of their intent to teach their children at home, yet a letter of intent often is submitted out of courtesy. New Jersey's regulations note that all children of compulsory school age must be in an instructional program equivalent to that provided in the public schools. In Texas, another state that's considered to have a low level of regulation, parents don't have to notify anyone of their intent to homeschool their children. Texas homeschools are considered private schools and aren't subject to state regulation.

States with moderate levels of regulation often require letters of intent to homeschool be submitted, as well as regular logs of instruction be kept, and other guidelines be followed. Florida, for example, requires that parents send a letter of intent to their local superintendent. Florida homeschoolers also have to log schoolwork and have the child annually evaluated using one of the methods of evaluation.

Other "moderate" states have different requirements of their homeschoolers. In South Carolina, parents who are intending to homeschool their children must have either a high school diploma or have passed the GED (general educational development) test. Parents have three choices when it comes to homeschooling in this state: (1) they can maintain instruction under the supervision of their local school district, which would vary by district, (2) they can homeschool under the direction of the South Carolina Association of Independent Home Schools (SCAIHS), which would require them to pay annual dues, have their child tested annually, and have their curriculum reviewed, or (3) they must be accountable to one of the state homeschooling associations.

States that are considered to have a high level of homeschooling regulation often require parents who teach their children at home to follow guidelines throughout the school year. Pennsylvania has a strict policy for homeschoolers and requires parents to submit a notarized affidavit of intent to homeschool, along with medical records and learning objectives for certain subjects. Note that the school only has the authority to say whether the required documentation was submitted, not to determine whether the homeschooling plan of instruction is acceptable or unacceptable. The parents also must keep records of instruction and of attendance during the year. At the end of the school year, the child must be evaluated by either a certified teacher or a licensed psychologist, a portfolio of schoolwork needs to be submitted, and in certain grades the child must take a standardized test. Also, parents who plan to teach their children at home must have a high school education. Pennsylvania, however, does offer another homeschooling option. Parents can have children homeschooled by a tutor who is a certified teacher, in which case the parents only need to submit the tutor's credentials and criminal record.

Parents intending to homeschool their children in New York, another state considered to have a high level of regulation, must file a letter indicating their intentions and submit an IHIP (Individualized Home Instruction Plan). As in Pennsylvania, the school doesn't have the authority to determine the acceptability of the IHIP, only whether information was submitted as outlined by the state. The parents also must submit quarterly reports during the year and engage the child in at least 900 hours of instruction for grades K–6. At the end of each school year, the homeschooled child must be assessed, which can mean taking a standardized assessment test in some years and having the parents provide a narrative of assessment in others. In Minnesota, another state that has a high level of regulation, parents must submit the names and birth dates of the children they plan to homeschool annually. The parents also must have a bachelor's degree, or else they will have to submit quarterly report cards to the school. Parents also must provide supporting documentation about the subject matter that is being taught, although the information needed may vary from school district to school district. In addition, homeschooled children in this state must be tested annually, but the school doesn't need to see the test results.

No matter what level of regulation your state has, there are ways to operate your homeschool with success. Here are a few tips as you negotiate the homeschooling waters:

- Be aware of what is a requirement and what isn't; you don't have to send extra forms and documentation if it's not required. Even if some schools ask for or prefer to see certain things—you don't have to comply if it's not legally required!
- All of these laws, rules, and regulations may seem like more trouble than they're worth. The Home School Legal Defense Association (HSLDA) can help in outlining your state's requirements; go to the association's Web site at *http://www.hslda.org*. For more information on your state's laws and related references, see the Homeschooling Online Resources that follow. They can help you find information on your specific state and may be able to direct you to local homeschooling groups.
- Veteran homeschoolers in your area can be a fountain of practical knowledge about the laws.

## Homeschooling Military Families

Frequently moving from location to location can be exhausting for families with one or more parent in the military. If you have school-age children, it can be even more complicated. Schools across states and U.S. schools in other countries often don't follow the same curriculum, and states often can have varying curriculum requirements for each grade.

The Department of Defense Dependent Schools (DoDDS) is responsible for the military educational system. There are three educational options for military families:

1. attend school with other military children
2. if in a foreign country, attend the local school in which the native language is spoken, although this option may require approval
3. homeschool

Homeschooling can provide consistency for families who have to relocate often. The move itself, along with the new culture your family will be exposed to, is a learning experience that can be incorporated into the curriculum. Note that military families that homeschool must abide by the laws of the area in which they reside, which may be different from where they claim residency for tax purposes. If your relocation takes your family abroad, one downside is the lack of curriculum resources available on short notice. Nonetheless, military homeschoolers may be able to use resources offered at base schools.

## Approaches and Curriculum

If you're reading this book you've probably already heard of many different approaches and methods to homeschooling, which some homeschoolers refer to as *unschooling* (see the Glossary for more information). It's important that you choose one approach or method that works best for you—there's no right or wrong way to homeschool!

The curriculum and materials that are used vary from person to person, but there are organizations that offer books, support, and materials to homeschoolers. Many homeschoolers find that a combination of methods works best. That's one of the reasons *Making the Grade* was created!

## Support Groups and Organizations

Homeschooling has become more popular, and the United States boasts a number of nationally recognized homeschooling organizations. Also, nearly every state has its own homeschooling organization to provide information on regulations in addition to other support. Many religious and ethnic groups also have their own homeschooling organizations.

## Homeschooling Online Resources

These are some of the online resources available for homeschoolers. You also can check your phone book for local organizations and resources.

### *National Organizations*

Alliance for Parental Involvement in Education
*http://www.croton.com/allpie/*

Alternative Education Resource Organization (AERO)
*http://www.edrev.org/links.htm*

American Homeschool Association (AHA)
*http://www.americanhomeschoolassociation.org/*

Home School Foundation
*http://www.homeschoolfoundation.org*

National Coalition of Alternative Community Schools
*http://www.ncacs.org/*

National Home Education Network (NHEN)
*http://www.nhen.org/*

National Home Education Research Institute (NHERI)
*http://www.nheri.org*

National Homeschooling Association (NHA)
*http://www.n-h-a.org*

### *Homeschooling and the Law*

Advocates for the Rights of Homeschoolers (ARH)
*http://www.geocities.com/arhfriends/*

Home School Legal Defense Association (HSLDA)
*http://www.hslda.org*

### *Children with Special Needs*

Children with Disabilities
*http://www.childrenwithdisabilities.ncjrs.org/*

Institutes for the Achievement of Human Potential (IAHP)
*http://www.iahp.org/*

National Challenged Homeschoolers Associated Network (NATHHAN)
*http://www.nathhan.com/*

### *Military Homeschooling*

Department of Defense Dependent Schools/Education Activity (DoDDS)
*http://www.odedodea.edu/*

### *Books, Supplies, Curriculum*

Federal Resources for Educational Excellence
*http://www.ed.gov/free/*

Home Schooling Homework
*http://www.dailyhomework.org/*

Home School Products
*http://www.homeschooldiscount.com/*

Homeschooler's Curriculum Swap
*http://theswap.com/*

HomeSchoolingSupply.com
*http://www.homeschoolingsupply.com/*

### *General Homeschooling Resources*

Family Unschoolers Network
*http://www.unschooling.org*

Home Education Magazine
*http://www.home-ed-magazine.com/*

Homeschool Central
*http://www.homeschoolcentral.com*

Homeschool Internet Yellow Pages
*http://www.homeschoolyellowpages.com/*

Homeschool World
*http://www.home-school.com/*

Homeschool.com
*http://www.homeschool.com/*

HSAdvisor.com
*http://www.hsadvisor.com/*

Unschooling.com
*http://www.unschooling.com/*

Waldorf Without Walls
*http://www.waldorfwithoutwalls.com/*

# Communicating Between Home and School

For homeschoolers, often there is limited contact with the schools beyond that which is required by the state. Yet a quick glance at your local schools will reveal opportunities, resources, and benefits that can offer you flexibility and that can supplement your child's total learning experience.

## Special Needs

If you have a child with special needs, such as dyslexia or ADHD (attention deficit hyperactivity disorder), taking advantage of the programs and services your public school provides can expand your support system and give you some relief in working with your child. In many instances, the easy access and little or no cost of these services makes this a viable option for homeschoolers.

Depending on your child's diagnosed needs, some school districts may offer full services and programs, while some may only provide consultations. In addition, some school districts' special education departments have established parent support networks that you may be able to participate in as a homeschooler. States and school districts vary in terms of what homeschoolers are allowed to participate in, so check with your local school administrator and then check with your state's regulations to verify your eligibility.

Two organizations, the Home School Legal Defense Association (HSLDA) and the National Challenged Homeschoolers Association Network (NATHHAN), offer a wide range of information and assistance on services and programs available for special needs children. Check them out on the Internet at *http://www.hslda.org* and *http://www.nathhan.com*. Your local homeschooling group—especially veteran homeschoolers—will have practical information you can use.

Additionally, some homeschooling parents combine the resources of a school with those offered by a private organization to maximize support.

## Gifted Children

If your child is considered gifted, your local public school may have programs available for students who require additional intellectual attention. Check with your local school administrator and your state's regulations first. In addition to providing information on special needs children, HSLDA and NATHHAN offer resources for parents of gifted children.

Don't be afraid to check out the colleges in your area, too. Many times colleges, especially community colleges, offer classes or onetime workshops that might be of interest to your child. Check with your local schools to see how you can take advantage of these opportunities.

## Extracurricular Activities

Locations of other homeschooling families in the area, schedules, and different homeschooling approaches can make creating clubs specifically for homeschoolers challenging. Nonetheless, extracurricular activities at your local schools can give your child opportunities for peer interaction, and it can help him or her develop new skills and interests that homeschooling situations can't always provide. For example, if your child has shown an interest in music and wants to play in a band, many communities don't have youth bands or orchestras (or if they do, the child must play at a certain level); in a school setting, however, your child might be able to play in the school band at his or her own level. Sometimes taking music lessons from a school's band leader is also an option.

Other extracurricular activities, such as Girl Scouts and Boy Scouts (or if your child is older, a language club or an academic club, such as one for math, science, or debate), might offer additional opportunities for your homeschooler to interact with his or her peers and have a worthwhile learning experience at the same time. These types of groups often need parent volunteers as leaders, which can provide you with additional interaction with the school. If your homeschooled child is interested in extracurricular athletics, towns might not offer community-based athletics at a competitive level, so participating in school sports may be an option to consider, especially for your older child.

Your school also might have other resources that are suited to your needs. For example, the school library may be a better place than your community library to go to for the materials you need. Many schools also have certain times of the week or season when the gymnasium is open to the community for use. And some schools even host special seasonal activities for students during holiday breaks. Contact your local school district before participating.

## Returning to School

If you plan on having your child return to school, taking advantage of the programs and opportunities offered can help ease the transition back into the classroom. Your child will already experience a sense of familiarity with his or her surroundings and peers, which can help smooth the transition to a different structure of learning.

# Meet Your Fifth Grader

The fifth-grade year is usually a time of agreeableness and smooth family relations in a child's life. A fifth grader is still enjoying the innocence of childhood and finding comfort in family routines while he or she takes the initial steps toward establishing an individual identity.

Of course, each child's development occurs according to his or her uniqueness and individual pattern of growth. Your child may progress slightly ahead of or behind the most common growth pattern or may even swing to one extreme or the other. In any case, having a solid understanding of the stages of child development and the usual social, emotional, physical, and mental growth patterns for a child between 10 and 11 and a half years old is very important for parents and teachers alike.

## Embrace Active Lifestyle

Fifth graders tend to enjoy themselves and maintain a "life is good" perspective. Of course, adults might have the same sunny attitude if we spent as much time out-of-doors playing games with friends as our fifth graders do. A child at this age is probably more interested in action than thought. Movement takes top priority. Fifth graders are compelled to be outdoors running, biking, and playing games that build their large motor skills. Your student will be especially attracted to playing close to home with the neighborhood children. There is a new drive to realize his or her potential physical abilities. Though not competitive with other children, he or she is physically competitive with himself or herself and is in a constant and wondrous process of discovering the answer to the question "What am I capable of doing?" It's important to allow ample time on a daily basis for the active instincts of your fifth grader to be expressed. Study time and lessons are important, but consideration needs to be made for this internal calling to move.

## Recognize Love of Nature

Another reason your fifth grader likes to be outdoors relates to a new awareness and appreciation of nature. A child at this age may be concerned about the environment and inspired to participate in conservation projects through your local forest preserve or nature center. You also may observe an interest in learning how to classify animals and an enthusiasm for seeing deer, birds, fish, and other animals in the wild. Your fifth grader may have a favorite animal about which he or she is passionate. If your family doesn't already have a pet, you may face a constant plea during this year to get one.

## Enjoy Family Relations

Fifth graders remain loyal to their families and generally don't show signs of desire to escape family influence. Favorite topics of writing include family and parents. Your fifth grader will choose the safety and emotional security of siding with a parent's opinion over a friend's. Though they may be harsh with siblings, fifth graders are usually pleasant to have around. A child in the fifth grade appreciates and strives for harmonious relations. A fifth grader doesn't like to be singled out as the best or the winner. He or she wants to do well and be as good as his or her peers but is concerned with how winning affects other people's feelings in the group.

## Present Clear Lines of Authority

Your fifth grader also is willing and in need of clear, structured authority and the guidance of straightforward standards and rules. Where discipline is concerned, the consequences for your fifth grader's unfavorable actions must be fair and relevant for him or her to understand and benefit from them. Your child will respond well to being informed about plans and decisions ahead of time so he or she can create appropriate expectations without disorienting surprises.

## Offer Guidance for Self-Control

A fifth grader is still unskilled at handling hurt feelings and his or her own anger. Deep feelings, both of affection and anger, tend to come in sudden outbursts. This inconsistency can undermine a fifth grader's friendly, sincere desire for camaraderie. Dealing appropriately with anger seems to be an especially challenging endeavor for fifth graders. Responses to angry feelings can be violent and may include foot stomping, yelling, kicking, and hitting. Your child prefers not to be cross, wants to be fair, and is eager to get along with everyone. In order to achieve this goal, he or she will need guidance and direction from caring adults who can teach him or her how to express feelings and communicate in respectful ways. Your fifth grader is open to input and willing to meet issues head on. Soon, he or she may not be so open. In fact, later, foot stomping may seem like a walk in the park compared to the trying attitudes of adolescence. Keep things in perspective and take full advantage of the opportunity to support and guide your child now.

## Understand Personal Habits

As your child romps his or her way through the fifth-grade year, expect resistance in the area of bathing. Generally a fifth grader doesn't want to come in to clean up. It may seem like his or her lifestyle has taken the tone of an outdoor camp, including a natural and accepted dismissal of daily hygiene. Your fifth grader's habits may seem completely inappropriate to you, but remember that he or she is experiencing a surge of kinetic energy through his or her body. There is a new awareness of the physical self in relation to the natural world. Your child is one with nature, his or her greatest love right now, and bathing is physically unappealing and contradictory to his or her senses. It can be helpful to set a regular schedule of "bath days" and bath times that can be enforced. Be assured that this stage won't last long and may change to the opposite extreme as your child matures.

Regarding fifth graders and clothing, the more comfortable and familiar the better. Old clothes and once-worn (or twice-worn or more!) clothes are the favorites and probably spend their unworn time crumpled on the floor. This will also change over the next one to two years. Fifth graders don't like to clean their rooms. Simple instructions to complete such as "make your bed," "hang up your clothes," and "pick up your projects" are often better received than the more general "clean your room." Your child will be better motivated to clean or do chores if he or she can work along with a helpful and directing adult. You may also notice that while the bed is unmade and the room is a mess, the picture of a favorite animal or sports team is placed meticulously on the wall.

In the area of food, your fifth grader may have favorite foods that he or she describes with a passion. Similarly, he or she may make dramatic refusals to certain foods using the words "I hate" and even making vomiting gestures. You will probably find that your fifth grader eats more than in the past and that he or she can eat at any time. Your child might lose interest in breakfast, however, and prefer to make this up with an extra snack before bed.

## Gauge Sexual Education Needs

The new awareness and physical changes that accompany your fifth grader's budding sexuality will produce different if not opposite reactions in boys and girls. A fifth-grade boy will tend toward obnoxiousness and humor concerning the subject of the body. Burping and jokes about elimination and other bodily functions are popular. He may retell sexual jokes that he has heard without understanding them. Although he may tell off-color sexual jokes, a fifth-grade boy tends to become more modest with his body when dressing or undressing. He will be curious about reproduction and may try to peek in on sisters or female peers to learn more—much to their horror.

Fifth-grade girls may be more private and prefer not to discuss much about sex, even with their families. Your female child might begin her menstrual cycle in fifth grade. While one fifth-grade girl may be eager to learn more about this, another may react with repulsion or be unexpectedly casual about the subject. A fifth-grade girl tends to be eager about breast growth and may want to experiment with a first bra, whether she needs one or not. Providing age-appropriate books about sex, reproduction, and babies that can be read in private may be a solution if your daughter is too embarrassed to talk directly to you about these topics. Follow up to see if she has questions, either verbally or with a special, private note.

## Encourage Thoughtful Observation

Mentally, a fifth-grade child is reality-bound, practical, and literal. He or she is more comfortable dealing with the here and now and the status quo. Your fifth grader's sense of humor will lean toward corny jokes, practical jokes, and puns. Because he or she still hasn't embraced abstract thought or ironic subtlety, your child's humor will probably be lost on you until he or she enters adolescence.

On a simple level, a fifth grader is good at grouping and understanding relationships and at gathering information based on up-front clues. He or she has become aware that different people have different lifestyles and diverse living habits. Your fifth-grade child may begin to comment, usually with neutrality, on the homes, possessions, and activities of the people down the street or in other countries. He or she may be interested in communicating more with people outside your family's cultural group.

## Balance Lesson Plans

Memorization comes easily to fifth graders and learning new facts can be a source of interest and amusement. At times your child may seem like a walking encyclopedia of unsolicited but interesting information. He or she will tend to grasp single-function math exercises easily but shy away from complex, multistep problems. For better or worse, most fifth-grade curricula do include some complex math functions and critical-thinking skills. The *Making the Grade* series offers a wide range of opportunities to modify or direct lessons to meet your child's needs. Your fifth grader will be naturally attracted to certain subjects and self-motivated to absorb new facts and information. Keep the emphasis on what he or she does know and go from there.

When doing lesson work with your fifth grader, keep in mind that he or she will appreciate knowing what is coming next and having a set lesson schedule. When teaching, you will need to provide ample opportunity for movement or action breaks in the study day, especially in the afternoon. Even if your child hasn't been a primarily kinesthetic, or movement oriented, learner in the past, incorporating more hands-on learning and movement is appropriate at this time. The *Making the Grade* series helps with this. Your fifth grader will want to please the teacher or parent, but his or her heart is called out to play, play, and play some more. Be conscientious of neighborhood play hours and schedule study time accordingly.

It's not uncommon for fifth graders to lose interest in reading during this year. Their energy has moved out of their heads and into their bodies in a big way. Reading books to your child is helpful. He or she may seem a bit old to be read to, but most children at this age still enjoy a book read aloud. Letting your fifth grader see you read on your own reinforces good reading habits and allows you to continue being a positive role model.

## Have Fun!

Enjoy your child during this year. He or she is interesting, full of information, and open to sharing. Chances are he or she has become a good talker and listener, too. This pleasing demeanor and loyalty to parents make your fifth grader very easy to be around. Make it a priority to have fun together. This is most likely the last year of innocence, agreeability, admiration, and eagerness to please before the contradictory adolescent stages begin. The positive reinforcement you instill now, together with the fond memories that you and your child create, will serve as a stabilizer for any potential turbulence in the future.

# Promoting Literacy

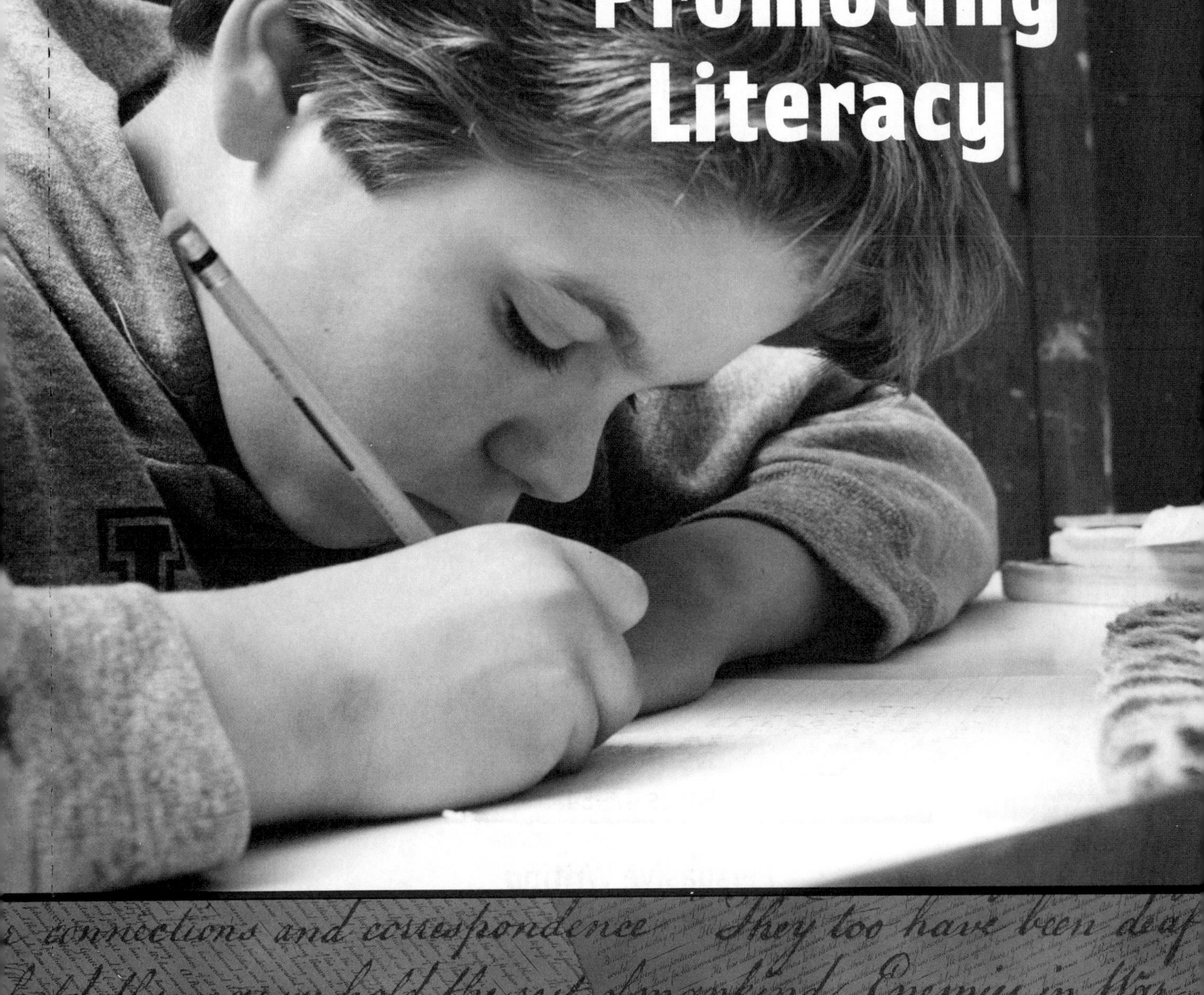

# Promoting Literacy

## Key Topics

TEACHING THE LESSON

# Understanding Narrative Fiction

*The art of storytelling will never diminish.*

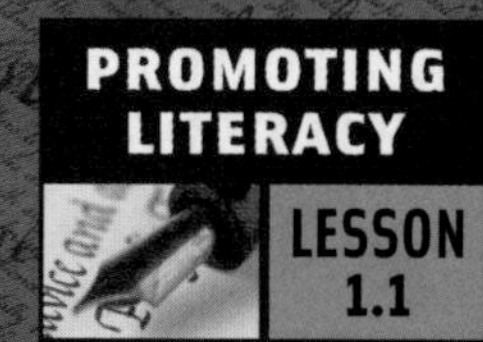


| OBJECTIVE | BACKGROUND | MATERIALS |
|---|---|---|
| To have your student orally deliver a narrative and then read a narrative | Oral storytelling is telling a tale using voice and gesture. Before the written word, oral storytelling was the method through which people learned their history, settled disagreements, and tried to make sense of the world around them. Storytelling was a way to entertain as well as inform. Acquiring oral skills is a good way for your student to prepare for writing. In this lesson, your student will learn how to tell a story, then he or she will read a narrative. | ■ Student Learning Pages 1.A–1.E |

## Let's Begin

**1** **CHOOSE A STORY** Explain that a storyteller needs to decide what story he or she would like to tell. Reveal that the story can be one of the following: a folktale he or she would like to retell; a story he or she has read or heard; or a personal story of something that happened to him or her. Ask your student what story he or she would like to tell.

**2** **REVEAL** Reveal that the story must have (1) characters, (2) a setting, and (3) a plot. Ask your student if he or she knows what these elements are.

**3** **EXPLAIN: CHARACTERS** Point out that characters are the people in the story. Characters also can be animals or objects that communicate, such as talking computers. Ask your student to name some characters in a story he or she might tell.

**4** **RELATE: SETTING** Relate that setting is where the story takes place. A story can have one setting or many different settings. Ask, *If you were telling a story about an astronaut, what setting or settings might be in your story? What might be the settings for a folktale? A personal story?*

**5** **EXPLAIN: PLOT** Explain that the plot of a story is made up of the events that happen. The events happen in a sequence: the

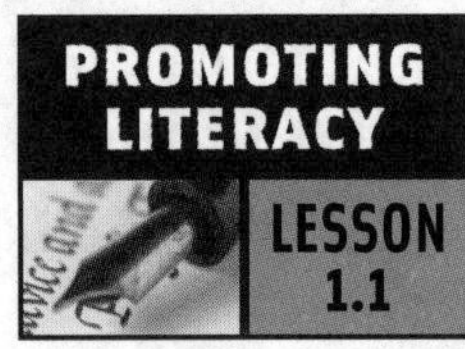

PROMOTING LITERACY

LESSON 1.1

beginning, middle, and end of the story. The plot also tells about the conflict, or problem, in the story and how it is resolved. Ask your student to name examples of problems that happen in stories.

**6** **ORGANIZE AND DISTRIBUTE** Distribute Student Learning Page 1.A. Tell your student that before he or she tells his or her story, it's helpful to use a time line to plan out the story.

**7** **PRESENT AN ORAL NARRATIVE** Have your student tell his or her story. Before he or she begins, encourage him or her to do the following:

1. Speak clearly and with vocal expression.
2. Use facial and body expressions to make the storytelling more lively.
3. Make eye contact with the listener or listeners.
4. Create different voices for characters to show who is speaking (if there is dialogue in the story).

**8** **ASSESS** Assess your student's understanding of presenting an oral narrative by reviewing the steps:

1. Choose a story.
2. Plan out the story events on a time line.
3. Tell the story clearly and with expression.

**9** **DISTRIBUTE** Distribute Student Learning Page 1.B. Allow your student time to read and do each activity. Then invite your student to retell part of his or her story, incorporating more body language.

**10** **DISTRIBUTE** Now distribute Student Learning Page 1.C. Have your student read the story then discuss. Ask, *What do you think of the author's writing?* Direct your student to explain why he or she thinks the passage is well written and enjoyable, or not. Ask, *What do you think will happen next in the story? Why?* [answers will vary] Then distribute Student Learning Page 1.D.

**FOR FURTHER READING**

*How and Why Stories: World Tales Kids Can Read and Tell,* by Martha Hamilton and Carol Lyon, ill. (August House Publishing, Inc., 1999).

*Storytelling for the Fun of It: A Handbook for Children,* by Vivian Dubrivin and Bobbi Shupe, ill. (Storycraft Publishing, 1999).

*Tradin' Tales with Grandpa: A Kid's Guide for Intergenerational Storytelling,* by Vivian Dubrivin and Bobbi Shupe, ill. (Storycraft Publishing, 2000).

# Branching Out

## TEACHING TIP

Learning oral skills is a good way for your student to rehearse for writing. A student who has to remember and organize details into a story will later find those details easier to capture in writing.

## CHECKING IN

One way to assess how well your student understands narrative is to ask how the oral and written narrative are the same and how they are different.

# Complete the Time Line

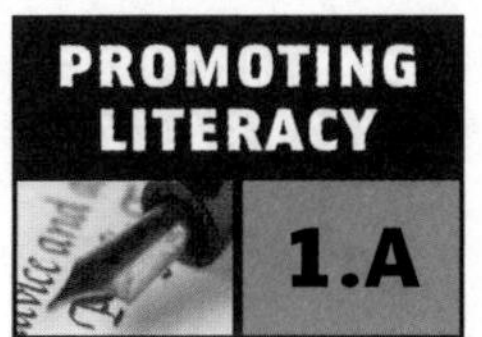


In order for a storyteller to tell a story, he or she must clearly know what happened. A time line can help you organize your events. After you have decided what story you will tell, complete the time line by writing the important events in your story in the order in which they occurred.

---

**Time Line of Events in Your Story**

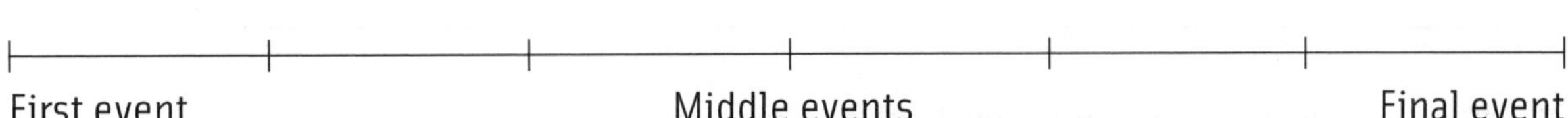

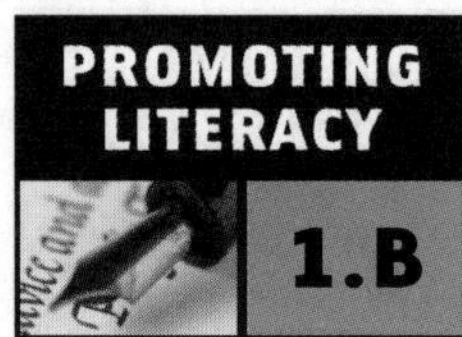


# Use Body Language

In everyday life, we speak with our bodies as well as our voices. How we stand, move, gesture, and use our eyes all communicate meaning. When you tell a story, you can let your body speak, too. Read each sentence and write how your body would speak.

---

1. "It was really scary in the dark forest!"

_______________________________________________

2. "Get over here, fast!"

_______________________________________________

3. "I'm so tired after running the race."

_______________________________________________

4. "Stay away! That's quicksand!"

_______________________________________________

5. "The puppy is so adorable!"

_______________________________________________

6. "Be quiet! The baby is asleep."

_______________________________________________

7. "She couldn't wait to open her birthday presents."

_______________________________________________

8. "Phew! It's hot!"

_______________________________________________

9. "It's so cold out here."

_______________________________________________

10. "I'm so sleepy after watching the movie."

_______________________________________________

# Understand Narrative Fiction

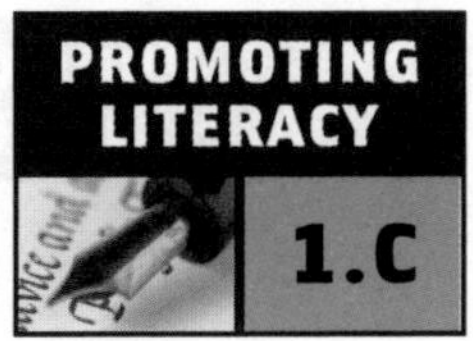


## The Library Card

by Jerry Spinelli

### Chapter 1

When my father said we were moving to a farm, I thought to myself, Okay, good. I was sick of the toilet that would never work. Sick of seeing my breath in winter in the bedroom. Sick of being afraid to open the kitchen cupboard because a rat might jump out, like it really did once.

So I was happy to come here, to a farm in Pennsylvania. Until I found out what kind of farm it was.

A mushroom farm.

I always hated mushrooms. In New York City that was easy to do: I just didn't eat them. I don't eat them here either, but I can't stop breathing, and that's where they get me. Because they stink.

Well, not the mushrooms themselves, but the stuff they grow in. It's not regular dirt, like any decent, normal plant. Oh no. They have to grow in poop. Horse poop to be exact.

There's piles of it all over. Heaps. Mountains. You can see the smell steaming off it. My father's boss laughed the first time he saw me holding my nose. It's only part poop, he said (except he said "manure"). He said they mix it with corncobs and other stuff. Big deal. They could mix it with Peppermint Patties and it would still smell like poop.

"Don't think of it that way," my mother tells me. "Think of it as the opposite. A perfume." She lifts her upper lip, sticks out her little finger, and says like a French lady, *"Eau de perfoom."* I laugh, and still smell poop.

Now, do these mountains of horse dung stay outside where they belong? Oh no. The workers shovel it inside, into long low buildings, because that's where mushrooms like to grow. In the dark.

(CONTINUED)

In spite of their taste, in spite of the smell, maybe I could stand to live with mushrooms if at least they grew in the sunshine like everything else. But they don't, and that makes them creepy, evil, the werewolves of the plant world. Sometimes I think they're in cahoots with the moon. Sometimes at night I feel them out there in their long low houses, silently oozing their little round white faces up out of their dark, smelly blankets: the moon and her million babies. I get the willies.

"It's your imagination running away with you," says my mother. Maybe so, but the stories I hear around here don't help either. Weird stories about mushrooms and their dark powers and how they can grow *anywhere,* wherever it's dark and there's the smallest speck of dirt. I had a nightmare once that I awoke to find them sprouting from between my toes.

So I never have to be told to take a shower; instead, I usually have to be told to get out. I try to keep my dark places lit up. I lie outside on a blanket in my bathing suit. I keep my arms upraised, I make sure both ears get a turn at the sun, and I spread my toes apart with jelly beans.

I don't think it's going to get better when school starts next week. I hear they call people like me "mushies."

Maybe I could stand all this if there was a library around. In New York City the library was only two blocks from our apartment. Whenever I felt bad, that's were I went. In fact, I went there when I felt good too. I was there every day. I got mad one time at Christmas when I found out the library was closed.

I loved my library card. It was all creased and smudged and spilled on, and the corners were rounded and furry. But it was the only official card I have ever had, and the reason it was so beat-up was because I carried it with me everywhere, because I never knew when I might need it. My mother said it was a good thing I had it too, letting me bring books home, because otherwise I would never leave the library, because I couldn't stop reading. She would have to bring my meals to the library and send along my stuffed red hippo so I could sleep right. We used to laugh about that.

I still have the card. Each day I stick it in my pocket, just like in New York City. But I'm in Mushroom Land now, and I haven't seen a library since we moved here.

(CONTINUED) 

# Chapter 2

When I woke up this morning a breeze was blowing *eau do perfoom* through my bedroom window. I knew I needed a break.

I decided to pack a lunch and take a hike. Then I figured, why wait till lunch? I put a cream cheese and jelly sandwich and an apple in a paper bag and announced to my mother what I was doing. I told her I would only go as far as the trees at the edge of the farm; you can see them from the house. She said take something to drink. I said I'm not going to be gone that long. She said be careful.

It was true—I didn't think I would be gone very long. I didn't expect to go past the trees. But I got there so fast, I thought, What kind of hike is that? And I could still smell the smell. So I took out my sandwich and kept walking. I guess my idea was to keep walking until I came to the end of the smell.

I walked through a field of cornstalk stubble, jumped over a little stream, climbed some fences, crossed some more fields, more mushroom farms, and always, steaming on the horizon, were the ever-present dark brown hills of *perfoom.* I finished the sandwich, finished the apple, and was starting to wish I had brought something to drink when I came to a road. I turned onto it.

I hadn't seen another person, and only a couple of cows since I left my house, and the road was just about as lonely. Every few minutes a truck roared by, and that was about it. It seemed like the rest of the world was smart enough to stay away from this place.

Mushroom Land is sort of hilly. The road dipped out of sight ahead of me, so I heard the next truck coming before I saw it. When it did come into view, it wasn't a truck after all, but a bus, green and white. I don't know why, but I stopped to watch it, and as it barreled down the road toward me I thought I must be having some sort of hallucination, those fumes were finally getting to me. Because I imagined I saw a word painted in big white letters across the green stripe above the wide window of the oncoming bus, and the word was

BOOKS

(CONTINUED) 

And then I jumped into my own hallucination. I was standing in the road waving my arms like a banshee, the bus blowing its horn and veering out to miss me, not slowing, not stopping. And then it was past me, gusting in my face—a bus without windows on the sides—and then brakes were screaming and gasping and half a city block beyond me the bus came to a halt, its two right wheels deep in blue roadside flowers. The squared-off top swayed against the sky.

The driver was a lady with a baseball cap and a T-shirt picturing a whale. She swiveled her seat to face me in the doorway.

The lady reached out and touched my shoulder. "What are you doing out here by yourself? Why were you waving us down?"

I told her about the hike and about looking up and seeing that word coming at me. "After that, I don't know. What kind of bus is this?"

She smiled and took my hand and pulled me all the way in. "It's a bookmobile."

 

PROMOTING LITERACY
LESSON 1.2

# Reading Historical Fiction

***It is said that history repeats itself; by learning about the past, we hope to avoid making the same mistakes in the future.***

| OBJECTIVE | BACKGROUND | MATERIALS |
|---|---|---|
| To have your student read historical fiction and write a fictional piece of his or her own | History lends itself to writers as a perfect setting for many stories. Historical fiction uses actual events, places, or people in fictional writing, which allows an author to both entertain and educate his or her readers. In this lesson, your student will read historical fiction and write his or her own historical fiction. | ■ Student Learning Pages 2.A–2.C |

**VOCABULARY**

**BOXCAR** a freight car, usually with sliding doors on the side

**BOWERY** a run-down area of New York City that, during the Great Depression, was filled with cheap restaurants and shops

**THREADBARE** having the fabric of clothing worn away so that the threads show

**FLOPHOUSES** cheap, broken-down hotels

## Let's Begin

**1** **BUILD BACKGROUND** Explain to your student that he or she will be reading a selection of historical fiction. This type of literature is a fictional story based on facts from a period in history. Explain that although points of the story may be factual, the tale that's told isn't real. Ask your student if he or she has read anything that could be considered historical fiction. Talk about why these books are considered historical fiction.

**2** **INTRODUCE** Share that the reading today is an excerpt from the book *Boxcar Molly: A Story from the Great Depression.* Explain that the Great Depression occurred in the 1930s in the United States, when the stock market crashed and many families were left poor and starving. Much of the nation suddenly became unemployed, and it was tough to find a job and earn money to buy things a family needed. Ask your student what he or she knows about the Great Depression. Then reveal that although the Depression was an actual historical event, the tale of Molly is fictional. To give your student a visual perspective of the Great Depression, check out photos of the time period on the

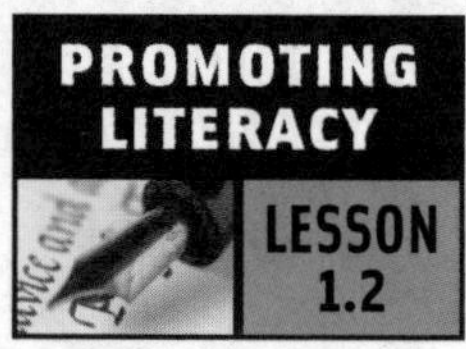


Library of Congress Web site at http://www.loc.gov. Note that because these are actual photos from the Depression, you may wish to preview them first in case they are disturbing.

**3** **DISTRIBUTE AND READ** Explain that in the story your student will be reading an excerpt from, Molly travels to various places riding in a **boxcar,** which is a freight car that often has sliding doors on the side. People could ride on trains in these freight cars, and the sliding doors made it easier for people to get on and off when the train stopped. Share that in this excerpt Molly and her traveling companion, Beanpole, are in New York City after having made their way on a freight train. Now distribute Student Learning Page 2.A.

**4** **REVIEW** Look back at the passage with your student for the words **Bowery, threadbare,** and **flophouses.** Explain that the Bowery was an area of New York City that, during the Depression, became run down and filled with cheap restaurants, bars, shops, and flophouses. Flophouses were broken-down hotels. Then reveal that threadbare describes clothing that has been worn away so that the threads show through.

**DID YOU KNOW?**

During the Great Depression, many people in the United States had no jobs, no homes, and little food to eat.

**5** **EXAMINE CHARACTERS** Have your student think about Molly and Beanpole. Ask, *What are some words to describe how Molly and Beanpole must have felt?* [possible answers: tired, lonely, courageous, scared, sad, hungry, anxious] Discuss.

**6** **MAKE THE CONNECTION** Tell your student that he or she will now write his or her own historical fiction. Invite your student to think of a historical event or time period. For ideas, have him or her look through the Social Studies lessons beginning on page 227. Then help your student research information about that period.

**7** **DISTRIBUTE** Distribute Student Learning Page 2.B. Have your student plan the characters, setting, and events of the story using this outline. Have your student begin drafting a story in his or her notebook, adding details to the basic events. Assist your student in proofreading and revising the story to complete a final draft.

**FOR FURTHER READING**

*Boxcar Molly: A Story from the Great Depression,* by James Riordan (Barron's Educational Series, Inc., 2002).

*Kids During the Great Depression,* by Lisa A. Wroble (PowerKids Press, 1999).

# Branching Out

## TEACHING TIP

If your student has shown an interest in this topic, have him or her read the entire book to see what happens after the excerpt.

## CHECKING IN

To assess your student's understanding of the story, ask him or her to describe in his or her own words what historical fiction is.

# Read Historical Fiction

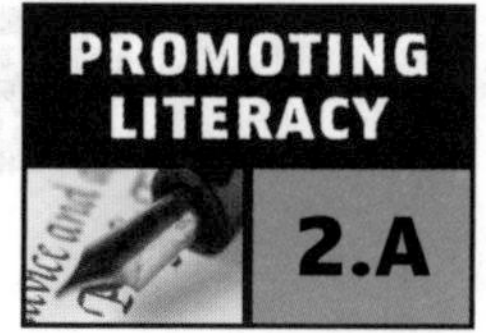


## Boxcar Molly: A Story from the Great Depression

by James Riordan

### Chapter 7

New York

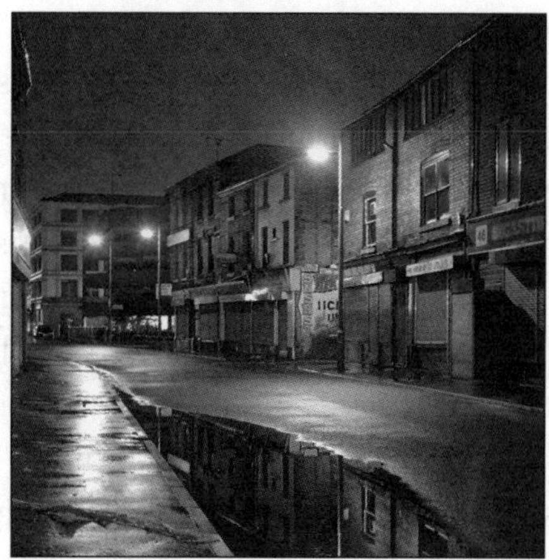

That afternoon in the winter of 1931, New York gave us a chilly welcome. It seemed too cold to rain, but it wasn't. The drops came down in slanting lines, driven by a bitter wind. The rainwater stood in pools in the railroad yard and along the shining streets.

Hands deep in pockets, collars high up around the ears, we headed for the Bowery where we'd heard there was a lodging house for the homeless. Beanpole had no idea if his uncle had received his letter informing him of our little social visit.

"We'll wait a couple of days and see how the land lies before we drop in on him," Beanpole said.

We had heard that five nights per month was the limit allowed at the Municipal Lodging House run by the New York City Department of Public Welfare. So we hoped for five nights' board until we descended on Beanpole's uncle. I couldn't help wondering if he would welcome visitors.

(CONTINUED) 

We headed for the lodging house, down on 25th Street near the East River. It wasn't hard to find. As we approached the **Bowery** we began to see little knots of people huddled in doorways or under bridges with the trains rumbling overhead. What with the rain and freezing wind, it was a bad time to be out, even if you were warmly dressed. These people weren't. Their shoes were broken, their clothes **threadbare.** They stared at us as we passed.

Now and then a joker had assembled half a dozen or more people about him. They would laugh noisily, unnaturally, whenever he reached the punchline of the joke. For most of the crowd, this was the only sound they made. These people were frightened, and frightened people keep silent.

Uneasily, Beanpole and I passed them by and turned a corner. We stopped dead in our tracks. Before us was a long line of men and women, three or sometimes four abreast, a block long, and wedged tightly together, so tightly that no one could get by.

I turned to Beanpole. "What's this about?" I asked.

"I guess that those at the front will eat tonight, and those at the back probably won't."

He was right. Every few minutes someone tried to break in at the front. From behind came a chorus of boos and jeers; the hungry and homeless disapproved of line jumpers.

Beanpole and I joined the line and got chatting to a middle-aged, barrel-chested man in front of us. He turned out to be an old hand at standing in line.

"The lodging house opens at four in the afternoon," he said in a deep growl; "so we've got an hour to kill before the line starts moving. It'll be twice as long by six. They take in one hundred and twenty-eight—not a single body more or less—every twenty-five minutes. That's the length of time it takes for one sitting in the dining room."

"What sort of grub do they serve up?" I asked.

"Each person gets a cup of coffee (in a tin mug, boiling hot), a big dish of stew (beef tonight, lamb tomorrow), and as much bread as he can eat. Anyone capable of downing a second helping of beef stew is welcome to it."

(CONTINUED) 

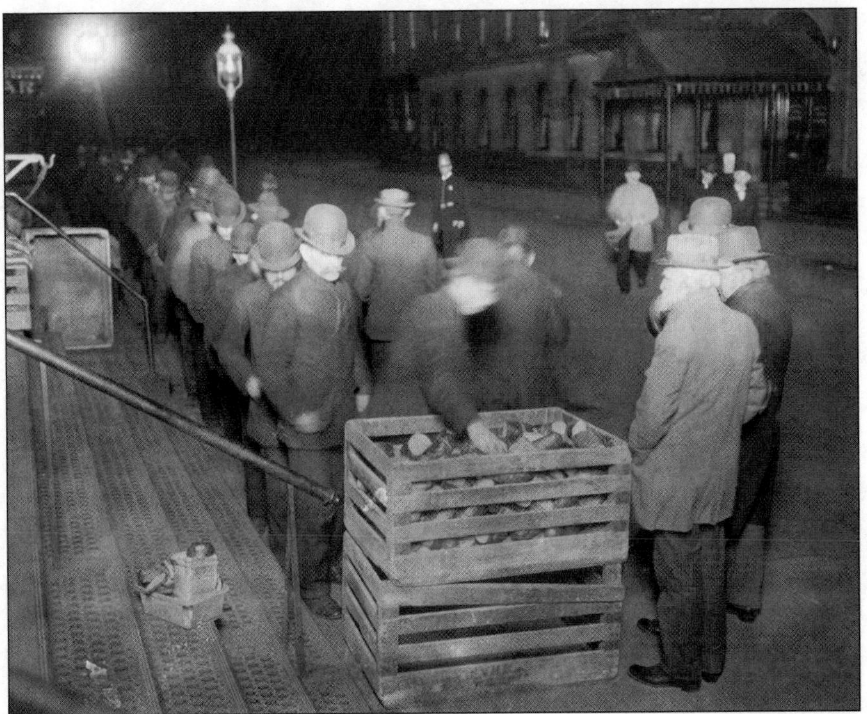

*During the Great Depression, people often waited in long lines to get food. This photo of a food line was taken in New York City.*

Our bellies started to rumble at the thought of it. As much food as we could eat!

"God, I'd sleep forever after a meal like that," said Beanpole with a grin.

"Me, I'm only here for the food," said our friend. "But if you want to stay the night, you're allowed seven hours' sleep."

"What happens if you don't get into the lodging?" asked Beanpole.

We were beginning to think the unthinkable—that we wouldn't make it that night.

"There are a few **flophouses.** And, of course, there's always the Salvation Army if you don't mind an ear bashing from Bible punchers. But there aren't nearly enough beds to go around."

"So where do people who don't get in go?" I asked, fearing I might find out pretty soon anyway.

(CONTINUED)

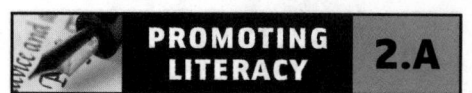

"Oh, they take in the city, walking around its squares and parks," he said with a wry smile. "It's a grand place, full of statues and bright lights: Times Square, Broadway, the Empire State Building, Central Park. Best of all are the public libraries—grand institutions for improving the mind, and warming the soul and seat of your pants! The only drawback is that there's nowhere to go when the libraries close."

As he was speaking, the line started to move, and everyone came to life.

"Don't lose your place," warned our new friend.

He need hardly have bothered. The line edged forward at a snail's pace. Four o'clock came and went. Six o'clock. Eight o'clock. We were still half a block away from food and board when the line stopped moving, and people began to drift away with slouched shoulders and a stiff walk.

 

# Write Historical Fiction

Read the outline. Then complete the outline with the setting, characters, and events of your historical fiction. Use your outline to write your story.

I. Setting
   A. Time period
   B. Place where the story happens

II. Characters
   A. Main character(s)
   B. Other character(s)

III. Events
   A. Event 1
   B. Event 2
   C. Other event(s)

I. Setting
   A. ______________________________
   B. ______________________________

II. Characters
   A. ______________________________
   B. ______________________________

III. Events
   A. ______________________________
   ______________________________
   B. ______________________________
   ______________________________
   C. ______________________________
   ______________________________

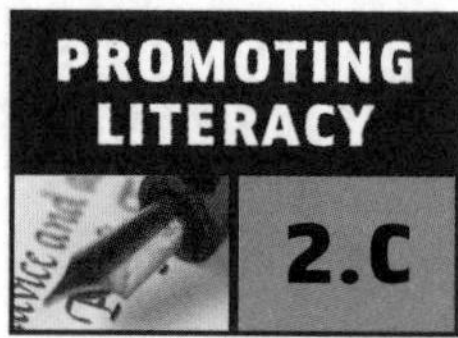


# What's Next? You Decide!

Now it's your turn to choose what to do next in the lesson. Read the activities and decide which one you want to do—you may want to try them all!

## Write a Letter

**STEPS**

Molly left her family to go look for work and support herself. She was suddenly in charge of her own life and very aware of the cruelty of the world.

- ❑ Suppose you're Molly. Write a letter to your family letting them know that you're safe.
- ❑ Include in your letter where you are and what you're doing. Also include what you've seen and how you feel.
- ❑ Then share your letter with a friend.

## Take Another Point of View

**STEPS**

*Boxcar Molly: A Story from the Great Depression* is told from Molly's point of view. "Point of view" means how a person sees things because of his or her age, job, and the place he or she lives. Suppose you're another character from the book, such as the middle-aged, barrel-chested man. Tell the story from his point of view.

- ❑ Before you begin, ask yourself, *How do you feel? What do you think of Molly?*
- ❑ Remember to keep your facts consistent with Molly's. Your opinions, feelings, and perspective may change.
- ❑ Then rewrite the story from the "new" point of view by supposing that you are now seeing the story through the eyes of the barrel-chested man. *How does he feel? What does he think about and do?*

## Create Your Own Boxcar

**MATERIALS**

- ❑ 1 shoebox
- ❑ 1 pair scissors
- ❑ glue
- ❑ 1 brown grocery bag

**STEPS**

Boxcar Molly traveled in a boxcar. The car provided transportation and shelter to those inside, but it wasn't fun to ride in. Design a boxcar that you'd like to live in for a few months.

- ❑ Find an empty shoebox that someone isn't using.
- ❑ Then cover it inside and outside with brown paper from a grocery bag.
- ❑ Fill it with things you'd need, such as blankets, and other things that you'd want to have with you.

# Reading Biographies

***Biographies can reveal a little bit about ourselves, too.***

| OBJECTIVE | BACKGROUND | MATERIALS |
|---|---|---|
| To have your student read an excerpt from a biography, explore the nature of biographies, and write a character sketch of his or her own | A biography tells about the difficulties a person had and how he or she overcame them. It also can reveal something about the reader. In this lesson, your student will read about Sojourner Truth, a courageous woman born into slavery who obtained her freedom by running away. Your student then will have the opportunity to write a character sketch, which is a detailed description of a certain person or character. | ■ Student Learning Pages 3.A–3.C<br>■ 1 dictionary |

**VOCABULARY**

**BIOGRAPHY** a true story of a person's life as told by another person
**DISMAL** dark and gloomy, horrible, dreadful
**PROSPEROUS** successful
**SOJOURN** a rest or to rest
**TRUTH** a fact or actuality

## Let's Begin

**1** **DISTRIBUTE AND PREVIEW** Distribute Student Learning Page 3.A. Tell your student that he or she will be reading a **biography.** Ask, *Is a biography fiction or nonfiction? How do you know?* [a biography is the story of a real person's life as told by another person]

**2** **EXPLAIN** Explain that Sojourner Truth was born a slave. Ask, *What do you think it was like to be an enslaved person in America? How did an enslaved person live? What rights did he or she have?* [slaves didn't have many rights and often were forced to work in harsh, unsafe conditions for long hours] After your student has given his or her responses, explain that he or she will learn more about how slaves were treated after reading a section of the biography, *Sojourner Truth and the Struggle for Freedom,* by Edward Beecher Claflin.

**3** **REVIEW** Explain the meanings of the words **dismal** and **prosperous.** Then ask what your student thinks **sojourn** means. Have him or her look the word up in the dictionary and write the definitions in his or her notebook. Then discuss the meaning

Combine this lesson with any of the Social Studies Lessons 4.7 to 4.10 to learn more about the history of slavery in the United States.

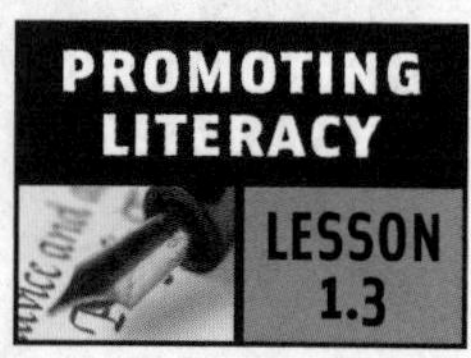

PROMOTING LITERACY

LESSON 1.3

of the word **truth.** Have your student consider the meanings and Sojourner Truth's name. Discuss how they could be related.

**4** **INTRODUCE THE STORY** Have your student read the first sentence of the excerpt. Ask, *Why do you think there was no exact record of Sojourner's birth date?* [possible answers could be that she was born long ago, and slaves probably weren't considered important enough at that time to keep records of their birth, and the people to whom her birth date might have been important may not have known how to read and write]

**DID YOU KNOW?**

The Underground Railroad was a secret system of helping slaves escape to freedom by hiding them in safe places as they made their way to the North.

**5** **INFER** After your student has read to the end of the excerpt, ask your student what it must have been like to be a slave. Then discuss.

**6** **COMPARE AND CONTRAST** Distribute Student Learning Page 3.B. Have your student complete the page and then discuss.

**7** **CONNECT** Now have your student think of someone he or she knows that he or she admires. Ask your student what qualities he or she likes about this person. Then have him or her write some notes about this person in his or her notebook, such as a physical description, what his or her likes and dislikes are, information about his or her family history, and anything else. Then tell your student that he or she is going to write a character sketch, or a detailed description, about this person.

**8** **GUIDE TO WRITE** Review the biography excerpt again with your student. Then assist your student in organizing his or her notes. Have him or her write his or her character sketch. Remember to give him or her enough time to write. Tell your student that he or she is a biographer!

# Branching Out

**FOR FURTHER READING**

*Journal of LeRoy Jeremiah Jones, a Fugitive Slave,* by K. J. Williams (1st Books Library, 2001).

*Minty: A Story of Young Harriet Tubman,* by Alan Schroeder and Rachel Axler (Viking Penguin, 2000).

*Sojourner Truth,* by Laura Spinale (Child's World, Inc., 1999).

## TEACHING TIPS

- ❑ Have your student read the rest of the book *Sojourner Truth and the Struggle for Freedom* by Edward Beecher Claflin.
- ❑ Have your student use the Internet to find more information about African-American history. Use key words such as *Underground Railroad* or *slavery in the United States* in the search engine of your choice.

## CHECKING IN

Assess your student's understanding of what he or she read by asking:

1. What kind of writing was the excerpt? Who was it about?
2. When did this person live? Where?
3. What difficulties did this person have?

# Explore Biographies

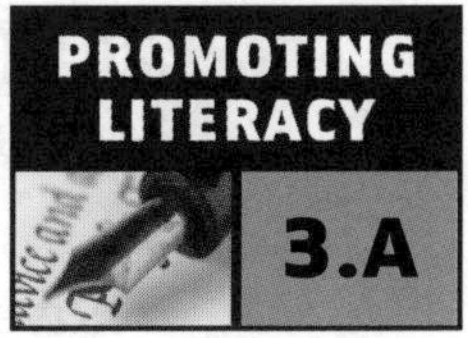


## Sojourner Truth and the Struggle for Freedom

by Edward Beecher Claflin

There is no exact record of Sojourner's birth date, but it was probably about 1797. She was born about fourteen years after the end of the American Revolution. Her original name was not Sojourner. It was Isabella, and her mother and father called her Belle. The first home she ever knew was the grim, dark cellar of a stately limestone house on the plantation of Charles Hardenbergh.

The Hardenberghs, wealthy Dutch landowners, owned nearly two million acres between the Hudson and Delaware

(CONTINUED)

Rivers in Ulster County, New York. The house where Belle lived was in the town of Hurley, about eighty miles north of New York City.

Colonel Hardenbergh owned a dozen slaves. Men, women, and children all slept together in the same dark cellar. This is how one writer described that room:

> It was a **dismal** chamber, its only lights consisting of a few panes of glass, through which the sun never shown. The space between the loose boards of the floor and the uneven earth below was often filled with mud and water. Inmates of both sexes and all ages slept on those damp boards, like horses, with a little straw and a blanket. Rheumatisms, fever-sores and palsies . . . racked the bodies of those fellow-slaves . . .

The first language that Belle learned was "low Dutch." This was the language first used by the Dutch immigrants who settled in New York. It was the language spoken by her master. Both her parents had names that sound strange to us, because they were in that language. Her father was called "Baumfree," which is low Dutch for "tree," and her mother was called "Mau-Mau Bett."

Mau-Mau Bett and Baumfree had ten children. But by the time Belle was born, only she and her younger brother Peter remained at the Hardenbergh's plantation. All other brothers and sisters had been sold. Slave children were considered the master's property. Whenever the master had slaves he did not need, he took the youngest or weakest to auction.

Mau-Mau Bett remembered all of Belle's brothers and sisters by name. At night, sitting in the damp cellar lit by a blazing pine knot, she would tell stories about the ones who had been taken away. With Belle and Peter at her knee, Mau-Mau Bett recalled the day when Belle's older brother and sister, Michael and Nancy, had been seized.

It had been a cold, snowy winter's day when Mau-Mau Bett lost Michael and Nancy. She recalled how Michael, who was just five years old, rose early to light the fire. As he knelt

(CONTINUED) 

warming his hands by the blazing twigs, he suddenly looked up. From outside the house came the brisk jingle of sleigh bells.

He was very excited. The arrival of a winter sleigh with prancing horses was a real event! Michael rushed up the stairs from the cellar onto the snowy drive.

A **prosperous** looking white man in a big fur coat got out of the sleigh and went into the house. As soon as the man was gone, Michael hopped up in the sleigh, hoping he would be taken for a ride.

When the driver emerged a few minutes later, he was carrying Michael's three-year-old sister Nancy. To Michael's delight, the man in the fur coat carried Nancy directly to the sleigh.

So they were *both* going for a ride!

But Michael's anticipation soon turned to horror. The driver did not put Nancy on the seat of the sleigh. Instead, he opened the box in back that was for holding luggage. He shoved Nancy inside and slammed the lid down.

(CONTINUED) 

As Nancy began to scream and cry, the driver bolted the lid shut.

Then he turned toward Michael.

Only then did Michael realize what was happening. This was a slave trader. Nancy had been sold! In terror, Michael turned and raced toward the cellar to hide.

The white man was too quick. With a single sweep of his arm he caught up the little boy, lifted the lid of the sleigh box, and hurled Michael inside with his sister.

Mounting the seat of the sleigh, the man in the fur coat touched his whip to the horses. Jangling bells mingled with the screams of Mau-Mau Bett's children as the sleigh pulled out of the yard and glided down the road.

Listening wide-eyed, Belle could imagine each moment of that dreadful day as Mau-Mau Bett told this story. The screams and pleas of her brother and sister rang in her ears as if she actually heard them. Even though she had never known Michael and Nancy, they were very much alive to her. Wherever they were now, they were still part of her family! Her mother loved those missing children so much that Sojourner could feel that ache in her own heart.

How could such a terrible thing happen?

Then a thought would occur to Belle that made her tremble and shake with fear. The same thing could happen to her!

She, Belle, belonged to Charles Hardenbergh. Mau-Mau Bett and Baumfree could not protect her. She was the possession of the man who lived upstairs in warm, well-furnished rooms with curtains at the windows. To him, Belle was just like his long-stemmed smoking pipe or his silk-embroidered armchair in his sitting room. He bought them and he could still sell them—and her—anytime he wanted to.

# Compare and Contrast

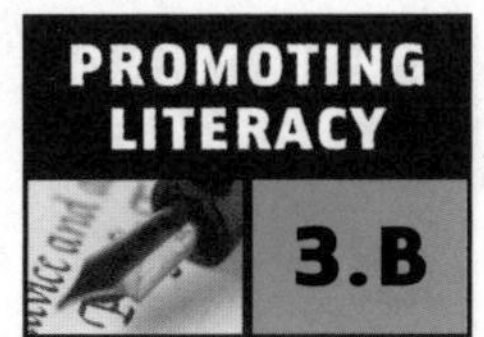


Compare and contrast what life was like for the Hardenbergh family and for the slaves on the plantation. Then on a separate sheet of paper draw a scene of what might be a typical day for either the Hardenbergh family or the slaves on the plantation.

**What Was Life Like?**

| Hardenbergh Family | Slaves on Plantation |
|---|---|
| 1. | 1. |
| 2. | 2. |
| 3. | 3. |

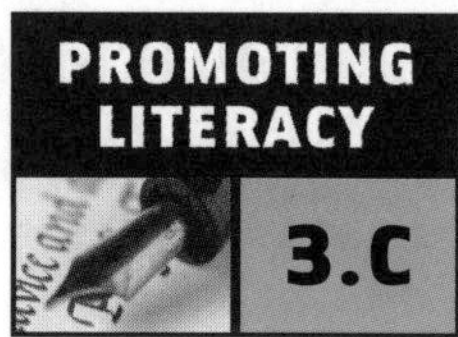


# What's Next? You Decide!

Now it's your turn to choose what to do next in the lesson. Read the activities and decide which one you want to do—you may want to try them both!

## Become a Reporter

### MATERIALS

- ❑ 1 blank cassette tape (optional)
- ❑ 1 portable cassette tape recorder (optional)

### STEPS

Become a reporter and interview someone from your community.

- ❑ Think about the people you've read or heard about in your community and choose someone you'd like to interview.
- ❑ Ask an adult's help and arrange to meet with this person.
- ❑ Write down about 10 to 20 questions you want to ask him or her before you go to the meeting.
- ❑ At the meeting, be sure to carefully write down what he or she says. If possible, tape record your interview to jog your memory later. Be sure to tell the person you'll be interviewing first.
- ❑ Once you get home, put together your notes and write an article about the person you interviewed. Then see if you can get your interview published in the local paper!

## Write an Introductory Letter

### STEPS

Do you have a friend or relative that lives far away? Write a letter to this person to introduce him or her to one of your local friends.

- ❑ Choose the person who is going to receive the letter. This should be a person whom you trust and know very well. If you don't know anyone who lives far away, then you can make up someone.
- ❑ Choose the friend you want to introduce in the letter. Be sure to ask permission to write about him or her.
- ❑ Make some notes in your notebook about what your friend looks like, enjoys doing, his or her family, and things you have done together.
- ❑ Write the introductory letter, being as specific and descriptive as possible. Remember, the person who gets the letter has never seen your friend before.
- ❑ Read your letter to an adult. Ask the adult if your letter is detailed enough. Make revisions to your letter if necessary.
- ❑ Send your letter. The next time your long-distance friend is in town, maybe the three of you can meet!

# Reading Poetry

*A poet is a painter whose brush is a pen.*

| OBJECTIVE | BACKGROUND | MATERIALS |
|---|---|---|
| To have your student read and understand poetry | Poetry is language that is used in a special way. In poems, poets don't only choose words for their meaning. Words are also chosen for the way they sound, for the images they suggest, and for the word pictures they create. Your student will read part of the famous poem about the ride of Paul Revere, *Paul Revere's Tale,* by Henry Wadsworth Longfellow. | ■ Student Learning Pages 4.A–4.B |

## VOCABULARY

**BELFRY** a tower or room for a bell
**RHYTHM** the repetition or pattern of syllables in a poem
**RHYME** two or more words that end in same or similar sounds
**STANZAS** groupings of lines of a poem that often have the same rhythm
**POEM** a composition written in verse; may incorporate a specific rhyme or rhythm
**SPAR** a pole that's part of a boat
**MAN-OF-WAR** a warship
**MOORINGS** places alongside a boat where objects, such as other watercraft, can be tied

# Let's Begin

**1** **PROVIDE BACKGROUND** Tell your student that he or she is about to read a poem about a historical event during the American Revolution against the British. Provide your student with some background information to help him or her comprehend the poem better. See Lessons 4.4 and 4.5 for historical information and activities about this time period.

**2** **EXPLAIN** Explain that on April 18, 1775, Revere was told to ride to Lexington, Massachusetts, to warn Samuel Adams and John Hancock that British troops were marching to arrest them. He rowed across the Charles River to Charlestown. From there he would be able to ride to Lexington. But first, he would need to know if the British troops would row "by sea" to Cambridge, or march "by land" out of Boston Neck. He had prearranged a set of signals with his associates across the river, in Boston, to hang

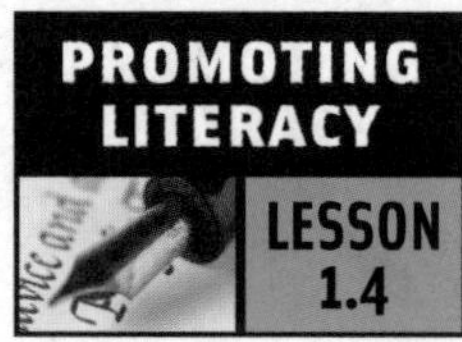

lanterns in the **belfry** of a church—one lantern if by land and two if by sea—before he went on his ride. Discuss why these signals were important.

**3** **INTRODUCE AND DISTRIBUTE** Explain that Henry Wadsworth Longfellow was a famous American poet and educator from New England who lived between 1807 and 1882. He is famous for the flowing **rhythm** and **rhyme** of his poetry and for being one of the first well-known poets to write about American themes. Distribute Student Learning Page 4.A. Tell your student that this is the first three **stanzas** of a famous, longer **poem** by Longfellow called *Paul Revere's Ride.* Have your student read the poem to himself or herself first. Then have your student read it aloud.

**4** **LISTEN** Tell your student that poetry often has a musical quality created by rhyme and use of rhythm. Encourage your student to listen to the repetition of sounds created by the rhyme as you read the poem aloud. Point out the rhyme and rhythm of other poems that your student might know. Then review the vocabulary words with your student.

**5** **DISCUSS** Draw your student's attention to the description of the British ship in the third stanza. Point out the words ***man-of-war,*** *phantom ship,* and *huge black hulk.* Ask, *What mood and feeling about the ship does the poet create?* [scary, powerful, waiting] Then draw your student's attention to the lines: "A phantom ship, with each mast and spar / Across the moon like a prison bar." Ask, *What are the mast and spar compared to?* [a prison bar] Ask, *Why do you think the poet has made this comparison?* [the ship represents England, which by controlling the colonies is in essence keeping the colonists prisoner]

**6** **CONTINUE** Have your student read the rest of the poem. See For Further Reading for titles of books.

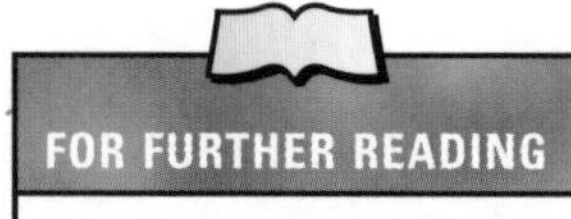

**FOR FURTHER READING**

*Lives: Poems About Famous Americans,* by Lee Bennett Hopkins and Leslie Straub, ill. (HarperCollins, 1999).

*Paul Revere,* by George E. Sullivan (Scholastic, Inc., 2000).

*Poetry for Young People: Robert Louis Stevenson,* by Frances Schoonmaker, ed., and Lucy Corvino, ill. (Sterling Publishing Co., 2000).

# Branching Out

## TEACHING TIP

Because poems tend to be more musical than prose, or writing using ordinary language, it's important to read a poem several times.

## CHECKING IN

Assess your student's understanding of reading a poem by asking, *In what ways is poetry different from prose, or language that's used in books, magazines, and newspapers?* [In prose, the writer mainly thinks about the meaning of the words. In a poem, the poet thinks about rhyme, rhythm, the music of the language, the images the language creates.]

# Read Poetry

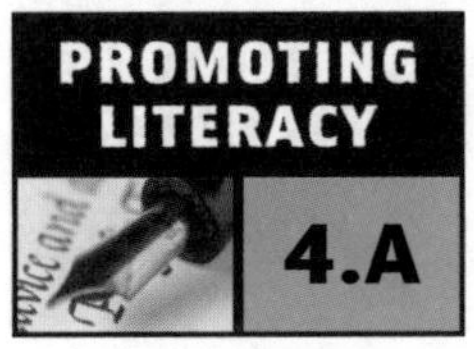


## Paul Revere's Ride

### by Henry Wadsworth Longfellow

Listen, my children, and you shall hear
Of the midnight ride of Paul Revere,
On the eighteenth of April, in Seventy-five;
Hardly a man is now alive
Who remembers that famous day and year.

He said to his friend, "If the British march
By land or sea from the town to-night,
Hang a lantern aloft in the **belfry** arch
Of the North Church tower as a signal light,—
One, if by land, and two, if by sea;
And I on the opposite shore will be,
Ready to ride and spread the alarm
Through every Middlesex village and farm
For the country folk to be up and to arm,"

Then he said, "Good night!" and with muffled oar
Silently rowed to the Charlestown shore,
Just as the moon rose over the bay,
Where swinging wide at her **moorings** lay
The Somerset, British **man-of-war;**
A phantom ship, with each mast and spar
Across the moon like a prison bar,
And a huge black hulk, that was magnified
By its own reflection in the tide.

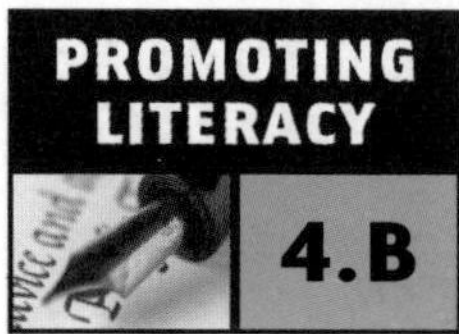


# What's Next? You Decide!

Now it's your turn to choose what to do next in the lesson. Read the activities and decide which one you want to do—you may want to try them all!

## Become a Poet

 **STEPS**

Imagine you're Longfellow and you're reading this poem to your fellow townsfolk during the time period in which it was written.

- ❑ Where do you think the poetry reading would take place? A town hall? A center square? What would you wear?
- ❑ Ask permission first and set up a room or an area of a room in which you'll read "your poem" to the townsfolk. Don't forget to decide on what you'd wear and how you'd look.
- ❑ Then invite townsfolk (your family, neighbors, and friends) to hear you read your poem!

## Write a Poem

**MATERIALS**

- ❑ 1 book of your favorite poems

**STEPS**

- ❑ Read a few poems that rhyme. Pay attention to the rhyming patterns and the rhythm.
- ❑ Choose one of the poems you like the best.
- ❑ Write your own poem that has the same rhyming pattern and number of lines per stanza.
- ❑ Think of your own idea for a subject to write about or use one of these:
  - A poem about a beautiful day
  - A poem about something you like to do and why
  - A poem that will make people laugh
- ❑ Share your poem with others. You may also want to illustrate your poem with pictures.

## Record Current Events with Poetry

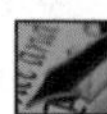 **STEPS**

Longfellow's poem was about an event. Think of a current event happening in your neighborhood, town, the nation, or the world and write a poem about it.

- ❑ What would your poem be about? Would your poem be directed at anyone in particular? What message would you want your poem to say?
- ❑ Remember that not every poem has to rhyme.
- ❑ Then, with an adult's help, see if you can get your poem published in a local newsletter or newspaper.

# Reading Drama

***Drama brings stories to life for an audience; it allows the audience to understand and relate to the characters on a personal level.***

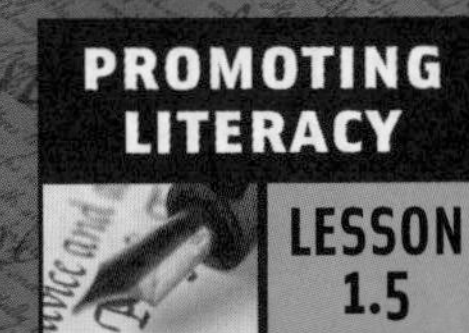


| OBJECTIVE | BACKGROUND | MATERIALS |
|---|---|---|
| To help your student recognize and understand the characteristics of drama by reading aloud a short play | Drama has been a popular form of literature for centuries. People enjoy going to plays for many reasons. Plays provide entertainment and allow us to connect with characters. They also provide an escape from the everyday world and allow us to look at situations from a different perspective. In this lesson, your student will read aloud a play and identify common characteristics of this form of literature. | ■ Student Learning Pages 5.A–5.C<br>■ 1 copy Sequence Chain, page 354 |

| VOCABULARY |
|---|
| **SCRIPT** a written version of what the characters will say and do |
| **CHARACTERS** the people in a play |
| **SETTING** the time and place that a play occurs |
| **PLOT** the basic story events in a play |
| **MOOD** the most prominent feeling of a play |
| **DIALOGUE** the words the characters say, written in a script following the name of the character who will say it |
| **STAGE DIRECTIONS** descriptions of action or how a character feels, often written in italics or parentheses |

## Let's Begin

**1** **INTRODUCE DRAMA** Ask your student to name his or her favorite movie. Explain that movies begin as scripts, in which the words that the characters say are written out. Plays are written in the same way. Most plays contain several components. Review the following drama vocabulary: **script, characters, setting, plot, mood, dialogue, stage directions.** Explain also that when reading aloud a play you don't need to speak the names of the characters when the names just indicate dialogue—you only have to speak the dialogue. The stage directions aren't read aloud either; they only give the person reading the play an idea of how to say the dialogue.

**2** **SET THE STAGE** Give your student a little background information on the play you are about to read. It's a dramatic version of a Russian legend called *The Sea King's Daughter.*

**ENRICH THE EXPERIENCE**

Point out to the students that all the movies and TV programs he or she watches began as scripts. The actors and actresses bring these scripts to life by reciting the dialogue and following the stage directions.

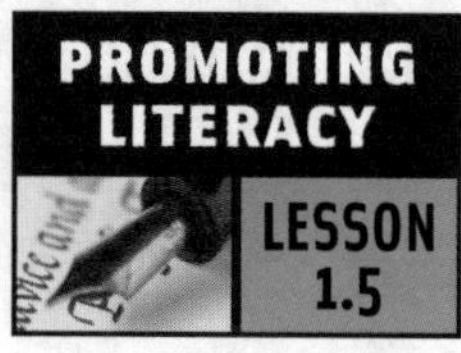

Because the reading is only an excerpt from the play, provide the following background:

> Sadko was a young musician who played music every day for a rich family, earning only a few coins for his service. He was very proud of his work and especially of his city, but he was lonely, and it made him sad that none of the rich women at the feasts would ever marry him because he was too poor. One day, while observing the River Volkhov, he wished that the river were a woman so he could marry it, for it was very beautiful and peaceful. Just then, the Sea King emerged from the water and invited Sadko to come to his underwater kingdom to play music at a feast.

3 **DISTRIBUTE** Invite your student to make a prediction about what might happen next. Ask him or her to give reasons to back up the prediction. Then distribute Student Learning Page 5.A. Explain that you will read some of the parts and the student will read some of the parts. Allow the student to decide which parts he or she would like to read. If possible, help him or her invent distinctive voices for the different characters he or she will be reading. Then read the play with your student.

4 **EXAMINE** Invite your student to examine the decision that Sadko was forced to make. Ask why it was a difficult decision to make. Distribute Student Learning Page 5.B and ask the student to complete the page. Discuss the student's answers and final decision. If possible, invite your student to contribute his or her own experience or background knowledge to his or her decision.

5 **STUDY** Ask your student to choose two characters from the play to study. Have him or her reread the parts of the play with those characters and make a list of adjectives that describe each. Discuss his or her responses, being sure that there is evidence in the play that supports each word.

**FOR FURTHER READING**

*Break a Leg!: The Kid's Guide to Acting and Stagecraft,* by Lise Friedman and Mary Dowdle, photo. (Workman Publishing Co., 2002).

*Magnificent Monologues for Kids,* by Chambers Stevens and Renee Rolle-Whatley, ed. (Sandcastle Publishing, 1999).

*Showtime! Over 75 Ways to Put On a Show,* by Reg Bolton (DK Publishing, 1998).

# Branching Out

## TEACHING TIP

It may be helpful to read the play more than once in order to get a better idea of the characters' personalities. During the first reading, your student will get an idea of the story line. In the second reading, he or she can put more feeling into the lines, because your student will have gained a better understanding of the characters.

## CHECKING IN

Assess the student's understanding of the story by distributing a copy of the Sequence Chain found on page 354. Ask him or her to fill in the important events in the order in which they occurred in the play.

# Discover Drama

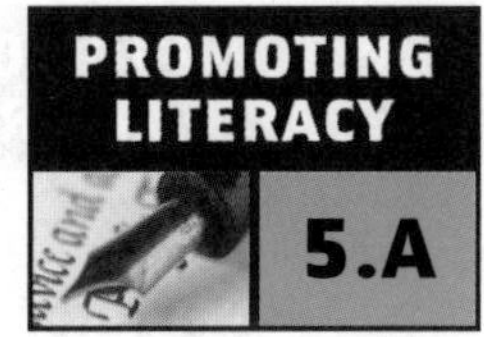


## The Sea King's Daughter
### A Russian Legend
**As told by Aaron Shepard**

**Narrator 1** The elegant room was filled with guests and royal attendants—herring and sprats, cod and flounder, gobies and sticklebacks, sand eels and sea scorpions, crabs and lobsters, starfish and squid, sea turtles and giant sturgeon.

**Sea King** You're just in time! Musician, come sit by me—and let the dance begin!

**Narrator 1** Sadko set his gusli on his lap and plucked a merry tune. Soon all the fish swam in graceful figures. The seafloor crawlers cavorted. The river maidens leaped and spun.

**Narrator 2** The King jumped to the center of the hall and joined the dance. His arms waved, his robe swirled, his hair streamed, his feet stamped.

**Sea King** Faster! Play faster!

**Narrator 1** Sadko played faster and the King's dance grew wilder. All the others stopped and watched in awe. Ever more madly did he move, whirling faster, leaping higher, stamping harder.

**Narrator 2** The Sea Queen whispered urgently,

**Sea Queen** Musician, end your tune! It seems to you the King merely dances in his hall. But above us, the sea is tossing ships like toys, and giant waves are breaking on the shore!

**Narrator 1** Alarmed, Sadko pulled a string until it snapped.

**Sadko** Your Majesty, my gusli is broken.

**Sea King** A shame.

**Narrator 2** . . . said the Sea King, winding to a stop.

**Sea King** I could have danced for days. But a fine fellow you are, Sadko. I think I'll marry you to one of my daughters and keep you here forever.

**Sadko** [*carefully*] Your Majesty, beneath the sea, your word is law. But this is not my home. I love my city of Novgorod.

**Sea King** Say no more about it! Now, behold your bride—the Princess Volkhova!

(CONTINUED)

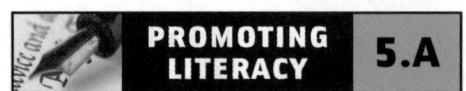

**Narrator 1** The princess stepped forward. Her green eyes were sparkling, and a soft smile graced her lips.

**Volkhova** Dearest Sadko, at last we can be together. For years I have thrilled to the music you've played on the shore.

**Sadko** [*in wonder*] Volkhova! You're as lovely as your river!

**Narrator 2** But the Sea Queen leaned over and said softly,

**Sea Queen** You are a good man, Sadko, so I will tell you the truth. If you but once kiss or embrace her, you can never return to your city again.

* * *

**Narrator 1** That night, Sadko longed to hold her, but time after time, the Queen's words came back to him—

**Sea Queen** [*voice only, offstage*] . . . never return to your city again . . .

**Volkhova** Dearest, why do you not embrace me?

**Sadko** [*stammering a little*] It is the custom of my city. We never kiss or embrace on the first night.

**Volkhova** [*sadly*] Then I fear you never will.

**Narrator 2** . . . and she turned away.

**Narrator 1** When Sadko awoke the next morning, he felt sunlight on his face. He opened his eyes and saw beside him not the Princess Volkhova but the River Volkhov. And behind him rose the walls of Novgorod!

**Sadko** My home.

**Narrator 2** . . . said Sadko, and he wept—perhaps for joy at his return, perhaps for sadness at his loss, perhaps for both.

* * *

**Narrator 1** The years were good to Sadko. With the money that remained to him, he bought a ship and goods enough to fill it. And so Sadko became a merchant, and in time, the richest man in Novgorod.

**Narrator 2** Yet sometimes still on a quiet evening he would walk out of the city alone, sit on the bank, and send his tinkling music over the water. And sometimes too a lovely head would rise from the river to listen—

**Narrator 1** or perhaps it was only the moonlight on the Volkhov.

# Examine Decision Making

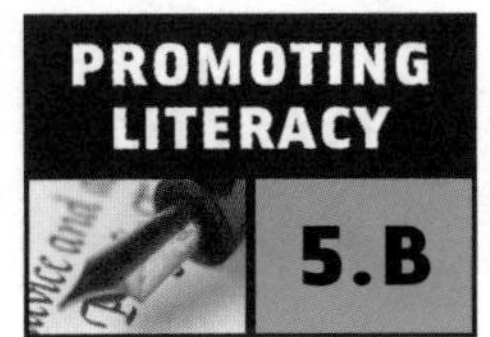


In *The Sea King's Daughter*, Sadko was forced to make a difficult decision. When faced with a decision like this, it's often helpful to make a list of the positive and negative effects of each choice. This sometimes makes it easier to "weigh" your options and see what the best decision would be. Complete the chart with the positive and negative effects of Sadko's decision, and then answer the question below.

| | Return to Novgorod | | Stay with Volkhova |
|---|---|---|---|
| + Positive Effects + | 1. | | 3. |
| – Negative Effects – | 2. | | 4. |

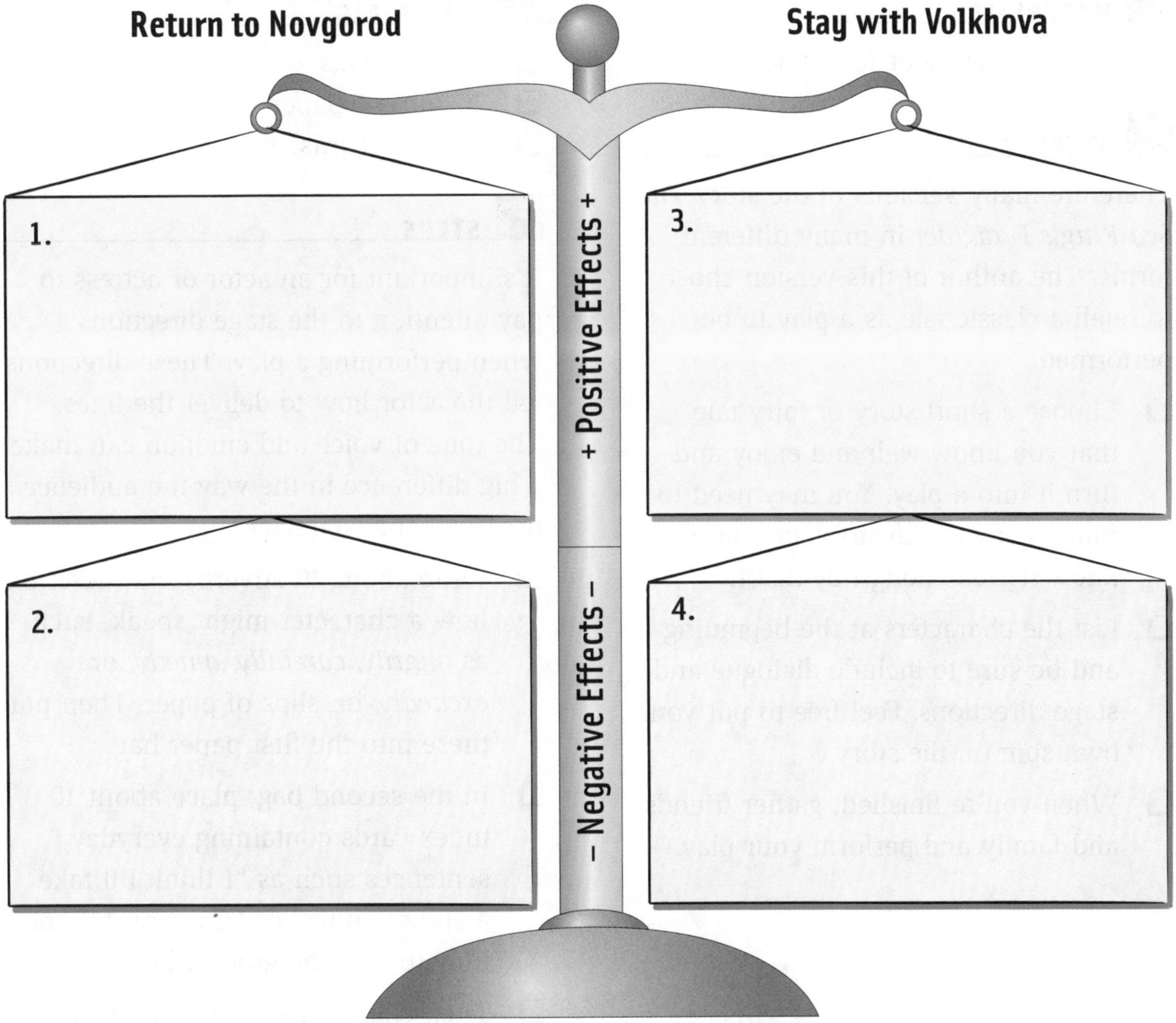

**If you were Sadko, what would you have done? Why? Use the information in the chart to support your decision.**

______________________________________________

______________________________________________

______________________________________________

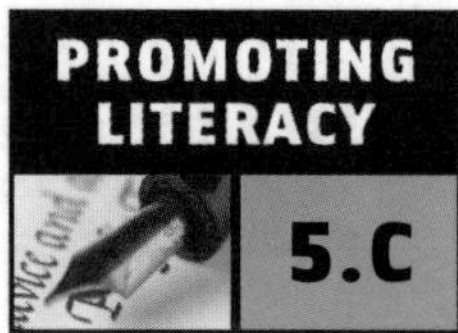


# What's Next? You Decide!

Now it's your turn to choose what to do next in the lesson. Read the activities and decide which one you want to do—you may want to try them both!

## Change Short Story to Drama

### MATERIALS

- ❑ 1 favorite story or fairy tale

### STEPS

There are many versions of the story *The Sea King's Daughter* in many different forms. The author of this version chose to retell a classic tale as a play to be performed.

- ❑ Choose a short story or fairy tale that you know well and enjoy and turn it into a play. You may need to find a copy of the story, or you may know it well enough by heart.
- ❑ List the characters at the beginning and be sure to include dialogue and stage directions. Feel free to put your own spin on the story.
- ❑ When you're finished, gather friends and family and perform your play.

## Read Stage Directions

### MATERIALS

- ❑ 2 paper bags
- ❑ 20 slips of paper
- ❑ 10 index cards

### STEPS

It's important for an actor or actress to pay attention to the stage directions when performing a play. These directions tell the actor how to deliver the lines. The tone of voice and emotion can make a big difference in the way the audience perceives the character.

- ❑ Write about 20 adverbs that describe how a character might speak, such as *angrily, carefully, quietly,* or *excitedly,* on slips of paper. Then put these into the first paper bag.
- ❑ In the second bag, place about 10 index cards containing everyday sentences such as "I think I'll take a shower now" or "Can you tell me how to find the grocery store?"
- ❑ Then choose a slip of paper from the first bag and a card from the second. Use the stage directions on the first slip of paper to read the sentence on the other slip of paper.
- ❑ You may want to find a friend to read the stage directions with, but be warned—some of the sentences will sound very silly.

TEACHING THE LESSON

# Using Parts of a Book

***If you know how a book is organized, you can find information in it quickly and easily.***

**PROMOTING LITERACY**

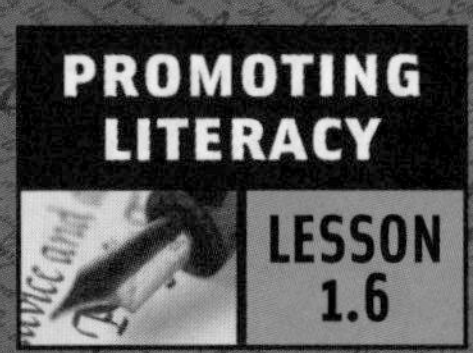

**LESSON 1.6**

| OBJECTIVE | BACKGROUND | MATERIALS |
|---|---|---|
| To have your student familiarize himself or herself with different parts of a book | Most books are organized in specific ways. In this lesson, your student will look at the title page, copyright page, table of contents, glossary, and index of a book and learn what each one contains. He or she also will learn to use a table of contents and an index to locate information in a book quickly and easily. | ■ Student Learning Pages 6.A–6.B<br>■ 1 book that contains a title page, a copyright page, a table of contents, a glossary, and an index |

**VOCABULARY**

**TITLE PAGE** the part of a book that shows who the author and publisher are

**COPYRIGHT PAGE** the part of a book that shows who published the book and when and where it was published

**TABLE OF CONTENTS** the part of a book that shows the titles of the chapters or sections of a book and the page numbers they begin on

**GLOSSARY** the part of a book that gives definitions for important words used in the book

**INDEX** the part of a book that lists topics covered in the book and the page numbers they can be found on

## Let's Begin

1 **DISPLAY** Show your student an example of a book that includes all of the parts mentioned in the vocabulary section above. Explain that these parts of a book provide information about the book. Then walk your student through each part of the book as outlined below, reviewing how each part can be used.

2 **EXPLAIN** Tell your student that the **title page** of a book is usually the first page on the inside of the book. Show him or her the title page of your book. Ask, *What information does this page show?* [the title and author of the book, the publisher of the book] Point out that sometimes the title page will also have other information, such as the name of an illustrator.

3 **REVEAL** Next show your student the **copyright page.** It's usually on the reverse side of the title page. Explain that the copyright page tells when the book was published, who published it, and where the publisher is located. Ask, *When was this book published?*

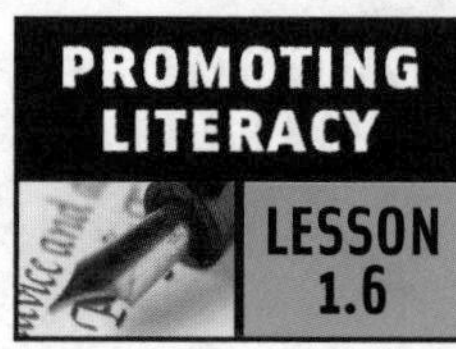


**4** **DISCUSS** Point out to your student that the **table of contents** usually follows the copyright page. Explain that the table of contents lists all the chapters in the book and the page number on which each chapter begins. It also sometimes lists the sections of each chapter and the page number on which each begins. Discuss the table of contents of your book with your student, asking such questions as *How many chapters are in this book? On which page does Chapter 3 begin? What is the title of Chapter 5?* Tell your student that for nonfiction books it's not always necessary to read the book from beginning to end. For example, point out that if you are looking for information on a specific subject, you can use the table of contents to find which chapter or chapters cover that subject, and then read just them!

**5** **EXPLAIN** Tell your student that some books have a **glossary** in the back of the book. Explain that a glossary provides definitions of important words that are used in the book. Review some of the entries in your book's glossary. Ask, *How can a glossary help a reader?* [it's easier to use the glossary than to look up a word in the dictionary; the definitions in a glossary will be specific to that book's subject; a reader may not always have a dictionary on hand]

**6** **DISCUSS** Point out to your student that the **index** is also in the back of a book. Explain that an index is a list of the topics covered in the book. The list is in alphabetical order, and beside each entry are the page numbers on which information about that topic can be found. Point out that indexes often have a number of subentries listed under a main entry. Tell your student that an index is more detailed than a table of contents, and that the topics covered are listed in alphabetical order to make it easier to find specific information in the book.

**7** **DISTRIBUTE** Distribute Student Learning Pages 6.A and 6.B. Have your student complete the activities.

# Branching Out

## TEACHING TIPS

- ❑ Make sure your student knows that in many ways the table of contents is the most important part of a book. From it you can get a good idea of what the book is about!
- ❑ You also can review the parts of this book, too!

## CHECKING IN

To check if your student understands the parts of a book, call out certain parts and have your student explain each part.

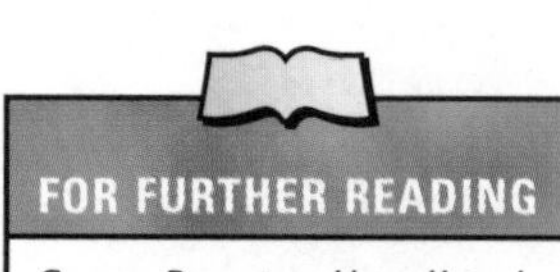

FOR FURTHER READING

*Score Booster Handbook for Reading and Language Arts*, by Tamim Ansary (Focused Learning, Ltd., 2000).

# Identify Parts of a Book

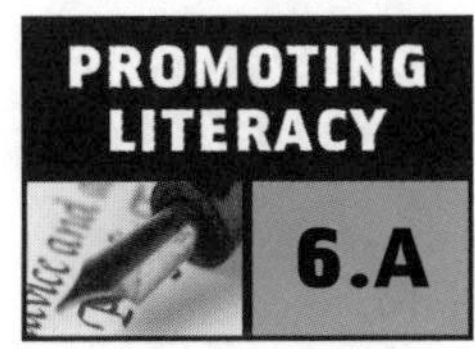


**PART A Read each question. Then write the letter of the part of the book where you would find that information.**

**A.** Title page
**B.** Copyright page
**C.** Table of contents
**D.** Glossary
**E.** Index

1. When the book was published ____________
2. The name of the author ____________
3. How many chapters are in the book ____________
4. The meaning of an important word ____________
5. An alphabetical list of the topics in the book ____________
6. The page on which each chapter begins ____________
7. The pages on which information about a topic is located ____________
8. The illustrator of the book ____________
9. The title of the book ____________
10. The titles of the chapters in the book ____________

**PART B Read the table of contents. Then answer the questions.**



11. What can you read about in Chapter 3? ____________
12. How many pages long is Chapter 1? ____________
13. In which chapter can you find out about traveling by boat? ____________
14. What kind of information will you find on pages 82–111? ____________
15. If you want to find out on which page you could read about the first astronaut in space, where would you look? ____________

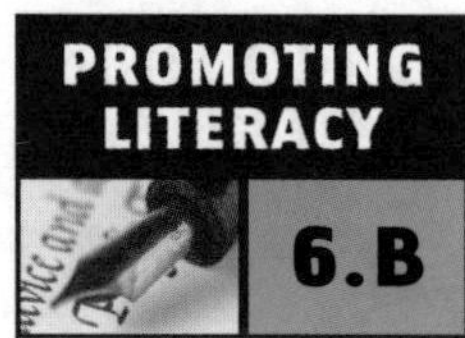


# Use an Index

Read this section of an index. Then answer the questions.

**Index**



1. Alexander Graham Bell was a famous inventor. On which page would you look to find out about some of the things he invented?

_______________

2. You want to find out about electric cars. On which page would you look?

_______________

3. Where would you look to find out about railway engines?

_______________

4. You want to find out how glass is made. On which page would you look?

_______________

# Using Primary Sources

***What better way is there to get as close as possible to a historical event or time period than by using primary sources?***

| OBJECTIVE | BACKGROUND | MATERIALS |
|---|---|---|
| To show your student how to identify and use primary sources | Authentic manuscripts and documents, artifacts, and photographs are all primary sources. Specific examples of primary sources include diaries, journals, letters, and memoirs. They may also include such physical artifacts as buildings, furniture, tools, clothing, and toys. In this lesson, your student will learn to distinguish, identify, and use primary sources. | ■ Student Learning Pages 7.A–7.B |

| VOCABULARY |
|---|
| **PRIMARY SOURCES** materials that give firsthand information about a historic event or time period |

## Let's Begin

**1** **EXPLAIN** Explain that **primary sources** give firsthand information about a historic event or time period. Tell your student to imagine that he or she is doing a report about what life was like during the time of the Civil War (1861–1865) in the United States. Point out that encyclopedias or history books about the war are not primary sources because they interpret or analyze history and are at least one step away from actual events.

*A photograph is a primary source.*

**2** **COMPARE** Ask your student, *Is there another way to find out about what life was like during the Civil War?* Lead your student to understand that he or she could look at letters, journals, speeches, and newspaper articles written by people during that time. Explain that these materials give firsthand information about what people thought and how they lived, and about how they viewed the events of their age. Explain that these materials are called primary sources.

**3** **DISCUSS** Ask, *How does a primary source bring you closer to what actually happened during a historic event?* [it lets you know the thoughts and feelings of historical people; it lets you know how news was reported then; photographs give information about how the people and settings actually looked] Give your

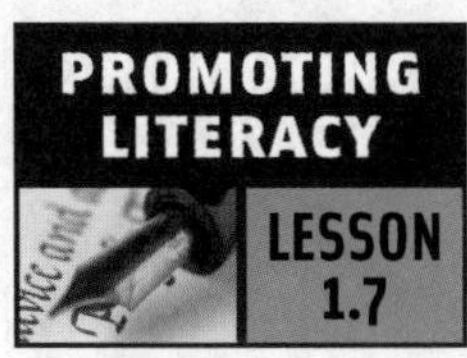


student a few examples of primary sources and ask him or her what he or she thinks might be learned from them. For example, ask, *What might be learned from a photograph of Civil War soldiers?* [what the uniforms were like; the soldiers' facial expressions might show their mood] Or ask, *What might be learned from a nurse's diary?* [it would not only show how people cared for the wounded during the Civil War, it would show what the nurse thought about what she was doing]

**ENRICH THE EXPERIENCE**

Explain to your student that language changes over time, and that language can provide a feeling or mood of the times. Let your student know that he or she may come across unfamiliar words or phrases when dealing with primary sources, but that he or she should take them as an opportunity to learn more about the time period they are from.

**4** **DISCUSS** Distribute Student Learning Page 7.A. Have your student complete Part A before writing a paragraph about what could be learned from the primary sources.

**5** **EXPAND** Discuss with your student that objects themselves also can be primary sources. For example, from the Civil War a uniform worn by a soldier, a rifle, or a flag could be a primary source. Point out that photographs of the uniform, rifle, and flag could serve as primary sources as well as the objects themselves.

# Branching Out

## TEACHING TIP

Ask your student to explain the difference between finding information from primary sources or from other sources such as encyclopedias or history books. Guide your student to understand that primary sources give more personal, firsthand information.

## CHECKING IN

Assess your student's understanding of primary sources by having him or her choose a historical subject, search the Internet or the library, and find two examples of primary sources for the subject.

**FOR FURTHER READING**

*Primary Sources Teaching Kit: Explorers,* by Karen Baicker (Scholastic, 2002).

*Primary Sources Teaching Kit: The Westward Movement,* by Karen Baicker (Scholastic, 2002).

*Seeking History: Teaching with Primary Sources in Grades 4–6,* by Monica Edinger (Heinemann, 2000).

# Identify Primary Sources

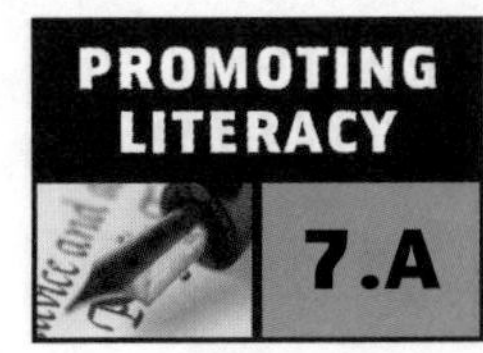


**PART A**

**Which of the following are primary sources? Put a check beside each one that you think is a primary source.**

_______ **1.** A photograph of a Boston street taken in 1897

_______ **2.** A recent magazine article about life at the end of the 1800s

_______ **3.** A journal written by a sea captain while at sea

_______ **4.** An encyclopedia entry about Magellan's sea voyages

_______ **5.** A political cartoon from the American Revolution

_______ **6.** A book about how Native Americans lived long ago

_______ **7.** A recording of Native American songs

_______ **8.** A fictional novel written about the Civil War

**PART B**

**Now write a short paragraph explaining what you think could be learned from each of these primary sources. Use your imagination!**

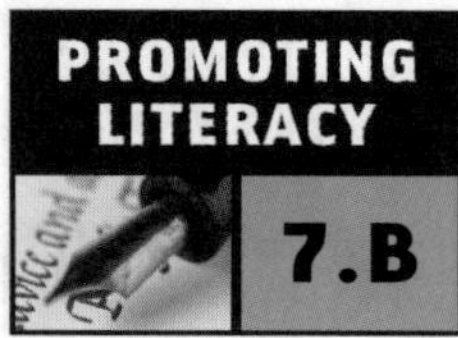
PROMOTING LITERACY 7.B

# What's Next? You Decide!

Now it's your turn to choose what to do next in the lesson. Read the activities and decide which one you want to do—you may want to try them both!

## Create a Time Capsule

### MATERIALS

- ❑ 1 plastic container
- ❑ various small personal objects

### STEPS

A time capsule is a locked container that is often buried underground for a number of years. When it's opened, it provides many primary sources for people researching our historical time period. Make your own time capsule for future researchers!

- ❑ First find a plastic container that you can bury in your backyard or on a plot of land. It should be able to keep out water. Ask an adult for help in choosing one if you need to.
- ❑ Then think about what information you want to give the people of the future. Which primary sources will get your message across?
- ❑ Decide which items you want to bury in your container.
- ❑ Pack up your time capsule and bury it! Remember to ask for permission before digging.

## Research Your Family

### MATERIALS

- ❑ old family letters and photographs

### STEPS

- ❑ Find original letters and photographs from ancestors.
- ❑ Use the primary sources you found to write a few paragraphs about your ancestors. Then answer these questions:
  - ❑ What did they look like?
  - ❑ How were they dressed?
  - ❑ What information do these sources give you?
  - ❑ What did they think about?
  - ❑ What was their life like?
  - ❑ What opinions did they have?

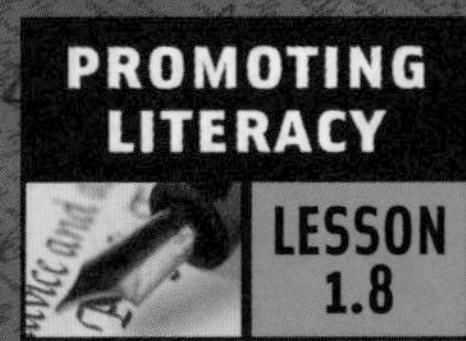


# Exploring Nonfiction Writing

***Nonfiction writers aim to relate real information in an engaging and interesting manner.***

| OBJECTIVE | BACKGROUND | MATERIALS |
|---|---|---|
| To help your student read and analyze nonfiction writing and write and present his or her own research report | Reading nonfiction writing is a crucial skill for gathering facts about a topic. To be knowledgeable about a subject, a student must be able to identify and understand facts. Reading nonfiction writing also helps a student in preparing research papers and oral reports on a variety of topics. In this lesson, your student will read and analyze a work of nonfiction writing. He or she also will use nonfiction research materials to write a research report and present a report orally. | ■ Student Learning Pages 8.A–8.C<br>■ 3–5 nonfiction pieces, such as magazine and newspaper articles and research books<br>■ 1 dictionary<br>■ 1 copy Venn Diagram, page 353 |

## VOCABULARY

**NONFICTION** literature that is not invented or imagined but based on actual events or perceptions
**ANALYZE** to study something by looking at its parts and their relationships
**REPORT** a written record or summary about an event, a person, or a thing
**CRUCIAL** necessary
**PRIMARY** first in importance
**PARALYZING** making powerless
**DENSE** thick or tightly compacted
**CAMOUFLAGED** disguised
**LAIRS** places to rest
**UNSUSPECTING** not expecting
**PRIMITIVE** simple
**DURABLE** able to last

# Let's Begin

**1** **GATHER** Gather together several **nonfiction** pieces, such as articles from reputable magazines and newspapers or research books. Then set them aside for Step 2.

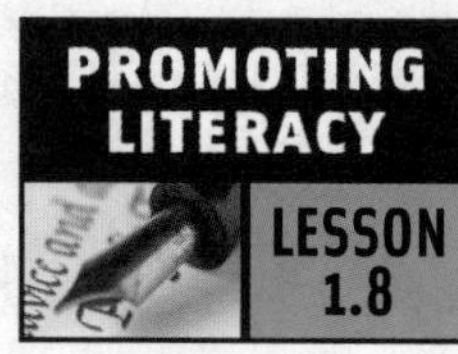


**2** **INTRODUCE NONFICTION WRITING** Invite your student to examine the pieces of nonfiction writing that you've gathered. Ask your student to think of reasons people might have to read these items. Help him or her to see that nonfiction writing is a valuable source of information about the world around us. We can read these things if we want to gather general information about a topic, or we can use them to research specific questions about a topic.

| What Do I Know? | |
|---|---|
| What Do I Want to Know? | |
| What Did I Learn? | |

**3** **DISTRIBUTE AND PREDICT** Distribute Student Learning Page 8.A. Invite your student to look at the title of the piece he or she will be reading in this lesson. Ask your student to predict what will be learned from reading the story. Then have him or her copy this chart into his or her notebook.

**4** **EXPLAIN** Explain that this is called a KWL Chart, and that it's a helpful way to organize and **analyze** information. This chart will help your student focus on main ideas and important facts in the reading. Point out that KWL stands for "know," "want to know," and "learn." When using a KWL chart, the first two rows are filled in at the beginning of the lesson and the bottom row is filled in at the end. This helps your student clarify what information he or she already knows and what new information has been discovered. First, have your student fill in the top row with facts that he or she already knows about spiders' silk. The middle row should be completed with questions about what your student wants to know about silk. After reading the selection, your student can fill in the bottom row with the things he or she learned. When your student has filled in the first two rows, discuss his or her responses.

**5** **READ AND ANALYZE** Read the selection together, stopping to answer questions or clarify confusions that may arise. When the student has finished reading, invite him or her to return to the KWL Chart. Ask the student to complete the right-hand column. If the reading answered any of his or her questions, the student should write the answers to them in the What Did I Learn? column. He or she should also write other important facts that the reading contained. Stress that only important facts should be listed here, because it's only a basic list of what was learned.

**6** **EXAMINE THE MAIN IDEA** Remind the student that a piece of writing usually has a main idea. The main idea refers to the most important point or idea that is presented in a piece of nonfiction. All of the facts in the story should work to support the main idea. Often the main idea is stated clearly; however, sometimes it can be more difficult to identify. Ask your student to skim the topics discussed throughout the passage. Help him or her write one or two topic sentences, or sentences that describe the main idea, that summarize what the author was trying to tell the reader. [spiders are unique in their silkmaking ability, and they use this ability in many ways] When the topic sentences have been formed, help your student find the details that supported this main idea.

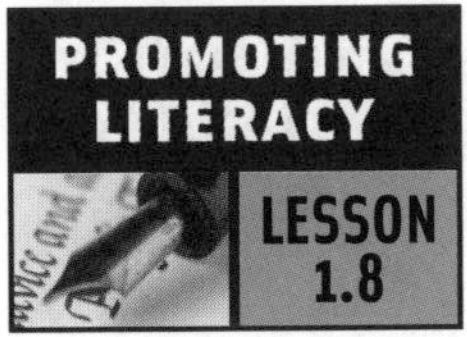


**7** **COMPARE AND CONTRAST** Distribute a copy of the Venn Diagram found on page 353. Invite your student to choose two types of spiders that were mentioned in the reading. Help him or her use this chart to compare the two types of spiders. Have the student write the name of one type of spider in each of the circles, then list the things that are the same about them in the overlapping section and the things that make them unique in the separate sections. Explain to the student that this is a good way to organize information when you're comparing two or more things.

**DID YOU KNOW?**

Spiders are carnivorous. They have eight legs and inject poison into their prey to kill it.

**8** **CHOOSE A TOPIC** Help your student find a topic that he or she would like to write a research paper about. Remind the student that a research paper presents facts about a particular topic. To choose a topic, have the student brainstorm by listing a few things he or she always has been curious about or wanted to learn more about. Help him or her select a topic that is narrow enough to write about.

**9** **TAKE NOTES** Once the topic has been selected, help your student find research information about the topic. Take him or her to a library to find books, encyclopedias, or magazines, or use the Internet to search for information. Encourage your student to find information that supports the main idea he or she would like to write about. Show your student how to take written notes. Have your student set aside several sheets of paper specifically for notes. Explain the importance of including the source and page number where each piece of information was found. Explain that this will help your student organize information and also allow him or her to easily go back to the source for more details if necessary. Tell the student that he or she won't have to use all of the information collected, but that if something looks like it might be useful it should be noted.

**10** **DISTRIBUTE** When the notetaking is complete and your student feels he or she has sufficient information to begin writing, distribute Student Learning Page 8.B. Explain to the student that it's helpful to organize ideas and information before beginning to write. Invite the student to write his or her main idea in the top box, then fill in the next tier of boxes with smaller topics,

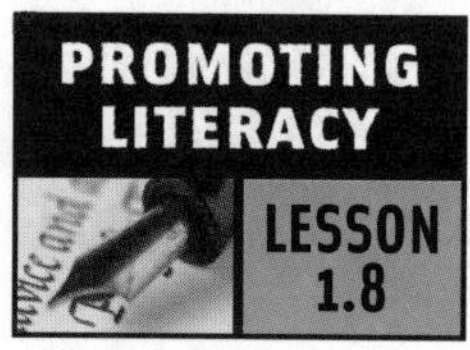


which may form topic sentences for separate paragraphs. Under each of these boxes, the student can list the supporting facts that back up the topic. In this way, your student can easily see the way his or her paper will be organized.

11 **WRITE** Allow time for your student to write a draft of his or her research paper. Remind him or her to use Student Learning Page 8.B as a guide.

12 **REVISE AND REWRITE** Have the student evaluate his or her rough draft. He or she should make sure that the supporting sentences work together to show that the topic sentence is true. Any irrelevant facts should be deleted. The student should also proofread the paper for capitalization, spelling, and punctuation errors. You may have to guide your student through the process of writing a **report.**

13 **PREPARE** Help your student prepare to present the research report in an oral presentation. Explain that an oral report must present the topic and supporting information in an interesting way that suits the audience. Before beginning, establish who the audience might be and how much it will know about the topic. Also assist your student in finding visual aids or other audiovisual devices to use with his or her report.

14 **PRESENT** Before your student presents the oral report, review the following points with him or her:

- Speak loudly and clearly.
- Make eye contact with the audience and use gestures and facial expressions that support your words.
- Use visual aids to help focus the audience's attention on key points as you speak.

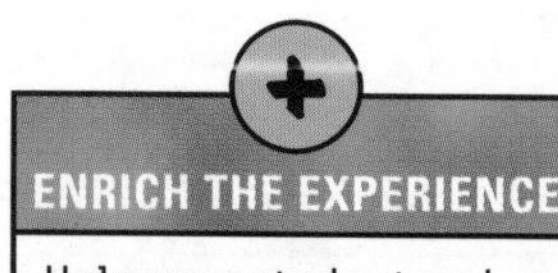

**ENRICH THE EXPERIENCE**

Help your student make the connection that later in life he or she may be asked to look at information and then fashion it into a report of some kind.

# Branching Out

## TEACHING TIP

Remind your student that in a research paper or informational presentation, it's important to relate facts. There is no place for opinions or feelings in this type of writing. The student should simply present facts.

## CHECKING IN

Assess your student's understanding of the importance of nonfiction by reviewing the useful purposes for this type of writing. Then talk about ways in which nonfiction can be used to write a report, which is something he or she will most likely do later in life.

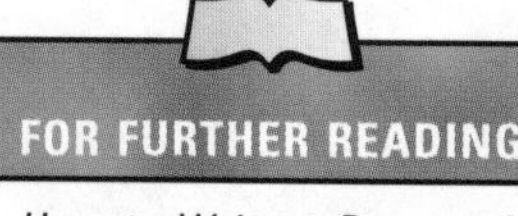

**FOR FURTHER READING**

*How to Write a Research Report,* by Kathleen Christopher Null (Teacher Created Materials, 1998).

*Researching Events,* by Maity Schrecengost (Highsmith Press, LLC, 1998).

# Explore Nonfiction Writing

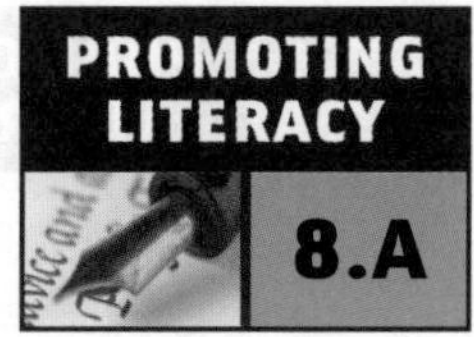


## Spider Silkmakers
## from *Animal Architecture*
### by Jennifer Owings Dewey

Spider silk has been used for centuries: to make nets for catching fish, to pack wounds, and to make the thin hairline sights on telescopes. People have learned that spider silk is one of nature's strongest fibers.

Silk is **crucial** to a spider's survival. It is used to snag and trap insects—the spider's **primary** prey. There are some kinds of insects that make silk in saliva glands inside their mouths during larval stages. But spiders are unique in making silk throughout their entire lives.

Spiders are master silkmakers. The silk is made in glands of the spider's body. At the tip of its abdomen are spinnerets, tiny bumps with holes from which the silk emerges. Some spiders can spin up to seven or eight varieties of silk, each one for a particular purpose.

Orb weavers are spiders named for the round webs they spin. An orb weaver building a web runs up, down, and across a shimmery network of silk. The spider's silk glands produce exactly the kind of silk it needs. Dry silk is used for the outer radius of the web. The center is made with sticky threads that trap insects and hold them in place until the spider attacks. Orb weavers use tough, gluey silk to wrap their insect victims before injecting them with a **paralyzing** poison.

Some tropical orb weavers spin colored silk to disguise their presence on a web. The patterns they weave into their webs perfectly match the patterns on their bodies.

Another species of spider, the cobweb weaver, combs its silk using the bristles on its back legs. Combing makes the silk fuzzy and **dense.** This creates a messy-looking cobweb, often found under stairs or in woodpiles. Cobwebs tangle and trap the spider's six-legged insect prey.

(CONTINUED)

"Trap-door spiders"—also called hairy mygalomorphs—make burrows in the ground with linings of soft silk and hinged lids of silk, sand, and saliva. The burrows are so well **camouflaged** that insects do not see them. Trap-door spiders wait in their **lairs** to jump out and grab a meal.

Spiders have developed other uses for silk, the wondrous fiber made in their bodies. "Spitting spiders" hurl masses of venom-soaked threads over **unsuspecting** insects. "Net-tossing" spiders hide in the grass and drop netlike webs on passing insects.

All but the most **primitive** spiders spin cocoons for their eggs. Most reserve their finest, softest silk to line these egg sacs and protect the delicate, tender spider eggs. Strong, waterproof silk is used for the outside of the egg sacs—making them **durable** and much more likely to survive, even under layers of winter snow. Spiderlings spend winter inside their egg sacs. Then they hatch in the spring, chewing their way free.

Spinning the egg sac is sometimes a spider's final silkmaking act, using up its silk glands forever. Without silk a spider dies, because it has no way to build traps and snares for insect prey.

# Organize and Plan Your Research Report

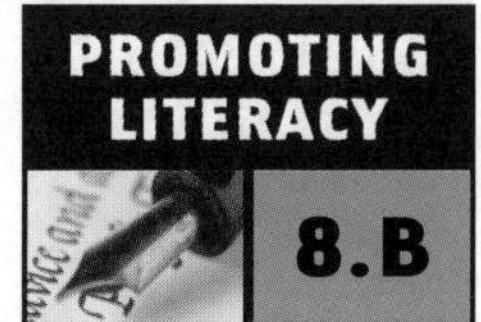


Complete the chart with your main idea, the smaller topics within the main idea, and the supporting details of the topic you've chosen for your research report.

**Main Idea**

**Smaller Topics**

**Supporting Details**

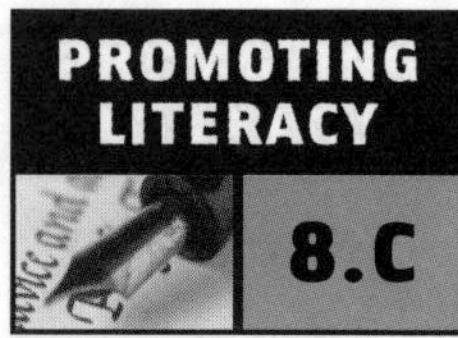


# What's Next? You Decide!

Now it's your turn to choose what to do next in the lesson. Read the activities and decide which one you want to do—you may want to try them both!

## Make a Nonfiction Collage

### MATERIALS

- ❑ 1 posterboard
- ❑ 2–4 magazines or newspapers with images of your topic
- ❑ construction paper
- ❑ 1 pair scissors
- ❑ markers

### STEPS

Create a collage of information and pictures about the topic of your research report.

- ❑ Choose some key phrases or facts that are very important to know about the topic.
- ❑ Write these words in different styles, colors, and sizes on the construction paper and cut them out.
- ❑ Then find images in magazines or newspapers and cut them out.
- ❑ When you have enough words and pictures, glue these onto the posterboard.
- ❑ Create a title and display your collage.

## Present a Mini Newscast

### MATERIALS

- ❑ 3 articles or reports on one news topic: newspaper, magazine, radio or television news

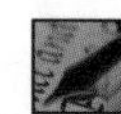

### STEPS

A news report is a type of nonfiction. Prepare an oral report using news sources and present it to your family.

- ❑ Choose a current event that is being reported in the news. Make sure the topic is interesting to you and that you feel enthusiastic about reporting on it.
- ❑ Find at least three articles or reports from different news sources and research the topic. Take notes and write down the sources of your information.
- ❑ Write a report that you can present orally. Keep all the information in your report factual and objective. Mention the source of important points in your report.
- ❑ Present your report to family members and/or friends. At the end, let your audience ask questions about your news. If there are any questions you can't answer, make a note of them. Tell the person you will research further and get back to him or her with the answer. Be sure to research and follow up on the question!

TEACHING THE LESSON

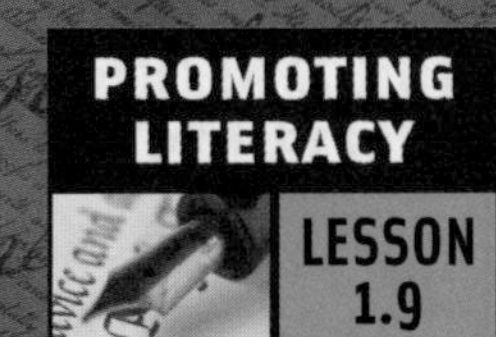


# Writing and Speaking to Persuade

*You may have an opinion, but if you can't give reasons that support it, it would be hard to convince others.*

| OBJECTIVE | BACKGROUND | MATERIALS |
|---|---|---|
| To have your student write and orally deliver a persuasive essay | Persuasive writing and speaking tries to convince the reader or listener to do something, to feel a certain way about something, or to think something. Your student will encounter persuasion throughout his or her life and may also be asked to persuade someone about something. In this lesson, your student will review examples of persuasion and then write and orally deliver a persuasive essay. | ■ Student Learning Pages 9.A–9.B<br>■ several letters to the editor from newspapers and/or magazines |

| VOCABULARY |
|---|
| **PERSUADE** to move someone to accept a certain position or belief<br>**CONVINCE** to bring someone to believe or agree |

## Let's Begin

**1** **PREVIEW** Tell your student that this lesson will show him or her how to **persuade** a reader or listener. Explain that when you persuade, you present your viewpoint about a topic and try to **convince** others to agree with you. Ask, *What are some examples of persuasion you have encountered?* [possible answer: advertisements and commercials] Now show your student some examples of persuasive writing in editorials or letters to the editor from newspapers or magazines. Discuss. Then distribute Student Learning Page 9.A. Have your student read it and then discuss. Refer to it as you teach the lesson.

**2** **BRAINSTORM TOPICS** Ask your student about topics, ideas, or products he or she feels strongly about—so strongly that he or she wants to persuade others to feel the same way. For example, he or she may believe strongly in recycling newspaper, glass, and plastic. Discuss these ideas with your student.

**3** **SELECT A TOPIC** Now have your student choose one topic or idea about which he or she feels the strongest and tell the

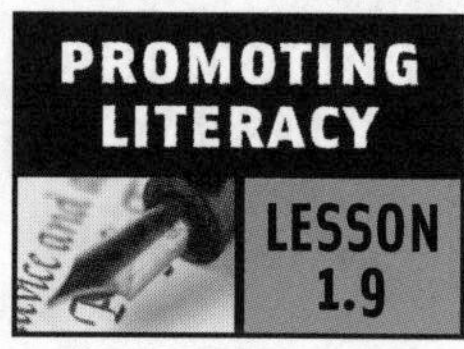


student that he or she will be writing a persuasive essay about it. Distribute Student Learning Page 9.B.

**4** **IDENTIFY PURPOSE AND AUDIENCE** Tell your student that once he or she has selected a topic, the next task is to decide what the purpose of the essay is. Ask, *What do you want to persuade others to do, feel, or think?* Together with your student, refer to the essay on Student Learning Page 9.A. Ask, *What is the purpose of the essay?* [to persuade readers to conserve water] The purpose of the essay is often found in the essay's introduction. Then tell your student that in order to **persuade** effectively, the writer should know to whom he or she is writing. Ask your student who would be the audience of his or her persuasive essay.

**5** **IDENTIFY INTRODUCTION AND CONCLUSION** Tell your student that the introduction lets the reader know what the writer is trying to **convince** readers to do, feel, or think, and that the conclusion is where the writer restates his or her point of view. Refer to the conclusion of the essay on Student Learning Page 9.A. Ask, *What does the writer tell the reader he or she should do?* [think of water as being precious and conserve it]

**6** **DRAFT, PROOF, AND WRITE** Tell your student that he or she now will write a persuasive essay on the topic he or she has chosen. Remind him or her to think of examples, reasons, and facts to support his or her point of view. Remember to give your student enough time to write a first draft. Then ask your student to proofread his or her essay, looking for grammatical errors or misspellings and also for any areas that could be clarified or arguments that could be strengthened. After proofreading, have your student write a final draft of the essay.

**FOR FURTHER READING**

*Persuasive Writing*, by Tara McCarthy (Scholastic Trade, 1999).

*Persuasive Writing, Grades 4–6*, by June Hetzel and Deborah McIntire (Creative Teaching Press, 1998).

*Persuasive Writing: Mini-Lessons, Strategies, Activities*, by Tara McCarthy and Drew Hires, ill. (Scholastic, Inc., 1998).

# Branching Out

## TEACHING TIP

In a persuasive essay, a writer also can present possible objections to his or her point of view and answer them.

## CHECKING IN

Assess your student's ability by reading and listening to his or her persuasive essay. Have a conversation with your student about what persuasion is and explore the persuasion he or she encounters. Ask him or her about what a persuasive essay or presentation might include.

# Read a Persuasive Essay

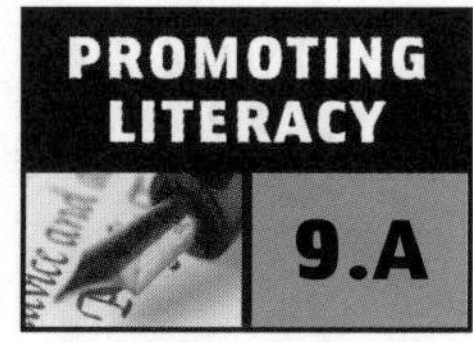


## The Importance of Conserving Water

Do you think there is a lot of water on this planet, and that there is no reason for people to worry about it? Well, you're right. There is a lot of water on Earth. As a matter of fact, Earth is sometimes called the "water planet" because 70 percent of it's covered with water. But only 3 percent of the world's water is freshwater—that's the kind of water people need to live. The world's freshwater supply is dwindling at a fast rate, however. There are now over 6 billion people on the planet, and many of them don't have enough access to freshwater. Pollution of water, droughts, and people wasting water are all endangering the freshwater supply needed for people, plants, and animals. Suppose you didn't have water to drink, bathe, or wash clothes. How would you feel? That's why it's so important for us to conserve water.

First of all, we can all start conserving water in the bathroom. Did you know that almost half of the water used in a typical home is used in the bathroom? So when you brush your teeth, don't keep the water running the entire time. Turn it off and on as you need it. When you shower, although the water feels good on your body, keep your showers as short as possible. And if a faucet leaks, it should be repaired as quickly as possible. Even one little leak in your kitchen sink can mean lots of lost water per year. Also, if you've noticed a leaky toilet, make sure you get that repaired, too.

Water conservation doesn't have to end with the bathroom. If you like to drink cold water from the faucet, keep a bottle of drinking water in the refrigerator instead. If you run the faucet to wash your fruits and vegetables, wash them in a bowl so that the faucet isn't running the entire time.

So the next time you brush your teeth or wash a piece of fruit, think of water as gold. Actually, water is more precious than gold, because you don't really need gold to live, but you do need water!

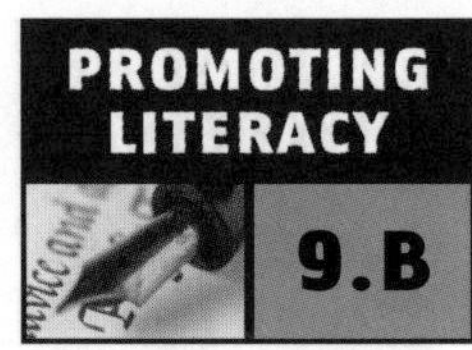


# Plan a Persuasive Essay

**Read each statement and complete the sentences.**

I want to persuade others to ____________________

____________________

____________________

____________________

____________________

My audience is ____________________

____________________

____________________

These are the reasons that support my point of view:

____ **1.** ____________________

____________________

____ **2.** ____________________

____________________

____ **3.** ____________________

____________________

____ **4.** ____________________

____________________

____ **5.** ____________________

____________________

____ **6.** ____________________

____________________

**Number your reasons in order from strongest (1) to weakest (6). When writing your persuasive essay, include the strongest points first.**

 

TEACHING THE LESSON

# Writing a Friendly Letter

***Writing a friendly letter is a thoughtful way to keep in touch with a friend or relative.***

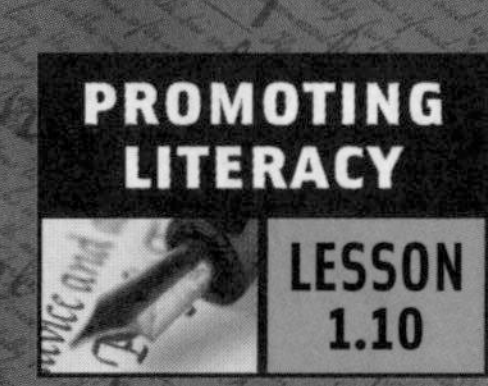


| OBJECTIVE | BACKGROUND | MATERIALS |
|---|---|---|
| To show your student how to write a friendly letter | There are many different kinds of letters. Business letters, request letters, and thank-you letters are a few examples. A friendly letter is an opportunity to share personal news and feelings. The tone of a friendly letter is informal. In this lesson, your student will learn how to write a friendly letter. | ■ Student Learning Pages 10.A–10.B<br>■ 1 pair scissors<br>■ glue or tape |

**VOCABULARY**

**INFORMAL** casual or familiar
**HEADING** the part of a friendly letter that includes the writer's address and the date the letter was written
**GREETING** the opening "hello" of a friendly letter
**BODY** the main part of a friendly letter where news, thoughts, and feelings are shared
**CLOSING** the final phrase of a friendly letter that expresses closeness with the person to whom the letter is written
**SIGNATURE** the final part of a friendly letter, the writer's handwritten name

## Let's Begin

1 **DISCUSS** Tell your student that a friendly, or **informal,** letter is a thoughtful way to share experiences, ideas, and feelings with friends and relatives. Ask, *Have you ever received a letter from a friend or relative? Who was it from? What kinds of things did you find out about in the letter? Did you enjoy reading the letter?* Discuss.

2 **SHOW** Show your student a friendly letter you have written, perhaps one to a relative your student knows. Use it as an example as you discuss the parts and tone of a friendly letter in this lesson.

3 **REVEAL** Point out to your student that the first part of a friendly letter is the **heading.** It includes the writer's address and the date the letter was written. Ask, *How is it helpful to the reader to include your address?* [then the reader knows where to write back to]

4 **EXPLAIN** Explain to your student that the **greeting** follows the heading. Tell your student that often writers use the word *dear* in a greeting, as in "Dear Mom," but that other words can be used, too.

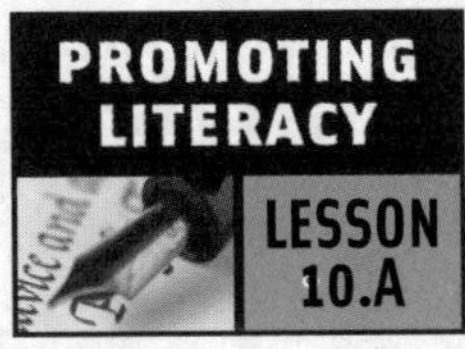


For example, you could write "Hello Mom," or even "Hi Mom,". Mention to your student that the greeting is followed by a comma.

**5** **DISCUSS** Tell your student that the **body** of the letter is next. It is where you relate your news and thoughts to whom you are writing. Make sure your student understands that the tone of a friendly letter is informal. Tell your student that he or she can write as if talking directly to the person, and that he or she should let his or her personality come through. Try to begin a friendly letter by saying something that shows you care about the person to whom you are writing. Then give some news about yourself or about people whom you both know, or share some personal thoughts or feelings. Ask, *What has happened to you lately that would be good news to share in a friendly letter?*

**6** **EXPLAIN** Point out that, like the greeting, the **closing** of a friendly letter can take many forms. For example, you can close a friendly letter with "Your friend," "Thinking of you," "Lots of love," and so on. Ask, *What other closings can you think of? Which do you prefer? Why?* Make sure your student understands that a closing should be sincere. Also note that the closing is followed by a comma. Next comes the final part of a friendly letter: the **signature.** Tell your student to sign friendly letters in his or her best handwriting. Distribute Student Learning Page 10.A and have your student complete the activity.

**7** **DISTRIBUTE AND WRITE** Distribute Student Learning Page 10.B and have your student write a friendly letter to someone he or she knows. It can be a friend, a relative, or whoever else is appropriate. Tell your student that if he or she is writing to a relative, the closing can reflect their relationship (such as "Your grandson," "Your niece," and so on). After your student has finished writing the draft of his or her letter, have him or her proofread it for grammar, spelling, capitalization, and punctuation errors. He or she should make all necessary corrections and rewrite a final draft.

# Branching Out

## TEACHING TIP

You may wish to take this opportunity to have your student begin a correspondence with a pen pal who lives far away.

## CHECKING IN

Assess your student's ability to write a friendly letter by reviewing the letter he or she wrote on Student Learning Page 10.B. Check that he or she provided the correct information in the five parts of the letter.

**FOR FURTHER READING**

*Creative Writing Ideas,* by Jo Ellen Moore and Joy Evans (Evan-Moor Educational Publishing, 1999).

*Intermediate Language Lessons,* by Emma Serl (Lost Classics Book Co., 2001).

# Unscramble the Letter

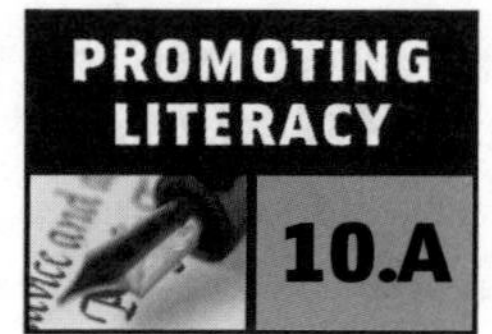


Read the different parts of a friendly letter. Unscramble them to make a complete letter. Cut out each part along the dotted line. Then arrange the parts in order and glue or tape them into your notebook.

Not much else to tell you right now. I hope you will write. Let me know how things are with you. Anything new?

280 Nevins Street
Brooklyn, New York 11217

Alicia

How are things in the old neighborhood? The move was OK. I never knew we had so much stuff until we had to pack and unpack it all! I like the new apartment where we live, but one thing I really miss is having a backyard. There is a big park nearby, though. Dad said that when the weather gets warm, we'll go play some catch. But if it snows enough, maybe we can go sledding. That's one good thing about living in a place where it snows!

January 5, 2003

Dear Meg,

I have been wanting to write you. I miss you. It seems like ages since we moved away. I don't need to tell you that I wish we could still hang out. I still think about some of the fun times.

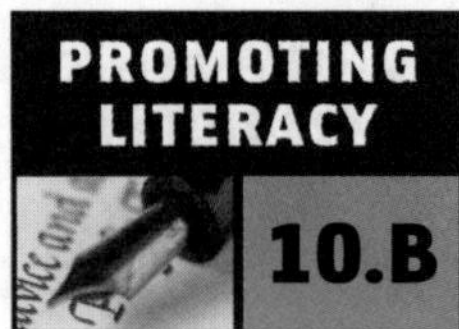


# Write a Friendly Letter

Think of someone you would like to write to. Use the letter outline below to write a rough draft. Share news and thoughts, and encourage the person to write you back. When you're finished, proofread your letter for any errors. Correct your mistakes and write a final draft. You may wish to copy your corrected letter onto a piece of stationery and then send it!

**Your address:** ______________________

______________________

**Today's date:** ______________________

**Greeting:**

______________________,

**Body:**

______________________

______________________

______________________

______________________

______________________

______________________

______________________

**Closing:** ______________________,

**Signature:**

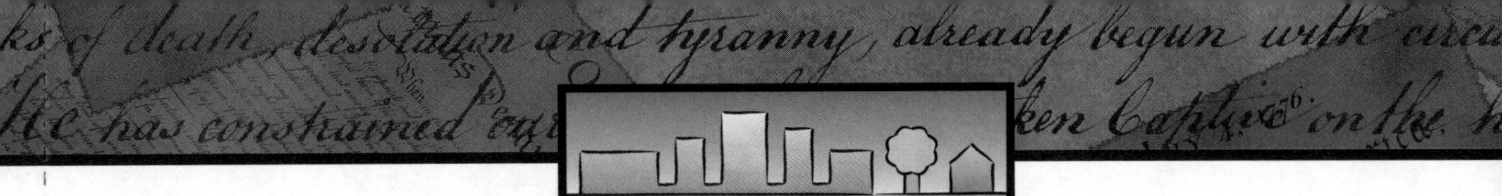

# In Your Community

**To reinforce the skills and concepts taught in this section, try one or more of these activities!**

### Storytelling to Children in Hospitals

Encourage your student to find some of his or her favorite storybooks that he or she would like to read to young children at a local hospital. Ask the hospital administrator before making the journey. You and your student also can read books aloud at a local senior citizens' center or at a local day care center. Be sure you or your child isn't coming down with a cold or the flu before going!

### Puppet Show

Ask your student to choose characters from his or her favorite childhood book. Then help him or her gather materials and supplies needed to make sock puppets for the characters. Have him or her write a script and create a stage. Then find a local day care center at which to have your student perform the puppet show. Make sure the story is okay for younger children first.

### Historical Fiction About Your Town

Help your student research your local town or region's history. Arrange to have your student meet with a historian or a librarian. Then have your student take this information and write a historical fiction story. Revisit Lesson 1.2 for pointers about this specific type of fiction.

### Real-World Writing

Arrange for your student to meet someone in your business community, such as a president or the chief operating officer of a company. Ask him or her to show your student what kinds of reports he or she writes and reads and what kinds of persuasion he or she encounters. Before the meeting, you may want to review Lessons 1.8 and 1.9 with your student. Help your student see the connection that what he or she is learning today will be valuable tomorrow.

### Your Town's Travel Brochure

Have your student make a travel brochure inviting others to visit your town. Contact your town hall, chamber of commerce, or convention and visitors bureau for photos, brochures, and other information to include in the brochure. Encourage your student to use as many primary sources as possible. See Lesson 1.7 for ideas. Assist your student in getting together the materials he or she may need to design and complete the brochure. Ask to have your local town hall, library, or convention and visitors bureau display it for others to see!

# We Have Learned

**Use this checklist to summarize what you and your student have accomplished in the Promoting Literacy section.**

- ❑ **Narrative Fiction**
- ❑ reading and analyzing narrative fiction
- ❑ characteristics of narrative fiction
- ❑ delivering oral narrative

- ❑ **Historical Fiction**
- ❑ reading and analyzing historical fiction
- ❑ characteristics of historical fiction
- ❑ writing a fictional story

- ❑ **Biography**
- ❑ reading and analyzing biography
- ❑ characteristics of biography
- ❑ writing a character sketch

- ❑ **Poetry**
- ❑ reading and analyzing poetry
- ❑ characteristics of poetry
- ❑ exploring rhyme and rhythm

- ❑ **Drama**
- ❑ reading and analyzing drama
- ❑ characteristics of drama
- ❑ exploring characters with dialogue

- ❑ **Reference Materials: Parts of Books and Primary Sources**
- ❑ identifying parts of books, using parts of books
- ❑ identifying primary sources, using primary sources
- ❑ evaluating primary sources

- ❑ **Research Report**
- ❑ reading and evaluating nonfiction
- ❑ writing a report
- ❑ delivering a report

- ❑ **Writing to Persuade**
- ❑ understanding persuasive writing
- ❑ delivering a persuasive presentation

- ❑ **Writing a Letter**
- ❑ understanding parts of a letter
- ❑ understanding tone and voice

**We have also learned:**

______________________________

______________________________

______________________________

______________________________

______________________________

______________________________

______________________________

______________________________

______________________________

______________________________

______________________________

# Math

# Math

## Key Topics

TEACHING THE LESSON

# Exploring Place Value of Whole Numbers and Decimals

***Without place value, how could you tell one from ten from a hundred?***

| OBJECTIVE | BACKGROUND | MATERIALS |
|---|---|---|
| To review for your student place value of whole numbers and then extend place value to decimals | Knowing how to read, write, and use numbers is a part of people's daily lives. Activities such as listening to the news, reading the newspaper, or following a recipe involve numbers—some of them very large. This lesson teaches place value through billions to your student and extends to using place value with decimals. | ■ Student Learning Pages 1.A–1.B<br>■ 1 newspaper or business magazine<br>■ 15–20 index cards<br>■ 1 number cube |

| VOCABULARY |
|---|
| **PLACE VALUE** the position of a digit in a number that gives its value |
| **PERIODS** in a number, groups of three digits separated by a comma |

# Let's Begin

## PLACE VALUE THROUGH BILLIONS

**1** **RELATE** Use your local newspaper or a business magazine to have your student find at least five examples of large numbers. Have your student write these numbers on a sheet of paper in his or her notebook. Ask, *How are these numbers used in the articles? How are these number written? What is the largest number you found? How do you say that number? What do these numbers tell you?*

**2** **REVIEW** Use one of the numbers to briefly review **place value** and **periods**—ones, tens, and hundreds in the ones period; thousands, ten thousands, and hundred thousands in the thousands period; and so on.

**3** **MODEL** Have your student prepare a place-value chart like the one at the top of the next page in his or her notebook. Use the same number from Step 2 to model the value of the digits in a

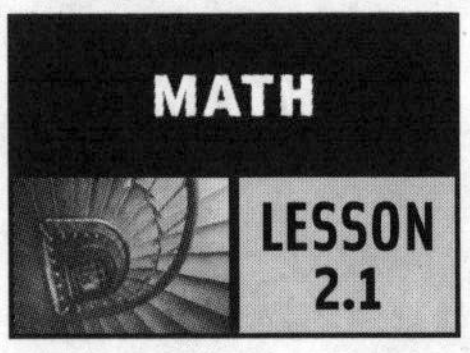

number. Write the numbers in the place-value chart and then read the number emphasizing the value of each digit. Have your student copy another number in the place-value chart and read the number emphasizing the value of each digit.

| Millions Period | | | Thousands Period | | | Ones Period | | |
|---|---|---|---|---|---|---|---|---|
| Hundred millions | Ten millions | Millions | Hundred thousands | Ten thousands | Thousands | Hundreds | Tens | Ones |
| | | | | | | | | |

4 **EXPLAIN AND REVIEW** Have your student copy the table below in his or her notebook. Use the numbers from the newspaper or magazine to review these three ways of writing numbers. Have your student write each number in standard form, word form, and expanded form.

| Forms for Writing Numbers | Example |
|---|---|
| Standard form | 2,357,368 |
| Word form | 2 million, 3 hundred fifty-seven thousand, 3 hundred sixty-eight |
| Expanded form | 2,000,000 + 300,000 + 50,000 + 7,000 + 300 + 60 + 8 |

5 **RELATE** Talk with your student about things in the world that occur in large quantities, such as millions and billions. Together, make a list on paper. [company stocks, populations of the world, animal or plant species, distances from and to planets]

6 **DISCUSS** Present this scenario to your student: *According to a study, as of April 2000 the state of California ranked No. 1 as having the largest population—33,871,648. In 1990, California was also ranked No. 1 with the largest population—29,760,021. That was a 13.8 percent increase in population.* Then ask, *How would you read these numbers? How would you write each number in the place-value chart?* Observe as your student reads and writes each number in the place-value chart.

7 **RESEARCH** Suggest that your student use resource books to find examples of numbers in millions and billions and list them in

 

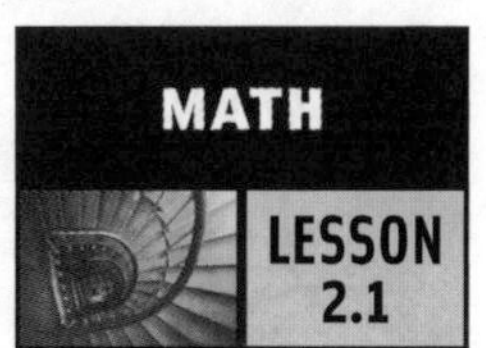


his or her notebook. Have your student add billions to the place-value chart.

**8** **PRACTICE** Have your student write these two numbers in his or her place-value chart: 378 billion; 281,546. Then have your student write the numbers in expanded form and read them.

**9** **COMPARE AND WRITE** Have your student use the numbers listed in his or her notebook to write examples of comparing large numbers using the greater than sign (>), the less than sign (<), and the equal sign (=). For example, your student might write 131,875 > 128,404 and 6,252 < 6,352.

**10** **PRACTICE** Have your student go to Questions 1–6 of Student Learning Page 1.A for more practice with place value.

## DECIMALS

**1** **EXPLORE** Mention that decimals can also be represented on a place-value chart. Remind your student that decimals are like fractions in that they represent values less than one. Ask, *Where you do often see decimals?* [money] *How would you show decimals on your place-value chart?* Have your student copy the chart below into his or her notebook.

| Hundreds | Tens | Ones | • | Tenths | Hundredths | Thousandths |
|---|---|---|---|---|---|---|
| | 1 | 3 | • | 8 | | |

**2** **DISCUSS** Talk about real-world situations other than money in which decimals are used. You may want to work together to find examples of decimals in resources such as newspapers, almanacs, and science and social studies books. Examples could include percent changes in data about population, baseball batting averages, unit prices on foods found in supermarkets, electric or gas bills, and distances.

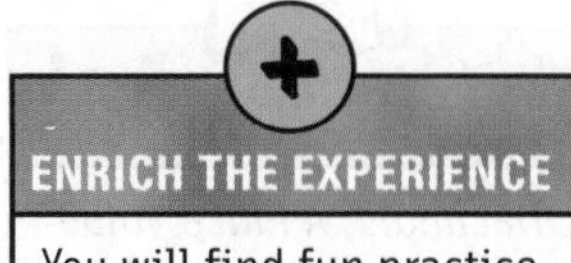

**ENRICH THE EXPERIENCE**

You will find fun practice games for place value with whole numbers and decimals online at http://www.funbrain.com.

**3** **ILLUSTRATE** Return to the scenario about California's population increase in Step 6. Use the 13.8 percent increase to discuss decimals. Explain that 0.8 is a decimal, meaning that it is less than one. Mention that although we often say "point 8," it means eight tenths. Use the place-value chart to show how to read the number. Say: *13 and 8 tenths.* The word *and* is a key word to signal that there is a part of a whole. Write five more numbers with decimals for your student to practice saying aloud.

**4** **EXPLORE** Use 13.8 again to explore exact and estimated numbers. Briefly review the rules for rounding numbers. [round up if the

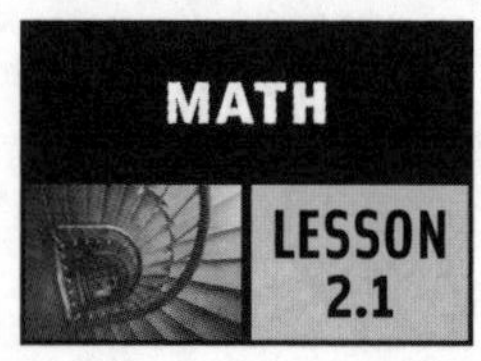

number is 5 or more; leave the number if it is less than 5] Ask, *What is 13.8 rounded to the nearest whole number?* [14] *How would you round 13.34?* [look at the digit in the tenths place and use the rules for rounding; 13]

**5** **PRACTICE** Have your student write these numbers in his or her notebook: 2.1, 3.78, 4.102, and 0.546. Then have your student write the numbers in expanded form and read them aloud. Next ask your student to write them in the place-value chart containing the decimal headings.

**6** **COMPARE AND WRITE** Have your student use the numbers listed in his or her notebook to write examples of comparing numbers with decimals using >, <, or =. Point out that a decimal number with more digits is not always larger than a number with less digits, as in 5 > 4.893.

**7** **PRACTICE** Have your student complete Student Learning Page 1.A for more practice with place value.

# Branching Out

## TEACHING TIP

You can create a flash-card game for your student to practice with. Write the standard form (2,568) of five numbers on each of five cards and the extended form (2,000 + 500 + 60 + 8) of the same five numbers on five more cards. Have your student play a matching or concentration game with the cards. Encourage your student to say the names of each number out loud for practice. He or she can play other games online at http://www.quia.com.

## CHECKING IN

Assess your student's understanding of place value by providing him or her with several numbers to write in standard form, word form, and expanded form. Use the same or different numbers to have your student write and solve two word problems, one that includes numbers in the millions or billions and another that includes decimals.

**FOR FURTHER READING**

*Decimals: A Place Value Approach,* by Linda Patriarca, Marilyn Scheffel, and Sheila Hedeman (Dale Seymour Publications, 1998).

*Mastering Essential Math Skills,* by Richard W. Fisher (Math Essentials, 1998).

*Math Made Easy: Fifth Grade Workbook,* by John Kennedy and Sean McArdle (DK Publishing, 2001).

# Compare Place Value

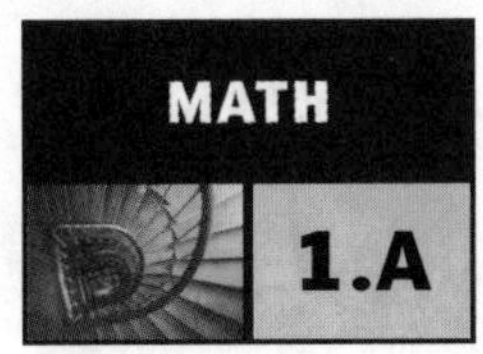


**Write the place value of the underlined digit.**

**1.** $2,\underline{1}06$ ________ **2.** $\underline{7}5,988$ ________ **3.** $\underline{5},567,342,212$ ________

**Compare each set of numbers using >, <, or =.**

**4.** 43,005 ____ 43,500 **5.** 812,345 ____ 802,545 **6.** 1,234,305 ____ 1,234,305

**Write the letter that represents each value.**

A B C D

0 1 2 3

**7.** 2.25 ____________ **8.** 1.25 ____________ **9.** 0.5 ____________

**Write the place value of the underlined digit.**

**10.** $2.\underline{3}4$ ____________ **11.** $8.6\underline{3}2$ ____________ **12.** $9.01\underline{1}$ ____________

**Write each in word form.**

**13.** 0.254 ______________________________

______________________________

**14.** 0.2 ______________________________

______________________________

**Write each fraction as a decimal.**

**15.** $\frac{750}{1,000}$ ____________

**16.** $\frac{4}{10}$ ____________

**17.** $\frac{42}{100}$ ____________

**18.** $\frac{6}{1,000}$ ____________

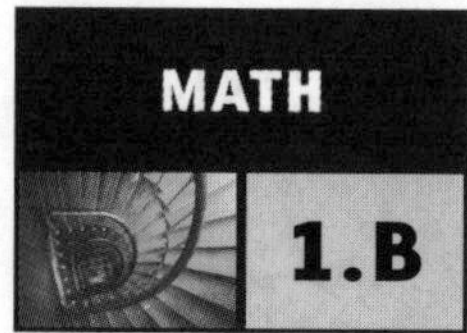
MATH 1.B

# What's Next? You Decide!

Now it's your turn to choose what to do next in the lesson. Read the activities and decide which one you want to do—you may want to try them both!

## Play Place Value

### MATERIALS

- ❑ 2–3 resource books
- ❑ 1 number cube labeled 1–6
- ❑ 11 index cards

### STEPS

This game requires two players.

- ❑ Use resources such as newspapers, magazines, almanacs, and science and social studies books to find articles that have large numbers or numbers with decimals. You will need to find 10 numbers. Write each number on its own index card.
- ❑ On a separate index card, write the numbers from the number cube, 1 through 6. This will be your key. Assign each number-cube number a place value that it can represent from hundredths to thousands (hundredths, tenths, ones, tens, hundreds, thousands). They do not need to be in order. For example, the number 1 on the cube could represent the tens place, and the number 6 on the cube could represent the hundredths place. Put the key card aside for reference.
- ❑ Shuffle the 10 other index cards.
- ❑ Choose an index card and roll the number cube.
- ❑ Take the number you rolled and find the place value it represents (look at the key card if you can't remember). Then find the value of the digit in that place in the number on the index card you chose. Write the value on a piece of paper.
- ❑ If the value of the digit is correctly written, score one point.
- ❑ Continue until all 10 numbers are used. Alternate play continues until a player wins 10 points.

## What Number Am I?

### MATERIALS

- ❑ 3–5 index cards

### STEPS

- ❑ Create some number riddles that use place value and are simple to guess. For example: This number has two digits. The sum of the digits is 12. The tens digit is 4. What number am I? (48)
- ❑ Write your riddles on separate index cards with the answers on the back.
- ❑ Share them with your family and friends.

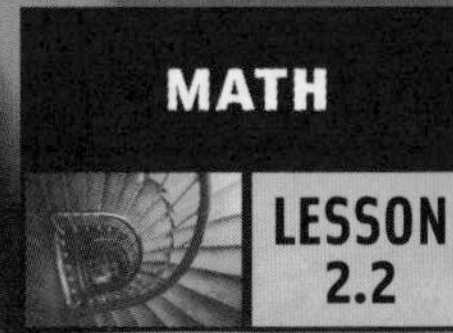


# Adding, Subtracting, and Estimating Whole Numbers and Decimals

***Sometimes getting the exact answer is important; other times, a rough estimate is all you need.***

| OBJECTIVE | BACKGROUND | MATERIALS |
|---|---|---|
| To show your student how to add, subtract, and estimate with whole numbers and decimals | Computing and estimating with whole numbers and decimals are skills your student will use throughout his or her life. Whether figuring gas mileage, comparing prices at the grocery store, or estimating the cost of monthly expenses, computing and estimating skills come into play. In this lesson, your student will apply addition and subtraction skills to larger numbers, estimation strategies, and adding and subtracting with decimals. | ■ Student Learning Pages 2.A–2.B |

**VOCABULARY**

**SUM** the answer of an addition problem
**ADDEND** the number to add in an addition problem
**ESTIMATING** calculating a rough or approximate answer
**DIFFERENCE** the answer of a subtraction problem
**DECIMAL** a number that uses a decimal point to express tenths, hundredths, thousandths, and so on

# Let's Begin

## PROPERTIES OF ADDITION

**1** **EXPLAIN** Talk with your student about activities that require a certain order or sequence. For example, when serving a meal it is important to put the dishes on the table before the food, but the order that the foods on your plate are eaten is not important. Remind your student that in addition the order in which the numbers are added does not change the **sum.** Show this example to your student: *4 + 5 = 9 and 5 + 4 = 9.* This example shows the Commutative Property of Addition.

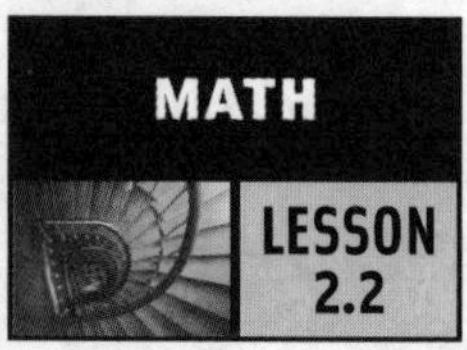


**2** **CONTINUE** Next, remind your student that in addition grouping the numbers in different ways does not change the sum. Tell your student that this is called the Associative Property of Addition. Show him or her this example: $2 + (5 + 4) = (2 + 5) + 4$. Remind your student that when parentheses are used in an equation the numbers in the parentheses are added first. The last property to review is the Zero Property of Addition. Remind your student that the sum of any number plus zero is the number itself. Ask him or her to give an example of this property [accept $x + 0 = x$]

**3** **ASK** Have your student write these equations in his or her notebook. Ask, *What property does each example show?*

| $3 + 0 = 3$ | $6 + (2 + 8) = (6 + 2) + 8$ | $7 + 3 = 10$ and $3 + 7 = 10$ |
|---|---|---|
| (Zero Property) | (Associative Property) | (Commutative Property) |

If your student identified the properties correctly, ask, *How did you know which property was shown by each example?* Encourage your student to tell how he or she remembered the properties. Have him or her write examples of his or her own. Check to make sure the examples he or she wrote are correct.

If your student didn't identify the properties correctly, guide him or her to identify the property for these examples and explain his or her choices.

| $4 + 0 = 4$ | $6 + 5 = 11$ and $5 + 6 = 11$ | $5 + (1 + 4) = (5 + 1) + 4$ |
|---|---|---|
| (Zero Property) | (Commutative Property) | (Associative Property) |
| $(2 + 3) + 7 = 2 + (3 + 7)$ | $8 + 0 = 8$ | $8 + 9 = 17$ and $9 + 8 = 17$ |
| (Associative Property) | (Zero Property) | (Commutative Property) |

**4** **RELATE** Explain that addition and subtraction are inverse operations. That means one reverses the other. It also means that subtraction can be used to check addition, and addition to check subtraction. Write the following examples on a sheet of paper. Discuss the examples with your student. Point out that subtracting an **addend** from the sum gives you the other addend, and that's how you know the sum is correct!

$$\begin{array}{r}13\\+\ 17\\\hline 30\end{array}\qquad\begin{array}{r}30\\-\ 17\\\hline 13\end{array}\qquad\begin{array}{r}758\\-\ 236\\\hline 522\end{array}\qquad\begin{array}{r}522\\+\ 236\\\hline 758\end{array}$$

Make up five similar addition and subtraction exercises for your student to complete for practice. Make sure that he or she uses addition to check subtraction exercises and subtraction to check addition exercises.

## ESTIMATION WITH SUMS AND DIFFERENCES

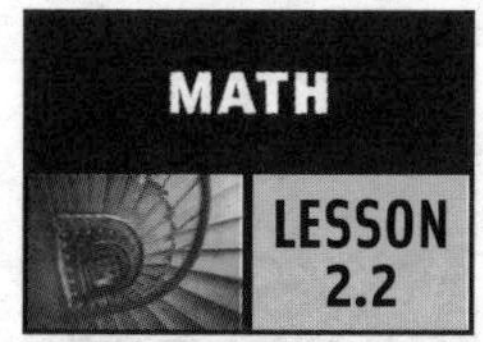


**1** **EXPLAIN** Tell your student that when **estimating,** rounding numbers makes them easier to add and subtract in your head. Review rounding rules. See Lesson 2.1 for more information. Explain that to round numbers to the nearest 10, look at the digit in the ones place. If the number is 5 or greater, round up; if it is less than 5, round down. Give your student these numbers to round to the nearest 10: 43 [40], 25 [30], 77 [80], and 21 [20]).

**2** **CONTINUE** Explain that to round to the nearest 100, check the digit in the tens place to see if it is 5 or more or less than 5. Have your student round these numbers to the nearest 100: 123 [100], 167 [200], 163 [200], and 145 [100]. Remind your student that rounding rules come in handy when adding and subtracting numbers in your head. Ask, *How would you estimate the sum of 27 + 34?* [round 27 up to 30 and 34 down to 30, add 30 + 30, equals 60, so 27 + 34 is about 60] *How would you estimate the* ***difference*** *of 47 − 16?* [round 47 up to 50 and 16 up to 20, subtract 50 − 20 equals 30, so 47 − 16 is about 30]

**3** **MODEL** Describe this scenario to your student: *You are at a sandwich shop with $2.50. You want a sandwich for $0.99 and a drink for $0.79. Tax is 8 cents per dollar.* Ask, *Do you have enough money to buy a sandwich and a drink?* Explain how you know. [yes; round $0.99 to $1.00 and round $0.79 to $0.80, that's $1.80, which can be rounded to $2.00; $2.00 + $0.16 for tax is less than $2.50]

**4** **REVIEW** If your student rounded the numbers and estimated correctly, ask, *How did you know to round up and add?* Encourage your student to tell what he or she knows about rounding rules and estimation. Write two or three similar examples on a sheet of paper for him or her to complete.

If your student did not round the numbers or estimate correctly, have him or her estimate the following answer:

$$\begin{array}{rcr} \$0.89 & \longrightarrow & \$1.00 \\ +\ \$2.77 & \longrightarrow & +\ \$3.00 \\ \hline \end{array}$$

Explain that the tenths place in both the numbers is more than 5, so both amounts are rounded up. The estimate is $4.00. Have your student use regular addition to find the exact answer. [$3.66] Talk with him or her about how close it is to the estimate.

## ADDITION OF NUMBERS TO TEN THOUSANDS

**1** **EXPLAIN** Does your student have a collection? Describe this scenario to your student: *David and Elliot both collect football cards. David has 1,878 cards and Elliot has 2,224. How many do they have in all?* [4,102 cards] Ask, *How would you solve this problem? What methods would you use?* Have your student solve the problem. Observe his or her method.

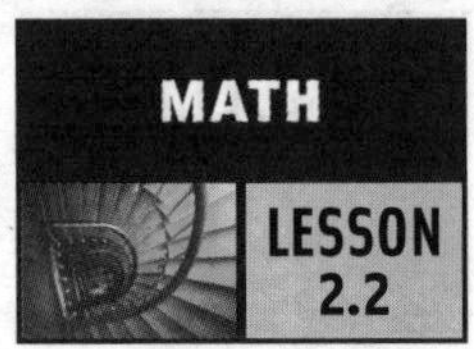


**2** **REVIEW** If your student solved the problem correctly, continue with adding greater numbers, for example: 12,368 + 23,479. Write five similar problems with five or more digits on a sheet of paper and have your student complete them. Discuss the different methods he or she could use to solve this problem. Talk about adding the numbers in his or her head, using pencil and paper to add, or using a calculator.

**3** **MODEL** If your student did not solve the problem correctly, show your student the steps for adding numbers greater than 1,000. While modeling each step, explain that the ones are added first (begin at the right). If the sum of the ones place is 10 or greater, you then regroup one ten to the tens column, as illustrated below. Then the tens are added and, if necessary, regrouped over to the hundreds, and so on.

| Add the ones and regroup if needed. | Add the tens and regroup if needed. | Add the hundreds and regroup if needed. | Add the thousands. |
|---|---|---|---|
| 1 | 11 | 1 11 | 1 11 |
| 1,878 | 1,878 | 1,878 | 1,878 |
| + 2,224 | + 2,224 | + 2,224 | + 2,224 |
| 2 | 02 | 102 | 4,102 |

Now have your student try again and check the answer with subtraction. Give similar exercises and observe as he or she completes them. Continue with exercises that have numbers to the ten-thousands place.

## SUBTRACTION OF LARGE NUMBERS

**1** **TRANSITION AND ASK** Use the football card scenario to review subtraction with large numbers. Have your student calculate how many more cards Elliot has. Ask, *How would you find the difference between 2,224 and 1,878?* [346] *What method would you use?* Ask your student to explain how he or she found the answer. Discuss.

**2** **REVIEW** If necessary, show your student specific steps for subtracting numbers greater than 1,000. Review how to begin with the ones place and borrow or regroup from the tens, hundreds, and thousands as needed.

| Set the ones and regroup as needed. | Subtract the tens and regroup as needed. | Subtract the hundreds and regroup as needed. | Subtract the thousands and regroup as needed. |
|---|---|---|---|
| 2 12 | 2 12 | 6 11 2 12 | 6 11 2 12 |
| 7,1~~3~~2 | 7,132 | ~~7~~,132 | 7,132 |
| − 2,224 | − 2,224 | − 2,224 | − 2,224 |
| 8 | 08 | 908 | 4,908 |

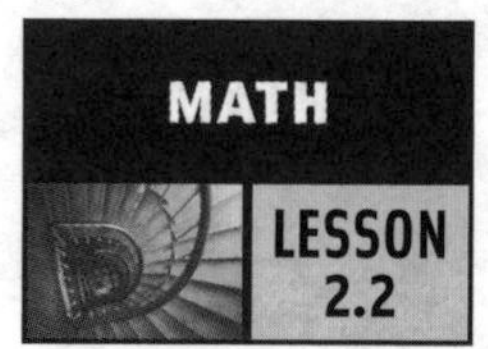


**3** **EXPAND** Have your student solve the following subtraction problem with numbers in the ten thousands: 23,479 − 12,368. Write five similar problems with numbers with five or more digits on a sheet of paper and have your student complete them. Observe his or her methods and review as needed. Distribute Student Learning Page 2.A. Have your student complete Part A for additional practice.

## MORE ESTIMATION STRATEGIES

**1** **EXPLAIN AND MODEL** Tell your student that there are different strategies for estimating. Explain how to use the front, or lead, digits of a number to make a quick estimate for addition problems of two or more numbers. Explain that this is called front-end estimation. Write the example below on a sheet of paper and walk through the exercise showing how to use the front digits to make a rough estimate.

**3**,219
**8**,932
\+ **3**,454

Rough estimate: 14,000

**2** **MODEL** Explain that the initial estimate can be refined by doing an adjusted estimate. Have your student look in the remaining digits for groupings of 1,000 or 500.

3,**219**
8,**932** → about 1,000
\+ 3,**454** → about 500

Adjusted estimate: 14,000 + 1,500 = 15,500

Ask your student to calculate the actual answer to the problem. [15,605] Point out that 15,500 is a reasonable estimate. Have your student complete Part B on Student Learning Page 2.A for more practice.

**3** **EXPLAIN** Explain to your student that another good strategy for doing mental-math estimates is to use compatible numbers. These are groups of numbers that are easy to compute mentally. Compatible numbers often end in 5 or 0. Using the example below, walk through the exercise and show your student how to adjust the numbers to make them compatible. Discuss why the numbers were adjusted up and down to make them compatible. Ask, *Why is 60 (and not 59) a compatible number in this problem?* [60 is a round number, which makes it easier to add in your head] Continue discussing the other numbers.

| **not compatible** | | **compatible** |
|---|---|---|
| 48 + 77 + 59 + 66 | → | 50 + 75 + 60 + 65 |

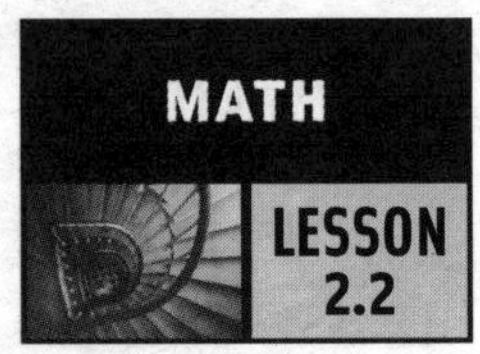

MATH

LESSON 2.2

## ADDITION AND SUBTRACTION OF DECIMALS

**1** **EXPLAIN** Present this **decimal** problem to your student: *Juana is a distance runner. While training for a race she ran 2.13 kilometers from the park to the train station and then 3.77 kilometers to the school. How far did she run?* [5.9 kilometers] Ask your student to solve this problem. Observe his or her method.

**2** **REVIEW** If your student solved the problem correctly, ask, *What did you do to solve this problem?* Discuss. If your student did not solve the problem correctly, review the steps for adding decimals. Explain that first the numbers need to be lined up by place value so that the decimals are aligned. Then complete the addition.

| **Line up the decimal points.** | **Add the hundredths and regroup if needed.** | **Add the tenths and regroup if needed.** | **Add the whole numbers.** |
|---|---|---|---|
| | 1 | 1 1 | 1 1 |
| 2.13 km | 2.13 km | 2.13 km | 2.13 km |
| + 3.97 km | + 3.97 km | + 3.97 km | + 3.97 km |
| | 0 | 10 | 6.10 km |

Have your student subtract to check the answer. [6.10 kilometers − 2.13 kilometers = 3.97 kilometers]

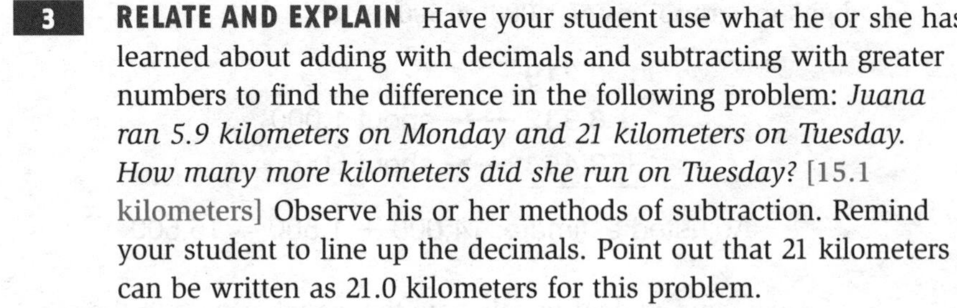

**3** **RELATE AND EXPLAIN** Have your student use what he or she has learned about adding with decimals and subtracting with greater numbers to find the difference in the following problem: *Juana ran 5.9 kilometers on Monday and 21 kilometers on Tuesday. How many more kilometers did she run on Tuesday?* [15.1 kilometers] Observe his or her methods of subtraction. Remind your student to line up the decimals. Point out that 21 kilometers can be written as 21.0 kilometers for this problem.

**FOR FURTHER READING**

*Fractions and Decimals: Grade 5*, by Carol Greens, Rika Spungin, and Linda Schulman Dacey (Dale Seymour, 1999).

*Math Bridge: 5th Grade*, by Jennifer Moore, Tracey Dankberg, and James Michael Orr (Rainbow Pub, 1999).

*Math Made Easy: Fifth Grade Workbook*, by John Kennedy and Sean McArdle (DK Publishing, 2001).

# Branching Out

## TEACHING TIP

Racing times are often shown in decimals and are a good source of real-world math problems. Have your student use the Internet to find some of the fastest times for runners in races of different lengths. Help him or her create math problems using different runners' race times.

## CHECKING IN

You can assess your student's understanding of computing and estimating by having him or her compare prices and costs of different items at a restaurant or grocery store. Have him or her identify the best value among grocery items or menu choices.

# Practice with Greater Numbers, Estimation

MATH 2.A

**PART A**

**Add and subtract. For more practice, on a separate sheet of paper subtract the odd-numbered problems and add the even-numbered problems.**

1. $\begin{array}{r} 38 \\ +\ 47 \\ \hline \end{array}$

2. $\begin{array}{r} 61 \\ -\ 26 \\ \hline \end{array}$

3. $\begin{array}{r} 436 \\ +\ 297 \\ \hline \end{array}$

4. $\begin{array}{r} 832 \\ -\ 379 \\ \hline \end{array}$

5. $\begin{array}{r} 6{,}589 \\ +\ 641 \\ \hline \end{array}$

6. $\begin{array}{r} 9{,}305 \\ -\ 2{,}794 \\ \hline \end{array}$

7. $\begin{array}{r} 12{,}375 \\ +\ 3{,}482 \\ \hline \end{array}$

8. $\begin{array}{r} 24{,}921 \\ -\ 11{,}179 \\ \hline \end{array}$

**PART B**

**Estimate the following sums using front-end estimation and adjusting.**

9. $\begin{array}{r} 4{,}212 \\ +\ 7{,}989 \\ \hline \end{array}$

10. $\begin{array}{r} 6{,}465 \\ +\ 520 \\ \hline \end{array}$

11. $\begin{array}{r} 10{,}089 \\ +\ 760 \\ \hline \end{array}$

12. $\begin{array}{r} 14{,}901 \\ +\ 827 \\ \hline \end{array}$

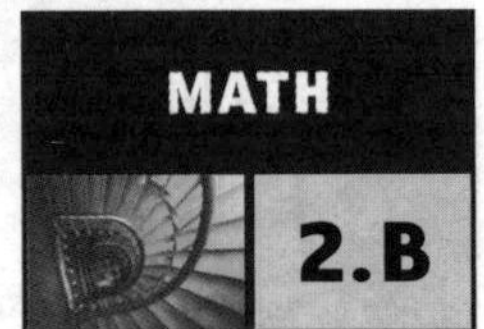


# What's Next? You Decide!

Now it's your turn to choose what to do next in the lesson. Read the activities and decide which one you want to do—you may want to try them both!

## Explore Equations

### STEPS

- ❑ Look at the numbers on both sides of the balance.
- ❑ Find the numbers that you could plug in to the boxes to balance the scale.
- ❑ Then on a separate sheet of paper make up some balance problems of your own.
- ❑ Draw balances with expressions on each pan like the one here.
- ❑ Invite a parent or friend to find the numbers to balance each scale.

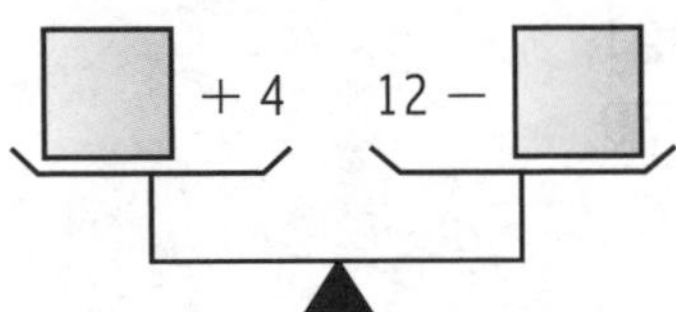


## Estimate at the Grocery Store

### MATERIALS

- ❑ 1 pocket-size notepad

### STEPS

Practice estimating decimals at the grocery store! Being able to come up with an estimated total cost for the groceries in your cart is a helpful skill to have.

- ❑ Ask an adult to take you along the next time he or she goes shopping for groceries. Bring a small notepad and pencil with you.
- ❑ Round the price of each item that is put in the cart to the nearest \$1.00 or \$.50.
- ❑ Use your notepad to keep a running total of the items. If you want, you can also try to keep the running total in your head.
- ❑ Before you go to the checkout line, estimate the total cost of the groceries in your cart. Write your estimate on your notepad.
- ❑ After you have checked out, compare your estimate to the actual cost of the groceries. Was your estimate accurate?

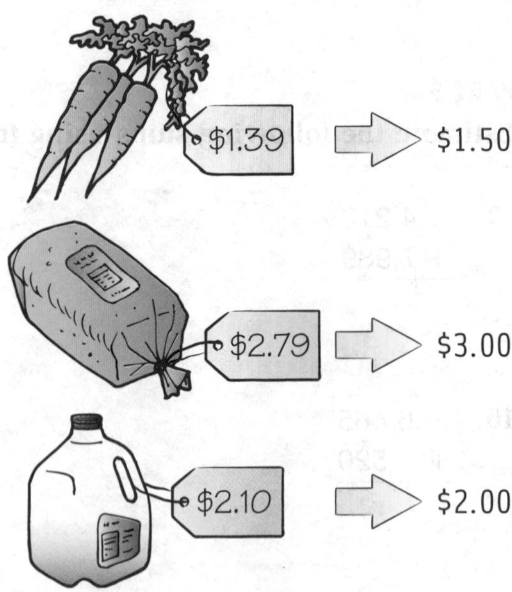

TEACHING THE LESSON

# Multiplying Whole Numbers

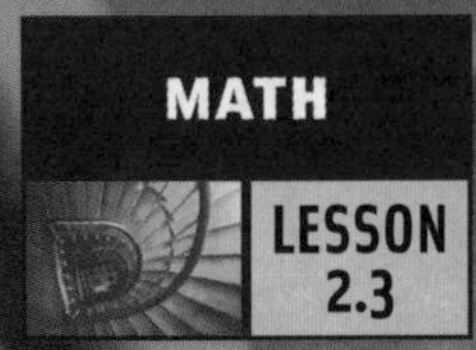


***M**ultiply, divide*
***A**dd, subtract to start.*
***T**hink of math*
***H**aving your interests at heart.*

| OBJECTIVE | BACKGROUND | MATERIALS |
|---|---|---|
| To reinforce and expand your student's multiplication skills | Knowing multiplication properties and patterns makes daily math quick and efficient. In this lesson, your student will study the properties of multiplication and the patterns for multiplying by tens as well as practice estimating. | ■ Student Learning Pages 3.A–3.B<br>■ 20 index cards<br>■ 1 die |

## Let's Begin

**1** **REVIEW AND DISCUSS** Briefly review the multiplication properties explained in the chart. Have your student copy this chart into his or her notebook to keep as a reference throughout the lesson.

| Multiplication Properties | Example |
|---|---|
| **Commutative Property** The order of the factors does not change the product. | $2 \times 5 = 5 \times 2 = 10$ |
| **Associative Property** The order of grouping factors does not change the product. | $6 \times (4 \times 3) = 72$<br>$(6 \times 4) \times 3 = 72$ |
| **Property of One** The product of any factor and one is the number itself. | $8 \times 1 = 8$ |
| **Zero Property** The product of zero and any factor is zero. | $9 \times 0 = 0$ |
| **Distributive Property** The product of multiplying the sum of two addends is the same as the sum of the products. | $2 \times 15 = (2 \times 10) + (2 \times 5)$<br>$(2 \times 10) + (2 \times 5) = 2 \times (10 + 5)$<br>$2 \times 15 = 20 + 10$<br>$30 = 30$ |

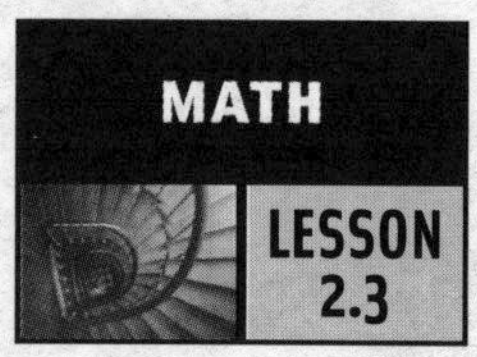

MATH

LESSON 2.3

| | × 10 | × 100 | × 1,000 |
|---|---|---|---|
| 4 | 40 | 400 | 4,000 |
| 7 | 70 | 700 | 7,000 |
| 9 | 90 | 900 | 9,000 |

**2** **EXPLORE** Mention that the Distributive Property of Multiplication will help when multiplying large numbers. Have your student copy the example 2 × 15 into his or her notebook. Use this scenario to illustrate the example: *A garden for planting sunflower seeds is 15 feet by 2 feet. How can you quickly find the area of the garden?* [multiply 2 × 10 and 2 × 5 and add the two products] Explain that multiplying 2 × 10 and 2 × 5 and then adding the two products is the same as multiplying 2 × (10 + 5).

**3** **RELATE** Review the chart from Step 1 with your student. Ask, *How can you tell that 4 × 10 equals 40 without doing the multiplication?* [since 4 × 1 = 4, 4 × 10 = 40] *What is the pattern?* [for multiples of 10, add one zero; for multiples of 100, add two zeros; for multiples of 1,000, add three zeros] Have your student complete Student Learning Page 3.A.

**4** **EXPLAIN AND MODEL** Point out that mastering basic multiplication facts and multiples of 10 will help when multiplying two- and three-digit numbers. Describe this scenario: *A package of sunflower seeds holds 89 seeds. If you plant 5 packages, how many sunflowers could grow?* Ask, *How will you solve the problem?* [multiply 89 × 5] *How will the Distributive Property of Multiplication help you?* [you can multiply 80 × 5 and then 9 × 5 and add the products] Use the steps in the chart below to model multiplying by a two-digit number. Then have your student multiply by a three-digit number.

| | | | |
|---|---|---|---|
| 1. | Multiply ones. | 4 tens and 5 ones | 9 × 5 = 45 |
| 2. | Multiply tens. | 4 hundreds | 80 × 5 = 400 |
| 3. | Add together. | 4 hundreds + 4 tens + 5 ones | 45 + 400 = 445 |
| Number of possible sunflowers: 445. | | | |

# Branching Out

## TEACHING TIP

Review rounding rules with your student as you go through the lesson.

## CHECKING IN

Assess your student's ability by providing him or her with the following multiplication problems: 32 × 7 and 628 × 3. Have your student explain the Distributive Property and use it to solve the first problem. For the second problem, have your student solve it using estimating rules.

**FOR FURTHER READING**

*Mastering Essential Math Skills,* by Richard W. Fisher (Math Essentials, 1998).

*The Best of Times: Math Strategies That Multiply,* by Greg Tang and Henry Briggs, ill. (Scholastic Trade, 2002).

# Multiply Whole Numbers

MATH
3.A

**Draw a line from the example to the multiplication property.**

1. $(4 \times 7) \times 5 = (7 \times 4) \times 5$
2. $3 \times 1 = 3$
3. $8 \times (2 \times 3) = (8 \times 2) \times 3$
4. $10 \times 0 = 0$
5. $9 \times 42 = (9 \times 40) + (9 \times 2)$

a. Associative
b. Commutative
c. Distributive
d. Property of One
e. Zero Property

**Use mental math to multiply. Write >, <, or =.**

6. $50 \times 90$ ______ $40 \times 200$
7. $30 \times 30$ ______ $20 \times 40$
8. $10 \times 60$ ______ $20 \times 30$

**Estimate the product.**

9. $57 \times 6 \approx$ ______
10. $22 \times 9 \approx$ ______
11. $982 \times 4 \approx$ ______

**Multiply. Show your work.**

12. $709 \times 4 =$ ______
13. $321 \times 2 =$ ______
14. $25 \times 25 =$ ______

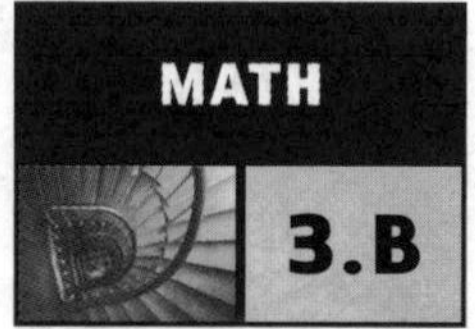

MATH 3.B

# What's Next? You Decide!

Now it's your turn to choose what to do next in the lesson. Read the activities and decide which one you want to do—you may want to try them both!

## Fun with Patterns

**STEPS**

Can you find the pattern? Follow the steps and see what happens.

- ❑ Write the product for each of the following:

  45 × 1,001 = ____________

  91 × 1,001 = ____________

  28 × 1,001 = ____________

- ❑ Look for a pattern. What do you notice?
- ❑ Multiply a two-digit number of your own by 1,001. What is the product?
- ❑ What is the pattern? Write a few sentences here about why the pattern works:

____________________________________

____________________________________

____________________________________

____________________________________

____________________________________

____________________________________

____________________________________

____________________________________

____________________________________

____________________________________

____________________________________

## Become a Chef

**STEPS**

You're a chef, and you're cooking a big dinner for 90 people.

- ❑ Look through cookbooks and find one of your favorite dinner recipes.
- ❑ Write all the ingredients in your notebook.
- ❑ Then look at how many portions the recipe is supposed to serve (4? 6? 8?).
- ❑ Depending on that number, figure out what you would need to multiply each ingredient by for 90 portions. You may have to ask an adult to help you.
- ❑ Multiply the ingredients by that number. Use a calculator to check your answer.
- ❑ Now find a recipe of one of your favorite desserts and do the same.
- ❑ For more multiplication fun, go to the store with an adult and calculate how much it would cost to buy the quantities of your ingredients.

TEACHING THE LESSON

# Dividing Whole Numbers

***Math Haiku***
*Dividing numbers*
*Is a skill to take you far*
*Wherever you go.*

| OBJECTIVE | BACKGROUND | MATERIALS |
|---|---|---|
| To have your student understand how to divide whole numbers and estimate quotients | Dividing whole numbers and estimating quotients are skills that are useful in everyday settings. This lesson explores division with whole numbers and uses estimation to determine whether quotients are too low or too high. | ■ Student Learning Pages 4.A–4.B |

**VOCABULARY**

**DIVIDEND** the number in a division problem that is being divided
**INVERSE** the opposite (division and multiplication are inverse operations)
**QUOTIENT** the answer in a division problem
**REMAINDER** the number that is left over in a division problem

# Let's Begin

**1** **REVIEW PRIOR KNOWLEDGE** Point out that to check a subtraction problem, you add. Ask, *To check an addition problem, what would you do?* [subtract] Explain that multiplication and division are also related. Ask, *If 4 × 3 = 12, how would you check your answer?* [divide 12 by 4 or divide 12 by 3] Point out that to check multiplication, you divide. To check division, you multiply.

**2** **PRACTICE** To illustrate the relationship between multiplication and division, have your student copy and solve the following equations in his or her notebook. For review, ask your student to identify the **dividend** in each division equation. [d: 72, e: 250, f: 3,600] Then have your student complete each equation and check the answers by the **inverse** operation.

$8 \times 3 = a$ $\quad 72 \div 9 = d$
$6 \times 30 = b$ $\quad 250 \div 5 = e$
$9 \times 600 = c$ $\quad 3{,}600 \div 4 = f$

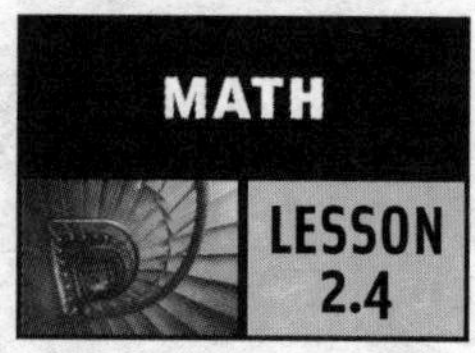


**3** **DISCUSS** Use the chart and discuss divisibility rules.

| **Divisibility Rules:** A whole number is divisible by |
|---|
| **2** if the number is even |
| **3** if the sum of its digits is divisible by 3 |
| **4** if the value of the last two digits is divisible by 4 |
| **5** if the last digit is 0 or 5 |
| **6** if the number is even and divisible by 3 |
| **9** if the sum of its digits is divisible by 9 |
| **10** if the last digit is 0 |

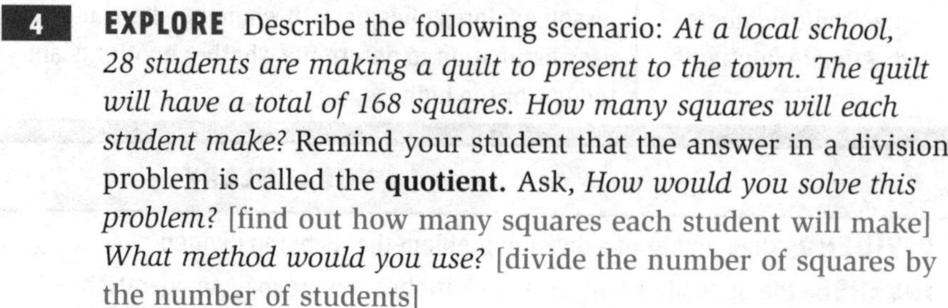

**4** **EXPLORE** Describe the following scenario: *At a local school, 28 students are making a quilt to present to the town. The quilt will have a total of 168 squares. How many squares will each student make?* Remind your student that the answer in a division problem is called the **quotient.** Ask, *How would you solve this problem?* [find out how many squares each student will make] *What method would you use?* [divide the number of squares by the number of students]

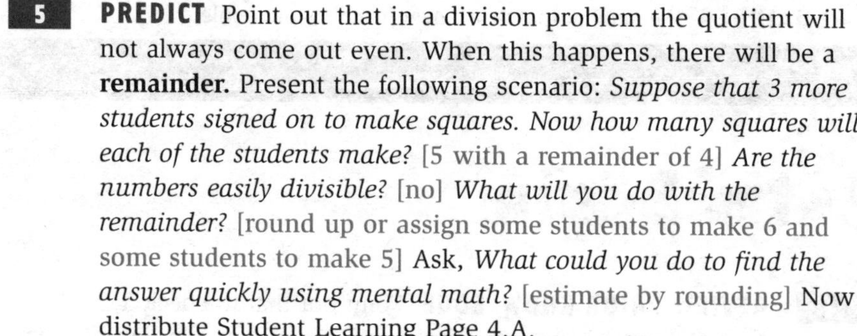

**5** **PREDICT** Point out that in a division problem the quotient will not always come out even. When this happens, there will be a **remainder.** Present the following scenario: *Suppose that 3 more students signed on to make squares. Now how many squares will each of the students make?* [5 with a remainder of 4] *Are the numbers easily divisible?* [no] *What will you do with the remainder?* [round up or assign some students to make 6 and some students to make 5] Ask, *What could you do to find the answer quickly using mental math?* [estimate by rounding] Now distribute Student Learning Page 4.A.

### FOR FURTHER READING

*Dazzling Division: Games and Activities That Make Math Easy and Fun,* by Lynette Long (John Wiley, 2000).

*Division Unplugged with Book,* by Emad Girgis and Glen Wyand, ill. (Jordan Music Productions, Inc., 1998).

*How to Tutor Multiplication, Division, and Fractions Arithmetic Workbook,* by Samuel L. Blumenfeld (Paradigm Company, 2001).

# Branching Out

## TEACHING TIP

Suggest that your student create word problems using ticket prices, such as finding how much each ticket costs if tickets for 14 people cost $126.

## CHECKING IN

Assess your student's ability with these three division problems.

423 ÷ 8 = ____ 4,685 ÷ 5 = ____ 1,267 ÷ 17 = ____

For each problem, ask, *What is the estimated quotient? What is the quotient? If there is a remainder, how will you interpret it?*

# Divide Whole Numbers and Estimate

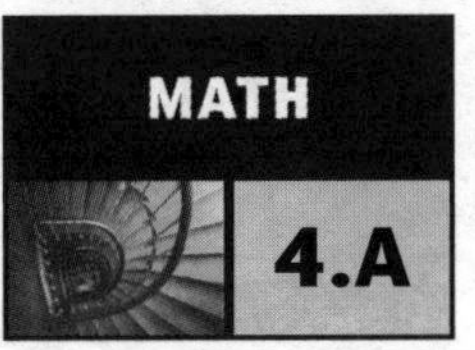


**Divide. Check your answer by multiplying.**

1. $5\overline{)75}$

2. $11\overline{)99}$

3. $15\overline{)225}$

4. $10\overline{)250}$

5. $8\overline{)960}$

6. $7\overline{)84}$

**Estimate the answer. Then divide. Tell whether your estimate is too high or too low.**

7. $7\overline{)89}$

8. $8\overline{)844}$

9. $6\overline{)543}$

10. $8\overline{)280}$

11. $6\overline{)27}$

12. $5\overline{)37}$

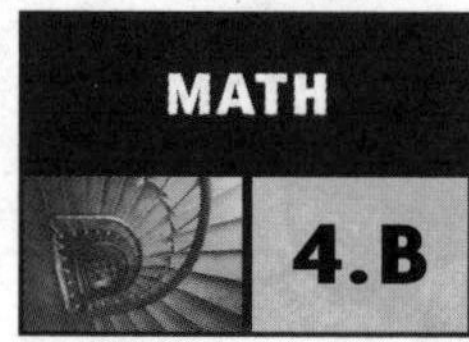


# Divide in the Town

The Davidson family has 6 people in it. Read each question. Then find the answer using division. Show your work.

Each day, if the people in the Davidson family . . .

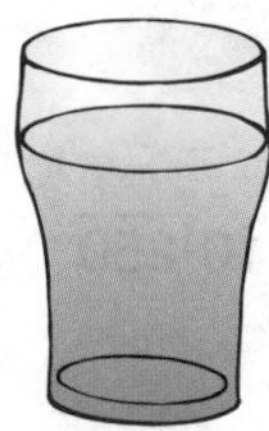

1. drank 48 glasses of water, how many glasses of water did each person drink per day?

_______________________________________________

2. ate 18 slices of bread, how many slices of bread did each person eat per day?

_______________________________________________

3. sneezed 30 times, how many times did each person sneeze per day?

_______________________________________________

4. tied their shoelaces 24 times, how many times did each person tie his or her shoelaces per day?

_______________________________________________

5. said "Thank you" 108 times, how many times did each person say "Thank you" per day?

_______________________________________________

6. walked 300 meters, how many meters did each person walk per day?

_______________________________________________

TEACHING THE LESSON

# Multiplying and Dividing Decimals

***Decimals are the universal language of fractions.***

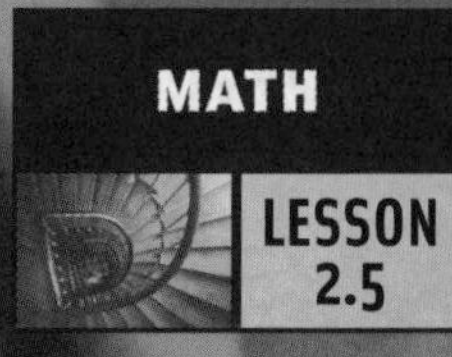


| OBJECTIVE | BACKGROUND | MATERIALS |
|---|---|---|
| To show your student how to multiply, divide, and estimate with decimals | Whether your student is calculating discounts, estimating the cost of multiple items, or computing data, knowing how to work with decimals comes in handy. This lesson applies the estimating, multiplying, and dividing skills your student already has to decimals. | ▪ Student Learning Pages 5.A–5.B<br>▪ 1 numbered die or 1 spinner numbered 1–6<br>▪ centimeter graph paper<br>▪ 5 index cards |

| VOCABULARY |
|---|
| **DECIMALS** numbers that use decimal points to express tenths, hundredths, thousandths, and so on<br>**PRODUCT** the answer to a multiplication problem<br>**DIVIDEND** the answer to a division problem |

# Let's Begin

## MULTIPLICATION OF DECIMALS AND WHOLE NUMBERS

**1** **REVIEW AND EXPLAIN** Review place value for **decimals** to the ten thousandths place with your student. Then explain that decimals can be rounded to make them easier to multiply in your head. Give your student these decimals to round to the nearest whole number: 24.8 [25], 6.97 [7], 2.5 [3], 9.62 [10], and 5.2 [5]. Ask, *How would you estimate the **product** of 26.8 × 4.1?* [round 26.8 up to 27 and 4.1 down to 4, multiply 27 × 4, that's 108, so 26.8 × 4.1 is about 108] Observe his or her method, then write two or three similar examples on a sheet of paper for him or her to complete. Check his or her work.

**2** **EXPLAIN** Does your student ever rearrange or add new furniture to his or her room? Describe this scenario to your student: *Cindy has six bookshelves lined up on two walls of her room. She wants to fit the bookshelves along one wall to make room for a new desk. Each bookshelf is 1.5 feet wide. The wall is 9.5 feet wide. Will the six bookshelves fit?*

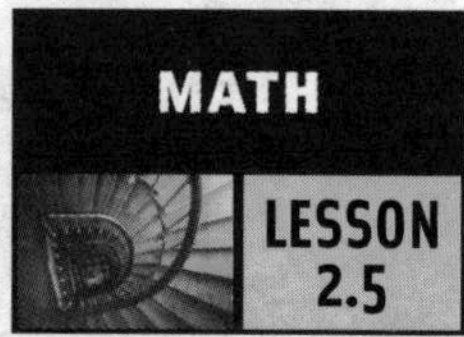


**3** **ASK** Ask, *How would you solve this problem?* [multiply the number of bookshelves by their width and compare it to the width of the wall] Have your student solve the problem. Observe his or her method.

If your student solved the problem correctly, ask, *What did you do to solve this problem?* Encourage him or her to explain that he or she multiplied the width of the bookshelves by the number of bookshelves, then compared the product [9 ft] to the width of the available wall space [9.5 ft] to find that the bookshelves will fit. Then ask, *How would you write the equation for this problem?* [1.5 ft × 6 = 9 ft]

If your student did not solve the problem correctly, write this example on a sheet of paper and walk your student through the exercise, showing how to multiply as with whole numbers. Point out that accurately counting the number of digits to the right of the decimal place in the factor so you can place the decimal point in the answer correctly is the most important step.

$$\begin{array}{r} 1.5 \\ \times\ 6 \\ \hline \end{array} \longrightarrow \text{Think: } \begin{array}{r} 15 \\ \times\ 6 \\ \hline 90 \end{array} \text{ tenths, which is 9}$$

In this exercise there is only one digit [5] to the right of the decimal, so count over once from the right in the answer to place the decimal [9.0]. Provide several similar exercises and observe as your student completes them. Continue with exercises that have numbers up to the ten thousands place.

**4** **PRACTICE** Model how to create practice problems with die or a number spinner. Roll the die to generate the tens, ones, and tenths digits of a decimal number and then roll again to generate a whole number. For example *12.3 × 4.* Have your student observe you create several problems. Then have your student use the die to write 10 problems in his or her notebook and find the products. Next, have your student try multiplying decimals with numbers in the hundredths place by whole numbers, for example: 12.45 × 8 or 56.92 × 3. Provide a calculator to check the answers.

**5** **CHART** Point out that when multiplying a decimal by 10, 100, or 1,000, a pattern helps to show where to write the decimal point. Help your student make a chart of multiplication facts for decimals to show the patterns. For example: 10 × 0.245 = 2.45, 10 × 2.45 = 24.5, 10 × 24.5 = 245, and 10 × 245 = 2,450. Do the same multiplying each number by 100 and 1,000 to finish the chart. Have your student find the pattern and discuss.

## MULTIPLICATION OF TWO DECIMALS

**1** **EXPLAIN** Explain that multiplying decimals by decimals is similar to multiplying whole numbers by whole numbers. Tell your student to consider this problem: *Cindy wants new carpet in her room. Her room is 9.5 feet wide and 10.5 feet long. How*

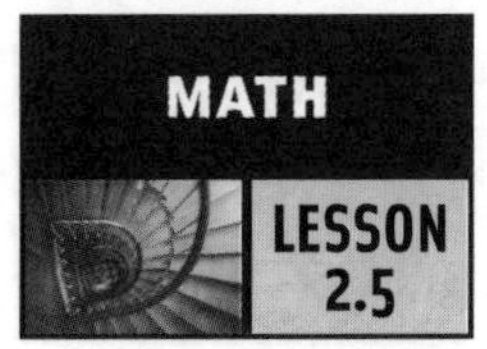


*can she find the area to discover how much carpet she needs?* [multiply the length times the width of the room: 10.5 ft × 9.5 ft = 99.75 ft] Have your student solve the problem while you observe his or her method. If he or she needs help with placing the decimal point, review how to place it correctly.

**2** **PRACTICE** Now go to Student Learning Page 5.A for additional practice.

**3** **MODEL AND WRITE** Review multiplying decimals with zeros in the product. Write the following example on a sheet of paper and walk your student through the exercise, showing how to insert zeros to show four decimal places.

| Multiply. | Insert four zeros to indicate four decimal places. Place the decimal point. |
|---|---|
| 0.03 | 0.03 |
| × 0.03 | × 0.03 |
| 9 | 0.0009 |

Write five similar exercises on index cards. Have your student pick a card, write the problem in his or her notebook, and solve.

## DIVISION OF DECIMALS AND WHOLE NUMBERS

**1** **EXPLAIN** Explain to your student that he or she can use decimal squares to illustrate dividing a decimal by a whole number. Show him or her how to shade a 10-by-10 square on graph paper to show 1 tenth and 1 hundredth as shown below. Explain that each 10-by-10 square equals 1 unit.

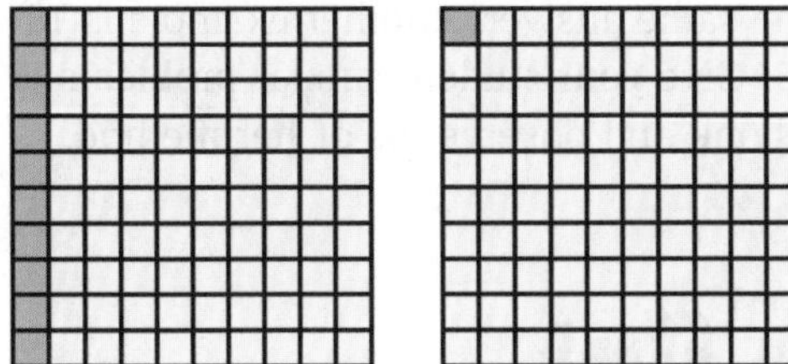

**2** **MODEL** Write 3.39 ÷ 3 on a sheet of paper. Use the decimal squares to walk your student through the problem. Shade decimal squares to represent 3.39 by shading three full 10 × 10 blocks and 39 squares in a fourth 10 × 10 block.

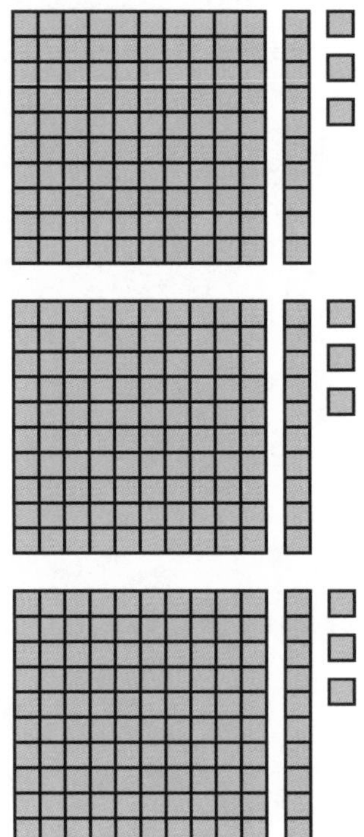

Cut out the three full squares and separate them into three piles. Then cut the 39 blocks into three groups of ten and three groups of three and divide between the three piles.

Ask, *What is the decimal name of each new group?* [1.13] *What is the answer to the problem?* [1.13] Have your student use decimal squares to solve the following problems: 4.04 ÷ 2, 9.63 ÷ 3, and 7.5 ÷ 5. Review his or her work.

3 **MODEL** Now show your student how to find 3.39 ÷ 3 using long division. Show your student how each whole and 13 hundredths relate to the graphs to place the decimal point in the answer.

**STEP 1**
Place a decimal point above the decimal point in the **dividend.**

$$3\overline{)3.39}$$

**STEP 2**
Divide as with whole numbers.

$$\begin{array}{r} 1.13 \\ 3\overline{)3.39} \\ 3\phantom{9} \\ \hline 39 \\ -\,39 \\ \hline 0 \end{array}$$

## DIVISION OF TWO DECIMALS

1 **EXPLAIN** Explain that when dividing a decimal by a decimal the equation can be simplified by using multiplication. Remind your student of the multiplication patterns he or she discovered when multiplying a decimal by 10, 100, or 1,000.

2 **REVEAL** Show him or her how to multiply both numbers in the phrase by 10 to change 1.25 ÷ 0.5 into 12.5 ÷ 5. Point out that 12.5 ÷ 5 and 1.25 ÷ 0.5 both equal 2.5. Explain that multiplying both numbers in a division problem by the same number creates a problem with the same answer. Another example is 10 ÷ 2 = 5 and 100 ÷ 20 = 5. Give your student similar problems to solve in his or her notebook and observe his or her method.

**FOR FURTHER READING**

*Delightful Decimals and Perfect Percents: Games That Make Math Easy and Fun,* by Lynette Long (John Wiley, 2002).

*Math Phonics—Fractions and Decimals Bonus Book,* by Marilyn B. Hein, Judy Mitchell, ed., and Ron Wheeler, ill. (Teaching and Learning Company, 2002).

# Branching Out

## TEACHING TIP

If your student struggles with multiplying or dividing with decimals, review easier exercises such as 7 × 0.9 or 8 ÷ 0.2, walking your student through each step. Continue with more difficult exercises.

## CHECKING IN

You can assess your student's understanding of working with decimals by having him or her solve real-world problems such as finding the total cost of bus fare for a group of seven at $1.75 each.

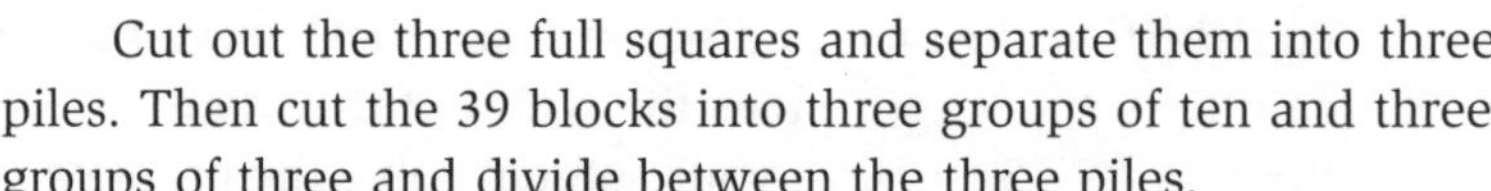

# Multiply with Decimals

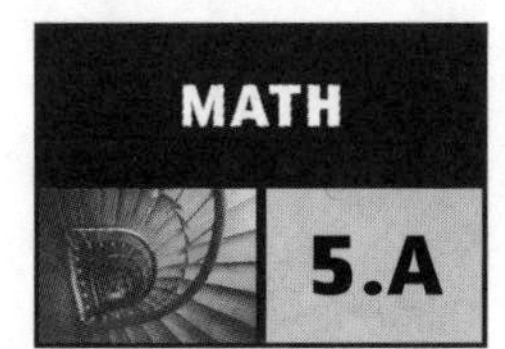


Estimate each answer in your head using rounding rules. Then multiply to find the actual answer.

1. $\begin{array}{r} 6.3 \\ \times\ 7.4 \\ \hline \end{array}$

2. $\begin{array}{r} 2.3 \\ \times\ 6.4 \\ \hline \end{array}$

3. $\begin{array}{r} 4.7 \\ \times\ 3.2 \\ \hline \end{array}$

4. $\begin{array}{r} 6.35 \\ \times\ 7.4 \\ \hline \end{array}$

5. $\begin{array}{r} 3.42 \\ \times\ 3.6 \\ \hline \end{array}$

6. $\begin{array}{r} 2.71 \\ \times\ 4.8 \\ \hline \end{array}$

7. $\begin{array}{r} 19.8 \\ \times\ 2.3 \\ \hline \end{array}$

8. $\begin{array}{r} 24.4 \\ \times\ 2.8 \\ \hline \end{array}$

9. $\begin{array}{r} 62.4 \\ \times\ 9.9 \\ \hline \end{array}$

10. $\begin{array}{r} 12.5 \\ \times\ 6.4 \\ \hline \end{array}$

11. $\begin{array}{r} 32.6 \\ \times\ 5.7 \\ \hline \end{array}$

12. $\begin{array}{r} 85.4 \\ \times\ 9.9 \\ \hline \end{array}$

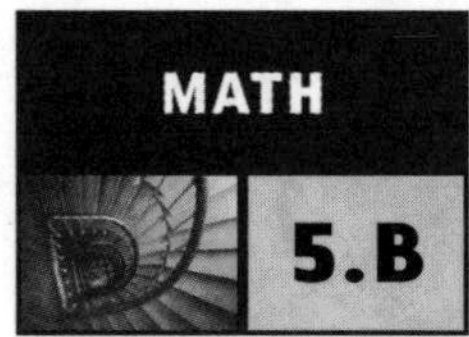


# What's Next? You Decide!

Now it's your turn to choose what to do next in the lesson. Read the activities and decide which one you want to do—you may want to try them both!

## Solve Multistep Problems

**STEPS**

Write your own multiplication or division word problems.

- ❑ Create problems that use more than one step to solve. Here is an example:

  A catalog sells baseball cards for $3.50 per set. If you order groups of 10, the cost is $3.00. What is the cheapest way to order enough sets for 18 team members? (order one group of 10 for $30.00 and one group of 8 for $28.00)

- ❑ Ask an adult or a friend to try your problems.
- ❑ Write your word problems here:

## Use Patterns to Divide with Decimals

**STEPS**

- ❑ Use a calculator to find each answer and complete the chart.

| |
|---|
| 2,870 ÷ 10 = 287 |
| 2,870 ÷ 100 = 28.7 |
| 2,870 ÷ 1,000 = |
| 287 ÷ 10 = 28.7 |
| 28.7 ÷ 100 = |
| 2.87 ÷ 1,000 = |
| 28.7 ÷ 10 = 2.87 |
| 0.00287 ÷ 100 = |
| 0.00287 ÷ 1,000 = |

- ❑ See if you can create your own division patterns.
- ❑ Share them with an adult.

TEACHING THE LESSON

# Working with Fractions

***Math is healthy exercise for the mind.***

| OBJECTIVE | BACKGROUND | MATERIALS |
|---|---|---|
| To help your student understand how to calculate equations with fractions and mixed numbers | Comfort and flexibility in working with fractions can add to your student's growing independence in daily living. This lesson applies the computing and estimating skills your student already has to fractions and mixed numbers. | ■ Student Learning Pages 6.A–6.D<br>■ 1 copy Grid, page 355<br>■ 8 strips of paper of equal size<br>■ colored pencils |

**VOCABULARY**

**DENOMINATOR** the bottom number in a fraction
**NUMERATOR** the top number in a fraction
**EQUIVALENT FRACTIONS** fractions that name the same number, such as $\frac{1}{2}$ and $\frac{3}{6}$
**LEAST COMMON MULTIPLE** (LCM) the smallest whole number that is a multiple of two or more chosen numbers
**GREATEST COMMON FACTOR** (GCF) the greatest whole number that is a factor of two or more chosen numbers
**PRIME NUMBER** an integer, not including 1, whose only factors are 1 and itself
**COMPOSITE NUMBER** an integer that is not prime
**MIXED NUMBER** a number that is the sum of a whole number and a fraction, such as $2\frac{2}{3}$
**RECIPROCAL** a fraction turned upside down

# Let's Begin

## FRACTION REVIEW

**1** **EXPLAIN** Explain that fractions describe part of one whole. Use the strips of paper to visually model the concept of fractions for your student. Explain to your student that all eight strips represent one whole. Each strip represents $\frac{1}{8}$; two strips represent $\frac{2}{8}$; and so on. Then share this example:

| 1 | |
|---|---|
| $\frac{1}{2}$ | |

| 1 | |
|---|---|
| $\frac{1}{2}$ | $\frac{1}{2}$ |

Point out that $\frac{1}{2}$ names one of two parts, while $\frac{2}{2}$ names two of two parts, or one whole. Ask, *How many wholes does $\frac{4}{4}$ name?* [one whole] Now, show your student the relationship between $\frac{1}{4}$, $\frac{2}{4}$, and $\frac{1}{2}$ in the diagram below. Discuss how fourths relate to one whole and $\frac{1}{2}$.

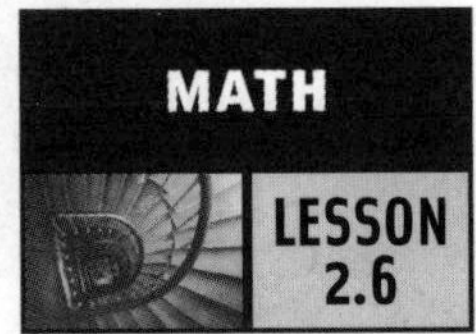


| 1 | | | |
|---|---|---|---|
| $\frac{1}{2}$ | | $\frac{1}{2}$ | |
| $\frac{1}{4}$ | $\frac{1}{4}$ | $\frac{1}{4}$ | $\frac{1}{4}$ |

**2** **COMPARE AND ASK** Show your student how to compare different fractions. Review the meanings of the following symbols: = means equals, > means greater than, < means less than. Ask, *Is $\frac{1}{4}$ greater or less than $\frac{1}{2}$?* [less than] Repeat this question with fractions of different sizes. Use drawings of circles or squares divided into sixths, eighths, or twelfths to illustrate the question. Point out that the greater the number of parts there are in a whole, the smaller each part is. Explain that the **denominator,** or bottom number, shows the size of the parts and the **numerator,** or top number, shows the number of parts.

## EQUIVALENT FRACTIONS

**1** **EXPLAIN** Tell your student that **equivalent fractions** use different numbers to represent the same value. Explain that equivalent fractions can be found by using a model or by multiplying or dividing the numerator and denominator by the same number [as long as it's not zero]. Tell your student that $\frac{3}{4}$ and $\frac{6}{8}$ are an example of equivalent fractions. Review the symbols in Step 2 above to compare fractions.

**2** **MODEL** Give your student a sheet of paper folded in three parts, or thirds. Ask him or her to color a third of it. Have him or her fold the paper back into thirds. Next have him or her fold the paper in half, adding one more fold. Ask, *How many parts will the whole have now?* [six] *How many will be shaded?* [two] Repeat this exercise with folding the paper in fourths then eighths, and halves then fourths. Have your student write the equations for each model in his or her notebook. [$\frac{1}{3} = \frac{2}{6}$, $\frac{1}{4} = \frac{2}{8}$, $\frac{1}{2} = \frac{2}{4}$]

**3** **MODEL** Show your student the following example for multiplying to find an equivalent fraction. Remind him or her that by multiplying the numerator and denominator by the same number (or a fraction representing one whole, such as $\frac{2}{2}$), an equivalent fraction is created. Point out that a fraction with the same number in the numerator and denominator, like $\frac{4}{4}$, is equal to the number 1. So multiplying a fraction by $\frac{4}{4}$ is like multiplying by 1.

$$\begin{array}{rr} 1 & 3 \\ \times 2 & \times 2 \\ \hline 2 & 6 \end{array} \qquad \begin{array}{rr} 1 & 3 \\ \times 4 & \times 4 \\ \hline 4 & 12 \end{array}$$

$$\frac{1}{3} = \frac{2}{6} = \frac{4}{12}$$

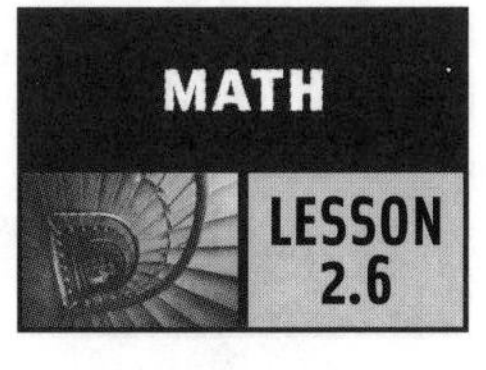


**4** **EXPLAIN AND PRACTICE** Show your student how to find the missing number in the equivalent-fraction equation $\frac{n}{3} = \frac{4}{12}$. Ask, *What do you have to do to 12 to get 3?* [divide by 4] *Now do the same thing to 4.* The missing number is 1.

$$\frac{n}{3} = \frac{4}{12}$$

$$l\overline{)12}^{\,3} \quad l = 4 \qquad 4\overline{)4}^{\,1} \quad n = 1$$

$$\frac{1}{3} = \frac{4}{12}$$

Have your student complete Student Learning Page 6.A for additional practice.

## COMMON DENOMINATORS AND ORDERING

**1** **EXPLAIN** Point out that it can be difficult to understand the relative values of two fractions if they have different denominators, such as $\frac{4}{6}$ and $\frac{3}{4}$. Tell your student that he or she can more easily compare the values of fractions by giving them a common denominator. Describe this scenario to your student: *Mike and his friend went hiking in the Smoky Mountains. Mike climbed $\frac{3}{4}$ of a mile and his friend climbed $\frac{4}{6}$ of a mile. Who climbed farther? How can you find out?*

**2** **MODEL** Tell your student that to rename the fractions with a common denominator you first have to find a common multiple. Remind your student how to find multiples of 4 and 6. Explain that the common denominator should be the **least common multiple (LCM),** or the lowest number, that is a multiple of both denominators. Ask, *What is the least common multiple of 4 and 6?* [12]

Multiples of 4 and 6:
**4:** 4, 8, 12 . . .
**6:** 6, 12 . . .

**3** **EXPLAIN** Tell your student that once he or she finds the least common multiple for the denominators, he or she can find the new numerators.

$$\frac{3}{4} = \frac{n}{12} \qquad \frac{4}{6} = \frac{n}{12}$$

Ask, *How many times does 4 go into 12?* [three times] Show your student how to multiply $\frac{3}{4} \times \frac{3}{3}$ to get $\frac{9}{12}$. Point out that $\frac{3}{4} = \frac{9}{12}$. Ask, *How many times does 6 go into 12?* [two times] Have your student do the multiplication to find that $\frac{4}{6} = \frac{8}{12}$. Discuss.

$$\frac{3}{4} \times \frac{3}{3} = \frac{9}{12} \qquad \frac{4}{6} \times \frac{2}{2} = \frac{8}{12}$$

To find out which fraction is greater, compare the numerators. Since 9 is greater than 8, $\frac{3}{4}$ of a mile is greater than $\frac{4}{6}$ of a mile. Mike climbed further than Sam!

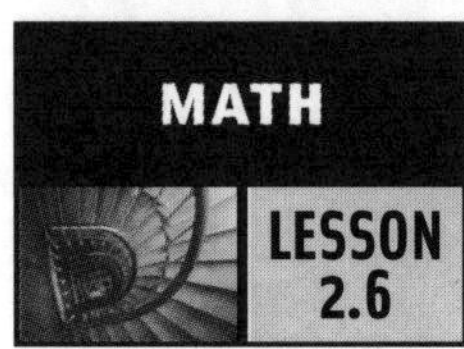

**4** **PRACTICE** Give your student more practice with comparing fractions by writing several fractions on index cards. Have him or her pick two cards at a time and find which fraction is greater, using the least common multiple to rename them as necessary.

**5** **EXPAND** Give your student the following fractions and have him or her order them from least to greatest by finding the least common multiple of the denominator and then comparing the numerators: $\frac{3}{4}$, $\frac{2}{8}$, $\frac{1}{2}$, $\frac{1}{3}$, $\frac{2}{3}$, $\frac{1}{6}$, $\frac{6}{8}$, and $\frac{1}{8}$. [least common multiple is 24; the order is $\frac{1}{8}$, $\frac{1}{6}$, $\frac{2}{8}$, $\frac{1}{3}$, $\frac{1}{2}$, $\frac{2}{3}$, $\frac{3}{4}$] Check his or her work and review as needed.

**6** **EXPLAIN** Explain that to compare and order mixed numbers, such as $\frac{2}{16}$, $2\frac{3}{8}$, and $2\frac{1}{4}$, look at the whole numbers first and order them, then rename the fractions with common denominators and put them in order. Point out that the mixed numbers in the example all have the same whole number, so your student can just compare the fractions to order the mixed numbers. Give him or her a few examples of mixed numbers that have different whole numbers, such as $3\frac{1}{2}$, $3\frac{2}{3}$, and $4\frac{1}{4}$. Discuss with your student how to compare and order them. Then give him or her a few more examples to complete in his or her notebook.

## ADDITION AND SUBTRACTION OF FRACTIONS

**1** **MODEL** Write the following example on a sheet of paper and walk your student through the exercise, showing how to add the numerators and use the same denominator.

$$\begin{array}{r} \frac{3}{6} \\ + \frac{2}{6} \\ \hline \frac{5}{6} \end{array}$$

$\frac{5}{6}$ → The denominators are the same, so write the denominator. Add the top numbers and write the sum above the denominator.

Continue with subtraction. Give your student the subtraction problem $\frac{5}{8} - \frac{3}{8}$. Walk him or her through the exercise, showing how to subtract the numerators and keep the denominator as with addition. Write five addition and subtraction exercises on index cards. Have your student pick cards, write the exercises in his or her notebook, and solve.

**2** **MODEL** Write the following example on a sheet of paper and walk your student through the exercise, showing how to rename the denominators using the least common multiple and then add the numerators.

$$\begin{array}{r} \frac{2}{4} \\ +\frac{2}{6} \\ \hline \frac{n}{12} \end{array}$$

→ The denominators are different. The least common multiple of 4 and 6 is 12, so write the least common denominator, 12.

$$\begin{array}{r} \frac{2}{4} = \frac{2 \times 3}{4 \times 3} = \frac{6}{12} \\ +\frac{2}{6} = \frac{2 \times 2}{6 \times 2} = \frac{4}{12} \\ \hline \frac{n}{12} \end{array}$$

→ Change the fractions to those with like denominators.

Add: $\frac{6}{12} + \frac{4}{12} = \frac{10}{12}$

**3** **REVEAL** Explain that $\frac{10}{12}$ is not in simplest form. This means that there is an equivalent fraction that uses smaller numbers that are factors of both the numerator and denominator. Have your student list the factors of 10 and 12 in order and find the largest number that is a factor of both numbers; this is the **greatest common factor (GCF).** [10: 1, 2, 5; 12: 1, 2, 3, 4, 6, 12; GCF = 2]

**4** **CONTINUE** Discuss the factors and guide your student to see that 2 is the greatest common factor of 10 and 12. Work with him or her to divide $\frac{10}{12}$ by $\frac{2}{2}$ to get $\frac{5}{6}$. Give him or her the following fractions to write in simplest form in his or her notebook: $\frac{15}{20}$, $\frac{5}{25}$, $\frac{6}{12}$, and $\frac{14}{21}$. Review his or her work.

**5** **EXPLAIN** Explain to your student that numbers are either prime or composite depending on their factors. When a number has only two factors, 1 and itself, it is called a **prime number.** A number with more than two factors is a **composite number.** The number 1 has only one factor so it is neither prime nor composite. Have your student find the prime and composite numbers from 2 to 10. Have him or her list the factors for each composite number. [prime: 2, 3, 5, 7; composite: 4 [1, 2, 4], 6 [1, 2, 3, 6], 8 [1, 2, 4, 8], 9 [1, 3, 9], 10 [1, 2, 5, 10]] Review his or her work.

**6** **DEMONSTRATE AND PRACTICE** Now give your student a subtraction problem with fractions: $\frac{6}{8} - \frac{3}{12}$. Walk your student through the exercise, showing how to rename the fractions with a common denominator and subtract the numerators as with addition. [least common multiple of 8 and 12 is 24; rename fractions as $\frac{18}{24} - \frac{6}{24}$] Remind him or her to write the answer in

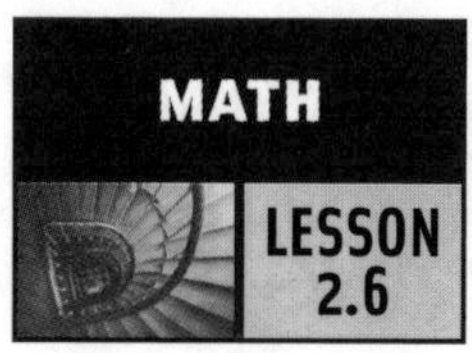


simplest form. [the answer is $\frac{12}{24}$; the GCF of 12 and 24 is 12, so the simplest form is $\frac{1}{2}$] Have your student complete Student Learning Page 6.B, Part A, for more practice.

## FRACTIONS GREATER THAN ONE

**1** **EXPLAIN** Introduce $\frac{5}{4}$. Explain that $\frac{5}{4}$ stands for 1 and $\frac{1}{4}$ more. This is called a **mixed number.** Point out that it can be thought of as $\frac{4}{4} + \frac{1}{4}$ and written $1\frac{1}{4}$. Have your student write a mixed number for $\frac{10}{8}$. [$1\frac{2}{8}$] Show him or her how to break the fraction into $\frac{8}{8} + \frac{2}{8}$, or $1\frac{2}{8}$.

**2** **MODEL** Write the mixed number $2\frac{1}{4}$ on a sheet of paper. Have your student find a fraction name for it. [$\frac{9}{4}$] Encourage him or her to use models such as buttons or to draw pictures to figure it out. Have your student copy the following fractions into his or her notebook and find their mixed-number names: $\frac{9}{7}$ [$1\frac{2}{7}$]; $\frac{3}{2}$ [$1\frac{1}{2}$]; $\frac{7}{2}$ [$3\frac{1}{2}$]; $\frac{12}{5}$ [$2\frac{2}{5}$]; and $\frac{8}{3}$ [$2\frac{2}{3}$].

## MIXED NUMBERS

**1** **EXPLAIN AND MODEL** Remind your student that a mixed number is a whole number with a fraction. Write the following example on a sheet of paper and walk your student through the exercise, showing how to find a common denominator, rename the mixed numbers, and then add the numerators.

$$\begin{array}{r} 6\frac{4}{16} \\ +\ 5\frac{3}{4} \\ \hline \end{array}$$

→ The fractions have different denominators. Find the least common multiple of 4 and 16.

$$\begin{array}{rcr} 6\frac{4}{16} & = & 6\frac{4}{16} \\ +\ 5\frac{3}{4} & = & +\ 5\frac{12}{16} \\ \hline & & 11\frac{16}{16} \end{array}$$

→ The least common multiple is 16. Multiply $\frac{3}{4} \times \frac{4}{4} = \frac{12}{16}$ and then add the numerators.

Remind your student that $\frac{16}{16} = 1$. Show him or her how to rename the answer.

$$11\frac{16}{16} = 11 + 1 = 12$$

**2** **DEMONSTRATE AND PRACTICE** Demonstrate subtraction with mixed numbers by walking your student through the following problem: $7\frac{6}{10} - 6\frac{2}{5}$. [$1\frac{2}{10}$ or $1\frac{1}{5}$] As with addition, show your student how to find a common denominator and subtract the numerators. Have your student complete Part B on Student Learning Page 6.B for practice. Ask your student to draw diagrams to show how he or she added or subtracted one or two problems.

 

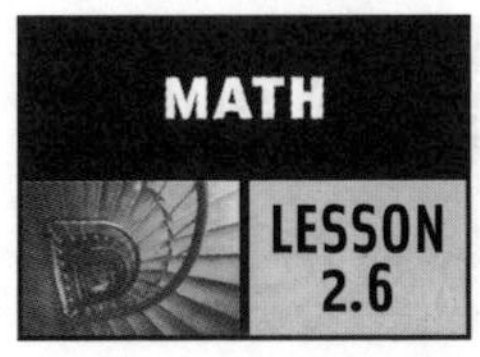


## MULTIPLICATION OF FRACTIONS

**1** **EXPLAIN** Explain that when multiplying, "times" means "of." Therefore, $3 \times 4$ means three groups of four. Point out that when a fraction is multiplied by another fraction, the product is a number less than either of the fractions. Ask, *Why do you think this is so?* [because a fraction is less than 1; consider that a half of a half is a fourth]

**2** **MODEL** Using the following example, show your student that the product of two fractions is found by multiplying the numerators and then multiplying the denominators.

$$\frac{3}{4} \times \frac{2}{3} = \frac{3 \times 2}{4 \times 3} = \frac{6}{12} \text{ or } \frac{1}{2}$$

**3** **EXPAND** Now show your student the following multiplication problem with a fraction and a mixed number:

$$2\frac{1}{2} \times \frac{1}{2}$$

Demonstrate how the distributive property of multiplication can be used to find the correct answer.

$$2\frac{1}{2} \times \frac{1}{2} = \left(\frac{2}{1} \times \frac{1}{2}\right) + \left(\frac{1}{2} \times \frac{1}{2}\right) = 1 + \frac{1}{4} = \frac{11}{4}$$

**4** **PRACTICE** Have your student multiply the following fractions in his or her notebook:

$$\frac{1}{5} \times \frac{2}{8}, \frac{1}{3} \times \frac{6}{7}, \frac{2}{5} \times \frac{4}{5}, \frac{3}{4} \times \frac{1}{2}, 3\frac{2}{3} \times \frac{1}{3}$$

[the products are $\frac{2}{40}$ or $\frac{1}{20}$, $\frac{6}{21}$ or $\frac{2}{7}$, $\frac{8}{25}$, $\frac{3}{8}$, $(3 \times \frac{1}{3}) + (\frac{2}{3} \times \frac{1}{3}) = 1\frac{2}{9}$] Check his or her work, and review.

## DIVISION OF FRACTIONS

**1** **EXPLAIN** Explain that the way to divide by a fraction is to multiply by its **reciprocal.** A reciprocal is a fraction turned upside down; $\frac{4}{5}$ is the reciprocal of $\frac{5}{4}$. Ask, *What is the reciprocal of $\frac{2}{3}$?* [$\frac{3}{2}$]

**2** **MODEL** Use the following example to model division with fractions. Point out that when a fraction is divided by a fraction, the answer, or quotient, is greater than the fraction being divided.

$$\frac{2}{3} \div \frac{3}{4} = \frac{2}{3} \times \frac{4}{3} = \frac{2 \times 4}{3 \times 3} = \frac{8}{9}$$

**3** **PRACTICE** Create five fraction division problems for your student to complete in his or her notebook. Review his or her work.

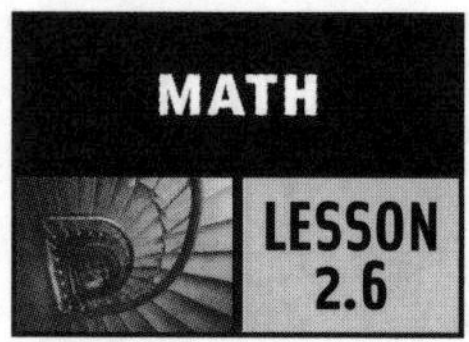


# Branching Out

## TEACHING TIP

When your student is working on his or her own, take time to make some of the fraction models your student will use in the lesson.

## CHECKING IN

You can assess your student's understanding of fractions by inviting him or her to cook with you when it's convenient. Invite him or her to convert recipes so that they will serve different numbers of people. Explain the different measurement units, then have him or her measure ingredients using only $\frac{1}{4}$- and $\frac{1}{3}$-cup measures.

**FOR FURTHER READING**

*Basic Computation Series 2000: Understanding Fractions,* by Loretta Taylor and Harold Taylor (Dale Seymour Publications, 2000).

*Math Practice Puzzles: Fractions and Decimals: Grades 4–6,* by Bob Olenych (Scholastic, Inc., 2002).

*Painless Fractions,* by Alyece Cummings and Laurie Hamilton, ill. (Barron's Educational Series, 1998).

# Find Equivalent Fractions

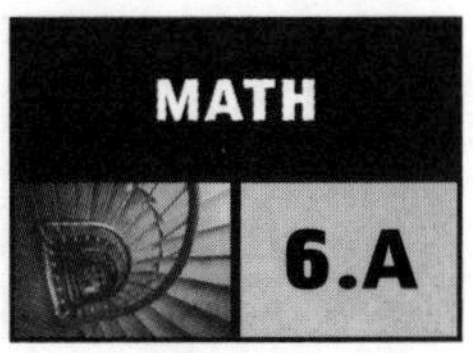


Find the missing number in the equivalent fractions.

1. $\frac{1}{3} = \frac{?}{6}$

   ? = ______

2. $\frac{2}{6} = \frac{?}{12}$

   ? = ______

3. $\frac{2}{9} = \frac{4}{?}$

   ? = ______

4. $\frac{5}{?} = \frac{10}{12}$

   ? = ______

5. $\frac{2}{3} = \frac{?}{18}$

   ? = ______

6. $\frac{6}{12} = \frac{12}{?}$

   ? = ______

7. $\frac{5}{?} = \frac{15}{30}$

   ? = ______

8. $\frac{?}{12} = \frac{8}{24}$

   ? = ______

9. $\frac{3}{5} = \frac{15}{?}$

   ? = ______

10. $\frac{3}{?} = \frac{12}{16}$

    ? = ______

11. $\frac{16}{28} = \frac{4}{?}$

    ? = ______

12. $\frac{25}{40} = \frac{?}{8}$

    ? = ______

**Now find three or more equivalent fractions for 1–12 and write them on a separate sheet of paper. Use models or draw pictures using a copy of the Grid found on page 355 if you want to.**

MATH 6.B

# Add and Subtract Fractions

**PART A** **Add or subtract. Find the common denominator if necessary. Write each answer in simplest form.**

1. $\frac{3}{4} - \frac{1}{4}$

4. $\frac{9}{10} + \frac{3}{15}$

2. $\frac{6}{9} + \frac{2}{9}$

5. $\frac{11}{12} - \frac{5}{6}$

3. $\frac{4}{7} - \frac{2}{14}$

6. $\frac{1}{5} + \frac{6}{25}$

**PART B** **Add or subtract.**

7. $2\frac{1}{3} + 3\frac{2}{3}$

10. $11\frac{9}{16} - 10\frac{1}{8}$

8. $8\frac{9}{10} - 6\frac{1}{5}$

11. $4\frac{7}{8} + 5\frac{1}{2}$

9. $1\frac{1}{2} + 2\frac{3}{6}$

12. $9\frac{1}{9} - 6\frac{1}{27}$

# Working with Ratios, Rates, Percents, and Probability

***What does math have to do with healthy eating? You may be surprised to find out.***

| OBJECTIVE | BACKGROUND | MATERIALS |
|---|---|---|
| To show your student what ratios, rates, percents, and probability are and how they relate to each other | Being able to understand rates and percents is important for making sound purchasing and investment decisions. In this lesson, your student will work with ratios, rates, scale drawing, percents, and probability. | ■ Student Learning Pages 7.A–7.B<br>■ 1 deck cards<br>■ 1 discount paper or store catalog<br>■ 1–3 maps of your country or region<br>■ 1 ruler |

**VOCABULARY**

**RATIO** the comparison of two numbers, such as 2 out of 3 or 2:3
**SCALE DRAWING** a proportional drawing of something that is larger or smaller than actual size
**RATE** the ratio of two measurements in different units
**UNIT RATE** a rate that has a denominator of 1
**PERCENT** a part of a whole that is expressed in hundredths
**PROBABILITY** the ratio of the number of ways an event can happen to the total number of possible outcomes

# Let's Begin

## RATIOS

**1** **EXPLAIN** When comparing two numbers that change at the same rate it is called a **ratio.** Present this scenario to your student: *Imagine that you and I are walking together. You take 3 steps each time I take 1 step. If we walk to the other side of the room, how many steps will you take if I take 5?* [15] Act it out with your student until he or she arrives at the right answer. Write 15 to 5. Explain that this is a ratio. Finding the simplest form of ratios is like finding the simplest form of a fraction. Tell your student that to find an equivalent ratio for 15 to 5 that is in its simplest form, divide each number by a common multiple, in this case 5, to get 3 to 1. Ratios can be written in any of these three ways: 3 to 1, $\frac{3}{1}$, and 3:1. Have your student write these three forms in his or her notebook. Ask your student to write another equivalent ratio. Review and discuss.

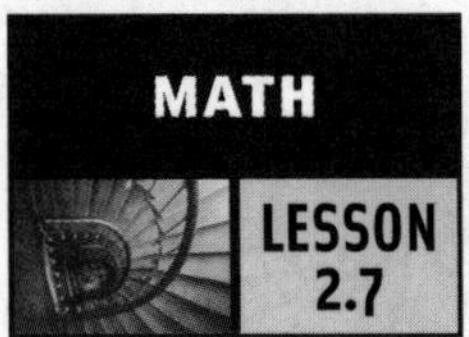


**2** **PRACTICE** Change the numbers in the above scenario to 6 steps to every 2. Write out the chart below (without the answers in brackets) on another sheet and have your student fill in the missing equivalent ratios. If your student has difficulty, remind him or her how multiplication and division are used to make equivalent fractions and that the same rule applies with ratios.

6:2
12: ____ [4]
18 to ____ [6]
[36] ____ :12
90: ____ [30]

## SCALE DRAWINGS

**1** **EXPLAIN** Explain that a **scale drawing** is used to represent something that is too large or small to be drawn in its actual size. Point out that a map is a scale drawing. Each map has a key or legend that shows the scale that it is drawn in, such as 1 inch = 100 miles. Look at several maps with your student. Ask, *Can you think of other ways scale drawings are used?* [by architects for building designs, by interior designers, by engineers to draw machines]

**2** **DISTRIBUTE** Have your student complete the exercises on Student Learning Page 7.A for practice working with scale drawings.

## RATES

**1** **EXPLORE** Present this scenario to your student: *A pack of 6 pens is $1.80. One pen is $0.25. How can you find out which is the better buy?* If your student needs a place to start, ask how much the pack of pens would be if each pen were $0.25. [$1.50] He or she will see that the single pen is the better buy. To help your student to divide $1.80 by 6, tell him or her to imagine taking $1.80 and spreading it equally among all 6 pens. Model and have your student copy the equation $1.80 ÷ 6 = $0.30. Explain that 6 pens per $1.80, or 1.8 dollars/6, is the **rate.** Then explain that a rate with 1 in the denominator [0.30/1] is called the **unit rate.** Have your student give examples of when knowing how to calculate a unit rate, such as a price per item, would be useful.

**2** **PRACTICE** Have your student copy the following prices into his or her notebook, figure the unit rate of the items, and identify the better buy.

**A.** 3 items for $5.00 or 4 for $6.00 [$1.67, $1.50]
**B.** 24 items for $25.95 or 12 for $10.99 [$1.08, $0.92]
**C.** 10 items for $9.99 or 6 for $4.99 [$0.99, $0.83]
**D.** 3 items for $2.50 or 2 for $1.75 [$0.83, $0.88]

## PERCENTS

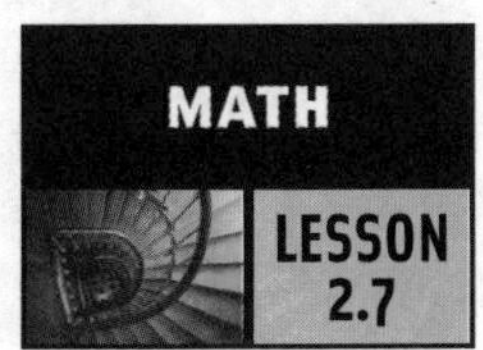


**1** **ASK** Ask, *How would you feel if you told a funny story and 8 people in the room laughed?* Guide your student to see that it depends on how many people were in the room. Your student would probably feel better if 8 out of 10 people liked the story rather than 8 out of 100. Ask, *What do you know about **percent**?* Let the student give information about where he or she has heard the word and what the symbol looks like. Explain that a percent is like a fraction whose denominator is always 100.

| FRACTION | DECIMAL | PERCENT |
|---|---|---|
| $\frac{4}{100}$ | .04 | 4% |
| $\frac{25}{100}$ | .25 | 25% |

**2** **MODEL** Have your student copy the relationship chart in his or her notebook. Ask your student to explain how to convert percents to decimals. [write the number and move the decimal point to the left two places] Draw a circle. Shade half the circle and ask your student what portion is shaded. [50%] Ask, *How can you write 50% as a decimal and a fraction?* [0.5 and $\frac{1}{2}$] Repeat this exercise with 75% of the circle shaded. Have your student add 50%, 75%, and their corresponding fractions and decimals to his or her chart.

**3** **EXPLORE** Look through a discount paper and notice how stores use percents. Ask, *How could you figure out how much 25% off would be for a bike that costs $100?* Before showing your student the formula, have your student arrive at the answer through common sense. Point out that 50% off would be one-half of $100, or $50. Explain that 25% off will be half of that. Ask, *How many groups of 25 are in 100? Think about a dollar and quarters.* [4] *Once your student sees that 25% off $100 is $25 off,* ask, *What operation could you perform with these numbers to get the same answer?* [divide $100 by 4, or multiply $100 by $\frac{1}{4}$ or 0.25]

**4** **MODEL AND PRACTICE** Have your student find the answer to the following problems. Ask, *What do you notice about finding 10% of a number?* [the answer is that number with the decimal point moved one place to the left]

25% of 60 [15] 10% of 24 [2.4]
75% of 50 [37.5] 10% of 240 [24]

**5** **PRACTICE** Remind your student to multiply when he or she hears "of" and point out that "is" stands for "equals." So the question "10 is what percent of 20?" can be written as $10 = n\% \times 20$. Ask the student to write an equation and solve these problems:

20 is what percent of 60? [33%]
45 is what percent of 100? [45%]

MATH

LESSON 2.7

## PROBABILITY

1 **EXPLORE** Look at a deck of cards with your student. Make sure he or she understands that there are 52 cards, split equally between red and black. Explain that the number of black and red cards will determine the **probability** of picking one or the other from the deck. Ask, *What is the probability of picking a red card?* [26 out of 52, or 1 out of 2, or $\frac{1}{2}$] *How many aces are there in the deck?* [4] *What is the probability of picking an ace?* [4 out of 52, or 1 out of 13, or $\frac{1}{13}$]

2 **MODEL** Model probability with a coin toss. Point out that there are two possible outcomes. Explain that the probability of tossing the coin and it landing tail side up is 1 out of 2 or 1 in 2. Ask, *What is the probability of landing two tails in two tosses? How could you use logic or common sense to find the answer?* Have your student make a tree diagram showing all the possible results of flipping a coin twice. Guide your student to see that the chance of flipping two tails in two flips (TT) is 1 out of 4 or 1 in 4. Then have your student draw the tree diagram for the probability of tossing tails three times in a row. Review and discuss.

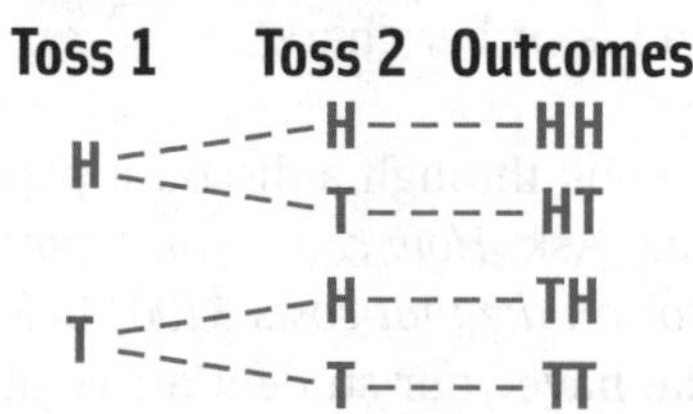


3 **REVEAL** Explain that multiplication is another way to find the answer. Each time a coin is tossed there is a 1 in 2 chance it will land on tails. The equivalent fraction is $\frac{1}{2}$, so multiply $\frac{1}{2}$ for the first flip by $\frac{1}{2}$ for the second flip. [$\frac{1}{2} \times \frac{1}{2} = \frac{1}{4}$] One out of 4 sets of two flips will be tails, tails.

# Branching Out

## TEACHING TIP

Get your student in the habit of asking himself or herself if an answer makes sense. Many math problems can be easily estimated.

## CHECKING IN

Ask your student to explain how understanding fractions and decimals helps to understand percents and vice versa. Have your student give examples. [40%, $\frac{40}{100}$, 0.4]

FOR FURTHER READING

*Skittle Riddles Math,* by Barbara McGrath (Charlesbridge Publishers, 2000).

*Grapes of Math,* by Greg Tang (Scholastic Press, 2001).

# Work with Scale Drawings

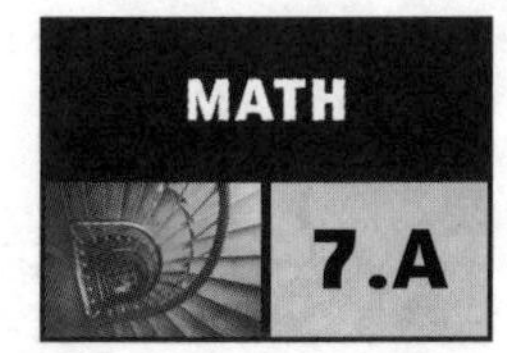


Use a ruler to complete the questions and add furniture to the scale drawing of a room.

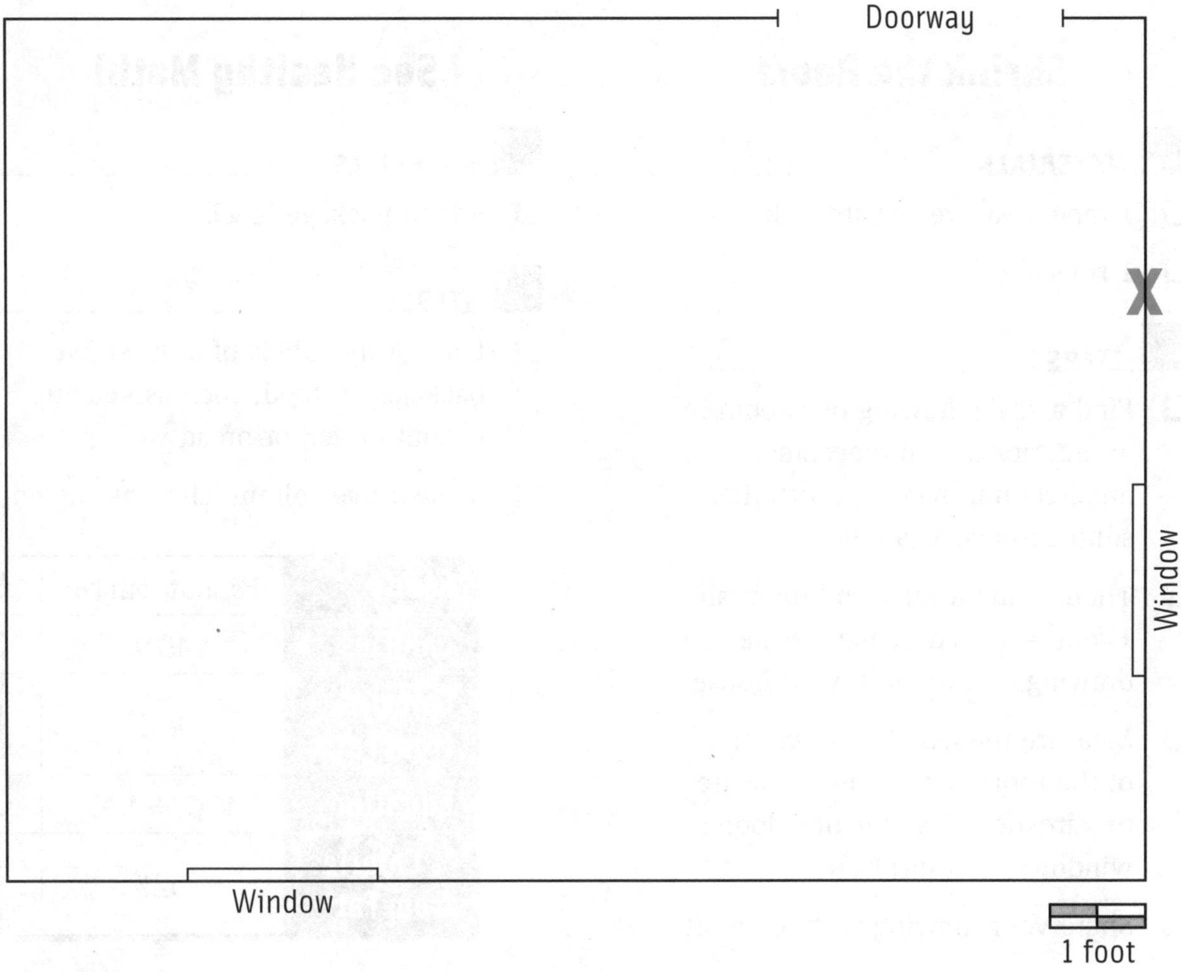

Doorway

X

Window

Window

1 foot

1. What is the scale of the drawing? ____________

2. What is the length and width of the room? ____________

3. How wide is each window? ____________

4. How many total feet of bookshelves could fit on each side of the window on the wall marked "x"? ____________

5. Add this furniture into the drawing. Be sure to draw each one to scale.

❑ Bed: 5 feet wide by 6 feet long
❑ Night table: $1\frac{1}{2}$ square feet
❑ Dresser: 4 feet long by $2\frac{1}{2}$ feet deep
❑ Bookshelf: 3 feet long by 1 foot deep

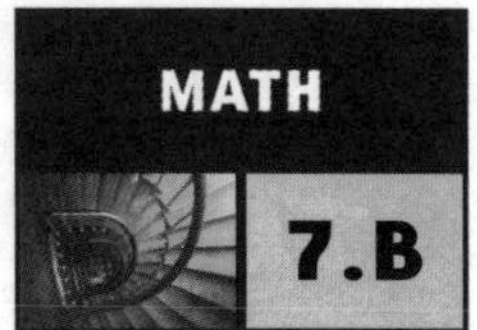


# What's Next? You Decide!

Now it's your turn to choose what to do next in the lesson. Read the activities and decide which one you want to do—you may want to try them both!

## Shrink the Room

### MATERIALS

- ❑ 1 tape measure or yardstick
- ❑ 1 ruler

### STEPS

- ❑ Find a scale drawing of a room in an interior design magazine, architectural magazine, or other source to use as a guide.
- ❑ Then, using a ruler and the scale 1 foot = 1 inch, make a scale drawing of a room in your house.
- ❑ Measure the length and width of the room with a tape measure or yardstick. Also include doors, windows, and furniture.
- ❑ Share your drawing with an adult.

## See Healthy Math!

### MATERIALS

- ❑ 5 food package labels

### STEPS

- ❑ Look at the labels of at least five packages of food, such as ketchup, peanut butter, or bread.
- ❑ Make a five-column chart as shown:

| Food | Peanut Butter | |
|---|---|---|
| Calories | 190 | |
| Calories from Fat | 100 | |
| Equation | 100 ÷ 190 | |
| % Calories from Fat | 52% | |

- ❑ If the food package shows fat grams only, multiply the fat grams by 9 to get calories from fat.
- ❑ In the fourth column, write the equation for calculating the percent of calories from fat. (Hint: divide the fat calories by the total calories.)
- ❑ Then write the percent of calories from fat in the last column.
- ❑ Write a general statement for each food, such as "About half the calories in peanut butter come from fat."

 

TEACHING THE LESSON

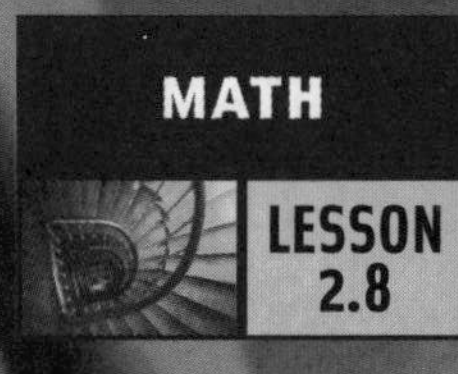


# Introducing Integers and Graphing Coordinates

***Every day is so filled with positive and negative integers that we hardly even notice them.***

| OBJECTIVE | BACKGROUND | MATERIALS |
| --- | --- | --- |
| To teach your student about integers and how to use them in graphing coordinates | Whether your student is learning about weather patterns, locating places on a globe, reading about sports, or calculating an allowance, he or she is using integers. This lesson will apply addition and subtraction skills to positive and negative whole numbers. This lesson will also apply the use of integers in making and interpreting coordinate graphs. | ■ Student Learning Pages 8.A–8.B |

| VOCABULARY |
| --- |
| **INTEGERS** the counting numbers, including zero, and their opposites |
| **EQUATION** a mathematical sentence that has an equal sign |

# Let's Begin

## INTRODUCE AND COMPARE INTEGERS

**1** **EXPLORE** Use the number line below to introduce **integers.** Call attention to the numbers to the right of zero and the arrow. The arrow means that the numbers continue. Explain that the numbers to the left of zero are less than zero and are called negative integers. The numbers to the right of zero are greater than zero and are called positive integers. Suggest that your student copy the number line in his or her notebook. Have your student circle −5 and +3 on the number line. Discuss which number is greater.

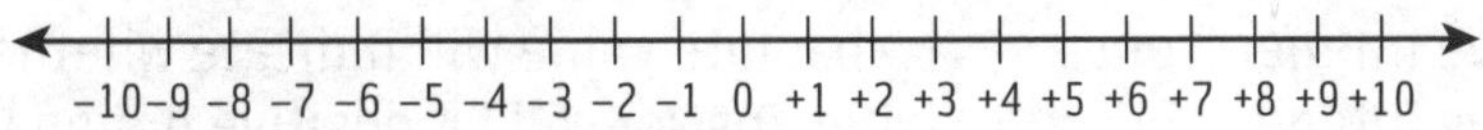


**2** **CONTINUE** Have your student underline −6 and +6 on the number line. Ask, *How many places are they from zero on the number line?* [6 to the left and 6 to the right] *Why are they opposites?* [each is located on either side of zero] Tell your student about absolute value, which is the "distance" a number

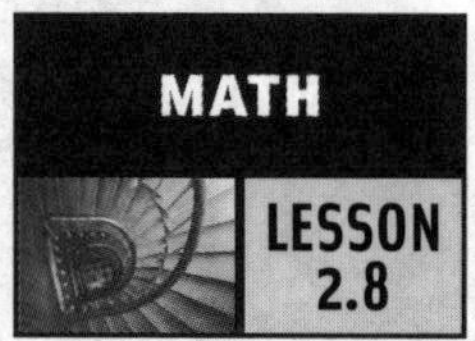

MATH

LESSON 2.8

is from zero. For example, −6 and +6 both have an absolute value of 6, because they are both 6 places from zero.

3 **RELATE AND COMPARE** Have your student make another number line in his or her notebook representing numbers from −20 to +20. Under the number line, have your student write the following numbers: −7, +12, −18, −2, +8. Ask your student to order the numbers from least to greatest. [−18, −7, −2, +8, +12] Then suggest that your student choose any five numbers from −20 to +20 and order them from least to greatest. Once your student has an understanding of ordering and comparing integers, explain that he or she can add and subtract integers.

## EVALUATE EXPRESSIONS

1 **EXPLORE AND MODEL** Use the number line to evaluate the following expressions with your student. Have your student copy these expressions into his or her notebook.

+4 + +5 (+9)    −7 + +5 (−2)

+8 − −2 (+10)    +3 − +5 (−2)

Using the number line, work together with your student to solve the expressions. Relate the following rules for adding and subtracting integers to your student. Tell your student to think of a negative sign as meaning "opposite." This means that when adding a negative number, you're basically subtracting the opposite of that number (+5 + −3 is the same as +5 − +3). It also means that when subtracting a negative number, because there are two negative signs, you are performing "the opposite

| | If | Then |
|---|---|---|
| **Adding integers** | both numbers are positive, | the sum will be positive. |
| | both numbers are negative, | the sum will be negative. |
| | one number is positive and the other is negative, | the number that has the greater absolute value will indicate whether the sum will be positive or negative. |
| **Subtracting integers** | you're subtracting a negative integer from a positive integer, | the answer will be positive. |
| | you're subtracting a negative integer from a negative integer, | the number that has the greater absolute value will indicate whether the answer will be positive or negative. |

| **Integer rules** | Adding a negative number is like subtracting a positive number. |
|---|---|
| | Subtracting a negative number is like adding a positive number. The minus signs cancel each other out. |

of the opposite," which is the same as adding the number (+5 − −3 is the same as +5 + +3).

When learning about integers, you may wish to show your student the rules for integers on the previous page. If you'd like, have your student copy the rules in his or her notebook. Suggest that your student provide an example next to each rule.

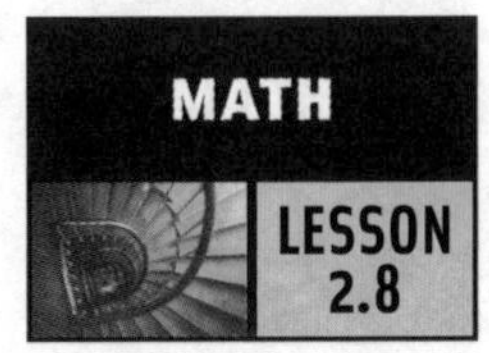


**2** **PRACTICE** Distribute Student Learning Page 8.A for more practice.

## INTEGER EQUATIONS

**1** **RELATE AND DISCUSS** Talk about places where your student has seen positive and negative numbers. Mention very cold temperatures or wind chill temperatures. Explain that one way to solve a problem about temperature is to use an **equation.** An equation is a mathematical expression that has an equal sign. [$1 + x = 2$] Help your student write one or two equations that relate to something he or she did this week. [had $2.00 and spent $0.50: $2.00 − $0.50 = $1.50]

**2** **ILLUSTRATE** Relate this word problem to your student: *The temperature at 5:00 P.M. was 17°F. The temperature was −7°F the next morning. How many degrees did the temperature drop?* Also ask, *How would you solve this problem?* [subtract the temperatures or use a number line to show temperature drop] *How would you write this expression as an equation?* [$17 - -7 = n$ or $17 - n = -7$]

In 1996, record low temperatures occurred from February 2 through February 4 in three states: Minnesota at −60°F, Iowa at −47°F, and Wisconsin at −55°F.

**3** **RELATE** Suppose that instead of the temperature dropping, the temperature rose from −7°F to 13°F. Ask, *How would you calculate the number of degrees the temperature rose?* [create an equation or use a number line to show temperature rise] *How would you write this equation?* [$-7 + n = 13$]

**4** **APPLY** Suggest that your student use the Internet or resource books to find the average high and low temperatures of a state or region. Have your student use the information to write one or more word problems about the temperatures. Then have your student write and solve an equation for each problem.

## COORDINATE GRAPHING

**1** **CONNECT AND EXPLORE** Provide your student with a sheet of graph paper. Have him or her draw a number line from −10 to +10. Under the number line have him or her draw a coordinate grid like the one on the next page. Discuss with your student how these two drawings are similar. Ask, *How are these alike?* [both have positive and negative numbers] *How do they differ?* [the coordinate grid has four sections with vertical and horizontal numbers; the coordinate grid has two lines instead of one]

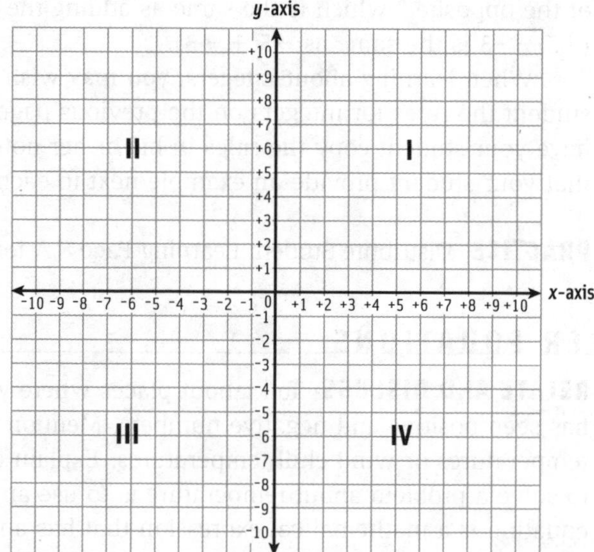


**2** **MODEL** Explain how the grid works. Use the terms *x*-axis and *y*-axis. Point to a number on the *x*-axis, such as +4, and a number on the *y*-axis, such as –6. Explain that together these two numbers make up an ordered pair. Call attention to the order of naming the coordinate pairs: the *x*-axis coordinate is named first, then the *y*-axis coordinate. Continue naming ordered pairs, such as (–8, +8), (+3, –2), and so on, while your student points to their locations on the grid. Introduce the term *quadrant.* Explain that a coordinate grid is divided into four sections called quadrants.

Distribute Student Learning Page 8.B for more practice.

# Branching Out

## TEACHING TIP

If you or your student need more help reviewing integers, try the Ask Dr. Math Web site at http://mathforum.org.

## CHECKING IN

Assess your student's ability by having him or her make and label from memory a number line from –10 to +10 and a coordinate grid from –10 to +10. Direct your student to add the labels: *x*-axis, *y*-axis, and quadrant numbers to the coordinate grid. Next, have your student solve this equation: $b = -18 + 3$. Then have your student label his or her grid with these ordered pairs: (+3, –1), (–4, +7), (+5, –5), and (–9, –3). Suggest that each ordered pair be given a letter.

**FOR FURTHER READING**

*Access to Math: Whole Numbers and Integers* (Globe Fearon, 1999).

*Great Graphs, Charts, and Tables That Build Real-Life Math Skills,* by Denise Kiernan (Scholastic, Inc., 2001).

*Scholastic Success with Charts, Tables, and Graphs,* by Michael Priestley (Scholastic, Inc., 2002).

# Use Integers and Number Lines

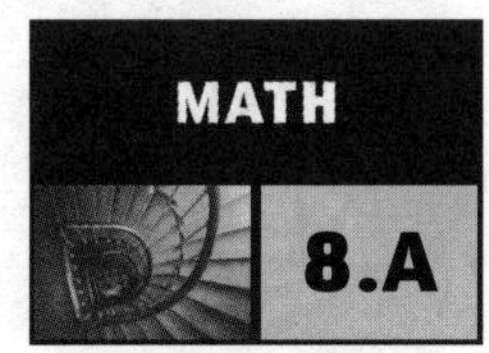


1. **In the space below, draw a number line from −10 to +10 and follow the directions.**

   **a.** Find +6 and label it *A*.

   **b.** Find −9 and label it *B*.

   **c.** Find 0 and label it *C*.

   **d.** Find −3 and label it *D*.

2. **Reorder the integers from least to greatest.**

   **a.** −4, +3, +10, −20, +8, +2 ____________________

   **b.** +27, +35, −2, +21, −10, −12 ____________________

   **c.** −9, −2, +2, +9, −6, +6 ____________________

3. **Reorder the integers from greatest to least.**

   **a.** −4, +3, +10, −20, +8, +2 ____________________

   **b.** +27, +35, −2, +21, −10, −12 ____________________

   **c.** −9, −2, +2, +9, −6, +6 ____________________

4. **Add or subtract.**

   **a.** −20 + +20 = ______

   **b.** +6 − −2 = ______

   **c.** +2 − +11 = ______

   **d.** +22 + +9 = ______

5. **Explain what sign the answer will have when you**

   **a.** add a positive integer and a negative integer. ____________________

   **b.** add a negative integer and a negative integer. ____________________

   **c.** subtract a negative integer from a positive integer. ____________________

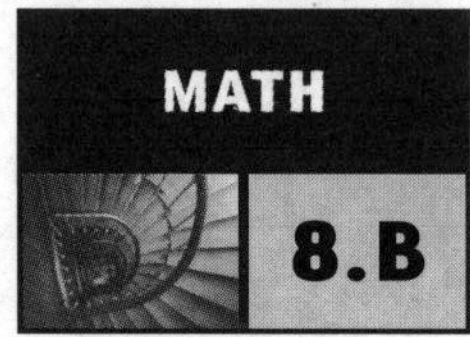


# Use Ordered Pairs and Coordinate Graphs

Draw and label a coordinate grid from −10 to +10. Label the *x*-axis, the *y*-axis, and the four quadrants.

**Use your coordinate grid to mark the following ordered pairs in the quadrants. Label the ordered pairs from *A* to *F* on the grid and then write their quadrant number on the lines.**

**A** (−8, +2) ____________

**B** (+3, +7) ____________

**C** (−5, +6) ____________

**D** (+9, −5) ____________

**E** (−1, −8) ____________

**F** (+1, −4) ____________

 

TEACHING THE LESSON

# Working with Graphs and Data

***A picture is worth a thousand words.***

| OBJECTIVE | BACKGROUND | MATERIALS |
|---|---|---|
| To help your student organize and display data | Graphs and charts are something your student will encounter throughout life. In this lesson, your student will learn that graphs can present information in a convenient way. Your student will also learn how to make graphs using data. | ■ Student Learning Pages 9.A–9.B<br>■ newspaper with graphs<br>■ 1 copy Grid, page 355<br>■ 2 crayons or pencils of different colors |

| VOCABULARY |
|---|
| **MEAN** a number that is the sum of a group of numbers divided by the total number of items in the group; the mathematical name for "average" |
| **DATA** information in the form of numbers |
| **MEDIAN** the middle number of a group of numbers arranged in order from least to greatest |
| **MODE** the number or numbers that are listed most often in a group of numbers |
| **RANGE** the difference between the greatest and least numbers in a group |

# Let's Begin

## MEAN, MEDIAN, MODE, AND RANGE

**1** **ASK** Ask, *What does the phrase "A picture is worth a thousand words" mean? What does it have to do with graphs?* Show your student a graph from a newspaper or magazine. Explain that graphs provide data or statistics at a glance. Introduce the idea of averages. Ask, *Where do we see averages everyday?* [weather page of newspaper, sports, business, and so on]

**2** **EXPLORE** Have the student look through a newspaper for graphs. Discuss the graphs with the student, pointing out the title of the graph, the information it displays, and the results. Ask, *Have you heard about baseball players having "averages"?* [have your student tell what he or she knows about averages] Explain that when people say, "His average is 300," it means that a player had hits 3 times out of 10 tries. (You may want to explain that the decimal point is moved over to the right to

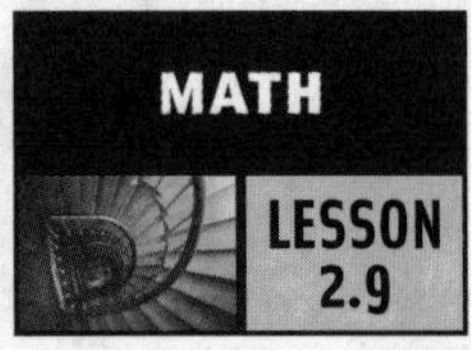

make the number bigger and therefore sound more interesting.) Tell your student that, in math, the average is called the **mean.**

3 **PRESENT** Have your student copy the following average temperature **data** for Chicago and Honolulu into his or her notebook.

**Average Temperature (°F)**

| | Jan. | Feb. | March | April | May | June | July |
|---|---|---|---|---|---|---|---|
| Chicago | 34 | 39 | 44 | 52 | 65 | 78 | 81 |
| Honolulu | 72 | 72 | 74 | 75 | 69 | 81 | 73 |

4 **EXPLAIN** Tell your student that when working with data and statistics there are four values that are important: mean, median, mode, and range. Explain that to find the mean temperature in Honolulu between January and July, add all the temperatures for Honolulu and divide the total by the amount of numbers, in this case seven. Review rounding rules with your student, then have your student find the mean. [73.7 rounded is 74]

5 **DESCRIBE** Explain that the **median** is the number that falls in the middle. If two numbers fall in the middle, then the median is the average of those two numbers. Have your student write the Honolulu temperatures horizontally from smallest to largest [69, 72, 72, 73, 74, 75, 81] and find the median. [73] Explain that the **mode** is the number repeated most often. Have your student find the mode. [72] Point out that if no number is repeated, there's no mode. Explain that the **range** of the data set is found by subtracting the smallest number from the largest. Have your student find the range. [81 − 69 = 12]

6 **PRACTICE** Have your student find the mean [56], median [52], mode [none], and range [47] from the graph for Chicago. What is misleading about the mean temperature for Chicago? [56 is the mean, but some months are much colder and some are much warmer]

7 **EXPLORE** Present another example of how the mean can be misleading. Ask, *The mean age of two people is 50. Can you guess their ages?* After your student has a chance to think of some possibilities, explain that they could be 49 and 51 or 1 and 99. Ask, *Why do you think it's important to know the range?* [because then you know how much difference there is between the numbers that make up the mean] Have your student complete the first part of Student Learning Page 9.A for more practice.

## BAR GRAPHS

1 **DESCRIBE** Explain that a bar graph is a type of graph that uses bars to show how different quantities compare. When there are

two sets of data, a double bar graph can be used. Ask, *How could you display the temperature data for Chicago and Honolulu so that someone looking at it could compare the temperatures in the two cities?* [use a double bar graph]

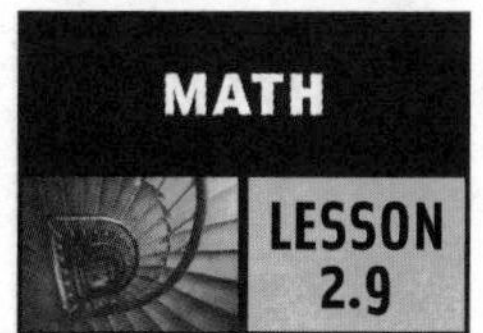


**2** **DRAW** Have your student make a double bar graph on a copy of the Grid from page 355 using the Chicago and Honolulu data. Give the following instructions:

1. Start at the bottom left. Create the horizontal axis with the seven months from January to July. Label the axis "Months."
2. Use colored pencils or crayons and assign one color to one city and another color to the other city.
3. Include a color key.
4. Label the vertical axis "Degrees Fahrenheit."
5. Make the vertical axis in 5-degree increments up to 90°.
6. Draw the bars into the graph to represent each month's temperature.
7. Give the graph a title.

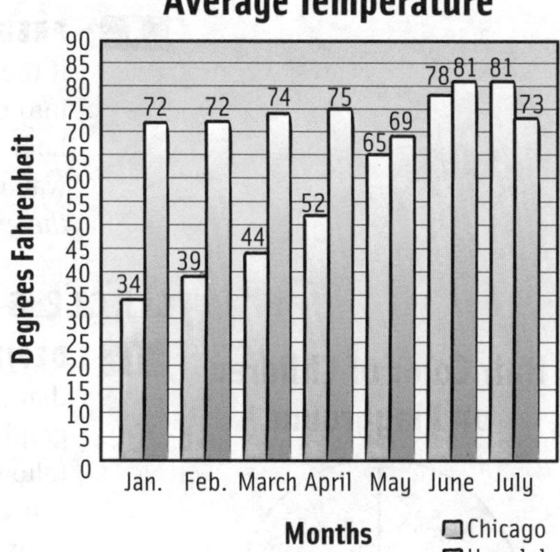


**3** **DISCUSS** Look at the graph together. Ask, *How would you compare the weather in the two cities? What can you say about the range of each city's temperatures?* [Chicago's weather has a wide range and gets a lot colder. Honolulu's temperature stays relatively steady] *Would you rather read a paragraph about this information or look at a graph? Why?* [look at a graph, because the visual data can be understood quickly]

**4** **EXPLORE** Point out that the way graphs are visually designed can change the way similar data is understood. Ask, *How could you remake this graph to convince someone that the weather in Honolulu and Chicago is not that different?* [make the range of temperatures on the vertical axis greater] *Who might be interested in the new graph?* [a Chicago store owner or tour guide] Discuss.

## LINE GRAPHS

**1** **EXPLAIN AND ASK** Explain that a line graph is a graph that uses lines to show changes or trends. Point out that to show something changing over time, it's best to use a line graph. Ask, *Let's say you wanted to record your height each year since you were five. How could you display the information? Would a bar graph be a good choice?* [no, bar graphs show how different amounts compare to each other] Show your student the line graph.

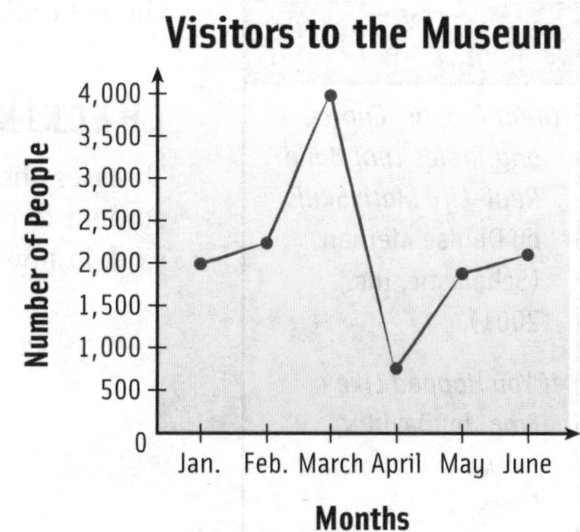

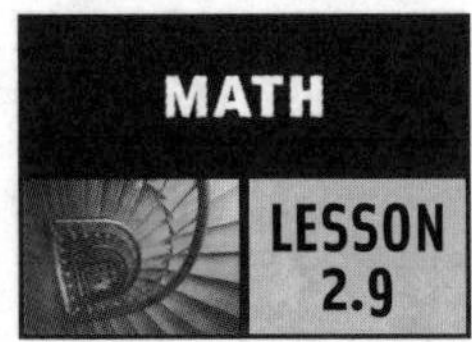

MATH

LESSON 2.9

**2** **EXPLORE** Start by reading the title and the axis labels. Notice how the number of people on the left is listed in quantities of 500. Tell your student that when numbering the quantities of something in a line graph, each quantity should be consistent in amount. In this case, the amount is 500. Ask, *Why do you think the numbers are arranged by five hundreds?* [too many visitors to label by ones, tens, or one hundreds]

**3** **PREDICT** Have your student imagine how the graph would look if the numbers of visitors on the vertical axis were broken down into one hundreds. [it would emphasize the differences more] Look back at the graphs from the newspapers and review the way each graph was made. Ask, *Could the data seem different if the graphs were made differently?* Discuss.

## CIRCLE GRAPHS

**1** **DEFINE** Tell your student that a circle graph is a type of graph that is used to show parts of a whole. Point out that circle graphs are also known as pie graphs. Show your student the following example of a circle graph. Explain that the graph shows the hair color of 30 children on a playground. Ask, *What color hair do most of the children have?* [brown]

**Hair Color of Children on Playground**

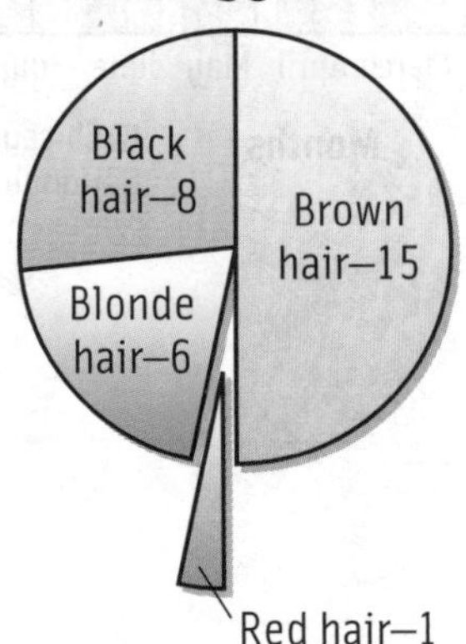


**2** **EXPLORE** Review the relationship between fractions and their equivalent percents with your student. Explain that information in circle graphs can also be expressed as a fraction or a percent. Ask, *If there are 30 children on the playground, what percent have brown hair?* [50%] *What percent have blonde hair?* [20%] *How are these written as fractions?* [$50\% = \frac{1}{2}$; $20\% = \frac{1}{5}$]

# Branching Out

## TEACHING TIP

Remind your student that once you get information from a graph, it's the reader's responsibility to study how the graph was put together so he or she isn't misled by how the information is displayed.

## CHECKING IN

To assess how well your student has understood graphs, ask your student to draw a general sketch of each graph from memory and explain how each is used best with data.

**FOR FURTHER READING**

*Great Graphs, Charts, and Tables That Build Real-Life Math Skills,* by Denise Kiernan (Scholastic, Inc., 2001).

*If You Hopped Like a Frog,* by David M. Schwartz (Scholastic Press, 1999).

# Interpret Data and Use Graphs

MATH

9.A

**PART A**

**Find the mean, median, mode, and range for each data set.**

12, 16, 10, 10

1. mean ______ 2. median ______ 3. mode ______ 4. range ______

4 lb, 5 lb, 6 lb, 3 lb, 17 lb

5. mean ______ 6. median ______ 7. mode ______ 8. range ______

**PART B**

**Create a circle graph that represents the different plants in Mrs. Henry's garden. She has 16 total acres. Eight acres of her garden are planted with flowers, 4 acres with tomatoes, 2 acres with corn, 1 acre with cucumbers, and 1 acre with herbs. Draw the graph in the circle pattern below. Then answer the questions.**

9. What percentage of the garden is corn? ______

10. What percentage is tomatoes? ______

11. What fraction can you write for the area where herbs are planted? ______

12. What fraction can you write for the combined areas of herbs and cucumbers? ______

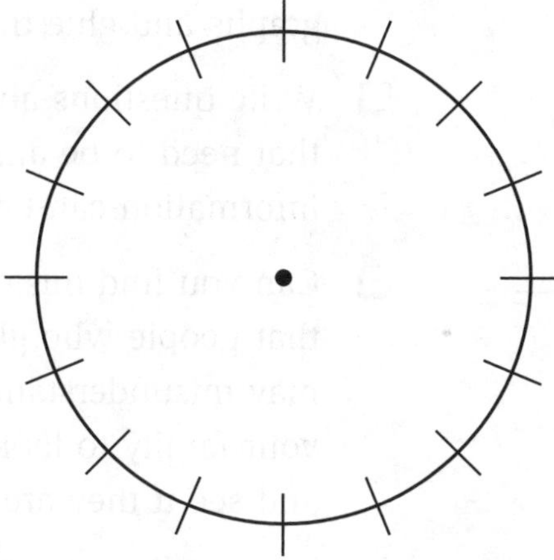

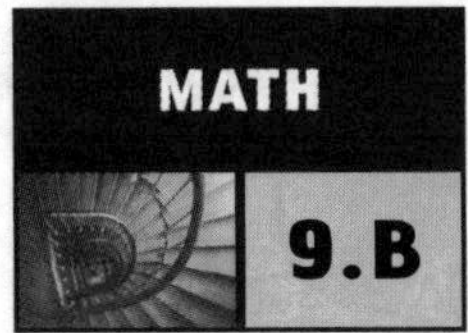


# What's Next? You Decide!

Now it's your turn to choose what to do next in the lesson. Read the activities and decide which one you want to do—you may want to try them all!

## Take Me Out to the Ball Game

### STEPS

Your town is thinking about buying a baseball team to play professionally, and you are on a committee that is in favor of having a team. The city wants to know if there's enough interest in baseball.

- ❑ Your committee took a survey of 100 people, asking them their favorite summer activities. The results were: 19—play golf; 30—go to a nature preserve; 36—go to sports events; 15—have a picnic.
- ❑ Create a bar graph showing the data in a way that would persuade the city to buy the team.
- ❑ Then review the results of the survey carefully. What could be misleading about the way the data was collected?
- ❑ Write your thoughts in your notebook and talk about them with an adult.

## Make a Sunrise Graph

### MATERIALS

- ❑ newspaper (optional)
- ❑ 1 copy Grid, page 355

### STEPS

- ❑ Use the local newspaper or the Internet to record the exact time of the sunrise for 10 days.
- ❑ Make a line graph to show the data. Label each axis and write a title for the graph.
- ❑ Study the graph. Do you see any patterns? Predict what the next 10 days will look like.
- ❑ Check your predictions against the data in the newspaper.
- ❑ Keep the graph for six months so you can look back at it when the seasons change. What do you notice about the change in daylight hours?

## Know the Media

### STEPS

- ❑ Look through magazines and newspapers for graphs. Cut out three graphs and glue them onto paper.
- ❑ Write questions about the graphs that need to be answered before the information can be fully understood.
- ❑ Can you find misleading information that people who glance at the graphs may misunderstand? Ask people in your family to look at the graphs and see if they are misled.

TEACHING THE LESSON

# Discovering Geometry

***Leonardo da Vinci, one of the greatest artists and scientists who ever lived, understood that math and art are inseparable.***

| OBJECTIVE | BACKGROUND | MATERIALS |
|---|---|---|
| To show your student geometric figures and concepts and how to relate them to his or her life | Geometry offers your student a chance to really "see" math. The shapes and concepts are often familiar to students, and they get excited relating objects in their world to math lessons. In this lesson, your student will learn how to identify and draw basic geometric forms. | ■ Student Learning Pages 10.A–10.D<br>■ 1 ruler<br>■ 2 identical forks |

# Let's Begin

## GEOMETRIC IDEAS

**1** **EXPLAIN** Explain that geometry is the study of lines and shapes. Find point *A* on the drawing below. In math, a line is a straight set of points that goes on forever in both directions. Ask, *Do you see a line in the picture?* [no] Explain that the areas from *A* to *C* or *A* to *B* are called line segments because they end on both sides at a point. Have your student find other line segments in the drawing. Ask, *Do you see any angles?* [yes] Explain that whenever lines intersect they form an angle. Ask, *How many angles do you see?* [six] When two lines meet at a common point, the point is called a vertex. Have your student count the vertices and compare that to the number of angles. [six angles, four vertices] Ask, *Why is there a difference?* [vertices can sometimes make two different angles] Explain that a ray in math is like a ray of sunshine. A ray is a line that has only one endpoint. Ask, *Do you see any rays in the drawing?* [no]

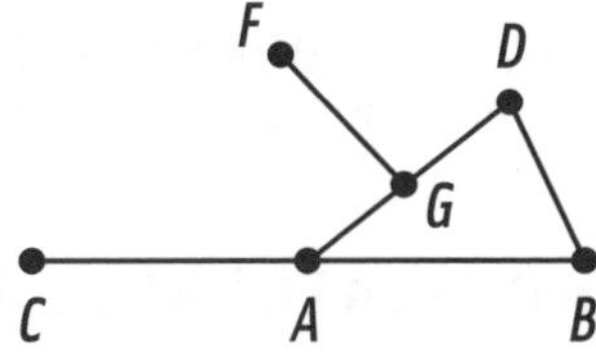


**2** **RELATE** Mention that a plane is a flat surface that goes on forever in every direction. Point out that a table or a sheet of paper is part of a plane. Have your student find three other examples of parts of planes in your home and list them in his or her notebook.

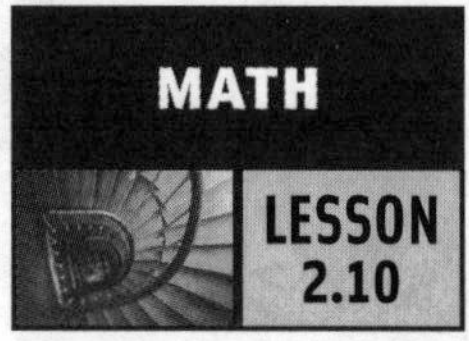


## ANGLES

**1** **ASK AND EXPLAIN** Ask, *Have you heard the phrase "He or she did a 180-degree turnaround"?* That means someone has completely changed. Have your student look at the line below. A line is a 180° angle. Ask, *Can you see why changing to the opposite way of thinking or acting is called "doing a 180"?*

**2** **EXPLAIN** Explain that perpendicular lines make two right angles. Ask, *If I cut this 180° angle exactly in half, what's the measurement of each of these angles?* [90°] Have your student take a square piece of paper and show that its corner can be fitted into the drawing of the right angle below. Explain that on a drawing a right angle will always be labeled with a small square, as in the picture.

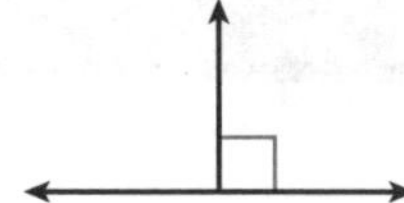

**3** **MODEL** Have your student bend his or her arm to form a right angle. A right angle is a 90° angle. Have the student bend his or her arm to make a smaller angle. Ask, *How many degrees is your angle now?* [any answer less than 90° and more than 0°] Explain that an angle that is smaller than 90 degrees is called an acute angle. Explain that any angle that is greater than 90° is called an obtuse angle.

**4** **DRAW AND EXPLAIN** In his or her notebook, have your student draw a line about five inches long with a ruler. Then ask him or her to draw another line that is exactly four inches away from that line. Point out that this can be done by marking two or three points that are the exact same distance from the line and then connecting them. Lines that stay the same distance apart forever are called parallel lines. Ask, *Will these lines ever cross?* [no] Then have your student draw two lines that do not cross on the paper but would if they went on forever. Ask, *Are these lines parallel?* [no] Explain that these are intersecting lines. Lines that cross to make a right angle are perpendicular. Have your student write several examples of parallel and perpendicular lines (e.g., lines of longitude and latitude) in his or her notebook.

## TRIANGLES, QUADRILATERALS, AND POLYGONS

**1** **PRACTICE AND DISTRIBUTE** Distribute Student Learning Page 10.A. Tell your student that in all triangles, whatever their type, the sum of the angles is 180°. Explain that a triangle with two perpendicular lines and one right angle is called a right triangle. Have your student draw a right triangle. Ask, *Drawing on what you know about right angles and the sum of the angles in a triangle, what might the measure of the other angles be?* [answer must be two angles, each smaller than 90°, that add up to 90°, such as 45° and 45° or 60° and 30°]

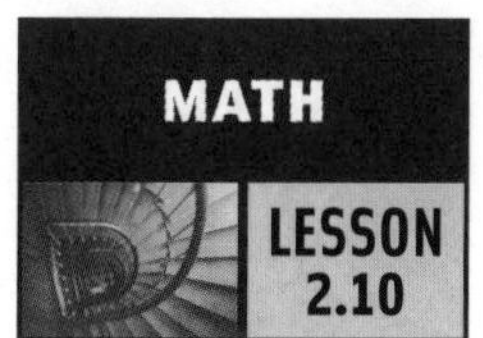


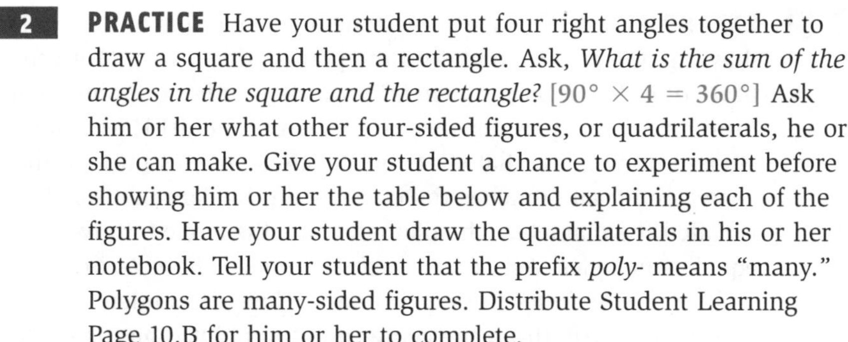

**2** **PRACTICE** Have your student put four right angles together to draw a square and then a rectangle. Ask, *What is the sum of the angles in the square and the rectangle?* [$90° \times 4 = 360°$] Ask him or her what other four-sided figures, or quadrilaterals, he or she can make. Give your student a chance to experiment before showing him or her the table below and explaining each of the figures. Have your student draw the quadrilaterals in his or her notebook. Tell your student that the prefix *poly-* means "many." Polygons are many-sided figures. Distribute Student Learning Page 10.B for him or her to complete.

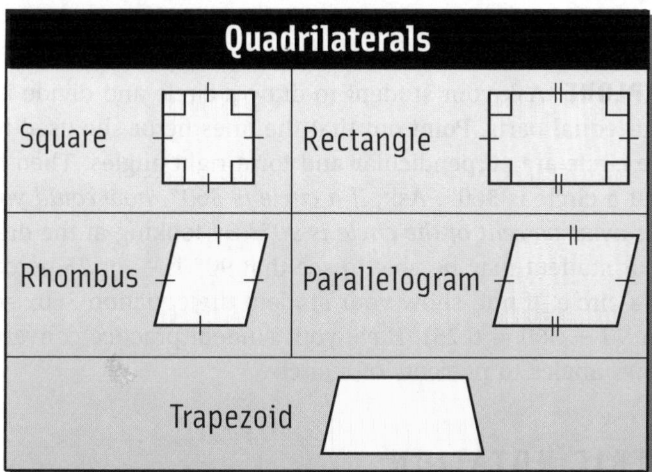


## CONGRUENCY AND FORMS

**1** **EXPLAIN** Take out two identical forks. Have your student look closely at them. Explain that the forks are congruent because they are exactly the same shape and size.

**2** **MODEL** Put one fork in a stationary position on top of a table. Give your student the second fork and ask him or her to slide it so it's in the same position. Explain that when you slide a figure or an object to change its position it's called a translation. Slide one fork into another position. For instance, face the tines in another direction. Ask, *Are the forks still congruent? Are they still the same size and shape?* [yes] Flip a fork over so that the tines are curved away from the table. Ask, *Are the forks still congruent?* [yes] Explain that when an object is flipped it is called a reflection.

## CIRCLES

**1** **DRAW** Have your student draw a point in the center of a piece of paper and label it *A*. Have him or her measure 10 points that are exactly three inches away from the center point and label three of the points *B, C,* and *D*. Ask, *What shape do you see appearing around the center point?* If your student does not see a circle, have him or her add a few more points using the same

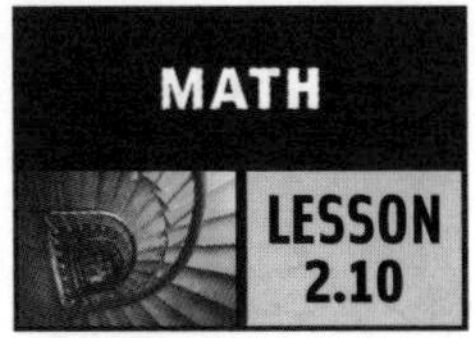

MATH

LESSON 2.10

method. Direct your student to draw the circle by connecting the dots.

**2** **EXPAND AND ASK** Have your student consider his or her circle drawing, the center point, and the points added. Ask, *Can you think of a definition for a circle?* [infinite number of points that form an arc of equal distance from a center point] Have your student draw a line that starts on the circle, passes through the center point, and touches the circle again. Explain that this line is called the diameter. The diameter cuts the circle into two equal semicircles. Ask, *Can you draw another diameter? How many can you draw?* [infinite amount] Have the student draw in line segment $\overline{AB}$ (from the center point to point $B$ on the circle). Explain that this line is called the radius. Have the student identify other examples of a radius.

**3** **EXPLORE** Ask your student to draw a circle and divide it into four equal parts. Point out that the lines he or she used to divide the circle are perpendicular and form right angles. Then mention that a circle is 360°. Ask, *If a circle is 360°, how could you find out what percent of the circle is 90°?* By looking at the drawing your student may be able to see that 90° is $\frac{1}{4}$, or 25 percent, of a circle. If not, show your student the equation $360x = 90$ (or $90 \div 360 = 0.25$). Have your student practice converting other angles to percents of a circle.

## GEOMETRIC NOTATION

**1** **EXPLAIN** Tell your student that there are standard symbols used in geometry to represent different figures. They are a kind of shorthand specific to geometry. Explain that one important symbol is for lines, and that you can indicate a line by putting a bar over the name of the line like so: $\overline{AB}$. Also, you can indicate an angle using an angle symbol like so: $\angle ABC$.

**2** **DISTRIBUTE** Distribute Student Learning Page 10.C to give your student practice using geometric notation.

# Branching Out

## TEACHING TIPS

Take a trip to an art museum or look through an art book. What does your student notice about the use of circles, polygons, and lines?

## CHECKING IN

To assess student understanding, ask your student to identify one example of each type of geometric figure mentioned in this lesson around the house.

**FOR FURTHER READING**

*Math Games and Activities*, by Claudia Zaslavsky (Chicago Review Press, 1998).

*Problem Solving and Logic*, by Marcia Miller and Martin Lee (Scholastic, 1998).

# Try Triangles

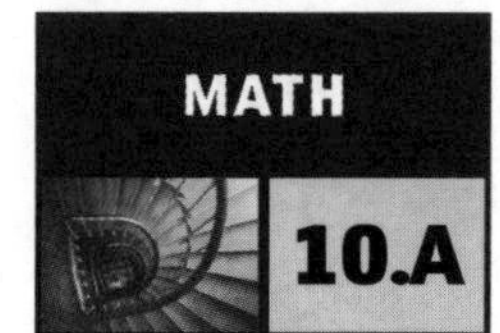


Use a ruler to draw an example of each type of triangle. Look at a reference book or on the Internet if you want to see an example.

| Type of Triangle | Description | Drawing |
| --- | --- | --- |
| Equilateral | All sides equal length | |
| Isosceles | 2 sides same length | |
| Scalene | No sides same length | |
| Acute | 3 acute angles | |
| Right | 1 right angle | |
| Obtuse | 1 obtuse angle | |

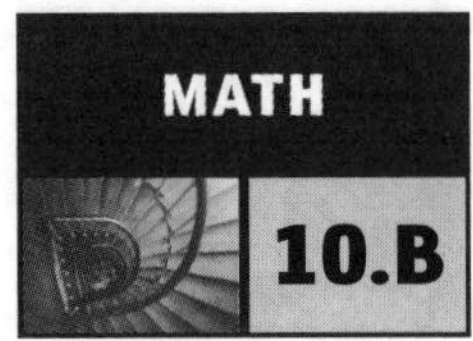


# Draw Polygons

Polygons are many-sided shapes. When a polygon has sides that are all the same length and has equal angles, it is called a regular polygon. Complete the table with regular polygons. Then draw your own polygon matching only the number of sides.

| | Number of Sides | Regular | Your Own |
|---|---|---|---|
| Pentagon | 5 | | |
| Hexagon | 6 | | |
| Heptagon | 7 | | |
| Octagon | 8 | | |
| Nonagon | 9 | | |
| Decagon | 10 | | |

 

# Use Geometric Notation

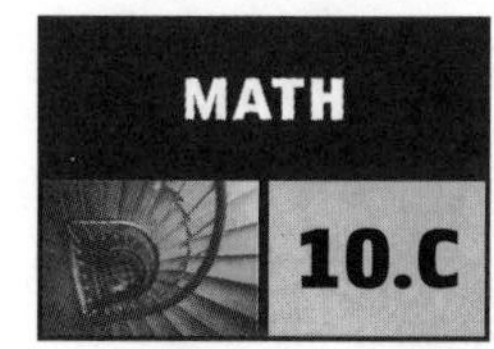


Read each question. Then answer the questions using geometric notation when possible.

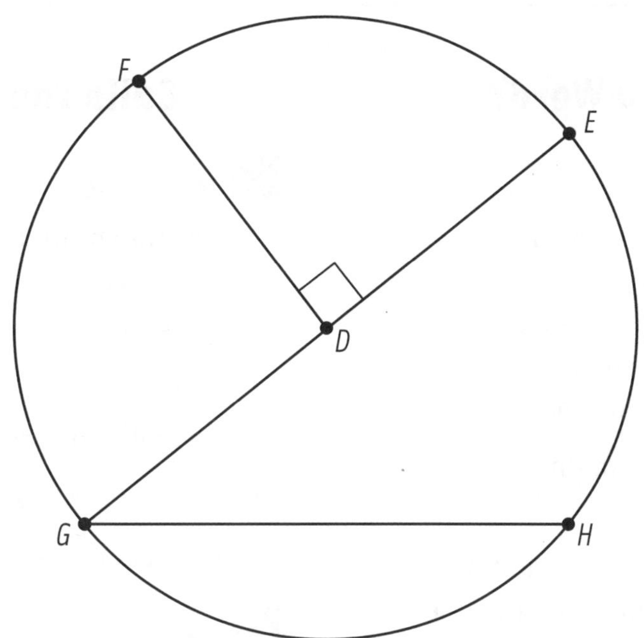


1. Which line represents the diameter? ____________

2. If the diameter is $5\frac{1}{2}$ inches, how long is the radius? ____________

3. What line represents the radius? ____________

4. Name three points that form a right angle. ____________

5. What kind of angle is *EGH*? ____________

6. What is line segment *GH* called? ____________

7. A friend tells you that chord *GH* is 6 inches long. You know that can't be right.

   Why? ______________________________________________

8. What is the length of line segment *DF*? ____________

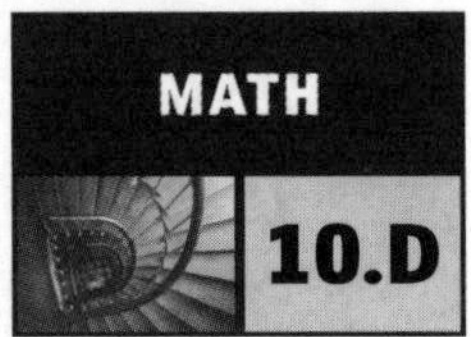


# What's Next? You Decide!

Now it's your turn to decide what to do next in the lesson. Read the activities and decide which one you want to do—you may want to try them both!

## What's in a Word?

### STEPS

- ❑ Think of words you already know or look in a dictionary to find words that begin with the same prefixes (*penta-*, *hexa-*, *hepta-*, and so on) as the names of the polygons listed below.
- ❑ Write a brief description of each word you list.
- ❑ Share your list with an adult and see if he or she can think of any other words.
  - Pentagon: 5 sides
  - Hexagon: 6 sides
  - Heptagon: 7 sides
  - Octagon: 8 sides
  - Nonagon: 9 sides
  - Decagon: 10 sides
- ❑ Now draw each of these shapes.

## Build the Pentagon

### MATERIALS

- ❑ several empty food boxes, sugar cubes, clay, or other building materials
- ❑ glue
- ❑ several paper clips
- ❑ 3–10 note cards
- ❑ markers or paint

### STEPS

Have you heard about a building called the Pentagon?

- ❑ Research on the Internet or at the library to learn about the building.
- ❑ Use what you learn to make a replica of the building from pudding boxes, sugar cubes, clay, or any other material you can think of.
- ❑ Glue the boxes together or fasten them with paper clips.
- ❑ Color or paint the building.
- ❑ Put the information you have learned about the Pentagon on note cards.
- ❑ Give a presentation for friends and family about your findings.
- ❑ Why do you think the building is called the Pentagon?

 

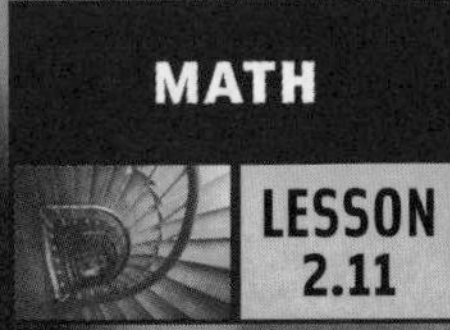


# Understanding Measurement

*Not a thing exists that can't be measured in some way.*

| OBJECTIVE | BACKGROUND | MATERIALS |
|---|---|---|
| To show your student how to use customary and metric units of measure and apply formulas to find perimeters, areas, volumes, and circumferences | Measuring skills are used for a variety of purposes in ordinary life. Whether your student enjoys cooking or craft projects, is an athlete or even just an observer of sports events, knowing how to choose the correct measuring tool for a given job and apply formulas appropriately will serve him or her well. This lesson reviews customary and metric units of measure and demonstrates how to apply formulas to find perimeters, areas, volumes, and circumferences. | ■ Student Learning Pages 11.A–11.B<br>■ 1 customary and 1 metric ruler<br>■ 1 tape measure<br>■ 1 yardstick/meterstick<br>■ measuring cups and spoons<br>■ 1 pan balance or scale<br>■ mass units |

## VOCABULARY

**LENGTH** the measure of the longest part of an object
**CAPACITY** how much a container or shape can hold
**WEIGHT** how heavy something is
**MASS** the amount of matter an object has
**SIZE** the bigness or physical bulk of an object; factor in choosing an appropriate measurement unit
**SHAPES** the spatial forms of objects
**AREA** the size of a flat surface
**WIDTH** the measure of an object taken at a right angle to the length in the horizontal plane
**PERIMETER** the distance around a figure other than a circle
**CIRCUMFERENCE** the distance around a circle
**VOLUME** the total space that is inside of a certain shape
**DIAMETER** a line drawn from one side of a circle to the other that goes through its center
**RADIUS** one half the length of a circle's diameter

# Let's Begin

## CUSTOMARY AND METRIC MEASUREMENT

**1** **EXPLAIN** Tell your student that there are various measurement systems. Remind him or her that the system used in the United States is called the customary system of measurement and that

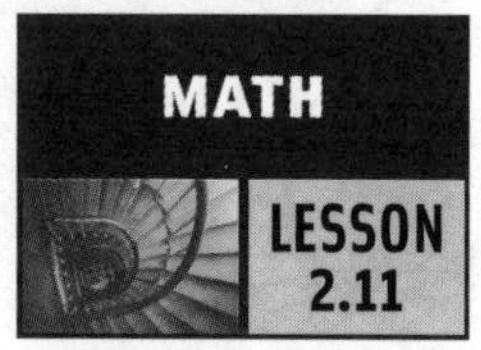


the metric system of measurement is used in most other countries worldwide. Review customary units and metric units with your student.

**Customary Units**

**Length**
1 foot (ft) = 12 inches (in.)
1 yard (yd) = 36 inches
1 yard = 3 feet
1 mile (mi) = 5,280 feet
1 mile = 1,760 yards

**Weight**
1 pound (lb) = 16 ounces (oz)
1 ton (T) = 2,000 pounds (lb)

**Capacity**
1 cup (c) = 8 fluid ounces (fl oz)
1 pint (pt) = 2 cups
1 quart (qt) = 2 pints
1 gallon (gal) = 4 quarts

**Metric Units**

**Length**
1 meter (m) = 1,000 millimeters (mm)
1 meter = 100 centimeters (cm)
1 meter = 10 decimeters
1 kilometer (km) = 1,000 meters (m)

**Mass**
1 gram (g) = 1,000 milligrams (mg)
1 kilogram (kg) = 1,000 grams
1 metric ton (t) = 1,000 kilograms

**Capacity**
1 liter (L) = 1,000 milliliters (mL)
1 kiloliter (kL) = 1,000 liters

**2** **DISCUSS** Talk with your student about the various tools used to measure different attributes of an object, for example, **length, capacity,** and **weight** or **mass.** Point out that measuring involves matching the unit of measure to what is being measured. For example, to measure length, first choose an appropriate unit, such as an inch or centimeter. Then line up several units next to the item you are measuring. This is why we created the ruler, measuring tape, yardstick, and meterstick.

**3** **EXPLAIN AND ASK** Explain the relationships between a mile and a kilometer, foot and yard, inch and centimeter. Have your student compare metric and customary units on rulers, a yardstick, and a meterstick. Ask, *What units are best to measure longer lengths and distances?* [foot, yard, mile, kilometer, meter] *What tools and units can you use to measure shorter lengths?* [metric and customary rulers; inch, millimeter, centimeter, decimeter]

**4** **MODEL AND EXPLORE** Model how to use a ruler and a meterstick or yardstick to measure the length of various objects of different sizes. Explain the reason you chose a certain size measurement tool. Show your student how to align the end of the measuring tool with the end of each item being measured to ensure the measures are accurate. Then have your student choose a measuring tool to measure various long and short items around your home and yard. Encourage him or her to estimate the length of each item before measuring it, and have him or her compare the estimate to the actual measure.

**5** **DISCUSS** Talk with your student about why he or she chose the measuring tool and the unit of measure for each item. Check to be sure that he or she chose the unit and tool that was most appropriate for each measuring task. Tell him or her that the choice of the tool and the **size** of the unit depends on the length or the distance to be measured. Help him or her understand that greater lengths and distances are easier to measure with larger units and that smaller units increase the precision of measurements. Using a ruler, meterstick, and yardstick review which measurement units are larger and smaller. Ask, *Should the distance around this room be measured in feet or inches?* [feet]

**6** **ASK** Ask, *What tools can you use to measure weight or mass?* [scale or balance] *What units of measure are used to measure large weights?* [ton] *What about lesser weights?* [pound, ounce] *Mass?* [kilogram, gram, metric ton]

**7** **DISCUSS** Talk with your student about how the size of an object is not the only thing that determines its weight or mass. Help him or her distinguish between the size of an object and its weight or mass.

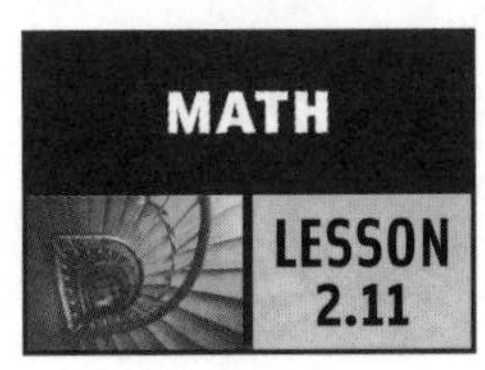


**8** **EXPLORE** Next have your student use a pan balance and mass units. Explain that the pan balance shows the mass of objects by balancing them against marked units of weight. Have him or her hold a gram and try to find objects that weigh the same amount. Repeat the process with different masses and objects. If you have a scale available, have your student explore weighing different objects to get a feel for weights from 1 to 16 ounces. Point out that 16 ounces is equal to 1 pound. Then ask him or her to find several items in your home that weight about 8 ounces. Repeat with another weight. Before you know it, your student will be able to lift an object and give a ballpark estimate of its weight!

**9** **ASK** Ask, *What tools can you use to measure capacity?* [measuring cups and spoons] *What units of measure are used to measure capacities?* [gallon, quart, pint, cup, liter, kiloliter, milliliter]

**10** **DISCUSS** Talk with your student about how to measure capacities when cooking. Point out that most recipes call for different ingredients (both wet and dry) that require measurements to specific capacities. Share some of your favorite recipes with your student. Encourage him or her to identify as many different capacities as possible.

**11** **ASK** Ask, *Can you think of times other than when cooking when it is common to measure capacities?* [when painting, washing floors and cars, watering plants, taking medicine]

**12** **EXPLORE** Help your student choose a recipe to try. Before he or she begins assembling measured ingredients, ask him or her to examine the measuring tools. Then observe your student to make sure that he or she chooses the appropriate tool for measuring each ingredient. Discuss why one tool is more appropriate than another.

## MEASUREMENT WITH SHAPES

**1** **REVEAL** Point out that sometimes it is important to be able to find and calculate the measurements of **shapes.** Give the example of painting a room and needing to figure out the total **area** of the walls so you can decide how much paint to buy. Explain that the formula to calculate the area of a square wall is area = **length** × **width,** or $A = l \times w$. Show your student the drawing of shapes and their area measures. Review the definitions for area, **perimeter, circumference, volume, diameter,** and **radius** listed in the beginning of the lesson with your student. Ask your student to draw a shape and shade in or mark the part that illustrates each definition in his or her notebook.

**Square**
Area = 4 sq ft

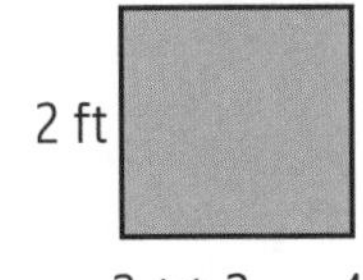


$2 \times 2 = 4$

**Rectangle**
Area = 6 sq ft

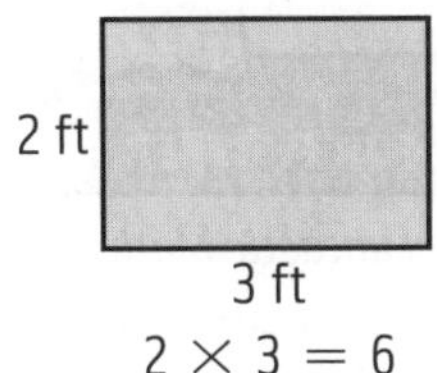


$2 \times 3 = 6$

**Triangle**
Area = 2 sq ft

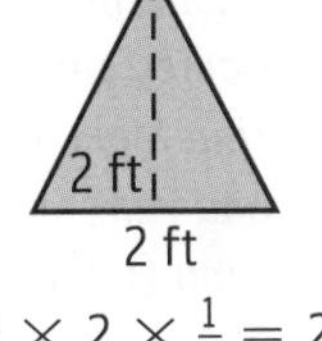


$2 \times 2 \times \frac{1}{2} = 2$

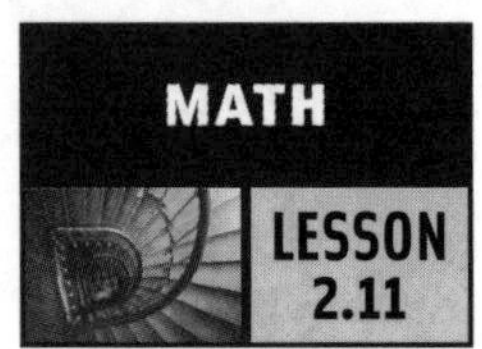


**2** **ASK** Ask, *Which measurements would be easier to get using a formula instead of a ruler?* [volume, area, circumference, perimeter] Have your student look up the formulas for each measurement and write them in his or her notebook. Discuss the different formulas and why they work. Have your student complete Student Learning Page 11.A for practice.

## TEMPERATURE AND TIME

**1** **EXPLAIN** Point out that the unit used to measure temperature is degrees. Explain that there are two different systems to measure temperature: Fahrenheit (°F) and Celsius (°C). Have your student copy the drawing below into his or her notebook. Have your student use the information in the drawing to estimate the temperatures for several different weather conditions. Ask, *If there is ice on the road, what temperature could it be in Celsius and Fahrenheit?* [0°C/32°F or below] *How about a summer day when you are comfortable in shorts?* [about 75°F/24°C] Discuss.

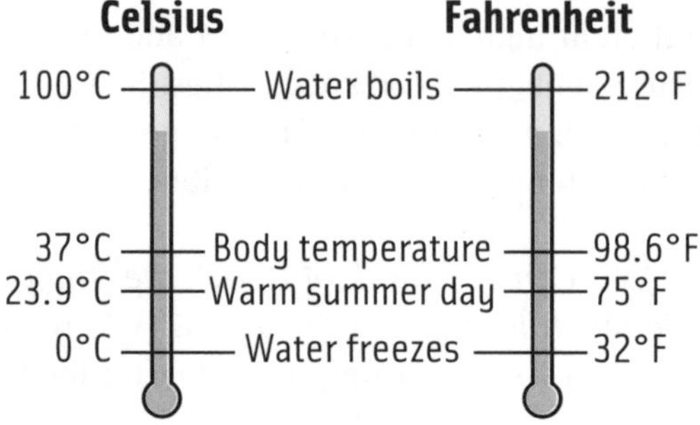


**2** **EXPLORE** Review units of time with your student (seconds, minutes, hours, days, months, years). Talk with him or her about situations in which timing to the second is critical, such as in gymnastics or other sports events. Have him or her use the library or search the Internet to find out how time has been measured throughout history.

**FOR FURTHER READING**

*Funtastic Math! Measurement and Geometry*, by Sarah Jane Brian and Marcia Miller (Scholastic Trade, 1999).

*Measurement Mania: Games and Activities That Make Math Easy and Fun*, by Lynette Long (John Wiley, 2001).

# Branching Out

## TEACHING TIP

If your student struggles with converting measurements, review easy examples such as converting inches to feet, walking your student through each step and increasing the difficulty of the examples.

## CHECKING IN

You can assess your student's understanding of working with measurement by having him or her complete a craft or cooking project that involves multiple measures as you observe.

# Use Measurements and Formulas

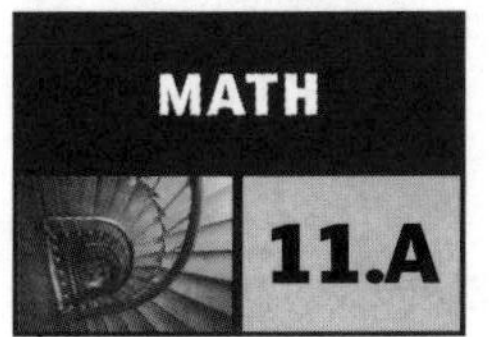


Complete the following measurements and formulas.

1. Measure the width and length of a doorway in your home. Be sure to choose an appropriate unit of measurement.

   $w$ = ______ $l$ = ______

2. Use the formula for area ($A = l \times w$) to find the area of the doorway.

   $A$ = ______

3. Measure the width, length, and height (or depth) of your kitchen sink using an appropriate unit of measurement.

   $w$ = ______ $l$ = ______ $h$ = ______

4. Use the formula for volume ($V = l \times w \times h$) to calculate the volume of the sink.

   $V$ = ______

5. Measure the length and width of a room in your home using an appropriate unit of measurement.

   Room ______ $l$ = ______ $w$ = ______

6. Use the formula for perimeter ($P = 2l + 2w$) to find the perimeter of the room.

   $P$ = ______

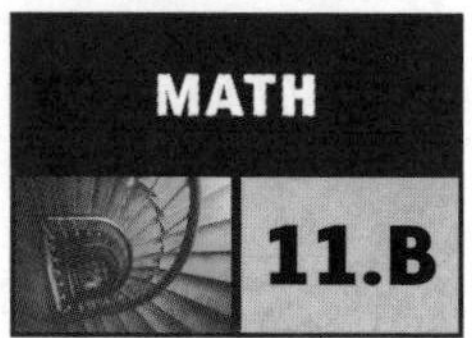


# What's Next? You Decide!

Now it's your turn to choose what to do next in the lesson. Read the activities and decide which one you want to do—you may want to try them both!

## Explore Circumference

### MATERIALS

- ❑ 3–4 pieces string
- ❑ 1 ruler
- ❑ 3–4 food or beverage cans of different sizes

### STEPS

How can you find the distance around a circle, or its circumference?

- ❑ Look at the top of the can. Notice that it's a circle.
- ❑ Use a ruler to measure across the top of the can to find the diameter of the circle. The diameter is the width of the fattest part of a circle.
- ❑ Then wrap the string around the can.
- ❑ Cut the string to match the distance around the can and use the ruler to find the string's length.
- ❑ Record the diameter and circumference in your notebook.
- ❑ Try it again with two or three cans of other sizes.
- ❑ Record all the diameters and circumferences in a table.
- ❑ What do you notice about the diameters and circumferences? Do you see a pattern? Talk about what you notice with an adult.

## Sense the Temperature

### MATERIALS

- ❑ 1 outdoor thermometer that shows °C and °F

### STEPS

- ❑ Place an outdoor thermometer outside where it's secure and easy to read.
- ❑ Check the temperature three times each day (morning, afternoon, and night) for three to five days in both Celsius and Fahrenheit.
- ❑ Keep a log of the temperatures, dates, and times in your notebook.
- ❑ For each temperature, write one or two sentences in the log about how the weather feels (cold, hot) and what kind of clothes you need to be comfortable.
- ❑ Next time you hear the weather forecast, you'll know how to dress for the temperature!

# In Your Community

**To reinforce the skills and concepts taught in this section, try one or more of these activities!**

## Lottery

Some states have a lottery, and some states have more than one type of lottery. Have your student find out what the odds or probability of winning the lottery are in your state. Then have him or her research and find the population of your town or region. Ask him or her to determine how many people in your community would win the lottery based on the findings.

## Graphs in the Newspaper

With your student contact your local newspaper. Find out where the researchers at the newspaper get the data for the graphs and charts they use. Be sure to ask if the researchers at the paper survey people or get information from another source. Then have your student choose a graph from the paper and have him or her do his or her own research about the same topic and see if he or she gets the same results.

## A Survey of Your Town

Ask your student if he or she has ever taken part in a survey. You might want to share your experiences of taking part in surveys. Have your student come up with a topic that he or she would like to know how the people in your community feel about. Encourage your student to look through the local paper for topics affecting your community, or perhaps look in the paper for a new product on the market. Then have your student come up with some questions about the topic that he or she will ask people in your neighborhood, on your block, or in your town. Have him or her collect the responses and make a chart or graph showing the results.

## Shopping Spree

Have your student select a foreign place that he or she would like to go to. Then have him or her look up the currency exchange rate in your local paper. Send your student on a shopping spree and have him or her pick out some items that he or she would like to buy for your home and then calculate how much they cost in the currency of the country he or she chose. Then have your student watch the exchange rate each day for two weeks. Have the student figure out which day he or she would get the most products for his or her money.

## University Math Visit

Arrange to have your student meet with the chairperson of the math department of a community college or another local college or university. Ask the chairperson to talk with your student about the different types of math classes offered, what types of careers use the math that's taught in the classes, and maybe give you and your student a tour of the math department. If time allows, have your student bring in some of the current math work he or she has been doing and have the chairperson show how that math is connected to a particular class.

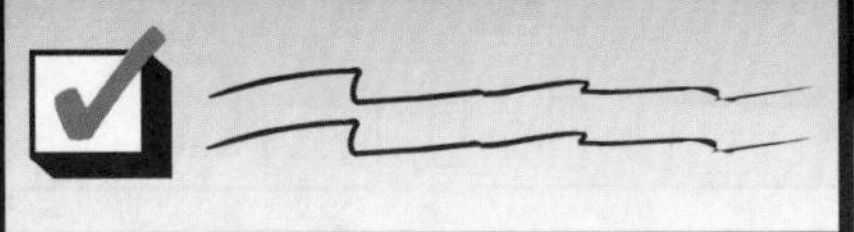

# We Have Learned

**Use this checklist to summarize what you and your student have accomplished in the Math section.**

- ❑ **Place Value and Whole Numbers**
- ❑ place value through thousandths, place value through billions
- ❑ greater than, less than, equal to
- ❑ place-value charts
- ❑ problem solving, estimating, rounding

- ❑ **Decimals**
- ❑ adding, subtracting, multiplying, dividing, estimating
- ❑ using money
- ❑ multiplying by whole numbers, multiplying by 10, 100, 1,000
- ❑ dividing by whole numbers, dividing by 10, 100, 1,000

- ❑ **Fractions**
- ❑ adding, subtracting, multiplying, dividing
- ❑ primes, composites, equivalents, fractions in simplest form
- ❑ common factors, common multiples
- ❑ finding fraction patterns, ordering fractions

- ❑ **Ratio, Percent, and Probability**
- ❑ ratios, rates, percents, probability
- ❑ relating percents, relating decimals, relating fractions
- ❑ predicting outcomes

- ❑ **Integers**
- ❑ comparing integers, ordering integers
- ❑ adding integers, subtracting integers
- ❑ evaluating expressions with integers

- ❑ **Graphs**
- ❑ graphing points in a coordinate plane
- ❑ ordered pairs, grouping
- ❑ axis ($x$ and $y$), quadrants

- ❑ **Data and Statistics**
- ❑ organizing data, displaying data
- ❑ making graphs, using graphs
- ❑ mean, median, range, mode

- ❑ **Geometry**
- ❑ measuring angles, classifying angles
- ❑ classification
- ❑ identifying figures, drawing figures
- ❑ congruent figures, transformations

- ❑ **Measurement**
- ❑ customary units, metric units
- ❑ length, capacity, mass, weight, area, perimeter, volume, diameter
- ❑ temperature, time
- ❑ measuring tools

**We have also learned:**

______________________________

______________________________

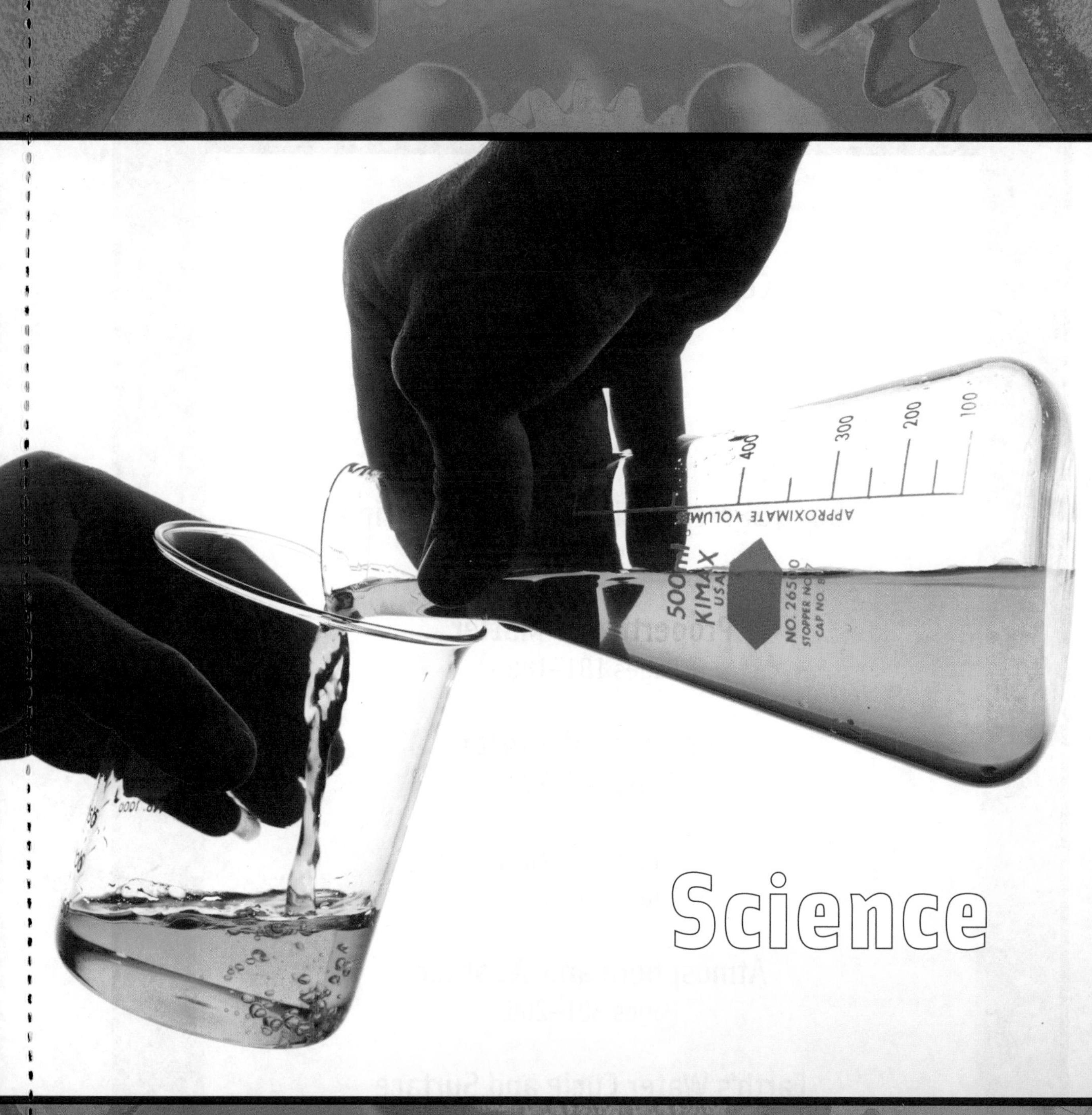
APPROXIMATE VOLUME
500ml
KIMAX
USA
400
300
200
100
NO. 26500
STOPPER NO.
CAP NO.

# Science

# Science

## Key Topics

# Understanding Cells

***All living things are made of cells. Each cell, like a microscopic factory, contains different structures that carry out a variety of tasks.***

| OBJECTIVE | BACKGROUND | MATERIALS |
|---|---|---|
| To help your student understand the nature of cells | Understanding cells will provide an important conceptual framework that your student will build on throughout his or her studies of life science. This lesson introduces your student to the development of the microscope, cell theory, and the structure and function of different types of cells. | ■ Student Learning Pages 1.A–1.C<br>■ 1 colored pencil<br>■ 1 medium-sized resealable plastic bag<br>■ 1 tablespoon petroleum jelly<br>■ various pieces of string, buttons, beans, beads, macaroni |

**VOCABULARY**

**EUKARYOTIC CELLS** cells, such as animal or plant cells, that have a nucleus

**ORGANELLES** structures within the cytoplasm of eukaryotic cells

**DNA** deoxyribonucleic acid; a substance in the nucleus of a cell that contains chemical instructions for everything that the cell does

**PROKARYOTIC CELLS** cells, such as bacteria cells or blue-green algae cells, that do not have a nucleus

# Let's Begin

## OBSERVING CELLS

**1** **ASK** Begin the lesson by using a KWL Chart. To create a KWL Chart, make a three-column chart on a sheet of paper or poster. In the first column, write "What I Know About Cells." In the second column, write "What I Want to Know About Cells." In the third column, write "What I Learned About Cells." Ask your student what he or she already knows about cells. Write everything your student knows about cells in the first column. Then ask your student what he or she would like to know about cells. Write that information in the second column. At the conclusion of the lesson, you can fill in the third column of the chart with what your student learns in the lesson.

**2** **EXPLAIN** Many people contributed to the discovery that living things are composed of cells. Scientists' observations and conclusions about cells became known as "the cell theory."

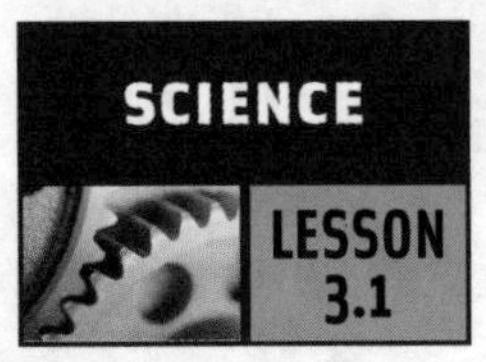


The major ideas of the cell theory are that all organisms are made of at least one cell, cells are the basic units of structure and function in all organisms, and all cells come from cells that already exist. To help your student understand the development of the ideas behind the cell theory, have him or her research the contributions of Robert Hooke, Theodor Schwann, Matthias Schlieden, and Rudolph Virchow. Ask your student to make a time line showing the development of the cell theory.

**DID YOU KNOW?**

A virus is not made up of cells. A virus is made of a piece of hereditary material covered by protein. Viruses reproduce inside living cells of other organisms.

**3** **RESEARCH** Cells were not discovered until the first microscopes were created and then improved. Have your student research the work Zacharias Janssen and Anton van Leeuwenhook did in the development of the microscope. Your student also might be interested in researching the different kinds of microscopes used today. Have your student read about how compound light microscopes, stereo microscopes, and electron microscopes work and how they are used. Ask your student to write a short paragraph about historic and present-day microscopes.

**4** **EXPLAIN** Tell your student that some organisms are one-celled, or unicellular. Bacteria and other microorganisms are unicellular. Plants and animals are made of many cells. Organisms with many cells are called multicellular organisms. Ask, *Are there more kinds of unicellular or multicellular organisms on Earth?* Have your student use reference sources such as books or Web sites to find the answer. [there are more kinds of multicellular organisms]

## EUKARYOTIC CELLS

**1** **EXPLAIN AND RESEARCH** Tell your student that plant and animal cells have much in common. Both of these types of cells are called **eukaryotic cells** because they have a nucleus. The nucleus is a cell's command center. It tells all of the other structures, or **organelles,** in the cell what to do. The nucleus also contains **DNA.** DNA, or deoxyribonucleic acid, contains chemical instructions for everything that the cell does. Have your student use reference sources and appropriate Web sites to learn more about DNA. Your student might be interested in finding out about the structure of DNA, how cells reproduce, and how DNA is analyzed and used as evidence in criminal proceedings.

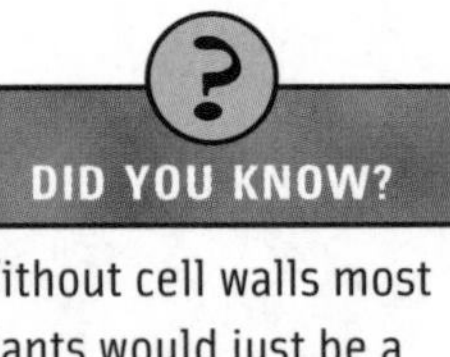

**DID YOU KNOW?**

Without cell walls most plants would just be a pile of green slime on the ground.

**2** **DIRECT AND DISTRIBUTE** Instruct your student to use reference sources to research plant and animal cells. Ask your student to discover organelles found in both plant and animal cells. Also ask your student to identify differences in plant and animal cells. Help your student see that plant cells, unlike animal cells, have a cell wall outside of the cell membrane. In addition, plant cells contain organelles called chloroplasts. Then distribute Student Learning Page 1.A and have your student write definitions for each cell structure in his or her own words. To help your student remember the functions of the different structures, encourage him or her to think of an analogy for each structure. For example, the nucleus is the "brain" of the cell.

 

**3** **DISTRIBUTE** Distribute Student Learning Page 1.B. Have your student complete the model. Provide any help he or she needs.

## PROKARYOTIC CELLS

**1** **EXPLAIN** Tell your student that **prokaryotic cells,** such as bacteria cells or blue-green algae, do not have a nucleus. Usually prokaryotic cells have a single molecule of DNA that floats inside the cell. Have your student use reference sources to draw and label a diagram of a bacteria cell on another piece of paper. Ask your student to compare the diagrams of the plant and animal cell on Student Learning Page 1.A to the bacteria cell. Ask your student to explain how the bacteria cell is similar to and different from each of the other cells. [similar: DNA directs protein production and heredity; different: bacteria have no nucleus] Ask your student to name structures that all three types of cells have in common. [cytoplasm, cell membrane]

**2** **RESEARCH** Ask your student what comes to mind when he or she thinks of bacteria. Many people think of bacteria as harmful organisms that make people sick. Ask your student to research ways that bacteria actually help people, such as aiding in the digestion of foods.

## CELLULAR RESPIRATION

**1** **EXPLAIN** Tell your student that all cells need energy to live. Ask your student how he or she gets the energy needed to read a book, walk, or play a game. Your student will probably know that humans get energy from food. Explain that after digesting a meal, food substances travel in the blood and into the cells. In the cells, the food is respired. This means that the food is broken down so that the energy is released and used. Have your student come up with a definition for *respire* in his or her own words.

**2** **EXPAND AND RESEARCH** Explain that in anaerobic respiration food substances are broken down without using oxygen. In this kind of respiration only a small amount of energy is released. In aerobic respiration, food substances are combined with oxygen. Carbon dioxide and water are produced as wastes. This type of respiration releases much more energy. We get most of the energy our bodies need from aerobic respiration. Instruct your student to read more about cellular respiration and the difference between aerobic and anaerobic respiration. Have your student write a paragraph describing aerobic and anaerobic cellular respiration on a separate sheet of paper. Discuss.

## CELLULAR RESPIRATION IN PLANTS

**1** **DISCOVER AND DIAGRAM** Ask your student how plants get food. Your student will probably remember that plants make their own food. Chloroplasts in plant cells take energy from the

**?**
**DID YOU KNOW?**

Cells are many different sizes. Mycoplasmas, a kind of bacteria, are known as the smallest free-living cell. A mycoplasma cell is about 0.1 micrometers long. The largest single cell that scientists know of is the ostrich egg. An ostrich egg can be about 10 inches long.

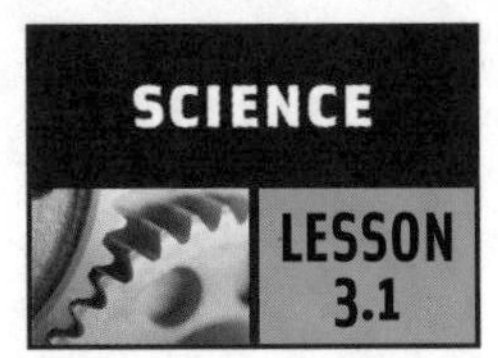


sun and convert it into sugars in a process called photosynthesis. During the day, a plant builds up food. Since the plant makes more food during the day than it breaks down, its leaves take in carbon dioxide. At night, photosynthesis stops and the plant breaks down more food and takes in oxygen. Encourage your student to find out more about plant respiration by researching the topic in reference sources. Then have your student write a paragraph describing the process. Review the paragraph together.

2 **CONCLUDE** To conclude the lesson, ask your student to review what he or she learned about cells. Write this information in the third column of the KWL Chart. Review the first two columns of the KWL Chart, which were completed at the beginning of the lesson. Ask your student if any of his or her original ideas have changed. Also ask your student if he or she learned everything he or she wanted to learn about cells. If there are any other ideas that your student is curious about, encourage him or her to do additional research. Your student could even write a research paper about one aspect of cells.

# Branching Out

## TEACHING TIP

If you have access to a microscope, consider purchasing slides of cells so that your student can actually see what cells look like. Another option is to make a slide of a green onion. Take a very small, thin slice from the base of the onion. Then put a drop of water on the slide and place the onion on top of the water. Smooth out any wrinkles with a toothpick. Place a coverslip on top of the onion. You can use a stain (such as iodine) to make the onion cells easier to see.

## CHECKING IN

Use the diagrams of plant and animal cells on Student Learning Page 1.A to assess how well your student understands cell structures and functions. Ask your student questions about the different cell structures. Ask him or her to explain how the different processes work. Your student's responses should help you assess how well he or she learned the lesson concepts.

**FOR FURTHER READING**

*The Cell Works (Microexplorers),* by Patrick A. Baeuerle and Norbert Lander (Barron's Juveniles, 1998).

*Cells (Science Concepts),* by Alvin Silverstein, Virginia B. Silverstein, and Laura Silverstein Nunn (Twenty-First Century Books, 2002).

*Cells and Systems (Life Processes),* by Holly Wallace and Anita Ganeri (Heinemann Library, 2001).

*The Way Life Works: A Science Lover's Illustrated Guide to How Life Grows, Develops, Reproduces, and Gets Along,* by Marlon Hoagland and Bert Dodson (Times Books, 1998).

# Define Cell Structures

Using what you remember from your research, write a definition in your own words for each cell part listed below. Then, if there are any definitions that you don't know, look them up in a dictionary, in an encyclopedia, or on the Internet to complete the list.

1. Cytoplasm ______________________
2. Plasma membrane ______________________
3. Cell wall ______________________
4. Nucleus ______________________
5. Golgi apparatus ______________________
6. Mitochondria ______________________
7. Chloroplast ______________________
8. Vacuole ______________________

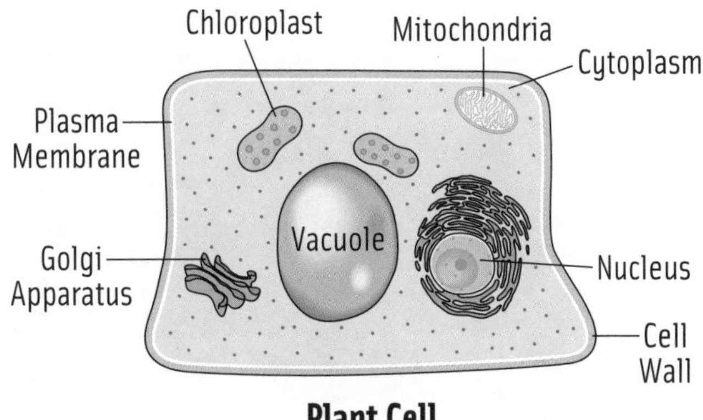


**Plant Cell**

# Create an Animal Cell Model

Read the materials and the steps. Then create an animal cell.

## MATERIALS

- ❑ 1 medium-sized resealable plastic bag
- ❑ 1 tablespoon petroleum jelly
- ❑ various pieces string, buttons, beads, beans, macaroni

## STEPS

1. Refer to Student Learning Page 1.A. Draw a cell at the bottom of this page and include the parts listed in this lesson. You will use this drawing to make your cell model.
2. Line the inside of the plastic bag with petroleum jelly to create the cell membrane and cytoplasm.
3. Look at the list of cell parts above and add beans, string, buttons, or other objects to represent each part. Use objects that look as realistic as possible to help you remember what they are.
4. Then give a short presentation to an adult, showing your cell model and explaining each of its parts.

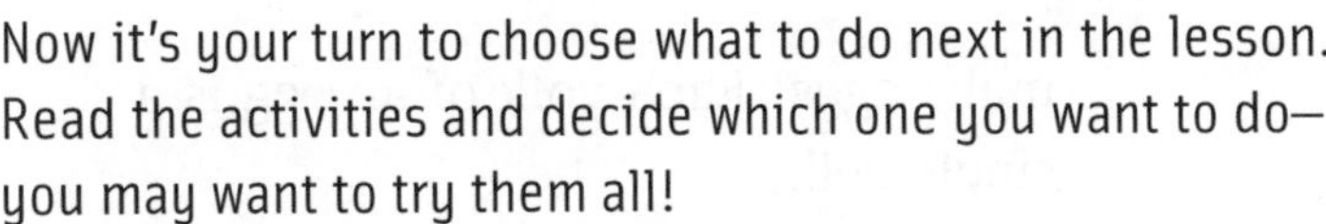

# What's Next? You Decide!

Now it's your turn to choose what to do next in the lesson. Read the activities and decide which one you want to do—you may want to try them all!

## Cell Life Cycle Comic Strip

### MATERIALS

- ❑ 2–3 sheets paper
- ❑ crayons, markers, or colored pencils

### STEPS

- ❑ Use the Internet or reference books to find out about mitosis, the process in which a cell reproduces into two identical cells.
- ❑ Then create a comic strip that shows how the process happens.
- ❑ Put each step of the process in its own panel.

## Observe Pond Organisms

### MATERIALS

- ❑ 1 cup water from a pond or another natural water source
- ❑ 1 microscope
- ❑ 2–3 microscope slides

### STEPS

- ❑ Ask a parent or an adult to help you collect water from a pond or another natural water source in your area.
- ❑ Put a drop of the water on a microscope slide and look at it under a microscope. You will probably want to make several slides.
- ❑ Draw pictures of what you observe.
- ❑ Use reference books to try to identify the kinds of organisms you see.

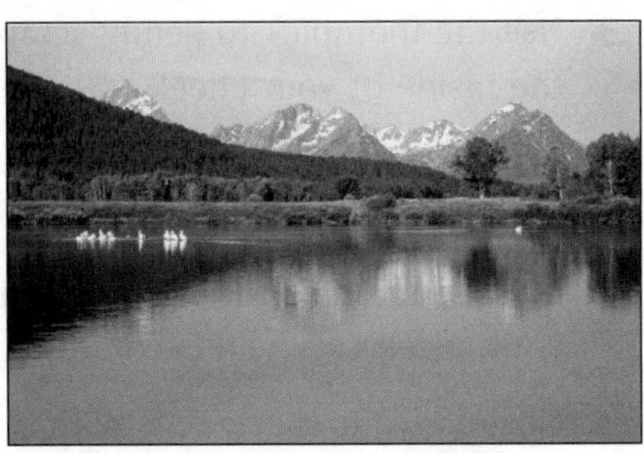

## Find Answers to Your Questions About Cells

### STEPS

- ❑ Write down all of the questions you have about cells.
- ❑ Then choose one or two questions to research. Look for answers in reference books, in magazine articles, and on appropriate Web sites.
- ❑ You might also consider writing a letter to a science professor in your area for help with your questions.

(CONTINUED) 

SCIENCE 1.C

## Observe a Cheek Cell

### MATERIALS

- ❑ 1 toothpick
- ❑ 1 microscope
- ❑ 1 drop iodine
- ❑ 1 microscope slide

### STEPS

- ❑ Place a drop of iodine on a slide.
- ❑ Use the toothpick to gently scrape the inside of your cheek.
- ❑ Place the tip of the toothpick into the iodine on the slide.
- ❑ Mix the toothpick and iodine so that your cheek cells will become stained.
- ❑ Observe your cheek cells with a microscope. Draw what you observe.
- ❑ Share your drawing with an adult.

## Cook with Cells

### MATERIALS

- ❑ 1–3 chicken eggs
- ❑ 1 frying pan
- ❑ 1 teaspoon cooking oil or butter
- ❑ 1 pinch salt and pepper
- ❑ 1 spatula

### STEPS

Did you know that you can cook a cell? People cook cells every day when they make eggs! Each yolk of an egg is a single cell.

- ❑ Work with an adult to do some cell-cooking experiments. What is your favorite way to eat egg cells? Scrambled, sunny-side up, or over easy? Season your cells with salt, pepper, or your favorite spice or sauce.
- ❑ After you have made a meal of cells, write a few sentences in your notebook about how you feel about eating eggs now that you know they are cells.
- ❑ Share your writing with an adult.

## Make a Microscope Manual

### STEPS

Microscopes are important science tools that must be used a certain way. Microscopes also must be properly cared for so that they can be used for a long time.

- ❑ Use reference books and appropriate Web sites to find out how to use and properly care for microscopes.
- ❑ Then create a book that shows others how to use and care for microscopes. Include illustrations to help your readers follow your instructions.

TEACHING THE LESSON

# Understanding Structures of Life

***Plants and animals are composed of cells. Cells make up tissues. Tissues make up organs. Organs make up organ systems.***

| OBJECTIVE | BACKGROUND | MATERIALS |
|---|---|---|
| To help your student understand the structures that make up plants and animals | Understanding the structure of plants and animals will build upon your student's knowledge of cells and prepare your student for later study of human body systems. In this lesson, your student will be introduced to tissues, organs, and organ systems in both plants and animals. | ■ Student Learning Pages 2.A–2.C |

**VOCABULARY**

**TISSUES** collections of similar cells that group together to perform a specific job

**XYLEM** a tissue in plants that carries water up from the roots and into the leaves

**PHLOEM** a tissue in plants that carries dissolved food substances down to the buds, shoots, and roots of a plant

**ORGAN** a structure that contains at least two types of tissues working together for a common purpose

**ORGAN SYSTEMS** systems in a plant or an animal that are made up of two or more organs that work together to do a job

# Let's Begin

## CELLS

**1** **REVIEW** Review with your student what he or she knows about plant and animal cells. Explain that cells come in many different sizes and shapes and perform many different jobs within an organism.

**2** **RESEARCH** Ask your student to research information about the following types of animal cells: nerve cells, red blood cells, muscle cells, fat cells, and skin cells. Instruct your student to draw the shape of each of these types of cells on a sheet of paper. Ask, *Why do you think the cells in our bodies come in different sizes and shapes?* Discuss.

**DID YOU KNOW?**

There are more than 200 types of cells in the human body. Some cells are worn out and replaced quickly. Others, such as brain cells, aren't replaced. That is one good reason to protect the brain by sticking with healthful habits and avoiding harmful chemical substances.

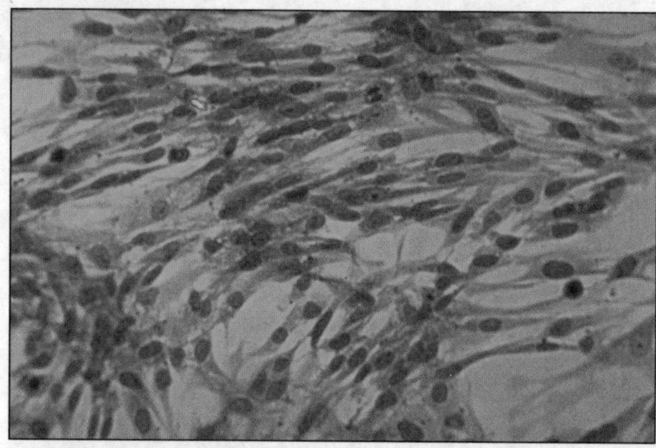

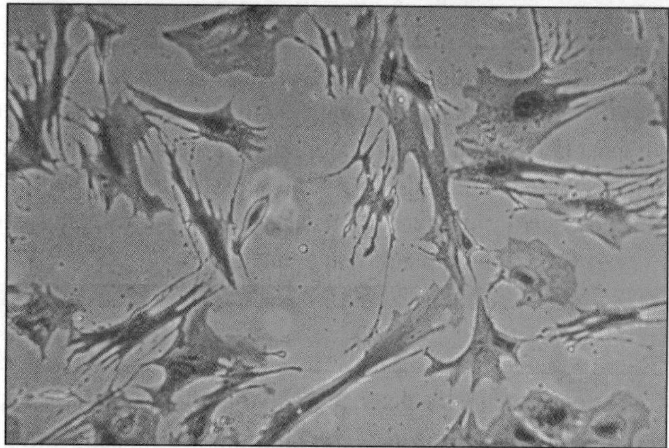

*Microscopic photos of new (top) and old (bottom) skin cells*

## TISSUES IN ANIMALS

**1** **EXPLAIN** Tell your student that cells group together in plants and animals to form **tissues.** Tissues are collections of similar cells that perform a specific job. Ask, *What are some examples of tissues in the human body?* [muscle tissue, nerve tissue, blood, ligaments, fat]

**2** **RESEARCH** Explain that human tissues are classified into four major groups: epithelial tissue, connective tissue, muscle tissue, and nerve tissue. Have your student research these different kinds of tissues and use what he or she learns to complete the chart on Student Learning Page 2.A.

**3** **DISCUSS** Discuss with your student what he or she knows about cancer. Your student probably knows that cancer is a disease, but he or she may not know exactly what happens when a person gets cancer. Have your student choose one form of cancer to learn more about. Your student can consult reference books, Web sites, or interview a doctor in your community to find out more about the disease. Ask your student to create an informative brochure about the disease, including how the disease works, is treated, and how to lessen the chances of developing cancer by eating healthful foods and exercising.

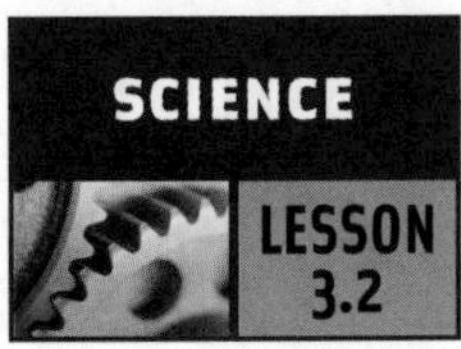


## TISSUES IN PLANTS

**1** **EXPLAIN** Tell your student that plants have tissues as well. **Xylem** and **phloem** are examples of tissues found in plants. Explain that water travels from the roots and up into the leaves of a plant through the xylem tissue. Dissolved food substances travel down the phloem tissue to the buds, shoots, and roots of a plant. Instruct your student to research these plant tissues.

**2** **ILLUSTRATE** Now have your student draw a diagram in his or her notebook showing the inside of a stem with labels indicating the xylem and phloem.

**DID YOU KNOW?**

Each day about 220 gallons of water are evaporated from a large tree's leaves. When this water is evaporated, more water is drawn up to take its place.

## ORGANS IN ANIMALS

**1** **EXPLAIN** Tell your student that after tissues, organs are the next level of organization in an animal or plant. An **organ** is a structure that contains at least two types of tissues working together for a common purpose. For example, the skin is an organ made up of epithelial tissue, connective tissue, nerve tissue, and muscle tissue. Ask, *Can you name other examples of organs found in animals?* [liver, kidneys, heart, brain, and so on]

**2** **RESEARCH** Have your student choose one organ in the human body to research. Ask your student to find out what kinds of tissues are found in the organ and then describe its structure and job. Have him or her draw a diagram of and list important facts about the organ.

## ORGANS IN PLANTS

**1** **REVEAL AND DIRECT** Explain that plants also have organs. A plant's organs include the roots, stem, and leaves. Instruct your student to use reference sources to label the diagram of a plant on Student Learning Page 2.B. He or she should add labels naming the different plant organs and telling what job each part does for the plant. Review his or her work and discuss.

**2** **RESEARCH** Tell your student that different kinds of plants have different types of roots, stems, and leaves. Accompany your student on a hike around your neighborhood, a local park, or a nature preserve. Your student can draw pictures of the different plants that he or she sees or collect leaves that have fallen on the ground. Then use reference sources to try and classify the plants that you saw together.

## ORGAN SYSTEMS IN ANIMALS

**1** **EXPLAIN** Tell your student that **organ systems** are made up of two or more organs that work together to do a job. For example, the role of the digestive system in animals is to break down food and absorb nutrients. The major organs in the human digestive

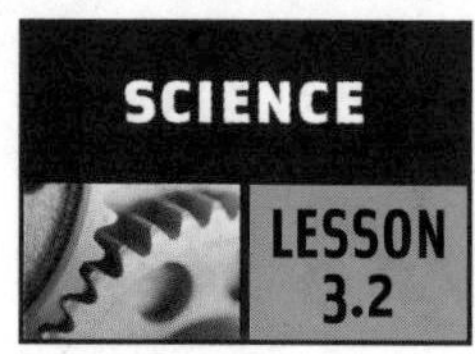


system include the mouth, esophagus, stomach, small intestine, and large intestine. Ask your student to look up other organ systems in the body and the organs that make up each organ system. Have him or her create a list of animal organ systems in a notebook.

**2** **RESEARCH** Ask your student to choose one organ system in the human body to research. Have him or her draw a diagram showing all of the organs within that organ system. Review the diagram with your student and discuss. Point out how all of the organs work together.

**3** **RELATE** Point out that the heart wouldn't function without the arteries and veins and that the lungs wouldn't function without the diaphragm or trachea. Explain that most organs are useless unless they're working as part of a system with other organs. A large intestine, for example, needs the help of the small intestine to function properly. Explain that organ systems are also dependent on each other. Ask, *Can you think of other examples of organs or organ systems that are dependent on each other?*

## ORGAN SYSTEMS IN PLANTS

**1** **EXPLAIN** Point out that plants also have organ systems. One organ system found in plants is the root system. Ask your student to research different kinds of root systems found in plants and their characteristics. Have your student make a list of plants that have each kind of root system.

**2** **EXPLORE** Spend some time together exploring a local park and try to find at least one plant for each different root system. You won't need to uproot the plants; simply look at the characteristics and shape of the leaves to identify the plants on the list.

**FOR FURTHER READING**

*Cancer (Lucent Overview Series)*, by Lisa Yount (Lucent Books, 1999).

*Guide to the Human Body: A Photographic Journey Through the Human Body*, by Richard Walker (DK Publishing, 2001).

*The World of Plant Life: An Inside Look*, by Gerald Legg, Steve Weston, and Jim Channell (Gareth Stevens, 2002).

# Branching Out

## TEACHING TIP

If possible, incorporate videos into your lesson. Videos and even medical programs on television about the human body can make learning about cells, tissues, and organs more interesting.

## CHECKING IN

To assess how well your student learned the concepts in this lesson, ask your student to create a picture book about tissues, organs, and systems based on what he or she learned. Your student can include illustrations of tissues, organs, and systems and definitions of each in his or her own words.

# Learn About Tissues in the Human Body

Complete the chart using your research about the four main kinds of tissues in the human body.

| Kind of Tissue | What It Does | Examples |
|---|---|---|
| Epithelial tissue | 1. | 2. |
| Connective tissue | 3. | 4. |
| Muscle tissue | 5. | 6. |
| Nerve tissue | 7. | 8. |

# Identify Plant Organs

Complete the diagram using reference sources. Write the name of each plant organ in the boxes and what job it does for the plant.

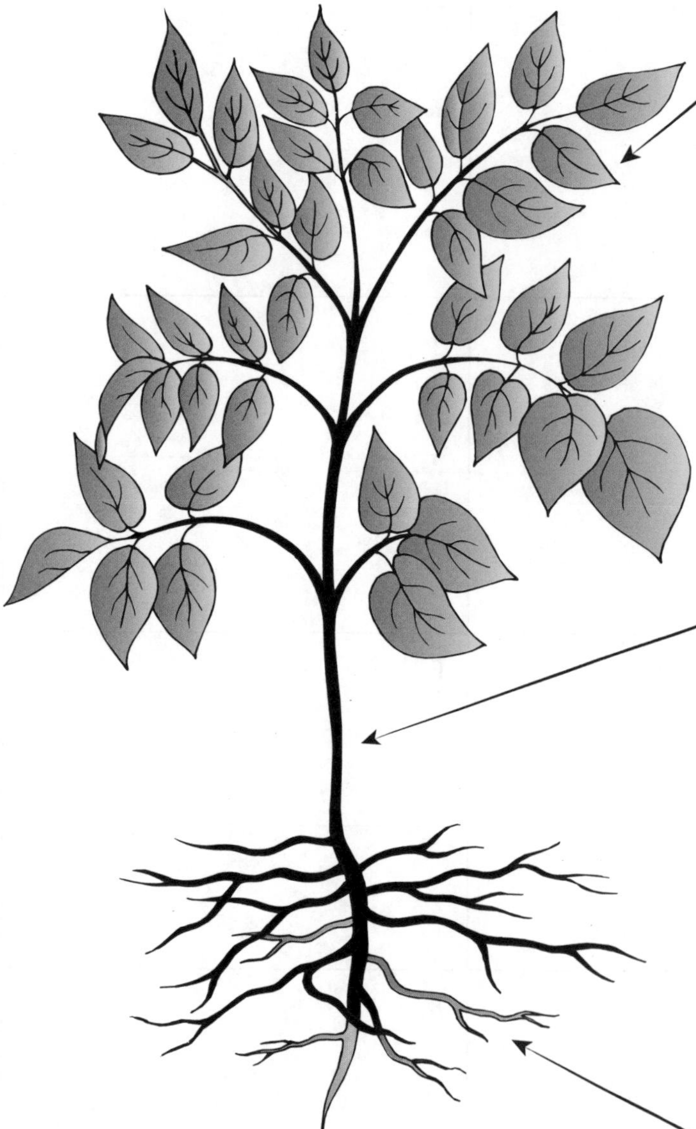

**1.**

| Name |
|---|
| Job |

**2.**

| Name |
|---|
| Job |

**3.**

| Name |
|---|
| Job |

# What's Next? You Decide!

Now it's your turn to choose what to do next in the lesson. Read the activities and decide which one you want to do—you may want to try them all!

## Observe Water Transport

### MATERIALS

- ❑ 1 celery stalk
- ❑ 1 paring knife
- ❑ 1 cutting board
- ❑ 1 glass water
- ❑ red food coloring

### STEPS

Complete this activity to observe how water moves up a stem through the xylem.

- ❑ Ask a parent or other adult to help you cut off the very end of a stalk of celery.
- ❑ Put five or six drops of red food coloring in a glass of water. The water should be very dark red.
- ❑ Place the celery stalk in the water with the end at the bottom of the glass.
- ❑ Predict what you think will happen and write your prediction in a notebook.
- ❑ The next day, observe the celery. Draw a conclusion about what happened and write the conclusion in your notebook.

## Write an Organ Donation Statement

### STEPS

- ❑ Look for books, magazine articles, and Web sites that discuss organ donation.
- ❑ Find out how donated organs are used. Read about people who have received donated organs and why people choose to donate their organs.
- ❑ Write a personal statement about why you would or would not be an organ donor and share it with your family.

## Compare Your Favorite Animals' Organs

### MATERIALS

- ❑ crayons, pencils, or markers

### STEPS

- ❑ Choose two of your favorite animals.
- ❑ Use reference sources to find out about their digestive organ system. What organs do the animals have in common? Are there any organs that are different or found in one animal and not the other?

(CONTINUED)

- ❑ Draw a diagram of each digestive system and label the parts.
- ❑ Write a paragraph about why you think the two digestive systems are the same or different. Do these animals live in different climates? Do they have different diets?
- ❑ Share your writing with an adult.

## Investigate Maple Syrup

### MATERIALS

- ❑ 1 book on the process of maple sugaring
- ❑ crayons or markers

### STEPS

Do you like maple syrup? Did you know that maple syrup comes from trees?

- ❑ Research the process of maple sugaring and removing sugar water from maple trees. Find out where maple syrup is harvested.
- ❑ Draw pictures of each stage in the maple sugaring process. Be sure to include captions that explain what is happening at each stage.
- ❑ Share your pictures and the story of maple syrup with an adult.

## Grow Tissues?

### STEPS

Much has been reported in the news in recent years about scientists' efforts to create tissues.

- ❑ Research the latest experiments scientists have done in this field.
- ❑ Read editorials on the topic.
- ❑ Decide what you think about the issue.
- ❑ Write a letter to the editor explaining your views on the issue. Be sure to back up your opinions with facts and to use reason and logic rather than just emotional appeals.
- ❑ When you are finished with your letter, you can mail it to your local newspaper if you like.

# Exploring Populations and Ecosystems

**Ecosystem Haiku**
***Plants and animals***
***interact with each other***
***an ecosystem.***

| OBJECTIVE | BACKGROUND | MATERIALS |
|---|---|---|
| To help your student learn about how animals and plants live together and interact, and how their behavior is affected by the world around them | Nothing lives on Earth in isolation; we are all products of a huge system of interactions with our environment, living and nonliving. In this lesson, your student will learn how ecosystems work and about some of the behaviors of animals and plants within them. | ■ Student Learning Pages 3.A–3.C<br>■ 1 copy Sequence Chain, page 354 |

## VOCABULARY

**ECOLOGISTS** people who study ecosystems
**BIOMES** regions on earth with particular types of climates
**ECOSYSTEMS** collections of living things in a particular place, plus the nonliving things in the environment that influence them
**COMMUNITIES** groups of populations in a certain area
**SPECIES** kinds of animals or plants
**POPULATIONS** groups of the same types of plants or animals in the same places
**ORGANISM** a living thing
**LIMITING FACTORS** things that prevent a population from getting larger
**CARRYING CAPACITY** the largest number of a species that an ecosystem can support over a long period of time
**PRODUCERS** organisms that come up with, or make, their own food
**CONSUMERS** organisms that eat other organisms
**DECOMPOSERS** organisms that eat the waste of, or eat, other organisms
**ADAPTATION** the way an organism adjusts to its environment
**STIMULI** (singular: stimulus) things that influence the behavior of living things
**TROPISM** when an organism reacts to stimuli involuntarily

# Let's Begin

**1** **ASK AND EXPLAIN** Ask your student, *Why do animals and plants live where they do?* [answers will vary; a starting point might be "because the places they live suit them" or a similar statement] Explain that **ecologists** are people who study **biomes** and their **ecosystems** to try to understand the ways that animals and plants interact with their environment. Ask your student if he or she knows what biomes and ecosystems might be from that sentence. Then reveal that an ecosystem is a collection of living things in an environment, plus the nonliving factors that influence them. A biome is a region on Earth with a particular type of climate.

*Located in the Sonoran Desert in Arizona, Columbia University's Biosphere 2 contains self-sustaining biomes that scientists use to study Earth's ecosystems. Biosphere 2 is open to visitors.*

**DID YOU KNOW?**

The prefix *bio-* comes from the Greek and means "life." *Eco-* is also from the Greek and means "house" or "habitat."

**2** **GO FURTHER** Mention that ecologists organize ecosystems into **communities** of different **species** that interact. A community is organized into **populations.** A population is all animals or plants of one species. Explain that an **organism** is a single "individual" within a population. Walk your student through these challenging definitions again. Then have your student give at least one example of this organization within an ecosystem. It may be necessary for him or her to do research to answer.

**3** **EXPLORE** Explain that when we talk of population, we usually mean human population of a certain area, such as the population of a town or city. The same is true of animals and plants. Reveal that the population of a place is always changing, and that some populations change more quickly than others. Ask, *How might*

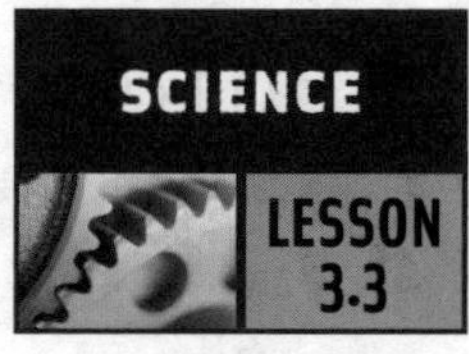


*populations of animals change in an area?* [births, deaths, migration, introduction or removal by humans]

Then challenge your student and ask, *What would **limiting factors** be on population growth in an area?* [living space, food, water] Explain that a limiting factor is something that prevents a population from getting larger. Some limiting factors can be indirect, too; for example, a forest fire burns trees, therefore birds have no nesting sites, so the bird population decreases. Then explain that the **carrying capacity** is the largest number of a species that an ecosystem can support over a long period of time. Together with your student see if you can come up with another example of an indirect limiting factor.

**4** **DISTRIBUTE AND PRACTICE** Distribute Student Learning Page 3.A and have your student do Steps 1 and 2.

**5** **EXPLAIN AND PRACTICE** Explain to your student that there can be all kinds of interaction between plants and animals in an ecosystem. For example, when a bear catches fish in a river, that's interaction. When a mosquito bites you, that's interaction. Or when a bird eats a berry, that's interaction. Have your student think of other interactions going on in his or her environment. You may have to prompt him or her with ideas to begin.

**6** **CONTINUE** Have your student return to Student Learning Page 3.A and complete Step 3.

**7** **DISTRIBUTE AND SHOW** Explain that a number of the interactions between organisms in an ecosystem involve the transfer of energy. Ask your student if he or she knows what the terms **producers, consumers,** and **decomposers** might mean. Show your student the diagram of the food web on Part A of Student Learning Page 3.B.

**8** **EXPLAIN** Explain that at the basic level, producers capture sunlight and use nutrients to make food. Consumers eat producers or eat other consumers that eat producers. Decomposers live off the dead bodies of organisms. Walk your student through the food web, then have him or her explain it back to you for further comprehension.

**9** **DRAW** Direct your student to Part B on Student Learning Page 3.B. Have him or her make a food web of the area he or she has already observed on Student Learning Page 3.A or of another ecosystem of his or her choosing. Then have him or her walk you through the web.

**10** **EXPLORE** Reveal that an ecosystem can undergo change. For example, a pond can dry up and then can become a meadow, which then later becomes a forest. Tell your student that this is a cycle of nature. Help your student think of another example of

**DID YOU KNOW?**

In addition to land ecosystems, there are water ecosystems: oceans, lakes, ponds, rivers, marshes, and bogs.

how an ecosystem can change, or think of another cycle of nature. [seasons, water cycle, moon cycle] Have your student make a copy of the Sequence Chain found on page 354 and chart the cycle.

**11** **REVIEW AND COMPARE** Review with your student other cycles of nature, such as the seasons, the moon, the water cycle, and the life cycles of different animals and plants. Then ask your student, *In what ways are they alike? Different?* Discuss.

**12** **EXPLORE AND WRITE** Tell your student that an **adaptation** of a plant or an animal is the way in which it adjusts to conditions in its environment. Have your student investigate this concept by using the example of the desert biome as found in the Sonoran Desert (southwestern United States and northern Mexico). Have your student research the plants and animals located in this area. Then ask him or her to list about six plants and animals that live there and note how each one has adapted to the hot, dry climate.

**13** **EXPLAIN AND MODEL** Explain to your student that plants make different types of adaptations to their environment compared to animals. These adaptations involve responding to light, heat, moisture, chemicals, electricity, and gravity. Changes of this sort are called **stimuli.** When an organism reacts to these changes automatically, that's called **tropism.** Help your student set up a simple experiment with two similar plants. Place one in a sunny windowsill, the other in a shady spot. Observe for several days. What happens? Then water one every day, keeping the soil moist. Let the soil dry out in the other. What happens now? Discuss.

**FOR FURTHER READING**

*Amazing Animals: Nature's Most Incredible Creatures,* Anthony D. Fredericks and Sneed B. Collard, eds. (Creative Publishing International, 2000).

*Animal Relationships and Animal Senses (Animal Survival Series),* by Michael Barre (Gareth Stevens, 1998).

*Exploding Ants: Amazing Facts About How Animals Adapt,* by Joanne Settel (Atheneum, 1999).

# Branching Out

## TEACHING TIP

When trying to help your student understand a concept, break down the idea into as many smaller parts as possible. Use notes and/or drawings to show the parts. When your student can envision them as parts of a whole, it's often easier to grasp the whole concept.

## CHECKING IN

To assess your student's understanding of ecosystems, adaptations, and behaviors, make up a set of flash cards and have your student provide definitions that explain how each concept actually works.

# Count Populations

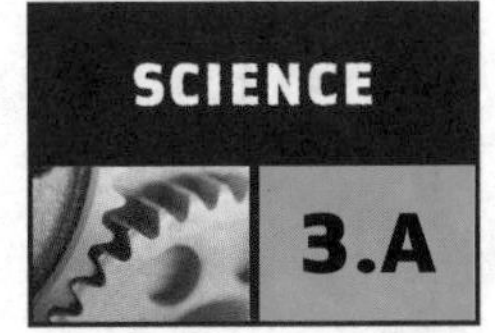


Choose an area around or near your home, such as a park or street block. Then follow the steps.

1. Take a count of the population of your chosen area. Make a list of each species of plants and animals (including humans) you see. Count or estimate how many of each species live in the area you have chosen.

2. Now try to figure out what you may **not** be able to see because it lives underground or is too tiny. Research what those organisms might be and estimate them in your population count.

3. Make a list of the species in your area that interact.

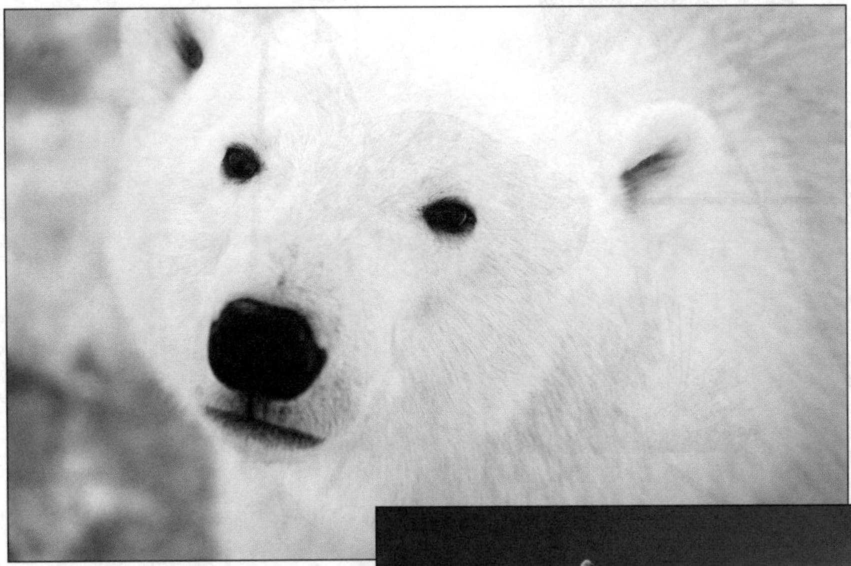

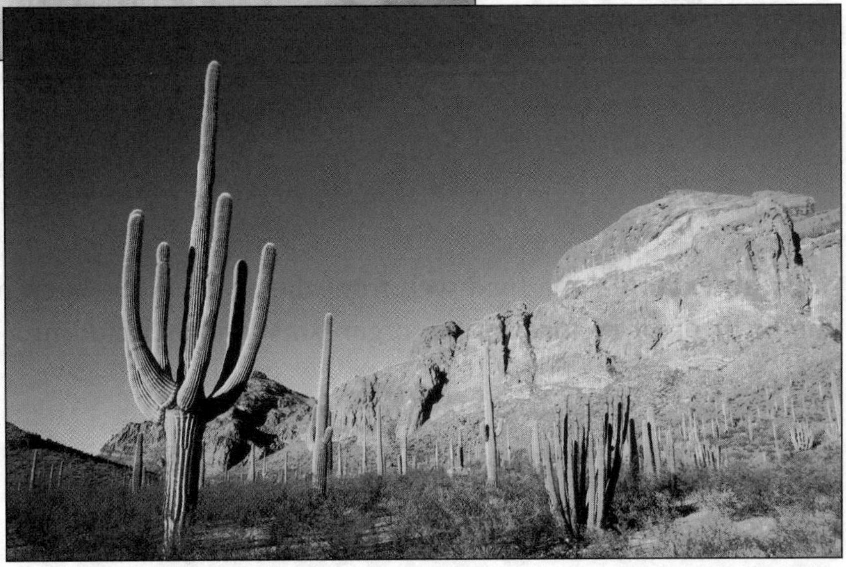

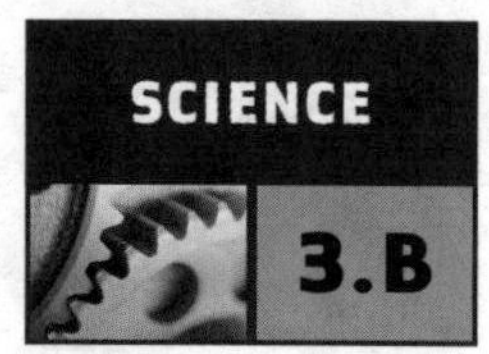


# Check Out the Web

**PART A**

**Examine the food web.**

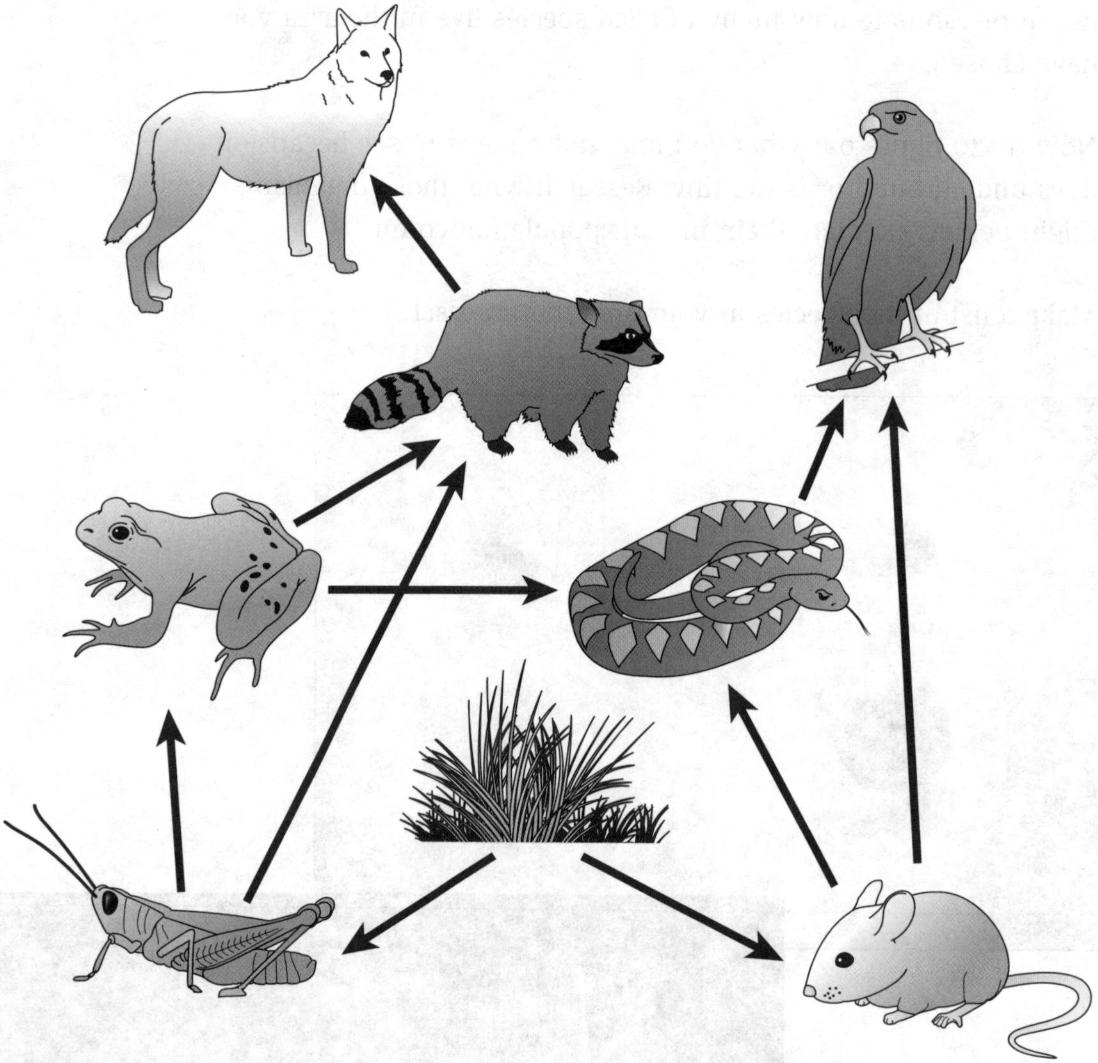

**PART B**

**Draw an example of a food web from the area you've been observing. Use cut-out photos or draw pictures of the organisms you're including.**

# What's Next? You Decide!

Now it's your turn to choose what to do next in the lesson. Read the activities and decide which one you want to do—you may want to try them all!

## Adapt to the Environment

### MATERIALS

- ❑ 24 index cards
- ❑ 1 pair scissors
- ❑ glue
- ❑ colored construction paper or patterned paper
- ❑ pictures of animals

### STEPS

Make your own matching game to play with a friend.

- ❑ Cut the index cards in half so that you've got 48 cards.
- ❑ On one side of 24 cards, draw or paste a picture of an animal. If you like, glue bright or patterned wrapping or other paper on the other side so you can't see what the animal is.
- ❑ On one side of the other half of the cards, write one way in which one animal from the first set of cards adapts to its environment. For example, on one card could be a picture of a chameleon, and on another card would be "changes color."
- ❑ Take turns matching an animal card with an adaptation card. If you make a match, keep the cards near you and take another turn—until you don't match anymore.
- ❑ Whoever winds up with the most matches wins.

## Live Under the Sea

### MATERIALS

- ❑ art materials of your choice (see below)

### STEPS

What is it like to live in a water ecosystem?

- ❑ Choose an ocean (seashore or deep ocean), a lake, a pond, a river, a marsh, or a bog.
- ❑ Research what interactions there are among the living and nonliving things in the ecosystem.
- ❑ Think about not just what your ecosystem is made of, but what it might **feel** like!
- ❑ Then find art materials and other supplies around the house (be sure to ask permission first) and create something that shows another person what it feels like to live under the sea.

(CONTINUED)

- ❑ Check out these ideas: If you think the deep ocean is a dark, scary, cold place, you might want to make a large, dark painting and play scary-sounding music when you show your artwork. Or if you think a lake is an active, happy place, you might want to create a dance for two fishes—one little and one big.

## Make Tropism Music

### MATERIALS

- ❑ 4 similar houseplants
- ❑ 1 ruler
- ❑ music of your choosing

### STEPS

Does music—and style of music—affect a plant's growth?

- ❑ Place four plants in a safe, quiet spot. Give them the same amount of light and water.
- ❑ Every night for two weeks, take two of the plants to a different room and play music for an hour. Make sure the temperatures of the rooms are similar. Choose similar music for all the nights—whatever kind you like.
- ❑ After one week, measure the plants and observe if the ones that have "listened" to music are taller and in otherwise better shape than the ones that haven't "listened" to music.
- ❑ Measure and observe again after two weeks. What are your findings?
- ❑ If you like, add a third pair of plants and play them a different kind of music.
- ❑ Compare the results. Can you draw any conclusions?

## Become Your Favorite Animal

### MATERIALS

- ❑ 1 sheet drawing paper
- ❑ colored pencils

### STEPS

- ❑ Choose your favorite animal.
- ❑ In your notebook, write details about it, such as what it looks like and its outer covering (is it fur?), what it eats, where it lives, and anything else you can think of.
- ❑ Then suppose you're this animal, but now you're located in a different place.
- ❑ Think about how you'd adapt. What food would you eat? What type of "house" would you have? How would you get along with the other animals and plants in your new location? Write these ideas in your notebook.
- ❑ Draw a picture of you in your new setting, showing your new foods, house, and other parts of your environment. Then show your picture to someone.

# Learning About Body Systems

*The body is one large system comprised of many smaller systems working in harmony.*

| OBJECTIVE | BACKGROUND | MATERIALS |
|---|---|---|
| To help your student understand how the systems of the body are structured and function | As your student more fully understands how the body systems work, he or she will be better prepared to make healthful decisions. This lesson introduces your student to the cardiovascular, digestive, excretory, skeletal, and muscular systems. | ■ Student Learning Pages 4.A–4.F<br>■ 1 piece cardboard at least 6-by-6-inches wide<br>■ 1 pair scissors<br>■ 20–30 drinking straws<br>■ 1 roll masking tape<br>■ 1 large lump modeling clay |

**VOCABULARY**

**CIRCULATORY SYSTEM** the body system that moves blood as well as oxygen, nutrients, carbon dioxide, and wastes through the body
**RESPIRATORY SYSTEM** the body system that helps move oxygen into the body and carbon dioxide out of the body
**DIGESTIVE SYSTEM** the body system that breaks down food into nutrients and wastes
**EXCRETORY SYSTEM** the body system that removes wastes from the body
**SKELETAL SYSTEM** the body system that supports and protects the body
**MUSCULAR SYSTEM** the body system that converts energy into movement

# Let's Begin

## CIRCULATORY SYSTEM

**1** **EXPLAIN** Explain to your student that the cardiovascular system is made up of two systems: the **circulatory system** and the **respiratory system.** The circulatory system is similar to a system of roads. The heart, blood, and vessels that make up the circulatory system move materials throughout the body. Direct your student to the KidsHealth Web site at http://www.kidshealth.org to find out more about the circulatory system.

**2** **GUIDE AND EXPLAIN** Distribute Student Learning Page 4.A. Have your student look at the diagram of the heart. Explain that the four chambers of the heart form two pumps. The right side

pumps oxygen-poor blood from the body to the lungs. The left side pumps oxygen-rich blood from the lungs to the body. Each pump is made up of two parts: an atrium on top and a ventricle on the bottom. Read the following information about how the blood flows through the heart. As you explain, have your student add arrows to the diagram to show the movement of blood in the heart.

During a heartbeat, the atrium contracts, pushing blood into the ventricle. A split second later the ventricle contracts, pushing blood out of the heart and into the arteries. Blood rich in carbon dioxide from the body enters the right atrium and goes into the lungs. Oxygen-rich blood from the lungs fills the left atrium and goes to the rest of the body.

**DID YOU KNOW?**

Over the course of the average lifetime, the heart beats more than 2.5 billion times without stopping.

## RESPIRATORY, DIGESTIVE, AND EXCRETORY SYSTEMS

**1** **DISTRIBUTE AND ASK** Distribute Student Learning Page 4.B. Ask your student to slowly breathe in and breathe out. Breathing is something we take for granted, but if we don't breathe we can't live. Explain to your student that the organs we use to breathe and that help us use oxygen are part of the respiratory system. You may want to go to the Web site http://www.innerbody.com or search for a book about the respiratory system. Have your student read about the respiratory system. Then have him or her draw a picture of the respiratory system on Student Learning Page 4.B.

**2** **EXPLORE** Ask your student to describe what happens to food after it is eaten. You and your student also can explore the **digestive system** at http://www.innerbody.com or look in a book for information about the digestion process. Distribute Student Learning Page 4.C. Have your student use what he or she learns about the digestive system to create a flowchart showing the process of digestion.

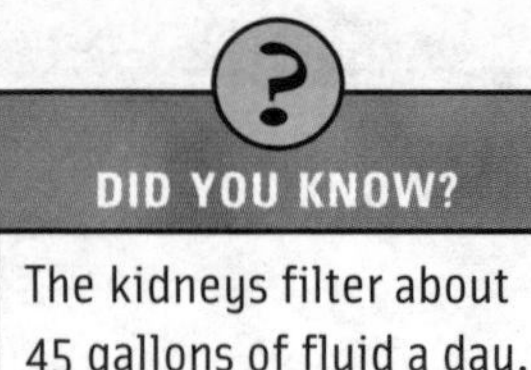

**DID YOU KNOW?**

The kidneys filter about 45 gallons of fluid a day.

**3** **DISCUSS** Ask your student what would happen if he or she never cleaned his or her room or took out the trash. While that might sound appealing at first, in reality your student would probably not like wading through the mounds of garbage or the smells that would result. Explain that our bodies must regularly get rid of wastes, too. Our **excretory system** does just that. After our cells get all the nutrients needed from the food we eat, they return what isn't needed to the blood. The blood carries these wastes to the kidneys. The kidneys filter the wastes and send urine to the bladder. Ask your student to research the excretory system. Have him or her find out about the relationship between the blood, kidneys, urine, and bladder and write a brief paragraph summarizing what he or she learned.

## SKELETAL SYSTEM

SCIENCE LESSON 3.4

**1** **PRESENT** Explain that our **skeletal system** shapes and supports our bodies. It protects our organs. Our bones store the minerals calcium and phosphorous and produce a supply of blood. Ask your student what our bodies would look like without skeletons. Have your student consider the main functions of the skeletal system. Discuss.

**2** **DISTRIBUTE AND DISCUSS** Distribute Student Learning Page 4.D. Have your student consider what bones are made of. Explain that even though bone looks solid, it isn't. Bone is actually made of three layers. The periosteum is a thin outer layer that is wrapped around a hard shell called compact bone. Compact bone grows in circles around hollow canals. Blood vessels in the canals supply food and oxygen to the bone cells. Beneath the compact bone is a spongy layer of minerals and bone marrow. Blood cells are made in the bone marrow. Even though bone isn't completely solid, it is very strong. Have your student follow the directions in the first half of Student Learning Page 4.D to create a model of a bone.

**3** **DIRECT** Tell your student that our skeletons are constructed in a way that allows us to move. Have your student try to walk while keeping his or her legs completely stiff and not bending. Ask, *How hard would it be to run or play if your legs were each a single bone? What if your spine were stiff and flat like a board?*

**4** **EXPLAIN** Have your student define the word *joint.* Explain that a joint is a place where two bones meet. Joints allow bones to move in certain directions but prevent them from moving in other ways. Tell your student that there are different kinds of joints. Then have your student complete Student Learning Page 4.D.

**DID YOU KNOW?**

No one is double-jointed. Some people are just more limber than others.

## MUSCULAR SYSTEM

**1** **DISCUSS AND DISTRIBUTE** Ask your student if anyone ever told him or her "don't move a muscle." Have your student try it. Explain that we can control many of the muscles in our **muscular system,** but there are some muscles we can't control. Explain that the muscles we can control are called skeletal muscles because they're attached to our bones with tissue called tendons. These muscles are also called voluntary muscles. The muscles we cannot control are called involuntary muscles. Tell your student that the heart is an involuntary muscle. Other involuntary muscles are called smooth muscles. The walls of blood vessels and the stomach are examples of smooth muscles. Explain that the muscles in blood vessels move blood through the vessels by contracting and relaxing in an involuntary pattern. Distribute Student Learning Page 4.E. Have your student use reference sources or Web sites to label the major muscles shown in the diagram.

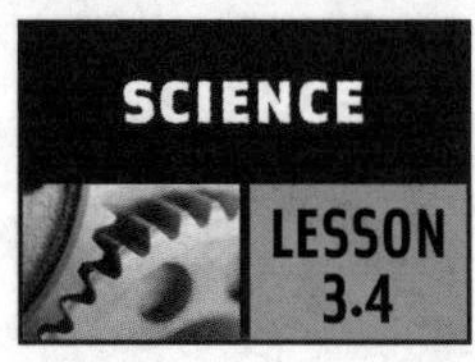


**2** **ASK** Have your student consider where muscles get the energy to move. Explain that blood vessels supply the muscles with fuel and oxygen and that nerves direct the muscles' actions. Without the proper fuel, muscles get tired and can't work. The digestive process puts nutrients into the blood that can be used by the muscles. Explain that to build large muscles he or she must use them. Regular exercise can help develop strong and fit muscles. Ask, *How do you think the food a marathon runner eats might be different from the food an average person eats?* Discuss.

# Branching Out

## TEACHING TIP

When teaching about body systems, it's helpful to provide models so that your student can get a better understanding of where organs and systems are located, what they look like, and how they function. Models can be purchased from educational supply companies, but it may be beneficial for your student to create models of his or her own.

## CHECKING IN

To assess how well your student has learned the body systems, engage in a dialogue about each of the systems. Ask your student questions such as, *What does the digestive system do? How is a circulatory system like a highway? What would happen to your body if you didn't have a skeletal system?* Let your student do the talking and ask follow-up questions only when necessary to clarify his or her understanding.

**FOR FURTHER READING**

*Eyewitness: The Human Body*, by Steve Parker (DK Publishing, 1999).

*Guide to the Human Body: A Photographic Journey Through the Human Body*, by Richard Walker (DK Publishing, 2001).

*Janice VanCleave's the Human Body for Every Kid: Easy Activities That Make Learning Science Fun*, by Janice VanCleave (EconoClad Books, 1999).

# Chart Blood Flow

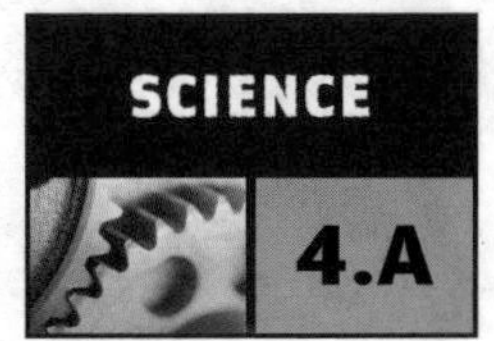


Study the diagram of the heart. Draw arrows on the diagram to show the direction of blood flowing through the heart. On the lines below, write a few sentences about how the heart, blood, and lungs work together to send oxygen to all parts of the body.

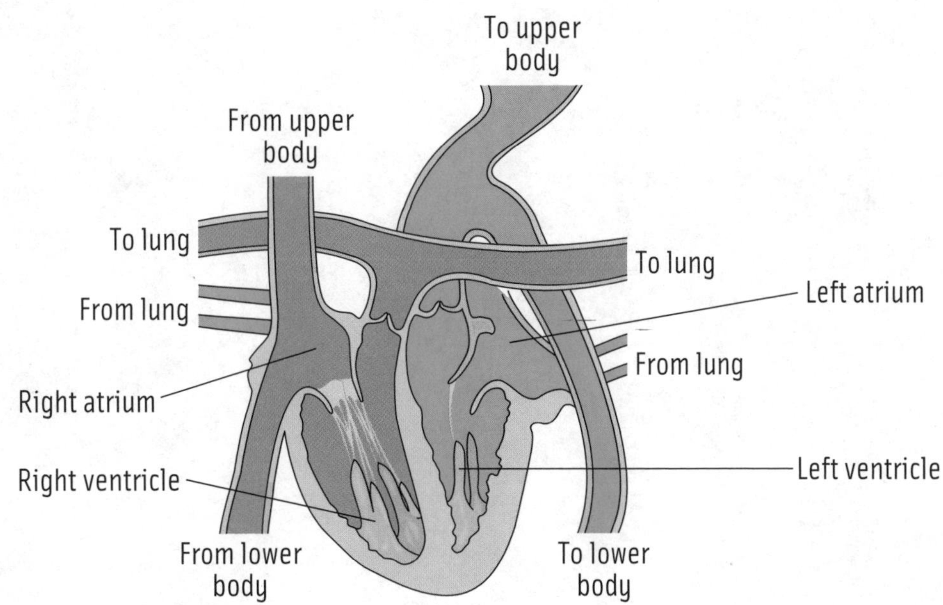

# Know Your Respiratory System

Using information from your research, draw a picture of your respiratory system. Label the nose, mouth, epiglottis, trachea, esophagus, lungs, and bronchi.

 

# Show the Process of Digestion

Use what you have learned in the lesson and through your research to create a flowchart showing the process of digestion in the space below.

If you need to, organize the layout of your flowchart on another piece of paper first. Be sure to include the jobs of the teeth, salivary glands, pharynx, esophagus, stomach, small intestine, large intestine, and rectum in the flowchart.

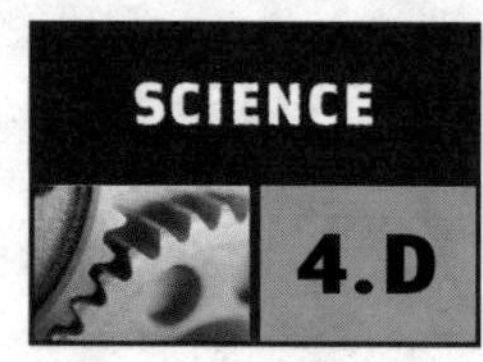


# Learn About Bones and Joints

## MATERIALS

- ❑ 1 piece cardboard at least 6 by 6 inches wide
- ❑ 1 pair scissors
- ❑ 20–30 drinking straws
- ❑ 1 roll tape
- ❑ 1 large lump modeling clay

## STEPS

1. Cut a piece of cardboard so that it is about six inches wide and as long as a drinking straw.
2. Attach two layers of drinking straws to the cardboard with tape.
3. Place a layer of modeling clay on top of the straws.
4. Roll the cardboard into a tube so that the straws and modeling clay are on the inside. Secure the tube with tape.
5. Answer the following questions in your notebook: What part of bone does the cardboard represent? What part of bone do the straws represent? What part of bone does the modeling clay represent?
6. Stand your bone model upright on a table and push on it with your hand. What can you conclude about bones? Write a few sentences in your notebook about what you noticed and learned.

**Use the drawings and descriptions of joint types to classify the following four joints: elbow, shoulder, neck, and thumb. Write the examples on the lines.**

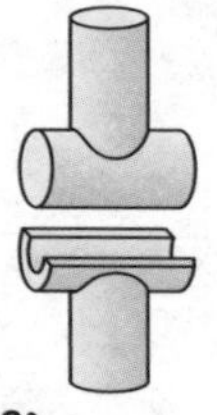

**Type:** Hinge joint
**Description:** Allows backward and forward movement
**Example from human body:**

______________

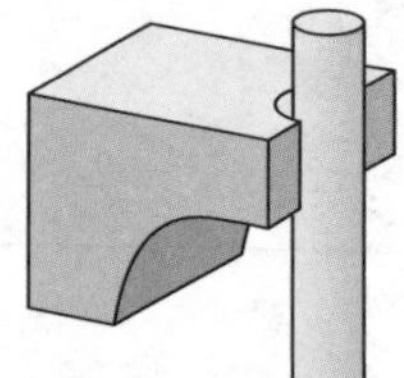

**Type:** Pivot joint
**Description:** Allows rotating movement
**Example from human body:**

______________

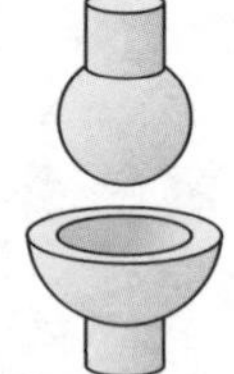

**Type:** Ball-and-socket joint
**Description:** Allows swinging movement
**Example from human body:**

______________

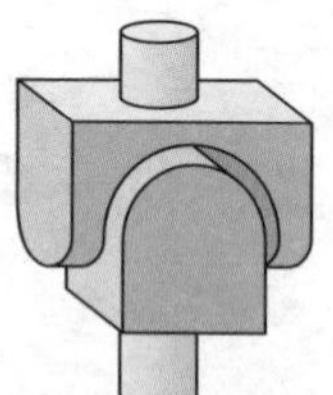

**Type:** Saddle joint
**Description:** Allows movement from side to side and back to front
**Example from human body:**

______________

# Locate the Major Muscles

Use a reference book or Web site to label these major muscles in the diagram below: biceps brachii, deltoid, gluteus maximus, hamstring, gastrocnemius, external oblique, latissimus dorsi, quadricep, tibialis anterior, rectus abdominus, pectoralis major, and triceps.

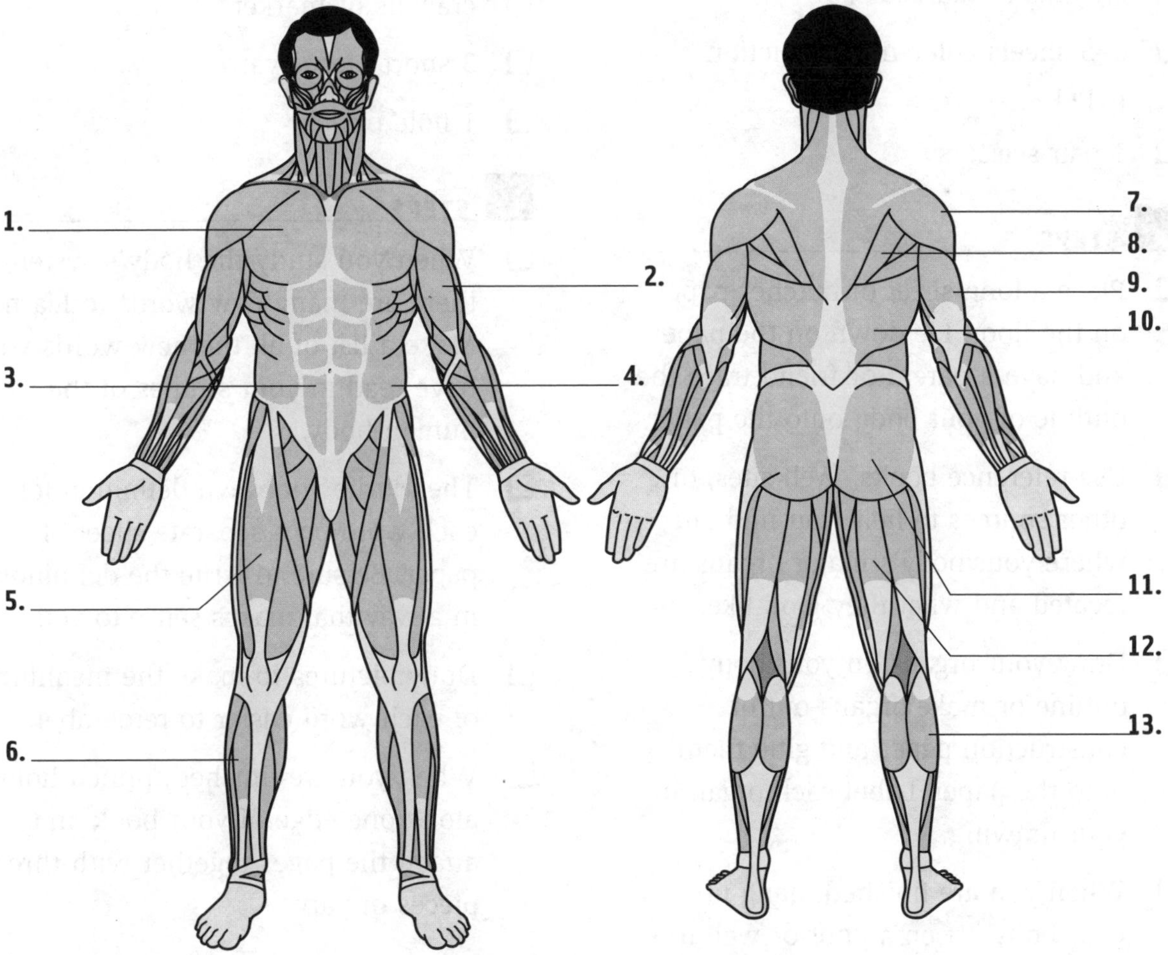

1. __________
2. __________
3. __________
4. __________
5. __________
6. __________
7. __________
8. __________
9. __________
10. __________
11. __________
12. __________
13. __________

SCIENCE 4.F

# What's Next? You Decide!

Now it's your turn to choose what to do next in the lesson. Read the activities and decide which one you want to do—you may want to try them both!

## Draw Your Body

### MATERIALS

- ❑ 1 sheet butcher paper as big as you are
- ❑ crayons or markers
- ❑ 3–5 sheets colored construction paper
- ❑ 1 pair scissors

### STEPS

- ❑ Place a long sheet of butcher paper on the floor. Lie down on the paper and have a parent or friend trace the outline of your body onto the paper.
- ❑ Use reference books, Web sites, or other sources to help you find out where your body's major organs are located and what they look like.
- ❑ Draw your organs on your body outline or make organs out of construction paper and glue them onto the paper. Label each organ in your drawing.
- ❑ When you are finished, hang up your body art on a door or wall to help you remember the names and locations of your body's organs.

## Learn the Language of the Body

### MATERIALS

- ❑ at least 7 sheets paper
- ❑ crayons or markers
- ❑ 3 short pieces yarn
- ❑ 1 hole punch

### STEPS

- ❑ When you study the body's systems, there are many new words to learn. Make a list of all the new words you have read in your studies of the human body.
- ❑ Then write your own definition for each word on a separate sheet of paper. Be sure to write the definitions in a way that makes sense to you.
- ❑ Draw pictures to make the meaning of each word easier to remember.
- ❑ When you are finished, punch holes along one edge of your book and attach the pages together with three pieces of yarn.

# Discovering Nutrition and Health

***Though health and happiness are not the same thing, you can't have the latter without the former.***

| OBJECTIVE | BACKGROUND | MATERIALS |
|---|---|---|
| To help your student understand the relationship between good nutrition and health and the benefits of exercise | Your family's choice of what to eat may depend on a lot of things: family background, schedule, whether you're at home or away, and personal taste. More and more, people are becoming aware of the health value of nutrition. People are also becoming aware that eating right isn't enough to maintain health. We also need appropriate exercise. In this lesson, your student will learn about the importance of making wise food choices and the value of exercise. | ■ Student Learning Pages 5.A–5.B<br>■ 1 ruler<br>■ 1 copy Web, page 354<br>■ colored pencils or markers<br>■ 1 body thermometer<br>■ 1 watch with second hand |

## VOCABULARY

**NUTRIENTS** substances in food that give your body energy and help cells grow and heal themselves
**ENERGY** the ability to do work or be active
**MOLECULES** the smallest bits of substances that have all their properties
**CARBON** a chemical element that is found in all living things
**HYDROGEN** the lightest chemical element; when combined with oxygen, it can make water
**OXYGEN** a chemical element that we need to breathe that makes up about one-fifth of air
**MALNUTRITION** a state in which a living thing is not getting the nutrition it needs
**CARBON DIOXIDE** a gas made of carbon and oxygen that your body creates and breathes out

# Let's Begin

**1** **REVEAL** Explain to your student that food contains six kinds of **nutrients:** proteins, carbohydrates, fats, vitamins, minerals, and water. Discuss what he or she already knows about foods that contain each of these nutrients. Then have your student explore your kitchen refrigerator, cabinets, and cupboards using food labels and reference books to learn more about what kinds of foods are high in various nutrients. Discuss the new information in light of what he or she already knows. Have your student write the major nutrients in two or three of his or her favorite foods in his or her notebook.

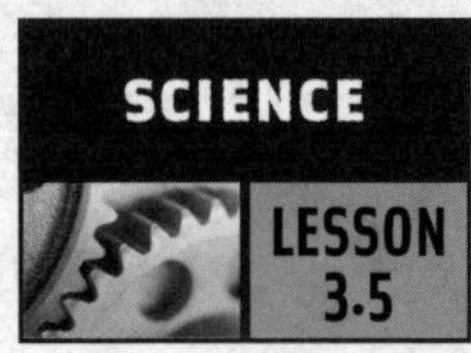


**2** **DISTRIBUTE** Distribute Student Learning Page 5.A. Have your student follow the directions for Step 1.

**3** **EXPLORE AND MODEL** Tell your student that carbohydrates are the main source of **energy** in a person's body. There are three kinds of carbohydrates: sugar, starch, and cellulose. Have your student find diagrams of **molecules** of each of them. Have him or her use three different kinds of dried beans or breakfast cereals to make models of the molecules. (One will represent **carbon,** one **hydrogen,** and one **oxygen.**) Have your student find out what role each of them plays in the body's digestion. Ask, *Why do you think sugar is the easiest to digest of the three kinds?* [because it is the easiest molecule to break down]

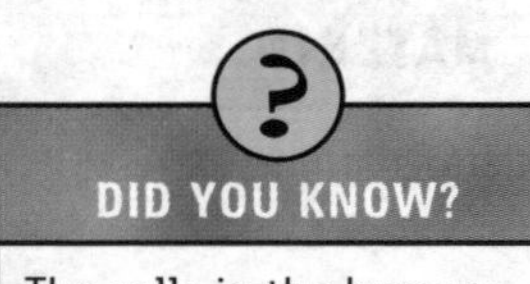

**DID YOU KNOW?**

The cells in the human body use sugar in the form of glucose.

**4** **RESEARCH** Have your student research how the body uses proteins, fats, vitamins, and minerals. Have him or her use the Web found on page 354 to record important information about each of these nutrients.

**5** **EXPLAIN AND COMPLETE** Explain that foods have different amounts of calories. A calorie is a measure of energy, specifically the energy required to raise the temperature of one kilogram of water one degree Celsius. All foods have a caloric value. Have your student find a table of calories in a cookbook, a book on nutrition, or on the Internet. Then have him or her return to Student Learning Page 5.A and complete Steps 2 and 3.

**6** **EXPLORE** Have your student find a recent diagram of the food guide pyramid that is created by the U.S. Department of Agriculture. Tell your student that over the last several decades, the food pyramid has changed as scientists have changed their ideas about what a person should eat. Mention that it is still under discussion and likely to change within his or her lifetime. Have your student use the current USDA pyramid to complete Step 4 on Student Learning Page 5.A.

**DID YOU KNOW?**

Some researchers think that kids who take nutritional supplements are healthier, stronger, and perform better in school than those who don't, especially if their eating habits are poor. So, kids, take your vitamins!

**7** **RESEARCH** Have your student find a list of major vitamins and how each one is used by the body. Have your student return to Student Learning Page 5.A and use this information to complete Steps 5 and 6.

**8** **DISCUSS AND MODEL** Discuss the benefits of good nutrition with your student. [your body is healthier, you maintain a proper weight, you have energy for your daily work, you grow properly, and so on] There is a saying "You are what you eat." Assuming this is true, have your student make a drawing of what he or she would look like, using food shapes as the parts of his or her body. Discuss, and have fun with this exercise!

**9** **EXPLAIN** Explain to your student that the body has different special needs for nutrients at different times. For example, it is important for the mineral density in bones to be as great as

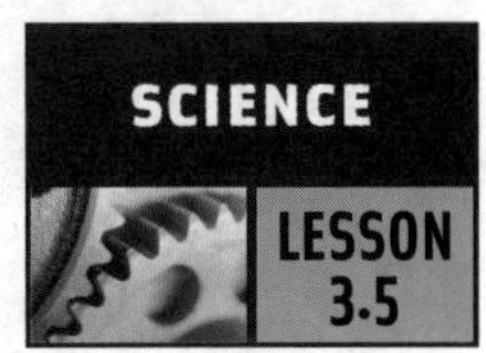


possible in order to prevent osteoporosis, a weakening of bones, in old age. Dairy products, which contain the highest usable amounts of the mineral calcium, are important during periods of growth. Scientists think that exercise also helps keep bones strong. Have your student check his or her research to find out how much calcium he or she should take in every day. If he or she isn't getting enough, discuss what foods can be added to the diet to get enough calcium.

**10** **RESEARCH AND WRITE** Explain that there are classic signs of different kinds of **malnutrition.** Have your student research these examples of malnutrition and make a chart or drawings that show each of the signs listed and what can be done to prevent them: xerosis, pellagra, goiter, scurvy, edema in legs, and lots of dental caries (cavities). Review the chart together.

**11** **RESEARCH AND WRITE** Explain that poor nutrition over time can cause disease. Have your student research one of the following diseases and its relationship to nutrition: diabetes (adult onset), heart disease, high blood pressure, gout, obesity, and stomach cancer. Ask your student to write a brief paragraph based on his or her research.

**12** **EXPLAIN AND CALCULATE** Tell your student that just as various foods give the body energy, any kind of activity the body does uses up energy. This intake and burning off of energy can be expressed in calories. The amount of calories you eat during the day, less what you use up in energy and produce in body wastes, equals the amount of weight that is added to the body. There are some activities that "burn" 300 calories per hour in a person weighing 100 pounds: dancing, bike riding, brisk walking, jumping rope, riding horses, shoveling show, and roller-skating. That's about six times more than you burn when you're sitting. To find the "burning" power of other activities and other weights, go to the Personal Health Zone Web site at http://www.personalhealthzone.com. Your student can plug in his or her exact weight, the activity he or she is doing, and the length of time—and get the calories burned. Have your student figure out how many calories he or she burns in a day while doing activities. (Don't forget sitting, eating, and sleeping!) Ask your student to record the calculations in his or her notebook. Discuss.

**13** **COMPARE** Tell your student that the human body tries to maintain a constant state even though changes in the environment are taking place. This state is called homeostasis. Some factors that affect homeostasis include body temperature, the amount of water and minerals in the body, blood sugar, oxygen, and **carbon dioxide** levels. The nervous system (brain, spinal cord, and nerves) and the endocrine system (hormones and certain organs) maintain homeostasis. Do an experiment with your student. Take your student's body temperature, the

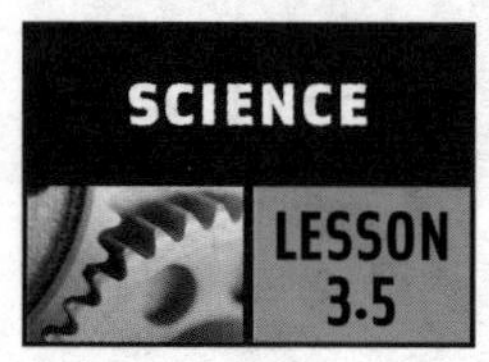

number of breaths per minute, and his or her heart rate (pulse) per minute. Take these measurements again after five minutes of running, jumping rope, aerobics, or other activity. Compare the results. Ask, *What happens when you exercise?* [certain things in your body change, such as temperature, breathing rate, perspiration, heart rate] *How does this relate to homeostasis?* [the changes are the body's responses so it can accommodate your exercise]

**14** **EXPLAIN AND MODEL** Explain that three measures of bodily health are endurance (the ability to keep up an activity), strength (the ability to move a muscle against an opposing force), and flexibility (the ability to move your joints and muscles). With your student, research exercises that are appropriate to his or her size, weight, and physical condition that will help him or her stay fit in each of these three areas. Work out a weekly exercise program that incorporates all three. If you like, have your student keep records of his or her exercises and chart the progress.

**FOR FURTHER READING**

*Fit Kids! The Complete Shape-up Program from Birth Through High School*, by Kenneth H. Cooper, M.D. (Boardman and Hudson, 1999).

*Food Rules! The Stuff You Munch, Its Crunch, Its Punch, and Why You Sometimes Lose Your Lunch*, by Bill Haduch (Puffin Books, 2001).

*Janice VanCleave's Food and Nutrition for Every Kid: Easy Activities That Make Learning Science Fun (Science for Every Kid Series)*, by Janice VanCleave (John Wiley and Sons, 1999).

*365 Activities for Fitness, Food, and Fun for the Whole Family*, by Julia E. Sweet (McGraw-Hill/Contemporary Books, 2001).

# Branching Out

## TEACHING TIP

When studying health topics such as eating and exercise, be sure to make the activities as hands-on as possible, especially for a student who learns well with a kinesthetic (movement and doing) learning style.

## CHECKING IN

To assess your student's understanding of nutrition and exercise, have him or her summarize these key points: kinds of nutrients, the food guide pyramid, nutrition's role in health, and the benefits of exercise. Have him or her explain how he or she incorporates this information into everyday living.

# Find Your Daily Bread

Read the steps and keep track of the food you eat in one day.

1. Use a ruler to make a chart like the one below on a separate sheet of paper. Keep track of all the foods you eat during the course of one day. Place a check mark in the column(s) under the nutrient(s) that each food contains.
2. For each of the foods you ate, figure the amount of calories it has. Record it on the chart and total the daily calories.
3. Look in a book or on the Internet for the amount of calories you should consume for your age, size, and level of activity. Is this about the same, more, or less than your total calories for the day? Figure out how many calories you need to add or subtract from your daily total to be in balance.
4. Use your diagram of the food guide pyramid to list the food group for each of the foods on your chart.
5. List on your chart the major vitamins found in each of the foods you ate.
6. If the amount of calories you consume in a day is already in balance, use the food pyramid and your lists of nutrients and vitamins to see how you might improve your diet and nutrition by exchanging some of the foods you eat for others.

If you want to increase the number of calories you consume in a day, use the pyramid and your lists as guides to figure out what the best foods to add would be. If you want to decrease the number of calories you consume in a day, use the pyramid and your lists as guides to figure out what you could cut out without losing important nutrients. Write down your ideas in your notebook, and discuss them with an adult.

| Food | Nutrients | | | | | | Calories | Major Vitamins | Food Group |
|---|---|---|---|---|---|---|---|---|---|
| | Protein | Carb. | Fat | Vit. | Min. | Water | | | |
| 2 slices white bread | ✓ | ✓ | ✓ | ✓ | ✓ | | 150 | B1, 2, 3 | |
| 1 cup apple juice | | ✓ | | ✓ | ✓ | ✓ | 120 | C | |
| 2 scrambled eggs | ✓ | ✓ | ✓ | ✓ | ✓ | ✓ | 220 | A, D, E, B1, 2, 3, 6, 9 | |
| 1 cup milk | ✓ | ✓ | ✓ | ✓ | ✓ | ✓ | 150 | A, C, D, E, B1, 2, 5, 6, 12 | |
| | | | | | | | | | |

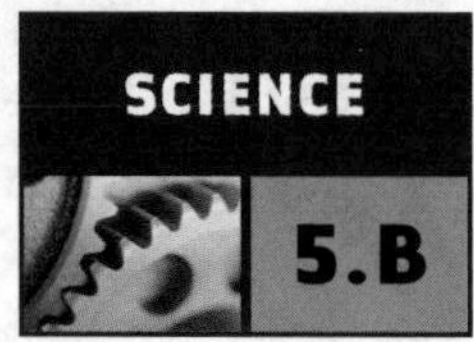


# What's Next? You Decide!

Now it's your turn to choose what to do next in the lesson. Read the activities and decide which one you want to do—you may want to try them both!

## Climb Aboard the Digestion Train

### MATERIALS

- ❑ 1 posterboard
- ❑ markers or colored pencils

### STEPS

How does your food get to where it's going? The digestive system is a fascinating part of your body.

- ❑ Investigate in a book or on the Internet to find the path that food takes once you place it in your mouth.
- ❑ Then imagine the whole thing as a train system. Draw it on posterboard as a transportation map with stations.
- ❑ Near each station, list the "attraction(s)"—the thing(s) that happen to the food there. Make sure to draw additional lines coming off the main one for food going to the bloodstream and to the urinary system.
- ❑ Share your drawing with an adult.

## Mind Your Minerals

### MATERIALS

- ❑ food magazines or supermarket circulars
- ❑ 1 pair scissors
- ❑ glue or tape
- ❑ 1–3 pieces string or 1 stapler

### STEPS

What minerals are in the foods you eat?

- ❑ Using information you learned in your research, make a list of the major minerals the body needs.
- ❑ Then look through magazines, newspaper flyers, or supermarket advertisements and cut out pictures of foods that provide each different mineral.
- ❑ Tape or glue your food pictures onto pieces of loose paper, one mineral per page.
- ❑ Write a sentence or two about each mineral and how it helps you stay healthy.
- ❑ Attach your pages together with string or staples to make a booklet.
- ❑ Share your booklet with your friends and family.

TEACHING THE LESSON

# Describing Matter

***Everything around us, from the rocks and grass under our feet, to the stars in the sky, even our own bodies, is made of matter.***

| OBJECTIVE | BACKGROUND | MATERIALS |
|---|---|---|
| To help your student understand how to classify and describe matter | Understanding the properties of matter helps us create and relate to our environment in a more beneficial way. In this lesson, your student will learn about the physical and chemical properties and states of matter, as well as how matter can be changed and measured. | ■ Student Learning Pages 6.A–6.B<br>■ 1 12-inch ruler<br>■ 1 large graduated cylinder<br>■ 1 pan balance<br>■ 1 outdoor thermometer |

**VOCABULARY**

**MATTER** anything that has mass and takes up space

**PHYSICAL PROPERTIES** properties of an object that can be observed without changing the identity of the object, such as color, size, shape, and density

**CHEMICAL PROPERTIES** characteristics of a substance that show whether it can undergo a chemical change

**BOILING POINT** the temperature at which a substance changes from a liquid to a gas

**MELTING POINT** the temperature at which a substance changes from a solid to a liquid

**HETEROGENEOUS MIXTURE** a mixture that contains two or more substances that can be identified by sight or with a microscope

**HOMOGENEOUS MIXTURE** a mixture made up of two or more substances that are evenly distributed

**COLLOID** a kind of heterogeneous mixture that does not separate once it has been mixed

# Let's Begin

## PHYSICAL AND CHEMICAL PROPERTIES

**1** **EXPLAIN** Explain to your student that **matter** is everywhere and that everything is made of matter. Matter can be described in many ways. Ask your student to describe an object in the room, such as a book, table, piece of bread, or pencil. Explain that characteristics such as color, shape, size, and density are examples of **physical properties.** Physical properties such as these can be observed without changing the object.

**2** **DISCUSS** Ask your student if he or she has ever seen medicine such as hydrogen peroxide that is sold in dark containers. Explain that the container reveals something about the **chemical properties** of the substance inside. The manufacturer uses that

**DID YOU KNOW?**

One way that matter can be described is by whether it is living or nonliving. Most matter in the universe is nonliving.

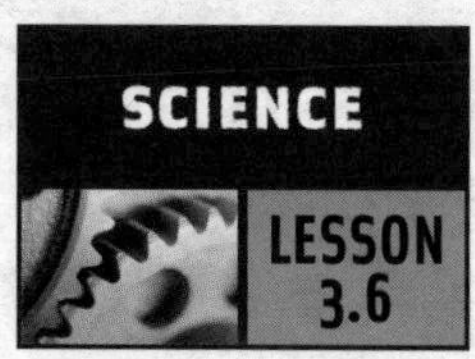


kind of container because the medicine will change if it's exposed to excess light. This is a chemical property. Your student may have also noticed information on product labels about the temperature range in which the product should be stored. This is also a chemical property. The product will change if it is stored at too high or too low of a temperature. Have your student look around your home for products and substances with light- or temperature-sensitive chemical properties. Ask him or her to list them in his or her notebook.

## PHYSICAL CHANGES AND CHEMICAL CHANGES AND REACTIONS

1 **ASK** Ask your student what happens when he or she gets a haircut. Is the hair chemically different? The hair is still made up of the same substances as before the haircut—it is simply shorter. Ask your student to think of other examples of physical changes. [painting a wall, mowing the grass in a yard, breaking a pencil]

2 **DISCUSS** Point out that a hard-boiled egg can't be changed back into a raw egg. Boiling the egg changes the chemical properties of the egg. Once the egg is cooked it can't be changed back to its original condition. Ask your student to list other chemical changes he or she has observed. [burning wood, spoiled food, rusted metal]

3 **EXPLAIN** Explain that a chemical reaction happens when a substance is broken apart and new substances are made from the pieces. A burning sparkler gives off a bright white light. This is an example of a chemical reaction. Other examples of chemical reactions include lighting a candle and the cold packs used to treat sprained ankles that are at room temperature until they are crushed. Ask your student to think of additional examples. Discuss.

## STATES OF MATTER

1 **REVEAL** Explain that matter can also be described by its state. The three common states of matter are solid, liquid, and gas. Explain that a solid has a definite shape that is difficult to change. The particles that make up a solid are closely packed together and can't move around. Then fill a glass with water, a liquid. Ask your student to pour the water into another container, such as a pitcher or bowl. Point out that because water is a liquid it takes on the shape of its container but it always takes the same amount of space. The particles in liquids attract each other and stick together. They slide past each other and move around. Next, ask your student to consider a helium balloon. Helium is a gas. Like a liquid, a gas does not have a shape of its own but takes on the shape of its container. The particles in gases are far apart and move quickly. Unlike a liquid, gases expand to fill the container. Ask your student to list examples of solids, liquids, and gases. Encourage your student to think about how these states are different.

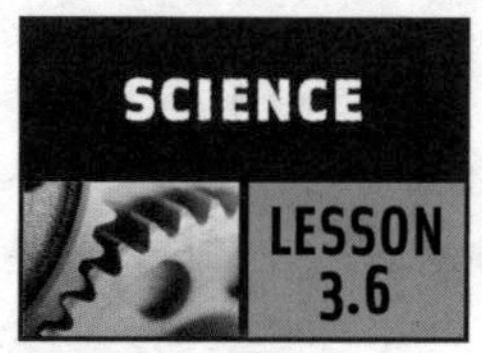


**2** **EXPLAIN** Point out that ice is frozen water, or water in a solid state. When the ice melts, it becomes water in a liquid state. If you boil water, steam results as the water changes from a liquid state to a gas state. Changes in states of matter are examples of physical changes because the identity of the substance does not change.

## BOILING POINT AND MELTING POINT

**1** **EXPLAIN** Tell your student that another way matter can be described is by its **boiling point** or **melting point.** The temperature at which a liquid changes into a gas is known as its boiling point. For example, water boils at 100°C or 212°F. The temperature at which a solid changes into a liquid is known as its melting point. The melting point of water (ice) is 0°C or 32°F.

**2** **RESEARCH** Explain that the boiling points and melting points of different substances vary. Ask your student to research the boiling and melting points of other common substances, such as oil and sugar. Have your student list them in his or her notebook. Discuss.

**DID YOU KNOW?**

Every pure substance has a constant boiling or melting point at normal air pressure. Adding other substances to a pure substance can change its boiling or melting point. For this reason, in northern climates people often add salt to icy and snowy roads. Adding salt lowers the melting point of the ice and snow. It makes the ice and snow melt much faster.

## MEASURING MATTER

**1** **DEMONSTRATE** Explain to your student that one common way scientists describe matter is by measuring it. Information about the metric system and how to measure length, mass, volume, and temperature is shown at the ThinkQuest Junior Web site at http://tqjunior.thinkquest.org/3804. Show your student how to use a ruler to measure length, a graduated cylinder to measure liquid volume, a pan balance to measure mass, and an outdoor thermometer to measure temperature.

**2** Now give your student an opportunity to practice measuring. Ask him or her to measure common objects, perhaps measuring the length of a book, the liquid volume of a glass of water, the mass of a quarter, and the temperature of the air outside. Have your student record the measurements in his or her notebook.

## MIXTURES

**1** **EXPLAIN** Explain that a **heterogeneous mixture** contains two or more substances that can be identified by sight or with the help of a microscope. A salad is an example of a heterogeneous mixture of vegetables. Explain that a **homogeneous mixture** is made up of two or more substances that are evenly distributed. Seawater is an example of a homogeneous mixture of salt and water. You can usually see through a homogenous mixture. The particles of salt can't be seen in the water even if you look with a microscope. Ask your student what kind of a mixture he or she thinks milk is. Tell him or her that milk is a mixture of water, protein, fats, and other substances. Milk is an example of a **colloid.** A colloid is a kind of heterogeneous mixture that does

**DID YOU KNOW?**

Oil and vinegar eventually separate after they're mixed. But if an emulsifier such as an egg yolk is added, the droplets of oil will float in the vinegar. Adding egg yolks produces a common emulsion called mayonnaise.

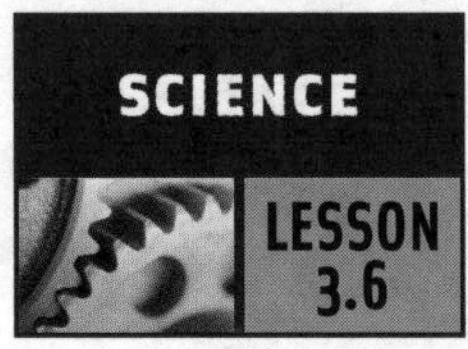

SCIENCE

LESSON 3.6

not separate once it has been mixed. Other examples of colloids are blood and gelatin. Ask your student to think of his or her own examples of these three different kinds of mixtures.

**2** **DISTRIBUTE** Distribute Student Learning Page 6.A. Instruct your student to go on a matter scavenger hunt by finding all of the examples listed.

# Branching Out

## TEACHING TIP

Many students are inherently curious about why things happen and love to try science experiments. You can find fun, hands-on science activities at the Exploratorium: Learning Studio Web site at http://www.exploratorium.edu and at the National Science Foundation: Family Activities Web site at http://www.nsf.gov.

## CHECKING IN

To assess your student's understanding of the properties of matter, ask your student to compare concepts such as the states of matter, physical and chemical properties, and physical and chemical changes. If your student struggles to explain the differences between these concepts, you can provide additional review.

**FOR FURTHER READING**

*Chemical Chaos*, by Nick Arnold and Tony De Saulles (Scholastic Paperbacks, 1998).

*Experiments with Solids, Liquids, and Gases*, by Salvatore Tocci (Scholastic Library Publishing, 2001).

*Eyewitness: Matter*, by Christopher Cooper (DK Publishing, 2000).

# Hunt for Matter

Go on a matter scavenger hunt around your house. Find these items and write what you find.

1. An object with a round shape ______________________
2. Two objects made of wood ______________________
3. A substance that can't be stored at a hot temperature ______________________
4. Two objects that have undergone physical changes ______________________
5. An object that has undergone a chemical change ______________________
6. Three solid objects ______________________
7. A gas ______________________
8. Three liquids ______________________
9. Two homogeneous mixtures ______________________
10. Two heterogeneous mixtures ______________________

# What's Next? You Decide!

Now it's your turn to choose what to do next in the lesson. Read the activities and decide which one you want to do— you may want to try them all!

## Experiment with Water

### MATERIALS

- ❑ 1 plastic container three-quarters full of hot water
- ❑ 1 plastic container three-quarters full of cold water
- ❑ 1 freezer
- ❑ 1 clock or timer

### STEPS

- ❑ Make a hypothesis, or educated guess, about whether hot water or cold water freezes faster.
- ❑ Then create an experiment to test your hypothesis. Write down what you did and saw.
- ❑ Was your hypothesis correct or incorrect?

## Learn the Science Behind Making Bread

### STEPS

- ❑ Have you ever thought about the science behind making bread? How does yeast make bread rise? Does making bread involve a chemical reaction?
- ❑ Read about making bread in reference books or on Web sites.
- ❑ Then try making your own bread!

## Is It Solid or Liquid?

### MATERIALS

- ❑ 1 cup cornstarch
- ❑ 1 bowl
- ❑ food coloring (optional)
- ❑ 1 glass water
- ❑ 1 newspaper

### STEPS

- ❑ Try this recipe for making a unique, gooey mixture. This can be very messy, so wear old clothes and spread newspaper on a table or counter to protect your work area.
- ❑ Put a cup of cornstarch in a bowl. Slowly stir small amounts of water into the cornstarch until it is thick like syrup. Add a drop or two of food coloring if you'd like.
- ❑ Now try some experiments. Squeeze the gooey mixture between two fingers. What happens? Can you shape it into a ball? What happens if you pour the mixture into another container?
- ❑ Do not eat the mixture. The substance you have created is called a non-neutonian fluid, or oobleck. Look at the library or on the Internet to learn more about this substance.

TEACHING THE LESSON

# Understanding Atoms and Elements

***Atoms, like building blocks, are the basic units that make up all of the matter in the universe.***

| OBJECTIVE | BACKGROUND | MATERIALS |
|---|---|---|
| To help your student understand the structure of matter | Understanding the structure of matter will give your student an important conceptual framework that he or she will build on as your student continues to study physical science. This lesson introduces your student to atoms, elements, molecules, compounds, and the periodic table. | ▪ Student Learning Pages 7.A–7.C<br>▪ 1 copy periodic table of elements |

**VOCABULARY**

**ATOMS** the smallest particles of an element
**PROTONS** particles in the nucleus of an atom with a positive charge
**NEUTRONS** neutral particles found in the nucleus of an atom
**ELECTRONS** negatively charged particles that move around the nucleus of an atom
**ELEMENT** a substance made up of only one kind of atom
**COMPOUNDS** substances made from atoms of two or more elements that have been chemically joined
**MOLECULE** the smallest unit of a compound; made up of combinations of atoms
**ATOMIC NUMBER** the number of protons in one atom of an element
**ATOMIC MASS** the number of protons plus the number of neutrons in one atom of an element

# Let's Begin

## ATOMS

**1** **ASK** Ask your student what he or she knows about **atoms.** Tell your student that all matter is made of microscopic particles called atoms. Atoms are so small that it would take millions of them to cover the period at the end of a sentence. Explain that much like cells are the building blocks of the tissues in our bodies, atoms are the building blocks of matter.

**2** **EXPLAIN** Tell your student that even though atoms are very small, they are composed of even smaller particles called **protons, neutrons,** and **electrons.** These particles each have

a different charge and location in the atom. Like a cell, an atom has a nucleus. The nucleus is made up of protons and neutrons. Protons have a positive charge and neutrons have a neutral charge. Because neutrons have no charge, the nucleus has a positive charge. Point out that most of the mass of an atom is in the nucleus. Electrons have a negative charge and are in constant motion, or orbit, around the nucleus. Ask, *How do you think the atom holds together if the electrons are moving all the time?* [the positive charge of the neutrons and negative charge of the electrons attract each other]

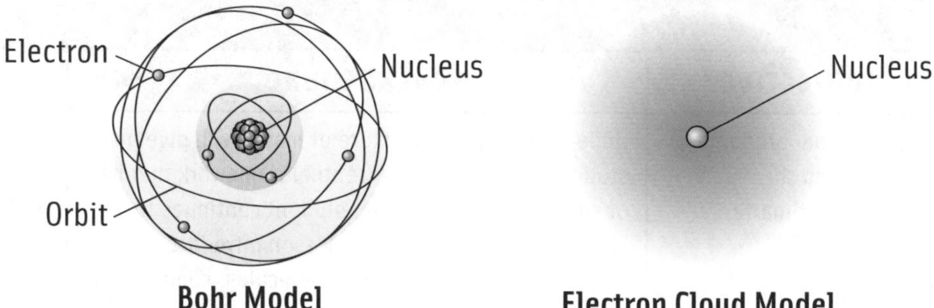


**Bohr Model** **Electron Cloud Model**

**3** **RESEARCH** Tell your student that more than two thousand years ago Greek thinkers proposed that atoms were the smallest parts of matter. Since then, many scientists have tried to create models, or form mental pictures, of what atoms might look like. Over the years, many different models have been proposed. Two of these models are the Bohr model and the electron cloud model. Instruct your student to use reference sources to research the various atomic models that have been proposed. Ask, *Which model is currently most adopted?* [electron cloud model]

## ELEMENTS

**1** **EXPLAIN** Tell your student that an **element** is a substance that is made of only one kind of atom. The copper in a penny is one example of an element. The element copper is made of pure copper atoms. Other examples of elements in pure form include neon found in some lighted signs, carbon used in a pencil point, and aluminum foil. Ask your student to name other elements.

**2** **RELATE** Explain that scientists created chemical symbols as an abbreviated way to write the name of an element. Chemical symbols consist of one capital letter or a capital letter along with one or two lowercase letters. The symbol for copper is Cu, the symbol for aluminum is Al, and the symbol for carbon is just C. Show your student a copy of the periodic table of elements and have him or her pick 10 or 12 elements and make flash cards to learn their chemical symbols. On one side of a flash card, have your student write a chemical symbol. On the other side of the flash card, have your student write the element name. Your student can also include an illustration or a key word that he or she associates with that element to help him or her remember what the element looks like or how it's used.

 

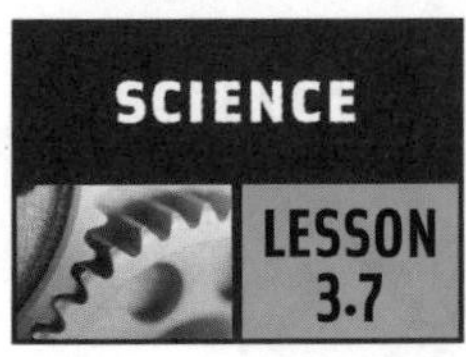


## COMPOUNDS AND MOLECULES

**1** **EXPLAIN AND RESEARCH** Tell your student that there are 118 known elements. Most things in the universe are made of combinations of elements that have been chemically joined. These combinations of elements are called **compounds.** For example, water is a compound ($H_2O$) made up of the elements hydrogen and oxygen. Compounds form during a chemical reaction. Usually the compounds formed will have different properties than the individual elements that formed them. Point out that sugar ($C_6H_{12}O_6$) is a compound made of carbon, hydrogen, and oxygen—a black solid and two gases that are neither white nor sweet. Have your student complete Student Learning Page 7.A to research other commonly found compounds.

**2** **DRAW AND DISCUSS** Explain that a **molecule** is the smallest unit of a compound. A molecule is made up of at least two atoms that join. For example, one molecule of water contains two hydrogen atoms and one oxygen atom. One molecule of sugar is made up of six carbon atoms, twelve hydrogen atoms, and six oxygen atoms. Have your student create a drawing in his or her notebook that illustrates how atoms, molecules, elements, and compounds relate to one another in size and complexity. Discuss.

## PERIODIC TABLE OF ELEMENTS

**1** **RELATE AND RESEARCH** During the late 1800s, a Russian chemist named Dmitry Mendeleyev was looking for a way to classify the elements. Mendeleyev studied the physical and chemical properties of all of the elements known at that time. Mendeleyev's organizational system is called the periodic table of elements. Ask your student to do additional research about Mendeleyev and his important contributions to chemistry. Ask, *Why did Mendeleyev's original periodic table of elements have blank spaces?* [because he predicted the existence of elements that weren't discovered yet]

**2** **REVEAL** Show your student a copy of the periodic table of elements again. Explain that each box in the table reveals information about an individual element: the atomic number, chemical symbol, name, and average atomic mass. The **atomic number** is the number of protons in one atom of an element. Point out that no two elements have the same atomic number. The **atomic mass** of an element is the average mass of the atoms of that element. It is also the number of protons plus the number of neutrons in one atom of an element. Ask, *What is the atomic mass of He?* [4] *What is its atomic number?* [2]

**3** **EXPAND** Tell your student that the periodic table of elements is arranged by groups and periods. The 18 vertical columns of the periodic table of elements are called groups. Elements in the same group have similar characteristics. Explain that the horizontal rows of the periodic table of elements are called periods. In general, the first element in a period is a solid and the

> **DID YOU KNOW?**
> After Mendeleyev predicted the existence of unknown elements, chemists who followed later discovered elements that fit the characteristics. Chemists continue to discover new elements today.

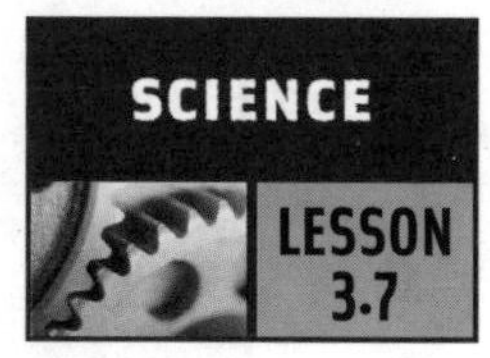

SCIENCE

LESSON 3.7

last element in a period is a gas. Atomic size decreases from left to right across a period, but atomic mass increases from left to right across a period. This means that atoms on the left side of a period are usually larger and more lightweight than the smaller and heavier atoms on the right side of a period. Ask, *Which do you think is larger based on the periodic table, an atom of argon (Ar) or an atom of sodium (Na)?* [sodium] *Which is heavier?* [argon]

## METALS AND NONMETALS

**1** **EXPLAIN** Some copies of the periodic table of elements include a line dividing the elements into metals, nonmetals, and metalloids. Some use colors to show this information. Point out to your student that most elements on the periodic table are metals. Characteristics of metals include shininess and being good conductors of heat and electricity. Point out the nonmetals on the periodic table. Characteristics of nonmetals include dullness and being poor conductors of heat and electricity. Elements called metalloids have properties of both metals and nonmetals. Have your student look at the table and find five examples of metals, nonmetals, and metalloids to write in his or her notebook.

**2** **ASK** Ask your student to consider why the periodic table of elements is helpful for scientists and how it makes learning about elements easier. Discuss.

**3** **PRACTICE** Have your student use the periodic table of elements to answer the questions on Student Learning Page 7.B.

**4** **REVIEW** To help your student review the major concepts of the lesson and remember the definitions of the vocabulary, have your student make an illustrated dictionary. Ask your student to create one page for each vocabulary word and any other important word or concept your student learned.

**FOR FURTHER READING**

*Adventures with Atoms and Molecules: Chemistry Experiments for Young People,* by Robert C. Mebane and Thomas R. Rybolt (Enslow Publishers, Inc., 1998).

*Eyewitness: Chemistry,* by Ann Newmark (DK Publishing, 2000).

*Mendeleyev's Dream: The Quest for the Elements,* by Paul Strathern (St. Martin's Press, 2001).

*What's the Matter?: The Story of Atoms and Molecules,* by Sunnie Kim, Lisa Melton, Dirk Wunderlich, ill., and Phil Ortiz, ill. (Science Kids, 2000).

# Branching Out

## TEACHING TIP

Atoms, elements, molecules, and compounds are abstract concepts that can be difficult to grasp. To help your student get a more concrete understanding of these concepts, incorporate the use of diagrams and models whenever possible in the lesson.

## CHECKING IN

To assess how well your student understands the concepts taught in this lesson, have your student teach the lesson back to you. Encourage your student to include each of the major concepts in the lesson and share as many details as possible.

# Research Compounds

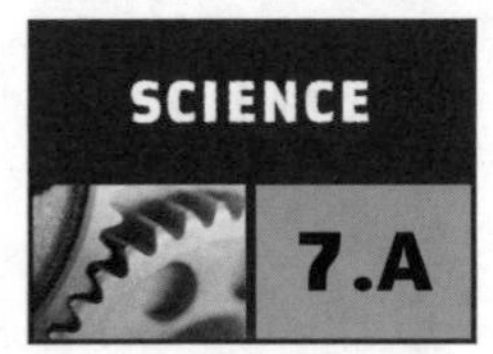


Find the chemical symbol and the molecules of these five compounds. Then choose four more compounds and complete the chart.

| | Compound | Chemical Symbol | Made of Molecules Of |
|---|---|---|---|
| 1. | Sugar | $C_6H_{12}O_6$ | carbon, hydrogen, |
| 2. | Table salt | | |
| 3. | Baking soda | | |
| 4. | Water | | |
| 5. | Hydrogen peroxide | | |
| 6. | Carbon dioxide | | |
| 7. | | | |
| 8. | | | |
| 9. | | | |
| 10. | | | |

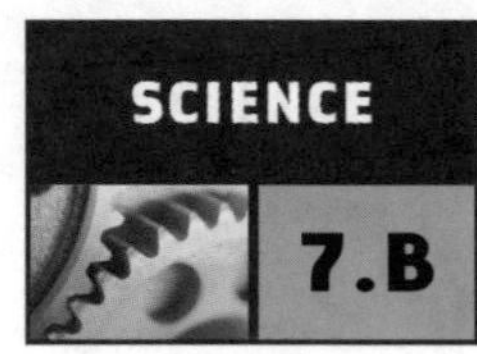


# Use the Periodic Table

Review the periodic table of elements. Then answer the questions.

1. Are more elements metals or nonmetals? ______
2. What is the chemical symbol for the element lead? ______
3. What is the atomic number for oxygen? ______
4. Are more elements artificially made or natural? ______
5. What is the atomic mass of the element calcium? ______
6. List three elements that are known to be radioactive.

______

______

______

7. List the elements that are gases at room temperature.

______

______

______

______

______

______

8. How many elements are shown in the periodic table? ______
9. List the names of the elements that have an unknown atomic mass.

______

______

______

______

10. Are more elements solid or liquid at room temperature? ______

# What's Next? You Decide!

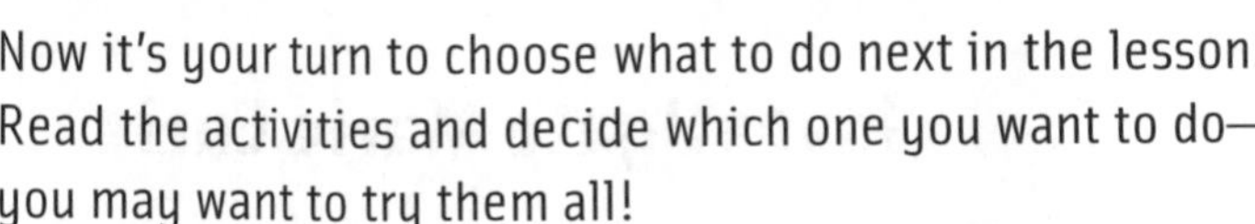

Now it's your turn to choose what to do next in the lesson. Read the activities and decide which one you want to do—you may want to try them all!

## Model an Atom

### MATERIALS

- ❑ 1 periodic table of elements
- ❑ 1 dark marker
- ❑ materials for model such as styrofoam balls, plastic balls, or golf balls
- ❑ pipe cleaners or wire
- ❑ glue

### STEPS

- ❑ Choose an element from the periodic table.
- ❑ Construct a model of an atom of that element. Be sure your model has the correct amount of protons, neutrons, and electrons.
- ❑ Draw the charge symbol (+ or –) on each with a marker.
- ❑ For help, look at the periodic table of elements in a reference book of atomic models or go to http://education.jlab.org/qa/atom_model.html.
- ❑ Share your model with an adult.

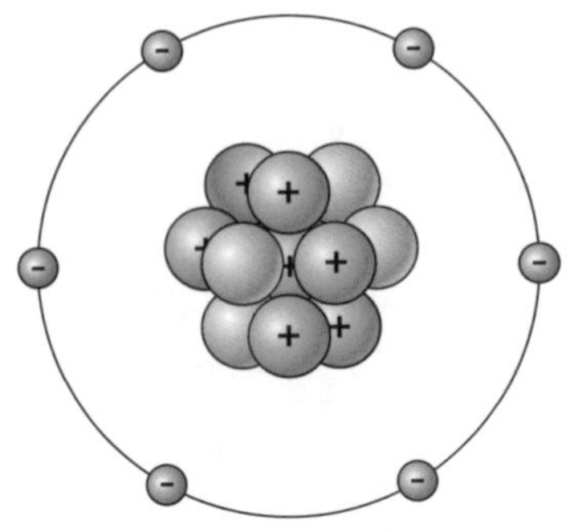

## Create a Presentation

### MATERIALS

- ❑ colored pencils, crayons, or markers
- ❑ posterboard or construction paper

### STEPS

- ❑ Research reference books or on the Internet to find out about how some atoms like to share electrons with other atoms and create bonds.
- ❑ Design a presentation for your family and teach them about atoms and bonding. Be sure to explain why atoms bond and the difference between ionic and covalent bonding.
- ❑ Create one or two drawings or pictures that will help your audience understand the presentation.
- ❑ Have your family gather around and learn about atoms. Have fun giving your presentation and encourage your audience to ask questions.

(CONTINUED) 

## Write Chemistry News

### STEPS

Use reference sources to find out more about how Dmitry Mendeleyev created the periodic table of elements.

- ❑ Write a newspaper story for a date in 1869, the year that the first periodic table of elements was published.
- ❑ Include all of the important details about Mendeleyev's important contribution to science.
- ❑ Don't forget to tell the who, what, when, where, why, and how of the story and to include a headline.
- ❑ Share the story with your family.

## Investigate Marie Curie

### STEPS

Marie Curie was a Noble Prize–winning chemist who discovered the radioactive elements polonium and radium.

- ❑ Research Curie and her accomplishments.
- ❑ Use what you find to write a biography about Curie's life and work.
- ❑ Have your biography explain how she discovered radium and polonium.
- ❑ Make an illustrated cover for the biography.
- ❑ Read the biography aloud to an adult.

TEACHING THE LESSON

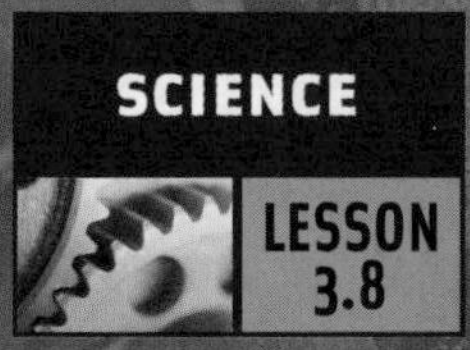


# Understanding Forms and Uses of Energy

*Everything we do, from running and playing to turning on a light, is dependent on energy.*

| OBJECTIVE | BACKGROUND | MATERIALS |
|---|---|---|
| To help your student understand the forms and uses of energy | This lesson introduces your student to the important concept of energy. Your student will learn about the forms of energy, the different ways energy is used, and the impact our use of energy has on the environment. | ■ Student Learning Pages 8.A–8.B<br>■ 1 copy Comparison Chart, page 353 |

**VOCABULARY**

**RADIANT ENERGY** energy that travels in the form of waves, such as sunlight
**THERMAL ENERGY** heat energy
**RENEWABLE** energy sources that can be used over and over again
**NONRENEWABLE** energy sources that can be used up or that take a long time to re-create themselves
**BIOMASS** a carbon-containing material that can be used as fuel
**FOSSIL FUELS** fuels formed underground over millions of years from the remains of dead plants and animals

# Let's Begin

## ENERGY

**1** **ASK** Ask your student what comes to mind when he or she hears the word *energy.* Have your student think of common expressions that include the word, such as "running out of energy" or "energy crisis." Discuss whether these expressions are accurate.

**2** **EXPLAIN** Tell your student that scientists define energy as the ability to do work. Nothing in our universe could live or move without energy. Some energy is stored energy, or potential energy. Some energy is working energy, or kinetic energy. For example, food contains chemical energy, which our bodies store until it is needed. Gasoline contains chemical energy that is stored until the key is turned in the ignition and the car starts. Ask, *What are other examples of stored energy?* [matches, cooking gas]

SCIENCE
LESSON 3.8

## FORMS AND USES OF ENERGY

**1** **EXPLAIN** Tell your student that energy comes in different forms. Most of the energy on Earth comes from the sun in the form of light. This type of energy travels in waves and is called **radiant energy.** When radiant energy from the sun reaches Earth's surface, some of it bounces back toward space and some is absorbed. Radiant energy that is absorbed becomes **thermal energy,** or heat energy. Using reference materials such as Earth-science books, have your student look up radiant energy and draw a diagram showing how this form of energy reaches Earth.

**2** **RESEARCH** Point out that other forms of energy include mechanical energy, electrical energy, chemical energy, and nuclear energy. Have your student make a copy of the Comparison Chart from page 353. Then have him or her research these different forms of energy and find their similarities and differences.

**3** **EXPLORE** Explain that we use energy in our daily lives. Ask, *How do you use energy throughout the day?* [possible answers: indoor light from electricity, refrigeration from electricity, electricity or gas to heat water or cook] Point out that all of this energy must have a source. Explain that some energy sources are **renewable** while others are **nonrenewable.**

## RENEWABLE RESOURCES

**1** **ASK** Ask, *What do you think renewable means?* Explain that renewable resources can be used over and over again. Renewable resources include solar energy, wind energy, hydroelectric energy, and geothermal energy. These resources are also called alternative resources because they're an alternative to the nonrenewable resources we use most.

*Wind farms generate energy for electricity.*

SCIENCE LESSON 3.8

**2** **RESEARCH AND COMPLETE** Ask your student to find out how each alternative energy source mentioned above works, as well as the pros and cons of using them. Then have your student use what he or she learns to complete the chart about renewable, alternative energy sources on Student Learning Page 8.A.

**3** **EXPLAIN** Explain that **biomass** is a renewable resource made from plant materials such as trees, grasses, and other crops. Ask your student to find out how this energy source is produced and used. Have your student research the latest experiments and outcomes in using biomass as an energy source. Have your student write a brief paragraph about what he or she learns. Discuss.

## NONRENEWABLE RESOURCES

**1** **DISCUSS** Explain that nonrenewable resources are energy sources that can be used up or can't be re-created in a short amount of time. Examples of nonrenewable resources include oil, natural gas, coal, and the element uranium used in nuclear power plants. Ask, *What is a problem with using nonrenewable energy sources?* [they are limited and can eventually run out; they also can create pollution]

**2** **EXPLAIN** Tell your student that oil, natural gas, and coal are called **fossil fuels.** These were formed over millions of years from heat and pressure on the remains of dead plants and animals. We get most of our energy from fossil fuels. Point out that gasoline is made from oil and that much of our electricity is produced using coal. Have your student research the details about how we use oil, natural gas, and coal on the Internet, with the U.S. Department of Energy, or using an almanac. Ask him or her to find out how much of each fuel source we use each year as a country and where it comes from.

**3** **RESEARCH** Have your student look for current articles about oil drilling in the United States. Ask your student to find articles that include different opinions on offshore oil drilling and proposals to drill in wildlife refuges. Ask, *Why do you think it can be difficult for nations to balance economic needs with environmental needs?* Talk about this with your student.

**4** **EXPLORE** Explain that nuclear energy is another popular energy source in the world. Have your student explore several reference books on nuclear power to find out how nuclear reactors work and what happens to nuclear waste. Your student also can contact the electric company to find out what percentage of your state's electrical energy comes from nuclear reactors. Ask your student to tell you about the pros and cons of using this energy source.

Nine out of every 10 tons of coal in the United States are used to generate electricity.

**5** **EXPLAIN** Tell your student that most power plants in the United States are powered by furnaces where coal or oil is burned.

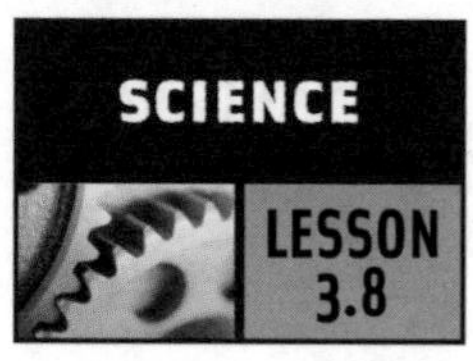

SCIENCE

LESSON 3.8

Electricity is produced when a furnace heats water, which produces steam. Have your student find the closest power plant to your town. Then help your student find what towns get energy from the power plant. See if you and your student can take a tour of the plant.

**6** **DISCUSS** Discuss with your student how power plants control pollution. Have your student research the changes that have taken place at power plants to lower the pollution produced from the plants.

## CONSERVATION OF ENERGY

**1** **DISCUSS** Discuss with your student what would happen if the United States were to run out of fossil fuels. Ask your student to give reasons that nonrenewable resources should be conserved and brainstorm ways to conserve fossil fuels. Remind your student that the electricity in our homes and businesses usually comes from power plants that use fossil fuels to produce electricity. Ask, *How can we conserve electric energy at home?* [turn off computers, televisions, and lights when leaving a room]

**2** **DISCUSS** Explain that conserving energy at home also helps reduce the costs of the electricity, water, and gas we use. Have your student use your family's electric bill to track electricity use in your home. Ask your student how the bill changes each month.

**3** **DESIGN** Have your student create a colorful and eye-catching poster illustrating and explaining his or her ideas about saving energy. Encourage your student to share his or her ideas with other family members and friends.

**DID YOU KNOW?**

An electric lightbulb converts less than 10 percent of the energy it uses into light. The rest of the energy is converted into heat.

**FOR FURTHER READING**

*Eyewitness: Energy,* by Jack Ahalloner and Clive Streeter (DK Publishing, 2000).

*From Oil to Gas (Start to Finish),* by Shannon Zemlicka (Lerner Publications Company, 2002).

*How to Split the Atom,* by Hazel Richardson and Scoular Anderson (Franklin Watts, 2001).

*Solar Power (Energy Forever Series),* by Ian S. Graham (Raintree/Steck Vaughn, 1999).

# Branching Out

## TEACHING TIP

Talking about how you and your family use energy in your home, such as turning on lights or keeping foods cold in the refrigerator, can make this sometimes difficult concept easier to understand.

## CHECKING IN

At the end of the lesson, ask your student to explain some of the concepts to you in his or her own words. If your student struggles to answer the questions or to explain his or her ideas, additional review may be necessary. Find out what part of the lesson your student is most excited about and relate your review to that topic.

# Understand Alternative Energy Sources

Complete the chart using what you've learned from your research about alternative energy sources.

| Alternative Energy Source | How It Works | Advantages | Disadvantages |
|---|---|---|---|
| **Solar energy** | 1. | 2. | 3. |
| **Wind energy** | 4. | 5. | 6. |
| **Hydroelectric energy** | 7. | 8. | 9. |
| **Geothermal energy** | 10. | 11. | 12. |

# What's Next? You Decide!

Now it's your turn to choose what to do next in the lesson. Read the activities and decide which one you want to do—you may want to try them both!

## Investigate Fossil Fuels

**MATERIALS**

- ❑ posterboard
- ❑ crayons or markers
- ❑ 2–4 old magazines

**STEPS**

- ❑ Choose one of the fossil fuels to research: coal, oil, or natural gas.
- ❑ Find out how the fuel forms and how it's processed and used.
- ❑ Find out how long supplies of the fuel are expected to last and identify advantages and disadvantages of using the fuel.
- ❑ Create a poster showing what you learned. Include magazine photos, pictures, or graphs in your poster.

## Experiment with Insulation

**MATERIALS**

- ❑ 3 small milk cartons
- ❑ plastic wrap, aluminum foil, or newspapers
- ❑ hot water
- ❑ 3–6 large rubber bands
- ❑ 3 thermometers
- ❑ 1 clock
- ❑ paper and pencil

**STEPS**

Insulation is used in homes to make them more energy efficient. It helps homes hold heat in winter and stay cool in summer. Try this experiment to compare how different insulation materials keep things warm.

- ❑ Fill three small milk cartons almost to the top with hot water from the tap. Be careful with the hot water.
- ❑ Choose two different insulation materials to test. Plastic wrap, aluminum foil, and newspaper are good examples.
- ❑ Wrap one kind of insulation around the milk carton. Leave space to insert a thermometer in the milk carton opening. Secure the insulation with rubber bands.
- ❑ Do the same with the second insulation material.
- ❑ Do not wrap any insulation material around the third milk carton.
- ❑ Insert a thermometer inside each milk carton. Use the rubber bands to make sure that the thermometer does not touch the bottom or sides of the milk carton. Try to keep the thermometers at the same height.
- ❑ Measure and record the temperature in each milk carton. Repeat every 10 minutes for an hour.

TEACHING THE LESSON

# Exploring Earth's Atmosphere and Weather

***There's a saying, "Everybody complains about the weather, but nobody does anything about it." You may not be able to change the weather, but at least you can understand it.***

| OBJECTIVE | BACKGROUND | MATERIALS |
|---|---|---|
| To help your student learn about Earth's atmosphere and the factors that cause changes in the weather | Earth is unique among the planets in the solar system with its life-supporting atmosphere and varied weather and climates. In this lesson, your student will learn details about Earth's atmosphere and weather, gaining an understanding of what he or she encounters daily. | ▪ Student Learning Pages 9.A–9.B<br>▪ 1 documentary film about severe storms in your area<br>▪ 1 fictional film about the same type of storm |

**VOCABULARY**

**ATMOSPHERE** the mixture of gases that surrounds Earth; the air

**OZONE LAYER** an area of the stratosphere that has a large amount of ozone, which helps protect us against harmful rays from the sun

**WEATHER** the state of the atmosphere (clear or cloudy, hot or cold, dry or wet, calm or stormy) at any given time

**AIR MASS** a large body of air that has the properties (warm, cool, dry, wet) of the area of Earth over which it develops

**FRONT** the border where two air masses meet

**CLIMATE** the weather patterns of a place over a long period of time

## Let's Begin

**1** **EXPLAIN AND DISCUSS** Have your student look at the chart below. Explain that we need oxygen to breathe, yet it makes up only about one-fifth of all the gas in the atmosphere. Explain that pollution from car exhausts and factories causes smog. Ask, *Why would smog make it harder to breathe?* [it disturbs the natural atmosphere, adding chemicals that shouldn't be there] Discuss what people can do to reduce smog.

**DID YOU KNOW?**

The atmosphere contains solids and liquids, too. The solids are dust, ice, and salt. Dust comes from the ground, ice is in the form of hail and snow, and salt is from ocean spray. Water is also in liquid form in clouds.

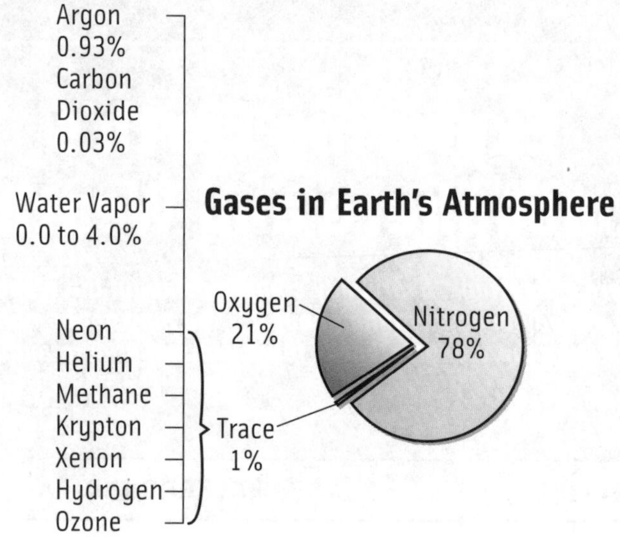


**2** **RELATE AND RESEARCH** Tell your student that Earth's **atmosphere** has five distinct layers: troposphere, stratosphere, mesosphere, thermosphere, and exosphere. Explain that an easy way to remember them is by understanding the meanings of their root words. *Tropo* means "change." It's the part of the atmosphere where weather changes take place. Remind your student about the tropism experiment about plant changes from Lesson 3.3. *Strato* means "layer." It's where the **ozone layer** is. *Meso* means "middle." *Thermo* means "heat." Temperatures increase as you go higher in the thermosphere. *Exo* means "outer." Have your student research the layers of the atmosphere and ask him or her to tell what natural and human activities go on in the various layers. [troposphere: weather, clouds, smog, plant and human life; stratosphere: ozone layer, jet stream, weather balloons; mesosphere: radio waves interact with ionosphere; thermosphere: auroras, meteor trails; exosphere: satellites/space shuttle orbits]

**3** **DESCRIBE** Tell your student that the sun is the source of all energy in Earth's atmosphere. When Earth receives energy from the sun, the atmosphere absorbs some of it, the land and water absorb some of it, and some of it bounces back into space. Ask, *What are some other things that the sun does?* [provides energy for plant photosynthesis, maintains Earth's atmosphere at a livable temperature]

**4** **EXPLAIN AND ASK** Explain that gravity causes the gases in the atmosphere to be pulled toward Earth. The closer to Earth's surface, the more the air molecules are compacted and the higher the air pressure. The higher you go up, the less the air molecules are compacted and the lower the air pressure. Ask, *Why do some people have trouble breathing in the mountains?* [the air pressure is lower; people take in less oxygen]

**5** **EXPLORE AND RESEARCH** Have your student investigate the four main measurements of air: temperature, humidity, pressure, and wind. Local newspapers are good sources for air measurements.

Then have him or her use the Internet or a reference book to research the instruments and scales that are used in these measurements. Suggest that your student make a chart showing the measurements. Also have him or her keep a list of adjectives that describe **weather**—for example, *hot, cold, gusty, foggy,* and *humid.*

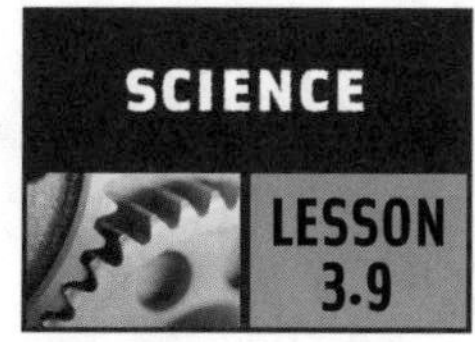


**6** **EXPLORE AND WRITE** Explain to your student that the sun heats Earth and its atmosphere unevenly. Look together at the drawing of Earth. Then ask, *Why is this so?* [Earth's surface is curved and its axis is tilted, so the sun's rays hit it at different angles; at the poles, the rays hit at a low angle and spread out] Discuss.

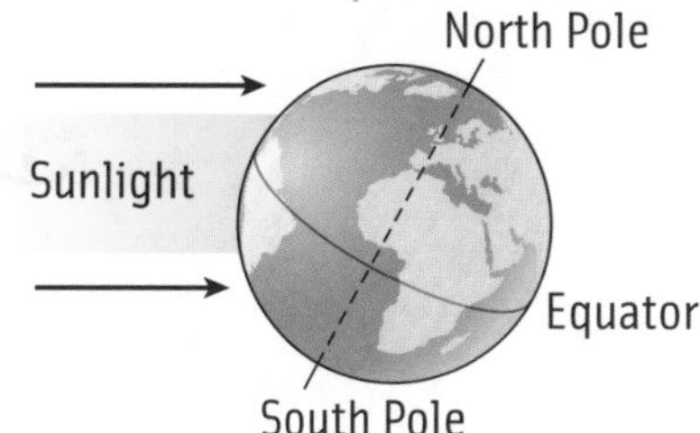


**7** **DISTRIBUTE** Distribute Student Learning Page 9.A. Have your student complete the exercise.

**8** **RESEARCH AND PREDICT** Ask, *How do you think you can predict the weather?* Your student may already know something about weather prediction, in which case you can discuss it. If not, tell him or her that you can't just look out the window, because weather keeps changing. Have your student look at a weather map in your local newspaper. Then have him or her use the key to interpret the map.

**9** **EXPLORE** Mention that an **air mass** can move; it's not stationary. When two air masses meet, the border where they meet is called a **front.** When a cold air mass comes upon a warm air mass, that's called a cold front. When a warm air mass moves in on a cold air mass, it's called a warm front. Have your student look at the weather map again and take note of the fronts. Then discuss.

**10** **OBSERVE** Have your student look at the clouds below. Have him or her research what each type of cloud suggests about the approaching weather.

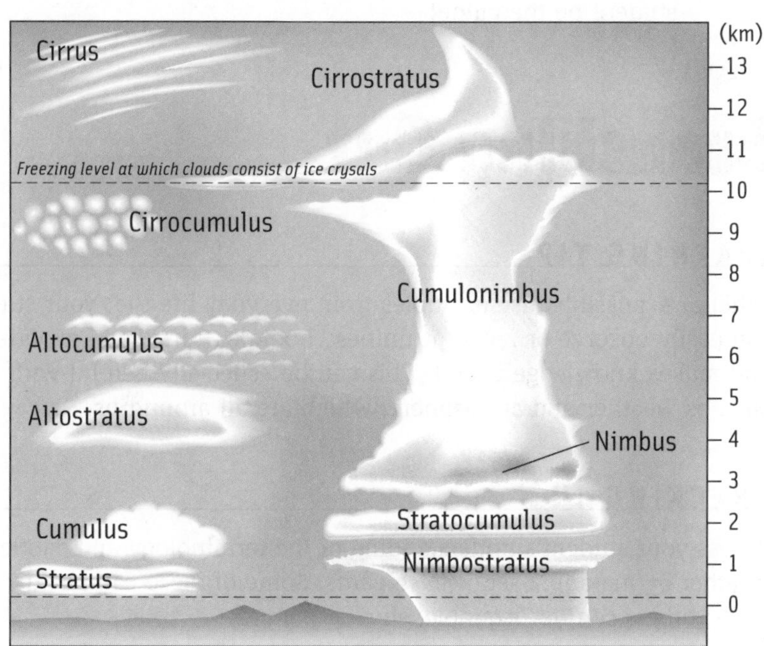

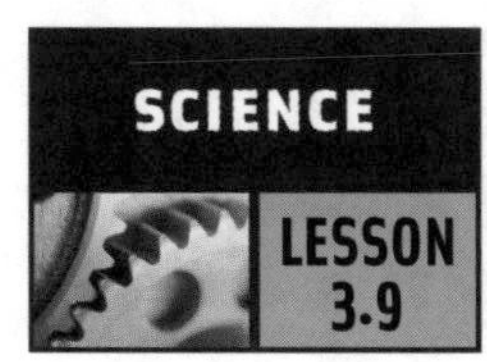

Have him or her decide if the cloud signs match the forecast from the newspaper in Step 8. Then ask your student to make a final prediction about tomorrow's weather. Have him or her review it the next day for accuracy. Ask, *Were there any surprises? What happened?* Discuss. You can have your student repeat these weather-predicting activities for as long as he or she is interested. Suggest keeping a weather log of predictions versus the actual weather.

11 **DISCUSS AND RESEARCH** Discuss with your student the kinds of severe weather you get where you live (tornadoes, hurricanes, thunderstorms, blizzards, and so on). Have him or her research the causes of the storm. Discuss why your area gets that kind of storm. Watch both a documentary and a fictional film made about one kind of severe weather. Discuss how realistic the fictional film was compared to the documentary. Talk about safety measures to take before and during different kinds of storms.

12 **EXPLAIN** Explain that wind can affect the weather, too. Reveal that besides the major wind patterns, there are smaller ones as well. Landforms such as mountains and valleys interfere with the flow of winds, especially westerlies. Seashores affect winds. Land heats up and cools off more quickly than water. This creates sea breezes that blow onshore during the day and land breezes that blow offshore at night.

13 **EXPLORE AND MODEL** Review the difference between weather and **climate.** Have your student study a world climate map and develop an understanding of the several kinds of climates. Have him or her locate where you are on the climate map. Ask, *What are the features of our climate?* Have your student write in his or her notebook. Then have him or her make a poster that shows when and how each feature appears during the course of a year where you live. The poster can take a variety of forms—let your student be the guide!

**FOR FURTHER READING**

*The Atlas of Natural Disasters,* by Jeff Groman (Friedman/Fairfax Publishing, 2002).

*Blizzard: The Storm That Changed America,* by Jim Murphy (Scholastic Trade, 2000).

*Clouds (Watts Library: Earth Science),* by Trudi Strain Trueit (Franklin Watts, 2002).

*Complete Weather Resource,* by Phillis Engelbreit (U*X*L, 1998).

*DK Guide to Weather,* by Michael Allaby (DK Publishing, 2000).

*El Niño: Stormy Weather for People and Wildlife,* by Caroline Arnold (Clarion, 1998).

*Eyewitness: Hurricane and Tornado,* by Jack Challoner (DK Publishing, 2000).

# Branching Out

## TEACHING TIP

Whenever possible, use examples from everyday life that your student can easily observe or recall. It unifies "book learning" and experience and makes knowledge useful. This can be especially helpful with topics such as weather and atmosphere, which are all around us.

## CHECKING IN

Assess your student's understanding of the terminology and subtleties of weather by making a set of flash cards. Some of these can be "definition" cards; others can, for example, show a picture.

 

# Understand Global Warming

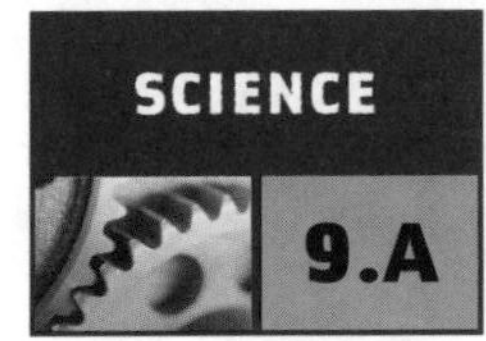


**PART A** Some scientists have predicted changes to Earth because of the thinning ozone layer. Changes include a rise in world temperatures, glaciers melting, and more. The changes have led to what some call global warming. Research possible causes and effects of global warming and then come up with solutions. Complete the chart with your findings.

**Global Warming**

| Causes | Effects | Solutions |
|---|---|---|
| | | |
| | | |
| | | |
| | | |

**PART B** Now write a letter to the editor of your local newspaper telling about the things your community can do to slow down global warming. Ask an adult to help you find the name and address of where to send your letter.

# What's Next? You Decide!

Now it's your turn to choose what to do next in the lesson. Read the activities and decide which one you want to do—you may want to try them both!

## Design a Brochure of Your Climate's Twin

### MATERIALS

- ❑ 1 copy Web, page 354
- ❑ 1 world climate map
- ❑ markers or colored pencils
- ❑ construction paper
- ❑ 2–5 travel sections of newspapers or magazines
- ❑ 1 pair scissors
- ❑ glue

### STEPS

What other places on Earth have climates similar to yours?

- ❑ Make a copy of the Web from page 354 and write the name of your town in the center circle. On the outer circles write words that describe your area's climate, such as *hot and dry.*
- ❑ Review what you wrote and find another climate similar to yours.
- ❑ Now find out the similarities—and the differences. For example, if the place you've chosen is in the Southern Hemisphere, the seasons will be at opposite times of the year.
- ❑ Design a travel brochure for your climate's twin.
- ❑ Locate pictures of the place you have chosen, and read about how the climate affects the people's lifestyles there.
- ❑ Cut out or draw pictures and maps. Highlight what you can do in different kinds of weather.
- ❑ As a challenge, see if you know someone from that climate and show him or her your brochure. Is it accurate?

## Broadcast Extreme Weather

### MATERIALS

- ❑ 1–3 posterboards
- ❑ markers

### STEPS

Do you know the coldest day in your town or state? What about the hottest?

- ❑ Work with an adult and contact a local newspaper's weather department. (Or perhaps check out your newspaper's Web site if it has one.)
- ❑ Find out the highest and lowest temperatures, the most rain and/or snow, the longest number of days of rain or snow in a row, the longest number of days in a row with and without sun, or whatever else you want!
- ❑ Then suppose all of those things happen in one day and give a funny weather broadcast to your family explaining what happened in the weather that day.
- ❑ Get creative and make colorful pictures or charts!

# Examining Water on Earth

***Earth has seawater to thank for its nickname, the Blue Planet.***

| OBJECTIVE | BACKGROUND | MATERIALS |
|---|---|---|
| To help your student learn about water and its importance on Earth's surface and in the atmosphere | Water is essential for life. In this lesson, your student will learn about the water cycle—the neverending process of water entering and leaving Earth's atmosphere. Most of the water on Earth lies in the 70 percent of its surface that is ocean. This vast saltwater expanse is largely unexplored, but in the future we may learn and use much more information about it. This lesson will primarily investigate the physical features and properties of the ocean. | ■ Student Learning Pages 10.A–10.B<br>■ water |

**VOCABULARY**

**GROUNDWATER** water absorbed by the ground, which supplies springs and wells and also seeps into oceans
**SEAWATER** saltwater in oceans and seas
**SATURATED** (of air) containing as much water as it can hold at a given temperature
**BREAKER** a wave that breaks, or collapses, along the shore
**TIDAL RANGE** the difference between the water level of a sea or an ocean at high and low tide
**OCEANOGRAPHY** the study of oceans, their plant and animal life, and their processes

## Let's Begin

**1** **EXPLAIN** Tell your student that oceans contain saltwater, which humans can't drink. Explain that oceans contain about 3.5 percent salts by volume. The most common salts are those containing sodium and chlorine, which we use in table salt. Scientists believe that oceans formed when water vapor from the first erupting volcanoes cooled enough to form storm clouds. The water in them fell as rain. It filled low places on Earth, called basins. Volcanoes—as well as **groundwater** and rivers—also add salts to ocean water. Have your student research the theory on how the oceans formed on the Internet or at the library.

**DID YOU KNOW?**

Other elements besides sodium and chlorine in **seawater** include magnesium, sulfur, calcium, and potassium.

**2** **EXPLAIN** Explain that every living thing needs water. Ninety-seven percent of the water on Earth is saltwater. Most living things can't use saltwater. Two-thirds of the Earth's freshwater is frozen at the North and South Poles. Only one percent of our total water is usable as it is. We find this usable water in lakes,

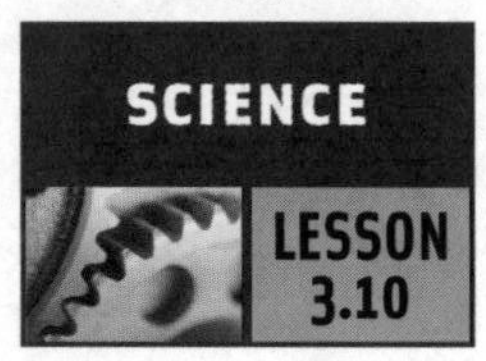


rivers, ponds, puddles, and below the ground. Water cycles through the atmosphere. By the process of evaporation, water on the surface becomes water vapor in the air. As it cools, it undergoes condensation, the formation of water droplets and clouds. When the clouds get heavy enough, the droplets in them fall back to Earth. This is called precipitation. Ask, *How does water get recycled through the atmosphere?* [through evaporation, condensation, and precipitation]

**DID YOU KNOW?**

What we usually think is steam coming out of a kettle is actually not. Real steam—at a temperature of 100°C—is invisible. What we see is water vapor that has already begun to cool.

**3** **MODEL** You and your student can make a model of the water cycle. Point out that since you will not be dependent on the sun to help water evaporate and droplets form clouds, your model will move a lot faster than the real water cycle. First, have your student put a large metal spoon in the freezer until it is ice cold. Fill a teakettle partway with water and place it on the stove to boil (evaporation). When the steam (water vapor) begins rising from the kettle, get the spoon and hold it above the spout. The cold spoon will make the steam condense and form water droplets. It will then begin to "rain" on the floor. Mop up your homemade rain with a rag or paper towel.

**4** **DISCUSS AND OBSERVE** Ask, *Why did the water condense when it hit the spoon?* [the air around the spoon was cooler, so it couldn't hold as much water vapor as the warmer air] Discuss this concept. Water vapor enters the air and fits between air molecules. At cooler temperatures, air and water-vapor molecules move more slowly. The water-vapor molecules can join together—that is, condense. Warmer air can hold more water vapor because the molecules move more quickly and don't join together.

**DID YOU KNOW?**

Depending on the temperature, water vapor evaporating into air that is already **saturated** will either turn back into water or will freeze into ice.

**5** **DEFINE AND OBSERVE** Tell your student that relative humidity is the measure of the amount of moisture in the air compared to the maximum amount it can contain *at a particular temperature.* The temperature at which the air can't hold any more moisture and water vapor condenses is called the dew point. Have your student fill a glass with ice water and watch what happens to the outside of the glass. Also have him or her observe the grass early in the morning. Ask, *What do you see? Why does it happen?* [condensation forms because the cold surface makes water vapor close to it turn back to liquid; on the grass it's called dew] Have your student look in the newspaper or on a Web site to find out the relative humidity and dew point in your area today.

**6** **COMPARE AND CONTRAST** Remind your student that air is always moving and that areas of the atmosphere differ in temperature. The uneven heating of air by the sun creates wind. In a similar way, the water in the ocean is always moving. That movement, or flow of ocean water, is called a current. It is like a river within the ocean. Just as warm air rises, warmer water—which is less dense than colder water—is closer to the ocean surface. There are different kinds of ocean currents. Have your student research three different types of ocean currents—surface currents, density currents, and upwelling—and write a sentence or two about each one in his or her notebook.

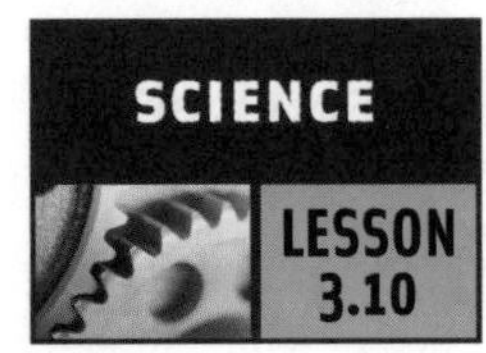


7 **DESCRIBE AND MODEL** Just as light and sound waves go through air, waves carry energy through water. Show your student the model of a wave below.

Explain that only the energy in an ocean wave moves forward, not the actual water. Have your student fill a bathtub or a large basin, place something that floats in the water, and use his or her hands to make a wave. Point out that after the wave calms down, just as the object is in the same place, the water is in the same place as it was before the wave. Particles of water move in a circle as the energy moves through them. The exception is a **breaker.** Have your student research breakers in a book or on a Web site. Ask, *What sport depends on breakers? Why? What happens to the water after a wave "breaks" on shore?* [surfing; in a breaker, the top of the wave moves faster than the bottom, helping the surfer ride to shore; gravity pulls the water back into the ocean]

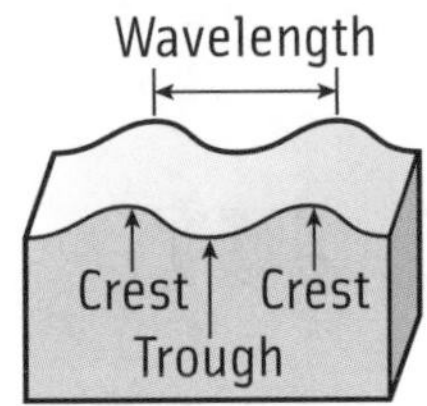


8 **EXPLAIN AND MODEL** Explain to your student that wind makes waves on the surface of a body of water by causing friction that moves the water along with it. There is another kind of giant wave, however, that is not caused by wind but by the effect of the gravity of the moon on Earth. This is called a tide. The tide is actually the crest of a long, long wave. To give your student an idea of how tides work, have him or her do the following: place a paper clip under a piece of paper. Then place another paper clip on top of the paper. Hold a magnet above the top clip. Ask, *What happens?* [the magnet should attract both paper clips] Although Earth is not flat like a piece of paper, this model is similar to what happens with the tide. The moon's gravity affects the water directly under the moon and the water on the opposite side of Earth *at the same time.* This causes a high tide on the side of Earth directly under the moon. Moreover, the moon's gravity also affects Earth, pulling it closer to the moon. This causes a bulge between Earth and the water on its side opposite from the moon, causing a high tide on the far side of Earth as well.

9 **RESEARCH** A high-and-low-tide cycle takes 12 hours and 25 minutes. So in a little more than a day there are two high and two low tides. Due to the size and shape of bays, gulfs, and other inlets of the ocean, however, some places have only one high and one low tide a day. Have your student research the **tidal range** in various places on Earth. Where is it the greatest?

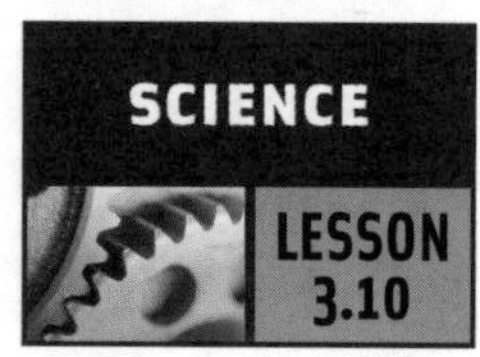


Where is it the least? Do you live along or near a coast? What is your tide cycle? What is your tidal range? Have your student write a brief paragraph answering these questions.

**10** **RESEARCH AND WRITE** Have your student find a map of the ocean floor in a book or on the Internet and study it. Have him or her write about the characteristics of the following landforms: continental shelf, continental slope, abyssal plain, midocean range, and trench. Ask your student to explain how the depth of each area of the ocean affects life there.

**11** **DISCUSS AND EXPLORE** Discuss with your student that the ocean is important to the world economy. People get oil and natural gas from under the continental shelf. They mine sand, metal, and diamonds from deposits left by rivers. In the future, mining might also take place in deepwater areas. Invite your student to imagine what this would be like. Have him or her research the obstacles to and requirements for sending people to the ocean's depths. Suggest that he or she use this information to write a fictional story about such an expedition.

**DID YOU KNOW?**

The tallest mountain on Earth (Mt. Everest) could sit in the deepest spot in the ocean (the Marianas Trench in the Pacific Ocean) and be covered by more than 6,000 feet of water.

# Branching Out

## TEACHING TIP

When studying a topic such as **oceanography,** which for the most part can't be investigated up close, it's helpful to use pictures or create models for important concepts and ideas.

## CHECKING IN

You can assess your student's understanding of concepts such as waves and tides by having him or her explain them in his or her own words, either orally or in short written statements. This shows a more thorough knowledge than being able to recognize facts in multiple-choice questions.

**FOR FURTHER READING**

*Eyewitness: Ocean,* by Miranda MacQuitty (DK Publishing, 2000).

*The Handy Ocean Answer Book,* by Thomas E. Svarney and Patricia Barnes-Svarney (Visible Ink Press, 1999).

*Oceans (Make It Work! Geography Series),* by Andrew Haslam and Barbara Taylor (Two-Can Publishing, 2000).

*What Makes an Ocean Wave? Questions and Answers About Oceans and Ocean Life,* by Melvin and Gilda Berger (Scholastic, Inc., 2001).

# Perform Experiments with Saltwater

Use this experiment to test the effects of temperature on evaporation.

## MATERIALS

- ❑ 4 microwave-safe bowls
- ❑ 4–6 cups water
- ❑ 12 tablespoons table salt
- ❑ 4 pieces masking tape

## STEPS

1. Fill each bowl with water.
2. Add three tablespoons of salt to each.
3. Number the bowls 1 through 4 with masking tape.
4. Place bowl No. 1 on a radiator or a sunny windowsill.
5. Place bowl No. 2 in a shady spot in the house.
6. Place bowl No. 3 in the refrigerator.
7. Place bowl No. 4 in the microwave, or empty its contents into a small pot and place over a low flame on the stove. (Get permission from an adult or ask for help.)
8. List the numbers of the bowls in order from the one you expect to evaporate first to the one you expect to evaporate last. Give your reasons.

   First: ______________________________

   Second: ______________________________

   Third: ______________________________

   Fourth: ______________________________

9. Are any of these evaporation methods a good way to remove salt from saltwater?

   Why or why not? ______________________________

   If not, try to think of a system that will remove the salt and leave desalted water and write your idea on the lines below. Would your system work for ocean water?

   Explain. ______________________________

   ______________________________

   ______________________________

# What's Next? You Decide!

Now it's your turn to choose what to do next in the lesson. Read the activities and decide which one you want to do—you may want to try them both!

## Check Out "Current" Events

### MATERIALS

- ❑ 1 map of the Atlantic Ocean showing the Gulf Stream
- ❑ 1 list of average high and low temperatures for January in European cities

### STEPS

- ❑ The Gulf Stream is a warm-ocean current that flows through the Atlantic Ocean. Research the Gulf Stream and find its path on a map of the Atlantic Ocean.
- ❑ Then use an almanac or the Internet (try http://www.accuweather.com) to find the average high and low temperatures of 6 to 10 cities in Europe, some near the Atlantic coast and some inland, but none along the Mediterranean Sea. You might include London, England; Paris, France; and Moscow, Russia.
- ❑ Make a list of cities and temperatures. How do they compare?
- ❑ If you like, research North American cities and compare the temperatures of cities along the Pacific coast with inland cities.

## Feel Tide Power!

### MATERIALS

- ❑ 1 sheet blank paper
- ❑ pencil, colored pencils, or markers

### STEPS

The energy from the ocean tide is strong enough in some places that it can be harnessed to produce electricity!

- ❑ Imagine a bay with a very high tidal range. At high tide, water washes against piers. Low tide exposes mudflats where many shore birds feed on sea creatures. When a dam is built at the entrance to the bay, water from high tide can be kept in the bay much longer. As the dam lets out the water, its flow can power machines that make electricity.
- ❑ Draw a picture of how you imagine a dam like this would look.
- ❑ Then, on a separate sheet of paper, write down reasons why you think it might be a good idea and why you think it might be a bad idea to build such a dam.

TEACHING THE LESSON

# Understanding Earth's Changing Surface

*If we take care of Earth and its resources, Earth will take care of us.*

| OBJECTIVE | BACKGROUND | MATERIALS |
| --- | --- | --- |
| To help your student learn about the surface of Earth, its resources, and the changes it undergoes over time | Mountains, glaciers, volcanoes, earthquakes . . . all are brought about by change on and deep within Earth's surface. Knowledge of what causes these events, together with an understanding of natural resources, will help give your student an appreciation of our fragile existence here on Earth. | ■ Student Learning Pages 11.A–11.B<br>■ 1 apple<br>■ 1 ice cube<br>■ 1 small ceramic or glass plate |

**VOCABULARY**

**CRUST** the outer layer of Earth
**CORE** the layer of Earth below the mantle that's made up of metal; the center of Earth
**MANTLE** the layer of Earth below the crust that's made up of hot, melted rock
**LITHOSPHERE** the layer of rock that includes the crust and part of the mantle
**PLATE TECTONICS** the theory that states that Earth's surface is made up of plates that are in constant motion
**EARTHQUAKES** sudden motions along breaks in Earth's crust
**VOLCANOES** openings in Earth's crust through which hot, melted rock goes out
**MAGMA** molten rock below Earth's surface
**LANDSLIDES** occasions when the ground moves down a slope or hill quickly
**GLACIERS** huge sheets of ice that move slowly
**NATURAL RESOURCE** a material or energy supplied by nature

## Let's Begin

**1** **ASK AND EXPLAIN** Ask your student, *Do you know what* terra firma *means?* [solid ground] Explain that this expression has long been used by travelers returning to land after an ocean voyage or a flight. Reveal that Earth isn't terra firma. Share that, in fact, even part of it that *is* solid is actually moving. Explain that this will become clear to your student as you study Earth's structure. Take an apple from the kitchen. Explain that Earth is made of layers. The outer layer, called the **crust,** which we live on, is about as thin relative to the rest of Earth as is the skin to the rest of the apple. Ask your student what he or she knows about the layers of Earth.

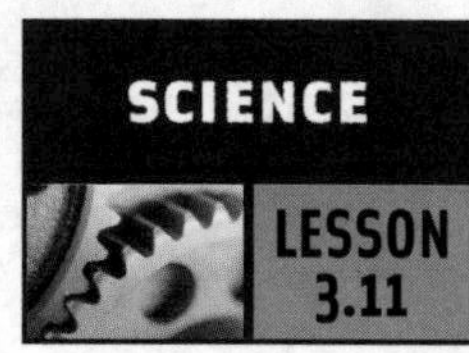


**2** **MODEL AND RESEARCH** Have your student help you construct a model of Earth's layers using real or imaginary food. Look at the drawing of Earth's layers for a guide. Think of something hot and solid for the inner **core** (perhaps a meatball). The outer core might be a thick layer of melted cheese. The **mantle** has three sublayers: an inner solid layer (perhaps some baked dough), a middle layer of red-hot rock that is sometimes solid and sometimes a thick liquid (tomato sauce with pieces of tomato), and another thin, solid layer (more dough). The outside, or crust, rests on the mantle and should have some cracks in it. Now have your student research what Earth's layers are actually made of.

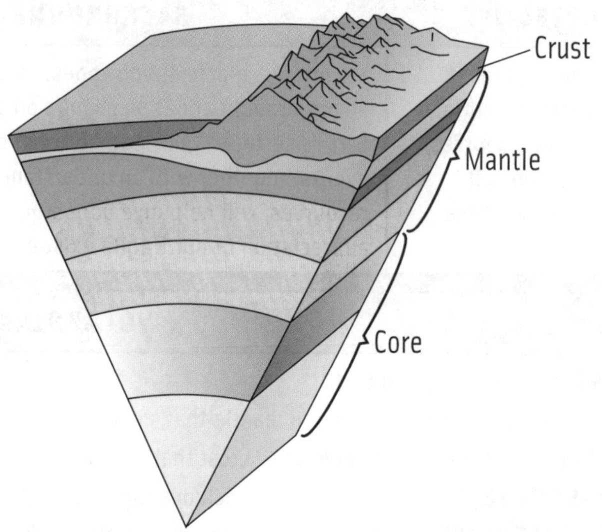


**3** **EXPLAIN** Explain that the **lithosphere,** which is the layer of rock that includes the crust and part of the mantle, is made up of about a dozen rigid plates of rock that are in constant motion. Tell your student that the arrangement of the crust and the upper mantle is responsible for activity on Earth's surface. As the pieces move (from less than an inch to more than two inches a year), the edges pass by one another in one of three ways: they spread apart, they come together, or they slide by. At the edges, or boundaries, between two plates, earthquakes, volcanoes, and mountain building occur. This is called the theory of **plate tectonics.** There is much evidence for the theory: the continents "fit" together like pieces of a puzzle, and the location of earthquakes and the formation of the Hawaiian Islands provide more evidence.

**DID YOU KNOW?**

Earthquakes are measured on a Richter scale, which is named after its inventor, Charles Richter. The higher the number, the stronger the quake.

**4** **DESCRIBE AND PREDICT** If you live in an area with frequent **earthquakes,** your student can probably describe an earthquake to you. If not, describe one to him or her. Explain that earthquakes are caused by huge blocks of rock that suddenly break apart. When the rocks break, they release a great amount of energy very quickly. The energy travels in waves in all directions from the center of the earthquake. Have him or her find out how a seismograph is used to help predict earthquakes. If your

student shows interest, have him or her research by checking out http://quake.wr.usgs.gov/4kids/, for example, to find interesting earthquake facts, the most recent earthquakes, and more.

5 **COMPARE AND CONTRAST** Like earthquakes, **volcanoes** occur most often along the boundaries of Earth's plates. In a volcano, **magma** from the mantle rises to the surface through underground spaces and surface cracks. Have your student research to find when the most recent volcano in the United States erupted.

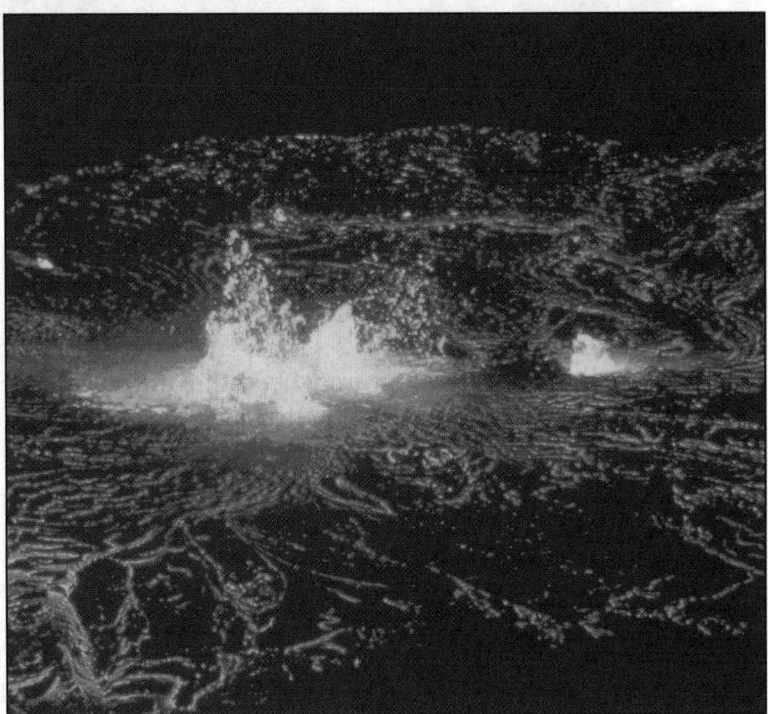

*Volcanoes occur most often along the boundaries of Earth's plates.*

6 **EXPLAIN AND RESEARCH** Explain that Earth's surface also is affected by **landslides.** These usually occur with other natural disasters, such as earthquakes, volcanoes, and floods. There have been landslides in all 50 states. Landslides can be very dangerous. Have your student research a landslide that happened near where you live in the reference section of the library or on the Internet. Have him or her find out what caused it and what is being done to prevent future slides.

7 **REVIEW AND MODEL** Review with your student that earthquakes, volcanoes, and landslides all change Earth's crust. Then introduce **glaciers.** Ask him or her what he or she knows about glaciers. Explain that a glacier is a huge sheet of ice that moves very slowly. You can model one theory of how a glacier moves: Take an ice cube out of the freezer and place it on a small plate. Leave it on a table for about a minute. Then ask, *What happens?* [ice begins to melt; a layer of water forms on the bottom; the ice can slip around the plate] This is how some scientists think a glacier moves—the great pressure of a glacier causes the ice at the bottom to melt, and the lower layers of the glacier slide over the water.

*As glaciers carved through land in what is now Montana, they helped create Hidden Lake at Glacier National Park.*

**8** **ASK AND DISCUSS** Mention that just as there are things on Earth's surface, such as mountains, lakes, and volcanoes, there are also things below Earth's surface. Ask your student to name some of the things we get from beneath Earth's surface. Some examples are gold, silver, and other metals; gems and other stones for jewelry; rock and clay for building; and fossil fuels. Ask your student if he or she knows what a fossil fuel is.

**9** **EXPLAIN AND WRITE** Explain to your student that a fossil fuel is a **natural resource.** Some examples are coal, oil, and natural gas—fuel that's found in nature. People use equipment to gather this fuel and make it suitable for us to use. Even though these occur naturally, sometimes people don't use them sensibly. For example, people use oil and gas in cars, which can pollute the air we breathe. Have your student research one of the major ways people pollute the environment. Then have him or her find the steps that can be taken to protect the environment from the pollutant.

**FOR FURTHER READING**

*Atlas of Earth (Atlas Library),* by Alexa Stace, Pauline Khng, and Dougal Dixon, ed. (Gareth Stevens, 2001).

*DK Guide to the Savage Earth,* by Trevor Day (DK Publishing, 2001).

*Earthquakes and Volcanoes (Reader's Digest Pathfinders),* by Lin Sutherland (Reader's Digest, 2000).

*Earth's Resources (Science Fact Files),* by Steve Parker (Raintree/Steck Vaughn, 2001).

# Branching Out

## TEACHING TIP

There are many videos available about Earth's layers, volcanoes, earthquakes, landslides, and glaciers that can enhance this lesson. You may want to preview them first.

## CHECKING IN

Assess your student's understanding of concepts concerning Earth, its changes, and its resources by having him or her role-play or act out parts of the lesson, such as plate tectonics, earthquakes, volcanoes, landslides, glaciers, using fossil fuels.

# Conserve, Reuse, Recycle

Conserve means "to save." Reuse means "to use again." Recycle means "to use something again for something else." Tour your home and find places where you can conserve, reuse, and recycle. Then set up a recycling center in your home.

## How to Conserve, Reuse, and Recycle

Do you know how to conserve, reuse, and recycle? You can conserve electricity by turning off the light when you leave a room. Or you can conserve water when brushing your teeth by turning off the water while you're brushing. You can reuse a shipping box by storing things in it or an old plastic tablecloth by cutting it up into strips to use as shelf liners. You can recycle newspapers so they're made into new paper products or aluminum cans so they're made into new aluminum products.

## Where to Conserve, Reuse, and Recycle

Take a "conserve, reuse, and recycle" tour of your home. Go room by room and list what you can conserve, reuse, and recycle. Make a separate checklist for conserving, reusing, and recycling.

## When to Conserve, Reuse, and Recycle

You can start conserving, reusing, and recycling right away. Show your checklists to an adult. Together with your family see how you can use the checklists to conserve, reuse, and recycle. With an adult, call your local recycling center and find out what it recycles and how items should be separated. Then create separate recycling bins in your home for newspaper (and/or office paper), aluminum, glass, and plastic. With your family, decide where you can place the bins for everyone to see and use.

# What's Next? You Decide!

Now it's your turn to choose what to do next in the lesson. Read the activities and decide which one you want to do—you may want to try them both!

## Become a Park Tour Guide

### STEPS

Give your family and friends a "tour" of a national park!

- ❑ Locate a U.S. national park that includes a volcano or has been formed by glaciers. If you need help finding one, go to the National Park Service Web site at http://www.nps.gov.
- ❑ Find out as much information as you can about the park, such as where your park's located, the history of the park, what there is to see and do at the park, what your park looks like, a map of the park, photographs, and anything else you can think of. Ask an adult for help if you'd like.
- ❑ With permission, choose a room or an area of a room to "become" your park. For example, your bedroom can become a park formed by glaciers: your bed is a lake, a lamp can be one of the unique types of animals found at the park, and the door to your bedroom is where visitors enter the park.
- ❑ Then give your family and friends a "tour" of the park. Be sure to include all of the unique things about the park in your tour.

## Start a Rock Collection

### MATERIALS

- ❑ 10–20 rocks
- ❑ 1 shallow box or box top
- ❑ 1 book about rocks

### STEPS

Earth's crust is made up of thousands of rocks. Start a rock collection to see what types of rocks are out there!

- ❑ Look around your home, your local park, or wherever. Be sure to ask permission first.
- ❑ Try to find different types of rocks. Choose some that are shiny, dull, rough, smooth, oddly shaped, of different colors, and with stripes.
- ❑ Make notes in your notebook about the details of each rock.
- ❑ Then display your rocks in the box top.
- ❑ Research your rocks and see what types of rocks you've found.
- ❑ Expand your collection throughout the year as you go to different places.

# Exploring Stars and the Solar System

***Space seems endless, as does our desire to explore it.***

| OBJECTIVE | BACKGROUND | MATERIALS |
|---|---|---|
| To have your student explore the nature of the solar system | Understanding the distances between planets, the hugeness of the sun, and the vastness of our universe can be both overwhelming and mysterious. This lesson will help make some of that mystery a bit more familiar to your student. | ■ Student Learning Pages 12.A–12.B<br>■ 1 tennis ball<br>■ 1 rubber band<br>■ 3 feet heavy cotton string |

| VOCABULARY |
|---|
| **ORBITS** repeated circular motions around a larger body |
| **ASTRONOMERS** scientists who study things outside Earth's atmosphere |
| **SOLAR SYSTEM** the sun and all bodies that orbit it |
| **STAR** a glowing body in the universe made of gas |

## Let's Begin

**1** **ASK AND MODEL** Ask, *Do you know why the moon* ***orbits*** *Earth?* [Earth's gravity keeps the lighter moon in orbit] Model how gravity works: Wrap a large rubber band around a tennis ball several times. Attach about three feet of string to the banded ball. Use the rubber band to help hold the string in place on the ball. Go outdoors with your student and find an open area of at least 20 square yards. Hold the loose end of the string and swing it around your head. Make sure all bystanders are a safe distance away. Build up speed so the ball circles your head more or less horizontally. Let go of the string. The ball flies off in a straight line. Point out to your student that you're like Earth, the ball is like the moon, and the tension in the string while you are swinging it is like the gravity that holds the moon in its orbit. Point out also that the sun's gravity keeps Earth and the other planets in their orbits, too. Then discuss.

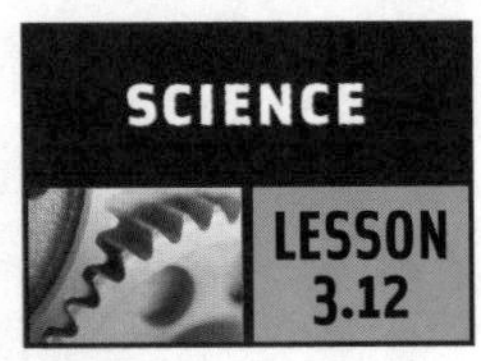


**2** **EXPLAIN AND MODEL** Explain that there is another type of movement that both the moon and Earth make: rotation on an axis. Have your student turn around slowly in a small circle while he or she also makes a large circle around you. You may have to demonstrate this. Make sure neither of you gets dizzy from spinning too fast! Ask, *What is one rotation of Earth on its axis?* [a day] Then ask, *What is one complete orbit of Earth around the sun?* [a year] Then have a conversation with your student explaining that the time of the moon's rotation is the same as its orbit. Because of that, we always see the same side of the moon.

**3** **RELATE** Relate that Earth's gravity enables us to live. It holds molecules in our atmosphere near the surface so we have air to breathe. The moon's gravity is so slight that it can't hold on to gases, so it has no atmosphere. The amount of gravity on a planet determines what something weighs there. To find out what something would weigh on a different planet, have your student multiply its Earth weight (or mass, which are the same) by the planet's gravity. Have your student select items from around the house—including himself or herself—and find out what they would weigh on other planets using the chart.

| Body | Gravity Compared to Earth |
|---|---|
| Moon | 0.17 |
| Mercury | 0.38 |
| Venus | 0.91 |
| Mars | 0.38 |
| Jupiter | 2.54 |
| Saturn | 1.08 |
| Uranus | 0.91 |
| Neptune | 1.19 |
| Pluto | 0.06 |

**4** **EXPLAIN AND EXPLORE** Explain that of the nine planets that orbit the sun, the surface of the smaller planets—Mercury, Venus, Earth, Mars, and Pluto—are solid, and the rest are gaseous (probably with a solid core). With your student, go to http://www.nasa.gov for interesting photos, information, and features of the solar system.

**5** **DESCRIBE AND WRITE** Have your student tell you what the sun looks like from Earth. [a small bright ball in the sky] Show your student this diagram of the sun. Explain how the sun has different areas and layers. Ask your student to research and write descriptions of each of the labeled areas. Then have him or her become the teacher and tell you how they all function together.

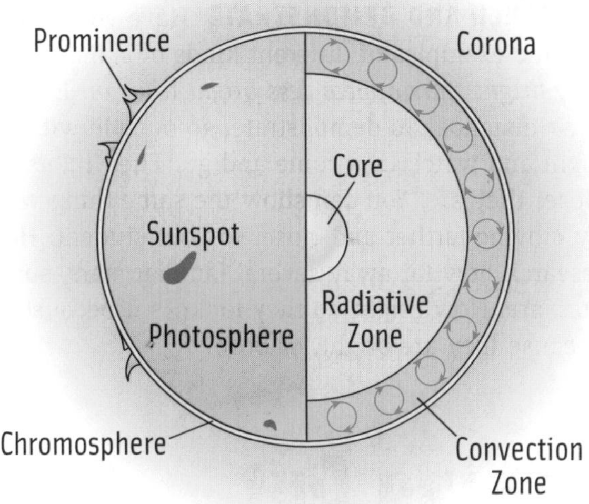

Other than Earth, the planets are named after Roman gods.

6 **TOUR** Explain to your student that scientists who study things outside Earth's atmosphere are called **astronomers.** Astronomers use instruments such as land-based and space-based telescopes and space probes to collect data from faraway objects. Together with your student locate the nearest observatory or large telescope. Research what scientists use it for, such as to look at one particular planet, to track comets, or something else. Arrange, if possible, to have you and your family take a tour of the observatory and talk with a scientist. Have your student prepare a list of questions before going.

7 **EXPLAIN** Explain to your student that the planets have been put into two categories based on where they are in relation to the sun. The two categories are inner planets and outer planets. The inner planets are Mercury, Venus, Earth, and Mars. The outer planets are Jupiter, Saturn, Uranus, Neptune, and Pluto. Have your student research one or two special features about each planet that make it unique. Then discuss.

8 **ASK AND DISCUSS** Ask, *Can you name any other objects in the **solar system** besides the planets?* Your student may or may not be able to think of any. At this point, there may still be some confusion about what is in and what is outside the solar system. Have your student look up the following solar system objects and describe them to you: comet, meteoroid, meteor, meteorite, and asteroid belt.

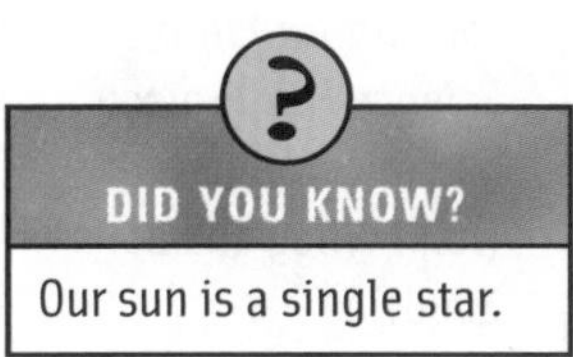


Our sun is a single star.

9 **EXPLAIN** Tell your student that a **star** is a hot ball of gas in space. Because it is hot, it gives off light of its own. Mention

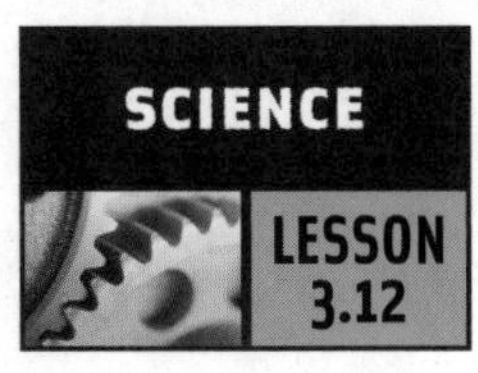

SCIENCE LESSON 3.12

that planets and moons don't give off their own light. The closest star to us is the sun, whose light takes just over eight minutes to reach Earth. Next to the sun, the closest star is Alpha Centauri, whose light takes 4.4 years to reach Earth. Ask your student what he or she knows about stars, such as those that make up the Big Dipper, and discuss.

**10** **RESEARCH AND DEMONSTRATE** Have your student research specific examples of different kinds of stars. Ask, *Why do some very bright stars appear less bright to us on Earth?* [because of their distance] To demonstrate, go outside with your student at night and watch cars come and go. Their lights are brighter the closer they are. You can show the same thing with a flashlight by moving farther and closer to your student. Have him or her research how far away several familiar stars, such as the North Star, are. How bright do they look? Is it because they are close, because they are bright, or both?

**FOR FURTHER READING**

*Comets, Asteroids, and Meteorites (Kaleidoscope: Space),* by Roy A. Gallant (Benchmark, 2000).

*Deep Space Astronomy,* by Gregory Vogt (Twenty-First Century Books, 1999).

*DK Space Encyclopedia,* by Nigel Henbest and Heather Couper (DK Publishing, 1999).

*Dot to Dot in the Sky,* by Joan Hinz (Whitecap Books, 2002).

*The Everything Kids' Space Book,* by Kathiann M. Kowalski (Adams Media Corporation, 2000).

*Janice VanCleave's A+ Projects in Astronomy,* by Janice VanCleave (John Wiley and Sons, 2001).

*Janice VanCleave's Solar System: Mind-Boggling Experiments You Can Turn into Science Fair Projects,* by Janice VanCleave (John Wiley and Sons, 2000).

# Branching Out

## TEACHING TIP

When studying a large body of knowledge that has a great deal of information, try to present it—and have your student present it—in as many different forms as possible: charts, drawings, time lines, graphs, tables, and so on. Check your local TV listings for shows on space, the planets, or the stars. Many libraries have videos on space, too.

## CHECKING IN

To assess your student's understanding of the solar system and the stars, have him or her tell you about space. Have him or her create charts or drawings that tell about the solar system, the planets, and the stars.

# Gazing at the Sky

Scientists have been studying the solar system for many years. Research information about the eight scientists below and make a room-sized time line of their discoveries.

**MATERIALS**

- ❑ 10 feet yarn or string
- ❑ construction paper
- ❑ markers
- ❑ 20 paper clips
- ❑ 1 pair scissors

**PART A**

**Research information about the eight scientists. For each scientist, find the date of birth, the date of death, and one important contribution each has made to the study of astronomy or space.**

Tycho Brahe: ______________________________

Nicolaus Copernicus: ______________________________

Galileo Galilei: ______________________________

Edmond Halley: ______________________________

Edwin Hubble: ______________________________

Johannes Kepler: ______________________________

Henrietta Leavitt: ______________________________

Ptolemy: ______________________________

**PART B**

**Using the construction paper, cut out shapes found in space, such as stars and planets. Write the information you found on the shapes—be sure to match the shape with the contribution. Take your yarn or string and tie it to two ends of the room, being careful not to break any objects in the room. Organize the dates of the scientists' discoveries, going in order of the earliest to the most recent. Then hang the shapes in order on the yarn or string using the paper clips.**

# What's Next? You Decide!

Now it's your turn to choose what to do next in the lesson. Read the activities and decide which one you want to do—you may want to try them both!

## Wish upon a Star

### MATERIALS

- ❑ 1 constellation chart for your area
- ❑ binoculars or telescope (optional)

### STEPS

Modern scientists have divided the night sky into 88 constellations. A constellation is a group of stars that look like they make a pattern in the sky. Identify constellations for yourself!

- ❑ Go to the library or search the Internet for a constellation chart for your area.
- ❑ Read the instructions for your location, the time of year, and the time of night for seeing stars.
- ❑ With permission, go outside on a clear night to a place where you can observe stars. It's fun to go with a friend or a family member.
- ❑ Start simple and locate a star or a constellation that's easy to find, such as the North Star or the Big Bear.
- ❑ If you want, find a book that has stories about how the constellations got their names. Pretty soon, you'll be a guide to the night sky.

## Chart a Month of the Moon

### MATERIALS

- ❑ 1 current calendar showing phases of the moon
- ❑ table of moon rising times or daily newspaper
- ❑ binoculars (optional)

### STEPS

- ❑ Look at the current month's calendar and find the days showing phases of the moon.
- ❑ In your notebook, make your own current calendar for the next 30 days.
- ❑ On your calendar, write what type of moon it will be on certain days. For example, on October 26 write "full moon."
- ❑ Every day, check for and note on your calendar the rising time of the moon. It will be around 15–20 minutes later each day. If possible, go outside and observe the moon in the sky. (Skip cloudy or rainy nights.) You also can check a daily newspaper for rising times of the moon.
- ❑ Then draw the shape of the moon that you see. Keep on checking on the moon until it has gone through all its phases. How many days has it taken?

# In Your Community

**To reinforce the skills and concepts taught in this section, try one or more of these activities!**

## Local Power Plant

Where is the nearest power plant to your home? Arrange a tour of a local power plant with your student. Have your student prepare questions for the tour. Example questions might include: What type of power is provided? What source does the plant use? Where does the source come from? How many households does the plant serve? Ask the tour guide to explain how the power from the plant gets to your home.

## Maple Syrup Farming

Does your student know that maple syrup comes from trees? Go to the local grocery store with your student and look on the bottle labels of the pure maple syrup. Where is the syrup from? If you live near an area where maple syrup is farmed, arrange for a visit to see the process firsthand. Have your student use reference materials to read about the process of maple sugaring and removing sugar water from maple trees and then create a list of questions he or she has. If you can't make the visit, arrange for a telephone interview with a maple syrup farmer. Your grocer may be able to help you find the farm's telephone number.

## Backyard Astronomy

You don't need complicated equipment to observe the nighttime sky. It is important, however, to get away from the light pollution in urban areas. A pair of binoculars is all your student needs to find and watch the constellations. Have your student look in your local newspaper or on the Internet for upcoming astronomical events, such as the Perseid meteor shower. If your student is interested in getting more involved, call a local planetarium to find the amateur astronomers in your area. Astronomy groups aren't uncommon and often meet on a regular basis.

## Museum of Natural History

Is your student interested in volcanoes, glaciers, earthquakes, or the forming of oceans? Find out about exhibits on the history and evolution of Earth's surface at your local museum of natural history. Plan an outing to the museum and have your student make a list of things he or she wants to learn about that day. You may want to review the information from Lesson 3.11 before you go. If there isn't a museum close to you, consider traveling to a nearby city to visit its museum and make the trip an adventure with your student!

## Ecosystem Restoration

Is there a local group that monitors wildlife in your area? Perhaps there is an ecosystem restoration project under way. If your student is interested in participating in a project like this, look on the Internet or call the park district to find out how he or she can get involved. If your student is interested in just learning more, see if you can arrange an interview for your student with one of the project leaders and a visit to the project site.

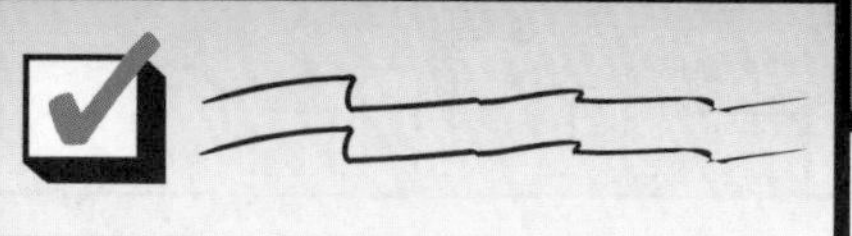

# We Have Learned

**Use this checklist to summarize what you and your student have accomplished in the Science section.**

- ❑ **Cells, Tissues, and Organs**
- ❑ early microscopes, cell study
- ❑ plant and animal cells and processes
- ❑ plant and animal tissues and organs
- ❑ functions of organ systems

- ❑ **Populations and Ecosystems**
- ❑ interaction among organisms in a community
- ❑ energy flow through an ecosystem
- ❑ plant and animal behavior and adaptation

- ❑ **Body Systems**
- ❑ cardiovascular system
- ❑ digestive system, excretory systems
- ❑ skeletal system, muscular systems

- ❑ **Nutrition, Exercise, and Health**
- ❑ energy, food, why nutrients are important
- ❑ physical fitness, strength, endurance

- ❑ **Physical and Chemical Properties of Matter**
- ❑ solid, liquid, gaseous states
- ❑ measuring length, mass, volume, temperature
- ❑ homogenous and heterogeneous mixtures and colloids

- ❑ **Structure of Matter**
- ❑ atoms, elements
- ❑ molecules, compounds
- ❑ periodic table, classifying matter

- ❑ **Forms and Uses of Energy**
- ❑ electricity, machines, fossil fuels, nuclear energy
- ❑ renewable energy and the environment

- ❑ **Earth's Atmosphere and Weather**
- ❑ sun and landforms affecting weather
- ❑ climate, weather prediction

- ❑ **Water on Earth**
- ❑ sources of saltwater and freshwater
- ❑ Earth's surface, atmosphere, water cycle
- ❑ oceanography

- ❑ **Earth's Crust, Mantle, and Core**
- ❑ volcanoes, earthquakes, landslides
- ❑ mountains, glaciers, continental shelves
- ❑ natural resources, fossil fuel, protecting the environment

- ❑ **Stars and the Solar System**
- ❑ Earth, moon, sun, gravity
- ❑ inner planets, outer planets
- ❑ stars, astronomers, telescopes

**We have also learned:**

______________________________

______________________________

# Social Studies

# Social Studies

## Key Topics

# Exploring Native Cultures of North America

***Discover the riches of the original American cultures.***

| OBJECTIVE | BACKGROUND | MATERIALS |
|---|---|---|
| To give your student appreciation for the great span and variety of native cultures that exist in the Americas | People have been living in North America for thousands of years. Today, many of our states, cities, and even streets are named after Native Americans. In this lesson, your student will learn about the different native cultures that thrived in North America and are still present today. | ■ Student Learning Pages 1.A–1.B<br>■ 1 copy Venn Diagram, page 353 |

| VOCABULARY |
|---|
| **CULTURES** the ways of life for particular groups of people |
| **WAMPUM** seashells tied together and worn as parts of belts or on strings |
| **RESERVATIONS** land that's been set aside by the U.S. government for native peoples to live on |
| **PUEBLO** a Native American people; *pueblo* is Spanish for "village" |
| **KACHINAS** special beings or spirits |

## Let's Begin

**1** **EXPLAIN** Explain that as early as 9000 B.C. there were human settlements in America experimenting with agriculture. Since that time, there have been many **cultures** in various parts of America. Cultures in the same area of the country often have similar ways of living. Past North American cultures that thrived include the peoples of the Southwestern Desert, Pacific Northwest, Eastern Woodlands, and Great Plains. Ask your student what he or she knows about Native Americans. Then show your student the map on the next page and refer to it throughout the lesson.

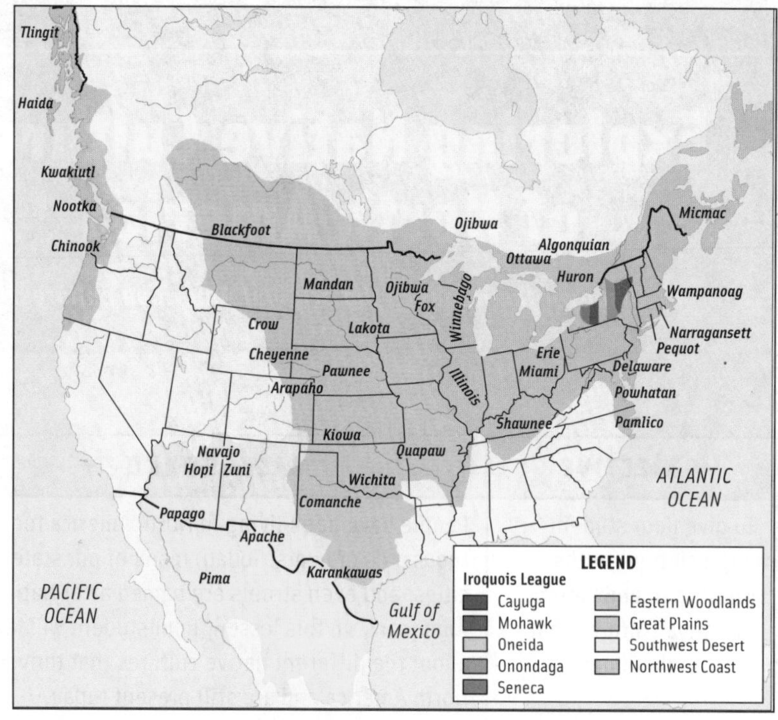


**2** **INTRODUCE THE EASTERN WOODLANDS** Together with your student look at the Eastern Woodlands area. Ask your student if he or she has heard of any of these Native American tribes. Explain that the peoples who lived in this area were dependent on the plentiful woods for firewood, hunting for food and clothing, and the rivers and lakes that were in the area for food and transportation. The water also helped their crops grow. Have your student research what animals they might have hunted and what crops they could have grown. Then ask, *What animals and vegetables did they eat?* [possible answers: deer, elk, corn, squash]

**3** **EXPLAIN** Mention that some of the people in this area were called the Iroquois. It's believed that in the 1500s five of the Iroquois tribes came together to form the Iroquois League, which was an organization formed to help govern and make decisions for all of the people in the league. The Iroquois League was made up of the Seneca, Oneida, Onondaga, Mohawk, and Cayuga, and later the Tuscarota. Reveal that the Iroquois League had a flag. Have your student find a picture of the flag and find what the symbols on it mean. Discuss.

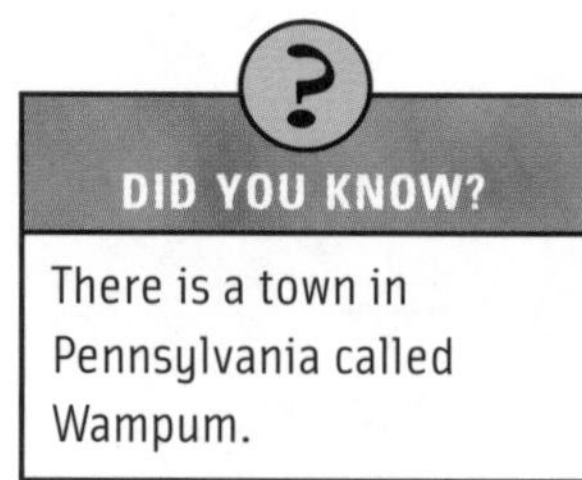


There is a town in Pennsylvania called Wampum.

**4** **REVEAL** Reveal that the Iroquois valued **wampum,** which were seashells that were polished, tied together, and then worn as part of belts or on strings. Wampum were used in ceremonies and given as gifts to mark important occasions, such as a marriage. Ask, *What item(s) do people use today as symbols of other things or in ceremonies?* [possible answers: wedding rings, friendship pins or bracelets, other jewelry]

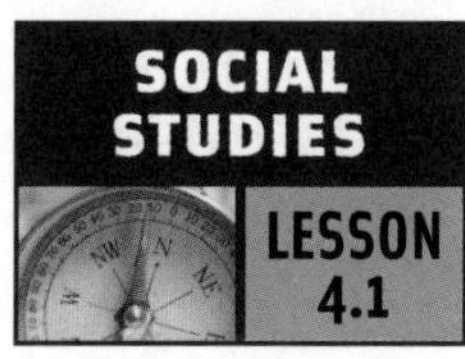


**5** **CONNECT** Share that Iroquois people exist today; many live on **reservations,** or land that's been set aside by the U.S. government for native peoples to live on. Have your student find the reservation nearest to your town. Encourage your student to find out what tribes live there and what are the challenges and privileges of living on a reservation today.

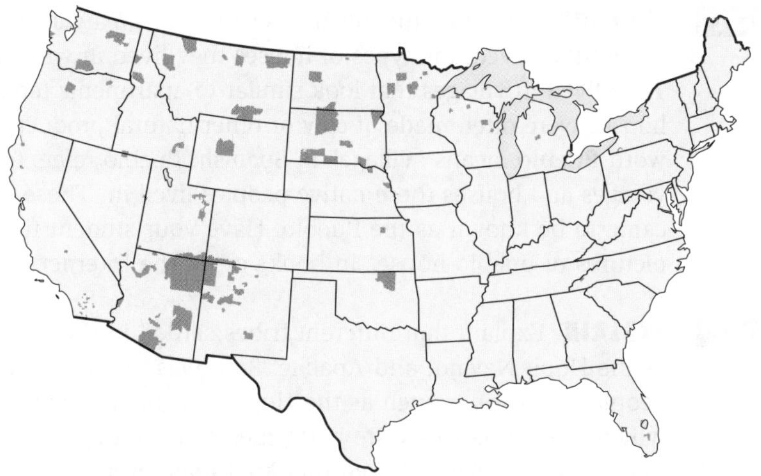

*Today, many Native Americans live on reservations. This map shows the locations of most of the Native American reservations.*

**6** **INTRODUCE THE GREAT PLAINS** Next, with your student look at the Great Plains area of the map from Step 1. The Great Plains are known for having land that is flat, grassy, and not filled with trees, unlike the woodland area of the East. Life on the Plains for native peoples included hunting and farming. Have a conversation with your student about what the challenges would be for people living in this area. If necessary, have your student research the Great Plains before discussing.

**7** **EXPLAIN** Explain that buffalo were very important to the native peoples of this region. They hunted them for food, used their fur and hide for clothing and blankets, and used other parts of the buffalo, too. For example, the horns could be made into bowls. Have your student research how the Great Plains people hunted buffalo. Then ask, *How did they hunt buffalo?* [often groups of hunters would follow buffalo; while on their travels they'd live in teepees] Discuss.

**8** **REVEAL** Share that two groups of Great Plains Native Americans that your student may have heard of are the Sioux and Cheyenne. Have your student choose one (or both) of these peoples and find out about how they lived, what types of houses they lived in, and how they used horses. Then discuss.

**9** **CONNECT** Explain that today many Cheyenne live on a reservation in Montana. They keep alive many of the ceremonies and traditions and perform them for the public. Go to http://www.cheyennetours.com to learn more about the Cheyenne today.

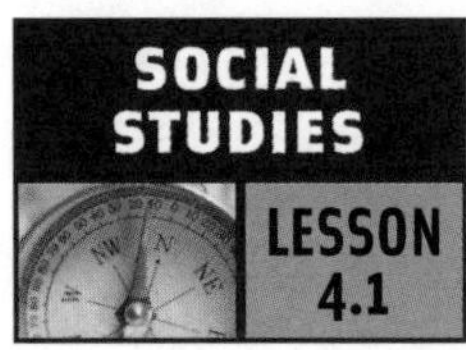


**10** **INTRODUCE THE SOUTHWESTERN DESERT** With your student, look at the Southwestern Desert area of the map. Explain that it's very hot and dry here with deserts. Mention that because it's very dry, the Southwest peoples lived differently than the tribes in the Eastern Woodlands and the Great Plains. Ask your student what he or she knows about the Southwest and discuss.

**11** **EXPLORE** Tell your student that because the area was dry where these tribes lived, the types of houses they lived in were different. They lived in villages that look similar to apartments today. The houses were often made of clay or other natural products. The word **Pueblo** means "village" in Spanish. Pueblo refers to the villages and houses these native peoples lived in. These people came to be known as the Pueblo. Have your student find pictures of pueblo houses in books or on the Internet.

**12** **EXPLAIN** Explain that different tribes settled in this area, such as the Hopi, Navajo, and Apache. Rain was important to these peoples, and tribes such as the Hopi often held ceremonies in which special dances were performed to encourage it to rain. The native peoples believed that **kachinas,** or special beings or spirits, could help them in bringing rain. Today, kachina figures, or dolls, are still made. Have your student research what spirits the kachinas represented and who makes them today.

**13** **CONNECT** Explain that today the Hopi and Navajo live on reservations in the Southwest. Reveal that during World War I and World War II the U.S. armed forces used a special code to communicate radio messages that the enemy could not understand. This special code came from Navajo and parts of other Native American languages. Encourage your student to research Navajo code talking on the Internet and say something to you in the code.

**14** **INTRODUCE THE PACIFIC NORTHWEST** Look at the Pacific Northwest area on the map with your student. Explain that this area was wooded, had plenty of water, and was filled with animals. The native peoples here didn't have to grow as many crops because they could hunt and gather much of their food. Have your student choose one of the peoples listed on the map. Then have him or her research what daily life was like. Encourage him or her to find the foods they ate, what their houses looked like, and what ceremonies were part of their life. Then discuss.

15 **DISCOVER** Ask your student what he or she knows about totem poles. Then tell him or her that people in this area often made totem poles. The peoples of the Northwest often carved them with images representing a family's ancestors. Help your student find different examples of totem poles and review them with him or her. Then have your student draw a design for a totem pole for a group or an organization that he or she belongs to.

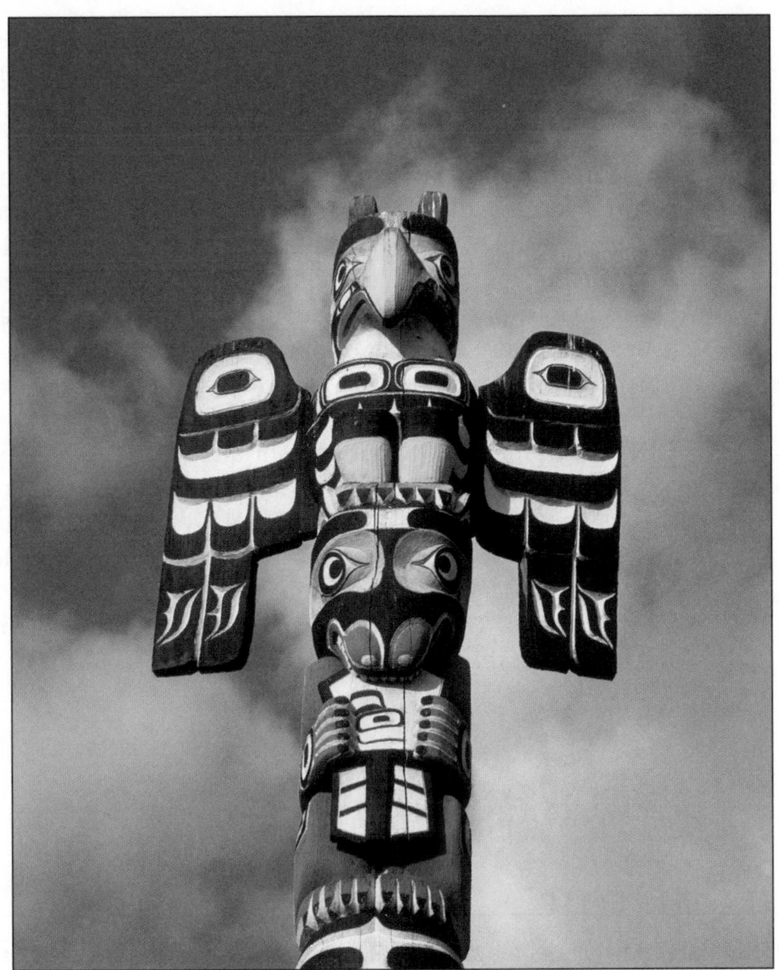

16 **CONNECT** Share with your student that one of the Northwest peoples who still exist today is the Kwakiutl. Have your student find out more about the Kwakiutl people if he or she hasn't already. Then have him or her discuss with you how these people's lifestyle has changed over the years.

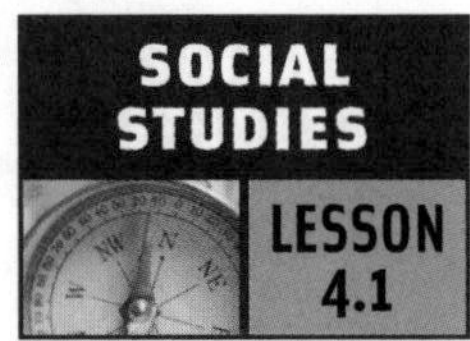


**17** **COMPARE** Now have your student choose two of the groups of Native Americans he or she has just learned about. Give your student a copy of the Venn Diagram found on page 353 or have your student draw the diagram in a notebook. Then have him or her compare and contrast details about the two groups. Remind your student to examine geographic location, climate, types of houses, food and water resources, customs and traditions, and government.

**18** **READ AND DISCUSS** Have your student go to the folklore section of the library and choose a Native American tale from one of the Native American groups he or she learned about in this lesson. Read the story together with your student. Then ask, *What elements of the story show us the culture this people had?* Discuss.

**19** **DISTRIBUTE AND WRITE** Distribute Student Learning Page 1.A. Have your student think about the native peoples he or she just learned about. Then have him or her complete the activity.

**20** **REVIEW AND CONNECT** Review with your student what he or she has learned about the different Native American tribes. Then challenge your student to find out about the Native Americans who lived in your area. Help your student to find any street names, parks, or rivers with Native American names. Find out if your local history museum or library has information on previous American peoples whom you and your student can explore.

**21** **CONTINUE** Share with your student that there are many native peoples still in America. Suggest to your student that he or she watch and listen for news about Native Americans on the television, radio, and newspaper. When news stories come up, have your student find the location of the mentioned event or tribe on a map. Then relate the story to the information he or she learned in this lesson.

**FOR FURTHER READING**

*A History of Us: The First Americans,* by Joy Hakim (Oxford University Press Children's Books, 2002).

*Native Americans: An Inside Look at the Tribes and Traditions,* by Laura Buller and Ranco Darren, contributor (DK Publishing, Inc., 2001).

*Pocahontas (In Their Own Words),* by George Sullivan (Scholastic Reference, 2002).

# Branching Out

## TEACHING TIP

There are many videos available about Native Americans that can add to this study. You may want to preview any video before showing it to the student.

## CHECKING IN

Discuss with your student what he or she has learned about the great variety of Native American cultures. Check to see that he or she can make distinctions between the tribes of the four regions by having your student draw a representation of each region.

# Write a Letter

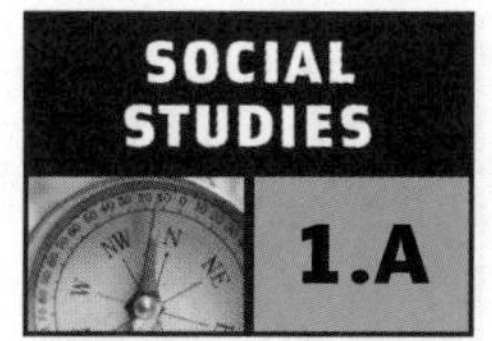


Suppose you're a member of one of the tribes you learned about in the lesson. Write a letter to a friend in another Native American tribe in a different region. In your letter, include information about what daily life is like for someone your age. Before you begin, read and answer the questions first. Write your letter on a separate sheet of paper.

## About Me

My name is: ______________________________

I live in this region: ______________________________

I am a member of this tribe: ______________________________

I eat these foods: ______________________________

The animals and plants in our region are: ______________________________

I live in a type of house called: ______________________________

I live in a house made of: ______________________________

I wear clothes made of: ______________________________

I sleep on this type of bed: ______________________________

During the day I do this: ______________________________

______________________________

During the day the rest of my family does this: ______________________________

______________________________

We have ceremonies for this: ______________________________

______________________________

In our ceremonies we do this: ______________________________

______________________________

I play these types of games: ______________________________

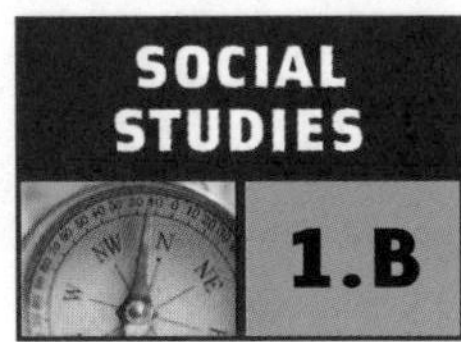


# What's Next? You Decide!

Now it's your turn to choose what to do next in the lesson. Read the activities and decide which one you want to do—you may want to try them both!

## Design Your Own Kachina Doll

### MATERIALS

- ❑ 1 cardboard paper towel tube
- ❑ 1 pair scissors
- ❑ tape
- ❑ 1 table tennis or plastic foam ball
- ❑ glue
- ❑ construction paper
- ❑ markers or paint
- ❑ glitter, buttons, beads, fabric

### STEPS

- ❑ Cut one slit in the paper towel tube about one-fourth to one-third of the way up. Then on the opposite side cut another slit the same length.
- ❑ At the end of the first slit, make a short cut lengthwise on either side of the slit. This will make a T. Do this for the other slit.
- ❑ Curve each of the cardboard flaps in to meet the flap on the opposite side. Tape them together. These will be your kachina's legs.
- ❑ Glue the table tennis ball to the top of the tube. If the tube is too small, cut short slits in the cardboard and fold back. Place the ball on top of the tube and glue the cardboard flaps to the ball. This will be your kachina's head.
- ❑ Use paint or markers to draw the doll's head on the ball. Use fabric or construction paper for the rest of the body. Then glue beads, buttons—whatever you want!

## Make a Family Totem Pole

### MATERIALS

- ❑ construction paper
- ❑ 1 cardboard paper towel tube
- ❑ 1 empty shoebox or other shallow box
- ❑ 1 pair scissors
- ❑ glue
- ❑ glitter, buttons, beads, yarn

### STEPS

- ❑ Find information about your current family members and ancestors.
- ❑ Cut a hole in the box large enough for the cardboard tube to fit. Place the tube into the hole to make sure it fits snugly. The box will keep your totem pole from falling over.
- ❑ Draw images and designs onto construction paper. Glue beads, glitter, and yarn to the construction paper.
- ❑ Glue the construction paper onto the totem pole.

# Following the Footsteps of the New World Explorers

***See the Americas as the early European explorers did.***

| OBJECTIVE | BACKGROUND | MATERIALS |
|---|---|---|
| To help your student understand how cultures came together as Europeans explored the Americas | Early explorers took difficult journeys. Some explorers were motivated by hopes of discovery, wealth, and power. Others sought to convert native people to their religion. Because of these explorers' travels and discoveries, the cultures of our ancestors were influenced in many ways. In this lesson, your student will see where and when they explored. | ■ Student Learning Pages 2.A–2.B<br>■ 1 copy Comparison Chart, page 353<br>■ colored pencils<br>■ 1 world map or globe |

## Let's Begin

**1** **EXPLAIN** Explain that the Vikings came to America before Christopher Columbus. Leif Ericsson was a Viking explorer who discovered Greenland. He heard that there was land farther west than Greenland. Sometime after 982, he and his crew landed on Newfoundland in present-day Canada. Archaeologists found the remains of a Viking settlement at L'Anse Aux Meadows in Newfoundland, Canada. Ask your student to research and find another Viking settlement. Then discuss.

**2** **RELATE AND COMPARE** Tell your student that although the Vikings had been to the Americas, the rest of Europe was unaware that the Americas existed. It was not until after Christopher Columbus sailed in 1492 that the rest of Europe learned about the Americas. Have your student write everything he or she knows about Christopher Columbus in one column on a copy of the Comparison Chart found on page 353. Then have your student research Columbus and fill in a second column. Ask, *How did your previous knowledge compare to what you learned? What surprised you?*

**3** **DISTRIBUTE** Distribute Student Learning Page 2.A. Discuss.

**DID YOU KNOW?**

Some Europeans who came to the New World forced Native Americans to give up their religion or enslaved them. Because many European diseases did not exist in the Americas, thousands of Native Americans died of smallpox and other illnesses that their bodies had no immunity to, or protection against.

*This drawing shows Hernán Cortés encountering Moctezuma II, the Aztec ruler of Mexico, in Tenochtitlan.*

**DID YOU KNOW?**

How did Native Americans originally travel to the Americas? Some scholars think that during the Ice Age, 40,000 to 10,000 years ago, there was a land bridge that connected Asia to North America close to where Alaska is today.

**FOR FURTHER READING**

*Christopher Columbus and the Discovery of the New World,* by Carole Gallagher (Chelsea House Publishing, 2000).

*Explorers and the New World,* by Eugene M. Wait (Nova Science Publishers, 2001).

*The Viking Explorers (Explorers of New Worlds),* by Jim Gallagher (Chelsea House Publishing, 2000).

4 **RELATE AND CONTRAST** Tell the student that Europeans and Native Americans found great differences in each other's cultures. The story of Hernán Cortés and the Aztec capital city of Tenochtitlan in present-day Mexico illustrates the frustrations the two peoples had. Have your student find information on Cortés and what happened in Tenochtitlan. Have your student use the Comparison Chart from the back of the book to contrast the two cultures.

5 **EXPLAIN AND IDENTIFY** Explain that before 1492, when Europe and America first made contact, Europeans had no potatoes, corn, cocoa (chocolate), peanuts, tomatoes, turkeys, beans, or sweet potatoes. These were native to the Americas. The Americans had no horses, cows, sheep, pigs, or wheat because they were native to Europe. Have your student think of some of his or her favorite meals. Ask, *What part of that meal would have been unavailable if you had been a European before 1492? What part of that meal would have been unavailable if you had been an American before 1492?*

# Branching Out

## TEACHING TIP

See if you can find some interesting stories or videos about the adventures of an explorer who is particularly interesting to your student.

## CHECKING IN

To see how well your student absorbed the information from the lesson, have a question-and-answer session covering the basic concepts of the lesson.

 

# Chart the Arrival of the Europeans

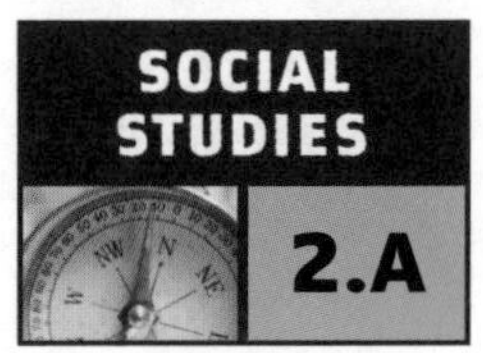


Put the explorations in order from earliest to most recent. Then on a separate sheet of paper make a time line and write each exploration in order. Write each entry in a different color, depending on the country from where the explorer came.

_____ **A.** Columbus, representing Spain, landed in America in 1492

_____ **B.** Spaniard Vasco Núñez de Balboa crossed the Isthmus of Panama to the Pacific in 1513

_____ **C.** Amerigo Vespucci, Italian, sailed to the east coast of South America in 1501

_____ **D.** In 1519, Hernán Cortés, Spanish, came to what is now Mexico

_____ **E.** Ferdinand Magellan, Portuguese, began an expedition around the world in 1519

_____ **F.** Around 1535, Spaniard Francisco Pizarro founded Lima, Peru

_____ **G.** Francisco Coronado, Spanish, explored the American Southwest in 1540

_____ **H.** Spaniard Alvar Núñez Cabeza de Vaca explored Texas in 1528

_____ **I.** Spaniard Hernando de Soto reached the Mississippi River in 1540

_____ **J.** Juan Ponce de Leon landed on the Florida peninsula in 1513

_____ **K.** English settlers landed on Roanoke Island in 1585

_____ **L.** In 1577, Francis Drake, English, began a voyage around the world

_____ **M.** In 1588, King Philip sent the Spanish Armada to attack an English fleet; the English won, establishing their right to settle part of the New World

_____ **N.** John Cabot, sailing for England, reached North America in 1497

_____ **O.** Jacques Cartier, French, reached Canada in 1534

_____ **P.** Giovanni da Verrazano, Italian, reached the Hudson River in 1524

_____ **Q.** Samuel de Champlain, French, explored the St. Lawrence River in 1603

_____ **R.** Henry Hudson, sailing for the Netherlands, explored the Atlantic coast of the present-day United States in 1690

_____ **S.** In 1624, settlers from the Netherlands began building a settlement on Manhattan Island

_____ **T.** Robert La Salle claimed all the land drained by the Mississippi River for France in 1682 and founded Louisiana

# What's Next? You Decide!

Now it's your turn to choose what to do next in the lesson. Read the activities and decide which one you want to do—you may want to try them all!

## Keep an Expedition Log

### MATERIALS

- ❑ stiff paper or thin cardboard
- ❑ 1 large needle
- ❑ heavy thread

### STEPS

Most explorers keep a record or log of everywhere they go and what they find there. Make your own log.

- ❑ Cut and fold paper to make a small book that you can keep in your pocket. Have an adult help you sew along the fold of the paper to hold the pages together.
- ❑ Glue a cover of stiff paper or thin cardboard onto your book.
- ❑ Write "Log" and the date on the cover.
- ❑ For at least three days, keep a log of everywhere you go, writing the time and a brief description of what happened.
- ❑ Read through your records. Share what you learned with an adult.

## Write a Saga

### STEPS

Vikings handed down long spoken tales called sagas.

- ❑ Think of an event that is significant to your family, perhaps a story of an adventure you had on vacation or the time you lost your dog in a storm.
- ❑ Write a long, detailed poem or story that tells about this event.
- ❑ Learn it well enough to tell it from memory. Practice using different voices, emotions, and gestures to make it more memorable for the audience.
- ❑ Recite your saga for your family!

## Plan a Menu

### MATERIALS

- ❑ 1–2 cookbooks

### STEPS

Plan a European or an American lunch or dinner menu limited to foods available before 1492.

- ❑ Look for recipes in cookbooks and make changes to ingredients to keep the menu true to pre-1492 times.
- ❑ Have an adult help you make the foods on your menu.
- ❑ Serve your menu along with a written explanation of the reasons you chose the foods you did. You can even request that your guests dress as if they were people living before 1492 and use only the type of utensils used then!

# Settling the Colonies

*No gains without pains.*
*—a common colonial saying*

| OBJECTIVE | BACKGROUND | MATERIALS |
|---|---|---|
| To help your student understand how the 13 English colonies were established in America | Each of the 13 English colonies has a different history and character. The reasons why they were founded are still reflected in the national values of the United States today. In this lesson, your student will learn about the reasons the early colonies were started, the challenges they faced, how they grew, and what daily life was like. | ■ Student Learning Pages 3.A–3.B<br>■ 1 copy Comparison Chart, page 353<br>■ 1 map of the territories of the French and Indian War |

## VOCABULARY

**SETTLEMENT** a place newly occupied by a group of people

**PERSECUTION** the act of causing someone to suffer because of a personal or religious belief

**DISSENTER** a person who disagrees with or rejects a common religion or social idea

**APPRENTICE** a person who pledges to learn someone's trade by working alongside him or her

**INDENTURED SERVANTS** people who agreed to work for a certain amount of time in exchange for a privilege, such as passage to America

**MISSIONS** places created by Christians to teach Christianity to native people

# Let's Begin

**1** **REVEAL** Explain that the first successful English **settlement** in America was called Jamestown and was settled in present-day Virginia in 1607. Jamestown was established as a business enterprise. People in England contributed money to help start the colony in hopes of making a profit. Instead of building houses and planting crops, the settlers spent their time and energy looking for gold. Many people starved and died of disease. John Smith was elected to lead the colony. He ordered colonists to build, plant, and work for their survival. Have your student research the settling of Jamestown, the land, the hardships, and the settlers' relationship with the native Powhatan tribe. Ask, *How was the relationship between the colonists and the Powhatan tribe?* [initially, the Powhatans saved the colonists from starvation, but there were problems later]

**DID YOU KNOW?**

Although we talk about Jamestown as being the first English colony, there was a colony before Jamestown. It was created on Roanoke Island in 1587. No one knows what happened to more than 100 Roanoke settlers. By 1590, they had all disappeared without a trace.

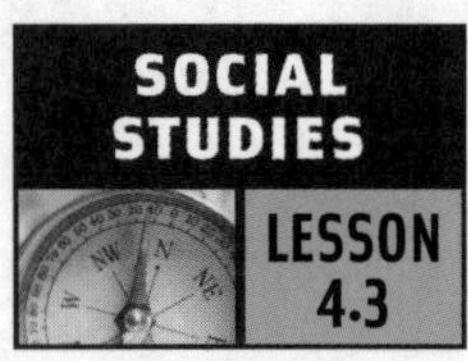


**2** **EXPAND** Point out that tobacco is a plant that originated in the Americas. Before coming to America, Europeans did not have tobacco. Around 1623, a Jamestown settler named John Rolfe raised a successful tobacco crop. The people of Jamestown began harvesting tobacco and selling it to England. Have your student find out about tobacco and Jamestown's growth, the first House of Burgesses, Jamestown government, and the marriage of John Rolfe and Pocahontas. Ask, *What did King James in England think about people using tobacco?* [he thought it was harmful and distasteful]

**DID YOU KNOW?**

The Pilgrims' Mayflower Compact was the plan for the government of their colony, which they named Plymouth. It called for "just and equal laws . . . for the general good of the colony." All the adult males who were aboard the *Mayflower* signed it, but none of the women were allowed to participate.

**3** **EXPLAIN** Tell your student that a group of people led by a man named William Bradford settled in Plymouth in 1620. These settlers are known as the Pilgrims because they came to America for religious reasons. They were looking for a home where they could practice their religious beliefs without **persecution** and protect their children from being taught outside their own faith. They had intended to settle close to Jamestown but their ship, the *Mayflower,* was blown off course. They landed further north on Cape Cod in present-day Massachusetts and set up their colony in Plymouth. Have your student research the reasons the Pilgrims came to America, the settling of Plymouth, the Mayflower Compact, and the help the settlers got from Samoset and the Wampanoag tribe. Point out that one of the first Thanksgivings was held in Plymouth.

**4** **COMPARE** Have your student compare the colonies of Jamestown and Plymouth. Suggest that he or she use the Comparison Chart found on page 353 to write the differences and similarities of the colonies. Ask your student to consider several categories, such as reason for colonizing, number of settlers, how they survived, and their relationship with native tribes. Discuss the similarities and differences together.

**DID YOU KNOW?**

The Pilgrims' Thanksgiving celebration with the Wampanoag tribe in 1621 is often thought of as the first Thanksgiving. However, around the same time other settlers in America were giving thanks, too, such as the Virginia settlers at Berkeley Plantation in 1619.

**5** **RELATE AND DISCUSS** Explain that just as religious freedom brought the Pilgrims to Plymouth it also brought another group called the Puritans in 1630. Their colony grew very rapidly, and sometimes there were disagreements about religious issues. Because of his dissension or disagreement, Roger Williams left the colony and founded Rhode Island in 1636. Anne Hutchinson, another **dissenter,** joined him. The people in Rhode Island had complete religious freedom. The same year, Thomas Hooker and 100 followers started the colony of Connecticut for the same reason. Have your student research one of these leaders. Ask, *What was this person like? How did he or she disagree with the Puritans? How did his or her insistence on religious freedom influence America today?*

**6** **DRAW AND IDENTIFY** Have your student review the map of the 13 colonies. Have him or her trace or draw the map in a notebook, labeling each colony with its name. Then ask your student to research the year and reason each colony was founded and to add it to his or her map.

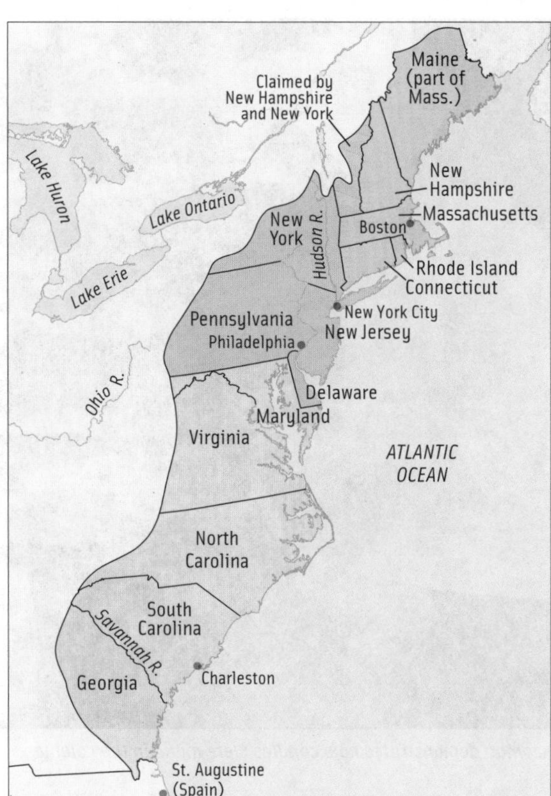


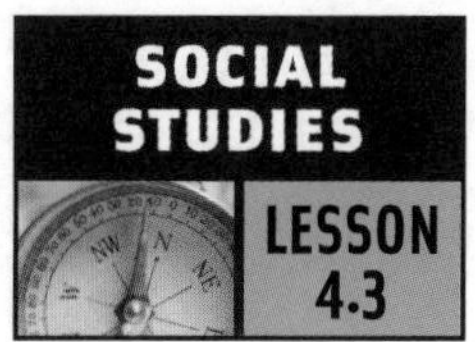


**7** **EXPLAIN AND COMPARE** Explain that the 13 colonies were divided into three regions: New England, Middle, and Southern. Have your student review these three regions on the map and make a list in his or her notebook of the colonies in each region. Have your student research the major crops, resources, type of soil, and plant life in each region. Ask, *What was the major crop in the Middle Colonies?* [wheat] *What major resources do you think came out of the New England Colonies?* [seafood, whaling, logging] *What conditions in the Southern Colonies made the area good for growing tobacco and rice?* [rich soil, a warm climate, and a long growing season]

**8** **DISTRIBUTE AND RESEARCH** Distribute Student Learning Page 3.A. Have your student use research sources to match the colony with its description. Discuss.

**9** **EXPLORE** Explain that in the colonies children had important jobs and worked hard just like the adults. On family farms, children had jobs such as gathering firewood, helping in the garden, making soap and candles, sewing, and cooking. In the colonial cities, children could find **apprentice** jobs such as shoemaker, blacksmith, fisherman, printer, surveyor, miller, merchant, surgeon, and dressmaker. Even though they worked hard, colonial children still had time for games and sports such as dancing, tag, hide-and-seek, sledding, and skating. Have your student find out more about apprenticeship in the colonies. Ask, *What skill would you like to be apprenticed in? Why?*

*A woman demonstrates how candles were made in the colonies.*

**10** **COMPARE** Have your student read more about everyday life in the colonial period. Explain that people had different lifestyles depending on whether they lived in cities or towns, on plantations, or on family farms. The largest cities at the time were Philadelphia, New York, Boston, and Charleston. Ask, *Which would be best for a person who wanted an apprenticeship?* [cities] *Which would have the fewest people?* [farms] *Which would have the most slaves?* [plantations]

**DID YOU KNOW?**

Elizabeth Lucas Pinckney, known as Eliza, was born in 1722 in England. As a child, she moved with her family to South Carolina. Her mother was sick and her father was a British officer, so at age 16 Eliza ran her family's plantation. She experimented with new crops, especially indigo, a plant that makes a blue dye. Soon South Carolina was famous for its indigo.

**11** **EXPLAIN** Tell your student that a man named Benjamin Franklin was an apprenticed printer and founded the first newspaper in Philadelphia. He also established the first hospital, public library, and volunteer fire department. He went on to become a famous scientist and an inventor and one of the founders of the U.S. government. Have your student research the life and accomplishments of Benjamin Franklin. Ask your student to write a script of one scene from Franklin's life. Encourage him or her to perform the scene in costume for your family.

**12** **EXPLAIN AND DISCUSS** Explain that there were two groups of people who were not free in the Americas, **indentured servants** and slaves. Some indentured servants agreed to work a set time in exchange for the voyage to the Americas. Others were prisoners. Many died of disease and overwork before they could become free. Slaves were captured in Africa and brought to work on plantations against their will. Slaves remained such for their entire lives unless they escaped. Have your student read about Benjamin Banneker, a talented craftsman, an activist, and the grandson of two escaped slaves.

**13** **DISCUSS** Explain that the Puritans wanted their children to learn to read so they could understand the Bible and the laws of the community. They started the first public school in the colonies in 1635. In 1647, leaders in Massachusetts required all towns to establish free public schools. No free schools existed in Europe at this time. Ask, *Do you think the leaders of Massachusetts had a good idea? Why?*

**14** **RELATE** Explain that religious freedom has always been an important part of American life. Remind your student that Massachusetts, Pennsylvania, Rhode Island, Connecticut, Maryland, and New Hampshire were all founded for religious reasons. In the 1700s, many Jewish and Christian people came to the 13 colonies to avoid being persecuted. In the 1730s, there was a movement in the Christian tradition called the Great Awakening. This movement revived the colonists' interest in religion. Protestant preachers traveled giving fervent sermons. New churches were built, religious colleges were started, and people were inspired to help one another. Ask, *How do you think the original values of religious freedom still can be seen in America today?* [separation of church and state, laws against religious discrimination, and so on]

**15** **DISCOVER** Explain that as the English colonies grew, more people began settling farther west. They crossed over the Appalachian Mountains and into the Ohio River valley. Soon conflict began. The French as well as the Native Americans had already claimed this land as their own. England demanded that the French leave the area. The French refused and in 1754 the French and Indian War began. Have your student review a map of the territories involved in the French and Indian War.

**16** **EXPLORE** The French won most of the early battles of the war. Leaders in Britain did not want to lose any land and decided to send more soldiers to America. With the help of the Iroquois tribe, the British were able to win the war in 1763. When English settlers continued to move onto the newly won British lands, the native people began to attack their settlements and forts. King George III didn't want to continue fighting a war with the Native Americans. To prevent future Native American attacks, he issued an official announcement to the colonists that they were not allowed to settle west of the Appalachian Mountains. The colonists did not agree with this new rule and tension grew between the colonies and Britain. Ask, *Why do you think the British might have been angry about the colonists eventually wanting their independence?* [because the British had spent so much money and risked lives defending the colonies in the war; because the colonies supported Britain's economy and trade and so on]

**17** **EXPLAIN** Point out that before the English began colonizing North America, Spain had set up colonies in present-day Mexico. In the 1600s, Spain was expanding its territory north from Mexico

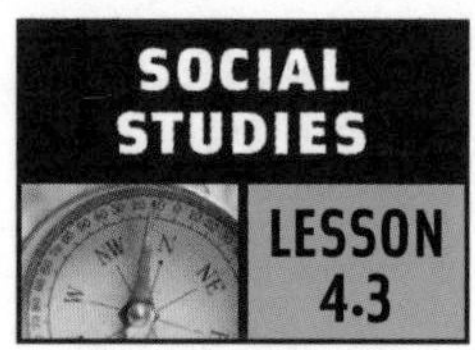


into what we know today as the southwestern United States. The settlers called this region New Mexico. There were many Native American tribes already living in this area, but the Spanish wanted to claim it for their own. The Spanish settlers disrupted the life of the tribal people and even enslaved some of them, especially the Pueblo tribe. Have your student research the Pueblo Revolt of 1680 when the Pueblo, Navajo, and Apache people drove the Spanish out of New Mexico. Ask, *Why do you think the lives of the Pueblo people were so disrupted by the Spanish?* [the Spanish had a goal of conquering and their culture was accustomed to wars, the Pueblo had a more passive culture]

**18** **RELATE** One of the ways the Spanish influenced the lives of the native people was through religion. The religious leaders wanted the native people to give up their traditional beliefs and learn about Christianity. The Catholic Church established many missions throughout what is now the southwestern and western United States. The **missions** were places where missionary priests lived and worked and where they attempted to convert the native peoples to Christianity. Have your student find out more about the growth of the missions in present-day Texas and California in the 1700s. Ask, *What do you think about the missionaries wanting to convert the Native Americans to Christianity?*

# Branching Out

## TEACHING TIP

Historical museums are an excellent way to help your student understand how the colonists lived. If there aren't any museums in your area, try finding a museum Internet site such as the Smithsonian at http://www.si.edu/.

## CHECKING IN

Show your student a map of the United States. Ask him or her to point out the New England Colonies, the Middle Colonies, and the Southern Colonies.

**FOR FURTHER READING**

*Life in the American Colonies,* by Ruth Dean and Melissa Thomson, eds. (Lucent Books, 1999).

*Life in the American Colonies: Daily Lifestyles of the Early Settlers,* by Jeanne M. Bracken (Discovery Enterprises, Ltd., 2001).

*America at the Time of Pocahontas: 1590 to 1754,* by Sally Senzell Isaacs (Heinemann Library, 1998).

# Name the Colony

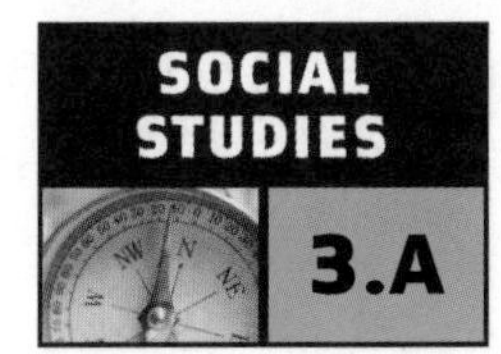


Use what you learned in the lesson and from your research to name the colony that matches each description.

1. This colony was first settled by the Dutch and called New Netherlands before King Charles II of England took it over and gave it to his brother, the Duke, as a gift.

   ______________________________

2. This colony was the last of the 13 colonies and was started by James Oglethorpe to help English people who were in jail because they owed money. ______________

3. This colony was the home of the Pilgrims and the Puritans. ______________

4. This colony was established for Catholics who had faced persecution in England and was named after the wife of King Charles I. ______________

5. This colony was the smallest of the colonies and the first to have total religious freedom. ______________

6. This colony was established by William Penn, a Quaker. ______________

7. This colony was started in 1636 by a Puritan dissenter, Thomas Hooker. It was located on a river with the same name. ______________

8. These two colonies were originally one colony that was granted to eight noblemen by King Charles II. ______________

9. This colony was originally part of New York before the duke of York gave it to two of his friends as a gift. ______________

10. Jamestown was the first settlement in this colony. ______________

11. This colony was originally the northern part of Massachusetts until 1691, when the king of England made it into a separate colony. ______________

12. This colony was created in 1701 and was originally the southern part of Pennsylvania. ______________

**Choose the colony where you would most like to have lived and write a paragraph about it in your notebook. Explain why you chose it and what life there was like.**

# What's Next? You Decide!

Now it's your turn to choose what to do next in the lesson. Read the activities and decide which one you want to do—you may want to try them both!

## Stir Up Some Hasty Pudding

### MATERIALS

- ❑ 1 cup cornmeal
- ❑ 1 medium-sized pot
- ❑ 2 cups water
- ❑ 1 teaspoon salt

### STEPS

Many of the first English settlers were able to survive by trading with the natives to get corn. Get permission and help from an adult to make this colonial food.

- ❑ Boil the water and salt in a pot.
- ❑ Sprinkle the cornmeal over the boiling water and stir constantly.
- ❑ Turn the heat down and simmer for 30 minutes, stirring occasionally.
- ❑ Serve your hasty pudding like oatmeal. Add milk, molasses, honey, or raisins. (Sugar was not available in colonial times.)
- ❑ Try cooling your pudding in the refrigerator, then cutting it into slices and frying them in a greased skillet.

## Re-create the First Thanksgiving

### MATERIALS

- ❑ 1 posterboard
- ❑ colored construction paper
- ❑ 1 pair scissors
- ❑ crayons or markers
- ❑ food magazines or supermarket flyers (optional)

### STEPS

One of the first Thanksgiving celebrations was held in Plymouth in 1621. The Pilgrims gave thanks for their first harvest and invited the people of the native Wampanoag tribe to join them. The party went on for three days!

- ❑ Find a book that talks about the Pilgrims' first Thanksgiving, and find out exactly what kind of foods they ate. You may be surprised.
- ❑ Read about the parades, games, and races they had to celebrate.
- ❑ Create a poster that shows the Pilgrims and Wampanoag at the celebration. Show the food they ate, the games they played, and the place they gathered. You can draw, cut pictures from magazines, and use colored construction paper for your poster.
- ❑ Share your poster with an adult.

# Understanding the Causes of the American Revolution

*No taxation without representation!*
*—a popular protest cry of the American Revolution*

| OBJECTIVE | BACKGROUND | MATERIALS |
| --- | --- | --- |
| To help your student trace the events, individuals, and movements that paved the way for an independent America | At some stage in every growth process, there is a time of finding autonomy. In most cases, autonomy requires a certain level of rebellion. This was certainly true for the young United States. In this lesson, your student will learn what led to the American Revolution. | ■ Student Learning Pages 4.A–4.B |

| VOCABULARY |
| --- |
| **PATRIOTS** people who love or defend their country, in this case the American colonies |
| **LOYALISTS** people who are loyal to something, in this case to the British government |
| **TARIFF** a tax paid on things purchased from another country |

## Let's Begin

**1** **EXPLAIN AND DISTRIBUTE** Explain that wars in the colonies, such as the French and Indian wars, had cost Britain money. Britain's government felt that if it had to defend the colonies, the colonies should pay. It began imposing taxes. The colonists felt that it wasn't their idea to fight the French and Indian wars, and that Britain should pay for its own wars. The British had also ordered the colonists to feed and house the British soldiers in their homes. Colonists called these orders The Intolerable Acts. Have your student research the actions of Britain and the colonies between 1767 and 1773 and then complete Student Learning Page 4.A.

**DID YOU KNOW?**

Among the people killed in the Boston Massacre was Crispus Attucks, an escaped slave who was leading fellow sailors in a protest against the British.

**2** **RELATE AND CONTRAST** Tell your student that in September 1774 representatives from 12 colonies (all except Georgia) met at the First Continental Congress in Philadelphia. Delegates voted to stop all trade with Britain until the Intolerable Acts were repealed. The delegates formed militias in each colony and agreed to meet again if necessary. The people who wanted to defend their rights were called **Patriots.** Tell your student that

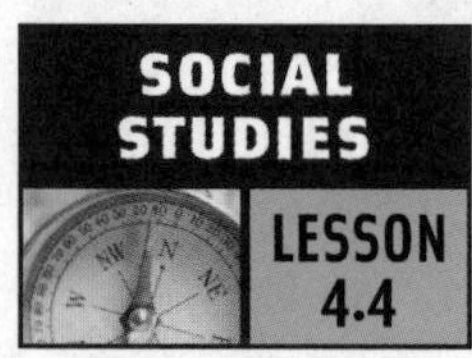


there were still many people in America who were loyal to Britain and King George. They were called **Loyalists.** Most of the Patriots considered themselves loyal. They hoped that Britain would listen to them and repeal the acts so they could continue to be British subjects. Ask, *What would Loyalists think of forming militias?* [they would think it was treason] *What would Patriots think if Britain refused to repeal the Intolerable Acts?* [they would think it was essential to fight]

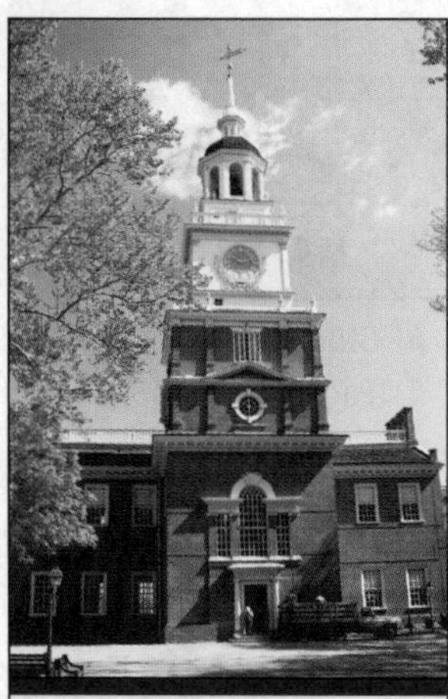

*Independence Hall, where the First and Second Continental Congresses met.*

**3** **RELATE AND MAP** Explain that in April 1775 the British were marching by night to Concord, a city northwest of Boston, to destroy weapons that Patriot militias were storing there and to arrest important patriot leaders. Paul Revere and others rode to warn the people living in the countryside. For more about Revere's ride, see Henry Wadsworth Longfellow's poem in Lesson 1.4. In the morning, British troops met Patriot minutemen at the Battle of Lexington. The British won but were delayed long enough at Lexington that patriot women had time to hide all the weapons and for patriot leaders to escape. Have your student read more about this important battle. Help your student find a map with Boston, Lexington, and Concord on it. Trace the movements of the various groups in this adventure.

**4** **RELATE AND DISCUSS** Tell your student that after the battle of Lexington delegates planned the Second Continental Congress for May 1775. There they formed the Continental Army and chose George Washington as general. They sent a letter called the Olive Branch Petition telling Britain they would be loyal if they could have more freedom. King George III would not read the petition. Ask, *Why do you think King George wouldn't read the Olive Branch Petition?* [he was angry that the colonists were defying his orders] *What did the Patriots do next?* [fight for independence]

**FOR FURTHER READING**

*Countdown to Independence: A Revolution of Ideas in England and Her American Colonies: 1760–1776,* by Natalie S. Bober (Atheneum, 2001).

*Events Leading to the American Revolution,* by Linda R. Wade (Abdo & Daughters, 2001).

*From Colonies to Country,* by Joy Hakim (Oxford University Press Children's Books, 1999).

**5** **ORGANIZE** Use Student Learning Page 4.A, the information from this lesson, and your student's research to make a time line together of the events leading to the American Revolution.

# Branching Out

## TEACHING TIP

Reading historic novels and biographies are good complements to the lesson.

## CHECKING IN

You can assess your student by asking him or her to list three events that led to the American Revolution and three things the Patriots did to try to settle their problem with Britain peacefully.

# Match Act and Reaction

SOCIAL STUDIES

4.A

Read each British action. Then read the Patriot reactions to these actions. Match each reaction to its action and write the correct letter.

## British Actions

_____ 1. Parliament passes the Stamp Act of 1765, saying that all printed documents (even playing cards) require a stamp to show the tax was paid.

_____ 2. Parliament repeals the Stamp Act but in 1767 passes the Townshend Acts, putting a **tariff** on paper, wool, tea, and other British products.

_____ 3. In 1768, British troops are stationed in Boston because of the resistance to the Townshend Acts.

_____ 4. On March 5, 1770, Parliament repeals the Townshend Acts because the boycott was hurting British merchants. It kept the tea tax.

_____ 5. The Tea Act of 1773 is passed. Colonists can only buy tea from the East India Company and still have to pay a tax.

_____ 6. Britain punishes Boston for the Tea Party. It sends soldiers into the city. Colonists are ordered to feed and house soldiers. The port of Boston is closed. The colonists call these the Intolerable Acts. People in Boston suffer.

## American Patriot Response

**A.** On December 16, 1773, the Sons of Liberty dress as Mohawk Indians, board ships, chop open tea chests, and throw tea into the harbor.

**B.** Americans from every colony send food, supplies, and money to Boston. Colonists begin identifying themselves as Patriots (rebels) or Loyalists (loyal to Britain). Leaders from 12 colonies meet to discuss what to do.

**C.** Colonists protest, "No taxation without representation!" Leaders from nine colonies meet. The Sons of Liberty burn stamps and threaten and attack stamp agents.

**D.** In 1772, the colonists form Committees of Correspondence in various towns all over the colonies. Committees send messages to each other by "express riders" such as Paul Revere.

**E.** Colonists boycott goods that have a tariff. The Daughters of Liberty make berry and herb teas and weave their own cloth to use instead of wool.

**F.** By 1770, fistfights between soldiers and colonists are frequent. When angry colonists surround soldiers on March 5, the soldiers fire. This is called the Boston Massacre.

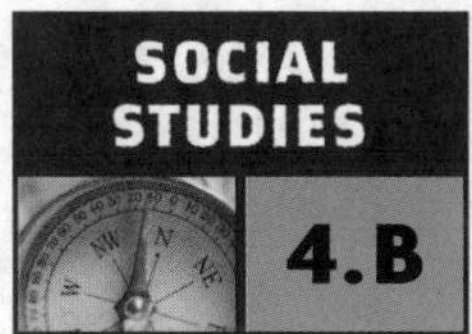


# What's Next? You Decide!

Now it's your turn to choose what to do next in the lesson. Read the activities and decide which one you want to do—you may want to try them all!

## Draw a Political Cartoon

**STEPS**

- ❑ Look at Benjamin Franklin's JOIN, or DIE cartoon. Notice that the parts of the snake are labeled with the initials of each colony. Franklin was trying to make the point that the colonies needed to unite as one to survive.
- ❑ Find other political cartoons in the newspaper. Figure out what each one is trying to say. If you need to, ask for an adult's help to understand the cartoons.
- ❑ Think of another possible political cartoon for this prerevolutionary period.
- ❑ Make a pencil drawing and revise as necessary. When it is ready, draw it in ink.

## Become a Revolutionary Character

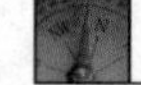

**STEPS**

- ❑ Research an important person of the prerevolutionary time.
- ❑ Write a script for that person as if he or she were talking. Have your character introduce himself or herself and tell about his or her life, particularly the part he or she played in preparing for the revolution.
- ❑ Dress in costume as the character, and act out your script for your family.

## Write a Historical Poem

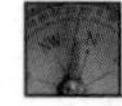

**STEPS**

In 1863, Henry Wadsworth Longfellow wrote about Paul Revere's midnight ride. The poem starts "Listen, my children, and you shall hear / Of the midnight ride of Paul Revere." (Check out Lesson 1.4 to read more of it.) Philis Wheatley was another poet in the 1700s.

- ❑ Find one or two of their poems to read, then write your own poem about an event in the lesson.
- ❑ Use any poetry style you like. In the 1700s, it was customary for poems to rhyme.

# Fighting the Revolution

***We, therefore, the representatives of the United States of America . . . declare that these United Colonies are, and of right ought to be, free and independent states.***
***—Declaration of Independence***

| OBJECTIVE | BACKGROUND | MATERIALS |
|---|---|---|
| To help your student follow the chain of events from the Declaration of Independence to the great battle of the American Revolution at Yorktown | The Declaration of Independence announced the colonists' intention to part from Britain. In this lesson, your student will find out how the American Revolution was fought and won. | ■ Student Learning Pages 5.A–5.B |

| VOCABULARY |
|---|
| **TREASON** disloyalty to one's country or government<br>**CONVICTIONS** strong beliefs or opinions a person has |

## Let's Begin

**1** **EXPLAIN** Explain that Patrick Henry was one of the earliest and most outspoken colonists who opposed King George III's taxes. After only two weeks as an elected representative in Virginia, Henry made a famous and bold speech that accused the king of trying to control America and destroy freedom. Many people accused Henry of **treason.** Point out that although other people felt the same way he did, they were afraid to speak out. The punishment for treason was hanging! Henry was brave enough to stand by his **convictions.** Have your student think of a time he or she had a strong opinion about something but knew that most other people did not agree. Ask, *How did that make you feel? What did you do?*

**2** **REVEAL** Explain that the purpose of the Declaration of Independence was to officially declare independence from Britain. It was written by Thomas Jefferson. He worked with Benjamin Franklin and John Adams and made several drafts before the final declaration was signed in 1776. Have your student research Jefferson, Franklin, Adams, and the story of the Declaration of Independence. Ask, *Why was it dangerous and risky to sign?* [because if the Americans lost to Britain, everyone who signed could be hanged]

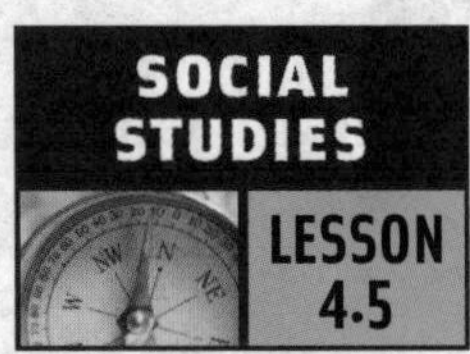


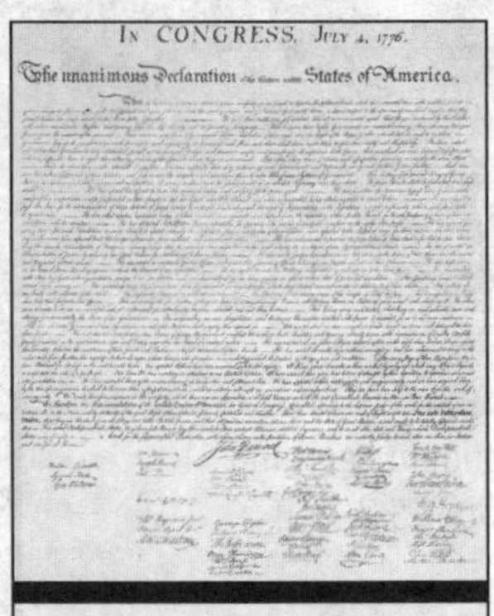

The Declaration of Independence

**3** **ANALYZE** Find a copy of the Declaration of Independence. Help your student write a sentence or two summarizing each paragraph. For each paragraph, ask, *What's the main idea?* Notice that the Declaration specifically mentions the king, King George III of Britain. Ask, *What do you think King George thought when he read this document? What part do you think upset him the most?* [answers will vary—he was angry enough to keep fighting a war]

**4** **EXPLAIN AND DISTRIBUTE** Distribute Student Learning Page 5.A. Explain that the American Revolution began in Lexington in 1775 and was not officially over until eight years later. Many battles were fought and other European countries besides Britain were involved. Have your student use a resource that describes the American Revolution to complete Student Learning Page 5.A.

**5** **EXPLAIN** Ask your student what he or she knows about George Washington. Explain that Washington was the commander of the American army during the Revolutionary War. Point out that before he became a general, he was a land surveyor and made maps of western Virginia. Have your student read more about George Washington's life and his role in the American Revolution. Ask, *How do you think his experience surveying land helped him lead his troops in the war?* [he was used to camping outdoors and could create good battle plans based on the land's terrain]

**6** **RELATE AND RESEARCH** Point out that many of the people who contributed to victory in the American Revolution were women. Martha Washington, Mary Ludwig Hays, and Deborah Sampson were on the front battle lines fighting and providing support. Phillis Wheatley was an African-American poet and former slave who published poems supporting the American Revolution. Have your student choose one of these women and find out the details of her contributions. Ask, *What inspires you the most about what this woman did?*

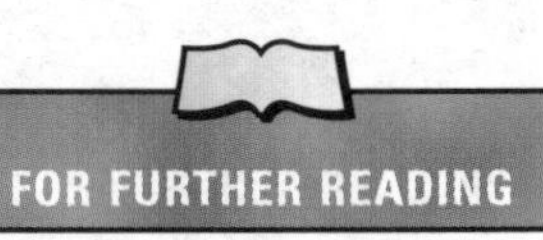

**FOR FURTHER READING**

*The American Revolution*, by Bruce Bliven and J. Thomas, ed. (Random House Childrens Pub., 2002).

*The American Revolution: "Give Me Liberty, or Give Me Death!"*, by Deborah Kent (Enslow Publishers, Inc., 2002).

*Eyewitness: American Revolution*, by Stuart Murray (DK Publishing, 2002).

# Branching Out

## TEACHING TIP

Have a historical atlas available for reference so that your student can trace where the events of the American Revolution occurred.

## CHECKING IN

Ask your student to tell you about two people who contributed to the American Revolution. Your student should be able to give details about each person and his or her contributions.

 

# Review the Battles of the Revolution

**PART A**

**Read each set of sentences. Then complete the sentences using one of the terms.**

Delaware
Valley Forge
Lexington
Treaty of Paris
Saratoga

1. After the Battles of ______________ and Concord, fought on April 19, 1775, the British victory was soured by Patriots shooting at them all the way back to Boston. Two hundred and fifty British soldiers died, compared to 50 Patriots.

2. Washington had his army cross the ______________ River in the dark on Christmas night of 1776. The next morning they surprised the German soldiers who were paid to fight for the British at Trenton, New Jersey, and took 1,000 prisoners.

3. The Battle of ______________ took several days in the fall of 1777. The British were low in supplies. Fresh soldiers kept reinforcing American troops. The British surrendered.

4. In late 1777, disease, hunger, and cold were the enemy at ______________. More than 2,500 men died.

5. In 1781, Nathanael Greene's tactic of forcing the British to chase him across North and South Carolina paid off when George Washington and the French navy helped him defeat Cornwallis. This was the last great battle, although it wasn't until 1783 that the ______________ officially ended the war.

**PART B**

**Choose one of the battles and read more about it in history books or on the Internet. On a separate sheet of paper, draw a scene from the battle. Your drawing can be a simple pencil sketch or a colorful poster. Be sure to show the details that made the battle important.**

# What's Next? You Decide!

Now it's your turn to choose what to do next in the lesson. Read the activities and decide which one you want to do—you may want to try them both!

## Write a Patriot Story

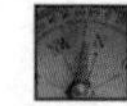

### STEPS

You are working for a family of Loyalists. No one knows that you are a Patriot. British officers come to have dinner with the family. You hear some news that will be very helpful to General George Washington and his army. You know he is camped in Pennsylvania, 20 miles from where you are. It would take you six hours to walk that far.

- ❑ Write a short story about how you would solve this problem and manage to warn General Washington. What risks would you have to take? What hardships would you have to face?
- ❑ Share your story with an adult.

## Figure the Math

### STEPS

Write five math word problems involving information about the American Revolution.

- ❑ Record the answers in a separate place.
- ❑ Give the problems to a friend to see if he or she can find the right answers.
- ❑ Example: The first battle of the American Revolution was in April 1775. General Cornwallis surrendered Yorktown in October 1781. The official peace came with the Treaty of Paris in 1783. About how long was the war? (6 years of fighting, 8 official years)

# Founding a New Nation

*Living free isn't easy.*

SOCIAL STUDIES

LESSON 4.6

| OBJECTIVE | BACKGROUND | MATERIALS |
|---|---|---|
| To help your student understand the difficult process of establishing a nation | The laws, government, and citizens' rights of the United States of America are based on our Constitution. Although written more than 200 years ago, it still serves us in our pursuit of life, liberty, and happiness. In this lesson, your student will learn how the Constitution of the United States came to be. | ■ Student Learning Pages 6.A–6.B |

**VOCABULARY**

**CONFEDERATION** a group that has agreed to unite
**LEGISLATIVE BRANCH** the part of an organization that has the power to make laws
**EXECUTIVE BRANCH** the part of an organization with power to administer and enforce laws
**JUDICIAL BRANCH** the part of an organization that interprets the laws
**COMPROMISE** a way to settle a disagreement or conflict in which each side gives up part of what it wants
**AMENDMENTS** additions or changes to the Constitution

## Let's Begin

1 **EXPLAIN AND RESEARCH** Explain that shortly after the Declaration of Independence was completed, the Continental Congress starting deciding how to run the country if the colonies won the war. The colonies adopted the Articles of **Confederation,** which outlined the new plan for the national government. Have your student research the Articles of Confederation. Discuss.

2 **RELATE** Tell your student that 55 representatives met in Philadelphia, Pennsylvania, in May 1787 to revise the Articles of Confederation. This meeting became known as the Constitutional Convention. Have your student research the problems and solutions discussed at the Constitutional Convention. Then have your student complete Student Learning Page 6.A.

3 **CHART** Explain that an important decision of the Continental Congress was to establish the **legislative, executive,** and **judicial branches** of the federal government, and create a system of

SOCIAL STUDIES
LESSON 4.6

checks and balances between each branch. Have your student study the chart of the checks and balances. Ask him or her what the job is for each branch.

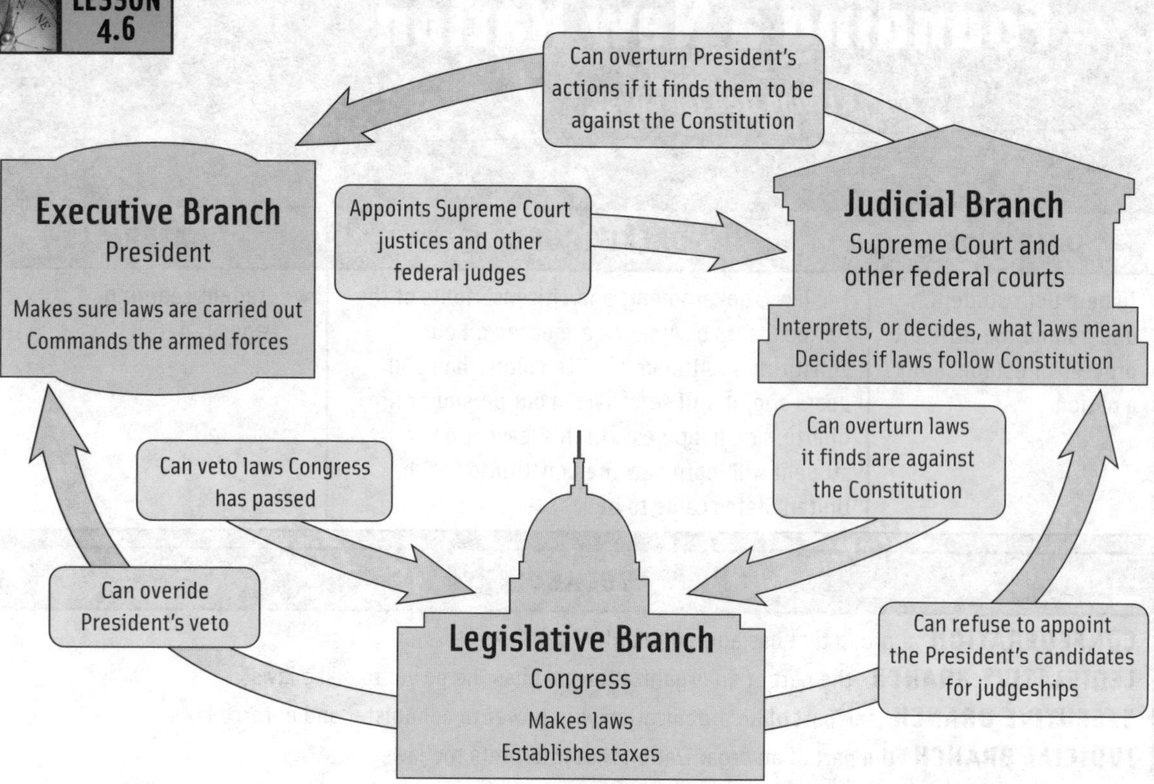
Can overturn President's actions if it finds them to be against the Constitution
Executive Branch
President
Makes sure laws are carried out
Commands the armed forces
Appoints Supreme Court justices and other federal judges
Judicial Branch
Supreme Court and other federal courts
Interprets, or decides, what laws mean
Decides if laws follow Constitution
Can overturn laws it finds are against the Constitution
Can veto laws Congress has passed
Can overide President's veto
Legislative Branch
Congress
Makes laws
Establishes taxes
Can refuse to appoint the President's candidates for judgeships

**4** **RELATE AND COMPARE** Tell your student that there were two main groups arguing over how the new government should be set up. The Federalists wanted a strong national government. The Antifederalists were worried that the government would not protect people's rights. Have your student compare their beliefs.

**5** **DISCUSS AND RESEARCH** Point out that the Constitution is a complex document involving **compromise** among many different ideas. The Bill of Rights added 10 **amendments,** or additions, to the Constitution. Have your student look up information on the Bill of Rights and give a brief list of what the 10 amendments are.

**FOR FURTHER READING**

*Sourcebook and Index: Documents That Shaped the American Nation* (Oxford University Press, 1999).

*Creating the Constitution: The People and Events That Formed the Nation,* Daniel Weidner, ed. (Enslow Publishers, Inc., 2002).

# Branching Out

## TEACHING TIP

Discuss with your student countries that are trying to set up new governments now.

## CHECKING IN

Ask your student what challenges Americans faced in setting up a new government that would work.

# Understand How the Constitution Was Created

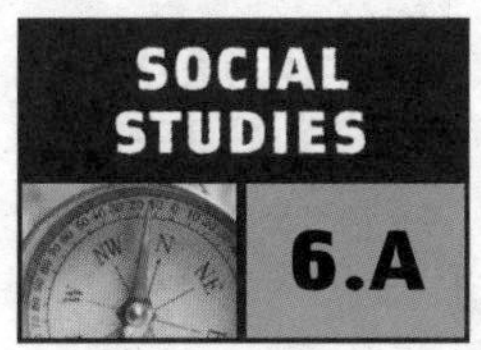


**PART A** **Read each problem. Then write the letter of the solution.**

## Problems

______ 1. The government had to be stronger. Some wanted to revise the Articles of Confederation. Others wanted to start over.

______ 2. The Virginia Plan proposed that states with larger populations, such as Virginia, should have more representatives than smaller ones. The New Jersey Plan proposed that each state have the same number of representatives, no matter what the size.

______ 3. How should populations be counted? Southern states wanted slaves to be counted when deciding how many representatives a state should have but not counted when it came to figuring taxes. Northern states with few slaves did not like this plan.

______ 4. Slavery caused another debate. Many wanted to outlaw it completely. Southern states were totally against that idea.

## Solutions

**A.** The delegates debated the Virginia and the New Jersey Plans for weeks. Roger Sherman of Connecticut suggested a compromise. Congress should be made up of two parts. One would be the Senate and the other the House of Representatives. The Senate would have two representatives for each state. In the House of Representatives, larger states would have more delegates.

**B.** The Three-Fifths Compromise said that enslaved people would count for three-fifths of a person for representation in Congress and for taxes.

**C.** As the delegates discussed what to do to strengthen the government, two plans developed. Both involved abandoning the Articles of Confederation and starting over.

**D.** Delegates agreed to take no action against slavery for 20 years.

**PART B** **Choose one of the problems listed. With a partner, hold a debate with each of you taking one side of the issue. Be sure to research the situation and ideas of each side in detail before your debate. Then switch sides and debate the issue again from the other point of view.**

# What's Next? You Decide!

Now it's your turn to choose what to do next in the lesson. Read the activities and decide which one you want to do—you may want to try them both!

## Take Minutes

### STEPS

People take minutes of a meeting so everyone has a record of what happened. The reason we know so much about the Constitutional Convention is that James Madison took careful notes of everything that happened.

- ❑ Choose a meeting in your home or community and practice taking minutes.
- ❑ Start by listing the date, time, place, and what type of meeting it is. Sometimes it is appropriate to write down the names of everyone who is there.
- ❑ List each topic that is brought up, write a brief description of any discussion, and record decisions.
- ❑ Rewrite or type a final draft of your minutes.
- ❑ Show them to someone else who was at the meeting, and ask if he or she thinks your minutes are accurate.

## Make a Woodcut

### MATERIALS

- ❑ cardboard
- ❑ 1 roller or paintbrush
- ❑ 1 pair scissors that can cut cardboard
- ❑ old newspaper
- ❑ 1 rolling pin
- ❑ glue
- ❑ ink or tempera paint

### STEPS

In early America, many of the pictures that were in books and newspapers were printed from woodcuts. You can use cardboard to make your own woodcut-style print.

- ❑ Cut a rectangle out of cardboard.
- ❑ Cut out a cardboard design that will fit within the rectangle. Your design can be a simple shape, such as a star, or something more detailed.
- ❑ Glue your design to the rectangle. The only thing that will "print" is the raised design.
- ❑ Cover your inking surface with newspaper.
- ❑ With a roller or paintbrush, cover the top of the cardboard "woodcut" with ink or paint. Lay it facing up on your surface and lay paper over it.
- ❑ Use a rolling pin to roll over the paper so that it makes contact with the ink or paint.
- ❑ Carefully remove the paper and set it aside to dry.
- ❑ Repeat the process to make as many prints as you want.

TEACHING THE LESSON

# Spreading Out Across the Continent

*Go west, young man!*

| OBJECTIVE | BACKGROUND | MATERIALS |
|---|---|---|
| To help your student understand the expansion and development of a new country | As the United States matured, it acquired new land, pioneers settled new places, and debates about slavery grew stronger. The nation's strength was tested with the War of 1812. In this lesson, your student will learn about how the young United States of America grew and will see the beginnings of the nation. | ■ Student Learning Pages 7.A–7.B<br>■ 1 copy Comparison Chart, page 353 |

| VOCABULARY |
|---|
| **DOCTRINE** a principle or position<br>**INDUSTRY** a process of systematic labor to make goods or provide services<br>**ABOLITIONISTS** people who wanted to abolish, or end, slavery |

## Let's Begin

**1** **EXPLAIN** Explain that in the early 1800s Americans moved further west, especially along the Ohio and Mississippi Rivers. They relied on the port in New Orleans to ship their goods to eastern ports and Europe. At that time, New Orleans was owned by the French. President Thomas Jefferson wanted to buy New Orleans. France decided to offer the entire Louisiana Territory. Have your student research the Louisiana Purchase. Ask, *Why did France sell more than New Orleans?* [to get money for its war against the British]

**2** **EXPLORE** President Jefferson sent an exploration party led by Captain Meriwether Lewis and William Clark to explore the new land. Jefferson wanted Lewis and Clark to find a water route to the Pacific Ocean, learn about the geography, soil, and climate of the new territory, and establish a neighborly relationship with the Native Americans they met. Have your student research the Lewis and Clark expedition. Ask, *What Native American woman*

**DID YOU KNOW?**

An invaluable member of the expedition was York, Clark's slave and childhood friend. After the expedition, York wanted his freedom. Clark refused.

*helped the expedition?* [Sacagawea] Have your student talk about two of the things Lewis and Clark saw in the West.

**3** **EXPLAIN AND RESEARCH** Explain that another event that affected the United States in the early 1800s was the war between France and Britain. Both countries tried to keep the United States from selling supplies to the other. The British began seizing U.S. trade ships and taking their goods and kidnapping U.S. sailors. U.S. trade with countries overseas became almost impossible. At first the United States didn't want to go to war, but tensions grew. In 1812, President Madison asked Congress to declare war on Britain. Have your student research the War of 1812. Ask, *Why do you think the United States was drawn into the war even though it started as a war between France and Britain?* [because the impact of the war at sea and actions of the British affected the ability of the United States to function]

Eli Whitney's cotton gin

**4** **REVEAL** Explain that in 1817, James Monroe became the fifth president of the United States. He purchased Florida from Spain and issued an important statement to European nations called the Monroe Doctrine. The **doctrine** warned against trying to create future colonies in the Americas. Have your student research the Monroe Doctrine and write a brief paragraph about how it affected United States and European relationships.

**5** **RESEARCH AND COMPARE** Explain that **industry** began to grow in the United States in the late 1700s. People began to leave their farm homes and move into towns to work and run new machines. Have your student research two of the following inventions that were important to developing industry: Eli Whitney's cotton gin, Cyrus McCormick's mechanical reaper, Robert Fulton's steam-powered boat, Peter Cooper's steam-powered locomotive, and Samuel Morse's telegraph. Ask him or her to fill out a Comparison Chart showing how things were done before and after the invention.

**FOR FURTHER READING**

*How We Crossed the West: The Adventures of Lewis and Clark,* by Rosalyn Schanzer (National Geographic Society, 2002).

*The Louisiana Purchase (Let Freedom Ring: Exploring the West),* by Elizabeth D. Jaffe (Bridgestone Books, 2002).

*The War of 1812 (Cornerstones of Freedom),* by Andrew Santella (Children's Press, 2000).

# Branching Out

## TEACHING TIP

Try role reversal with your student. After he or she has researched a topic, ask your student to give you the lesson and ask questions.

## CHECKING IN

Ask the student to tell you about three events or issues of this time period, who the important people were, and the outcomes.

# Map the Expansion of a Country

Look at the map. On a separate sheet of paper, create a time line that shows when the different regions joined the United States. Then write a paragraph describing how three of the regions came to be part of the United States.

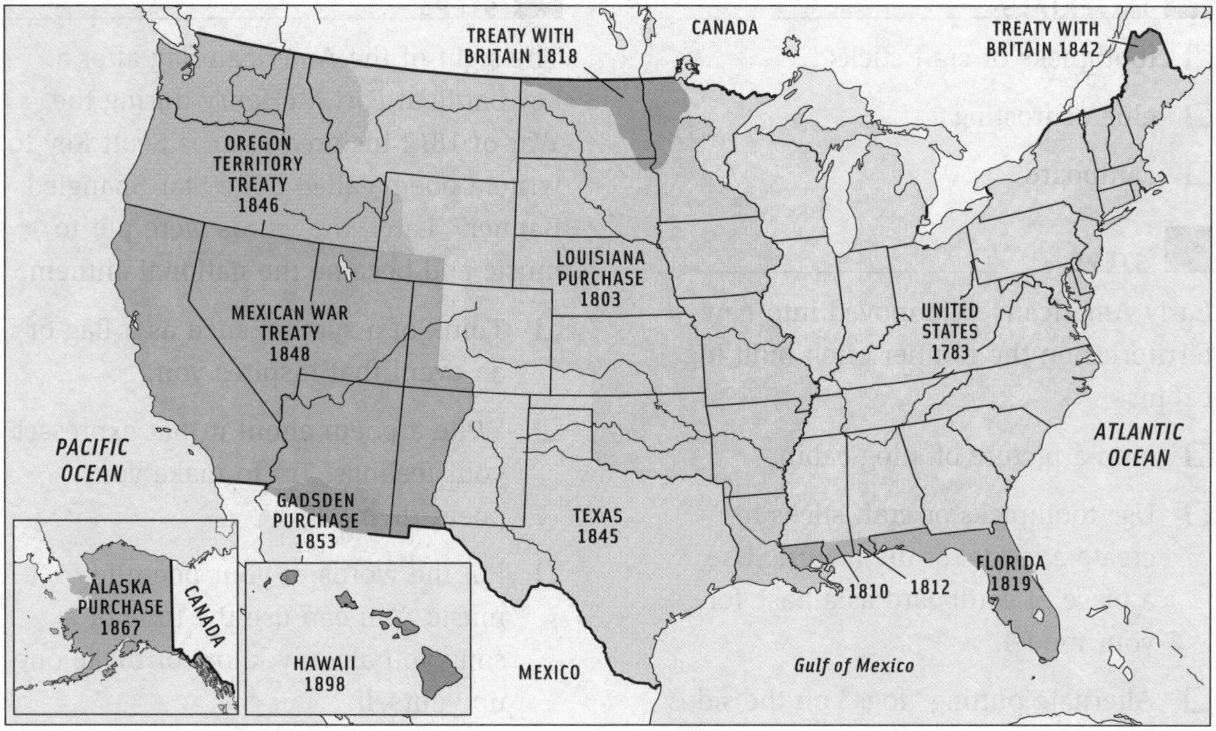

# What's Next? You Decide!

Now it's your turn to choose what to do next in the lesson. Read the activities and decide which one you want to do—you may want to try them both!

## Make a Log Cabin

### MATERIALS

- ❑ toothpicks or craft sticks
- ❑ glue or frosting
- ❑ cardboard

### STEPS

Early Americans who moved into new territories on the frontier often built log cabins.

- ❑ Find a picture of a log cabin.
- ❑ Use toothpicks or craft sticks to create a model of the picture. Use a piece of cardboard as a base for your model.
- ❑ Alternate putting "logs" on the sides and on the front and back walls.
- ❑ Use glue to hold each layer together.
- ❑ Research a story about early American pioneers. Share the story with an adult and show him or her your model log cabin.

## Write Your Own Anthem

### STEPS

The sight of the American flag after a key battle at Fort McHenry during the War of 1812 inspired Francis Scott Key to write a poem called "The Star-Spangled Banner." Later, the words were put to music and became the national anthem.

- ❑ Think of a symbol such as a flag or an event that inspires you.
- ❑ Write a poem about it that expresses your feelings. Try to make your poem rhyme.
- ❑ Put the words of your poem to music. You can use the tune of a song you already know or make one up yourself.
- ❑ Sing your anthem for your family and friends.

# Traveling the Road to Civil War

***Compromise until you can compromise no more.***

| OBJECTIVE | BACKGROUND | MATERIALS |
|---|---|---|
| To help your student understand the complex issues that led to the Civil War | The question of slavery had been delayed when the U.S. Constitution was written. As time went on, the North and the South developed increasingly different views about it. In this lesson, your student will see how the country tried to compromise and how difficult it can be for a country to solve problems. | ■ Student Learning Pages 8.A–8.B |

**VOCABULARY**

**SLAVERY** a social and an economic system in which people are forced to give up their freedom and work for a master

**COMPROMISE** a way to settle a disagreement or conflict in which each side gives up part of what it wants

**FUGITIVE** a person who is on the run or trying to escape

**TERRITORIES** a land belonging to a country but not yet made into a state or province

## Let's Begin

**1** **EXPLAIN** Explain to the student that as the United States grew **slavery** and the opposition to slavery became issues that affected every political decision. In 1819, there were 11 free states and 11 slave states in the Union. The people of Missouri wanted to become the 23rd state and the 12th slave state. Free states did not want to be outnumbered. John C. Calhoun of South Carolina said that slavery was a state issue and that states had the right to make decisions about their own way of life. Finally, Senator Henry Clay of Kentucky proposed the Missouri Compromise. Have your student look up what that **compromise** was and find a map that shows the Missouri Compromise line.

**2** **DISCUSS** Tell the student that for 30 years the Missouri Compromise worked. All new states north of the line were admitted as free states, and all states south of the line were admitted as slave states. In 1849, however, there were 15 free states and 15 slave states. California applied for statehood. Henry Clay proposed another compromise. Have your student read about the Compromise of 1850 and the **Fugitive** Slave Law.

Ask, *What was the compromise?* [California could be a free state if the North would accept the Fugitive Slave Law]

**3** **READ AND DISCUSS** Tell your student that eventually the discussions in Congress about these issues became very heated. People had strong feelings on both sides. Without the Compromise of 1850, the North and South would have split then over the issue of slavery. The people who opposed slavery were willing to compromise because they wanted to keep the country together. Ask, *How would you have felt if you were a member of Congress during this time? What would you have done?*

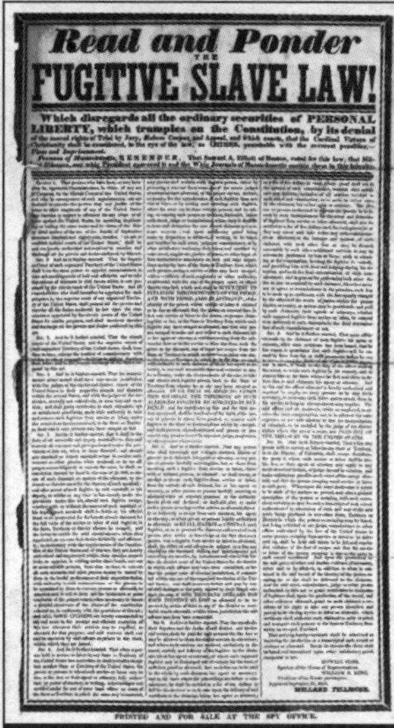
Read and Ponder
THE
FUGITIVE SLAVE LAW!

*Many Northerners were upset by the Fugitive Slave Law.*

**4** **RELATE** Explain that in 1854 another decision challenged the Missouri Compromise. Senator Stephen Douglas of Illinois proposed that Nebraska become two **territories.** Both would be free territories because they were above the line drawn in the Missouri Compromise. Southerners felt this was unfair. Congress passed the Kansas-Nebraska Act, which left the decision to the popular vote by the people in the territories. Have your student look up this act. Ask, *What were the consequences of this act?* [Kansas voted to be a slave territory; Northerners said the voting had been unfair; violence broke out] *What does that say about what might happen in the future?* [people were passionate enough about slavery to resort to violence or war]

**5** **RELATE AND COMPARE** Many Americans were content to keep compromising on the issue of slavery. Three things helped change that: Harriet Beecher Stowe wrote a novel, Dred Scott lost a court case, and John Brown tried to start a revolution. Have your student research each of these people and make a cause-and-effect chart. Your student should list these three events on one side of a paper and on the other side list many of the effects that happened. Remember that the same event can have different effects for different people.

**FOR FURTHER READING**

*Before the Creek Ran Red,* by Carolyn Reeder (Harper Collins Children's Books, 2003).

*Days of Jubilee: The End of Slavery in the United States,* by Patricia C. McKissack and Fredrick L. McKissack (Scholastic, Inc., 2003).

*Slavery and the Coming of the Civil War: 1831–1861,* by Christopher Collier and James Lincoln Collier (Benchmark Books, 2000).

# Branching Out

## TEACHING TIP

If your student has difficulty thinking of causes and effects, guide him or her by asking questions or by sharing an effect you notice to get him or her started.

## CHECKING IN

Ask, *How did Americans try to compromise over the issue of slavery?* The student should be able to list at least two ways.

 

# Understand the Causes of War

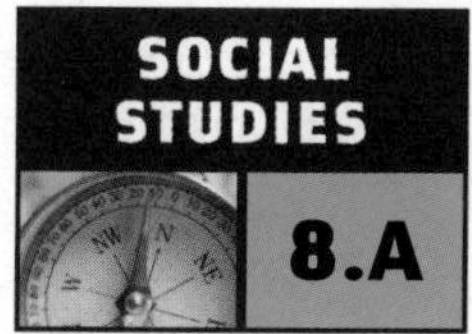


**PART A Read each question and write the letter of the answer.**

**A.** John Brown

**B.** Harriet Beecher Stowe

**C.** Dred Scott

**D.** Missouri

**E.** Kansas-Nebraska Act

**F.** California

_______ **1.** What state was the 23rd state admitted to the Union?

_______ **2.** The Fugitive Slave Law was passed so that which state could be admitted to the Union?

_______ **3.** Kansas was called "bleeding Kansas" because of what compromise?

_______ **4.** Who wrote the book *Uncle Tom's Cabin*?

_______ **5.** Which former slave went to court to try to get his freedom because he had lived in Illinois, a free state?

_______ **6.** Who tried to steal weapons from Harpers Ferry, Virginia?

**PART B Choose one of the events from Part A and become a reporter. Write a news article that explains the importance of the event, the outcome, and the people involved. Share your article with an adult.**

# What's Next? You Decide!

Now it's your turn to choose what to do next in the lesson. Read the activities and decide which one you want to do—you may want to try them both!

## Experience the Power of Speaking

### MATERIALS

- ❑ 3–10 index cards

### STEPS

Henry Clay, Frederick Douglass, Daniel Webster, and Sojourner Truth all influenced the way people thought by making public speeches.

- ❑ Research a speech from this time period that you agree with or write your own speech. Possible Internet sources include http://douglassarchives.org/ or http://www.sojournertruth.org.
- ❑ Learn your speech so that you can deliver it smoothly, with feeling and excitement.
- ❑ Try not to read the speech word for word. Instead, use index cards and make notes to help you remember the main points and the order you want to say them.
- ❑ Present it to an audience.
- ❑ Get feedback from your audience. Ask them if your speech was convincing and offer to answer any questions they have.

## Practice Compromising

### STEPS

Is there an issue that you and someone else regularly disagree about? It might be who gets the comics section of the newspaper first, or who has to do a certain chore at home.

- ❑ Write down what is important to you about the issue and what you think is important to the other person.
- ❑ See if there are any areas where you would be willing to offer a compromise.
- ❑ Approach the other person with your compromise suggestion.
- ❑ Discuss options with the other person, giving him or her plenty of time to think about other possibilities.
- ❑ If you start to get angry, calm yourself down. If you both feel strongly about the issue, you will need to be committed to working it out.
- ❑ Once you have reached a compromise, write it down and have the other person look it over to make sure you both agree.
- ❑ Sign the written compromise and keep it in a safe place.

# Marching to the Civil War

*There are no winners in war.*

| OBJECTIVE | BACKGROUND | MATERIALS |
|---|---|---|
| To help your student follow the sequence of events in the Civil War | The Civil War saw the nation fighting against itself. In this lesson, your student will follow the events of the Civil War, including learning what led to it, and see how war can tear apart a country and families. | ■ Student Learning Pages 9.A–9.B<br>■ 1 present-day map of the United States<br>■ 1 copy Grid, page 355 |

| VOCABULARY |
|---|
| **CIVIL WAR** a war between parts of the same country<br>**SECTIONALISM** the feeling that certain sections' interests are important<br>**ABOLITIONISTS** people who wanted to abolish, or end, slavery<br>**SECEDE** to withdraw as a member or ally<br>**EMANCIPATE** to free someone or something |

## Let's Begin

**1** **INTRODUCE AND DISCUSS** Mention that the **Civil War** between the North and the South began on April 12, 1861, and ended on April 9, 1865. Offer background about the time period by explaining that in the mid-1800s the North was much more industrialized than the South. This means that there were more businesses, factories, and workers in the North. In the South, life was centered around the plantation and the economy was based on agriculture. The differences between the North and South led to what was called **sectionalism,** which was the feeling that the country was split into sections and didn't have any common interests. Ask, *How would sectionalism lead to people deciding to stop working together?* [they feel so different they feel they should each go their own way] Discuss.

**2** **EXPLAIN** Explain that among the differences between the North and South, slavery was an important difference. Slavery wasn't allowed in the North as it was in the South. Plantations grew crops, such as cotton, and relied on slaves to keep them running. By the 1850s, most Northern states had passed laws stating that slavery was illegal. Slaves were treated cruelly and didn't have the

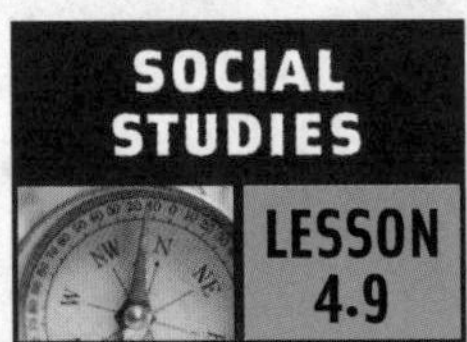


same rights as others. People who wanted to end slavery were called **abolitionists.** Reveal to your student that three famous abolitionists were Harriet Tubman, Nat Turner, and Harriet Beecher Stowe. Have your student research on the Internet or in books to find out what they did to help end slavery. Then discuss.

**3** **SHARE** Mention that many people tried to help free slaves. Ask your student what he or she knows of the Underground Railroad. Explain that the Underground Railroad was a secret system of helping slaves escape to freedom by hiding them in safe places as they made their way to the North. If you haven't already, have your student go to Lesson 1.3 for the biography of Sojourner Truth, who helped with the Underground Railroad. Mention that the Underground Railroad helped thousands of slaves escape to the North. Have your student go to http://www.nationalgeographic.org, where he or she can follow the journey of a slave going through the Underground Railroad. Have your student trace a route of the Underground Railroad on a present-day map of the United States.

Abraham Lincoln

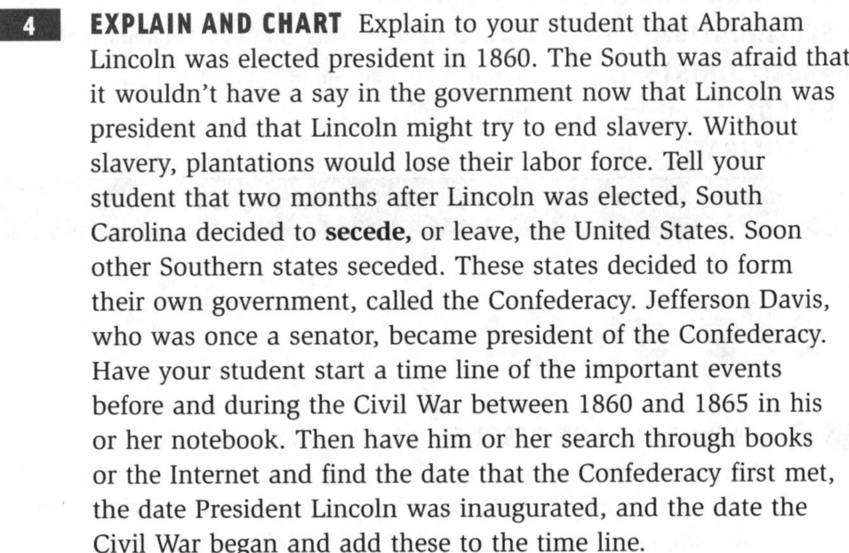

**4** **EXPLAIN AND CHART** Explain to your student that Abraham Lincoln was elected president in 1860. The South was afraid that it wouldn't have a say in the government now that Lincoln was president and that Lincoln might try to end slavery. Without slavery, plantations would lose their labor force. Tell your student that two months after Lincoln was elected, South Carolina decided to **secede,** or leave, the United States. Soon other Southern states seceded. These states decided to form their own government, called the Confederacy. Jefferson Davis, who was once a senator, became president of the Confederacy. Have your student start a time line of the important events before and during the Civil War between 1860 and 1865 in his or her notebook. Then have him or her search through books or the Internet and find the date that the Confederacy first met, the date President Lincoln was inaugurated, and the date the Civil War began and add these to the time line.

Jefferson Davis

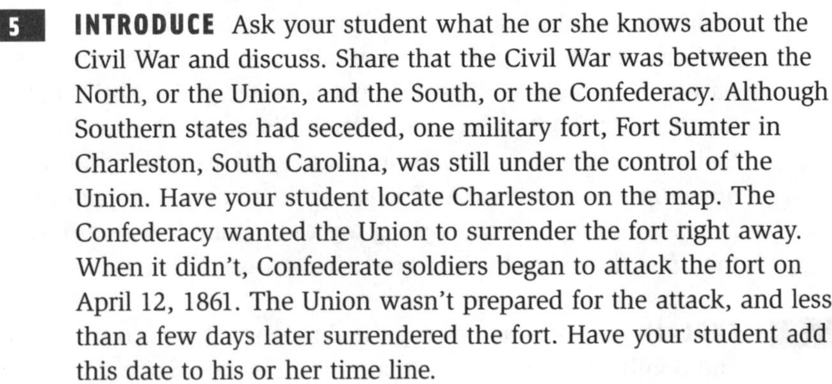

**5** **INTRODUCE** Ask your student what he or she knows about the Civil War and discuss. Share that the Civil War was between the North, or the Union, and the South, or the Confederacy. Although Southern states had seceded, one military fort, Fort Sumter in Charleston, South Carolina, was still under the control of the Union. Have your student locate Charleston on the map. The Confederacy wanted the Union to surrender the fort right away. When it didn't, Confederate soldiers began to attack the fort on April 12, 1861. The Union wasn't prepared for the attack, and less than a few days later surrendered the fort. Have your student add this date to his or her time line.

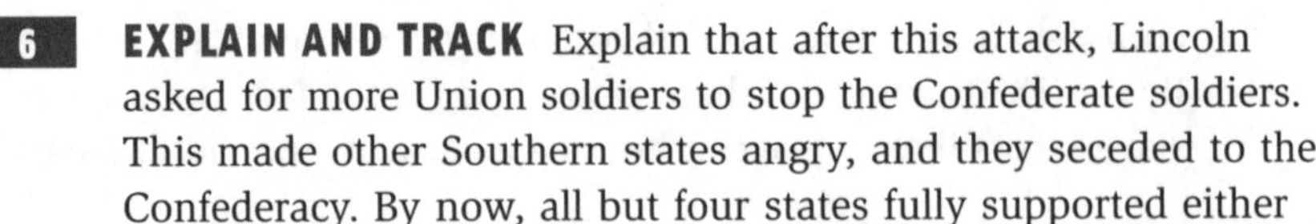

**6** **EXPLAIN AND TRACK** Explain that after this attack, Lincoln asked for more Union soldiers to stop the Confederate soldiers. This made other Southern states angry, and they seceded to the Confederacy. By now, all but four states fully supported either the Union or the Confederacy. Share that the four remaining states, Delaware, Kentucky, Maryland, and Missouri, were called border states. Then explain that West Virginia broke away from Virginia to join the Union. Have your student locate and track these on the map.

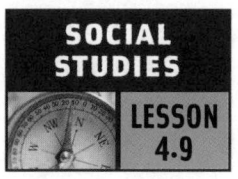

## Union and Confederacy During the Civil War

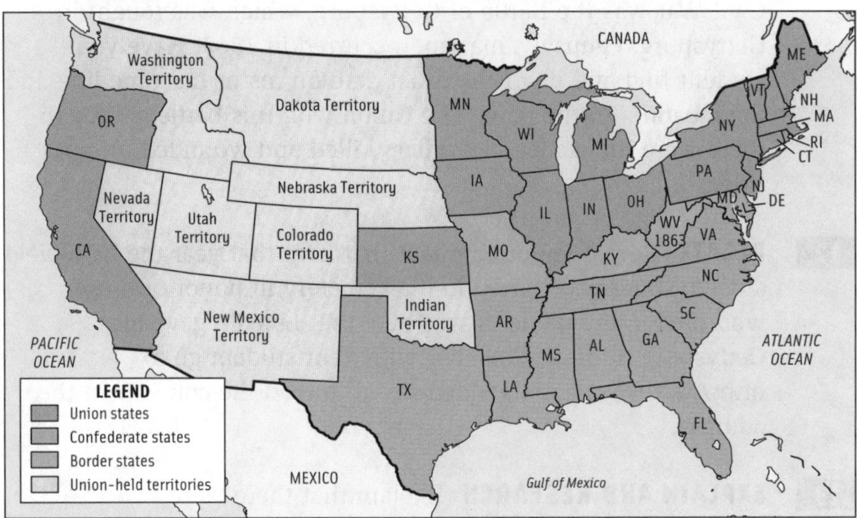


**7** **CONNECT** Explain that the Civil War was an emotional time for the country. Sometimes families had members fighting on different sides of the war. Have your student read the letters of soldiers and their families during the Civil War. Reproductions of letters can be found on the Internet at http://www.civilwarletters.com.

**8** **RESEARCH AND COMPARE** Have your student research important people in the Civil War, such as Confederate General Robert E. Lee, Union General Ulysses S. Grant, Matthew Brady, Frederick Douglass, William Lloyd Garrison, Belle Boyd, and Clara Barton. Explain that not just soldiers were important in the Civil War—many men and women helped with gathering supplies, offering medicine, and more.

**9** **EXPLAIN AND RESEARCH** Explain that one important early battle in the Civil War was the First Battle of Bull Run (called the Battle of Manassas by the Confederacy), which occurred in 1861. This battle is important because at first the Union was winning, but then the Confederates eventually won. Have your student locate this town on the map, and then have him or her research the exact date of this battle and chart it on his or her time line.

**10** **DISCUSS** Tell your student that at first Lincoln's goal was to keep the Union together. By 1862, though, Lincoln came to believe that he had to **emancipate,** or free, the slaves to win the war. In January of that year, Lincoln gave the Emancipation Proclamation. Reveal that the Emancipation Proclamation was a formal statement

from Lincoln that said that all slaves in the Confederacy were free. Go to http://www.archives.gov and enter "Emancipation Proclamation" into the Search function to read the contents of this statement.

**ENRICH THE EXPERIENCE**

Have a conversation with your student about the importance of having freedom.

**11** **EXPLAIN AND MAP** Explain that the war continued even after the Emancipation Proclamation. Another important battle of the Civil War was the Battle of Gettysburg, which was fought in Gettysburg, Pennsylvania, and occurred in 1863. Have your student find and chart the exact date on his or her time line and the location on the map. The Union won this battle, although there were thousands of soldiers killed and wounded on both sides.

**12** **RELATE** Reveal to your student that later that year the battlefield at Gettysburg was turned into a cemetery in honor of those who died in the battle. It was here that Lincoln gave his Gettysburg Address. Together with your student go to http://www.gettysburgaddress.com to read the contents of the address.

**13** **EXPLAIN AND RESEARCH** Explain that there were two important incidents toward the end of the Civil War that led to the Confederacy's downfall. In 1864, Union General William Tecumseh Sherman overtook Atlanta, Georgia, and then later Savannah, Georgia. Have your student locate these places on the map and then find the exact dates and chart them on the time line. Then have your student research three other important battles of the Civil War—the Battle of Antietam, the Second Battle of Bull Run, and the Battle of Vicksburg—and find their locations on the map and chart them on the time line.

**14** **REVIEW** Review with your student the map and time line. Then have him or her add this: Appomattox Court House, Virginia, April 9, 1865. This was the date that Union General Grant and Confederate General Lee met. Lee surrendered to the Union.

**FOR FURTHER READING**

*Eyewitness: Civil War,* by John Stanchak (DK Publishing, 2000).

*Fields of Fury: The American Civil War,* by James M. McPherson (Atheneum, 2002).

*Scholastic Encyclopedia of the Civil War,* by Catherine Clinton (Scholastic Trade, 1999).

# Branching Out

## TEACHING TIP

Let your student guide you to what interests him or her about the Civil War.

## CHECKING IN

Assess your student by asking him or her why the Civil War began. Encourage him or her to "teach" the lesson back to you.

# Take Sides

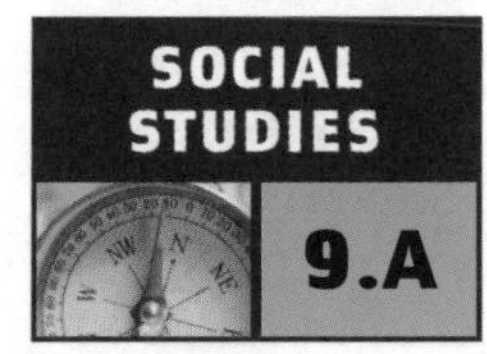


Read each Civil War–related term. Decide if it belongs with the North or the South. Write each term on the correct side. Then see if you can create a crossword puzzle using some of the terms. Write clues for the terms you've chosen.

- ❑ abolitionists
- ❑ Abraham Lincoln
- ❑ Confederacy
- ❑ industrialization was increasing quickly here
- ❑ victory at Fort Sumter
- ❑ victory at Battle of Gettysburg
- ❑ seceded states
- ❑ Jefferson Davis
- ❑ Robert E. Lee
- ❑ victory at Battle of First Bull Run
- ❑ Union victory at Savannah, Georgia
- ❑ plantations important here
- ❑ Ulysses S. Grant

| Civil War Terms | |
|---|---|
| **North** | **South** |
| | |

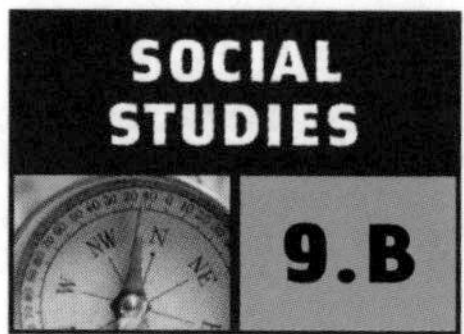


# What's Next? You Decide!

Now it's your turn to choose what to do next in the lesson. Read the activities and decide which one you want to do—you may want to try them both!

## Make Music

### MATERIALS

- ❑ 1 kazoo (optional)
- ❑ 1 piano or other instrument (optional)

### STEPS

Sing a song from the Civil War with your kazoo!

- ❑ Research in books or on the Internet for a song from the Civil War, such as "Dixie" or "The Battle Hymn of the Republic."
- ❑ Learn the words or learn how to play the song on the piano or with a kazoo.
- ❑ Practice until the song sounds polished and then play it for someone. If you live in an area where there is a lot of Civil War history, have an adult help you arrange to play it at a community historical event.

## Draw or Sculpt It

### MATERIALS

- ❑ colored pencils or fine markers
- ❑ modeling clay (optional)
- ❑ cardboard for sculpture base (optional)

### STEPS

Make a Civil War drawing or sculpture.

- ❑ Choose a battle scene or a person doing something during the Civil War and sketch it on paper. For example, include soldiers in battle, or perhaps a nurse tending to the wounded, or even a spy sneaking through the fields.
- ❑ Remember to try to show the emotion of the people involved.
- ❑ After your sketch is complete, you can fill it in with color and detail or choose one scene and sculpt it in clay.
- ❑ Give your artwork a title and sign it.
- ❑ See if your local library would like to display it!

# Understanding the Reconstruction

***A man convinced against his will is of the same opinion still.***

| OBJECTIVE | BACKGROUND | MATERIALS |
|---|---|---|
| To help your student understand how America changed after the Civil War | The period of Reconstruction was an important time for the United States. In this lesson, your student will learn about the struggle to reunite the nation and follow through on the promise of emancipation. | ▪ Student Learning Pages 10.A–10.B<br>▪ 1 copy Comparison Chart, page 353 |

| VOCABULARY |
|---|
| **ASSASSINATED** killed suddenly or secretly<br>**RECONSTRUCTION** the reorganization of the Southern American states back into the Union<br>**IMPEACHMENT** when charges of illegal actions are brought against an elected official |

# Let's Begin

**1** **EXPLAIN** Explain that President Abraham Lincoln was **assassinated** on the night of April 14, 1865. Have the student research what happened that night. Because of the assassination, Lincoln was not able to carry out his **Reconstruction** plans to reunite the North and South. Vice President Andrew Johnson, who was from the South, became the president and created his own plan. Under Johnson's plan, in order to be readmitted to the Union each Southern state needed to form a new state government, pledge to obey all federal laws, and deal fairly with newly freed African-Americans. By 1865, Johnson felt the Southern states had all met the requirements. Ask, *How do you think the fact that Johnson was from the South influenced his Reconstruction plan?* [his plan was easier on the South; he had sympathy for the South]

**DID YOU KNOW?**

In response to the Reconstruction Plan, a group of white Southerners formed the Ku Klux Klan, a secret society that would intimidate African-Americans and other minorities.

**2** **OBSERVE** Explain that there is a folk saying that says "A man convinced against his will is of the same opinion still." Have your student copy this saying into his or her notebook. Talk together about what it means. With slavery outlawed, Southern

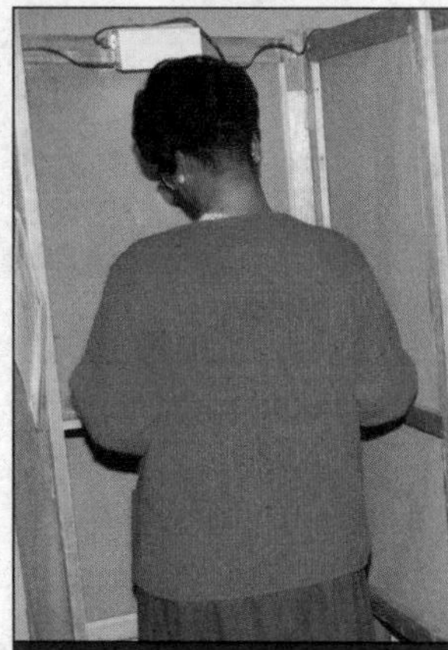

*The Fifteenth Amendment granted African-Americans the right to vote.*

**DID YOU KNOW?**

In 1870, the Fifteenth Amendment gave African-American men the right to vote. It would be 50 years before women were given the right to vote in 1920.

**FOR FURTHER READING**

*A History of US, Reconstruction and Reform, 1865–1870,* by Joy Hakim (Oxford University Press, 2002).

*Rebuilding After the Civil War,* by Judith Peacock (Bridgestone Books, 2002).

*Reconstruction: The Years Following the Civil War,* by Linda R. Wade (Abdo & Daughters, 1998).

states passed laws called black codes. African-Americans could not vote, act as jurors, own guns, own land, or take certain jobs. Ask, *How do the black codes show that the folk saying is right?* [many Southerners still believed that black people were not equal to them and were unwilling to give former slaves the full rights of citizenship]

3 **EXPLAIN AND COMPARE** Explain that Congress was angry about the black codes. Congress made a new Reconstruction plan and sent federal troops to the South to enforce it. Military governors repealed the black codes and set heavy taxes to rebuild railroads and encourage new businesses, such as factories, to replace the old slave-dependent economy. Southerners resented Northerners who moved south to do business, calling them carpetbaggers because of their cloth suitcases. The Freedmen's Bureau was created and built hospitals and schools for newly freed people. Two African-Americans became U.S. senators, Hiram R. Revels and Blanche K. Bruce. Twenty African-Americans were elected to the House of Representatives. Ask, *How do you think this made the Southerners feel?*

4 **SUMMARIZE** Explain that after the Civil War between 1865 and 1870 three amendments were added to the Constitution. These amendments abolished slavery and guaranteed equal rights for former slaves and people of all races. Ask your student to look up the Thirteenth, Fourteenth, and Fifteenth Amendments to the Constitution. Talk together about what each amendment means.

5 **DISTRIBUTE AND COMPARE** By 1870, all former Confederate states were readmitted to the Union. By 1877, federal troops left the South. Immediately people began to work around the Fourteenth and Fifteenth Amendments, passing Jim Crow laws, charging poll taxes, and requiring reading tests before voting. Then have your student complete Student Learning Page 10.A.

# Branching Out

## TEACHING TIP

The topics covered in this lesson may be emotionally charged for your student. Introduce each new item slowly, and take time to address your student's questions or concerns about slavery or any other issues.

## CHECKING IN

Ask your student to mention two differences between Johnson's Reconstruction plan and Congress's Reconstruction plan.

# Explore the Reconstruction

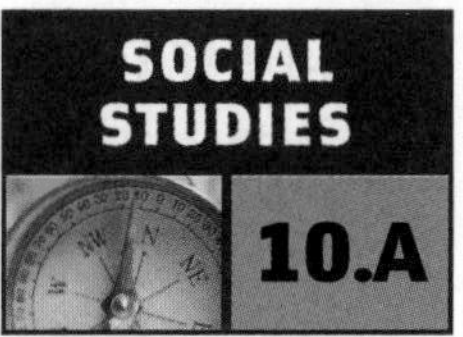


Write in the correct letters of the causes and effects.

| Cause | Effect |
|---|---|
| The South loses the war. | 1. ______ |
| 2. ______ | Andrew Johnson must carry out Reconstruction. |
| The South passes black codes. | 3. ______ |
| 4. ______ | Much of the South resents the military government. |
| Taxes are imposed for rebuilding. | 5. ______ |
| 6. ______ | Southerners resent carpetbaggers. |
| 7. ______ | The Ku Klux Klan is formed. |
| Andrew Johnson opposes the Fourteenth Amendment. | 8. ______ |
| Reconstruction ends. | 9. ______ |

**A.** The South passes Jim Crow laws.
**B.** Congress impeaches Johnson.
**C.** Congress sets up military governments.
**D.** Abraham Lincoln dies.
**E.** Congress passes a new Reconstruction plan.
**F.** Northerners come to the South for business.
**G.** The South must be readmitted to the Union.
**H.** The people in the South resent the new taxes.
**I.** Black codes are repealed.

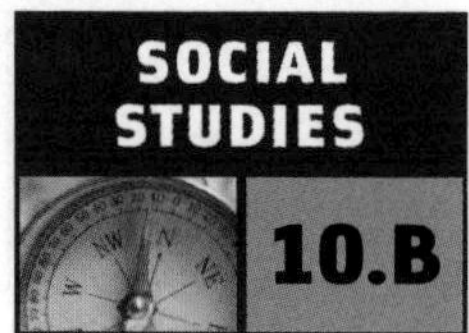


# What's Next? You Decide!

Now it's your turn to choose what to do next in the lesson. Read the activities and decide which one you want to do—you may want to try them both!

## Design a Reading Lesson Plan

### STEPS

The Freedmen's Bureau was created to help newly freed people after the war.

- ❑ You are a teacher hired by the Freedmen's Bureau. You are teaching children and grown-ups to read. Most of your students have never been to school before.
- ❑ Write down what you will teach first. Perhaps you want to start with the alphabet, or teach the sounds of the vowels. This is called a lesson plan.
- ❑ After you write your lesson plan, think of several activities or exercises that go with your lesson plan.
- ❑ Then write down how you will make sure the students have understood the lesson.
- ❑ Share your lesson plan with an adult. Then teach your lesson plan to a friend.

## Build a Model Railroad

### MATERIALS

- ❑ cardboard
- ❑ colored pencils or markers
- ❑ heavy paper or posterboard
- ❑ twigs, cotton, sand for landscape
- ❑ 6–10 buttons or bottle caps
- ❑ glue
- ❑ modeling clay
- ❑ paint and brushes

### STEPS

Railroads were very important in rebuilding the South and restarting the economy.

- ❑ Research the railroad during Reconstruction and find a few pictures to give you some ideas.
- ❑ Use a model train set or make your own out of cardboard and paper, buttons, or bottle caps.
- ❑ Build a model train scene that has trees, houses, and other details showing how things might have looked in a Southern train station during Reconstruction. You can use cardboard for the foundation, model clay to hold up the trees, and thick paper to make the houses.

 

TEACHING THE LESSON

SOCIAL STUDIES

LESSON 4.11

# Expanding Westward

***New places and new opportunities for some, great change for others.***

| OBJECTIVE | BACKGROUND | MATERIALS |
|---|---|---|
| To help your student understand how the western United States was settled | Going west became easier and more attractive for Americans with the growth of railroads, opportunity to own farmland, and new inventions in agriculture and communication. In this lesson, your student will learn about how the western United States was settled to the Great Plains and Pacific Ocean. | ■ Student Learning Pages 11.A–11.B<br>■ 1 U.S. map |

### VOCABULARY

**WAGON TRAINS** groups of people traveling across the country in a long line of covered wagons pulled by horses and oxen

**TRANSCONTINENTAL** reaching across the continent

**HOMESTEADERS** people who took advantage of the Homestead Act and turned a piece of land on the Great Plains into a farm

**IMMIGRANTS** people who move from one country to another country

**RESERVATIONS** land that's been set aside by the U.S. government for native peoples to live on

## Let's Begin

**1** **REVIEW AND EXPLAIN** Look at a United States map with your student. Talk about what the western frontier was like in 1830, before the Mexican-American War. Explain that many Native Americans lived in the West on the Great Plains, in the Rocky Mountains, and on the West Coast. Some had lived there for centuries; others had come when their lands in the East were taken over by the European settlers. There were also a few mountain men in the West. These men were French, English, American, Native American, and free African-American men who made their living by trapping animals and selling their fur. Point out that at this time most of the land west of the Rocky Mountains was not part of the United States. Ask, *What country did most of the western land belong to in 1830?* [Mexico]

**2** **EXPLORE** Explain that in 1846 the United States and Britain signed a treaty that settled the border between the northwestern United States, which was called Oregon Country, and Canada. People in the East heard news that the land there was beautiful and good for farming. Many decided to travel across the country to begin new lives in the Northwest. Explain that they traveled in groups of covered wagons called **wagon trains** along a 2,000-mile route called the Oregon Trail. The travelers had to survive the weather, dangerous river crossings, accidents, and sickness. Other hazards included attacks by Native American groups or armed robbers. Have your student look up the Oregon Trail. Follow the trail together on a map. Ask, *What types of land did travelers have to cross on the Oregon Trail?* [rivers, mountains, plains] *If a wagon train averaged 20 miles a day, how many days would it take to travel the entire trail?* [100] *Why did people want to move to Oregon?* [adventure, good land]

*Groups of settlers traveled the Oregon Trail in wagon trains.*

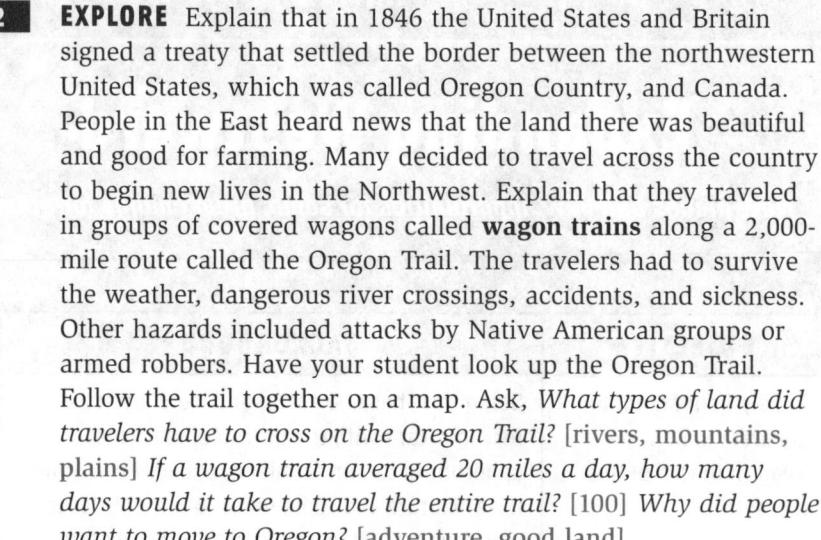

**3** **RELATE** Tell your student that in 1848 gold was accidentally discovered in a stream in California. Word spread quickly. Word of mouth and letters back to the East gave Easterners "gold fever." People from other countries even came to look for gold. In 1849, more than 80,000 people arrived in California looking to strike it rich. Historians call this the California gold rush. Ask, *Why do you think miners were called forty-niners?* [many arrived in 1849]

**4** **EXPLAIN** Explain that in 1845 there were 15,000 people in California and that by 1850 there were 93,000. Very few got rich by finding gold. Supplies were in demand and prices were high. What little gold most miners found was spent on basic food and supplies. Some people did make money by starting businesses. Levi Strauss, who emigrated from Germany in 1850, made tough pants held together with metal rivets. Ask, *What do you think a person needs to create a successful business?* [there is an existing need for their goods or services; an original idea; to be in the right place at the right time]

**5** **REVEAL AND RESEARCH** Explain that at first there was very little communication between the people in the East and West. Then, in 1860, the Pony Express began delivering mail across the country in only 10 days. Have your student look up the Pony Express to see how this was possible. Have him or her write a brief paragraph describing how the Pony Express worked.

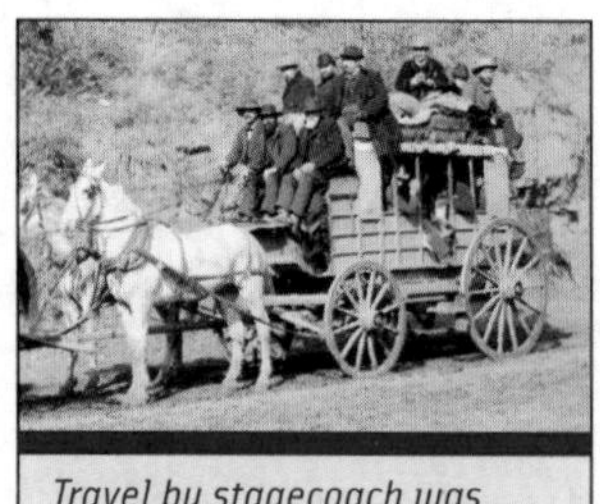
*Travel by stagecoach was rough and uncomfortable, but it provided an opportunity to see the beauty of the West.*

**6** **COMPARE** Explain that soon after the Pony Express began an inventor named Samuel Morse invented the telegraph. The telegraph could send electronic messages across the country in minutes. Ask your student to research the invention and development of the telegraph. Have him or her compare the **transcontinental** telegraph to the Pony Express. *How did the use of the telegraph affect the Pony Express?* [it put the Pony Express out of business]

 

SOCIAL STUDIES LESSON 4.11

7 **RELATE AND DISCUSS** Explain that railroads also changed the way people traveled and how goods were shipped. In 1862, two different railroad companies began a race to build a railroad all the way to the Pacific Coast. The two companies involved were the Union Pacific and the Central Pacific. Point out that the labor of former Civil War soldiers, former slaves, and Irish, German, and Chinese immigrants made this huge construction project possible. Many people died in dynamite accidents while blasting through rock to make tunnels. Finally, on May 10, 1869, the transcontinental railroad was complete. People could travel from the East Coast to the West Coast in less than 10 days. By 1893, there were several transcontinental railroad lines. Have your student look on a map of the United States and choose a place he or she would like to visit. Then help your student obtain a railroad map and trace the rail route that goes closest to the destination.

8 **CONTRAST** Ask your student to consider why most people who went west chose to travel all the way to California or Oregon instead of settling along the way. Explain that the land between the Mississippi River and the Rocky Mountains is called the Great Plains. The plains were a flat, dry grassland, great for buffalo to live on but not for farming. Halfway through the Civil War, Congress decided to do something about this. It passed the Homestead Act. Have your student look up the Homestead Act and tell why it helped settle the Great Plains area.

9 **DISCUSS** Tell your student that the Homestead Act inspired many people to settle on the western plains. Homesteading, however, was not easy. The grasses of the Great Plains extended deep into the soil. **Homesteaders** had to dig past the grass, called sod. This is why the farmers of the Great Plains were called sodbusters. Many of the settlers had no farming experience. There were many other challenges from nature: tornadoes, hailstorms, flooding, droughts, prairie fires, blizzards, ice storms, and clouds of grasshoppers that could eat all the crops. Many settlers abandoned the land before their five years were up. Have your student suppose he or she is a settler taking advantage of the Homestead Act. Ask your student to write a letter to a family member in the East describing the land and daily life, or make a pencil or an ink drawing of a homestead.

10 **EXPLAIN** Point out that even though some homesteaders left their land and returned to eastern cities and towns, the opportunity to own farmland attracted other people to take their places. These people not only came from the eastern United States but from European countries as well. The new **immigrants** brought new farming skills and seeds for crops that grew well in the soil of the Great Plains. Explain that many former slaves from the South, who called themselves Exodusters, also took advantage of the Homestead Act. They mostly settled in Kansas and Nebraska. They took their name from the Book of Exodus in the Bible, in which Moses leads his people out of slavery. African-American settlers

founded the town of Nicodemus, Kansas. Have your student read more about the contributions European and African-American homesteaders made to the establishment of American life on the Great Plains.

**11** **RELATE** Explain that the creation of machines and tools made farming easier and more productive for the homesteaders. Have your student research the inventions that changed plains farming. Ask, *How did these new tools and crops change people's lives?*

**12** **EXPLAIN** Point out that in 1830 the majority of people living in the western United States were Native Americans. The Native American tribes that roamed the Great Plains followed the buffalo and depended on the great herds for their food, clothing, and shelter. As the railroad brought more settlers west and ranchers began fencing in their land, the buffalo started disappearing. Railroad workers killed buffalo for food, and others began shooting buffalo for sport or for their hides. The drop in buffalo population and increase in homesteaders was threatening the Native American way of life. The interests of the United States and the Native Americans were in conflict. The government wanted the Native Americans to move onto specific areas of land that had been set aside for them. These were called **reservations.** Ask, *How do you think moving onto a reservation would change the Native Americans' way of life?* [they would not be able to hunt freely or move across the land freely]

*Today you can still see windmills on farms in the Great Plains.*

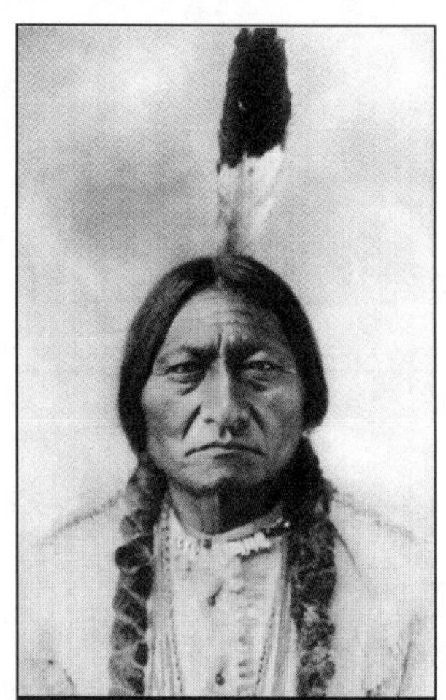
*Lakota tribal leader Sitting Bull refused to sell the Black Hills to the United States government.*

# Branching Out

## TEACHING TIP

There are many topics in this lesson. Encourage your student to further explore the area(s) he or she is most interested in.

## CHECKING IN

Show your student a United States map. Have him or her point out at least two western regions and explain how they got settled.

**FOR FURTHER READING**

*The Quest for California's Gold,* by James P. Burger (Powerkids Press, 2002).

*Westward Expansion: Making of America,* by Dale Anderson (Raintree/Steck-Vaughn, 2000).

# Write Their Stories

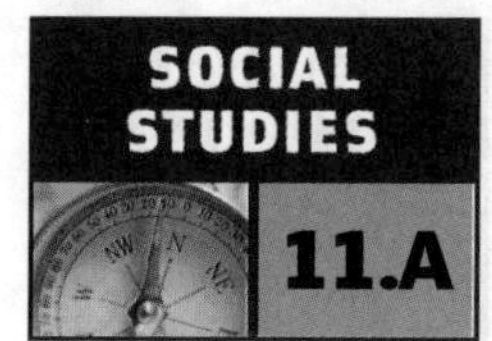


Read the description of each child. Then write a brief paragraph about the boy or girl. Describe what brought the family to the western United States, details about daily life, what he or she hears the family talk about, and how he or she feels. Research and use an extra sheet of paper if you need to.

1. Martha, an 11-year-old American girl from Illinois who is traveling with her family to Oregon Country on the Oregon Trail in 1846

2. Red Bird, a Lakota Sioux Native American boy who lives with his tribe on a reservation in the Black Hills in 1874

3. Elizabeth, a 10-year-old African-American girl from Alabama whose family now has a farm in Nebraska on the Great Plains

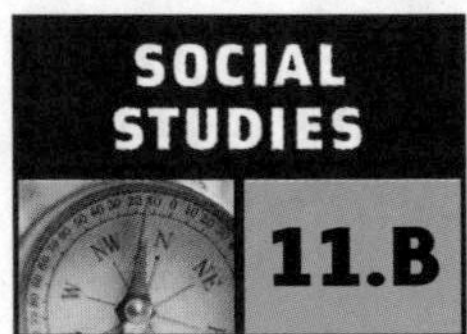


# What's Next? You Decide!

Now it's your turn to choose what to do next in the lesson. Read the activities and decide which one you want to do—you may want to try them both!

## Make Butter

### MATERIALS

- ❑ 1 pint heavy cream
- ❑ 1 clear plastic container with lid
- ❑ salt (optional)

### STEPS

The early settlers had to make all of their own food—including butter. Try making your own butter.

- ❑ Put the cream in a container with a lid.
- ❑ Shake the container quickly until the cream is white and thick. This is whipped cream.
- ❑ Keep shaking the container until yellow butter forms. It will be surrounded by thin milky liquid. This may take several minutes.
- ❑ Sprinkle salt onto the butter if you like. Press the butter with a spoon and pour off the liquid. This liquid is fresh buttermilk. Try it if you want!
- ❑ Add a little water to the butter. Swirl the water around, then pour it off and press the butter again. When no more liquid comes out, the butter is ready.
- ❑ Shape your butter and put it on a butter dish. You can stir some honey into it and make honey butter.
- ❑ Spread the butter on your favorite bread or biscuits and share it with your family!

## Model the Oregon Trail

### MATERIALS

- ❑ 1 map Oregon Trail that shows rivers, valleys, and mountains
- ❑ modeling clay or salt dough (recipe below)
- ❑ craft paint and paintbrush
- ❑ 1 flat piece cardboard or wood

**Salt Dough** Ask an adult for help in making this recipe before you begin. Simmer 1 cup salt, $\frac{1}{2}$ cup cornstarch, and $\frac{2}{3}$ cup water over low heat, stirring constantly until thick. Remove from heat and cool. Knead well.

### STEPS

Make a three-dimensional or relief map of the Oregon Trail.

- ❑ Put a thin layer of clay or salt dough over a cardboard or wood base.
- ❑ Study the map of the Oregon Trail and draw a sketch of it lightly onto the clay. Add more clay or dough to show where the mountains begin and where the highest points are.
- ❑ Carve grooves to represent the rivers.
- ❑ When you are finished, let the map dry completely.
- ❑ Paint the map—including a line for the Oregon Trail.
- ❑ Share your map with your friends and family.

TEACHING THE LESSON

# Reforming America

*If we want to, we can find a better way.*

| OBJECTIVE | BACKGROUND | MATERIALS |
|---|---|---|
| To give your student an appreciation of the reforms and inventions that helped the United States grow and improve | New industries brought big business and power to America. American farmers and immigrants from Europe came to work in the factories. The fast growth of industrial society created problems that required reform. In this lesson, your student will learn about how the nation grew, changed, and worked through these problems. | ■ Student Learning Pages 12.A–12.B<br>■ 1 map North and South America |

## VOCABULARY

**INDUSTRY** a specific system of labor to create a product or products
**SWEATSHOPS** factories where workers have long hours, unhealthy conditions, and low wages
**UNIONS** groups of people, usually laborers, uniting in a common cause
**STRIKE** an action in which workers refuse to work until their demands are met
**TENEMENTS** run-down apartment houses in a poor section of a large city
**PREJUDICE** a judgment based on a preconceived idea, a belief, or an opinion
**REFORMS** changes that are made to improve something that is not working well
**ANTITRUST LAWS** laws that prevent single companies from having too much control
**MUCKRAKERS** people who look for scandal or injustice and write about it
**ISTHMUS** a narrow area of land connecting two larger areas of land
**STOCK MARKET** an organized place where stocks are bought and sold

# Let's Begin

1 **EXPLAIN AND RESEARCH** Explain that in the late 1700s the Industrial Revolution began in the United States. Previously, most people farmed for a living and made the things they needed by hand. Then machines were invented. Machines needed workers to run them. Jobs opened up in the cities, and people moved from their farms. A man named Francis Cabot Lowell created one of the largest factories in Boston in 1812. Point out that although most of our products today are made in factories, in the early 1800s this was a revolutionary change. Explain that most of the workers in the factory were young women who came from nearby farms for the opportunity to earn money. Ask, *How would it change a person's life to leave*

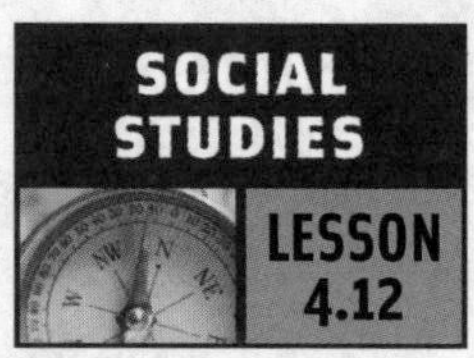


*a farm and go to work in a factory?* [more crowded with people, being paid to work for the first time, working required hours, buying food instead of growing it]

**2** **EXPLAIN** Tell your student that while **industry** was growing, inventors were finding better systems and materials. Several businessmen grew their companies and became very rich. When an English inventor developed the Bessemer process of making steel in 1856, Andrew Carnegie began making steel at the then lowest possible price. He bought mines, ships, and railroads so he could keep costs low. He paid his workers as small a wage as possible. He became one of the world's richest people. Explain that when oil was found in 1859 in western Pennsylvania, John D. Rockefeller used methods similar to Carnegie's to build the oil industry and also became extremely rich. This period in history is sometimes called the Gilded Age because of the many people who became wealthy in business. Have your student research one of the men who became wealthy in business during the Gilded Age and write a paragraph about what he did.

**DID YOU KNOW?**

At the end of his life, Andrew Carnegie donated millions of dollars to build public libraries and to help other causes.

**3** **EXPLAIN AND DISTRIBUTE** Explain that other new inventions, such as the electric lightbulb and the telephone, changed the way Americans lived and worked. Between 1856 and 1903, inventors created new processes and machines that have evolved into what we use today. Have your student research the inventions of this time and complete the time line on Student Learning Page 12.A.

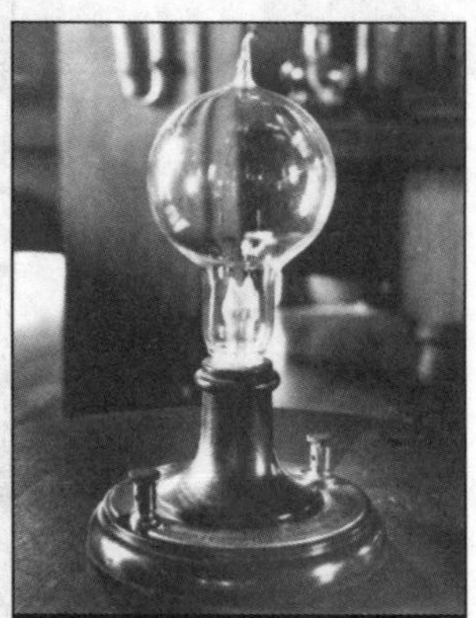

*Of all Thomas Edison's inventions, the electric lightbulb was the most difficult to complete.*

**4** **DISCOVER** Tell your student about the saying "Necessity is the mother of invention." Ask your student to explain what he or she thinks this saying means. Suggest that your student consider his or her daily routine and think of an invention that might solve a problem or make something easier to do. Encourage your student to take time thinking about this and to write down or draw any ideas in a notebook.

**5** **RELATE AND DISCUSS** Tell your student that businesses wanted to produce goods as cheaply as possible and did not always treat their workers well. Workers at one of Carnegie's steel mills worked 12 hours a day, had only two vacation days a year, and earned 10 dollars a week. Children also worked, doing dangerous jobs in cotton mills and coal mines. Their parents needed the money. Explain that unsafe working conditions endangered workers. Some factories were called **sweatshops** because the women there worked in crowded conditions with lots of sewing machines. Managers did not listen to the concerns of the workers. Have your student research what happened in 1911 at the Triangle Shirtwaist Company, a sweatshop in New York where 146 people were killed. Ask, *Why did the factory managers and owners treat people poorly?* [because they were mostly worried about making money]

*Alexander Graham Bell is best known for his invention of the telephone.*

*In the early 1800s, many children worked in factories.*

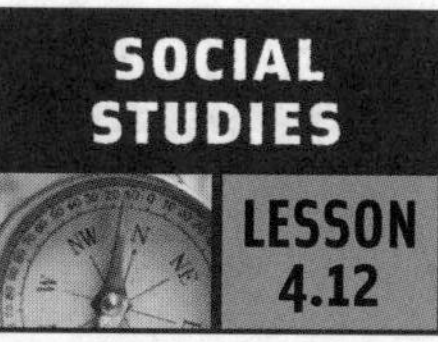

**DID YOU KNOW?**

Thomas Edison is famous for inventing the lightbulb. However, the bulb he invented could only burn for two days. Lewis Latimer, an African-American inventor, invented a bulb that could last much longer.

**6** **EXPLORE** Explain that eventually factory workers banded together into labor **unions.** Samuel Gompers was a teenager working in a cigar factory when he realized that workers would have more power if they organized into a group. He helped form a union of cigar factory workers. When owners cut workers' wages in 1877, Gompers led a **strike.** This was the beginning of the labor movement and the organization of the American Federation of Labor (AFL) in 1886. After a lot of hard work, many strikes, and even bloodshed and death, most industries finally got an eight-hour workday and safer conditions. The government also made child labor illegal. Explain that in 1894 Congress declared Labor Day a national holiday because of the contributions of workers. Have your student research the work of Gompers and the details of the labor movement. Ask him or her to take notes and present an oral overview of what he or she learned.

*Lewis Latimer improved on Thomas Edison's lightbulb.*

*Between 1860 and 1910, millions of people came from Europe to the United States as immigrants.*

**DID YOU KNOW?**

Another well-known labor organizer was Mary Harris Jones. When she was in her 50s, she began encouraging the miners in the Appalachian Mountains to join the union. She worked for the labor cause into her 90s. The miners called her Mother Jones.

**7** **EXPLAIN AND DISCUSS** Explain that in the 1800s and early 1900s many people came to the United States from Europe hoping to find work and better lives. They came from countries such as Ireland, Germany, Sweden, Italy, Austria-Hungary, and

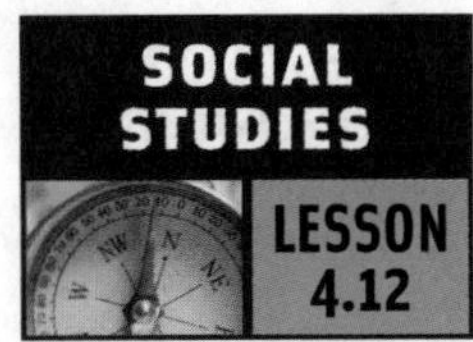


Russia. At that time, there were so many immigrants moving to cities to work in the factories that housing was hard to find. Whole families often crowded into **tenements,** which were buildings divided into small rooms or apartments. Eight people might live in one or two rooms. Some tenements didn't have heat or windows, or even indoor bathrooms. Have your student consider what it would have been like to live in a tenement apartment. Discuss.

**8** **RELATE** Point out that immigrants also faced **prejudice,** which is when people make judgments about a person based on their culture or race or another general characteristic without knowing the person. Some businesses posted signs that said things such as "No Irish need apply." Immigrants who didn't speak English faced the challenge of learning the language. Ask, *How do you feel about the way the immigrants lived? If you could do something to help, would you? What would you do?*

*Jane Addams started Hull House in Chicago in 1889.*

**9** **RESEARCH AND REPORT** Tell your student that some people did work to help immigrants. In 1889, a woman named Jane Addams rented an old house in Chicago called Hull House. Have your student look up Addams and find out what she did with the house and how her idea spread to other cities. Have your student write down three ways that she helped immigrants and poor people.

**10** **EXPLORE** Explain that even after the United States had stretched from coast to coast it kept expanding. In 1867, the Russian government sold Alaska to the United States for two cents an acre. Another addition to the country was the Hawaiian Islands. Americans established sugarcane and pineapple plantations in Hawaii in the 1800s. Have your student locate Hawaii on a map and read about Queen Liliuokalani. Have your student write the date of Alaska's and Hawaii's addition to the United States on his or her time line.

**11** **EXPLAIN AND ILLUSTRATE** Explain that Cuba was once a Spanish colony. In 1895, the Cuban people revolted. Spain reacted by imprisoning many Cuban people so they could not fight. Point out that people in the United States were upset because they believed in the right of the people to choose their government. Americans also didn't want to lose their many businesses in Cuba. The United States sent a military battleship to Cuba to protect American interests. There was an accidental explosion on the ship, but newspapers reported that Spain had caused the explosion. The United States blamed Spain and declared war in 1898. Have your student research the Spanish-American War and Theodore Roosevelt. Ask, *What was the outcome of the war?* [the United States won; Cuba gained independence from Spain; the United States got control of Puerto Rico, Guam, and the Philippines]

**12** **RELATE AND RESEARCH** Explain that because the United States won the Spanish-American War it was considered a world power.

 

Tell your student that Theodore Roosevelt's leadership in the Spanish-American War made him popular in the United States. Roosevelt was elected vice president and became president after William McKinley was assassinated. Roosevelt is well known for creating many important **reforms** for the country while he was the president, including **antitrust laws** and food safety laws, and establishing new national parks. Have your student read a biographical sketch of Roosevelt and write down six interesting facts about his life. Ask, *How did Roosevelt's childhood experiences affect the way he treated people as a leader?* [he was sick and weak as a child, and as an adult wanted to help less fortunate people]

13 **EXPLAIN AND DISCUSS** Explain that the Progressives were reformers who believed in progress and thought that life should become better. Some Progressives were writers. They wrote about problems that needed fixing. They were called **muckrakers** because they saw the muck and pointed it out. President Roosevelt agreed with the Progressives. Because a muckraker named Ida Tarbell wrote articles about Rockefeller's Standard Oil Company controlling the industry, President Roosevelt was inspired to create reforms that broke up large companies that controlled entire industries. Because a muckraker named Upton Sinclair wrote a book about the dirty conditions in meatpacking plants, laws were proposed that would make food safer and cleaner. Ask, *How does speaking about problems in the world help improve people's lives?* [it makes people more aware; it inspires people to help; it inspires people to speak out about other problems]

14 **MAP AND RESEARCH** Have your student look at a map of North and South America and find Panama. Have your student trace the sailing route from the Atlantic coast of the United States to the Pacific Coast around Cape Horn in South America. Then have him or her trace the route using the **Isthmus** of Panama. President Roosevelt wanted to build a canal across the Isthmus of Panama to create a shorter route for American shipping. Explain that there were many challenges. First, the United States had to get control of the land, which was owned by Columbia at the time. Second, disease-carrying mosquitoes lived in the rain forest where the canal was to be built. Third, the rain forest, mountains, swamps, and mud made digging a canal difficult. Have your student look up the Panama Canal to find out how these three problems were solved and when the canal was finally finished. [1914]

15 **RELATE AND REPORT** As businesses grew, cities grew. New York and Chicago began constructing office buildings so tall they "scraped the sky." Boston built the first underground train, a subway, in 1897. Electric streetcars were popular for transportation. In the early 1900s, automobiles joined horse-drawn carriages and wagons. People who first came to the cities, whether from the farm or a faraway country, often felt as if they had stepped into another world. Have your student look for photographs or illustrations of city streets in the early 1900s

showing the first skyscrapers, subway stations, automobiles, and streetcars. Ask, *What differences do you notice between today's city streets and the streets in the 1900s?* [now there are more automobiles, taller buildings, and large buses and trucks]

*Steel made from the Bessemer process made it possible to build skyscrapers.*

16 **EXPAND** Point out that when large numbers of people began streaming into the cities, it caused many problems. There was not enough clean water, garbage began to pile up in the streets, people walking on unlit night streets were often robbed or had their pockets picked, and poorly constructed tenement buildings caused many deaths due to fire. Explain that the people who lived in the cities spoke out to the city governments and forced them to make improvements. Laws called building codes, which required all new buildings to have plumbing and fire escapes, were passed. Factories were built away from residential areas to cut down on air pollution. Have your student read about city life in the 1800s and how it changed after 1880. Ask him or her to give an oral summary, and discuss the things that he or she found most interesting.

17 **EXPLORE** Explain that the growth of business also helped the growth of art and culture. In large cities where there was a lot of money, museums, opera houses, and concert halls were built. Ask, *Why do you think the growth of industry helps the growth of culture?* [because when there is prosperity all the money isn't being used for survival and some can be spent on the arts and entertainment]

18 **EXPLAIN AND EXPLORE** Explain that, as industry grew and businesses began to make more money, some companies began selling shares of stock, or percent ownership, of the company. Companies use the money they get from selling stock to expand their companies. As a company grows, the stocks become more valuable and people make a profit. Explain that in the early 1900s more corporations began selling stock and the **stock market** opened. Have your student research the history of the stock market to find out more information.

**FOR FURTHER READING**

*The Gilded Age: A History in Documents,* by Janette Thomas Greenwood, ed. (Oxford University Press Children's Books, 2000).

*Remember the Maine: The Spanish-American War Begins,* by Tim McNeese (Morgan Reynolds, 2001).

# Branching Out

## TEACHING TIP

Point out that the conflict between unions and business management doesn't have one correct answer. Help your student see that there are advantages to low-cost goods and to treating workers well.

## CHECKING IN

Ask your student how big business changed the way America worked. Your student should be able to explain how stocks were sold and traded, how cities grew, and that unions developed to defend workers' rights.

 

# Create a Time Line

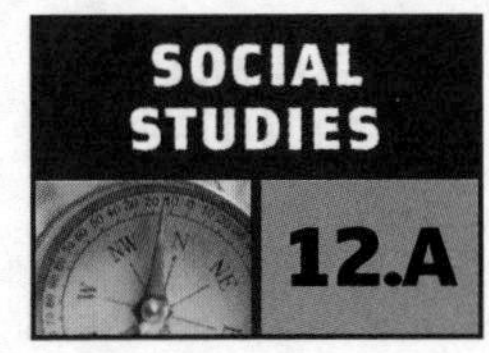


**PART A Find the dates of these inventions. Then write the dates, the inventions, and the inventors on the time line. Add other important dates from the lesson to the time line.**

Typewriter—Christopher Latham Sholes

Automobile—Henry Ford

Telephone—Alexander Graham Bell

Electric lightbulb—Thomas Edison and Lewis Latimer

Radio—Guglielmo Marconi

Airplane—Orville and Wilbur Wright

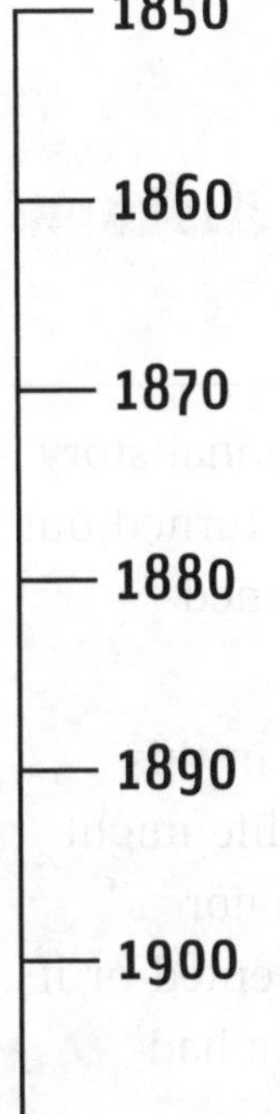


**PART B Now choose two inventions. On a separate sheet of paper, write a paragraph about how they changed the way people live.**

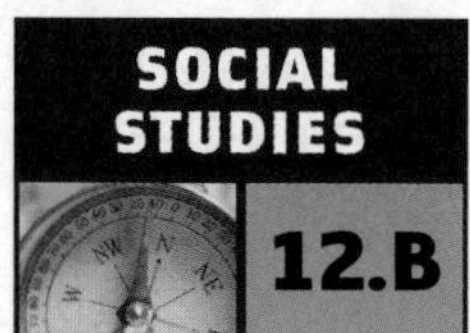


# What's Next? You Decide!

Now it's your turn to choose what to do next in the lesson. Read the activities and decide which one you want to do—you may want to try them all!

## Play the Stock Market

### MATERIALS

- ❑ current stock market listing from the newspaper or Internet

### STEPS

- ❑ Look through a stock market listing and choose a company you think would be worth investing in. Write down the stock that you decide to "buy."
- ❑ Research the company on the Internet or at the library and see when it was started and how it has been performing.
- ❑ Check your stock's price each day for three days and write it down. Then check again after one week and after one month.
- ❑ Write a few sentences in your notebook about how the stock price rose or fell during that time. Was it what you expected?

## Survey Household Inventions

### STEPS

- ❑ Divide a piece of paper into three columns.
- ❑ At the top of the first column write "Before 1800." At the top of the second column write "After 1800." Above the third column write a question mark.
- ❑ Walk through your house and look at your household machines and appliances. Write the name of each machine in one of the columns according to when it was invented. If you aren't sure which column it goes in, put it under the question mark and then research it.
- ❑ When you are done with the survey, write a report on what you found. Which column had the most items? What did you learn?

## Write an Alternative History

### STEPS

An alternative history is a fictional story about how things would have turned out if a historical event had happened differently.

- ❑ Review what you learned in this lesson. Think about how life might be different for you if a major invention hadn't been invented or if one of the historical events had turned out differently.
- ❑ Write a short story that begins with one of the situations from the lesson but ends in a different way.
- ❑ Share your story with an adult.

# In Your Community

**To reinforce the skills and concepts taught in this section, try one or more of these activities!**

## Historical Weavers and Looms

Explain that before and during the American Revolution, cloth-making machines weren't invented yet. Women wove most of the fabric on looms. With your student visit a museum or historical society that has a loom. Some art schools also may have working looms. If possible, arrange for a demonstration. Then, at home, have your student create his or her own miniature loom. Use a small piece of cardboard as the loom and yarn for thread so your student can experiment with the process of weaving. Your student also might be interested in visiting a museum where a modern textile machine is on display.

## Letter or Petition for a Cause

The independence and evolution of the United States was fueled by the bravery of the citizens who spoke out for what they believed in. Is there something that your student has a concern for or an opinion about? Perhaps a political, an environmental, or a social issue? Encourage him or her to write a letter to a newspaper, local organization, or political leader expressing his or her opinion and suggesting possibilities for change. Your student might even be interested in writing a petition for a specific change he or she would like to see and collecting signatures from people in your community.

## Political Demonstration Experience

Political and social demonstrations are legal in the United States, and they happen frequently. Keep an eye out for a nearby rally or gathering. If you can, attend the demonstration with your student so he or she can see a nonviolent way some people express their opinions and rally support for a cause. If there aren't any gatherings near your town, watch or read about a demonstration in Washington, D.C., or another capital city. Observe how many people are there, the message or goal of the demonstration, and how the peace is kept. How do the people express themselves? By speaking, reciting poetry, playing music, marching, yelling, chanting? Take some time to discuss the event with your student. Encourage him or her to research the history of the issue that prompted the demonstration and find out the opinions of both sides.

## First European to See Your Neighborhood

Have your student research the first European explorer to travel to your part of the country. When did the explorer arrive? What country was he or she from? Did the explorer travel by land or water? Did he or she have help from Native Americans? Encourage your student to try and find a source that includes the explorer's travel notes, if available, and to read about what the land and people were like firsthand. See if you can arrange to have your student talk with a local historian.

## Local Train Ride

Have your student research your local rail system. Have him or her study a local rail map and find the location of the closest passenger rail station. Visit the train station together. If you like, take a train ride and try to arrange an interview with the train conductor. Have your student prepare his or her questions beforehand.

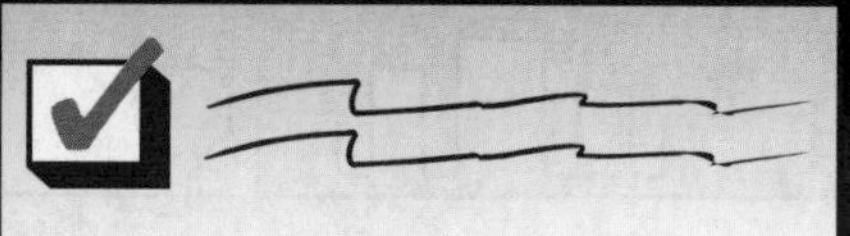

# We Have Learned

**Use this checklist to summarize what you and your student have accomplished in the Social Studies section.**

- ❑ **Native Americans**
- ❑ Southwestern desert, Pacific Northwest
- ❑ East Woodlands, Great Plains

- ❑ **European Exploration in America**
- ❑ Vikings and ice age explorers
- ❑ Spanish, British, and French

- ❑ **American Colonies**
- ❑ early Jamestown, Plymouth
- ❑ everyday colonial life, religion of the 13 colonies
- ❑ Spanish missions, French and Indian Wars

- ❑ **Conflicts with Britain**
- ❑ Stamp Act, Townshend Acts
- ❑ taxes on tea, Boston Tea Party
- ❑ First and Second Continental Congress

- ❑ **American Revolution**
- ❑ Declaration of Independence
- ❑ important people
- ❑ important battles

- ❑ **Post American Revolution**
- ❑ Articles of Confederation
- ❑ Constitution, Bill of Rights
- ❑ three branches of government

- ❑ **New U.S. Territories**
- ❑ Louisiana Purchase, Lewis and Clark
- ❑ War of 1812
- ❑ slavery and Underground Railroad

- ❑ **Civil War**
- ❑ Kansas-Nebraska Act
- ❑ fighting in Congress
- ❑ Dred Scott
- ❑ important battles
- ❑ Emancipation Proclamation, Gettysburg Address

- ❑ **Reconstruction**
- ❑ Lincoln assassination, impeachment of president
- ❑ thirteenth amendment, fourteenth amendment, fifteenth amendment
- ❑ rebuilding of North and South, railroads and factories

- ❑ **Western Expansion**
- ❑ railroads, homesteading
- ❑ policies toward Native Americans
- ❑ California gold rush, Oregon Trail, Pony Express

- ❑ **National Growth and Reform**
- ❑ Industrial Revolution, European immigration
- ❑ Teddy Roosevelt, rise of big business, national power
- ❑ growth of cities, stock market

**We have also learned:**

____________________________

____________________________

**Read each question and answer choices that follow. Circle the letter of the correct answer.**

1. Which of the following is an example of oral storytelling?
   - **A** a story you hear from another person
   - **B** a story passed verbally through generations
   - **C** a story told using voice and gestures
   - **D** a story spoken for increased understanding

2. Which of the following is NOT an important part of oral storytelling?
   - **A** making eye contact with your listeners
   - **B** matching your purpose to the listeners
   - **C** editing for spelling, capitalization, and punctuation
   - **D** organizing the delivery of your message

3. While telling a story, you should—
   - **A** explain differences between facts and opinions.
   - **B** properly use gestures and nonverbal language.
   - **C** speak with as little emotion as possible.
   - **D** keep your voice at a conversational level.

4. Which type of writing is presented in first person?
   - **A** research report
   - **B** biography
   - **C** autobiography
   - **D** dramatic play

5. Which type of writing includes a list of sources?
   - **A** biography
   - **B** research report
   - **C** drama
   - **D** historical fiction

6. Which of the following are common features of poetry?
   - **A** chronology and description
   - **B** cause and effect
   - **C** compare and contrast
   - **D** stanzas and rhythm

7. Which type of writing convinces others to accept an opinion?
   - **A** autobiography
   - **B** persuasive writing
   - **C** explanatory writing
   - **D** narrative

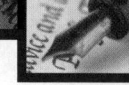

**8.** In the writing process, an outline is part of—

**A** choosing a topic.

**B** publishing the paper.

**C** proofreading and revising the draft.

**D** organizing and planning the paper.

**9.** Part of proofreading and revising your paper should include—

**A** adding details from further research.

**B** deciding on the best way to publish.

**C** checking for grammatical errors.

**D** organizing information for presentation.

**10.** The final step in the writing process is—

**A** choosing an ending topic for support.

**B** proofreading and revising your facts.

**C** publishing and presenting your paper.

**D** adding details for clearer meaning.

**Read the sentences in the box. Decide which type of writing it is. Circle the letter of the correct answer.**

11. The party was a kaleidoscope of colors. The food and decorations were shades of green, gold, red, and blue. Even the musicians wore brightly colored suits.

A descriptive
B explanatory
C persuasive
D drama

12. I walked outside to view the excitement. When I looked down the street, I saw a flock of geese blocking the road. It took almost an hour for the traffic to clear once the geese had gone.

A research report
B dramatic reading
C narrative
D poetry

13. This car has a three-year bumper-to-bumper warranty. You should buy this car because it is the safest for your family.

A narrative
B persuasive
C explanatory
D descriptive

14. Silas K. Smythe grew up in Baltimore, Maryland. As a teen, he learned to work hard for what he wanted.

A biography
B persuasive
C explanatory
D autobiography

**Read each selection. Read the questions and answer choices that go with each selection. Circle the letter of the correct answer.**

**Use for 15–18.**

The 110th Annual Jackson County Fair was scheduled to begin tonight. It was the premier family attraction, offering a wide variety of exhibits, foods, entertainment, rides, and hands-on activities. The fair was known to offer something for everyone. The fun included a working farm and petting zoo, rides, contests, and games.

Agnes brimmed with anticipation. This year she was chosen to perform a song at the fair's opening ceremony. Agnes had chosen a song that she considered soothing and appropriate. She had practiced her song every day with her uncle, Ramon. He accompanied her on guitar. Agnes was careful to sing every note just right. She also made sure that she sang at the same pace that her uncle played on the guitar.

Now, Agnes had one problem. Her grandparents and great aunt Anna were scheduled to fly in for her singing debut. However, their plane was late. Agnes was scheduled to go on stage in five minutes. She couldn't bear singing without her entire family present. Agnes wanted this to be a memorable occasion for everyone in her family.

Four minutes passed. Agnes made her way to the stage. As she approached it, her stomach curled at the thought of her grandparents missing her song. Agnes steadied herself at the microphone. She sadly looked out into the audience. Once her eyes focused, she couldn't believe who she saw standing in the front row. Agnes smiled widely and motioned for her uncle to begin playing.

**15.** Which of the following titles best represents this selection?

**A** *Agnes's Song*

**B** *A Day at the Fair*

**C** *Practice Makes Perfect*

**D** *A Song for the Family*

**16.** What can you conclude about the Jackson County Fair?

**A** It is a big town event.

**B** It happens once every two years.

**C** Activities for adults are limited.

**D** Few people attend it.

**17.** Agnes's family can best be described as—

**A** bothersome.

**B** supportive.

**C** careless.

**D** inconsiderate.

**18.** Which of the following words most nearly means the same as the underlined word in the sentence below?

> Agnes's grandparents and great aunt Anna are flying in for her singing <u>debut.</u>

**A** first appearance

**B** first tryout

**C** latest effort

**D** latest performance

**Use for 19–24.**

**Lazy, Hazy Summer Day**

I sit on the pier—shoes kicked off—
down by the edge of the beach
The wind is quiet for now, the
clouds appear within my reach
The children are building sandcastles
nearby
I build them too, using the clouds in
the sky

The sound of the water is relaxing
as it travels onto the shore and
then out
I close my eyes just for a moment,
listening to the great lake's shout
I contain the prickly, pale sand
parading underneath my feet
I attempt to count each pointed
grain as if it were a special treat

I inhale the smell of the lake,
absorbing the season's exiting
calm
I feel order and peace within me,
the world rests within my palm
It's time to begin my journey home
as the day draws near an end
I bid you farewell lazy, hazy
summer day—I'll see you next
year, good friend

**19.** "Lazy, Hazy Summer Day" can best be described as a—

**A** narrative.

**B** biography.

**C** drama.

**D** poem.

**20.** How is the selection arranged?

**A** by paragraphs

**B** by stanzas

**C** in time-order sequence

**D** in order of events described

**21.** Where does the selection take place?

**A** in the park

**B** at the beach

**C** on the lake

**D** near a house

**22.** Based on the selection, you can conclude—

**A** it is near the end of summer.

**B** summer has just begun.

**C** the speaker lives in a place that is warm all year.

**D** the speaker rejects the idea of changing seasons.

**23.** The words **prickly, pale,** and **parading** are special because they—

**A** produce a rhyming pattern.

**B** begin with the letter *p*.

**C** describe the sand.

**D** end with the same sound.

**24.** You can best predict the speaker will—

**A** stay later at the beach.

**B** visit the beach again.

**C** build another sandcastle.

**D** make a new friend.

**Read the sentences in the box. Decide the best way to write the underlined sentences. Circle the letter of the correct answer.**

**25.** Peter plays the guitar. <u>He has been playing for six years he enjoys playing music.</u>

**A** He has been playing for six years, he enjoys playing music.

**B** He has been playing for six years. He enjoys playing music.

**C** He has been playing. For six years he enjoys playing music.

**D** Correct as written

**26.** Hoshi is taking a cooking class. <u>So far she has learned to cook the following items. Chicken pot pie and zucchini bread.</u>

**A** So far she has learned to cook the following items, chicken pot pie and zucchini bread.

**B** So far she has learned to cook the following items: chicken pot pie and zucchini bread.

**C** So far she has learned to cook the following items. Chicken pot pie. And zucchini bread.

**D** Correct as written

**27.** Mr. Suarez asked each student to name his or her favorite animal. <u>Giles said my favorite animal is a dog.</u>

**A** Giles "said my favorite animal is a dog."

**B** "Giles said my favorite animal is a dog."

**C** Giles said, "My favorite animal is a dog."

**D** Correct as written

**28.** <u>Sylvia's family has two pets. A cat and a hamster.</u> Sylvia's job is to feed the hamster.

**A** Sylvia's family has two pets; a cat and a hamster.

**B** Sylvia's family has two pets, a cat and a hamster.

**C** Sylvia's family has two pets a cat and a hamster.

**D** Correct as written

**Use for 29–31.**

**Marta's Plan**

Marta was miserable. It was almost the end of her first day at her new school, and she hadn't made one new friend. Although she smiled and greeted the other students, no one seemed to pick up on her gestures of friendship. Marta pondered her situation. She decided to try one more time, using a new plan. Marta was hopeful that it would work. Marta approached a group of students who were trading books. They were discussing their next book club meeting. Marta asked the group for suggestions on great books to read. The group invited Marta to join their book club. Marta agreed. She was thrilled her plan worked.

**29.** What is the main idea of the selection?

______________________________

______________________________

______________________________

**30.** What do you think will happen next in the story? Support your answer using details from the selection.

______________________________

______________________________

______________________________

**31.** Fill in the story map to describe Marta throughout the selection.

Turning Point

| Marta at Beginning of Story | Event That Caused Marta to Change | Marta at End of Story |
|---|---|---|
| | | |

Use for 32–36.

*George Horace Gallup*

**George Horace Gallup**

Have you ever wanted to find out what members of your family like to eat most often? Have you ever wondered which books were the most popular at your local library? Opinion polls could help you find out the answers to these questions. Opinion polls are surveys given to a certain group of people to find out their opinions, views, and interests. One of the most renowned leaders of opinion polls is George Horace Gallup.

George Horace Gallup was born on November 18, 1901, in a small town in Iowa. He attended school in Iowa, studying journalism. After completing college, Gallup pursued a career as an instructor of journalism, working for several universities. In 1935, he formed his first polling company, the American Institute of Public Opinion (also known as the Gallup Poll). Here, Gallup surveyed a wide sample of the population. He carefully noted his sample population's opinions and views on different issues. He firmly believed that polls were logical methods of obtaining information on the opinions of people. Furthermore, he felt that polls provided politicians with an accurate gauge of society's thoughts, feelings, and perspectives on many topics. He shared his beliefs with others. By 1944, Gallup was a major leader in public opinion polling. This was largely due to his dedication and hard work and his achieving higher rates of accuracy in polling results than any other person in his field. Gallup was particularly famous for his accuracy in preelection polls. He received many honors for his achievements in opinion polls. The Gallup polling methods are still used today.

**32.** *George Horace Gallup* is a biography. What features of a biography are used in this selection?

________________________________

________________________________

________________________________

**33.** What is the main idea of the selection?

________________________________

________________________________

________________________________

**34.** How might George Gallup's training in journalism have helped him with his polling?

______________________________

______________________________

______________________________

**35.** Read the sentences below. Write the meanings of the underlined words in each sentence.

> He firmly believed that polls were <u>logical</u> methods of obtaining information on the opinions of people.

______________________________

> This was largely due to his <u>dedication</u> and hard work and his achieving higher rates of accuracy in polling results than any other person in his field.

______________________________

**36.** Complete the map at the top of the next column about George Horace Gallup.

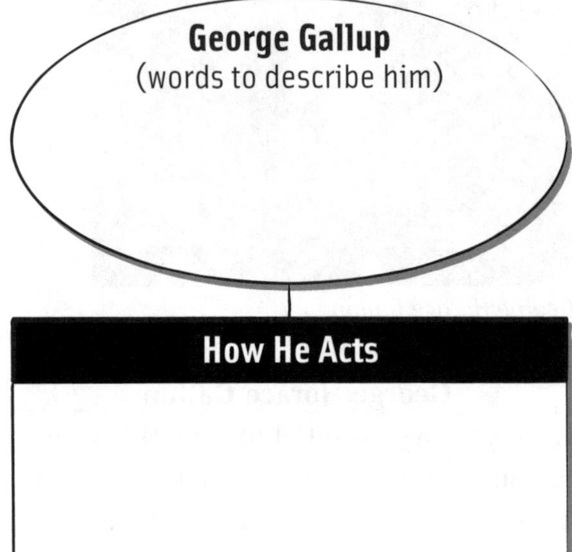

What He Does
1. Goes to school for journalism
2. Teaches
3. Invents opinion poll that is very accurate
4. Shares beliefs
George Gallup
(words to describe him)
How He Acts


Use the map to write a character sketch of George Horace Gallup.

______________________________

______________________________

______________________________

______________________________

______________________________

______________________________

______________________________

______________________________

**Use for 37–38.**

**Dinner Decisions**

*Scene 1—In the home of Beth and Chuck.*

1. **Beth:** What do you want for dinner?
2. *Chuck places his index finger on his chin as he thinks about the question.*
3. **Chuck:** How about a vegetable pizza?
4. **Beth:** Sounds terrific! Let's go because I'm starving.
5. *Beth and Chuck exit through the front door of the house.*

**37.** What do Lines 2 and 5 show?

**38.** What type of writing is *Dinner Decisions*? What tells you this? Use examples from the selection in your answer.

**Read each sentence. Rewrite the sentence using a synonym for the underlined word.**

**39.** The little girl was <u>silent</u> about how the accident happened.

**40.** They <u>enjoyed</u> the nonstop action of the movie.

**41.** He replied with the <u>proper</u> answer.

**42.** The bottom <u>portion</u> of my receipt is missing.

**Read each sentence. Write the correct pronoun to complete each sentence.**

**43.** Natasha wants to invite everyone __________ knows to the party.

**44.** Miguel helped __________ to more of the mashed potatoes.

**45.** Marcus and Melvin are pleased that __________ friend can visit longer.

**46.** Four of the basketball players forgot __________ uniforms.

**47.** Rewrite the paragraph. Use correct grammar, spelling, capitalization, and punctuation.

| Daniel really wants to visit texas. His friend Adam lives in abeline. The closet Daniel have ever been to Texas was when he visits Oklahoma with his family? There are three cities Daniel wants to visit in Texas. They are abeline Dallas, and Corpus christi He hopes to visit this citys soon. |
|---|

________________________________________

**48.** Read the letter. Write the words from the box to fill in the missing parts of the letter.

__________________

__________________

Today I got a new bike. I was thrilled. It is gold and black, which are the colors that I wanted. Dad said that he will take me riding on the bike trail in a few weeks. Maybe you can come with us when you visit this summer.

__________________

__________________

| Dear Randall,<br>Your cousin Raphael<br>Sincerely,<br>May 30 |
|---|

**49.** Choose one of the following types of writing and construct a well-organized essay. Write an introduction, several paragraphs, and a conclusion. You have 15 minutes to complete your essay.

- Explanatory
- Persuasive
- Historical fiction

**Read each question and answer choice that follows. Circle the letter of the correct answer.**

**1.** What is the place value of 9 in 432,789,054?

**A** hundred millions
**B** ten millions
**C** thousands
**D** ten thousands

**2.** Round 24,597,421 to the nearest million.

**A** 25,000,000
**B** 24,600,000
**C** 24,597,000
**D** 20,000,000

**3.** Round 29.0472 to the nearest hundredth.

**A** 30
**B** 29.0
**C** 29.05
**D** 29.047

**4.** $-12 + 3 =$

**A** −15
**B** −10
**C** −9
**D** −6

**5.** $-4 - 6 =$

**A** −10
**B** −2
**C** 2
**D** 10

**6.** $6.23 + 12.87 =$

**A** 18.01
**B** 18.1
**C** 19.01
**D** 19.1

**7.** $8.07 - 2.49 =$

**A** 6.58
**B** 6.42
**C** 5.58
**D** 5.42

**8.** $36{,}459 + 89{,}674 =$

**A** 126,023
**B** 126,033
**C** 126,123
**D** 126,133

**9.** $12{,}304{,}561 - 6{,}897{,}305 =$

**A** 5,406,246
**B** 5,406,256
**C** 5,407,246
**D** 5,407,256

**10.** $798 \times 37 =$

**A** 29,326
**B** 29,426
**C** 29,526
**D** 29,626

**11.** $45 \times n = 225$

**A** 4

**B** 5

**C** 10

**D** 15

**12.** $274 \div 7 =$

**A** 37

**B** 37 R1

**C** 39

**D** 39 R1

**13.** $n \div 8 = 342$

**A** 2,736

**B** 2,766

**C** 2,826

**D** 2,836

**14.** $9.08 \times 2.7 =$

**A** 18.516

**B** 18.56

**C** 24.516

**D** 24.56

**15.** $18 \times 9.8 =$

**A** 162.8

**B** 168.4

**C** 176.4

**D** 178.8

**16.** $14.44 \div 4 =$

**A** 3.51

**B** 3.61

**C** 3.71

**D** 3.81

**17.** $18.13 \div 3.7 =$

**A** 4.6

**B** 4.7

**C** 4.8

**D** 4.9

**18.** $\frac{4}{10} =$

**A** 4.0

**B** 0.4

**C** 0.04

**D** 0.004

**19.** $0.07 =$

**A** $\frac{7}{10}$

**B** $\frac{7}{100}$

**C** $\frac{7}{1,000}$

**D** $\frac{7}{10,000}$

**20.** $\frac{3}{4} + \frac{5}{8} =$

**A** $1\frac{1}{8}$

**B** $1\frac{1}{4}$

**C** $1\frac{3}{8}$

**D** $1\frac{3}{4}$

21. $2\frac{3}{5} + \frac{3}{5} =$

A $3$

B $3\frac{1}{5}$

C $3\frac{2}{5}$

D $3\frac{3}{5}$

22. $\frac{5}{7} - \frac{2}{7} =$

A $\frac{1}{7}$

B $\frac{2}{7}$

C $\frac{3}{7}$

D $\frac{4}{7}$

23. $\frac{3}{4} - \frac{1}{4} =$

A $\frac{3}{4}$

B $\frac{1}{4}$

C $\frac{1}{2}$

D $\frac{3}{4}$

24. $\frac{5}{6} \div 8 =$

A $4\frac{1}{3}$

B $4\frac{2}{3}$

C $5\frac{2}{3}$

D $6\frac{2}{3}$

25. $\frac{3}{4} \div 7\frac{1}{2} =$

A $5\frac{5}{8}$

B $5\frac{7}{8}$

C $6\frac{1}{8}$

D $6\frac{3}{8}$

26. $\frac{1}{3} \div \frac{3}{4} =$

A $\frac{2}{3}$

B $\frac{2}{4}$

C $\frac{1}{8}$

D $\frac{4}{9}$

27. $\frac{1}{2} \div \frac{1}{4} =$

A 1

B 2

C 3

D 4

28. Which ratio is equivalent to 3:4?

A 6:4

B 3:8

C 9:12

D 9:8

**Read each question. Write the answers. Show your work.**

**29.** Classify each angle shown.

**30.** Classify each triangle shown.

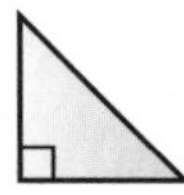

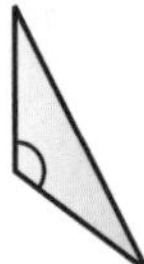

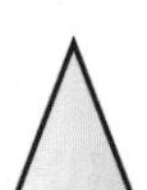

**31.** Label each quadrilateral shown.

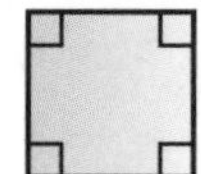

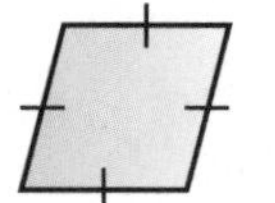

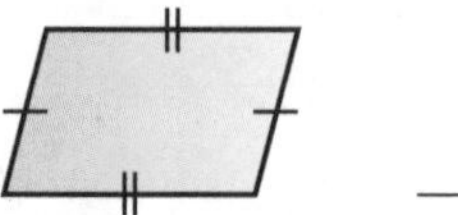

**32.** Find the perimeter. Show your work in solving the problem. ______

**Rectangle**

7 in.

4 in. 4 in.

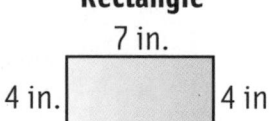

7 in.

**33.** Order from greatest to least.
45,729 45,972 45,297 45,792

______

**34.** Order from least to greatest.
2.340 2.034 2.304 2.043

______

35. Write an expression for 15 more than a number.

____________________

36. Darcey is 14 years old. She is 4 years older than Pamela. Write an equation for Pamela's age. How old is Pamela?

____________________

37. Hector bought 6 notebooks at $0.99 each. Estimate how much Hector spent. Show your work.

____________________

38. Alec bought a book for $6.99, another book for $3.50, and a math game for $12.88. Write a math problem to show Alec's total. Solve the problem.

____________________

39. Veronica had $4.50. She bought a pen for $1.23 and an eraser for $0.76. How much did she have left? Write a math problem to show how much Veronica had left. Solve the problem.

____________________

40. Write the greatest common factors of the numbers below.

12 and 18 __________

36 and 48 __________

13 and 18 __________

41. List four common multiples of 4 and 6.

______ ______ ______ ______

42. Convert each measure.

3,000 meters = ______ kilometers

90 minutes = ______ seconds

100 centimeters = ______ decimeters

72 hours = ______ days

43. List three fractions equivalent to $\frac{2}{3}$.

______ ______ ______

44. Order from least to greatest.

$\frac{19}{16}$ $\frac{11}{8}$ $1\frac{1}{4}$ $1\frac{1}{8}$

____________________

45. Write 45% as a fraction in simplest form and as a decimal.

__________ __________

**46.** Write a fraction to show the probability of the spinner landing on 3.

---

**47.** Carmen found a pair of pants for $24.99. They were on sale for 15% off. Estimate the cost of the pants. Show your work.

---

**48.** Graph each point on the coordinate plane.

(0, 4) (1, 5) (–3, 3) (–2, –4) (5, –3)

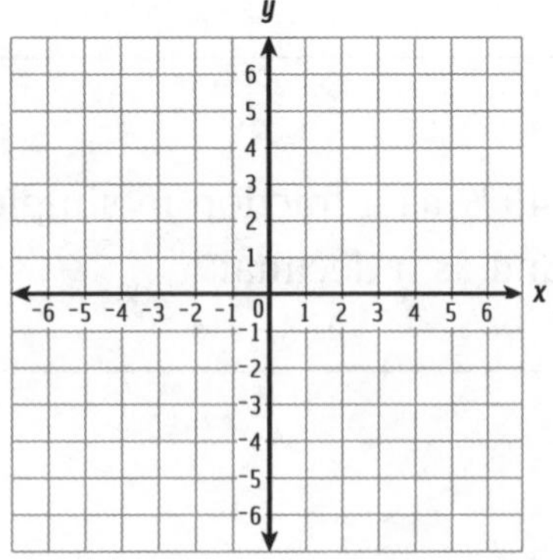


**49.** Make a bar graph showing the amount of rain in each month.

| Month | Rainfall (in inches) |
|---|---|
| April | $2\frac{4}{10}$ |
| May | $2\frac{7}{10}$ |
| June | $2\frac{1}{10}$ |
| July | $2\frac{9}{10}$ |

Show bar graph:

**50.** The chart shows the height in inches of 10 students in Mr. Lee's class. Find the mean, median, range, and mode of the data.

| Name | Height (in inches) |
|---|---|
| Mabel | 62 |
| Pablo | 58 |
| Norah | 56 |
| Murray | 61 |
| Phoebe | 60 |
| Lucas | 58 |
| Opal | 60 |
| Kurt | 55 |
| Raquel | 59 |
| Jerome | 58 |

Mean: ______________

Median: ______________

Range: ______________

Mode: ______________

**51.** The chart shows the test scores on last week's math test. What was the average score? Tell how you found your answer.

**Test Scores**

| | | | | |
|---|---|---|---|---|
| 82 | 96 | 84 | 92 | 76 |
| 68 | 75 | 65 | 88 | 84 |
| 71 | 78 | 93 | 98 | 92 |
| 82 | 83 | 90 | 80 | 81 |

Average score: ______________

__________________________________

__________________________________

__________________________________

__________________________________

__________________________________

__________________________________

__________________________________

__________________________________

__________________________________

**52.** Draw a number line and plot each integer.

–5, 6, –3, –4, 3, 1, 0, –2, 2

**53.** Frank has three shirts: white, gray, and black. He has four ties: red, blue, green, and yellow. Draw a tree diagram to show how many different combinations of shirts and ties Frank can wear.

**54.** Find the volume of the rectangular prism.

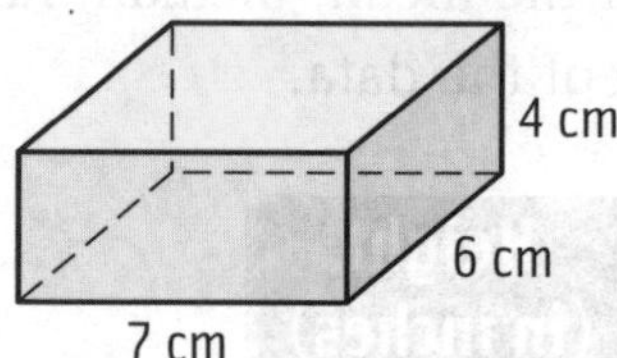


______________________________

**55.** Find the area of the triangle.

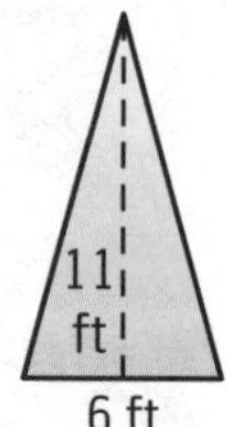


______________________________

**56.** Draw a square with an area of 36 $m^2$. Label the length of each side.

**Read each question and answer choice that follows. Circle the letter of the correct answer.**

1. A cell that has no nucleus is called a __________ cell.
   **A** prokaryotic
   **B** eukaryotic
   **C** cytoplasmic
   **D** organelle

2. In the water cycle, in what process does water in a lake become water vapor in the air?
   **A** condensation
   **B** evaporation
   **C** precipitation
   **D** transpiration

3. Another name for snow and rain is—
   **A** condensation.
   **B** evaporation.
   **C** precipitation.
   **D** transpiration.

4. What is the temperature at which a substance changes from a liquid to a gas?
   **A** freezing point
   **B** condensing point
   **C** boiling point
   **D** melting point

5. In an ecosystem, producers use the sun's energy to produce food. Which of the following is a producer in forest ecosystems?
   **A** tree
   **B** owl
   **C** bacteria
   **D** mouse

6. Which diagram shows the layers of Earth correctly labeled?

A

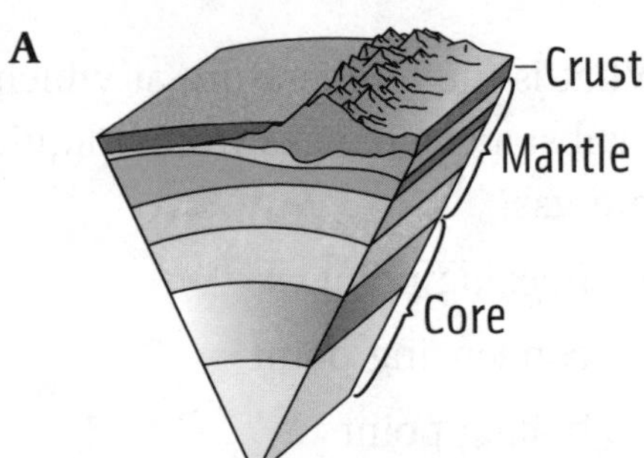


B

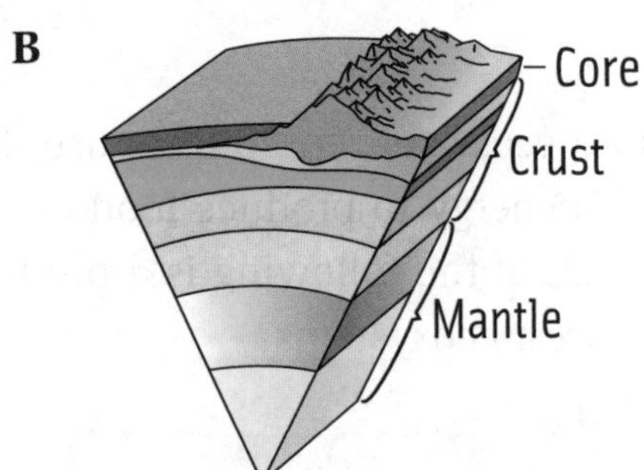


C

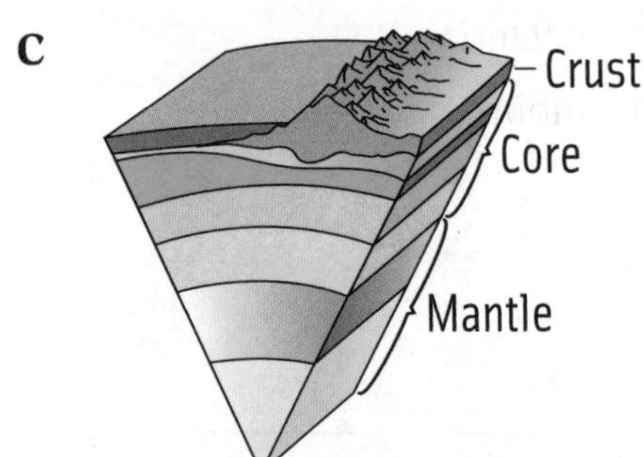


D

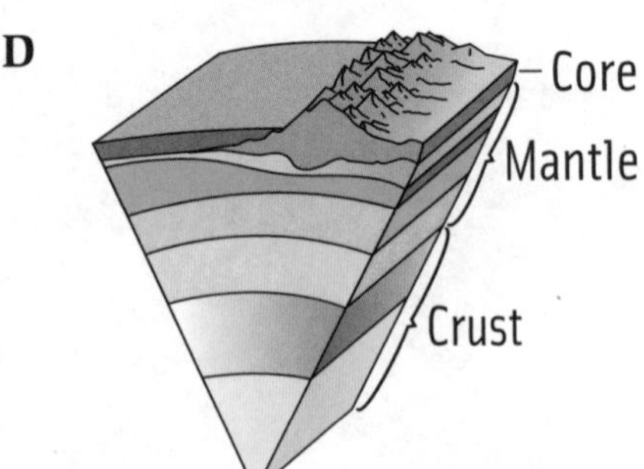


7. What keeps Earth in orbit?
   **A** the sun's gravity
   **B** the moon's rotation
   **C** the gravity of the inner planets
   **D** the gravity of the outer planets

8. Why do some stars look brighter than others?
   **A** they have different orbits
   **B** they are at different distances from Earth
   **C** they have different amounts of gravity
   **D** they have different revolutions

9. What is the smallest unit of a compound?
   **A** molecule
   **B** element
   **C** particle
   **D** cell

10. An atom has a nucleus. The nucleus is made up of—
    **A** cells and molecules.
    **B** molecules and neutrons.
    **C** protons and neutrons.
    **D** electrons and neutrons.

**11.** In Tomika's plant experiment, the plant leaves involuntarily moved toward the light. This is called—

**A** tropism.

**B** stimulus.

**C** response.

**D** adaptation.

**12.** A chameleon changing colors to match its environment is an example of—

**A** tropism.

**B** stimulus.

**C** stimuli.

**D** adaptation.

**13.** Which is a nonrenewable source of energy?

**A** fossil fuel

**B** solar energy

**C** wind energy

**D** hydroelectric power

**14.** Which is NOT a function of the skeletal system?

**A** protects the organs of the body

**B** filters wastes from the blood

**C** produces red blood cells

**D** stores minerals

**15.** The circle graph shows the relative amounts of different components in the air we breathe. What label should be placed in the blank?

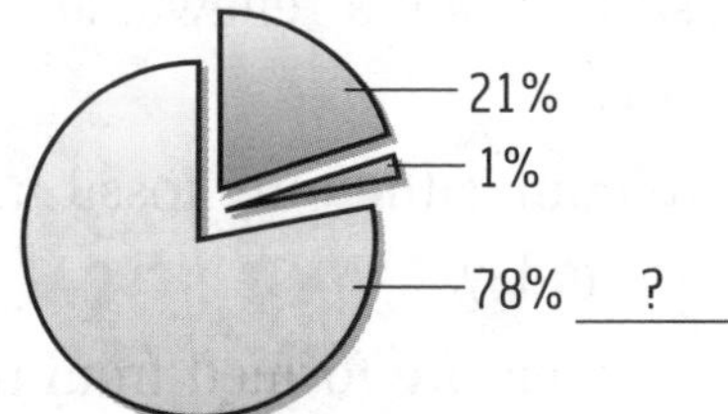


**A** carbon dioxide

**B** oxygen

**C** hydrogen

**D** nitrogen

**16.** What is the largest number of a species that an ecosystem can support?

**A** carrying capacity

**B** community

**C** population

**D** biome

**17.** What is an example of a limiting factor of an ecosystem?

**A** biome

**B** tropism

**C** food

**D** species

**18.** Which statement about fossil fuels is true?

**A** Fossil fuels are the result of heat and pressure acting on rock.

**B** Fossil fuels are a renewable resource.

**C** Petroleum is the only fossil fuel in use today.

**D** Fossil fuels are formed from the remains of living organisms.

**19.** Roberta wants to make sure she is eating a nutritious diet. What is the best strategy for her to follow?

**A** eat food from only one section of the food pyramid

**B** follow diets printed in magazines

**C** try to eat a variety of foods every day

**D** eat anything as long as it is low in fat

**20.** What system allows the body to use the energy and nutrients in food for life processes?

**A** digestive system

**B** circulatory system

**C** skeletal system

**D** respiratory system

**21.** Which definition best describes **tissues**?

**A** collections of similar cells that group together to perform a specific job

**B** systems in organisms that are made up of two or more organs that work together to do a job

**C** structures within the cytoplasm of cells

**D** substances in the nucleus of cells that contain "instructions" for the cells

**22.** Erica filled a beaker with sand and salt. She stirred until the two substances were thoroughly mixed. What is the best description of the contents of the beaker?

**A** colloid

**B** homogeneous mixture

**C** heterogeneous mixture

**D** solution

**Read each selection and the questions that follow. Answer the questions in complete sentences.**

**Use for 23–24.**

The muscular system of the human body contains some muscles that we can control. These are called voluntary muscles. It also contains some that we can't. These are called involuntary muscles.

**23.** Look at the picture. What are three actions being performed by involuntary muscles in the girl's body?

______________________________

______________________________

______________________________

**24.** What are three actions being performed by voluntary muscles in the girl's body?

______________________________

______________________________

______________________________

**25.** Three important environmental concerns are the use of resources, human population growth, and pollution. Write a paragraph that describes how the use of resources and pollution are connected to human population growth.

______________________________

______________________________

______________________________

______________________________

______________________________

______________________________

**26.** The cells of your body require oxygen in order to carry out their functions. Name two different organ systems involved in the process of getting oxygen to your cells. Write a paragraph that describes the role of each of these organ systems in getting oxygen to your cells.

______________________________

______________________________

______________________________

______________________________

______________________________

______________________________

**27.** Earth's surface changes over time. Describe how earthquakes, volcanoes, and glaciers can change Earth's surface.

______________________________

______________________________

______________________________

______________________________

______________________________

______________________________

**28.** Choose two natural resources. Describe two ways that humans can wisely use each of the natural resources you chose.

______________________________

______________________________

______________________________

______________________________

______________________________

______________________________

**Use for 29–30.**

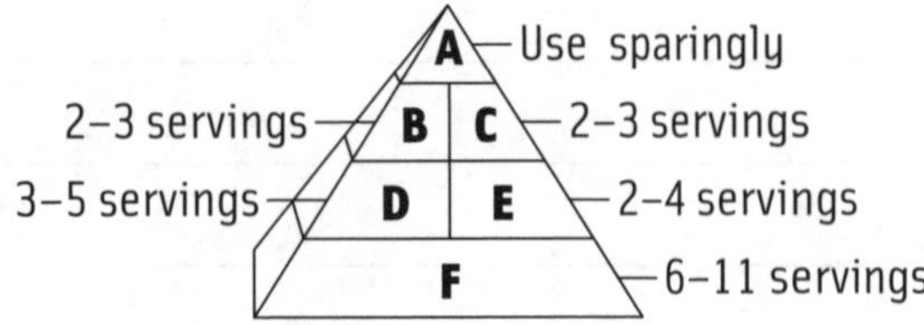


**29.** The food guide pyramid indicates the number of servings from each group of foods that should be eaten each day. Add the labels to the food guide pyramid.

**A** ______________________________

**B** ______________________________

**C** ______________________________

**D** ______________________________

**E** ______________________________

**F** ______________________________

**30.** Using the food guide pyramid is a good way to ensure that your body gets the nutrients you need. Give an example of a disease that can occur if your body does not get the nutrients it needs. Then tell which nutrient is related to this disease and what foods can be eaten regularly to avoid getting this disease.

______________________________

______________________________

______________________________

______________________________

______________________________

______________________________

______________________________

______________________________

______________________________

Use for 31–32.

| Type of Energy | How It Works |
|---|---|
| Solar energy | |
| Wind energy | |
| Hydroelectric energy | |

**31.** Complete the table by describing how each type of energy works.

**32.** Choose one source of energy from the table and write a paragraph that describes the positive and negative effects of this type of energy. Include at least one positive and one negative effect.

**Use for 33–34.**

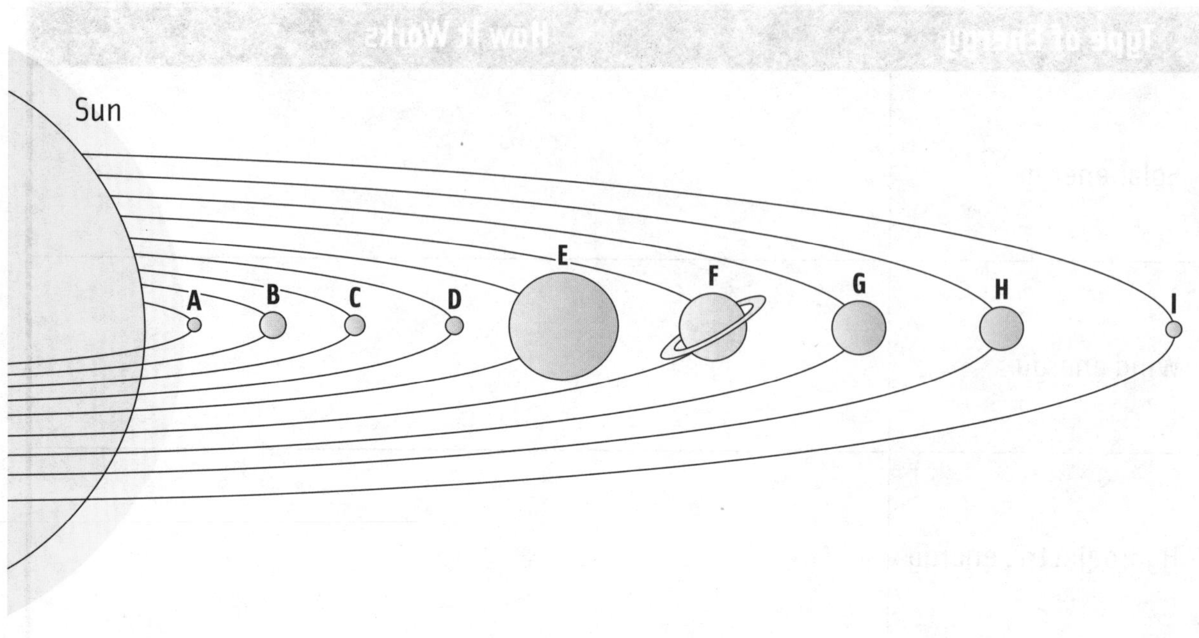


**33.** Label each planet in this diagram of the solar system.

A ______________________ F ______________________

B ______________________ G ______________________

C ______________________ H ______________________

D ______________________ I ______________________

E ______________________

**34.** List the inner planets and the outer planets.

| **Inner Planets** | **Outer Planets** |
|---|---|
| ______________________ | ______________________ |
| ______________________ | ______________________ |
| ______________________ | ______________________ |
| ______________________ | ______________________ |
| | ______________________ |

**Read each question and answer choice that follows. Circle the letter of the correct answer.**

**1.** Juan Ponce de Léon was an explorer from—

**A** France.

**B** Great Britain.

**C** Spain.

**D** America.

**2.** What problem did European explorers face in the Americas?

**A** There was an overcrowding of European explorers.

**B** There were too many fine riches to store.

**C** There were bitter disagreements with the Native Americans.

**D** The taxes were too high.

**3.** All were established regions of the colonies EXCEPT—

**A** Northern Alliance.

**B** Middle.

**C** Southern.

**D** New England.

**4.** The Jamestown colony thrived because of—

**A** cotton.

**B** rice.

**C** corn.

**D** tobacco.

**5.** What was the cause of the French and Indian War?

**A** dispute over territory in North America

**B** dispute over slave ownership

**C** dispute over territory in France

**D** dispute over the Suez Canal

**6.** Which of these placed a tax on most printed materials?

**A** Intolerable Acts

**B** Townshend Acts

**C** Stamp Act

**D** Tea Act

**7.** Who was chosen to write the Declaration of Independence?

**A** Thomas Jefferson

**B** Benjamin Franklin

**C** Patrick Henry

**D** King George

**8.** George Washington was a key person in which war?

**A** Pacific-Northwest War

**B** American Revolution

**C** Mexican-American War

**D** Civil War

9. 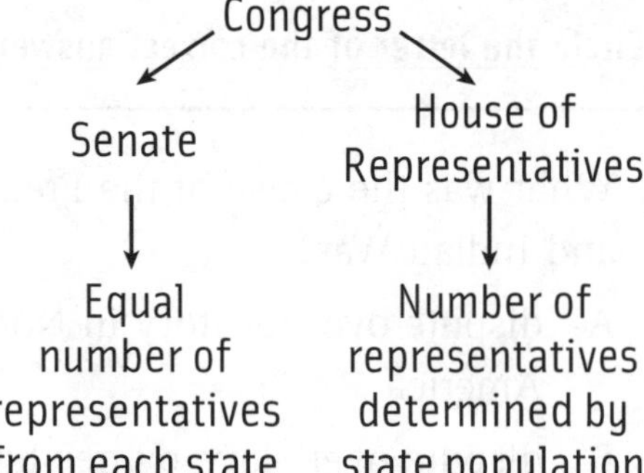


This diagram shows a—

A dictatorship.

B monarchy.

C legislature.

D judicial system.

10. The Articles of Confederation established—

A a powerful military.

B three branches of government.

C judges with unlimited authority.

D a monarchy.

11. What ended the War of 1812?

A Treaty of Ghent

B Emancipation Proclamation

C Declaration of Independence

D Treaty of Paris

12. Who led the Underground Railroad?

A Nat Turner

B Frederick Douglass

C Harriet Tubman

D Sojourner Truth

13. Which act allowed states to vote separately on the inclusion of slavery?

A Alien and Sedition Act

B Kansas-Nebraska Act

C Townshend Act

D Coercive Act

14. Where did the first battle of the Civil War occur?

A Lexington

B Concord

C Fort Sumter

D Fort Wayne

15. The Emancipation Proclamation—

A freed all slaves.

B upheld slavery.

C freed slaves in the Confederate states.

D upheld slavery in the Confederate states.

16. Which constitutional amendment abolished slavery?

A first

B fifth

C thirteenth

D twenty-first

17. Which area of the South's economy was most important during Reconstruction?
    - A bank business
    - B postal system
    - C raising livestock
    - D railroads

18. Which of these promoted the settlement of the West?
    - A Homestead Act
    - B Enforcement Act
    - C Great Compromise
    - D Compromise of 1877

19. The path that many settlers took out west was called the—
    - A Oregon Country.
    - B Oregon Trail.
    - C Canada Country.
    - D Canada Trail.

20. Who helped organize labor unions?
    - A Samuel Gompers
    - B Francis Cabot Lowell
    - C President Theodore Roosevelt
    - D Andrew Carnegie

**Read each selection and the questions that follow. Answer the questions in complete sentences.**

21. What was the significance of Paul Revere's ride in 1775?

_______________________________

_______________________________

_______________________________

22. Explain the Lewis and Clark expedition. Name two other people who helped in the Lewis and Clark expedition.

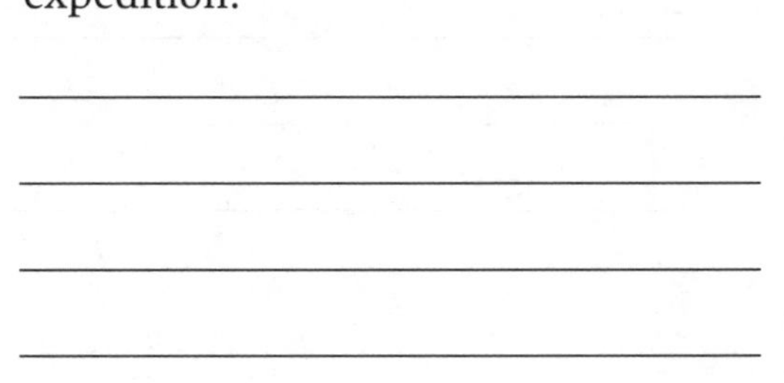

23. Plot the following events on the time line: the Missouri Compromise, John Brown's rebellion, the Dred Scott court case, the Kansas-Nebraska Act, the Compromise of 1850, and Harriet Beecher Stowe's novel.

24. Who were indentured servants? How were they similar to slaves? How were they different from slaves?

______________________

______________________

______________________

______________________

25. What two important events happened at Gettysburg, Pennsylvania?

______________________

______________________

______________________

______________________

26. Who was Jane Addams? How did she help immigrants and poor people?

______________________

______________________

______________________

______________________

27. What was the Guilded Age?

______________________

______________________

______________________

28. List the major invention of each inventor.

Eli Whitney: ______________________

Robert Fulton: ______________________

Samuel Morse: ______________________

**Use for 29–30.**

We the People of the United States, in Order to form a more perfect Union, establish Justice, insure domestic Tranquility, provide for the common defense, promote the general Welfare, and secure the Blessings of Liberty to ourselves and our Posterity, do ordain and establish this Constitution for the United States of America.

29. What is the title of this selection?

______________________

30. Describe the three branches of government that help the United States keep true to this document.

______________________

______________________

______________________

______________________

______________________

______________________

**Read each selection in Part A and answer the questions. Then read the directions in Part B and write your essay.**

## Part A: Short Answer

### Use for 31–32.

Today "the American Dream" is to work hard and become wealthy, important, and famous. Many American Indians had a completely different attitude. They traded extensively, and some of them became very rich. But they refused to accumulate wealth, and acquired it mainly to give it away in shows of generosity. They thought the white Americans' habit of accumulating food and possessions was greedy and they suspected that someone who stored up wealth was a witch! Similarly, American Indians developed a way of government that was completely different from that found in European societies. Some Europeans even claimed that they had no government at all, but others conceded that—though they were impossible for white Americans to understand—American Indian ways seemed to work quite well for American Indians.

**31.** How did American Indian views on wealth differ from those of Europeans?

________________________________

________________________________

________________________________

________________________________

________________________________

________________________________

________________________________

________________________________

________________________________

**32.** Why did Europeans consider American Indians to have no government?

________________________________

________________________________

________________________________

________________________________

________________________________

________________________________

________________________________

________________________________

________________________________

**Use for 33–34.**

The American Indians did not wage war for the same reasons as the white man. They did not do it to gain land, for they believed that no man could own the land, fighting instead for resources. They did not fight in armies like Europeans, and they believed that their first duty was to preserve their culture, tribal beliefs, and families. Although American Indians had fought each other for as long as Europeans had, battles were not as bloody before the arrival of the Europeans and their superior military technology.

**33.** How did American Indian beliefs about land differ from those of European settlers?

______________________________

______________________________

______________________________

______________________________

______________________________

**34.** How did European technology affect the way wars were fought?

______________________________

______________________________

______________________________

______________________________

______________________________

**Use for 35–36.**

The coming of the white settlers brought disaster for the American Indians. . . . The Sioux chief Luther Standing Bear summed up their struggles with the white man: *"Only to the white man was Nature 'a wilderness,' and only to him was the land 'infested' with 'wild' animals and 'savage' people. To us it was tame. Not until the hairy man from the east came and with brutal frenzy heaped injustices upon our people did the 'Wild West' begin for us."*

**35.** How did American Indian views of nature differ from those of the European settlers?

______________________________

______________________________

______________________________

______________________________

______________________________

**36.** Why were the American Indians unsuccessful in their fight against the European settlers?

______________________________

______________________________

______________________________

______________________________

______________________________

## Part B: Essay

**Write an essay using the information from the selections. You may also use your knowledge of social studies. Include an introduction, two supporting paragraphs, and a conclusion.**

**37.** Support this statement in your essay:
The European settlers' way of life differed significantly from the American Indians' way of life and resulted in conflict between the two groups.

# Assessment Answers

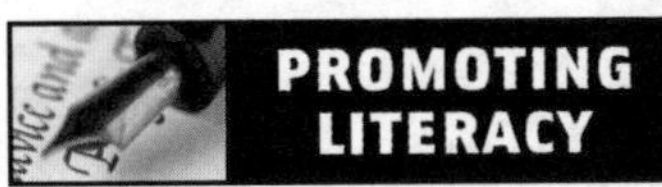

**PROMOTING LITERACY**

1. C
2. C
3. B
4. C
5. B
6. D
7. B
8. D
9. C
10. C
11. A
12. C
13. B
14. A
15. D
16. A
17. B
18. A
19. D
20. B
21. B
22. A
23. B
24. B
25. B
26. B
27. C
28. B
29. The main idea of the selection is that Marta was miserable at her new school until she created a plan to make friends.
30. Answers will vary. Possible answer: Marta will become friends with members of the book club and will be happy at her new school.
31. Marta at beginning of story: Marta is miserable because she hasn't made friends at her new school; Event that caused Marta to change: Marta came up with a plan when she saw a group of students sharing books; Marta at end of story: Marta is happy that her plan worked, as it seems she is on her way to making friends.
32. The features of a biography used in this selection are that it is told in the third person and that the life of another person is written about using dates and chronological order.
33. The main idea is that George Gallup created a poll that accurately surveyed the opinions of the population.
34. Answers will vary. Possible answer: As a journalism student, he might have learned how to ask the right kinds of questions to get the information needed from people.
35. Logical: sensible, reasonable; dedication: loyalty, devotion
36. Answers will vary. Possible answer: What he does: George Gallup goes to school to study journalism, becomes a teacher, and develops an accurate method of polling opinions that is still used today; How he acts: Gallup is careful, creative, and dedicated.
37. Answers will vary. Possible answer: Chuck is someone who is fun to be around. There is never a dull moment with Chuck in the room.

### *Scoring Rubric for Question 38:*

**4 POINTS**
The student demonstrates a complete understanding of a drama by identifying the selection as a drama and accurately listing the features of a drama.

**3 POINTS**
The student demonstrates a nearly complete understanding of a drama by identifying the selection as a drama and accurately listing the features of a drama.

**2 POINTS**
The student demonstrates a partial understanding of a drama by identifying the selection as a drama and by accurately listing a feature of a drama.

**1 POINT**
The student demonstrates little understanding of a drama by identifying the selection as a drama but does not accurately list the features of a drama.

**0 POINTS**
The student fails to demonstrate any understanding of a drama or its features.

39. Answers will vary. Possible answer: The girl was quiet about how the accident happened.
40. Answers will vary. Possible answer: They liked the nonstop action of the movie.
41. Answers will vary. Possible answer: He replied with the correct answer.
42. Answers will vary. Possible answer: The bottom part of my receipt is missing.
43. she
44. himself
45. their
46. their

# Assessment Answers

***Scoring Rubric for Question 47:***

**4 POINTS**

The student demonstrates a complete understanding of grammar, spelling, punctuation, and capitalization.

Example: Daniel really wants to visit Texas. His friend Adam lives in Abeline. The closest Daniel has ever been to Texas was when he visited Oklahoma with his family. There are three cities Daniel wants to visit in Texas: Abeline, Dallas, and Corpus Christi. He hopes to visit these cities soon.

**3 POINTS**

The student demonstrates a substantial understanding of grammar, spelling, punctuation, and capitalization, with a few errors.

**2 POINTS**

The student demonstrates adequate understanding of grammar, spelling, punctuation, and capitalization, with many significant errors.

**1 POINT**

The student demonstrates a limited understanding of grammar, spelling, punctuation, and capitalization, only incorporating a few correct changes.

**0 POINTS**

The student demonstrates no understanding of grammar, spelling, punctuation, and capitalization.

***Scoring Rubric for Question 48:***

**4 POINTS**

The student demonstrates a complete understanding of friendly letter writing, attending to correct placement of all four letter parts.

May 30

Dear Randall,

Today I got a new bike. I was thrilled. It is gold and black, which are the colors that I wanted. Dad said that he will take me riding on the bike trail in a few weeks. Maybe you can come with us when you visit this summer.

Sincerely,
Your cousin Raphael

**3 POINTS**

The student demonstrates a nearly complete understanding of friendly letter writing, attending to correct placement of three letter parts.

**2 POINTS**

The student demonstrates a partial understanding of friendly letter writing, with correct placement of two letter parts.

**1 POINT**

The student demonstrates little understanding of friendly letter writing, with correct placement of one letter part.

**0 POINTS**

The student demonstrates no understanding of friendly letter writing.

***Scoring Rubric for Question 49:***

**4 POINTS**

The essay is well-organized with a clear introduction, body, and conclusion. There are no errors in grammar, spelling, punctuation, or capitalization.

**3 POINTS**

The essay has an introduction, body, and conclusion. There are a few minor errors in grammar, spelling, punctuation, and capitalization.

**2 POINTS**

The essay lacks clear organization. There are significant errors in grammar, spelling, punctuation, and capitalization.

**1 POINT**

The essay lacks any organization. There are numerous errors in grammar, spelling, punctuation, and capitalization.

**0 POINTS**

The student demonstrates no understanding of how to organize an essay. There are so many errors in grammar, spelling, punctuation, and capitalization that the essay is unreadable.

## MATH

1. C
2. A
3. C
4. C
5. A
6. D
7. C
8. D
9. D
10. C

# Assessment Answers

11. B
12. D
13. A
14. C
15. C
16. B
17. D
18. B
19. B
20. C
21. B
22. C
23. C
24. D
25. A
26. D
27. B
28. C
29. Angles shown in order: acute, right, and obtuse
30. Triangles shown in order: right, obtuse, and acute
31. Quadrilaterals shown in order: square, rhombus, and parallelogram
32. $7 \times 4 = 28$ inches
33. 45,972; 45,792; 45,729; 45,297
34. 2.034, 2.043, 2.304, 2.340
35. $n + 15$
36. $n + 4 = 14$; Pamela is 10 years old.
37. $6 \times \$1.00 = \$6.00$
38. $\$6.99 + \$3.50 + \$12.88 = \$23.37$
39. $\$4.50 - \$1.23 - \$0.76 = \$2.51$
40. Greatest common factors in order of items: 6, 12, 1
41. 12, 24, 36, 48
42. 300,000 kilometers
    1,000 decimeters
    5,400 seconds
    3 days
43. Possible answer: $\frac{4}{6}, \frac{6}{9}, \frac{8}{12}$
44. $1\frac{1}{8}, \frac{19}{16}, 1\frac{1}{4}, \frac{11}{8}$
45. $\frac{9}{20}$; 0.45
46. $\frac{3}{8}$
47. \$24.99 rounded = \$25
    $15\% = 0.15$
    $\$25 \times 0.15 = \$3.75$
    $\$25 - \$3.75 = \$21.25$

48.
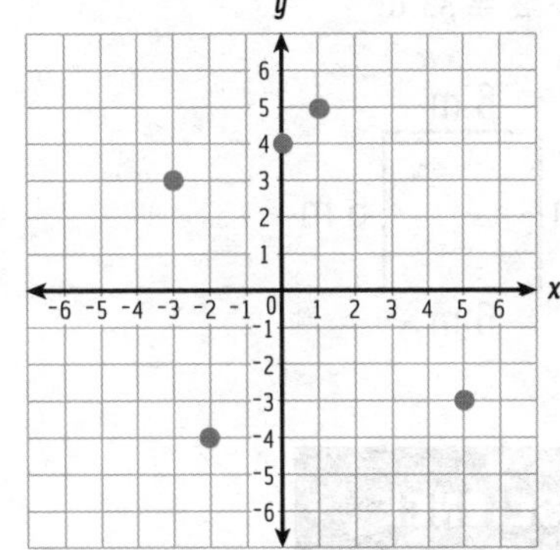


49.
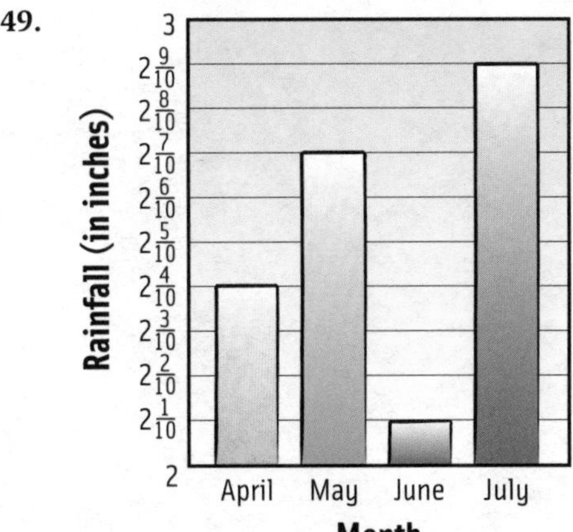


50. mean: 58.7 inches; median: 58.5 inches; range: 7 inches; mode: 58 inches
51. 82.9. Possible response: I took the sum of all of the math scores and divided it by the number of scores shown.
52. −7 −6 −5 −4 −3 −2 −1 0 1 2 3 4 5 6 7

53.
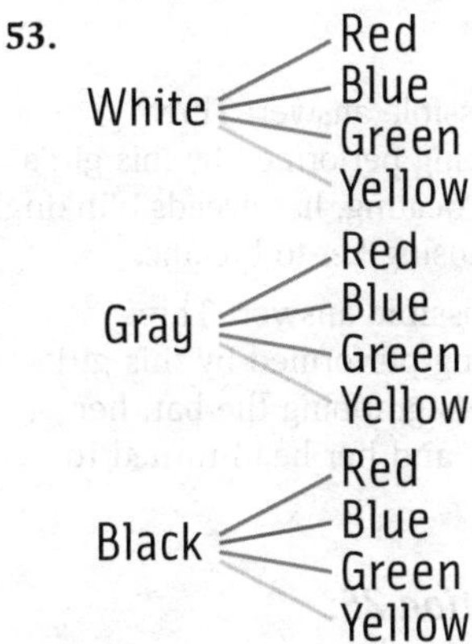


54. $7 \times 6 \times 4 = 168$ cm$^3$

# Assessment Answers

55. $(11 \times 6) \div 2 = 33\ ft^2$

56. 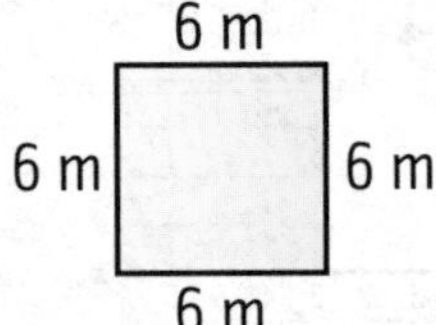

## SCIENCE

1. A
2. B
3. C
4. C
5. A
6. A
7. A
8. B
9. A
10. C
11. A
12. D
13. A
14. B
15. D
16. A
17. C
18. D
19. C
20. A
21. A
22. B
23. Answers will vary. Possible answer: Three involuntary actions being performed by this girl's muscles are her heart beating, her eyelids blinking, and her diaphragm causing her to breathe.
24. Answers will vary. Possible answer: Three voluntary actions being performed by this girl's muscles are her fingers grabbing the bat, her arms holding the bat, and her head turned to look at the pitcher.

### *Scoring Rubric for Question 25:*

**4 POINTS**
The paragraph shows the student understands that resource use and pollution are a function of human population growth. When human population increases, both resource use and pollution increase.

**3 POINTS**
The paragraph shows some understanding that these categories of environmental concern are related, and that the size of the human population does affect the other categories.

**2 POINTS**
The paragraph indicates an understanding of these environmental concerns but doesn't clearly point out the relationship between them.

**1 POINT**
The paragraph indicates little understanding of these environmental concerns.

**0 POINTS**
The paragraph indicates no understanding of these environmental concerns.

### *Scoring Rubric for Question 26:*

**4 POINTS**
The paragraph correctly names two systems involved in getting oxygen to the cells of the body and correctly describes their functions. For example, two systems involved in getting oxygen to the cells are the muscular system and the respiratory system. The respiratory system is responsible for oxygen being drawn into the lungs; the muscular system is responsible for the beating of the heart, which sends the oxygenated blood through the body.

**3 POINTS**
The paragraph correctly names two systems responsible for the delivery of oxygen to the cells but does not accurately or clearly describe their functions.

**2 POINTS**
The paragraph correctly names one system responsible for the delivery of oxygen to the cells and accurately or clearly describes its function.

**1 POINT**
The paragraph correctly names one system responsible for the delivery of oxygen to the cells but does not accurately or clearly describe its function.

**0 POINTS**
The paragraph does not correctly name a system and does not accurately describe the function of any system.

27. Answers will vary. Possible answer: Earthquakes are caused by huge blocks of rock that suddenly break apart. The ground underneath us changes. In a volcano, magma from the mantle comes to the surface through underground spaces and

surface cracks. The magma can spread over the ground and harden. A glacier is a huge sheet of ice that moves very slowly. As it moves, it moves ground and land. The holes left from a glacier can become lakes. The ground that has piled up can become mountains.

28. Answers will vary. Possible answer: Water: We can save water in our homes by not running the water when we don't need to. We also can clean up lakes that have been polluted so that fish, animals, and plants can use them again. Oil: We can carpool. We can make cars that use less gasoline.
29. From bottom to top and left to right, the labels should read: breads, grains, and rice; vegetables; fruits; milk, yogurt; meats, eggs, nuts, and poultry; fats, oils, and sweets.
30. Answers will vary. Possible answer: Anemia is a disease that results from low levels of iron. Foods that can be eaten regularly to avoid anemia are leafy, dark-green vegetables and liver.
31. Solar energy: sunlight goes into special machines; these machines convert the sunlight into electricity. Wind energy: the wind makes the blades on a windmill move; the movement of the wind blades makes another machine move that can, for example, move water or create electricity. Hydroelectric energy:
water goes from a higher place to a lower place, like in a dam; the force of the water moving can be connected to a machine that can make electricity.

### *Scoring Rubric for Question 32:*

The paragraph correctly describes at least one positive effect and one negative effect for the type of energy chosen and shows an understanding of the type of energy.

**3 POINTS**
The paragraph correctly describes at least one positive effect or one negative effect for the type of energy chosen and shows some understanding of the type of energy.

**2 POINTS**
The paragraph correctly describes at least one positive effect or one negative effect for the type of energy chosen and shows little understanding of the type of energy.

**1 POINT**
The paragraph describes at least one positive effect or one negative effect for the type of energy chosen but does not show an understanding of the type of energy.

**0 POINTS**
The paragraph does not correctly describe at least one positive effect or one negative effect for the type of energy chosen and does not show an understanding of the type of energy.

33. Left to right: A. Mercury, B. Venus, C. Earth, D. Mars, E. Jupiter, F. Saturn, G. Uranus, H. Neptune, I. Pluto
34. Inner planets: Mercury, Venus, Earth, Mars; Outer planets: Jupiter, Saturn, Uranus, Neptune, Pluto

## SOCIAL STUDIES

1. C
2. C
3. A
4. D
5. A
6. C
7. A
8. B
9. C
10. B
11. A
12. C
13. B
14. C
15. C
16. C
17. D
18. A
19. B
20. A
21. The significance of Paul Revere's ride was that it warned the people in the countryside that the British planned to destroy patriot weapons and might arrest patriot leaders.

# Assessment Answers

### *Scoring Rubric for Question 22:*

**2 POINTS**

The student answers both questions correctly by showing a complete understanding of the Lewis and Clark expedition *and* naming the two people who helped Lewis and Clark.

Example: In May 1804, Meriwether Lewis and William Clark led an expedition of about 45 men to map out the size and/or boundaries of the Louisiana Territory as ordered by President Thomas Jefferson. Sacagewea and Clark's slave, York, helped in the expedition.

**1 POINT**

The student answers one of the questions correctly.

**0 POINTS**

The student answers neither question correctly or fails to answer the questions.

23. 1820: the Missouri Compromise; 1850: the Compromise of 1850; 1852: Harriet Beecher Stowe's novel; 1854: the Kansas-Nebraska Act; 1857: the Dred Scott court case; 1859: John Brown's rebellion

### *Scoring Rubric for Question 24:*

**2 POINTS**

The student answers both questions correctly by showing an understanding of indentured servants and naming the similarities and differences between indentured servants and slaves.

Example: Indentured servants were individuals who agreed to work for a period of time in exchange for voyage to the Americas. The indentured servants and slaves were alike in that they both worked very hard and rarely became free persons. They were different in that the indentured servants came to the Americas of their own free will, whereas slaves were brought to the Americas by force.

**1 POINT**

The student answers one of the questions correctly.

**0 POINTS**

The student answers both questions incorrectly or fails to answer the questions.

25. Two important events: (1) One of the Civil War battles was fought there, with the Union winning the battle; (2) Gettysburg was later turned into a cemetery to honor those who lost their lives during the Gettysburg Battle, and Lincoln gave his famous Gettysburg Address there.

26. Jane Addams established Hull House in Chicago. She helped the immigrants and poor people by assisting them with needed services such as an employment agency, day care, housing, and adult-education classes.

27. The Guilded Age was the term used to indicate that a small layer of wealth covered the poverty and corruption in most of society.

28. Eli Whitney: cotton gin; Robert Fulton: steam-powered boat; Samuel Morse: telegraph

29. Preamble to the United States Constitution

### *Scoring Rubric for Question 30:*

**4 POINTS**

The student demonstrates a complete understanding of the organization of the U.S. government into three branches, outlining the role of the executive branch, the judicial branch, and the legislative branch.

**3 POINTS**

The student demonstrates a partial understanding of the organization of the U.S. government into branches, describing the roles of two of the three branches of government.

**2 POINTS**

The student demonstrates a limited understanding of the organization of the U.S. government into branches, describing the role of one of the three branches of government.

**1 POINT**

The student demonstrates a limited understanding of the organization of the U.S. government into branches but does not describe any of the three branches.

**0 POINTS**

The student demonstrates no understanding of the organization of the U.S. government and its branches.

31. European settlers accumulated wealth, but American Indians believed this was greedy.

32. European settlers could not understand how the American Indian government worked, so they assumed the American Indians had no government at all.

33. European settlers were concerned with ownership of land, but American Indians believed that humans could not own the land.

34. The European settlers' advanced weapons made battles bloodier.

35. American Indians viewed nature as tame, while European settlers saw it as wild and dangerous.

36. Answers will vary. Possible answer: The American Indians were unable to overcome the injustices of the European settlers, which changed their lives forever.

### *Scoring Rubric for Question 37:*

**4 POINTS**
The essay is well written, well organized, and demonstrates a clear understanding of the lifestyles of the American Indians and the European settlers. It clearly contrasts their ways of life and describes how this led to conflict.

**3 POINTS**
The essay has a few minor flaws in grammar and organization but demonstrates a good understanding of the way of life of the American Indians and the European settlers and their conflict.

**2 POINTS**
The essay has some significant flaws in grammar and organization. It demonstrates some understanding of the way of life of American Indians and European settlers and their conflict.

**1 POINT**
The essay has major flaws in grammar and organization. There is very little understanding of the way of life of the American Indians and European settlers and their conflict.

**0 POINTS**
The essay shows no understanding of the way of life of the American Indians and European settlers and their conflict *or* the student fails to answer the question or writes off topic.

# Answers

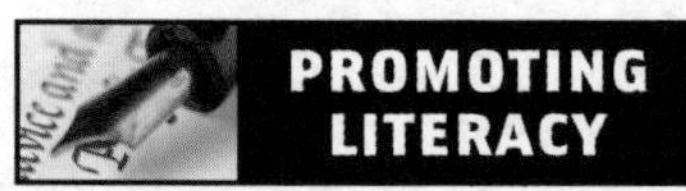


## Lesson 1.1 *Student Learning Page 1.A*

Time line should note important story events in order.

### *Student Learning Page 1.D*

Two characteristics should be chosen and examples given for each. Answers will vary.

independent: goes to the library alone, makes her own lunch, takes a walk alone

smart: reads a lot of books, able to explain and defend her opinions

funny: describes the things she doesn't like in a humorous way; makes the reader laugh

imaginative: compares the mushrooms to moon babies; describes mushrooms as werewolves; thinks mushrooms will grow from the dirt in her toes

## Lesson 1.2 *Student Learning Page 2.B*

Answers will vary. Outline should be filled in completely.

## Lesson 1.3 *Student Learning Page 3.B*

Answers will vary. Possible answers:

Hardenberghs: were wealthy, owned land and slaves; lived in a stately home in warm, well-furnished rooms; could buy and sell slaves

Slaves: were crammed into a small, dark, damp room; could be sold at any time; had no rights; family could be broken up

## Lesson 1.5 *Student Learning Page 5.B*

Answers will vary. Possible answers:

1. living in the home he loves; creating a successful business
2. never being able to embrace Volkhova; feeling lonely
3. being loved by a beautiful princess; getting married
4. never being able to return home to Novgorod; missing his home

## Lesson 1.6 *Student Learning Page 6.A*

1. B
2. A
3. C
4. D
5. E
6. C
7. E
8. A
9. A
10. C
11. Air travel
12. 10 pages
13. Chapter 2
14. Meanings of important words in the book
15. The index, which is on page 112

### *Student Learning Page 6.B*

1. Page 117
2. Page 87
3. Page 124
4. Page 69

## Lesson 1.7 *Student Learning Page 7.A*

1. primary source
2. not a primary source
3. primary source
4. not a primary source
5. primary source
6. not a primary source
7. primary source
8. not a primary source

## Lesson 1.8 *Student Learning Page 8.B*

Answers will vary. Chart should be filled in accurately, with the main idea, smaller topics, and supporting details.

## Lesson 1.9 *Student Learning Page 9.B*

Answers will vary. Topic, audience, and reasons should be completed.

# Answers

## Lesson 1.10 *Student Learning Page 10.A*

The unscrambled letter is:

January 5, 2003
280 Nevins . . .

Dear Meg,

I have been wanting. . . .

How are things in the old. . . .

Now much else to tell. . . .

Your friend,
Alicia

### *Student Learning Page 10.B*

The information in the letter should be accurate, and the tone should be informal.

## Lesson 2.1 *Student Learning Page 1.A*

1. hundreds
2. ten thousands
3. billions
4. <
5. >
6. =
7. D
8. B
9. A
10. tenths
11. hundredths
12. thousandths
13. two hundred fifty-four thousandths
14. two tenths
15. 0.00750
16. 0.4
17. 0.42
18. 0.006

## Lesson 2.2 *Student Learning Page 2.A*

1. 85
2. 35
3. 733
4. 453
5. 7,230
6. 6,511
7. 15,857
8. 13,742
9. 12,000
10. 7,000
11. 11,000
12. 16,000

## Lesson 2.3 *Student Learning Page 3.A*

1. Commutative
2. Property of One
3. Associative
4. Zero Property
5. Distributive
6. <
7. >
8. =
9. 360
10. 180
11. 4,000
12. 2,836
13. 642
14. 625

## Lesson 2.4 *Student Learning Page 4.A*

1. 15
2. 9
3. 15
4. 25
5. 120
6. 12

7–12. Estimates will vary. Actual answers are given.

7. 12 R5
8. 105 R4
9. 90 R3
10. 35
11. 4 R5
12. 7 R2

# Answers

### *Student Learning Page 4.B*

1. 8
2. 3
3. 5
4. 4
5. 18
6. 50

### Lesson 2.5 *Student Learning Page 5.A*

1. 46.62; estimate: 42
2. 14.72; estimate: 12
3. 15.04; estimate: 15
4. 46.99; estimate: 42
5. 12.312; estimate: 12
6. 13.008; estimate: 15
7. 45.54; estimate: 40
8. 68.32; estimate: 72
9. 617.76; estimate: 620
10. 80; estimate: 78
11. 185.82; estimate: 198
12. 845.46; estimate: 850

### Lesson 2.6 *Student Learning Page 6.A*

1. 2
2. 4
3. 18
4. 6
5. 12
6. 24
7. 10
8. 4
9. 25
10. 4
11. 7
12. 5

### *Student Learning Page 6.B*

Prime numbers from 2–50: 2, 3, 5, 7, 11, 13, 17, 19, 23, 29, 31, 37, 41, 43, 47

### *Student Learning Page 6.C*

1. $\frac{2}{4}$
2. $\frac{8}{9}$
3. $\frac{3}{7}$
4. $1\frac{1}{6}$
5. $\frac{1}{12}$
6. $\frac{11}{25}$
7. 6
8. $2\frac{7}{10}$
9. 4
10. $1\frac{7}{16}$
11. $10\frac{3}{8}$
12. $3\frac{2}{27}$

### Lesson 2.7 *Student Learning Page 7.A*

1. 1 foot = $\frac{1}{2}$ inch
2. 12 feet long, 9 feet wide
3. 2 feet
4. 7 feet
5. Objects should be drawn correctly.

### Lesson 2.8 *Student Learning Page 8.A*

1. Number line from −10 to +10 should be drawn with points labeled correctly.
2. **a.** −20, −4, +2, +3, +8, +10
   **b.** −12, −10, −2, +21, +27, +35
   **c.** −9, −6, −2, +2, +6, +9
3. **a.** +10, +8, +3, +2, −4, −20
   **b.** +35, +27, +21, −2, −10, −12
   **c.** +9, +6, +2, −2, −6, −9
4. **a.** 0
   **b.** +8
   **c.** −9
   **d.** +31
5. **a.** The number with the greater absolute value tells whether the sum will be positive or negative.
   **b.** The sum will be negative.
   **c.** The answer will be positive.

### *Student Learning Page 8.B*

Coordinate grid with labels and quadrants should be drawn correctly.

*A* in quadrant II
*B* in quadrant I
*C* in quadrant II
*D* in quadrant IV
*E* in quadrant III
*F* in quadrant IV

## Lesson 2.9 *Student Learning Page 9.A*

1. 12
2. 11
3. 10
4. 6
5. 7
6. 5
7. none
8. 14
9. 12.5%
10. 25%
11. $\frac{1}{16}$
12. $\frac{2}{16}$ or $\frac{1}{8}$

## Lesson 2.10 *Student Learning Page 10.A*

Triangles should be drawn correctly.

### *Student Learning Page 10.B*

Polygons should be drawn correctly.

### *Student Learning Page 10.C*

1. $\overline{GE}$
2. 2.75 or $2\frac{3}{4}$ inches
3. $\overline{DG}$ or $\overline{DE}$ or $\overline{DF}$
4. $\angle EDF$ or $\angle GDF$
5. acute
6. a chord
7. A chord can't be longer than the diameter.
8. $2\frac{3}{4}$ inches (half the diameter)

### *Student Learning Page 10.D*

**What's in a Word?**

Answers will vary. Possible answers:

1. pentagram—a five-pointed star
2. hexabasic—a science word meaning six atoms
3. heptameter—a verse with seven measures
4. octave—eight notes
5. nonagenarian—a 90-year-old person
6. decade—10 years

## Lesson 2.11 *Student Learning Page 11.A*

Answers will vary. Possible answers:

**1–2.** Answers should be in feet or meters.

**3–4.** Answers should be in inches or centimeters.

**5–6.** Answers should be in feet or meters.

## Lesson 3.1 *Student Learning Page 1.A*

1. cytoplasm—a jellylike fluid inside a cell containing organelles
2. plasma membrane—a thin layer that surrounds a cell and holds everything inside; it also controls what goes into and out of a cell
3. cell wall—a stiff wall made of cellulose surrounding a plant cell that helps a plant maintain its shape
4. nucleus—a cell's command center; it contains chemical instructions called DNA (deoxyribonucleic acid) for everything a cell does
5. golgi apparatus—a group of membranes that sort incoming proteins for use in other parts of the cell
6. mitochondria—tiny organelles that break down food molecules so the cell has energy to live
7. chloroplast—organelle in plant cells that converts energy from the sun into sugars
8. vacuole—bubble inside a cell that stores the molecules a cell needs to survive; vacuoles store food, water, oil, and waste products

Model of animal cell should be completed correctly.

## Lesson 3.2 *Student Learning Page 2.A*

1. Serves as linings in different parts of the body; helps keep organs in place and protected
2. outer layer of skin, inside of mouth, inside of stomach, tissue surrounding organs
3. adds support and structure to the body
4. inner layers of skin, tendons, ligaments, cartilage, bone, fat, blood
5. contracts allowing movement
6. muscles throughout the body
7. generates and conducts electrical signals in the body
8. neurons, glial cells

### *Student Learning Page 2.B*

1. leaves—collect and convert sunlight into sugars; take in carbon dioxide and give off oxygen

# Answers

2. stem—support the plant; transport water to leaves and sugars to roots
3. roots—absorb water and nutrients; anchor the plant to keep it from moving

## Lesson 3.3 *Student Learning Page 3.A*

Answers will vary. Population should be counted accurately for the area chosen. Species should be identified correctly.

### *Student Learning Page 3.B*

Answers will vary. Food web and food web example should be identified and drawn accurately.

## Lesson 3.4 *Student Learning Page 4.A*

Arrows should show correctly the flow of blood through the heart.

### *Student Learning Page 4.B*

Diagram of the respiratory system should be drawn and labeled correctly.

### *Student Learning Page 4.C*

Flowchart showing the process of digestion should be shown. All major steps should be included.

### *Student Learning Page 4.D*

Bone model should be complete and all questions answered; cardboard: periosteum (the outer layer of bone); straws: compact bone; modeling clay: minerals and bone marrow

elbow: hinge; shoulder: ball-and-socket; neck: pivot; thumb: saddle

### *Student Learning Page 4.E*

The following should be labeled in diagram:

1. pectoralis major
2. biceps brachii
3. rectus abdominus
4. external oblique
5. quadricep
6. tibialis anterior
7. deltoid
8. trapezius
9. tricep
10. latissimus dorsi
11. gluteus maximus
12. hamstring
13. gastrocnemius

## Lesson 3.5 *Student Learning Page 5.A*

Answers will vary.

## Lesson 3.6 *Student Learning Page 6.A*

Answers will vary. Possible answers:

1. baseball
2. table, chair
3. milk
4. old clothes, cut-up paper
5. lit candle
6. soap, door, ice
7. steam
8. water, oil, juice
9. air, lemonade
10. chocolate chip cookie, soil

## Lesson 3.7 *Student Learning Page 7.A*

2. table salt; NaCl; sodium and chlorine
3. baking soda; $NaHCO_3$; sodium, hydrogen, carbon, and oxygen
4. water; $H_2O$; hydrogen and oxygen
5. hydrogen peroxide; $H_2O_2$; hydrogen and oxygen
6. carbon dioxide; $CO_2$; carbon and oxygen

7–10. Answers will vary.

### *Student Learning Page 7.B*

1. More elements are metals.
2. The chemical symbol for lead is Pb.
3. The atomic number for oxygen is 8.
4. More elements are natural.
5. The atomic weight of calcium is 40.
6. Possible answers include radon, radium, and uranium.
7. hydrogen, helium, nitrogen, oxygen, fluorine, neon, chlorine, argon, krypton, xenon, and radon
8. 118 elements
9. ununtrium, ununpentium, ununhexium, ununseptium, and ununoctium
10. More elements are solid.

## Lesson 3.8 *Student Learning Page 8.A*

1. Devices collect solar energy and convert it into electricity, or solar heating systems heat air or water.
2. No pollution. Answers will vary.

3. Sunlight that hits Earth isn't constant. To collect useful amounts requires a large area. Answers will vary.
4. Blades of a wind turbine "catch" the wind and the blades of the turbine spin. This generates electricity.
5. Wind turbines produce no pollution. The United States has many locations where wind turbines could be used. Answers will vary.
6. Wind turbines can be noisy. Answers will vary.
7. Moving water flows through a pipe and pushes against a turbine (turning the blades) to produce electricity.
8. It's inexpensive. It produces no pollution. Answers will vary.
9. Affects natural habitats. Answers will vary.
10. In places where Earth's crust has trapped steam and hot water, people drill into the crust, allowing heat to escape as steam or hot water. The steam turns a turbine that generates electricity.
11. Produces less pollution than fossil fuels. Answers will vary.
12. Few places have geothermal energy. People must be close to source. Has a minor impact on soil. Answers will vary.

## Lesson 3.9 *Student Learning Page 9.A*

Answers will vary. Possible answers:

1. increase of carbon dioxide and nitrous oxide in atmosphere, increase use of fossil fuel, loss of plant life from deforestation
2. polar ice caps begin to melt, sea level rises, flooding, rain patterns change
3. reforestation, reduce use of fossil fuels, increase use of wind, solar energy, and hydro energy

## Lesson 3.10 *Student Learning Page 10.A*

8. No. 4, No. 1, No. 2, No. 3. Heat causes more rapid evaporation.
9. No, because none of them has a way of capturing the water that is evaporating. Designs will vary. None of them will work for ocean water, because it contains salts other than "table" salt. It would need more steps to separate other chemicals.

## *Student Learning Page 10.B*

**Check Out "Current" Events**

European cities near the Atlantic (London, Dublin, etc.) have milder January temperatures than inland cities. North American cities near the Pacific (Seattle, Washington; Portland, Oregon; etc.) have milder winter temperatures than inland cities.

## Lesson 3.11 *Student Learning Page 11.A*

Recycling center should reflect correctly the recycling options in your community.

## Lesson 3.12 *Student Learning Page 12.A*

Answers about contributions will vary.

Brahe: (1546–1601); discovered and corrected errors in the standard astronomical tables; discovered supernova located in the constellation of Cassiopeia

Copernicus: (1473–1543); developed an important theory of planetary movement

Galileo: (1564–1642); first astronomer to use a telescope

Halley: (1656–1742); first to calculate the orbit of the comet named after him (Halley's Comet)

Hubble: (1889–1953); founder of "extragalactic" astronomy; discovered galaxies beyond the Milky Way Galaxy

Kepler: (1571–1630); formulated three laws: First, the orbits of Earth and other planets of the solar system are elliptical in shape; Second, the planets travel faster the closer they are to the sun; Third, the size of a planet and length of time that planet takes to orbit the sun are related

Leavitt: (1868–1921); discovered more than 2,400 stars (about half of the total known in her day)

Ptolemy: (ca. 100–ca. 170); believed the sun and the planets orbited around Earth

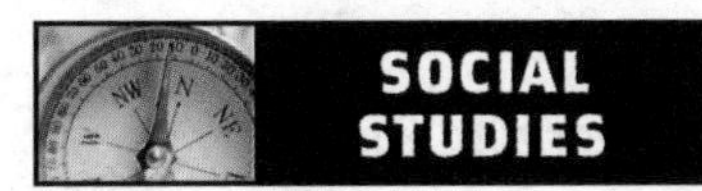

# SOCIAL STUDIES

## Lesson 4.1 *Student Learning Page 1.A*

Answers will vary. Details about his or her Native American lifestyle should be accurate.

# Answers

## Lesson 4.2 *Student Learning Page 2.A*

Time line order: A, N, C, B, J, D, E, P, H, O, F, G, I, L, K, M, Q, S, T, R

## Lesson 4.3 *Student Learning Page 3.A*

1. New York
2. Georgia
3. Massachusetts
4. Maryland
5. Rhode Island
6. Pennsylvania
7. Connecticut
8. North and South Carolina
9. New Jersey
10. Virginia
11. New Hampshire
12. Delaware

## Lesson 4.4 *Student Learning Page 4.A*

1. C
2. E
3. F
4. D
5. A
6. B

## Lesson 4.5 *Student Learning Page 5.A*

1. Lexington
2. Delaware
3. Saratoga
4. Valley Forge
5. Treaty of Paris

Drawing of battle should be completed correctly.

## Lesson 4.6 *Student Learning Page 6.A*

1. C
2. A
3. B
4. D

## Lesson 4.7 *Student Learning Page 7.A*

Time line and paragraph should be completed accurately.

## Lesson 4.8 *Student Learning Page 8.A*

1. D
2. F
3. E
4. B
5. C
6. A

## Lesson 4.9 *Student Learning Page 9.A*

North: abolitionists, Abraham Lincoln, industrialization was increasing quickly here, Ulysses S. Grant, victory at Battle of Gettysburg, Union victory at Savannah, Georgia

South: Confederacy, Jefferson Davis, plantations important here, Robert E. Lee, victory at Fort Sumter, victory at Battle of First Bull Run, seceded states

## Lesson 4.10 *Student Learning Page 10.A*

1. G
2. D
3. E
4. C
5. H
6. F
7. I
8. B
9. A

## Lesson 4.11 *Student Learning Page 11.A*

Answers will vary. Possible answers:

1. Martha's family has heard good things about the land and opportunity in Oregon Country. The trip is long and sometimes there is bad weather. Some people have gotten sick. She has seen buffalo and mountains and crossed a river.
2. Red Bird probably has heard her parents talk of the days when they lived further east. Now she is hearing angry talk about many white men coming to the Black Hills. She is afraid there is going to be a war.
3. Elizabeth and her parents are Exodusters, homesteaders who came from the South. Her parents were slaves freed after the Civil War.

## Lesson 4.12 *Student Learning Page 12.A*

Typewriter: 1873; Telephone: 1876; Electric lightbulb: 1879; Automobile: 1885; Radio: 1895; Airplane: 1903

# GLOSSARY

***Like any other specialty area, teaching and homeschooling have their own unique vocabulary. We've included some terms we thought might be helpful.***

***accelerated learning***
when a student completes a certain set of lessons faster than most students; this can happen due to a student's natural motivation or in a more structured manner, such as continuing lessons throughout the year versus taking the summer off

***assessment***
a review of a student's learning progress and comprehension; traditionally done through tests or grades; assessments in progressive learning environments such as homeschooling take on many different forms, including summary discussions, demonstrative projects, and oral questions and answers; formalized assessment is included in this book, beginning on page 295

***auditory learner***
an individual who absorbs new information most effectively by listening; an auditory learner will remember information that is spoken or related through sound such as musical lyrics, reading aloud, or audiocassettes

***child-centered learning***
a type of learning in which the teaching style places the child at the center of his or her learning, meaning that a child begins and proceeds with new subjects, such as reading, as he or she is ready; this style of teaching requires intimate awareness of the student by the teacher

***correlated to state standards***
a phrase that means that something meets or exceeds a particular state's mandatory educational requirements for the intended grade level

***critical thinking skill***
the ability to assess information, make independent judgments, and draw conclusions; this skill is independent of and goes beyond the memorized information that a student has learned

***curriculum***
an ordered list of specific topics of study that is used as a teaching plan

***distance learning***
a type of instruction in which classes are completed at a different physical location than at the school that offers them; formerly known as correspondence classes, this term now includes video and Internet classes

***graphic organizer***
a way to visually organize information for the purpose of learning enhancement; usually referring to charts and graphs, these can be useful for visual learners; several graphic organizers are included in this book: Venn Diagram, Comparison Chart, Web, and Sequence Chain

***inclusive***
a homeschool group that is inclusive and welcomes anyone who homeschools regardless of religious or educational beliefs or practices; as homeschooling becomes more popular, more inclusive groups have been formed; in the traditional classroom setting, an inclusive school is focused on reaching out to the increasingly diverse student populations to provide a supportive and quality education to all students regardless of economic status, gender, race, or disability

***kinesthetic learner***

an individual who absorbs new information most effectively through experience; a kinesthetic learner will understand information by completing hands-on exercises, doing, and moving

***learning style***

the singular manner and rate that each child naturally pursues his or her education; educators have identified three primary ways of describing learning styles: audio, kinesthetic, and visual

***lesson plan***

a detailed description of the part of the curriculum one is planning to teach on a certain day

***multicultural***

adapted to relate to diverse cultures; many teachers incorporate multicultural learning materials into their lessons to encourage exposure to different traditions

***"real" books***

books you get at the library or the bookstore that aren't textbooks; some homeschoolers work almost exclusively from real books and don't use textbooks at all; this book provides a curriculum that's based on reading and research with real books

***scoring rubric***

a measurement tool used to assess student work that includes a system of scoring levels of performance; scoring rubrics are used with some lessons in this book and with the formalized assessment section in the back of this book

***self-directed learner***

an individual who is free to pursue education by his or her own means and guidance versus through traditional classes or schools; a term often used in homeschool literature

***self-teaching***

when an individual naturally learns about a topic of particular interest on his or her own, without formal instruction and usually as a result of natural attraction to or talent in the subject matter

***standardized test***

a test is considered standardized when it is given in the same manner, with the same directions to students of the same grade level across a school district, state, or country; the test shows how your student is doing compared to others in the same group; the assessment section beginning on page 295 offers examples of standardized test questions

***teaching strategy***

a creative way to motivate and inspire students, such as using a visual aid, entertaining or humorous delivery, interactive activity, or theme-based lessons; if your student is bored, he or she might benefit from a change in teaching strategies

***unschooling***

a teaching philosophy first identified by educator John Holt that's based on the idea that, as a homeschool parent, you may proceed however you see fit as long as there is confidence that your child is learning; works under the assertion that textbook-type teaching can dull a child's natural zest for learning and the belief that a student will learn more when he or she is engaged, uninterrupted, and enjoying what he or she is learning

***visual learner***

an individual who absorbs new information most effectively through the sense of sight; a visual learner will comprehend information by reading, watching a video, using a visual computer program, and looking at pictures in books

***Waldorf***

a method of education that was developed by Rudolph Steiner and attempts to teach the whole child: physical, emotional, and academic; Waldorf schools are located throughout the country, and there is also a network of Waldorf homeschoolers

## Venn Diagram

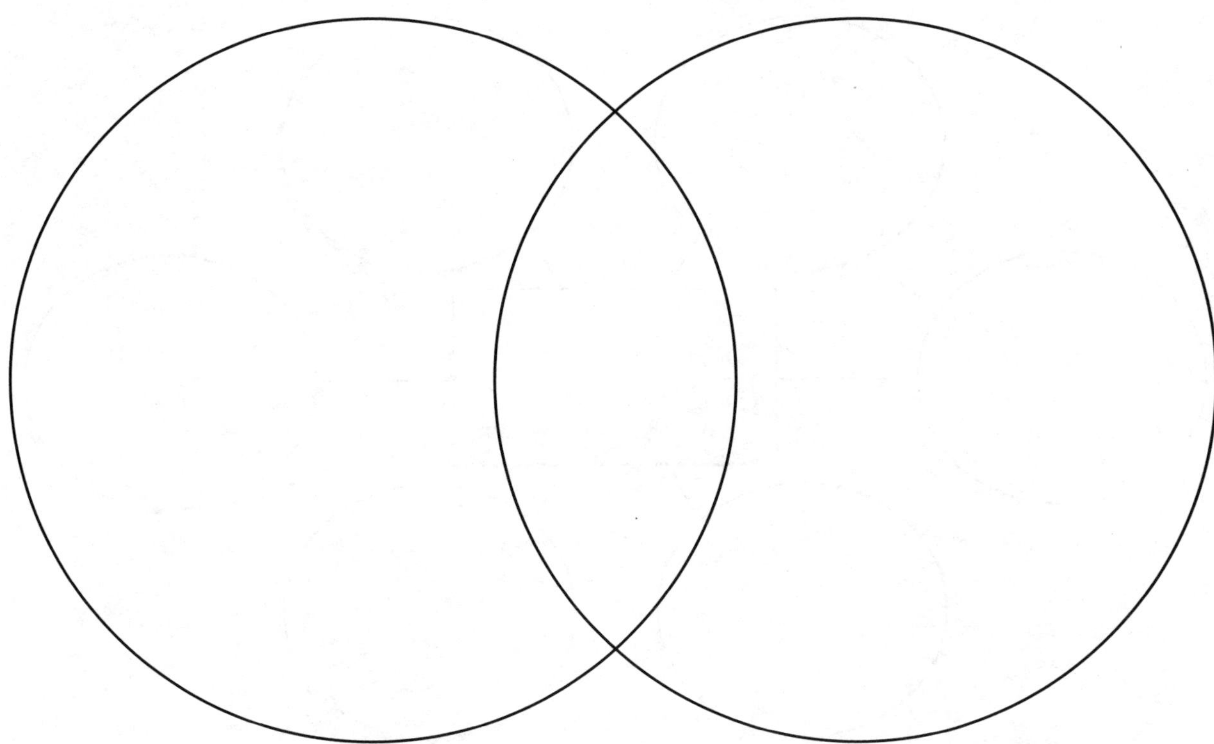

## Comparison Chart

| **Issue:** ______________ | **A:** ______________ | **B:** ______________ |
|---|---|---|
| I. | 1. | 2. |
| II. | 3. | 4. |
| III. | 5. | 6. |

## Web

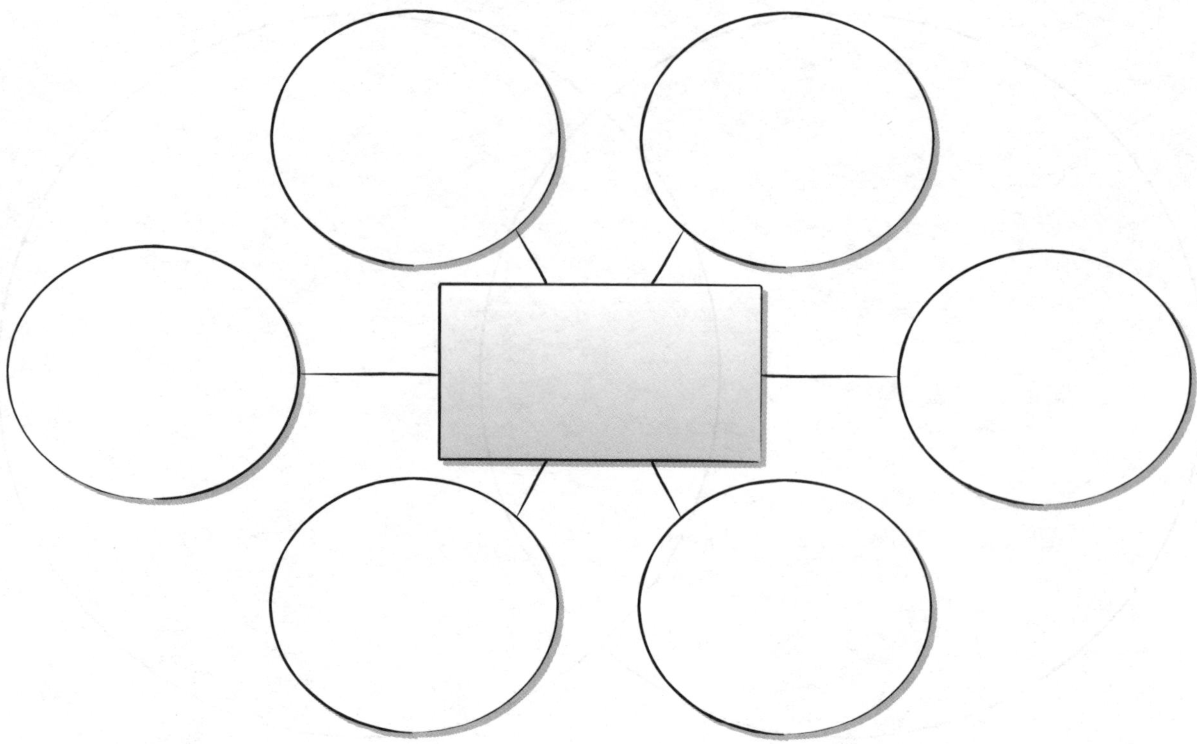

## Sequence Chain

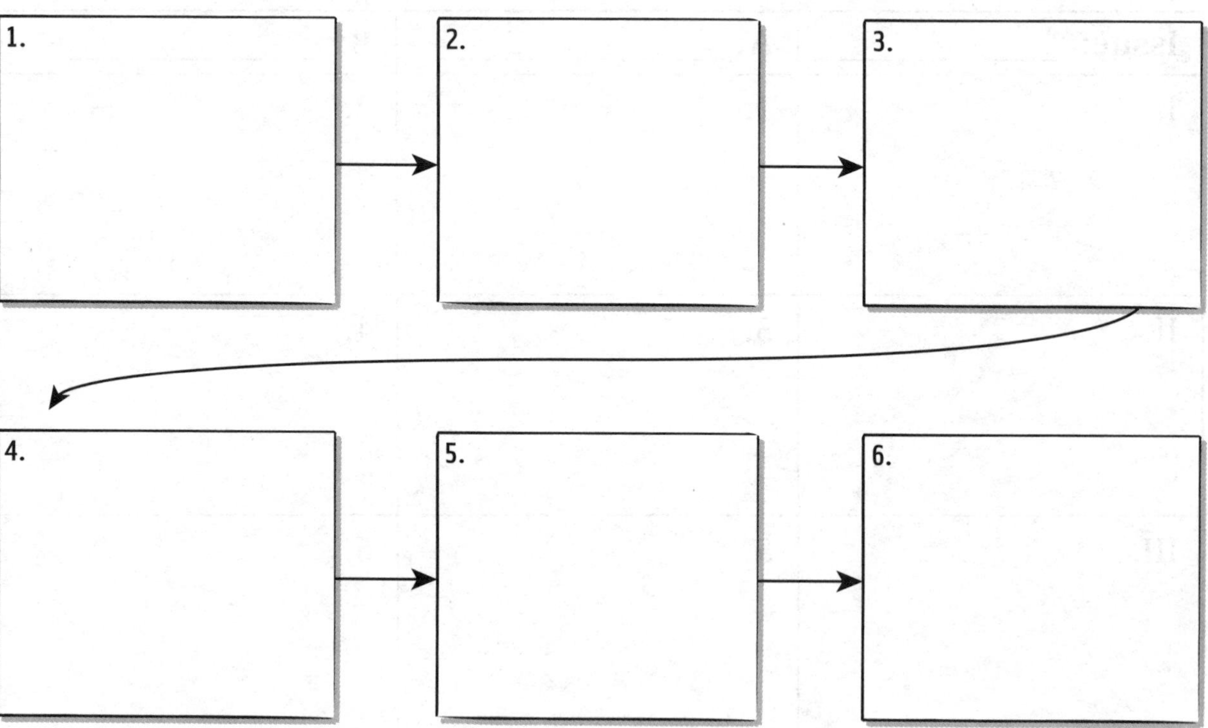

# Grid

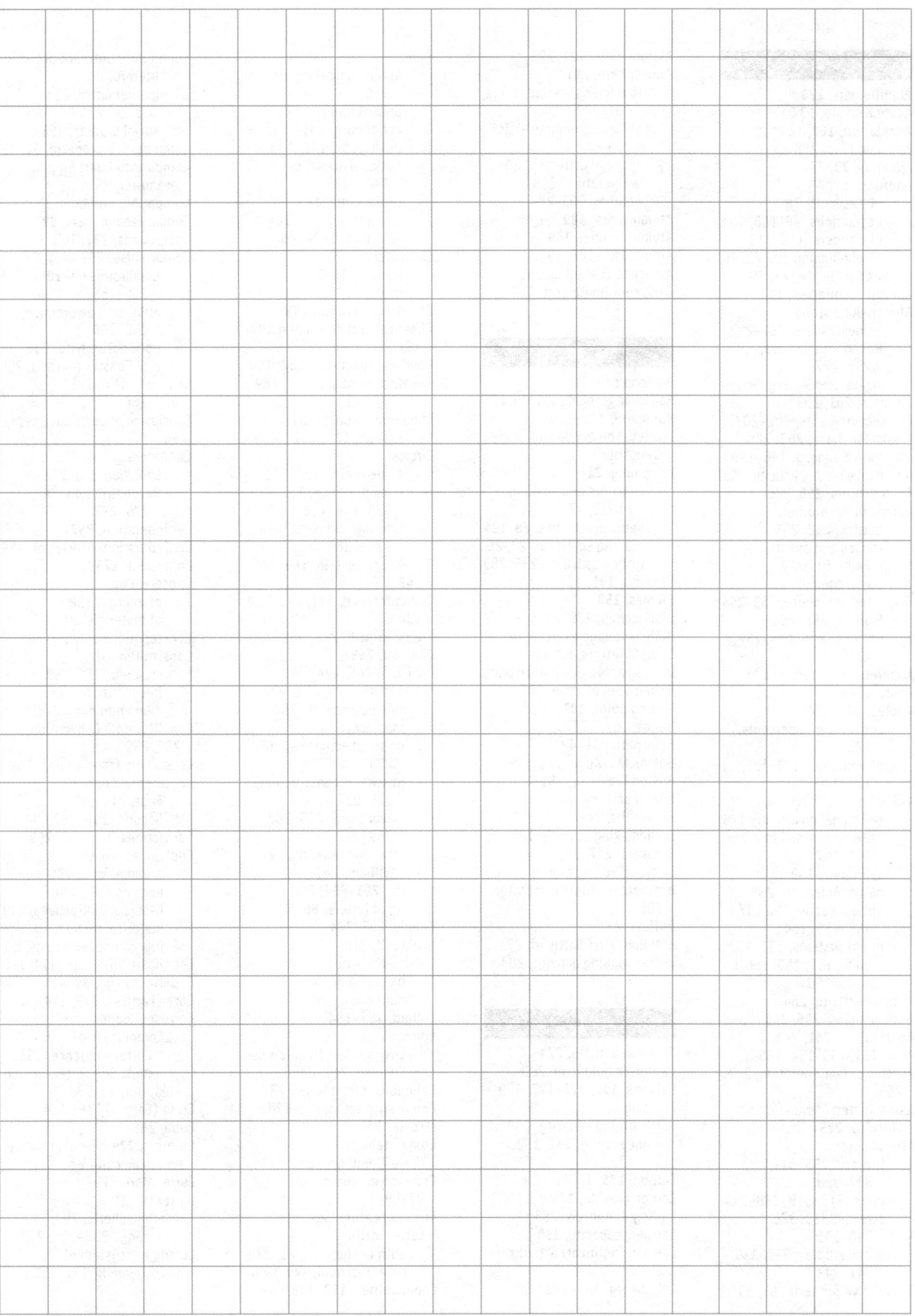

# Index

*Note: Page numbers in bold indicate the definition of a term.*



 

# Index

*Note: Page numbers in bold indicate the definition of a term.*

# Index

*Note: Page numbers in bold indicate the definition of a term.*

# Index

*Note: Page numbers in bold indicate the definition of a term.*

# Index

*Note: Page numbers in bold indicate the definition of a term.*

# Index

*Note: Page numbers in bold indicate the definition of a term.*



## X



## Z

# Credits

## Art & Photo Credits

### *Promoting Literacy*
**Background:** National Archives and Records Administration
**Icon:** © PhotoDisc
**Opener (page 1):** © PhotoDisc
**Page 3:** © PhotoDisc; **5:** PP/FA, Inc.; **10:** Carol Stutz Illustration; **14:** © Bettmann/CORBIS; **15:** © David Toase/Getty Images; **23:** © Bettmann/CORBIS; **25:** © Photodisc Collection/Getty Images; **27, 37, 41, 42:** PP/FA, Inc.; **43:** © PhotoDisc; **48:** Precision Graphics; **49:** © Royalty-Free/CORBIS; **52:** Carol Stutz Illustration; **53:** PP/FA, Inc.; **61:** Precision Graphics

### *Math*
**Background/Icon:** © Mel Curtis/Getty Images
**Opener (page 65):** © PhotoDisc
**Page 68, 69, 71:** Precision Graphics; **75:** © Royalty-Free/CORBIS; **80 (left):** Precision Graphics; **80 (right):** Carol Stutz Illustration; **81, 82 (top):** Precision Graphics; **82 (bottom):** PP/FA, Inc.; **84:** Carol Stutz Illustration; **86:** Precision Graphics; **86:** © PhotoDisc; **88:** Carol Stutz Illustration; **91, 92, 94, 95, 96:** Precision Graphics; **106:** © PhotoDisc; **108, 109:** Precision Graphics; **110:** PP/FA, Inc.; **111, 112, 114, 118, 119, 120, 121, 123:** Precision Graphics; **124 (top):** PP/FA, Inc.; **124 (bottom), 125:** Precision Graphics; **127, 128:** PP/FA, Inc.; **129, 132, 133, 134:** Precision Graphics

### *Science*
**Background/Icon:** © PhotoDisc
**Opener (page 139):** © PhotoDisc
**Page 145:** Precision Graphics; **147:** © John Wang/Getty Images; **150:** © Dan McCoy/Rainbow/Picture Quest; **153:** PP/FA, Inc.; **154:** Carol Stutz Illustration; **158:** © James Marshall/CORBIS; **161:** © Royalty-Free/CORBIS; **162, 169, 172, 173, 179:** Precision Graphics; **185:** Image Source; **188:** Precision Graphics; **191:** PP/FA, Inc.; **193:** Precision Graphics; **196:** © CORBIS; **199:** PP/FA, Inc.; **202, 203:** Precision Graphics; **205:** PP/FA, Inc.; **209, 214:** Precision Graphics; **215:** National Park Service; **216:** Glacier National Park; **217:** Carol Stutz Illustration; **219:** © CORBIS; **220, 221:** Precision Graphics

### *Social Studies*
**Background/Icon:** © PhotoDisc
**Opener (page 227):** © PhotoDisc
**Page 230:** Mapping Specialists, Ltd.; **232:** © Tom Bean/CORBIS; **233:** © Jim Zuckerman/CORBIS; **236:** Carol Stutz Illustration; **238:** © CORBIS; **243:** Mapping Specialists, Ltd.; **244:** © Wolfgang Kaehler/CORBIS; **250:** © Royalty-Free/CORBIS; **252:** © CORBIS; **254:** National Archives and Records Administration; **256:** Carol Stutz Illustration; **258:** Precision Graphics; **262:** © Bettmann/CORBIS; **263:** Mapping Specialists, Ltd.; **266, 270:** © CORBIS; **271:** Mapping Specialists, Ltd.; **273:** Precision Graphics; **276:** © Photodisc Collection/Getty Images; **280 (top):** © Royalty-Free/CORBIS; **280 (bottom):** Library of Congress, Prints & Photographs Division, LC-USZ62-5073; **282 (top):** © PhotoDisc; **282 (bottom):** © Bettmann/CORBIS; **286 (top):** U.S. Department of the Interior, National Park Service, Edison National Historic Site; **286 (bottom):** © Bettmann/CORBIS; **287 (right):** U.S. Department of the Interior, National Park Service, Edison National Historic Site; **287 (top):** Library of Congress, Prints & Photographs Division, LC-USZ62-16724; **287 (bottom):** Library of Congress, Prints & Photographs Division, LC-USZ62-95433; **288:** © Bettmann/CORBIS; **290:** © Royalty-Free/CORBIS; **291:** Precision Graphics

**Page 299:** Carol Stutz Illustration; **302:** PP/FA, Inc.; **303:** © Bettmann/CORBIS; **304:** PP/FA, Inc.; **314, 316 (top left, top right):** Precision Graphics; **316 (bottom):** PP/FA, Inc.; **317, 318, 320, 321 (right):** Precision Graphics; **321 (left), 323:** Carol Stutz Illustration; **324, 325, 326, 328, 329, 339, 340:** Precision Graphics; **353, 354, 355:** PP/FA, Inc.

## Literature Credits

7–10, from THE LIBRARY CARD by Jerry Spinelli. Copyright © 1997 by Jerry Spinelli. Reprinted by permission of Scholastic Inc.

15–18, from *Boxcar Molly: A Story from the Great Depression* by James Riordan. Text copyright © 2001 by James Riordan. Reprinted by arrangement with Hodder Children's Books.

23–26, from *Sojourner Truth and the Struggle for Freedom* by Edward Beecher Claflin. Copyright © 1987 by Eisen, Durwood & Co., Inc. Reprinted by arrangement with Barron's Educational Series, Inc.

31, from *The Complete Poetical Works of Henry Wadsworth Longfellow* by Henry Wadsworth Longfellow. Published by Houghton Mifflin Company, 1902.

35–36, copyright 1997, 2002 Aaron Shepard. Adapted by the author from the picture book published by Atheneum Books for Young Readers, New York, 1997. For the complete script, visit www.aaronshep.com.

51–52, from *ANIMAL ARCHITECTURE* by Jennifer Owings Dewey. Published by Orchard Books, an imprint of Scholastic Inc. Copyright © 1991 by Jennifer Owings Dewey. Reprinted by permission.

331–332, from *North American Indian Life*. U.S. edition copyright © 2000 by Barron's Educational Series, Inc. Reprinted by arrangement with Barron's Educational Series, Inc.

# HAPPINESS IS . . .

As I've been pondering the subject of happiness this morning—an elusive and seemingly unattainable state for so many—I am led to these words of Jesus:

> If any man would come after me, let him deny himself and take up his cross and follow me . . .
>
> Matthew 16:24–25 RSV

I believe the secret of happiness lies imbedded in those words, painful though they appear to be . . . When any of us embarks on the pursuit of happiness for ourselves, it eludes us. When we become absorbed in something demanding and worthwhile above and beyond ourselves, happiness seems to be there as a by-product of the self-giving . . .

*Other Avon Books by*
**Catherine Marshall**

BEYOND OUR SELVES
CATHERINE MARSHALL'S STORY BIBLE
CHRISTY
THE HELPER
JULIE
A MAN CALLED PETER
SOMETHING MORE
TO LIVE AGAIN

# CATHERINE MARSHALL

# A Closer Walk

## A Spiritual Lifeline To God

Edited by Leonard E. LeSourd

AVON
PUBLISHERS OF BARD, CAMELOT, DISCUS AND FLARE BOOKS

AVON BOOKS
A division of
The Hearst Corporation
105 Madison Avenue
New York, New York 10016


Published by arrangement with Chosen Books
Library of Congress Catalog Card Number: 86-10045
ISBN: 0-380-70390-4



First Avon Printing: December 1987



Printed in the U.S.A.

K-R 10 9 8 7 6 5 4 3 2 1

*I am weak but Thou art strong*
*Jesus, keep me from all wrong;*
*I'll be satisfied as long*
*As I walk, dear Lord, close to Thee.*

*Just a closer walk with Thee*
*Grant it, Jesus, if You please;*
*Daily walking close to Thee*
*Let it be, dear Lord, let it be.*

# ACKNOWLEDGMENTS

Special thanks go to Jeanne Sevigny, Catherine's trusted secretary and close friend of fourteen years, who not only did the typing of Catherine's handwritten journal items, but served as advisor on the selection of material used in this book. Also to Regina Trollinger and Yvonne Burgan for their secretarial skills.

A big debt of gratitude to Elizabeth Sherrill, whose book expertise guided Catherine for twenty-two years through the writing of *Beyond Our Selves*, *Christy*, *Adventures in Prayer*, *Something More*, *Meeting God At Every Turn*, and *Julie*, and who edited the editor of this manuscript with her usual sensitivity and brilliance.

# CONTENTS

# Using This Book . . . On Your Own Walk

For you—as it has for me—*A Closer Walk* can become not so much a book as a traveling companion, inviting us to share the rough places and the mountain tops with a fellow pilgrim, Catherine Marshall.

In personal journals kept during her most creative years as a writer, wife, and mother, Catherine recorded her encounters with such roadblocks as . . .

Criticalness
The Poverty Complex
Resentment
The Dry Period
Chronic Worry
Illness

Most importantly, she described also the "way through," which she found in the Scriptures.

Throughout her journey, the Bible was the traveler's staff on which Catherine leaned. From every page shines her commitment to daily Bible reading—and her faithfulness in applying what she read to that day's need.

If you're like me, two things will happen as you make this pilgrimage with Catherine. Your own Bible reading will become more focused, more personal, infinitely more exciting. And you will be nudged to start your own "travel diary."

This was exactly the impact on Len LeSourd, after reading the first of these entries. Before he married Catherine, Len recalls today, he had never thought of putting his own spiritual struggles down on paper—certainly not *as* he was living through them.

Shortly after their marriage in 1959, however, a moving van delivered Catherine's possessions to their first home. Len watched in husbandly amusement as Catherine hovered over one particular carton, clearly attaching more value to it than to the clothes, dishes, and pieces of furniture that arrived along with it.

"My journals," Catherine explained.

When Len still looked blank, she drew from the box a dark green volume, four inches by seven, with "Year Book 1934" stamped on the front. Catherine had filled the book with reactions to campus life that sophomore year at Agnes Scott College in Georgia. Three more green journals in the box covered the years through 1937.

There was a five-year diary for 1938–42, recording Catherine's soul-searching as she met and eventually married Peter Marshall. Journals of various shapes and colors detailed her years as Peter's wife: the birth of their son, her own serious illness, the loss of her young husband. As a widow in the 1950s, Catherine entered her spiritual questing in a succession of spiral-bound notebooks.

In growing astonishment, Len helped Catherine store the volumes on a shelf. What discipline and devotion these thousands of pages represented! Where would a person find the time?

Len soon found out. Early in the morning, Catherine would take from a dresser drawer a bright red hardcover *Daily Reminder.* No amount of fatigue from the previous day spent corralling three small stepchildren, no pleas from a sleepy husband, could keep her from this daily appointment-in-writing with God.

When Catherine finally allowed Len to read some current entries, he understood her commitment to the discipline. These were more than simply prayer records, more even than the joyful recording of answers. The act of writing itself was part of Catherine's relationship with God; it helped define her needs, focus her prayers, act out her trust.

Len soon joined her in this early morning time and began keeping a prayer record of his own. His approach was somewhat different from Catherine's. Each individual's format, style, and frequency will of course be unique. But right from the start Len discovered the secret that Catherine had known for years: *putting prayer issues on paper* eliminates the vagueness that so often diffuses personal devotions.

Her lively new family, Len confesses, sometimes made it difficult for Catherine to keep a set time of day for her journal. Before long she was making her entries at any and every moment when the dust settled.

But make them she did. For the next twenty-three years Catherine poured her hopes and dreams, questions asked of God and answers received from Him, into the growing collection of *Daily Reminders.* The current volume accompanied the LeSourds on trips, appeared in the laundry room and at the breakfast table. When Catherine's pen was stilled on March 18, 1983, these journals were her rich legacy to Len, with instructions to disclose the contents with wisdom and discretion.

*A Closer Walk* is the result.

It will remain only "someone else's story," however, unless you and I come along.

Elizabeth Sherrill

# A Woman Called Catherine

The first time I saw Catherine was on December 1, 1955, at a luncheon in the Waldorf Astoria ballroom, where she was to receive the Salvation Army's 1955 Award for her contributions to "the spiritual life of her time." A poll that year had listed her as one of the ten most admired women in America. As the dignitaries, mostly men, filed onto the stage, Catherine, overshadowed by their physical presence, looked small, fragile, a bit overwhelmed.

I stared at her more closely. What was the secret of her sudden propulsion onto the national stage? Writing a best-selling religious book like *A Man Called Peter* couldn't do it alone. Watching her animated gestures as she conversed with master of ceremonies Walter Hoving (president of prestigious Tiffany's), noting her trim figure and stylish grooming, I decided that she was a phenomenon—a devout preacher's wife who had also won the admiration of nonbelievers.

How had she done it?

I listened carefully to Catherine's speech that described the "supernatural intervention of God" at Dunkirk during World War II. *Unlikely subject for a sophisticated New York City gathering,* I thought to myself. But she avoided religious clichés and held her audience. *A high voltage, spiritual woman, but with worldly wisdom,* I concluded.

Some months later Catherine was invited to speak at our Young Adult Group at the Marble Collegiate Church. There, I met her face to face for the first time, bathed for a short moment in her warm smile and controlled intensity. Yet, too, a shyness. In her speech I liked the practical way she applied biblical truths to her personal struggles.

As the editor of *Guideposts,* I wrote and asked her if she would write a piece for our small inspirational magazine, which had just reached a circulation of one hundred thousand. We talked over the phone about it. Her article "How You Can Receive God's Guidance" sparked eager reader response.

In 1957 I was functioning in the role of single parent, trying to rear three small children in Carmel, New York, while commuting over a hundred miles each day to work in New York City. It was a lonely, difficult time for me. One night I poured out my agony to God and laid before Him my need for a wife. Then, remembering Catherine's article on guidance, I took out a yellow pad, prepared to write down the names of any possible mates He might suggest.

Catherine's name popped into my mind.

It seemed almost ludicrous to tie Catherine Marshall to my plea for a partner. "That can't be your idea, Lord," I said, dismissing the thought.

Then I recalled Catherine's book *To Live Again* and the chapter that had entranced me—"They Walk in Wistfulness." In it she had given a poignant answer to a doctor's question about her emotional well-being. I reread the chapter and came to these words:

> Do you really want to know what it feels like to be a widow? God made men and women for each other. Any other way of life is wrong; because it is abnormal. The last few months it's been like having a gnawing

hunger, a haunting wistfulness at the center of life. I can forget about it for short periods—ignore it sometimes. But it's always there—always—and I'm afraid not even you can prescribe any pills that can cure it.

Elsewhere in that same chapter she wrote:

The need is to love and to be loved—that ultimate of life. Could I, and all those like me who walk the earth in wistfulness, find the way to trust God even for that?

Suddenly I knew that Catherine and I had something in common—loneliness. But so little else, it seemed. The whole idea was ridiculous.

I ticked off the reasons why.

First and foremost, who would want to follow the Peter and Catherine act? Their romance and marriage had entranced and stirred millions of people through her best-selling book; more millions had been captivated by the beautifully-done movie of *A Man Called Peter.*

Why would I want to marry a super-spiritual Christian celebrity? Who was almost five years older than I was?

Even more to the point, why would Catherine, at age forty-four, even supposing she should be attracted to me as an individual, want to marry a man who was rearing three small children?

Looked at logically, the idea of Catherine and me pairing up made little sense from any standpoint.

But . . . a voice deep inside reminded me, God is not bound by logic.

The least I could do was give it one good shot, I decided. If God was in it, I'd soon know. So I called Catherine, said *Guideposts* was looking for another article (true), and asked her if I could come to Washington and take her out for dinner. Requesting a dinner date should signal to her that I had more in mind than just an article.

She parried that proposal with the suggestion we make it lunch.

Strike one.

I took a plane from New York to Washington, rented a car, and drove to her town house just off Wisconsin Avenue. Catherine emerged, wearing a dark blue dress with white collar and cuffs; silver earrings and a diamond brooch added distinct feminine touches. A lovely woman. Something quickened inside me.

Lunch at a Georgetown restaurant, however, was a letdown. Catherine was friendly and full of ideas for an article. Yet she neatly sidestepped all probing into her personal life. She was the consummate professional.

Strike two.

I drove her back to her town house, prepared to say goodbye and dismiss once and for all any thoughts of a personal relationship. Just before opening the car door, I happened to ask her a question regarding the Holy Spirit. It was as if I had found the combination to a valuable safe. An excited conversation followed that lasted for another half hour. Our two spirits had touched, then been ignited.

I was still at bat.

A week or so later I wrote to Catherine, asking if I could see her on the way back from an upcoming trip to California. With my plans a bit uncertain, I listed two possible dates, told her I would telephone beforehand. There wasn't time before I left for the coast for her to reply.

I did call Catherine from California—several times—but got no answer. The morning I was to fly from Los Angeles to Washington I called again—still nobody there. Then I came to a conclusion.

*This is ridiculous. Catherine has no interest in me personally. I'm being silly to pursue this. Besides, she's not even home.*

I changed my reservation from Washington to New York, flew home, and decided to forget the inner nudging that I should seek a romance with Catherine.

Strike three?

No, not quite. A foul tip, perhaps, that the catcher dropped. Several days later I received a letter from Catherine. "What happened to you?" she wrote. "You asked me to hold two dates. I did, but you never appeared. Or called. Is anything wrong?"

I was startled. Then stimulated. Catherine was obviously annoyed with me. But that was not all bad. In fact, it was many moons better than indifference.

In a spirit of contrition, I started to call Catherine, then stopped. A new, more direct approach was needed. *Drop your editorial front, Len; don't be defensive. Approach her man to woman.* In this vein, I wrote her a letter.

In *Meeting God At Every Turn* Catherine describes how she reacted to this change of style in me:

> There was nothing of the professional editor about the letter I received from Len several days later. "I would like to know you better," he wrote. "How do you react to this idea? We'll choose a day, and then you write on your calendar three letters: F U N. I'll pick you up in the morning in my car and we'll just take off to the beach or the mountains or whatever."
>
> The letter seemed deliberately couched to say, "If you're interested in pursuing this relationship, let's have a go at it. If not, then tell me so right now."
>
> I liked the approach. We set a day in early August. Len telephoned the night before from a Washington motel to say that he would call for me at 10:30 the next morning. He was delighted when I suggested fixing a picnic lunch.
>
> The next morning turned out to be a beautiful summer day, not too hot. When I met Len at my front door, I found myself slipping easily into the adventur-

ous mood he had suggested. He put the picnic basket in the trunk of his car and we climbed into the front seat. "What do you prefer," he asked casually, "ocean or mountains?"

"I would choose the mountains," I replied.

"Which direction?"

I aimed him west toward Skyline Drive. As we drove along, I studied this fortyish editor sitting beside me. He was of medium height; dark hair beginning to gray; lithe, athletic figure. His gray-blue eyes were direct, warm, the lids often crinkling with humor. He was a good conversationalist, probing but relaxed. I relaxed, too. It was going to be a good day.

It was a good day, an amazing day. We talked for almost eleven hours straight. All my resistance to following the Peter Marshall romance, to her "super spirituality" and to our age difference dissolved in my astonishment over Catherine's physical warmth, simplicity, and earthy good humor. I was overwhelmed by the idea that God had perceived all this beforehand and had brought us together. During that one astounding day I fell in love with Catherine and began to think ahead toward marriage.

Catherine was slower in coming to this conclusion. She had to face more obstacles than I did. Mine had been mostly ego problems. Hers were substantive: taking on three small children, turning at a right angle to the life that had seemed to stretch so comfortably and predictably ahead of her—for which her dream house was even then being built. This home in Bethesda, Maryland, was to be ready for occupancy within a few months; Catherine had personally designed it to meet her career-woman needs.

That she was able to overcome these obstacles had to be the Lord's doing. For weeks she prayed, probed the Scriptures. And it was during this time of her intense searching that I began to find answers to the question I asked myself at that Salvation Army luncheon: What was the special charisma in this woman that had captured both believers and nonbelievers?

First, a down-to-earth quality that shunned subterfuge and embraced candor and openness. Ever since the success of *A Man Called Peter*, people had tried to put her on a spiritual pedestal. She resisted, refused to play the role of guru, insisted that she was a struggler for truth like everyone else.

Second, the spirit of adventure. She saw her faith in this light. Jesus was bold, imaginative, unpredictable. God's plan for each life was unique, did not fit any set formula. Both the death of her first husband and the rebirth of love interest in her life were totally unexpected, yet within the illimitable providence of the God she knew.

Third, vulnerability. Catherine was honest about her flaws, admitting her inadequacies in such areas as child rearing and certain social situations. Result: she learned from her mistakes. This quality also made her open to editorial advice in every book she wrote but one, and that one had to be abandoned.

I learned a lot about Catherine during this period, but the deeper secret of her success eluded me. That first date, rambling along the Skyline Drive, was in early August; we were married three months later on November 14, 1959.

Catherine had huge adjustments to make. She sold her Washington dream house to move to Chappaqua, forty miles north of New York City, so that I could continue to commute to my job at *Guideposts* in the city. My children—Linda, ten; Chester, six; Jeffrey, three—had been through a deeply unsettling two years, adjusting to a variety of housekeepers. They had mixed feelings toward moving into a new house, and especially toward "the new Mommie that Daddy's bringing home."

Catherine's son, Peter John, nineteen, was going through a period of rebellion at Yale. It's hard enough for a young person to cope with one celebrity parent, but Peter's father and mother both were "Christian personages.'' Peter told us one day with a straight face that when he graduated he wanted to be a beach boy at Virginia Beach.

Catherine and I had so many things to pray about that we began to rise an hour early each morning to read the Bible and seek answers together. Her current journal lay open beside us in these pre-dawn prayer times, recording our changing needs, His unchanging faithfulness.

Our togetherness as an author-editor team was tested early in our marriage. Catherine had already been working over a year researching her novel *Christy* and had written some fifty or so pages. One day she handed me her manuscript. Outside of her typist, I would be the first to read it. I started in with much anticipation.

Two hours later I faced a dilemma. The manuscript was wordy, short on action—yes, a bit dull. Conversation between mountain people was almost undecipherable because of Catherine's attempt to spell out the dialect as she had heard it. On the plus side, the characters were truly believable. Should I tell her the whole truth, or just center on the good things I saw in the manuscript?

Drawing a deep breath, I told her the truth as I saw it. She flinched for a moment, then stared at me with a new light in her eyes. ''You're right on all counts,'' she admitted. ''I felt it was weak, but hoped somehow I was too close to it to see its strengths.'' She sighed, ''Let's start with the mountain dialect.''

Thus did I pass the first crucial test of our professional relationship. If I had been less than honest, she would have eventually gotten the needed critique from Ed Kuhn, her McGraw-Hill editor. But she and I were full collaborators at work, now, as well as in the home.

As the years passed Catherine and I, as a writer-editor team, became more and more productive: between us we were responsible for nearly one hundred *Guideposts* articles and more than thirty published books. There were dozens of appearances as a speaking team; numerous courses conducted together on Christian subjects, highlighting the movement of the Holy Spirit.

I have one major regret about all this. We didn't take enough time to smell the flowers, to learn what it really means to take a vacation. We went from deadline to deadline, from crisis to crisis, dealing with what had to be done, forgetting too often to mark on our calendar those letters F U N. I feel deeply convicted about this, but the truth is that Catherine and I were workaholics.

During our twenty-three years of marriage I did discover the secrets behind her extraordinary gifts of communication. There were two. One came out through the dedication she showed in rearing my three young children—despite lungs that never operated at more than seventy-five percent normal capacity. It emerged as she struggled for the precise descriptive phrase in her writing, as she sought the exactly right color for a living room chair, in her search for tonal perfection in stereo music. She tried to lift the sights of her family and friends by planting dreams in our hearts of achievements that appeared beyond us.

This reach toward excellence was a part of everything she did.

One example, I'll never forget. Catherine was preparing a dinner party for special friends. The day before, she asked me to drive her to Falls Church just outside of Washington—an hour's trip. "Some errands," she told me.

One errand, as it turned out. At a bakery, which sold a certain kind of macaroons. As we drove about Falls Church looking for this bakery in steamy weather, I fought off a growing irritation.

"Catherine, why are these macaroons so important to you?"

"I have a great recipe for grinding them into a wonderful sauce."

"A sauce! For what?"

"For the fruit compote I'm planning for dessert."

I turned and looked at her in amazement. "We're taking three hours out of a day, in terrible heat, to drive through miserable traffic to buy a bag of macaroons so people can pour a little sauce on their dessert!"

"That's right," she said. "It's the sauce that makes the dessert."

That was Catherine. She gave herself unreservedly to what she was doing, would settle for nothing but one hundred percent, was one-eyed in the scriptural sense whether it was writing, speaking, painting, decorating, preparing meals, building family life.

Her intensity spilled over into everything and I loved to watch it erupt. One night during the late 1960s, she strode into our bedroom where I was reading and began to pace the floor, face furious. "What's happened?" I asked in alarm.

She didn't answer right away, just stared at me with tears in her eyes. "I'm so upset I can hardly speak," she said.

"Over what?"

"Viet Nam! We shouldn't be fighting there. It's wrong . . . wrong . . . wrong. God will punish us for this."

I looked at her in amazement, surprised again at the emotion she poured into her convictions that could focus one moment on a child's poor study habits, the next on a war ten thousand miles away.

But there's another more profound reason for Catherine's extraordinary accomplishments. Her love of Jesus, expressed through a love affair with Scripture.

Bibles were scattered throughout our house . . . all editions, plus reference books and concordances. We often went to bed, turned out the light, and listened to a chapter of Scripture on tape. If she could have found a way to spread Bible passages on a slice of bread, Catherine would have devoured it.

When upset or under spiritual assault or in physical pain, Catherine would go to her office, kneel by her chair, and open her Bible to the fifty-third chapter of Isaiah, or the ninety-first Psalm, or the second chapter of Acts, or the eighth chapter of Romans. She would read, then pray, then read, then pray some more. She liked to pray with the Bible clutched in her hands; it gave her strength. She would rest her case on its promises. Catherine didn't read the Bible for solace or inspiration, but to have an encounter with the Lord. Sometimes she emerged from these sessions contrite, sometimes at peace, sometimes still in turmoil. I think these were the most intense moments of her life.

All of Catherine's Bibles are marked with underlinings; color shadings make certain passages almost leap out at you. Question marks and exclamation points dot page after page. A long comment will be scribbled at the top or bottom or along the side. Sometimes "Yes! Yes! Yes!" indicates Catherine's exuberant confirmation of a teaching.

Some of her happiest moments were when she was preparing a Bible study for one of our classes or for a writing project. She chose our king-size bed for this adventure, propping herself up with pillows, while Bibles, reference books, a thesaurus, a concordance, and yellow pads were spread all about her.

Catherine's passion for the Word permeated her whole life. It undergirded her writing. It formed a base for us as a married team in the making of family decisions. It provided substance to her counseling of people through the mail. I'm convinced it was also the basis for her inner vitality, her charisma, and the mantle of authority she wore with some reluctance.

Her grappling with the Word mostly took place in the early morning hours, as she fed her questions and discoveries into her journals. Material from these writings—her "closer walk" with her Lord—provides the content for this book. They cover our struggles in bringing together two broken homes, learning to relate to children and stepchildren—and later, our relationship to their spouses and our grandchildren.

What shines through Catherine's words is that Christian growth and adventuring never stop. The search for more of the truth is endlessly absorbing: the promises God holds out are worth every moment of struggle, the "walk" never arrives at some static, fixed point, but leads on into ever deeper intimacy with God.

*A Closer Walk* is the record of Catherine's encounters with the Lord of Scripture along the way, most appearing in print for the first time. The book is divided into six sections that move chronologically from our early life together as a family, through Christian creativity and growth, into spiritual warfare, to the final triumph of her death.

Years before Catherine died, we had talked about the probability that I would outlive her. Since I had worked so closely with her on every writing project, she knew we were in accord on one basic principle—no book of her writings would see print unless it measured up to her standard of excellence. The principal guardians of this standard were to be myself and her long-time friend and editorial advisor, Elizabeth Sherrill, whose talents we both admire so much and who has carefully gone over this manuscript.

May this book bless you who read it, and stimulate you to seek "a closer walk" with Jesus.

Leonard E. LeSourd

# Section One

# The Home As His Classroom

*Upon returning from our honeymoon in late 1959, Catherine and I confronted all the problems and adjustments involved in bringing together two broken homes. Catherine's greatest self-doubt centered around the responsibility for mothering three young stepchildren. (Her son, Peter John Marshall, was attending college.) Always a perfectionist, she felt she lacked the patient, accepting qualities of an ideal mother.*

*The early morning time when we sought answers together in the Bible became lifeblood for Catherine. Time and again from Scripture she drew insight and answers. Praying together in advance of the inevitable conflicts and confrontations solidified our marriage. It is hard to stay upset or angry at your mate when you are sitting up in bed side by side, holding hands, reading God's Word.*

*The setting for the following episodes was an eight-room home in Chappaqua, New York, a suburban community some forty miles north of New York City, where we lived for the first five years of our marriage.*

*LL*

1

# A New Way to See Jesus

As Len and I begin our new life together, I'm enjoying a new way to read the New Testament—undoubtedly a way known to many Christians through the centuries but new to me: during my early morning devotions I'm reading the words as if Jesus were speaking directly to me.

At the time of my discovery, I was going through the Gospels consecutively, desiring above all else to get a vivid portrait of Jesus. And a portrait emerged all right, not so much what He looked like, as the characteristics of His person. I discovered in Him one who is totally alive—physically stalwart, emotionally sensitive. Humor, I definitely found. And grief—not for Himself, but for others' hurts and the tragic havoc that sin brings. And love, an amazing love that pours out of Him with never any effort to hide it or dam it up. Yet it is a love with steel in it.

Over and over I have come upon this steel—a note of stringency in Jesus' conversation and His way of dealing with people that, for the most part, seems alien to the teaching in our churches today. Never have I found a trace of coddling or compromising or self-protectiveness in Him.

For example, there was the Pharisee who asked Jesus to lunch at his house. Jesus accepted. But if there was anything pleasant about the conversation around the table, we were not told so in Luke's account. Indeed, centuries later, the words all but blister the page:

> But woe to you Pharisees! for you tithe mint and rue and every herb, and neglect justice and the love of God . . . you love the best seat in the synagogues and salutations in the market places . . . you are like graves which are not seen, and men walk over them without knowing it.
>
> Luke 11:42–44 RSV

It is clear that Christ chose to tell this particular man and his guests the simple, straightforward truth rather than keeping quiet or being socially correct. That takes courage of a rare sort, and Jesus must have known full well that it could lead only to a cross.

There is an unexpected dividend from reading the New Testament as if Jesus were speaking to me: when I look away from the problems in my new marriage to turn my full attention to Jesus, He proves Himself alive by concerning Himself with my life, family, and friends and talking to me about these matters morning after morning.

Last week, for example, as I read the twelfth chapter of Luke, it was as though Jesus were saying:

> Beware of pretending before the family to be something you are not, or to have attained spiritual values that you have not attained. This is hypocrisy. And nothing is more futile than trying to keep anything secret. There is nothing covered up among family members that is not going to be uncovered.

Later in the same chapter He seemed to tell me:

> You think that because members of your family believe in Me, all should be peaceful and serene. Not so. My presence is not going to bring sweet peace and an easy time. On occasions, My thoughts and My way will bring severe discord. Do not be surprised when this happens. Realize that out of temporary disharmony—if it includes honest facing-up—comes growth for each member of the family and a further knitting together in Me.

This new way of letting Jesus speak to me may help me relate to a new neighbor too. She's asked me to assist in a community project in which I do not believe. I was puzzled as to how to handle the situation without hurting her feelings. In the eleventh chapter of Luke I heard:

> You think that you do not want to tell your neighbor the truth because you do not want to hurt her. The real reason is that you want to protect yourself from her displeasure, or antagonism. It is wrong to keep quiet because you care more about her friendship (or anyone else's) than you care about her growth in Me. That is just another way of putting yourself first.

What are the results of these meditations? Increased honesty in our family has already led to more openness toward God in the lives of two of our children. I find that I'm less threatened by family arguments. So far I have not found the way or the courage to be honest with my friend. I ducked out of the project through an excuse.

But this I can say—the resurrected Jesus is a continual reality in my life. How can I ever find words to express the joy of His presence?

# 2

# STEPMOTHERING

This morning I am pondering my bizarre dream of last night to see if the Lord is telling me something through it:

In my dream a small animal emerged from a swelling near my shoulder. Looking more closely, I saw that the animal was wounded. "Those cuts will have to be sewn up," I thought, and then I woke up.

As I listened for God's word about the dream, I recalled how both Len and I have referred to the two small boys as being like bear cubs the way they roll and romp about the family room. Yesterday they broke a vase doing this. I have to admit that sometimes the children "get under my skin." Obviously the Lord is pointing out that changes need to be made in my attitude.

Part of what Len and I have to resolve comes down to the proper order he places on his new wife and his children by a previous marriage. All the stepmother tales in fairy stories and folklore tell us that we are confronting something basic and difficult here.

Len's emotions toward his flesh and blood are *so* strong that perhaps it is against nature for him to try to put his wife first. In his mind, he's done this, but his instinctive emotion is to defend and protect his children. Yet not to put the wife first is to risk disaster in the marriage.

I turned to the nineteenth chapter of Matthew:

> For this reason a man shall leave his father and mother and be joined to his wife, and the two shall become one.
>
> Matthew 19:5 RSV

Fortunately, Len and I can pray together and can talk over these problems. I was able to tell him about my dream without fearing he would use it against me. We are learning to admit our weaknesses to each other.

3

# Around the Dinner Table

After much experimentation, Len and I have settled on the evening meal as the ideal time and place for growing as a family. Mornings are too pressured, evenings too filled with school work, meetings, phone calls.

Being at the dinner table each night of the week is a command performance for Len and myself, Linda, Chester, and Jeff. No TV dinners in front of the tube. No dinners for our children at friends' houses except on weekends. A major effort by Len and me to keep our professional activities from interfering with this time.

The meal begins with grace, and the children do most of the praying, learning to overcome shyness until they can talk to God easily. Soon I hope we'll learn to say grace just as naturally when we eat as a family in restaurants.

Len and I try not to dominate the ensuing conversation, but draw out each child. "What did you learn today in school, Chester? . . . Which teacher do you like the most, Linda? . . . Who is your best friend, Jeff?"

Criticism in this setting, we learned, quenches fragile spirits; it's better saved for one-on-one encounters. After dinner there's a reading from Scripture and family prayer around the table. One of our main objectives is to show Jesus as so engaging a Person that we would all enjoy it if He joined us at the table.

"Jesus had a sense of humor," I mentioned once.

This seemed to surprise the children so the next night I came to the table armed with examples from Scripture. About the hypocrisy of the Pharisees He said, "You blind guides, straining out a gnat and swallowing a camel" (Matthew 23:24 RSV).

This is the humor of exaggeration, I explained, pointing out that Jesus' humor was always for a purpose. Sometimes it was His bridge to an individual He would otherwise have had trouble reaching. Most often it was to illuminate a truth.

There was the occasion when Christ joshed His disciples about spiritual timidity: "Is a lamp brought in to be put under a bushel, or under a bed?" (Mark 4:21 RSV). The point He was making: "I need disciples who don't hide their light."

When the apostles became too impressed with the crowds Jesus was drawing, knowing full well that crowds gather for many reasons, Jesus commented dryly, "Wherever the carcass lies, there will the vultures gather" (Matthew 24:28 MOFFATT).

Once we reread the Gospels, watching for Christ's wit, we find it everywhere. "Can one blind man be guide to another blind man? Surely they will both fall into the ditch" (Luke 6:39 PHILLIPS). Or the comment made about the rich man who valued his possessions too much. "It is easier for a camel to go through the eye of a needle than for a rich man to enter the kingdom of God" (Luke 18:25 NEB).

To awaken people at every level of their being, Jesus used every weapon of language and communication to achieve His goals; most effective were the humorous thrust and banter about those who put on airs and think more highly of themselves than they should. Jesus sees all our incongruities and absurdities, and He laughs along with us.

As the result of these dinner table discussions, we're all finding that our spontaneity and fervor in worshiping Him increase. Our goal with the children: to help them see in Christ an incredible Man with that rare blend found nowhere else—purity, strength, compassion, and sparkling humor.

# 4

# Loving the Unlovely

As I look out over the bright greenery of our backyard this morning, I realize how hard it is for me to love people, even members of my own family, when I disapprove of their behavior. I know this is wrong, Lord Jesus, because You demonstrated time after time that it is possible, even necessary, to love people without judgment.

There was the woman taken in adultery and about to be stoned when You asked the mob surrounding her, "If any one of you is without sin, let him be the first to throw a stone at her." As You told her to go and sin no more, I could almost hear the caring quality of Your voice. Likewise with the woman You met at the well, the one who had had five husbands. Uncondemning love was in Your manner.

I have no trouble forgiving certain people, but recently I have seen that the forgiveness is not complete in Your eyes until I can love them too.

Ever since we moved here to Chappaqua, Marilyn[1] has been a thorn in my side. She's overbearing, overweight, and always overreacting. Her criticalness rubs me raw. Forgive her, sure. Love her, so hard for me. We can't manufacture love, can we? Until now I haven't even been willing for *You* to love Marilyn *through* me.

[1]Not her real name.

Queer about love . . . Is it a quality so of a piece that when we deliberately withhold it from any single human being, we deny love itself and, in the end, are rendered incapable of loving?

So last night, down on my knees in Len's presence, I confessed all this. With Len and You as witnesses, I'm giving You permission to give me the gift of love for Marilyn.

But this morning I'm not willing to stop there; I would like to be able to love people the way You love them. In Your Word this morning I came across some verses that give me a handle on how.

In 2 Peter 1, the apostle rejoices in the "precious and very great promises" by which we may be "partakers of the divine nature." Then he gives us a ladder of seven steps leading to this high goal:

1) To faith, add *virtue.* (v. 5)
2) To virtue, add *knowledge.* (v. 5)
3) To knowledge, add *self-control.* (v. 6)
4) To self-control, add *steadfastness.* (v. 6)
5) To steadfastness, add *godliness.* (v. 6)
6) To godliness, add *brotherly affection.* (v. 7)
7) To brotherly affection will then be added, *love.* (v. 7)

"For if these things are yours and abound," Peter concludes, "they keep you from being ineffective or unfruitful in the knowledge of our Lord Jesus Christ" (v. 8, RSV).

I want to climb that ladder, Lord, to be able to know You and love You more than ever before.

# 5

# SEEKING EXCELLENCE

I've been troubled about Linda's school work. Considering her high IQ she's not doing anything like her best. Last night at the dinner table I told her about one of my favorite Bible verses, which appears no less than three times in the Old Testament: He maketh my feet like hinds' feet, and setteth me upon my high places (Psalm 18:32–33, 2 Samuel 22:33–34, and Habakkuk 3:19 KJV).

"What in the world does that mean?" she asked, with a frown on her freckled face.

To answer, I told her about a friend of mine. . . .

When I was six years old, this family friend whom we called "Auntie Chamberlain" purchased the book *Hiawatha* for me. But this was no ordinary copy. It had hand-cut paper, beautiful illustrations, a pronouncing vocabulary for difficult Indian names, even a section for handicraft projects.

She had searched all over town to find it. And this was so typical of Auntie Chamberlain—a woman who gave herself totally to life. Auntie Chamberlain taught me the importance of doing every task with my whole heart. Soon I discovered that family games—like Parcheesi—were the most fun when played with total enthusiasm and concentration. Piano lessons took on added luster when I not only learned to read a piece of music, but also memorized it. School assignments were more fun when I did more than the minimum required.

I found that something more important than good grades came from this approach: a deep inner satisfaction, a glow, a happiness. And conversely, I discovered that when I undertook any project halfheartedly, the result was usually half successful.

Later on, while living in Washington, I saw to my delight this "Auntie Chamberlain quality" in another individual—Dr. Lida Earhart. She, too, gave all of herself to whatever task she undertook and had been the first woman to attain the rank of full professor at Columbia University. After retiring, she came to Washington to live and regularly attended services at our New York Avenue Presbyterian Church.

One day someone asked Miss Earhart to give a talk on the Book of Job at the monthly meeting of the church women's association. This was probably a tossed-off invitation, with the usual kind of talk expected. But the talk turned out to be far from usual. For two months Miss Earhart had studied the Book of Job. She had researched the archeological features of the time of Job and his contemporaries. She had read biblical scholars' analyses of the book. She had pondered deeply the book's theme: the problem of evil in our world. The result was one of the most memorable presentations I ever have heard.

Even more remarkable, she had done all that work for an ordinary church meeting. Nothing extraordinary had been asked or expected. Yet she knew *the secret of hinds' feet.*

"What is the secret?" Linda asked.

"The rear feet of the female red deer, known also as the *hind,*" I said, "step in precisely the same spot where the front feet have just been. Every motion of the hind is followed through with this same single-focused consistency, making it the most sure-footed of all mountain animals."

As the feet of the female deer are to the mountains, I told her, so is the mind of man to the heights of life. "Ask yourself—how many things have I done with single-minded devotion, nothing held back?"

"Not many," she admitted.

"It's not easy in our modern world," I agreed, "to make our lives like hinds' feet. Too much today is done with minimal effort. This attitude can begin with school work done sloppily—but there's no joy in halfhearted efforts."

Linda listened with real interest to this biblical simile. Lord, make it come alive in her life!

# 6

# THE CONTAGION OF JOY

As I absorb the Gospels this September morning, I'm seeing Jesus so clearly as a vital young Man who loved life and was filled with joy.

I'm influenced no doubt by my experience last month [August 1961] at a conference of The Fellowship of Christian Athletes in Estes Park, Colorado, where I spoke to the wives of the coaches and leaders. I never had seen so much muscle and maleness packed into one area. During the entire week there was a virile, vibrant atmosphere. And who was the central figure? Jesus Christ!

Of primary interest to me was the involvement of my son Peter, who had graduated from Yale the previous June. Peter admitted his purpose in coming to the conference was to get close to nationally known athletes. "I'm not interested in hearing any Sunday school stories," he told Len and me. During high school and college to my great dismay he had rejected his Christian heritage.

Instead of Sunday school stories, Peter heard some of the biggest names in sports unashamedly tell how they had found joy in the Christian faith. From the beginning my son was swept along in the excitement of young men singing, shouting, laughing, competing, and praying together. By the fourth day he was literally catapulted into making a personal commitment of his life to Jesus Christ as Savior and Lord.

"It is an awesome thing when you meet Jesus for the first time," he told me later. Gone was his bored, know-it-all attitude, in its place a new aliveness. A decision to enter Princeton Theological Seminary followed a few weeks later.

It makes me eager to take a fresh look at the qualities of the One who has such an attraction for young people—in His time and ours. The Gospel picture of Him is of a joyous man with a buoyant zest for life. The New Testament in one place describes Him as "anointed . . . with the oil of gladness" (Hebrews 1:9 KJV).

As I read through the Gospels, I see that Jesus had quite a bit to say about joy. We are *not* invited to a relationship that will take away our fun but asked to "enter into the joy of [our] Lord" (Matthew 25:21 KJV). The purpose of His coming to earth, Jesus said, was in order that our *joy might be full!* (John 15:11 KJV).

No wonder the young in the full tide of life adored Him and left everything to be with Him! And the young today still respond to the lure of adventure and the giving of their all to a cause. That is why the stringency and the sacrifice called for by movements like the Peace Corps have so much appeal.

I can see that Jesus drew men and women into the Kingdom by promising them two things: first, trouble—hardship, danger; and second, joy. But what curious alchemy is this that He can make even danger and hardship seem joyous? He understands things about human nature that we grasp only dimly: few of us are really challenged by the promise of soft living, by an emphasis on me-first, or by a life of easy compromise.

Christ still asks for one's total surrender and then promises His gift of full, overflowing joy. It was that Spirit of joy that I felt in the young people at Estes Park. It was this Spirit that captured my son and turned his life around.

7

# QUENCHING A CHILD'S SPIRIT

After three years of marriage, Len and I are groping for wisdom in relating to each of our children. Gradually we have become aware that family life is God's classroom for shaping us into the kind of people He wants us to be.

God often speaks to me through dreams. Last night, for example, I dreamed I was talking to Jeff, our irrepressible six-year-old. In my right hand was a bottle of what looked like baby aspirin. Jeff and I were having one of our typical confrontations. In the dream, however, I lost my temper and somehow the bottle hit one of his eyes. He cried and to my alarm I saw on my hand fluid from his eye.

The next scene was of Len carrying Jeff into our bedroom, where I was standing by the window. Sitting on his father's knee, Jeff took his forefinger and ran it around his eye socket. I looked and—to my horror—there was no eye there.

"Let's get him to an eye doctor fast!" I urged.

Len's stance was his usual patient tolerance, though now full of sadness. "It's too late. There's no eye there."

I was overcome with grief—then, to my great relief, I woke up.

This morning when I asked the Lord if He was telling me something through this dream, I was led to one of Jesus' teachings in the Sermon on the Mount.

> The eye is the lamp of the body. So, if your eye is sound, your whole body will be full of light.
>
> Matthew 6:22 RSV

Then came His gentle but firm correction to me. I had been putting out, quenching, some of Jeff's light by the way I had been treating him.

Convicted of my sin, I confessed immediately the specific ways I have been quenching the light in Jeff: (1) Through losing my temper (quite inexcusable); (2) dominating him because I'm bigger; (3) not demonstrating enough love for Jeff.

I asked for and received God's forgiveness for these sins. Then I sought out Jeff, hugged him, and asked his forgiveness.

"That's okay, Mom," he said with a grin. Pause. "Can I have Rodney over for lunch today?"

*Several weeks later:* I dreamed again last night about Jeff. This time he and Chester were tumbling about on the back porch. Suddenly Jeff lost his balance and fell down the steps, his head striking the pavement below.

The next picture was of Jeff being carried off on a stretcher covered with blankets neatly tucked in, with his head heavily bandaged. And in my dream, suddenly I realized how much *I loved this little guy.*

# 8

# MALNUTRITION OF THE SPIRIT

The problems that arise in second marriages are more than I could ever have imagined. Being a new mother to three young children is exhausting, leaving little time for creative writing. There are times when life seems to go gray; I have no zest for anything.

When this happened last week I recognized my problem: *malnutrition of the spirit.*

It was Carol, my friend from California, who had made me aware months ago that spiritual undernourishment can be quite as real as physical starvation. When I first met Carol, it was obvious that she had problems, but not the usual ones. She had a happy marriage; no major troubles with her three children; everything fine economically; no health difficulties.

But she felt tired all the time from the daily routine. "Nothing is much fun anymore," she had said. "I have so little energy that no undertaking seems worth attempting. What's wrong with me?"

An hour and much talk later, I had a sudden inspiration: could it be that Carol's inner spirit was starving to death?

Taking up my Bible, I turned to the Old Testament story of Daniel. I read to her about how Daniel was in exile in the king's palace. "His windows being open in his chamber toward Jerusalem, he kneeled upon his knees three times a day, and prayed, and gave thanks before his God, as he did aforetime" (Daniel 6:10 KJV).

"We have three meals a day," I suggested. "Perhaps we need spiritual food three times a day too."

"But what *is* spiritual food? And how do you take it?" Carol asked.

"Jesus said that His words are spirit and life indeed. He used metaphor upon metaphor to tell us that His Spirit is our life substance. He described himself as 'living water' and 'the bread of life.' Meeting Him in Scripture is like an intravenous feeding from His Spirit to our spirit," I replied.

"So," I challenged Carol, "would you be willing to try spiritual food in the form of life-giving Bible verses three times a day for one month?"

At a Christian bookstore Carol found an "Inspiration Box" of paper capsules, each containing a verse of Scripture. They were to be taken daily as spiritual vitamins. (This word "vitamin" means "life substance.")

Later, with another spiritually undernourished friend, we decided that an additional blessing came when we took the time ourselves to dig through Scripture and put together a homemade card file of spiritual vitamins.

So last week I produced a "Vitamin Box" of dozens of favorite passages for my new family. I used a concordance and looked up words such as *strength, food, bread, water, hunger,* and *thirst.* Other cards were culled from Christ's own words. Now before blessing the food at each meal, we pass the box, and one of the children chooses a card to read aloud. The nourishment is most effective when the life-giving words of Scripture are memorized and so become the permanent possessions of mind and heart.

> But they that wait upon the Lord shall renew their strength; they shall mount up with wings as eagles; they shall run, and not be weary; and they shall walk, and not faint.
>
> Isaiah 40:31 KJV

> For the Lord disciplines the man he loves. . . . So up with your listless hands! Strengthen your weak knees! And make straight paths for your feet.
>
> Hebrews 12:6, 12–13, MOFFATT

> Oh that men would praise the Lord for his goodness, and for his wonderful works to the children of men! For he satisfieth the longing soul, and filleth the hungry soul with goodness.
>
> Psalm 107:8–9 KJV

> . . . My grace is sufficient for thee: for my strength is made perfect in weakness.
>
> 2 Corinthians 12:9 KJV

By saturating my mind with these and other verses, I find that the grayness lifts, the spirit is infused with spiritual food, and I am ready to meet any difficulty that comes along.

9

# Early Morning Time

*Awake my soul, and with the sun*
*Thy daily stage of duty run;*
*Shake off dull sloth, and joyful rise*
*To pay the morning sacrifice!*

*Shine on me, Lord, new life impart,*
*Fresh ardors kindle in my heart;*
*One ray of Thine all-quickening light*
*Dispels the clouds and dark of night.*
*Thomas Ken (1637–1711)*

As Len and I arise at 6:00 A.M. this morning, I find the above verses help move me from "dull sloth" to "fresh ardors." Then in Psalm 5, I read:

> Give ear to my words, O Lord, consider my meditation. Hearken unto the voice of my cry. . . . My voice shalt thou hear in the morning, O Lord; in the morning will I direct my prayer unto thee, and will look up.
> Psalm 5:1–3 KJV

God, who created heaven and earth, will hear *my* voice? The King of the universe will consider *my* meditation?

Oh, thank You, Lord, for the undreamed-of opportunity of this audience with the King! Anyone who has a favor to ask of an earthly monarch has no chance of having his request granted until he makes his wish known to the king. That *could* be second-hand—generally is, in protocol-bound human societies. What a privilege to have an audience in person! Yet this is the status and the honor You allow each of us, Lord.

Even more privileged is he so in favor with the King that he is allowed as long as he wishes to be with the One he loves, listen to Him, watch Him, bask in His presence. In earthly courts, such a one would be considered favored indeed, and the courts we're invited to enter are of an "infinite majesty." Just to say "Thank You" seems inadequate. This morning I make it a welling, swelling gratitude!

# 10

# Subject One to Another

This week I've been focusing my thoughts and prayers on the fifth chapter of Ephesians.

> Wives be subject—be submissive and adapt yourselves—to your own husbands as [a service] to the Lord. For the husband is head of the wife as Christ is the Head of the church. . . . As the church is subject to Christ, so let wives also be subject in everything to their husbands.
>
> Ephesians 5:22–24 AMPLIFIED

Like many women, I've struggled with conflicting emotions over the current emphasis on "submission." Especially when I hear of a case, as I did last week, of a husband who used this passage in Ephesians to intimidate his wife and force her to accept and condone his own adultery with another woman. An extreme situation, of course, but one of many instances where the basic truth of Scripture is violated or distorted when taken out of context.

For example, the admonition "Wives, submit to your husbands" is coupled in Ephesians with, "Husbands, love your wives, as Christ loved the church and gave Himself up for her'' (v. 25). Yet this complementary verse is frequently overlooked.

This week's Bible focus was promoted by a letter:

"I am having a mighty struggle with my role as a Christian wife," the woman wrote. "Something inside of me literally rebels at the words—obey, submit, subject! At times I have considered the apostle Paul to be a male chauvinist. Also, I can't believe that my loving heavenly Father, as I personally know Him, would want me to be as completely and blindly submissive as these Scriptures seem to indicate.

"I realize my resentment and selfishness is sin, yet when I try to submit to my husband, I end up feeling angry and hypocritical. Or like a spiritless dumb animal. How do I understand and accept this teaching?"

To answer this question, I've taken time to review my own relationship as a wife to Len, study the Ephesians chapter, then talk and pray some more with my husband.

When we were first married, Len suggested that I assume spiritual responsibility for our home. This seemed wrong to me. It went against a number of scriptural teachings. Also I doubted that Len's two sons would respond to this; they would perhaps see religion as "a woman's thing." In fact, Chester, the elder son, who is gifted in all sports, sees God the Father primarily through his own athletic father. Once Len and I began to search the Bible together in the early mornings, he saw for himself that he should take spiritual leadership of our home and did so.

But there's more. As we study Ephesians 5, we're beginning to believe that this may be one of the most misinterpreted chapters in the New Testament. Nor do we believe that St. Paul was any kind of male chauvinist.

Much light is shed when we investigate the background against which Paul was teaching. He had come out of Judaism, a patriarchal system where women were considered their husbands' property. Still, Jewish women were better off than most. In the other countries around the Mediterranean basin of Paul's day, wives had no political or social status whatever, were allowed no education, no activity beyond the home. In the Greek world, for instance, groups of single young women were trained to provide the social and sex life of Greek husbands whose wives stayed at home, did the menial tasks, and cared for the children.

In Ephesians, chapters four through six, Paul is speaking out against this immoral system and is trying to teach new Ephesian Christians how they should relate to one another. It is only against this pagan backdrop that we can see how revolutionary Paul's "Husbands, love your wives" was! Not only was Paul not against women, he, like his Master before him, was teaching that women are equally children of the Father and as such are to be respected and beloved. At that time this was a radically new approach to women.

In the end we're discovering that the hub upon which the Ephesian "submission" passages turn is the statement that introduces them: "Be subject to one another out of reverence for Christ" (Ephesians 5:21 AMPLIFIED). This is the irreducible minimum of Paul's instructions to all Christians—male or female.

What is coming out of Len's and my seeking prayers on this subject can be described as a triangle of authority more than a pecking order. God is at the apex of the triangle; the husband and wife are equally positioned at the lower corners. Thus both mates are equal in His sight, equally beloved by Him, equally committed to each other and to Him.

We're finding "Be subject to one another out of reverence for Christ" to be intensely practical. It means a spirit of mutual respect, a willingness to listen. It means giving—and sometimes giving in—on the part of both of us, since sometimes God gives His direction through Len, at other times through me. Most importantly, at the peak of the triangle God Himself has to be acknowledged as the final Authority in the home.

In thinking further about the subject this morning, I realize that I want for our home everything in that Ephesians chapter. I want Len to be its spiritual head. I want him to be a husband whom I can love and trust and submit to in the biblical sense. I want him to love me as Jesus loves the Church, to love me as he would love his own body. I also want to "respect, reverence, honor, love, and esteem him exceedingly."

# Section Two

# Adventuresome Living

*Travel is often called "the door to adventure." Catherine and I had our share of this kind of excitement. During the early years of our marriage we visited Uganda, Kenya, the Holy Land, drove through central Europe, painted with oils on the beaches of Bora Bora and Moréa in the South Pacific, shared stories with missionaries in such remote places as Tonga, Fiji, and Tahiti, ministered to groups in Samoa and Australia.*

*Yet the real adventure for us was always spiritual: testing scriptural truths, exploring different kinds of prayer, sharing in fellowship groups, teaching together from the Bible. The base for the first five years of our marriage was Chappaqua, New York. When Northern winters caused increasing congestion of Catherine's lungs, we moved to Boynton Beach, Florida, in November 1964.*

*The first of our children to marry was Peter, who met Edith Wallis at Princeton Theological Seminary. They were married on May 29, 1966, and their daughter, Mary Elizabeth Marshall, was born on March 1, 1969.*

*During these years life was tumultuous, demanding, often exhausting. With God in charge of our lives, there was the never-ending suspense of wondering what He had in store for us next.*

*LL*

# 1

# THE PRAYER OF AGREEMENT

I am impressed this morning with the power in a Scripture verse about prayer.

When my son Peter accepted an invitation to give a speech in Kansas City, I had a telephone call from a dentist in that city who was on the sponsoring committee. This man asked me to pray for the meeting and that Peter's message would be God's topic for this particular audience at this particular time.

The dentist and I decided to claim the promise of Jesus in Matthew 18:19–20 RSV:

> "If two of you agree on earth about anything they ask, it will be done for them by my Father in heaven. For where two or three are gathered in my name, there am I in the midst of them."

In heartfelt accord, my caller and I asked God that His word only be spoken at the upcoming gathering.

Peter's talk was in the newly decorated ballroom of the largest hotel in Kansas City, with six hundred people in attendance. The audience were both Christians and non-Christians, a cross section of civic Kansas City.

Len and I learned later that just before Peter was to speak a black man with a powerful voice sang "There Is a Balm in Gilead." This got to everyone, especially Peter.

On the table beside him were the notes of the prepared speech, which he had in fact planned to use. After hearing the song, he shoved aside his papers, rose, and picked up the theme of the song for his talk. For one hour and fifteen minutes he laid out before that Kansas City audience Jesus Christ as *the* "balm in Gilead."

The room was so quiet (according to the dentist) that not even the usual coughing and respiratory upheavals were in evidence. A doctor friend, not particularly religious, who was there as the guest of the dentist, told him afterwards, "I've never witnessed or heard anything like it. It was so quiet that I was almost afraid to breathe."

I asked the dentist, "But, speaking that long extemporaneously, didn't Peter ramble or repeat himself?"

"Not once," he answered. "However you tie it, Catherine, when anyone can hold six hundred people *that* attentive for an hour and a quarter—that had to be God."

What neither Peter nor the dentist knows is that "There Is a Balm in Gilead" was one of the favorite songs of Peter's father. He had sung it in a quartet during his seminary days. He sometimes sang it as a duet in Westminster Church in Atlanta. When he was pastor of the New York Avenue Church in Washington, it was one of the favorite numbers of Charlie Beaschler's great massed choirs. Now, through that singer in Kansas City, God has used it again to bring His message to a hurting world.

# 2

# HAPPINESS IS . . .

As I've been pondering the subject of happiness this morning—an elusive and seemingly unattainable state for so many—I am led to these words of Jesus:

> If any man would come after me, let him deny himself and take up his cross and follow me. For whoever would save his life will lose it, and whoever loses his life for my sake will find it.
>
> Matthew 16:24–25 RSV

I believe the secret of happiness lies imbedded in those words, painful though they appear to be. How else explain radiant people like the young man who sat in our living room and described how his six-year-old boy had died in his arms from leukemia. Today this man finds fulfillment in giving himself totally to helping college students. Or the woman I visited recently whose husband had turned out to be a homosexual and demanded a divorce. Some years later, this woman also lost her eyesight. Yet she is a cheerful, loving person, fully self-supporting.

You might say that such people almost have a right to be unhappy. That they are not, lies in the way they spend themselves for others.

I have observed that when any of us embarks on the pursuit of happiness for ourselves, it eludes us. Often I've asked myself why. It must be because happiness comes to us only as a dividend. When we become absorbed in something demanding and worthwhile above and beyond ourselves, happiness seems to be there as a by-product of the self-giving.

That should not be a startling truth, yet I'm surprised at how few people understand and accept it. Have we made a god of happiness? Have we been brainwashed by ads assuring us "Happiness is . . ."—usually a big, shiny, new gadget?

Perhaps our national preoccupation with happiness dates from these words in the Declaration of Independence:

> . . . All men are . . . endowed by their Creator with certain unalienable rights, [and] among these are life, liberty and *the pursuit of happiness* [italics added].

Now, I have always had immense admiration for Thomas Jefferson, author of these words. And until recently I never questioned them. But (and my apologies to you, Mr. Jefferson) I do question them as I see more and more people interpret "the pursuit of happiness" as a license to grab for power or money or physical pleasure.

The truth, as I see it, is that not one of us has "an unalienable right" to anything, not even to life itself. We did nothing to bring about our birth, and we are dependent for the next breath we draw on the grace of God. How arrogant and ungrateful we must seem to our Creator when we demand our "rights."

I think of Mary and Harold Brinig—a remarkable couple who found the true basis of happiness some years ago. Having moved to Chicago where they had no friends, they became irritable with each other and unhappy. While seeking help from the Bible one day, they were struck by these words of Jesus:

> You did not choose me, but I chose you and appointed you that you should go and bear fruit and that your fruit should abide . . .
>
> John 15:16 RSV

Somehow that passage was like light penetrating their darkness: much of their unhappiness, they realized, was caused by self-centeredness. Could Jesus be choosing them for service? But practically speaking, how could this happen in a big city like Chicago?

The first person they encountered after this revelation was the waitress who served them in a nearby restaurant. She apologized for giving slow service, admitted she was new in the city and miserable. They invited her to visit them in their apartment after work.

"You did not choose me, but I chose you. . . ." A widower in the next apartment was the second person they befriended. Soon a dozen people were meeting together once a week for conversation and prayer.

Out of these meetings grew a project called Adventures in Friendship. Before long, scores of people were involved in seeking the lonely and the shut-ins throughout the whole area. Needless to say, Mary and Harold Brinig had become so absorbed in the needs of others that their own life was enriched beyond anything I can describe. Happiness found them.

This Chicago experience prepared the Brinigs for a thirty-five-year team ministry at the Marble Collegiate Church in New York City that resulted in spiritually rejuvenated lives for thousands of people, including my husband, Len.

3

# The Power of *Let*

While reading a manuscript by Mrs. John Peters (wife of the founder of World Neighbors), I was intrigued by one episode in particular. Losing his footing in the bathroom, her husband struck his head on the ceramic soap dish. One ear was almost severed and he was bleeding profusely when Mrs. Peters heard his cries and came to his aid.

Despite her shock at the sight of so much blood, the Spirit took over and enabled her to speak with authority. She heard herself saying, "Let the bleeding stop immediately. Let there be no infection. Let there be no pain. Let there be no scarring."

Mrs. Peters made no comment on the experience other than to report that, gloriously, the bleeding stopped. There was no infection. Almost no pain. No scars. But something about these "Lets" stuck like glue to my mind.

I realized that it was the same word God had used in creating our world. "*Let* there be light," . . . and so on.

Jesus to His disciples:

> *Let* your light so shine before men, that they may see your good works, and glorify your Father which is in heaven.
>
> Matthew 5:16 KJV

And if the house is worthy, *let* your peace come upon it; but if it is not worthy, *let* your peace return to you.
Matthew 10:13 RSV

Paul used it too:

*Let* this mind be in you, which was also in Christ Jesus.
Philippians 2:5 KJV

What, I wondered, is the significance of this word for us?

Author Harold Hill gave me the missing insight. " 'Let' is a word of tremendous faith with volumes of meaning poured into it," he told me. "It *assumes* the total love and good will of the Father. It *assumes* that heaven is crammed with good gifts that the Father desires to give His children. The 'let' is saying, 'Father, I give to You permission to do so-and-so for us down here on earth. I allow it.' "

It also assumes an almost preposterous humility on God's part—that He should wait for our permission to bestow wonderful gifts on us! How amazing!

Worlds of meaning behind this three-letter word . . . *let.*

4

# The Poverty Complex

I'm going through one of those "money anxiety" periods this morning, Lord, so I know I've taken my eyes off You and placed them squarely on worldly matters.

The sad thing is that I know better. Only the other day I was expressing my incredulity over a famous financier who committed suicide when his wealth diminished from fifty million to ten million. It seemed inconceivable that a man could feel desperate about money when he still possessed ten million dollars. Wealth, clearly, is a matter of attitude.

So once again I go through the process of replacing fear with faith in connection with Your provision.

*First*, I need to remind myself that You control all of earth's material resources. Most of us do not really believe this. Yet from cover to cover the Bible declares it:

> The earth is the Lord's and the fulness thereof. . . .
>
> Psalm 24:1 KJV

> But my God shall supply all your need according to his riches. . . .
>
> Philippians 4:19 KJV

If I truly believe that I am a child of a King, then my fear will disappear. Worrying would be the sure sign that I did not believe God's ownership of earth's resources. To think myself a pauper is to deny either the King's riches or my being His beloved child.

*Second,* I can think about Mary Welch. Born in a log cabin on a run-down farm in west Texas, even after she became a Christian she found it difficult to shed her poverty complex. A turning point for her came when she was in St. Paul, Minnesota, on a speaking trip as the guest of a wealthy woman. As she was preparing to take a bath before dinner, she drew her customary three inches of water in the tub.

Her hostess happened to look into the tub. "You're not intending to take a bath in that tiny amount of water?"

"Why not? That's all I ever use."

"This isn't Texas, Mary," her hostess chided her. "There's no shortage of water here. Minnesota has ten *thousand* lakes."

Mary realized that she had just gotten a sharp insight about herself. She watched the water nearly fill the tub. Then she lathered herself with soap—marveling at all she was wasting. That night before she went to sleep she asked God to register His Perfect Adequacy on her subconscious and clear out all her deep-rooted beliefs in shortages.

Soon after, Mary realized that even her skinny, ninety-pound body looked like a shortage of woman. She took a piece of soft soap and, in a full-length mirror, drew an outline of her ideal measurements. Then she packed most of her size-three dresses to send to an orphanage.

Her mother caught her at the packing and didn't approve at all. "You've never had much. You worked too hard to get those clothes to give them away. Besides, suppose you *don't* gain weight?"

But Mary realized that she could not pray for one thing and make provisions for another. Furthermore, she had discovered what she calls the "law of the Golden Initiative": the secret of receiving is to give—even out of poverty. In fact, the more sunk we are in visions of lack, the greater need we have to start giving.

So the dresses went off to the orphanage. "And within that year," Mary reports, "I measured exactly what I had pictured and prepared for—size nine."

*The third thing* I'm to do is to remind myself of that moment of decision I faced some weeks after Peter Marshall's death in 1949. The trustees of his church gave me a bleak financial report of how little insurance money there was. They advised me to take a full-time job to support Peter John and myself.

You, Lord, encouraged me to write, with the promise that if I trusted You, all my needs would be met. I took Your challenge and how greatly have You blessed me! Thank you, Lord. Praise You! Forgive me for my lack of faith.

# 5

# Forward, Like Gideon!

This morning, Len and I dragged ourselves out of bed at 6:00 A.M. for our morning prayer time. After the long drive from Evergreen Farm in Virginia to southern Florida, I'm exhausted. Our suitcases are still packed. But there's a meeting of our church committee on Christian education this afternoon that Len insists we attend.

I'm fighting off resentment as well as fatigue. I want to get back to my writing. Meetings drain me. Bore me. Len wants us to teach a class on the Holy Spirit this winter to a group that is resistant to what is happening across the country today, frightened by the excesses of some of the "Jesus people," by speaking in tongues and so on. Len looks at this class as an adventure. I'm full of doubts as to whether we can handle it.

Is it coincidence that I have been reading the Book of Judges? Today it was the story of Gideon. Such fascinating reading! So jam-packed full of truths and insights!

For instance, Gideon certainly had no idea that he was anyone special in God's sight or in man's. He lived at a low point in Israel's history when the people had forsaken Jehovah and were worshiping idols.

Yet God sent an angel to Gideon with the message, "The Lord is with you, you mighty man of [fearless] courage" (Judges 6:12 AMPLIFIED).

There's immense humor in this greeting. For the "mighty man of courage" was at that moment hiding out in a winepress for fear of the Midiänites.

And his reaction to the angel's appearance was doubt and confusion. "If the Lord is with us, why is all this befallen us?" (v. 13).

The answer was a strange one. The angel did not rebuke Gideon for answering back with unbelief. Instead, he repeated, "Go in this your might, and you shall save Israel from the hand of Midian. Have I not sent you?" (v. 14).

Again Gideon sounds like anything but a hero. He replies, in effect, "Who, me? Save Israel? Surely you must be kidding. My clan is the poorest in Israel and I'm the least in my father's house, the youngest son, the one everyone picks on."

The Lord's answer is, "Surely, I will be with you, and you shall smite the Midianites as one man" (v. 16).

Only after the angel disappears does Gideon seem to realize that he has actually been in the presence of an angel. His reaction to this, characteristically, is downbeat all the way. He might have been thrilled and begun praising God. Instead, he says, "Alas, O Lord God! For now I have seen the Angel of the Lord face to face!" (v. 22).

Never on God's side, however, is there anything but patient understanding of Gideon's doubt and unbelief. "Peace be to you; do not fear, you shall not die" (v. 23).

Then begins a series of clear-cut instructions from the Lord. First, Gideon is to tear down two idols.

The "mighty man of courage" obeys, but does it at night because he's so scared of his own clan, even of his father and brothers.

In fact, his father sticks up for him before the townspeople.

But Gideon is full of doubt still. Only after elaborate further signs and reassurances from Jehovah will he consent to take command of the Israelite forces. And then the point of the story becomes clear: it is God's strength and His alone that delivers us. For God persuades Gideon to reduce his warriors from 22,000 to 300. And it is this small army that routs the Midianites.

The clear message for today that I receive from this reading is that God is going to show me that I can rely on Him alone—for physical strength as for every other need. So thank You, Lord, for the meeting I will go to this afternoon, hence no nap today. Thank You for the challenge of teaching a class on the Holy Spirit. Full speed ahead, O Gideon!

6

# Small Needs

After the Bible study I gave last week on praying for all our needs, no matter how small, one woman took sharp issue with me.

"Asking for small things is being selfish," she remonstrated, "and self-centered prayers just aren't answered. I think we should pray only about *spiritual* needs. Besides, the God who runs the universe can't be bothered with individual wishes."

I could only reply that this was not Jesus' viewpoint as presented in the Gospels: both by teaching and by action He impressed upon us that no need is too trivial for His attention.

I've combed Scripture for examples and there are many, such as: The wine needed at a wedding feast (John 2:1–11); a dying sparrow (Matthew 10:29); a lost lamb (Luke 15:3–7).

These vignettes, scattered through the Gospels like little patches of gold dust, say to us, "No creaturely need is outside the scope of prayer."

As if to emphasize the same thought, the apostle Paul adds:

> Do not fret or have any anxiety about anything, but in every circumstance and in everything by prayer and pe-

tition [definite requests] with thanksgiving continue to make your wants known to God.

Philippians 4:6 AMPLIFIED

Now obviously not all our human wants are genuine needs. Moreover, we are often so selfish and shortsighted that the granting of some wants would not be good for us. But I believe that Scripture invites us to talk over all our concerns and dreams with our Father, then leave the outcome to His wisdom.

Just before Christmas we had a wonderful example of His loving involvement in the everyday-ness of life. My son Peter was laboring to build an elaborate miniature horse stable for his daughter, Mary Elizabeth. Hour after hour, he closeted himself in the basement putting it together. Especially time-consuming was the process of covering the roof with tiny shingles of almost paper-thin plywood. As the laborious work of positioning and gluing proceeded, it became apparent that he was going to run out of shingles.

Peter called all manner of hobby stores in the area. Nobody had any.

He even called the company in Texas that made the shingles. Yes, they could get them to him in time by special plane service for about $100. Too costly.

Finally, Peter found a hobby store up the road that had half of one package. The owner's wife had been using them for some project and had that many left. This was still not enough to complete the roof, but Peter decided to pick up those that were available.

As he drove off I breathed up a quiet little prayer about this. Immediately I had a mental picture—a little drama really—of Peter walking into the hobby store and the owner saying, "I have a surprise for you. I found another package of those shingles."

Peter came back home beaming. What I had "seen" as I prayed was exactly what had happened. He had more than enough to finish the roof.

A very small prayer request for what many would consider a superficial need. Yet this little episode gave all of us a heartwarming glimpse of the Father's careful provision for the small details of our lives—and of the adventure He means each moment in His world to be!

7

# Homemade Bread

I am troubled about a quality of blandness in our nation today, a lack of creativity. It's apparent in our leaders. Most gear their lives to television ratings, are afraid to take stands on issues. Movies and stage plays focus on sex and violence, with little originality. Sex so dominates advertising and the arts that it has become commonplace, almost boring.

Jesus lashed out at the spiritless quality in the people of His time:

> I know thy works, that thou art neither cold nor hot: I would thou wert cold or hot. So, then, because thou art lukewarm, and neither cold nor hot, I will spew thee out of my mouth.
>
> Revelation 3:15–16 KJV

One of our new neighbors is no longer trapped in a bland way of life. Yet for the first twelve years of her marriage, Cynthia felt she was losing her identity in an endless procession of social events and chauffeuring of children.

During one cocktail party, Cynthia decided to limit herself to ginger ale and made some discoveries—not especially pleasant: "I saw our crowd through new eyes," she told me. "No one was really saying anything. Most sentences were never even finished. There was a lot of laughter over—well, nothing at all. All at once I began to ask questions about what we call 'the good life.'

"What was so good about it?

"But," she continued, "what was I to do? If my husband and I ducked those invitations, we'd be thought snobbish and eventually dropped. But if we went, we would have to drink, otherwise how could we stand the emptiness?"

In a search for answers, Cynthia set aside an hour each day for meditation. As she did this over a period of weeks there came to her the realization that she was being met in this quiet hour, at her point of need, by something more than her own thoughts and her own psyche, by Someone who loved her and who insisted that His love must be passed on to her family and her friends.

Cynthia began to bake bread regularly, finding this ancient female ritual deeply satisfying. "You can't imagine how many enemies I slay and repressions I get rid of as I knead that bread," she says.

Instead of letting the children dash away from the dinner table for television, the evening meal has become a time for family sharing. Family Game Night once a week has become a creative substitute for television.

A new strength developed in Cynthia in regard to her children. I have heard her tell her astonished eleven-year-old that he is going to walk to Little League one way each practice day, and calmly state to her nine-year-old daughter that she certainly is not going to buy her any "training" bras.

"I've discovered that real love for our children has to go beyond catering to their every whim—or we turn them into tyrannical little princes and princesses," Cynthia said. "They, too, have to find their own inner resources. And how can they, if I do for them the things that they could do for themselves?"

Recognizing that some of her friends were as bored as she with the typical cocktail party, she began experimenting with some new types of entertaining. One evening after a buffet supper, a hand-picked group listened spellbound to a play on the radio, "The Murder Trial of William Palmer, Surgeon." Cynthia had supplied each guest with a paperback copy of the play to follow as they listened. The evening was a big hit, especially with the men.

"I realized one day that my church had little more meaning for me than did our country club," Cynthia said. "I called our pastor and asked if there was a Bible study."

That's what brought Cynthia and her husband to our house, where eight couples were already meeting twice a month to find ways to relate the Bible to some everyday problems we were all facing. Out of this experience has come a new level of shared concerns for us all and the exciting discovery of answers sought out together.

As I ponder Cynthia's story, I've concluded that we don't have to settle for blandness in life; God, who is the Author of creativity, is ready to make a dull life adventuresome the moment we allow His Holy Spirit to go to work inside us.

# Section Three

# Christian Growth

*There is a misconception in the minds of many believers that successful communicators of the faith speak from some Mt. Olympus of perfection—that it is only because these Christian superstars have overcome their faults and weaknesses that they are able to minister to others in a mighty way.*

*Not true. Those most used of God often have struggled or are struggling with one or more major weaknesses. It is often just because of a weakness that these people have much to share.*

*Dr. Norman Vincent Peale frankly admits that only due to his own fears and doubts and tensions was he able to minister so effectively to others with similar problems. A study of Christian leaders down through the ages reveals that most of them battled major weaknesses.*

*So it was with Catherine. The Lord gave her major gifts in the area of communication that catapulted her into the public eye. But when people tried to place her on a pedestal, she refused, knowing that God alone deserves to be exalted. Instead, she wrote openly about her struggles, her mistakes, her flaws.*

*In her journals she was ruthless with herself. The following excerpts indicate how hard she struggled to overcome certain weaknesses, how seriously she took the matter of our need to grow spiritually.*

*A lesson learned was an inadequately thought-through novel she began in 1969 and abandoned two-and-a-half years later. It was titled* Gloria. *The loss of time and energy on this manuscript weighed on Catherine for years.*

*LL*

1

# Dealing with a Major Mistake

Last week I needed to be alone for a few days to think and pray. The mistake I made in deciding to write the novel *Gloria* has shaken my confidence. The shelved manuscript is like a death in the family.

What went wrong?

I needed to find some answers about this—and about other troubling areas in my life. So I made arrangements to spend two days at the Cenacle, a Roman Catholic Retreat House several miles away in Lantana, Florida. Len dropped me off Sunday at 8:00 P.M.

The next morning after breakfast I sat for a while in a lawn chair out under an ancient mango tree. Through the curving trunks of the coconut palms I had a glimpse of the Intracoastal Waterway. The grounds were alive with bird calls.

A sound new to me was the creaking of the tall, tall bamboo that borders part of the property. The bamboo, too, was ancient. The slender branches writhed and creaked as they rubbed against one another in the barely perceptible breeze. The creaking reminded me of the grating of a long-unused hinge, as of a door being opened after many years. The foliage was still delicate and lacy as it was when the bamboo was young.

Leaf patterns were all across the grass. Squirrels raced up and down trees. A cardinal kept whistling, "Cheer! Cheer!"

I had thought that I wanted guidance on certain family matters and whether there was some way to resurrect *Gloria*. But when I talked briefly with Sister Forman at breakfast, her advice was to seek Christ and Him alone and let Him decide what He wanted to talk to me about.

That morning the first thought dropped into my mind was the single word *edification*. "Think on edification," He seemed to be saying, "what builds the members of the family up in love, perfecting them into the body of Christ."

The focus throughout the morning was largely on my home situation. (Perhaps the conclusion to be drawn is that it's essential that I get this right with Christ before I can write *anything* worthwhile.)

Soon I found myself turning to the book of John. As I read, the Holy Spirit showed me that I had fallen hook, line, and sinker for one of Satan's oldest and most-used tricks: looking steadily at the difficulty instead of at Jesus. I had listened, really paid attention to Old Scratch's suggestions—every one of them, I fear—as to the size and intractability of my problems. The Comforter told me that all of this had been Satan's technique for discouraging me unduly and that I must *never* fall for this temptation again.

Next I was shown that my husband, my children, and my grandchildren are not mine, but God's. He's not only as concerned as I am for them, but loves them far more than I ever could. Therefore, I was to take my possessive, self-centered hands off—strictly off. So, in an act of relinquishment, I did this.

Then came a beautiful touch. I was reading in the Psalms when suddenly these words leapt from the page:

> The Lord will perfect that which concerns me . . . forsake not the works of Your own hands.
>
> Psalm 138:8 AMPLIFIED

I could—and did—claim this promise promptly for my family. Years ago the Lord began a work in these lives. It's His business to perfect what He started. He has promised that He will. I've claimed and accepted that promise. It's as good as done. My heart is steadily rejoicing. Weights and weights have been lifted from me.

The focus that afternoon turned from my home situation to my failure with *Gloria.* What do You have to tell me about this, Lord?

I was led to this passages in Numbers:

> . . . the people . . . spoke against God and against Moses, and said, "Why have you brought us up out of Egypt to die in the desert? There is no bread! There is no water! And we detest this miserable food!"
>
> Then the Lord sent venomous snakes among them; they bit the people and many Israelites died. The people came to Moses and said, "We sinned when we spoke against the Lord and against you. Pray that the Lord will take the snakes away from us." So Moses prayed for the people.
>
> The Lord said to Moses, "Make a snake and put it up on a pole; anyone who is bitten can look at it and live." So Moses made a bronze snake and put it up on a pole. Then when anyone was bitten by a snake and looked at the bronze snake, he lived.
>
> Numbers 21:4–9 NIV

It didn't take long for me to get the point: God told Moses that the people were to take that which had hurt them and lift it up to Him. He would then turn even a snake into blessing and victory. Thus the "snake" in our life can be redeemed and turned to power.

In this way does God deal with our mistakes and sins. I had made a mistake in undertaking the novel *Gloria.* I had not heeded the advice of experts like Elizabeth Sherrill and Len; even my mother had expressed strong reservations. But God would find a way to turn a bad experience into good.

Even more to the point: when any one of us has made a wrong (or even doubtful) turning in our lives through arrogance or lack of trust or impatience or fear—or what not—God will show us a way out. Therefore, I am to turn off all negative thoughts about this wrong decision and accept fully my situation as it is now, as God's will for me now. I am to place the present situation in His hands for Him to use fully for my spiritual growth and for the "edification" of all concerned. Further, I am to do this joyfully.

2

# The Servant Role

The message I am getting today from Jesus is the servant role that He wants to play in the lives of every one of us. The following passages reveal to me the extent of His passion to *serve* us because He loves us so much:

> . . . the Son of man came not to be waited on but to serve, and to give His life as a ransom for many . . . .
>
> Matthew 20:28 AMPLIFIED
>
> . . . I am in your midst as one who serves.
>
> Luke 22:27 AMPLIFIED

In the early days of my walk with Him, when I was experimenting day by day with hearing the Inner Voice, I had a hard time believing that His guidance was for *my* benefit, never His own. I still can hardly grasp this.

When He wrapped a towel around his waist, poured water into a basin, and began to wash his disciples' feet (see John 13:4–5), Simon Peter objected that this was beneath the dignity of the Master. *We* the disciples are to be the servants, I want to insist along with Peter. But Jesus answered him, "If I do not wash you, you have no part in me."

This is a stunning and stupendous thought. Unless I can believe in *this much* love for me, unless I can and will accept Him with faith as my servant as well as my God, unless I truly know that it's *my* good He seeks, not His glory (He already has all of that He can use for all eternity), *then I cannot have his companionship.*

What an amazing revelation!

# 3

# Why Do We Judge Others?

I am determined to dig in on the matter of my critical nature. I do not like it. It's negative; yes, often destructive. Jesus warned us not to be judgmental. So did Paul:

> Then let us no more pass judgment on one another, but rather decide never to put a stumbling block or hindrance in the way.
>
> Romans 14:13 RSV

I have tried to excuse myself by saying that one must evaluate situations and people. It won't wash. It still comes out judging, a haughty superiority, which is the opposite of love.

With Jesus' help I want to go back to my childhood to see if I can find the root cause for this fault of mine:

He is showing me a little girl who was supersensitive in the sense that she would rather die than be laughed at or found unacceptable by her peers, and most of all, by the adults around her. When she didn't make friends as quickly as other children, she tried to persuade herself that she was superior to others her age.

She got by with this superiority syndrome in school because she received top grades, especially in writing and speech courses. She yearned to be like classmates who were outgoing, witty, and popular, but since she had none of these personality traits, she convinced herself that these were lesser qualities while those of the mind and spirit were somehow on a higher plane.

When she left her small hometown for college, nothing changed in her approach to other people. Because she felt inferior socially, she looked with secret disapproval at those who danced, played cards, and went to drinking parties, all denied to her as a preacher's child.

Superiority breeds contempt. And contempt breeds criticalness. And my criticalness cut me off from other people. Even when I said nothing, made no comment at all, people would tell me they could feel my unkind judgment of them. I was miserable about this quality in me, yet trapped by it.

Along with all this, ironically enough, went an acute sensitivity to any criticalness of me. The Holy Spirit pointed out to me how *deeply* the least tiny bit of unacceptance rankles, causing a wound that festers on, year after year. Incidents, so small that a healthy reaction on my part should have been amusement and then prompt dismissal of the incident from mind, are remembered—still with an emotional sting attached—years later.

For instance . . . soon after I was married to Peter Marshall, I remember a woman friend commenting about my hands, "Well, they aren't beautiful, but at least they're capable-looking."

The pronouncement that my hands weren't pretty has stuck; ever since, it made me reluctant to have a manicurist do my nails.

This is, of course, acute oversensitivity, which, in turn, is the sure sign of acute self-centeredness . . . the same hypersensitivity and self-protectiveness that had led me to take refuge in an assumed superiority to others—with the accompanying right to stand in judgment on them.

Being oversensitive, I am quick to pick it up in others and relate to it. Once when a judge at the Junior Miss Pageant in Mobile, Alabama, I found myself intrigued by the contestant with the highest academic average of all fifty girls. When she came to the five judges for her ten-minute interview, I watched her with deep interest.

One question asked her was: "If you could pick out one person in any field of endeavor in our world today whom you admire most, whom would you pick?"

She hesitated a moment and then said loud and clear, "Jesus Christ."

Two of the judges responded almost simultaneously, "Oh, we mean a living person."

The girl felt rebuked. Her eyes filled with tears; she choked up and never could get herself under control during the rest of the interview. I ached for her. I wanted to hug her and tell her I loved her reply, that to me, as to her, Jesus *was* a living person.

Later, though, I wondered if her extreme sensitivity had caused her to put all her efforts into getting top grades—thereby avoiding, as I had, the far riskier confrontation of equal-to-equal.

How do we sensitive, critical people deal with our condition? I had one very direct answer from the Lord recently after I had loosed a blast of angry criticism at one of our national leaders at the luncheon table. God said to me, "Do not criticize at all" (1 Corinthians 4:5 MOFFATT). "You spread negativism around you and pollute your own atmosphere when you do so. Turn your criticism and your indignation to good use by praying for that leader right now."

A good handle for me to grasp!

# 4

# A Fast on Criticalness

The Lord continues to deal with me about my critical spirit, convicting me that I have been wrong to judge any person or situation:

> Do not judge, or you too will be judged. For in the same way you judge others, you will be judged, and with the measure you use, it will be measured to you.
>
> Matthew 7:1–2 NIV

One morning last week He gave me an assignment: *for one day I was to go on a "fast" from criticism. I was not to criticize anybody about anything.*

Into my mind crowded all the usual objections. "But then what happens to value judgments? You Yourself, Lord, spoke of 'righteous judgment.' How could society operate without standards and limits?"

All such resistance was brushed aside. "Just obey Me without questioning: an absolute fast on any critical statements for this day."

As I pondered this assignment I realized there was an even humorous side to this kind of fast. What did the Lord want to show me?

For the first half of the day, I simply felt a void, almost as if I had been wiped out as a person. This was especially true at lunch with my husband, Len, my mother, son Jeff and my secretary, Jeanne Sevigny, present. Several topics came up (school prayer, abortion, the ERA amendment) about which I had definite opinions. I listened to the others and kept silent. Barbed comments on the tip of my tongue about certain world leaders were suppressed. In our talkative family no one seemed to notice.

Bemused, I noticed that my comments were not missed. The federal government, the judicial system, and the institutional church could apparently get along fine without my penetrating observations. But still I didn't see what this fast on criticism was accomplishing—until mid-afternoon.

For several years I had been praying for one talented young man whose life had gotten sidetracked. Perhaps my prayers for him had been too negative. That afternoon, a specific, positive vision for this life was dropped into my mind with God's unmistakable hallmark on it—joy.

Ideas began to flow in a way I had not experienced in years. Now it was apparent what the Lord wanted me to see. My critical nature had not corrected a single one of the multitudinous things I found fault with. What it *had* done was to stifle my own creativity—in prayer, in relationships, perhaps even in writing—ideas that He wanted to give me.

Last Sunday night in a Bible study group, I told of my Day's Fast experiment. The response was startling. Many admitted that criticalness was the chief problem in their offices, or in their marriages, or with their teenage children.

My own character flaw here is not going to be corrected overnight. But in thinking this problem through the past few days, I find the most solid scriptural basis possible for dealing with it. (The Greek word translated "judge" in King James, becomes "criticize" in Moffatt.)

All through the Sermon on the Mount, Jesus sets Himself squarely against our seeing other people and life situations through this negative lens.

What He is showing me so far can be summed up as follows:

1) A critical spirit focuses us on ourselves and makes us unhappy. We lose perspective and humor.
2) A critical spirit blocks the positive creative thoughts God longs to give us.
3) A critical spirit can prevent good relationships between individuals and often produces retaliatory criticalness.
4) Criticalness blocks the work of the Spirit of God: love, good will, mercy.
5) Whenever we see something genuinely wrong in another person's behavior, rather than criticize him or her directly, or—far worse—gripe about him behind his back, we should ask the Spirit of God to do the correction needed.

Convicted of the true destructiveness of a critical mindset, on my knees I am repeating this prayer: "Lord, I repent of this sin of judgment. I am deeply sorry for having committed so gross an offense against You and against myself so continually. I claim Your promise of forgiveness and seek a new beginning."

# 5

# THOU FOOL

I visited my friend Virginia Lively in Belle Glade, Florida, on Sunday afternoon. Out of several hours of prayer together came—among other things—the conviction that my relationship with and attitude to B—— needs to be corrected by Jesus, especially in the spiritual realm.

This morning, Lord, You brought to my remembrance Your words, "Whosoever shall say to his brother . . . Thou fool, shall be in danger of hell fire" (Matthew 5:22 KJV).

Well, I have certainly been saying that of B——, and thinking it. How clearly I see this now, Lord, as the sin of spiritual and intellectual pride. So I confess this sin of mental and verbal judgment. I ask You to forgive me for my arrogance and to cleanse me. Bring my attitude toward, my every thought of, my every reaction toward, and my every word about or to B—— in line with Your view of her.

Cleanse me of every holier-than-thou stance. Since I am "hidden in Christ," then my opinion of anyone doesn't matter. Only Jesus' opinion matters.

Thank You, Lord, for Your acceptance of this confession. Thank You for Your forgiveness. Thank You for the beginning right now of a new relationship with B——.

Thank You for dealing with her in Your all-seeing love. Thank You for lifting the burden of resentment and judging from me. I *do* feel tons lighter already. Thank You!!

# 6

# Jesus Makes the Decisions

Yesterday I began trying to get back to a real *quiet time* in the early morning. My directive was, "Never mind about reading. Spend the time getting in touch with Jesus directly."

For a couple of days prior to this the Holy Spirit had dropped a curious clause from Scripture into my mind and heart: "And the government shall be upon [Jesus'] shoulder . . ." (Isaiah 9:6 KJV). I had never thought of this in relation to the government of *my* life. Suddenly it spoke volumes to me . . . the responsibility of my life is now His, the burden *He* will carry. He will make the decisions, the right decisions. What a relief: what joy to turn it over to Him.

Yesterday I mostly just asked Him questions, knowing that sooner or later in His time, He will answer them. He well knows my questioning spirit. I don't think He minds that.

Having posed my questions, I left them there, in His hands . . . and felt sweet peace flow into my spirit.

A while ago I was told that I was to refrain from criticism for one month, a fast of the tongue. Now I am directed to extend this curbing of my faultfinding into the thought area.

The Spirit reminded me of Jesus' words, "Sufficient unto the day is the evil thereof." Clearly then, Jesus recognizes the evil all around us in our daily walk. Simply, for the time being, I am not to let my mind dwell there. The Spirit also showed me that the tidiness of my possessions and papers has a direct bearing on my peace on the inside. Rather than let this chore weigh on me as an added pressure, though, I am to let Him direct me *when* to undertake straightening up my things.

# 7

# THE DRY PERIOD

I've been off on a familiar barren road recently and need to get down on paper the steps I took to get back on the main highway. I'm talking about the *dry period.* The state is always much the same for me: shriveled and lonely on the inside. I can't do any writing. I'm unable to accomplish much of anything, just going through the motions of life and barely able to do that. Worst of all—shut off from God.

In her book *Mysticism,* Evelyn Underhill points out that such experiences are a necessary part of the Christian walk.

> For those who have trod the Christian way for some time, a spiritual and psychic fatigue occasionally creeps in and overcomes one. In this state one knows anew the helplessness of us humans. Yet here, for a time, we are in a worse state than at the beginning of our Christian walk. For at that early stage, along with the helplessness, there was the sure and wonderful knowledge of God's adequacy.
>
> Now the skies seem totally deaf; no glorious light breaks through at all. Nothing, inside or outside, seems to work. If one can ride it through on sheer blind faith, just hanging onto the rock of salvation, *then* it has to

pass, and we go on into an advanced state in the spiritual life.

The reason this dry state is necessary, she points out, is that we have to find anew our need, become desperate in a new way, in order to get on with the next stage in our Christian development.

We know that physically and emotionally the developing self advances through a series of growth spurts interspersed with pauses on plateaus. Apparently, the same process holds in the spiritual life.

So the way out of this latest dry period for me began with an admission of my helplessness. And not just a grudging acknowledgment, but a trusting and expectant *acceptance*, relying on Jesus' promise that *His* strength is made perfect in *my* weakness (see 2 Corinthians 12:9).

Next, I was not only to bear this dry and barren stretch of life, but actually to *thank* God for it. My praise to Him lacked enthusiasm at first, but as always the Psalms supplied the words I could not. (Psalms 95, 100, 103 are some of my favorites.) Gradually my cup began to fill and my spirit to loosen.

The last step was to show someone I loved them; in this case it was a visit to a bed-bound neighbor.

Before going back to my writing, I asked the Holy Spirit for specific help in setting up the story sequences in my novel. Soon a wonderful thing began to happen. I could feel my creative nature thrusting down its rootlets in search of the life-giving Water at some deep level in my being. Bit by bit, episode by episode, I watched the lineaments of the story line emerging in my mind. It was as if I could see the bulbs I planted in the ground last fall begin their growth in the cold and the dark. Even the creative process that formed the earth, I reflected, began in *darkness*.

It takes acceptance and praise and outgoing love for me to emerge from a dry period, but, oh, the exhilaration that follows!

# 8

# To Forgive . . . and Forget

This morning I had to face up to the fact that I still had a bad attitude toward a woman who is constantly attacking me and my writings. On taking it to the Lord, I received two insights:

(1) The reason I am so upset is that *I haven't forgiven her completely.* I've made stabs at this in the past, but as she comes to my mind I have an almost physical sensation, as of iron bars pressing against my chest. The Lord showed me that on the other side of these bars was a woman, a human being, who needed to be freed. So, on my knees before Him, I went through a process of unreservedly forgiving her by an act of my will. I confessed my feelings about her and asked God to make the forgiveness real.

(2) My job was not finished, however, He told me, until *I can forget what she has done.*

"But *how can* I do that, Lord?"

*Your will is greater than your memory, Catherine. Rebuke the painful memory and cast it out in the name of Jesus.*

I was to ". . . bring into captivity every thought to the obedience of Christ" (2 Corinthians 10:5 KJV). Then to ask forgiveness for hanging onto these memories (we tend to stab ourselves again and again with old, hurtful episodes), and ask for an alarm system on the door of my mind whenever the memory tries to creep back.

From henceforth I am to look at this woman—*and at anyone else who has ever hurt me*—with eyes of compassion and love, concentrating on the potential they have for good. Only thus will I be able to see them as Jesus does.

"But Lord . . . will this approach bring about changes in them?"

*That's between them and Me. You will have peace.*

9

# THE KEY TO OBEDIENCE

Am struggling this morning with the seeming contradiction between Jesus' constant stress on *obedience* as crucial to Christian growth, over against the reality of "grace," which is the "unmerited favor of God."

Obedience would seem to be our going up the ladder step by step, not earning our way exactly, while continually dependent on still putting forth our own efforts. Whereas the teaching all through the Bible is that it is God who always takes the initiative with us. All of God's good gifts are given by pure grace; there is no way we can deserve a single one of them.

So—exactly where and how does obedience fit into this?

I'm beginning to see that the missing key here is Love. The chief characteristic of love is wanting to do what pleases the beloved. The analogy Jesus used most often was filial love: He meant His relationship to His Father to be the pattern for *our* relationship to Him (Jesus). Jesus' obedience was not the result of gritted teeth and grim determination, but the natural outworking of love: "I do as the Father has commanded me, so that the world may know (be convinced) that I love the Father . . ." (John 14:31 AMPLIFIED).

When we truly love someone, our focus is on *him* or *her*, not on ourselves. And our constant thought is, "What can I do to give this beloved person joy? To please him? To ease his path? To minister to him?"

It staggers my mind to think that I can in any way minister to Jesus, or gladden His heart. Yet this is the gracious message of the Gospel, which always puts the emphasis on love:

> "We love Him, because He first loved us" (1 John 4:19 AMPLIFIED).

God's grace, God's initiative.

> ". . . If a person [really] loves Me, he will keep My word—obey My teaching" (John 14:23 AMPLIFIED).

Our natural, unforced response.

# 10

# Worry: Be Gone

This morning I awoke full of worry about the future, with Len having resigned from his job as editor of *Guideposts*. Len and I were in agreement about this step, and he is enthusiastic about going into book publishing with John and Elizabeth Sherrill, but I see so many obstacles ahead, especially when his salary check stops coming.

Then the Lord directed me to the fourth chapter of Philippians, particularly to verse 8 (AMPLIFIED, italics added):

> . . . whatever is worthy of reverence . . .
> is honorable and seemly . . .
> is just . . .
> is pure . . .
> is lovely and lovable . . .
> is kind and winsome and gracious,
> if there is any
> virtue . . .
> excellence . . .
> anything worthy of praise,
> [we are to] think on
> and weigh
> and take account of these things—
> *fix* your minds on them.

Now this might seem to be the worst kind of not facing reality were it not for the fact that earlier in the same chapter Paul has already exhorted us (v. 6) to pray about *everything*, to pour our hearts out to the Heavenly Father with "definite requests."

My problem is that having done this, having laid my concern before the Father, I get the feeling that if I do not frequently return to it in my mind and keep "worrying" it, much as a dog would a bone, then there certainly can be no chance of solving it. It's a feeling that it would actually be irresponsible or frivolous *not* to do this—wrong to think about other things, and go my merry way while a major problem faces us.

I slip into the worry stance in spite of telling myself over and over that God is the problem-solver, that we can confidently leave our situation in His hands. I know what I should do, yet emotionally and practically I do not act out this letting go. This morning God seems to be pointing out chapter four in Philippians as a blueprint for handling crises His way:

1) Regardless of any circumstances, we are to *rejoice in the Lord always.*
2) We are *not* to fret or have anxiety about *anything.*
3) We are to pray about everything, making our needs and wants known unto God.
4) We are to be content with our earthly lot, whatever it is.
5) We are to guard our thoughts, think only upon upbeat, positive things—nothing negative. If we will do the above, then we are promised:
   a) God's peace . . . shall garrison and mount guard over our hearts and minds in Christ Jesus.
   b) Christ will "infuse inner strength into us"—that is, "We will be self-sufficient in Christ's sufficiency."

*LL Note: God honored our leap of faith into book publishing. Chosen Books, from its inception, produced books that made a major impact on both the Christian and secular world.*

# 11

# HIS PEACE

This morning the Lord asked me to look up the Scripture verse "the things that belong unto thy peace." With the help of a concordance, I found it in Luke 19:41–42 KJV. The scene is a hill overlooking Jerusalem.

> . . . [Jesus] beheld the city, and wept over it, Saying If thou hadst known, even thou, at least in this thy day, the things which belong unto thy peace! but now they are hid from thine eyes.

Lord, what do You want me to understand from this? What are the things that belong to my peace?

Surely, this ties in with the "rest" that was the other message given me this morning.

> There remaineth, therefore, a rest to the people of God. For he that is entered into his rest, he also hath ceased from his own works. . . .
>
> Hebrews 4:9–10 KJV

In the midst of disquiet about so many things in our life right now—my trying to make progress on my novel, the Chosen Books situation in general, my declining eyesight due to cataracts, poor sleep, etc., the message Jesus wants me to have today seems to be simply, "Peace! Rest in Me. I am here to give you, Catherine, the precious gift of peace of mind and spirit."

How glorious! He confirms it in Scripture after Scripture (italics added):

> May grace (God's favor) and *peace* (which is perfect well-being, all necessary good, all spiritual prosperity and freedom from fears and agitating passions and moral conflicts), be multiplied to you. . . .
>
> 2 Peter 1:2 AMPLIFIED

> For though the mountains should depart and the hills be shaken or removed, yet My love and kindness shall not depart from you, nor shall My covenant of peace and completeness be removed, says the Lord, Who has compassion on you.
>
> Isaiah 54:10 AMPLIFIED

Praise You, Lord Jesus! Praise You!!

*The next day* . . .

I discovered yesterday that the beautiful freedom the Lord gave me in His gracious promises of "peace" carried along with it the joy of a moment-by-moment obedience.

That is, during the day I made the discovery that I had departed from the habit of looking directly to Jesus for the answer to small daily decisions; that the only way I will keep a pliable, obedient spirit in the larger decisions, is to look to Him and *to obey* in the smaller ones.

I had slipped badly on that. I'm always getting hung up on the tension, or seeming tension, between freedom in Christ Jesus and obedience.

James, however, makes this connection beautifully:

> But the man who looks intently into the perfect law that gives freedom, and continues to do this, not forgetting what he has heard, but doing it—he will be blessed in what he does.
>
> James 1:25 NIV

Or to approach all this another way. I see that Satan has small chance of getting at us—of accusing us and destroying our rest (as he has with me so often over "small" things like sleeping pills, or the lipstick issue I faced years ago on Cape Cod) when we are faithful in present-moment obedience, steadily looking to Jesus, asking, "Shall I do this? Or not?"—and then obeying.

Thus this obedience *results* in liberty—and the two go hand in hand.

# 12

# IDOLATRY

A couple of days ago Len and I had a heated discussion about the subject matter for the Tuesday evening Bible class and how we were going to teach it. He did not accept—or even understand—what I was saying, and it annoyed me that I could not get my point across.

That night I had a dream in which I was pursued by photographers. Flattered, I allowed them to take a series of pictures. When they appeared in print, I was horrified. The photos were obnoxious, nasty, almost obscene. To my eyes, the pictures clearly said, "She's a big show-off."

Through the dream I believe God was revealing to me my arrogance and self-righteousness about my *opinions*. I saw that this has always been one of my problems with the children, Linda especially. "Love me, love my opinions!" Ideas are very, very important to me, and I consider *my* ideas uncommonly valuable.

How ironic that the very passage over which Len and I disagreed—the giving of the Law to Moses—included as the first Commandment of all: *Thou shalt have no other gods before me* (Exodus 20:3 KJV).

Before bedtime that night I confessed to God and to Len my idolatry of my own passionately held convictions.

# 13

# Self-Denial

Last night at bedtime I ate several pieces of candy, which was wrong from every point of view: pure gratification of self's momentary desire.

This morning I could not worship the Lord. Something was coming between us. Then the Spirit spoke gently, "*Deny yourself* . . . pick up your cross daily and follow Me." It was as if He were putting His finger on the words "Deny yourself." I had never noticed them particularly in that passage. I wasn't even certain those two words were there. So I looked up the verse; they were there all right. I also got illumination on the rest of the passage: "For whoever wants to save his [higher, spiritual, eternal] life, will lose [the lower, natural, temporal life which is lived (only) on earth]" (Mark 8:35 AMPLIFIED).

I saw that Jesus is here simply stating a fact of life. If I want to lose weight, I must give up the lower desire for stuffing my mouth in order to attain the higher desire of a fit, healthy body.

If I want to write a book, I must give up the use of my time for other things.

For the first time I glimpse the rationale of certain spiritual exercises, such as fasting.

Lord, teach me!

# 14

# Self-Denial: The Teaching Goes On

An insight today on how to make the denial of some small pleasure not only less painful but even an almost joyous event.

Up to this point in my life, whenever I've thought I was hearing the Lord's voice telling me to give up something that I loved, I could—and often would—drag my feet for weeks and months. Often I've had to pray the laggard's prayer, "O Lord, make me willing to be made willing." Almost always I've thought of obedience to the Lord as really quite painful.

But now after so many years of my Christian walk, a change is taking place within me. Jesus is becoming much more real to me as a person. I believe that what has been happening to me recently is the beginning of the direct fulfillment of this passage (italics added):

> The person who has My commands and keeps them is the one who [really] loves Me, and whoever [really] loves Me will be loved by My Father. And I [too] will

> love him and *will show* (reveal, manifest) *Myself to him—I will let Myself be clearly seen by him and make Myself real to him.*
>
> John 14:21 AMPLIFIED

For quite a stretch I've been getting the message that Jesus was displeased with my 5:00 to 6:00 P.M. "Happy Hour," a time for relaxed reading or listening to music, when I sip a glass of sherry. At first I thought He wanted me to give up the sherry. Lately I've seen that it isn't so much what He wants me to give up, but that He wants me to be active physically during this hour, to walk or work in the garden. I had let myself become too lazy and sedentary, and too rigid about this 5:00 to 6:00 P.M. pattern. *I* like my ruts. *He* wants me active, and above all, flexible.

Then He began teaching me about *how* He goes about changing long-standing habits. It's part of the outworking of the great promise,

> This is the covenant which I will make with the house of Israel after those days, says the Lord: I will put my law . . . upon their hearts; and I will be their God, and they shall be my people.
>
> Jeremiah 31:33 RSV

I had never before tied this promise to the problems connected with habit changing. I have no addiction to alcohol or smoking, or sweets, for instance, but I ache for certain persons I know who do. I see now how He helps us with these ingrained patterns when we ask Him for help. What happens is that *our* tastes begin to change. Something that we liked a lot suddenly is not so appealing. When we understand *how* He works and that this *is* the Lord Himself working, then we can stop resisting our own changing tastes, thank Him, and flow with the new direction of the tide.

It's a marvelous plan only He could have thought of, for there is no pain in ceasing to do what we no longer care to do.

# 15

# THE TEMPTATION OF THINGS

I've been through a small siege of temptation to worldliness that I'm almost embarrassed to write about—and yet feel I should.

From the time I was a small girl I've loved pretty, feminine things, especially jewelry. Nothing very unusual or terribly wrong about that. For most of my life I could not afford jewelry, so it was no issue.

Even when in recent years I could afford some jewelry, the Depression syndrome that permeated my family for many years has kept me frugal. One day a check for several hundred dollars arrived that I hadn't expected. "Now I can get those gold earrings," I said to myself.

So I began making trips to jewelry stores looking for the exactly right earrings. Then an inner restlessness began to ruffle me. So I started to argue with God.

"Lord, are You telling me that earrings are too frivolous?"

Silence.

"It isn't as though I'm buying them from my tithe funds. I mean, the money is extra. I hadn't expected it."

Silence.

"Lord, I've spent much more for a rug or a piece of furniture without this guilt complex. Now, really, isn't this inner disquiet just my Puritan, Depression-born complex?"

Then came the gentle response:

*I'm concerned over the inordinate amount of time you've given to this in your thought life.*

At once I was led to the apostle John's comment on worldliness and his warning about the "delight of the eyes":

> Do not love or cherish the world or the things that are in the world. If any one loves the world, love for the Father is not in him.
>
> For all that is in the world, the lust of the flesh [craving for sensual gratification], and the lust of the eyes [greedy longings of the mind] and the pride of life [assurance in one's own resources or in the stability of earthly things]—these do not come from the Father but from the world [itself].
>
> And the world passes away and disappears . . .
>
> 1 John 2:15–17 AMPLIFIED

Here John is taking us into the higher reaches of spirituality. He doesn't use the word "sin"; he doesn't mention Satan. He's concerned with whether we realize the extent of God's love for us—and how much love for God there is in us.

The crux of it: the love exchange between God and me is going to suffer if I focus too much on worldly things.

16

# Fear of Man

The Lord is having me look at something this morning that is very unsettling. It came first through the following verse:

> The fear of man bringeth a snare: but whoso putteth his trust in the Lord shall be safe.
>
> Proverbs 29:25 KJV

I don't fear man in a physical way, but do I fear his disapproval of me? In other words, how much do I try to please other people instead of looking to God alone for His approval? Certainly, there is enormous pressure on all of us to be accepted and approved by others. But God wants us to resist this pressure. Consider the tragedy of the religious leaders of Jesus' day:

> Among the chief rulers also many believed on him; but because of the Pharisees they did not confess him, lest they should be put out of the synagogue: For they loved the praise of men more than the praise of God.
>
> John 12:42–43 KJV

Even Peter, soon to be leader of the earliest church, denied knowing Jesus at all following His arrest, simply to remain in the good graces of a motley crowd gathered around a bonfire. Peter was no coward. When the soldiers had come to seize Jesus, he had grabbed a sword and cut off the ear of one of them. So it wasn't his life Peter feared for here, but the ridicule and judgment and opinions of others.

We are told that in our daily task—whatever our vocation or profession or daily round—we are to seek to please God more than man:

> Servants, obey in all things your masters according to the flesh; not with eyeservice, as menpleasers; but in singleness of heart, fearing God.
>
> Colossians 3:22 KJV

The thought comes that my tendency to be critical of others springs out of the soil of what-people-will-think. What we are, we see in others. I am judgmental, therefore I expect others to be the same.

Jesus was simply stating a law of life when He told us, ". . . judge [and] ye shall be judged: and with what measure ye mete, it shall be measured to you" (Matthew 7:2 KJV). Put this way, judging others constantly cultivates more soil for the thistles of fear-of-man to grow in.

Judgmentalism is an attempt to ward off this fear by standing in a superior place. Self thinks that when it can get there first and judge before others can state their opinions, it can forestall others' criticisms. Of course, self is mistaken, since the very opposite happens—judging draws the judgment of others.

Two passages of Scripture, personalized for this specific fear, are helping me overcome my exaggerated concern for man's approval:

Fear not [the opinions of others]: for I have redeemed thee; I have called thee by thy name; thou art mine.

Isaiah 43:1 KJV

When thou passest through the waters [of ridicule], I will be with thee; and through the rivers [of rejection], they shall not overflow thee: when thou walkest through the fire [of contempt], thou shalt not be burned; neither shall the flame kindle upon thee.

Isaiah 43:2 KJV

# 17

# Immersed in a Horse Trough

I want to get down in my journal the fascinating experience Len and I had this past weekend. At the urging of our friend Virginia Lively we drove to Clewiston, Florida, about sixty miles from our home here in Boynton Beach. Virginia had gone through what she called a "believer's baptism" in the Episcopal church there. She described it as "a beautiful, cleansing, and healing experience" and urged us to consider doing it.

For months now I have read with fascination about the Jesus people, a California phenomenon. Most seem to be young, former members of the drug culture, who, after a "believer's baptism" in the Pacific Ocean, experience an almost total change of lifestyle.

Virginia's conviction was that every Christian should have the opportunity of undergoing baptism *following* his or her personal decision for Christ. She had been baptized as a very young child in her own Episcopal church and had accepted this sacrament as valid, but she believes that, ideally, we should be "dedicated" to God as babies, then have a "water baptism" later when we are ready to accept Jesus on our own.

I spent a morning digging out Scripture references to baptism, coming on one archetype I'd never noticed:

> For Christ . . . was put to death in the body but made alive by the Spirit, through whom also he went and preached to the spirits in prison who disobeyed long ago when God waited patiently in the days of Noah while the ark was being built. In it only a few people, eight in all, were saved through water, and this water symbolizes baptism that now saves you also—not the removal of dirt from the body but the pledge of a good conscience toward God . . .
>
> 1 Peter 3:18–21 NIV

Since the subject of baptism has always divided Christians, at first Len and I felt a certain wariness about accepting Virginia's invitation. Then John and Elizabeth (Tib) Sherrill (our close friends and associates at *Guideposts* magazine) arrived for a visit and expressed interest. All four of us had been baptized as infants, long before we could remember. We were convinced that the performance of this sacrament on our behalfs had been complete and theologically adequate in every way. We all agreed, however, that we didn't want to miss anything that the Lord might have for us right now. The Sherrills, LeSourds, my friend Freddie Koch, and her daughter Claudia drove from our home in Boynton Beach last Saturday for a spiritual adventure. In Clewiston we located the home of the Episcopal rector. Virginia Lively had arrived there a few minutes earlier.

The first thing that happened was between John Sherrill and me. Our relationship had become strained through some theological differences. While we sat together in the rector's living room, John began speaking about his fear of change. Twice when there had been major upheavals in his life he had developed cancer. He confessed apprehension of a recurrence in the face of upcoming changes in his and Tib's situation.

At Virginia's urging, he recollected his childhood and talked about the little-boy John—skinny, non-athletic, not popular with the "in" crowd—and tears filled my eyes. How I identified with him there. A new love for John filled me and I went over and hugged him. The reconciliation was complete and almost instantaneous.

Next we went to the nearby Episcopal church, a small sanctuary set in a grove of Florida pine trees. In the vestibule of the church had been placed a galvanized iron horse trough, the stickers from the feed store still visible on one end. A hose, connected to a water spigot outside, ran through the open screen door and was filling the trough. This was to be the setting for the baptism.

First, we sat down in the sanctuary and sang some appropriate hymns. The Episcopal priest, in slacks and sports shirt, prayed, then explained the significance of a believer's baptism: that it was not necessary for salvation, but an opportunity for confession, asking and receiving forgiveness, then making a new commitment of our lives to Jesus. This would open us to a fresh infusion of the Holy Spirit with the resulting new love and joy and power that comes when Jesus indwells us.

As we changed into bathing suits, each of us pondered the areas in our lives where confession and forgiveness were needed. This was done quietly with God, with our spouses, or openly with the rector. The Sherrills led the way, first Tib, then John being immersed.

Afterwards John said softly to Tibby, "Now that we have left our old persons at the bottom of the horse trough and are new creatures, don't you think we ought to get married again?"

The two of them, barefoot, water dripping from their hair and bathing suits, stood before the altar, pledging themselves to one another again. Len and I followed . . . into the horse trough and then to the altar for a reaffirmation of our marriage vows, our eyes brimming with tears.

The next morning, after we got home, we found just outside our front door an elaborate "Just Married" sign which Claudia Koch—who had been wide-eyed during the ceremonies—had made and sometime during the night left at our door.

# Section Four

# His Strength in Our Weakness

*At one point during our courtship, Catherine voiced a concern over her health, saying she doubted that she had more than five years to live. I "pooh-poohed" this, pointing to her own mother's robust health at age sixty-seven.*

*Both of us were wrong. Catherine lived twenty-three years more, but her death at sixty-nine was far short of her mother's life span (Mother Wood is now ninety-four).*

*And for all of those twenty-three years Catherine battled a debilitating emphysema that sapped her energy and sometimes left her gasping for breath after even so simple an exertion as climbing a flight of stairs. New York winters brought on severe bronchitis. Our move to Boynton Beach, Florida, doubtless prolonged her life, but it did not solve her health problems. Along the way she won a battle over sleeping pills—until her last years when sleeplessness once more turned her nights into a spiritual battleground.*

*Prayers for Catherine's healing throughout our marriage lifted her, strengthened her, but never totally healed her. "Why?" she asked over and over. The enigma of why some are healed, some are not, frustrated Catherine all her life.*

*But she never stopped struggling for answers. And out of the struggle came—not the robust health she yearned for, but a daily, growing intimacy with God that became far more precious than any amount of physical stamina. Her constant companion on this closer walk . . . the Bible.*

*LL*

# 1

# TRUSTING GOD

Today this verse in Psalm 37 spoke to me:

> Commit your way to the Lord—roll and repose [each care of] your load on Him; trust (lean on, rely on and be confident) also in Him, and He will bring it to pass.
>
> Psalm 37:5 AMPLIFIED

This is my husband Len's favorite verse of the entire Bible. He has leaned on this passage in recent years while making the switch from editing a magazine to publishing Christian books.

There is much in Scripture stressing our need to have faith in God. The above verse takes us a step further. It not only admonishes us to trust, it promises that when we do, God will act in a supernatural way to answer our need. Dwell on that for a moment. We trust, God acts. A mind-blowing premise.

Yet total, all-out trust on our part is not as easy as it first seems. There are periods when God's face is shrouded, when His dealings with us will *appear* as if He does not care, when He seems not to be acting like a true Father. Can we then hang onto the fact of His love and His faithfulness and that He *is* a prayer-answering God?

Can we get to the point Habakkuk reached: "Though the fig tree does not blossom, and there be no fruit on the vines . . . Yet I will rejoice in the Lord . . . !" (Habakkuk 3:17–18 AMPLIFIED).

Can we, *at the moment* when His face is hidden, exult in the God of our salvation? "The Lord God is my strength, my personal bravery and my invincible army" (v. 19).

Last Saturday morning Len had a chance to demonstrate the principle of trust in a difficult situation. He awoke with a very bad throat condition; could hardly speak. Yet he was supposed to give a talk that morning at a men's prayer breakfast in the local Lutheran church.

Before he left for the church I anointed him with oil, placed my hand on his throat, and asked the Lord to do a healing work in Len for the glory of God.

During the breakfast preceding Len's speech, however, he told me later, his voice got worse and worse until there was little left but a croak. The Lutheran pastor suggested turning the gathering into a discussion group, giving Len the chance to bow out. But no, my husband would at least try.

So Len stood up and uttered a rasping, halting first sentence, literally plunging ahead on faith. Suddenly, he reported afterwards, his voice cleared. From then on, for thirty-odd minutes, the message poured out with no cough, hardly even a clearing of the throat. The Holy Spirit had simply taken over. In the question period afterwards, still no problem with his throat.

But when he returned home, Len's voice was once again a painful whisper.

What fascinated me in this episode is how biblical it is: as the symptoms get worse, the temptation is there to "give up" and not to trust Jesus. We must resist that temptation in the midst of our very real human helplessness, "roll" the entire burden onto His shoulders, as He bade us do, step out and *take the first step* with bare, no-evidence-at-all faith.

And lo, He does take over gloriously, doing what we literally cannot do for ourselves.

2

# LORD, I RESENT . . .

> Thank [God] in everything—no matter what the circumstances may be, be thankful and give thanks; for this is the will of God for you [who are] in Christ Jesus . . .
>
> 1 Thessalonians 5:18 AMPLIFIED

Yesterday morning in my prayer time, God showed me that if I wanted more vitality for my work hours, I had to deal with the following resentments that were smoldering inside me.

I resent my lack of social graces in certain situations, which I'm inclined to blame on my childhood years when I too often fled social encounters.

I resent the fact that I'm such a poor sleeper. I can see that resentment produces tension and, of course, accumulated tension through the day is one reason I'm not sleeping better.

Here at Evergreen Farm there are so many stairs to climb, and outside, hills and more hills, which I cannot mount because of my breathlessness. This condition is a constant embarrassment and the central thorn in my flesh. I resent my damaged lungs.

I see this morning that there are deeper resentments still: that of creeping old age, being progressively shut down, as it were, and, of course, out there—death. Have I not always resented the fact of death, even though I have total belief in and expectancy about the life after death?

How can I come to terms with all this?

The answer came in the above verse. I am to praise God for *all* things, regardless of where they seem to originate. Doing this, He points out, is the key to receiving the blessings of God. Praise will wash away my resentments. I've known this, accepted it, even written about praise. But as I began praising Him yesterday, my efforts were wooden.

Then came these thoughts: I was to ignore my feelings and act on the principle. I was to do it despite the lack of joy—simply because God told me to. True praise grows out of the recognition and acknowledgment that in His time God will bring good out of bad. There is the intolerable situation on the one hand and the fulfillment of Romans 8:28 on the other hand. ("All things work together for good. . . .") By an act of will and through imagination and with faith, I am to turn my back on the bad and face the good, and begin actively to praise God for it as Scripture commands.

Shortly after this insight, my cleaning woman called in to say that she was not coming. Praised God for this, though mechanically.

Following that, joy began spilling over into the tiny everydayness of my life. Walked by a vase of beautiful roses from our garden and buried my nose in the fragrance, saying, "Praise You, Lord, for such beauty!"

Stepped onto our patio for a moment to listen to the birds singing. "Praise You, Lord, for all Your creatures."

Then came the feeling that all these small acts put together—little trickles of praise—were running together, beginning to form a river of praise.

Continued to praise God for *all* things, good and bad. All setbacks, frustrations, and resentments.

Praise You, Lord, for my awkwardness in certain social situations.

Praise You, Lord, that I have trouble sleeping.

Praise You, Lord, for my weak lungs.

Praise You, Lord, for creeping old age.

Praise You, Lord, for the death that comes to all of us.

This morning I actually woke up with praise swelling in my heart. Only later did I realize I had slept through the entire night! Cannot remember when I last did this! Awakened by the coffee pot going on. Imagine! Praise God indeed!

# 3

# Do I Really Want to Get Well?

My heart is heavy this morning as I think of Rosalind. She is almost bedridden now with asthma. We went to pray for her healing yesterday, but she was more interested in talking about her ailments than in receiving Christ's love and power. How tragic!

This morning I turned again to the Gospel of John for the story of the man at the Pool of Bethesda who had been ill for thirty-eight years. As I read, I pretended I was there in Jerusalem myself, watching in the shadow of one of those great arched colonnades around the long pool. I could shut my eyes and see the scene as if it were happening today.

The man in this account is a chronic invalid, probably in his fifties or sixties. The stone floor around the large pool is crowded with the pallets of the crippled and the blind. But this man has been there longer than any. He is now the old-timer; his illness has virtually become his career and status symbol.

Now Jesus appears, threading His way through the porticos. He looks into the eyes of the sick man: "Do you want to become well?" (John 5:6 AMPLIFIED).

It seems a ridiculous question on the surface. Wouldn't anyone want to be healed of a physical handicap? But surprisingly the invalid begins to stammer excuses.

"Sir," he replies to Jesus, "it's just that I haven't anybody to put me into the pool when the angel of healing is present. While I'm trying to get there, somebody else always gets into the water first."

As I read these words I knew that this sick man's problem was Rosalind's problem too. He thought he wanted healing, but even to his own ears his rationalizations must sound hollow. Yet those amazing eyes boring into his hold no contempt. Rather, Jesus issues a loving directive in a voice that rings with authority. "Pick up your bed and walk."

This is the moment of truth. I could picture the emotions moving across the pinched features: surprise, consternation, doubt, awareness, hope, then resolution. The man scrambles to his feet, picks up his bedroll, a well man.

How much this story says to me every time I read it—and can say to anyone who finds his fervent petitions unanswered. The principle here is: True prayer is dominant desire. If the person is divided in his real yearnings, he will experience emptiness and frustration.

I still remember vividly the three years in the 1940s when I myself was bedridden. Little by little I had come to enjoy my quiet life. I thought that I yearned for healing, but in fact I was not ready to shoulder the full responsibilities of vigorous health.

Only when I asked the Lord to mend my inner confusion was I able to go all-out in prayer. The healing of my physical disability followed.

Since that experience, I have been able to perceive this divided self as a major stumbling block to many people. I think of my friend in Washington, Jessie, who had been praying long and hard for her husband to be healed of alcoholism. Jessie was spiritually minded, her husband worldly and cynical. He was contemptuous of his wife's frequent trips to retreats and church meetings.

Several of us met regularly to pray with Jessie that her husband would encounter the living Christ for himself. Thanks to a group of vital Christian men, this came about, gloriously. John became a recovered alcoholic and a changed man.

The surprise was Jessie's reaction. Her criticism of John continued unabated. For the first time we, her friends, suspected the divided will in Jessie. Our suspicions were confirmed one night when one of the women suggested that Jessie thank God for so great an answer to our prayers for John.

Jessie could not do it. The words would not come. Then we understood. For years Jessie's prayers for John had gone unanswered because she had enjoyed standing above John on her pedestal marked "spiritual." Admired by friends for her suffering and patience with an alcoholic husband, she came to enjoy her martyr role. Therefore, the unsuspected desire of her deepest being had canceled out the prayer of her lips for John's conversion. Only when she was able to see this divided self and surrender it to God was she able to work out a better relationship with her husband.

It is so clear to me this morning. The divided self can defeat us in every area. Like finding the right job. When we hear the job-seeker insist on a string of specific conditions regarding salary, hours, pension, geographic location—we will often find a cleavage in his aspirations.

Fortunately, there is something we can do about the contradictions inside us.

First, we can present our long-standing, unanswered prayers to God for analysis. If there is any division of will deep inside, He will put His finger on it. This will hurt. We will be shocked—even as the man at the pool was, even as Jessie was.

Second, we can acknowledge this inner inconsistency and present it, without cringing or making excuses, to

God for healing, asking Him to bring our conscious and subconscious minds into harmony. At this point He will almost always issue us a directive as Jesus did the man at the poolside. He asks that we prove our wholeheartedness by obedience. The moment that we rise to obey Him, we discover a great fact: that the word of God and the work of God are one. His words *are* life—with power to restore the atrophied will, to quicken pallid desire, to resurrect us from the graveclothes of a half-dead existence.

# 4

# To Live in the Present Moment

I want to record this morning that I did something yesterday, November 5, 1978, I do too seldom. For a period of time I lived fully in the present moment. What a healing this was for my spirit.

It happened in church. Six members of our family were sitting in the same pew.

Beside me was my tall son Peter, then his beautiful wife, Edith, and their two children, Mary Elizabeth and Peter Jonathan; on my other side, Len—so faithful, so solid. And we were all healthy and together and of one mind in the Lord. Great surges of gratitude washed over me and I was happier than I have been in a long time.

The Spirit seemed to say, "Bask in the moment. No matter that the future may hold problems. This is yours."

I did bask. It was golden.

My thankfulness flowed beyond the church walls. I thanked Him for my mother—now eighty-seven—who is still with us with her serene, cheerful disposition. How blessed I am, Lord, to have had You choose such a woman to bear me! I thank You for her lifelong gentleness . . . her womanliness, her unwavering faithfulness, her vision that always could lift our dreams on wings and send them flying beyond drudgery or mundane circumstances.

And for Len's three children, grown now, all Christians, each on the right path to his or her own fulfillment. How grateful I am for what they have taught me.

At that beautiful moment God seemed to be shining a light on each member of my family, saying, "See what I have wrought. Enjoy them, be thankful for them, for everything I make is good."

And my response this morning is to thank Him and praise Him in these words I find in His book:

> Give thanks to the Lord, for he is good; his love endures forever.
>
> Psalm 107:1 NIV

> O Lord my God, you are very great; you are clothed with splendor and majesty.
>
> Psalm 104:1 NIV

> Shout for joy to the Lord, all the earth. Worship the Lord with gladness; come before him with joyful songs. . . . Enter his gates with thanksgiving and his courts with praise; give thanks to him and praise his name.
>
> Psalm 100:1–2, 4 NIV

> Thanks be to God! He gives us the victory through our Lord Jesus Christ.
>
> 1 Corinthians 15:57 NIV

# 5

# Helplessness

When I was still not asleep last night about 1:00 A.M., I swallowed one mild sleeping pill. No sleep! At five minutes to three, feeling empty, I got up, went to the kitchen, ate two Ritz crackers with peanut butter, drank a paper cup full of milk, and went back to bed.

Still no sleep! About 4:00 A.M., I took a second sleeping pill. It had no effect at all. I saw dawn break and finally got up.

I got down on my knees and prayed something like, "Lord, You have promised to talk to Your friends. Would you tell me what this is all about?"

I drank a cup of coffee in bed, had my quiet time—Bible reading, etc. No answer from Him. Dead silence.

Got down on my knees again and prayed. No response.

Or . . . was I simply not listening to the message He was speaking? As I was dressing, light began to dawn: He wants to demonstrate to me that I really am helpless without Him, that I really am dependent on Him *even for the sleeping pills to work.* Jesus put it this way:

> Apart from Me—cut off from vital union with Me—you can do nothing.
>
> John 15:5 AMPLIFIED

Since I am stubborn, He has been forced to bring this oh, so-very-basic truth home to me the hard way.

It was on the subject of sleep—the subject *I* wanted to know about—that He was silent. He did not promise me a thing, not that I would sleep beautifully without the sleeping pills, nor that I would sleep *with* them, this afternoon or tonight; nothing. Apparently, He wants me to place this whole area trustingly into His hands, believing that He loves me and wants me to be full of the vitality that comes from adequate sleep. Total dependence, that's the all-important lesson He wants me to learn. For regardless of what I do or do not do, whether I'm in a period of trusting Him or of pulling away, *He* never forgets that I belong to Him, that my life has been paid for with a price. *He* never lets me go!

This is such a *tremendous* base fact to know and to build on and to lean on.

Praise God for this tough experience!

# 6

# Spiritual Preparation for Surgery

This morning I can look back over the past weeks and see so clearly how God works in adversity. It began over a month ago with the doctor's words, "You're going to need surgery. . . ."

The procedure was "routine," he assured me, the problem most likely "minor," but no casual approach could soften the impact of the next sentence: "Of course, we never know what we'll find." Statistics on cancer then followed. "With this type of ovarian cyst, the percentage of malignancy is . . ."

Thus began a month's battle with fear. As I drove home from the doctor's office that beautiful September afternoon, the brilliant color of the autumn leaves seemed tarnished. How is it, I marveled, that bad news has a way of invading human life so suddenly? Trouble rings no warning bells. Adversity and sorrow stalk into life on rubber soles.

"Fear is lack of faith," I told myself. "It dishonors God." But then I discovered that I could not handle fear any more than I could mastermind any other strong emotion.

As Len and I talked over my situation, our first reaction was the very human one: "Is this operation really necessary?" However "routine" such surgery might be for the doctor, my inadequate lungs make any use of anesthesia a questionable risk. On the medical level, a second opinion seemed the wise course. We pursued this; the second examination confirmed the first.

Next came our conviction that we needed to pose the same question in prayer: "Lord, what is Your will? Do You want to handle my case through prayer alone?"

After all, Scripture provides clear directives and means of grace, which we ignore to our own detriment. From James 5:13–15: prayer with a group of fellow Christians, followed by the laying on of hands and/or anointing with oil by church elders or spiritual leaders. From 1 Corinthians 11:23–30: prayer at the altar rail of a church by a priest or pastor, with the laying on of hands and/or Communion.

How wonderful it is when God wants to move in this direct manner, and the way is clear for Him to do so! This is what happened to John Sherrill back in 1960 when a suspicious lump was discovered in John's neck and an operation scheduled to remove it. Since a melanoma cancer had been surgically removed from his ear two years before, John asked his rector for the ancient laying-on-of-hands ministry of the Episcopal Church.

Twenty-four hours later, when the famous cancer specialist at New York's Memorial Hospital operated, all he could find was a tiny, dried-up nodule. No lump, no malignancy. I know of other instances equally dramatic, where God has chosen to heal without medical intervention.

In my case, a group of fellow Christians began to meet with Len and me for prayer at 7:30 each morning. My crisis was their crisis. After two weeks in which we sought God's healing, I went for still one more examination. The doctor found no change. More intensive prayer followed; with it came the assurance that I was to go ahead with the operation, that my lungs would withstand the strain, and that there would be no cancer.

Apparently this was one of those times when God wishes us to make use of the skilled hands of surgeons. (God may have other purposes too, of course, such as some personal contact in the hospital He wishes us to make for Him.)

The next step in preparation came over the long-distance telephone from a Christian physician in North Carolina. "Over several years," he told me, "I have seen an incredible difference in the patient's post-operative condition between those who saturate surgery with prayer and those who don't. Most anyone facing surgery has fears. We can't just will them away. But God can handle our fears.

"Another thing," he went on. "Those undergirded with prayer often escape sticky little complications and just sail through the recovery. They even heal faster."

What helped me most of all during those long hours the night before the operation were two Scripture verses. The first promise spoke to fear:

> Fear not; [there is nothing to fear]. . . . For I, the Lord your God, hold your right hand; I, Who say to you, Fear not, I will help you!
>
> Isaiah 41:10, 13 AMPLIFIED

The second Scripture was a promise from the Psalms:

> Though I walk in the midst of trouble, thou wilt revive me . . . thy right hand shall save me.
>
> Psalm 138:7 KJV

As I read these reassuring words, a clear picture was dropped into my mind, childlike in its simplicity: the Lord would be standing on the right side of the operating table, facing me, looking into my eyes.

*Of course.* He would have to be in that position since the Isaiah promise was that He would hold my right hand, and the promise from the Psalms was that by *His* right hand, He would save me. *How beautiful!* I thought.

At ten minutes to eight the next morning, Len and our daughter, Linda, who had flown down from Washington, arrived at my hospital room just as an orderly appeared to roll me to the operating room.

"A quick prayer," Len said. He had no sooner said, "Amen" than the telephone rang. It was our dear friend, the Reverend Joe Bishop. "I can't believe this split-second timing," I told him. "The orderly is here to take me to surgery."

"Then time for one more prayer," Joe said. His loving benediction was all around us as we left the room.

All through the corridors Len and Linda walked beside the stretcher, right up to the anteroom.

As I was wheeled into the operating room I was given a beautiful three-part promise, one from each Person of the Trinity:

God the Father would hold me in His everlasting arms.
Jesus would take my right hand in His.
From the moment I lost consciousness, the Holy Spirit would be my Breath of life.

After that, suddenly I found that fear was nowhere around.

*LL Note: The cyst was benign. Catherine had a recovery as swift and uneventful as the North Carolina doctor predicted.*

# 7

# My Yoke Is Easy

For many years I have pondered the following words of Jesus, wanting to bear them out in my life, repeatedly falling short:

> Come to Me, all you who labor and are heavy-laden and over burdened, and I will cause you to rest—I will ease and relieve and refresh your souls.
>
> Take My yoke upon you, and learn of Me; for I am gentle (meek) and humble (lowly) in heart, and you will find rest—relief, ease and refreshment and recreation and blessed quiet—for your souls.
>
> For My yoke is wholesome (useful, good)—not harsh, hard, sharp or pressing, but comfortable, gracious and pleasant; and My burden is light and easy to be borne.
>
> Matthew 11:28–30 AMPLIFIED

Then at age sixty-five I was given a whole new perception of these verses through my friend, Roberta Dorr, author of the novel *Bathsheba*. During a visit at our home, she told me of the miracle-healing of her doctor-husband from supposedly incurable Hodgkins disease.

The diagnosis was made while her husband, David, was still in surgical residency. Having a laid-back temperament, David accepted the verdict of a very limited life span and went about his work.

But Roberta has a different nature—always seeking to understand, always questioning, always a fighter. She resisted the idea of losing her beloved husband and seeing their three small children grow up without a father. She and her husband had just filled out the final papers and were ready for an appointment to a hospital in Africa when the diagnosis was made final. Why, she asked over and over, had this happened?

No answer came. Until at last, with total relinquishment she asked God the right question, "How do You want me to pray about my husband?"

One morning shortly afterward, this thought was planted in her mind: "Pray that your husband will be able to *use* for the good of others the medical training he has been given."

As soon as Roberta prayed *this* prayer, the tremendous burden lifted from her heart. She had discovered that the yoke Jesus offered really did bring peace; by praying *His* prayer, sharing with Him His concern for all of suffering humanity, she was able to repose her load on His great strength. One year later the doctors at Johns Hopkins were astonished during a periodic test to discover no trace of disease in David. They were frank to say that they did not understand what had happened. Three years later, they dismissed him entirely, still unable to explain it. The disease never reappeared, but during the four years of "waiting," David completed a surgical residency that was to change his life. Instead of going to Africa, he went to the Gaza Strip where he was desperately needed as a surgeon.

It was while the Dorrs were on a medical mission to the Middle East that Roberta had further illumination about what it means to be yoked together with Jesus. (The Dorrs spent a total of seventeen years in Yemen and

Gaza.) Perhaps seeing double-yoked oxen working the fields helped bring the truth home to her.

Roberta had always thought of these verses in Matthew as a metaphor of Jesus helping her with *her* projects, *her* life—plowing *her* field, so to speak.

Then one day the Lord said to her something like this: "No, you have it all wrong—backwards. Drop your plans. At the beginning of each day simply ask to be yoked with Me for *My* work, to plow *My* field. Then you will find that the yoke fits perfectly and that the burden truly is light."

I've thought a lot about Roberta's experience. First, David's healing. Did it happen in part because David was so involved in ministering to other people that he didn't have time to dwell on his own illness? Did he not only find refreshment in serving his Lord, but healing as well?

Not the whole answer, of course, but a clue toward that great mystery of how and why miraculous healings take place.

Second, there's much for me to ponder about the injunction Roberta received to "drop her plans" and listen for God's plan for her.

Again I'm back to relinquishment. Time after time I've laid my concerns, questions, doubts, plans, on God's altar. The problem for me is leaving them there.

At age sixty-five I still have that determination to take charge of my life, to prove that I can still do everything I did when I was twenty. I still want God to applaud my good works. It's so ridiculous! No wonder I have trouble sleeping and breathing.

Meanwhile, God waits patiently for me to come to Him, forgetting my agenda, so that I can hear what He has in mind for me.

Is it possible for an opinionated woman in her autumn years to become like a child and sit at the feet of Jesus with one idea—to hear what He will say?

8

# The Joy of the Lord Shall Be Your Strength

For weeks now I have been so discouraged about the quality of my writing that I wonder if I am capable of doing another novel. Is *Christy* to be the only one?

The new novel I've been working on is set in western Pennsylvania during the 1930s. So far it seems lifeless. The characters aren't real to me yet.

Yesterday was the low point as I struggled to get words on paper. I had a mental picture of myself as a lost, crying sheep at the bottom of a very deep pit. Then with startling clarity these words of Jesus flooded my thinking:

> I tell you the truth, I am the gate for the sheep . . . whoever enters through me will be saved. He will come in and go out, and find pasture.
>
> John 10:7–9 NIV

How like Jesus to rescue people like me, not because we have done, or are currently doing, one solitary thing to deserve it. I sought Him and last night He reached down and, with His shepherd's crook, physically and spiritually lifted me out of the pit. Today He is comforting me even as He puts renewed strength into me.

It happened through a dream, fragments of which remained in my mind upon awakening.

In the dream I had a basket in my hands decorated around the rim and sides with flowers and leaves. I was having to "redo" the decorations. As I took off the old ones I was surprised to find how easy they were to remove. But there was an even greater surprise: I *expected* the flowers to be artificial ones, but found them not only real flowers, but surprisingly fresh.

When I awoke there was a joy and a release springing from deep in my spirit and my heart was full of praise.

The message of the dream appeared to be not only my own readiness to begin work on the novel again, but even divine approval of the timing. And the ease with which the bunches of flowers were removed from the basket and the fact that they were *fresh*, seemed to say, "The task of revision will not be as difficult as you have thought, and you will find the material fresh."

I have long known that my writing is never truly on target unless I feel at some point, while in the process of getting words on paper, that certain hallmark of joy within. The scene I am attempting to write may be quite a serious one, but the touchstone of joy must be there—or else I'm working in my own strength, not His.

It will take a little while to turn around a habit of negative thinking about this book—but Jesus is beginning to do that for me this morning. In fact, He who *always* gives to us "more abundantly than we could ask or think" has given me a glimpse of *His* vision for this novel.

I had been realizing the last few days, as I have been doing a quick rereading of the words already written, that I am at the same point in this book I was with *A Man Called Peter* when I received the devastating critique: "You haven't yet gotten *inside* the man Peter."

It was after I fell into a pit of discouragement over that remark that God told me, "No man's life has ultimate significance apart from what that man's life shows about God." So I re-outlined Peter's story *that* way.

Now God is telling me to think of the novel like this: We are living in a time when evil and trouble seem rampant. Every person I know has *trouble* of some kind.

So I am to separate the strands of the different kinds of trouble in the novel, and see what God's solution is to each one. For instance, we have

Economic trouble—I am writing of the Depression times, the 30s.

Emotional depression—Ken, the father, with his conviction that he is a failure.

Ecological trouble—powerful financial interests ignore environmental danger signs.

Natural disaster—the final flood. What is God saying here? To us today?

I'm going to have to listen to the Inner Voice *very* carefully to "get" all this, but praise God, oh, how I praise Him for this revelation! For He is saying, "Yes, yes, of *course* I want you to write this book. Yes, yes, it has an important message for our time."

Oh, thank You, Lord. Thank You for the return of joy to my life!

# 9

# THE INTERCESSORS

Yesterday this Scriptural passage seemed to leap out at me:

> And he [the Lord] saw that there was no man, and wondered that there was no intercessor. . . .
>
> Isaiah 59:16 KJV

Then came a rather startling bit of guidance from the Lord (I want to check this out with others). He seemed to be asking me to set up an intercession ministry that would consist chiefly of people with the desire and the faith to pray for others, and the time to devote to it—like many of the elderly, or handicapped, or those who earnestly want to be used by God but can't figure out *how* to be useful within the limitations of family demands, geographical location, etc.

To these intercessors would be forwarded the letters and requests we receive from those who need prayer—with names removed, of course—to whom it could mean everything to know that other people are lifting them up. My conscience hurts me when people write for prayer and I can give so little time to each one, for there are so many.

It would mean an incredible job of collation and feedback, a lot of postage, probably a newsletter with real input on the subject of intercessory prayer. Since this is a phase of prayer about which I know least, I'm surprised the Lord would lay this upon me.

*LL Note: This was Catherine's first journal notation (June 1, 1980) about intercessory prayer; her guidance grew stronger with the passing weeks. From this single verse in Isaiah has grown the Intercessors prayer movement, launched in the fall of 1980 as a part of the nonprofit organization Breakthrough, Inc. (Lincoln, Virginia 22078). As of April 1, 1986, there were 1500 intercessors enrolled to handle the thousands of prayer requests received each year. The newsletter (put out eight times a year) was being mailed to 12,000 people involved in intercession.*

# Section Five

# Spiritual Warfare

*Early in our marriage Catherine and I went through periods when we seemed to be up against a kind of unexplained opposition: there would be a series of breakdowns in our household equipment; times when all the children misbehaved for no apparent reason; work would be constantly interrupted; and we would feel a heaviness in our spirits. At first we tried to examine these happenings logically; then as we learned more about the dark powers and principalities at work in the world we realized that on occasion we were under a form of satanic attack.*

*When Catherine was writing* Beyond Our Selves, *she reported the spirit of opposition in her office as being almost palpable. No wonder, since this book more than any other of hers helped people move from unbelief or an uncertain faith into making a commitment to Jesus Christ as Lord.*

*As we learned more about "the enemy" and his cohorts, we were able to pray against those dark spirits, reducing their effectiveness. But we were never free from them. In fact as the years went by, we accepted the fact that for all of us engaged in Christian service, there is never-ending spiritual warfare.*

*In the final years of her life, as her body weakened from a series of ailments, Catherine had a daily battle with the dark forces. Rebuking the enemy in the name of Jesus was the best weapon for reclaiming the creative atmosphere to do our work, to minister to others, to protect our home environment.*

*But we could never relax our vigilance.*

*LL*

# 1

# FEAR

Last night I had a vivid dream. . . . While driving a car, I became terrified of what was ahead. With no clear idea of what the problem was, I could not seem to keep from doing the very worst thing possible—*closing my eyes as I drove.*

Then I was driving over a concrete road with about three inches of very clear water on it. There was still overwhelming fear in me. I awoke in panic.

As I pondered it this morning, the message of the dream would appear to be that my actual danger is very small—shallow water. Thus my real problem is fear itself. Fear of many things, including God Himself.

He scolded me for this—gently—this morning, reminding me that fear is one of Satan's tools. The *fear of God*—the wrong kind, that is, fearfulness rather than awe—is something I have struggled with for so many, many years. And I sense that many believing people are like me, unable to love and praise their Heavenly Father fully because of fear—often a fear of punishment.

Then I remembered something that Jesus did. Knowing that all people struggle with fear, He often prefaced what He was about to say to His fellow humans with the words, "Fear not."

Therefore my prayer is, "Lord, I hand my fears over to You, fears of all kinds. Fear of You is actually a kind of blasphemy against Your character. I'm sorry. Forgive me."

In answer to my prayer, a line from an old hymn, "Take it to the Lord in prayer," began running through my mind. The Spirit said very clearly, "Why do you think I am reminding you of these words? *Pay attention to every line of these verses.* Learn to bring everything directly to Me instead of allowing so many worrying wonderings."

*What a Friend we have in Jesus*
*All our sins and griefs to bear!*
*What a privilege to carry*
*Everything to God in prayer.*
*O what peace we often forfeit,*
*O what needless pain we bear,*
*All because we do not carry*
*Everything to God in prayer.*

*Have we trials and temptations?*
*Is there trouble anywhere?*
*We should never be discouraged—*
*Take it to the Lord in prayer.*
*Can we find a friend so faithful*
*Who will all our sorrows share?*
*Jesus knows our every weakness—*
*Take it to the Lord in prayer.*

*Are we weak and heavy-laden*
*Cumbered with a load of care?*
*Precious Saviour, still our refuge—*
*Take it to the Lord in prayer.*
*Do thy friends despise, forsake thee?*

*Take it to the Lord in prayer;*
*In His arms He'll take and shield thee—*
*Thou wilt find a solace there.*
*Joseph Scriven (1819–1886)*

2

# Fear of Death

A visit from Betty Malz this week has forced me to do something I keep putting off—examining my attitude about death.

After returning to life from twenty-eight minutes of being dead (*My Glimpse of Eternity*), Betty is so full of *details* of what life will be in eternity, as well as bubbling over with stories of remarkable answers to prayer, that being with her is like a feast.

Yet our conversation several nights ago highlighted my own wrong emotional orientation to death. Though I know intellectually that Jesus *did* conquer death, though I believe with my mind in immortality, my emotions deny this. Somewhere back in my childhood certain experiences planted firmly the conviction that death is our enemy, to be hated and fought every step of the way. By the time I was in my teens, I was writing poetry full of emotional rebellion about the brevity of our lives here and how pathetically unfair that is.

I slept almost none at all night before last, finding in myself a deep unrest about all this.

Yesterday morning as I prayed about it, I remembered a New Testament verse about those "who for fear of death are in bondage all their lives." This seemed such an exact description of me that I thought, *I'd like to take a look at that verse.* Whereupon the Helper clearly said (in my thoughts), *Look in Hebrews.*

So I turned to that book, not having the least idea *where* in Hebrews. I found the verse in the second chapter, fifteenth verse.

Verse fourteen talks about what Jesus did for us on the Cross:

> . . . that by [going through] death He might bring to nought and make of no effect him who had the power of death, that is, the devil.

Verse fifteen:

> And also that He might deliver and completely set free all those who through the (haunting) fear of death were held in bondage throughout the whole course of their lives.
>
> AMPLIFIED

How to the point! I decided that I had been in emotional bondage to the fear of death long enough, that Satan had used this as a way of stirring up doubt and confusion in me. All of which has interfered with my having full fellowship with the Father.

So I made a date with Betty Malz and Len for 4:30 yesterday afternoon and in prayer together we claimed my freedom, asking that Jesus fulfill His promise "to deliver and completely set free."

Last night at the church meeting where Betty spoke, one of the hymns we sang was "Be Still, My Soul." The words were like a Night Letter straight from the heart of God in answer to my claiming prayer in the afternoon (italics added).

> Be still, my soul—the Lord is on thy side!
> Bear patiently the cross of grief or pain;

Leave to thy God to order and provide—
*In every change* He faithful will remain.

Be still, my soul—thy best, thy Heavenly Friend
Through thorny ways leads to a joyful end.

Be still, my soul—thy God doth undertake
*To guide the future as He has the past,*
Thy hope, thy confidence let nothing shake—
All now mysterious shall be bright at last . . .

# 3

# SELF-DISSATISFACTION

Last night I dreamed I was making a telephone call from a department store pay phone. There was immense trouble, though, about finding the number. I could not locate the yellow pages of the directory. Then I thought that I might have the number written in one of two notebooks in my handbag. But the two notebooks kept getting mixed up, and as I would find the page, someone else would push into the phone booth ahead of me, and my finger would slip out of place in the little notebook. Once I located the number, only to find it so blurry that I could not read it.

The message my unconscious seems to be playing back to me—confusion. Not enough order in my life, or even in my pocketbook.

This morning as I sought answers in prayer to a number of problems, the same spirit of confusion seemed to settle upon me. Quickly I asked for His help. After a few moments I was led to Psalm 78. These verses hit me:

> He divided the sea and led them through. . . . He guided them with the cloud by day and with light from the fire all night. He split the rocks in the desert and gave them water as abundant as the seas. . . . But they continued to sin against him rebelling in the desert

against the Most High. They willfully put God to the test by demanding the food they craved.

vv. 13–18 NIV

. . . and his wrath rose against Israel, for they did not believe in God or trust in his deliverance.

vv. 21–22 NIV

Was I full of doubts and questions and criticism like the Israelites? Yes, I had to admit I was. How can I be free of this, Lord?

These words of reassurance came:

"Thou art my beloved child, Catherine. Rest in that love. . . . Simply rest in it. Bathe in it. Stop asking so many questions. Stop all this probing, taking your spiritual temperature. Does the Lord want me to do this? Or that? Is this right? Is that right? This is the source of the confusion you are feeling.

"You *are* My child, My disciple. I accepted you long ago—*as you are*—as you are growing.

"You are *still* accepted. Nothing is between us from My side, only yours! Grasp that by faith and all else will follow.

"The nervous probing is Satan's doing, to unsettle you, to confuse you, to knock you off the base of your belief.

"Let My joy flow through you unimpeded, even though you do not feel it at first. *Let it flow. Be not afraid.* That joy will sweep away your fear and uncertainties.

"Stop accusing yourself, Catherine. Turn any such thoughts over to Me instantly. They come from Satan, not from Me.

"Place yourself in My hands as though you were an infant. Let *Me* handle your questions, the tattered remnants of your unbelief, your growth in My *grace*—not My stringency.

"Grace . . . grace . . . grace. Love . . . love . . . love. I came *not* to judge or to condemn. *All* accusation comes from the enemy.

"Open the floodgates that My love can bathe you and that the living water may flow through you to others."

# 4

# FREE FROM BONDAGE

Sarah, a woman in our Tuesday night group at church, told us the following experience.

For years she had been struggling to quit smoking. She would get down to two packs a week, then back up to three, endlessly defeated. Her conscience hurt her about the grip that cigarettes had on her.

Sarah sat on the front row the night Len did a Bible study on how the Holy Spirit can free us from any habit that binds us and keeps us from a close relationship to Jesus. The Scripture he focused on:

> For if you live according to the sinful nature, you will die; but if by the Spirit you put to death the misdeeds of the body, you will live, because those who are led by the Spirit of God are sons of God.
>
> Romans 8:13–14 NIV

In his talk, Len included alcohol, drugs, cigarettes, food, and sex as pitfalls for the compulsive personality. Sarah told us later that she began to associate Len with her cigarette struggle.

One night Sarah had a short, vivid dream in which Len was present. Then she saw a hand with a lighted cigarette between the fingers. The fingers began vigorously and repeatedly tamping out the cigarette. With that the dream ended.

When Sarah awoke the next morning she pondered whether the meaning of the dream could be as obvious as it seemed. Scarcely thinking, she reached for her package of cigarettes. There was a single cigarette left. She lighted it, but it tasted different, not at all good. She tamped it out and has had no desire to smoke since. Her tastes, her desire-world itself, had been transformed by the Spirit.

Later Len and I shared with the group the following steps we use in praying for someone in the grip of addiction:

1. In the name of Jesus move against the powers of darkness that have attached themselves to R——'s mind and will.
2. With Christ's authority, drive these forces back a day at a time. Persist. No matter how long it takes; refuse to be discouraged.
3. Once you have captured any piece of ground in R——'s mind from the enemy, occupy it with a declaration of faith, telling Satan he cannot return.
4. When R—— has been released from an addiction, pray for his salvation and his infilling by the Holy Spirit.

We also suggested that anyone who, like Sarah, has been released from addiction, hold onto the following verse:

> Stand fast therefore in the liberty wherewith Christ hath made us free, and be not entangled again with the yoke of bondage.
>
> Galatians 5:1 KJV

# 5

# SATAN'S BEST WEAPON

There is an oft-repeated story about the time Satan gathered his co-workers together for a strategy session. The purpose: find more effective ways to tempt Christians into sin.

One evil spirit said, "Let's set before them the delights of sin."

Satan shook his head. "That works up to a point, but not with the strong believers."

Another incubus suggested, "We can show them that virtue is costly."

Satan again shook his head. "They know that the rewards are worth it."

The third little demon had a knowing look in his eye. "Let's bring discouragement to their souls."

"Now you have it!" cried Satan. "Discouragement is the weapon!"

How true it is! Right now I am worn down by lack of sleep. I thought I had won a victory over sleeplessness and dependence on sleeping pills six years ago. But lately I've been in the pit of despair. Nor has going back to a mild sleeping pill helped.

This morning I want to put on paper what it is like to try and sleep. I go to bed fatigued, yet am not able to let go. The sleep mechanism of the frontal lobe of my brain is apparently all askew. It's as if the stay-alert function is working overtime—night and day. Even at moments when, out of total weariness, I am about to drop off, the brain sends the message, "Wake up!" and I jerk to.

There is a constant tiredness behind my eyes, lids are heavy as if pressing the eyes back into the head.

I cannot find any comfortable position in bed. Make elaborate arrangements with pillows and sheet, but no sooner settled than I am moving again. What to do with the arms to keep them from aching? How to place my neck?

My face itches and I must scratch. There's a cramp in one leg and I flex and unflex my toes. The sheet is scratching my chin. Right arm is hot. Finally, I tumble to the fact that there can be no sleep until I lie perfectly still for a while. Yet it's agony to force myself to do so.

The nights seem endless. How can they be so long?

When I do—toward dawn—drop off, the "sleep start" wakens me abruptly. A muscle in a leg gives a sudden jerk.

I have come to hate the bed, yet am drawn to it, always hopeful. Isn't it man's *natural* state to sleep? Lord, I'm exhausted and discouraged.

So many times discouragement has been the doorway through which the powers of evil have flooded into my situation. For discouragement says, "My problem is bigger than God, who is not adequate to handle my particular need. So herewith I take my eyes off God, bow down before my problem, and give myself to it."

In digging through Scripture on this subject, I have discovered that no matter how difficult the situation, Jesus' attitude was always a calm, "Courage, My son, My daughter. Have no fear. There is nothing here that My Father cannot handle."

It was not that Jesus minimized the problem, but rather that His faith was a magnet for God's power. He knew that *no* problem was any match for the Lord God Almighty.

I confess now that I am discouraged because I have been relying on myself rather than on You, Lord; I have expected something from myself and am deeply disappointed not to find it there. I want to think that I can handle things myself . . . succeed better . . . do more than others.

In *The Practice of the Presence of God,* Brother Lawrence writes that he was never upset when he had failed in some duty. He simply confessed his fault, saying to God, "I shall never do otherwise, if You leave me to myself; it is You who must hinder my failing and mend what is amiss." After this admission, he gave himself no further uneasiness about it.

What the devil wants us to do, of course, is to focus on our failure rather than on Jesus. For when we keep our eyes on Him, we find that no problem—of the 1st century or the 20th—has ever defeated Him.

Jesus never encountered a human situation that discouraged Him. Sickness and disease? Jesus healed a man blind from birth . . . a woman who'd had an issue of blood for twelve years . . . another bent double with arthritis for eighteen years. At not one of these cases did Jesus look with despairing heart.

Did sin get Him down? Never, no matter how heinous. Jesus insisted that He had come into the world not to condemn us, but to save us (John 8:15; 12:47). His attitude was that any time spent in condemnation, in wallowing in old sins and regrets, in recriminations, in kicking ourselves around, is wasted time.

The woman taken in adultery, He forgave and restored—immediately.

Zaccheus had spent a lifetime in greed and grasping. Yet Jesus told him, "*This* day has salvation come to thy house."

Jesus' word in any situation was one of encouragement:

To the paralytic borne by four: "Courage, My son!"

To the ruler of the synagogue whose daughter was dying: ‘‘Have no fear, only believe, and she shall get well.’’

To Martha, grieving over her dead brother: ‘‘Said I not unto thee, that if thou wouldst believe, thou shouldst see the glory of God?’’

Hear that, Satan? In the name of Jesus, I kick you and discouragement out of my life.

6

# THE OTHER SIDE OF THE MOUNTAIN

Yesterday David Hill from Dallas telephoned and was on for forty-five minutes. David has had an escape from some sort of cult. He is unmarried, thirty-two or thirty-three, and has been a Christian for eight years. *What* a mature Christian he is for an eight-year-old!

He has had quite a bit of experience with spiritual warfare, and one of the helpful facts he gave me is that when we're engaged in these battles energy is sapped from us and we are *very* prone to depression. *Exactly* my state for the last two months!

He also painted a very vivid picture of Genesis 22. As Abraham and Isaac were toiling up Mount Moriah, Satan must have been tempting Abraham every few minutes. "Surely you did not hear God correctly! Sacrifice your son and heir? Why should you do such an evil thing? Why, Isaac was God's special gift to you in your wife's old age. You're probably just getting senile, etc., etc."

But at *that very moment* that Abraham was struggling with his thoughts, the ram was traveling up the *other* side of the Mount, and God was preparing the way of escape.

David's message was, God always is working on the "ram part"—the escape, God's own way out.

# 7

# Knowing the Enemy

How much better we will withstand Satan's assaults when we're wise to his tactics! Thus, these past few days I've been searching the Bible for insights as to the forces—within and without—arrayed against us.

*The Serpent's Strategy:*

First of all the serpent's objective was to call God a liar, to contradict His Word, to tell Eve—and us—"His Word is not so." It was because Eve believed the serpent as over against God that the Fall came (Genesis 3:2–4).

The serpent's second strategy was to tell Eve, in effect, "God is out to take away or withhold something good from you."

The third trick was to tempt the woman into letting the forbidden fruit play upon her senses. She put herself in the way of the temptation, walked around it, looked at it, toyed with it (Genesis 3:6).

Three curve balls—and Eve struck out.

*The Immediate Results* of her sin:

1. Eve wanted fellowship in her disobedience. She felt at once the sense of isolation that sin brings. Inevitably when we do wrong we want to drag other people down with us. So Eve gave the fruit to Adam to eat (v. 6).

2. Innocence was gone. Both the man and the woman knew they were naked.

3. They had no desire for fellowship with God; ran from Him; in fact, hid themselves from Him (Genesis 3:8).

4. They knew fear (v. 10).

5. They knew shame (vv. 7–10).

6. Each blamed his sin on someone else:
Adam—on Eve (v. 12).
Eve—on the serpent (v. 13).

*The Far-reaching Results:*

1. Woman is reduced to a subordinate position to man.

2. In sorrow and pain and difficulty will the reproduction process take place. Moreover, woman will be something of a slave to her sexual desire for her husband (v. 16).

3. Man shall till the ground, which will be stubborn in producing for him. He will get food by the sweat of his brow (vv. 17–19).

4. Death enters life—"To dust thou shalt return" (v. 19).

5. Adam and Eve begin to wear clothing, symbol of perpetual loss of innocence (v. 21).

6. They are driven from the Garden and the Tree of Life (vv. 23–24).

*How seriously did Jesus take demons?*

Apparently very seriously indeed. When He sent the first group of disciples on the first mission, His charge to them was:

First: Preaching
Second: Casting out demons (Mark 3:14–15).

The demons always seemed to have recognized:

1. *Who Jesus was* (Mark 1:24, 34; 3:11; 5:7).

2. *That Jesus was against them all the way.*

3. *That they had to obey Him* (Mark 1:25–28, 5:12–13).

*Jesus' dealing with demons:*

1. He rebuked them (Mark 1:25).
2. He then gave them a direct order (Mark 1:25, 5:8).
3. He charged them not to reveal who He was (Mark 3:12).

*The result for the possessed individual:*

1. He is often buffeted and thrown about (Mark 1:26).
2. But the demon obeys Jesus and departs (Mark 1:26).

These further insights have come as I pondered Satan's inroads into my own heart and will:

1. When we rejoice over, or look for, or repeat with relish negative news, then we have placed ourselves on the side of evil.
2. It is possible to take this negative stance so often with regard to situations and persons that this becomes a way of life. Negative thinking is really a weapon of Satan. *We* call it "realism"; Christ calls it "not believing the truth."
3. We do not realize how definitely our mind-set—that is, what the mind picks out from all the news to highlight—reveals *whose* side we're really on.
4. Even after we have accepted Jesus and asked Him to come and live within us, Satan will keep trying to persuade us that the flesh is dominant and must be obeyed. Satan will also feed us the lie that "that's human nature" and there's nothing we can do about it.
5. The response to Satan's attacks has to be *faith*. When I became Jesus' woman, a series of marvelous things happened—whether the effects are visible yet or not. Among them, as I accepted the atoning work of Jesus for me, I was unshackled on the inside from my bondage to the flesh, freed from the ascendancy of flesh over spirit (Romans 8:2). Paul says that when we accept this wonderful liberation by faith, and begin to live it out, we find that the flesh now *has* to obey the spirit, that Satan

has been subdued, overcome, deprived of his power (Romans 8:3). Realizing this, we need only allow the Holy Spirit to lead the way, step by step, obedient act by obedient act, like a conquering General victoriously marching ahead (Romans 8:9–16).

# 8

# OFFENSIVE WARFARE

Yesterday I read a pamphlet by Ralph Mahoney, editor of *World Map Digest,* who makes the following powerful points about spiritual warfare:

1. "On this rock I will build my church, and the gates of hell will not overcome it" (Matthew 16:18 NIV).

Now, gates are stationary. *They* are fixed in place, stay put. Therefore, the "gates of hell" cannot move against us. So Jesus has to mean that His church is to take the offensive against the citadel of Satan.

The picture (according to Mahoney) is of a victorious Church laying siege to hell and breaking down the gates to release its prisoners.

2. "That enemy of yours, the devil, roams around like a lion roaring [in fierce hunger], seeking someone to seize upon and devour" (1 Peter 5:8 AMPLIFIED). Peter did not write those words to scare us to death, says Mahoney. For the key word is *like* the lion. Satan is always an imitator, a fake, a bluff, a counterfeit. He *isn't* a lion. His claws were drawn out at Calvary.

3. The real Lion is Jesus, "the Lion of the tribe of Judah" (Revelation 5:5 AMPLIFIED). We Christians have no strength or ability in ourselves for fighting Satan, or for pulling down gates, or anything else.

But as we allow the Lion of Judah to live in us, we take on the nature of Him who is the real Lion. Our weapons—fickle and weak of themselves—pass through God and become mighty enough to make hell itself tremble with fear.

# 9

# CONVERSATIONS WITH GOD

*LL Note: As she learned more and more about confronting Satan with his lies and deceit, rebuking him daily, and seeking to hear the voice of the Lord, the answers from Him became clearer and clearer. Here are excerpts from Catherine's 1981 journal:*

"Lord, I need Your help in so many areas. How can I better hear Your voice?"

*You need to begin listening in the absolute quiet as you did during that summer long ago on Cape Cod. Remember how you lay on the daybed in the living room, pen and notebook in hand, in absolute stillness? I spoke to you then—and will again.*

*A morning Quiet Time should be that—not simply reading in this book or that. What I, your Lord, have to say to you is more important than the best wisdom of any author.*

"Lord, my novel goes so slowly. The words I put on paper seem so wooden. I need Your Help."

*I am glad you have asked Me to be your editor. Turn to Me each time you begin writing for specific directions. If you want real creativity, follow My inner directives.*

*Now, start reading 2 Corinthians and I'll have more to say to you.*

"Lord, I wince at 2 Corinthians 2:9: obedience in all things. How do I achieve that? I feel like such a failure in that area."

*Child—you always take life too seriously—with too heavy a spirit, too anxious a mien. A true child of Mine has no need to worry so. You act as if you think you have to do everything yourself, as if I, your Burden Bearer, am not with you at all. Do you really think that honors Me?*

*Do you not see the egotism in all this? Satan has gotten a toehold in this attitude-area in you, and you have failed to recognize it so that you can deal with it. He is the one who wants you burdened down, fatigued, feeling overwhelmed with work.*

"Lord, what a gorgeous revelation! Thank You, thank You. . . . But how do I kick the old boy out and let You turn these wrong attitudes around?"

*By recognizing Satan's lies. For example, he wants you to think that your everyday life is monotonous and dull. The very opposite is true. Satan's aim is always to turn your eyes to the world. That's not for you. Even during that brief period in Washington when you thought you were making a little progress into Washington social life, it wasn't for you and would have garnered you husks had you achieved it. Forget it! Permanently! Your life is fascinating, with pleasant surprises every day. Praise Me for the richness of the life I have given you.*

*Each time you feel a negative attitude building up inside yourself, refuse to accept it. Recognize the satanic source of it, reject it, and turn to Me.*

"Lord, there are doubts in me this morning. I admit it. Doubts that what I am writing down here is really You speaking and not just my wishful thinking or what I think You would say. How can I be sure?"

*Proof in the world of the spirit never comes in the same way as in the material world. Don't try to transfer the techniques of what you call "evidence" from the one realm to the other.*

*Trust the Holy Spirit to be the link between us, to speak My words, transfer them to you—and He will. Was there not a sureness and a joy and a knowledge of My benediction on you yesterday that you have not known in a long time?*

"Yes, there was, Lord. But there are so many things I want and need to talk over with You that it's going to take all eternity to do it."

*Your endless curiosity, which at its best is real seeking, is from Me. Don't fight it. Those who seek Me, do find. Remember? "The poor in spirit". . . . Always I am ready to receive any questing. I bless you and love you beyond comprehension.*

"Lord, I know that discouragement is from Satan, that I have no business being discouraged under any circumstances. But I am troubled about my novel. I don't feel I can finish it. How do I keep from giving into those down feelings?"

*Patience, Catherine, patience. Don't be dismayed. What's happening to you is only a ripple, a little wave on a big sea. This too will pass. The hostages do come home. The prodigal does return. Joy cometh in the morning.*

*Take a deep breath, look to Me, and be glad. Smile again. The sky has not fallen in.*

*In other words, keep at it.*

"Thank You, Lord. And thank You that the Spirit gave me this verse from Psalm 31 yesterday: 'My times are in Your hand' (v. 15 AMPLIFIED)."

* * *

"Lord, what I read in Tournier's *The Healing of Persons* is exciting to me because I have long sought the answer to the problem of 'scruples,' of why I am the sort of person who is always finding some one little thing wrong in my life that I am convinced stands between me and You. I feel very guilty about having to go back to sleeping pills, even though they are the mildest available. So, Lord, the question I ask today: Am I exaggerating a minor problem, my scruple of the moment—sleeping pills—in order not to have to face up to something much more important that You really want me to look at?"

*Do you not see that your love of sleep and your desire to escape into sleep is, in large part—and always has been—because you are reluctant to give more of yourself in love for others?*

"What a revelation, Lord! But how do I go about letting You change something as ingrained in me as this? It would be asking You to change a lifelong habit pattern. Also, I'd be afraid that going the people route really would knock out my writing."

*I told you that My yoke is easy and My burden is light, didn't I? My burden was and is and always has been love of people, love of you, Catherine. You've never believed Me that this burden is light. You'll find that this is so only as you allow Me to take you by the hand and lead you out. Are you willing?*

"Yes, Lord."

"Lord, are there other sins You want me to look at, which I have perhaps avoided facing up to, by the smoke screen of small 'scruples'? What I long for is that love of You, and the realization of Your love for me, become the motivating factor in my obedience."

*Ah, if only you knew how much I love you! If only you knew what love surrounds you from the "cloud of witnesses" here with Me—your father, your brother, and Peter. If only you knew how many prayers are constantly flowing for you. How grateful you should be for the waves of good will flowing to you constantly from those who read your books.*

*Relax into My love. Allow Me to love you. There are times when a mother wants to hold her child. No words need pass between them, just the feel of love. This morning let Me love you like that. Let all spiritual strain and tension go. Relax in Me.*

"How beautiful, Lord. I do!"

"Lord, is there any particular word You want to speak to me this morning?"

*Your life has become unbalanced, Catherine, hence your boredom. You need to cook, to garden, to shop, to exercise more, to be with people more. The more you retreat into the idea-world away from people, the more unreal your Christianity and your relationship with Me will become—even though in such retreat you might think that you were being more spiritual.*

"I had almost no sleep last night, Lord. This morning I am full of fears again."

*Read the 91st Psalm, Catherine, and absorb it into your bone and marrow and bloodstream and mind and heart and spirit.*

*I will deliver Catherine. . . .*

*I will set her on high because she knows and understands My name, has a personal knowledge of My mercy, My love, My kindness. You, Catherine, are to trust and rely on Me, knowing that I will never forsake you.*

*You, Catherine, will call upon Me, and I will answer you; I will be with you in trouble, I will deliver you and honor you.*

*One fearful of the water can never get over the fear by standing on the bank shivering, consumed by the fear. . . .*

*I will not force one to do anything. . . .*

*Take the first step toward Me. Trust My love for you. Trust . . . trust!*

# Section Six

# The Final Victory

*Early in 1982 Catherine realized her time on earth was limited. The emphysema in her lungs had been slowly reducing her vitality. Walking up a flight of stairs was a major undertaking. Talking to people, meetings, shopping drained her.*

*Saddest of all to see was how her growing breathlessness affected her mornings, the cream time for manuscript work she looked forward to so much. I would watch her go resolutely into her office at 9:00* A.M. *Forty minutes later I would hear her return to our bedroom. Once I confronted her there as she lay listlessly on the bed.*

*Tears welled up in her eyes. "I try to concentrate," she said. "The inner drive is gone. I don't have it anymore."*

*Then she would rail at herself for being a quitter, get up, and try again. My dilemma was: Should I prod her into doing what was painful and hard, or let her drift into invalidism?*

*The answer soon became clear. Catherine's basic competitiveness, her battling nature, her spirit of adventure, and her curiosity about life could not, should not be allowed to die. Catherine would never have forgiven me if I had encouraged her to let go of all this.*

*So we waged spiritual war against the forces of darkness and the enemy's subtle enticements to give in to weakness. The coffee-pot alarm continued to be set for 6:30* A.M. *The day began with an hour of Scripture reading, prayer, and journal entries. During the morning, work continued on the novel* Julie. *Commitments to our prayer and fellowship groups were kept. We ended the day in prayer, when I anointed Catherine with oil, taking a stand against ill health, asking for sharpness of thinking and a healing of body and spirit.*

*LL*

# 1

# HIS UNFINISHED WORK IN ME

Dreamed last night about death. I don't relish putting this one on paper, but since it *has* to be worked through with the Lord, I suppose I must.

I was in a country where certain citizens were being exterminated by order of the state. One got one's notice and came to a special "office" in which were three booths, side by side. In one of these you were given a shot, like a dog being "put to sleep." Afterwards you were carted off to a back room where the bodies were stacked.

Apparently my number had come up. When I got to the office, I noticed that there were stacks and stacks of dirty dishes in the three booths. I sought to stall my death by offering eagerly to wash all the dishes. The attendant said, "Sure, go ahead. I don't blame you. Just don't tell any of the others that I agreed."

I started to wash a stack of plates, saying to myself, "There's always the chance of something happening to intervene, a national emergency or something." Then I woke up.

So now that I have put this dream on paper, Lord, what does it mean—and what do I do about it?

As I waited for some response, a name came to mind—*John Wesley.* Tuttle's book on Wesley was in the stack of unread books on my night table. I picked it up and soon discovered that Wesley and I shared a dread of death as the Great Enemy. Wesley's fear surfaced dramatically in 1735 during a crossing of the Atlantic to Georgia. There were heavy storms at sea and the small wooden ship at times seemed doomed. Most on board, including the crew, were terror-struck. The only ones who remained calm were a group of German Moravian Christians.

Seeing the strength of these Christians as they faced death, Wesley knew he must work through his problem. In reviewing his walk of faith, he realized he had espoused a life of *asceticism,* which took four forms:

1. Self-denial. (He lived frugally in order to give money to the poor.)
2. Solitude.
3. Works of charity. (Including visits to the terrible prisons of the time where he prayed with condemned men.)
4. Interior life as exemplified by the great mystics.

Now Wesley had to admit that while each of these disciplines had a place in Christian life, not one of them dealt with his fear of death. Finally he began to see that this fear was not from God, as the mystics maintained, but from Satan.

Soon after these discoveries John Wesley had his personal experience of the Holy Spirit at Aldersgate. He was back against the basic New Testament proposition: There is no road to God except via faith in the finished work of Jesus Christ on the Cross. Joy flooded in and gradually his fear of death dropped away as the totality of these triumphant words of Jesus sank into his being:

In My Father's house there are many dwelling places (homes). If it were not so, I would have told you, for I am going away to prepare a place for you.

And when (if) I go and make ready a place for you, I will come back again and will take you to Myself, that where I am you may be also.

John 14:2–3 AMPLIFIED

I know that the Holy Spirit has much unfinished work to do inside me about my attitude toward death. I need this, and I will myself to desire it.

2

# Our Servant Role

I was the recipient of a beautiful and touching act last night that reverberates through my prayer time this morning. Myra Gertz, a friend and member of our church fellowship group, asked if she could drop in for a short visit.

As we talked I could see that she had something on her mind and was struggling how to say it. Finally she did.

"Catherine, I feel a bit foolish, but the Lord told me to come over and wash your feet. I don't know what this is all about and I've never done this before, but the Voice was very emphatic."

I was startled. My inner reaction was, *Oh, no! Surely, this is not necessary.* But our group had been learning to respect these nudges from the Spirit. "We certainly want to obey the Lord, Myra," I agreed.

Soon she was on the floor in front of me with towels and a basin of water. She removed my stockings and shoes and gently began washing my feet.

Tears filled my eyes as I felt the presence of the Lord through Myra. He had instigated this, just as He had done with His disciples two thousand years ago.

I was the needy one all right. My fatigue level had never been lower.

"Catherine, the Lord wants you to know He loves you deeply," Myra said as she finished drying my feet. "May I pray for you now?"

"Of course."

She did, asking for a healing in every part of me—mind, spirit, emotions, and body. A deep feeling of peace spread over me. "Thank you for being faithful, Myra," I said as she left.

This morning I read through the Scripture account of this act by Jesus in the New Testament book of John:

> When he had finished washing their feet, (Jesus) put on his clothes and returned to his place. "Do you understand what I have done for you?" he asked them.
>
> "You call me 'Teacher' and 'Lord,' and rightly so, for that is what I am. Now that I, your Lord and Teacher, have washed your feet, you also should wash one another's feet. I have set you an example that you should do as I have done for you. I tell you the truth, no servant is greater than his master, nor is a messenger greater than the one who sent him. Now that you know these things, you will be blessed if you do them."
>
> John 13:12–17 NIV

*I have set you an example that you should do as I have done for you. . . .* Myra had been obedient to this instruction of Jesus, although I can imagine what she went through, wondering if it would seem overemotional to me.

And it did, at first. But how I needed it. I was hurting. Jesus knew this, wanted to demonstrate His love for me and chose Myra as His vessel. If she had not been faithful, a beautiful inner healing experience would not have happened.

# 3

# Body Language

> I beseech you therefore, brethren . . . that ye present your bodies a living sacrifice, holy, acceptable unto God, which is your reasonable service.
>
> Romans 12:1 KJV

Reading the Bible yesterday afternoon, I felt an inner nudge to stop and reread this verse. I was conscious that I resisted this idea of offering my body as a sacrifice. Why? Because I suspected it could mean more speaking and traveling, more stress and pressure, with consequent loss of sleep at night, and no chance to recoup with daytime naps.

What is so bad about this is that I'm not really trusting the Lord with my physical body—and that's an awful confession. God expects his followers to be willing to be expendable; I've been circling around this point of total trust in a kind of spiritual holding pattern, unwilling to lay down my body as "a living sacrifice." I'm constantly protecting myself, succumbing too quickly to the temptation to stop my work and lie down for a while.

The conviction then came that I must be willing—and tell God so—to have the self with which I was born, the particular bundle of talents, predispositions, preferences, tastes—all that constitutes me—nailed to the Cross with Jesus, actually die and be buried with Him.

*But,* a voice inside me argued, *didn't I do just this when I became a Christian?* Jesus assured me, however, that this was a new step of dying to the self that so loves body comforts and beautiful things, that longs to escape the demands and entanglements of other people.

Much of that self *I dislike* (Romans 7:15–25). But a lot of what constitutes "me" I like very much. I've been "me," and lived with "me," and put up with "me" a long time. To lay this self on the altar would indeed be a death.

I remembered Jesus' words about "counting the cost" (Luke 14:28). Was I really willing to take myself to the Cross, die and be buried—not having any idea what sort of person would rise with Jesus on the third day?

I went through agony thinking about this, with a lot of tears.

Scripture says that Jesus resolutely and willingly turned His face to the Cross for "the joy that was set before Him" (Hebrews 12:2).

I finally told Jesus that I was going forward with this because I knew He *was* going to have His way with me, now or in the next life.

I got down on my knees in my office by the daybed at 4:40 P.M. and offered up my body to Him as a living sacrifice.

As a result, I must now be obedient hour by hour, day by day, and *not* hold back. This means seeing the indwelling Spirit so residing in my mortal flesh that I am willing to spend myself totally for others, as He did. It means letting *all* self go—everything in my desire world—whenever it cuts across His higher priorities.

No wonder we can do no mighty works until the surrender is this complete. Until Jesus has been allowed to come and make His home in me like *that,* I will be praying for others, doing His work, in *my* name and in *my* nature rather than in His.

The apostle John puts it this way:

> He laid down His [own] life for us; and we ought to lay [our] lives down for [those who are our] brothers in [Him].
>
> 1 John 3:16 AMPLIFIED

*LL Note: Six months of creativity followed during which Catherine made an important breakthrough with her novel* Julie, *ministered to several in our prayer group, made several speeches. The two of us drove together from Florida to our farm in Virginia for a month, then flew back to Florida to continue work on her novel.*

# 4

# SELF-PITY

This morning I took to the Lord a matter that has troubled me for the past two years or so. Sudden tears. I've never been a person who cries often. I generally keep my emotions in check, perhaps more than I should. Recently though, bouts of unpredictable weeping.

The Lord has graciously shown me this morning the why of tears being just under the surface of these past weeks—*self-pity*. In reality, I am weeping for myself.

I weep because of what is happening to me physically. First, my energy level has again dropped to such a degree that it is literally a chore to put one foot before the other. Added to that, worse breathlessness than I've ever known. Sometimes even sitting or lying in bed, I wonder if I'm going to be able to take the next breath. This makes the stairs and hills at Evergreen Farm an agony.

Most puzzling, after years of battling sleeplessness, suddenly I can hardly stay awake. I must check out with the doctor whether this is an overreaction to the new arthritis drug they are giving me.

Or is it possible that, through lack of oxygen to the brain, I am coming into early senility? Hideous thought! For the first time since early girlhood I have no desire to read at night. During church yesterday, I could scarcely keep my eyes open.

Lord, help!

I am led to this verse:

> . . . I know . . . Whom I have believed . . . and I am [positively] persuaded that He is able to guard and keep that which has been entrusted to me and which I have committed [to Him] until that day.
>
> 2 Timothy 1:12 AMPLIFIED

Since self-pity is a sin, then clearly it has to be dealt with as a sin. A sin because since I belong to Jesus, it is He who has control over my life. Thus He overrules everything that He "allows" to happen to me—overrules it for *good.*

My part is to trust Him as a loving Heavenly Father in each of these adverse circumstances. I am to watch expectantly for the "good" . . . the new adventure He has for me . . . the open door I am to go through toward the better way to which He is leading me.

So, given all that, what is there to have self-pity about?

I see that there is a self-discipline to practice during the days ahead: Each time I am tempted toward despairing self-pity, I am to rebuke it, reject it, and turn immediately to praise.

# 5

# Crisis Time

*On July 9, 1982, Catherine was so weak that we had her taken by ambulance to Bethesda Memorial Hospital in Boynton Beach, Florida. Tests showed an alarming carbon dioxide content in her body because of shallow breathing, and she was placed in the Intensive Care Unit. Respirator tubes led through her mouth to her lungs; she was fed through an IV tube in her nose. Machines handled all her body functions. Family members could visit her for no more than fifteen-minute periods three times a day.*

*Because the tubes in her mouth and nose made it hard to wear glasses, she found it difficult to read the small print of her Bible. A gray 10 by 7-inch notebook that she had filled over the years with Bible promises (see p. 191) in large handwriting became her spiritual lifeline.*

*The prognosis for her recovery was not good. Doctors could offer no hope that her breathing capacity would improve enough for her to be taken off the respirator. It appeared that Catherine's last days would be spent in the Intensive Care Unit, unable to speak, communicating only through a note pad. Here is a sample of her scribbled comments as the painful weeks passed:*

I never knew how frustrating it can be not to be able to speak a word.

I can only move my head about six inches because of that tube in my nose. Lying all night in that one position is torture.

Each little thing is so difficult. It's tough to be getting weaker and weaker and thinner and thinner.

The progress from day to day depends on the blood gases test they take . . . they're running out of places on my arms to draw blood, I bruise so easily.

Remember those old-fashioned cardboard fans people used in church? See if you can find one at home. It gets so hot here at night.

This has been a lonely day. Shifting personnel each with little knowledge of my situation. Sense some are hostile toward Christians. Wish I was a better witness to them for Jesus.

I'm taking twice as many breaths per minute as I should. How do I retrain my body?

I feel that something has to give today. I'm so miserable that I don't see how I can take much more.

It seemed that the Lord was promising me last night that Romans 8:28 would be fulfilled and that I was to begin praising Him. "I believe. Help my unbelief."

Had a crisis with the IV. They spent two hours trying to get it to work. When I began praying they found the answer.

Prayed about my dread of nights. Discovered why I can't really relax. I'm a chronic thinker and a "what-if-er." Prayed to change.

Imagine, four weeks without a shampoo! I dare not look in the mirror. Will be horrified.

Last night the simple thought, "Be still and know that I am God," pulled me through.

*On July 24 at 7:30 A.M., my telephone rang: a male nurse reported that Catherine wanted to see me right away. "Don't be alarmed," he said. "It's not a medical emergency. Your wife has something to tell you that she feels is important."*

*I awoke Peter and Jeff (the family members then on hand) and we drove immediately to the hospital. Catherine greeted us with great excitement in her eyes and reported through written notes that during the night she had felt the Lord's presence there in her Intensive Care cubicle! With His presence came the assurance that she was being healed.*

*Confirmation came in the next blood tests, which showed a definite decrease in the carbon dioxide content in her body. Day by day the improvement continued. Just as doctors had been unable to explain Catherine's sudden loss of breathing capacity, so too were they baffled when it returned. One doctor said it had to be the power of prayer.*

*One by one the tubes came out. The ventilator was wheeled away. On August 11, Catherine was moved out of the Intensive Care Unit; she had been there thirty-two days. Nine days later, on August 20th, a rejoicing husband brought her home.*

*Catherine had been through a dehumanizing process in Intensive Care and had lost twenty-five pounds. The recuperation was agonizingly slow as members of the family took turns coming to Florida to help her recover. Meanwhile, Catherine resumed her journal entries.*

*LL*

# 6

# CRUCIFIED WITH JESUS

In many ways my thirty-two-day stint in the Intensive Care Unit of Bethesda Hospital was a crucifixion experience. Soon after I arrived there, the Lord reminded me of the act I had performed (through Romans 12:1) of offering forever my defective body, along with all my faculties, as a living sacrifice on His Cross.

While lying on my back, hour after hour, unable to read or talk, I had plenty of time to reflect on the study I did awhile ago on the "Humanity of Jesus." Through it I saw that His humanness for thirty-three years on earth was *real;* that He was as helpless, as "out of control" of circumstances, as we are. All this was in order for Him to be the Wayshower, the true and very practical Captain of our salvation.

I also perceived that during this earthly walk, *the* guiding principle of Jesus' life was "what pleases My Father in heaven, never what *I* want to do."

In the intervening months since I made this study, several things have been happening: (1) the Holy Spirit has been doing a steady softening and melting process within me. This has meant that the plights of other persons presented to me, mostly through correspondence, have been laid on my heart with a new urgency; (2) During this same period my own circumstances have not only been taken out of my control, but also have gone in directions contrary to anything *I* would wish.

At what point in the Christian walk are we *actually* "crucified with Him"? At what point is the mortal self dead on His cross and buried with Him?

In my case, I concluded, dying to self has been going on for some time. For me it has been a slow, torturous, lingering death indeed—no doubt because I have been resisting all the way. I'm reasonably sure that it need not be this drawn out and this painful, if the believer really understands what is going on and why, and assents to it in his will. Yet I do think it's something we have to walk through all the way and *feel.* Death on a Cross hurts.

Early the morning of July 24 (fifteen days after entering the hospital) the climax came for me. I was in a semi-conscious, dreaming state when I felt myself literally hanging on the Cross with Jesus. There was no pain from the nails in my hands or feet; only a suffocating, crushing weight on my chest as my entire body dragged downwards. I knew I was close to death, but strangely there was absolutely no fear.

As the weight on the rib cage grew unendurable, however, I was aware of a dark presence, as well as that of Jesus. A fierce struggle with some evil force ensued. Again and again I rebuked the dark power and ordered him to be gone. He didn't leave easily, but leave he did at last.

Then—so gently—Jesus picked me up and removed me from the Cross. As He did so, three words came to me: "The Great Exchange." Later I realized this is what theologians call "the substitutionary atonement," meaning that every sinful thing in our lives was dealt with in Christ's finished work on His Cross. At the moment I knew only that the crushing weight had lifted from my ribs.

I awoke the next morning very excited, feeling that a miracle had taken place in my body. This is the note saved by Len I wrote to the nurse:

> Please grant me this one request! I want to see my family, now! My husband first. Please call him. 732-6352.
>
> My husband, my son Peter, my son Jeffrey. I want all of them. I want no medication before they get here. I'll "calm down" to suit you.

When Len, Peter, and Jeffrey arrived, through notes I told them about my death, that at one point in my struggle with that dark force, it seemed my body parts were burnt up and lying in pieces around the room. The turning point came when way down deep I cried, "Jesus! Lord. My Lord." And He came and was with me. And He healed me.

My family was very responsive, but I think they wondered if it was a hallucination brought on by low oxygen levels in the brain. The key would be the next blood gases test.

When the doctor arrived at my bedside the next day, he was all smiles. "The carbon dioxide is way down!" he reported. And then we all celebrated!

What transpired on the Cross two thousand years ago has taken on sparkling new meaning for me. We are accustomed to thinking that Jesus carried only our sins on the Cross, but Scripture makes it equally clear that He bore all our sicknesses and diseases there too. . . .

> When evening came, they brought to Him (Jesus) many who were under the power of demons, and He drove out the spirits with a word, and restored to health all who were sick; And thus He fulfilled what was spoken by the prophet Isaiah, He Himself took our weaknesses and infirmities and bore away our diseases.
>
> Matthew 8:16–17 (Isaiah 53:4) AMPLIFIED

Len asked me the other night what I considered the chief significance of my crucifixion experience.

"I'm not sure yet," I replied. "I was close to death and the Lord returned me to life. He must have had a reason."

"Do you know what that might be?"

"There are a number of things I'm supposed to do. Finish my novel was one. Even more important: work on some bruised relationships." Then it struck me. "I've had a crucifixion, but not a resurrection."

Len wouldn't accept this. "You emerged from a dark valley into the light. Wasn't that a resurrection?"

"Not entirely. My breathing was restored to what it was last spring, but that's far from normal. My lungs have still not been completely healed."

"Consider this, Catherine," Len replied. "You've operated with little more than half your normal lung power for almost forty years. But look at all you've accomplished. Maybe, like Paul, God's given you a thorn in the flesh for a reason."

Lord, how much more I have to learn!

7

# Doing Grief Work

How grateful I am for Robert Bonham's[1] visits during my recuperation! What a sensitive counselor and friend! His gifts of wisdom and discernment are balm to my spirit.

After I told him how discouraged I am over the slowness of my recovery and the suspicion that my voice may be permanently damaged, it came out last week that Bob feels I am doing *grief* work.

The minute he spoke the word "grief," it rang a bell within me. He said that whenever we encounter a major shift or change in life, of necessity it involves separation from things well-known and comfortable (whether completely desirable or not), and this entails loss.

When I asked him to spell this out as he saw it in my situation, he ticked off the following:

*Loss of identity in the Intensive Care Unit (ICU).* Rings, bracelets, etc., removed and placed in hospital safe. Only individuation is a plastic identification bracelet on patient's left wrist.

[1]At the time the Reverend Robert Bonham was Director of the Christian Institute of Healing at New Covenant Church, Pompano Beach, Florida.

*Loss of dignity.* Emergency conditions in ICU rule out privacy. Tendency on part of nurses is to deal with bodies, not persons.

*Loss of speech for so long.* Respirator tubes in mouth mean communication is curtailed.

*The possibility of loss of life.* Death is common and frequent in ICU. Dependency on machines underscores the fragility of life.

*Loss of mental ability and memory.* Reduced oxygen in brain brings on confusion.

As he talked a flood of emotion ran through me. I saw the physical stripping of possessions that takes place in any hospital as more devastating than I had acknowledged. It says, in part, that any so-called success one has had is now of no consequence. That comes off too. Raiment is a hospital gown—the same garment for everyone. One is just a *body* headed for life or death.

I know now what my husband Peter meant when he was asked what he had learned from his first heart attack. His reply, "I have learned that the kingdom of God can go on without Peter Marshall."

In the same way I learned in the hospital that everyone can get along quite well without my opinions or "insights" or teaching. Even my wedding ring, symbol of marriage to Len, the closest earthly relationship, was taken away. The experience left me feeling not only helpless but worthless—a digit. The danger here, of course, is that this sense of nonentity can lead one into the pit of despair. It can render one unable not only to accept God's unqualified love, but also the love of other people.

Bob's complete assurance that "this too will pass" was very heartening. He had no answer, though, to my question as to what I can do to make the grief work shorter. Simply that I am to trust God and listen.

This morning I had this word from the Spirit. He tells me to praise and rejoice. He brings to mind the Scripture song we've sung so often at church:

> Rejoice in the Lord always; again I will say Rejoice.
>
> Philippians 4:4 RSV

Rejoice!

That I can enjoy music again through my stereo record-player. I actually got up and played the piano a bit—"Breathe on me, breath of God. . . ."

Rejoice!

Telephoned T. and confessed my lack of love and understanding about several matters. A time of renewed fellowship and reconciliation.

Rejoice!

For patient Len and faithful family . . . for the Intercessors . . . for all who prayed . . . for my doctors and the hospital personnel.

Rejoice!

Linda and I are so close now. She drove down to be with me for a week, bringing a gift of four mats and four napkins for the dining-room table. "Use them," she urged. The point is that Len and the doctor have insisted on my getting out of bed and eating at the table.

Rejoice!

Mary Moncur discovered a tree with mangos out of season. Also fresh grapefruit. And our lime tree is so full that Mary will spend all morning squeezing and freezing them.

Praise You, Lord, for Bob Bonham giving up half of every Saturday to be with me.

Praise You, Lord, for bringing out all the fears that are clinging around the fear of death—so that I can deal with them.

Praise You, Lord, for allowing me to have those experiences in Intensive Care, and for pulling me back from death.

# 8

# Receiving Love

God continues to heal me. This morning He gave me a walloping message about the fact that I have not always been able to receive other people's love and so cannot receive Jesus' love. This revelation was sparked by a hassle with Len last night in our bedroom when I was complaining about members of the household who are shielding me about family situations, finances, and decisions that involve my manuscripts and affairs.

Len became quite agitated; finally with tears in his eyes he said, "Catherine, the doctors have told us that you need time to recover from being at death's door. What we're doing is for your protection, out of our love for you. Don't you realize that we almost lost you?" With that, his voice broke with a show of emotion such as I have rarely seen in our marriage.

This morning I awoke with the full impact of Len's deep feeling sweeping over me. How often, I wondered, do men in our society shortchange themselves and their families by letting a "macho" front cover up a sensitive nature underneath? The conviction came too, though, that I have not been open enough to love. I've often had trouble accepting the feelings Len did express. The affection and gratitude of friends and readers, too.

"Read 1 Corinthians 13," the Spirit nudged.

Those verses lay it out for me even more stringently than Len did last night:

> Love is patient, love is kind. It does not envy, it does not boast, it is not proud. It is not rude, it is not self-seeking, it is not easily angered, it keeps no record of wrongs. Love does not delight in evil but rejoices with the truth. It always protects, always trusts, always hopes, always perseveres.
>
> 1 Corinthians 13:4–7 NIV

I see further that, while my act of laying my body on the altar as "a living sacrifice" was a good first step, it was not enough for: "Though I give my body to be burned and have not love, it profiteth me nothing" (v. 3).

Now comes further revelation, even as I write. Following the 1944 experience of Jesus' healing Presence in my room after I was bedridden for almost three years, I nevertheless lacked something. I've always supposed it was sufficient faith to make the healing complete.

But suppose it was *love* that was missing, not faith. Oh, obedience was not altogether there either, but obedience would have followed love.

"Lord, I rejoice. Lord, I capitulate. Lord, let Your love—and Len's and the love of those around me, each member of my family, and all the love of far-flung friends through my books—*take over.*"

# 9

# Grief Work Continued—The Healing of Memories

Today I shared with Bob Bonham what I have only flicked at with Len: that is the strange negativism I'm feeling about myself. Lately I keep seeing the underside of things, tend to concentrate on the downbeat.

I'm aware too of a loosening of the hold that *things* have on me. I could care less about fixing up Evergreen Farm or the Florida house—redecorating, repairing, restoring—whereas I used to be very much on top of all of this.

Bob interpreted these observations positively by telling me that this is a normal part of recuperation, that the "grief work" needs to go on. He sees too that God is showing me how to *die to self.* The indifference to *things* is simply one manifestation of this. As the culmination of this process, Bob sees that self will eventually be given back to me in a new way.

Even as I write this, the Spirit gives me a further insight—I am to take the lassitude, the wanting to lie down and take oxygen, the lack of motivation and will power to get on with diaphragm exercises, as part and yet another proof of this "death." The crucifixion experience at the hospital was real.

The above, positively seen, is that Catherine is dead and my dependence upon *Jesus'* motivation and *His* strength is more real than ever.

After reassuring me that my negativism is a part of the recovery process, Bob Bonham then sought to lead me through the healing of some memories that lie at the root of my fear of physical death.

Bob asked me to begin this session by seeking "contact" with Jesus. For example, I might ask to feel the touch of His hand on mine. Then I was to let Jesus lead me back to the memory He wanted to heal.

The first one, curiously, was the time I was walking in the woods as a young girl and stepped on something in the leaves. To my horror I saw that it was a dead bird. The dread of that experience has obviously clung to me ever since.

The second was the time our family went to a relative's funeral in Johnson City, Tennessee. The body of Uncle John Herndon was in a coffin open for viewing. This was my first look at a dead person. The stark coldness of my uncle's face numbed me.

The third was a real surprise—the "living death" of my grandmother Sarah Wood for whom I was named. Grandmother, for the last part of her life, stayed in her bedroom, where she would allow no window opened. To me she appeared sealed in a tomb.

Bob had me continue to seek contact with Jesus who repeatedly reassured me that death was a doorway experience, that the body was shed as an old, worn-out garment while the inner person, the essential being, went joyously through the door into eternal life.

The whole process took over an hour.

After Bob Bonham left I remembered that Agnes Sanford in her book *The Healing Gifts of the Spirit* had a chapter entitled "The Healing of the Memories." I found the book in my library, turned to that chapter and was stopped by this sentence:

"The truth is that any wound to the soul so deep that it is not healed by our own self-searching and prayers is inevitably connected with a subconscious awareness of sin."

We find the same connection in the Bible! Jesus died for our *sins*. Yet in Isaiah 53:4 we are told, "Surely he hath borne our griefs."

So there is a sense in which sin equals, or is tantamount to, grief.

Which is why the healing of memories is bound up with the forgiveness of sins.

While pondering all this, I recalled my mother's statement to me several years ago, how it distressed her, after Peter's death, the way I would spend hours talking over lofty "spiritual matters" with our housekeeper while my nine-year-old son, Peter John, playing alone in his bedroom, desperately needed my attention, time, and love.

A picture came to mind. It is an actual photo. Peter John is half-squatting on the floor of his bedroom, his toys around him, his big eyes solemn, bewildered, seeking.

With sudden tears I confessed my "heavenly-mindedness" as a sin and asked Jesus' forgiveness.

Next I asked Jesus to go back in time and take that little boy with the hurt, bewildered eyes in His arms. Then to sit there on the bedroom floor beside him, playing with him, ministering the healing needed to Peter John's lonely heart.

"Thank You, Lord, that all time—past, present, and future—is 'right now' with You. Therefore, that little boy is available to Your healing presence, even as the little girl Catherine is. I claim especially Your power to 'cleanse me from all unrighteousness.' Thank You for

Your great promise 'to restore . . . the years that the locust has eaten' (Joel 2:25 AMPLIFIED), both for Peter and for me.''

After this prayer I felt the love of Jesus washing over my body like a benediction.

What the Spirit has been doing for me through Bob Bonham is remarkable. Each time I believe I have plumbed the depths of peace and joy in the Christian life, there is more . . . more . . . more! My spirit bounds and leaps and overflows with thanksgiving so that I struggle for any way at all to express it! The fact that Jesus would love each individual *that much*—me—regardless of worth, regardless of performance turned in, regardless of anything, is *so* amazing. No wonder He was raised to the right hand of the Father and crowned with glory and honor!!

10

# Keeping My Eyes Upon Jesus

Fell on my face yesterday. Breathing was laborious. Did very little walking. Could not do the exercises. Was discouraged and disheartened and bored.

I knew the cause of all this. A letter came from my doctor, putting names and tags to my "chronic" illness for use in Medicare forms. It sounded so final that I began looking at *this*, accepting it, settling down to it.

I also opened the door to fear. Not so much fear of death because I've actually, finally worked through that. This time it was a fear that I would let down the readers of my books who expect me to be an example of victorious faith.

In my session with Bob Bonham we traced the roots of this fear of letting people down, back to my childhood. What came out was that my father's praising me so highly when I played the piano for his prayer meetings, or made top grades in school, eventually created in me the feeling that I *had* to achieve in order to have his love.

As the years passed this feeling was extended to other members of my family, to friends, even to God. Added to this was the belief that because I have been so public in my life as a Christian, if I did not measure up to what

Jesus expected of me, I would not only let Him down, but that people "out there" would think less of *Him;* that Jesus' reputation would actually suffer.

Put in so many words, this is obviously ridiculous! But that's what came out. So yesterday was a total setback for me.

This morning I sought the Lord's forgiveness and was told something like this, most emphatically:

"Catherine, take your eyes off yourself, off your symptoms, off your fears and center your attention on Me. Look at *Me.* Keep looking at Me.

"Allow Me to be your Doctor. This is My will. I *do* know how to give you health. I made you. I know how to mend you.

"Why do you think I healed everyone who came to Me in the days of My flesh? Out of overflowing mercy. I had only to see any human being blind or crippled or sick or in pain to want to set the wrong situation right as quickly as possible.

"I have told you in My Word (Hebrews) that as man's High Priest I am able—and want—to '*run*' to the assistance of those who cry to Me."

In my answering prayer, I said, "Lord, I do cry to You. I give You permission to change me on the inside, to strengthen my flabby spiritual muscles, to reverse the direction of my gaze, to make me eager to look at You only.

"I know You want a resurrection thrust inside me and an end to my doubts and negative thinking. In the wake of this will come new life and health. If not on this earth, then I will go into the next life with the differentness that You want for me."

Then Jesus led me to the sixteenth chapter of John where I was stopped by this magnificent verse:

> . . . it is profitable—good, expedient, advantageous—for you that I go away. Because if I do not go away, the Comforter (Counselor, Helper, Advocate, Interces-

sor, Strengthener, Standby) will not come to you—into close fellowship with you . . .

John 16:7 AMPLIFIED

These are the blessed functions of the Holy Spirit promised by Jesus:

*Counselor* (He gives wisdom to the simple.)
*Helper* (He lifts us over every obstacle.)
*Advocate* (He is our personal lawyer to "take us on" and plead our case.)
*Intercessor* (He stands before the throne of grace.)
*Strengthener* (He gives us vitality and courage.)
*Standby* (He is always at our side.)

How can a one of us get along without any of those things!

Then glorious verse 33 (italic added):

I have told you these things so that *in Me* you may have perfect peace and confidence. In the world you have tribulation and trials and distress and frustration; but be of good cheer—take courage, be confident, certain, undaunted—for I have overcome the world. —I have deprived it of power to harm, have conquered it [for you].

# 11

# RESURRECTION

*Thanks to Pastor Robert Bonham and the ministry of other loving friends and family, Catherine made good progress during September, October, and November 1982. To my amazement she decided we should accept the invitation to fly to Cape Cod to spend Thanksgiving with her son Peter, his wife, Edith, and their three children, Mary Elizabeth, thirteen, Peter Jonathan, nine, and David Christopher, two. Mother Wood, ninety-one, insisted she would go too.*

*There were moments of hilarity en route. Since Catherine and her mother both needed wheelchairs to traverse airport terminals, I took over when porters were not available, jockeying both wheelchairs through gates and up and down ramps.*

*It was Catherine's first visit to the Marshalls' new home, a joyous family time with four generations interacting, sometimes peacefully, sometimes through tensions that bubbled with creativity.*

*At Christmastime, our own home was the scene of another family reunion. Chet and his wife, Susan, arrived with our new grandson, Jacob LeSourd, joined by Linda and Phil Lader and our younger son, Jeff. Christmas had been a time when the perfectionist in Catherine ran her ragged with holiday preparations. Now for the first time in twenty-three years, Catherine let others run the show and simply enjoyed herself. Gift-giving and elaborate meals had been reduced, allowing more time for games and family talk.*

*At the beginning of 1983 Catherine set several goals for herself. An 800-page draft of the novel had been completed, but needed months of work to sharpen characterization.*

*She wanted to resume writing for each issue of* The Intercessors *newsletter.*

*And do an article about her mother for a* Guideposts *series on aging.*

*At the end of January, however, she underwent a cataract operation. From her journal:*

February 9th . . . I am staggering under what the eye surgeon said to me yesterday during a routine checkup following the cataract surgery: "You are sick from head to toe." I did not have to accept this verdict, but I did. Now I really have to ditch it—with the Spirit's help and by God's grace. This verse has truly helped me:

> And if the Spirit of Him Who raised up Jesus from the dead dwells in you, [then] He Who raised up Christ Jesus from the dead will also restore to life your mortal (short-lived, perishable) bodies through His Spirit Who dwells in you.
>
> Romans 8:11 AMPLIFIED

February 24th . . . Have hit a new low. I am quite out of breath—indeed, gasping for air—just in walking from room to room. My doctor could find no obvious cause for the trouble yesterday. Today it hit me. . . . Once again the doctors neither know what is wrong, nor how to help me. So . . . I am backed up against Jesus' help.

March 9th . . . In my Quiet Time, this thought: my hospital experience of the crucifixion was centered on the matter of breathing. This morning the Holy Spirit reminded me once again: "Jesus took your breathing problem into His own body on the Cross so that from henceforth *He* is your life-breath."

*With great heaviness of spirit I drove Catherine to Bethesda Memorial Hospital on March 11th, where she was admitted for more tests. We made light of it. "Just a few days," I assured her.*

*Silently, however, I was recalling another hospital episode almost twelve years before. A daughter, Amy Catherine, had been born to Peter and Edith Marshall and been given her grandmother's name. The baby, however, was genetically damaged in lungs, kidneys, and brain. Doctors at Children's Hospital in Boston offered no hope.*

*Friends from around the country gathered to pray for little Amy's healing. God answered the prayers, but not the way we expected. Healings occurred . . . in the people who came to pray. Amy Catherine died.*

*Catherine was desolate for months. "What went wrong?" she wept.*

*Eventually, she saw it—nothing went wrong! God is a sovereign God. We can plead with Him, bargain with Him, rail at Him, and claim anything and everything in His name. In return God overwhelms us with His blessings, but retains the decisions about "times and seasons" in His hands.*

*Here is Catherine's last journal entry made in the hospital:*

March 12th . . . The blood test yesterday showed carbon dioxide level in my blood too high, but not dangerous; not enough oxygen in the blood, however. Another problem seems to be anemia.

This morning Jesus told me once again: "Keep your eyes off yourself and look steadily at Me. I love you. I know how to mend you."

*That very day Catherine was taken to the same Intensive Care Unit where she had spent so many weeks last summer, and put on a respirator. Shortly after midnight on March 18, Catherine's heart stopped beating. The Lord had come to take her with Him to experience the joyous resurrection she missed last summer.*

In the hours and days that followed, the Lord seemed to place all of us in the family under His special love and protection; plus a necessary degree of numbness. The calls, letters, cards, flowers, and food that flowed in warmed and nourished us.

Two triumphant occasions followed: the burial service in National Presbyterian Church, Washington, D.C., conducted by its pastor and Catherine's close friend, Dr. Louis Evans, Jr., with her son, Peter John Marshall.

And the memorial service at the New Covenant Presbyterian Church, Pompano Beach, Florida. Pastors George Callahan along with Dr. William Earnhart (church elder and Catherine's personal physician) shared their memories of a great lady.

Robert Bonham, the man who for so many hours ministered healing to Catherine as pastor and friend, spoke these words at this same service:

"During Catherine's funeral in the National Presbyterian Church, my eyes went to some beautiful stained glass windows through which the sun was shining. I thought of Jesus telling His disciples, 'You are the light of the world.' Catherine as a 20th century follower put her light on a lamp stand so that all might see.

"I looked at the glass in those windows and thought about all the pieces therein. There were dark pieces and light pieces, all kinds of colors blended together. I thought about the suffering experiences that Catherine had early in her life and recently in the hospital. These were deep, deep colors. Her body never was able to keep up with her mind and her spirit. It always hauled her back.

"There were, of course, the brighter colors, the rose tints of love and warmth—the giving of her heart to those in her family and to everyone she touched. Those colors went out across the United States and throughout the world. I remember years back when I was at the University of Illinois, one of the professors there had a hydrocephalic child. He told me that he had called Catherine up long distance and had asked her to pray for his child. She did and the child was healed. All the way to Illinois, and other places far and near, went those pieces of radiating light—warm, bright, healing colors falling on the lives of people.

"There were so many pieces in her life—the books that she and the Lord wrote—the articles for *Guideposts* and other magazines. She wrote nothing that did not have all of her heart and mind in it as well as the heart and mind of Christ. Starting *The Intercessors* not long ago, she and Leonard mobilized prayer warriors across the nation to bring help to many people. Her family represents warm, glowing pieces of glass in the mosaic of her life. Likewise her many friends who kept calling when she died and could not believe that this had happened.

"A surprising thing about a stained glass window is that when the light is not shining through, it comes across as dull. Have you ever looked at a stained glass window when there is no light behind it? You cannot see what is in it. Catherine always had Christ's light shining through her life. As the light of Jesus radiated through the stained glass mosaic of her life, all of us who were within sight of it got blessed.

"When the sun goes down, the horizon stays bright for a long time. There is going to be a long afterglow to Catherine Marshall LeSourd's life. The books that were written will go on to become classics in Christian literature. The articles will go on helping people. There are things she has written that will yet find their way into print to bless us. Her touches on our lives will live on, ministering to my children, and my children's children.

"In the last page of her book *To Live Again*, Catherine wrote these words as she faced life without her husband, Peter: 'At moments when the future is completely obscured, can any one of us afford to go to meet our tomorrows with dragging feet? God had been in the past, then He would be in the future, too. Always He had brought adventure, high hopes, unexpected friends, new ventures that broke old patterns. Then in my future must lie more goodness, more mercy, more adventures, more friends. Across the hills, light was breaking through the storm clouds. Suddenly, just ahead of the car an incandescent, iridescent rainbow appeared, hung there shimmering. I hadn't seen a rainbow for a long time.' And then Catherine's last sentence, 'I drove steadily into the light.'

"Catherine is doing that right now—moving steadily into the Light."

# Catherine's Scriptural Lifeline

Early in her marriage to Len, Catherine formed the habit of copying into a gray 10 by 7 inch notebook the Bible verses that helped most in health or household crises. Over the years the pages filled to become a kind of scriptural lifeline. In the summer of 1982, when she was in the Intensive Care Unit, too ill to read the handwritten entries herself, a member of her family or close friend would read them to her. Here are 41 verses[1] to which she clung with ever-growing assurance:

> Behold, I am the Lord, the God of all flesh; is there anything too hard for Me?
>
> Jeremiah 32:27

> The grass withers, the flower fades, but the word of our God will stand for ever.
>
> Isaiah 40:8

> He has bestowed on us His precious and exceedingly great promises, so that through them you may escape

[1]All passages from the Amplified Bible unless otherwise noted.

(by flight) from the moral decay (rottenness and corruption) that is in the world because of covetousness (lust and greed), and become sharers (partakers) of the divine nature.

2 Peter 1:4

God is faithful—reliable, trustworthy and [therefore] ever true to His promise, and He can be depended on; by Him you were called into companionship and participation with His Son, Jesus Christ our Lord.

1 Corinthians 1:9

So shall my word be that goeth forth out of my mouth: it shall not return unto me void, but it shall accomplish that which I please, and it shall prosper in the thing whereto I sent it.

Isaiah 55:11 KJV

And if the Spirit of Him Who raised up Jesus from the dead dwells in you, [then] He Who raised up Christ Jesus from the dead will also restore to life your mortal (short-lived, perishable) bodies through His Spirit Who dwells in you.

Romans 8:11

So too the (Holy) Spirit comes to our aid and bears us up in our weakness; for we do not know what prayer to offer nor how to offer it worthily as we ought, but the Spirit Himself goes to meet our supplication and pleads in our behalf with unspeakable yearnings and groanings too deep for utterance.

Romans 8:26

And we know that all things work together for good to them that love God, to them who are the called according to his purpose.

Romans 8:28 KJV

I know that whatsoever God doeth, it shall be for ever: nothing can be put to it, nor anything taken from it: and God doeth it, that men should fear before him.

Ecclesiastes 3:14 KJV

For the Lord is our judge, the Lord is our law-giver, the Lord is our king; He will save us.

Isaiah 33:22

For I, the Lord your God, hold your right hand; I, Who say to you, Fear not, I will help you!

Isaiah 41:13

For God's gifts and His call are irrevocable—He never withdraws them when once they are given, and He does not change His mind about those to whom He gives His grace or to whom He sends His call.

Romans 11:29

When the enemy shall come in like a flood, the Spirit of the Lord will lift up a standard against him and put him to flight—for He will come like a rushing stream which the breath of the Lord drives.

Isaiah 59:19

But God is faithful [to His Word and to His compassionate nature], and He [can be trusted] not to let you be tempted . . . beyond your ability and strength of resistance and power to endure, but with the temptation He will [always] also provide the way out—the means of escape to a landing place—that you may be capable and strong and powerful patiently to bear up under it.

1 Corinthians 10:13

The Lord redeems the life of His servants, and none of those who take refuge and trust in Him shall be condemned or held guilty.

Psalm 34:22

Though I walk in the midst of trouble, You will revive me; You will stretch forth Your hand against the wrath of my enemies, and Your right hand will save me.

Psalm 138:7

The Lord also will be a refuge and a high tower for the oppressed, a refuge and a stronghold in times of trouble [high cost, destitution and desperation].

Psalm 9:9

And He will establish you to the end—keep you steadfast, give you strength, and guarantee your vindication, that is, be your warrant against all accusation or indictment—[so that you will be] guiltless and irreproachable in the day of our Lord Jesus Christ, the Messiah.

1 Corinthians 1:8

He will swallow up death in victory—He will abolish death forever; and the Lord God will wipe away tears from off all faces; and the reproach of His people He will take away from off all the earth; for the Lord has spoken it.

Isaiah 25:8

Fear not; for I am with you; do not . . . be dismayed, for I am your God. I will strengthen and harden you [to difficulties]; yes, I will help you; yes, I will hold you up and retain you with My victorious right hand of rightness and justice.

Isaiah 41:10

I have called you by your name, you are Mine. When you pass through the waters I will be with you, and through the rivers they shall not overwhelm you; when you walk through the fire you shall not be burned . . . nor shall the flame kindle upon you. For I am the Lord your God, the Holy One of Israel, your Savior . . .

Isaiah 43:1–3

For though the mountains should depart and the hills be shaken or removed, yet My love and kindness shall not depart from you, nor shall My covenant of peace and completeness be removed, says the Lord, Who has compassion on you.

Isaiah 54:10

For thus saith the Lord God, the Holy One of Israel; In returning and rest shall ye be saved; in quietness and in confidence shall be your strength.

Isaiah 30:15 KJV

In the world you have tribulation and trials and distress and frustration; but be of good cheer—take courage, be confident, certain, undaunted—for I have overcome the world. —I have deprived it of power to harm, have conquered it [for you].

John 16:33

I assure you, most solemnly I tell you, the person whose ears are open to My words—who listens to My message—and believes and trusts in and clings to and relies on Him Who sent Me has (possesses now) eternal life. And he does not come into judgment—does not incur sentence of judgment, will not come under condemnation—but he has already passed over out of death into life.

John 5:24

Do not fret or have any anxiety about anything, but in every circumstance and in everything by prayer and petition [definite requests] with thanksgiving continue to make your wants known to God. And God's peace . . . which transcends all understanding, shall garrison and mount guard over your hearts and minds in Christ Jesus.

Philippians 4:6–7

But they that wait upon the Lord shall renew their strength; they shall mount up with wings as eagles; they shall run, and not be weary; and they shall walk, and not faint.

Isaiah 40:31 KJV

Whoever takes a drink of the water that I will give him shall never, no never, be thirsty any more. But the water that I will give him shall become a spring of water welling up (flowing, bubbling) continually within him unto eternal life.

John 4:14

My sheep hear my voice, and I know them, and they follow me: And I give unto them eternal life; and they shall never perish, neither shall any man pluck them out of my hand. My Father, which gave them me, is greater than all; and no man is able to pluck them out of my Father's hand. I and My Father are one.

John 10:27–30 KJV

Keep and protect me, O God, for in You I have found refuge, and in You do I put my trust and hide myself. . . . my body too shall rest and confidently dwell in safety.

Psalm 16:1,9

In the day when I called, You answered me, and strengthened me with strength (might and inflexibility) [to temptation] in my inner self.

Psalm 138:3

Now the Lord is the Spirit, and where the Spirit of the

Lord is, there is liberty—emancipation from bondage, freedom.

2 Corinthians 3:17

(For the weapons of our warfare are not carnal, but mighty through God to the pulling down of strongholds;) Casting down imaginations, and every high thing that exalteth itself against the knowledge of God, and bringing into captivity every thought to the obedience of Christ.

2 Corinthians 10:4–5 KJV

Behold God, my salvation! I will trust and not be afraid, for the Lord God is my strength and song; yes, He has become my salvation. Therefore with joy will you draw water from the wells of salvation.

Isaiah 12:2–3

Rejoice in the Lord always—delight, gladden yourselves in Him; again I say, Rejoice!

Philippians 4:4

Although the fig tree shall not blossom, neither shall fruit be in the vines; the labour of the olive shall fail, and the fields shall yield no meat; the flock shall be cut off from the fold, and there shall be no herd in the stalls: Yet I will rejoice in the Lord, I will joy in the God of my salvation. The Lord God is my strength, and he will make my feet like hinds' feet, and he will make me to walk upon mine high places.

Habakkuk 3:17–19 KJV

Heal me, O Lord, and I shall be healed; save me, and I shall be saved; for You are my praise.

Jeremiah 17:14

Thou wilt keep him in perfect peace, whose mind is stayed on thee: because he trusteth in thee.

Isaiah 26:3 KJV

Our inner selves wait [earnestly] for the Lord; He is our help and our shield. For in Him does our heart rejoice, because we have trusted (relied on and been confident) in His holy name.

Psalm 33:20–21

. . . for He (God) Himself has said, I will not in any way fail you nor give you up nor leave you without support. [I will] not . . . in any degree leave you helpless, nor forsake nor let [you] down [relax My hold on you]. —Assuredly not!

Hebrews 13:5

For I am persuaded beyond doubt—am sure—that neither death, nor life, nor angels, nor principalities, nor things impending and threatening, nor things to come, nor powers, Nor height, nor depth, nor anything else in all creation will be able to separate us from the love of God which is in Christ Jesus our Lord.

Romans 8:38–39

# Encyclopedia Brown's First Book of Puzzles and Games

# Encyclopedia Brown's First Book of Puzzles and Games

BY JIM RAZZI

Based upon the Encyclopedia Brown Series
created by Donald J. Sobol

A BANTAM SKYLARK BOOK

ENCYCLOPEDIA BROWN'S FIRST BOOK
OF PUZZLES AND GAMES

*A Bantam Skylark Book / published by arrangement with
Elsevier/Nelson Books*

*Bantam Skylark edition / February 1980*



ISBN 0-553-15058-8

*Published simultaneously in the United States and Canada*

---

*Bantam Books are published by Bantam Books, Inc. Its trademark, consisting of the words "Bantam Books" and the portrayal of a bantam, is Registered in U.S. Patent and Trademark Office and in other countries. Marca Registrada. Bantam Books, Inc., 666 Fifth Avenue, New York, New York 10019.*

---

PRINTED IN THE UNITED STATES OF AMERICA

0 9 8 7 6 5 4 3 2 1

## Introduction

Here's Encyclopedia and all the gang in their first *Puzzles and Games Book.* Now you can have more fun with America's Sherlock Holmes in sneakers.

There are clues to spot, codes to crack, mazes to solve, word games, picture puzzles and lots more! It's all here, so grab a pencil and your wits for hours of stimulating, brain-teasing fun!

## *Crime Wave*

It's a sleepy day in Idaville but even so, Encyclopedia Brown has observed four crimes taking place. Can you spot them?

## ***The Line Up***

Chief Brown, Encyclopedia's father, has just caught Spider Spinoza, the jewel thief. He's in the line-up on the next page. A detective had been trailing him all day and gave this report to Chief Brown:

"I first observed Spider Spinoza in a drugstore, buying a comb. I knew that he was probably up to no good, so I followed him. After the drugstore, he went to an eye doctor to have his eyeglasses cleaned. He left the eye doctor and walked down 3rd Street. It started to rain just then and Spider opened his umbrella. I then observed him going into a jewelry store. While in the jewelry store, he stole a number of items while the owner was busy with another customer. He put these items in his jacket pocket and ran out of the store. It was then that I identified myself as a policeman and nabbed him."

Now that you know the detective's report, tell us who is Spider Spinoza, A, B, C, D or E?

A
B
C
D
E

## *Match the Prints*

Encyclopedia Brown is trying to match up some fingerprints. See if you can help. In the fingerprints below, only two are exactly alike. Which are they?

## ***Encyclopedia meets The Brain***

Brains Malloy was the brainiest kid in Idaville next to Encyclopedia. Some say that it was even. So to settle the question, Brains sent a message to Encyclopedia. The message explained itself and after a few hard looks, Encyclopedia got it. Can you? Here is the message that Brains sent.

**$\frac{\text{STAND}}{\text{I}}$ THAT YOU $\frac{\text{NEVER}}{\text{LOOK}}$ A CLUE.**

**IF $\frac{\text{STAND}}{\text{YOU CAN}}$ THIS MESSAGE, I WILL**

**BELIEVE THAT AND ADMIT YOU ARE SMARTER THAN I AM.**

**BRAINS MALLOY**

## ***Prehistoric Word Find***

In *The Case of the Cave Drawings,* a dishonest teenager tries to cash in on phony prehistoric paintings. But Encyclopedia spots the fake when he realizes that dinosaurs and cavemen don't mix. In the word find below, however, we did mix cavemen and dinosaurs. They're all hidden, of course, so you'll have to find them. You can go forward, backward, vertically, horizontally and diagonally. Draw a pencil line around each word as you find it. Look for: LIZARD, PREHISTORIC, CLUB, DINOSAUR, VOLCANO, EARTHQUAKE, SPEAR, FIRE, SUN, CAVEMAN, MAMMAL and ROC (a legendary giant bird).

| | | | | | | | | | | | |
|---|---|---|---|---|---|---|---|---|---|---|---|
| E | A | R | T | H | A | R | I | F | L | O | P |
| R | V | O | L | A | C | O | R | L | I | R | P |
| U | O | D | S | A | E | U | A | A | Z | R | R |
| O | L | U | V | C | A | V | E | M | A | N | E |
| S | P | E | R | S | R | O | P | M | R | I | H |
| O | M | T | O | L | T | L | S | A | D | D | I |
| N | A | N | C | A | H | C | I | M | C | R | S |
| I | I | L | O | M | Q | A | H | L | H | R | T |
| D | U | N | M | S | U | N | E | T | A | A | O |
| B | I | A | A | E | A | O | I | A | R | Z | R |
| D | M | U | R | A | K | A | P | I | I | I | I |
| S | O | N | I | M | E | V | A | C | F | L | C |

## *Clue Code*

Here's one of Encyclopedia's "Clue Codes." He's sure that none of the Tigers would be smart enough to get the message if they ever found it.

Here is how it works:
□ stands for a consonant (T,N,C,S etc.)
☆ stands for a vowel (A,E,I etc.)
Now from the clues, guess the words and then read the message downward.

| | | | | |
|---|---|---|---|---|
| □☆☆□ | = | (To come together) | = | ___________ |
| □☆ | = | (Meaning myself) | = | ___________ |
| ☆□ | = | (Inside) | = | ___________ |
| □□☆ | = | (Definite article) | = | ___________ |
| ☆□□ | = | (Not young) | = | ___________ |
| □☆□□ | = | (A farm building) | = | ___________ |
| □☆□☆□□□ | = | (This evening) | = | ___________ |

## Sea Monster

In *The Case of the Red Boat,* Encyclopedia and his father go out fishing and end up netting a pair of thieves.

They were lucky they didn't meet up with this monster while on the water. Which monster? Well, it's an eight-armed creature of the deep. If you can guess its name, put it on the dashed lines below. Now take a pencil and shade in all the areas below that have the letters that make up that name. __ __ __ __ __ __ __

## ***Short Cut Maze***

Encyclopedia wants to take a short cut to his home across the fenced-in backyards. See if you can find the shortest route to his home. Begin at START and find your way to HOME. You cannot cross any lines. Here's a hint: The shortest way will pass by only four houses.

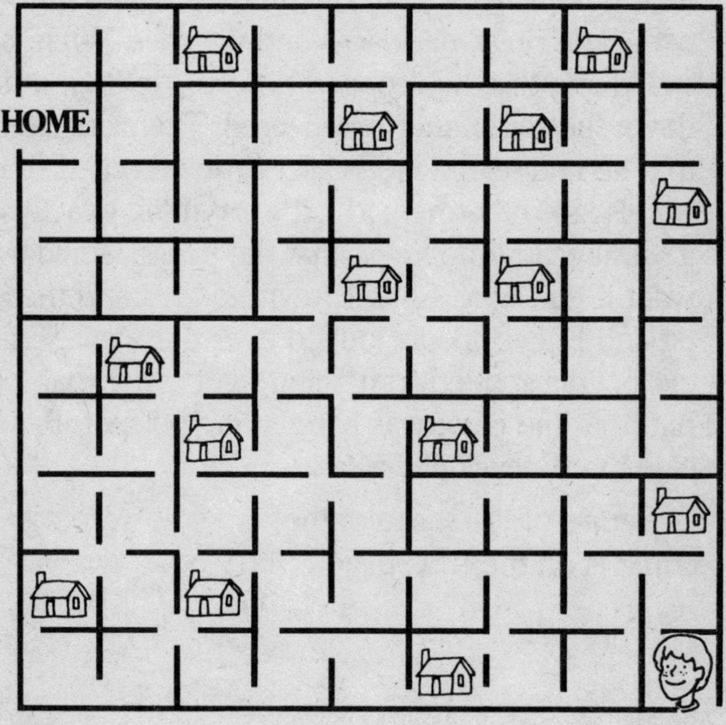

## *Spot the Clue*

A jewelry store has been robbed and Chief Brown and Encyclopedia hurry to the scene. When they get there, a store clerk explains what happened. He was there alone, he says, because the owner had gone out to lunch. Suddenly, he continued, while he was in the back of the store, someone outside threw a brick through the window. The window breaker reached in and grabbed some rings, necklaces and watches. While he was doing this, he dropped his cap. He then ran down the street and disappeared. The clerk said that he had telephoned Chief Brown immediately. He also said that he had left everything exactly as it was because he knew that the police would want it that way. Chief Brown nodded and then he and Encyclopedia looked over the scene. Encyclopedia spotted something right away that told him that the clerk was lying. Can you spot the clue that Encyclopedia saw?

A picture of the scene of the crime is on the next page.

JEWELRY STO

## *Bugs Bugs Brown*

Bugs Meany, who was always trying to bug Encyclopedia Brown and get even with him, made up these trick stories. In each story, there is one mistake. Bugs told the stories to Encyclopedia Brown in front of a group of kids, hoping that Encyclopedia would make a fool of himself. Encyclopedia of course found the mistake in each story. Can you? Here are the stories:

Late Lucy Washburn lived in a lovely, one-leveled ranch-style house on Elm Street. They called her Late Lucy because she was never on time for anything. One day, she had a date to go skate boarding with Ruth Phillips at three o'clock that afternoon. She had some chores to take care of first, however, and before she knew it, it was ten minutes to three and she wasn't ready yet. Lucy made up her mind not to be late this time, though. She rushed around as if she were doing the latest dance, the hop, skip and jump, and was finished just as Punctual Phillips rang the doorbell. Lucy ran down the stairs and opened the door. It was exactly three o'clock. Lucy was all out of breath but she had made it on time for once!

*

Mario Piccolo was the star catcher of the Idaville Little League baseball team. The team had worked out all day and Mario was dog-tired when he returned home that night. He decided to turn in early and get a lot of sleep. The next day was the big game with the Baystown Bashers and Mario wanted to be good and rested. So at nine o'clock that night, he went up to his bedroom, laid his mitt on his bedside table, and quickly put on his pajamas. He set the alarm on his big alarm clock to go off at nine-thirty the next morning. The alarm always woke him up. No sooner had his head hit the pillow then he was fast asleep. At fifteen minutes past nine, a car's horn honked loudly outside Mario's window but he didn't hear a thing. The next thing he knew it was nine-thirty, the alarm was ringing and the sun was shining. Mario picked up his catcher's mitt from the table and thought about the coming game. It was going to be tough, but he was sure they would win.

## *Name the Case*

A mis-typed note gave Encyclopedia the answer to this sparkling gem of a case. To find out which case it was, solve the acrostic puzzle.

Here is what to do: Guess the words from the clues, and write the letters in the spaces above the numbers. Then transfer the letters to the same numbered boxes in the grid on the next page. You will then find the name of the case.

1. Bugs Meany is a _ _ _ _ _ member
   1 21 19 3 20
2. Opposite of fat _ _ _ _
   10 2 14 18
3. Another word for enemy _ _ _
   9 8 7
4. His Majesty's Ship _ _ _
   11 13 15
5. Encyclopedia hung this outside his garage. _ _ _ _
   6 17 23 22
6. What Encyclopedia loved to work on _ _ _ _
   4 5 16 12

| 1 | 2 | 3 | 4 | 5 | 6 | 7 | 8 | 9 | 10 | 11 | 12 |
|---|---|---|---|---|---|---|---|---|---|---|---|
| 13 | 14 | 15 | 16 | 17 | 18 | 19 | 20 | 21 | 22 | 23 | |

## *The Case of the Busy Chief*

Chief Brown had to go to various places on his way home from the Idaville Police Station. He was a busy man so he asked his son, Encyclopedia, to find out the best way he could go to all the places. Encyclopedia solved the problem by drawing a map of the roads that led to all the places. He then traced a route on the roads with a pencil that passed through each place. He never passed the the same place twice, however, and he never went back over his line. Can you do it?

Begin at START and end at FINISH.

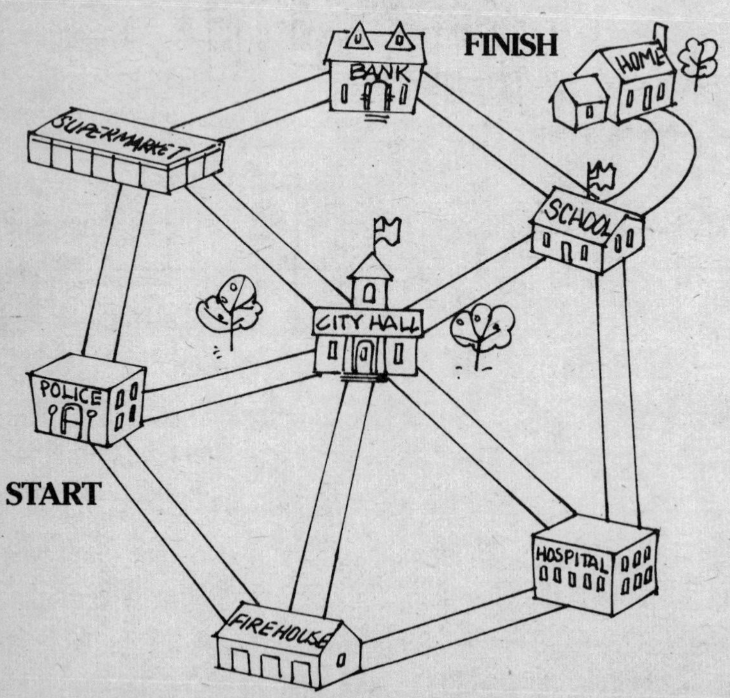

## *What's in a Name?*

Billy Stein was a very scientific kid. So it was no surprise when he came into Encyclopedia's garage one summer morning and said: "I would like to hire you to find my pet *eight-legged wingless arachnid.* I've lost it and it was more fun than a barrel of *simians.* I used to have *a warm-blooded vertebrate covered with feathers* but it died. I then owned a *mammal with leathery wings* but it slept a lot in the daytime, so I gave it away. I then bought a *scaly, limbless long-bodied reptile* but it became lost in the grass. Before I lost my latest pet, I had an *aquatic and land mollusk with a spiral shell* but it was too boring to play with. Do you think you can find my pet?

Encyclopedia said that he would give it a try. Sally Kimball just looked at Encyclopedia Brown with her mouth open.

"Do you know what he was talking about?" she asked in wonder. "Sure," answered Encyclopedia, "Don't you?"

If you know the animals that are italicized above. write them in order below.

1.__________ 3.__________ 5.__________

2.__________ 4.__________ 6.__________

P. S. If you don't know the animals, look up the answers and then have fun trying them out on your friends.

## *Movie Crossword*

In *The Case of the Missing Statue*, Chief Brown and Encyclopedia try to help a movie star. But it seemed that her problem was just a big act to get attention. Pay attention to this movie crossword and see if you can solve it and be in the spotlight.

***ACROSS***

1. Movie city
7. North America (abbr.)
8. Murder movie
9. Mother
12. Travolta or Redford
15. Movie monster
16. Famous actors and actresses
18. Slim
21. Setting of movie or play
22. Nickel (symbol)
23. Cinemascope is seen on what? (2 wds.)

***DOWN***

2. Not young
3. Shoot-'em-up movie
4. Before two
5. Betcha can't do it!
6. Cougar
10. Sophia Loren or Suzanne Somers
11. Twelve o'clock
13. Sherlock Holmes or Inspector Clouseau
14. Outdoor movie
17. Movie film wheels
19. Baseball team (how many?)
20. Batman sound

NOW PLAYING
1
2
3
4
5
6
7
8
9
10
11
12
13
14
15
16
17
18
19
20
21
22
23

## *Pinball Wizard*

Tilt Wilson is the pinball champ of Idaville. He has a high score of 140 points. One day, Sally Kimball challenged him to a game and beat him! See if you can beat Tilt's high score of 140 yourself.

Here is how to play:

Start at the STAR, and with a light pencil line, find your way to the FINISH. When you pass through a numbered opening add that number to your score. You cannot cross over your own line and you can't go through the same opening twice otherwise, TILT!

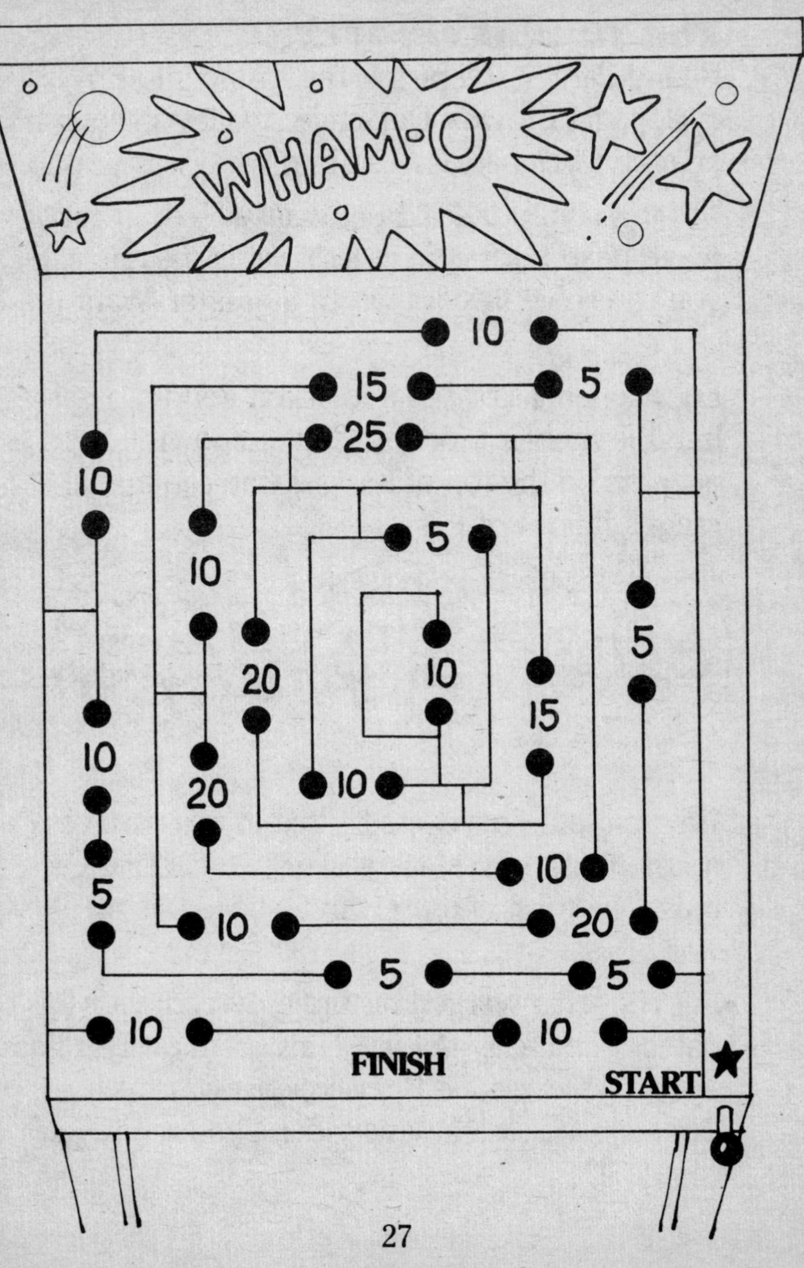
WHAM-O
10
15
5
25
10
10
5
5
10
20
10
15
10
10
20
10
10
5
10
20
5
5
5
10
10
FINISH
START

## *The Two-Bit Mystery*

Benny Parker, the puzzle nut, came into Encyclopedia Brown's Detective Agency shaking his head. Encyclopedia asked him what was wrong.

"It's this coin puzzle," Benny answered, "I can't make head nor tail of it! It's driving me crazy. If you can solve this, it's worth a quarter. Want the case?"

Encyclopedia said yes and asked Benny to tell him the problem. Benny plunked down three quarters on the top of the gasoline can and arranged them like this:

He then told Encyclopedia that in three moves, no more, no less, turning over two coins at each move, he must end up with all heads facing upward.

Encyclopedia worked his brain overtime for this one but he finally got it. Benny went away a happy puzzle-lover and Encyclopedia was twenty-five cents richer. Now why don't you see if you can do it?

## Letter-Wise

Sally Kimball, Encyclopedia's partner, wrote down these letters on a slip of paper. Each letter stands for the name of something and there is a natural sequence to them. There is one last letter missing. Can you tell us what it is? Here are the letters:

**M T W T F S ?**

If you got that one, try this next one that Encyclopedia Brown wrote down. Each letter below represents a number: Can you tell us what the next letter should be?

**O T T F F S S ?**

### *Crazy Graffiti*

The latest party game in Idaville is crazy graffiti. The idea is to figure out what the words really stand for. It can be the name of a famous person, an object or a common saying. For instance, number 3 stands for "double time." Now try to guess the rest.

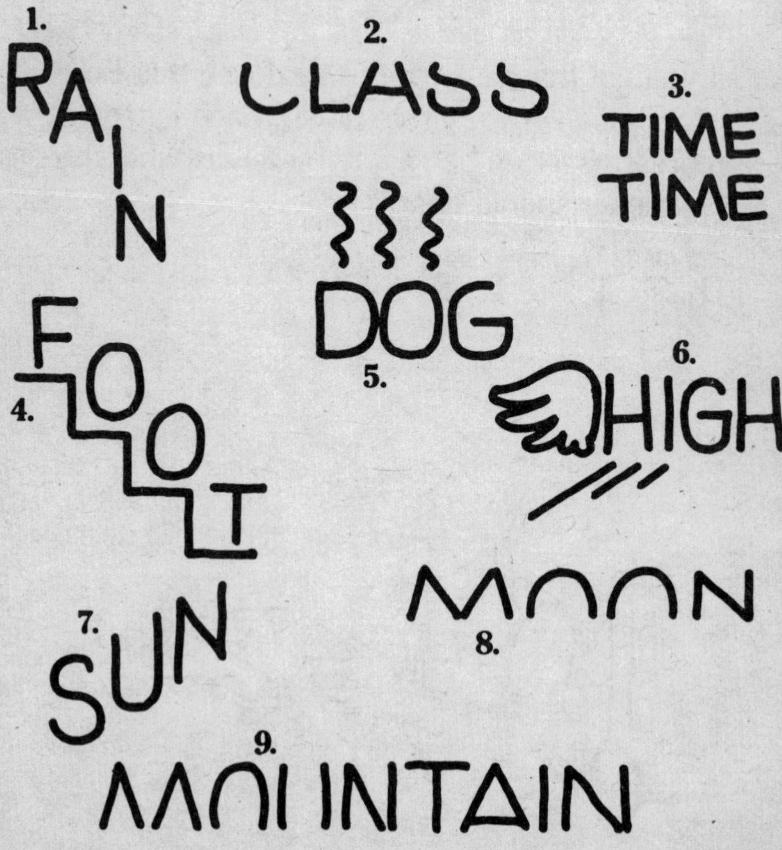

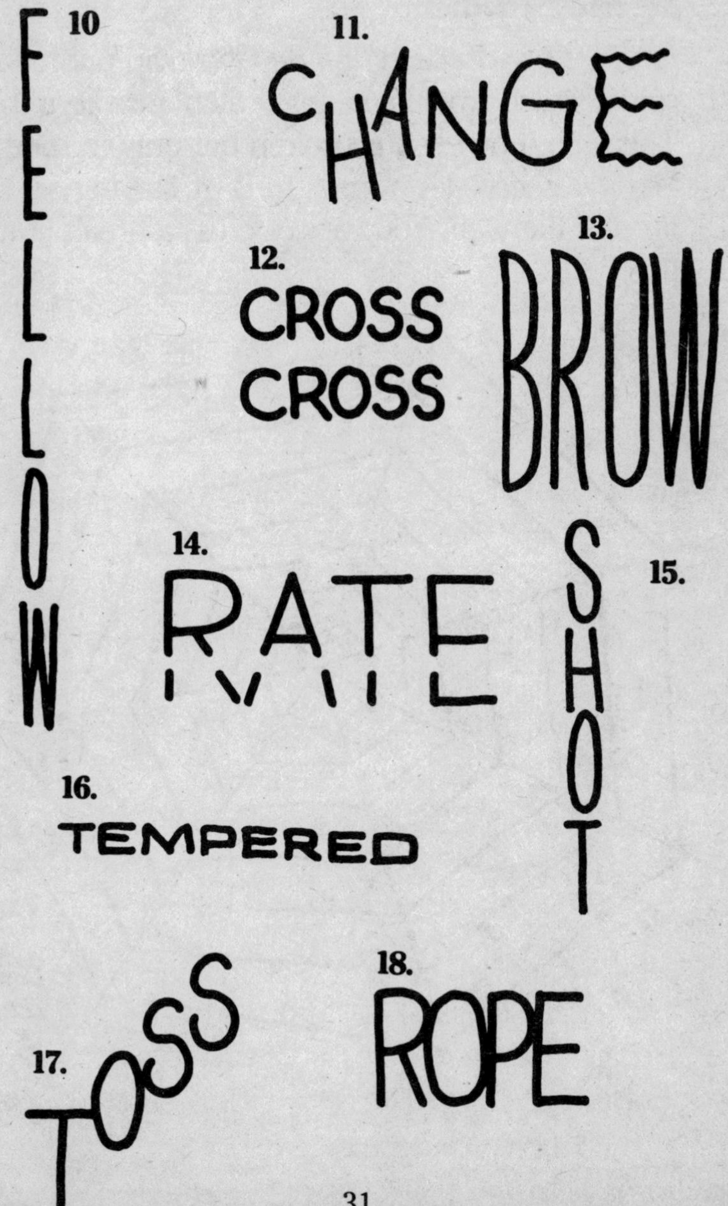
FELLOW
10
11.
CHANGE
12.
CROSS
CROSS
13.
BROW
14.
RATE
SHOT
15.
16.
TEMPERED
17.
TOSS
18.
ROPE

## Spider Maze

In *The Case of the Whistling Ghost,* an unbroken spider's web was the clue to catch a camera thief. This web, however, *is* broken but only in spots. See if you can get from A to B by staying on the lines of the web. You cannot cross a break in a line.

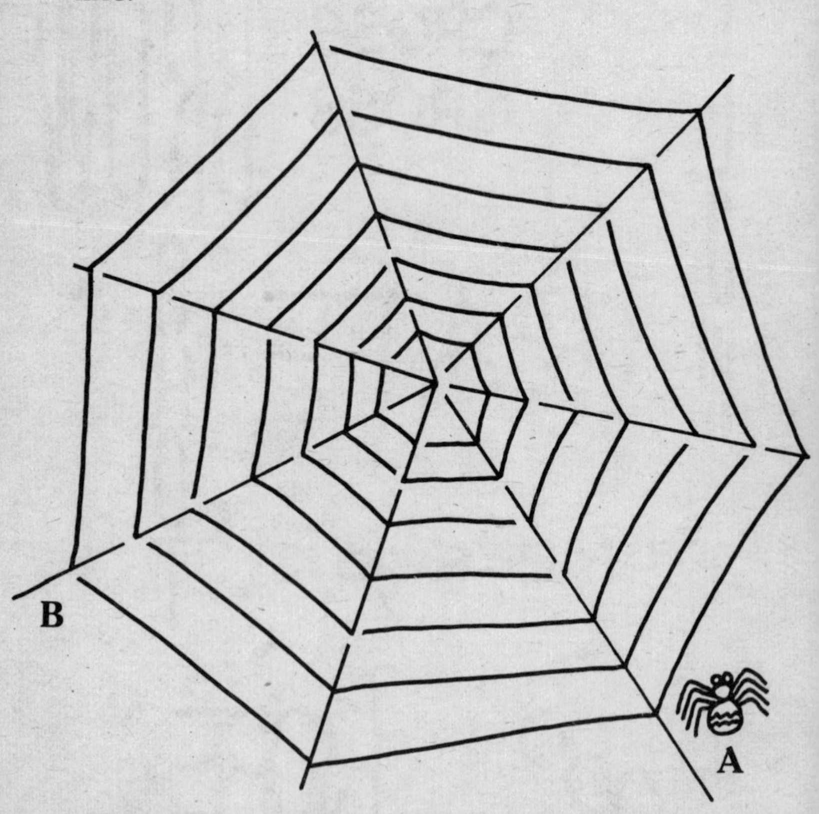

## *A Visual Trick*

Roscoe Kippers is Idaville's amateur kid magician. He likes to come up with optical illusions to show his friends. Here's one that he just came up with.

What to do:

There is a hidden message in the jumble of lines below. To see it, just hold the page at an angle away from you and close one eye. Look in the direction of the arrow, beginning at START and move around clockwise. Can you see the message?

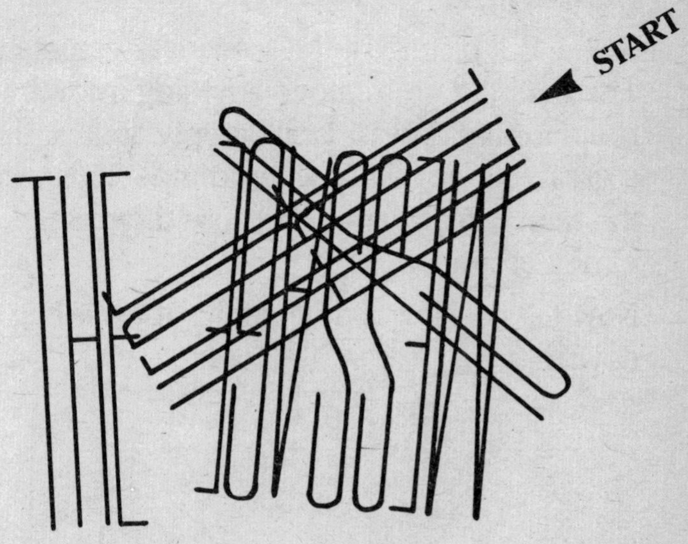

## *A Short Mystery*

See if you can solve a mystery just like Encyclopedia Brown would.

Here is the mystery:

A short man was in an empty room. There was a cloth bag hanging from a hook near the ceiling. The short man had money hidden in the bag. He was much too short to reach the bag by himself and there was absolutely no other furniture or manmade object in the room. Yet the man reached up slowly and took the bag off the hook with his hand.

Below is a picture of the scene a few hours later. The man did not remove anything from the room in that time. It is still empty. In fact, there is a great, big puddle of water on the floor which the man can't clean up because there is not even a mop around.

Now tell us. How did he get his money bag down?

## *Witness to the Crime*

Encyclopedia Brown was just coming out of the Beefy Burger Palace when he witnessed this bank robbery. He carefully noted a number of things as a good witness should. Later, when his father, Chief Brown, asked him some questions, Encyclopedia was ready with the answers.

Now see if you can do the same. Study the picture of the robbery below and try to remember all the details. Then turn the page and answer the questions. Don't peek back.

1. How many robbers were there?________________

2. What was the license number of the getaway car?________________

3. What time did the robbery take place?________________

4. What was the name of the bank that was robbed?________________

5. At what avenue and street was the getaway car parked?________________

6. The robber getting into the car:

   A. Was he masked?________________

   B. Did he wear a hat?________________

   C. Was his shirt striped or checked?________________

   D. Did he wear sunglasses?________________

   E. Was he armed?________________

7. What's the address of the bank?________________

## *Cryptograms*

One of Encyclopedia Brown's favorite pastimes is solving cryptograms. A cryptogram is a code in which other letters are substituted for the real letters of the alphabet. Now, of course, in any one cryptogram, you don't know yet which letters stand for the real letters. You have to figure it out a little at a time by trial and error. It's not as hard as it sounds. For instance, a single letter standing alone will usually stand for I or A. A group of three letters occurring frequently throughout the cryptogram, will usually be AND or THE. These are used frequently in sentences. Two letters together will probably be AS, DO, IS, IT, OF and so on.

As you start getting some letters, you will then get parts of words. Then you can guess what the rest of the letters are. For example, if you figured out that G I O K I L stood for D O C T O ? so far; you can guess that the last L will stand for R and the word would be D O C T O R. Now of course you know that all the other L's in the cryptogram stand for R also. You also know that all G's stand for D, all I's for O and so on.

Now let's start off on an easy one. The statement below in cryptogram code will tell you a fact about cryptograms. Decode the statement in the lines underneath. Since this is your first one, we will give you some hints to start you off.

Here they are: H=C, L=G, W=R, Z=U, X=S, P=K, D=Y, G=B, F=A.

Now here's the cryptogram

**NK DTZ YFPJ YMJ YNRJ**

__ ___ ____ ___ ____

**FSI YWTZGQJ YT IT**

___ ________ __ __

**YMJR, HWDUYTLWFRX**

____, ____________

**FWJ KZS!**

___ ___!

After you've solved this one, turn the page for a longer one.

## *Space-Age Nursery Rhyme*

Here's a cryptogram of an old nursery rhyme. It has a Space-Age surprise in it that is not in the original. Solve the cryptogram and you'll see what we mean.

Here's some hints: U=I, P=D, X=L, V=J.

TQK, PUPPXQ, PUPPXQ,

___, ______, ______,

FTQ OMF MZP FTQ

___ ___ ___ ___

RUPPXQ, FTQ OAI

______, ___ ___

VGYBQP AHQD FTQ

______ ____ ___

YAAZ, FTQ MEFDAZMGF

____, ___ _________

XMGSTQP FA EQQ EGOT

_______ __ ___ ____

EBADF, MZP FTQ PUET

_____, ___ ___ ____

DMZ MIMK IUFT FTQ

___ ____ ____ ___

EBAAZ.

_____

## Seeing Stars

Bugs Meany is selling copies of a photograph that he says was taken by a famous astronomer. It shows the moon and stars, and the astronomer has personally autographed each one. When Encyclopedia Brown sees the photo, however, he tells everyone that it's a fake and no astronomer ever took that picture. How did he know?
Here is the photo.

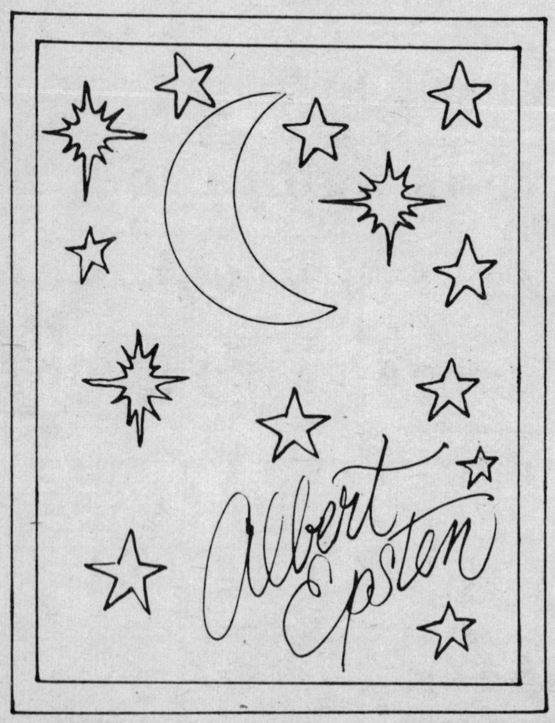

## *Encyclopedia Brown Word Maze*

In this word maze you must find words by drawing a continuous line from letter to letter until you spell the word. For example, we have found the word TIGER for you. You can go forward, backward, up, down, horizontally, vertically and diagonally. However, you cannot jump over any letter. Starting anywhere you want to, find: ENCYCLOPEDIA, BUGS MEANY (one word in the maze), IDAVILLE, SALLY KIMBALL (one word), CHIEF BROWN (one word).

| | | | | | | | |
|---|---|---|---|---|---|---|---|
| E | N | B | G | M | E | D | I |
| Y | C | U | S | A | N | A | L |
| P | C | L | I | T | Y | V | L |
| E | O | R | E | G | L | I | A |
| C | D | I | A | L | E | B | M |
| H | I | O | W | N | L | Y | I |
| E | F | B | R | S | A | L | K |

## ***Indian Word Find***

In *The Case of the Bitter Drink,* the Daughters of the Pioneers hold Indian trials. One of the tests is to drink something really bitter and not make a face. One of the Braves, however, cheats by freezing his mouth, but Encyclopedia finds him out in the end.

Now in the word find below, there are hidden words relating to Indians. You can go forward, backward, vertically, horizontally and diagonally. Draw a pencil line around each word as you find it. Look for: WAMPUM, WARPATH, TOMAHAWK, MOCCASIN, TOMTOM, FEATHER, ARROW, DRUM, BUFFALO, BRAVES and TEPEE.

| O | L | A | F | U | B | T | O | N | U | R | D |
|---|---|---|---|---|---|---|---|---|---|---|---|
| F | E | A | T | H | E | A | R | R | O | A | A |
| O | W | A | M | P | U | M | R | W | K | M | V |
| M | H | R | E | A | E | A | T | W | S | O | A |
| N | T | T | E | P | E | E | A | O | E | C | R |
| U | A | F | E | A | T | H | E | R | V | C | B |
| R | P | T | R | R | A | R | A | R | A | A | E |
| D | R | U | M | M | O | V | O | A | R | S | T |
| R | A | D | O | L | A | F | F | U | B | I | A |
| A | W | T | O | M | T | O | M | O | T | N | P |
| W | A | N | R | U | M | O | W | O | M | E | R |
| B | R | A | V | E | T | O | M | T | O | N | A |
| M | A | C | C | A | S | I | N | O | T | A | W |

## *Be a Police Artist*

Below you will find a witness's description of a man seen robbing a house. See if you can help Encyclopedia Brown get a picture of the suspect. Here is what to do: Read the description and draw in the missing parts. When you have finished, turn to the answer section to see how close your picture comes to the real person.

Here is the description:

"He had dark, curly hair and wore eyeglasses. He also had a large nose and a small mustache. His chin was square."

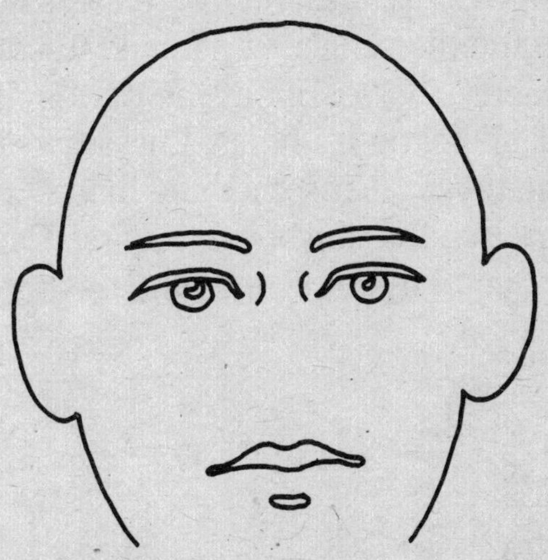

## *Spot the Clue*

This incident happened when Encyclopedia and his father, Chief Brown, were vacationing on a ranch out West. It seemed that the ranch boss had sent a payroll messenger out to the cowboys on the range. It was payday and he was carrying nearly a thousand dollars. A short while later, however, the messenger, who was a tall, thin cowboy, came riding back to the ranch. He was on a different horse. He shouted that he had been robbed. The ranch boss asked what had happened. The cowboy messenger told him that he had been held up by a big cowboy, even taller than he was. The bandit had then made him change horses because the messenger's horse was faster. So the messenger was forced to come back on the bandit's horse. But as the cowboy told his story, still sitting on his horse, Encyclopedia noticed something. That something made Encyclopedia sure that the cowboy was lying. Can you spot the clue in the picture on the next page?

## Name Game

Fill in the names going across in the grid below by following the clues. When you're finished, find Encyclopedia Brown's real first name hiding somewhere in the grid. Circle it with a pencil when you do.

**ACROSS**

1. First name of Brown's junior partner (girl)
2. Girl's name associated with Christmas
3. Boy's name. Rhymes with ferry
4. Last name of the leader of the Tigers
5. Informal form of Louis

| | | | | |
|---|---|---|---|---|
| 1. S | | | | |
| 2. C | | | | |
| 3. J | | | | |
| 4. M | | | | |
| 5. L | | | | |

## *Treasure Island*

Tubby Jones ran up to Encyclopedia Brown's garage one summer morning all out of breath. "I'm going to be rich!" he yelled, waving a map. He showed Encyclopedia Brown an old treasure map he had found on the beach. It had instructions on where treasure could be found on Gull Island, right off the coast. Encyclopedia studied the map and then said: "Save your breath, Tubby, this map's a fake." How did Encyclopedia know?

Here is a picture of the map.

## Trapped!

Encyclopedia and his friends are lost in Carson's Caverns. They took a wrong turn somewhere. Now they don't know which way is out and to top it off, they haven't even seen anything yet. But Encyclopedia saves the day. Not only does he lead the gang out but they manage to see every cavern along the way.
Think you can do it?

Here's what to do:

Take a pencil and start at Cavern A. Draw a continuous line through the tunnels that passes through each cavern only once. You cannot visit the same cavern twice and you cannot cross your own line. You must end up at exit E.

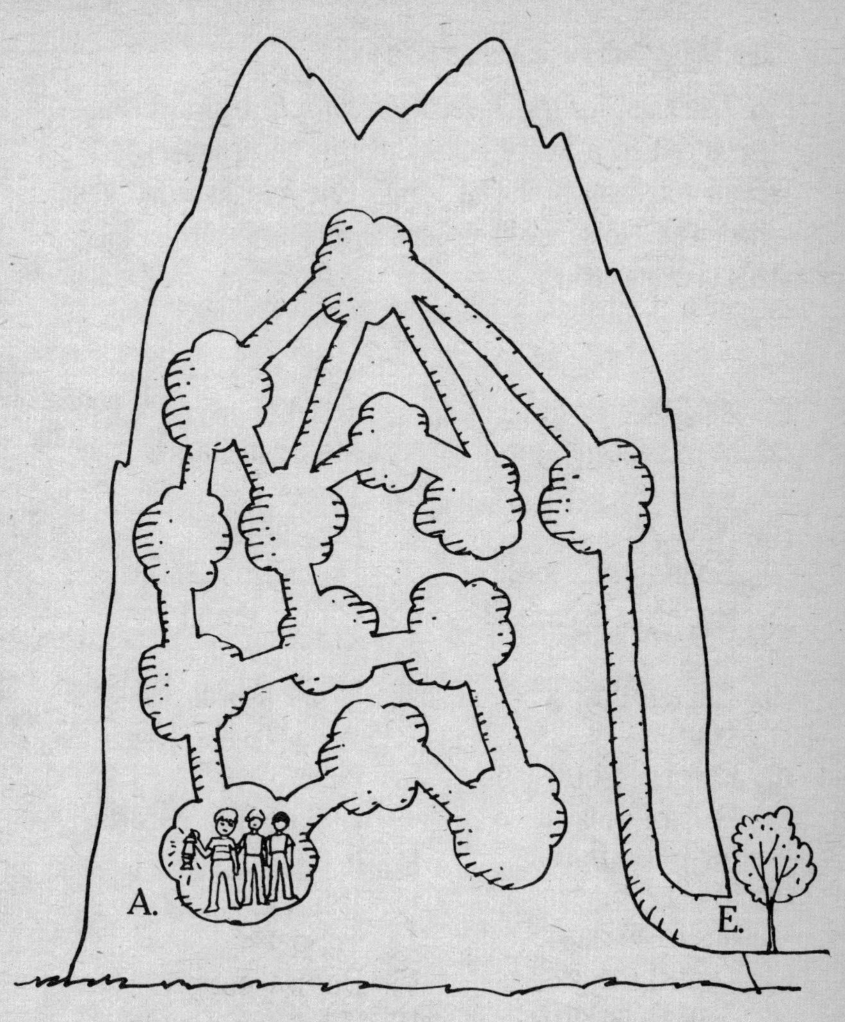
A.
E.

## *Bullfighter Crossword*

In *The Case of the Boy Bullfighter,* a trained dog turns out to a lot of bull. But the gang is treated to an exciting bullfight while Encyclopedia solves the case. Now see if you're brave enough to face this crossword.

**ACROSS**

2. What a bullfighter must be!
4. Not on
6. Bullfighter's tool
8. Event in Spanish arena
9. Bullfighting country
10. Color for bull
12. Part of bull given for good fight
14. The bull going after the cape
16. One-third of Santa's laugh
17. Reduce in length
20. A bull will do this before he charges
21. Bullring cheer
22. Not strong

**DOWN**

1. Mexican bandit
2. Places for bullfights
3. Bullfight stadium
5. High-pitched instrument
6. What a bull will do
7. Near
9. Bullfighters parade
11. In
13. What it will do in Spain
15. Bull's weapons
18. What the picador rides
19. Slow, easy run

1
2
3
4
5
6
7
8
9
10
11
12
13
14
15
16
17
18
19
20
21
22

## ***Spot the Clue***

Melvin Moore came running up to Encyclopedia Brown for help. Jack Evinrode had been stealing his gas again! Encyclopedia asked him to explain. Melvin said that Jack Evinrode had a small boat with an outboard motor in the back. He said that he had suspected Jack of stealing gasoline from his boathouse for a while now. He knew that Jack was always spending money on other things so he never had enough to buy gas with. Now it seems that Melvin had actually seen him stealing gasoline that morning. It was now late afternoon. Encyclopedia went down to the dock with Melvin to look for Jack. Just as they got there, they saw Jack tying up his boat. They went over and Melvin demanded that Jack pay for the gas he stole. Jack denied stealing any gas from Melvin and said that as a matter of fact, he had very little gas in his motor.

"That's because you used it all up!" shouted Melvin. Jack said that it wasn't true. He said that, in fact, he had been rowing all day because he had so little gas. He showed Melvin and Encyclopedia two long oars. It was then that Encyclopedia noticed something that tripped Jack up. Can you spot the clue in the picture on the next page?

## *From Boats to Oats*

Encyclopedia loves boating and horseback riding, so it's no surprise that he loves this word game.

Here's what to do:

Just change one letter in each word below that relates to boating so that each word becomes a new word that relates to horses.

**PADDLE — ____________**

**SPAR — ____________**

**MATE — ____________**

**BOAT — ____________**

**SAIL — ____________**

# Answers

*Crime Wave, page 7*

The four crimes are:
1. Car going the wrong way on a one-way street
2. Boy throwing litter on the sidewalk
3. Same boy crossing street when light says DON'T WALK
4. Posters up on wall that says POST NO BILLS

P. S. If you thought that the van was parked illegally at the NO PARKING sign, remember it says 10 PM.

*The Line-Up, pages 8 & 9*

Spider Spinoza is "B." If you didn't get it, read the report again and you'll see that all the others are eliminated for one reason or another. For example, the bald man wouldn't have bought a comb, and so on.

*Match the Prints, page 10*

Numbers 2 and 8 are exactly alike

*Encyclopedia meets The Brain, page 11*

The message reads:
I UNDERSTAND THAT YOU NEVER OVERLOOK A CLUE. IF YOU CAN UNDERSTAND THIS MESSAGE, I WILL BELIEVE THAT AND ADMIT YOU ARE SMARTER THAN I AM.

# Answers

*Prehistoric Word Find, page 12*

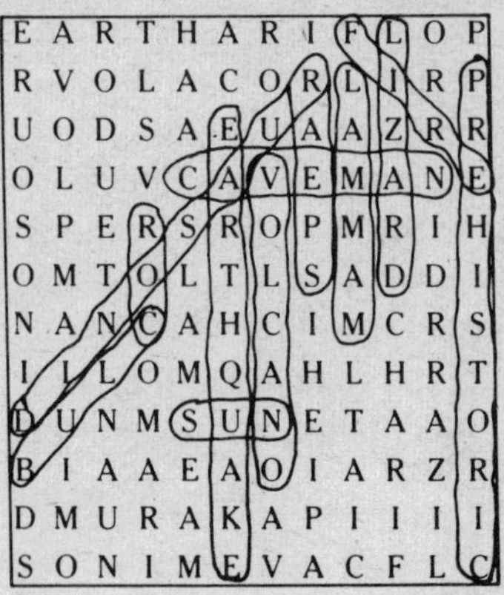


*Clue Code, page 13*

The message reads: MEET
ME
IN
THE
OLD
BARN
TONIGHT

*Sea Monster, page 14*

*OCTOPUS*

## Answers

*Short-Cut Maze, page 15*

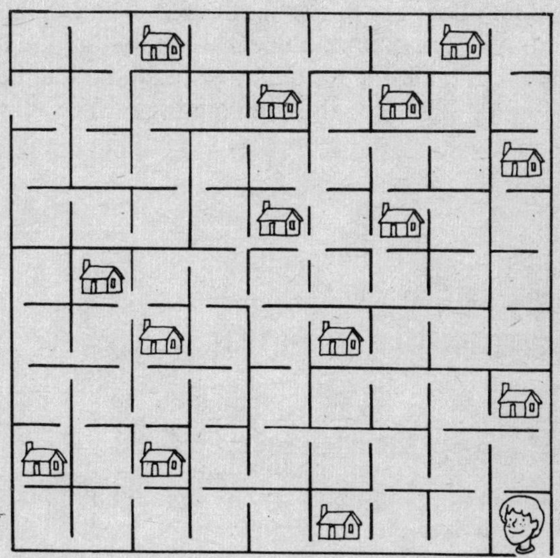

*Spot the Clue, pages 16 & 17*

Encyclopedia saw that the brick was *outside* the window. If the brick had been thrown through the window from the outside, as the clerk stated, it would have been *inside* the store. Remember, the clerk said that he left everything exactly the way it was.

When caught in his lie, the clerk confessed that he threw the brick from inside the store. He then stole the jewelry himself and made up the story about the thief and the dropped cap.

## Answers

*Bugs Bugs Brown, pages 18 & 19*

Lucy could not *run down the stairs* because, as was stated at the beginning of the story, she lived in a one-level house.

If Mario set his alarm to go off at 9:30 at 9:00 that night, the alarm would go off in a half hour from then. The clock doesn't know PM from AM of course. Since it was said that the *alarm* always woke him up, it means that he woke up a half hour later, or 9:30 PM. Therefore the sun couldn't have been shining.

*Name the Case, pages 20 & 21*

1. TIGER, 2. THIN, 3. FOE, 4. HMS, 5. SIGN, 6. CASE

| T | H | E | C | A | S | E | O | F | T | H | E |
|---|---|---|---|---|---|---|---|---|---|---|---|
| M | I | S | S | I | N | G | R | I | N | G | ■ |

*The Case of the Busy Chief, page 22*

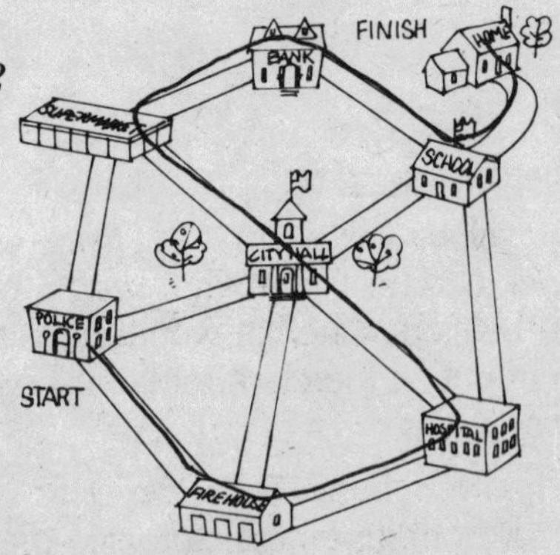


*What's in a Name?, page 23*

1. Spider, 2. Monkeys, 3. Bird, 4. Bat, 5. Snake, 6. Snail

# Answers

*Movie Crossword, pages 24 & 25*

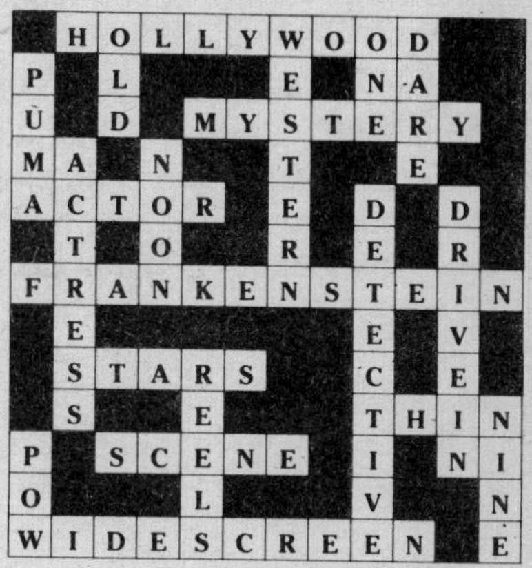

*Pinball Wizard, pages 26 & 27*

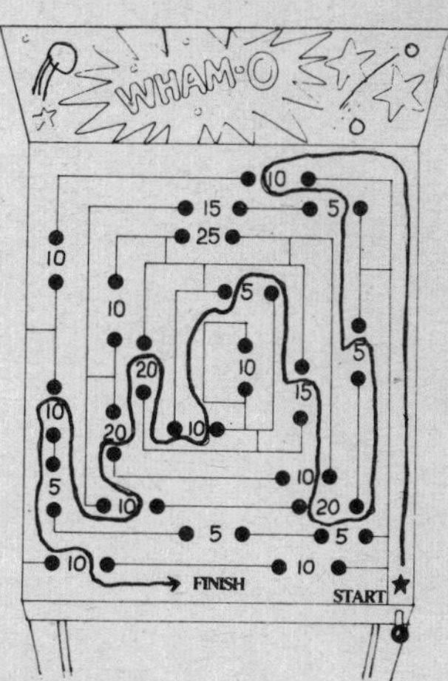


*The Two-Bit Mystery, page 28*

First move: Turn over the first and second coins.
Second move: Turn over the first and third coins.
Third move: Turn over the first and second coins.

*Letter-Wise, page 29*

S. The letters stand for the days of the week.
E. The letters stand for: ONE, TWO, THREE, FOUR, and so on.

# Answers

*Crazy Graffiti, pages 30 & 31*

1. Rainfall 2. Lower class 4. Footsteps 5. Hot Dog
6. Flying high 7. Sunrise 8. Half moon 9. Mountain top
10. Longfellow 11. Loose change 12 High brow
13. Double-cross 14. Cut-rate 15. Long shot
16. Short-tempered 17. Tightrope 18. Toss-up

*Spider Maze, page 32*

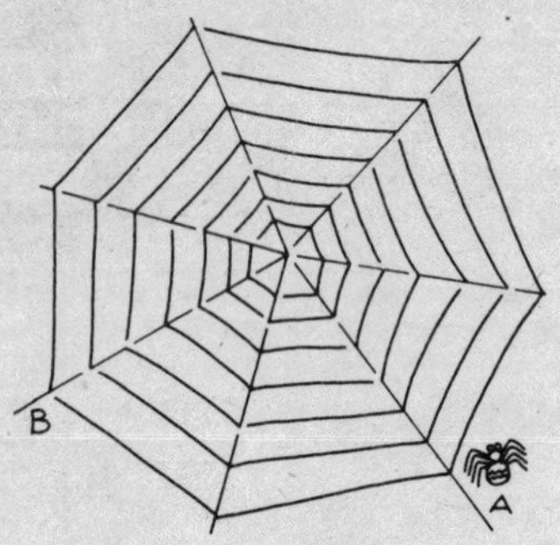


*A Visual Trick, page 33*

The message reads: HERE IS THE MESSAGE

*A Short Mystery, page 34*

He stood on a big block of ice that was in the room.
The puddle of water was from the ice when it melted.

*Witness to the Crime!, pages 35 & 36*

1. 2, 2. 3592, 3. Three O'clock, 4. Idaville First National Bank.
5. Holly Ave. & 4th St, 6. A. Yes, B. Yes, C. Striped,
D. No, E. Yes, 7. 960 Holly Ave.

# Answers

*Cryptograms, pages 37, 38 & 39*

IF YOU TAKE THE TIME
AND TROUBLE TO DO
THEM, CRYPTOGRAMS
ARE FUN!

HEY, DIDDLE, DIDDLE,
THE CAT AND THE
FIDDLE, THE COW
JUMPED OVER THE
MOON, THE ASTRONAUT
LAUGHED TO SEE SUCH
SPORT, AND THE DISH
RAN AWAY WITH THE
SPOON.

*Seeing Stars, page 40*

The stars could never be seen inside the moon's crescent as shown. The moon would cover them since that part is solid but just in shadow.

*Encyclopedia Brown Word Maze, page 41*

| E | N | B | G | M | E | D | I |
|---|---|---|---|---|---|---|---|
| Y | C | U | S | A | N | A | L |
| P | C | L | I | T | Y | V | L |
| E | O | R | E | G | L | I | A |
| C | D | I | A | L | E | B | M |
| H | I | O | W | N | L | Y | I |
| E | F | B | R | S | A | L | K |

## Answers

*Indian Word Find, page 42*

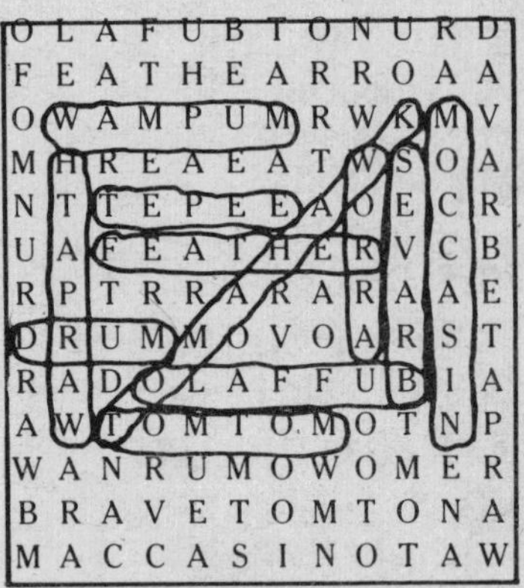

*Be a Police Artist, page 43*

*Spot the Clue, pages 44 & 45*

Encyclopedia noticed that the stirrup on the horse was short. Too short even for the messenger. If the bandit was even taller, then it couldn't have been a tall bandit's horse. When caught in his lie, the messenger confessed that he and his friend, Shorty Smith, had planned it to look like a robbery. They were to meet later and divide the money.

# Answers

*Name Game, page 46*

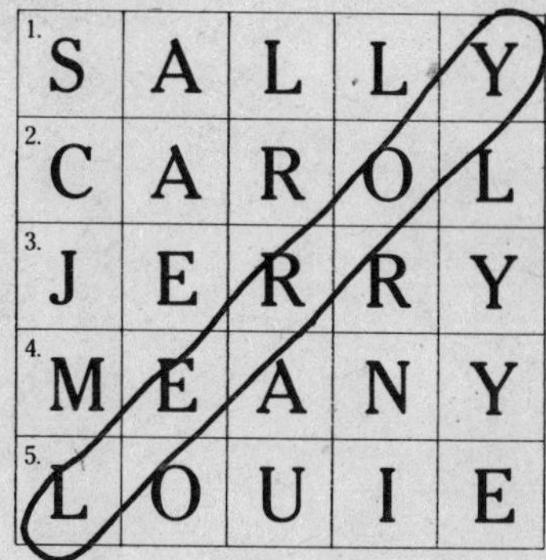


*Treasure Island, page 47*

By looking at the compass points on the map, Encyclopedia noticed that all the trees were WEST of the rocks. Since the sun rises in the East, in *EARLY MORN* the shadows of the trees would all be facing away from the rocks in the opposite direction. Therefore none of the rocks could *TAKE THE FIRST SHADE OF A TREE.*

*Trapped!, pages 48 & 49*

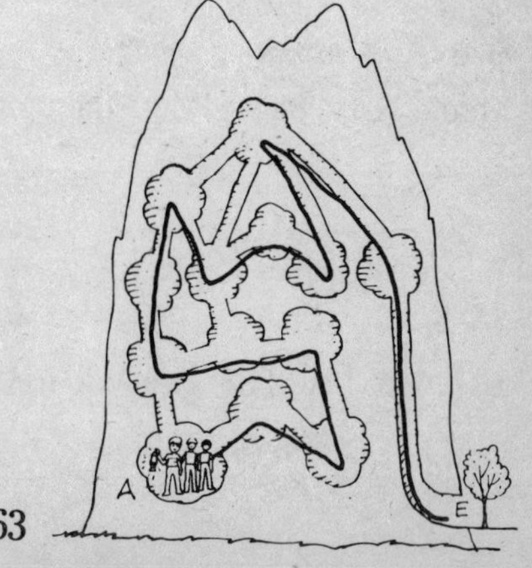

# Answers

*Bullfighter Crossword, pages 50 & 51*

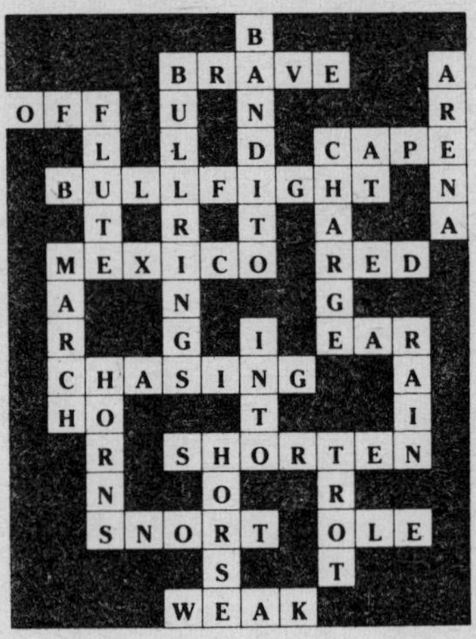

*Spot the Clue, pages 52 & 53*

Encyclopedia noticed that Jack's boat had no oarlocks. It's practically impossible to row a boat without oarlocks, much less row it around all day. When caught in his lie, Jack confessed to stealing the gas.

*From Boats to Oats, page 54*

Saddle, Spur, Mare, Boot, Tail

If you enjoyed this book, look for the other *Encyclopedia Brown's Puzzles and Games* books at your favorite bookstore.

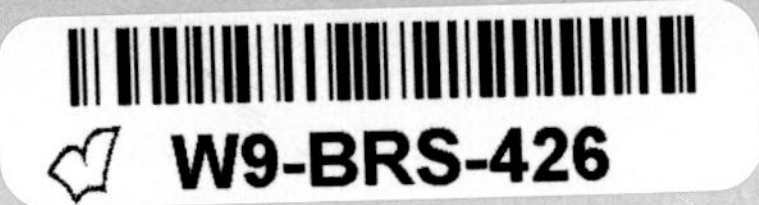


# MR. TUCKET

OTHER YEARLING BOOKS BY GARY PAULSEN
YOU WILL ENJOY:

THE BOY WHO OWNED THE SCHOOL
THE COOKCAMP
THE MONUMENT
THE VOYAGE OF THE *FROG*
THE WINTER ROOM
THE RIVER
THE HAYMEADOW
The Culpepper Adventure Series
World of Adventure Series

YEARLING BOOKS are designed especially to entertain and enlighten young people. Patricia Reilly Giff, consultant to this series, received her bachelor's degree from Marymount College and a master's degree in history from St. John's University. She holds a Professional Diploma in Reading and a Doctorate of Humane Letters from Hofstra University. She was a teacher and reading consultant for many years, and is the author of numerous books for young readers.

For a complete listing of all Yearling titles, write to
Dell Readers Service,
P.O. Box 1045,
South Holland, IL 60473.

# MR. TUCKET

—— Gary Paulsen ——

A Yearling Book

Published by
Bantam Doubleday Dell Books for Young Readers
a division of
Bantam Doubleday Dell Publishing Group, Inc.
1540 Broadway
New York, New York 10036



ISBN: 0-440-41133-5

Reprinted by arrangement with Delacorte Press

Printed in the United States of America

December 1995

10 9 8 7 6 5 4 3 2 1 OPM

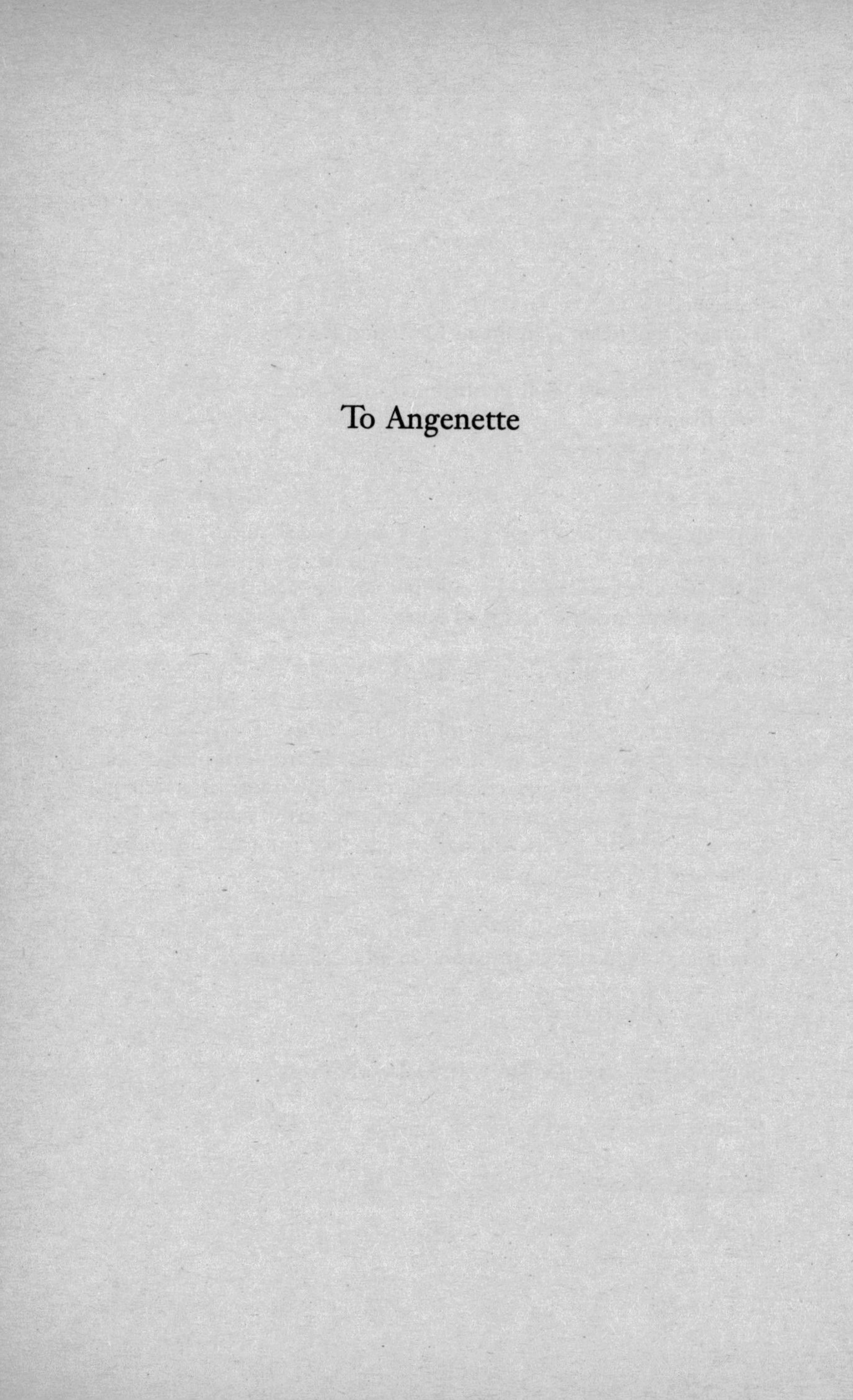

To Angenette

# Chapter One

**Francis Alphonse Tucket** came back to life slowly. He didn't open his eyes. He didn't want to open his eyes until he remembered everything that had happened.

Yesterday had been Francis's fourteenth birthday, and he had celebrated it quietly. Usually his mother and father—and even his nine-year-old sister Rebecca—made a big thing of birthdays. They had friends in, and a giant cake cooked to perfection on his mother's huge wood-burning stove, and by four in the afternoon everybody was so full of homemade ice cream and cake they couldn't move.

But that was how it had been on the farm in Missouri, where they had had the big house and barn. Yesterday they had celebrated Francis's birthday on the tailgate of a Conestoga wagon at the foothills of the Rocky Mountains. It was June 13, 1848—a warm summer Tuesday in a new country and they were with a wagon train on its way to Oregon. Francis, on awakening that morning, thought that even without any sort of birthday party, it would be his best birthday yet. How many boys of fourteen had ever seen drawings of the Rockies, let alone the real thing? That was an adventure in itself, not to mention crossing the great Kansas plains and watching the train scout, Mr. Ballard, hunt buffalo for the wagon train.

But then there had been a party—or at least a sort of party. As the wagons had squared away for the day's journey westward, Francis's mother called him from helping his father hitch some oxen to the yoke and tongue of the wagon. He went to the rear, where she was, and there, sitting on the tailgate, was a cake. He had no idea how she had done it—her stove was way back in Missouri, too heavy for the wagon. And he had not seen her doing anything special on the buffalo-chip fire that morning—but there it was, a cake. And easily one of the nicest cakes he'd ever seen.

"Happy fourteenth birthday, Alphonse," she said, with a smile. She had always called him Alphonse. His father always called him Francis.

For a long moment he didn't answer, just stood staring at the cake. Then he thanked her, knowing it would do no good to ask her how she'd done it. She would just answer, "Where there's a will, there's a way," as she always explained things that seemed impossible to Francis.

"Would you like a piece now?" she asked. "Or would you rather wait until tonight? The train is going to stop early today. Mr. Ballard wants to check all the wagons before we get to the mountains."

He wanted a piece so badly his mouth was watering, but he knew that wasn't what she expected, so he hid his eagerness. "We could have a sort of party," he suggested. "I could ask Ike and Max over and maybe offer them some cake." Ike and Max were the only other two boys in the train. There were five girls, but they kind of kept to themselves after Max threw a garter snake on one of them.

"That's a good idea," his mother said, nodding. "I'll wrap it in muslin and save it for this evening."

He could tell that he had pleased her. In all

truth, he didn't really want to share the cake with Ike and Max. Oh, they were nice enough, but they weren't really friends. It just happened that they were the only other boys, and Francis was more or less forced to do things with them. Ike would have been all right except that he talked funny and did things in an odd way. He said "thee" and "thou" and his folks always made him wear black clothes and a black flat-brimmed hat. Francis's father had said they were Quakers from the East somewhere, and that they all talked like that, but Francis still found it hard to get used to somebody calling him "friend" all the time.

Max was an out-and-out bully, and Francis wouldn't talk to him at all under normal conditions. But in the wagon train he had to. Max kept finding him when the wagons stopped for the night, and it was either talk or fight. They had fought several times, before Francis had found it easier to talk.

And in fighting they were pretty evenly matched. Their worst fight had taken place the time Max had teased Ike—short for Ichabod. Ike wouldn't fight, no matter how many bad names Max called him. Finally Max had hit Ike on the shoulder. That had made Francis mad and he'd torn into Max and given him a bloody nose, which got him a licking from his father that night, but he didn't care. The licking hadn't been much—he knew his father was doing it because there was no other way to keep Max's mother from complaining all over the train—and his father hadn't used a switch the way he did when Francis did something really bad. He had used his hand, and had smacked only twice, lightly, hiding a grin.

So Francis wasn't all that eager to share his cake with Ike and Max, but it pleased his mother—and he hadn't expected a cake anyway.

The idea of getting a present wasn't even on his mind that Tuesday morning. The nearest store was over five hundred miles away and he knew, or thought he knew, every item in the wagon. He'd helped load it, and there hadn't been any presents, or anything that had looked like presents. But they'd fooled him again. When he got back to the front of the wagon, to help his father finish with the oxen, he was handed a long, thin bundle wrapped in butcher's paper.

"Happy birthday, Francis," his father said, smiling. "We figured that it was about time you had one of these."

Francis was really puzzled, until his fingers tore away some of the paper. He didn't need to unwrap it all to know what it was. Already the sun hit a brass fitting, some dark, hand-rubbed walnut, and the brown sheen of polished steel.

"A rifle." His voice was soft. "A *new* rifle. But how . . . I mean, I helped load the wagon, and I didn't see it."

"The Petersons carried it in their wagon for me," his father said. "I brought it over to ours last night while you were sleeping. Do you like it?"

By this time Francis had torn off the rest of the paper and was finding it hard to keep from bouncing in excitement.

"It's a Lancaster," his father explained. "I think probably the only one of its kind. I thought about buying you a Hawkens in St. Louis, but they only make heavy rifles that fire heavy balls. When I talked to Mr. Lancaster, he said that a smaller caliber was more accurate, and with just a bit more powder, gave as much power as a big ball. Oh, the bullet mold, percussion caps, and powder flask are still in Mr. Peterson's wagon."

Francis could do nothing but stare at the rifle. Its stock, going only halfway up the barrel and bound to the metal with hand-forged brass bands, was of burled walnut. The lock, hammer, and trigger had been case-hardened in new oil, so they looked like etched marble instead of steel, and the barrel was the deepest, richest brown he had ever seen. The whole weapon had been made smaller than a full-sized rifle—just right for a fourteen-year-old boy. Even the sights, full elk-horn design for easy sighting, seemed to be in miniature.

"You mean . . ." Francis hesitated. There was really no way he could express enough thanks. "Did you really have this made just for me?"

"Then you do like it," his father said, smiling again. "I was worried about that. I thought maybe you wouldn't think too much of owning a rifle." His eyes crinkled. "I'm sure there must be a couple of thousand things a boy would rather own than a rifle—"

"I don't know about other boys," Francis interrupted. "But there isn't even one thing *I'd* want before a rifle. I've been wanting a rifle of my own ever since Mr. Ballard took me out and taught me how to shoot his buffalo gun."

They laughed, both of them remembering how the first shot Francis had taken with the scout's big .60-caliber gun had knocked him back on his rear.

"Well, you don't have to worry about getting knocked over with this one," his father assured Francis. "This is only a .40 caliber. Mr. Lancaster said it was fast, but wouldn't kick too much. The only way to find out is to shoot it, I guess. Why don't you go over to the Petersons' wagon and get the mold, caps, and powder? There's also a bag of lead balls already molded. Then when we pull out, you can drop back of the last wagon and practice shooting buffalo chips."

"Alone?" Francis asked.

"I don't see why not. You know how to handle a weapon—I watched you the other day with Mr. Ballard. Just make sure you don't shoot toward the train. It wouldn't do to break somebody's prize punch bowl."

Francis grinned. The only one in the wagon train foolish enough to carry a punch bowl had been Max's mother—and she bragged about it every chance she got. No, it wouldn't do to break it—especially if *he* did it.

"I'll be careful," Francis said, and started for the Petersons' wagon.

"And make sure you don't stray out of sight," his father called. "Mr. Ballard says there've been some Pawnee in this area. They might like to get their hands on that little rifle of yours."

This time they both smiled. The idea of Indians being around was pretty funny. All across the Kansas plains there had been talk of Indian trouble, and everybody worried about the Comanches. And they hadn't, not once in the whole trip, even seen a feather—let alone an Indian. Francis was almost disappointed. He had looked forward to seeing Indians nearly as much as seeing the mountains.

Francis dropped back from the rear of the train, and failed to notice that he was falling too far back. His forgetfulness was caused by the little rifle. Shooting it was a dream. He couldn't seem to miss, and it didn't kick at all. He got so engrossed in firing it that he didn't see the last wagon pull far ahead.

He lay still now, and tried to remember exactly what happened. He had fired about ten times, he knew, liking the little rifle more each time. On the eleventh or so shot, as he was loading, a large brown hand had clamped itself over his mouth.

His rifle had been grabbed first. There had been seven Indians—six young men and an older warrior. Probably a hunting party, because they hadn't been wearing paint. Then Francis made his first mistake; instead of just relaxing and biding his time until he could get a chance to escape, he fought them. Kicking and swinging and biting, more out of fear than courage, he had given the seven Pawnees a rough few minutes. Finally they'd hit him, just a little tap in back of his ear with his own rifle butt, and he had fallen like a stone.

They had ridden all that day, with Francis draped head-down across the old man's lap, bouncing like a sack of meal. He had passed into and out of consciousness on the trip, and had no idea where they finally dropped him—except that it was a dark and smelly place.

Now it was time to open his eyes. He opened them—then shut them as fast as he could.

Sitting above him, giving him a toothless grin, was the ugliest old person he'd ever seen—he couldn't tell at first if it was a man or a woman. Just a wrinkled face and toothless mouth that smiled when Francis's eyes came open.

# Chapter Two

**Francis's camp life** with the Pawnees began that very morning. The old woman—as it turned out—was the wife of the old man who had been with the hunting party. She tied a rope around his neck and dragged him around the camp like a new puppy. At each lodge she would stop and call the whole family out. Then she would point at Francis and gabble something he couldn't understand. He guessed that she was bragging about her new "son." But he didn't much like what followed. The women would pinch his arms and push his lips back to look at his teeth, while the children—if there were any at the lodge—came out and kicked him.

Francis didn't stand for it at first. When another boy his age kicked him, he kicked right back, and landed a fairly good blow. This made all the adults laugh, but his "mother" shook her head and pulled his neck rope so tight it nearly strangled him. He figured finally that it was easier to play along and let them kick him. For the present it was enough just to stay alive and learn as much as possible about the Pawnees. He might need the information later to escape. And he would escape; he was sure of it. Either alone, or with somebody from the train—probably Mr. Ballard—who would come to rescue him.

In the meantime, he might as well make it as easy as possible on himself. To this end, he smiled at his new "mother."

That was his second mistake. Immediately she returned the smile and took the rope off his neck. That much he liked. But before he could get accustomed to the freedom of movement, three young Indian boys jumped him, and he had to fight like a demon just to stay on his feet. It would have been pretty fair if just one of the young Indians had tackled him. But with three of them climbing all over him Francis had no choice but to fight back any way he could—which meant hitting, biting, and kicking.

What surprised and angered him most was that none of the elders—not even his "mother"—made any move to stop the fight. Instead they just gathered around and cheered. None of them, it seemed, was on Francis's side, and this didn't help him keep his temper. Neither did the fact that he knew he couldn't win against the three boys. After the first five minutes, he decided that if he was going to lose anyway, he might as well do as much damage as possible on the way down. He picked the largest of the Indian boys and went after him. The other two might as well not have been there. One jumped on his back and another grabbed at his legs, but it was all too late to save the boy Francis had concentrated on—he was underneath Francis when the other two forced him down. And for every blow the two boys should have landed, Francis gave the Indian boy under him one on the nose. Even if they killed him for it, he was going to make that boy sorry he'd ever picked a fight.

"Hoka-ha!"

Francis didn't hear the yell, but the two boys on top of him jumped away. Francis just kept hammering away at the boy beneath him, who had now curled into a ball and covered his head with his arms.

"Hoka-ha," came the gruff voice a second time.

"It is enough! You fight with fists—the way a girl fights."

Francis felt himself lifted roughly by the back of his belt and dropped in the dirt. Immediately he swung around and attacked the man who had lifted him. He was struck such a blow that it knocked him head over heels.

"It is *enough*! I will not say it again."

Francis wiped his eyes with the back of his hand. He had expected to see a tall, or at least a strong-looking man. Instead he found himself looking at a short, wiry Indian with his hair in one braid. At the bottom of the braid there was one feather, hanging straight down. The man wore plain buckskins, unbeaded moccasins, and carried a rifle in his left hand. It was Francis's rifle.

"Enough my foot," he said, glaring up at the Indian. "They started it, not me. You want to start knocking somebody around, why not give *them* a lick or two? And if you're so tough, why do you have to steal rifles from boys?"

In a sudden hush of the people gathered around the fighting area, Francis watched in horror as the Indian raised the muzzle of the rifle until it pointed dead between his eyes.

"Bravery in youth is a good thing," the Indian said. He wasn't smiling. "It is not good to be stupid, little white-eyed wolf. It is stupid to insult the man who holds your gun. It is stupid to insult your elders. If you do it again, I will kill you."

The Indian let the rifle down easily and spun away. Francis watched him go, kneeling there in the dirt. He had never seen such a pure, cold look in a man's eyes, and he knew that he would have to be very careful whenever the one-braided warrior was around.

# Chapter Three

**Three weeks after** he came to the Pawnee camp, Francis learned that the brave who had threatened to kill him, and had purchased the rifle for two good horses from the old man who had led the party, was named Braid. Braid was a war leader. He was not a chief, but any time there was a need for a raid, Braid was the man who led the war party. In camp he was just another warrior, except that he was so mean that many people feared him. He had the scalps of many "victories" braided around the doorway to his lodge. He did not dress in finery, the way many warriors did, because he didn't need to impress anybody. His scalps did that for him.

Francis hated Braid more than anything on earth. He watched him lead out a big party of more than forty warriors. They were gone all that day and through the night until the next morning.

When they returned it was obvious that they had been on a big raid. Four of the braves were dead, draped across their horses. More were wounded. But even while the women of the dead men sent up their wailing and covered their faces with ashes, the rest of the tribe prepared for dancing and celebration.

One of the braves, Francis saw, had a scalp with blond hair. The party must have made a raid against a group of white people, and the only white people in the area were in his wagon train. It sickened him to realize that Braid had probably used *his* rifle to shoot at them.

Braid sought out Francis immediately upon the return of the raiding party.

"They will not be coming for you," the wiry Indian said smirking. "Not now, not ever. I have given them reason to fear the Pawnees. They will not risk fighting us for one stupid little white-eyes."

Francis knew he was telling the truth. They would not be coming for him. Not because they feared these Indians, but because they would think he was dead. The train would lick its wounds and head on for Oregon without him. He would have to find a way to escape on his own.

But Braid hadn't finished yet. The warrior dug into his buckskins, pulled out something, and threw it down in front of Francis.

"I brought this for a girl child," he said. "But perhaps you would enjoy playing with it more."

Francis stared at the object in the dirt. Only one thing kept him from screaming and attacking Braid —and that was the knowledge that it would do no good.

What Braid had thrown down was a small china doll. It was a pretty doll, fashioned after a woman going to a ball.

There was only one thing wrong with the doll— its nose had been broken off. Francis remembered exactly how that had happened. He had been teasing Rebecca, as he did sometimes, and in a fit of anger she had thrown the doll at him. She had missed him, and the doll had hit the corner of the stove and the nose had broken off. It was his sister's doll—Rebecca's doll.

That night, during the dancing and celebration, Francis tried to escape. They caught him not ten feet from the lodge and tied him up.

The next morning they let him loose, and that evening he tried to get away again. This time his "mother" beat him across the backs of his legs with a dried willow cane.

So Francis gave up the idea of escaping for a while. They were watching him too closely.

After his third week there, a large council meeting was held and the tribe decided to move the village. Francis had to help dismantle the lodge and load it on the travois in back of the horses—normally considered woman work, as was gathering wood—but he didn't mind because the work took his mind off the terrible situation he was in.

He did mind the direction the band took when they had finished packing, however. Strung in a long line, with much barking of camp dogs, the file headed due northeast—away from the direction of the wagon train.

I'll have to get all the way to Oregon, Francis thought glumly as he trudged along beside the travois, before I'll find out about Rebecca. That is, if I find a way to escape.

It didn't cheer him either to find that the movement of the tribe—almost twenty miles a day—almost doubled the speed that the wagon train made.

They traveled for ten days, and then put up a new camp on the southern edge of the Black Hills, the village winter ground—the place of sweet water and good hunting.

Strangely, Francis liked the Black Hills even more than he had liked the Rockies. The Black Hills were not only fine to look at—with their dark ridges and green meadows—but good to live with as well.

And it was here that Francis met Mr. Grimes.

It happened early one morning. Francis had just finished fetching wood and was bending down over the fire, built outside the lodge because the days were still quite warm, when it seemed every dog in camp started barking at once. Francis turned to see what all the noise was about, and there, riding into the middle of the Pawnee camp as though it were the main street of St. Louis, was a white man with only one arm.

It was, Francis learned from one of the Indian boys, Mr. Jason Grimes.

[illegible]

the village [illegible] the place of [illegible]
and [illegible]

[illegible] the Black Hills [illegible]

[illegible]

# Chapter Four

**There are certain things** that are always easy to remember because of the way they happen. Francis's first sight of Mr. Jason Grimes was like that. He would remember it always because of the way Mr. Grimes ignored the Pawnees. It was not an easy thing to do. The Indian dogs were snapping at the hooves of his horses and pack mules, and the squaws and children were so thick all around him that he only showed from the waist up. Yet he ignored them, threading his horse carefully, gracefully around the noisy women and children, looking off in space as though they didn't exist. He made quite a figure as he rode, straight backed, moving easily with the horse's roll. Francis got more of an impression of a piece of timber bolted to a saddle than a man—until he looked at Mr. Grimes's face. It was a thin face, and almost as dark as an Indian's, except that it bore a bushy beard and mustache. He had thin lips and washed-out blue eyes, and on top of his head he wore a dashing but dusty derby, set slightly back, with one long feather sticking straight up from the band. He had on fringed but otherwise not very fancy buckskins, plain moccasins, and no belt.

The last thing Francis noted was that Mr. Grimes's left arm was gone. He carried his rifle, wrapped in a buckskin case, with the same hand that loosely held his horse's reins, and the fact that he had no left arm didn't seem to bother him at all. It seemed almost natural, as though he would have looked odd *with* a left arm.

Francis realized suddenly that he was staring with his mouth open. He shut it. He moved forward through the crowd around the mountain man.

"Hey," he called. "Hey, over here. I'm a *captive*!" The word sounded funny when he said it, but he saw that the mountain man had heard, for he looked down from his horse quickly, then back up.

Francis wasn't sure, but he thought the derby-topped head had shaken left to right just once—as though telling him to be quiet.

Then he couldn't see anything more because his "mother" found him and dropped a noose over his head. She dragged him back, cackling happily, and led him into a corner of the lodge.

With his hands tied in back of him and his ankles lashed firmly together, Francis had plenty of time to think. Most of his thoughts were about the mountain man. How could he come into the Pawnee camp and not be harmed? And *why* had he come? Was he a friend of the Indians?

There were no answers in that dark corner of the lodge, but one thing was plain. The Pawnee weren't going to kill the mountain man. Just the opposite—his arrival was to be the reason for a full day of celebrating. Francis heard all the preparations, and with this knowledge, his heart sank. Any man that friendly with the Pawnees wouldn't be likely to offer him help in escaping.

All that day he lay in the lodge, wondering. He got no food and no water. By nine that night, when the dancing had reached its full frenzy, he at last fell asleep.

Francis wasn't sure of the time when he opened his eyes, but it was either very late that same night or very early the following morning. He did know why he had awakened. There was a calloused hand clamped over his mouth, and in the darkness of the lodge, he could make out the shape of a derby.

It was the mountain man.

Francis felt the bushy beard against his ear, and heard a whisper.

"Don't move. No sound. Just blink your eyes if you hear me and are wide awake."

Francis blinked, and the hand was taken off his mouth.

"Can you ride?" the mountain man asked, still whispering hoarsely.

Francis nodded.

"Good. In back of the lodge you'll find a little black mare I swiped from the Pawnee herd. Walk her out of camp with your hand over her muzzle. When you're safely out of camp, get on her and ride as hard as you can with the North Star on your right shoulder—" He stopped suddenly as Francis's "mother," across the lodge, turned in her sleep. In a second he continued, "If you ride hard enough, and don't hit a hole somewhere, dawn will catch you at a small creek. Take the mare right into the middle of the creek and head upstream. Keep going in the water until you think you're going to drop, then go another ten miles. If you stop, they'll get you. Now, did you understand all that?"

Francis nodded again, "Where will you be?" he asked, rubbing his wrists, which the mountain man had cut loose while he was talking.

"Why, I'll be sitting right here in camp," the mountain man answered, chuckling softly, "eating a good breakfast, wondering whether or not they've caught you. If they don't, I'll see you in a couple of days. Now, are you going to sit and jaw all night or get riding?"

Francis took it for the command it was. Thirty seconds later he was leading the little mare quietly out of the village hoping with all his heart that he smelled enough like an Indian not to upset the dogs.

A minute after that he was on her back, wishing he'd never told a lie in his life. The only time he'd ever been on a horse was when he'd ridden a work-horse while his father plowed. That had only been at a walk, and with a lot of harness straps to hang on to.

The little black mare didn't even have a blanket on her back and she only had two speeds—dead stop and full run.

# Chapter Five

**Francis got his first mouthful** of dirt not a hundred paces from where he got on the little black mare. Luckily, he had figured on falling off, and had taken the precaution of wrapping her jaw rope tightly around his hand. When he hit the ground, she dragged him only a couple of yards. He didn't have time to moan about his scraped elbows and knees. He didn't have time for anything but to get on again.

The second time he made nearly three hundred shattering yards before sliding off her side and bouncing on the rocks of a dry streambed. The trouble was that the mare was so fat—it was like trying to ride a nail keg.

He didn't discover the secret until he had fallen off three more times, removing more and more skin from his elbows and knees each time. Then he remembered how the mountain man had ridden—stiff backed, but loose, almost relaxed, where he joined the horse. Francis still bounced around a lot, but all his bouncing was straight up and down—not off to the side. And once he'd learned to relax, Francis found riding the black mare exciting.

Never had he been so purely thrilled. Her dainty head came down, her ears folded back along her flattened neck, and she really flew. Francis didn't try to turn her, as long as she kept in the right general direction—due west—and he forgot everything in the roar of wind and drumming thunder of her hoofs.

Just at false dawn, when the first grayness made faint shadows under trees, the mare streaked out onto a large meadow. It was entirely flat, and she picked up speed when she hit its edge. Francis, content in the knowledge that she wouldn't have to dodge around rocks and trees for a while, relaxed even more and loosened his hold on her mane.

When she hit the water, he went off over her

head, and when he got up, found he was neck deep in muck. The creek ran straight down the middle of the meadow. When he finally managed to scrape the mud from his eyes, the mare was nowhere to be seen. He had dropped the jaw rope, and she had gone on. He couldn't even hear her hooves. He wanted to look for her, then realized he hadn't time for that. This was the stream the mountain man had been talking about. Horse or not, his orders had been definite—head up the middle of the stream, and don't stop.

He stepped deeper into the water, but didn't start upstream immediately. He felt sad that the mare was gone. He would have liked to keep her awhile, and though he didn't think much of the Pawnees he admired their horses.

"Thank you," he said quietly, looking off into the darkness. "Thank you, little mare. It was a good ride."

And he started walking in the water, only vaguely aware of the chill.

Real dawn caught him nearly four miles up the stream. He had long since left the meadow behind, and the stream was now bordered by thick scrub pine trees. He was very tired, and ached all over from his many falls from the mare. But he knew that if he stopped before getting far enough up-stream, he might not meet the mountain man again.

So he kept walking; not in miles, or even yards, but in steps. All day long he did that. He quit thinking of food early in the morning; it did nothing but make him hungry. And somehow, without his having been aware of the passing of a day, evening found him still trudging, still moving. He didn't know how far he'd come, only hoped it was far enough.

Just as the first night birds began dipping and wheeling over the stream for insects, Francis Alphonse Tucket pulled himself onto the bank beneath a clump of overhanging willows and dropped like a bag of sand.

In five seconds, wet clothes and all, he wouldn't have heard the Indians even if they beat their drums right next to his head.

# Chapter Six

**Francis awakened** to a heavenly smell—the aroma of boiling coffee. He was afraid that if he opened his eyes, the smell of coffee would vanish. But when a full ten seconds had passed, and the smell was still there, he knew he hadn't been dreaming.

He sat up and saw the mountain man sitting over a small fire about ten feet away. His back was to Francis, but he spoke at once without turning around.

" 'Bout time you opened up a mite—day's half gone already. You sleep like a fancy city man."

Francis stretched, wincing at the pain in his legs. That would be from the little mare, and the pain in his arms would be from falling on them, and the pain in his knees from the rocks he had landed on, but the pain in his stomach was from hunger. "How did you know I was awake?" he asked after a moment.

"Your breathing changed. When you quit sucking wind like an old buffalo, I figured you were coming around."

"You've sure got good ears."

"I'm alive. You don't stay that way long out here unless you can hear a little."

Francis filed away that advice, and got up. Everything in him hurt with the movement. He didn't believe anything could be that stiff and still be alive.

"I thought you said you could ride." The mountain man chuckled.

"I did all right," Francis answered defensively.

"If you mean you made it alive, I guess you did at that. But I wouldn't call what happened to your hands and knees all right. Seems to me you lost a little hide. Still, you pulled a good trick with that mare—sending her off ahead while you came upstream." His chuckle turned to an outright laugh. "I followed Braid and five or six others for a while when they came after you. Unless I miss my guess, they're down on the Powder River somewhere, *still* after that mare."

"I didn't plan it," Francis cut in. "I fell off."

"Eh?"

"I said I fell off her when she hit the stream. I fell off and she kept right on going without me."

"That's sort of what I figured, but I thought it would be better if you said it. Kinda keep the air clean around here, if we talk straight." He turned and faced Francis for the first time. "You know, that lie about knowing how to ride could have got us both killed last night, don't you? They could have caught you, and worked you over a bit, and the first thing you know you would have been telling them all about my getting a horse for you. Don't go shaking your head. I know you wouldn't want to talk. But I've seen the Pawnees make a man tell stories he didn't even *know*. So from now on you just tell me what you know is straight, and that'll keep us *both* out of trouble. What's your name?"

"Francis Alphonse Tucket."

"I said it would be better if we kept everything *straight*, boy. Now what's your handle?"

"I wasn't lying. My name really *is* Francis Alphonse Tucket. Honest."

"Let me put it another way. What do you go by? I mean, haven't you got a sort of short name they call you?"

Francis thought a minute, then shook his head. "My mother always called me Alphonse, and my father called me Francis. I guess you can take your pick."

The trapper shook his head. "I'm sorry, and nothing against your folks, understand, but I don't like either of them. They don't hit my tongue right. Tell you what. My name is Jason Grimes. You call me Mr. Grimes, and I'll call you Mr. Tucket—that should keep us both happy. Is that all right with you?"

Francis shrugged. "Suits me fine, Mr. Grimes."

"Good. Now then, Mr. Tucket, why don't you hobble your crippled body over here and have a sip of coffee? There's nothing like a touch of coffee to take the sharp edge off an empty belly. After that I'll give you a little venison jerky, and while you're chewing that you can tell me how you came to be the son of that old Pawnee lady."

Francis had tried coffee before, stolen from his mother's stove with sugar in it and he took some in a gulp. It was bitter and he nearly spit it out. But the heat of it felt good and seemed to take away some of the ache in his stomach.

The jerky was as tough as an old boot. While he chewed it—and it took *some* chewing—he told Mr. Grimes about the adventure, starting with the wagon train and the rifle.

He finished his tale by telling how Braid had thrown the doll down in front of him.

Mr. Grimes nodded when Francis finished. "That Braid is a mean one. Back before I made friends with the Pawnees by bringing them powder and lead every time I came through, Braid and I had one bush-ripper of a fight. Knives, hatchets—the whole works. I guess it lasted over an hour, and when it was done, he had one scar down his back and I had lost an arm."

"You mean Braid took your arm off?" Francis asked.

"No, he just cut it good. But it got infected later and I had a doctor in St. Louis whack it off before it poisoned my whole body. It makes for some pretty tight talking whenever I come into his village. Braid hasn't forgotten his scar a bit, and every time I come in he asks me to wrestle. Oh, and speaking of wrestling, I've got something for you. Won it from Braid yesterday wrestling—he made the mistake of tying one arm behind his back to make the fight more fair. He was too stupid to realize that I get a lot of all kinds of practice with only one arm, so I whipped him pretty easy."

As he talked, Mr. Grimes went to his saddle and pulled out a blanket wrapped around something. He carefully unrolled the blanket and handed Francis his rifle, mold, powder, and caps.

"My rifle!"

"Yup, and a sweet little shooter she is, too. I knew it was yours when you started telling me about getting it for your birthday. Seeing as how it looks like we'll be riding together for a while—at least until I teach you enough so's you can make Oregon on your own—we'll take a couple of days off and I'll teach you to shoot it."

"I can shoot," Francis said.

"Well, maybe you can, and maybe you can't. But just reading signs makes your story look thin."

"What do you mean?" Francis asked.

"I mean if you *really* knew how to shoot that rifle, it wouldn't have been seven Pawnees jumping you that day by the wagon train. It would only have been five, and maybe just four—and those four would have been thinking seriously about going home without you. *That's* what I mean."

# Chapter Seven

"No-ah, Mr. Tucket, that isn't quite the way it's done."

It was the first time Mr. Grimes used the long, drawn-out negative answer to something Francis had messed up. But it wasn't to be the last. In fact, he would use that long no, as Francis thought of it, about ten times to every short nod, which was the way the mountain man approved of anything.

It was the afternoon of the day Francis and Mr. Grimes had met at the stream. Francis had just loaded and fired his gun as instructed by Mr.

Grimes. He felt that he'd done all right. A piece of wood more than thirty yards distant had turned to splinters with his shot. And it *had* been the piece of wood he was shooting at.

"What did I do wrong?" he asked. "I hit the piece of wood, didn't I?" There was just a thin bit of annoyance in his voice.

Mr. Grimes smiled and hooked his right hand in back of his neck, stretching. "Well, now, that's just about what *everybody* says—when they don't know about rifles." He mimicked Francis, " 'I hit the piece of wood, didn't I?' And yes, you did, Mr. Tucket. You hit the piece of wood. But how many times more can you hit it? Go ahead, load up and have at it. Pick another piece of wood out there and hit it for me, will you?"

Francis loaded, aimed, and fired at a buffalo chip about forty yards away. He missed. He tried twice more and missed both times.

Mr. Grimes nodded. "It's this way. You're holding that thing like it was an old rag. Your arms are loose, you're slopping your cheek against the stock, you're grabbing with your hands—and that's all wrong. You'll hit once or twice that way, if you're lucky. But the real trick of shooting a decent gun is to be able to put about four out of five balls in the same place, or nearly so. Now, Mr. Tucket, we'll see if we can't do a little reshaping of that crippled body of yours . . ."

He wasn't fooling. In the next five minutes Francis felt as though both his arms had been broken. Mr. Grimes pulled Francis's right elbow up so high the shoulder popped, and he jerked the left elbow down, directly beneath the barrel of the rifle.

"And don't grab with that left hand on the stock. Just make a baby cradle with your fingers and let the rifle sleep in it."

Francis nodded. It hurt, standing that way, but he could see how it made for more consistent shooting.

"All right, Mr. Tucket, load up and fire again."

Francis didn't start hitting right away, but at least his shots were falling in the same general area. He turned after four shots. "How's that?"

Mr. Grimes nodded. "All right, but you're taking too long to reload."

"What do you mean, too long? It was just a couple of seconds between shots." Actually it was more like a minute. But that wasn't what Mr. Grimes meant.

"It's this way, Mr. Tucket. What would you do if Braid came riding up the creek right now?"

"Why, I'd . . ." Francis blushed. He was standing with an empty rifle. If Braid, or any other threat, for that matter, came riding up the creek, Francis knew it would take him at least thirty seconds to load.

"That's right, Mr. Tucket. You'd be tied like a cow before you got powder down the bore. Every time you shoot, no matter whether you're shooting at buffalo chips or buffalo, you load as soon as the ball leaves the barrel. Carrying an empty rifle is about like carrying an empty water skin. When you get really thirsty, Mr. Tucket, you can't drink air."

Francis smiled sheepishly. "I guess I've got a lot to learn, haven't I?"

"Ayup, Mr. Tucket, you have a lot to learn, but you're coming along. Now let's clean that little shooter of yours and try some rapid firing. That's what really separates the men, or boys, for that matter, from their scalps in this country—not being able to shoot *fast.*"

Cleaning the rifle was easy. Francis just cupped creek water in his hand and poured it down the barrel, swabbed it with a piece of patch on the end of his ramrod, then greased the bore.

"Now this is how we'll do it," Mr. Grimes told him, fetching his own rifle from his saddle. "We'll have a sort of contest. We'll start at the same time, and the one who gets the most shots off while I count to ten will get out of working tonight—getting wood and cooking some of the jerky. Does that suit you, Mr. Tucket?"

Francis nodded. He didn't see how he could lose, shooting against a one-armed man.

"All right, Mr. Tucket. Go!"

"But you don't even have your rifle out of its case, Mr. Grimes," Francis said. "You aren't even ready."

"Just giving you the benefit of a little head start, Mr. Tucket. Ready? Go!"

They both fired at the same instant. Mr. Grimes had just flipped his rifle and fired, one-armed, before its buckskin case hit the ground.

"One," he said, starting the count.

Francis worked frantically. From his flask he poured powder into his cupped palm, then he emptied the roughly measured powder down the bore.

"Two."

As Francis was placing the patch across the mouth of the bore, he heard the roar of Mr. Grimes's Hawkens. He couldn't believe it. He put the ball on the patch, and drew the ramrod from its cradle beneath the barrel. He started the ball down with his thumb . . .

"Three."

. . . and put the ramrod on top of it. As he slammed the ball home he heard the mighty

Hawkens roar again. Mr. Grimes had fired three to his one. Francis capped the nipple, raised the rifle . . .

"Four."

. . . and fired. As his second shot tore a buffalo chip to pieces, the Hawkens belched fire a fourth time. It was too much for Francis. He lowered his rifle and watched Mr. Grimes.

"Five."

Mr. Grimes raised his Hawkens and fired. Number five. Five shots in the time it had taken Francis to make two. Clearly, Francis had missed something.

"Six."

Mr. Grimes lowered the Hawkens and held it between his knees. In one fluid motion he poured powder from the flask at his side down the barrel directly—without measuring—and brought the muzzle of the rifle up to his mouth. From his lips he spit a ball into the muzzle. Without a patch, it slid freely down, needing no ramrod. He slammed the butt of the rifle on the ground, to seat the ball, and from the space between his fingers pulled a percussion cap. It fitted quickly on the nipple, the Hawkens came up, and . . .

"Seven."

. . . smoke again poured out over the grass.

Mr. Grimes lowered his rifle and grinned. "I don't guess I have to go all the way to ten after all."

"But that wasn't fair," Francis said. "You didn't patch your balls, or measure your powder—"

"Now, now, Mr. Tucket. The word 'fair' is pretty loose. What's not fair in St. Louis at a turkey shoot might *be* fair when you're up against five or six Comanch." He cut the word "Comanche" off. "Out here people sort of think of 'fair' meaning the same as 'alive.' Savvy?"

Francis smiled. "Savvy. 'Fair' means that I'm going to gather wood and cook jerky."

"You *are* coming along, Mr. Tucket," the mountain man said, grinning again. "Ten, fifteen years, if you're still alive, you'll be the best wood gatherer in the Black Hills . . ."

# Chapter Eight

THEY LEFT EARLY the next morning. Francis would have liked to stay on for a few more days, but Mr. Grimes saddled his big sorrel gelding just after coffee with the air of a man who has somewhere to go, and Francis, stiff or not, knew better than to make any other suggestions.

"Come on up, Mr. Tucket. Let's see how old Footloose carries double."

As it turned out, old Footloose carried double almost as well as he carried single. Francis was given the job of holding the rope that led back to the pack mules. They followed nicely—showing none of the stubbornness Francis thought mules were supposed to show—and under a lightly clouded sky they made their way at a slow walk toward the southwest.

If Francis had expected a lot of conversation as they rode, he would have been sadly disappointed. Mr. Grimes was of the thinking that when he had something to say, he said it—usually with a bit of pepper thrown in. But when there wasn't anything to talk about, two or three hours might pass without a word coming from his bearded face.

Francis had close to a hundred questions he wanted to ask, but he didn't say anything for nearly two hours. In that time they had passed out of the main part of the pine forests and were winding down a dry-bottom canyon. It was an extremely pleasant place, even without water. Both sides of the canyon were of gray rock, and were high enough to keep the mid-morning sun from reaching Francis's back. Occasionally he could hear magpies chattering, and twice he heard the drumming of grouse, beating their wings on rotten logs. Even the sound of the sorrel's shod hooves, ringing off the rock walls, seemed natural and nice.

There was something bothering Francis, however, that kept him from enjoying these things the way he might have. Part of it was Rebecca—and not knowing about her. But it was Mr. Grimes that upset him more, and finally, as the sorrel brought them out of the canyon and back into the sun, Francis spoke up.

"Mr. Grimes, how is it that you're so friendly with the Pawnees—I mean, with Braid having caused you to lose your arm and all? I would think you'd be downright mad, or at least not friendly enough to bring them powder and lead."

Mr. Grimes snorted, and Francis could see the mountain man's back jerk as he began to laugh. "Honestly, Mr. Tucket, you do ask the mulish questions, don't you? I'll bet you spend the rest of your days looking gift horses in their mouths."

"What do you mean?"

"You want me to answer that? Or would you rather figure it out for yourself?" the mountain man said. "It seems simple to me. If I hadn't been 'friendly with the Pawnees' as you put it, you'd be back there with a rope around your neck, getting whipped."

"I'm sorry," Francis murmured. "It was a dumb thing to ask—"

"But since you asked," Mr. Grimes cut in, "I think maybe I ought to answer it. You think I ought to be mad at Braid on account of my arm. Well, Braid can't help the way he was made, no more than you or me. The Pawnees call themselves 'The People.' They live with the land. If you put it in our talk, that means they live by nature—the same nature that makes a she-bear gut you if you mess with her cubs. Braid costing me my arm is about the same as if a she-bear took it. I couldn't get mad at a bear and I couldn't get mad at Braid, and I couldn't hate the whole Pawnee tribe because of a mistake."

"You call losing an arm a *mistake*?" Francis asked.

"Yes, sir. I should have got Braid before he got my arm—not doing it was a mistake."

"How can you talk about killing Braid when you don't hate him, aren't even mad at him?"

"Now be careful, Mr. Tucket. Asking a question is one thing—even when it's a dumb question. But now you're picking, and picking is what St. Louis city folk do . . ."

"No—I mean it. In the wagon train and at Braid's village, I fought a lot. But I couldn't *really* fight unless I got good and mad. Now you make it all sound so cool and calm—I just don't understand, that's all."

Mr. Grimes laughed. "Let me put it another way. I live by trapping, mostly beaver. Sometimes I trap on Pawnee land, sometimes not. When I *do* trap on Pawnee land, it figures that I'd want to do it without getting my hair lifted, so I bring them something they need—powder and lead—and I don't get mad. I get something—beaver pelts—and the Pawnees get something. We all stay happy. Well, maybe not happy—but alive."

Francis couldn't help himself. "Why do you have to bring them powder and lead? They turn right around and use it on white people—like my folks. That doesn't seem right to me . . ."

Francis felt the trapper stiffen in the saddle. He bit his tongue, and thought that he fully deserved getting knocked on the ground and left for the Indians.

Gradually the stiffness went away. Without turning, and in a dead-even voice, Mr. Grimes said, "I guess we'd better ride quiet for a while."

For nearly an hour there was only the sound of the sorrel's hooves and bird calls and their own breathing. Francis called himself many kinds of a fool in that time.

When the silence was at last broken, it was Mr. Grimes who spoke.

"You've been through a lot in the past month or so, and I guess maybe I ought to take that into consideration a mite—"

"No," Francis interrupted, glad of the chance to

speak. "I was dumb. I'm sorry—I shouldn't have talked that way."

"Well, I'm going to say something to you that I shouldn't have to say. I'm not a war maker. I don't want to kill Pawnees, and I don't want to kill whites. If they want to kill each other, that's something else again. I ride right down the middle. And if my powder and lead is used to kill whites, I'm sorry. But it's not my fault. That same powder and lead would kill a lot of buffalo and antelope—and that's how most of it is used. Some mountain men and traders bring the Indians whiskey—if you want to pick yourself a *real* fight, go after those men."

"But I didn't mean—"

"And don't come clawing at me. I've killed a few Indians in my time, and I'll probably kill a few more. I may even put Braid under, someday, or he may kill me. But you can make money on this: If I *do* kill Braid, it won't be because he has something I want, like land. I'll leave that to the farmers—your people. And that's the last I want to hear about it."

He quit talking as suddenly as he'd begun. Again the silence was thick and painful. There was nothing Francis could say, and he knew it, and the knowledge made him even sadder.

"Mr. Grimes," he asked, "where are we going?"

"You mean today, or next month?"

"Well, today, I guess. I thought if we happened to be going near a settlement of some kind in the next few days, you could drop me off."

The mountain man nodded. "If that's what you want. We'll be getting to a settlement tonight—or at least the only kind of settlement they have out here. You can drop off there if you want to. I think Standing Bear would be right proud to have you stay awhile—"

"Standing Bear?" Francis cut in. "Who's he?"

"He's the head of the settlement. I was thinking earlier of swinging by there and picking up a horse for you. Of course now that you want to stop, we'll just drop in and forget about the horse . . ."

"What kind of a settlement is it?"

"Well, it's not really a settlement. More like what you'd call a camp. Out here we call it something else."

"What do you call it?"

"A village," the mountain man answered, chuckling. "Out here we call it a Sioux village. You sure do pick the funniest places to want to stay, Mr. Tucket."

# Chapter Nine

**Francis tried** not to be afraid when the Sioux village came into view. He had seen only one type of Indian so far, the mean type. And he knew that the Pawnee tribe was the not-too-distant cousin of the Sioux. Thoughts of recapture took the place of his faith in Mr. Grimes's judgment, and Francis went cold all over.

"Easy, Mr. Tucket," the mountain man said without turning. "This is like a show. You saw me come into the Pawnee village—we do the same thing here. Act easy."

Francis took his cue from Mr. Grimes. He stiffened his back and tried to remember something not related to where he was now. His mind settled on the birthday cake his mother had made, and looking straight ahead—neither down nor left nor right—he pictured it in exact detail.

The clamor in the village was deafening. Chief Standing Bear's group had an even noisier bunch of dogs than the Pawnees, and the children's howling was earshattering. Francis marveled at the sorrel and the mules. They paid no more attention to the screaming than did their master except that once a mule took aim and nearly drove a dog's head through his rear end with a rear hoof.

Finally, when they had woven their way to about the center of the village, Mr. Grimes pulled lightly on the reins and stopped.

"Standing Bear," the mountain man called.

Francis watched as a small channel opened in the crowd to the right and an Indian, who limped, came through. He was short, bowlegged, and stocky, but he moved with a smoothness that made Francis think immediately of a cat. It must be Standing Bear, Francis thought, and he was not smiling. When he was five feet from the sorrel, his right hand came up slowly, and with as much grace as he used walking.

Mr. Grimes shrugged, said something in Sioux to the chief, received an answer, and laughed.

"I *thought* it was a mite tight," he said to Francis. "Braid sent word ahead and asked Standing Bear to hold you if the Sioux found you. That's interesting since the Pawnee and Sioux are usually enemies—I guess he made a small peace with this village because catching you is so important. It would seem, Mr. Tucket, that you hurt his prestige—the black mare was Braid's personal mount. You sure do things in spades when you get loose, don't you? Taking a war leader's prize horse and all."

"Me?" Francis said. "*I* didn't take—"

"Now, now, Mr. Tucket. Just leave sleeping dogs alone. Old Standing Bear here thinks you must be one go-getter of a young warrior—bucking a big war leader and all. The Sioux think it's the funniest joke they ever heard, so why don't you just play along?"

All the time he had been talking to Francis, Mr. Grimes hadn't stopped looking and smiling at Standing Bear. He said something in Sioux, laughed again when Standing Bear answered, and nodded. "Raise your right hand, Mr. Tucket, the way standing Bear put up his."

Francis complied. "What did you say to him?"

"I told him you were the toughest fighter in the

Black Hills, that you were clever as the fox, that your heart was the heart of a mountain lion."

"You said all that about me?"

"Don't let it go to your head, Mr. Tucket. Indians don't take anybody's word on anything. Standing Bear says that he has a pretty tough boy in *his* village—"

"Oh, no . . ."

"Oh, yes, Mr. Tucket. It seems that your wrestling days aren't over yet." He turned and again said something to Standing Bear in Sioux.

"*Now* what did you tell him?" Francis asked.

"I just said that you weren't afraid of his boy, sort of."

"What do you mean, 'sort of'?"

"I said you were so sure of winning that you'd bet your rifle against a good pony and a set of buckskins."

"You did *what*?"

"Now don't get rattled, Mr. Tucket. Didn't those Pawnee boys teach you *anything* about wrestling?"

Francis's eyes scanned the crowd around them, looking for his possible competitor. "Yes, Mr. Grimes, the Pawnees *did* teach me something about wrestling."

"Well, then . . ."

"They taught me how to lose."

There were certain formalities that had to be observed before the match. Mr. Grimes had also brought the Sioux powder and lead. Francis watched him loosen the pack on one of the mules and remove a small keg. It couldn't have been more than a two-pound keg of powder, but the way the Sioux carried on, it could well have been two hundred pounds of triple-fine.

"They can't make it," Mr. Grimes told Francis. "So the only way they can get powder is to buy it, or get it as a gift, or steal it."

After distributing the powder there was more talk, and *still* more talk with Standing Bear. Francis almost went to sleep on the sorrel just listening to him. By this time all of the women had disappeared, the children had backed out of the circle of men, and Mr. Grimes seemed to be the only one listening to Standing Bear. The sun set while he was talking, the evening chill seeped into Francis's back, fires began to flare up around camp, the smell of buffalo cooking touched his nostrils, and *still* Standing Bear talked on.

Finally the Indian's voice stopped.

Mr. Grimes said something briefly in Sioux. The Indian replied, just as briefly. Mr. Grimes nodded, and turned to Francis. "Better get down and stretch a bit. Footloose is probably tired, too."

Francis slid off to the left and fell flat on his face. Both his legs were asleep.

Mr. Grimes muttered something in Sioux and all the warriors laughed.

"What did you say?" Francis asked.

"I told them you were saving your legs for the match."

"Well, if it hadn't been for old, old chief windbag there, my legs probably wouldn't have fallen asleep," Francis said grumpily, flexing his knees. "What was he talking about, anyway?"

"Well, he said that his lands reach to where it is always cold in the North, to where great waters end the land in the East, as far as all the ducks and geese and small birds fly in the cold of the end of the time of the sun—"

"Couldn't you cut it down a bit?" Francis asked. "I'm hungry."

"He said I could trap beaver on Sioux land. I thanked him. Then he said I was welcome. Then you fell off the horse—"

"All right. I understood that part. Now do I get a chance to eat before I lose my rifle?"

"Sure do, Mr. Tucket, prime buffalo. But I don't know as I like this negative thinking you're doing.

Cheer up a mite. They probably won't have but a midget against you. Why not think instead of owning a pony and some good buckskins?"

"I told you. I'm too good at losing."

Many things were stacked up against Francis's chances of winning the pony and buckskins. First, he was so hungry that when food was finally offered him, in the form of a large slab of hot buffalo meat, he ate until he could barely stand.

Then, too, two days hadn't completely worn out the stiffness in his legs, hips, and arms. And riding all day on the rounded haunch of the sorrel was hardly good training for wrestling. But the main obstacle was the Indian boy Standing Bear had picked to fight him. He was not a midget, he wasn't even small.

Francis stood on one side of a circle of braves. At his side, silent as usual, was Mr. Grimes. Across from him, and just inside the circle, was the Indian boy—a good thirty feet away.

He was about four inches taller than Francis, and he weighed about ten pounds more than Francis's one hundred and thirty-five pounds. And *he* hadn't spent the whole day riding on the sorrel.

"This is going to be murder," Francis whispered to Mr. Grimes. "Pure murder."

"I'm glad to see your confidence returning, Mr.

Tucket. Just a few minutes ago you were ready to give up. Now you're talking about killing him."

"I meant it the other way."

"Oh."

Francis looked across the circle. A large fire had been built to one side, and in the light he could see two men smearing something on the other boy.

"What are they doing to him?" Francis asked.

"Greasing him," Mr. Grimes answered. "And it's about time you took your shirt off."

"You mean I've got to do that?"

"No, you don't, Mr. Tucket. But the grease is going to make it harder to hold him than a wet catfish. It seems sensible to me that you'd sort of feel like doing the same thing."

Francis took off his shirt slowly, and Mr. Grimes covered him from the waist up with cold buffalo grease.

"It stinks," Francis complained.

"Don't say that too loud." Mr. Grimes chuckled. "They think it smells nice—like perfume."

More wood was thrown on the fire. Into the center of the circle stepped Standing Bear. He looked first at the Indian boy and seemed to snort something in Sioux. The Indian boy smiled and nodded. Standing Bear turned to Francis and snorted the same thing.

"Nod and grin," Mr. Grimes told him. "He's asking if you're ready."

Francis nodded and smiled, at least halfheartedly. He didn't really feel ready.

Standing Bear snorted some more, then spoke for a full five minutes.

"He's spouting the rules," Mr. Grimes said. "No biting, no hitting with the closed hand, no hitting with elbows or knees, humph, I didn't know that."

"Know what?"

"They allow kicking, but not with the toes. You have to curve your toes under and kick with the top of your foot. I guess you'd better take your boots off, Mr. Tucket. It wouldn't be fair to kick him with boots on."

Francis sighed resignedly and stooped to remove his boots. You might know they'd allow kicking, he thought. In truth, his boots were in tatters, but he felt odd barefoot.

"The rest of the rules are simple. You fight in the circle and stay out of the fire. If one of you falls or is thrown out of the circle, he gets thrown right back in and the fight goes on. The match ends when one of you says uncle—go." Mr. Grimes pushed Francis into the ring. The other boy had already entered from the other side.

Francis had wrestled a lot with the Pawnee boys, but he was hardly ready for this Sioux terror. With a loud scream the Indian boy, grinning widely, bounced across the clearing, spun lightly on his left leg, and placed the instep of his right foot dead in the center of Francis's still-undigested buffalo, hard.

It was a kick solid enough to drop an ox. Francis went down with his hands doubled over his stomach and a look of complete surprise on his face.

The Sioux boy landed on him like a cougar—a smiling cougar—and Francis's arm was twisted up his back and his face was mashed in the dirt.

A loud collective grunt issued from around the circle. It was going to be a quick fight, and the Sioux boy would have a fine new rifle. This white boy must have been terribly lucky in his dealings with the warrior Braid.

But Francis wasn't quitting, in spite of being out of breath, and having a mouth full of dirt. The arm lock looked wicked but it didn't hurt much. The Indian had failed to twist the arm enough to make it painful, and his mistake gave Francis much needed time to catch his breath. Then he used a trick he'd learned fighting with Max. He totally and completely relaxed, even the arm the Indian boy was holding. It worked. The Sioux wrestler felt the relaxing, and took the opportunity to change his hold.

It was what Francis had hoped for. With a mighty heave, he arched his back upward and threw the Sioux boy. Then he scrambled and landed, as hard as he could, on top of the boy, grabbed him around the neck and leg, and arched his back.

Another grunt came from the crowd. Maybe the fight would go on for a while yet. Francis heard Mr. Grimes on the side: "Well done, Mr. Tucket."

In almost any other match it would have been the end, for the Indian was all but paralyzed. Francis was on the boy's back, pulling him up at both ends, and he couldn't move.

But because of the grease, Francis couldn't maintain his hold. His hand slipped from the boy's neck, the Indian rolled over, and before Francis really knew what had happened, *he* was in the dirt.

This time Francis saw something new in the Indian's eyes. It was respect. Whereas he had jumped in screaming the first time, he now circled warily as the two regained their feet.

This was Francis's kind of fighting. The circling, looking for a weakness, was how he had learned to wrestle with white boys, and he noticed now a weakness in the Indian. He favored his right leg, the one Francis had twisted.

It was simple, then. All Francis had to do was feint to the left, then come in hard on the right.

The Indian boy would be slow that way, and Francis could get a neck hold, usually a match-stopper.

He feinted, and came in on the right, and the Indian boy was waiting for him. The weak leg had been only a bait, and Francis ran straight into a backhanded slap across his windpipe. It stopped his breathing again, and in the brief second that he hesitated, the Indian tripped him and used Francis's own hold—the reverse back arch. But there was a new twist. Instead of grabbing Francis around the neck, the Indian boy wrapped his fingers in Francis's hair, where there was no grease.

Still another grunt came from the crowd. Surely this would be the end of the match. The white boy couldn't move, and he couldn't get away. Some of the men even turned to go back to their lodges.

Francis *couldn't* move. He tried relaxing again, but the trick didn't work a second time. The Indian boy had him. It wasn't over, though, after all. Mr. Grimes leaned over from the edge of the circle and whispered: "Mr. Tucket, there's been talk of keeping you for Braid if you don't put up a better fight."

Francis didn't really believe him. It was the sort of thing Mr. Grimes would say just to get him riled. But he wasn't quite sure. The Indians did some funny things, and the thought of being sent back to Braid's camp was a terrible thought.

The Indian boy did something completely natural. He spat to get the dust out of his mouth. He didn't spit at or on Francis. But the spit landed about four inches in front of his eyes.

Francis saw pink, then red, and finally just fire. "Now you didn't have to go and do *that*," he yelled in English.

Later not even Mr. Grimes could tell how Francis got out of the hold. But get out of the hold he did, and within thirty seconds it was pretty clear to the crowd that one angry white boy was going to be a pony and a set of buckskins richer. His twist to get out of the hold knocked the Indian boy on his back in the dirt, and Francis, acting more from instinct than logic, made what Mr. Grimes later called a "goat leap." He jumped high in the air and, in an almost perfect swan dive, landed headfirst in the center of the Indian's stomach. Before the boy could regain his breath, Francis had flopped down and wrapped a scissors hold around his chest. Five seconds passed, then ten, and on the fifteenth second—Mr. Grimes had been counting—the Indian boy gasped his defeat. "That's enough, Mr. Tucket," Mr. Grimes called.

Francis released the boy immediately, no longer angry. He stood, and was surprised to see the Indian boy smiling up at him. On the spur of the moment, he leaned down and helped the still-gasping boy to get up. Around the circle there were many grunts of approval.

The Indian, as soon as his breathing settled down, began jabbering and laughing right away. Francis turned to Mr. Grimes.

"What's he saying?"

"He's saying it was well worth a pony to learn that new trick—he means that business of butting."

"Well, I'm glad he's happy," Francis said, laughing also. "And you can tell him that I learned something myself." He rubbed his back. "I may have won a pony, but I don't think I'll be riding it right away . . ."

# Chapter Ten

**Francis couldn't figure out** what to do. First he decided he wanted to stay on at Standing Bear's village, but then he found that he wanted to go on with Mr. Grimes. He had announced that he wouldn't be able to ride the pony for a while, but even so Mr. Grimes shook him awake at dawn the next morning.

"Come on, Mr. Tucket. There's a horse to be picked out, and we have to be on our way today. I swear, you sleep like a bear in winter."

Actually, there wasn't "a horse to be picked

out." Standing Bear had already done the picking—and true to Indian form, he had chosen the best pony in the corral.

She was a mare, and except for a white splotch of hair across her rump in the shape of a bird's wing, she was as black as the night. Standing Bear pointed to her with pride, smiled, and talked in Sioux to Mr. Grimes, who reported to Francis:

"He says he picked the pony for two reasons. One, she is good. Two, he hears you have a special liking for black mares. That's a joke and you should laugh."

Francis laughed.

Standing Bear talked some more.

"He says that she's been trained to hunt buffalo, and you should steer her with you knees. Nod and smile."

Francis nodded and smiled at the chief. It wasn't what he'd normally call a smiling morning. The sun wasn't warm yet, he hadn't gone to sleep until well past midnight, and he wouldn't have made it from his borrowed buffalo-robe bed to the corral if Mr. Grimes hadn't half dragged him. It seemed like all he had done since getting lost from the wagon train was get stiffer and stiffer.

Standing Bear acknowledged Francis's smile. He said something in Sioux.

"The pony is now yours," Mr. Grimes translated. "You can take her to your lodge—I guess he means where you slept last night, up by old Footloose."

The mare had a rope halter. Francis opened the corral gate and tried to grab the halter. She backed away, mixing in with some other ponies. He looked questioningly at Mr. Grimes. "How do I catch her?"

"You could run her down," the mountain man answered.

Francis gave him a nasty look. He could barely walk. At that moment, Mr. Grimes stepped into the corral with a horsehide rope. He flipped it out once, twice, and on the third try the noose fell over the mare's head. She stopped then at the feel of the rope on her neck and Francis hobbled up to her.

"Come on, Mr. Tucket," said the mountain man. "Climb on. Let's see how she takes to your weight."

"But, Mr. Grimes . . ." Francis complained. "I'm like a board. Give me a day or two to loosen up—"

"The best way to loosen up is to move a bit. Now climb on, before Standing Bear gets the thought you don't *like* his pony."

All the time he had been talking, Mr. Grimes

was fashioning from a second piece of rope a war bridle—a slipknot—around the mare's lower jaw.

In two tries, Francis managed to get his stomach over the back of the mare. He swiveled slowly until his legs hung down either side, then sat up, straight and stiff.

"Please, little pony," he said quietly, "remember my condition."

The strange part was that the pony *did* seem to understand. She didn't move quickly, or buck, or even tremble. And when Mr. Grimes handed him the end of the war-bridle rope, she walked toward the gate as meekly as a kitten.

It was Standing Bear who caused the trouble. Just as Francis and the pony came through the gate, the Sioux chief picked up a switch, moved behind the mare, and brought the switch down across the white splotch on her rump.

"Eeeeyah!" he yelled.

Actually, as Mr. Grimes pointed out later, Francis should have thanked the old chief, because what happened next loosened Francis in a hurry. But when that switch landed, he was too surprised to do anything but grab the mane of the black mare and close his eyes.

The mare became a dark comet, flashing through the middle of the awakening Sioux village like a fast wind. She knocked dogs out of the way and cleared cooking fires—jumping completely over one old woman kneeling over a pot of food. Through all this, Francis managed somehow to stay on her back.

When the mare reached the edge of the village, she stopped. Francis naturally kept on going, and finally *he* stopped with his face buried in a pile of still raw buffalo hides, but his troubles weren't over yet.

Coming hot on the heels of the little mare was the old woman, throwing rocks as fast as she could. Francis might be a good wrestler, and very smart to outwit Braid—but *nobody* jumped a horse over the old woman and her cook fire and got away with it.

Francis was quick to recognize disaster. Forgetting the mare, he made a dash back toward the safety of Mr. Grimes.

Mr. Grimes wasn't offering much safety. In fact, he wasn't offering anything. He and Standing Bear were wrapped over the top of the pole of the corral, laughing till tears ran down their cheeks.

"Keep it up, Mr. Tucket," the trapper said, as Francis ran by. "She's gaining on you."

Within a hundred yards Francis outran the old woman *and* her deadly rocks, and had also managed to kick away about ten of the camp dogs that had been snapping at his heels.

"Jokers," he mumbled, returning to the corral. The mare had walked back, looking as meek as she had before the wild ride. "Real jokers. I bet you get a lot of laughs out of throwing people off cliffs."

"Now, Mr. Tucket. Old Standing Bear just wanted you to know you were getting a pony that knew how to *run.*" The mountain man was barely holding back laughter. "Besides, look how loose you are. You might as well be an old washrag . . ."

Francis nodded, looking down at himself. "And I look like one, too." But his anger weakened fast, and he smiled. The truth was he *had* loosened up.

"We'll stop early today," Mr. Grimes said. "I feel like some fresh antelope. And you can just carry your buckskins until then, so you can take a bath and start all new."

"I guess I will go with you," Francis said.

"Oh. Well, that depends, Mr. Tucket."

"On what?"

"On whether or not you can spend half a day riding downwind of me. You smell positively ripe from those hides."

# Chapter Eleven

**Noon found the two riders** almost ten miles from the Sioux village. They were on the edge of a small stream, and Francis was only too glad when Mr. Grimes called a halt at a clearing.

"While you're stripping and taking a bath," the mountain man said, "I'll scout up ahead for some meat. There's a mesa about two miles on down where there's usually an antelope or two."

Francis nodded. They picketed the mules, and Mr. Grimes rode off.

Warm, with little or no breeze dancing through

the cottonwoods along the stream, it was truly a day made for swimming. Francis hit the water before the mountain man was out of sight. It was cold—spring fed in the hills somewhere—but the cold only made it all the more refreshing. He played around for a while, diving and splashing in a deep pool, and then scrubbed himself, using his shirt for a washcloth.

He climbed out of the stream and let the sun dry him as he lay on his back. He'd come a long way, he thought. Not in miles—he doubted that he was much closer to Oregon than when the Pawnees had captured him. But in time and knowledge, he'd come what seemed like a thousand years. He'd seen and done more than most people did all their lives, and he was only fourteen.

Presently he was dry, so he unwrapped the buckskins from one of the mule packs on the ground. They were plain, like Mr. Grimes's, and for the same reason. You could hide easier without a lot of colored beads to give you away. Actually, the buckskins had been made as a hunting suit for the boy he had wrestled. But they were new and hadn't been used yet and they fit Francis. The pants stopped at his ankles and fitted tightly to his hips and legs—following the principle of most Indian dress that a belt was good for nothing but cutting into your stomach when you bent over. The buckskin shirt had one set of fringes across the chest, was open at the throat, and its bottom fell almost a foot below his waist.

Mr. Grimes had thought ahead. There were no pockets in the buckskins, so he had procured for Francis a "possibles" sack to hold his flask and shooting equipment. This hung from a strap over his shoulder. Mr. Grimes had also picked up a pair of plain, ankle-high moccasins for him.

When Francis finished dressing, he looked nothing like the boy who had left St. Louis with the wagon train. The buckskins, even new, gave him the appearance of belonging more to the plains than to a settlement. His face was weathered and tan, and his hair—usually kept short by his mother—fell well below his ears.

He smiled, thinking of how he must look. It's too bad I don't have a mirror, he told himself. I probably look like a young Mr. Grimes. The idea strangely pleased him, and his smile widened as he carried his old clothes across the stream and buried them beneath a rotten log. He felt as though he was burying his past life.

He came back across the stream just as Mr. Grimes returned. He stopped the sorrel but did not dismount.

"Well, well, Mr. Tucket. I near mistook you for Jim Bridger. Probably would have if you didn't have brown hair. Jim is turning gray at the temples."

Francis felt a blush sweep over his face.

Mr. Grimes didn't miss it. "I was going to ask you to shoot an antelope for me—but now I don't know. A red face stands out just a mite, and you might scare them away. Howsomever, if you can pull yourself up on the mare one more time, maybe I can offer you a little sport."

Francis wheeled away, glad for the chance to do something. Mr. Grimes had the darndest way of *noticing* everything. Francis untied the mare, slipped her war bridle up tight, and with his rifle in one hand, jumped on her back. He took the reins in his other hand.

Mr. Grimes loped out of camp and Francis jabbed his heels into the mare's ribs to catch up. They rode side by side for twenty minutes, and then pulled up sharply on the edge of what Francis first took to be a cliff. Below them lay an immense level plain, as green as a hay field and twice as flat. Far out on the opposite side of the mesa Francis could see fifteen or twenty brown specks.

"Antelope, Mr. Tucket—or dinner, depending on how you look at it. I'd like you to shoot me a nice young buck—"

"From *here*?" Francis interrupted. "Why, they're at least two miles away."

"No-ah, Mr. Tucket. Not from here. You leave your mare up here with me and you climb down there. Then you hide and"—he dug in his saddlebags and produced a piece of white cloth—"and wave this around for a while. It's an old Indian trick. They get curious about what you're wiggling and come to see what it is. *Then* you shoot one—and make sure he's a young buck. The old ones get old by running a lot—and that makes them tough."

Francis took the rag, slid off his horse, and looked down the cliff. Actually it was a steep slide, and could be descended fairly easily.

"Why are you sending me down?" he asked. "I've never shot an antelope . . ."

"That's just why, Mr. Tucket. That's just why. Now you'd better get going—we've only got about seven hours of daylight left." His voice was sarcastic.

Francis looked across the mesa at the antelope and shrugged. He was sure asked to do a lot of funny things. He started down the slide.

Going down was easy, and it wasn't as far as it looked. In fifteen minutes he was at the bottom, in back of a small rise, and lying on his stomach waving the rag in the air.

Francis couldn't see the antelope, and as the seconds turned into minutes, he wasn't completely sure that the antelope could see his waving rag. He raised carefully up on his elbows in the grass, but could see nothing. Turning, he looked up at the slide—hoping to see Mr. Grimes calling him back. Again, he saw nothing.

This is silly, he thought. I don't even know what's happening. The antelope probably ran off when I started down the slide. He raised up again. Still nothing. The grass was so high—it was like a wall around him. He started to get up, then fell back. The only thing keeping him still was fear of ridicule by the mountain man. Francis's orders had been specific: bring back a young buck. Getting up now could ruin it, but if the antelope *had* run off, it was stupid to stay down in the grass all afternoon. He waved the rag again.

That's when the thought hit him: this was all a joke. Mr. Grimes was a great one for jokes. Like sending him down to wave a rag around in a bunch of grass, telling him, of all things, that the antelope would *come* to him. And he'd fallen for it—lock, stock, and barrel. He shook his head. Wouldn't he ever learn?

Again he started to get up, and that's when he saw the antelope. There were two of them. One was quite a bit larger than the other. They were both males, and they had seen Francis move.

Even so, they stood still, absolutely still, not even blinking their eyes.

Francis took in a shallow breath, held it, and leapt to his feet, swinging up his rifle. But as fast as he was, the antelope were faster. In the seeming twitch of two white tails, they were doing close to forty miles an hour, dead away from Francis.

He fired, remembering at the last second to aim at the smaller buck. It wasn't a particularly difficult shot, but Francis was rattled, and he felt certain he'd missed. Yet the young antelope pitched forward and fell.

Francis couldn't believe his eyes. He reloaded at once and walked up to the buck. No second shot was needed; the antelope had been hit in the back of the head, just below the horn base. Francis grabbed him by the horns and began pulling him toward the slide. It was a long haul up, and he was sweating by the time he reached the top where Mr. Grimes was waiting.

"Well, Mr. Tucket. You seem to have done all right down there." The mountain man was grinning, and he fetched a knife from his saddlebag. He made one neat cut down the middle of the dead buck and removed the entrails. He saved the liver and heart and left the rest. "The coyotes will get the leavings. I wasn't sure how you'd do. You can tell a lot about a man when he's hunting antelope. It's the waiting. A lot of 'em get nervous and start fidgeting around. I've known grown men to actually stand up and scare 'em away."

Francis blushed again. "Well," he began, "I can see how something like that could happen. I mean, I almost . . ."

"Generally speaking, though," the mountain man went on as though he hadn't heard, "if a man makes it through once, you don't have to worry about him. He'll pull his load when the time comes, and that's all you can ask of any man."

"I *was* a little nervous," Francis said quietly.

"Well, it didn't hurt your shooting a lot," Mr. Grimes said, pointing toward the antelope's head. "I'd call that a right smart shot."

"I thought I'd missed."

Mr. Grimes nodded. "That happens sometimes. You never know till the smoke clears." There was something about his voice; he seemed to be talking around something. Francis caught it but didn't say anything. By that time Mr. Grimes had a small, smokeless fire going and had spitted the liver.

They ate it when its edge was just turning brown, cutting it in thin strips with Mr. Grimes's knife. Francis thought he had never tasted anything so rich and delicious.

After eating the liver, they returned to the camp by the stream and roasted a whole rear quarter of the buck. Then they spent most of the rest of the afternoon and evening cutting off slices and eating them. By dark, they had consumed close to twelve pounds of fresh meat. Mr. Grimes wrapped the rest in the main part of the antelope's skin and put it in one of the mule packs.

"It doesn't really get good for two or three days," he said. "And if it's well wrapped, it'll keep for more than a week."

They doused the fire and turned in early. Mr. Grimes was asleep as soon as his head hit the saddle.

Francis lay for a time thinking. There was something bothering him and it took him almost five minutes to realize what it was. Then he got up, quietly, and fished one of his rifle balls out of his "possibles" sack. He found the antelope's head where Mr. Grimes had left it, and in the moonless dark he turned it over and put the ball in the hole in the back of the head.

As he suspected, it was much too large a hole to have been made by his rifle. He dropped the head and returned to his bed. From now on, he thought, if that man says up is down and day is night, I'll believe him. Anybody who can make a shot like that, timing it to go off at the same time as another rifle, and hit a running antelope at two—no, three hundred yards, *can't* be wrong.

It was a comforting thought. Francis went to sleep smiling.

# Chapter Twelve

**For a week** they rode at an easy pace, saving the horses. Still they made close to a hundred miles before Mr. Grimes pulled up on the seventh evening.

"How do you feel about a little night riding, Mr. Tucket?" he asked.

"All right," Francis answered. "Why?"

"I sort of figured we could make Spot Johnnie's before turning in. Be nice to have a decent meal and sleep loose for a change."

Francis had no idea what he was talking about.

Not once had he mentioned this Spot Johnnie, but Francis decided not to question the mountain man.

"And we can grain the horses. Especially that mare of yours."

So they rode on. There was half a moon to furnish some light and sometime toward midnight Mr. Grimes pointed down at a light in a shallow valley.

"Spot Johnnie's," he said. "Now when we go in, you stay right out to the side of me—so's it doesn't look like you're sneaking. Okay?"

Francis nodded. They started down, angled across a flat meadow, and approached three log buildings. When they were still a hundred feet from the cabins, Mr. Grimes stopped.

"Ease that hammer down with your thumb, Spot," he said in a voice so low it was almost a whisper. "It's Jason Grimes."

Francis hadn't seen or heard a thing, so it was to his utter and complete surprise that the figure of a man arose suddenly beside him—not five feet away. He jumped.

"Dang it all, Jason," the man said, laughing and shaking his head. "You sure do ruin a man's fun. I was planning to let you get all the way up to the building, and then take that pretty hat of yours off, feather and all."

"That's why I stopped," Mr. Grimes answered.

"Got me a friend here who doesn't understand that kind of fun. He might just put a ball in your gizzard by mistake."

Rather than stop to talk, they kept on riding slowly, and Spot Johnnie walked between them. They pulled up at the front cabin. Light was leaking out around the hide windows, and in its glow, Francis got his first look at Spot Johnnie as Mr. Grimes introduced them. There wasn't really much to see. He could have been fifty or a hundred. He had a gray beard and long hair that hung well past his shoulders, and he wore beaded buckskins. There was no hat on his head; instead he wore a beaded headband to keep his hair out of his eyes. His rifle was a Hawkens. Francis liked him at once—there was a nice sound in his speech, a sort of easy confidence, and his eyes looked merry all the time.

"Figured you were always pretty much of a loner, Jason," Spot said, eyeing Francis. "How'd you come by picking up a cub?"

While Mr. Grimes explained about Francis, a boy of perhaps ten years of age came out of the cabin and took the horses around back. Then the three of them went inside.

At first, the inside of the cabin made Francis homesick. It was all so warm and cheerful. Two children were playing on the floor beneath a huge wooden table. There was a fire in the fireplace, although it wasn't at all cold. On one side of the cabin there were beds, arranged in bunk fashion, and all around the walls hung blankets and jackets and old moccasins. It looked like a home. And then, suddenly, he wasn't so homesick anymore—leaning over a big kettle near the fireplace was a large Indian woman.

It startled him to see the woman, not in a lodge, but in a house. She must be Johnnie's wife, he knew, but he caught himself staring just the same. She made him think of the Pawnee village.

As if reading his mind, Spot Johnnie suddenly spoke up. "And this is my family, Mr. Tucket. That's my wife, Bird Dance, over by the fire, and under the table are Jared and John, and the boy you saw outside was Clarence."

The boys under the table didn't look out. But Bird Dance turned from the fire, smiled, and said in perfect English, "How do you do. I'm sure you must be hungry after riding all day. Please sit down and have some stew and biscuits."

Francis managed to hide his surprise. He smiled —he liked her at once—and turned to the table. Mr. Grimes was already sitting there with Spot.

"How've you been making out, Spot?" Mr. Grimes asked.

"Fit," came the answer. "Pure fit and prime. Got me a full warehouse of furs and a wagon or two due next week from St. Louis to pick 'em up. Been a good year, and it might be a better one next. And you?"

"So-so," Mr. Grimes answered. "Found me a new hole last winter that I figure on trying before snow comes. What you giving for near-prime pelts this year, Spot?"

"You mean in money or trade?"

"Money."

"Two dollars—if it's a big one."

"Seems kinda low . . ."

"I might go three, if I knew the trapper and knew he wasn't out just to give me his culls."

"Fair enough. You got yourself a deal. Now, about provisions. You got everything?"

"All but sugar. It's running three dollars a pint —*wholesale.* So I've put off ordering it, hoping it would go down a mite."

"Fine. We'll need the usual. Your oldest boy can put it together tomorrow. In the meantime, I've got some questions that need answering."

They had to stop talking to eat the stew and biscuits, which proved to be worth at least a ten-day ride. Francis ate four bowls of stew and half a dozen fresh biscuits before Bird Dance cleared the table.

"Now," Spot said, lighting a pipe and propping his legs on a small three-legged stool. "What kind of questions you got, Jason?"

"About Indians, Spot. There's something downright funny going on and I can't pin it down. Take Braid, for instance—"

"*You* take him," Spot cut in. "I've had enough of that skunk to hold me for all my days."

"What happened?"

"Nothing—to me. But Braid's thinking of taking over the whole Pawnee nation, way it looks, and for nothing but war. He was here a while back asking for things—powder, mostly, and caps. Only he didn't ask for 'em the way a man might. He said, 'The *Pawnee* want powder and the *Pawnee* want caps,' just like he was talking for the whole tribe. I don't like it."

"I thought he was getting a little feisty," Mr. Grimes said.

"It's not just things like taking this boy," Spot said, gesturing toward Francis. "That's bad enough. But Braid's also been raiding. There've been two wagon trains through here, and they both lost some people to Pawnees being led by Braid."

"Those two trains," Francis said, interrupting, "did any of the people in them mention losing a little girl?"

Spot scratched his head. "No . . . mostly they didn't want to talk about those they'd lost, so they didn't talk about the Indians much at all. One woman—I think it was a brown-haired woman—asked me if the Indians always killed captives. She was pretty broken up about losing a boy—"

"I'm that boy," Francis said. "She's my mother." He sighed. Then at least his mother was alive, and most likely his father. "She didn't mention a girl named Rebecca?"

"Nope—at least not that I recollect. But as I said, the people mostly didn't talk about the raid."

They were silent for a while, thinking. Francis was imagining the muscled figure of Braid nestled just over his rifle's sights.

"Braid's stupid," Spot continued after a minute or two. "He's talking about making a clean sweep, or so I hear, and driving all whites from Pawnee territory."

"That's a bit strong," Mr. Grimes said. "He might hit a train or two, but I don't think he'll bother us—I mean you and me. It would only hurt him to put us under—he'd get no more trade."

"All the same," Spot said, "if I were you, and I knew Braid was around somewhere, I'd make sure I had my shoulder blades covered by a tree."

Mr. Grimes shrugged. "I do that anyway—just

natural. But I don't like this other thing much. If there's anything worse than one mad Pawnee, it's a hundred mad Pawnees. Braid's stirring up a war, maybe. Not so good . . ." His voice trailed off.

And that finished any talk for another thirty minutes or so, while they ate and drank *still* more. Francis had thought he was full, but he was fast changing his eating patterns. He was learning that when you *can* eat, you eat. It might be a couple of days before you got a chance to eat again.

"Just one question," Mr. Grimes said around a mouthful of biscuit. "What's the story on the Crows? I spent a week coming across their stomping grounds and didn't see a one. Usually I get shot at at least once."

"I don't know," Spot answered. "But there's been word they found a big herd of buffalo and spent the summer living in back of the herd. I also heard they've broken up a bit—too many war chiefs or something—and that there's a bunch of small bands out, just taking what they can get when they can get it. But you know the Crows: if you see 'em, more'n likely you're going to have to fight 'em." Spot leaned back and sighed. "Enough of that—I think it's time for a game. Or are you scared? I figured you'd probably given up—seeing how bad I whipped you last time."

"*Whipped* me?" snorted Mr. Grimes. "Did you hear that, Mr. Tucket? This old spot-head thinks he whipped me. Waugh! Drag out the plank and we'll see who whips who in this pond."

"Stakes?" Spot asked, laughing.

"One prime pelt—which I haven't got—against three pints of sugar—which you haven't got. Suit you?"

"Why not? I can always use another pelt."

"Ho—you sure are the one for talk. Where's that plank?"

Spot turned and fetched a flat board from the wall. The board was about two feet long, and at either end a heavy leather thong was lashed. Francis could make neither head nor tail of it, even when Spot put the board down in front of Mr. Grimes and seated himself opposite. The children had been put to bed, but Spot's wife came over from a stool by the fire. She was smiling, and kept smiling while she took their right arms and placed them on the board. When the arms were in such a position that the back of Mr. Grimes's hand was against the back of Spot's, she brought the leather thongs up and around and lashed their elbows in place. Now their arms could move neither forward nor backward, nor up at the elbow.

The two men, with their hands still back-to-back, hooked thumbs. Mr. Grimes looked at Spot, Spot returned the look, they both nodded, and the woman said, "Go!"

It didn't seem to be much of a match at first. The object of the contest was to twist your arm and drag your opponent's thumb down to the board by twisting *his* arm. At the start, Spot got the jump. Mr. Grimes didn't stop him until his thumb was almost mashed into the board, and then only by an effort that made all the cords in his neck stand out.

They hung like that for a long time, grinning at each other, their breath coming in rasps. Then, ever so slowly, Mr. Grimes started to push Spot's thumb back up. The thumbs stopped again when they were straight up, swung back and forth for a period of ten seconds, then suddenly plunged down until Spot's thumb touched the board.

"Ahh!" he said. "Where'd you get all *that*?"

"Been practicing," Mr. Grimes answered. "Figuring the way you whipped me last time . . ."

"Ha! Woman?" Spot called. "Fetch this badger three pints of brown sugar—not that he earned it, understand, but a deal is a deal."

"Seems there's a snake around here somewhere," Mr. Grimes said, grinning. "I thought you didn't have any sugar?"

"Nope—said I didn't *order* any," Spot answered.

"Lots of difference. Besides, you trying to tell me you don't have a single pelt out there in your pack somewheres?"

"Nope—got *three* I saved from last year."

Francis stared at them. The betting didn't make any sense. They both bet something they said they didn't have, but which they really did have. He was going to ask about it, but just then Mr. Grimes suggested getting some sleep and Francis, who had been sitting with the warm glow of the fire on his back and an extremely full stomach, realized that if he so much as blinked, he would be asleep.

He staggered to the warm corner by the fire, where Spot told him to go, and was soon dead to the world.

# Chapter Thirteen

**Mr. Grimes and Francis** stayed with Spot Johnnie for three days. They had meant to leave sooner, but things kept happening. First there was a joke shooting match between Mr. Grimes and Spot —a joke match because neither of them really tried to win. All they did was trick shooting; kind of show-off stuff, Francis thought. Like Spot throwing a piece of mud in the air, then stooping to pick up his rifle and shooting the mud before it hit the ground. And Mr. Grimes shooting a big rock over five hundred yards away, hitting it three times in a row.

Then the shooting match led to a wrestling match, and the wrestling match led to a giant dinner and warm sun to lie around in and a swim down in the creek by the stable, and before Francis really thought about it at all, three days had disappeared. On the morning of the fourth day, they rose early, packed the mules, and started out.

They were about half a mile from the buildings when they saw the wagons. Mr. Grimes saw them first, as usual.

"Farmers, Mr. Tucket," he said, pointing back past Spot Johnnie's place. Two wagons were visible coming down into the valley, crawling along. They were a good three miles away, but Francis could make out the men walking alongside the oxen. "It could be your chance—if they're going to Oregon. Most likely they are."

Francis didn't understand at first. He wasn't really thinking of himself in connection with wagons. And when he finally caught the mountain man's meaning, somehow it made him feel sad. Still, he nodded. "I guess so—that is, if they wouldn't mind taking a boy along."

"I think they'd probably be happy to have that extra gun," Mr. Grimes said, "especially if Braid's going to do some kicking up."

There was a long moment. The morning sun

caught the mare's mane and made it look almost blue. And how would you like to slow down to ten miles a day, little mare? Francis found himself thinking. How would you like to eat oxen dust and be tied with other horses at night? He looked again at the wagons. There were five showing now—five plodding wagons settled into the ruts across the prairie.

And he didn't want to be with them; not with the dust and the slow wagons and all the people carrying punch bowls. There was more to it now—more than if he were just another train boy. He knew more. He knew Indians, and how to shoot, and how to wrestle—

"You sure do seem to be in powerful thought, Mr. Tucket," Mr. Grimes cut in. "A man would think you're having trouble making up your mind . . ."

There was that, too, Francis thought. How can I just keep going with the mountain man? Mr. Grimes has his own way of life. It's a wild and exciting life, but is it the kind of life for me—for the rest of my life?

Francis shook his head in bewilderment. Then, slowly, he turned toward the wagons.

"Of course"—Mr. Grimes stopped him—"you've got to figure those people are maybe pretty dumb. They won't make Oregon anyways—at least not *this* winter. Here it is early fall, and they're only this far. Way I figure it, they'll be spending winter about halfway there—somewhere in the west part of Dakota Country, where it gets cold."

Francis looked at him. Was the mountain man telling him to stay? Or was he just ridiculing the "farmers" for being dumb?

"Now me," Mr. Grimes continued, his face still blank, "I figure on spending my winter not far from here—where the snow won't get *too* much higher'n a horse and I don't have to worry about much except a few stray Crows. If I get lucky and fill out on beaver fast, I just might come down here and spend the winter with Spot."

"Are you trying to tell me that I'd be better off staying with you through the winter than I would be if I joined that particular wagon train?"

"No-ah, Mr. Tucket, that isn't quite right. I'm not trying to tell you anything. It's your mind, you make it up . . ."

Francis nodded.

". . . but I'd hate to think I plucked you from Braid just so's you could turn out dumb."

Francis felt warm all over—warmer than the morning sun could have made him feel. He hefted his rifle, turned the little mare once more and almost—but not quite—laughed in relief. The truth was he didn't want to leave and it had been handled for him.

Mr. Grimes clucked at the sorrel and moved ahead. He didn't look back—not at the wagons or at Francis. He rode straight, his derby and feather aimed dead ahead.

Francis caught up. He didn't look back at the train either. It might as well not have been there. He felt that he should thank the mountain man, but what could he say? A straight "thank you" would probably only make him snort.

"The way I figured it, Mr. Grimes," he said finally, his eyes straight ahead, "if a guy's gotta spend a winter, he might as well spend it the best way he can . . ."

The mountain man smiled.

# Chapter Fourteen

TWO DAYS AWAY from Spot Johnnie's, Mr. Grimes stopped on the edge of a deep canyon.

"From here on, Mr. Tucket, we'll see no more people—Indians or otherwise."

Francis nodded, and believed him. They wound down a narrow trail to the bottom of the canyon. It was a dark place, with sheer walls and a thick forested floor, and in the bottom was a narrow stream. Mr. Grimes put his sorrel in the middle of this, and instructed Francis to do the same with his mare.

"We go up it awhile," he said, "and that's how we make *sure* we don't see any people."

That "awhile" proved to be two days long. When they camped at night, Mr. Grimes didn't allow a fire. And in the mornings, when they got ready to leave, he went around brushing out signs of their horses and making the campsite look as though they'd never been there.

At the end of the second day, they moved away from the stream. The canyon had widened into a valley more than ten miles across, and Mr. Grimes headed toward the right—or northern—edge. The forest was much thicker, the ground softer, but still he allowed no traces of their presence to remain at any campsite. His sharp eyes missed nothing, and he left no trail. Where the horses' hooves sank into the ground, he painstakingly pushed sticks under the depressions to raise them. When a twig was broken, he rubbed dirt on the broken end to make it look old.

"It's still pretty plain," he explained to Francis, standing over a hoof mark that Francis couldn't see even though he knew where it lay. "But in a couple of days, the best Kiowa tracker in the world couldn't find us—and neither will another trapper."

"Why are you being so careful?" Francis asked. He was tired of going slow.

"You heard the reasons just now, Mr. Tucket. One is the trappers. It's not that I'm greedy, at least no more than the next. But there's just enough beaver where we're headed to keep a man going, so long as he doesn't clean 'em out in one season. I wouldn't clean 'em out—and neither would another *good* trapper . . ."

"Then what are you worried about?"

"Every man who traps beaver isn't all that thoughtful. We come up here and take out a catch, and if somebody follows us who doesn't think about next season, he might clean out the beaver—lock, stock, and prime pelt. So I'm careful. I'm not worried, Mr. Tucket, just careful."

"All right, that's one reason. What's the other?"

"Indians; Crows, to be exact. We're on the edge of their country, and they're kind of unpredictable. We're going to be spread up and down the canyon, traps all over, and if they find out we're up here, they can make it mean for us. So we're careful about them, too. Any *other* questions, Mr. Tucket?"

"No, sir."

When they finally got where they were going—a shallow meadow about three miles wide and ten miles long, leading away from the canyon—Francis could see the reason for caution. Down the middle of the meadow was a long string of beaver ponds, one joined to the next by a short neck of water. Francis knew nothing of beaver, but he guessed there were probably hundreds of them.

Mr. Grimes led the way up the meadow, and it took them one whole day of slow riding to get to the northern end, and the sound of the beaver, slapping their tails against the water, stayed ahead of them all the way.

"Well, Mr. Tucket," the mountain man said, when they finally stopped, "I make it out to be a pretty fair season for us. What say we make a home?"

First they had to build a house, and although it wasn't much more than a large lean-to, it seemed like a house by the time the roof was finally finished. Mr. Grimes gave Francis an ax from one of the mule packs, and he cut all the poles for the lean-to while the mountain man did what he called the "count" on the beaver stream. It took Francis the better part of a week to cut enough long timbers for the walls and roof, and during that time, he saw Mr. Grimes only in the evenings and early mornings.

At first it didn't bother him. There was a job to be done, and Francis, with his two good arms, was better equipped to do it. But by the fourth day he felt irritated because it seemed to him that the mountain man was just taking a vacation while he put up the house. Over morning coffee, he said, "What are you doing out there all day? Not that I really care, understand. But a guy has to learn—"

Mr. Grimes snorted and then sipped his coffee. "Seems to me you *ought* to care. I mean, I'm out there just resting on my stomach along the creek while you slave away on our castle. *I'd* care. But if I tell you, will you promise not to laugh?"

"Sure."

"I'm counting the grown beaver in each pond, one at a time."

Francis didn't laugh, because he didn't understand. "Why are you counting them?" he asked.

"So when we start taking 'em, we'll know how many we can take out of each pond without ruining it. Of course, trapping all the beaver in the world won't help us if we don't have a house to dry the pelts in . . ."

Francis didn't ask any more questions. Instead he got the house up, back in the trees along the meadow, and Mr. Grimes finished his count just in time to help with the last poles on the roof. Then they put up a small pole corral for the horses and mules, and when that was finished, they moved in. Now, Mr. Grimes explained, there was nothing to do but wait.

"It's like this, Mr. Tucket," he said. "There are

two times to trap beaver. In late fall and early spring. In the fall, you catch them when their coats are turning prime—getting ready for the cold. In the spring, you catch them before they lose their winter pelts. Now I prefer to catch them in the fall —and I'll let you guess why."

Francis thought for a minute, then shrugged. "I don't know. Is the market better?"

"True, but that's not really why. If you take a mother beaver in the spring, you might take her just after she's had young. You not only trap the mother, but kill the young because you take away their milk. If I take her in the fall, her babies—the kits— haven't even started yet and I only kill one beaver—"

"But what's the difference?" Francis interrupted. "I mean, she's still gone, and she still can't have the kits."

"Right. But beaver mate up in the fall, and they mate for life. If I trap a female in the fall, the male that would have mated with her goes on and finds another. It all works out, Mr. Tucket, it all works out."

Francis thought about it, nodded, then asked, "When do we get started?"

"About two weeks after the first cold snap, when their pelts firm up. I figure down here, in the bottom of this canyon, we ought to see some cold before long."

It was true, Francis knew. Most of the aspens had taken on a golden hue, and the scrub oaks were already losing some leaves. The days were still warm but the nights had a way of turning cold, and moving out in the morning from beneath the warm buffalo robe Mr. Grimes had given him got harder each day. Also, the fact that there was little to do made it hard to get up.

Francis found you either had too much to do, or nothing. When there was nothing, his thoughts turned always to his mother and father, and he wondered how they were doing in Oregon. He missed them, but for some strange reason, he missed Rebecca more. She had always been sort of a nuisance to him, following him when he wanted to be alone, asking him dumb questions—this made him smile when he thought of some of the questions he asked Mr. Grimes—and yet he missed her.

Finally the cold weather came. One morning, Francis crawled out of his buffalo robe and the world was a land of crisp whiteness. Frost covered everything. Mr. Grimes was already up, humming—of all things—while he sharpened his skinning and fleshing knife.

"To work, Mr. Tucket," he announced. "Our holiday's over."

Now they had just two weeks to cut enough bait sticks—short pieces of green aspen—store them along the stream, plan the trap line, make skin-drying hoops of the same green aspen, and sort and "purify" the traps.

And with all this work to be done, company arrived. Francis, for a change, saw them first, but only because Mr. Grimes was out cutting bait sticks. Francis was in front of the hut, lashing some drying hoops together with thongs of fresh rawhide from a deer that had wandered into their camp. Across the meadow came four horses. Two of them were being led, and two of them were being ridden. They were quite far away, too far to identify the riders as anything but men, too far away to allow any wild guessing. But even so, Francis made a wild guess and decided they were Crows.

All of this took just five seconds. On the sixth second, he was in the house, looking out through an opening in its side. His cheek lay against the stock of his rifle, the hammer was back, a percussion cap covered the nipple, the barrel was charged, and his finger was on the trigger.

The two men rode, as though drawn by an invisible cord, straight toward the cabin.

# Chapter Fifteen

When the men and horses were still some two hundred yards away, they stopped. One man dismounted and studied the soft ground of the meadow. He turned and said something to the man who was still mounted, and then swung back into his saddle. From the way he dismounted and mounted and the way they rode, Francis now realized that they weren't Indians. More than likely, especially since they had pack horses, they were trappers.

He eased up from the rifle, but only a little.

They could still be up to no good, and it didn't hurt to be ready. He watched for some sign of their intentions—and got it when they were just a hundred yards from the house.

One of them slipped his rifle from its buckskin case and laid the gun across his lap. The other then did the same, and Francis could feel the hair on his neck rise. Nobody dropping in for a friendly visit would make a point of coming armed and ready.

His cheek went back to the stock of his rifle. He wanted to run out back and get the mountain man, but he didn't know how far he'd have to go. And if he left the pack mules and all their equipment alone, even for a minute, everything might be gone by the time they got back.

No, he couldn't leave. There was nothing else to do—he would simply have to stay and try to bluff them out.

Approximately thirty yards from the house, the two men stopped. They were about twenty feet apart, sitting their horses loosely, but both of their rifles were aimed in the general direction of the lean-to. Francis could make out their features easily. One of them was rather short and bearded. The other was lean, also bearded, fairly tall, and it was he who leaned forward in the saddle and called:

"Yo, the house! Anybody home?"

Francis said nothing. He watched.

"Up there! The house!" the man called again. "Anybody home?"

They were getting uneasy. Francis could tell by the way the lean one angled his rifle upward as he talked. Even at that range, the muzzle looked like a cave. Might as well say something, he thought, before they just fire away.

"Who are you, and what do you want?" he called, trying to make his voice sound gruff and older.

"Name's Bridger," answered the lean one. "Jim—to people who come into the light. This here's my partner, Jake Barnes. And all we want is a little hospitality."

Sure, thought Francis—you're Jim Bridger and I'm Kit Carson. If you really are Jim Bridger, you sure wouldn't just amble blind into a trap like this. How do you know I'm not an Indian? You could have been following anybody's tracks.

"You lost your tongue in there?" the lean one yelled again. "I said that the name's Bridger . . ."

"I heard you," Francis answered. The man was lying. He was sure of it. He brought up the front sight of his rifle. It made him feel funny, aiming at a man. But he'd been caught off guard once—by Braid—and it wasn't going to happen twice. "I'm not sure I believe it. Can you prove you're Jim Bridger?"

"*Prove?* What's to prove? I'm just sitting here, ain't I? I said I was Bridger, didn't I? What more do you need?"

There it was. He said he was Bridger, but Francis was positive he was lying, and so they were stalemated. There was nothing to do but wait for Mr. Grimes.

"If you're *really* Jim Bridger," Francis called, "you won't mind just sitting there for a while—"

"What for?"

"Until—until somebody comes who can tell me if that's the truth."

"And what if I decide to ride off? Or come plowing *at* you?"

"I've got a gun on you."

"I figured *that.*"

"I'll use it."

"Maybe. When's this man coming?"

"Soon."

"What's his name?"

"You don't need to know."

"All right. I'll wait for a spell. But if he doesn't come soon, and I mean *soon*, you better figure on using that gun."

The minutes dragged. The sun got hotter, and flies began buzzing around the horses.

He had no idea how long Mr. Grimes would be gone, Francis realized. Somehow, half an hour crawled past. It was the longest half hour of his life. And Bridger—or the man who said he was Bridger—didn't help any. If he had gotten nervous, or started to move around, Francis would have felt better. But he didn't. He just sat his horse—cool, calm, waiting. And the smaller man did the same.

Forty minutes passed, fifty, then an hour was gone. And that was enough.

The lean one moved. He straightened in his saddle and called. "Time's up. I haven't got ten years to waste. Now I'm gonna turn around and ride out of here. My partner's coming with me. I don't think you'll touch anything off—but if you do, you'll get only one of us. And the other one will get you, just as sure as winter's coming."

This was it then; the test. Francis reset his sight. It would be suicide to let the man go. He and his partner might ride off a mile, turn around, and sneak back to kill them at night.

Even as the lean one turned his horse, and the partner followed suit, Francis knew he couldn't do it. It was one thing to shoot somebody who was attacking you, but to just come out and shoot a man because you thought he might be lying—

"Jim Bridger!" the voice was loud, cutting through Francis's thoughts. It came from the side of the clearing he couldn't see, but he knew that voice. It belonged to Jason Grimes. "You figuring on riding out of here without taking a cup of coffee with an old friend?"

The two men stopped their horses. "I figured you was up here somewhere," the lean one said. "And to be downright truthful about it all, I *did* stop for some coffee. I figured old Jason Grimes was as good as the next for a free spot of java. But before you get all relaxed about us stopping for a while, maybe you ought to know there's a two-legged terror in that shack over there with a gun on us. Shouldn't we ask *him* about stopping?"

"What . . . ?" Mr. Grimes turned to the building. "Oh . . . how long you been here?"

"Seems like ten years," Jake Barnes said. "Maybe an hour, really."

"And Mr. Tucket kept you at bay all that time?"

"Who?" Jim Bridger asked.

"Mr. Tucket." Mr. Grimes turned again to the building. "Mr. Tucket, come on out here and meet the men you've been holding."

So it *was* Bridger. Francis felt like an idiot. Still,

he couldn't stay out of sight forever. He stepped out of the doorway and walked toward the horses.

"Why, it's ain't nothing but a cub." Jim Bridger snorted. "Jake, we've been sitting here worried about a *cub.*"

That broke the ice, and the two men dismounted, grinning at Francis.

"Where'd you get him?" Bridger asked.

While Francis made a fire, Mr. Grimes told the two mountain men about him. By the time the explanation was finished, the coffee was ready, and they all sipped it and chewed on venison. After that, the men smoked and Francis sat quietly thinking. There was something bothering him. Finally he could hold it no longer.

"Mr. Bridger," he asked, "how did you find us?"

"Why, we just followed your trail, boy. Easy as following a herd of buffalo. But don't worry. We covered tracks coming in—ours *and* yours."

Francis looked at Mr. Grimes. He was smiling.

"Ho!" he exclaimed. "You're feeding Mr. Tucket a nettle. Bad for his liver. The fact is, Mr. Tucket, there's another meadow like this up a ways that belongs to Mr. Bridger. I found this one last year about the same time he found his. We met coming out, so he knew I'd be here about now. Unless I miss my guess, he's on his way up there now."

Bridger nodded. "Caught, cold turkey. Boy, never lie in front of Jason Grimes. You'll lose every time. Say"—he turned to Mr. Grimes—"how are you and Braid getting on lately?"

That triggered off another round of talk. They covered the Indian tribes—Pawnee, Sioux, and finally, while Francis made another pot of coffee, the Crow.

"You might be extra careful when you go out," Bridger told Mr. Grimes. "We saw some fresh Crow sign down at the mouth of the valley. Whole tribe—man, woman, child, and dog. Looking for a wintering ground, I reckon, so they probably won't bother you. But I don't think they'd pass up a chance at those rifles if they ran across you."

Mr. Grimes nodded. "The Crows and the weather—you can't tell about either one. But I think I'd take a blizzard to a Crow any day . . ."

Francis listened to them intently. His stomach was full of warm coffee and jerky, evening was coming down, the fire felt good, and he was in the company of a living legend—Jim Bridger. What more could he ask? Why think about such unpleasant things as snowstorms or Indians at a time like this? Better just to listen, because someday he would want to tell his family everything about this meeting with the fabulous Jim Bridger.

# Chapter Sixteen

**Bridger and his partner** pulled out early the following morning. Before they were even out of sight, Mr. Grimes said, "Back to work. We lost a good part of a day, Mr. Tucket, and we couldn't afford it."

He walked out of camp to get more bait sticks, and Francis went back to work on the drying hoops.

Actually, they were fairly simple to make. He took a slim piece of springy willow or aspen, eight feet long, and bent it into a circle about three feet across. Then he lashed the ends together with wet, green rawhide that seemed to shrink when it dried and made the two ends of the willow become one piece. After a beaver was skinned, the hide was put in this hoop and with lacing around the sides pulled toward the edges so that when it was dry it would be a hard plate of hide with fur on one side.

Mr. Grimes wanted two hundred of these hoops. Francis ran out of rawhide that evening on the fiftieth hoop. He told Mr. Grimes about it.

"Well, Mr. Tucket, the woods are full of deer and you've got a rifle. Seems like a fairly simple problem to me . . ."

So the next morning Francis walked quietly through the pine glades, glad of a chance to get away from the lean-to. Not three hundred yards from the house, he stopped on the edge of a small clearing, just to enjoy the morning, and found himself facing a nice three-point buck.

There was the deer, and there was Francis, with perhaps fifty feet between them. He raised his rifle, aimed at the buck's shoulder, and squeezed the trigger. The little Lancaster cracked sharply—higher and faster sounding than Mr. Grimes's big bull gun—and the deer took two steps forward, sagging as he walked, and fell. Francis reloaded, as cool as though he were shooting buffalo chips, and aimed at the deer's head. He fired again and it was over.

He started forward, then, remembering what he'd been taught, stopped and reloaded again.

And he suddenly started shaking all over, as though he had a chill. He couldn't even walk right and had to sit down. It was silly, but he was nervous about the deer—nervous and rattled. He didn't know what it was—he just had to sit down for a minute.

When he got up, it was as though it had never happened. He grabbed the deer by its rack and dragged it back to camp. There he skinned it and cut the wet hide into strips half an inch wide. By late afternoon, he was again making hoops, the incident all but forgotten.

Mr. Grimes came in at about four o'clock, his arm full of sticks, and Francis told him about the deer.

"Buck fever, Mr. Tucket—or, as some call it, gun jaw. Most people get it the first time they think about shooting anything bigger than a rabbit. Usually it only hits a man once or twice—and then only if he's had time to think about it. You're lucky."

"Why?"

" 'Cause some get it *before* they shoot. They can't even pull the trigger. I watched one man—and this is pure gospel—stand up against a bear that didn't like him at all, and all he did was aim his rifle and say, 'Bang.' "

"You mean he didn't shoot?"

"Nope. Didn't even draw his hammer. If I hadn't been there to kill the bear, that man would have been nothing in a second or two. Unless the bear could understand English. Hah!"

But Francis couldn't laugh at the joke. He remembered shaking all over, and he hoped that when the time came—*if* it came—for him to face something dangerous, he wouldn't do something dumb like saying "Bang."

By the end of the week the hoops were finished, and Mr. Grimes had gathered all the bait sticks. Next came the traps. There were fifty of them—big, double-springed traps with bait-pan trips. They all had to be smoked over a low fire of green aspen to take away the smell of man. So Francis was put in charge of the smoking fire, working ten traps at a time. They were hung over the fire with a long pole and taken off with a forked stick. Once smoked, they could not be touched by human hands.

After the traps were smoked, they were hung three to a stick, so that Mr. Grimes could carry them to the individual ponds without touching them.

About halfway through the second week of

working, as if on demand, cold settled in and held for a few hours. The next morning, Mr. Grimes reported that they'd start trapping that day.

"There'll be ice on the ponds," he said. "That makes it easier. The beaver sort of give themselves away by cutting holes in the ice. All you have to do is drop a trap in the hole and wait. They come right into it. Even if the ice melts off—and it probably will before the day is out—they still use the same place. Sort of like you'd use a hallway in a house."

While he talked, he was working, lashing bait sticks and trap sticks to a long aspen pole. This pole, with twenty-one traps, he handed to Francis. Then he made another one, just like the first.

They rode out toward the first pond well before noon. Francis was almost excited. All this labor, and now he would actually see what they'd been working toward. And, he thought, just maybe, the back-breaking labor would slack off a bit.

They dismounted at the first pond, and sure enough, despite the fact that it was turning out to be a fairly warm day, the pond was covered by a thin layer of ice. At one point, near the dam of sticks and mud along the bank, there was a broken, jagged hole about two feet across. In this hole the mountain man placed one trap, set, on a pole that angled down into the water and stuck in the mud on the bottom. The trap was well under water and above the trap he tied several bait sticks to the pole with rawhide.

"But won't the beaver see the trap?" Francis asked.

"He'll see it, all right," came the answer, gruff and short. "But he won't take *notice*, Mr. Tucket. At least not till he steps in the trap. Old Daddy Beaver goes more by his nose than his eyes, and if you smoked these traps right, he'll think that piece of iron is another hunk of wood."

So it went, pond by pond. It was nearly dark when they finished the fourteenth pond. Francis had done nothing but hand out traps and bait sticks, and yet he was exhausted—and more than ready to head back for the house and a warm fire.

Mr. Grimes headed back to the first pond.

"They're good enough to let us trap 'em, Mr. Tucket," he said. "The least we can do is keep up."

"You mean there'll be one trapped already?" Francis asked.

"More than one, or I miss my guess."

And of course, he was right. The first pond yielded one, same with the second, nothing in the third, one in the fourth and so on. By midnight or so, with Francis all but falling off his mare, they had eleven prime beaver.

Mr. Grimes had reset all the traps, and although he didn't say anything, Francis was living in a quiet horror that they might start all over again, and *again*, and just keep going until they had two hundred beaver.

But the trapper headed his sorrel back to camp. Once there, after the fire was going and coffee started, he went to work skinning the beaver. And Francis, who could think of nothing but crawling into his big buffalo robe and forgetting everything, was told to stay up and stretch the hides on the hoops.

By eight in the morning—with no sleep—they had finished the twenty-six beaver they had trapped.

"We sleep till noon, Mr. Tucket," the mountain man announced. "Then we start over. And we've got more work now, because after this haul, we'll have to move the traps."

Francis didn't hear the last words about more work. He was asleep.

At noon he didn't want to get up. He wouldn't have wanted to rise with fifteen hours of sleep, but with just four, he almost *couldn't* get up. Mr. Grimes dumped cold water on his face and he did get up, sputtering, and after a little fresh venison, they started again.

Francis lost all track of time. It didn't seem possible to him that human beings could live and work on such an insane schedule. Work at midnight, go to bed at dawn. Get up in four hours and work some more. Ride out with traps and bait sticks, come back with dead, wet beaver. Skin and stretch. Sleep. Eat while you worked, while you rode. Set traps. Close your eyes for what seemed like a second, then open them and work again.

Finally, Mr. Grimes stopped. Five days could have passed, or maybe five years—Francis didn't know. All he knew was that two hundred beaver pelts were hanging and drying inside the house. It was impossible not to know that, for their stench was overpowering.

"We sleep now, Mr. Tucket, as long as we want," the trapper said, grinning. Francis was standing in front of him, almost falling down. "The pelts have to dry for a week at least. I'll wake you at the end of the week."

Oh, no, you won't, Francis thought, grabbing his buffalo robe and heading upwind of the building. Not in a week. I won't even be *started* catching up in a week. Wake me in January sometime, or maybe next spring. Better yet, don't *ever* wake me.

# Chapter Seventeen

THE WEEK OF IDLE RESTING that Mr. Grimes had promised Francis never took place, but it wasn't the mountain man's fault.

What happened to ruin the week was the sudden arrival of more "company." But this time, the company didn't consist of friends of Jason Grimes. They arrived on the third day after all the pelts had been hung to dry.

Contrary to what he had thought, Francis didn't sleep even for a day. After ten hours of solid snoring, he was up gathering wood. And by the second day, he was practically bored stiff.

"Don't fret on so much, Mr. Tucket," the trapper said when Francis began grumbling. "A man would think you wanted to go back to work. Rest up a mite. There'll be plenty to do."

Francis snorted. "I wouldn't even mind some more trapping. It's better than just sitting around, getting soft."

"Ah, Mr. Tucket, relax. Trap more beaver and you'd just have to sit around for another week. These things take time."

So Francis had dreamed up things to do. He made bullets—when he already had enough to stand off a small army. He took to riding around the meadow along the stream, not going anywhere in particular, just riding.

And he was riding on the morning of the third day, out along the stream, just angling across it, not paying much attention to what he was doing, when something whistled past his cheek, brushing him lightly—almost like a fly. He reached his hand up absently, and at that instant, the horse stepped on a rock and stumbled.

The sudden movement saved Francis's life. The second arrow—which would have hit him squarely in the middle of the chest—whirred past and buried itself in the muck of a beaver dam ten yards upstream.

"Heeah!" Francis screamed, and at the same second fired his rifle in the air. He had two purposes in mind for shooting the rifle. First, it would warn Mr. Grimes. Second, it would get the mare running.

And run she did. Like a little bomb going off beneath Francis, she was out of the stream and at a full gallop in the space of one breath, while he clung to her back like a flea.

She ran straight ahead, and luckily she happened to be pointed toward the camp. But unluckily, she was also pointed toward the Indians, who were hidden in the brush along the stream *between* Francis and the camp, and she took him right through the middle of them.

Francis hadn't seen the Indians, and suddenly he was ten feet away from all five of them. They were five Crows painted for war, ready, and wanting one thing—to make Francis look like a porcupine.

Arrows whistled by him, and Francis felt as though the world had suddenly gone crazy. Painted faces popped up in front of him, screeched, loosed a feathered missile, and disappeared. Somebody fired a gun right by his face, and it deafened him. He felt a hand grab at his leg, and he managed to shake it off. Another hand came up; he clubbed it down with his empty rifle and—he was free!

He was out of the ring of faces and arrows, flying along with the mare.

He looked back. He had seen no horses, but he knew that the Indians wouldn't be too far from their mounts. It was nearly two miles to camp—two long miles. His horse was well fed and with any kind of a lead, he could probably beat them.

He studied the ground ahead. It was smooth, grassy—ideal for running. He looked back again, and saw that two Indians were mounted and starting after him. As he watched, three others burst out of a stand of willows near where they'd jumped Francis.

It would be a chase. Francis studied his lead—a hundred yards, no more. And he was holding an empty rifle. I *have* to beat them, he thought. He had a good mount in his Indian pony, but the Crows were also riding Indian ponies. It stood to reason that out of five ponies, at least one would be as fast or faster than his. He couldn't expect miracles *all* the time.

Sure enough, one of the ponies was as fast as his little mare. But two others were faster, and they gained rapidly. Before he'd covered half a mile, they had cut his hundred-yard lead in half.

Francis leaned forward. "Run! If I ever needed speed, I need it now."

She was full-out already. She put her ears back and stretched an inch or two, but it didn't help much.

Another half mile, he thought, watching the two Indians gaining on him, and they'll be alongside of me. Then what?

Forty yards now, and one of the Indians raised his bow and loosed an arrow.

Francis, looking back, saw the arrow rise in a slow arc and fall toward him. He felt his stomach tighten as his eyes followed its course.

It fell short—by ten yards or so. The Indian fitted another arrow to the bow and aimed.

He's getting the range, Francis thought. Only thirty yards separated them now.

Francis nudged his pony just as the Indian shot his second arrow. The mare veered to the left, still at a dead run, and the arrow missed.

Twenty yards now. They can't miss again, he thought. Not at this short range.

Only fifteen yards, and now two Indians raised their bows.

"No!" Francis cried. "You can't . . ."

Then he heard it. Far off—a noise like the sound of muted thunder. A second later, he heard something whisper over his head, and the lead Indian fell from his horse.

The second Indian veered aside—releasing his arrow at the same time, but missing Francis.

The Hawkens—the great Hawkens of Jason Grimes had done it again.

Francis eased up a bit and looked for the mountain man. It was still almost a quarter of a mile to camp—an impossible range, an impossible shot.

Now Francis saw him—a speck that was leaning against a tree by the camp. At this range it was impossible to tell what the mountain man was doing, but in a moment Francis knew. A cloud of smoke jumped out in front of him, and the sound of a shot followed.

Francis whirled to watch the Indians. One of the ponies somersaulted, throwing his rider heavily.

That still left three. And those three stopped, dismounted, and hid behind the available cover.

Francis dropped down to a canter. It was safe now, and the mare was blowing pretty hard. Even so, it wasn't but a few moments before he was dismounting at the camp.

Mr. Grimes was smiling. "I do declare, Mr. Tucket. You sure pick some mighty funny people to be horse racing with. If you were all *that* hard up for something to do, I might have raced you myself. You didn't have to go and find a bunch of Crows."

"Well, you know how it is," Francis answered, returning the smile, though he was shaking inside and felt a little sick to his stomach. "I was getting pretty bored, just sitting around all the time. A fellow needs *some* action now and then."

"Used to be that way myself, before I lost my arm. Still, I wish you'd come and ask me before you do those things." He pointed at the Indians in the field. One of them had mounted and was heading away at a run. The mountain man shrugged. "No sense doing any more fancy shooting. One of them would be bound to get away."

"Where is he going?" Francis asked.

"For help, Mr. Tucket. And I expect not too far, the way he's riding. Well, you *said* you wanted something to do—some action. Unless I miss my guess, before long you're going to get all the action you ever wanted. Unless . . ."

"Unless what?"

"Unless we run, Mr. Tucket. And stay ahead."

"But we can't run," Francis said. "There are two of them left, watching us. They'd know right where we went."

"I swear, Mr. Tucket, you're getting smarter every day. So it appears that what we've got to do is get rid of those two Indians in the field."

"We?"

"Sure. Were you figuring on doing it all by yourself?"

Francis looked out across the meadow. Two ponies stood grazing almost a mile away. But the Indians weren't in sight. They could be anywhere, everywhere.

"How do we do it?"

"Simple, Mr. Tucket. We just walk out there until they shoot at us, then we shoot back."

Francis suddenly remembered that his rifle was empty. He reloaded it quickly.

"All right, Mr. Tucket, let's go. We don't have all day."

The mountain man started walking out across the meadow, his rifle draped casually across his shoulder. He looked for all the world as though he were just going for a morning stroll, or perhaps to hunt rabbits.

Except these rabbits, Francis thought, hurrying to catch up, aren't like normal rabbits. These rabbits shoot back.

# Chapter Eighteen

**Francis would never forget** that morning "walk." He was afraid, and as they walked closer to where he thought the two Indians were, he became more and *more* afraid. His forehead ran with sweat, and it was all he could do to keep from stopping, or turning, or yelling. But he didn't, he couldn't, because the mountain man was really depending on him.

"You take the one on the right when they jump us, Mr. Tucket," Mr. Grimes said, in his usual casual voice, as they walked. "I'll do my best on the left one."

So Francis couldn't afford to let fear dominate his actions. If he froze up, or ran, it could mean the death of Mr. Grimes. If he missed, or shot a second late, Mr. Grimes would be gone.

He tried to calm down so he could watch the grass for movement, or see any signs in the soft dirt. But his fear was too real. And then Mr. Grimes stopped, held up his hand, and said, "Mind now, Mr. Tucket. They're close. I can feel 'em."

Francis couldn't feel anything. All he could think was that somehow, some way, they had walked *past* the Indians and he would get an arrow in his back any second.

"Now!"

That's all he heard—that shout from Mr. Grimes. From then on, everything was automatic. In front of them, not ten feet away, two painted faces and bronze chests rose. Two arrows were pulled back on taut strings. Two Indian throats let out a roaring sound.

Francis fired without aiming. He just pointed his rifle in the general direction of the Indian on his right side and pulled the trigger; then he turned and ran.

He ran until he stumbled and fell, and then he

lay on the ground and was sick. Sick from fear, and sick from having fired his rifle at a man, no matter the man's intent.

Mr. Grimes came up to him a moment later.

"Did—did I?"

"Did you shoot him?"

Francis nodded.

"Yes, Mr. Tucket, and a fair shot it was, too. It kept him occupied long enough for me to finish him."

"You mean I didn't—kill—him?"

"Nope. You only winged him. Creased him along the head. But it was enough to give him something else to think about till I could get in close."

Francis sat up. The grass was still cool, but the sun felt good. Better, far better than it had a few moments before. "We did it, eh, Mr. Grimes?"

"No-ah, Mr. Tucket, that isn't quite true. We did *part* of it. We still have to get out of this place before that brave comes back. And the longer you sit there, the more likely it is some brave's gonna wind up with your hair for a dance tonight . . ."

"Aren't you forgetting something?" Francis asked. "One of those Indians was thrown by his pony and that Indian is still around. He'll follow us."

"Not without a horse, he won't. And we're going to have their horses under beaver pelts. Now quit your jawing."

At a fast trot the mountain man was heading back toward the camp. Francis followed him. Once there, Mr. Grimes started on the beaver pelts, which were still damp, but dry enough to lash into bundles to be tied across the horses. He told Francis to mount up and go after the Indian ponies.

It took only a few minutes. His mare still smelled all right to the Indian ponies, so they didn't shy away when he approached. But he had one bad moment, after he had gathered up the four ponies. While he was walking them back to camp, he rode past the Indian who had been thrown.

He was sitting on the ground, and if eyes could kill, Francis would have been dead. The Indian was trying to draw his bow, but Francis could see that an injured shoulder wouldn't allow this action. In addition, one of his legs was twisted under him. Francis rode past quietly.

Mr. Grimes had been working like a fiend. All the pelts were lashed into bundles of twenty-five, stacked and waiting. The mules had been cut loose and scared off.

"Why don't we use the mules?" Francis asked.

"Too slow," came the quick answer. "And

they'd need grain to move faster. Indian ponies can do it on grass—and we're going to be needing some speed."

That was the last word spoken for over an hour. Working hard, Mr. Grimes and Francis tied the pelts in bundles across the ponies. They were a bit skittish at first—smelling the almost-green hides—but Mr. Grimes kept them tied close to trees until their eyes quit rolling and they stopped blowing.

Then he and Francis mounted their horses and rode out. It had been almost two hours since the brave had gone for help. If the rest of the tribe were within fifteen miles of the camp, the brave and more warriors could be back any second.

Francis and Mr. Grimes rode hard, holding the horses at a steady lope. The Indian ponies kept up easily, and since the temperature had dropped considerably, it was cool enough to allow a decent run without heating the horses too much. South, down the canyon, in the direction they were heading, clouds were building into a gray wall that indicated snow or rain.

Twenty minutes later, back at the cabin, ten Crow braves dismounted and briefly studied the campsite and surrounding area.

They found many things. By feeling the manure

left by the horses and finding it still warm, they knew that Mr. Grimes and Francis had only a short lead. By noting all the beaver traps left behind, they suspected that the two were running in fear.

The leader of the party, an old man—not too old to ride but old enough to have wisdom—smiled at two of the younger men, who were ready to ride their ponies into the ground to catch Mr. Grimes and Francis.

"Let us stay here for a time and help Laughing Pony fix his shoulder and leg, then we will go. We will still have them before daybreak tomorrow."

The young men shook their heads and grumbled but did as he told them to do.

# Chapter Nineteen

**It was almost** as if the storm had been waiting for them. Mr. Grimes led, pulling two pack horses and Francis followed pulling two more out into the prairie away from the mouth of the canyon and the snow took on more force, coming so fast that it quickly covered the horses and packs. Francis looked back and could see no trace of any tracks—the snow blew in as fast as they were made—and he smiled.

It was silly to keep going now, when surely their tracks would be blotted by the snow.

Mr. Grimes rode on. To be sure, he eased the pace a bit—impossible not to, the way the wind was driving at them—but he didn't stop.

Another hour passed. The snow was heavier, thicker. It was hard for Francis to see the short ten feet to Mr. Grimes. The temperature had dropped ten or fifteen degrees, and it was now near freezing. Francis took turns with his hands in handling the reins, holding one beneath his shirt to warm while the other got numb on the reins.

And *still* they ran. The world became a mixture of thudding hoofs, howling wind, and slashing snow. Twice, Francis had to force himself to resist cutting loose the two pack horses following him. He had tied their lead lines around his waist, and they kept pulling at him, holding him back, snagging at him.

There was no telling how long Mr. Grimes would have pushed them. He might have tried to ride the storm out. But finally, the little mare decided for them.

One second she was running almost smooth, and the next she was tumbling down under Francis, throwing him clear as she collapsed. He screamed, and luckily Mr. Grimes heard him.

By the time the mountain man had wheeled and stopped, Francis was getting up from the snow. The mare was on her feet, too, but sagging and with her head nearly on the ground. She had run just short of breaking her heart.

Francis loosened the pack horses' lead lines from his waist and looked up, through the snow and wind, at the mountain man, who was still mounted. He could see the verdict on the man's frost-covered face.

"No!" Francis screamed. "I'm not leaving her!"

"Mr. Tucket . . ."

"I'm not leaving her!" Francis repeated. He knew how foolish it sounded. They were out in the open in a violent storm, but he was going to stay with his horse. He didn't care. She hadn't flinched when those five Crows jumped him. *He* wasn't going to leave her to die in a blizzard just for a few beaver pelts.

"Mr. Tucket . . ."

"No!"

Then a strange thing happened. From what Francis knew of Mr. Grimes, he half expected the trapper to go off and leave him alone. Or hit him on the head and carry him.

Mr. Grimes dismounted, hunched his back into the wind, and smiled.

"I do declare, Mr. Tucket, you sure do pick the funniest times to be stubborn. I just hope that when

I get down, you'll be this hot about staying around with me . . ."

Francis realized he was crying. He wasn't sure why. He was tired, but he had won—at least sort of won. There was a lot of snow, and a lot of wind, and he was cold—but it wasn't that kind of crying. He just felt choked. He turned away.

"And now, Mr. Tucket, if we're ever going to see what the world is like *after* this humdinger, we'd better get to work. Help me get these horses around."

Mr. Grimes put all the horses, nose-to-tail, in a tight circle. Then he cut the beaver pelts loose from the Indian ponies and put the packs in the middle of the circle of horses.

"Now hobble 'em," he said, tying a piece of lead rope around one of the ponies' front ankles. "Hobble 'em tight."

Francis worked fast. In no time, all the horses, including his own, were hobbled tight—front and rear.

Then Mr. Grimes went around the circle on the outside and began pushing the horses over, toward the center. When he was done, all of them were lying on their sides, with their backs leaving only a small circle of empty space around the beaver pelts. Mr. Grimes went around and pulled all the horses' front and back legs together and hog-tied them. Now they couldn't get up, no matter how hard they tried.

"And now, Mr. Tucket, why don't you and me catch up on a little sleep?"

Stepping over the horses to the center, he motioned Francis to do the same. They cleared off the snow in a little empty space, and began covering it with beaver pelts cut loose from the packs.

They used almost half of the two hundred near-dry pelts, fur-side up, and when they'd finished, the circle of space was completely covered with warm fur. They lay down and covered themselves with the remaining pelts.

It was a cozy, warm place. The horses' backs gave off heat and stifled the sound of the wind. Francis was almost asleep as he put the last pelt in place. In a few seconds, just as he was drifting off, he heard the hoarse snore of the mountain man next to him.

# Chapter Twenty

**Francis didn't know** for sure how long they slept in their horseflesh shelter. Perhaps ten hours. Then they lay awake for a time, not talking, just listening to the wind whistling, and fell asleep again. The second time he awakened, Francis could hear nothing but his own breathing and the gentle sighing of the horses. There was no wind, no lashing snow. He stretched as much as the cramped space would allow, and felt Mr. Grimes move near him.

"Well, Mr. Tucket," the mountain man said, "should we see what it's like outside?"

Outside it was so white, so bright and dazzling that Francis had to close his eyes for a minute to keep from getting a headache. They had a bit of trouble getting out of their home—the snow had drifted nearly four feet deep over them—but once out, Francis was amazed to feel the warmth of the sun.

Mr. Grimes didn't allow him much time to marvel at things, or even over the fact that they were still alive.

"Come on, Mr. Tucket, we've got to put these horses back on their feet and get to Spot Johnnie's. We're not in clover yet . . ."

Getting the horses up turned out to be quite a job. They were stiff—Mr. Grimes said the only reason they hadn't frozen to death was that the snow had made a sort of blanket around them—and before they could stand, the circulation had to be rubbed back into their legs.

Once up, the mounts had to be walked back and forth through the snow to loosen them up some more. It was nearly an hour before Francis and Mr. Grimes loaded the beaver pelts and started off.

They had ridden hard—even in the storm—and Francis was surprised to find that they were much farther along than he had thought—well out of the main river valley they had tried to follow out of the canyon country and back up on the plains. It was a good thing, too. The deep snow in the bottom of the valley made it almost impossible to ride, and the horses floundered again and again.

Once they had fought their way to the top of the bluff wall—where the wind had swept the snow along—the going was much easier. There were drifts now and then, but they rode around the really big pileups.

It was cold—almost zero—but without the wind, and with the sun on his back, Francis felt fine. His mare was in good shape again, and the world was a bright new land—crisp, clean, alive. Steam boiled out of the ponies' nostrils.

They rode slowly most of the morning, letting the horses stop to graze now and then, and early in the afternoon, Mr. Grimes called a halt near a stand of brush.

"Why are we stopping so soon?" Francis asked. "We could make another ten miles before dark."

"And freeze to death, Mr. Tucket? They wouldn't find us until spring—if then. We're stopping to build a lean-to out of those willows and get a fire going. We're stopping to eat—if you can find some meat around here somewhere—*and* we're stopping to let this sun work on those beaver pelts for a spell. That take care of your question?"

Francis nodded, sliding from the mare. They cut the pelts loose and spread them, fur-side up to dry the moisture out of them. Then they tethered the horses, and Mr. Grimes took his knife and cut small willow poles for a shelter. Francis shouldered his rifle and ambled off in search of game.

They had been seeing rabbits all morning—jackrabbits in the open places, and cottontails in the brushy beds of streams. In only a few minutes he had got two of the bigger jackrabbits and was carrying them back to camp. There he found a cozy, three-sided bungalow waiting, with a roaring fire in front of it.

Mr. Grimes was standing near the fire, warming himself, and Francis smiled. It all looked like a picture his father had hung up in their barn back in Missouri. The picture showed an old lumberjack, in the middle of the woods, standing over a small fire warming his hands and grinning, while in the background, a bear was sneaking out of the lumberjack's tent with a side of bacon.

"You're sure grinning a lot, Mr. Tucket," the mountain man said with a snort. "Especially for someone who couldn't do any better than a couple of scruffy rabbits. I was sort of figuring on you bringing back an antelope or two . . ."

Francis told him about the picture in the barn, and Mr. Grimes snorted again.

"Must have been an eastern bear. Out here we've got grizzlies, at least up in the peaks. If a grizzly decided to take a side of bacon, he'd like as not take it over your body." While he talked, he was dressing out the rabbits and spitting them over the fire. Before long, they were sizzling and hissing.

They ate quietly—the rabbit meat so tough Francis thought his moccasins might be easier to chew—and after polishing off both rabbits, Mr. Grimes gathered up some of the pelts for the lean-to while Francis led the horses to a clear spot nearby so they could graze.

The afternoon turned to dark early, and with the darkness they heaped wood on the fire and went to sleep, wrapped in beaver pelts.

The next morning they were up before the sun. By first light—still stiff and a bit cold—they were riding. They rode at a good clip most of the day. By late afternoon, Francis could see smoke on the horizon, and he pointed it out to Mr. Grimes.

"I see it, Mr. Tucket. Spot Johnnie's, unless I miss my guess or took a wrong turn somewhere. Only . . ."

"Only what?"

"Only there seems to be a bit more smoke than

there should. Let's see if we can get a run out of these ponies."

He kicked Footloose in the ribs and upped his stride. Francis kneed his mare into a following gallop and the pack horses kept up.

There had been something different in the mountain man's voice—a hardness that wasn't usually there, not even when the Crows had jumped them. Francis wasn't sure, but he thought it was the first time he'd ever heard Mr. Grimes sound even a little alarmed.

And the smoke got thicker as they neared.

# Chapter Twenty-one

**ON THE RIDGE** overlooking Spot Johnnie's Mr. Grimes pulled to a stop. Francis reined in beside him a second later. What met their eyes was total carnage.

Down below, *all* the buildings were on fire—including the storage sheds—and they were burning so fiercely that the snow around them was melted for more than a hundred feet.

Around the house area could be seen small humps, like gray rocks, scattered here and there. There were perhaps twenty of these humps, and with sudden shock, Francis realized that they were bodies. They rode down toward the house.

"Pawnees," Mr. Grimes said, examining several bodies. "Braid and his boys."

Above the burning trading post, toward the east about two miles, they now saw a wagon train of twenty or more wagons. These were not arranged in a circle, but scattered this way and that, and two of the wagons were burning. They looked like small torches in the snow.

Mr. Grimes heeled Footloose and started at a walk toward the house. His rifle was balanced across his lap, and his back was slouched in a way Francis had never seen.

Francis followed. The pack horses automatically followed and slowly the procession approached the trading post.

There were bodies of Pawnee Indians everywhere. They lay as they had fallen, some running, some stretched out as though sleeping.

"I count twenty-three," Mr. Grimes said. His voice was hollow. "Old Spot put up one whale of a fight."

They dismounted and searched the ground around the post, but could not find the bodies of Spot or his family.

"Maybe they got away," Francis offered, "and made it over to the wagon train."

"No-ah, Mr. Tucket. That's a nice thought, but there are too many dead braves around here. They wouldn't have let Spot get away."

"But they aren't out here . . ." Francis's voice trailed off as his eyes went to the still-burning house. The fire was roaring now, as the pitch in the log walls started to burn.

"In—in there?" Francis asked, pointing to the flames. "Spot . . . ?"

Mr. Grimes gave a short nod. He stood for a moment, watching the fire, breathing deeply. Then he broke off and studied the dead Indians on the ground.

"What are you looking for?" Francis asked.

The mountain man didn't answer. Presently he finished his examination, looked off across the hills, and mounted.

"C'mon, Mr. Tucket, let's go talk to the farmers."

When they were a hundred yards from the wagon train, three men came out to meet them. Two of them held rifles at the ready; the other one —in the middle—a stocky man with red hair and a red face, did the talking.

Mr. Grimes dismounted again. "They hit you long ago?" he asked.

"Maybe an hour, maybe more. Fifteen or so came down on our wagons and another forty jumped the trading post."

"You lose many men?"

"Two. Thing is, they kept us hopping while they nailed the post. We couldn't get out to help . . ."

Mr. Grimes nodded. "They were after powder. Did—did anyone get out of the house?"

The stocky man shook his head. "At least, if they did, we didn't see 'em. Friends of yours?"

Mr. Grimes was quiet, staring at the snow-covered hills.

"I know how you feel," the man went on. "One of the two we lost was my brother . . ."

There was silence for a while. Francis realized that the stocky man was crying, but that his lips were moving back and forth in anger.

Mr. Grimes broke the silence. "Well, it appears that the time has come to do something about Braid." He turned to look at Francis. "Remember me telling you, Mr. Tucket, that if I ever did kill Braid, it wouldn't be because he had something I wanted. This is different, Mr. Tucket, very different."

He walked over to Footloose, removed the saddle, threw it on the ground, and mounted bareback. "What's your name?" he asked the stocky man.

"Groves. Ben Groves."

"Well, Mr. Groves, I'd take it kindly if you'd keep you eyes on Mr. Tucket, the boy here, for me."

"Now wait a minute—" Francis began.

"There's a fair chance I won't be coming back from this ride," Mr. Grimes went on, ignoring Francis. "Fact is, he's kinda headstrong, and if somebody doesn't watch him, he's likely to do just about anything. Understand me, Mr. Groves?"

The redheaded man nodded. He motioned to the other two men, and before Francis could move, they had grabbed him, pulled him from his horse, and were holding him fast.

"Hey!" he yelled. "Wait a minute! Mr. Grimes, you can't just go out there and jump a whole tribe of Pawnee." He tried to wiggle free but failed. "They'll—they'll kill you. That's dumb. You can't do that, Mr. Grimes. You can't be dumb. You wouldn't let *me* be dumb . . ."

"Now, now, Mr. Tucket. You're rattling on, and that won't do at all. Mr. Groves, if I don't come back by morning, my saddle, all those beaver pelts, and the ponies belong to the boy. I'd be happy if you'd make sure he gets them—not, of course, that anybody'd be foolish enough to try to take them away from him."

"No!" Francis yelled.

"Also," the mountain man continued, "would your train be going to Oregon?"

Mr. Groves nodded. "The Willamette Valley."

"The boy's got folks out there. You might take him with you—maybe make him work his way."

"No! No!"

"I'll do everything you ask," the farmer answered. "I'll hand deliver him, with his pelts, to his folks if you want. But I'd rather be riding out with you . . ."

"No-ah, Mr. Groves. It just takes one. Two, and they'd kill us both. One, and I might get close enough—by insulting Braid."

"No!" Francis screamed again. "Even if you win, you lose. For what? There's no reason to die. It's done, Mr. Grimes—and done is done."

"And now, Mr. Tucket." The mountain man turned at last to Francis. "Before I go—and I don't want you getting some kind of swelled head out of this—I'd like to say it's been sort of fun having you around. Be seeing you . . ."

He wheeled his horse and started off, northeast, riding loose and fast.

"Mr. Grimes, come back!" Francis yelled after him. "Come back, come back, come back . . ."

But Footloose, without the saddle, gained speed rapidly and before Francis could think the mountain man had vanished in the dying evening light.

# — Chapter Twenty-two —

FRANCIS RODE HARD.

It was a strange mount, but he now knew how to ride well enough to stay on almost any horse. This one was a big black—long legged and fresh. And stolen.

An hour after Mr. Grimes had gone, just after moonrise, Mr. Groves had made the mistake of not watching Francis closely. In a flash, he had run to the corral, thrown a war bridle on the black, and with nothing but his rifle, had left the camp.

The trail cut in the snow and lighted by the half

moon was easy to follow. But the hour lead Mr. Grimes had on him worried Francis. Footloose had been tired, it was true, but without a saddle—and considering also that Footloose was a big horse—it was entirely possible that Mr. Grimes would catch up to the Pawnees before Francis could catch up to him.

Francis drove the horse hard. Every time the black even thought of slowing, he laid his rifle barrel with a vengeance across the gelding's rump. What, exactly, he was going to do when and if he caught up with the mountain man, Francis wasn't sure. Try to stop him, of course, but—if he couldn't talk Mr. Grimes out of tangling with Braid, then at least help him. Two guns were always better than one.

Two hours of riding brought the moon higher and made it practically as light as day when it was actually almost ten o'clock at night.

Ten o'clock, Francis thought, goading the black to even longer strides. How I've changed. There was a time when ten o'clock at night meant getting wrapped in a huge quilt and bundled into bed, and feeling the warmth leave my face as the fire in the wood stove died. Died. There was a time when I didn't even think of things that died. I didn't know anything about all this killing. Nothing died, ever, except a farm animal now and then.

He pushed these thoughts from his mind. They were making him afraid—afraid that he might not catch up.

There would be times, later, when he would wonder about all the little things that kept him from reaching Mr. Grimes in time. If he had beat the black harder, or tried to make his break from the wagon train earlier . . .

As it was, he was only a split second late—the time that it takes a man to pull a trigger. He rode over a rise, and there, in a small, flat meadow, were Braid and Mr. Grimes.

They were riding hard at each other and, in the moonlight, the snow flying up around their horses as they closed looked like the fine spray thrown up in front of a ship. They were both stripped to the waist and carrying rifles. When the horses were fifty feet apart, the two men fired. Francis saw the rifles flash and both men tumble from their horse.

They had fired at the same instant, and the one-armed and one-braided men landed within ten feet of each other.

Francis's mind went blank when the mountain man fell from his horse. He rode up, dismounted, and if he noticed the fifteen mounted warriors on the other side of the battlefield, he gave no sign of it. He didn't care.

"Howdy, Mr. Tucket," the mountain man said, wincing as he pulled himself to a sitting position. His shoulder was turning red. "I sort of figured you'd be along. Glad you could make it in time for the fun . . ." He winced again.

Francis tore his shirt off and wrapped it around the shoulder. Mr. Grimes pushed him away. "No-ah, Mr. Tucket. Not done yet." He propped himself on one knee, then slowly stood, grunting, weaving.

"What do you mean?" Francis asked. "Braid's dead." He pointed to where the Indian lay in the snow. The mounted warriors were now around the body in a half circle. "It's done."

"Not done yet," Mr. Grimes repeated, staggering. He pulled out his skinning knife. "One more thing to do." Weaving drunkenly, he made his way to the body of his enemy. Then he leaned down.

"No!" Francis screamed. "You *can't* . . ." He ran and pulled the mountain man away. This, somehow, was worse than all the rest. To kill Braid was one thing, perhaps even right, in the cold-blooded justice that ruled the prairie. But not this—this animal thing.

"*Can't,* Mr. Tucket?" Mr. Grimes said, laughing

hoarsely. "And why not? He would have done the same to me . . ."

Francis stared in horror, then turned away. Many things were suddenly clear to him, and the biggest was that Mr. Grimes was right. He *could* do what he was doing, simply because he was ruled by the same law that ruled Braid. He was of the prairie, the land, the mountains—and was, in a way, a kind of animal. It was not wrong—not for Jason Grimes.

But for Francis Alphonse Tucket? For someone from a farm in Missouri? For someone with a family waiting in Oregon?

There were different rules for different people. One set for Mr. Grimes, but, Francis thought, as he reached his horse, there was a different set for him. He was *not* and did not want to be a "mountain man."

He mounted the horse. Mr. Grimes would be all right, he knew. The fight had been fair in the Indians' eyes, and besides, they wanted to keep on trading for powder. No, the Indians wouldn't kill Mr. Grimes, and his shoulder would heal. Soon he would be trapping again.

But this time without me, Francis told himself, squaring his shoulders. He wiped his eyes with the back of his hand. A boy named Francis Alphonse Tucket might stay and live wild and follow the beaver ponds. But Francis Alphonse Tucket wasn't a boy anymore. Jason Grimes had made that boy *Mr.* Tucket and Mr. Tucket was going to Oregon, to his family, to his kind of life—to his set of rules.

Francis slapped the horse as hard as he could and headed for the wagon train. And somehow he knew he'd better not look back at Mr. Grimes—not even to wave a good-bye.

**Gary Paulsen** is the distinguished author of many critically acclaimed books for young people, including three Newbery Honor Books, *The Winter Room*, *Hatchet*, and *Dogsong*. His most recent books for Delacorte Press are *The Monument*, *The River*, and *The Haymeadow*, which won The Western Writers of America Golden Spur Award. He and his wife have houses in Wyoming, New Mexico, and Minnesota.

# Teacher's Manual and Key

# SPANISH IS FUN

## BOOK A

*Heywood Wald, PhD*

When ordering this book, please specify either **N 448 T**
or SPANISH IS FUN, BOOK A, TEACHER'S MANUAL

AMSCO SCHOOL PUBLICATIONS, INC.
315 Hudson Street / New York, N.Y. 10013

# Cassettes

The Cassette program comprises four two-sided cassettes providing practice in vocabulary, structure, listening, and speaking. The voices are those of native speakers of several Latin-American countries.

Each of the twenty lessons in the book includes the following materials on the cassettes:

Optional oral exercises in four-phased sequences: cue—pause for student response—correct response by native speaker—pause for student repetition.

The narrative or playlet at normal speed.

Questions or completions based on the narrative or playlet in four-phased sequences.

The conversation, first at normal speed, then by phrases with pauses for student repetition.

The Cassettes (Ordering Code N 456 C) are available separately from the publisher. A cassette script is included.

ISBN 0-87720-532-9



Printed in the United States of America

# Introduction

This *Teacher's Manual and Key for* SPANISH IS FUN, BOOK A, includes the following:

- Suggestions for presenting the key sections of the lessons.
- Supplementary explanatory notes that teachers may wish to use in suitable classroom contexts.
- Optional oral exercises not printed in the student text, designed to practice and test the audiolingual skills.
- A complete Key to all blank slots in the structural sections, all exercises, and all games and puzzles.

### Vocabulary

We recommend that teachers present approximately half of the lesson vocabulary in one class session. With the aid of supplementary materials (such as pictures and objects), teachers can direct students to repeat two or three times in unison the name of the item in Spanish. Students may then be prompted by gestures and intonation to respond individually to simple questions:

**¿Es un lápiz? – Sí, es un lápiz.**
**¿Es un libro? – No, es un lápiz.**
**¿Qué es? – Es un lápiz.**

As the course progresses and students become more proficient, questions may increase in number and difficulty. Teachers may also wish to recognize varying degrees of readiness among students by individualizing the cue-response sequences.

### Structures

Structure is presented inductively in order to encourage students to discover and formulate their own conclusions about grammatical principles. The sequences of questions and directed responses about structure include open "slots" for completion by students. This device is designed to motivate students to observe, compare, reason, and form conclusions. Immediate reinforcement is provided through the completed statements of the structural principles involved. We recommend that the oral exercises in this *Manual* be given immediately after the presentation of structures.

## Actividades

The exercises (which may be done both orally and in writing) are closely integrated with the learning materials in that they follow directly after the materials to which they apply. The exercises are designed to make students work actively in the language—hence, **actividades**—whether they practice vocabulary, structure, conversation, or writing. Systematic recycling of lexical and structural elements helps reinforce all materials and develops increasing proficiency as the course progresses.

## Reading

The narratives or playlets feature new vocabulary and structural elements and reinforce previously learned grammar and expressions. Marginal glosses give the meanings of new words. Although these narratives and playlets are intended chiefly to develop reading skill, they are equally suitable for practice in listening comprehension, speaking, and—through the accompanying **actividades**—writing.

To maintain class interest, each reading passage may be divided into appropriate segments and presented in different ways: the teacher reads; the class repeats phrases in unison after the teacher; individual students are called on to read or repeat; and others.

New vocabulary may be practiced before the reading passage is presented by demonstration through gestures, props, or simple explanation in Spanish by means of synonyms or antonyms. As a last resort, English may be used briefly by the teacher to assure comprehension.

Each reading piece is followed by **actividades** of various types to test comprehension: true-and-false, with students supplying the correct information for a false statement; completions; questions and answers, which may be done orally or in writing. Teachers may wish to expand upon the **actividades** provided in the book by personalizing the materials in addition to those in the text.

## Conversation

The situational dialogs are intended for additional communicative practice. The utterances are kept short in order to encourage mastery if not memorization.

We suggest that teachers introduce the conversation through dramatization and gestures as well as with visual aids. Encourage students to repeat each line of dialog in unison. If a line is too long, it may be broken into logical parts. Roles may be assigned to groups and individual students and then reversed or reassigned, so that every student has an opportunity to participate. Students may be called upon to articulate and dramatize their own dialogs by changing words and phrases from the original. Teachers may wish to check comprehension by means of an oral exercise.

### Diálogo — Información personal

The lesson conversations are accompanied by exercises designed to reinforce comprehension and speaking. The **Diálogo** exercises, which may be done orally or in writing, provide assimilation practice of the conversation. From this springboard, the primary goal—the ability to apply acquired language skills freely—is developed through the **Información personal** materials, in which students are encouraged to express themselves about their own lives and experiences. We have provided sample responses for these exercises in the Key.

# Spanish Pronunciation

The introductory section of this *Manual* consists of a guide to Spanish pronunciation. We recommend that vowel, consonant, and vowel-combination sounds be practiced as preliminary exercises and as they occur in the lessons. To overcome self-consciousness, students may be asked to practice pronunciation several times in unison. The class may then be divided into halves, then thirds, and then rows for the purpose of repetition, ending with recital by individual students. Teachers may wish to distribute copies of the pronunciation guide to their students.

| SPANISH LETTERS | ENGLISH SOUNDS | EXAMPLES |
|---|---|---|
| **a** | *a* (*father*) | c**a**s**a** (KAH-sah) |
| **e** | *ay* (*day*) | m**e**sa (MAY-sah)* |
| **i** | *ee* (*meet*) | l**i**bro (LEE-broh) |
| **o** | *o* (*open*) | f**o**t**o** (FOH-toh) |

* Without the glide to the [i] sound.

| SPANISH LETTERS | ENGLISH SOUNDS | EXAMPLES |
|---|---|---|
| **u** | *oo* (*tooth*) | m**u**cho (MOO-choh) |
| **b, v** | *b* (*boy*) | **b**anco (BAN-koh), **v**aso (BAH-soh) |
| **c** (before **a, o, u**) | *c* (*cat*) | **c**ampo (KAM-poh), **c**osa (KOH-sah) |
| **c** (before **e, i**) | *c* (*cent*) | **c**entral (sen-TRAHL), **c**inco (SEEN-koh) |
| **cc** | ks sound (*accept*) | a**cc**ión (ahk-see-OHN) |
| **g** (before **a, o, u**) | *g* (*go*) | **g**afas (GAH-fahs), **g**oma (GOH-mah) |
| **g** (before **e, i**) | approximately like *h* (*hot*) | **g**eneral (he-neh-RAHL) |
| **h** | always silent | **h**asta (AHS-tah) |
| **j** | approximately like *h* (*hot*) | **j**ardín (hahr-DEEN) |
| **l** | *l* (*lamp*) | **l**ámpara (LAHM-pah-rah) |
| **ll** | approximately like *y* (*yes*) | caba**ll**o (kah-BAH-yoh) |
| **ñ** | *ny* (*canyon*) | a**ñ**o (AH-nyoh) |
| **qu** | *k* (*keep*) | **qu**e (kay) |
| **r** | trilled once | ca**r**o (KAH-roh) |
| **rr** (or **r** at beginning of a word) | trilled strongly | **r**ico (RREE-koh), pe**rr**o (PEH-rroh) |
| **s** | *s* (*see*) | ro**s**a (ROH-sah) |
| **x** (before a consonant) | *s* (*see*) | e**x**tra (ES-trah) |
| **x** (before a vowel) | *ks* (*socks*) | e**x**amen (ek-SAH-men) |
| **y** | *y* (*yes*) | **y**o (yoh) |
| **y** (by itself, meaning "and") | *ee* (*meet*) | **y** (ee) |
| **z** | *s* (*see*) | **z**apato (sah-PAH-toh) |

SOME VOWEL COMBINATIONS

| | | |
|---|---|---|
| **ai, ay** | *i* (*kite*) | **ai**re (I-re), h**ay** (I) |
| **au** | *ow* (*how*) | **au**to (OW-toh) |
| **ei, ey** | *ey* (*they*) | r**ei**na (REY-nah), r**ey** |
| **oi, oy** | *oy* (*boy*) | **oi**ga (OY-gah), v**oy** |

# Primera Parte

## Lección 1

**Notes:** The first lesson presents cognates. This workable Spanish vocabulary is designed to give students a feeling of confidence right from the start. We suggest that each column of words be practiced separately for pronunciation and meaning. Students should learn each noun with its definite article. After correct pronunciation has been mastered, teachers may wish to practice words by means of gestures, pictures, or other visual cues. The Optional Oral Exercises in this *Manual* and the **actividades** in the student's book reinforce comprehension and acquisition and allow for personalization of the material. By the end of this first lesson, students should already have a sense of accomplishment and success.

### Optional Oral Exercises

**A.** Repeat each noun with the definite article:

1. cine
2. fiesta
3. niño
4. flor
5. hotel
6. libro
7. bicicleta
8. animal
9. familia
10. clase

*Key*

1. *el cine*
2. *la fiesta*
3. *el niño*
4. *la flor*
5. *el hotel*
6. *el libro*
7. *la bicicleta*
8. *el animal*
9. *la familia*
10. *la clase*

**B.** Form a complete sentence, using the adjectives given:

EXAMPLE: moderno **El hospital es moderno.**

1. inteligente
2. interesante
3. horrible
4. natural
5. tropical
6. popular
7. importante
8. grande

*KEY* (Sample responses)

1. *El estudiante es inteligente.*
2. *El libro es interesante.*
3. *El dragón es horrible.*
4. *La fruta es natural.*
5. *El insecto es tropical.*
6. *La actriz es popular.*
7. *La familia es importante.*
8. *La casa es grande.*

**C.** Give the English meaning of each of the following sentences:

1. La escuela es grande.
2. El automóvil es necesario.
3. La música es popular.
4. El doctor es famoso.
5. El periódico es importante.
6. El aeropuerto es moderno.
7. La clase es interesante.
8. El cereal es delicioso.
9. El perro es inteligente.
10. El color es horrible.

*KEY* (These answers may be oral or written):

1. *The school is big.*
2. *The car is necessary.*
3. *The music is popular.*
4. *The doctor is famous.*
5. *The newspaper is important.*
6. *The airport is modern.*
7. *The class is interesting.*
8. *The cereal is delicious.*
9. *The dog is intelligent.*
10. *The color is horrible.*

## Key to Actividades

**A**

1. *el gato*
2. *el insecto*
3. *la bicicleta*
4. *el hotel*
5. *el camello*
6. *el barbero*
7. *la escuela*
8. *el periódico*
9. *la rosa*
10. *el dragón*

**B**

1. *la pluma*
2. *el piano*
3. *el doctor*
4. *la televisión*
5. *la bicicleta*
6. *el libro*
7. *el perro*
8. *la lámpara*
9. *el café*
10. *la fruta*
11. *el pollo*
12. *el cine*
13. *el banco*
14. *el automóvil*
15. *el tren*
16. *el calendario*
17. *el disco*
18. *el hospital*

**C.**

1. *la*
2. *el*
3. *la*
4. *el*
5. *el*
6. *el*
7. *el*
8. *la*
9. *la*
10. *el*
11. *la*
12. *el*
13. *el*
14. *la*
15. *el*
16. *el*

**D** (Sample responses)

1. *importante, famoso, popular, americano*
2. *tropical, natural, grande*
3. *grande, terrible*
4. *delicioso, americano*
5. *rápido, importante, americano*
6. *popular, famoso, americano, importante*
7. *natural, popular*
8. *rápido*
9. *grande, popular, tropical*
10. *americano, famoso, popular, importante*

**E**

1. *No*
2. *Sí*
3. *Sí*
4. *Sí*
5. *Sí*

**F** (Sample responses)

1. *clase, casa, escuela, iglesia*
2. *actor, hombre, amigo*
3. *clase, escuela, familia*
4. *tren, automóvil*
5. *niña, profesora, madre, actriz*
6. *automóvil, taxi, banco*
7. *actriz, princesa, iglesia, mujer*
8. *hotel, hospital, aeropuerto*
9. *chocolate, café, pollo*

**Información personal** (Sample responses)

*Yo soy grande.*
*Yo soy inteligente.*
*Yo soy popular.*
*Yo soy terrible.*
*Yo soy estudiante.*

## Lección 2

**Notes:** As an interesting motivational device for this lesson, you may wish to introduce the vocabulary and story with a picture of your family and speak briefly about it in Spanish. Students may also be encouraged to bring pictures of their families and talk about them in class.

## Key to Structures

**3** . . . In Spanish, if a noun ends in a vowel (**a, e, i, o, u**), add the letter *s* to the singular form of the noun to make it plural.

**4** . . . Do the nouns in Group I end in a vowel? *No*. How do they end? *In a consonant*. What letters do you add to make them plural? *es*. Here's the rule: In Spanish, if a noun ends in a consonant (for example **l, n, r**), add the letters *es* to the singular form of the noun to make it plural.

**5** Now underline all the words in Group I that mean "the." Look carefully at Group II, and do the same and fill in the rest of the rule:

The plural form of **el** is *los.*
The plural form of **la** is *las.*
**los** and **las** mean *the.*

## Optional Oral Exercises

**A.** Repeat each noun with the definite article:

1. hombres
2. abuela
3. tigre
4. perros
5. blusas
6. disco
7. madres
8. automóviles
9. ambulancia
10. hijo

*KEY*

1. *los hombres*
2. *la abuela*
3. *el tigre*
4. *los perros*
5. *las blusas*
6. *el disco*
7. *las madres*
8. *los automóviles*
9. *la ambulancia*
10. *el hijo*

**B.** Change from singular to plural:

1. el actor
2. la abuela
3. la familia
4. la flor
5. el auto
6. el amigo
7. el animal
8. la lámpara
9. la mujer
10. el teatro

*KEY*

1. *los actores*
2. *las abuelas*
3. *las familias*
4. *las flores*
5. *los autos*
6. *los amigos*
7. *los animales*
8. *las lámparas*
9. *las mujeres*
10. *los teatros*

## Key to Actividades

**A**

1. *el abuelo*
2. *el hermano*
3. *los padres*
4. *la hermana*
5. *el gato*
6. *los abuelos*
7. *la madre*
8. *el perro*
9. *la abuela*
10. *el padre*

**B**

1. *la abuela*
2. *el hermano*
3. *la hija*
4. *el padre*
5. *el gato*
6. *el abuelo*
7. *la madre*
8. *el perro*

**C**

1. *Sí.*
2. *No. Carlos y María son los hijos.*
3. *Sí.*
4. *Sí.*
5. *No. Antonio es el padre.*
6. *Sí.*
7. *Sí.*
8. *No. Es mi abuelo.*

**D**

1. *los*
2. *el*
3. *los*
4. *las*
5. *la*
6. *los*
7. *los*
8. *el*
9. *la*
10. *la*
11. *la*
12. *las*
13. *la*
14. *los*
15. *las*
16. *la*
17. *el*
18. *el*
19. *los*
20. *el*

**E**

1. *los padres*
2. *los colores*
3. *los trenes*
4. *las blusas*
5. *los autos*
6. *las ambulancias*
7. *los tigres*
8. *los hombres*
9. *los niños*
10. *los profesores*
11. *las hijas*
12. *los animales*
13. *las clases*
14. *las rosas*
15. *los abuelos*
16. *los platos*
17. *las bicicletas*
18. *las mujeres*
19. *las flores*
20. *los cines*

**F**

1. *la familia*
2. *los hijos*
3. *el gato*
4. *el hijo*
5. *la madre*
6. *los abuelos*
7. *los padres*
8. *la hija*
9. *el perro*

**Información personal** (Sample responses)

Me llamo: *Carlos/Susana Rojas*
Madre: *Mi madre se llama Luisa.*
Padre: *Mi padre se llama Ernesto.*
Hermano(s): *Mi hermano se llama Roberto.*
Hermana(s): *Mi hermana se llama Patricia.*
Abuelo(s): *Mi abuelo se llama Alberto.*
Abuela(s): *Mi abuela se llama Ana.*
Perro(s): *Mi perro se llama Tigre.*
Gato(s): *Mi gato se llama Caramelo.*

**Diálogo**

Buenos *días*. ¿Cómo te *llamas*?

*Buenos* días. Me *llamo* Alicia.

*Me* llamo Ramón. ¿*Cómo* estás, Alicia?

*Bien*, gracias. ¿Y *tú*?

*Regular*. Hasta *la vista*, Alicia.

*Adiós*, Ramón. Hasta *mañana*.

# Lección 3

**Notes:** Classroom objects may serve as motivational devices for this lesson. Apply the optional oral exercises about the definite article with the vocabulary in this and previous lessons before proceeding to the indefinite article.

The lesson narrative may serve as a point of departure for a simple, personalized conversation about your class.

## Key to Structures

**3** Look at the story again. There are two new little words that you read several times. Can you find these two new words? They are *un* and *una*.

**4** Let's start by comparing the two groups of nouns. Are the nouns in Group I masculine or feminine? *Masculine*. How do you know? *el is used*. What does **el** mean? *the*. Now look at Group II. Which word has replaced **el**? *un*. What does **un** mean? *a*.

**5** . . . Are the nouns in Group I masculine or feminine? *Feminine*. How do you know? *la is used*. What does **la** mean? *the*. Now look at Group II. Which word has replaced **la**? *una*. What does **una** mean? *a*.

## Optional Oral Exercises

**A.** Repeat each noun with the definite article:

1. mesa
2. ventana
3. profesor
4. escuela
5. papel
6. diccionario
7. cuaderno
8. alumna
9. lápiz
10. pizarra

*KEY*

1. *la mesa*
2. *la ventana*
3. *el profesor*
4. *la escuela*
5. *el papel*
6. *el diccionario*
7. *el cuaderno*
8. *la alumna*
9. *el lápiz*
10. *la pizarra*

**B.** Change to plural:

1. la puerta
2. el alumno
3. la profesora
4. la lección
5. el libro
6. el doctor
7. el muchacho
8. la pluma
9. el papel
10. la persona

*KEY*

1. *las puertas*
2. *los alumnos*
3. *las profesoras*
4. *las lecciones*
5. *los libros*
6. *los doctores*
7. *los muchachos*
8. *las plumas*
9. *los papeles*
10. *las personas*

**C.** Change the definite article to the indefinite article **un** or **una:**

EXAMPLE: **el** lápiz  **un** lápiz

1. la muchacha
2. la mesa
3. el hermano
4. el diccionario
5. la ventana
6. el parque
7. la clase
8. el cuaderno
9. el gato
10. la hija

*KEY*

1. *una muchacha*
2. *una mesa*
3. *un hermano*
4. *un diccionario*
5. *una ventana*
6. *un parque*
7. *una clase*
8. *un cuaderno*
9. *un gato*
10. *una hija*

## Key to Actividades

**A**

1. *el libro*
2. *la alumna*
3. *el lápiz*
4. *la ventana*
5. *la escuela*
6. *el papel*
7. *el alumno*
8. *la pizarra*
9. *la profesora*
10. *la pluma*
11. *la puerta*
12. *el profesor*

**B**

1. *los*
2. *la*
3. *el*
4. *la*
5. *los*
6. *las*
7. *los*
8. *la*
9. *el*
10. *la*

**C**

1. *No. La clase de español es interesante.*
2. *No. La profesora de la clase se llama Carmen López.*
3. *No. Pedro y Juana son alumnos.*
4. *No. El padre de Juana es doctor.*
5. *Sí.*

**D**

1. *la profesora*
2. *una pluma, un lápiz y muchos libros.*
3. *muchos alumnos*
4. *profesora*
5. *doctor*

**E**

1. *doctor*
2. *un doctor mexicano*
3. *profesora*
4. *una profesora interesante*
5. *alumno/estudiante*
6. *un alumno inteligente*
7. *actriz*
8. *una actriz popular*

**F**

1. *una pluma*
2. *un alumno*
3. *un libro*
4. *una profesora*
5. *un papel*
6. *una pizarra*
7. *una ventana*
8. *una mesa*
9. *un lápiz*
10. *una puerta*

**G**
1. *una lección*
2. *un alumno*
3. *una niña*
4. *un profesor*
5. *un parque*
6. *una escuela*
7. *un abuelo*
8. *un hijo*

**H**
1. *una*
2. *un*
3. *un*
4. *un*
5. *un*
6. *una*
7. *una*
8. *una*
9. *una*
10. *una*
11. *una*
12. *una*
13. *un*
14. *un*
15. *una*
16. *un*

**Preguntas personales** (Sample responses)

1. *El profesor / la profesora está en la clase.*
2. *Mi profesor se llama señor López.*
3. *Mi pluma está en la mesa.*
4. *Mis libros están en casa.*
5. *Mis papeles están aquí.*

**Información personal** (Sample responses)

1. *una pluma*
2. *un diccionario*
3. *un libro*
4. *un cuaderno*
5. *un lápiz*
6. *papel*

**Diálogo**

Buenos días, Federico.

*Buenos días, Señorita López.*

¿Dónde está tu libro de español?

*Aquí está mi libro, Señorita López.*

Muy bien. ¿Y tu lápiz?

*Aquí está mi lápiz.*

Tú estás muy bien preparado, Federico.

*Gracias. El español es mi clase favorita.*

# Lección 4

**Notes:** Teachers may wish to have students act out various verbs in this lesson. Students say in Spanish what they are doing or have others guess what they are doing. Students should use verbs in complete sentences to describe the actions.

Teachers may also cue students (or have students cue one another), using intonation to pose questions. Example: **¿Tú hablas?** A student answers: **Yo hablo.** The entire class may then respond in unison: **Él/Ella habla.** Or: **¿Ustedes hablan? – Nosotros hablamos. – Ellos/Ellas hablan.**

## Key to Structures

**3** . . . Now can you do one? Take the verb **comprar** (*to buy*). Remove the **-ar,** look at the subjects and add the correct endings:

| | |
|---|---|
| yo compr*o* | nosotros compr*amos* |
| tú compr*as* | ustedes compr*an* |
| usted compr*a* | ellos/ellas compr*an* |
| él compr*a* | |
| ella compr*a* | |

## Optional Oral Exercises

**A.** Repeat the sentence with the correct pronoun for the subject you hear:

1. Rosa estudia español.
2. David y yo compramos libros.
3. José y Juan hablan francés.
4. Carmen y Susana trabajan en el mercado.
5. El hombre entra en el restaurante.
6. Los alumnos contestan en la clase.
7. El perro pasa por el parque.
8. La niña mira la televisión.
9. Las muchachas bailan en la discoteca.
10. Roberto visita a la abuela.

*KEY*

1. *Ella estudia español.*
2. *Nosotros compramos libros.*
3. *Ellos hablan francés.*
4. *Ellas trabajan en el mercado.*
5. *Él entra en el restaurante.*
6. *Ellos contestan en la clase.*
7. *Él pasa por el parque.*
8. *Ella mira la televisión.*
9. *Ellas bailan en la discoteca.*
10. *Él visita a la abuela.*

**B.** Express the verb with the subject you hear:

| | | | |
|---|---|---|---|
| 1. mirar: | nosotros | 6. comprar: | tú |
| 2. hablar: | ustedes | 7. contestar: | ellos |
| 3. bailar: | yo | 8. trabajar: | el padre |
| 4. estudiar: | el alumno | 9. usar: | usted |
| 5. preguntar: | Alicia | 10. visitar: | las hijas |

*KEY*

1. *nosotros miramos*
2. *ustedes hablan*
3. *yo bailo*
4. *el alumno estudia*
5. *Alicia pregunta*
6. *tú compras*
7. *ellos contestan*
8. *el padre trabaja*
9. *usted usa*
10. *las hijas visitan*

## Key to Actividades

**A**

1. *usted*
2. *tú*
3. *usted*
4. *ustedes*
5. *tú*
6. *ustedes*
7. *tú*
8. *ustedes*

**B**

| | |
|---|---|
| 1. *yo* | *I answer* |
| 2. *tú* | *you buy* |
| 3. *yo* | *I enter* |
| 4. *ustedes, ellos, ellas* | *you study, they study* |
| 5. *usted, él, ella* | *you work, he works, she works* |
| 6. *ustedes, ellos, ellas* | *you use, they use* |
| 7. *yo* | *I ask* |
| 8. *tú* | *you visit* |

**C**

1. *uso*
2. *trabajas*
3. *contesta*
4. *pregunta*
5. *escucha*
6. *visitamos*
7. *pasan*
8. *entramos*

**D**

1. *hablo*
2. *trabajas*
3. *compramos*
4. *entran*
5. *estudian*
6. *pasa*
7. *visito*
8. *escuchas*
9. *contestamos*
10. *usa*

**E**
1. *No. la señorita Pacheco trabaja en una escuela.*
2. *No. Los alumnos estudian español.*
3. *No. La profesora usa muchos libros y papeles.*
4. *No. Yo escucho bien.*
5. *No. La profesora pregunta y yo contesto.*
6. *No. La señorita Pacheco es una profesora muy buena.*
7. *No. Los alumnos estudian mucho.*
8. *No. Cuando la profesora habla, los alumnos escuchan.*
9. *No. Los alumnos estudian inglés y matemáticas.*

**F**
1. *El profesor pregunta.*
2. *Usted compra una rosa.*
3. *Yo escucho.*
4. *Nosotros entramos.*
5. *Los hombres trabajan.*
6. *Ellos hablan español.*
7. *Los animales pasan.*
8. *Los estudiantes contestan.*

## Diálogo

Yo deseo *bailar*.

Aquí hay una *discoteca*.

¿Vamos a entrar?

Sí, deseo una buena *mesa*.

Aquí hay una mesa *magnífica*.

Yo deseo *hablar* con el muchacho rubio.

Yo deseo bailar con el muchacho moreno y *guapo*.

¡*Vamos*! ¡Buena *suerte*!

## Información personal (Sample responses)

*Yo hablo por teléfono.*
*Yo entro en la casa.*
*Yo miro la televisión.*
*Yo escucho la radio.*
*Yo estudio la lección.*
*Yo compro el libro.*
*Yo contesto en la clase.*

# Repaso I (Lecciones 1–4)

## Key to Actividades

**A**

1. *madre*
2. *amiga*
3. *abuelos*
4. *flor*
5. *disco*
6. *lápiz*
7. *gato*
8. *pluma*
9. *libro*
10. *mesa*
11. *alumno*
12. *hija*
13. *papel*
14. *pollo*
15. *hombres*
16. *niña*
17. *perro*
18. *estudiante*

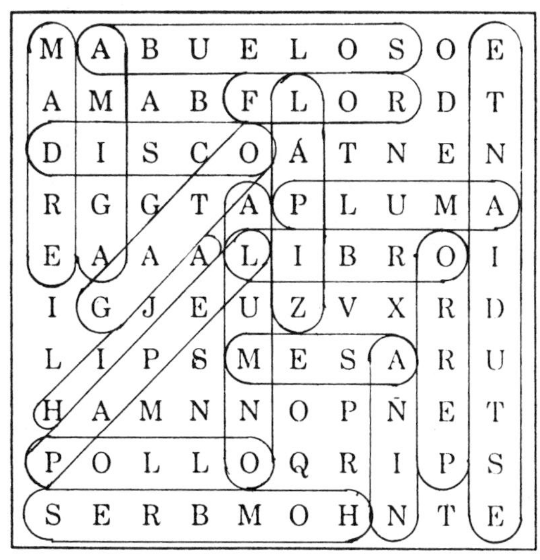


**B**

1. *un libro*
2. *un lápiz*
3. *una pluma*
4. *un papel*
5. *una pizarra*
6. *una alumna*
7. *una profesora*
8. *un diccionario*
9. *un calendario*
10. *una ventana*

**C**

1. *mira*
2. *visitamos*
3. *contestan*
4. *uso*
5. *trabaja*
6. *preguntan*
7. *entra*
8. *compran*
9. *pasan*
10. *habla*

**D** El español es *FABULOSO*.

1. *P R O* **F** *E S O R*
2. *C* **A** *S A*
3. *A* **B** *U E L O S*
4. *A* **U** *T O M Ó V I L*
5. *F A M I* **L** *I A*
6. *D* **O** *C T O R*
7. *D I* **S** *C O*
8. *N I Ñ* **O**

**E** Pepe es un *muchacho*. Él estudia español en la *escuela*. La *madre* de Pepe se llama Isabel. El *padre* se llama Jorge. El padre es *doctor*. Él trabaja en un *hospital*. La madre de Pepe es *profesora*. Ella trabaja en una *escuela* moderna. Pepe estudia en una *escuela* grande. En la *clase* usa muchas cosas: un *lápiz*, una *pluma*, un *libro* y *papel*. En la *casa* de Pepe hay dos animales. Amigo es un *perro*, y Patitas es un *gato*.

# Segunda Parte

## Lección 5

**Notes:** The techniques for verb practice used in Lesson 4 may be repeated in Lesson 5. Now, however, students should also answer in the negative and form questions using inversion. Although question words such as **¿cómo?**, **¿cuándo?**, **¿dónde?**, **¿adónde?**, **¿por qué?** occur throughout the book, students should not be required to use them actively. These terms are beyond the level and scope of this text.

Point out that in colloquial Spanish we may sometimes ask questions without inversion. Examples: **¿Alicia estudia español? ¿Tú hablas francés?**

### Key to Structures

**1** . . . Do you see what's happening here? If you want to make a sentence negative in Spanish, what word is placed directly in front of the verb? *no* . If you wrote **no**, you are correct.

### Optional Oral Exercises

**A.** Express the verb with the subject you hear:

1. escuchar: él
2. preguntar: nosotros
3. entrar: Pablo y Olga
4. mirar: tú
5. practicar: María y Alicia
6. cantar: la señorita
7. bailar: Daniel
8. contestar: la profesora
9. pasar: usted
10. trabajar: ustedes
11. usar: yo
12. hablar: tú

*KEY*

1. *él escucha*
2. *nosotros preguntamos*
3. *Pablo y Olga entran*
4. *tú miras*
5. *María y Alicia practican*
6. *la señorita canta*
7. *Daniel baila*
8. *la profesora contesta*
9. *usted pasa*
10. *ustedes trabajan*
11. *yo uso*
12. *tú hablas*

**B.** Make these sentences negative:

1. Nosotros escuchamos la radio.
2. Los alumnos estudian español.
3. Ana compra un disco.
4. El doctor trabaja en el hospital.
5. Yo canto bien.
6. Tú usas el automóvil.
7. Ustedes hablan mucho.
8. Luis necesita dinero.
9. Nosotros practicamos la lección.
10. Usted desea una bicicleta.
11. Él entra en la clase.
12. Ellas bailan en la fiesta.

*KEY*

1. *Nosotros no escuchamos la radio.*
2. *Los alumnos no estudian español.*
3. *Ana no compra un disco.*
4. *El doctor no trabaja en el hospital.*
5. *Yo no canto bien.*
6. *Tú no usas el automóvil.*
7. *Ustedes no hablan mucho.*
8. *Luis no necesita dinero.*
9. *Nosotros no practicamos la lección.*
10. *Usted no desea una bicicleta.*
11. *Él no entra en la clase.*
12. *Ellas no bailan en la fiesta.*

**C.** Change these sentences to questions:

1. Nosotros escuchamos la radio.
2. Los alumnos estudian español.
3. Ana compra un disco.
4. El doctor trabaja en el hospital.
5. Yo canto bien.
6. Tú usas el automóvil.
7. Ustedes hablan mucho.
8. Luis necesita dinero.
9. Nosotros practicamos la lección.

10. Usted desea una bicicleta.
11. Él entra en la clase.
12. Ellas bailan en la fiesta.

*KEY*

1. *¿Escuchamos nosotros la radio?*
2. *¿Estudian los alumnos español?*
3. *¿Compra Ana un disco?*
4. *¿Trabaja el doctor en el hospital?*
5. *¿Canto yo bien?*
6. *¿Usas tú el automóvil?*
7. *¿Hablan ustedes mucho?*
8. *¿Necesita Luis dinero?*
9. *¿Practicamos nosotros la lección?*
10. *¿Desea usted una bicicleta?*
11. *¿Entra él en la clase?*
12. *¿Bailan ellas en la fiesta?*

**D.** Directed dialog. Student #1 asks the question, student #2 responds, class responds in unison.

Pregúntele a un alumno (una alumna, unos alumnos, unas alumnas) si él (ella, ellos, ellas)

1. baila(n) bien
2. contesta(n) en clase
3. mira(n) la televisión
4. estudia(n) en casa
5. compra(n) muchos discos
6. practica(n) las lecciones
7. desea(n) un automóvil
8. pregunta(n) mucho

*KEY*

| STUDENT #1 | STUDENT #2 |
|---|---|
| 1. *¿Bailas tú bien?* <br> *¿Baila(n) usted(es) bien?* | *Sí, yo bailo/nosotros bailamos bien.* |
| 2. *¿Contestas tú en clase?* <br> *¿Contesta(n) usted(es) en clase?* | *Sí, yo contesto/nosotros contestamos en clase.* |
| 3. *¿Miras tú la televisión?* <br> *¿Mira(n) usted(es) la televisión?* | *Sí, yo miro/nosotros miramos la televisión.* |

| | |
|---|---|
| 4. *¿Estudias tú en casa?*<br>*¿Estudia(n) usted(es) en casa?* | *Sí, yo estudio/nosotros estudiamos en casa.* |
| 5. *¿Compras tú muchos discos?*<br>*¿Compra(n) usted(es) muchos discos?* | *Sí, yo compro/nosotros compramos muchos discos.* |
| 6. *¿Practicas tú las lecciones?*<br>*¿Practica(n) usted(es) las lecciones?* | *Sí, yo practico/nosotros practicamos las lecciones.* |
| 7. *¿Deseas tú un automóvil?*<br>*¿Desea(n) usted(es) un automóvil?* | *Sí, yo deseo/nosotros deseamos un automóvil.* |
| 8. *¿Preguntas tú mucho?*<br>*¿Pregunta(n) usted(es) mucho?* | *Sí, yo pregunto/ nosotros preguntamos mucho.* |

NOTE: The procedure for the directed dialog may be extended to practice (a) negative and (b) third-person singular and plural verb forms.

EXAMPLES: (a) *¿Hablas tú francés? No, yo no hablo francés.*
(b) *Pregúntele a Pablo si María habla español.*
Student #1: *¿Habla María español?*
Student #2: *Sí, ella habla español.*
Class in unison: *Sí, ella habla español.*

## Key to Actividades

**A**

1. *Yo no hablo.*
   *I don't speak. I am not speaking.*
2. *Ustedes no usan papeles.*
   *You don't use papers. You are not using papers.*
3. *Tú no contestas.*
   *You don't answer. You are not answering.*
4. *Ellos no escuchan.*
   *They don't listen. They are not listening.*
5. *María no baila.*
   *María doesn't dance. María isn't dancing.*
6. *Los automóviles no pasan.*
   *The cars don't pass. The cars are not passing.*

7. *Ella no practica.*
   *She doesn't practice. She isn't practicing.*
8. *La profesora no trabaja.*
   *The teacher doesn't work. The teacher isn't working.*
9. *El actor no entra.*
   *The actor doesn't enter. The actor isn't entering.*
10. *Los padres no preguntan.*
    *The parents don't ask. The parents are not asking.*

**B**

1. *¿Pregunta usted?*
   *Do you ask? Are you asking?*
2. *¿Contestan los muchachos?*
   *Do the boys answer? Are the boys answering?*
3. *¿Entra el amigo?*
   *Does the friend enter? Is the friend entering?*
4. *¿Canta la madre?*
   *Does the mother sing? Is the mother singing?*
5. *¿Compran los hombres?*
   *Do the men buy? Are the men buying?*
6. *¿Visita el hermano?*
   *Does the brother visit? Is the brother visiting?*
7. *¿Practican las hijas?*
   *Do the daughters practice? Are the daughters practicing?*
8. *¿Escucha el médico?*
   *Does the doctor listen? Is the doctor listening?*
9. *¿Trabaja la mujer?*
   *Does the woman work? Is the woman working?*
10. *¿Bailamos nosotras?*
    *Do we dance? Are we dancing?*

**C**

| | | | | | |
|---|---|---|---|---|---|
| 1. *c* | 3. *g* | 5. *j* | 7. *k* | 9. *e* | 11. *a* |
| 2. *d* | 4. *h* | 6. *b* | 8. *i* | 10. *l* | 12. *f* |

**D** (Sample responses)

1. *Sí, el automóvil es importante en América.*
2. *Sí, los médicos usan automóviles.*
3. *Yo necesito un automóvil para ir a la escuela.*
   *Yo no necesito un automóvil.*
4. *Un automóvil necesita mucha gasolina.*
5. *Necesito un garaje para un automóvil.*

**E** 1. *¿Escucha usted?*
2. *¿Compra usted una lámpara?*
3. *¿Mira usted la foto (grafía)?*

**F** 1. *¿Miras tú la televisión?*
2. *¿Practicas tú el piano?*
3. *¿Usas tú la (una) pluma?*

**Preguntas personales** (Sample responses)

1. *Sí, bailo bien.*
2. *No, no canto en la clase.*
3. *Sí, hablo español.*
4. *Sí, escucho con atención.*

**Información personal** (Sample responses)

*Yo estudio las lecciones en casa.*
*Yo pregunto mucho en clase.*
*Yo escucho cuando el profesor (la profesora) habla.*
*Yo practico el español.*
*Yo no visito a muchos amigos.*
*Yo no escucho mucho la radio.*
*Yo trabajo mucho.*

**Diálogo**

Buenas tardes, señor. ¿Qué desea Ud.?

*Buenas tardes. Necesito un automóvil.*

Está bien. ¿Grande o pequeño?

*Un automóvil pequeño. Es para ir al supermercado.*

¿Desea Ud. un auto nuevo o usado?

*Usado, si es bueno.*

Claro. Aquí tiene un automóvil bueno por poco dinero.

*¡Perfecto!*

# Lección 6

**Notes:** To practice the numbers from 1 to 30, students may use a calendar, guess people's ages in pictures, count play money, recite phone numbers, or formulate simple mathematical problems that other students answer in complete Spanish sentences.

## Optional Oral Exercises

**A.** Write down the number you hear:

1. siete
2. trece
3. veinte
4. diez y seis
5. doce
6. cuatro
7. nueve
8. quince
9. treinta
10. veinte y ocho

*KEY*

1. *7*
2. *13*
3. *20*
4. *16*
5. *12*
6. *4*
7. *9*
8. *15*
9. *30*
10. *28*

**B.** Give the number that comes after the number you hear:

1. diez
2. dos
3. cinco
4. veinte
5. veinte y tres
6. siete
7. catorce
8. veinte y seis
9. doce
10. veinte y nueve

*KEY*

1. *once*
2. *tres*
3. *seis*
4. *veinte y uno*
5. *veinte y cuatro*
6. *ocho*
7. *quince*
8. *veinte y siete*
9. *trece*
10. *treinta*

**C.** Give the number that comes before the number you hear:

1. diez y siete
2. cuatro
3. diez
4. trece
5. veinte y seis
6. veinte y tres
7. uno
8. diez y seis
9. veinte
10. dos

*KEY*

1. *diez y seis*
2. *tres*
3. *nueve*
4. *doce*
5. *veinte y cinco*
6. *veinte y dos*
7. *cero*
8. *quince*
9. *diez y nueve*
10. *uno*

**D.** ¿Cuántos son

1. tres y cuatro?
2. treinta menos diez?
3. dos por cuatro?
4. veinte menos cinco?
5. treinta dividido por tres?
6. dos por ocho?
7. veinte menos seis?
8. veinte dividido por cuatro?

*KEY*

1. *Tres y cuatro son siete.*
2. *Treinta menos diez son veinte.*
3. *Dos por cuatro son ocho.*
4. *Veinte menos cinco son quince.*
5. *Treinta dividido por tres son diez.*
6. *Dos por ocho son diez y seis.*
7. *Veinte menos seis son catorce.*
8. *Veinte dividido por cuatro son cinco.*

**E.** Have students articulate their own math problems to the class.

## Key to Actividades

**A** 1. *4* 2. *2* 3. *13* 4. *20* 5. *18* 6. *15* 7. *5* 8. *9*

**B** *veinte y siete*
*quince*
*doce*
*siete*
*catorce*
*veinte y nueve*
*dos*
*once*

**C**
1. *cuatro–cinco–seis–tres–dos–siete–ocho*
2. *ocho–siete–nueve–cuatro–seis–dos–uno*
3. *siete–tres–siete–tres–cuatro–cinco–seis*
4. *cuatro–cinco–cinco–seis–siete–cuatro–tres*
5. *seis–dos–cero–dos–nueve–ocho–siete*
6. *cero–ocho–cero–dos–cinco–tres–nueve*

**D**
1. *siete*
2. *seis*
3. *un billete de lotería*
4. *veinte*
5. *diez y siete*
6. *último*

**E**
1. veinte y tres *23*
2. once *11*
3. siete *7*
4. veinte y cuatro *24*
5. diez y seis *16*
6. diez y nueve *19*
7. quince *15*
8. veinte y ocho *28*
9. doce *12*
10. cinco *5*

**F**
1. 14 *catorce*
2. 22 *veinte y dos*
3. 6 *seis*
4. 17 *diez y siete*
5. 30 *treinta*
6. 21 *veinte y uno*
7. 8 *ocho*
8. 4 *cuatro*
9. 13 *trece*
10. 29 *veinte y nueve*

**G**
1. $5 + 5 = 10$
2. $20 - 5 = 15$
3. $9 \times 2 = 18$
4. $6 + 3 = 9$
5. $4 \div 2 = 2$
6. $17 - 16 = 1$
7. $11 \times 1 = 11$
8. $20 \div 5 = 4$
9. $18 \div 2 = 9$
10. $16 + 3 = 19$

**H**
1. *Dos y tres son cinco.*
2. *Nueve menos dos son siete.*
3. *Cuatro por cuatro son diez y seis.*
4. *Ocho dividido por dos son cuatro.*
5. *Veinte y dos y tres son veinte y cinco.*
6. *Diez menos cinco son cinco.*
7. *Veinte y cuatro y cinco son veinte y nueve.*
8. *Seis dividido por tres son dos.*
9. *Diez y once son veinte y uno.*
10. *Diez y ocho menos siete son once.*

**I**
1. (a) *dos*
2. (b) *once*
3. (c) *dos*
4. (a) *ocho*
5. (a) *quince*
6. (b) *uno*
7. (c) *nueve*
8. (a) *uno*
9. (b) *doce*
10. (c) *dos*

**J**
1. *Diez y cinco son quince.*
   *Quince y siete son veinte y dos.*
   *Veinte y dos y ocho son treinta.*
2. *Seis y siete son trece.*
   *Trece y cuatro son diez y siete.*
   *Diez y siete y doce son veinte y nueve.*

3. *Trece y ocho son once.*
   *Once y diez son veinte y uno.*
   *Veinte y uno y dos son veinte y tres.*
4. *Trece y once son veinte y cuatro.*
   *Veinte y cuatro y tres son veinte y siete.*
   *Veinte y siete y uno son veinte y ocho.*

**Diálogo**

*¿Cuántos son tres y cuatro?*

¡Uy! Tres y cuatro son seis.

*¿Cuántos son quince menos cinco?*

Quince menos cinco son nueve.

*¿Cuántos son veinte dividido por dos?*

Veinte dividido por dos son once.

*¿Qué te pasa hoy?*

Es imposible hacer cálculos con este vendaje.

**Información personal** (Sample responses)

1. *trece años*
2. *dos hermanos*
3. *una hermana*
4. *seis miembros*
5. *uno*
6. *tres–tres–cinco*
7. *seis–tres–uno–ocho–dos–cuatro–cero*

# Lección 7

**Notes:** The techniques suggested in Lessons 4 and 5 may also be applied in this lesson on **-er** verbs. Individualized cue-response sequences should be encouraged wherever possible.

### Key to Structures

**2** Here are eight more action words. You have probably noticed that these verbs don't end in **-ar** but in *-er* .

**4** . . . What is the extra word in the Spanish sentences that has no equivalent in the English sentences? *a* .

## Optional Oral Exercises

**A.** Express the correct verb form with the subject you hear:

| | | | |
|---|---|---|---|
| 1. ver: | nosotros | 6. vender: | usted |
| 2. comprender: | yo | 7. comer: | Pablo y Roberto |
| 3. leer: | Rosita | 8. correr: | el gato |
| 4. beber: | el niño | 9. aprender: | ustedes |
| 5. responder: | tú | 10. saber: | tú |

*KEY*

1. *nosotros vemos*
2. *yo comprendo*
3. *Rosita lee*
4. *el niño bebe*
5. *tú respondes*
6. *usted vende*
7. *Pablo y Roberto comen*
8. *el gato corre*
9. *ustedes aprenden*
10. *tú sabes*

**B.** Make the following sentences negative:

1. Yo leo en español.
2. Juan aprende la lección.
3. Usted vende flores.
4. Nosotros comemos muchas frutas.
5. Tú respondes la pregunta.
6. Ustedes saben bailar bien.
7. La niña corre a la casa.
8. Las madres comprenden a los hijos.
9. Yo veo a Pablo en la escuela.
10. Él bebe rápidamente.

*KEY*

1. *Yo no leo en español.*
2. *Juan no aprende la lección.*
3. *Usted no vende flores.*
4. *Nosotros no comemos muchas frutas.*
5. *Tú no respondes la pregunta.*
6. *Ustedes no saben bailar bien.*
7. *La niña no corre a la casa.*
8. *Las madres no comprenden a los hijos.*
9. *Yo no veo a Pablo en la escuela.*
10. *Él no bebe rápidamente.*

**C.** Change the following sentences to questions:

1. Yo leo en español.
2. Juan aprende la lección.
3. Usted vende flores.
4. Nosotros comemos muchas frutas.
5. Tú respondes la pregunta.
6. Ustedes saben bailar bien.
7. La niña corre a la casa.
8. Las madres comprenden a los hijos.
9. Yo veo a Pablo en la escuela.
10. Él bebe rápidamente.

*KEY*

1. *¿Leo yo en español?*
2. *¿Aprende Juan la lección?*
3. *¿Vende usted flores?*
4. *¿Comemos nosotros muchas frutas?*
5. *¿Respondes tú la pregunta?*
6. *¿Saben ustedes bailar bien?*
7. *¿Corre la niña a la casa?*
8. *¿Comprenden las madres a los hijos?*
9. *¿Veo yo a Pablo en la escuela?*
10. *¿Bebe él rápidamente?*

## Key to Actividades

| | | | | | |
|---|---|---|---|---|---|
| **A** | yo | *aprendo* | *comprendo* | *leo* | *veo* |
| | tú | *aprendes* | *comprendes* | *lees* | *ves* |
| | usted | *aprende* | *comprende* | *lee* | *ve* |
| | él | *aprende* | *comprende* | *lee* | *ve* |
| | ella | *aprende* | *comprende* | *lee* | *ve* |
| | nosotros | *aprendemos* | *comprendemos* | *leemos* | *vemos* |
| | ustedes | *aprenden* | *comprenden* | *leen* | *ven* |
| | ellos | *aprenden* | *comprenden* | *leen* | *ven* |
| | ellas | *aprenden* | *comprenden* | *leen* | *ven* |

NOTE TO TEACHERS: Songs provide a pleasant opportunity for practice in pronunciation and reinforcement of lexical and structural elements. [Teachers may also wish to consult *Vamos a cantar* (*Sing and Learn Spanish*), by Harriet Barnett and Betty M. Barlow, Shawnee Press, Inc., Delaware Water Gap, PA 18327.]

**Mi familia feliz**

(To the melody of "My bonnie lies over the ocean")

Yo tengo un padre muy bueno,
Mi madre es buena también,
Y ellos están muy contentos
Porque yo aprendo muy bien.

Hola, hola,
Hola, buenos días, ¿qué tal?, ¿qué tal?
Hola, hola,
Hola, buenos días, ¿qué tal?

**B**
1. Comprendemos la lección.
2. Comprendemos *al* ~~el~~ presidente.
3. Yo no veo *a* la muchacha.
4. Yo no veo el billete.
5. Los alumnos escuchan el disco.
6. Los alumnos escuchan *a* la señora Montano.
7. María visita *al* ~~el~~ director.
8. María visita la clase.
9. No comprendo *a* la profesora.
10. No comprendo la pregunta.

**C**
1. *de once años*
2. *el gato*
3. *comida*
4. *ve a Lupita*
5. *comprende*

**D**
1. *visitamos*
2. *vende*
3. *practicas*
4. *lee*
5. *responde*
6. *usan*
7. *aprenden*
8. *trabaja*
9. *veo*
10. *corre*

**E** 1. *Nosotros no visitamos a la profesora.*
2. *Pedro no vende billetes de lotería.*
3. *Tú no practicas la lección.*
4. *Usted no lee el periódico.*
5. *Mi hermano no responde en español.*
6. *Ellos no usan muchos libros.*
7. *Ustedes no aprenden rápidamente.*
8. *Mi padre no trabaja en una escuela moderna.*
9. *Yo no veo a mi gato en el jardín.*
10. *Ella no corre a la tienda con su perro.*

**F** 1. *¿Visitamos nosotros a la profesora?*
2. *¿Vende Pedro billetes de lotería?*
3. *¿Practicas tú la lección?*
4. *¿Lee usted el periódico?*
5. *¿Responde mi hermano en español?*
6. *¿Usan ellos muchos libros?*
7. *¿Aprenden ustedes rápidamente?*
8. *¿Trabaja mi padre en una escuela moderna?*
9. *¿Veo yo a mi gato en el jardín?*
10. *¿Corre ella a la tienda con su perro?*

**G** 1. *El perro sabe bailar.*
2. *Nosotras leemos un libro.*
3. *Vemos el avión.*
4. *El muchacho vende periódicos.*
5. *El gato come.*
6. *El hombre bebe el café.*
7. *Los alumnos aprenden mucho.*
8. *Ellos corren al cine.*
9. *Yo respondo en la clase.*
10. *La muchacha no comprende.*

**H** 1. *yo*
2. *tú*
3. *nosotros*
4. *ustedes/ellos/ellas*
5. *usted/él/ella*
6. *usted/él/ella*
7. *yo*
8. *ustedes/ellos/ellas*
9. *nosotros*
10. *tú*

**Información personal** (Sample responses)

1. *rápidamente*
2. *muchas frutas*
3. *en el parque*
4. *las preguntas en la clase*
5. *en un restaurante*
6. *música popular*

**Diálogo**

Hola, Susana. ¿Adónde vas?

*Voy con mi gato Chiquito al parque.*

Es un gato bonito. ¿Es inteligente?

*Oh, sí. Él comprende mucho.*

Yo prefiero a mi perro, Rambolito.

*Es un animal muy pequeño.*

Sí, pero no come mucho.

*Yo prefiero a mi gato. Hasta luego, Roberto.*

# Lección 8

**Notes:** The vocabulary in this lesson may be practiced—in addition to the **actividades**—by having students describe television and literary characters, people and objects in newspapers and magazines, and classroom objects.

### Key to Structures

**4** . . . Notice that an adjective in Spanish agrees in gender with the person it describes. Which letter do the masculine forms of the adjective end in? *o* . Which letter do the feminine forms of the adjective end in? *a* .

**5** . . . We change the letter *o* to *a* .

**7** . . . What do you notice about the adjectives in both columns? *They are the same* .

**8 . . .**

| | |
|---|---|
| rico | *ricos* |
| perfecto | *perfectos* |
| moreno | *morenos* |
| elegante | *elegantes* |
| interesante | *interesantes* |

Look at Group I. How many people are we describing? *one* . Look at Group II. How many people are we describing? *more than one* . Which letter did we have to add to the adjective to show that we are describing more than one? We added the letter *s* .

**9 . . .**

| | |
|---|---|
| rica | *ricas* |
| perfecta | *perfectas* |
| morena | *morenas* |
| elegante | *elegantes* |
| interesante | *interesantes* |

Look at Group I. What is the gender of the noun we are describing? *feminine* . How many people are we describing in Group I? *one* . Now look at Group II. How many feminine people are we describing? *more than one* . Which letter did we have to add to the adjective to show that we are describing more than one? We added the letter *s* .

**10. . .**

| | |
|---|---|
| difícil | *difíciles* |
| fácil | *fáciles* |

Which letters did we have to add to the adjectives in Group I to show that we are describing more than one? We added the letters *es* .

## Optional Oral Exercises

**A.** Complete the second sentence with the correct form of the adjective.

1. El chocolate es delicioso. La banana es ____.
2. El actor es famoso. La actriz es ____.
3. El muchacho es romántico. La muchacha es ____.
4. Roberto es rico. Juanita es ____.
5. El padre es moreno. La hija es ____.
6. El lápiz es pequeño. La pluma es ____.
7. El abuelo es viejo. La abuela es ____.

8. El hotel es magnífico. La escuela es ____.
9. El hermano es rubio. La hermana es ____.
10. El animal es feo. La casa es ____.

*KEY*

1. *deliciosa*
2. *famosa*
3. *romántica*
4. *rica*
5. *morena*
6. *pequeña*
7. *vieja*
8. *magnífica*
9. *rubia*
10. *fea*

**B.** Complete the second sentence with the correct form of the adjective:

1. El elefante es grande. El tigre es ____.
2. El deporte es importante. La música es ____.
3. El español no es difícil. La lección no es ____.
4. Pablo es popular. Carmen es ____.
5. El libro es interesante. La clase es ____.

*KEY*

1. *grande*
2. *importante*
3. *difícil*
4. *popular*
5. *interesante*

**C.** Change to plural:

| EXAMPLE: | él es pequeño | **ellos son pequeños** |
| --- | --- | --- |
| | ella es pequeña | **ellas son pequeñas** |

1. Él es gordo.
2. Él es moreno.
3. Él es pobre.
4. Él es feo.
5. Él es americano.
6. Ella es bonita.
7. Ella es flaca.
8. Ella es vieja.
9. Ella es inteligente.
10. Ella as rubia.

*KEY*

1. *Ellos son gordos.*
2. *Ellos son morenos.*
3. *Ellos son pobres.*
4. *Ellos son feos.*
5. *Ellos son americanos.*
6. *Ellas son bonitas.*
7. *Ellas son flacas.*
8. *Ellas son viejas.*
9. *Ellas son inteligentes.*
10. *Ellas son rubias.*

**D.** Change to plural:

EXAMPLE: la música popular **las músicas populares**

1. la muchacha joven
2. la lección fácil
3. el libro difícil
4. la fruta tropical
5. el automóvil español

*KEY*

1. *las muchachas jóvenes*
2. *las lecciones fáciles*
3. *los libros difíciles*
4. *las frutas tropicales*
5. *los automóviles españoles*

## Key to Actividades

**A**
1. *American*
2. *comfortable*
3. *delicious*
4. *different*
5. *elegant*
6. *stupid*
7. *excellent*
8. *famous*
9. *horrible*
10. *important*
11. *intelligent*
12. *interesting*
13. *magnificent*
14 *modern*
15. *necessary*
16. *ordinary*
17. *perfect*
18. *popular*
19. *romantic*
20. *tropical*

**B**
1. *americano*
2. *pequeño*
3. *moreno*
4. *inteligente*
5. *popular*
6. *perfecto*

**C**
1. *americano*
2. *pequeño y moreno*
3. *inteligente*
4. *baila*
5. *perfecto*

**D**
1. *americana*
2. *pequeña*
3. *morena*
4. *inteligente*
5. *popular*
6. *perfecta*

**E**
1. *americana*
2. *pequeña y morena*
3. *inteligente*
4. *los deportes*
5. *perfecta*

**F**
1. *rubio*
2. *rica*
3. *viejo*
4. *famosa*
5. *moreno*
6. *flaca*

**G**
1. *rápido*
2. *deliciosa*
3. *romántico*
4. *moderna*
5. *necesario*
6. *magnífica*

**H**
1. *americana*
2. *bonita*
3. *ordinaria*
4. *morena*
5. *feo*
6. *rápido*
7. *vieja*
8. *pequeño*
9. *perfecto*
10. *romántica*

**I**
1. *popular*
2. *grande*
3. *fácil*
4. *interesante*
5. *tropical*

**J**
1. *grande*
2. *bonita*
3. *ricos*
4. *difíciles*
5. *tropicales*
6. *pequeño*
7. *inteligente*
8. *italiano*
9. *perfecta*
10. *importante*

**K**
1. *el animal grande*
2. *el libro importante*
3. *la señora rica*
4. *el hombre viejo*
5. *la alumna popular*
6. *los gatos gordos*
7. *el muchacho pobre*
8. *las mesas pequeñas*
9. *el trabajo fácil*
10. *las muchachas flacas*

**L**
1. *moderna*
2. *elegantes*
3. *difíciles*
4. *rápidos*
5. *viejo*
6. *importante*
7. *pequeñas*
8. *ordinaria*
9. *pobre*
10. *bonitas*

**Información personal** (Sample responses)

1. *Yo soy popular.*
2. *Yo soy inteligente.*
3. *Yo soy rubio.*
4. *Yo soy grande.*
5. *Yo soy flaco.*

**Diálogo**

Buenos días, Señor Ponce.

*Buenos días, Señor Martínez. ¿Cómo está usted?*

Muy bien, gracias. ¿Y usted?

*Así así. ¡Qué muchacho tan magnífico!*

Gracias. Él es tan grande, tan inteligente, tan popular . . .

*Y tan contento.*

Como su padre.

*¡Madre mía!*

# Repaso II (Lecciones 5–8)

## Key to Actividades

**A**

1. *bebo*
2. *come*
3. *leen*
4. *comprende*
5. *corren*
6. *aprende*
7. *vende*
8. *ve*
9. *responde*

**B**

| 9 adjectives | | 4 verbs | 3 nouns | 2 numbers |
|---|---|---|---|---|
| *moderno* | *fácil* | *ver* | *mundo* | *veinte* |
| *gordo* | *pobre* | *correr* | *jardín* | *dos* |
| *rico* | *rubio* | *leer* | *flor* | |
| *bonito* | *americano* | *comer* | | |
| *feo* | | | | |

**C**

**D** 1. *Carmen* 2. *Ramón* 3. *Micaela* 4. *Juanito*

**E** dos = *TRABAJO FÁCIL*
tres = *FORTUNA GRANDE*
cuatro = *UN AUTO MODERNO*
cinco = *CASA BONITA*
seis = *VIDA CONTENTA*
siete = *MUCHOS AMIGOS*

**F** Yo vivo en una *ciudad* grande. En mi ciudad hay *hoteles* modernos, *restaurantes* excelentes, *cines* nuevos y *parques* bonitos. En los parques hay muchas *flores*. Para ir a las secciones diferentes de la *ciudad*, los *muchachos* y las *muchachas*, los *hombres* y las *mujeres* usan varios métodos de transporte. Carmen usa el *tren*, Jorge el *autobús*. Lupita toma un *taxi* y Raúl tiene un *automóvil* pequeño. Juanito y su hermana Lolita van a la *escuela* en *bicicleta*.

**G**
1. *veinte y siete*
2. *veinte y dos, catorce, treinta*
3. *quince*
4. *diez y seis*
5. *cuatro, tres, seis, ocho, cinco, siete*
6. *veinte y uno*

# Tercera Parte

## Lección 9

**Notes:** Ask students to identify the professions of various famous people or to guess a profession being acted out by a student. Using forms of **ser** introduced in this lesson, students may describe themselves, friends, acquaintances, and various professions.

### Optional Oral Exercises

**A.** Express the correct form of the verb **ser** with the subject you hear:

1. usted
2. los muchachos
3. Raúl
4. tú
5. ella
6. ustedes
7. yo
8. Ana
9. nosotros
10. Susana y Carmen

*KEY*

1. *usted es*
2. *los muchachos son*
3. *Raúl es*
4. *tú eres*
5. *ella es*
6. *ustedes son*
7. *yo soy*
8. *Ana es*
9. *nosotros somos*
10. *Susana y Carmen son*

**B.** Make the following sentences negative:

1. Las muchachas son americanas.
2. Usted es abogado.
3. Tú eres rubio.
4. Nosotros somos amigos.
5. Enrique y Marcos son populares.
6. Marta es pequeña.
7. Yo soy dentista.
8. Ellos son cubanos.
9. El perro es inteligente.
10. Ustedes son elegantes.

*KEY*

1. *Las muchachas no son americanas.*
2. *Usted no es abogado.*
3. *Tú no eres rubio.*
4. *Nosotros no somos amigos.*
5. *Enrique y Marcos no son populares.*
6. *Marta no es pequeña.*
7. *Yo no soy dentista.*
8. *Ellos no son cubanos.*
9. *El perro no es inteligente.*
10. *Ustedes no son elegantes.*

**C.** Change the following sentences to questions:

1. Las muchachas son americanas.
2. Usted es abogado.
3. Tú eres rubio.
4. Nosotros somos amigos.
5. Enrique y Marcos son populares.
6. Marta es pequeña.
7. Yo soy dentista.
8. Ellos son cubanos.
9. El perro es inteligente.
10. Ustedes son elegantes.

*KEY*

1. *¿Son las muchachas americanas?*
2. *¿Es usted abogado?*
3. *¿Eres tú rubio?*
4. *¿Somos nosotros amigos?*
5. *¿Son Enrique y Marcos populares?*
6. *¿Es Marta pequeña?*
7. *¿Soy yo dentista?*
8. *¿Son ellos cubanos?*
9. *¿Es el perro inteligente?*
10. *¿Son ustedes elegantes?*

**D.** Directed dialog (See Lesson 5, Optional Oral Exercise D, for procedure.)

Pregúntele a un alumno (una alumna) si él (ella) es

1. tímido (-a)
2. popular
3. romántico (-a)
4. inteligente
5. rico (-a)
6. colombiano (-a)
7. grande
8. joven
9. moreno (-a)
10. perfecto (-a)

*KEY*

| | STUDENT #1 | STUDENT #2 |
|---|---|---|
| 1. | *¿Eres tímido (-a)?* *¿Es usted tímido (-a)?* | *Sí, soy tímido (-a)* |
| 2. | *¿Eres popular?* *¿Es usted popular?* | *Sí, soy popular.* |
| 3. | *¿Eres romántico (-a)?* *¿Es usted romántico (-a)?* | *Sí, soy romántico (-a).* |
| 4. | *¿Eres inteligente?* *¿Es usted inteligente?* | *Sí, soy inteligente.* |
| 5. | *¿Eres rico (-a)?* *¿Es usted rico (-a)?* | *Sí, soy rico (-a).* |
| 6. | *¿Eres colombiano (-a)?* *¿Es usted colombiano (-a)?* | *Sí, soy colombiano.* |
| 7. | *¿Eres grande?* *¿Es usted grande?* | *Sí, soy grande.* |
| 8. | *¿Eres joven?* *¿Es usted joven?* | *Sí, soy joven.* |
| 9. | *¿Eres moreno (-a)?* *¿Es usted moreno (-a)?* | *Sí, soy moreno (-a).* |
| 10. | *¿Eres perfecto (-a)?* *¿Es usted perfecto (-a)?* | *Sí, soy perfecto (-a).* |

NOTE: The procedure for the directed dialog may be extended to negative, plural, and third-person verb forms.

## Key to Actividades

**A**
1. *un médico*
2. *una dentista*
3. *un policía*
4. *una enfermera*
5. *una profesora*
6. *un secretario*
7. *una abogada*
8. *un cartero*

**B** 1. *una secretaria*
2. *un profesor*
3. *una médica*
4. *un dentista*
5. *un abogado*
6. *una policía*

**C** (Sample responses)

NOTE TO TEACHERS: You may wish at this point to have students review the omission of the indefinite article on page 38 of the textbook.

1. ____ *es actriz.*
2. ____ *es enfermera.*
3. ____ *es médico.*
4. ____ *es dentista.*
5. ____ *es cartero.*

**D** 1. *es*
2. *soy*
3. *es*
4. *es*
5. *es*
6. *son*
7. *son*
8. *son*
9. *somos*
10. *es*

**E** 1. *Manuel no es mexicano.*
2. *Yo no soy cartero.*
3. *Ella no es secretaria.*
4. *¿No es Ud. abogado?*
5. *María no es dentista.*
6. *Mis padres no son médicos.*
7. *Ellos no son gordos.*
8. *¿No son Uds. los hermanos de José?*
9. *Nosotros no somos importantes.*
10. *El policía no es joven.*

**F** 1. *Tú eres moreno.*
2. *Ud. es importante.*
3. *Nosotras somos bonitas.*
4. *Amigo es mi perro.*
5. *Ellos son pequeños.*
6. *Ellas son flacas.*
7. *Ella es rica.*
8. *Yo soy inteligente.*

**G** 1. *Juanita Campos es una alumna nueva./ El señor Fernández es el profesor de la clase.*
2. *Cierto.*
3. *Cierto.*
4. *El padre de Juanita trabaja en un garaje. Es mecánico.*

5. *Juanita es colombiana.*
6. *La madre de Juanita trabaja en un hospital.*
7. *Juanita habla español en casa.*
8. *Cierto.*

**H**

1. *Juanita Campos es una alumna nueva./ Juanita Campos es una niña colombiana.*
2. *Juanita habla español.*
3. *Sí, el señor Fernández habla español.*
4. *La madre de Juanita trabaja en un hospital.*
5. *Juanita es colombiana.*

**Preguntas personales** (Sample responses)

1. *Soy muy inteligente.*
2. *Soy grande.*
3. *Soy rubio/rubia.*
4. *Soy flaco/flaca.*

**Información personal** (Sample responses)

1. *Un actor es famoso. Trabaja en el cine o en el teatro.*
2. *Un médico es importante. Trabaja en el hospital.*
3. *Una dentista es necesaria. Es rica.*
4. *Un profesor es inteligente. Trabaja en una escuela.*
5. *Una abogada es importante. Estudia y sabe mucho.*
6. *Una secretaria es necesaria. Trabaja en una oficina.*
7. *Un mecánico es importante. Trabaja en un garaje.*

**Diálogo**

¿Quién es?

*Es mi hermana.*

¿Ella es profesora?

*No, es policía.*

¿Y tu hermano?

*Es actor.*

¿Y tú?

*Yo soy alumno.*

# Lección 10

**Notes:** The techniques used in Lessons 4 and 5 may be applied in this lesson on **-ir** verbs. To stimulate conversation, personalized questions may be extended beyond those provided in the text.

## Key to Structures

**2** . . .

| | |
|---|---|
| yo abr*o* | nosotros / nosotras } abr*imos* |
| tú abr*es* | |
| Ud. abr*e* | Uds. abr*en* |
| él abr*e* | ellos / ellas } abr*en* |
| ella abr*e* | |

## Optional Oral Exercises

**A.** Express the correct verb form with the subject you hear:

1. escribir: los alumnos
2. abrir: él
3. salir: yo
4. cubrir: usted
5. dividir: la niña
6. vivir: ellas
7. recibir: nosotros
8. salir: tú
9. sufrir: ustedes
10. dividir: los amigos

*KEY*

1. *los alumnos escriben*
2. *él abre*
3. *yo salgo*
4. *usted cubre*
5. *la niña divide*
6. *ellas viven*
7. *nosotros recibimos*
8. *tú sales*
9. *ustedes sufren*
10. *los amigos dividen*

**B.** Make the following sentences negative:

1. Alicia vive en España.
2. La secretaria sale de la oficina.
3. Nosotros cubrimos el automóvil.
4. Yo salgo con los amigos.
5. Usted sufre mucho.
6. Rosa y Ana dividen los números por dos.
7. La muchacha cubre la ventana.

8. El profesor abre el libro.
9. Ustedes reciben chocolates.
10. Nosotros escribimos a los abuelos.

*KEY*

1. *Alicia no vive en España.*
2. *La secretaria no sale de la oficina.*
3. *Nosotros no cubrimos el automóvil.*
4. *Yo no salgo con los amigos.*
5. *Usted no sufre mucho.*
6. *Rosa y Ana no dividen los números por dos.*
7. *La muchacha no cubre la ventana.*
8. *El profesor no abre el libro.*
9. *Ustedes no reciben chocolates.*
10. *Nosotros no escribimos a los abuelos.*

**C.** Change the following sentences to questions:

1. Alicia vive en España.
2. La secretaria sale de la oficina.
3. Nosotros cubrimos el automóvil.
4. Yo salgo con los amigos.
5. Usted sufre mucho.
6. Rosa y Ana dividen los números por dos.
7. La muchacha cubre la ventana.
8. El profesor abre el libro.
9. Ustedes reciben chocolates.
10. Nosotros escribimos a los abuelos.

*KEY*

1. *¿Vive Alicia en España?*
2. *¿Sale la secretaria de la oficina?*
3. *¿Cubrimos nosotros el automóvil?*
4. *¿Salgo yo con los amigos?*
5. *¿Sufre usted mucho?*
6. *¿Dividen Rosa y Ana los números por dos?*
7. *¿Cubre la muchacha la ventana?*
8. *¿Abre el profesor el libro?*
9. *¿Reciben ustedes chocolates?*
10. *¿Escribimos nosotros a los abuelos?*

**D.** Directed dialog (See Lesson 5, Optional Oral Exercise D, for procedure.)

Pregúntele a un alumno (una alumna) si él (ella)

1. recibe el periódico
2. abre los libros en casa
3. sale de la escuela ahora
4. escribe a los amigos
5. sufre mucho

*KEY*

| | STUDENT #1 | STUDENT #2 |
|---|---|---|
| 1. | *¿Recibes el periódico?* | *Sí, recibo el periódico.* |
| 2. | *¿Abres los libros en casa?* | *Sí, yo abro los libros en casa.* |
| 3. | *¿Sales de la escuela ahora?* | *No, no salgo de la escuela ahora.* |
| 4. | *¿Escribes a los amigos?* | *Sí, yo escribo a los amigos.* |
| 5. | *¿Sufres mucho?* | *No, no sufro mucho.* |

## Key to Actividades

**A**

| | | | | |
|---|---|---|---|---|
| yo | *cubro* | *divido* | *recibo* | *sufro* |
| tú | *cubres* | *divides* | *recibes* | *sufres* |
| usted | *cubre* | *divide* | *recibe* | *sufre* |
| él | *cubre* | *divide* | *recibe* | *sufre* |
| ella | *cubre* | *divide* | *recibe* | *sufre* |
| nosotros | *cubrimos* | *dividimos* | *recibimos* | *sufrimos* |
| ustedes | *cubren* | *dividen* | *reciben* | *sufren* |
| ellos | *cubren* | *dividen* | *reciben* | *sufren* |
| ellas | *cubren* | *dividen* | *reciben* | *sufren* |

**B**

1. *Tú vives con tu familia.*
2. *Ellas sufren mucho.*
3. *Ud. cubre la mesa.*
4. *Yo recibo una bicicleta.*
5. *Él abre la ventana.*
6. *Nosotros dividimos las frutas.*

**C**

1. *j*
2. *i*
3. *b*
4. *g*
5. *k*
6. *l*
7. *o*
8. *n*
9. *d*
10. *m*
11. *f*
12. *h*
13. *e*
14. *a*
15. *c*

**D**

1. *salen. They are leaving (They leave) tomorrow.*
2. *salgo de. I'm leaving the class.*
3. *sale. She is going out (goes out) with her dog.*

4. *sales de. When do you leave (are you leaving) the house?*
5. *salen. Are you going out now? (Are you leaving now?)*
6. *salimos. We are leaving (we leave) (we are going out) today.*
7. *sale de. You aren't leaving (you don't leave) the house.*

**E** 1. *a* 2. *a* 3. *c* 4. *a* 5. *a* 6. *b* 7. *a* 8. *c* 9. *c* 10. *a*

**F** 1. *salgo* 2. *saben* 3. *son* 4. *visito* 5. *responde* 6. *reciben* 7. *bebes* 8. *abre* 9. *vivimos* 10. *deseo*

**G**

| -ar verbs | -er verbs | -ir verbs |
|---|---|---|
| *comprar* | *comer* | *vivir* |
| *visitar* | *beber* | |
| *trabajar* | *comprender* | |

**H** 1. (d) *amigas* 2. (c) *vive en* 3. (d) *nuevo* 4. (a) *dos* 5. (c) *el hospital* 6. (a) *hermanas* 7. (b) *una oficina* 8. (d) *come* 9. (d) *médico* 10. (b) *radios*

**I** La familia de Paco *vive* bien. Ellos *viven* en una casa *magnífica*. Hay dos *hermanas*: Carmen y Rosa. Una es *enfermera* y la otra es *secretaria*. Ellas siempre *compran* ropa *bonita*. La familia *come* y *bebe* bien. Siempre hay mucha *comida* en la *mesa*. El padre *trabaja* en un *supermercado*.

**Diálogo**

Hola, Manuel. ¿Cómo estás?

*Sufro mucho.*

¿Por qué?

*Tengo mucho trabajo.*

¿Qué haces?

*Escribo una historia.*

Es fácil. ¿Sabes tú cosas de toda la familia?

*¡Claro que sí! Pero hay ocho personas.*

**Información personal** (Sample responses)

1. *José/Susana*
2. *americano/americana*
3. *en la ciudad de*
4. *nuevo/viejo/grande*
5. *un hermano y dos hermanas*
6. *David, Ana y Luisa*
7. *bonita/fea*
8. *mecánico/médico*
9. *cinco/seis*
10. *moderna/interesante*

# Lección 11

**Notes:** We suggest that the teachers act out (or have students act out)—even to the point of exaggeration—various states of being, conditions, or situations to help students learn and practice the uses of **estar** and **ser.** Apply the vocabulary learned through Lesson 10.

Practice in forms of **estar** and **ser** may involve first-person statements **(Ahora yo estoy triste. Nosotros somos ricos.)**; second-person questions, with answers (**¿Estás contenta? — Sí, estoy contenta. ¿Es Ud. profesora? — No, soy estudiante.**); and third-person descriptions (**El café está frío. Las muchachas son gordas.**).

## Optional Oral Exercises

**A.** Express the correct form of the verb **estar** with the subject you hear:

1. el padre
2. nosotros
3. Carmen y Alicia
4. yo
5. ellos
6. ustedes
7. la señora
8. tú
9. Juan
10. usted

*KEY*

1. *el padre está*
2. *nosotros estamos*
3. *Carmen y Alicia están*
4. *yo estoy*
5. *ellos están*
6. *ustedes están*
7. *la señora está*
8. *tú estás*
9. *Juan está*
10. *usted está*

**B.** Make the following sentences negative:

1. Yo estoy triste.
2. Usted está cansado.
3. El restaurante está abierto.
4. Ellas están en Puerto Rico.
5. La abuela está enferma.
6. Ustedes están en la clase.
7. Tú estás muy bien.
8. Nosotros estamos sentados.
9. El café está muy caliente.
10. Ella está en la oficina.

*KEY*

1. *Yo no estoy triste.*
2. *Usted no está cansado.*
3. *El restaurante no está abierto.*
4. *Ellas no están en Puerto Rico.*
5. *La abuela no está enferma.*
6. *Ustedes no están en la clase.*
7. *Tú no estás muy bien.*
8. *Nosotros no estamos sentados.*
9. *El café no está muy caliente.*
10. *Ella no está en la oficina.*

**C.** Change the following sentences to questions:

1. Yo estoy triste.
2. Usted está cansado.
3. El restaurante está abierto.
4. Ellas están en Puerto Rico.
5. La abuela está enferma.
6. Ustedes están en la clase.
7. Tú estás muy bien.
8. Nosotros estamos sentados.
9. El café está muy caliente.
10. Ella está en la oficina.

*KEY*

1. *¿Estoy yo triste?*
2. *¿Está usted cansado?*
3. *¿Está el restaurante abierto?*
4. *¿Están ellas en Puerto Rico?*
5. *¿Está la abuela enferma?*
6. *¿Están ustedes en la clase?*
7. *¿Estás tú muy bien?*
8. *¿Estamos nosotros sentados?*
9. *¿Está el café muy caliente?*
10. *¿Está ella en la oficina?*

**D.** Directed dialog (See Lesson 5, Optional Oral Exercise D, for procedure.)

Pregúntele a un alumno (una alumna) si

1. está bien.
2. la ventana está abierta.
3. la profesora está en la clase.
4. está contento (-a).
5. está sentado (-a).
6. está enfermo (-a).
7. está en Canadá.
8. la profesora está sentada.
9. está cansado (-a).
10. está en la clase de español.

*KEY*

| | STUDENT #1 | STUDENT #2 |
|---|---|---|
| 1. | *¿Estás bien? / ¿Está Ud. bien?* | *Sí, estoy bien.* |
| 2. | *¿Está la ventana abierta?* | *No, la ventana no está abierta.* |
| 3. | *¿Está la profesora en la clase?* | *Sí, la profesora está en la clase.* |
| 4. | *¿Estás contento (-a)?* | *Sí, estoy contento (-a).* |
| 5. | *¿Estás sentado (-a)?* | *Sí, estoy sentado (-a).* |
| 6. | *¿Estás enfermo (-a)?* | *No, no estoy enfermo (-a).* |
| 7. | *¿Estás en Canadá?* | *No, no estoy en Canadá.* |
| 8. | *¿Está la profesora sentada?* | *Sí, la profesora está sentada.* |
| 9. | *¿Estás cansado (-a)?* | *No, no estoy cansado (-a).* |
| 10. | *¿Estás en la clase de español?* | *Sí, estoy en la clase de español.* |

# *Buenos días*

(To the melody of "Frère Jacques")

The singers can be divided into four groups. The first group begins at 1; the second begins with "Buenos días" when the first group is at 2; the third group begins at 1 when the first group is at 3, and the fourth begins when the first group is at 4. Each group stops after singing the entire canon twice.

## Key to Actividades

**A**

1. *están (location)*
2. *está (health)*
3. *estamos (temporary condition)*
4. *está (health)*
5. *están (health)*
6. *está (location)*
7. *está (temporary condition)*
8. *están (temporary condition)*
9. *estoy (temporary condition)*
10. *está (health)*

**B**

1. *El médico está en el hospital.*
2. *Ellas son abogadas.*
3. *Mi abuelo es carpintero.*
4. *El agua está caliente.*
5. *Nosotros somos americanos.*
6. *¿Es María gorda?*

**C**

1. *está*
2. *soy*
3. *es*
4. *está*
5. *están*
6. *son*
7. *es*
8. *estamos*
9. *es*
10. *son*

**D**

1. *está*
2. *casa, enferma*
3. *sufre*
4. *médico*
5. *está*
6. *es*
7. *estás, estás*
8. *es*
9. *hay*
10. *está*

**Preguntas personales** (Sample responses)

1. *Sí, estoy contento (contenta) cuando hay clases.*
2. *No, yo no sufro en la clase de español.*
3. *No, no deseo mirar la televisión todo el día.*
4. *Sí, soy joven y guapo (bonita).*

**Información personal** (Sample responses)

1. *Sí*
2. *Sí*
3. *No*
4. *No*
5. *No*
6. *No*
7. *No*
8. *No*
9. *Sí*
10. *Sí*

**Diálogo**

¿Cómo *estás*, niña?

Estoy *enferma.*

¿Qué *pasa?*

No deseo *comer.*

Tienes *un resfriado.*

¿Necesito *una medicina?*

No, pero no vas *a la escuela mañana.*

*Muchas gracias*, doctora.

# Lección 12

**Notes:** This lesson dealing with "how to tell time" has been organized in such a way that teachers can progress as quickly or as slowly as class readiness requires. The basic clock patterns are presented one at a time, along with separate sets of **actividades.** A large model clock may be useful for audiolingual practice. Personalized conversation may be encouraged by having students pass the clock around while they ask each other when they perform certain activities.

## Key to Structures

**1** . . .
7:00 *Son las siete* .
8:00 *Son las ocho* .
9:00 *Son las nueve* .
10:00 *Son las diez* .
11:00 *Son las once* .
12:00 *Son las doce* .

**2** How do you say "What time is it?" in Spanish? *¿Qué hora es?* . What are the words for "it is" when saying "it is one o'clock"? *Es la* . What are the words for "it is" when saying any other hour? *Son las* . How do you say "It is noon"? *Es mediodía* . How do you say "It is midnight?" *Es medianoche* .

**3** . . .
5:05 *Son las cinco y cinco* .
6:05 *Son las seis y cinco* .
7:05 *Son las siete y cinco* .
8:05 *Son las ocho y cinco* .

**4** . . .
7:10 *Son las siete y diez.*
8:10 *Son las ocho y diez.*
10:20 *Son las diez y veinte.*
1:25 *Es la una y veinte y cinco.*

How do you express time after the hour? *We use y and add the minutes.*

. . .
3:06 *Son las tres y seis.*
4:13 *Son las cuatro y trece.*
5:22 *Son las cinco y veinte y dos.*

**5** . . . 4:55 *Son las cinco menos cinco.*
5:55 *Son las seis menos cinco.*
6:55 *Son las siete menos cinco.*

**6** . . . 6:50 *Son las siete menos diez.*
12:35 *Es la una menos veinte y cinco.*

How do you express time before the hour? *We use menos and subtract the minutes from the next hour.*

. . . 7:44 *Son las ocho menos diez y seis.*
8:51 *Son las nueve menos nueve.*

**7** . . . 5:15 *Son las cinco y cuarto.*
6:15 *Son las seis y cuarto.*
7:15 *Son las siete y cuarto.*
8:15 *Son las ocho y cuarto.*
4:45 *Son las cinco menos cuarto.*
5:45 *Son las seis menos cuarto.*
6:45 *Son las siete menos cuarto.*
7:45 *Son las ocho menos cuarto.*

What is the special word for "a quarter"? *cuarto* . How do you say "a quarter after"? *y cuarto* . How do you say " a quarter before"? *menos cuarto* .

**8** . . . 5:30 *Son las cinco y media.*
6:30 *Son las seis y media.*
7:30 *Son las siete y media.*
8:30 *Son las ocho y media.*

What is the special word for "half past"? *media* . How do you express "half past the hour"? *y media* .

**9** . . . If you want to express "at" a certain time, which Spanish word must you use before the time? *a* .

**10** . . . How do you express "in the morning" or "A.M." in Spanish? *de la mañana* . How do you express "in the afternoon" or "P.M."? *de la tarde* . How do you express "in the evening" or "P.M"? *de la noche* .

## Optional Oral Exercises

**A.** Give these times in Spanish: (Teacher may give the times in English or display them on a clock.)

1. 3:05
2. 6:35
3. 9:20
4. 4:45
5. 7:30
6. 10:50
7. 2:10
8. 5:15
9. 11:55
10. 1:40
11. 12:25
12. 9:55

*KEY*

1. *Son las tres y cinco.*
2. *Son las siete menos veinte y cinco.*
3. *Son las nueve y veinte.*
4. *Son las cinco menos cuarto.*
5. *Son las siete y media.*
6. *Son las once menos diez.*
7. *Son las dos y diez.*
8. *Son las cinco y cuarto.*
9. *Son las doce menos cinco.*
10. *Son las dos menos veinte.*
11. *Son las doce y veinte y cinco.*
12. *Son las diez menos cinco.*

**B.** Write the time you hear:

1. Son las seis menos cuarto.
2. Son las diez y veinte y cinco.
3. Son las doce y media.
4. Son las ocho menos veinte.
5. Son las tres y diez.
6. Son las nueve menos cinco.
7. Son las cuatro y cuarto.
8. Son las dos y veinte.
9. Son las cinco menos diez.
10. Es la una y cinco.
11. Son las siete menos veinte.
12. Es mediodía.

*KEY*

1. *5:45*
2. *10:25*
3. *12:30*
4. *7:40*
5. *3:10*
6. *8:55*
7. *4:15*
8. *2:20*
9. *4:50*
10. *1:05*
11. *6:40*
12. *12:00*

## Key to Actividades

**A**

1. *1:45*
2. *7:30*
3. *11:10*
4. *12:15*
5. *1:15*
6. *9:20*
7. *2:50*
8. *4:35*
9. *10:13*
10. *3:31*

**B**

1. *Son las tres y veinte.*
2. *Son las diez menos cinco.*
3. *Son las cuatro y media.*
4. *Son las once menos cuarto.*
5. *Son las siete menos veinte y cinco.*
6. *Son las dos y veinte y cinco.*
7. *Son las dos menos diez.*
8. *Es la una menos veinte.*
9. *Son las cinco y diez y seis.*
10. *Son las nueve menos diez y ocho.*

**C**

1. *Son las tres menos diez.*
2. *Es la una y diez.*
3. *Son las diez menos veinte y cinco.*
4. *Son las seis y veinte.*
5. *Son las cuatro y cuarto.*
6. *Son las siete y veinte y cinco.*
7. *Son las once menos cuarto.*
8. *Son las tres y cinco.*
9. *Son las doce y media.*
10. *Son las seis menos veinte.*

**D**

**E** 1. *Son las siete menos veinte y cinco de la noche.*
2. *Son las dos y cuarto de la mañana.*
3. *Son las cuatro menos cuarto de la tarde.*
4. *Son las ocho menos cinco de la mañana.*
5. *Son las diez y veinte y cinco de la noche.*
6. *Son las cinco y diez de la tarde.*

**F**

1. *b*
2. *c*
3. *a*
4. *c*
5. *a*
6. *b*
7. *c*
8. *b*
9. *c*
10. *a*

**G** 1. *Francisco habla con Pepe y Rosita.*
2. *En el reloj de Pepe son las nueve y media.*
3. *Es imposible. En mi reloj son las diez.*
4. *Francisco tiene un examen en la clase de inglés.*
5. *El señor López está ausente.*

**Información personal** (Sample responses)

1. *las ocho de la mañana.*
2. *las dos menos cinco de la tarde.*
3. *las siete de la noche.*
4. *las ocho de la noche.*
5. *las seis y media de la tarde.*

**Diálogo**

¿Qué *hora* es?

Son *las cuatro y cuarto*. ¿Por qué?

Hay un *programa* importante en la *televisión* a las seis.

*¿Qué* programa?

Una *película* cómica.

*¿Cómo* se llama la película?

La *sorpresa* de Drácula.

Deseo *ver* la película *también*.

# Repaso III (Lecciones 9–12)

**Key to Actividades**

**A**

Solution: D E N T I S T A

**B**

1. *salen*
2. *recibe*
3. *abre*
4. *cubrimos*
5. *vives*
6. *escribe*
7. *dividen*
8. *sufro*

**C** 1. S E **C** R E T A R I A
2. M U C **H** A C H A
3. P **O** L I C Í A
4. A **C** T O R
5. A B **O** G A D O
6. F A M I **L** I A
7. M E S **A**
8. F I E S **T** A
9. B A R B **E** R O

**D** *Soledad, vamos al parque mañana a las tres de la tarde. Carlos.*

**E**

| Adjectives | Verbs |
|---|---|
| *inteligente* | *beber* |
| *moderno* | *cubrir* |
| *excelente* | *ver* |
| *delicioso* | *vender* |
| *fácil* | *sufrir* |
| *estúpido* | *leer* |
| *rico* | *salir* |
| *bonito* | |
| *perfecto* | |
| *interesante* | |
| *elegante* | |
| *feo* | |

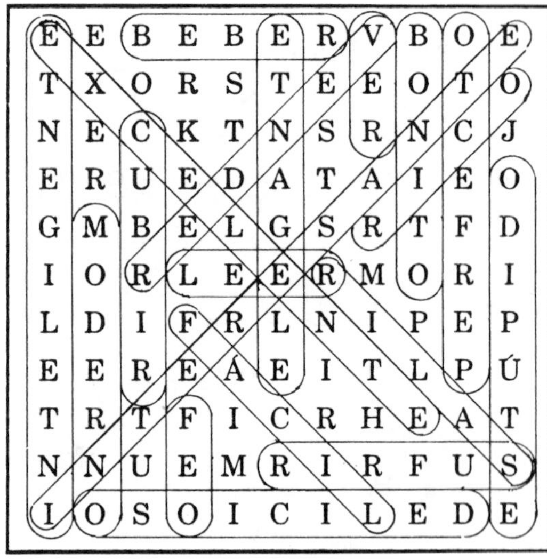

**F**
1. *Ella es abogada.*
2. *Ellos están enfermos.*
3. *Él está cansado.*
4. *Ellos son policías.*
5. *Ella es profesora.*
6. *Él está triste.*
7. *La puerta está abierta.*
8. *Ellos son jóvenes.*
9. *Ellos son ricos.*
10. *Ellos están en el parque.*

**G** El señor Fernández es *profesor* en una *escuela* moderna. Es el primer día de clases. Una *niña* de diez años entra en la *clase*. Ella está muy *triste*; no está *contenta*. «¿Cómo te llamas?», pregunta el *profesor*. «Me llamo Juanita», contesta la *niña*. «¿Habla Ud. español?» «Sí, todos los *niños/muchachos* y las *niñas/muchachas* de la clase hablan español.» Ahora Juanita está *contenta*. «¿Qué hace tu padre?», pregunta el *profesor*. «Mi padre es *mecánico* y mi madre es *enfermera*. Ella trabaja en un *hospital*.» «Vas a aprender mucho en la *clase*.» «Gracias, señor profesor.»

## Achievement Test I (Lessons 1–12)

**1**

1. *la rosa, la flor*
2. *el lápiz*
3. *el gato*
4. *los padres*
5. *la escuela*
6. *el dinero*
7. *la bicicleta*
8. *la casa*
9. *la puerta*
10. *el perro*

**2**

1. *Cierto.*
2. *El elefante es un animal grande.*
3. *El médico trabaja en un hospital.*
4. *Los gatos son inteligentes.*
5. *Comemos las bananas.*

**3**

| | el | la | los | las |
|---|---|---|---|---|
| 1. automóvil | ✓ | | | |
| 2. televisiones | | | | ✓ |
| 3. trenes | | | ✓ | |
| 4. lección | | ✓ | | |
| 5. doctor | ✓ | | | |

**4**

| | un | una |
|---|---|---|
| 1. hijo | ✓ | |
| 2. periódico | ✓ | |
| 3. fruta | | ✓ |
| 4. actriz | | ✓ |
| 5. tienda | | ✓ |

**5**

1. trece *13*
2. veinte y seis *26*
3. cuatro *4*
4. veinte y uno *21*
5. diez y siete *17*
6. doce *12*
7. diez y nueve *19*
8. catorce *14*
9. veinte y dos *22*
10. once *11*

**6**

| | tú | usted |
|---|---|---|
| 1. el profesor López | | ✓ |
| 2. Silvia | ✓ | |
| 3. la señora Campos | | ✓ |
| 4. un hermano | ✓ | |
| 5. el doctor Gómez | | ✓ |

**7**

1. *Son las cinco y veinte.*
2. *Son las nueve menos cinco.*
3. *Son las cuatro y diez.*
4. *Son las ocho menos cuarto.*
5. *Son las once y media.*
6. *Son las tres menos diez.*
7. *Son las seis y veinte y cinco.*
8. *Son las dos y cinco.*
9. *Son las siete menos veinte.*
10. *Son las diez menos veinte y cinco.*

**8**

1. *moderna*
2. *nuevo*
3. *gordos*
4. *bonitas*
5. *rubia*
6. *inteligentes*
7. *pequeñas*
8. *española*
9. *fea*
10. *rico*

**9**

1. *compro*
2. *lee*
3. *abres*
4. *aprende*
5. *bailamos*
6. *recibe*
7. *cubre*
8. *contesta*
9. *ve*
10. *miramos*

**10**

1. *La enfermera no trabaja mucho.*
2. *Los niños no pasan.*
3. *Tú no hablas bien.*
4. *Ella no escucha la música.*
5. *Ellos no miran la lección.*

**11**

6. *¿Comprende Ud. español?*
7. *¿Bailan ustedes bien?*
8. *¿Como yo?*
9. *¿Estudias tú mucho?*
10. *¿Aprende la mujer?*

**12**

1. *está*
2. *estamos*
3. *es*
4. *está*
5. *son*
6. *es*
7. *está*
8. *soy*
9. *está*
10. *están*

**13** 1. *(a)* 2. *(b)* 3. *(b)* 4. *(a)* 5. *(d)*

**14** 1. *(b)* 2. *(c)* 3. *(d)* 4. *(a)* 5. *(b)*

# Cuarta Parte

## Lección 13

**Notes:** A game of "Simon says," or a funny Halloween movable scarecrow or similar figure may help students learn and practice the parts of the body.

To practice forms of **tener,** students may talk about the things they possess, using vocabulary from this and earlier lessons.

### Optional Oral Exercises

**A. ¿Qué es esto?** (Teacher points to parts of the body indicated in the Key.)

*KEY*

1. *Es la mano.*
2. *Es la cabeza.*
3. *Es la boca.*
4. *Es la nariz.*
5. *Son los ojos.*
6. *Es la pierna.*
7. *Es el pie.*
8. *Es la cara.*

**B.** Express the correct form of the verb **tener** with the subject you hear:

1. usted
2. yo
3. los padres
4. tú
5. Roberto
6. ustedes
7. nosotros
8. María y Víctor
9. ella
10. ellas

*KEY*

1. *usted tiene*
2. *yo tengo*
3. *los padres tienen*
4. *tú tienes*
5. *Roberto tiene*
6. *ustedes tienen*
7. *nosotros tenemos*
8. *María y Víctor tienen*
9. *ella tiene*
10. *ellas tienen*

**C.** Make the following sentences negative:

1. Él tiene el cuaderno.
2. Nosotros tenemos los papeles.

3. Ellas tienen el pelo rubio.
4. Yo tengo la nariz grande.
5. Usted tiene un hermano.
6. Vicente tiene los ojos bonitos.
7. José y Ana tienen hambre.
8. El perro tiene sed.
9. Ustedes tienen quince años.
10. Tú tienes un examen hoy.

*KEY*

1. *Él no tiene el cuaderno.*
2. *Nosotros no tenemos los papeles.*
3. *Ellas no tienen el pelo rubio.*
4. *Yo no tengo la nariz grande.*
5. *Usted no tiene un hermano.*
6. *Vicente no tiene los ojos bonitos.*
7. *José y Ana no tienen hambre.*
8. *El perro no tiene sed.*
9. *Ustedes no tienen quince años.*
10. *Tú no tienes un examen hoy.*

**D.** Change the following sentences to questions:

1. Él tiene el cuaderno.
2. Nosotros tenemos los papeles.
3. Ellas tienen el pelo rubio.
4. Yo tengo la nariz grande.
5. Usted tiene un hermano.
6. Vicente tiene los ojos bonitos.
7. José y Ana tienen hambre.
8. El perro tiene sed.
9. Ustedes tienen quince años.
10. Tú tienes un examen hoy.

*KEY*

1. *¿Tiene él el cuaderno?*
2. *¿Tenemos nosotros los papeles?*
3. *¿Tienen ellas el pelo rubio?*
4. *¿Tengo yo la nariz grande?*

5. *¿Tiene usted un hermano?*
6. *¿Tiene Vicente los ojos bonitos?*
7. *¿Tienen José y Ana hambre?*
8. *¿Tiene el perro sed?*
9. *¿Tienen ustedes quince años?*
10. *¿Tienes tú un examen hoy?*

**E.** Directed dialog (See Lesson 5, Optional Oral Exercise D, for procedure.)

Pregúntele a un alumno (una alumna, unos alumnos, unas alumnas) si él (ella, ellos, ellas) tiene(n)

1. hambre
2. sed
3. sueño
4. calor
5. frío

*KEY*

| STUDENT #1 | STUDENT #2 |
|---|---|
| 1. *¿Tienes hambre?* / *¿Tiene usted hambre?* | *Sí, tengo hambre.* |
| *¿Tienen ustedes hambre?* | *Sí, tenemos hambre.* |
| 2. *¿Tienes sed?* / *¿Tiene usted sed?* | *Sí, tengo sed.* |
| *¿Tienen ustedes sed?* | *Sí, tenemos sed.* |
| 3. *¿Tienes sueño?* / *¿Tiene usted sueño?* | *Sí, tengo sueño.* |
| *¿Tienen ustedes sueño?* | *Sí, tenemos sueño.* |
| 4. *¿Tienes calor?* / *¿Tiene usted calor?* | *No, no tengo calor.* |
| *¿Tienen ustedes calor?* | *No, no tenemos calor.* |
| 5. *¿Tienes frío?* / *¿Tiene usted frío?* | *No, no tengo frío.* |
| *¿Tienen ustedes frío?* | *No, no tenemos frío.* |

## Key to Actividades

**A**
1. *la mano*
2. *la oreja*
3. *la boca*
4. *los ojos*
5. *la cara*
6. *la cabeza*
7. *la nariz*
8. *el brazo*
9. *el pelo*
10. *el pie*
11. *la pierna*
12. *el dedo*

**B**
1. *la cabeza*
2. *la nariz*
3. *la boca*
4. *los ojos*
5. *la oreja*
6. *la cara*

**C**
1. *el pelo*
2. *la pierna*
3. *el brazo*
4. *la mano*
5. *el dedo*
6. *el pie*

**D**
1. *mirar*
2. *correr, bailar*
3. *trabajar*
4. *hablar*
5. *bailar, correr*
6. *escuchar*
7. *escribir*

**E**
1. *Es un laboratorio en el pueblo de Transformia.*
2. *Todos los habitantes están tristes.*
3. *El león, Feroz, no puede combatir más al dictador.*
4. *Carlota tiene una idea fantástica.*
5. *Cierto.*
6. *Autómata es capaz de destruir a Decepcionador.*
7. *Autómata quiere hablar.*
8. *Autómata se parece a ____.*

**F**

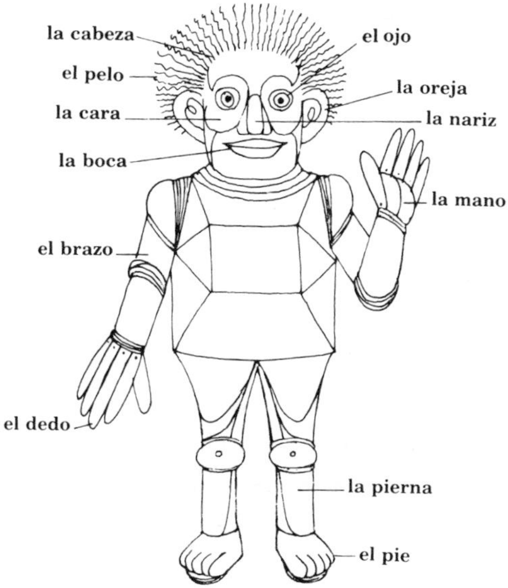

la cabeza
el ojo
el pelo
la oreja
la cara
la nariz
la boca
la mano
el brazo
el dedo
la pierna
el pie

**G**
1. *nosotros*
2. *ustedes/ellos/ellas*
3. *yo*
4. *usted/él/ella*
5. *tú*

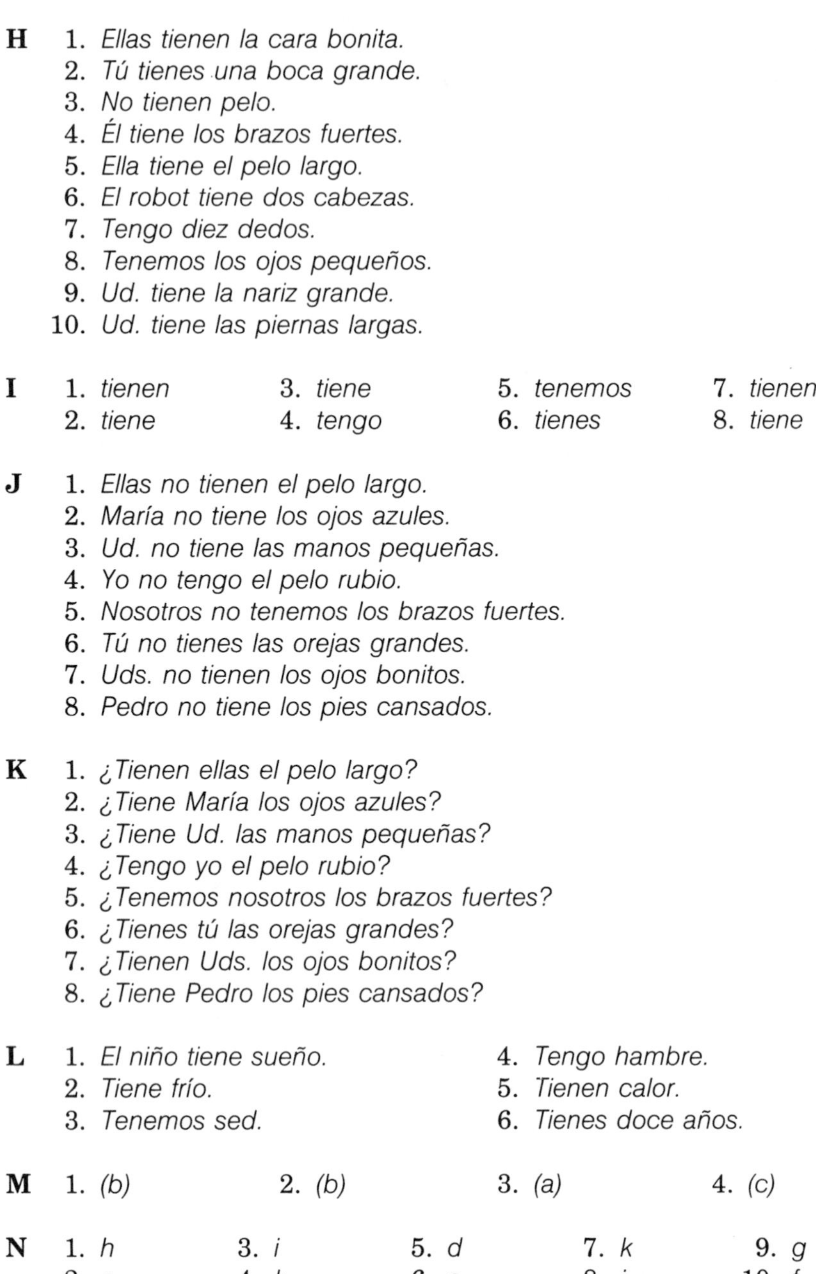

**H**
1. *Ellas tienen la cara bonita.*
2. *Tú tienes una boca grande.*
3. *No tienen pelo.*
4. *Él tiene los brazos fuertes.*
5. *Ella tiene el pelo largo.*
6. *El robot tiene dos cabezas.*
7. *Tengo diez dedos.*
8. *Tenemos los ojos pequeños.*
9. *Ud. tiene la nariz grande.*
10. *Ud. tiene las piernas largas.*

**I**
1. *tienen*
2. *tiene*
3. *tiene*
4. *tengo*
5. *tenemos*
6. *tienes*
7. *tienen*
8. *tiene*

**J**
1. *Ellas no tienen el pelo largo.*
2. *María no tiene los ojos azules.*
3. *Ud. no tiene las manos pequeñas.*
4. *Yo no tengo el pelo rubio.*
5. *Nosotros no tenemos los brazos fuertes.*
6. *Tú no tienes las orejas grandes.*
7. *Uds. no tienen los ojos bonitos.*
8. *Pedro no tiene los pies cansados.*

**K**
1. *¿Tienen ellas el pelo largo?*
2. *¿Tiene María los ojos azules?*
3. *¿Tiene Ud. las manos pequeñas?*
4. *¿Tengo yo el pelo rubio?*
5. *¿Tenemos nosotros los brazos fuertes?*
6. *¿Tienes tú las orejas grandes?*
7. *¿Tienen Uds. los ojos bonitos?*
8. *¿Tiene Pedro los pies cansados?*

**L**
1. *El niño tiene sueño.*
2. *Tiene frío.*
3. *Tenemos sed.*
4. *Tengo hambre.*
5. *Tienen calor.*
6. *Tienes doce años.*

**M**
1. *(b)*
2. *(b)*
3. *(a)*
4. *(c)*

**N**
1. *h*
2. *a*
3. *i*
4. *b*
5. *d*
6. *c*
7. *k*
8. *j*
9. *g*
10. *f*

**O**
1. *Tengo hambre.*
2. *Tú tienes sueño.*
3. *Ellos (Ellas) tienen frío.*
4. *Tenemos razón.*
5. *Usted tiene sed.*

**Diálogo**

1. *Tengo dolor de garganta.*
2. *Tengo dolor de piernas.*
3. *Tengo dolor de cabeza.*
4. *Tengo dolor de brazos.*
5. *Tengo dolor de oído.*

**Preguntas personales** (Sample responses)

1. *Tengo catorce años.*
2. *Sí, tengo hambre.*
3. *No, no tengo siempre razón.*
4. *Tengo sueño a las once de la noche.*

**Información personal** (Sample responses)

1. *El robot tiene los brazos largos.*
2. *Él no tiene pelo.*
3. *Él es inteligente y habla español.*

# Lección 14

**Notes:** Use the calendar and weather scenes to practice the days, months, and seasons. These topics lend themselves to extended personalized conversation about which days, months, and seasons students prefer and why.

In this context, students should not be expected to use expressions with the verb **hacer,** which will be presented later, in Lesson 19. The conversations on pages 254–255 and 261–262 in the text and the accompanying **actividades,** along with the personalized practice on pages 256, 263, and 268, provide sufficient models for oral expression.

### Key to Structures

**6** **. . .** Can you fill in the blanks? To express the date, use: **Es** + *el* + *number* + *de* + *month*. **. . .** To express the date when speaking of the first day of the month use: **Es** + *el* + *primero* + *de* + *month*. If you want to include the day of the week: **Es lunes, el tres de mayo: Es** + *day*, + *el* + *number* + *de* + *month*.

## Optional Oral Exercises

**A.** Give the day that comes before the day you hear:

1. domingo
2. viernes
3. sábado
4. martes
5. jueves
6. lunes
7. miércoles

*KEY*

1. *sábado*
2. *jueves*
3. *viernes*
4. *lunes*
5. *miércoles*
6. *domingo*
7. *martes*

**B.** Give the day that comes after the day you hear:

1. viernes
2. sábado
3. martes
4. domingo
5. lunes
6. miércoles
7. jueves

*KEY*

1. *sábado*
2. *domingo*
3. *miércoles*
4. *lunes*
5. *martes*
6. *jueves*
7. *viernes*

**C.** Give the month that comes before the month you hear:

1. mayo
2. noviembre
3. agosto
4. junio
5. febrero
6. octubre
7. julio
8. septiembre
9. enero
10. marzo
11. diciembre
12. abril

*KEY*

1. *abril*
2. *octubre*
3. *julio*
4. *mayo*
5. *enero*
6. *septiembre*
7. *junio*
8. *agosto*
9. *diciembre*
10. *febrero*
11. *noviembre*
12. *marzo*

**D.** Give the month that comes after the month you hear:

1. mayo
2. agosto
3. febrero
4. octubre
5. junio
6. noviembre
7. enero
8. septiembre
9. abril
10. diciembre
11. marzo
12. julio

*KEY*

1. *junio*
2. *septiembre*
3. *marzo*
4. *noviembre*
5. *julio*
6. *diciembre*
7. *febrero*
8. *octubre*
9. *mayo*
10. *enero*
11. *abril*
12. *agosto*

**E** **¿Cuál es la fecha de hoy?** (Give the date in English or point to the date on a calendar):

1. Friday, May 5
2. Thursday, April 22
3. Tuesday, July 30
4. Saturday, January 12
5. Sunday, March 1
6. Monday, August 16
7. Wednesday, June 11

*KEY*

1. *Hoy es viernes, el cinco de mayo.*
2. *Hoy es jueves, el veinte y dos de abril.*
3. *Hoy es martes, el treinta de julio.*
4. *Hoy es sábado, el doce de enero.*
5. *Hoy es domingo, el primero de marzo.*
6. *Hoy es lunes, el diez y seis de agosto.*
7. *Hoy es miércoles, el once de junio.*

**F.** Give the seasons for these months:

1. marzo
2. octubre
3. agosto
4. enero
5. septiembre
6. mayo
7. diciembre
8. junio
9. febrero
10. abril
11. noviembre
12. julio

*KEY*

1. *la primavera*
2. *el otoño*
3. *el verano*
4. *el invierno*
5. *el otoño*
6. *la primavera*
7. *el invierno*
8. *el verano*
9. *el invierno*
10. *la primavera*
11. *el otoño*
12. *el verano*

## Key to Actividades

**A**

1. *domingo*
2. *jueves*
3. *sábado*
4. *martes*
5. *miércoles*
6. *viernes*
7. *lunes*

**B** 1. *lunes / miércoles* 2. *miércoles / viernes* 3. *viernes / domingo* 4. *domingo / martes*

**C** 1. *d* 2. *e* 3. *f* 4. *a* 5. *b* 6. *c*

**D**
1. *Tiene un match de tenis con un amigo.*
2. *Está siempre contenta.*
3. *Tiene una clase especial después de las clases en la escuela.*
4. *Ve una película con las amigas.*
5. *Quiere dormir.*
6. *Mira el fútbol en la televisión.*

**E** (Sample response)

*El sábado. Salgo con los amigos al cine.*

**F**
1. *septiembre*
2. *mayo*
3. *diciembre*
4. *junio/julio*
5. *noviembre*
6. *marzo*
7. *julio/junio*
8. *abril*
9. *febrero*
10. *agosto*
11. *octubre*
12. *enero*

**G**
1. *julio / septiembre*
2. *octubre / diciembre*
3. *enero / marzo*
4. *abril / junio*
5. *agosto / octubre*
6. *noviembre / enero*
7. *febrero / abril*
8. *mayo / julio*

**H**

| la primavera | el verano | el otoño | el invierno |
|---|---|---|---|
| *marzo* | *junio* | *septiembre* | *diciembre* |
| *abril* | *julio* | *octubre* | *enero* |
| *mayo* | *agosto* | *noviembre* | *febrero* |

**I** 1. *el otoño* 2. *la primavera* 3. *el verano* 4. *el invierno*

**J**
1. *f*
2. *h*
3. *d*
4. *c*
5. *g*
6. *b*
7. *a*
8. *e*

**K**
1. *En mayo me gustan las flores bonitas.*
2. *En julio y agosto me gustan las vacaciones.*
3. *En diciembre me gusta la Navidad.*
4. *En julio quiero ir a la playa.*

5. *En octubre quiero jugar al fútbol.*
6. *En septiembre me gustan mis clases en la escuela.*
7. *En enero quiero esquiar.*
8. *En abril quiero ir al parque.*

**L** (Sample responses)

*El verano. Me gusta ir a la playa.*
*Julio y agosto. Me gustan las vacaciones.*

**M**

| | | |
|---|---|---|
| 1. *la primavera* | 5. *la primavera* | 9. *la primavera* |
| 2. *el verano* | 6. *el verano* | 10. *el verano* |
| 3. *el invierno* | 7. *el otoño* | 11. *el otoño* |
| 4. *el otoño* | 8. *el invierno* | 12. *el invierno* |

**N**

1. *Es el cuatro de junio.*
2. *Es el once de enero.*
3. *Es el quince de mayo.*
4. *Es el veinte y uno de diciembre.*
5. *Es el veinte y siete de septiembre.*
6. *Es el treinta de abril.*
7. *Es martes, el catorce de febrero.*
8. *Es jueves, el siete de agosto.*
9. *Es domingo, el treinta y uno de marzo.*
10. *Es lunes, el primero de noviembre.*
11. *Es miércoles, el diez y seis de julio.*
12. *Es sábado, el trece de octubre.*

**O** (Sample responses)

1. *el veinte y nueve de septiembre*
2. *el cuatro de julio*
3. *el veinte y siete de noviembre*
4. *el veinte y cinco de diciembre*
5. *el primero de enero*

**Diálogo** (Sample responses)

*Es diciembre.*
*Tenemos vacaciones y me gusta esquiar.*
*¿Cómo celebras tu cumpleaños?*
*¡Qué suerte! Mi cumpleaños es el once de enero y tengo clases.*

**Información personal** (Sample responses)

1. *Hoy es viernes, el primero de marzo.*
2. *Mi cumpleaños es el doce de julio.*
3. *Mi estación favorita es la primavera.*
4. *Tengo frío en el invierno.*
5. *Tengo calor en el verano.*

# Lección 15

**Notes:** Use pictures of the parts of a house (or even a dollhouse) to introduce or practice the vocabulary in this lesson. Practice the possessive adjectives introduced here with all suitable lexical elements learned up to this point. Directed-dialog techniques previously suggested for verb practice are equally suitable for possessives:

| | |
|---|---|
| TEACHER OR STUDENT #1: | **Pregúntele a un alumno (una alumna) si es su libro.** |
| STUDENT #2: | **¿Es tu (su) libro?** |
| STUDENT #3: | **Sí, es mi libro.** |
| CLASS IN UNISON: | **Es su libro.** |

This procedure may also be used with negative responses, plural forms, or any combination of possessives:

| | |
|---|---|
| TEACHER OR STUDENT #1: | **Pregúntele a un alumno (una alumna) si son sus libros.** |
| STUDENT #2: | **¿Son tus (sus) libros?** |
| STUDENT #3: | **No, no son mis libros.** |
| CLASS IN UNISON: | **No son sus libros.** |

### Key to Structures

**2** . . . Look at the nouns in Group I. Underline them. Are these nouns singular or plural? *singular* . What does **mi** mean? *my* . Now look at Group II. Which word has replaced **mi** from Group I? *mis* . What does **mis** mean? *my* .

**3** . . . What do **tu** and **tus** mean? *your* . When do you use **tu?** *before a singular noun* . When do you use **tus?** *before a plural noun* . When you use **tu** or **tus,** are you being familiar or formal? *familiar* .

**4** . . . When do you use **su?** *before a singular noun* . When do you use **sus?** *before a plural noun* .

**5** . . . Which subject pronouns do **nuestro, nuestros, nuestra, nuestras** bring to mind? *nosotros, nosotras* . What do **nuestro, nuestros, nuestra, nuestras** mean? *our* .
When do you use **nuestro?** *before a masculine singular noun.*
**nuestros?** *before a masculine plural noun.*
**nuestra?** *before a feminine singular noun.*
**nuestras?** *before a feminine plural noun.*

## Optional Oral Exercises

**A.** Repeat the sentence using the possessive adjective **mi** or **mis** in place of the definite article:

1. Es la madre.
2. Es la cama.
3. Son las sillas.
4. Es el apartamento.
5. Son los hermanos.
6. Es la lámpara.
7. Es el sofá.
8. Son los consejeros.

*KEY*

1. *Es mi madre.*
2. *Es mi cama.*
3. *Son mis sillas.*
4. *Es mi apartamento.*
5. *Son mis hermanos.*
6. *Es mi lámpara.*
7. *Es mi sofá.*
8. *Son mis consejeros.*

**B.** Repeat the sentence using the possessive adjective **tu** or **tus** in place of the definite article:

1. Es el amigo.
2. Son las hermanas.
3. Es la casa.
4. Es el dormitorio.
5. Son los abuelos.
6. Es el profesor.
7. Es el gato.
8. Son las fotos.

*KEY*

1. *Es tu amigo.*
2. *Son tus hermanas.*
3. *Es tu casa.*
4. *Es tu dormitorio.*
5. *Son tus abuelos.*
6. *Es tu profesor.*
7. *Es tu gato.*
8. *Son tus fotos.*

**C.** Repeat the sentence using the possessive adjective **nuestro, nuestra, nuestros,** or **nuestras** in place of the definite article:

1. Es la televisión.
2. Es el cuarto de baño.
3. Son las bicicletas.
4. Es la comida.
5. Son los cuadernos.
6. Son las amigas.
7. Es el comedor.
8. Son los padres.

*KEY*

1. *Es nuestra televisión.*
2. *Es nuestro cuarto de baño.*
3. *Son nuestras bicicletas.*
4. *Es nuestra comida.*
5. *Son nuestros cuadernos.*
6. *Son nuestras amigas.*
7. *Es nuestro comedor.*
8. *Son nuestros padres.*

**D.** Change the sentence to express possession with the possessive adjective **su** or **sus:**

1. Es el hijo del señor Campos.
2. Son los abuelos de Rosa.
3. Es el disco de Roberto.
4. Es la casa de los señores Gómez.
5. Son las hermanas de Pablo.
6. Es el profesor de ustedes.
7. Son los lápices de usted.
8. Es la cama de Felipe.

*KEY*

1. *Es su hijo.*
2. *Son sus abuelos.*
3. *Es su disco.*
4. *Es su casa.*
5. *Son sus hermanas.*
6. *Es su profesor.*
7. *Son sus lápices.*
8. *Es su cama.*

**E.** Directed dialog (See Lesson 5, Optional Oral Exercise D, for procedure.)

Pregúntele a un alumno (una alumna) si él (ella)

1. tiene su dormitorio.
2. estudia sus lecciones.
3. trabaja en su casa.
4. sale con sus hermanos.
5. usa su diccionario.
6. vende sus libros viejos.

| STUDENT #1 | STUDENT #2 |
|---|---|
| 1. *¿Tienes tu dormitorio?*<br>*¿Tiene usted su dormitorio?* | *Sí, tengo mi dormitorio.* |
| 2. *¿Estudias tus lecciones?*<br>*¿Estudia usted sus lecciones?* | *Sí, estudio mis lecciones.* |
| 3. *¿Trabajas en tu casa?*<br>*¿Trabaja usted en su casa?* | *Sí, trabajo en mi casa.* |
| 4. *¿Sales con tus hermanos?*<br>*¿Sale usted con sus hermanos?* | *Sí, salgo con mis hermanos.* |
| 5. *¿Usas tu diccionario?*<br>*¿Usa usted su diccionario?* | *Sí, uso mi diccionario.* |
| 6. *¿Vendes tus libros viejos?*<br>*¿Vende usted sus libros viejos?* | *Sí, vendo mis libros viejos.* |

NOTE: This procedure may also be used with negative responses and any combination of possessives.

## Key to Actividades

**A**
1. *el cuarto de baño*
2. *la cama*
3. *la silla*
4. *el sofá*
5. *el apartamento*
6. *la lámpara*
7. *la casa*
8. *la cocina*
9. *el dormitorio*
10. *la mesa*

**B** (Sample responses)
1. *en la sala*
2. *en la sala*
3. *en la sala*
4. *en la sala*
5. *en el comedor*
6. *en el dormitorio*
7. *en la sala*
8. *en el dormitorio*
9. *en la cocina*
10. *en la sala*
11. *en el dormitorio*
12. *en la cocina*

**C**
1. *mi*
2. *mis*
3. *mi*
4. *mis*
5. *mis*
6. *mis*
7. *mi*
8. *mi*
9. *mis*
10. *mi*

**D** 1. *mi abuela* 2. *mi hermana* 3. *mi abuela* 4. *mis hermanos* 5. *mis abuelos*

**E** 1. *tu* 2. *tu* 3. *tus* 4. *tus* 5. *tu* 6. *tus* 7. *tu* 8. *tus* 9. *tu* 10. *tus*

**F** 1. *su* 2. *su* 3. *sus* 4. *su* 5. *su* 6. *sus* 7. *sus* 8. *su* 9. *su* 10. *sus*

**G** 1. *su madre* 2. *su madre* 3. *su padre* 4. *sus hijos* 5. *su flor* 6. *su secretaria* 7. *sus automóviles* 8. *su médico* 9. *sus lámparas* 10. *su abuelo*

**H** 1. *nuestra* 2. *nuestros* 3. *nuestra* 4. *nuestro* 5. *nuestras* 6. *nuestros* 7. *nuestra* 8. *nuestro* 9. *nuestros* 10. *nuestras*

**I** 1. *mis* 2. *tu* 3. *nuestros* 4. *sus* 5. *sus* 6. *mi* 7. *su* 8. *su* 9. *nuestro* 10. *tus*

**J** 1. *nuestras escuelas* 2. *tu periódico* 3. *mi automóvil* 4. *sus profesores* 5. *su médico* 6. *nuestra ciudad* 7. *sus amigas* 8. *mi dinero* 9. *tus discos* 10. *nuestra sala*

**K** 1. *estupendo* 2. *sus amigos* 3. *el fútbol* 4. *excelentes* 5. *su padre* 6. *su madre y sus hermanas* 7. *sus consejeros* 8. *sus reglas* 9. *horrible* 10. *premios*

**Diálogo**

¡Ayúdame!

¿Dónde está mi *lápiz* ?

Tu *lápiz* está sobre *la mesa.*

¿Dónde está mi *bolso* ?

Tu *bolso* está sobre *la cama.*

¿Dónde están mis *libros* ?

Tus *libros* están sobre *la televisión.*

¿Dónde está mi *dinero* ?

Tienes tu *dinero* en tus *manos.*

# Lección 16

**Notes:** Mastery of numbers to 100 can be achieved through counting by 2s, 3s, 4s, 5s, and so on; by counting play money (preferably Spanish); or by having students give simple math problems to one another.

### Optional Oral Exercises

**A.** Write down the number you hear in Spanish:

1. veinte y tres
2. cuarenta y siete
3. sesenta y ocho
4. cincuenta y cuatro
5. treinta y dos
6. setenta y dos
7. ochenta y cinco
8. trece
9. noventa y seis
10. ciento

*KEY*

1. *23*
2. *47*
3. *68*
4. *54*
5. *32*
6. *72*
7. *85*
8. *13*
9. *96*
10. *100*

**B.** Give the number that comes after the number you hear:

1. veinte y seis
2. cuarenta
3. sesenta y dos
4. diez
5. cincuenta y cuatro
6. treinta y ocho
7. noventa y nueve
8. noventa y uno
9. setenta y tres
10. ochenta y siete

*KEY*

1. *veinte y siete*
2. *cuarenta y uno*
3. *sesenta y tres*
4. *once*
5. *cincuenta y cinco*
6. *treinta y nueve*
7. *ciento*
8. *noventa y dos*
9. *setenta y cuatro*
10. *ochenta y ocho*

**C.** Give the number that comes before the number you hear:

1. cincuenta y nueve
2. cuarenta
3. noventa y seis
4. veinte y tres
5. ochenta y uno
6. sesenta y siete
7. diez y seis
8. ochenta y cuatro
9. setenta y siete
10. treinta y cinco

*KEY*

1. *cincuenta y ocho*
2. *treinta y nueve*
3. *noventa y cinco*
4. *veinte y dos*
5. *ochenta*
6. *sesenta y seis*
7. *quince*
8. *ochenta y tres*
9. *setenta y seis*
10. *treinta y cuatro*

**D.** ¿Cuántos son

1. veinte y treinta?
2. ciento menos cuarenta?
3. ochenta dividido por dos?
4. dos por siete?
5. treinta y cincuenta?
6. sesenta menos treinta?
7. ciento dividido por cinco?
8. siete por once?

*KEY*

1. *Veinte y treinta son cincuenta.*
2. *Ciento menos cuarenta son sesenta.*
3. *Ochenta dividido por dos son cuarenta.*
4. *Dos por siete son catorce.*
5. *Treinta y cincuenta son ochenta.*
6. *Sesenta menos treinta son treinta.*
7. *Ciento dividido por cinco son veinte.*
8. *Siete por once son setenta y siete.*

## Key to Actividades

**A** 1. *23* 2. *47* 3. *31* 4. *16* 5. *14* 6. *59* 7. *12* 8. *62* 9. *15* 10. *13* 11. *11* 12. *7*

**B** 1. *80* 2. *43* 3. *71* 4. *24* 5. *57* 6. *61* 7. *35* 8. *84* 9. *16* 10. *90*

**C**
1. ochenta y uno *81*
2. sesenta y cinco *65*
3. noventa y seis *96*
4. cincuenta y tres *53*
5. veinte y ocho *28*
6. setenta y nueve *79*
7. noventa y dos *92*
8. cuarenta y cuatro *44*
9. treinta *30*
10. ochenta y siete *87*

**D** NOTE TO TEACHERS: Have students say the numbers out loud as they connect the dots.

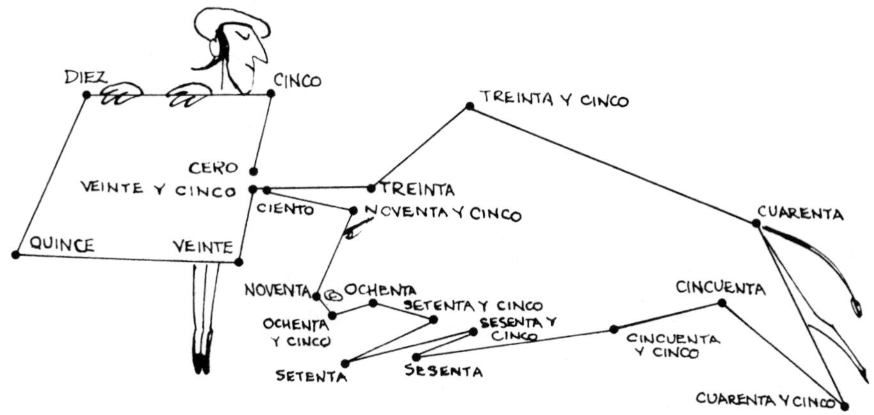

**E** 1. *Él arregla el automóvil de la Sra. Ramírez.*
2. *Él prepara la comida para su madre.*
3. *Él cuida a los cuatro niños de los González.*
4. *Él pasea el perro del Sr. Santiago.*

**F**

| | EL DINERO | | EL TOTAL |
|---|---|---|---|
| El banco | veinte y tres | dólares | *$23* |
| La Sra. Ramírez | *cuarenta* | dólares | *$40* |
| La madre | *catorce × cuatro = cincuenta y seis* | dólares | *$56* |
| Los González | *doce × tres = treinta y seis* | dólares | *$36* |
| El Sr. Santiago | *quince* | dólares | *$15* |
| | | | *$170* |

| | |
|---|---|
| El dinero de Jaimito: | *ciento setenta dólares* |
| La grabadora: | *ciento cincuenta y nueve dólares* |
| Jaimito tiene todavía: | *once dólares* |

**G** 1. *cincuenta, ochenta, ochenta*
2. *trece, seis, diez*
3. *veinte y siete, treinta, catorce*
4. *veinte, doce, siete*

**H** 1. *trece*
2. *catorce*
3. *quince*
4. *veinte y nueve*
5. *treinta*
6. *cuarenta*
7. *cincuenta*
8. *sesenta*
9. *setenta y dos*
10. *noventa y cinco*

**I** 1. *doce*
2. *cuarenta y nueve*
3. *setenta y ocho*
4. *ochenta*
5. *diez y nueve*
6. *sesenta y tres*
7. *catorce*
8. *treinta y seis*
9. *veinte y cuatro*
10. *ochenta y siete*
11. *cincuenta y uno*
12. *noventa y tres*
13. *quince*
14. *setenta y seis*
15. *noventa y nueve*

**Diálogo**

Setenta y uno, setenta y dos, setenta y tres . . .

*¿Qué haces?*

Cuento . . . ochenta y uno, ochenta y dos, ochenta y tres . . .

*¿Qué cuentas?*

Cuento las horas, noventa y uno . . .

*¿Qué horas cuentas?*

Cuento las horas hasta mi fiesta de sorpresa.

*Quiero ayudarte.*

**Información personal** (Sample responses)

1. a. *ocho + siete = quince*
   b. *ciento − diez = noventa*
   c. *cinco × seis = treinta*
   d. *cuarenta y nueve ÷ siete = siete*
2. a. *setenta y ocho*
   b. *noventa y cinco*
   c. *treinta*
   d. *cuarenta*

# Repaso IV (Lecciones 13–16)

## Key to Actividades

**A**

1. *R O B O* **T**
2. *P* **E** *L O*
3. **N** *A R I Z*
4. *D O M I N* **G** *O*
5. **O** *R E J A*
6. *F E C* **H** *A*
7. *B R* **A** *Z O*
8. **M** *A N O*
9. **B** *O C A*
10. *P I E* **R** *N A*
11. *P I* **E**

**B**

| A | M | O | R |
|---|---|---|---|
| 1 | 15 | 18 | 21 |

| D | I | N | E | R | O |
|---|---|---|---|---|---|
| 5 | 10 | 16 | 6 | 21 | 18 |

| V | A | C | A | C | I | O | N | E | S |
|---|---|---|---|---|---|---|---|---|---|
| 26 | 1 | 3 | 1 | 3 | 10 | 18 | 16 | 6 | 23 |

| P | R | O | F | E | S | O | R | A |
|---|---|---|---|---|---|---|---|---|
| 19 | 21 | 18 | 7 | 6 | 23 | 18 | 21 | 1 |

| M | I | LL | O | N | A | R | I | O | S |
|---|---|---|---|---|---|---|---|---|---|
| 15 | 10 | 14 | 18 | 16 | 1 | 21 | 10 | 18 | 23 |

**C**

1. *Él tiene frío.*
2. *Él tiene dolor de cabeza.*
3. *Ella tiene hambre.*
4. *Él tiene sueño.*
5. *Él tiene sed.*
6. *Ella tiene calor.*

**D**

```
  M I É R C O L E S   J U L I O        
  A                   U   U   C        
  R                   N   N   T        
  T   V           M   I   E   U     H  
  E N E R O     M A Y O   S Á B A D O  
  S   R   T   D   R           R     R  
      A   O   O   Z   J U E V E S   A  
  S   N   Ñ   M   O         I          
P E R O   O   I             E          
  M           N O V I E M B R E        
  A       P   G             N       S  
I N V I E R N O             E       E  
  A       I           A G O S T O   P  
          M           B             T  
      D Í A           R             I  
          V         D I C I E M B R E  
          E           L             M  
          R                 M       B  
    E S T A C I Ó N       F E B R E R O
                            S       E  
```

**E** 1. *Es el cuatro de julio.*
2. *Es el primero de enero.*
3. *Es el doce de febrero.*
4. *Es el treinta y uno de octubre.*

**F** 1. *Es una fotografía de su madre.*
2. *Es una fotografía de sus abuelos.*
3. *Es una fotografía de su abuelo.*
4. *Es una fotografía de tu perro.*
5. *Es una fotografía de sus padres.*
6. *Es una fotografía de mi madre.*
7. *Es una fotografía de tu familia.*
8. *Es una fotografía de su padre.*
9. *Es una fotografía de su gato.*

**G**

| | | | |
|---|---|---|---|
| 1. *cocina* | 4. *dormitorio* | 1. *cara* | 7. *nariz* |
| 2. *lámpara* | 5. *sofá* | 2. *garganta* | 8. *cabeza* |
| 3. *comedor* | 6. *silla* | 3. *dedo* | 9. *oreja* |
| 4. *sala* | 8. *cama* | 4. *boca* | 10. *mano* |
| | | 5. *pie* | 11. *ojo* |
| | | 6. *pierna* | 12. *brazo* |

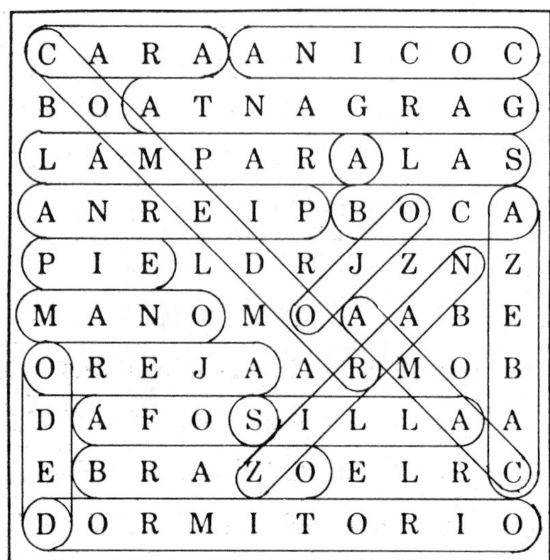

**H** El pobre Paco está *enfermo*. Él va al *médico* con su *madre*. El *médico/doctor* trabaja en el *hospital*. Él examina al *muchacho*. Él examina los *ojos*, la *boca*, la *nariz* y los *oídos* de Paco. El *doctor* pregunta: «¿Tienes dolor de *cabeza*?» Paco dice: «Sí.» El *doctor* dice: «Paco, tienes gripe. Necesitas estar en *cama* una *semana*. No debes ir a la *escuela*.» Paco está *triste*. A él le gusta la *clase* de español.

# Quinta Parte

## Lección 17

**Notes:** Empty food containers or pictures may supplement the illustrations in this lesson on food. Encourage students to speak about foods they like or do not like, those they eat in school and those they prepare at home. This lesson provides opportunities for Spanish, Mexican, or other hispanic food sampling, a make-believe meal or a picnic in class.

Teachers may wish, consistent with student readiness, to use a wall map of Spain, Central America, or South America to point out areas with which certain foods and dishes are identified. Students may also be asked to draw maps and locate the areas and specialties on them.

Ask students which things they like. Example: **¿Te gusta el helado de chocolate o de vainilla?** Student answers: **Me gusta el helado de chocolate. No me gusta el helado de vainilla.**

### Key to Structures

**2** . . . How many are referred to in each example in Group I? *one*. How many are referred to in the examples in Group II? *more than one*. What do both **me gusta** and **me gustan** mean? *I like*.

**6** . . . Who is doing the liking in the first example? *Roberto*. Who is doing the liking in the second example? *los alumnos*. What little word did we put before **Roberto** and **los alumnos?** *a*.

### Optional Oral Exercises

**A.** Tell someone in Spanish that you like the following foods:

1. la ensalada
2. el pescado
3. las legumbres
4. el helado de chocolate
5. las papas fritas
6. la sopa
7. el jugo de naranja
8. la leche
9. el pan
10. el queso
11. las frutas
12. la carne

*KEY*

1. *Me gusta la ensalada.*
2. *Me gusta el pescado.*
3. *Me gustan las legumbres.*
4. *Me gusta el helado de chocolate.*
5. *Me gustan las papas fritas.*
6. *Me gusta la sopa.*
7. *Me gusta el jugo de naranja.*
8. *Me gusta la leche.*
9. *Me gusta el pan.*
10. *Me gusta el queso.*
11. *Me gustan las frutas.*
12. *Me gusta la carne.*

**B.** Make the following sentences negative:

1. Me gusta el sandwich de queso.
2. Te gustan las salchichas.
3. Le gusta comer mucho.
4. Nos gusta el invierno.
5. Les gusta la música ruidosa.

*KEY*

1. *No me gusta el sandwich de queso.*
2. *No te gustan las salchichas.*
3. *No le gusta comer mucho.*
4. *No nos gusta el invierno.*
5. *No les gusta la música ruidosa.*

**C.** Directed dialog (See Lesson 5, Optional Oral Exercise D, for procedure.)

Pregúntele a un alumno (una alumna) si a él (ella) le gusta(n)

1. estudiar español.
2. comer en un restaurante.
3. los huevos duros.
4. el cine.
5. las fiestas.
6. el café.
7. comprar discos.
8. mirar la televisión.
9. los helados.
10. sus amigos.

*KEY* (Sample responses)

| | STUDENT #1 | STUDENT #2 |
|---|---|---|
| 1. | *¿Te gusta estudiar español?* | *Sí, me gusta estudiar español.* |
| 2. | *¿Te gusta comer en un restaurante?* | *Sí, me gusta comer en un restaurante.* |
| 3. | *¿Te gustan los huevos duros?* | *No, no me gustan los huevos duros.* |
| 4. | *¿Te gusta el cine?* | *Sí, me gusta el cine.* |
| 5. | *¿Te gustan las fiestas?* | *Sí, me gustan las fiestas.* |
| 6. | *¿Te gusta el café?* | *No, no me gusta el café.* |
| 7. | *¿Te gusta comprar discos?* | *Sí, me gusta comprar discos.* |
| 8. | *¿Te gusta mirar la televisión?* | *No, no me gusta mirar la televisión.* |
| 9. | *¿Te gustan los helados?* | *Sí, me gustan los helados.* |
| 10. | *¿Te gustan tus amigos?* | *Sí, me gustan mis amigos.* |

## Key to Actividades

**A**

1. *el pan*
2. *el helado*
3. *el queso*
4. *la carne*
5. *la leche*
6. *la ensalada*
7. *el jugo de naranja*
8. *el pescado*

**B**

1. *la sopa*
2. *el agua*
3. *las frutas*
4. *las legumbres*
5. *los sandwiches*
6. *el pollo*
7. *las papas*
8. *la salchicha*

**C**

1. *el*
2. *el*
3. *la*
4. *las*
5. *la*
6. *los*
7. *el*
8. *el*
9. *el*
10. *la*
11. *la*
12. *el*
13. *las*
14. *el*
15. *las*
16. *la*

**D**

1. *gusta*
2. *gustan*
3. *gustan*
4. *gusta*
5. *gusta*
6. *gustan*

**E**
1. *Me gusta la profesora.*
2. *Le gusta (mirar) la televisión.*
3. *Nos gusta comer.*
4. *Le gusta hablar mucho.*
5. *Les gusta cantar.*
6. *Te gusta el helado.*
7. *Le gustan los automóviles.*
8. *Les gustan los gatos.*
9. *Les gusta el cine.*
10. *Le gustan los libros.*

**F**
1. *No me gusta la profesora.*
2. *No le gusta (mirar) la televisión.*
3. *No nos gusta comer.*
4. *No le gusta hablar mucho.*
5. *No les gusta cantar.*
6. *No te gusta el helado.*
7. *No le gustan los automóviles.*
8. *No les gustan los gatos.*
9. *No les gusta el cine.*
10. *No le gustan los libros.*

**G**
1. *j*
2. *g*
3. *e*
4. *c*
5. *a*
6. *i*
7. *b*
8. *f*

**H**
1. *quieres / ensalada*
2. *quiere frutas*
3. *quieren / docena / huevos*
4. *quiere / perro*
5. *queremos pan*
6. *quiere / helado*
7. *quieren / vaso / leche*
8. *quiero / dinero*

**I** (Sample responses)

1. *una ensalada mixta de lechuga y tomate con huevos duros y una soda.*
2. *el arroz con pollo o una hamburguesa con queso y papas fritas o un bistec con puré de papas.*
3. *quiere / jugo de naranja.*
4. *carne*
5. *vegetariano*

**Preguntas personales** (Sample responses)

1. *Si tengo hambre, me gusta comer un sandwich.*
2. *No, no me gustan las legumbres.*
3. *Sí, me gustan las frutas.*
4. *No me gusta comer pescado.*
5. *Me gusta el helado de chocolate.*

**Información personal** (Sample responses)

1. *bistec con papas fritas*
2. *pollo con legumbres*
3. *ensalada mixta con huevos duros*
4. *sandwiches de carne con lechuga y tomate*
5. *pescado frito*

**Diálogo** (Sample responses)

Buenos días, señores. Aquí está el menú.

*Gracias. ¿Cuál es la especialidad del día?*

Hay un pescado magnífico.

*No nos gusta el pescado.*

Tenemos sandwiches excelentes.

*No nos gustan los sandwiches.*

¿Qué quieren comer Uds., entonces?

*Queremos dos hamburguesas con queso y papas fritas.*

# Lección 18

**Notes:** Articles of clothing hung on a clothesline or rope across the front of the classroom (or pictures of such articles) will be useful in introducing and practicing the vocabulary in this lesson. Both the teacher and students may use crayons or colored paper to practice the names of colors. The two lexical groups (clothes and colors) combine naturally for such practice. Students may be asked to describe what they are wearing or what is shown in magazine advertisements. This practice also involves the reinforcement of possessive adjectives. The teacher may ask a student: **¿Tu camisa es azul?** The student answers: **No, mi camisa no es azul. Es blanca.** Or the teacher asks: **¿Tu blusa es roja?** The student answers: **No es roja. Es negra.** Agreement of adjectives is a natural part of such practice.

## Optional Oral Exercises

**A.** Repeat each noun with the correct definite article:

1. sombrero
2. guantes
3. ropa
4. zapatos
5. vestido
6. blusa
7. suéter
8. medias
9. pantalones
10. traje

*KEY*

1. *el sombrero*
2. *los guantes*
3. *la ropa*
4. *los zapatos*
5. *el vestido*
6. *la blusa*
7. *el suéter*
8. *las medias*
9. *los pantalones*
10. *el traje*

**B.** Form sentences with the following words, using the correct Spanish for *my*: (The teacher may hold up a piece of colored paper and a small article of clothing or an illustration.)

EXAMPLE: blusa — blanca **Mi blusa es blanca.**

1. sombrero — gris
2. pantalones — blancos
3. camisa — rosada
4. chaqueta — azul
5. suéter — amarillo
6. corbata — roja
7. guantes — negros
8. falda — anaranjada
9. medias — azules
10. abrigo — verde

*KEY*

1. *Mi sombrero es gris.*
2. *Mis pantalones son blancos.*
3. *Mi camisa es rosada.*
4. *Mi chaqueta es azul.*
5. *Mi suéter es amarillo.*
6. *Mi corbata es roja.*
7. *Mis guantes son negros.*
8. *Mi falda es anaranjada.*
9. *Mis medias son azules.*
10. *Mi abrigo es verde.*

## Key to Actividades

**A**

NOTE TO TEACHERS: You may wish to tell students that **medias cortas** is equivalent to *socks* in Spanish America. **Calcetines** is rarely used.

**B**

1. *el sombrero*
2. *la chaqueta*
3. *el vestido*
4. *los zapatos*
5. *los pantalones*
6. *la falda*
7. *la blusa*
8. *las medias*
9. *el abrigo*
10. *la camisa*
11. *los guantes*
12. *el suéter*
13. *la corbata*
14. *el traje*
15. *la ropa*

**C**

1. *el sombrero blanco*
2. *el vestido rojo*
3. *el suéter amarillo*
4. *el abrigo negro*
5. *la blusa anaranjada*
6. *la camisa azul*
7. *el traje pardo/castaño*
8. *la falda verde*

**D** 1. *pantalones rojos*
2. *vestidos blancos*
3. *trajes grises*
4. *blusas amarillas*
5. *zapatos negros*
6. *medias azules*
7. *camisas rosadas*
8. *corbatas pardas/castañas*

**E** 1. *El señor Romero es el profesor de español.*
2. *Es un profesor con mucha imaginación.*
3. *Da una lección sobre la ropa y los colores.*
4. *Da un ejercicio interesante.*
5. *Cierto.*
6. *Los alumnos preparan ropa diferente.*
7. *El premio es un disco de música española.*
8. *La ropa diferente es extraordinaria.*

**Diálogo** (Sample responses)

Señor, busco *una camisa rosada*.

Aquí está.

Y quiero también *un suéter rojo*.

¿Le gustan los colores populares?

Sí. Me gusta *la ropa de muchos colores*.

Bueno. Es necesario pagar inmediatamente.

**Información personal** (Sample responses)

1. *Me gustan las faldas negras.*
2. *Me gusta un vestido blanco.*
3. *Me gusta un abrigo gris.*
4. *Me gustan los guantes rojos.*
5. *Me gusta un suéter de muchos colores.*

# Lección 19

**Notes:** Use pictures and a calendar to practice the vocabulary in this lesson. The optional oral exercises for this lesson suggest techniques for practicing **hacer** in different contexts.

## Key to Structures

**3** . . .

| | |
|---|---|
| yo *hago* | nosotros } *hacemos* |
| tú *haces* | nosotras } *hacemos* |
| Ud. *hace* | Uds. *hacen* |
| él *hace* | ellos *hacen* |
| ella *hace* | ellas *hacen* |

## Optional Oral Exercises

**A.** Answer the following questions in complete Spanish sentences:

1. ¿Qué tiempo hace en la primavera?
2. ¿Qué tiempo hace en el otoño?
3. ¿Qué tiempo hace en el invierno?
4. ¿Qué tiempo hace en el verano?

*KEY*

1. *Hace buen tiempo en la primavera.*
2. *Hace viento en el otoño.*
3. *Hace frío en el invierno.*
4. *Hace calor en el verano.*

**B.** Tell in which season the following weather occurs:

1. Hace mal tiempo.
2. Hace buen tiempo.
3. Llueve.
4. Hace sol.
5. Hace calor.
6. Hace viento.
7. Nieva.
8. Hace frío.

*KEY*

1. *Hace mal tiempo en el otoño.*
2. *Hace buen tiempo en la primavera.*
3. *Llueve en la primavera.*
4. *Hace sol en el verano.*
5. *Hace calor en el verano.*
6. *Hace viento en el otoño.*
7. *Nieva en el invierno.*
8. *Hace frío en el invierno.*

**C.** Express the correct form of the verb **hacer** with the subject you hear:

1. ellos
2. nosotros
3. María
4. yo
5. ella
6. ustedes
7. tú
8. Juan
9. usted
10. Carmen y Rosa

*KEY*

1. *ellos hacen*
2. *nosotros hacemos*
3. *María hace*
4. *yo hago*
5. *ella hace*
6. *ustedes hacen*
7. *tú haces*
8. *Juan hace*
9. *usted hace*
10. *Carmen y Rosa hacen*

**D.** Make the following sentences negative:

1. Ellos hacen las tareas.
2. Mi madre hace la comida.
3. Ricardo hace un sandwich de queso.
4. Tú haces muecas.
5. Yo hago una figura de nieve.
6. Nosotros hacemos una ensalada.
7. Hace calor hoy.
8. La profesora hace muchas preguntas.
9. Usted hace su cama.
10. Ustedes hacen un pastel.

*KEY*

1. *Ellos no hacen las tareas.*
2. *Mi madre no hace la comida.*
3. *Ricardo no hace un sandwich de queso.*
4. *Tú no haces muecas.*
5. *Yo no hago una figura de nieve.*
6. *Nosotros no hacemos una ensalada.*
7. *No hace calor hoy.*
8. *La profesora no hace muchas preguntas.*
9. *Usted no hace su cama.*
10. *Ustedes no hacen un pastel.*

**E.** Change the following sentences to questions:

1. Ellos hacen las tareas.
2. Mi madre hace la comida.
3. Ricardo hace un sandwich de queso.
4. Tú haces muecas.
5. Yo hago una figura de nieve.
6. Nosotros hacemos una ensalada.
7. Hace calor hoy.
8. La profesora hace muchas preguntas.
9. Usted hace su cama.
10. Ustedes hacen un pastel.

*KEY*

1. *¿Hacen ellos las tareas?*
2. *¿Hace mi madre la comida?*
3. *¿Hace Ricardo un sandwich de queso?*
4. *¿Haces tú muecas?*
5. *¿Hago yo una figura de nieve?*
6. *¿Hacemos nosotros una ensalada?*
7. *¿Hace calor hoy?*
8. *¿Hace la profesora muchas preguntas?*
9. *¿Hace usted su cama?*
10. *¿Hacen ustedes un pastel?*

**F.** Make the following sentences negative:

1. Yo voy al supermercado.
2. Carmen y Rosa van al cine.
3. Los niños van a la playa.
4. El profesor va a la escuela.
5. Mi hermana va al teatro.
6. Ustedes van a la fiesta.
7. Tú vas al aeropuerto.
8. Nosotros vamos a España.
9. Usted va a su apartamento.
10. Mis padres van al restaurante.

*KEY*

1. *Yo no voy al supermercado.*
2. *Carmen y Rosa no van al cine.*
3. *Los niños no van a la playa.*
4. *El profesor no va a la escuela.*
5. *Mi hermana no va al teatro.*
6. *Ustedes no van a la fiesta.*
7. *Tú no vas al aeropuerto.*
8. *Nosotros no vamos a España.*
9. *Usted no va a su apartamento.*
10. *Mis padres no van al restaurante.*

**G.** Directed dialog (See Lesson 5, Optional Oral Exercise D, for procedure.)

Pregúntele a un alumno (una alumna)

1. qué tiempo hace hoy.
2. dónde hace sus tareas.
3. qué hace en el invierno.
4. qué hace en el verano.
5. si hace su cama.
6. si va a la playa en agosto.
7. si va al cine con sus amigos.
8. si hace fresco en el verano.
9. si va a la escuela en automóvil.
10. si hace sus tareas inmediatamente.

*KEY*

| | STUDENT #1 | STUDENT #2 |
|---|---|---|
| 1. | *¿Qué tiempo hace hoy?* | *Hoy hace viento.* |
| 2. | *¿Dónde haces tus tareas?* | *Hago mis tareas en casa.* |
| 3. | *¿Qué haces en el invierno?* | *Voy a esquiar en el invierno.* |
| 4. | *¿Qué haces en el verano?* | *Voy a un campamento en el verano.* |
| 5. | *¿Haces tu cama?* | *No, no hago mi cama.* |
| 6. | *¿Vas a la playa en agosto?* | *No, no voy a la playa en agosto.* |
| 7. | *¿Vas al cine con tus amigos?* | *Sí, voy al cine con mis amigos.* |

8. *¿Hace fresco en el verano?* — *No, no hace fresco en el verano.*
9. *¿Vas a la escuela en automóvil?* — *Sí, voy a la escuela en automóvil.*
10. *¿Haces tus tareas inmediatamente?* — *Sí, hago mis tareas inmediatamente.*

Teachers may wish to expand upon these procedures with more personalized materials.

## Key to Actividades

**A**

1. *Hace buen tiempo.*
2. *Nieva.*
3. *Hace mal tiempo.*
4. *Llueve.*
5. *Hace calor.*
6. *Hace viento.*
7. *Hace frío.*
8. *Hace sol.*

**B**

1. *Nieva.*
2. *Hace buen tiempo.*
3. *Hace viento.*
4. *Hace calor.*
5. *Hace mal tiempo.*
6. *Hace frío.*
7. *Llueve.*
8. *Hace sol.*

**C**

1. *Luis*
2. *invierno*
3. *a casa*
4. *chocolate*
5. *nieva*
6. *figura de nieve*
7. *esquiar*
8. *miedo*
9. *bolas de nieve*
10. *muecas*

**D**

1. *Hacen una figura de nieve.*
2. *¿Por qué haces muecas?*
3. *Ellas hacen tortillas.*
4. *Hace calor.*
5. *Hace buen tiempo.*
6. *Hago mis tareas.*

**E** (Sample responses)

1. *Hoy hace buen tiempo.*
2. *Voy a la playa cuando hace calor.*
3. *Voy a esquiar en el invierno.*
4. *Hago mis tareas a las ocho de la noche.*
5. *Mis amigos y yo hacemos bolas de nieve en el invierno.*

**F** 1. *van* 2. *van* 3. *va* 4. *va* 5. *voy* 6. *va* 7. *vamos* 8. *vas*

**Información personal** (Sample responses)

1. *Hace buen tiempo.*
2. *Nieva y hace mucho frío.*
3. *Llueve y hace fresco.*
4. *Hace sol.*

**Diálogo** (Sample responses)

*¿Qué tiempo hace hoy?*

Hace mucho calor.

*¿Por qué haces muecas?*

No me gusta el verano.

*¿Quieres jugar al fútbol en el parque?*

No me gustan los deportes. Tengo miedo del sol.

*Entonces vamos a tomar un helado.*

Bueno. ¡Vamos!

# Lección 20

**Notes:** Teachers may prefer to present the vocabulary in this lesson in two parts, depending on the level of readiness of the class. Use pictures to help with class practice.

## Optional Oral Exercises

**A.** Repeat each noun with the definite article:

1. mono
2. cochino
3. vaca
4. caballo
5. león
6. tigre
7. gallina
8. elefante
9. pato
10. pez

*KEY*

1. *el mono*
2. *el cochino*
3. *la vaca*
4. *el caballo*
5. *el león*
6. *el tigre*
7. *la gallina*
8. *el elefante*
9. *el pato*
10. *el pez*

**B.** Express the correct form of the verb **decir** with the subject you hear:

1. nosotros
2. yo
3. usted
4. Roberto
5. el periódico
6. mis abuelos
7. tú
8. ustedes
9. el médico
10. ellas

*KEY*

1. *nosotros decimos*
2. *yo digo*
3. *usted dice*
4. *Roberto dice*
5. *el periódico dice*
6. *mis abuelos dicen*
7. *tú dices*
8. *ustedes dicen*
9. *el médico dice*
10. *ellas dicen*

**C.** Make these sentences negative:

1. Él dice que el español es difícil.
2. Nosotros decimos la verdad.
3. La radio dice que hace frío.
4. Ustedes dicen que van al parque.
5. Yo digo muchas cosas.
6. Rosa y Carlos dicen que son amigos.
7. Usted dice que quiere salir.
8. La niña dice que quiere comer.
9. Ellos dicen que tienen dinero.
10. Tú dices que estás enfermo.

*KEY*

1. *Él no dice que el español es difícil.*
2. *Nosotros no decimos la verdad.*
3. *La radio no dice que hace frío.*
4. *Ustedes no dicen que van al parque.*
5. *Yo no digo muchas cosas.*
6. *Rosa y Carlos no dicen que son amigos.*
7. *Usted no dice que quiere salir.*
8. *La niña no dice que quiere comer.*
9. *Ellos no dicen que tienen dinero.*
10. *Tú no dices que estás enfermo.*

**D.** Change these sentences to questions:

1. Él dice que el español es difícil.
2. Nosotros decimos la verdad.
3. La radio dice que hace frío.
4. Ustedes dicen que van al parque.
5. Yo digo muchas cosas.
6. Rosa y Carlos dicen que son amigos.
7. Usted dice que quiere salir.
8. La niña dice que quiere comer.
9. Ellos dicen que tienen dinero.
10. Tú dices que estás enfermo.

*KEY*

1. *¿Dice él que el español es difícil?*
2. *¿Decimos nosotros la verdad?*
3. *¿Dice la radio que hace frío?*
4. *¿Dicen ustedes que van al parque?*
5. *¿Digo yo muchas cosas?*
6. *¿Dicen Rosa y Carlos que son amigos?*
7. *¿Dice usted que quiere salir?*
8. *¿Dice la niña que quiere comer?*
9. *¿Dicen ellos que tienen dinero?*
10. *¿Dices tú que estás enfermo?*

**E.** Directed dialog (See Lesson 5, Optional Oral Exercise D, for procedure.)

Pregúntele a un alumno (una alumna) si

1. le gustan los animales.
2. va al parque zoológico.
3. dice siempre la verdad.
4. tiene peces en casa.
5. los leones son grandes.
6. quiere tener un caballo.
7. dice que hoy es domingo.
8. dice que el mono es feroz.
9. tiene un perro inteligente.
10. dice que el pato vive en el agua.

| | STUDENT #1 | STUDENT #2 |
|---|---|---|
| 1. | *¿Te gustan los animales?* | *Sí, me gustan los animales.* |
| 2. | *¿Vas al parque zoológico?* | *Sí, voy al parque zoológico.* |
| 3. | *¿Dices siempre la verdad?* | *No, no digo siempre la verdad.* |
| 4. | *¿Tienes peces en casa?* | *No, no tengo peces en casa.* |
| 5. | *¿Son los leones grandes?* | *Sí, los leones son grandes.* |
| 6. | *¿Quieres tener un caballo?* | *Sí, quiero tener un caballo.* |
| 7. | *¿Dices que hoy es domingo?* | *No, no digo que hoy es domingo.* |
| 8. | *¿Dices que el mono es feroz?* | *No, no digo que el mono es feroz.* |
| 9. | *¿Tienes un perro inteligente?* | *Sí, tengo un perro inteligente.* |
| 10. | *¿Dices que el pato vive en el agua?* | *Sí, digo que el pato vive en el agua.* |

## Key to Actividades

**A**
1. *el perro*
2. *el cochino*
3. *el caballo*
4. *el león*
5. *la vaca*
6. *el gato*
7. *el mono*
8. *el tigre*
9. *el elefante*
10. *la gallina*

**B**

| | | | |
|---|---|---|---|
| *el gato* | *el pez* | *la vaca* | *el mono* |
| *el perro* | | *el caballo* | *el león* |
| | | *la gallina* | *el tigre* |
| | | *el cochino* | *el elefante* |
| | | *el pato* | |

**C**
1. *c*
2. *g*
3. *i*
4. *h*
5. *a*
6. *j*
7. *f*
8. *d*
9. *e*
10. *b*

**D**
1. *Yo veo un caballo.*
2. *Yo veo un cochino.*
3. *Yo veo una gallina.*
4. *Yo veo un gato.*
5. *Yo veo un perro.*
6. *Yo veo una vaca.*

**E**

1. *la vaca*
2. *el león*
3. *el cochino*
4. *el elefante*
5. *el tigre*
6. *el gato*
7. *el mono*
8. *el caballo*
9. *el perro*
10. *la gallina*

**F**

1. *¿Por qué es simpática?*
2. *¿Cuándo da la pata?*
3. *¿Cómo juega su perra?*
4. *¿Qué come?*
5. *¿Dónde juega?*
6. *¿A quién ama?*

**G**

1. *digo*
2. *dice*
3. *dicen*
4. *decimos*
5. *dices*

**H**

1. *Digo que hoy es lunes.*
2. *María dice que tenemos mucho tiempo.*
3. *La radio dice que va a llover mañana.*
4. *¿Tú dices que tienes razón?*
5. *¿Qué decimos a la profesora si no hacemos nuestras tareas?*
6. *Dicen que el examen es muy difícil.*

**Información personal** (Sample responses)

*Mi animal favorito es el caballo.*
*Es grande y fuerte.*
*Corre rápidamente.*
*Es inteligente.*
*Es pardo y blanco.*

**Diálogo**

1. *¿Con quién hablas?*
2. *Hablo con mis amigos, Esmeralda y Tornado.*
3. *¿Qué les dices?*
4. *Les digo que me gustan mucho.*
5. *¿Qué responden?*
6. *No dicen nada.*
7. *¿Por qué no?*
8. *¡Son mi vaca y mi caballo!*

# Repaso V (Lecciones 17–20)

## Key to Actividades

**A**
1. *el teatro*
2. *la estación de policía*
3. *la tienda de bicicletas*
4. *el cine*
5. *el restaurante «Cuatro Estaciones»*
6. *la tienda de frutas*
7. *el garaje*
8. *el almacén «Gran Chic»*
9. *el parque zoológico*
10. *el correo*
11. *el supermercado*
12. *el café «A Gusto»*

**B**

H (E) (L) A D O

E N (S) A (L) A D A

H A (M) (B) U R (G) U E S (A)

(S) (U) P (E) R M E (R) C A D O

LAS LEGUMBRES.

V E S (T) I (D) O

M (E) D (I) A S

C (A) M I S (A)

P (A) N T A (L) O (N) E S

A LA TIENDA.

**C**

| | | | | | | | | | | | | | | | | | | |
|---|---|---|---|---|---|---|---|---|---|---|---|---|---|---|---|---|---|---|
| 1 D | E | 2 C | I | M | O | S | | | 3 V | | 4 Q | U | E | R | E | M | O | 5 S |
| E | | I | | | | | | | E | | U | | | | | | | U |
| 6 P | A | N | T | 7 A | L | O | N | E | S | | E | | | | | 8 C | | P |
| O | | E | | M | | | | | T | | S | | | 9 T | R | A | J | E |
| R | | | 10 V | A | N | | | | I | | O | | | | | M | | R |
| 11 T | U | | | R | | 12 N | O | | D | | | | | 13 B | | I | | M |
| E | | 14 G | R | I | S | | | 15 C | O | C | H | I | N | O | | S | | E |
| S | | | | L | | | | | | | | | | T | | A | | R |
| | 16 S | Í | | 17 L | E | 18 G | U | 19 M | B | 20 R | E | S | | A | | | | C |
| | O | | | O | | A | | O | | O | | | | S | | | | A |
| | P | | | | | 21 T | A | N | | J | | | | | | 22 V | | D |
| | 23 A | B | R | I | G | O | | O | | O | | 24 P | E | S | C | A | D | O |

**D**

1. *queso*
2. *helado*
3. *leche*
4. *agua*
5. *ensalada*
6. *pescado*
7. *pollo*
8. *carne*
9. *jugo de naranja*
10. *huevos*
11. *sopa*
12. *bistec*
13. *legumbre*
14. *fruta*
15. *sandwiches*
16. *papas*
17. *salchichas*
18. *pan*
19. *café*

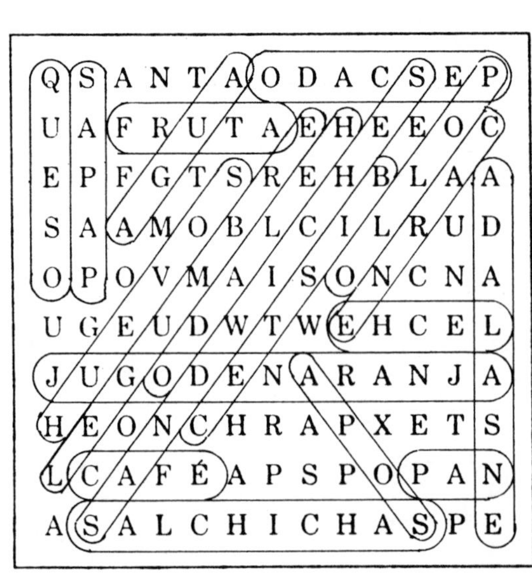

**E** 1. **R** **O** *P* *A*
1 2

2. **M** **E** *D* *I* *A* *S*
3 4

3. **B** **L** **U** *S* *A*
5 6 7

4. **Z** *A* *P* **A** *T* *O* **S**
8 9 10

5. *C* **O** **R** *B* *A* *T* *A*
11 12

**Solution: un**

| S | O | M | B | R | E | R | O | | A | Z | U | L |
|---|---|---|---|---|---|---|---|---|---|---|---|---|
| 10 | 11 | 3 | 5 | 1 | 4 | 12 | 2 | | 9 | 8 | 7 | 6 |

**F** Todo el mundo habla del *tiempo*. Siempre preguntan: ¿Qué *tiempo* hace? En el *invierno*, hace mucho *frío*. Llevamos un *abrigo* y *guantes*. En la *primavera* y en el *otoño* hace *fresco* y llevamos una *chaqueta*. En el *verano* hace mucho *calor*. No necesitamos mucha *ropa*. Vamos a la *playa*. Hay mucho *sol* y no hay *nieve*. ¿Cuál es tu estación favorita? ¿Es la *primavera*, el *verano*, el *otoño* o el *invierno*?

Hay una *fiesta* en la *casa* de Jorge. Las *muchachas* y los *muchachos* llegan a la *casa* a *las ocho*. Escuchan *discos,* *bailan* y *comen*. La *madre* y el *padre* sirven *sandwiches*, *ensalada*, *frutas*, *pan*, *queso*, *jugo de naranja* y *helado*. Es el cumpleaños de Jorge. Desde hoy, el *veinte y uno de septiembre*, Jorge tiene *catorce* años.

## Achievement Test II (Lessons 13–20)

**1**
1. *la ropa*
2. *el apartamento*
3. *el helado*
4. *la cocina*
5. *la gallina*
6. *la boca*
7. *el traje*
8. *la vaca*
9. *la mano*
10. *el dinero*

**2** 1. treinta y ocho *38*
2. ochenta y cuatro *84*
3. cincuenta y uno *51*
4. noventa y tres *93*
5. setenta y seis *76*

**3** 1. *mis* 3. *tus* 5. *sus*
2. *su* 4. *nuestras*

**4**

| | |
|---|---|
| 1. Es el veinte y dos de abril. | *It's April 22.* |
| 2. Es el quince de julio. | *It's July 15.* |
| 3. Es el treinta de octubre. | *It's October 30.* |
| 4. Es el catorce de enero. | *It's January 14.* |
| 5. Es el primero de marzo. | *It's March 1.* |

**5**

| | |
|---|---|
| 1. Es miércoles. | *It's Wednesday.* |
| 2. Es domingo. | *It's Sunday.* |
| 3. Es jueves. | *It's Thursday.* |
| 4. Es martes. | *It's Tuesday.* |
| 5. Es viernes. | *It's Friday.* |

**6**

| | |
|---|---|
| 1. ¿Cuál es la fecha de hoy? | 1. *a* |
| 2. ¿Cómo está usted? | 2. *c* |
| 3. ¿En qué estación estamos? | 3. *b* |
| 4. ¿Qué tiempo hace? | 4. *b* |
| 5. ¿Cuántos años tienes? | 5. *a* |

**7** 1. *Hace viento.*
2. *Hace frío.*
3. *Hace sol.*
4. *Hace mal tiempo. / Llueve.*
5. *Nieva.*
6. *Hace buen tiempo. / Hace calor.*

**8** 1. *Es el invierno.* 3. *Es la primavera.*
2. *Es el otoño.* 4. *Es el verano.*

**9**

1. *tengo*
2. *tenemos*
3. *tienes*
4. *tiene*
5. *tiene*
6. *tienen*
7. *Hace*
8. *haces*
9. *hago*
10. *hacen*
11. *hace*
12. *hacemos*
13. *gusta*
14. *gusta*
15. *gustan*
16. *gusta*
17. *gustan*
18. *gusta*
19. *van*
20. *voy*
21. *vamos*
22. *Va*
23. *vas*
24. *van*
25. *dice*
26. *digo*
27. *decimos*
28. *dicen*
29. *dicen*
30. *dices*

**10**

1. *blanco*
2. *rojos*
3. *negra*
4. *azules*
5. *amarillo*
6. *pardas/castañas*
7. *anaranjada*
8. *verdes*
9. *grises*
10. *rosadas*

**11**

1. *d*
2. *c*
3. *b*
4. *a*
5. *c*

**12**

1. *(b)*
2. *(a)*
3. *(d)*
4. *(d)*
5. *(c)*

# Real-Life Couples: Why They Eloped

"We both felt a traditional wedding wasn't appropriate for who we are."

"A friend who had just eloped called from the islands and said, 'You guys should do it. It was perfect!'"

"It seemed like we were doing things to make other people happy, not us."

"It was the second marriage for both of us, and we didn't want to put our parents through the hassle or expense."

"I jokingly said, 'Let's go to Vegas,' and she agreed."

"I have a friend whose mother got upset because the number of people on one side of the church didn't equal the number on the other side. I couldn't deal with situations like that!"

"Money was an issue. As we were planning, we kept calculating how much it would cost."

"We had been living together for a long time, so getting married wasn't a big deal, just something to do in public."

*If any of these sound familiar, then this is the book for you!*

Scott Shaw &
Lynn Beahan

Bantam Books
NEW YORK TORONTO
LONDON SYDNEY AUCKLAND

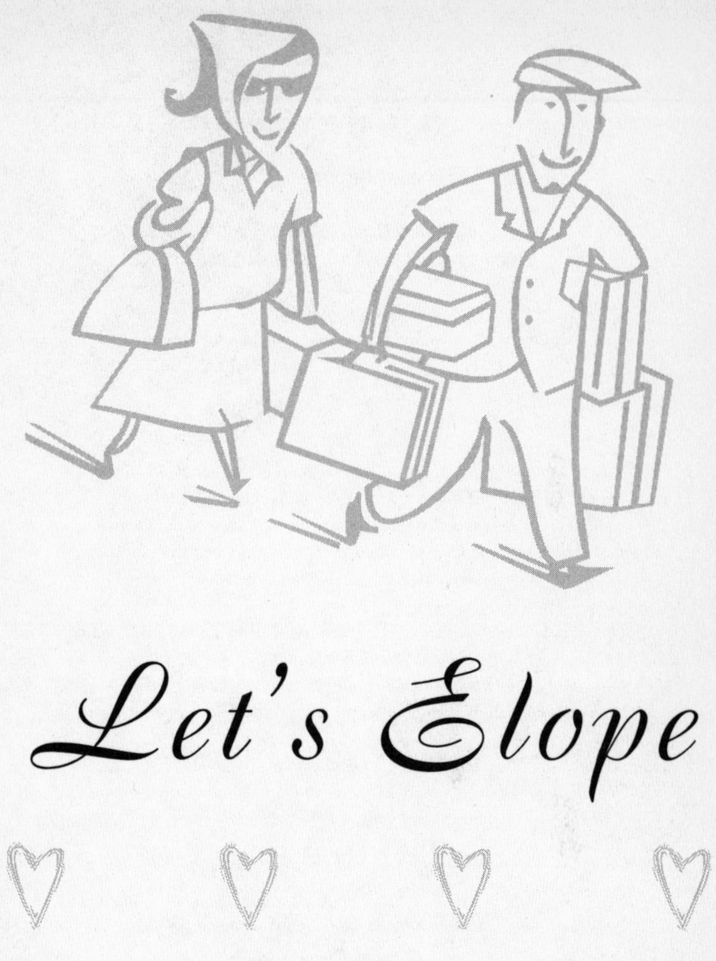

# Let's Elope

♡ ♡ ♡ ♡

THE DEFINITIVE GUIDE TO ELOPING, DESTINATION WEDDINGS, AND OTHER CREATIVE WEDDING OPTIONS

LET'S ELOPE

PUBLISHING HISTORY
Bantam trade paperback / January 2001



*Book design by Jennifer Ann Daddio*



Library of Congress Cataloging-in-Publication Data
Shaw, Scott.
Let's elope : the definitive guide to eloping, destination weddings, and other creative weddings / Scott Shaw and Lynn Beahan.
p. cm.
ISBN 0-553-38082-6 (pbk.)
1. Weddings—Planning. 2. Elopement. 3. Destination weddings.
I. Beahan, Lynn, 1968– II. Title.
HQ745.B42 2001
395.2'2—dc21 00-059913

*Published simultaneously in the United States and Canada*

---

Bantam Books are published by Bantam Books, a division of Random House, Inc. Its trademark, consisting of the words "Bantam Books" and the portrayal of a rooster, is Registered in U.S. Patent and Trademark Office and in other countries. Marca Registrada. Bantam Books, 1540 Broadway, New York, New York 10036.

---

PRINTED IN THE UNITED STATES OF AMERICA

FFG 10 9 8 7 6 5 4 3

**elope:** (1) to run away secretly; especially, to leave one's home to marry a lover. (2) to run away, to escape, to abscond. (3) *a delightful and perfectly sensible alternative to large traditional weddings.*

*To Camille and Harris,*
*our patient partners*

# Acknowledgments

The authors would like to thank the following individuals for their invaluable help and support in making this book: Marnie Cochran for her encouragement and guidance when this book was still at the idea stage; Jessica Jones and Christine Brooks for making this book possible; Mary Stapp for her research assistance; Kathleen Jayes at Bantam-Dell for her editing expertise, and her assistant Jamie Ehrlich; Stacey Glick at Jane Dystel Literary Agency for helping to launch our idea; John Heebink for his sportsmanship; Barbara Whitehill and Andrea Rotondo for their insight to the world of alternative weddings; Catherine Kerr for her wedding Web world knowledge; Ken, Carol, and Kathleen Beahan for their basement, phone line, and PC; all of the couples who shared their stories with us; and Elvis.

# Contents

# *Introduction*

At first I thought it was a mistake. A half hour of earnest searching in my local Barnes and Noble had yielded 100-plus books on how to plan a nice, traditional wedding. Beautiful coffee table books on wedding flowers, thick wedding organizers with two checklists per chapter, even three different books on how to give a wedding toast. But nothing on elopement. Not even a mention in *Miss Manners' Guide to Excruciatingly Correct Behavior* (though she does tell you how to wear a Phi Beta Kappa key and how to behave when you're a guest at the White House).

"This doesn't make sense," I told my fiancée. "A zillion people must elope every year. Do you think they just wing it?"

"Perhaps they're just sold out of eloping books," she suggested. "Let's ask at the counter."

"Hmmm . . . I'm sure we must have something," the clerk said, frowning, as he peered into the computer screen. "Some friends just eloped and they couldn't plan a reception at McDonald's—they must have gotten some help."

We chose not to take his remarks personally. We're perfectly capable adults and felt sure we could have figured it out ourselves in a pinch. But why reinvent the wheel? Why not grab a few helpful hints on how to do it, maybe some ideas about where to go, and definitely some advice on how to handle our parents. Not to mention the whole etiquette thing. What are you supposed to do about announcements? And what's the deal with gifts when you elope? One of us had been married before, but all the hoopla and rules surrounding that event didn't seem to apply to eloping.

"Sorry, I guess no one's written a book on eloping," the clerk said finally.

Bingo! The lightbulb lit up. Thirty minutes later, after a quick search at Amazon.com produced the same result—zilch!—I'd found my calling for the next year (after my own elopement and honeymoon, of course).

Eloping, I quickly discovered, is like politics. Everyone has an opinion on the subject. The first four people my fiancée and I talked to—our parents—certainly did. To our surprise, they liked the idea very much. We found lots of elopement fans, in fact, including a large number of couples that *wish* they had eloped. Others on their way to the altar wouldn't consider the subject, although sometimes their fiancés and parents perked up when they heard what we were working on! "Couldn't you just print a draft and leave it lying around?" they asked. "Maybe he'll read it and change his mind." We also discovered that as with politics, there are a great many "undecideds" out there; couples that like the idea but that are concerned they might regret skipping the "Big Traditional Wedding."

My co-writer, Lynn, and I wrote this book with the needs of these different audiences in mind. It is largely a how-to guide, with a sprinkling of true-life stories and collected wisdom. Those of you born to elope can skip right to the practical stuff. If you're undecided, you might want to look at all the hybrid elopement-wedding options we describe; couples are having more fun than you could imagine reinventing (breaking?)

the rules every day. And those of you who assume you'll end up with a big wedding should pay special attention to chapter 1, "Why You Should Elope." Read it carefully.

Why do we want to change someone's mind about something so personal? For a simple, compelling reason: not a single person we interviewed had a moment's regret about eloping. Not one. Whether they eloped for fun, to save money, or to stave off family conflicts, they all were—and still are—delighted with their choice. We agree wholeheartedly: keep it simple, have fun, and be yourself.

*—Scott Shaw*

# A Word About Stereotypes

It is difficult to write about eloping, weddings, and families without bumping into the classic stereotypes: the overeager bride; the inattentive "whatever-you-want" groom; the mother of the bride intent on throwing the wedding *she* never had; or the desperate-to-avoid-conflict father of the bride (or the status-conscious father who views the wedding as a business networking event). None of these stereotypes are wholly true, and yet there is enough truth that we still recognize them.

While researching this book, we encountered exceptions to the stereotypes: overanxious grooms and reluctant brides; brides' mothers who openly suggested eloping; and fathers who put their foot down and insisted on a big wedding.

That said, we have still chosen to use some of the more traditional stereotypes here, primarily because they're familiar; we recognize and understand the situations and characters instantly. But feel free to substitute genders and roles as you wish, ignoring those that seem out of place, and adapting our advice to your own lives and families.

PART ONE

# Eloping 101

# 1. Why You Should Elope

Couples that've eloped can often pinpoint the exact moment when the idea hit them: the night they came home late from work and cringed at a stack of wedding planners on their bedside table; the phone call from Mom or Dad asking them how the invitation list was coming along; or the end-of-month bill-paying session when they just couldn't make things add up. One of them turns to the other and says the magic words: "Why don't we just elope?"

"Wouldn't that be nice!" they agree as they return to the Dreaded Wedding Checklist. But for those who take the idea seriously, something changes. The pressure's off, a cloud has been lifted, and all of a sudden wedding planning feels more the way you hoped it would: romantic, fun, and exciting. Of course it does! That's because you really are *planning* now, not just following someone else's instructions. All of a sudden it's *your* wedding again, and ideas race through your head: a barefoot wedding on a tropical beach; on a mountaintop surrounded by wildflowers; in Vegas, surrounded by the friends you *really* love (and Elvis, of course); or in a small country chapel with just your parents and siblings as witnesses. Anything is possible, but most of all the opportunity to express yourself, to celebrate one of the most important events of your life in the way you want.

## But I Want a Big Wedding!

OK. Go ahead and say it. Scream it at the top of your lungs if that helps. But let's examine what you really want: a romantic, memorable occasion that you can celebrate with your family and close friends, right? Perfectly reasonable, except that you won't get those warm, fuzzy feelings from a traditional big wedding.

For starters, romance and large crowds don't go together. And memories? Sorry. In bride-time your wedding day lasts 15 minutes. Then—whoosh!—it's gone. That's why people hire photographers, to prove it really happened. Otherwise you'd swear somebody drugged you and tossed you in a limo. Before you dismiss this as a plot to steal your dreams, listen to what the unrivaled master of the event has to say:

> *You out there in bride-land, you sweet thing: are you planning your wedding so that it will be perfect in every detail? Do you expect it to be the happiest day of your life? Miss Manners sincerely hopes not.*
>
> MISS MANNERS' GUIDE TO EXCRUCIATINGLY CORRECT BEHAVIOR

"My goodness! Who on earth is she talking about?" you ask. "Not me! *My* wedding will certainly be different!" Of course it will be different. Just not in the way you think it will. Listen to Miss Manners. She knows what she's talking about. Big weddings are like a family vacation to Mount Everest: a year of painstaking preparation, an exhausting hike to base camp, and then the mad scramble to the summit while the weather holds. When you arrive at the top there's a momentary sense of terrific accomplishment—I did it! But you're hungry, tired, and sick to death of your traveling companions. After a quick glimpse in all directions, you're ready to get the heck home.

Don't let yourself be swayed by the reassuring tones of those "perfect wedding" planners, either, the ones you rushed to buy the day after you got engaged. If anything, their two checklists per chapter should set off warning bells. Do you really want a wedding that requires endless preparation, faultless execution, plus a healthy dose of luck?

We hope we've gotten to you in time, because the point of no return comes quickly with traditional weddings, usually

## What Is a Big Wedding, Anyway?

This is a subject of great debate. At first glance it would seem to be a question of numbers, but there is wide disagreement on which numbers to use. We've heard couples talk enthusiastically about their "small wedding," then casually let drop that they're struggling to keep the guest list under 500. Get serious. In our view anything over 50 guests constitutes a big wedding. That's the point at which you've gone beyond your immediate family and closest friends. You are now hosting a public event, with all the attendant duties and complications.

But numbers don't tell the whole story. A big wedding is defined as much by style as by sheer numbers. A casual clambake wedding for 100 may be less stressful than a formal dinner for 40. The operative words are *stress* and *planning*. Too much of the latter induces the former. A good rule of thumb: planning a wedding should be easier than moving. You start two months before, make five or six phone calls, and keep your guest and to-do lists at one page each.

within weeks of the engagement announcement. A date is picked, a flurry of phone calls go out to friends and relatives, a site is booked, and before you know it you're committed. You can't turn back and so you have to rationalize the misery. The groom who hates to-do lists starts professing a newfound joy for organizing; the bride who detests balancing her checkbook pretends to enjoy managing a $25,000 budget. And both of you realize that your post-college independence has been an illusion; Mom and Dad have been lurking in the background all these years, readying themselves for this—the crowning event of parent-child conflict.

## DOES IT HAVE TO BE STRESSFUL?

Unfortunately, yes. The devil's in the details, and nowhere is this old saying more true than in planning a big wedding. Details mean decisions—thousands of them! You start with the big decisions: how many guests to have; where to hold it; whom to invite; what to wear; what sort of flowers; what music to play; and what food to serve. "OK, I can handle these," you tell yourself. "I'm a grown-up who makes big decisions every day." Ah, but wedding decisions aren't like business decisions, where you make up your mind and move on to the next problem. Wedding decisions are inextricably linked together in a NASA-like decision tree of infinite permutations. Again and again you'll find yourself revising plans and revisiting prior decisions in light of new facts.

Take flowers, for example. This seemingly safe and easy area is actually fraught with complexity. You start with an idea for a complex centerpiece on each table, only to find out that (a) you can't get the flowers you wanted after all, or (b) you can't afford the prices charged by professional arrangers. So now you're considering other options. But that may mean rethinking the whole table layout, the color of the table linens or—God forbid!—the bridesmaids' dresses. While you're at it you'll probably want to go back and take a second look at the other flowers you've picked for the church, buffet table, or elsewhere. And, of course, you'll have to rework the budget. If your solution is now to have a friend or relative do the flowers, you've just added a whole new set of items to your list, and anxieties to your life.

Multiply this complexity by the sheer number of decisions you have to make and mounting an Everest expedition starts to look like a trip to the grocery store. Whom to invite, for example, is not 150 decisions on whom to invite, but 1,500 decisions on whom *not* to invite. Or more, since Palm Pilots and e-mail mean everyone's staying in touch these days. By the time you're done you'll feel like an admissions director at an Ivy League college. Of course, you can expand the size of the group (something Harvard can't do for its entering class), but then you'll have to cull through your reject list all over again to see who makes the second cut. If all of this sounds ridiculous, ask a friend who's gone through List Hell.

Just sitting all by yourself in a room for a few weeks to make all of these decisions would be exhausting work. Now factor in discussion, debate, and full-fledged argument on 100 or more of these decisions. Suddenly your fiancé is looking more and more like an ex you'd rather forget and you're vowing never to let your mother near any offspring of yours. Think we're exaggerating? Listen again to Miss Manners. Planning a wedding, she advises, is "an excellent opportunity for the couple to learn how to placate others and negotiate compromise, surely requirements for family life." Well said, but she's putting it a bit too delicately. The truth is, planning a wedding is a difficult, stressful exercise that makes no one happy.

Adding insult to injury, just when you think you're done, after you've made all your decisions and compromises, fate steps in to play a few tricks. It rains the day of your wedding, or the caterer's truck breaks down, or the staff doesn't show. Or, or, or . . . something always goes wrong. The guests won't care, they'll have a good time anyway. But imperfections, however trivial, are hard for the bride to ignore after months of detailed planning. Understandably, she lets it get to her, spoiling an otherwise delightful party. Just listen to Jill K, a professional wedding photographer: "I photograph a lot of weddings. At almost every wedding something goes wrong that depresses the bride by the end of the night."

## SO WHY DO WE PUT OURSELVES THROUGH THIS?

Cynics might call it a conspiracy masterminded by the $32 billion a year wedding industry. That's a bit harsh, though. If it is a conspiracy, it is largely a well-intentioned one. Starting with your parents, who meant well when they read you those bedtime stories about Cinderella, Snow White, Sleeping Beauty, and their princes. They still mean well, in fact. That's why they've suddenly jumped back into your life. They, along with everyone else who has an opinion about your wedding (which is everyone you know, and some you don't), are just thinking of your happiness. The problem is, it's too much of a good thing; too many good thoughts coming your way, an information and opinion overload that's only gotten worse with e-mail.

Further confusing matters, there's a paradoxical conspiracy of silence surrounding big weddings. Yes, everyone has an opinion, but they're also keeping secrets from you. No one wants to rain on your party by telling you that your wedding sounds identical to the last five weddings they went to, or that they argued incessantly with their fiancé or parents before their own wedding. No, they'll lie, or politely feign enthusiasm. But pour your friends enough wine and in private they might loosen up, might confess that if they had it all to do over again they'd elope in a heartbeat. Public statements are another matter, however. Only rarely will you see a big wedding bride break ranks to express regret. The most famous, of course, was Princess Diana. She called her wedding day one of the most miserable days of her life, and not just because she and Charles flubbed their lines. What does that tell you, that the most famous bride of the century, whose wedding mesmerized the whole world, didn't enjoy her day?

## *Then There's the Money Issue*

Money probably wasn't high on Lady Di's list of wedding problems, but for most people the financial burden of a big wedding adds an extra layer of stress. Conflict can arise, too, if the bride and groom find themselves at odds with their parents, or with each other, on how—or how much—to spend. And even under the best of circumstances, developing and managing a large budget can be an unfamiliar and unwelcome burden.

Just how large a budget are we talking about? Well, *Brides*

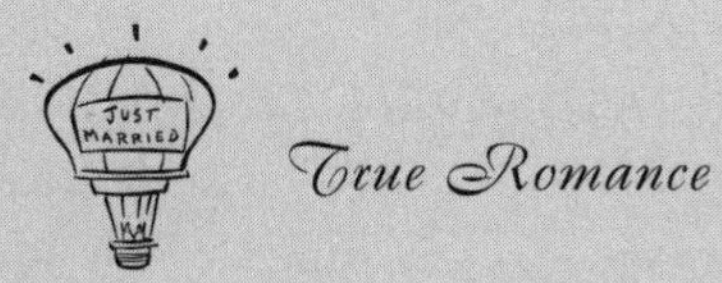


### *True Romance*

*Frankly, Scarlett, I'm in love with someone else . . .*
Clark Gable and Carole Lombard, perhaps one of Hollywood's most romantic couples, eloped in March 1939. Their romance began in 1936 when both were at a formal ball called The White Mayfair Ball. Although earlier they had filmed a movie together and seemed to be interested in each other at that time, they had an argument and no romance followed. The morning after their "remeeting" at the ball, Gable awoke to doves flying about his hotel room. Lombard had ordered the doves and Gable knew he had another chance with her. In March 1939, when taking a few days off from filming *Gone with the Wind*, Gable showed that he really didn't "give a damn" about Scarlett, and he and Lombard eloped to Kingman, Arizona.

magazine puts the average cost of a wedding at just over $17,000. But that's just an average. As you'll see in the following pages, it's amazingly easy to spend twice that much. Either way, we're talking big numbers. Big enough to make anyone think twice.

For some couples the discussion starts and ends with the money issue: if they can't have the wedding they want, they'd rather elope. Others opt for planning a simpler wedding. Increasingly, though, even couples that *can* afford a big wedding are looking at the cost and reconsidering. And why shouldn't they? Young people are more savvy about finances these days. They crunch numbers at work and at home, juggling their mutual funds, 401k investments, stock options, and cafeteria-style benefit plans. It's only natural for them to look at the cost of a big wedding. What else could they be doing with that money? (We have some suggestions, and a helpful way to calculate opportunity cost, in the following pages.)

Two demographic trends are also pushing people to look more closely at the cost of large weddings. The first is that couples are waiting longer to get married. According to the U.S. Census Bureau, the average age of first marriages in 1958 was 23 for men and 20 for women. In 1998, 40 years later, the numbers were 27 for men and 25 for women. Those four to five extra years work both ways. Couples may be better off financially today, but they're also closer to life's big-ticket commitments—a house, kids, and retirement. Of course they'll consider what else they could do with the money they would spend on a wedding. The second trend is the high rate of divorce and remarriage. Memories may last forever, but if the marriage didn't then it's hard not

The first known cash advance to pay for a wedding was recorded in 32 B.C. when the bride's father mortgaged his olive crop for 10 years to pay for the festivities.

to regret that $50,000 first wedding. On the positive side, once you've had a big wedding you don't need, or want, another one.

### WHAT A BIG WEDDING REALLY COSTS

Before we go any further, let's deal with that $17,000 national average. The problem as we see it is that no one wants to have an average wedding. So that $17,000 is more like a base price. But, of course, couples want *all* the options on their special day. So to help you understand what *your* wedding would cost (and how easily costs can spiral out of control), we decided to compare the cost of an "average" and a "real" wedding.

You might be surprised to hear that it actually turned out to be a difficult assignment. Although all the big wedding books have chapters on budgeting, with lots of advice and fill-in-the-blank forms, not one of them actually adds up all the costs. Oh, they'll point out that a photographer might cost from $250 to $1,500, or that caterers might charge you from $50 to $200 per guest, but they won't fill in the blanks for you. They won't come right out and tell you that a big wedding costs more than a nice car. Conspiracy theorists might say they don't want you to know until it's too late, until after you've taken the plunge by booking a caterer or country club. More likely the editors of these books are just being polite. They don't want to be the ones to tell you that you can't have the wedding of your dreams for $8,000.

For our sample budget we decided on 125 guests, including three bridesmaids and three groomsmen. While most budget work sheets (and the $17,000 national average) don't include the rehearsal dinner, we decided to add $3,500 to pay for it. Another reason our budget is higher is because we live in Washington, D.C., and because we used the average, not the lowest, estimates from vendors. We freely admit you could do better by driving harder bargains, or if you live in a smaller city. And we aren't saying you can't pull off a $17,000 wedding in Manhattan (or find ways to spend $100,000 in a small town). But generally, in the bigger cities and suburban areas you *will* have to work at it harder. You'll also have to do it alone, since neither budget includes a wedding consultant. Sorry, at these prices you're on your own.

## *A Tale of Two Budgets*

| | National Average | Real Wedding |
|---|---|---|
| Stationery | $ 340 | $ 600 |
| Invitations, announcements, thank-you notes, reply cards, at-home, and pew cards. | | |
| Photography | 1,275 | 2,000 |
| Formal portraits (engagement and wedding), wedding album, albums for parents, extra prints, video of wedding. | | |
| Reception | 8,500 | 15,200 |
| Food, beverages, wedding cake, service, gratuities, taxes, valet, coat check, police, room rental charges. | ($68 per person) | ($122 per person) |
| Music | 1,394 | 2,500 |
| Church/synagogue and reception. | | |
| Bridal Attire | 1,861 | 3,500 |
| Dress, headpiece, and veil; undergarments, jewelry; shoes and trousseau; groom's attire and accessories. | | |
| Transportation/Lodging | 323 | 750 |
| Limousines, parking, shuttles, bride/groom's suite. | | |

| | | |
|---|---|---|
| Wedding Parties | 0 | 3,500 |
| Bridal luncheon, rehearsal dinner, out-of-town guest events. | | |
| Ceremony | 476 | 750 |
| Church/synagogue fees, officiant, assistants, maintenance staff, sexton. | | |
| Gifts | 340 | 500 |
| Bridesmaids, groomsmen, maid of honor, best man. | | |
| Flowers | 1,045 | 2,000 |
| At ceremony, bouquets, corsages, at reception. | | |
| Extras | 0 | 500 |
| Monogrammed napkins/matches, favors, groom's cake, birdseed. | | |
| Wedding Rings | 340 | 700 |
| Tips, Taxes, and Miscellaneous | 1,106 | 1,500 |
| Total Estimated Cost: | 17,000 | 34,000 |
| Total Cost per Guest: | $136 | $272 |

## GETTING BY ON LESS

Weddings are a bit like automobiles: you get what you pay for (reliability and style going hand in hand with price), and both seem to start at about $17,000 these days. So you're not going to get a new BMW or a perfect wedding for $8,000. And beware of shortcuts: champagne expectations on a Kool-Aid budget backfire every time. You shouldn't invite people to a 7 P.M. wedding and then not serve them dinner, or host a country club wedding with a cash bar. We aren't saying you *can't* (it's your wedding, you can do whatever you want). But it *is* out of the ordinary and some of your guests may take offense. You say you don't care? Well, then, you may also want to consider the following cost-saving tips from one budget-minded wedding planner:

• Hire high-school musicians.
• Use preprinted fill-in-the-blank invitations.
• Hold your wedding midweek in winter.
• Double up with another bride to save on decorations.

It is not our place to judge, but none of these ideas appeal to us. We think it's wiser to adjust your expectations. Not downward, but laterally. Think "out of the box," as the business consultants are so fond of suggesting. Instead of trying to pull off a $50,000 wedding on a $5,000 budget, why not throw a spectacular $5,000 wedding? For that amount of money you can host a lovely garden wedding with light sandwiches, chilled white table wine, and games for the children. Or an intimate at-home service followed by a dinner party reception for 30 guests at an elegant restaurant. Both would be delightful and different, and your guests will be much more likely to have fun and remember it fondly. You will, too.

## THE INDIRECT COSTS OF BIG WEDDINGS

Before you start rationalizing about how $34,000 (or $17,000) isn't so much money after all (I'll just keep my car for another five years), you need to look at some of the other costs involved with big weddings. The physical and emotional strain on you, your fiancé, and family goes without saying. But what about your guests? What will it cost *them* to attend your wedding? Their time, of course. But also a great deal of money.

Let's start with a quick quiz: how many of your 125 guests live within a three-hour drive? Maybe half? OK, so that leaves 62.5 people who need airline tickets, hotel rooms, and perhaps a new outfit. Figure the average out-of-town guest will spend $600 (a reasonable, by no means extravagant, estimate), and you've just spent $37,500 of their money. Wow, that was easy, wasn't it? And that's not including any gifts, which could add another $10,000 to their bill. Add it up and your friends and

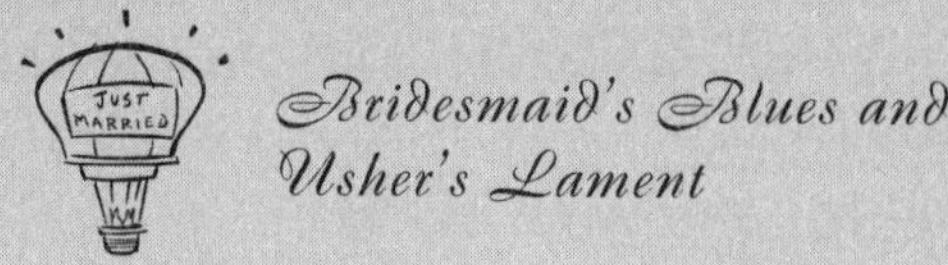

## Bridesmaid's Blues and Usher's Lament

The traditional wedding is a vicious circle of cross-commitments and IOUs. In fact, the system depends on it. How else could you convince young people to shell out a big chunk of their earnings—and most of their vacation time—racing from one wedding to another? No wonder the airports are so crowded! A bit of math will reveal just how serious this problem is: if the average bride has six attendants (and the average groom six ushers), then it stands to reason that the average young person will be in at least six weddings herself, not including her own. Now multiply that by $800 or so in usher/bridesmaid expenses and you're almost up to $5,000. Talk about opportunity cost! Imagine what kind of returns you could get if you diverted that $5,000 into a long-term savings account: $158,036 in 30 years, to be exact.

But forget about the money for a second. Look at this issue in human terms: all of us have a limited amount of free time, and more than enough stress, in our lives. So why would you want to take from the former and add to the latter? Misery may love company, but if you really loved your friends you wouldn't do this to them.

"But that's not fair!" you protest. "I flew to Albany (no mean feat in itself) and bought an aqua chiffon dress to be in *her* wedding." Well, that was nice of you. But two wrongs still don't make a right. Put yourself in your prospective bridesmaid's shoes for a moment (and we're not talking about dyed lavender pumps). Would she rather (a) spend a long weekend somewhere romantic with her significant other, or (b) fly cross-country and spend three days in an airport hotel, readying herself to march down an aisle in a $200 bridesmaid's dress she'll never wear again?

family are spending almost $50,000 of their own money. It's a wonder newlywed couples receive gifts at all!

### YOUR MILLION-DOLLAR WEDDING

In an era when everyone wants to be a millionaire, few seem to understand that a million dollars is right in front of them as they thumb through those thick wedding planners. Really! Imagine for a minute you took that $34,000 and invested it. Maybe you opened an account with Charles Schwab, say, with a cute little name like "The Wedding Fund." Thirty years later, just when you're ready to retire, you and your sweetheart will **have more than a million dollars** waiting for you! ($1,074,644 to be exact, assuming a 12.2 percent annual return, which is what the Standard & Poor's index has averaged over the last 50 years).

Wow. Kind of makes you stop and think, doesn't it? You could buy a beach house, a pied-à-terre in Paris, or send the kids to college without having to save a nickel. And before you argue that inflation would make that million worth a bit less (it would, but even with a 3 percent inflation rate, you'd have $442,739 worth of buying power in today's dollars), remember: you wouldn't have *anything* left at all if you'd done the big wedding.

Here's a simple exercise:

1. Take your preliminary wedding budget.
2. Add 50 percent. That's the real number anyway.
3. Round your budget off to the closest $5,000.
4. Find the corresponding row on the chart below and read across to find out how much you're giving up by insisting on the big wedding.
5. Buy a bottle of wine. Drink it with your fiancé and make a list of all the fun things you could do with that money besides hosting a wedding.

## *The 30-Year Wedding Fund*

| Initial Investment | Interest Rate 5% | 10% | 12.2% | 15% |
|---|---|---|---|---|
| *$5,000* | $21,609 | $87,241 | $158,036 | $331,059 |
| *$10,000* | 43,219 | 174,494 | 316,072 | 662,117 |
| *$15,000* | 64,829 | 261,741 | 474,108 | 993,177 |
| ***$17,000*** | 73,473 | 296,640 | **537,322** | 1,125,600 |
| *$20,000* | 86,439 | 348,988 | 632,144 | 1,324,235 |
| *$25,000* | 108,048 | 436,235 | 790,179 | 1,655,294 |
| *$30,000* | 129,658 | 523,482 | 948,215 | 1,986,353 |
| ***$34,000*** | 146,946 | 593,280 | **1,074,644** | 2,251,200 |
| *$50,000* | 216,097 | 872,470 | 1,580,359 | 3,310,589 |

### *Paris for a Lifetime!*

Of all the wonderful things you could do with $34,000, we like this one best. It's a simple plan devised by sentimental fools who think that *staying* married is the real goal. Even if you threw away every other argument for elopement in this book, the Paris Plan should still get you. And if your fiancé is the stick-in-the-mud, if he is insisting on the big wedding, then you should put him to the test. If he says no to the Paris Plan, you need to take a serious look at what you're getting yourself into.

Here's how it works: just tuck the $34,000 away in your Schwab account for 10 years and you'll have $88,187 (assuming a 10 percent return). At that point just the interest on your nest egg ($4,409, assuming a 5 percent return) would pay for a week in Paris *every year for the rest of your life*! It's not quite enough to bring the kids along, of course, but is that really such a bad thing?

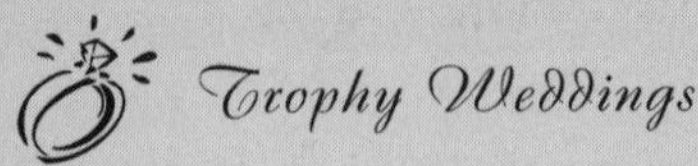

## Trophy Weddings

For professional wedding-watchers it's a great sport to see just how far some people will go. The answer is *very far* and *too far*, as evidenced by the "Trophy Wedding." This is big-game hunting in a jet-set jungle, where a handful of ultra-elite wedding planners lead their clients deeper and deeper into forbidden territory, their reputations dependent on providing something new and different—the ultimate wedding. Money, of course, is no object, and Europe is a favorite destination for American couples looking to bag their dream wedding. According to *The New York Times*, one wedding started with 450 guests in Paris and ended five days later in Marrakech, Morocco, with guests transported by private jets. At a smaller wedding in Venice, the 160 guests required the services of a fleet of private water taxis to attend nine events in four days, with two wedding planners coordinating the flotillas and parties. And at yet another wedding the cake was flown in by private jet.

Clearly, something or someone is out of control here. The budgets certainly are. Wedding planners estimate that a multiday splurge for a European wedding costs "anywhere from $100,000 to several million," a range that leaves plenty of room for unforeseen contingencies, like sending jets to pick up cakes. The dark underside of these trophy weddings? The guests' wallets. Said one 26-year-old who attended several trophy weddings in a row, "I feel like I have to go to them. They're your friends. But I'm broke now." Guests at another trophy wedding estimated they spent $4,000—not including the cost of a wedding gift, new outfits, or the nanny they brought along for their toddler. After one or two of these even the most affluent of guests might consider asking if they can hitch a ride with the cake next time.

## BUT MY PARENTS ARE PAYING FOR THE WEDDING

It's nice that they've offered. Before you take them up on their offer, however, you'd better consider the consequences. For one thing, you're not exactly getting off scot-free. If someone offered you $34,000 to spend all your waking hours for the next nine months in a conflict-management seminar, would you instantly accept? You might also consider that your parents have already done a great deal for you. Wouldn't it be nice to just thank them for their offer, but suggest they spend it on themselves? Lastly, you might consider—though never aloud, and not for long—that your parents might repay your thoughtfulness with a gift of their own. And if that gift takes the form of a check, and that check just happens to equal the cost of a wedding, well, isn't that a coincidence!

## WHAT ABOUT JUST ASKING THEM FOR THE MONEY?

No, never, strike that thought from your mind. Do not for a moment imagine that you are "owed" a wedding or its monetary equivalent. Your parents' money is *their* money, not yours. And while they might be willing to spend some of it on your long-awaited wedding, they might also (quite reasonably) feel that writing you a check doesn't quite do the same thing for them. In fact, they are just as likely to feel that you have deprived them of something special (see chapter 6, "How to Convince Everyone Else"). It is perfectly reasonable to analyze the economic impact of your wedding if you're paying for it, thoughtful of you to consider the impact on your parents if they're paying, but never acceptable to bargain with or blackmail your parents.

## WHAT ABOUT THE LOOT?

Fess up. You've been wondering, haven't you? "What am I giving up if I elope?" For some couples it's not even the dollar value of the gifts, but the curiosity factor: "Dawn, tell us what's behind door number two for Amy and John!" But going through with a big wedding to satisfy either curiosity or greed is a huge mistake. Here are three sound arguments to prove this point:

*Loot Argument No.1: Gifts Are Not a Legal Right*

It may be customary for guests to give gifts, but it is not a legal requirement. (If you really wanted to get logical you could argue that the guest who has just spent $1,000 to attend your wedding should not be expected to shell out another $100 or so for a gift. *She* should be sent home with a gift!) And although you may feel like gifts are your just rewards for putting yourselves through the difficulties of planning a big wedding, that, too, is an unacceptable argument.

*Loot Argument No.2: You're Better Off Buying the Loot Yourself Anyway*

Getting married for the loot is not only pathetic, but it's also a bad deal; right up there with selling Manhattan for the equivalent of $24 (in gewgaws and the Indian currency). Think about it: why would you spend $17,000 (much less $34,000!) for a garage full of questionable merchandise that falls into two categories: useless items and overpriced necessities. Certainly you'd never pay retail for any of this, assuming you'd even buy it in the first place. "But I'm not paying for it," you say, "what do I care if it's overpriced?" Aren't you, though? Your wedding isn't exactly free, and the time spent planning it must count for something. No, if you're lusting after loot, you'd be better off skipping the wedding and buying it yourself.

*Loot Argument No.3: You'll Get the Goods Anyway!*

We can now lift your spirits: in all likelihood you will still be showered with gifts following your elopement. And irony of ironies, you may actually get *better* gifts! It's true: there is simply no limit to the gratitude some people will show at being spared a big wedding. If you follow our advice on quietly registering and including your "at-home" address on the wedding announcement, you will soon be on a first-name basis with your local UPS driver.

### A MACROECONOMIC PERSPECTIVE

For those who appreciate the big, big picture, it's fun to consider the macroeconomic cost of traditional weddings. The logical conclusion is frightening: big weddings are sapping our national economy and threatening our long-term survival. Seriously? Well, look at the numbers: start with the two million people a year who get married. That works out to a million weddings. Say a quarter of these are elopements or small weddings (more after this book comes out, of course). That leaves 750,000 traditional weddings. Using *Brides* magazine's average cost of $17,000, we're talking $12 billion a year in direct wedding expenses. Add another $18 billion to $20 billion spent by guests and we're over $30 billion. And that number doesn't begin to account for the lost productivity. Just think about all those people planning and attending big weddings; how many million hours are spent? Does anyone's calculator even go that high? Granted, the wedding industry employs a good number of people. But in this era of low unemployment some employers would love to tap into this labor pool. And just imagine—the impending social security crisis could be solved overnight if newlywed couples could invest $17,000 tax free for their retirement in a WED-IRA account!

# 2.

# A Short History of Elopement

*Flashback: 17th century, the English countryside.*

*A young woman—it's you!—sits by an open hearth, eyes straining as she struggles to finish a difficult piece of needlepoint. Suddenly the door bursts open. It's Edward, the second son of a neighboring landowner, and he is breathing heavily. Time is short. Your wedding to Edward's older brother is tomorrow, and your father is expected back soon. Edward reaches out and you rise shakily, not sure your legs will hold. Edward's smile gives you strength. (His older brother may inherit everything, but thank goodness Edward has the looks in the family.) He picks you up and carries you to his waiting horse. As you gallop away his best friends—his groomsmen—cover your retreat. You're terrified and elated at the same time. But the deed is done—you've eloped!*

There you have it. Eloping has always been the romantic first cousin to traditional weddings, dating from an era when marriages were arranged and brides had little say in the matter. Today it's still a viable strategy for defeating parents' well-intentioned matrimonial plans. Only now it's not so much about *whom* you marry, as *how* you get married. The principle's the

## *Gretna Green*

In 1754 the English Parliament tightened marriage laws, requiring parental consent for the marriage of minors. That sent off a stampede to Scotland, where the age of consent was only 16. Gretna Green happened to be the first village on the Scottish side of the border, and conveniently located on the main road from London. The blacksmith's shop at the village center soon became Gretna Green's best-known venue for quick marriages, and sparked a long tradition of "Anvil Priests," so named because the blacksmiths performed many of the ceremonies. These unlicensed officiants made much of the symbolism, declaring that just as hot metals were married under great stress and heat, so, too, were unions "forged" in the blacksmith's shop bound to endure.

Gretna Green attracted its share of scandal, including a well-publicized incident involving the tenth earl of Westmoreland, an impoverished aristocrat, and his lover, Sarah Anne Child, the daughter of a rich London banker.

"Suppose you were in love with a girl and her father refused his consent to the union? What would you do?" the young earl asked Sarah's father one evening. Mr. Child replied: "Why, run away to Gretna Green, of course!"

The earl took Mr. Child at his word and snuck off with Sarah in the night. Enraged, Mr. Child followed them north, catching up with them on the Scottish border. The banker shot the earl's lead carriage horse but the couple cut the dead horse from its traces and escaped with the three remaining horses pulling their carriage. An accomplice sabotaged the banker's carriage and hours later the couple was married at the blacksmith's shop.

Over the next century Parliament and the church tried various measures to stop the flood of couples fleeing to Gretna Green. None worked, however, and Gretna Green continued to thrive as the Las Vegas of the British Isles. Today Gretna Green continues to attract couples, with more than 4,000 a year making the pilgrimage to the original blacksmith's shop. There couples can still be married, with the sharp clank of an anvil pronouncing the union solid. For more information on Gretna Green, its history, and how to get married there, visit **gretnagreen.co.uk** on the Web.

same, though: eloping is about people taking charge of their own lives, for better or for worse.

## *Evolution of the Modern Wedding*

The modern wedding, which celebrates romance and commitment in the company of friends and family, is a relatively new invention. Until the mid–19th century, weddings marked an economic union, with a corresponding emphasis on contracts and dowries. If a party was thrown at all, it was likely to be held on the night of the contract signing rather than on the wedding night. Engagements were also shorter, two or three months at most, just long enough to work out those sticky contractual details. And until the late 19th century, most weddings were held at the bride's home, a simple affair involving just the families, the local priest, and a home-cooked meal afterward.

Of course, if you came from a wealthy or royal family it was another matter. The goal then (as now?) was to impress one's peers with a limitless display of wealth. And as the industrial age transformed England and America, a new class of wealthy industrialists sought to imitate the nobility's homes, clothing, and customs. Weddings became a splendid opportunity to show off in all three arenas.

The emerging middle class sought, in turn, to copy upper-class manners and styles. A new invention, the etiquette book, arrived on the scene to help them. These books helped the middle class maneuver through the minefield of unwritten social customs that had governed upper-class society for generations. Advice on weddings, the penultimate social event—and minefield—was especially sought after and dispensed. Here's an excerpt from the *Bride's Book of Etiquette,* circa 1930:

> *In planning a wedding, three factors must be considered—the means and social position of the bride, the groom, and their families; the wishes of the bride and groom; the dignity which the occasion demands.*
>
> *Social custom requires that the wedding conform to the position of the persons directly interested. It is the worst possible taste to turn the occasion into an elaborate social function, far beyond the means of the bride's parents. Such weddings invite ridicule. The most beautiful weddings and those which linger longest in the memory of guests are the simplest affairs, so carefully managed that there is no confusion, no evidence of anxiety on the part of the bride or her family.*
>
> *The wishes of the bride and groom should be consulted next, and*

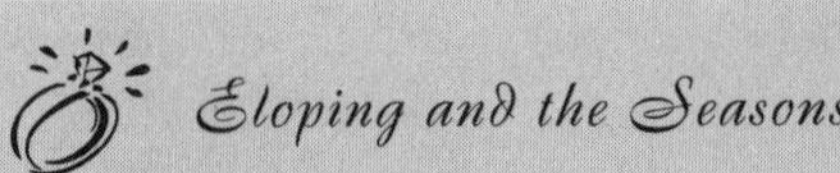


The south Wales god of the underworld, Gwynn ap Nudd, was in love with Creiddylad. However, Creiddylad eloped with Gwythr ap Greidawl, which infuriated Gwynn, as the two had often fought over Creiddylad. Gwynn abducted Creiddylad and the two fought once again. The fight over Creiddylad began on May Day and is said to represent the seasonal contest between summer and winter.

*their choice between a small, simple wedding and a large function should be accepted. Very often this, the greatest day in the lives of a young couple, is clouded by the domination or social ambition of a well-meaning but thoughtless and selfish family.*

*BRIDE'S BOOK OF ETIQUETTE*
ANN STEESE RICHARDSON
NEW YORK: HARPER AND BROTHERS

In the ordering of priorities you can see the evolution of the modern wedding. The fact that the bride and groom's wishes come second—after the families' social position—seems somewhat anachronistic today. But at least the couples' wishes made it

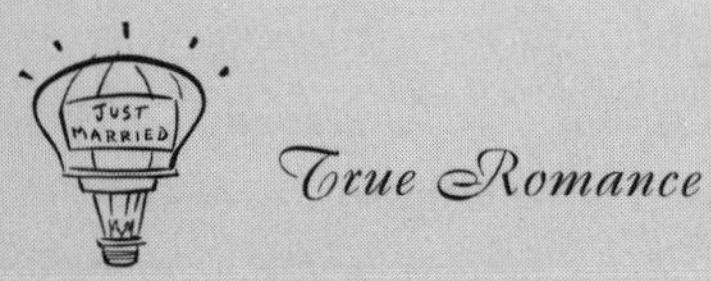


*True Romance*

*Poetry in Motion:*
*Robert Browning and Elizabeth Barrett*

Elizabeth Barrett was a reclusive, bedridden, unmarried poet when Robert Browning began a correspondence with her in 1845. Due to a back injury when she was a child, Elizabeth was an invalid who lived with her very protective and jealous father. Browning, a poet himself, although at the time not as famous as Elizabeth, admired her work and became interested in her as more than a pen pal. They continued writing a series of love letters that led to a secret engagement and then elopement to Italy in 1846. They were married for 15 years until Elizabeth died in Robert's arms in 1861. Browning went on to become a famous writer. He died in Venice in 1889 and was buried in Poet's Corner at Westminster Abbey.

onto the list. In previous centuries a couple may not have had any say in their own wedding, including whom they'd be marrying.

## Eloping Comes of Age

The 1960s and '70s opened the door for the next developments in wedding customs. Couples eager to challenge old ways, and their parents, pushed the nontraditional wedding into the mainstream. Often this amounted to little more than a cosmetic makeover; a change in costume, vows, and menu (no meat, please). But the underlying structure of the traditional wedding, a ceremony followed by a large reception, lived on. Eloping remained in the shadows, the more extreme option for dealing with irreconcilable family disagreements. But beginning in the 1980s and 1990s, eloping became a legitimate third option unto itself, less a reactionary alternative and more of a positive affirmation. Couples waiting longer to get married, and couples who'd already done the traditional or even nontraditional wedding, played a big part in this. More confident and affluent, but not necessarily anti-anything, they simply decided that eloping was more meaningful—and more fun.

These trendsetters also blurred the lines between weddings and elopement. Is it an elopement when you tell people beforehand? When you do a small family-only service, followed by a huge bash at your local dive bar when you return from your honeymoon? And what about a surprise wedding? Is that a form of elopement?

Yes, yes, and yes. The modern definition of eloping is simply this: *anything other than a large, traditional, structured wedding.* In the next chapter we'll explore some of these other ideas, and hear from couples who tried them.

# 3.

# What Are Your Options?

Perhaps one reason so many couples choose traditional weddings is that there's precious little advice out there on what the other options are. "All roads lead to Rome," the ancients used to say, a sentiment seemingly shared by most wedding planners.

Nonsense. You have more choices than you realize.

## 1. True Elopements

The true elopement is characterized by minimal planning, total surprise, and no guests. Nothing could be simpler—you swing by the courthouse and then go straight to the airport, stopping only to drop your announcement cards in a mailbox. Pack a bathing suit, but leave behind all the stresses and worries. You'll have some explaining to do upon your return, of course, but not to your analyst or accountant, who'll appreciate that you're both sane and solvent.

True elopements actually come in two varieties, in-town and getaway.

*The In-Town Elopement:*
It doesn't get any easier than this; you could pull it off on your lunch break. All you're really doing is stripping a $34,000 wedding down to the bare-bones, minimum legal requirements. In most states it's a two-step process:

1. Go to your local county courthouse to pick up a marriage license. Call first, though. Some counties and states have a waiting period and a few still require blood tests.

2. Find a minister, justice of the peace, or other duly appointed person to perform the actual service and sign the license. Haven't been to church lately? No problem. Most marriage license offices keep a list of close-by officers of the court who can meet you on the courthouse steps.

That's it. You're married. If one of you wants to change your name you'll have to make a second trip to the courthouse afterward. But otherwise, you're done.

*The Getaway Elopement:*
Hands down, Las Vegas is the easiest option. All you have to do is prove you're over 18 and pay $35. The same rules (or lack thereof) apply on the Nevada side of Lake Tahoe, where you'll get a slightly more refined experience. The other 49 states have widely differing requirements. Hawaii, for example, has no waiting period, but Wisconsin requires six months. Some states will waive their requirement for out-of-towners and others will help by mailing you a marriage license application in advance. To find out what the local rules are, call the marriage license office for the city or county in which you plan to get married, or check out their Web site (see chapter 7, "Start with the Web").

Marrying abroad is another matter. Some countries make it easy, while others make it terribly difficult. Keep in mind that in order for you to be lawfully married when you get home,

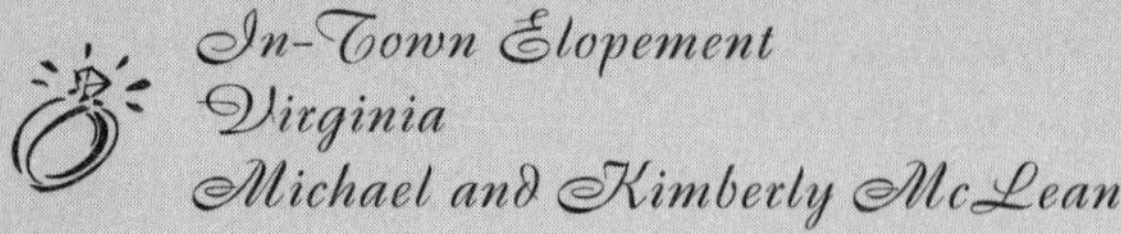

## In-Town Elopement
## Virginia
## Michael and Kimberly McLean

*Background*

**Michael:** Kimberly and I were already engaged but didn't want to put our families through the hassle of a wedding and buying gifts. We'd both been married before and wanted something more intimate this time, something just between us. Ironically, we'd both received our final divorce papers on Valentine's Day. So we decided to change the meaning of Valentine's Day for us and chose that day to get married.

*The Plan*

**Michael:** Since Kimberly had moved back into her parents' house after her divorce, and we weren't going to tell anyone until afterward, we had to be a bit sneaky about the plan. I'm in the Marines and Kimberly's in the Navy, so we thought that it would be appropriate to use a military chaplain. I found one who was a Navy captain, and also a chaplain licensed to perform marriage ceremonies in Virginia. He agreed to marry us in his house.

*The Big Day*

**Kimberly:** Michael left work early the day of our wedding and came to my house to get changed. Wouldn't you know it, my dad came home for lunch that day, which he never does, and asked us what we were getting dressed up for! We told him we had dinner plans, which seemed a bit strange since it was snowing like crazy. But he accepted our answer and we headed out into the blizzard. As we walked up to the chaplain's house I remember my shoe heel kept getting stuck in the snow. The Captain had prepared a simple but moving ceremony, with his wife as our witness. It was an emotional moment for us, especially since both our prior marriages had ended exactly one year earlier. Afterward we went to a photography studio to have a wedding portrait done, and then on to dinner in a quiet restaurant.

*The News*

**Michael:** Kim told her parents the next day. They were shocked but they approved of our marriage and quickly congratulated us. I waited to tell my parents until I had a chance to see them in person. They were happy, too. And our friends know we're a fun-loving, impulsive couple, so they found it appropriate.

*Looking Back*

We have no regrets. You think about it every once in a while, but then you look at all the work that goes into a wedding. Everyone is under stress and there are always catastrophes. We're *so glad* we did what we did, plus it saved us a lot of money.

your wedding abroad must follow the legal requirements of the country in which you were married. "When in Rome . . ." is the rule here. So if you follow the Italian rules you're done. You don't even have to register your marriage when you get back. Unfortunately, this is easier said than done, as Italy's marriage laws are among the more stringent in Europe (see part 2, "Where to Elope"). One final caveat: If you choose to get married abroad, be sure to bring home an extra copy of your official marriage license and put it somewhere safe. Ten years from now, when you need a new copy, a foreign marriage bureau may not be as accommodating as your local courthouse.

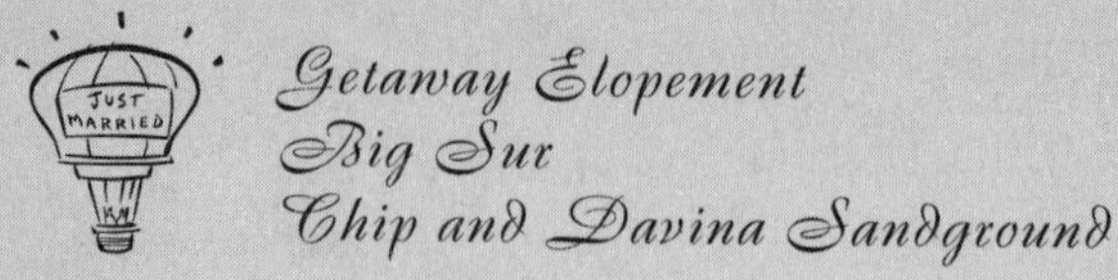


## Getaway Elopement
## Big Sur
## Chip and Davina Sandground

*Background*

**Chip:** Davina wanted to elope from the very beginning. Soon after we moved to San Francisco we started looking for places to get married, but found it very frustrating. Every place we liked was already booked six months ahead and every time we thought we might have found a place, another couple had snatched it up. Then we talked to a friend of ours from New York who was telling us how she had recently run away to the islands and she said, "You guys should elope–it was perfect!" We looked at each other and said, "Why the heck not!"

*The Plan*

**Chip:** We booked a room at an inn in Big Sur, one of Davina's favorite places. It must be a popular place to get married, because the hotel concierge turned out to be a licensed justice of the peace! She sent us sample vows and encouraged us to customize the service, which we did. We then booked the photographer she recommended and bought flowers from their florist in Carmel. We got a marriage license in San Francisco, which we needed to do a number of days before the ceremony took place.

*The Big Day*

**Davina:** The day of our wedding we left San Francisco in a misty rain that lasted until we arrived in Big Sur. We got to the inn and dressed at a leisurely pace for the big event. The photographer showed up about 30 minutes before the ceremony to take pictures. Then the concierge/justice of the peace showed up and took us to a small clearing overlooking the Pacific. The photographer shot photos of the wedding, which turned out to be incredibly personal and heartfelt. After the wedding we went back to the room to sign the legal certificates and to drink some champagne with the photographer and the concierge. We lit a fire and laughed about the fact that no one had a clue we were married! Then we went to dinner in the hotel's dining room that overlooks the ocean, a beautiful setting. There, Chip ran into an old friend and his wife who were celebrating their tenth wedding anniversary. They were the first people to hear our news. The rest of the weekend passed like a dream.

*The News*

**Davina:** Sunday morning we called my parents in England to break the news. That was not quite as easy as everything else. My mom was upset that my dad didn't have the opportunity to give me away and they were both surprised and sort of speechless. Chip's parents, who are divorced, took it much better.

*Back Home*

**Chip:** We decided that we would have a party in San Francisco when we got back. We invited 80 people, including both sets of parents, who hadn't met yet. We even had a small "rehearsal dinner" the night before. Both parties were wonderful. We had taken dance lessons and dazzled everyone with our moves at the big party. We decided on a delayed honeymoon to Africa and arranged to fly through England, where Davina's parents live. They hosted a party for us there and we finally got our chance to have a big traditional wedding cake. A few months later, my guy friends took me out in New York and we had a "bachelor party" night.

*Looking Back*

We feel we had the best of all worlds—we got to do everything and in our own order and with the time to enjoy it all. Our parents really got into it, especially at the parties where we danced all night. In retrospect, the experience was entirely positive. We definitely have no regrets.

## 2. *Hybrid Wedding-Elopements*

Hybrid wedding-elopements are often the perfect choice for those who want to elope but can't quite work up the nerve. Hybrids come in all shapes and sizes. They are generally characterized by a simple service and at least one great party to celebrate the nuptials. Of course the ceremony and the party don't have to be on the same day. Waiting a few days, or even weeks, can give you a chance to relax and enjoy planning your wild party.

*The Courthouse with Friends or Family Elopement:*

This is an in-town true elopement with a twist—your family or friends are there as your witnesses. From the courthouse you can head straight to the airport, or back to the office. A more thoughtful option, however, is to take your witnesses to lunch or dinner afterward.

*The Surprise Wedding:*

Laugh all you want, but this option has it all: a dramatic burst of excitement as you make your entrance in a dreamy

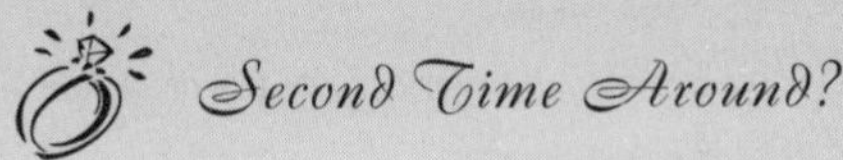

### Second Time Around?

At the minimum, most states require that you provide the exact date of your divorce. Others may want to see a copy of your divorce decree—don't leave home without it!

gown, a minimum of planning hassles, *and* you still get to share your special day with your family and friends. Some couples dive straight into this option; others choose it only when the pressure of planning their wedding has gotten to be too much.

The surprise wedding requires a pretense for a party. Birthday parties are a favorite excuse, but a party to celebrate your engagement is even better. That way no one will wonder about the odd guest list. Either way, someone makes excuses for your absence as the guests trickle in. "She's still getting dressed," if the party's at your house, or, "She's running late" if it's somewhere else. (No one will question this at an engagement party, since all brides-to-be are chronically time-challenged.) Meanwhile, the minister is hiding in a spare bedroom, or chatting up the super in the basement of your apartment building. Finally, when everyone's arrived, someone surreptitiously hits the play button, the *Wedding March* comes on, and you sweep into the room!

A delightful twist on the surprise wedding is to make it a double surprise wedding. A friend, your fiancé, or even your parents organize a "surprise" birthday party for you. Just imagine the fun as you turn the tables on your guests, arriving all decked out in white with a minister in tow! Plus there's a nice personal benefit with the double surprise wedding: your spouse is much less likely to forget your wedding anniversary since it falls on your birthday.

Caution: do not attempt a surprise wedding without telling your parents beforehand if: (a) they never show up to any party you invite them to, (b) either of them has a heart condition, or

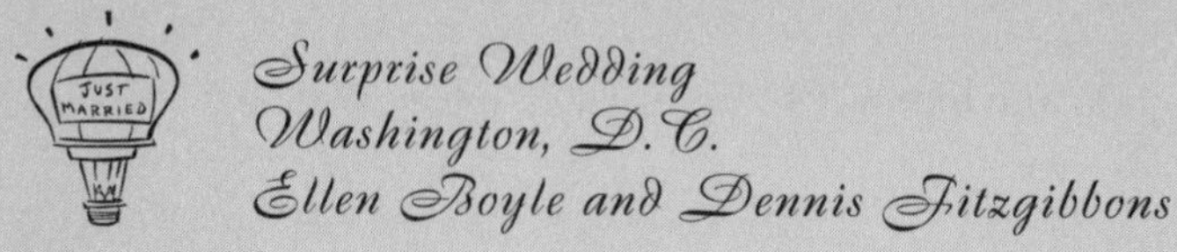


## Surprise Wedding
## Washington, D.C.
## Ellen Boyle and Dennis Fitzgibbons

*Background*

**Ellen:** We had been living together for a number of years and weren't wild about doing a big traditional wedding. We wanted something that would be more intimate, more us, and more fun! Our solution was a 120-person surprise wedding, using my upcoming 40th birthday as a cover story. Dennis took charge of the invitations and pretended to be organizing a surprise birthday party for me. He used a post office box as return address for the RSVPs and asked guests to wear creative black tie. Only our immediate family and one or two friends knew about the surprise-within-a-surprise party plan.

*The Big Day*

The party was held on the top floor of an elegant downtown Washington office building, in a space designed for large receptions and functions. The invitations had asked people to show up promptly at 7:30 and wear creative black tie. So no one thought it unusual that Dennis was in a tuxedo. And because it was my 40th birthday, no one questioned why my parents were there. It was the perfect setup! At 7:30 on the nose, Dennis announced, "It's time for the surprise!" Then the band began to play *Here Comes the Bride* as I walked into the room wearing my wedding gown. Shrieks and laughter followed me up to the makeshift altar. I think most of the guests were in shock during the short service, but they rallied and the rest of the evening was a riot. The story of our wedding quickly made its way around Capitol Hill, where Dennis and I both work, and for weeks afterward people would come up to us and say, "Oh my God, we heard about that wedding!"

*Looking Back*
We thought a surprise wedding would be easy to pull off, but it took more work than we expected. I can see now why people could take forever to plan a wedding, or why they just elope. We have no regrets, though, and I would absolutely recommend it. My sisters would, too—they were happy because they didn't have to wear matching dresses!

(c) your mother has been pressing you for months to hold a big wedding and you see this as a quick way to win the argument.

*The Progressive Elopement:*
This option is so named because of its similarity to a progressive dinner party, a wonderful 1950s pastime that sadly has fallen out of favor in recent decades. Here's how these work: you sneak off for the actual vows and then organize (or let others organize) a series of parties afterward. This is a particularly nifty idea if you and your fiancé are the product of nomadic households; for example, if both sets of parents have moved from where you grew up and you and your fiancé have migrated to a big city since college. With a progressive wedding you can have parties in five cities! (Both of your hometowns, both sets of parents' new hometowns, plus wherever you live now.) The airlines won't like this because you two are the only ones doing any traveling. But your guests will shower you with gratitude and presents because you're saving them a fortune.

*The Last-Minute "Escape" Elopement:*
These are more common than you'd guess. Halfway through the wedding-planning nightmare you and your fiancé

look at each other and ask the obvious question: "Why are we doing this?" At that point, of course, everyone already knows you're getting married. You may even have booked a reception site, caterers, and a band. But fear not—it's never too late. Off you go to a nice weekend in Vegas. You'll come back rested, married, and ready to party. You keep the reception just like you'd planned, only now it's a stress-free party.

What about the guests? No problem, especially if you'd planned a service and reception at one site. In that case you could just surprise them! Show up in white for the party, with a ring already on your finger. On the other hand, if you planned a church service first, you will need to drop a short note to your guests letting them know that the reception is on, but for them to skip the church. A postcard featuring your elopement destination would be particularly appropriate. It might say something like this:

*Dear Friends,*
*Well, we just couldn't wait! John and I got married last weekend in Las Vegas. But the party's still on for December 12 and we hope you'll join us for a celebration of our marriage.*

*Love, Cindy*

*P.S. Elvis lives! In fact, he married us—wait till you see the pictures!*

Or the more formal approach:

DOCTOR AND MRS. ARCHIBOLD SMYTHE
ANNOUNCE WITH PLEASURE
THE MARRIAGE OF THEIR DAUGHTER
MELISSA ANNE
TO
MR. JOSEPH FIELDING.
THE RECEPTION IN THEIR HONOR
WILL BE HELD AS SCHEDULED
ON THE 24TH OF FEBRUARY
AT THE MILBOURNE COUNTRY CLUB.

## *Last-Minute Escape Elopement*
## *Las Vegas*
## *Tim and Lois Rauner*

*Background*

**Lois:** We're sort of traditional; maybe that's where we got into trouble. I wanted a wedding done with everything just right. But as we began to plan our wedding it seemed that every decision got us further away from what we wanted and closer to some sort of convention-style event. I expected the planning to be fun and it wasn't. To top it off, my friends said, "Oh just wait, it gets worse!" It seemed like we were doing everything to make other people happy.

In addition to the general hassle factor of planning the wedding, we were also having problems because we weren't the same religion; I'm Baptist and Tim is Catholic. Both churches were willing to work with us, but more work on top of wedding planning just seemed overwhelming. So when Tim jokingly said one night, "Hey, let's go to Vegas," I said, "Sure!"

*The Plan*

**Tim:** As soon as we made the decision to elope it felt like a huge burden had been lifted from our backs. We did have one problem, though: we'd already booked the country club and put down a deposit for a 300-person reception. We decided to go ahead with that party, but sneak off to Las Vegas a month or so ahead of time. Our first thought was to get married in a hot-air balloon in the desert outside Las Vegas. But the only day the balloon company had available was April Fools' and that didn't seem like a good idea.

*The Big Day*

**Lois:** In the end we just hopped a flight to Vegas and opened the Yellow Pages. The first ads for wedding chapels seemed too tacky, so we opted for a justice of the peace instead. He married us in his office; I was wearing blue jeans and afterward we went to a casino where we actually won money! For the big party back home we got all dressed up; Tim wore a tux and I wore a wedding dress. We had it all—a wedding cake, a band, and our friends even threw rice on us afterward. The only thing missing was the stress. The party was totally relaxed and fun and I think people had an especially great time because it was so different.

*Looking Back*

**Lois:** One thing that surprised us was how many people came up to us at the reception to say that they wished they had done the same thing. Especially women! I was shocked. After talking to a couple of my girlfriends I felt that I had narrowly escaped disaster. Other people told us how they had eloped, too. It's like there is a secret club of elopers out there. They're careful not to hurt the feelings of couples who have done the traditional thing, or those who have their heart set on a big wedding. But if you ask them, all the elopers will tell you it's the only way to go. We have no regrets *at all*.

## 3. Intimate Weddings

Purists will argue that intimate weddings have no place in a book on elopement. That's silly. *Anything* that saves you the headache and stress of a big wedding deserves consideration. Here's a sampler of ideas to consider:

*The At-Home Wedding:*

This is a perfectly charming and acceptable alternative to the big wedding. It is usually a family-only affair, plus a dozen or so close friends, at most. Dinner afterward can be buffet-style or casual in the backyard. Be careful, however. Many big weddings begin life as small at-home weddings. Unless you keep a tight rein on the guest list it can easily spiral out of control.

*The Country Wedding Weekend:*

This is a lot easier, cheaper, and more rewarding than you might think. With a few phone calls to reserve a country inn, discuss the menu, and arrange for a justice of the peace, you're done. Your guests arrive Friday in time for cocktails, followed by a casual nonrehearsal dinner. Saturday's free for walks or a bit of antiquing. Then at 5 P.M. everyone gathers in the parlor or on the porch for the ceremony. Afterward you can sip champagne before wandering in for dinner. Sunday, after a nice, big country-style brunch, your guests head home. Relaxing, romantic, and indulgent—what more could you ask for?

The cost of a country wedding weekend may also surprise you, even at a four-star inn. For around $10,000 you can pick up the bill for everything, including rooms, for a 20-person wedding party. If your guests pay their own way you can do it for a lot less, just the cost of the two dinners and your ceremony. Either way it's a bargain.

Here are some suggestions: avoid inns that are too small or don't have full-time (and talented!) chefs. With so much riding on the quality of the inn, you're far better off paying more for experience and quality. Since many inns open their dining room to the general public, make sure they have a private dining room to accommodate your party. Don't hesitate to ask even the most elegant inn for a discount. Most will happily oblige if you're booking all or most of their rooms.

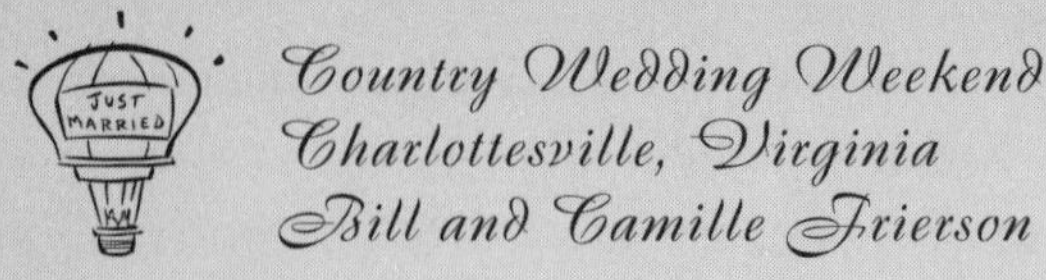


## Country Wedding Weekend
## Charlottesville, Virginia
## Bill and Camille Frierson

*Background*

**Camille:** Bill had been married before, an enormous wedding with 400 guests, and didn't want that again. He would have gone along with a big wedding if I had wanted it, but I didn't want that at all. I've always dreaded a big wedding. Maybe that's why I was 32 before I got married! I'm from Nashville and in the South there's no such thing as a small wedding. By the time you're done with aunts, uncles, and cousins you're already over 100 guests. And that's before you start on your friends, your parents' friends, and his parents' friends. We weren't interested in the rounds of parties that people throw and everyone getting involved in each other's lives. I just couldn't have faced it and my mother and I would have killed each other.

*The Plan*

**Bill:** We decided to do our elopement-wedding in Charlottesville, Virginia. It's a beautiful place only two hours away from Washington, and Camille went to college there. There are dozens of fantastic small inns and bed-and-breakfasts. We wanted to find a place with enough rooms for our families and to take it over for a whole weekend. We found two in a guidebook and went to Charlottesville for a weekend to scout out our choices. We found one that would give us the whole inn for the weekend so we booked it; the other we reserved for our rehearsal dinner.

*The Big Day*

**Camille:** We had a beautiful day with a clear blue sky. Monticello, Jefferson's home, was close by, so we took the whole group there in the morning. We had lunch in town and everyone did his own thing in the afternoon. The wedding itself was intimate and romantic. The parlor where we were married had high ceilings and was full of antiques. It felt like we were back in Monticello in Jefferson's living room. The county sheriff whom the inn had recommended married us and he used a short service that he wrote himself. We loved it. After the ceremony, we had champagne while a pianist played and then we moved into the dining room. Just like the night before, the combination of an intimate private room, a roaring fire, and fantastic food made the evening perfect.

*Looking Back*
**Camille:** When I tell my single girlfriends about it they get dreamy-eyed, and when I tell my married girlfriends who did the big wedding thing, they get a sad look on their faces. I know we made the right call.

**Bill:** Camille's parents were very generous and paid for the whole weekend for both families. Everyone left feeling pampered and happy.

*The Dinner Party Wedding:*

This is like the country wedding weekend without the country or weekend parts. Instead you invite 20 or 30 guests to your wedding. The ceremony can be at the same place as the dinner party, or at a nearby church (preferably a small one, appropriate to the size of your group). Afterward there's a catered dinner at someone's house (any house but yours will do) or a favorite restaurant (again, insist on a private dining room to make it special).

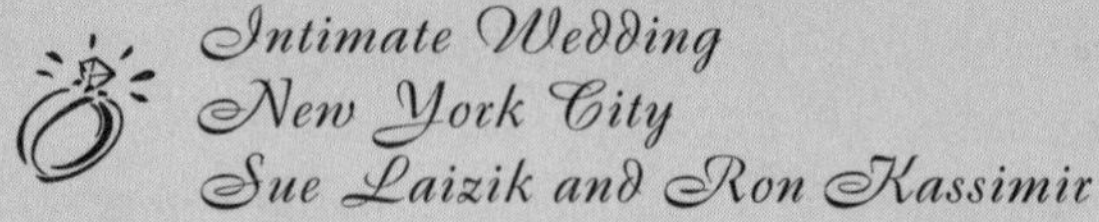

Intimate Wedding
New York City
Sue Laizik and Ron Kassimir


*Background*

We started out trying to plan a bigger wedding but didn't get too far. We're just not the type of people who thrive on making decisions and, to be honest, we couldn't care less about all the details. That's not how we live, so why would we get married that way? We also kept wondering how much all this would cost us. So we decided to do something smaller and more intimate instead.

*The Plan*

One night we went to check out the Terrace Restaurant on the Upper West Side. As soon as we walked in we *knew* this was the place. We spoke to the owners, they agreed, and that's all the planning we did! We invited both of our immediate families and some friends. I bought some postcards at Urban Outfitters that had pretty pictures of flowers on them and sent them out to family. To our friends we sent different postcards with a photo of an old-fashioned couple on it and the words "two more victims." At one point during all of this, my mother gave me some money and told me to spend it on the wedding, or anything else I wanted.

*The Big Day*

For the ceremony both of us wore suits. There were 26 people present. A woman my yoga teacher recommended performed the service. We were married on the terrace, then came into the restaurant for cocktails and dinner. For good luck and to stick with Jewish tradition, Ron's mother made us break the glass. It was like having a really nice evening out—with a wedding as an appetizer! Afterward we sent out announcements, little cards I made on the laser printer. Everyone's reaction was great and four months later we threw ourselves a casual party at a local club. We had a "no gifts" policy, but people brought them anyway and some family members sent checks.

*Looking Back*

What we did really reflected us. I was relaxed and got to talk to everybody. It was a social occasion, not something stiff and unpleasant. I've even worn my white suit several times since. My advice would be that if there's any inkling of a doubt, have a small wedding, not a big one.

*The Yacht Wedding:*

When you charter a yacht for a 3- or 4-hour wedding cruise you combine the best aspects of the country wedding weekend with the dinner party wedding. You are hosting something elegant and different, yet your guests still get to sleep in their own beds. Organizing a yacht wedding is very easy, no more difficult than reserving a private room at a restaurant. The cost is roughly comparable, too, starting at $2,000 to $3,000 for a 30-person event. Most charter yacht services can provide a list of licensed officiants they work with. (For more details see part 2, "Where to Elope.")

## 4. *Destination Weddings*

Destination weddings are becoming enormously popular, and for good reason. They are the perfect solution for couples that want to avoid a traditional wedding but that still want to include family and friends in their special day. Technically, the country wedding weekend would fall into the destination wedding category. But destination weddings usually involve more than just a short drive from home, and the guest list may be larger than just the immediate family.

Destination weddings can be loads of fun. Guests get to combine your wedding with a vacation and they tend to really get into the spirit of the event. For the bride and groom this enthusiasm is a welcome change from the lethargy of some wedding guests. And if your guests pay their own way, the wedding won't cost you much more than a nice vacation. (Your airfare doesn't count, since that comes out of your honeymoon budget.)

The drawback to destination weddings? Your guests are exactly that: *your* guests. Some people travel better than others, a point worth considering as you make up your invitation list, but all of your guests will require some hand-holding. You should enlist the hotel's staff to help you as often as you can. But ultimately, from sunburns to child care, your guests' problems are *your* problems.

We have divided destination weddings into three categories, small, large, and cruise-ship weddings.

*The Small Destination Wedding:*

Small destination weddings usually combine a romantic locale and a guest list hovering between 20 and 25 people. Any fewer and you'll feel like people are tagging along on your honeymoon; any more and you'll wear yourself out with the logistics. A group this size is easy to organize (especially since some of them will be traveling as couples) and you'll get a chance to spend quality time with all your guests.

*The Large Destination Wedding:*

Larger groups obviously require larger facilities and more coordination. It is also harder to predict the appetites, needs, or wishes of 50 to 100 people. For all of these reasons, resort

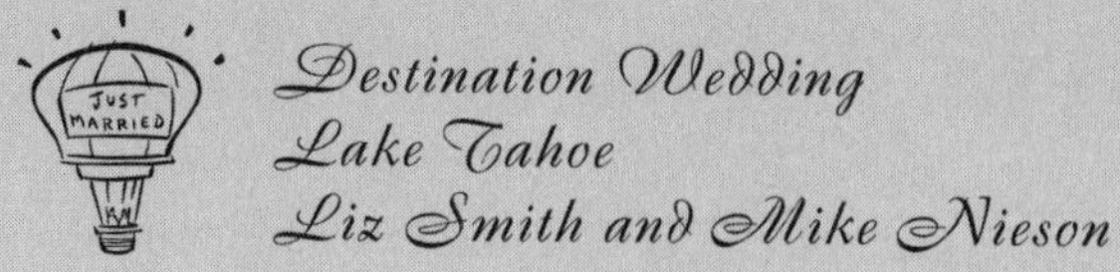


## Destination Wedding
## Lake Tahoe
## Liz Smith and Mike Nieson

*Background*

**Mike:** We were planning to get married but weren't sure what to do. We knew that wedding planning can create a lot of animosity and we wanted to skip all of that. We thought, let's go to a place that we love and whoever can make it, can make it. We decided on Tahoe, where we had both been before. We also knew that it was not uncommon to get married there. Tahoe is kind of a wedding Mecca, like Reno but not so "casino-y"—it fit our style. So we talked to the people at the Hyatt on the lake and set up a reception there. Then we sent out invitations announcing what we were going to do and just said, "Call us if you can make it."

*The Big Day*

**Liz:** I had a real dress. We also had a wedding cake and a photographer. We were married by a justice of the peace in a beautiful room; it was all windows and overlooked the lake. Although almost 40 people came, it still felt like a very intimate gathering. Afterward we had a reception in the hotel. The entire wedding cost us $3,000, which paid for everything except alcohol, airfare, and the hotel. Several people incorporated the wedding into their vacation and stayed for a week. When we returned we threw a party where we showed the video and pictures of the wedding. We even had a similar dinner—carved turkey. A good friend of mine came up to me and said that she had spent a ton of money on their wedding and if she could do it over again, she would have gone to Tahoe, too.

*Looking Back*
**Liz:** I have no regrets. A friend of mine who is still in debt from her wedding said, "Gosh, it was just one day, and two years later I'm still paying it off." People seem to get so caught up in their weddings that they lose perspective. That's not what we wanted to do.

hotels are an ideal choice for large destination weddings. The resort's staff has done this 100 times before, and most resorts have a full-time social director who performs many of the services for which you'd have to pay a wedding consultant. The downside of large resort weddings is that you won't have the facilities all to yourself. This may not seem like a big deal, but try to imagine sharing the hotel with a group of vacationing college students or screaming children, because it may happen.

The single most important piece of advice in planning a resort wedding is to get *recent* references. Every resort has a brochure that looks pretty. But what you see isn't necessarily what you'll get. Some rooms are better than others, staff comes and goes, and, in the tropics, storms take their toll. Talking to someone who had her wedding there recently will give you a good feel for whether the hotel can live up to your expectations.

You should try to visit the resort before you make your final decision (if at all possible). A quick $1,000, three-day trip may seem extravagant, but not when you consider what's at stake. Your guests are about to spend $50,000 at the resort. How would you feel if you showed up to find the hotel was undergoing major renovations?

With regard to costs, you might be surprised to learn that resort weddings are usually a good deal. The prices of overseas resorts can be competitive with most American hotels. Be sure to work out every last possible charge ahead of time, however. Once there, you and your guests are prisoners of the hotel. The room rates are an obvious cost you'll want to confirm in writing. But other expenses, like overpriced drinks or 22 percent across-the-board service charges can quickly leave your guests feeling resentful—of both the hotel and *you*!

You can avoid this problem by negotiating perks in advance for your guests. Taxes are usually non-negotiable, but everything else is fair game, so ask for: reduced service charges on room rentals (the 18 percent to 22 percent charge on dining room service or room service charges are probably not negotiable, however); reduced rate for excursions and water-sports rentals; and happy-hour bar prices around the clock for your guests. None of this will cost you anything and your guests will love you for it. And don't forget yourself! Most hotels will give the bridal couple a free room if they bring along a large group.

Obviously, your bargaining position won't be too strong if you're looking at a Christmas wedding in the tropics. But most

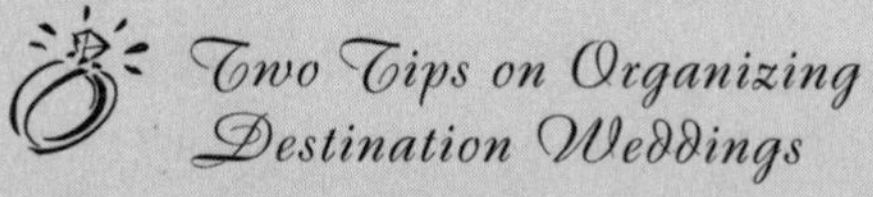

### Two Tips on Organizing Destination Weddings

- Don't overschedule people or events. People can get burned out quickly on each other's company. So provide plenty of ideas and guidance, but keep the formal group activities to a minimum.
- Be careful with the size of your guest list; *do not* assume that the difficulty and expense of getting there will do the job of paring your list down. Quite the opposite. According to several destination wedding planners, it's a strange-but-true phenomenon that people who would otherwise skip your in-town wedding will happily fly halfway around the world at their own expense to watch you get married.

## Destination Wedding
## Jamaica
## Gigi and Kurt Ehlers

*Background*

**Gigi:** We never really had a desire for a big wedding, perhaps because my parents are German, and Europeans don't have big weddings. So we were thinking of something smaller, maybe 75 people, when we first started looking. We looked at a country club, but the estimate we got from them was $10,000! Then I heard of a friend talking about her wedding in Jamaica and I thought it was worth looking into the idea.

*The Plan*

A travel agent researched it for us and found a resort in Jamaica that could accommodate both families and singles. She also found us a couples-only resort on the same island that we could go to afterward for a private honeymoon. The resort we chose to get married at was used to doing weddings and even had a wedding coordinator. The wedding package cost $350 and you could choose a morning, afternoon, or sunset wedding. For our guests there were plenty of activities to do all day long—golf, scuba, and excursions.

*The Big Day*

We were married outside, standing under a trellis with flowers on it. A local minister performed the service. It was short, only 15 minutes. They had taped music (you could choose from the *Wedding March* or some Kenny G song, so we went with Kenny G) and there was a videographer and a photographer. After the ceremony we signed the certificate and licenses and then went to dinner with all our guests. When we got home to the States we threw a big cookout at the Jersey Shore in July for the other relatives and friends who couldn't make it. They loved hearing about what we did.

*Looking Back*

Since our wedding we've been to a couple of traditional weddings, and each time we've come away glad that we got married in Jamaica. It was so easy and there was no stress involved. We got to spend four days with our friends and family, and people got to relax and have a good time. We have no regrets and would definitely recommend it.

resorts do have lull periods even in winter. They'll be much more willing to negotiate for bookings then. A final note concerning airfares: your travel agent can work out a group discount for more popular resort areas, but you—and especially your guests—will need to plan as far in advance as possible.

*The Cruise-Ship Wedding:*

On late-night TV stations across the country, *The Love Boat* sails forever. Maybe that's why shipboard weddings have become so popular in recent years. Almost all of the major cruise lines have special wedding coordinators and the newest cruise ships even come equipped with special wedding chapels.

Technically speaking, shipboard weddings are just large destination weddings, only the destination is moving. Not too fast, thankfully, and on the newer, giant cruise ships seasickness is almost unheard of. The size of these ships is a mixed blessing, though. Not only do you have to share the ship with 1,500 strangers, but you may also be sharing the ship with a dozen other bridal parties.

The popularity of cruise-ship weddings is simple to explain:

(1) their experienced full-time wedding coordinators make it easy, (2) it's different, and (3) you know what you're getting. This last point is particularly attractive. The service, accommodations, and food on board cruise ships are on par with better resorts or hotels. So if you can get over the "other people" thing (and remember, you wouldn't have a hotel or resort all to yourself, either), then a shipboard wedding may make perfect sense. There is one major drawback, however. Cruise lines, the good ones anyway, book early and they aren't cheap. They also won't negotiate with you the way a smaller resort might. (For more information see part 2, "Where to Elope.")

## 5. *Theme Weddings and Other Offbeat Ideas*

The range of options here is broad, from a wedding in costume to an undersea scuba wedding where vows are exchanged on an erasable board (though presumably the commitment is no less binding). Theme weddings are easy to visualize, but for some of the other ideas presented below you would be wise to talk with someone who's hosted a similar wedding. Before you embark on a white-water rafting wedding adventure, for example, you'll want to be sure you know what you and your guests are in for.

*The Theme Wedding:*

Theme weddings are a close relative of the destination wedding, and an equally popular trend these days. In fact, the line is sometimes blurred between the two. A masked ball wedding in Venice would qualify as both a theme wedding and a destination wedding. So, too, would a Cinderella wedding at Disney World. And if your guests are asked to wear blue suede shoes to the Vegas Chapel of Love, then you're also doing a themed destination wedding.

Typically the decorations and menu are themed, and guests

are asked to come in costume. It may sound silly but it works. Guests treat a theme wedding as more of a party, not another solemn wedding and predictable reception. The hosts usually find it easier to relax, too, and the day will stand out in everyone's memories.

Some other themes to consider: Western-style, Halloween, beach party, New Year's Eve, or Roaring Twenties with beaded dresses and slicked back hair. Perhaps enough time has even passed to do a '60s wedding. Imagine a bride gliding toward the altar in a tie-dyed wedding gown, with Jerry Garcia's vocals setting the mood.

*The Offbeat Wedding:*

This is a final catch-all category for the truly adventurous. The rule here? Anything goes! Want to get married underwater on a tropical reef? No problem. Aloft in a hot-air balloon? Sure—unless your minister has acrophobia. You can also get married on a white-water rafting expedition, on horseback in Colorado, host a ski wedding, or take your vows in a chapel at Yosemite National Park. In Las Vegas you can even get married in a drive-through wedding chapel. About the only thing that hasn't been done yet is an on-line wedding, and that's probably just a matter of time.

The common denominator with all of these options is that they express the lifestyle and passions of the couple. What a nice and romantic idea! And as unorthodox (and downright wacky) as some of these options might appear, they are all more fun than a traditional wedding. Your guests won't be bored, and your wedding album won't be filled with the usual photos.

## *The Test of Time*

Whatever option you choose, you can take comfort in knowing that elopers never look back. None of the couples we interviewed (including dozens whose stories didn't make it into the final version of this book) expressed any regrets about their decision to elope. That makes us wonder if perhaps marriages that begin with an elopement might even hold up better over time. But in the absence of a formal study, we can only provide anecdotal evidence, including this tale of a couple who eloped more than 40 years ago:

### *Joe and Kathie Costello*

*Background*

**Kathie:** We met when we were in the seventh grade and started dating when we were sophomores in high school. We didn't go to the same school (both of us were in Catholic schools on Staten Island), but I would see him at the pool. He wore his father's wool bathing suit with a belt. I always felt bad for him 'cause it looked so goofy. My two older sisters had been married in the two years prior and had big weddings, and I knew I didn't want a big wedding like they'd had. Plus, Joe's mother didn't like me because I was taking "her son" away and we knew she would never approve of a wedding.

*The Plan*

We decided we needed to tie the knot after high school graduation. Joe had a four-year scholarship playing basketball at Wagner College on Staten Island and I went to work at the phone company. So we went down to Elkton, Maryland, on a Monday with another couple that was planning to do the same thing. We filled out the paperwork, got the license, and made an appointment for later that week with the justice of the peace.

*The Big Day*
We didn't tell anyone, just drove back to Elkton on Friday and got married. We gave each other wedding bands that cost $25. Then we drove back to New York City and had a Chinese dinner.

*Back Home*
We still wanted to have a church wedding, even though we'd eloped. So before we told anyone we spoke to our priest. No surprise there, the first thing he said was, "You need to tell your parents." My parents were OK with it and came with us to speak to Joe's parents. Joe's mother was *not* happy. The first thing she did was to take away the new car they'd given him for graduation. Then she tried to ban all of Joe's family members from attending our church wedding. But his father came, and others from his father's side of the family.

*Looking Back*
We have no regrets. They say that if you get married young, it doesn't work. Well, look at us! We've been married 42 years and have 8 children and 19 grandchildren. I'd say it worked out just fine.

# Which One's Right for You?

There *is* a right wedding for every couple. The trick is in discovering which one suits you both. Maybe this little quiz can help:

**1. This is a second wedding for one or both of us: Yes No**

If you or your partner has been married before, eloping is a natural choice. At least one of you has already done the big wedding and can tell the other what he's *not* missing. Most of the options discussed in the previous chapter will work for second-timers. But the humor, even silliness, of a **surprise wedding** appeals to us. It is as though you're saying, "We care enough to make a public commitment, and want you to be a part of it, but we aren't terribly concerned about formalities here." Given that one or both of you have been down this road before, this emphasis on substance over style seems appropriate.

**2. I can keep my mouth shut: Yes No It Depends**

If you answer no, **a surprise wedding** is definitely out. Perhaps the best solution is to agree to elope, but let your partner keep the manner, date, and destination to herself. That way you can't possibly spill the beans. You may also wish to consider a **progressive wedding-elopement.** This option, at least, plays upon your strengths: the more people you tell in advance, the more parties they'll throw upon your return.

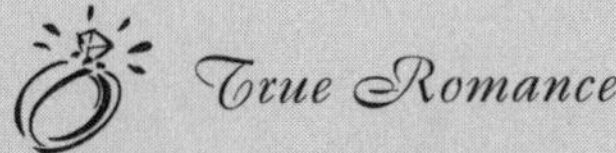

*Sweet 16s: Percy Bysshe Shelley*

Percy Bysshe Shelley, famous radical political writer of the early 1800s, first caused a scandal when he married 16-year-old Harriet Westbrook, the daughter of a coffee-house keeper. They eloped to Scotland and Shelley's father never forgave him for creating such a scene. Shelley moved to Ireland and became known for his revolutionary speeches on politics and religion. He later returned to England and met fellow revolutionary thinker William Godwin. Shelley was struggling financially, so Godwin invited Shelley and his wife to live in his home. Shelley started to feel that Harriet was not able to share his intellectual pursuits and they separated. Shelley then became intrigued with Godwin's 16-year-old daughter, Mary, and they became secret lovers. Godwin disapproved of the romance and in July 1814, the couple eloped to France. Mary Shelley went on to become an author and wrote the famous horror story *Frankenstein*.

**3. I'm an impulsive person: Yes No Sometimes**

On the face of it, eloping would seem to best suit impulsive people. But nonimpulsive people are also good candidates for elopement. Why? Because their orderly minds quickly take stock of the mountain of work involved with a big wedding, causing them to recoil in horror. And because nonimpulsive people are often good at keeping secrets, they are ideally suited to **true elopements**.

For the impulsive couple (which, by definition, includes any couple in which at least one person is impulsive), a **surprise wedding** works great, or even turning a normal family vacation into a **surprise-destination wedding**. In fact, the impulsive couple can get away with any kind of wedding—except the traditional kind.

**4. I care what my parents think: Always Sometimes Never**

"Never" and "always" are both problematic answers, and more the province of psychologists. So let's assume the "sometimes" position: you are not out to hurt your parents deliberately, but neither is their happiness your first concern after climbing out of bed each morning. In fact, you have negotiated a workable truce with your parents over the years: they stay out of your checkbook and bedroom, you show up for most major holidays. Marriage and weddings, unfortunately, intrude into both of these sacred domains. You are—or soon will be—sleeping with this other person, and you may need money from your parents to make this new development legal. Meanwhile, your nuptial plans now intersect your parents' lives in two other areas: their social status (or aspirations) and their dormant parental emotions. No wonder so many couples cave in. We would never advise a rash elopement resulting in ruptured parental relations, but you should not feel compelled to accept a big wedding if you don't want one. Really, what you need to do is get away from the "either-or" argument. What about a third option? One that gives them a chance to witness the wedding but spares you the stress of a lavish shindig. Any of the **hybrids** should work here, and while they might not be an easy sell, the *threat* of a **true elopement** should ensure your parents' ultimate cooperation.

**5. We love adventures: Yes No**
**I do, but he or she doesn't**

Your upcoming wedding provides a splendid opportunity to begin exploring these differences. Often the more adventurous partner defers, as in, "I wanted to get married atop Kilimanjaro, but she hates camping so we did it at the country club." Such a shame. They could have done both, had a lovely, albeit small and informal, service outdoors (if not at 19,000 feet) and then, in the best tradition of explorers, hosted an evening at "the club" some weeks or months later.

A **small destination wedding** is also an appealing choice. The adventurous partner gets to shake her or his fist at convention, while the other partner gets to plan a delightful wedding for 30 in Paris or Santa Fe. A fair enough trade, and a good lesson in compromise to start the marriage off on the right note.

**6. Our budget is: $17,000-plus A lot less**
**What's a budget?**

If you can afford the $17,000-plus cost of the average big wedding, then the world is your oyster. A **small destination wed-**

**ding,** an **elegant in-town elopement**, or even a sunset **yacht wedding** can all be done for half of this amount. Thus you have the luxury of considering your choice as consequence of personalities, style, and preferences.

Do not despair, however, if you answered "a lot less." Eloping and chronic cash flow shortages are time-honored partners. Clearly, a **true elopement** would work. Or perhaps an **at-home wedding**. Either way, you'll be spending what money you have on yourself, and not on trying to impress or entertain strangers. Perhaps you set aside a little money for a few charming dinner parties at your house or apartment upon your return. You could cook favorite dishes from your honeymoon locale, and perhaps send your guests home with a picture of you and your beloved taken in situ. This is so much more creative and fun than struggling to throw a big bash on a small budget.

Now, for the budget-less: are your circumstances terribly strained, and a budget therefore pointless? If that is the case, a **true elopement,** if only a quick journey to the courthouse and rain check on the honeymoon, is just the ticket. Or is it that you

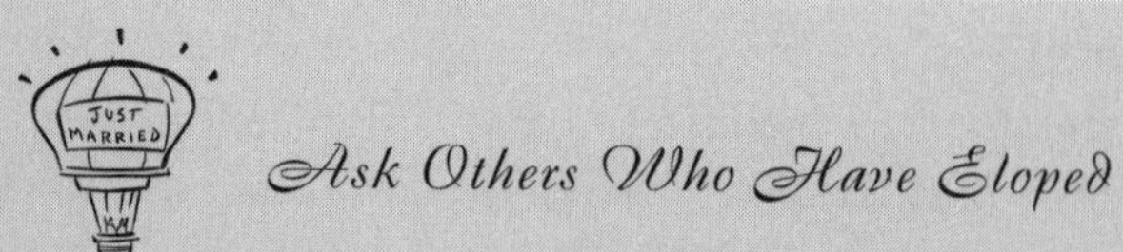


### Ask Others Who Have Eloped

If you're teetering between two options, track down someone who's already done the ones you're interested in. It may take some work, but not as much as you think. For starters, people are *always* happy to tell you about their weddings. Especially those who venture outside the traditional paths. A mass e-mail to friends will get the ball rolling, or you can explore the bulletin board sections of any wedding Web site.

have never had to worry about money? If the la
describes your situation, then a call to your travel ag
order. Paris is always delightful, and first class on Air F
a cozy way to speed your elopement. As an added
France's lengthy residency requirement (see part 2, "W
Elope") means you'll be there at least a month. What a s

# 5. The Etiquette of Eloping

Is elopement etiquette an oxymoron? Not at all. In fact, the less traditional your wedding, the more important etiquette becomes. Attention to etiquette, which is really just a set of courtesies and customs, will help people come to terms with your unorthodox decision to elope.

## Announcing Your Engagement

Once upon a time engagement announcements were an important part of the social food chain. Picnics, cocktail parties, and formal dinners, hosted by family and friends, would fill the weeks and months leading up to the wedding. Thus the engagement announcement served as advance notice, a "clear your calendar!" warning to the same group that would later receive wedding invitations.

Couples that intend to elope should, for a number of reasons, revive the custom of engagement announcements. To begin with, why deny yourself the limelight, your "five minutes of fame"? When you announce your engagement you are sim-

ply taking a well-deserved bow in public. A second reason is that your engagement announcements will serve notice that what is about to follow is not a shotgun wedding or an impetuous act. Of course your friends and family won't know what you've got planned until after the fact. But when they do hear that you eloped, they'll be less shocked and skeptical.

Inviting your parents to announce your engagement, as is customary, is a particularly smart move when you're planning to elope. The very nature of elopement carries an unspoken hint that parental wishes are being thwarted. But a traditionally worded announcement, one that includes your parents on the card, will be remembered after you elope. Recipients will understand that your marriage, if not your choice of *how* to get married, was not against your parents' wishes. Inviting your parents to announce your engagement can also be a conciliatory act if they're upset with your decision (which assumes that you've told them, of course). You may not care about social niceties but they might. The same logic holds true, maybe more so, if you're *not* planning to tell your parents. Encouraging them to send out engagement announcements allows them to save face with their friends later: "Oh, sure. We knew all along they were going to elope!"

The style of an engagement card is up to you, but for all the reasons mentioned above, traditional is better when you plan to elope.

DR. AND MRS. RICHARD THORNHILL
ANNOUNCE WITH PLEASURE
THE ENGAGEMENT OF THEIR DAUGHTER
SARAH EMILY
TO MR. JOSEPH ROGERS

The familiar copperplate script on cream-colored card stock has a reassuring effect on people. And yes, you *should* buy nice ones—why not, with all the money you're about to save by eloping!

## Engagement Parties

Engagement parties are loads of fun, and there's no reason you should miss out on them just because you intend to elope. In fact, they are usually much more fun than the actual wedding itself, certainly for the bride and groom. You get all the attention with none of the stress. Engagement parties are also another way of publicly demonstrating that you have thought through this decision to get married and that your parents approve. In fact, engagement parties thrown by your parents for their friends will go a long way in assuaging any residual disappointment Mom and Dad may have about your plans to elope.

One fun trick is to play it coy with the admiring crowd at all your engagement parties. "No, we haven't set a date yet. Who knows, we might just elope!" Or you can get downright mischievous, "Well, we were thinking of the country club, but they can only accommodate 800, you know." This is particularly fun if Dad's in on the joke. He will bask in the pitying glances directed at him all night long, and his friends will pick up his bar tab for months, right up until the day you elope.

## Announcing the Wedding (After the Fact)

If you skipped the engagement announcements, then after-the-fact wedding announcements are essential. Not only do you need to inform people of the change in your marital status, but you can also suggest parental approval, or at least after-the-fact acceptance, of your actions.

Even if you did mail engagement announcements, you still need to send wedding announcements to the same list of people. Why? Because otherwise they'll keep waiting for the wedding invitation (or worse, think they've lost it: "Honey, have you come across an invitation for Joannie Smith's wedding? Maybe I should call Nancy."). Thus the wedding announcements tell your friends and family that although they weren't there to witness the event, you actually *did* complete the engagement successfully.

Wedding announcements also serve the practical function of telling people where you'll now be living. This is done by listing your new marital address in the lower left corner of the card, under the words *At Home*. You can also enclose a separate "At-Home" card. Both methods accomplish the same goal and, incidentally, provide an address should the recipient wish to send you a congratulatory note or gift.

In style, wedding announcement cards look exactly like a wedding invitation, with a slight change in wording. Thus, "Dr. and Mrs. Richard Thornhill *request the pleasure of your company* . . ." becomes, "Dr. and Mrs. Richard Thornhill *announce with pleasure the marriage of* . . ." You might also add a touch of detail concerning the wedding itself: "The couple were married on June 24th at the bride's family home in Maine." Or, "The couple were married on June 24th by Mr. Elvis Presley in Las Vegas, Nevada."

One final note: superstition (and common sense) dictate that you wait until *after* you are married to mail your announcements. Just as with larger, traditional weddings, those magic words—*till death do us part*—have occasionally caused a last-minute change of heart.

## Newspaper Announcements

Placing an announcement in the local papers before or after your wedding sends the same message as engagement and wedding announcements, only to a larger audience. You can play it straight, leaving Elvis out altogether. Or you can have some fun: "The couple were married on January 26th in Ocho Rios,

Jamaica. The groom wore black surfer trunks and the bride a lace bikini with red polka dots."

## The Church or Synagogue

Legally speaking, you don't need a blessing from anyone to get married. Not from your parents (assuming you're over 18) and not from God, either. Ministers and rabbis are just two of several professionals, along with justices of the peace and other officers of the court, who are legally empowered to perform a marriage ceremony.

But what you *have* to do, and what you *should* do, are not the same thing. Sharing your little secret with your minister (or priest, rabbi, or other spiritual leader) is both a wise and a thoughtful course of action. The most obvious reason is to make sure that your church will recognize your marriage after the fact. It is much easier, and more pleasant, to discuss your church's position before you elope. Some churches may welcome you back with open arms. Others require a formal church ceremony or marriage blessing. And certain denominations, or even ministers acting on their own, may insist that you and your spouse attend their premarriage counseling programs.

On a personal level, your minister is likely to appreciate your consideration in confiding in him. The advance warning also leaves him in a better position, and more inclined, to help smooth over any problems you might face with your family upon your return. You need not worry about ministers spilling the beans, either—keeping secrets is part of their job description. And you may be surprised to find your minister more understanding than you expected. After all, he's witnessed more than his share of wedding stress and conflict over the years. He will certainly understand your decision, and may secretly even approve of it.

*A Love Written in the Stars (and Stripes): Betsy Ross*

Betsy (Griscom) Ross was raised in a strict Quaker family in Pennsylvania. She was serving an apprenticeship as an upholsterer when she met and fell in love with John Ross, an Episcopalian. They eloped, but Betsy suffered the consequences. She was "read out" of the Quaker meeting house for marrying an Episcopalian, which cut her off completely from her religious community and her family. Soon after, at the request of Congress, Betsy Ross sewed the first Stars and Stripes flag for the new United States of America.

## The Ceremony

Remember that when you go to the courthouse you're just applying for a license to get married. The actual ceremony must be performed by someone authorized in that jurisdiction (foreign weddings are another story; see part 2, "Where to Elope"). But unlike a church wedding, where you may be limited to selected readings, you're in charge of the show here. You can write your own vows, borrow someone else's, or leave it to the minister or justice of the peace to come up with something.

## Registering for Gifts

We left this for last, a reward for those who paid attention to the finer points of etiquette. Registering for gifts is a subject sure to elicit differing opinions. Some will find it inappropriate. They believe that wedding gifts are given as a token of appreciation for being invited as guests to a wedding. Others, and we include ourselves here, believe otherwise. You're getting married, a joyous occasion. If your friends and family want to send you gifts, why shouldn't you give them some guidance? Guidance, though, nothing more. As with more traditional weddings, your guests are under no obligation to buy you anything. It is never appropriate to drop hints, either, by including registry information with wedding announcements. Just let human nature take its course. You will be pleasantly surprised.

# 6.

# How to Convince Everyone Else

You're convinced, right? Good. So now we just have to tackle everyone else. Fortunately we can narrow this down a bit, since you don't have to convince *everyone* else. Just a couple of important people, like your fiancé and maybe your parents. Your friends (see below) will take the news of your elopement in stride, and perhaps with relief. As for your distant relatives, who cares?

## Start with Your Fiancé

This is the obvious place to begin as failure on this front means you're done. But despite the high stakes, don't even think about recruiting allies, like his brother or sister, to help argue your case. If it ever comes out that you approached them first—and it will, since everything eventually comes out in a marriage—this will be seen as the highest act of disloyalty and betrayal: "How could you go behind my back!" Trust us: you don't want to go there.

So how do you raise the subject? Carefully. Leave yourself

plenty of wiggle room should you encounter resistance. Gentlemen, in particular, take note: some, though certainly not all, women interpret a lack of enthusiasm for a big wedding to mean a lack of enthusiasm for the marriage in general. You'll want to avoid this implication at all costs.

Specifically, how you approach your partner depends on his or her temperament and expectations. If your fiancée broke out a hidden stash of bridal magazines the night you proposed, then you might have a problem. But if she changes the subject every time you mention the need to "get started on this wedding stuff," then it might be a very short, easy conversation. "You too? Great! Let's do it!"

Fortify yourself with this fact: every sane couple talks about eloping at some point. Unfortunately, it's usually not until they're knee deep in wedding preparations. Thus the conversation is often wistful and short:

"Gee, I wish we'd just eloped."

"Yeah, me too. Would you please pass me some more envelopes to address?"

We maintain that it's *never* too late to elope (see Last-Minute "Escape" Elopement in chapter 3), but we do understand that the decision gets harder as time passes, as commitments are made, and as money is spent. All the more reason to raise the subject now.

OK, to get the ball rolling quickly—before the country club is booked—you'll need a couple of choice opening lines. You can write your own or take your pick of these:

### THE SOFT SELL

"Honey, call me crazy, but I've been thinking, how would you feel about just eloping?" Then, quickly, before they have a chance to respond, throw out some of the reasons to skip the big wedding: "It just seems to me that our relationship doesn't need all this stress, and we could certainly use the money we'd save."

### THE DIRECT APPROACH

"Sweetheart, this is insane. Why don't we just elope?"

### THE BOWL-THEM-OVER-WITH-STATISTICS PLAY

"Can you believe it? Someone at the office said they read that 3 out of 10 couples are choosing to elope these days, and 4 out of 5 brides said they'd elope if they had to do it all over again! But what really blew me away was that 9 out of 10 fathers said they'd rather write a check and skip the wedding altogether."

No, these are not verifiable statistics. How could they be? Nobody compiles surveys like this. It doesn't matter. The beauty of this approach is that you can appear skeptical yourself, even as you raise the subject.

### THE DANGLING QUERY

"Did you hear that so-and-so eloped? I wonder why they did that?"

### THE COWARDLY APPROACH

Leave a brown paper–wrapped copy of this book in the mailbox.

### WHAT IF THEY VETO THE IDEA IN 10 SECONDS FLAT?

Tough luck. That "for better or for worse" stuff includes how you get to the altar. Cheer up, though. You're not the first person to go through this. You could try again in a couple of weeks, but by then your die-hard big wedding advocate may have already booked the band.

## *Dealing with Your Parents*

### SHOULD WE TELL THEM BEFOREHAND?

This is one of life's classic "damned-if-you-do and damned-if-you-don't" dilemmas. Discussing the matter beforehand can complicate matters by inviting their objections (see below). Not involving them poses another problem. If you secretly elope, you've not only deprived them of the big wedding, but also hurt their feelings and displayed a lack of trust, telling them in effect that you didn't think they'd support you. This can be the stuff of decades-long grudges. Use your best judgment.

### HOW TO RAISE THE SUBJECT

Note we said, *raise*. Diplomacy should be the order of the day here. Far better to ease them into the idea rather than announce that you've made up your mind. Use gentle phrases like, "We're comfortable with the idea of eloping," or, "We just can't see ourselves doing a big wedding." Your parents may surprise you and say, "That sounds terribly sensible, dear." But even if they appear upset or disappointed, odds are they'll come around to it once they've had a chance to think things through. Ultimately it's your wedding (or nonwedding) and you will need to put your foot down. But there's no need to take a confrontational approach from the outset.

There are three situations, however, in which it is completely acceptable to leave your parents in the dark about your plans to elope:

1. When you know they will make your life miserable and fight you bitterly right up to the day you elope.
2. When you haven't spoken to your parents in years anyway, and don't particularly want them to be part of your future life.
3. When your parents are lighthearted lovers themselves and will actually delight in your secret elopement. You lucky person.

### BUT MY PARENTS WILL KILL ME!

Maybe not. Here you are thinking their fondest wish is to see you walking down the aisle in white. So why is Mom smiling as you stutter over the e-word: *elopement.* Why is Dad reaching for his

## True Romance

*Living High on the Hope: Evalyn Walsh and Edward Beale McLean*

Evalyn Walsh, the owner of the Hope Diamond, was the feisty daughter of an Irish immigrant who struck gold. Her family was living in Washington, D.C., where she met the heir to the *Washington Post* fortune, Edward Beale McLean. The two eloped in 1908, against her family's advice. Then they went on a three-month honeymoon to Europe and the Middle East with $200,000 from Evalyn's father, so he must not have been too upset. By the end of their trip, they ran out of money, but Evalyn's father just cabled some more to the couple in Paris. It seems that since Evalyn saved her father the expense of an elaborate wedding, he was very generous with his wedding "presents."

checkbook so quickly? "Oh, no!" he says, offering a token resistance, "I was *so* looking forward to a big wedding!" Then quickly, before you change your mind, "How much did you say you want?"

What's happening here is that your parents are proving, once again, that they are wiser than you thought. They may be delighted to write a check for your elopement simply because elopements, unlike big weddings, can't run over budget. Your father might also be thrilled to buy his way out of a year's worth of agony and conflict on the home front. None of this means your father doesn't love you. He does. And he'll happily walk you down the aisle if you want. But given the choice, his practical side may show through. He'll do the arithmetic, calculate pain and suffering, add in punitive damages, and whip out that checkbook faster than you can imagine.

What about Mom? Well, traditionally she has been the higher authority on weddings, so if Mom wants a big wedding, then Dad will probably take her side, or go to a neutral corner. That's to be expected. After all, he still has to live with your mother after you're gone. Here's the good news, though—Mom may think eloping is a great idea. "Excuse me?" you say. "You don't know *my* mother!" True enough, but maybe your mom has been telling you what she thinks you want to hear. Privately, she may be as relieved as Dad to hear she's off the hook. Times have changed for mothers of the bride, after all. Most of them work, so running around for nine months looking for the perfect veil isn't exactly the mother-daughter bonding experience it once was. Plus if Mom's already "done" a wedding for one of your sisters, she may have gotten the wedding bug out of her system. Either everything went perfectly and she does not want to tempt fate again or, more likely, it wasn't as wonderful as she'd hoped for.

## OVERCOMING OBJECTIONS

The catch with being less than forceful about your intention to elope is that you're opening the door to parental objections. The best-laid plans can founder here in the face of parental disapproval: good-bye, Paris, hello, Aunt Mildred. But we hope you know your parents well enough to anticipate their arguments and thus prepare your counterarguments. Below are the top-five parental objections and advice on how to handle them:

*Objection Number One: But We Want to Be There!*

Of course they do! They've generally invested more than a quarter of a century raising you. Now they just want to see their child walk down the aisle. Is that too much to ask? Maybe. It all depends on which aisle we're talking about. Will any aisle do? Or must it be a cathedral-like setting, with silk runners and pews packed with strange faces? Fortunately, it's a snap to find out: just invite Mom and Dad to the courthouse

### The Money Issue, Again

Just a gentle reminder not to confuse the issues when you sit down with your parents. It is wholly inappropriate to suggest, or imply, that you expect your parents to give you any of the money they would have spent on the wedding. Presumably you have decided that eloping is the right thing to do. If your parents offer to pay for your elopement, with perhaps a little something left over, that's one thing. But you should never ask for money or become upset if it isn't offered.

Many couples elope to spare their parents the expense, or the awkwardness surrounding a discussion about money when circumstances are limited. But here, too, you need to be careful. This is an expense they have anticipated for a long time, and they may be crushed to get a postcard saying you've eloped. That said, talking to your parents beforehand carries its own risks. If they sense that you're eloping for their sake, but that you'd actually prefer a big wedding, they're likely to feel guilty. Better, perhaps, to tell a white lie. Use work and the stress of planning a big wedding as your excuse, and let their reaction guide your decision.

to be your witnesses. If all they *really* want is to watch you get married, this should solve the problem.

Sometimes, though, the "We Want to Be There!" argument is just a smoke screen, in which case inviting them to the courthouse amounts to calling their bluff. When they decline that invitation you'll need to find out what the *real* problem is. It may be that your mother is one of those parents—and there are still plenty of them out there—who believe that their daughters owe them a wedding. But why? What do they *really* want here? The answer usually rests in one of these other four objections:

### *Objection Number Two: What Will the Neighbors Think?*

No one will ever admit it, but social status is often the driving force behind big weddings. Since the beginning of time parents have used their children's weddings as an opportunity to remind vassals and business associates of their wealth and importance. Fortunately there's an easy way to counter this urge: allow your parents to throw you a ridiculously lavish reception *after* you've returned from your honeymoon. That might feel like you're caving in, but don't worry—you're not. There is a world of difference between a fun party for 500 and a formal wedding reception for 500. Especially if you're the bride. Opt for the fun party and you escape the pressures of your wedding day, plus all the attendant rules and hoopla. Most important, your mother can plan this whole event without your involvement. All you have to do is show up and have fun.

If your parents don't buy into the reception idea right away, you might want to invoke fear and fashion. Fear, by reminding them that even the best-planned weddings have been known to fall apart. "Remember So-and-So's wedding?" you say sweetly. "Everything went wrong, even though they spent $100,000 and hired Arturo Europa from New York to plan it," (long pause). "God, her poor mother, everyone still feels sorry for her!" (Pause again, then turn on the positive spin.) "But Blazie Smith—you know her, don't you? Well, she and her husband—he owns XYZ Computers—they eloped to Bali and then threw a fabulous party when they got back. Everyone was talking about how great it was. I hear they got the idea from a friend in London. Supposedly someone in the royal family eloped last year. And you know what? Queen Elizabeth sent her a note afterward, saying she thought it was a terribly sensible thing to do!" OK, so maybe that's pushing it a bit. But you get the idea. (Besides, what's your mom going to do, call Buckingham Palace to see if it's true?)

Finally, if your parents still won't budge, you can always

lay a trap for them. Pretend to go along at first with Mom's plans. But just before she books the country club, smilingly put your foot down on a couple of points: insist on an unconventional service and a vegan, alcohol-free reception. That should do it.

*Objection Number Three: Your Parents Want a Big Wedding Because They Didn't Have One*

This one's easy. All you need do is to prove to your parents that they didn't miss out on anything. Encourage them to talk to friends who've suffered through a few big weddings, then toss them a bone—ask them to throw the 500-person party when you return. In the end, of course, you can also just be honest: "Mom and Dad, this is *my* wedding, OK? And this is what *I* want." This argument has actually worked once or twice.

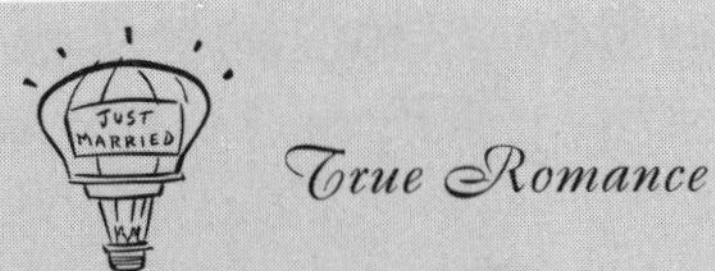


True Romance

*Muskrat Love?*

Daryl "The Captain" Dragon and Toni Tennille were married shortly after their song "Love Will Keep Us Together" reached number one in summer 1975. But Tennille describes it as more of a legal transaction. Her mother wanted the live-in couple to be legally married before the reporters started calling. So, the Captain and Tennille went to the Silver Queen Casino and Wedding Chapel in Virginia City, Nevada, picked up two witnesses (one who was eating his lunch in the saloon), and got married. They returned to the chapel to renew their vows 20 years later. Love *did* keep them together.

### *Objection Number Four: What Will the Groom's Family Think of Us?*

This comes up from time to time, especially if the groom comes from a wealthy family. In this situation, the bride's parents feel they are obligated to throw a lavish wedding, even if they don't want one or can't afford to. One hopes the groom's parents are not only wealthy but well mannered; the last thing they'd want is to bankrupt their future in-laws. The solution here is to break the news of the planned elopement *first* to the groom's parents. They might not be thrilled either—eloping just isn't done in some social circles—but once the shock wears off they can usually be enlisted in the cause. A nice little note from them to the bride's parents, commiserating but indicating acceptance of the proposed elopement, should do the trick. This officially lets the bride's parents off the social hook. There's actually a nice little bonus here, too. Now each family can host a reception in their hometown, and in a style each feels comfortable with. One couple that eloped to the Caribbean came back to a black-tie party in Kansas City, followed by a clambake in Boston.

### *Objection Number Five: It's My Last Chance to Control Your Life!*

Just once it would be nice if parents fessed up to this. Fat chance. But when you've reasoned your way through all the other arguments, this naked grasp for power is what you're left with. You have two choices: (1) yet another knock-down-drag-out fight (which you'll lose because control freaks live for battles like this), or, (2) you can elope. Forgetting all the romantic and financial reasons presented in this book, it is situations like this that have kept the "anvil priests" (see page 23) and their brethren busy over the years.

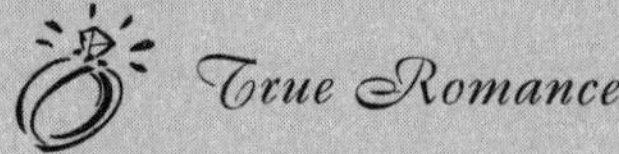

### True Romance

*Come on Down!!*

Bob Barker, the host of the successful game show *The Price Is Right,* is also one who didn't go for the traditional wedding. When Barker was 15 he asked a fellow classmate, Dorothy Jo, to an Ella Fitzgerald concert. They fell in love. Barker and Dorothy Jo eloped in St. Louis in 1945 when Barker, then 21, was on leave as a Navy pilot. "We fell in love as kids, and we stayed in love."

PART TWO

# *Where to Elope*

# 7. Start with the Web

The Web has quickly emerged as an indispensable resource for would-be elopers. Despite its clutter (yes, you could also waste all the time you've saved by not doing a traditional wedding, just surfing the Web), it's a gold mine of valuable information. Here are just a few ways the Web can help:

- You can research the legal requirements for getting married in any city, state, or country.
- You can get great ideas about places to elope or honeymoon, and then dig down to find out-of-the way hotels, B&Bs, or resorts.
- You can find great deals in travel (last-minute airline e-savers are tailor-made for impulsive elopers!), hotels, even wedding dresses if you want to elope in white.
- You can swap war stories with others who eloped, or read about the travails of those who did big traditional weddings.
- You can even create a home page with pictures and stories about your elopement for all your friends and family to share.

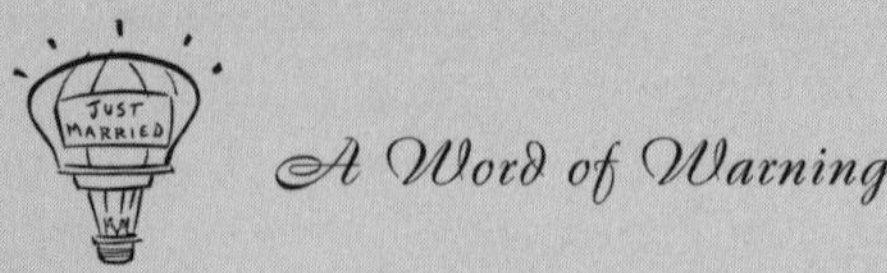


### A Word of Warning

Type "wedding," "elope," or "bride" into any search engine and you'll get buried with hits. To complicate matters further, most of these sites are geared to traditional weddings. Bridal magazines, wedding-planning consultants, and all the other industry players are on the Web these days, eager for a piece of that $32 billion prize. Given their vested interest in pushing you down the aisle, don't expect feature articles on the wisdom of eloping. But don't write off these wedding sites, either. Their honeymoon tips and gift registry services are useful, and even the practical wedding advice may be helpful if you're planning a hybrid wedding-elopement.

## Where to Find Help on the Web

### RESEARCHING MARRIAGE LICENSE REQUIREMENTS ON THE WEB

*The United States*

You need specific requirements for the county where you plan to get married. That information is usually available on-line and most counties use a standardized address format beginning with "co" then adding the county name and postal abbreviation for the state: **www.co.countyname.state.us** (e.g., **www.co.sacramento.ca.us**). If you don't know the name of the county, however, then start with a state government Web search. All 50 states use standardized Web address format with their two-letter postal initial: **www.state.XX.us** (e.g., **www.state.ca.us** for California). The state sites will connect you to the city or county you're looking for.

*International*

Depending on the country, you may be able to get the information you need from a hotel, a travel agency, or a wedding planner. (**HeartofEurope.com**, for example, provides marriage license requirements for—you guessed it!—most European countries.) But it is essential to double-check information with an official source, either a consulate in a major U.S. city, or the country's embassy in Washington, D.C. Embassy phone numbers can be obtained through directory assistance for area code 202. **Consulate.Travel.com.hk** also maintains a Web directory of all consulate and embassy phone, fax, e-mail, and Web addresses worldwide.

## WEDDING WEB SITES

Some of these sites are sponsored by bridal magazines, others are entirely Web-based. All have budget planners, checklists, bulletin boards, honeymoon travel centers, advice columns, and links to gift registries. The best feature of these sites, though, is the bulletin boards. Go to them when you're wavering, when you're not quite sure you can go through with this. A quick 30 minutes spent reading war stories will give you fresh resolve!

*LetsElope.com*

OK, we're biased. This is our site. Until we created it there was no all-purpose site devoted exclusively to eloping. At our site you can: share feedback and ideas with others who have eloped; participate in our on-line surveys; e-mail thorny questions about eloping to our Etiquette Advisor; or surf around the Destinations board.

Our favorite feature? You can send someone a copy of this book wrapped in brown paper with no return address.

*Other Wedding Web Sites*

| | |
|---|---|
| **TheKnot.com** | First big wedding Web site, offers a biweekly newsletter and |

| | |
|---|---|
| | allows couples to create their own personalized wedding page (as do most other all-purpose sites) |
| **Modernbride.com** | Offshoot of *Modern Bride* magazine, good feature articles and archives |
| **Weddingnetwork.com** | All-purpose site, editorial content by *Modern Bride* |
| **Weddings.com** | All-purpose site created by **Della.com**, an on-line gift registry |
| **Weddingpages.com** | All-purpose site |
| **WeddingChannel.com** | All-purpose site that also hosts *Bride's* magazine on-line and gift registries with some large stores like Macy's |
| **Brides.com** | Home page for *Bride's* magazine, editorial archives, and links to other wedding sites |

## GIFT REGISTRY

On-line gift registry may prove to be the most valuable contribution of the Web to modern civilization. Couples can now mix and match their requests from a variety of stores and monitor their haul on an hourly basis. For wedding guests—the ones spending the money—it's not terribly different from the old days when you called a store, gave them your charge card number, and told them how much you wanted to spend. But now you can actually see what you're buying. That should spare you the embarrassing scene when you show up at the newlyweds' home and don't recognize your own gift.

All of the major department stores have on-line registries, as do many specialty retailers. More recently a number of reg-

*Hint*

To find a retailer's wedding registry site, try adding a dot com to the store's name. If that doesn't work, type the store's name into your search engine. And if you still come up empty, call the store directly (or its 800 number) and ask them for the Web address.

istry-only sites have appeared, including **e.Wish.com** and **Della.com** (which also has **della.weddings.com**). You can access specific retailers directly (e.g., **macys.com**) or through one of the all-purpose wedding sites or on-line registries. The advantage of not going directly to the retailer's own site is that a couple can create a list of items from lots of stores. For the truly lazy or unimaginative, **TheKnot.com** will even create a list for you based on a quick lifestyle survey. (Sample question: "The perfect weekend with your honey would involve: (a) pizza and a video, (b) the great outdoors and sleeping under the stars, (c) the three C's: cappuccino, croissants, and cinema.")

### WOMEN'S SITES

**iVillage.com** and **Women.com** are two of the better-known sites addressing a broad array of women's issues. The wedding and marriage advice you'll find here, in articles, on bulletin boards, or in chat rooms, tends to come with a more mature slant than the mainstream wedding-only sites. **iVillage** has links to **Della.com,** a major wedding registry. **Women.com** has a link to **TheKnot.com,** a major all-purpose wedding site.

## TRAVEL AND DESTINATIONS

Eloping generally involves travel, if not to actually get married, then usually for the honeymoon part. Either way, the Web's perfect for doing your travel homework. Two tips, however:

- As you research destinations, you are better off ignoring the wedding angle, at least initially. Why? Because typing "elope" or "honeymoon" into any search engine will leave you buried under a mountain of "Special Honeymoon Offers" from packaged tour and resort operators. Stick to general-purpose travel sites on major portals such as AOL or Yahoo! Both of these have plenty of links to other guides such as Fodor's, Lonely Planet, or smaller guidebook publishers. Or try a specialty travel site like **concierge.com** (romantic getaways and adventure travel) or **KarenBrown.com** (European small hotels).
- Once you know *where* you want to elope you can get specific wedding-related information from hotel operators, official government information sites (for legal requirements), or from locally based wedding-planning consultants (which you can also find on the Web).

# 8.

# Wedding Packages

Due to the popularity of hassle-free weddings and eloping, many resorts, hotels, travel planners, and cruise ships offer wedding packages. In some cases, such as all-inclusive resorts, your wedding ceremony may be "free" if you are honeymooning at the resort. On the other hand, wedding packages can cost up to $2,000 to $3,000 if you are planning a small destination wedding with guests, followed by a reception. The basic rule of wedding packages is similar to planning a big wedding; each added amenity will increase the price.

Following are samples of various wedding packages, from "basic" to "deluxe." If you decide to go with a wedding package, make sure to ask your hotel, wedding planner, or justice of the peace for a list of exactly what is included in the cost of your ceremony:

## Basic Wedding Package

Short consultation and location assistance
Minister and marriage ceremony
Marriage license processing

## One-Step-Up Wedding Package

Consultation and location assistance
Round-trip transportation to and from wedding site
Location fee (e.g., church fee, if applicable)
Bridal bouquet and boutonniere
Taped music
Professional photography (you may have to have the film developed yourselves)
Champagne
One-tier wedding cake
Marriage license processing

## Deluxe Wedding Package

Consultation and location assistance
Rehearsal the night before ceremony
Round-trip transportation in a stretch limo, horse and buggy, or whatever, to and from wedding site
Location fee (e.g., church fee, if applicable)
Bridal bouquet and boutonniere, flowers for attendants
Professional photography package (they develop the film for you)
Live music
Champagne
Wedding cake
Dinner reception for couple and guests after the ceremony
Marriage license processing
Wedding video (may be extra)
Wedding album (may be extra)

## Shipboard Wedding Package

One- to three-hour day trip on the water
Wedding ceremony
Bottle of champagne

One-tier wedding cake
Bridal bouquet and boutonniere
Marriage license processing

Packages can make your wedding easy. One of the best features of a wedding package is the marriage license processing. This can save you hours of time. Remember to ask if you need to supply witnesses or if they can be supplied for you. If you are getting married at a resort, ask if you have your choice of locations or if ceremonies are only performed on the grounds of the resort. Also keep in mind that although most of these packages can be available with a day's notice, you may not be able to obtain a marriage license without spending 24 to 72 hours in your destination country. Research the marriage license requirements before you schedule your wedding. Also note that the prices of packages will not include gratuities that are normally given to the wedding officiant, limo driver, and anyone else involved in the planning.

If you want a hassle-free wedding in the midst of a wonderful vacation, go with the wedding package option and leave the coordinating to someone else.

# 9. Old Favorites

## ♡ Atlantic City

Nicknamed "America's Favorite Playground," Atlantic City is the number-one day-tripping destination in the world. Located on the Jersey Shore, Atlantic City is known for its casinos providing 24-hour gambling and entertainment. Atlantic City also has beaches and golf courses for those not inclined to press their luck at the roulette table. There are no freestanding wedding chapels in Atlantic City for walk-in weddings, but there are plenty of places to tie the knot.

### FUN IDEAS AND SITES

- At a nearby winery
- At a casino
- On the greens at a golf resort
- On the beach
- On the boardwalk
- In a luxury hotel

## WEDDING PACKAGES

Most listings providing information about wedding packages are located in the neighboring towns of Atlantic City. **The Renault Winery,** in Egg Harbor, New Jersey, offers two packages, one in the Vintage Room for 30 to 200 people and one in the Grand Ballroom for 150 to 300 people. You can contact the Renault Winery through their Web site for pricing information. Other locations offering wedding packages are the **Tomasello Winery, Sweetwater Casino,** and **Mayer's Inn and Marina,** and for those of you who want a high-tech experience, **The Showbarn.** If you are looking for assistance planning a very small gathering, or a theme wedding, contact one of the planners listed below.

## WEB SITE AND CONTACT INFO

*Planners/Services*

- **atlanticcityweddings.com:** Very helpful information about getting married in Atlantic City, vendor lists, reception halls, and more. Also provides links to venues that provide wedding packages.
- **www.njwedding.com:** the Internet wedding directory of New Jersey.
- **Elegant Occasions**
  Denville, NJ
  (973) 361–9200
  Elegwed204@aol.com
  Specializing in Weekend Warrior and destination weddings in Atlantic City.
- **Now and Forever Bridal Consulting**
  Philadelphia, PA
  (215) 467–6663
  Bridal consulting service for South Jersey; can do theme weddings.
- **Enchanting Affairs**
  Rockaway, NJ

(973) 586–7906
Professional wedding planners in New Jersey.

- **blueheronpines.com:** Blue Heron Pines Golf Course site. (609) 965–1800
- **renaultwinery.com:** Renault Winery site. (609) 965–2111
- **tomasellowinery.com:** Tomasello Winery site. (800) MMM-WINE
- **mayersinn.com:** Mayer's Inn and Marina site. (609) 927–3100
- **smithvillenj.com/the showbarn/weddings:** The Showbarn site. (609) 748–7799

*Tourism*

- **library.atlantic.city.lib.nj.us/ac/:** The official city site for Atlantic City.
- **atlantic-city-hotels.net:** Atlantic City Hotels and Casinos Online.
- **Greater Atlantic City Chamber of Commerce**
  1125 Atlantic Avenue
  Atlantic City, NJ 08401
  (609) 345–5600

*License Info*

- **atlanticcityweddings.com:** Lists license requirements and information about permits for beach and boardwalk weddings.
- **Atlantic City—City Hall**
  Room 507
  1301 Bacharach Boulevard
  Atlantic City, NJ 08401
  (609) 347–5410
- **Atlantic City Parks and Recreation:** Call for details and prices on permits for weddings in public spaces. (609) 347–5427

## ♡ *Lake Tahoe*

Lake Tahoe is a historically famous spot for laid-back weddings and elopements. Located on the border of California and Nevada, its rich scenery consists of mountains, lakes, and beaches that provide gorgeous backdrops for a wedding ceremony in any season. Gambling is legal on the Nevada side for those who want to test their luck. Skiing, sledding, sailing, and hiking are all available for the nature lovers.

### FUN IDEAS AND SITES

- **Chapel weddings:** Lake Tahoe has several freestanding wedding chapels. Other chapels are part of a resort with preferential booking and special rates for resort guests. If you decide to go with a freestanding chapel, be sure to call ahead to check availability.
- **Emerald Bay:** You can have your ceremony on a 200-foot bluff overlooking the lake and out of view from tourists.
- **Top of the Heavenly Tram:** Take a tram to and from your wedding site, 2,000 feet above Lake Tahoe.
- **Regan Beach:** Get married on a wooden deck that overhangs the lake or in a grassy park surrounded by tall evergreens.
- **Horse-drawn sleigh:** You and your wedding party can take a sleigh ride to a beautiful meadow overlooking the lake.
- **Ski weddings:** A little bit trickier to arrange, but most resorts or the chamber of commerce Web sites recommend wedding planners to help out.

### WEDDING PACKAGES

**Cloud 9** offers a bargain package for the Basic Wedding costing $95. Prices increase as more amenities are added. The Romance Wedding Package costs $599 and includes a day cruise.

Skiing packages are also available. Check with your hotel to find out whether they offer their own wedding packages.

## WEB SITE AND CONTACT INFO

*Planners/Services*

- **weddingstahoe.com:** Site provides information on wedding vendors, ceremony locations, chapels, aerial weddings, and boat weddings as well as a message board.
- **tahoeweddinginfo.com:** Web site for a wedding coordinator and referral service.
  (800) 417–3148
  (530) 573–6044
- **cloud9-wedding-inn.com:** Site for Cloud 9 Weddings, who provide wedding ceremonies/services at their inn.

*Services on the Lake*

- **M.S. Dixie II Paddle Wheeler**
  Zephyr Cove, NV
  (775) 588–3508
- **The Party Boat**
  South Lake Tahoe, CA
  (530) 544–8888
- **Hornblower's Tahoe Queen**
  South Lake Tahoe, CA
  (530) 541–3364
- **Woodwind Sailing**
  Stateline, NV
  (775) 588–3000
- **North Tahoe Cruises—*Tahoe Gal***
  Tahoe City, CA
  (800) 218–2464

*Tourism*

- **tahoevacationguide.com:** The *Tahoe Vacation Guide* Web site that provides information on Tahoe activities: skiing, casinos, nightlife, cruises, and resorts.
  (800) MY TAHOE

*License Info*

- **El Dorado County Clerk (for California-side marriage licenses)**
  3368 Lake Tahoe Boulevard
  Suite #108
  South Lake Tahoe, CA 96150
  (530) 573–3409
- **Douglas County Clerk/Lake Tahoe (for Nevada-side marriage licenses)**
  County Administration Building/Sheriff's Office
  Hwy. 50, Stateline, NV 89449
  (775) 588–7100

## Las Vegas

Las Vegas and eloping are synonymous for good reason: getting married in Vegas is easy, fast, and stress-free. It can also be incredibly tacky, but that's half the attraction for most couples. Call it the pendulum effect: having decided to forgo the country club and custom-fitted dresses, couples head to the desert and hire Elvis to pronounce the vows.

Besides the intrigue of having a Vegas wedding (and a good story to tell your kids), there are four practical reasons to consider Las Vegas:

1. **Cost:** Under $200 in most cases. More if you want something special, but competition among the chapels and hotels keeps the prices reasonable for all budgets.

2. **Ease:** Really, it couldn't get any easier. One phone call and the limo picks you up. And that's assuming you even have to leave your hotel!
3. **No red tape:** You can get married with no waiting period, no blood test, and the license office is open 365 days a year (and 24 hours a day on weekends).
4. **Fun:** Vegas rocks around the clock with gambling, big-name shows, even fun activities for kids. Whatever else you can say about Vegas—it's not boring. And skipping all that wedding planning back home makes it all the sweeter.

## NEVADA WEDDING HISTORY

Vegas weddings first became popular—and achieved notoriety—in the decades before no-fault divorce, and before churches developed a more tolerant position on second marriages. In those pre-Elvis days Nevada was the only state where quickie divorces and weddings were possible. Vegas lost that legal monopoly in recent decades. Now it's almost as easy to get married in any of the other 49 states. But the mystique still holds; a "Vegas Wedding" symbolizes a certain swaggering, devil-may-care attitude toward social convention. Meanwhile, Las Vegas has developed a new monopoly, as the unrivaled center of the fast-and-easy theme-wedding universe.

## LEGAL REQUIREMENTS

Very simple, as long as you're both over 18. Just show up at the courthouse with $35 and your driver's license or passport. You do not need copies of divorce papers from any previous marriage, but you will need to tell the clerk when and where the divorce was registered. The Clark County Courthouse is open from 8 A.M. to midnight Sunday through Thursday, and 24 hours a day Friday and Saturday. No blood test, waiting periods, or appointments are necessary. The courthouse is located at 200 South Third Street, and the phone number is (702) 455-4415.

### If at First You Don't Succeed...

Mickey Rooney was married eight times in Las Vegas to eight different women:

1. 1942: Ava Gardner
2. 1944: Betty Jane Rase
3. 1948: Martha Vickers
4. 1952: Elaine Mahnken
5. 1958: Barbara Ann Thompson
6. 1967: Marge Lane
7. 1969: Carolyn Hockett
8. 1978: January Chamberlain

## FUN IDEAS AND SITES

There are four ways to get married in Vegas:

- **On the courthouse steps:** Or anywhere else in town, by a duly authorized officer of the court, such as a justice of the peace. Basically, someone will meet you at the courthouse and perform the actual ceremony after you take care of the paperwork. The cost is approximately $100. A list of authorized persons can be obtained from the clerk's office.
- **Hotels:** For a long time the wedding chapels had the matrimony business to themselves. But in recent years big-name hotels have begun to compete, offering their own wedding packages. In general, hotel weddings are a bit more sedate, although most do offer a limited menu of theme weddings (and everyone in Vegas can get you Elvis). Prices are competitive with chapels, too, running

approximately $600 to $800 for a basic ceremony with fewer than 20 guests. Hotels make the most sense for those who want a touch more class than the typical chapel (do you really want to bump into Spock on your way out?) or for those who are planning to have a larger number of guests. A more elaborate ceremony and large private reception can easily be arranged at any hotel—for an additional fee, of course. Note: most hotels require at least 10 days advance reservations.

- **Wedding chapels:** Wedding chapels still have the upper hand over hotels for those looking for something out of the ordinary. And while it's smart to reserve ahead at wedding chapels (particularly for theme weddings) it is not a requirement as it is at most hotels. Wedding chapels are spread throughout Las Vegas but most are easily accessible from the Strip. Limo service to and from your hotel is always included in the total cost of wedding packages. Non-theme wedding packages begin at $175 at most chapels; theme weddings run $600 to $800. (Extra characters, such as a full complement of *Star Trek* look-alikes, will cost you an extra $50 to $75 each.) Some of the most popular theme wedding options include: Rock & Roll (Elvis), Gangster, Western, Beach Party, Intergalactic (*Star Trek*), Egyptian, Gothic, and Sports-themed. If you're not in a rush it's actually worth staying around after your own Wild West wedding to watch the chapel pit crew work at Indy speeds to transform the chapel into an Egyptian tomb for the next group.
- **Outdoors:** Hot-air balloon and helicopter weddings are popular and easily arranged. The cost is roughly $1,000. Other outdoor options include Red Rocks Canyon, river and lake weddings, or mountaintop weddings in the nearby Sierra Nevada. All of these can be arranged through any of the major Las Vegas wedding service companies.

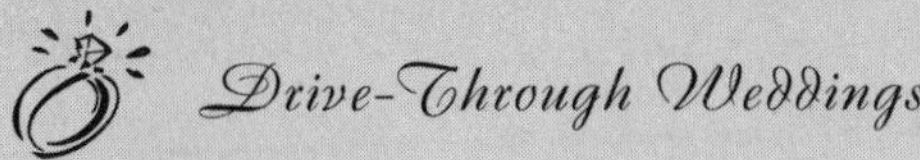

## Drive-Through Weddings

Yes, only in Las Vegas. Faster than you can get in and out of most hamburger joints you can get married in the drive-through lane at *A Special Memory Wedding Chapel.* One couple didn't even drive up to the window, they in-line skated along with the rest of their wedding party. Imagine, a workout and wedding, all in one.

### HELPFUL HINTS

Las Vegas's wedding planners are real pros and can arrange almost anything you want on short notice. But if you want something special, you'd be wise to do some research beforehand. Las Vegas can be a bit overwhelming when you first arrive and it may take a day or two just to get your bearings. If a quick, simple service is more your speed, any hotel front desk can arrange a wedding service or direct you to a nearby chapel.

When you pick your chapel, find out if there is just one wedding area or if they have several chapels within the chapel. You may have your choice of several wedding atmospheres within one location. Be specific about your music preferences. If you have a special song you want played, your chapel may have a recording of that. If not, they'll happily let you bring your own tape or CD.

Shop around. There are plenty of wedding consultants in Vegas that can help you orchestrate your wedding. The city is full of entertainers, DJs, limo services, dress shops, photographers, and florists, and most will work with you on short notice. You may want to call for a free copy of *The Perfect Wedding Guide for Las Vegas*. It is full of ads, along with helpful phone numbers, photos, and Web sites. Call (702) 871–8083 or visit their Web site **perfectweddingguide.com** to order a copy.

## *Top-15 Celebrity Elopements in Vegas*

**1943:** Betty Grable married bandleader Harry James at the Little Church of the West.

**1949:** Zsa Zsa Gabor married actor George Sanders at the Little Church of the West.

**1954:** Kirk Douglas married Ann Buydens at the Sahara Hotel (they are still married).

**1955:** Joan Crawford married Alfred Steele (CEO of Pepsi-Cola) at the Flamingo Hotel.

**1957:** Steve Lawrence married Eydie Gorme at the home of the owner of the old El Rancho Hotel. Paul Newman married Joanne Woodward at the El Rancho Hotel.

**1963:** Bette White married Allen Ludden at the Sands Hotel.

**1965:** Judy Garland married Mark Herron at the Little Church of the West.

**1966:** Frank Sinatra married Mia Farrow at the Sands.

**1967:** Elvis Presley married Priscilla Anne Beaulieu in a suite at the Aladdin Hotel. Ann-Margret married Roger Smith at the Riviera Hotel.

**1968:** Wayne Newton married Elaine Okamura at the Flamingo Hotel.

**1972:** George Hamilton married Alana Collins at the Las Vegas Hilton. Following their divorce, Alana married rock star Rod Stewart.

**1989:** Michael Jordan married Juanita Vanoy at The Little White Chapel.

**1998:** Dennis Rodman married Carmen Electra at Little Chapel of the Flowers.

## WEB SITE AND CONTACT INFO

And just when you thought they couldn't make it any easier, the Internet came along. The information superhighway runs right through Vegas, so now you can preview facilities, different packages and pricing, and ceremony options. Below is a listing of chapels, resorts, and wedding-planning companies.

*Freestanding Wedding Chapels*

- **Viva Las Vegas Wedding Chapel**
  **vivalasvegasweddings.com**
  (800) 574–4450
- **Chapel Orleans**
  **orleanscasino.com**
  (888) 365–7111
  (702) 365–7555
- **Little Chapel of the Flowers**
  **littlechapel.com**
  (800) 843–2410
  (702) 735–4331
- **Candlelight Wedding Chapel**
  **candlelight.v1net.com**
  (800) 962–1818
  (702) 735–4179
- **Silver Bells Wedding Chapel**
  **www.silverbell.com**
  (800) 221–8492
  (702) 382–3726
- **Little White Wedding Chapel**
  **alittlewhitechapel.com**
  (800) 545–8111
- **Wedding Bells Chapel**
  **lasvegasweddingbells.com**
  (702) 731-BELL
  (800) 305–9040

- **A Special Memory Wedding Chapel**
  **aspecialmemory.com**
  (800) 962–7798
  (702) 384–2211

*Resorts and Casino Chapels*

- **New York New York Wedding Chapel**
  (800) 652-NYNY
  (702) 740–6626
- **Forever Grand at the MGM Grand**
  (800) 646–5530
- **Chapel by the Bay at Mandalay Bay**
  (702) 632–7278
- **Caesar's Palace Wedding Chapel**
  **caesars.com**
  (702) 731–7111
  (877) 279–3334
- **Paris Wedding Chapel**
  **Paris-lv.com**
  (877) 650–5021
- **Bellagio Hotel Wedding Chapel**
  **bellagiolasvegas.com**
  (888) 987–3344
  (702) 693–7700
- **Circus Circus Chapel of the Fountains**
  (800) 444-CIRCUS
- **Monte Carlo Resort and Casino Wedding Chapel**
  (800) 311–8999
- **Treasure Island Wedding Chapels**
  (800) 944–7444
  (702) 894–7111
- **Aladdin Resort and Casino**
  (800) 634–3424
  (702) 736–0111

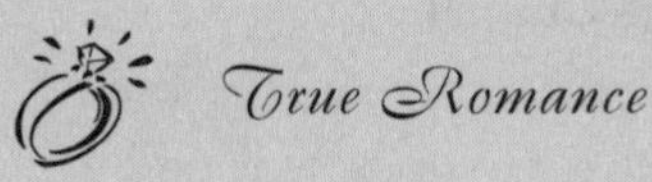


*To Plan or Not to Plan: John and Melissa vs. Kevin and Betsy*

You don't need a year in advance to plan your Vegas wedding/elopement. John and Melissa Merklinger were planning a trip to Vegas, just for fun, and decided ahead of time that they would tie the knot while they were there. They told no one. Melissa took a white dress and John packed khakis and a shirt, and that was all the planning they did. They arrived in Vegas on a Tuesday. The following Friday, they woke up and said, "Should we get married today?" decided it was a good day, and opened the Yellow Pages. They chose the first chapel listing they saw with a full-page ad. They called and arranged their afternoon. They were picked up in a limo, which took them to get their marriage license. The limo then took them to a local jeweler and they walked out with wedding rings. Then they went to the chapel where the chaplain was waiting, and they were married. The package at the time cost $210, not including wedding bands and an extra $30 to pay the chaplain. They called their families to inform them of the news and continued on with their vacation, as a married couple.

Kevin and Betsy, 35, had both been married before. They began to plan a backyard wedding at their place in Los Angeles, but when the planning started and they were adding up the costs, they thought it was too expensive and too much hassle. So two weeks before flying to Vegas, they called their friends and invited them to their wedding at Caesar's Palace. There were 25 people in attendance. The guests met at one of the bars before the ceremony for cocktails then all went upstairs to Caesar's Neptune Villa—The Palace Chapel, for the ceremony. Betsy wore a blue dress,

Kevin a suit. The ceremony was short, the reverend talked about how the two had met (at a RATT concert), said the wedding vows, and then a guitar-playing Elvis showed up to sing "Viva Las Vegas" as the newly married couple walked down the aisle and out the door to enjoy the night with their friends in the casino. Kevin and Betsy did some planning for their wedding and were able to have a good-sized group of people attend, as well as reserve the chapel at Caesar's and find Elvis (although his arrival was a surprise for Betsy).

- **Tropicana Resort and Casino**
  (800) 634–4000
  (702) 739–2222
- **Riviera Resort and Casino**
  (800) 634–6753
  (702) 734–5110

*License Info*

- **Clark County Courthouse**
  200 South Third Street
  (702) 455–4415

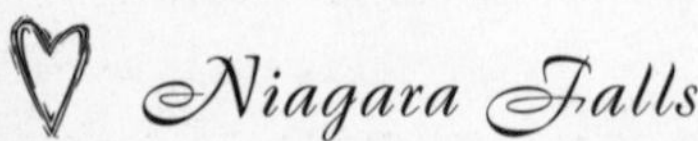

## Niagara Falls

Often called the "Honeymoon Capital of the World," Niagara Falls divides New York State and Canada, providing a natural wonder for the eyes to see and plenty of spots to elope. The popularity of Niagara Falls for a wedding dates from the 1800s when Jerome Bonaparte (Napoléon's younger brother) and his bride went to the Falls, as well as Theodosia Burr (daughter of Aaron Burr) and her groom.

## FUN IDEAS AND SITES

- **Niagara Wedding Chapel:** Built in 1991, the first "one-stop" chapel in the Falls.
- **Observation Tower:** Overlooks the Falls and is ideal for intimate weddings.
- **Scenic settings around the Falls:** There are many different locations to choose from. When you arrive in town go to the Falls and just pick the spot! It's really that easy. Prospect Point or Luna Island are popular spots.
- **Wintergarden:** This is a lush enclosed botanical garden that is recommended more for pictures than for a ceremony. It is a public building visited by many tourists, so privacy is not guaranteed.
- **Oakes Inn:** You can exchange vows here in the Fallsview Chapel located on the Observation Deck, which overlooks both the Canadian and the American Falls.
- **Countryside Wedding:** The Wayside Chapel is located on the Niagara Parkway and it is the only authentic miniature chapel of its kind in the Niagara area. It is located 10 minutes from Niagara Falls.
- **Gazebo wedding:** The town of Niagara on the Lake, once voted Canada's prettiest town, has a gazebo that overlooks Lake Ontario and Old Fort Niagara, perfect for exchanging vows.
- **Victorian town of Niagara on the Lake:** This town is nearby to the Falls and offers several different backdrops for a wedding as well as lodging and restaurants.

## WEDDING PACKAGES

The **Niagara Falls Wedding Chapel** (Niagara Falls, New York) offers packages from The Romantic Get Away for $99 to the Super Deluxe for $399. **The Wedding Company of Niagara** offers packages ranging from $225 to $450; they perform wedding services in their chapel or at any other location "land, air, or sea."

## WEB SITE AND CONTACT INFO

*Planners/Services*

- **vaxxine.com/weddings:** Site for The Wedding Company of Niagara.
- **occasionsniagara.com:** Basic wedding information for Niagara Falls.
- **niagarafallslive.com:** More information on Niagara Falls with a wedding link.
- **The Niagara Falls Wedding Chapel**
  (800) 785–LOVE (5683)

*Tourism*

- **niagarafallstourism.com:** Niagara Falls Visitors and Conventions Bureau Site.
- **nflschamber.com:** Chamber of Commerce site.
- **The Niagara Falls Chamber of Commerce (Ontario)**
  (905) 374–3666
- **Parks and Recreation for the Town of Niagara on the Lake**
  (905) 468–3266

*License Info*

- **Clerks Department—Niagara Falls City Hall**
  4310 Queen Street
  P.O. Box 1023
  Niagara Falls, Ontario L2E 6X5
  (905) 356–7521

# Other Romantic Destinations

## Disney

Although Goofy, Pluto, and Mickey come to mind when you think of Disney, more than 10,000 couples in the past five years have chosen Disney as their wedding spot. You can have a resort setting or a theme wedding. Since the folks at Disney specialize in entertainment, they offer many options. You can have an intimate wedding at Disney for the two of you (and several guests) or a large affair with a long guest list. If Disney can pull off a daily fireworks display, parades, and a jug band made of singing bears, they can grant you your wish for a "Fairy Tale Wedding." Disney has its own wedding department, which includes a sales team, wedding coordinator, chefs, caterers, DJs, florists, makeup artists, and baby-sitters.

### FUN IDEAS AND SITES

- The wedding pavilion in Disney World. It is surrounded by water and has a view of Cinderella's Castle.

- Sea Breeze Point at Disney's Boardwalk.
- The Wedding Gazebo at Disney's Yacht Club Resort.
- Sunrise Terrace at Disney's Wilderness Lodge.
- Sunset Pointe at Disney's Polynesian Resort.

## WEDDING PACKAGES

### *The Intimate Wedding vs. the Custom Wedding*

Disney offers two types of weddings: the **Intimate Wedding** and the **Custom Wedding.** Disney classifies an Intimate Wedding as anything with fewer than 15 people in attendance. For more than 15 people, Disney suggests a custom wedding that will be more expensive but will include more "extras." **Intimate weddings** can be planned on very short notice and are often the choice of elopers. The basic Intimate Wedding package costs approximately $3,000. You can add to the standard Intimate Wedding package by upgrading to the Deluxe Intimate Wedding ($3,154) or the Premium Intimate Wedding ($3,656). Just ask your wedding coordinator. **Custom weddings**, on the other hand, are uniquely tailored to your desires. The folks at Disney are entertainment specialists and can pretty much do anything, with the motto, "If your heart is in your dream, no request is too extreme." Even if your theme has nothing to do with Disney characters or settings, they can execute it. One couple asked Disney to re-create the street on which they had met in Paris. So the folks at Disney re-created the block using a photograph that the couple provided. It's nice to know they can indulge you, but you probably won't need this kind of attention. Disney has hundreds of locations throughout the various parks and at the resorts to provide elegant, lush, or "goofy" backgrounds for your ceremony.

### *Theme Weddings at Disney*

The most common theme wedding at Disney is the Cinderella/Prince Charming wedding. The couple actually dresses up as Cinderella and Prince Charming (he can be on a horse) and exchange vows in front of Cinderella's castle. No wicked stepmothers or singing mice, but you *can* have a ball if you like. Theme weddings are considered a type of custom wedding and prices will vary on these. Be sure to ask for some ballpark figures when deciding what you want.

## HELPFUL HINTS

*How to Plan a Disney Wedding*

Once you have decided to get married at Disney, half of the work is over. Couples who planned Disney weddings describe the process as "fun" (ask most brides if "fun" is how they would describe making wedding arrangements). Call Fairy Tale Weddings at (407) 828–3400 and speak to a sales manager. They will be able to answer all of your questions. It is recommended that months before your wedding you take a trip to the park to see the grounds and facilities. However, if that is not possible, the sales team can send you photos, videos, and all sorts of information about Disney weddings. When you decide on a wedding

Disney characters are not allowed to participate in your ceremony. They cannot walk you down the aisle or officiate. However, they can greet you after your ceremony and can show up at your reception. You can also hire other theme park characters to be incorporated into your weekend. For example, the actors who play the obnoxious tourists that entertain you while you wait in line for rides at MGM (aka the "MGM Tourists") can be hired for your reception, if you feel your group lacks obnoxious wedding guests.

scenario, the sales manager will be prepared to establish your budget based on your decisions and you can work from there.

If you are planning an intimate wedding, be aware that you cannot sign a contract with Disney until eight months before the wedding date. So if you are seriously planning ahead, talk about that with your sales manager.

Once your contract is signed, you will be assigned a wedding coordinator and the planning begins. Ask your wedding coordinator about "Save the Date" card mailings. They will send out the cards to your guest list in true Disney style. Disney will offer your guests discount room rates they are entitled to as guests at your wedding. If you travel to the park, you will meet with your coordinator and a representative from each department in the wedding world: floral, entertainment, food, and more. You will also have a cake tasting. If you are presenting the chef with a specific recipe for an entrée, you can schedule a food tasting as well. If you are having something more basic, such as steak, chicken, or shrimp, a tasting won't be provided. If you meet with your coordinator on-site, plan to spend at least a few hours discussing your plans and talking with the different representatives from each area.

You can schedule a park photo session before the park opens to feel like you are the only ones in the Magic Kingdom. If you do this, realize that you will be getting up at the crack of dawn to be picture perfect for your shoot. If you are an all-night partyer, you may want to drop this idea.

Many brides recommend a trip to the spa at the Grand Floridian sometime before the wedding ceremony. This is a full-service spa offering everything from manicures to hair styling. You can also find hair salons (one being Ivy Trellis at the Grand Floridian) to have your hair perfectly coiffed for the big day. If you have a wedding party, treat the girls to some pre-event pampering.

Some couples choose to select their favorite Disney wedding tunes to be a part of their wedding. Some suggestions are:

- "Rebekah and Doobie," also known as the Cinderella Fanfare.
- Selections from the *Heigh-Ho! Mozart CD,* which features favorite Disney tunes in the style of great classical composers.
- "Bibidy Bobbidy Bach" is another favorite.

*Elopements or Weddings on Short Notice*

An intimate wedding can be planned on very short notice, with the same attention from a coordinator as the "full-fledged" weddings. A few weeks in advance are usually required, but if you are at Disney and decide that you are in the mood to tie the knot, call the Fairy Tale Weddings Department. You will most likely be accommodated. You can send out wedding announcements right from the park! That beats the usual "Hello from Mickey and Minnie" postcard any day.

*Fancy Footwear: The Famous Glass Slipper*

For those of you who want more than photo memories of your event, you can find glass slippers to take home with you. Your coordinator can get a small glass slipper and have your names engraved in it for about $40. The Crystal Shop at Walt Disney World is another place to find your slipper. Custom Glass Etching offers glass slippers and can be found on the Web at **glassetcher.com.** If you really want to play the part and wear your glass slippers, you can find clear vinyl "crystal"-looking pumps on the Web at **bridalshoes.com.**

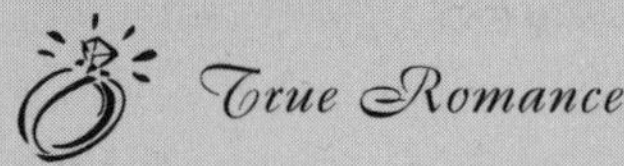

*A Wedding at Disney: Andrea and Leonard*

Andrea and Leonard were one of the first couples to get married at Disney World in September 1994. Andrea describes it as the most magical day of their lives. Andrea is from Boston and always dreamed of an old-fashioned New England wedding. Her husband is from a small seacoast town in New Hampshire and had also always envisioned a maritime New England wedding. They got what they dreamed about with their Disney wedding. The ambience of a seacoast resort was found at the Yacht Club at Disney, which was designed to replicate turn-of-the-century sea resorts once found on Martha's Vineyard and Nantucket. The Group Travel department at Disney offered their guests highly discounted room rates and park discounts so that 30 of their friends could afford this vacation. Andrea and Leonard did all of their wedding planning over the phone with their wedding coordinator and were happy to meet him when they arrived. Andrea was thrilled with the way the event was handled. "By the time our wedding day rolled around, Bill (the coordinator) knew exactly what we wanted and saw to it that each detail was executed perfectly," she says. Their ceremony was performed at the wedding gazebo where a flute and guitar played several songs. After the I-do's, everyone gathered at Martha's Vineyard lounge at the Beach Club where they threw a cocktail reception. The food was great. After the cocktails, everyone went to a luncheon at Ariel's, where the food received great reviews. Then they rented a pontoon boat with a smaller group of friends. The couple celebrated long into the night, and the bride commented, "Cinderella never had it this good."

#### WEB SITE AND CONTACT INFO

- **disney.com:** Disney Online: The Official Disney Web site. Click on the section on Fairy Tale Weddings for your wedding information.
- **getawayweddings.com:** The "Unofficial Disney Wedding Guide." Although Disney does not sponsor this site, their wedding department supports it. You will find more detailed information about how to plan a wedding at Disney, plus added features such as message boards, an e-mail contact (a Disney bride herself), firsthand stories of Disney weddings, couples' reviews of their Disney wedding, and access to the *Disneymooners* page.
- **hiddenmickeys.org:** Another helpful site sponsored by the Hidden Mickeys.
- **wdw4adults.com:** Walt Disney World for Adults.

## ♡ Grand Canyon

The immense beauty of the Grand Canyon, the gorge of the Colorado River, draws more than three million people each year and it is one of the single most amazing geological wonders in the world. Located in northwest Arizona, it is more than 1 mile deep, 4 to 18 miles wide, and more than 150 miles long. It's also a magical place to get married.

#### FUN IDEAS AND SITES

- On Navajo Bridge
- At Peach Springs (the gateway to the Grand Canyon caverns)
- Atop Mather Point (major vista overlook)
- At Phantom Ranch, the midpoint of the Bright Angel Trail
- In a hot-air balloon
- In a helicoptor
- In an airplane
- Ceremony by a medicine man

## WEDDING PACKAGES

**Grand Canyon Marketing** offers unique wedding packages for weddings both in the air or on the ground. Helicopter weddings are available for $795 and $1,145, depending on how long you want to stay in the air. If you do not like to hover, try an airplane wedding that costs $795 for a 60-minute flight. On land, you can have a Navajo Blessing Ceremony, where your ceremony is performed by a medicine man for $775, or a Cowboy Shotgun Wedding that includes a singing cowboy for $575.

## WEB SITE AND CONTACT INFO

### *Planners/Services*

- **gcanyon.com:** This Web site is sponsored by Grand Canyon Marketing and lists several wedding packages offered by local businesses. Here you can find additional information on weddings in the air and theme weddings.

### *Tourism*

- **maintour.com/arizona/grand:** General tourist information about the Grand Canyon.
- **grandcanyontourcompany.com:** Grand Canyon Tour Company: air tours, vbus tours, helicopter tours, hiking tours, rafting tours.
- **nps.gov/grca:** Official Grand Canyon Web site hosted by the National Park Service.
- **thecanyon.com:** Grand Canyon National Park site.

### *License Info*

- **state.az.us:** The state site for Arizona listing county sites where marriage license information can be obtained (go to the FAQ section of the site).
  Note: All backcountry trips and camping require a permit that can be obtained by writing or calling:

**Grand Canyon National Park**
P.O. Box 129
Grand Canyon, AZ 86023
(520) 638–7875

## Maine

Lighthouses, rocky shores, seagulls, and lobsters all come to mind when you think of coastal Maine. And don't forget getting married. The mountains of Acadia National Park provide a beautiful backdrop for those choosing to marry on the shore. Maine is a haven for campers, hikers, fishermen, whale watchers, seafood lovers, and couples looking for a scenic spot to tie the knot.

### FUN IDEAS AND SITES

- On a whale-watching cruise
- Lobster bake
- Acadia National Park
- On a rocky shoreline
- At the end of a pier
- In a stone mansion overlooking the ocean
- In a stone chapel
- On a lobster boat

### WEDDING PACKAGES

You will find many wedding-related Web sites for Maine but very few prices. **Weddings by the Sea** is one company that offers wedding packages for groups of up to 24 people. You will want to contact a wedding planner or call a hotel or B&B where you plan to stay and see if they have wedding packages. Use the Web as your research tool and then do price shopping by e-mail or phone.

*Planners/Services*

- **maineweddings.com:** This wedding provider's site also lists other Maine wedding-related sites.
- **maineweddingbythesea.com:** Lists places to marry in Sullivan.
  P.O. Box 290
  Sullivan, ME 04664
  (207) 422–4771
- **neweddingsolutions.com:** A Maine wedding directory organized by region.
- **alltimefavorites.com/maine:** Maine wedding and event-planning resource directory.
- **Wedding Solutions, Inc.**
  P.O. Box 451
  Bath, ME 04530
  (207) 443–4800
- **Wedding & Event Central**
  172 Route 1
  Scarborough, ME 04074
  (207) 883–9673
- **Gilfedders Wedding Consultants**
  5 Arbutus Avenue
  Old Orchard, ME 04064
  (207) 934–8399
- **Weddings by Simone Consultants**
  Windham, ME 04062
  (207) 892–2260
- **Sally Bullard**
  (207) 633–3372
  (800) 662–1245 ext. 66
- **A Maine Wedding**
  P.O. Box 127 East
  Boothbay, ME 04544

*Tourism*

- **maineguide.com:** A Maine Resource Guide, gives regional information, accommodation listings, and basic tourist information.

*License Info*

- **Department of Human Services, Vital Records** (207) 287–3181
- **state.me.us:** Web site with marriage license information; you need to do a site search for "marriage license."

## Mall of America

The Mall of America is the biggest mall in the United States. The Chapel of Love at the Mall of America in Bloomington, Minnesota, is located on the third floor (next to Bloomingdale's) and is open seven days a week. More than 2,000 couples have been married in the Chapel's 70-seat indoor garden. It's quick, easy, and affordable. If you can't take time off from work for a honeymoon, take the rest of the day off and enjoy some of the Mall of America's other features, such as a roller coaster and a full-size zoo.

### WEDDING PACKAGES

The **Chapel of Love** offers five wedding packages and a vow-renewal package. The simplest and least expensive package is the Dream Wedding, which ranges in price from $239 to $339, depending on the day of the week you get married. The Premiere is the top-end package, which costs between $639 and $739, depending again on which day you wed.

### WEB SITE AND CONTACT INFO

*Planners/Services*

- **chapeloflove.com:** The official Chapel of Love Web site.
  (800) 299–LOVE (5683)

*Tourism*

- **mallofamerica.com:** The Web site of the Mall of America.

*License Info*

- **City of Bloomington Information Desk**
  (952) 948–8700

## *Martha's Vineyard and Nantucket*

Located off Cape Cod, in Massachusetts, Martha's Vineyard and Nantucket are two lovely, romantic islands, with lighthouses, historic homes, and beautiful beaches. Martha's Vineyard is a haven for artists and a getaway for celebrities. Here you can see colonial farms and Victorian gingerbread-style homes along stacked stone walls. Nantucket lies 30 miles further out at sea and is known for its pristine beaches, cool ocean breezes, and cobblestone streets lined with historic homes. Both islands are popular tourist spots in the summer months.

### FUN IDEAS AND SITES

- Clambake reception
- Lobster bake reception
- Ceremony at the foot of a lighthouse
- Beach wedding
- Ceremony in a Victorian home
- Wedding on a private yacht

## WEDDING PACKAGES

Martha's Vineyard and Nantucket aren't typical "wedding package" destinations. But weddings are a cottage industry on both islands and the local wedding planners can make it easy. For a simple do-it-yourself elopement, you can make your own package by getting your marriage license, calling a justice of the peace or minister, and picking a spot on the beach. It will be economical and stress-free. Then pick your favorite lobster house for your postwedding meal.

## WEB SITE AND CONTACT INFO

### MARTHA'S VINEYARD

*Planners/Services*

- **The Wedding Network of Martha's Vineyard**
  6 South Water Street
  Edgartown, MA 02539
  (508) 627–8232
- **Martha's Vineyard Weddings**
  P.O. Box 120
  West Tisbury, MA 02575
  (508) 693–7272
  (508) 693–4051
- **An Island Affair**
  Patricia A. Blanc
  481P Hidden Cove
  Edgartown, MA 02539
  (508) 693–5176
  Vera Thornton
  Edgartown, MA 02539
  (508) 627–1000
- **With Grace**
  P.O. Box 2622
  Vineyard Haven, MA 02568
  (508) 696–6406

- **Captain Flanders' House**
  North Road, Box 384
  Chilmark, MA 02535
  (508) 645–3123
- **Dr. Daniel Fisher House**
  **Old Whaling Church**
  99 Main Street, Box 5277
  Edgartown, MA 02539
  (508) 627–8017
  (508) 627–4440
- **Harborside Inn**
  Box 67
  Edgartown, MA 02539
  (508) 627–4321
- **Harborview Hotel**
  131 N. Water Street
  Edgartown, MA 02539
  (508) 627–7000
- **The Hob Knob Inn**
  128 Main Street
  Edgartown, MA 02539
  (508) 627–9510
- **Jonathan Munroe House**
  100 Main Street
  Edgartown, MA 02539
  (508) 627–5536
- **Lambert's Cove Country Inn**
  Lambert's Cove Road, West Tisbury
  Mail: RR 1, Box 422,
  Vineyard Haven, MA 02568
  (508) 693–2298
- **O'Brien's Serious Seafood Grill**
  137 Main Street
  Edgartown, MA 02539
  (508) 627–5850

- **mvclambake.com—Martha's Vineyard Clambake Company**
  P.O. Box 9000
  Edgartown, MA 02539
  (800) 828-6936
  (508) 627-8809

*Tourism*

- **mvol.com:** Martha's Vineyard On-line, click on "weddings" for vendor lists and other tourism-related listings.
- **mvy.com:** Martha's Vineyard Chamber of Commerce Web site.
  P.O. Box 1698
  Beach Road
  Vineyard Haven, MA 02568
  (508) 693-0085

## NANTUCKET

*Planners/Services*

- **Lori Corry & Co.**
  Nantucket
  (508) 325-0063
- **Petals & Rice**
  4 Quince Street
  Nantucket, MA 02554
  (508) 228-3053
  (508) 325-5570
- **A Taste of Nantucket**
  Box 2875
  Nantucket, MA 02584
  (508) 228-9200

- **Emily Pihl**
  Box 3229
  Nantucket, MA 02584
  (508) 228–2700
- **Heaven Can Wait**
  Accommodation Service
  Box 622,
  Siasconset, MA 02564
  (508) 257–4000
- **Let's Have An Affair**
  64 Pocomo Road
  Nantucket, MA 02554
  (508) 228–4205
- **Waterfront Wedding**
  37 Cliff Road
  Nantucket, MA 02554
  (508) 228–4114

*Tourism*

- **Nantucket Island Chamber of Commerce**
  48 Main Street, Dept. 1I
  Nantucket Island, MA 02554
  (508) 228–1700

*License Info*

- **state.ma.us:** Site where you can find marriage license requirements.

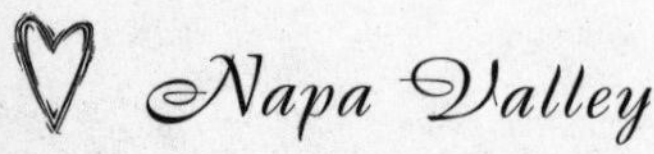

## Napa Valley

Vineyards, winery caves, and historic gardens are popular spots for small ceremonies in Napa Valley. Located just outside San Francisco, Napa Valley is a beautiful escape from the city, accessible by car, and a wonderful place to unwind with a glass of your favorite chardonnay. You can spend hours tasting wines at the many famous wineries or lose yourselves in a drive through the Valley. The buildings are beautiful and the scenery is stunning. You can stay in San Francisco and make Napa a day trip to exchange your vows or stay right in Napa Valley, which has many hotels, inns, and bed-and-breakfasts to choose from. And if you want a church wedding, there are several quaint churches available for your ceremony, as well.

### FUN IDEAS AND SITES

- Rent a winery building after hours
- Hot-air balloon
- Ceremony at a spa
- Private estate
- Wine-tasting reception
- Bed-and-breakfast ceremony

### WEDDING PACKAGES

Wedding packages in Napa Valley are not standardized. Visit the sites of wedding planners listed below and figure out your budget and what you have in mind. Napa Valley planners will customize your wedding. There are no set packages.

### WEB SITE AND CONTACT INFO

*Planners/Services*

- **napavalley.com:** Has a special section called "Plan-a-Wedding" with lists of vendors in the area (photographers, entertainment, planners, locations, etc).
- **winecountrywedding.com:** Web site for The Main Event, Wine Country Wedding and Event Planners.
  P.O. Box 3827
  Napa, CA 94558
  (707) 253–8160
- **winecountryassociates.com:** Site for Wine Country Weddings.
  (707) 945–1314

- **nvaloft.com:** Site for a family of hot-air balloon companies that include:
  Above the West Ballooning
  (800) 627–2759
  Adventures Aloft
  (800) 944–4408
  Balloon Aviation
  (800) 367–6272
- **Affectionate Arrangements**
  1149 Rancho Drive
  Napa, CA 94558
- **All Great Occasions**
  Kimberly Bailey
  P.O. Box 419
  Napa, CA 94559
- **Napa Valley Weddings**
  Caroline Templeton
  P.O. Box 6376
  Napa, CA 94581
  (707) 224–1824
- **Wedding Ministries/Enchanting Elopements**
  3416 Yount Avenue
  Napa, CA 94558

*Tourism*

- **winecountryliving.com:** The site for the Napa Valley Tourist Bureau, which includes a section on Wine Country Weddings.
  488 Washington Street
  Yountville, CA 94599
  (707) 258–1957
- **napavalleyonline.com:** Information about Napa Valley including lists of service providers, bed-and-breakfasts, hotels, etc.

*License Info*

- **County Clerk/Recorder's Office**
  **co.napa.us/departments/recorder.htm**
  P.O. Box 298
  Napa, CA 94559
  (707) 253–4246

## ♡ *New Orleans*

New Orleans, also known as the Big Easy, is one of the largest ports in the United States and home to the famous Mardi Gras celebration, Dixieland jazz, the French Quarter, Cajun cooking, and voodoo. Situated in southeast Louisiana on the Gulf of Mexico, it has the feeling of the tropics. The city is built on drained swampland and the humidity can get up to 96 percent in the summer months, so plan your wardrobe and activities accordingly. Variety is the spice of life in this culturally diverse city offering a number of options for weddings.

### FUN IDEAS AND SITES

- City Park Botanical Gardens
- French Quarter courtyard
- A bayou
- Bourbon Street
- St. Charles Avenue mansions
- Paddlewheel riverboat down the Mississippi
- Museum of Art
- Horse-and-carriage ride
- Audubon Zoo
- Riverwalk Fountain
- Jackson Square
- Moonwalk on the Mississippi

### WEDDING PACKAGES

**The Wedding Ministry** offers various wedding packages in New Orleans. Their most basic packages are priced as low as

$70. Their basic Church Wedding Package is $375. The prices go up from there depending on location and "extras." **Grand Occasions** specializes in planning weddings in New Orleans for couples from out of state; they accommodate all budgets, but you will have to call to find out specific package fees.

## WEB SITE AND CONTACT INFO

### *Planners/Services*

- **grandoccasions.net:** Grand Occasions wedding planners Web site.
- **theweddingministry.com**: Wedding services offered by an ordained minister.

### *Tourism*

- **neworleanscvb.com:** New Orleans Metropolitan Convention & Visitors Bureau.
  1520 Sugar Bowl Drive
  New Orleans, LA 70112
  (504) 566–5011
  (800) 672–6124
- **gnofn.org/chamber:** New Orleans Regional Chamber of Commerce.
  Suite 1700, 601 Poniards Street
  New Orleans, LA 70130
  (504) 527–6900
- **louisianatravel.com:** Louisiana Office of Tourism.
  P.O. Box 94291
  Baton Rouge, LA 70804
  (225) 342–8100
  (800) 633–6979

### *License Info*

Below is a listing of where you can obtain a marriage license in New Orleans.

- **Jefferson Parish**
  (East Bank)
  Joseph S. Yenni Building
  1221 Elmwood Park Boulevard
  Elmwood Industrial Park
  Clerk of Court, Room 603
  (504) 736–6390
- **Jefferson Parish**
  (West Bank)
  Gretna Courthouse
  Second and Derbigny
  Clerk of Court, Third Floor
  Gretna
  (504) 364–2922
  (504) 364–2923
- **Orleans Parish**
  325 Loyola Avenue, Room 102
  New Orleans, LA 70112
  (504) 568–5182

## ♡ *San Juan Islands*

The San Juan Islands are located in Washington State. Unlike many neighboring islands, the San Juan Islands see 247 days of sunshine a year on average. The islands are only accessible by air or boat. The Washington State Ferry is the most popular way to reach the islands. Once on the islands, you can occupy yourselves by whale watching, biking, kayaking, or visiting the national and state parks. The beauty and seclusion of the islands make them a romantic place to get married.

### FUN IDEAS AND SITES

- Ceremony on the bluffs, under Cattle Point Lighthouse
- Wed at one of the many B&Bs

- Private country garden of Wood Duck Ponds
- Roche Harbor Resort ceremony
- On the grounds of British Camp

## WEDDING PACKAGES

**Wood Duck Ponds** at Friday Harbor can provide an intimate setting for two or larger spaces to accommodate groups. Their basic wedding package, including usage of the grounds, parking, bridal suite, and rehearsal the night before, costs $1,500. Go to the San Juan Island Chamber of Commerce Web site and click on the "Special Interest" section. It has links to resorts, B&Bs, and other wedding-related businesses you can e-mail directly for more price information.

## WEB SITE AND CONTACT INFO

### *Planners/Services*

- **woodduckponds.com:** Wood Duck Ponds Web site.
  42 Wood Duck Lane
  Friday Harbor, WA 98250
  (360) 378–2356
- **rocheharbor.com:** Roche Harbor Resort and Marina Web site.
  P.O. Box 4001
  Roche Harbor, WA 98250
  (360) 378–2155
  (800) 451–8910

### *Tourism*

- **sanjuanisland.org:** The official Web site of the San Juan Islands Chamber of Commerce.
  P.O. Box 98
  Friday Harbor, WA 98250
  (360) 378–5240

*License Info*

- **Thurston County Clerk's Office**
  (360) 786–5430

##  *Yosemite National Park*

Yosemite National Park sits in the heart of California's Sierra Nevada and some call it the most beautiful national park in the United States. You will find giant sequoia trees, famous rock formations, glaciers, domes, rivers, mountains, and spectacular waterfalls. There is an elevation change of 11,000 feet between the valley and the high country. It is a popular park for avid rock climbers, hang gliders, hikers, and the occasional couple getting married.

### FUN IDEAS AND SITES

- **In Yosemite Valley**
  Lower Falls
  Swinging Bridge Picnic Area
  Cathedral Beach Picnic Area
  Bridal Veil Falls
- **In Wawona**
  Wawona Point
  Glacier Point
- **In Tuolomne**
  Soda Springs
  Tenaya Beach
  Tuolomne Lodge Area
  Big Oak Flat
  Tuolomne Grove
- **Yosemite Community Church (Chapel)**

Note: As all of the above listings are public areas, you may find crowds, especially during mealtimes in the picnic areas. Sites are available on a first-come, first-serve basis. If your wedding party is less than 10 people, however, you are not limited to certain locations, except open meadow areas.

## WEDDING PACKAGES

Wedding packages are offered by **Yosemite Weddings** (Web site and address below) in a number of locations including El Capitan, Yosemite, and the Half Dome Yosemite Chapel. Call for prices. Be aware that you must apply for a permit to be wed in the park (contact information below). The application costs $50 and the permit, upon approval, costs $100; both are nonrefundable.

## WEB SITE AND CONTACT INFO

*Planners/Services*

- **mariposa.yosemite.net:** Site for wedding planning services in Yosemite National Park.
- **nps.gov:** Site for the National Park Service listing rules and regulations for getting married in Yosemite National Park; has a wedding application form you can print and send in to the park service.
- **yosemitepark.com:** Click on "events/weddings" and you will find lodging information, venues for wedding receptions, and prices for receptions.
- **Yosemite Concession Services**
  Special Functions
  (559) 253–5673
- **Yosemite Community Chapel**
  P.O. Box 456
  Yosemite National Park, CA 95389
- **Yosemite Weddings**
  4548 Triangle Road
  Mariposa, CA 95338
  (209) 742–6633
  (209) 966–3036

*Tourism*

- **nps.com/yose:** National Park Service site for Yosemite National Park; lists wedding information and rules.
- **National Park Service**
  (209) 372–0200

*License Info*

- **state.ca.us:** The state site for California. Since Yosemite National Park covers several counties (Wawona and Tuolomne), marriage license requirements for park wedding sites may differ. Search for the specific county on the state site and you will find the county clerk's office contact information.

# 11. Eloping to the Tropics

Sun, sea, and sand have always drawn couples to the tropics. In fact, those visions of warm beaches and cold rum drinks are often the only thing that makes the final big wedding week bearable. But there's no need to punish yourself before collecting the reward. Why not skip the big wedding altogether and head straight for the sun?

The first thing you need to decide is whether you want to get married in the islands or just honeymoon there. The latter is easier, obviously, but many Caribbean islands make it fairly simple to get married, as well. It may be a bit more legwork than Vegas, but nowhere near as complicated as some European countries (see chapter 14, "Europe"). If you're drawn to the idea, you'll also need to decide whether it's just going to be the two of you, or if it is going to be a small destination wedding with friends and family tagging along. That's not hard to arrange, but it will influence your choice of destinations. A small romantic hideaway isn't the place for your sister's toddlers, and most couples-only resorts don't want your single friends (or children). The biggest decision of all is to think about what kind of experience you want. There are some very different options here, ranging from remote privacy to Mardi Gras–like communal fun. It's all a question of what you're up for—or think you'll be up for—when the day arrives. Here's a brief rundown of your options, with details and contact information for domestic and foreign tropical locales in the pages that follow.

## All-in-One Resorts

Talk about easy. These resorts are designed from the ground up to make your elopement easy. Three big companies—Sandals, SuperClubs, and Couples—dominate this market, each with several properties scattered around the Caribbean. They all have experienced full-time wedding coordinators on staff and all offer a one-price package for everything. Many couples choose to bring along another couple to be their best man and maid of honor, but generally speaking these aren't places to drag Aunt Sally and Uncle Walter (certainly not with their kids). The atmosphere at these resorts is somewhere between a great party and a romantic dinner, depending on how much you want to talk to other couples. Keep in mind, though, that these are fairly large resorts, so although they're geared for honeymooners, the privacy factor isn't what you might get at a smaller resort.

### SANDALS

Self-described as a "Tropical Hideaway," Sandals resorts are located on four different islands and are created exclusively for couples. For one price, the following is included: unlimited liquor, gourmet dining in a total of 42 restaurants, luxurious accommodations including suites with their own concierge service, and land and water sports (including golf, waterskiing, and scuba diving). Sandals resorts are located in Jamaica, Antigua, St. Lucia, and The Bahamas.

## WEDDING PACKAGES

Sandals has Weddingmoon packages, where they have combined the wedding and the honeymoon, offering guests one all-inclusive package. These packages start at $750. Couples getting married at Sandals must be staying at the resort and there is an additional fee for wedding guests attending your ceremony who are not staying at the resort.

## WEB SITE AND CONTACT INFO

- **sandals.com:** Official Sandals Web site, with a section on weddings.
- **Sandals Weddings Department**
  (888) SANDALS

## SUPERCLUBS

SuperClubs are a group of all-inclusive resorts located in Jamaica and The Bahamas. There are eight SuperClubs resorts that offer wedding packages. Some SuperClubs are for couples only, but others can accommodate singles and families.

### *Locations*

- **Boscobel Beach,** near Ocho Rios, Jamaica. This SuperClub is the Caribbean's only superinclusive resort for families.
- **Breezes Bahamas** is located in Nassau, The Bahamas.
- **Breezes Montego Bay** is in Jamaica.
- **Breezes Golf and Beach Resort** is located 40 miles outside of Montego Bay, Jamaica, and caters to golfers, tennis players, and sports enthusiasts.
- **Grand Lido Negril** in Negril, Jamaica, is an AAA Four-Diamond Resort, catering more to luxury vacations.
- **Grand Lido Sans Souci** is another AAA Four-Diamond Resort located in Ocho Rios, Jamaica.
- **Hedonism II** is located in Negril, Jamaica.

- **Hedonism III** is for singles and couples (over 18 years old) and is located in St. Anne, Jamaica.

## WEDDING PACKAGES

If you choose one of the honeymoon packages at a SuperClub and stay a minimum of three nights, the cost of your wedding ceremony at the club is included. Prices vary based on your length of stay. SuperClubs does offer the seventh night free if you stay for six nights. They also offer discounts on future visits if you have your wedding at SuperClubs. Visit the Web site to see all eight resorts and the wedding package details.

## WEB SITE AND CONTACT INFO

- **superclubs.com:** Official SuperClubs Web site.
  P.O. Box 61, Kingston 4
  Jamaica, W.I.
  (877) GO-SUPER
  (954) 925–0925

## COUPLES

Couples Resorts are all-inclusive resorts for couples only. At Couples Resorts, weddings are performed Monday through Saturday. The first wedding is performed at 9 A.M. and the last wedding is at 4 P.M. The entire wedding lasts one hour. The average length of the actual ceremony is 10 minutes. Vows are standard. The wedding date may be confirmed before making hotel reservations. Guests must call the sales department at the hotel to arrange the wedding. On arrival at the hotel the guests must go to the sales office to make final arrangements. The wedding coordinator will arrange the location of the ceremony with the guests.

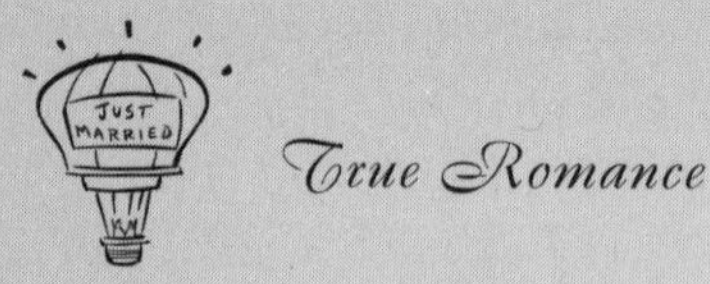


## True Romance

*Gigi and Kurt Ehlers*

Gigi and Kurt originally wanted a medium-sized "normal" wedding, but Gigi heard from a friend about her wedding in Jamaica and it sounded like a great idea. They had looked at a country club but didn't want to go into debt, preferring to spend their money on a honeymoon.

"We stayed at a place that could accommodate families and singles. They had done a lot of weddings there and it was cost-effective," says Gigi.

Kurt and Gigi had 14 guests at their wedding and everyone had a great time. They were married on Friday night and most of their guests stayed until Monday. Everyone hung out together on Saturday and Sunday and golfed. The wedding coordinator at the hotel took care of everything. "We were married by a minister on the island; it was a 15-minute ceremony. We had taped music. We were under a trellis with flowers and there were chairs set up for the guests. After the ceremony, we had champagne and cake. We got the wedding video the next day (it's not that great, because it was done in one day, but we like it). After the ceremony, we signed the certificate and license and went to dinner," says Gigi. Kurt continues, "We have no regrets and would definitely recommend it—without a doubt!"

### WEDDING PACKAGES

If you stay at a Couples resort for six nights or longer, the cost of your wedding at the resort is included in the overall price for your stay.

*Location:* Jamaica only

**WEB SITE AND CONTACT INFO**

- **couples-jamaica.com:** The Official Couples Web site.
- **Couples Hotel Sales Office**
  (876) 975-4271

## *Other Resorts*

Other resort hotels have several advantages, and a couple of disadvantages, compared to the couples-only option. Obviously, they work better if you're planning a destination wedding that involves children or unmarried friends or family. There's also a lot more variety in choosing the kind of accommodations and experience you want. The Caribbean is filled with resorts that run the gamut from 25 rooms to 200 rooms, from $150 a night to $1,000 a night. If you both like to scuba dive, or would like to learn, there are diving resorts. Or you can find ones that offer great golf, spectacular food, and just about anything else you want. The drawback of resorts is also a potential plus: the other guests. Unlike at a couples-only resort, you may be the only honeymooners. That will make you feel special and the staff will probably pamper you a bit extra. But it also means you may have a young family in the room next door. The best way to resolve this is by having a nice chat with the resort when you (or your travel agent) book the rooms. Make sure they know it's your honeymoon and that you'd like a nice quiet part of the hotel. If you're inclined to mix a wedding and honeymoon, be absolutely sure to discuss this with the resort manager before you book the rooms. Some can accommodate you easily. Others will be learning on the job how to arrange weddings—not a reassuring prospect. A smart idea is to ask for references from two or three couples that were married there recently.

## Hideaway Hotels and Private Homes

Hideaway hotels are a very nice option, though they tend to be a bit more pricey. But you do get what you pay for—a smaller hotel, a better staff-to-guest ratio, and usually more charm, character, and privacy. You'll need to hunt down these hotels, though. They tend to advertise only in the high-end travel magazines, if at all, and they book early with their regular, returning guests. Be sure to have a long discussion with them and ask for references if you're looking to get married while you're staying at the hotel.

Private homes are an increasingly popular idea, and more affordable than you'd think. On some islands, like St. Barts or Harbor Island (The Bahamas), the supply of charming small homes for rent far outstrips the number of hotel rooms. And the price of a weeklong rental is usually half to two-thirds the cost of staying in a hotel. You won't get meals of course (unless you arrange for a cook ahead of time, which can be done), but that leaves you with the option of dining out, which can be nice when it's just the two of you alone all day. And the *alone* part—the privacy you get with a house all to yourself, especially if it comes with a pool—is the real attraction. To combine a villa/private house rental with a wedding, you'll need to find someone on the island who knows the ropes. Start with the property agent who's renting you the house.

Hideaway hotels and private homes are available in many tropical destinations. The Internet is the best place to begin your research, as you can see pictures of the locations and compare prices. Remember to ask the people running the hotel or villa if they allow weddings at their location and if so, could they help you coordinate your wedding.

### WEB SITE AND CONTACT INFO

- **virtualcities.com:** A site listing bed-and-breakfasts, inns, and small hotels in the United States and the Caribbean.

- **greatrentals.com:** Lists over 1,700 vacation rentals in the U.S. and abroad. Includes homes, cottages, villas, cabins, resorts, and houseboats.
- **vacationrentalnet.com:** Worldwide vacation rentals.
- **mundacatravel.com:** Private home rentals in the Mexican Caribbean and in Cuba.
- **bahamasweb.com:** Site for Bahamas home rentals.

*Mexico*

- **Casa Piazza of La Punta**
  Manzanillo, Mexico
  9,000-square-foot luxury vacation villa located on the tip of the Santiago Peninsula; 5 bedrooms
  (888) 8-CASA-81
  E-mail: scott@casapiazza.com
- **Puesta del Sol II—sunset 2 & 3**
  Cozumel, Mexico
  Three- and four-bedroom units on the water, each with private bath, sundeck, and private swimming pool
  (3109) 351–2652
  E-mail: fennell.tom@mcleod.net
- **Ajijic Bed and Breakfast**
  Jalisco, Mexico
  Mexican inn with six garden rooms in the village of Ajijic
  52 (376) 6–03–83
  E-mail: ajijic@infosel.net.mx

*Caribbean*

- **Nisbet Plantation**
  Nevis, Caribbean
  Plantation-style cottages (wedding packages available)
  **caribbeans.com/2nevis**

- **Caribbean Paradise Inn**
  Turks and Caicos, British West Indies
  Sixteen rooms designed for indoor and outdoor living; 250-yard walk from the water
  (649) 946–5020
  E-mail: inn@paradise.tc
- **Oasis Marigot's Ocean Cottage**
  Castries, St. Lucia, West Indies
  Two-story inn with four self-contained apartments
  (800) 263–4202
  E-mail: info@oasismarigot.com
- **The Great House**
  Castries, St. Lucia, West Indies
  Elegant residence, accommodates six guests in three rooms, all with their own bathroom
  (800) 263–4202
  E-mail: info@oasismarigot.com

## *Tropical Destinations (U.S.A.)*

### ♡ *Hawaii*

Waterfalls, brightly colored flowers, crashing waves, high mountains, Polynesian cooking, floral patterns, Don Ho, leis and beaches all come to mind when we think of Hawaii. An exotic paradise comprised of six major islands in the South Pacific makes Hawaii a popular spot for tourists throughout the year. For the beach enthusiast there are white-sand beaches for sunning and coral reefs for snorkeling. For the sports enthusiast, there are golf courses, tennis courts, and water sports. Temperatures in Hawaii range from 60 degrees to 90 degrees all year long. Each Hawaiian island is rich in culture and tradition. Choose from the Big Island of Hawaii, Kauai, Oahu, Maui, Molokai, or Lanai. You won't be disappointed in what you find.

## FUN IDEAS AND SITES

- On an offshore island
- On a sailboat or Windjammer cruise
- White Ginger Falls: A 75-foot waterfall that can be the backdrop for your ceremony
- Botanical gardens
- Ualakaa Park in Mount Tantalus—offers a spectacular view stretching to the Waianew Mountains
- Underwater

## WEDDING PACKAGES

**Affordable Weddings of Hawaii** offers packages ranging from $95 for the Kamaaina Package to $245 for their Gardenia Package. They can also arrange dinners, flowers, limo service, and ceremonies at several different and exotic locations. If you are interested in an ocean theme, **Above Heaven's Gate** offers Weddings at Sea starting at $595 and also performs Underwater Weddings for $495 (for certified divers only). The **Old Hawaii Wedding Chapel** in Honolulu has a Complete Wedding for $199. Visit any of the Web sites listed below and they will provide more specific information on Hawaii wedding packages. Weddings can be performed on every Hawaiian island. To narrow things down, choose your island first, and then pick your wedding location.

## WEB SITE AND CONTACT INFO

*Planners/Services*

- **wedhawaii.com:** Site for Affordable Weddings of Hawaii, good for information gathering and price shopping.
- **bluehawaiiweddings.com:** Blue Hawaii Weddings is a full-service wedding coordination company specializing in wedding planning and honeymoons in Hawaii.

- **hawaiibride.com:** *Hawaii Bride and Groom* magazine on-line.
- **hawaiiweddings.com:** Above Heaven's Gate wedding providers, specializing in weddings in unique locations.
- **hawaii-weddings.com:** Site for Aloha Beautiful Weddings, offering a variety of wedding packages.

*Tourism*

- **state.hi.us:** Excellent site with information about Hawaii and requirements for getting married in Hawaii.
- **gohawaii.com:** Web site of the Hawaii Visitors and Conventions Bureau. Has a section specifically on weddings and also great information on the Hawaiian Islands.
- **Hawaii Visitors and Convention Bureau**
  (808) 923–1811

*License Info*

For a pamphlet entitled "Getting Married," published by the state of Hawaii, write to:

- **State of Hawaii Department of Health**
  Marriage License Office
  P.O. Box 3378
  Honolulu, HI 96801
  (808) 586–4544
  (808) 586–4410

## ♡ Key West

Key West is a great choice for eloping. Easy to get to from the East Coast, Key West has charm, plenty of sunshine, and dozens of romantic B&Bs for your honeymoon pleasure. Key West works well for small destination weddings, too. There are plenty of accommodations available and lots of interesting sights that your guests can explore on their own. The town is compact, making group events easy to organize. Another idea is to make Key West your destination: start in Miami and drive down through the Keys, staying overnight along the way. You can celebrate your arrival in Key West with a sunset wedding cruise around the island.

### FUN IDEAS AND SITES

- The Ernest Hemingway Home and Museum: A beautifully landscaped property, owned by Hemingway from 1931 to 1961, available for private weddings. The grounds can accommodate small or large groups, and a tour of the house itself is included for your guests.
- Audubon House and Tropical Gardens: An 1840s home providing a gorgeous backdrop for a wedding. The gardens hold a variety of orchids and bromeliads and there is an early 19th-century nursery that provides a historic look into gardening.
- Wedding cruises: Key West is known for its gorgeous tropical waters and the local custom of gathering to watch the sun set at the Mallory Square docks. Combining these two elements into a sunset wedding cruise is quickly becoming a new tradition in Key West.
- Ft. Zachary Taylor State Park: Said to have the "most beautiful beach on the island" shaded by Australian pine trees.

### WEDDING PACKAGES

There are numerous wedding packages offered in Key West. **Dial M for Matrimony** has packages on both land and sea. Onshore wedding packages range from the Simply for You at $75 to the Love in Bloom, which is $325. If you want to exchange vows on the water, prices range from $275 for the Wedding at Sea, to the Classic Elegance, which ranges from $450 for the sunset cruise to $800 for a full-day cruise. **Blue Moon**

**Wedding Services** has a Sailboat for Two wedding for $165 and the *Dreamchaser* sailboat has wedding packages starting at $295. Go to the Web sites (listed below) for these wedding service providers where you can see photos of locations and vessels before you show up.

## WEB SITE AND CONTACT INFO

*Planners/Services*

- **dialm.net:** Dial M for Matrimony Web site.
  (800) 670–0385
- **Blue Moon Wedding Services**
  (301) 294–6674
- **dreamchasercharters.com:** Site for *Dreamchaser* trimaran.
- **audubonhouse.com:** The Web site for the Audubon House.
  (877) 281-BIRD
- **The Ernest Hemingway Home and Museum**
  (305) 294–1136
- **reefchief.com:** Schooner *Reef Chief* site for Weddings at Sea.

*Tourism*

- **keywest.com:** Site that lists everything Key West has to offer. You can click on a section called "Services and Weddings," where you'll find links for hotels, charter yachts, and other wedding-related service providers.
- **floridakeys.com:** General information on the Florida Keys.

*License Info*

- **The Key West Clerk of the Court**
  500 Whitehead Street
  Key West, FL 33030
  (305) 294–4641

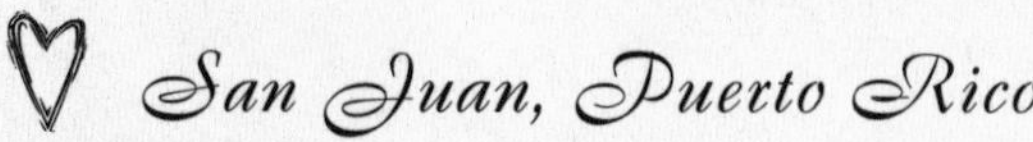

## San Juan, Puerto Rico

San Juan is the largest city and principal seaport of Puerto Rico, as well as the main manufacturing, financial, cultural, and tourist center of Puerto Rico. Old San Juan, the historic part of the city, lies on a small island connected to the mainland by bridges. Its narrow, crooked streets are lined with restaurants, shops, and buildings constructed during the 16th and 17th centuries. On the mainland, high-rise luxury hotels line the white-sand beaches. Natives speak mostly Spanish, but you'll find that everyone in the tourist industry speaks fluent English. San Juan is charming, exciting, and a romantic place for a wedding.

### FUN IDEAS AND SITES

- In a church in Old San Juan
- On a local beach
- In the rain forest (El Yunque)
- Town Square
- On a cruise ship about to depart
- On a private boat

### WEDDING PACKAGES

**A Wedding for You** has several wedding packages in Puerto Rico. You can have an onboard wedding, with the ship's permission, starting at $600. If you are a landlubber, the Romantic Island Wedding is available for $800.

## WEB SITE AND CONTACT INFO

*Planners/Services*

- **aweddingforyou.com:** Wedding planners offering packages in Puerto Rico. Good site to browse and see prices of various packages.

*Tourism*

- **camarapr.coqui.net:** The Web site for the Puerto Rico Chamber of Commerce.
  Chamber of Commerce of Puerto Rico
  P.O. Box 9024033
  San Juan, PR 00902–4033
  (787) 721–6060
- **wepa.com:** Information about the island and the process of getting married in Puerto Rico.

*License Info*

- **Department of Health**
  Demographic Registry Office
  Box 11854
  Fernandez Juncos Station
  Santurce, Puerto Rico 00910
  (787) 728–7980
- **escapetopuertorico.com:** Lists marriage requirements for Puerto Rico.

## ♡ U.S. Virgin Islands

Located in the Caribbean, the U.S. Virgin Islands are surrounded by sparkling blue water and are a popular site for vacationers, cruises, and honeymooners. Each island—St. Croix, St. Thomas, and St. John—offers spectacular backdrops for wedding ceremonies and has all of the amenities you need. The official language is English, and the U.S. dollar is the currency used.

### ST. CROIX

This is the largest of the U.S. Virgin Islands spanning an area of 82 square miles. The island has two distinct towns to visit: Christiansted and Frederiksted, as well as a tropical rain forest.

### ST. THOMAS

The port of Charlotte Amalie, which is the capital of the U.S. Virgin Islands, is the most popular cruise port in the Caribbean. Upon entering the harbor, you can see the pastel-colored houses in the hills and the colorful boats lined up on the waterfront.

### ST. JOHN

St. John is the smallest of the Virgin Islands, just 28 square miles in area, but it may be the most spectacular. Not the shopping mecca of its neighbors, two-thirds of St. John is a U.S. national park where you can see unspoiled Caribbean countryside and wildlife. You can tour the park by safari bus or Jeep.

### FUN IDEAS AND SITES

- Underwater party on a submarine
- Take a helicopter to the isolated Hans Lollik
- Ceremony on a private yacht
- Wed on the grounds of a private villa

### WEDDING PACKAGES

**A Wedding for You** offers wedding packages on all three islands. You can arrange to have a wedding on board a private boat for $700 (off of St. Croix). If you prefer to wed on the beach or in a garden, there are wedding packages available for $900 (in St. Croix). These prices will vary if you choose St. John or St. Thomas. You can e-mail A Wedding for You from their Web site to request price quotes for wedding packages on the various islands.

## WEB SITE AND CONTACT INFO

*Planners/Services*

- **marriott.vi:** Click on "weddings" and you will find information for Weddings in Paradise wedding planners.
- **cstyle.co.vi:** Web site for Caribbean Style Weddings.
- **usvi.net/seaside:** Page for Seaside Weddings wedding planners.
- **wedusvi.com:** Web site for Fantasia Weddings wedding planners.
- **st-thomas.com/wed:** Weddings the Island Way wedding planners site.

*Tourism*

- **usvi.net:** Site with basic tourist information for St. John, St. Thomas, and St. Croix, also has a wedding section.

*License Info*

- **wedaway.com:** Web site that gives you the marriage license requirements for getting married in the U.S. Virgin Islands and other foreign destinations.
- **To marry on St. Thomas or St. John contact:**
  The Territorial Court of the Virgin Islands
  P.O. Box 70
  St. Thomas, U.S. Virgin Islands 00804
  (340) 774–6680, ext. 6434
- **To marry on St. Croix contact:**
  Family Division
  Territorial Court of the Virgin Islands
  P.O. Box 929
  Christiansted, St. Croix, USVI 00821
  (340) 778–9750

- **Virgin Island Tourist Information:**
  Call and ask for a free "Getting Married in the United States Virgin Islands" kit, which includes a license application and guidelines, plus a detailed list of consultants, vendors, and houses of worship.
  (800) 372-USVI, from the United States

## *Tropical Destinations (Foreign)*

### ♡ *The Bahamas*

The Bahamas consists of 700 islands situated only 50 miles off the coast of Florida (less than an hour plane flight). Newcomers to the islands of The Bahamas quickly realize that they have stumbled upon not one, but many diverse destinations. Nassau is the most cosmopolitan of the islands, while Inagua is a desertlike sanctuary for wildlife. The Bahamas is easy to get to and an easy place to get married. English is the official language and the Bahamian dollar is the currency used.

#### FUN IDEAS AND SITES

- In the water among the dolphins
- In a national park
- On a Nassau hillside overlooking the sea
- In a tiny fishing village in Eleuthera
- On the pink sand of Harbour Island
- In a historical church
- In the 14th-century "French Cloisters" on Paradise Island

#### WEDDING PACKAGES

**Wedding Circles** offers wedding packages starting at $975 for the Simply Bahamian to $4,875 for the Ultimate Bahamian. If you are interested in a ceremony with dolphins on the Blue

*Jimmy and Tracey Blank*

Jimmy and Tracey Blank were married in The Bahamas in October 1996. They had been living together for five years and after Jimmy had a bout with cancer, they realized that they wanted to be married and they wanted to have hassle-free planning. "We had been through so much with my health that we really couldn't foresee stressing ourselves out over planning a wedding, an occasion celebrating our love. We love the islands and we love relaxing, so we decided to go to The Bahamas," Jimmy says. Tracey continues, "I had just finished my master's degree and we couldn't really afford a big ceremony. Plus, it really wasn't our style. We told people that we were going to get married there but we didn't invite anyone. We needed a vacation ourselves after the illness, and at the end of my master's, so we decided to make our wedding part of our trip. Since we had lived together for so long, we didn't think we needed anyone there to witness our commitment to each other; it was obvious that we were committed." Jimmy sums it up, "We have no regrets. We had a simple ceremony all planned by the hotel. We had a week under the sun doing whatever we wanted to do. It was beautiful, it was romantic, it was affordable, and it was us."

Lagoon, you can have the Bahamian Splash for $3,500. Don't forget there are all-inclusive resorts in The Bahamas that offer wedding packages. Or, do it yourself without all of the bells and whistles; the two of you, a beach, and a minister.

*Planners/Services*

- **bahamasweddingplanners.com:** Site for Wedding Circles wedding planners.
- **(888) NUPTUAL:** They will send you a free brochure about weddings and honeymoons in The Bahamas.

*Tourism*

- **webcenter.travelocity-dest.aol.com:** Informational Web site about The Bahamas, includes information on the history of The Bahamas, highlights of the different islands, weather trends, things to do, and other basic tourism information.
- **all-travel.net:** Go to "The Bahamas" section of this site for a directory of hotels in The Bahamas including photos, rates, and contact information.

*License Info*

- **For Nassau, Paradise Island, and the Out Islands:**
  Registrar General
  P.O. Box N-532
  Nassau, Bahamas
  (242) 322–3316
- **For Grand Bahama Island:**
  Assistant Registrar General's office
  (242) 352–4934
- **wedaway.com:** Web site that provides lists of marriage license requirements in locations outside the United States (go to "Bahamas").

*Bahamas Tourist Offices in the United States*

- **Chicago**
  (773) 693–1500

- **Dallas**
  (214) 742–1886
- **Los Angeles**
  (213) 385–0033
- **Miami**
  (305) 932–0051
  (305) 937–0585
- **New York**
  (212) 758–2777

*Tourist Offices in The Bahamas*

- **Head Office**
  P.O. Box N 3701
  Nassau
  (242) 322–7500
- **Grand Bahama**
  International Bazaar
  (242) 352–8356
  (242) 352–8044

## ♡ *Barbados*

Originally settled by the British, Barbados is a sophisticated gem in the Caribbean. The island is known for enchanting colonial towns, stately homes, quaint cottages, green countryside, English traditions (teatime and all-day cricket matches), fine dining, and upscale duty-free shopping (Barbados is considered the duty-free center of the eastern Caribbean). Rum is abundant, with more than 1,000 rum shops. English is the official language and the Barbados dollar is the currency used.

### FUN IDEAS AND SITES

- Private yacht or sailboat
- Harrison's Cave: An underground cave geographically located in the center of Barbados

- Beach wedding
- Island safari wedding

## WEDDING PACKAGES

There are plenty of wedding packages available in Barbados. **The Bougainvillea Beach Resort** offers the Best Wedding Package for $485. The **Crane Hotel** weddings start at $600 for hotel guests. Visit the Web sites listed below for lists of hotels that offer wedding packages as well as wedding planners who have put together wedding packages. Although many of the Web sites don't list prices, all have request forms where you can write for rates. Also keep in mind that you can lower the price of your ceremony by not choosing all of the amenities offered within a package and creating your own, just with the basics.

## WEB SITE AND CONTACT INFO

### *Planners/Services*

- **barbados.org:** Web site for the Barbados Tourism Authority. Has a list of wedding planners and services they offer; hotels that have wedding packages (for both guests and nonguests); and frequently asked questions about getting married in Barbados.
- **funbarbados.com:** On-line travel guide that lists wedding packages and services as well as general tourist information about Barbados.

### *Tourism*

- **Barbados Tourism Authority—Barbados Office**
  Harbour Road
  Bridgetown, Barbados
  (246) 427–2623

- **Barbados Tourism Authority—U.S.A. Office**
  3440 Wilshire Boulevard, Suite 1215
  Los Angeles, CA 90010
  (213) 380–2198
  (213) 380–2199

*License Info*

- **funbarbados.com:** This site lists documentation needed for obtaining a marriage license in Barbados.
- **Ministry of Home Affairs**
  General Post Office Building, 5th Floor
  Bridgetown, Barbados
  (246) 228–8950

## Belize: Ambergris Caye

Ambergris Caye (pronounced "key") is the largest of 200 cays that surround the coastline of Belize. Ambergris Caye is 25 miles long and just over a mile wide. It is located just off the tip of Mexico's Yucatán Peninsula in the shallow and clear waters of the Caribbean. It is known for excellent snorkeling, scuba diving, and fishing. English is the official language, but you will also hear English Creole, Spanish, and Garifuna. The Belizean dollar is the currency used. Please note that Belizean ATMs will not accept foreign cards.

### FUN IDEAS AND SITES

- Beach wedding
- Ceremony on a private boat
- Ceremony at Maruba Resort Jungle Spa

*Planners/Services*

- **belizeweddings.com:** Service providers for weddings in Belize. May be able to not only coordinate your ceremony, but also assist you with the paperwork.
- **www.traveltourbelize.com:** On the Weddings in Paradise page you can e-mail them directly to help in your planning.

*Tourism*

- **ambergriscaye.com:** An excellent site packed with photos and information about Ambergris Caye, as well as other regions of Belize. Also lists marriage requirements for Belize.

*License Info*

- **General Registry in Belize City**
  (501) 2–77377
- **Solicitor General's office in Belmopan**
  (501) 8–22154

## Bermuda

Once belonging to Britain's empire, Bermuda remains true to its roots as a self-governing, dependent territory. Bermuda is comprised of more than 150 small islands and islets located in the West Atlantic. Bermuda is famous for its pink sand beaches. Inland you can drive through green hills and stop off at high cliffs overlooking the sea. If you aren't a beach bum, you can spend your time playing golf on one of Bermuda's eight golf courses. The nearest land to Bermuda is Cape Hatteras, North Carolina, 600 miles to the west. English is the official language, and the Bermuda dollar is the currency used. The

Bermuda dollar is pegged to the U.S. dollar on an equal (one-to-one) basis. This means that U.S. currency is accepted at shops, restaurants, and hotels at equal (face) value.

### FUN IDEAS AND SITES

- Ceremony at a golf resort
- Sunset ceremony on the beach
- Ceremony on a private yacht or boat charter

### WEDDING PACKAGES

Prices can run the gamut if you are planning a wedding in Bermuda. **A Wedding for You, Inc.,** has packages ranging from $750 for an Onboard Wedding on a private boat to $1,175 for a shoreside wedding. **Bermuda Wedding Associates** has a basic package for $1,500, with the option of paying extra to be married in a church, to travel in a horse and carriage, or to "rent" witnesses.

### WEB SITE AND CONTACT INFO

*Planners/Services*

- **toptens.com:** Site for Bermuda Wedding Associates. This site contains wedding packages as well as frequently asked questions about the legalities of getting married in Bermuda.
- **aweddingforyou.com:** A Wedding for You, Inc., destination wedding planners.
  10860 Southwest 38th Drive
  Davie, FL 33328–1328
  (800) 929–4198
  (954) 472–0320
- **Bermuda Wedding and Special Events**
  Shelly A. Hamill, Professional Bridal Consultant
  P.O. Box CR 228
  Hamilton Parish, CR BX, Bermuda
  (441) 236–7471
  E-mail: shamill@ibl.bm

- **The Bridal Suite**
  Park Road, Suite 7
  Hamilton, HM 09, Bermuda
  (441) 292–2025
  Mailing address:
  P.O. Box HM 3180
  Hamilton, HM NX, Bermuda
  E-mail: wedding@ibl.bm
- **The Wedding Salon, Ltd.**
  U.S. mailing address:
  2312 Trellis Court
  Raleigh, NC 27604
  (919) 217–4395
  Bermuda mailing address:
  86 Spanish Point Road #10
  Pembroke HM 02, Bermuda
  (441) 292–5677

*Tourism*

- **virtualvoyages.com:** Bermuda Information and things-to-do site.
- **bermudatourism.org:** Bermuda Department of Tourism Web site.

*License Info*

- **toptens.com:** Lists legal requirements for getting married in Bermuda.

## Cayman Islands

The Cayman Islands is a British Crown Colony located in the western Caribbean, a mere 70-minute flight direct from Miami. The island country consists of Grand Cayman, the largest and most populous of the trio; and the Sister Islands of Cayman Brac and Little Cayman, which lie approximately 89 miles east-northeast of

Grand Cayman and are separated from each other by a channel about seven miles wide. English is the official language. You may detect a "brogue" that reflects the people's Welsh, Scottish, and English heritage. The Cayman Islands has its own currency,

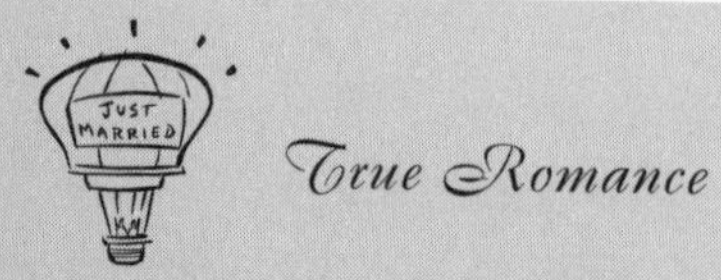


### True Romance

*Gayle and Todd Wheeler*

Gayle and Todd were married in Bermuda on June 4, 1993. Originally they were planning a small ceremony in Boston for New Year's Eve, but it was more expensive than they anticipated and they worried about asking family to travel to Boston in the winter, as the weather is unreliable. They had traveled to Bermuda twice together before and had seen people get married there. Even though they were living in Massachusetts, they decided to get married in Bermuda. When they arrived, they encountered a lot of problems with the original hotel they had booked (which was under new management since the last time they stayed there, (two) years earlier). But once they changed hotels, all went well.

They were wed in the Botanical Gardens, arriving there by horse and buggy. The minister wore Bermuda shorts and a T-shirt at their 5 P.M. wedding. They wrote their own vows and the minister gave his traditional ceremony.

"My advice is not to book a place sight unseen or without knowing everything they offer and without seeing pictures," says Gayle. "We hadn't stayed in our hotel for two years and when we got there, it was a disaster. The minister who married us found the Botanical Gardens for us and helped arrange our transportation. He was wonderful."

first issued in 1972, whose basic unit is the dollar. The CI dollar has a fixed exchange rate with the U.S. dollar of CI$1.00 equals US$1.25. Or, the U.S. dollar equals CI $.80. Best of all, there is *no need for visitors to exchange their U.S. dollars into local currency.*

### FUN IDEAS AND SITES

- Sunset ceremony on Seven Mile Beach
- Ceremony on a sailboat or private yacht
- Ceremony inside a grand old house

### WEDDING PACKAGES

**A Wedding for You** offers wedding packages in the Cayman Islands. You can have a ceremony aboard a ship for $600, or have it on at Seven Mile Beach for $900. A Wedding for You can also arrange for you to have a Grand Old House Gazebo Wedding for $900.

### WEB SITE AND CONTACT INFO

*Planners/Services*

- **aweddingforyou.com:** A Wedding for You Web site offers wedding packages for Grand Cayman and other destinations.

*Tourism*

- **caymanislands.ky**: Official Web site of the Cayman Islands Department of Tourism.
- **Cayman Islands Department of Tourism Headquarters**
  The Pavilion, Cricket Square
  Elgin Avenue, George Town
  P.O. Box 67 GT
  Grand Cayman, BWI
  (345) 949–0623

*License Info*

- **Government Information Services:** A brochure, "Getting Married in the Cayman Islands," containing complete guidelines and information can be obtained by writing Government Information Services.
  Cricket Square
  Grand Cayman
  (345) 949–8092
- **Chief Secretary's Office:** Call for a marriage license application.
  4th Floor (Room 406)
  Government Administration Building
  George Town
  (345) 949–7900

## Fiji

The Fiji archipelago is located in the South Pacific. In the days of sailing ships it was known as The Cannibal Isles and carefully avoided by mariners because of its fierce warriors and treacherous waters. Fiji consists of 333 islands, and natives boast that the islands get sunshine almost every day, making it great for swimming and sunning. The Great Sea Reef, one of the world's largest barrier reefs, is located in Fiji, making it an excellent destination for scuba divers and snorkelers. Lobster, crab, and clams fresh from the sea are always on the menu at the resorts. If you are running away to get married, why not run far and tie the knot in Fiji? English is the official language. Fijian and Hindustani are spoken as well. The national currency is the Fiji dollar, which is divided into 100 cents and trades independently on the foreign-exchange markets. Overseas currency is widely accepted in the form of cash or traveler's checks. Most international credit cards are also accepted at resorts and major shops.

### FUN IDEAS AND SITES

- Beach wedding wearing traditional Fijian wedding attire
- Ceremony on Turtle Island, where *The Blue Lagoon* was filmed
- Ceremony on a private boat

### WEDDING PACKAGES

There are numerous wedding packages offered by resorts on the Islands of Fiji. You can choose your island or choose your resort, and then look into a wedding package. You can get married in Musket Cove for as little as $300 or have a resort wedding with friends if you want to spend a few thousand dollars. There are plenty of Web sites to surf that list wedding packages in Fiji.

### WEB SITE AND CONTACT INFO

*Planners/Services*

- **nukubati.com:** Site that lists wedding packages offered on Nukubati Island.
- **castawayisland.com:** Site for Castaway Island Resort that has a section on wedding packages.
- **fiji-islands.com:** The Fiji Escapes Travel Web site, which lists a variety of wedding packages at different resorts and islands, including prices.
- **tropicalislandvacation.com:** Site that provides information about getting married in Fiji and focuses on several resorts.

*Tourism*

- **fijiislands.org:** Fiji Islands Travel and Accommodation Guide—Fiji Visitors Bureau
- **South Pacific Holidays Fiji**
  (877) SEE-FIJI (from the United States and Canada)
  (360) 944–1712
  E-mail: sph@spac.com

*License Info*

- **Registrar General**
  Births, Deaths, and Marriages
  Suva, Fiji
  (679) 315–178
- **wedaway.com:** Site providing the legal requirements for getting married in Fiji and other destinations abroad.

## Cook Islands

The Cook Islands are made up of 15 islands scattered over 2.5 million square miles in the South Pacific. They are set in a secluded corner of the South Pacific, directly south of the Hawaiian Islands and approximately an hour's flight from Tahiti. The main islands are Rarotonga and Aitutaki; however all but two of the Cook Islands are accessible by air. English is the official language. The Cook Islands unit of currency is the New Zealand dollar. This is supplemented by some Cook Island coins: $1, $2, and $5. The coins are not negotiable outside the Cook Islands, but make for interesting souvenirs. New Zealand dollars may be purchased at the airport, ANZ or Westpac bank, or the Western Union Office, downtown Avarua. Note that there are no ATMs in the Cook Islands. Money transfers may be sent to the Cook Islands from anywhere in the world via Western Union Money Transfer Service.

### FUN IDEAS AND SITES

- Muri Beach, Rarotonga
- Koromiri Island
- Ceremony on a glass-bottom boat, sipping champagne
- Wear traditional Polynesian wedding attire
- Botanical Gardens
- Uninhabited island
- Local church

## WEDDING PACKAGES

Packages are offered by many resorts in the Cook Islands. There are also wedding planners in the islands to assist you in coordinating your ceremony. **Jetsave Travel** offers several wedding packages, starting with the Simple Wedding for $1,034 and the Deluxe Wedding for $2,058. **Rarotonga Resort** has wedding packages ranging from $686 for The Promise package to the Wedding Made in Heaven for $6,439.

## WEB SITE AND CONTACT INFO

*Planners/Services*

- **jetsave.co.ck:** Jetsave Travel's guide to the Cook Islands, includes wedding section.
  P.O. Box 40
  Rarotonga, Cook Islands
  (682) 27–707
- **edgewater.co.ck:** Web site for the Edgewater resort, located in Rarotonga. This resort offers wedding packages.
- **rarotongan.co.uk:** Web site for the Rarotonga Resort, which lists its six wedding packages, including prices.

*Tourism*

- **cook-islands.com:** The official tourism site for the Cook Islands, also has wedding information.
- **webcentral.co.ck:** Tourist information site for the Cook Islands, with a section on weddings.

*License Info*

- **Registrar's Department**
  Department of Justice and Lands
  P.O. Box 11
  Rarotonga, Cook Islands
  E-mail: offices@justice.gov.ck

- **cook-islands.com:** The official tourism Web site of the Cook Islands; click "honeymoons" and you can find the legal requirements for getting married.

## *St. Kitts, Caribbean*

The island of St. Kitts is located in the Eastern Caribbean, south of St. Martin and west of Antigua. It measures only 23 miles long with a population of 35,000. Here you won't find the crowds of more popular resort areas, but you will find the beauty. Accommodations on the islands range from private villas to large hotels. Some activities available on St. Kitts include boating, snorkeling, scuba diving, golfing, and gambling at the casinos. St. Kitts is a hidden gem in the Caribbean, still somewhat unknown by tourists and therefore an excellent choice for an elopement. English is the official language. The official currency is the Eastern Caribbean dollar, which is fixed to the U.S. dollar. U.S. currency, traveler's checks, and major credit cards are welcome everywhere.

### FUN IDEAS AND SITES

- A day cruise through the volcanic islands
- On a white sand beach at the southern tip of St. Kitts
- Ottley's Plantation Inn
- Water-ski to your beach of choice
- Horseback ride to a spot in the rain forest

### WEDDING PACKAGES

**Birdrock Beach Hotel** offers wedding packages starting at $500. You will need to e-mail or call the other hotels to find out about their wedding packages.

*Planners/Services*

- **caribbeans.com:** Has lists of accommodations in St. Kitts and lists which hotels offer wedding services, with links to each hotel so you can inquire about packages and prices.

*Tourism*

- **stkitts-nevis.com:** Official travel guide for St. Kitts and Nevis.
- **St. Kitts and Nevis Tourism Office**
  414 East 75th Street, 5th Floor
  New York, NY 10021
  (800) 582–6208
  (212) 535–1234
- **St. Kitts and Nevis Department of Tourism**
  Department of Tourism
  Pelican Mall, Bay Road
  P.O. Box 132
  Basseterre, St. Kitts, WI
  (869) 465–2620/4040
  e-mail: mintc&e@caribsurf.com

*License Info*

- **wedaway.com:** Legal requirements for getting married in St. Kitts and basic facts about the island.

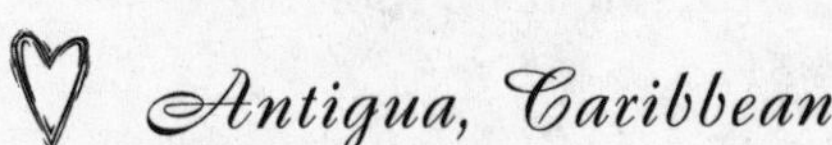

Antigua Island is the largest of the British Leeward Islands (108 square miles) in the Caribbean. It is renowned among sailors around the world for its rich nautical history. Not only do sunbathers travel to the island, but history buffs go there as well. There are 366 beaches on the island; that's one for every day of the year, and one left over, as the locals say. Some beaches are deserted, while others are occupied by windsurfers and snorkelers. Most hotels in Antigua offer wedding and honeymoon packages. There are no residency requirements to get married there. English is the official language, and the Eastern Caribbean dollar is the currency used.

## FUN IDEAS AND SITES

- Nelson's Dockyard National Park
- Rendezvous Bay Beach
- On a sailboat out of English Harbour
- Fort Berkeley
- Monk's Hill

## WEB SITE AND CONTACT INFO

### *Planners/Services*

- **caribbeans.com:** Web site featuring Caribbean locations with a section on romantic destinations that lists hotels offering wedding packages. Click on the Antigua page.

### *Tourism*

- **Antigua Tourism Office** (in Antigua)
  Long Street, St. John's
  Antigua, WI
  (268) 462–0480
- **Antigua and Barbuda Department of Tourism**
  610 Fifth Avenue, Suite 311
  New York, NY 10020
  (212) 541–4117
- **Antigua and Barbuda Department of Tourism and Trade**
  25 S.E. 2nd Avenue, Suite 300
  Miami, FL 33131
  (305) 381–6762

*License Info*

- **interknowledge.com/antigua-barbuda:** Web site containing all of the information you need for getting married in Antigua and Barbuda, including fees and addresses.

## ♡ *Tonga, South Seas*

If you have travel time (15-hour flight from Los Angeles) and want a truly different experience for your wedding, visit the island of Tonga in the South Seas. It is actually the Kingdom of Tonga and is a sailor's paradise, as there are plenty of small surrounding islands where you may drop anchor and bask in the sun. There is excellent year-round surfing and superb coral reef diving. If you don't want to watch the smaller fish under the water, go on a whale-watching day trip, as the waters of Vava'u are a breeding refuge for Humpback whales during the months of June through November. The people are friendly and the attitude is laid back. English is widely spoken, as well as Tongan. The currency used is Tonga Pa'anga (TOP).

### FUN IDEAS AND SITES

- On a whale watching tour
- Take a seaplane to an uninhabited island
- In a limestone sea cave
- On a plantation
- At the base of a volcano

### WEB SITE AND CONTACT INFO

*Planners/Services*

- **southseaislands.com:** Basic tourist information about Tonga including listing of accommodations you can contact to inquire about wedding packages.

*Tourism*

- **tongaonline.com:** Web site with basic tourist information and links to hotel sites.
- **vacations.tvb.com.gov.to:** Official Web site of the Tonga Visitor's Bureau.
- **hotelguide.com:** Site that lists hotels all over the world (with a section on Tonga), hotel ratings, and room rates.
- **Tonga Visitors Bureau Representative**
  4805 Driftwood Court
  El Sobrante, CA 94803–1805
  (510) 233–1381
  (510) 768–6227
  E-mail: tonga@value.net

*License Info*

- **Consulate of Tonga**
  360 Post Street, Suite 604
  San Francisco, CA 94108
  (415) 781–0365
  E-mail: tania@sfconsulate.gov.to

# 12.

# Weddings on the Water

Getting married on the water is becoming a popular choice for couples. You can choose to get wed on the waves in two ways: on a commercial cruise ship as part of your cruise vacation, or on a private sailboat or yacht for a day trip.

## Cruise-Ship Weddings

Basic shipboard wedding packages typically cost $600 to $800, in addition to cruise fare, which typically runs from $100 to $200 per person, per day. The wedding package usually includes a civil ceremony in a private location, photographs, flowers, champagne, and wedding cake for two. Additional services are available at extra charge, including: elaborate photography, video services, catering, live music, flowers, transportation, beauty appointments, larger wedding cakes, tuxedo rentals, invitations, marriage license processing, and religious officiants and ceremonies in different languages.

Cruise-line weddings normally take place on board before the ship sets sail or at one of the ship's ports of call. Ceremonies are *not* performed at sea or by the ship's captain (except onboard Princess Cruises' *Grand Princess*). Marriages are instead performed by a nondenominational minister or a civil officiant. Couples can write their own vows, bring their own music, and choose whatever attire they wish: formal, casual, theme, or even swimsuits!

Many cruise lines discourage outside deck weddings, mainly for privacy reasons. While locations inside can be reserved for a bridal party, outside decks must remain open to the public. But brides should also take into consideration the risk of rain or extreme heat in the tropics that can be damaging to their dress, hairstyle, and spirits. Noise is also a concern, from passing boats, the ship's public-address system, or other passengers and staff.

Once the ship sails, the ship's host or hostess is the bridal couple's contact. He or she will provide details on any special activities planned for newlyweds, such as a honeymooner's party, where onboard couples have an opportunity to meet.

## PLANNING A SHIPBOARD WEDDING

Planning a shipboard wedding starts with a call to the cruise line's wedding coordinator. (Note: some cruise lines handle wedding planning in-house, others contract with outside wedding service companies. In-house is generally preferable—you certainly don't want the shipboard staff blaming someone else for a mix-up on your big day! In either case, make sure you ask plenty of questions and get everything in writing.) The wedding planners take care of everything, including fees, licenses, documentation, and time and location of the ceremony. Most cruise ships offer a number of different options for wedding locations, ranging from an intimate library, a spotlight location on deck (though with restrictions and warnings—see above), or in one of the ship's lounges for larger weddings.

Most cruise lines require couples to reserve their cruise through a travel agent before booking their wedding package with the cruise line itself. The cruise lines' Web sites can direct you to a travel agent close to you. Barbara Whitehill has worked as a wedding coordinator for several cruise lines and now works as a cruise-only wedding consultant. Visit her Web site at **www.theweddingexperience.com** or call her at (305) 577–3358. You can also visit one of the many cruise-only travel agents on the Web. These include: **Cruise.com, AffordableCruise.com, BestPriceCruises.com,** and **CruiseCompany.net** (this site has a helpful guide to all major cruise lines, plus a number of specialty lines with distinctive ships or destinations). To be safe, be sure you contact the cruise line's wedding department to ensure the availability of a wedding date before placing the deposit for your cruise. Due to limited space, wedding reservations are normally allocated on a first-come, first-serve basis. Full payment for the wedding on most cruise lines is due at time of booking.

## QUESTIONS TO ASK

- Does the cruise line arrange weddings? (Some smaller lines, such as Windjammer Cruises, will direct you to a travel agent or wedding planner at most of their ports of call. This may add a bit of anxiety if you want more of a "plan.")
- Does the cruise line operate its own wedding department or does it contract with an outside wedding planning company?

## CAUTION

- Be careful to match your expectations and budget with the ship's itinerary, amenities, and passenger profile. If you're looking for a romantic getaway you may not want to be booked on a cruise with a family-oriented theme or a fraternity reunion. If you dislike sunny, hot weather, you'll be happier cruising to Alaska than to the Caribbean. And if you don't like crowds, a state-of-the-art 1,500-passenger ship might not suit you too well, either.

## LISTING OF MAJOR CRUISE LINES

*Royal Caribbean International*
**royalcaribbean.com**
(888) 933–7225

- Offers Royal Romance Weddings with packages starting at $800.
- Performed more than 1,300 weddings in 1999.
- Will have a wedding Skylight Chapel on its new ship, the *Voyager of the Seas*. *Legend of the Seas* and *Splendour of the Seas* have golf courses—and weddings can be held on the course.
- Destinations: The Bahamas, Caribbean, Mexico, Hawaii, Alaska, Europe, transatlantic.
- Large ships, well run, activities for people of all ages. Prices from $100 to $200 per person, per day.

*Carnival Cruise Lines*
**Carnival.com**
(800) 933–4968

- Offer wedding packages starting at $575.
- Held more than 2,000 weddings in 1999.
- Destinations: The Bahamas, Caribbean, Mexico.
- The Fun Ship cruise line, casual style with large modern ships. Prices from $100 to $200 per person, per day.

*Princess Cruise Lines*
**princesscruises.com**
(800) PRINCES

- The original *Love Boat* cruise line. At Sea wedding packages start at $1,400.
- Princess is currently the only cruise line that offers wed-

dings at sea, and they are held only on the *Grand Princess,* sailing to the Mediterranean and Caribbean. The ceremony is performed in their special wedding chapel, Hearts & Minds, and is officiated by the ship's captain.

- Destinations: The Bahamas, Caribbean, Mexico, Hawaii, Alaska, Europe, transatlantic, Pacific.
- Premium cruise line, with prices from $150 to $400 per person, per day.

*Norwegian Cruise Line*
**ncl.com**
(800) 327–7030

- Offers wedding packages starting at $875.
- Destinations: Europe, Hawaii, Bermuda, Alaska, Caribbean, Mexico, South America, Hawaii, transatlantic.
- Intimate, modern ships with an emphasis on service. Prices from $100 to $200 per person, per day.

*Disney Cruise Line*
**disneycruise.com**
(800) 951–3532

- Destination: The Bahamas.
- Large ships, family oriented. Prices from $100 to $200 per person, per day.

*Premier Cruises*
**premiercruises.com**
(800) 990–7770

- Destinations: The Bahamas, Caribbean, Mediterranean, Canada.
- Well-maintained, vintage ships from the golden era of cruising. (Not to be confused with Premier's Big Red

Boat, which offers family-oriented value cruises on larger ships out of Port Canaveral.) Prices from $75 to $150 per person, per day.

*Holland America Line*
**hollandamerica.com**
(877) 724–5425

- Destinations: Europe, Alaska, Caribbean, Mexico, South America, Canada, New England.
- Premium, elegant cruise line with a semiformal yet relaxed atmosphere. Prices from $150 to $400 per person, per day.

*American Hawaii Cruises*
**cruisehawaii.com**
(800) 765–7000

- Romance in Paradise packages starting at $695 (requires a deposit to hold the date). Flowers for the brides (lei and lei po'o [headpiece]) and lei for the groom.
- The ceremony is performed in the ports of Honolulu, Kauai, or Maui with a limit of three weddings per cruise.
- Destinations: Hawaii (interisland) only. Well-maintained, vintage-style ships. Prices from $100 to $200 per person, per day.

*Windjammer Cruises*
**windjammer.com**
(800) 327–2601

- The original adult beach party cruise on tall-masted sailing ships.
- They do not have a structured wedding program, but do

offer honeymoon specials (with a 50-percent-off return coupon).

- Destinations: Windward/Leeward Islands of the Caribbean.

## *Yacht and Sailboat Weddings*

This is a very fun option with lots of room for variety: a sailboat service for a small group; a black-tie dinner on board an elegant yacht; or a "beach party" cruise for several hundred.

Isn't this wildly expensive? Well, not nearly as expensive as the big wedding you just skipped. Some Web sites offer sample packages so you can compare prices. Most Web sites have a "contact us" section or an information sheet where you can tell the company what you are looking for and they can send you a price quote via e-mail. Below are listed just some of the charter companies out there. If you are eloping to the islands, you will probably be able to arrange something simple when you get there; there are many day charters available. Just make sure you are aware of the marriage license requirements of whatever port you are in. You don't want to get married on someone's boat on a romantic sunset cruise only to find that, once home, your marriage doesn't really count at all.

Listed below are some charter companies that offer weddings on board. If you are researching this on your own, look for boats that offer "Special Events," "Corporate Parties," etc. They are the ones that can hold a number of guests and are equipped with food and beverage services.

## *Within the United States*

### CALIFORNIA

*Bay Breeze Charters*

Based in the San Francisco Bay Area, this charter company allows you to exchange your vows with the Golden Gate Bridge as your background. You can later stop at Angel Island for photos or a barbecue party. You can bring your own minister or have the captain perform your ceremony. The crew of Bay Breeze Charters will assist you in planning all aspects of your ceremony, intimate or with a group.

**Bay Breeze Charters**
1001 Bridgeway #154
Sausalito, CA 94965
(415) 331–1851
(800) 849–9256
**sailsbay.com**

*Pacific Avalon Yacht Charters*

Long Beach and Newport Beach

This group specializes in "pleasure cruises for all occasions," which includes weddings. The yachts can hold groups of 2 to 400 people. They offer several wedding packages from $5,000 to $6,500, depending on the number of people and the day of the week (Sunday and Friday versus Saturday). The packages include the use of the yacht, catering, the minister, beverages (soft drinks and coffee), wedding cake, music, photographer, flowers, and parking.

**Pacific Avalon Yacht Charters**
Long Beach
Dock #4
Rainbow Harbor
(562) 628–1931

Newport Beach
3404 Via Oporto #103
(949) 673–8545
**epayc.com**

## DELAWARE

*Ceremonies at Sea*

Ceremonies at Sea is based in Rehoboth Beach, Delaware, and provides boats and yachts for special occasions. For any budget or location, simple to elegant, they can help arrange the event to fit your needs.

**Woodcock Enterprises**
9 James A Street
Rehoboth Beach, DE 19971–2014
(302) 227–7066

## FLORIDA

*Seacoast Yacht Charter Cruises*

This outfitter has four boats to choose from, both sailboats and powerboats (up to 53 feet long). They cruise Florida's West Coast on the Gulf of Mexico. They can arrange for food on board or you can bring your own. Call for more information about wedding ceremonies on board and what parts of the coordination they will cover for you.

**Seacoast Yacht Charter Cruises (west-central Florida)**
Anclote Isles Marina
331 Anclote Road
Tarpon Springs, FL 34689
(800) 322–6070

**Seacoast Yacht Charter Cruises (southwest Florida)**
Tarpon Point Marina
1430 Rose Garden Road
Cape Coral, FL 33914
(800) 468–1807
**seacoastcharters.com**

## ILLINOIS

*Anita Dee Yacht Charters*

Based in Chicago, this outfitter has two yachts to choose from. They have their own caterer, Elegant Edge Distinctive Catering, on board to prepare food for you and your guests as you depart from Navy Pier on Lake Michigan.

*Anita Dee Yacht Charters*
2000 North Racine
Chicago, IL 60614
(773) 281–1300
**anitadee.com**

## MARYLAND

*The Liberte Schooner, Inc.*

You can have your wedding on *The Liberte* in Annapolis, Maryland, or in Falmouth, Cape Cod, Massachusetts. You can visit their Web site for shots of brides and grooms getting married on their decks.
(410) 263–8234
**members.aol.com/theliberte**

## MASSACHUSETTS

*Princess Yacht Charters*

Based in Boston Harbor, Princess Yacht Charters can accommodate groups of all sizes. They are available to do weddings and can provide full liquor services on board.

Princess Yacht Charters, Ltd.
60 Rowes Wharf
Boston, MA 02110
(617) 951–2460
**princessyacht.com**

## NEVADA

*The Tahoe Star*

This 54-foot yacht is the private yacht of gaming legend William Harrah. Built for luxury, this vessel has a full-service bar and offers a yacht menu featuring hors d'oeuvres and delicious buffets. The *Tahoe Star* also provides dockside service to many lakeside restaurants.

Harrah's Tahoe
P.O. Box 8
Stateline, NV 89449–0008
Attn: *Tahoe Star* Charters
**tahoestar.com**
Phone for Wedding Coordinators
(800) Say-I-Do-To
(800) 729–4362

## NEW YORK

*World Yacht*

If you want to go small and fancy or big and fancy, World Yacht, anchored on the Hudson River, caters to all types of special events, including weddings. They have a fleet of five restaurant yachts available for private charter. Each varies in accommodation, rental fee, and catering requirements, according to the yacht selected, month of the year and day of the week. E-mail them from their Web site, they are prompt with their reply.

World Yacht
Private Parties Line
(212) 630–8800
(800) 498–4276
**worldyacht.com**

### TEXAS

*Ultra Sailing Charters*

Ultra Sailing Charters sails on Clear Lake and Galveston Bay in Texas. You can have a lavish dinner or a simple sail on this luxury trimaran. You can arrange to have your wedding ceremony and meal on board, or exchange vows on the water and cruise to a restaurant to eat and celebrate on land. The *Ultra* is the largest U.S. Coast Guard–certified passenger-carrying sailing yacht in the state of Texas and can carry up to 49 passengers.

Ultra Sailing Charters, L.C.
2732 Lighthouse Drive
Nassau Bay, Texas 77058
(281) 333–2063
**home.flash.net/~ultratr**

## *Outside of the U.S.*

### PUERTO VALLARTA, MEXICO

*Alegre Cruises Fine Dining and Charters*

Located in Puerto Vallarta, Mexico, Alegre Charters offers day and sunset cruises where you can eat, drink, and dance. They have a staff that can assist you in your wedding planning on one of their boats or on the beach.

Alegre Cruises
Puerto Vallarta, Jalisco
Mexico
(3) 22 3–02–06
(3) 22 2–51–65
**alegre-cruises.com**

## VIRGIN ISLANDS, ST. JOHN

*Gypsy Spirit II*

This 34-foot DuFour yacht sails around St. John and the Virgin Islands and can provide a memorable site for your wedding. There is a maximum of six passengers allowed on board, so you would have a rather intimate ceremony. This ship has its own reverend and arrangements can be made by contacting him through the ship.

Gypsy Spirit II
P.O. Box 776
St. John, VI
(340) 771–1364
**vi-fun-n-sun.com/gypsy**

## INTERNATIONAL

*Five Star Charters International Yachts*

This company is based in Sausalito, California but offers services in the Caribbean and also in Greece/Turkey, South Pacific/Cook Islands, Europe/French Riviera, USA: East and West Coast yachting available.

They have a sister catering company, Five Star Catering, which serves the San Francisco Bay Area and Five Star charters leaving from that port. This company represents 500 yachts worldwide so if your destination is not listed above or on the Web site, be sure to call and see if they have a boat where you want to go.

Five Star Charters
85 Liberty Ship Way #112
Sausalito, CA 94965
(415) 332-7187
**baydelta.com**

# 13. Mexico

Viva Mexico! As a neighbor of the United States, Mexico is an easy-to-reach destination that offers beaches, mountains, ancient ruins, shopping, and restaurants as well as plenty of places to get married. You could go for a quick weekend in the Yucatán Peninsula or spend two weeks visiting Mayan ruin sites. The food is good, the people are friendly, and you will find that many speak English. Mexico also has spectacular beaches on the Pacific Coast and in the Gulf.

**Cancún** and **Cozumel** are located where the Gulf of Mexico meets the Caribbean. Cancún is on the tip of Mexico's Yucatán Peninsula and Cozumel is a neighboring island just a 30-minute flight away. Both destinations have white-sand beaches, clear blue water, and plenty of sunshine. Cancún is a fast-paced, young persons' resort, while Cozumel is a bit more relaxed. Cozumel has some of the best scuba diving and snorkeling in the country.

If you are thinking about heading to the Pacific Coast, there are several places that stand out. **Acapulco** is famous for its culture and history. The water and beaches aren't as outstanding as Cancún, but the hotels, private homes, and villas are astounding. There are great restaurants, plenty of shopping, and active nightlife.

**Puerto Vallarta** has more of an international feel to the city, with its cobblestone streets leading the way to trendy boutiques. You can take a Jeep ride into the jungle or bask in the sun on the beach all day.

Other less populated beaches, and more for those who like to "rough it," are the beaches in the **Oaxaca** region of Mexico such as **Puerto Escondido** and **Puerto Angel.** Here you can watch world-class surfers test their skills in the crashing waves. You can rent a no-frills bungalow on the beach or stay in a private villa. You'll see a mixture of the resort crowd and the backpacking crowd.

Inland Mexico provides some excellent sightseeing. Visits to Mayan ruins scattered throughout the country make exciting day trips. Go to the rain forest region of **Chiapas** and camp out by **Palenque** to hear the howler monkeys roar at night. If camping is not your style, the city of **Oaxaca** is a cultural paradise filled with shops and restaurants and home to the Monte Alban ruins. Also nestled in the mountains of Mexico you will find charming cities such as **San Miguel de Allende** and **San Cristobal de las Casas**, where you can sit at a café on the town square, visit museums, or hike to nearby churches. If you want a more cosmopolitan feel, you can spend weeks checking out **Mexico City.** Restaurants, museums, shops, theater, and dance are among the many activities that can keep a couple busy.

Getting married in Mexico is easy. While each federal district has its rules and regulations, most are pretty relaxed. Basic documentation is necessary for both civil and religious ceremonies. Spanish is the official language, but English is widely spoken. The currency is the nuevo peso (MXP).

## WEB SITE AND CONTACT INFO

*Planners/Services*

- **paradiseweddings.com:** Web site for Paradise Weddings, which provides wedding packages in the Yucatán. They can do a simple, intimate wedding or a ceremony plus a party afterward for you and your guests.
- **dreamweavers.com:** Information on "dream weddings," with several listings in Mexico.

*Tourism*

- **travelnotes.cc:** Marriage information in Mexico as well as lists of private villas where you can stay. Each listing provides a photo and price.
- **virtualcities.com:** A directory of B&Bs, small inns, and small hotels with listings in Mexico.
- **mexico-travel.com:** Mexico's interactive tourism site.
- **Mexico Tourism Offices in the United States**
  405 Park Avenue, Suite 1401
  New York, NY 10022
  (212) 421–6655

  1911 Pennsylvania Avenue
  Washington, DC 20005
  (202) 728–1750

*License Info*

- **quicklink.com/mexico/requisitos/marriage.htm:** Lists legal marriage requirements for getting married in Mexico.
- **wedaway.com:** Here you can find information about marriage license requirements in Mexico as well as in other foreign destinations.

- **Oficina del Registro Civil (Civil Registrar's Office in Mexico)**
  Arcos de Belen y Doctor Andrade
  06720 Mexico, D.F.
  52 (0)5–578 7140

# 14. Europe

Now we're talking! With all the money you've saved by skipping your big wedding, you can indulge yourself with the ultimate elopement and honeymoon. Paris, Venice, the moors of Scotland, the Côte d'Azur, Italy's Amalfi coast—the options for a European elopement or small destination wedding are endless.

Unfortunately, the paperwork can be endless too, or at least it may seem like that. With the exception of Gretna Green in Scotland (see page 203), getting married in Europe requires some serious advance planning. In predominantly Catholic countries, such as Ireland, France, and Italy, the church continues to influence the process more heavily than back home in the United States. But even in Protestant countries the rules are simply more complicated. Hey, they don't call it the Old World for nothing! That said, Europe is still very popular for eloping. Start by contacting the embassy or consulate office of the country that you'd like to get married in. They will walk you through the particulars. Even then, you may wish to consider using the services of a local wedding planner who can interpret these rules and make things happen on time.

There are two informative Web sites that list the legal requirements for getting married abroad: **www.heartofeurope.com** has "legal pages" listing the ins and outs of tying the knot in England, Scotland, Italy, Northern Ireland, the Republic of Ireland, France, Finland, Belgium, the Netherlands, Austria, Switzerland, and Spain. If you can't find what you are looking for at that site, try **www.wedaway.com.** They provide resources to help you plan your wedding away. The site includes a Quick Guide, a summary of legal requirements for a long list of countries outside of the U.S.

So where should you elope to in Europe? Following is a sampling of ideas.

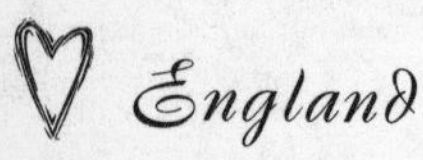

## England

If you want to go to Europe on the shortest flight to a place where everyone speaks the Queen's English, then England is the place for you. Airfares to London are more reasonable than ever. You can stay in London and check out Westminster Abbey, Big Ben, and Buckingham Palace. Or go to the English countryside and learn the true meaning of "beautiful gardens." Whatever you decide, England is full of exciting places to get married and pubs where you can celebrate your union. The currency used is the British pound.

### FUN IDEAS AND SITES

- **London Zoo in Regents Park:** The London Zoo has two rooms for wedding ceremonies: the Raffles Suite and the Regency Room. You cannot see the animals from these rooms, but you can have drinks and appetizers in one of the animal houses.
- **Bentley Wildfowl and Motor Museum:** Interesting museum that is home to a collection of 100 species of wild

fowl as well as one of Britain's finest collections of vintage cars. Weddings can be held in the gallery and receptions in a tent on the lawn.

- **Naworth Castle:** You can have your dream medieval wedding in the great hall of this castle. The castle is situated in the hills of Cumbria, in sight of the Scottish border.
- **Rivers Nightclub and Boaters Restaurant:** If you are more of a "clubber," this might be the place for you. It is a pub-restaurant and nightclub that was originally a 1930s tearoom.
- **007 Bond Street:** If you always wanted to be Bond, James Bond, you can have your very own 007 wedding at this theme pub. The pub's first floor is full of Bond memorabilia and upstairs is Moneypenny's Nightclub. There are a number of packages that include room hire, drinks, a buffet or sit-down meal, and so on. And they have their "License to Wed."
- **The Richmond Gate Hotel and Restaurant:** Only seven miles west of central London, Richmond-Upon-Thames is a charming town along the River Thames. The Richmond Gate Hotel is a four-star hotel in the style of an English country house. There are three marriage rooms, which can accommodate 10 to 70 seated guests, depending on the time of day and your needs.
- **Leez Priory:** Another site outside of London is Leez Priory, a 15th-century Tudor manor, located on 40 acres of land in Essex. You can rent out the entire building or just a room for a small group.

## WEB SITE AND CONTACT INFO

*Planners/Services*

- **wedding-services.demon.co.uk/marriage:** This site lists wedding services available for people planning weddings throughout the United Kingdom.

- **weddingguideuk.com:** This site is an excellent resource for wedding legalities, venues, advice, prices, and consultants. This on-line magazine has a great list of venues throughout the United Kingdom that shows photos of each location and has an information request form for each locale.
- **weddings.co.uk:** Information on "Brilliant and Unusual Wedding Venues," extensive listings of venues and wedding services provided all over the United Kingdom, plus wedding-related articles and information on wedding finances.
- **London Zoo**
  Regents Park
  London NW1 4RY
  0171 586 3339
- **Bentley Wildfowl and Motor Museum**
  Halland
  Lews
  East Sussex BN8 5AF
  01825 840 573
- **Naworth Castle**
  Naworth
  Cumbria CA8 2HF
  016977–3229
- **007 Bond Street**
  Bond Gate
  Nuneaton
  Warwickshire CV11 4DA
  01203 347 563
- **Richmond Gate Hotel**
  Richmond-Upon-Thames
  Surrey TW10 6RP
  United Kingdom
  0181–940 0061

- **Leez Priory**
  Hertford End
  Chelmsford
  Essex CM3 1JP
  United Kingdom
  44 (0) 1245–362555

*Tourism*

- **travelfileAOL.com:** Site for AOL's travel file on England, includes images, videos, and accommodation information.
- **webguideengland.com:** This site is an Internet directory and Web guide for England.

*License Info*

- **weddings.co.uk:** Lists legal requirements for marriages in the United Kingdom.
- **The Family Records Centre**
  1 Myddleton Street
  London EC1R 1UW
  44 (0) 181–392 5300
- **British Information Services**
  845 Third Avenue
  New York, NY 10022
  (212) 745–0200

## ♡ France

When we think of France, we think of Paris, the Eiffel Tower, fields of lavender, and couples in love walking hand-in-hand down the Champs-Elysées. However, it is quite difficult, if not impossible, to elope in France without serious advance planning. If you can swing it, however, a ceremony in one of the wine regions, in a charming village, or at the base of the Eiffel Tower

*A Duel for Love: Richard Brinsley Sheridan*

Richard Brinsley Sheridan is known to the theater world for writing comedies, including *The Rivals* and *The School for Scandal.* In 1772 Sheridan eloped to France with Elizabeth Linley. After they were married in Calais, the girl's father caught up with them. As a result of Sheridan's sneaky behavior, Elizabeth's father challenged Sheridan to a duel. The fight took place and Sheridan was seriously wounded. But he recovered and soon qualified to become a lawyer. Elizabeth's father gave permission for the couple to marry "officially."

would surely be something to remember. The official language is French, and the currency is the French franc (FF).

## FUN IDEAS AND SITES

- **Barge It:** What about a barge ride for romance? Spend a day taking in the lush scenery of France while the crew prepares a gourmet meal, serves you French wine, and lets you off somewhere to exchange vows, or wed on deck. Barge cruises can be as active or restful as you want them to be, and they can last a few hours to a week.
- **Cruise the French Riviera:** Marry in a fishing village and later enjoy your wedding lunch in one of the finest restaurants on the French Riviera.
- **Monaco Yacht Wedding:** Want to play royalty for the day? Try having your ceremony on a yacht in the port of Monaco. Have a ceremony and a meal on board, then cruise up the coast of the Côte d'Azur to take in the beauty of Monaco.

- **Maison Opéra, Paris:** This opera house was built between 1865 and 1870 and is available for small wedding ceremonies. You can celebrate your wedding in the Salon Rouge, which you may recognize, since Franco Zeffirelli reproduced this room for the film *La Traviata.*
- **Montmartre, Espace Dalí:** This building is dedicated to the great 20th-century artist Salvador Dalí. Located among some of the best Dalí works, there is a chapel front where you can exchange vows.
- **Château des Ormeaux, Nazelles:** The Château des Ormeaux was the residence of the Marquise de Maintenon's husband, the French poet Paul Scarron. It overlooks the Loire Valley in the heart of the Châteaux area. Wedding packages include one or two nights in the château and the visit to Amboise. The landlord of the château performs the ceremony.
- **Champs-Elysées:** Get married on the most famous avenue in the world.
- **Palais des Papes, Avignon:** This is the pope's Palace in Avignon, known as the center of the Christian world in the 14th century. It is considered to be the largest Gothic palace in Europe and has been the home of nine popes. Wedding ceremonies are performed in the Four Windows Room.
- **Villa Ephrussi de Rothschild, Saint Jean Cap Ferrat:** This palace, built between 1905 and 1912 by Baronne Ephrussi de Rothschild, sits on the Peninsula of Cap Ferrat. There are salons and gardens with views of the sea where you can have your wedding ceremony.
- **Hôtel Le Méridien—Beach Plaza, Monte Carlo:** If you like gambling and luxury, you will be at home in Monte Carlo. The Hôtel Le Méridien allows couples staying at the hotel to have an outdoor ceremony on the private beach of the hotel.

*Planners/Services*

- **weddingsabroad.com:** Web site for Weddings Abroad, wedding planners that coordinate a number of weddings in France, mostly in Paris, Provence, and Côte d'Azur (locations mentioned above). They can also do cruise weddings. Also lists legal requirements for getting married in France.
- **Lanikai.com:** Web site for Lanikai Charter Barge Cruises in France.
- **Perso.wanadoo.fr/barge.elisabeth/barge.elisabeth.htm:** Web page of the Elisabeth barge, photos, rates, route map.

*Tourism*

- **france-travelguide.com:** Tourism site for France. The Web site has French vocabulary lists, information about regions, helpful hints, and links.
- **allexperts.com/travel/france.shtml:** Web site where "veteran" travelers answer questions about traveling in France.
- **vive-la-france.org:** Web site with tips and ideas to plan your next trip to France. Information on culture, regions, accommodations, and more. Site also has bulletin boards and a hotel search engine.

*License Info*

- **heartofeurope.com:** Web site with legal requirements for obtaining a marriage license in France as well as other European countries.

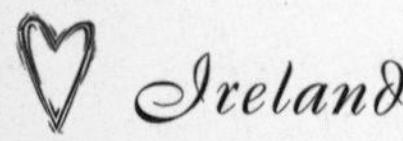

## Ireland

Ireland has some of the most stringent residency requirements in Europe, making it all but impossible to elope there on impulse (unless you're willing to stay for a month). Some of the paperwork can be done in advance, however, and for some couples the work is well worth the chance to get married in such a remarkable country. Its natural beauty, rich history, and the warmth of its people make it quite special. English is spoken, and the currency is the punt, often called a "pound" as in the United Kingdom.

### FUN IDEAS AND SITES

- **Fitzpatrick Castle:** Located in Dublin, this majestic 18th-century castle is the perfect place to have your wedding.
- **Beaufield Mews:** Located just 10 minutes south of Dublin on the road to Wicklow, there is still only one wedding held per day in the restaurant here. An original cobbled courtyard and ancient trees surround this quaint 18th-century restaurant and antique shop. The hayloft seats up to 60 guests and the coach house up to 130.
- **Finnstown Country House Hotel:** This hotel is set on 50 acres of woodland and is regarded as one of the finest manor houses in Dublin and is ideal for small wedding receptions.

### WEB SITE AND CONTACT INFO

*Planners/Services*

- **weddingsinireland.com:** Site for Weddings in Ireland wedding coordinators; you pick the city, they can help you find the locations and people you need.
- **wed-ireland.com:** This site has suggestions for wedding services, venues, and needs for the bride and groom. Lots of advertisements but a good place to start to see what is available.
- **irish-weddings.com:** This site has a list of wedding service providers and thorough hotel listings.

- **iwd.ie:** This is the site for *Irish Wedding Diary,* an Irish wedding magazine on-line. There is a list of locations for weddings and receptions such as the ones listed above (Beaufield Mews, Finnstown Country House Hotel) including photos and contact information.
- **iwc.ie:** The site for Irish Wedding Coordinators, specializing in coordinating your wedding in Ireland.
- **irelandnow.com:** This site explains Irish wedding traditions.
- **fitzpatrickhotels.com:** This site helps you plan your wedding in Fitzpatrick Castle, Fitzpatrick Cork, or Fitzpatrick Bunrattey.

*Tourism*

- **ireland.travel.ie/home/index.asp:** Site for Ireland's Tourist Board.
- **all-ireland.com:** Web site for All Ireland Travel.
- **irelandtravel.co.uk/home/index.asp:** Tourism site for Ireland listing accommodations, things to do, and so on.

*License Info*

- **goireland.about.com:** This is **about.com**'s guide to getting married in Ireland and lists legal requirements for getting married in Ireland.
- **irelandnow.com:** Click on their "Making It Legal" page and you'll find the requirements to obtain a marriage license in Ireland.

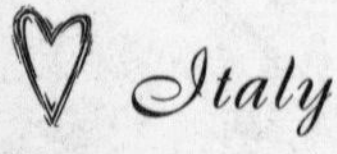

## Italy

Italy is a very romantic place to tie the knot. It offers gorgeous settings from the hills of Tuscany to Vatican City. You can get married in a beautiful church, in the Alps, or near a Roman ruin. The options are endless. The official language is standard Italian and numerous dialects. Currency used is the lira.

### FUN IDEAS AND SITES

In **Florence** you can marry in the Sala Rosa in the famous Palazzo Vecchio, which once belonged to Cosimo de'Medici; you can celebrate your wedding in the presence of the Amigeri (traditional guards of Florence) with 16th-century Renaissance music playing in the background. For a religious blessing, the famous cathedral in the nearby hill town of **Fiesole** is a charming spot. If you want luxury, check out the five-star Grand Hotel Villa Cora, where you can have your wedding in the Sala Blue and then stay for your honeymoon.

When in **Rome**, do as the Romans do and have a wedding blessing in the middle of the Roman Forum. Or, go within the third-century walls of the famous Baths of Caracalla where you will find an ex-convent from the 16th century. Rome is a city of modern, ancient, and medieval architecture, so you won't be limited to one style of surrounding.

**Tuscany** and **Umbria**, two regions just a few hours north of Rome, expand your options even further. There are literally hundreds of postcard-perfect small towns, such as San Gimignano or Cortona, from which to choose. Close by you'll find magnificent villas, which you can rent by the week (or month!) for yourselves or your guests. The **Chianti** region within Tuscany offers a dozen or so small towns famous for their wineries. **San Marino** is one of them, a wonderful spot that is filled with treasures like historic sites, castles, and spectacular views of the towns below. If you want a view of the ocean, the **Amalfi Coast** is a beautiful stretch of Italian shoreline with clinging cliff-side roads and tiled towns. Classical ruins, strong traditions, and enchanting beaches make this region popular for vacationers looking for serenity and couples looking for a special place to get married.

And then there is **Venice.** This city is known for its winding canals, ancient bridges, gondolas, St. Mark's square, and lovers. Venice has dozens of churches, from the simplest chapels to gorgeous cathedrals. And within the cathedrals there are private chapels suitable for smaller groups or just a couple and their witnesses. Now imagine a gondola waiting for you outside the church. Or a fleet of elegant water taxis to whisk your guests to a reception at a Renaissance palace on the Grand Canal. Everything about Venice speaks of romance, with just one caveat: stay away in summer! Alas, this advice is true for Florence and Rome, too (and Paris and London for that matter). Tourists besiege all the major cities during the months of June, July, and August (and into early September). In the smaller towns of Italy this won't be much of a problem. Once again, a local wedding planner can offer advice and perhaps recommend some off-the-beaten-path options for summer weddings.

## WEB SITE AND CONTACT INFO

*Planners/Services*

- **weddingsinitaly.com:** Site for Weddings in Italy, a company specializing in both types of services, civil and religious, as well as receptions and honeymoons throughout Italy.
  Regency San Marino SRL
  Via Ventotto Luglio 124
  47031 Borgomaggiore
  Repubblica di San Marino
  378875392

*Tourism*

- **emmeti.it:** Welcome to Italy, Travel and Tourism site.
- **lowpricetravel.net/europe/italy.html:** On-line reservation site for hotels, motels, cars, and airlines.

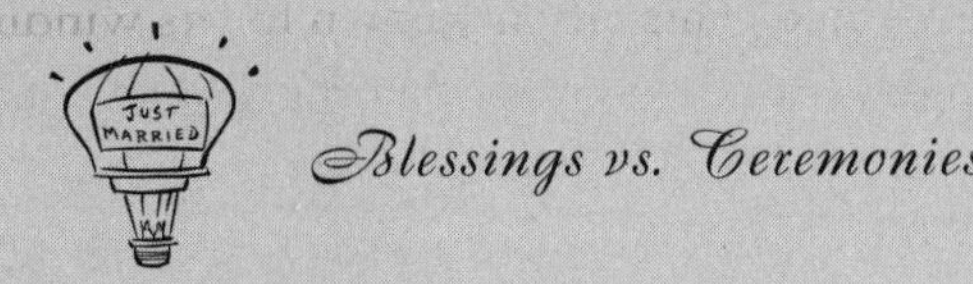


### *Blessings vs. Ceremonies*

As you surf the Web for ideas you'll notice that in some locations marriage "blessings" are allowed, but not the actual ceremony. This is largely a church matter, once again. Put simply, if you want to have a Catholic ceremony in Italy you need to be married in a church. The good news? There are thousands of churches in Italy to choose from! And finding a romantic spot for a small reception (if you're bringing along any friends or family) is just as easy. Just be sure to make your reservations well in advance, as many of these centuries-old churches, palaces, and private homes frequently close for much-needed repairs.

- **freedom-tour.com/italy:** Site for personalized tours to Italy. Offers information on hotels, car rentals, flights, transfers, limousine, English-language schools, and excursions.
- **goitaly.about.com:** This site lists hotels, villa rentals, restaurants, and events as well as maps and tips for trip planning to Italy.
- **all-travel.net/italy:** A quick guide about resources on the Net about Italy.

*License Info*

- **weddingsabroad.com:** Site where you can find information on how to obtain a marriage license in Italy.

## *Scotland*

Scotland has three great advantages for would-be elopers: first, it is easier to get married in Scotland than almost anyplace else

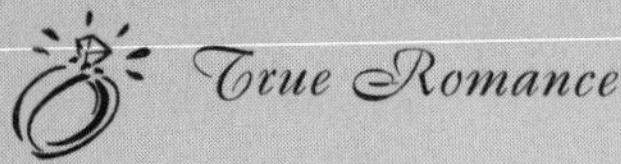


*The Romantic Warrior: Giuseppe Garibaldi*

Giuseppe Garibaldi was a 19th-century adventurer and self-taught military genius who led the fight for Italy's unification, and who played a starring role in other independence struggles in Europe and Latin America. He originally wanted to be a sailor and joined the Sardinian navy, going to South America and offering his services to the province of Rio Grande, which was rebelling against the emperor of Brazil. He called himself a guerrilla warrior and privateer and was once suspended by his wrists for two hours for an attempted prison escape. Later he returned to Italy and headed a group of volunteers against the Austrians. In the midst of all this, he eloped with the "beautiful Creole" Anita Riveira de Siloba, who joined him in his campaigns and with whom he had three children. Garibaldi went on to fight for many other causes throughout Europe and died in 1882.

in Europe. Second, everyone speaks English (albeit with an accent that may make it seem otherwise). Third, Scotland is starkly beautiful. Its sheer cliffs, spectacular countryside, grand homes and castles, and charming small villages and chapels conspire to create a strangely romantic aura. English and Gaelic are both spoken. The currency is the British pound.

## FUN IDEAS AND SITES

- Dundas Castle
  South Queensferry, Edinburgh, Scotland
  Built in 1818, Dundas Castle has a spectacular view of the River Forth, the Pentland Hills, and the beautiful countryside that surrounds the castle. This historic castle

is available for weddings for up to 100 guests, which can be held in the Great Hall of the "Auld Keep" or in more intimate parts of the old castle.

- Gretna Hall Hotel
  Gretna Green, Scotland
  Built in 1710, the Gretna Hall Hotel is the largest and oldest hotel in Gretna Green, close to the original blacksmith's shop where the famous "anvil marriages" gave Gretna Green its reputation as a magnet for couples eloping. You can hold your ceremony in the hotel, or at the blacksmith's shop with a small reception afterward at the hotel.
- In an old Scottish church
- At a golf resort
- In front of Edinburgh Castle

## WEB SITE AND CONTACT INFO

*Planners/Services*

- **Litu.com:** The official Web site for Litú Weddings wedding planners. They explain what they can arrange for you and include an informative article entitled "Getting Married in Scotland," which explains Scottish wedding tradition.
- **Scotland-info.co.uk/weddings:** Highland Wedding Belles wedding planners Web site.
  Janis MacLean
  25 Millcraig Road
  Dingwall, Ross-shire IV 159PS
  Scotland
  44 (0) 1349 867665

*Tourism*

- **nationaltrustofscotland.com:** Web site for National Trust for Scotland and Historic Scotland. They list many castles, stately homes, and historic sites throughout Scotland, which are available for private functions. Local wedding planner references are also available.

- **brideshead.co.uk:** Site featuring country houses all over the United Kingdom where you can have your wedding.
- **Dundas Castle**
  South Queensferry, Edinburgh
  EH30 9SP
  Scotland
  44 (0) 131–319 2039
  E-mail: EDundasCastle@WeddingGuideUK.com
- **weddingguideuk.com/GretnaHall.html**–Gretna Hall Hotel Web site
  Gretna Green
  Dumfriesshire
  DG16 5DY
  Scotland
  44 (0) 1462–337

*License Info*

- **General Register Office for Scotland**
  Ladywell House, Ladywell Road
  Edinburgh
  EH12 7TF
  Scotland
  44 (0) 131–334 0380
  E-mail: marriage@gro-scotland.gov.uk
- **open.gov.uk/gros/groshome.htm:** Web site for the General Register Office for Scotland, where you can find the requirements for obtaining a marriage license.

SCOTT SHAW, a native of Florida, now lives in Washington, D.C., where he works with start-up companies. He eloped in 1997, and has since decided that start-ups and eloping have much in common. The motivation and key to success for both are simple, he believes: "Conserve cash, move fast, and have fun." To that, he adds that in either endeavor "going public" too early is usually a mistake.

LYNN BEAHAN is a writer and marketing consultant. She plans to take some of her own advice when she ties the knot. (After all, she wrote the book.) Lynn lives outside of Philadelphia, PA.

# PRENTICE-HALL FOUNDATIONS OF FINANCE SERIES

**John C. Burton**
*The Management of Working Capital*

**Alan Coleman**
*Financial Management of Financial Institutions*

**Herbert E. Dougall**
*Capital Markets and Institutions, 2nd ed.*

**Robert K. Jaedicke and Robert T. Sprouse**
*Accounting Flows: Income, Funds, and Cash*

**James T. S. Porterfield**
*Investment Decisions and Capital Costs*

**Alexander A. Robichek and Stewart C. Myers**
*Optimal Financing Decisions*

**Ezra Solomon and Jaime C. Laya**
*Measuring Investment Worth*

**James C. Van Horne**
*The Function and Analysis of Capital Market Rates*

**J. Fred Weston**
*The Scope and Methodology of Finance*

**Clark Francis and Stephen H. Archer**
*Portfolio Analysis*

PRENTICE-HALL FOUNDATIONS OF FINANCE SERIES

**Ezra Solomon,** *Editor*

# Optimal Financing Decisions

**Alexander A. Robichek**

*Associate Professor of Business Administration*
*Graduate School of Business*
*Stanford University*

**Stewart C. Myers**

*Graduate School of Business*
*Stanford University*

Prentice-Hall, Inc., Englewood Cliffs, New Jersey

Library of Congress Catalog Card No. 65-23567

Printed in the United States of America (63811-C)

Current printing (last digit):

11 10 9 8 7

PRENTICE-HALL INTERNATIONAL, INC., *London*
PRENTICE-HALL OF AUSTRALIA, PTY., LTD., *Sydney*
PRENTICE-HALL OF CANADA, LTD., *Toronto*
PRENTICE-HALL OF INDIA (PRIVATE) LTD., *New Delhi*
PRENTICE-HALL OF JAPAN, INC., *Tokyo*

# Editor's Note

The subject matter of Financial Management is in the process of rapid change. A growing analytical content, virtually nonexistent ten years ago, has displaced the earlier descriptive treatment as the center of emphasis in the field.

These developments have created problems both for teachers and students. On the one hand, recent and current thinking, which is addressed to basic questions that cut across traditional divisions of the subject matter, does not fit neatly into the older structure of academic courses and texts in Corporate Finance. On the other hand, the new developments have not yet stabilized and as a result have not yet reached the degree of certainty, lucidity, and freedom from controversy that would permit all of them to be captured within a single, straightforward treatment at the textbook level. Indeed, given the present rate of change, it will be years before such a development can be expected.

One solution to the problem, which the present Foundations of Finance Series tries to provide, is to cover the major components of the subject through short independent studies. These individual essays provide a vehicle through which the writer can concentrate on a single sequence of ideas and thus communicate some of the excitement of current thinking and controversy. For the teacher and student, the separate self-contained books provide up-to-date surveys of current thinking on each sub-area covered, and at the same time permit maximum flexibility in course and curriculum design.

EZRA SOLOMON

*Stanford University, 1965*

# Preface

This book presents a systematic application of financial theory to the problem of the firm's financing decisions. Although important theoretical points are developed in the course of our exposition, the book does not present theory for its own sake. Instead, theory is organized to shed light on the complex web of circumstance within which a financial manager must act.

There are two reasons for this strategy. First, the scope of this book is limited to the financing, as distinct from the investment, decision. No general theory of finance can separate financing and investment, even under the qualifications in this book. Thus any discussion of financial theory for its own sake would be incomplete. Second, we wish to avoid the common polarization of theory and practice. The very phrase "theory *versus* practice" is insidious: We intend to take a middle road insofar as this is possible, even at the expense of the unalloyed satisfactions that belong to the pure theoretician and the "practical man."

We assume a practical knowledge of finance equivalent to that provided by an introductory course in corporation finance. Any lack of understanding of the terms we use or of the institutional factors to which we refer can be remedied by consulting an introductory text. We also assume a modest expertise in economic reasoning. Our hope is that the book will be useful to a variety of readers—that is, students in economics and finance, both at the graduate and undergraduate levels; teachers of finance and economics who want a concise summary of recent developments in financial theory; and the financial managers who must actually make the decisions this book analyzes.

The first chapter describes the functions and objectives of financial management and briefly considers various other approaches to financial theory. Chapter II defines the financial variables in a simplified economic setting—for example, the present value concept, rates of return, and differing interpretations of income. The next two chapters consider two issues central to the financing decision: the choice between debt and equity financing and the problem of dividend policies. These problems introduce related problems of market imperfections, uncertainty, and growth. Chapter V presents a detailed analysis of the effects of uncertainty on the financing decision and permits us to establish a valuation formula based on more rigorous and general theoretical foundations. The next chapter presents a framework for financial decision making with special emphasis on the role that the financial manager's judgment must play in reaching a decision. Factors such as inflation, taxes, and transactions costs are discussed. Chapters VII and VIII look at aspects of the short- and long-term financing decisions, respectively, as "subproblems" of the general framework established in Chapter VI. The last two chapters should be read as a progress report on quantitative techniques and are intended to reduce guess work in financial decision making.

The authors wish to thank members of the faculty and students of the Stanford Graduate School of Business, as well as several personal friends. To mention any single person for his comments and encouragement would be to slight many others, so we shall restrict specific citation to our typists: Sally MacKinnon, Famah Andrew, and Elizabeth Bannister.

This book reflects research and study partially underwritten by the Ford Foundation. The conclusions and opinions of the authors are not necessarily those of the Ford Foundation.

A.A.R.

S.C.M.

# Table of Contents

# Introduction: The Functions and Objectives of Finance

In finance, there is no such thing as disembodied knowledge. Our understanding of financial theory, such as it is, must be accompanied by an understanding of how this knowledge relates to other activities of the firm and of the world at large. As there is no neat boundary between these activities and the problems which comprise the subject matter of finance, our investigation must begin with definitions.

In this introductory chapter, therefore, we shall state these problems and make clear the point of view implicit in our discussion. This requires answers to three basic questions.

1. What are the functions of finance, and with which of these functions is this book concerned?
2. Functions presuppose goals: What is the objective of financial management?
3. Which of the various possible approaches to financial problems does this book use?

## The Functions of Finance

Solomon[1] has described the modern approach to financial management as the attempt to provide answers to these questions:

1. What specific assets should an enterprise acquire?

[1] Ezra Solomon, *The Theory of Financial Management* (New York: Columbia University Press, 1963), p. 8.

2. What total volume of funds should an enterprise commit?
3. How should the funds required be financed?

The finance *function* is to determine the answers to these questions.

In this book, the first two questions will be referred to jointly as the *investment* decision, the third as the *financing* decision. We shall be concerned primarily with the financing decision, the limited scope of this book requiring us to take the investment decision as given in most instances. However, the investment and financing decisions are obviously interrelated, as we shall be reminding the reader from time to time. In fact, maximizing the firm's objectives requires simultaneous consideration of all three of the preceding questions.

But there is more to the finance function than has been implied thus far. Probably if we were to choose one characteristic which differentiated finance from other business fields such as marketing, production, organizational behavior, and so on, that characteristic would be time. All financial decisions require an estimate of future events—often not just what will happen next month or next year, but also the events of ten, twenty or more years in the future. Our knowledge of such events ranges from a fair degree of certainty to guesses which we can only hope are educated.

These fundamental problems of time and uncertainty lead us to consider the problem of financial *theory* in a somewhat different light than the finance *function*. Financial theory may be defined as the investigation of how best to carry out the finance function, subject to the problems posed by time and uncertainty.

This distinction is important because this book is mainly concerned with financial theory. Any description of how the finance function may be carried out in practice is necessarily subsidiary. The book is "practical" in the sense that the authors have not assumed away important problems, but theoretical in its approach to these problems.

To summarize, in this book we shall attempt to discover how best to make the *financing* decision in light of the fundamental theoretical problems posed by time and uncertainty.

## The Objective of Finance

This book assumes that the *objective* of the financial manager is to *maximize the value of the firm to its stockholders.*

In these words the objective is too vague to be operationally useful, but later chapters will examine in some detail how this value is to be determined. Here we are mainly concerned with explaining what is meant by this objective and why it was chosen.

For one thing, we do not mean to imply that the financial manager is the only person who should pursue this objective. In fact, the term *financial manager* is used merely as a convenient label for any executive who makes financial decisions. We are implying, however, that this objective should be taken as the goal of the firm's financial policy for the purposes of our discussion.

A short digression on the types of over-all objectives which the corporation may pursue may help to put this in the proper context. Generally speaking, three types of goals may be distinguished: company-oriented goals, stockholder-oriented goals, and goals with an essentially ideological foundation. Our objective is, of course, stockholder-oriented.

Ideological goals reflect particular convictions about the proper role of the corporation in the American social and economic system. One business leader described the proper goal of the corporation as conducting "the affairs of the corporation in such a way as to maintain an *equitable and working balance* among the claims of the various directly interested groups—stockholders, employees, customers, and the public at large."[2] Now it is an extremely difficult task to specify exactly how this balance is to be achieved—a task which is obviously impossible even to discuss here. But achieving this balance may well conflict with the goal of maximizing value as perceived by shareholders. For our purposes, pursuit of such ideological goals is likely to affect the financing decision either (a) by imposing *constraints* on financing alternatives, in the same way as the law constrains many business activities; or (b) by requiring a particular *distribution* of the value created by the firm's activities (including the financing decision) among the "various directly interested groups." As an example of the latter point, suppose especially astute financing decisions raised the firm's cash flow in a given year. The extra funds might be distributed entirely as dividends; or, alternatively, "an equitable and working balance" might be obtained by distributing part of the funds as dividends, and the rest in the form of lower prices, higher wages, etc.

In the case where constraints are imposed, we can reformulate our financial objective as "to maximize the value of the firm to the shareholders, subject to the relevant constraints." In the case where a different distribution of value is required, a financial manager might not be able to pursue policies which maximized value as perceived by shareholders. Still, an estimate of what this maximum value *would be if optimal financing policies were pursued* is an essential item of information, for we cannot confidently say that a particular financing decision "balances" the interests of stockholders with those of other

---

[2] Frank Abrams, quoted in E. S. Mason, "The Apologetics of Managerialism," *Journal of Business*, XXXI, No. 1 (1958), 3. (Italics in the original.)

interested parties without an estimate of how much stockholders suffer by virtue of that decision.

We may conclude, therefore, that the conception of a corporation as "balancing" its various social responsibilities does not compromise the usefulness of an investigation into the factors which maximize the value of a corporation to its stockholders.

At the other extreme from the "balancing" corporation is the situation where the firm's objective is company-oriented—i.e., to some extent the firm is viewed by its managers as an end in itself. To be sure, few executives will be found explicitly promulgating such a goal. But the wide separation between the owners and managers of large American firms has led to consistent speculation that managers are serving their own ends rather than the shareholders'. For instance, it has been argued that firms try to maximize sales, subject to a constraint in that a "satisfactory" rate of profit must be achieved on invested capital.[3] The managers of such a firm presumably bask in the prestige and market power which sheer company size provides, while the extra costs of such a maximum-effort sales drive are subtracted from funds that otherwise would be available as dividends.

On the other hand, decisions which are in effect company-oriented (in the sense that they do not serve the owners' interests) may be made simply because managers are careless in evaluating the effects of decisions on stockholders' value. For instance, a company might decide to introduce product *A* on the reasoning that this is necessary to "keep the company competitive in market *B*." Whose interests does this decision serve? Perhaps the stockholders'; but it could easily be that, from the stockholders' point of view, the cost or extra risk of "keeping competitive" outweighs the value of the expected benefits.

To the extent that company-oriented policies are simply a matter of poor communication of shareholder preferences to managers, the objective which this book assumes is entirely appropriate. To the manager who pursues company-oriented policies as a matter of policy, unshakable habit, or simple apathy with regard to shareholder interests, many parts of this book will seem out of focus, if not irrelevant.

## Approaches to the Valuation Problem

Accepting a stockholder-oriented objective as a criterion for decision-making requires *predictions* of the effects of proposed financing alternatives on investors' perceptions of value. Predictions, in

[3] See William J. Baumol, *Business Behavior, Value and Growth* (New York: Macmillan, 1959).

turn, require a knowledge of what determines value to investors—in particular the effects of those factors which are decision variables from the point of view of the financial manager.

If a company's owners are also its managers, or if there are only a few stockholders, then this prediction requires at most only a modest survey. But in large American corporations, which typically have thousands of shareholders, making a survey for each important financial decision is out of the question. In such cases the direct lines of communication between stockholders and financial managers become tenuous and undependable, so that in general the market price of a firm's shares must be used as an indication of economic value to shareholders. For most purposes, however, the market price is likely to be sufficient.

This book's approach to valuation is *normative*; that is, we will erect a theory of how rational investors *should* value stocks, basing our theory on realistic but generalized assumptions about stockholder attitudes and market characteristics. With this theoretical framework in mind, the financial manager could in principle trace out the effects of his alternative actions on value. In practice, of course, he will inevitably experience both difficulties in applying the framework and exceptions to the assumptions on which the framework is based. In any case, the *strategy* behind the normative approach should be clear.

There are other approaches to this fundamental problem of valuation, however, which are complementary to our normative strategy. For instance, most general textbooks in finance are *descriptive*. They present a survey of the alternatives commonly open to the financial manager, of the financial environment in which the firm must operate, and of the way financial decisions are actually made. They serve as good introductions to enlightened financial practice.

A second alternative approach which is more specifically related to the problem of valuation is the procedures that have been developed for security analysis. A security analyst typically does not work with the theoretical models of a normative approach. In order to arrive at a recommendation to buy, sell, or hold a particular security, he generally sifts through a wide range of historical data, trends, and forecasts, applies rules of thumb of varying degrees of sophistication, ponders the situation, and then makes his judgment. The logic involved is often murky, but security analysts can hardly be criticized for not using conceptually rigorous tools when these tools do not yet exist.

A financial manager cannot help but profit by some knowledge of the decision-making techniques used in security analysis, since these techniques undoubtedly have significant effects on the perceived value of stocks. But many of the techniques of security analysis are of little direct use as financial decision-making tools in the firm because of the difference in the points of view of financial managers and security analysts. For example, estimating future earnings per share based on aggregate data and imperfect information is a technique commonly applied by security analysts; yet, the financial manager, who has direct access to internal information, often would use an entirely different approach.

The security analyst may be said to take a *pragmatic* approach to the problem of valuation. Such an approach concentrates on the search for rules of thumb and simplified decision techniques which *work* with regard to present problems and readily available data.

If present techniques of security analysis worked perfectly, there would be no reason for our present investigation. Such perfect techniques are nowhere in sight, however.

Users of both normative and pragmatic approaches to finance seek improvement in financial practice. The normative strategy, however, rests in the belief that there is a logical structure in financial affairs which, as we come to understand it, will erode the difference between pragmatic and normative approaches. It is this belief which justifies emphasizing theory and eschewing premature simplifications.

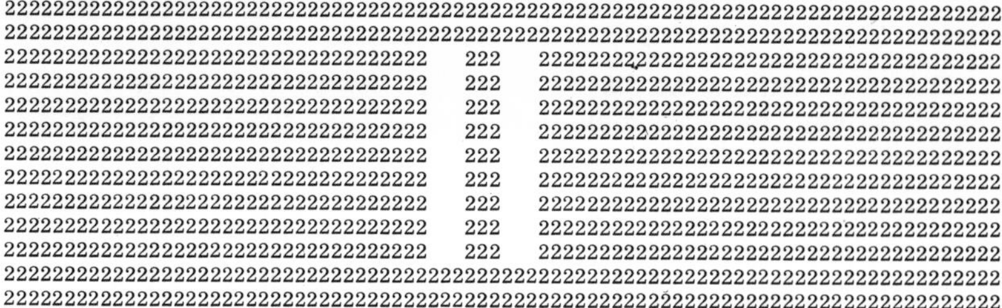

# The Economic Basis for the Financial Variables

In this chapter we attempt to secure a clear understanding of the assumptions and variables which underlie most of the arguments of financial theory. This is an important task because these concepts are really the tools of the trade of financial management, the means by which we hope to discover some logical order in financial problems. Thus we begin at the beginning—that is to say, with the simplest possible assumptions.

The discussion will move from a look at the characteristics of perfect and imperfect markets to a discussion of techniques of evaluating patterns of cash flow over time. The economic basis for the idea of income will then be presented. The chapter concludes with a short introduction to the role of risk and uncertainty in financial analysis.

## Perfect and Imperfect Markets

Very often market imperfections are presented as if they were exceptions from a more general case. This is, of course, not so; there is no such thing as an absolutely perfect market. When we say "perfect markets are assumed except for . . . ," the idea of a perfect market is being used as a standard. Thus it is important to know what is meant by the term.

When we speak of perfect markets, usually we mean perfect capital markets. One recent article has summarized the requirements as follows:

> In "perfect capital markets" no buyer or seller (or issuer) of securities is large enough for his transactions to have an appreciable impact on the then ruling price. All traders have equal and costless access to information about the ruling price and about all other relevant characteristics of shares .... No brokerage fees, transfer taxes or other transaction costs are incurred when securities are bought, sold, or issued.[1]

Also, there must be no taxes, or at least no taxes the imposition of which would change economic decisions.

It is tautological to say that a rational trader will manage his economic assets so as to maximize the satisfaction he derives from them. For our purposes, however, it is reasonable to transfer this definition of rational behavior into the context of two variables: risk and expected monetary value. If we keep risk constant for a moment, the concept of "rational behavior" follows from the supposition that any investor will prefer more monetary value to less, and will act only in his own interests—that is, he will try to maximize the monetary value of the assets he owns.

Discussion couched in terms of perfect markets (and most discussion of imperfect ones, for that matter) assumes that such maximizing behavior is universal.

We can temporarily avoid the problem of risk by assuming certainty—that is, by assuming that all actual or potential investors have exact and complete knowledge of future events. This implies that everyone is in complete agreement regarding all future events and, in particular, regarding future income, cash flows, dividends, and stock prices.

The differences between the world of perfect markets and certainty and reality are either obvious or will become so later. Two comments, however, are apposite at this point:

1. Given perfect markets and certainty, there is no difference whatever between any of the possible forms of financing, and therefore there is essentially no financing decision. In particular, there is no difference between debt and equity. Where uncertainty exists, equity investment is usually considered more risky than investment

---

[1] Merton H. Miller and Franco Modigliani, "Dividend Policy, Growth and the Valuation of Shares," *Journal of Business*, XXXIV, No. 4 (1961), 412.

in the bonds of the same company; on the other hand, the expected return on equity funds is normally higher. But if there is no difference in risk, stocks and bonds cannot sell at prices at which they yield different rates of return.

2. The foregoing assumptions have said nothing about all the activities of the economy that take place outside capital markets. Under conditions of certainty, one need not be too uncomfortable with this omission, since we can suppose that the effects of any interactions with the rest of the economy will be foreseen. This will not do, however, in other situations. For the most part, for instance, the market rate of interest is assumed given, whereas from a broader point of view such variables are the result of monetary and fiscal policy, the business cycle, international capital flows, and many other factors. We are usually justified in assuming such variables as given when viewing the financing problem from the viewpoint of a single firm, whose actions have little effect on them. But the more general problem always lurks in the background.

## Value Under Perfect Markets and Certainty

Given the assumptions of perfect markets and certainty, the capital market in equilibrium will have some unique rate of interest, $i$, and an investment $I_o$ can always be invested at a rate of $i$ per cent per annum. A person investing $I_o$ in, say, government bonds, could realize an amount $V_t = I_o(1 + i)^t$ at the end of year $t$. From another point of view, a person could borrow against future value at the same rate $i$.

The basic interest rate or "opportunity cost" $i$ establishes the time value of money, a concept by which we can compare the present value of amounts received at different times in the future. If $i$ is constant for all future periods, then the value of $F_{t+1}$ in period $t$ will be $F_{t+1}/(1 + i)$. In this case the cash flow $F_{t+1}$ is said to be *discounted* to period $t$ by the factor $1/(1 + i)$. In general, the present value of an investment is the sum of the future cash flows, $F_t$, received as a result of this investment, discounted to the present, minus the value of funds invested in period $t = 0$. That is, $PV = V_0 - I_0$, where $PV$ equals the present value of the investment.

In this case $V_0$ can be defined as the value of the investment at the end of period $t = 0$—that is, after all the decisions of period $t = 0$—dividends, financing, investment, etc.—have been carried out. Although it is sometimes convenient to speak of cash flows as occurring during period $t$, we will value cash flows as if they all occur simultaneously at the end of the period. If $V_0$ is defined in this manner, then

(2-1) $$V_0 = \sum_{t=1}^{\infty} \frac{F_t}{(1+i)^t}.$$

Since $PV = V_0 - I_0$, we can write

$$PV = \sum_{t=1}^{\infty} \frac{F_t}{(1+i)^t} - I_0.$$

More generally, we can set $-I_0 = F_0$, so that

(2-2) $$PV = \sum_{t=1}^{\infty} \frac{F_t}{(1+i)^t} + \frac{F_0}{(1+i)^0} = \sum_{t=0}^{\infty} \frac{F_t}{(1+i)^t}.$$

Equation (2-1) is actually a simplification of the case where the discount rate itself varies with time. (This simplification is often used but sometimes not justified.) Where $i_\tau$ expresses the discount rate for the period $\tau$, Eq. (2-1) is written:

(2-3) $$V_0 = \sum_{t=1}^{\infty} \frac{F_t}{\prod_{\tau=1}^{t} (1+i_\tau)}$$

where $\prod_{\tau=1}^{t} (1+i_\tau)$ denotes the product $(1+i_1)(1+i_2)\ldots(1+i_t)$.

Given a pattern of future cash flows, we can say that they represent a rate of return of exactly $i$ if $PV$ is zero. If the investment earns a return greater than (or less than) $i$, the present value $PV$ will be greater than (or less than) zero. Thus the profitability of an investment can be judged by its present value.

An alternative measure of profitability is the internal rate of return or "true yield," $r$. Given a series of future cash flows, $r$ is defined as the solution rate of discount in Eq. (2-4) below:

(2-4) $$PV = \sum_{t=0}^{\infty} \frac{F_t}{(1+r)^t} = 0.$$

The present value and the internal rate of return measures of profitability are not equivalent tools for measuring investment value, as many authors have noted.[2] The important difference for present

[2] For a discussion, see Ezra Solomon, *The Theory of Financial Management* (New York: Columbia University Press, 1963), Chap. 10, and J. Hirshleifer, "On the Theory of the Optimal Investment Decision," *Journal of Political Economy*, LXIV, No. 4 (1958), 329–352.

purposes is that the measures give different results when used as a basis for defining income.

## The Notion of Income

Income from the point of view of the shareholders of the firm may be defined as the increment in the shareholders' personal wealth as a result of their ownership of the firm's stock over a specified period. In the present context, "wealth" is measured by monetary value, since the assumption of certainty abstracts from risk.

To trace out the implications of this definition, suppose a group of investors contributes a total of $I_0$ dollars for $N$ shares of stock of some corporation. The total value of the company at this point is just $I_0$. Suppose $I_0$ is invested in a project of limited life, terminating in some period $t = t^*$. Immediately after the investment is made, the value of the firm to the shareholders is

$$V_0 = \sum_{t=1}^{t^*} \frac{F_t}{(1+i)^t} = \sum_{t=1}^{\infty} \frac{F_t}{(1+i)^t}. \tag{2-5}$$

It is assumed that cash returns to this investment are paid to the shareholders as dividends, and that $i$ is constant over time.

If the investment will earn a rate of return greater than $i$, then $V_0 > I_0$, and there is an immediate increase in the value of the company's stock as soon as the company is committed to the investment. This increase in value represents income. The income in year zero, $Y_0$, would be given by $V_0 - I_0$, or, since $I_0$ is a negative cash flow, $V_0 + F_0$. This income is a "windfall gain," which accrues to the owners of the firm as a result of their being able to invest in a project that is more profitable than the standard market rate. We shall assume, purely as a matter of convention, that the windfall gain is realized at the end of period $t = 0$.

Once the windfall gain is realized through the increase in value of the owners' stock, income will continue to be realized at a rate of exactly $i$ on the value of their equity for the remainder of the project's life. It follows from the discounted present value (DPV) definition of wealth that the income of any period $j$ is the net cash flow $F_j$ plus the appreciation (or minus the depreciation) in value during the period—value in this context being defined by Eq. (2-5). Therefore,

$$Y_j = F_j + (V_j - V_{j-1}). \tag{2-6}$$

Now, a necessary condition for capital market equilibrium is that the company earn at a rate just equal to $i$ once the windfall gains have been realized. Thus we have equation (2-7)[3]

(2-7) $$Y_j = iV_{j-1} = F_j + (V_j - V_{j-1}).$$

If $iV_{j-1} < F_j + V_j - V_{j-1}$, then investors could realize a rate greater than $i$ by buying the stock in $t = j - 1$ and holding it for one period. The resulting arbitrage process would raise the price of the stock until the equality (2-7) held. Conversely, if $iV_{j-1} > F_j + V_j - V_{j-1}$, the stock would be overpriced in $t = j - 1$, and it would pay stockholders to sell their shares and invest the proceeds at the market rate $i$. This would tend to drive down the price of the stock in $t = j - 1$. Equation (2-7) must hold, therefore, under our present assumptions of perfect markets and conditions of certainty.

The *DPV* approach to value and income is one facet of a more general theory of the valuation of shares in the market. The central idea of this theory is given by Eq. (2-3), and the development of this central idea underlies a large part of this volume. Our position is that the objective of financial management should be to maximize the value of the company to present shareholders. In the case at hand, as well as in most other cases where less restrictive assumptions hold, market price of the stock reflects this value.

In any case where value is determined by the *DPV* approach, the *DPV* notion of income is clearly the appropriate one.[4] We should, however, establish that different ways of looking at income and wealth result in substantially different ways of reporting the results of a given investment and cash flow pattern.

---

[3] We can prove Eq. (2-7) as follows. Using the general definition of present value, we can write

$$V_{j-1} = \sum_{t=j}^{\infty} \frac{F_t}{(1+i)^{t-j+1}} = \frac{F_j}{(1+i)} + \sum_{t=j+1}^{\infty} \frac{F_t}{(1+i)^{t-j+1}}.$$

Multiplying both sides by $(1 + i)$,

$$(1+i)V_{j-i} = F_j + \sum_{t=j+1}^{\infty} \frac{F_t}{(1+i)^{t-j}} = F_j + V_j;$$

or

$$V_j = (1+i)V_{j-1} - F_j.$$

Substituting this result in Eq. (2-6), we can easily obtain the proof:

$$Y_j = F_j + (1+i)V_{j-1} - F_j - V_{j-1};$$

$$Y_j = iV_{j-1}$$

[4] Our conclusions have been accepted on a theoretical basis by other authors, e.g., Diran Bodenhorn, "A Cash Flow Concept of Profit," *Journal of Finance*, XIX, No. 1 (1964), 24*f*., and Edgar O. Edwards and Philip W. Bell, *The Theory and Measurement of Business Income*, (Berkeley: University of California Press, 1964), pp. 39*ff*.

One such divergent method is the accounting process. We need not review it here except to remark that basing income on historical data rather than expectations is antipodal to the notion of *DPV*-based income.

Another way in which wealth as monetary value may be viewed, which has a certain common-sense appeal, is based on the internal rate of return (*IRR*) basis for evaluating profitability. This method defines wealth as "owner-contributed funds plus the return on these funds at the internal rate of return less withdrawals." Specifically, for the same hypothetical company investing $I_0$, assume that the return on this investment will be $r > i$. We can define the owners' wealth or "investment," $I_j$, in any period $j$ as:

$$I_j = I_0(1 + r)^j - \sum_{t=1}^{j} F_t(1 + r)^{j-t}, \tag{2-8}$$

where the variables $F_t$ represent dividends paid to the owners. According to this concept, income in period $j$ is given by $Y_j = rI_{j-1}$.

Rather than working through all the implications of this notion formally, we will present a more or less realistic example of how the different interpretations of income would work out if applied to a hypothetical investment project.

Assume $I_0$ consists of a total outlay of $100,000, $60,000 of this for equipment (depreciated on a straight line basis) and $40,000 for working capital. The investment project will last three years, i.e., $t^* = 3$. Table 2-1 shows accounting income and funds flow for the project. It is again assumed that cash returns on this investment are paid out to stockholders and not reinvested in the firm; also, the discount rate is set at $i = 0.10$.

We can solve Eq. (2-4) to obtain $r = 0.25$. Table 2-2 sets out the figures obtained for income and wealth in periods zero to three by applying the *DPV*, *IRR*, and accounting approaches. The *DPV* approach gives a windfall gain in $t = 0$ of $35,049; neither of the other approaches indicates that any income is realized during this period. Wealth, at the end of $t = 0$, is $135,049 where the *DPV* method is used, and $100,000 in each of the other cases. (Wealth is $V_j$ in the *DPV* method, $I_j$ in the *IRR* method, and the book value of equity in the accounting method.)

For the *DPV* method, the reported income in period 1 is $13,505, which is 10 per cent of the wealth at the beginning of that period. Since $25,000 is paid out to the shareholders, the value at the end of period 1 must be less than at the end of period 0—that is, $123,554 is less than $135,049. The income in period 2 is 10 per cent of $123,554 and so on.

The wealth at the beginning of period 1 under the *IRR* approach is $100,000, since the actual increase in the stockholders' value is

**Table 2–1**

**A. Accounting Income Statements**

| | $t = 0$ | $t = 1$ | $t = 2$ | $t = t^* = 3$ |
|---|---|---|---|---|
| Revenues | 0 | 75,000 | 200,000 | 170,000 |
| Expenses before depreciation | 0 | 60,000 | 105,000 | 80,000 |
| Gross income | 0 | 15,000 | 95,000 | 90,000 |
| Depreciation | 0 | 20,000 | 20,000 | 20,000 |
| Net income (loss) | 0 | (5,000) | 75,000 | 70,000 |
| Taxes (50% rate) | 0 | 0 | 35,000[a] | 35,000 |
| Net income (loss) after taxes | 0 | (5,000) | 40,000 | 35,000 |

**B. Funds Flow Statements**

| | $t = 0$ | $t = 1$ | $t = 2$ | $t = t^* = 3$ |
|---|---|---|---|---|
| Funds from operations[b] | | 15,000 | 60,000 | 55,000 |
| Less: investment in fixed assets | −60,000 | | | |
| Less: investment in working capital[c] | −40,000 | +10,000 | −15,000 | +45,000 |
| Net cash flow | −100,000 | +25,000 | +45,000 | +100,000 |

[a] Net of tax carry forward from loss in $t = 1$.
[b] That is, revenues minus expenses requiring funds or, equivalently, net income plus depreciation.
[c] A negative sign denotes an addition to working capital, a positive sign a reduction.

not reported. Income in this period is figured at 25 per cent of wealth, or $25,000. By chance, exactly this amount is paid out. Income in period 2 is 25 per cent of the remaining wealth, again $25,000, but in this case $45,000 is paid out, leaving a smaller base for period 3 income.

The accounting approach warns of a substantial loss in period 1—the accounting figures are merely transferred from Table 2-1—but indicates substantially higher income in later periods.

Under the *DPV* approach, as more and more of the project's returns are paid out, the value of the stock declines, and consequently the income earned by the firm declines (even though the stockholders' *personal* wealth may be continually increasing). Income figures obtained by other methods, however, do not follow this pattern and, as a consequence, are not related in any simple way to the value of the firm's stock.

## Table 2–2: Reported Income and Wealth

| Period | Item | *DPV*[a] | *IRR*[b] | Accounting |
|---|---|---|---|---|
| 0 | Initial investment | 100,000 | 100,000 | 100,000 |
| | Windfall gain income | 35,049 | — | — |
| | Total wealth[c] | 135,049 | 100,000 | 100,000 |
| 1 | Income for period | 13,505 | 25,000 | (5,000) |
| | Wealth before cash distribution | 148,554 | 125,000 | 95,000 |
| | Cash distribution | 25,000 | 25,000 | 25,000 |
| | Total wealth | 123,554 | 100,000 | 70,000 |
| 2 | Income for period | 12,355 | 25,000 | 40,000 |
| | Wealth before cash distribution | 135,909 | 125,000 | 110,000 |
| | Cash distribution | 45,000 | 45,000 | 45,000 |
| | Total wealth | 90,909 | 80,000 | 65,000 |
| 3 | Income for period | 9,091 | 20,000 | 35,000 |
| | Wealth before cash distribution | 100,000 | 100,000 | 100,000 |
| | Cash distribution | 100,000 | 100,000 | 100,000 |
| | Wealth | 0 | 0 | 0 |

[a] *DPV* = "discounted present value" basis.
[b] *IRR* = "internal rate of return" basis.
[c] "Wealth" is wealth remaining in the firm at the end of the period. The term has nothing to do with stockholders' personal wealth.

Table 2-3 summarizes the income reported by the three methods. It will be noted that the total income reported over the three-year period is the same in every case; only the timing of the reported income differs.

## Table 2–3: Results of Applying Different Notions of Income

| | $t = 0$ | $t = 1$ | $t = 2$ | $t = t^* = 3$ | Total |
|---|---|---|---|---|---|
| *IRR* basis | 0 | 25,000 | 25,000 | 20,000 | 70,000 |
| Accounting basis | 0 | (5,000) | 40,000 | 35,000 | 70,000 |
| *DPV* Basis: | | | | | |
| Windfall gain | 35,049 | — | — | — | 35,049 |
| Ordinary income | 0 | 13,505 | 12,355 | 9,091 | 34,951 |
| Total | 35,049 | 13,505 | 12,355 | 9,091 | 70,000 |

This is not to say that, for purposes other than the financing decision, alternate concepts of income may not be useful or necessary or both; but in wrestling with the financing decision, we must look at income from the shareholders' point of view—this is the basic reason why the *DPV* approach is preferable.

The broad outlines of modern financial theory follow from these interpretations of income and value. Assume certainty still holds and the firm has the opportunity to invest in a series of independent projects. Since the criterion is the maximization of the present value of a share of stock to present stockholders (given by the discounted present value of future cash flows, under present assumptions), the firm will invest in a series of projects as long as the marginal rate of return on investment is at least $i$. That is, the firm will invest in all projects with a non-negative present value. Any further investment or disinvestment will lower the value of the shares. Since the firm can borrow or lend freely at the market interest rate, we can be assured that it will in fact reach this equilibrium position. The problem of dividend policy does not arise—the firm will pay out whatever portion of its net positive cash flows it cannot invest internally to earn at least the market rate $i$. The stockholder is indifferent to the pattern of the distribution of these payouts over time, since he can borrow or lend to distribute present value over time in any desired pattern.

## Risk and Uncertainty[5]

That the discounted present value notion is based on expectations is both a great advantage and a conspicuous weakness of the approach. The weakness, unfortunately, cannot be avoided: we know that companies are valued on expectations of future events. Purchase of even the most conservative security involves a judgment of the probable future performance of whatever organization stands behind it. The central role of expectations applies *a fortiori* to growth stocks, for which the historical record is less likely to be a reliable indication of probable future performance.

Thus the discounted present value notion, though exact in concept, is often fuzzy in use. From some points of view—e.g., accounting—it may be necessary to use procedures which are exact in use but fuzzy in concept.

In dealing with risk and uncertainty we can assume that some future outcomes can be assigned a definite probability distribution—for instance, the possible outcomes of a spin of a roulette wheel. In

[5] Risk and uncertainty are discussed in some detail in Chapter 5. The terms are introduced here in anticipation of their use in Chapters 3 and 4.

other cases—for instance, the sales of a new product—no specific probability distribution can be assigned with absolute confidence. In cases of the latter type, we often speak of subjective probability distributions as reflecting beliefs about the future. We have no reason, however, to suppose that different persons' subjective probability distributions will be identical.

For any probability distribution, subjective or otherwise, the mean of the distribution will be spoken of as the "expected value" (for instance, $E(F_t)$ denotes the expected value of net cash flows in period $t$). The level of risk connected with an expected value is normally assumed to be a positive function of the variance of its distribution, or some other measure of dispersion. This is, of course, an imperfect, proxy measure of the actual risk as perceived by the investor.

The important factors, it should be emphasized, are the expectations actually held by investors. In the first place, these may vary because (a) the information available to different investors varies in amount or quality or because (b) the investors evaluate the same information differently, arriving at different subjective probabilities for various possible outcomes. Besides these differences, investors' actions may differ because (a) they have different attitudes toward risk or because (b) they may expect other investors to behave "irrationally." As an example of the latter point, an investor may buy a stock which he considers overpriced, if he expects that purchases by other investors will push the price of the stock still higher in the short run.

Normally it is assumed that investors are averse to risk—i.e., that the expected equilibrium rate of return of the stock of a risky corporation will be higher than that of a less risky firm, and that the expected return of any stock will be higher than the market rate of interest on a riskless investment, say government bonds. We shall adopt this assumption for the time being; its plausibility and implications will be examined in more detail in Chapter 5.

Customarily a distinction is made between "business risk" and "financial risk." Business risk is the risk inherent in the physical operations of the firm; it arises simply from the inability to insure absolutely stable sales, costs, and profits. The corporation cannot be entirely protected from the vicissitudes of the market. Business risk exists independently of the means by which the firm is financed.

Financial risk is added to business risk when a corporation, instead of meeting all capital requirements with equity funds, borrows a portion of its needs. Borrowing increases risk in two ways. First, borrowing means that the company must meet fixed interest charges and principal repayment schedules or face bankruptcy. Second, to the extent that borrowing is used, the fluctuations of the annual net cash flow available for payment of dividends or for reinvestment will be greater as a proportion of the stockholders' investment.

To see this, imagine a company with all-equity financing. The managers and shareholders of the company expect certain average sales, cash flows, capital requirements, etc. They also expect some fluctuations around these expected values. The stockholders are interested in the fluctuations of the net cash flow that will be available for dividends and reinvestment—a measure of the risk inherent in these fluctuations would be, say, $\sigma_{F_t}/E_t$, the standard deviation of net annual cash flows divided by the value of the stockholders' equity investment in the firm. Now, the shareholders could elect to have the firm pay larger dividends and borrow to meet capital requirements. Since the interest cost on the borrowed funds is most likely less than the over-all return the firm is expected to earn on its capital, the expected return on the shareholders' remaining equity value would rise. On the other hand, the ratio $\sigma_{F_t}/E_t$ would also rise, since $E_t$ would fall if the extra dividends were paid.

The stockholders are, in short, faced with a tradeoff between risk and return. This tradeoff is the central problem of finance.

## Constant Expected Yearly Income

As a note to our discussion of income, one simplified application of the *DPV* concept under conditions of uncertainty will be presented. This case, which we term constant expected yearly income, is a useful expositional device, appearing again and again in the literature.

If a company has a given cash flow $X$ in $t = 1$, we will suppose that by reinvesting some portion of this cash flow, say $Z$ dollars, it can assure $F_2 = X$ in year two. If it continues reinvesting $Z$ in every year, the managers expect that net cash flow can be maintained at a constant average figure. Therefore, the expected value $(X - Z) = F_t$ is a constant for all future periods, *given* the decision to reinvest $Z$ per year. The values of the firm in years $j$ and $j + 1$ therefore are, respectively:

$$V_j = \sum_{t=j+1}^{\infty} \frac{F_t}{(1 + \rho)^{t-j}}, \tag{2-9}$$

$$V_{j+1} = \sum_{t=j+2}^{\infty} \frac{F_t}{(1 + \rho)^{t-(j+1)}}. \tag{2-10}$$

Note that we introduced the discount rate $\rho$ in place of $i$, the market rate of discount on riskless investments. Since we have assumed investors are averse to risk, the higher the risk of a stream of expected cash flows, the lower the present value of this stream to investors.

This is equivalent to saying that investors "require" a rate of return $\rho$ which is greater than the riskless rate $i$.[6]

It is apparent from Eqs. (2-9) and (2-10) that the value of this firm's shares will not change from period to period. Applying the same reasoning by which we derived Eq. (2-7), we can deduce that the expected *DPV* income in any period is the net expected cash flow for that period, i.e., $F_t$. According to the manager's estimates, therefore, $F_t$ is the mean of the probability distribution of income in any period, i.e., $E(F_t)$. And, assuming the shareholders agree with the managers, their expected yearly dividend, $F_t$, establishes the value of the company in a simpler way than before—that is, Eqs. (2-9) and (2-10) reduce to

$$V_t = V_{t+1} = \frac{Y_t}{\rho} = \frac{F_t}{\rho}. \qquad (2\text{-}11)$$

The simplicity of this formulation makes it useful in discussing various financial problems. However, the assumption of perpetual reinvestment, and especially the use of a constant required discount rate, restricts any analysis to one aspect of the more general problem with which we are faced.

---

[6] Using this "required rate of discount" is common procedure in financial literature. We shall temporarily adopt this approach, although Chapter 5 below reveals that a required discount rate cannot be used in general to *measure* risk. However, this does not affect the substance of the argument of the following two chapters.

# 3

# The General Problem of Capital Structure

IN REVIEWING the scholarly literature relevant to the financing decision, this chapter and the next enter a slightly more organic world than that of the last chapter. Despite some equations and occasional intricacies of logic, the goal of the various writers discussed here has been the practical one of understanding capital markets.

The first point to make is that this goal has been only partially achieved. As evidence we need only cite the pervasive argument about the degree to which certain sets of assumptions describe capital markets. For instance, it is obvious that capital markets are not strictly perfect markets, but just how imperfect they are is an open question. If capital markets were really understood, such arguments would be frivolous. For present purposes, therefore, the goal is not complete understanding but an account of the state of the art of financial theory.

Basically, this chapter discusses the choice between debt and equity in terms of the confrontation between the Modigliani–Miller and "traditional" hypotheses.[1] We will also touch on several corollary aspects of financial theory.

---

[1] The Modigliani-Miller hypothesis is that of their article, "The Cost of Capital, Corporation Finance and the Theory of Investment," *American Economic Review*, XLVIII, No. 3 (1958), 261–297, reprinted in Ezra Solomon, ed., *The Management*

### The Relation of Price to Leverage

We have seen that under conditions of certainty and perfect markets there is no difference between debt and equity. The problem of debt as a substitute for equity only arises when uncertainty obtains. With this in mind, and dropping the assumption of certainty, we can ask whether there is some combination of debt and equity which will, *ceteris paribus*, maximize the stockholders' value per share. For present purposes we can define value as the market price of common stock.

The "traditional" view on this question is that the stockholders' value per share can be increased by judicious use of debt. The other position, (expounded by Modigliani and Miller, "MM" hereafter) implies that, in the absence of taxes on corporate income, the value of a firm is independent of the proportion of debt to total capitalization.

Suppose a firm has a fixed set of assets which can be expected to produce a constant expected yearly income, $\bar{Y}$, with no debt in its capital structure. We will consider the effects of financing these assets with different proportions of debt to equity. Let $L$ and $E$ represent the market values of debt and equity, respectively. Define $\lambda$, a measure of leverage, as $L/E$, and $V$, the total market value of the company, as $L + E$.

The MM hypothesis is that the total value of the company is fixed by the amount of $\bar{Y}$ and the uncertainty connected with this income, and is not in any way dependent on $\lambda$. Therefore we have their Proposition I, which states that with respect to leverage,

$$V = \frac{\bar{Y}}{\rho} = \text{a constant,} \tag{3-1}$$

where $\rho$ is the company's over-all *cost of capital.*

The market demands a rate of return (rate of interest) $i$ on $L$, and the stockholders' required rate of return on $E$ is $k$. Now the company's over-all cost of capital, $\rho$, can be expressed as:

$$\rho = i\frac{L}{V} + k\frac{E}{V}. \tag{3-2}$$

Since $\bar{Y} = iL + kE$, this is equivalent to $\rho = \bar{Y}/V$.

---

*of Corporate Capital* (New York: Free Press of Glencoe, 1959). Page references in subsequent footnotes are to the latter version. The traditional position has been argued by authors too numerous to list here in full, though some representative authors will be discussed later in this chapter. For an exposition of the traditional position more complete than undertaken here, see Ezra Solomon, *The Theory of Financial Management* (New York: Columbia University Press, 1963), pp. 92–98.

Assuming that $V$ is in fact constant, let us consider the substitution of debt for equity in the firm's capital structure. For instance, suppose that a company has $n$ shares of stock outstanding, and that market price, $P$, of a share is \$1.00. The firm now issues \$1.00 of extra debt and uses the proceeds to repurchase one share of stock. It is apparent that, if the total value of the company is unchanged by this substitution, then the price per share of the company's stock cannot change. That is,

$$V = L_0 + nP = (L_0 + 1.00) + (n - 1)P$$

implies that $P$ is constant and equal to \$1.00. Thus the MM position also implies that the value of a share of stock is independent of leverage, given $\bar{Y}$.

The traditional position states that, as a company replaces equity with debt, $P$ and $V$ may rise for "reasonable" levels of debt, and then fall if leverage becomes unreasonably high.

To put this another way, if $V$ is constant, then by Eq. (3-1), $\rho$ is constant; if $V$ varies with leverage according to the pattern of the traditional position, then $\rho$ is a shallow, "U-shaped" function of $\lambda$. Figure 3-1 summarizes these relations.

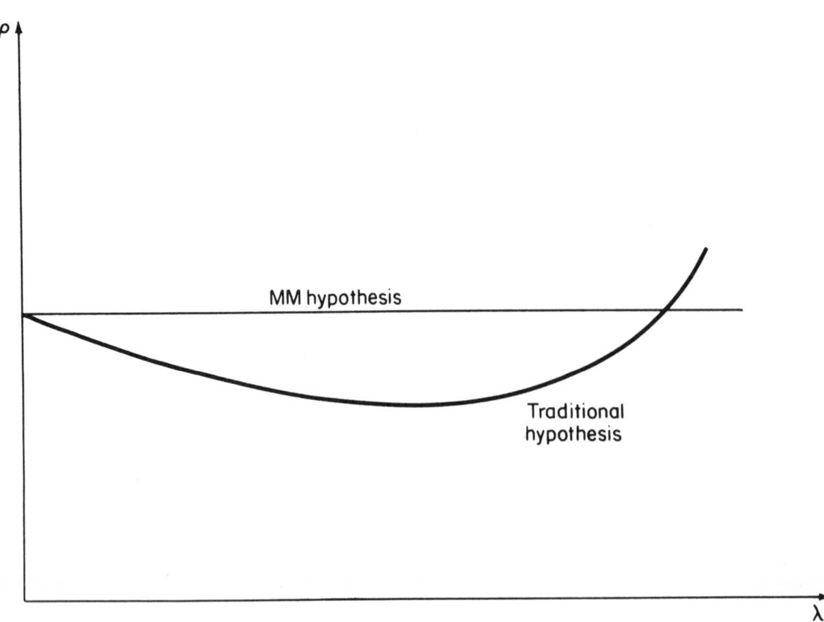


FIG. 3–1

## Assumptions of the MM Model

Here as elsewhere, the assumptions behind the MM model are crucial. The assumptions of the MM model are:

1. Firms can be grouped into homogeneous risk classes. Firms in a given risk class need not be the same size, but the subjective probability distributions assigned to the firms' expected values of $\bar{Y}$ must be such that all investors value all the firms in the class at the same rate of return $\rho$. We are in effect assuming that investors "require" the same rate of return for all firms whose expected income is regarded by investors as identically risky.[2]

2. MM interpret $\bar{Y}$ in the following manner. First, let us define $\chi[Y(t)]$ as a joint probability distribution for the incomes in all future years, $Y_1$, $Y_2$, $Y_3$, . . . . The variable $Y$ is the average of the values in this series. Even though $Y_1$, $Y_2$, $Y_3$, . . . may be an infinite series, we can be sure that $Y$ approaches some finite value by assuming, as MM seem to, that the mean of the probability distribution of *each* $Y_t$ is constant and the variance of each is finite. Thus MM define their constant expected yearly income as $\bar{Y} = E(Y)$. Strictly speaking, $Y$ is not a random variable, since there is a definite, "true" value for $Y$. We speak of $Y$ as if it were a random variable because we do not know what this true value is. In effect, we are using past and present income as data in a sampling process to make an inference about the value of $Y$, and as the profits of the firm are observed over the years, stockholders may well change their best estimate of what $Y$ is. The uncertainty of investors concerning the reliability of this "best estimate," $\bar{Y}$, means that risk in a world conforming to the MM assumptions exists in a rather special sense. The risk to investors depends not only on the random fluctuations of $Y_t$, but also in the possibility that the actual value of $Y$ may turn out to be different than their "best estimate," $\bar{Y} = E(Y)$.

3. MM assume that all present and prospective investors have arrived at identical estimates of average expected income $\bar{Y}$.

4. Stocks and bonds are assumed to be traded in perfect markets. This means, among other things, that individuals can borrow substantial amounts at the same rate of interest charged corporations.

5. In their initial model, MM assume that there are no taxes on corporate income.

---

[2] Actually, it does not follow that risk can be adequately represented by a single "required rate of return." We will demonstrate this fact in Chapter 5. This is not a serious objection when we use simplified models that assume constant expected future income, but it raises serious problems when we try to identify "homogeneous risk classes" in practice.

## The Proof of MM's Proposition I

Under these conditions MM prove that if the value, $V$, of two firms with identical $\bar{Y}$ and in the same risk class differs, it will be advantageous for investors to arbitrage so as to bring the values of the corporations into equality, regardless of any differences in the firms' leverage.

Consider two hypothetical companies $A$ and $B$. $A$ has all-equity financing and is valued at \$10,000. $B$ has \$4,000 of debt outstanding and is valued at \$11,000, \$1,000 more than $A$. Each, however, has the same expected income, $\bar{Y}$ = \$1,000, and is in the same risk class. The relevant aspects of the two companies are summarized in Table 3-1.

**Table 3–1**

| *Variable* | *Company A* | *Company B* |
|---|---|---|
| $\bar{Y}$ | 1,000 | 1,000 |
| $L$ | — | 4,000 |
| $i$ | — | 0.04 |
| $iL$ | — | 160 |
| $kE$ | 1,000 | 840 |
| $k$ | 0.10 | 0.12 |
| $E$ | 10,000 | 7,000 |
| $V$ | 10,000 | 11,000 |

The reason the values of the two companies are not equal is that the market value of company $B$'s stock is too high; according to MM, the value of $B$'s equity should be \$6,000, returning $k = 0.14$.

Now, suppose a stockholder in $B$ owned 1/100 of the shares of that company. MM argue that it will pay this shareholder to rearrange his holdings in such a way as to cause downward pressure on the price of the stock of company $B$.

The shareholder would sell his shares, netting \$70. Note that $\lambda$ for company $B$ is 4/7. Now the stockholder borrows \$40, so that his personal leverage is the same as that of his old equity in company $B$. He invests the total, \$110, in the stock of $A$. Since $k = 0.10$ for $A$, the investor receives a net return of \$9.60 on his new investment (that is, dividends of \$11 minus interest charges of \$1.60, since $i = 0.04$). His old investment earned only \$8.40.

If the risk of the new portfolio to the investor is no greater, it will be rational for him to arbitrage in this manner, and, since other stockholders will do likewise, $E$ for company $B$ must tend to the equilibrium value established by the MM hypothesis, \$6,000. MM contend that the risk is in fact the same, since (a) the estimate of the risk in the unlevered earnings stream $\bar{Y}$ is the same for all shareholders, and (b) the proportion of debt to equity is the same whether the debt is held by the company or by the arbitraging investor.

One important implication of the arbitrage process is illustrated by this example. The arbitrage, as MM see it, will lower the price of company $B$'s stock, but *will not* raise the price of company $A$'s. This is because the required rate of return on an unlevered company is taken as fixed by the market, in much the same way that the interest rate is taken as given. Thus for the arbitrage process to work exactly as outlined here, company $B$ must be out of line not only with company $A$, but with the equilibrium of the capital market as well. In other words, we have assumed that company $A$'s cost of capital $\rho$ is the equilibrium market rate for the risk class to which companies $A$ and $B$ belong.

The reader can verify that the arbitrage process would work if this situation were reversed, i.e., if company $A$ happened to be out of line with the market as a whole. Suppose that this were so and that the price of company $A$'s stock were higher than that of company $B$'s stock. In this case a stockholder in $A$ would sell his stock and buy a *mixture* of the stocks and bonds of company $B$—this is the only way an investor could maintain a constant degree of risk in his personal investment.

The essence of the MM argument is that arbitrage processes of the types examined above will establish a market equilibrium in which the total value of a firm will depend only on investors' estimates of the firm's business risk and its expected future income. The general condition for this equilibrium to exist is that *no two claims to expected future cash receipts considered to be identical in risk can sell at prices such that the expected rates of return on the claims differ.* From the point of view of the firm, it often seems natural to suppose that a claim may be *either* a bond *or* a stock. MM's recognition of the fact that claims may be *combinations* of corporate debt, personal debt and equity is an important insight. Under their assumptions, the proof of their Proposition I follows readily. Even though this proof may not follow under different assumptions, this insight remains important.

## Criticism of the MM Assumptions

The assertion that investors can arbitrage without increasing the risk of their investment portfolios is obviously crucial for MM's argument, and criticism of this idea has been important to the arguments of the authors supporting the traditional position.[3] We can

[3] See, for example, Diran Bodenhorn, "On the Problem of Capital Budgeting," *Journal of Finance*, XIV, No. 4 (1959), 473–492, and David Durand, "The Cost of Capital in an Imperfect Market: A Reply to Modigliani and Miller," *American Economic Review*, XLIX, No. 4 (1959), 646–655.

summarize their objections as follows:

1. In practice, borrowing rates for corporations and individuals differ—presumably because of the corporations' greater creditworthiness.

2. From the standpoint of the individual shareholder, there may be less risk in corporate than in personal borrowing (for an equivalent amount of leverage). For instance, in the event of default on corporate bonds, the stockholder has the protection of limited liability. For personal borrowing, he does not. Other objections might be raised. What about the possibility of margin calls? Does the investor have sufficient funds to meet interest payments on personal debt if the company has a bad year and pays no dividends at all?

3. Defining risk only in terms of (a) the corporate risk class and (b) the degree of personal or corporate leverage may not be adequate; a more sophisticated investigation might reveal other factors not included in the MM argument. The risk of bankruptcy is one such factor.

4. Transactions costs or taxes might hinder the arbitrage mechanism. We should expect such things as brokerage fees for the buying and selling of stock to be significant, especially for investors with small holdings. The capital gains tax may act as a similar sort of transactions cost in many cases.

The observation that the MM assumptions with regard to the risk of arbitrage do not hold in general casts doubt on the universal applicability of the theory. However, it is not necessary for *every* shareholder to arbitrage: a few active traders might bring the values into line. Thus it is difficult to determine what weight should be given to the traditionalists' objections. Market imperfections are a matter of degree, and we must ask what degree of imperfection is "enough" to negate the MM argument. As MM have noted,

> No amount of *a priori* speculation [can] ever settle the question of how close the substitutability is between homemade and corporate leverage, to say nothing of how close it would have to be to prevent any significant discrepancy from emerging.[4]

## The Behavior of *k* and *i*

Before coming to any final judgment on the validity of the MM hypothesis, it will be useful to trace out some of the further implications of their Proposition I. In particular, the behavior of the required rates of return on debt and equity as a function of $\lambda$ is important,

---

[4] F. Modigliani and M. H. Miller, "The Cost of Capital, Corporation Finance, and the Theory of Investment: Reply," *American Economic Review*, XLIX, No. 4 (1959), 657.

since this behavior has been the subject of most of the tests of the MM propositions.[5]

Normally, the rate of interest on debt is taken as given by the market. Assuming $i$ is given, we can derive the value of $k$ implied by the MM analysis. By definition,

$$\bar{Y} = iL + kE,$$

so

$$k = \frac{\bar{Y} - iL}{E}. \tag{3-3}$$

We know from Eq. (3-1) that $\bar{Y} = \rho(L + E)$, since $L + E = V$. Substituting in Eq. (3-3),

$$k = \frac{\rho(E + L) - iL}{E},$$

or

$$k = \rho + (\rho - i)\frac{L}{E} = \rho + (\rho - i)\lambda. \tag{3-4}$$

This equation, which is MM's Proposition II, establishes the behavior of $k$, given $\lambda$ and $i$. This relationship is shown graphically in Fig. 3-2. As Fig. 3-2 shows, the required $k$ will increase linearly as a

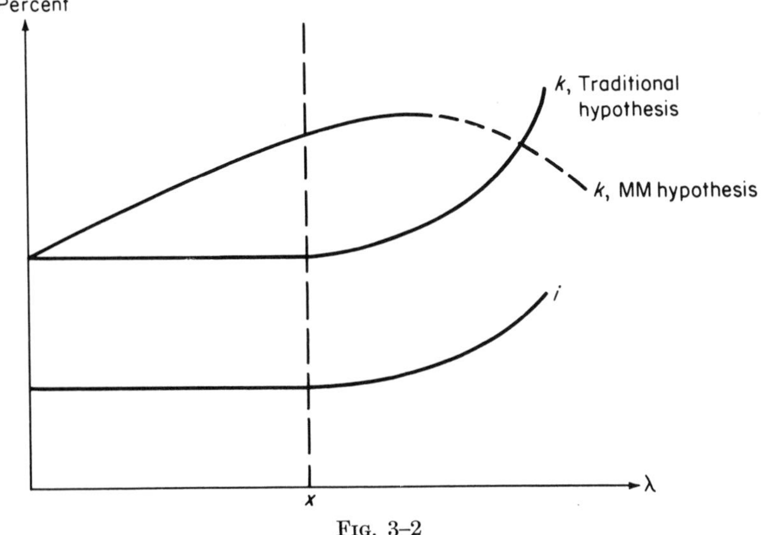


FIG. 3–2

[5] The use of "required rates of return" for debt and equity is subject to the same objections as thinking of the cost of capital as the required rate of return on the firm as a whole. See Note 2 for this chapter.

function of $\lambda$ as long as $i$ is constant. If $i$ rises at higher levels of leverage (the region to the right of the vertical dotted line in Fig. 3-2), $k$ will increase at a decreasing rate, and according to MM *may even decline* if $i$ is sufficiently high.[6]

Following the traditional approach, also shown in Fig. 3-2, we would reason that the required $k$ does not increase materially for low values of $\lambda$, but that it rises sharply as leverage increases. This would result in the U-shaped curve for $\rho$ shown in Fig. 3-1.

Since the required $k$ depends on $i$, it is important that we specify exactly how this interest rate is to be measured. Boness[7] points out that the *promised* yields on risky bonds are not likely to be correct measures of the interest a firm's creditors *expect* to receive. The promised yield on risky bonds presumably includes some premium to compensate for possible default of the bonds' interest, principal, or both. If creditors' estimates of the value of expected returns were unaffected by risk, we could expect this premium exactly to offset the expected value of default losses. In this case the *expected* rate of interest would be exactly equal to the riskless rate, established, for instance, by the yield on government bonds of comparable maturities.[8] However, such an expected rate can be no greater than the promised rate.

If lenders do not expect to receive the promised rate, is there any reason for stockholders to expect to pay this amount? In the case of default on a corporation's debt, the firm's stockholders have limited liability. If stockholders regard default as possible, the expected rate of interest from their viewpoint as debtors will be less than the rate promised by the corporation.

Although there is no simple way of specifying what the expected rate is, the Boness point is a valid one. We shall therefore define the interest rate, $i$, as an expected rate of interest which is, moreover, judged identical by both bondholders and stockholders.

If the stockholders of a company expect the company to pay the creditors exactly the rate the creditors expect to get, the behavior of $k$ and $i$ remains as shown in Fig. 3-2. The relevant figure from all points of view is the expected rate of interest.

In general, of course, it is not obvious that the expectations of stockholders and creditors will coincide. Whether they do or not is a question of fact. When all variables are changing—and, in fact, they do change—the entire problem of expectations is a thorny one. For

[6] Modigliani and Miller, "The Cost of Capital, Corporation Finance and the Theory of Investment," *op. cit.*, pp. 161–62.

[7] A. J. Boness, "A Pedagogic Note on the Cost of Capital," *Journal of Finance*, XIX, No. 1 (1964), 99–106.

[8] The government bonds will be riskless only if there is no uncertainty about the possibility of inflation. We shall assume in this chapter that there is no such uncertainty.

instance the interest rate, however it is measured, is not constant—it varies with business conditions, the nation's monetary policy, and many other factors. For many decisions,[9] an expected value for the future market interest rate must be used. This estimate is subject to the same sort of uncertainty as are estimates of income. As long as expectations are uniformly held and can be considered constant for purposes of analysis, they are tractable as variables. However, we should remember that expectations do change in ways we cannot yet systematically explain before assuming any particular model is in any sense "true."

Still another aspect of the concept of an expected interest rate must be noted, however. Our discussion would be clear enough if it were not for certain ambiguities in the idea of "risk" or "probability" of default. If the company issued income bonds, on which interest is paid only to the extent that income is earned in a given year, there would be no problem. Here the risk of default can be evaluated in a straightforward manner from the expected probability distribution of future yearly earnings.

For normal types of debt, however, the probability of default is more difficult to estimate. The fact that a particular year's income is below interest requirements does not necessarily mean disaster. If expectations regarding the ultimate value of the firm remain unchanged, the year's low income can be dismissed as a random fluctuation, and the interest payments met by borrowing against the firm's long-run value.

Even if such unused borrowing capacity is not available, the company can forego the reinvestment of part or all of the internally generated funds not considered income, i.e., depreciation charges, or it can liquidate part of its assets. Thus, in a crisis situation, the cash flow a firm can generate is the paramount factor in the risk of default that year; the future value of the firm, of course, might be compromised by drastic methods of obtaining funds. We only mention such complications at this point.

In any case, henceforth the variable $i$ will be defined as the rate creditors *expect* to receive and the company (and its stockholders) *expect* to have to pay.

## A Presentation of the Traditional Position

Thus far we have not fully investigated the logic behind the traditional position. One presentation of the theory—that of Schwartz[10]—

[9] E.g., when the company must plan to refinance debt in the future.

[10] Eli Schwartz, "The Theory of the Capital Structure of the Firm," *Journal of Finance*, XIV, No. 1 (1959), 18–39. We have changed Schwartz's presentation to suit our purposes here, but we believe his basic ideas are retained, though we have been forced to omit discussion of many of Schwartz's contributions.

discusses the problem in somewhat different terms than we have used, but the change in context will prepare the way for some further observations on the choice between debt and equity.

Consider the case where the amount of capital required to support a firm's activities is essentially fixed—for instance, a new corporation formed to exploit a certain opportunity requiring an investment $I_0$. The owners of the new company must decide how best to finance their requirements—that is, the best proportion of debt to equity in the firm's beginning capitalization. One determinant of the decision is the dollar value of expected dividends relative to the stockholders' investment, $I_E$. Let $I_L$ be the portion financed by debt.

Now, the total investment is fixed, since $I_L + I_E = I_0$. Also, let $\bar{Y}$, the constant expected yearly income before interest, equal $rI_0$, where $r$ is the internal rate of return on $I_0$. Finally, if there is no reinvestment of earnings as determined by the internal rate of return method,[11] then the yearly dividend expected by shareholders is a constant, $\bar{D}$, given by:

$$\bar{D} = \bar{Y} - iI_L = hI_E. \tag{3-5}$$

Here we use $h$ as the expected dividend return per dollar of the shareholders' initially contributed capital.

By setting up the problem in this way, we can derive an expression for $h$ that is parallel to Eq. (3-4), which describes $k$ as a function of $L/E$. That is,

$$h = \frac{r(I_E + I_L) - iI_L}{I_E},$$

or

$$h = r + (r - i)\frac{I_L}{I_E}. \tag{3-6}$$

This shows that with a constant $r$, $h$ will increase with the ratio of debt capital to equity capital, assuming $r$ is greater than $i$. If the spread between $r$ and $i$ is constant, $h$ is a linear function of $I_L/I_E$. If the interest rate rises with increasing proportions of debt, then $h$ will increase at a decreasing rate.

In thinking of the corporation's capital needs as fixed, we have isolated the effect of the financing decision on the stockholders' dividend return. Of course, this is rarely possible in reality, since financing and investment decisions are usually closely intertwined.

Also, as we have seen, there is normally a tradeoff between expected returns and financial risk. This tradeoff is not considered in Eq. (3-6). The next section will discuss the choice between risk and the dividend return, $h$.

---

[11] See our discussion of Chapter 2.

## The Traditional Position: The Tradeoff Between Risk and Expected Dividend Return

We shall now superimpose the tradeoff between risk and expected dividend return, $h$, on the example of the previous section.

Figure 3-3 describes this tradeoff. Suppose the company has a degree of leverage such that the owner of a share of stock expects to receive a return $h$ in dividends with a degree of risk indicated by point $x$ on the abcissa of Fig. 3-3. This stockholder's position is thus defined by point $A$.

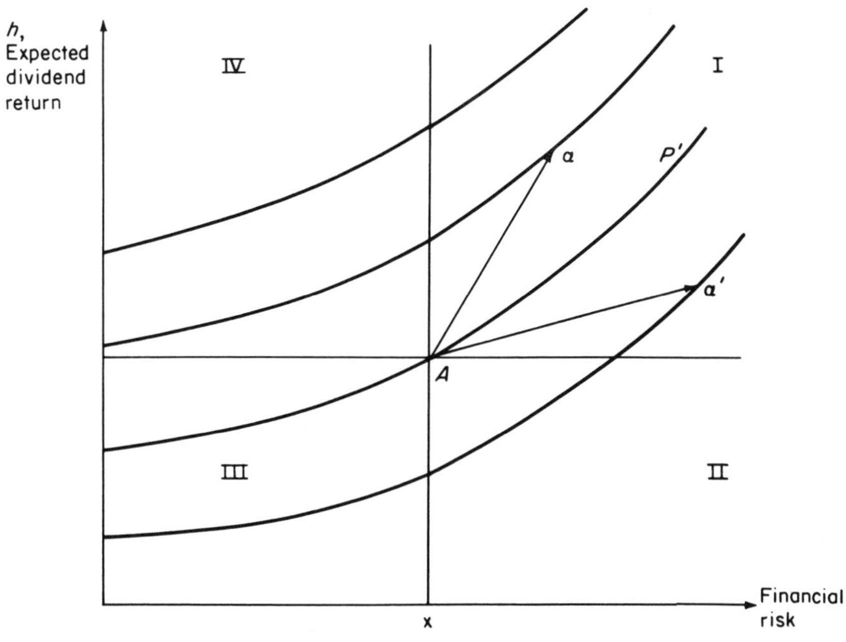


FIG. 3–3

If the stockholder has opportunities to change this position and is averse to risk, he will:

1. Always take advantage of opportunities in quadrant IV—such opportunities offer more expected income and less risk.
2. Never move into quadrant II, since these opportunities would offer both less expected income and more risk.
3. Sometimes take advantage of opportunities in quadrants I and III.

We can say, however, that there is a series of points, including $A$, in quadrants I and III between which the investor is indifferent. The *indifference curve* $P'$ describes these points. Any position above an indifference curve is preferred to positions on the curve, while positions on the indifference curve are preferred to positions below it.

By choosing different starting points we can (at least conceptually) generate a series of these indifference curves. Four are indicated in Fig. 3-3. We follow normal usage and assume they are convex.

Following this reasoning, it is clear that the investor would take advantage of the opportunity $\alpha$, since it is on a higher indifference curve (i.e., one which cuts through quadrant IV). He would not take advantage of the opportunity $\alpha'$, which is on a lower indifference curve (i.e., one which cuts through quadrant II).

Under present assumptions, these indifference curves may be viewed as defining the share price of a stock. For if two stocks offering different combinations of risk and expected dividend return sell at the same price in a perfect market, it follows that investors are indifferent between them.[12] If changes in a firm's financial policies result in a new combination of risk and expected dividend return, the price of the firm's stock will remain unchanged only if this new combination lies on the same indifference curve as the combination expected by investors before the new policies were announced. According to this reasoning, the market price of the firm's stock is *maximized* when investors expect a combination of risk and expected return which is on the highest possible indifference curve.

The indifference curves are redrawn in Fig. 3-4, where financial risk is indicated by $I_L/I_E$ as used in Eq. (3-6). $I_L$ and $I_E$ can be thought of as contributions of debt and equity holders, respectively, to the firm's total capital investment $I_0$. If the required rate of interest rises with leverage, the expected dividend return on the stockholders' investment will vary with $I_L/I_E$ as shown by curve $HH$ in Fig. 3-4. It can be seen that the highest share price possible is achieved at point $A$, where $h$ as a function of $I_L/I_E$ is tangent to the indifference curve $P'''$. The traditional position argues that, at lower levels of debt, stockholders would be willing to accept greater risk in return for higher expected dividends made possible by increasing the proportion of debt to equity in the firm's capitalization; at higher levels of debt, the increased expected dividends would not offset the greater risk created by the substitution of debt for equity.

Schwartz's approach therefore implies the traditional position. Further, we can argue that $A$ must be located somewhere in the range of financial risk represented by $OB$ in Fig. 3-4. The optimum point $A$ could not be to the right of $B$ (on the dotted segment of $HH$), since this would require stockholders simultaneously to accept a smaller amount of expected dividends *and* greater risk than at point $B$. This is inconsistent with the present analysis, which assumes risk aversion.

---

[12] Assuming the market is in equilibrium.

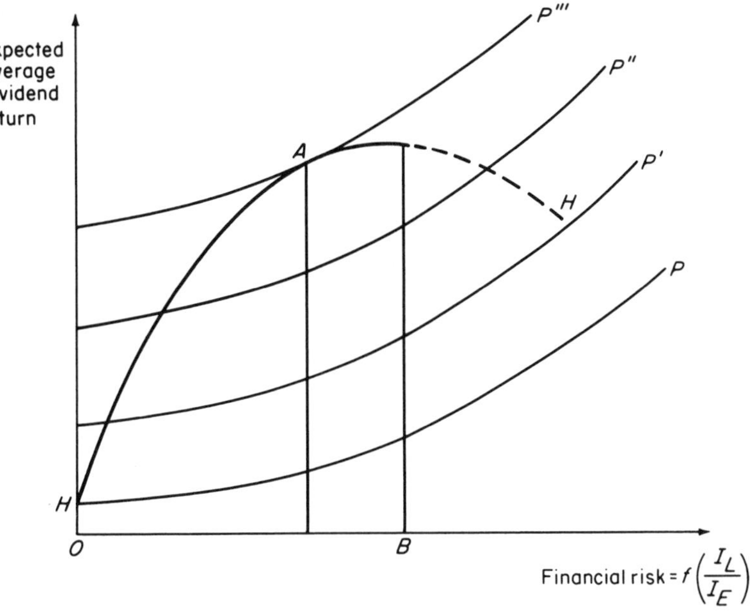


Fig. 3–4

In this context, the comparison with the MM conclusions is striking. The MM argument implies a constant market price for the stock given the expected income stream $\bar{Y}$. If we remember that in Fig. 3-4 the indifference curves can be thought of as constant market price curves, the MM analysis would imply that *HH* can itself be an indifference curve, since the market price of the firm's stock would be unchanged along it. In general, the indifference curves in Fig. 3-4 would be concave if all the MM conclusions hold.

Which argument, then, are we to accept—the traditional one or MM's? Each model's conclusions follow from the assumptions that the model itself makes. On a theoretical basis, the decision must go to the MM model, since its assumptions are more general. MM recognize the possibility of investors holding combinations of bonds, stocks, and personal borrowing. The traditional model does not, in spite of the fact that in a perfect market it pays investors to engage in an MM-type arbitrage if stock prices actually behave in the manner described by the traditional model. On a theoretical basis, the issue is as simple as that.

In practice, of course, it is not always clear which set of assumptions is more appropriate. We noted earlier in this chapter that market imperfections may interfere with the arbitrage process. But for the moment let us continue in assuming perfect markets and return to Fig. 3-4. We have stated that the MM model implies a constant market price of the firm's shares along curve *HH*. But for high degrees of leverage (to the right of *B* in Fig. 3-4) the *HH* curve declines. If this were possible, then we would be forced to conclude that investors, whom we have thus far assumed averse to risk, are willing to accept a lower dividend return as leverage and financial risk increase.

Let us restate this problem in terms of the MM model. We concluded above that the expected interest rate was likely to rise as a function of $\lambda$ as $\lambda$ rose beyond some critical point. Beyond this critical $\lambda$ debt will be exposed to some risk of default. If the MM proposition II holds and the expected rate of interest does rise, $k$ will rise at a decreasing rate as a function of $\lambda$. In fact, MM have stated[13] that *i may rise fast enough to cause* k *to decline* even if Proposition II holds. Such a situation is shown in Fig. 3-2 by the dashed portion of the $k$ curve for the MM hypothesis.

MM's statement that $k$ may decline with leverage for highly levered companies has been a basis for criticism of their assumptions.[14] They justify this possibility by arguing that some investors prefer risk, and thus would be willing to accept the riskier but higher-priced shares.

One obvious objection to the possibility of a declining $k$ is that it would be irrational for a company to add debt in such a way as to decrease the stockholders' expected return; however, this begs the question, since we cannot arbitrarily rule out errors of judgment. The basic contradiction remains. If MM's proposition II holds and interest costs rise at a great enough rate, then it is possible for $k$ to decline if leverage and financial risk are increasing. But this conflicts with the notion that investors are averse to risk created by leverage.

We shall argue in the next section that this seeming contradiction is illusory, since under the assumptions of risk aversion and perfect markets the interest rate *cannot behave in such a way as to cause* k *to decline*. We believe this will resolve an important theoretical objection to the MM propositions.

## The Relation between k and Leverage

In the appendix to this chapter we establish that, if the MM propositions hold, the necessary condition for $k$ to decline as debt is

---

[13] Modigliani and Miller, "The Cost of Capital, Corporation Finance and the Theory of Investment," *op. cit.*, p. 161.

[14] Notably by Ezra Solomon, "Leverage and the Cost of Capital," *Journal of Finance*, XVII, No. 2 (1963), 273–279.

substituted for equity is that $m$, the marginal interest rate, be greater than $k$. Is this possible? To put the question in another way, is it possible for capital markets to be at an equilibrium position in which the required rate of return on equity is a decreasing function of leverage?

Consider the instance where, as debt is substituted for equity in the firm's capitalization, each increment of debt is subordinated to all previous debt. Thus for any increment $\Delta L$, the risk position of all previous debt is unchanged, and $m$ is simply the interest cost of $\Delta L$ divided by $\Delta L$. Can the interest rate of $\Delta L$ be greater than the stockholders' expected return, $k$, *when the holders of* $\Delta$L *are in a preferred position to equity with regard to all cash flows and assets of the company?* It *cannot* if investors are averse to risk and perfect markets exist. In this case, then, $m < k$, and $k$ therefore cannot decline.

This conclusion holds even if we do not assume that each increment of debt is subordinate to all previous debt. This is so because for any degree of leverage, given the underlying business risk of the corporation, the average interest rate on a firm's debt is determined solely by the market's equilibrium structure of yields with respect to risk. The composition of the firm's debt is immaterial, since under present assumptions no two claims to future cash receipts considered to be identical in risk can sell at prices such that the expected rate of return on the claims differs. A "claim" in this context refers to all the securities which make up the firm's total outstanding debt. Consequently, the manner in which a firm's debt is divided among various classes of senior or junior securities does not affect average interest costs for the debt as a whole.

This conclusion is based on the same reasoning used to establish MM's propositions. Moreover, an arbitrage mechanism similar to what MM describe can also be applied to the *debt* of firms similar in business risk and leverage.

For instance, consider two companies, identical in all respects except that one has only one class of debt, while the other has several with various degrees of privilege or seniority. An investor could buy a cross section of the debt of the second company, dividing his purchases among the various classes of debt according to the ratio of the market value of each class of debt to the total debt of the company. By so doing, the investor would obtain a portfolio with exactly the same risk as a bond of the first company. If the average interest rate on the debt of the two companies differed, it would pay investors to arbitrage between the bonds of the first company and a portfolio of the bonds of the second company.

An important corollary of the above argument is that in perfect markets a company cannot reduce the over-all cost of its debt by issuing any particular combination of senior and junior securities.

The cost of borrowing depends only on business risk and the degree to which a firm is leveraged. Thus we can be assured that the behavior of average and marginal interest rates will not be affected by the composition of the firm's debt.

We have therefore proved that under present assumptions $k$ cannot be a declining function of leverage when debt is substituted for equity. We can complete this discussion by relaxing the assumption that $V$ and $\bar{Y}$ are constant, and considering cases where debt is added not to replace equity but for investment.[15]

If a growing company remains in the same risk class, defined by $\rho$, and earns a rate of return $r = \rho$ on all new investment,[16] we can deduce the behavior of $k$ and $i$ as follows.

Suppose some company $A$ expands so that $V_2 = V_1(1 + g)$.[17] We could imagine the company expanding by first increasing both $E_1$ and $L_1$ by a factor of $(1 + g)$, and, second, substituting debt for equity so that $L_2 - L_1 = gV_1$. Thus all of the expansion would ultimately be financed with debt. During the first step, $k_1 = k_2$ and $i_1 = i_2$, since the risk classes of both debt and equity are unchanged. Since $k$ cannot fall as debt is substituted for equity if the prices of company $A$'s stock and bonds are in equilibrium with respect to capital markets, it follows that $k$ cannot decline for the case where debt is added for expansion purposes.

To put this another way, if the above conclusion did not hold, then it would be possible for some firm $B$, larger than but in the same risk class as firm $A$, to lower the rate of return expected by its shareholders by substituting debt for equity. But we have already shown that $k$ cannot decline when leverage is increased by this route. For our analysis, the average and marginal interest rates are therefore established independently of our choice of "substitution" or "expansion" models.

---

[15] *Idem.*

[16] Unless an investment decision has already been discounted by the market, it probably *will* affect the risk class of a company. That is, if the extra investment gives a constant expected yearly income $\Delta\bar{Y}$, the standard deviation of $Y_2 = Y_1 + \Delta Y$ will be the same proportion of total expected income *only if* the random variable $\Delta Y$ is perfectly correlated with $Y_1$. Of course, other measures of risk are possible; but the point here is that we cannot say the company's business risk is constant without some assumption as to the intercorrelation of $Y_1$ and $\Delta Y$. Such an assumption will hold in reality only by coincidence.

Similarly, the rate of return on new investment could easily be greater than $\rho$, resulting in a windfall profit and a rise in price of the investing company's stock. Under such favorable conditions, the stockholders would be able to absorb interest costs where $m > \rho$ *and* realize a net rise in their expected return $k$, as long as $m$ is less than $r$.

[17] Under the stated conditions, the change in the market value of the firm, $\Delta V$, is equal to the amount of additional funds invested in the firm, $\Delta L$.

## Comments and Qualifications

In the previous section we have cleared up one apparent inconsistency in the MM argument. But if we can now accept their reasoning more wholeheartedly, does it follow that the financial manager can ignore the choice between debt and equity as irrelevant to the firm's stockholders? This is the implication of the MM argument, since if their propositions hold, the market price of the company's shares is unaffected by the degree of leverage.

However, we cannot regard the choice between debt and equity as irrelevant in practice. The fact that the assumptions made so far in this chapter cannot all hold in practice means that both dangers and opportunities exist for the financial manager in the choice between debt and equity.

It is conceivable, for instance, that because of changed expectations, temporary disequilibrium, or mistaken judgment, some company $A$ puts itself in a position such that the marginal interest rate of added debt is greater than $k$. Immediately we have a paradox. First, if MM's propositions hold, $k$ falls. In this situation it pays risk-averting stockholders to sell their shares, since other stocks offer not only higher returns but less risk—e.g., stocks comparable to company $A$ stock before the debt was added. But if this happens, the price of the stock, and therefore the market value of the firm as a whole, declines, setting an MM-type arbitrage process into motion. This induces arbitraging investors to purchase the stocks *and* bonds of the company and causes *upward* pressure on the stock price. Thus two seemingly reasonable adjustments of company $A$ securities with respect to market equilibrium lead to opposite consequences.

How is this paradox to be resolved? If the average interest rates charged the company are out of line with those of the market as a whole (i.e., too high for the risks involved), the market yield will adjust and resolve the paradox.[18] That is, immediately after the new debt is issued, its market value will rise above its issue price, and the yield will fall until it is in line with the rate the market actually requires. If this happens, however, the MM conclusions hold *only if the price of the firm's stock falls.* This in turn will cause the stockholders' return, $k$, to rise sufficiently to resolve the initial paradox.

---

[18] If the average interest rate *is* in line with the market rate structure, then we can only conclude that this structure itself is in disequilibrium. The above paradox cannot be resolved without a change in either $\rho$ or the interest rate—in other words, without a change in the entire structure of rates with respect to risk. There is a *general* disequilibrium in capital markets, rather than a *partial* disequilibrium of the firm with respect to capital markets. How a general equilibrium is reached in this case cannot be our concern here. For the purposes of this book, the market structure of yields over time must be taken from the point of view of the financial manager, i.e., as given.

It must be emphasized, however, that *the paradox is resolved at the stockholders' expense.* While the value of the firm as a whole is unaffected by the financial manager's mistake in agreeing to pay excessive interest, the proportion of this value represented by the stockholders' equity will be less than what it would have been if the firm had obtained an interest rate on its bonds equal to the rate actually required by the market.

Having presented an example of the dangers which may lurk in the choice between debt and equity, we should note that opportunities also may exist. A shrewd financial manager might be able to borrow at a cost lower than the market equilibrium rate of interest. In this case the value of the debt would eventually fall, and the firm's stockholders would realize a gain at the expense of its creditors.

These dangers and opportunities of course exist at any degree of leverage, not just in the region where the marginal interest rate is close to $k$. Paying an interest rate different from the one the market actually requires on a marginal dollar of debt affects the value of a highly leveraged company in the same way as the value of a company with little debt in its capital structure.

It is important to distinguish between the behavior of $V$, the value of the firm as a whole, and $P$, the value of a share of the firm's equity. As the two examples we have just presented demonstrate, $P$ can fluctuate even when $V$ is constant. When we accept the MM assumptions of perfect markets, we do not imply that capital markets will forever remain in a stable equilibrium. There will be continual adjustments—adjustments which create both dangers and opportunities for financial managers. Furthermore, when we retreat from the simplified assumptions used in the foregoing discussion, both the dangers and opportunities undoubtedly increase.

## The Effect of Corporate Income Taxes[19]

Thus far we have assumed that corporate taxes do not exist and that all of the firm's income is paid out either to stockholders or bondholders of the firm.

Now we shall suppose that $\bar{Y}$, the firm's expected annual income before interest and taxes, is taxed at a rate $T$ by the government. Define $\bar{Y}_T$ as the firm's expected yearly income after taxes but including interest payments. For an unleveraged firm, it is clear that $\bar{Y}_T = (1 - T)\bar{Y}$. More generally,

$$\bar{Y}_T = (1 - T)(\bar{Y} - iL) + iL$$

$$\bar{Y}_T = (1 - T)\bar{Y} + TiL. \tag{3-7}$$

[19] See F. Modigliani and M. H. Miller, "Corporate Income Taxes and the Cost of Capital: A Correction," *American Economic Review*, LIII, No. 3 (1963), 433–442.

Since the portion of $\bar{Y}$ paid in interest is not taxed, leverage increases the proportion of $\bar{Y}$ expected to be paid out as interest and/or dividends. Equation (3-7) reflects this fact: the term $TiL$ may be regarded as a "bonus" or "rebate," in the form of lower effective interest costs, to stockholders of leveraged firms.

We can specify the effect of this rebate on the value of the firm to its shareholders by first considering the market value of an unleveraged firm whose after-tax earnings $(1 - T)\bar{Y}$ are valued by investors at a rate $\rho_0$. As before, this required rate of return is determined by the investors' estimates of the riskiness of $\bar{Y}$. The value of the unleveraged firm will be simply

$$V_T = \frac{(1 - T)\bar{Y}}{\rho_0}. \tag{3-8}$$

If debt is substituted for equity in the firm's capitalization, the total value of the firm will be increased by the capitalized value of the "bonus" $TiL$. If $i_T$ is the rate of capitalization which investors assign to $TiL$, then $V_T$ for a leveraged firm is given by

$$V_T = \frac{(1 - T)\bar{Y}}{\rho_0} + \frac{TiL}{i_T}. \tag{3-9}$$

Normally we would expect $i_T$ to equal $i$, since fluctuations in the "bonus" income $TiL$ are exactly determined by fluctuations in the interest actually paid, so that investors' estimates of the risk, if any, of $TiL$ should be the same as the risk of expected interest payments $iL$. Certainly if the firm's bonds are considered riskless, both $i_T$ and $i$ will be equal to $\bar{i}$, the riskless rate of interest. In general, if the attitudes toward risk of bondholders and shareholders are the same, we would expect $i_T$ to be approximately equal to $i$, so that $V_T$ is approximately

$$V_T \cong \frac{(1 - T)\bar{Y}}{\rho_0} + TL. \tag{3-10}$$

This result has important implications from several points of view. First, it is obvious from Eq. (3-9) or (3-10) that the total value of the firm increases with leverage because of the tax effect. This is equivalent to saying that the firm's *after-tax cost of capital*, defined by $\rho_T = \bar{Y}_T/V_T$, *declines* with leverage. Second, since the "bonus" value, $TL$, created by the corporate tax effect is directly reflected in the equity value of the firm, we can conclude that increasing leverage increases the value of the firm to its shareholders; in fact, if the expected interest rate on debt is considered the same by both stockholders and bondholders, then Eq. (3-9) seems to imply that debt financing would always be preferable to equity financing. Carrying this to its logical extreme, we might suppose that an all-debt firm would be the ideal, and that in practice we would observe all financial managers trying to obtain as much debt financing as possible. The fact that all financial managers do not act in this way poses an important problem for the MM propositions.

### Why Debt May Be a Disadvantage

Is it reasonable to suppose that debt financing should always be preferred to equity financing? Our common sense says no. In this section we shall examine conditions under which debt financing may not be advantageous.

One might argue that market imperfections prevent the full operation of the arbitrage process MM describe. In this case we would not expect MM's Proposition I to hold in real life. Instead, we would postulate the traditional U-shaped cost of capital curve (shown in Figure 3-1). In this case, the disadvantages of debt financing at high degrees of leverage are obvious.

However, there may be alternative lines of argument. MM assume that investors' estimates of the amount and riskiness of $\bar{Y}$, the firm's expected earnings before interest and taxes, are unchanged by the firm's choice between debt and equity. This assumption may be incorrect.

Suppose investors expect an unleveraged firm to earn a constant expected income, $\bar{Y}$. If these expectations are to be realized, then the firm will have to reinvest a portion of its annual cash flows in order to maintain its income-producing assets. This does not mean that the investment is certain to be made in the expected amount, since fluctuations in $Y_t$, the firm's actual future income, will largely determine the firm's future investment decision. For instance, if $Y_t$ turns out to be consistently larger than the estimate $\bar{Y}$, it would be reasonable to expect the firm to increase its yearly investment in order to expand the firm further. On the other hand, if actual earnings are consistently less than the original estimate $\bar{Y}$, then we might expect the firm's managers to take a more conservative approach to reinvesting the firm's actual future cash flows. Moreover, the actual investment decisions of, say, some future period $\tau$ will partly determine the firm's actual income for periods $\tau + 1$, $\tau + 2$, $\tau + 3$, etc.

It may be that the examples given in the preceding paragraph do not correctly describe the expected changes in the firm's investment decision when actual earnings differ from estimated earnings $\bar{Y}$. But estimates of the amount and riskiness of $\bar{Y}$ must reflect some assumptions regarding the expected *strategy* of the firm's managers when confronted with unexpected developments.

Now let us pose this question: is there any reason to expect a firm's future investment strategy to be changed by the substitution of debt for equity in the firm's capital structure?

The answer to this question is yes if a highly leveraged firm may be forced to pass up profitable investments which an unleveraged, but otherwise identical, firm would be able to undertake. Let us consider the case, therefore, of a highly leveraged firm which finds itself in a situation where insufficient funds are on hand to meet mandatory payments to creditors and to make all planned investments. In order to simplify exposition, we will temporarily assume the absence of corporate income taxes.

Now we can consider two of the alternative courses of action open to the leveraged firm.

1. The firm may not undertake all planned investment. If the present value of these foregone investments is positive, however, then the total value of the firm will decline.

2. But in perfect markets, there would be no reason to reduce planned investment, since additional financing would always be available at the cost of capital, $\rho$. A reduction in the firm's planned investment, therefore, would occur only if market imperfections limit the financing available to the firm at the cost of capital.

These market imperfections seem to exist, however, especially for highly leveraged firms which experience poor operating results. As MM themselves note, difficulties in borrowing may arise because of restrictions imposed by creditors on the financial policies of the firm (these restrictions presumably raise the real cost of borrowing for the firm), or because of the unwillingness of institutional investors to lend funds to "unsound" concerns.[20] Similar considerations apply to possible new issues of equity shares.

The attempt to issue stock in the face of poor operating results may well be interpreted as a sign of weakness by the market. If this is the case, prospective shareholders would be willing to purchase the firm's stock only at a substantial discount from the "intrinsic" value of the shares. Clearly, the existence of such market imperfections raises the possibility of an interruption in the firm's planned investment.

Of course, we would expect financial managers to attempt to avoid situations in which the value of the firm would be reduced because of unavailability or high cost of additional financing. High-risk investments could be avoided, for instance, or dividends could be reduced in order to build up a liquid balance of cash or marketable securities. These alternatives, however, represent changes in the

---

[20] MM note this possibility in a footnote to their original paper. See "The Cost of Capital, Corporation Finance and the Theory of Investment," p. 160, footnote 18.

firm's investment strategy. Moreover, either alternative is likely to reduce the over-all profitability of the firm's investment.

Of course, we cannot be certain that increased leverage will actually lead to a change in the firm's investment plans. But the likelihood of such an interruption will increase as leverage is increased. And since the firm's earnings are likely to decline if such interruptions actually occur, we hypothesize that $\bar{Y}$, the investor's estimate of *average* earnings, will be a *decreasing* function of leverage.

This reasoning, of course, is only an example of how leverage might affect a firm's value. To reach general conclusions a complete dynamic model would have to be constructed—an undertaking which must be postponed.[21] But this example is sufficient to show that MM's assumed separation of the investment and financing decisions is not valid in general.

## A Suggested Reconciliation of the MM and Traditional Positions

The example of the previous section also raises the possibility that the effect of leverage on value is approximately as the traditional position predicts. Suppose a firm increases leverage by substituting debt for equity. The value of the firm will tend to increase with leverage because of the "bonus" received in the form of lower corporate taxes. On the other hand, as the company adds debt, the increased likelihood of possible interruptions of the firm's planned reinvestment would tend to lower the value of the firm. For firms which are highly leveraged, we would expect the effect of these interruptions on investors' estimates of $\bar{Y}$ to be substantial—perhaps substantial enough so that the value of the firm would *decline* for further increases in leverage, despite the "bonus" created by lower taxes. We can hypothesize, therefore, that $V_T$, the total value of the firm, will at first be an increasing function of leverage, but that $V_T$ will be a decreasing function of leverage for highly leveraged companies.

If we assume initially that investors do not revise their estimates of the riskiness of $\bar{Y}$ as leverage is increased, the preceding hypothesis regarding the behavior of $V_T$ as a function of leverage implies that an optimal degree of leverage may exist even under conditions in which the MM propositions hold. Notice that the term *optimal* here refers to that degree of leverage which will maximize the over-all *value* of the corporation. The firm's cost of capital may not be minimized at this optimal position.

---

[21] A more complete dynamic model should include, for example, the manner in which inflation affects the choice between debt and equity. Inflation would decrease the real value of the debt of a leveraged firm. Thus, stockholders of a leveraged firm would gain relative to the stockholders of an unleveraged firm. This consideration would qualify our hypothesis about the relationship between leverage and $\bar{Y}$. We will discuss inflation in more detail in Chapter 6.

MM state that the firm's after-tax cost of capital will be given by

$$\rho_T = \frac{\bar{Y}_T}{V_T} \tag{3-11}$$

where $V_T$ is defined by Eq. (3-9), and $\bar{Y}_T$ is the firm's income after taxes but including interest payments. MM assume that $\bar{Y}_T$ is given by Eq. (3-7), that is

$$\bar{Y}_T = (1 - T)\bar{Y} + TiL \tag{3-7}$$

where $\bar{Y}$ is a constant. But suppose we rewrite Eq. (3-7) as

$$\bar{Y}_T = (1 - T)\bar{Y}(\lambda) + TiL \tag{3-7a}$$

where $\bar{Y} = \bar{Y}(\lambda)$ is assumed to decline with $\lambda$ for high degrees of leverage. As we explained in the example of the previous section, stockholders' estimates of $\bar{Y}$ may decline because of the possibility of the firm's having to interrupt future investments in order to meet interest payments.

Values of $\bar{Y}_T$ and $\bar{Y}$ under the MM assumptions are plotted as solid lines in Fig. 3-5. Dotted curves show the behavior of $\bar{Y}_T(\lambda)$ and

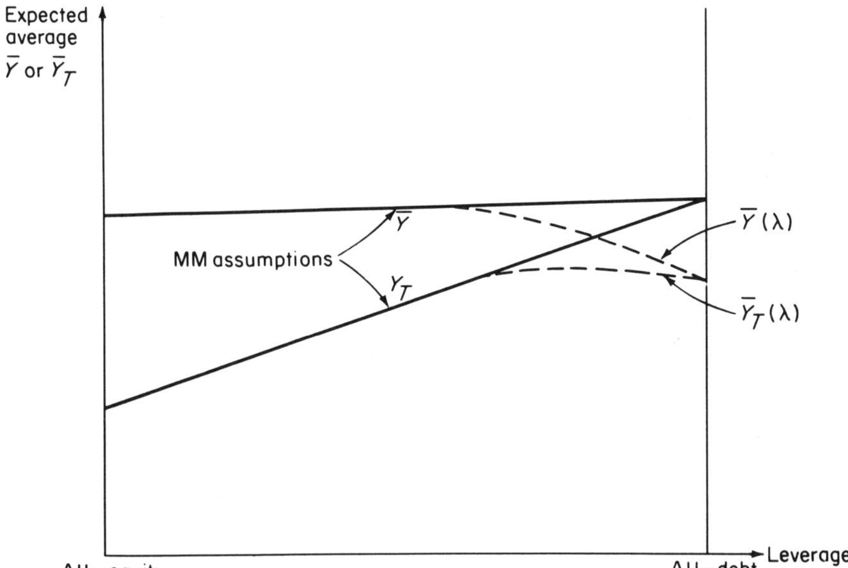


FIG. 3–5

$\bar{Y}(\lambda)$ on the assumption that investors' estimates of $\bar{Y}(\lambda)$ decrease if the firm is highly leveraged.[22]

Now, let us look again at Eq. (3-10), which expresses $V_T$ as a function of $\bar{Y}$ and leverage. If $\bar{Y} = \bar{Y}(\lambda)$,

$$V_T = \frac{(1 - T)\,\bar{Y}(\lambda)}{\rho_0} + TL. \tag{3-10a}$$

It is apparent from Eq. (3-10a) that if

$$\frac{(1 - T)}{\rho_0}\frac{d\bar{Y}(\lambda)}{dL} > T,$$

then $V_T$ will be a declining function of leverage. If we knew the function $\bar{Y} = \bar{Y}(\lambda)$, we could specify the optimal degree of leverage by the following condition:

$$\frac{(1 - T)}{\rho_0}\frac{d\bar{Y}(\lambda)}{dL} = T. \tag{3-12}$$

However, even though the MM assumptions are incorrect when $\bar{Y}$ is a function of leverage, their reasoning still applies once the degree of leverage and $\bar{Y}(\lambda)$ are given. That is, even though $\bar{Y}_T$ and $V_T$ may change in ways MM did not consider, the ratio $\rho_T = \bar{Y}_T/V_T$ should be as MM predict for the degree of leverage ultimately reached. In general, the firm's cost of capital, $\rho_T$, is not a reliable index of changes in the firm's over-all value.

Now let us suppose that investors change their estimates of the firm's risk class as leverage is increased. It seems reasonable to say that $\bar{Y}$ would appear more risky—at least it is hard to imagine instances where the possibility of interruption of the firm's investment plans would make prospective earnings less risky than before. In this case, the cost of capital of highly leveraged companies would be higher than predicted by MM, which would make it even more likely that $V_T$ would ultimately become a decreasing function of leverage. In fact, it is possible that changes in investors' estimates of the riskiness of $\bar{Y}$ would be substantial enough so that a firm's cost of capital would actually rise as a function of leverage, despite the MM predictions.

Of course these hypotheses will remain speculative until more general dynamic models can be derived. However, they are a plausible reconciliation of the MM logic and traditional conclusions. In the next section we shall examine the empirical data on the MM propositions with these hypotheses in mind.

---

[22] Note that $\bar{Y}$ could decline even in the absence of corporate taxes; the conclusions of this section would apply *a fortiori* in a taxless world.

## Testing the MM Propositions

Having discussed the MM propositions, it is time to turn the investigation to the complex realities with which the financial manager has to deal. Reality is fine if one knows what is real and what isn't; unfortunately, in this case we are not quite sure.

What evidence we do have has been obtained by trying to find a pattern operating in conjunction with, and perhaps hidden by, many other factors—changing expectations, the effects of the business cycle and fiscal and monetary policies, changes in investment opportunities, inflation or deflation, etc.

In testing, it is these "other factors" that raise the least tractable difficulties. The investigator cannot hope to eliminate their effects. Instead, he must attempt to design his experiment so that these other factors will affect the results randomly. If there are nonrandom factors operating, their effect cannot be expected to "cancel out," even if very large samples are used. In such cases the experiment will be biased and inconclusive.

The very fact that such random and nonrandom factors exist, however, makes it clear that, even if we could resolve the MM controversy, we would be unable to specify the complete rules for the financing decision. While the academician is often justified in considering a problem *ceteris paribus*, a financial officer cannot. Of course this is not to say that the resolution of the controversy would not be a great help in financial management.

In their original paper, MM cite two studies that seem to support their argument that the cost of capital is independent of leverage.[23] The two samples tested were a group of 43 large electric utilities and a group of 42 oil companies.

To test Proposition I, $\rho_T$ was plotted against leverage for the two samples. For both samples, $\rho_T$ was found to be nearly constant, with values of 5.3 per cent for the electric utilities sample and 8.5 per cent for the oil companies. The regression equations had a slight upward slope, but this was too small to be statistically significant. Thus these data do not support the traditional position. However, these results are also inconsistent with MM's revised hypothesis that the cost of capital declines with leverage.[24]

MM regard their results as suggestive, rather than conclusive, and doubtless are not surprised that their tests have been criticized.

---

[23] Modigliani and Miller, "The Cost of Capital, Corporation Finance and the Theory of Investment," *op. cit.*, pp. 167–173.

[24] Modigliani and Miller, "Corporate Income Taxes and the Cost of Capital: A Correction," *op. cit.*, is a revision of their original article, in which MM assumed that $\rho_T$ was constant.

The difficulties in testing make it a formidable task to provide conclusive proof or rebuttal to the MM propositions. It will be instructive to look at some of these difficulties, since they are good examples of the "other factors" that affect financial decisions.

The first problem is that of measuring the variables. For instance, expected average income, $\bar{Y}$, does not appear in annual reports, as accounting measures are based on historical data. Yet we know that stock values reflect expectations, even if accounting figures often do not. If a company reports an accounting loss, the value of the stock rarely drops to zero; stockholders normally have some expectations of future value despite the reported loss. We might be able to impute expectations from the market value of the stock if we knew the stockholders' required rate of return. Unfortunately this is exactly what we are looking for.

The problem of measurement is not restricted to income. For instance, in a fluctuating stock and bond market, how are we to arrive at a single value for the stock price of a company, or the interest rate on its bonds? What if interest rates are expected to change in the future? Can we assume that inaccuracies because of these difficulties will cancel out for a sufficiently large sample, or is there a possibility that such inaccuracies will bias the results? Should we try to exclude cases which appear "abnormal"?

Another problem in testing is: how can one be sure that all the companies of a given sample are of a given risk class?[25] The dilemma an experimentor faces is that in order to make his sample more homogeneous as to risk, he will probably have to reduce sample size, thus jeopardizing the statistical value of the test.

Probably the most comprehensive test of the MM propositions has been made by Barges,[26] using samples from the railroad, department store, and cement industries. His results indicate a U-shaped cost of capital function.

The weight we give his results, however, depends to a large extent on the reasonableness of his use of book values rather than market values to measure $L$ and $E$. Barges argues that the use of market value introduces a bias in testing[27]; that is, there is a tendency to confuse business risk with financial risk. Suppose we observe a company in two successive years. In year 1, $\lambda = 0.5$ and $k = 0.10$. In year 2, $\lambda = 0.6$ and $k = 0.12$. One interpretation would be that, because of a greater debt obligation, financial risk has increased to

---

[25] As we shall show in Chapter 5, this problem is even more difficult than we imply here, since single discount rates are generally not adequate measures of risk.

[26] Alexander Barges, *The Effect of Capital Structure on the Cost of Capital* (Englewood Cliffs, N.J.: Prentice-Hall, 1963).

[27] *Ibid.*, p. 26–29.

the extent that stockholders demand an extra 2 per cent on their equity. Barges would argue, however, that the following could have occurred. Suppose business conditions change in year 2 in such a way that investors decide that this company is more risky than before, even though expected *average* future earnings are the same. The value of the company's stock declines, and $k$ rises as a consequence. And since $\lambda$ equals the ratio of the *market* values of debt and equity, $\lambda$ will have risen. In this case measuring leverage in terms of market values is clearly misleading, since the company's debt obligations as a proportion of expected income have not changed.

From another point of view, companies which actually are in different risk classes may appear to conform to MM's Proposition II if leverage is defined in terms of market values and the companies are erroneously assumed to be in the same risk class.

Barges's use of book values tends to eliminate this kind of bias, which might favor the MM hypothesis. In fact, his results seem to indicate this bias exists.

On the other hand, the use of book values in the original MM tests made no statistical difference. Also, book values for equity are notoriously arbitrary figures. For instance, accounting procedures add current retained earnings to a cumulative sum of past retained earnings, without adjustment for change in the value of the dollar, so that book values are often substantially less than market values. Has Barges really tested the MM hypothesis, or has he chosen an easier target?

Barges attempts to evade any possible biases in the book value measures by using data from three industries, using different measures of financial risk, and testing various subsamples of the original data. He finds no bias.

Subject to these qualifications, then, Barges's tests indicate that the cost of capital is a U-shaped function of leverage. He concludes that the MM propositions are disproved.

Barges is correct in stating that his results seem to vindicate the conclusions of the traditional position, but it is not clear that the logic of the MM argument need be cast aside. It seems possible that ultimately we shall be able to have our (theoretical) cake and eat it too, since we demonstrated in the previous section that investors' estimates of the amount and riskiness of expected earnings may change as a function of leverage, affecting the value of the firm and its cost of capital even where the MM propositions hold.

Perhaps ironically, both the MM and traditional positions now seem to point to the same conclusion: that there is some degree of leverage which will maximize the value of the firm. This is an important conclusion, even though we cannot pinpoint which combination of debt and equity financing is optimal.

## A Concluding Remark

Since the first MM article, the controversy over the cost of capital has attracted the attention of a great many writers. The heat of their arguments, however, is less surprising that the paucity of writings supporting the MM position, since the resolution of the issues MM raised is by no means obvious. We are convinced that the impulse to disagree—regardless of the formal reasoning behind the disagreement—partly lies in the reluctance to accept the conclusion that the controversy itself merely illustrates: the narrowness of our systematic understanding of corporate finance. Until recently, knowledge in this area rested largely on experience, and experience had become a pedantic teacher.

It is extremely important, therefore, to attempt to keep in mind what we do not know.

## Appendix

In this appendix we show that, in order for $k$ to decline as debt is substituted for equity, the marginal rate of interest, $m$, must exceed $k$.

The total interest expected to be paid by the corporation is simply $iL$. Thus the marginal rate is given by

$$m = \frac{d(iL)}{dL} = i + L\frac{di}{dL}. \tag{3A-1}$$

We can rewrite Eq. (3-2) as:

$$\rho V = iL + kE. \tag{3A-2}$$

The general differential equation of Eq. (3A-2) is

$$V d\rho + \rho dV = idL + Ldi + kdE + Edk. \tag{3A-3}$$

If the MM propositions hold, $\rho$ and $V$ are constants, $dV = 0$, and $d\rho = 0$. Also, since we are considering the substitution of debt for equity, $dL = -dE$. Thus Eq. (3A-3) reduces to

$$0 = idL + Ldi + Edk - kdL. \tag{3A-4}$$

To specify the point beyond which $k$ declines, we set $dk = 0$ and solve. The necessary condition is

$$k = i + L\frac{di}{dL} = m. \tag{3A-5}$$

Solomon[28] arrives at a different condition for $k$ to decline, that is that $m > \rho$. The difference arises from his considering the case where debt is added to a constant equity base. In this case $dV = dL$ and $dE = 0$. Since Solomon also assumes the firm stays in the same risk class, $d\rho = 0$. From Eq. (3A-3), therefore, we have

$$\rho dL = Ldi + idL + Edk. \tag{3A-6}$$

Setting $dk = 0$, this reduces to Solomon's result, i.e.,

$$\rho = i + L\frac{di}{dL} = m. \tag{3A-7}$$

---

28 Ezra Solomon, "Leverage and the Cost of Capital," *op cit.*

# 4

# Dividends, Growth, and Market Imperfections

The previous chapter dealt at some length with the interrelation of debt and equity financing and the valuation of equity shares. In this chapter our examination of the financing decision is broadened by the introduction of dividends as a variable. In turn, this introduces the problem of investment, since if earnings are not entirely paid out as dividends (as was assumed above), they must perforce be reinvested. Reinvestment, moreover, introduces the problem of growth.

It can be shown that, in perfect markets, dividend policy is irrelevant to the price of the stock *if* investment is given. Our considering dividends in the sense in which they do make a difference therefore introduces market imperfections.

Thus in four ways—consideration of dividends, investment, growth, and market imperfections—this chapter will be concerned with a more complicated and more "practical" world.

## Do Dividends Affect Share Valuation?

The problem of dividend policy does not arise when perfect markets and certainty obtain. In that case the value of the equity of a company is simply the present value of the company's future cash flows, net of interest charges. The company will pay out these cash flows as dividends only when it can no longer reinvest them at a rate greater than or equal to the market interest rate. This interest rate, it will be remembered, is unique, and applies to all financing, lending, and investment decisions.

Of course, under conditions of certainty it is difficult to imagine how investment opportunities could exist which would yield a return greater than this interest rate. Under certainty, there would be no reward for foresight, no premium for accepting risk (because there is no risk), and no privileged opportunities (because in a perfect market these would have been taken advantage of long ago). The reason the assumption of certainty is useful is not because it is realistic —since it is impossible—but because it is easier to understand some of the broader concepts if we assume that people act *as if* there were certainty.

Given perfect markets and certainty, rational shareholders will expect financial managers to maximize the present value of cash dividends. The problem in this case is to find the optimal investment plan. Once this optimal plan is established, dividend policy follows as a by-product. Therefore, dividend policy is irrelevant to the choice of an optimal investment plan. In other words, stockholders will be indifferent to alternative investment plans that represent identical present value even if the alternative plans entail radically different patterns of dividend payment. This will be so because a stockholder can distribute the present value of these dividends in any time pattern. He can lend the dividends at the market rate of interest if he wants to defer their consumption; if he wishes to consume before the dividends are actually paid, he can either sell a portion of his stock or borrow the required amount, using the future dividends as collateral. As a result of these opportunities open to the shareholder, the dividend decision need depend on the investment decision and nothing else.

Now suppose that the amount of future dividends is uncertain, but that all investors agree on the *expected* amount and risk of these dividends—in other words, on the "risk class" of the expected dividend stream. We will also assume that the new investments a firm undertakes do not change the firm's risk class, and that the firm is unleveraged.[1]

Like MM[2] and Lintner,[3] we can argue that under these or equivalent assumptions dividend policy does not make any difference *once the*

---

[1] These two assumptions simplify exposition but do not compromise the argument. Of course, the optimal financing decision in practice will reflect considerations of risk and leverage as well as dividend policy. We shall consider the combined effect of these considerations in Chapter 6.

[2] M. H. Miller and F. Modigliani, "Dividend Policy, Growth, and the Valuation of Shares," *Journal of Business*, XXXIV, No. 4 (1961), 411–433.

[3] John Lintner, "Dividends, Earnings, Leverage, Stock Prices and the Supply of Capital to Corporations," *Review of Economics and Statistics*, XLIV, No. 3 (1962), 243–269.

*investment decision is made for the present and all future periods.* We will present a simplified version of their arguments here.

Suppose a hypothetical firm expects constant average earnings and is financed entirely by equity capital. Normally the firm pays out all its earnings as dividends and reinvests that amount of cash equal to depreciation charges. The firm suddenly has the opportunity to invest an amount of cash greater than depreciation charges in period $t = 0$. This investment can be financed either by an issue of additional stock to new investors or by a reduction of the normal dividend.

The additional investment, $I_0$, will, with appropriate reinvestment of a portion of the cash flows it produces, give a constant expected yearly increment to income, $\Delta\bar{Y}$. We will suppose that $\Delta\bar{Y}/k$ is enough greater than $I_0$ so that there is no question that the investment will be adopted.[4] Without saying anything about financing, therefore, we know that the value of the company in $t = 1$ will be $(\bar{Y} + \Delta\bar{Y})/k$.[5]

The value of the company has increased by more than $I_0$. But this increase will occur as soon as the plans for the investment decision are made known and therefore will be reflected in the value of stock held by the initial shareholders before the investment actually takes place; this "windfall gain" income due to the favorable investment opportunity takes place regardless of the financing decision.

Since the relevant objective here is value to the initial shareholders, it is appropriate to look at this hypothetical financing decision from their viewpoint. It will be shown that the present value of the stock held by the initial shareholders is identical whether present dividends are cut or new stock issued and therefore that dividend policy makes no difference in this case. In other words, the choice between financing by retained earnings or new stock issue is moot.

Denote the value of the company to the initial shareholders at time $t = 0$ by $E_0'$. If the investment opportunity had not occurred,

$$E_0' = D_0 + \frac{E_1'}{(1 + k)}\,.$$

---

[4] For an all-equity firm, $k = \rho$. Since the discussion of this chapter will concentrate on the value of dividend streams to shareholders, $k$ will be used, where applicable, rather than $\rho$. It should also be noted that there are conceptual problems in the use of the discount rate $k$ as a "required rate of return," as we shall show in Chapter 5. The present argument is unaffected, as it could be recast in terms of the "certainty equivalent" of $\bar{Y}$, in which case the riskless rate of interest would be used for discounting. The meaning of "certainty equivalent" is explained in Chapter 5.

[5] We assume that returns to the investment $I_0$ will not begin until $t = 1$. Also, remember that we assume $\bar{Y}$ and $(\bar{Y} + \Delta\bar{Y})$ to be in the same risk class.

Since $E_1' = \bar{Y}/k$,

$$E_0' = D_0 + \frac{\bar{Y}/k}{(1+k)} = D_0 + \frac{\bar{Y}}{k(1-k)}. \tag{4-1}$$

If it has been decided to issue new equity to provide the needed funds for the investment $I_0$, then the dividend in $t = 0$ is $D_0 = Y_0$, and

$$E_0' = Y_0 + \frac{\bar{Y} + (\Delta\bar{Y} - \bar{A})}{k(1+k)}. \tag{4-2}$$

where $\bar{A}$ is the constant expected return required by the *new shareholders* over time.

If it is decided to reduce the dividend and not to issue new stock, then the alternative value for $E_0'$ is

$$E_0' = Y_0 - I_0 + \frac{\bar{Y} + \Delta\bar{Y}}{k(1+k)}. \tag{4-3}$$

Obviously, $E_0'$ is the same under the two alternatives only if

$$I_0 = \frac{\bar{A}}{k(1+k)}.$$

If the new shareholders discount future returns of this company at the *same rate* $k$ as the original shareholders, then *in period* $t = 1$ the value of the newly issued shares will be the capitalized value of expected dividends—that is, $\bar{A}/k$. But since the new shareholders will not receive any dividends until period $t = 1$, the value of the new shares at $t = 0$ will be less by a factor of $1/(1+k)$. Thus $I_0$, the amount new shareholders will contribute if promised an annual dividend $\bar{A}$ starting at $t = 1$, will be

$$I_0 = \frac{\bar{A}}{k(1+k)}. \tag{4-4}$$

If the new shareholders require a rate of return greater (or less) than $k$, then a higher (or lower) stream of promised earnings $\bar{A}$ will be required, making the issue of new stock less (or more) attractive to present shareholders. But if the same rate $k$ is demanded, then the initial stockholders will indeed be indifferent to the two financing alternatives, since it will be true that

$$I_0 = \frac{\bar{A}}{k(1+k)}.$$

We have used the simple case where investment gives a constant expected yearly income, but the proof would follow for any future cash flow pattern.[6]

Under present assumptions, our proof that the value of the firm is independent of dividend policy means that any reduction in current dividends paid to the original shareholders will be exactly offset by a capital gain realized by these shareholders. In other words, dividend policy cannot affect the over-all value of the firm—it can only affect the form in which this value is realized.

## Why Dividend Policy May Affect the Value of the Company to Its Shareholders

The proof of the previous section has assumed that the investment plan of the firm is given for the present and future periods and that all present and prospective shareholders require the same rate of return $k$.

We could argue that dividend policies affect value to present shareholders if these policies change as a result of changes in the firm's investment plan. This is an incorrect argument, however, since dividend policy becomes irrelevant *once the revised investment plan is made known to investors.*

However, dividend policies would make a difference in valuation if present and prospective stockholders disagreed as to the present value of expected future earnings, given the investment decision. In this case, in order to obtain $I_0$ from an issue of new stock, the company might have to promise a return of more than (or less than) $\bar{A}$ to the new stockholders, in which case the original shareholders would not be indifferent to the two given financing alternatives.

Moreover, if market imperfections exist, it is possible that investors will value certain *patterns* of dividend payment more highly than others. For instance, suppose investors depend on dividends to support present consumption expenditures, and that if dividends are postponed, the stockholders are not able or willing to borrow against the (increased) future dividends and not willing to sell a portion of their stock. For instance, the risk involved in borrowing might be greater for a small stockholder than for the company; or such a shareholder might not be able to borrow except at a rate greater than $k$. This shareholder might also be unwilling to sell part of his stock holdings if, for instance, he thought the stock were undervalued in the market, or because of tax considerations.

The implication for the company is that, when these or similar market imperfections obtain, dividend policy does affect value and

[6] For a more extensive discussion, see Miller and Modigliani, *op. cit.*

that certain patterns of dividend payouts are worth more to investors than others. We can list several other possible considerations that imply the same conclusion:

1. In general, a company that foregoes present dividends does so in order to increase the present value of future dividends. In doing so, however, it is shifting the time pattern of the company's future dividends further into the future. Gordon[7] and Walter,[8] among others, have suggested that dividends expected in the near future are normally less risky than those expected farther in the future. If we assume risk aversion, dividends expected in the far future might therefore be discounted at a higher rate to compensate for the extra risk. This adds another dimension to the dividend-investment decision, one which we shall discuss more fully later in this chapter and in Chapter 5.

2. We have assumed that the stockholder can always reinvest dividends at a rate of return $k$. This may not be strictly true. For one thing, he must pay personal income taxes on the dividends he receives. Transaction costs, such as broker's fees, further reduce the portion of the dividend which the stockholder can reinvest. From another point of view, underwriting costs of a new stock issue would lead to similar complications.

3. Differential tax rates may affect the dividend decision. Since capital gains rates are lower than ordinary income tax rates for all taxpayers, stockholders would prefer a dollar's worth of price appreciation to a dollar's worth of dividends. From the point of view of the shareholders, emphasis on "growth" rather than current dividends would appear to be preferable if sufficiently profitable investment alternatives are available to the firm.

4. If expectations of future prospects of a company are variable, what factors are most likely to cause these expectations to change? One such factor is dividend policy. In many cases, the raising or lowering of dividends is regarded by investors as a signal of how management views a company's prospects. Therefore lowering dividends could cause the price of a stock to fall, even if the foregone dividends are used for investment which is expected to produce more than adequate returns.

5. We can add a final item to this list by restating a point. One of the crucial assumptions in the proof that "dividend policy does not affect value" was that all present and prospective shareholders agree

---

[7] M. J. Gordon, *The Investment, Financing, and Valuation of the Corporation* (Homewood, Ill.: Richard D. Irwin, 1962), Chapter 5. Also see Gordon's article, "Optical Investment and Financing Policy," *Journal of Finance*, XVIII, No. 2 (1963), 264–272.

[8] J. E. Walter, "Dividend Policy: Its Influence on the Value of the Enterprise," *Journal of Finance*, XVIII, No. 2 (1963), 280–291.

on the risk class and prospects of the company. In practice, this is unlikely. Both the information available to shareholders and their subjective evaluations of this information are likely to vary. Moreover, we would expect that those persons whose estimates of a particular company's prospects are most favorable would already have purchased that company's stock. In this case, the buyers of a new stock issue would be less optimistic and would demand a relatively higher proportion of the future earnings as a return on their investment.

Although some patterns of dividend payment may be more desirable than others from the point of view of investors, it should not be concluded that the financial manager is never justified in departing from a "desirable" pattern. Considered in a vacuum, some shifts in dividend policy may reduce the value of the firm to its shareholders—for instance, a sudden reduction in dividends might have this effect if a policy of stable dividends had been followed in the past. However, if in this case the foregone dividends are reinvested in a sufficiently profitable project, the *net* change in the value of the firm to its shareholders resulting from a shift in dividend policy in conjunction with the new investment will be positive. The net change in value is precisely what the financial manager must consider. In short, dividend policies and investment opportunities must be considered simultaneously if the optimal financial decision is to be reached.

## Dividends and Earnings as a Basis for Stock Values

In most of the initial part of this chapter, we have assumed that all earnings are paid out as dividends. If only a portion of earnings is distributed, what is the result? On this issue we are faced with (at least) two apparently contrasting views. On the one hand, Graham, Dodd, and Cottle write:

> This predominant role of dividends has found full reflection in a generally accepted theory of investment value which states that a common stock is worth the sum of all the dividends to be paid on it in the future, each discounted to its present worth.[9]

As an example of another point of view, we can cite MM:

> . . . as long as management is presumed to be acting in the best interest of the stockholders, retained earnings can be regarded as equivalent to a fully subscribed, pre-emptive issue of common stock. Hence, for

[9] B. Graham, D. L. Dodd, and S. Cottle, *Security Analysis: Principles and Techniques* (4th ed.) (New York: McGraw-Hill 1962), pp. 480–481.

present purposes, the division of the stream between cash dividends and retained earnings in any period is a mere detail.[10]

The question raised here is: what do investors "really" evaluate when deciding whether to purchase the stock of a given company? Or, accepting the concept of discounted present value, what "returns" are to be discounted—earnings or dividends?

This book assumes the value of a share of stock is the discounted present value of the dividends expected to be paid to the owners of that share. The purpose of this section is to show why this assumption is acceptable.

But first let us clear the ground by eliminating a fertile source of confusion that arises because we have generally represented the value of each of the $n$ shares of a firm's stock by $P = (1/n)(\bar{Y}/k)$ or $P = (1/n)(\bar{D}/k)$. This was possible only because the expected value of $\bar{Y}$ or $\bar{D}$ was treated as constant for the indefinite future. For instance, in the MM model discussed in the last chapter we assumed, in effect, that expected future earnings were constant and entirely distributed as dividends. In this case, $\bar{D} = \bar{Y}$, and

$$P = \frac{1}{n} \sum_{t=1}^{\infty} \frac{\bar{Y}}{(1+k)^t} = \frac{1}{n} \sum_{t=1}^{\infty} \frac{\bar{D}}{(1+k)^t} \tag{4-5}$$

is equivalent to

$$P = \frac{1}{n}\frac{\bar{Y}}{k} = \frac{1}{n}\frac{\bar{D}}{k}\,. \tag{4-6}$$

However, this simplified case will rarely obtain. We cannot expect the price of stock to depend on current earnings or current dividends alone. Nor does observing the ratio $D_t/nP_t$ or $Y_t/nP_t$ at a given time $t$ necessarily constitute an observation of the stockholders' "required rate of return" $k$.

This point is widely recognized; still, since expectations are hard to come by in any exact form, current earnings and/or dividends are often used for "practical purposes" as a basis for valuation.

In any case, there is no reason to be surprised if some stocks sell at prices such that the observed dividend yield, $D_t/nP_t$, is low in comparison with other observed market rates of return. Our presumption would be that $P_t$ is high, because the value at time $t$ of dividends

[10] F. Modigliani and M. H. Miller, "The Cost of Capital, Corporation Finance, and the Theory of Investment," *American Economic Review*, XLVIII, No. 3 (1958), 261–297, reprinted in E. Solomon, ed., *The Management of Corporate Capital* (New York: Free Press of Glencoe, 1959), p. 154. This statement is, of course, taken out of context, and the reader should not attempt to infer from it the logic of the MM position.

expected in subsequent periods is high. In a rough way, "growth stocks" may be said to illustrate this situation.

Now, at the beginning of this section we quoted MM's statement that "the division of the [earnings] stream between cash dividends and retained earnings is a mere detail." We have seen this is so, given the conditions under which dividend policy makes no difference. But even if these conditions hold, are we then justified in postulating that the value of a share of stock is the discounted present value of the stock's *pro rata* share of the firm's expected future earnings, $\bar{Y}_t$? The answer is no. As MM themselves argue, such a postulate involves double counting.[11] This fallacy hinges on the fact that the actual income in any future period $t$, $Y_t$, is likely to represent in part a return to earnings reinvested in previous periods. In other words, a firm which reinvests a portion of a given period's earnings makes a sacrifice in the hope of future returns. If the present value of these returns outweighs the sacrifice, then the value of the firm increases. But we are clearly not justified in assuming that the value of the firm is increased by the amount of the investment *and* by the present value of the returns expected because the investment is made.

It turns out that if we adjust for this double counting we are led back to the "dividend model" of stock value.

This will become clearer if we examine the total cash flow of a firm in any given year, $F_t$. The main sources and uses of $F_t$ are as follows:

1. One source is funds from operations, net of taxes and changes in invested capital, which we shall designate $C_t$. This will normally be a source of funds, i.e., $C_t > 0$.
2. Another source is funds contributed by new borrowing or stock issues, less any repayment of principal of loans. We will represent this source or use by $Z_t$.
3. The firm's gross investment, $I_t$, normally is a use of funds. That is, in most cases $I_t$ will be positive as funds are absorbed by replacement of worn-out or obsolescent machines, by purchase of new capital equipment, or by increases in working capital requirements. But it can easily happen that $I_t < 0$—e.g., if a firm sells a part of its assets or because of a reduction in working capital requirements. As the adjective "gross" implies, $I_t$ includes no adjustment for depreciation.
4. A portion of $F_t$ may be paid out as interest to present and/or future creditors. This amount, using our previous notation, is $i_tL_t$.
5. A portion of $F_t$ may be paid as dividends to the owners of additional shares, if any, created by stock issue between period zero and period $t$. Call this amount $A_t$, where $A_t \geqq 0$.

[11] Miller and Modigliani, "Dividend Policy, Growth and the Valuation of Shares," *op. cit.*, p. 420. The same point has been made by Diran Bodenhorn, "On the Problems of Capital Budgeting," *Journal of Finance*, XIV, No. 4 (1959), 473–492 and Lintner, *op. cit.*, especially pp. 248*ff*.

6. The remainder of $F_t$ is simply the dividends, $D_t$, paid to the shares of stock in existence at time zero. Now we can write the equality of sources and uses as

$$Z_t + C_t = D_t + I_t + A_t + i_t L_t$$

or

$$D_t = C_t - i_t L_t - A_t - I_t + Z_t. \tag{4-7}$$

From the point of view of investors evaluating a firm's stock at time zero, we can thus say that $\bar{D}_t$, the dividend expected to be paid at time $t$, will be the total expected cash flow of the firm less expected amounts of interest payments, dividend payments to holders of new shares issued after time zero but before time $t$, and investment expenditures. Similarly, the value of one of the $n$ original shares at time zero may be defined by

$$P_0 = \frac{1}{n} \sum_{t=1}^{\infty} \frac{\bar{D}_t}{(1 + k)^t} = \frac{1}{n} \sum_{t=1}^{\infty} \frac{\bar{F}_t - i_t \bar{L}_t - \bar{A}_t - \bar{I}_t}{(1 + k)^t}, \tag{4-8}$$

where we interpret $k$ as the investors' "required rate of return."

Parenthetically, we could derive a more general version of Eq. (4-8) if we discounted by the factor $1/(1 + k_t)^t$, where $k_t$ applies *only* to the expected dividend $\bar{D}_t$, $k_{t+1}$ *only* to $\bar{D}_{t+1}$, and so on. This will be discussed further in Chapter 5. For present purposes, Eq. (4-8) in effect assumes the less general case where $k_1 = k_2 = \ldots = k_t = \ldots = k_\infty$.

Now suppose the firm's accounting procedures generate some arbitrary depreciation figure $W_t$, for period $t$. Then, adding $(+W_t - W_t)$ to the right-hand side of Eq. (4-7) and grouping the terms, we have

$$D_t = (C_t - i_t L_t - W_t) - (I_t - W_t - Z_t) - A_t. \tag{4-9}$$

But the accounting income of the firm, $Y_t$, is given by $Y_t = (C_t - i_t L_t - W_t)$. Moreover, the term $(I_t - W_t - F_t)$ is that proportion of gross investment which must be financed with *retained earnings*, since retained earnings are by definition reinvested.

Let $\bar{Y}_t^R$ represent the amount of earnings stockholders expect to be reinvested. Then we can rewrite Eq. (4-8) as

$$P_0 = \frac{1}{n} \sum_{t=1}^{\infty} \frac{\bar{D}_t}{(1 + k)^t} = \frac{1}{n} \sum_{t=1}^{\infty} \frac{\bar{Y}_t - \bar{Y}_t^R - \bar{A}_t}{(1 + k)^t}. \tag{4-10}$$

It is precisely in this sense that the dividend and earnings "approaches" to valuation are equivalent.[12] This is so because Eq. (4-10)

[12] MM and Lintner reach essentially this conclusion. See MM's "Dividend Policy, Growth and the Valuation of Shares," *op. cit.*, pp. 418*ff.*, and Lintner, *op. cit.*

avoids the double-counting fallacy which invalidates the naïve earnings approach, and, moreover, because the validity of Eq. (4-10) is largely protected from the vagaries of accounting practice, since expected depreciation, $\bar{W}_t$, can vary widely under "generally accepted accounting principles without affecting Eq. (4–10)."

Although the "sophisticated" earnings approach embodied in Eq. (4-10) is as valid as the dividends approach, we shall assume subsequently that the value of a share of stock is given by the discounted present value of expected future dividends. This allows a single starting point for the discussion to come.

## The Problem of Growth in General

Thus far we have not dealt with growth *qua* growth. As will become apparent, growth raises both opportunities and problems for analysis of stock prices and the financing decision. This section will focus on the most comprehensive work in this area, M. J. Gordon's *The Investment, Financing and Valuation of the Corporation.* An outline of his basic model follows.[13]

Assume a company that retains a constant proportion, $b$, of earnings in the present and every future period, and that investment in any period adds a constant increment to earnings in every subsequent period. Let $r$, the return to new investment, be this increment to income divided by the incremental investment. This $r$ is also assumed to be a constant. Also, assume that the company finances its investments entirely by retained earnings. Then,

$$D_t = (1 - b) Y_t,$$

and

$$Y_{t+1} = Y_t + rbY_t = Y_t(1 + rb)$$

at every point in the future. Note that $bY_t$ is the proportion of earnings reinvested, and that $rbY_t$ is the incremental earnings to this investment. This implies a constant growth rate, $rb$, for earnings, so that

$$Y_t = Y_0(1 + rb)^t \cong Y_0e^{rbt}. \tag{4-11}$$

---

[13] Gordon, *The Investment, Financing and Valuation of the Corporation*, Chapter 3. The model was first proposed in M. J. Gordon and Eli Shapiro, "Capital Equipment Analysis: The Required Rate of Profit," *Management Science*, III (1956), 102–110. The article is reprinted in Solomon, *The Management of Corporate Capital, op. cit.*

If the value of the firm in year zero is the present value of all future dividends, discounted at a constant rate $k$, then we can write $V_0$ as

$$V_0 = \int_0^\infty D_t e^{-kt}\, dt. \tag{4-12}$$

Substituting from Eq. (4-11) gives:

$$V_0 = \int_0^\infty (1 - b)\, Y_0 e^{rbt} e^{-kt}\, dt.$$

If $k$ is greater than $rb$, we can integrate to obtain:

$$V_0 = \frac{(1 - b)\, Y_0}{k - rb}. \tag{4-13}$$

Alternatively, if $V_0$ is known, $k$ can be determined.

$$k = \frac{(1 - b)\, Y_0}{V_0} + br = d + br, \tag{4-14}$$

where $d$ is the current dividend yield.

This model's particular merit is that it gives a measure of stock prices in terms of current, rather than expected, values of $r$, $b$, and $Y_t$. These current values could presumably be gleaned from readily available data. This is not to say that expectations have been ignored; instead, Gordon has offered a hypothesis of how expectations of future dividends are reflected in current prices.

In his empirical work, however, Gordon has made substantial modifications to the model embodied in Eqs. (4-13) and (4-14). To see why more sophisticated models are necessary, we shall examine some central features of the simple model at this point.

First, the model assumes not only that shares are valued at the discounted present value of expected future dividends but also that payout ratios are constant for all future periods. Thus if all current earnings are reinvested, the simple model would assume that $b = 1$ for all future periods. But if $b$ is constant and equal to one, no dividends can be expected at any time; accordingly, Eq. (4-13) would predict that $V_0 = 0$. But experience contradicts such a prediction, since we often observe that stocks which pay no current dividends sell at positive prices.

Gordon's model also recognizes that the dividend decision is the obverse of the investment decision. We can therefore differentiate Eq. (4-13) with respect to $b$, the proportion of earnings retained and invested. If $k$ and $r$ are independent of $b$, this gives

$$\frac{\partial V_0}{\partial b} = \frac{Y_0}{(k - br)^2} \cdot (r - k). \tag{4-15}$$

Note that if $r = k$, $V_0$ is independent of the amount retained. If $r < k$, then Eq. (4-15) indicates that the firm ought to pay out all of its earnings in dividends; i.e., the optimal value of $b$ is zero. If $r > k$, the firm ought to reinvest all earnings; i.e., the optimal value of $b$ is one. In fact, in this case the model could be interpreted as predicting that the company would expand without limit, since new stock could be issued at a cost of only $k$ to shareholders, assuming prospective shareholders shared the initial shareholders' expectations and attitudes toward risk.

This prediction, of course, is also at odds with common sense. The next section of this chapter, therefore, will take another look at the assumptions of the simple Gordon model.

## Gordon's Assumptions in the Simple Growth Model

The crucial assumptions of the simple model presented in the previous section were: (a) that a constant proportion of earnings will be reinvested in all future periods, (b) that a constant rate of return is earned on all future investments of the firm, and (c) that expected dividends are discounted at a constant required rate of return, $k$. Let us examine each of these assumptions in turn.

In general, a constant payout ratio may be fairly realistic, since the research of Lintner,[14] for instance, has shown that corporations usually have a target payout ratio to which they adhere fairly closely over the long run. (This does not necessarily mean that this is good policy for these companies, however.)

The assumption of a constant rate of return $r$ is more at odds with normal conceptions—the relationship usually assumed is that $r$ declines with the volume of investment, since the most profitable investments are presumably undertaken first. The idea of a constant $r$ would be more palatable if we looked at it from the point of view of the stockholder, who may not have any clear idea of how $r$ varies with investment and therefore might regard this variable as a long-run, average rate of return, divorced from the returns of individual investment projects.

We may begin discussion of the third assumption by noting that Gordon's model can only be derived if $k$ is greater than $rb$. In Eq.

[14] John Lintner, "Distribution of Incomes of Corporations Between Dividends, Retained Earnings and Taxation," *American Economic Review*, XLIV, No. 2 (1956), 97–113.

(4-13), for instance, it can be seen that as the value of $rb$ approaches $k$, the price of the stock approaches infinity. In the long run it is hard to imagine the case where the expected growth rate is greater than $k$, since if companies continued to grow at a rate $rb > k$, eventually the rate $k$ would itself change. Therefore this restriction, at least in the long run, is not likely to cause enormous amounts of trouble.

But we cannot rely on "the long run" to remove this problem completely. Financial managers frequently have the opportunity to invest in individual projects earning a rate $r > k$, and we should not be surprised in practice to find some companies which can earn an *average* rate $r > k$ on new projects. But if this is so and $r$ is constant, Eq. (4-13) indicates that the price of the stock can be made infinite by choice of an appropriate retention rate.[15] Since an infinite stock price is impossible, in such a case the simple Gordon model is of little use for financial decision-making.

There are two reasonable ways to preserve the model's operational usefulness. These are either to assume that $r$ is a decreasing function of $b$, or that $k$ is an increasing function of $b$. Gordon emphasizes the latter "solution," arguing that higher present investment at the expense of dividends shifts the pattern of dividend payout farther into the future, thus increasing $k$, since the over-all riskiness of the stock's expected stream of dividends is increased.

It will be useful to state this more precisely. Gordon implies that returns expected in the near future are normally less risky than returns expected in the far future; that is, the returns expected to a given investment ten years hence will, *ceteris paribus*, be more risky than expected returns five years hence, simply because we can foresee the future only hazily and the distant future hardly at all.

Thus in Eq. (4-13) we have one variable $k$ to describe risks and time preference with respect to a shifting, complicated pattern of expected future dividends. Clearly, we must interpret $k$ as a combination measure reflecting this pattern. Specifically, define the rate $k_t$ as the rate of discount the stockholder applies *only* to $\bar{D}_t$. Thus $k_{t+1}$ is relevant *only* to the evaluation of $\bar{D}_{t+1}$, $k_{t+2}$ is relevant *only* to $\bar{D}_{t+2}$, and so on. Then we can determine some *composite discount rate*, $\hat{k}$, such that

$$(4\text{-}16) \qquad V_0 = \sum_{t=1}^{\infty} \frac{\bar{D}_t}{(1 + k_t)^t} = \sum_{t=1}^{\infty} \frac{\bar{D}_t}{(1 + \hat{k})^t}.$$

Strictly speaking, it is this composite rate which should be used in Gordon's model.

Gordon's model is thus unrealistic in that it describes the shareholder as actually using a single discount rate $\hat{k}$ to evaluate expected

[15] See Bodenhorn, *op. cit.*, p. 487.

dividends, rather than the whole spectrum of rates $k_t$ that actually may be relevant. We have, therefore, no guarantee that $\hat{k}$ can actually be observed; furthermore, as we shall see in Chapter 5, the use of a single, constant discount rate can lead to serious errors in decision-making.

In any case, Gordon drops the assumption of a constant discount rate, arguing instead that the rates $k_t$ tend to rise for periods that are farther in the future. If this is so, the composite discount rate will normally rise as present dividends are reduced to allow greater investment expenditures.

Gordon uses this conclusion to propose another approach to a problem discussed before—i.e., whether dividend policy makes any difference. He argues that, since $\hat{k}$ is likely to be a positive function of $b$, the shifting of the pattern of dividend payouts usually does make a difference. MM would reply that the distant dividends are more risky only because investments with distant returns are normally more risky, and that dividend policy remains a mere detail once the firm's investment plan is given.[16]

## Empirical Tests and Problems of Measurement

Empirical proof or disproof of theoretical work such as Gordon's is extremely difficult—so difficult, in fact, that, although a good deal of empirical work has been done,[17] we can report no consensus on which of the theoretical conclusions of this chapter actually hold in practice. Because of the complex statistical issues involved, we can do little here to resolve these empirical problems.

Nevertheless, it is important to emphasize why these problems exist. Probably their most important cause is that theories of stock valuation are all based to some extent on variables which cannot be measured directly—that is, the expectations of investors regarding the amount and risk of future dividends. Thus to be meaningful, empirical investigations must make some assumptions about what aspects of the historical record provide useful clues to investors' expectations. Several items widely regarded as clues are discussed in this section.

One obvious clue would seem to be the amount of earnings retained and reinvested. If a firm is acting in the best interests of its shareholders, future dividends expected from investment of a dollar of

---

16 The reader can examine this "controversy" in more detail by contrasting the arguments of Gordon, "Optimal Investment and Financing Policy," *op. cit.*, and Miller and Modigliani, "Dividend Policy, Growth and the Valuation of Shares," *op. cit.*, pp. 424*ff*.

17 Readers interested in pursuing this subject further will find the authors mentioned in this section a good introduction and a source of further references.

retained earnings should be worth at least as much as a dollar of dividends—otherwise the funds should not be reinvested. But straightforward statistical tests tend to show that dividends are "worth more" to stockholders than retained earnings, so much so that a popular security analysis text has given dividends four times the weight of earnings in a "rule of thumb" valuation formula.[18] Faced with these results, we must conclude either that (a) our theories are only partially adequate, or (b) that retained earnings do not provide as simple a clue to investors' expectations as has been supposed. Although the former conclusion will inevitably be true, Irwin Friend and Marshall Puckett arrive at the latter conclusion in a recent article. They argue that, when certain statistical biases and problems have been overcome, "there is little basis for the customary view that . . . a dollar of dividends has several times the impact on price of a dollar of retained earnings."[19] However, the route to their conclusions is not, as scholars are fond of saying, "intuitively obvious."

Another useful clue can be found in historical rates of growth of dividends or earnings, since it seems reasonable that investors will tend to extrapolate past rates of growth in estimating the trend of future dividends. Gordon takes this approach, of course, since his basic model assumes a constant rate of growth for all future periods. In fact, in Gordon's empirical tests the clue provided by past rates of growth turns out to be highly significant in explaining variations in share prices.[20]

One item for which direct clues are particularly scarce is the risk which investors impute to expected dividends. Expectations of risk are particularly elusive because there is only one "true" dividend, $D_t$; we cannot observe, say, random variations of $D_t$ about some mean value, even though we often use "subjective probability distributions" to describe investors' estimates of risk. The risk of an expected dividend is an entirely subjective element, which disappears when the dividend is paid.

Ultimately, we can observe risk only insofar as it affects value. It is from this point of view that the "required rate of return" is often used as an indicator of investors' estimates of risk. The reasoning is that the greater the perceived risk of expected dividends, the lower the present value of these dividends to investors. Equation (4-16) is then used to derive a composite rate $\hat{k}$ that is supposed to measure the degree to which risk affects value. But as we noted when the com-

[18] Graham, Dodd, and Cottle, *op. cit.*, p. 518.

[19] Irwin Friend and Marshall Puckett, "Dividends and Stock Prices," *American Economic Review*, LIV, No. 5 (1964), 656–682. Quotation on p. 680.

[20] For Gordon's results, see *The Investment, Financing, and Valuation of the Corporation*, *op. cit.*, pp. 167*ff*. Also, see Burton G. Malkiel, "Equity Yields, Growth and the Structure of Share Prices," *American Economic Review*, LIII (1963), 1004–1031, for a discussion of growth.

posite rate was introduced, $\hat{k}$ may not be observable, since it is an artificial "weighted average" of the individual rates $k_t$ that are generally considered relevant to valuation. This difficulty is a symptom of our naïve treatment of risk in Chapters 3 and 4; a more complete discussion of risk and uncertainty will be undertaken in the next chapter.

Some other factors that seem to be clues to investors' estimates of risk have been identified, however. Gordon, for instance, finds that company size, liquidity of assets, and past stability of earnings seem to affect stock prices[21]; that is, it appears that investors regard the expected dividends of large, liquid, and historically stable companies as relatively less risky than those of companies without these characteristics. Benishay's work[22] corroborates Gordon's findings with regard to size and earnings stability.

## Conclusion

We have now covered most of the theoretical ideas that have been advanced to deal with the traditional concerns of corporate finance. So many variables are relevant to these topics that our treatment has necessarily been variegated. However, all the topics are similar in two respects. First, they are unified by the objective of financial management that we have assumed in investigating them. This unifying theme will be further developed in Chapter 6. Second, behind our discussion of these topics there is a common problem which we have not yet faced squarely. This problem is to determine more precisely the effects of uncertainty on value. We shall turn to this task in the next chapter.

---

[21] Gordon, *The Investment, Financing, and Valuation of the Corporation*, *op. cit.*, pp. 167*ff*.

[22] Haskel Benishay, "Variability in Earnings-Price Ratios of Corporate Equities," *American Economic Review*, LI, No. 1 (1961), 81–94.

# 5

# Uncertainty and Value

Risk and uncertainty have played an important, but submerged, role in the preceding chapters. We have made various assumptions to fit various arguments, but however reasonable these assumptions seemed in previous contexts, it is time for an exposé. It will quickly become apparent that financial theory provides a far from exact description of the manner in which risk and uncertainty affect financial decisions.

Our explanation of the effects of risk and uncertainty on finance is generally plausible but vague. Unfortunately, present techniques do not allow a precise "solution" to the problems created by risk and uncertainty. Even the *measurement* of risk poses problems. But at the end of this chapter we will be able to reformulate under conditions of uncertainty the concepts of income and value introduced in Chapter 2.[1]

## Introductory Comments on Risk and Uncertainty

One way to avoid the problem of uncertainty is to assume that decisions are based only on expected values. This is another way of

---

[1] The discussion of risk and uncertainty in this chapter is far from all-inclusive, as frequent reference to other works indicates. The present chapter is best regarded as an introduction to these topics.

saying that decision makers, whether management or stockholders, are indifferent to risk—an assumption positing an antiseptic world in which people would act as if expected returns were certain to be realized. Normally, however, a subjective element is inescapable. The postulate that some Mr. X is averse to risk is a statement about his attitudes. These attitudes cannot be regarded mechanistically: we can object if the attitudes are self-contradictory, or if they ignore relevant information, but we cannot object just because they may, in our opinion, be "unreasonable." (That is, we can say very little in the latter case without imposing an essentially *moral* judgment on Mr. X.)

This is not presented as philosophy but to point out that, although we can in some cases develop "measures" of attitudes, such measures never have the same concreteness as saying, "Mr. X weighs 170 lbs." "Measures of attitudes," in fact, is a potentially misleading phrase, since such measuring systems are attempts to describe and predict Mr. X's actions in given situations and are not intended to "explain" his attitudes in any way.

In this chapter, we shall take as given subjective estimates of both the expected values of future returns and the probability distributions of these returns. The dispersion of the subjective probability distribution may be thought of as varying inversely with the degree of confidence of a decision maker regarding his estimate.

Temporarily, however, we shall relinquish the use of the present value concept. This is necessary because the present value of, say, expected future dividends to a stockholder depends in part on the risk perceived by the stockholder; and risk is precisely the problem at hand.

In assuming subjective estimates of expected future values and probability distributions of these expected values, we have in effect sidestepped the distinction made by many authors between risk and uncertainty. Formally, risk refers to random events, the robability distribution of which is known. Uncertainty in the formal sense refers to cases where probability distributions are not known and thus are not wholly meaningful.[2] Where uncertainty in this sense holds, analyses in terms of expected values and probability distributions are not

---

[2] R. D. Luce and H. Raiffa, *Games and Decisions: Introduction and Critical Survey* (New York: John Wiley & Sons, 1957), p. 13. According to their classification, this chapter's subject matter would be neither risk nor uncertainty but a combination of the two. The past performance and present characteristics of companies, securities, and markets normally provide *some* information as to the relative likelihoods of possible future outcomes, even though probability distributions cannot be assigned with absolute confidence. Thus, although uncertainty in the formal sense is likely to be present in most financing decisions, we will deal with risk and uncertainty in an essentially parallel manner, and the formal distinction between the terms will not be rigorously maintained.

on firm ground. Financial decisions are perhaps best regarded as subject to a *mixture* of risk and uncertainty in the formal sense of these terms. That is, subjective estimates of expected values and their probability distributions imply at least *partial* uncertainty in the formal sense.

We assume, in spite of this, that stockholders are willing to base their actions on these subjective estimates. To be sure, this rules out some other approaches to decision-making under uncertainty.[3] On the other hand, although subjective estimates are of questionable usefulness in some instances, other approaches are not overwhelmingly superior and would require a substantial detour from our main argument.

## The Basis for Risk Aversion

Regardless of their disagreement on most other issues, the authors discussed thus far have been practically unanimous in the opinion that investors by and large are averse to risk. For example, MM define a required rate of return, $\rho$, for an unleveraged equity stream of a given risk class. It is clear from their exposition that they expect $\rho$ to be greater than the riskless rate of interest; the only possible reason is risk aversion. The traditional position on the problem of capital structure also assumes risk aversion.

Risk aversion can be formally defined as follows: a person is averse to risk in a given situation if, given the choice between two returns with the same expected monetary value, he chooses the alternative with the less risk, risk being defined, for the time being, as some function of the dispersion of the subjective probability distributions of the expected returns.

Risk aversion has a strong introspective basis. Nearly everyone buys some sort of insurance, and the fact that insurance companies make money indicates that, on the average, the expected present value of an investment in insurance is negative. Few people would gamble their life savings in a poker game, even on an especially good hand.

Consider Fig. 5-1, which will serve as an introduction to the concept of utility. Let us reintroduce Mr. X, whose utility function, $U = g(M)$, is plotted against monetary value, $M$, to be received in a given future year. Assuming that Mr. X can consistently express his preferences as to various values of $M$, we can construct a utility curve that summarizes these preferences.

---

[3] That is, approaches which do not depend on the direct use of probability distributions—e.g., the minimax criterion, the "potential surprise" approach, etc. See Luce and Raiffa, *op. cit.*, Chapter 13, for a more complete discussion.

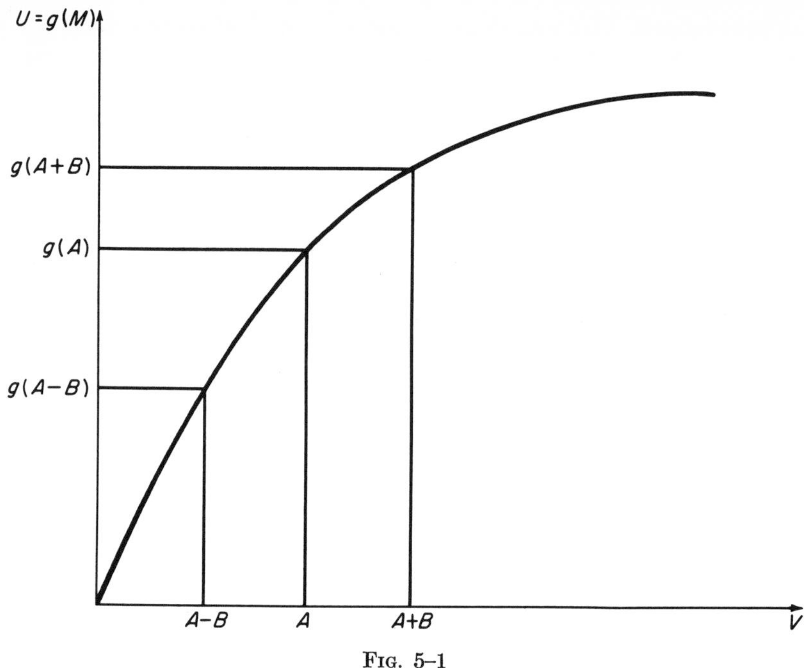


FIG. 5–1

Drawing the curve $U = g(M)$ upward-sloping and convex to the origin reflects two assumptions: (a) Mr. X always prefers a higher amount to a lower one; and (b) each successive identical positive increment of money is "worth less" to Mr. X than the preceding increment. In other words the marginal utility of money is declining, although it is always positive.[4]

Suppose Mr. X has an income $A$ in a given year, and is offered the chance to bet the amount $B$ on the flip of a fair coin. The expected value of this bet is zero, since the possibilities of winning or losing $B$ are equally probable. The possible loss of utility, $g(A) - g(A - B)$, however, is greater than the possible gain, $g(A + B) - g(A)$, because of the shape of the utility curve. Thus Mr. X's expected utility declines if the gamble is accepted. Fig. 5-1 shows this situation.

Therefore the assumption of a utility function and declining marginal utility of $M$ is sufficient to establish risk aversion.

---

[4] For a justification, see Jack Hirshleifer, "The Investment Decision Under Uncertainty" (mimeo., University of California at Los Angeles, 1964), pp. 18–19. Pages 26–37 of Hirshleifer's article discuss a classic work in this area, i.e., M. Friedman and L. J. Savage, "The Utility Analysis of Choices Involving Risk," *Journal of Political Economy*, LVI (1948) 279–304, reprinted in American Economic Association (G. J. Stigler and K. E. Boulding, eds.) *Readings in Price Theory* (Homewood, Ill.: Richard D. Irwin, 1952).

Unfortunately, assuming risk aversion in general is prevented by the simple observation that people do gamble, even though most gambling is undertaken at moderately unfavorable odds. Gambling is the most obvious case in which attempting to describe a person's preferences in terms of monetary income versus risk may be shortsighted. For many of us, there is a certain pleasurable thrill in gambling. It seems reasonable enough to suppose that, for many people, the satisfactions of gambling *qua* gambling are sufficient to overcome basic attitudes of risk aversion, especially when the sums involved are small compared with the gambler's total personal wealth. At the other extreme, a person with a family to support who earns $5,000 yearly would be considered neurotic (at least) if he bet $5,000 on a flip of a coin.

In any case, we cannot deny that stockholders may not be averse to risk. The existence of gambling is one reason why management should be cautious in imputing attitudes toward risk to stockholders. There are other reasons for caution. For example, letting Mr. X assume the role of a hypothetical shareholder:

1. Mr. X and management may not agree on the degree of risk inherent in a given proposal or situation. After all, the riskiness of the firm must be evaluated by a subjective judgment of whatever information is available, and both the subjective judgment and the information available to different observers may vary. Mr. X might be much more willing to bet large sums if he thought the dice were loaded in his favor.
2. If Mr. X were a millionaire with large holdings of many companies' common stocks, he would probably have attitudes toward risk quite different from those of a small stockholder whose equity in a given company is a large part of his total wealth.

## The Utility Function[5]

Obviously, risk and uncertainty are complex and slippery subjects. Thus far, we have resolved sample problems by assuming complete knowledge—shown, for instance, by an indifference map—of the preferences of stockholders such as the hypothetical Mr. X.

Practically speaking, it is rarely possible for a financial manager to know the preferences of stockholders regarding every project or financing decision. Except in a very closely held company, a poll

[5] For a more rigorous and comprehensive summary of the meaning of utility, see Luce and Raiffa, *op. cit.*, Chapter 2. Other useful introductions to this subject are Armen A. Alchian, "The Meaning of Utility Measurement," *American Economic Review*, XLIII, No. 1 (1953), 26–50, and Robert Schlaifer, *Probability and Statistics for Business Decisions* (New York: McGraw-Hill, 1959), Chapter 2.

or vote is out of the question for all except the most momentous decisions.

In order to maximize the value of a company's stock to its shareholders, a financial manager must have some way of systematizing and summarizing stockholder preferences. One approach is to use a utility function, which theoretically could provide a description of an *individual's* preferences such that maximization of the utility function would coincide with the maximization of the value of the stock to that individual. Such a measure, linked with the basic objective of financial management, would be an extremely valuable decision-making tool. Unfortunately, the utility approach is not at present practical for financial decision-making. The concept is of more than academic interest, however, since (a) it may find future use, and (b) because of the general problems exposed by discussion of the concept.

Suppose Mr. X must choose between three alternative "projects"[6] that will return certain payoffs $P1$, $P2$, and $P3$, at some future date. Mr. X decides he prefers $P3$ to $P2$, and $P2$ to $P1$.

**Table 5–1**

| | | Measure | | |
|---|---|---|---|---|
| *Payoff* | *Utility* | *A* | *B* | *C* |
| $P1$ | $U(P_1)$ | 1.0 | 10.0 | 0.10 |
| $P2$ | $U(P_2)$ | 2.0 | 25.0 | 0.15 |
| $P3$ | $U(P_3)$ | 3.0 | 30.0 | 0.30 |

Numerical measures of "utility" which reflect this preference ordering can easily be obtained. For example, consider Table 5-1. The *only* requirement here is that the measure chosen should reflect the order of preference unambiguously. The above measures are *ordinal* measures, requiring that $U(P_3) > U(P_2) > U(P_1)$ for measures $A$, $B$, and $C$. But any of the measures $A$, $B$, or $C$ is equally acceptable.

Unfortunately, an ordinal measure is of little use for more complicated decisions—the choice, for instance, between a project with a certain return of $P2$ and one with an equal chance of returning $P1$ or $P3$. Multiplying the utilities of $P1$ and $P3$ by 0.5 and adding the results gives no meaningful figure for "expected utility," since each of the measures $A$, $B$, and $C$ indicates a different decision.

---

[6] The term "project" will be used to refer to any given, feasible decision alternative.

In cases like this, where the ordinal measure of utility is useless, a *cardinal* measure of utility is needed, one which permits a comparison of "projects" whose outcomes are uncertain. In order to obtain this, we must be able to specify the range of possible outcomes or payoffs $A_0, A_1, A_2, \ldots, A_r$, for a given project, and the probability of occurrence of each outcome $A_i$. For financial decisions, the probabilities would be assigned to each outcome $A_i$ on the basis of partially subjective judgments.

If we assume that Mr. X is able to estimate the probability of any outcome $A_i$ if a given project is undertaken, and that his preferences regarding the possible outcomes are "consistent," then a cardinal utility measure can be derived for that project.

The following assumptions are necessary to ensure that Mr. X's preferences are "consistent."

1. Mr. X must be able to supply us with a consistent, transitive ordering of his preferences; i.e., Mr. X must be able to decide whether he prefers any possible outcome $A_i$ to $A_j$, or whether he is indifferent between the two outcomes. If a sufficient number of such decisions are made, we should arrive at a complete ordering of Mr. X's preferences. For this ordering to be transitive, we require that, if $A_i$ is preferred to $A_j$, and $A_j$ is preferred to $A_k$, then $A_i$ is preferred to $A_k$.

2. Define $A_0$ and $A_r$ as the most and the least desirable outcomes. We require that Mr. X be indifferent between any outcome $A_i$ and some lottery with only two possible outcomes $A_0$ and $A_r$; i.e., there is some probability $p$ such that Mr. X is indifferent between the certain return $A_i$ and the lottery with an expected value $pA_0 + (1 - p)A_r$. In addition, $A_i$ and $pA_0 + (1 - p)A_r$ must be perfect substitutes from Mr. X's point of view in the context of any possible decision.

3. Mr. X prefers a lottery promising $pA_0 + (1 - p)A_r$ to another promising $qA_0 + (1 - q)A_r$ if and only if $p > q$.

4. Last, we must require that Mr. X be indifferent between any "compound" (i.e., sequential) lottery or decision-making process and a simple lottery or decision if the mean and subjective probability distribution of the ultimate outcome are identical for the simple and compound cases.

Assumption 4 is as good a place as any for beginning to point out the problems inherent in these seemingly reasonable assumptions. For instance, a compound decision might involve investing in a sequence of two projects, the proceeds from the first being used to finance the second. The combination of the two projects has a series of possible outcomes at a specified future date, and a subjective probability distribution is assigned to these final outcomes, derived from combinations of the probabilities of success of the two projects considered separately. Would this compound project be equally as attractive as a single project with the same possible ultimate outcomes and the same subjective probability distribution? Perhaps not: for instance, the decision maker might prefer the compound project if the success or failure of the first stage of the project reduced his uncertainty about the final outcome while the second stage was in progress.

We could question the reasonableness of assumption 2 by suggesting a situation like the following. Imagine a case where the worst possible outcome means severe personal hardship. To a small, unincorporated businessman, for instance, a substantial loss might mean bankruptcy, going on relief, a hungry family, etc. Similarly, the cessation of dividends that are essential income for stockholders might inflict severe hardship. Does it really make sense to speak of a hypothetical lottery in which there is some probability that this worst possible alternative could occur in the same breath with outcomes involving only moderate stakes? Could a meaningful choice be made?

Other objections have been raised to the assumptions necessary to establish a cardinal utility function, but they need not be mentioned here.[7] It is sufficient that a note of caution has been injected.

## The Concept of Utility and Financing Decisions

The modern concept of utility is part of a trend toward much more rigorous examination of the problems of risk and rational choice. There has been essentially no practical use of the utility concept, however. For one thing, where there are many possible outcomes, interviewing to establish an order of preference among them is an arduous task. The utility notion may find more concrete use in the future; for the present, however, it is probably more to the point to consider some pivotal problem areas suspended somewhere between theory and practice.

One problem is this: we have assumed the existence of probability distributions for certain possible outcomes that are simultaneously subjective and concretely specified. But it is doubtful whether most people actually make decisions in terms of even simple, discrete probability distributions. Rather, decisions may be made on the basis of vague concepts of likelihood and an amorphous factor called judgment. Given these habitual approaches, we should hardly be surprised if an attempt to obtain a probability distribution from a person's beliefs about a complicated set of possible outcomes leads to contradictions. Some apparent contradictions would often arise simply because of the human prerogative of changing one's mind. Further information, the consideration of new alternatives, or just

---

[7] For a more complete discussion, see Luce and Raiffa, *op. cit.*, Chapter 2.

rumination may lead to a change of opinion. The attempt to derive a preference ordering may in itself assist such rethinking by presenting new alternatives or by exposing contradictions.

Of course, part of the difficulty with this concept stems from a lack of familiarity. We should not expect to find the concept of the subjective probability distribution among the customary furniture of stockholders' brains. It is used as a way of providing an explicit and rigorous logical framework for decision-making. It is a tool, the use of which is justified only if it works, and tools are always "artificial" at first.

Another major problem stemming from the above discussion is the impossibility of interpersonal comparisons of utility. Economic theory considers this a cardinal sin, which we have no intention of committing.

Suppose a certain decision is worth 40 units of utility on stockholder X's utility scale but would result in a loss of 20 units on stockholder Y's scale. A financial manager would *not* be justified in going ahead, arguing that "total utility" would be increased. In the first place, a cardinal utility function merely describes preferences; it cannot be said to have any measurable relation with satisfaction, even if quantities of that ephemeral concept could be defined. Even if satisfaction could be measured, however, making one person better off at the expense of another remains an essentially moral decision. Such judgments are indeed made but without the support of economic reasoning.

This raises a fundamental question about the objectives of financial management. In light of the foregoing discussion, what is the meaning of the phrase, "maximize the value of the corporation's stock as perceived by the shareholders"? If the value of the stock is looked at in terms of utility, this statement is meaningless.

It is true that the choice of an appropriate objective is sometimes intractable in terms of economic reasoning. An extreme example is the case where there are only a few shareholders, the preferences of these shareholders differ, and the stock is not traded frequently enough to establish a dependable market price. In such a case, the financial manager has little choice but to refer important alternatives to the stockholders. Corporation law provides essentially political procedures for resolving such conflicts.

When the stock is widely traded and there is a definite market price, the problem is somewhat simpler. *Even though a given decision decreases the "value" of the stock to an investor, he will be better off if, as a result of the decision, the stock price rises above the original "value" of the stock to this investor.* If this condition is satisfied, such an investor can sell his stock and be better off as a result of the company's decision.

Given perfect markets and equilibrium, this condition will hold whenever market price rises, since at equilibrium every investor's valuation of a marginal share of the stock will be equal to the market price.[8] In this case, *any* increase in market price benefits *every* stockholder, regardless of how any individual investor's estimate of the stock's value changes.

Unfortunately, absolutely perfect markets do not exist. Imperfections are important particularly with respect to stockholders who are "locked in" to their holdings because of tax reasons, desire to preserve voting rights, or simple inertia. If the preferences of such shareholders differ significantly from those of more active traders, the objective of maximizing market price may not be appropriate.

We can sum up in an example. Suppose Mr. X's personal valuation of a share of a given company's stock is $70, but that the market price $P_0$ is $60. The company then makes a financing decision which decreases the value of the stock to Mr. X to $65 but results in a second market price, $P_1 > P_0$. Now, if $P_1$ is $69, Mr. X is worse off; if $P_1$ is $71, he is better off, since he can sell the stock at $1 more than the original value of the stock to him. However, if for some reason Mr. X cannot sell the stock, then he is worse off regardless of any rise in the market price, since his personal estimate of the value of the stock has fallen to $65.

We do not want to overemphasize these problems: compared to other markets, the stock market has relatively few imperfections, and its responsiveness is usually fairly good. For practical purposes, maximizing the market price of the company's stock is normally the appropriate objective for financial management. Caution is necessary, however, when pursuit of this objective appears to go against the wishes of a locked-in minority of shareholders. And, of course, we are assuming that pursuit does not include short-run inflations of stock prices by use of misleading information, market operations, or similar methods.

## Risk from the Investor's Point of View

No doubt nearly everyone has an introspective idea of what risk is. In fact, this common understanding is the only justification for our delaying so long the discussion of the factors which actually determine the risk of a stock from the point of view of an investor. But this discussion becomes necessary as soon as we are confronted with the problem of specifying how the value of the firm to its stock-

---

[8] This is simply the condition for an investor to be in equilibrium with regard to his personal stock holdings. In perfect markets, we can assume that every investor will adjust his holdings until this condition is satisfied.

holders is affected by risk and uncertainty. From the point of view of the investor, what does the term *risk* mean?

As a first approximation, we might say that risk is a positive function of the dispersion of the subjective probability distribution of expected dividends. The greater the dispersion, the greater the risk. This conforms with our common-sense notions of what risk is. Moreover, it would seem reasonable to use the customary measures of dispersion—i.e., the standard deviation or variance of the subjective probability distribution—to measure risk.

Following this reasoning, consider two companies that are expected to pay identical dividends in all future years. These dividends have been assigned subjective probability distributions by investors such that the standard deviations of the distributions are also identical for the two companies. Are we justified in concluding that the value of the equity of the two companies is the same?

The answer to this question is maybe. The above reasoning is not necessarily wrong, but it requires qualification.

In the first place, it is possible for probability distributions with identical means and standard deviations to be substantially different in form. Figure 5-2 shows two possible distributions which have (approximately) the same mean and variance.

Knowledge of the mean and standard deviation of these distributions is helpful but not sufficient. It will be remembered that the concept of utility cannot be directly applied to the valuation of a risky "project" unless a specific probability can be assigned to each possible outcome. The knowledge of the mean and standard devia-

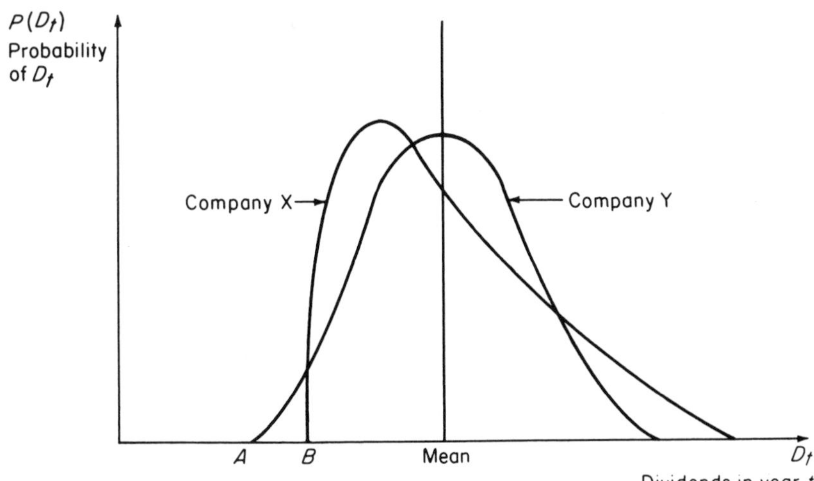


FIG. 5–2

tion of a subjective probability distribution does not in general permit this specification.

To put it another way, suppose that Fig. 5-2 shows the subjective probability distributions of a certain year's expected dividends for two hypothetical companies. We have labeled the two distributions as belonging to Company X and Company Y. While it is possible for Company Y's dividend to fall in the range *AB* in Fig. 5-2, the probability that Company X's dividend will be this low is zero—that is, investors believe that it is impossible for Company X's dividend to fall below *B*.

Now, if low dividends mean substantial personal hardships for stockholders, the stock of Company X might be considered more valuable by investors than that of Company Y.

On the other hand, we might argue that the higher modal or "most likely" dividend payment of Company Y would tend to make that company's stock more valuable. In general, we may conclude that the standard deviation assigned to expected dividends cannot be used as a complete explanation of risk.

A second qualification may be suggested by the following question. Which of the following alternatives would an investor who is averse to risk choose: (a) a bet of $1,000 on the flip of a fair coin, or (b) ten bets of $100 each on ten separate flips of a fair coin? The expected return of the two alternatives is the same—i.e., zero. But under the second alternative, the investor could reasonably expect the gains and losses of the ten separate bets to "cancel out," so that his final gain or loss would most probably be smaller than under the first alternative. Thus the second alternative would be the rational choice if the investor is averse to risk.

This is the familiar argument for diversification and against "putting all your eggs in one basket." It applies directly to the investor. The over-all risk of an investor's *portfolio* depends on the extent to which the returns of the various individual securities he owns "cancel out." From the point of view of an investor, the value of a particular stock partly depends on the extent to which fluctuations in the returns on the stock are correlated with the fluctuations in the returns of the other securities he holds.[9]

[9] Modern quantitative techniques have been applied to this problem from the investor's point of view. The pioneering work is that of H. Markowitz, *Portfolio Selection*, Monograph 16, Cowles Foundation for Research in Economics at Yale University (New York: John Wiley & Sons, 1959). Simplified expositions of the principles involved may be found in A. D. Martin, Jr., "Mathematical Programming of Portfolio Selections," *Management Science*, I, No. 2 (1954), 152–166, and H. Markowitz, "Portfolio Selection," *Journal of Finance*, VII, No. 1 (1952), 77–91. The implications for the firm's financial decisions, however, have not been worked out quantitatively, although an impressive beginning is made by William F. Sharpe, "Capital Asset Prices: A Theory of Market Equilibrium under Conditions of Risk," *Journal of Finance*, XIX, No. 3 (1964), 425–442.

In summarizing these remarks, we can specify three broad factors which determine the riskiness of a stock to an investor: (a) the dispersion of the subjective probability distribution assigned to expected dividends, (b) the form of this distribution, and (c) the extent to which random variations in the dividends are correlated with the variations in returns of other investment opportunities.

Strictly speaking, the listing of these three factors which determine risk does not constitute a *definition* of risk. In effect, we have been using the term *risk* to refer to a variety of factors which affect value. Their common characteristic is that they are relevant only when the assumption of certainty is discarded.

Fortunately, the financial manager is interested in risk only insofar as it affects value, so that for present purposes we can beg the ultimate question of definition with a clear conscience. This allows us to turn to the question of how risk is to be accounted for in the framework of financial management.

### Uncertainty and Present Value

Previous sections of this chapter have summarized what systematic understanding we have of a series of questions that in practice are solved by varying mixtures of assumption and judgment. We have, insofar as possible, justified the normal assumption of risk aversion; explored the bridges (notably the modern concept of utility) between decision-making and the preferences decisions are supposed to reflect; reconsidered the over-all objective for financial management, and discussed the factors determining risk from the point of view of the investor. The state of the art is such that foolproof procedures for dealing with uncertainty do not exist, but hopefully knowledge of the problems involved will forestall errors of reasoning, if not of judgment.

Thus far, the time element has been ignored. These concluding sections will reintroduce it, reconciling—at least on a theoretical basis—uncertainty with the concept of present value. As before, we shall assume that the expected results of present actions can be predicted, in particular the expected dividends per share and the probability distribution of these dividends. Management's objective is to choose those financing and investment decisions which are expected to produce the most valuable stream of expected future dividends. We can take this objective as equivalent to maximizing the present price of the company's stock.

From the discussion of Chapters 3 and 4, we might infer that the market price of a common share would be given by

(5-1) $$P_0 = \sum_{t=1}^{\infty} \frac{\bar{D}_t}{\prod_{\tau=1}^{t} (1 + k_\tau)}$$

where $\bar{D}_t$ is now defined as the expected dividend per share in year $t$. Since both business and financial risks are reflected in dividends, Eq. (5-1) assumes that investors discount the dividend stream at "required" rates $k_\tau$, which are greater than the riskless rates of interest. The greater the over-all risk, the greater the spread between $k_\tau$ and the riskless rate $\bar{i}_\tau$.

Although use of "required rates of discount" may be a convenient shorthand for the purpose of discussing some topics, using this approach to *measure* the effect of risk on present value leads to serious contradictions, as will be shown.[10]

Fortunately, an alternative path is open—the use of the *certainty equivalent* of expected dividends[11]—the basic idea of certainty equivalents being simply that, whatever the risk of an expected dividend, there is some factor, $\alpha_t$, where $0 \leqq \alpha_t \leqq 1$, such that the risk-averting investor is indifferent between $\bar{D}_t$ and a dividend $D_t^* = \alpha_t \bar{D}_t$ which is certain to be paid. If we knew the investor's utility function for

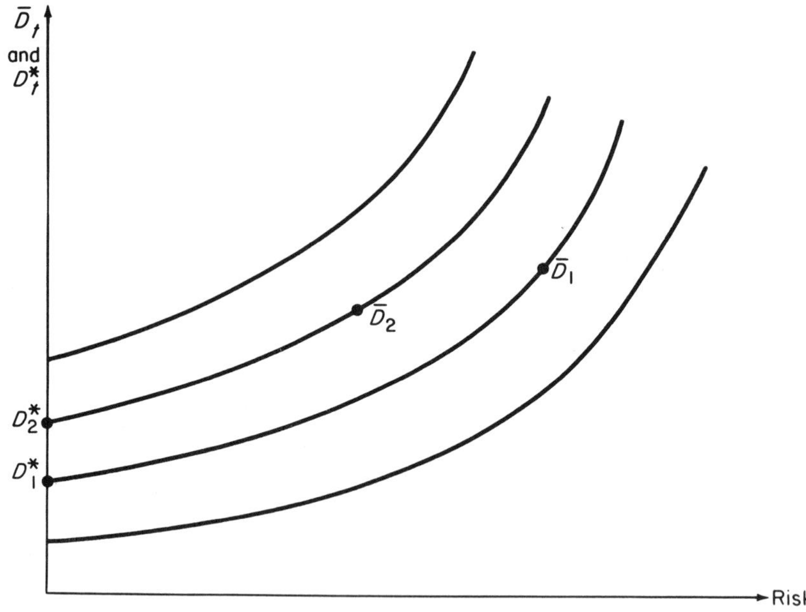


FIG. 5-3

[10] The authors are grateful to Professor Howard Raiffa for planting in their minds the seed of doubt on this subject. Any errors of logic in the exposition are the authors' own.

[11] The idea of certainty equivalents has found wide use in theoretical financial literature. See, for instance, Friedrick and Vera Lutz, *The Theory of Investment of the Firm* (Princeton, N.J.: Princeton University Press, 1951), Chapter 15.

dividends in year $t$, the equivalence could easily be determined. The factor $\alpha_t$ is intended to summarize the effects of risk on value. In terms of the remarks of the previous section, we can deduce that $\alpha_t$ will be larger to the extent that (a) the dispersion of the subjective probability distribution assigned to the expected dividend is low; (b) the form of the distribution is attractive to the investor, and (c) random variations in dividends are expected to cancel out with variations in the returns of other investments held by the investor.

As a numerical example, suppose a stockholder estimates $\bar{D}_t$ to be \$15. We could hypothetically offer him a choice between this uncertain \$15 and some certain income. The certain income for which the stockholder would exchange $\bar{D}_t$ is $D_t^*$. If $D_t^*$ is, say, \$10, then $\alpha_t$ is $\frac{2}{3}$.

Figure 5-3 shows a series of what have been called certainty equivalence curves; these are merely indifference curves between certain dividends and progressively more risky dividends. For instance, in Fig. 5-3, $D_1^*$ is equivalent in value to $\bar{D}_1$.

Putting the problem in this context implies the question: "What price would an investor pay for the certain stream of dividends $D_1^*$, $D_2^*$, $D_3^*$, etc.?" The answer is the present value of the certain dividend stream discounted at the riskless rate of interest. That is,

$$P_0 = \sum_{t=1}^{\infty} \frac{D_t^*}{\prod_{\tau=1}^{t} (1 + \bar{i}_\tau)} = \sum_{t=1}^{\infty} \frac{\alpha_t \bar{D}_t}{\prod_{\tau=1}^{\infty} (1 + \bar{i}_\tau)}. \tag{5-2}$$

Since there are alternative, essentially riskless investments returning $\bar{i}_\tau$—e.g., government bonds—it is clear that, given perfect markets and identical expectations and attitudes toward risk on the part of investors, $P_0$ would be the equilibrium price of the stock. Even if expectations and attitudes toward risk differ among investors, Eq. (5-2) still defines the value of the stock to any individual.

On the face of it, Eqs. (5-1) and (5-2) may seem to be merely different paths to the same answer, differing only in mathematical formulation. Any such impression, however, is illusory.

Consider again the preceding example, where $\bar{D}_t = \$15$, $D_t^* = \$10$, and $\alpha_t = \frac{2}{3}$. We shall add the stipulation that $\bar{D}_t = \bar{D}_3$—that is, one dividend is expected three years hence—and that the relevant riskless interest rates are $\bar{i}_1 = 0.05$, $\bar{i}_2 = 0.04$, $\bar{i}_3 = 0.03$. Given this information, we can easily compute $P_0$, which in this example is the present value of $\bar{D}_3$ at $t = 0$. That is, using Eq. (5-2),

$$P_0 = \frac{\alpha_t \bar{D}_3}{\prod_{\tau=1}^{3} (1 + \bar{i}_\tau)} = \frac{\frac{2}{3}(15)}{(1.05)(1.04)(1.03)} = 8.89.$$

However, if we tried to use Eq. (5-1) to determine $P_0$, we would have no way of determining $k_1$, $k_2$, and $k_3$, the short-term future rates. We can deduce that

$$\alpha_t \prod_{\tau=1}^{3} (1 + k_\tau) = \prod_{\tau=1}^{3} (1 + \bar{\imath}_\tau),$$

but this equation leaves the values of the $k_\tau$'s indeterminate. In other words, the preceding equation has an infinite number of possible solutions $(k_1, k_2, k_3)$, even when $\alpha_t$ and the $\bar{\imath}_\tau$'s are known. In view of this fact we can ask whether the idea of the series of rates $k_1, k_2, \ldots k_\tau$ has any meaning whatsoever. How is one to observe them?

Normally, of course, the product $\prod_{\tau=1}^{t} (1 + k_\tau)$ is not used for discounting; authors generally assume some constant rate $k$ (perhaps referring to the "more general case" where $k_\tau$ is not constant). Normal usage also assumes that $k$ is determined by two factors: investors' attitudes toward risk and the underlying riskless rate. We can show, however, that $k$ cannot satisfactorily be defined by these two factors.

Consider the expected future dividends $\bar{D}_t$ and $\bar{D}_{t+1}$, which are equal in magnitude *and* are considered equally risky by investors; i.e., the investors' certainty equivalents $D_t^*$ and $D_{t+1}^*$ are equal. Thus $\alpha_t = \alpha_{t+1}$, since

$$\alpha_t = \frac{D_t^*}{\bar{D}_t} = \frac{D_{t+1}^*}{\bar{D}_{t+1}} = \alpha_{t+1}.$$

For simplicity of exposition, let us also assume that $\bar{\imath}_\tau$ is constant for all $\tau \leqq t + 1$.

If the "risk-adjusted" discount rate approach is valid, Eq. (5-1) must give the same results as Eq. (5-2).[12] For period $t$,

$$\frac{D_t^*}{(1 + \bar{\imath})^t} = \frac{\bar{D}_t}{(1 + k)^t} = \frac{(1/\alpha_t)D_t^*}{(1 + k)^t}.$$

Therefore,

$$\alpha_t = \frac{(1 + \bar{\imath})^t}{(1 + k)^t}. \tag{5-3}$$

By similar reasoning, for period $t + 1$,

$$\alpha_{t+1} = \frac{(1 + \bar{\imath})^{t+1}}{(1 + k)^{t+1}} = \frac{(1 + \bar{\imath})^t(1 + \bar{\imath})}{(1 + k)^t(1 + k)}. \tag{5-4}$$

---

[12] By *definition* the stockholder must be indifferent between the stream of risky dividends and the value of the stock $P_0$ as given by Eq. (5–2).

*Since* $\alpha_t = \alpha_{t+1}$, *unless* $(1 + k) = (1 + \bar{\imath})$, Eqs. (5-3) *and* (5-4) *are contradictory;* and it is hardly reasonable that $(1 + k) = (1 + \bar{\imath})$, since $k$ is supposed to be greater than the riskless rate $\bar{\imath}$ to "compensate" for the riskiness of $\bar{D}_t$ and $\bar{D}_{t+1}$.

The only way to escape this contradiction would be to define separate "average" discount rates $k_t$ for *every* future year. That is, $k_t$ would apply *only* to $D_t$, $k_{t+1}$ would apply *only* to $\bar{D}_{t+1}$, etc. Then Eqs. (5-3) and (5-4) could be restated as

$$\alpha_t = \frac{(1 + \bar{\imath})^t}{(1 + k_t)^t} \tag{5-5}$$

and

$$\alpha_{t+1} = \frac{(1 + \bar{\imath})^{t+1}}{(1 + k_{t+1})^{t+1}} \tag{5-6}$$

without contradiction. But this means that $k_1, k_2, \ldots, k_{t+1}$ cannot be identical *even if the expected dividends to which they apply are considered equally risky.* The converse also holds and is perhaps more striking: if $k_1 = k_2 = \ldots = k_{t+1}$, then the expected dividends $\bar{D}_1, \bar{D}_2, \ldots, \bar{D}_{t+1}$ cannot be equally risky. That is, $\alpha_t$ is not constant. This conclusion is completely at odds with the normal assumption that "a constant discount rate implies constant risk."

## Use of Discount Rates in Practice

Perhaps it is premature to conclude that the "risk-adjusted required rate of return" approach is completely useless for financial decision-making. For instance, the use of a discount rate to reflect risk may have some advantage in that it is simple and familiar. Moreover, in certain special cases, the use of a constant discount rate may be theoretically justified.

From Eq. (5-5) we know that in any period $t$,

$$\alpha_t = \frac{(1 + \bar{\imath})^t}{(1 + k_t)^t}$$

where the riskless rate of interest $\bar{\imath}$ is assumed constant over time, and $k_t$ is the "average" rate of discount which applies only to period $t$. In order to use a constant rate of discount, $k$, in the valuation process, the average rates must be the same for all periods, i.e., $k_1 = k_2 = \ldots k_\infty$. It is apparent from Eq. (5-5) that this condition will be satisfied only if $\alpha_t$ is given by

$$\alpha_t = \frac{(1 + \bar{\imath})^t}{(1 + k_t)^t} = \frac{(1 + \bar{\imath})^t}{(1 + k)^t} \tag{5-7}$$

where $k_t = k$ is constant over time. Equation (5-7) implies that $\alpha_t$ *decreases* at a constant rate over time. In other words, we can find some constant discount rate $k$ which is an unambiguous measure of return under risk if and only if the risk of expected returns (as measured by the factor $\alpha_t$) increases at a constant rate as a function of the time at which the returns are expected to be achieved.

For instance, suppose $\alpha_0$ is 1.0 and the riskiness of future returns is expected to increase over time in such a way that $\alpha_t$ decreases at 10 per cent per annum. Then $\alpha_1 = 0.9\alpha_0 = 0.90$; $\alpha_2 = 0.9\alpha_1 = 0.81$; etc. Now, we can deduce from Eq. (5-7) that

$$\alpha_{t+1} = \alpha_t \frac{(1 + \bar{\imath})}{(1 + k)} \tag{5-8}$$

if the conditions for $k_t$ to be constant over time are satisfied. Thus, in the present example,

$$\alpha_2 = \frac{(1 + \bar{\imath})}{(1 + k)} \alpha_1,$$

and if $\bar{\imath} = 0.04$, then

$$0.81 = 0.9 \left(\frac{1.04}{1 + k}\right).$$

Solving this, we find that $k$ must equal approximately 15.6 per cent.

Although the use of a constant discount rate to measure risk may be justified under certain assumptions, it should be clear that serious decision-making errors may result if the discount rate approach is used where these assumptions do not apply.

For instance, suppose $\alpha_t$ and $\bar{\imath}$ are constant over time. Then the "average" rates $k_t$ must *decrease* with time. To illustrate, consider an infinite stream of expected dividends such that $\bar{D}_t = \bar{D} = 15$, $\alpha_t = \alpha = \frac{2}{3}$ and $\bar{\imath} = 0.04$. Then, by use of Eq. (5-2),

$$P_0 = \frac{\frac{2}{3}(15)}{(1 + 0.04)} + \frac{\frac{2}{3}(15)}{(1 + 0.04)^2} + \cdots + \frac{\frac{2}{3}(15)}{(1 + 0.04)^\infty}$$

$$= \frac{10}{0.04} = 250.00.$$

Now, we can find some "required composite rate of return," $\hat{k}$, such that the discounted value of the stream of *expected* dividends $\bar{D}_t$ will be 250.00. In this case

$$\hat{k} = \frac{\bar{D}}{P_0} = \frac{15}{250} = 0.06. \tag{5-9}$$

For comparison, values for the individual average $k_t$'s can be derived as follows: the present value of $\bar{D}_1$ as given by the certainty equivalent approach is

$$PV(\bar{D}_1) = \frac{\frac{2}{3}(15)}{1.04} = 9.615.$$

This present value must be identical regardless of the discounting procedure employed. Therefore,

$$PV(\bar{D}_1) = 9.615 = \frac{\bar{D}_1}{1 + k_1} = \frac{15}{1 + k_1},$$

and

$$k_1 = \frac{15}{9.615} - 1 = 0.56.$$

Similarly, "average" $k_t$'s can be derived for subsequent periods. The value of $k_t$ will decline with $t$, and as $t$ approaches infinity, $k_t$ will approach the riskless rate $\bar{\imath}$.

Suppose the financial manager expects that a reduction of \$1.00 in dividends per share in $t = 0$ will allow increasing dividends per share by \$1.50 in $t = 1$. This alternative provides an expected return of 50 per cent. However, he estimates that the risk of this expected change in $\bar{D}_1$ is subject to the same risks as dividends in general, so that $\alpha_1$ remains at $\frac{2}{3}$. Using the certainty equivalent approach, the net present value to shareholders of the investment would be

$$\frac{\alpha_1(\Delta\bar{D}_1)}{1 + \bar{\imath}} - \Delta\bar{D}_0 = \frac{\frac{2}{3}(1.50)}{1.04} - 1 \cong -0.0385.$$

Obviously, this is not an acceptable decision, as use of the discount rate criterion with $k_1 = 0.56$ would confirm. But discounting at the "required composite rate of return" $\hat{k} = 0.06$ would lead to an incorrect decision. In fact, using $\hat{k} = 0.06$, the foregoing proposition would appear to have a net present value of \$0.41—a dramatic distortion of its actual value. In general, we must conclude as we did above: a single discount rate is not always adequate to express risk.

The certainty equivalent approach avoids such ambiguities by proceeding directly from the ideas of rational choice outlined in this chapter. The basic determinant of stock value is stockholder preferences. The certainty equivalent approach summarizes these preferences directly, the discount rate approach indirectly; this difference is at the roots of the latter method's difficulties.

## The Realization of Income over Time

As we noted earlier in this chapter, the practical objective of financial management is usually to maximize the market value of the firm's stock. In terms of the financial decision-making process, we can say that any financing decision ultimately depends on predictions of the change in market price which would result from the adoption of a given financing alternative; that is, the financial manager must principally be concerned with *changes* in the value of the firm to its stockholders.

Any investigation of these changes in value, however, essentially is an investigation of the pattern in which stockholders realize income over time. In fact, income from the point of view of a shareholder may be *defined* as the increment in his personal wealth resulting from his ownership of the stock over a specified period.

In Chapter 2 we developed a concept of income based on discounted present value under the highly artificial assumptions of perfect markets and certainty. In this section we shall develop a generalized description of income from the shareholder's point of view; these concepts will be more specifically related to market price fluctuations in the next chapter.

We shall begin with this basic proposition: the income realized by the firm's stockholders in any period $t = j$ will be equal, in the absence of new investment, to dividend payments plus or minus any changes in the value of the firm to the shareholders, i.e.,

$$Y_j = D_j + V_j - V_{j-1} \tag{5-10}$$

where $Y_j$ represents the income realized in period $j$, $D_j$ the dividends paid out by the firm, and $(V_j - V_{j-1})$ the change in the market value of the firm's outstanding shares.

We shall now investigate the determinants of $Y_j$ as seen through the eyes of Mr. X, whom we take as representing the attitudes of present and prospective shareholders. As a first approximation, assume that Mr. X's estimates of $\bar{D}_{j+1}, \bar{D}_{j+2}, \ldots, \bar{D}_\infty$ and $\alpha_{j+1}, \alpha_{j+2}, \ldots, \alpha_\infty$ are the same in period $j$ as they were in period $j - 1$. If the riskless rate of interest, $\bar{i}$, is constant, then Eq. (5-10) may be rewritten as[13]

(5-11) $$Y_j = D_j - \alpha_j \bar{D}_j + \bar{\imath} V_{j-1}.$$

This gives us the realized income in period $j$ in terms of the actual dividend paid, the riskless rate of interest, the value of the stock in period $j - 1$, and the stockholder's estimate in period $j - 1$ of the expected value and certainty equivalent of period $j$.

Equation (5-11) is closely related to the simplified expression for income developed in Chapter 2 with the assumption of certainty. In fact, if all expected future dividends are certain to be paid, then $\bar{D}_t = D_t$ and $\alpha_t = 1$ for all future periods, so that Eq. (5-11) reduces to

(5-12) $$Y_j = \bar{\imath} V_{j-1}.$$

This is the same conclusion we reached in Chapter 2.

Unfortunately Eq. (5-11) is an oversimplification. It rests on our assumption that Mr. X will *not* expect his estimates of $\alpha_t$ and $\bar{D}_t$ to change over time—an assumption we cannot expect to hold in general.

To illustrate, let us consider the manner in which the value of a risky return $\bar{D}_{t^*}$ may be expected to change over time. We are assuming that $\bar{D}_{t^*}$ represents at any given time Mr. X's best estimate of the payment he expects to receive at time $t^*$. Let us choose period $j - 1$ as a starting point.

Now a hypothetical investor, such as Mr. X, may expect his estimate $\bar{D}_{t^*}$ to change, but we assume he has no way of *predicting* how

---

[13] This can be proved as follows. If $\bar{\imath}$ is constant, we can write, using Eq. (5-2),

$$V_{j-1} = \sum_{t=j}^{\infty} \frac{\alpha_t \bar{D}_t}{(1+\bar{\imath})^{t-j+1}} = \frac{\alpha_j \bar{D}_j}{(1+\bar{\imath})} + \sum_{t=j+1}^{\infty} \frac{\alpha_t \bar{D}_t}{(1+\bar{\imath})^{t-j+1}}.$$

Multiplying both sides by $(1 + \bar{\imath})$,

$$(1+\bar{\imath})V_{j-1} = \alpha_j \bar{D}_j + \sum_{t=j+1}^{\infty} \frac{\alpha_t \bar{D}_t}{(1+\bar{\imath})^{t-j}}$$

$$= \alpha_j \bar{D}_j + V_j;$$

$$V_j = (1+\bar{\imath})V_{j-1} - \alpha_j \bar{D}_j.$$

Substituting in Eq. (5-10),

$$Y_j = D_j + (1+\bar{\imath})V_{j-1} - \alpha_j \bar{D}_j - V_{j-1};$$

(5-11) $$Y_j = D_j - \alpha_j \bar{D}_j + \bar{\imath} V_{j-1}.$$

This proof could be easily extended if $\bar{\imath}$ is variable with time. In this case income would be given by

(5-11a) $$Y_j = D_j - \alpha_j \bar{D}_j - \bar{\imath}_j V_{j-1}.$$

As we shall note below, however, Eq. (5-11) is derived on the assumption that $\alpha_t$ and $\bar{D}_t$ are unchanged for $t = j + 1$, $t = j + 2$, $\ldots$, $t = \infty$.

his estimate $\bar{D}_{t^*}$ will change, and therefore has no reason to expect it to rise rather than fall or vice versa. For if he were able to predict how a given estimate would change, then that estimate would not be his *best estimate.* Anything less than the best estimate an investor makes in period $j - 1$ is therefore assumed irrelevant to any decisions made in that period.

However, Mr. X also assigns some $\alpha_{t^*}$ to $\bar{D}_{t^*}$ in period $j - 1$ to reflect the perceived riskiness of the expected return; moreover, it is possible for estimates of $\alpha_{t^*}$ to change over time. Let us define ${}_\tau\bar{\alpha}_{t^*}$ as the expected value of $\alpha_{t^*}$ in period $\tau$, where $\tau \leqq t^*$. That is, if at time $j - 1$ Mr. X expects that the appropriate certainty equivalent of $\bar{D}_{t^*}$ will be $0.8\bar{D}_{t^*}$ in period $\tau$, then ${}_\tau\alpha_{t^*} = 0.8$. Of course, by the time period $\tau$ actually arrives, Mr. X may have a different opinion of the riskiness of $\bar{D}_{t^*}$. In general, ${}_\tau\bar{\alpha}_{t^*}$ need not equal the value of $\alpha_{t^*}$ which the investor actually assigns to $\bar{D}_{t^*}$ on the basis of the evidence available at period $\tau$. Furthermore, ${}_\tau\bar{\alpha}_{t^*}$ need not equal $\alpha_{t^*}$ as assigned at time $j - 1$.

The manner in which ${}_\tau\bar{\alpha}_{t^*}$ varies over time for $j \leqq \tau \leqq t^*$ will depend on the way in which the actual return to be received at time $t^*$, i.e., $D_{t^*}$, is determined. Consider three hypothetical examples: (a) $D_{t^*}$ is determined by a flip of a coin at time $t^*$; (b) $D_{t^*}$ depends on whether a firm obtains a crucial contract at time $j$; and (c) $D_{t^*}$ depends on the over-all rate of growth of a firm's earnings between period $j - 1$ and $t^*$. In case (a) *no uncertainty is resolved until period* $t^*$ when the coin is tossed; in case (b) a large part of the uncertainty *is expected to be resolved in period j;* and in case (c) uncertainty would be *expected to be resolved gradually over time.* In any case, however, we know that the amount of the actual dividend will become certain

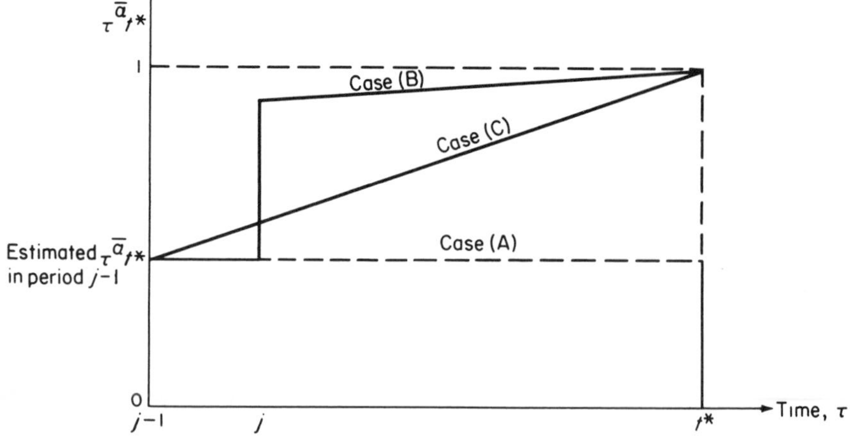


FIG. 5–4

sooner or later. In other words, we know that at period $\tau = t^*$, ${}_\tau\bar{\alpha}_{t^*} = \alpha_{t^*} = 1$. Figure 5-4 illustrates these three cases by plotting the changes in ${}_\tau\bar{\alpha}_{t^*}$ with time that Mr. X might reasonably predict at time $j - 1$.

As $\alpha_{t^*}$ rises for future dividends, however, so does value as defined by Eq. (5-2); and since income is defined in terms of value, an expected rise in ${}_\tau\bar{\alpha}_{t^*}$ represents expected income to the shareholder. We can include this in Eq. (5-11) by writing

$$(5\text{-}13) \quad Y_j = D_j - \alpha_j\bar{D}_j + \bar{\imath}V_{j-1} + [E(V_j) - \tilde{V}_j] + [V_j - E(V_j)].$$

In Eq. (5-13), $E(V_j)$ is Mr. X's expectation (at time $j - 1$) of the value of the stock at time $j$. In terms of Mr. X's estimates made at time $j - 1$, we can define $E(V_j)$ by

$$(5\text{-}14) \qquad E(V_j) = \sum_{t=j+1}^{\infty} \frac{{}_j\bar{\alpha}_t\bar{D}_t}{(1 + \bar{\imath})^t}.$$

The variable $\tilde{V}_j$ represents the value of the stock to Mr. X at time $j$ on the assumption that uncertainty regarding $D_{j+1}$, $D_{j+2}$, $D_{j+3}$, etc., has in no way been resolved between time $j - 1$ and time $j$.[14] We may define it as

$$(5\text{-}15) \qquad \tilde{V}_j = \sum_{t=j+1}^{\infty} \frac{{}_{j-1}\bar{\alpha}_t\bar{D}_t}{(1 + \bar{\imath})^t}.$$

As before, the term $V_j$ indicates the *actual* value of the stock to the investor at time $j$.

Equation (5-13) may now be interpreted. The term $E(V_j) - \tilde{V}_j$ represents the income the investor expects to receive in period $j$ as uncertainty is resolved with respect to periods $j + 1$, $j + 2$, $j + 3$, etc. However, Mr. X's estimates regarding these periods may not change in exactly the manner that he anticipated at time $j - 1$. Thus the term $[V_j - E(V_j)]$ is introduced to represent the effect of unanticipated changes in valuation on the income actually realized in period $j$.

We can regard Eq. (5-13) in its entirety as representing the total income actually realized in period $j$. However, it is also useful to examine the income Mr. X *expects* to realize in period $j$. By definition, an investor at time $j - 1$ will expect his best estimates of expected dividends and stock value to be realized in period $j$. In general, we may define an investor's *expected income* during the period $t = j - 1$

---

[14] Mathematically, $\tilde{V}_j$ can also be expressed as $(1 + \bar{\imath})V_{j-1} - \alpha_j\bar{D}_j$. This term appears in the preceding note, since $V_j = \tilde{V}_j$ under the assumptions used in deriving Eq. (5-11).

to $t = j$ as

$$\bar{Y}_j = \bar{D}_j + E(V_j) - E(V_{j-1}). \tag{5-16}$$

To put this more precisely, if Mr. X's expectations turn out to be exactly right, then $D_j = \bar{D}_j$ and $E(V_j) = V_j$, so that we may derive an investor's expected income from Eq. (5-13) as

$$\bar{Y}_j = (1 - \alpha_j)\bar{D}_j + \bar{i}V_{j-1} + [E(V_j) - \tilde{V}_j]. \tag{5-17}$$

If a stock is completely riskless, then $\alpha_j = 1$ and $E(V_j) = \tilde{V}_j$ and the total income expected (and realized) in period $j$ is just $\bar{i}V_{j-1}$.[15] Therefore we may interpret the sum of the terms $(1 - \alpha_j)\bar{D}_j$ and $[E(V_j) - \tilde{V}_j]$ as Mr. X's *expected income for risk-bearing* during the period from time $j - 1$ to time $j$.

Finally, we can observe from comparison of Eqs. (5-13) and (5-17) that expected income will differ from realized income to the extent that $D_j$ and $V_j$ differ from $\bar{D}_j$ and $E(V_j)$, respectively.

## An Illustration

The concepts discussed in the two preceding sections are so complex that an example illustrating the major points in the argument may be helpful.

We shall consider a company which is expected to pay dividends in periods $t = 1$, $t = 2$, and $t = 3$, but no dividends in subsequent periods. (Eliminating the subsequent dividends simplifies the necessary calculations.) Suppose Mr. X has arrived at estimates of the amount and riskiness of the three expected dividends. These estimates are shown in Table 5–2.

**Table 5–2**

| | | |
|---|---|---|
| $\bar{D}_1 = 100$ | $\bar{D}_2 = 200$ | $\bar{D}_3 = 400$ |
| $\alpha_1 = 0.9$ | $\alpha_2 = 0.8$ | $\alpha_3 = 0.7$ |
| | ${}_1\bar{\alpha}_2 = 0.9$ | ${}_1\bar{\alpha}_3 = 0.8$ |
| | | ${}_2\bar{\alpha}_3 = 0.9$ |

We shall briefly review the notation used in Table 5-2. The variables $\alpha_t$ are the coefficients which "deflate" the expected dividend $\bar{D}_t$ to its certainty equivalent. Thus the certainty equivalent of $\bar{D}_t$ is $\alpha_t\bar{D}_t$. The variables ${}_\tau\bar{\alpha}_t$ are the "certainty equivalent coefficients" that the investor at time $t = 0$ expects he will use in his valuation of the stock at the end of period $\tau$. For this example, Mr. X expects that at the end of period $\tau = 1$ he will estimate $\alpha_3$ to be 0.8; thus ${}_1\bar{\alpha}_3$ is 0.8.

[15] This was our conclusion in Chapter 2 and in Eq. (5-12).

If we assume a constant riskless rate of interest, $\bar{i} = 0.04$, the value of the stock to Mr. X in period $t = 0$ is given by Eq. (5-2):

$$V_0 = \frac{0.9(100)}{(1 + 0.04)} + \frac{0.8(200)}{(1 + 0.04)^2} + \frac{0.7(400)}{(1 + 0.04)^3} = 483.39.$$

The expected value of the stock to Mr. X at the end of period 1 can be obtained by use of Eq. (5-14):

$$E(V_1) = \frac{0.9(200)}{(1 + 0.04)} + \frac{0.8(400)}{(1 + 0.04)^2} = 468.93.$$

We can also use Eq. (5-14) to obtain the expected value of the stock at the end of period 2:

$$E(V_2) = \frac{0.9(400)}{(1 + 0.04)} = 346.15.$$

Using Eq. (5-16), we can now obtain the income Mr. X expects to obtain in periods 1, 2, and 3.

$$\bar{Y}_1 = 100 + 468.93 - 483.39 = 85.55$$

$$\bar{Y}_2 = 200 + 346.15 - 468.93 = 77.22$$

$$\bar{Y}_3 = 400 + 0 - 346.15 = 53.85$$

Using Eq. (5-17), we find the expected incomes $\bar{Y}_1$, $\bar{Y}_2$, and $\bar{Y}_3$ may in turn be expressed as the sum of two components: the income which would have been received if the expected dividends were certain to be received, and the expected income for risk-bearing. This is done in Table 5-3, which includes in parentheses expected "rates of return" for the various periods. These "rates of return" are obtained simply by dividing the income expected in a given period by the expected value of the stock at the end of the preceding period.

**Table 5–3**

| | *Period 1* | *Period 2* | *Period 3* |
|---|---|---|---|
| Expected income if the dividends were certain | 19.34 (0.04) | 18.76 (0.04) | 13.85 (0.04) |
| Expected income for risk-bearing | 66.21 (0.137) | 58.46 (0.125) | 40.00 (0.116) |
| Total expected income | 85.55 (0.177) | 77.22 (0.165) | 53.85 (0.156) |

Table 5-3 shows, among other things, that the total expected "rate of return" varies from period to period. Thus a single "composite discount rate," $\hat{k}$, could not be used in this problem without distorting our results. To be sure, the distortion might not be significant for some practical purposes, but the logical error involved cannot be corrected by the appeal to practicality. In any case, the interested reader will be able to construct examples in which the distortion is substantial.

To continue, note that Eq. (5-17) allows us to divide the expected income for risk-bearing for any given period into two components: the resolution of uncertainty with respect to dividends expected in that period, and the resolution of uncertainty with respect to dividends expected in subsequent periods. This requires computation of $\tilde{V}_t$, the expected value of the stock if no resolution of uncertainty with respect to subsequent dividends takes place during that period.[16] Using Eq. (5-15),

$$\tilde{V}_1 = \frac{0.8(200)}{(1 + 0.04)} + \frac{0.7(400)}{(1 + 0.04)^2} = 412.72;$$

$$\tilde{V}_2 = \frac{0.8(400)}{(1 + 0.04)} = 307.69.$$

Table 5-4 summarizes the components of expected income for risk bearing.

Taken together, Tables 5-3 and 5-4 completely summarize the income Mr. X expects to receive over time.

**Table 5–4**

| | *Period 1* | *Period 2* | *Period 3* |
|---|---|---|---|
| Expected income for risk bearing due to: | | | |
| (a) uncertainty of the amount $D_t$ | 10.00 | 20.00 | 40.00 |
| (b) expected resolution of uncertainty for subsequent dividends | 56.21 | 38.46 | 0 |
| Total | 66.21 | 58.46 | 40.00 |

## Conclusion

In the preceding section we demonstrated that the pattern in which stockholders realize income over time depends not only on

[16] But assuming that uncertainty *will* be resolved in the preceding periods according to Mr. X's expectations at period $t = 0$.

concrete factors such as dividend payments and the interest rate but also on the extent to which stockholders' expectations change over time. The problems posed by treating expectations as variable are especially difficult because we have no assurance that expectations will change in a stable and predictable pattern. In fact, Eq. (5-13), which sums up our conclusions with regard to income and uncertainty, places essentially no restrictions on the kinds of patterns that might occur.

Of course, further information often allows a financial manager to make more specific predictions. The distinction between the three cases illustrated in Chapter 4 was a realistic example. Also, less general models of valuation frequently embody fairly reasonable, although restrictive, assumptions about the pattern in which income is realized. For instance, the idea of constant expected income used by MM is consistent with unique "required rates of return" if we make the additional assumption that the $\alpha_t$'s assigned to expected dividends[17] vary over time in the manner specified by Eq. (5-8). This is not necessarily unrealistic, since it implies merely that the uncertainty attached to particular dividends is expected to be resolved at a fairly constant rate over time. A similar assumption could be made to justify use of a constant $\hat{k}$ in the Gordon dividend model that was described in Chapter 4.

But the most important result of this chapter is that the models discussed in Chapters 3 and 4 are useful but not completely general descriptions of the considerations that affect the value of stocks as investments. How are we to interpret the concept of a "risk class" when MM define it in terms of a unique "required rate of return"? What is the meaning of the term *cost of capital?* Is there any reason to suppose that we can observe $\hat{k}$, the stockholders' rate of discount, as defined by Gordon? Can the certainty equivalent factors $\alpha_t$ be given sufficient empirical meaning to be useful in practice? These are open questions; and although the arguments of these and the other authors discussed remain useful and important, the financial manager must use considerable caution in applying them.

---

[17] MM assumed that all income was paid out as dividends.

# 6

# A Normative Framework for Finance

THE FIRST five chapters of this book have covered financial theory in seven-league boots, or, to use a more modern metaphor, by jet, seven miles up. From such a height, colors blend, roads straighten, the fields of the Midwest achieve an astonishing regularity, and even in such a disruption as the Rocky Mountains a certain north-south logic can be ascertained.

The sad fact, however, is that the financial manager is earthbound. From seven miles up, we can inform him of the nature of alternative destinations, tell him, in a rough sense, how to get there, and note the likely hazards of the journey. But there is very little basis on which to inform him whether the traffic in Omaha is bad today.

Thus the use of the word *framework* in this chapter's title, rather than *model* or *solution procedure*—the latter terms are presumptuous. The purpose of this chapter is to tie together what we know about finance by indicating the likely relations between the major variables affecting the financing decision. These variables include both those previously discussed, such as income, leverage, dividends, growth and uncertainty, and further considerations such as capital constraints, taxes, inflation, and transaction and issue costs. Insofar as possible, we will attempt to integrate these factors in an objective function based on the basic valuation formula discussed in Chapter 5.

By making a wide-ranging survey of factors affecting the financing decision, this chapter attempts to put the reader in the shoes of the financial manager and to establish some appreciation of the nature of the over-all decision that must be made. Determining the effects of leverage, risk, market imperfections, etc., is difficult enough. Determining the combined effect of all these factors on the value of the firm to its shareholders is a problem of compound difficulty; as we shall see, in practice none of these factors can be considered apart from the effects of the others.

Our problem would be substantially simpler if the financial manager also happened to be the sole owner. But we must be primarily concerned with the case where the financial manager must act in the interests of many shareholders, and where problems of communication become crucial. For instance, the value of the company to its shareholders cannot be maximized if their attitudes toward risk are misunderstood by the financial manager. As this chapter shall show, the channels of communication normally are not simple or direct.

Because of the complexity of the over-all problem, the available conceptual tools are not adequate to provide the solution for the optimal financing decision in general. We have every reason to suppose that an optimal financing decision exists, but the financial manager can rarely specify this decision exactly. This chapter describes the nature of the judgment the financial manager must make.

## Review of the Basic Valuation Formula

In Chapter 5 we arrived at the following formula for the value of the equity shares of a firm.[1]

$$P_0 = \sum_{t=1}^{\infty} \frac{\alpha_t \bar{D}_t}{\prod_{\tau=1}^{t} (1 + \bar{\imath}_\tau)} \tag{6-1}$$

Let us review the conclusions that Eq. (6-1) embodies. First, it conforms to the discounted present value approach presented in Chapter 2. Second, it reflects the conclusion of Chapter 4 that expected dividends are the appropriate basis for establishing stock value. Third, it adheres to the certainty equivalent approach to uncertainty. Last, strictly speaking, Eq. (6-1) applies only to an *individual* shareholder's expectations and attitudes toward risk. Thus, in using the formula to represent the market price of the firm's stock, we are establishing the fiction that "the market" or a "representative investor" behaves according to certain expectations and risk attitudes.

---

[1] See p. 81.

Since for most purposes, market price can be taken as a measure of the value of the firm to its stockholders, this fiction will usually not affect financial decisions, although the cautionary comments of Chapter 5 are still germane.[2]

Equation (6-1) embodies no conclusions about the relation between financial leverage and value. We will turn to this point later in this chapter.

## The Optimal Financing Decision Under Conditions of Certainty

Many of the considerations which this chapter discusses can be most conveniently introduced if certainty is assumed. Temporarily, therefore, let us modify Eq. (6-1) so that $\alpha_t = 1$ and $\alpha_t\bar{D}_t = \bar{D}_t = D_t$, where the simple $D_t$ represents the dividend expected (and certain) in year $t$. Therefore we can write

$$P_0 = \sum_{t=1}^{\infty} \frac{D_t}{\prod_{\tau=1}^{t} (1 + \bar{\imath}_\tau)}, \tag{6-2}$$

which, except for notation, is identical to Eq. (2-3). Under conditions of perfect markets and certainty, application of this formula establishes both the investment plan and the financing requirements of the firm. The company will plan to invest in all projects, present and future, with a non-negative net present value.[3] This investment plan establishes the firm's financing requirements for all future periods, and two simple decision rules specify the optimal financing decision:

1. Pay out as dividends any cash on hand that is not required for the firm's planned investment.
2. Obtain any required funds by stock issue at the instant they are needed for investment. (We are not considering borrowing, because there is no difference between debt and equity under conditions of certainty in perfect markets.)

These two rules are the whole story under these simplified assumptions. The stockholder is indifferent to the pattern in which dividends are distributed over time, since he can borrow against or lend present or future dividends so as to distribute present value over time in any desired pattern. And we can be assured that funds required for investment would be instantaneously available in any required amount at the rates $\bar{\imath}_\tau$.

In order to illustrate how these two rules would be applied, a simple pattern of *cumulative* financing requirements is plotted over time in

---

[2] See p. 75*f*.

[3] When projects are not independent, the firm will accept those projects which, in combination, will result in the maximum present value attainable.

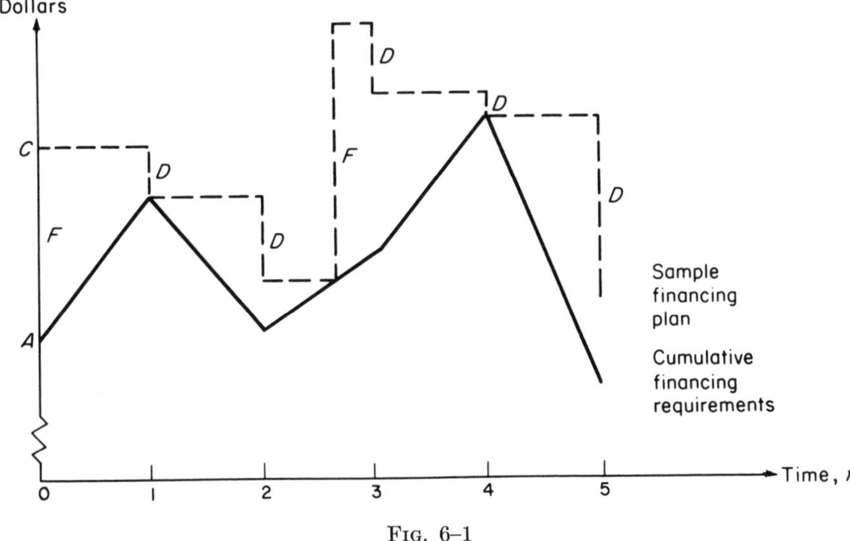


FIG. 6–1

Fig. 6-1. This schedule is the sum of the expected annual cash flows of projects undertaken by a hypothetical firm. The cumulative requirements line is drawn upward-sloping when the firm's investments absorb capital, and downward-sloping when the net cash flows from these investments are positive. In this example, net cash flows are negative in the year from $t = 0$ to $t = 1$; positive from $t = 1$ to $t = 2$; negative from $t = 2$ to $t = 4$, and positive for the last year shown. We assume there is no cash on hand at $t = 0$.

Given perfect markets and certainty, we can apply the two financing rules stated in the previous section to come up with a financing plan. Note that the rules imply also that the firm's cash balance will always be zero, since the first rule directs the financial manager immediately to pay out any available cash as dividends. ("Available" in this context means "not needed to meet the cumulative financing requirements.") It should be emphasized that, under these assumptions, there is no need even for a "minimum cash balance," since funds may be obtained instantaneously when needed. Therefore, from $t = 0$ to $t = 1$ the company will issue equity shares day by day throughout the year in amounts just sufficient to keep up with the increasing financial requirements. Then in the year from $t = 1$ to $t = 2$, the firm will pay dividends day by day as the firm's operations make the funds available. Similarly, the firm will issue stock from $t = 2$ to $t = 4$, pay dividends from $t = 4$ to $t = 5$, and so on.

Thus if we were to plot a "cumulative financing plan" for the firm (i.e., cumulative proceeds from sale of stock minus cumulative dividend payments) such a schedule would coincide exactly with the schedule of cumulative financing requirements over time.

Before considering other factors which affect the financing decisions, a few comments on this simple case may be helpful. First, note that the costs of financing are the same for all investment projects: this allows a legitimate separation of the investment and financing decisions. If, however, different investment plans imply different financing costs relative to the amounts invested, such a separation is not legitimate. The latter case is, of course, the realistic one. Financing costs depend on both the business and the financial risk of the corporation, and the investment decision largely determines business risk. It is equally true that the investment decision depends on the financing decision, as the use of the "cost of capital" rule to evaluate investment projects suggests. In order to maximize value, therefore, the firm's investment and financing plans must normally be chosen simultaneously.

For the purposes of this book, and quite often in practice, it is appropriate to consider the financing decision *given* the financing requirements established by an investment plan. If we assume that an optimal financing plan can be derived for any investment plan, then considering various investment plans *cum* optimal financing plans would allow the best combination to be selected. Moreover, even when absolutely optimal policies cannot be precisely identified, an iterative decision-making process may result in an investment-financing plan which approximates the optimum one. For example, given a proposed investment plan, we could imagine a financial manager concluding that financing costs could be reduced if financial requirements were modified. A new investment plan could then be drawn up, the financial alternatives re-evaluated, and so on. By such a process of trial and error a better approximation of the optimal investment-financing decision could be achieved. This process obviously requires consideration of the financing decision with the investment decision (temporarily) assumed given.

It is interesting to note that the investment decision is often considered taking the financing decision as given. This occurs not only in the context of the trial-and-error process described; in practice we often find companies with a very restricted set of feasible financing alternatives. Also, the use of a single "cost of capital" for investment decisions implicitly takes the financing decision as given.[4]

---

[4] This implicit assumption may lead to errors where the cost of capital concept is naïvely used. For examples, see Alexander A. Robichek and John G. MacDonald, "The Cost of Capital Concept: Potential Use and Misuse," *Financial Executive*, June 1965, p. 20 *ff*. Indeed, the concept itself is on somewhat shaky ground in light of our conclusions in Chapter 5 above—i.e., that a single discount rate was not adequate to describe the riskiness of various investments.

## Other Factors in the Financing Decision under Certainty

Of course it is quite absurd to imagine 365 different stock issues in the course of a year—that is, it is absurd to ignore "transaction costs" of these issues. Transaction costs are the first of several factors that qualify the two simple financing rules given above. Although these factors introduce market imperfections, the assumption of certainty will be retained.

### Transaction Costs

There are two kinds of "costs" in obtaining capital. First, there is the required return of the investors, i.e., the interest or dividends, usually lumped under the rubric "cost of capital." The second variety is what we call "transaction costs,"[5] e.g., paperwork, brokerage fees, filing with the Securities and Exchange Commission (S.E.C.), etc. To a substantial extent, the latter costs are fixed. For instance, the paperwork in sending out a dividend check for $2 or one for $100 is the same; the S.E.C. requires essentially the same steps whether a stock issue is expected to yield proceeds of $500,000 or $5,000,000. Usually the firm can reduce total transaction costs by selling equity shares or declaring dividends in greater amounts but less frequently. On the other hand, there is a cost to the shareholders if the firm holds balances of idle cash or short-term securities which could earn greater returns if invested elsewhere. The objective in trading off these lost returns against transaction costs is to achieve the lowest over-all cost of financing; *ceteris paribus*, this would maximize stockholder value as defined by Eq. (6-2).

A sample financing plan (not necessarily an optimal one) that takes transaction costs into account is plotted as the dashed line in Fig. 6-1. The firm's cash balance is indicated by the vertical difference between the dashed and solid lines (i.e., cumulative financing obtained less cumulative financing requirements equals cash balance). In this example we have assumed that some dividend is paid each year and that transaction costs in issuing stock are substantial. The firm begins with total capitalization $OA$, but immediately sells shares (F) to obtain $AC$ at $t = 0$, then pays dividends $(D)$ at $t = 1$ and $t = 2$. Another stock issue $(F)$ is required between $t = 2$ and $t = 3$. Dividends $(D)$ continue to be paid yearly.

The idea behind such a financing plan is to reduce the total transaction costs of financing. This is done, however, at the expense of

---

[5] For a more formal discussion which considers the effects of transactions costs, see John Lintner, "Dividends, Earnings, Leverage, Stock Prices and the Supply of Capital to Corporations," *Review of Economic and Statistics*, XLIV, No. 3 (1962), 243–269.

leaving sizeable cash balances idle or invested in short-term securities earning a relatively low rate of return.

## Inflation

Common stocks are widely regarded as a "hedge" against inflation. Of course, debt interest and principal repayments are fixed in monetary terms. But it is assumed that the money earnings and dividends of corporations rise with the general price level, partially or completely offsetting any decline in the *real* value of the dollar amount of the original dividend expectations. In fact, it is conceivable that the *real* value of expected dividends will rise in inflationary conditions.

We can incorporate this in our analysis as follows. Assume that the market is suddenly informed that inflation will take place in the future. Define $\eta_\tau$ as the expected (and known) yearly rate of inflation of the general price level in year $t = \tau$. Under perfect markets and certainty, this will be reflected in the riskless rate of interest, $\bar{\imath}_\tau$, so that $(1 + \bar{\imath}_\tau) = (1 + i_\tau^*)(1 + \eta_\tau)$, where $i_\tau^*$ is the "pure" interest rate in year $t = \tau$. Let $\beta_\tau$ be the percentage change in $D_t$ induced by inflation in year $t = \tau$, where $D_t$ is redefined as the dividend that the stockholders would receive *if no inflation whatsoever were expected*. We can rewrite Eq. (6-2) as

$$P_0 = \sum_{t=1}^{\infty} \frac{D_t \prod_{\tau=1}^{t} (1 + \beta_\tau)}{\prod_{\tau=1}^{t} [(1 + i_\tau^*)(1 + \eta_\tau)]}. \tag{6-3}$$

Notice that the price of the stock will be unaffected by a change in the rate of inflation if $\eta_\tau = \beta_\tau$ for all future periods, rise if $\beta_\tau > \eta_\tau$, and fall if $\beta_\tau < \eta_\tau$. It is possible, of course, that $\beta_\tau > \eta_\tau$ for some periods but not for others, in which case the impact on value must be computed from Eq. (6-3). In all cases, the effects of inflation on the value of the firm could be determined if the variables of Eq. (6-3) were known.

## Personal Income Taxes

Since the investor's personal tax rate determines the amount of "after-tax" expected dividends, it would seem that the higher an investor's personal tax rate, the less the value of a given stream of expected dividends to him. The simplicity of this statement is misleading, however. It is impossible to specify exactly the effect of personal tax rates on financing decisions without additional and restrictive assumptions.

One approach would be to recast Eq. (6-2) so that both expected dividends *and* the riskless interest rate are on an after-tax basis, and assume that the personal tax rate may vary between individuals and over time. If we let $T_\tau$ represent the personal tax rate applicable to a given shareholder at time $t = \tau$, then we could recast Eq. (6-2) in a form such as

$$P_0 = \sum_{t=1}^{\infty} \frac{(1 - T_t)\, D_t}{\prod_{\tau=1}^{t} [1 + \bar{i}_\tau (1 - T_\tau)]} . \tag{6-4}$$

Equation (6-4) is, however, only one possible alternative, since the denominator of the valuation equation may take many different forms on an after-tax basis. The denominator is an opportunity cost, established by the highest after-tax rate of return which can be obtained on a riskless investment. The alternatives available here are rather complicated. Equation (6-4) assumes that the relevant alternative is for the individual investor to buy taxable, riskless securities maturing at time $t$, promising $\bar{i}_\tau$ for periods 1 to $t$, and to reinvest the yearly interest payments. Since the interest payments would represent taxable income to the investor, the full amount of these interest payments would not be available for reinvestment. Personal tax payments would reduce funds available for reinvestment by a factor of $(1 - T_\tau)$, and the yearly growth rate of the funds invested in taxable, riskless securities would be only $\bar{i}_\tau\,(1 - T_\tau)$ in each year $\tau$.

On the other hand, personal taxes are irrelevant for many large institutional investors—for instance, pension funds—whose interest and dividend income is not taxed.

Still another possibility might be that the rate of return on highest grade tax-exempt bonds is the opportunity cost. It is a slight distortion to assume that such bonds are completely riskless, but this assumption could be made as an approximation. Suppose the interest rate were 3 per cent on tax-exempt municipals and 4 per cent on taxable government bonds of comparable maturity. If an investor's personal tax rate were less than 25 per cent, he could earn an after-tax return of more than 3 per cent on taxable government bonds, and municipal bonds would be irrelevant to the valuation of his stock holdings. If his personal tax rate were greater than 25 per cent, taxable government bonds would be irrelevant to his personal investment decision.

We could introduce some after-tax discount rate in the valuation formula, but in view of the impossibility of specifying a unique rate for all investors we believe it simpler, and probably no less accurate, to exclude the effect of personal taxes by assuming that "the market," or the "average investor" behaves *as if* $\bar{i}_\tau$ were the relevant *pre-tax* riskless discount rate. For most widely held companies, we believe this to be an acceptable fiction.

However, in some instances the financial manager will find it advisable to adjust his decisions to special tax considerations. For instance, suppose a large proportion of the firm's shares to be held by a Mr. W (W for wealthy). The tax rate on Mr. W's dividends is so high that the value of a given stream of future dividends to him (discounted at the tax-free municipal bond rate) is lower than the market value of this same stream. What would be the optimal financing decision for the firm from the point of view of Mr. W? It is clear that Mr. W would always prefer to receive a *given* amount of income in the form of capital gains (which are taxed at a lower rate than ordinary income) rather than dividends. From his point of view it might well be desirable for the firm to reinvest present dividends, even if the after-tax value to him of the increment to expected dividends is less than the after-tax value of present dividends foregone. Such a strategy would be attractive to Mr. W if (and only if) he expects market price to rise so that his expected proceeds from the sale of the shares net of capital gains taxes are increased by an amount greater than the after-tax value of the present dividend foregone.[6] It does *not* follow, however, than an investor should always attempt to realize income in the form of capital gains merely because the capital gains tax rate is lower than the effective personal tax rate. As the example of Mr. W illustrates, the choice is not simply dependent on the relevant tax rates but also on the difference between the market price and the investor's personal valuation of the stock. The objective is to obtain the highest value after all taxes.

## Stockholder Time Preferences in Imperfect Markets

We have argued that in perfect markets, stockholders would be indifferent to the different time patterns in which dividends could be paid, since they could always either reinvest the dividends or sell a part of their stock holdings to achieve any desired pattern of consumption over time. However, in imperfect markets, stockholders may often be unable or unwilling to act in order to redistribute present value over time in the optimal pattern.

This factor is frequently significant for financial decision-making. Suppose, for example, that Mr. X has purchased stock with the expectation of a stable dividend income, but the company in which he has invested is considering financing a new investment project by

[6] Of course, if the other stockholders of the firm shared the opinion of Mr. W and the market, reinvesting the present dividends would be to their advantage also. Furthermore, the firm should not ignore the possibility of repurchasing its own stock, where this alternative is legally available.

decreasing current dividends. Suppose also that Mr. X has arranged his personal investment plan so that his expected dividends are optimally distributed over time. If the company changes its dividend pattern (which from the point of view of Mr. X was optimal), the value of the stock to Mr. X will change if he is not able to adjust his stock holdings so as to achieve again the optimal pattern of personal income. To the extent that he is not able so to adjust,[7] the value of the stock to Mr. X will be lower than the potential value as described by Eq. (6-2). We may represent this effect by $\gamma_t$, where $\gamma_t = 1$ if the dividend policy of the firm is optimal from the stockholder's point of view, or the stockholder can adjust without cost to the desired pattern, but $\gamma_t < 1$ to the extent that Mr. X's desired pattern of dividends cannot be achieved. We could thus rewrite Eq. (6-2) as

$$P_0 = \sum_{t=1}^{\infty} \frac{\gamma_t D_t}{\prod_{\tau=1}^{t} (1 + \bar{i}_\tau)} . \tag{6-5}$$

## Constraints on Financing Alternatives

For issues discussed in previous chapters, it has been sufficient to speak in terms of the broad categories of debt and equity, and to assume that the proportions of each could be varied at will. In practice, a financial manager must choose between many types of financing. In doing so he is likely to find as many varieties of constraints.

For example, many corporations have adopted a financing policy of not issuing new equity shares. Now, as an unimpeachable constraint on financial policy this is not in the best interest of stockholders. If the expected present value of investing the funds contributed by a stock issue is greater than the present value of dividends promised to new shareholders, then the present value of dividends expected by the original shareholders will be increased in spite of the "dilution." Thus there is little point in making an *a priori* judgment against a stock issue. Nevertheless, if the reaction of present stockholders is such that any issue of new stock would reduce the perceived value of their shares, the financial manager is forced to treat this factor as a constraint.

Another common constraint is the desire of one or a small group of stockholders to retain, say, 51 per cent of outstanding shares in order to retain managerial control of the firm. This would impose a constraint on the amount of new shares that could be issued.

The problem of control often arises in another guise when creditors seek to impose restraints on company policies in order to protect

---

[7] If he is able to adjust but the adjustment is costly, the same conclusion follows.

investments that are, from their point of view, uncomfortably risky. For instance, a bank may not lend to a firm unless working capital is kept above a certain figure, or if accounts receivable are already factored.

There may be other forms of contraints—e.g., government regulations, considerations of the company's social responsibilities—but in most cases these are more relevant to the investment decision, and thus may be ignored for present purposes. Sometimes, however, financing alternatives may be constrained by such considerations.

As long as the constraints can be precisely specified, the financial problem can be solved by various programming approaches under conditions of certainty.[8] In some cases certainty may be assumed in practice—e.g., Chapter 7 discusses a solution to the short-term financing problem under this assumption and subject to a set of constraints on financing alternatives.

## The Choice Between Debt and Equity Reconsidered

It will be helpful, partly as a review, to set out the ways in which the choice between debt and equity financing affects value.

In Chapter 3, our examination of leverage led us to the conclusion that leverage affects value because:

1. Corporate income is taxed.

And probably because:

2. Certain types of market imperfections restrict the MM arbitrage process.
3. The investment strategy of the firm may be changed by leverage. (We chiefly discussed the example in which future investment plans are changed because of fixed debt obligations.)

In addition, the discussion in this chapter of the various factors which affect the financing decision allows us to add other items to the list:

4. Since debt contracts are made in monetary rather than real terms, changing expectations of inflation may affect the relative desirability of debt and equity financing.

---

[8] See, for instance, A. Charnes, W. W. Cooper and M. H. Miller, "Application of Linear Programming to Financial Budgeting and the Cost of Funds," *Journal of Business*, XXXII, No. 1 (1959), 20–46, reprinted in Ezra Solomon, ed., *The Management of Corporate Capital* (New York: Free Press of Glencoe, 1959); also H. Martin Weingartner, *Mathematical Programming and the Analysis of Capital Budgeting Problems* (Englewood Cliffs, N.J.: Prentice-Hall, 1963). We will return to some aspects of this problem in Chapters 7 and 8.

5. A firm may be able to borrow only if it accepts constraints on subsequent financial decisions.
6. Transaction costs in borrowing may be different than the transaction costs of other financing alternatives.
7. Changes in borrowing may be the means by which particular patterns of dividend payments can be obtained (although we must be careful not to suppose that either the end or the means always represent optimal financing policy).

Perhaps still other factors will affect the debt-equity decision in certain circumstances. But until we can predict with greater precision how value is affected by the seven items listed here, it seems pointless to go further. And as long as we have gone this far in confessing ignorance, we might as well note another unsolved problem. This lies in the fact that the MM argument is largely presented in terms of "required rates of return." As was shown in Chapter 5, these rates of return are not related to risk in any unambiguous way. To be sure, use of these rates is justified under certain assumptions,[9] but unless we make these assumptions many statements made in the simplified world of the MM model are difficult to interpret in general. Related problems arise when we try to observe required rates of return in practice.[10]

These problems of the MM model exemplify a chronic ailment of financial theory—our lack of understanding of how financial theory can be used and interpreted. MM need not be singled out for special criticism, since problems of use and interpretation are not present only in their model.

Nevertheless, it seems reasonable to conclude tentatively that neither the all-equity nor the very highly leveraged firm represents optimal financing policy. The all-equity firm cannot benefit from the "bonus" created by leverage because of corporate taxes. On the other hand, a firm which replaces more and more equity with debt would sooner or later be confronted with another consideration—that is, possible interruption of future investment plans because of the existence of high, fixed debt charges. As explained in Chapter 3, these considerations would suffice to define a range of optimal or near-optimal leverage. Other considerations, such as those introduced in this chapter, will of course affect the optimal financing decision with respect to leverage.

---

[9] See the conclusion to Chapter 5.

[10] That is, the rate of return actually realized by stockholders in each period will not in general be equal to an unique "required rate of return," even if all relevant variables actually turn out exactly as stockholders estimated. For example, see our illustrative example, p. 90 above.

## Reintroducing Uncertainty in the Objective Function

Early in this chapter we assumed certainty in order to introduce several additional factors relevant to the financing decision. Reintroducing uncertainty is, however, simple enough, at least from a mathematical viewpoint. Rewriting Eq. (6-1) and introducing the modifications discussed in Eqs. (6-3), (6-4), and (6-5), we have

$$P_0 = \sum_{t=1}^{\infty} \frac{\gamma_t \alpha_t \bar{D}_t \prod_{\tau=1}^{t} (1 + \bar{\beta}_\tau)}{\prod_{\tau=1}^{t} [(1 + i_\tau^*)(1 + \eta_\tau)]} . \tag{6-6}$$

The substitution of $\alpha_t$ (the risk-adjustment factor) and $\bar{D}_t$ (the expected dividend in the absence of inflation) for $D_t$ is straightforward; it follows from the discussion of Chapter 5. A complication enters, however, when we recognize that the adjustment for inflation must be thought of in terms of expected values $\bar{\beta}_\tau$, since no investor knows with certainty how dividends will be affected by expected inflation (or deflation).[11] The uncertainty associated with $\bar{\beta}_\tau$—and consequently with the *real* value of the expected dividend—will be reflected in $\alpha_t$.[12]

An alternative approach to inflation is possible. Let $\bar{D}_t$ be redefined as the expected dividend if investors' current expectations of future inflation turn out to be exactly correct. Now we can rewrite Eq. (6-6) somewhat more concisely:

$$P_0 = \sum_{t=1}^{\infty} \frac{\gamma_t \alpha_t \bar{D}_t}{\prod_{\tau=1}^{t} (1 + i_\tau^*)(1 + \eta_t)} = \sum_{t=1}^{\infty} \frac{\gamma_t \alpha_t \bar{D}_t}{\prod_{\tau=1}^{t} (1 + \bar{i}_\tau)} . \tag{6-6a}$$

The information included in Eq. (6-6) by use of the term

$$\prod_{\tau=1}^{t} (1 + \bar{\beta}_\tau)$$

is still relevant, however, in estimating the effect on value if *actual* inflation turns out to be different from *expected* inflation. The cer-

---

[11] Note that the variables $\eta_\tau$ represent the market reaction to expectations of inflation, as reflected in the yields of riskless bonds. It is, of course, difficult to observe the effects of $i_\tau^*$ and $\eta_\tau$ separately, but one does not need to: knowledge of the rates $\bar{i}_\tau$ is sufficient for the purposes of Eq. (6-6).

[12] We are ignoring one complication. If $\bar{\beta}_\tau > \eta_\tau$, and inflation actually occurs at the rate $\eta_\tau$ in $t = \tau$, the firm will find that it has extra funds available for dividends in that year. However, the firm may decide to reinvest these funds; that is to say, the firm's reinvestment plan, which we have taken as given, may be changed because of changing expectations of inflation. This factor could be incorporated into our analysis but at a cost in complexity that does not seem warranted.

tainty equivalent factor $\alpha_t$ will still be affected by investors' uncertainty about the factors $\beta_\tau$.

A similar comment must be made regarding transaction costs. (Although these costs are not included separately in Eq. (6-6), they will affect value by affecting $\bar{D}_t$ and sometimes $\alpha_t$.) Because of the time required to execute financing decisions, and because of the short-term volatility of stock and bond prices, uncertainty with respect to market behavior affects transaction costs. If a financial manager has planned a bond issue, it is obviously to the advantage of the present stockholders of the company to sell these bonds when interest rates are as low as possible. Similarly, *ceteris paribus*, sale of new equity shares to other than present shareholders is best made when the price of the company's stock is at the highest possible point. However, in most procedures there is an inevitable lag between the final decision to issue stocks and the time at which the issue is actually sold, and stock prices or interest rates may change in the interim.

Uncertainty as to the behavior of stock prices or interest rates may be an important factor, especially for smaller or less well-known companies for which the acceptability of a stock or bond issue to prospective investors is not assured. A financial manager is sometimes able to eliminate risk by issuing securities through an underwriter, but this is expensive since flotation costs may amount to 15 per cent or more of gross proceeds of an issue.[13] The greater part of these costs must be interpreted as insurance against market uncertainty.

No extended discussion is needed here on the other factors introduced above. Our symbol for the effect of the expected pattern of dividends, $\gamma_t$, can be defined by the optimal pattern of *expected* dividends $\bar{D}_t$. And, although programming approaches to some types of constrained financial decisions under conditions of uncertainty are available, they are sufficiently arcane that we feel justified in merely referring the interested reader to them.[14]

## Uncertainty and Observation of Financial Variables

The central thread of this book has been the objective of maximizing the value of a firm's common equity to its present stockholders. This chapter has, in effect, restated this objective as the

---

[13] Securities and Exchange Commission, *Costs of Flotation of Corporate Securities* (Washington, D.C.: U.S. Government Printing Office, 1957), p. 19*ff*.

[14] For instance, A. Charnes and W. W. Cooper, "Chance Constrained Programming," *Management Science*, VI, No. 1 (1959), 73–79; G. Danzig, "Linear Programming under Uncertainty," *Management Science*, I, Nos. 3 and 4 (1955), 197–206; and S. E. Elmaghraby, "An Approach to Linear Programming under Uncertainty," *Operations Research*, VII, No. 2 (1959), 208–216.

following: maximize market value of the equity as given by

$$P_0 = \sum_{t=1}^{\infty} \frac{\gamma_t \alpha_t \bar{D}_t}{\prod_{\tau=1}^{t} (1 + \bar{i}_\tau)}, \tag{6-6a}$$

subject to various constraints, and the adaptation of financing and investment plans to special tax situations of stockholders, if these seem relevant.

Including an equation in a normative statement immediately requires a disclaimer in an age so enamoured of computation as ours. We do not expect the financial manager to be able to *compute* the optimal financing decision, at least in the foreseeable future.

Why not? The variables in Eq. (6-6) are not ephemera: their effect on value is well supported by intuition and accepted in practical discussion. We can be fairly sure of the manner in which the variables in Eq. (6-6) are related to $P_0$. For example, if investors are averse to risk, and the perceived riskiness of future dividends rises, $\alpha_t$ and consequently $P_0$ will fall; if $\bar{\beta}_\tau$ rises and $\eta_\tau$ remains constant, then $P_0$ will rise; and so on. The problem in computation lies not in the implausibility of Eq. (6-6) but in separating the effects of the independent variables on $P_0$. We rarely can *observe* the effects of a change in $P_0$ caused by one of the independent variables under the necessary assumption that all other relevant variables are constant.

Consider what happens when stock prices fall as it becomes evident that the economy is entering a period of recession. It is plausible to suppose that the "average stockholder" is affected by all of the following considerations:

1. Human nature being what it is, expectations of future dividends are revised downward.
2. At the same time, these dividends seem riskier than they did in the optimism of a bull market.
3. Fears of inflation diminish in a recession; if the stock was attractive on this score during the expansionary phase of the business cycle, its value during a recession decreases.
4. During recessionary periods, we may expect the average stockholder to become less venturesome, and to prefer stocks with a stable dividend payment over other stocks.
5. Interest rates normally fall in a recession.

If the business cycle moves into a strong expansionary stage, we would expect exactly the opposite reaction in each case. In either situation, all six of the independent variables are likely to act in concert, which makes it extremely difficult to deduce their separate impacts on value. We must, moreover, look at the independent variables in terms of expectations, which compounds the problem of observation.

We believe Eq. (6-6), and the discussion it summarizes, to be useful to the financial manager in two ways:

1. It explicitly states the nature of the relationship between a set of variables and the objective of financial management.
2. It is always useful to try to determine "what would happen if . . . ?" Working out the value of an equity share as given by Eq. (6-6) on the basis of management's predictions of dividends and "reasonable" assumed values for the other financial variables is of value both in (a) making explicit the assumptions which financial decisions embody, and in (b) determining the "sensitivity" of these decisions to possible errors in these assumptions. That is to say, use of this approach allows us explicitly to consider questions such as the following: "If stockholders are more averse to risk than we suppose, would our over-all financial plan be changed, and if so, in what degree?"

In short, we are trying to build a framework within which a financial manager can use his judgment most effectively. However, before accepting this framework, we must emphasize the basic assumption that underlies Eq. (6-6). This assumption can be presented in either of two forms. One of these is to assume that, in general, investors consciously attempt to act in a way that is "rational" from an economic point of view, and that, if the stockholders' attitudes, expectations, and opportunities could be adequately described, maximizing Eq. (6-6) is equivalent to maximizing the value of the firm to its present shareholders. An equivalent but somewhat weaker assumption merely holds that "the market" behaves as if this were so.

Undoubtedly there will be exceptions to these assumptions, but we believe them to be the best basis for financial theory now available.

### Some Comments on the Role of Judgment in Financial Management

There is nothing irrational about changing one's mind. Thus there is nothing necessarily irrational behind the dramatic reversals of opinion sometimes observed in the stock market. Often factors that significantly affect the value of a firm's stock may become apparent to many investors all at once. A series of such revelations would cause substantial, and entirely justified, fluctuations in stock price. Considering the number of independent variables that affect the value of a share of stock, we would expect price fluctuation to be the rule, rather than the exception, in a rational but uncertain world.

Nevertheless, the existence of price fluctuations means that financial managers must exercise a particular sort of judgment. Many price fluctuations may *seem* irrational to the financial manager, who is often in a better position than the average investor to estimate many determinants of intrinsic stock value, and who in any case rarely revises his estimates of the relevant financial variables on a day-to-day basis.

It is clear that financing decisions cannot be adjusted in response to daily fluctuations in market price. Even the dramatic reversals of investor opinion mentioned at the beginning of this section need not cause a change in financing decisions. If the price of a stock falls off sharply in the course of a general market panic, a financial manager would rightly hesitate to interpret the price change as a rejection of his financial policies. On the other hand, in some cases, dramatic price changes may vindicate financial policy. A financial manager would be justifiably heartened if the price of his company's stock shot up after the announcement of a new dividend policy.

Clearly, all price fluctuations cannot be assumed to be of equal importance. The interpretation of price changes is largely a matter of judgment, and there will always be difficult borderline cases. The market itself, however, offers some clues. Fundamental changes in the value of a company's shares as perceived by stockholders are likely to be reflected in some or all of the following ways:

1. Shifts in the price of the company's stock relative to comparable companies—e.g., other companies in the same industry.
2. A trend in the price of the stock different from that of the market as a whole.
3. Any significant price change that appears to be permanent deserves an attempt at explanation by the financial manager.
4. A price change that appears to follow from a financing or investment decision. Such changes are in a sense "predictable:" e.g., financial managers should be especially attentive to any changes in market price subsequent to the announcement of a new dividend policy.

From another point of view, fluctuations may be evaluated in terms of expected and unexpected changes in market price. In terms of the present example, the announcement of a new dividend policy is expected to increase the value of the firm to its stockholders. If the price of the stock does rise after the announcement, then all is well; if the price falls, however, a fundamental rethinking of financial policy should follow.

Of course we cannot attempt to predict all price fluctuations, even though we have theoretical explanations of what determines changes in value over time.[15] But even modest attempts to predict broad trends in stock value will be useful to financial management, not only as a means of evaluating price fluctuations but also as a means of "checking out" management's assumptions regarding stockholders' attitudes and expectations. There is always the temptation for the

---

[15] This subject was discussed at length in Chapter 5.

financial manager to act on the basis of what he feels investors *should* want, rather than on the basis of their actual preferences.

Of course, a financial manager may on occasion find that policies that he considers unquestionably desirable run counter to investors' attitudes or expectations. It may be that stockholders, if better informed, would accept these policies. In some instances, the financial manager may take it upon himself to make the necessary information about company policies available; or, he may feel that trends in economic conditions or in the company's operating performance will soon make the desirability of these policies clear. If, however, the financial manager judges the stockholders' attitudes or expectations to be permanent, then he should modify financial policies so that *value as the stockholders perceive it* is maximized.

Finally, we must again remark that market price is not always the appropriate measure of value to stockholders, e.g., where the stock is not widely traded, or where market imperfections prevent free trading of the stock by some shareholders.[16] In such instances, the normal goal of maximizing market price must be pursued with appropriate qualifications.

## Summary

As a concluding note, we must again emphasize what this chapter has attempted to achieve. First, we have established a framework in which the optimal financing decision can be made with regard to combinations of investment-financing alternatives. Insofar as possible, we have included in the framework all factors which we feel significantly affect the value of a firm's stock to investors. Second, by describing the sort of judgments required in financial decision making, we have made clear the practical difficulties of identifying the optimal financing decision.

The complex interrelationships of the elements included in the framework and the problems of specifying investor attitudes and expectations are such that the optimum financing decision can only rarely be exactly specified. It may be discouraging to many readers to reflect on the demands made by the world on the financial manager's judgment—and mistakes will surely be made. However, glossing over the problems involved would have made them no less formidable.

In a sense, this chapter is this book's center of gravity. It synthesizes what we have learned from the theoretical discussions of previous chapters, and it sets the stage for the more practical discussions of financial problems that follow. In the next chapter the short-term financing decision will be considered as a subproblem of the framework we have established here. Chapter 8 will present some specific approaches to aspects of the long-term financing problem.

---

[16] See our discussion, pp. 75*ff*.

# The Short-Term Financing Decision

THE GENERALIZED discussion of Chapter VI could not help but emphasize our present inability to "solve" the over-all financing problem. This chapter stands as a counterweight to the last one in that it illustrates how an important *subproblem*—that is, the problem of short-term financing—can be "solved."

## Defining the Subproblem

We could imagine a financial manager formulating this subproblem in the following manner. Suppose at time $t_0$ management proposes an investment plan which, if undertaken in addition to the company's present operations, would result in the estimated cumulative funds requirement over time indicated by the line $I_0E$ in Fig. 7-1. At $t_0$, the firm's balance sheet shows an amount $OI_0$ invested in the firm's operations and a cash balance $DI_0$. The financial manager observes a long-run growth in the annual minimum cumulative funds requirement, shown in Fig. 7-1 by the line $I_0C$. A fairly regular seasonal cash requirement is predicted in addition to these minimum requirements. Finally, short-term predictions of sales, collections of accounts receivable, inventory requirements, etc., have been assembled to predict a month-to-month cash flow pattern for the period between $t_0$ and $t_1$. This is shown by the portion of $I_0E$ between $t_0$ and $t_1$.

The pattern of short-term financing is determined by the expected month-to-month funds requirement. The actual amounts of required financing in the short term, however, depend on two long-term decisions. First, the long-term investment decision affects the amount of cash required from all sources. In the example shown in Fig. 7-1, for instance, estimated peak funds requirements are expected to increase. Second, long-term financing can provide various proportions of the firm's expected total needs. Suppose long-term sources provide funds amounting to the line $AB$ in Fig. 7-1; in this case there would be no expected need for short-term financing whatsoever. Or, long-term funds could be obtained amounting to the line $I_0C$, in which case the entire expected seasonal fluctuation would have to be financed with short-term instruments. The most common case is somewhere between these two extremes, although we ought not to rule out the possibility of financing "long-term requirements"—that is, funds in amounts below the line $I_0C$—by short-term instruments.

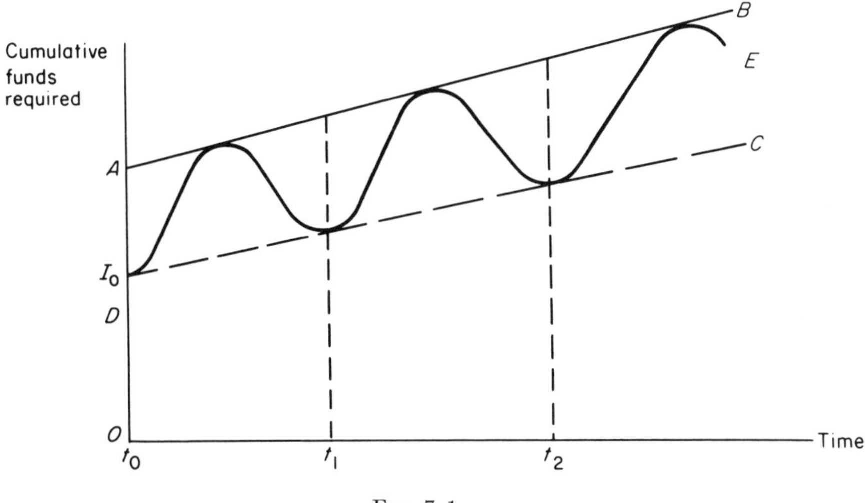


FIG. 7-1

The effect of such considerations is to separate the financing problem into two separate questions. First, what should be the proportions of short and long-term financing in the firm's capital structure? Second, once these proportions have been chosen, what is the optimal way to finance the short-term requirement? The subproblem of short-term finance is to find an answer to the second question.

Obviously these questions are not independent. The relative cost and risk of short- versus long-term debt will determine their proportions in the firm's optimal capital structure; that is, the answer to the second question partly determines the answer to the first. In order to find the over-all optimum, the solutions to the two questions must be found simultaneously.

In practice, the financial manager will attempt to improve the firm's financing plan by considering possible marginal changes in the existing financing mix. Estimating the costs and risks of various short-term financing plans is obviously essential to this process of gradual improvement. Even more important, the financial manager must arrange to meet the *actual* short-term requirements of the firm on a month-to-month basis—he cannot postpone this task while the search for the best over-all financial plan proceeds.

We shall discuss the short-term financing subproblem in some detail in the remainder of this chapter. A fairly realistic example is presented which can be solved using linear programming.[1] The example takes the short-term financing requirement as given. Moreover, the risk of the various alternatives is assumed constant (with some qualifications). That is, the risk of short-term financing is assumed to be chiefly dependent on the *amount* of short-term financing relative to the remainder of the firm's capitalization, not on the means by which the short-term requirement is actually met.

The decision problem which we will consider excludes autonomous financing, i.e., financing generated automatically by the investment decision. For example, it may be customary for suppliers not to require immediate cash payment or for employees to be paid on a monthly basis. The financial decision maker must be cognizant of these autonomous sources because they affect the amount of external financing which must be provided by financial management. Our concern here is with the financing needed over and above the autonomous sources.

## A Typical Short-Term Financing Problem

If one alternative is clearly superior to all others the short-term financing problem is easily resolved by accepting that alternative. Sometimes, for example, the company may be able to obtain all the

---

[1] This chapter is an adaptation of A. A. Robichek, D. Teichroew and J. M. Jones, "Optimal Short Term Financing Decision," *Management Science*, forthcoming. The details of the mathematical formulation are not presented here.

We should note, also, that other authors have developed computational techniques applicable to the short-term financing problem. See, for example, A. Charnes, W. W. Cooper and M. H. Miller, "Application of Linear Programming to Financial Budgeting and the Costing of Funds," *Journal of Business*, XXXII, No. 1 (1959), reprinted in Ezra Solomon, ed., *The Management of Corporate Capital* (New York: The Macmillan Company, Free Press of Glencoe, 1959); and W. Beranek, *Analysis for Financial Decisions* (Homewood, Illinois: Richard D. Irwin, Inc., 1963), Chap. XI, XIII, and XIV.

funds it needs under a favorable line of credit. More frequent, however, is the situation where either one alternative is not superior in every respect or where various constraints limit the feasible solutions. In these instances, the financial decision maker must select a "financing package."

Consider the problem faced by a financial officer who has prepared the short-term cash budget presented in Table 7-1. This detailed budget is summarized by Fig. 7-2, which shows month-to-month changes in the firm's cumulative short-term funds requirement.

We shall now describe this problem in somewhat more detail.

## The Cash Budget

Table 7-1 shows, by periods, for twelve periods: total receipts (line 6), total disbursements (line 12), the difference between receipts and disbursements as adjusted by the required change in minimum operating cash balances (line 15), and finally the cumulative cash requirements (line 16). Financial costs of obtaining funds to meet these requirements are not included in the budget.

Only two basic types of cash receipts are considered for this particular example: (1) collections of accounts receivable and (2) all other receipts, which include sources such as cash sales, proceeds from sale of capital equipment, etc. The detail underlying the determination of the collections of accounts receivable is shown. The financial officer normally does not have any control over the rate of sales, the pattern of collections on accounts receivable, or over "other receipts." However, he is able to use the accounts receivable as security in order to obtain funds.

Similarly, two types of disbursements are shown in the table: (1) payments for purchases, and (2) all other disbursements, including

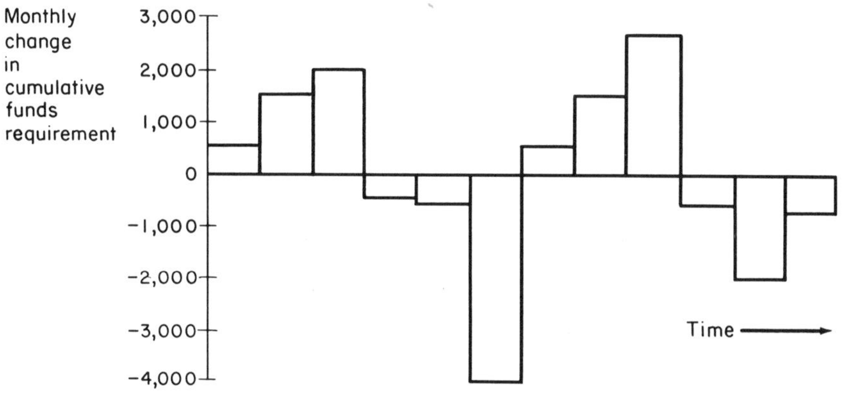


FIG. 7–2

## Table 7–1: Cash Budget (Millions of dollars)

**(Bracketed figures denote need to obtain funds and unbracketed figures denote excess cash.)**

| *Receipts* | | *Periods* | | | | | | | | | | | |
|---|---|---|---|---|---|---|---|---|---|---|---|---|---|
| | | 1 | 2 | 3 | 4 | 5 | 6 | 7 | 8 | 9 | 10 | 11 | 12 |
| Line 1: | Accounts Receivable—Beginning | 3.0 | 3.0 | 4.5 | 4.25 | 4.25 | 2.0 | 3.5 | 4.5 | 4.5 | 4.25 | 3.5 | 2.5 |
| Line 2: | +Sales on Accounts Receivable | 2.0 | 3.0 | 2.5 | 2.5 | 1.75 | 3.0 | 3.0 | 3.0 | 2.25 | 2.25 | 2.0 | 2.5 |
| Line 3: | −Accounts Receivable—End | 3.0 | 4.5 | 4.25 | 4.25 | 2.0 | 3.5 | 4.5 | 4.5 | 4.25 | 3.5 | 2.5 | 3.5 |
| Line 4: | Collections on Accounts Receivable | 2.0 | 1.5 | 2.75 | 2.5 | 4.0 | 1.5 | 2.0 | 3.0 | 2.5 | 3.0 | 3.0 | 1.5 |
| Line 5: | Other Receipts (Cash sales, etc.) | 1.5 | 1.0 | 1.25 | 2.0 | 1.0 | 4.8 | 1.0 | 1.0 | 1.0 | 1.6 | 1.9 | 1.7 |
| Line 6: | Total Receipts | 3.5 | 2.5 | 4.0 | 4.5 | 5.0 | 6.3 | 3.0 | 4.0 | 3.5 | 4.6 | 4.9 | 3.2 |
| *Disbursements* | | | | | | | | | | | | | |
| Line 7: | Accounts Payable—Beginning | 2.0 | 2.0 | 2.5 | 2.5 | 2.5 | 1.0 | 1.0 | 2.0 | 2.5 | 2.5 | 1.5 | 1.0 |
| Line 8: | +Purchases (Net) | 2.0 | 2.5 | 2.5 | 2.5 | 1.0 | 1.0 | 2.0 | 2.5 | 2.5 | 1.5 | 1.0 | 2.0 |
| Line 9: | −Accounts Payable—End | 2.0 | 2.5 | 2.5 | 2.5 | 1.0 | 1.0 | 2.0 | 2.5 | 2.5 | 1.5 | 1.0 | 2.0 |
| Line 10: | Payments for Purchases | 2.0 | 2.0 | 2.5 | 2.5 | 2.5 | 1.0 | 1.0 | 2.0 | 2.5 | 2.5 | 1.5 | 1.0 |
| Line 11: | Other Disbursements | 2.0 | 2.0 | 3.4 | 1.5 | 1.9 | 1.4 | 2.5 | 3.5 | 3.6 | 1.5 | 1.5 | 1.5 |
| Line 12: | Total Disbursements | 4.0 | 4.0 | 5.9 | 4.0 | 4.4 | 2.4 | 3.5 | 5.5 | 6.1 | 4.0 | 3.0 | 2.5 |
| Line 13: | Receipts—Disbursements | (0.5) | (1.5) | (1.9) | 0.5 | 0.6 | 3.9 | (0.5) | (1.5) | (2.6) | 0.6 | 1.9 | 0.7 |
| Line 14: | Change in Minimum Operating Cash Balance | | | (0.1) | | | 0.1 | | | (0.1) | | 0.1 | |
| Line 15: | Cash Requirement for Period Before Interest and Compensating Balance | (0.5) | (1.5) | (2.0) | 0.5 | 0.6 | 4.0 | (0.5) | (1.5) | (2.7) | (0.6) | 2.0 | 0.7 |
| Line 16: | Cumulative Requirement Before Interest and Compensating Balance | (0.5) | (2.0) | (4.0) | (3.5) | (2.9) | 1.1 | 0.6 | (0.9) | (3.6) | (3.0) | (1.0) | (0.3) |
| Line 17: | Memo—Minimum Operating Cash Balance | 0.1 | 0.1 | 0.2 | 0.2 | 0.2 | 0.1 | 0.1 | 0.1 | 0.2 | 0.2 | 0.1 | 0.1 |

payments to creditors on outstanding debts. Again, the financial officer normally does not have any control over the rate of purchases or other disbursements. However, he does have control over when payments are actually made on accounts payable.

Changes in the minimum operating cash balances (line 14) are obtained by taking the differences from one period to the next in the minimum operating cash balance, line 17 of Table 7-1. The cumulative cash requirement before interest and compensating balance at the end of any period (line 16) is merely the sum of the adjusted cash requirements for all previous periods.

## Financial Alternatives

The next step in formulating the problem is to examine the alternatives open to the financial officer, and to determine the costs and the constraints associated with these alternatives. In the description of the alternatives we shall assume that all cash transactions, with one exception, take place at the beginning of the periods. The exception is the collection of accounts receivable, and is explained in detail below.

*Unsecured line of credit* The company has available an unsecured line of credit with a bank which permits it to borrow up to $1,500,000. The bank requires a compensating cash balance of not less than 20 per cent of the amount actually borrowed under the line of credit; the operating cash balance is available to meet this requirement. The interest rate on this line of credit is 0.9 per cent per period. Money can be borrowed or repaid at the beginning of each period.

*Pledging of accounts receivable* The firm can pledge its accounts receivable as security for a bank loan. The amount available under this alternative is limited to a maximum of $3,750,000. The bank will lend up to 80 per cent of the face value of pledged accounts receivable. A portion of the accounts receivable outstanding at the beginning of the period is repaid in the normal course of the business during the period. It is assumed that 30 per cent of these accounts are repaid at a uniform rate during the period; therefore in order to fulfill the requirements at the beginning of a period, it is necessary to borrow $1 for each $.85 of average requirements. The total cost of borrowing under this alternative is 1.4 per cent per period of the average amount of loan outstanding.

Normally the bank will not allow the company to have an unsecured line of credit and at the same time pledge its accounts receivable on an additional loan, nor does it encourage frequent switches from one to the other.

*Stretching of accounts payable* The financial officer, at his option, may stretch (i.e., delay) payments on accounts payable. In the preparation of the cash budget, it was assumed that the purchases were paid in time to obtain the discounts offered by many suppliers for prompt payment. If the payments are stretched the discounts cannot be taken. These foregone discounts then become an additional cost to the firm. The discount loss, on the average, amounts to $3\frac{1}{2}$ per cent if the payments are stretched one period. The financial officer may stretch up to 80 per cent of payments in the period in which they first become due. Once the accounts payable are stretched, the financial officer may decide to stretch them for one additional period at no loss of discount. However, this amount is limited to 75 per cent of the amount already stretched for one period.

Although the stretching of payments for an additional period involves no further loss of discounts, it does involve the loss of good will on the part of the creditors. A loss of confidence on the part of creditors may also occur if the company is inconsistent in its payments policy. A creditor becomes concerned when a company, which has been taking the discount, suddenly delays payments for two periods.

*Term loan* The firm has an offer of a term loan from its bank, which must be taken out at the beginning of the initial period under consideration. It is limited to amounts between $500,000 and $2,000,000. The principal of the loan must be repaid in ten equal installments; the first installment is due six periods after the loan is initially taken out, and the subsequent installments are due at six-period intervals. No speed-up of payments is possible. If the firm takes out a term loan, the bank insists on further constraints on the amount borrowed if at the same time the firm uses either the line of credit or pledging of accounts receivable. The maximum total borrowing if the term loan and a line of credit is used is $2,500,000. The maximum total borrowing if a term loan is used and receivables are pledged is $4,500,000. The interest rate on the term loan is 0.8 per cent per period. In addition, the bank requires certain restrictions on company operations, such as limitations on officers' salaries, dividend payments, and capital expenditures.

*Investment of excess cash* The financial officer may invest any cash in excess of the minimum operating cash balance in short term securities which yield a rate of return of 0.4 per cent per period. It is assumed that no transaction costs are associated with investing or disinvesting in these short-term securities.

*Combinations of these alternatives* The financial officer may use any combination of the alternatives listed above, except that the bank will not permit the use of alternative 1, that is, the line of credit, in combination with alternative 2, that is, the pledging of accounts receivable. Also, a switch between these two alternatives during the periods under consideration is not acceptable.

## Formulating the Objective

The problem that has been considered above is a typical short-term financing problem of a business subject to seasonal cash-flow patterns. The immediate decision that faces the financial officer is whether to take out a term loan and if this is done, in what amount. Furthermore, at the beginning of each period he must decide how to acquire additional cash if it is needed or what to do with excess cash if any is available.

Taking the cash budget as given and the rates as stated, the financial officer can compute the costs of any proposed decision. As a first approximation, suppose that he prefers to use the plan that has the minimum explicit cost. A few trial calculations are sufficient to show that the optimum decision is not obvious. Should the term loan be used? Should the financial manager use the line of credit or stretch accounts payable? Given the various constraints, what financing plans are feasible?

A further complication is introduced when we admit that the decision of the financial manager is usually not based solely on the explicit interest costs. He must also consider "qualitative" factors. For instance, stretching payables involves a loss of the confidence of creditors and the term loan requires some bothersome restrictions on company operations. A term loan is also a long-range commitment that may affect the company's financial risk and/or prevent it from taking advantage of other financing opportunities if interest rates change. These "qualitative" factors arise because of our inability completely to separate the short-term financing subproblem from the firm's over-all financial plan. In the case at hand, it is possible that minimization of explicit interest costs within the context of the short-term subproblem may actually *decrease* the net value of the stockholders' equity because of deleterious side-effects.

One particular example of such side-effects provides an illustration of the interrelationship between the long- and short-term financing decisions. This side-effect arises because of the arbitrarily limited period of time under consideration in the short-term problem. Suppose the firm in our example adopts a short-term financing plan which minimizes explicit interest costs. If everything turns out as expected, the result will be a particular financing mix at the end of the twelve-month "planning horizon." However, it does not follow that this ending financing mix is the best starting point for periods beyond the planning horizon. For instance, the financing alternatives available in subsequent periods would be reduced if accounts payable were stretched to the maximum allowable extent at the end of the initial twelve months.

We can approach this problem in one of two ways. One way is to extend the planning horizon. By this means we could explicitly analyze the short-term subproblem over a longer period—say, fifteen months. The trouble with this approach is that we are faced with the same problem at the end of the new planning horizon as we were at the end of the old one. That is, the financing mix planned for the fifteenth month may not be best for the financial needs of months sixteen, seventeen, eighteen, etc. Moreover, although the analysis is made more complete by extension of the planning horizon, the expanded problem is more difficult to solve.

Therefore, in view of the difficulties in specifying an "optimal" horizon, we have arbitrarily set the short-term planning horizon at the customary twelve months. Instead of extending the planning horizon to take into account the effects of the short-term plan on subsequent periods, we are supposing that the financial manager can make an estimate of the desired ending financial mix. *Implicit costs* will be assigned if the planned ending mix differs from this desired mix.

The choice of the desired financing mix will depend on the conditions expected to prevail after the planning horizon. Probably this decision will be based partly on judgment and partly on explicit analysis. It is, of course, a shortcut—but a shortcut which allows us to avoid complicating our initial subproblem to the extent that it becomes unsolvable. In this sense, such shortcut methods are eminently practical.

Now we can go ahead to assign implicit costs (or credits) in order to incorporate in our problem the "qualitative" factors discussed above. These costs will be expressed as rates per period. First the qualitative disadvantages in the stretching of payables and in the term loan will be incorporated into the problem through the use of implicit costs, which will be added to the explicit costs of funds obtained by the term loan or by stretching accounts payable. In our example, these implicit cost rates are assumed constant. The rates are:

1.0 per cent/period = implicit cost of ill will to creditors
when payments are stretched
more than one period.
.3 per cent/period = implicit costs of the term loan.

Second, we will specify "end" explicit costs (or credits) to be proportional to the amounts by which certain ending balances in the financing plan differ from what these items would be if the financing plan resulted in the desired ending mix. For instance, in our example, .4 per cent of the amount of the term loan outstanding in the last period under consideration is entered as a cost. The complete list of end cost percentages follows:

.5 per cent = "end" cost for line of credit.
.6 per cent = "end" cost for pledged receivables.
1.0 per cent = "end" cost for stretched payables.
.4 per cent = "end" cost for term loan.
.3 per cent = "end" credit for excess cash available because of the term loan.

For simplicity's sake, we have assumed in our example that the desired ending financing mix is exactly the same as the beginning mix.

Now, finally, we can specify our objective function: the objective is to minimize total relevant costs, that is, explicit plus implicit costs, subject to the quantitative restrictions of the problem.

## A Note on Assumptions

In the formulation of this example a number of assumptions were made explicitly or implicitly. At this point it will be helpful to restate them and summarize their justification.

The first three are primarily for convenience and can be modified if the extra complications are considered worthwhile.

1. All transactions except collection of accounts receivable occur at the beginning of a period (or the end of the previous period). In practice many of the decisions are in fact made at the beginning of a period, though transactions occur continuously. This point is not crucial, since increased accuracy can be obtained, if desired, by dividing the total time into shorter periods.
2. Interest on money borrowed in any period is added to cash requirements at the beginning of the next period.
3. The term loan is available only at the beginning of the first period.

The next four assumptions involve more difficult conceptual or computational problems.

4. It has been assumed that the costs of the various alternatives are proportional to the amount borrowed. There is no provision for fixed transaction costs of, say, initiating a term loan or a line of credit.
5. The qualitative factors are incorporated by assigning implicit costs which are proportional to the amount borrowed. In practice, these costs must be included, but they cannot be readily estimated.
6. The model is terminated after a finite number of periods.
7. All parameters and requirements are assumed known with certainty at the time the initial decisions are made. We will discuss ways of treating uncertainty within the subproblem we have defined after examing the linear programming solution to the problem we have formulated.

**Table 7–2: Minimum Total Relevant Costs Under Various Alternatives**

| | | | | | Implicit Costs | | | Total Relevant Cost |
|---|---|---|---|---|---|---|---|---|
| *Case* | *Term Loan* | *Line of Credit* | *Pledging* | *Interest Cost* | *Stretching* | *Term Loan* | *End Condition* | *Explicit Plus Implicit* |
| 1 | 1,111,111 | yes | no | 281,741 | 23,121 | 37,997 | 2,727 | 345,586 |
| 2 | 1,176,642 | no | yes | 270,150 | 0,204 | 40,242 | 2,750 | 313,346 |
| 3 | — | yes | no | 366,710 | 50,033 | — | 3,503 | 420,246 |
| 4 | — | no | yes | 342,299 | 13,378 | — | 4,471 | 360,148 |
| 5 | 500,000 | yes | no | 318,296 | 33,453 | 17,100 | 2,616 | 371,465 |
| 6 | 500,000 | no | yes | 301,293 | 5,773 | 17,100 | 2,828 | 326,995 |
| 7 | 1,000,000 | yes | no | 284,886 | 24,078 | 34,200 | 2,637 | 345,801 |
| 8 | 1,000,000 | no | yes | 276,136 | 0,412 | 34,200 | 2,611 | 313,359 |
| 9 | 2,000,000 | yes | no | 288,382 | 18,459 | 68,400 | 3,537 | 378,778 |
| 10 | 2,000,000 | no | yes | 256,914 | 0 | 68,400 | 3,443 | 328,757 |

## The Solution to the Example Problem

This section discusses the solution to the example problem presented above. The solution was obtained by use of a linear programming algorithm.[2]

The minimum "total relevant costs" for a number of cases are shown in Table 7-2. The first case is the optimal financing plan using the line of credit; the second case is the optimal plan if pledging of accounts receivable is used.

In addition, the minimum cost solutions for eight cases with *fixed* term loans of 0.0, 0.5, 1, and 2 million dollars were computed with either the line of credit or the pledging of receivables. For each of the cases, Table 7-2 shows relevant costs.

As can be seen in Table 7-2, the optimum solution for this problem is achieved by using a term loan of $1,176,642 in combination with pledging of accounts receivable (Case 2). For this case, the total relevant costs are $313,346 over the twelve-month planning period. The optimum solution to the problem would be different if, instead of minimizing total relevant costs, only explicit interest costs were minimized. For example, the explicit interest in the optimum solution with the $2,000,000 term loan and pledging (Case 10) is less than the explicit interest for the optimum case (Case 2).

A detailed statement for the optimum solution, that is, Case 2, is given in Table 7-3. The table shows first the requirements as they were given in line 15 of Table 7-1, and the net interest paid under the optimum solution. The net interest is added to the requirements to give the adjusted requirements. Next are shown the borrowings under pledged receivables, stretched payables, and term loan, and the gross new borrowing. The repayments under each of the alternatives and the net new borrowing are then shown. Subtracting the change in the excess cash balance from the net new borrowing gives a remainder which is exactly equal to the adjusted requirements. Thus, the cash requirements are met. The implicit costs are not shown since they do not affect the cash flows. It is easy to verify that the solution shown in Table 7-3 is feasible; i.e., it satisfies all the constraints stated above.

## Marginal Costs and Their Use

In addition to the explicit optimum solutions given in Table 7-2, the linear programming approach can also be used to determine answers to other questions. For instance, management may wish to choose a nonoptimal solution because of some factor not included in the model. In this case, knowing the linear programming optimum

[2] See Robichek, Teichroew and Jones, "Optimal Short Term Financing Decision," for a detailed description of solution procedures.

## Table 7–3 (Case 2): Detailed Statement of the Optimum Solution for Case 2, Pledging + Optimum Term Loan

| *Period* | 1 | 2 | 3 | 4 | 5 | 6 | 7 | 8 | 9 | 10 | 11 | 12 |
|---|---|---|---|---|---|---|---|---|---|---|---|---|
| Requirement | (500,000) | (1,500,000) | (2,000,000) | 500,000 | 600,000 | 4,000,000 | (500,000) | (1,500,000) | (2,700,000) | 600,000 | 2,000,000 | 700,000 |
| *Interest* | | | | | | | | | | | | |
| Pledging of Receivables | — | — | (11,621) | (39,548) | (33,328) | (25,812) | — | — | — | (37,919) | (30,168) | (2,709) |
| Stretched Payables | — | — | — | (919) | — | — | — | — | — | — | — | — |
| Term Loan | — | (9,413) | (9,413) | (9,413) | (9,413) | (9,413) | (9,413) | (8,472) | (8,472) | (8,472) | (8,472) | (8,472) |
| Less: Income | — | 2,707 | — | — | — | — | 8,484 | 6,010 | — | — | — | — |
| Total Interest | — | (6,706) | (21,034) | (49,880) | (42,741) | (35,225) | (929) | (2,462) | (8,472) | (46,391) | (38,640) | (11,181) |
| Adjusted Reqt. for Period | (500,000) | (1,506,706) | (2,021,034) | 450,120 | 557,259 | 3,964,775 | (500,929) | (1,502,462) | (2,708,472) | 553,609 | 1,961,360 | 688,819 |
| *New Borrowing* | | | | | | | | | | | | |
| Pledging | — | 830,064 | 2,243,809 | 403,208 | 177,295 | — | — | — | 2,708,472 | 258,932 | — | — |
| Stretching | — | — | 26,244 | — | — | — | — | — | — | — | — | — |
| Term Loan | 1,176,642 | — | — | — | — | — | — | — | — | — | — | — |
| Total New Borrowing | 1,176,642 | 830,064 | 2,270,053 | 403,208 | 177,295 | — | — | — | 2,708,472 | 258,932 | — | — |
| *Repayments* | | | | | | | | | | | | |
| Pledging | — | — | (249,019) | (847,456) | (714,182) | (1,843,720) | — | — | — | (812,541) | (1,961,360) | (193,503) |
| Stretching | — | — | — | (5,872) | (20,372) | — | — | — | — | — | — | — |
| Term Loan | — | — | — | — | — | — | (117,664) | — | — | — | — | — |
| Total Repayment | — | — | (249,019) | (853,328) | (734,554) | (1,843,720) | (117,664) | — | — | (812,541) | (1,961,360) | (193,503) |
| Net New Borrowing | 1,176,642 | 830,064 | 2,021,034 | (450,120) | (557,259) | (1,843,720) | (117,664) | — | 2,708,472 | (553,609) | (1,961,360) | (193,503) |
| Change in Excess Cash | (676,642) | 676,642 | — | — | — | (2,121,055) | 618,593 | 1,502,462 | — | — | — | (495,316) |
| Reqt. Financed | 500,000 | 1,506,706 | 2,021,034 | (450,120) | (557,259) | (3,964,775) | 500,929 | 1,502,462 | 2,708,472 | (553,609) | (1,961,360) | (688,819) |

will enable management to determine the opportunity cost of the alternative.

On the other hand, management may wish to consider changes in other variables under its control; for example, management may consider delaying capital expenditures included in the cash budget or changing some of the management-imposed constraints. Or, management may wish to request changes in the parameters not under its control, such as maximum limits on the various loans. For all of these purposes, management can make use of the "marginal costs" generated by the linear programming solution. These marginal costs measure the effect of small changes in the various parameters on the total relevant costs.

We will illustrate the potential value of marginal costs with two examples based on the linear programming solution for Case 2. For instance, management might consider stretching $1,000 of payables a second time in period 6, a course of action which is nonoptimal. Using the marginal cost values we can determine that this action would add $5.71 to the total relevant costs. Or, management may wish to negotiate a change in the constraint on total borrowing ($4,500,000 in this case). At the margin the raising of the constraint by $1,000 would decrease total relevant costs by $16.24.

## Uncertainty

In general, the optimum solution to this short-term financing problem can be obtained only by solving the linear programming problem. There is no simple decision rule which will always give the optimum, even under the assumption that all requirements, variables and constraints are known with certainty. In practice, moreover, this assumption does not hold. The purpose of this section is to examine the changes in approach which may be used to take uncertainty into account.[3]

There are several ways in which the linear programming model described above can be useful for decision making under uncertainty.

First, the linear programming solution provides management with the alternative which minimizes planned cost. If management, because of uncertainty, considers a financial decision which does not minimize planned cost, the extra cost can be thought of as the "cost of insurance against uncertainty." Of course, the decision maker must then decide whether the extra cost is justified.

Second, the linear programming approach can be used to examine the implications of changes in estimated requirements, variables or constraints. For instance, a number of runs could be made to test the

[3] The approaches to uncertainty which we shall examine here retain use of the linear programming algorithm. Other approaches may be used: for instance, Beranek discusses what is essentially a dynamic programming approach. See, Beranek, *Analysis for Financial Decisions*, Chap. XI.

effect of possible divergences from forecasted requirements. Or, if probability distributions can be estimated for the various elements of the subproblem, available simulation techniques can be used to develop quantitative measures of risk. We shall examine such techniques further in Chapter VIII.

Third, the linear programming model can be looked at as minimizing *expected* cost if the expected values of various variables and requirements are used. Constraints and minimum cash requirements can then be arranged so that the over-all solution meets minimum "safety" requirements. Management might require that reserve borrowing power be retained for emergencies in the form of an unused line of credit. Or, the size of the minimum cash balance might be adjusted to provide a liquid cushion against risk.

Fourth, implicit costs can be introduced to offset possible effects of the short-term financing decision on the value of the stockholders' expected dividend stream.

## Conclusion

Theory and practice intersect at the point of decision. In this chapter we have attempted to illuminate this point of intersection by detailed presentation of a realistic example—that is, the subproblem of short-term finance.

The reason for considering subproblems is that the over-all financing problem is too complex to be analyzed all at once. The financial manager must therefore attempt to break down the over-all problem into manageable parts.

However, our example illustrated that special difficulties arise when we consider subproblems one by one. First, any definition of the boundaries of a subproblem will inevitably be arbitrary. In our example, we discovered that it is by no means clear where the line between short and long-term financing should be drawn. Second, it is never easy to specify completely the costs of alternative financing plans. The assignment of implicit costs is entirely a matter of judgement in some cases.

In defining subproblems, the financial manager must make a choice between manageability and realism. Solutions may always be obtained if subproblems are defined narrowly enough, but financial managers are right to distrust such solutions in broader contexts. The temptation, therefore, is to expand the problem, making it both more realistic but also harder to solve.

Which, then, is better: a precise answer to a narrow subproblem, or a fuzzy answer to a more complex and realistic subproblem? Unfortunately, we cannot say in general. All we can say is the obvious: that is, that the answer to this question depends on the complexity of the situation and the adequacy of the available solution procedures.

# The Long-Term Financing Decision

We have stated that the objective of this book is not to propound financial theory *qua* theory, but to organize financial theory in such a way as to shed light on the practical problems faced by the financial manager. The only practical means to this end, however, is to break down the over-all problem of finance into manageable parts or subproblems.

In Chapter 7, we investigated the subproblem of short-term finance. In this chapter, we shall turn our attention to various parts of the long-term financing decision. We shall assume, as we have throughout this book, that the firm's investment decision may be taken as given. Thus our objective is to finance the funds requirements created by the firm's investments in such a way as to maximize the value of the firm to its shareholders.

We have, of course, already considered the most basic issues in the long-term financing problem—that is, the choice between debt and equity and the problem of dividend policy—in Chapters 3 and 4. But our analysis has thus far been a trifle abstract.

In this chapter we will discuss a series of more specific topics and procedures. Broadly speaking, our presentation is divided into two parts. In the first part of the chapter, we will investigate a series of practical questions, such as:

1. Are book value figures useful for financial decision making?
2. Under what conditions is maximizing the total market value of the firm equivalent to maximizing the value of the firm to its original shareholders?
3. What is the best procedure for a firm wishing to repurchase a portion of its outstanding shares?
4. How might a financial manager go about determining the optimal combination of the various long-term financing instruments—specifically, preferred stock and senior and subordinated debt—given the amount of common equity and the financial needs?

The second part of the chapter discusses procedures for generating and analyzing the information necessary to evaluate possible financial strategies under conditions of uncertainty. (Uncertainty exists, after all, only because we cannot obtain perfect information.) We shall discuss simulation procedures and heuristic techniques—common sense approaches to the analysis of problems when information is imperfect.

## The Choice Between Debt and Equity Revisited

This section and the four that follow examine a series of practical topics relevant to the long-term financing decision. Since these topics are in themselves only loosely related, it will be helpful to discuss them all in the context of a somewhat larger, but familiar, problem: the choice between debt and equity.

Therefore let us reintroduce the debt-equity problem in a highly simplified form, as follows. We shall assume:[1]

1. That the size of the firm is constant, and that investors expect the firm to generate a constant average yearly income, $\bar{Y}$.
2. That investors' estimates of $\bar{Y}$ are unaffected by leverage.
3. That there are no taxes on corporate income.
4. That uncertainty, as reflected in the certainty equivalent coefficients, $\alpha_t$, is resolved at a constant rate over time. That is, for any year, $t$, $\alpha_t = \alpha_o e^{-bt}$, where $b$ is a constant between zero and one. When this assumption holds, we can temporarily revert to the simplified mathematical notation of Chapter 3, using a constant "required rate of return," $k$, to discount the dividends which present shareholders expect to receive.[2]
5. The firm pays out all earnings as either interest payments or dividends.

[1] These assumptions will rarely hold in practice, of course. More realistic assumptions are used in Chapter 3 and later in this chapter.

[2] In this case $k = \bar{i} + b$, where $\bar{i}$ is the riskless rate of interest and $b$ is the rate at which uncertainty as reflected in the $\alpha_t$'s is resolved over time. See our discussion in Chapter 5, p. 84.

6. All present and prospective shareholders agree on the firm's expected average earnings, $\bar{Y}$, and on the "risk class" of the firm. If new equity shares are issued, the buyers of these shares will require the same rate, $k$, as the firm's original shareholders.[3] In other words, the firm's original shareholders can always obtain equity capital at a market rate of $k$.

In this case, the objective is to maximize the total market value of the firm, $V$. By definition, $V = L + E$, where $L$ and $E$ are the market values of debt and equity, respectively. If $i$ is the interest rate of debt, we can redefine $V$ as

$$V = L + \frac{\bar{Y} - iL}{k}. \tag{8-1}$$

The term $\frac{\bar{Y} - iL}{k}$ is simply the capitalized value of expected dividend payments.

Both $i$ and $k$ depend on the level of $L$. The condition for maximum $V$ as a function of the level of debt is obtained by differentiating (8-1) with respect to $L$. The result follows:

$$i + L\frac{di}{dL} = k - \frac{dk}{dL}\left(\frac{\bar{Y} - iL}{k}\right). \tag{8-2}$$

We can interpret (8-2) as follows. As debt is substituted for equity (remember that $\bar{Y}$ is constant), the maximum $V$ is reached at the point where the marginal interest rate on debt—the left side of (8-2)—is equal to the shareholders' "required" rate $k$ minus the rate of change in the value of the equity caused by the rise in $k$ as a result of the added debt. If the marginal interest rate is less than the right side of (8-2), then the value of the firm will increase if additional debt is added. If the marginal interest rate exceeds the right side, $V$ will increase if the amount of debt is reduced.

We recall from Chapter 3 that the firm's over-all cost of capital, $\rho$, can be expressed as

$$\rho = i\frac{L}{V} + k\frac{E}{V}, \tag{8-3}$$

where $\bar{Y} = iL + kE$. The reader may verify that the conditions for minimizing $\rho$ are identical to the conditions for maximizing $V$. We would expect that since

$$V = \frac{\bar{Y}}{\rho}, \tag{8-4}$$

and $\bar{Y}$ was presumed to be a constant.

[3] Assuming the risk class of the firm is unchanged.

## The Use of Book Values in Financial Decisions

The reader should note that (8-3) defines the firm's cost of capital, $\rho$, in terms of the ratios of the market values of debt and equity to $V$, the total market value of the firm. We know from practical experience, however, that many financial decision makers pay close attention to balance sheet values of debt and equity. Also, a number of authors who discuss the cost of capital imply book value percentages in their exposition.[4] It will be worth while, therefore, to determine whether the use of book values for debt and equity affects the results obtained in the last section.

Consider a new firm which is being formed by Mr. X as the sole shareholder. The firm requires an initial amount of capital $I_o$. We can define, along the lines of the discussion in Chapter 2, the net discounted present value created by the formation of the firm as

$$DPV = V - I_o. \tag{8-5}$$

The total book value of the firm will be just $I_o$. Thus the amount $DPV$, the "windfall gain" Mr. X receives, is simply equal to the difference between the market and book values of the firm. The conditions for maximum $DPV$ are of course identical to those for maximum $V$.

Now let us define $z$ as the proportion of total book value, $I_o$, represented by debt. Dividing both sides of (8-1) by $I_o$, we obtain

$$\frac{V}{I_o} = z + \frac{\dfrac{\bar{Y}}{I_o} - iz}{k}. \tag{8-6}$$

Taking $z$ as the decision variable, we can proceed as before to determine the necessary conditions for maximizing $V$. Differentiating (8-6) with respect to $z$, we find these conditions are:

$$i + z\frac{di}{dz} = k - \frac{dk}{dz}\left[\frac{\dfrac{\bar{Y}}{I_o} - iz}{k}\right]. \tag{8-7}$$

Equation (8-7) is, of course, equivalent to Eq. (8-2), in the sense that both equations imply the same total amount of debt in the firm's capital structure. However, the optimum degree of leverage as measured by $z$ will not necessarily equal the ratio of debt to the total market value of the firm. In fact, $z$ will equal $L/V$ if and only if, by

[4] For example, see R. W. Johnson, *Financial Management*, 2nd ed. (Boston: Allyn & Bacon, Inc., 1962), Chapter 8; P. Hunt, C. Williams, and G. Donaldson, *Basic Business Finance*, Rev. Ed. (Homewood, Ill.: Richard D. Irwin, Inc., 1961), Chapter 21; and others.

some coincidence, $I_o = V$. Thus a statement such as "the optimal proportion of debt in the firm's capital structure is 40 per cent" has little meaning unless we specify whether book or market values are used as the basis for measurement.

Furthermore, if the over-all cost of capital is defined in terms of book value—that is, as

$$\rho(\text{book}) = iz + (1 - z)k \tag{8-8}$$

—then the weighted average cost of capital so defined will not equal the cost of capital as defined by (8-3) unless $V = I_o$. Because of the difference between book and market values, for a given capital structure $\rho$ (book) will *understate* the real cost of capital $\rho$ if market value exceeds book value, and *overstate* it if the converse holds. Minimizing $\rho$ (book), therefore, will *not* in general be equivalent to maximizing the over-all market value of the firm. In view of its undependable behavior, there is little point in using $\rho$ (book) at all.

This is not to say that book values may not be useful in other contexts. If creditors pay close attention to book value figures, it may be easier to estimate how the interest rates charged the firm vary as a function of leverage if book value measures are used. In terms of our present example, a financial manager might find it easier to use Eq. (8-7) rather than Eq. (8-2) in attempting to determine the optimal amount of leverage. But the financial manager should remember that book figures are usually very poor measures of the value of the firm to its shareholders.

## An Example

Suppose the following information is available to the financial manager of a firm:

$$\bar{Y} = 100{,}000, \text{ a constant.}$$

$$I_o = 900{,}000, \text{ a constant.}$$

$$i = .03 + .08z^2.$$

$$k = .10 + .15z^2.$$

where $z = L/I_o$, and the other variables are defined as in the preceding sections. In this section we will work out optimal financing decisions for these highly simplified relationships. The determinants of $i$, the interest rate charged the firm, and of $k$, the stockholders' required rate of return, are of course considerably more complex than indicated here;[5] but the relationships assumed will be sufficient to illustrate several important points.

[5] For example, see L. Fisher, "Determinants of Risk Premiums on Corporate Bonds," *Journal of Political Economy*, LXVII, No. 3 (1959) 217–237.

A simple iterative computer routine was used to determine the answers to three questions:[6]

1. If the objective is to maximize $V$, the total value of the firm, what should be the proportion of debt in the firm's capital structure?
2. Is the minimization of $\rho$(book) equivalent to maximizing $V$?
3. At what level of debt will $P$, the market price of the firm's stock, be maximized, assuming the book value of each share outstanding is $100?

The answers to these questions are given in Table 8-1.

**Table 8–1**

| | $z$ | $V$ | $\rho$ | $\rho$(book) | $P$ |
|---|---|---|---|---|---|
| 1. Maximum $V$: | .23 | 1,067,833 | .0937 | .0910 | 124.22 |
| 2. Minimum $\rho$(book): | .295 | 1,063,200 | .0941 | .0906 | 125.72 |
| 3. Maximum $P$: | .38 | 1,047,156 | .0955 | .0912 | 126.37 |

Assume to begin with that our hypothetical firm is financed entirely with equity capital. Then the importance of the first result should be obvious: the maximization of $V$, the total value of the firm, will also maximize the wealth of its shareholders. Suppose the firm issues bonds up to the point where $z = .23$, paying out the proceeds as "bonus" dividends to the shareholders. By doing this, debt would be substituted for equity in the firm's capitalization up to the point where $V$ is maximized. Since $z = L/I_o$, the amount of debt issued will be given by $L = zI_o = .23(900{,}000) = 207{,}000$. In effect, therefore, 23 per cent, or $207,000, of the shareholders' original contributed capital will be returned to them. The total value of the shareholders' equity after the dividend is distributed will be $E = V - L = 1{,}067{,}833 - 207{,}000 = 860{,}833$.

The resulting change in the shareholders' personal wealth can now be summarized:

**Table 8–2**

| | $E$ | *Bonus Dividend Paid* | *Wealth of Stockholders* |
|---|---|---|---|
| 1. For the original all-equity firm: | 1,000,000 | 0 | 1,000,000 |
| 2. After optimal capital structure is achieved: | 860,833 | 207,000 | 1,067,833 |
| 3. Net change: | −139,167 | +207,000 | +67,833 |

[6] The iterative solutions were tested to verify that the mathematical conditions for the optimum are satisfied. The verifications are not presented here. The interested reader may wish to verify the conditions as an exercise.

It is clear that the shareholders will realize the entire increase in value due to the attainment of the optimal capital structure.

Of course, we have described only one route by which this optimal capital structure might be attained. Another alternative would be for the firm to use the proceeds of the bond issue to repurchase and retire a portion of the firm's outstanding stock.

But if the firm is owned by more than one shareholder, a problem arises: what repurchase price is fair to all of the firm's shareholders? Obviously, there will be no "bonus" dividend in this case; instead, the entire increase in the total value of the firm due to the substitution of debt for equity will be realized as a capital gain.

Assume the initial price of the shares reflects the value of the firm to its shareholders before any changes in capital structure are made. If the firm announces the intended change in capital structure, the market price of all shares will then adjust to reflect the expected increase in equity value. If the firm then proceeds to repurchase the stock, this increase in value will be equitably shared by all stockholders.

On the other hand, if the firm keeps its plans secret, those stockholders who sell on the assumption that the firm does not intend to change its capital structure receive less than fair value. Those who retain their shares will realize a disproportionately large capital gain once the firm's financing plans become known.

This point is of considerable practical importance, since many large firms are repurchasing their stock in the open market, apparently for tax reasons.[7] These companies are probably penalizing the selling shareholders if these shareholders are unaware that the firm itself is the purchaser.

We can now turn to the second question our example was designed to illustrate. Only a brief comment will be required.

Since the true cost of capital, $\rho$, is simply defined as the ratio $\bar{Y}/V$, and since $\bar{Y}$ is constant, $\rho$ will be minimized when $V$ is maximized. Thus in our example, the minimum true cost of capital is achieved at $z = .23$. However, as is shown in Table 8-1, $\rho$ (book) is not minimized at this degree of leverage. Furthermore, for $z = .23$, $\rho$ (book) $=$ .0910—an understatement of the true cost of capital.

Finally, Table 8-1 gives us the answer to the third question posed at the beginning of this section. It tells us that $P$, the market price per share, is maximized when $z = .38$—a considerably higher level of debt than is desirable if the objective is to maximize the total value of the firm. The values obtained for $P$ assume that shares were originally issued at an arbitrary book value of $100 per share. This

[7] For a discussion of this topic see E. F. Brigham, "The Profitability of a Firm's Purchase of Its Own Common Stock," *California Management Review*, VII, No. 2 (1964) 69–76.

allows us to calculate the number of outstanding shares required for any degree of leverage.

It is important to understand why $V$ and $P$ are not maximized at the same degree of leverage. As shown in Table 8-1, when $z = .23$, the total market value of the firm's equity is $E = 860{,}833$. We have assumed that there is one share outstanding for every $100 of book-value equity. Thus when $z = .23$, the book value of equity is $693,000, and 6,930 shares will be outstanding. The market price, $P$, is defined as

$$P = \frac{\bar{Y} - iL}{N \cdot k} = \frac{E}{N} \tag{8-9}$$

where $N$ = the number of shares outstanding. Thus when $V$ is maximized,

$$P = \frac{E}{N} = \frac{860{,}833}{6{,}930} = \$124.22.$$

By similar reasoning, when $z = .38$, the book value of equity will be $558,000, so that $N = 5{,}580$. Thus

$$P = \frac{E}{N} = \frac{705{,}156}{5{,}580} = \$126.37.$$

Of course this maximum value of $P$ has little relevance to the shareholders of a going concern. In this case, any windfall gain created by the formation of the firm would be already reflected in the market value of the outstanding shares. Therefore, it would not pay the shareholders of the firm to increase leverage beyond the point where $z = .23$. (The interested reader can confirm this by recalculating the figures in Table 8-2 for $z = .38$.)

In certain special cases, however, issuing an amount of debt such that $z = .38$ is the optimal financing decision. Suppose Mr. X is the *founder* of the hypothetical firm we have been discussing. Assume also that:

1. Mr. X has only a limited amount of personal capital—e.g., $100,000.
2. Other investors have funds available but insist that they be allowed to purchase the firm's stock on exactly the same terms as Mr. X. In effect, the other investors demand a *pro rata* share of any windfall gain created by the formation of the firm.

If the purchase price of the shares is arbitrarily set at $100, then Mr. X will be able to purchase 1,000 shares. For additional financing, he must choose between debt and additional equity to be held by other investors. Mr. X's objective is obvious: his personal wealth will be maximized by that financing decision which maximizes the market price of his 1,000 shares. The optimal financing decision thus requires leverage so that $z = .38$. This decision will allow Mr. X to achieve the largest possible windfall gain on his personal investment.

The last problem discussed above is common in practice. For example, the organizers of a bank are legally prevented from issuing promotional shares. If the reader decides to form a bank, he will be in the same position as Mr. X.

### Earnings Per Share and the Multiplier

As long as we are concerned with practical issues, it may be useful to mention an approach to valuation widely used in security analysis. This is the concept of the multiplier, which relates earnings per share to market price.

Let $M$ be the multiplier, defined by $M = P/EPS$, where $EPS$ represents current earnings per share. Obviously, we can always find *some* value for $M$ such that $M(EPS) = P$. But security analysts usually have definite ideas about the appropriate multiplier for a particular stock. Our problem is to determine the economic meaning of "appropriate."

One way in which the multiplier is useful is as a way of comparing the relative prices of different stocks. As a rule of thumb, it makes sense to say that the stock of companies which have similar growth prospects and are regarded as equally risky should have roughly the same ratio of price to current earnings—i.e., roughly the same multiplier. Thus if a company's stock sells at a multiplier which is substantially lower than that of similar companies, the security analyst would strongly suspect that the stock was "undervalued" by the market.

Knowledge of what investors regard as appropriate multipliers is also useful to a firm's financial manager when estimates of the future price of the firm's stock are needed. As we shall show later in this chapter, projecting and evaluating the results of alternative financing strategies usually requires estimates of the price at which new shares can be issued in future years. If the firm's yearly earnings have been projected, an estimate of the "appropriate" multipliers is equivalent to a rough estimate of future share prices.

In some cases, multipliers can be easily derived from the concepts presented in this book. The example we will give here closely resembles the Gordon model presented in Chapter 4. If we assume, as Gordon does, a valuation equation which is continuous in time, then we can rewrite a simplified version of our fundamental valuation equation (6-6a) as

$$P_o = \int_0^\infty \alpha_t \bar{D}_t \exp(-\bar{i}t)\, dt. \tag{8-10}$$

If we assume a constant growth rate in expected dividends, $g$, then

$$\bar{D}_t = D_o e^{gt},$$

so that (8-10) can be expressed as

$$P_o = \int_0^\infty \alpha_t D_o \exp\left[-(\bar{\imath} - g)t\right] dt \tag{8-11}$$

Now, suppose uncertainty, as reflected in the $\alpha_t$'s, varies over time in the following way:

$$\alpha_t = \alpha_o \exp(-ct),$$

where $c$ is a constant. This expression would follow if we assumed that uncertainty as measured by $\alpha_t$ is typically resolved at a constant rate over time. Assuming that $\alpha_o = 1$, then

$$P_o = \int_0^\infty D_o \exp\left[-(\bar{\imath} + c - g)t\right] dt. \tag{8-12}$$

If $c + \bar{\imath} > g$, we can integrate to obtain

$$P_o = \frac{D_o}{\bar{\imath} + c - g}. \tag{8-13}$$

If $b_o$ is the payout ratio in period $t = 0$, then

$$D_o = b_o\left[\frac{(Y_o - iL)(1 - T)}{N}\right],$$

where the term in brackets is earnings per share after interest and taxes. If we rewrite (8-13) as

$$P_o = \frac{b_o[(Y_o - iL)(1 - T)]}{(\bar{\imath} + c - g)N}, \tag{8-14}$$

then it is clear that the market multiplier will be given by

$$M = \frac{b_o}{\bar{\imath} + c - g}. \tag{8-15}$$

These results are interesting in several respects. First, Eq. (8-13), the expression for the value of a share to the shareholders, is closely related to the solution of the Gordon model, Eq. (4-10), although the assumptions of the Gordon model differ from those used here.

Second, since we have assumed here that uncertainty as measured by $\alpha_t$ is resolved at a constant rate over time, the use of a required rate of return is justified. This rate will be given by $k = \bar{\imath} + c$.

Third, our results can be used to point out a commonly made mistake in the measurement of this "required" rate of return for purposes of capital budgeting. Many writers recommend that this required rate be estimated by the reciprocal of the multiplier. But even when the use of a single rate, $k$, is valid, it is not true in general that $k = 1/M$. Under the assumptions used in deriving (8-15), $k = 1/M$ only if either $b_0 = 1$ and $g = 0$ (i. e., all earnings are paid out as dividends and the earnings are not expected to grow over time) or $b = 1 - g/k$. Otherwise the use of the inverse of the multiplier as an estimate of $k$ is not valid.

## Optimal Financing Mix Given the Amount of Common Equity

The discussion of the preceding sections was limited to the choice between debt and equity. However, a number of different forms of debt exist, as well as preferred stocks. In this section we will present an example illustrating the decision problem of selecting the optimal combination of the various forms of debt and preferred stock *given* the portion of the long-term needs which is to be financed by common equity and short-term financing.

We will assume for the purposes of this example that an optimum combination of the various types of debt and preferred stock does exist, despite our proof in Chapter 3 that such an optimum cannot exist in perfect markets. However, where sufficiently perfect markets do not obtain, the decision problem is relevant. Although research is needed in this area, we can observe that many firms have complicated capital structures, and that the various forms of subordinated debt are finding increasing use.

For purposes of our example we will assume that problems connected with debt maturities and with timing of the issues can be ignored. Furthermore, we assume that the various possible financing combinations do not affect the "risk class" of the common stock as perceived by the market. Given these assumptions, the objective is to arrive at the combination of various forms of debt and preferred stock which minimizes the cost of interest and preferred stock dividends. This optimal combination will maximize the value of the stock, since we are increasing the expected return to the common shares while not changing any other variable in the fundamental valuation equation (6-6a).

A number of factors contribute to the complexity of the financing mix problem. For example, the interest rates on the various forms of debt are interrelated; thus the rate on senior debt depends in part on how much subordinated debt the firm has and vice versa. Also, a number of constraints are typically imposed on the firm by its creditors.

The general problem can be stated as follows. Let $L_j$ and $i_j$ denote, respectively, the amount and the interest cost of the debt (or preferred stock) of type $j$. The total cost ($TC$) is given by

$$TC = \sum_{j=1}^{m} i_j L_j,$$

where $m$ is the total number of financing sources considered. The objective is to minimize $TC$ subject to the constraint

$$L = \sum_{j=1}^{m} L_j,$$

where $L$ represents the total amount to be financed with debt and preferred stock. That is, the total need must be satisfied by the combination of the various forms of financing.

Our illustrative example is based on the financing mix problem faced by the typical large commercial finance company. The assets of these companies normally exceed \$1 billion. We assume, as noted above, that the firm has decided what proportion of its needs will be financed with short-term financing and common equity, and that the resulting funds requirement to be financed with long-term capital amounts to \$1 billion. Thus $L = 1{,}000{,}000{,}000$. The firm is considering the following alternative sources of capital:

$L_1$ = senior debt,

$L_2$ = subordinated debt,

$L_3$ = capital notes (that is, junior subordinated debt), and

$L_4$ = preferred stock.

For a variety of reasons, a number of constraints are imposed. These are summarized below, with $E$ denoting the book value of common equity:

$$L_3 \leq .5\ (L_4 + E).$$

$$L_2 \leq .5\ (L_3 + L_4 + E), \text{ and}$$

$$L_1 \leq 1.5\ (L_2 + L_3 + L_4 + E).$$

These constraints impose limits on the amounts of debt of various types that can be used. For example, the first constraint limits the amount of capital notes to one half of the sum of the preferred stock and common equity. Note, however, that there is no limit on the amount of preferred stock.

For this example we will assume that $E = 200{,}000{,}000$ and that the following interest rate relationships prevail:

$$i_1 = .045 + .030\left(\frac{L_1}{L}\right)^2,$$

$$i_2 = i_1 + .0005 + (.0760 - i_1 - .0005)\left(\frac{L_2}{L - L_1}\right)^2,$$

$$i_3 = i_2 + .0005 + (.0770 - i_2 - .0005)\left(\frac{L_3}{L - L_1 - L_2}\right)^2, \text{ and}$$

$$i_4 = .090 + .005\left(\frac{L_1 + L_2 + L_3}{L}\right).$$

The interest rate relationships are for purposes of illustration only: they are intended to be realistic but are not derived from actual data. The "rate" on preferred stock is adjusted to reflect the fact that dividends on preferred are not deductible for tax purposes. The equation for $i_4$ implies that if preferred stock is used to finance the entire need and if the corporate tax rate is 50 per cent, dividend yield to the investor is 4.5 per cent. The yield is somewhat higher if debt is used to meet a portion of the financing needs. This relationship approximates the prevailing yields on preferred stocks.

The objective is to select the financing mix which will minimize interest costs. Mathematically speaking, the problem is one of minimizing an objective function with nonlinear functional relationships, subject to linear constraints. Analytic techniques to solve this type of problem are not widely available and, in general, are quite complex.[8] For this reason, we have employed a simple iterative computer technique. Basically the approach assumed that the constraints with respect to the use of subordinate debt and capital notes are binding in the optimal solution. The routine then worked out the costs of the various types of debt and preferred stock. The lowest cost combination obtained was then tested by using proportions of $L_2$ and $L_3$ just below those permitted by the constraints.

Of course, this approach does not absolutely guarantee that the solution obtained by the iterative method is in fact the optimal solution. However, if we had serious doubts as to the value of the iterative solution we could then resort to more sophisticated computer routines.

---

[8] Professor Robert Wilson of the Graduate School of Business, Stanford University, has developed a routine which can solve the type of problem discussed here. But, we have not attempted to employ his routine for our example.

Table 8-3 summarizes the solution obtained by the iterative procedure:

**Table 8–3**

| | *Interest Rate* ($i_j$) | *Amount* ($L_j$) |
|---|---|---|
| $L_1$ (Senior debt): | .051083 | 450.3 |
| $L_2$ (Subordinated debt): | .056629 | 249.9 |
| $L_3$ (Capital notes): | .063266 | 166.6 |
| $L_4$ (Preferred stock): | .094334 | 133.2 |
| | | 1,000.0 |

Using the figures in Table 8-3 we can compute the average interest rate on the total financing, $i_a$, as follows:

$$\begin{aligned} i_a &= i_1 \frac{L_1}{L} + i_2 \frac{L_2}{L} + i_3 \frac{L_3}{L} + i_4 \frac{L_4}{L} \\ &= (.051083)(.4503) + (.056629)(.2499) \\ &\qquad + (.063266)(.1666) + (.094334)(.1332) \\ &= .0602597. \end{aligned}$$

The total cost, $TC$, is merely the average interest cost multiplied by the total financing need. In this case

$$TC = i_a L = (.0602597)(1{,}000{,}000{,}000) = 60{,}259{,}700.$$

In this particular solution, the constraints with respect to $L_2$ and $L_3$ were binding; the constraint pertaining to $L_1$ was not. That is, we used all the permissible amounts of $L_2$ and $L_3$ given the amount of equity and the chosen amount of preferred stock; we did not use all of the senior debt which could have been employed. The reader can verify that the constraints are in fact observed.

An appealing feature of mathematical models is that a unique answer to the problem is obtained. It is, therefore, especially important to understand fully the assumptions upon which the model rests. Some of the assumptions may be questioned before implementing the "optimal" solution. In the above illustration, for example, will the "optimum" structure be flexible enough to withstand cyclic change which may affect a number of the variables and parameters of the model? How rigid are the constraints used in the model? What provision, if any, should be made for future refinancing?

## Dynamic Aspects of the Long-Term Financing Decision

In preceding sections of this chapter we have made some simplifying assumptions with respect to the pattern of expected cash flows.

Although cash flows were recognized as uncertain, their expectation was assumed constant over time. This assumption enabled us to demonstrate how certain mathematical techniques might be used to arrive at the optimal financing decision. The demonstration was not merely a mathematical exercise; some practical situations exist where the techniques, or variations thereof, may be very useful. For instance, firms with relatively stable earnings streams over time may use calculus to estimate the debt-equity combination which would lead to highest market value for the firm's shares.

In this section we shall see that removal of the assumption of constant expected cash flow complicates the decision considerably. No longer can we apply calculus or programming methods to generate *the* optimum solution. The problem is such that it cannot be "solved" with existing quantitative methodology.

There are two elements of the long-term financing problem under these more general conditions. The first is the generation of the information necessary for decision making. Information regarding expected future cash flows is not readily available; furthermore, the cash flows will depend on the financing strategies which are adopted. The second element of the problem concerns the evaluation of the information and the selection of a particular strategy.[9]

In the context of this volume, we need information which will enable us to maximize the value of the firm to its shareholders, as given by the objective function (6-6a). We will use *simulation* to generate the relevant financial information and the *heuristic* technique to evaluate it.

Simulation refers to the systematic projection of results under alternative assumptions.[10] In this chapter, simulation will be used to project expected dividends and market prices under varying sets of assumptions and alternative financing strategies. The heuristic approach refers to the decision making process where the best of a restricted set of reasonable strategies is adopted, where "reasonableness" is determined by judgment.[11]

---

[9] The optimal strategy does not have to be a simple one such as "use 30 per cent debt." It may include provisions for changes in policy over time and for conditional actions depending on the course of future events.

[10] For examples of simulation techniques, see J. W. Forrester, *Industrial Dynamics* (Cambridge, Mass.: The Massachusetts Institute of Technology Press, 1961); or Charles P. Bonini, *Simulation of Information and Decision Systems in the Firm* (Englewood Cliffs, N. J.: Prentice-Hall, Inc., 1963).

[11] For example, decision theorists have used the heuristic approach to program computers to play chess. In chess, after a number of moves have been played, the possible alternative moves are many. Furthermore, in response to each move the opponent has a number of possible counter-moves, and so on. Rather than have the computer evaluate *all* possible moves, counter-moves, counter-counter-moves, etc., the computer is programmed to select only a limited number of reasonable moves for evaluation. The "obviously poor" moves are rejected without going through the evaluation process.

Simulation and the heuristic approach are often combined if the alternatives involve multiple decisions over time. For example, the expected results of a selected set of reasonable alternative strategies may be projected or simulated over time. The financial manager would then select the strategy for which the simulated results best meet the objective. Of course, the heuristic approach can also be used in conjunction with an optimization technique such as linear programming or differential calculus. For instance, we may define heuristically the set of feasible strategies and then select one of these strategies by linear programming.

In practice, financial managers have employed some variation of the simulation-heuristic approach for years. For example, any long-range cash forecast which assumes a particular financial strategy belongs in this category. Thus, the financial decision maker's experience should enable him to select a group of financing strategies which are not "obviously poor." Still, even this group will usually contain a large number of alternatives. Those who have prepared long-range financial forecasts know the time-consuming nature of the process. Imagine the time necessary to prepare 500 or more forecasts under different assumptions. Fortunately, computers reduce the work required: simulation processes can be programmed with relative ease.

We shall now describe a general simulation-heuristic approach to the long-term financing decision, under the assumption that the outcomes of the financial variables depend only on the chosen strategies and are not subject to random variations. Simulation with variables subject to given subjective probability distributions will be the topic of a later section. In the next section, an example will be used to illustrate the method described here.

The procedure can be conveniently separated into four stages:

Stage 1.

This stage is the projection of financing requirements. The financial manager must:

(a) Select the time period (for example, one year) and a planning horizon.
(b) Specify certain preliminary financing alternatives, such as tentative dividend policy.
(c) Project the expected cash flows under the assumption that the investment decision is given. This projection requires careful study. For example, in order to construct the simulation procedure it may be necessary to estimate the relationship between inventories and fixed assets. The preliminary financial needs over time (a negative need indicating a forecasted excess of cash) are the output of stage 1.

Stage 2.

The heuristic approach is introduced in this stage. The decision maker must choose a set of financing strategies to simulate, basing his selection on the expected cash requirements over time and on his knowledge of alternatives available to the firm. The strategies must specify:

(a) the type of financing instrument to issue—for example, debt, preferred stock, or common stock;
(b) timing of issues—that is, when to issue the specific securities;
(c) maturity of the issues;
(d) expected interest rates on debt and dividend rate on preferred;
(e) possible revisions in dividend policy.

For instance, one possible strategy would be to:

(a) issue $10 million of 20-year debentures at the end of year 2 at an expected interest cost of 5 per cent, with a $500,000 sinking fund requirement per annum;
(b) raise $24 million in year 5 by issuing 2,000,000 shares of common at an expected price of $12 per share;
(c) change dividend policy from paying 70 per cent of reported earnings to 60 per cent of earnings.

The number of strategies which can be tested is limitless. Thus, judgment must be exercised because excessive information is not only costly to obtain but may lead to inefficient use of the decision maker's time. The output of stage 2 should include all the information which will assist the decision maker in making his final selection. For example, it may include expected dividends and earnings over time, various financial ratios, etc.

Stage 3.

In this stage the interrelations of the financing and the investment decisions must be considered. Given the results obtained in stage 2, the decision maker may conclude that none of the strategies is acceptable. Thus, he may change some of the basic inputs, such as the preliminary investment decision. Or he may introduce a set of constraints into the model; for example, projects which result in reported accounting losses in the early years may be deferred if reported accounting income falls below some minimum target value. Also, the decision maker may simulate the impact of modified strategies if these appear promising. Given the revised set of conditions, the process outlined under stage 2 is merely repeated.

Stage 4.

This final stage is also the most difficult one. The decision maker must select one of the alternative strategies. The criterion for the choice is deceptively simple: maximize value to shareholders. However, applying the criterion is difficult indeed. We need only recall the discussion of valuation in Chapter 6 to show that we can offer no easy solution. The decision maker must attempt to identify the differential impact of the alternative strategies on the elements of the valuation equation (6-6a).

## Example of the Simulation-Heuristic Approach

The example in this section will illustrate how financial information can be generated and evaluated for alternative "reasonable" financing strategies. The illustration is based on publicly available data for a utility company.

This example is presented in order to demonstrate the method described in the preceding section. Consequently, expediency has been substituted for realism in defining some of the simulation relationships. For example, the assets were grouped into only two categories: plant and other assets. Also, where applicable, historical statistical relationships were used to provide simulated values. In practice, these historical relationships may or may not be close approximations to expected relationships. The firm, of course, could generate better and more detailed information from internal data.

Our reasons for choosing a public utility company are the following: (a) the company's investment decision is largely independent of its financing decision; that is, investments depend primarily on the economic growth of the area served by the utility—all needed investments are undertaken and financed by best available means; (b) the company is expected to be in periodic need of external long-term capital; (c) the company employs all the principal forms of long-term finance: debt, preferred stock, and common equity.

### Simulation Stage 1

A time period of one year was chosen, with a planning horizon of ten years. The simulation model estimated financial needs by projecting pro-forma balance sheets. The steps in the simulation model were as follows:

(a) Estimated plant requirements were projected assuming a growth rate in output and plant of 5.5 per cent per annum. This rate was based on various published forecasts.
(b) Other assets and current liabilities were projected on the basis of their past statistical relationship to plant.

(c) The level of long-term capital required to support the forecasted growth was determined by subtracting current liabilities from the funds required for plant and other assets.
(d) The level of long-term capital available in the absence of new financing was determined (more on this item later).
(e) The estimated long-term financial needs were computed by subtracting the estimated level of available capital without new financing from the estimated level of required capital.

Of course, a great deal of additional information (acquired either by investigation or assumption) must be specified in order to construct the simulation model. In our example, for instance, we assumed the following:

1. The principal of long-term debt was assumed to mature at the rate of 5 per cent per annum; that is, we assumed an average maturity of 20 years for the debt, with equal annual retirements.
2. At the beginning of the simulation, the company had some debt outstanding with coupon rates below expected long-run average interest costs. For this reason, the average interest rate on all long-term debt was projected to increase slightly over time and then level off at 4.5 per cent beginning in year four.
3. The amount of preferred stock was held constant during the first stage of the simulation. Also held constant at 5.24 per cent was the dividend rate on preferred.
4. A constant average rate of return of 6.25 per cent (net of all taxes) was assumed on required capital.
5. The preliminary dividend policy on common was assumed to be the annual payment of a dividend equal to $66\frac{2}{3}$ per cent of reported earnings to the common equity. Of course, this assumption is in itself a strategy; it was reevaluated in the subsequent stages.
6. Regression analysis was used to identify the relationships between plant on the one hand and other assets and current liabilities on the other.

It may be helpful to describe in more detail how financing from internal sources was incorporated in the simulation model. First, the "preliminary" yearly earnings to common were generated to provide an estimate of the increase in common equity due to retention of earnings. Then the estimated preliminary retained earnings for each period were added to the common equity existing at the beginning of the time period to arrive at the estimate of total common equity at the end of the time period in the absence of new common stock issues. Finally, the estimated level of total long-term capital in the firm without new long-term financing was obtained by adding the estimated end-of-period long-term debt, preferred stock, and common equity. This quantity was then subtracted from required total long-term capital to obtain the preliminary financial needs. Table

8-4 gives the forecasted financial requirements for years one through ten:

**Table 8–4**
**(millions of dollars)**

| | *Year* | | | | | | | | | |
|---|---|---|---|---|---|---|---|---|---|---|
| Estimated Need: | *1* | *2* | *3* | *4* | *5* | *6* | *7* | *8* | *9* | *10* |
| For period | 211 | 220 | 212 | 226 | 239 | 254 | 269 | 285 | 302 | 320 |
| Cumulative | 211 | 431 | 643 | 869 | 1,108 | 1,362 | 1,631 | 1,916 | 2,218 | 2,538 |

## Simulation Stage 2

The first decision which must be made in this stage concerns the type of information desired as the output of the simulation. In this particular example we needed information which would be useful in attempting to maximize the present value of future dividends expected by present shareholders. Therefore the primary output of the simulation was a forecast of dividends per share over time. In addition, the output included earnings per share and the expected market price per share at the end of the horizon period.

We chose a set of eight "reasonable" financial strategies to simulate. The major characteristics of the individual strategies are summarized below:

*Strategy S–1* Maintain the ratios of the various forms of financing to total long-term capital at the current level. Specifically, these ratios were: debt, 50.5 per cent; preferred stock, 13.2 per cent; and common equity, 36.3 per cent.

In addition, we assumed that market price of common stock over time is related to earnings per share and that the price-earnings ratio remains constant at 17.

*Strategy S–2* Raise the percentage of debt .5 per cent per annum to a maximum of 55 per cent. Do not issue any new preferred stock. Assume price-earnings ratio constant at 17.

*Strategy S–3* Raise the percentage of debt as in S–2 above. Maintain preferred stock at a constant 13.2 per cent of capitalization. Assume price-earnings ratio constant at 17.

*Strategy S–4* Same as S–3, except that the price-earnings ratio is assumed to decline linearly from 17 to 16 in ten years.

*Strategy S–5* Same as S–2, except for the constraint that the percentage of preferred stock must be maintained at or above 10 per cent of total capitalization.

*Strategy S–6* Same as S–4, except that the dividend policy on common stock is changed. The total dividend paid to all common shareholders is maintained at a level not less than the amount paid in year zero, but the dividend is raised only after the increase does not require the issue of new common stock.

*Strategy S–7* Same as S–6, except that no new common stock is issued.

*Strategy S–8* Same as S–1, except that no new common stock is issued.

For the sake of simplicity, the varying combinations of capital structure were assumed not to affect the interest rate which the firm had to pay on its long-term debt. Table 8-5 summarizes the simulation output of stage 2.

**Table 8–5: Output of Simulation Stage 2**

| | | *Strategies* | | | | | | | |
|---|---|---|---|---|---|---|---|---|---|
| | | *S–1* | *S–2* | *S–3* | *S–4* | *S–5* | *S–6* | *S–7* | *S–8* |
| Estimated Dividends: | | | | | | | | | |
| Year | 1 | 1.09 | 1.08 | 1.09 | 1.09 | 1.08 | 1.13 | 0.54 | 0.53 |
| | 2 | 1.12 | 1.11 | 1.13 | 1.13 | 1.11 | 1.11 | 0.96 | 0.71 |
| | 3 | 1.15 | 1.15 | 1.16 | 1.16 | 1.15 | 1.10 | 1.00 | 0.72 |
| | 4 | 1.17 | 1.17 | 1.19 | 1.19 | 1.17 | 1.09 | 1.03 | 0.73 |
| | 5 | 1.22 | 1.22 | 1.24 | 1.24 | 1.22 | 1.09 | 1.09 | 0.79 |
| | 6 | 1.27 | 1.27 | 1.29 | 1.29 | 1.28 | 1.11 | 1.15 | 0.82 |
| | 7 | 1.31 | 1.31 | 1.35 | 1.35 | 1.31 | 1.18 | 1.22 | 0.87 |
| | 8 | 1.37 | 1.37 | 1.40 | 1.41 | 1.38 | 1.25 | 1.30 | 0.92 |
| | 9 | 1.42 | 1.43 | 1.47 | 1.46 | 1.44 | 1.33 | 1.39 | 0.97 |
| | 10 | 1.48 | 1.49 | 1.53 | 1.52 | 1.50 | 1.42 | 1.47 | 1.03 |
| Estimated market price— Year 10 | | 37.57 | 37.74 | 38.93 | 36.64 | 38.25 | 38.08 | 39.52 | 44.54 |

For each strategy the estimated market price of the shares at the end of year 10 was obtained by multiplying estimated earnings per share for year ten by the price-earnings ratio assumed for the particular strategy.

Finally, it should be re-emphasized that the naïve share valuation model based on a price-earnings relationship was used because it was simple to handle for purposes of illustration. In practice, the valuation problem must be handled with great care.

Simulation Stage 3

Possible revisions of the investment decision and the impact of these revisions on financial needs were not considered in this illustration. Also, no additional strategies were investigated.

Simulation Stage 4

The next section will consider the problem of selecting one of the strategies on the basis of the simulated results.

## The Evaluation of Alternative Strategies

The information pertaining to the eight strategies must now be evaluated and one of the strategies must be selected. The choice of a particular strategy does not preclude the possibility that the strategy may be changed as conditions change over time. As a matter of fact, the financial decision process requires a continuous re-evaluation of past decisions.

We recall from Chapter 6 the valuation equation (6-6a):

$$P_o = \sum_{t=1}^{\infty} \frac{\gamma_t \alpha_t \bar{D}_t}{\prod_{\tau=1}^{t} (1 + \bar{i}_\tau)}. \tag{6-6a}$$

For purposes of our example, we assumed the modified objective function below:

$$P_o = \sum_{t=1}^{10} \frac{\alpha_t \bar{D}_t}{(1 + \bar{i})^t} + \frac{\alpha_v \bar{P}_{10}}{(1 + \bar{i})^{10}}, \tag{8-16}$$

where $\bar{P}_{10}$ denotes the expected market price at end of period 10, as given in Table 8-5.

Equation (8-16) differs from (6-6a) in three ways. First, it disregards the impact on value of the time preference factor $\gamma_t$. In practice, this omission may lead to errors in valuation. For example, strategies S–6, S–7, and S–8 call for dividend policies which are radically different from the policy followed by the company in the past. These changes in dividend policy may have a profound effect on the value of the stock through the $\gamma_t$ factor, which reflects the shareholders' time preference for dividends. Second, the choice of the time-horizon model made it necessary to specify a certainty equivalent factor for forecasted market price at the end of year ten. This factor is denoted by $\alpha_v$ in Eq. (8-16). The manner in which $\alpha_v$ was determined will be described below. Finally, a constant $\bar{i}$ was used as the discount rate.

**Table 8–6: Values of $\bar{P}_o$ Using Linearly Declining $\alpha_t$'s**

($\alpha_t = 1 - at$)

| | Strategies | | | | | | | |
|---|---|---|---|---|---|---|---|---|
| *a* | *1*† | *2*† | *3*† | *4** | *5*† | *6** | *7** | *8*† |
| .005 | 32.62 | 32.72 | 33.63 | 32.23 | 33.06 | 32.36 | 32.56 | 33.34 |
| .01 | 30.49 | 30.58 | 31.43 | 30.14 | 30.90 | 30.22 | 30.36 | 30.96 |
| .015 | 28.36 | 28.44 | 29.23 | 28.05 | 28.73 | 28.09 | 28.15 | 28.58 |
| .02 | 26.24 | 26.31 | 27.02 | 25.96 | 26.57 | 25.95 | 25.94 | 26.20 |
| .025 | 24.11 | 24.17 | 24.82 | 23.87 | 24.40 | 23.82 | 23.74 | 23.81 |
| .03 | 21.98 | 22.03 | 22.62 | 21.78 | 22.24 | 21.68 | 21.53 | 21.43 |
| .035 | 19.85 | 19.89 | 20.41 | 19.69 | 20.07 | 19.55 | 19.32 | 19.05 |
| .04 | 17.72 | 17.75 | 18.21 | 17.60 | 17.91 | 17.41 | 17.12 | 16.67 |
| .045 | 15.59 | 15.61 | 16.00 | 15.51 | 15.74 | 15.28 | 14.91 | 14.28 |
| .05 | 13.46 | 13.47 | 13.80 | 13.42 | 13.58 | 13.14 | 12.70 | 11.90 |

* P/E ratio of 16 assumed.
† P/E ratio of 17 assumed.

The values of $\bar{P}_o$ for the eight strategies are shown in Tables 8-6 and 8-7, under alternate assumptions regarding the values of $\alpha_t$ over time. The specific functional relationships assumed for $\alpha_t$ are shown in the respective tables; $\alpha_t$ was assumed to decline linearly in Table 8-6 and exponentially in Table 8-7. The following assumptions were made in deriving the values for both tables: $\bar{i} = 4.25$ per cent and $\alpha_v = \alpha_{15}$. The first assumption was for convenience; we could have easily included a riskless discount rate which varied over time. The second assumption relates to our earlier comments on the subject of naïve valuation models. By setting $\alpha_v = \alpha_{15}$ we simply implied

**Table 8–7: Values of $\bar{P}_o$ Using Exponentially Declining $\alpha_t$'s**

($\alpha_t = e^{-bt}$)

| | Strategies | | | | | | | |
|---|---|---|---|---|---|---|---|---|
| *b* | *1*† | *2*† | *3*† | *4** | *5*† | *6** | *7** | *8*† |
| .01 | 30.78 | 30.87 | 31.72 | 30.42 | 31.18 | 30.15 | 30.65 | 31.29 |
| .02 | 27.32 | 27.39 | 28.14 | 27.02 | 27.67 | 27.04 | 27.08 | 27.44 |
| .03 | 24.30 | 24.37 | 25.03 | 24.06 | 24.61 | 24.03 | 23.96 | 24.11 |
| .04 | 21.68 | 21.73 | 22.31 | 21.48 | 21.94 | 21.40 | 21.26 | 21.22 |
| .05 | 19.38 | 19.43 | 19.94 | 19.22 | 19.61 | 19.11 | 18.90 | 18.71 |
| .06 | 17.38 | 17.42 | 17.87 | 17.25 | 17.57 | 17.11 | 16.84 | 16.54 |
| .07 | 15.63 | 15.66 | 16.06 | 15.52 | 15.79 | 15.37 | 15.04 | 14.64 |
| .08 | 14.09 | 14.11 | 14.47 | 14.01 | 14.23 | 13.84 | 13.47 | 13.00 |
| .09 | 12.74 | 12.76 | 13.08 | 12.68 | 12.86 | 12.50 | 12.10 | 11.56 |
| .10 | 11.56 | 11.58 | 11.86 | 11.52 | 11.66 | 11.33 | 10.89 | 10.31 |

* P/E ratio of 16 assumed.
† P/E ratio of 17 assumed.

that the certainty equivalent factor pertaining to the forecasted end-of-horizon market value is relatively less than the factor for the forecasted dividend in that year. This was done because of the fact that the projected market value reflects the discounted value of expected dividends after the planning horizon and thus may be subject to a greater degree of uncertainty than the expected dividend in the horizon year.

For purposes of our example, we did not define a unique function over time for $\alpha_t$, because of the difficulty of identifying this relationship in practice. Consequently, we did not derive a unique "optimal" solution. Instead we hypothesized two general relationships and then calculated the impact on $P_o$ of changes in the basic parameter of the $\alpha_t$ functions. This enabled us to measure the consequences of incorrect choice. Also, we wanted to illustrate the wide range of possible approaches to the final evaluation process.

Examination of Tables 8-6 and 8-7 discloses that, if we assume that all strategies lead to *equal* certainty equivalent factors in all years, strategy S–3 dominates all other strategies for the range of the parameters "*a*" and "*b*" in the tables. That is, the value $P_o$ is greater for strategy S–3 than for any other strategy for *all* parameter values in the tables.

Thus, if we accept as valid: (a) all of the assumptions underlying our simulation model, (b) the functional relationships for $\alpha_t$, and (c) equal certainty equivalent factors for all strategies, then strategy S–3 is the best of the strategies evaluated. In this sense, it is "optimal."

But, we may doubt the validity of certain assumptions. For example, the various strategies may lead to different perceived risk characteristics for the expected dividend stream. Therefore, the parameter values for "*a*" or "*b*" need not be identical for all strategies even if the functional relationship for $\alpha_t$ is correctly identified. For instance, referring to Table 8-7, a value of $22.31 is derived if we conclude that the most likely value for "*b*" for strategy S–3 is .04. If we decide that "*b*" is .03 for strategy S–4, we obtain a value of $24.06. In this case strategy S–4 would be preferred to strategy S–3. Similar comparisons can be made for the other strategies. The "best" strategy is the one which has the highest value after all factors are evaluated.

In order to compare the approach based on certainty equivalents with the one based on the "required risk-adjusted discount rate," $k$, we computed the values of $P_o$ as a function of the rate $k$. The values for the eight strategies as functions of $k$ are summarized in Table 8-8.

Again strategy S–3 appears as the dominant strategy in the absence of differences in risk. Indeed, we could have predicted this result based on the results given in Table 8-7, since, as was shown

**Table 8–8: Values of $\bar{P}_0$ Using a Composite Discount Rate $k$**

| | *Strategies* | | | | | | | |
|---|---|---|---|---|---|---|---|---|
| $k$ | *1*† | *2*† | *3*† | *4** | *5*† | *6** | *7** | *8*† |
| .05 | 32.66 | 32.76 | 33.67 | 32.26 | 33.10 | 32.40 | 32.62 | 33.44 |
| .06 | 30.10 | 30.19 | 31.03 | 29.74 | 30.50 | 29.85 | 29.98 | 30.66 |
| .07 | 27.78 | 27.86 | 28.63 | 27.46 | 28.14 | 27.54 | 27.60 | 28.14 |
| .08 | 25.68 | 25.75 | 26.45 | 25.39 | 26.00 | 25.44 | 25.44 | 25.86 |
| .09 | 23.76 | 23.83 | 24.47 | 23.50 | 24.06 | 23.53 | 23.47 | 23.79 |
| .10 | 22.02 | 22.08 | 22.68 | 21.79 | 22.29 | 21.80 | 21.69 | 21.92 |
| .11 | 20.44 | 20.49 | 21.04 | 20.23 | 20.69 | 20.22 | 20.07 | 20.21 |
| .12 | 18.99 | 19.04 | 19.55 | 18.81 | 19.22 | 18.79 | 18.59 | 18.67 |

* P/E of 16 assumed.
† P/E of 17 assumed.

before, the evaluation approach using an exponentially declining $\alpha_t$ and the one using a composite discount rate $k$ are directly related.

The preceding illustration was based on a company which is expected to have continued needs for external long-term capital. In practice, many firms are not in this position. Some firms may find that the simulation output in stage 1 projects an excess of long-term capital. Here, the financial decision maker must concern himself with the best possible future uses for these excess funds. Alternative strategies in this case may include increases in dividends, changes in investment policy, possible repurchase of the company's common stock, or retirement of long-term debt and preferred stock.

## Simulation and Uncertainty

The three preceding sections illustrated the application of simulation and heuristic techniques to the long-term financing decision. Although we referred to uncertainty, especially as it related to the ultimate choice of a financial strategy, the approach was essentially deterministic. That is, the simulation output was dependent only on the specified functional relationships and the simulated strategy, not on chance.

In practice, of course, the probability that the actual results will exactly equal these forecasts is essentially zero. Since the degree of uncertainty is a major factor in the evaluation of strategies, the financial manager must develop all possible information about the reliability of the forecasted financial results.

Discussions of how such information might be systematically generated are lacking in the present literature, although many authors discuss parts of the general problem. For instance, some authors have assigned special importance to the conditions resulting in the minimum possible cash flow over time. Thus, Donaldson in his analysis of corporate debt capacity suggests the determination of a "recession cash flow."[12] Donaldson uses this information as an index of the risk of cash inadequacy in a recession and as a "rough measure of the impact of debt servicing on this risk." He proceeds to provide a "basis for relating the commonly used and highly generalized rules of thumb [with respect to debt capacity] to the financial circumstances of the individual industry and firm."[13]

Donaldson's analysis is excellent, as far as it goes. The principal shortcoming lies in his failure to specify an objective and then relate the analysis to this objective. Still, the volume is well worth reading; it complements our analysis by providing important insight into practical aspects of financial decision making.

Solomon suggests that the maximum amount of long-term debt should be set so that the firm is able to meet all the debt obligations (interest and principal) even if it is assumed that the firm will generate cash at the minimum possible rate over the uncertain future.[14] Actually, Solomon discusses individual projects and not the firm as a whole, but the generalization to the firm is implied in his analysis. Solomon's recommendation assumes a particular attitude toward risk by the firm's equity holders. However, risk attitudes of stockholder groups vary. If the firm's shareholders, fully aware of the risks involved, are in favor of adding debt beyond the point suggested by Solomon, then, in our opinion, management should act accordingly.

A common sense approach to the evaluation of uncertainty is to rerun the simulation using revised sets of assumptions in the model. We used essentially this approach in the last section in evaluating the effects of different assumptions about the certainty equivalent coefficients, $\alpha_t$.

The so-called Monte Carlo method is a systematic way of investigating the implications of uncertainty for the financial variables. Instead of specifying directly the values for the relevant variables in the simulation model, as we have done in the preceding section, the Monte Carlo approach uses assumed probability distributions for the variables. For instance, in our example the specified annual growth rate in plant of 5.5 per cent was an estimate of the most likely rate. Will there be a significant difference in the financial needs of Company P if the actual future growth rate is greater than or less than 5.5 per cent in any one year? The impact of varying growth rates can be investigated by estimating a probability distribution for the rates over time and then generating a series of "actual"

---

[12] Gordon Donaldson, *Corporate Debt Capacity* (Cambridge, Mass.: Harvard University, 1961), p. 191.

[13] Donaldson, *Corporate Debt Capacity*, p. 218.

[14] Ezra Solomon, "Measuring a Company's Cost of Capital," in E. Solomon, ed., *The Management of Corporate Capital*, pp. 139–40.

values by means of random numbers.[15] In this way the impact of uncertain events is simulated in as unbiased a manner as possible. Similarly, probability distributions can be specified for other relevant variables and their "actual" values determined for purposes of simulation. If desired, covariances can be used to simulate interrelationships between variables.

As applied to financial planning, the Monte Carlo method enables the decision maker to study the effects on financial needs of random and/or systematic variations from the expected values of the variables. Also, the method can provide quantitative measures of the risk of cash inadequacy. However, Monte Carlo simulation requires more preparation than the straightforward simulation method described in the preceding section. For instance, we must specify the probability distributions of the variables as well as the manner in which the variables relate to each other. The programming problem is more complex, but not materially so; a number of computer subroutines are available for use in a Monte Carlo simulation. We have, on a number of occasions, successfully used Monte Carlo simulation to derive financial forecasts, where the output included not only the expected needs over time but also the variance of the needs.

Once the probability distributions and their interrelations are specified, the decision maker must decide on the type of output he desires from the first stage. For example, the output may include complete listings of all relevant variables for a limited number of simulation runs. Or, alternatively, a large number of runs, say 100, could be made and the output used to estimate the means and the standard deviations for any or all of the variables of the model. Both types of output mentioned above provide useful information for financial decision making. The value of the information will be discussed below.

Figures 8-1a and 8-1b illustrate possible outputs of several simulation runs for two hypothetical companies—Company A and Company B. The output shown is the estimated periodic financial need over time. The figures show important differences in the expected pattern of funds needs. In the case of Company A, it appears that the firm's needs are strongly correlated over time; that is, the pattern of requirements depends to a large extent on the needs of the preceding periods. A utility company may have such a pattern of needs, since its requirements depend heavily on the long-run economic growth of the area it serves. On the whole, the output indicates a rising need over time on the average.

---

[15] The Monte Carlo method is described in most books dealing with operations research. For one description, see M. Sasieni, A. Yaspan, and L. Friedman, *Operations Research—Methods and Problems* (New York: John Wiley & Sons, Inc., 1959), pp. 58–67.

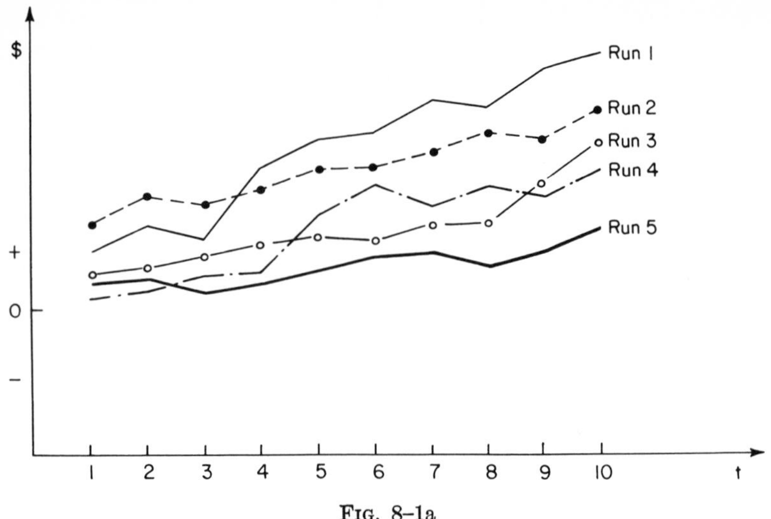


FIG. 8–1a

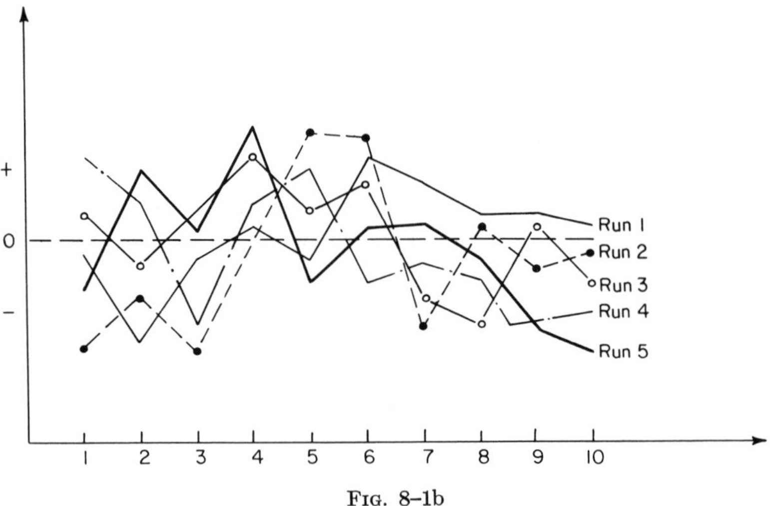


FIG. 8–1b

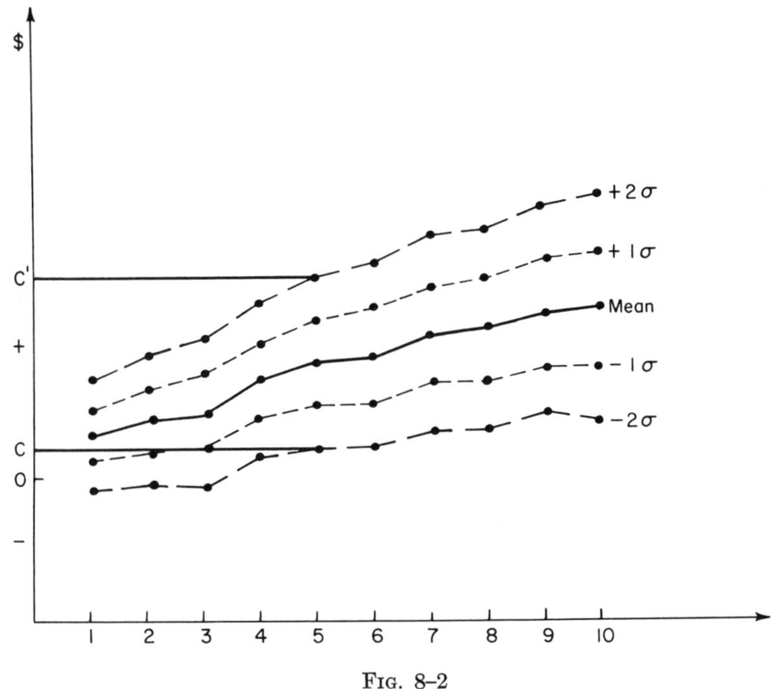


FIG. 8–2

On the other hand, the output for Company B describes an entirely different situation. An intertemporal correlation of needs is not observable. Also, the average of the needs over time appears to decline and excess funds may eventually be available.

Figure 8-2 illustrates a type of output which provides values of the means and the standard deviations of the periodic financial needs. The financial decision maker of this company—say Company C—is given quantitative measures of the degree of possible variation of future financial needs. For example, if the resulting distributions of needs over time approximate the normal distribution, then there is a 95 per cent chance that the financial requirement in period 3 of Figure 8-2 will be between C and C'.[16]

The foregoing analysis has a number of implications for financial planning. For example, in selecting the financial strategies to simulate in stage 2, the decision maker must consider the firm's ability to adjust its financial plan over time if forecasts are not realized. For instance, note that in the case of Company A, a departure from the

[16] For the normal probability distribution, 95 per cent of the area under the probability function is in the range between the mean minus two standard deviations and the mean plus two standard deviations.

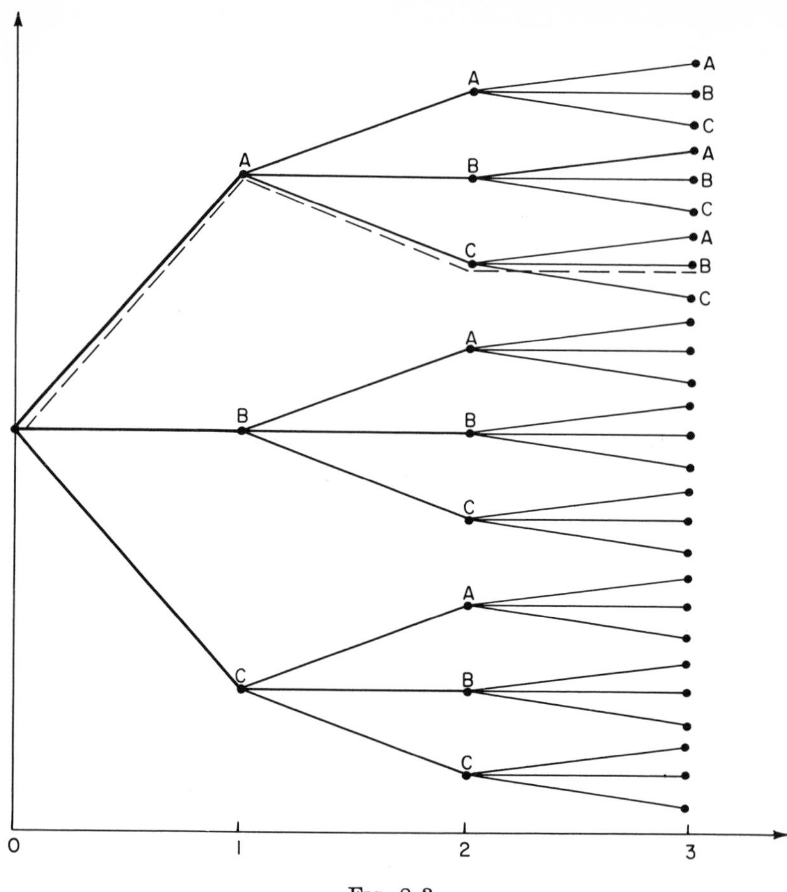


FIG. 8–3

expected financial needs in one period tends to lead to further departures in subsequent periods; no such correlation appears to exist in the case of Company B. We may hypothesize that the financial officer of Company B will find it advantageous to design financing strategies which are highly flexible. For Company A, on the other hand, a high degree of short-run flexibility does not seem to be necessary.

The idea of flexibility can be discussed with greater precision in terms of *conditional* strategies, that is, strategies providing for alternative courses of action depending on the actual events of preceding periods. For example, one such conditional strategy for the public utility simulation may be specified as follows: if actual needs for the preceding period are 20 per cent or more below forecasts, use course of action C; if actual needs exceed forecasts by 20 per cent or more, use course of action A; if actual needs fall within 20 per cent of forecasts, use course of action B.

Figure 8-3 illustrates how the simulation process would work for three periods for the conditional strategy just described. In period one, a random event is generated from a specified probability distribution. This chance event determines the difference between actual and forecasted needs and thus whether course of action A, B, or C is chosen. Given this choice, another chance event is generated (a different probability distribution may be used, since the results of period one are likely to affect subsequent forecasts). The choice between A, B, or C is then made again, and so on. The result is a "decision tree," and each simulation run can follow any path along the tree. One such hypothetical path is shown by the dotted line in Figure 8-3; in this case, the path followed is the sequence of actions A, C, B. One can easily see that the number of possible paths becomes extremely large as we extend the planning horizon.

In general, conditional strategies can be designed to dampen the variations in forecasted needs over time; that is, the relative variations are usually larger if only unconditional strategies are used. Once the decision maker has selected the conditional strategies to simulate, the approach reverts to the procedure used in the deterministic case. However, in addition to forecasting dividends and earnings, the model can provide measures of risk for the relevant variables. Thus, the output may also include standard deviations for expected dividends and measures of intertemporal correlation over time.

Measures of risk can be especially useful in providing an estimate for the relative values of the $\alpha_t$'s, that is, the risk coefficients in Eq. (6-6a). The usefulness and the shortcomings of the standard deviation as a measure of risk were discussed in Chapter 5. Measures of intertemporal correlation, that is, measures of the manner in which the variables are related to each other over time for the various simulation runs, also provide relevant information for decision making. For example, the yearly dividends for two companies may have the same expectations and standard deviations over time, but need not be evaluated in the same way. For instance, a simulated strategy might result in a pattern of dividends similar to the pattern of funds requirements shown in Figure 8-1a, while another simulated strategy might yield a pattern similar to the one shown in Figure 8-1b. If the second strategy were followed, stockholders could be reasonably confident that random variations in dividends would "cancel out" over time. There would be no such assurance, however, if the first strategy were followed.

Finally, certain methods which were mentioned in Chapter 6—mathematical techniques designed to handle problems under conditions of uncertainty—may find increasing application in the final evaluation stage. Such a constraint can be expressed as follows: the probability that the dividends fall below some specified minimum level should be less than, say, 1 per cent.

Still, the objective remains the same: maximize the value of the firm to the present shareholders.

## Concluding Remarks

In the preface, we stated that the objective of this volume was to present a systematic application of financial theory to the practical problem of the firm's financing decision. The objective was attained only in part; for instance, our "systematic" applications often rested on artificial assumptions regarding the financial environment. Nevertheless, we feel that the volume is a necessary first step.

Certainly it can be said that further research is needed. Questions such as the following need empirical investigation:

1. What is the relationship between the firm's financing decision and the interest rate which the market requires on the firm's debt?
2. Can the risk and time preference coefficients in the valuation equation of Chapter 6, i.e., the $\alpha_t$'s and $\gamma_t$'s, be measured?
3. Is our normative valuation formula a useful way to represent the value of common stock to investors in real life?

An old African proverb says, "Do not test the depth of a river with both feet." In this book, we disregarded this message and often proposed different approaches to financial theory from those encountered in the current literature. We are confident that we have identified the variables which are relevant in financial decision making. We are less certain as to whether our formulation of the interrelationships is useful. Only time will tell.

# Index

# Heigh-Ho! Heigh-Ho!

**Funny,**
**Insightful,**
**Encouraging**
**and Sometimes Painful**

**QUOTES ABOUT WORK**

**by Terry Sullivan and Al Gini**

**ACTA Publications**
**Chicago, Illinois**

*Heigh-Ho! Heigh-Ho!*
*Funny, Insightful, Encouraging and Sometimes Painful Quotes about Work*
by Terry Sullivan and Al Gini

Al Gini is Associate Professor of Philosophy at Loyola University of Chicago and Managing Editor of *Business Ethics Quarterly.*
Terry Sullivan is a freelance writer whose work appears in *GQ Magazine* and *Chicago Magazine.* He is the editor of the *DePaul University Magazine.*

Edited by Gregory F. Augustine Pierce
Artwork by Isz
Typesetting by Garrison Publications

When known, occupations and nationalities (if not American) of the original authors, written sources of their quotes, and birth and death dates of those known to be deceased are given. Quotations not in the public domain have been used under the concept of "fair use" and "calculated risk" and remain the property of the original copyright holders. Bible quotes are from the New Revised Standard Version. 
4848 N. Clark Street
Chicago, IL 60640
312-271-1030
Year 99 98 97 96 95 94
Printing 6 5 4 3 2 1
ISBN: 0-87946-094-6
Library of Congress Number: 94-076846
Printed in the United States of America

# TABLE OF CONTENTS

# DEDICATION

To the countless men and women across America who, having been asked what they'd do if they won $36,000,000 in the lottery, tell reporters they would have no intention of quitting their jobs.

* * *

And special thanks to Patricia C. Haskell and Colin Hubbard for *their* good work.

# INTRODUCTION

> Sounds like a personal problem. See the Chaplain.
>
> Hubert E. Davis

Who, you might ask, is Hubert E. Davis? No, he isn't someone you ought to know; he's a former boss of mine and his quote above is the inspiration for this collection. It was his usual response when faced with an office problem he preferred not to deal with. Genuinely insurmountable problems, on the other hand, those which neither he nor anyone else could resolve, were met with a smile and his observation that, "Life is a vale of tears." Hubert was quotable, in a vaguely ecclesiastical way. What he inspired in us was an inquiry into all those other quotable people on the subject of work. Fiction, scholarship, movies, theater, religion—the whole mess of written and spoken culture is awash in wisdom about our daily toil, and nobody has collected it in one place for those of us who need some snappy reply for the boss or some profound insight for our own souls. Hence: *Heigh Ho! Heigh Ho!*

This title phrase is, you'll recall, part of the cheerful ditty the seven dwarves sang while heading off to work the mine every morning. "Whistle while you work," they suggested. What we forget is that the dwarves were self-employed and that at least one of them was Dopey. (Probably the one who wrote the song.) Scrooge's beleaguered clerk Bob Cratchit, you'll also remember, was not self-employed, and he didn't whistle at work, at least not until his boss had had a spirit-induced change of heart. Let us learn from these examples.

Lyricists regularly give us advice about work. "Get a job," some demented tunesmith of the Fifties insisted, almost certainly the father of a teenager. That, I suppose, is decent advice, but what are the odds anyone would work on the railroad all the livelong day, *just* to pass the time away?

Some people, of course, are happy in their work. Some of them are lucky, others are artists—defined by John Dewey as people who get paid to do what they would do anyway. Some others are artists of their own psyches—folks who can manage to make the best of any situation and wring a measure of satisfaction from the humblest, most back- and spirit-breaking occupations. For at least as many, however, work's a chain gang—from the modern stoop-laborers hunkered in the glow of a million cathode ray tubes to untold legions asking us if we'd like fries with that. And all of them, the happy and the numb, harbor a dream of some kind about their work.

Another old colleague of mine, Harvey Irlen, genuinely understood work and the people who did it. He knew we all wanted the perfect job, the corner office, the money, the power, the satisfaction. He knew that we were all buying those lottery tickets, waiting for the Bluebird of Happiness to land in our over-mortgaged tree. On the wall of his office, however, there hung an illustration titled, "The Bluebird of Learning to Live with It."

To help give you some perspective on learning to live with it, we've collected the accumulated wisdom of some people who have thought long and hard about work and some whose insights were quick and fleeting, if no less valuable. So take this book to work, lock yourself in the bathroom, and *read* all about what you're supposed to be *doing*.

*T. S.*

# CHAPTER 1
# Work—A Definition

What is this thing called work? There are short answers. Work is anything you have to do, whether you have to do it for money or not. Work is that thing that goes bump in the morning, that thing you have to do because your grandparents didn't buy Xerox stock or downtown Atlanta real estate when they were giving it away. Or it's the thing you have to do because, well, you just have to do it.

Work is stupefying, fun, hard to start, hard to quit, live and on Memorex, by turns. It's the thing that fills in the blanks—it doesn't have a definition, it *is* a definition. And the definitions are as many as there are jobs and people who hold them. Henry Ford went to work, and so did the guy who wired the first turn signals on the line in Dearborn. They both had opinions about the automobile business, and they both were right.

Nobody wants to work, until there isn't any work to do. Then everybody wants to work. Chances are you're as confused as the rest of us. This chapter may help—or it may confuse you more. Either way, you'll still have to go to work tomorrow. Unless you don't.

WORK

Nothing is really work unless you would rather be doing something else.

JAMES M. BARRIE, ENGLISH WRITER, 1860-1937

Some people like work, some people hate it, most try not to think about it when they don't have to. But everybody's got feelings and opinions about it—very few of which can be repeated in mixed company.

LARRY OLIVE, BUSINESSMAN

You can't eat for eight hours a day, nor drink for eight hours a day--all you can do for eight hours is work! Which is the reason man makes himself and everybody else so miserable and unhappy.

WILLIAM FAULKNER, NOVELIST, 1897-1962

I think everybody should have a career. Careers give you money and a place to go during weekdays when there's nothing good on television.

DAVE BARRY, HUMORIST

Our work should keep us from the three great evils: boredom, vice and poverty.

VOLTAIRE, FRENCH PHILOSOPHER, 1694-1778, *CANDIDE*

Work is not primarily a thing one does to live, but the thing one lives to do. It is, or should be, the full expression of the worker's faculties, the thing in which he finds spiritual, mental and bodily satisfaction, and the medium in which he offers himself to God.

DOROTHY L. SAYERS, ENGLISH NOVELIST, 1893-1957

Contentment is work so engrossing that you do not know that you are working.

Donald Hall, poet, *Life Work*

By working faithfully eight hours a day, you may eventually get to be a boss and work twelve hours a day.

Robert Frost, poet, 1874-1963

Work is prayer. Work is also stink. Therefore stink is prayer.

Aldous Huxley, English essayist, 1894-1963

By sitting quietly in your neat rows for long periods of time doing exactly what you are told in school, you are preparing to sit quietly in neat rows for long periods of time doing exactly what you are told as an adult. And remember: if you stay in school for years and years, you'll delay (for a while) your worst working fears.

MATT GROENING, CARTOONIST, *LIFE IN HELL*

Anyone can do any amount of work, provided it isn't the work he's supposed to be doing at that moment.

ROBERT BENCHLEY, HUMORIST, 1889-1945

No race can prosper until it learns there is as much dignity in tilling a field as in writing a poem.

BOOKER T. WASHINGTON, EDUCATOR, 1856-1915

. . . as a path to happiness, work is not highly prized by men. They do not strive after it as they do other possibilities of satisfaction. The great majority of people only work under the stress of necessity, and this natural human aversion to work raises most difficult social issues.

SIGMUND FREUD, AUSTRIAN PSYCHOLOGIST, 1856-1939, *CIVILIZATION AND ITS DISCONTENTS*

I do not like work even when some-one else does it.

MARK TWAIN, HUMORIST, 1835-1910

"People mutht be amuthed. They can't be alwayth a learning, nor yet they can't be alwayth a working. They an't made for it."

(CHARACTER MR. SLEARY) CHARLES DICKENS, ENGLISH NOVELIST, 1812-1870, *HARD TIMES*

The man whose whole life is spent performing a few simple operations generally becomes as stupid and ignorant as it is possible for a human creature to become.

Adam Smith, english economist, 1723-1790, *The Wealth of Nations*

I think most of us are looking for a calling, not a job. Most of us, like the assembly line worker, have jobs that are too small for our spirit. Jobs are not big enough for people.

Studs Terkel, journalist, *Working*

To say a man holds a job is to misstate the fact. The job holds the man.

James Gould Cozzens

The routine of our daily work has too often served as deep, dumb, deaf sleep, a refuge from two of life's most crucial states of being—keen awakedness to the needs of others and equal awakedness to the transcendent, which only comes in some state of loitering, dallying, tarrying, goofing off.

Francine du Plessix-Gray, french essayist,
"in praise of idleness"

Everything considered, work is less boring than amusing oneself.

Charles Baudelaire, french poet, 1821-1867

Labour without joy is base. Labour without sorrow is base. Sorrow without labour is base. Joy without labour is base.

John Ruskin, english writer, 1819-1900

The secret of life is to have a task, something you bring everything to, every minute of the day for your whole life. And the most important thing is—it must be something you cannot possibly do!

HENRY MOORE, ENGLISH SCULPTOR, 1898-1986

To labor is to pray.

ST. BENEDICT, ITALIAN MONK, 480-543

When men work they recognize one another as brothers.

M.D. CHENU, O.P, FRENCH THEOLOGIAN

Work is much more fun than fun.

NOEL COWARD, ENGLISH PLAYWRIGHT, 1899-1973

Work which remains permeated with the play attitude is art . . . .

JOHN DEWEY, PHILOSOPHER, 1859-1952, *ART AS EXPERIENCE*

The most fortunate people of all . . . are those for whom the line between work and play gets rubbed out, for whom work is pleasure and pleasure is in work.

JOSEPH EPSTEIN, ESSAYIST, *THE AMERICAN SCHOLAR*

The dignity and honor which work communicates to people is derived not from the object achieved but from the person's actual enjoyment in the process, that is, from the labor of one's hands and mind.

JOHN PAUL II, POPE, *LABOREM EXERCENS*

The right to work [is] the most precious liberty that man possesses. Man has indeed as much right to work as he has to live, to be free, to own property.

William O. Douglas, u.s. supreme court justice, 1898-1980

As individuals express their lives, so they are. What [individuals]. . . are . . . coincides with their production, both with what they produce and with how they produce. The nature of individuals thus depends on the material conditions determining their production.

Karl Marx, german philosopher, 1818-1883
*The German Ideology*

Do your work.
Do your work.
That is how I shall know you.

Ralph Waldo Emerson, essayist, 1803-1882

1) Work should not damage, degrade, humiliate, exhaust, stultify, or persistently bore the worker;

2) It should interest and satisfy him;

3) It should utilize many of the valued skills and abilities he already possess and provide opportunity for him to acquire others;

4) It should enhance, or at least leave unimpaired, his interest and ability to perform other major life roles—as husband or wife, parent, citizen, and friend; and

5) It should fulfill the instrumental purpose of getting a living, in terms acceptable to him.

Robert L. Kahn, sociologist

Man labors. Man must work to survive as a being with biological needs. But since work is an activity which demands cooperation, man must create an organization of labor, and in fact a community in which members speak the same language, develop common values, and produce symbols that sustain their cooperation. Labor is thus highly personal and at the same time wholly social.

Gregory Baum, canadian theologian, *The Priority of Labor*

Labor is prior to, and independent of, capital. Capital is only the fruit of labor, and could never have existed if labor had not first existed. Labor is the superior of capital, and deserves much the higher consideration.

Abraham Lincoln, 16th president of the united States, 1809-1865

Work is of two kinds: first, altering the position of matter at or near the earth's surface relative to other matter; second, telling other people to do so. The first kind is unpleasant and ill-paid; the second is pleasant and highly paid.

BERTRAND RUSSELL, ENGLISH PHILOSOPHER, 1872-1970

"Sex is a sublimation of the work instinct . . . ."

(CHARACTER MORRIS ZAPP) DAVID LODGE, NOVELIST, *SMALL WORLD*

We don't consider manual work as a curse, or even a necessity, not even as a means of making a living. We consider it as a high human function, as a basis of human life, the most dignified thing in the life of the human being, and which ought to be free, creative. Men ought to be proud of it.

DAVID BEN-GURION, ISRAELI PRIME MINISTER, 1886-1973

He who considers his work beneath him will be above doing it well.

ALEXANDER CHASE

You can buy a man's time; you can buy his physical presence at a given place; you can even buy a measured number of his skilled muscular motions per hour. But you can not buy enthusiasm...you can not buy loyalty...you can not buy the devotion of hearts, minds, or souls. You must earn these.

CLARENCE FRANCIS, BUSINESSMAN

". . . What I hated about working wasn't the working, it was the working for."

(CHARACTER SKY DIAL) MICHAEL DORRIS, NOVELIST, *WORKING MEN*

Morality requires that businesses offer meaningful work because morality requires that all individuals have a right to a meaningful life.

JOANNE B. CIULLA, PHILOSOPHER

When a great many people are unable to find work, unemployment results.

CALVIN COOLIDGE, 30TH PRESIDENT OF THE UNITED STATES, 1872-1933

The worst part of my job is: Not knowing who you are when you're out of work.

MICHAEL RICHARDS, ACTOR

Being out of work . . . is the surest path to self-loathing.

JOSEPH EPSTEIN, ESSAYIST, *THE AMERICAN SCHOLAR*

# CHAPTER 2
## Workwise: Things We Learn On The Job

We learn more about work at work than we ever learned about it in school. These days the crowd from the management suite are listening to the folks on the factory floor, but if you want the straight skinny, you'll listen to what people say under their breath in both places. For that matter, you'll probably learn more going through the paper in the copy room wastebasket than you ever will trying to follow what the consultants are pointing at on that overhead projector. But pay attention anyway.

The words of the prophets aren't written on the subway walls anymore, they're in the fine print of employment contracts. Get ready to be downsized, rightsized or re-engineered and you may be able to avoid it altogether. Or you may be ready to step up as a consultant, specializing in downsizing. In any case, education is wonderful thing. You're idling on the shoulder of the information interstate and we want you to learn a few things about work so you can play in the traffic.

Keep the pedal to the metal and your ear to the keyhole.

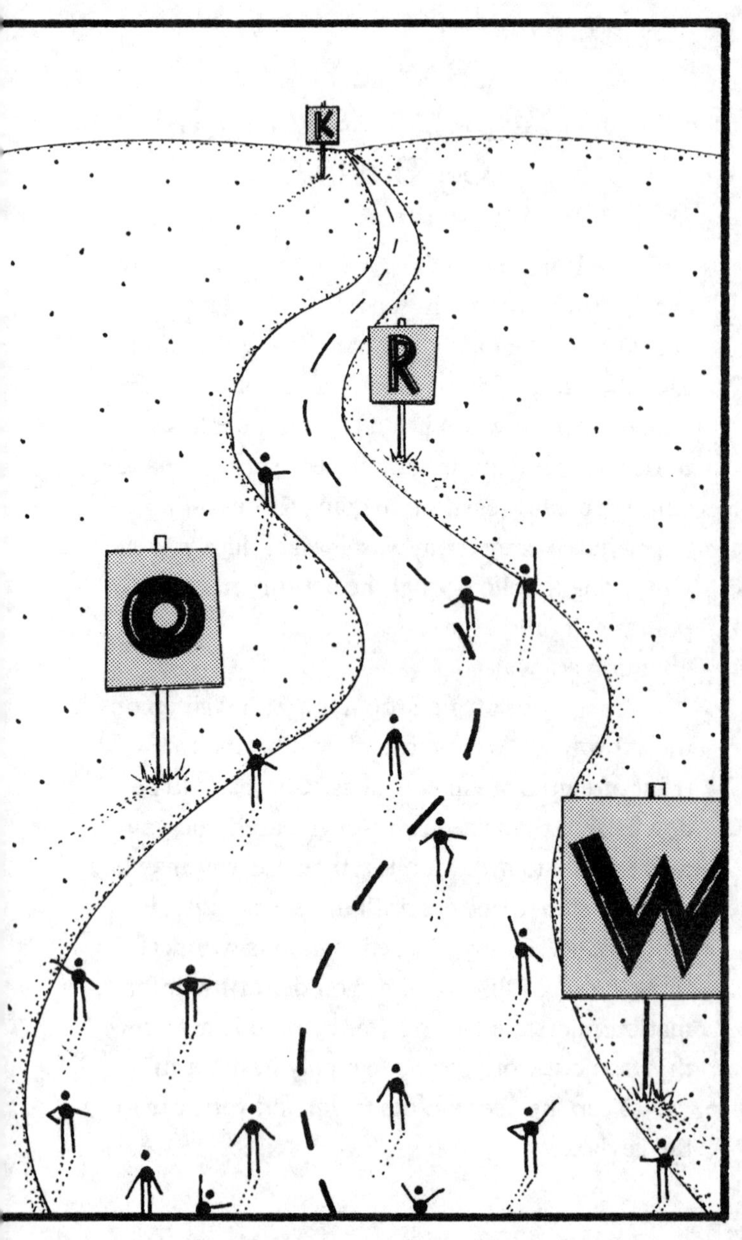
K
R
O
W

There are people who can make the creation of poetry or the leadership of a large university or corporation seem loathsome, and then there are people who can make the job of porter or waitress seem a good and useful thing.

JOSEPH EPSTEIN, ESSAYIST, *THE AMERICAN SCHOLAR*

Any work that is untrue to its own technique is a living lie.

DORTHY L. SAYERS, ENGLISH NOVELIST, 1893-1882

That which we persist in doing becomes easier—not that the nature of the task has changed, but our ability to do has increased.

RALPH WALDO EMERSON, ESSAYIST, 1803-1882

Having a good job is not the same as doing a good job.

ROBERT L. KAHN, SOCIOLOGIST

If my film makes one more person miserable, I've done my job.

WOODY ALLEN, FILMMAKER

I played football the only way I knew. If you have the football and 11 guys are after you, if you're smart, you'll run. It was no big deal.

RED GRANGE, FOOTBALL PLAYER, 1903-1991

A journalist is someone who would if he could, but he can't, so he tells those who already can how they should.

CLIFF TEMPLE, ENGLISH JOURNALIST

"Fighting was tough, but at least there were rules. The rounds were three minutes long with a minute of rest in between. You did not kick, bite or punch in the balls. You did not rabbit punch or hit a man when he was down. You did not punch after the bell. There were ropes that limited the world, that brought the world down to that twenty-foot square where you fought another man. You used your body and your mind, but there were rules. Not like life."

(CHARACTER BOBBY FALLON) PETER HAMILL, NOVELIST,
*FLESH AND BLOOD*

We missed a lot of tackles.

VINCE COLEMAN, FOOTBALL PLAYER, ON HIS TEAM'S 81-0 LOSS

We just need to work on some fundamentals.

GILBERT ALVAREZ, HIGH SCHOOL BASKETBALL COACH,
EXPLAINING A 136-7 LOSS

I can't play perfect every day.

TEDDY MARTINEZ, BASEBALL PLAYER, ON COMMITTING 5 ERRORS IN 5 GAMES

Coach, I don't know and I don't care.

JEFF WILKENS, BASKETBALL PLAYER, WHEN ASKED IF HIS POOR PERFORMANCE IN A GAME WAS DUE TO IGNORANCE OR APATHY

Baseball pays more, and you get hit less.

OLD SPORTS DICTUM

You work 16 straight Sundays and if you're lucky, you get to work some more.

WARREN MOON, FOOTBALL PLAYER, ON HIS PROFESSION

I couldn't face one more hotel, one more airport or another tennis club. I wasn't enjoying it anymore. My friends were so jealous, but it's not like you get to see anything. It's only a job.

ANGELICA GALVADON, TENNIS PLAYER, ON HER RETIREMENT FROM THE WOMEN'S TOUR AT AGE 17

I don't try to intimidate anybody *before* a fight. That's nonsense. I intimidate people by hitting them.

MIKE TYSON, BOXER

A professional is someone who tells you something you already know and makes it sound confusing.

AUTHOR UNKNOWN

Clergyman, n. A man who undertakes the management of our spiritual affairs as a method of bettering his temporal ones.

AMBROSE BIERCE, HUMORIST, 1842-1914

I've been digging about four graves per week for 40 years. That makes approximately 8,000 graves I've dug.

PAUL TRUMPF, GRAVEDIGGER

I've been working in show business for 86 years . . . . Listen, when I started, the only types of entertainment we had were vaudeville, the burlesque, minstrel shows, the theater, silent movies and the hole in the wall between our bathroom and the Wisnewsky's bedroom. The hole in the wall was the most popular.

GEORGE BURNS, COMEDIAN

I never work on anything. Dedication is such a weird word after all, after Albert Schweitzer and people like that. That's dedication, when you give your whole life. No one dedicates themselves to anything anymore.

Ringo Starr, english musician

"I can't think when I sell shoes. I just have to sail along in some kind of a blind passion of greed. Just let the criminal instinct in me take over. I don't know what would happen to a guy in this business if he had a conscience. Fortunately, I have none whatsoever."

(character marty hansen) Thomas Blonty, *The Competitor*

"Salesmen . . . are a vigorous, fun-loving bunch when they are not suffering abdominal cramps . . . ."

(character bob slocum) Joseph Heller, *Something Happened*

In Washington, D.C., where I live, there actually *are* more lawyers than people.

Sandra Day O'Connor, u.s. supreme court justice

Scrubbing floors and emptying bedpans have just as much dignity as there is in any work done in this country—including my own.

Richard Nixon, 37th president of the united states

Life to me is black and white. There are no grays.

Sam Jones, executioner at Angola (Louisiana) state prison

Cops see people at their worst and the worst kind of people.

Joseph Waumbaugh, novelist

Cops know things you and I don't. It's knowledge crafted out of years spent on the street, sizing up and dealing with the volatile, cunning, confused, comic, tragic, often goofy behavior of human beings from every social, economic, and mental level, and it's knowledge won as a by-product of investigating criminal specialties such as homicide, sex crimes, property crimes, and narcotics. A cop who works traffic has peered deeper into the recesses of the human psyche than most shrinks. A cop who works homicide, or sex crimes, will tell you things Dostoyevski only guessed at.

CONNIE FLETCHER, SOCIOLOGIST, *WHAT COPS KNOW*

Every waking and sleeping moment, my nightmare is the fact that I will give an order that will cause countless numbers of human beings to lose their lives. I don't want my troops to die. I don't want my troops to be maimed. It's an intensely personal, emotional thing for me. Any decision you have to make that involves the loss of human life is nothing you do lightly. I agonize over it.

H. NORMAN SCHWARZKOPF, U.S.ARMY GENERAL

A doctor can bury his mistakes but an architect can only advise his client to plant vines.

FRANK LLOYD WRIGHT, ARCHITECT, 1869-1959

Let everyone sweep in front of his own door, and the whole world will be clean.

JOHANN WOLFGANG VON GOETHE, GERMAN POET, 1749-1832

In a completely rational society, the best of us would be teachers and the rest of us would have to settle for something else.

LEE IACOCCA, BUSINESSMAN

It's not good, we will lose our jobs.

UNIDENTIFIED EAST GERMAN BORDER GUARD,
ON THE TEARING DOWN OF THE BERLIN WALL

"A job. Mama, a job? I open and close car doors all day long. I drive a man around in his limousine and I say, 'Yes, sir; no, sir; very good, sir; shall I take the Drive, sir?' Mama, that ain't no kind of job . . . that ain't nothing at all. Mama, I don't know if I can make you understand.

(CHARACTER WALTER LEE YOUNGER) LORRAINE HANSBERRY, PLAYWRIGHT,
*A RAISIN IN THE SUN*

It is conventional to complain about work, and complaining is usually bragging.

DONALD HALL, POET, *LIFE WORK*

# CHAPTER 3
## Work As Identity, Work As Necessity

You are what you eat, but you have to work to eat in the first place. More likely, you are what you do—or so some of the best brains in the philosophy, psychology and sociology games tell us. Japanese corporate culture tells us the same thing: Your identity is on your business card, salaryperson. I have a title, therefore I am. If you don't like who you are, it seems, change what you do. Here's a test. What do Michelangelo, George Patton, Queen Victoria, Ty Cobb, Gertrude Stein, and Vlad the Impaler have in common?

Answer: You remember what they did.

"Just Do It," Nike (the shoe company, not the Greek god) said, and they have a point. If you're going to work, people are going to use your job to describe you. And you are going to use your job to describe yourself. Make sure you like what you have to say.

Don't just sit there, do something.

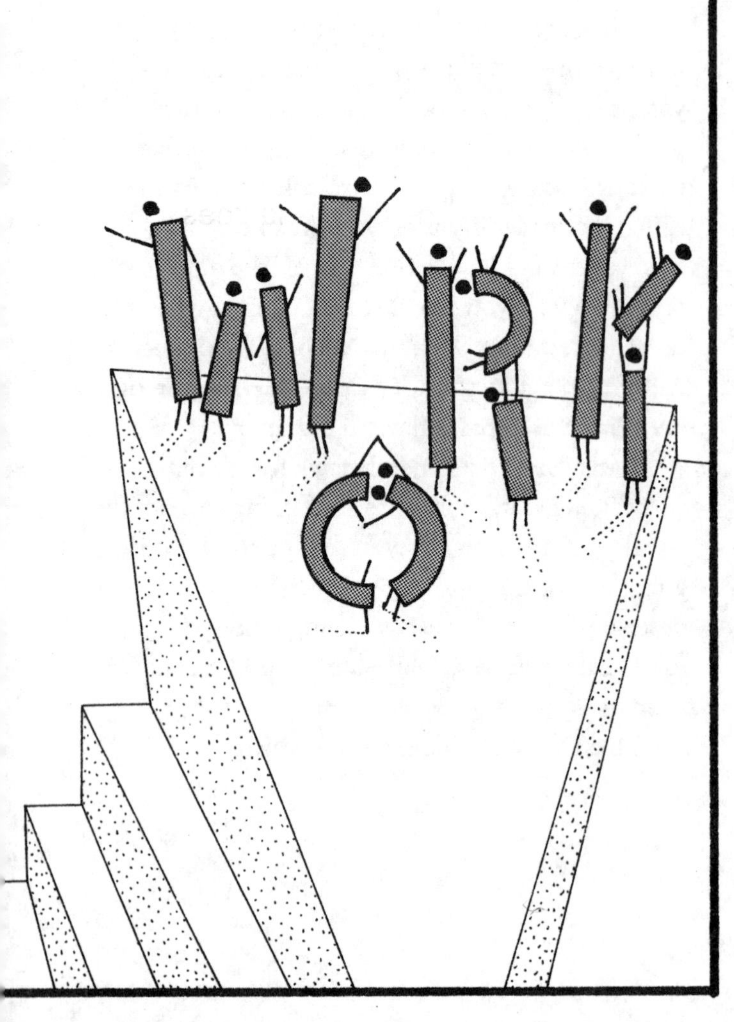

I don't do it for therapy. I do it because that's what I've always done. What's your alternative? Stay in bed or work.

FRANK ZAPPA, MUSCIAN 1943-1993

A man is what he does and does well. That's one thing I learned in my life.

ELIA KAZAN, NOVELIST, *THE ARRANGEMENT*

Career and identity are inextricably bound up: Indeed they are almost equivalent.

DOUGLAS LABIER, SOCIOLOGIST, *MODERN MADNESS: THE EMOTIONAL FALLOUT OF SUCCESS*

When love and skill work together, expect a masterpiece.

JOHN RUSKIN, ENGLISH WRITER, 1819-1900

I don't needs the money, I needs the work.

Jimmy Durante, comedian, when asked why he continued to perform into his eighties, 1893-1980

Work and love—these are the basics. Without them there is neurosis.

Theodore Reik, Austrian-American psychoanalyst, 1880-1969, *Of Love and Lust*

Good for the body is the work of the body, and good for the soul is the work of the soul, and good for either is the work of the other.

Henry David Thoreau, essayist, 1817-1862

Something real, cool and solid lies before you; something unromantic as Monday morning, when all who have to work wake with the consciousness that they must rise and betake themselves thereto.

CHARLOTTE BRONTË, ENGLISH NOVELIST, 1816-1855, PRELUDE TO *SHIRLEY*

Work, like food, is a necessity.

LEO TOLSTOY, RUSSIAN NOVELIST, 1828-1910

Labor is the axis of human self-making.

GREGORY BAUM, CANADIAN THEOLOGIAN, *THE PRIORITY OF LABOR*

I believe in the dignity of labor, whether with head or hand; that the world owes no man a living but that it owes every man an opportunity to make a living.

JOHN D. ROCKEFELLER, JR., BUSINESSMAN, 1874-1960

A person's activities determine his self-identity, and in western culture paid employment is, rightly or wrongly, the main activity by which we define and assess ourselves and others.

Robert L. Kahn, sociologist

The personal commitment of a man to his skill, the intellectual commitment and emotional commitment working together as one, has made the ascent of man.

Jacob Bronowski, anthropologist, 1908-1974,
*The Ascent of Man*

Since modern man experiences himself both as the seller and as the commodity to be sold on the market, his self-esteem depends on conditions beyond his control. If he is successful, he is valuable; if he is not, he is worthless.

Erich Fromm, german psychologist, 1900-1980,
*The Revolution of Hope*

"Men like to work. It's a funny thing, but they do. They may moan about it every Monday morning, they may agitate for shorter hours and longer holidays, but they need to work for their self-respect."

(CHARACTER VIC WILCOX) DAVID LODGE, NOVELIST, *NICE WORK*

I am convinced that it is not fear of death, of our lives ending, that haunts our sleep so much as the fear that our lives will not have mattered, that as far as the world is concerned we might as well never have lived. What we miss in our lives, no matter how much we have, is that sense of meaning.

HAROLD KUSHNER, RABBI, *WHEN ALL YOU'VE EVER WANTED ISN'T ENOUGH*

Work is integral to the whole tapestry of our lives. If we have no happiness or joy within ourselves how can there be any at work? 'The world is as we are' is the old Hindu saying. As we enhance our self-esteem, so we enhance our working lives.

MARSHA SINETAR, PSYCHOLOGIST, *DO WHAT YOU LOVE, THE MONEY WILL FOLLOW*

In work not only should matter gain in nobility, but man himself should not experience a lowering of his nobility in the work being done.

JOHN PAUL II, POPE, *LABOREM EXERCENS*

Through work, man actualizes himself; man becomes the one he is meant to be...man appears as one who becomes truly himself through his work. For in work a person expresses himself, assumes responsibility for his world, and prepares his own and society's future.

GREGORY BAUM, CANADIAN THEOLOGIAN, *THE PRIORITY OF LABOR*

Men love to think they can lose themselves in work.

MARLANE MEYER, PLAYWRIGHT, *THE GEOGRAPHY OF LUCK*

If all of life were a job, and all that man could get out of it wages, then you'd have to admit that the wages just weren't high enough.

JOSEPH CONRAD, POLISH-ENGLISH NOVELIST, 1857-1924

Good work is work that ennobles the product as it ennobles the producer.

E. F. SCHUMACHER, ECONOMIST, 1911-1973, *GOOD WORK*

Bad work follow ye as long as ye live.

JAMES RUSSELL LOWELL, POET, 1819-1891

At the level of mental health, interesting work is a requirement of adult life.

ADINA SCHWARTZ, PHILOSOPHER

Adults need meaningful work in the same way that children need interesting play in order to fulfill themselves as persons.

AL GINI, PHILOSOPHER

Work: The doing is as important as what gets done, the making as valuable as the made.

THEODORE ROSZAK, HISTORIAN, *PERSON/PLANET*

For men, the center of life is the self and the work.

CAROL GILLIGAN, PSYCHOLOGIST, *IN A DIFFERENT VOICE*

A man out of work is a stranger to himself.

ROLLO MAY, PSYCHOLOGIST

For my father's generation job satisfaction meant—"Hey, be satisfied you gotta job!"

CHRISTOPHER CIMINO, BUSINESSMAN

After 50 years of living, it occurs to me that the most significant thing people do is go to work, whether it is to go to work on their novel or the assembly plant or fixing somebody's teeth.

THOMAS MCGUANE, NOVELIST

"I wanted to think about—What? Who I was? Who I wasn't? The words mean everything and nothing at the same time. I was a lawyer, but that was the only thing I was certain I was. Didn't other people have better I.D. than just their jobs?"

(CHARACTER NELL BERMAN) JUDITH ROSSNER, NOVELIST,
*HIS LITTLE WOMEN*

To put one brick upon another,
Add a third, and then a fourth,
Leaves no time to wonder whether
What you do has any worth.
But to sit with bricks around you
While the winds of heaven bawl
Weighing what you should or
  can do
Leaves no doubt of it at all.

PHILIP LARKIN, ENGLISH POET, 1922-1985, *TOADS REVISITED*

No man is born into the world
  whose work
Is not born with him; there is
  always work,
And tools to work withal, for
  those who will;
And blessed are the
  horny hands of toil.

JAMES RUSSELL LOWELL, POET, 1819-1991,
*A GLANCE BEHIND THE CURTAIN*

To every reproach I know but one answer, namely, to go again to my work. "But you neglect your relations." Too true, then I will work the harder. "But you have no genius." Yes, then I will work the harder. "But you have detached yourself from people: you must regain some positive relation." Yes, I will work the harder.

RALPH WALDO EMERSON, ESSAYIST, 1803-1882

# CHAPTER 4
## Choosing A Career

Door number 1. Pick a card, any card. Welcome to the employment merry-go-round, where anybody can grab the brass ring, but it can turn your finger green if you're not careful.

Every day, millions begin the search, poring over classified ads and reading posters on the walls of employment agencies and college placement offices, searching for the perfect job. Millions more sit on coffee breaks trying to figure a way out of their current perfect job into one that doesn't cause quite so much stomach pain.

Meanwhile, millions more leap from bed eager for another day on the job. Are they lucky, or do they know something we don't? Is the fault in the stars, or ourselves? Why do some get the lady while others get the tiger? What if the tiger is choosing among the doors in the first place?

Learn to relax and love the randomness of it all, or learn a little something from people who have been there . . . and back.

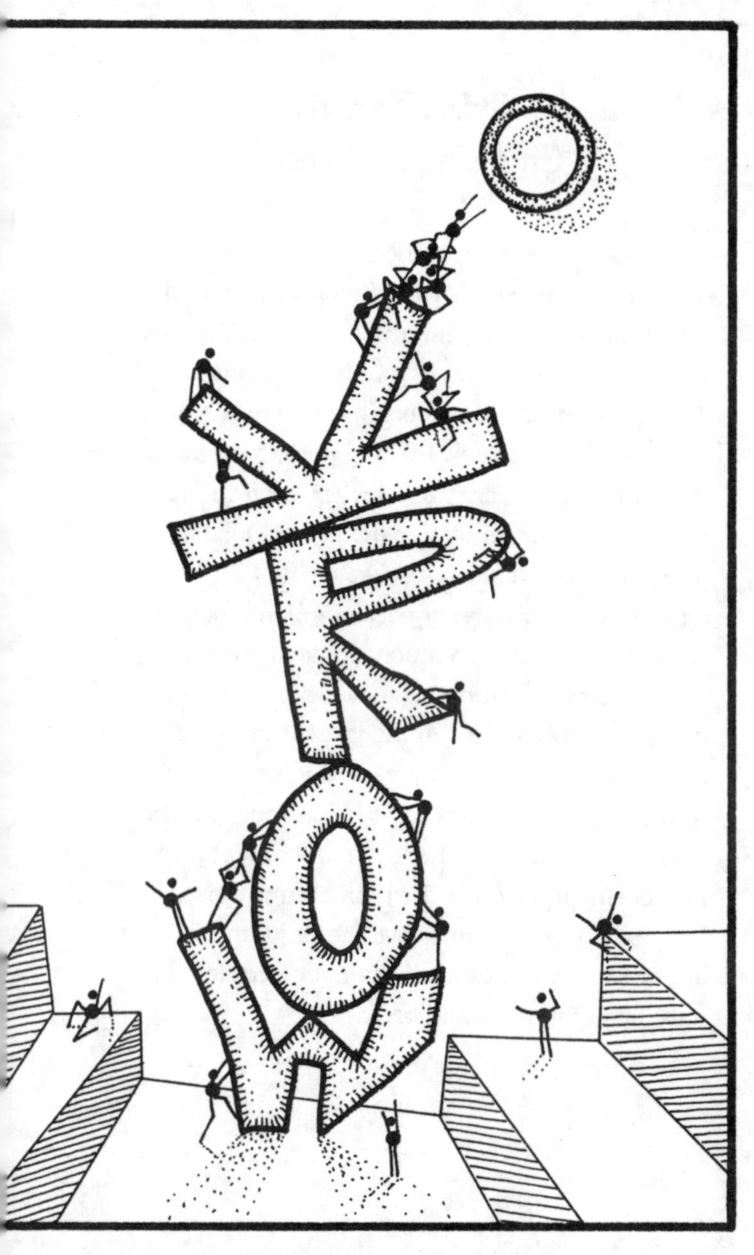

The only job you start out at the top on is digging a ditch.

William Ensley, carpenter

My father was a human cannonball who used to go around country fairs and rodeos being shot out of a cannon. He used to say, "Go to college or be a cannonball."

Bob Kuechenberg, football player, on his motivation for attending college

One of the great paradoxes of human development is that we are required to make crucial choices (about careers and work) before we have the knowledge, judgment and self-understanding to choose wisely. Yet if we put off these choices until we feel truly ready, the delay may produce other and greater costs.

Daniel J. Levinson, psychologist, *Seasons of a Man's Life*

I'll tell you a secret—adults don't know what they want to do for a living. That's why they`re always asking kids what they want to be when they grow up—they're looking for ideas.

PAULA POUNDSTONE, COMEDIAN

If I would be a young man again and had to decide how to make my living, I would not try to become a scientist or scholar or teacher. I would rather choose to be a plumber or a peddler, in the hope to find that modest degree of independence still available under present circumstances.

ALBERT EINSTEIN, PHYSICIST, 1879-1955

People, like plants, may need to be repotted occasionally, at least until the pot is big enough for the specimen to grow without stunting."

ROBERT FORD, BUSINESSMAN, ON CHANGING JOBS

When I was young I worked on a farm. Then I decided to study the law. After that, I never worked again.

CLARENCE DARROW, LAWYER, 1857-1938

Lionel viewed acting as a trade like any other and was fond of saying that had their father been a plumber, he and John would have undoubtedly flushed drains for a living.

MARGOT PETERS, BIOGRAPHER, *THE HOUSE OF BARRYMORE*

Strictly speaking the worker who drains sewers to protect humanity from unhealthy miasmas is a very useful member of society, whereas the theologian who seeks to befog the brain with supernatural, transcendental doctrines is an extremely harmful individual.

AUGUST BEBEL, GERMAN PHILOSOPHER, 1840-1913,
*DIE FRAU UND DER SOZIALISMUS*

I didn't raise my kid to be a catcher.

ROCKY MARCIANO'S MOTHER, WHEN HER SON CHOSE BOXING OVER BASEBALL

The policeman is the little boy who grew up to be what he said he was going to be.

RAYMOND BURR, ACTOR, 1917-1993

If it falls to your lot to be a street sweeper, sweep streets like Michelangelo carved marble. Sweep streets as Shakespeare wrote pictures. Sweep streets so well that all the hosts of heaven will have to say, "Here lives the streetsweeper who did his job well."

MARTIN LUTHER KING, JR., CIVIL RIGHTS LEADER, 1929-1968

# CHAPTER 5
## The Joy Of Work

Work is like shaving—if you don't do it every day, you're a bum. At least that's what I read on the sexist sign above the grill in a truck-stop on the Ohio Turnpike once. That doesn't mean work can't be fun. Michael Jordan had fun at work, because he knew how good he was. Dan Quayle had fun at work, because he knew how lucky he was. You can have fun at work too, but always test the audience first—is it yourself, your boss, your colleagues, your customers, your competitors . . . or all of the above?.

Richard Nixon did not have fun at work; Jack Kennedy did. What do we learn from this? Never mind. Concentrate instead on the silliness of work. Imagine what the world would be like if nobody did some jobs? Imagine a world free of corn flakes, newspapers, muffler parts, taxicabs, cosmetic surgery, disposable coffee cups, philosophy, inkjet printers, accounting, etc., etc. There, that isn't so bad, is it? We'd all survive, and you'd still find something to do.

Stop worrying and learn to love your job. Pay no attention to that man behind the screen.

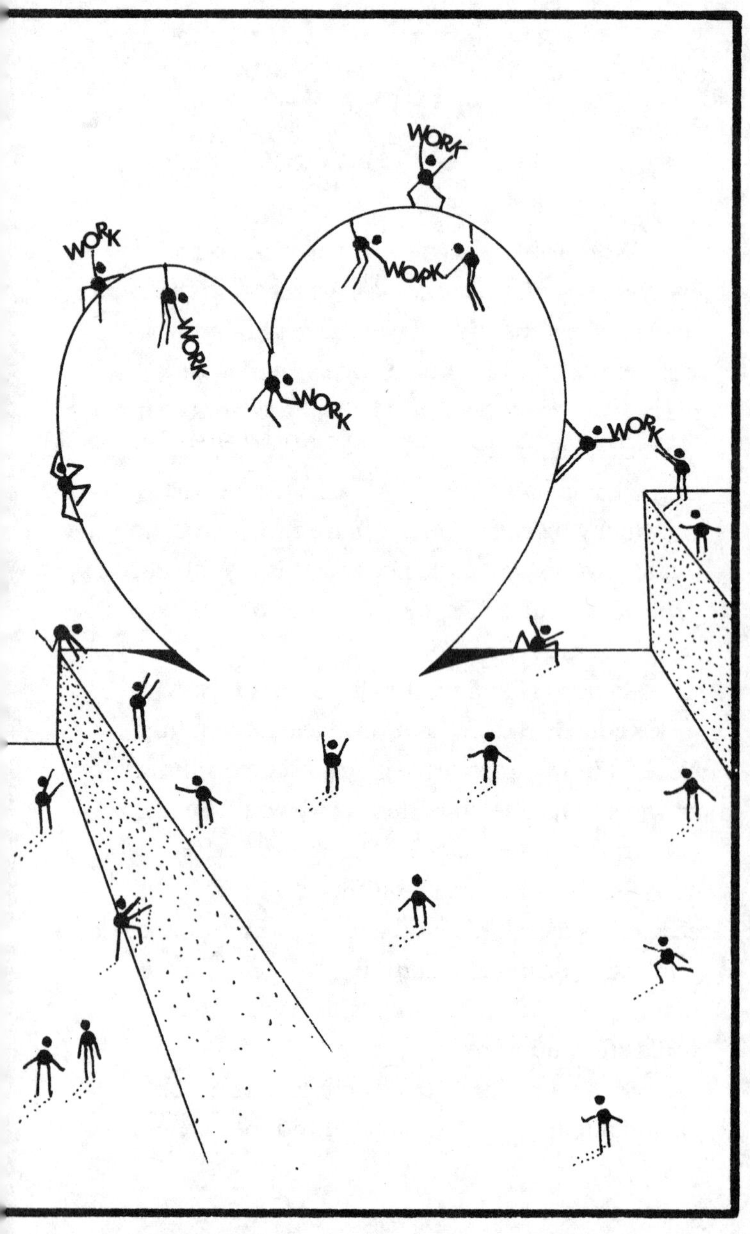
WORK
WORK
WORK
WORK
WORK
WORK

A man can do only what he can do. But if he does that each day he can sleep at night and do it again the next day.

ALBERT SCHWEITZER, DOCTOR, 1875-1965

The only happy people I know are the ones who are working well at something they consider important.

ABRAHAM MASLOW, PSYCHOLOGIST, 1908-1970, *EUPSYCHIAN MANAGEMENT*

". . . the secret of life . . . [is] to make your living at what you want to do."

(CHARACTER ARNOLD TRITELBAUM) ELIA KAZAN, NOVELIST, *THE ARRANGEMENT*

Happiness is loving what you do, even if you don't do it well.

GEORGE BURNS, COMEDIAN

Happiness lies not in the mere possession of money; it lies in the joy of achievement, in the thrill of creative effort. The joy and moral stimulation of work no longer must be forgotten in the mad chase after evanescent profits.

FRANKLIN DELANO ROOSEVELT, 32ND PRESIDENT OF THE UNITED STATES, 1882-1945

"In every job that must be done, there is an element of fun."

(CHARACTER MARY POPPINS) RICHARD MORTON SHERMAN, LYRICIST, "JUST A SPOONFULL OF SUGAR"

(The) willing acceptance of one's work is what makes life bearable.

VOLTAIRE, FRENCH PHILOSOPHER, 1694-1778, *CANDIDE*

Coaching is what I like to do, where I belong. I read I was supposed to go into broadcasting next season, but I know some coaches who became first-class jerks as analysts. Plus, the feeling I got coaching this last season in Chicago, you can't get that in any office, or any TV booth.

MIKE DITKA, FOOTBALL COACH, BEFORE HE BECAME A SPORTS BROADCASTER

A cowboy is someone who loves his work. Since the hours are long—ten to fifteen hours a day—and the pay is $30 he has to. What's required of him is an odd mixture of physical vigor and maternalism. His part of the beef-raising industry is to birth and nurture calves and take care of their mothers. For the most part his work is done on horseback and in a lifetime he sees and comes to know more animals than people.

GRETEL EHRLICH, ESSAYIST, *THE SOLACE OF OPEN SPACES*

I haven't got time to be tired.

Wilhelm I, emperor of Germany, 1797-1888

The reason I love conducting is that I love the people I conduct, and I love the people for whom we play....it's the most potent love affair you can have in your life.

Leonard Bernstein, conductor, 1918-1990

I don't play golf, I don't go to the movies.  I get up at 3 o'clock every morning, and I haven't missed a day in 10 years.  I've got tunnel vision about my work.  I train horses.  It's the only thing I do with my life.

D. Wayne Lukas, horse trainer

I play and have fun. Just like I did when I was a kid. To me, baseball is going out and playing. You still do everything—hit, run and catch—the same. It's fun.

KEN GRIFFEY, JR., BASEBALL PLAYER

"Down at the plant, I'm doing a job. And when I die, somebody else will be doing this job. And when he dies, somebody else will do it. I dunno. Makes you feel great to be a part of something like that."

(CHARACTER HOMER SIMPSON) MATT GROENING, CARTOONIST, *THE SIMPSONS*

It requires a certain kind of mind to see beauty in a hamburger bun. Yet is it any more unusual to find grace in the texture and softly curved silhouette of a bun than to reflect lovingly on...the arrangement of textures and colors in a butterfly's wing?

RAY KROC, BUSINESSMAN, 1902-1984

When you are making a success of something, it's not work. It's a way of life. You enjoy yourself because you are making your contribution to the world.

ANDY GRANATELLI, AUTO RACING DRIVER

Good science consists largely of play disguised as serious work.

EDMUND WILSON, LITERARY CRITIC, 1895-1972

To win, you have to get people who want more out of life than a paycheck. I didn't come here for the money. I can make more money in two weeks of speaking engagements than I can by coaching here for a year or more.

GEORGE ALLEN, FOOTBALL COACH, 1922-1990

A good job not only has to pay well, it also has to offer hope.

JAMES BALDWIN, NOVELIST, 1924-1987

If I didn't have writing. I'd be running down the street hurling grenades in people's faces.

PAUL FUSSELL, ESSAYIST

"I started to love boxing: hitting people, making them miss, seeing them fall. And it wasn't just the fighting. I began to love the rest of it: the sweating, the rope skipping, the smell of damp concrete in the gym, the sound of the other fighters grunting when they dug punches into the heavy bags."

(CHARACTER BOBBY FALLON) PETER HAMILL, NOVELIST,
*FLESH AND BLOOD*

My job is like working in the park; it doesn't affect me . . . .

PAUL TRUMPF, GRAVEDIGGER

"Other cops put in their nine hours and go home to their families twenty miles from town and that's it, but guys like me, why I got nobody and I want nobody. I do my living on my beat."

(CHARACTER BAMPER MORGAN) JOSEPH WAUMBAUGH, NOVELIST,
*THE BLUE KNIGHT*

I make deals at home. It's what I do.

Donald Trump, businessman, when asked what he does to relax

You don't have to be exceptionally intelligent to do what I do.

Harry Caray, baseball announcer

I'm appalled at how easy the business is.

Dan Dierdorf, football player, on his new career in broadcasting

Despite everything that's happened, it's still the best job I ever had.

Sydney Biddle Barrows, former madame, on the escort service she operated

There's an old story about three workers breaking up rocks. When the first was asked what he was doing, he replied, "Making little ones out of big ones;" the second said, "Making a living;" and the third, "Building a cathedral." While each of these answers was, of course, accurate, I hope to convince the reader that the third answer was "true"—that is, more faithful to our commonly shared potential of humanness.

JOHN JULIAN RYAN, THEOLOGIAN

No amount of pay ever made a good soldier, a good teacher, a good artist, or a good workman.

JOHN RUSKIN, ENGLISH WRITER, 1819-1900

# CHAPTER 6
## How To Succeed

Just remember these eleven words: "Yes, Dad went to Harvard Law. That's where he met Mom." Remember also that Horatio Alger was fictional, but Bill Gates is real. Opportunity doesn't knock anymore, it just leaves an E-Mail message. And a lot of people forget to check their screens.

There are as many ways to succeed as there are suckers born, but you do want to make it to retirement unindicted. Hard work will get you there, sometimes. Sometimes a little carefully selected boot-licking will do the same. Genius helps. An eye for the main chance helps more. Dumb luck never hurt anybody. IBM had it right with their corporate motto: Think. Then somebody else thought harder.

Best to try everything. Think hard, work hard, apply some carefully considered hypocrisy ("that's a nice tie"), stay low, move fast, and don't be afraid to take a chance.

You have the right to the pursuit of happiness. Catching it is another matter. But you also have the right to sing the blues. Read on.

W
O
R
K

There's only one surefire way to succeed in business: make something people want, make it well, and make it in one size.

HENRY FORD, BUSINESSMAN, 1863-1947

Rules to live by at work: (1) You never go around your boss. (2) You tell your boss what he wants to hear, even when your boss claims that he wants dissenting views. (3) If your boss wants something dropped, you drop it. (4) You are sensitive to your boss's wishes so that you anticipate what he wants; you don't force him, in other words, to act as boss. (5) Your job is not to report something that your boss does not want reported, but rather to cover it up. You do what your job requires, and you keep your mouth shut.

ROBERT JACKALL, SOCIOLOGIST, *MORAL MAZES*

Don't confuse fame with success. One is Madonna; the other is Helen Keller.

ERMA BOMBECK, HUMORIST

". . . the secret of life . . . [is] to make your living at what you want to do."

(CHARACTER EDDIE ANDERSON) ELIA KAZAN, NOVELIST, *THE ARRANGEMENT*

Don't play what you know. Play what you hear.

MILES DAVIS, MUSICIAN, 1926-1991

"There ain't nothin' matters less than what you did yesterday."

(CHARACTER T.D. DAVIS) PETER DEXTER, NOVELIST, *GOD'S POCKET*

Above all, be loyal to your superior's agenda.

JOHN DELOREAN, BUSINESSMAN, SUMMARIZING THE CORPORATE PHILOSOPHY OF ROGER SMITH, CEO OF GENERAL MOTORS

What we want in our . . . business executive is somebody who demands the absolute best in everything, somebody who is never satisfied, somebody who, if he had been in charge of decorating the Sistine Chapel, would have said "This is a good fresco, Michelangelo, but I want a better fresco, and I want it by tomorrow morning."

DAVE BARRY, HUMORIST

"I have a wife and children, and business, as they say, is business. . . . I get up, I go, I lie a little, I peddle a little, I watch the rules, I talk the talk. We fellas have those offices high up there so we can catch the wind and go with it, however it blows."

(CHARACTER ARNOLD BURNS) HERB GARDNER, PLAYWRIGHT,
*A THOUSAND CLOWNS*

No one ever got very far by working a 40-hour week. Most of the notable people I know are trying to manage a 40-hour day.

CHANNING POLLOCK

Q: How many people work in your office?
A: About half of them.

AUTHOR UNKNOWN

Unless you are willing to drench yourself in your work beyond the capacity of the average man, you are just not cut out for positions at the top.

J.C. PENNEY, 1875-1971, BUSINESSMAN

Opportunity is missed by most people because it is dressed in overalls and looks like work.

THOMAS ALVA EDISON, INVENTOR, 1847-1931

To youth I have but three words of counsel—work, work, work.

OTTO VON BISMARCK, CHANCELLOR OF GERMANY, 1815-1898

It takes work to take over.

ED SHURNA, COMMUNITY ORGANIZER

Eighty percent of success is showing up.

WOODY ALLEN, FILMMAKER

Do what you love. The money will follow.

MARSHA SINETAR, PSYCHOLOGIST, *DO WHAT YOU LOVE, THE MONEY WILL FOLLOW*

"Most American success originates in an obstetrician's hands: if he pulls you out of a woman who is in the right marriage, your future is assured."

(CHARACTER OWNEY MORRISON) JIMMY BRESLIN, NOVELIST, *TABLE MONEY*

You have to take your ego, put it in your back pocket and zip it. If you're waiting for someone to tell you what a good job you're doing, you'll wait a long time.

JIM COVERT, FOOTBALL PLAYER

My grandfather once told me that there are two kinds of people: those who do the work and those who take the credit. He told me to try to be in the first group; there was less competition there.

INDIRA GANDHI, PRIME MINISTER OF INDIA, 1917-1984

There is no such thing as a bad client.

JERRY DELLA FEMINA, ADVERTISING EXECUTIVE, *FROM THE FOLKS WHO GAVE YOU PEARL HARBOR*

I don't want any yes-men around me. I want everybody to tell me the truth even if it costs them their jobs.

SAMUEL GOLDWYN, PRODUCER, 1882-1974

"He used to be a yes man but he got himself some guts and now he goes around saying 'maybe' to everyone."

(CHARACTER MURRAY BURNS) HERB GARDNER, PLAYWRIGHT, *A THOUSAND CLOWNS*

Get a lot while you're young.

JOHN G. HOPPE, SR., REALTOR, ON THE SECRET TO BUSINESS SUCCESS

Well, you take one day off, and you're thinking, "Boy, this is great. . . ." Then you take two days off, and then three. To me, comedy is like lifting weights; once you start, if you don't do it every day, everything begins to atrophy and you wind up a big fat pig. And it's not exactly unrewarding work. You say to yourself, "I can stay home and watch Jake and the Fatman, or I can make $25,000."

Jay Leno, comedian, on why he works so hard

Success is the one unpardonable sin against one's fellows.

Ambrose Bierce, humorist, 1842-1914

Try not to become a man of success but rather try to become a man of value.

Albert Einstein, physicist, 1879-1955

I've always wanted to win, that's what it's all about. If I hadn't wanted to win, I wouldn't even have gotten in on this thing. I would have gotten a job at Montgomery Ward instead.

George Allen, football coach, 1922-1990

Don't wait for your ship to come in; swim out to it.

Author unknown

If you don't want to work, you have to work to earn enough money so that you won't have to work.

Ogden Nash, essayist, 1902-1971

Nothing in this world can take the place of persistence. Talent will not; nothing is more common than unsuccessful men with talent. Genius will not; unrewarded genius is almost a proverb. Education will not; the world is full of educated derelicts. Persistence and determination alone are omnipotent.

CALVIN COOLIDGE, 30TH PRESIDENT OF THE UNITED STATES, 1872-1933

Politics is not a bad profession. If you succeed, there are many rewards; if you disgrace yourself, you can always write a book.

RONALD REAGAN, 40TH PRESIDENT OF THE UNITED STATES

# CHAPTER 7
# Up The Organization

You are a cog in a well-oiled wheel. Sometimes the other cogs resent you. Stop worrying, that's what cogs do best.

The trick is to be a bigger cog; get the "you are here" arrow a little higher on the organizational chart. This is not easy, but it can be done. You can wait it out—that's why God made attrition. You can work it out—become a better cog. You can help rewrite the chart—if you can get hold of the magic marker. You can quit and redesign your own wheel—but be prepared to be a lonely cog, with no other cogs to work late with you when the project is due in the morning.

No matter which strategy you choose, the important thing is to understand organizations. They are alive; they need to be fed, watered, and kept warm. Find out what they eat. Feed them. Accounting firms like neatness, law firms like money, universities like words, advertising agencies like attention, governments like loyalty.

Nobody likes surprises.

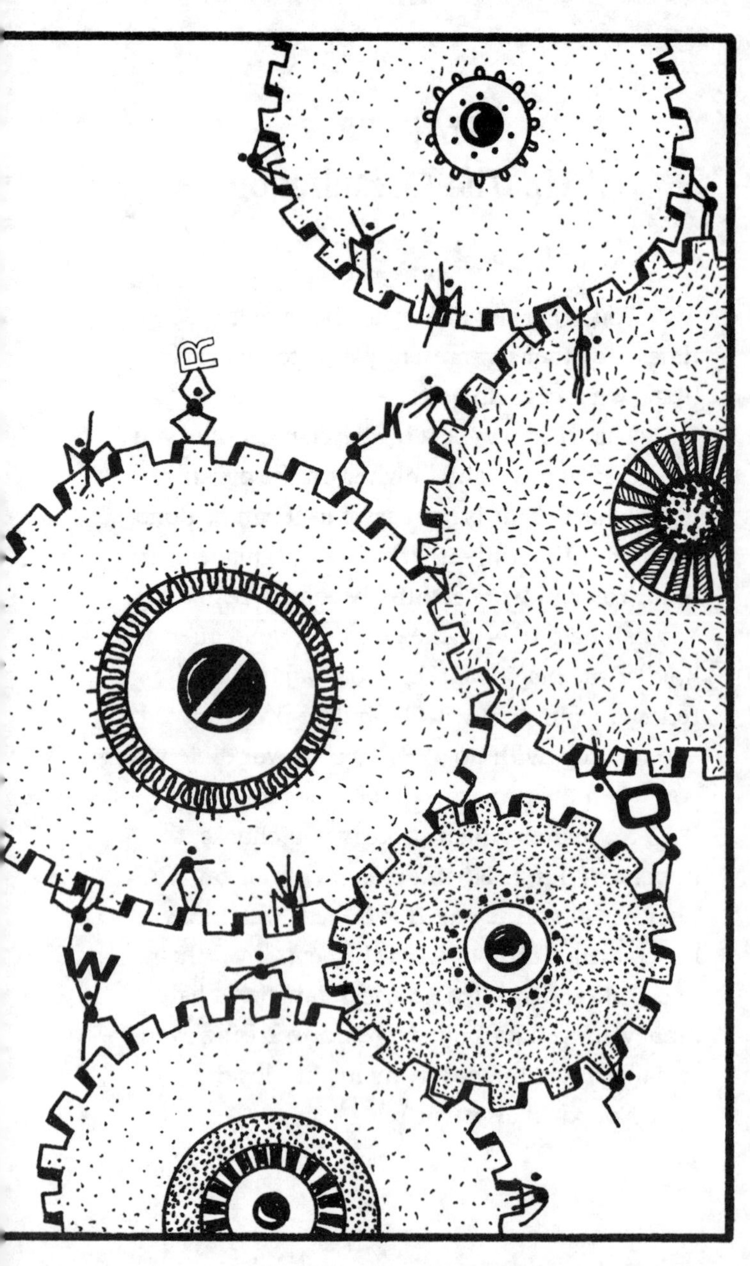
R
K
O
W

All professions are conspiracies against the laity.

George Bernard Shaw, writer, 1856-1950

The business of America is business.

Calvin Coolidge, 30th president of the United States, 1872-1933

In the corporate world, 1,000 "Attaboys" are wiped away with one "Oh, shit!"

Robert Jackall, sociologist, *Moral Mazes*

Don't work for the company, work for yourself.

Soichiro Honda, Japanese businessman, 1906-1991

If we face a recession, we should not lay off employees; the company should sacrifice a profit. It's management's risk and management's responsibility. Employees are not guilty; why should they suffer?

AKIO MORITA, JAPANESE BUSINESSMAN, BEFORE HIS COMPANY BEGAN LAYING OFF WORKERS

If you work for yourself you do it for your own amusement, which is all right; if you work for others, you reap nothing but ingratitude.

GUY DE MAUPASSANT, FRENCH NOVELIST, 1850-1893

Accomplishing the impossible means only that the boss will add it to your regular duties.

DOUG LARSON

"Most people are kept in line by fear of loss. It's the great disciplinary force of the Establishment."

(CHARACTER MARJIE MARVIN) JOHN KENNETH GALBRAITH, ECONOMIST, *A TENURED PROFESSOR*

The tie that binds men and women in work organizations today, particularly at the professional and managerial levels, is narrow self interest, rather than a sense of mutual obligation and responsibility.

A. ZALENZNICK, BUSINESS EDUCATOR

If we didn't have bonuses, we wouldn't have had anybody working for us.

STEVEN ANREDER, STOCKBROKER, ON HIS FIRM'S LAST-MINUTE MULTIMILLION-DOLLAR PAYOUT JUST BEFORE FILING FOR BANKRUPTCY

The higher up the ladder people went in the conglomerate . . . the bigger their desks became and the less paper and other impedimenta they had on them.

DAVID LODGE, NOVELIST, *NICE WORK*

Corporations behave more like humans than most people think, including many of the people who run them. Often reckless in youth, the successful ones also grow fat and sclerotic in middle age, foolish, even addled in their dotage.

JAMES KROHE, JR., JOURNALIST

People cannot be trusted to do their jobs if they do not know how. And if they have incompetent leaders, the coefficient of the mistrust is the number of those leaders multiplied by the number of people who report to them.

JOHN O. WHITNEY, MANAGEMENT CONSULTANT, *THE TRUST FACTOR*

Even if the rules devised by bureaucracy are outstandingly humane, nobody likes to be ruled by rules, that is to say, by people whose answer to every complaint is: I did not make the rules; I am merely applying them.

E.F. SCHUMACHER, ECONOMIST, 1911-1973, *SMALL IS BEAUTIFUL*

Management is, in fact, a sacred trust in which the well-being of other people is put in your care during most of their waking hours. It is a trust placed upon you first by those who put you in the job, but more important than that, it is a trust placed upon you after you get the job by those whom you are to manage.

JAMES A. AUTRY, BUSINESSMAN, *LOVE AND PROFIT*

When I order abandon ship, it doesn't matter what time I leave. Abandon is for everybody. If some people like to stay, they can stay.

YIANNIS AVRANAS, CAPTAIN OF THE CRUISE SHIP OCEANOS, WHICH SANK IN THE INDIAN OCEAN, ON WHY HE LEFT IN A LIFEBOAT WHILE HUNDREDS OF PASSENGERS WERE STILL ABOARD

Good executives never put off until tomorrow what they can get some-one else to do today.

RED LONGWELL, BUSINESSMAN

The definition of an administrator . . . is someone who knows what he can get away with.

AMANDA CROSS, NOVELIST, *A TRAP FOR FOOLS*

We pretend to work, and they pretend to pay us.

POPULAR ADAGE IN FORMER SOVIET UNION

"You're not supposed to strike an employee. We have rules about that."

(CHARACTER BABE WILLIAMS) RICHARD ADLER, PLAYWRIGHT, *THE PAJAMA GAME*

It takes geniuses to build businesses and idiots to run them.

JOSEPH BROOKS, BUSINESSMAN

The question, who ought to be boss, is like asking who ought to be the tenor in the quartet. Obviously, the man who can sing tenor.

HENRY FORD, BUSINESSMAN, 1863-1947

"You think too much, boss."

(CHARACTER ZORBA), NIKOS KAZANTZAKIS, NOVELIST, 1883-1957, *ZORBA THE GREEK*

The harder you work, the luckier you get.

GARY PLAYER, GOLFER

Productivity comes from commitment not from authority.

W. L. GORE, BUSINESSMAN

"The reason people wanted to be supervisors was so that they wouldn't have to do what they did to get there . . . ."

(CHARACTER COLEMAN PEETS) PETER DEXTER, NOVELIST,
*GOD'S POCKET*

If people feel they have control over their destinies they will persist at tasks.

TOM PETERS AND ROBERT WATERMAN, MANAGEMENT CONSULTANTS,
*IN SEARCH OF EXCELLENCE*

# CHAPTER 8
# Money

Life is not Monopoly—you don't get anything for passing go. You do get what you pay for, whether you pay in sweat, marketing plans, jury summations or repaired fenders. And money is usually *what* you get.

Time isn't money. If it were, you could pay for your groceries by hanging out at the check-out lane for a while. And money isn't how you keep score, although if you don't have any you don't even get to play.

So what is money? It's how the people you work for say Have a Nice Day. It's what you get—besides that occasional warm glow inside—for doing a good job. But try to avoid the mistaken notion that money actually measures anyone's worth. If it did, Madonna would be a better person than Mother Teresa. On the other hand, remember your car payments and heed Sophie Tucker's words: " I've been rich and I've been poor; rich is better."

Money may be the root of all evil, but we still use it to pay the piper. Honk if you want to call the tune.

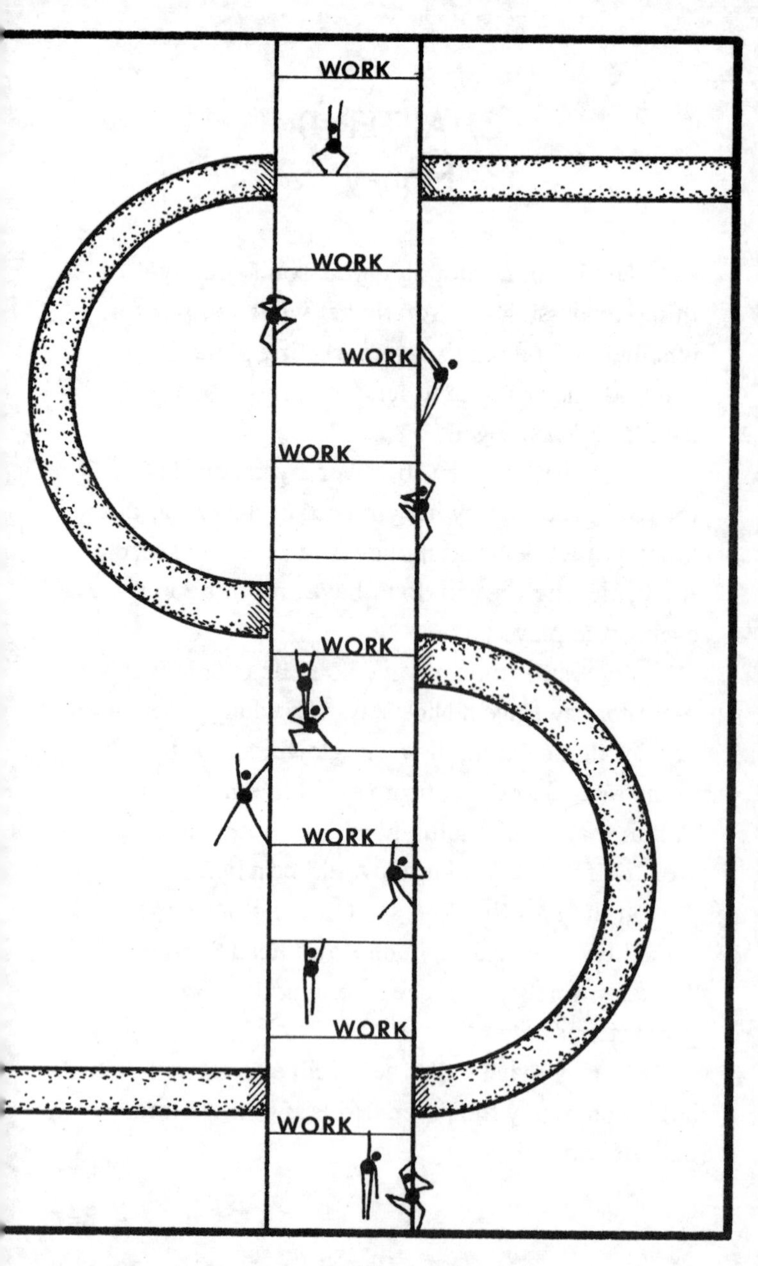
WORK
WORK
WORK
WORK
WORK
WORK
WORK
WORK

"I learned long ago that there's nothing intrinsically wrong with being out of work. It's being out of money that's the problem."

(CHARACTER MARK RENZLER) PAUL ENGLEMAN, NOVELIST, *WHO SHOT LONGSHOT SAM?*

It isn't necessary to be rich and famous to be happy. It's only necessary to be rich.

ALAN ALDA, ACTOR

A man who has a million dollars is as well off as if he were rich.

JOHN JACOB ASTOR, BUSINESSMAN, 1763-1848

I've been rich, and I've been poor; rich is better.

SOPHIE TUCKER, SINGER, 1884-1966

Why do you think the lottery is so popular? Do you think anybody would play if the super payoff was a job on the night shift in a meat-packing plant? People play it so if they win they can be rich and idle. Like I told you years ago—if work is so good, how come they have to pay us to do it?

Mike Royko, columnist

Young people, nowadays, imagine money is everything and when they grow older they know it.

Oscar Wilde, Irish poet, 1854-1900

Whoever said that money can't buy you happiness, didn't know where to shop.

Jackie Gleason, comedian, 1916-1987

The easiest job I ever tackled in this world is that of making money. It is, in fact, almost as easy as losing it. Almost, but not quite.

H. L. Mencken, journalist, 1880-1956

---

I think greed is healthy. You can be greedy and still feel good about yourself.

Ivan Boesky, businessman, before pleading guilty to insider trading

It is, after all, a sound instinct which puts business below the professions, and burdens the business man with a social inferiority that he can never quite shake off, even in America. The business man, in fact, acquiesces in this assumption of his inferiority even when he protests against it. He is the only man above the hangman and the scavenger who is forever apologizing for his occupation. He is the only one who always seeks to make it appear, when he attains the object of his labors, i.e., the making of a great deal of money, that it was not the object of his labors.

H. L. MENCKEN, JOURNALIST 1880-1956

Business is a good game—lots of competition and a minimum of rules. You keep score with money.

NOLAN BUSHNELL, BUSINESSMAN

Wall Street has its own measure of worth. . . . The measure is not rectitude, not public virtue, not personal saintliness, not intelligence, not even personal hygiene, though that is a commendable thing after a long day in the shirt-sleeved trading room. The measure is simple and inescapable: it is dollars having been earned and being accumulated.

JOHN KENNETH GALBRAITH, ECONOMIST

Little ol' boy in the Panhandle told me the other day you can still make a small fortune in agriculture. Problem is, you got to start with a large one.

JIM HIGHTOWER, POLITICIAN

Americans know more about how to make a living than how to live.

HENRY DAVID THOREAU, ESSAYIST, 1817-1862

There's no reason we should be making more than a philosophy professor.

SUSAN GETZENDANNER, LAWYER

"Banking isn't just money-making. Banking is starting new businesses and saving old ones. Banking is helping the right man over a bad time. Banking is keeping the heart of the economy pumping. If you don't feel that way about it, you ought to quit and become a stock-broker."

(CHARACTER PERCY PRIME) LOUIS AUCHINCLOSS, NOVELIST, *THE EMBEZZLER*

I tend to doubt that the quality of policemen would become greatly improved if the job paid vastly more money, yet I have a hunch that the quality of doctors and lawyers might rise if they were paid less.

JOSEPH EPSTEIN, ESSAYIST, *THE AMERICAN SCHOLAR*

The bad thing is that by the time somebody comes to me, they are pretty far up the creek. The good thing is they will pay almost anything.

BRENDAN SULLIVAN, LAWYER

I know the public gets mad and jealous. I can understand it. But it's not like the Pirates are going to give the money to the homeless if they don't give it to Barry Bonds.

HUBIE BROOKS, BASEBALL PLAYER, ON DISCONTENT OVER ANOTHER PLAYER'S $2.3 MILLION SALARY

The possession of goods, whether acquired aggressively by one's own exertion or passively by transmission through inheritance from others, becomes a conventional basis of reputability. The possession of wealth, which was at the outset valued simply as an evidence of efficiency, becomes, in popular apprehension, itself a meritorious act. Wealth is now itself intrinsically honorable and confers honor on its possessor.

THORSTEIN VEBLEN, SOCIOLOGIST, 1857-1929,
*THEORY OF THE LEISURE CLASS*

Money is like an arm or leg—use it or lose it.

HENRY FORD, BUSINESSMAN, 1863-1947

Moderation has been declared a virtue so as to curb the ambition of the great and console lesser folk for their lack of fortune and merit.

AUTHOR UNKNOWN

When a man has had to work so hard to get money, why should he impose on himself the further hardship of trying to save it?

DON HEROLD

We forget what gives money its value—that someone exchanged work for it.

NEAL O'HARA

"No matter how hard you climb, there are always the rich above you, who got there without effort. Lucky stiffs, holding you down, making you discontent so you buy more of the crap advertised on television."

(CHARACTER HARRY "RABBIT" ANGSTROM) JOHN UPDIKE, NOVELIST, *RABBIT AT REST*

I'm not going to give any of it back.

BUD BLACK, BASEBALL PLAYER ON HIS $10 MILLION, 4-YEAR CONTRACT, DESPITE A CAREER RECORD OF 83-82

They had the drawn, brittle look that comes from a lifetime of doing work you don't love, then finding out you're a million dollars in debt to boot.

GRETEL EHRLICH, ESSAYIST, *THE SOLACE OF OPEN SPACES*, ON A FARMING COUPLE AT THE AUCTION OF THEIR FARM

# CHAPTER 9
## Take This Job And Shove It

A winner never quits and a quitter never wins? Einstein quit the patent office. Rocky Marciano quit while he was ahead. Even Princess Di quit. The little-engine-that-could never quit, but then it was the little-engine-that-*could.* The little-engine-that-*couldn't* would have been wise to look for a flatter road-bed.

Quitting is as quitting does—sometimes it pays and sometimes it doesn't. It's best to have another job, but it's essential to have a plan. It's also necessary to remember that while your boss can say you're *unfired,* you probably can't say you *unquit.* They don't have to let you play unless it's your bat.

That said, there is comfort in harboring thoughts of dramatic departures. Something indefinable is gained by writing the resignation letter that never gets sent. (Do it at home, lock the drawer, and destroy all diskettes.) Practice your speech in the bathroom, but don't deliver it.

Meanwhile, work on your resume and keep buying those lottery tickets.

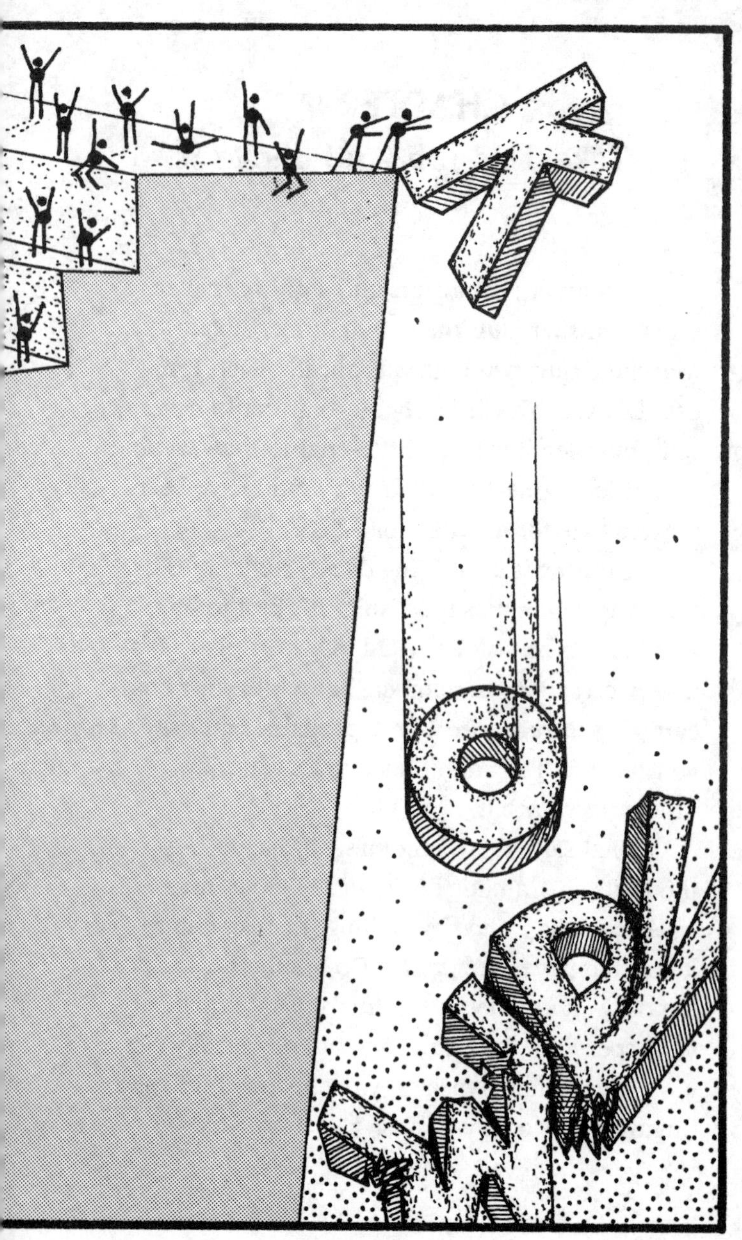

Why should I let this toad work
Squat on my life?

PHILIP LARKIN, ENGLISH POET, 1922-1985, *TOADS*

Man's first disobedience resulted in the curse of work.

JOHN MILTON, ENGLISH POET, 1608-1674

To the Greeks, work was a curse and nothing else.

ADRIANO TILGHER, PHILOSOPHER, 1887-1941,
*HOMO FABER: WORK THROUGH THE AGES*

My father taught me to work, but not to love it. I never did like to work, and I don't deny it. I'd rather read, tell stories, crack jokes, talk, laugh—anything but work.

ABRAHAM LINCOLN, 16TH PRESIDENT OF UNITED STATES, 1809-1865

Work is the curse of the drinking class.

OSCAR WILDE, IRISH POET, 1854-1900

You gotta work all your life, but you don't gotta enjoy it.

AUTHOR UNKNOWN, "NORTHERN LIGHTS," FOLK SONG

My dad . . . didn't like his work. But he was a Depression kid. To him, any work was good work. He figured the best thing he could do for his family was to work himself to death. And he did. He died at 62.

LARRY HEINEMANN, NOVELIST

Labor is the curse of the world and nobody can meddle with it without becoming proportionately brutified.

NATHANIEL HAWTHORNE, NOVELIST, 1804-1864

The gods had condemned Sisyphus to ceaselessly rolling a rock to the top of a mountain, whence the stone would fall back of its own weight. They had thought with some reason that there is no more dreaded punishment than futile and hopeless labor . . . .

ALBERT CAMUS, FRENCH PHILOSOPHER, 1913-1960

There is nothing more discouraging than having a barrel beside you with 10,000 bolts in it and using them all up. Then you get a barrel with another 10,000 bolts.

CHARLES R. WALKER AND ROBERT H. GUEST, MANAGEMENT CONSULTANTS, *THE MAN ON THE ASSEMBLY LINE*

The main thing is to never, ever work. I just sit around all day doing what Americans call hanging out.

QUENTIN CRISP, ENGLISH ACTOR

A lot of nonsense is spoken about work. Some of the finest men I've known were the laziest. Never work because it's expected of you. Find out how much work you must do to live and be happy. Don't do any more.

James Michener, novelist, *Fires of Spring*

I have never liked work. To me a job is an invasion of privacy.

Danny McGoorty, construction worker

Work is something adults did to punish kids for growing up.

Bob Fenster, novelist, *The Last Page*

I didn't want to work. It was as simple as that. I distrusted work, disliked it. I thought it was a very bad thing that the human race had unfortunately invented for itself.

AGATHA CHRISTIE, ENGLISH NOVELIST, 1891-1976

Work is for cowards.

V. J. PUCKETT, POOL HUSTLER

Times have changed. Forty years ago people worked 12 hours a day, and it was called economic slavery. Now they work 14 hours a day and it's called moonlighting.

ROBERT ORBEN

Without work, all life goes rotten, but when work is soulless, life stifles and dies.

ALBERT CAMUS, FRENCH PHILOSOPHER, 1913-60

When work is utterly disagreeable and week awaits weekend, our delight in recreation reveals our misery.

Donald Hall, poet, *Life Work*

If you have a job without aggravations, you don't have a job.

Malcolm Forbes, businessman, 1919-1990

"If work was a good thing the rich would have it all and not let you do it."

(character Manuel) Elmore Leonard, novelist, *Split Images*

We're like gerbils. We're in a cage, running around and around.

Tom Brokaw, television reporter, on T.V. anchorpeople

The trouble with the rat race is that, even if you win, you're still a rat.

LILY TOMLIN, COMEDIAN

The first thing happens at work: When the arm starts moving, the brain stops.

UNIDENTIFIED STEELWORKER

That job will kill you.  I'm serious. That job will kill you.

EUGENE SAWYER, POLITICIAN, ON BEING THE MAYOR OF CHICAGO

More men are killed by overwork than the importance of this world justifies.

RUDYARD KIPLING, ENGLISH WRITER, 1865-1936

"I need a job; I'm used to getting up every morning, going someplace and hating it."

(CHARACTER GLORIA) IVY AUSTIN, COMEDIAN, ON *THE AMERICAN RADIO THEATER OF THE AIR*

If it were not for the demands made upon me by my business, I would provide living proof that a man can live quite happily for decades without ever doing any work.

J. PAUL GETTY, BUSINESSMAN, 1892-1976

It is not labor in itself that is repugnant to man; it is not the natural necessity for exertion which is a curse. It is only labor which produces nothing—exertion of which he cannot see the result.

HENRY GEORGE, ENGLISH LABOR LEADER, 1839-1897

"Whatever you do, don't get a job. Don't work in an office. When you wake up in the morning, be where you want to be."

JOHN GUARE, PLAYWRIGHT, QUOTING ADVICE FROM HIS FATHER

---

"In my department, there are six people who are afraid of me, and one small secretary who is afraid of all of us. I have one other person working for me who is not afraid of anyone, not even me, and I would fire him quickly, but I am afraid of him."

(CHARACTER BOB SLOCUM) JOSEPH HELLER, NOVELIST,
*SOMETHING HAPPENED*

Work is external to the worker...it is not part of his nature; and consequently, he does not fulfill himself in his work but denies himself, has a feeling of misery rather than well-being, does not develop freely his mental and physical energies but is physically exhausted and mentally debased. The worker feels himself at home only during his leisure hours, whereas at work he feels homeless. His work is not voluntary but imposed forced labor. It is not the satisfaction of a need, but only a means of satisfying other needs.

KARL MARX, GERMAN PHILOSOPHER, 1818-1883,
*THE ECONOMIC AND PHILOSOPHICAL MANUSCRIPTS OF 1844*

# CHAPTER 10
## Hard Work, Working Harder

By the sweat of your brow shall you live. Sorry, that's the legacy. You could, of course, work smart, as they say. You'll discover, however, that working smart is hard work. There are shortcuts to success, but they're difficult too. A lazy nose gathers no grindstones.

Lift that barge, tote that spreadsheet. Get a little greedy and you land in a minimum-security facility—just ask some of the folks in the savings and loan business. The good news is that working your fingers to, or near, the bone will get you ahead. But that's also the bad news.

On the other hand, sometimes success is a piece of cake. The trick is always the same—if it doesn't feel like work, grab it. It's more important to have the right job than a good job, or maybe the right job is always a good job. Make a serious effort never to do anything you're not good at, unless you don't have any choice. And while your doing what you have no choice about, figure out what you *are* good at. Then try to get hired to do *that*.

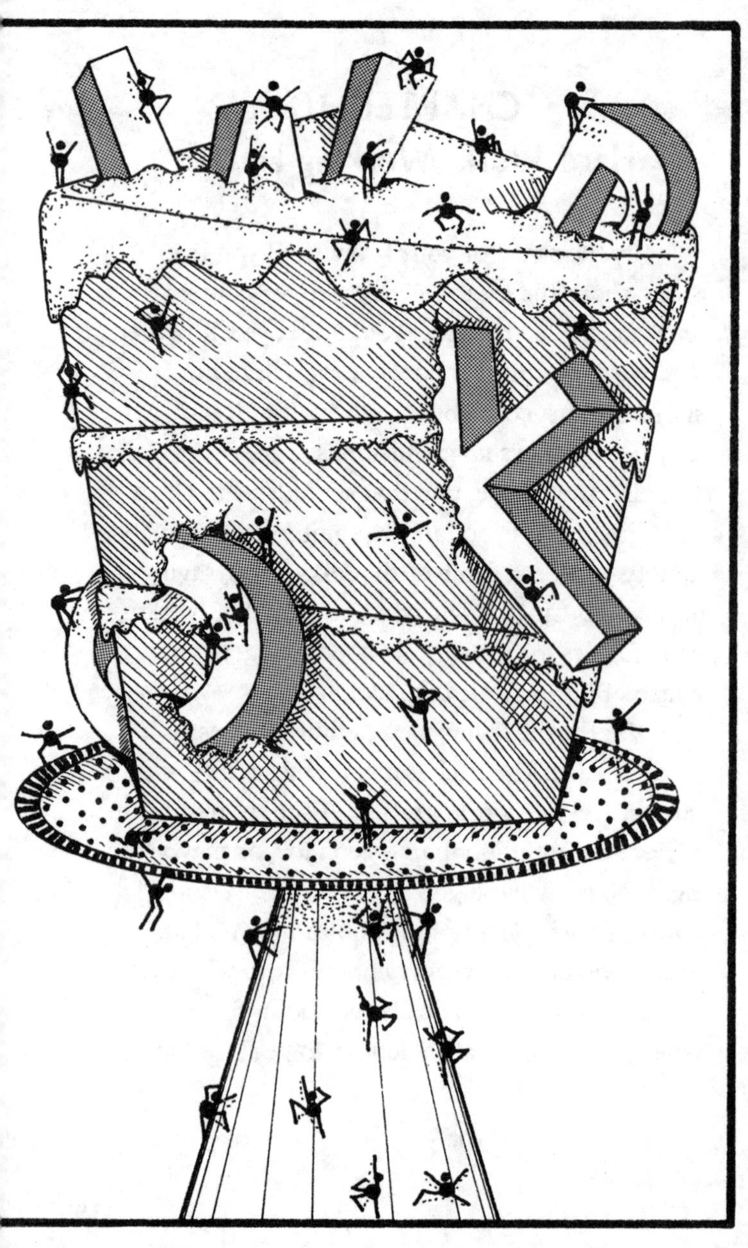

Most people like hard work. Particularly when they are paying for it.

FRANKLIN P. JONES

The Secret of Success: 1.) Get a job. 2.) Get a better job. 3.) Get an even better job. 4.) Repeat as often as necessary.

MATT GROENING, CARTOONIST, *WORK IS HELL*

"Work, work, work. Nothing means anything except work. You can do anything if you say you're doing it for work."

(CHARACTER ROSE "TWO" KORZA) BILL GRIFFITH, NOVELIST, *TIME FOR FRANKIE COOLIN*

When men are employed, they are best contented; for on the days they worked they were good-natured and cheerful, and, with the consciousness of having done a good day's work, they spent the evening jollily; but on their idle days they were mutinous and quarrelsome.

Benjamin Franklin, politician, 1706-1790

The society that scorns excellence in plumbing because it is a humble activity, yet accepts shoddiness in philosophy because it is an exalted activity, will have neither good plumbing nor good philosophy, and as a result neither its pipes nor its theories will hold water.

John Gardner, politician

I oppose suicide on the grounds that it represents a wish to stop working.

JOHANN FICHTE, GERMAN PHILOSOPHER, 1762-1814

Do not tell me how hard you work. Tell me how much you get done.

JAMES J. LING, BUSINESSMAN

Hey, did you ever notice when you don't go to lunch you really feel better because you think you're working so hard?

JERRY DELLA FEMINA, ADVERTISING EXECUTIVE, *FROM THE FOLKS WHO GAVE YOU PEARL HARBOR*

When a man tells you that he got rich through hard work, ask him whose.

DON MARQUIS, NEWSPAPER COLUMNIST, 1878-1937

"Don't you ever feel like work?" a lazy boy was asked, and he answered, "Yes, sir, but I do without."

SALVADOR DE MARDARIAGA

Nothing so impairs intellectual achievement as exposure to physical activity.

RALPH WALDO EMERSON, ESSAYIST, 1803-1882

Thinking is the hardest work there is, which is the probable reason why so few engage in it.

HENRY FORD, BUSNESSMAN, 1863-1947

No one has a right to sit down and feel hopeless. There's too much work to do.

DOROTHY DAY, SOCIAL ACTIVIST, 1897-1980

It's better to burn out than to fade away.

NEIL YOUNG, MUSICIAN

When I played pro football, I never set out to hurt anybody deliberately. Unless it was, you know, important. Like a league game or something.

DICK BUTKUS, FOOTBALL PLAYER

Writing a column is really very easy, you just open a vein and let it bleed out onto the paper.

RED SMITH, COLUMNIST, 1905-1992

I'm trying to do too much and I'm thinking too much, and I'm thinking about trying to do too much.

TONY GUY, BASKETBALL PLAYER, ON HIS SHOOTING SLUMP

Those who stay late at work, *always* make a point of mentioning it. They may get to the top, but they left everything else behind several years ago. You don't get there without giving up a lot.

Paul Weingarten, journalist, "The Not-Me Generation"

"Workaholics get bad press," says one hard worker who asked to remain anonymous. "The assumption," said the workaholic, who owns her own business, "is that all we do is work and that we do it to the exclusion of our family and friends. That's not true." Although she admits she works "all the time" and that her husband also is a workaholic, she says they always make time for each other and their child. "Being a workaholic," she insists, "does not mean you have a psychotic commitment. I take energy I get from work and put it into the rest of my life. It's a nice, big, round circle."

Carol Kleiman, columnist

Working hard and workaholism are not the same. Workaholics crave work as if it were an addictive drug and are ground down, not energized, by their lives.

DENNIS TOPOLNICKI, PSYCHOLOGIST

Workaholism is one of the only addictions in society that we boast about, that we're proud of, that we actually support.

DIANE FASSEL, SOCIOLOGIST, *WORKING OURSELVES TO DEATH*

I never did anything worth doing by accident; nor did any of my inventions come by accident; they came by work.

THOMAS ALVA EDISON, INVENTOR, 1847-1931

I believe in work, hard work and long hours of work. Men do not break down from overwork, but from worry and dissipation.

CHARLES E. HUGHES, SOCIOLOGIST

For the work addict, the job is like a chocolate factory for the overeater. It is as if an active alcoholic were going to work in a saloon. . . . What is more, you get paid for it.

DIANE FASSEL, SOCIOLOGIST, *WORKING OURSELVES TO DEATH*

Though proponents of a kinder, gentler workplace stress family values and the importance of relaxation, most firms still like to have a workaholic at the helm.

CAROL KLEIMAN, COLUMNIST

I don't know. I don't see her that much.

RAY PERKINS, FOOTBALL COACH, ON WHETHER HIS WIFE DISAPPROVES OF HIS 18-HOUR WORKDAYS.

Industry need not wish, and he that lives upon hopes will die fasting. There are no gains without pains. He that hath a trade hath an estate, and he that hath a calling hath an office or profit and honor; but then the trade must be worked at, and the calling followed, or neither the estate nor the office will enable us to pay our taxes. If we are industrious, we shall never starve; for, at the working man's house hunger looks in, but dares not enter. Nor will the bailiff or the constable enter, for industry pay debts, while idleness and neglect increase them.

BENJAMIN FRANKLIN, POLITICIAN, 1706-1790

Upheavals at work can be more traumatic than, say, a divorce, because many people don't spend all that much time with their spouse anyway.

RONNI SANDROFF, PSYCHOLOGIST

Work loads that are incompatible with family life are themselves a kind of toxin—to men as well as women, and ultimately to businesses as well as families.

BARBARA EHRENREICH AND DEIRDRE ENGLISH, ESSAYISTS, "BLOWING THE WHISTLE ON THE MOMMY TRACK"

The name for those who work as hard at fun as they do at work is "playaholics." Playaholics feel the pressure to use time off as effectively as time on the job. They conduct their leisure activities as they do their professional affairs, with every moment structured. They're driven by activity rather than by pleasure.

Peter Dickens, business consultant

Hard work . . . builds character. This notion carries less conviction because business people, and our society as a whole, have little patience with those who, even though they work hard, make a habit of finishing out of the money.

Robert Jackall, sociologist, *Moral Mazes*

# CHAPTER 11
## Holy And Ancient Texts

Someday they'll discover a set of scrolls in the desert with Sanskrit want ads for prophets: "Position Available—self-starter, experience less important than ability to motivate, good communication skills, must be free to travel."

Of course prophets work. Even the Pope works. It's a good job, but it's still a job: going to meetings, blessing people in the square, pontificating. Popes, prophets, philosophers, they all work, mostly at thankless tasks, and a lot of them have had something to say on the subject.

Collected here are a few tidbits from those boys in the back room, the oldies but goodies that make sense because they've always made sense. Never be afraid of eternal verities; there's no truth like an old truth. Think of them as the original text of *In Search of Excellence.*

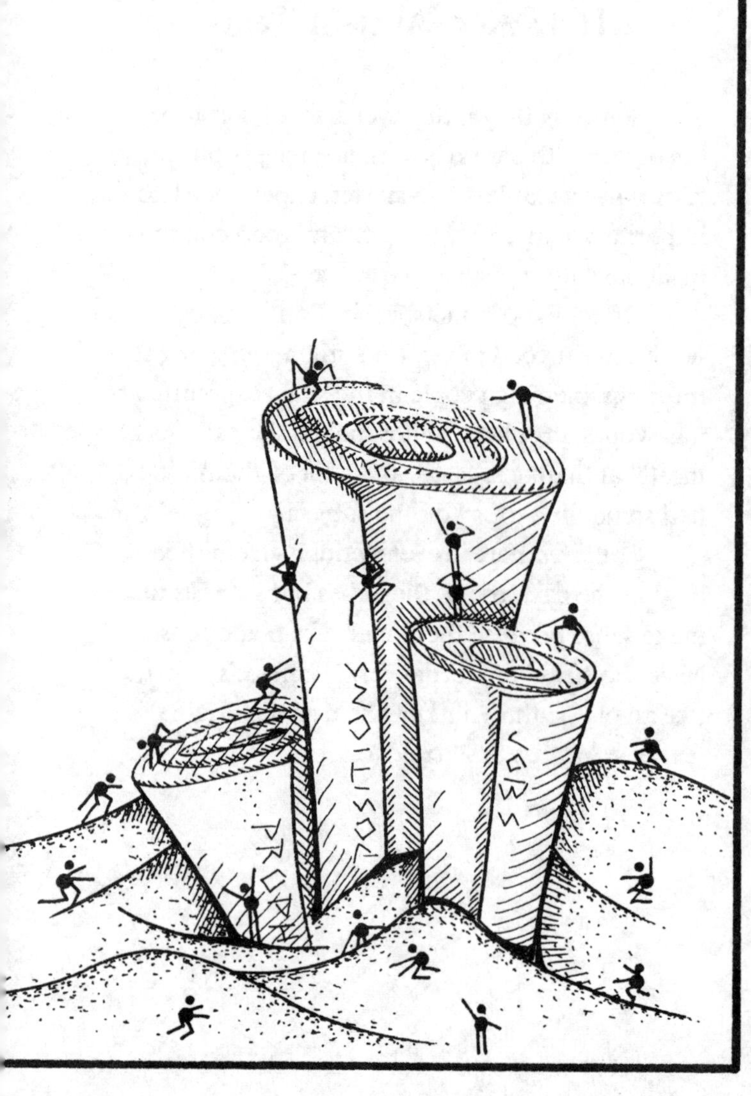
POSITIONS
JOBS

Labor conquers all things.

VIRGIL, ROMAN POET, 70-19 B.C.

I hated all my toil in which I had toiled under the sun, seeing that I must leave it to those who come after me.

ECCLESIASTES 2:18

Man is born to labor, as a bird to fly.

PIUS XI, POPE, *1857-1939, QUADRAGESIMO ANNO*

Work is not a curse, it is a blessing from God who calls man to rule the earth and transform it, so that the divine work of creation may continue with man's intelligence and effort.

JOHN PAUL II, POPE, *LABOREN EXERCENS*

Anyone unwilling to work should not eat.

2 Thessalonians 3:10

Nothing is so certain as that the evils of idleness can be shaken off by hard work.

Seneca, roman philosopher, 4 B.C.—65 A.D.

Remember that the life of this world is but a sport and a pastime.

Koran, LVII 19

It is God's gift that all should eat and drink and take pleasure in all their toil.

Ecclesiastes 3:13

Work done in the spirit of service has been raised to the level of worship.

ABDUL-BAHA, SON OF BAHA U UAH, PROPHET-FOUNDER OF THE BAHAI FAITH

Never was good work done without much trouble.

CHINESE PROVERB

Like good stewards of the manifold grace of God, serve one another with whatever gift each of you has received.

I PETER 4:10

Whatever your task, put yourselves into it, as done for the Lord and not for your masters.

COLOSSIANS 3:23

This is what I have seen to be good: it is fitting to eat and drink and find enjoyment in all the toil with which one toils under the sun.

ECCLESIASTES 5:18

Even if tomorrow I knew the world would go to pieces I would still plant my apple tree.

MARTIN LUTHER, GERMAN THEOLOGIAN, 1483-1546

A man can't get rich if he takes proper care of his family.

NAVAJO SAYING

A slack hand causes poverty, but the hand of the diligent makes rich.

PROVERBS 10:4

Those who till their land will have plenty of food, but those who follow worthless pursuits have no sense.

PROVERBS 12:11

If man does not find his food like the animals and birds but must earn it, that is due to sin.

TALMUD

Sweat is the ornament of virtue's face.

HESIOD, GREEK POET, 8TH CENTURY B.C.

By the sweat of your face you shall eat bread.

GENESIS 3:19

Work is the worship of the Lord. Do not make any distinction between menial and respectable work.

SWAMI SIVANANDA, HINDU THEOLOGIAN, 1887-1963

The Four Sins Crying to Heaven for Vengeance: Willful Murder, Sodomy, Oppression of the Poor, Defrauding Laborers of Their Wages.

THE PENNY CATECHISM

# CHAPTER 12
# Women And Work

The gray flannel suit is now gender-free. And about time. There are now two generations of women who know exactly how much (or how little) fun all those guys are having downtown every day. Turns out to be some of each, of course, but now there are no secrets in the corporate gameroom and everybody gets a chance to play.

Advice for men: Practice senseless acts of androgyny. The guys at the office aren't just guys anymore; half of them have heard all those jokes and the other half don't want to. And which half is which isn't as clear as you think it is, and it never was. Things are not more complicated, they're just more obvious.

Advice for women: Practice ignoring the jerks. And try not to emulate the successful jerks. There is no level playing field, but it's not always clear which way the ground's sloping. Figure out who the players are, keep a scorecard.

W w O o R r K K

Whatever women do they must do twice as well as men to be thought half as good. Luckily this is not difficult.

CHARLOTTE WHITTON, WRITER

Women can have fame and fortune, office affairs, silicon injections, and dazzling designer clothes....But the one thing they can't have, apparently, is a man who shares the work at home.

HELEN GURLEY BROWN, EDITOR

If, as I did, you took all the Fifties good mothering advice too seriously, you could get the impression that a child deprived of its mother's full-time focus might climb towers twenty years later and start shooting up the citizenry. The headlines would say, Mother Chose Work, Kid Goes Berserk.

JUDITH WAX, ESSAYIST, 1932-1979, *STARTING IN THE MIDDLE*

Among primitive people (as perhaps among those not so primitive) males are commonly inclined to leave drudge work to females.

EDMUND F. BYRNE, PHILOSOPHER, *WORK, INC.*

Why would any woman choose to be a chief financial officer rather than a tull-time mother?

EDMUND PRATT, BUSINESSMAN

. . . work that is not paid lacks significance, much as we might wish it otherwise.

ROBERT KAHN, SOCIOLOGIST, *WORK AND HEALTH*

Make [your employers] understand that you are in their service as workers, not as women.

AUTHOR UNKNOWN, IN *THE REVOLUTION* (WOMAN SUFFERAGE NEWSPAPER), OCTOBER 8, 1868

There is a “his” and “hers” to the economic development of the United States. In the latter part of the nineteenth century, it was mainly men who were drawn off the farm into paid, industrial work and who changed their way of life and their identity. At that point in history, men became more different from their fathers than women became from their mothers. Today the economic arrow points at women; it is a women who are being drawn into wage work, and women who are undergoing changes in their way of life and identity. Women are departing more from their mothers’ and grandmothers’ way of life, men are doing so less.

ARLIE HOCHSCHILD, SOCIOLOGIST, *THE SECOND SHIFT*

Our great-grandfathers were certainly not horrified by automation. After all, they did provide the ribbed washboard, the crossbuck saw, the spinning wheel, and other labor-saving devices in order to enable great-grandma to do the work of three hired girls.

ERICH FROMM, PHILOSOPHER, 1900-1980

. . . women have always worked: for most social classes, the era of forced leisure for women was brief, insofar as it existed, and in all the history of men's brutality to women, men have never punished women so much as when—in city and suburb, at different historical moments according to social class, from the eighteenth century into the twentieth—men removed from women the necessity or convention of work equal in quantity and importance to men's work.

DONALD HALL, POET, *LIFE WORK*

I believe in the natural family order where the man works and the woman stays home and raises the kids. It's what the people want and what they will get if I am elected governor.

LARRY FORGY, POLITICIAN

Family life will never be ennobling until the central horror of the dependence of women on men is done away with.

GEORGE BERNARD SHAW, IRISH WRITER, 1856-1950

I would lose every shred of credibility with my male colleagues if I told them I needed time with my children. In their world, needing time with children doesn't count as a 'real' reason for any decision about your job. So I told them my husband got a more lucrative offer in Boston. They understood that. They said, 'Oh, Boston. That sounds good.'

Ann Myerson, businesswoman, *Working Women*

The lack of any kind of mandated benefits around childbirth is the biggest single reason why women are doing so badly in the workplace. Unless you support women in their roles as mothers, you will never get equality of opportunity.

Sylvia Hewlett, economist, *The Lesser Life: The Myth of Women's Liberation in America*

Why do moms have a monopoly on guilt? You never read any stories about dads who feel guilty about leaving their kids in day care.

CYNDA MORGAN, BUSINESSWOMAN

He loved his children but he could not stay home with them. His job had stretches of pressure, of grinding routine and psychic bombardment, but it was a treat to come to work after spending a day while Rita was away and the kids were in his care, their demands, their fights, their ferocious, insatiable energy pushing him rather quickly past exhaustion and into a state of jittery rage.

CHARLES DICKENSON, NOVELIST, *RUMOR HAS IT*

It's all right to take time off to baby a client, just so long as it's not your *own* child.

ARLIE HOCHSCHILD, SOCIOLOGIST, *THE SECOND SHIFT*

The birth of the second child is the moment when even the most dedicated career woman is sorely tried to keep everything in motion at once.

ERMA BOMBECK, COLUMNIST

What's all this talk about women wanting a career? I've always had a career, or at least a job. And I didn't have any choice about it either!

JOSEPHINE SALLY PALMERI, SECRETARY, 1919-1993

If woman are to participate fully in corporate life and find meaning in both home and family, the work must change and families must be seen by everyone, including government and corporations, as the responsibility of both men and women. The solution will be nearer when a man can confidently take the morning off to attend a third grade play.

Al Gini, philosopher, "Woman's Work: Seeking Identity Through Occupation"

It's no wonder that so many of the best mystery and detective novels are written by women; for what is so seldom true in the ragged cloth of women's real life is true in these engaging parables: blame is righteously assigned, justice and truth triumph—there are no loose ends.

Barbara Grizzuti Harrison, essayist, *Off-Center*

Don't go for it. Hire some schmuck to go for it. (This is known as managerial style.)

ALICE KAHN, ESSAYIST, *MULTILPLE SARCASM*

Success is something I will dress for when I get there, and not until.

FRAN LEBOWITZ, HUMORIST, *SOCIAL STUDIES*

Prostitution is caused not by female depravity and male licentiousness but by underpaying, undervaluing, and overworking women so shamelessly that the poorest are forced to respond to prostitution to keep body and soul together.

GEORGE BERNARD SHAW, IRISH WRITER, 1856-1950

When the history of the last quarter of the 20th century in the U.S. is written, scholars may well conclude that the nation's most important social development has been the rise to positions of power and influence of its most vigorous majority: American women.

Anthony Taylor, management consultant

Dear Ms. Ellerbee:

I like your program. I even like you. But I was wondering where you got such a wimpy last name?

Dear Sir:

From a man, where else?

Linda Ellerbee, television journalist, *And So It Goes, Adventures in Television*

# CHAPTER 13
## Retirement

You've got to start out like you can hold out. Which means that if you want to get to retirement, figure out now how to work hard and like it. It will make the long haul feel a lot shorter. Sneaks up on you anyway, retirement does; ask anyone who owns one.

The trick, of course, is to retire early . . . or not at all. If you're stuck with your shoulder to an particularly recalcitrant wheel, consider that early retirement offer—or invest in high-risk stocks.

*Or,* start looking for a better wheel. The happiest people are the ones who get paid to do what they want to do. They're the ones who never retire or don't notice when they do. The best jobs don't even have a retirement plan: Pope, Queen, Supreme Court Justice, Rolling Stone.

Stick with your job until you learn to love it, or leave it the first chance you get. Then find a job doing something you won't want to stop doing and die in harness. Picasso didn't retire to play golf, why should you?

WORK

eT

i

RE

m

In this society, women retire, men die.

MARGARET MEAD, ANTHROPOLOGIST, 1901-1978

I think I'll work all my life. When you're having fun, why stop having fun?

HELEN THOMAS, JOURNALIST

I don't want to achieve immortality through my work. I want to achieve it through not dying.

WOODY ALLEN, FILMMAKER

You've probably been wondering how I manage to totter on at the advanced age of eighty-two . . . . I do have a strong motivation for keeping fit—I want to go on working as long as I can.

REX HARRISON, ENGLISH ACTOR, 1908-1990

Next year will be my 30th doing the NFL with CBS. I don't have any plans to retire. I enjoy what I do. I don't know how many people are lucky enough to have a job where they really, really can't wait to get to work. It's almost like playing. You build yourself up for a peak performance. Then it's a new week, and you do it all over again.

Pat Summerall, television sportscaster, just before CBS lost the rights to broadcast National Football League games

I have reached the time of my life when I don't have to work with anyone who is not as happy to work with me.

Georg Solti, Hungarian conductor

I'm against retiring. The thing that keeps a man alive is having something to do. Sitting in a rocker never appealed to me. Golf or fishing isn't as much fun as working.

"COLONEL" HARLAN SANDERS, BUSINESSMAN, 1890-1980

I'll retire in two more years, but after that I'd like to continue to work here in the summer. Winters are getting kind of hard. After 10 years of that I'll stay home and look out the window and let the other guys work. It's better to quit when you're ahead. Don't wait until they carry you out!

PAUL TRUMPF, GRAVEDIGGER

It's a grind trying to beat those 60-year-old kids out there.

SAM SNEAD, GOLFER, ON WHY HE DECLINED TO PLAY ON THE PGA SENIOR TOUR AT AGE 77

Tears? Nah. Guys who cry are the ones who feel they didn't get it all done. This bottle's empty. Nothing left to pour.

DAN HAMPTON, FOOTBALL PLAYER, ON HIS RETIREMENT

I'm Ma Rainey . . . mother of Beale Street. I'm 78 years old. Ain't never had enough of nothing, and it's too damn late now.

EPITAPH IN ELMWOOD CEMETERY, MEMPHIS, TENNESSEE

You lose an awful lot of speed between 80 and 86.

RUTH ROTHFARB, ON WHY IT WOULD BE TOUGH TO BEAT HER BEST MARATHON TIME SET SIX YEARS EARLIER AT AGE 80

Sit on my rear end.

THURGOOD MARSHALL, U.S. SUPREME COURT JUSTICE, 1908-1993,
WHEN ASKED WHAT HE WAS GOING TO DO
AFTER HE RETIRED

By the time you've made it, you've had it.

MALCOLM FORBES, BUSINESSMAN, 1919-1990

Well, for one thing, I find that I no longer win every golf game I play.

GEORGE BUSH, 41ST PRESIDENT OF THE UNITED STATES,
ON HIS LIFE AFTER BEING VOTED OUT OF OFFICE

I must study politics and war, that my sons have the liberty to study mathematics and philosophy. My sons ought to study mathematics and philosophy, geography, natural history, and naval architecture, in order to give their children the right to study painting, poetry, music, architecture, statuary, tapestry, and porcelain.

JOHN ADAMS, SECOND PRESIDENT OF THE UNITED STATES, 1735-1818

Why, into the usual vices of the romantic idealist: into sloth and melancholy . . . into love and marriage and the begetting of children, into the strenuous maneuvers of earning a living without living to earn, into travel and play and music and drink and talk and laughter, into saving the world—but saving the world was only a hobby. Into watching cloud formations float across our planetary skies. But mostly into sloth and melancholy, and I don't regret a moment of it.

EDWARD ABBEY, NOVELIST, WHEN ASKED "WHERE HAVE THE YEARS GONE?"

# INDEX

# Help us with the next edition of Heigh-Ho! Heigh-Ho!

Which quotes did we miss? Which did we blow? We'd like to know. If you have more information on the sources of the quotations in this book or have a favorite quote on work that you would like to see included, please copy and fill out this form (use additional paper if necessary) and mail it to us.

The quote by ________________ on page___ should read:

______________________________________________

______________________________________________

It should be attributed to ______________________

The author's occupation is/was ____________________

The author's nationality is ______________________

The dates of the author's birth and death are ____________

The printed source for the quote is ________________

The following additional quote should be included:

______________________________________________

______________________________________________

It should be attributed to ______________________

The author's occupation is/was ____________________

The author's nationality is ______________________

The dates of the author's birth and death are ____________

The printed source for the quote is ________________

Optional:

Your name ______________________________

Address ________________________________

City/State/Zip ___________________________

Telephone ______________________________

Mail to: Heigh-Ho! Heigh-Ho!
c/o ACTA Publications
4848 N. Clark Street
Chicago, IL 60640

# "FASCINATING . . . HIGHLY ATMOSPHERIC . . . A LUSH, HYPNOTIC SETTING."

## —*Detroit News/Free Press*

"Highly recommended . . . A thriller filled with a wealth of legal detail and realistic characters that will appeal to Phillip Margolin fans."

—*Library Journal*

"Siegel is a talented, compelling, enjoyable writer."

—*San Francisco Chronicle*

"A winning story packed with bizarre plot twists, high-octane action, bizarre characters, and a slam-bang finish. A thumbs-up choice for mystery fans."

—*Booklist*

"Despite its sleepy appearance, the tiny hamlet of El Nido, Calif., harbors terrible secrets. . . . Siegel beautifully captures the flavor of scandal in a small community—the knowing looks, the awkward silences, the amateur attempts at coverup."

—*Publishers Weekly*

Also by Barry Siegel

THE PERFECT WITNESS*
A DEATH IN WHITE BEAR LAKE*
SHADES OF GRAY

**Published by The Ballantine Publishing Group*

# ACTUAL INNOCENCE

Barry Siegel

BALLANTINE BOOKS • NEW YORK

A Ballantine Book
Published by The Ballantine Publishing Group
 Published in the United States by The Ballantine Publishing Group, a division of Random House, Inc., New York, and simultaneously in Canada by Random House of Canada Limited, Toronto.



www.randomhouse.com/BB/

Library of Congress Catalog Card Number: 00-110315

ISBN: 0-345-41310-5

Manufactured in the United States of America

First Hardcover Edition: October 1999
First Mass Market Edition: January 2001

10 9 8 7 6 5 4 3 2 1

To the memory of my mother,
and her enduring love of family

# ONE

The phone rang yet again. Greg Monarch reached for it, but his hand stopped short. His head ached so badly, he could barely see across his desk. He'd been reading case files since dawn, preparing for three trials at once. Now he longed only for a dim silence. Closing his eyes, he imagined himself back in Pecho Rancho State Park, where he'd spent the weekend. Eight thousand acres of lost Central California coastland. Hidden coves, wooded stream canyons, golden poppy fields . . .

At least the phone had stopped ringing.

Greg rose from his chair and walked to the window. Through the pane, he studied the creek winding past La Graciosa's central plaza. It was dusk, the sky a pale pink glow. Shoppers and families were gathering on the town plaza, local farmers were spreading their apples and avocados on the backs of pickup trucks, children were tossing bread crumbs to ducks at the creek's edge. Greg turned back to his desk. His head still hurt, but he could see now.

He almost wished he couldn't. There, on the desk's edge, sat the embossed, gold-lettered card. The invitation to the Chumash County Criminal Bar Association's annual awards dinner. And, beside it, the announcement of this year's Lawyer of the Year: Greg Monarch.

The Sullivan murder trial, the Plaskow business, the Danny McCloud case—Monarch had cultivated a singular reputation on the Central Coast. He'd won his share of acquittals, he'd shown his instinct for doing what was needed, but he'd not lunged for the spotlight. No showboating on TV, no tell-all books, no unctuous self-promotion. "His efforts have well served the legal community and the public at large," went the citation to be presented at tonight's dinner. "Greg Monarch has provided a standard of excellence for all others in his profession."

What would he say when it came time for his acceptance speech? Greg glanced at a legal pad where, during breaks from his trial preparation, he'd been trying to scribble out some comments. *We all play a critical role, a necessary role. . . . Without a zealous adversary for the defense, the system breaks down. . . . What's at stake is the integrity of the law as an institution. . . . What's at stake is the state's interest in a just society. . . .*

It was there Greg had lost his thread. He picked up a pen, started anew.

*What's at stake is the mask of propriety. The defense attorney provides the mask. The defense attorney's unfettered advocacy of his client validates what the state does. . . . Without the defense attorney, the state would look mighty bad indeed. . . .*

Greg stopped, put down his pen. That wouldn't do. No. He'd have to wing it. He'd ad-lib from the podium.

Greg was reaching for his coat when he heard a knock at the door in his anteroom. He ignored it. His office was closed; he was already late. The knock came again, three hard raps, insistently. Greg turned toward the door. Four, five, six.

"Monarch?" The man calling from the street was offering more a greeting than a question. The voice sounded patrician, and familiar. "Monarch, I know you're there. Let me in."

Greg wished he could ignore this summons. It wasn't every day, though, that Judge Daniel Solman came knocking at a lawyer's door. Solman, the chief federal district judge for the Central California region, could be found more often at a public podium, speaking before hundreds, if not thousands. That was so even back at Chumash State, where he and Greg had been passing friends and classmates, sharing the occasional teacher and lecture hall. Student government had been Solman's province in those days, and his stepping-stone. It was a shame really that he'd gotten himself appointed a federal judge seven years ago, for that development, however lustrous, had derailed a promising political career. The United States District Court did not offer Solman enough opportunities to orate.

No, he couldn't ignore Judge Solman. Greg reached for the doorknob.

"Evening, Judge," he said. "I was just heading out."

"Won't keep you long," Solman began, stepping inside without invitation.

Greg studied his guest. The sweeping breadth of the forehead, the mane of curly gray hair, the cast of the mouth, and the expression in his lively eyes all portrayed an uncommon flair—hardly the sensibility of a judge. Without his robes, Daniel Solman suggested a thriving entrepreneur more than a man of the law. He favored Italian crepe wools, cashmere blazers, hand-sewn calfskin moccasins. Greg wondered where he bought his clothes.

"In town for the weekend, and on my way to the county bar dinner," the judge was saying now. "Saw your light still on, so thought I'd stop by. Just an impulse. Had a notion you might be interested in what's crossed my desk."

"Did you?"

"Yes. . . . Quite a curious habeas corpus petition. Pro se, handwritten, pauper, rather hapless. Right up your alley, in other words. Another poor, vulnerable lass, fighting institutional power."

Greg took a step back from Solman. Despite his flip manner, the judge didn't appear all that relaxed. It was so unusual for him to show up like this. "Wouldn't say that's exactly my alley," Greg said. "Why come to me?"

"She needs a lawyer if she's going to proceed." Solman peered at Greg with curiosity. "And . . . well, Monarch, she's sort of asked for you."

Greg showed only mild interest. So many prisoners sent

him urgent pleas these days. Urgent pleas and densely packed boxes of documents. "Sort of? What do you mean?"

"She attached a note to her petition, requesting that a copy be sent to Greg Monarch."

"But her petition has already been written and filed. She doesn't need me."

"This petition won't get her through the door."

"Why do you think anything will?"

Solman's eyes roamed about Greg's small unadorned office. "Well now, that's just the question. Probably not. Probably she has no chance at all. Still, the way she puts things, the way she writes . . . Hard to explain. You'll see if you take a look. No federal judge would act on this as it is, but—"

"What's she in for?"

The question stopped Solman for a moment. "Murder one," he offered finally, sounding uneasy with the notion. "Slashed an old man's throat, it seems, out by a riverbank in the El Nido Valley. One moonlit night five years ago. She's been losing appeals ever since."

As well she should, Greg reasoned. Why should throat slashers win their appeals? Why should murderers walk free? "Sorry, Judge, I've had my fill of death-row cases." He paused. "I've had my fill of defending killers."

Solman looked now as if he regretted this unplanned visit. "I understand," he said with sudden conviction. "Don't blame you." He stepped toward the door. "It was just something I thought you should see. As I say, I stopped by on impulse. Maybe because of the time issue . . . I'll be off now."

"Time issue?" Greg asked. "What do you mean?"

Solman slowly turned back to him. "She's only six months from the executioner. They've set the date. This is her last appeal."

Greg, without thinking, glanced at his watch. Habeas petitions were a particular quagmire. Unwinding the past with virtually no chance of getting anywhere. Courts weren't even interested anymore whether your client was innocent, just as long as the judges and prosecutors dotted all their *i*'s. Not more than a hundred out of ten thousand federal habeas petitions even won review each year, and of those, maybe four or five prevailed. A miserable waste of time.

"Sorry, Judge," Greg said. "Still not interested. My plate's pretty full. Our dedicated prosecutor here in Chumash County keeps throwing new criminal cases at me. I take it he's anxious to keep me gainfully employed. That leaves little time for a no-chance dance down a dead-end road. Give it to some eager young kid just out of law school."

Solman nodded his agreement but seemed lost in thought. He stood at the door, hand on the knob, not moving. Greg had never known Solman to cerebrate like this.

"Tell you what," the judge finally suggested. "I'm going to send this woman's petition over to your office by messenger. We'll slip it through your mail slot, despite your full plate. Read it with your nightcap this evening. Send it back tomorrow morning if you're not interested."

"That's just what I'll do," Greg promised.

He walked down the brick path that followed the creek as it wound through La Graciosa. The evening air cleared Greg's head. From time to time, he paused to smell the jacaranda and watch the creek roll by. When others passed, he called out the casual greetings common in a small town. *Hey there . . . Been a while . . . Well, how you doing?* Two assistant prosecutors, knowing where he was headed, stopped to congratulate him and urge him to enjoy his night in the spotlight. "I intend to do just that," he informed them with a grin. "Just like every night."

*The way she puts it, the way she writes.* What an odd thing for Solman to say. *Hard to explain.* Greg, striding quickly now, shook off the judge's words.

The Apple Canyon Inn, that's where they were having this dinner. At the foot of Carmel Street, where the creek sank into an underground tunnel and began its ten-mile journey to the sea. Just five blocks away. Greg straightened his tie and ran a hand through short sandy hair. In this stretch, he had the creek path largely to himself. Through the rear windows of bars and cafés that backed onto the creek, he could see familiar faces leaning into the evening's first Graciosa Brew. Laughter and the lilting sound of a piano drifted through the perennial haze that gripped La Graciosa most evenings. Greg smelled camphor at the creek's edge, kelp from the sea ten miles distant. La Graciosa hadn't changed yet, he thought with satisfaction. The coastal mountain range still held back the world. So did the fog. For the time being, this town remained a lost outpost. Ranching, farming, fishing, that was it. That, and just enough transgression to keep a criminal defense attorney occupied.

He stood finally before the Apple Canyon Inn. Unsure whether to reflect a town forged in the Spanish-mission era, or one ripened in frontier ranching days, the inn had chosen a compromise: adobe and tile mixed freely with split timber. Yellow light poured from a bank of paned windows. Inside, scattered about the lobby, Greg could see dozens of lawyers lifting glasses to their lips. If nothing else, the criminal bar of Chumash County knew how to bend an elbow.

"Well, if it isn't Greg Monarch himself." A large damp hand gripped Greg's shoulder, a red meaty face loomed near his ear. Against his will, Greg inhaled Jerry Belson's whiskey breath. Jerry Belson, the ex-cop turned shoddy criminal defense lawyer. Greg had savaged him in the Sullivan trial. Why would Belson be so solicitous now? Was that what the Lawyer of the Year Award got you?

"Just a little winded," Greg muttered, hoping to avoid a conversation. "Long walk. Need to sit down. See you inside."

Breaking free of Belson's grip, Greg pushed through the inn's front door. More hands reached for him, more faces loomed. He grinned gamely, nodding and waving at those he knew. Arms propelled him forward. *Glad to see you, Greg. . . . Way to go, Greg. . . . Congratulations . . . Terrific . . .* At least now he was among close, valued colleagues. Tim Ruthman, Ron Carson, Jenny Blair, Art Parrish, all the usual gang. They were his compadres, lawyers renowned for their defense of everyone from white-collar swindlers to odd fellows waving knives under the downtown bridge. Ruthman was Greg's favorite. A big bear of a man with a bushy mustache and a constantly amused expression, Tim took his job seriously, but not himself.

"You sure you don't want to go fishing tonight instead?" Ruthman whispered in Greg's ear.

"You're reading my mind," Greg said. "My boat's bobbing on the lake, waiting for us."

"Looks like they're waiting for you here, too."

"If only you guys hadn't voted for me."

"If only you hadn't won all those cases."

Greg hesitated, weighing a response. Before he could speak, he felt a hand on his shoulder, pulling him away from Ruthman.

"This way, Greg. We need you up on the dais soon. Running a bit late."

Jonathan Clamber, president of the criminal bar association, twitched as he spoke. Rapid eye blinks, jaw clenches, that's how he got whenever timetables weren't being met. Clamber had Greg by the elbow. Together they weaved through the crowd.

"There'll be a few kickoff speeches," Clamber was saying. "Usual stuff. Membership drive, booster numbers, telegram from the governor. Still waiting on the president, not sure whether that son of a bitch will deliver on time. Then we do a couple toasts, a couple small change awards. After that, I do the presentation speech for the Lawyer of the Year Award. When I finish, you stand up."

Clamber peered at Greg, who appeared to be searching the room for something. "You listening to me, Monarch? You look distracted."

Greg offered what he hoped resembled an obliging smile. "Nice to see you too, Jonathan. Sorry I was late. A bit overwhelmed by work, that's all. Three cases that act as if they mean to end up inside a courtroom."

Clamber regarded Greg now with open irritation. He'd

never been part of Greg Monarch's fan club. Hadn't even voted for him. Greg's courtroom style at times was a bit too audacious for Clamber's meticulous taste. "You could work on your attitude, Monarch. Should be grateful about this award. Lucky you're getting it."

"Yes, quite lucky. Much obliged."

"You don't look terribly appreciative, Monarch."

"Appearances can be deceiving."

Clamber's hands flexed. "If I had my way, you'd be pleading before the state bar ethics crowd, not accepting awards."

"Take comfort, Jonathan. Someday you may very well have your way."

They both knew Greg had won the bar association's annual award by a rather narrow margin. After they tallied the executive board's vote, two of the more straitlaced members clucked loudly in dismay, and one particularly crotchety septuagenarian stomped out in protest.

"Monarch, piece of advice." Clamber placed a tight wiry hand on Greg's shoulder. "Keep your acceptance speech short."

Greg tried his best to appear appreciative as he sat on the dais. He was a tall, rangy man with angular features, dark watchful eyes, and the long graceful fingers of a pianist. He raised those fingers to his brow now. Bright lights blazed in his face, so before him the crowd of five hundred appeared mainly as shadows. Only occasionally did a decipherable face swim into view. Yet clearly he was among friends and admirers, despite Clamber's venom. Out of their mouths came lavish praise for him.

For him, and for themselves as well. Speaker after speaker hailed their profession without qualm or censure. Everything merited an anecdote, everything drew enthusiastic huzzahs. Greg scanned the crowd, peering into a dark sea of murmuring voices. He saw Judge Solman near the front, nodding amiably at him. Halfway back, his once-close companion, the federal prosecutor Kimberly Rosen, offered a faint wink. In the rear, standing against the wall among the local journalists, the *News-Times* reporter Jimmy O'Brien waved a wide chunky hand. Greg lifted his eyes to the dinner hall's windows, which gave onto a side street just off the corner of Carmel. Nearly a full moon tonight, he realized. The lake would be shimmering.

Then it was time for the guest of honor to speak. Greg moved slowly toward the microphone, still composing his comments. He gripped the lectern with two hands and drew a breath. "We toil in a noble cause," he began. "You honor me too much." The rest he managed by rote, drawing from dozens of speeches he'd delivered over the years. *The pursuit of justice cannot be reduced to storytelling. . . . A trial is a search for truth. . . . We need to recommit ourselves to the faith that the state must prove, with honest evidence, its case against the accused. . . . The defense attorney who walks into the courtroom honestly defending the guilty also defends the innocent. He preserves the system. He makes the powerful state always prove its case against the powerless. . . .*

Enthusiastic applause interrupted Greg twice. When he finished, hands clasped his shoulders, voices murmured praise in his ear. Greg backed away from those surrounding him even as he offered his thanks. *Yes . . . Certainly . . . How kind of you . . . Much appreciated . . .* Spotting an exit at the rear of the podium, he inched toward it. *Could use some fresh air for a moment . . . Been working all day . . . Need to clear my head . . .* In a lull, finding himself alone, he turned to the door. Tim Ruthman, watching from the corner, knowing what he was up to, waved him on with a broad grin. Before many others noticed, Greg was gone.

Outside, the creek beckoned. Greg stood on the path above its bank, listening to the sound of water slapping against earthen barriers. He turned finally and began the short trek to his creekside cottage. Reaching La Graciosa's plaza, he decided instead to stop at his office. There he paced through the suite of rooms, unsure what he was seeking. He paused at the window. Slowly he sank onto the upholstered reading chair beside his desk. Only then did he spot the long manila envelope lying on the ground below the mail slot, just inside his office door. He studied it for a moment, puzzled, before recalling Judge Solman's peculiar visit. There it was: the habeas petition.

Greg rose, reached for the envelope, settled at his desk. So thin, he thought, holding the bundle in his hand. Not at all like a lawyer's legal brief, especially when a life was at stake. So devoid of a lawyer's voluminous oratory, a lawyer's ceaseless cascade of arguments and citations. Instead, no doubt, just as the judge promised: a simple hapless plea.

Greg pulled the document from the envelope. Only nine pages in all. Handwritten, but not sloppy. Straight lines, perfect circles, elegant curls. This woman had printed her words as if inscribing invitations to a birthday party. For all that, the substance of her message looked drearily commonplace. Four previous appeals denied, the last by the state supreme court. Each rejection issued after ventilation of the usual claims: newly discovered evidence, prosecutorial misconduct, ineffective defense counsel. Judges must yawn, seeing this type of stuff day in and day out.

Yet Judge Solman hadn't yawned; Solman had come knocking at his door. Greg leafed again through the nine pages, trying to gauge what the judge had seen. Was it the handwriting itself, the sense of a real person making this plea rather than a lawyer? Or was it the aura of something feminine in the curl of the letters? Something female and urgent and full of yearning? Or had Solman just never before read a forlorn plea from a guilty soul sitting on death row?

Greg flipped back to the document's front page. He scanned past the legal phrases, searching for this woman's name. He squinted, running a finger from line to line. Then he froze.

*Sarah Marion Trant, Petitioner, v. Mr. Bryce Chalmers, Superintendent, Respondent.*

Sarah Marion Trant. Sarah Trant.

Greg closed his eyes.

Sarah Trant.

Did Judge Solman do this purposefully? Did Solman know? How could he? Sarah had come along well after law school, many months after his shared classrooms with the judge.

Greg sat in the dark, fighting off memories. Sarah on the night they met, Sarah on the night they parted. Both times, her bright hazel eyes so urgent and hungry, so full of hope. *What a fight that was, Greg, what a scene. . . . I fear that irrevocable things have happened. . . . What should we do? . . . I don't want to feel such pain, I don't want to be confused. . . . I'll say goodbye to you for now. . . . Maybe we can face each other in the future on sturdier ground. . . . Oh, Greg, don't marry anyone, all right? . . . There is no one better than you. . . .*

An asylum, that's where he'd always imagined Sarah might end up. Instead, she'd landed in state prison. Slash an old man's throat on a dark riverbank? Yes, he had to admit . . . he'd seen that possibility in her. She could do that.

Again he leafed through the habeas petition. There was nothing there, nothing to suggest anything but yet another murderer who desired escape from the consequences of her actions. Yet another killer who wanted him to win for her. Why was Sarah turning to him after all these years? Reaching the end of the document, Greg stopped. There, stuck on the back page, he noticed Sarah's personal plea, scrawled on a small yellow card. *Please send copy of this to Greg Monarch in La Graciosa.* That's all it said.

Greg stared at the words, then rose and began to pace again. Through a narrow winding mountain pass—that's where El Nido lay, that's how you got there. A remote oak-thick river valley, some sixty miles southeast of La Graciosa, well across the county line. With his dad, Greg had hiked and fished there often in his youth. Less frequently, but always with rekindled memories, he'd returned in recent years. Didn't he even know a lawyer out there?

Greg studied the bare walls of his office. He tried to sit down but couldn't keep still. Three cases he had, all coming to trial. Unless they could be postponed. He reached for his phone. "Goddamn it, Judge," he snapped into Solman's answering machine. "What are you doing to me?"

# TWO

The Chumash Dunes were wondrous. Those great white mounds, reaching south along the coast from Pirate's Beach, rose like an apparition in the misty drizzle. Greg, kicking a sturdy broad-shouldered roan into a gallop, felt the cold dank wind in his face as he threaded through a grove of willow and poplar, then opened onto the beach and flew across the hard sand at the surf's edge. Before him Sarah led the way, her long dark hair wild in the breeze. *There's something about you,* she murmured when they stopped to rest. *Something that I can't understand completely. The way you move, the way you won't give up, the way I know you'd fight for your beliefs.* Her cool smooth palm moved gently across his face. *You are one of a kind, Greg. . . . I know you understand about wonder. . . . I trust you. . . . I love you so much. . . .*

Greg awoke with a start, smelling gas fumes, or perhaps leaking oil. For a moment he thought of returning to his dream, but found he could not. One side of his head throbbed; something sticky clung to his face.

He stirred, pulled himself into a sitting position. In his car, that's where he was. On the side of a road, peering into a lush forest. The windshield cracked, shards of glass on the seat beside him. Greg recalled leaving La Graciosa early on the Saturday morning after the awards dinner. The drive toward El Nido; a treacherous mountain pass; a low rising sun in his eyes; a jolting collision. Nothing more. Greg slowly climbed out of his car. Now he grasped what had happened. Half awake, distracted, blinded by the sun, he'd cracked into a thick tree trunk fallen across his path. His car sat twisted on the road's shoulder. Greg's hand rose to his face, tracing the sticky substance on his forehead. Blood. No wonder his head hurt.

Greg looked about. He was standing on a wooded ridge in the high foothills of the El Nido Valley. Some hundred feet below him, in an oak-thick mountain gorge, a clear pebbly trout stream coursed through a tumble of rust-colored boulders. At one bend, he spotted a solitary fly fisherman, knee-deep in the water, casting upstream into the current. At the next bend, he watched a woman swimming lazily across the river. A woman who now was rising, naked and willowy and distracted, from the deep blue-green pool where she'd been bathing. Rivulets of water, sparkling in the morning sun, ran down her back. She reached up and unpinned her hair, which fell, a tousled tawny mane, to her shoulders. Then, like a deer sensing a foreign presence in the wind, she looked up and spotted Greg. For a moment she stood still. Slowly, her eyes still on him, she reached for her clothes. Pulling a pale green dress over her damp body, she ran a hand through her hair. Turning, she began to climb out of the creek bed.

Greg turned too, and crossed the road. There a long steep slope rose to a yet higher plateau. He drew a breath, fighting off a wave of dizzy nausea. Then he scrambled up the slope, using tree roots as footholds. At the crest, facing to the southeast, he lifted his eyes to the vast El Nido Valley. It rolled before him to the horizon, ten miles long and three miles wide. Magnificent dense live oak forests backed up to towering seven-thousand-foot mountains ribbed with gray sandstone; pale morning sunlight played through deep foliage-thick ravines; dark green orchards climbed foothill slopes abundant with orange trees, avocado bushes, and grapevines. In the mid-distance rose the century-old tile roofs of El Nido Village, the valley's solitary town. No more than seven thousand dwelled there, perhaps another thirty thousand in the surrounding countryside. Coming from a misty coastal region, Greg marveled at this barricaded valley's startling clarity. In all his visits here, he'd never seen fog.

He pivoted away from the vista. He'd have to hike his way

out, that much seemed certain. The descent down the slope, grasping tree branches, proved more treacherous but half as long as the trip up. Stepping past his battered car, he began walking up the mountain road. Around a bend, it turned from pavement to dirt. A hundred yards farther, it narrowed into a path. Then came a shed, and beyond it a splintered wooden gate, blocking his way. On the gate sat a board bearing hand-lettered words: DO NOT TRESPASS—PRIVATE PROPERTY.

Greg climbed over the gate, trying to ignore his aching head. He was now moving across what looked to be a vast empty campus of some sort. He circled structures, peered into windows. A central brick building, two wooden lodge houses, a half-dozen cottages, a kitchen and mess hall, a football field, sports equipment, boxes and supplies. No people, though. No sign of life, only its residue.

Greg stopped before one of the lodge houses. Through a window he saw folding chairs, a long table, a dais, a white board. He stepped closer. Smudges discolored the board where someone had dragged a rag, wiping out whatever had been written. Greg squinted; through the blur, he thought he saw a trace of words, but the lines and curls had no shape, no meaning he could discern. He turned and walked on. A pair of boots lying on the porch before a cottage caught his eye. They were knee-high rubbers, black with blue trim, meant for backcountry travel in deep snow. Men wore such boots in the far north, from Minnesota to Maine, not in Central California. Yet here they were. Greg looked through the cottage's window. In the small corner room, a single bed, a thin mattress, no sheets. In the main room, hanging on a hook, three pairs of white overalls. Also a fireplace, laid with fresh wood.

Greg meandered, listening for noises, hearing none. The utter silence felt like a presence, something alive, something watching. Nothing moved, though. No breeze here. No birds either. The sky was empty. Ancient oaks, ringing the campus, stood still in fields crowded with vines and mosses. Greg felt a sudden desire to get out of this place.

He turned, hiked toward the far end of the complex. Past another wooden gate and No Trespassing sign, he found himself in a wooded field. He followed a small dry wash to a ledge of sandrock and leaned against it. A piece of the sandrock broke off in his hand. It reeked strangely of rotten eggs. Greg looked down at his feet. He was standing on a dark tarlike material. Asphaltum, he judged, asphaltum that had seeped from a canyon wall. He kicked over the thick rotting trunk of a fallen oak tree. In the furrow it had created sat a pool of pale green liquid. He bent to study this peculiar fluid.

"Get up." The words sounded like a command, not a suggestion.

Lifting his head, Greg stared into the barrel of a rifle. Behind it stood a stout man with a ragged reddish-brown beard. The shirttails from his brown flannel shirt hung over a pair of denim overalls. He spat at Greg's feet.

"Get up, turn around, back out. You're trespassing."

Greg looked back and forth between the rifle and the dark tarry ground. "Trespassing on what?" he asked.

Past the abandoned camp, the mountain path broadened again. Heeding the rifleman's brusque command, Greg followed that road as it descended through two miles of sharp switchbacks. Around a final turn, the forest suddenly opened into a rolling meadow bordered by a low wooden fence. Studying the horizon, Greg realized he was standing at the edge of a vast ranch that reached across much of the valley floor. On a rise to the south stood a two-story structure made of stone and timber. It looked to Greg more like a hunting lodge than a home.

Twenty minutes later, he knocked at its front door. Dusty sweat glistened on the neck of the Latino who opened the door. He appeared to be fresh from the fields, but didn't hold himself like a ranch hand. He wore a straw hat, and had piercing brown eyes, and gnawed on a toothpick.

"May I see the master of the house?" Greg asked, offering his business card.

"There is no master," the man replied without glancing at the card. "We've got a mistress." He studied Greg's bloodied forehead for a moment, then ushered him into a cavernous room filled with furniture made of walnut and leather. "I'm Alex Ramirez," he said. "I'm the ranch foreman. You wait here."

Left alone, Greg glanced about the room. It had to be at least fifty feet long, he estimated, and thirty wide. The high beamed ceilings were made of polished oak logs. On one wall hung a large oil painting, the obvious portrait of a patriarch: Fierce, deep-socketed, ice-blue eyes stared out from under thick eyebrows, as if examining and judging those standing before him. A floor-to-ceiling brick fireplace occupied much of a second wall, a huge picture window a third. Through it Greg could see half of the El Nido Valley.

Edward Sanborn, it suddenly occurred to Greg. The oil portrait was of Edward P. Sanborn, the legendary founder of El Nido. How dim he'd been not to make the connection.

"Welcome to El Nido, Mr. Monarch. I'm Diana Sanborn."

Greg turned from the window. She appeared to be about seventy, a robust seventy. Her long loose gray hair spilled to her shoulders from under a dirty white cowboy hat; her scuffed black cowboy boots poked out from a long flowing lavender skirt. Her smile warmed the room. Her voice sounded like champagne.

"I've already been welcomed," Greg said.

Diana Sanborn's eyes danced with anticipation. She had high cheekbones and a generous mouth. "Tell me," she said. "Tell me who has welcomed you."

"He didn't introduce himself. Just waved a rifle, ordered me to stop trespassing, pointed me toward your ranch. An abandoned camp of some sort, down the road a couple of miles. That's where I left my car."

Greg's answer was not, it appeared, what Diana Sanborn had expected, or wanted. She no longer looked the least amused. "Left your car, Mr. Monarch?"

"I had an automobile accident. I didn't notice a tree trunk across the road."

Stepping closer to Greg, Diana Sanborn now could see the gash at the side of his forehead. "My goodness, Mr. Monarch, you're injured."

"Just a cut. It's stopped bleeding already. I'm okay."

"Alex," the old lady called. "Alex, bring us washcloths and hot water." Then to Greg she said, "Lose your way, Mr. Monarch?"

Without knowing exactly why, Greg felt uneasy. "No," he replied. "Just got blinded by the rising sun in my eyes."

Diana Sanborn's eyebrows arched. "Just what were you doing out on the edge of my property?"

Greg hesitated. For all her warmth, this grand woman couldn't mask the hint of interrogation in her voice. "Taking a drive, Mrs. Sanborn. Clearing my head."

"A drive to clear your head? That sounds marvelous, Mr. Monarch. So far from home, though."

"I had a lot to clear."

Sanborn's rich laughter filled the room. "Okay, I give up. Why don't you simply tell me what brings you to El Nido?"

"Must I?"

Sanborn's smile revealed a row of gleaming white teeth. "Strangers do not usually come here, Mr. Monarch."

They settled on the veranda before a sloping lawn densely treed with live oak and sycamore. Beyond, Sanborn Ranch reached toward the foothills. Alex brought hot washcloths; a thin dark Latina brought iced tea and biscuits. "I'll talk first," Diana volunteered.

She'd grown up on this ranch, her mother and father distant figures to her, world travelers whom she hardly knew. She was raised by servants and her widowed grandfather. Yes, her grandfather was Edward Sanborn, the valley's honored patron. She'd married twice and divorced twice. With no male family members surviving, she ran the ranch herself now, helped by a foreman and small crew. She rode through her pastures, inspecting the stock, making notes for the boys. She counted how many deer she spotted. She watched to see whether the turkeys were here or gone. She looked to see if she had any quail.

"Just a real country life, Mr. Monarch. A real country life I wish dearly to preserve."

"You think it's threatened?"

Sanborn studied him. "No, I don't. But we remain always vigilant. Wouldn't you agree that is wise?"

Greg's forehead still throbbed. He had no interest in parrying with this lady. "Mrs. Sanborn, I'll be direct. Whatever your concerns about preserving your valley, I can assure you I'm not here to aggravate them. As you know from my card, I'm a lawyer from La Graciosa. I drove out here to see someone at the state prison. Just passing through, don't even intend to spend the night. That is, if I can get a little help here. You think I possibly could make a couple of calls? And maybe get a ride down to the village?"

At those words, Diana Sanborn turned toward the horizon and fell silent. When she next spoke, her voice had gone dry.

"Someone at the prison, Mr. Monarch?"

Beads of sweat dripped down Greg's face. He suddenly felt hot and cold at once. The room tilted before him. "Yes," he said. "Sarah Trant."

Squinting through his pain, Greg could only vaguely see Sanborn now as she jumped to her feet. "Bless your heart, Mr. Monarch," he could hear her saying as he drifted away. "You just rest yourself. We'll get you help right away. Don't you worry, we'll get you all straightened out."

Greg awoke to find a narrow, pinched face hanging above him. Light from a window glinted off small gimlet eyes. The man was short and wiry, and smelled vaguely of aftershave lotion. On his hip he packed a holstered revolver. It took Greg a moment to realize he wore a uniform.

"Sheriff Roy Rimmer," the face offered by way of introduction. "Sheriff of El Nido County."

Greg slowly pushed himself into a sitting position. They were still on the veranda where he'd settled with Diana Sanborn, but the mistress of the house was nowhere to be seen. Greg glanced up at the sky. Late morning, he guessed. He'd been out at least an hour.

"Greg Monarch," he said. "Citizen of Chumash County."

"You're being too modest, Mr. Monarch. Such a celebrated

lawyer, the toast of the Central Coast. They even gave you an award last night, didn't they? Right there in La Graciosa. We've made a couple of calls. You have quite a reputation."

Greg studied the sheriff. Rimmer suggested to him a man who always sat on the edge of his chair, if he sat at all.

"Don't believe everything you hear," Greg advised.

"It would be hard to do that, Mr. Monarch. After all, so much of what we hear sounds downright inconceivable."

Greg at last found his head clear and pain free. The nap had done some good. "I understand what you mean, Sheriff. Things I hear also sound downright inconceivable."

"Hear about what, Monarch?"

Greg pushed himself to his feet. A raspy edge had seeped into Rimmer's voice. El Nido no longer was feeling so insulated. "What happened to the 'mister,' Sheriff? I was getting used to it."

Rimmer took a step closer. The sheriff's head was level with Greg's chest. "Cracked your car up pretty bad down the road," Rimmer said. "Must have been quite a party over there in La Graciosa. Maybe you drank a bit too much. Maybe you inhaled something. Who knows about those Chumash County defense lawyers. It's a little late now, but maybe a blood test will tell us a story."

"Then again," Greg said, "maybe a few photographs of the accident scene will reveal a negligent county that leaves fallen tree trunks lying across public roads. Good idea, Sheriff. Let's do a real thorough investigation."

Rimmer's eyes grew more fixed. "Ms. Sanborn says you've come here to see Sarah Trant over at the prison."

"That's right."

"That may be a problem. She's in solitary confinement. Don't believe you can just arrive over there. At least not with first-degree murderers. You've got to arrange visits. Write the warden, set it up."

"In solitary? What for?"

"Wouldn't know. But that Trant woman, she's trouble. Always has been. Making a ruckus, I'm sure."

That was probably true, Greg thought. Sarah certainly was

trouble. He bent over and put his mouth next to Rimmer's left ear. "County sheriffs have squat to do with state prisons," he said. "So get out of my face. I mean to get over to the prison one way or another. I mean to see Sarah Trant today."

Rimmer jerked his head back. "Sorry, Monarch. Don't think that's possible."

"Tell you what," Greg offered, walking to a phone he'd spotted in an alcove off the veranda. "Let's call the federal judge who sent me Trant's habeas petition. Let's tell Judge Solman that the sheriff of El Nido County says I can't see a state murder convict about a federal matter."

Greg picked up the phone, started punching numbers. "What's all this based on? Just why is it I can't see her? Want to make sure I get it right for the judge."

Rimmer reached Greg's side in two steps and took the phone from his hand. "Okay, Monarch," he said. "We'll let you have your little visit."

More than anything else, geography protected El Nido. Cradled by mountain ranges on all sides, the valley offered no approach other than through a narrow pass. The access road from La Graciosa first curved past El Nido Lake at the basin's high northwest end, then descended through the La Luna foothills in a southeasterly slant toward the center of the valley floor. There rose the village, eight blocks of shops and cafés running along Main Street. To the south of this hub, a pergola led into sixty-acre Sanborn Park. To the north, stately old ranch houses filled the wooded slope that fronted the La Lunas. A walk from those residential foothills through the village, then into the park, and down to its southern border at El Nido Creek required no more than twenty minutes.

Even to the east, farther into the valley, where distances might be described in miles rather than blocks, a bike would do as well as a car. Just past the village, all signs of commerce gave way to lush citrus groves, interrupted only by a few isolated homes. Diana Sanborn's white timber lodge sat out there, on a bluff some two miles beyond the hamlet. On the far backside of her ranch, the valley narrowed into increasingly rugged terrain as it ascended to the foothills and the abandoned camp Greg had traversed. On the village side, El Nido Creek formed the ranch's southwest boundary as it flowed toward town. Throw an inner tube in there, Greg thought, and you could float all the way through Sanborn Park.

He didn't have an inner tube, though. Instead he had Sheriff Rimmer's patrol car, with Rimmer behind the wheel. They were winding their way west from Sanborn Ranch, through groves abundant with oranges and avocados and peaches. In an instant they were entering El Nido Village and moving slowly down Main Street. The place, Greg noted with appreciation, had hardly changed at all. As it had for one hundred years, a tile-roofed Spanish arcade spanned the long block across from Sanborn Park, sheltering a familiar mix of art galleries and dress shops, bookstores and folk-music cafés. There was the homemade ice cream stand he'd loved as a boy, and the dimly lit Gaucho Tavern he'd wondered about. There was the toy store, and the tea shop, and the well-stocked newsstand. At the end of the block, the tile and adobe U.S. Post Office tower remained El Nido's tallest structure, reaching sixty-five feet into the air.

Just past that tower, Sheriff Rimmer turned left, then right onto Old Brook Road, which closely followed El Nido Creek as both rolled to the west. Greg studied the rippling water, preparing himself. Three miles down this bygone wagon trail, Sarah Trant resided in the state penitentiary.

Greg thought the La Luna Women's Correctional Center a site more suitable for respite than punishment. It sat on 160 acres of wooded tableland at the mouth of the valley, barely within the county's boundary. Dappled sunshine graced the front of the low whitewashed adobe buildings; El Nido Creek meandered along the prison's southern border; century-old sycamores shaded rolling green lawns. Only a barbed-wire fence and four security booths at each corner of the property marred the effect.

Rimmer drove Greg past the sentries. At a double wall of iron gates just inside the prison's entry hall, the sheriff reluctantly handed him off to a dour-looking prison guard, who led him to a small office. Thirty minutes of paperwork followed under the eyes of a clerk who pointed silently at where he wanted signatures. Then a second guard led Greg to a bare, fluorescent-lit holding area. "Wait here," he instructed as he turned on his heel.

They called his name a full hour later. He rose and headed toward the double gates. The first wall slid open, then slammed shut behind him as he stepped inside. He stood in what amounted to a large barred cell as a guard, hidden from view, took his time hitting the button that activated the second gate. When it opened finally, Greg walked into the heart of the prison. A female guard escorted him down a hallway to a compact interview room. There, hanging from the ceiling, a bare bright bulb lit pale green walls. Using his handkerchief, Greg reached up and unscrewed the bulb. The weak yellow hallway light seeping through a small window was enough. He wanted shadows for his reunion with Sarah Trant.

What would she look like these twenty years later? He couldn't say. He knew only that she'd still be searching for something.

"Counsel for the defense, I presume? My savior?"

Standing in the doorway, backlit by the hallway's dim illumination, Sarah for a moment appeared to Greg much as she had two decades before. The loose thick auburn hair fell across her shoulders. The intense hazel eyes sparkled with amused challenge. A thin white cotton shift clung to a still-slender body. Sarah watched him, hands on hips. He'd phoned ahead so that she'd be prepared.

"Not your savior, Sarah," Greg said. "Never was much good at that."

"You'll get no argument from me there."

He waved her to a chair. The guard retreated, closing the interview-room door. Greg studied the woman before him. Closer up, Sarah did not appear quite as she had when he'd last seen her. The years showed under her eyes, and at the corners of her mouth. A flicker of exuberance still played across her face, but so too did something else. Greg's heart sank. Sarah looked as if a part of her were missing.

They'd met the summer after he'd finished law school, she a graduate writing program. Both of them at loose ends, he not yet committed to being a lawyer, she not prepared for what it took to write. Living in rented single rooms on the rough edge of Clam Beach, their two cramped units part of a peeling wood-frame complex that stared out at a wind-whipped sea. Neither of them knew where they were headed, or what to do with themselves, so they spent their days at the water's edge, their evenings in bed with bottles of wine. She electrified him back then—she and her abandon and her unreasonable appetites. They were forever devising schemes, plunging into projects, scouring the Central Coast, meeting strange characters, gawking at the phantasmagoria. There were nights they never slept, nights they roamed the vast lost Chumash Dunes, nights they talked endlessly and made love and swam naked under a black starlit sky. Sarah so hungry, lying in the sand, her legs wrapped around him, crying and moaning, beating on his chest, holding him tightly inside her. . . . It didn't matter that she was constantly, even then, longing after something ineffable. For a time, it all seemed possible, it all seemed within their reach.

Her decline came slowly, over many months, as her writing stalled and Greg turned to his budding law practice. She still radiated delight and humor in most situations, but also an uncomfortable, growing urgency. Hers was a vibrant desolation, full of game resolve, and it moved Greg in ways he couldn't explain. When she started turning to him for solutions—seeking in him an energy she could appropriate—he tried his best. He yearned to see her once more striding cockily through her world. In time, though, he realized neither he nor anyone could provide what she sought. When Sarah also came to understand this much, her tremulous search turned frantic.

She began moving repeatedly, lurching from one apartment to another along the Central California coast, furiously arranging rooms for writing that never seemed to satisfy. *Just try to show me that I can provide you with things,* she begged Greg. *With information, with visions. Let me feel courageous sometimes. Let me have a hand in things. You've got to understand that I'm strong. . . . I'm just full of stories, I'm a whole big panorama, and I want to* feel *that way. . . . Sometimes I feel overshadowed by you. . . .*

Near the end, after he'd opened his own small law office in La Graciosa, he'd come home at night to find her waiting in his rented house. She'd stare impatiently at him, as if she were expecting something, as if she meant to siphon out his insides. She'd pull him onto her smooth flat belly, shake him, try to draw blows from him. She'd gobble Libriums, hunch over her typewriter, struggle to write the stories she felt so full of. She'd jump into her battered green Mustang, gun the engine, roar aimlessly north up Highway 101.

One day late in their third summer, with Greg in the passenger seat, she didn't stop driving until they were in Canada. It was as if she couldn't stop, was afraid to stop. Hour after hour they hurtled up the coast, pausing only for gas and sandwiches. I have friends up there, Sarah told Greg. Friends on an island off Vancouver. We'll go visit, it'll be such a surprise, these guys will love to see us. Greg nodded his agreement, as uncertain as he was excited by her wild, unstoppable quest.

When they finally arrived on that island off Vancouver, though, their hosts didn't appear particularly enchanted. They were a gray-haired couple, busy with their garden and pickling. How Sarah knew them, Greg never did learn. After an oddly strained hour in the living room, the lady of the house tactfully handed her visitors a bottle of homemade blueberry wine and sent them on their way. Greg and Sarah ended up at a dark, drafty motel on a side street half a mile from the shore.

It was there, with nowhere else to ricochet, that Sarah finally unraveled. Greg sometimes thought she consciously chose to let go that night. More often, though, he imagined her charging full speed toward a precipice, unable to brake, plunging helplessly over the edge. Whatever its provenance, the descent didn't take long. Greg went out for ice and hamburgers. When he returned, she was crouched in a corner of their room, glowering at the motel manager's fat, lazy brown cat. Glowering, and clutching a twelve-inch carving knife she'd found in their kitchenette's back drawer.

"He's trying to kill me," Sarah hissed, waving her knife at the cat. "I have to get him first."

In the gloom it took Greg a moment to see she was stark naked. Her jeans and blouse lay crumpled by her side; she sat cross-legged, her long dark hair falling across full, milk-white breasts. He moved toward her, reaching for the knife. Realizing his intent, she leapt up and dived for the cat, swinging the blade in a broad sweeping arc. The cat hissed and jumped away. Sarah followed, wielding the knife like a dagger. From corner to corner they pounced, cat screeching, Sarah thrusting, until Greg finally tackled his winsome hazel-eyed girl and pinned her to the ground. That he felt aroused in this moment, lying atop Sarah's naked heaving body, he never told anyone. To the counselors and doctors who eventually appeared, that evening and in the following weeks, he confined himself to the facts as best he knew them.

"Oh, Greg," Sarah sighed on the morning they finally took her to a private psychiatric clinic. "I can't figure it out, Greg. I can't figure out how to get back."

At first he came by regularly, but as time passed his visits dwindled, then ceased. Eventually she moved to a sort of halfway house, then out on her own. For a while, living by herself, she wrote him letters.

*At three this morning, I drove around Berkeley, winding up at the House of Pancakes for coffee and fresh fruit. The only fresh fruit was a banana, but I ordered it anyway. The waitress brought it to me sliced up, with a little pitcher of half-and-half. It was nice. I ate it slowly, reading through my brown phone book that I take everywhere. I longed for you. And before the banana and phone book, before all this, I longed for you. On my birthday I cried myself to sleep longing for your body to hold. You probably don't believe me. And even if you do, it doesn't matter. Your willpower is stronger than mine. And knowing you, I knew that it would be this way. You won't allow yourself to be confused. I am such a fool. . . .*

After the letters stopped, he still occasionally found a postcard from her in his mailbox, usually reporting on one environmental cause or another she was promoting at the time. Once she sent him a newspaper clipping about her monthlong sojourn in the high branches of a thousand-year-old redwood that a lumber company wanted to cut down. Surrounded by an Earth First! crowd, she gradually receded into her own story. Years passed. The postcards tapered off. He lost track of her.

"Been a while," Greg said. "Hasn't it, Sarah?"

She offered a nervous little laugh. "That's not much of an opener, Greg."

"I was trying to start slowly."

"Expected something more interesting from you. Something like, 'Still waving knives around, Sarah?' That would be an icebreaker."

Greg watched how she held herself. Legs crossed and jaw pitched forward, resting now on her closed fist. As if she were willing herself to remain cogent. "Still Sarah, I see. Still Sarah after all these years."

"And what about you? Still Greg?"

He didn't know how to answer that one. He'd wanted her to need him those long years ago. He'd savored her need, he'd grown strong on her need. Yet she'd drained him, too. Drained him, and nearly unhinged him. He learned from her the dangers of misreading voracious hunger as allure. He learned from her the need to keep hold of himself. He'd learned from her the need to fend off certain types of unbridled emotional tumult.

"Sarah, you should know something. A federal judge sent me your habeas petition because you requested that I get a copy. He didn't realize we once knew each other. He just thought I'd be interested. I am, Sarah. As always. That's not changed. But I can't help. . . . I can't get involved. We're way past all that. I came here only because you asked for me. I'm not staying. I'll get your petition to the right lawyer."

Sarah looked at him through lowered eyelashes. "Don't even want to hear my story? Don't even want to hear how I ended up in this place?"

Greg glanced around the room. The skeptical smile, the longing in her eyes . . . He'd been seduced back then as much by her uncertainty as by her sensuousness. "Well, yes . . . ," he said. "Sure I do."

"Where do we start?"

Greg took a deep breath. "Why don't we start with whether you're still waving knives around."

For a moment, Sarah didn't appear to register what he'd said. Then she did, and it was as if the ground had collapsed under her. Her eyes slid swiftly from allure to anxiety to something dark and muddled. She wrapped her arms around her body. The sudden transformation startled Greg, even though he'd seen it often before. In an instant, Sarah became the girl he'd glimpsed at the end of their time together.

"Maybe so," Sarah whispered. "Maybe I am still waving knives."

She began to talk, her voice halting and faint, as if coming from somewhere far away. Her story started not in El Nido but in the woods of Northern California. She'd found her place there, she wanted Greg to know. She'd found meaning, reasons, a way to live. She'd fought for clean rivers, old-growth redwood forests, riparian watersheds, spotted owls. She'd joined groups that shared her concerns, she'd met comrades equally full of passion. With them she'd challenged corporations, educated homeowners, marched, picketed, traveled the state. Then, finally, a half-dozen years ago, she'd set off on her own and arrived in El Nido. For a time, she thought she'd fit in here. Then it all unraveled.

"Brewster Tomaz," she said. "That's who they say I killed."

"Who was he?"

"A sour prune, that's who he was. A crazy, mean-faced old geologist. Always glaring and hollering at us. Once he drove his pickup straight at us as we stood by the creek. Another time—"

"Who's 'us'?" Greg asked. "You and who else?"

The question seemed to sadden Sarah. "I wasn't alone," she said softly. "At least not at the start."

"Let's go back to the start."

She closed her eyes, then opened them. "It began when ModoCorp came to El Nido. Big company out of San Francisco. Bought a gorgeous chunk of wilderness up in the foothills, announced plans to build a world-class health spa. Lot of folks in the valley sided with them, especially after they hired Brewster Tomaz to promote their cause. But not everyone. Not me. There were demonstrations. Confrontations down at the river, lots of pushing and shoving. One time . . ."

Sarah stopped and turned away.

"One time what, Sarah?"

"I don't want to say."

"Tell me."

"I . . . I think . . . One time I pushed Brewster and he fell backward into the water."

"What day was that, Sarah?"

Sarah frowned, nibbled at her lip. "It was the night of the murder. But I ran off right after that. Brewster was alive then. I didn't cut his throat."

"Yet you've been found guilty of doing just that."

"And sentenced to death . . . Six months to go."

As often with her, he felt baffled. What had happened? Was she really a killer? He couldn't ask. No defense attorney wants to hear a confession that will later handcuff him in court. *A defense attorney shouldn't hear what he doesn't need to know.* "Not just a verdict," Greg managed to say. "Four appellate rejections."

She studied her hands. "I think I've been framed."

"You think?"

Sarah looked up at him now, her eyes glistening with dismay. "I'm confused, Greg. I didn't kill Brewster. But I imagined it. I imagined slashing his throat."

Greg rose from his chair. He'd walked this road before. "Okay Sarah, okay," was all he could think to say.

"Won't you help me?"

"Someone will help you."

"No, Greg. No. You."

Greg had reached the interview room door. He yanked it open. "Not me," he said.

Outside the prison, Greg stood blinking in the afternoon sunlight. A steady breeze pushed warm air against his face, reminding him of how dry and hot the valley could be. He began walking down a long gravel pathway, toward the sentry booth and the barbed-wire gate. Although his head no longer hurt, he found he had to step carefully to keep his balance. When he reached the prison's gate, he glanced about.

"I suspect you need a ride, Mr. Monarch."

Peering into the glare, Greg recognized Diana Sanborn. She stood leaning against a white rusted Dodge pickup that had its best years well behind it. She had a booted foot propped on the side fender, an arm stretched toward the roof. Her cowboy hat hung around her neck.

"What I need is a way out of El Nido," he said. "Just want to get my car fixed and drive away."

Diana patted her pickup as if it were a horse. "I'm so sorry, Mr. Monarch, I'm afraid that's not possible. We're having your car towed up here right now. But it's Saturday. We have no auto shops in El Nido, no parts. Also no taxi service."

"No rentals?"

"I'm afraid not."

"Then I'll call a friend. Someone from Chumash County."

"If you wish," Diana said. She hesitated. "I apologize about the sheriff. I thought it best to summon him because of your injury, and the automobile accident."

"Yet another warm El Nido welcoming party. Your valley teems with hospitality."

"You two left the ranch so suddenly, I didn't know you were departing. Otherwise I would have said goodbye."

"That's why you were waiting for me here? To say goodbye?"

"No, that's not why." Diana pushed herself off the pickup and stepped toward Greg. He saw something in her expression now that he couldn't read. "Please accept my hospitality," she said. "Please stay the weekend in El Nido."

Greg tried to take a step, but staggered instead. Diana, a yard from him, reached out to lend support. Leaning against her, he felt oddly comforted.

"Besides," Diana Sanborn said. "You are in no condition to travel."

# THREE

Standing before the oil portrait of his hostess's forebear, Greg tried to imagine how El Nido must have looked to Edward P. Sanborn when he first rode into this valley near the turn of the century. The perpetual play of sunlight, the towering mountains, the warm dry air—he would have seen that, and more. Rather than the dusty truck farms and immaculate ranch houses and pockets of weathered cottages that now decorated the valley, the country beyond the small hamlet would have offered a vast solitude, acre after acre unbroken by human habitation. Grizzlies and mountain lions, but no people at all.

Greg's eyes moved slowly down Edward Sanborn's portrait to a small bronze plaque discreetly positioned under its thick walnut frame. He began to read. *It is difficult for newcomers to the valley to realize what Mr. Sanborn's generosity has meant, because they cannot visualize what existed before his day.* Below those words was verse:

*There came to the El Nido Valley*
*The peaceful El Nido*
*A decade or so ago*
*A man rich in goods and gold*
*And rich in the love of the beautiful . . .*

It was late Saturday afternoon. Greg had been in El Nido less than a day, but felt himself already affected. The world beyond the valley had started to slip away. Greg recalled feeling that same sensation as a boy whenever he came here. He and his father, alone in a rowboat on El Nido Lake. They could talk in ways they never did back at home, sharing thoughts normally hidden, forgetting boundaries, achieving a fragile connection. Greg welcomed the chance to revisit that time, that place. He had no intention of representing Sarah Trant, yet he'd protested only momentarily before accepting Diana's invitation to stay the weekend.

From the living-room wall where Edward Sanborn's portrait hung, Greg walked to a small side room, just off Diana's veranda. She'd offered him this alcove for his personal use during his brief stay. Sunlight poured through a picture window giving onto a view of the El Nido Valley. In one corner there was a desk and phone, in another a lamp and reading chair. *Your private place to think, or work, or whatever it is you do,* Diana had explained, her voice a bright trill that left Greg struggling yet again to read her. Something about his presence in El Nido clearly unnerved this woman, yet she appeared curiously driven to keep him in the valley. She'd even summoned her personal physician to tend to his head wound.

Greg sat down at the desk, then turned again to the foot-high pile of news articles that he'd found an hour before in a bottom drawer while casually exploring his temporary domain. Whether Diana had purposefully placed them there, or simply forgotten where she'd stored them, he could not say. All he knew was that the small weekly newspaper's accounts of how Sarah Trant came to be on death row made for interesting reading.

Once more, Greg leafed through them. He'd assembled what had been a haphazard pile into chronological order. Viewed that way, he could see that the story began—as Sarah said—not with the cranky old geologist Brewster Tomaz's murder, but months before, with the arrival of ModoCorp. With the arrival, to be exact, of Charles Whit, identified as founder and managing director of ModoCorp. Sarah had mentioned the company, but not the man. And she hadn't mentioned that the "gorgeous chunk of wilderness" they bought was a long-closed thirty-six-acre religious complex called Camp Mahrah. Greg studied the newspaper map that located this camp. Here's where he must have cracked up his car. Here's where the rifleman welcomed him to El Nido.

Greg kept reading. Fronted by a public relations team, Whit had showered El Nido with soaring but vague talk about a world-class health spa at Camp Mahrah. There'd been town hall meetings, slide shows, and what looked to be Whit's calculated insinuation into the community. Whit had bought a home in the rustic El Nido neighborhood called Woodland, originally developed by Edward Sanborn. He'd paid calls to bankers, small-business merchants, local civic leaders, the Lions Club. He'd made the circuit of various Sunday church services. He'd bought the grand champion hog at El Nido County's livestock auction. He'd contributed to the Little League, the Firemen's Association, the El Nido High School's "Project Graduation." He'd donated $500 toward a scholarship for the newly crowned Miss El Nido.

Most important, he'd hired Brewster Tomaz.

Greg had to admit that was an astute move. Tomaz, the articles made clear, was a well-known El Nido native, born and raised in the valley, amusing and cantankerous at once, and much appreciated for both traits. He'd lived alone almost his entire seventy-three years, yet nearly everyone considered his solitary nature a mark of hardy individualism rather than misanthropy. They particularly respected Tomaz for his unmatched knowledge of the region. He knew the valley's terrain as well as anyone. With Tomaz on board, ModoCorp had gained both respectability and instant roots in the community. Support for the health spa at Camp Mahrah gradually mounted.

Yet why would a man like Tomaz sign on with an outfit such as ModoCorp? Greg studied the geologist's photos, as if his face might offer an answer. He saw only an old man's withered scowl. Sarah was right; Tomaz did indeed resemble a prune. A bloated prune, with a broad sunburned forehead and a perpetual five-day beard. Colorful and eccentric and amusing, yes, but to Greg there also was a look of menace about him. In almost every photo, the crusty old coot's thin lips curled in a manner that suggested genuine contempt; one color snapshot revealed cold pale blue eyes aimed with distaste at a subject beyond the camera's range.

*Big plans for El Nido.* That's what Sarah had said. *Confrontations at the river, pushing and shoving.* In the later articles, Greg saw what she meant. ModoCorp, having won provisional approval to clear their land, ostensibly for fire-control purposes, had suddenly rolled in a bulldozer with no advance notice and cut a new road through state forestland. Then they'd fenced off the segment of a public hiking and equestrian trail that crossed a corner of Camp Mahrah. Finally, they'd started digging diversion channels where El Nido Creek bordered their property high in the foothills. It had been a dry year in El Nido, so even Brewster Tomaz's involvement couldn't keep a few eyebrows from rising over this threat to a central source of valley water. Only after Charles Whit made clear they intended merely to construct an auxiliary water supply, again for firefighting purposes, did the valley's anxiety wane. Not Sarah's, though.

Here, Greg saw, was where she really started waving her banner. Speeches at local Grange meetings, petitions for restraining orders, demonstrations at the entrance of Camp Mahrah, confrontations at the El Nido Creek diversion site—Sarah was always present, and usually alone. A majority of citizens were behind ModoCorp by then. Despite some trepidation, even El Nido's city fathers, pushed by merchants hungry for growing tourist dollars, had voted to support the planned health spa. Sarah's strident objections were offending just about the entire community.

Greg read on. There'd been several face-to-face encounters between Sarah and Brewster Tomaz. Once the two had even ended up in a shoving match in front of ModoCorp's bulldozer, and Sarah had evidently gotten the best of him. Greg cringed as he studied the photo of Tomaz sprawled in El Nido Creek that day; it looked too much like foreshadowing. ModoCorp had finally gone to the local magistrate's court seeking an injunction against her physical intrusions. There was no way around the matter: It appeared that Sarah by then was just about stalking the quaint old geologist.

Flipping through the clips, Greg reached the murder itself.

It happened just past dusk on a chilly December evening, not near Camp Mahrah, but rather, at the stretch of El Nido Creek that formed the southern boundary of Sanborn Park. There'd been a concert that night in the park, one of a monthly series offered free by the amateur El Nido Band. A commotion at the river was heard. Then Brewster Tomaz's body was found, floating facedown in the rippling water. Accidental drowning, it might have seemed at first. Until they turned the body over and saw the geologist's slashed throat.

From the accounts before Greg, it did not appear authorities took more than a few hours to arrest Sarah Trant. No wonder: Who else was known to be hounding the victim, who else was known to have pushed him into the river, who else in all the valley would slash a man's neck ear to ear? In her statements to police, Sarah readily admitted that she'd been down at the river, that she'd confronted and argued there with Brewster Tomaz, that she'd once again pushed Tomaz into the water. That was all, though. She'd run off after that, she insisted, and had never looked back.

Perhaps the jury might have believed her, perhaps not. It was hard to say, because before those twelve citizens could commence deliberating, a final surprise witness had stepped forward for the prosecution. A witness who claimed to have rushed to the dying geologist's side. A witness who claimed that she heard Brewster Tomaz, with his last breath, whisper: "Sarah did this, Sarah had a knife."

Greg once more studied the accompanying photo of the witness. She'd been five years younger then, the face a bit thinner, the hair not quite as gray. Looking at her high cheekbones and wide dark amused eyes, he could easily imagine her as a young woman driving men to distraction as she walked the streets of El Nido. Now she was unnerving him. . . . Just how, he wondered, did Diana Sanborn come to be the star prosecution witness who sealed Sarah Trant's fate?

"An interesting read?"

Greg looked up to see Alex Ramirez staring at him from

the doorway. The ranch foreman apparently had the run of Diana's house.

"A puzzling read," Greg said.

"Yes, I suspect it is for you."

"Not for you?"

Alex shrugged. "I'm a little closer to it."

"What do you mean?"

Alex showed nothing in his expression. "I just mean I'm from here, I'm from El Nido. Fourth generation. My family has worked this land—other people's land—for more than a century. I understand this valley as an outsider could not."

"You must understand the valley to grasp the meaning of this murder case?"

"It wouldn't hurt. It was a fight over development of the valley that led to this killing, and there have been many such fights before. Each has its own story . . . but there are patterns."

On impulse Greg said, "Tell me about this place. I want to know."

"It wouldn't be of interest to you."

"Yes it would."

"You think so?" Alex was studying him with curiosity.

"Yes."

Alex pulled up a chair, sat down. He'd needed little persuading. He spoke warmly now, plainly savoring the memories, and the chance to recount them.

The Chumash were El Nido's original inhabitants, he began. They lived in peace, eating grain and berries, acorns and fish. Didn't own the land, though. The missions held title, then the Mexican government, which began handing out parcels to political favorites. Rancho El Nido, almost eighteen thousand acres in all, went to Federico Alvera in 1837. Title changed hands a half-dozen times over the next quarter century. Speculators made quick profits, then moved on. For a time it looked as if El Nido would fall to progress. Entrepreneurs built health spas around the region's natural hot springs. Wildcatters sank oil wells in ravines where petroleum seeped from crevices. Eastern settlers fueled a frantic land rush, doubling property values within weeks, then doubling them again.

Alex's eyes gleamed with pleasure at the thought of what followed. "That boom in 1887 lasted just months. The health spas had to shut their doors for lack of business, and the prospectors withdrew for lack of oil. No one much minded in the valley. By the turn of the century, El Nido had returned to being what it is now."

"Which is . . . ?" Greg asked.

Alex looked at Greg as if he should know. "A forgotten valley," he said.

"When did Edward Sanborn show up?"

"Just about then. Around 1901, I'd say. Came from Michigan. Made a fortune there manufacturing ball bearings or something. He favored progress also, but of his own sort. Looked at what was just another dusty western village and hired an architect. They built that arcade on Main Street."

"Spanish-mission style," Greg said.

"That's right."

"The post office tower and the El Nido Valley Inn had the same architect?"

"Right again," Alex said.

"Then there's Sanborn Park," Greg said. "Sixty acres of woodland right in the middle of the village. Edward Sanborn's gift to the valley. My father called it 'the soul of El Nido.' "

Alex appeared to appreciate that description. "If Sanborn had let them," he said, "they would have renamed the whole town after him. When he died, he willed millions of dollars to all sorts of groups across the valley. Folks staged a county-wide celebration over that. Called it 'Sanborn Day.' "

"That's where the plaque came from? The one below his portrait?"

"Yes."

They both fell silent. Greg tried to sort out his thoughts.

"So Alex," he asked after a while. "What does all this history have to do with Brewster Tomaz's murder? You also have insights about that?"

"No . . . just questions."

"Such as?"

"Why you're here."

Greg felt a growing interest in this ranch foreman. "Certainly," he said, "your boss has explained."

"Explain more. What draws you to Sarah Trant's case?"

"I'm not drawn to it," Greg said. "I'll be leaving on Monday."

At that, Alex appeared confused. "You're not drawn to it?"

"Why should I be?"

Alex looked over his shoulder, then rose and reached to close the door to the room. He stepped toward Greg. "No reason, really . . ." He stopped, frowning. "You've seen the autopsy report, I assume? And the autopsy photos?"

Greg shook his head. "What's the point? A habeas petition is about procedural errors and constitutional violations. You don't reinvestigate murders in federal court. You don't redo the trial."

Alex backed toward the door. "I see. Of course. That's what I thought. No point. No point at all."

*No point at all.* Greg had heard those words before, connected to another case. A notorious case. Sitting alone at dusk in Diana Sanborn's guest office, the memory filled his mind. Not just to defend a mentally unstable killer, but to keep him from being arrested, to let him walk the streets of La Graciosa undetected—Greg had to agree with his critics, such was not a commonplace legal maneuver.

The phone call had come unexpectedly, at home one Sunday morning, almost five years before. Within minutes, he'd found himself standing in a gas station parking lot, listening to a gawky man in gray work clothes confess to an unsolved homicide. "I did it," Jason Pine reported shyly. "Killed that store clerk last night. Thought she was my ex-girlfriend. No point at all."

Greg never could figure out just why he didn't walk away right then. From news accounts, he knew about the shooting of Mary Ann Michaels, single mother of two little kids, up at the 7-Eleven on Crocker Highway. Itinerants on drugs usually committed that type of crime; only they would try to steal the few bucks not kept in a safe at a convenience store. Jason Pine didn't look like a druggie, though. With his unnerving smile and stiffly held arms and sideburns cut above his ears, Pine looked to Greg like a mental case. A mental case who had not yet managed to wipe out his ex-girlfriend.

By then, though, Pine also looked like his client. At least it seemed that way to Greg. He'd agreed to meet this man, he'd listened to his story. Greg felt ethically and legally bound to keep his client's confession confidential. Only if Pine directly threatened to kill someone could Greg inform authorities. Pine hadn't gone that far. He talked only of what he'd done to a store clerk, not what he might do to an ex-girlfriend.

Greg let him come to his office the next day. There Pine told his story at even greater length. He was thirty-three. He'd been under psychological treatment since he was fifteen. He'd stopped taking his Prozac and lithium after watching a TV counselor say drugs do bad things to you. He'd also stopped going to his therapist. He'd grown so lonely. That's why he tried to visit his former girlfriend. She ran him off. He drank beer all night, then started driving around, looking for her. Drove around until he came to that 7-Eleven. The clerk there was making a pot of coffee, just as his ex-girlfriend used to do. He pulled the trigger five times. He was horrified at what he'd done. He understood all too well he was ill. Sitting in bars, he watched everyone having a good time. He fantasized about being part of that. He knew he was different. He knew he was alone.

Greg scrawled on a yellow pad as Pine spoke. They would put him in prison, Greg knew. Pine was flat out crazy, but they'd put him behind bars forever if he talked. Better to get him committed to a hospital, get him examined. That would take him off the streets but still protect his rights. As long as the state asked for the exam, whatever Pine said to a doctor in the hospital was usable only on the issue of sanity, not guilt or innocence.

Goddamn Dennis Taylor. If only the Chumash County district attorney had agreed from the start to this plan, they wouldn't all have twisted in the wind for so long. Taylor wouldn't buy Greg's ploy, though. He had his own job, which was to build the best possible prosecutable case. He knew just how to do that, too—exploit Greg's desire to get his client off the streets. It became a high-stakes chess game. For two months, he and the DA two-stepped down their fine frightening line, Greg insisting he'd reveal his client's identity only for a hospital commitment, the DA insisting he'd take him only under arrest, each waiting for the other to blink.

"Monarch, forget it," Taylor snapped one day. "I'm not going to just pick up this guy and commit him based on your hearsay. I don't know who the guy is, even. Don't have a probable cause to hold him. If we got to trial, what's my case? Don't have one. You're a great lawyer, Greg, but how the hell you know this guy is crazy?"

Taylor rolled a pencil across his desk then, and looked out the window. "I believe there's a public-safety exception to the confidentiality privilege," he said. "If there's a threat to public safety, you can violate confidentiality. You can share this."

"Bull," Greg snorted. "Where'd you pull that out of?"

In the end, they'd called the hot line at the California state bar's board of professional responsibility. They'd laid out the deal to an ethics counselor, talking together on the speakerphone. Then they'd asked, Who's right? Is there a public-safety exception?

No doubt about it, the state expert declared. The defense attorney is right. There's no exception. Mr. Monarch can't betray his client.

Greg leafed through the El Nido directory, then picked up the phone and punched in the residential number of Reginald Dodge. By newspaper accounts, Dodge had served as Sarah Trant's defense counsel at her state murder trial. On this early Saturday evening, Greg couldn't imagine El Nido citizens being anywhere but home. In this case, at least, his intuition proved right. Dodge answered on the second ring.

"Dodge here," he said.

Greg tried to imagine this man on the other end of the phone line. A criminal defense attorney in a place such as El Nido must spend most of his time doing—what? Car radio thefts, dope smokers in Sanborn Park, the occasional domestic squabble, that's what filled the police blotter reprinted in the valley's weekly newspaper. A murder trial must have been an extraordinary experience for him. In fact, it likely had been his first and only.

"Mr. Dodge, my name is Greg Monarch. I'm a lawyer from La Graciosa, here in El Nido for the weekend—"

Dodge interrupted. "Yes, Mr. Monarch, so I've heard. This is a small town. Your arrival has been noted."

"Then you know I'm here because of Sarah Trant's habeas petition?"

In the silence that followed, Greg thought he could hear the clink of ice cubes in a glass.

"Yessir," Dodge finally replied. "That I know." His voice sounded overly hearty.

"I'm wondering if I might browse a bit through your case files. Just to get up to speed. Especially interested in the autopsy report and photos on Brewster Tomaz."

Again a silence, and the clink of ice cubes. "Well, now," Dodge began. He was having trouble forming his words. "That would be difficult. Five years ago, that trial was. Those files got stored away long ago. Not sure where, tell the truth. That would take a while, track all that down. You'd be long gone by then."

"Maybe not," Greg said. "I like the air here."

Dodge erupted in a spasm of coughing. When he stopped he made the gulping noise of a man hungry for oxygen. "Watch out for her, Monarch, watch out for that woman. Sarah Trant told me six different stories. Never knew what she'd be saying day to day."

"The autopsy report," Greg said. "Surely that's public record. It would be much easier getting it from you than from the DA."

"Don't have it. That's the honest truth. Gave it to the pathologist who was going to testify for the defense, so he could prepare his expert testimony. Never got it back."

"What do you mean 'going to testify'?"

A bitter laugh came from somewhere deep in Dodge's throat. "Well, he did testify. But it's a matter of debate whether it was for the defense."

"Who called him as a witness?"

It sounded as if Dodge were draining his glass. "The defense called him, Mr. Monarch. I called him."

Dr. Grant Montrose also answered his own phone when Greg punched in his number. "Yes, yes, this is Dr. Montrose," he snapped. "Who is this?"

The pathologist sounded like a busy man, or at least a harried one. He had a vague accent that Greg couldn't place.

"Greg Monarch here. I'm a lawyer from La Graciosa, here in El Nido for a day trying to help Sarah Trant with an appeal."

"What can I do for you, Mr. Monarch?" Montrose didn't sound any more surprised by his call than did Dodge.

"I need a copy of the autopsy report on Brewster Tomaz. Sarah's trial attorney tells me he sent his copy to you. Since for the time being at least I'm Sarah's lawyer, I'd like to get it back."

Montrose cleared his throat. Greg imagined someone rotund, with a pompous air and a monocle. Maybe a rug on his head.

"Well, Mr. Monarch," the pathologist said, "I don't know if I can give that to you. There are certain rules we have to follow. There's something called discovery, isn't there? If I just send you the autopsy report, we'd be going way outside that process."

Greg labored to keep his tone reasonable. "Dr. Montrose, I commend your concern about the discovery process. But the autopsy report and photographs would have come into the case even before the trial. They're part of the public record now. Sarah's lawyer had them, Sarah's lawyer gave them to you so you could prepare your testimony. They're actually part of Sarah's property, if you think about it. You just never got around to returning them."

A long pause. "Well, I don't know," Montrose said finally. "I don't think I can do this without getting the district attorney's approval. Why don't you just ask the DA for a copy?"

Greg stared out Diana's window toward the El Nido Valley. Dusk had turned to a pitch-black hue. He could no longer see where he was. Of course, he could call the DA. But why was this pathologist being so resistant?

"Dr. Montrose, wouldn't it be easier if you just pulled it from your files and sent me a copy?"

"Well, I don't know. We have to watch how we do these things. Anyway, I purge my files. Like everyone does. I may have thrown it away."

"Dr. Montrose, Sarah Trant needs the report and photos. What gives here? Why are you withholding them?"

Montrose's tone shifted now. Pomposity gave way to a certain high-pitched alarm. "Was she granted a new trial? Is that why you want this stuff?"

"No, not yet. But she's aiming for one." Greg could hear footsteps, as if Montrose were pacing about his phone. He continued. "Doctor, you were retained by Sarah Trant. You were given these documents by Sarah's lawyer."

"No!" Montrose cried. "No, I was not hired by Sarah Trant. I was hired by the state."

"Well now, you may have been paid by the state, Doctor, but you were paid to assist Sarah Trant."

"No, Mr. Monarch. I was paid by the state to analyze evidence fairly."

Greg tried to speak gently. Montrose, for all his bluster, sounded scared. "Why are you doing this, Doctor?"

Montrose lacked the polish to carry off what he was attempting. He couldn't contain himself any longer: "Because I've been directed by the DA's office not to release either the autopsy report or photos to you, that's why. I've been directed. I've been ordered."

"Who in the DA's office?" Greg asked.

"The district attorney himself. James Mashburn."

Greg stiffened in his chair. He'd lost track of affairs here in this remote valley. He'd thought Karl Jackson was still the DA. But that couldn't be, come to think of it. Jackson was a state judge now. *James Mashburn.* Greg had once known a lawyer by that name. A lawyer who'd left La Graciosa years ago for the inland valleys. For El Nido, in fact. Yes. It must be him.

Looking about in the darkened room, Greg now realized that Alex Ramirez was standing in the doorway, listening to his half of the conversation. Slowly, he placed the receiver back on the phone without bothering with farewells.

"Tell me, Alex," he said. "Just how big is this?"

# FOUR

Peering through the big picture window in his office, El Nido County District Attorney James Mashburn watched three laughing seven-year-old girls splash in the public fountain that fronted Sanborn Park. The fountain was an abstract free-form structure, but to Mashburn it looked like a woman bent over with one hand cupped, as if she were playing craps. He'd always wanted to hang big fake dice from her fingers.

"Mashburn, may I ask if you're listening to me?"

Slowly, the DA turned from the window. Sheriff Roy Rimmer's narrow, insistent face hadn't gone away. There it was still, floating in the air on the far side of the room. Mashburn had inherited that face when he first took office. By then Rimmer had been the El Nido County sheriff for a decade, and knew way too much about the valley to be ignored. The truth was, Mashburn needed Rimmer. Especially when he began, the DA had lacked a natural bent for the harsher aspects of prosecuting. He'd also lacked the grasp of El Nido that only a native possessed. Rimmer was his hammer. Also, his eyes and ears.

"Are you there, Jim?" Rimmer asked again. "Are you with me?"

Mashburn ran a hand through his salt-and-pepper beard. He was a sturdy man, pushing fifty now, with a high forehead, a perpetual frown, and dark wary eyes. "I'm here, Roy. Whether I'm with you is another matter."

"Okay, then. I'll settle for that right now. What I'm saying is, this Monarch fellow is out of control. Christ sake, look at these goddamn letters he's sending to the judge. Jesus. We have to respond, Jim. We have to do something to head this off."

As Rimmer talked, the DA thumbed again through Greg's correspondence. *This Monarch fellow.* To the sheriff, he was a stranger. Not to Mashburn, though. What he most recalled about Monarch was the way he drummed his fingers on the bar counter as they worked a pitcher of beer.

They'd never been friends. Not even colleagues, really. But for one summer they'd held a similar hand of cards. It must have been a dozen years ago. Mashburn still thought of those days with appreciation. He'd been on the other side then, working as a criminal defense attorney. His client, and Monarch's, were both targets of a Chumash County grand jury probe. The prosecutor thought one or the other might be the killer in a tangled drug deal gone wrong. The prosecutor had no real evidence, just a desire to charge someone. So he tried playing Monarch against Mashburn, dangling immunity, threatening death row, inviting either to deliver a client willing to sing. Usually, someone caved in such a situation, lunging after their self-interests. But not this time. One evening, Monarch hauled Mashburn to a funky old tavern called JB's Red Rooster, poured a vat of Graciosa Brew into him, and proposed they trust each other. For once, he urged, let's stand together.

What do you have in mind? Mashburn asked.

Monarch didn't answer at first. He tapped his fingers on the bar in that manner he had, humming along to the tune being pounded out by the piano player. Only after the music stopped did he turn back to Mashburn. A joint defense agreement, he said then. We negotiate a joint defense agreement.

It had been a clever suggestion, Mashburn had to admit. Each of them, in that way, could legitimately inform the other what the DA had been asking their client, and what their client had told the DA. Joint defense agreements invariably made it more difficult for authorities to flip a target. They countered the government's standard divide-and-conquer strategy in criminal cases.

"Helps level the playing field" was how Greg put it at JB's

that night. "All those case agents and detectives and prosecutors get to share information. Why don't we?"

Stonewalling, of course, was another way to put it. Circling the wagons. A conspiracy backing up the original conspiracy that triggered the initial investigation. A way for wrongdoers to learn whether their version of events was fitting with other witnesses'. As DA in El Nido County, Mashburn had been forced to deal with such ploys more than once. Goddamn frustrating as hell, that's how he saw them now.

Not back then, though. Back then, the Chumash County DA had no recourse but to let both their clients go. The two defense lawyers toasted their success with a hike at dusk into the Chumash Dunes. Not long after, Mashburn moved inland to El Nido and started on the path that led to the DA's office. He hadn't seen or heard from Monarch in more than a decade.

Mashburn turned his attention back to Greg's letters. He knew less than he should about this whole Sarah Trant situation. Brewster Tomaz had been murdered well before he took office. It had been his predecessor Karl Jackson's prosecution, and Sheriff Rimmer's investigation. Just as well, really. He didn't want his thumbprints on this one. The whole case gave off a bad odor. The stink was there even though Sarah Trant's guilt seemed perfectly obvious. Take the matter of footprints along the riverbank, for just one example. The police in their official reports described only those of Brewster Tomaz and Sarah Trant, but the forensic technician's account—which Mashburn found in the investigative file—also included mention of a third set. Boot prints, to be precise. The left boot had distinctive half-soled nail marks, rows of tacks pounded in diagonally across the half-sole. Those prints held obvious importance. Yet the defense attorney Reggie Dodge had never introduced them at trial. Mashburn suspected Dodge had never been told about them. Mashburn wondered what else Dodge hadn't been told.

With irritation, the DA tossed Monarch's letters back on a desk already filled with a jumble of documents. He could see the cause for Sheriff Rimmer's concern. Greg Monarch still knew how to play his hand. He'd gone home after his first weekend in El Nido but hadn't backed off. From Chumash County he'd fired off letters and phone calls for a good week. He wasn't representing Sarah Trant, he explained to those few willing to ask. He was just poking around, helping out for the moment.

His first letter had gone to Dr. Grant Montrose, the pathologist who'd testified for the defense at Sarah Trant's trial. *The purpose of this letter is to confirm our telephone conversation last Saturday. I called to ask if you would give me a copy of the autopsy report and photos on Brewster Tomaz. You refused. "I wasn't hired by Sarah Trant, I was hired by the state," you told me. You also told me that you'd been "ordered" by the El Nido County DA's office not to provide anything. If you feel that the above inaccurately reflects our conversation, please so inform me in writing within seventy-two hours. If I don't hear from you, I'll assume that you agree with everything set forth in this letter.*

It was, Mashburn knew, the last line, under Greg Monarch's signature, that most bothered Rimmer:

*cc: The Honorable Daniel Solman*

Monarch had copied this letter to the federal judge.

And not just that letter; he'd copied everything he'd written. Including letters he'd sent to Mashburn.

*Dear DA James Mashburn . . . I am writing to confirm certain instructions that your office has given to Dr. Montrose. The doctor has refused to provide me the autopsy report and photos on Brewster Tomaz. He has told me he can't do so without your express approval. He has also told me that you instructed him not to provide me those documents. I trust you agree with this account. If you disagree . . .*

Again, there at the bottom, was *cc: The Honorable Daniel Solman.*

Mashburn's mouth started to curve into an appreciative smile. Then he caught himself, and quickly shook all expression off his face. He was a professional, after all. A prosecutor. His job, like it or not, was to represent the state and fight this habeas petition. His job was to protect the conviction his colleagues had won. You have to take a stand to be a prosecutor, or else you never get anything done. You can't be a prosecutor if you shrink from making the calls or fighting the battles. And once you're fighting, you simply can't entertain the possibility of being wrong. You have to act certain, even if you aren't. Goddamn hardass certain.

"Okay, Roy," Mashburn said. "So if it were up to you, which it isn't, how would you respond?"

Rimmer paced across the room, his hands clasped behind his back. "We deny everything, first off. We simply must, Jim. We deny his accounts of our conversations."

Mashburn nodded, and turned back to his picture window. The little girls were still splashing in the fountain. "I see. Yes, of course. That makes perfect sense, Rimmer. Except for one thing. Monarch is absolutely right. He hasn't managed to get anything from us. We've stonewalled him quite nicely. How do we explain that?"

Rimmer flushed with exasperation. "We never said we wouldn't provide him documents, Jim. We told him we'd be happy to hand over anything, provided he had a subpoena."

Mashburn kept his eyes on the window. "Of course, you know Greg Monarch can't issue subpoenas, or, in this situation, get anyone else to issue them."

Rimmer walked to Mashburn's side. "Oh really?" he said. "I didn't realize that. I'm not a lawyer, after all."

Mashburn turned on him. "Let's cut the bullshit, Rimmer. For whatever reasons, you guys obviously rigged this one from start to finish, even though it looks like you damn well had the right target. You should have played it straight, you would have won anyway, but you didn't. Now I have to clean up your mess. That I'll do, because that's my goddamn job. I can't just blow this off. I'm not going to put a murderer back on the streets. But I don't like this game."

Rimmer offered a faint smile. "I knew I could count on you, Jim."

Mashburn picked up the letter he'd drafted in response to Greg Monarch's foray. Greg had kept it formal in his correspondence, not acknowledging any connection, so he'd done the same.

*Dear Mr. Monarch: I am by copy of this note advising Judge Solman that the information contained in your letter is utterly false. I have never directed Dr. Montrose to withhold documents from you. I question why you are copying the judge on correspondence of this nature. . . .*

"This ought to do it," the DA said.

As Rimmer scanned the page, his smile widened into a look of unbounded delight. "Very nice, Jim," he said. "Yes, this ought to do it."

At dusk, as the valley sky turned slowly from gold to pink, the bell atop the U.S. Post Office tower began to toll, signaling the start of the weekly El Nido Band concert. Parents watching their children splash in Sanborn Park's public fountain turned to listen. So did teenagers racing mountain bikes down the park's dirt pathways, and folks riding horses along its equestrian trail. Soon, families bearing beach chairs and coolers were strolling toward the open lawn that surrounded Sanborn Park's redwood bandstand. Under a spreading oak, two stout ladies from the Heritage Club sold homemade popcorn and lemonade.

It was the Sunday evening of Greg's second weekend in El Nido. His last evening, he told himself. He'd won postponements in his three most pressing cases, and farmed out other matters to Tim Ruthman, but the calls summoning him home kept coming. He couldn't stay away from La Graciosa for long. He'd stirred things up as much as he could here. He'd rattled a few cages, he'd alerted Judge Solman to the hint of funny business. Tomorrow he'd hand Sarah off to a local lawyer or the county public defender.

For the moment, though, he stood to one side of the concert bandstand, watching and remembering. There'd been past evenings like this one. He and his father, on a blanket, humming along to the unabashedly corny tunes. They'd felt a little odd, like spies intruding on a closed world. They'd also rolled their eyes in those moments when the town came close to reminding them of a stage set straight out of *The Music Man*. Yet they'd always been warmly welcomed by El Nido's natives, and that felt authentic. It was easy, Greg found now, to spot those longtime residents of El Nido amid the valley's more recent arrivals. They entered the park not with their families but in separate groups—men, women, children. From newspaper photos, Greg recognized El Nido's mayor, eighty-two-year-old Sam Rabe. He was leaning against one side of the bandstand, scratching his bristly white beard and spitting tobacco juice into the high grass. His wife Tammy Rabe loomed a few steps behind him. Greg could hear her booming out instructions on where to sit—"You over there, now don't argue, you to that corner"—as her two-inch silver crescent-moon earrings clanked and her five coral-and-turquoise rings glittered. Not one citizen passing her way objected to his assignment; at 205 pounds—much of those stuffed this evening into a pair of improbably tight Levi's—the mayor's wife did not brook much dispute.

Diana Sanborn had invited Greg to attend this concert. He'd dropped by Sanborn Ranch that morning, hoping for a final visit with the mistress of the house. He'd found her at the breakfast table, picking at a bowl of fresh blueberries. She'd seemed softer there in the morning light, less overpowering. She'd walked him around the ranch, explaining how she monitored the moods of her livestock. Pointing out the protected rise where she often watched the sunset, she talked of the peculiar pink light that filled El Nido's skies at dusk. "We will be doing our best imitation of *The Music Man* tonight in the park," she'd said finally, as if she'd overheard Greg and his father. "Come see for yourself." Now, returned to the public stage, wearing her trademark granny dress with boots and a cowboy hat, Diana stood in the center of the park crying *bless your heart* to half the population of El Nido. Greg watched her for a while, then glanced at the tall slender woman standing beside her. She was, Greg saw, already studying him.

She held his gaze. Her emerald dress matched her eyes. They were intriguing eyes, enormous and full of feeling. She had an oval face framed by a tangle of light brown hair, and the type of mouth that looked as if it were always on the edge of an arriving smile. She could be thirty, Greg thought, maybe thirty-five.

Diana waved him over. "Mr. Monarch, someone for you to meet," she sang out. "Jasmine Gest, Greg Monarch. Jas is quite our glamorous star. Writes articles and columns for the *El Nido News*. Also writes short stories and poems, which one day will surely be published. She even finds time to volunteer at El Nido's historical museum. She does it all. While Greg, alas"—here Diana whooped loudly—"is limited to being a lawyer."

Jas smiled faintly at Diana's words. She looked down, then up at Greg. "We've met already," she said.

It took Greg a moment to understand. Then he realized: Here was the woman he'd seen bathing at the river on his first morning in El Nido. She appeared as coolly composed now as she had then.

"You were an inspiring introduction to El Nido," he said.

Jas rolled her eyes. "You have me at a disadvantage. You know more about me than I know of you."

*Bless your heart, bless your heart.* From twenty yards away, they both heard Diana's cries. Without their noticing, she'd drifted off.

Jas kept looking at Greg. There was something in her manner, he thought. Something he recognized.

"Not bad," he said. "Even in a dress."

Jas winced. "Come on, you can do better than that."

"I was trying to be subtle."

"Oh yes, subtle indeed." Jas waved her hand above and behind her. "So subtle it went right over my head."

"I'll work on that."

She didn't respond. It took Greg a moment to realize that he'd lost Jasmine's attention. Following where her gaze had turned, he saw a big broad-shouldered man moving through the crowd. From his newspaper photos, Greg recognized Charles Whit. The managing director of ModoCorp was looking over the heads of those around him, surveying the crowd. Whit had never left El Nido after Brewster Tomaz's death, even though the murder appeared to have derailed his plans. He still talked occasionally about a world-class health mecca, but he no longer made any effort to get it built. *When the time is right,* he told folks now. Those who probed further heard complicated explanations about prohibitive economics in a limited market. To the merchants and bankers and anyone else in El Nido blessed with the least business sense, it sounded as if Whit no longer really intended to build a spa at Camp Mahrah. Given that, his continued residency in the valley represented something of a mystery.

Whit walked with a slight limp and carried a thick walnut cane, which he appeared to use mainly for clearing a path and pointing at folks. His face and neck and hands were the color of weathered copper, his light-gray eyes a striking contrast. The sun and wind had bleached his hair and wrinkled his skin, obscuring his age. He looked like a man who lived outdoors. He also looked like a man accustomed to giving orders. His eyes registered intelligence but not emotion; his cold steady smile had no root.

For all that, what most struck folks in El Nido about Whit was his eerily far-reaching knowledge of their community. He seemed to know something about almost everyone in town. How Ed Snell's grandpa drowned crossing the flooded El Nido Creek; how Constable Thomas Bell ended up locking himself in his own jail one night; how old George Garson robbed El Nido Bank in March 1916 while pretending to be showering at the adjacent Boxer Club. In the early going, Whit had entertained people by repeating such tales over beers at the Gaucho Tavern. Eventually, though, his mastery of their histories had started making some folks feel uneasy. So had the whiff of Christianity that in time began coloring Whit's conversation. *Christ is the center of my life,* he'd taken to declaring publicly in recent months. *If it's not right, I don't do it.* Such talk didn't sit very well with El Nido folks. Nor, for that matter, did Whit's insistent way of making you say hello back to him. The truth was, just about everything connected to Charles Whit had started to disturb a certain element in the valley.

"He irritates me, waving all friendly." It was the mayor's wife Tammy Rabe, who, with Diana Sanborn, had silently sidled up to where Greg now stood with Jas. "He did that at the public springs when I was swimming. 'Why don't you kiss my ass,' I said. He knows I don't want him waving at me."

Diana whooped and slapped Tammy's back. Just then, Whit spotted the three women. He grinned, and waggled his cane back and forth.

The El Nido Band began to tune up. They were an amateur group, pulled together from whichever local citizens had even the slightest bent for music. Teachers, carpenters, ranch hands, all sat side by side on the bandstand gripping their instruments. One played the trumpet, another the flute, a third kettledrums. There was a clarinet, an oboe, a bassoon, an alto sax, a French horn, a trombone, a tuba, a string bass. Families on the lawn started humming and clapping as the players launched tentatively into their first tune. A fourteen-year-old girl with straw-colored hair took the microphone. *Oh Nido, oh Nido, where the stars they shine so bright . . .*

"Charming little song, isn't it?" Charles Whit's voice was low and full of gravel. He was standing at Greg's elbow, watching the bandstand. "This your first visit to El Nido, Mr. Monarch?"

Greg studied the man before speaking. Whit's gray eyes seemed to have gone dead on him. He held his head at a truculent angle.

"I've visited before," Greg said finally. "But not for a while."

"What brings you here now?"

"I can't imagine you don't know. Everyone else seems to, even before I tell them."

"I wouldn't ask if I knew."

Greg turned back to the bandstand. "Okay, Mr. Whit. The sunshine brings me."

"Valley can get mighty hot."

"I'm partial to heat."

Whit smiled but didn't look amused. "Yes, so I hear.

Understand you're an attorney. Criminal defense. Pretty big name over in Chumash County."

"It's a small county," Greg pointed out. "Easy to stand out."

The band kicked into its second tune, drums and tuba leading the way. Greg thought he recognized "You'll Never Walk Alone." Whit leaned over, spoke into his ear. "You planning to stick around El Nido long, Mr. Monarch?"

"I haven't decided. What about you?"

Whit moved his mouth even closer to Greg's ear now. "I haven't decided either."

"Yet you still consider Camp Mahrah worth protecting."

"It's an expensive investment."

"Armed guards to protect an abandoned camp?"

A trace of humor began to creep into Whit's expression. "Just a caretaker, Mr. Monarch."

"A caretaker with a rifle and an attitude."

"My caretaker's manners are misleading. They're not what they seem."

"What ever is?"

Whit looked genuinely delighted. He reached out, placed a muscular hand on Greg's shoulder. "We may get along yet," he said.

As the band played on, Greg wandered through Sanborn Park, retreating ever farther from the music, losing himself finally in the thick stands of live oak that filled the park's lonely interior. He heard water running in the dark, then, with help from the moonlight, found the creek. He settled on its bank and leaned back.

What his father had most admired about the citizens of El Nido was their quiet, unforced sense of purpose. Growing oranges and running cattle involved certain verities and imperatives that left no room for much questioning. You rose, pulled on your boots, went to work, and saw the fruit of your labor. *It must keep the mind so steady,* his father would say with that fixed, inward look of his. Yet Dr. Paul A. Monarch never once thought of dwelling forever in what looked to be such an innocently bucolic province. El Nido to him was a place to visit and imagine, nothing more.

The crack of a twig drew Greg from his thoughts. He heard her voice before he could see her. "Thought I spotted you wander off this way," she said, sliding down the bank to where he sat. Jas Gest ran a hand through her hair. The moonlight glinted off her emerald-green eyes. "Figured maybe you could use some company."

"I came out here to think," Greg replied.

"About . . . ?"

He studied her. "What it must have been like," he said finally, "for you to watch Sarah Trant's trial."

Jas blinked with surprise. She settled on the bank next to Greg. "How do you know I watched the trial?"

"You pore through enough piles of old news clips, you start to notice the bylines."

"I'm delighted you noticed."

"What did *you* notice? I mean, back then, five years ago, at the trial?"

Jas shrugged. "Big deal to have a murder trial of any kind here in the valley, but this one looked open-and-shut. Sarah Trant was the obvious suspect. They had a watertight case against her."

"Why did you choose to write so much about it?"

"Trials fascinate me. Especially murder trials. They tell a lot about people."

"You want to know about people?"

"Not particularly," Jas said. "I just like occasional confirmation of my worldview."

"Which is . . . ?"

Jas drew lines in the dirt at the creek's edge. "Let's save that for later."

"You expect there'll be a later?"

"Oh yes."

Greg found he couldn't look away from her. "Tell me," he asked. "How long have you been in El Nido?"

She shook her head. "Enough about me, okay?"

"Okay," Greg said. "Let's talk about Sarah Trant, then."

"Yes. Let's."

"You know Sarah? You spent time with Sarah?"

"I know her, yes. Not well, though. We weren't close."

"What does that mean?"

"We took a couple of hikes together. Drinks at the Gaucho Tavern sometimes. Single women need to buddy up over there to fend off the cowboys."

Greg chose his next words carefully. "Tell me, Jasmine. . . . What was Sarah like with you?"

Despite his caution, irritation showed in Jas's eyes. "What are you asking? Whether she ever acted like a murderer?"

Greg tried again. "Just wanted to know her state of mind. The Sarah I know cycles in and out. Sometimes she's there with you, sometimes she's lost."

Jas's expression softened. "Yes," she agreed. "Yes, that's Sarah."

Greg pushed himself up off the riverbank. "You could help me."

"How so?"

"Show me where they found Brewster Tomaz's body. Show me the murder site."

They rose silently and stepped carefully along the creek's moonlit bank, winding farther into the woodland. In the distance, the El Nido Band's music grew ever fainter. *This valley of ours . . . This valley so serene . . .* The forest closed overhead, obscuring the moon. They slipped on round worn boulders at the water's edge, they tripped over tree roots bulging from the ground. Greg struggled to keep his bearings. It all felt so overgrown here, so untended. Looking straight ahead, he found himself staring directly into a towering wall of dense foliage. He heard no sound now but for the wind in the oaks. "Have we lost our way?" he asked.

Jas looked amused. She was standing at the edge of the bank, one hand on her hip. "Not yet, Counselor," she said. "That moment may come, but not yet." She waved her other hand toward the water. "Here's where they found Brewster. Facedown, half in the creek, half out."

Greg turned to where she was pointing. The low bank,

sheer elsewhere along the creek, here sloped gradually to the water, forming a flat crescent of bare earth. Like a small beach, Greg thought. From this spot a person could easily bend over and splash his face. Or dive in for a swim. That notion drew Greg's eyes to Jas. For a moment he recalled her rising from the creek on his first morning in El Nido. She looked at him as if she knew what he was thinking.

"Which way in the water?" he asked. "Head facing which way?"

"Head in the water, feet up on the bank."

Greg walked about, surveying the setting. He tried to imagine Sarah here, tried to imagine Sarah bent at the water's edge, slashing Brewster Tomaz's throat ear to ear. It wasn't that he couldn't conceive of someone committing such a brutal act; over the years his clients had exposed him to all manner of human possibility. It was the notion of Sarah doing it that gave him pause. From where could she have summoned not just the needed physical force but the savage volition?

Greg wished again that he had the autopsy report and photos. He hadn't expected to be denied for so long. Jim Mashburn still hadn't acquiesced. Such resistance, from a former colleague no less, aroused Greg's interest even more than the contents of the report itself.

"How could this have happened?" he asked Jas. "What was the state's theory at trial?"

"Theory at trial, Counselor? Or what happened? Which one?"

"Good point. I meant, what do they say Sarah did?"

Jas walked to his side, an arch look in her eyes. She suddenly pushed him hard, her open palms against his chest. Greg's feet slipped out from under him as he fell on the soft earth, landing on his back. In an instant Jas was on her knees above him, straddling his torso. Her curled right hand pounded into his hip once, twice, three times. Then the hand rose to his throat. Jas's fingernails dragged across his neck.

"That's how," she said. "You catch a man unawares, a woman Sarah's size could do just about anything."

Greg stared up at her. She still had him pinned. He could feel her thighs gripping his waist. “Brewster was a big man,” he said.

“An old big man.” Jas only now began to rise off of Greg. “An old man caught unawares.”

Greg grabbed her right hand to hold her where she was. He pulled her hand back to his hip. “Why did you first whack me here?”

Jas shrugged. “Don’t know. Just an impulse, I guess.”

Greg shifted his hips, moving against her. She stayed with him. “Kind of curious,” he said. “I don’t know many women capable of slashing a grown man’s throat.”

Jas finally pulled away from his grip and rose to her feet. “You should get out more.”

James Mashburn longed for a cigarette, but not even he, the elected district attorney of El Nido, could light up in the county building. They’d made the whole place smoke-free a year before. Reading the sentiment of the community, Mashburn hadn’t opposed the move publicly, but among associates he railed against the lunacies of the politically correct crowd. Why couldn’t he smoke a goddamn cigarette in the privacy of his own office? Did they fear he’d pollute Roy Rimmer’s virgin lungs as the sheriff sat plotting tactics half a football field down a hallway? It just didn’t make sense.

The peal of Mashburn’s private phone line interrupted his thoughts. From the blinking lights on the panel before him, he could see it was Sheriff Rimmer, calling from down that hallway. He reached for the phone, then dropped his hand and instead looked about his office. There were times when this place made him feel weary, but he liked being a prosecutor. He felt suited for his job, even if he had more or less tumbled into it. He’d started out thinking he’d be a cop, of all things. Working as an Army Airborne MP had been fun. Jumping out of planes, driving fast cars, having patrol dogs as partners—what more could a nineteen-year-old want? Police science in college had felt different, though. He’d quickly switched to an English major, figuring he’d go to law school and become a criminal defense attorney. That's exactly how it worked out, at least for a while. It wasn't a bad role—he liked playing the maverick, he liked working for himself—but he gradually tired of saving so many loathsome characters from their just desserts. Once he tried prosecuting, he found he enjoyed it. Trials and cops were better than writing briefs. Helping victims felt good.

The ringing had stopped for a moment. Now it began again. Reluctantly, Mashburn punched the speaker button. "Yes, Roy," he said. "What is it you want?"

"What do I want?" Rimmer was sputtering. "For one thing, Jim, it would be nice if you answered when I buzzed."

"Done. What else?"

"Some strategy. We need to talk."

Mashburn felt a headache coming on. Rimmer loved mapping strategy more than anyone he knew. "What's this about, Roy?"

"A visitor who wants to come see you."

"A visitor?"

"Yes, a visitor. Our friend from Chumash County has called. Greg Monarch wants a meeting."

Mashburn tried to fight off the feeling of dread tugging at him. He'd been avoiding Monarch daily, yet expecting him. "I suppose he's still after the autopsy documents."

"No doubt," Rimmer said. "Maybe more, though. We spotted him at the band concert last night. Watched him for a while. Then he and Jas Gest headed toward the creek."

"Jas Gest? . . . Where on the creek?"

"Where do you think? The murder site, Jim. The spot on the creek where Sarah Trant murdered Brewster Tomaz."

Mashburn studied a crack in the ceiling above him. You could phrase that differently, he thought. You could say simply, the spot where Tomaz was murdered. Most probably, Sarah Trant had killed Tomaz. Most certainly, in fact. Yet Mashburn had been around courtrooms long enough not to place excessive faith in a jury's verdict. "Oh, that spot," he said. "Where you conducted such a fair and thorough investigation."

"How about focusing, Jim? Greg Monarch wants to come

over this afternoon. We need to hold him off. Run him in circles while we get fortified. I'll tell him you're not available."

Mashburn flipped a pencil end to end, and watched it roll off his desk. He wondered how Greg had weathered the years. "But I am available," he said.

Not until he'd been ushered into the district attorney's office did Greg entirely recall his days with James Mashburn. There'd been so many cases since then, so many lawyers, so many moments. He'd needed the sight of Mashburn standing before him to bring everything back. Then he remembered clearly. He remembered a pitcher of Graciosa Brew at JB's, a corner table by the woodstove, a bargain struck as the piano player's wife, Shirley, sang in the background.

*How can I know you won't flip on me?* That's what Mashburn had asked him that night.

*Better to rely on me than the DA.* That's how he'd answered.

They'd raised glasses then. They'd trusted each other. And because they did, they'd stopped the Chumash County DA, Dennis Taylor. Whether they should have was another matter. Both their clients, as Greg recalled, had gone on to ever-larger drug deals and ever-more-monstrous acts of brutality.

"Welcome to El Nido County," Mashburn said. "Been a long time, Greg."

"Yes," Greg said. "A long time."

At Mashburn's side, Sheriff Rimmer looked back and forth at the two lawyers. "You know each other?"

"Many years ago," Mashburn said. "For just a month or two. A case in Chumash County."

"You've come a long way," Greg said. "You're a prosecutor now."

Mashburn pointed him to a seat and settled behind his desk. "Yes, I'm a prosecutor."

Greg tried to adjust to that notion. Back when he knew him, Mashburn had not seemed the type. He'd lacked the necessary hubris. He wasn't nearly absolute enough to rise before a jury, point to the defendant, and declare without question or qualm that this—this—is the face of a murderer. Maybe such conduct didn't require hubris, though. Maybe Mashburn needed only a pure and unconflicted heart to do his job.

"So what can we do for you, Monarch?"

The question, coming as it did from Sheriff Rimmer, annoyed Greg. He looked at Mashburn. "Is there a reason why the sheriff has joined us today?"

"I wasn't in office during the Trant trial," Mashburn said, "and my predecessor is now a state judge. So I asked Roy to be here because he handled the investigation."

"I see," Greg said. "Well, then. Maybe the sheriff can explain why the DA's office told Dr. Montrose he shouldn't give me Brewster Tomaz's autopsy report and photos unless he was subpoenaed."

Mashburn responded quickly and sharply. "That's not true, Greg, and we have so informed Judge Solman. When Dr. Montrose contacted me, I advised him that he was a defense witness at Trant's trial, and the DA's office therefore had no voice in how he dealt with you."

"That's not what Montrose told me," Greg said.

Mashburn started to answer, but Rimmer spoke first. "So as not to disappoint you, Monarch, perhaps we should make this perfectly clear right now. We're not going to relitigate a state murder trial. That's not what a federal habeas proceeding is about. Autopsy reports, crime-scene reports, none of that is relevant to a habeas action. You don't start poring over the basic evidence in a habeas. You know that, Monarch. Or you ought to."

Greg dipped his head in apology. "Forgive me, Sheriff. I'm not as well versed in habeas actions as you seem to be. Just feeling my way."

Rimmer nodded vigorously, as if they were in utter agreement. "You're not even representing Sarah Trant, as I understand it. You say you're just poking around. Yet you're copying all your letters to a federal judge. Just what exactly are you doing, Monarch?"

"I thought he'd be interested."

"You shouldn't be sending him letters like that."

Greg rose, walked to Jim Mashburn's desk, and put his

hand on the DA's phone. "You're right," he said. "Mail takes so much time. Let's call Judge Solman instead. Let's have a phone conference right now."

Rimmer stepped toward Greg, but Mashburn got to him first. "Okay, Greg," the DA said. "Okay."

From a file cabinet, Mashburn pulled out a large manila envelope and tossed it onto his desk. Greg picked it up. "Feels kind of thin, gentlemen."

Rimmer gripped the edge of the desk as if to keep himself steady. "That's everything. Autopsy report and photos, just as you asked. So let's not hail the judge once again, okay?"

Greg began to pull documents from the envelope. "What about crime-scene photos?"

"No." Rimmer was at Greg's side. "That's part of the investigative file. That's not part of what was handed over to the defense. And that's certainly not anything ripe for habeas review."

By now, Greg had the autopsy photos on the desk before him. He picked up one and looked more closely. "My God," he said.

Brewster Tomaz's neck wound went all the way to the bone of the spinal cord. It was almost six inches side to side, two inches in width, and at least an inch and a half deep. Everything inside Tomaz's throat appeared to have been severed.

"Nasty gash there," Greg said.

"Precisely," Rimmer replied. "That's what we call murder."

Greg scanned the six-page autopsy report. Then, more slowly, he reread the words on page two. *The slashing wound extends from the skin of the center of the throat down to the anterior surface of the vertebral column. This wound involves the skin, subcutaneous tissues, skeletal muscle, small vessels and nerves, and cuts the larynx in half in such a way that the epiglottis is separated from the rest of the larynx. The esophagus is also cut completely. . . . However, the wound does not involve the carotid arteries. . . .*

Greg turned back to the photo. His father hadn't been a surgeon, just a plain country doctor serving La Graciosa for thirty-five years. But growing up in his home, Greg had learned a good deal about anatomy. The practice of criminal law had also, from time to time, provided him an education about the insides of dead people's bodies. He'd seen slashed throats before. He knew the location of the carotid artery, he knew what it looked like. Brewster's was cut in half.

"Think your coroner missed something," Greg said.

Mashburn frowned. "What are you talking about?"

"Looks to me like you have a cut carotid artery here. But your autopsy report says no."

"Autopsy was done by the county pathologist," Rimmer said. "Assisted by a throat specialist. You know more than they do?"

Greg flipped back through the autopsy report.

*There is moderate rigor mortis and no lividity. . . . The abdomen is scaphoid and on palpitation no organs are felt. . . . The upper portion of the left thigh shows a stab wound that ends in the bony tissues of the pelvis. . . .*

There it was, on page four. *The cardiovascular system is devoid of any blood and the vessels appear to be empty, confirming the fact that the decedent must have bled profusely preceding death. . . .*

"Mr. Tomaz lost all his blood," Greg said. "That usually means you've opened up a main vessel." He looked back at the photo. The blood around Tomaz was a bright red. "And the color of the blood indicates it's freshly oxygenated. Which means it came from an artery. An artery close to the heart."

Mashburn rose, walked around his desk, glanced at the photo. The DA appeared to need a cigarette. "What's your point, Greg? Why does this matter to you so much?"

Greg put a finger on the photo and ran it along the victim's throat. "The vagus and laryngeal nerves run up the neck right there, right beside the left carotid artery. If the left artery is severed, so are those nerves."

Rimmer slapped the desk with the palm of his hand. "So the nerves were cut. Cause of death for Tomaz was a cut throat, isn't that the point? Wouldn't you agree?"

"Yes, of course," Greg said. "I was just wondering. . . ."

"What were you wondering?" Mashburn asked. He looked as if he truly wanted to know.

"It's just that these nerves are rather important," Greg said.

"How so?"

"You need them to talk. Cutting those nerves makes speech immediately impossible."

"So?" Rimmer demanded. "So . . . ?"

"So what I'm wondering," Greg said, "is how a dying Brewster Tomaz could have told Diana Sanborn that 'Sarah did it.' "

Rimmer's face had turned putty white, yet his eyes still seethed. "You're not a doctor, Monarch. You're not an expert pathologist. We had one on the stand. He said Tomaz could have talked."

"Dr. Montrose?" Greg asked. "That would have been Dr. Montrose?"

Mashburn glanced at his sheriff. "What does it matter who it was, Greg? None of this is ripe for habeas. We didn't just have experts say he could talk, we had jurors agree. You don't get to retry a murder case at a federal habeas hearing. You know that, Greg. You're wasting your time."

Greg began stuffing the documents back into the manila envelope. Mashburn, he knew, had a point. Both Congress and the Supreme Court had been narrowing the habeas window for years. It was hard enough even to get a hearing. To actually win relief was almost impossible. To get a federal judge to review old evidence was unheard of. *Barefoot v. Estelle*—that no doubt was the Supreme Court decision Mashburn would wave around if they ever really got going on this. *Barefoot,* invoking the "presumption of finality," declared that "the role of federal habeas proceedings is secondary and limited. . . . Federal courts are not forums in which to relitigate trials."

Yet Greg wondered: What if—just possibly—Sarah really was innocent? What if, for once, he had a case he really ought to win?

It shouldn't matter, he knew that. Sarah had a right to defend herself even if guilty. A writ of habeas corpus allowed state prisoners to seek release not because they were innocent, but because the government had unfairly convicted them. Greg, though, cared little about unfair convictions. He'd had his fill of milking procedural errors and technical violations. He knew it was wrongheaded for any self-respecting defense attorney, but he cared only about actual innocence.

*Actual innocence.* That opened the federal courtroom door like no other claim. That opened all sorts of doors.

Greg tossed the manila envelope across the table to Mashburn. "You're right, Jim, no doubt I am wasting my time," he said, heading for the hallway. "But at least now I understand why you've been so protective of this autopsy report."

# FIVE

In the dark silence of her bed, Diana Sanborn twisted and turned restlessly, waiting for the night to end. As usual, it seemed to go on forever, trapping Diana in her memories.

They weren't all bad ones. All these years later, so much about growing up in El Nido still warmed her insides. Sharing a saddle with her grandfather when she was five, riding with his thick arms wrapped tightly around her. Owning her own mare at twelve. Going to May Day parties, sitting in the little brick schoolhouse. Listening to the stentorian if slightly off-key village blacksmith lead Sunday choir. Glimpsing a pair of booted feet sticking out from under the swinging door at Barney's Saloon, proof positive of an actual barroom shoot-out. Watching the first coming of the Southern Pacific train, rolling along the new sixteen-mile El Nido spur, heralded by trumpets and grand parties.

Diana often used to ride her mare Candy out to meet the train. One day when she didn't get to the stables fast enough, Candy took off on her own at the sound of the railroad's whistle. Diana found her down by the station, without rider or saddle, dutifully greeting passengers. Such a sight never fazed those who rode the El Nido spur. They were accustomed to all manner of irregularity. Sometimes the railroad engineers halted the train in the middle of fields to go duck hunting. Sometimes they made unscheduled stops to pick up passengers near their farms. Sometimes they let everyone pile out to pick apricots.

El Nido meant "the nest" in Spanish, and that's how Diana, growing up, had felt about her valley. She couldn't remember precisely when she lost that feeling of protection. It had vanished in increments—beginning no doubt with Thanksgiving Day, the year she was eight.

It was, as she recalled, the coldest day of a frigid winter. Icy rain had fallen in the valley the night before; at day's break, snow lay heavily on the mountaintops. As usual Diana's parents were somewhere else, traveling in Europe, and her grandfather had business in San Francisco. So she spent the holiday with the Halder family. The Halders lived not far from the Sanborn ranch, their home set in an abundant orange orchard at the foot of the La Luna Mountain Range. Diana loved that home, where a half-dozen children were always scrambling about. Jenny Halder, just a month younger than Diana, was her best friend. For hours on end, they played together in worlds entirely of their own creation.

The Halders' ten-year-old boy, Kenny, was the one who first started talking about the snow that Thanksgiving morning. He wanted to roll in the bright white drifts covering the ridge above the Halder residence. After much begging, his older brother Charles agreed to take him up the slope. No more than a mile trek; they'd be back well before dinner. Jenny decided to join them, but Diana, helping Mrs. Halder roll out a blueberry pie, chose to stay in the warm kitchen. Jenny giggled and waved at her as she left the house. Three bustling hours passed, with the Thanksgiving feast almost ready to serve, before the Halders grasped that the children hadn't returned. Calls were made, alarms rung, a search team formed. Not until early next morning did they find the tracks in the snow where the trio had stopped and played. Not until midmorning did they find the three children's bodies at the bottom of Shady Canyon. They sat huddled together, frozen to death, the Halder home barely visible in the distance.

Kenny had slipped and broken an ankle, that's what the coroner eventually decided. He couldn't walk. Charles had carried him a ways, then stopped to rest. He'd taken off his own coat and wrapped it about his little brother. Jenny had curled up on Charles's lap. Then they'd grown drowsy as the chill air slowed their blood. Gradually, gently, they'd fallen asleep.

Diana roused herself and glanced over at the clock atop her nightstand. With relief she saw it was, at last, five. A reasonable time to rise; her usual time to rise.

Diana climbed out of bed and moved to the window that looked out on the valley. She yanked open the thick, heavy drapes. Sunrise, her old friend. The brightening sky so cool and light and full of promise. El Nido followed an east-west configuration, uncommon in this reach of the California coast, where most ranges trended north-south. That, as Diana never tired of explaining to visitors, was why they enjoyed such exceptional sunshine for a deep valley. Gentle now in the early morning, lingering later in the pink-hued evening skies—Diana treasured the valley's light more than anything in her life.

She wrapped a soft terry-cloth robe about her and settled at a small oak desk in the corner of her bedroom. From a drawer she pulled out a thick leather-bound journal. Only here at dawn did she find it possible to put her thoughts on paper. She wrote almost every morning. At times she focused on recent events, at times distant ones, but always she sought understanding for how she now felt. Today she tried to record her memories of when El Nido began to change. She wrote slowly, laboring over her words, pausing often. After a while, she put down her pen and reached for a hairbrush. So much remained confusing. In her own mind, it was after Jenny died that the mood in El Nido shifted. Yet she understood this was her own particularly narrow way of viewing matters. For the grown-ups, other incidents certainly cast longer shadows.

Some happened well before her time, at the turn of the century or before. From her grandfather's stories, Diana knew there once came a big bearded man, digging holes. Then a rush of others, full of all sorts of plans for developing the valley. None of them lasted, of course. Eventually, Edward Sanborn and his esteemed Committee of Ten managed to quiet everything down; those they called "the demons of discord" all departed. Yet the demons left a lasting impact. Even as a ten-year-old, Diana was aware that certain folks turned their heads or looked down as they passed each other along the Main Street arcade. Conversations would begin with homey ebullience, then at mention of one thing or another, trail off. People who were once content, it seemed to Diana, had soured just a little.

They'd saved El Nido. That's what her grandfather always reminded her. El Nido hadn't been ruined.

Nor would it be ruined now, she told herself. Diana picked up her pen again. Before she could resume writing, a knock at her bedroom door interrupted the mistress of Sanborn Ranch. "Come on in, Alex, I'm decent," Diana called out.

Her foreman walked in balancing a tray in one hand. On it was Diana's customary breakfast—a pot of herbal tea, a glass of juice freshly squeezed from El Nido Valley oranges, and dry wheat toast. Alex put the tray at Diana's side. "Morning," he said. "I'm off to mend fence today up near the Signal Trail ravine, but thought you'd want to hear the news first."

Diana poured the tea, squeezed in a touch of honey, stirred. "By all means."

Alex placed a cloth napkin by her side. "It looks like Greg Monarch is going to stay," he said.

Diana kept stirring her tea. "Stay? Whatever do you mean?"

"Stay on the case, I mean. Represent Sarah Trant."

The cup in Diana's hand wobbled; tea spilled on the table. She grabbed the napkin and began rubbing the spot. Then her hand stilled, and she sat silently, staring out her window at a small herd of cattle. Greg Monarch's arrival in El Nido had alarmed her from that very first morning. Yet she had not wanted him to leave. Such conflict was no stranger to Diana, and also no comfort. Echoes from all quarters and all eras regularly competed for her attention. As usual, her grandfather spoke loudest. Diana pointed to the phone. "We certainly need to defuse Mr. Monarch, don't we now? Dial up Sheriff Rimmer, will you, Alex, please?"

Alex didn't move.

"Do it, Alex," Diana ordered. "Call the sheriff."

Still, the foreman stood where he was. He looked hard at her. "Why?" he asked.

Diana searched for an answer. For a moment, she considered wrapping her response in anger. *Such insolence, Alex.* But she and her foreman had been through too much together for posturing. "We've been over all this before," she finally said. "I'm counting on you, Alex."

He picked up the receiver. Not until the phone was ringing in his ear did Diana change her mind. She reached over then and pressed down the receiver buttons. The loudest voice, Diana had decided, couldn't drown out all the others. "Bless your heart, Alex," she said. "Let's not make that call just now."

Alex showed no expression as he put down the handset. "What about Greg Monarch?" he asked.

"Yes," Diana replied. "What about Greg Monarch?"

This time they brought Sarah to the attorney's conference room in handcuffs. The prison guard shrugged when Greg questioned their necessity. "She's a dangerous lady," he explained. "Dangerous to all of us."

Sarah didn't respond. She'd been dancing in her cell when they came to get her. Dancing and singing. *Summertime, and the living is easy . . .* She knew the guards had been watching, but didn't care. It made her feel powerful in a way. She swayed and tossed her hair, let her shift climb up her thigh. Through the two small windows, she could see the guards tugging at their trousers and shifting on their feet. Powerful, yes. That's how she felt. Even free.

"Sarah, I've decided to represent you," Greg said. "I've decided I'll help you with this habeas petition."

Sarah stared blankly at him. "Ah," she offered. "Well, now."

Greg leaned forward. "You hear me, Sarah?"

Sarah allowed a winsome smile to spread slowly across her face. She reached for Greg's hand. It had been so easy to draw him in those many years ago. He'd been so ready to let go. To choose danger and abandon over cautious endurance. To be foolish rather than dead. He'd made it to shore since then, she could see that easily enough. Now he hung back, at least from her. She felt so tempted to roil him once more, to knock him off balance. To let him feel again her disarray . . . hers, and his too. *Here's to the crazy ones, Greg. The misfits and troublemakers. What's the proper template, anyway? What's normal? Who's to say?*

And yet . . . she couldn't do that to Greg. She felt too protective of him. Disorder wasn't in his best interests these days. She admired his focused drive, his refusal to compromise or unravel. She respected his carefulness about human relations and other people's lives. She'd grown so tired of weak men whining in coffee shops to her. She loved Greg for being different from all the others. Besides—she needed a first-rate lawyer just now, not a partner in chaos.

"Yes, of course I hear you," Sarah replied. "You're going to rescue me. Isn't that what you said? How nice, after all these years."

Greg stared at their entwined hands. "Can't promise a rescue, Sarah. My obligations will keep me in La Graciosa much of the time, and habeas pleas are remote long shots anyway. Just going to be your lawyer. We'll try our best."

Sarah began caressing his hand. Then she lifted his fingers to her lips. "Yes, our best," she murmured. "Our very best."

Through the window, the guard was staring intently at them. Greg pulled his hand from Sarah's grasp. "Listen carefully," he said. "I tried to visit your trial attorney, Reggie Dodge, but couldn't get to him. Bedridden and feverish, his wife says. Maybe pneumonia. So I really need you. Talk to me about Diana Sanborn. Why would she pin Brewster Tomaz's murder on you? Why would she say she heard Tomaz making a dying declaration?"

Sarah ran a hand through her thick dark hair. "Why indeed?"

"Do you know Diana? What's your connection?"

Sarah started to answer, then stopped. An image of Diana on horseback filled her mind. That's how they'd met. Sarah on her knees, Diana atop a spirited roan. A cowgirl, that's what Sarah had fancied herself when she signed on at the Sanborn Ranch. Alex Ramirez had assured her she could handle the job. He'd assured her she would get the hang of waking before dawn to milk the cows, then laying the kitchen fire and starting breakfast for all the hands. She'd been at it for three weeks when Diana rode up one day.

"You're not cut out for this type of work," Diana barked. "Come on in the house."

They talked that first morning about El Nido. The boom and bust of a century before, Diana's grandfather, dry oil wells, Modo-Corp's plans, Charles Whit and Brewster Tomaz. Diana liked her spirit right off, her spirit and what Diana called her "passion to preserve." Diana wanted Sarah to be her special aide in the continuing struggle to protect El Nido. Diana's eyes blazed when she talked of this struggle. Some people felt overwhelmed in her presence, overwhelmed by her grand enthusiasms. Not Sarah, though. Diana's example reminded her how to stride down streets by herself, how to take everything in, how to imagine all sorts of stories and notions. Diana returned to her a sense of bravado. Diana saw her and heard her; Diana understood her. Maybe too well, it was true. Sometimes Sarah felt at Diana's mercy. Those moments always passed, though. Diana helped quiet the noise in her mind. Diana helped still the voices.

*Keep up the fight . . . resist the temptation to turn inward.* That was Diana's clarion call. Sometimes the "fight" seemed to imply something abstract and universal. Other times it sounded as if Diana were talking specifically about El Nido. She'd grown so tired of people being mistreated, Diana told Sarah over and over. Especially because of money. *Where there's a possibility of making millions, you can justify anything. But some things are right, some things are wrong. Always will be. When you victimize people for your own gain, that's wrong. Always will be.*

Sarah felt like standing and applauding sometimes when Diana talked. Sarah felt like doing anything for her.

"So you want to know my connection to Diana Sanborn?"

Sarah shot Greg a look full of challenge. "That's hard to describe. I worked on her ranch for a while. We talked sometimes. She urged me not to seek insulation from the world. What do you think of such advice, Gregory?"

He shifted in his chair. It had been a recurrent theme in their time together: Sarah's insatiable appetite for exposure. *Let's go for it, Greg. We can have it all.* Truth was, he'd felt the same; her passions roused his own. Too much so, on occasion. Her turmoil matched something within himself, forming a combustible mix. Together they were volatile, turbulent. They could argue over anything—which friends to visit, how to spend the weekend—but the subtext was always the drive to define themselves. One night in the car she whacked him across the head so hard he almost drove off the road; another night, at a beach party, he straight-armed her into a trash can before an audience of dozens. They reconciled with equal fervor: Using her key to his cottage, she'd crawl into his bed just before dawn, her voice thick, her eyes half closed with desire. They were addicted to each other, caught in an endless, compulsive cycle of embrace and retreat, ardor and combat. He'd had to seal himself off from her finally. Either that, or lose his mind.

"Sounds like a smart idea to me," he said. "Sounds like Diana Sanborn understands you."

"Understands me." Sarah chewed on those words. "Understands me," she said again.

Greg tried to seize the opening. "Given your connection with her, why would she say she heard Brewster Tomaz's dying declaration?"

"Perhaps because it's true. Perhaps because she did hear him."

"I don't think that's possible."

"What you think doesn't matter, Greg. My own expert witness said differently. My own witness, right at my trial."

"Why is that, Sarah? Why did Dr. Montrose flip on you?"

"Who knows."

"I need your help here, Sarah, if you want mine. We have six months, just half a year."

Sarah studied the floor. "I guess the prosecutor got to Dr. Montrose. That's what Reggie told me."

"How so? What happened?"

"I . . . I don't know. That's just what Reggie said."

"What else do you remember, Sarah?"

She pulled back from him. "Why . . . what for?"

"We have a chance here, Sarah."

"No. There's no chance."

"Yes, Sarah."

Tears rolled down Sarah's cheeks. Something wild showed in her eyes. "You're not going away this time?"

Greg hesitated, trying to craft an honest answer. "No," he said finally. "I'm not going away."

Alex Ramirez asked Pablo to move by gently squeezing with his thighs. The whiskey-brown quarter horse had a lot of personality, but was in a cooperative mood today. He stepped toward the dozen heifers cringing before them. Alex lazily flicked the end of a coiled rope. He felt more at home in this moment than in any other his days offered.

Alex's father, and his father before him, had been among the proud California *vaqueros* who showed the others how to manage cattle in the New World. It was not an easy task. Lacking the proper grasses or hemp for rope, they made their own rawhide *reatas*; to rope cattle with these *reatas* required months of practice. Then you needed the right horse. *Quebrar el Caballo*—to break the horse—did not mean to break the spirit of the horse but to train it for the uses for which the rider might need it. The horse a rider chose for the day would depend on whether he planned to be roping, rodeoing, or cutting beef.

Patience, practice, observation—all were needed to earn the name *vaquero*. So was a particular way of looking at the world. Alex's grandfather, who was said to have roped three grizzlies in one day with nothing but his *reata*, often told him: A *vaquero* had a way of believing that if something went haywire he was lucky it wasn't worse, and if things went right, he was also lucky.

As he herded the cows into the Sanborn Ranch corral, Alex reminded himself of his grandfather's saying. Yes, that was the way to look at Brewster Tomaz's murder and Sarah Trant's prosecution. Things could have been worse. Brewster Tomaz could have lived, for instance. The notion roiled Alex. Never had a man so offended him. In middle age, Tomaz at least had managed to season his cranky bombast with lively stories about the valley, thereby winning considerable favor in El Nido. But in his later years, an intractable bile seeped into him that—to Alex's mind, at least—no narrative could redeem. Tomaz acquired pounds and wrinkles and flaps of skin, and in his expression, recurring traces of disdain. He showed up everywhere, at town meetings and park concerts and pancake breakfasts, as if he were an occupying army. He spoke little at these gatherings, mainly watching with blank pale-blue eyes. Many still respected him from a careful distance, yet even Diana Sanborn shrank from him in public. Particularly Diana.

"Hey there."

Alex started at the sight of Greg Monarch standing by the corral fence, then quickly regained his composure. He popped a toothpick between his teeth and rode toward Greg. "Hey there," he said back.

"I was looking for the mistress of the house. But no one answered at the front door."

Alex nodded, chewed on his toothpick, pushed back his straw hat. "Well, then," he said, "I guess she's not home."

Greg reached over and patted Alex's horse on his sweaty neck. Minutes before, pounding on the thick oak double doors of the main ranch house, he'd sensed someone inside watching him. He'd stepped back after a while and looked up. A pair of second-story window shutters stood open; what appeared to be a shadow played on the edge of a pale blue curtain that fluttered slowly in the wind.

"Either that," Greg said, "or maybe she's just not available?"

Alex offered a shrug that suggested he was not inclined to bicker over words. "Or not available," he agreed.

"I was hoping to get some information."

Alex glanced over at the main house. For a moment, he tugged at his saddle's straps. Then he pulled the toothpick from his mouth and tossed it to the ground. "So you want to talk to me instead?"

They sat on great blocks of hay in the barn. Outside, a hot breeze rustled through the bright sun-drenched valley; in here, all was cool and dim. "You looked quite at home," Greg began, pointing to the corral. "That is an art."

Alex accepted the praise with ease. "First you need to get your ideas across to your horse. I learned from my ancestors."

Greg searched his memory. "*Jineta*—isn't that what it's called?"

Alex smiled faintly at this reference to a centuries-old heritage of horse training. "Yes, that's right. My great-uncle Felipe often used that word." Then he added, "I hear you are staying. I hear you are Sarah Trant's lawyer."

"Looks that way."

"So now you're drawn to this case?"

"You could say that." Greg studied Alex. The foreman, so laconic and self-assured, held himself as if he owned the valley. "I'm trying to understand what happened here," Greg continued. "Five years ago. When Brewster Tomaz was killed, when Sarah was arrested."

"It's not complicated. People here don't like development much, but took a liking to the idea of a health spa at Camp Mahrah instead of something like an industrial plant. Sarah Trant didn't share that liking. Started acting really *loca*. Shouting, pushing, demonstrating. Brewster was her biggest target. Harassed him like crazy. When he turns up floating in the river with a slashed throat, it was obvious who did it. Jury stayed out, what, forty minutes?"

"I think it was forty-five."

"There you go."

Greg plucked at the bale of hay he sat on. "Tell me about Charles Whit and ModoCorp."

"Whit's a mighty sharp fellow. Mighty impressive . . . Can't say the same about his buddies, though."

"How so?"

"When Whit first came to town, he had a skinny young guy and a fat old guy with him. Public relations team, he called them. Hell. Maybe they do good with pencil and paper, but when they got out here in the country, they didn't know much. They tried to drive a Suburban across a creek that I row across. I know I can't cross water in a motor vehicle."

Alex paused, shook his head, continued. "This was middle of summer, pretty hot. The fat one is about 220 pounds, I'd say. Pretty round. Clearly he's sat at a desk a long time. No doubt has a four-year college degree. He walked a mile to ask me for help. I went to pull him out. That skinny fellow was waiting for us. I gave him a chain. He walks out in the water, hooks it to that nice chrome bumper. I tell him, someone will be mad when I yank that bumper off. Better hook it to the frame instead."

Alex pushed his straw hat to the back of his head, nodding at Greg. "That little skinny fella. He probably has a four-year degree too."

Greg stifled a smile. "Tell me about Diana and Sarah."

"What's to tell?"

"A good deal, I think."

Alex fell silent. The heel of his boots began to dig into the bale of hay. "That's not something I know about," he said finally.

"Why?"

Alex worked some more at the bale. "They spent time together alone."

"They were friends?"

"What can I say? One was the employer, the other a summer hire."

"Tell me about Diana's testimony. She heard Brewster Tomaz say that Sarah did it?"

Alex looked away. "Yes she did."

Greg spoke slowly now. "I think Sarah was framed. . . . I think you know that."

Alex removed his straw hat and started slapping it on his thigh. "Don't know any such thing."

"Then why did you tell me to get a look at the autopsy reports?"

"I just asked if you'd seen it. I was just talkin'. Diana Sanborn heard Brewster, that much is certain."

"How'd that happen?"

"Several of them, half a dozen I think, ran down from the concert when they heard the cries at the creek. The others stood back a few yards, but Diana, because she knew him, rushed to Brewster. Took him in her arms, cradled his head. That's when he talked. Low raspy whisper, hard to make out, but she heard him."

Alex stared hard at Greg and repeated: "She heard him."

Greg rose to leave. "Well, then," he said, "that's that."

It required only a drive through the valley to realize there was more than one El Nido. Beyond the hamlet, the scattering of modern ranch-style houses that now sat amid the lush citrus groves offered an oddly suburban retreat for professionals wishing to flee the coastal fog. Closer in, on dusty side streets at the edges of the central arcade, small faded wood-frame homes provided housing for a mix of laborers, artists, lost souls, and wizened seniors. To the east, vast spreads reached toward Upper El Nido, some working ranches filled with livestock, others the estates of gentlemen farmers who, as a hobby, irrigated row after row of fruit trees. Such different stations and ways of life produced a certain tension, but not as much as an outsider might expect. Shared values, not obvious divisions, were what most colored the regular afternoon gatherings in Sanborn Park.

There, off to one side of the bandstand, Mayor Sam Rabe and his wife, Tammy, held court daily. El Nido had no smoke-filled backrooms. The mayor dispensed licenses and permits right on the sloping lawn, while citizens gave him a piece of their mind. Unneeded stop signs, speeding cars, blocked drainage ditches—whatever annoyed you received immediate attention, and often resolution.

An hour after his visit with Alex Ramirez, Greg sat on a bench by the Sanborn Park bandstand, listening to that day's litany of complaints. The town's beautification statute irritated one red-faced homeowner, who wondered whether he needed the city council's permission to paint his house. A vandal's theft of flowers and ornaments from the 150-year-old El Nido cemetery dismayed an elderly couple. The biggest ruckus came from a half-dozen citizens enraged over a rancher's newly built fence across a popular hiking trail. To Greg the six protesters, varying in age and manner, appeared to be a cross section of the El Nido community. Nothing, he reasoned, could unite these folks like a blocked hiking trail.

"May I join you?"

Greg looked up to see Jasmine Gest standing before him. She sat down before he could answer. "Word is, you're staying," she said. "You're going to handle Sarah's appeal."

"That's right."

"Well, then, maybe I can help."

Greg studied Jas. She acted so sure of herself, so comfortable in her world. He sensed something else, though. "Why do you want to help?"

"For one thing, I know Sarah."

"You weren't close. That's what you told me."

"I know her, though."

"You two don't seem to have much in common."

"You have X-ray eyes? You can see straight inside us?"

"I think so."

Jas appeared intrigued by the notion. She faced him straight on now. "Yes, I think so too. . . . Maybe I should wear lead underwear or something."

"Or maybe I should look away."

"No. . . . Don't do that."

Greg tried to regain his train of thought. "Okay, then . . . We were talking about Sarah. Could you explain a bit about Sarah here in the valley?"

Jas took her time, watching Tammy Rabe smother an El Nido citizen with a bear hug. Then she said, "Sarah didn't understand

El Nido. She caught the love of nature here but didn't see that underneath it, just about everyone is a landowner. Everyone has an investment. Shopping centers and car dealerships may be a sin to these people, but El Nido needs something to goose its economy. Just ask the poor merchants under the Arcade."

"A health spa brings in tourists with thick wallets."

"Precisely. Sarah missed that. Whit and ModoCorp were the devil to her. She didn't realize they were potential saviors to lots of people here."

"No one told her?"

"They tried. I tried. Jesus. You should have seen her this one night at the Gaucho Tavern. Really decked out, by the way. A drop-dead-sexy minidress. Dancing with the cowboys, singing, having a grand old time. She and the cowboys. Then Sarah sees Brewster Tomaz over in a corner booth with Charles Whit. Rushes over, starts in on them. Tomaz laughs and says something crude. So she picks up a glass of whiskey and tosses it in his face. If I hadn't hustled her out of there then, I don't know what would have happened."

Tammy Rabe was waving a finger in someone's face now. Sam Rabe looked as if he were taking a nap. "Tell me, Jas," Greg asked. "Were there other times you saw Sarah attack Tomaz like that?"

Jas glared. "What difference does that make? She has rights, Greg. No matter what, she still deserves a fair shake in court. She still deserves your help."

The sun hung low in the El Nido sky by the time Greg left Sanborn Park. He meant to return to La Graciosa this evening, and his cottage on Graciosa Creek. Both his law practice and his friends beckoned. There'd been three messages on his voice mail from Tim Ruthman, who was covering for him on a drug bust, and two from his buddy Jimmy O'Brien, urging his company on a fishing trip. *Come on, Monarch, the bass are practically jumping into the boat. . . .* Then there'd been the reminder from Cindy Seaman over at the county probation department. *We're supposed to have dinner to-*

*gether one night this week. . . . You didn't forget, now, did you, Gregory?* He hadn't. First, though, he had one more stop in El Nido. He drove east through the village, past the arcade and post office, plunging quickly into the citrus groves. Where the road curved right to Sanborn Ranch, he instead turned left, onto a gravel path that climbed into the foothills on the north side of the valley.

If only Sarah were really innocent, Greg thought. He so much wanted her to be innocent. So much needed her to be innocent. Sarah was unstable, Sarah acted crazy, but that alone didn't make her a killer. El Nido regarded her as a killer, that's what made her one. . . . And yet, he had to admit . . . Sarah was capable of irrational acts. He'd seen enough in their time together. There'd been moments when she utterly alarmed him. There'd been moments when he couldn't begin to explain what she was doing.

Greg had reached the higher foothills now, in the rugged far end of the valley. Upper El Nido looked to him like the eroded course of an ancient stream. A ridge dotted with purple lupine and a scattered stand of live oaks separated it from the main valley. Facing west down the length of the basin, Greg gazed at foothills thick with cottonwood and white alder and sycamore, ceanothus and sage and manzanita. Closer, in the twilight, he saw a fast-moving creek tumbling from on high and bending sharply eastward, its banks decorated with strange black bands. Beyond, an emerald meadow shone through the open forest. Here was the El Nido of old, the El Nido that Greg had hiked with his father, the El Nido where Greg came to know his father.

*Old Alder Road.* Greg spotted the sign he'd been searching for. He turned down what seemed more a path than a road. After a quarter mile, he parked and began to hike into a narrow wooded canyon. Hearing the earth crunch under his feet, he looked down and saw he was again walking on black asphaltum. Oil oozing from cracks in the canyon walls had hardened into something that suggested a volcanic lava flow. Greg spotted the bones of several coyotes and deer. They'd been caught, he imagined, in the thick tarry flow.

The same crunching sound again claimed his attention. This time, though, it came not from under his feet but from somewhere behind him, off in the woods. Greg stood still and tried not to breathe. He could hear now only the chatter of birds in the forest. It wasn't pleasant to think you were being followed. Yet he felt certain there was someone behind him, back along the trail. The birds were convincing him. Another lesson from his father: Birds were brazen liars in certain matters, but they never lied to each other concerning the activities of man.

Greg heard the crunching again. One step, two, three. He turned around, peered through the trees, saw nothing. He moved off the path, into the edge of the forest. The silence bothered him almost as much as the noise. An annoyed landowner would come charging at a suspected trespasser. Who would hang back like this, trailing but hidden?

Greg walked back onto the path. He took a step, then another. A breeze drifted through the tree branches. Then came the crack of a twig. Greg swung around toward the sound. In a small clearing, some hundred feet away, two startled deer, mother and fawn, stood staring at him. Suddenly they bolted, bounding over a wild hedge of willows. Greg waited, but heard nothing more. There was nothing else to do. He turned and continued up the path.

At its end, Greg came to a small wood-frame cabin. *One Alder Road,* that was the address he'd found in the El Nido directory. Home of Buster Lloyd, El Nido's solitary paramedic. They called him an emergency medical technician, actually, an EMT. *EMT Buster Lloyd*—those were the words the coroner had scrawled near the bottom of the autopsy report on Brewster Tomaz. *EMT Buster Lloyd, first medical response on scene.* Nothing more. Greg had spotted the note just before leaving the DA's office. He'd never seen that name mentioned before or since.

Lloyd opened the door before Greg could knock. He was rail thin, over six feet tall, with a ponytail and a bushy beard. He squinted at the presence of a stranger.

"Buster Lloyd?" Greg asked.

"That's me. Who are you?"

"My name is Greg Monarch. I'm a lawyer, representing Sarah Trant."

"Who's that?"

"The woman convicted of killing Brewster Tomaz."

"Oh yeah, yeah. Tomaz. Boy, was his throat cut."

"That's just what I wanted to ask you about. What can you tell me about his injury? Do you remember what you saw?"

"Do I remember. Jesus, yes. That was the nastiest wound you would ever want to see. Cut straight to the bone of the spinal cord. Everything sliced up. Just about everything you got in your neck."

"Carotid artery?"

"Sure. Carotid, epiglottis, everything."

Greg tried to sound casual. "Did you know that the autopsy report said the carotid wasn't involved?"

Lloyd took two steps back into his cabin. You didn't get much work as an EMT, Greg imagined, if you bucked the county coroner. "What?" Lloyd said. "No, hell, I didn't . . . I mean . . . Maybe I was wrong. . . ."

Greg tried another tack. "Was Brewster Tomaz able to talk when you got to him?"

Lloyd snorted. "Talk? You kidding? I cut your left carotid, that side of your brain starts dying instantly. We're talking maybe one second. And the left side of your brain controls speech. You can't talk without your left hemisphere. . . . Talking? Hell. I cut your left carotid, you're unconscious in seconds, dead in five minutes."

Greg suspected the answer to his next question before he asked it. "Buster, why didn't you tell the police any of this when they interviewed you after Tomaz's murder?"

Lloyd regarded him now as if he were a madman. "Tell the police?"

"There's a police report summarizing your interview, but there's nothing in it about talking or carotid arteries."

Lloyd clawed at his beard. "A police report on my interview? How could that be?"

"What do you mean, Buster?"

"The police never interviewed me. Nobody interviewed me. You're the first person to ask me about Brewster Tomaz's death."

# SIX

Sheriff Roy Rimmer wiped his brow and tried to will himself to remain calm. If only Jim Mashburn could see things his way. Jim couldn't, though. Either that, or Jim didn't want to.

They were sitting in the DA's office. Out the window, Rimmer could hear children playing in the Sanborn Park fountain. The shrill noise annoyed him. How could Mashburn work in such a setting? It didn't seem possible. Nor did it seem possible for Mashburn to disregard him so often. Couldn't Mashburn see how fortunate he was to have a county sheriff with such a grasp of the law? Particularly the law as it functioned in El Nido County?

"Excuse me, Jim, but are you listening to me?"

Mashburn turned from the window. The sheriff's question appeared to summon the DA back to the matter at hand. There it sat on Mashburn's desk: Sarah Trant's amended habeas petition. This one, drafted by Greg Monarch, offered professionally printed blocks of type instead of graceful schoolgirl curls. Now it looked like a legal brief rather than an invitation to a birthday party. More important, it raised the stakes. No longer was Trant simply claiming the usual reasons—procedural errors, ineffectiveness of counsel—for why she merited a new trial. This revised petition, in no uncertain terms, accused the DA's office of enough "flagrant prosecutorial misconduct" to create a situation of "manifest injustice." What's more, it flatly declared Sarah Trant innocent.

Mashburn lifted the petition and began to read Monarch's words out loud: "The criminal justice system has utterly failed Sarah Trant. Police and the prosecution, having decided she was guilty, set out to create a world of evidence in support of their theory. They altered reports, hid boot prints, tampered with witnesses. . . ."

Rimmer reached over and pulled the petition from Mashburn's hands. "You going to memorize that, Jim?" he asked. "Or do something about it?"

"Do something about it?" Mashburn yanked the petition back from Rimmer, rolled it into a cylinder, and began slapping it against his desk. "What do you suggest, Roy?"

Rimmer, staring at his empty hand, fought an impulse to lunge again for the document. His palm stung from what felt like a paper cut. Goddamn Mashburn. Who the hell did he think he was? Mashburn didn't even come from this valley. Mashburn was an outsider who'd moved from the coast and got himself elected DA because of a relative's political sway. What did Mashburn know about El Nido?

People with family money, people with privilege. Ever since he was a boy, Rimmer had watched them prance blissfully across the valley. So unlike Rimmer's own life. His family went back four generations in El Nido, but they'd lost their land decades ago. From his grandparents' time on, they'd worked for other people. Rimmer, in his youth, had tried to break that pattern. He'd scraped together every penny he had and bought a patch of land back up in the foothills. He meant to grow citrus, and raise cattle, and build a fine home. It had never worked out, though. He couldn't get financing, he couldn't get permits and variances, he couldn't get anything. The previous owners had never told him about the restrictive covenants that came attached to his land. They'd misled him about the quality of the soil as well, and the availability of water.

He'd ended up in law enforcement. The sheriff's department had an opening. Eventually he ran for sheriff and won. It hadn't been a half-bad move in the end. The pace of the sheriff's department suited him. He was out, moving around the county, meeting people. That was certainly better than sitting behind a desk or a plow all day long. Now people looked up to him, admired him, responded to him. Now people listened to him.

Rimmer came to Mashburn's side. "What do I suggest, Jim? I have all sorts of suggestions."

"Such as what, Roy? Going back and retrying Sarah Trant the right way?"

"Damnit, Jim, she was guilty. And she got convicted. That is the right way."

Mashburn turned on him so suddenly, Rimmer instinctively took a step back and raised a protective hand. "Did Reggie Dodge know all he should have at the trial?" the DA demanded. "Did he get everything the defense was entitled to?"

Rimmer held his ground now. "Monarch is claiming actual innocence. *Actual innocence.* That is a crock."

"So why did my predecessor spin this one, Roy? He didn't need to. As you say, Sarah Trant is flat-out guilty. Karl Jackson had a solid case. Just what exactly in the goddamn hell happened here?"

Rimmer didn't answer at first. He squeezed his hands into fists and began pacing the room. "Karl Jackson needed more than a case," he offered.

"What are you talking about?"

"Doesn't matter at this point. We have to stop this Monarch fellow. Stop Monarch, and rein in that half-berserk federal judge."

"How do you propose to stop a federal judge, Roy?"

"Watch me," the sheriff said. He reached for the phone and punched in a number. "Rimmer here," he murmured. "Get me Whit. Pronto."

Alex Ramirez sank slowly to his knees beside the broad brown carcass. She looked strangely hale, he thought, as if she were simply sleeping on the bank of El Nido Creek. Yet this heifer was quite dead. Just like the two others.

Alex fought a mounting sense of unease. He rose and surveyed this southwestern reach of Sanborn Ranch, as if searching in the landscape for an answer. When he'd found that first cow down by a bend of the creek, he hadn't known what to think. Hoof-and-mouth, an insecticide, a predator, nothing made sense. Old Dr. Pitts, their local veterinarian, didn't have a clue. Alex didn't like to lose even one head from his herds, so he'd called the state health boys right away. They'd shown up within hours, poking and prodding and taking all manner of samples. They'd been a garrulous friendly bunch at that first visit, full of promises and reassurances. Then they'd disappeared, and clammed up. Alex had never managed to get a written report from them, or even a clear word on the phone. No one would tell him what killed his cow.

Now there were three dead.

Alex raised a hand to his hat. The wind was up today, a real blow flowing down off the mountains. He turned toward Sanborn Lodge. Bury it, Diana had ordered after they'd found the first one. Bury it and fence off that stretch of the creek. He'd never known Diana to act in such a manner. With much protest, he'd followed her command, but had not stopped puzzling. No strangers with bags of poison could have visited Sanborn Ranch without his knowledge. Whatever killed his cows had to be in the soil or the water right here on the ranch. Just what, though?

In his frustration, Alex had twice hiked down to the river to study the area where the cows died. One time he plowed up the earth, only to find layers and layers of the rich fertile soil for which all of El Nido was renowned. Another time he took creek water to the county's one private lab, only to have the folks there tell him he had a crystal-clear stream on his property. Yet there had to be something. There had to be.

On impulse, Alex lunged now at the dark brown earth. He began clawing at the stream bank, tunneling into the thick mud. Nothing but rich El Nido Valley soil, nothing poisonous, nothing evil . . . He dug deeper, rending the creek bank, throwing clumps of dirt into the air. It was senseless, he knew, but he didn't care. If only he could find an answer. If only—

A strange smell stopped him suddenly. Something offensive, like the odor of rotten eggs. He started to rise, but faltered. In an instant he was feeling dizzy and nauseated. His eyes hurt. So did his nose and throat and head. He crawled to the creek and retched until he had only dry heaves to offer. For a while he lay there, not moving. When he finally felt strong enough, he rose and lurched toward his pickup truck. By the time he made it to Sanborn Lodge, he was feeling fully recovered.

"Something made me sick out there," he informed Diana Sanborn.

He was pacing before her as she sat stiffly in a chair by her great-room fireplace.

"Whatever are you talking about?" Diana asked. There was steel in her voice. "You look just fine to me, Alex."

He stared hard at her. "We've got to deal with this," he insisted. "We have to understand why our cows died."

She stared back. "Perhaps you didn't hear me, Alex. I said you looked just fine."

He gave up then, suddenly realizing his misjudgment. He was being foolish, of course, to challenge her. He knew why she didn't want to face this matter. There was no swaying her. He would have to let her be.

Diana Sanborn walked along El Nido's Main Street arcade as if leading a procession. Past the ice-cream shop that offered nary a scoop of nonfat yogurt, past the bookstore that featured ponytailed folksingers in the back room, past the guitar shop whose proprietor plucked "This Land Is Your Land" from his front door. . . . Diana cherished all she saw. She waved furiously, she stomped her cowboy boots, she cried out greetings.

Only Tammy Rabe, the bounteous mayor's wife, was brave enough to block Diana's way. The two women found themselves facing each other in front of the El Nido Realty window. Photos there, of Spanish cottages and wood-frame cabins and six-thousand-square-foot ranch homes, offered newcomers to the valley the promise of an enchanted retreat. Neither Diana nor Tammy gave them a glance.

"What do you know about this Monarch lawyer?" Tammy asked over the jangle of her bracelets and earrings. "I hear he's filed some petition, and Sarah Trant is getting a new trial. We thought this was all settled."

Diana hung on to her hearty demeanor. "Now, don't go getting so riled, Tammy. A petition was filed, but that doesn't mean she gets a new trial. Doesn't even mean she gets a hearing. We will see. Nothing to worry about right now. Nothing to do."

Tammy gripped Diana's arm. "If this blows up—"

"Hush now." Diana put her hand on Tammy's mouth. "You're too loud. And too worried."

At the end of the arcade, Diana reached her pickup truck. In an instant she was barreling along Main Street. Then she was turning onto narrow, wooded Old Brook Road. She exhaled, happy to be offstage finally. Out her window Diana could see El Nido Creek flowing by. Two miles to the east, Brewster Tomaz had breathed his last in these waters. A mile to the west, Sarah Trant counted her days.

The prison was Diana's destination. She stopped in a parking lot that overlooked the low whitewashed adobe complex, but remained in her truck. From the driver's seat, she studied the view before her. There'd been a health spa here once, she knew. Yet another of the many enterprises that had failed during her grandfather's time. The wildcatters had it even worse than the health nuts back then. Not a single well came in, despite all the auspicious reports about El Nido's fabulous oil springs. Flow those springs did, unceasing sluggish streams pouring out of the mountainsides, day after day, covering acres of land, crossing roads, literally paving them with asphaltum for hundreds of yards. Yet it was a heavy thick crude they yielded, with no apparent commercial value. What's more, their abundance was illusory; the prospectors eventually concluded that the oil seeped from shallow pockets near the surface, not great reserves deep in the earth. In the end, the springs mainly constituted a problem: All kinds of stock would get stuck in the tarry matter, leaving their bones as a warning to others. Farmers detested the stuff, speaking of "tar flat" as they would a trespassing horse thief. Each year they made a great show of burning the flow, making a wick out of a handful of hay. As a young child, Diana recalled gaping at a fierce blaze as high as a church.

That image vaguely troubled her. Why, she wondered angrily, must memories of the past always affect her so? She smacked at her dashboard as if to chase away her demons. *Don't give in to yourself,* she muttered. *Don't give in.* Snapping open her purse, she reached for a tissue and wiped her eyes. She turned to stare at the prison's windows. Through which one might she spot Sarah? Through which one might she learn how poor Sarah was faring?

"You okay, Ms. Sanborn?"

Diana jumped at the question, then turned to find Greg Monarch at her window. "What are you doing, Mr. Monarch? Following me?"

"Actually, my client resides inside."

"Yes, of course. That is true."

Greg bent down so his head was level with Diana's. "You visit the state prison often?"

"I go everywhere in El Nido, Mr. Monarch. I have friends everywhere."

Greg nodded as if that made sense. "The other day, I came to the ranch with a question for you. You weren't in."

"So ask it now, Mr. Monarch. Now that we've just happened to bump into each other like this."

"Okay, I will." Greg rested an arm on the pickup's windowsill. "Ms. Sanborn, are you certain you heard Brewster Tomaz's dying declaration?"

"Whatever do you mean?"

"Those few minutes when you held him in your arms, when you cradled his head. Did he really talk to you?"

Diana twisted in her seat to face him squarely. "Yes, he most certainly did."

"It's just that his throat was cut so badly, I don't think he could have said a word."

"Are you a doctor, Mr. Monarch?"

"No—"

"Well then, perhaps we should place our trust in the pathologists who conducted the autopsy, and thought Brewster capable of speech."

"Perhaps we should," Greg said. He studied this ebullient gray-haired lady rancher. Diana's cowboy hat sat on the seat by her side; her right boot rested lightly on the truck's accelerator pedal. "One other thing," he continued. "As I understand it from looking at the trial record, first time this dying declaration got mentioned in a police report is three weeks after the murder. Ms. Sanborn, why didn't you tell the sheriff's detectives about it right away?"

Diana turned to the prison. Her eyes scanned a row of windows set in the low adobe wall. "I was trying to protect Sarah," she said finally. "I cared about her. I didn't want her in such trouble."

"What changed your mind?"

Diana glanced at her watch, then reached for the key in her ignition. "My conscience, Mr. Monarch. My grandfather brought me up to be truthful. So I had to tell the truth. Now, please excuse me. I must go."

Greg leaned through her open window. "You looked troubled a moment ago. Also a product of your conscience?"

Diana started to turn her ignition but stopped. She settled back in the truck's seat, examining Greg's face. Then she reached into her purse, pulled out an envelope, and handed it to him. "A first for me," she said. "My first anonymous blackmail letter. Received it this morning."

Greg took the envelope from her outstretched hand. From it he pulled a single sheet of paper. *I demand restitution,* the unknown correspondent declared in hand-printed block letters. *I demand restitution for wrongs done my forebears in years gone by. Make amends, or I will kill you.*

"What's this about?" he asked. "What wrongs?"

Diana shrugged. "Who knows? The world is filled with wrongs."

At dusk, Jasmine Gest rode her charcoal Appaloosa, Dusty, along the equestrian trail that snaked through Sanborn Park.

Just minutes from El Nido's main street, she was trotting through a densely treed forest that screened out all sights and sounds of the village. Normally this ride settled her mind, but not now. Memories of Sarah Trant's trial tugged at her. Such was one effect of Greg Monarch's arrival in the valley.

She'd thought it a distressing yet obvious affair. During the trial no one doubted Sarah's guilt, not even Jas. Especially not Jas, given what she knew about Sarah. She'd never told anyone the most damning things. Such as how Sarah zealously tracked Brewster Tomaz's movements through the valley, and how Sarah once took a steak knife to photos of the crusty old geologist. And how Sarah came unnaturally alive—eyes blazing, face flushed—in those moments when she talked of her campaign against ModoCorp. The fact was, sitting in the courtroom, not even Sarah herself had appeared to lay claim to actual innocence. Defiant, that's how she'd acted. Also peculiar. Each day she dressed up for her trial: special hats, colorful scarves, black stockings, rouge and lipstick. As if she were an actress playing a role. She kept glancing around at the spectators, while just about ignoring her lawyer. The more Jas thought about it, the more it seemed that Sarah had been expecting something—something or someone—throughout the proceeding. She'd appeared downright disappointed in the trial's final hours. As if events had not gone as planned.

Dr. Montrose's testimony definitely hadn't gone as planned. Reggie Dodge looked absolutely stricken when the pathologist started saying that Tomaz could have talked. Not even as lame a lawyer as Reggie Dodge would have called Montrose if he'd seen that coming. So what had happened there? Jas made a mental note to look into the matter. She also made a mental note to share her thoughts with Greg Monarch.

Jas had to admit that she found Monarch captivating. The way he watched her . . . He looked at her as if they were fellow travelers. He looked at her in a manner that compelled her to look back. He—

A commotion through the trees, over by the fountain, interrupted Jas's reflections. She could hear children crying. Jas reined Dusty in, then rode off the trail. Halfway across the park, she saw that a teenager, skateboarding, had collided with two toddlers. Parents were scrambling, but no one seemed seriously hurt. Jas started to turn back, then stopped. On a bench to the side of the fountain, she'd spotted a man hunched over in thought. A tall lean man with sandy hair. He seemed so coiled, even in repose. All skin and nerves and sense organs and brain. Greg Monarch. Just the fellow she wanted to see.

Watching parents deal with salty tears and skinned knees, Greg didn't notice Jasmine until she was twenty yards away. She rode easily. Her jeans had a hole in one knee, her flannel shirt spilled out at the back. She dismounted with a quick springy jump. The green eyes opened wide, full of welcome.

"I was just thinking of you," she said.

"And I of you."

"Oh sure."

"Truth."

"Okay, then. . . . You go first."

"Okay," Greg agreed. "I was thinking about the night of the concert here in the park. Down by the creek, you said 'enough about me.' You said, 'later.' Now it's later."

"Aha. So you want my story. That it?"

"Sort of."

Looking amused, Jas settled on the bench beside him. "I've got no notches on my belt. That's my deep dark secret. No notches."

"Notches?"

"You know . . . marriages, divorces, baby announcements, marriage counseling bills, separation agreements, restraining orders . . . Nothing."

"Somehow, this doesn't surprise me."

"That obvious, huh?"

"Let's say you don't strike me as being part of the mainstream."

"You neither."

"No."

"There are times I'd like to be. . . . It's shameful what I sometimes long for."

"Do tell."

"In certain reckless moments, I find myself wanting to be like Barbara Stanwyck in *The Big Valley*. You know, with four strapping sons and all that. I want to pop cake into a groom's mouth and dodge rice. I want meddling in-laws."

"I won't tell anyone."

"I know it's unrealistic."

"You need to lower your expectations."

Jas laughed. Her hand reached out and came to rest on his forearm. "I lay low on the subject of notches usually. I realize how fragile men are. It's dangerous to confide mixed fantasies about *The Big Valley* and shared child custody. This makes you appear jumpy, and if there's one thing you shouldn't be these days, it's jumpy."

"I suppose you're right." Greg felt her fingers warm his skin. It was true—when she rode up, he'd been thinking of her. But also of Sarah. Meeting Sarah again after all these years had rekindled a welter of feelings he'd long kept at bay. Too many feelings, too many alarms, too many lessons. Now here was Jas, so stirring in her own way. He couldn't go there, not now. He needed to keep his senses about him. Yet he imagined Jas would be of genuine help in a place such as El Nido. Obliged to shuttle between La Graciosa and this valley, he'd not managed to gain full entry. He needed an escort.

"Shall we share our other thoughts?" he asked. "About the murder case?"

Jas patted his arm, then pulled her hand away. "Good idea. We were getting too serious here."

"Diana Sanborn," Greg began. "She's on my mind. A singular woman. Her testimony put Sarah away, yet she offered me her guest room."

Jas shook her head. "Not sure you should make too much of that. Diana Sanborn considers herself the grand hostess of El Nido. Her hospitality is automatic, and universal."

"She's a troubled hostess just now."

"What do you mean?"

"She was looking upset earlier today. I found her sitting in her truck, over by the prison."

"Upset about what?"

Greg, wondering whether to mention the blackmail letter, decided to hold back. "I think she has an enemy right now. Someone who worries her. Someone who has threatened her."

Jas gave him an odd look. "If Brewster Tomaz were still alive, I'd say him."

"Tomaz?"

"He was a real mean one underneath that crusty curmudgeon routine. It would especially come out in the Gaucho Tavern late at night, after he'd had a pitcher of beer. He'd get in just about anyone's face. Especially a woman if she didn't take kindly to him. He'd get downright scary sometimes. There were nights in there I thought he was going to smack someone good."

"But why would you think of him particularly as Diana's enemy?"

"Hard to explain. Something in the way they acted when they found themselves in the same room together. He'd glare at her, and she . . . well, she'd almost recoil. . . . Usually this happened at town meetings, when they were arguing over land-use issues. Diana loves the El Nido Valley. I don't think Tomaz really did, for all his knowledge of this place. So maybe that explains it."

"Maybe," Greg said. "At any rate, Tomaz is dead. Who else might threaten Diana?"

Jas fell silent. "ModoCorp . . . Charles Whit," she offered finally. Then she seemed to have second thoughts. "I mean, I don't really know. But that's a possibility."

Greg slid closer to her. "Tell me what you do know."

The bell started tolling atop the post office tower. After striking the hour, it continued, sounding the notes of a song that Greg couldn't quite recognize. Pedestrians and park visitors stopped to listen as they watched the sun settle below the tree line.

"What do you say we relocate?" Jas said.

Greg trailed in his car as Jas rode Dusty back to the stables. From there they drove west out Old Brook Road. They crossed over the highway leading to the ocean and La Graciosa, turning north into the mountains. The road narrowed and curved. Here the thick stands of oak gave way to open meadows and cultivated farmland. Greg watched a man working his field, guiding a battered red plow, a kerchief tied around his head. Two children ran up to him just then, hollering. Greg couldn't hear their words, but imagined they were calling him to supper.

"Over there." Jas was pointing down a dirt road that curved off to the left. Greg followed it around a sharp bend, then suddenly found himself staring at a long oval body of water that glowed under the darkening pink sky. Mountains thick with oak and sycamore cradled it on all sides; this was the only road in. "Welcome to El Nido Lake," Jas said.

Greg looked around at his past. There, to the west, in that shaded cove, was where he had often fished with his father. "I've been here before," he said.

They settled on a patch of pebbly shore just as the sun's last blush disappeared behind a ridge. "We were talking about ModoCorp," Greg reminded her. "ModoCorp and Charles Whit."

Jas began tossing pebbles into the water. "Something funny between them and Diana. Something I'm not sure about."

"How so?"

"She never opposed them, not openly. Certainly not after Whit won over most of El Nido. Whatever's best for the valley, that's all you'd hear her say. But she got in their way, I think. She and her foreman."

"Alex?"

"You've met Alex?"

Greg nodded. He tried to hide his surprise at what he was

hearing. "I didn't realize they opposed Whit's group. How do you mean, got in their way?"

"Tangled with them somehow. You could just tell. Whit and Diana at a meeting, their eyes would meet sometimes, and it wasn't what you'd call friendly. Tense like. Alex made it worse. Sometimes I thought he and Whit would maybe throw a punch or two."

"What kind of meetings?"

Jas pulled her knees up under her chin and wrapped her arms around them. "Town hall meetings, mainly. They're held monthly, right in the mayor's living room. Quite a scene when Whit came. He with his PR team, everyone else so quiet and polite. Given Whit's size and manner and all, I guess only a drunk would dare to start an argument."

"What would Whit say?"

"Not much of anything. His PR boys usually did the talking, while he watched the crowd with those eyes of his."

"And the PR team's line . . . ?"

"The usual hooha. 'By telling the truth we hope everyone will be able to make a decision based on factual, accurate information and less on emotion.' Never got more precise. Always talked about a 'world-class health spa' but never showed us the plans. 'This will be good for everyone' was as specific as it got."

"How'd that play in the valley?"

"Tell you the truth, most just looked at Whit kind of blankly, especially in the early going. As I said, who's going to argue? He always had big loose-leaf notebooks full of tax-base growth projections with him, but no one ever touched them. A lot of the guys just leaned against Sam Rabe's walls with their arms folded, or walked the hallways with their hands shoved in their pockets. I don't think people really knew what to say. Except for Alex Ramirez."

Jas grinned at the memory. "I can still see him at the very first meeting with Whit . . . squatting against the wall, rolling a rubber ball to one of Sam Rabe's mangy mutts as Whit's guys talked on and on. Whit finally steps in and says, 'It's important that everyone who has a question about this project be given an opportunity to have all their questions answered.' Alex, still rolling the ball, his eyes on Sam Rabe's mutt, asks, 'What will you do if people oppose you?'

"For a minute, I don't think Whit knows what to say. Then he answers, 'Why . . . we'll pack up and leave.' So then Alex looks around the room and asks, 'Who here wants this man to stay in El Nido?' No one speaks or moves. I mean it. Hands stay in pockets, arms remain folded. I think most folks just didn't know what to think. They weren't for or against, and surely didn't want to get in the middle of those two guys. That's how people are in El Nido. Alex runs with it, though. 'Well, now,' he says finally. 'Mr. Whit, I guess you got your answer.'

"That's when the bad blood started, right then. Whit kind of smiles at Alex in that empty way he has. 'We'll see,' Whit says as he gathers his books and walks out. 'We will see how everyone feels.' A week later, Whit hired Brewster Tomaz."

It was Greg's turn to toss pebbles into the water. The pink sky had deepened to magenta, then black; moonlight glinted off the lake. Somewhere a loon called. "What about Diana and Whit?" he asked. "You ever see them go at it?"

Jas thought, then nodded. "The Camp Mahrah acreage, like everything around here, derives from Spanish land grant days. Somewhere during all the land swaps and sales, the Sanborn family ended up with an easement across Camp Mahrah land. It had been granted many decades ago, so the Sanborns could get to their caliche mines over by the sandstone cliffs."

"Caliche?"

"Limestone gravel. They once used it in road building around El Nido, but no longer. It's been many years since caliche was worth anything. For that matter, the Sanborns' caliche probably was mined out long ago. Legally, though, the easement still exists. I can remember Diana just whooping at one meeting, that way she has. 'Way I see it,' she declared, 'the Sanborn family still needs access to its valuable caliche mines.' Then, late one night, to underscore that point, Alex trailered the ranch's backhoe right up the mountain and commenced to do a spot of caliche mining."

Jas laughed out loud. "He really mined that mountain. Swear to God."

Greg turned Jas's story around in his mind. He tried to fill in the dots, tried to weave a persuasive theory. But he'd somehow lost the thread. "What does all this amount to?" he asked. "Did Alex or Diana ever do anything that really stopped Whit?"

"Nope, can't say they did. Just gave him a little trouble at the meetings. Eventually, to no one's surprise, Diana lined up on Whit's side. Like I told you, a quality health spa would help the valley, add value to everyone's holdings. It was economics and market studies that stopped the spa, as far as I understand, not local opposition. El Nido is too isolated to draw a big enough crowd, it seems. To most folks' regret."

"So why do you think ModoCorp might be threatening Diana?"

"Don't know, really. I just tossed that out without really thinking. Sort of an instinct, based on what I saw at those early meetings. Now that you ask, I'm probably wrong. They almost act like allies now."

Greg kept throwing pebbles into the water. "What about Sarah? Where does she fit in?"

"Come on," Jas said. "She was stalking Brewster. She pushed the old man in the water."

Greg suddenly felt hollow. "You think Sarah is guilty, don't you?"

"Sure, but so what if she is?"

Greg could see both indignation and moonlight in Jas's eyes. "What do you mean?" he asked.

"I mean, maybe something terribly wrong still happened here even if she is guilty."

Greg waited, but Jas said nothing more. Instead, she looked at him steadily, in a way that made the heat rise in his face. He held her gaze for a moment, wondering whether she looked at all men like that. Then, sensing something moving, he turned toward the lake. A strange object, a black lump, bobbed in the water at the shore's edge. Greg rose and approached it. With a stick, he pulled it to the pebble beach.

Not just black, Greg saw now. It was black with a green metallic sheen, a not-uncommon coloring for the type of cormorant found in Central California waters. Greg studied the dead bird. The long hooked bill, the large fully webbed feet, the short strong legs—the cormorant was well equipped to dive for food, and to swim once it hit the water.

Not this one, though. Greg placed his hands on the bird's wet feathers, ran his fingers across its back. Then he rubbed his fingers together.

"Oil," he said, gazing at the water. "There must be a slick out there somewhere."

Near midnight, after a solitary dinner at the Rancho Café in El Nido Village, Greg drove the winding mountain pass that led to La Graciosa. A bright moonlit sky showed him the way. He had a promising plea-bargain conference scheduled with the Chumash County DA the next afternoon, then plans to meet Jimmy O'Brien at JB's Red Rooster Tavern. The eagerness he felt, heading home, surprised him.

*Something terribly wrong still happened here.*

Jas's words echoed in his mind. The El Nido DA's office most certainly had played this one fast and loose. Yet cops and prosecutors were always doing that. Most times, they knew they had the guilty party and simply wanted to make sure the jurors did also. That was wrong, of course—the state didn't get to put people away just because they were guilty, the state first had to prove their guilt. Still, there were certain moments when Greg wondered: What was worse, that or letting dangerous killers walk the streets of our cities?

He shuddered at a memory. Jason Pine suddenly disappearing one night . . . Jason Pine on a clandestine manic prowl through Chumash County. At dawn, he showed up at his terrified aunt's apartment, hollering and slamming things about. Only then did Greg turn him in, only then did he finally bring Pine down to the sheriff's office. It wasn't enough.

When the DA learned Pine would talk only to doctors, not detectives, he responded with an ace card. *He won't talk, we've got nothing on him, so we're turning him loose.* Greg responded with his own ace card—a phone call to his reporter pal Jimmy O'Brien. *Want a good story about the DA letting a killer walk free?* A week later, Jason Pine ended up just where Greg wished him—in the Chumash County Mental Health Institute. Thanks to his clever attorney, there was no jail for Pine, just a bed and a window. That, and a prospect for release.

The scent of kelp disrupted Greg's reverie. He'd reached La Graciosa, wrapped as usual in a blanket of fog. His house, a half mile upcreek from the town square, rose like a promise before him. He parked and walked inside. On the way to the deck, he stopped to check for phone messages.

There was one. The voice on the machine sounded cheerful and familiar. It was, Greg recognized instantly, Julia Brass, Judge Daniel Solman's clerk. She wanted him to know that Judge Solman had reviewed his amended habeas petition on behalf of Sarah Trant. Reviewed it, and found it worth consideration.

*Judge Solman has scheduled a status conference,* Julia advised. *He wants all lawyers in his chambers first thing tomorrow morning.*

# SEVEN

U.S. District Judge Daniel Solman rifled impatiently through the untidy pile of documents strewn on the credenza behind his desk. Such disarray annoyed him, yet he had little means to achieve order. These days he worked, literally, out of a suitcase. A colossal once-in-a-hundred-years storm, followed soon after by a moderate 4.4 earthquake, had left his customary federal quarters uninhabitable for eighteen months now. He'd been obliged to toil in temporary offices, and to travel, like a roving circuit magistrate, to hearings in outlying districts.

At least the Chumash County Courthouse, where he'd installed himself today for the purpose of considering Sarah Trant's habeas petition, offered the advantage of being located in his hometown. Solman had grown up in La Graciosa and attended Chumash State. He always welcomed the chance to revisit his roots. That the county courthouse occupied a former house of God made the return all the more pleasurable. Solman enjoyed sitting in the two-hundred-year-old *asistencia* and imagining its early use as assistant chapel for Mission San Luis Obispo de Tolosa to the north.

"Judge Solman?"

He examined the unfamiliar intercom box on his desk, looking for a button to press. Each office he sat in these days had a different tangle of machinery to decipher. "Yes, Julia?" he said finally, his hand loosely cupping the side of the box.

That seemed to work: Julia heard him. "The lawyers are present now," she said. "Jim Mashburn from El Nido County, Greg Monarch for the petitioner."

Solman stared at the papers spread on the desk before him.

He wasn't sure why he'd urged Sarah Trant's habeas petition on Monarch that first night, and he certainly couldn't say why he'd taken matters a step further, to this status conference. He felt almost as if he were following an involuntary instinct, one that ran contrary to his normal bent. Yes, it was true, the initial impetus had come from Sarah Trant herself, from Trant's request that Monarch get a copy of her petition. Yet he would have sent her handwritten plea to Greg even if the prisoner hadn't asked. It was Greg's kind of case. From the mid-distance that their acquaintanceship provided, Solman had privately followed Monarch's course through the law with admiration. He wasn't the least like him; he didn't share Monarch's brand of brooding diligence, nor his affinity for abject souls and likely transgressors. Yet Greg moved him in some way. Greg, he had to admit, embodied something he lacked.

"Okay, Julia," the judge said. "I'm ready. Send them in."

Walking side by side with Mashburn into Judge Solman's quarters, Greg puzzled over the DA's manner. In the judge's waiting room, Jim had shifted about in his chair, struggling to make small talk, avoiding eye contact. For a moment Greg had imagined him feeling qualms about Trant's case. Yet now that didn't seem to be the case.

Settling into chairs before Judge Solman, Mashburn projected aggressive certitude, not ambivalence. "I'll be happy to," he said when Solman invited him to go first. He pulled a sheaf of papers from his briefcase and began. "Your Honor . . . What are we doing here? The petitioner is basically seeking a retrial. Boil all this down"—here Mashburn waved at the petition in Solman's hands—"and what she's doing is asking you, a federal judge, to retry her case. She's asking you to usurp a state judge's role."

Solman looked back and forth at the lawyers. "Isn't that what a federal habeas claim is all about?"

"No, sir." Mashburn rifled through the papers clutched in his hand. "I won't read everything we've cited in our response brief, just a bit from this most relevant Supreme Court decision."

Solman rolled his eyes. "Why do I think I'm going to hear a few lines from *Barefoot v. Estelle* at this moment?"

" 'A presumption of finality,' " Mashburn said with emphasis. He looked over at Greg, then turned back to the judge. "That's what *Barefoot* talks about. 'The role of federal habeas proceedings is secondary and limited. . . . Federal courts are not forums in which to relitigate trials—' "

Solman held up a hand. "I know the language, you needn't go on. You can just brief me on all that."

Mashburn blinked back his frustration. "That's my case in a nutshell, Your Honor. If you know the language of *Barefoot*, you know my case."

"Well, then," Solman said, "I guess I know your case." He turned to Greg. "Let's move on. Mr. Monarch, you want to take a turn?"

Greg weighed his response. He saw he had Solman with him for some reason. Yet—knowing his college classmate to be a cautious and politically minded jurist—he still felt the need to supply the judge with a solid rationale for favoring Sarah's plea.

"Yes, Your Honor, I'll speak just for a moment," Greg said. "I think it's important for the Court to keep in mind that Sarah Trant is claiming actual innocence. That changes the equation a bit, Your Honor. *Barefoot* isn't the controlling case then. The key is *Schlup v. Delo*. No matter what procedural defaults you've got, no matter what you've waived or failed to raise earlier, Schlup lets you in the door if your case involves a fundamental miscarriage of justice. And *Schlup* says the federal district court isn't bound by the rules of admissibility that would govern at trial. The claim of actual innocence allows the habeas court also to consider relevant evidence that was either excluded or unavailable at trial."

Greg let a faint smile show as he looked back and forth between Mashburn and Solman. "We've got lots of that type of evidence, Your Honor. We're not entitled to retry everything in a federal court, but by claiming actual innocence we're allowed to show you evidence the trial judge and jury never saw. We get to pursue the truth for once, rather than just argue process. We get a chance to prove our claims."

"Excuse me, Greg." Mashburn was twisting in his chair, facing him. "You haven't raised these claims in the state system yet. You haven't exhausted your appeals in the California courts, which have jurisdiction over your client, and over all crimes of murder within the state's boundaries. You have no business in a federal court."

Greg shook his head. "Two years ago, the California legislature amended its statutes to exclude actual innocence as a basis for certain appeals. By doing so, I would argue that the state in effect relinquished its jurisdiction over claims such as Sarah's, and placed them squarely in the federal forum."

"How can you say—" Mashburn began.

"Besides," Greg interrupted, "even if the state were willing to hear Sarah's latest appeal, I don't believe her rights would be protected. It's El Nido County, after all, where this would eventually get remanded under a state proceeding. And I don't believe El Nido can be trusted to treat Sarah Trant fairly. I don't believe El Nido can guarantee Ms. Trant the basic protections of the U.S. Constitution."

Anger welled in Mashburn's face. "What do you mean by that, Greg? Just what do you mean?"

Greg remained still. In their brief time working together, he'd found Jim neither dim nor unprincipled. Back then, Mashburn had made sure they played by the proper rules. So why not now? How could Jim so earnestly dispatch Sarah Trant to the executioner? Didn't he see that neither of them really knew the truth?

"I mean something is going on in your valley," Greg said. "Somebody framed Sarah Trant but good, Jim. Somebody wanted Sarah in prison."

"For Christ's sake," Mashburn snapped. "She killed a man, Greg. That's why she's in prison. She killed Brewster Tomaz."

"No," Greg said. "That's not why."

Solman interrupted. "Gentlemen, let's stick to the legal issues for the moment, okay?"

Both lawyers turned to face him. Solman reached for the habeas petition on his desk. "Mr. Monarch has thrown in the usual language you find in these things," he said. " 'There are situations where the criminal justice system fails'—that's a nice hoary chestnut, don't you all think?"

Mashburn grabbed at that opening. "Fails for whom? For the accused, or for the victims? Or for all of us? I would argue that—"

Solman again held up a hand to stop the DA. "Point is granted. Hoary chestnut discarded." The judge leafed through the petition's pages. "But there's more than hoary chestnuts in here, isn't there? You've got a very funny-looking autopsy report in here, don't you? And you've got a very funny-looking defense expert, don't you? That pathologist sounds more like a witness for the prosecution—"

"Your Honor." This time Mashburn was interrupting Solman. "No fewer than four California trial and appellate judges have reviewed all this and found no merit to Trant's claims. Do you propose setting yourself above them? Do you think you have a right to ignore all their findings?"

Solman chewed on that. Mashburn's words appeared to affect him. "Well, not ignore," he said. "Just review."

Mashburn had the look of a gambler now. "This is what riles the public, Your Honor. Murderers kill, murderers get convicted. Then come years of judicial delay. People are angry at federal intrusion into state affairs, people are genuinely distressed about violent crime. That's why you've got campaigns against federal judges these days. That's why you've got U.S. senators talking about ending lifetime tenure." Mashburn was almost out of his chair. "And that, Your Honor, is why you get citizens talking about impeaching federal judges."

Greg watched Solman as Mashburn spoke. The judge's expression had started to shift; his judicial air and sense of command were fading. Greg wasn't altogether surprised. He'd occasionally seen Solman dance near the edge of an adventurous act, but he'd always backed off eventually, settling for the assurance of established forms.

"You raise a valid issue, Mr. Mashburn," Solman said finally. "It is also true that our Congress and Supreme Court don't want the habeas process overused. They've narrowed the window, haven't they? They don't want state convicts to get bite after bite at the federal apple. Only one bite, they say. Convicts should get only one bite—"

"Your Honor, that's just the point." Greg was now sitting on the edge of his chair too. He'd been waiting for the conversation to reach this moment. "If you deny Sarah Trant's petition, she won't get another chance. She will have taken her one bite of the apple."

"You sure of that?" Solman asked, looking puzzled.

"It's in that new 1996 federal law. The Antiterrorism and Effective Death Penalty Act. One bite, that's what the AEDPA dictates. A single federal habeas petition, no more. If you deny her, Sarah Trant would need approval from the court of appeals to return to federal court. And if they say no, that's it. She can't take it to the Supreme Court."

"Judge—" Mashburn tried to interrupt.

Again Greg wouldn't let him: "Do you want to close the door like that, Your Honor? Would that not be constitutionally intolerable?"

"The law is the law—" Once more Mashburn couldn't finish a sentence. Greg was on his feet now.

"That's just it, Your Honor. The law is the law. The U.S. Constitution, the Fourteenth Amendment, due process—"

"Okay, that's enough." Solman waved them both off. Greg sat down, studying the judge. Solman was acting uneasy, as a man of caution and custom will when faced with making a genuine choice. Yet even as Greg watched him, Solman appeared to gather himself and will himself forward.

"Your office shouldn't have rigged it so much." The judge was frowning at Mashburn as he spoke. "Two or three crooked angles, fine, you're making sure the guilty don't walk. But it looks like your office crossed every damn line here."

"Your Honor—" Mashburn began.

"Gentlemen," Solman interrupted. "I've decided to schedule an evidentiary hearing on Sarah Trant's habeas petition."

Each time Greg visited Sarah now at the La Luna Women's Correctional Center, he surveyed the other prisoners gathered in the communal visiting area. They came from all over the state, fed into this medium-security facility by faceless bureaucrats at a distant dispatching center. Some had the sickly pallor and hard worn faces of career cons, while some looked so fresh and vulnerable Greg wondered how they'd survive a week in this place. Drug convictions brought the majority here; often that meant they'd done a boyfriend's bidding. Either that, or they were here because they attempted to kill a boyfriend. Most people would be surprised to learn how many women tried to take contracts out on the men who beat them day and night.

Greg usually found the same guard standing by the door of the interview room where he met with Sarah. He was not a particularly menacing man, with his narrow shoulders and concave chest and big ears, but he had a habit of staring at Sarah with absolutely no expression. Once, when Greg tired of this routine, he taped a piece of paper over the interview room's small window. It worked for twenty minutes. Then the guard knocked and told him he had to take the paper down. Today, Greg thought of trying that maneuver again. As usual, their sentinel was watching them ceaselessly. With her back to the door, Sarah didn't seem to notice, but Greg sensed she felt his presence.

"Do you understand what I'm saying?" Greg asked. "Sarah, the judge has granted us a hearing. We're going to court. He's going to consider your petition."

Sarah nibbled at her lip. "May I talk a little?" she asked. "I so much want to talk to you."

Greg steeled himself, uncertain where she was heading. He slowly sank into a chair. "What, Sarah?"

"You're afraid of me, aren't you?"

Involuntarily, Greg leaned back. Sarah's hands rested on

the table that separated them. They looked so scarred, like an old woman's. Or like those of someone who'd made too many frenzied attempts to escape from locked rooms. "You matter to me," he said. "That's how I feel."

She ignored his response. "I know one of the reasons you're afraid of me. It's because I haven't met the terms of my contract. You know, like in *Mr. Sammler's Planet*. Remember us reading Bellow together? The prayer over that nephew? I haven't done that. I haven't taken hold of my life—"

"Sarah . . ." Greg tried to interrupt.

She wouldn't let him. "I've never been very good at that business. I've preferred being naive, being an enthralled wide-eyed dupe. To some men, like yourself, it's a charming attitude in a woman. I understand. It can be funny. It can make the days seem more interesting. But somewhere along the line this mechanism can break down. It did with me. I know that I loved myself more when I was twenty-two than I have ever since."

Greg thought of Sarah at twenty-two. He loved her then too. He loved her that summer morning when she pointed her battered Mustang toward Canada and said *Come on, let's go*. Yet he had to admit he'd harbored other feelings as well. She was forever reciting her same string of stories, wanting him always to listen with wonder. . . . She never could get them down on paper, though. She could never get anything down on paper. *I can't organize your interior,* he'd told her more than once. *We occupy our own rooms.*

"You did make the days more interesting," he said now. "Still do."

Sarah lowered her eyes, then raised them. "That last summer, Greg. You remember?"

"Of course."

"That last visit we had, when I came to you from the halfway house?"

"Yes, I recall."

"I drove away that day feeling like I'd tried to sell you a broken watch. I hadn't meant to sell anything. I wanted to voice a faint hope for our future. That's all. But then the tears came. So messy, so awful. Jesus. What a way to part. Sorry."

Greg reached for her weathered hand. "Nothing to be sorry about."

Sarah grasped his hands in her own but said nothing more. It looked to Greg as if she were listening to voices he couldn't hear.

"So," she said suddenly. "We get to have a hearing. The judge has given us a hearing."

Greg answered quickly, eager to keep her with him. "Yes, and not just a hearing. I asked for the right to depose state witnesses, and to conduct unlimited discovery. Judge Solman agreed. Because of 'unusual circumstances,' he said."

"What does this mean?"

"It means we get to see everything the state has on your case, Sarah. They only had to disclose a part of their files back at the time of your trial. Now they have to hand over all they've got."

Sarah closed her eyes. She squeezed Greg's hands. Then, with one finger, she traced the lines in his palms. Realizing she was silently sobbing, Greg put an arm around her shoulders. "What more can you tell me about the night of the murder, Sarah? Down by the river, you say you confronted Tomaz, pushed him in the water, then ran off. Did you see anyone else?"

She looked as if she was going to answer, but didn't. Instead she began to hum, then sing softly. *Bewitched, bothered, and bewildered* . . . Greg despaired. He grasped her by the shoulders, pulled her toward him, and held her close, as if that would keep her from slipping away.

"Sarah, Sarah. Listen to me. While you were running from the river, where was Diana Sanborn? Did you see Diana?"

*Bewitched, bothered, and bewildered* . . . As Sarah sang, she ran her hand along Greg's neck. The feel of her fingers on his skin set him on edge. For a moment he was back with her, ricocheting up the coast on a hot summer night. "Sarah," he said. "Sarah."

A faint click and flash of light startled Greg out of his daze.

He looked up, following the sound, and found himself staring, through a window, into the mirthless eyes of the thin gray guard. In the man's hands was a small automatic Nikon, which he held propped against the window, the open lens aimed at Greg and Sarah.

"Guess what?" Greg advised his client. "We've just had our picture taken."

# EIGHT

Great flocks of blackbirds circled in the darkening sky. Wild-eyed deer, hares with astonishing ears, strangely crested quail, the sheer sullen walls of the La Lunas—taken together, they suggested an undiscovered world. Greg was riding a quarter horse named Harley up the Santa Theresa trail into Upper El Nido. Beside him Diana Sanborn sat her saddle squarely, as though it were a bench, with a silvered and tasseled strap tied across her lap. She'd blanched when he showed up unannounced at her front door. Then she'd said, "Come see my valley at dusk."

They stopped and dismounted above the steep drop that divided El Nido. Below them, the basin filled with an exceptional color of pink streaked with purple. Thin bands of light scaled the mountain faces, turning red-gold at the crest. Cottonwood and white alder and sycamore, ceanothus and sage and manzanita, prickly pear and yucca and abundant lupines—Greg's eyes roamed eagerly across the tableau.

"Here, we are *on* the El Nido," Diana said, her arm sweeping toward the horizon. "Not in, but on. Here's the El Nido known by its settlers. For others, for those in cars who follow the roads, El Nido puts on a disguise. You and I are seeing El Nido as it really is. If you stay here for long, Mr. Monarch, you will come to love El Nido as I do."

Greg said, "It makes you want to bow down to Mother Nature."

"There is more than Nature to thank for all this."

Greg looked at her but said nothing. He wondered if she'd intended such an edge in her voice.

"Places are shaped by how we behave, wouldn't you say, Mr. Monarch?" Diana was smiling now, dipping her head, looking recovered. The impish mischief in her eyes stripped twenty years away.

"I'd say everything's shaped by how we behave," he replied. "And why don't you call me Greg."

Diana clapped her hands. "Yes! Actions have consequences. A place's character and tradition, for instance. That's one consequence, wouldn't you say? One event connects to the next in a way that gives a place a particular . . . history."

"Yes, one event connects to the next," Greg agreed. "That I couldn't deny."

They sat in silence on a narrow ledge, studying the vista. It was almost dark now. Lights from the village twinkled in the distance. "You may call me Diana," she announced.

"Okay, Diana. So what's really going on in El Nido?"

"Whatever do you mean?"

"ModoCorp, Charles Whit, a health spa that gets talked about but never built. Even though everyone seems to want it. Everyone but you, that is."

Diana smiled. "Goodness, Greg. Your mind has been wandering far from Sarah Trant's cause."

"Has it?"

Diana clung to her smile. "I've never been opposed to ModoCorp's plans. Just certain details. That is customary in these affairs. I'm quite eager for El Nido to grow, as long as it happens in a suitable manner. It has to grow, in fact, or it shall die."

"Sarah thought otherwise."

"Yes," Diana said, her smile now slipping away. "Sarah did."

"And Sarah worked for you?"

"For a summer. Hired on as a ranch hand, wasn't suited for that. Didn't last."

"Isn't there more to it, Diana?"

"What do you mean?"

"You two had a bond of sorts."

Diana looked steadily at him. She drew a breath. "Yes, you're right. . . . Sarah is full of passion. Sarah burns brightly. She has a soul that I recognize."

"It pained you to have to testify against her?"

"I almost didn't, it bothered me so much."

"Yet you did."

"Yes . . . I did."

Greg studied the basin below them. It had been another hot, dry day, the warm air pushed through the valley by a ceaseless breeze. Now though, without the sun, he felt chilled. He pulled his jacket collar tighter around his neck. "Why did you ask me to stay in El Nido, Diana? Why offer me your guest room that first weekend? What do you want?"

Diana rose, walked to her mare, began to pat her neck. Next she adjusted the horse's reins, tightened a buckle, checked a stirrup. Then she untwisted the silvered tasseled saddle strap. When she finally turned back to Greg, she seemed to be weighing something. "What I want you can't do," she said.

Greg came to her side. "Try me."

She looked at him without speaking. Twice she began to talk but didn't. She closed her eyes, then opened them. Finally, she said, "I want someone to fix the past."

Diana told her story as they rode back down the hill. She talked first about the winter she turned eight. She talked about a girl named Jenny, and a Thanksgiving hike in the snow, and three children huddled together against the arctic cold. Then she sighed and said, "I want to tell you more. I want to tell you about my sixteenth summer."

Greg, not knowing how to respond, simply nodded. They rode in silence, he waiting, she studying the sky. After half a mile, Diana began. She spoke slowly, measuring her words.

That summer, she said, a young man came to work on her grandfather's ranch. He was so unlike the others: not a boy at all, but a brooding, tightly wound twenty-four-year-old. She couldn't stop looking at him. He had pale blue eyes and jet-black hair. Sometimes he let her tag along as he toured the ranch, drilling holes and testing soil conditions for her grandfather. When he rested, he'd even talk to her a bit. She listened mostly, but in time found herself responding. It thrilled and scared her at once, how she opened herself to him.

Then he turned on her—so suddenly, she never saw it coming. One night on the ridge, with too much whiskey in his stomach, and maybe too many of her words in his ear, all that moody intensity turned to anger. He slapped her once over something tart she said. Then he slapped her again, harder. When she cried, his eyes brightened and his hand curled into a fist. He yanked her shirt open, then went for her jeans. She couldn't tell which hurt more, the blows to her head or him ramming into her. At his climax he rose above her, propped up on his hands, hollering and swiping at her. For a moment Diana didn't know if she was being raped or murdered.

She never told anyone. Even as he was climbing off her, she knew she wouldn't. She had no choice really, since she well understood what would follow if she did. Her grandfather would kill her attacker on the spot, the instant he heard what had happened. Then he'd be charged with murder. Charged and maybe even convicted. Not even Edward Sanborn could kill his employees at will.

So the ranch hand stayed on, monitoring soil conditions for Edward Sanborn for almost eight years. When he left them, it was for another job just five miles farther into the valley. He never moved from El Nido. Year in and year out, first on her grandfather's ranch, then later on the streets of the village, Diana found herself obliged to pass silently by her attacker. Occasionally he'd nod a greeting, which she had to return.

"Thus both of us aged over the decades, silently sharing a secret," Diana concluded. "Now, isn't that a quaint love story?"

They'd reached the stables at Sanborn Ranch. Greg wondered why she'd chosen to tell him all this. "Is he still around?" he asked.

Diana offered an odd, faraway smile. "Alas, no. He passed on a while back. He's just a memory now. Although a persistent one."

Alex, approaching from the corral, greeted them and helped Diana dismount. She started toward the main house as Greg headed for his car. Then she turned and called to him. "You might as well know, Greg. My take on human nature is not all that favorable. Especially men's."

As she studied the documents spread across the table, Jasmine Gest could feel his eyes on her. Sheriff Roy Rimmer was not being in the least lascivious, yet something in his manner made Jas tug at her black miniskirt. She wished she'd worn something else today. Rimmer turned away finally. Jas clutched at the buttons of her gray wool sweater.

Ah well, she thought. She had Greg Monarch beside her. She looked to him now for support.

"Sheriff," Greg was saying. "Should we repeat the question again? Are you having trouble concentrating today?"

The three, along with a staff lawyer from the DA's office named Donald Taub, were seated in a rented conference room at the El Nido Inn. The petitioner may conduct discovery and depose state witnesses, Judge Solman had ruled. So that's what they were doing. Greg had enlisted Jas as a temporary assistant to help sort through documents. They'd been at it three weeks now. Each day, they'd learned something new.

First came the intriguing revelation that Dr. Montrose's income from serving as a state expert witness had ballooned in the year after Sarah's trial—from $5,000 to $35,000. Then came a curious police report that made mention of a bloodstained blue-checked kerchief found just downstream from the murder site. Then an extraordinary report describing distinctive boot prints—a half-sole with diagonal nails—spotted on the creek bank right beside Tomaz's body. Finally—most astonishing of all—the account of one Judith Daniels, an El

Nido spinster who'd reached the murder scene just behind Diana Sanborn.

A never-produced investigative file told the story. Half a year after the murder—one month before Sarah's trial—Judith Daniels had called the sheriff's department. *I saw someone that night,* she'd informed Sheriff Rimmer. *Someone running into the brush on the far side of the creek. Someone much taller and bulkier than Sarah. I saw him get as far as the yonder alder tree. Then he flat-out disappeared.*

When he first found this report, Greg felt as if he'd stumbled on a hidden world, a parallel universe that operated by its own set of rules. Even in a system known for unconscionable deception, he didn't see how the prosecution could have kept this from Reggie Dodge.

"Sorry," Rimmer was saying. "Perhaps I am having trouble concentrating today. Please repeat the question."

Greg leaned over so as to get squarely into Rimmer's line of sight. "The question is, how did these police reports not get turned over to the defense? Why was none of this revealed at Sarah's trial?"

Rimmer couldn't hide his irritation. "Those weren't official police reports. Those were just internal memos among our investigators. Sorting out what was legitimate evidence, that's what they were doing. Also, what was exculpatory. If it's not exculpatory, it doesn't have to be disclosed."

"The testimony of an eyewitness is not evidence, Sheriff Rimmer? And not exculpatory?"

Rimmer offered a condescending smile. "You're not from here, Mr. Monarch. Otherwise you'd know that Judith Daniels isn't right in the head. She's the village oddball. You lived here, you'd know that."

"The boot prints, the kerchief?"

"Prints were two days old, the kerchief months old. Not from the murder night."

Greg tapped the table with a pencil. "Sheriff, just what does constitute something worth mentioning in an official police report?"

Rimmer surveyed the room, as if looking for an example in a corner of the El Nido Inn. The strain of being required to answer this La Graciosa lawyer's questions for three uninterrupted hours showed now in the set of his jaw and the clench of his fists. The sheriff's eyes finally lighted on Jas. "Well, now," he said. "Say if Jas here were attacked on the way to this deposition . . . Say she was raped . . . That would be a report. We'd write that up as a formal report."

Greg rose, and Rimmer started out of his chair too. The DA's lawyer, silent in a corner until now, jumped between them. "Okay, now, okay," Taub said. "Let's all settle down."

Greg remained on his feet. He reached for a pile of the documents they'd gained through discovery. "Sheriff, here is what you call a formal police report, I take it. It summarizes your department's interviews with Diana Sanborn on the night of the murder, and then again two weeks later. This, you agree, is a police report?"

Rimmer sat back down. So did Greg. "Yes, sir," the sheriff said. "That's a report."

"You know what's not in here, Sheriff? What's not in this formal police report?"

"No, sir."

"What's not in here is anything about Diana Sanborn saying she heard the victim's dying declaration."

Rimmer looked bored. "So it didn't get written down right away . . . That's not a secret, Monarch. Reggie Dodge worked that angle quite a bit during the murder trial, without getting anywhere."

Greg leaned forward. "Well, let's work it a little bit more, Sheriff. Are you saying you wouldn't have put it in a report that Diana heard a dying declaration?"

"For chrissake, Monarch, it eventually got written up. Take a look at those later reports."

"Three weeks later, to be exact."

"Okay, fine, three weeks. It's in there, isn't it?"

"Sheriff!" Greg snapped. "You think this kind of stuff is going to play once we get in a federal courtroom?"

Rimmer grinned. "That depends who the judge is," he said. "And who the lawyers are."

At dusk on the day of Sheriff Rimmer's deposition, Greg and Jas drove to an Italian farm family's café that stood among the avocado orchards a mile outside El Nido Village. "Best pizza and spaghetti in the West," she'd promised. With a bottle of Chianti, and a sky washed pale gold, and an outdoor table sheltered by a hundred-year-old live oak, Greg was willing to agree.

"They rigged the case, pure and simple," Jas said. "Isn't that right?"

Greg curled pasta onto his fork. "Pure and simple."

"Do you have what you need?"

"What I need is a new trial for Sarah. No way to know whether I have that. Judges don't issue habeas writs very often. No matter what's happened. Just like everyone else, they accept that cops and prosecutors cook their cases. As long as they haven't framed someone obviously innocent, judges usually let them have their way."

"Even Judge Solman?"

"Oh, I think particularly Judge Solman."

"But Solman granted you a hearing."

"That doesn't mean he'll issue a writ. Most who get to a habeas hearing still end up having their petitions denied."

"That's what you expect?"

"No. . . . Not at all."

Greg started tapping the table with his fingers. Jas studied his hands. "What, then?" she asked.

"Can't say yet. Too murky to expect anything . . . We just need to be aware of what's going on."

"I can't imagine you being unaware," she said. "Of anything."

He looked at her. "The folks who rolled Reggie Dodge aren't going to lie down now just because I came to town waving a habeas petition."

"No, I suppose not."

They sat in silence then, sipping their wine.

"What did you and Sarah talk about?" Greg asked.

"Sarah and I? . . . When?"

"Those times you were together. Those hikes you mentioned, those drinks at the Gaucho."

Jas's eyes danced. "You imagining some juicy girl talk, maybe? That what you had in mind?"

"Just asking . . ."

"The latest shoe styles . . . that's what we talked about. Hair news. Health tips were also big."

"Okay, okay." Greg held up his hands in surrender. "This is getting too serious again. Back to the case."

"I'm ready."

"One thing we need to do," he said. "That's ask Reggie Dodge about all these reports he supposedly never saw. We need to go over what he knew, what they didn't tell him. His testimony will be critical for us. He gives us the key to dozens of violations."

"You haven't talked to him yet?"

"I keep trying, but can't get past his wife. She insists he's still too weak to talk. Flat on his back. The pneumonia, or whatever it is, lingers. I stopped by his house yesterday but couldn't get a foot in the door. She won't even put him on the phone."

"I happen to know Mrs. Dodge fairly well," Jas said. "From the museum. Why don't I call her, see if that works? We could maybe visit them after dinner. They don't live far from here."

While Jas went to the pay phone, Greg watched a hawk float down the valley on a current of air, following the setting sun to the sea. Twice he twisted in his seat, sensing someone watching from the dense woodland beyond the café. Both times he saw nothing but trees.

"Oh God, Greg." Jas was at his side now, ashen. "I . . . Oh . . ."

"What, Jas?"

"It's Reggie Dodge."

"What?"

"He's dead. Died in his sleep last night. His wife found him in bed this morning."

"Dead of what?"

Jas exhaled slowly. "They don't know. The coroner has no idea."

# NINE

Diana Sanborn labored to project the gusto that she knew was expected of her. Her surroundings didn't help, though. This weathered cabin, no doubt a charming retreat half a century ago, now stank of mildew and something fouler. Out a small window she could see only dust and rusting machinery and a barren landscape. She longed to be home at Sanborn Ranch, alone in her bedroom with her journal.

She wasn't alone, though. Nor home. Diana surveyed the room. Charles Whit stood in one corner, smiling without appearing the least amused. Sheriff Rimmer sat in a rocking chair by the fireplace, rapidly pitching back and forth. Near the front door, James Mashburn sifted through a briefcase, looking distracted.

"Sorry to call you all here in such conditions," Whit was saying. "But we seem to have a problem."

They were gathered at Camp Mahrah on a blustery Sunday afternoon. Diana wondered at the original use of this cabin. It wasn't big enough to be a dormitory for the children, not lavish enough for the supervisors. The head counselor's quarters? The cook's? Outside, she could hear the wind howling through the oaks. The campus sat on a plateau, ringed by a forest thick with vines and moss. No one could see in, no one could see out. Each time she visited here, Diana felt uneasy.

"A problem." Roy Rimmer contemplated those words. "No, not a problem. It's an absolute catastrophe. If Greg Monarch gets another week of discovery, the whole goddamn package is going to unravel. Just what is going on? Monarch was supposed to be stopped long ago."

"Yes," Whit agreed. "That was the plan."

Both men turned to Mashburn. The DA glared back at them. "We wouldn't need a plan if you folks hadn't made such a goddamn mess of things to start with."

"Be that as it may—" Whit began.

"You're right," Mashburn interrupted. "Be that as it may, I now have a job to do. I tried to stop Monarch, just as we discussed. Went to two conferences with Judge Solman. Second one we even brought the attorney general with us, for chrissake. Solman wouldn't back down. We couldn't push him off this."

"We have to." Rimmer was up out of his chair now. "We've got to stop the bleeding."

"Excuse me, gentlemen." Diana offered a puzzled, ingenuous smile. "What more is there hidden away in your mysterious files?"

Mashburn leaned forward, hands on knees. "I ask the same question, Roy. Some of what's come out so far is news to me. Is there more to come? Pray share with us."

Rimmer waved him off. "It's not the documents I'm worried about now. It's Sarah Trant's mouth. And you, Ms. Sanborn, should worry as much about that as any of us."

Diana didn't look worried. "I don't believe Mr. Monarch has a clue about our situation in El Nido. He simply wants to rescue Sarah."

Whit poked at the fire with the tip of his cane. "Why do you say that, Ms. Sanborn? If I may inquire."

"We've spoken. He's never asked about El Nido. And Sarah's not talking, I'm sure of that."

Whit turned from the fire. "Why are you so sure?"

"Because Sarah doesn't really have anything to tell."

"She knows," Rimmer interjected. "She knows."

"But she doesn't know she knows," Diana said. "Bless her heart."

Whit sat down next to Diana. "Not good enough, Ms. Sanborn. I require considerably greater reassurance, as do my colleagues. We want Monarch out of El Nido, we want an end to this unexpected habeas proceeding. Otherwise, we quite reasonably fear, everything will blow wide open."

*Everything.* Diana turned that word over in her mind. So much it could encompass. *Everything.* By that did they mean the moment in El Nido history when Edward P. Sanborn so decisively dispatched the demons of discord? Or did they mean, more generally, that moment when life soured in El Nido? Moments, rather; there were more than one, of course.

"Mr. Whit," Diana said. "You talk as if you own this whole valley."

Whit stared at her. He waved an arm. "From yon mountain to yon mountain, I ought to."

"And from heaven to hell, Mr. Whit?"

Whit's smile did not register in his light gray eyes. "I'm sure you understand we need to quell this, Ms. Sanborn. Otherwise, it may be the end for all of us and, I'm afraid, for your cherished El Nido."

"Why make this point to me?" Diana asked, sounding irritated. "You and your colleagues are the ones with the power to quell this."

"And quell it we will, Ms. Sanborn. Don't you worry, given the stakes. I seek only your continued support in this effort. You've been with us for so long, it would be a shame to lose you."

Diana gazed steadily at Whit. "Yes," she said. "That would be a shame."

Whit moved his face closer to hers. "It's just that you've been so hospitable to Greg Monarch since his arrival. You offered him your guest room and your doctor. You visit with him. You seem to want him around."

"I was simply being a human being that first weekend, hard as that might be to understand. He'd been in an accident, he needed medical attention."

"And since then, Ms. Sanborn?"

"You and I are of different generations, Mr. Whit, and, forgive me, different backgrounds. Perhaps that's why you find my manners peculiar."

Whit rose and walked to the fireplace. He stood with his

broad back to the flames, warming his hands. "I'm sure that must be it. I hope so, at least. My colleagues and I, we would feel just devastated if you abandoned us."

A man's holler out in the yard interrupted them. Through the window they could see Camp Mahrah's burly caretaker waving for his boss to come outside. "Please excuse me," Whit said as he headed for the door. "Always something to attend to around here."

"Mr. Whit," Diana called, just as he was about to step outside. "What are your plans these days for Camp Mahrah?"

Whit stopped, turned. "Maybe I'll develop all this as a religious center," he said. "Now that Christ has become the center of my life, that might just be its best purpose."

Alex Ramirez studied the bull fuming at him from the far corner of the corral. He thought hard about tailing him, but questioned whether his horse possessed the necessary sensibility today. Pablo knew what to do, but he did not always wish to work in such close concert with the one who rode him—or anyone, for that matter. Alex respected and understood that impulse. He turned away from the bull. He'd leave him be for now. He'd leave them all be. Alex faced into the wind and turned up his collar. The animals were skittish today, anyway. This was a real blow. Up to fifty miles an hour, he judged.

A cloud of dust kicked up by the winds caught his attention. It was moving toward him, down the dirt road that led from Sanborn Ranch to Camp Mahrah. Then the dust lifted for an instant, and he saw under it Diana's white pickup, bouncing and lurching among the potholes. She was driving faster than the wind.

"Alex!" She called to him even before she climbed out of the truck. "Alex, over here. Get out of this blasted gale."

They sat in the pickup, watching a wall of live oaks bending with each gust. "Whit is agitated," she said. "And Whit is suspicious."

Alex looked unimpressed as Diana described her meeting

at Camp Mahrah. When she finished, he popped a toothpick into his mouth. "What can Whit do?" he asked.

"Dear God," Diana sputtered. "You proud Latino men."

"Whit doesn't run the federal courts."

"But Whit has associates, Alex."

"We never see them."

"No, and I suspect we never will. But they're thinking of us."

Alex looked at her with raised eyebrows.

"They would be devastated if I abandoned them," Diana said. "That's what Whit told me. Devastated."

"Just like Sarah Trant was?"

"Alex! Dear God."

"We have become part of something that is not good."

She turned on him. "We're in the right here, Alex. We have a just cause. Sometimes that requires sacrifices."

"Human sacrifices?"

Diana glared at him. "It's more complicated than that. As you very well know, Alex."

"You can say so," he replied, "if you want."

Diana swung away from him and stared out the window. The bowed trees stood at nearly a forty-five-degree angle now. "I received another anonymous letter yesterday," she said. "Same message."

Greg watched Sarah through the small window that gave onto the prisoner's meeting room. Usually they brought her to him; this time she was waiting. She appeared calm today.

"Watch out for her," said the guard at Greg's side. "She's dangerous."

Greg looked at him. It was the thin one with big ears again. "I've been so advised by your buddies more than once. I've got it now, I think."

The guard's face remained blank. "Reminders never hurt."

"Are you assigned full-time to Sarah Trant?" Greg asked. "You always seem to be around."

"Only when you're here, Mr. Monarch."

"I see," Greg said as the door to the meeting room swung open for him. "Much obliged for your guidance."

Sarah looked up at his entry. Her long dark hair, parted in the middle, framed a face full of hope. He was right about the calm he'd sensed at the window. He prayed that it might prove a good day for Sarah to talk.

"How are you doing?"

She offered a rueful smile. "Not throwing knives around today."

"Come on, now, you never did."

She raised her eyebrows. "Even I remember a certain motel room on a Canadian island."

"I meant here, in El Nido."

Sarah started to respond, then stopped. She looked down at her feet and clasped her hands together. "You sound so certain."

Greg searched for the right response. No, he wasn't certain. He just wanted to be certain. "You were framed, Sarah. . . ." That much was surely true. "Through discovery and depositions, we've been seeing all the evidence they held back at your trial."

"All the evidence?"

"Do you remember a blue-checked kerchief, Sarah?"

She looked wary now. "No . . . no."

"Who was wearing boots that night?"

"I . . . No one . . . I don't know. . . ."

"Why did Diana Sanborn want you convicted for Brewster Tomaz's murder?"

"She didn't, she didn't!" Sarah bit off the words, then looked dismayed at her outburst.

"Why do you say that, Sarah? What do you mean? What reason do you have to defend Diana?"

Sarah didn't answer. Slowly her eyes lost their focus. She rose from her chair, humming and swaying to a private rhythm. "Diana," she said. "I think something happened to Diana long ago."

"Has she told you?"

"No. . . . No. . . . I just sensed it."

Greg reached to still her. "I care more about what happened five years ago," he said. "At the river, between the two of you."

Sarah stopped humming. She looked at him. "I pushed Brewster Tomaz in the river, then ran away."

"Where was Diana?"

"I didn't see Diana."

"Why did Brewster Tomaz say it was you who cut him?"

Sarah stepped closer and wrapped her arms around him, as if she meant them to dance. "Maybe Brewster wanted to get me in trouble."

Greg held her off, gripping her arms at the elbows. "This won't do, Sarah. Your habeas hearing starts next week. You have less than six months to go. You need to stay with me."

Sarah studied his tightly curled fingers. "During Easter services that first year after we parted, I wrote a letter to you in my head and started to cry. The guy with me thought I was touched by all the banners and trumpets and the choir. I was saying goodbye to you. . . ."

"Sarah—what did Reggie Dodge tell you during the trial? What did he know about Tomaz's murder? What did he get from the prosecutors?"

"I have no idea. He barely spoke to me. Why don't you ask him?"

Greg slowed down now. He cupped her face with his hands. "Sarah, I can't ask him. Reggie Dodge is dead. He died last week, before I could talk to him. Some rare type of infection, they say."

That news appeared to undo her. She slumped into Greg's arms with a small cry, and stood close against him. "Oh my," she said. He held her now, trying to soothe. She responded, pressing against him, clinging to him.

Despite himself, Greg became aware that he could feel her thighs and breasts. A memory rose of the day he tackled her on the motel floor and lay atop her. Alarmed at his own feelings, he tried to move her away, but she wrapped herself tighter around him. "Sarah," he said. "Sarah."

Just then an arm reached between them. Following the arm

came the prison guard's bony face. "Now, now," he said. "There'll be none of that in this prison."

After entering the El Nido basin on the main highway from La Graciosa, it was possible to swing south onto Old Brook Road and use it to approach the village. Greg, traveling back and forth between La Graciosa and El Nido, found he favored this more scenic if winding route. Old Brook Road ascended slowly to the east, winding gracefully as it followed El Nido Creek, whose clear sparkling waters it crossed and recrossed twelve times in four miles. At points the road passed under high banks fringed with giant sycamores, and at others it opened out into gentle dells dotted here and there with weathered farmhouses. Then, past the village, at Tiger Canyon, the outlet to upper El Nido, Old Brook hooked to the north and climbed sharply into the La Luna foothills.

Driving this route late on the day of his encounter with Sarah, Greg stopped and looked back over his shoulder when he reached the Tiger juncture. All of the lower El Nido Valley spread before him, luminous under a long blue sky. The setting didn't please him. He felt too confined, hemmed in as he was by a sheer oak-covered cliff on one side and the brooding mass called Gunpowder Mountain on the other. He had no choice, though. By Greg's reading of the county map, a gravel spur off this end of Old Brook provided a back way into Camp Mahrah. He wanted to revisit the camp before the habeas hearing began, preferably without being evicted so quickly this time. He sensed that Charles Whit's machinations up there had a bearing on Sarah's fate.

Greg mulled the tenuous links. Sarah Trant had openly fought against Whit and ModoCorp. Diana Sanborn had fought them too, but didn't want it to seem that way now. Diana and Sarah once had some sort of bond. What had happened? If Brewster Tomaz didn't make a dying declaration, then why did Diana belatedly step forward with such a claim? There must be something in all this, Greg told himself. Something that explained why El Nido County had found Sarah Trant guilty of first-degree murder.

Or maybe not: Perhaps it was simpler. Perhaps he once again was defending a murderer, and once again was trying to convince himself otherwise. In truth, Sarah herself wasn't claiming innocence with much vigor. Sarah was conveniently going away whenever Greg pressed her. Games within games. That's what he'd been drawn into. And what if he won those games? Might another unstable killer end up walking the streets of a bucolic Central California town? Perfect, Greg thought. Maybe he could bag another Lawyer of the Year Award to boot.

Thus occupied, Greg didn't at first notice the car trailing him far in the distance. Only as it began to close on him did he catch its image in his rearview mirror. Since there was no turnoff on this cliffside road, and the gravelly curves made speeding up a reckless maneuver, Greg slowed down instead. He wanted to see who was following him.

Whoever it was, he didn't appear to be in a hurry. Each time the two cars rounded another bend they were closer together, but not by much. Watching in his rearview mirror, Greg measured the slowly narrowing gap. Not until they were fifty feet apart did he spot the big red spotlights set in the other car's rear window. He had a black-and-white on his tail. Property of the El Nido County Sheriff's Department.

Yet the man behind the wheel didn't look like a sheriff's deputy. At twenty feet, Greg could see him clearly. He had a fat face and a ragged reddish-brown beard. He was wearing what looked to be overalls. Greg had the sense he'd seen him before, but couldn't place where. He also had the sense that this wasn't the spot to get reacquainted.

Greg punched his accelerator, exploding in a cloud of dust and pebbles. Going into the first curve, he kept his foot on the gas. By the second bend he'd lost sight of the black-and-white. At the third he saw a dirt road off to the right that climbed into the mountains. A cattle guard blocked it. Greg braked hard, jumped out, threw open the gate. Once through it, he stopped and pulled the gate shut. Then he again hit the gas.

Ten minutes down the road, Greg decided he'd lost both the

black-and-white and his way. He didn't know where he was. Yet the meadows and slopes looked familiar. He tried to envision the route he'd followed in the past half hour. It occurred to him he'd traveled in a wide arc, a sort of half-circle. He must now be in the foothills to the north of El Nido Village, heading southwest. He was, in other words, approaching the back end of Sanborn Ranch.

Ten minutes more and he was there. With an odd sense of appreciation, he drove down the trail that led toward the Sanborn stables, and then beyond to the main house. He parked near the barn and climbed out of his car, feeling as if he'd reached a sanctuary. Diana greeted him at the door to the kitchen.

"Glad you're home . . ." Greg began to say. Then he noticed Diana's expression. She appeared distraught.

"Sheriff Rimmer is looking for you," she said.

"Tell me about it. I've been in a chase—"

"Greg, you don't understand. One of the guards, out at the prison. He's saying he saw you have improper physical contact with Sarah Trant."

Greg's throat went dry. He tried to speak but couldn't.

"They've filed a report about you," Diana said. "Sheriff Rimmer has it in his mind to charge you with sexual misconduct."

# TEN

Jasmine Gest, loping atop the Appaloosa she called Dusty, felt his eyes from one hundred yards away. Instantly, she sensed he was waiting for her. Fred Darvill, the wizened but still sharp-tongued eighty-year-old proprietor of El Nido Antiques, was not the sort to wander along the equestrian trail in Sanborn Park. He would more likely be found beside the spittoon in the Gaucho Tavern, or else beside his calculator and ledgers. Whiskey and profits, that's what interested the old coot. Except for now, on this warm autumn afternoon. Jas shifted in her saddle. What did he want with her?

"Hey there, Jasmine," Darvill called out. "Pretty sunset isn't it?"

Jas reluctantly reined in Dusty. Besides running his antique shop, Darvill served as curator at the local historical museum. She worked for him in a sense, although without getting paid, at least not in money. What he provided her was an acute ear on various rumblings in the community.

"Actually," she said, "I'd call it your average sunset."

Darvill spit a gob of tobacco-stained saliva onto the edge of the horse path, then suddenly launched into a volley of sneezing. Bent over, a red handkerchief to his nose, he heaved and snorted. With a bald sunburned head and a scratchy five-day-old white beard, he suggested to Jas a miner fresh from the Sierra foothills. "Damn allergies," Darvill muttered when he'd finished. "Happens whenever I even walk through the park."

Jas shook her head in sympathy. Darvill was an eccentric curmudgeon, but at least he could spin some droll tales, and he meant no harm. Born and raised in El Nido, he knew more about the valley's history than anyone, and cared about it in a way far different from his fellow merchants. Jas wasn't sure, but thought he'd even sided with Sarah Trant during some of her confrontations with ModoCorp.

"So why are you in the park, Mr. Darvill?"

The old man extracted a folded manila envelope from his jacket pocket and pressed it into Jas's hand. His eyes glinted. "The welfare of El Nido, that's why I'm here, Jasmine."

Jas glanced at the envelope but didn't open it. "I'm afraid you've lost me. What is this?"

Darvill moved closer and began to stroke her horse's neck. "Cattle . . . that's what it is. Dead cattle."

Jas searched her memory. "Is this museum business, Mr. Darvill?"

The old man started sneezing again. Bent over nearly double, he looked as if he were suffocating. Jas jumped off Dusty and came to his side. He reached for her arm to steady himself. His eyes had turned red and watery, yet still they showed a spark. "Not museum business, no, Jasmine. Newspaper business. Something for you to write about."

"Something for me—"

Darvill waved her off. "Got to get out of here, Jas. Damn pollen is going to kill me." He turned away, then looked back over his shoulder. "You didn't get this stuff from me, didn't even see me. But read what's in there. See what you think."

She watched him hobble down the path, then tore open the envelope he'd left her. From it she pulled out four typed pages and three photographs. Dead cattle, he'd said, and that's what the photos showed. Jas studied the pages. "CALIFORNIA DEPT. OF AGRICULTURE," read the uppercase words at the top of each sheet. Then, under it: "Confidential Document. Not For Public Release."

Jas looked up, searching the park for a sign of Darvill, but he'd disappeared. She turned back to the pages and began reading. Each page described in fine detail the death of a single cow. Three dead heifers, total. All in the El Nido Valley over the past six months. All at Sanborn Ranch.

Jas couldn't follow the technical jargon that filled most of the pages. She could tell only that they'd taken samples and performed tests, vainly searching for a cause of the deaths. One of the cows had lungs filled with fluid, but the two others had simply ceased breathing; it was as if their brains had stopped sending signals to inhale and exhale. *Precise explanation unavailable* is how the state bureaucrats put it. On each page, that same conclusion: *Precise explanation unavailable.*

That was all. Reaching the end of the report, Jas flipped back through the pages to the start and read them again. Obscure and qualify, that was the timeworn hallmark of state bureaucrats. Yet even for them, this report stood out. They didn't want to speculate, they weren't sure, they didn't really know. *Precise explanation unavailable.* That's all they could say.

Jas mounted Dusty and kicked her into a fast lope. Darvill was certainly right about one thing. This was something for her to write about.

After rereading Jas's article while sitting by the fountain in Sanborn Park, Greg walked across the street and along the Arcade. At the entrance to Gaucho's Tavern he stopped. From inside the bar he thought he heard the voice of Alex Ramirez. Greg stepped through Gaucho's swinging door. The room before him was dark and narrow, packed with six billiards tables, side by side. Off to the right, a chipped oak bar ran the length of the room. In the rear, a big-screen TV filled the back wall.

There was Alex, on the TV screen. He had to admit, Alex was effective. Greg ordered a Graciosa Brew and settled on a stool at the end of the bar nearest the screen. Alex stood before the camera without artifice: the cowboy hat pushed back on his head, the toothpick rolling slowly in his mouth, the eyes full of deadpan pride. "The state scientists came down and investigated. They found no explanation. We suspect some sort of virus. Just one of those things. It's not unknown. If you run cattle as long as my family, you see these things. . . ."

You did indeed, Greg thought. In Chumash County, he recalled from his history lessons, a brutal drought wiped out some three hundred thousand head between 1862 and 1864, leaving bleached bones strewn throughout the arroyos. It also left many cattle-baron families bereft. As the local historians told it, a young ranchero who lost everything hitched his wildest horse to a buckboard one windy moonlit night and rattled out of town, watched only by a solitary fevered old woman, propped up by her window. Out near the fog-enshrouded Clam Beach cliffs, it was said, he whipped his horse to a frenzy, then plunged with it over the rim to the wet rocks below, leaving only a broken wheel at the cliff's edge as a farewell note.

Greg found himself trying to sort out his thoughts about Diana Sanborn. She wasn't an ally; she was, in truth, an adversary, the person whose testimony put Sarah on death row. Yet he felt an inexplicable concern for her. A threatening blackmail letter, now three dead cows: What was going on? Why was this woman under siege?

Glancing up at the TV, Greg saw that Diana had joined Alex. "The state tells us a precise explanation is unavailable . . . ," she was saying. "Surely this will pass. . . . We live in a grand unspoilt valley . . ."

Greg sensed someone at his elbow. He turned to find Jasmine Gest on the stool beside him. They'd been regularly crossing paths like this, without apparent plan. Greg knew the contact wasn't as random as it seemed.

"What do you think?" Jas asked. "You believe them?"

"No, I don't. I wonder, though."

"About what?"

"Diana Sanborn seems to me a woman in need of help."

Jas regarded him with amused skepticism. "Not an appropriate feeling for Sarah Trant's lawyer, I'd say. Diana Sanborn is Sarah's worst enemy."

Greg put his bottle down. He'd grown accustomed to sparring with her. "Thanks for the input. But I think I'm still capable of deciding which of my feelings is appropriate."

"Ooooh," she said. "Such vehemence."

"I'm just trying to sort things out, Jas."

"You need to do your sorting all alone? God, Greg . . . Don't tell me you're one of those men who still needs his space."

"What I need," he said, "is more information."

She instantly turned serious. "Such as?"

"Diana and Sarah. Tell me more about the two of them together."

Jas mulled his question before speaking. "From what I can tell," she said finally, "Diana was Sarah's Svengali. Sarah adored her, worshiped her. Would do anything Diana asked."

"Why? What was Diana's hold on her?"

"You would need a shrink to answer that one. All I know is, Sarah changed around Diana. Got so sparkly, and focused, too. Especially when Diana did her grand-old-lady turn. The gracious-yet-commanding stuff. Sarah really came alive then."

"That displeased you?"

Jas lifted a beer to her lips. "It's just that sometimes I got the sense Diana was manipulating Sarah."

"Maybe she was helping Sarah. Galvanizing her. There are moments when Sarah needs that."

Jas tapped the bar counter. "You see all sides and possibilities, don't you, Greg? Nothing is ever black-and-white."

"What about you? Your world is lit by bright clarity?"

"Sometimes, yes, sometimes things are clear."

"So that's your worldview. At the park that first night, you said 'let's save it for later.' I've been waiting ever since."

"Sorry . . . You're still waiting."

"A bit more complicated than bright clarity?"

"Oh yes."

"Tell me about it."

"You have a few days?"

"I could find them."

"Warning . . . I'm a handful."

"I bet."

"Do you?"

Greg studied her. "You blame Diana for Sarah's situation?"

he asked. "You think Diana egged her on? Set her against ModoCorp and Tomaz?"

She looked away. "Wouldn't say that exactly. Sarah had her own ax to grind, after all. She didn't need Diana to get her marching and shoving. . . . And yet, who knows? . . . I wonder . . ."

"Aha." Greg gave her a look full of mock surprise. "The matter is shaded, then."

Jas started to respond, but new voices distracted them. They glanced back at the TV. Alex and Diana had been replaced by a twenty-second "bright" concerning volunteer crafts programs in El Nido's elementary schools. Greg imagined himself up there on the screen, cornered by the camera as the anchor warned about "alarming charges" of sexual misconduct at the women's prison.

"You're right about one thing," he told Jas. "I do see all possibilities."

The post office tower bell chimed the seven o'clock hour as Greg walked through Sanborn Park. Dusk once again was falling. On the equestrian trail, a scattering of riders and bicyclists dodged the occasional walker. Greg realized that he'd grown accustomed to the rhythms of this town.

At the edge of the park's west boundary, he stopped. He was standing before the county administrative building. In the window of the district attorney's suite, he saw lights still burning. He studied them for a minute, then pushed open the building's front door. The staff had gone home for the night; he had the hallways to himself. He knocked at Jim Mashburn's door. The DA opened it himself, looking distracted. The sleeves of his brown cardigan were pushed up above his elbows. A pair of reading glasses sat on the bridge of his nose. In the gloom, Mashburn squinted. "Greg," he sputtered. "What are you doing here?"

"Saw your light on, thought we might chat for a minute."

Mashburn stood in silence. His displeasure was palpable. "Way to do that is to make an appointment. Call my office tomorrow."

Greg put a hand on the door to keep it open. "Come on, Jim. We need to talk."

Mashburn looked about, as if searching for a means of escape. He put a hand on his side of the door. For a moment they stood like that, gauging the pressure each could feel from the other. Then Mashburn shrugged, and waved Greg inside.

They sat across from each other, Mashburn barricaded behind a desk piled high with transcripts and briefs. Greg wondered what he'd find in those stacks if given the chance to explore. The federal discovery process had yielded multiple revelations, but surely Mashburn hadn't handed over everything.

"How are things in Chumash County?" Mashburn asked. "You still have that house on the creek?"

"Still there. But our buddy Dennis Taylor, as you know, has moved on. From Chumash County DA to state attorney general, just as he always planned."

"Yes. . . . Yes, I see Dennis from time to time."

"Ever remind Taylor of the summer you tussled with him over his grand jury probe?"

Mashburn held up a hand in protest. "*We* tussled with him. The summer *we* tussled with him."

"Yes, that's right. The two of us."

Mashburn rose and turned toward the window that gave onto a view of Sanborn Park. In the dark, illuminated only by a solitary streetlight's yellow flicker, the fountain looked like an apparition. "Hell of a lot has passed under the bridge since then."

Greg watched him. The moon lit one side of Mashburn's face; the other remained in shadows. "You were going to quit the law, I thought. Change your whole life. A new direction."

Mashburn turned toward him. "And you were going to stop defending killers. Told me you were sick of all that. That day we hiked in the dunes."

Greg reflected. He remembered an honest camaraderie with Mashburn, but he didn't recall saying such a thing. What did it matter, anyway? Whatever he'd said, they were just words, uttered years ago.

"I've had the chance to look at the responses you filed in federal court," Greg advised. "I'm wondering about them."

Mashburn stared at him. "Wondering what, Greg?"

"Whether you really want to make such representations to Judge Solman."

Mashburn walked back to his desk and sat down. "Stop, Greg. This is how it's done. You want to challenge the state's claims, do it in court. You're wasting our time."

Greg studied the DA. Yes, they had talked that day. After celebrating their victory over the local Chumash County prosecutor, they'd imagined other lives they might live. It had been just an afternoon's fantasy. Yet they had talked.

Greg said, "You claim in your response that Diana Sanborn right away told deputies about Tomaz's dying declaration. Right there at the river. On the very first night. Yet this isn't reflected in the initial police reports. It's also not what was represented five years ago at Sarah's trial. Or to me at any time since I started taking depositions."

Mashburn rubbed his temples, looking irritated. "That's all explained in my response, Greg. There was a lot of confusion back then about what was said when, to whom. One of the key deputy sheriffs went on medical leave because of a heart attack right after Tomaz's death, so files got mislaid and communications broke down. We've just now found that deputy's original handwritten notes. He spoke to Ms. Sanborn that first night. Looking at his notes, we found that he recorded mention by Diana of a dying declaration. It just didn't get into a formal report for a few days."

"Oh, come on, Jim . . ."

Mashburn held his hands palm up. "We have an affidavit from the deputy about this, Greg. We have a document expert affirming the handwritten notes are genuine, and five years old."

"And what do you think, Jim?"

"What do you mean?"

"You think this is how it happened?"

"Yes. . . . Damnit Greg, it can be proven."

"How do you know what happened?"

"How do I know? I have all this evidence. I have—"

"Jim, come on. You weren't there at the time, you weren't the DA. Where's it coming from?"

Mashburn hesitated. "Sheriff Rimmer," he said. "It's Roy's story."

Greg said nothing.

"But damnit, Greg, we also have Diana Sanborn. She agrees she spoke to this deputy."

Greg couldn't hide his surprise. "Diana? She goes along with this?"

Mashburn allowed himself a small, tight grin. "She most certainly does. We have an affidavit."

"You do? When did she sign it?"

"Just last week."

Greg labored to understand. To him, Diana had openly admitted making a belated report about the dying declaration. *I was trying to protect Sarah.* Why switch tales now? "How'd you get to her, Jim?"

Mashburn flushed. "I resent that, Greg."

Greg didn't care. An angry James Mashburn would be better than this fellow. "Something lopsided here, Mr. DA. Something to investigate, maybe."

"You're way out of bounds, Greg—"

"One other thing," Greg said. "How do you sleep at night?"

Mashburn rose from his chair and started around his desk. Greg rose too. The DA stopped inches from him. "You sanctimonious hypocrite," Mashburn said. "A man of your morals shouldn't point fingers at anyone else."

"My morals?"

Mashburn's expression had turned stony. "Sheriff Rimmer tells me you were caught handling your client in the interview room. Just about to wet your willie, way Rimmer tells it."

"Yet another bit of fiction from the El Nido County sheriff."

"Everyone spins stories but you, Greg? Is that how it works?"

"How can you stand side by side with someone like Rimmer?"

Mashburn pointed Greg toward the door. "To be a prosecutor you have to make choices," he said. "You have to decide. And I've decided. I'm filing charges against you."

# ELEVEN

Hot fierce winds roared through the El Nido Valley on the morning Sarah Trant's hearing was to start. The smell of sage and greasewood filled the air; the usual sound of birds had given way to the occasional buzz of a deerfly. Diana Sanborn, rising from a troubled sleep, immediately sensed something amiss. At her window, she pulled back the thick drapes. In the distance, at the far northwest side of the valley, she saw an ominous pall of reddish-brown smoke rising from the towering La Luna Mountain Range. It had been a dry year, and now, in October, the brush and timber were crackle dry. If prevailing winds shifted, Diana calculated, the fire might reach the valley by late afternoon.

She turned her ear to the window. On hot days you could hear the post office bell for miles. As she expected, it was tolling now. That bell always sounded at the report of a fire. The alarm brought out all the able-bodied men in El Nido, Alex among them. They'd soon be gathering at the edge of Sanborn Park, their arms full of backpacks and axes and water bottles.

Diana's thoughts drifted to other fires, long-ago fires in El Nido. She was seven when the most ferocious one nearly destroyed the entire valley. Her grandfather depended on her help even then. That first afternoon she filled buckets and rolled out garden hoses while Edward Sanborn consulted with his ranch crew and the local rangers. They all ate supper that evening under a big oak tree with the aid of a kerosene lantern. Then they hiked to the top of the highest hill on the ranch to inspect the distant blaze. The others all looked worried, so Diana matched their expression. Privately, though, she exulted at the thrilling wall of flames.

While they watched, the wind shifted suddenly toward the valley floor. By nine P.M. the fire, blown into unburned brush and timber along the hillside, had flared. By ten it had traveled eight miles, and was licking at the edge of El Nido's northernmost residential district. Diana's grandfather gathered tools and blankets, kissed her goodbye, and headed off to fight the flames.

The second day remained a blur to Diana. She remembered only a solid overcast of smoke over the entire valley, with no sun visible. She remembered almost everyone in El Nido madly fleeing from the valley by auto, buckboard, horse, and foot. Most of all, she remembered her grandfather returning to their ranch and staying put, refusing to believe that a fire would have the effrontery to burn him out.

By afternoon, their end of the valley was just about deserted but for Edward Sanborn's family and crew. By nine the trees and sky all around them glowed red. By ten the winds were howling at thirty miles an hour and the live oaks had begun to steam. Diana cried then, no longer so thrilled, but still her grandfather stood his ground. Not until nearly midnight, with the fire cresting the ridge just two miles from the ranch, did the winds shift, carrying flames back across already-blackened acreage. Without fuel, the hungry fire began to abate. "I knew we wouldn't be burnt out," Edward Sanborn told Diana, holding his granddaughter tightly in his arms. "I wasn't going to let that happen to us."

From her window Diana surveyed her perfect valley. Nothing stirred yet. No glowing red branches, no steaming oaks, no howling gale. Perhaps the winds would hold, perhaps the fire wouldn't reach them. To her surprise, Diana felt the slightest twinge of regret at that notion. Maybe El Nido needed a cleansing fire. A fire that consumed their history and legacy. A fire that allowed them all to start afresh.

Diana shook off such thoughts and turned her eyes to the mountain pass that led to Chumash County. Just sixty miles through that pass, Sarah Trant's hearing was about to begin in

La Graciosa's auxiliary courtroom. Diana tried to imagine that vintage chamber, with Sarah sitting beside Greg Monarch at the petitioner's table. She tried also to imagine herself in that room. On which day, she wondered, would Greg Monarch call her to the witness stand?

"Well now, gentlemen," Judge Solman was saying, "it looks like we have some preliminary business to handle. Make yourselves at home. Sit down."

They were standing in Solman's chambers, Greg Monarch and James Mashburn. The two settled into chairs before the judge's desk. Greg had never felt personally warm toward Solman, nor connected to him by bonds of taste or outlook. At this moment, though, he keenly appreciated that Solman would be presiding over Sarah's hearing.

"I'd ask that this conference be under seal," Greg began.

Solman held up a hand. "Let's hear first what it's about, okay? Then I'll decide. Does the DA's office want to start?"

Mashburn reached for a file, opened it, studied the pages before him. "The problem we have here," he said, "is that there's an issue concerning Mr. Monarch. A prison guard reports he saw him, well, having intimate contact with Sarah Trant."

Solman flinched at those words ever so slightly, but enough for Greg to notice. His hand moved to his forehead. "What?" he asked.

Mashburn kept his eyes on the pages in his hand. "The guard described what he saw to his supervisor, who brought it to us. We feel we can't just sit on this."

"Is that so?" Solman asked.

"Yes. . . . We feel this needs to be revealed."

"Let me see the guard's report," Solman commanded.

From the file on his lap, the DA handed over a two-page document. Solman scanned it, then reread it more slowly.

"Why?" the judge asked. "Why do you feel this needs to be revealed?"

"At the very least because it speaks to the character of the petitioner's lawyer. More important, it may mean Greg can't continue in this proceeding. We may very well choose to file charges against him."

Solman turned to Greg with raised eyebrows.

"First, I dispute every word in this report," Greg said. "Second, the DA's office has never even questioned me about these charges. They've just been waving the report in my face. Mr. Mashburn says he 'may very well' file charges. I respectfully submit that's garbage. He's trying to force me off the case."

Solman took off his reading glasses and squeezed the bridge of his nose. "Is that what you're trying to do, Mr. Mashburn?"

"No, Your Honor. That's not what I'm trying to do. My intent is twofold. One is to enforce the laws of El Nido County. The other is to protect this case's integrity. We go forward with Greg on the case, Sarah Trant would have a great basis for an appeal. Incompetent defense counsel due to inappropriate emotional involvement . . . I can hear Ms. Trant's next attorney shouting such words even now."

Solman again studied the guard's report. He held the document as a shield between him and the lawyers. "Inapproriate emotional involvement?" he asked. "What exactly do you mean, Mr. Mashburn?"

The DA glanced at Greg. "It's not just what happened at the prison, Your Honor. We've learned that Greg and Sarah once had a relationship. They were lovers. They—"

"What the hell are you doing, Jim?" Greg was half out of his seat, his voice rising. "I don't know where you 'learned' that. . . . Actually, I can imagine. . . . But it's no secret, and nothing that needs hiding. It happened more than twenty years ago. It's irrelevant now. You know that, Jim. You know that perfectly well."

Solman was looking at Greg. "So that's why Sarah asked for you. . . ."

Greg ignored him. "Tell me, Jim. . . . Have your investigators interviewed Sarah Trant? Has Sarah confirmed the guard's report?"

Mashburn scowled. "She denied it. What else is she going

to do? She loses her attorney otherwise. Perhaps her attorney even warned her that might happen if she talked. Perhaps—"

"Wait a minute," Judge Solman interrupted. "She's not making any accusation at all? She's disputing the accusation?"

Mashburn shifted in his seat. "Yes, sir, but—"

"So what's this about?" Solman interrupted again. "What are you doing?"

"As I said, we're enforcing our county's laws, and protecting our case."

The judge hesitated, tapping his desk with a pencil. His gaze swung from the DA to the defense attorney, then back again. The sight of Solman momentarily wavering reminded Greg that this man had that quality in him.

"Sorry, Mr. Mashburn," the judge said finally. "Your county's laws are of no concern at a federal habeas proceeding."

"But protecting our case does matter here, Your Honor. If this goes to appeal—"

"Okay, now." Solman waved Mashburn off. "I'll tell you what. I see what you have here, and I'm just not going to get into it. This is a federal habeas proceeding. You think you can pin a sex charge on Greg, give it a try. Go file over there in El Nido County Court. It's your prerogative. Give it a try."

Mashburn stuffed the guard's report back into his file as if it were contaminated. "Yes, Your Honor," he snapped. "We might just do that."

Greg stood up.

"Gentlemen," the judge declared, "we'll begin the hearing after lunch."

Rising from their creekside table at Stella's Café, Greg and Jas could smell smoke in the air. Their eyes instinctively traveled to the vast distant mountain range that separated La Graciosa from the hot inland valleys. The edge of an ugly brown cloud showed over the range's crest. A helicopter hovered silently off to one side. "Seems well to the north," Jas said. "Don't think that's near El Nido."

Greg didn't appear to hear her. "The one who puzzles me," he said, "is Mashburn. How could he be doing this? Defending the characters who prosecuted Sarah. Waving a phony charge at me. As if he doesn't have a conscience at all."

Slowly, Jas turned away from the mountains. "Of course, Mashburn might say the same about you. Defending an obvious killer. Playing games with the legal system. Obscuring the truth."

"Yes," Greg agreed. "He might."

She put a hand on his arm. "Jim Mashburn is no more sure of his role than you are. You both question what you're doing. You both have a conscience problem."

"Only in the law," Greg said, "would we call it a problem."

They'd spent the lunch hour analyzing the merits of Sarah's case. Despite everything damning he'd uncovered during discovery, Greg wanted more. A mind so inclined could still think Sarah looked mighty guilty. It would, Greg reasoned, finally come down to Brewster Tomaz's dying declaration, and that was the problem. Greg had managed to find a respected forensic pathologist who didn't think an expiring Tomaz could speak, but his was a qualified judgment. What with all the blood in the autopsy photos, Dr. Oscar Quagler, the medical examiner for San Luis, could only infer that Tomaz's carotid was cut. Which left the state a nice hole through which to run their own experts. The two doctors who did the autopsy would swear that the carotid hadn't been cut, and Dr. Montrose would agree with them that speech was possible. They'd end up with a stalemate, in other words. Nothing conclusive for either of them. Yet each lawyer would act as if he had God on his side.

Mashburn, of course, had someone of almost equal importance. *We also have Diana.* That's how Mashburn had put it. *We also have Diana.*

"Jas," Greg said as they walked the creekside pathway toward La Graciosa's courthouse, "that piece you wrote about the dead cattle at Sanborn Ranch. What's the inside story? What didn't you share with El Nido's citizens?"

Jas sniffed the air and glanced back at the mountain range. "Nothing more to know. I wrote what I had."

They were at La Graciosa's town square, in front of the

courthouse. Greg looked at his watch. "We have time. Let's sit for a while."

They settled on a bench near the creek. The plaza was popular at midday. Shoppers and office workers strolled at the water's edge, lounged near the bear fountain, ate sandwiches under spreading sycamores. Here and there, someone called out to Greg, waving. The newspaperman Jimmy O'Brien, as usual full of exuberant bombast, came over to complain. *Small-minded editors don't want me to cover your hearing, damnit. Nothing to do with Chumash County, they say. What the hell. Got something else even bigger right now. Tell you about it tonight* . . . Then Tim Ruthman headed his way, openly seeking congratulations. Two days before, he'd won Greg's drug case for him.

"Just keep passing those potheads to me," Ruthman grinned. "Helps pay the kid's orthodontia bills."

Greg smiled back with genuine appreciation. Ruthman, with his broad shoulders and thick mustache gone half to gray, looked more like an aging linebacker than a lawyer. Yet he knew how to work a courtroom. Greg truly needed him, now that the habeas hearing was under way. "Might just have to do that, Tim. Going to be tied up before Judge Solman for a while. In fact, I'll call you later today. Two more files need moving off my desk."

Ruthman glanced at Jas with open curiosity. Greg made the introductions without explaining who she was. Ruthman shot Greg a sideways wink as he turned and left. Jas laughed. "That's okay, Greg," she said. "I like being a mystery."

They gazed out at the creek. Below them, at the water's edge, a mother was helping her young daughter feed bread crumbs to a trio of hungry ducks. Greg watched as the birds grabbed their morsels, then drifted downstream. *Birds in the water.* The image tugged at him. He'd sat with Jas once before, watching a bird in the water. But it was a dead bird. A dead cormorant mired in an oil slick in the middle of El Nido Lake. Dead birds, then dead cattle.

"Explain to me again about El Nido's oil, Jas."

"What exactly do you want to know?"

"You told me at the lake how it oozed everywhere but wasn't worth anything. Low-grade unusable oil, and only in surface pockets. Drove all the oil prospectors to ruin a century ago."

"Yes. That's true. But it took some of them a long time to realize they'd failed. Lots of stuff about that in our historical museum. Memoirs, records, deeds. Come by sometime, I'll show you. Because I volunteer there, they let me roam at will."

"I'll do that when there's time. Just give me an overview right now."

"Not sure I can. Trouble is, I haven't really read that stuff closely. Didn't appear terribly interesting, to tell you the truth. A bunch of failures, a bunch of false turns in El Nido's history. It wasn't the valley's destiny, it's not what El Nido is about."

"What do you mean?"

"I mean visions of oil fields quickly faded after one false boom." Jas chewed on that, then continued. "You know, it's really something. Had El Nido's history been different, had the experts found the petroleum that they expected, the valley might be full of oil rigs instead of farms and orchards."

Greg was still staring at the creek. "It is something, isn't it?"

Jas watched him as if waiting for a signal, or another question. When none came, she moved closer to him on the bench.

"Why are you asking about this, Greg? What's it about?"

"Probably nothing."

Jas moved closer yet. She looked at him frankly, but he wouldn't meet her gaze. "What's with you?" she asked.

He kept his eyes on the moving water. "Sarah's execution date."

Jas raised a hand to his chin and turned his face toward her. "Who disappointed you so badly?" she asked. "Or did she scare you?"

"Let's go," Greg said, rising from the bench. "The hearing is about to start."

* * *

On the way to the courtroom, Greg stopped to visit Sarah in her prison cell. With regret, he pointedly asked a guard to remain in full sight just outside the barred window. Sarah sat on her cot in a simple white cotton dress and sandals. She looked uncomfortable.

"They came and questioned me," she said. "About you. About you and me."

"Yes, I know. They're trying to knock me off the case."

Sarah raised her hand to her mouth. "How could they do that?"

"They're threatening to charge me with sexual contact with you, Sarah."

"They call that sexual contact? Jesus . . ."

"It's okay," Greg said. "Don't bother. It won't come to anything."

"The hearing . . . ?"

"It's about to start. They'll be bringing you into the courtroom in a few minutes."

"What am I supposed to say?"

Greg glanced at the guard watching them, then moved closer to Sarah, lowering his voice. "If I call you to the stand, you're to tell what happened. Don't hide anything, don't change anything. Just tell the truth. You pushed Tomaz, he fell in the river, you ran off, you saw no one else."

"I . . . but . . . I . . ."

"Don't worry. You won't be called right away," Greg said. "And maybe not at all."

"Oh . . ."

"Sarah, tell me something." Greg kneeled down to where she sat. "Did Diana Sanborn ever talk to you about oil in the El Nido Valley?"

That question transformed Sarah; her eyes grew focused and fierce. "No," she said. "We never talked about any such thing."

There'd be no jury this time, just a solitary federal judge. Greg, entering the *asistencia*'s courtroom, reflexively turned his eyes to the empty bench where Solman soon would be sitting.

He didn't expect this judge, or any judge, to guarantee him justice—only a level playing field. He'd do the rest himself.

Greg glanced around. No more than a handful of spectators had claimed seats; the other lawyers and Sarah Trant had yet to arrive. Chumash County's auxiliary courtroom occupied what had been, a century before, the *asistencia*'s modest church. It had a vaulted and beamed ceiling, but was compact and narrow, only twenty-five feet in width, with seats for just 150 in twelve rows. Not the usual venue for a federal proceeding; instead of dark walnut walls and thick carpets, this one offered whitewashed plaster and pink-hued, hand-laid cement. It would be odd, arguing a federal habeas here in La Graciosa.

"I hope you understand I had to do that, Greg."

James Mashburn was standing at his end of the attorney's table, unpacking his briefcase.

"Do what?" Greg asked, acting mystified.

"Protect my case."

"That's what you call what happened in Solman's chambers?"

Mashburn threw a stack of files on the table. "Yes, damnit, that's what I call it."

"Then why hope for my understanding? It's all perfectly clear, isn't it, Jim?"

Mashburn's frown showed more unease than anger. He took a step back. His tone softened. "What do you say, Greg. Shall we get on with this hearing?"

"Soon as Judge Solman gets here."

The DA, leafing through papers now, kept his head down. "I heard something over lunch. Heard there's a problem with Solman."

At first Greg didn't register Mashburn's words. Then he did. He turned to the DA. "A problem? What do you mean?" Greg started toward Mashburn, but stopped when he saw Sarah Trant being led his way. She kept glancing about, as if trying to understand her surroundings. Gone were the focused, fierce eyes.

"He had some out-of-town visitors with him in his chambers," Mashburn said. "Fainted or something, right in front of them. A van full of paramedics came, then a doctor. For a while they weren't sure whether he could preside at this hearing."

"All rise!" the court bailiff called out.

Through the door leading to the judges' chambers came a pale stiff figure wrapped in black robes. He reached the bench and stopped for a moment, surveying the courtroom. The judge's robes billowed and opened enough for Greg to see the hints of Solman's fine charcoal-gray suit. Standing before them with narrowed eyes and a stiffly set jaw, Solman suggested a man determined to stay his course. He wouldn't look at Greg.

"Good afternoon," Solman said. "Sorry for the delay. I was taken dizzy in my chambers. They say I'm just fine now."

"Your Honor . . ." Greg started to approach the bench, framing his motion as he walked. Something had happened in the judge's chambers, something had transformed Solman. "I would like—"

"Don't bother, Mr. Monarch." Solman was waving him away, his mouth pinched with annoyance. "There's no point filing a motion to delay. I've been given a clean bill of health. I most certainly will be presiding at this habeas hearing."

# TWELVE

"Answer me, please. Did you not see that the left carotid artery had been totally severed?" In face of the witness's silence, Greg repeated his question. "Did you not see that the carotid had been cut?"

The petitioner went first at a habeas hearing, and Greg had started with Buster Lloyd, the emergency medical technician who'd examined Tomaz's bloodied body. Lloyd had cut his ponytail and bushy beard, so he looked nothing like the mountain man Greg had met weeks before at the end of Old Alder Road. He suggested now an eager junior executive at a bustling health maintenance organization. Which, in fact, he was. Health Shield, a giant Central California HMO, had hired him a month before, offering a lucrative post overseeing all operations in El Nido County.

"There was so much blood," Lloyd finally replied, frowning over Greg's question. "I couldn't really make it out clearly."

Greg nodded as if that were precisely the response he wanted. This was the third time Lloyd had ducked him. He'd expected something like this. They'd flipped Reggie Dodge's witnesses, so why not his? He just hadn't known which ones they'd get.

"But it was severed," Greg said. "To me, in your deposition, you said it was severed."

Another pause. "I'm not sure. . . . Yes . . . well . . ."

"Mr. Lloyd, you are under oath."

Without expression, Buster stared out into the courtroom. "I wasn't in a position right up close to his neck. I . . . I don't remember specifically seeing exactly the left carotid artery."

Greg approached, and stood within inches of the witness. "Would it refresh your recollection if you looked at what you told me in your deposition?"

This time the pause stretched on for twenty seconds. It didn't appear as if Buster would answer.

"Your deposition," Greg said finally. "Where you were also under oath?"

"Okay . . . yes."

Greg handed him his deposition and pointed at the relevant lines. Lloyd read, then looked up.

"Well, okay, yes," he said. "I recall saying that."

"But the question is, does it refresh your recollection of actually seeing the severed artery?"

Lloyd frowned and started to stroke the beard he'd shaved off. "We didn't explore the wound. We didn't open it up. There was so much blood."

"In your deposition you said—"

"But I never told the police that," Lloyd interrupted. "I never told them I saw a cut carotid."

Greg leaned against the witness stand railing as if he were this man's neighbor. "Mr. Lloyd, do you recall telling me that the police never even interviewed you after Brewster Tomaz's murder?"

Lloyd made a show of great puzzlement. "But there's a police report, Mr. Monarch. A police report of their interview with me."

Greg tried a flash of anger. "You're under oath, Mr. Lloyd. Yes or no. Didn't you say the police never interviewed—"

Mashburn interrupted: "Your Honor, I object. Asked and answered. He's badgering his own witness."

Greg headed for his chair before Solman could respond. "That's okay," he said. "No more questions."

Buster was only the start. Witness after witness took the stand sounding not the least like the people Greg had deposed.

They qualified where they'd once been certain; they were vague where they'd once been precise. A deputy sheriff couldn't recall just where along the river he'd seen the strange boot prints with nailed half-soles. An audio technician couldn't explain the odd clicks heard on a taped interview with Sarah Trant. An evidence clerk wasn't sure she'd ever seen various now-missing photos of the murder scene. *It's possible but not likely. . . . It's hard to say. . . . The photos are blurry. I wasn't there. . . .* Greg hammered them hard, reading passages from their depositions, pointing out discrepancies between their words then and now. He'd deposed everyone he could find for just this reason: to pin them down before they were turned. Yet even with their previous testimony before them, the witnesses frowned and coughed and shifted about. *It's hard to say. . . . I wasn't there. . . .*

"This reminds me of my murder trial," Sarah whispered during a brief lull. "Exactly the same. Poor Reggie. He hadn't a clue."

"We've got a clue," Greg replied, "but we've still got some terribly malleable witnesses."

"They're denying their own words. . . ."

"Yes. Plenty of baffled good ol' boy aplomb . . . Plays well in most courtrooms."

Greg was sitting as if coiled for attack, drumming his fingers on the attorney's table. Sarah looked at him with pleading eyes. "Thank God you're not confused, Greg. . . . Please don't get confused."

Greg watched as Mashburn poured two spoons of sugar into his coffee, then reached for a peach Danish. They were in Judge Solman's chambers on the third morning of the hearing. Solman sipped a cup of tea behind his desk. Greg drank water.

"What's this about, Greg?" Solman asked. His voice now had a nervous edge to it almost constantly. "I'd like to keep these private sessions in chambers to a minimum. Public has a right to know what's going on."

*What is this about.* Greg wondered how to answer. The night before, he'd visited the spinster Judith Daniels to arrange her transportation to this hearing. Judith Daniels, the critical eyewitness who'd seen someone other than Sarah Trant fleeing upriver at the time of the murder. She'd not been called or even revealed during Sarah's initial murder trial, yet she'd been cooperative over the past few weeks with Greg and Jas. Coherent, too. Pot of fresh-brewed coffee always on the stove, like someone's grandmother. Sometimes a plate of just-baked chocolate-chip cookies. A round butterball of a woman with gray-black hair pulled into a bun. A little flighty maybe, a little jumpy, what with her odd quavering laugh and her eyes constantly darting about. But always certain of what she'd seen. *A figure in a slicker. Bigger than Sarah Trant. Ran like a man, hopped right across the river. Headed toward the yonder alder tree. Saw his body clearly in the moonlight. Not his face, though.*

Always eager to tell everyone, too. Until last evening, that is. *I can't, Mr. Monarch. No, I won't.* That's what she'd cried out, over and over. *I can't. I won't.* Greg tried to reason with her, tried to inquire, but to no end. The whole time, Judith Daniels stayed in her kitchen, slowly wiping her countertop with a wet dishcloth. No coffee, no cookies. Her countertop bare, bleached of all content.

"Your Honor," Greg said, "we have a new issue that just came up. It's about a critical eyewitness. For weeks she's been saying she would testify. Last night I visited her, to arrange for her to be here, and she just flatly refused. All of a sudden. I asked her why. She said that she'd been called on by Roy Rimmer."

"Roy Rimmer?" the judge asked.

Mashburn splashed coffee on the carpet as he leaned forward to explain. "He's the El Nido County sheriff, Your Honor."

"Rimmer came to see her and just got her very, very scared," Greg continued. "Asked her questions about what she saw at the creek, what she was going to say at the hearing, was she sure of her testimony, did she know what perjury was. She's not a stable woman to begin with, and Rimmer put her over the edge. Now she says she won't testify unless she can do it in chambers and there's an absolute guarantee her name won't be in the press."

"Your Honor," Mashburn said. "May I speak?"

The judge turned to him. "Yes, please do."

"First of all, Counsel here has given me no advance notice of this, so I have not checked into the facts of the matter. But I do know that Rimmer was planning to visit Judith Daniels. That is something we don't apologize about. She was obviously a potential witness at this hearing. She hasn't been deposed. We have a fair right to go out and talk to her regarding what her testimony was going to be. I don't believe the El Nido sheriff would threaten her or anyone like that. I resent that suggestion, in fact. I resent that greatly. This was fair exercise of our right. Nothing more."

Greg looked at the DA. "Jim, just how can you say what the sheriff did or didn't do?"

"He's under my direction. He functions as investigator for the DA's office. He does what I wish."

"What you wish. Well—"

"Enough." Judge Solman spoke sharply. "You two are supposed to address me, not each other."

"Your Honor—" Greg began.

"Enough," Judge Solman repeated. He frowned as he shifted in his chair. "Let me understand this, Greg. You're claiming that the prosecution has tampered with a defense witness?"

"That's exactly what I'm saying, Judge."

"This is outrageous, Your Honor." Mashburn's voice was rising. "He offers no proof. The sheriff has a right to visit this woman. An absolute right—"

Solman held up a hand to stop him. He glanced back and forth at the two lawyers. His frown had deepened into dismay.

"Greg," the judge said, "I think you've got an overactive imagination. Certainly Ms. Daniels has nothing to fear from

El Nido authorities, or from testifying here in our courtroom. Tell her that, Greg. Tell her that it's not possible to believe otherwise about an entire county like El Nido."

"And if that doesn't work?"

The judge went stone-faced on him. "If that doesn't work, Greg, I can't help you. This is a public proceeding. I will not hold private testimony in chambers. And I certainly won't seal any testimony. And much as I wish, I can't control the press."

"You'd rather lose this witness's testimony?" Greg asked.

Judge Solman looked at him with vacant eyes. "You lose it, Greg. Not me."

Alex Ramirez wiped the hot wet back of his neck and glanced at the darkening evening sky. Ashes had started to fall, resembling nothing so much as flakes of snow. If only they were, he thought. The wind had increased and swung about, taking the fire once more into burning ground. Trees and bushes glowed red in the distance. For three days now the blaze had been whirling like this in erratic patterns, driven by chaotic gusts. Turning back on itself, pushing toward the coast, lunging again into the valley . . . To Alex, it looked as if the flames were taunting El Nido.

How did this start? he wondered. A hunter's unextinguished campfire perhaps, or a carelessly discarded cigarette. Word was, a boy on Gunpowder Mountain first noticed the smoke at seven that first morning. Someone else saw a wisp at eight. But for both of them, the nearest telephone was miles away. Not until the Gunpowder Lookout spotted it did word of the fire reach the Forest Service. Since then, they'd matched every move of the fire with a well-timed counteroffensive. Shock troops charged its smoking flanks; special crews slashed firebreaks through thick chaparral; roaming units wiped up hot spots and set backfires; an airborne tanker dropped gallons of retardant. All this in one of the roughest portions of the La Luna Mountains, a country inaccessible except by trail, with only a few roads touching its valley borders.

They might just win, Alex thought. For all its disordered fury, the fire ran only 6,700 acres that first day, and 3,500 the second, far less than truly big conflagrations in this region. They had more than three hundred men now in the battle, and fifty miles of fortified fire line. The south side of the blaze was under control. Maybe it would never reach El Nido; maybe it would never reach Camp Mahrah. By reflex, Alex turned and looked through the pass toward Sanborn Ranch.

*You can't let this fire reach the camp.* That's what Diana had told him. Alex tried to imagine what might follow if he failed, but quickly shook off the thought. At least, he reminded himself, these flames were distracting everyone from Sarah Trant's hearing.

Greg approached the witness stand to continue his questioning of Dr. Oscar Quagler. The medical examiner from San Luis was highly esteemed throughout Central California, and frequently sought as an expert witness. Usually, though, he testified for the state. Getting him for Sarah's side had been a valuable coup. At least it had seemed that way until today.

"No, not exactly," the forensic pathologist was saying. "I couldn't possibly be that definite."

Greg held the man's own letter in his hands. A letter in which Quagler stated that he didn't believe Brewster Tomaz could have made a dying declaration. *I can't say with medical certainty he couldn't talk. But I'm willing to testify that I believe he didn't make that dying declaration about your client. I can honestly say I don't believe he was able to speak.*

"Doctor," Greg asked, "isn't it your opinion that Brewster Tomaz was unable to make a dying declaration?"

"No," the doctor repeated. "I couldn't be that definite. . . . You never know."

Greg rolled up the letter and began to tap it on the witness stand railing. "Let's go over this once more," he suggested. "Regarding the injuries to Brewster Tomaz's neck, and their effect on his ability to speak . . . As I understand your prior statements, you feel that the ability of Brewster Tomaz to speak was eliminated as a result of the injuries that he suffered. Is that not true, Dr. Quagler? Is that not the case?"

"Objection." Mashburn remained seated. "He's leading, Your Honor. Also, asked and answered."

Judge Solman addressed Greg without looking at him. "Mr. Monarch, what do you say we just allow the experts to tell us what they think, okay?"

Greg stared at the judge. Solman kept his head down, scribbling on a legal pad. Greg started pacing across the front of the courtroom, fighting for time.

He no longer wanted Dr. Quagler to say what he thought. Yet he had little recourse. This was his own witness, he'd called him to the stand. He studied the man now as if he'd never seen him before. The acclaimed pathologist had narrow sloped shoulders, a wispy mustache, and the look in his eye of a nervous feline. Had he always displayed that tic in his right cheek?

"Okay, Doctor," Greg proposed. "Let's make one more attempt here. Please tell the Court what effect you think the injuries had on the victim's ability to speak."

"It would have been compromised but not eliminated," Quagler said.

Greg moved closer to the doctor. "Not eliminated?"

Quagler's tic began jerking with added intensity. "That is correct. Not eliminated."

Greg suddenly felt empathy for the late Reggie Dodge. Dodge with Dr. Montrose, he with Dr. Quagler. They were kindred souls now. He pivoted from the witness stand. "No more questions," he said.

Solman tapped his gavel. "It's almost five, and a Friday at that. I think we've done enough for our first week. We'll reconvene Monday morning at nine."

As he rose from the bench, the judge finally glanced over at Greg. He appeared to be searching for something to say.

"Counselor, you had some problems with that witness," he offered.

"Yes," Greg replied. "Not often that a habeas petitioner puts on a witness to bolster the state's case."

Solman looked away. "You are quite the maverick, Greg. Quite the maverick."

Greg and Jas silently poked at salads as they sat on the creek-side deck of Stella's Café in La Graciosa. What once had been wisps of smoke curling above the distant mountain range were now great mushroom-shaped clouds. The wind had picked up but had no fixed direction. It swirled about crazily, undecided where to go. The smell of burnt timber filled the air.

"I take it things aren't going so well," Jas said.

"So well?"

Jas slowly put her fork down. They'd spent time together this week in La Graciosa. Breakfast at the Apple Canyon Inn, where she was staying while covering the hearing. Lunch on the plaza. Dinner at Stella's. At the start, Greg had talked with animation about everything from El Nido history to trial strategy to his childhood in Chumash County. Listening and watching, Jas had seen such passion stored in his eyes. He'd gone away from her, though, as the week unfolded.

"I mean the witnesses," Jas said. "They're flipping on you, aren't they?"

Greg was watching the dark mushroom clouds. He didn't answer. An hour before, he'd tried to visit Judge Solman in his chambers. An ex parte talk, without the DA present, was against the rules, but not uncommon with Daniel Solman. Greg had made it only to the judge's door. There a clerk had blocked his way. *The judge is occupied.* That's what she'd told Greg. *He can't see you alone, anyway.*

"Earth to Greg, Earth to Greg. Come in, please."

He turned to her. "Sorry, just drifting there."

"I was asking about the witnesses."

"Yes, they're flipping. Not surprising, though. It all makes sense. It's all to be expected."

"I see." Jas tried out her tone of sardonic challenge. "So you're the wise man here."

"No, not wise. Just aware."

He'd known for quite a long time, after all. That first weekend in El Nido, trying to get an autopsy report. *How big is this?* he'd asked Alex. Right from then, he'd sensed what might happen. Witnesses scared into perjury were the least of it. Prison guards trapping him in Sarah's arms, civilians in police cars chasing him through the mountains, armed men circling Camp Mahrah. Even that wasn't everything.

Greg shivered in the night air. He pulled his coat collar tighter around him. Jas's arch expression turned to concern. She put a hand on his arm. "Are you okay, Greg? Are you ill?"

*Ill.* The word jabbed at him. Reggie Dodge was dead, Daniel Solman fainting and furiously backpedaling. That was part of it too, of course. This wasn't just a legal battle. They were in a war.

"Don't worry, Jas. I'm fine."

"Greg . . ." Her hand came to rest on his neck. "You want my worldview now?"

He turned his attention to her. "You bet. . . . I've asked more than once."

"Despite how I act, not everything is so terribly clear to me."

"I know, Jas."

"At times I feel like someone who doesn't belong in the world where she's dwelling. Like someone separate from the life she's living. Like I'm acting all the time."

"You're not as alone as you feel."

"Greg . . . I've done this for so long, I'm not always sure who I am."

"I understand."

"Yes, I think you do."

Her gaze was direct, and full of feeling. No, Greg thought. She couldn't possibly look at all men like that. It would be so easy to let go with Jas. So easy once more to lose himself.

"I have a trip to make tonight," he said. "I'm going back to El Nido."

It was strange. That was the only way to put it. The fire now advancing directly toward El Nido didn't appear to require customary fuel. Flames exploded in burnt-out clearings and jumped well beyond the tree line; they looked as if they were feeding upon themselves. That, at least, was how it seemed to Greg as he drove on Old Brook Road, winding along the river's edge. You couldn't get all the way into the valley by the main route, which was blocked by rangers and fire trucks, but this ancient wagon trail remained open. In the dark, Greg listened to the winds slap the creek against its banks. At least there'd been no lives lost fighting this fire. Just one major injury, that's what Jas had reported over dinner.

A firefighter. He fell over a thirty-foot cliff in Pascual Canyon, breaking his leg. Possible internal damage. They carried him on an improvised stretcher to a nearby fire camp, but from there only a hiking trail led out of the mountains. They tried to airlift him, but the smoke and winds prevented landing a helicopter. Unwilling to wait, they instead carried the man to a tunnel at the nearby El Nido Lake dam. Through that tunnel there ran a pipeline that supplied water to El Nido Village, and beside the pipeline, a narrow-gauge railway, used by tram cars during the building of the dam. They put the injured firefighter on one of those cars and drove him through three miles of tunnel to the portal, where an ambulance was waiting. Hours of mountain hiking over sixty miles of rough terrain were cut to minutes. "There's lots of tunnels like that in the valley," Jas had said. "What a way of escape."

Greg had to admit, it was ingenious. So ingenious, in fact, that the thought of it wouldn't leave his mind. *Ways of escape.* As Jas said, El Nido was full of them.

Old Brook Road curved to the north now, toward the center of El Nido Village. Following it, Greg found himself at the rear edge of Sanborn Park. He parked and hiked through woodland, guided by smoke-filtered moonlight. He was looking for the spot on the river where they'd found Brewster Tomaz, the spot Jas had shown him weeks earlier. It wasn't hard to find. So many citizens of the valley had come to inspect it, they'd trampled a lush ravine into a bare clearing. Greg stood on the bank there and stared across the river. After a moment he moved fifty feet downstream to a narrow shallow bend, where he waded to the other side, jumping on boulders when he could, stepping in the icy water when he had to. Then he climbed a slope, heading toward the base of El Nido's foothills.

*I saw him get as far as the yonder alder tree. Then he flat-out disappeared.* That's what Judith Daniels had told Sheriff Rimmer about the strange figure who fled the murder scene. That's also what she'd told Greg more recently, before she'd grown too scared to talk at all. Greg surveyed his surroundings, squinting in the murky light. Live oaks and sycamore filled the forest. He stepped among them, branches scratching his face, twigs snapping under his feet. In the distance he could hear sirens. Then, off to the right, he saw it: A tree unlike the others in this stand. There were the coarsely toothed three-inch leaves, dark green above, paler green beneath; there the ascending branches with pendulous tips. White alders grew so fast along stream banks in the California foothills. This one, Greg estimated, was eighty feet tall, with a forty-foot spread. He turned back toward the river; up on this slope the tree most certainly was visible from the far bank. *Yonder alder tree.* Here it was, not fifty feet from the base of the foothills.

Greg hiked to it, then circled it. Again he circled it, widening his arc. Then a third time, and a fourth. The fifth turn carried him into thick brush at the start of the foothills. The sixth turn brought him to an opening in that brush. Greg knelt and pushed through it with his head and shoulders. Before him a dark cavern stretched into the bowels of the mountain. Greg pulled a small flashlight from his pocket and stepped inside.

The tunnel smelled of rotten eggs, recalling for Greg his first morning in El Nido. Asphaltum crackled under his feet, another reminder. Greg stepped gingerly, wincing at the odor. The tunnel curved, hooking to the left. He must be circling the village now, arcing to the east end. Greg walked on until he estimated he'd covered a good two miles.

He slowed, then stopped. Time to rest. Greg rubbed his eyes. They felt so irritated. So did his nose and throat. He began to cough and gasp. He sank to the floor. There he sat, trying to focus.

Sarah was at the river that night, she didn't deny it. Maybe she'd even been there when Tomaz was murdered. But she didn't do it. No, couldn't have. Someone else did. Someone who escaped through this tunnel. Someone who . . .

Greg lost his train of thought. His head ached. He felt dizzy, and nauseated. He fought for each breath.

*Someone who . . .*

Greg closed his eyes. Then he forced them open. No, he didn't want to fall asleep in here. He tried to stand, but failed. He tried again, pushing himself off the tunnel's floor, grabbing at an outcropping. This time he made it to his feet. He still couldn't breathe without laboring. Less than a mile to go, he calculated. Maybe only half a mile. Greg put one foot in front of the other.

At first he staggered, then he didn't. Here in this last stretch the tunnel broadened and the ceiling lifted. Greg slowly stood upright, and found he could breathe more easily. With each step his head cleared. After five minutes, the dizziness and nausea passed. He looked around with eyes no longer burning. A rusted old pipeline, he now saw, ran along one side of the tunnel. He lifted his head to follow where it led. In the distance he spotted something bright. He stopped and shut off his flashlight. Then he laughed. Literally, here was a light at the end of the tunnel. Moonlight.

Reaching the portal, Greg stepped out of the tunnel and inhaled the night air. He was standing in a thicket of chaparral. Clearing a path with his hands, he slowly made his way down a wooded slope. Then he was in a clearing. A hundred yards off rose the Sanborn Ranch's tall red barn. Greg started walking toward the adjoining bunkhouse. He closed the distance silently. At the bunkhouse porch, he climbed three steps. He stopped, stood still. Before him was the usual inventory of saddles, shovels, gasoline jugs, and coils of rope. Greg had not a clue what he was looking for.

Then, under a bench on the far corner of the porch, he saw a pair of muddy boots. Greg reached for them, lifted them, turned them over. He'd expected the left boot to have rows of tacks pounded in diagonally across the half-sole. It didn't, though. The soles of both boots were smooth, unblemished. Greg ran his hand over them, feeling the glossy leather.

"What a surprise, Greg."

He turned slowly toward the voice. Diana Sanborn stood in the clearing before the bunkhouse, lit from behind by the moon and a high distant ridge glowing red with flames. Her long lavender skirt billowed in the wind. "Likewise," Greg said.

"Why would it be a surprise to you, Greg? This is my property, after all. I belong here."

"I meant the affidavit you gave Mashburn the other day. Swearing that you'd told the detectives about Brewster's dying declaration right then on the murder night."

Diana climbed the steps to the porch, came to Greg's side. She reached out and took the boots from his hands. "My goodness," she said. "These are so muddy. These certainly need cleaning."

"What happened the night of Tomaz's murder, Diana?"

Her eyes danced, her long gray hair whirled in the hot wind. "Bless your heart, Greg. What happened is not the point, is it? What we say happened, what we believe happened, that's the point."

"So goes the philosophy of the El Nido Valley?"

"So goes the philosophy everywhere, Greg. You know that. You are quite celebrated for knowing that, in fact. You win awards for knowing that."

Greg started to respond, then checked himself. She kept talking. "It's okay, don't you see, Greg? Everyone else here is playing that game. You won't get far unless you do too. So declare Sarah Trant innocent. Bless your heart. Believe Sarah Trant innocent."

Greg blinked as ashes from the sky filled his eyes. "Who wore these boots on the murder night, Diana?"

She looked at the objects in her hand. "These? These boots are two years old, as you no doubt can tell. They didn't exist on the night Brewster died."

"I reached your ranch through a tunnel. Ended over there in the chaparral. Started at an alder tree just beyond the murder site."

The ashes were falling on Diana too, on her shoulders and hands and eyelashes. She didn't notice, or chose not to bother with them. "My grandfather used to pipe water from the river through that tunnel. Long ago, a century ago. It's been abandoned for at least fifty years."

"I got sick in there, almost passed out."

"No wonder. There must be precious little air in such a godforsaken place. You shouldn't have gone in that tunnel. No one with any sense would."

"It smells of rotten eggs in there."

Finally, a trace of anxiety showed in Diana's eyes. For a moment Greg thought he'd penetrated her armor. Then he followed her gaze. She was looking at the sloping hill behind the bunkhouse. A wall of flames had jumped a canyon and cleared the hill's crest. "I would think that a spectacular sight," Diana said, "if it weren't a scant two miles from my home."

# THIRTEEN

Sheriff Roy Rimmer paused to regain his breath. Sweat dampened the back of his uniform and dripped from his forehead down his gaunt cheeks. He didn't mind all the exertion. A fire in the valley demanded everything the sheriff's department had to give. In such a grave situation, the citizens of El Nido needed him even more than normally. They were seeking him out, calling to him, imploring him. There were roadways to keep clear, animals to rescue, families to evacuate. Rimmer hadn't stopped in hours.

Some forty-eight hours, to be exact. For two days now they'd been fighting the blaze as you did every chaparral fire in this reach of California. They flew airplanes for reconnaissance; they built camps at strategic points; they set up radio communication. For a good while, it all made little difference. While the citizens of El Nido watched and packed and loaded their cars, the firefighters found themselves struggling to stop a force of nature. The blaze, growing more focused as it marched into the valley, made spectacular runs into the higher, rougher backcountry. Several fire lines were lost, and two camps destroyed; once, a team of men were temporarily trapped by flames. Yet finally, man's wile and grit prevailed. They assumed command, they beat back nature. The fire still burned, but it was dying now. The gales had ceased, the humidity had risen. Each hour the fire burned more slowly, each hour they pinched it a little closer.

Rimmer loved the action. He didn't mind that his own role, in the end, had mainly involved traffic control. He'd been part of the battle. He'd fought the fire. So now he rested. Wiping his brow with a soiled handkerchief, he stood on a knoll near the far northeast edge of Sanborn Ranch, looking to the south.

Diana Sanborn's house rose in the distance, unscathed. Behind it, shrouded in a smoky haze, Rimmer could see the Sanborn barn and stables, also untouched. Down in the village, they told stories of how Diana and the La Graciosa lawyer stood their ground that first night, hanging wet sheets in front of windows, hosing down the barn, stomping out microfires. Rimmer didn't buy all that talk, though. The wind had shifted for Diana, that's what really happened. Just as it had for her grandfather decades before.

Rimmer wondered at the old lady's good fortune. The fire had crept to within yards of her buildings, right down to the clearing where she'd planted a small grove of orange trees. The round ripe fruit still filled green-leafed branches; from a distance they suggested to Rimmer a hallowed golden shield protecting the Sanborn legacy. Of course, he knew they were just oranges. He understood that much. He understood also that citrus trees were always the last vegetation to burn in the valley. Yet elsewhere, they'd gone up in flames. Elsewhere everything had burned.

Rimmer turned his back to the Sanborn house and surveyed the La Luna foothills to the north. Up there, for instance. Up at Camp Mahrah. Rimmer squinted, and shielded his eyes with one hand. Yes, you could see the camp's shadowy outline now. The fire had thinned the thick oak forest that surrounded Mahrah's flanks, the brooding cathedral-dark forest that protected and hid what existed within. For those who knew where to position themselves, and where to look, Charles Whit's property stood exposed.

Rimmer studied the scene with mounting worry. He could see the scorched brick common house, still standing. He could see the charred remains of two wooden lodge houses. He could see the kitchen and mess hall, apparently untouched. What else? Rimmer scanned slowly across the campus. Just as he had feared. There they were, barely visible through the forest, if only to the educated eye: Camp Mahrah's ancient oil wells and refinery.

Rimmer couldn't imagine how Charles Whit was going to respond. Whit usually maintained a mastery over himself, but this . . . It could very well throw the man into a frenzy. Whit had made it perfectly plain to him more than once that the rusty primitive oil wells of Camp Mahrah had to remain hidden. Rimmer didn't understand why, but sensed the reasons sprang from somewhere deep inside Whit. Whenever Whit talked about those oil wells, he grew so agitated. Pacing about, punching the floor with his cane, glowering at whoever stood before him . . .

*What do you imagine happened up here, Roy? Why do you think the old pioneer wildcatters couldn't make a go of it when this land was theirs? They had these wells, they had a pipeline, they had a future . . . Something peculiar happened here, Roy. . . . Something terribly wrong.*

Sometimes Rimmer would join in, to show his empathy, to let Whit know that the two of them shared similar sensibilities. *Yes, it was left for others to grow rich in the El Nido Valley. . . . Then proclaim that no one else could do the same . . .*

Whit always seemed to like that comment. In those moments, at least, Whit appeared to regard Rimmer with something approaching appreciation.

The sheriff, staring again at the tenebrous outline of Camp Mahrah, moved along the knoll now to gain other vistas. Suddenly he became aware that someone was standing behind him, off to the left. His hand darted to his revolver; he whirled to face his stalker. Then he saw who it was, and his hand dropped to his side.

"Morning, Sheriff," Greg Monarch said. "What a splendid view we have up here."

Under a thick cloud of smoke that hung over the valley like a heavy gray lid, dozens of families huddled in the rolling green sanctuary of Sanborn Park. By noon, residents from all over the valley had poured into the center of town, some on foot or horses, others driving soot-covered automobiles. They were returning, not fleeing. They came now to swap war stories, and reclaim their town, and give thanks that this hadn't been among their more cataclysmic fires. A six-year-old boy displayed his prized crayon set, a Christmas gift from a favorite uncle, all melted like water. A woman of the mountains named Harriet Parker—a packer and hunter who could throw a diamond hitch as well as any man—talked of being nearly trapped by flames while leading a loaded pack train up a narrow canyon trail. With aplomb, a teenage girl told of skinny-dipping in a meadow stream as ashes fell and a fire engine, siren blaring, roared along the canyon road across the river. A father of six with a red face and a round belly recounted how he'd thought to escape the flames by riding his horse into an open barren field, only to have the fire explode about him anyway.

Greg Monarch listened to them all as he wound his way through the crowd. He settled finally on a bench near the Sanborn Park fountain. By necessity, Judge Solman had postponed the hearing. With the main mountain pass blocked, travel between El Nido and La Graciosa required a lengthy circuitous route. Sarah Trant, most of the witnesses, and all the lawyers "are sitting on the wrong side of the hill," Solman declared. Greg didn't argue in the least. He welcomed the delay.

Sweat darkened the front of his shirt. He'd been hiking as the day warmed up, but not aimlessly. He'd shadowed Roy Rimmer to that knoll after spotting him near the Sanborn property. There he'd followed Rimmer's gaze and seen the oil rigs. He'd seen also the look in Rimmer's eyes. When the sheriff left, he'd climbed the trail to Camp Mahrah.

Embers strewn across the ground still glowed faintly when he reached the campus. Burnt, toppled trees lay here and there amid blackened columns of oak and sycamore. Yet the fire had targeted its prey selectively; a good part of

Camp Mahrah remained insulated by a thick green forest. Apart from the smell of burnt timber, the place to Greg felt much as it had during his first visit. Still no signs of life, no noises, no birds, no breeze. He toured the campus more slowly this time. There, as before, were a pair of knee-high rubbers, but now Greg saw they weren't a solitary pair. A row of these backcountry boots lined a wall inside a storage shed. On hooks above them hung an equal number of the white overalls Greg had once spotted through a window. They were thick, with zippered seals at the cuffs. Yards of steel chain lay coiled there also, and odd lengths of iron piping. In the brick central hall, Greg discovered a floor-to-ceiling cabinet stocked full of canned goods and bottled water. Outside, he found that Mahrah's playing fields had survived unsinged.

He turned and plunged farther into the untended camp wilderness, away from the cottages and open meadows. A trail took him ever deeper into the smoldering forest. He climbed, descended, forded a shallow stream. Suddenly he was in a small clearing. The oil wells and refinery rose before him, more rusted than charred. Six wells, of a sort Greg had never seen but in old photos. In their day, they'd been steam-driven affairs that could not have reached more than five hundred feet into the earth. The refinery looked even more primitive. It was essentially a still, cylindrical in shape, made of cast iron, with worms for condensing the vapors, and agitators to treat the oils. It could have held no more than a thousand gallons at a time, Greg estimated.

He took a step forward and suddenly faltered. Again, the smell of rotten eggs overwhelmed him. He found it difficult to draw a breath. Knowing where this experience was headed, he turned and lurched out of the field. Nearly blinded by tearing eyes, he found himself half sliding down a gentle slope. With the heels of his hands, he braked, and came to rest in a sitting position. He wiped his eyes, struggling to regain vision. He peered out at his surroundings.

Farther down the slope, where the ground leveled into a

plain, he could see now a mammoth earthen pit, open but contained by a low levee. The pit appeared to be full of muddy water. Greg lifted his eyes. In the distance he could see four other pits, dotting a plain that was a good mile wide, maybe two miles long. The smell of rotten eggs was even stronger here than at the wells. Greg felt his head swimming. He fought to breathe. With concentrated effort he pushed himself to his feet and began his climb back up the slope. It took him fifteen minutes to make it to the cool still of Camp Mahrah's playing field.

"So, Greg Monarch, this is where you went."

Greg looked up from his park bench to find Jas Gest standing above him, hands on her hips. "With a few stops along the way," he said.

"I hope it isn't too forward if I say I was worried."

"I can handle that much brass from you, I think."

"Oh, there's plenty more where that came from."

"I'm well aware."

Jas smiled at that. "Okay, mister. Out of touch for two days in a valley full of fire . . . Sounds kind of interesting. Tell me about it."

Greg surveyed the park full of people, saying nothing.

"Come on," Jas urged.

Greg considered. He did need someone to confide in about the case. He couldn't deny that any longer. "I found a tunnel," he said.

"Yes?"

"A tunnel that leads from the river to the Sanborn Ranch."

It was Jas's turn to glance around the park. "There are dozens of old abandoned tunnels around here. That one was probably Edward Sanborn's water supply at one time."

"Precisely what Diana said."

"So?"

"It starts just up the bank from where Tomaz was killed."

Jas looked amused. "You have a theory? You think the murderer escaped through that tunnel?"

"It's possible."

Jas shook her head. "But not likely. That tunnel, all those old tunnels, were sealed up until about three years ago. The city engineers opened them up then because they were worried about accumulated gases. It was big news here at the time, fair amount of controversy. I wrote an article for the newspaper."

"I didn't know that," Greg said, unable to hide his disappointment.

"No, I guess you didn't. . . . What an adventurer you are. Where else have you been?"

"Camp Mahrah."

This time he had Jas's interest. "Mahrah? Why did you go up there?"

"I followed your Sheriff Rimmer up a trail this morning. Watched him studying the camp from a knoll. He seemed intrigued by what he was seeing. That intrigued me."

"Why? Nothing's going on up there. Whit doesn't even talk about development plans anymore. The camp's been abandoned for years."

"People meet there, though. People work there, stay there."

"How can you say that?"

"There was a conference of some sort up there just weeks ago."

"What are you talking about, Greg?"

"I'm talking about folding chairs, a long table, a dais, a freshly smudged white board."

"What an imagination."

"Also a fireplace, freshly laid with wood."

"You saw all this today?"

"Actually, I saw most of it the first morning I arrived in El Nido." He looked at her with appreciation. "The morning I saw you at the river."

"Oh, that morning."

A commotion off to the side interrupted them. Sam Rabe had climbed up on the bandstand with a megaphone in hand. The mayor was shouting announcements about road conditions, weather forecasts, temporary shelters, financial aid.

Below him, Tammy Rabe appeared and began circulating through the crowd, her arms full of brochures and forms. Neighbors called to each other and reached for everything Tammy had to offer. A sliver of sunlight poked through the smoke. Somewhere in the park a boy tossed a Frisbee into the air.

"One thing I didn't see that first morning," Greg said. "Antique oil wells and a funny little refinery setup."

"Oil wells? . . . Where?"

"Up in Camp Mahrah's foothills. They've always been hidden by a forest of oaks. But the fire thinned the forest. You can catch a glimpse from Sanborn Ranch if you get in just the right place."

Jas started to say something, then stopped, realizing they weren't alone. She and Greg turned at the same instant to see Tammy Rabe standing directly behind them. She reminded Greg of a volcano about to erupt.

"What's always been hidden?" she demanded, stepping around to face them. "You can catch a glimpse of what, Mr. Monarch?"

He considered deflecting her, but decided not to. "Oil wells up in Camp Mahrah. Oil wells and a small refinery."

"How could you—" Tammy Rabe didn't finish her question.

Greg answered anyway. "The fire has deprived them of their cover, I'm afraid."

Tammy Rabe said nothing now. She looked back and forth at Greg and Jas, then up at the bandstand where her husband still was reading announcements. Her silver crescent earrings jangled as she whipped her head about. Her coral rings reminded Greg of iron knuckles. Finally she moved her thick red lips to within inches of their ears. "You two have stirred things up enough here in El Nido," she murmured. "You're making El Nido look bad. You're going to destroy El Nido."

"That's not my aim," Greg said.

Tammy Rabe appeared to be struggling to find the right expression. "Be careful, Mr. Monarch," she said finally. "While you are in El Nido, I advise you to be very careful."

Alexander Moss, proprietor of El Nido's first livery stable, served also as the village's first constable. Reasoning that every town should have a jail, he built one in 1874 in his backyard, using stucco, timber, and tile. Moss was also the town's undertaker, though; he ended up using the jail more to store coffins than house criminals. Later, when a larger prison was erected behind Sanborn Park, the city fathers lifted Moss's jail off its foundation and transported the structure to a site beside El Nido's first church. Eventually Fred Darvill, in his role as historical society curator, claimed it for use as a modest local museum.

Greg had to duck his head as he passed now through the jail's doorway. Jas instinctively took his hand to lead him in the gloom. They stepped carefully through corridors filled with boxes, reaching finally the open room at the building's center. It had white walls lined by shelves, and, in its center, a long bare table. At one end sat Fred Darvill, waiting for them.

"Come on in," he grumbled, rising from his chair. "I'll bring you what you're after."

A piece of El Nido's history, that's what Greg had asked for. The history of El Nido's nineteenth-century oil boom and bust. Jas had urged him days before to visit the museum. He'd brushed aside her suggestion, meaning to follow that notion when he had time. For this he kicked himself now. He wasn't yet sure, but he suspected he should have started here.

Darvill shuffled back into the room bearing three thick brown expandable files. He placed them on the table, keeping his hand on them. The room's fluorescent light glinted off his bald sunburned head. He looked vaguely uncomfortable.

"This is everything," he said. "Like I told Jas, there's not a whole helluva lot." He pulled a paisley blue handkerchief from his pocket and wiped his nose. "At least not in the official record."

"You have allergies in here too, Fred?" Jas asked.

"Dust," he muttered. "Drives me nuts."

Still Darvill kept his hand on the files. Greg held out a hand. Darvill stared at him. "Why do you want to see this stuff, son?"

"I'm just curious about El Nido's history."

Darvill suddenly launched into a volley of sneezing. A fine mist from his nose evaded the handkerchief in his hand, landing instead on the files sitting before him. Darvill wiped them with the side of his arm, then, with a shrug, pushed them across the table.

Greg started pulling the pages from the files. Here were ancient news clippings, private correspondence, personal reminiscences, oral histories; here were dozens of voices speaking from the grave about a bygone time in El Nido. Greg rifled eagerly through the documents, scanning passages. He paused finally over a memoir titled simply "The Capitalist." He began to read.

> There was a man they called the capitalist once in El Nido. A big bearded fellow by the name of Wallace Barley. He owned a fleet of whaling vessels which sailed out of San Francisco Bay. Late in the nineteenth century, Barley heard about the oil seepages to the south, in the mountains behind El Nido, and decided to investigate. What he saw—oil struggling to the surface at every crevice, running down the slopes like rivers—astounded him. Barley scraped together every penny he could and started drilling. The first well came up dry, then a second, a third, a fourth, a fifth. The sixth was make or break for him. He drilled down 550 feet, and in came a gusher. It was a thick tarry gusher, though: not the least usable. Undaunted, Barley built a refinery, thinking he could produce commercial-grade oil. But Barley knew little about building and operating a refinery. A fire soon destroyed his. Barley rebuilt, and refined, and proudly sent his first shipment of one hundred barrels to the East Coast. Only to have his good name

marred when that shipment for reasons unknown disappeared en route. Barley tried instead to sell to the West Coast, but failed again when cheaper and better-quality eastern oil flooded the Pacific market. . . . To continue, Barley now needed new financing, which he pursued with unbounded vigor. Then certain East Coast refiners appeared in El Nido and sank their own wells. All came up dry or clogged with thick tarry goo. Word of the easterners' failure thoroughly debunked talk of a vast oil field in El Nido. Everyone's financing—Wallace Barley's included—quickly evaporated. Even in the face of ruin Barley tried to continue, but then his rebuilt refinery exploded for a second time. Broke and despairing, he finally gave up. They say he went mad and died of a morphine overdose, alone in an El Nido boardinghouse. . . .

Greg flipped through the documents. Here were reports on those that followed Barley. *Others bought his land and drilled where Barley first recovered oil. Very few wells had to be drilled, actually, as the oil was easily obtained from tunnels dug into the mountainside seepages. . . . In 1886 a pipeline was laid from a refinery in the El Nido foothills to the shores of Clam Beach in Chumash County. . . .*

Yet the results apparently weren't satisfactory. *This type of oil, the scientists decided, would never serve commercial uses. A large natural flow of surface oil cannot be regarded as a favorable indication of the existence of large oil deposits below, and heavy accumulations of asphaltum are a still less favorable indication. . . . After four years and $200,000, the prospectors lost their enthusiasm for oil. . . .*

Here, Greg saw, was where Edward Sanborn made his appearance. He'd been quietly buying up as much of the prospectors' land as he could get his hands on. Now he proposed his dream of an "agrarian paradise." *An agrarian paradise anchored by a choice, verdant oak-thick residential development on five hundred acres to the north of town. "Woodland," they called it. Instead of oil wells, graceful*

*Spanish homes and acres of citrus spread throughout the valley. Thus did El Nido evolve as a truly isolated land. . . .*

A gnarled hand on his arm interrupted Greg. "Interesting reading?" Fred Darvill asked.

Greg looked up. He thought he saw mischief in the old man's ancient eyes. "Yes," he said. "I think so."

# FOURTEEN

"Okay now, Sheriff, let's go back to the evening of the murder."

"Yes, sir."

For a moment Greg Monarch let Roy Rimmer ponder those critical hours on his own. He turned slowly, walked to the lawyers' table, picked up a file, flipped through pages. The sheriff's studied deference was getting on his nerves.

"Now, then," Greg continued. "At Sarah Trant's trial you testified that when you went down to the river that night, went to search the river—"

"Yes, sir . . ."

"—that you were specifically looking for footprints. Isn't that right?"

"Yes, sir."

"Good . . . Glad we agree on that much."

In truth, Greg wasn't glad about anything. He chafed at the need to be in this courtroom. With the fire thoroughly contained, Judge Solman had resumed the habeas hearing long before he could finish pursuing all that still intrigued him in El Nido. Clearly, Brewster Tomaz's murder and Sarah Trant's prosecution were mere props in some larger contest that stretched well beyond the Camp Mahrah conflict. To save Sarah, Greg needed to uncover everything that remained hidden to him in El Nido. Yet there was little chance to do so within the confines of this habeas hearing. He planned to feel his way, kick up some dust, keep his eyes open—and hope Judge Solman didn't hold too tight a rein.

"Now, then," Greg continued. "Sheriff Rimmer, isn't it

true that at Sarah's trial you testified that you found only her footprints and Tomaz's at the river?"

"Yes, sir."

"And that was a flat-out lie, wasn't it, Sheriff Rimmer?"

Rimmer started to show some flash, then regained control of himself. He reached for a glass of water. "Not at the time, sir. When I testified at the trial, I totally forgot about the other set of boot prints we'd found."

"I see," Greg said. "So you went to the river that evening looking for footprints. You already answered yes to that. Do you want to change that answer?"

"No." Rimmer stared at Greg. "I went there looking for footprints."

"Okay. Besides the footprints of Sarah Trant and Brewster Tomaz, you found a third set, did you not? Boot prints?"

"Not the ones I was looking for. Those were old ones—"

"Hold on," Greg interrupted. "Please just answer my questions. That last required only a yes or no. Now. You saw a set of boot prints and you thought, Well, those aren't the ones I'm looking for. Is that your testimony?"

Rimmer went back to sipping his water. "Yes, it is."

"Tell me, Sheriff. Did you misunderstand the defense attorney's question at Sarah's murder trial? Is that your testimony?"

"No, I understood the question. I just had totally forgotten about the boot prints. If I'd remembered, I would have answered differently."

Greg frowned and paced. As he passed the lawyer's table, Sarah caught his eye. In her expression he saw growing hope. He touched her shoulder, then wheeled toward the witness stand. "Okay, I see. Okay. So you forgot about the prints. Let's just accept what you're saying, let's assume that it's true. But you surely would have put it in a report right then, right after you first saw the boot prints. Wouldn't you?"

Rimmer turned to James Mashburn with a silent command in his eyes. Greg stepped between them. Next Rimmer glanced up at the judge. Solman's hand rested on his gavel.

"Wouldn't you, Sheriff?" Greg demanded. "Wouldn't you put it in a report?"

"I supervise, Mr. Monarch. I wasn't the one actually on the line down there in charge of the operation. I wasn't the one writing the reports."

"So you didn't do a report on what you found at the river?"

"No."

"Did you take notes?"

"Yes. . . ."

Before Greg could frame his next question, Judge Solman intervened. "Excuse me, Counselor, may I contribute here?"

In a habeas proceeding, federal judges were allowed and often did interrogate witnesses directly. Solman had made little use of this power so far. Now, apparently, he meant to. Greg fumed. He'd been on a roll. Apparently, too much of one.

"Of course, Your Honor," he said.

Solman leaned forward, nodded at Rimmer. "Sheriff, didn't someone write up a report about these boot prints?"

Rimmer nodded vigorously. "Yes, Your Honor, the forensic technician did it. There was a forensic write-up on those prints."

"And was there a reason why you didn't consider that forensic write-up to be of any importance?"

"Yes, sir. The forensic team told us those prints were three days old. They could tell because there'd been a freeze earlier in the week. The prints were set in icy mud. I'm not sure of all the technical details, but it's in the report, which you have among our submissions. Bottom line is, we knew they weren't from the murder night."

"And did you make this report available to Ms. Trant's defense attorney?"

Rimmer appeared shocked at the question. "Of course, Your Honor. . . . I handed it to Reggie Dodge myself."

"Did Mr. Dodge ever bring it up again?"

"No, sir. He seemed to agree the boot prints weren't relevant. He said something like, 'Well, this isn't anything.' Never heard any more from him about it."

Judge Solman removed his reading glasses, wiped them,

put them back on, and turned to Greg. "Counselor, you may continue. But I wouldn't use up much more time on this matter if I were you."

Greg stared at Solman. The judge looked away and began scribbling on a pad. Greg turned next to James Mashburn. The district attorney was busily leafing through a sheaf of documents.

"Okay, then," Greg said slowly. "I'm finished with this witness."

Detective Gary Goolan, Rimmer's chief deputy, moved to the witness stand with the measured, cautious look of a trusted second-in-command. He had thick black brows and a sparse mustache that barely covered the top of his thinly pressed lips. He kept glancing about, as if casing the courtroom. When he sat down, he remained, in the manner of his boss, on the edge of the chair.

"Detective Goolan," Greg began. "Can we agree that you interviewed Diana Sanborn on the night of the murder?"

"No, sir."

"You didn't interview her?"

"No, sir, I just talked to her."

Greg labored to maintain an even tone. "All right then . . . So you talked to her, you didn't conduct a formal interview."

"Yes, sir."

"In your conversation, did you hear Ms. Sanborn say that Brewster Tomaz had made a dying declaration, that Tomaz had said 'Sarah did it'?"

"In those exact words?"

Greg leaned closer to his witness. "You can answer that yes or no, Detective."

"The problem is, because I got sick, I didn't—"

"So what you're saying is, as far as you recall, Diana Sanborn didn't tell you Brewster Tomaz made a dying declaration about Sarah?"

"I didn't say that."

"You have no idea one way or the other?"

"I wouldn't put it that way."

It had been a long time since Greg felt the impulse to lunge at a witness. Over the years, he'd stifled that unfortunate tendency. Yet now, just for a passing moment, he imagined closing his fingers tightly around Goolan's neck. "Okay," he said. "Diana Sanborn's story. That would have been an important thing for you to put in your police report, would it not?"

"Yes, sir."

"So . . ." Greg walked to the lawyer's table, rifled through a file, pulled out a document. "So, let's look at your police report. Do you see what you wrote? Please read it for us, this part right here."

Goolan frowned, put on a pair of reading glasses. "Diana Sanborn was yelling, 'Oh my God, Brewster Tomaz is dead, someone cut Brewster's throat. . . .' "

Greg stopped him. "You wrote that?"

"Yes, sir."

"You didn't write that Diana Sanborn reported that Tomaz had spoken and identified the killer?"

"No."

"You didn't write it because it never happened?"

"No, that's not why. You can't—"

"Detective," Greg interrupted. "Let's look at your final report. The one you wrote two weeks after the murder. Still there's no mention of Diana Sanborn reporting Tomaz's dying declaration."

"That's right, I didn't make a reference to it."

"And you didn't make a reference because Diana Sanborn never told you anything about a dying declaration?"

"That's not so. . . . There's a reason. . . . I'd like to—"

"Yes or no, Detective, yes or no."

"I can't answer that yes or no. Do you want me to explain why—"

"Yes or no." Greg slapped the railing of the witness stand. "Yes or no."

"Hold on, now, Counselor." On the bench, Judge Solman was leaning forward, gavel in hand. "May I intervene here once again?"

Greg ignored him. “Is it your testimony, Detective, that if Diana Sanborn told you about a dying declaration, you would not have put it down in your report? Is that your testimony? Yes or no?”

Solman was banging his gavel now. “That’s enough, Counselor, that’s enough. If you don’t mind, I’d like to get involved.”

“Of course, Your Honor.” Greg marched back to the lawyers’ table. “Go right ahead, Your Honor. Get involved, Your Honor.”

“You’re risking contempt, Mr. Monarch. Let me warn you, if you continue in this way, you’re going to put me into a position where this will have to get quite unpleasant. Do you understand that?”

Greg felt Sarah’s hand on his arm. She squeezed his wrist, imploring him silently. “Yes, Your Honor,” he said. “I understand.”

Solman offered a thin smile. “Good, then. That’s excellent, Mr. Monarch.” He turned to the witness. “Detective Goolan, I have just a couple of questions.”

“Yes, Your Honor. . . . Whatever you want to know.”

“Detective Goolan, do I understand correctly that you suffered a heart attack shortly after Brewster Tomaz’s murder?”

“Yes, Your Honor. Just hours after. The next morning. I went on medical leave.”

“Did this situation affect how you handled reports about Tomaz’s murder?”

“Yes, Your Honor. I lost track of things. I had notes that never got written up. There were things I was going to tell Sheriff Rimmer that never got told.”

Judge Solman held up a document. “This is the El Nido County district attorney’s prehearing response to the petitioner’s discovery questions. This page here”—Solman pulled out a flagged sheet—“is a copy of your original handwritten notes from the evening of the murder?”

“Yes, sir.”

Solman pointed to a paragraph. “Could you read this passage for us?”

Goolan took the page from him and again put on his

reading glasses. " 'Diana Sanborn told me she heard Brewster Tomaz make a dying declaration. She told me Tomaz said "Sarah did it. . . ." ' "

"Your Honor, I object!" Greg was on his feet, and half shouting. "Who knows when these notes were written? Who knows whether this is an authentic document? I must register my formal protest about what's going on here. You're not even waiting for the state to make its case. You're doing Jim Mashburn's work for him. With all due respect, Your Honor, it seems clear that you've become a partisan for the respondent. Exception, Your Honor. I wish to—"

"Mr. Monarch!" Solman interrupted him with a bang of his gavel. Cold fury showed in his eyes. "Mr. Monarch, let's make something perfectly clear. I'm the custodian of the legal system here. We are seeking the truth in this courtroom. Nothing more or less. You want to get some points in the record for an appellate panel to read, you better make sure you're within bounds. Do you understand me? I won't have pyrotechnics in this courtroom."

Greg started to respond, but again felt Sarah's hand. This time she had his elbow, and was tugging. "You made your point," she whispered. Her eyes glinted with fear.

"Yes, Your Honor," Greg said. "I understand."

The judge was still clenching his gavel. "Mr. Mashburn, you want to be heard on this?"

The DA rose slowly. He glanced at Greg, then quickly away. "Your Honor, as you know from our response, we have a document expert affirming the handwritten notes as genuine and five years old. We also have a sworn affidavit from Detective Goolan. And—well, I hesitate to present the respondent's case out of turn here, but we will also have quite a critical witness who will corroborate Detective Goolan."

Solman raised an eyebrow. "That would be . . . ?"

Mashburn spoke so softly, Greg could barely hear him. "That would be Diana Sanborn."

During the lunch hour on the resumed hearing's fifth day, Greg sat on a bench in La Graciosa's central plaza, savoring the lively scene before him. There was his old pal Alison Davana, strolling along the creek with a man Greg didn't recognize. There was Cindy Seamon from the probation department, chatting excitedly to a group of friends. There was Dave Murphy, the piano player at JB's Tavern, lounging in the sun with eyes half-closed. To them and others, Greg waved greetings. When he spotted two colleagues from the county defense bar, Ron Carson and Art Parrish, he called them over.

"Hey, stranger," Parrish began, with his usual deadpan delivery. "You in semiretirement? This your permanent park bench?"

"Retirement wouldn't be such a bad idea just now," Greg replied.

Parrish turned serious. "Hear Solman is giving you a rough time . . . Whatever we can do to help."

"Ditto," Carson offered. "If not with the habeas, with your other cases."

Parrish was tall and thin, and afflicted with a nervous blink. Except for an excessive fondness for Irish whiskey, Greg thought him a first-rate lawyer. Carson, shorter and calmer, and entirely sober, made up with dedication what he lacked in acuity. "Thanks, guys," Greg said. "Tim Ruthman has taken over what needs immediate attention. I'll holler if he starts sinking."

By now the plaza was teeming. A moment after Parrish and Carson left, Jimmy O'Brien stopped by. Then came a neighbor who lived two cottages down on the creek. Then a former client who'd managed to deflect a securities fraud charge. Not until half past one, with the plaza finally clearing, did Greg find himself alone. An untasted ham and cheese sandwich rested in his hands. His mind remained, as it had this entire afternoon, on Judge Solman.

No longer did Greg find his chief obstacle to be recalcitrant witnesses. Forensic technicians with bad memories were nothing compared to Solman's combative involvement. Solman wasn't just being cautious now. He was fighting Greg over every piece of evidence, he was leading witnesses with coercive questions, he was rolling his eyes at testimony he didn't like. Not even Reggie Dodge had to face someone like this federal judge. Greg longed to counter Solman in some fashion. Either that, or steer him into reversible error.

Greg rose and began stepping rapidly along the creek path. He had no destination, just the need to release energy. Maybe he'd follow the creek all the way to Pirate's Beach. Maybe he'd plunge into the dunes. Maybe he'd scale every last one of those majestic unspoiled mounds.

If only he could talk to Jas. It surprised him that he felt this need, but he did. When she told him she wouldn't be attending the hearing this week, he'd raised no objection. Now he wished he had.

Other business, she'd said. He wondered. Their last time together, after they'd locked up the historical museum, they'd had trouble talking. Over drinks at the Gaucho Tavern, she'd grown ever more quiet. They weren't arguing, not in their words at least. Just in their moods. He'd sensed her impatience. *There are times you hold back,* she'd pointed out. She'd tried to joke about it—*You sure do like heading for the train, mister*—but he'd heard no humor in her voice.

There was much he'd wanted to say in response. How not heading for the train had once cost him dearly. How he'd nearly come unhinged over another woman. How he'd learned the need to keep his balance. How, even so, he didn't always head for the train.

He'd not said any of that, though. Instead he'd told her, "Sarah's on death row. I have work to do in El Nido."

She'd smiled then, a mysterious, amused glint in her eyes. *So do I,* she'd said softly, as if reassuring him. With that she rose, ran a palm across his neck, and walked out. He hadn't heard from her since. He'd tried calling her twice in the past forty-eight hours, but hadn't reached her.

Greg, far down the creekside path, was nearly trotting now. On the outskirts of town, he followed Graciosa Creek as it curved into a narrow, densely treed glen. Dappled woodland sunlight filtered through the oaks, played off the rippling water here, giving this quiet hollow the feel of a hidden sanctuary. Greg settled on a rocky ledge beside the water.

If only he'd talked to her at the Gaucho. If only he'd explained. She would have understood. . . .

The sound of twigs cracking farther up the creek startled Greg out of his reverie. Through the thick shield of branches, he saw a man approaching. He was walking slowly, as if lost in thought. His head was down, his hands thrust in his pockets. Then he stopped, and lifted his eyes to the sky in the manner of a supplicant. Greg froze. Of all the places for Judge Solman to spend his lunch hour, how could he choose this glen?

Solman suddenly turned off the trail and scrambled through a ravine. Greg listened to the sound of his receding steps. Perhaps, Greg told himself, the judge simply hadn't seen him.

James Mashburn stared at Greg as they settled at either end of the lawyer's table. Judge Solman hadn't come out of his chambers yet for the afternoon session. Nor had the motley scattering of courtroom spectators—the bored, the curious, the morbid—returned from lunch. Greg and the El Nido County DA had an empty chamber to themselves.

"Are you even going to put on a case?" Greg asked. "Wouldn't it be sort of redundant after everything the judge has done?"

Mashburn wouldn't take the bait. "Don't you worry, Greg. You better believe we'll put on a case."

"With Diana Sanborn as your star witness?"

Mashburn hesitated. "Well, you heard me say as much to the judge."

"Anyone else?"

"What do you mean?"

"How about Judith Daniels, for instance? Even if she is a batty spinster."

Mashburn frowned. "You heard the judge in chambers. You heard him say he wanted everything done in open court. Daniels won't testify in here, you know that."

Greg slid over to the chair directly adjacent to Mashburn. "Aren't you curious, though? Goddamn it, Jim, don't you wonder about what she saw?"

Mashburn's frown deepened to a scowl. Spectators had started drifting into the courtroom. The DA tried to keep his voice low. "This isn't an academic inquiry, for chrissake. I'm a prosecutor. You're a defense attorney."

"You're an officer of the court, Jim."

Mashburn rose and started to walk away. Then he turned back. Some of the spectators were studying them now. "You act as if only you have truth on your side, Greg. It's not that simple. You can argue the evidence more than one way. You say Tomaz couldn't talk, I have two doctors who insist his carotid artery wasn't cut. You jump up and down about those boot prints, I have a forensics tech who says they were days old. You think we cooked a detective's notes, I have a document expert who says they're golden. That's what courts are for, goddamn it. That's what trials are about."

"Settle down, Jim." Greg enjoyed seeing Mashburn agitated. "I was just asking whether you were curious."

Mashburn slapped the table. "This whole goddamn circus shouldn't even be in federal court. Solman made a mistake granting Trant a hearing. From his conduct, it appears he realizes that now. You think he's on my side, but maybe he's just trying to correct his course."

"They rigged Sarah's trial, Jim."

"Jesus Christ . . . We've gone over this before with Solman—"

"Tell me this," Greg interrupted. "Why do you think so many people want Sarah to be guilty? Why have so many people gone to such trouble to make sure Sarah is guilty?"

The noise of a door swinging open interrupted them. A guard was leading Sarah toward their table. Behind him, the court bailiff appeared. "All rise," he shouted. Out from his chambers strode the Honorable Daniel Solman.

"Mr. Monarch," the judge said as he settled at the bench. "Where are you in your case?"

"At the end of my rope." That failed to draw even a

glimmer from Solman, so Greg continued. "I had hoped to include Judith Daniels in my case, but as you know, we can't get her to testify in open court."

"Then she won't be testifying at all," Solman said. "Isn't that what we decided?"

"Yes, Your Honor."

"Anything else for the petitioner?"

Greg hesitated. He'd hacked away at the case from all sorts of angles. He could keep hacking, but saw no point in fighting further on the present level. If they were going to prevail, it would be through means he didn't yet have at hand. Mashburn would certainly call Diana Sanborn and the ex-prosecutor Karl Jackson; if not, Greg could get them as hostile rebuttal witnesses. That left only Sarah Trant. He'd been putting off to the last minute a decision on whether to call her to the stand. Her effectiveness would hinge on which Sarah chose to appear. Greg couldn't be sure whether he'd be putting on a winsome plain-speaking woman or a muddled babbler. It really wouldn't matter, anyway. Both Sarahs—all the various Sarahs—were vague about the murder night. The notion of exposing any of them to Mashburn's cross made Greg shudder.

"Your Honor," he said. "We may wish to call Sarah Trant and certain other witnesses as rebuttal, after we hear the state's case. With the understanding that we may do so, the petitioner rests."

Solman nodded his assent without looking up. "Ready with your first witness?" he asked James Mashburn.

On they came. Two executives from ModoCorp, a forensic technician, a document expert, two doctors, three sheriff's deputies, Roy Rimmer recalled for the state, a half-dozen El Nido residents who'd seen Sarah Trant's conduct about town. Each witness spoke with assurance and precision, each witness had a story to tell.

They talked of how Sarah Trant had stalked and taunted Brewster Tomaz for months. They reported how Sarah Trant twice shoved Brewster Tomaz in full public view down by the river. One witness thought she'd overheard Sarah Trant actually plotting to waylay Tomaz. The ModoCorp executives told how they'd been forced to seek an injunction against her physical intrusions. The two doctors declared themselves certain Tomaz's carotid artery had not been cut.

Sarah Trant admitted being down at the river, the detectives pointed out. She admitted arguing with Brewster Tomaz. She admitted pushing him into the creek.

"Actual innocence?" James Mashburn asked each investigator. "Detective, have you at any moment considered the possibility that Sarah Trant is actually innocent?"

"No, sir," each replied. "I never have seen any reason to consider that possibility."

Greg parried as best he could when it came his turn to cross-examine, but his mind was focused elsewhere. Diana Sanborn and Judge Karl Jackson would be the centerpiece of the DA's case, he reasoned; on them and no one else this hearing would turn. When would their turns come? What would they say? By the time Greg approached the stand to begin the cross of yet another El Nido State Park ranger, he was feeling almost as restless as the spectators sitting behind him.

It was late on Friday afternoon. Up on the bench, Judge Solman examined his watch. Greg intended only a quick, routine interrogation. Ranger Willie Wilton was a minor player, after all. He'd once encountered Sarah at a demonstration against ModoCorp. Mashburn had questioned him for just fifteen minutes, getting him to describe his observations of Sarah at the demonstration, and his efforts to calm her.

"Ranger Wilton," Greg began. "Did you ever write up a report documenting your encounter with Sarah Trant?"

"A report?"

Wilton appeared to be turning that notion over in his mind. He had thin graying hair pulled back in a ponytail, and pale brown eyes filled with concern. He'd been wavering over almost every question, as if he weren't accustomed to being interrogated.

"Yes, Ranger. A report."

"Well, no, sir."

"Okay. For the purposes of this hearing, were you ever asked to put in writing your memories of the demonstration?"

"No, sir."

"Did you talk to anybody involved in El Nido County law enforcement? In the sheriff's or the DA's office?"

Wilton turned wary now. "When?" he asked.

"At any time, sir. At any time."

"Well . . ." Wilton hesitated. "A couple days ago, yes."

Greg put down the file he'd been thumbing through. Wilton suddenly had all of his attention.

"To whom?" Greg asked.

"To . . . well, to Sheriff Roy Rimmer."

Greg squeezed Sarah's shoulder, then slowly approached the witness stand. He studied Wilton. "Where were you when you had this conversation?"

"In the sheriff's office."

Judge Solman interrupted before Greg could continue. "We're nearing five o'clock, Mr. Monarch. How much longer do you intend to go on?"

"I'm not sure, Your Honor. Not long." Greg struggled to sound obeisant. "Please let me continue."

Solman glanced again at his watch. "Okay, but let's not get bogged down here."

No sir, Greg thought. We won't get bogged down.

"Ranger Wilton, who called this meeting?"

Wilton shifted in his chair. "Sheriff Rimmer," he muttered.

"Speak up, please," Greg said. "The court reporter needs to hear you."

"Sheriff Rimmer."

"What did he say to you?"

"He asked me if I had been called to testify at this hearing."

"And what did you say?"

"Yes."

"Anything else?"

"No. We decided that we shouldn't talk about it to each other since we both were going to testify."

"I see. How admirable. You were both being so very scrupulous."

Greg nodded, paced. He felt Judge Solman's impatient eyes on him but refused to look up. Greg sensed something within his grasp, but didn't know what. He turned back to the witness. "Tell me this, Ranger. Did you and the sheriff talk about anything else while you were in his office?"

Wilton swallowed hard. "Anything else?"

"Yes, Deputy. Anything else?"

"No, sir." Wilton glanced up at the judge. "I swear to that, Your Honor. Swear to God."

Greg moved his mouth near the witness's ear. "Ranger Wilton, you've sworn to everything you say here. You took an oath before you sat down."

"Okay, well. Okay. No is the answer."

It was like reeling in a big catch without knowing what you had on your line, Greg thought. He tried to reconstruct; he tried to grasp just what had caused Sheriff Rimmer to summon such a minor witness for obvious coaching. A thought occurred to him.

"Ranger Wilton, have you ever encountered Sarah Trant other than at that one demonstration back in October of—"

Wilton interrupted before Greg could finish his question. "I know what you're asking about," he cried.

Greg walked slowly to the witness's side. He tried not to show his confusion. "What is it I'm asking about, Ranger Wilton?"

"Object, Your Honor." Mashburn was on his feet now. "The witness isn't being responsive. There's been no question asked. This isn't—"

"There is a question," Greg interrupted. "I've asked him what it is that I'm asking him about. That's a question."

Judge Solman wavered. "It does seem to be a question. . . . Mr. DA, you want to be heard further?"

For a passing moment, Mashburn looked as if he were weighing options. Then he said, "I repeat my objection. . . . Monarch can't go fishing like this. He's got to ask a specific question."

Greg moved to the lawyers' table. He suddenly felt Sarah's finger on the back of his hand. He leaned down as if to study his notes, his head beside his client's. *Christmas Day six years ago,* she whispered.

Greg rose and turned to the witness before the judge could speak. "Isn't it true, Ranger Wilton, that you encountered Sarah Christmas Day six years ago?"

Wilton's eyes were fixed on Sarah now as if she were the only person in the room. "You're asking about the El Nido Lake campground, aren't you? That day when this woman came up to me to complain about her dog?"

Greg nodded vigorously. "Yes, that's it, Ranger Wilton. Tell me about that day, tell me about Sarah and her dog."

"It's just not true—" Wilton stopped himself as he looked over at Mashburn. "I mean, what's there to tell?"

Greg leaned down again to study his notes. Sarah's mouth barely moved. *Oil in the lake.*

Greg rose and approached the witness. "What's not true, Ranger?"

Desperation showed in Wilton's eyes now. "There's nothing to tell. . . . That's what I meant to say."

"Nothing to tell?" Greg repeated. He leaned closer to Wilton. "Ranger Wilton, don't you want to tell us about the oil in the lake?"

Wilton flinched at those words. "It's not true," he insisted. "Not true."

"Again I ask, Ranger. What's not true?"

Mashburn was rising to object again, but Wilton spoke first. "Okay, yes," he blurted. "She did say her dog had tramped around in some thick patches of crude oil at the edge of the lake. But I swear, she never told me that she'd seen oil spurting into the lake. She never told me about all the oil she saw gushing into the lake. I would have reported that, I would've told someone—"

"Your Honor!" Mashburn was charging the bench. "None of this is relevant, this is way far afield, I move all this be stricken, I—"

"—Sarah Trant never told me," Ranger Wilton continued. "I would have reported it, I never heard her—"

Solman banged his gavel. "Enough," he shouted. "Everyone stop."

At the lawyers' table, Greg clutched Sarah's hand as he waited for silence to fall. "Your Honor," he said when it came. "I ask for another delay of this hearing. There's obviously much I still don't know about the prosecution of Sarah Trant."

# FIFTEEN

This time Greg kept a table between him and Sarah Trant. He'd wanted a chaperone, too, but still couldn't find Jas. It wasn't that she was missing. Neighbors had seen her on early-morning hikes, a storekeeper down the street had sold her fresh produce. Yet she was never home when he called.

His impulse was to go after her, knock on her door, make demands, declare something. He didn't have the time, though. Judge Solman—grumpily allowing that the state had withheld evidence about the ranger "even if its relevance is unclear"—had granted him a recess, but for only seventy-two hours. That, plus a weekend. Greg had five days.

Sarah held the key, or at least one of them. She sat now with one hand to her brow, watching him. The thin fluorescent bulb in the prison interview room was blinking off and on.

"I had a dream last night," she said.

"What about?"

"We were on the beach. . . . In the dunes . . ."

"You want to tell me more?"

Just then the light flickering overhead gave out entirely. Sarah sat in shadows, lit only by the glimmer from the window that opened onto the hallway. "No," she said. "There's no point."

"Okay, then . . ."

"Greg . . ."

"What?"

"I admire you so much. How you are. How you're handling

yourself in the courtroom. How you're fighting for me. But don't let the rest of you go flat. Clear all the hurdles."

Greg leaned back in his chair. "Let's talk about the El Nido Lake campground."

Much to his relief, recognition showed in Sarah's face. "What we got the ranger to babble about yesterday?" she asked. "At the hearing?"

"Yes. Your dog, an oil patch, the ranger."

She ran a hand through her long dark hair. "I cued you on that, but didn't really understand what was going on. Why does it matter? What does it have to do with my habeas hearing?"

"I don't know," Greg said. "Let's walk through that day and see if we can figure this out."

Sarah fell silent. He waited. This had been their way so long ago. Sometimes moods moved through her like summer squalls. There was nothing to do then but stick around and bide your time. If you were of a mind to.

"What a day that was," Sarah was saying now. "So sunny and crisp. With a deep-blue sky and those thick cumulus clouds. Billowy white balls that looked like cotton candy . . ."

She stopped, distracted by the image. Greg reached out and lightly touched her hand. "Go on, Sarah."

She stared at his fingers where they brushed her palm. "My dog was playing at the edge of the lake," she continued. "Came back to me caked in a thick crude oil. Big ugly patches of the stuff were floating right at the edge of the lake. I complained to the ranger. Didn't do any good, not that I thought it would. Just wanted to tell someone. Just wanted to blow off a little."

"Was there more, Sarah?"

"More?"

"On the witness stand, the ranger. He talked about oil gushing into the lake. *She never told me about all the oil she saw gushing into the lake.* That's what he said. What was he talking about?"

"I . . . well . . ." She was pulling away again.

"Sarah, did you see oil gushing into the lake?"

"What are you after?" Her face twisted with anxiety. "All that happened long before the murder."

Greg gripped her hands firmly now. Hell with the guards, hell with the accusations. "I have a better question. Why don't you want to talk about this? Why haven't you ever told anyone about the oil at the lake that day?"

"But I did—" Sarah blurted the words out, then stopped herself.

"Who?" Greg demanded. "Who did you tell?"

"I . . . I . . ." Sarah hesitated.

"Talk to me, Sarah. Talk to me or I'm walking out of here for good."

"Diana Sanborn." Sarah, in her terror, almost shouted the words. "I told Diana. But she didn't want to hear about it, she didn't want anyone to hear. She told me to keep it quiet. She told me absolutely not to tell anyone else."

"Diana?" Greg chewed on that. "Did she say why?"

"No. . . . She was quite definite, though."

Greg had Sarah by the forearms now. He pulled her closer. "Sarah, I don't have answers, just ideas. But I know this is important. The ranger was alarmed, he thought he was being accused—"

"Well, he was." Sarah bit off the words. Her anger, Greg saw with appreciation, was stronger than her fear.

"Accused of what?"

"Accused of screwing up big time. Yes, I saw oil gushing, just pouring into the lake from somewhere off at the far bank. I told that ranger about it . . . oh, I hollered. He just ignored me, didn't seem to care. Or maybe didn't believe me. It was horrible, Greg. Hundreds of gallons, I imagine. Maybe more. All through the wetlands, up on the sand. A big slick about two hundred yards offshore . . ."

Tears filled Sarah's eyes. "The birds, that was the worst to me. Heron, egrets, sandpipers, ducks. All of them caked with that heavy sticky oil. They've got two endangered species out there, damnit. The California brown pelican and the snowy plover. Don't know what happened to them. Just terrible, so awful . . ."

"Sarah," Greg said. "Tell me exactly. How did the ranger respond when you told him?"

"Like he didn't want to know, like he—" Sarah stopped. She turned to Greg with sudden surprise.

"What, Sarah?"

"It just occurred to me," she said. "I've been thinking all this time that he didn't care, didn't want to know. But that's not it, really. . . . It was more like he already knew."

Greg squeezed her hands so hard, she winced. "Could you see where the oil was gushing from?"

"That's the other thing that was odd. No, I couldn't see. The oil was coming from nowhere, just bubbling up from a marshy edge of the lake. So I went to investigate. Waded right in there. Dug around with my hands. So weird what I found—"

"How about an underground pipe?" Greg asked. "An ancient, rusty pipe, in the weeds or under the water?"

Sarah looked startled. "How did you know?"

"Over there, right in that spot."

Sheriff Roy Rimmer glanced at the small narrow glen where Charles Whit was pointing. They'd been walking through Camp Mahrah for an hour now, reliving the fire, assessing the remaining damage, contemplating what still needed fixing. The smell of wood smoke filled the air. Their boots crunched on charred oak branches.

"Eleven dead deer huddled together in that one spot," Whit said. "Quite a sight. Then you had all the doves. Looked like they were sleeping. Flames never touched them. All those beauties, suffocated by fire gases."

Rimmer turned away from the glen. He didn't care about the deer and the doves. To him the only part of the natural world up here that mattered were the mountain trout streams. He did like to fish. Damn fire probably ruined that, though. The trout would suffer severely this coming winter. Might die out completely when the rains carried the ashes and lye from the burned areas into the creeks.

"Your concern for the animals of the forest is touching," Rimmer said. "I thought you'd be more worried about those oil wells, now that you can see them from the Sanborn plateau."

Whit stopped at the mention of the oil wells. Yet to Rimmer's disappointment, he showed little in the way of real dismay. "Who'd ever be up there looking?" Whit asked.

Rimmer hitched up his trousers and tried to wipe tarry ashes off his shoes. "Greg Monarch, for one. Remember? He came up behind me. Must have followed me up there."

"You're not even sure he saw the wells, though. You don't know what he saw."

"He could have seen them. Can't get around that."

Whit still didn't react. "Nothing really to look at, anyway, Roy. Just part of El Nido's historical walking tour. A reminder of the past."

Whit resumed his trek through the camp. Rimmer trailed after, nursing a simmering resentment. He'd thought he might be able to affect Whit a bit today. But he could see now that it would take more than a little taunting to wipe the cold, empty look off this fellow's face.

"The past has links to the present," Rimmer said. "I think maybe Monarch is starting to figure that out."

Whit stopped again. "What do you mean? . . . Why do you say that?"

Rimmer took his time answering. First there was more ash to wipe off his boots. Then there was a horizon to study. "It's more than intuition," he said finally. "Mashburn briefed me about the hearing. Seems our prosecutor made the clever decision to put that El Nido Lake ranger on the witness stand. What's his name. Wilton."

Whit showed something now. Concern, Rimmer thought. Not alarm yet. But there was concern.

"Willie Wilton?" Whit asked.

"Yessir. Late yesterday, Mashburn puts Wilton on the stand to talk about a demonstration or something. But Wilton has other matters on his mind."

"Such as?"

"Christmas Day at El Nido Lake."

Whit flushed. Even in the forest gloom of Camp Mahrah, Rimmer could see his wrinkled coppery forehead darken with anger. "Mashburn asked him about Christmas Day?" Whit asked.

"No, no. Our friend Wilton just blurted it all out on his own."

"Jesus Christ."

Yes. Now Rimmer could detect alarm in Whit. Alarm was an unpleasant feeling, but surely it was preferable to what Whit usually showed. Over the months, the sheriff had grown unavoidably bothered by Whit's manner. The smile that seemed more like a sneer, the empty expression that hid such guile. There were times when Rimmer wanted to slam Whit's face against a tree trunk. He couldn't, though. His own fate, after all, was intricately tied to Whit's.

Not just Whit's, actually. Also to Whit's colleagues' up north. Maybe someday Rimmer would be one of them. He'd like that. They saw the big picture, just as he did. They aimed high, just as he did. High, indeed. Those ModoCorp folks were reaching to the goddamn sky. Their computer server alone cost more than a million bucks. The Auspex, they called it. The Auspex something or other. First one of its kind went to NASA to guide space shuttles. Second went to ModoCorp.

Whit had briefed him on all this at the start, when they were wooing him. Rimmer had to admit, he'd been impressed.

All that stuff about exploring under the Gulf of Mexico, for instance. Miles into the earth's crust, searching for oil on a continental shelf that had already been intensively drilled. Searching for oil—and finding it. Yet not with drills. No. Instead, ModoCorp used computer technology. *We're taking the wildness out of wildcatting,* that's what Whit had said. *A petroleum company without rigs or roughnecks. A goddamn virtual energy company.*

At the least, it was an invisible one. Just an inconspicuous San Francisco office suite with a discreet nameplate on the door. Never a press release, never a public statement. Founded by Whit, first run as his one-man shop, then "grown" with the help of nameless investors. To be more precise, "absorbed" by a conglomerate, but with Whit still running his own show. That's how Whit put it. *People don't know we even exist,* he'd chortled. *People don't know how real we are.* Real—and, as Rimmer saw it, brilliant.

First they bought huge volumes of digitized seismic data. Then they hired the best geologists and gave them all the computer power they needed to analyze that data. Bingo. Without breaking a sweat they were finding new oil reservoirs in areas the major energy companies thought were uneconomical or all tapped out.

Whit had taken Rimmer up to ModoCorp's headquarters once. Obviously it was to soften him up, to get him on board, but even so, the visit was really something. A silent room full of earnest young college grads staring at computer screens. Some kind of green carpet covered the walls. An air-filtration system hummed softly up in the ceiling. Walking down an aisle, Whit stopped at one of the monitors, pointing at a display full of jagged lines and rich colors.

The fellow working that computer looked up with an eager, proud grin. *It's a topographic view of sandstone,* he explained. *See the lighter-colored areas? That's where the reflected sound shows a higher probability of finding petroleum. . . . Way down it is. Ten thousand feet under the seafloor . . .*

Then someone in an expensive gray suit stopped by. Thomas, just Thomas. Thomas, and a handshake. Thomas had dark slicked-back hair and pink cheeks. He also had his lines down cold. On and on he went, as if Rimmer were a venture capitalist with a pocket full of cash.

"It works so beautifully," Thomas explained. "Ships bounce sound signals off underground formations. We buy up the result. Enough 3-D seismic data to cover, say, the entire continental shelf of the Pacific Coast. Our computers translate the data. We scan for the best prospects. Then we buy leases. Either that or make deals with those who hold the mineral rights. It's all so low cost. A buyer's market right now."

Beaming over that notion, Thomas started to move on. Then he turned back, gripped by an afterthought, or maybe something he saw in Rimmer's eyes. "This isn't just about us making money, of course. You should understand that, Sheriff. This creates a new balance of economic power. Instead of cringing at OPEC threats, the rest of the world can now impose its own embargo on Iraqi oil. Instead of worrying about rising oil prices, we can expect prices to fall to their lowest level in years. This is a godsend for our country, Sheriff Rimmer. A godsend."

Rimmer spoke up then, to show them he was wise to their ways, and a not-unsophisticated player himself. "I assume that's why you have so much support in the right places?"

Standing at Thomas's side, Charles Whit intervened with a glacial smile. "You assume correctly," he said. "And that, my good Sheriff, is why we so much expect your support as well."

Eventually they'd gained it. Why not? When they first came to him, saying they wanted to buy his wretched piece of land adjacent to Camp Mahrah, he thought they were joking or something. As far as he knew, his rocky acreage on the backside of the camp wasn't worth a red cent. He'd long ago given up hope of growing anything up there. In fact, he'd given up hope of ever unloading the miserable property. Now these ModoCorp fellows were offering him a figure that was ten times the land's assessed value. He resisted initially, not trusting them. That's when Whit escorted him to San Francisco. We will make you a partner with us, they told him there at the ModoCorp headquarters. You will prosper in the El Nido Valley.

Rimmer wasn't that gullible. "Why do you need me?" he asked.

*We need your land as an approach and staging area. . . . And we need your support as the sheriff of El Nido County.*

"My support as sheriff?"

*Just in case we ever run into any trouble . . . It helps to have the law on your side.*

Why not indeed? Why shouldn't he prosper as so many others had in the El Nido Valley? Besides, as the ModoCorp folks pointed out, this wasn't just about making money. This was a godsend for our country. The welfare of the nation mattered a great deal to Rimmer. He couldn't let everyone down.

"What did that damn ranger say exactly?" Whit was demanding now. They'd reached the edge of Camp Mahrah's playing fields. "What did Willie Wilton say?"

Rimmer held up two open palms. "I wasn't there . . . but some reporters were. Three of them, in fact. This is going to make the Sunday papers, I'm afraid. . . . You can read all about it tomorrow."

Finally, undisguised dismay spread across Whit's broad, weathered face. Rimmer exulted. "Should we sit down for a moment?" the sheriff proposed. "You look so under the weather."

Walking through Sanborn Park, Greg found himself no longer able to enjoy its charms. Conversations stopped or slowed down as he passed, and heads turned away. Here and there, someone glared openly at him. The latest news reports about Sarah's hearing had roiled people. More than a few citizens, in fact, had felt compelled to fire off agitated letters to the editor.

*What in God's name does El Nido Lake have to do with Miss Sarah Trant killing Brewster Tomaz? . . . How could this murderess tarnish the reputation of our beautiful lake? . . . Ours is an unspoilt valley, no matter what that killer says. . . . Why doesn't this big-shot La Graciosa lawyer go pay attention to his own county . . . ?*

Greg took this mainly as proud and protective folks blowing off steam, yet it was clear he'd crossed a certain line. He no longer was just battling the sheriff and DA. He now had adversaries scattered throughout the community. To be pitted against the valley's citizens in this manner gave him no satisfaction at all.

It didn't help that Jas still hadn't surfaced. It had been more than a week since they talked. Twice Greg had visited her home, a rented adobe bungalow just off Main Street. It didn't look as if she'd been there for several days. He couldn't deny it: He longed to know where she'd gone; he longed to know she was okay.

"Well, my goodness, look who we have here. Bless your heart, Greg, where have you been?"

Diana Sanborn had approached from behind. He hadn't seen her coming, but he'd expected her. He knew she walked the equestrian trail most afternoons at this hour. He'd counted on them crossing paths. They'd done so hardly at all since the night he helped her beat back the flames licking at her back door. Greg didn't know whether her circumvention was by accident or design.

"I've been at a federal hearing in La Graciosa most of the time, remember?" he said. "How about you?"

She laughed as gaily as she could manage. "Just counting my cows."

Greg hesitated. Talking in any manner to the state's star witness opened him to potential charges of tampering. Talking to such a witness about her coming testimony opened him to certain charges. Yet they'd merely bumped into each other in the middle of Sanborn Park. So random an encounter. So public.

"I imagined you'd also be spending a bit of time preparing for your testimony at the hearing," he said. "James Mashburn has promised us we'd be seeing you in the courtroom."

All hint of gaiety drained from Diana's expression. "What's there to prepare for? When I'm called to the stand, I shall simply tell what I saw and heard."

"Mashburn says he's got you on board."

"No one has me, Gregory."

"Mashburn must be mistaken, then."

Diana started to speak, then stopped. She peered at him with pensive eyes. "You must be sorry you ever came to El Nido," she said finally. "Everything is more complicated than you imagined. And now people are turning on you."

"Are they?"

"They're writing letters. They're talking."

"What are they saying?"

"They're just muttering. The one thing that unites everyone here is the valley itself. You cast the valley in a bad light, you have a big crowd against you."

"What does that mean?"

Diana glanced up the equestrian trail. "There's been talk, that's all I know."

"Is this a warning? Are you the appointed messenger, Diana?"

She looked genuinely bothered by that suggestion. "Far from it . . . I'm actually concerned for you, if you must know."

"That's reassuring to hear."

Diana said nothing in response. Greg wondered whether he'd managed to offend her. Then he saw she was merely distracted. Diana's eyes were locked on something across the street, under the Arcade. Greg followed her gaze. It took him a moment, then he saw what drew her attention: Jasmine Gest. Jas was striding with determination, as if on her way to an urgent appointment.

He reached her just as she was passing the open doorway of the Gaucho Tavern. His hand on her elbow stopped her. "You've been missing in action," he said.

She exhaled slowly. "It's called free rein, Greg."

"Just wondered what happened to you."

"Why? I'm not accountable to you. What's it to you where I go or what I do?"

Greg started to respond, but at that moment a laughing teenage couple collided with Greg. Then a mother with a double stroller forced him to the edge of the sidewalk. Greg regained his hold on Jas's elbow and guided her toward the entrance to the Gaucho Tavern. She tried to stop, bracing herself against his pressure. He ignored her resistance and pushed harder. In an instant they were standing inside the bar.

A half-dozen East Valley ranch hands looked up from their pool tables.

"This is coercion, Greg. You're forcing me."

"Go ahead, slap me if you want."

"Not what I had in mind."

"Let's sit over there. In the corner booth."

He kept his hand on her elbow, but she walked with him now under her own power. As they settled in the booth, Greg waved to the bartender, who'd been watching them with a sullen stare. "Couple of Graciosa Brews," he called. "You know, that foreign beer from Chumash County."

Jas laughed softly. "Feisty today, I see. Good. Showing your anger is good for you."

"I'll show you anger," he said. "Damnit, what's been going on?"

"Talk to me, Greg. Don't bark commands."

She worked on her beer, watching him over the edge of her glass.

"Okay," he said. "I was worried. Thought something might have happened to you."

"Aha. We raised that flat line on your electrocardiogram, that it? Well, we can lower it, too. Raise it and lower it . . . Raise it and lower it . . ."

He looked at her with amusement now. "To have so much power must be intoxicating."

"I got tired of hanging around," Jas said next. "Waiting for you to welcome me in. Set out on my own. It was an interesting experience."

"What have you been doing?"

"Working on an article, Greg. Doing my job. Investigating."

"The topic being . . . ?"

Jas licked the beer's foam off the edge of her glass. "The topic being Sarah Trant at El Nido Lake on Christmas Day."

Greg struggled to understand. "You weren't at the hearing. . . ."

She looked now as if she wanted to slide closer to him in the booth. She didn't, though. "I talked to people who were.

Couldn't believe the ranger blurting all that out. Sounded intriguing. I decided to chase after it a little. Kept me out of the county for a while. So being gone wasn't just a way to annoy you." Jas smiled. "Though I confess I didn't mind that effect."

Greg tried to think of what to say next. That she hadn't been in jeopardy, that she instead had simply struck out on her own, left him with a confusing mix of feelings. "So," he said finally. "What did your independent investigation turn up?"

"Why, Greg, I was wondering if you would ever ask."

He waved for two more beers. She pulled notes from a pocket.

It was clear, Jas began, that Sarah Trant had indeed spotted an oil spill on Christmas Day. There'd been some talk about oil at the lake, it hadn't been a total secret. Nor had it been a big deal. Maybe a couple hundred gallons, that's what Jas had heard. The routine, perennial seeping from the crevices of the valley's foothills. An independent contractor's cleanup crew worked it one night behind barricaded roads. Portable lights, bulldozers, skiffs pulling booms, skimmers sucking oil—they had it cleaned up by dawn.

"Lots of equipment and manpower for two hundred gallons of routine seepage," Greg said.

"They roll out the artillery here when the wetlands are threatened."

"All the same . . ."

Jas regarded Greg with appreciation. "Very good, Greg. There is more to this. I've been holding back."

"It wasn't just natural seepage, was it?"

"No, I don't think it was." Jas, despite herself, slid closer to Greg. "Get this now. Way I hear, it involves Charles Whit and ModoCorp. I'm told they'd been retooling those old oil wells up in Camp Mahrah. Don't know why, those holes are all dry. In fact, I always thought those holes never did come in. Still, that's what I'm told. They were fiddling with the wells, must have pumped up a bit of oil somewhere. Because they had oil running in a pipeline. And you know what that pipeline did?

Burst on them. Whatever the cause . . . corrosion, stress from vibrations . . . the pipeline ruptured."

Greg's eyes flickered now in the dark of the tavern. His second beer sat untouched before him. "What kind of pipeline?"

"A gathering line of some sort, I hear. Gravity-fed, low-pressure. Meant mainly to carry crude from one storage area to another. Buried just eight inches underground. Except who knows? There's no regulation, no mapping, no permits. I tried to check. Get this, Greg. There's no record of the Camp Mahrah pipeline on file anywhere in our state government. It's not shown on the county's maps of oil and natural-gas pipelines."

"A ghost pipeline?"

"Something like that."

Greg knew the region of the spill. That's where he'd fished with his father. They might have cleaned up the mess right away, but it would take a long time for the lake and wetlands to recover. Years, maybe. Oil kills insects, which disrupts the food chain. Also, oil can seep into the soil, then resurface and create a new slick. Greg thought of the dead cormorant he'd found floating out at the lake. He imagined dozens more had died. Maybe hundreds. It was a migratory zone out there, after all. Who knew the full impact of ModoCorp's decision to fiddle with ancient oil wells.

"Where's the state of California on this?" Greg asked.

"Good question. Initial response came from the Department of Fish and Game. They've got a special section just for oil spills. Their guys showed up immediately. Then they disappeared. Backed away. Hands off."

Greg was momentarily empty of questions. They sat in silence for a while.

Then Jas said, "It's kind of funny."

"What is?"

"While I was poking around in the archives on this, I came across clips about another oil spill. At nearly the same time. End of that year. At the ocean, northwest of El Nido. The Chumash Dunes region. In the dunes, on the beach, out to sea. That one was much bigger. . . . Thousands of gallons . . . I'm sure you recall."

Greg put down his beer. He most certainly did. Nearly seven miles of his beach had been damaged. His dunes. His wildlife habitat. His refuge. "People walking on the beach were coming back with feet just black with oil," he said. "Campers, bathers, the dune buggy crowd, they all abandoned the place. Even the surfers left."

"Yes, it was pretty bad."

"So what about it? Why bring that up?"

"Don't know, just thought it odd. Initial reports had state investigators speculating that the spill came from the oil wells they've got on floating stations two miles out to sea. But from what I can tell, they never confirmed that, never pinned that down. In later reports, their language always remained kind of vague. Maybe that's just how bureaucrats express themselves."

Greg knew the answer to his next question, yet still asked: "Remind me. This ocean spill, how close was it to the end of the year?"

"Two days after Christmas."

Greg spun his glass around on the table. "I wonder."

Jas stilled his hand with the tips of her fingers. "Greg, there's something I want to know."

He looked at her, waiting.

"How come you took this case?" she asked.

"Thought I explained. Judge Solman sent me the habeas petition."

"But why did he do that?"

Greg studied his glass. "Sarah asked him to."

"Sarah knew you?"

"Yes."

"You two go back a ways?"

Greg raised his eyes to hers. "Way back."

She covered his hand with her own. "It was Sarah who let you down?"

"I wouldn't put it that way."

"Do you worry I'll go crazy like she did? Is that it, Greg?

You think all complicated, impetuous women end up off their rockers?"

He stared at her without answering. She held his gaze. "You did good work," Greg said finally. "But hey, Jas, come on. Don't go away like that again."

Stepping slowly and awkwardly, Greg walked backward toward the shore of El Nido Lake. That was the only way to move with all the gear he had on. A full-length quarter-inch wet suit and hood, a wraparound tempered-glass mask, a BCD inflatable bladder jacket, a twenty-two-pound weight belt, a Brut regulator, a snorkel, gloves, boots . . . What made walking particularly challenging were the giant adjustable ribbed scuba fins on his feet and the full seventy-two-cubic-foot air tank on his back. It wasn't possible to move or enter the water gracefully with full scuba gear on.

So Greg didn't try. He lurched without concern, looking over his shoulder as he moved deeper into the water. The lake reached to his shoulders, his neck, his forehead. He waved at Jas waiting on the shore, then began his feet-first descent by exhaling and slowly deflating the BCD jacket. Down he went into the heart of the lake.

This was the only way Greg knew to test his theory quickly. Were the El Nido Lake oil spill and the Chumash Dunes slick somehow connected? Had someone diverted the lake oil to the ocean, so it wouldn't be noticed in the valley? If so, that meant there must be some sort of bypass system at the lake, some sort of underwater pump tied to a pipeline that drained to the sea. Probably it was a pump normally used to divert runoff irrigation water, but Greg couldn't say for sure; nowhere did the public record indicate anything about such a setup.

Surveying the lake from the shore, Greg had spotted a small wooden shed on the water's edge, securely padlocked and nearly hidden by high weeds. That's where the motor would be, Greg reasoned, if there was one. Fifteen feet from it a utility pole rose from the ground with a small metal box attached to one side. A control panel, perhaps, with a simple on-off switch. Yes; Greg felt certain. Someone must have turned on the pump after the spill began. No one was going to confirm that theory for him, of course. Certainly not within the few hours he had left before Sarah's hearing resumed. He'd have to do his own verifying.

Greg could see the lake bottom now. He pumped air into his BCD to halt his descent. He hung suspended in the water above the floor, neither floating nor sinking. He looked around. Water is eight hundred times more dense than air, and that made for differences. Greg had gradually lost much of the world's light during his descent. Colors had been absorbed, one by one. First red, then orange, then yellow. The deeper Greg went, the darker and less colorful. Red and orange and yellow objects appeared brownish, gray, black. They also appeared larger and closer than they were: Light traveled at a different speed in water, magnifying objects by 25 percent.

A heavy clanking sound off to his left caused Greg to flinch. Was it really off to his left, though? Sound traveled four times faster in water, which made it hard to tell just where it was coming from. To Greg, the noise he heard seemed to come from everywhere around him. He weighed the matter for a moment, then let it drop. He flicked one fin in the water and began to swim.

He'd learned scuba diving from his father in the waters near the Channel Islands, south of La Graciosa and the Chumash Dunes. When Greg had proved himself there, in the frigid, surging murk off Central California, his father took him to the clear still waters of Hawaii and the South Pacific. It wasn't the gear or culture of scuba that induced them to don wet suits and air tanks, but rather, the underwater world that diving made accessible. Majestic lava archways, brilliant coral formations, eels and sea urchins, sea turtles and white-tip sharks . . . All dwelling in a universe so still and insulated, so unlike the one they inhabited above the water's surface.

Diving didn't just allow relaxation, it required it. To swim about without fatigue in water's greater density, you had to let go. Rapid and jerky movements just wasted energy. Nice and easy, that was the way to move. Breathing worked the same way. If you took quick shallow breaths, you weren't getting much fresh air, or conserving what you had in your tank. To dwell underwater, you had to breathe slowly and deeply.

Calm it down, Greg reminded himself. Ease off . . . Inhale . . . Deep, slow . . . Exhale . . . Slower still . . . He was swaying effortlessly through the water now, following the circumference of the lake, orienting himself. If he had his bearings, the shed should be just over there, in that inlet. Did he have his bearings, though? It was hard to keep his focus in this world. Everything so muted and uncanny. Only largemouth bass and catfish for company. You don't swim fast or work hard down here, you—

Suddenly Greg saw it. Over to the right, by a sloping bank thick with willows. A pipe descending toward the lake bottom; a steel cylinder, maybe fourteen inches in diameter. Supported, it appeared, by a four-cornered structure made of wooden pilings. The pilings continued to the bottom of the lake; the pipe stopped some five feet off the bottom. Its end flared, and sat on a concrete base.

Greg flipped a fin and moved closer. This flared end, he saw now, was something attached to the pipe. It had a wide opening covered by a slotted grate. An intake head, Greg realized. If he was right, there would be a propeller shaft running down the inside of this pipe.

Greg swam closer yet. If he could stick his face inside the opening, he should be able to see the propeller and pump unit itself. The pump wasn't on, so there was no danger of being sucked in. Even if it were, the grate would protect him.

He had the pipe in his hand now. He moved down its length to the opening. He peered through the slots. Yes, just as he'd imagined. There it was, the shaft, the propeller—

Then he saw nothing. The blow came suddenly, something hard and unyielding cracking against the back of his head. At the same instant he heard a roar, and felt the pump's voracious suction pulling at his head, his regulator, his face mask. Greg dove and kicked away. Silt churned from the lake bottom clouded the water and his vision. Yet he'd be sightless anyway; his mask had been knocked off his face, and the human eye needs air before it to function. The roar grew louder, filling Greg's ears. Where it came from he didn't know.

Nor, Greg suddenly realized, did he know where his regulator was. His mouthpiece had been knocked away from his face. Greg had no way to breathe. A sense of suffocation gripped him. Stay calm, he told himself. He knew how to recover a regulator. The arm sweep, that's what you did. Greg lowered his right shoulder, then extended his arm out to his side and behind him until he could touch his tank. He swept his arm forward while extended, feeling for the regulator hose, waiting for it to hit his arm.

It never did. Greg's panic mounted. Was there no regulator hose there? He reached back directly now to where the hose was attached to the first stage. Nothing. The pump must have ripped it away.

He had no time to think anymore. In an instant, Greg unbuckled his weight belt and began inflating his BCD jacket. A buoyant emergency ascent, they called it. Last option in a disaster. As he began to rise, Greg looked forty feet up to the surface. He started to exhale, continuously, slowly. Make the sound, he told himself. A-a-a-a-h-h-h. Don't stop, keep exhaling. He'd have plenty of air to spare; the air compressed in his lungs would expand as he rose. Not only could he keep exhaling, he had to. Otherwise his lungs would explode.

A-a-a-a-h-h-h. He was halfway there now, twenty feet to go, then fifteen. Greg felt dizzy, his head ached. A-a-a-a-h. He thought of his father, who taught him this ascent, who taught him its greatest value: to know you could do it; to know you didn't need your air.

A-a-a-a-h-h-h. Five feet now. Through the water, he could see the blue sky. It must be a dream, but Greg thought he could see something else as well. Jasmine Gest's face. Oh Lord, what was that? Jas's hands, reaching for him?

I should have gone down with you, she kept saying. I should have watched over you. I shouldn't have gone away. Don't you worry, though. You're just fine. Take it easy, now. Keep still. Keep calm. Breathe easy. Nice and easy. Come on, now, Greg. . . .

Jas gently coaxed him back as they lay on the lakeshore. She'd peeled down his wet suit, pulled off his hood and gloves. Her drenched dress clung to her body. Her hair, loose and wild, brushed his face. He was supposed to feel confused in the aftermath of this, that's what the books said. He should have lowered alertness, unclear thinking, visual problems. Yet he didn't. He saw Jas plainly, saw her on her knees straddling him, saw her wet dress hitched up to her hips. When she leaned down, her breasts touched his cheek. He felt the press of her thighs, the stiffness of her nipples. He started to shiver. Jas, noticing, turned him on his left side and propped up his legs with the scuba equipment. Then she lay down beside him, wrapping herself around him.

"I don't have a blanket," she explained. "Trying to keep you warm."

"You're doing a fine job."

When the shivering stopped, he pulled her closer and kissed her. She tasted of the lake and the grass and something else, and she responded with an urgency that overwhelmed him. He felt her tongue on his neck, his ears, his chest. Then she rolled on top of him and pressed herself against him. She began pulling at his wet suit. Now he did feel light-headed. "Jas . . . ," he said.

Suddenly she stopped. She sat up, and looked around the lake with a worried air.

Greg watched her pull her knees to her chest and wrap her arms around her legs. The sun was drying out her dress, but it still clung to her. Buttons ran down the dress's front, holding the thin cloth together.

"What happened down there?" she asked. "Who's out there? We're not alone, are we?"

Greg moved closer to her. He hadn't wanted to dwell on that possibility just now. Perhaps the pump was on a timer and his assailant was an inanimate object; the blow to his head had been so unyielding. "Not sure," he said. "I may have cracked into a submerged boulder or log, for all I know."

She exhaled slowly. "I wish that were true," she said. Her voice was thick.

He felt her breath on his neck, he felt his blood pound. "Jas—"

She stayed him with a hand on his chest, then sat silently, gazing out at the lake. "Did you find what you were after?"

"Yes. . . ." He tried to gather himself. "An electric power pump, from what I could tell. The kind they use to lift large volumes of water at flood-control and irrigation stations. Thing like that lifts so much so fast, it creates a vortex. I can imagine what happened. Vortex pulled the water down, skimmed the oil off the top, just like scum in a bathtub. Then through a pipeline to the sea . . . Jas, all those thousands of gallons of crude out near the Chumash Dunes, I bet they came from here. I bet they came from El Nido, not from offshore wells."

Jas's brow wrinkled. "How could that be? El Nido is a dry hole once you get past all the tar and surface seepage."

Greg couldn't keep his eyes off the rising hem of her dress. He gently touched her bare, damp thigh. Her skin felt even smoother than he'd imagined. "I don't think so," he said. "The first day I came here, the proof was right before me. Up at Camp Mahrah. Not just asphaltum, but also a pool of oil. Then later, the fire burning away from the tree line, the fire burning in bare fields. El Nido's boom and bust. Wallace Barley's strange chain of disasters. Jas, there's oil under El Nido. Always has been. Real oil."

Jas watched Greg's hand as it now moved slowly along her leg. "I don't get it," she said. "I can understand covering up a spill. But if there's oil in the valley, why would ModoCorp hide it? Why not just pump it out and make a few hundred million?"

"I'm not sure. . . . But if I can find the answer, I think I'll know why so many people in El Nido wanted Sarah Trant convicted of murder."

"And how will you—"

Greg stopped her with a palm at her mouth. He pulled her to him by her shoulders. He reached for the top button of her dress. When he tugged at it, to his surprise all the buttons gave way. The dress fell open. Jas's mouth curved into a languid smile. "How'd you do that?" she asked.

# SIXTEEN

Greg Monarch, by now familiar with the rhythms of a day in El Nido, approached Sanborn Ranch during that stretch of the afternoon when Diana customarily visited the village. Even then, he chose the backroad that led him most directly to the corrals and stables. He found Alex in his private quarters, hard by the ranch hands' bunkhouse.

"Time to talk," Greg said.

Alex was sitting on a frayed brown cotton sofa in a front room that faced toward the Sanborn barn. In the kitchen, a pile of dirty plates and pots tottered by the sink.

"About what?" Alex asked.

"Rotten eggs and dead cows."

"Rotten eggs?"

"The smell of rotten eggs."

Greg saw he had Alex now. The foreman glanced through a big picture window at the main house. "She's not here right now," he said. "But she'll be back soon."

Just north of the ranch they found the trailhead for a little-used route into the foothills. For half an hour they hiked in silence, through a land still untamed despite the nearby village. The prickly pear and yucca, the scarlet lupines and golden poppies, the oaks and sycamores and towering mountains—everything declared itself boldly. At dusk the two men stopped on a knoll above a sheer drop, watching the El Nido basin fill with color.

This land, Greg imagined, must so delight Alex Ramirez.

"In my family," Alex said, "there are many stories of strange acts."

"Tell me about them."

Alex lifted his eyes to the sky. "An uncle who thought his wife's heart resided on the wrong side of her chest, who took to pounding on her chest to put it right. A cousin who imagined himself able to cure all human diseases. A grandfather who sold two-hundred-dollar-an-acre land for one hundred."

"Why did he do that?"

"Because he felt it a shame that poor deserving men were compelled to do without simply because they lacked money."

"Is that such a strange notion?"

Alex smiled with appreciation. "You are right, I didn't think my grandfather so terribly strange. All the same, the telling of his story draws much clucking and eye rolling in my family."

Greg waited a moment, then said, "I myself have a strange story to tell."

Alex settled on the flat edge of a smooth gray boulder. "Okay. . . . Tell me your strange story."

Greg talked first of the asphaltum and pooled petroleum at Camp Mahrah, then of the oil spill at El Nido Lake. Lastly, he spoke about the tunnel that ran from the creek to the back of the Sanborn property. "I almost passed out in there. The smell of rotten eggs was overpowering. I found that same odor up at Camp Mahrah."

Alex said nothing at first. "A strange tale indeed," he finally offered. "But what of it?"

"That is my question for you, Alex."

In the gloom, Greg imagined his companion struggling, imagined a show of anxiety in his eyes. Perhaps not, though. "I have no answer" is all Alex would say.

"Let me talk more, then."

"Okay."

"There is oil under El Nido. Always has been, even though the boom went bust a century ago. And there's something else. Something that makes it not a good idea for this oil to be pumped right now. Something that few here want known."

"Okay."

"Something that you know about, Alex."

The foreman turned to him. "Why do you say that?"

"The dead cows on your ranch, Alex. You are too good a foreman to look the other way about them. You know why they died."

"No. . . ."

"Yes. And why they died is part of the mystery that no one wants known. Isn't that so?"

Alex rose and walked to the far corner of the knoll. He stood at the edge of the sheer drop. For an irrational instant Greg feared the foreman might jump. Then Alex turned toward him.

"There was a time when I thought myself capable of doing anything for this land," Alex said. "For this land, and for Diana Sanborn."

"It is always hard to know our limits and capabilities."

Silence then. On Alex's face, Greg could see the debate waging within.

"I will tell you another strange story," Alex said.

"Okay."

"It's true, I wouldn't just look the other way when my cattle die. I didn't. No one would ever give me answers, though. The state health guys came and went without ever telling me anything. Private labs were no help either. So one morning, I went out to examine the soil on my own. Down by the river, down where the cows died."

"What did you find?"

"Nothing, not a thing. I got sick, though. Really sick."

"Let me guess. You felt dizzy and nauseated. Your eyes hurt. So did your nose and throat and head. You had trouble breathing."

"Exactly."

"And . . . ?"

"You're right, there is more. I smelled something there at the river, just before I got sick. The odor of rotten eggs."

"What's your theory, Alex?"

"That's where you're wrong. I truly don't have one. I don't

know why the cows died. They just stopped breathing. No one will tell me why."

"What does Diana Sanborn think?"

Alex stared out at the valley, saying nothing.

"Diana has enemies, Alex. She's in trouble. I can help her, but first I need to know what this is all about."

"You're not her friend."

"No, not exactly. But I am also not her enemy. Which is more than others can say."

"That's true," Alex agreed. He turned slowly from his view of the valley, and studied Greg as if taking his full measure. In that moment, something appeared to give way in him. He sighed and pushed back his hat. "Yes," he said, "she is in trouble."

"Tell me."

"I went to Diana straight from the river, that morning I got sick. Rushed to the house, found her in that sitting chair by her fireplace."

"Near where her grandfather's portrait hangs."

"Yes, with Edward Sanborn watching us from above. I was so full of myself. We've got to find out why these cows died, I told her. We've got to find out why the state health guys backed away."

"Diana's response?"

"Hardly any at all. It took me only a short while to realize why."

Greg waited for Alex to continue, but the silence stretched on. "I need to know, Alex."

"One more strange story."

"One more," Greg agreed.

Alex began to pace along the knoll. "In the early days of oil exploration in the El Nido Valley . . . Let's say you're right, that back then there really was oil here, not just dry wells."

"Okay," Greg agreed again. "Let's say."

"Let's say that oil was carried through a track of secret underground pipes from inland reservoirs all the way to the ocean. Let's say those pipes began to leak. Began to leak, and kept leaking. For thirty years, forty, maybe fifty."

"That's a long time."

"Let's say that as a result, a subsurface plume of oil formed in the center of El Nido Village. Right along Main Street and the Arcade, right through Sanborn Park. Then eastward toward Sanborn Ranch. Accumulated slowly, year after year."

"That would . . ." Greg stopped himself, waiting.

Alex continued. "Let's say a half-dozen years ago a newly arrived would-be developer in El Nido bought up a nice chunk of land in the foothills. Let's say this developer started bulldozing away. Let's say this developer stumbled upon evidence of that plume. Stumbled upon it, and realized it came from his property, from his oil wells, from his pipelines."

It was Greg's turn to stare out at the valley. "That's a problem for the developer, isn't it? He's responsible, as landowner and assignee?"

"Exactly. But it's a problem not just for him. It's a problem for the whole community. Who wants teams of overdressed strangers fanning across Main Street, waving probes and monitors at the Arcade and Sanborn Park? Who wants an environmental-impact report calling for the whole village to be torn apart? Who wants an enormous excavation? Minimize disruption, that's what everyone wants. Save the town. Maybe treat the plume with concrete and chemicals. Maybe try bioremediation."

"Or maybe do nothing," Greg said. He thought of Diana riding across her ranch one windblown evening, beating back the fireballs threatening to destroy her home. "No doubt many here would rather take their chances living quietly above an oil plume than dealing with the publicity and lawsuits and destruction of their town."

Alex was relaxed enough now to show a tentative smile. "You better believe it," he said. "Diana took me to one of their meetings. Pretty private gathering, up at Camp Mahrah. The sheriff, Charles Whit, the Rabes, the Arcade shop owners. Some talked about having to feed their families. Others kept insisting the hazard was overblown. Everyone agreed on one thing: They wanted the town to stay as it is. They didn't want

El Nido torn up. They wanted to keep the plume secret. Fact is, they downright insisted."

"ModoCorp and the townsfolk were on the same bus? Each side, for their own reasons?"

"Exactly. Suddenly, if reluctantly, everyone had common interests."

"Is it possible just to sit on this? Is the town safe to live in?"

Alex stopped pacing and sat down next to Greg. "So many voices on that. You've got the ecology types wailing on about all sorts of hazards. Then you've got the shopowners pointing out that they've had this plume thing for decades with no problems. Fact is, ModoCorp and Diana both paid for private studies, and neither came up with any direct evidence linking the plume to health hazards in El Nido. So yeah, maybe the town is safe despite the plume."

*No direct evidence.* Greg mulled that. "The plume doesn't explain the dead cows?"

"No, don't see how it could. But Diana assumed it did. That's why she resisted when I came barging in on her. That's why she wanted to ignore the whole business. She feared that if we started digging too far into the cows' deaths, the trail would lead to the plume. She preferred just to bury the cows."

"You couldn't explain to her . . . ?"

"Not that easy. Fact is, she's right. No matter the true cause of their deaths, the cows would probably lead to the plume, what with all the digging and testing. And Diana isn't at her most rational when facing that possibility."

Alex laughed with dark, rueful eyes. "Thing is," he continued, "even though she paid for a study, she doesn't really acknowledge the plume even exists. I once tried to talk it all out with her. She cut me off with a wave of her hand. 'Alex,' she said, 'it's just not true. If there were a plume, it could very well extend under Sanborn Ranch as well as El Nido Village.' She rose then and went to stand under the portrait of her grandfather. 'So,' she told me, 'there is no plume.' "

Alex fell silent. Greg asked, "You agreed with her finally?"

"How'd you know?" Alex looked at him as if beseeching his approval. "There was something in the way Diana stood there, insisting on the world being as she wished. I didn't want her to be wrong. I didn't want her to be vanquished."

"I understand."

"I know nothing else, Monarch. I don't know why the cows died."

"Can anyone else help us?"

Alex thought on that, then suddenly sat up straight. "One of the state health boys who came out to the ranch. An inspector for the environmental agency. He didn't act like the others. Looked like something was bothering him. He tried to talk to me one day, but his buddies kept interrupting, getting between us. Never saw him again, he wasn't with them their next visit. I forgot about him."

"His name, Alex?"

The foreman drew a breath. "He never told me."

James Mashburn, standing by his office window, peering out at Sanborn Park's central fountain, tried to ignore the sound of Sheriff Rimmer's impatient pacing. If I stay here long enough, he told himself, Roy might just disappear.

"Come on, Jim, we need to start throwing elbows now," Rimmer was saying. "Monarch is tripping up our witnesses. He's roaming all over the place, he's casting lines everywhere. This is maddening. This is—"

"This is a lesson," Mashburn interrupted, turning from the window. "That's what it is, Roy. Just think how a lousy last-gasp handwritten habeas petition has brought everything to the brink of utter exposure. Sort of gives you a new regard for habeas petitions, doesn't it?"

Rimmer didn't look appreciative. "We should have shut Monarch down a long time ago. That was the plan. It was a good plan. We covered all the bases. We got everyone from Diana Sanborn to Judge Solman on board. But Monarch keeps twirling around like a windup toy with a perpetual spring."

"He does," Mashburn agreed, "doesn't he."

Rimmer moved to his side. "This is my county. I'm expected to keep things running properly. I'm expected to keep the lid on this."

"Who exactly expects that of you, Roy?"

Rimmer stared at the DA. "What do you understand about it all?" he said in a low voice. "What does Greg Monarch understand? You're just a pair of lawyers. Just two men enslaved by a bunch of written rules. Rules that people never followed. Rules that people violated all the time. Rules that never, ever applied in El Nido."

Mashburn turned away and walked back to the window. Rimmer had a point, he thought. He and Greg were bound by the rule of law. Also by a sense of their roles in the system. *You could argue the evidence more than one way.* That's what he'd told Greg when they were debating in the courtroom. He'd meant it, he could defend that stance any day. Yet what of Greg's questions? *Aren't you curious, Jim? . . . Why do you think so many people want Sarah to be guilty?* If only he could forge his own role. Not every day, not forever, but of a moment. When that was needed.

"Don't worry, Roy," Mashburn said. "You're right. The legal system does bind me. As long as I'm the DA, I'll do my goddamn job. I'll defend the state's case. I'll be your advocate."

"Okay, then," Rimmer said, looking unsure how to take Mashburn's pledge. "What are you going to do?"

"Try to win . . . Try to stop Greg Monarch."

Rimmer thought on that, then asked, "What ever happened to the sexual-misconduct charges you were going to bring against him?"

The mention of that complaint made Mashburn cringe. "Chrissake, Roy. You know perfectly well we were just trying to harass him with that. Not even Judge Solman would go for it. If I filed in county court, it wouldn't come to anything until long after this habeas hearing ended. Probably wouldn't come to anything ever."

"Yes, no doubt," Rimmer said. "But Monarch hasn't stopped

handling her in the meeting rooms. We've got a couple more moments on tape. They like to touch each other."

For a moment Mashburn entertained the notion of wrapping his fingers around the sheriff's bony neck. Instead he asked, "You're videotaping him now?"

"Whatever it takes, Jim."

"You put him on notice you're doing this?"

"Come on, now, Jim. What would be the point of that?"

Mashburn spoke slowly, stretching out each word: "To . . . make . . . it . . . legal."

"We don't need a legal tape. We just need something that convinces Monarch to back off."

Mashburn offered a faint smile. "Sorry, Roy. But I think that highly unlikely."

Rimmer studied the DA. "You sound so appreciative of Monarch. You part of his team, Jim? You know what else he's got planned?"

Mashburn lifted a document from his desk and waved it at the sheriff. "Don't have to be part of his team to see what's coming. Just need to look at the schedule when we resume the hearing next week."

"What?" Rimmer asked.

"If I don't call Karl Jackson to the stand, Monarch is going to, as a hostile rebuttal witness for the petitioner."

"Judge Jackson?"

"That's right, Roy. Your buddy. The fellow who prosecuted Sarah Trant for murder. The Honorable Karl Jackson."

At dawn in her bedroom, Diana Sanborn opened her journal and once again began to write. Her sleep had been filled with such vivid, precise dreams in recent weeks. Her mare Candy, the railroad, little Jenny Holder, her violent blue-eyed beau—the wondrous kaleidoscope, at once dark and exciting, hardly ever stopped now inside her mind. It was as if something was coming that required her to review her life, something apocalyptic. Diana felt it in her bones.

Not just her bones, though. She had more tangible evidence. Charles Whit and Sheriff Rimmer, for one thing. That gracious duo had dropped by to tell her of Greg Monarch's adventure in El Nido Lake. The postman had come too, with a third anonymous letter, this one even more threatening than the others. *You will die if you don't make amends. You will die if you don't provide restitution. . . .* Finally, there'd been Greg Monarch's visit.

Not to see her, though. Sitting her horse on a knoll off to the east, where she'd ridden to check on a dozen calves and their moms, she'd watched Greg roll quietly up to Alex Ramirez's quarters. Then she'd watched them hike off together into the foothills. They'd been gone three hours. She'd been waiting ever since for Alex to tell her about the visit, but he hadn't. Alex's silence terrified Diana. *I am alone now,* she wrote in her journal. *There is so much to hold together. It is all coming apart. Maybe that is best. . . .*

She stopped, put down her pen. *Maybe that is best.* She'd written those words once before in this journal. When Greg Monarch came, when Greg Monarch decided to stay and represent Sarah Trant. She'd imagined then a painless resolution, but of course that had been foolish on her part. There were prices to pay, consequences of actions, always and forever. To save El Nido, she'd forsaken a young woman whom she cared for. To save El Nido, she'd forged a bond with her enemies, she'd ignored the valley's poisonous plume, she'd let her cows die. And everything for naught, finally: To tear down the prison bars confining Sarah, it looked as if Greg Monarch was going to dismantle all of El Nido.

What would Edward Sanborn make of that? Edward Sanborn, who in a public treatise once wrote that "it is the right and duty of a community to take such steps as may seem right against whatever is harmful to its welfare." *Whatever tends to retard the progress of a community should be looked upon as a public enemy, and the public have the right to rise up and abolish the enemy. . . .*

More and more frequently now, Diana found herself thinking of her grandfather, and those wondrous days when he was so vital and resolute. Neither storms nor anything else in nature could prevent him from going where he would.

Whether in a saddle or a buckboard, he galloped across the plains, using his whip when need be. Which wasn't often, for his horses heeded him. They knew his voice, which seemed to inspire them to courage and trust. He had a similar effect on people. Once, after dinner, though the night was blustery and bitterly cold, he hitched up the horse and took Diana for a sleigh ride. The wind howled with fury, but the winter stars were very bright, and the sleigh bells made a haunting sound. Diana was bundled up to the nose, sitting beside her grandfather, where nothing, for that one evening, could get at her.

Diana closed her journal. Sheriff Rimmer advised that Mashburn was saving her until last. Yet Rimmer also warned that Greg Monarch might call her to the witness stand himself. Which process would be easier? Or did it really matter? Either way, there was no denying that the demons of discord had returned to El Nido Valley. Or rather, the descendant of those demons. She knew from where her anonymous letters came. She knew who was writing them. Diana picked up her pen again and opened the journal. *Here is my pledge: I shall take such steps as may seem right. . . . El Nido will prevail. . . .*

As they walked along the Arcade, Greg reached out to place a protective hand on the small of Jas's back. To his regret, he saw that she, by association, now also drew cold, hostile glances. At this moment, Sam and Tammy Rabe were staring at them from across the street, where they stood before the park fountain. Jas noticed but didn't appear to care.

"Where else can we explore El Nido's history?" he asked her.

"I'm not sure."

The oil wells of Camp Mahrah and Diana Sanborn's anonymous letters were tugging at Greg's mind. There was a link between the two, he was certain of that. A link that he suspected went a long way toward explaining Diana's role in Sarah Trant's prosecution.

Greg suddenly stopped in midstep, struck by a notion. "Doesn't El Nido have a cemetery?"

They were there inside of ten minutes. The small overgrown plot of land sat in the heart of the oak-thick residential area called Woodland—Edward Sanborn's Woodland. Surrounded by a low stone wall and a wild lilac hedge, the El Nido cemetery suggested nothing so much as a quaint country garden. Large oaks spread their protective limbs over hundred-year-old graves. A rickety windmill and pump—donated by a young widow a century ago to "keep our city of the dead green"—irrigated the park's lush gardens.

In a way, Greg thought, here was a history of El Nido no one could dispute. With Jas at his side, he stepped slowly through the cemetery, reading tombstones in the still afternoon. The cemetery accepted its first four customers in 1870, and most tombstone dates were from the nineteenth century. Some markers were merely native stone with names of beloved ones scratched into them. Others were broken wooden crosses with fading, barely visible letters. Yet there were also some large granite headstones that bestowed recognition on entire families. You could, it occurred to Greg, piece together entire lineages from the words and dates in this cemetery. If not the story of an entire community.

"Look over there in the Alexander family plot," Jas said, pointing. "Julie Alexander. Not yet sixteen when she died in June 1897, one day before she was scheduled to speak at a state convention of the Women's Christian Temperance League in Chumash County. Largest funeral procession ever seen in El Nido up until that time." Jas swung her hand down another row. "There's Miriam Dayton. Twice widowed, eighty-four when she died, a tiny, nearly deaf gnome so stooped she was almost bent double. There's pictures of her in our files, and letters about her. Such sad anxious eyes. Spent her days knitting string washcloths, gathering eucalyptus bark for kindling, and waiting at the window for family members to return from horse-and-buggy rides. Yet she championed women's right to vote. Voted for the first time months before she died."

Greg turned to Jas. "You know everyone's history here?"

"Well, some . . ."

Greg pointed to a marker.

"That's James Boulin. Dead at age seventy-five of an accidental gunshot wound after overcoming a terrible case of tuberculosis. Took a ride in his pal Paul Wilson's new car. There was a shotgun lying on the seat. Wilson braked, the gun fell to the floor and went off."

Greg pointed to another marker.

"Wyman Williams, dead at twenty-eight because he got his dander up. Lost money in a card game at Hank Sidney's billiard parlor. Was still angry the next day, decided to take his losses out on the proprietor. Waited in an alley for Sidney to walk by on his way home for lunch, as he did every day. Except Sidney skipped lunch that day. So Williams finally came charging through the pool hall's front door, waving a gun. Sidney grabbed his own pistol and shot Williams to death on the spot."

Greg turned away from Jas and walked through the aisles, reading markers. There was the Wheelers' family plot, the Bullards', the Crowleys', the Danielsons', the Stillmans'. He stopped finally at a plot marked by a simple gray rectangle of granite. Here it was, what he was after. The Barley family plot. Wallace Barley's grave. Greg bent to study the nearly illegible names.

There was Lawrence P. Barley, who died in 1862. That must have been Wally's father, Greg reasoned.

There was Wallace Barley himself. Died in 1902.

Wally's wife Glenda, 1911.

Their son Thomas Barley . . . Another son, Jonathan Barley . . . Greg's eyes stopped at the name of their daughter. Gretchen Barley. Gretchen Barley Whitschenson. Born in 1890, married to one Joseph Whitschenson in 1915. Died in 1955.

*Whitschenson.* Could a later descendant have shortened that last name?

Greg's eyes moved farther down the granite rock, but there

were no more names. That was it. The last addition to the Barley family plot had come more than four decades ago.

"Jas," Greg said. "You know anything about Wallace Barley's daughter Gretchen?"

Jas didn't answer. Greg looked up but couldn't spot her. He rose and started pacing through the cemetery. The foliage was so dense here, he couldn't see from row to row. Where had she gone? These disappearing acts were getting on his nerves. He glanced up at the empty road. He thought he heard something pushing through the brush. "Jas," he called, fighting a wisp of panic. "Jas."

She rose suddenly from behind a hedge at the end of the cemetery where she'd been on her knees, studying a splintery marker. She lifted a hand that was holding a bunch of withered leaves. "Here," she said. "Over here."

Greg tried to hide the alarm he'd felt. "I was asking whether you knew anything about Wallace Barley's daughter Gretchen."

"Got me on that one. Nothing about her in the archives. Far as I can tell, the Barleys didn't stay in El Nido long after Wallace died. I think I saw somewhere that the daughter moved to San Francisco."

Greg walked to her side. "Would you recall seeing anything about her own family? About her having a son?"

"Not likely we'd have reports like that from San Francisco. Why are you asking this? What's the point?"

"There probably is none," Greg said. "But let's take one more look at what Fred Darvill's got over at the museum."

This time they didn't seek Darvill's guidance. Jas used her own set of keys to enter the closed museum. Greg took one wall of shelves, she another. For two hours they combed the stacks, flipping through mountains of files, not knowing what they were looking for. *General El Nido History,* read the label on one shelf. *Oil Exploration,* read another. Neither offered anything Greg hadn't seen before.

"I think Darvill showed you all there is," Jas said finally.

Greg didn't appear to hear her. He was striding down corridors now, his eyes surveying the building, his hands testing doorknobs. One led to a utility closet, another to a bathroom, a third to a small office. At a fourth, Greg stopped. The knob wouldn't turn. "This one is locked," he said.

"It's just a storage room, Greg."

"Can you open it?"

She fumbled with her set of keys, trying one, then another. The third key fit. She pulled open the door to a small room thick with dust and a musty smell. Stacks of boxes filled the chamber, reaching almost to the ceiling. "Over the years," she explained, "people from across the valley have dumped stuff with us when they moved away, or when their parents died off. We've never had much of a staff, so these boxes have just accumulated. Mostly household memorabilia. The idea has always been to index and organize everything one day. Don't know when that day will come, though."

Two at a time, Greg carried the boxes out to the museum's central chamber. Then he began pulling open the top flaps. He'd hoped to find some order to what he saw inside the boxes, but instead he found jumbles of dusty, yellowing documents that looked as if they'd been thrown in haphazardly during intermittent efforts at housecleaning. His hands moved through chaos. News clips, receipts, and scribbled notes mingled with faded photos, birthday cards, land deeds, someone's employment contract. Greg picked up pieces of paper, straining to read pale illegible words. Nothing had meaning, nothing had import. Greg turned from one box to the other, moving faster now, fighting a growing unease. How many hours did he have left? It was late Friday. Just two days, forty-eight hours—

"Look at this." Jas was standing over the far box, holding a thick brown expandable file. With a large blue marker, someone had written three words on its side. "Committee of Ten," Jas read. She handed the file to Greg. "Sounds interesting, doesn't it?"

Greg opened the file. The pages were as crackly and yellowing as the others. The impatient handwriting slanted across the page at an angle, often spilling into the margins or curling sideways. Yet here was order. At last. Someone had felt compelled to keep a journal. Dates, a chronology, a narrative . . . A voice from the past, telling a story. It wasn't a story that Greg found surprising.

The early meetings among Edward Sanborn and his Committee of Ten. Their anxious concern at the encroaching oil wildcatters. Their passion to preserve and defend El Nido. Their love for their verdant oak-thick valley. And so their threats, their bribes. And their growing efforts at sabotage.

Setting the fire that destroyed Wallace Barley's first refinery. Arranging for Barley's oil shipment, bound for the East Coast, to be dumped in Panama. Flooding Barley's Pacific Coast market with cheaper eastern oil, shipped at deeply discounted rates by cooperative railroad men. Finally, the arrival in El Nido of East Coast refiners with ties to Edward Sanborn. East Coast refiners determined to keep hold of their monopoly, determined to squelch potential competition from Central California.

They bought land adjacent to Barley's. They sank phony wells that had to come up dry. They debunked talk of vast oil fields in El Nido. They discouraged financiers and other prospectors.

Still Barley struggled on, so the Committee of Ten blew up his refinery a second time. At last Barley gave up, broke and despairing.

*Barley's wagon roads instead led the way for the next folks,* wrote the anonymous memoirist. *Stouthearted adventurers in search of a home . . .*

Greg was turning through the pages so quickly now, he almost missed the quickly scribbled coda. It was just a single sheet, an afterthought at the bottom of a thick stack of pages.

*Wallace Barley's descendants had to sell their land after his death. Yet for reasons unknown, they retained the mineral rights, despite all efforts of the Committee to purchase them. Edward Sanborn, in his final months, still talked of his failure in this matter. By then he'd watched the rights pass from one generation to the next. It was as if this family meant to keep a memory. . . .*

Greg studied those words. *One generation to the next.*

"Hey there," Jas called, waving her own stack of photos at the other side of the room. "More spoils . . . Look at these."

One by one he held them to the light. So faded, the black-and-white tones a blurred brownish tinge. Here were memories of a different sort—memories of Sanborn Ranch. Filtered, it seemed, through the lens of someone who worked there. He'd taken a few shots of his employers—there was a teenaged Diana with her grandfather—yet most captured the ranch hands relaxing in their bunkhouse, or toiling in a corral.

Greg moved slowly through the photos. A cattle drive, cowboys on horseback, someone sitting on a fence staring moodily at the camera, someone with a rope—Greg stopped, then flipped back to the photo of the moody young man on the fence. He had surly eyes and jet-black hair, and—yes—beside him, Edward Sanborn's granddaughter. Her fresh lively face was turned not to the camera but to him. *A brooding, tightly wound twenty-four-year-old.* Diana Sanborn's beau. It had to be. When had the assault come? Just after this photo was taken? Slowly, Greg turned the photo over. There, in light blue ink, in the right bottom corner, someone had scrawled something. Greg squinted at the pale letters and moved toward the window to get a better light over his shoulder.

The slam of a door stopped him. "What are you two doing in here?" a voice demanded. Greg turned to see Fred Darvill standing on the far side of the room. The old man's hands were shaking. His eyes looked as if they'd rolled halfway back in his head. Darvill took a step, then lunged toward Greg in a paroxysm of throat-rattling dismay. Greg stuffed the photo in his back pocket, grabbed the Committee of Ten file, and pushed Jasmine toward the exit.

"We've worn out our welcome," he whispered.

At first they couldn't open the front door. Greg vainly tried to yank back a jammed dead bolt. Darvill was closing on them with outstretched arms. Without effect, Greg slammed his shoulder against the thick oak panel. Jas pulled him away, flashing a key. In an instant she had the door open.

"After you," she said.

# SEVENTEEN

When Greg reached his room at the El Nido Inn just before ten P.M., he pulled off his dust-covered clothes and stood under a hot shower. He regretted that Jas hadn't stayed with him. *Somebody to see,* she'd explained as she drove off. He imagined her now beside him, and in that instant felt the warm water coursing down his body, kneading his muscles, releasing what held him.

"Are things complicated enough for you now?" she'd asked after they'd managed to escape from the museum.

They were standing then on the sidewalk outside Sanborn Park, catching their breath. Greg was rubbing his shoulder, where he'd slammed it against the door. "Getting there," he said.

Jas looked back at the museum. "I may have lost my volunteer job."

"What made Darvill so angry?"

"I don't think he was angry. More like scared, or upset."

"About what?"

"I'm not sure. Darvill doesn't scare usually. He also isn't one to keep things hidden. In fact, he shares things with me."

"But he also cares mightily about this valley, I presume."

"Yes," Jas said. "That's true."

Greg was toweling himself off, recollecting that exchange, when his telephone rang. Jas, on a cell phone, sounded like a distant, broken echo. Greg strained to hear. *In the canyon . . . I'm going to Judith Daniels's house . . . Just to try . . . Woman to woman might work . . . Will let you know . . .* Then they lost the connection. The canyons had swallowed her up. Greg fought to quell his sense of dread. He wished he hadn't talked to Jas about his critical need for the dotty spinster's testimony. He didn't want her going out alone like this. She wouldn't likely mind him, though, if he tried to call her off.

An hour later, the phone rang again as Greg was sitting on his balcony, staring at a moonless sky. He glanced at his watch as he lunged to answer it. Almost midnight. He would tell her—

"Is this Greg Monarch?" The man's voice on the other end sounded tentative. Greg struggled to adjust.

"Yes. . . . Yes. . . . Who is this?"

"Sorry, did I wake you?"

"No, but . . ."

"Didn't think I would."

"Who is this?"

"Name is Jeremy Rollins."

Greg searched his memory. "Do I know you?"

"No, no you don't. Not directly. But we have certain interests in common."

"Forgive me, Mr. Rollins, but is this going to become a guessing game? I'm too tired for that just now."

"It's you who must forgive me. I'm being too oblique. Sorry, I'm not accustomed to this sort of thing. I tried to talk to that ranch foreman weeks ago, but didn't do any better back then with him."

"Ranch foreman?"

"Yes . . . out at the Sanborn place."

"Alex Ramirez?"

"Yes . . . that was his name."

A notion occurred to Greg. "Mr. Rollins, are you by chance an agent with the state environmental agency? Are you the one who came out to inspect the dead cows?"

"Very good guess, Mr. Monarch. Except I'm no longer with the state. Quit a month ago."

"Reached retirement age?"

"The age of discontent, I'd call it."

"Alex talked of you but never knew your name."

"He managed to track me down, nonetheless. . . . Don't know how, but he reached me yesterday. Urged me to call you. Said you wanted to know more about the Sanborn cows."

Greg suddenly realized he'd never eaten dinner. "Mr. Rollins, I'm famished. Want to join me for a hamburger?"

They met at the all-night diner on the canyon road leading from Chumash County into the valley. A ragged mix of bikers up late and fishermen up early had the place half filled. Greg guided Rollins to a corner booth and sat with his back to the wall. Two billiards tables stood off to their right, unused and unkempt, scarred by dozens of cigarette burns. One rough plank wall featured snakeskins and steer horns, another a twenty-pound stuffed bass. Biting into his hamburger, Greg kept his eyes on Rollins.

He had gray skin and a long narrow face, and resembled the career technocrat he was. Close-cropped white hair, a short-sleeved shirt, a tentative manner . . . Yet something in Rollins's eyes set him apart. An indignation, Greg thought. Beneath his composed demeanor, Rollins appeared to be deeply offended by something.

"So I understand you're here in El Nido defending Sarah Trant," Rollins was saying.

"Yes. . . . And I also find myself indulging in some historical research."

Rollins offered a skittish smile but didn't say anything. Greg tried to prod him. "I appreciate you calling me," he offered. "I've been wanting to meet you."

"Yeah," Rollins said, stirring a cup of coffee. "That's what Alex Ramirez told me."

"Okay, then. So can we talk?"

Rollins twisted around to survey the café. He drummed his fingers on the table. He rearranged a pile of sugar cubes. "I don't think so. This was a mistake, calling you."

Greg leaned forward, willing to gamble. "I know about the oil plume under El Nido. Shall we start there?"

Rollins looked surprised. "You know about the plume?"

Greg hesitated. He preferred collecting information to dispensing. "They've kept a pretty tight lid on it," he said. "A community secret."

"Yes, they have."

"So how do you know about the plume?"

Rollins knocked over his pile of sugar cubes. "A couple of scientists I know were hired privately to do some tests. Their contracts called for strict confidentiality, which for the most part they observed with due diligence."

"As I understand," Greg said, happy to be collecting again, "the plume developed from a leaking pipeline."

"Yes. . . . Slow leak from carrier lines."

"From how far back?"

"Maybe as much as half a century, when they were still prospecting for oil in El Nido. Leaked for decades." Rollins's eyes roamed around the café as he spoke. "But that plume is of no concern to me."

"Why not?"

"I've seen the private studies my colleagues did. No evidence of any danger, none at all. It isn't a refined by-product . . . just pooled oil that's been sitting there for decades, causing no pattern of harm. Believe me, if there were real dangers, I'd be the first to holler."

Maybe Alex's instincts were right, then, Greg thought. "So why all the hand-wringing?"

Rollins regarded him with exasperation. "Because even with these environmental red herrings, you always have certain terribly vocal folks wailing about toxic contamination. Some of them have heartfelt political agendas, but lots are just after a pot of gold. Commercial landlords, especially. They suddenly sound like tree huggers when they smell a chance to replace their weathered old shacks with four stories of brand-spanking-new stucco, courtesy of a bailout or settlement. There's no stopping them once they get their lawyers yelling about lawsuits and liability. I've seen this happen. One really fine funky old beach town not far from here just got ripped apart for no good reason other than the landlords' desire to go upscale."

Rollins began tapping the table with his knuckles. "Don't

you get it, Mr. Monarch? El Nido has plenty good reason to hide the plume even if it's not harmful to anyone."

Greg studied Rollins, trying to assess what he saw in this man's cautious indignant eyes. "So why did Diana Sanborn's cows die?" he asked.

Rollins frowned, looked over his shoulder again. The café was nearly full now. Fishermen heading for the lake, farmers rising before the roosters, insomniacs seeking solace. Here and there, a face turned toward their booth.

"If the plume doesn't explain the dead cows," Greg continued, "it also doesn't explain why you're so angry."

"You're right . . . it doesn't."

A waitress suddenly appeared before them, offering a coffeepot. Rollins flinched; Greg waved her away. "What, then?" he asked.

Rollins began kneading his neck. "You'd think a place like this would be empty at such an hour."

"Not with so many folks trying to catch fish. You want bass, you've got to wake up before they do."

Rollins chewed on those words for a while. Then he shrugged and began to speak, keeping his voice low.

"Soon as I got out to the Sanborn Ranch, I had a notion what was up. Cows don't just stop breathing usually. They don't just lie down and die without any sign of disease, or anything toxic in the water or land. The wind was really up that day. A real blow, coming down from the foothills. Hard to ignore the odor of rotten eggs in the air. You put those two together, cows that stop breathing and a rotten-egg smell, well, it was pretty plain. At least to me."

"What?"

"Hydrogen sulfide, I figured. Hard to prove, though. They found nothing in the soil or water. They wouldn't. It would be in the air. That day for sure. Other days too, no doubt. But not all the time."

"Hydrogen sulfide? What's that? Where would it come from?"

"It's an air contaminant common in oil fields and refineries. Develops from petroleum refining, among other things. Highly toxic, quite colorless."

"And reeking of rotten eggs?"

"Even at low concentrations. Inhalation is the common route into the body. Passes easily from the lungs into the bloodstream."

"Symptoms include irritation of the eyes, nose, throat? Headache, dizziness, nausea, breathing difficulty?"

Rollins peered at him with curiosity. "Sounds like you've had your own encounter with the stuff. Probably in low dosages, though. In higher exposures, you get shock, convulsions, coma, and death. It can kill quickly, I tell you. It's a neurotoxin. Builds up in the blood, poisons the nerve and brain cells. Wrecks the centers of the brain that control breathing. Your lungs stop working. You die of asphyxiation. You can be overcome in seconds."

Greg slowly breathed in and out, involuntarily checking his lungs. "Twice I've smelled that rotten-egg odor. Up at Camp Mahrah. Then in a tunnel leading to the Sanborn ranch. Both times it went away as I kept moving."

Concern showed in Rollins's eyes now. "Stuff can deaden a person's sense of smell. Make him unaware he's being exposed. If the rotten-egg odor disappears, it may not necessarily mean exposure has stopped. It's said in oil refineries, if you think you've caught the smell of hydrogen sulfide and then it goes away, you're probably already on your way down."

Greg started to mull that, then decided not to. "The dead cows," he asked. "Couldn't they have been tested?"

"There's no specific, medically useful test for the presence of hydrogen sulfide in blood and urine. Tests will only show the resulting damage done to the brain and nerves and organs. We could have done that. I wanted to run those tests. But I got overruled by my supervisors at state health. I argued, even had some sympathetic ears. Then it went up the ladder, and we got stopped. Not just stopped, actually. Silenced. Total blackout ordered."

"Why?"

Rollins offered a faint smile. "I can only speculate."

Greg gazed out the café's front window. The sky had a hue to it that promised the coming sunrise. The more resolute fishermen, he imagined, already would be standing in their boats, casting. "So let's speculate," he said.

Rollins leaned across the table, his voice even lower now. "Like I told you, the wind was blowing down from the foothills that day. Down from the Camp Mahrah acreage, to be precise. Those cows on the creek were in a direct line from the camp. So that's where I think the hydrogen sulfide came from."

"What would the stuff be doing up there?"

"Remember, now, you get hydrogen sulfide as part of the by-product waste of petroleum refining. Oil companies have to dump that waste somewhere." Rollins once more scanned the café, then turned back to Greg. "My guess is that ModoCorp has been using Camp Mahrah as a dumping ground for toxic waste. From all their other oil fields along the Gulf and Pacific Coast. It would be easy. They've got isolated private routes in from the backside of their property. They could have moved hundreds of truckloads over the past five years. Maybe thousands."

"Why?"

"They have to put it somewhere, and have few choices. Oil waste, it's a multimillion-dollar business in its own right."

"I mean, why El Nido?"

"We've just discussed one possible reason. The plume. Hard to keep that covered up once they start openly pumping oil. Probably not enough oil in this valley to warrant the risk, at any rate. Maybe they never really meant to pump oil here. Could be they always planned Camp Mahrah as their central waste dump. It's the perfect spot for it, after all. Remote, heavily forested, small population, low density . . . It's a place where no one would notice what ModoCorp was doing."

An image suddenly rose in Greg's mind from the day he hiked alone into Camp Mahrah. He half sliding down a gentle slope, landing near a huge earthen pit full of muddy water.

The overwhelming odor of rotten eggs, the protective white overalls, the tall rubber boots . . .

"I think I've seen part of that waste dump," Greg said.

Dimensions and colors mattered most to the former state health agent. Greg tried his best to describe for Rollins what he'd observed that day through dizzy watering eyes. When he finished, Rollins slapped the table with an open palm.

"I'm willing to bet that El Nido citizens have a poisonous dump site hard by their lovely town." Rollins was still trying to talk quietly, but his voice was rising. "Besides the immediate dangers, you've got the potential long-term impact. Birth defects, cancer, kidney problems, respiratory troubles, eye ailments, chest pain, memory loss, headaches, trembling, depression . . . They've all been linked to this stuff. So much possibility here . . . And the folks don't have a blessed clue."

Greg labored to understand. "Doesn't ModoCorp have to tell someone? Doesn't this get regulated?"

Disgust showed in Rollins's eyes. "There's a huge gorgeous loophole in the hazardous-waste laws that exempts the oil industry from federal regulation. Some twenty years ago, Big Oil's lobbyists pushed a sweetheart deal through Congress. Lets them pump toxic waste out of a well, label it 'nonhazardous,' and dump it near towns without warning a soul. They don't even have to know what's in the waste. All they have to do is say this waste came out of ground where they sank oil wells. In any other industry, federal law would require the same waste to be trapped, labeled, and handled as hazardous material. But not the oil industry. That's how broad the loophole is. Nothing like it in federal law."

The crowd in the restaurant had thinned out now. The sun, low in the sky, reached through the café's window, warming the front tables. It would be a scorcher today, Greg imagined. "So this isn't just going on in El Nido?" he asked.

"Happens all over the place in oil country. You've got more than fifty thousand oil fields producing waste that's got to go somewhere. The individual states could do their own regulating, but they're usually sitting deep in the oil companies' pockets. Result is, folks in thousands of communities end up having no idea what they've got in their backyards."

"Until an ill wind blows some of the stuff off site?"

Rollins looked at his watch, then suddenly rose to leave. "Precisely," he said.

Through bleary eyes, from fifty yards away, driving down Main Street, Greg spotted Jas Gest's car in the parking lot of the El Nido Inn. Relief mixed with a feeling of overwhelming exhaustion. He hadn't slept all night, and couldn't now. It was nearly nine on a bright, cloudless Sunday morning. Too bright, the sun harsh and relentless, already leaving no shadows. He had just twenty-four hours to go before the hearing resumed. One day to turn everything around.

There was no point, he understood now, to arguing either the law or the evidence. They weren't going to let him win that way. He could orate as much as he wished about the Fourteenth Amendment and due process. It would get them nowhere. Nor would trying to prove Sarah's innocence. Actual innocence . . . What a crock. He needed a hammer, that's what he needed.

Greg braked hard as he peered into the bright light. There she was, outside the motel, rushing toward him as he pulled into the parking lot. Something, he suddenly realized, was wrong. Jas nearly tripped in her haste to reach him. At his car, on the passenger's side, she grabbed the door handle, yanked, then collapsed on the seat beside him.

"Some guy followed me out to Judith Daniels's house," she gasped. "Got on my tail halfway through the canyon. I floored it, but he caught up. God, Greg, he nearly rammed me. . . . I could see him in the mirror. A fat red face, a big ragged beard. He was staring at me. His eyes were so awful. . . . I started looping onto backroads, but he kept coming. Damnit, Greg—"

"You got away finally?"

"Yes, but only after—"

"Did you get to Judith Daniels?"

"No, I couldn't. . . . I came back, I circled around on the old fire road, that's where I lost him. . . ."

He helped her out of the car and led her to his room at the inn. She paced about in agitation, then sank onto the bed. He came to her, sat beside her, put his hands on her shoulders. "Are you okay, Jas?" he asked.

"I'll be fine . . . now that you're here."

He began to rub her temples. His fingers moved gently along the side of her face, then down her neck and along her spine. She turned toward him, and the palms of his hands brushed her breasts. She arched her shoulder blades and moaned softly with parted lips. He stopped, and rose from the bed. "I'm sorry, Jas . . . I'll be back, I'm not heading for the train. . . . But I can't stay right now."

She grasped his hands. "Why . . . ?"

"There's someone I have to see."

# EIGHTEEN

As if coming into a new country, Greg drove with slow watchful eyes through the lush orchards of El Nido's east end. The abundance startled him, for he hadn't been by this way for some time. He'd grown accustomed to approaching Diana Sanborn's property from the dusty, curving backroads. This Sunday morning he would be arriving through the main gate.

They had Sarah Trant in solitary confinement now. Assaulting a prison guard, they said. Sure, maybe so, that certainly was possible. He had no time to argue or sort it out, though. It wasn't Sarah he needed, anyway.

Diana would see him, Greg was sure of that. She had to see him. *We have Diana Sanborn,* Mashburn claimed. No. Not yet.

Greg parked in the gravel clearing to the side of the house, then climbed the steps to a wide planked front porch. As he was trying to decide between knocking or using the bell, Diana suddenly opened the door. She seemed startled to find him before her. At her side stood a young girl. Maybe ten years old, Greg gauged. Gentle blue eyes, a guileless face, long dark-blond hair pulled into a ponytail. They didn't look related.

"This is not a convenient time," Diana said quickly. "We're in a sort of a rush, I'm afraid. We're on our way out."

"You and I need to talk, Diana."

"It will have to wait."

"It can't wait."

Diana regarded him with a mix of irritation and unease. "This is Ashley. The daughter of my ranch hand Edward. I'm afraid her pet pig is gravely ill. I know something about pigs, so she has come to enlist my aid. There's no time to waste."

Greg looked back and forth at the girl and the woman. He'd raised a pig once as a boy, he and his father in the home where he grew up, high in the wooded mountainside above La Graciosa. "I know something about those fellows myself," he said. "Let me help."

Ashley's pigpen sat at the bottom of an old orchard below a trio of ranch hands' cabins. It was a splintered wood-frame structure, painted a faded blue, fronted by a small fenced yard and shaded by a handful of orange trees. Through a small window Greg, with appreciation, could see sawdust on the floor. Sawdust was nice to root in, and made a warm bed.

"Winnie just didn't show up for supper," Ashley said. She had a tremor in her voice. "She's never missed a full trough."

Just then a small round pig emerged from the shed. She stood listlessly in the middle of the yard, regarding them with blank eyes.

"This is Winnie?" Greg asked.

"Actually," Ashley replied, "her full name is Winnifred P. Wombly."

"Almost certainly she's just plugged up," Diana said. "An injection of soapy water will fix that."

"I'd try two ounces of castor oil first," Greg said. "If that doesn't work, go to the soapy water."

Diana and Ashley both looked at him. "How enchanting," Diana said. "Our award-winning lawyer also knows pigs." To Ashley she suggested, "Why don't you run over to the bunkhouse and find us some castor oil."

Greg added, "And some clothesline. Just in case."

Ashley said, "Won't need to be tying up Winnie. Promise you that."

"Okay, then," Greg agreed. "No clothesline."

Greg watched the girl run off, then took Diana by the arm and guided her to a redwood bench by the low rail fence. "Let's sit here," he said.

The view from their perch was of Diana's western range. Grazing cows meandered sluggishly, looking for shade. The sun had climbed higher. It was nearing noon. What did he have left? Greg wondered. Twenty hours?

"Sarah's hearing resumes tomorrow," he said. "It will be a critical week."

"I imagine so."

"At first I focused only on the law and the evidence. I knew little about El Nido. I didn't understand what had happened here. What was happening."

Diana showed nothing. "Happened here?"

"Come on, Diana. When I first came, you wanted me to stay in the valley. You had a reason."

"Happened here?" Diana repeated the words as if they would yield their own meaning.

The sound of Ashley's feet on the gravel road stopped them. She came running through the gate into the pigpen's yard, waving a small bottle of castor oil. In her other hand she held a length of clothesline. On her face was a small sheepish grin. "Just in case," she said.

Then Ashley reached down, grabbed Winnie by both her front legs, and upset her quickly. As Winnie opened her mouth to protest, Ashley turned the oil into her throat. The pig gave off a scream, high-pitched and hysterical, but it didn't last long. When Ashley released her legs, Winnie righted herself. The corners of her mouth turned up in a set smile. She stood her ground, studying them, as oil dripped from her lips. Ashley gently scratched her.

"Hope that works," Diana said. "Otherwise we're gonna have to try an enema."

Ashley came to her side. The girl raised her arms and offered Diana a shy, tentative hug. The mistress of Sanborn Ranch hugged back. "Bless your heart," Diana said. "Don't you worry, Winnie will be just fine."

From one of the cabins, they could hear someone calling Ashley now. The girl let go of Diana and turned to Winnie, who got from her a less tentative hug. Then she started out of the pigpen yard. "Thanks to you too, Mr. Monarch," Ashley called as she danced through the gate.

"The ways she moves," Greg said. "She reminds me of a ballerina."

Diana had a faraway look in her eyes. "She reminds me of myself."

Greg chose his words carefully. "You must want so much to preserve the valley for someone like her. As your grandfather did for you."

"Yes . . ." Diana began. Then she caught herself. "What precisely do you mean, Gregory?"

"The Committee of Ten. Wallace Barley. The refinery fires. The lost Panama shipment. The Eastern refiners and the phony dry wells . . . I know about it all."

"Oh, do you?" Diana didn't flinch. "How, may I ask?"

"There are amateur historians aplenty in the valley, it seems, who like to keep journals. Their families tend to dump boxes of memorabilia at the historical museum. There's much interesting reading to be found there, if you're willing to poke around in the storage room."

Dismay started to color Diana's expression. Then, through what seemed an act of will, she smiled grandly and swept her arm all about her, following the horizon. "Yes," she said. "My grandfather and his colleagues left us quite a legacy."

Greg spoke gently. "Maybe we can right wrongs, Diana, and still protect your valley."

Diana rose at those words and strode across the yard. She led Winnie back into the pigpen, then reached for a rake and fussed with the sawdust. Next she checked the food trough and refilled the water bucket. That done, she looked about, fixed on an orange tree, and began pulling ripe fruit off the branches. Finally, she turned to Greg.

"Is that possible?" she asked. "Is that really possible?"

"Yes, Diana. We can do this. We need to do this."

Diana studied Greg, then dropped the oranges at her feet. She slowly moved back to her seat beside him. "I've not managed to pull it off by myself," she said. "Doing right and protecting my valley appear to be mutually exclusive goals."

"Diana . . . Tell me what you've done. Tell me what's happened."

"You tell me something first."

"What's that?"

"How is Sarah doing?"

Greg spoke softly. "She's as you might expect someone in her situation."

"Does she . . . does she speak of me ever?"

"She defends you, Diana. She protects you."

Diana sat in silence for a moment, mulling Greg's words. Then she began. "I had to protect the valley. At first that meant resisting ModoCorp. At those early meetings, Alex and I, we did rather nicely. Had them stalled a bit, claiming easements over camp property. Then they hired Brewster."

"The game changed with Tomaz," Greg said. "Then some more when they rolled their bulldozers and discovered the plume."

This time Diana did flinch. "You know also about the plume?"

"Yes."

She waited for him to explain how he knew, but Greg sat still. Slowly, her shoulders sagged. Her body seemed to leak air. "So . . . ," she said. "It's out."

"No. Only I know. It's not out."

"Only you?"

"Yes."

As she weighed those words, Diana regained her vigor. He'd given her some room to maneuver. "Yes," she said. "The game changed. I couldn't let anyone know. Couldn't allow El Nido to be torn up."

"That gave ModoCorp leverage over you."

"Yes. Now we were partners of a sort. We had mutual interests suddenly. For different reasons, none of us could let the plume become public knowledge."

"Then came the oil spill at El Nido Lake."

Diana slapped the bench. "They were such fools. Fiddled with the old wells. Didn't understand about those pipes up there. Didn't realize they were rotted into nothing."

"A big oil spill would tell everyone there was oil in the valley. Which would cause certain folks to take a closer look, and no doubt discover the plume. Within months you'd have both a massive excavation and state-of-the-art oil wells. All across El Nido."

"Yes, precisely. Which was unthinkable, of course. So I didn't want the spill known any more than did Charles Whit."

"Thank goodness for the bypass pump. Only you would have known how to divert the oil from the lake."

Diana again looked startled at what Greg knew. "No," she said slowly. "Not only me."

Greg mulled that, then suddenly understood. "Brewster Tomaz. He would have known."

"Very good, Gregory. Yes, Brewster knew. He knew also that the bypass took it all the way to a submarine pipe that ran half a mile into the sea. They once used that pipe to transport oil directly to tankers sitting offshore. With a little cooperation from state investigators, you could make it look like the spill came from the ocean to the shore. Very nice solution."

"If only Sarah hadn't seen the leak," Greg said. "If only Sarah hadn't started yelling at state rangers."

"Just so," Diana agreed.

"At least you were able to keep her quiet. Good thing you had such sway over Sarah when she came to you with her news."

"She told you about that? . . . Well, yes, it was a good thing." Diana looked unsettled, as if something had been left unsaid.

Again Greg made the leap with her. "Sarah wasn't the only problem, was she? There was someone else perfectly willing to expose El Nido's oil secrets. Someone else who threatened everyone's interests."

Diana regarded Greg with open admiration now. "I am impressed, Gregory. Yes. Brewster Tomaz had an armlock on all of us. Brewster would never miss the chance to take advantage of people when he could. It was a lifetime habit of his, far as I can tell. Regarding El Nido's oil, he understood he was in an enviable position. He threatened to reveal the plume's existence. He blackmailed me."

"And he also played it against Whit and ModoCorp?"

"Yes."

"Anyone could have killed Tomaz. Everyone had a reason."

Diana offered a mirthless laugh. "You could say that."

"Diana," Greg pleaded. "What happened?"

She looked at him without artifice. "Whoever killed him had to. Sometimes that's the way it works. You do what's needed to make things as they should be."

"Who does? Who does what's needed?"

"We were all down at the river that night. I was there. Alex, Sarah, Whit, Rimmer. Half of El Nido. Choose whom you wish."

"El Nido chose Sarah."

"Yes."

"Why?"

Diana began fussing over the hem of her long skirt, pulling at a loose thread. "I tried to say I'd seen a strange hooded man rushing away. I tried to say that at the start."

"Tried?"

"Yes. Sheriff Rimmer wasn't interested."

"He wanted Sarah?"

"He and whomever he reports to."

"Why?"

"Oh goodness, Gregory." Diana couldn't hide her exasperation. "They had all sorts of reasons. She had to be defused. She'd seen the oil leak, she was yelling at rangers, who knew how long I could keep her quiet. They had to get her out of circulation. What's more, maybe even more important, she provided a clean, uncomplicated explanation for Brewster's murder. Sarah's guilt was the simplest to prove, the most obvious. You didn't have to bring in plumes and oil spills to explain her as the murderer. She was an eco-terrorist who'd been stalking Brewster. She was also an outsider. She was making El Nido look bad." Diana offered a rueful smile. "As you are, Gregory."

Greg tried not to sound like an accuser. "You went along with this, Diana?"

She hung on to her smile. "Sometimes, my dear Gregory,

you must align yourself with folks who don't exactly warm your heart."

"Especially if they threaten to kill you."

"Whatever do you mean . . . ?"

"The blackmail letters."

Diana's smile evaporated. "You've figured that out too?"

"I've been prowling around your local cemetery. From what I saw there, I'm willing to bet that Charles Whit is Wallace Barley's grandson. Born to Barley's daughter, Gretchen. He wrote the letters, didn't he? He or someone who works for him."

Diana rose again from their bench and walked about the pigpen. She studied the horizon. "That's a fair surmise," she said. "Gretchen married a fellow in San Francisco named Joseph Whitschenson. Their son, if they had one, might logically have shortened his name."

"You've been fighting your grandfather's battles anew."

"Yes."

"Diana," Greg said. "I need to know. They wanted a dying declaration from Tomaz. . . . So you gave them one?"

She kept her eyes on the horizon. "Yes. . . . Yes I did."

Greg tried to hide his dismay.

"For all our needs," Diana was saying. "For the sake of El Nido. Sometimes we must cross lines. . . ."

"Where do you draw those lines, Diana? How do you decide?"

"You tell me, Greg. You're the expert. You win awards for crossing lines."

He forced himself to stay on track. "Who killed Brewster Tomaz? You? Whit? Rimmer?"

Diana's rich laugh filled the air much as it had his first day in El Nido. "Here's where it really gets amusing, Greg. The truth is, Sarah killed Brewster."

"How can you say . . . ?"

"I saw her do it. I went to the river with her."

"You were with her?"

"No, I hung back. I stayed at the edge of the woods. Brewster was making outrageous demands, insisting on his 'just desserts,' threatening to reveal everything. I'm afraid my response may have egged Sarah on. But I didn't realize what she was going to do. Honestly, I didn't."

Greg struggled to absorb Diana's words. He didn't believe her. And yet he knew she could be telling the truth. "What you're saying, then, is that Whit and Rimmer framed a guilty person?"

"Exactly. They didn't realize it, though. They didn't really know who killed Brewster. They just wanted the simplest story, and they also wanted Sarah put away. To achieve that, they thought they needed me to create a tale. They didn't. I neglected to disabuse them of that notion."

Greg's mind reeled. Sarah was guilty, Sarah did it. Sarah killed Tomaz. Okay, then. He could believe that. So what, though? They'd still framed her. You couldn't just ignore due process, the Fourteenth Amendment, the United States Constitution. A human being was sitting in jail facing execution based on what they'd done. A dangerously unstable human being, perhaps. Yet who finally was the greater threat? Sarah, or those who put her away?

"This is wrong," he said. "Diana, you know it's wrong. That's why you wanted me to stay in El Nido. You wanted me to fix the mess you made."

Something showed in Diana's eyes at that. A longing, Greg thought. A need. Yet she beat it back. "It's also wrong to destroy El Nido," she insisted. "My grandfather. He did what he had to. So did I. We can't let anyone destroy our valley."

Listening to Diana, the obvious suddenly occurred to Greg: The mistress of Sanborn Ranch didn't know about the waste dump. ModoCorp wouldn't have shared that part of their business with her; they'd have lost her if they had. He saw finally his path. Of course. It was the only way.

"That's right," he said quickly. "But that's precisely what Whit's gang is doing, Diana. Right now. Destroying El Nido. Why do you think your cows died?"

"The plume . . ."

"No, not the plume. The plume is only a theoretical hazard, with no proven effect. Hydrogen sulfide killed your cows, not old pooled oil. Hydrogen sulfide, blowing in the air from ModoCorp's waste dump."

"Waste dump . . . ?"

"Diana, they're dumping oil waste into Camp Mahrah from all their operations up and down the West Coast."

"What nonsense. That couldn't be. They'd need a dozen permits—"

"No, Diana. Whole thing is legal. They don't have to ask or tell anyone."

"A waste dump? . . . In El Nido?"

"It's true, Diana. . . . They need to be stopped."

Diana was trembling now. "Sarah's still guilty. Sarah killed Brewster."

"I need your help, Diana. We need to get this out."

"No!" Diana's eyes blazed with fear. "No one can know about the plume. . . . No one can tear up El Nido."

Greg exulted. Surely, he had her. "You have no choice, then," he said gently. "You give me what I need, or everyone will know about El Nido's plume."

"No choice?" Diana cried. "You're wrong there, Gregory. We always have a choice."

# NINETEEN

They saw each other in the same instant. James Mashburn glanced up from the bench where he sat just as Greg Monarch turned his way. They nodded. Then Greg moved toward the El Nido County DA.

It was Sunday evening on La Graciosa's central plaza, a dormant time in the life of Greg's hometown. He relished the sense of repose the plaza offered at the end of a weekend. By then the weekly Thursday night farmer's market—with its blockaded roadway and makeshift produce stands and outdoor barbecue grills—had receded in memory. The plaza and surrounding avenues were swept clean, posters removed, benches replaced. Not a store clerk or shopper stirred. In the window of Stella's Café, Greg could see waitresses stacking chairs and wiping tables.

He'd be home soon, Greg told himself. Sarah Trant's hearing was to resume in the morning, in the *asistencia* that stood as it had for two hundred years on the far side of the plaza. Whatever was to happen would come this week.

"The game's almost over," Greg said to Mashburn. "Almost time to count our chips."

The DA slid over on the bench, offering Greg a seat. "Not a game, Greg. Not any kind of game."

"No. . . . Of course not."

They sat in silence for a moment, watching the creek. Greg wondered if Mashburn had the same absurd impulse he had just then, which was to talk strategy together, to plot jointly how they would conduct matters when the hearing resumed in the morning. Of course, if he shared all he knew with

Mashburn, at the end of the tale Sarah would still be the one who murdered Brewster Tomaz. A framed murderer, but a murderer nonetheless. Without actual innocence, Greg felt he had nothing, despite what the laws of the land promised.

Something else now occurred to Greg. To tell more, to tell Mashburn why they'd framed Sarah, to tell about ModoCorp and oil plumes and waste dumps, he would need to betray Diana Sanborn. Greg, to his surprise, found himself incapable of doing so. He wouldn't be the cause of El Nido's ruin.

"You've shown me nothing new, Greg." Mashburn sounded more sorrowful than combative. "I've been willing to listen, okay? But all I've seen is the same old stuff. Yes, they were sloppy. Yes, they cut some corners and polished a few rough spots. But that's not extraordinary. You know that."

Greg looked about the plaza. "You aren't offended by what you've seen, Jim?"

Mashburn started to respond, then stopped. In Jim's expression, Greg thought he saw feelings not unlike his own. The DA looked as if he wanted to share concerns and impulses. The DA looked as if he longed to feel at least a shred of valor.

"Well, Greg," he said. "Of course I've seen things that offend me. What the hell, though. I often do. It's certainly not unusual. You don't want to be offended, don't look too closely at how we seek justice in this world."

"There are other ways to avoid being offended."

"Sure there are. But they all involve lying down on the job."

"Maybe that's what's needed sometimes."

"Can the crap, Greg. You want *me* to lie down. You'd never do the same. Never."

"What if you flat-out knew you were nailing an innocent person?"

"That's not the case here, Greg."

"You don't know."

"Chrissake, Greg, you're all tangled up with this woman. You can't see—"

"Tell me this," Greg proposed. "If Reggie Dodge had

known about the boot prints, do you think he could have put on a better case? Or if Reggie Dodge had known about Judith Daniels's eyewitness account? Or if Reggie Dodge hadn't faced belated recollections about a dying declaration—"

Mashburn leapt up from the bench. "Enough, Greg. For the love of God. Sarah Trant's appeals have been filled with these arguments for years. They don't make her innocent. She killed that old man, damnit. Face facts, Greg. Face that your ex-lover is a killer."

"Now, wait—"

"No, you wait. I'm not lying down for you. We're adversaries, Greg. That's how it works. You don't like the rules, don't play in the game. There's no right or wrong. Just winners and losers . . ."

Greg stopped fighting. It was dark now on the plaza, and empty. He sat still on the bench, looking up at Mashburn, taking the measure of this man. What he saw gave him reassurance. "Come on, Jim," he said. "I know you don't believe that."

From the window of his chambers in the *asistencia*, Judge Solman watched Greg Monarch and James Mashburn talking in the plaza. When the two lawyers rose and parted, Solman returned to his desk and the files before him. He'd come here on this Sunday evening seeking a moment alone before the habeas hearing resumed in the morning. He wanted to consider how he'd ended up in such a regretful position.

If he had it to do over, he never would have stopped by Greg Monarch's office with that handwritten habeas petition. What compelled him to do so? Solman couldn't fix on a satisfactory answer. Of course, he was facing the question with hindsight now. At the start he hadn't the slightest notion of the quagmire attached to this petition. If he had, he might very well have shredded Sarah Trant's sorry little plea the instant he received it.

He hadn't shredded it, though. Instead, he'd walked it over to Greg. He couldn't turn back the clock now; he had to continue forward, as they all did. That, unavoidably, had been among the several matters he'd been pondering these past five days. He hadn't granted Greg a delay just because the state withheld evidence. He'd needed his own respite. He'd bought time for himself as well as for the defense attorney.

He'd seen such outrage in Greg's eyes these past weeks. Sitting in the courtroom, it had been hard to look down at that man after a while. Solman had found himself turning away, scribbling on his legal pad, staring at the ceiling . . . anything but gaze upon the consequences of his own chosen conduct.

He wished he could reverse course now. He wished he could stop what he was doing. He couldn't, though. There were too many forces at play. Too many forces to defy. He saw no means of escape.

Jasmine Gest came to Greg later that night as he sat on his deck at home, watching Graciosa Creek flow by. There'd been no plan or phone call. She just showed up and settled beside him on his redwood swing.

"You mind?" she said. "I need a place to stay during the hearing."

"And if I did . . . ?"

"I would leave."

He pulled her to him. "Don't leave."

Jas's hand moved to his neck. Her lips brushed his ear. "Then don't go away anymore. Especially when I'm gasping for breath in a motel room. Moaning, too. Gasping and moaning."

"A deal."

They sat in silence. Greg knew he hadn't managed to hide his apprehension from her. These days, he rarely could hide anything from her.

"What will happen tomorrow?" she asked.

"Hard to say."

"You have a plan, though."

"Is that a question?"

"No," Jas said. "It's not a question."

Greg ran a hand through her hair. "You think you're so smart."

"I know you."

"Funny . . . I don't."

"I know that too."

Greg's hand roamed down her back, coming to rest on her hip. He could feel her thigh through the thin cotton dress. "Yeah, sure, I have a plan. I always have a plan."

She studied him. "Want to talk about it? Tell me what bothers you so?"

"What bothers me," Greg said, "is what always bothers me."

Jas hesitated, then spoke. "Tell me about Jason Pine. Tell me the end of that story."

It was so like her to do that, Greg thought. To make such a leap. To know where he was.

"Okay," he said. "Jason Pine." As he began, it occurred to him that he'd never told anyone the end of the story.

It really was a nice bit of courtroom handiwork, Greg had to admit. At Pine's murder trial, he couldn't even get Jason's mother or minister to testify on his behalf. Nor could he call a medical expert to the stand, for the court provided no funds to hire one. All he had going for him—to counter three state doctors' testimony that the defendant was drunk on the murder night, not mentally ill—were the records from Pine's twenty-two-month stay at a private psychiatric hospital in Delaware. Only by chance did Greg, poring through those handwritten sheets, notice certain tenuous references to "pseudopsychopathic schizophrenia." The term meant nothing, really. It could be applied broadly and subjectively to anyone a doctor thought might have some characteristics of a schizophrenic. Or rather, it once could be applied. No longer; the American Psychiatric Association dropped it as a recognized diagnosis the very year Pine was being treated in Delaware.

Normally, Greg wouldn't have been able to get these Delaware records admitted without testimony from the doctor who wrote them up. It was here Greg undeniably hornswaggled the district attorney. "Come on, Taylor," he'd urged. "Defense has no money to fly in experts. Let me use the records. Stipulate their entry into evidence." Maybe Taylor was overconfident, maybe Taylor foolishly succumbed to a sense of fair play. For whatever reason, he agreed. Which decision—Greg couldn't help observe—had its own consequence. Putting the records into evidence meant Greg could talk about them in his closing argument. Any good lawyer can testify better than an expert—that was a maxim learned in law school, then over and over in the courtroom. Greg certainly proved its verity at Pine's trial.

"Ladies and gentlemen," he told the jury, "we don't have a psychiatrist who is going to testify today. The defendant is indigent. He can't afford to fly in experts. You noticed that, unlike the state, we didn't have a psychiatrist testifying for the defense. What we do have are all the psychiatric records, which we furnished you, entered into evidence. In those records you can see mention of many things. An alcoholic abusive father, a depressive mother, early-childhood trauma, an overindulgent grandmother, antisocial behavior. But most important, there are diagnoses. Doctors diagnosed him. Doctors called him mentally ill."

*Pseudopsychopathic schizophrenia*—over and over in his closing, Greg repeated that term, until it sounded like an ominous threat. Dates and times, explanations, narratives. *Pseudopsychopathic schizophrenia.* Then, with perfect timing, he backed away from that meaningless phrase. It's up to you to decide whether Jason is sane, Greg told the jurors. Just because a psychologist or psychiatrist or other expert says he's competent or not, that doesn't change things. It's up to you. Here's what you need to think about: Would a normal person do what Jason Pine did? Would you or your friends or relatives? *This murder was so horrible, nobody in their right mind could have done that. Nobody in their right mind.*

After deliberating for just two hours, the jurors unanimously agreed. Pine, declared insane, went back to the mental hospital instead of prison. To the mental hospital, where a doctor soon declared that he wasn't insane after all. Where a doctor eventually insisted they therefore had to let Pine go.

* * *

"That's just what a judge felt obliged to do in the end," Greg told Jas. "Jason Pine walked free because I convinced a jury he was insane, when he wasn't. Six months later, he strolled into another convenience store. Again he thought he saw his ex-girlfriend, and again he pulled the trigger. A bullet to the heart. This one had no children, at least."

Jas put her arms around his neck and curled against him on the redwood swing. "It's not your fault Greg. You did nothing wrong. You did precisely what you were supposed to do."

Greg felt the warm pressure of her body. He clung to her with a sort of desperation.

"I know that," he said. "And I'm going to do it again."

# TWENTY

On a dark fogbound morning such as this one, there was nothing to be seen of La Graciosa's central plaza. Now all the familiar objects that normally provided Greg his bearings were hidden. The park benches, the bear statue, the winding creek, even the *asistencia* itself, had vanished behind a thick gray wall. Greg moved slowly toward the courthouse, stepping with care.

It was nearly half past eight on Monday. Sarah Trant's habeas hearing was to resume in forty minutes. Greg wanted to talk once more with his client; they'd brought her from the El Nido state prison late the evening before. Feeling gravel underfoot, he turned up the unpaved path that circled to the sheriff's private jailhouse entrance at the rear of the building. A guard led him down a hallway toward her cell. It had been days since he'd seen her. Days that had emphatically challenged his own understanding of her role in Brewster Tomaz's death. He no longer was certain how to approach his client. *A defense attorney shouldn't hear what he doesn't need to know.* Greg, though, longed to know everything.

"How nice," Sarah said. "My savior has returned."

She was sitting on the edge of a cot. The effect of her tenure in solitary confinement showed. She blinked with uncertainty.

"Not sure you should call me that, Sarah."

"Oh." His tone stopped her. "What's changed?"

He held back, reluctant to take her where they had to go. He cast about for other topics. "Did you really assault a guard?"

She looked away. "That skinny guard with big ears tried to

get handsy when I was alone on mop brigade outside the mess hall. Told me I should be nice to him. Nice to him like . . ."

"Like what?"

"Like I was nice to my attorney."

"What happened next?"

"I pushed him away and got out of there. That was all. An obvious case of assault on my part. So yes, I confess. I'm guilty."

Greg drew a breath. "Sarah," he asked. "You want to confess to anything else?"

Confusion showed in her expression now. "Confess . . . What do you mean?"

A ray of sunlight reached through the cell's small window, warming the side of Greg's face. He could see a patch of blue sky. The fog was lifting. "Sarah, the thing is, Diana Sanborn says she went down to the river with you that night. She says she stayed back at the edge of the woods. She says she saw you kill Brewster Tomaz."

Sarah sat still for a moment. Then she rose from her cot and walked to the window. She wrapped her hands around the iron bars that kept her from the plaza. "I pushed him into the river, I know I did that," she said. "I also know I ran off afterwards."

"You're not certain what happened between those two moments, are you, Sarah? You've never been certain. Whenever we've gone over that night, you've acted confused."

"I imagine slashing his throat . . . there's a vision in my mind." She began to weep. "I couldn't have, though. How could I?"

He came to her and held her in his arms. "In your mind, Sarah. You sometimes can't separate your dreams from reality, can you?"

"I think I can, but sometimes . . . Oh, Greg, it gets confusing. It gets so scary."

"Why would you have charged Tomaz with a knife that night, Sarah? Can you remember how this started?"

"He was going to ruin El Nido. He was helping ModoCorp. I had to stop him. . . ."

"That night, though. What happened that night?"

"Diana . . . she was so tormented by Tomaz. He was threatening her, scaring her. He was hurting her so much . . . I just—" Sarah stopped and turned away. "That's all I remember."

He pulled her back to him, cupping her face in his hands. He stroked her cheeks, searching for understanding in the feel of her skin. Sarah changed around Diana, that's what Jas had told him. Diana had a hold on her. Enthralled her with the history of the valley, her grandfather, unspoiled Eden. Sarah, wide-eyed, lapped it up. Greg could see why, given Diana's subtext. Good and evil sharply defined in an otherwise bewildering universe. A world of unblemished clarity, high purpose, intricate meaning. That's what Diana offered Sarah. Just what Sarah always wanted. Diana fed Sarah's eternal hunger.

"She's not your friend," Greg said. "Diana betrayed you. She gave you up for the murder."

Sarah twisted out of his arms, turned back to the window. "That's not true," she said. "Diana is my friend."

Emerging from his chambers, Judge Solman walked slowly to the bench, keeping his head down and his eyes averted from all who'd gathered for Sarah Trant's habeas hearing. When he did finally speak, he offered only a brusque greeting, then began leafing through documents.

"Your Honor—" James Mashburn began.

"I trust we're all up to speed now?" Solman interrupted. "Are we ready to get to the end of this proceeding?"

"Yes, Your Honor," Mashburn replied. "The state has been ready for some time now."

Solman glanced vaguely at the petitioner's side of the table. "Your Honor," Greg said. "I'm ready to proceed."

Solman nodded at Mashburn. "Call your next witness."

"I call Judge Karl Jackson."

The former prosecutor of El Nido County was a tall, thin man with an oddly serene manner. Watching him stride through the courtroom toward the witness stand, Greg Monarch searched vainly for any sign of menace. Karl Jackson had the look of one who would make a good drinking companion any evening at the Gaucho Tavern. He'd grown up in El Nido County, Greg knew that much. After law school at Berkeley, he'd opened a private practice, but after four years had joined the DA's office. He'd worked his way up, year by year. Eventually he ran for the office of district attorney and won. He was reelected six times. Then the governor appointed him to the state bench.

"Judge Jackson," Mashburn began. "Good morning."

"Good morning," Jackson replied, with the tone of one who thought it indeed was.

The two of them, the former and present district attorneys, proceeded to engage in a gracious dance. Mashburn had decided to call Jackson to the stand himself, rather than wait for Greg. Now he lobbed softball questions, guiding Jackson carefully through the prosecution of Sarah Trant. Why he'd chosen to charge her, why he'd disregarded certain pieces of evidence, why he thought it unnecessary to share various matters with the defense attorney. Most central to all his reasoning, Jackson explained, was Brewster Tomaz's dying declaration.

Here the witness pointedly looked up at Judge Solman, sharing a collegial moment. He had the victim naming his killer, Jackson pointed out, and a highly respected member of the community hearing him do so. What more could you want? The jury had listened, the jury had delivered a verdict. That's how the system worked. It wasn't the district attorney who convicted Sarah Trant. It wasn't El Nido County, or the state of California. It was a jury of twelve El Nido citizens. God bless the jury system. What could be preferable? What could be a more wonderful defense against abuse?

When it finally came time for his cross, Greg approached this witness with deliberation. He didn't expect to make his case on Jackson's back; that would come later today. Nor did he expect Solman to let him get too far. For the moment, his aim was simpler. He wanted this good honorable man to explain himself.

"Judge Jackson," Greg began. "You were the prosecuting attorney in the murder trial of Sarah Trant?"

"That's correct."

"And you were involved from the start, right?"

"From the night Brewster Tomaz was murdered."

"You asked for a murder in the first degree verdict, correct?"

"Correct."

"And you asked for the death penalty, right?"

"We had a death-penalty hearing, that is correct."

"Well," Greg said, moving closer to his witness. "You asked for the death penalty. You didn't have the hearing by accident, did you?"

For the first time, some of the contented geniality slid off of Jackson. "No, we didn't. Right. We filed a notice."

"Okay, then." Greg circled around to the lawyers' table, picked up a file, then turned back to the witness stand. "To start out with, I'd like to review what you didn't do as part of your job of prosecuting Sarah Trant and asking for the death penalty. You didn't, Judge Jackson, think that the extra set of boot prints found at the murder site were significant in any way? Is that what you indicated on direct? Is that still your testimony, Judge?"

Jackson frowned now. "That doesn't capture the context," he said. "But yes, at the start of the trial the boot prints were not considered a significant issue."

"Do you recall looking at those prints yourself?"

"It's hard to say. I had the sheriff's office—"

"Yes or no, Judge. You never looked at the boot prints that you decided weren't significant in a death-penalty murder trial?"

"I can't imagine that I didn't. . . . But I have no specific recollection of looking at them."

"Isn't it a fact that you depended on Sheriff Rimmer to determine what you were shown concerning the crime-scene evidence?"

Jackson reached for a glass of water. "That's how it always worked. He had control of the evidence. I visited him, or he came to me and showed me what he had."

"You looked only at what Sheriff Rimmer showed you, is that your testimony?"

"I asked to see everything, and I assumed that Sheriff Rimmer showed me everything. I know of no reason for him not to show me everything."

"I ask you again, Judge. Did you or did you not see those boot prints?"

"To the best of my recollection . . . I have no specific recollection."

"Do you recall conferring with the forensics tech who decided they were three days old?"

"There again, I'm not sure. The sheriff's office handled that."

"Yes or no, Judge."

Now Jackson looked as if he wanted to slam a gavel down somewhere. Up on the bench, Judge Solman reached for his. "I can't imagine I didn't," the witness said again. "But I have no specific recollection."

"Do you recall sharing the matter of the extra boot prints with Sarah Trant's trial attorney, Reginald Dodge?"

"As I understood it, Sheriff Rimmer provided Dodge with those prints."

"Do you have any independent knowledge that Dodge was provided those prints?"

"I can't imagine he wasn't."

"Yes or no, Judge."

"Okay, no, I have no independent recollection."

So it went for much of the morning. *I can't imagine . . . I have no independent recollection . . . The sheriff handled that . . .* By midday, Greg had heard his fill of slippery responses. This good, honorable man was not explaining himself in the least. Out of the corner of his eye, Greg watched Mashburn absorb his predecessor's performance. What did Jim think? What could Jim possibly think?

Just past noon, Greg approached Jackson with his final set of questions. "And you didn't believe it was worthwhile to look at photos from the murder site yourself?" he asked. "To see if what the police told you was the truth?"

"I didn't think they reflected a contested issue."

Greg moved his mouth near Jackson's ear. "You've been a lawyer long enough to know that when I ask a question you're supposed to answer it. Isn't that right, Judge Jackson?"

The witness glanced up at the bench. "Yes," he said evenly. "Of course."

Solman shifted about, and Greg tensed, preparing for his intervention. It didn't come, though. Solman was busily scribbling something on a pad before him. Greg tried to read the judge's expression. He realized now that Solman hadn't intervened all morning. Was he going to give him room to roam today?

"Is there a chance," Greg asked Jackson, "that you just preferred not to know what the sheriff's detectives were up to?"

"No, sir." A tinge of pink showed around Jackson's jowls.

"Okay, then," Greg suggested. "Let's talk for a moment about the so-called dying declaration. Detective Gary Goolan has told us he heard from Ms. Sanborn about this right away, on the night of the murder, but just didn't manage to get it into his reports until weeks later. Does that sound believable to you?"

"As I understand it, he did tell his colleagues. Then he—"

"No, no. I don't think that comes close to being a responsive answer. Please answer my question."

"Detective Goolan did report what he'd heard—"

"We seem to be having some problems with the acoustics in here," Greg interrupted. "Let me try again. Yes or no, does that sound believable to you?"

Jackson summoned a faint smile. "Yes, it does."

"Do you still have confidence in his account of Diana Sanborn's statement to him?"

"Yes, I do."

"You are telling us you don't find anything unusual about anything in that statement?"

Jackson looked up at Judge Solman again. Greg followed his glance. To his surprise, Solman was frowning at the witness.

"Yes or no," Greg said. "Yes or no, Judge Jackson."

"No. . . . I don't find anything unusual."

Greg slapped the railing before him. "Tell me, Judge Jackson, do you think this is some kind of sport?"

"No, I don't, sir. . . . Absolutely not, sir."

"Do you realize that Sarah Trant sits here facing execution based on the evidence you put on? Do you realize that?"

"Yes, of course I do."

"You sit here and defend this type of evidence?"

"Yes, I am defending it."

"Are you telling us the truth, Judge Jackson? Are you telling us the whole truth? Are you telling us nothing but the truth?"

"Yes, sir." Jackson's eyes blazed. "Yes, sir, I most certainly am."

"Is Sarah Trant really the greatest menace in this courtroom? Is there possibly someone else here who represents an even greater peril?"

Mashburn jumped up. "Objection, objection!"

Solman was finally reaching for his gavel. "That's enough, Mr. Monarch. . . . You're pushing too far now. . . . You must stay on track."

"I am on track," Greg insisted. "Judge Jackson, isn't it true you withheld the boot prints from Reggie Dodge? Isn't it true you withheld Judith Daniels's eyewitness account? Isn't—"

"You only need turn over material to the defense that's exculpatory," Jackson interrupted. "We followed the law."

"The law? . . . The law?"

"Yes, the law," Jackson said. "The California Rules of Criminal Procedure—"

"No!" Greg thundered. "Excuse me. We're talking here about something called the United States Constitution. We're talking about the Fourteenth Amendment. We're talking about due process of law. That's what we're talking about. Are we not, Judge Jackson? Are we not—"

"Objection!" Mashburn called. "Objection."

"That's quite enough," the judge declared. "Stop, everyone, stop. I've been giving you latitude today, Mr. Monarch, but you're way out of bounds now—"

"It's not me who's out of bounds," Greg snapped. "Tell that to this witness. Tell that—"

"Counselor!" Solman was banging his gavel. "That's quite enough. If you can't settle down, I'll throw you in jail. Don't think I won't, Mr. Monarch. Don't make that mistake."

Behind him, Greg could hear Sarah sobbing. "Greg," she gasped. "Please . . . I need you. . . ." He turned and walked back to the lawyers' table, his eyes on Jim Mashburn. At least he'd had an impact, that much he could see. To the judge he said, "You're right, Your Honor. That is quite enough. No more questions."

At the lunch break, Greg picked up a tri-tip sandwich at Stella's Café, then hiked along Graciosa Creek, following it to where it curved into the narrow wooded glen that had become his sanctuary during the hearing. He'd retreated more than once to this quiet hollow, where the sunlight filtered through the oaks and played off the rippling water. He sat in his customary spot, on a rocky ledge beside the water, and waited.

The sound he was hoping for, of someone stepping through the surrounding thicket, came just moments later. Then the form of a man appeared out of the dense brush. He was walking quickly, as if in a hurry to reach a destination. When he saw Greg, he froze. This time, though, he didn't turn and flee.

"Well now, Greg," Judge Solman said, trying to hide his fluster. "I didn't know we had a common interest in shady glens."

"I did," Greg said. "I've seen you here before, more than once. Several times, in fact, during the lunch hour. Not a bad way to escape from the hearing."

"I've not seen you."

"I think you did, once at least. At the start of the hearing. I was sitting on this very ledge. You turned off the trail and slipped down that ravine over there. Since then, I've made sure to keep out of your way."

Solman's fluster deepened into embarrassment. "Well, okay, Greg. Yes. It would have been improper for us to meet."

"Yet we need to, don't we?"

"What do you mean?"

Greg weighed his words, not sure how to pursue the opening he sensed. "You sure have sandbagged me, Judge. What was it you said? *Just thought you might be interested in what's crossed my desk. . . . The way she puts things . . . This is her last chance.* Jesus. Thought you'd meet me halfway, at least. You granted the hearing, after all. Now you're thinking of throwing me in jail."

Solman stood where he was, unwilling to close the distance between them. "We can't be talking like this. Alone, without the other lawyers. It's against all the rules."

"I'm delighted to hear that you are so concerned with rules," Greg said.

Solman took two steps toward him. "Listen to me, Greg. Getting a habeas hearing doesn't mean you automatically win. You put on evidence, so does the state. I thought your gal had some interesting business in her petition. The state has answers, though. And you, Greg, have a temper. Any judge would be reining you in as I do. Some judges would already have you behind bars."

Greg studied the creek. "How'd they get to you?" he asked after a while. "Tell me, Judge. What did it take?"

Solman advanced now, stood above him. A vein had started throbbing in his neck. "Elemental principles of law and government in this country," he said. "That's what got to me, Greg. Those principles restrain federal intrusion into a state's affairs. Look at what the Ninth Circuit just said the other month in rejecting that *Delaney* habeas: 'We are sensitive to the independence of the California courts and of that state's sovereignty.' "

"Oh, come on, Judge—"

"No," Solman interrupted. "You can't just blow up the fundamental balance of power between state and federal courts. You can't dismantle the entire underpinning of the legal system."

Greg stared at Solman. "You've got to act, because the state won't, Judge. The state won't because it's they who created this gross injustice."

Solman looked away. "Fine. Then keep arguing your case. Do the best you can. We'll see where it leads."

"There's no jury, Daniel. It's going to be up to you."

Solman tugged at his collar. "I'm trying to keep things on track. That's all. On track. There will be a reviewable record out of this. I need to pass appellate review."

"Hey, Daniel." Greg spoke quietly, straining to keep a tone of argument out of his voice. "Don't you dream sometimes of just doing the right thing?"

Solman began absentmindedly touching the pulsing vein on his neck. "The right thing," he said. "As if that were a fixed object that we all could recognize. It's not, though. Unsettling as it may be to you, trials rarely yield incontestable truth. We traffic in the world of reasonable doubt."

"Come on, Daniel. You gave me my seventy-two-hour delay, which I needed. And today, on the bench, you gave me some leeway. You also looked quite unhappy with Karl Jackson. Acts of a man with a conscience, I'd say."

"You read too much into my gestures."

"No, I don't buy that. Something has happened. What turned you back to me? The sheriff's testimony? Karl Jackson's? Or was it all those long hours of thinking over the past five days?"

Solman held up a warning hand. "I haven't turned back to you, Greg."

"Then you're lined up with a bad sort on this one."

"Bad sort, perhaps," the judge said. "But they include just about every big hitter in the state."

"Well beyond California, actually. Big hitters all across the country, from what I can tell. I still didn't expect this of you. Back in law school, you were ever the politician on the podium. But you stood for something, Daniel. You were a leader."

Solman looked as if he'd received a body blow. He turned and walked toward the water. There he stood, examining the creek. "No, I didn't expect this of me either," he offered finally. "Maybe that's what I've been thinking about during the recess. . . . On top of that, it didn't help today to see a respected judge disgrace himself on the witness stand."

"Tell me, Daniel, during your thinking, you reach any conclusions?"

Solman held his hands cupped together as if in prayer. "Nothing so certain, I'm afraid. Only questions occur to me, not answers. It occurs to me, for instance, that maybe I shouldn't have ever accepted appointment to the bench. I wonder now if I made a mistake. Be honest, Greg. Back in law school, did I strike you as having a particularly wise and noble judicial bent?"

"Well, I . . ." Greg, face-to-face with this man, found he couldn't lie. "Not really, Daniel. Sorry. I must confess."

Solman nodded his absolution. "It is a hard thing to admit . . . but I'm not a particularly brave person."

"I'm going to help you be one," Greg said. "In court this afternoon, I'll give you what you need."

Solman was pacing now, and didn't look as if he'd heard Greg. "I thought Sarah Trant's was a curious plea, maybe even a worthwhile plea. I concede that. I thought it might intrigue you, and, well, to be honest, I guess the notion of arousing your concern attracted me. But there was so much I didn't know. If only I'd understood back then what a tangled box we were opening."

"It is tangled," Greg agreed. "But we're going to untangle it. You'll have good reason to rule for Sarah. You won't even have a choice."

Solman stepped to where Greg sat on the ledge, and settled beside him. "I realize some people are willing to lose everything in the defense of what they deem to be right and just. Not me, though. Can you understand, Greg? I don't wish to lose everything."

"Of course I understand. But you won't lose at all."

"Besides," Solman continued. "Who knows what's right and just?"

Greg kept his eyes on the creek. "Yes, precisely. Who knows?"

Diana Sanborn lingered in La Graciosa's plaza, just as they'd planned. She strolled about, stopping to look at the sculpture of a bear, then the ducks in the creek, then the face of the two-hundred-year-old *asistencia*. She'd not been here very often, for she only rarely ventured from the valley. She found La Graciosa's central core pleasing. Like El Nido, it had weathered the forces of time. This plaza reminded her of El Nido's arcade. Without the oil plume, she surmised.

Instead they had fog. She'd nearly caught her death this morning, accustomed as she was to rising in a warm dry valley. The sun finally had burned off the heavy mist, yet still Diana felt a chill. She pulled her scarf more securely around her neck and let her mind drift. It wasn't, she had to admit, entirely accurate to describe the El Nido Valley as dry. They didn't have fog, but they did, in rare moments, have legendary cloudbursts. In her twelfth year, Diana had seen one. She could recall it now with as much clarity as ever.

The clouds that day had been gathering in a great black bank in the west for some hours. Thick masses piled up on the already accumulated clouds, until they seemed miles thick, dark and threatening. On the opposite side, from the northeast, loomed a similar bank of clouds. As the hours passed, the dense masses advanced on each other. The winds seemed to cease, but higher up among the clouds, Diana could hear a low brooding roar. The roar deepened then, and the leaves rustled. At first a few drops fell, as large as rocks. Soon they came faster and so thickly that Diana couldn't see fifty feet away. Small ravines were waist-deep in water, the flat ground a good inch. Still a greater roar could be heard. Down the channel of El Nido Creek came a wall of water five feet high and a hundred feet wide, sweeping everything in its course.

A cloudburst, it was later explained to Diana, was simply a point of condensation between two opposing currents of air, both saturated with moisture and suspended for some time over a small territory. Yet to Diana that day it had looked like the end of the world. In a certain reach of the El Nido Valley, she still could see the cloudburst's history written in the pile of rocks that covered nearly a four-square-mile canyon. At the mouth of the canyon, the debris remained over one hundred feet deep. They estimated that some one hundred million cubic yards of earth and rocks were swept away that day. It was hard to imagine the force of a torrent that could, in an hour or two, cast forth such a mass. Yet Diana had seen it with her own eyes.

The sound of steps pulled Diana from her reverie. Looking up, she saw James Mashburn exiting the *asistencia* by the side door he always used. Diana turned quickly and cut across the plaza at an angle that would intersect with the DA's path toward Stella's Café. They met in the center, near the bear sculpture, just as Diana had calculated.

"Mr. Mashburn," she sang out. "How nice to encounter you. How convenient, in fact. There is something we need to talk about."

Mashburn regarded his star witness with puzzlement. They'd gone over Diana's testimony ten days before. He thought they had everything nailed down. She'd told her story without a hitch during the practices. "Need to talk about?" he asked. "What do you mean?"

"It's about my testimony this afternoon. I must talk to you before that happens."

Puzzlement gave way to concern. Mashburn took Diana by the elbow, guided her toward Stella's. "Come," he said. "We'll get a quiet table on the deck."

They sat near the railing, with the creek drifting by at their feet. Each poked at a salad. Diana threw bread crumbs to the ducks on the stream's bank while Mashburn watched and fidgeted. Theirs had always been more a respectful relationship than a close one. That Mashburn wasn't a native of El Nido didn't help. In truth, Sheriff Rimmer had handled most of the contacts with Diana. He'd prepped her for this hearing, just as he had for the original trial. Mashburn had monitored them from afar, as if disdaining that type of involvement. Diana couldn't recall when they'd been alone together like this.

"I've been thinking about the evening of the murder," she began.

Mashburn froze, a forkful of lettuce halfway to his mouth.

"So much I blocked off, so much I couldn't bear thinking about. So much going on, everyone in a frenzy. A person gets confused. It's hard. . . ."

Mashburn leaned forward. "Diana, what are you saying?"

She reached for a handkerchief in her purse. She dabbed at her eyes, then began.

It didn't happen as she told them at the trial, Diana explained. She didn't just come upon Brewster after he'd been attacked. She was standing in the woods beyond the creek. She saw Sarah down at the river. Sarah with Brewster. She saw Sarah push Brewster in the water. But then Sarah ran off, just as she has always claimed. Someone else came running up. A man; at least she assumed it was a man. Taller and bulkier than Sarah. Broad shoulders, thick forearms. She couldn't see his face. He had a hooded jacket tied tightly over his head. He also had a knife. She saw it glint in the moonlight when he lifted it to the sky. She couldn't see what he did with the knife. Only that he lifted it. Then he ran off too. Not in the direction Sarah went. Across the river, into the brush on the far side. Got as far as the big alder tree over there. Then he flat-out disappeared.

Mashburn by now had put his fork down. "Why didn't you tell us this before?" he demanded. "Back then, at the time of the murder?"

Diana found a dry spot of her handkerchief and applied it to her eyes again. "I did. . . . I'm afraid I most certainly did."

Mashburn looked both furious and in great pain.

"I told all this to Sheriff Rimmer back then," Diana continued. "He came to me saying that the spinster Judith Daniels had seen a third person, a man, running from the river. I started to tell him that I had too. Sheriff Rimmer stopped me. He told me not to dwell on that. They had so much evidence pointing toward Sarah Trant, so much evidence putting Sarah at the murder site. Since we all knew Sarah did it, we shouldn't muddy things up. Besides, that

Judith Daniels, everyone knew she was a dotty old lady, terribly disturbed. Wouldn't be a reliable witness in any case. We were better to forget the third man. Better to stick with Sarah."

Tears were rolling down Diana's cheeks now. Mashburn, seeing that her handkerchief was a sodden ball, handed her his napkin.

"I let Sheriff Rimmer convince me," Diana said. "I don't know why. Then I forgot about it. No, that's not so. I put it aside. I put it away. Until now . . ."

Mashburn reached for his glass of water. "Tomaz's dying declaration . . . Are you saying you didn't hear that?"

Diana put down the napkin and rearranged herself in her chair. "I heard Brewster. Yet the memory haunts me now. He was whispering, gasping. Something awfully guttural . . ."

Diana hesitated, as if lost in a memory. Mashburn leaned forward. "Go on," he urged.

Diana nodded her thanks for the encouragement. "The truth of the matter is that I now think Brewster was just making noises, to which I applied meaning."

Mashburn sat back in his chair. He felt about for his napkin, then realized Diana had it. She, noticing, handed him her clean one. He dipped it in his water glass, wiped it on the back of his neck.

"Your story," he said. "It fits exactly with Judith Daniels's."

"Yes," Diana agreed. "Also with Sarah Trant's testimony at her trial."

"You're . . . You . . ." Mashburn was having trouble speaking. Diana waited for him. "If this is true," he continued after a moment, "your account knocks out the entire underlying theory of the trial. It's an entirely new story. It . . . it changes the theory of the case."

"I'm afraid so. But I felt I needed to tell you. This has weighed so awfully on me."

Mashburn's expression hardened suddenly. "Maybe you're lying. How can I believe you? You're telling me you committed perjury back at the trial. Why not assume you're lying now? It certainly is possible. Likely, even. No, I'm sorry,

Diana. You just can't be trusted anymore. What you're telling me is worthless."

Diana sighed. "I realized you would feel that way, Mr. Mashburn, even though it was your own sheriff who coerced me. Yet I have corroboration for my account."

"Corroboration?"

"Yes. My foreman, Alex Ramirez. He was with me that evening. He was standing beside me in the woods."

"Your foreman . . . ?" Mashburn fell silent, lost in thought. Slowly, his look of wary concern faded. To her surprise, Diana thought she saw a glint in his eyes now. "Are you sure of all this?" he asked finally. "Let's hear it again."

By the time Diana finished walking a second time through her story, Mashburn was drumming his fingers on the table. He rose suddenly. "It's going to come out anyway," he told Diana. "So let's get it over with."

The conference in Judge Daniel Solman's chambers began at 1:30 P.M. Mashburn sat off to one side, Greg between Diana and Sarah. The two women traded tentative, fragile glances, while from across his vast desk, Solman gazed at everyone with uncertainty. "I don't know what this is about," he said slowly. "How do you want to proceed, Mr. Mashburn? You asked for this conference."

The DA nodded at the court reporter seated in a corner of the room. "This should all be on the record," he suggested.

"It is," Solman assured him. "Don't you worry."

"Fine," Mashburn said. "We're prepared to start, then. I'm just going to ask Ms. Sanborn to speak to the Court."

"So we should swear her in?" the judge asked.

Mashburn glanced at Greg, but Monarch was studiously riffling through a file. "I guess that's a matter for the Court to decide," the DA said. "Perhaps I should explain. Walking to lunch today, I encountered Diana Sanborn out on the plaza. She needed to speak with me, she said. We went over to Stella's, sat on the deck. She seemed terribly upset. Terribly. So maybe we should just hear from Ms. Sanborn."

"Will she be making representations of fact?" Solman asked.

"I would have to say that is correct, Your Honor."

"Fine," Solman said. "Ms. Sanborn, would you kindly raise your right hand? . . . Do you swear to tell the truth, the whole truth, and nothing but the truth, so help you God?"

In her grandest voice Diana declared, "Yes, I do."

"Okay, Ms. Sanborn," Solman said. "What would you like to say to the Court?"

For the third time on this Monday, Diana Sanborn walked through her story, this time before a judge and court reporter.

*Someone else came running up. A man, taller and bulkier than Sarah . . . I told all this to Sheriff Rimmer back then. . . . He told me not to dwell on that. . . . I let Sheriff Rimmer convince me. . . . Then I put it aside. . . .*

As she spoke, Judge Solman sat ever straighter in his chair. He reached for a pen and a legal pad. His eyes, at first fixed on Diana, slowly moved to Greg. He kept them there until Greg looked up at him. Solman finally interrupted Diana. "The dying declaration, Ms. Sanborn? Did you hear that or not?"

Diana softly exhaled. "I heard something, Your Honor. But as I reflect back now, I'm sure it was only a meaningless noise, a dying gasp. I'm afraid I applied the meaning. Either that, or maybe Brewster just meant Sarah was there, Sarah pushed him. . . . It was all so unclear. . . . I'm sorry."

Judge Solman frowned. "You testified at the murder trial with such certainty, Ms. Sanborn."

Diana pulled the handkerchief from her purse, dabbed at her eyes. "I am so sorry. I'm afraid I let Sheriff Rimmer influence me. It was he who took all my statements. It was he who prepared me for my testimony. I'm not accustomed to murders and courtrooms. . . ."

To Greg's left, Sarah was sobbing now, stretching her arms out toward Diana. To Greg's right, Diana was blinking back tears and turning to Sarah. Solman looked back and forth at them. Then his eyes returned to Greg. "Very interesting, Mr. Monarch," the judge said. "Fascinating."

Greg tried not to show anything. Jim had bought Diana's

new tale, that much was certain. It looked as if Judge Solman was heading that way also. Mashburn no more had the instincts of a prosecutor than Solman had a feel for the bench. Their sense of conflict was all Greg needed. That, plus Diana. Diana, the mistress of Sanborn Ranch, the virtuoso of high theater.

Who could say whether Diana was committing perjury in Judge Solman's chambers? Is there not always doubt? Is not evaluating such a matter up to a jury or judge? It didn't matter anyway, Greg told himself. Lawyers regularly strive to fool jurors and judges, so how absurd to worry about a witness's possible perjury. The ethical distinction between lying to jurors and pulling the wool over their eyes was surely a fine one. All Greg knew was his own role. He was Sarah Trant's champion against a hostile world.

Greg leaned forward. "Your Honor," he said, "I think the record should reflect that Diana Sanborn's testimony here is totally consistent with what Judith Daniels told police soon after the murder. It is also totally consistent with what Sarah Trant has always said."

Judge Solman allowed just the barest glimmer of appreciation. "Yes," he agreed. "I suppose the record should reflect that much, shouldn't it?" Then he asked, "Anything further, Mr. Mashburn?"

"No, Your Honor. I felt I had the obligation to offer this—"

"Well, then," Greg interrupted. "Does that mean we now come to the question of relief, Your Honor?"

"Relief . . . ?" Solman blinked in confusion.

Greg turned to the DA. "Jim, tell me this. Does the State intend to continue defending this case?"

Mashburn appeared as perplexed as the judge, and also wary. "Now, wait just a minute," he said. "I didn't come here to surrender. No, sir. I'm still representing the State. I believe I have two obligations. One is total candor with the Court—"

"Which you have consistently offered," Solman said. "Unlike the sheriff of El Nido County."

"I've tried . . ." Mashburn spoke now as if stepping

through a minefield. "But it was Ms. Sanborn. . . . I would have come forward anyway, but it was Ms. Sanborn—"

"Excuse me," Greg interrupted. "I guess I'm having a little trouble hearing in here. What was it we said about relief for my client?"

Solman finally took Greg's cue. "It does seem clear now that the petitioner is entitled to relief, Mr. Mashburn. The only question is, how much?"

"It seems clear?" Mashburn sputtered. "The only question is how much?"

"I believe that's what I said," Judge Solman murmured.

The DA stared hard at Greg, realizing finally where this was heading. "We're going to make our own rules of the game?" he asked. "Is that it, Greg? Rules we can believe in?"

"It's an idea."

Mashburn sat in silence for a long moment. Then he drew a breath and swung toward the judge. "Okay," he said. "I'll give a little here. . . . Yes. . . . Obviously there is some relief justified in this particular case. Yes. . . . I agree relief is warranted, and I think we're talking now—"

"About what relief," Solman said.

"Yes," Mashburn agreed. "What relief."

"May I propose something?" Greg asked.

The DA and judge turned to him. "Given what we've heard here," Greg said, "I ask that the Court consider releasing Sarah Trant outright at this point. I ask that the Court find Sarah Trant, by clear and convincing evidence, actually innocent of Brewster Tomaz's murder."

A silence fell in Judge Solman's chambers. No one appeared to know what to say. Sarah Trant and Diana Sanborn fussed with their handkerchiefs. Daniel Solman and James Mashburn gaped at Greg.

So Greg continued: "Given what we know about Sheriff Rimmer's conduct, there's clearly no basis for holding her. You've got witness tampering, suborning perjury, hiding critical evidence. . . . Just about everything but a dying declaration by Brewster Tomaz. If I may say so, Sheriff Rimmer merits a trial here, not Sarah Trant."

"But . . ." Judge Solman rubbed his temples, trying to keep up with Greg. "Customarily, if I were to issue this writ, if I were to grant the habeas petition, you'd get not freedom but a new murder trial in state court. Mr. Monarch, convicted murderers just don't walk out the door at a federal habeas hearing."

"Yes, Your Honor," Greg agreed. "Not normally. But this is an exceptional case. We're not only looking at outrageous prosecutorial misconduct. We're looking at a petitioner's actual innocence. We're asking that Sarah Trant walk free not because she was unfairly convicted, but because she didn't kill Brewster Tomaz."

Solman examined Greg now as if finally seeing him revealed. He said nothing for a moment. Then he turned his attention to the DA. "Mr. Mashburn, what do you say? Mr. Monarch raises an interesting question, doesn't he? You have a response?"

Mashburn's mouth opened but no words came. He was still a prosecutor, despite everything. "You mean we just let her go?" he asked finally. "She walks? How can—"

Solman interrupted. "It needn't be put just like that. What I'm thinking is, I issue the writ. Then the district attorney's office simply decides against retrying the case. Nice and easy. No need, then, for judicial dramatics."

"Hold on, now," Mashburn said. "How in heaven could I not retry—"

Solman interrupted again. "The question is, how are you going to defend this? How could you retry her if I grant this habeas appeal? All your evidence is tainted, everything Roy Rimmer touched. You don't have a dying declaration. Instead you have a mystery man fleeing across the creek."

Still Mashburn held back. "Your Honor, I said relief was warranted, but I never said—"

This time Greg interrupted. "Jim, after what you've heard, you really want to win here? That's what you want?"

Those words stopped the DA. Mashburn turned slowly to Greg. Amused recognition crept across his face. "I thought there weren't winners and losers in this game, Greg. Just right and wrong."

"Only if you say so, Jim."

Mashburn rose and paced about. He stopped at the window that gave onto a view of La Graciosa's plaza. There he stood, his back to the room, his hand on a pane of glass. When he finally turned around, he was beaming. "Well, hell," he said. "Yes . . . I say so."

Solman regarded the two lawyers with wonder and open relief. "I don't believe we're any longer in an adversarial relationship here," he said. "For the record, we'll still hold oral argument tomorrow as to what precisely the relief should involve. But I can tell you right now, I'm planning to issue the writ. I'm also planning to declare Sarah Trant actually innocent. Counselors, are we in agreement on that plan?"

"Yes, Your Honor," Greg said.

All faces swung to the El Nido County DA. "So are we agreed, Mr. Mashburn?" Judge Solman asked.

Mashburn's eyes were fixed on Greg. Without turning his head, he spoke to Solman. "I don't see how I can object, Your Honor."

# TWENTY-ONE

From his stool at the bar of JB's Red Rooster Tavern, Greg nursed a whiskey as he listened to the saloon's piano player, Dave Murphy, pound out his brand of country blues. Anytime now, Greg knew, Dave's wife, Shirley, would appear, ready to sing by his side. No doubt Jimmy O'Brien would come barreling in. Some of the local lawyers would be there, certainly Tim Ruthman. Maybe Alison and Cindy. Even Kim Rosen might show up. He'd not been to JB's in months. With satisfaction, Greg saw it hadn't changed a bit. The ancient mahogany and maple bar, the billiards tables, the potbellied stove, the kerosene lamp, the branding irons, the steer horns . . . JB's was permanently frozen in time. So, too, were Greg's memories of the place. He'd celebrated more than one courtroom victory here, and fought with more than one woman.

Tonight was an occasion for celebration. They were almost at the finish line. Mashburn had caved, Solman was on board. Very likely, Sarah would walk tomorrow. Sarah's actual innocence demanded as much; actual innocence opened so many doors. Yet Greg didn't feel like celebrating just yet.

"You lost me somewhere."

Greg looked up to find Jas Gest on the next stool. "I told you to meet me here," he said.

"I don't mean that, Greg. I mean, you lost me in that courtroom. What happened today? You're behind closed doors in the judge's chambers for half the afternoon, then the hearing is postponed again."

Greg signaled the bartender to pour Jas a glass of white

wine. He tried to look casual and pleased at the same time. "We had a breakthrough today. Diana Sanborn came forward with a revised story. Seems not Sarah but a strange hooded fellow is the killer. Fits exactly with Judith Daniels's account. Diana saw him running from the river waving a knife, but was persuaded by Sheriff Rimmer to forget that bit of information."

Jas's eyes widened. "My God . . . She just came forward. . . . How did that happen?"

Greg nursed his drink. "Actually, she approached Mashburn with it during the lunch hour. He felt obliged to take it to the judge. That's why we were in his chambers."

Jas was studying him now. "I see. . . . So you just learned of this in his chambers?"

"That's right."

"Must have been quite a surprise."

"It was that."

"Wonder what moved Diana to flip."

"Her conscience, maybe?"

Jas nodded, lost in thought. "So where are things now?"

"I've asked the judge to issue the writ. Also to release Sarah outright. Solman will grant these requests tomorrow."

"How can you be sure?"

"Mashburn didn't object. Mashburn agreed relief was due."

Jas let out a low whistle. "Now I see why you win awards." She looked as if she wanted to say more, but didn't. Instead she waved for a second round of drinks. At the piano, Dave was launching into a tune Greg recognized. "Angel from Montgomery." With appreciation, he turned to watch Shirley at the microphone.

"Well, then, Greg, we should celebrate tonight, shouldn't we?" Jas was tugging at his arm. "Let's dance."

He held her closely, feeling her against him as they moved with the music. His eyes roamed the room, though. They weren't finished, he was sure of that. This wasn't over.

Jas's right hand was sliding down to his hip now; she was slapping playfully at his haunch. In an instant, the gesture reminded Greg of another day. They by the creek in the park, she pushing him down and straddling him, simulating the murder . . . Slapping at his hip before slashing his throat. Why had she done that?

"Jas, did you ever read the autopsy report on Tomaz?"

"Yeah, sure."

"Besides the slashed neck, wasn't there something else?"

Jas looked oddly at him. "Yes. . . . Remember? . . . The left hip, a knife wound into the pelvis bone . . ."

"The bone?"

"I'm sure of it. At the trial, I remember hearing that the tip of the blade broke off into the bone."

He'd missed that, or forgotten it, so intent was he on the carotid artery.

Jas patted the side of his head. "Poor boy. Just can't stop taking it apart, can you? Come on, relax. You've won, Greg."

No, he hadn't. Not yet.

He stopped dancing. "Where's Diana?"

"Why should I know?"

"She's staying where you are, at the El Nido Inn. I told her to come over here with you. Didn't you see her?"

Now Jas stopped dancing also. "I did see her," she said. "But she wasn't heading this way."

"Where was she?"

"She was at the front desk, checking out."

A full moon guided Diana Sanborn through the wooded, curving mountain pass. She required no light, though. She could find El Nido blindfolded.

She rolled her window down as she drove, wanting to feel the breeze on her face. The air gained a growing clarity as she plunged ever deeper into the canyon. She'd go back to the coast tomorrow, she'd finish the job she'd started for Greg Monarch. But tonight she needed to sleep in El Nido.

What a job it had been. Diana wondered how her grandfather's obligations compared. Would he have gone as far as she had? Most certainly, if obliged. He recognized no limits. Once, he and another rancher, crossing a vast plain in a small buckboard, came to a deep and wide wash barring their way home. It was late in the day; driving around the wash would involve a matter of miles and several hours' travel, taking them far into the night. *I'm not going around it*—that's what Edward Sanborn declared. The other rancher, frightened out of his wits, leapt from the buckboard just as Diana's grandfather put the whip to his team. An instant later, in unity, horses, carriage, and driver bounded over the wash. Edward Sanborn made it home in time for dinner.

He never chose his battles unwisely, though. No doubt her grandfather would have managed to avoid the situation she faced. Diana hadn't realized it would come to this. A step at a time, that's how they'd been drawn in, until she couldn't retreat. Would she ever be forgiven?

Diana was descending now into the El Nido Valley. She drove through the village, empty and unlit at this hour, then plunged into the citrus groves of the East End. Sanborn Ranch's gates rose before her in a welcoming embrace. She parked behind the main house, smelling the air as she climbed out of her pickup. She glanced over at Alex's bungalow. The lights were off, which by itself was not odd. But where was Alex's truck? With regret, Diana turned to the house. What a shame he was out. She had an urge to talk to him.

Diana flipped on lights as she moved through her kitchen and pantry. In the great room, she stopped before the portrait of Edward Sanborn. Those potent ice-blue eyes so often had focused on her. She'd basked in the attention, yet in truth she'd also squirmed at times. She could never hide from her grandfather. He saw everything. Everything, that is, but what happened to her one moonlit evening in the summer of her sixteenth year. It would have appalled Diana's grandfather to learn of his ignorance regarding this matter. Yet knowledge would have been worse. All these decades later, Diana remained sure of that.

She wrapped her arms about her. A chill had settled in the valley this evening. Diana glanced at the great stone fireplace. Someone had laid it with oak logs and kindling. How nice of Alex, or whichever ranch hand thought to do this. Diana struck a long stick match against the mantel and touched it to the kindling. The fire grew quickly in the crackle-dry wood. Diana sat on the hearth, drawing warmth as she stared into the flames.

Then she heard a sound. Not exactly of footsteps, she thought. More of a thump, as if something had fallen to the ground. Upstairs, she judged. Almost directly above her. She started to rise and look up. So it was only out of the corner of an eye, turned sideways, that she saw the flames suddenly erupt. They leapt toward her with a raucous roar. Scorching heat washed over her, then pain of a sort she'd never felt before. All she could see was a bright white light. She was on the ground now, rolling away from the fireplace. She thought she heard a pounding on a door. Something red and wet was falling down her forehead, down her nose. The flames had stopped barking at her, at least. She lay still, waiting for the pain to cease.

Just past dawn, in the first pink light of day, Greg descended into the El Nido Valley. La Graciosa had been fogbound when he left; here all was crystal clear. On impulse he pulled over to the side of the road. Not until he climbed out of his car did he realize this was where he'd collided with a tree trunk on that first morning he came into the valley. Over there was where he stood, watching Jasmine Gest rise slowly from a blue-green lagoon. Greg walked over to look once again at that bend in the river. He was in no particular rush.

They had Diana in a private room at the El Nido Community Hospital. She'd survive, they'd reassured him. In a good deal of pain right now, though, and not yet ready for visitors. It could have been much worse. A nasty scalp wound, a moderate concussion, but only first-degree burns, mainly along the side of her body. Luckily, the blast had blown her away from the flames. It was James Mashburn who'd first given Greg the news, calling him at JB's Tavern. Mashburn in turn had heard about it from Sheriff Rimmer.

The firewood had exploded on her, that's what they figured.

The logs had been packed with black mining powder. It was an old ranch trick to booby-trap logs like that when you suspect someone is stealing your firewood. Soon enough, a stove or fireplace explodes in the thief's home, and you've got your culprit. One of Diana's hands, knowing that full cords had been disappearing from ranches all around the valley, must have packed some of their wood. Then somehow those logs had ended up in the main-house fireplace, instead of stacked outside as bait. Hell of an accident.

Greg would have to wait to see Diana. Maybe by the end of the day, they'd told him. Or maybe tomorrow. That would be soon enough. He had other business to transact first anyway. From the ledge where he stood, Greg scanned the creek coursing a hundred feet below him. A fly fisherman caught his attention, just as one had on his first day. There were no naked willowy bathers about this morning, though. Greg lifted his eyes to the horizon. So little had changed. The ravines and orchards and vines, the pale morning sunlight. Greg turned back to his car.

They'd be waiting for him at the entrance to Camp Mahrah. That's what Charles Whit and Roy Rimmer had told him when he'd reached them late last night. One hour past dawn, they'd said. He was early. No doubt they would be also.

Where the road turned to dirt and narrowed into a path, Greg parked his car and began walking. At the splintered wooden gate with the hand-lettered Do Not Trespass sign, he waited only for a moment. Then he stepped around the barrier. New growth, he saw, had already started to obscure the fire that had scorched this part of the valley. Burgeoning willows overwhelmed blackened columns of oak and sycamore, promising a needed food source for the wildlife that fed on them. Someone had made sure to rebuild the watershed structure. They'd replaced culverts and set stone to buffer runoff areas. Greg eyed with appreciation the bales of straw, the boulders, the check dams, the armored stream banks. Whoever ran this camp knew how to manage the land.

"Welcome to Camp Mahrah, Mr. Monarch."

Charles Whit had suddenly appeared fifty feet in front of him without notice. He somehow filled more space than even his considerable size dictated. Greg stepped toward him, then stopped as he noticed Sheriff Rimmer well off to his right, standing in the shade of a spreading oak. "Why don't we all gather together," Greg suggested.

Whit offered his cold, steady smile. "An excellent idea," he said. "Both of you, please join me. We'll walk to the lodge."

They fell in line together, Whit commanding the center. Even with his limp and cane, he moved along at a pace that required the others to step quickly. As they walked, Rimmer aimed fierce looks at Greg, but Whit kept his eye on where he was headed. They were in the heart of the campus now, passing along the side of the playing field. There was no evidence of a fire here at all; they'd reseeded with abundance. All the charred buildings had been stripped and rebuilt with fresh timber. As before, a strange silence filled Camp Mahrah. Greg looked up at an empty sky and sniffed, but couldn't detect even the hint of rotten eggs. There was no wind today, so perhaps that made a difference.

Whit pointed the way to one of the lodge houses. Greg recognized it as the one where, through a window, he'd seen the evidence of a meeting long ago. Whit stood at its door, holding open a front screen. Greg had Sheriff Rimmer at his back. Reluctantly, he stepped into the room. The two other men followed him, then closed the door.

Whit pointed to a rocking chair by the fireplace. "You ought to find that comfortable, Mr. Monarch."

Greg waited for the others to sit down before settling into the rocker. They were in straight-backed chairs, placed just far enough apart that he needed to swing his head to look at one, then the other. He pulled his rocker back to gain a wider perspective.

"On the phone last night you spoke of an urgent matter we needed to discuss," Whit said. "So let's discuss."

Greg looked back and forth at the two men. "Yes," he agreed. "Let's discuss."

Rimmer erupted. "Are we to guess what this is about, Monarch? What is this, Twenty Questions?"

"More like Jeopardy," Greg replied. "Wouldn't you say?"

Whit's smile grew wider, even as he fixed Greg with empty gray eyes. "Just what do you mean?"

"For a remote insulated valley, there's been so much danger. Sudden deaths such as Reggie Dodge's. Little accidents such as mine while diving out at El Nido Lake. Now Diana Sanborn's fireplace explodes on her. The mayor should put up a sign at the city limits. Something like, 'Hazardous Zone, Proceed at Your Own Risk.' "

Rimmer was shifting restlessly in his chair. Whit moved not at all, but looked even more impatient. "I don't mean to sound rude," Whit said. "But get to the point, Mr. Monarch."

Greg rose and walked to the fireplace, where he put a foot on the hearth, a hand on the mantel. "The point," he said, "is that it's time to call your dogs off."

Rimmer started to respond, but Whit waved him into silence, then turned to Greg. "Mr. Monarch, when I first met you at the park during that band concert, I told you we might get along yet. I still feel that way. You do your job well. I like that. I admire talent and discipline almost as much as I appreciate the willingness to do what's needed. I see now why you are so celebrated in Chumash County."

Greg ran his hand along the fireplace mantel as he looked past the seated men to the window behind them. A stand of oaks shaded and obscured his view. He could see only the corner of another lodge house, and the edge of the distant playing field. That and, for a passing moment, what had appeared to be the outline of someone moving slowly among the trees. It occurred to Greg that he needed to speak his piece as quickly as possible.

"I know everything now," he said. "The plume, the oil spill, Brewster Tomaz's blackmail efforts, the alliance with Diana, the need to defuse Sarah." Greg looked hard at Whit. "I also know about the waste dump."

Until those last words, Whit had appeared entirely at ease. Mention of the waste dump drew a response, though. The wrinkled skin reddened around his receding forehead. "You're making a mistake here," Whit cautioned. "Be aware, Mr. Monarch. You are involving yourself with forces you should avoid."

"I'd be more than happy to take a wide detour," Greg said. "That's why I've asked to speak to you."

As Whit digested those words, he relaxed once again. "A deal . . . That's what you're here to offer, isn't it, Mr. Monarch?"

"Precisely." Greg left the fireplace, returned to his rocker. "As I say, you call off your dogs. That means Diana Sanborn is safe to walk the streets of El Nido, and so is Sarah Trant when Judge Solman releases her."

"Which," Whit interrupted, "I understand he plans to do this very day."

"If I can get back to La Graciosa in time. We may need another day or two."

Whit appeared lost in thought. "Yes. . . . Well, Ms. Trant's release does alter matters, doesn't it? . . . But I interrupted you, I'm afraid. Please continue."

"Calling off the dogs also means you withdraw your considerable pressure from the DA's office." Greg thought of Judge Solman. "And from the entire legal system, for that matter. On their own, the judge decides whether to issue a writ, and the DA decides whether to retry."

"I'm flattered, but you overestimate our powers."

"I don't think so."

"You also ask for a lot."

"I'm not finished. You also seal off the old wells up here in Camp Mahrah, and dismantle the pumps."

Whit studied Greg with fascination. "You are amazing, Mr. Monarch."

"Something else," Greg continued. "You shut down the waste dump, rehabilitate the land, and do something worthwhile with Camp Mahrah. Develop a regional park, or make that world-class health spa a reality, not just a decoy."

Sheriff Rimmer was on his feet now, advancing toward

Greg. "Are you mad, Monarch?" he demanded. "There's oil under here. This is my chance. . . . You can't—"

From where he sat, Whit stopped Rimmer with the end of his cane. "Take it easy, Roy," he advised, pointing the sheriff back to his chair. "You had best sit down."

Rimmer glowered but slowly complied. Whit turned back to Greg.

"Anything else, Mr. Monarch? Have we reached the end of your list?"

"Just one more thing. Sheriff Rimmer here. He's served his county nobly all these years. He deserves a restful retirement. That would surely please him more than facing the conspiracy and obstruction of justice charges that Judge Solman no doubt is presently contemplating."

Whit brandished his cane before Rimmer could respond. The sheriff gripped the arms of his chair, staring wide-eyed at the two men before him, but said nothing.

Whit asked, "And in exchange for all this, Mr. Monarch?"

"Silence."

"Can you elaborate a little?"

"Silence about the plume, to begin with. That will save your people about four hundred million dollars in cleanup costs and criminal fines. And silence about the waste dump. That will save your people many times more dollars . . . lots more."

Whit's eyes traveled to the window now. Greg followed his glance. He saw nothing but the trees rustling in a slight breeze. "The waste dump is a perfectly legal operation," Whit observed. "Nothing to hide."

"Then why is it run as a clandestine operation through the backroads? Why doesn't anyone in El Nido know about it? Why go to such lengths to conceal everything?"

"ModoCorp is a privately held company. It needn't make public all that it does."

Greg slowly rocked back and forth. "My turn for appreciation. You are being so ingenious, Mr. Whit . . . but also a little incomplete."

"Am I?"

"The dumping is legal," Greg said, "but only because there's a gaping loophole in the hazardous-waste laws. No one really knows about this loophole. Got passed without anyone paying attention. It starts getting into the news, people start getting aware, there'll be hell to pay. At the least, enormous pressure to reverse things, change the law, kill the loophole. It would ruin the game for everyone. That's why you need the waste dump kept secret. That's why you and your colleagues at ModoCorp will value my silence. You people surely don't want to ruin your sweetheart deal."

"You presume much about our wants."

"Not just your wants, actually. It's a far bigger game, isn't it?"

Whit couldn't stop himself from gloating. It showed in his tone, and in his eyes. "You're right, Mr. Monarch. It is far bigger. There are national interests involved, reaching to the highest levels. That's precisely why I advised you against getting involved. So many interests, so much power, so much money. You're trying to take on all sorts of forces. You're—"

"Actually," Greg interrupted, "it's you and your ModoCorp colleagues who will be taking on these forces if we can't come to terms here."

Whit stared at Greg. "What do you mean?"

"I mean you'll have a nasty problem if you blow everyone's sweetheart deal just because of your little situation in El Nido. Not only ModoCorp has a compelling interest in keeping this thing covered up. Mr. Whit, to put it plainly, you let this blow, you'll make lots of powerful folks very unhappy. I imagine you won't fare well."

"And . . ." Whit's eyes looked as if they'd momentarily gone out of focus. "And . . . how exactly would you make it blow? Who would pay attention outside of the valley if you start hollering? No one cares about El Nido's waste dump. This isn't big news anywhere else."

Greg continued his rocking. He made a note in his mind to buy a chair just like this one for his house. He found the rhythm soothing. "What if, say, someone threatens to leap off a La Luna mountain cliff in protest of your waste dump? A few people, actually. A devout core from El Nido who would do anything to preserve their valley. That would make for quite a public relations mess, wouldn't you say?"

"Preposterous."

Greg smiled. "I'm afraid that Sarah Trant and her friends are precisely that. . . . Sarah loves how that native Colombian tribe hog-tied Occidental with just such threats of mass suicide. . . . And remember, Sarah will soon be out of jail."

"The U'wa tribe," Whit muttered, recognizing the reference. He was unable to hide his dismay. He glanced again at the window. Greg, trying to follow his gaze, saw only trees.

"As you might imagine," Whit disclosed, "we're not alone up here at Camp Mahrah. This lodge house is surrounded."

"Yes," Greg said. "As I might imagine."

Whit turned to him. "They swindled my family, you know. The community of El Nido, a century ago. They stole our legacy, and utterly destroyed my grandfather. We've been brutalized by these lovely folks."

"That was long ago. Those who hurt your family aren't alive."

"Their descendants are."

"Yes," Greg agreed. "And they appear as determined as their forebears to preserve this valley."

Whit flared at that, but didn't argue the point. "My family kept the mineral rights, God knows why. By the time they passed down to me, I was already doing quite well in the oil business. I'd taken on 'investors.' I'd been 'absorbed,' as they say. I had partners just loaded with supercomputers and high-tech geeks. We were in the Gulf, and laying plans for the Pacific Coast. I didn't need El Nido Valley for the money. Coming here, buying Camp Mahrah, settling in, it mainly meant a chance to vindicate my grandfather, to reclaim finally what was his due."

"Forgive me," Greg said. "But wasn't it also a chance for retribution?"

Whit shifted in his chair. "Yes, Mr. Monarch, yes it was."

"No matter what it took?"

Whit looked at him steadily. "Yes."

"Sending threatening blackmail letters through the U.S. mail is a federal crime that carries grave consequences."

"For those who do it."

"Or those who cause it to be done."

"If such a link can be proven."

"Yes," Greg said. "But given what we now know, that shouldn't be too difficult."

The tips of Whit's fingers, gripping his cane, had turned white. "You are good, Monarch. But this isn't enough. You're not holding a full hand."

"How about motive. Does that round things out?"

"Motive?"

"Brewster Tomaz knew about the plume and the waste dump. No doubt he knew much more. He was threatening you. He was blackmailing you."

Whit started tapping his cane on the floor. "Such speculation . . ."

"You had the motive. You had reason to kill him."

"Sarah Trant's on trial, no one else—"

"Unless new evidence is introduced."

Whit raised his cane and pointed it at Greg. "This is all a bluff."

"You will prosper no matter what happens here, Mr. Whit. . . . Maybe the two grandchildren can work something out."

"The two grandchildren?"

"You and Diana."

Whit was adrift now. His cane hung loosely in his hand. "A waste dump instead of oil wells . . . Necessary in my business, and even appropriate for this blasted place . . . But not what I'd counted on. That hadn't been the original plan."

"It couldn't have been what your grandfather wanted here."

Whit sat in silence, staring out the window. Then he turned to Greg. "I wasn't sure what we'd be doing with you."

"I understand."

"Now I know."

"Yes?"

Still the smile didn't show in Whit's pale gray eyes. White teeth flashed, though. "We're going to make a deal with you," he said.

# TWENTY-TWO

Higher and higher she flew, first her feet reaching toward the sky, then her head. Long dark hair billowed in the wind. Intense hazel eyes danced with glee. "Oh my," Sarah Trant called out. "Yeeha . . ."

From a bench by the fountain in Sanborn Park, Greg and Jas watched as Sarah pitched back and forth on one of the park's playground swings. She'd tried the jungle gym already, and the merry-go-round, and the hanging bars. Jas wanted to join her, but Greg, for the moment, was keeping a hand on her arm.

"My savior," Sarah had sighed when Greg met her at the prison gate this morning. Following the briefest of final oral arguments, it had taken Solman only twenty-four hours to issue his writ and declare Sarah's actual innocence. Late that same afternoon, Mashburn had announced he wouldn't retry Sarah Trant. They'd led Sarah down a corridor to freedom at dawn the next day.

"My savior," she repeated to Greg as he drove away from the prison.

"For once," he said. "Finally."

"Just in time," she said, laughing.

He glanced at her sideways then, and saw the familiar flicker of exuberance play across her face. He raised a hand to her cheek and gently brushed the hair from her eyes. For an eager moment he imagined her restored. Her manner vaguely unsettled him, though. When he tried to talk to her about the future, she simply nodded and sighed and clung to him.

"ModoCorp is packing up and going away from El Nido," he told her just before they reached Sanborn Park. "No more oil spills, no more anything. There's going to be a regional park up at Camp Mahrah."

"Who do we fight, then?" she asked. "Who do we go after?"

The courts no longer had jurisdiction over her. Greg had placed a call, so far unanswered, to El Nido's one group-care home. He'd try again later in the day. He'd do whatever was needed. "Sarah," he said. "The battle has ended. No more speeches, no more demonstrations, no more talking. We settle down. We keep a low profile. We fight no one."

She looked as if she was sulking, but said nothing more. In an instant she was out the door and at the playground.

"A complicated, impetuous woman," Jas observed as Sarah headed now toward the fountain.

Greg turned from Sarah to Jas. "They're everywhere," he said.

"You have a problem with that?"

Greg spoke softly. "Not at all."

She put a hand on his wrist. "Something terribly wrong happened here, Greg. You fixed it."

"Yes . . . I suppose I did."

"You did good, Greg."

He wrapped her in his arms. "Okay, Jas . . . thank you. . . . Everything's fine."

An angry cry interrupted them. They looked up to find Sarah dancing in the fountain, bare legs flashing, her skirt hitched up to her hips. An outraged matron with two young children in tow was shouting alarms at this display. Jas started giggling as she and Greg jumped up to intervene. "You know what?" she said. "I think Sarah and I have some things in common."

From Sanborn Park, Greg once more drove through El Nido's abundant East End. He soaked up everything with hungry eyes, for he didn't think he'd be passing by this way again anytime soon. The sun hung low in the sky. Another dusk was painting the valley brilliant shades of pink and purple. It wasn't hard for Greg to imagine why people came to El Nido and decided to stay. He wished them all well, them and their protected valley.

The gateway to Sanborn Ranch now rose before Greg. He drove through and parked as usual in the back. This time, though, he knocked at the front entrance, as he had on the day he first met Diana Sanborn.

Alex Ramirez opened the door. He gazed at Greg with dark, solemn eyes. "They brought her from the hospital late this morning," he said. "She's waiting for you."

Greg followed a nurse who led him up a curving flight of stairs and down a corridor. He entered Diana's bedroom by himself. For a moment he hung back at the door, watching her. She lay slightly propped up in her bed, breathing heavily. Her face was swollen, her forehead and arms wrapped in thick white bandages. She peered up at him, first with groggy eyes, then with recognition.

"What you must think of me," Diana whispered.

"And you of me."

She tried to smile, but it looked more like a grimace. "We are a pair."

"A victorious pair."

"Yes, so I've been told," Diana agreed. "I must say I'm very impressed at your achievements."

"Our achievements. You were magnificent with Mashburn and Solman."

She stared deep into Greg's eyes now. "Okay, our achievements. Yet I was simply righting my wrongs. I want you to know how anguished I've been about Sarah. What I did was required, it was mandated by people with power over me. But I never imagined she'd end up on death row."

"She was guilty," Greg said. "You weren't framing an innocent person."

A faint tremor played across Diana's face. "Yes. . . . Still . . . that's no rationale. . . . I never could sleep at night after her trial. I stayed awake for long hours, writing in my journal. Then, finally, you arrived." Diana reached for his hand. "I was so happy when you came to the valley. Scared, but happy also. I saw a way out of this."

Greg pulled up a chair and sat down beside Diana's bed. He spoke as gently as he could. "There's more to it," he said. "Isn't there, Diana?"

She closed her eyes. Minutes passed. Greg waited. He glanced at the nurse hovering in the hallway. When he turned back to Diana, she was watching him with eyes now wide open and crystal clear. "Of course there's more," she said. "Isn't there always?"

"It wasn't just your valley you were protecting by handing over Sarah, was it?"

"What do you mean?"

"You were protecting the one person who mattered to you more than anyone in the valley. The person who cared most about you, the person who would do anything for you."

"My goodness . . . ," she murmured.

"Alex killed Brewster, didn't he, Diana?"

"That's preposterous. . . ."

"It had to be a man. The hip wound, the broken blade tip in Brewster's hip. Only a man was strong enough to do that."

"Oh dear, Gregory . . . There are many men in El Nido Valley. There is, for example, our mysterious hooded fellow with the broad shoulders."

"The boots in the bunkhouse . . . The tunnel."

"All explained, all discounted. Besides, why would Alex kill Brewster?"

"For you, Diana. Because he thought that's what you wanted."

"I wanted a cranky old geologist killed over a land dispute?"

"He wasn't just a cranky old geologist, Diana. Was he?"

She maneuvered to sit up. He helped her with an arm around her back, and a pillow. Then he pulled a photo from his jacket pocket. As he held it before her, she gasped.

"Recognize that young man sitting on the fence? Recognize your brooding, high-strung beau with the jet-black hair?"

"Where did you . . . ?"

"In the boxes at the historical museum. Fred Darvill came charging at me just as I was studying this one, so I stuck it in my pocket and didn't get around to looking at the back until this past weekend."

"The back . . . ?"

He turned the photo over, held it before Diana. "As you can see, somebody scribbled the names of those in the photo."

She peered, then sank onto her pillow, once again closing her eyes.

"Brewster Tomaz," Greg said. "That's the young man's name, as I read it. I should have realized. You said your young man drilled holes and tested soil conditions for your father. A budding geologist. Of course. Funny how time plays tricks. I looked at our murder victim always as a grizzled old goat. I never thought of him as being a young man once. Yet he was. As were you a young woman. By my calculation, he would have been twenty-four when you were sixteen."

Diana opened her eyes. "Yes, that's right. That's how old we were."

"After all these years . . ."

"He was going to ravage me again. Twice. At both the start and end of my life."

"Alex knew what he'd done to you back then?"

"Yes, Alex knew. . . . But, Greg, you must understand. . . . So did Sarah."

"All three of you were down there at the river that night with Tomaz. Sarah argued with him, then pushed him in the river and ran off. What followed wasn't planned. Brewster threatened you, no doubt. On impulse, full of passion, Alex advanced toward him. You stayed back, watching your foreman until he fled across the river. Then you ran to Brewster yourself. Maybe to sneer at his dying face, maybe to make sure he was dead. That would have been understandable.

But others were approaching now. So you scooped him up, held him in your arms. In an instant, you had to choose. You were frantic, you were torn. But above all, you feared for Alex. You had to protect Alex. So you pointed the police toward Sarah."

Diana's laugh sounded utterly genuine. "My goodness, Gregory. You surely do love stories, don't you? But don't you see, however you figure this, it's still just a story. That's how you lawyers build cases. You weave narratives to ensure someone's conviction or acquittal. Or—" Diana gazed at Greg with tender eyes. "Or sometimes, to make things be the way you wish them to be. Bless your heart, Greg. You so much want Sarah to be innocent. So this is your story."

"And you so much wish Alex to be innocent."

"Indeed," Diana agreed. "The fact is, we could devise all sorts of narratives regarding Brewster Tomaz's death. Any of them could be right or wrong. Who knows? You'll never reach truth in this, Greg. Only a verdict."

"That's not enough for me."

Diana's face filled with sympathy. "Oh, Gregory, I do understand. We need to make clear who the victims and villains are, don't we? The world being so confusing, it needs that much clarity at least. So let's say this, shall we: Justice was served, whoever killed Brewster Tomaz."

Greg lifted his eyes to her bedroom's picture window. In the distance he could see the mountain pass leading to La Graciosa. He'd be home by dusk. "Okay," Greg agreed. "Let's say that."

Then he turned to her. "Tell me this at least, Diana. . . . What have I done here?"

Her grand smile filled the room now. She whooped with pleasure as she waved at the wondrous vista. "You have restored my faith in mankind, that's what you've done, Gregory. You have shown us the way. You have shown us how to protect ourselves. You have saved El Nido."

With effort, she reached up from her pillows and threw

her bandaged arms around Greg. "Bless our hearts," she said. "We were such innocents until you came to our valley."

The story of a town that wanted to forget, and those who wouldn't let them...

## A DEATH IN WHITE BEAR LAKE

The True Chronicle of an All-American Town

"A masterfully depicted true-crime tale... This perceptive analysis of the case by a *Los Angeles Times* reporter is stirring."

—*Publishers Weekly*

# Complete World Bartender Guide

Edited by Bob Sennett

BANTAM BOOKS
Toronto / New York / London / Sydney

COMPLETE WORLD BARTENDER GUIDE
The Standard Reference to 2000 Drinks

*A Bantam Book / published by arrangement with Poorhouse Press*

*PRINTING HISTORY*

*Poorhouse edition published September 1977*
*6 printings through August 1979*

*Appeared in Condensed form by Profile Books-Q Publications Minature Book*

*Bantam Edition / September 1981*



ISBN 0-553-14897-4

*Published simultaneously in the United States and Canada*

---

*Bantam Books are published by Bantam Books, Inc. Its trademark, consisting of the words "Bantam Books" and the portrayal of a bantam, is Registered in U.S. Patent and Trademark Office and in other countries. Marca Registrada. Bantam Books, Inc., 666 Fifth Avenue, New York, New York 10103.*

---

PRINTED IN THE UNITED STATES OF AMERICA

0 9 8 7 6 5 4

# Contents

# INTRODUCTION

The Complete Bartender's Guide presents a compendium of popular cocktails and beverages for easy reference.

Drink recipes are listed alphabetically by their common names. The rear index orders the drinks by liquor ingredient.

The recipes are culled from professional bartenders, commercial distillers, and private collections. The Complete Guide is a valuable and comprehensive resource.

We, the editors, acknowledge the public health hazard of drinking alcohol in excess.

For this reason, we have included a section entitled "Responsible Drinking" which outlines some aspects of alcohol abuse.

We offer the Guide as a service to those who have achieved an understanding of alcohol as an intoxicant, and who have established by good judgment when drinking is appropriate for them.

# *TIPS FOR BARTENDERS*

## GLASSES

Use freshly washed glassware. Place glasses face down on a thin towel for drying. Use a stemmed glass for cocktails served with no ice so that the hand holding the glass will not warm the drink.

## FROSTING A GLASS

Keep in a refrigerator (or bury in shaved ice) until glass is frosted.
To "sugar-frost" glass, wet the rim of a pre-chilled glass with lime or lemon then dip into powdered sugar, or salt per recipe.

## CHILLING A GLASS

Refrigerate or fill each glass with shaved or crushed ice before mixing. Shake out the melted ice before pouring the drink.

## SHAKE AND BLENDING

Drinks containing fruit juices, sugar, eggs, cream etc. should be well shaken. To attain a frothy quality, use an electric blender. Also use a blender for punches, sours and fruit and egg drinks.

## STIRRING

Stir drinks with clear liquors including ice. Stir drinks containing a carbonated mixer very gently. Don't stir liqueurs.

## ADDING SUGAR

Sugar should be put in the mixing glass first, then add the liquor. Powered sugar is best used with alcohol because it dissolves easily with alcohol at low temperatures. Some bartenders prefer syrup because it blends instantly. Store syrup in bottles and keep cool. If you want to make your own, here's how: dissolve one pound of granulated sugar in one-half pint of hot water. Stir slowly adding water to make desired quantity (usually one pint).

## USING ICE

Ice goes into the mixing glass, shaker or drinking glass before drink. Use cubes, as a rule, for old fashioneds, highballs or any on-the-rocks drinks. Cracked or cubed ice is best for stirring and shaking. Crushed or shaved ice for frappes and other tall drinks or for sipping drinks through straws.

## BITTERS

Only a dash or two. Made from combinations of roots, barks, berries and herbs. They are aromatic and bitter in taste.

The four brands below are most popular:

| | |
|---|---|
| ANGOSTURA BITTERS | made in Trinidad |
| ABBOTT'S AGED BITTERS | made in Baltimore |
| PEYCHAUD'S BITTERS | made in New Orleans |
| ORANGE BITTERS | made in England |

## TWIST OR PEEL

When using a twist of lemon peel, rub outer skin of peel around the rim of the glass to coat it with its natural oil. Add some of its oil to the drink by twisting the peel over the glass. Then add the peel itself.

## FRUIT OR JUICES

Wash fruit first. Slices should be 3/8″ thick and slit up the center to saddle on rim of glass. Keep garnishes on a bed of ice or in a cool place. In drinks containing fruit juices you must pour in the liquor last.

## SERVING BEER

Chill beer like champagne; surround with ice cubes and turn gently a few times. Don't serve it *too* cold for it goes flat. Don't shake bottle or can before opening. Open gently to prevent gushing. Once opened, serve promptly! Don't tilt glass to allow beer to slide slowly down side! Instead, pour beer into center of glass, holding bottle or can at a high angle until a head comes up. Then pour beer more slowly. Most people prefer a firm head, about 1″ deep.

## EGGS

To separate the white of an egg from its yolk, crack open on the edge of the glass, then shift the yolk back and forth from one half shell to the other until all the white drops into the glass. Always put the egg into the mixing glass before the liquor. When shaker is used include (cubed or cracked) ice to help blend the egg with the other ingredients.

## SERVING

When serving the same cocktail for more than one, mix the drinks in one batch. Set up all the glasses in a row and partially fill each glass (half). Then go back and top off each glass.

## TO FLAME LIQUOR

(Brandy, Rum, Gin, Whiskey)
Prewarm the glass, vessel and liquor. First preheat one spoon of liquor over a flame and set afire. Then pour flaming liquor carefully into remainder. It will set the rest aflame.

## THE STRAINER

Strain cocktails into serving glasses with a wire strainer.

## VERMOUTH

Vermouth is a white appetizer wine. It is often flavored with about forty different herbs, roots, berries, flowers and seeds. There are many vermouth brand labels, each with its own formula. The dry (French) has a light gold color and has a nutty flavor. Sweet (Italian) vermouth has a more syrupy quality. Keep bottle corked or it will go stale.

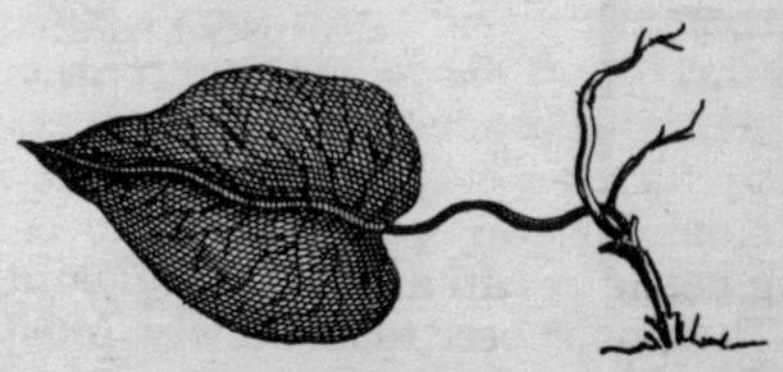

# *BAR TOOLS AND GLASSES*

A glass hierarchy still exists at most public bars, but times are changing and particularly in home bars people have learned to be more flexible.

These are the glasses and tools you will need to fill most requests. Keep in mind that these are only guidelines because the styles of glasses constantly change.

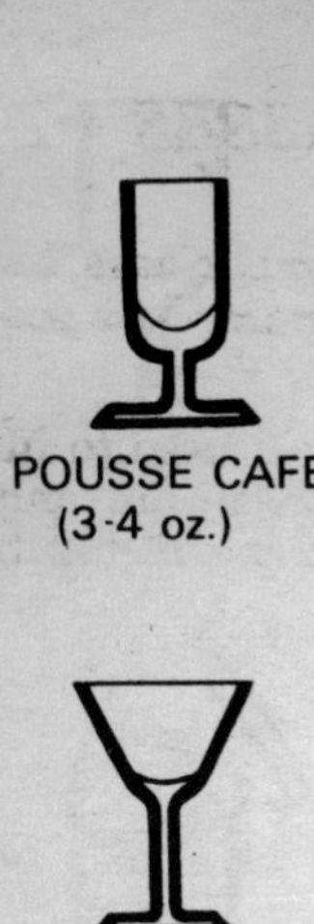
POUSSE CAFE
(3-4 oz.)

CORDIAL
(PONY)
( 1-2 oz.)

SHERRY
(2 oz.)

PARFAIT

COCKTAIL
( 3 ½ oz.)

BRANDY
(3 oz.)

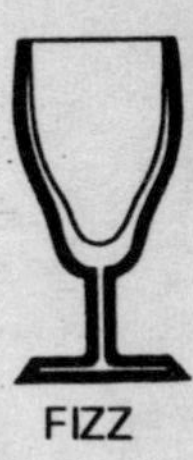
FIZZ

SOUR
(5 oz.)

OLD FASHIONED
(6 - 8 oz.)

BIG
OLD FASHIONED
(15 - 16 oz.)

SNIFTER

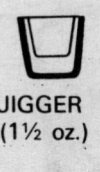

TALL COLLINS
(10 - 14 oz.)

JIGGER
(1½ oz.)

HIGHBALL
(8 oz.)

MARTINI
( 4 oz.)

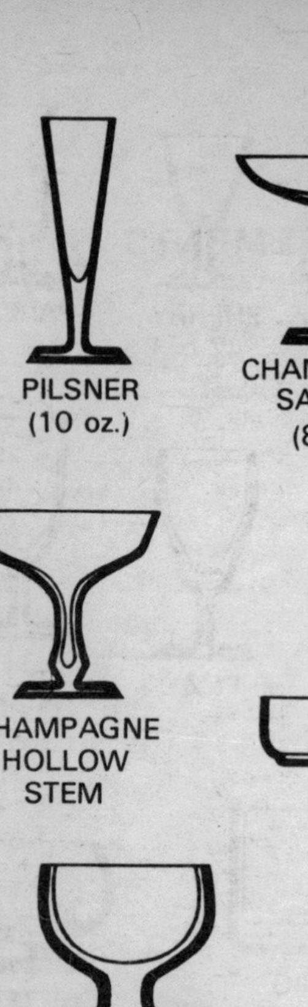

PILSNER
(10 oz.)

CHAMPAGNE
SAUCER
(8 oz.)

WINE
( 4 - 5 oz.)

CHAMPAGNE
HOLLOW
STEM

PUNCH BOWL
AND CUP

BEER GOBLET

EGG NOG

MUG
(10 oz.)

LARGE
MIXING
PITCHER
AND
LONG
HANDLED
SPOON

# MEASUREMENTS

| | Standard | Metric |
|---|---|---|
| 1 Dash | 1/32 ounce | 0.9 ml. |
| 1 Teaspoon | ⅛ ounce | 3.7 ml. |
| 1 Tablespoon | ⅜ ounce | 11.1 ml. |
| 1 Pony | 1 ounce | 29.5 ml. |
| 1 Jigger | 1½ ounces | 44.5 ml. |
| 1 Wineglass | 4 ounces | 119ml |
| 1 Split | 6 ounces | 177 ml. |
| 1 Cup | 8 ounces | 257 ml. |
| 1 Miniature (nip) | 2 ounces | 59.2 ml. |
| 1 Half Pint | 8 ounces | 257 ml. |
| 1 Tenth | 12.8 ounces | 378.88 ml. |
| 1 Pint | 16 ounces | 472 ml. |
| 1 Fifth | 25.6 ounces | 755.2 ml. |
| 1 Quart | 32 ounces | 944 ml. |
| 1 Imperial Quart | 38.4 ounces | 1.137 liter |
| 1 Half Gallon | 64 ounces | 1.894 liter |
| 1 Gallon | 128 ounces | 3.789 liter |
| Dry Wine and Champagne | | |
| Split (¼ bottle) | 6 oz. | 177 ml. |
| "Pint" (½ bottle) | 12 oz. | 375.2 ml. |
| "Quart" (1 bottle) | 25 oz. | 739.0 ml. |
| Magnum (2 bottles) | 52 oz. | 1.534 liter |
| Jeroboam (4 bottles) | 104 oz. | 3.078 liter |
| Tappit-hen | 128 oz. | 3.788 liter |
| Rehoboam (6 bottles) | | 4.434 liter |
| Methuselah (8 bottles) | | 5.912 liter |
| Salmanazar (12 bottles) | | 8.868 liter |
| Balthazar (16 bottles) | | 11.829 liter |
| Nebuchadnezzar (20 bottles) | | 14.780 liter |
| Demijohn (4.9 gallons) | | 18.66 liter |

# *STOCKING & PLANNING*

Stocking for parties depends on the nature of the occasion and the kind of party, type of people, etc. Here is a general plan based on the experienced of commercial distilleries.

## THE BASIC STOCK FOR THE HOME BAR

**WHISKEYS** Two bottles each of a good Scotch, bourbon and a serviceable blended whiskey.

**GINS** A bottle or two of good old American gin will do fine.

**VODKA** Vodka goes fast. Keep a few good-sized bottles around.

**RUMS** One super-dark Jamaican, one virgin white Puerto Rican and one Bacardi for special occasions.

**BRANDIES** Start with a bottle of fine cognac, add a bottle or two of good, inexpensive mixing brandies and one or two fruit brandies . . . apricot and blackberry are very popular.

**LIQUEURS** It's best to have a bottle of coffee liqueur, a bottle of Grand Marnier and a bottle of creme de cassis. In addition (and by nationality) lay in:

ITALIAN: Galliano, Tuaca
DANISH: Aquavit, Cherry Heering
DUTCH: Curacao, Creme Yvette, Kummel
FRENCH: Chartreuse, Benedictine
SCOTCH: Drambuie
BRITISH: Sloe Gin

Last, but not least, you should have a bottle of dry vermouth, a bottle of sweet vermouth and a wide assortment of bitters . . . Angostura, Orange, Abbott's Aged and Peychaud's.

# PLANNING

The chart below is what commercial distillers generally estimate as the yield per bottle.

## DRINKS PER BOTTLE (FIFTH)

(For quarts add 20% to number of drinks)

| RUM | PORT | WHISKEY |
|---|---|---|
| 16 Daiquiris | 16 Drinks | 16 Highballs |
| 12 Rum Collins | | 14 Manhattans |
| 12 Rum Coolers | | 16 Sours |
| | | 16 Old Fashioneds |

| GIN | LIQUEURS | SHERRY |
|---|---|---|
| 16 Tom Collins | 30 Cocktails | 16 Drinks |
| 14 Martinis | 20 Frappes | |
| 16 Fizzes | | |

| DRY VERMOUTH | SWEET VERMOUTH |
|---|---|
| 56 Martinis | 28 Manhattans |

CHAMPAGNE AND SPARKLING WINES

7 Drinks

## PARTIES

| NO. OF PEOPLE | COCKTAIL PARTY (2 HOURS) | DINNER (2 HOURS) |
|---|---|---|
| 4 | 12 Drinks | 8 Cocktails<br>8 Glasses of Wine |
| 6 | 18 Drinks | 12 Cocktails<br>12 Glasses of Wine<br>6 Liqueurs |
| 8 | 24 Drinks | 16 Cocktails<br>16 Glasses of Wine<br>8 Liqueurs |

# MINI-DICTIONARY

**ABSINTHE**- cordial with anise seed (licorice) flavor; contains wormwood (which is banned by the U.S. government). ABISANTE, ABSON, ANISETTE, HERBSAINT, MISTRA, OJEN, OXYGENE, PERNOD are substitutes.

**ADES**—Served tall with ice and garnished with slices of fruit. Mainly made with sweetened lemon or lime juice and a variety of liquors and filled with plain or soda water.

**AGE**—Often this is used as a measure of quality. It is not always dependable because rate of aging and ingredients are a factor too.

**ALCOHOL** ($C_2H_5OH$)—Common to all liquor. Ethyl alcohol, spirits distilled from grain, grape, fruit and cane are most common.

**ALE**—Heavier and more bitter than lager.

**AMER PICON**—A French cordial, bitter, orange-flavored, made from quinine and spices.

**AMERICAN BLENDED LIGHT WHISKEYS**—An American whiskey category. Contains 20 per cent straight whiskeys (at 100 proof) and 80 per cent of American light whiskey.

**AMERICAN BRANDY**—Generally distilled in California. It is usually produced by the same firms that grow the grapes. They distill, age, blend, bottle and market the brandies under their own brand names.

**AMERICAN WHISKEY**—The United States produces over thirty-three distinct types of whiskey.

**ANISETTE**—A cordial made from the anise seed, licorice flavor.

**APPLE BRANDY, APPLE JACK OR CALVADOS**—Distilled from apple cider. Calvados is produced only in Normandy, France.

**ARMAGNAC**—A type of brandy produced only in the Armagnac region of France.

**BEER**—A fermented malt beverage.

**BENEDICTINE**—A cordial made from a secret herb formula. Benedictine monks first made this liqueur.

**BITTERS**—A very concentrated flavoring agent made from roots, barks, herbs and/or berries.

**BLENDED WHISKEY**—Combines straight whiskeys with neutral grain spirits. Straight whiskey dominates the mix by 20%. Sold at 80 proof.

**BLEND OF STRAIGHT WHISKEYS**—Two or more straight whiskeys blended together and excludes neutral grain spirits.

**BOCK BEER, PORTER AND STOUT**—Heavier, darker, richer and sweeter than either lager beer or ale in that order. About 6% alcohol.

**BOTTLED-in-BOND WHISKEY**—Straight whiskey, usually bourbon or rye, produced under government control and supervision. Bonded whiskey must be at least four years old, bottled at 100 proof and produced in one distilling by the same distiller. It must be sorted and bottled at a bonded warehouse under government supervision.

**BOURBON WHISKEY**—Distilled from grain mash containing 51 per cent corn and aged more than four years in new (charred) oak barrels. Amber color. Bourbon gets its name from Bourbon County in Kentucky where it originated. Illinois, Indiana, Ohio, Pennsylvania, Tennessee and Missouri also produce bourbon.

**BRANDY**—Made (distilled) from a fermented mash of grapes or fruit. Generally they are aged in oak casks and bottled at 80 or 84 proof.

**BUCKS**—Made with an ounce or so of liquor and lemon juice plus ginger ale, and topped with a twist of lemon.

**CANADIAN WHISKEY**—A blended whiskey. Distilled from rye, corn and barley. Produced only in Canada under government control. Canadian whiskey sold in this country is at least four years old. Lighter than American whiskey, it is sold at 80 proof.

**CHARTREUSE**—A cordial made from herb liqueurs (either yellow or green). Carthusian monks originated this.

**COGNAC**—A type of brandy produced only in the Cognac region of France.

**COBBLERS**—Tall drinks generally served in a large goblet with shaved ice, fruit and liquor, decorated with berries, fresh fruit and a sprig of mint. Served with a straw.

**COLLINS**—Tall, cool punch-like drinks. Tom and John are best known. Any basic liquor with juice of lemon or lime, over ice cubes in a frosted 12-oz.

highball glass. Sugar and soda water added. Garnished with lemon slice and a cherry.

**COOLERS**—A tall drink made with different types of liquor, flavoring, cracked ice, carbonated beverage and fruit rinds.

**CORDIAL**—A liquor (or liqueur) made by mixing or redistilling neutral spirits. Fruits, flowers, herbs, seeds, roots, plants or juices are used and a sweetening is added. Most cordials are sweet, colorful and highly concentrated. Many are made from secret recipes and processes.

**CREME**—A cordial with a very high sugar content. It s cream-like consistency gives it its prefix. It comes in the following combinations:
CREME DE CACAO—from cacao and vanilla beans
CREME DE CASSIS—from black currants
CREME DE MENTHE—from mint
CREME YVETTE—from violets

**CUPS**—Made with brandy and Triple Sec, together with sweet wine, dry champagne or cider. Mixed in glass pitchers with ice cubes, served in stemmed claret glasses.

**CURACAO**—A cordial made of dried orange peel. It comes from the Dutch West Indies.

**DAISIES**—Large cocktails made of liquor, grenadine or any other cordial with lemon or lime juice. Shaken with ice and served in a stein, metal cup or old fashioned glass over ice cubes, decorated with fruit.

**DRY GIN**—Gin that is very low in sweetness.

**DUBONNET**—An aperitif wine made from aromatics. It has a quinine taste and is mostly made in France.

**EGG NOG**—First achieved popularity in the American Colonies in 1775. The word "noggin" is an English word for small drinking cup. The liquors usually used in egg nog have historically been rum and brandy. Whiskey, sherry, ale and cider can also be used. It is basically a combination of eggs, milk and liquor.

**FIXES**—A drink mixed in the serving glass. Sometimes another name for highball. Served over lots of ice.

**FIZZES**—Made from liquor, citrus juices and sugar. Shaken with ice and strained into small highball glasses. Soda ("Fizz") water is then added. Any carbonated beverage, even champagne, may be used. Some add egg whites or yolks.

**FLAVORED VODKA**—American origin. Generally served straight or in mixed drinks. It is sweetened and flavored, usually with orange, lemon, lime or grape. Sold at 70 proof.

**FLIPS**—An egg nog and fizz combination. Made with liquor, egg and sugar with shaved ice, shaken well. Strained into short stemmed flip glasses for serving. Sprinkled with nutmeg.

**FRAPPES**—Small drinks. Several liqueurs combined and poured over shaved or crushed ice.

**FRUIT BRANDIES**—Fruit flavored liqueurs produced from blackberries, peaches, apricots, cherries and ginger. They are usually brandy-based at 70 to 80 proof.

**GIN**—Distilled from grain. Juniper berries and other botanicals give it its flavor. Most gin is colorless. Some gins appear golden or straw-color because of aging in barrels. Gin is bottled at proofs varying from 80 to 94.

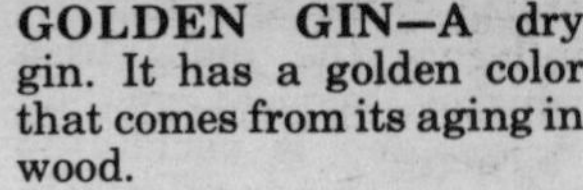

**GOLDEN GIN**—A dry gin. It has a golden color that comes from its aging in wood.

**GRAIN NEUTRAL SPIRITS**—(Alcohol distilled from grain at 190 proof. Used in blended whiskeys for making gin and vodka and other liquors. It is almost tasteless and colorless.

**GRENADINE**—A flavoring for drinks. It is made from pomegranates.

**HEAVY-BODIED RUMS**—Dark, sweet with a pungent bouquet and a rich molasses-like body. They come from Jamaica, Demerara (British Guiana), Martinique, Trinidad, Barbados and New England.

**HIGHBALLS**—Any liquor served with ice, soda, plain water, ginger ale or other carbonated liquids.

**HOLLAND, GENEVA OR SCHIEDAM GINS**—These are highly flavored and rich in aromatic oils. They are made in Holland where gin originated.

**HOT DRINKS**—Made with liquor in any beverage. Served piping hot and not much liquor.

**IRISH WHISKEY**—A blend that contains barley malt whiskeys and grain whiskeys. The malt is dried in coal-fired kilns. The aroma of the fires does not influence the malt. Irish whiskey is heavier than Scotch and is usually 86 proof. It is produced only in Ireland.

**JULEPS**—Made with Kentucky bourbon and fresh mint leaves (muddled, crushed or whole). May also be made with rye, brandy, gin, rum or champagne. Served with shaved ice in an ice-frosted glass with a mint or fruit garnish and a straw.

**KENTUCKY WHISKEY**—A blend of straight bottled whiskies. Distilled in Kentucky.

**KUMMEL**—A cordial liqueur made from caraway and anise seeds with herb flavors added.

**LIGHT-BODIED RUMS**—Dry with slight molasses flavor. They come from Puerto Rico, Cuba and the Virgin Islands, Dominican Republic, Haiti, Venezuela, Mexico, Hawaii and the Philippines.

**LAGER BEER**—(3.6% alcohol) is the most popular beer.

**LIGHT WHISKEY**—A type of American whiskey produced at 160 to 189 proof, stored at least four years in used, charred oak containers. Light in flavor and smooth tasting. Color varies from clear to amber.

**LONDON DRY GIN**—Accepted as a generic term but originated in England. It sometimes appears on American-made labels.

**MARASCHINO**—A liqueur made from cherries. These cherries come from Dalmatia, Yugoslovia.

**OLD TOM GIN**—A gin that contains sugar syrup. It is made in England.

**PASSION FRUIT (PASSIONOLA)**—A mix made from the Passion Flower. It is nonalcoholic.

**PERNOD**—A liqueur, anise-flavored and used as an absinthe substitute.

**PEPPERMINT SCHNAPPS**—A creme de menthe that is rather light in body.

**POUSSE-CAFES**—Made from several cordials and liqueurs poured in series so that one floats atop another. Each has a different color and specific weight that permits "floating."

**PROOF**—The measure of the strength of the alcohol. One (degree) proof equals one-half of 1 per cent of alcohol. For example: 80 proof equals 40 per cent alcohol. Whiskey sold outside of America has been of more moderate, lower proofs. U.S. made whiskey and brandy is usually 80 proof.

**PUNCHES**—Citrus juices with two or more liquors or wines. Served cold. Hot punches use milk, eggs and cream.

**RICKEYS**—Made with lime, cracked ice, soda or any carbonated beverage and whiskey, gin, rum or brandy. Served with the rind of lime. Similar to a collins or sour.

**ROCK AND RYE**—A fruit juice that combines rock candy, rye whiskey and fruit slices.

**RUM**—Made by distilling the fermented juice of sugar cane, cane syrup and molasses at 190 proof (160 proof for New England rum). It is bottled and sold at 80 proof. Aged in uncharred barrels, it picks up very little color. Caramel is added to create dark rums. Most rums are a blend of several kinds.

**RYE WHISKEY**—Distilled from a grain mash of 80 per cent corn. It is usually aged in re-used charred oak barrels.

**SANGAREES**—Made with whiskey, gin, rum, or brandy, with port wine floated on top, or with wine, ale, porter or stout, with a sprinkle of nutmeg. Actually a tall, sweet, old fashioned (without bitters).

**SCOTCH WHISKEY**—Blended whiskies from native barley grain and Scottish pot stills. All Scotch blends contain malt whiskey and grain whiskey. The smoky flavor comes from drying malted barley over peat fires. Produced only in Scotland. Exported Scotch is at least four years old and is usualy 80 to 86 proof.

**SLINGS**—Made like sangarees with the addition of lemon juice and a twist of lemon peel. Served in an old fashioned glass.

**SLOE GIN**—A liqueur made from blackthorn bush (sloe) berries.

**SWEDISH PUNCH**—A liqueur made from Batavia Arak rum, tea, lemon and spices. Sometimes comes as ARRACK PUNCH AND CALORIC PUNCH. Swedish origin.

**SMASHES**—Small juleps. Served in old fashioned glasses. Made with muddled sugar, ice cubes, whiskey, gin, rum or brandy and soda. Garnished with sprigs of mint and fruit.

**SOURS**—Made of lemon juice, ice, sugar, with any basic liquor. Similar to a highly concentrated punch.

Decorated with lemon slice and cherry.

**STRAIGHT WHISKEY**—A whiskey that is distilled from grain but not blended with neutral grain spirits or any other whiskey and aged in charred oak barrels for at least two years.

**SWIZZLE STICK**—A twig with a few forked branches on its end. It is usually inserted into the glass or pitcher and twirled rapidly between the hands. Used in cool drinks of lime, sugar, liquor, bitters, which are packed with shaved ice.

**TEQUILLA**—A distillate of the sap of the century plant. Sometimes called "Cactus Whiskey."

**TODDIES**—Served hot or cold. A lump or teaspoon of sugar dissolved in a little hot water, with liquor, ice or hot water added and stirred. Served with clove, nutmeg, cinnamon or lemon peel.

**TRIPLE SEC**—A cordial similar to Curacao but less sweet and colorless.

**VACUUM-DISTILLED GIN**—Distilled in glass-lined vacuum stills at low temperature, about 90°, to preserve the light, volatile flavors and aromas without the bitterness found in other gins.

**VODKA**—A refined and filtered liquor distilled at 190 proof and bottled for sale at 80 to 110 proof. Originally made in Russia from potatoes. It is usually distilled from corn and wheat in the United States. The differences between various vodkas depends on the types of grains used and the distilling and filtering processes. Most American vodkas are filtered through activated charcoal. Vodka is colorless, tasteless and odorless. It is not aged.

**WHISKEY**—Made from grains like corn, rye, barley, or wheat. It is distilled from a fermented mash of the grain, then aged in oak barrels. At this stage it is a water-colored liquid. During the aging period, it gradually attains its amber color, flavor and aroma. It is bottled and sold at 80 proof. Whiskey of each country is distinct from that of the others because of local grain characteristics, distillation techniques and formulas. Scotland, Ireland, U.S. and Canada are major producers.

**WINE**—Made from the fermented juice of grapes. If another fruit is used it appears on the label. Under 14 to 21 per cent.

**ZUBROVKA**—A Polish vodka in which European "buffalo" grass is steeped to give it a pale yellow color and a slight aroma.

# *POUSSE-CAFES*

Pousse-cafes appeal to the artist in every bartender; they are layered, colorful drinks made with liqueurs of different specific gravities.

Pour over the rounded surface of a teaspoon to spread each cordial or brandy slowly and evenly over the one below without mixing. Try inserting a glass stirring rod into the glass and then slowly pour each ingredient down the rod.

Pour all ingredients in exactly the order given in the recipe.

Following is a list of beautiful suggestions. Pour them into your pony glass *in the order* listed . . . or they will not quite float.

- GREEN CREME DE MENTHE, GALLIANO, BLACKBERRY LIQUEUR AND KIRSCHWASSER.
- CREME DE NOYAUX, ANISETTE, TUACA AND WHIPPED CREAM
- GRENADINE, WHITE CREME DE CACAO, TRIPLE SEC AND FORBIDDEN FRUIT.
- BANANA LIQUEUR, CHERRY HEERING AND COGNAC.
- PEACH LIQUEUR, KIRSCH AND PERNOD.

Each liqueur has a specific weight. The lighter ones float atop the heavier. So, the idea is to put the heaviest into the glass first, then the next lightest and so on. The following chart lists the weights of the most popular liqueurs used in Pousse-cafes.

| Liqueur | Weight |
|---|---|
| ANISETTE LIQUEUR red or white (50 Proof) | 17.8 |
| CREME de NOYAUX (50 Proof) | 17.7 |
| CREME de MENTHE green, white or gold (60 Proof) | 15.9 |
| CREME de BANANA (50 Proof) | 15.0 |
| CREME de CACAO brown or white (50 Proof) | 15.0 |
| GOLD LIQUEUR (50 Proof) | 15.0 |
| MARASCHINO LIQUEUR (50 Proof) | 14.9 |
| COFFEE LIQUEUR (50 Proof) | 14.2 |
| CHERRY LIQUEUR (48 Proof) | 12.7 |
| PARFAIT AMOUR (50 Proof) | 12.7 |
| BLUE CURACAO (60 Proof) | 11.7 |
| BLACKBERRY LIQUEUR (50 Proof) | 11.2 |
| APRICOT LIQUEUR (58 Proof) | 10.0 |
| DRY ORANGE CURACAO (60 Proof) | 9.8 |
| TRIPLE SEC (60 Proof) | 9.8 |
| COFFEE FLAVORED BRANDY (70 Proof) | 9.0 |
| LIQUEUR MONASTIQUE (78 Proof) | 7.9 |
| PEACH FLAVORED BRANDY (70 Proof) | 7.0 |
| CHERRY FLAVORED BRANDY (70 Proof) | 6.8 |
| BLACKBERRY FLAVORED BRANDY (70 Proof) | 6.7 |
| APRICOT FLAVORED BRANDY (70 Proof) | 6.6 |
| ROCK & RYE LIQUEUR (60 Proof) | 6.5 |
| GINGER FLAVORED BRANDY (70 Proof) | 6.4 |
| PEPPERMINT SCHNAPPS (60 Proof) | 5.2 |
| KUMMEL (78 Proof) | 4.2 |
| PEACH LIQUEUR (60 Proof) | 4.1 |
| SLOE GIN (60 Proof) | 4.0 |

## WINES

[illegible]

## AMERICAN WINES

[illegible] as cocktails, Sherry and Vermouth [illegible]

# WINES

Wine has been gaining a lot of popularity recently, and every bartender should have some knowledge of the basics of buying and serving wine.

The first thing you should know when looking for a wine is what *class* of wine you want. Most wines fit into one of five classes: appetizer, red, white, dessert, and sparkling.

Once you have determined the class of wine you want, the next step is to decide on the *generic type* of wine. Names like Burgundy and champagne were derived from the districts in which the wine was originally produced. As these wines became famous all over the world, the names came to be associated with any wine that was similar to the original, regardless of where it came from, These names are now the standard terms to describes types of wines.

A further distinction in wine selection is the *varietal type*. This refers to the name of the principal grape variety used in the wine. A Burgundy type wine can be made with many different combinations of grapes. Each combination will have the general characteristics of a Burgundy, but will have its own unique flavor. For examples, a *Gamay* wine is a Burgundy type wine made with California Gamay grapes. As you come to know wines, you will not only develop preferences for different generic types, but also different varietal types.

The following is a more extensive description of the classes of wines and listings of the characteristics of the more popular American types of wines.

## APPETIZER WINES

Served before meals or as cocktails. Sherry and Vermouth are most popular.

Sherry has a nutty flavor, comes in sweet medium or dry (In dry wines all or most of the sugar has fermented into alcholol.) and ranges in color from pale to dark amber. The alcohol content of Sherry is around 20 per cent. Sherry may be served chilled or not according to taste.

Vermouth is wine flavored with herbs. There are two types; dry (French) and sweet (Italian). Alcohol content is between 15 per cent and 20 per cent. Vermouth is usually "on the rocks."

## TABLE WINES (RED)

Usually dry and served with main-course red meat or dark fowl dishes. The two types, Burgundy and claret (claret is the English name for Bordeaux), usually have an alcohol content of 12 per cent. Serve at room temperature or below it. About one hour before serving, draw the cork from the bottle to allow the wine to "breathe."

A third type of red wine called Rose goes pleasantly with any food and should be served chilled.

## TABLE WINES (WHITE)

These run from extremely dry to sweet and are best with white meats, fowl and seafood. Serve chilled. The three types of white table wines, sauterne, Rhine and white Burgundy, have the same alcoholic content as red table wines.

French sauternes are white wines that are somewhat sweet. American sauternes are dry, medium and sweet. Sweet sauternes are best with desserts.

German white table wines range from sweet to dry. American Rhine wines are dry and light-bodied, pale gold in color.

American white Burgundy table wines are like the white Burgundy wines of France. They are less tart than the Rhine wines but have a fruity flavor and body.

## DESSERT WINES

Sweet, full-bodied wines served with desserts and as afternoon refreshments. Their alcoholic content is around 20 per cent. They come in port, white port, muscatel and Tokay types.

## SPARKLING WINES

The most popular types are champagne and sparkling Burgundy. They are both effervescent. Champagne ranges from completely dry (usually labeled "Brut"), semi-dry (labeled "Extra Dry," "Dry" or "Sec,") and sweet (usually labeled "Doux"). Served before dinner with or without appetizers; with almost any dinner entree; and with dessert. It comes in straw color, pink or red. Always serve chilled.

Sparkling Burgundy is red and somewhat dry. Serve chilled with red meats and game.

## *AMERICAN WINES*

Listed below are wines made in America which have over the years become popular. Professional bartenders report a growing preference for them over some European wines.

## RED TABLE WINES

BARBERA: Italian type. *Varietal.* California. Robust and fruity. Excellent with Italian food.

BURGUNDY: Burgundy type. *Generic.* California, Ohio, and New York. Serve with red meats, game or cheese.

CABERNET or CABERNET SAUVIGNON: Claret type. *Varietal.* California. Rich and fruity. Serve with red and white meats and fowl.

CHARBONO: Italian type. *Varietal.* California. Similar to Barbera. Fine with Italian meals.

CHIANTI: Italian type *Generic*. California and East. American brands are not made from the same grapes as Italian Chianti. Dry, fruity and slightly tart. Goes with Italian foods.

CLARET: Claret (Bordeaux) type. *Generic*. California. and New York. Soft and fruity. Goes with red meats and fowl.

GAMAY: Burgundy type. *Varietal*. California. Soft, fragrant. Serve with red meats and cheese.

GAMAY ROSE: Rose type *Varietal*. California. Light. Serve chilled with all foods.

GRENACHE ROSE: Rose type. *Varietal*. California. Fruity fragrance. Serve chilled with all foods.

GRIGNOLINO: Italian type. *Varietal*. California. Similar to Barbera but more tart. Serve with red meats and Italian food.

MOURESTAL: Claret type *Varietal*. California. Medium body, soft with fruity aroma. Serve with red meats or fowl.

PINOT NOIR: Burgundy type. *Varietal*. California. Full-bodied, robust. Serve with red meats, game or cheese.

ROSE: Rose type. California. Light and fruity. Serve chilled with any food.

ZINFANDEL: Claret type. *Varietal*. California. Light-bodied, tart, aromatic with a fruity bouquet. A luncheon or dinner wine.

## WHITE TABLE WINES

CHABLIS: White Burgundy type. *Generic*. California and New York. Light and fruity. Pale amber. Serve chilled with seafoods, white meats, and fowl.

DELWARE: Rhine wine type. *Varietal.* New York and Ohio. Fruity with a spicy bouquet. Serve chilled with seafood, fowl.

DUTCHESS: Rhine wine type. *Varietal.* New York. Very dry, light and slightly tart. Serve with seafood and fowl. Chill.

DRY SEMILLON: Sauterne type. *Varietal.* California. Fruity and medium full-bodied. A dinner wine for chicken, seafood and white meats. Chill.

FOLLE BLANCHE: White Burgundy type. *Varietal.* California. A dry and delicate wine. It is thin-bodied,, similar to a French Chablis. Serve with seafood and fowl. Chill.

GEWURZTRAMINER: Rhine or Alsatian type. *Varietal.* California. Aromatic with a spicy flavor. Serve chilled.

GREY RIESLING: Rhine wine type. *Varietal.* California. Soft, mild, and light in body. Serve chilled with seafood, fowl, and light entrees.

HAUTE SAUTERNE: Sauterne type. *Generic.* California, Ohio, New York. Sweet. A dessert wine.

JOHANNISBERG RIESLING: Rhine wine type. *Varietal.* California. Fragrant and fruity. Excellent with seafood and fowl. Serve chilled.

MOSELLE: Rhine wine type. *Generic.* California. Serve chilled with seafood and fowl.

PINOT BLANC: White Burgundy type. *Varietal.* California. Fragrant, lively and dry. Serve chilled with seafood and chicken.

PINOT CHARDONNAY: White Burgundy type. *Varietal.* California. Aromatic, rich body. Serve chilled with seafood and chicken.

RHINE: Rhine wine type. *Generic.* California. New York, and Ohio. Often made from table grapes. Serve with seafood and fowl.

RIESLING: Rhine wine type. *Generic.* California, New York, and Ohio. Dry, fresh and clean. Serve chilled with seafood and fowl.

SAUTERNE: Sauterne type *Generic.* California, Ohio, and New York. Varies from sweet to dry. Serve chilled.

SAUVIGNON BLANC: Sauterne type. *Varietal.* California. Fruity, extremely dry and full-bodied. Serve with almost any meal, but best with shellfish and fowl. There is also a semi-sweet Sauvignon Blanc which goes with chicken. The sweet goes with desserts. Serve chilled.

SWEET SEMILLON: Sauterne type *Varietal.* California. Rich, full-bodied, fairly sweet. Serve chilled with desserts. Excellent in punches and cups.

SYLVANER: Rhine wine type. *Varietal.* California. Light and a little tart. Goes well with seafood. Serve chilled.

TRAMINER: Rhine type. *Varietal.* California. A dry wine, fragrant and flowery in flavor. Serve chilled with chicken, seafoods, and veal.

WHITE PINOT: White Burgundy type. *Varietal.* California. Sometimes called Pinot Blanc. Made from the Chenin Blanc grape in California. Dry, light and fruity. Serve chilled with seafood, fowl, and light meats.

## WHITE WINES

**CALIFORNIA AND NEW YORK**
Chablis
Rhine Wine
Riesling

**NEW YORK**
Lake Delaware
Lake Dutchess
Lake Diana
Elvira
Iona

**CALIFORNIA**
Johannisberger Riesling
Sylvaner
Traminer
Folle Blanche
Sauvignon Blanc

**OHIO**
Lake Erie Island
Delaware

## SAUTERNES (DRY)

**CALIFORNIA AND NEW YORK**
Dry Sauterne

**OHIO**
Isle St. George

**CALIFORNIA**
Pinot Chardonay
Pinot Blanc
Dry Semillon
Chateau Beaulieu

## SAUTERNES (MED. SWEET—SWEET)

**CALIFORNIA AND NEW YORK**
Sauterne
Haut Sauterne

**CALIFORNIA**
Sweet Semillon

**NEW YORK**
Lake Niagara

## RED WINES

CALIFORNIA AND NEW YORK
Burgundy
Claret

NEW YORK
Lake Isabella

CALIFORNIA
Barbera
Charbono
Zinfandel
Pinot Noir
Gamay
Caberet

---

## CHAMPAGNES

NEW YORK
Gold Seal Brut
Vindemy Brut Special
Great Western Brut Special

CALIFORNIA
Almaden Brut
Korbel Brut

---

## THE MAJOR EUROPEAN WINE DISTRICTS

### FRANCE

| BURGUNDY | LOIRE | BORDEAUX |
|---|---|---|
| Chablis | Muscadet | Medoe |
| Cote de Nuits | Anjou | Pomerol |
| Cote de Beaune | Saumur | St. Emilion |
| Chalonnats | Bourqueil, Chinnon | Graves |
| Maconnais | Vouvray | Sauternes |
| Beaujolais | Pouilly-Fume | |
| | Sancerre | |

RHONES

| | | |
|---|---|---|
| Chateauneuf-du Pape | Cote Rotie<br>Hermitage | Travel |

### ITALY

| | | |
|---|---|---|
| Oxvieto-Est!Est!!Est!!! | Piedmont | Valpolicella |
| The Marches | Barolo | Emillia |
| Verdicchio | Lombardy | Lambrusco |
| Latium | Valtellina | Tuscany |
| Frascati | Veneto | Chientl |
| Campania | Soave Bardolino | Umbria |
| Lacryma Christi | | |

### GERMANY

| | | |
|---|---|---|
| Mosel, Saar | Rheingau | Rheinpfalz |
| Ruwer | Rheinhessen | Franconia |

### SWITZERLAND

| | | |
|---|---|---|
| Neuchatel | Vaud | Valais |
| | Ticino | |

## LIQUEURS (CORDIALS)

There are over a hundred cordials on the market of which many are the special concoctions of the manufacturers known only in their own locality.

Cordials may be divided into two general categories: fruit and plant. However, some seem to fall into both. A green chartreuse can contain up to 250 ingredients. Calisay, made in Spain, contains over 125 different herbs, plants and fruits.

A cordial is an artificial liquor or spirit made by either maceration or infusion. In maceration, fruits and plants are steeped in brandy, or rectified spirit, for about six to eight months. Then other ingredients are added. In infusion; the alcohol is mixed with juice of fresh crushed fruit, spiced and sweetened. Or the oils of various plants may be mixed with alcohol, diluted with water, sweetened with sugar. Cordials prepared by the maceration method are more highly regarded by experts.

APRICOT BRANDY (ABRICOTINE): A brandy made from small French apricots.

ABSINTHE: The classic original is scarce. Traditionally it contained wormwood, claimed to be a narcotic. Modern Absinthe, minus wormwood, comes under the trade names Herbsaint or Pernod, and both are popular flavoring agents.

ANISETTE: Compounded from anise-seed oil and the oil of bitter almonds, dissolved in strong spirits.

BENEDICTINE: Made of a variety of herbs and cognac brandy. Originated by a Benedictine monk in Fecamp, France, over 400 years ago. It is still made there.

CHARTREUSE, GREEN OR YELLOW: Made in Tarragona, Spain, today, but originated in France over 300 years ago. A secret recipe of the Carthusian fathers. The yellow contains 120 ingredients (110 proof). The green is made from 250 ingredients (110 proof).

CHERRY HEERING: Made in Copenhagen, Denmark, of cherries, spice, sugar, brandy.

COUINTREAU: Sweeter than white curacao and triple sec which are similar in flavor. Made from fine brandy, with orange peel as the principal base.

CREME DE CACAO: Made from cacao beans and brandy.

CREME DE CASSIS: Made from black currants, steeped in brandy and sweetened with syrup. Called an aperitif in France, a vermouth cassis is made with equal parts of creme de cassis, dry vermouth and sparkling spring water.

CREME DE MENTHE: Made of cognac and fresh peppermint leaves. It comes in white and green.

CREME DE NOYAU: A compound of brandy, bitter almonds, nutmeg, mace and the kernals of apricot or peach pits.

CREME DE ROSE: Made of aromatic seeds and brandy and sweetened with rose petals.

CREME YVETTE: Made the same way as creme de rose, with violet petals substituted for the rose petals. Aromatic.

CURACAO: Made of bitter green orange, mace, cloves and cinnamon and sweetened with wine brandy.

DRAMBUIE: Made from Scotch whisky and wild honey.

FALERNUM: Prepared from West Indian herbs, limes and rum. Alcoholic content only 6 per cent. Sweet flavored.

FLOR ALPINA: Italian. Comes in a tall bottle containing a stalk of the tree, crystalline with a heavy encrüstation of sugar. Sweet flavored.

FRAISETTE: Made of alcoholic syrup, white wine and strawberries.

FRAMBOISE: Made from raspberries, it has a high alcohol content.

GOLDWASSER: It's French name is Eau de Vie de Cantzig. It's German name is Danzig Goldwasser. The French is a distillation of fruit peels, herbs and spices with an alcohol base. The German has a caraway-seed flavor. Both have flecks of gold-leaf added. Reputed to be the oldest cordial made. It was first produced in Italy.

GRAND MARNIER: Composed of white curacao and fine champagne.

KUMMEL: Flavored with caraway and cumin seeds. Supposed to have originated in Russia but popular in Germany. Kummel means caraway seed in German.

MARASCHINO: Made with sour cherries and honey. It is white in color and is used as a flavoring agent. It bears no relationship to the popular red maraschino cherries.

PARFAIT AMOUR: Highly perfumed and very sweet made of citron, cinnamon, coriander and brandy.

PRUNELLE: Made from small Burgundian prunes and brandy.

SLIVOVITZ: Made from plums, fermented and distilled. High proof.

STREGA: Italian. Made of orange peel, spices and strong spirits. Very sweet.

SUZE LIQUEUR: Compounded from gentian, a bitter-flavored root supposed to have some medicinal qualities. In the final blending, the bitterness disappears, but the pleasant gentian flavor remains.

---

# RESPONSIBLE DRINKING

Two-thirds of all Americans drink alcoholic beverages. Most of these people do not misuse alcohol.

But 9 million men and women are abusers.

It is unclear whether the reader of this brief article is likely to have a drinking problem; regardless, precaution taken by each and every drinker is a healthy measure.

Drinking patterns vary among people, and abuse must be judged in terms of the individual; however it can generally be stated that:

Drinking becomes a problem when it is associated repeatedly with psychological, physical, or social difficulties.

Without elaborating the long term effects that heavy drinking will have on the body, it should be known that like any other drug, addiction is a potential hazard. Also, an excess of alcohol will effect organs such as the brain, the heart, the liver.

Behavior patterns may be warning signs of misuse. If the day is frequently begun with a drink, if a drink is needed to perform at work, if friends or relatives complain about drinking, or if unusual events (such as memory losses or reckless behavior) occur while drinking, it may be time to seek professional advice.

## WHAT CAN I, AS A BARTENDER, DO TO FOSTER RESPONSIBLE DRINKING?

1. Provide food with drinks, such as dairy products, fish, and meats.
2. Do not push loaded drinks onto your guests; do not insist on refilling a cocktail.
3. Offer non-alcoholic substitutes, such as fruit, vegetable, or soft drinks as attractive alternatives.
4. Do not arrange parties just for drinking; have plenty of other activities planned.

**DRIVING:** The risks of driving while intoxicated are demonstrated by statistics: many fatal road accidents are caused by drunk drivers.

The state limit is a blood alcohol concentration of 0.10%. This represents about two drinks taken within an hour by a man of 150 pounds.

The following chart is a useful barometer of drinking. One drink is equal to about 1.5 oz. of whisky, 5 oz. of wine or 2 bottles of beer. The shaded area indicated the range beyond the legal limit, when the pleasurable (innocuous) effects of alcohol yield to serious impairments of judgment and behavior.

Note that for each hour after drinking has stopped, .015 can be subtracted from the blood concentration, as this is the rate of elimination.

| | DRINKS | | | | | |
|---|---|---|---|---|---|---|
| Body Weight | 1 | 2 | 3 | 4 | 5 | 6 |
| 100 lbs. | .038 | .075 | .113 | .150 | .188 | .225 |
| 120 " | .031 | .063 | .094 | .125 | .156 | .188 |
| 140 " | .027 | .054 | .080 | .107 | .134 | .161 |
| 160 " | .023 | .047 | .070 | .094 | .117 | .141 |
| 180 " | .021 | .042 | .063 | .083 | .104 | .124 |
| 200 " | .019 | .038 | .056 | .075 | .094 | .113 |
| 220 " | .017 | .034 | .051 | .068 | .085 | .102 |
| 240 " | .016 | .031 | .047 | .063 | .078 | .094 |

# RECIPES

# A-Z

Use a bartender's mixing glass whenever the instructions state "combine" ingredients. Strain the drink from the mixing glass into the drinking glass suggested by the illustration alongside the ingredients.

NOTE: The number of glasses or cups shown alongside a recipe do not necessarily indicate the quantity of drinks the recipe will produce.

---

## A-1 PICK-ME-UP

1 pint dark rum
1 lb. rock candy
1 doz. eggs
1 doz. lemons

*Squeeze the juice of the lemons into a crock pot; add the eggs broken in their shells. Cover with a damp cloth and allow to stand for several days. (The shells will dissolve.) When ready strain through cheesecloth into another pot. Combine the rum and the rock candy in a saucepan; boil with a quart of water until smooth. Combine with the egg mixture and bottle for future use.*

## A.J.

1½ oz. apple brandy
1½ oz. unsweetened grapefruit juice
A few drops grenadine

*Combine with ice; shake well. Strain and add ice.*

## ABBEY

1½ oz. gin
1½ oz. orange juice
1-2 dashes orange bitters

*Combine with ice; shake. Strain over ice, top with a cherry.*

## ABBEY COCKTAIL

1½ oz. gin
¾ oz. orange juice
¼ oz. sweet vermouth
1-2 dashes of Angostura bitters

*Combine with ice; shake. Strain, add ice, top with a cherry.*

**ABERDEEN ANGUS**

2 oz. Scotch
1 oz. Drambuie
1 tbs. honey
2 tsp. lime juice

*Combine the Scotch and the honey; stir until smooth. Add the lime juice. Warm the Drambuie over a low flame, turn out on a ladle; ignite and pour into the mug. Stir and serve immediately.*

**ABSINTHE SUISSESSE**

1½ oz. absinthe substitute
1 egg white
Several drops of anisette, white creme de menthe
A few drops of orange flower water

*Combine with ice; shake well. Strain straight up.*

**ACADIAN MEAD**

2 quarts honey
12 oz. boiling water

*Dissolve the honey with the water in a crock pot; allow to ferment before bottling and sealing.*

**ACAPULCO**

1¾ oz. rum
¼ oz. Triple Sec
1 egg white
½ oz. lime juice
Sugar to taste
Mint leaves

*Combine with ice; shake into pre-chilled glass. Strain. Add ice and top with one or two mint leaves, partially torn.*

**ADAM AND EVE**

1 oz. gin
1 oz. cognac
1 oz. Forbidden Fruit
A few drops lemon juice

*Combine with ice; shake. Strain over ice.*

**ADDINGTON**

1½ oz. sweet vermouth
1½ oz. dry vermouth
Club soda

*Combine everything (except the soda) with ice and shake. Strain; add ice and soda. Add a twist of lemon, plus the peel.*

**ADMIRAL COCKTAIL**

1 oz. bourbon
1½ oz. dry vermouth
½ lemon

*Combine with ice; shake. Strain. Squeeze in the lemon's juice, stir, and drop in the peel. Add ice.*

## ADONIS

2 oz. dry sherry
1 oz. sweet vermouth
1-2 dashes orange bitters

*Combine with ice; shake. Strain over ice.*

## AFFINITY

¾ oz. Scotch
¾ oz. sweet vermouth
¾ oz. dry vermouth
A few dashes of Angostura bitters

*Combine with ice; shake. Strain. Add ice, and a twist of lemon plus peel, and top with a cherry.*

*For an* **AFFINITY COCKTAIL** *use ¾ oz. dry sherry and ¾ oz. port instead of vermouth.*

## AFTER DINNER

1½ oz. apricot brandy
1½ oz. curacao
2 oz. lime juice

*Combine with ice; shake. Strain. Add a twist of lime and ice. Drop in the peel.*

## AFTER DINNER SPECIAL

¾ oz. cherry brandy
1½ oz. Swedish Punch
1 oz. lime juice

*Combine with ice; shake. Strain over ice.*

## AIRMAIL SPECIAL

*Follow the recipe for an* **AMERICAN FLYER,** *substituting a teaspoon of honey for the sugar. Shake extra well.*

## AL LONG'S SPECIAL HOT TODDY

2 oz. Drambuie
2 oz. Scotch
1 oz. raspberry syrup
1 tbs. lime juice
3 oz. water

*Combine in a saucepan. Bring to a boil. Serve hot.*

## ALABAMA

¾ oz. brandy
¾ oz. curacao
1 oz. lime juice
½ tsp. sugar

*Combine with ice; shake. Strain. Add ice, and a twist of orange. Drop in the peel.*

## ALABAZAM

2 oz. cognac
2 tsp. sugar syrup
1 tbs. curacao
1 tsp. lemon juice
1-2 dashes orange bitters

*Combine with ice; shake well. Strain and add ice.*

## ALASKA

1½ oz. gin
¾ oz. yellow chartreuse
1-2 dashes orange bitters

*Combine with ice; shake very well. Strain over ice.*

## ALBERMARLE FIZZ

2 oz. dry gin
½ lemon
1 tsp. sugar
1 tsp. raspberry syrup
Club soda
Sugar

*Over three cubes of ice, add gin, squeeze in the juice of the lemon. Add sugar and the raspberry syrup and stir well. Fill glass with club soda.*

## ALE FLIP

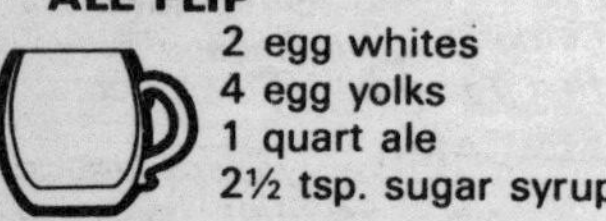

2 egg whites
4 egg yolks
1 quart ale
2½ tsp. sugar syrup

*Beat the egg whites until creamy; beat the egg yolks, and combine the two, adding the sugar syrup. Pour the ale into a saucepan and bring to a boil. Gradually add the egg mixture to the boiling ale, stirring it constantly. Remove from heat and transfer between two pitchers vigorously to build a frothy head. Balance out the brew between the pitchers, dust with nutmeg, and serve steaming hot.*

## ALE SANGAREE

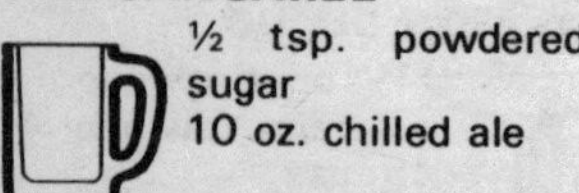

½ tsp. powdered sugar
10 oz. chilled ale

*Dissolve the sugar in with a few drops of water. Add the ale and dust with nutmeg.*

## ALEXANDER WITH PRUNELLE

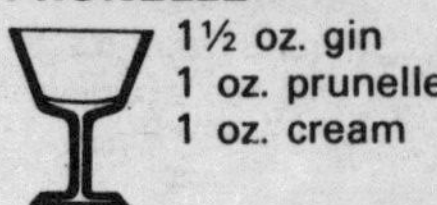

1½ oz. gin
1 oz. prunelle
1 oz. cream

*Combine with ice; shake well. Strain, and dust with cinnamon.*

## ALEXANDER YOUNG

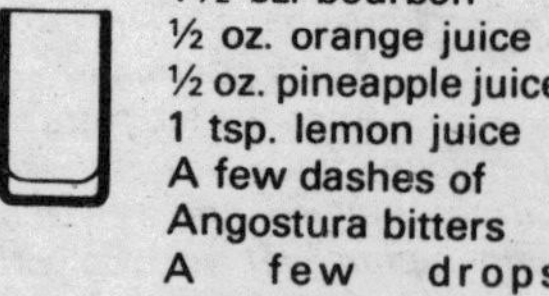

1½ oz. bourbon
½ oz. orange juice
½ oz. pineapple juice
1 tsp. lemon juice
A few dashes of Angostura bitters
A few drops grenadine

*Combine with ice; shake well. Strain over crushed ice.*

## ALFONSO SPECIAL

¾ oz. dry gin
1½ oz. Grand Marnier
A few drops sweet vermouth and dry vermouth
A few dashes of Angostura bitters

*Combine with ice; shake. Strain and add ice.*

## ALGONQUIN

2 oz. rye
1 oz. dry vermouth
1 oz. pineapple juice

*Combine with ice; shake. Strain and add ice.*

**ALL-WHITE FRAPPE**

1 oz. anisette
1 oz. white creme de cacao
½ oz. white creme de menthe
1 oz. lemon juice

*Combine with ice; shake well. Strain over crushed ice.*

**ALLEN**

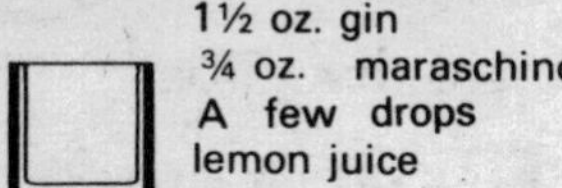

1½ oz. gin
¾ oz. maraschino
A few drops lemon juice

*Combine with ice, shake well. Strain and add ice.*

**ALLIES**

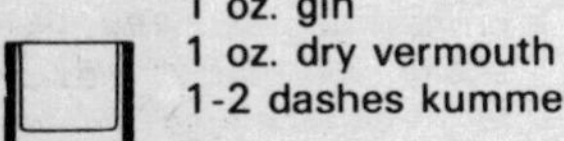

1 oz. gin
1 oz. dry vermouth
1-2 dashes kummel

*Combine with ice; shake well. Strain and add ice.*
*For a* **BERLINER**, *increase the gin, halve the vermouth, and add ¼ oz. of lemon juice.*

**ALMOND COCKTAIL**

2 oz. gin
1 oz. dry vermouth
A pair of almonds, peeled
A crushed peach kernel
½ tsp. powdered sugar
1 tsp. kirsch
1 tsp. peach brandy

*Warm the gin; add the almonds, sugar, and kernel. Allow to cool; add the remaining ingredients and stir. Strain and add ice.*

**AMABILE BEONE**

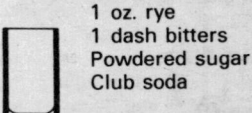

1 oz. Drambuie
2 oz. green creme de menthe
A few drops Pernod
Sugar

*Combine with ice; shake well. Strain. "Sugar Frost" glass. Coat the rim with Pernod, and dip it in sugar.*

**AMARANTH**

1 oz. rye
1 dash bitters
Powdered sugar
Club soda

*Combine the rye, any kind of bitters, and a dash of powdered sugar in a glass. Stir well. Add ice and fill with club soda.*

**AMBASSADOR**

2 oz. tequila
Orange juice

*Pour the tequila into glass, add ice and orange juice. Add 1 oz. of sugar syrup to sweeten.*

**AMBER CLOUD**

1½ oz. cognac
2 tbs. Galliano

*Combine with ice; shake well. Pour over crushed ice.*

**AMBROSIA FOR TWO**

3 oz. brandy
3 oz. apple brandy
Several drops of raspberry syrup
Champagne

*Combine the brandies and the syrup with ice; shake. Strain into two pre-chilled wine glasses. Fill each glass with champagne and stir.*

**AMER PICON COOLER**

1½ oz. Amer Picon
1 oz. gin
½ oz. cherry liqueur
1 tsp. sugar syrup
1 tsp. lemon juice
Club soda

*Combine with ice; shake well. Strain. Add ice and club soda.*

**AMERICAN BEAUTY**

¾ oz. brandy
¾ oz. dry vermouth
¾ oz. orange juice
¼ oz. white creme de menthe
1 oz. port
A few drops grenadine

*Combine with ice; shake well. Strain. Carefully add port, tipping the glass so that the port floats on top.*

**AMERICAN FLYER**

1½ oz. Bacardi
1½ tsp. lime juice
A pinch sugar
Champagne

*Combine the rum, juice and sugar with ice; shake. Strain; fill the glass with champagne.*

**AMERICAN LEGION MARGUERITA**

2 oz. tequila
1 oz. Cointreau
½ oz. lemon juice
½ oz. lime juice
Salt

*Combine with ice; shake well. Moisten serving glass rim with water and frost with salt. Strain.*

**AMERICAN ROSE**

1½ oz. brandy
1 tsp. grenadine
½ ripe peach, skinned and masked
A few drops Pernod
Champagne

*Combine the brandy, Pernod, grenadine, ice and peach; shake extremely well. Fill large glass with crushed ice and strain in the drink. Add the champagne.*

**AMERICANA**

¼ oz. 100-proof bourbon
½ tsp. sugar
1-2 dashes bitters
Champagne
I peach slice

*Combine the bourbon, bitters and sugar. Stir until the sugar is dissolved. Add champagne and a slice of peach.*

**AMERICANO**

1¼ oz. Campari
1¼ oz. sweet vermouth
Club soda

*Combine everything except the soda with ice. Strain, add ice and fill with club soda.*

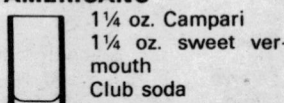

## AMONTILLADO COCKTAIL

1 oz. Amontillado
1 oz. Dubonnet

*Combine in a wide champagne glass; stir gently. Touch it up with a twist of lemon and add ice.*

## ANCHORS AWEIGH

1 oz. bourbon
2 tbs. heavy cream
2 tsp. apiece Triple Sec, peach brandy and maraschino
A few drops cherry juice

*Combine with ice; shake well. Strain and serve straight up.*

## ANDALUSIA

1½ oz. dry sherry
½ oz. cognac
½ oz. white rum
A few dashes of Angostura bitters

*Combine with ice; shake well. Strain and add ice.*

## ANDALUSIAN WINE

1 pint red wine
1 pint water
Sugar to taste
Lemon slices

*Combine in a pitcher; fill with ice.*

## ANGEL FACE

1 oz. dry gin
1 oz. apricot brandy
1 oz. apple brandy

*Combine with ice; shake well. Strain and add ice.*

## ANGEL'S DELIGHT

¼ oz. grenadine
¼ oz. Triple Sec
¼ oz. Creme Yvette
¼ oz. cream

*Carefully add in above order, tipping glass so ingredients float on top of each other.*

## ANGEL'S RUM PUNCH

1 bottle Jamaican rum
1 quart milk
1 tsp. honey

*Combine; stir gently to dissolve the honey. Serve with ice; stir a few times to frost the glass before drinking.*

## ANGEL'S TIP

1 oz. dark creme de cacao
½ oz. heavy cream

*Pour the creme de cacao into a pony glass, tip it and carefully add the cream, floating it on top.*
*For a* **KING ALPHONSE** *spear a maraschino cherry and bridge it over serving glass.*

## ANGEL'S WINGS

½ oz. creme de violette
½ oz. raspberry syrup
½ oz. maraschino

*Pour each ingredient as shown, tipping glass so that the ingredients do not mix but float on top of each other.*

### ANGELICA RATAFIA

4 small bunches angelica stalks, with leaves
1 tbs. whole angelica seeds
Nutmeg, ground cinnamon, crushed cloves
4 lbs. sugar

*Pound the angelica stalks and leaves on the bottom of a crock pot; add the seeds and spices and store in a cool place for two months. Strain. Boil the sugar in enough water to make a syrup; combine with the spiced angelica; stir well and re-strain; bottle for future use.*

---

### ANGLER'S COCKTAIL

1½ oz. dry gin
A few drops of grenadine
1-2 dashes Angostura bitters
1-2 dashes orange bitters

*Combine with ice; shake. Strain. Add ice if desired.*

### ANISE VODKA

1 pint vodka
2 oz. whole anise seeds
2 oz. rock candy

*Combine in a large bottle; seal tightly and allow to stand at room temperature for at least one week. Strain clean and re-bottle for future use.*

### ANKLE BREAKER

1½ oz. cherry brandy
1 oz. lime juice
1 oz. 151-proof rum
2 tsp. sugar syrup

*Combine with ice, shake well. Strain over ice.*

### ANNE

1½ oz. apple brandy
¾ oz. Cointreau
¾ oz. Dubonnet
1-2 dashes Angostura bitters

*Combine without ice; stir until well-blended. Pour over ice, decorate with one red and one green cherry, a slice of orange and a slice of lime.*

---

### ANISETTE DE BORDEAUX

7 oz. whole, green anise seeds
3 oz. star anise seeds
1½ oz. fine tea
1 tbs. apiece ground coriander and fennel
10 pints sugar
3½ gallons cooking alcohol

*Pound the anise seeds into a powder; combine with the remaining spices and steep in the alcohol for two weeks. Strain. Boil the sugar in enough water to make a thick syrup; mix with anisette. Bottle and store in a cool place until fermented. Strain and re-bottle for future use.*

## ANNIVERSARY PUNCH

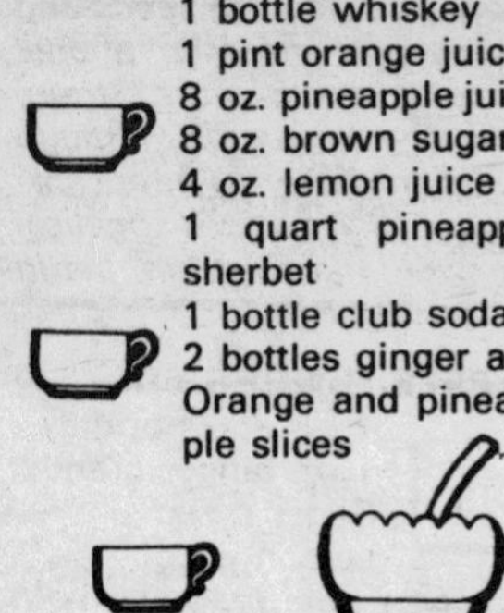

1 bottle whiskey
1 pint orange juice
8 oz. pineapple juice
8 oz. brown sugar
4 oz. lemon juice
1 quart pineapple sherbet
1 bottle club soda
2 bottles ginger ale
Orange and pineapple slices

*Combine everything except the sherbet, sodas and garnishes; stir well. Before serving, add the ginger ale and soda. Use the sherbet instead of ice; garnish with cherries.*

## APPENDECTOMY

6 oz. gin
1½ oz. lime juice
¾ oz. Grand Marnier
1 egg white

*Combine with ice; shake exhremely well. Serves two. Strain into a goblet or split in two old-fashioned glasses over ice.*

## APPENDICITIS

12 oz. gin
3 oz. lemon juice
1½ oz. curacao
1 whole egg

*Combine with ice; shake extremely well. Serves four.*

## APPLE BLOW

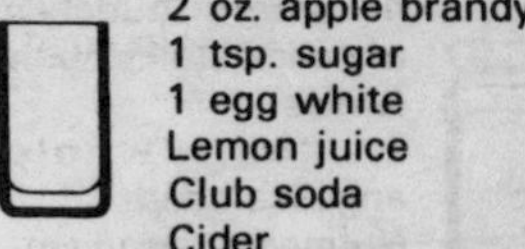

2 oz. apple brandy
1 tsp. sugar
1 egg white
Lemon juice
Club soda
Cider

*In a mixing glass filled with ice, combine the apple brandy, sugar, egg white and several drops of lemon juice. Shake well. Strain over ice into a glass and fill with half soda and half cider.*
*For an* **APPLE BLOW FIZZ,** omit the cider and fill the glass entirely with soda.

## APPLE BRANDY COCKTAIL

1½ oz. apple brandy
½ tsp. grenadine
½ tsp. lemon juice

*Combine with ice; shake well. Strain and add ice.*
*For an* **APPLE BRANDY SOUR**, *increase the brandy, eliminate the grenadine and strain straight up.*

## APPLE BRANDY COOLER

2 oz. brandy
1 oz. white rum
1 tsp. lime juice
Apple juice
1 tsp. Jamaican rum

*Combine the brandy, rum and lime juice with ice, then almost fill the glass with apple juice and stir well. Float the Jamaican rum on top. Top with a slice of lime.*

**APPLE BRANDY HIGHBALL**

2 oz. apple brandy
Ginger ale

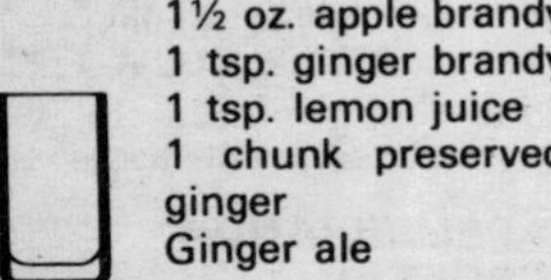

*Pour the apple brandy over ice. Add ginger ale and a twist of lemon. Stir well.*

**APPLE BUCK**

1½ oz. apple brandy
1 tsp. ginger brandy
1 tsp. lemon juice
1 chunk preserved ginger
Ginger ale

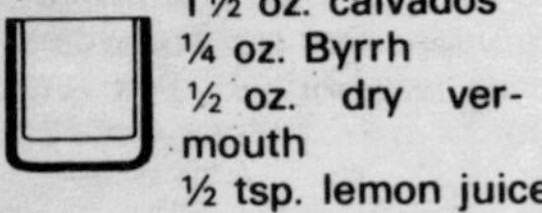

*With ice, combine the apple brandy, ginger brandy and lemon juice; shake well. Strain over ice, fill with ginger ale. Top with the preserved ginger.*

**APPLE BYRRH**

1½ oz. calvados
¼ oz. Byrrh
½ oz. dry vermouth
½ tsp. lemon juice

*Combine with ice; shake well. Strain. Add ice and a twist of lemon, plus the peel.*

**APPLE COCKTAIL**

2 oz. brandy
1 oz. apple brandy

*Combine with ice; shake well. Strain and add ice.*

**APPLE DUBONNET**

1½ oz. calvados
1½ oz. Dubonnet

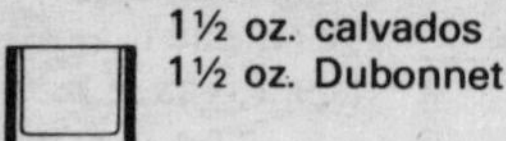

*Combine with ice; shake well. Strain, add ice and top with a slice of lemon.*

**APPLE GINGER FIX**

1 oz. apple brandy
1 oz. ginger brandy
Sugar syrup
Lemon juice

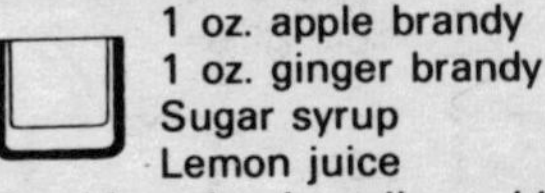

*Combine the brandies with ice. Add several drops of sugar syrup and a teaspoon of lemon juice; shake well. Strain over crushed ice. Top with a slice of lemon.*

**APPLE GINGER SANGAREE**

1½ oz. apple brandy
½ oz. green ginger wine

*Combine with ice; shake well. Strain, add ice and decorate with an orange slice.*

**APPLE KNOCKER**

2½ oz. apple brandy
3 oz. orange juice
½ oz. sweet vermouth
1 tsp. lemon juice
1½ tsp. sugar syrup

*Combine with ice; shake well. Strain with crushed ice.*

## APPLE LILLET

1½ oz. calvados
1½ oz. Lillet

*Combine with ice; shake well. Strain, add ice, and top with an orange slice.*

## APPLE RUM RICKEY

¾ oz. apple brandy
¾ oz. white rum
Club soda

*Combine the rum and the brandy with ice; shake well. Strain over ice into a glass and fill with club soda. Add a twist of orange and lime; stir and drop the peels into the drink.*

## APPLE SMILE

1½ oz. gin
1 tbs. apple brandy
2 tsp. lime juice
A few drops grenadine

*Combine with ice; shake well. Strain and add ice.*

## APPLE SWIZZLE

1½ oz. apple brandy
1 oz. white rum
1 tsp. lime juice
1 tsp. powdered sugar
A few dashes of Angostura bitters

*Combine with ice; shake well. Strain over crushed ice.*

---

## APPLE WINE

4 lbs. apples
1½ lbs. sugar

*Slice the apples in their skins; place them in a large pot and add 1 gal. of water which has been boiled clean and cooled. Store at room temperature for at least a week, stirring every day. Strain the juice a bit and allow to stand until the sugar dissolves naturally. Pour off into bottles; seal and allow to ferment for a week to ten days.*

---

## APPLE STRAWBERRY CORDIAL

1 dozen apples
½ peck strawberries
1 lb. brown sugar
Whiskey
Allspice, nutmeg, mace

*Peel and core the apples. Simmer them in a pint of water for several minutes; add the spices and simmer twice as long. Add the strawberries and the sugar, plus approximately five more cups of water and simmer several more minutes. Allow to cool; strain and double the amount of liquid with whiskey. Bottle for future use.*

**APPLECAR**

¾ oz. apple brandy
¾ oz. curacao
1 tbs. lemon juice

*Combine with ice; shake well. Strain and add ice. Cointreau can be used instead of curacao.*

**APPLEHAWK**

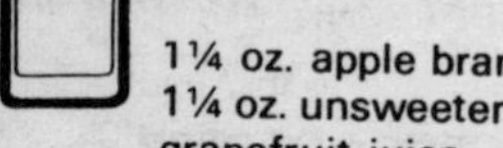

1¼ oz. apple brandy
1¼ oz. unsweetened grapefruit juice
½ tsp. sugar syrup

*Combine with ice; shake well. Strain and add ice.*

---

**APPLEJACK NO. 1**

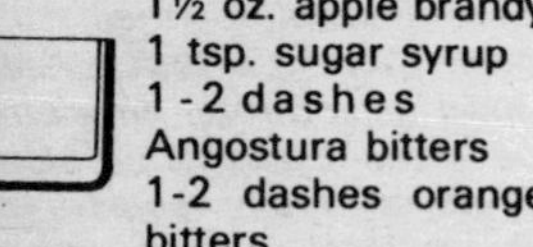

1½ oz. apple brandy
1 tsp. sugar syrup
1-2 dashes Angostura bitters
1-2 dashes orange bitters

*Combine the brandy and the sugar syrup with ice. Add bitters; shake well. Strain and add ice.*

**APPLEJACK NO. 2**

Substitute ½ oz. sweet vermouth for the sugar syrup.

**APPLEJACK ALGONQUIN**

1½ oz. apple brandy
1 tsp. baked apple
1 cube sugar
Nutmeg

*In a glass, combine apple brandy and the baked apple. Drop in the sugar; fill with hot water and stir well. Garnish with nutmeg.*

**APPLEJACK COCKTAIL**

2 oz. apple brandy
¼ oz. curacao
1 tsp. powdered sugar
1½ tbs. lime juice

*Combine with ice; shake well. Strain over crushed ice.*

**APPLEJACK PUNCH**

2 bottles apple juice
1 bottle ginger ale
1 bottle vodka
1 pint orange juice
Mint sprigs

*Combine everything except the mint and ginger ale in a large punch bowl; stir well. Add the ginger ale plus chunks of ice. Decorate with mint.*

**APPLEJACK RABBIT**

1½ oz. apple brandy
½ oz. lemon juice
½ oz. lime juice
½ tsp. maple syrup

*Combine with ice; shake very well. Dip glass rim in water or maple syrup and line with sugar. Strain in the drink and add ice.*

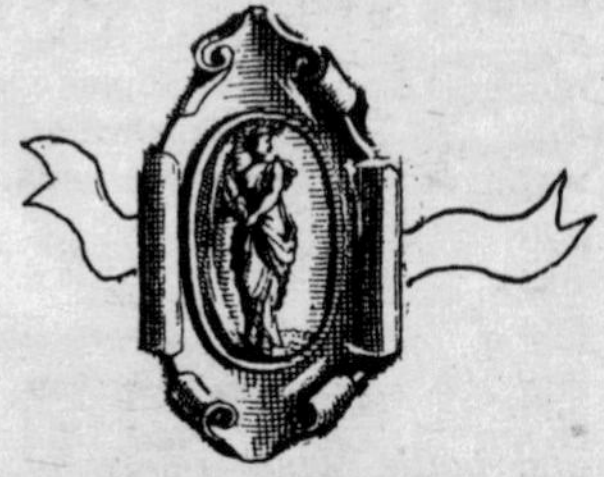

## APPLEJACK SOUR

2 oz. apple brandy
½ oz. lemon juice
1½ tsp. sugar syrup

*Combine with ice; shake well. Strain into a sour glass and serve straight up or in an old-fashioned glass over ice.*

*For a* **SOUR RED APPLE-JACK,** *add a few drops of grenadine and a few drops of lime juice, halving the sugar.*

## APRICOT ANISE FIZZ

1 ¾ oz. gin
½ oz. apricot brandy
¼ oz. anisette
1 tsp. lemon juice
Club soda
½ apricot

*Combine with ice; shake well. Strain and add ice. Almost fill with club soda. Add a twist of lemon, drop in the peel and stir. Add the apricot.*

## APRICOT BRANDY

1 lb. apricots
1 lb. sugar
4 oz. brandy

*Boil the apricots whole in enough water to cover them; lower heat and simmer until tender. Remove the skins. Boil the sugar in enough water to make a syrup and pour it over the apricots. Allow to stand for at least a day. Pour out into a jug or large bottle; add the brandy, seal and store a year. Strain and bottle when ready for future use.*

## APRICOT BRANDY

2 oz. apricot brandy
Several drops grenadine
Club soda

*Pour the apricot brandy into glass. Add the grenadine and ice; stir well. Fill with club soda. Twist in a lemon and an orange peel. Top with fruit slices.*

## APRICOT COOLER

1¼ oz. apricot brandy
¾ oz. lemon juice
1 tbs. sugar syrup
1 peeled, pitted apricot

*Cook and cool the apricot. Mash well and put in a mixing glass filled with ice, along with the apricot brandy, the lemon juice and the sugar syrup. Shake extremely well. Pour unstrained into glass and serve with a straw.*

---

## APRICOT FIZZ

2 oz. apricot brandy
1 tsp. lemon juice
1 tsp. powdered sugar
Club soda

*Combine brandy, juice and sugar with ice; shake well. Strain, add ice and fill with club soda. Top with fruit slices.*

**APRICOT LADY**

1 oz. apricot brandy
1½ oz. white rum
½ tsp. curacao
1 tsp. lime juice
1 egg white

*Combine in an ice-filled mixing glass; shake very well. Strain over crushed ice. Top with an orange slice.*

**APRICOT NO. 1**

2 oz. apricot brandy
1 oz. orange juice
1 oz. lemon juice
A few drops gin

*Combine with ice, shake well. Strain and add ice.*

**APRICOT NOG**

4 oz. white rum
4 oz. heavy cream
4 oz. apricot nectar
2 oz. apricot brandy
1 egg, well beaten
4 oz. crushed ice

*Combine in blender at a high speed until smooth. Serve garnished with nutmeg.*

**APRICOT PIE**

1 oz. white rum
1 oz. sweet vermouth
¼ oz. apricot brandy
½ tsp. lemon juice
Several drops grenadine

*Combine in a mixing glass filled with ice; shake well. Strain, add ice and twist in an orange peel.*

**APRICOT VODKA**

1 lb. apricots, peeled and pitted
3 cups cooking alcohol
2 cups sugar
Grated lemon rinds

*Boil the sugar in enough water to make a syrup; add the apricots and simmer for several minutes. Strain and allow to cool. Add the alcohol, 2 cups of water and the rinds; pour off into a bottle and store for at least a month. Strain and re-bottle for future use when ready.*

**AQUAVIT FIZZ**

5 oz. aquavit
1 oz. Cherry Heering
2 tbs. sugar syrup
1 oz. lemon juice
1 egg white
Club soda

*Combine (except soda) with ice; shake well. Strain and fill with club soda. Serves two.*

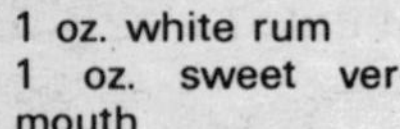

**AQUAVIT RICKEY**

1½ oz. aquavit
1 tsp. kummel
Club soda

*Combine aquavit and kummel in a highball glass, add ice and fill with club soda. Squeeze a slice of lime into the drink, drop in the peel and stir well.*

## AQUEDUCT

1½ oz. vodka
¼ oz. curacao
¼ oz. apricot liqueur
1 tsp. lime juice

*Combine with ice; shake well. Strain, add ice and a twist of orange.*

## ARCHBISHOP PUNCH

1 bottle claret
1 large orange
6 cloves
Sugar

*Stick the cloves into the orange and bake in a medium-hot oven (300°). When the orange browns, remove it, quarter it, take out the seeds and place it in a saucepan. Pour in the bottle of claret, and a tablespoon of sugar; simmer until steaming. Serve hot.*

*For a* **BRANDY BISHOP** *pour ⅛ oz. of Brandy into each mug when serving.*

---

## ARGENTINE JULEP

1 oz. brandy
1 oz. light claret
1 oz. orange juice
1 oz. pineapple juice
¼ oz. Cointreau
A mint sprig

*Combine (except mint) with ice. Add sugar; shake well. Strain over crushed ice. Top with an orange slice and a mint sprig.*

## ARRACK PUNCH

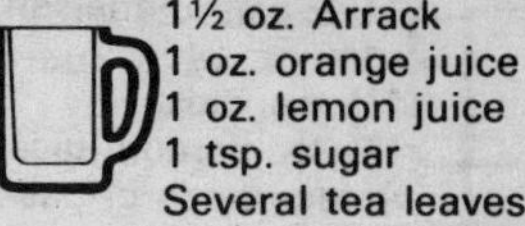

1½ oz. Arrack
1 oz. orange juice
1 oz. lemon juice
1 tsp. sugar
Several tea leaves

*Combine the Arrack, juices and sugar in a large mug. Add boiling water; infuse with dark tea several minutes. Stir well. Decorate with pineapple slice.*

## ARTILLERY

2 oz. gin
¾ oz. sweet vermouth
A few dashes of Angostura bitters

*Combine with ice; shake well. Strain, add ice and twist in a lemon peel.*

## ARTILLERY PUNCH

1 gallon hard cider
1 bottle bourbon
1 bottle dark rum
1 quart orange juice
1 quart strawberries
6 large pineapples
1 dozen bottles champagne

*Slice the pineapple; cut out all the meat. Squeeze and save all the juice. Slice and squeeze the strawberries; combine the juice with the pineapple and orange juice in a large punch bowl. Add the rum, whiskey and cider; stir well and allow to stand overnight. Add the champagne plus ice when ready to serve.*

**ASTRONAUT**

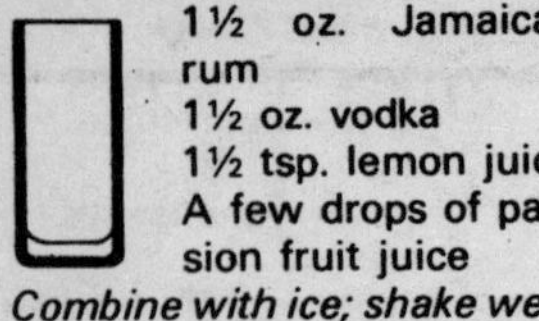

1½ oz. Jamaican rum
1½ oz. vodka
1½ tsp. lemon juice
A few drops of passion fruit juice

*Combine with ice; shake well. Strain and add ice. Touch it up with lemon and drop in the peel.*

**AUNT AGATHA**

2 oz. white rum
4 oz. orange juice
1 dash Angostura bitters

*Pour the rum and the orange juice into a wide glass. Stir gently and then drop in a few cubes of ice. Float the Angostura bitters on top.*

---

**AUNT BETSY'S FAVORITE**

1 bottle dry red wine
2 cups dark port
1 cup brandy
4 tsp. sugar
Peels of two oranges
6 cloves
12 cinnamon sticks

*Combine the wines and brandy in a saucepan. Add the sugar, peels, cloves and cinnamon sticks. Heat slowly and do not bring to a boil. Serves 10-12.*

**AUNT JEMIMA**

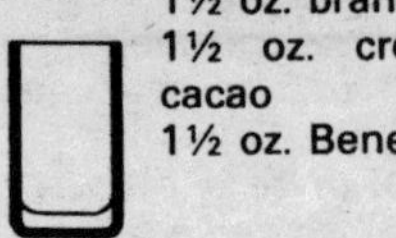

1½ oz. brandy
1½ oz. creme de cacao
1½ oz. Benedictine

*Combine, carefully tilting the glass so that each ingredient floats upon the other.*

**AVIATION**

2 oz. gin
½ oz. lemon juice
¼ oz. maraschino

*Combine with ice; shake very well. Strain and add ice.*

**AZTEC PUNCH**

5 gallons grapefruit juice
1 gallon tequila
3 cups lemon juice
1 cup sugar syrup
2 quarts dark tea

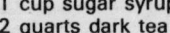

*Combine in a large punch bowl and add a block of ice before serving.*

## YOUR OWN RECIPE

# YOUR OWN RECIPE

Use a bartender's mixing glass whenever the instructions state "combine" ingredients. Strain the drink from the mixing glass into the drinking glass suggested by the illustration alongside the ingredients.

# B

The glass pictured for each drink is our suggestion; other drinking cups may be used as well.

---

## B & B

1 oz. Benedictine
1 oz. brandy

*Stir together, serve straight up.*

## B & B COLLINS

2 oz. cognac
1 tbs. sugar syrup
1 tsp. lemon juice
1 tsp. Benedictine
Club soda

*Combine cognac, juice and sugar syrup with ice; shake well. Strain, add ice, almost fill with club soda. Stir gently. Float Benedictine on top. Decorate with lemon slice.*

---

## B.V.D.

¾ oz. dry gin, white rum and dry vermouth

*Combine with ice; shake well. Strain and add ice.*

## BACARDI SPECIAL

1½ oz. Bacardi
1 oz. lime juice
¾ oz. gin
1 tsp. grenadine

*Combine with ice; shake well. Strain and add ice.*

## BACHELOR'S BAIT

2 oz. gin
½ tsp. grenadine
1-2 dashes orange bitters
1 egg white

*Combine with ice; shake extremely well. Strain and add ice.*

## BADMINTON

1 bottle red wine
2 oz. sugar
A pinch of nutmeg
Cucumber slices
½ pint club soda

*Combine the wine and sugar in a pitcher; stir until the sugar is dissolved. Add plenty of ice. Garnish with nutmeg; decorate with cucumber slices. Add the soda before serving.*

**BAIRN**

1½ oz. Scotch
¾ oz. Cointreau
1-2 dashes orange bitters

*Combine with ice; shake well.*

**BALI HAI**

1 oz. gin
1 oz. white rum
1 oz. okolehao
1 oz. lemon juice
3 oz. lime juice
Champagne

*Combine everything except the champagne with ice; shake well. Strain over crushed ice. Add several drops champagne.*

**BALTIMORE BRACER**

1 oz. brandy
1 oz. anisette
1 egg white

*Combine with ice; shake extremely well. Strain and add ice.*

**BANANA BIRD**

1 oz. bourbon
1 oz. heavy cream
2 tsp. creme de banana
2 tsp. Triple Sec

*Combine with ice; shake very well. Drain into a sour glass straight up.*

**BANANA CHARTREUSE**

4 bananas, barely ripe
4 oz. yellow chartreuse
Butter
Ground ginger

*Peel the bananas. Slice them into quarters; first the long way, then in half. Saute the banana slices in a generous amount of butter; sprinkle with ginger and pour the chartreuse over them. Ignite; burn for no more than sixty seconds and serve at once.*

**BALTIMORE EGG NOG**

½ pint cognac, Jamaican rum, apple brandy and peach brandy
1 doz. eggs
½ lb. sugar
1½ quarts milk
1 pint ice cream (any flavor)
½ pint heavy cream

*Separate eggs. Lightly beat yolks in a large saucepan; add liquors and heat until eggs are cooked. Gently beat in sugar, milk, ice cream and heavy cream. Cool and refrigerate. A half-hour before serving, beat egg whites until stiff and fold into the dessert. Top with nutmeg or cinnamon. Serves 4-6.*

## BANANA COCKTAIL

1¼ oz. vodka
1 tsp. banana liqueur
½ lime
Club soda
Mint sprigs

*Combine the vodka and banana liquer with ice; shake well. Strain, squeeze in the lime and drop in the peel. Add ice and fill with club soda. Stir gently and top with sprigs of mint.*

## BANANA DAIQUIRI

2 oz. white rum
1½ tsp. lime juice
1 tsp. banana liqueur
½ banana, sliced
4 oz. crushed ice

*Combine in an electric blender; blend at a low speed for no more than 15 seconds. Strain.*

## BANANA MANGO

1½ oz. white rum
½ oz. mango nectar
¾ tsp. banana liqueur
2 tsp. lime juice
1 mango slice

*Combine with ice; shake well. Strain, add ice. Top with mango slice.*

## BANANA RUM FRAPPE

½ oz. white rum
½ oz. banana liqueur
½ oz. orange juice

*Combine with ice; shake well. Strain over crushed ice.*

## BANANA SQUASH

4 oz. white rum
3 tsp. lime juice
2 brown bananas, sliced
6 oz. crushed ice

*Soak the banana slices with the rum in a deep bowl for several hours. Combine this with the lime juice and ice in a blender at a high speed for 15 seconds. Turn out straight up. (Bananas can be browned by storing in a refrigerator.)*

## BANANA VODKA

1 pint vodka
1 ripe banana, peeled and sliced
1 lemon, sliced in the skin
12 oz. rock candy

*Combine in a large bottle; seal tightly and allow to stand at room temperature for at least a week, or until all the rock candy has dissolved. Shake gently at least once each day. Strain when ready, squeeze in the lemon juice and re-bottle for future use.*

## BANSHEE

1 oz. white creme de cacao
1 oz. creme de banana
1 oz. light cream

*Combine with ice; shake very well. Strain. Serve straight up.*

**BARBARY COAST**

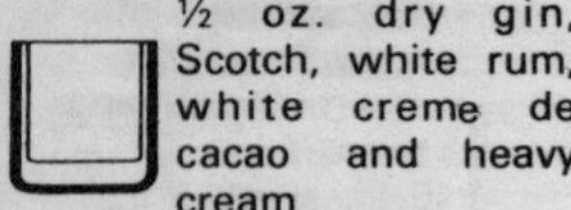

½ oz. dry gin, Scotch, white rum, white creme de cacao and heavy cream

*Combine with ice; shake very well. Strain and add ice.*

**BARLEY CIDER**

12 gallons sweet cider
5 lb. brown sugar
2 lb. raisins
2 quarts barley
2 oz. olive oil

*Combine in a large wooden cask; stir well. Seal and allow to ferment. When ready, strain off into another cask to age.*

**BARNUM**

1½ oz. gin
½ oz. apricot brandy
A few dashes of Angostura bitters
A few drops lemon juice

*Combine with ice; shake well. Strain and add ice.*

**BARTON SPECIAL**

1½ oz. calvados
¾ oz. Scotch
¾ oz. dry gin

*Combine with ice; shake well. Strain, add ice and a twist of lemon; drop in the peel.*

**BATIDO DE PINA**

2½ oz. white rum
2/3 cup crushed pineapple
1 tsp. powdered sugar

*Combine the rum with the crushed pineapple in an electric blender; blend until smooth.*

**BAYARD FIZZ**

2 oz. gin
2 tsp. maraschino
1 tsp. lemon juice
1 tsp. raspberry syrup
2 raspberries
Club soda

*Combine (except the soda and the raspberries) with ice; shake well. Strain and add ice. Fill with soda. Stir gently. Float raspberries on top.*

**BARROSA CUP**

1 bottle blackberry brandy
1 bottle peach brandy
1 pint cherry whiskey, dark curacao and maraschino
4 oz. sherry and kummel
3 oz. sugar
1 tsp. almond extract
Lemon rinds, cucumber peels
1 pint champagne

*Combine everything except the champagne; stir until blended. Strain clean. Add champagne plus chunks of ice before serving.*

## BAYBERRY PUNCH

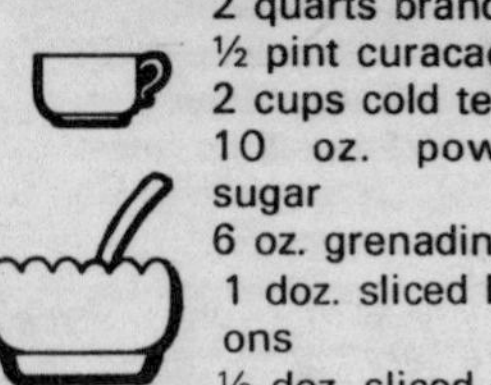

2 quarts brandy
½ pint curacao
2 cups cold tea
10 oz. powdered sugar
6 oz. grenadine
1 doz. sliced lemons
½ doz. sliced oranges

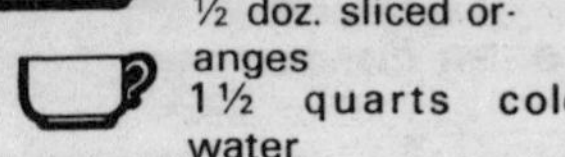

1½ quarts cold water

*Combine in a large punch bowl; mix well. Add ice a half-hour before serving. Fruit slices can be squeezed in before mixing, if desired.*

## BAYOU

1¾ oz. brandy
2 tsp. lime juice
1 tsp. mango nectar
Several drops peach liqueur
1 peach slice

*Combine (except peach slice) with ice; shake well. Strain and add ice. Top with peach slice.*

## BAYOU BEER

*There are any number of ways to make beer. This is one.*

1 oz. hops
A cake of yeast
1 lb. molasses

*Combine in a large saucepan; bring to a boil and stir constantly. Allow to cool and ferment before bottling in a crock pot or stone jug, (it should only take a few days).*

## BEACHCOMBER

1½ oz. rum
1 tsp. lime juice
1 tsp. Triple Sec
Several drops maraschino
Sugar

*Combine with ice; shake well. Line the rim of glass with water, press it in sugar. Strain in drink, add ice.*

## BEACHCOMBER'S BRACER

1 oz. white rum
1 tbs. orange curacao
1 tbs. bourbon
1 tsp. powdered sugar
A few dashes of Angostura bitters
Lemon juice

*Dissolve the sugar with a few drops of lemon juice in a mug; add the remaining ingredients. Fill the mug with boiling water and stir well.*

## BEACHCOMBER'S GOLD

1½ oz. white rum
½ oz. dry vermouth
½ oz. sweet vermouth

*Combine with ice; shake well. Strain; add crushed ice.*

## BEAUTY SPOT

1 oz. dry gin
½ oz. sweet vermouth
½ oz. dry vermouth
1 tsp. orange juice
1 drop grenadine

*Combine everything except grenadine with ice; shake well. Pour grenadine into small glass; add ice, strain in the drink. Do not stir.*

**BEE'S KISS**

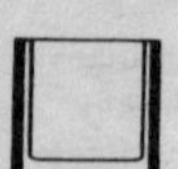

1½ oz. white rum
1tsp. honey
1 tsp. heavy cream

*Combine with ice; shake very well. Strain and add ice.*

---

**BEE-BEE**

Bourbon
Honey
The skins of 2 oranges, 3 lemons and 4 limes

*Dice fruit skins and place in the coffee receptacle of a percolator. Pour several teaspoons of honey over the skins and percolate in bourbon. Serve hot.*

---

**BEEF AND BULL**

2 oz. beef bouillon
1 oz. bourbon
Cucumber slices
A pinch salt

*Combine everything except the cucumber slices with ice; shake well. Strain with ice; garnish with cucumber.*

**BEER BUSTER**

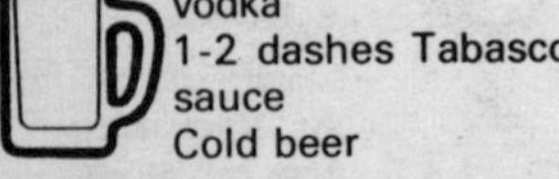

2 oz. cold, 100-proof vodka
1-2 dashes Tabasco sauce
Cold beer

*Pour vodka into a beer mug. Add Tabasco sauce; fill the mug with cold beer and stir.*

**BEER PANACHEE**

10 oz. beer
12 oz. lime soda
2 tbs. sugar
1 tsp. lime juice

*Combine with chunks of ice before serving; stir to blend.*

**BEER PUNCH**

10 oz. beer
12 oz. grapefruit or orange juice
1 bottle ginger ale
4 oz. sugar
2 tbs. lime juice

*Combine with chunks of ice before serving; stir gently.*

**BELLINI PUNCH**

Peaches
Iced champagne
1 tbs. lemon juice
Sugar

*Puree enough peaches to generously fill bottom of a small punch bowl. Add three times as much champagne, plus the lemon juice and sugar to taste. Stir very well.*

**BELMONT**

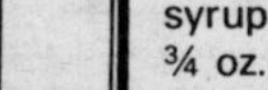

2 oz. gin
½ oz. raspberry syrup
¾ oz. heavy cream

*Combine with ice; shake very well. Strain; add ice.*

## BELVUE EGG NOG

1 doz. eggs
1 cup sugar
1 pint cognac
½ pint Jamaican rum
½ pint heavy cream
1 pint milk

*Separate the eggs. Beat yolks well; add sugar, cognac and rum. Stir until smooth and well-blended. Whip the heavy cream; add milk. Beat egg whites until stiff; fold cream mixture and stiff egg whites into the liquor. Season with nutmeg and refrigerate until ready to serve. For a less sweet eggnog, don't whip the cream, halve the sugar and add a little more cognac.*

---

## BENEDICT

1 oz. Scotch
1oz. Benedictine
Ginger ale

*Over a few cubes of ice pour the Scotch and the Benedictine. Fill glass with ginger ale and stir.*

## BENEDICTINE COCKTAIL

3 oz. Benedictine
A few dashes of Angostura bitters
Powdered sugar
½ lemon

*Combine Benedictine with bitters. Shake only a few seconds. Rub the lemon around the rim of a glass and press the rim in powdered sugar. Drop a cherry into the glass; add the Benedictine plus ice.*

## BENNETT

2 oz. gin
1½ oz. lime juice
A few dashes of Angostura bitters
1 tsp. powdered sugar

*Combine with ice; shake well. Strain and add ice.*

## BERMUDA BOUQUET

1½ oz. dry gin
1 oz. apricot brandy
1 tsp. powdered sugar
½ tsp. grenadine
½ tsp. curacao

*Combine with ice; shake well. Strain. Add ice, a twist of orange; drop in the peels.*

## BERMUDA HIGHBALL

1 oz. gin
1 oz. brandy
1 oz. dry vermouth
Club soda

*Combine the gin, brandy and vermouth; add ice and fill with club soda; stir gently.*

## BERMUDA ROSE

1½ oz. gin
1 tbs. lime juice
A few drops of grenadine
A few drops apricot brandy

*Combine with ice; shake well. Strain and add ice.*

## BETSY ROSS

1½ oz. brandy
1½ oz. port
A few drops curacao
A few dashes of Angostura bitters
Combine with ice; shake well. Strain. Add ice.

## BETTY COCKTAIL

1½ oz. dry gin
½ oz. Swedish Punch
½ lemon

*Fill a small glass with ice; pour in the gin and Swedish Punch. Squeeze in the lemon; drop in the peel and stir well.*

## BETWEEN THE SHEETS

1 oz. brandy
1 oz. Cointreau
1 oz. white rum
1 tsp. lemon juice

*Combine with ice; shake well. Strain and add ice.*

## BIG APPLE

1 oz. apple brandy
3 oz. apple juice
3 tbs. baked apple
A pinch ground ginger

*Heat the juice and the ginger; simmer for a few minutes. Warm a glass tumbler; add the baked apple. Pour the apple brandy into a ladle; ignite and pour over the baked apple. Put out the fire with the warm, spiced juice. Stir gently. Serve warm with a spoon to eat the apple.*

## BIG JOHN'S SPECIAL

2 oz. grapefruit juice
2 tbs. gin
1 tbs. vodka
1 tbs. orange juice
A few drops orange flower water
A few maraschino cherries
A few drops cherry juice
An orange slice, cut into small pieces
2 oz. crushed ice

*Combine in a blender at a high speed until smooth. Serve unstrained.*

## BILLY TAYLOR

2 oz. gin
1½ oz. lime juice
1 tsp.powdered sugar
Club soda

*Combine everything except the club soda with ice; shake well. Strain; add ice and fill the glass with club soda.*

## BIMBO PUNCH

1½ quarts brandy
6 large lemons
1 lb. sugar

*Slice the lemons and steep in the brandy overnight. Strain the brandy out. Dissolve the sugar in enough boiling water to make a watery syrup; cool; add to the brandy, and refrigerate. One-half hour before serving, pour the punch into a large bowl filled with chunks of ice and decorate with slices of fruit.*

## BIRD OF PARADISE

2 oz. gin
2 tbs. lemon juice
1 tsp. powdered sugar
1 tsp. grenadine
1 egg white
Club soda

*Combine (except the soda) with ice; shake extremely well. Strain. Add ice and fill with soda.*

---

## BISCAYNE

1 oz. gin
½ oz. white rum
½ oz. Forbidden Fruit
1 tsp. lime juice

*Combine with ice; shake well. Strain and add ice. Decorate with lime slice.*

## BISHOP

2 oz. orange juice
1½ oz. lemon juice
1 tsp. powdered sugar
1 tsp. rum
Burgundy

*Half fill glass with crushed ice; combine the orange juice, lemon juice and powdered sugar. Almost fill glass with Burgundy and stir well. Float rum on top and decorate with orange slice.*

## BISHOP'S COCKTAIL

2 oz. gin
2 oz. ginger wine

*Combine with ice; shake well. Strain and add ice.*

## BITTER BANANA COOLER

1½ oz. white rum
2 oz. pineapple juice
½ oz. lime juice
1-2 dashes Peychaud's bitters
½ banana, sliced
Lemon
4 oz. crushed ice

*Combine (except soda) in an electric blender; blend at a low speed for no more than 15 seconds. Strain, add more ice and fill with soda.*

---

## BITTER LEMON COOLER

1½ oz. dry vermouth
1 oz. dry gin
1 tsp. lemon juice
1 tsp. raspberry syrup
Lemon soda

*Combine (except the soda) with ice; shake well. Strain; add ice and fill with soda. Add a twist of lemon; stir and drop in the peel.*

## BITTERSWEET

1¼ oz. sweet vermouth
1¼ oz. dry vermouth
1-2 dashes Angostura bitters
1-2 dashes orange bitters

*Combine with ice; shake well. Strain into a martini glass straight up or in an old-fashioned glass filled with ice. Add a twist of orange and drop in the peel.*

## BLACK BEAUTY

3 oz. blackberry liqueur
1 tbs. lime juice

*Combine with ice; shake well. Strain into a chilled champagne glass straight up.*

## BLACK DAIQUIRI

1½ oz. Jamaican rum
2 tsp. lime juice
1 tsp. honey

*Combine with ice; shake very well. Strain into a sour glass.*

## BLACK EYE

1½ oz. vodka
2 tsp. blackberry brandy
2 tbs. lime juice

*Combine with ice; shake well. Strain straight up. Decorate with a slice of lime.*

## BLACK HAWK

1¼ oz. whiskey
1½ oz. sloe gin

*Combine with ice; shake well. Strain into a martini glass straight up or over ice in an old-fashioned glass. Top with a cherry.*

## BLACK PEARL

1½ oz. gold rum
1 tsp. apricot brandy
2 tsp. pineapple juice
1 tsp. Jamaican rum

*Combine with ice; shake well. Strain. Serve straight up.*

## BLACK RUSSIAN

1½ oz. vodka
¾ oz. Kahlua

*Combine with ice; shake well. Strain and add ice. For a* **BLACK MAGIC** *add a few drops of lemon juice before shaking.*

## BLACK STRIPE

3 oz. Jamaican rum
1 tsp. dark molasses

*Mix the rum with the molasses in a mug. Fill the mug with boiling water; add a twist of lemon and stir very well. Serve hot.*

## BLACK VELVET

Fill a tall glass with equal parts champagne and stout. Stir gently.

## BLACKBERRY CORDIAL

½ gallon blackberry juice
1 pint cognac
4 cups sugar
Ground cloves
Allspice

*Combine everything except the cognac in a large saucepan; bring to a boil several times, stirring occasionally. Add the brandy and bottle, cork and seal the cordial while still hot. Store in a cool, dark place for several months. Eight quarts of blackberries can be used to extract ½ gallon of juice, if you wish to start from scratch.*

## BLACKBERRY COOLER

1½ oz. blackberry brandy
½ oz. lemon juice
Club soda

*Combine the brandy and lemon juice; add ice and fill with club soda. Stir well.*

## BLACKBERRY WINE

½ peck crushed blackberries
1 gallon hot water
Sugar

*Combine the crushed berries with the water in a large crock pot and allow to stand for two days. Strain and add three parts sugar for each part juice; stir, seal and allow to stand for several months.*

## BLACKJACK

1¼ oz. kirsch
1¼ oz. iced coffee
A few drops brandy

*Combine the kirsch and the coffee in a wide champagne glass filled with crushed ice. Add the brandy and gently stir.*

## BLACKTHORN

1½ oz. Irish whiskey
1½ oz. dry vermouth
Several drops Pernod
Several dashes Angostura bitters

*Combine with ice; shake well. Strain and add ice. Sloe gin can be used instead of the whiskey.*

## BLANCHE

1 oz. Cointreau
1 oz. white curacao
1 oz. anisette

*Combine with ice; shake well. Strain and add ice.*

**BLENDED COMFORT**

2 oz. whiskey
1 oz. Southern Comfort
1 oz. orange juice
½ oz. dry vermouth
2 tbs. lemon juice
¼ peach, skinned
4 oz. crushed ice

*Combine in an electric blender; blend at a low speed no more than 15 seconds. Strain and fill glass with crushed ice. Top with a lemon slice and an orange slice.*

**BLENHEIM**

1 oz. apple brandy
½ oz. apricot brandy
1 tbs. lemon juice
1 tsp. grenadine
1-2 dashes Angostura bitters

*Combine with ice; shake well. Strain and add ice.*

**BLENTON**

2 oz. gin
Several drops dry vermouth
1-2 dashes Angostura bitters

*Pour the gin into a mixing glass filled with ice; add the vermouth and bitters. Shake well. Strain. Add a twist of lemon and drop in the peel.*

**BLINKER**

1½ oz. rye
2 oz. grapefruit juice
1 tbs. grenadine

*Combine with ice; shake well. Strain and add ice.*

**BLIZZARD**

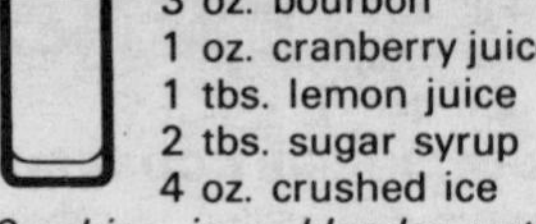

3 oz. bourbon
1 oz. cranberry juice
1 tbs. lemon juice
2 tbs. sugar syrup
4 oz. crushed ice

*Combine in a blender until the drink is thick. Serve straight up.*

**BLOOD AND SAND**

¾ oz. Scotch, cherry brandy, sweet vermouth and orange juice

*Combine with ice; shake well. Strain and add ice.*

**BLOODHOUND**

1 oz. gin
½ oz. sweet vermouth
½ oz. dry vermouth
1 tsp. strawberry liqueur
1 strawberry

*Combine everything except the strawberry with ice; shake well. Strain and add ice. Top with the strawberry.*

**BLOODY MARIANA**

2 oz. vodka
6 oz. V-8 vegetable juice
1 tsp. lime juice
A few drops Tabasco sauce
A few drops Worchestershire sauce
A pinch of white pepper
A pinch of celery salt
A pinch of oregano

*Combine with ice; shake. Strain and add ice.*

**BLOODY MARY**

1½ oz. vodka
3 oz. tomato juice
1 tbs. lemon juice
Several drops Worchestershire sauce
Several drops Tabasco sauce

*Combine with ice; shake well. Strain and serve straight up. Add salt and pepper to taste. For a* **BLOODY MARIE** *halve the lemon juice and add several drops of Pernod. For a* **BLOODY MARIA** *use tequila instead of vodka.*

---

**BLUE ANGEL**

½ oz. blue curacao, vanilla parfait, brandy and heavy cream

*Combine with ice; shake very well. Strain and serve straight up.*

**BLUE BELL**

1½ oz. whiskey
1 tbs. dry vermouth
1-2 dashes Angostura bitters

*Combine with ice; shake well. Strain and add ice.*

**BLUE MOON**

1½ oz. gin
¾ oz. dry vermouth
1-2 dashes orange bitters
1-2 dashes Creme Yvette

*Combine with ice; shake well. Strain and add ice.*

**BLUE MOUNTAIN**

1½ oz. Ja
rum
1½ oz. orang
¾ Tia Maria
¾ oz. vodka

*Combine with ice; shake well. Strain and add ice.*

**BLUE PACIFIC**

3 oz. dry gin
A few drops of dry vermouth
1-2 dashes vodka
1-2 dashes blue food coloring

*Combine without ice; stir until blended. Pour out over ice. Decorate with a black olive.*

**BLUE SHARK**

1½ oz. tequila
1½ oz. vodka
1-2 dashes blue food coloring

*Combine with ice; shake well. Strain and add ice.*

**BLUE TAIL FLY**

1½ oz. blue curacao
1 tbs. white creme de cacao
1 tbs. light cream

*Combine with ice; shake very well. Strain. Serve over ice.*

## BLUEBERRY CORDIAL

1 quart blueberries
12 oz. sugar
whiskey

*Boil the berries for at least half an hour in enough water to cover them. Add the sugar; stir and allow to simmer until thick. Strain the syrup clean and add the same amount of whiskey as syrup. Stir well. Bottle and seal to use as a cordial.*

## BLUEBERRY RUM FIZZ

2½ oz. white rum
½ oz. Triple Sec
1 tbs. lemon juice
1 tsp. blueberry syrup
A few blueberries
Club soda

*Combine (except the soda and blueberries) with ice; shake well. Strain; add ice and fill glass with soda. Top with blueberries and a lemon slice.*

## BLUEBIRD

2½ oz gin
½ oz. curacao
Several dashes Angostura bitters

*Combine with ice; shake well. Strain and add ice. Add a twist of lemon and drop in the peel. Top with a cherry.*

## BLUEBLAZER

3 oz. Scotch
3 oz. boiling water
Powdered sugar

*Pour the Scotch into one mug, the boiling water in another. Ignite the Scotch; toss the burning liquor and the water from mug to mug. When throughly mixed, the mixture will look like a stream of fire. Pour it all into one of the mugs; add a teaspoon of powdered sugar and a twist of lemon. Stir and wait until it cools enough to drink.*

## BOB DANBY

2 oz. Dubonnet
1 oz. strong brandy

*Combine with ice; shake well. Strain and add ice.*

## BOBBY BURNS

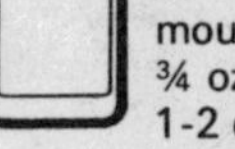

1½ oz. Scotch
¾ oz. sweet vermouth
¾ oz. dry vermouth
1-2 dashes Benedictine

*Combine with ice; shake well. Strain and add ice. For a sweeter drink, increase the Benedictine to a teaspoon and omit the dry vermouth.*

---

## BOILERMAKER

*Drink 2 oz.of whiskey straight up and wash it down with a large mug of beer. The whiskey and the beer can be combined in a highball glass, if desired. Scotch can be used instead of blended whiskey.*

*For a* **DOG'S NOSE** *substitute gin for the whiskey and mix with the beer.*

**BOLERO**

1½ oz. white rum
¾ oz. apple brandy
Several drops sweet vermouth

*Combine with ice; shake well. Strain and add ice. Add a twist of lemon and drop in the peel.*

**BOLO**

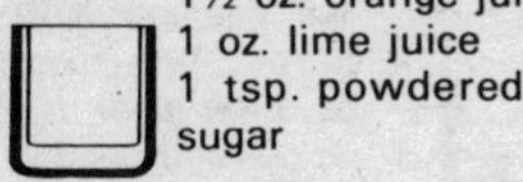

3 oz. white rum
1½ oz. orange juice
1 oz. lime juice
1 tsp. powdered sugar

*Combine with ice; shake well. Strain and add ice.*

**BOMB**

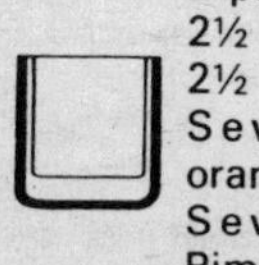

2 pints sherry
2½ oz. Cointreau
2½ oz. orange juice
Several dashes orange bitters
Several dashes Pimento Dram
Olives

*Combine with ice and stir very well. Serve with crushed ice. Top each glass with an olive.*

**BOMBAY**

1 oz. brandy
1 oz. sweet vermouth
½ oz. dry vermouth
1-2 dashes curacao
A few drops Pernod

*Combine with ice; shake well. Strain and add ice.*

**BOMBAY PUNCH**

1 bottle cognac
1 bottle dry sherry
4 oz. curacao
4 oz. maraschino
9 oz. lemon juice
Sugar to taste
2 bottles club soda
4 bottles champagne

*Combine all but the champagne and soda. Add the champagne and soda, plus ice.*

---

**BOMBE GLACEE TULLAMORE**

1 quart vanilla ice cream
1 pint coffee ice cream
4 oz. Irish Mist
1 tsp. almond extract

*Line the sides of a bombe or similar deep dish with the coffee ice cream. In a separate bowl, combine the Irish Mist and vanilla ice cream; stir until well-blended. Add the almond extract. Pack the ice cream and liqueur into the coffee ice cream mold; freeze. Keep frozen until ready to use.*

---

**BONNIE PRINCE**

1¼ oz. gin
½ oz. Lillet
Several drops Drambuie

*Combine with ice; shake well. Strain and add ice. Add more Drambuie, if you want a stronger drink.*

**BONSONI**

3 oz. sweet vermouth
1½ tbs. Fernet Branca
1-2 dashes sugar syrup
1-2 dashes Pernod

*Combine with ice; shake well. Strain and add ice. For a less sweet drink, eliminate the sugar syrup and the Pernod.*

---

**BOOMERANG**

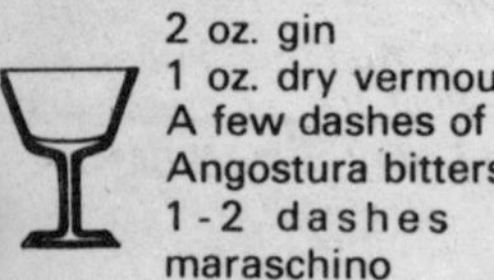

2 oz. gin
1 oz. dry vermouth
A few dashes of Angostura bitters
1-2 dashes maraschino

*Combine with ice; shake well. Strain. Add a twist of lemon and drop in the peel. Serve straight up.*

**BOOSTER**

2½ oz. brandy
¼ oz. curacao
1 egg white

*Combine with ice; shake extremely well. Strain and add ice. Dust with nutmeg.*

**BORDEN CHASE**

1½ oz. Scotch
½ oz. sweet vermouth
1-2 dashes orange bitters
Several drops Pernod

*Combine with ice; shake well. Strain and add ice.*

**BORINQUEN**

1½ oz. white rum
½ oz. orange juice
½ oz. passion fruit juice
1 tbs. lime juice
1 tsp. high-proof rum
Gardenia or jasmine flowers

*Combine with ice; shake well. Strain over crushed ice; decorate with gardenia or jasmine. For a thicker drink, mix all the ingredients in an electric blender with ½ cup crushed ice.*

**BOSOM CARESSER**

½ oz. Madeira
¼ oz. brandy
¼ oz. curacao
1 tsp. grenadine
1 egg yolk

*Combine with ice; shake extremely well. Strain; serve straight up.*

**BOSTON COCKTAIL**

1 oz. dry gin
1 oz. apricot brandy
1 tsp. lemon juice
1 tsp. grenadine

*Combine with ice; shake well. Strain and add ice.*

## BOSTON FISH HOUSE PUNCH

1½ quarts Jamaican rum
1 bottle brandy
4 oz. peach brandy
3 quarts champagne
4 oz. sugar syrup
2 oz. lime juice
2 oz. lemon juice

*Combine the sugar syrup, lemon juice and lime juice in a large punch bowl. Add the rum, brandies and champagne; stir gently. Serve over ice.*

## BOSTON SIDECAR

1 oz. brandy
1 oz. rum
1 oz. Triple Sec
1 tbs. lime juice

*Combine with ice; shake well. Strain and add ice.*

## BOSTON SOUR

2 oz. whiskey
1½ oz. lemon juice
1 tsp. powdered sugar
1 egg white
Club soda

*Combine (except the soda) with ice; shake well. Strain, add ice and fill the glass with club soda. Top with a lemon slice and a cherry.*

## BOURBON A LA CREME

2 oz. bourbon
1 oz. dark creme de cacao
1-2 vanilla beans

*Combine with ice and allow to stand in the refrigerator for at least one hour. When ready, shake well and strain straight up.*

## BOURBON AND EGG SOUR

2 oz. bourbon
1½ tsp. lemon juice
1 tsp. powdered sugar
1 egg
Several drops of bitters (Angostura touched up with rum and maraschino is best)

*Combine with ice; shake well. Strain.*

## BOURBON BRANCA

2 oz. bourbon
1 tsp. Fernet Branca

*Combine in an old-fashioned glass; stir well. Add ice. Touch it up with a twist of lemon.*

---

## BOURBON CARDINAL

1½ oz. 100-proof bourbon
1 tbs. grapefruit juice
1 tbs. cranberry juice
1 tbs. sugar syrup
2 tsp. lemon juice
A few drops cherry juice

*Combine with ice; shake well. Strain. Serve straight up; decorate with a pair of maraschino cherries.*

## BOURBON COLLINS

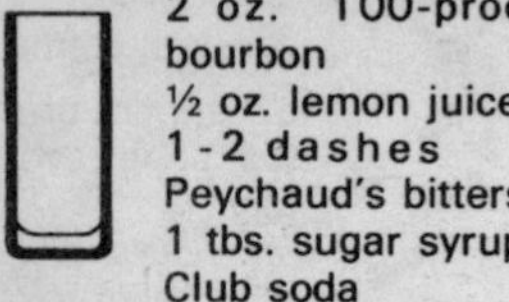

2 oz. 100-proof bourbon
½ oz. lemon juice
1-2 dashes Peychaud's bitters
1 tbs. sugar syrup
Club soda

*Combine (except the soda) with ice; shake well. Strain, add ice and fill with soda. Top with a lemon slice.*

## BOURBON DAISY

2 oz. bourbon
1 tbs. lemon juice
1 tsp. grenadine
1 tsp. Southern Comfort
Club soda
1 pineapple stick

*Combine the bourbon, lemon juice and grenadine with ice; shake well. Strain, add ice and fill with soda. Float the Sourthern Comfort on top and top with a slice of orange and the pineapple stick.*

## BOURBON EGG NOG

1 doz. eggs
1½ cups sugar
1 quart heavy cream
1 quart milk
1 quart bourbon

*Separate the eggs. Combine the yolks with sugar and beat until well-blended. In another bowl, beat the heavy cream until stiff but not whipped; add the milk and slowly stir in the bourbon. Combine this with the yolks. Beat the egg whites until stiff and fold them into the egg nog. Refrigerate until ready to serve. Dust with nutmeg.*

## BOURBON PUNCH

1 quart bourbon
4 oz. grenadine
4 oz. sugar
3 oz. lemon juice
6 oz. orange juice
1 quart club soda

*Dissolve the sugar with the fruit juices. Add the grenadine and the whiskey and stir until blended.*

## BOURBON SLOE GIN

1½ oz. bourbon
½ oz. sloe gin
½ oz. lemon juice
1 tsp. sugar syrup

*Combine with ice; shake well. Strain over crushed ice. Top with a lemon slice and a peach slice.*

## BOURBON SOUR

2 oz. bourbon
2 tbs. lemon juice
2 tsp. sugar syrup

*Combine with ice; shake well. Strain straight up; decorate with a slice of orange.*

## BOURBONVILLE

1½ oz. bourbon
1½ tsp. lime juice
Club soda

*Combine the bourbon and the lime juice with ice; shake well. Strain; add ice and fill the glass with soda. Touch it up with a twist of lime.*

### BOURGOGNE A L'ORANGE

2 bottles Burgundy
2 oranges
1 cup sugar
Cloves

*In a wide bowl, combine the soft, inner skins of the oranges with the sugar. Pour in 4 oz. of boiling water and allow to stand for at least 15 minutes.*
*Squeeze in the juice of half of one orange and strain the mixture into a large saucepan. Add the Burgundy. Heat and stir; do not bring to a boil. Serve hot. Decorate each mug with slices of orange stuck with cloves.*

### BOXCAR

1¼ oz. Cointreau
1¼ oz. gin
1 tsp. lime juice
1 egg white
1-2 dashes grenadine
Sugar

*Combine with ice; shake extremely well. Line the rim of a glass with water and press it in sugar. Strain in the drink straight up.*

### BRANDIED APRICOT

1½ oz. brandy
½ oz. apricot brandy
2 tsp. lemon juice

*Combine with ice; shake well. Strain, add ice and a twist of orange; drop in the peel.*

### BRANDIED APRICOT FLIP

1½ oz. brandy
1 oz. apricot brandy
1 tbs. sugar syrup
1 egg

*Combine with ice; shake extremely well. Strain into a small glass straight up. Dust with nutmeg.*

### BRANDIED BANANA COLLINS

1½ oz. brandy
1 oz. banana liqueur
2 tsp. lemon juice
Club soda
1 banana slice

*Combine (except the soda and banana slice) with ice; shake well. Strain, add ice and fill with club soda. Decorate with the banana slice and a lemon slice.*

### BRANDIED BOAT

1 oz. dark port
1 oz. brandy
2 tsp. lemon juice
1 tsp. maraschino

*Combine with ice; shake well. Strain and add ice. Decorate with and orange slice.*

### BRANDIED CORDIAL MEDOC

1½ oz. brandy
½ oz. Cordial Medoc
2 tsp. lemon juice

*Combine with ice; shake well. Strain and add ice. Add a twist of lemon and drop in the peel.*

**BRANDIED GINGER**

1 oz. brandy
½ oz. ginger brandy
1 tsp. lime juice
1 tsp. orange juice
1 chunk ginger

*Combine (except the ginger chunk) with ice; shake well. Strain and add ice. Decorate with the ginger.*

**BRANDIED MADEIRA**

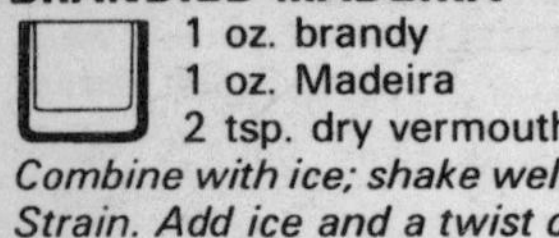

1 oz. brandy
1 oz. Madeira
2 tsp. dry vermouth

*Combine with ice; shake well. Strain. Add ice and a twist of lemon; drop in the peel.*

**BRANDIED PEACH FIZZ**

2 oz. brandy
2 tsp. peach brandy
2 tsp. lemon juice
1½ tsp. sugar syrup
1 tsp. banana liqueur
Club soda
1 peach slice

*Combine everything except the soda and the peach slice with ice; shake well. Strain, add ice and fill with soda. Decorate with peach slice.*
*For a* **BRANDIED PEACH SLING**, *eliminate the banana liqueur, put peach slice into the drink.*

**BRANDIED MOCHA PUNCH**

1 quart hot dark coffee
1 quart hot chocolate
10 oz. brandy
Whipped cream
Chocolate chips
Cinnamon

*Combine the coffee and hot chocolate in a large punch bowl and allow to cool. Stir in the brandy and add ice. Decorate with whipped cream, chocolate chips and cinnamon. Serve over ice, making sure each gets a bit of the garnish.*

**BRANDIED NIGHT**

1¼ oz. brandy
1 oz. gin
Several drops dry vermouth
1 olive

*Combine (except the olive) with ice; shake well. Strain and decorate with the olive. Serve straight up.*

**BRANDY ALEXANDER**

1½ oz. brandy
1 oz. dark creme de cacao
1 oz. heavy cream

*Combine with ice; shake well. Strain and serve straight up. For an* **ALEXANDER'S SISTER**, *substitute Kahlua for the dark creme de cacao.*

**BRANDY AND AMER PICON**

2 oz. cognac
2 tsp. Amer Picon

*Combine with ice; shake well. Strain and add ice. Add a twist of lemon and a twist of orange; drop in the peels.*

**BRANDY APRICOT FRAPPE**

¾ oz. brandy
½ oz. apricot brandy
¼ oz. creme de noyaux

*Combine with ice; shake well. Strain over crushed ice.*

**BRANDY BERRY FIX**

2 oz. brandy
2 tsp. lemon juice
1½ tsp. sugar syrup
1 tsp. strawberry liqueur

*Combine with ice; shake well. Strain over crushed ice.*

**BRANDY BLAZER**

2 oz. brandy
1 cube of sugar

*Place the sugar cube on the bottom of a small, wide bowl. Pour in the brandy and stir until the sugar is dissolved. Add a twist of lemon and a twist of orange; ignite for a few seconds. Extinguish the blaze and serve hot, strain and serve straight up.*

**BRANDY BOAT**

2 oz. brandy
2 tsp. sugar syrup
1 tsp. pineapple juice
1 tsp. lemon juice
Several drops lime juice
A few drops rum
Club soda
Fruit slices

*Combine (except the rum, soda and fruit slices) with ice; shake well. Strain. Add a few drops of club soda and fill with crushed ice. Float the rum on top; decorate with fruit slices.*

**BRANDY BUCK**

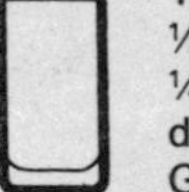

1½ oz. brandy
½ oz. lemon juice
¼ oz. white creme de menthe
Ginger ale
Seedless grapes

*Combine (except the ginger ale and grapes) with ice; shake well. Strain, add ice and fill with ginger ale. Decorate with a couple of seedless grapes.*

**BRANDY CHAMPARELLE**

¼ oz. curacao, yellow chartreuse, anisette and brandy

*Combine and stir gently.*

/

### BRANDY COBBLER

1½ oz. brandy
2 tsp. curacao
2 tsp. lemon juice
1½ tsp. sugar syrup
1 tsp. kirschwasser
1 pineapple stick

*Combine (except the pineapple stick) with ice; shake well. Strain over crushed ice. Top with the pineapple stick.*

### BRANDY CRUSTA

2 oz. brandy
2 tsp. curacao
2 tsp. lemon juice
1 tsp. maraschino
1-2 dashes bitters
1 spiral lemon peel

*Combine (except the lemon peel) with ice; shake well. Strain over ice and lemon peel.*

### BRANDY DAISY

2 oz. brandy
1 tbs. lemon juice
2 tsp. grenadine
Skinned, pressed peaches
Cooked apples and apricots

*Combine the brandy, lemon juice and grenadine with ice; shake well. Strain. Add the peaches, apples and apricots.*

### BRANDY EGG NOG

2½ oz. brandy
1 cup milk
1 egg
2 tbs.powdered sugar

*Combine with ice; shake extremely well. Strain and garnish with nutmeg. Serve straight up.*

### BRANDY FINO

1½ oz. brandy
2 tsp. dry sherry
2 tsp. Drambuie

*Combine with ice; shake well. Strain. Add ice and a twist of lemon; drop in the peel. Decorate with an orange slice.*

### BRANDY FIX

1¼ oz. brandy
¾ oz. cherry brandy
1 tsp. lime juice
1 tsp. sugar syrup

*Combine with ice; shake well. Strain over crushed ice and serve with a straw.*

### BRANDY FIZZ

1¼ oz. brandy
1 tbs. lemon juice
2 tsp. sugar syrup
Several dashes yellow chartreuse
Club soda

*Combine all but the soda with ice; shake well. Strain, add ice and fill with soda.*

### BRANDY FLIP

2 oz. brandy
1 tsp. sugar syrup
½ tsp. curacao
1-2 dashes bitters
1 mint sprig

*Combine (except the mint) with ice; shake well. Strain and add ice. Add a twist of lemon and drop in the peel; top with mint.*

## BRANDY GRUEL

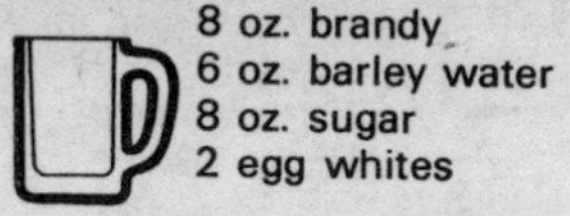

8 oz. brandy
6 oz. barley water
8 oz. sugar
2 egg whites

*Combine the barley water with the sugar plus a few teaspoons of boiling water in a saucepan. Slowly add the brandy, stirring constantly. Allow to cool. In a separate bowl, beat the egg whites until foamy; then fold them into the gruel. Serve in large mugs.*

## BRANDY HOT TODDY

2 oz. brandy
1 cube sugar

*Drop the sugar cube in a mug and fill 2/3 with boiling water. Add the brandy and stir until the sugar is completely dissolved. Add a twist of lemon; drop in the peel. Garnish with nutmeg; serve steaming hot.*

## BRANDY MILK PUNCH

2 oz. brandy
8 oz. milk
1 tsp. powdered sugar

*Combine with ice; shake well. Strain over ice and garnish with nutmeg.*

## BRANDY MINT FIZZ

2 oz. brandy
½ oz. white creme de menthe
¼ oz. white creme de cacao
2 tsp. lemon juice
1 tsp. sugar syrup
Club soda
Mint leaves

*Combine everything except the soda and the mint with ice; shake well. Strain, add ice and fill with soda. Decorate with mint leaves, partially torn.*

## BRANDY MINT FLOAT

1½ oz. white creme de menthe
1 tbs. brandy

*Pour the creme de menthe over ice in a small liqueur glass; carefully float the brandy.*

## BRANDY MINT JULEP

3 oz. brandy
1 oz. sugar syrup
Mint sprigs
Fruit slices

*Place a few sprigs of mint on the bottom of a wide glass. Pour in the sugar syrup and crush the leaves in it. Add the brandy. Fill with crushed ice, packing the ice as solidly as possible and stirring until very cold. Decorate with fruit and serve with a straw.*

## BRANDY OLD FASHIONED

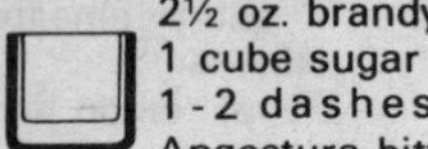

2½ oz. brandy
1 cube sugar
1-2 dashes Angostura bitters

*Combine the bitters, a twist of lemon and sugar cube. Pour in the brandy and stir until the sugar is completely dissolved. Add ice.*

## BRANDY PUNCH

3 quarts brandy
8 oz. Jamaican rum
3 oz. lemon juice
1 oz. curacao
1 gallon water
Sliced raspberries, chopped pineapple, and orange slices

*Combine everything except the fruit in a large punch bowl; sugar to taste and stir well. Decorate with the fruit. A half-hour before serving, add ice. Serve very cold.*

## BRANDY SANGAREE

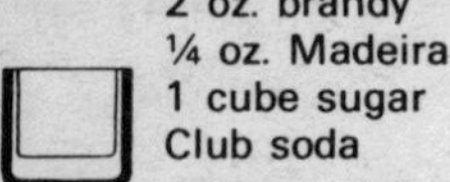

2 oz. brandy
¼ oz. Madeira
1 cube sugar
Club soda

*Dissolve sugar cube in a tablespoon of club soda. Pour in the brandy and the Madeira; add a few more drops of soda. Stir well and add ice. Garnish with nutmeg. Add a twist of orange and drop in the peel.*

## BRANDY SHRUB

10 oz. lemon juice
1 quart brandy
1 quart sherry
1½ lb. sugar
Lemon peels

*Place the peels in a large bowl. Add the lemon juice and the brandy; stir and allow to stand at room temperature at least 3 days. When ready, pour in the sherry. Add the sugar and stir until the sugar is completely dissolved. Strain into a large pitcher and refrigerate until ready to serve.*

## BRANDY SOUR

2 oz. brandy
2 tsp. lemon juice
1 tsp. orange juice
1 tsp. sugar syrup

*Combine with ice; shake well. Strain, decorate with a lemon slice and serve straight up.*

## BRANDY STEW

4 oz. cognac
2 oz. sugar
1 tbs. butter
Grated nutmeg, ground cloves, cinnamon and allspice

*Dissolve the sugar with the butter over low heat in a large saucepan; add the spices and simmer several minutes before adding the cognac. Stir constantly and do not allow the cognac to burn. Serve immediately.*

## BRANDY STINGER

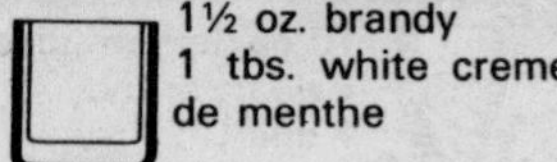

1½ oz. brandy
1 tbs. white creme de menthe

*Combine with ice; shake well. Strain into an old-fashioned glass and add ice. Touch it up with a twist of lemon.*

---

## BRANDY TIPPLE

16 oz. dark coffee, warm
8 oz. cognac
1 oz. sugar syrup
2 eggs

*Beat the eggs; add the syrup, cognac and coffee. Shake well with ice until cool. Turn out over ice.*

## BRAWNY BROTH

1 oz. vodka
A pinch of pepper
A pinch of salt
A lemon slice
1 packet powdered beef bouillon

*Combine; fill mug with boiling water and stir well.*

## BRAZIL

1½ oz. sherry
1½ oz. dry vermouth
A few drops Pernod
1-2 dashes Angostura bitters

*Combine with ice; shake well. Strain and add ice. Add a twist of lemon and drop in the peel.*

## BRIDE'S BOWL

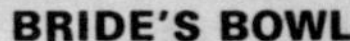

3 bottles gold rum
1 quart pineapple juice
2 cups lemon juice
2 cups sugar
1 pint whole strawberries
Pineapple chunks
2 bottles club soda

*Boil the sugar with enough water to make a syrup; combine with fruit chunks and juices and stir to blend. Pour in the rum and store in the refrigerator for a few hours. Add the soda plus chunks of ice before serving; float the strawberries.*

## BRIGHTON PUNCH

1 oz. bourbon
1 oz. cognac
¾ oz. Benedictine
2 tsp. lemon juice
Club soda

*Combine (except the club soda) with ice; shake well. Strain, add ice and fill with soda. Decorate with an orange slice and a lemon slice*

## BRITISH ATOLL

1 oz. dry gin
1 oz. creme de banana
1 oz. orange juice

*Combine with ice; shake well.*

**BRITTANY**

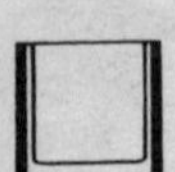

1½ oz. gin
2 tsp. Amer Picon
1 tsp. orange juice
1 tsp. lemon juice

*Combine with ice and a twist of orange; drop in the peel.*

**BROKEN SPUR**

1½ oz. white port
1 tsp. dry gin
1 tsp. anisette
1 tsp. sweet vermouth
1 egg yolk

*Combine with ice; shake extremely well. Strain and add ice.*

**BRONX COCKTAIL**

1½ oz. gin
1 oz. lemon juice
2 tsp. orange juice
2 tsp. dry vermouth
2 tsp. sweet vermouth

*Combine with ice; shake well. Strain and add ice.*
*For a* **BLOODY BRONX COCKTAIL** *substitute the juice of ¼ blood orange for the orange juice.*

**BRONX SILVER**

1 oz. dry gin
1 tbs. orange juice
2 tsp. dry vermouth
1 egg white

*Combine with ice; shake extremely well. Strain and add ice.*

**BROUSSARD'S ORANGE BRULOT**

1 orange
2 cubes sugar
Brandy

*Make cups out of the orange by slicing the skin around its circumference (without cutting the fruit) and sliding the skin away gently with a spoon. Drop a cube of sugar into each cup; pour in as much brandy as you wish and ignite. Stir gently while burning; drink when cooled. Brandy burns best when previously warmed.*
*For a* **LIZARD SKIN** *do not ignite brandy.*

**BROWN**

1¼ oz. bourbon
1¼ oz. dry vermouth
1-2 dashes orange bitters

*Combine with ice; shake well. Strain and add ice.*

**BRUNELLE**

1 oz. Pernod
3 oz. lemon juice
1½ tsp. powdered sugar

*Combine with ice; shake well. Strain and add ice.*

**BUBY**

2 oz. gin
3 tbs. lemon juice
1 tsp. grenadine

*Combine with ice; shake well. Strain and add ice.*

## BUDDHA PUNCH

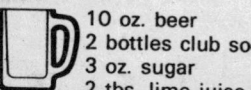

8 oz. red wine
5 oz. orange juice
5 oz. lemon juice
2½ oz. curacao
2½ oz. Jamaican rum
A few dashes of Angostura bitters
16 oz. club soda
1 bottle champagne
Fruit slices
Mint leaves

*Combine (except soda, champagne and garnishes) in a large punch bowl; stir well. Just before serving, add the soda, champagne and ice. Decorate with the fruit and mint leaves.*

## BUL

10 oz. beer
2 bottles club soda
3 oz. sugar
2 tbs. lime juice

*Combine with chunks of ice before serving; stir gently to blend.*

## BULL'S MILK

1½ oz. brandy
1 oz. rum
8 oz. milk
1 tsp. powdered sugar

*Combine with ice; shake well. Strain and add ice. Dust with nutmeg and cinnamon.*

## BULLSHOT

1 dash Worcestershire sauce
4 oz. beef bouillion
1½ oz. vodka

*Combine; add ice and a twist of lemon.*

## BUNNY BONANZA

1½ oz. tequila
1 oz. apple brandy
2 tsp. lemon juice
1½ tsp. sugar syrup
½ tsp. curacao

*Combine with ice; shake well. Strain, add ice and decorate with lemon slice*

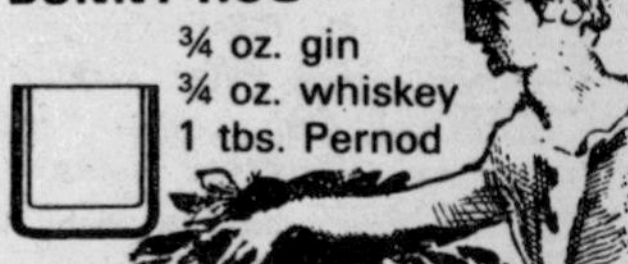

## BUNNY HUG

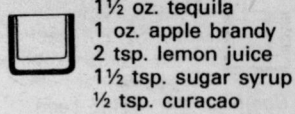

¾ oz. gin
¾ oz. whiskey
1 tbs. Pernod

*Combine with ice; shake well. Strain and add ice.*

## BUNNY MOTHER

1½ oz. vodka
1½ tbs. lemon juice
1½ tbs. orange juice
1½ tsp. sugar syrup
1 tsp. Cointreau
1 tsp. grenadine

*Combine (except the Cointreau) with ice; shake well. Strain and add ice. Float the Cointreau on top and decorate with a slice of orange and a cherry.*

## BURGUNDY COCKTAIL

3 oz. Burgundy
1 oz. brandy
Several drops of maraschino

*Combine with ice; shake well. Strain straight up. Decorate with a slice of lemon.*

## BURGUNDY CUP

2½ oz. whiskey
1¼ oz. curacao
1¼ oz. Benedictine
3 oz. sugar
8 oz. club soda
1½ bottles Burgundy

*Combine the whiskey, curacao and Benedictine in a large pitcher; add the sugar and stir until the sugar is completely dissolved. Add the Burgundy, club soda and ice. Decorate with fruit slices.*

## BURNING BLUE MOUNTAIN

5 oz. Jamaican rum
2 tsp. powdered sugar
The rind of one orange and one lime, in pieces
A lemon peel

*Warm the rum in a wide chafing dish. Add the sugar and fruit rinds; stir until the sugar has dissolved. Ignite and serve. Ladle out with a long-handled spoon.*

---

## BURGUNDY PUNCH

2 bottles Burgundy
8 oz. port
5 oz. orange juice
4 tsp. lemon juice
2 quarts cold bottled water
Sugar
Cucumber slices

*Combine the Burgundy, port and juices in a large punch bowl; sugar to taste and stir well. Add the water and ice just before serving; top with cucumber slices.*

---

## BURLESQUE

1 oz. bourbon
1 tsp. parfait amour
2 tsp. lemon juice
2 tsp. Triple Sec

*Combine with ice; shake well. Strain. Serve straight up.*

## BUSHRANGER

1 oz. Dubonnet
1 oz. white rum
A few dashes of Angostura bitters

*Combine with ice; shake well. Strain. Add ice and a twist of lemon; drop in the peel.*

## BYCULLA

1 oz. sherry
1 oz. port
1 tbs. curacao
1 tbs. ginger wine

*Combine with ice; shake well. Strain and add ice.*

## YOUR OWN RECIPE

## YOUR OWN RECIPE

Use a bartender's mixing glass whenever the instructions state "combine" ingredients. Strain the drink from the mixing glass into the drinking glass suggested by the illustration alongside the ingredients.

NOTE: The number of glasses or cups shown alongside a recipe do not necessarily indicate the quantity of drinks the recipe will produce.

---

**CABARET**

1 oz. dry gin
1 oz. Dubonnet
A few dashes of Angostura bitters
A few drops Pernod

*Combine with ice; shake well. Strain and add ice. Top with a cherry.*

**CABARET NO. 2**

1½ oz. gin
½ tsp. dry vermouth
A few dashes of Angostura bitters
A few drops Benedictine

*Combine with ice; shake well. Strain and add ice. Top with a cherry.*

**CABLEGRAM**

2 oz. whiskey
1 tsp. powdered sugar
1 tsp. lemon juice
Ginger ale

*Combine (except the ginger ale) with ice; shake well. Strain, add ice, and fill the glass with ginger ale.*

**CADIZ**

¾ oz. amontillado
¾ oz. blackberry liqueur
2 tsp. Triple Sec
2 tsp. heavy cream

*Combine with ice; shake very well. Strain and add ice.*

**CAFE BRULOT**

8 oz. brandy
1 pint boiling coffee
2 sugar cubes
6 cloves
1 chopped vanilla bean
1 cinnamon stick

*Pour the brandy into a small, wide bowl. Add one cube of sugar, cloves, and vanilla. Toss in a cinnamon stick and slices of orange and lemon; stir well. Pour in the coffee. Dunk the remaining cube of sugar in brandy; place the cube on a spoon, ignite it, and dip the spoon into the bowl, igniting the punch. Serve hot.*

**CAFE CACAO**

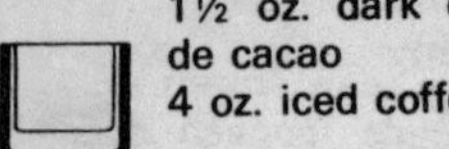

1½ oz. dark creme de cacao
4 oz. iced coffee

*Combine. Stir gently.*

**CAFE COCKTAIL**

1½ oz. dark, iced coffee
1½ tsp. sugar syrup
¾ oz. dark creme de cacao
¾ oz. cognac

*Combine with ice; shake well. Strain, add ice and a twist of lemon.*

**CAFE DE PARIS**

2 oz. gin
¼ oz. heavy cream
1 egg white
Several drops Pernod

*Combine with ice; shake extremely well. Strain and add ice.*

**CAFE DIABLE**

4 cups hot, strong coffee
6 oz. cognac
1 oz. sugar
Whole cloves, cinnamon sticks
Grated orange and lemon rinds

*Combine the sugar, rinds, and spices in a chafing dish. Add all but 1 tablespoon of the cognac; ignite the remaining spoon of cognac and slowly enter it into the sugar. Allow to burn until the sugar has dissolved. Pour in the coffee; stir, and serve.*

**CAFE GROG**

2 oz. Jamaican rum
¾ oz. brandy
1-2 cubes sugar
4 oz. hot black coffee

*Combine. Stir well. Add a twist of lemon.*

**CAJUN NOG**

2 bottles whiskey
8 oz. Jamaican rum
Vanilla ice cream
Nutmeg
6 eggs
4 oz. brown sugar

*Separate the eggs. Combine the yolks with the brown sugar; stir until smooth. Carefully add the whiskey and the rum to this egg mixture, stirring constantly. Refrigerate. Beat the egg whites in another bowl until stiff. Serve cold. Top each glass with a spoon of ice cream and dust with nutmeg.*

## CALIFORNIA PUNCH

2 bottles California Sauterne
2 bottles California champagne
1 quart orange sherbet
2 6-oz. cans frozen orange juice concentrate
1 6-oz. can frozen lemonade concentrate
Orange slices, whole strawberries

*Combine the frozen fruit juice concentrates with the Sauterne in a large punch bowl; stir well to blend. Add the champagne immediately before serving. Use the sherbet instead of or in conjunction with chunks of ice; garnish with the orange slices and strawberries.*

---

## CAMBRIDGE MILK PUNCH

2 quarts milk
1 pint rum
8 oz. brandy
8 oz. sugar, in cubes
2 eggs, well-beaten
Grated lemon rind

*Combine the milk, sugar cubes, and rinds in a saucepan; bring to a boil, stirring constantly until the sugar dissolves. Strain out the peels. Remove from heat; add the eggs, rum, and brandy. Beat until foamy and serve in pre-warmed mugs.*

## CAMPFIRE BRULOT

1 bottle brandy
A pot of hot coffee
Cinnamon sticks, whole colves, soft shelled nuts, lemon and orange peels, nutmeg

*Ideal for the camper. Pour the brandy into an iron pot or small kettle; add the spices and ignite. Slowly pour in the coffee while the liquor burns; cool and enjoy.*

## CANADIAN

1½ oz. curacao
1½ oz. lemon juice
1 tsp. powdered sugar
Several dashes Jamaican rum

*Combine with ice; shake well. Strain and add ice.*

## CANADIAN AND CAMPARI

1 oz. Canadian whiskey
1 oz. dry vermouth
2 tsp. Campari

*Combine with ice; shake well. Strain and add ice. Add a twist of lemon.*

## CANADIAN APPLE

1½ oz. Canadian whiskey
½ oz. calvados
1½ tsp. sugar syrup
1 tsp. lemon juice
1-2 dashes cinnamon

*Combine with ice; shake well. Strain and add ice. Decorate with lemon slice.*

## CANADIAN BLACKBERRY FIX

1½ oz. Canadian whiskey
½ oz. blackberry liqueur
2 tsp. lemon juice
1 tsp. sugar syrup
1 blackberry

*Combine with ice; shake well. Strain over tightly packed crushed ice. Decorate with a lemon slice and a blackberry.*

## CANADIAN CHERRY

1½ oz. Canadian whiskey
½ oz. Cherry Heering
1 tsp. lemon juice
1 tsp. orange juice
Sugar

*Combine with ice; shake well. Sugar frost glass with Cherry Heering. Strain in the drink and add ice.*

## CANADIAN DAISY

14 oz. Canadian whiskey
2 tsp. lemon juice
1 tsp. raspberry syrup
Club soda
Whole raspberries
1 tsp. brandy

*Combine the whiskey, juice, and syrup with ice; shake well. Strain. Add ice. Fill with club soda. Decorate with raspberries and float the brandy.*

## CANADIAN OLD FASHIONED

1½ oz. Canadian whiskey
½ tsp. curacao
Several drops lemon juice
1-2 dashes Angostura bitters

*Combine with ice; shake well. Strain and add ice. Add a twist of lemon and of orange.*

## CANADIAN PINEAPPLE

1½ oz. Canadian whiskey
2 tsp. pineapple juice
2 tsp. lemon juice
Several drops maraschino
1 pineapple stick

*Combine with ice; shake well. Strain and add ice. Top it with the pineapple stick.*

## CAPE CODDER

2 oz. vodka
1 tbs. lime juice
Cranberry juice

*Combine the vodka and lime juice. Stir. Add ice and fill the glass with cranberry juice; stir again until the glass begins to frost.*

## CAPRI

1½ oz. white creme de cacao
2 tbs. blue curacao
1 tbs. green creme de menthe

*Combine with ice; shake well. Strain and add ice.*

**CAPRICE**

2 oz. gin
1 oz. sweet vermouth
1 oz. Campari

*Combine with ice; shake well. Strain into a martini glass straight up.*

**CARA SPOSA**

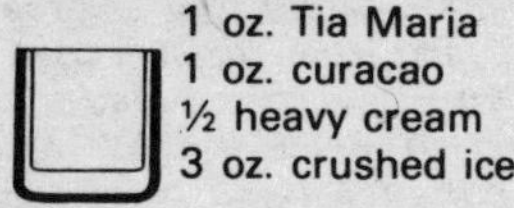

1 oz. Tia Maria
1 oz. curacao
½ heavy cream
3 oz. crushed ice

*Combine in a blender at a low speed for 15 seconds. Strain and serve straight up.*

**CARDINAL COCKTAIL**

2 oz. white rum
1½ tbs. lime juice
1 tsp. almond extract
1 tsp. grenadine
1 tsp. Triple Sec

*Combine with ice; shake well. Strain and add ice. Top with a lime slice.*

**CARDINAL PUNCH**

1 bottle champagne
2 quarts claret
1 quart club soda
1 pint brandy
1 pint Jamaican rum
8 oz. sweet vermouth
6 oz. powdered sugar
3 cups lemon juice

*Combine all but soda and champagne, stir with ice. When ready to serve, add soda and champagne; top with fruit slices.*

**CARIB COCKTAIL**

1½ oz. white rum
1 oz. lime juice
1 oz. pineapple juice

*Combine with ice; shake well. Strain and add ice.*

**CARIBBEAN CHAMPAGNE**

4 oz. champagne
½ tsp. white rum
½ tsp. banana liqueur
1-2 dashes orange bitters
1 banana slice

*Combine (except the banana slice) in a wide champagne glass straight up; stir gently. Decorate with the slice of banana. Crushed ice optional.*

**CARIBBEAN COCKTAIL**

2 oz. white rum
8 oz. pineapple juice
2 tbs. lime juice
1 oz. sugar syrup
1-2 dashes orange bitters
Club soda

*Combine (except the soda) with ice; shake. Strain; add ice and soda.*

**CARIBBEAN JOY**

1½ oz. Scotch
2 tsp. lime juice
1 tsp. powdered sugar
Several drops Cointreau

*Combine with ice; shake well. Strain and add ice.*

## CARIOCA COOLER

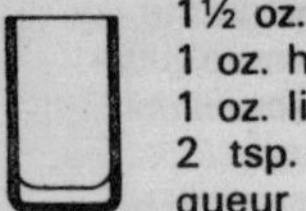

1½ oz. white rum
1 oz. honey
1 oz. lime juice
2 tsp. mandarin liqueur
2 oz. crushed ice

*Combine in a blender at a high speed for 10 seconds. Strain into a pre-chilled glass filled with crushed ice. Top with a slice of lime.*

## CARLTON

3 oz. orange juice
2 tbs. Grand Marnier
1 egg white
A few drops of peach bitters
Champagne

*Combine everything except the champagne with ice; shake very well. Strain; add champagne and stir gently. Decorate with a cherry.*

## CAROLINA

3 oz. Centenario or aged tequila
1 oz. heavy cream
1½ tsp. grenadine
Several drops vanilla extract
1 egg white

*Combine with ice; shake well. Strain; serve straight up. Dust with cinnamon. Top with cherry.*

## CARROL

1½ oz. brandy
1 tbs. sweet vermouth

*Combine with ice; shake well. Strain and add ice. Top with a cherry.*

## CARROT WINE

4 lbs. carrots, pared clean
2 oz. hops
3 lbs. sugar, moistened in water
1 tbs. yeast

*Boil the carrots in 1 gal. of water for 15 minutes; add the hops and boil another 10 minutes. Strain into a large pot; add the moist sugar. When lukewarm, spread the yeast on a slice of toast and drop the toast and yeast into the pot. Seal and allow to ferment for a day and a half. When fermented, strain clean and seal up in bottles. Store for at least a month before using.*

## CASA BLANCA

2 oz. Jamaican rum
1 tsp. lime juice
A few dashes of Angostura bitters
A few drops of curacao
A few drops of maraschino

*Combine with ice; shake well. Strain and add ice.*

## CASA BLANCA SPECIAL

2 oz. dark rum
3 tsp. sugar syrup
3 tsp. lime juice
1 tsp. apiece of Cointreau, cherry brandy. and grenadine
1-2 dashes Angostura bitters

*Combine with ice; shake well. Strain. Decorate with a cherry and a slice of orange.*

**CASINO**

2 oz. gin
½ tsp. maraschino
1-2 dashes orange bitters
A few drops lemon juice

*Combine with ice; shake well. Strain and add ice.*

**CASSIS PUNCH**

13 bottles white wine
4 oz. creme de cassis
2 cups strawberries

*Steep the strawberries in the creme de cassis for 1-2 hours before serving. Strain the creme de cassis. Add the wine plus chunks of ice. Float the strawberries.*

**CASTLE DIP**

1½ oz. apple brandy
1½ oz. white creme de menthe
A few drops Pernod

*Combine with ice; shake well. Strain and add ice.*

**CASTLE SPECIAL**

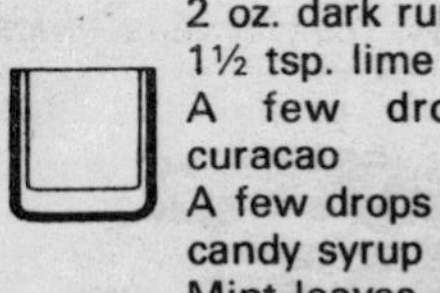

2 oz. dark rum
1½ tsp. lime juice
A few drops of curacao
A few drops of rock candy syrup
Mint leaves

*Combine (except the mint leaves) with ice; shake. Strain and add ice. Top with mint.*

**CELERY WINE**

1 large bunch of celery
3 lb. sugar
2 cakes of yeast, moistened
Lemon slices

*Boil the celery in a gallon of water for at least 15 minutes. Strain and allow to cool; combine with the sugar, lemon slices, and the yeast and store in a warm place for several days. Re-strain; seal in a crock pot and allow to ferment for several weeks. Store in bottles for future use.*

**CHABLIS COOLER**

1 oz. vodka
2 tsp. grenadine
2 tsp. lemon juice
A few drops vanilla extract
Chablis
Sugar

*Sugar frost the glass. Pour in all the ingredients except the Chablis and stir well. Add ice and fill with Chablis.*

**CHABLIS CUP**

1 bottle Chablis
4 oz. Grand Marnier
4 oz. kirsch
2½ cups sliced peaches, strawberries, lemons, and oranges
Mint sprigs

*Combine all but the Chablis and mint. Refrigerate for one hour. When ready, pour the fruit in. Top with mint.*

### CHAMPAGNE AND APPLE PUNCH

2 quarts apple juice
2 bottles white rum
2 bottles champagne
1 tbs. Angostura bitters

*Combine the juice, rum, and bitters. Stir. Add the champagne plus chunks of ice before serving; stir very gently to mix.*

### CHAMPAGNE BAYOU

2 oz. gin
2 tsp. sugar syrup
1 tsp. lemon juice
Champagne

*Combine the gin, syrup, and juice with ice; shake well. Strain, add ice and fill the glass with champagne. Flavored brandies can be used instead of the gin.*

### CHAMPAGNE BRUNCH PUNCH

2 bottles cognac
8 oz. curacao
12 oz. orange juice
9 oz. lemon juice
8 oz. grenadine
Sugar to taste
Orange peels, in spirals
1 bottle champagne

*Combine everything except the champagne; stir well. Add the champagne plus chunks of ice before serving.*

### CHAMPAGNE CASSIS

*Serve your champagne as always, adding a few drops of creme de cassis.*

### CHAMPAGNE CIDER

9 gallons hard cider
2½ pints maple syrup
1½ pints cooking alcohol
1 cup skimmed milk
A few drops apiece orange flower water and neroli

*Combine the cider, maple syrup, and alcohol in a wooden cask; seal and store for several weeks. When ready, skim the surface clean; add the milk, flower water, and neroli. Stir well and bottle. Store the bottles on their sides for aeration.*

### CHAMPAGNE COOLER

1 oz. brandy
1 oz. Cointreau
Champagne
Mint sprigs

*Pour the brandy and the Cointreau over packed crushed ice. Fill with champagne and stir. Top with mint sprigs.*

## CHAMPAGNE CUP

2 oz. brandy
2 oz. curacao
1 pint club soda
1 bottle champagne
Slices of pineapple and strawberries
Cucumber peels

*Combine the brandy and the curacao with ice; add the fruit slices and peels. Stir well. Pour in the soda and the champagne before serving.*

## CHAMPAGNE JULEP

1½ oz. brandy
1 tbs. sugar syrup
Champagne
A few mint sprigs

*Crush the mint in the sugar syrup on the bottom of a glass. Fill with crushed ice; add the brandy. Pour in the champagne. Stir gently. Decorate with more sprigs of mint.*

## CHAMPAGNE POLONAISE

Blackberry liqueur
1 tsp. blackberry brandy
Cognac
Several drops champagne
Sugar

*Sugar frost a glass with a little blackberry liqueur. Pour in the brandy; add the cognac. Fill with champagne and gently stir.*

## CHAMPAGNE PUNCH

4 bottles champagne
1 quart club soda
1 pint curacao
1 pint brandy
8 oz. maraschino
8 oz. powdered sugar
3 cups lemon juice

*Combine all except the champagne. Stir well. Add the soda plus chunks of ice before serving.*

*There are many variations to a* **CHAMPAGNE PUNCH:** *You can substitute rum for the brandy, halve the lemon juice and add orange juice to make it up, and add pineapple juice for the maraschino (omitting the curacao and club soda).*

*If you like the taste of other liquors with champagne, make the punch with rum, brandy, and bourbon (a bottle each), halving the champagne and the sugar, and using orange juice instead of the lemon juice altogether. Seal it with 1 quart of strong cold tea instead of the club soda. Orange bitters can be added for a zingier punch. Fruit slices are for topping.*

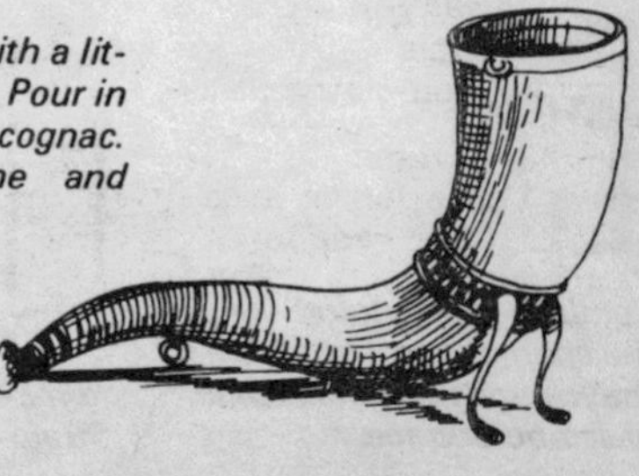

Ancient Royal Drinking Horn

**CHAMPAGNE SHERBET PUNCH**

2 bottles chilled champagne
1 quart lemon sherbet
1 bottle chilled sauterne

*Place the sherbet in the center of a punch bowl. Pour the champagne and sauterne around it. Serve with a scoop, putting half sherbet and half wine into each glass.*

**CHAMPAGNE ST. MORITZ**

1 tbs. dry gin
1 tbs. apricot brandy
1 tbs. orange juice
Champagne

*Combine everything except the champagne with ice; shake well. Strain into a wide champagne glass straight up. Fill with champagne and stir.*

**CHANCELLOR**

1½ oz. Scotch
1½ tsp. dry vermouth
1½ tsp. port
1-2 dashes bitters

*Combine with ice; shake well. Strain and add ice.*

**CHANTICLEER**

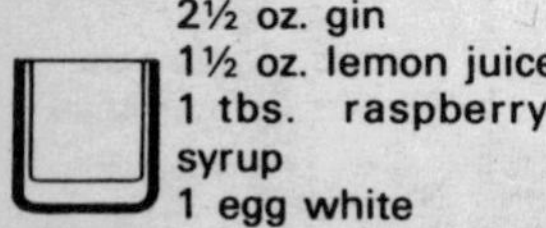

2½ oz. gin
1½ oz. lemon juice
1 tbs. raspberry syrup
1 egg white

*Combine with ice; shake well. Strain and add ice.*

**CHAPALA**

1½ oz. tequila
2 tsp. orange juice
lemon juice, and grenadine
A few drops orange flower water

*Combine with ice; shake well. Strain and add ice. Top with an orange slice.*

---

**CHAPEL HILL**

1½ oz. whiskey
½ oz. curacao
2 tsp. lemon juice

*Combine with ice; shake well. Strain and add ice. Top with an orange slice.*

---

**CHARLES**

1½ oz. brandy
1½ oz. sweet vermouth
A few dashes of Angostura bitters

*Combine with ice; shake well. Strain and add ice.*

**CHARLIE CHAPLIN**

2½ oz. sloe gin
2½ oz. apricot brandy
1½ tbs. lime juice

*Combine with ice; shake well. Strain over crushed ice.*

## CHARTREUSE CHAMPAGNE

4 oz. champagne
Several drops green chartreuse
Several drops cognac

*Combine and gently stir. Add a twist of lemon.*

## CHARTREUSE COGNAC FRAPPE

1 tbs. yellow chartreuse
1 tbs. cognac
Lemon soda

*Combine with ice; shake well. Strain, add ice, and fill with lemon soda. Decorate with an orange slice.*

## CHATEAU D'ISSOGNE

1½ oz. bourbon
1½ oz. sweet vermouth
1 tbs. aquavit
A few drops of Campari

*Combine with ice; shake well. Strain straight up.*

## CHATHAM

1¼ oz. gin
2 tsp. ginger brandy
1 tsp. lemon juice
1 piece preserved ginger

*Combine the gin, brandy, and lemon juice with ice. Shake well. Strain, add ice, and drop in the piece of ginger.*

## CHATHAM ARTILLERY PUNCH

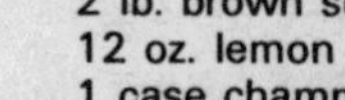

1½ gallons rose wine
1½ quarts rye
1 quart brandy
1½ gallons dark iced tea
½ gallon rum
1 quart dry gin
8 oz. Benedictine
1½ gallons orange juice
2 lb. brown sugar
12 oz. lemon juice
1 case champagne

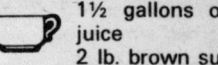

*Combine everything but the champagne in a large punch bowl; refrigerate for at least 48 hours. Before serving, pour in the champagne, add chunks of ice, and stir.*

## CHAUNCEY

½ oz. rye
½ oz. gin
½ oz. sweet vermouth
½ oz. brandy
1-2 dashes orange bitters

*Combine with ice; shake well. Strain and add ice.*

## CHELSEA SIDECAR

1½ oz. gin
1 tbs. Triple Sec
1 tbs. lemon juice

*Combine with ice, shake well. Strain and add ice.*

## CHERRY BLOSSOM

1½ oz. brandy
1 tbs. cherry liqueur
A few drops of curacao
A few drops of grenadine
½ oz. lemon juice
Sugar

*Combine. Shake with ice. Sugar frost the glass with cherry brandy. Strain in the drink.*

## CHERRY BOUNCE

1 quart Jamaican rum
5 pints whole cherries
Brown sugar

*Muddle the cherries (unstoned). Pour the rum over them and allow to stand at room temperature for at least one week. After this time, strain the drink clean; add brown sugar to taste, and allow to stand another week before serving. Serve over ice.*

## CHERRY COBBLER

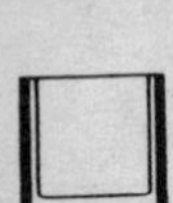

1½ oz. gin
2 tsp. Cherry Heering
2 tsp. creme de cassis
2 tsp. lemon juice
1½ tsp. sugar syrup

*Combine the liquors, lemon juice, and sugar syrup with ice; shake well. Strain over ice. Decorate with a lemon slice and a cherry.*

## CHERRY DAIQUIRI

1½ oz. white rum
2 tsp. lime juice
2 tsp. cherry liqueur
A few drops kirsch

*Combine with ice; shake well. Strain, add ice and a twist of lime.*

## CHERRY GINGER FRAPPE

1 oz. cherry liqueur
1 tsp. kirschwasser
1 tsp. ginger brandy
1 piece preserved ginger

*Combine the liquors without ice and mix well. Pour over crushed ice. Spear a cherry and the ginger on a toothpick and bridge the pick across the drink.*

## CHERRY RUM FIX

1½ oz. vodka
2 tsp. Cherry Heering
2 tsp. lemon juice
1 tsp. sugar

*Into 2 oz. of water, add the sugar and stir until completely dissolved. Fill with crushed ice and pour in the vodka, Cherry Heering, and lemon juice. Decorate with a lemon slice.*

## CHERRY SLING

1½ oz. gin
2 tsp. Cherry Karise
2 tsp. lime juice

*Combine with ice; shake well. Strain and add ice.*

### CHICAGO

1½ oz. brandy
A few drops curacao
Powdered sugar
1-2 dashes
Angostura bitters
Champagne
Sugar

*Combine the brandy, curacao, and bitters with ice. Shake well. Sugar frost the glass with lemon juice. Strain in the drink and fill with champagne.*

### CHICAGO BOMB

2 oz. vanilla ice cream
1 tsp. white creme de cacao
1 tsp. green creme de menthe

*Combine in a blender at a high speed for a few seconds. Serve straight up.*

### CHICAGO FIZZ

1 oz. white rum
1 oz. port
1½ tsp. lemon juice
1 tsp. powdered sugar
1 egg white
Club soda

*Combine (except the club soda) with ice; shake well. Strain, add ice, and fill the glass with club soda.*

### CHINA

2 oz. gold rum
1 tsp. curacao
A few drops grenadine
A few drops passion fruit juice
A few dashes of Angostura bitters

*Combine with ice; shake well. Strain and add ice.*

### CHINESE COCKTAIL

1½ oz. Jamaican rum
1 tbs. grenadine
A few dashes curacao
A few dashes maraschino
1-2 dashes
Angostura bitters

*Combine with ice; shake well. Strain and add ice.*

### CHIQUITA

1½ oz. vodka
2 tsp. banana liqueur
2 tsp. lime juice
2 oz. sliced bananas
1 tsp. sugar
2 oz. crushed ice

*Combine in a blender at a low speed for 15 seconds. Strain and serve straight up.*

### CHIQUITA PUNCH

¾ oz. banana liqueur
¾ oz. orange juice
¾ oz. heavy cream
1 tsp. grenadine
6 oz. crushed ice

*Combine in a blender at a high speed for 15 seconds. Strain and serve straight up.*

## CHOCOLATE EGG NOG

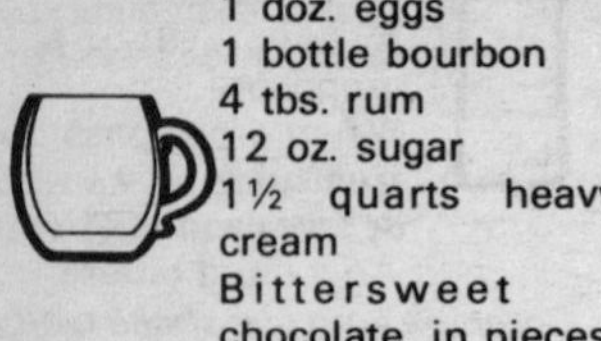

1 doz. eggs
1 bottle bourbon
4 tbs. rum
12 oz. sugar
1½ quarts heavy cream
Bittersweet chocolate, in pieces

*Separate the eggs. Beat the yolks with 1 cup of the sugar; add the bourbon and the rum in small amounts, stirring constantly. Beat the egg whites with the remaining sugar until stiff; whip the cream. Fold them both carefull into the nog. Garnish with the chocolate.*

## CHOCOLATE ORANGE FRAPPE

1 oz. white creme de cacao
1 oz. orange juice
1 tsp. Roiano

*Combine without ice; pour over crushed ice.*

## CHOCOLATE RUM

1 oz. white rum
2 tsp. white creme de cacao
2 tsp. white creme de menthe
2 tsp. heavy cream
1 tsp. high-proof rum

*Combine the white rum and creams with ice; shake well. Strain and add ice. Float the high-proof rum on top.*

## CHOCOLATE SOLDIER

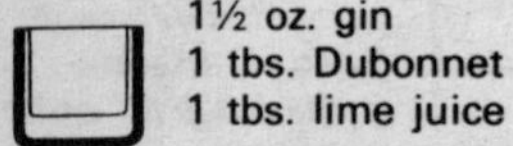

1½ oz. gin
1 tbs. Dubonnet
1 tbs. lime juice

*Combine with ice; shake well. Strain and add ice.*

## CHRISTMAS DELIGHT

10 oz. white rum
3 egg yolks
8 oz. sugar
1 tsp. vanilla extract
14 oz. undiluted evaporated milk

*Combine the yolks and the sugar in a saucepan; slowly add the milk and stir until smooth. Heat for no more than two minutes, stirring rapidly. Remove from heat; add the vanilla and the rum. Stir well.*

## CHRISTMAS RUM PUNCH

½ gallon cider
1 bottle Jamaican rum
½ doz. oranges
Cloves
Sugar
Cinnamon
Nutmeg

*Stick the oranges with cloves and bake until the oranges begin to brown. Slice the oranges and place them in a large punch bowl; pour in the rum and add sugar to taste. Ignite; extinguish with the cider after a few minutes. Garnish with cinnamon and nutmeg; serve hot.*

## CHRISTMAS TEA PUNCH

2 bottles red wine
1 bottle dark rum
3 cups hot tea
2 lbs. sugar
3 oz. orange juice
1 oz. lemon juice

*Combine the wine, juices, tea, and all but one oz. of the rum; heat thoroughly but do not allow to boil. Turn out into a large chafing dish; add all but 2 oz. sugar and stir until the sugar has dissolved. Combine the leftover sugar and rum in a ladle; ignite and infuse into the warm punch. Serve immediately.*

## CHRISTMAS WINE

2 gallon bottles red wine
1 bottle port
1 pint brandy
1 lemon, stuck with cloves
Grated tangerine peels
Some ginger, mace, nutmeg, and cinnamon

*Combine in a large saucepan; heat thoroughly but do not allow to boil. Serve warm in mugs.*

## CHRISTOPHER'S MOTHER

2 oz. gin
1 oz. white rum
2 tsp. orange juice
1 tsp. lemon juice
A few drops of whiskey

*Combine with ice; shake well. Strain and add ice.*

## CHRYSANTHEMUM

2 tbs. dry vermouth
2 tbs. Benedictine
Several dashes Pernod

*Combine with ice; shake well. Strain, add ice and a twist of orange.*

## CHURCHILL

1½ oz. Scotch
½ oz. Cointreau
½ oz. sweet vermouth
2 tsp. lime juice

*Combine with ice; shake well. Strain and add ice.*

## CIDER CUP

1 quart cider
2 tbs. maraschino
2 tbs. brandy
12 oz. club soda

*Combine all the ingredients in a large pitcher with ice cubes. Garnish with a twist of lemon or orange; stir.*

## CIDER HEADACHE MEDICINE

1 quart hard cider
2 oz. whole white mustard seeds
2 oz. whole burdock seeds
1 horse-radish root, cut into small pieces

*Combine in a large jar or bottle; cover tightly. Allow to stand for several hours before using. Drink in moderation.*

## CIDER NIGHT CAP

½ gallon hard cider
3 oz. powdered sugar
9 eggs, separated
Grated nutmeg, allspice

*Combine the egg yolks with the sugar; beat until creamy. In a separate bowl, beat the whites until foamy; combine with the sweetened yolks in a large bowl. Heat the cider in a large saucepan; when it begins to boil pour it over the eggs, stirring constantly. Top with the garnishes and serve in mugs.*

## CIDER SYLLABUB

1 pint hard cider
1 pint heavy cream
4 oz. brandy
2 egg whites
2 oz. sugar
Grated lemon rind; tsp. lemon juice

*Combine the brandy with the cider in a large crock; add the lemon juice, rind, and sugar. Stir very well to blend and store in a cool place overnight. When ready, beat together the cream and egg whites until thick and fold into the cider.*

## CIDER POSSET

1 quart heavy cream
1 pint cider
8 oz. Madeira
10 egg yolks
4 egg whites
Grated nutmeg

*Combine the cream and the cider in a saucepan; beat the yolks and the whites in separate bowls until thick and creamy and add to the cider and cream. Pour in the Madeira and nutmeg to taste and simmer over low heat until saucy; do not allow to boil. Serve warmed in mugs.*

## CIDER SMASH

2 oz. brandy
1 tbs. powdered sugar
Pineapple chunks
Lemon slices
Cider

*Dissolve the sugar with the brandy; add fruit slices plus plenty of crushed ice. Fill the glass with cider and stir gently.*

## CITY SLICKER

1½ oz. brandy
¾ oz. curacao

*Combine with ice; shake well. Strain and add ice.*

## CITRONELLE

The rinds of 3 doz. lemons
The rinds of 5 oranges
6 cups of sugar
1 gallon cooking alcohol
Ground cloves, nutmeg

*Grate the rinds and combine in a pot with ground cloves and the alcohol. Seal the pot and allow to steep for at least two weeks. Strain clean and add the sugar, diluted in a quart of water. Bottle and store in a cool, dark place.*

---

## CLARET COBBLER

1 tsp. powdered sugar
1 tsp. lemon juice
A few drops of maraschino
Claret
1 oz. crushed ice
1 pineapple stick

*Over crushed ice, add sugar, lemon juice, and maraschino. Stir well. Fill with claret. Top with pineapple.*

---

## CLARET COCKTAIL

1 oz. claret
1 oz. brandy
1 tsp. curacao
1 tsp. lemon
½ tsp. anisette

*Combine with ice; shake well. Strain and add ice and a twist of orange.*

## CLARET COOLER

4 oz. claret
1 oz. orange juice
2 tsp. brandy
2 tsp. lemon juice
3 oz. club soda
1 long sliver orange rind

*Pour the wine, brandy, soda, and juices over ice and stir well. Drop in the orange rind and add a twist of lemon.*

## CLARET CUP

1 bottle claret
1 bottle club soda
8 oz. sherry
2½ oz. Triple Sec
2½ oz. brandy
1 lemon rind, pared
Powdered sugar
Fruit slices
Fresh mint

*Combine in a small punch bowl and stir well. Add powdered sugar to taste. Decorate with fruit and mint. Let stand a few hours before serving.*

## CLARET FRUIT CUP

1 bottle claret
3 oz. orange juice
3 tsp. lemon juice
Grated lemon rind
1½ oz. sugar
2 oz. brandy
1 cucumber slice
2 bottles club soda

*Soak the claret with the sugar in a punch bowl for at least one hour. Stir and add the juices and brandy. Garnish with the rinds. When ready to serve, add the soda plus enough crushed ice to fill the bowl and stir gently.*

**CLARET PUNCH**

3 cups lemon juice
1 cup powdered sugar
3 quarts claret
8 oz. curacao
8 oz. brandy
1 quart club soda
Fruit slices

*In a large punch bowl, combine the lemon juice with the sugar. Stir vigorously to dissolve sugar. Pour in the wine, curacao, brandy, and soda. Stir. Top with fruit. Add chunks of ice a half-hour before serving.*

**CLARET RUM COOLER**

3 oz. claret
1 oz. white
2 tsp. kirschwasser
2 tsp. Falernum
1 strawberry

*Combine with ice; stir well. Drop in the strawberry or add a twist of orange.*

**CLARIDGE COCKTAIL**

¾ oz. dry gin
¾ oz. dry vermouth
2 tsp. apricot brandy
2 tsp. Triple Sec

*Combine with ice; shake well. Strain and add ice.*

**CLASSIC**

1½ oz. brandy
2 tsp. lemon juice
1 tsp. maraschino
1 tsp. curacao

*Combine with ice; shake well. Strain and add ice.*

**CLOISTER**

1½ oz. gin
2 tsp. grapefruit juice
1 tsp. lemon juice
1 tsp. yellow chartreuse

*Combine with ice; shake well. Strain and add ice.*

**CLOVER CLUB**

1½ oz. gin
2 tbs. lime juice
2 tbs. grenadine
1 egg white

*Combine with ice; shake well. Strain and add ice.*

**CLOVER CLUB ROYAL**

1½ oz. gin
1 tbs. lemon juice
1 tsp. grenadine
½ egg yolk

*Combine with ice; shake well. Strain and add ice.*

**CLUB MARTINI**

1½ oz. gin
2 tsp. sweet vermouth

*Combine with ice; shake well. Strain. Decorate with an olive and serve straight up.*

**COCICE**

1½ oz. white rum
1 oz. coconut milk
1 tsp. sugar syrup
6 oz. crushed ice

*Combine in a blender at a high speed for 25 seconds. Pour out straight up.*

**COCONUT BRANDY BOWL**

3 oz. brandy
1½ banana liqueur
2 large coconuts
Crushed ice

*Slice off the eyes of the coconuts; drain and save the milk. Gouge out the meat of the coconuts; saving as much milk from that as possible. Combine the brandy, banana liqueur, and all the coconut milk in a blender with 3-4 oz. of crushed ice. Blend at a high speed for 15 seconds. Serve the drink in the two coconut shells.*

**COCONUT COOLER**

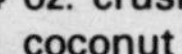

1½ oz. white rum
1 oz. cream of coconut
1 oz. heavy cream
4 oz. crushed ice
1 coconut

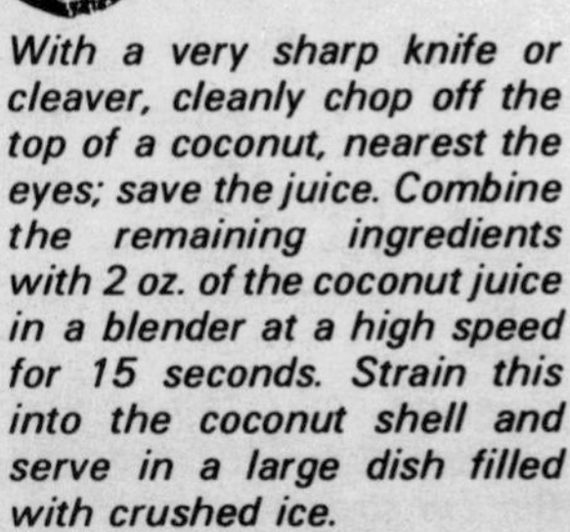

*With a very sharp knife or cleaver, cleanly chop off the top of a coconut, nearest the eyes; save the juice. Combine the remaining ingredients with 2 oz. of the coconut juice in a blender at a high speed for 15 seconds. Strain this into the coconut shell and serve in a large dish filled with crushed ice.*

**COCONUT CORDIAL**

White rum
Sugar
A large coconut

*Slice off the eye of the coconut and drain. Fill the coconut with water and measure the amount of water you put in. Combine the rum and sugar (at a ratio of 2:1) to equal the amount of water. Stir until the sugar has dissolved and pour it into the coconut. Seal it with wax and store at room temperature for at least a month. Uncork and bottle. Serve as a cordial.*

**COCONUT GIN**

1½ oz. gin
2 tsp. lemon juice
1 tsp. maraschino
1 tsp. cream of coconut

*Combine with ice; shake. Strain and add ice.*

**COCONUT GROVE COOLER**

1½ oz. bourbon
2 tsp. apiece of orange juice, lemon juice, orange curacao, grenadine, and pineapple juice
1 tsp. Passionola

*Combine with ice; shake well. Strain over crushed ice. Decorate with orange and pineapple slices, a cherry, and a mint sprig.*

## COCONUT RUM

1 large coconut
Brown sugar

*Slice off the eyes of the coconut and drain out the milk. Fill with brown sugar and seal very tightly. Allow the sugar in the coconut ferment in a cool, dark place for several months. When ready, you will be able to smell and taste a most delicate, coconut-scented rum. Serve pieces of coconut meat on the side.*

## COCONUT TEQUILA

1½ oz. tequila
2 tsp. lemon juice
2 tsp. cream of coconut
1 tsp. maraschino
4 oz. crushed ice

*Combine in a blender at a low speed for 15 seconds. Strain and serve straight up.*

## COEXISTENCE COLLINS

2 oz. vodka
2 tsp. lemon juice
1½ tsp. sugar syrup
1 tsp. kummel
1 cucumber peel
Club soda

*Combine the vodka, juice, sugar, and kummel with ice; shake well. Strain, add ice, and fill with club soda. Top with the cucumber peel and a twist of lemon.*

## COFFEE ALEXANDER

1½ oz. brandy or gin
1 oz. Galacafe
1 oz. heavy cream
Sugar

*Wet the rim of a glass with Galacafe and press in sugar. Combine all the liquids and shake in a mixing glass. Strain into the frosted glass.*

## COFFEE BLAZER

1 tbs. coffee liqueur
1 tbs. cognac
Sugar
Lemon slice
Hot coffee
Whipped cream

*Warm the coffee liqueur and cognac over a low flame. Line the rim of an old-fashioned glass with the juice of the lemon slice; press it in sugar and drop in the slice. Warm the glass to melt the sugar; pour in the warmed liquor and ignite. Pour in the coffee; stir well. Garnish with whipped cream.*

## COFFEE COCKTAIL

1½ oz. apple brandy
1½ oz. port
1 egg yolk
1 oz. coffee

*Combine with ice; shake. Strain and add ice. Top with nutmeg.*

### COFFEE COOLER

1½ oz. vodka
1 oz. heavy cream
1 oz. Kahlua
1½ tsp. sugar syrup
4 oz. iced coffee
1 scoop coffee ice cream

*Combine all (except ice cream) with ice; shake. Strain, add ice and the ice cream.*

### COFFEE EGG NOG

1½ oz. whiskey
1 oz. Kahlua
2 tsp. heavy cream
1½ tsp. sugar syrup
1 egg
½ tsp. instant coffee
4 oz. milk
Ground coriander

*Combine all (except the coriander) with ice; shake. Strain and add ice. Dust with coriander.*

### COFFEE FLIP

1½ oz. cognac
1 oz. port
1½ tsp. sugar syrup
1 egg
1 oz. coffee

*Combine with ice; shake. Strain. Dust with nutmeg and serve straight up.*

### COFFEE GRAND MARNIER

¾ oz. Kahlua
¾ oz. Grand Marnier
1 tbs. orange juice

*Combine without ice.; stir well. Pour over crushed ice. Top with an orange slice.*

### COFFEE GRASSHOPPER

¾ oz. coffee liqueur
¾ oz. white creme de menthe
¾ oz. heavy cream

*Combine with ice; shake very well. Strain and add ice.*

### COFFEE KIRSCH

1 oz. kirsch
1 egg white
4 oz. coffee
A pinch of sugar

*Combine with ice; shake well. Strain and add ice.*

### COFFEE LIQUEUR

5 cups cooking alcohol
4 lb. sugar
8 oz. brewed ground coffee beans

*Combine the coffee with 1 cup of alcohol in a pot; allow to stand for at least one week. Boil the sugar in water to make a syrup; remove from heat. Add the unused alcohol and the prepared coffee; stir, strain, and bottle. Store for several months before using.*

---

### COFFEE NO. 2

1½ oz. brandy
1 tbs. port
1-2 dashes curacao
1 tsp. sugar syrup
1 egg yolk
1 oz. coffee

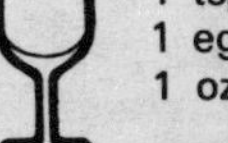

*Combine with ice; shake well. Strain and add ice; garnish with nutmeg.*

## COFFEE ROIANO

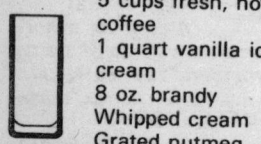

1½ oz. Roiano
2 tsp. coffee liqueur
2 tsp. cream
3 oz. crushed ice

*Combine in a blender at a low speed for 15 seconds. Strain and serve straight up.*

---

## COFFEE VIENNESE

5 cups fresh, hot coffee
1 quart vanilla ice cream
8 oz. brandy
Whipped cream
Grated nutmeg

*Combine the coffee and the brandy in a large chafing dish to keep hot. Fill several tall glasses with alternate layers of brandy and coffee and scoops of ice cream, stirring to blend until every glass is almost full. Garnish with whipped cream dusted with nutmeg.*

## COGNAC MINT FRAPPE

1 oz. green creme de menthe
1 tsp. cognac
Mint leaves, partially torn

*Combine the creme de menthe and the cognac without ice; stir well. Pour over crushed ice; top with the mint leaves.*

## COKE AND DAGGER

2 oz. Jamuican rum
Cola
1-2 drops orange bitters

*Combine the rum and the bitters. Stir well. Add ice and fill with cola; stir gently. Touch it up with a twist of orange.*

## COLD APPLE TODDY

1 quart apple brandy
1 pint peach brandy
1 pint sherry
1 doz. apples
10 oz. sugar
2 quarts boiling water

*Bake the apples; mash while hot. Add the sugar and boiling water and stir well. Pour in the brandies; stir. Cover and allow to cool. Strain when cool, add the sherry, and serve over ice.*

## COLD DECK

1½ oz. brandy
¾ oz. sweet vermouth
¾ oz. white creme de menthe
1-2 dashes Pernod

*Combine with ice; shake well. Strain and add ice.*

## COLD DUCK

2 bottles Moselle
1 bottle champagne
1½ oz. lemon juice
3 oz. sugar
1 large lemon

*Dissolve the sugar with the lemon juice on the bottom of a large punch bowl; add the Moselle and stir gently. Carefully peel the lemon in one long, spiral strip. Hook the end of the peel over the side of the bowl and place the whole, peeled lemon in the wine. Add the champagne before serving.*

## COLD IRISH

1½ oz. Irish whiskey
½ oz. Irish Mist
A few drops creme de cacao
Whipped cream
Coffee soda

*Pour the whiskey and the Irish Mist over ice. Fill with coffee soda and stir. Touch up the whipped cream with the creme de cacao and use it to top the drink.*

## COLD WINE FLIP

3 oz. claret, burgundy, or sherry
1 egg
1 tsp. powdered sugar

*Combine the wine and the egg with ice; shake well. Dissolve the sugar with a few drops of water. Strain over ice and stir gently. Garnish with nutmeg.*

## COLONIAL CAUDLE

1 pint white wine
8 oz. sugar
8 oz. oatmeal water
3 tsp. orange juice
Grated lemon rind

*Simmer the oatmeal water with lemon rinds (to taste) for several minutes. Strain clean into a separate bowl. Add the sugar, orange juice, and wine; stir until well-blended. Serve in mugs.*

## COLONIAL TEA PUNCH

12 lemons, thinly peeled
1 quart dark iced tea
1 quart Jamaican rum
1½ oz. brandy
12 oz. sugar

*Combine the juice of the lemons, their peels, the tea, and the sugar. Steep for 1-2 hours. Then, a half-hour before serving add the rum, brandy, and chunks of ice.*

## COLUMBIA SKIN

1 lemon, thinly peeled
9 oz. Scotch
2 cups boiling water

*Slice the fruit and place its peels and the slices on the bottom of a small, heat-proof pitcher. Pour in the Scotch and the boiling water; stir. Serve hot, topped with lemon slices.*

## COLUMBIA SKIN NO. 2

3 oz. rum
1½ oz. lemon juice
1 tsp. curacao
2 cubes sugar
1 tbs. water

*Combine in a saucepan; heat and stir but do not boil. Pour out into a warm glass; serve hot. Brandy or gin can be used for the rum.*

## COMBO

2½ oz. dry vermouth
¼ oz. cognac
½ tsp. curacao
1 tsp. sugar syrup
A few dashes of Angostura bitters

*Combine with ice; shake. Strain and add ice.*

## COMMODORE

1 oz. bourbon
1 oz. dark creme de cacao
1 oz. lemon juice
1-2 dashes grenadine

*Combine with ice; shake well. Strain and serve straight up.*

## COMMONWEALTH

1¾ oz. Canadian whiskey
½ oz. Van der Hum liqueur
1 tsp. lemon juice

*Combine with ice; shake well. Strain; add ice and a twist of orange.*

## CONCHITA

1 oz. tequila
1 oz. grapefruit juice
A few drops lemon juice

*Combine with ice; shake well. Strain and add ice.*

## CONCH SHELL

4 oz. white rum
2 tsp. lime juice

*Combine with ice; shake well. Strain and add ice.*

---

## CONNECTICUT SYLLABUB

*This one is from the first cookbook ever published in New England, written by Miss Amelia Simonds of Hartford: "Sweeten a quart of cyder with refined sugar, grate nutmeg into it, then milk your cow into your liquor."*

## CONSTANT COMMENT PUNCH

1 quart tea, iced
1 pint orange juice
8 oz. lemon juice
8 oz. sugar
1 bottle ginger ale
Bourbon
Fruit slices, cherries, mint sprigs

*Combine everything except the soda, bourbon, and garnishes. Stir well to blend. Add the ginger ale plus ice before serving; top with the fruit slices, cherries, and mint. Spike the punch with bourbon to taste.*

## CONSTANTIA PUNCH

1 bottle claret
4 oz. Van der Hum
4 oz. brandy liqueur
7 oz. sugar
Whole cloves
1 orange, peeled and sliced

*Combine the wine with the orange slices, sugar, and cloves in a saucepan; heat thoroughly but do not allow to boil. Add 1 pint of already boiling water plus the brandy liqueur and the Van der Hum and stir well. Allow to cool and serve garnished with nutmeg.*

## CONTINENTAL SOUR

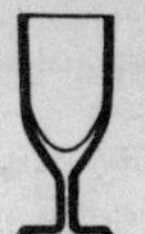

1¼ oz. rye
1½ tbs. lemon juice
1 tsp. sugar syrup
1 egg white
1 tbs. claret

*Combine (except the claret) with ice; shake extremely well. Strain, add ice, and float the claret on top.*

## COOCH BEHAR

1½ oz. pepper vodka
3 oz. tomato juice

*Combine with ice; shake well. Strain and add ice.*
*To make your own pepper vodka, drop a hot chili pepper into a bottle of vodka and let it stand for a week or so.*

## COOL COLONEL

1½ oz. bourbon
1 oz. Southern Comfort
3 oz. dark iced tea
½ oz. lemon juice
3 tsp. sugar syrup
Club soda

*Combine all (except the soda); add ice and stir well. Splash in some soda and add a twist of lemon.*

## CONSTITUTION FLIP

1 pint hard cider
2 oz. rock candy
1 egg
Whole cloves
A cinnamon stick

*Crush the rock candy and the cinnamon stick together into a powder; add to the cider and stir well. Beat in an egg; stir briskly until the drink foams. Serve in two large mugs; heat with a hot mulling poker.*

## COOL CUP

1 quart cider
1½ cups sherry
1 large lemon
6 oz. sugar, in cubes
Grated nutmeg
Mint sprigs

*Peel the lemon; rub the cubes against the rinds until the cubes turn yellow. Drop them on the bottom of a large pitcher; squeeze the juice of the fruit over them and stir until dissolved. Add the cider, sherry, and nutmeg; stir well. Top with mint.*

## COPA DE ORO

1 oz. gold rum
3 tsp. lime juice
2 tsp. sugar syrup
A few drops of maraschino
3 oz. crushed ice
A few drops Pernod

*Combine everything except the Pernod in a blender at a high speed for 10 seconds. Strain into a deep-dish champagne glass straight up. Float the Pernod.*

## COPENHAGEN

1 oz. gin
1 oz. aquavit
1 tsp. dry vermouth

*Combine with ice; shake well. Strain and add ice. Top with an olive.*

## COPENHAGEN SPECIAL

1 oz. aquavit
1 oz. Arrack
1½ tbs. lemon juice

*Combine with ice; shake well. Strain and add ice.*

## CORDIAL MEDOC CUP

1 oz. Cordial Medoc
½ oz. cognac
1½ tbs. lemon juice
1 tsp. sugar syrup
Champagne

*Combine all (except the champagne) with ice; shake. Strain, add ice, and fill with champagne. Top with a slice of orange.*

## CORDIAL MEDOC SOUR

1½ oz. gin
½ oz. Cordial Medoc
2 tsp. lemon juice

*Combine with ice; shake well. Strain. Top with a slice of orange and serve straight up.*

## CORKSCREW

1½ oz. white rum
½ oz. peach liqueur
2 tsp. dry vermouth

*Combine with ice; shake well. Strain and add ice. Top with a lime slice.*

## CORSON

1½ oz. sherry
1½ oz. gin
1 oz. lemon juice
A few drops of sweet vermouth, dry vermouth, curacao, cherry brandy, and white creme de cacao

*Combine with ice; shake well. Strain and add ice.*

### COSTA DEL SOL

2 oz. gin
1 oz. apricot brandy
1 oz. Cointreau

*Combine with ice; shake well. Strain straight up.*

### COTE D'AZUR COOLER

1 oz. brandy
2 tsp. lemon juice
2 tsp. pineapple juice
A few drops of maraschino
Club soda

*Combine all except the club soda with ice; shake well. Strain straight; add soda and stir.*

### COUCOU CUMBER

1½ oz. vodka
2 tsp. sugar syrup
1 tsp. Pernod
1 large cucumber

*Combine everything except the cucumber with ice; shake well. Slice one end off the cucumber, use an apple corer on the other end to hollow out all the meat. Strain in the drink; add crushed ice to fill the cucumber, and serve on a flat dish for support.*

### COUNSELLOR'S CUP

8 oz. cognac
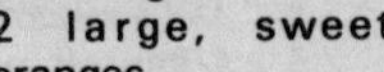
2 large, sweet oranges
4 oz. sugar, in cubes
3 tsp. lemon juice

*Peel the oranges; rub the sugar cubes against the rinds until they turn orange. Combine the cubes in a pint of water in a large saucepan; bring to a boil. Lower heat and simmer. Squeeze in the juice of the oranges; add the lemon juice, and bring back to a boil; stir well. As soon as it boils, remove from heat and pour into a heatproof bowl; add the cognac and stir. Serve immediately in warmed mugs.*

### CRANBERRY CHRISTMAS PUNCH

1 quart cranberry juice
1 bottle Sauterne
8 oz. brandy
Sugar
Lemon slices
1 bottle club soda

*Combine the wine, juice, brandy, and lemon slices in a large pot; stir well and allow to stand, covered, at room temperature for several hours. Add sugar to taste if needed. Turn out into a large punch bowl; add the soda plus chunks of ice before serving.*

## CREAM AND COFFEE PUNCH

1 quart vanilla ice cream
½ bottle Jamaican rum
3 quarts hot dark coffee

*Place the ice cream in a punch bowl; add the coffee and stir until the ice cream has melted. Pour in the rum and add ice.*

## CREAMY ORANGE

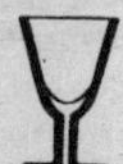

1 oz. cream sherry
1 oz. orange juice
2 tsp. heavy cream
2 tsp. brandy

*Combine with ice; shake very well. Strain and add ice.*

## CREAMY SCREWDRIVER

2 oz. vodka
6 oz. orange
1 egg yolk
1½ tsp. sugar syrup
¾ cup crushed ice

*Combine in a blender at low speed for 15 seconds. Strain over ice.*

## CREME DE CACAO

1 lb. cacao beans
2 cups sugar
2 bottles brandy
1 tbs. vanilla extract

*Roast the beans until nearly charred; soak in the brandy for a week. Boil the sugar in water to make a thick syrup; allow it to cool and then combine with the brandy. Add the vanilla extract; strain and bottle for future use.*

## CREME DE LAURIER

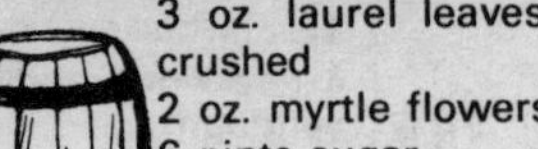

3 oz. laurel leaves, crushed
2 oz. myrtle flowers
6 pints sugar
Whole cloves, chopped nutmeg
3 bottles brandy

*Pound and blend the laurel leaves, myrtle flowers, cloves, and nutmeg; pour the brandy over them. Boil the sugar in enough water to make a syrup; allow to cool and combine with the spiced brandy. Strain and bottle for future use.*

## CREME DE MENTHE

1 lb. mint sprigs, as fresh as possible
7 pints cognac
4 pints sugar
2 tbs. peppermint extract
Grated lemon rinds

*Wash the mint sprigs; chop into fine pieces. Combine with the lemon rinds in a flat bowl; pound as finely as possible. Soak in the brandy for a week. Strain; distill, and add the peppermint extract. Boil the sugar in enough water to make a syrup; allow to cool. Add to the brandy and stand for a half-hour. Strain and bottle for future use.*

## CREOLE

1 oz. whiskey
1 oz. sweet vermouth
1-2 dashes Amer Picon
1-2 dashes Benedictine

*Combine with ice; shake well. Strain. Add ice and a twist of lemon.*

## CREOLE CHAMPAGNE PUNCH

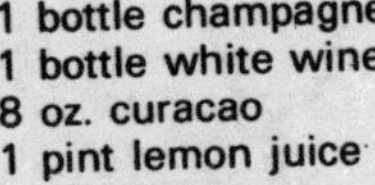

1 bottle champagne
1 bottle white wine
8 oz. curacao
1 pint lemon juice
2 cups sugar
1 pineapple, half grated, half sliced
Whole strawberries
2 bottles club soda

*Dissolve the sugar with the lemon juice. Add the wine, champagne, and curacao. Stir well. Garnish with the grated and sliced pineapple and the strawberries. Add the soda plus chunks of ice before serving; stir to blend.*

## CREOLE DOWNFALL

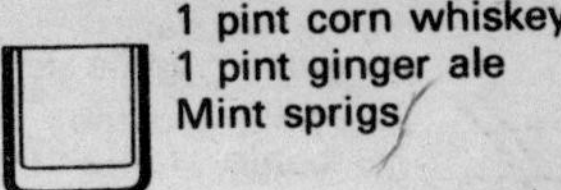

1 pint corn whiskey
1 pint ginger ale
Mint sprigs

*Muddle the mint in a large jar; add the whiskey and the ginger ale. Seal the jar tightly and refrigerate for at least a week. Serve straight up or as a mixer like straight whiskey.*

## CREOLE LADY

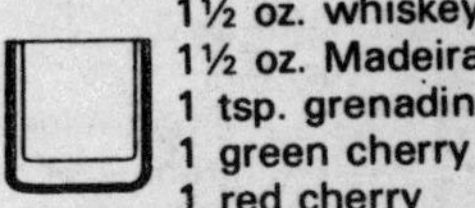

1½ oz. whiskey
1½ oz. Madeira
1 tsp. grenadine
1 green cherry
1 red cherry

*Combine with ice; shake well. Strain and add ice. Top with the cherries.*

## CREOLE WHITE WINE PUNCH

2½ bottle Sauterne
1 pint lemon juice
8 oz. brandy
2 cup sugar
Grated and sliced pineapple
Cherries, mint sprigs
1 bottle club soda

*Combine everything except the soda, wine, and mint leaves and allow to stand at room temperature for one hour. Add the wine and soda plus chunks of ice*

## CREOLE CLARET PUNCH

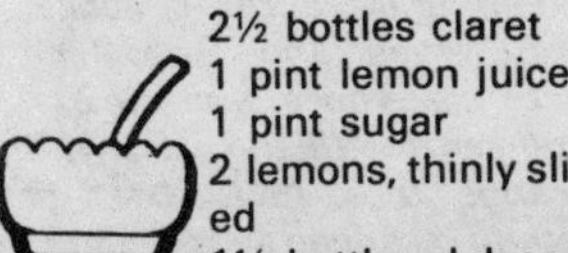

2½ bottles claret
1 pint lemon juice
1 pint sugar
2 lemons, thinly slic-ed
1½ bottles club soda

*Combine everything except the soda; stir well. Add the soda plus chunks of ice before serving.*

**CRIMEAN CUP**

16 oz. cognac
8 oz. dark rum
8 oz. maraschino
3 oz. sugar
10 oz. lemon juice
3 cup sugar syrup
2 tsp. almond extract
Grated lemon rinds
2 bottles club soda
2 bottles champagne

*Muddle the rinds with the sugar. Add the lemon juice and the soda; stir until the sugar is dissolved. Add the sugar syrup and beat until foamy. Pour in the cognac, maraschino, and rum and allow to stand until marinated. Add the champagne plus chunks of ice.*

---

**CRIMSON**

2 oz. gin
1 oz. port
½ oz. lemon juice
1 tsp. grenadine

*Combine the gin, juice, and grenadine with ice; shake well. Strain; add ice and float the port.*

**CUBAN SPECIAL**

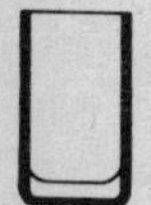

1 oz. white rum
½ tsp. curacao
¾ oz. pineapple juice
¾ oz. lime juice
1 pineapple stick

*Combine (except the pineapple stick) with ice; shake well. Strain, add ice and decorate with the pinapple.*

**CUCUMBER CHAMPAGNE**

1 oz. Benedictine
2 tsp. lemon juice
8 oz. champagne
1 long, narrow cucumber peel

*Pour the Benedictine and lemon juice over the peel. Add the champagne and stir gently. Let it stand a bit.*

**CULROSS**

1½ oz. gold rum
½ oz. Lillet
1 tsp. apricot brandy
1 tsp. lime juice

*Combine with ice; shake well. Strain and add ice.*

**CUPID**

3 oz. sherry
1 egg
1 tsp. powdered sugar
1 pinch cayenne pepper

*Combine with ice; shake extremely well. Strain and add ice.*

**CURACAO COOLER**

1 oz. blue curacao
1 oz. vodka
2 tsp. lime juice
2 tsp. lemon juice
Orange juice

*Combine the curacao, vodka, and lemon and lime juice with ice; shake well. Strain, add ice, and fill the glass with orange juice. Add a twist of lemon, orange, and/or lime.*

# YOUR OWN RECIPE

# YOUR OWN RECIPE

Use a bartender's mixing glass whenever the instructions state "combine" ingredients. Strain the drink from the mixing glass into the drinking glass suggested by the illustration alongside the ingredients.

## DAFFODIL

1 oz. apple brandy
1 oz. white port
2 tsp. apricot brandy
2 tsp. lemon juice
Yellow gumdrops

*Combine everything except the gumdrops with ice; shake well. Strain straight up. Cut the gumdrops and use toothpicks to spear them; then bridge the glass with the speared gumdrops.*

## DAIQUIRI

2 oz. white rum
1 oz. lime juice
1 tsp. sugar syrup

*Combine with ice; shake well. Strain and add ice.*

## DAISY

2 oz. tequila
2 tsp. lemon juice
2 tsp. grenadine
2 tsp. club soda

*Combine with ice; shake well. Strain and add ice.*

## DAMN THE WEATHER

1 oz. gin
2 tsp. sweet vermouth
2 tsp. orange juice
1 tsp. curacao

*Combine with ice; shake well. Strain and add ice.*

## DAMSON WINE

7 lb. damsons
2 lb. sugar
4 oz. brandy
1 oz. yeast, spread on a piece of toast

*Slice the fruit; place them in a large pot and pour in a gallon of boiling water. Close tightly and allow to stand for several days; stir occasionally. Strain out the juice into a separate pot; add the sugar and brandy plus the yeast on toast. Seal and allow to ferment. Strain when ready and store a year before used.*

## DANCING LEPRECHAUN

1½ oz. Irish Whiskey
1½ oz. lemon juice
Club soda
Ginger ale

*Combine the whiskey and the juice; shake with ice. Strain and add ice. Fill the glass with equal parts soda and ginger ale; stir gently. Touch it up with a twist of lemon.*

## DANIEL DE ORO

1 oz. tequila
Orange juice
½ tsp. Creme Damiana

*Pour the tequila into a glass; add ice and fill with orange juice. Top it off with the Creme Damiana.*

## DANISH GIN FIZZ

1½ oz. gin
½ oz. Cherry Herring
2 tsp. lime juice
1 tsp. kirschwasser
1½ tsp. sugar syrup
Club soda

*Combine all (except the soda) with ice; shake well. Strain, add ice and fill the glass with club soda. Add a lime slice.*

## DANNY'S SPECIAL

2 oz. bourbon
1 oz. Cointreau
3 tbs. lemon juice
1 tsp. Grand Marnier

*Combine with ice; shake well. Strain and add plenty of ice.*

## DARE COCKTAIL

¾ oz. dry vermouth
¾ oz. dry gin
1 tbs. apricot brandy
1 tsp. lemon juice

*Combine with ice; shake well. Strain and add ice.*

## DE RIGUEUR

1 oz. whiskey
2 tsp. grapefruit juice
2 tsp. honey

*Combine with ice; shake and strain. Serve over ice.*

## DEAUVILLE

¾ oz. brandy
¾ oz. apple brandy
¾ oz. Cointreau or Triple Sec
1½ tbs. lemon juice

*Combine with ice; shake well. Strain and add ice.*

## DEEP SEA

1 oz. Old Tom gin
1 oz. dry vermouth
1-2 dashes Pernod
1-2 dashes orange bitters
1 olive

*Combine with ice; shake well. Strain, add ice and a twist of lemon.*

---

## DELTA

1½ oz. whiskey
½ oz. Southern Comfort
2 tsp. lime juice
1 tsp. sugar syrup
1 peach slice

*Combine all but the peach with ice; shake well. Strain and add ice. Top with the peach.*

## DEMPSEY

1 oz. gin
1 oz. apple brandy
1-2 dashes Pernod
1 - 2 dashes grenadine

*Combine with ice; shake well. Strain over ice.*

## DEPTH BOMB

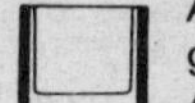

1¼ oz. apple brandy
1¼ oz. brandy
A few drops of grenadine
A few drops lemon juice

*Combine with ice; shake well. Strain and add ice.*

## DERBY NO. 1

1½ oz. gin
1-2 dashes peach bitters
Mint sprigs

*Combine the gin and the bitters with ice; shake well. Strain and add ice. Decorate with mint.*

## DERBY NO.2

1 oz. whiskey
2 tsp. sweet vermouth
2 tsp. white curacao
1½ tbs. lime juice
1 mint leaf

*Combine all but the mint leaf with ice; shake well. Strain and add ice. Decorate with the mint.*

## DERBY DAIQUIRI

1½ oz. white rum
1 oz. orange juice
2 tsp. lime juice
2 tsp. sugar syrup
3 oz. crushed ice

*Combine in a blender at a low speed for 15 seconds. Strain and serve straight up.*

## DERBY FIZZ

1½ oz. whiskey
1½ tsp. sugar syrup
1 tsp. lemon juice
1 egg
A few drops of curacao
Club soda

*Combine (except the soda) with ice; shake well. Strain, add ice, and club soda.*

## DERBY RUM FIX

2 oz. white rum
2 tsp. lime juice
1½ tsp. sugar syrup
1 oz. orange juice

*Combine without ice; stir. Strain over crushed ice. Decorate with a slice of orange and a cherry.*

## DEVIL'S TAIL

1½ oz. gold rum
1 oz. vodka
2 tsp. lime juice
2 tsp. grenadine
1 tsp. apricot liqueur
3 oz. crushed ice

*Combine in a blender at a low speed for 15 seconds. Strain, add a twist of lime and serve straight up.*

## DEWBERRY CORDIAL

1 quart dewberries
1 gallon water
1.5 lb. sugar
A cake of yeast

*Mash the berries and combine them with the water in a large crock pot. Add the sugar and yeast and stir until blended. Allow to ferment for at least one month before straining and re-bottling it as a liqueur.*

## DIABLO

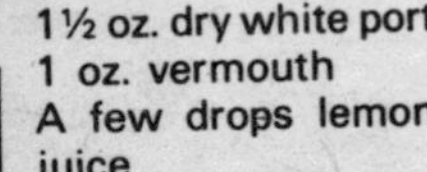

1½ oz. dry white port
1 oz. vermouth
A few drops lemon juice

*Combine with ice; shake well. Strain, add ice and a twist of lemon.*

---

## DIAMOND PUNCH

1 bottle champagne
6 oz. raspberry syrup
4 oz. gin
2 oz. orange juice
3 tsp. lemon juice
3 tsp. lime juice

*Combine with chunks of ice before serving.*

## DIANA

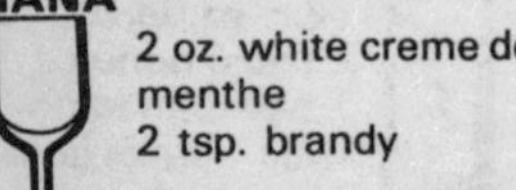

2 oz. white creme de menthe
2 tsp. brandy

*Pack a small wine glass with crushed ice and pour in the creme de menth. Float the brandy.*

## DIKI-DIKI

2 oz. apple brandy
2 tsp. grapefruit juice
2 tsp. dry gin

*Combine with ice; shake well. Strain and add ice.*

## DINAH

1½ oz. whiskey
¾ oz. lemon juice
½ tsp. powdered sugar

*Combine. Shake with ice. Pour on ice. Decorate with mint.*

## DIPLOMAT

3 oz. dry vermouth
1 oz. sweet vermouth
A few drops of maraschino

*Combine with ice; shake very well. Strain and add ice.*

## DIPLOMAT SPECIAL

2 oz. Scotch
1 tbs. dry vermouth
Several drops Pernod

*Combine with ice; shake well. Strain into a pre-chilled martini glass, straight up; add a twist of lemon.*

Ancient Wooden cup... British. Called a QUAIGH

**DIXIE**

¾ oz. gin
1½ oz. orange juice
2 tsp. Pernod
2 tsp. dry vermouth
1-2 dashes grenadine

*Combine with ice; shake. Strain and add ice.*

**DIXIE WHISKEY**

2 oz. whiskey
¼ oz. lemon juice
½ tsp. powdered sugar
½ tsp. white creme de menthe
A few drops curacao

*Combine with ice; shake. Strain and add ice.*

**DOBBS**

White creme de menthe
Fernet Branca

*Pour the creme de menthe into a glass filled with crushed ice. Top with few dashes of Fernet Branca.*

**DOCTOR**

1½ oz. Swedish Punch
2 oz. lime juice

*Combine with ice; shake. Strain and add ice.*

**DOCTOR FUNK**

3 oz. Jamaican rum
¾ oz. lemon juice
1 tbs. Pernod
1 tsp. grenadine
1 tsp. powdered sugar
Club soda
1 small lime

*Squeeze the lime into a mixing glass; drop in the fruit. Add ice and everything else except the soda; shake well. Strain; add ice and club soda.*

**DOLORES**

¾ oz. cherry brandy
¾ oz. creme de cacao
¾ oz. Spanish brandy
1 egg white

*Combine with ice; shake extremely well. Strain and add ice.*

**DOOLITTLE SPECIAL**

1¼ oz. whiskey
A few dashes sugar syrup
½ lemon

*Muddle the lemon on the bottom of a glass; add the whiskey, sugar, and ice. Stir.*

**DORADO COCKTAIL**

2 oz. tequila
1½ oz. lemon juice
1 tbs. honey

*Combine with ice; shake well. Strain and add ice.*

## DOUBLE DERBY

2½ oz. bourbon
2 oz. strong iced tea
2 oz. claret
1½ tbs. red currant syrup
1½ tbs. orange juice
2 tsp. lemon juice

*Combine; add ice and stir very well. Decorate with a slice of orange. Heat the red currant jelly in a teaspoon with warm water to make the syrup. Stir again.*

## DOUBLE STANDARD SOUR

¾ oz. whiskey
¾ oz. dry gin
1½ tsp. lemon juice
½ tsp. powdered sugar
½ tsp. grenadine

*Combine with ice; shake. Strain straight up and decorate with a slice of lemon and a cherry.*

## DRAGOON PUNCH

3 pints porter stout
3 pints ale
½ pint brandy
½ pint sherry
4 oz. sugar syrup
3 lemons, sliced
2 bottles champagne

*Combine all but the champagne. Stir well. A half-hour before serving, add the champagne and chunks of ice.*

## DREAM COCKTAIL

1½ oz. brandy
1 tsp. curacao
A few drops anisette

*Combine with ice; shake well. Strain and add ice.*

## DRY COLD DECK

1¾ oz. brandy
2 tsp. dry vermouth
1 tsp. white creme de menthe

*Combine with ice; shake well. Strain and add ice.*

## DRY MANHATTAN COOLER

2 oz. whiskey
1 oz. dry vermouth
2 oz. orange juice
2 tsp. lemon juice
2 tsp. almond extract
Club soda

*Combine all but the soda. Shake with ice. Strain. Pour on ice.*

## DRY VERMOUTH COBBLER

3 oz. dry vermouth
3 oz. club soda

*Half-fill a glass with crushed ice. Add the vermouth and soda; stir well. Top with a lemon slice.*

**DUBARRY COCKTAIL**

¾ oz. dry vermouth
1½ oz. gin
Several drops Pernod
1-2 dashes bitters

*Strain and add ice.*

**DUBONNET COCKTAIL**

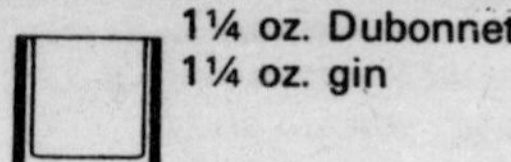

1¼ oz. Dubonnet
1¼ oz. gin

*Combine with ice; shake. Strain. Add ice and a twist of lemon.*

**DUBONNET FIZZ**

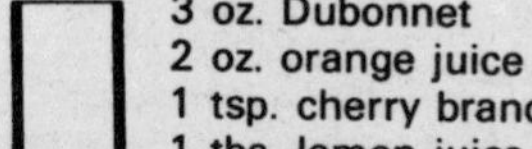

3 oz. Dubonnet
2 oz. orange juice
1 tsp. cherry brandy
1 tbs. lemon juice
Club soda

*Combine (except the soda) with ice; shake. Strain, add ice, and club soda. Top with a lemon slice and a cherry. For an extra kick, add 1 teaspoon of kirschwasser.*

**DUBONNET MANHATTEN**

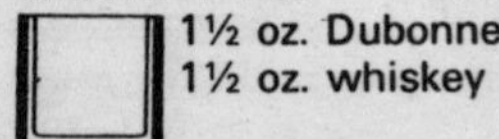

1½ oz. Dubonnet
1½ oz. whiskey

*Combine with ice; shake well. Strain. Add ice and top with a cherry.*

**DUBONNET ON THE ROCKS**

*Twist a lemon peel into a glass; drop in the peel. Add ice and Dubonnet. Stir well.*

**DUBONNET PUNCH**

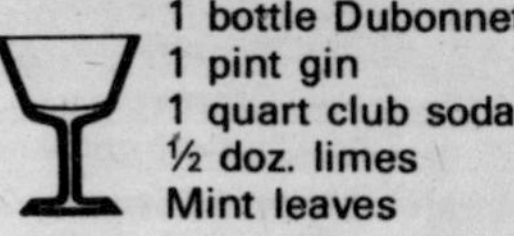

1 bottle Dubonnet
1 pint gin
1 quart club soda
½ doz. limes
Mint leaves

*Combine the juice of the limes, the Dubonnet, and the gin in a pitcher. Add the lime rinds, club soda, and ice. Serve with crushed ice and mint leaves.*

**DUCHESS**

¾ oz. Pernod
¾ oz. dry vermouth
¾ oz. sweet vermouth

*Combine with ice; shake well. Strain and add ice.*

**DUKE OF MARLBOROUGH**

1½ oz. sherry
1½ oz. sweet vermouth
2 oz. lime juice
Several dashes raspberry syrup

*Combine with ice; shake. Strain and add ice.*

**DULCET**

1 oz. vodka
2 tsp. curacao
2 tsp. anisette
2 tsp. apricot liqueur
1 tsp. lemon juice
½ brandied apricot

*Combine all but the apricot with ice; shake well. Strain and add ice and the apricot.*

**DUNDEE**

1 oz. gin
2 tbs. Scotch
2 tsp. Drambuie
1 tsp. lemon juice

*Combine with ice; shake well. Strain and add ice. Decorate with a cherry and a twist of lemon.*

**DURANGO**

1½ oz. tequila
2 tbs. grapefruit juice
1 tsp. almond extract
Mint sprigs
Calistoga spring water

*Combine the tequila, juice, and almond extract with ice; shake well. Strain into a large tumbler; add ice and fill with spring water. Garnish with mint.*

**DUTCH TRADEWINDS**

1½ oz. gin
1 tbs. curacao
3 tbs. lemon juice
1 egg white
1 tsp. sugar syrup

*Combine with ice; shake very well. Strain and add ice.*

English Tankard 1600

# YOUR OWN RECIPE

# YOUR OWN RECIPE

Use a bartender's mixing glass whenever the instructions state "combine" ingredients. Strain the drink from the mixing glass into the drinking glass suggested by the illustration alongside the ingredients.

NOTE: The number of glasses or cups shown alongside a recipe do not necessarily indicate the quantity of drinks the recipe will produce.

---

**EARTHQUAKE**

1½ oz. tequila
1 tsp. grenadine
2 strawberries
1-2 dashes orange bitters
3 oz. crushed ice

*Combine in a blender at a high speed for 15 seconds. Strain straight up with a lime slice and a strawberry.*

**EAST INDIA**

1½ oz. brandy
1 tsp. pineapple juice
1 tsp. red curacao
A few dashes of Angostura bitters

*Combine with ice; shake well. Strain and add ice.*

**EAST INDIAN SPECIAL**

1½ oz. sherry
1½ oz. dry vermouth
1-2 dashes orange bitters

*Combine with ice; shake well. Strain and add ice.*
*(A few variations: reduce the sherry; use peach bitters instead of orange bitters and garnish with mint; touch up with maraschino.)*

**ECLIPSE**

1½ oz. sloe gin
1 oz. gin
2 tsp. grenadine
1 cherry

*Combine the gins with ice; shake well. Drop the cherry into a glass and cover it with grenadine. Carefully strain in the gins so that they float on the grenadine; add a twist of orange.*

**EGG AND WINE**

1 oz. sherry
1 egg
1 tbs. sugar
Grated nutmeg

*Separate the egg. Beat the yolk with the sugar until creamy; add the sherry and stir well. Beat the white until stiff. Fold the whites with the wine mixture into a wine glass; top with nutmeg.*

## EGG LEMONADE

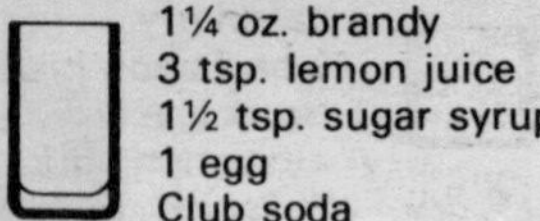

1¼ oz. brandy
3 tsp. lemon juice
1½ tsp. sugar syrup
1 egg
Club soda

*Combine all but the soda with ice. Shake extremely well. Strain; add ice and fill with club soda.*

---

## EGG NOG FOR ONE

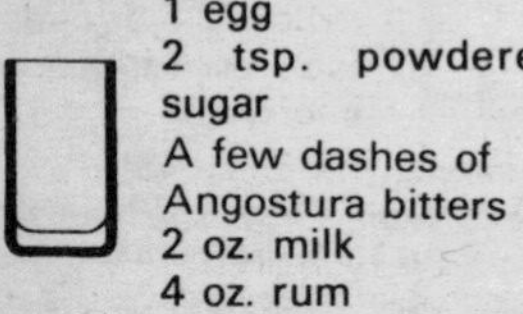

1 egg
2 tsp. powdered sugar
A few dashes of Angostura bitters
2 oz. milk
4 oz. rum

*Heat the rum, but do not boil. Break the egg into a serving glass; add the sugar, bitters, and milk. Pour in the hot rum and stir well. Serve hot.*

---

## EGG NOG NASHVILLE

1 quart bourbon
1 pint Jamaican rum
1 pint brandy
3 quarts heavy cream
2 cups sugar
18 eggs, separated

*Combine the liquors and egg yolks; stir well. Combine the cream and sugar; blend into the liquor mixture. Beat the egg whites until stiff and gently fold them in. Garnish with cloves and nutmeg.*

## EGG SOUR

1½ oz. brandy
1½ oz. curacao
2 tbs. lemon juice
1 tsp. powdered sugar
1 egg

*Combine with ice; shake extremely well. Strain and add ice.*

## EL DIABLO

1½ oz. tequila
½ oz. creme de cassis
1½ tsp. lime juice
Ginger ale

*Pour the lime juice into a glass. Add the tequila and creme de cassis; drop in a few ice cubes and ginger ale. Stir gently; add a lime twist.*

## EL PRESIDENTE

1½ oz. white rum
½ oz. curacao
2 tsp. dry vermouth
1-2 dashes grenadine

*Combine with ice; shake. Strain and add ice.*

## EL YUNQUE

1½ oz. white rum
2 tsp. lemon juice
A few drops of green creme de menthe
Pineapple juice

*Combine everything except the pineapple juice with ice; shake well. Strain over ice and fill with juice.*

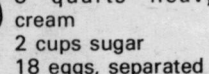

**ELK**

1 oz. dry gin
1 oz. Prunelle
A few drops dry vermouth

*Combine with ice; shake well. Strain and add ice.*

**ELK'S OWN**

1½ oz. rye
¾ oz. port
1 tbs. lemon juice
1 egg white
1 tsp. powdered sugar
1 pineapple stick

*Combine (except the pineapple stick) with ice; shake well. Strain and add ice; decorate with the pineapple.*

**EMERALD ISLE**

2 oz. dry gin
1 tsp. green creme de menthe
A few dashes of Angostura bitters

*Combine with ice; shake. Strain and add ice.*

---

**EMPIRE PEACH**

3 bottles chilled Moselle, one sparkling
2 large peaches
2 tbs. powdered sugar

*Place peeled peaches on the bottom of a pitcher. Add one bottle of plain Moselle and sugar; stir and refrigerate for at least a half-hour. Just before serving, add the other two bottles of Moselle.*

**ENGLISH BOLO**

4 oz. sherry
1½ oz. lemon juice
1 tsp. sugar
A cinnamon stick

*Muddle the sugar and the lemon juice with a cinnamon stick in a small tumbler. Add the sherry and stir. Serve straight up—stick and all.*

**ENGLISH CHRISTMAS PUNCH**

2 bottles red wine
1 quart dark tea
3 oz. orange juice
3 tsp. lemon juice
2 lb. sugar
1 bottle rum

*Combine all but the sugar and rum in a large saucepan and heat thoroughly. Strain into a punch bowl. Place the sugar in a shallow pan and soak it in some of the rum. Ignite it over the punch, pour it in, and add the rest of the rum. Stir well.*

**ENGLISH HOT PUNCH**

1 pint rum
½ pint brandy
2 large lemons
1 orange
Several sugar cubes

*Peel the fruit; rub the sugar cubes in the rinds until the cubes take no more color. Combine the colored cubes with 2 or 3 more oz. cane sugar in a large punch bowl; squeeze in the juice of the fruit meats and add 1½ pints of boiling water. Stir until all the sugar is dissolved. Pour in the rum and the brandy. Serve while warm.*

## ENGLISH MULE

1½ oz. gin
3 oz. green ginger wine
2½ oz. orange juice
Club soda
A chunk of preserved ginger

*Combine (except soda and ginger) with ice; shake well. Strain into glass; add ice and club soda. Stir gently. Decorate with ginger.*

## ENGLISH ROYAL PUNCH

1 pint cognac
1 pint dark tea
½ pint Jamaican rum
3 oz. curacao
3 oz. Arrack
3 oz. lime juice
4 oz. sugar
1 lemon, sliced
4 egg whites

*Combine all but the egg whites in a large saucepan and heat well (don't boil). Beat the egg whites until stiff and fold into the punch. Serve hot.*

## EVE

Pink champagne
1 tbs. cognac
2 tsp. sugar
2 tsp. curacao
Several drops of Pernod

*Pour the Pernod drops into a wide champagne glass; turn the glass to coat its sides. Pour in the cognac; soak the sugar with the curacao until the sugar has dissolved and add to the cognac; stir gently. Fill the glass with champagne.*

## EVERGLADES SPECIAL

1 oz. white rum
1 oz. white creme de cacao
1 oz. light cream
2 tsp. coffee liqueur

*Combine with ice; shake. Strain. Fill with ice.*

## EVERYBODY'S RUSH

1½ oz. Irish whiskey
1 tsp. green chartreuse
A few dashes creme de menthe

*Combine with ice; shake well. Strain and add ice.*

---

## EWING

*A straight shot of rye with a dash or two of Angostura bitters on top.*

## EYE-OPENER

1½ oz. white rum
1 tsp. curacao
1 tsp. white creme de cacao
Several drops Pernod
1 tsp. sugar syrup
1 egg yolk

*Combine with ice; shake extremely well. Strain and add ice.*

# YOUR OWN RECIPE

# YOUR OWN RECIPE

Use a bartender's mixing glass whenever the instructions state "combine" ingredients. Strain the drink from the mixing glass into the drinking glass suggested by the illustration alongside the ingredients.

NOTE: The number of glasses or cups shown alongside a recipe do not necessarily indicate the quantity of drinks the recipe will produce.

---

**FAIR AND WARMER**

1½ oz. white rum
1 tbs. sweet vermouth
1-2 dashes curacao

*Combine with ice; shake well. Strain, add ice and a twist of lemon; drop in the peel.*

**FAIRY BELLE**

2 oz. gin
2 tsp. apricot brandy
1 tsp. grenadine
1 egg white

*Combine with ice; shake well. Strain and add ice.*

**FALLEN ANGEL**

3 oz. gin
3 oz. lime juice
1-2 dashes green creme de menthe
A few dashes of Angostura bitters

*Combine with ice; shake well. Strain and add ice. Decorate with a cherry.*

**FANCIULLI**

1½ oz. bourbon
1 tbs. sweet vermouth
1 tbs. Fernet Branca

*Combine with ice; shake well. Strain over crushed ice.*

**FANCY BRANDY**

2 oz. brandy
A few drops curacao
½ tsp. sugar syrup
A few dashes of Angostura bitters

*Combine with ice; shake well. Strain, add ice and a twist of lemon; drop in the peel. Whiskey or gin can be substituted for the brandy.*

**FANTASIO**

1 oz. brandy
1 tbs. dry vermouth
1 tsp. white creme de cacao
1 tsp. maraschino

*Combine with ice; shake well. Strain and add ice.*

**FARMER'S COCKTAIL**

1 oz. dry gin
2 tsp. dry vermouth
2 tsp. sweet vermouth
A few dashes of Angostura bitters

*Combine with ice; shake well. Strain and add ice.*

**FAVORITE**

¾ oz. gin
¾ oz. dry vermouth
¾ oz. apricot brandy
A few drops lemon juice

*Combine with ice; shake well. Strain and add ice.*

**FEMINA**

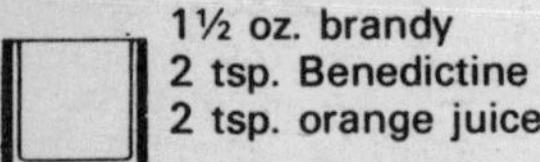

1½ oz. brandy
2 tsp. Benedictine
2 tsp. orange juice

*Combine with ice; shake well. Strain and add ice. Decorate with an orange slice.*

**FERN GULLY**

1 oz. Jamaican rum
1 oz. white rum
2 tsp. cream of coconut
2 tsp. orange juice
2 tsp. lime juice
1 tsp. almond extract
3 oz. crushed ice

*Combine in a blender at a low speed for no more than 15 seconds. Strain and serve straight up.*

**FERN GULLY FIZZ**

1 oz. Jamaican rum
1 oz. white rum
1 oz. pineapple juice
1 tbs. lime juice
1 fresh pineapple slice
Club soda

*Combine the rums and juices with ice; shake well. Strain, add ice, and fill with soda. Decorate with pineapple.*

**FERNET BRANCA**

2 oz. gin
2 tsp. sweet vermouth
2 tsp. Fernet Branca

*Combine with ice; shake well. Strain and add ice.*
*For a* **FIFTH AVENUE**, *add more vermouth and Fernet Branca at the expense of the gin.*

**FESTIVAL**

¾ oz. dark creme de cacao
¾ oz. heavy cream
1 tbs. apricot brandy
1 tsp. grenadine

*Combine with ice; shake well. Strain and add ice.*

**FESTIVE WINE CUP**

1 bottle white wine
2 oz. brandy
1 oz. sugar
1 pint club soda
Slices of peaches and strawberries
Mint sprigs

*Combine the wine, brandy, and sugar. Stir until the sugar has dissolved. Add the club soda before serving. Top with fruit slices and mint.*

**FESTOONERS' HIGH TEA**

1 bottle whiskey
1 bottle Angelica wine
1 bottle champagne
4 oz. curacao
5 oz. lemon juice
2 quarts lemon juice
2 quarts iced, green tea

*Combine and add chunks of ice. Decorate with lemon rinds and fruit slices.*

**FIFTY-FIFTY**

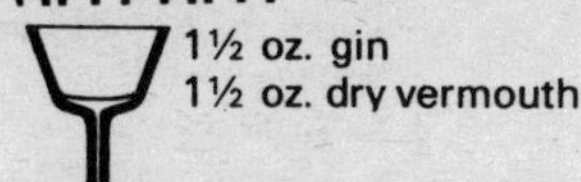

1½ oz. gin
1½ oz. dry vermouth

*Combine with ice; shake well. Strain. Decorate with an olive, and serve straight up.*

**FIG LEAF FLIP**

1½ oz. sweet vermouth
1 oz. white rum
1½ tbs. lime juice
A few dashes of Angostura bitters

*Combine with ice; shake well. Strain and add ice. Top with a cherry.*

**FINO**

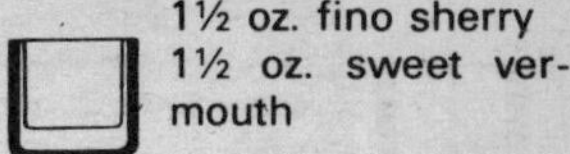

1½ oz. fino sherry
1½ oz. sweet vermouth

*Combine with ice; shake well. Strain. Decorate with a lemon slice.*

**FINO MARTINI**

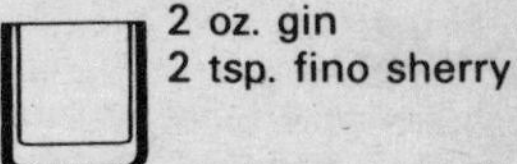

2 oz. gin
2 tsp. fino sherry

*Combine with ice; shake well. Strain. Add ice and a twist of lemon.*

**FINO RICKEY**

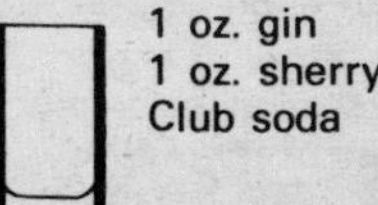

1 oz. gin
1 oz. sherry
Club soda

*Combine the sherry and gin. Add ice, fill with club soda, and stir. Add a twist of lime; drop in the peel.*

**FIORD**

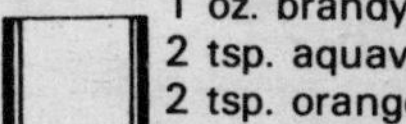

1 oz. brandy
2 tsp. aquavit
2 tsp. orange juice
2 tsp. lime juice
1 tsp. grenadine

*Combine with ice; shake well. Strain and add ice.*

## FISH HOUSE PUNCH

1½ quarts brandy
1 pint peach brandy
1 pint rum
1 quart dark iced tea
1 quart club soda
8 oz. powdered sugar
1½ pints lemon juice

*In a large punch bowl, dissolve the sugar in the lemon juice; add ice and combine the remaining ingredients. Decorate with slices of fruit. There are many variations of* **FISH HOUSE PUNCHES.** *You could use white and gold rums in place of half the brandy, and 9 oz. of frozen lemonade concentrate instead of the lemon juice (eliminating the sugar and adding a quart of water). Or use white wine and a cup of water instead of the tea.*

## FISH HOUSE PUNCH AU NATUREL

*Follow your favorite* **FISH HOUSE PUNCH** *recipe, substituting bottled mineral or spring water for the tea.*

## FISH HOUSE PUNCH NO. 2

2 bottles Jamaican rum
1 bottle lemon juice
1 bottle cognac
4 oz. peach brandy
12 oz. sugar

*Dissolve the sugar in enough water to make syrup; combine with the lemon juice in a large punch bowl and stir. Add the rum, cognac, and brandy; allow to stand an hour or two.*

## FIREMAN'S SOUR

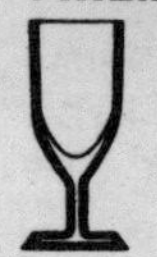

1½ oz. white rum
2 oz. lime juice
2 tsp. grenadine
1 tsp. sugar syrup
Club soda

*Combine everything except the club soda with ice; shake well. Strain and spritz it with soda. Serve straight up.*

## FLAG

1½ oz. apricot brandy
1 oz. claret
1 tsp. Creme Yvette
A few dashes of curacao

*Combine the brandy and curacao with ice; shake well. Over the Creme Yvette carefully strain in the brandy and curacao so that it floats on top of the Creme Yvette. Top with the claret.*

## FLAMES OVER NEW JERSEY

1 quart apple brandy
A few dashes of Angostura bitters
8 oz. sugar

*Warm the brandy and combine it with the bitters and the sugar in a punch bowl. Stir until the sugar is dissolved. Ignite at the table. Extinguish with a quart of boiling water; stir and serve hot.*

**FLAMING GLOGG**

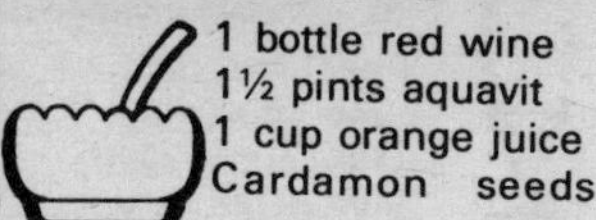

1 bottle red wine
1½ pints aquavit
1 cup orange juice
Cardamon seeds, whole cloves, cinnamon sticks

Blanched almonds, raisins, dried figs
Grated orange rinds
Sugar (to taste)

*Combine everything except ¾ cup of the aquavit in a large pot; heat but do not allow to boil. Simmer several minutes. Serve unstrained over a chafing dish or similar warmer. Add the remaining aquavit and stir.*

**FLOATING TORCH for the FLAMING GLOGG**

½ large grapefruit
6 oz. aquavit
Sugar

*Carefully pare the meat of the fruit; do not puncture the skin. Line the rim of the fruit with a few drops of aquavit; press it in sugar. Warm the remaining aquavit. Float the grapefruit in the* **FLAMING GLOGG;** *pour in the aquavit (even if it overflows) and ignite. When flame subsides, overturn the grapefruit shell. Do not allow the aquavit to burn too long.*

**FLAMING HOT BUTTERED RUM**

*Follow the recipe for* **HOT BUTTERED RUM.** *Just before serving, tip a few drops of 151-proof rum over a few pinches of sugar in a ladle. Warm the ladle over the hot buttered rum; then ignite the rum and sugar and infuse into the drink. Drink at once.*

**FLAMING PETER**

1 oz. vodka
1 oz. Cherry Herring
2 tsp. dry vermouth
2 tsp. orange juice

*Combine with ice; shake well. Strain and add ice.*

**FLAMINGO COCKTAIL**

1¼ oz. dry gin
½ oz. apricot brandy
1½ tsp. lime juice
1 tsp. grenadine

*Combine with ice; shake well. Strain and add ice.*

**FLINTLOCK**

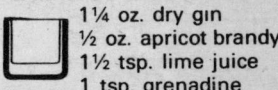

1½ oz. bourbon
½ oz. apple brandy
1 tsp. lemon juice
Several drops grenadine
1-2 dashes white creme de menthe

*Combine with ice; shake well. Strain and add ice.*

## FLORADORA

2 oz. gin
2 oz. lime juice
1 tsp. sugar syrup
1 tbs. grenadine
1 tsp. sugar syrup
Club soda

*Combine (except the soda) with ice. Strain over crushed ice and fill with soda.*

## FLORIDA

1¼ oz. orange juice
½ oz. gin
1 tsp. kirschwasser
1 tsp. Triple Sec
1 tsp. lemon juice

*Combine with ice; shake well. Strain and add ice.*

## FLORIDA PUNCH

1½ oz. rum
1½ oz. orange juice
1½ oz. grapefruit juice
¾ oz. brandy

*Combine with ice; shake well. Strain and add ice.*

## FLORIDIAN

1½ oz. dry vermouth
2 oz. grapefruit juice
2 tsp. Forbidden Fruit
1 tsp. Falernum
1-2 dashes orange bitters

*Combine with ice; shake well. Strain and add ice. Top with a lemon slice.*

## FLORIDIAN COCKTAIL

1 oz. sweet vermouth
¾ oz. rye
1 tsp. Amer Picon
1 tsp. sugar syrup
½ tsp. curacao
1-2 dashes orange bitters

*Combine with ice; shake well. Strain and add ice.*

## FLYING DUTCHMAN

*Pour just enough curacao into a glass to coat its side. Add 2 oz. cold gin.*

## FLYING GRASSHOPPER

1 oz. vodka
2 tsp. green creme de menthe
2 tsp. white creme de menthe

*Combine with ice; shake well. Strain and add ice.*

## FLYING SCOTCHMAN

1 oz. Scotch
1 oz. sweet vermouth
A few drops sugar syrup
A few dashes of Angostura bitters

*Combine with ice; shake well. Strain and add ice.*

## FOGGY DAY

1½ oz. gin
1 tsp. Pernod
1 lemon slice

*Combine the gin and Pernod with ice; shake well. Rub the lemon slice around the rim of a glass, then drop it in. Strain in the drink and add ice.*

**FOGHORN**

3 oz. gin
Ginger beer

*Pour the gin into a glass, add ice and fill with beer. Decorate with a lemon slice.*

**FORESTER**

1 oz. bourbon
1 tsp. cherry juice
1 tsp. lemon juice

*Combine with ice; shake well. Strain and add ice. Decorate with a cherry.*

**FORT LAUDERDALE**

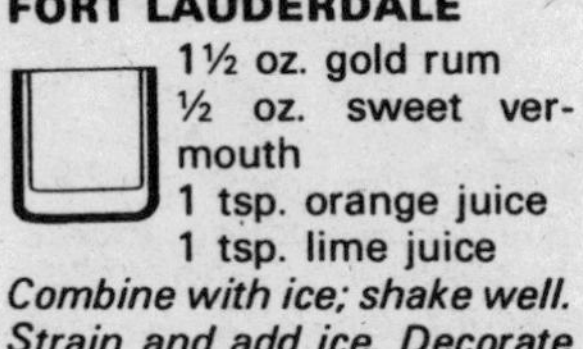

1½ oz. gold rum
½ oz. sweet vermouth
1 tsp. orange juice
1 tsp. lime juice

*Combine with ice; shake well. Strain and add ice. Decorate with a slice of orange.*

**FOUR SECTORS**

1 oz. bourbon
1 oz. vodka
1 oz. Grand Marnier
1 oz. unsweetened lime juice
A few dashes of Angostura bitters

*Combine with ice; shake well. Strain and add ice. Garnish with slices of fruit, a slice of cucumber, and a cherry.*

**FOX RIVER**

1½ oz. rye
2 tsp. dark creme de cacao
A few drops peach bitters

*Combine with ice; shake well. Strain. Add ice and a twist of lemon; drop in the peel.*

**FOXHOUND**

1½ oz. brandy
2 tsp. cranberry juice
1 tsp. kummel
1 tsp. lemon juice

*Combine with ice; shake well. Strain and add ice. Decorate with a lemon slice.*

**FRAISE FIZZ**

1½ oz. gin
1 oz. Chambery fraise
2 tsp. lemon juice
1½ tsp. sugar syrup
1 large strawberry
Club soda

*Combine (except the strawberry and the soda) with ice; shake well. Strain, add ice and fill with soda. Add a twist of lemon and drop in the peel. Top with a strawberry.*

**FRANCES ANN**

1 oz. Scotch
½ oz. Cherry Herring
1 tsp. dry vermouth

*Combine with ice; shake well. Strain and add ice.*

## FRANKENJACK COCKTAIL

1 oz. dry gin
½ oz. apricot brandy
1 tbs. dry vermouth
1 tsp. Triple Sec

*Combine with ice; shake well. Strain and add ice. Decorate with a cherry. Cointreau can be substituted for the Triple Sec.*

## FRAPPES

*Any liqueur can be prepared as a* **FRAPPE**. *Simply pour 1½ oz. of your favorite — Pernod, white or green creme de menthe, creme de noyaux — into a glass filled with crushed ice.*

## FREE SILVER

1½ oz. Old Tom gin
¾ oz. Jamaican rum
1 tbs. lemon juice
1 tsp. sugar syrup
1 oz. milk
Club soda

*Combine all but the club soda with ice; shake well. Strain; add ice and fill with soda.*

## FRENCH APPETIZER

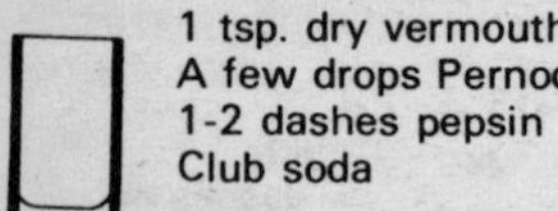

1 tsp. dry vermouth
A few drops Pernod
1-2 dashes pepsin
Club soda

*Combine the vermouth, Pernod, and pepsin with a few ice cubes; stir well. Strain over crushed ice; fill the tumbler with soda and stir.*

## FRENCH CHAMPAGNE PUNCH

1 bottle imported French champagne
1 bottle white wine
1 pint cognac
1 bottle club soda

*Combine; add large chunks of ice before serving. Garnish with fruit slices.*

---

## FRENCH CIDER CUP

1 quart hard cider
2 oz. cognac
2 oz. curacao
2 oz. powdered sugar
12 oz. club soda
Orange slices
Mint sprigs

*Combine everything except the soda and garnishes. Stir well. Add plenty of ice and the soda before serving. Top with the orange slices and mint.*

---

## FRENCH FOAM

¼ oz. brandy
¼ oz. kirschwasser
1½ tsp. sugar syrup
A few dashes of Angostura bitters
Champagne
Lemon sherbet

*Combine all but the champagne and the sherbet in a glass; stir well. Fill the glass part way with champagne. Float a small scoop of sherbet on top. Pour more champagne over it until the glass is full.*

**FRENCH GREEN DRAGON**

1½ oz. cognac
1½ oz. green chartreuse

*Combine with ice; shake well. Strain and add ice.*

**FRENCH PUNCH**

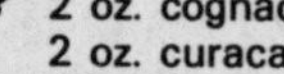
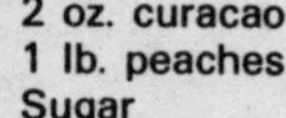

3 bottles Rhine wine
1 bottle champagne
2 oz. cognac
2 oz. curacao
1 lb. peaches
Sugar

*Peel and slice the peaches; combine with enough sugar to barely cover them in a large punch bowl. Add the Rhine wine and allow to stand for at least one hour. Add the remaining ingredients plus chunks of ice.*

**FRENCH RIVIERA**

2 oz. rye
1 oz. apricot brandy
1 tsp. lemon juice

*Combine with ice; shake well. Strain and add ice. Top with a cherry.*

**FRENCH 75**

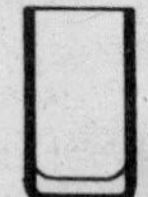

1½ oz. cognac
1½ tsp. lemon juice
½ tsp. powdered sugar
Champagne

*Combine (except the champagne) with ice; shake well. Strain; add ice and fill with champagne. Add a twist of lemon.*

**FRENCH VERMOUTH AND CURACAO**

3 oz. dry vermouth
1½ oz. curacao
Club soda

*Into the vermouth and the curacao, add ice; fill with club soda, and stir gently.*

**FRISCO**

2 oz. Benedictine
1 oz. lemon juice
Rye

*Combine the Benedictine and lemon juice; add plenty of ice and fill with rye. Stir well. For more delicate palates, a* **FRISCO** *can be made of equal parts Benedictine and bourbon, adding a twist of lemon instead of the juice.*

**FRISCO SOUR**

2 oz. whiskey
1 tbs. lemon juice
1 tbs. lime juice
2 tsp. grenadine
Club soda

*Combine all but the soda with ice; shake well. Strain. Fill with club soda and decorate with fruit slices. Serve straight up.*

**FROBISHER**

2 oz. gin
A few dashes of Angostura bitters
Champagne

*Combine the gin and the bitters; add ice and fill with champagne. Add a twist of lemon.*

**FROSTBITE**

1 oz. tequila
2 oz. heavy cream
2 tsp. white creme de cacao
3 oz. crushed ice

*Combine in a blender at a low speed no more than 15 seconds. Strain and serve straight up.*

**FROSTED COFFEE PUNCH**

3 pints strong, iced coffee
8 oz. Jamaican rum
4 oz. sugar
5 pints vanilla ice cream
2 cups whipped cream

*Dissolve the sugar with the coffee. Add the rum and ice cream and stir until smooth. Top with whipped cream.*

**FROSTED MINT COCOA**

4 oz. cocoa
6 oz. sugar
5 cups milk
1½ pints vanilla ice cream
Several drops white creme de menthe

*Combine the cocoa and sugar with a cup of boiling water in a saucepan; simmer for several minutes. Warm the milk in a double boiler; add the cocoa and creme de menthe. Stir well and allow to cool. Combine the cocoa with the ice cream; blend until smooth.*

**FROSTY VINE**

2 oz. vanilla ice cream
1 oz. brandy
1 oz. port

*Combine in a blender at high speed until smooth. Serve straight up.*

**FROTH BLOWER COCKTAIL**

2 oz. dry gin
1 egg white
1 tsp. grenadine

*Combine with ice; shake well. Strain and add ice.*

**FROTHY DAWN COCKTAIL**

1½ oz. white rum
1 oz. orange juice
2 tsp. Falernum
1 tsp. maraschino

*Combine with ice; shake well. Strain and add ice.*

**FROUPE**

1½ oz. brandy
1½ oz. sweet vermouth
1 tsp. Benedictine

*Combine with ice; shake well. Strain and add ice.*

## FROZEN DRINKS

*All frozen are made basically the same way: Combine the ingredients in an electric blender, add 3 oz. of crushed ice, and blend at a low speed for no more than 15 seconds. Strain the drink into a wide champagne glass and serve straight up.*

### FROZEN APPLE

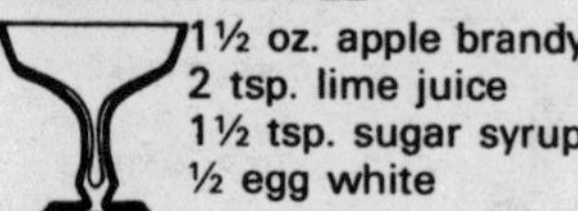

1½ oz. apple brandy
2 tsp. lime juice
1½ tsp. sugar syrup
½ egg white

### FROZEN APPLE AND BANANA

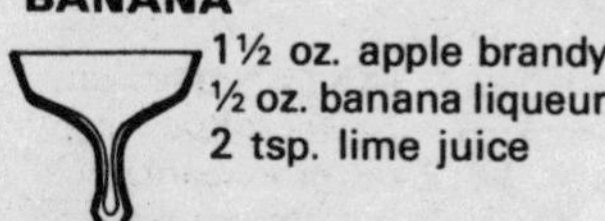

1½ oz. apple brandy
½ oz. banana liqueur
2 tsp. lime juice

*Garnish with a slice of banana.*

### FROZEN APPLE DAIQUIRI

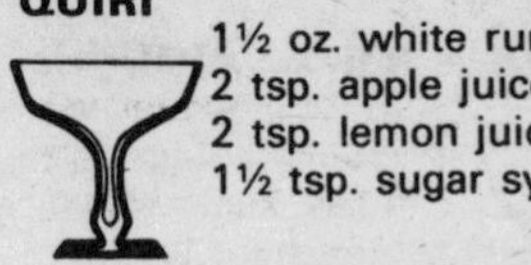

1½ oz. white rum
2 tsp. apple juice
2 tsp. lemon juice
1½ tsp. sugar syrup

*Garnish with an apple wedge.*

### FROZEN AQUAVIT

1½ oz. aquavit
2 tsp. lime juice
1½ tsp. sugar syrup
1 tsp. kirschwasser
½ egg white

*Add one extra oz. of crushed ice.*

### FROZEN BERKELEY

1½ oz. white rum
½ oz. California brandy
2 tsp. passion fruit juice

### FROZEN BLACK CURRENT

1 oz. creme de cassis
1 oz. pineapple juice
2 tsp. brandy

*Garnish with a slice of orange.*

### FROZEN BLACKBERRY TEQUILA

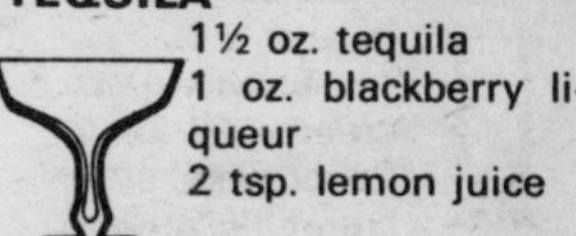

1½ oz. tequila
1 oz. blackberry liqueur
2 tsp. lemon juice

*Garnish with a slice of lemon.*

### FROZEN BRANDY AND PORT

1 oz. brandy
¾ oz. port
1 egg
1 tsp. powdered sugar

*Garnish with nutmeg.*

**FROZEN BRANDY AND RUM**

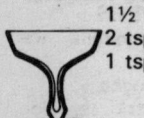

1½ oz. brandy
1 oz. rum
2 tsp. lemon juice
2 tsp. sugar syrup
1 egg yolk

**FROZEN DAIQUIRI**

1½ oz. white rum
2 tsp. lime juice
1 tsp. sugar syrup

*Add an extra oz. of crushed ice. Serve with a straw and top with a teaspoon of 151-proof rum.*

**FROZEN GUAVA DAIQUIRI**

1½ oz. white rum
1 oz. guava nectar
2 tsp. lime juice
1 tsp. banana liqueur

**FROZEN GUAVA-ORANGE DAIQUIRI**

1½ oz. white rum
¾ oz. guava syrup
2 tsp. orange juice
2 tsp. lime juice

**FROZEN JULEP**

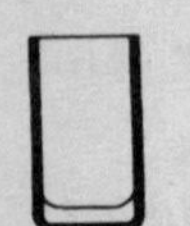

2 oz. bourbon
1 oz. lemon juice
1 oz. sugar syrup
Several mint sprigs, crushed
6 oz. crushed ice

*Combine in a blender at high speed for 20 seconds. Serve straight up. Top with a cherry and a mint sprig.*

**FROZEN LIME DAIQUIRI**

2 oz. white rum
2 tsp. lime liqueur
2 tsp. lime juice

*Add a twist of lime in the glass and drop in the peel.*

**FROZEN MANGO-LIME DAIQUIRI**

1½ oz. white rum
1 oz. mango nectar
2 tsp. lime liqueur
2 tsp. lime juice

*Garnish with a slice of mango.*

**FROZEN MATADOR**

1 oz. tequila
2 oz. pineapple juice
2 tsp. lime juice

*Garnish with a pineapple stick*

**FROZEN MINT DAIQUIRI**

2 oz. white rum
2 tsp. lime juice
1½ tsp. sugar syrup
½ doz. mint leaves

*Add an extra oz. of crushed ice*

**FROZEN PASSION FRUIT DAIQUIRI**

1½ oz. white rum
½ oz. passion fruit syrup
2 tsp. lime juice
2 tsp. orange juice
1 tsp. lemon juice

## FROZEN PEACH DAIQUIRI

1½ oz. white rum
2 oz. frozen peaches, thawed and sliced.

*Save the syrup from the frozen peaches and add 2 teaspoons into the blender.*

## FROZEN PINEAPPLE DAIQUIRI

1½ oz. white rum
2 tsp. lime juice
1 tsp sugar syrup
2 canned pineapple rings, sliced and drained

## FROZEN RUM HONEY

2 oz. 151-proof rum
½ oz. honey
2 tsp. lemon juice

*Combine in a blender at a high speed for no more than 15 seconds. Strain. Add ice.*

## FROZEN RUSSIAN APPLE

1½ oz. vodka
¼ oz. calvados
2 tsp. lime juice
1 tsp. sugar syrup
2 oz. chopped apples

*Put one less oz. of chopped ice in the blender.*

## FROZEN SESAME DAIQUIRI

1½ oz. rum
½ oz. sesame syrup
2 tsp. lime juice
2 tsp. dry vermouth
2 tsp. orange juice

## FROZEN SOURSOP DAIQUIRI

1½ oz. white rum
¼ oz. Jamaican rum
1 oz. soursop (guanabana) nectar
1 tsp. lime juice
2 oz. bananas

## FROZEN STEPPES

2 oz. vanilla ice cream
2 tbs. vodka
1 tbs. dark creme de cacao

*Combine in a blender at a high speed until smooth. Serve straight up.*

## FULL HOUSE

¾ oz. apple whiskey
¾ oz. Benedictine
¾ oz. yellow chartreuse
A few dashes of Angostura bitters

*Combine with ice; shake well. Strain and add ice.*

U.S. COLONIAL "Stone Jugg" or "Fflander"

# YOUR OWN RECIPE

# YOUR OWN RECIPE

# YOUR OWN RECIPE

Use a bartender's mixing glass whenever the instructions state "combine" ingredients. Strain the drink from the mixing glass into the drinking glass suggested by the illustration alongside the ingredients.

The glass pictured for each drink is our suggestion; other drinking cups may be used as well.

# G

---

## GASLIGHT

1½ oz. Scotch
2 tsp. sweet vermouth
1-2 dashes orange curacao
A few drops Drambuie

*Combine (except the Drambuie) with ice; shake well. Strain, add ice and a twist of orange, and pour the Drambuie on top.*

## GAUGUIN

2 oz. white rum
2 tsp. passion fruit syrup
2 tsp. lemon juice
1 tsp. lime juice
3 oz. crushed ice

*Combine in a blender at a low speed for 15 seconds. Strain straight up and add a cherry.*

## GAZETTE

1½ oz. brandy
1 oz. sweet vermouth
1 tsp. lemon juice
1 tsp. sugar syrup

*Combine with ice; shake. Strain and add ice.*

## GEISHA

2 oz. bourbon
1 oz. sake
2 tsp. sugar syrup
1½ tsp. lemon juice

*Combine with ice; shake well. Strain; add ice. Decorate with a cherry.*

## GENERAL HARRISON'S EGGNOG

1 egg
1 tsp. powdered sugar
Claret

*Combine the egg and sugar with ice; shake extremely well. Strain. Add claret. Dust with nutmeg.*

## GENOA

¾ oz. gin
¾ oz. grappa
2 tsp. sambuca
2 tsp. dry vermouth

*Combine with ice; shake well. Strain and add ice and an olive.*

**GENTLE BULL**

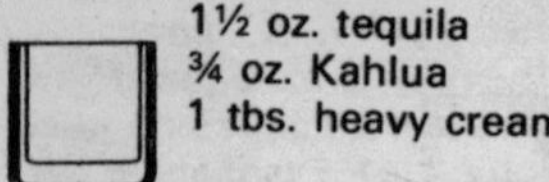

1½ oz. tequila
¾ oz. Kahlua
1 tbs. heavy cream

*Combine with ice; shake well. Strain and add ice.*

**GENTLE JOHN**

1¼ oz. Scotch
A few drops dry vermouth
A few drops Cointreau
1-2 dashes orange bitters

*Combine with ice; shake well. Strain and add ice.*

**GEORGIA RUM COOLER**

2½ oz. white rum
2 tsp. lemon juice
1 tsp. grenadine
1 tsp. Falernum
1 tsp. salted peanuts
4 oz. crushed ice
Club soda

*Combine (except the soda) in a blender at a high speed for 30 seconds. Strain, add ice, and soda. Dust with cinnamon.*

**GIBSON**

2½ oz. gin
A few drops dry vermouth
1 cocktail onion

*Combine the gin and vermouth and stir well. Top with the onion.*

**GILDED ORANGE**

2 oz. gin
3 tbs. orange juice
2 tsp. dark rum
2 tsp. sugar syrup
A few drops lemon juice
1-2 dashes almond extract

*Combine with ice; shake well. Strain and add ice.*

**GILROY**

¾ oz. gin
¾ oz. cherry brandy
2 tsp. dry vermouth
2 tsp. lemon juice
1-2 dashes orange bitters

*Combine with ice; shake well. Strain and add ice.*

**GIMLET**

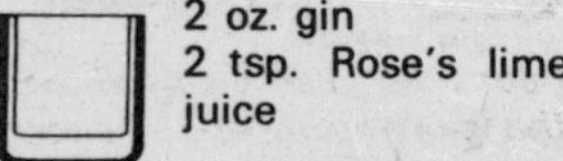

2 oz. gin
2 tsp. Rose's lime juice

*Combine with ice; shake well. Strain and add ice.*

**GIN ALOHA**

1½ oz. gin
½ oz. unsweetened pineapple juice
1 tsp. curacao
A few dashes orange bitters

*Combine with ice; shake well. Strain; add ice and a cherry.*

**GIN AND CAMPARI**

1½ oz. gin
1½ oz. Campari

*Combine with ice; shake. Strain. Add ice and a twist of orange.*

**GIN AND LIME**

1½ oz. gin
½ lime
2 tsp. orange juice
1 tsp. Rose's lime juice

*Pour lime juice over ice; add the gin and juices and shake well. Strain. Add ice and a twist of lime.*

**GIN AND SIN**

2 oz. gin
1 tbs. Cinzano

*Combine and stir. Serve straight up.*

**GIN AND TONIC**

2½ oz. gin
Tonic water

*Pour the gin; add ice, tonic and a twist of lemon. Or use sherry instead of gin.*

**GIN AQUAVIT**

1½ oz. gin
½ oz. aquavit
2 tsp. lemon juice
1½ tsp. sugar syrup
1 tsp. heavy cream
½ egg white

*Combine with ice; shake extremely well. Strain and add ice.*

**GIN BENEDICTINE SANGAREE**

1¼ oz. gin
¼ oz. Benedictine
2 tsp. grapefruit juice

*Combine with ice; shake well. Strain, add ice and a slice of lemon and garnish with nutmeg.*

**GIN BOWL**

1 gallon dry white wine
1 bottle gin
8 oz. iced green tea
Lemon slices

*Combine and stir well. Add chunks of ice before serving. To strengthen, add a cup of Jamaican rum.*

**GIN CASSIS**

1½ oz. gin
2 tsp. lemon juice
2 tsp. creme de cassis

*Combine with ice; shake well. Strain and add ice.*

**GIN COCO**

Gin
1 coconut

*Open the coconut and save the juice. Add one part gin for every two parts coconut juice; stir and serve over ice.*

**GIN DAIQUIRI**

1½ oz. gin
½ oz. white rum
2 tsp. lime juice
1 tsp. sugar syrup

*Combine with ice; shake well. Strain and add ice.*

**GIN DAISY**

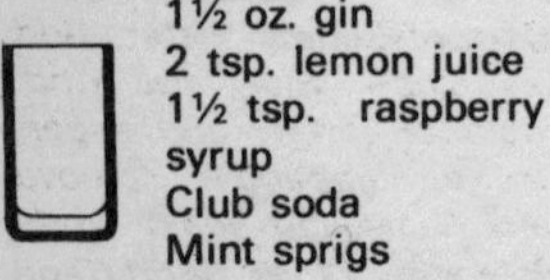

1½ oz. gin
2 tsp. lemon juice
1½ tsp. raspberry syrup
Club soda
Mint sprigs

*Combine the gin, juice, and syrup with ice; shake well. Strain; add ice and club soda. Top with the mint or a lemon slice.*

**GIN FIZZ**

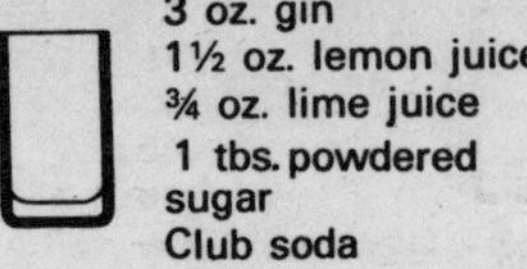

3 oz. gin
1½ oz. lemon juice
¾ oz. lime juice
1 tbs. powdered sugar
Club soda

*Combine (except the soda) with ice; shake well. Strain; add ice and soda.*

**GIN MINT FIZZ**

2 oz. gin
2 tsp. lemon juice
1½ tsp. sugar syrup
1 tsp. white creme de menthe
Mint leaves

*Combine (except the mint leaves) with ice; shake well. Strain over crushed ice and top with mint leaves, partially torn.*

**GIN OLD-FASHIONED**

1½ oz. gin
½ tsp. sugar syrup
A few dashes of Angostura bitters

*Combine and stir. Add ice and a twist of lemon.*

**GIN PUNCH**

8 oz. gin
4 oz. maraschino
2 oz. lemon juice
Grated lemon rind
2 oz. sugar syrup
1 bottle ginger ale

*Combine everything except the ale. Stir well. Add the ale plus chunks of ice before serving.*

**GIN RICKEY**

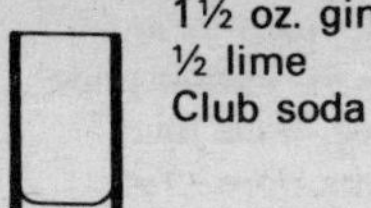

1½ oz. gin
½ lime
Club soda

*Pour the gin; add ice and club soda. Squeeze in the lime; include the rind and stir.*

**GIN RISQUE**

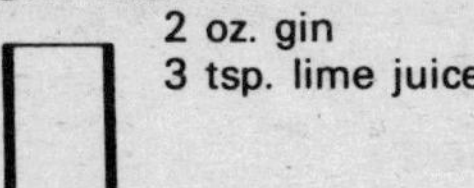

2 oz. gin
3 tsp. lime juice

*Combine with ice; shake. Strain; add plenty of ice and fill the glass with cold water. Touch it up with a twist of lime.*

**GIN SIDECAR**

1½ oz. high-proof gin
1 oz. Triple Sec
1 oz. lemon juice

*Combine with ice; shake. Strain and add ice.*

**GIN SOUTHERN**

1½ oz. gin
½ oz. Southern Comfort
1 tsp. lemon juice
1 tsp. grapefruit juice

*Combine with ice; shake well. Strain and add ice.*

**GIN SWIZZLE**

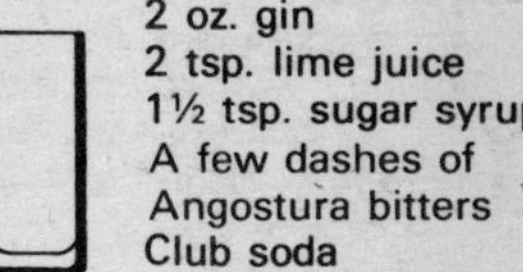

2 oz. gin
2 tsp. lime juice
1½ tsp. sugar syrup
A few dashes of Angostura bitters
Club soda

*Combine (except the soda) with ice; shake well. Strain; add ice and club soda.*

**GIN WITH A WEDGE**

*Pour 2 oz. gin into an old-fashioned glass; fill the glass with ice. Drop a thick orange slice into the glass; stir it well with the gin and ice to flavor the drink and frost the glass.*

**GINGER BEER**

1½ oz. ginger
1½ oz. cream of tartar
3 tsp. lemon juice
Grated lemon rind
3 cups of sugar
1 tsp. dry active yeast, dissolved in a few drops of water

*Pound the ginger into a powder; combine with a gallon of boiling water. Add the lemon juice and rind, cream of tartar, and sugar, stirring constantly. Remove from heat; add yeast when lukewarm. Close tightly and allow to stand for several hours. Strain and seal tightly in bottles. Store in a cool, dark place.*

## GINGER HIGHBALL

1½ oz. whiskey
A large chunk fresh ginger root
Club soda

*Pour the whiskey into a highball glass; squeeze the ginger root through a garlic press above it. Add ice and fill with soda; stir.*

## GINGER MARTINI

*Fix your favorite martini in a mixing glass; add a sliver of dried ginger root and let it sit a few minutes. Add ice, shake, and strain straight up.*

## GINGER RUM TEA

1½ oz. rum
A chunk of preserved ginger
A cup of hot tea

*Pour the rum into the tea; add the ginger and stir. This drink can be served iced.*

## GINGERSNAP

3 oz. vodka
1 oz. ginger wine
Club soda

*Combine the vodka and wine, add ice and stir gently. Add soda.*

## GLACIER

1 oz. brandy
2 tsp. Parfait Amour
1½ tsp. lemon juice
1½ tsp. lime juice
A few drops of rock candy syrup

*Combine with ice; shake. Strain and add ice.*

## GLAD EYE

1½ oz. Pernod
¾ oz. peppermint

*Combine with ice; shake well. Strain and add ice.*

## GLASGOW

1½ oz. Scotch
1 tbs. lemon juice
1 tsp. dry vermouth
1 tsp. almond extract

*Combine with ice; shake well. Strain and add ice.*

## GLOGG

1 bottle port
1 bottle Madeira
1 bottle medium dry sherry
½ bottle dry red wine
4 oz. warm brandy
8 oz. sugar cubes
1 cup raisins
1
almonds
1 doz. cloves
1 cinnamon stick
A few cardamom seeds

*Combine everything except the sugar, brandy, raisins, and nuts in a large saucepan and heat. Place the sugar cubes in a shallow pan above the glogg; pour the brandy over the cubes and ignite. Extinguish the brandy by dipping the contents of the pan into the glogg. Stir until the sugar is completely dissolved. Serve in mugs; garnish each with a few of the almonds and raisins.*

**GLOOM CHASER**

½ oz. Grand Marnier
½ oz. curacao
2 tsp. lemon juice
2 tsp. grenadine

*Combine with ice; shake well. Strain and add ice.*

**GLOOM LIFTER**

1¼ oz. whiskey
2 tsp. raspberry syrup
1½ tsp. lemon juice
1 tsp. sugar syrup
½ tsp. brandy
A small portion of egg white

*Combine with ice; shake extremely well. Strain and add ice.*

**GLOW WINE**

2 bottles claret
8 oz. sugar
½ doz. cloves
The peels of ½ lemon, sliced
A few dashes cinnamon

*Combine in a large saucepan and boil. Serve immediately. Top with an orange slice.*

**GLUEWEIN**

6 oz. claret
3 cubes sugar
1 cinnamon stick
1 clove

*Combine in a small saucepan and bring to a boil. Serve in a large mug steaming hot. Cider can be used instead of claret; add a dash of rum or apple brandy.*

**GOLD CADILLAC**

¾ oz. white creme de cacao
¾ oz. heavy cream
¾ oz. Galliano
3 oz. crushed ice

*Combine in a blender at a low speed for 15 seconds. Strain straight up.*

**GOLDEN DAWN**

1 oz. apple brandy
1 oz. apricot brandy
1 oz. dry gin
A few drops orange juice
A few drops grenadine

*Combine (except the grenadine) with ice; shake well. Strain. Add ice and then the grenadine; do not stir.*

**GOLDEN DAZE**

1½ oz. dry gin
1 oz. orange juice
¾ oz. apricot brandy

*Combine with ice; shake well. Strain and add ice.*

**GOLDEN DRAGON**

1 tbs. yellow chartreuse
1 tsp. brandy

*Float the brandy over the chartreuse.*

**GOLDEN FROG**

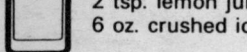

½ oz. vodka
½ oz. Galliano
2 tsp. Strega
2 tsp. lemon juice
6 oz. crushed ice

*Combine in a blender at a high speed for 15 seconds. Strain and add ice.*

**GOLDEN GATE**

¾ oz. white rum
¾ oz. gin
2 tsp. lemon juice
2 tsp. white creme de cacao
1 tsp. 151-proof rum
A few drops Falernum

*Combine with ice; shake well. Strain and add ice. Top with an orange slice.*

**GOLDEN GIN FIZZ**

2½ oz. gin
1½ tbs. lemon juice
2½ tsp. sugar syrup
1 egg yolk
Club soda

*Combine (except the soda) with ice; shake well. Strain; add ice and soda. Top with a lemon slice and nutmeg.*

**GOLDEN GLOW**

1¼ oz. bourbon
2 tbs. orange juice
2 tsp. lemon juice
1½ tsp. sugar syrup
A few drops Jamaican rum
Grenadine

*Combine (except the grenadine) with ice; shake. Strain straight up over a few drops of grenadine.*

**GOLDEN HORNET**

1½ oz. gin
½ oz. amontillado
2 tsp. Scotch

*Combine the gin and amontillado with ice; shake. Strain. Add ice and a twist of lemon; float the Scotch on top.*

**GOLDEN RETRIEVER PUNCH**

1 pint apricot syrup
1 pint lime juice
3 pints orange juice
3 quarts club soda

*Combine in a large punch bowl. Add chunks of ice immediately before serving.*

**GOLDEN SCREW**

1 oz. gin
2 oz. orange juice
A few dashes of Angostura bitters

*Combine, add ice, and stir well.*
*For a* **SCREWDRIVER**, *use vodka instead of gin and no bitters.*

## GOLDEN SLIPPER

1 oz. yellow chartreuse
1 oz. apricot brandy
1 egg yolk

*Combine with ice; shake well. Strain and add ice.*

## GOLF MARTINI

1½ oz. gin
2 tsp. dry vermouth
A few dashes of Angostura bitters

*Combine straight up and gently stir. Add an olive.*

## GOOD NIGHT ALL

1 gallon beer
8 oz. honey
A few pinches pepper and ground cloves
1 pinch ground ginger
2 cinnamon sticks

*Combine the beer and honey in a saucepan; heat until the honey is completely dissolved. Place the spices in an infuser and steep them in the beer overnight. Serve hot.*

## GOSSIP'S CUP

12 oz. ale
1½ oz. cognac
1 tsp. brown sugar
Grated lemon rind
A pinch of ginger and nutmeg

*Combine in a saucepan; heat but do not allow to boil. Serve in mugs. Add extra garnish if you wish.*

## GOURMET MARTINI

1½ oz. gin
2 tsp. dry vermouth
A few drops Campari

*Combine straight up; stir.*

## GRANADA

1 oz. fino sherry
1 oz. brandy
2 tsp. curacao
Tonic water

*Combine (except the tonic) with ice; shake. Strain; add ice and tonic. Top with an orange slice.*

## GRAND CENTRAL

1½ oz. bourbon
1 tsp. sugar syrup
A few dashes of Angostura bitters

*Combine with ice; shake well. Strain and add ice.*

## GRAND EGG NOG

4 oz. Grand Marnier
4 oz. each white rum and brandy
4 oz. sugar
3 eggs, separated
1 quart milk
1 pint cream
Grated nutmeg

*Beat the sugar with the yolks. Slowly add the rum, brandy, and Grand Marnier, stirring constantly. Cool in the refrigerator for a few hours, stirring occasionally. When ready, slowly add the milk, again stirring constantly. Whip the cream; beat the whites until stiff. Fold them into the nog. Garnish with nutmeg.*

## GRAND MARNIER QUETSCH

1 oz. Grand Marnier
1 tsp. quetsch plum brandy
1 tsp. orange juice

*Combine without ice; stir well. Pour over crushed ice. Add a lemon slice.*

## GRAND ORANGE BLOSSOM

1½ oz. gin
2 tbs. orange juice
1 tbs. Grand Marnier
1 tsp. sugar syrup

*Combine with ice; shake well. Strain and add ice.*

## GRAND PASSION

2 oz. gin
1 oz. passion fruit nectar
1-2 dashes Angostura bitters

*Combine with ice; shake well. Strain and add ice.*

## GRAND ROYAL FIZZ

2 oz. gin
1 oz. orange juice
1 oz. lemon juice
2 tsp. heavy cream
1 tsp. powdered sugar
A few drops of maraschino
Club soda

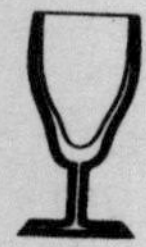

*Combine (except soda) with ice. Strain; add ice and soda.*

## GRAND SLAM

2 oz. Swedish Punch
2 tsp. sweet vermouth
2 tsp. dry vermouth

*Combine with ice; shake. Strain and add ice.*

## GRANVILLE

1½ oz. gin
1 tsp. Grand Marnier
1 tsp. calvados
1 tsp. lemon juice

*Combine with ice; shake. Strain and add ice.*

## GRAPEFRUIT BEER

½ doz. grapefruit
12 oz. dry active yeast

*Peel and slice the grapefruit; combine with 3 gals. of hot water in a large crock pot. Allow to cool; add the yeast. Seal and allow to ferment. Bottle immediately after fermentation.*

## GRAPEFRUIT COCKTAIL

1½ oz. dry gin
1½ oz. grapefruit juice
1 tsp. maraschino

*Combine with ice; shake. Strain and add ice. Add a cherry.*

**GRAPEFRUIT COOLER**

2 oz. whiskey
4 oz. unsweetened grapefruit juice
2 tsp. red currant syrup
1 tsp. lemon juice

*Combine with ice; shake. Strain; add plenty of ice and a slice of lemon or orange.*

**GRAPEFRUIT HIGHBALL**

1½ oz. Puerto Rican rum
Grapefruit juice

*Pour the rum into a highball glass; add ice and fill with grapefruit juice. Stir well.*

**GRAPEFRUIT NOG**

1½ oz. brandy
4 oz. unsweetened grapefruit juice
1 tbs. lemon juice
1 tbs. honey
1 egg
4 oz. crushed ice

*Combine in a blender at a low speed for 20 seconds. Strain and add lots of ice.*

**GRAPPA STREGA**

1 oz. grappa
1 oz. Strega
1 tsp. lemon juice
1 tsp. orange juice

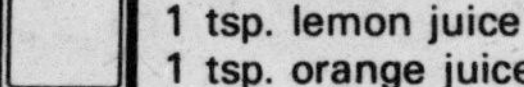

*Combine with ice; shake. Strain. Add ice and a twist of lemon.*

**GRASSHOPPER**

1 oz. green creme de menthe
1 oz. white creme de cacao
1 oz. heavy cream

*Combine with ice; shake well. Strain straight up. For a* **MEXICAN GRASSHOPPER** *use Kahlua instead of creme de cacao.*

---

**GREAT SECRET**

1½ oz. gin
2 tsp. Lillet
1-2 dashes Angostura bitters

*Combine with ice; shake. Strain. Add ice and a twist of orange.*

**GREEK BUCK**

1½ oz. Metaxa brandy
2 tsp. lemon juice
1 tsp. ouzo
Ginger ale

*Combine the brandy and lemon juice with ice; shake. Strain; add ice, ginger ale, and a slice of lemon. Float the ouzo on top.*

**GREENBACK**

2 oz. gin
2 tsp. lime juice
1 tsp. green creme de menthe

*Combine with ice; shake. Strain and add ice.*

## GREEN DEVIL

1½ oz. gin
1 tsp. green creme de menthe
2 tsp. lime juice
Mint sprigs

*Combine (except mint) with ice; shake well. Strain, add ice and mint.*

## GREEN DRAGON

1½ oz. dry gin
1 oz. green creme de menthe

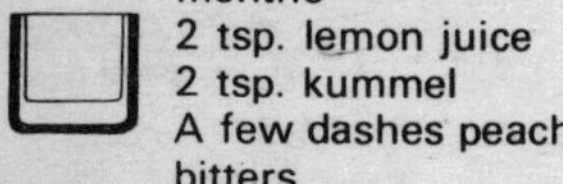

2 tsp. lemon juice
2 tsp. kummel
A few dashes peach bitters

*Combine with ice; shake. Strain and add ice.*

## GREEN FIRE

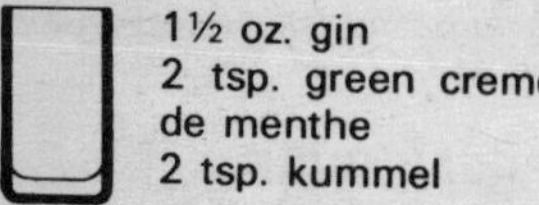

1½ oz. gin
2 tsp. green creme de menthe
2 tsp. kummel

*Combine with ice; shake well. Strain and add ice.*

## GREEN ROOM

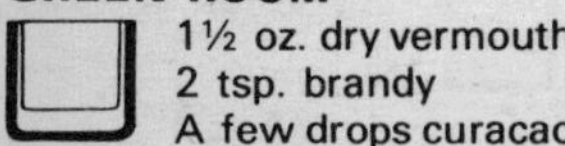

1½ oz. dry vermouth
2 tsp. brandy
A few drops curacao

*Combine with ice; shake. Strain and add ice.*

## GRENADINE RICKEY

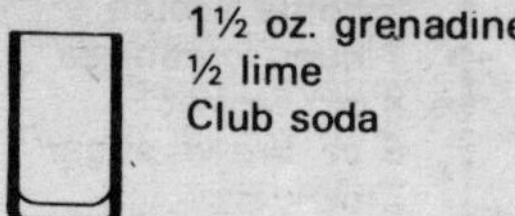

1½ oz. grenadine
½ lime
Club soda

*Squeeze the lime into a glass; add the rind, the grenadine and a few cubes of ice. Add club soda and stir.*

## GROG

2 oz. Jamaican rum
1 tbs. lemon juice
1 cube sugar
A few cloves
1 cinnamon stick

*Combine in a mug; fill with boiling water and stir until the sugar is completely dissolved. Add a twist of lemon. Serve hot.*

## GUANABANA

1½ oz. white rum
1½ tbs. soursop (guanabana) nectar
1 tsp. lime juice

*Combine with ice; shake. Strain and add ice.*

## GUARDSMAN'S PUNCH

1 bottle Scotch
1 pint green tea
6 oz. brandy
½ cup sugar
1 oz. port
The peels of 1 lemon, sliced

*Combine in a large saucepan. Heat, but do not boil; serve steaming hot.*

## GUARDSMAN'S PUNCH II

1 bottle Scotch
1 quart green tea
8 oz. cognac
8 oz. brown sugar
2 oz. port
Grated lemon peels

*Combine the tea, sugar, and grated peels in a large pot; heat and stir until the sugar has dissolved. Add the port and Scotch; stir well. Heat a ladle-full of the cognac over low heat; ignite and infuse the punch. Add the rest of the cognac and serve immediately.*

## GUAVA COOLER

2 oz. vodka
2 tbs. guava nectar
2 tsp. sugar syrup

*Combine with ice; shake well. Strain and add ice.*

## GUAVA WATER

1½ oz. rum
1½ oz. guava nectar
2 tsp. lemon juice
2 tsp. pineapple juice
2 tsp. maraschino
1 tsp. sugar syrup
1 guava shell
Club soda

*Combine (except the shell and the soda) with ice; shake. Strain; add ice and club soda. Top with the guava shell or a slice of lemon.*

## GYPSY

2 oz. vodka
2 tsp. Benedictine
1 tsp. lemon juice
1 tsp. orange juice

*Combine with ice; shake. Strain and add ice. Top with a slice of orange.*

Ale Jug
1800
(United States)

# YOUR OWN RECIPE

# YOUR OWN RECIPE

# YOUR OWN RECIPE

Use a bartender's mixing glass whenever the instructions state "combine" ingredients. Strain the drink from the mixing glass into the drinking glass suggested by the illustration alongside the ingredients.

The glass pictured for each drink is our suggestion; other drinking cups may be used as well.

---

### HABITANT COCKTAIL

1½ oz. Canadian whiskey
1 oz. lemon juice
1 tsp. maple syrup

*Combine with ice; shake. Strain and add ice. Top with a slice of orange and a cherry.*

### HABIT ROUGE

1½ oz. gin
2 tbs. grapefruit juice
2 oz. cranberry juice
1 tsp. honey
2 oz. crushed ice

*Combine in blender at a high speed until the consistency of snow. Serve unstrained.*

### HAPA TIQI

1 oz. white rum
1 oz. orange juice
1 tbs. lemon juice
2 tsp. brandy
1 tsp. almond extract
Gardenia blossoms

*Combine everything except the blossoms with ice; shake well. Strain over plenty of ice. Garnish with gardenia.*

### HAPPY APPLE RUM TWIST

1½ oz. white rum
3 oz. coder
1 oz. lemon juice

*Combine with ice; shake. Strain. Add ice and a twist of lime with its peel.*

### HAPPY HOUR PUNCH

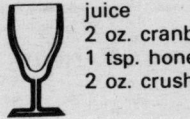

1 fifth Southern Comfort
8 oz. pineapple juice
8 oz. grapefruit juice
4 oz. lemon juice
4 bottles champagne
Orange slices

*Combine (except the champagne) in a large punch bowl; decorate with slices of orange. Add the champagne and chunks of ice immediately before serving.*

### HARBORMASTER SWIZZLE

2½ oz. Jamaican rum
1½ tsp. lime juice
1½ tsp. sugar syrup
Several dashes of Demarara bitters

*Combine with ice; shake well. Strain over crushed ice; add cold water to fill. Stir gently until the glass begins to frost.*

**HARLEM**

1½ oz. dry gin
1 tbs. pineapple juice
A few chunks canned pineapple
A few drops maraschino

*Combine with ice; shake well. Strain and add ice.*

**HARRITY**

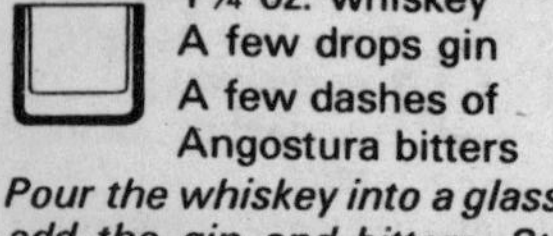

1¼ oz. whiskey
A few drops gin
A few dashes of Angostura bitters

*Pour the whiskey into a glass; add the gin and bitters. Stir well and add ice.*

**HARRY LAUDER**

1¼ oz. Scotch
1¼ oz. sweet vermouth
½ tsp. sugar syrup

*Combine with ice; shake well. Strain and add ice.*

**HARVARD**

1½ oz. brandy
1 tbs. sweet vermouth
2 tsp. lemon juice
1 tsp. grenadine
A few dashes of Angostura bitters

*Combine with ice; shake well. Strain and add ice.*

**HARVARD COOLER**

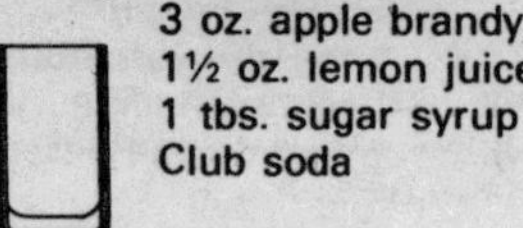

3 oz. apple brandy
1½ oz. lemon juice
1 tbs. sugar syrup
Club soda

*Combine (except the soda) with ice; shake. Strain; add ice and club soda.*

**HARVARD WINE**

1 oz. dry vermouth
1 tbs. brandy
1-2 dashes orange bitters
Club soda

*Combine (except the soda) with ice; shake. Strain; add ice and soda.*

---

**HARVEY WALLBANGER**

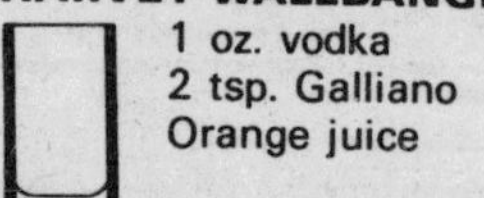

1 oz. vodka
2 tsp. Galliano
Orange juice

*Pour the vodka into a tall glass; add ice and almost fill the glass with orange juice. Float the Galliano on top.*

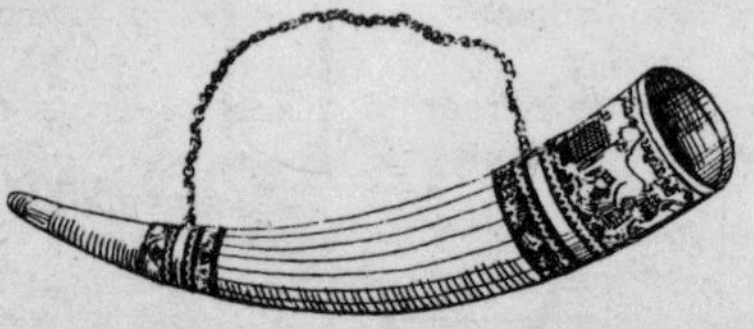

## HASTY COCKTAIL

1½ oz. dry gin
1 tbs. dry vermouth
1 tsp. grenadine
A few drops Pernod

*Combine with ice; shake. Strain and add ice.*

## HAVANA

1 oz. apricot brandy
½ oz. gin
2 tsp. Swedish Punch
A few drops lemon juice

*Combine with ice; shake. Strain and add ice.*

## HAVANA CLUB

1½ oz. white rum
1 tbs. dry vermouth

*Combine with ice; shake. Strain and add ice.*

## HAVANA DAIQUIRI

2 oz. white rum
1 oz. lemon juice
1 tbs. banana liqueur
1 tsp. sugar syrup

*Combine with ice; shake well. Strain and add ice.*

## HAWAIIAN

1½ oz. gin
1 tbs. pineapple juice
1 egg white
1-2 dashes orange bitters

*Combine with ice; shake well. Strain and add ice. This can also be made with a tablespoon of curacao and a tablespoon of orange juice instead of the pineapple juice and the egg white.*

## HAWAIIAN CHAMPAGNE PUNCH

1 pint rum
1 pint brandy
1 pint lemon juice
4 oz. curacao
4 oz. marashino
3 cups powdered sugar
3 large pineapples
4 bottles champagne

*Pare the meat out of the pineapples; crush and combine with the powdered sugar in a bowl. Allow to stand for a few hours. Turn out into a large punch bowl; add everything except the champagne. Stir well and allow to stand overnight. Add the champagne plus chunks of ice immediately before serving.*

## HAWAIIAN COFFEE

1 cup iced coffee
8 oz. coffee ice cream
4 oz. pineapple juice
2 oz. white rum

*Combine in blender at a high speed until smooth. Split between two tall glasses.*

## HAWAIIAN DAISY

1½ oz. white rum
2 tsp. pineapple juice
1 tsp. lime juice
1 tsp. grenadine
1 tsp. 151-proof rum
1 chunk papaya
Club soda

*Combine (except the rum, papaya, and the soda) with ice; shake. Strain; add ice and club soda. Decorate with the papaya and float the rum on top.*

---

## HAWAIIAN EYE

1½ oz. bourbon
1 oz. each of vodka, Kahlua, and heavy cream
2 tsp. Pernod
1 egg white
2 oz. cherry juice
3 oz. crushed ice

*Combine in a blender at a high speed for 15 seconds. Strain straight up. Decorate with slices of pineapple and a cherry.*

## HAWAIIAN HIGHBALL

3 oz. Irish whiskey
2 tsp. pineapple juice
1 tsp. lemon juice
club soda

*Combine the whiskey with the juices; add ice and fill with soda. Stir gently.*

## HAYMAKER'S SWITCHEL

1 pint brandy
2 quarts water
6 oz. vinegar
4 oz. molasses
8 oz. brown sugar
1 pinch of ginger

*Combine; stir until the sugar is dissolved and the vinegar is dispersed. Add ice before serving.*

## HEARNS

¾ oz. bourbon
¾ oz. sweet vermouth
¾ oz. Pernod
A few dashes of Angostura bitters

*Combine with ice; shake. Strain and add ice.*

## HEART WARMER

3 oz. cognac
1 egg yolk
A pinch of paprika

*Combine with ice; shake extremely well. Strain over ice.*

## HEATHER

1½ oz. Scotch
Several drops dry vermouth
A few dashes of Angostura bitters

*Combine with ice; shake well. Strain and add ice.*

## HESITATION

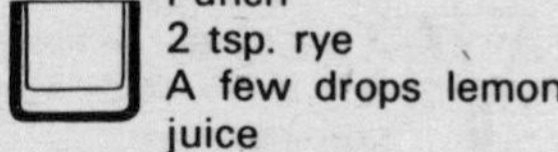

1½ oz. Swedish Punch
2 tsp. rye
A few drops lemon juice

*Combine with ice; shake. Strain and add ice.*

---

## HET PINT

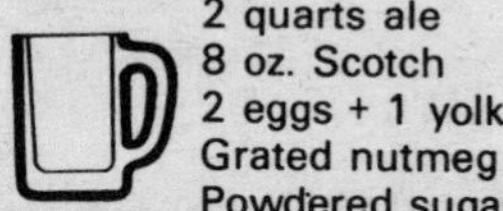

2 quarts ale
8 oz. Scotch
2 eggs + 1 yolk
Grated nutmeg
Powdered sugar

*Combine the ale and nutmeg in a saucepan; add sugar to taste and bring to a boil. Lower the heat. Beat the eggs; add the yolk and combine with the hot ale; stir constantly. Add the Scotch. Pour the brew mug-to-mug to build up a head; serve while still foamy and hot.*

## HIBISCUS CUG

2 oz. white rum
1 oz. Cointreau
1½ tsp. lime juice
1 tsp. Pernod
3 oz. crushed ice
Hibiscus blossoms

*Combine in a blender at high speed for 15 seconds. Turn out straight up; serve with a straw. Decorate with hibiscus.*

## HIGH HAT

1 oz. Cherry Herring
4 oz. rye
3 tbs. lemon juice

*Combine with ice; shake. Strain and add ice.*

## HIGHLAND BITTERS

2 tbs. gentian root
2 tsp. orange peels
1 tsp. camomile flowers
1 tsp. cinnamon
2 cloves
1 oz. coriander seeds
2 bottles Scotch

*Pound the spices until fine and mix well; add them to the Scotch. Store in tightly sealed pots or bottles for two weeks before drinking.*

## HIGHLAND FLING

1½ oz. Scotch
3 oz. milk
1 tsp. powdered sugar

*Combine with ice; shake well. Strain and add ice. Dust with nutmeg.*

## HIGHLAND FLING NO 2.

1½ oz. Scotch
1 tbs. sweet vermouth
1-2 dashes orange bitters

*Combine with ice; shake. Strain and add ice plus an olive.*

## HIPPOCRAS

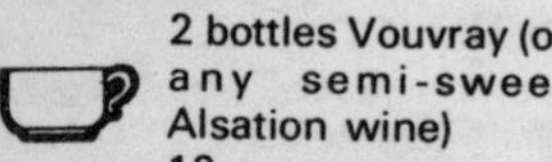

2 bottles Vouvray (or any semi-sweet Alsation wine)
12 oz. sugar
2 lemons, quartered
1 tsp. mace
A few pinches freshly ground white pepper
2 cinnamon sticks

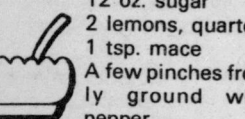

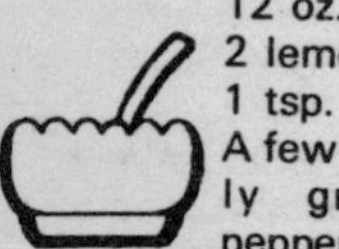

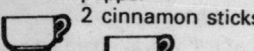

*Combine the wine and the sugar in a punch bowl and stir until the sugar is completely dissolved. Squeeze in the lemons and drop in the rinds. Add the spices and chunks of ice; allow them some time to blend before serving.*

## HIT AND RUN

2 oz. gin
1 tbs. port
A few drops of anisette

*Combine with ice; shake. Strain and add ice.*

## HOFFMAN HOUSE

1½ oz. dry gin
1 tbs. dry vermouth
1-2 dashes orange bitters

*Combine with ice; shake. Strain straight up and add an olive.*

## HOLIDAY

1½ oz. tequila
2 tsp. lemon juice
A few drops grenadine
1 green cherry

*Combine (except the cherry) with ice; shake well. Strain straight up and add a cherry.*

## HOLIDAY EGGNOG

1 pint rye
1 oz. Jamaican rum
6 eggs
6 oz. sugar
1 pint heavy cream
1 pint milk

*Separate the eggs; beat 4 oz. of sugar with the yolks and save the rest for the whites. In a large bowl, combine the milk and the cream with the yolks. Add the rye; allow it to stand for a few hours. Just before serving, beat the egg whites, add the remaining sugar, and fold this into the nog. Dust with nutmeg.*

**HOLLAND HOUSE**

1½ oz. gin
2 tsp. dry vermouth
1 tbs. lemon juice
A few drops maraschino
1 pineapple slice, chopped

*Combine with ice; shake well. Strain and add ice.*

**HONEYBEE**

2 oz. white rum
2 tsp. lemon juice
1 tbs. honey

*Combine with ice; shake well. Strain and add ice.*

---

**HONEYDEW COOLER**

1½ oz. gin
1 tbs. lemon juice
1 tbs. heavy cream
1 tsp. sugar syrup
A few drops Pernod
3 oz. honeydew, diced
4 oz. crushed ice
Club soda

*Combine (except the soda) in a blender at a low speed for 20 seconds. Strain; add ice and a splash of soda.*

---

**HONEYMOON**

1½ oz. apple brandy
1½ oz. lemon juice
3 tsp. Benedictine
A few drops curacao

*Combine with ice; shake. Strain and add ice.*

**HONEYSUCKLE**

1½ oz. gold rum
1 oz. lime juice
1 tsp. honey

*Combine with ice; shake. Strain and add ice.*

**HONOLULU**

1 oz. gin
1 oz. Benedictine
1 tbs. maraschino

*Combine with ice; shake. Strain and add ice.*

**HONOLULU PUNCH**

1 pint brandy
1 pint Jamaican rum
1 cup lemon juice
2 ripe pineapples
6 oz. sugar
4 bottles champagne

*Peel and grate the pineapples; place in a large punch bowl, sprinkle with the sugar, and allow to stand for at least one hour. Add the juice, brandy, and rum and refrigerate overnight. Just before serving, add the champagne and chunks of ice.*

**HONORABLE**

¾ oz. bourbon
¾ oz. sweet vermouth
¾ oz. dry vermouth

*Combine with ice; shake. Strain and add ice.*

## HOOPLA

½ oz. Cointreau
½ oz. Lillet
2 tsp. lemon juice
2 tsp. brandy

*Combine with ice; shake. Strain and add ice.*

## HOOT MON

1 oz. Scotch
½ oz. Lillet
2 tsp. sweet vermouth

*Combine with ice; shake. Strain and add ice.*

## HOP FROG

1 oz. brandy
2 oz. lime juice

*Combine with ice; shake. Strain and add ice.*

## HOP TOAD

¾ oz. white rum
¾ oz. apricot brandy
1 tbs. lime juice

*Combine with ice; shake well. Strain and add ice.*

## HOPPEL POPPEL

8 oz. dark rum
5 oz. sugar
4 egg yolks
1 tsp. vanilla extract
1 quart milk

*Combine the yolks and the sugar; beat until creamy. Heat but do not scald the milk in a separate saucepan. Add the egg mixture plus the vanilla; stir constantly. Pour in the rum. Serve warm in mugs. Garnish with nutmeg.*

## HORSECAR

1 oz. rye
1½ tbs. sweet vermouth
1½ tbs. dry vermouth
1-2 dashes Angostura bitters

*Combine with ice; shake. Strain and add ice. Top with a cherry.*

---

## HORSE MARY

1½ oz. vodka
5 oz. tomato juice
1½ tsp. lemon juice
2 tsp. grated horse radish
1 egg white
A few drops of Worchestershire sauce
A few drops of Tabasco sauce
Salt and pepper to taste

*Combine; shake with ice. Strain straight up.*

---

## HORSE'S NECK

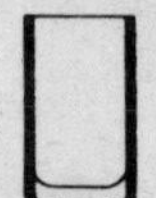

2½ oz. whiskey
1 lemon
Ginger ale

*Carefully peel the lemon so that the peel turns out one long spiral strip. Pour out the whiskey; drop in the spiral peel. Add ice and ginger ale. Squeeze in a few drops of the lemon's juice and gently stir. Gin can be used instead of whiskey.*

### HOT APPLE TODDY

2 oz. apple brandy
2 oz. hot baked apple
2 tsp. cider

*Combine in a heated mug; fill with very hot water and stir. Dust with nutmeg.*

### HOT BRANDY

4 oz. brandy
1 tsp. sugar

*Dissolve the sugar in a mug with a few drops of hot water. Pour in the brandy and fill with boiling water. Top with nutmeg.*

### HOT BRICK TODDY

2 oz. whiskey
1 tsp. sweet butter
1 tsp. powdered sugar
1 tbs. hot water
1 dash cinnamon

*Combine (except the whiskey) and stir until well-blended. Add the whiskey and boiling water.*

### HOT BUTTERED COMFORT

1¼ oz. Southern Comfort
1 cinnamon stick
1 lemon slice
1 pat butter

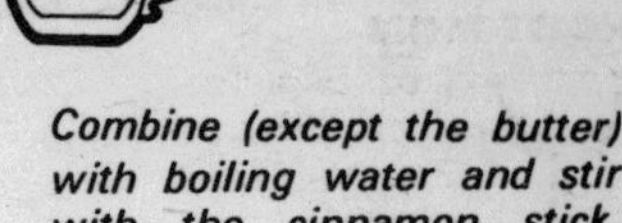

*Combine (except the butter) with boiling water and stir with the cinnamon stick. Float the butter on top.*

### HOT BUTTERED RUM

2½ oz. Jamaican rum
1 tbs. sweet butter
6-8 oz. cider
1 lemon slice
1 cinnamon stick
Cloves

*Combine (except the cider and butter) in a warmed mug. Add hot cider to the spiced rum. Top with butter and nutmeg.*

### HOT BUTTERED APPLEJACK

1 quart cider
4 oz. apple brandy
4 oz. powdered sugar
Cinnamon sticks
Butter

*Heat the cider but do not boil. Serve into four mugs; add an oz. of apple brandy, an oz. of sugar, a cinnamon stick, and a pat of butter. Top with nutmeg, add a twist of lemon, and stir.*

## HOT BUTTERED RUM DE CACAO

2 oz. Jamaican rum
1 oz. dark creme de cacao
2 tsp. brown sugar
Whole cloves, a cinnamon stick, nutmeg
Butter

*Combine the spices and sugar in a warm mug; add a little boiling water and allow to steep a minute or two. Add the rum and creme de cacao; fill the mug with boiling water and stir well. Touch it up with a twist of lemons. Top it with a spot of butter.*

## HOT BUTTERED TODDY

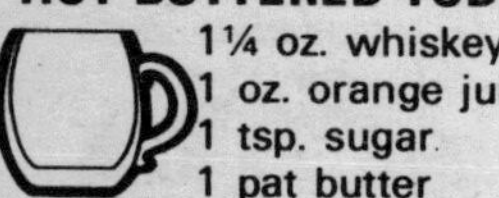

1¼ oz. whiskey
1 oz. orange juice
1 tsp. sugar
1 pat butter

*Combine (except the butter) with hot water and stir well. Top it off with the butter.*

## HOT CREOLE

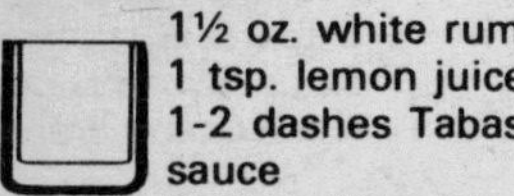

1½ oz. white rum
1 tsp. lemon juice
1-2 dashes Tabasco sauce
Cold beef bouillon

*Combine (except the bouillon), then add ice and bouillon. Stir well. Top with salt and pepper to taste.*

## HOT GIN TODDY

2½ oz. gin
1½ oz. lemon juice
2 cubes sugar

*Combine the sugar and the lemon juice; stir until the sugar is completely dissolved. Add the gin and boiling water. Top with a lemon slice.*

## HOT IRISH PUNCH

4 oz. Irish whiskey
2 cubes sugar
A few drops lemon juice

*Combine the sugar with a few drops of hot water; stir until the sugar is completely dissolved. Add the whiskey and lemon juice to the hot water and stir. Top with a lemon slice and nutmeg.*

## HOT JAMAICAN GROG

1½ oz. Jamaican rum
1 tsp. sugar
A slice of lemon
Whole cloves

*Place the sugar, lemon slice, and cloves in a mug; add the rum and fill the mug with boiling water. Stir and allow to steep for a few minutes. Drink piping hot.*

### HOT LOCOMOTIVE

6 oz. Burgundy
2 tbs. honey
1 tbs. sugar syrup
1 tbs. curacao
1 egg yolk

*Combine the egg yolk, sugar, and honey without ice; stir well. Pour the curacao and the Burgundy into a saucepan; add the honey/egg mixture and heat until boiling, stirring constantly. Serve steaming hot. Top with lemon slice and cinnamon.*

### HOT MILK PUNCH

2 oz. rum
2 oz. brandy
1 tsp. powdered sugar
Hot milk

*Combine and stir very well. Top with nutmeg.*

### HOT MINT BURGUNDY DELIGHT

3 oz. hot Burgundy
6 fresh mint leaves
1½ tbs. sugar syrup
1 lemon peel
A few drops maraschino
1 cinnamon stick

*Muddle the mint leaves with the sugar syrup. Add the lemon peel, maraschino, cinnamon stick, and Burgundy; stir well. Add boiling water.*

### HOT POT

1 pint bourbon
1 pint rum
8 oz. brandy
2 quarts milk
2 quarts heavy cream
2 cups sugar
1 dozen egg yolks
Ginger, cinnamon, nutmeg and salt
Whole cloves, brown sugar

*Combine the yolk and the sugar in a large bowl; beat until creamy. Add the milk and the cream plus the spices and stir to blend. Turn out into a large pot or cauldron; add the liquors and heat until thick. Do not allow to boil; stir constantly. Serve hot in mugs.*

### HOT PUNCH

1 bottle whiskey
1 bottle dark rum
1 bottle Benedictine
1 bottle cherry brandy
1 pint light tea
Sliced bananas, grapes, apples, lemons

*Simmer the sliced fruit with the sugar and spices in the tea for several hours. Add the liquors and keep warm until ready to serve.*

**HOT RUM**

4 oz. Jamaican rum
1½ tsp. lemon juice
2 cubes sugar

*Dissolve the sugar with a few drops of hot water. Add the rum and the lemon juice; fill with hot water and stir. Garnish with cinnamon.*

**HOT RUM PUNCH**

1 pint gold rum
4 oz. cognac
4 oz. kummel
4 oz. Benedictine
1 orange, peeled and sliced
1 lemon, peeled and sliced.

*Combine; add sugar to taste. Add 3 pints of boiling water; stir well.*

**HOT RYE**

2½ oz. rye
1 cube sugar

*Dissolve the sugar with a few drops of hot water; add the rye and top with cinnamon. Serve with a small pitcher of hot water and a slice of lemon on the side.*

**HOT SCOTCH**

4 oz. Scotch
1-2 cubes sugar

*Dissolve the sugar with a few drops of hot water; add the Scotch and hot water. Add twist of lemon slice and the peel; top with nutmeg.*

**HOT SPICED PORT**

1½ oz. port
1 sugar cube
Whole cloves, allspice
A pinch nutmeg
Grated lemon rind

*Dissolve the sugar with a few drops of warm water in a mug; add the spices and port and fill the mug with boiling water. Stir well. Garnish with the grated rind plus extra nutmeg if you like. Sherry Madeira, brandy, rum, or claret can be used instead of the port.*

**HOT SPICED RUM**

1¼ oz. Jamaican rum
2 tsp. sugar
2 tsp. butter
A few dashes ground cloves and cinnamon

*Combine with boiling water and stir well.*

---

**HOT SPICED WINE**

1 bottle Burgundy
4 oz. hot sugar syrup
Ground cloves and cinnamon
Cinnamon sticks

*Heat the bottle of Burgundy in a pot of water, but do not boil. Pour it into a pitcher with the hot sugar syrup; add the powdered spices and stir. Serve with a cinnamon stick or slices of fruit.*

## HOT TEA PUNCH

1 pint gold gum
1 pint brandy
3 pints hot tea
2 oranges, sliced
1 lemon, sliced

*Combine in a large saucepan; add sugar to taste and heat. Serve steaming hot.*

## HOT WHISKEY TODDY

2 oz. whiskey
1 cube sugar

*Dissolve the sugar with a few drops of hot water. Pour in the whiskey and boiling water; stir well. Top with lemon slice and nutmeg.*

## HOT WINE PUNCH

1 bottle red wine
3 tsp. sugar
Cloves
Cinnamon sticks
1 lemon rind, sliced

*Combine the sugar with a cup of boiling water in a saucepan and stir until completely dissolved. Add the spices, rind, and wine; bring to a second boil. Serve hot.*

## HOTEL PLAZA

¾ oz. dry gin
1 tbs. sweet vermouth
1 tbs. dry vermouth
1 slice pineapple, crushed

*Combine with ice; shake. Strain and add ice.*

## HPW

1½ oz. gin
2 tsp. dry vermouth
2 tsp. sweet vermouth

*Combine with ice; shake. Strain. Add ice and a twist of orange; add the peel.*

## HUDSON BAY

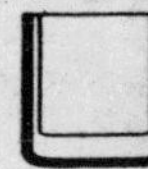

1 oz. gin
½ oz. cherry liqueur
2 tsp. orange juice
1 tsp. lime juice
1 tsp. 151-proof rum

*Combine with ice; shake. Strain and add ice. Top with lime slice.*

## HOT ZOMBIE

2 oz. gold rum
1 oz. apiece dark rum, 151-proof rum, and orange curacao
1 oz. apiece orange and lemon juice
A few drops grenadine
A few drops Pernod
Hot tea

*Combine the fruit juices and grenadine; add a little tea and mix well. Add the gold and dark rums, curacao, and Pernod. Heat the 151-proof rum in a ladle; ignite and infuse in the mug. Extinquish, stir well, and serve hot.*

**HUNDRED PERCENT**

1½ oz. Swedish Punch
1 tsp. lemon juice
1 tsp. orange juice
1-2 dashes grenadine

*Combine with ice; shake. Strain and add ice.*

**HUNTER'S COCKTAIL**

1½ oz. rye
1 tbs. cherry brandy

*Combine straight up; stir to blend. Decorate with a cherry.*

**HUNTINGTON SPECIAL**

1½ oz. gin
2 tsp. lemon juice
1 tsp. grenadine

*Combine with ice; shake. Strain and add ice.*

**HUNTSMAN**

1½ oz. Vodka
2 tsp. Jamaican rum
1½ tsp. lime juice
1-2 pinches powdered sugar

*Combine with ice; shake well. Strain and add ice.*

**HURRICANE**

1 oz. white rum
1 oz. gold rum
2 tsp. passion fruit syrup
2 tsp. lime juice.

*Combine with ice; shake. Strain and add ice.*

**HURRICANE COOLER**

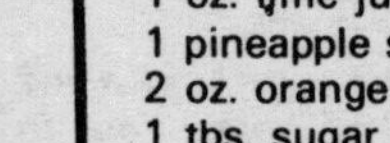

1 oz. white rum
1 oz. Jamaican rum
1 oz. lime juice
1 pineapple stick
2 oz. orange juice
1 tbs. sugar syrup
2 tsp. orange bitters
A few drops of Pernod

*Combine with ice; shake well. Strain over crushed ice. Decorate with the pineapple stick and a cherry.*

**HUSTLER**

2 oz. bourbon
1 oz. orange curacao
1 oz. sweet vermouth
2 tsp. lime juice

*Combine with ice; shake well. Strain and add ice.*

Swiss Hand-Carved Wooden Tankard

# YOUR OWN RECIPE

# YOUR OWN RECIPE

Use a bartender's mixing glass whenever the instructions state "combine" ingredients. Strain the drink from the mixing glass into the drinking glass suggested by the illustration alongside the ingredients.

---

**ICEBERG**

2 oz. orange sherbet
1 oz. Galliano
2 tsp. Cointreau

*Combine in a blender until smooth. Serve straight up.*

**ICEBREAKER**

2 oz. tequila
2 oz. grapefruit juice
1 tbs. grenadine
2 tsp. Cointreau
4 oz. crushed ice

*Combine in a blender at a low speed for 15 seconds. Strain straight up.*

**ICED COFFEE COCKTAIL**

1½ oz. Jamaican rum
1½ oz. iced coffee
2 tsp. dark creme de cacao
1 tsp. sugar

*Combine with ice; shake well. Strain and add ice. Decorate with a cherry.*

**ICED COFFEE PUNCH**

1 gallon iced coffee
1 quart vanilla ice cream
2 quarts light cream
8 oz. sugar
2 oz. Jamaican rum

*Combine the sugar with the coffee; refrigerate until very cold. When ready to serve, place the ice cream in the center of a large punch bowl; pour in the coffee, rum and cream. Stir until smooth and well blended.*

**ICED RUM COFFEE**

1½ oz. white rum
1 tsp. Jamaican rum
2 tbs. whipped cream
6 oz. iced black coffee
Sugar

*Combine the rums and the coffee; sugar to taste. Fill the glass with ice and top with the whipped cream.*

**ICED COFFEE FILLIP**

1-2 tsp. Tia Maria
8 oz. iced black coffee

*Pour the coffee. Add ice and the Tia Maria; stir well.*

## ICED RUM TEA

1½ oz. white rum
2 tsp. 151-proof rum
1 tsp. Falernum
1 tsp. lemon juice
1 tsp. sugar
6 oz. iced dark tea
Mint leaves

*Combine (except the mint leaves); allow to stand a few minutes before filling the glass with ice. Stir well. Garnish with mint leaves, partially torn, and a slice of lemon.*

## IL MAGNIFICO

¾ oz. Tuaca
¾ oz. curacao
1 tbs. heavy cream
3 oz. crushed ice

*Combine in a blender at a low speed for 15 seconds. Strain straight up.*

## IMPERIAL

1½ oz. dry gin
1½ oz. dry vermouth
A few dashes of maraschino
A few dashes of Angostura bitters

*Combine with ice; shake. Strain and add ice and top with an olive.*

## INCOME TAX COCKTAIL

1 oz. dry gin
1 tbs. orange juice
1 tsp. dry vermouth
1 tsp. sweet vermouth
A few dashes of Angostura bitters

*Combine with ice; shake. Strain and add ice.*

## INDEPENDENCE DAY PUNCH

2 quarts bourbon
1 pint pineapple juice
8 oz. lime juice
4 bottles club soda

*Combine everything except the soda; stir until well blended. Add the soda plus chunks of ice.*

## INDEPENDENCE SWIZZLE

2 oz. Trinidad rum
2 tsp. lime juice
A few dashes Angostura bitters
1 tsp. honey
1 tsp. sugar

*Combine; stir until the sugar and honey are blended well. Add ice and twirl to partially melt the ice. Repeat and keep adding ice until the glass is full.*

## INDIAN RIVER

1½ oz. whiskey
2 tsp. unsweetened grapefruit juice
1 tsp. raspberry liqueur
1 tsp. sweet vermouth

*Combine with ice; shake. Strain and add ice.*

**INSTANT EGG NOG**

2 quarts vanilla ice cream
1 bottle bourbon
4 oz. Jamaican rum

*Place the ice cream in a punch bowl; add the bourbon and rum and stir until the ice cream has melted and blended with the liquors. Dust with nutmeg.*

**INTERNATIONAL**

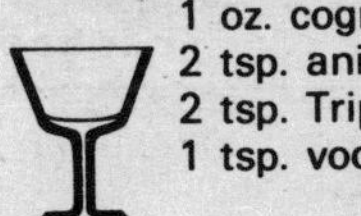

1 oz. cognac
2 tsp. anisette
2 tsp. Triple Sec
1 tsp. vodka

*Combine with ice; shake well. Strain straight up.*

**IQUIQUE COCKTAIL**

4 oz. gin
1 oz. lemon juice
3 tsp. powdered sugar
Several drops of Angostura bitters

*Combine with ice; shake. Strain and add ice.*

**IRISH**

1¼ oz. Irish whiskey
A few drops Pernod
A few drops curacao
1-2 dashes maraschino
1-2 dashes Angostura bitters

*Combine with ice; shake. Strain. Add ice and a twist of orange plus the peel.*

**IRISH-CANADIAN SANGAREE**

1¼ oz. Canadian whiskey
2 tsp. Irish Mist
1 tsp. orange juice
1 tsp. lemon juice

*Combine and stir well. Add ice and dust with nutmeg.*

**IRISH COFFEE**

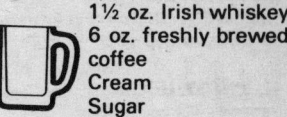

1½ oz. Irish whiskey
6 oz. freshly brewed coffee
Cream
Sugar

*Sweeten the coffee to taste; add the whiskey and stir. Float cream on top.*

**IRISH COOLER**

3 oz. Irish whiskey
Club soda

*Pour; add ice, soda, and a twist of lemon plus the peel.*

**IRISH COW**

1½ oz. Irish whiskey
8 oz. hot milk
1 tsp. sugar

*Pour the milk into a glass; add the sugar and whiskey. Stir well.*

## IRISH CRESTA

1 oz. Irish whiskey
2 tsp. Irish Mist
2 tsp. orange juice
1 egg white

*Combine with ice; shake well. Strain and add ice.*

## IRISH EYES

2 oz. green creme de menthe
2 oz. heavy cream
2 tbs. Irish whiskey

*Combine with ice; shake. Strain straight up and decorate with a cherry.*

## IRISH FIX

2 oz. Irish whiskey
2 tsp. Irish Mist
2 tsp. lemon juice
1 tsp. sugar

*Dissolve the sugar with a few drops of hot water in a glass. Add whiskey and lemon juice; fill with crushed ice and stir well. Add slices of orange and lemon and float the Irish Mist on top.*

## IRISH FIZZ

2½ oz. Irish whiskey
1½ tsp. lemon juice
1 tsp. curacao
½ tsp. sugar
Club soda

*Combine (except the soda) with ice; shake. Strain; add ice and club soda.*

## IRISH SHILLELAGH

1½ oz. Irish whiskey
½ oz. sloe gin
1½ oz. lemon juice
2 tsp. white rum
1 tsp. sugar
2 peach slices, chopped
2 raspberries
1 strawberry
1 cherry

*Combine (except the berries and cherry) with ice; shake. Strain and add ice. Add the fruit to decorate.*

## ISLE OF THE BLESSED COCONUT

1½ oz. white rum
2 tsp. cream of coconut
2 tsp. lime juice
1 tsp. lemon juice
1 tsp. orange juice
1 tsp. sugar syrup
3 oz. crushed ice
Coconut slices

*Combine (except the coconut slices) in a blender at a low speed for 15 seconds. Strain straight up. Serve with the coconut slices on the side.*

## ITALIAN APERITIF

3 oz. Punt e Mes
A few drops sweet vermouth
A few drops Campari

*Pour the Punt e Mes over ice into a small goblet. Add the vermouth and the Campari; stir gently. Touch it up with a squeeze of lemon plus the peel; garnish with slice of lemon.*

# YOUR OWN RECIPE

# YOUR OWN RECIPE

Use a bartender's mixing glass whenever the instructions state "combine" ingredients. Strain the drink from the mixing glass into the drinking glass suggested by the illustration alongside the ingredients.

The glass pictured for each drink is our suggestion; other drinking cups may be used as well.

# J

---

### JACKALOPE

1 bottle Bourbon
8 oz. sugar
1 doz. lemons

*Slice the lemons in half; squeeze the juice into a large pot. Add the rinds plus the bourbon and sugar; stir until smooth. Close the pot and refrigerate overnight. Strain clean when ready to use; serve over ice.*

### JACKIE O. 'S ROSE

1 oz. white rum
2 tsp. orange Cointreau
2 tsp. lime juice
1 tsp. sugar syrup

*Combine with ice; shake. Strain over crushed ice.*

### JACK-IN-THE-BOX

1¼ oz. apple brandy
2 tsp. pineapple juice
1½ tsp. lemon juice
A few dashes of Angostura bitters

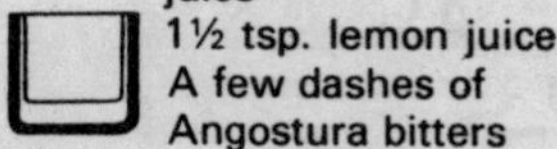

*Combine with ice; shake. Strain and add ice.*

### JACK THE GRIPPER

1 bottle apple brandy
8 oz. sugar
2 tbs. Angostura bitters
3 tsp. lemon juice
Cinnamon sticks
Grated lemon peel

*Combine the brandy, sugar, and bitters in a large saucepan; heat and stir until the sugar has dissolved. Simmer with a few cinnamon sticks and lemon peels for several minutes. Just before serving; ignite. Extinguish the flames with a few spritzes of boiling water. Serve at once, piping hot, in mugs.*

### JADE

1¾ gold rum
1½ tsp. lime juice
1½ tsp. sugar syrup
Several drops green creme de menthe
Several drops curacao

*Combine with ice; shake. Strain and add ice. Decorate with a lime slice.*

## JAMAICA GINGER

1½ oz. white rum
½ oz. Jamaican rum
2 tsp. 151-proof rum
2 tsp. Falernum
2 tsp. lime juice
Ginger beer
1 pineapple slice dipped into white creme de menthe
1 chunk ginger

*Combine the rums, Falernum, and juice with ice; shake well. Strain add ice, and fill with ginger beer. Decorate with the pineapple and ginger.*

## JAMAICA GLOW

1½ oz. gin
½ oz. dry red wine
2 tsp. orange juice
1 tsp. Jamaican rum

*Combine with ice; shake. Strain over ice. Top with a lime slice.*

## JAMAICAN ELEGANCE

1½ oz. Jamaican rum
½ oz. brandy
1 tbs. lime juice
2 tsp. pineapple juice
1 tsp. sugar syrup

*Combine with ice; shake. Strain and add plenty of ice. Top with a lemon slice.*

## JAMAICAN GINGER BEER

5 oz. Jamaican ginger
2 oz. honey
2 oz. lime juice
1 egg white
24 oz. sugar
1 cake of yeast
2 quarts water
A few drops of Angostura bitters

*Combine the ginger, sugar, honey, water, and lime juice in a large pot. Add the yeast and the egg white; stir to blend. Allow to stand in a cool, dark place for several days. When ready, strain through cheesecloth; add more sugar to taste, plus bitters. Bottle and refrigerate until ready to use.*

## JAMAICAN HOT TEA PUNCH

1 pint Jamaican rum
1 pint brandy
2 oranges, sliced
1 lime, sliced
3 pints hot tea
Sugar and spices

*Combine in a saucepan, heat slowly and stir. Add sugar to taste; spices if you wish.*

## JAMAICAN SHANDY

1 bottle Red Stripe beer
1 pt. ginger beer, ice cold

*Combine stir gently. Serve over ice.*

**JAMOCHA**

1½ oz. Jamaican rum
½ tsp. sugar
A pinch of cinnamon
1 tbs. of whipped cream
Freshly brewed coffee

*Combine the rum, sugar, and cinnamon in a mug; fill the mug with coffee and stir. Top with the whipped cream.*

---

**JAPALAC**

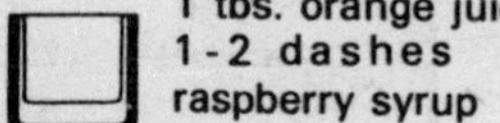

1¼ oz. rye
1¼ oz. dry vermouth
1 tbs. orange juice
1-2 dashes raspberry syrup

*Combine with ice; shake. Strain and add ice.*

**JAPANESE COCKTAIL**

2 oz. brandy
1 tsp. lime juice
1 tsp. almond extract
A few dashes of Angostura bitters

*Combine with ice; shake. Strain and add ice, a twist of lime, and the peel.*

**JAPANESE FIZZ**

2¼ oz. whiskey
¾ oz. port
2 tsp. lemon juice
1½ tsp. sugar syrup
Club soda
1 pineapple stick

*Combine (except the soda and pineapple stick) with ice; shake well. Strain, add ice and soda. Add the twist of orange, plus its peel. Top with the pineapple stick.*

**JAVA COOLER**

1½ oz. gin
1½ tsp. lemon juice
A few dashes of Angostura bitters
Tonic water

*Add the lime juice, bitters, and gin over ice; stir well. Fill with tonic.*

**JEFFERSON DAVIS PUNCH**

12 bottles claret
2 bottles sherry
½ bottle brandy
½ pint Jamaican rum
1½ pints lemon juice
8 oz. maraschino
3 bottles ginger ale
6 bottles club soda
3 lb. sugar

*Dissolve the sugar in some water to make it syrup; combine (except the ginger ale and soda) and stir. Top with slices of lemon and orange. Allow to stand overnight. Add the soda and ginger ale, plus ice, before serving.*

**JERSEY DEVIL**

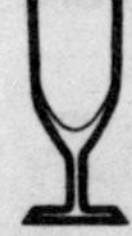

1½ oz. apple brandy
1 oz. cranberry juice
2 tbs. lime juice
2 tsp. Cointreau
1 tsp. sugar syrup
An apple slice

*Combine with ice: shake well. Strain decorate with apple slice.*

**JERSEY LIGHTNING**

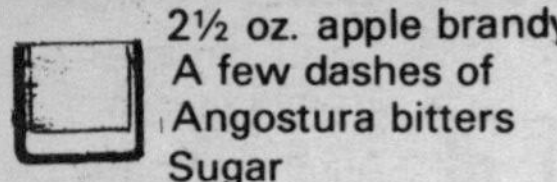

2½ oz. apple brandy
A few dashes of Angostura bitters
Sugar

*Combine with ice. Sugar to taste. Strain and add ice.*

**JERSEY MUG**

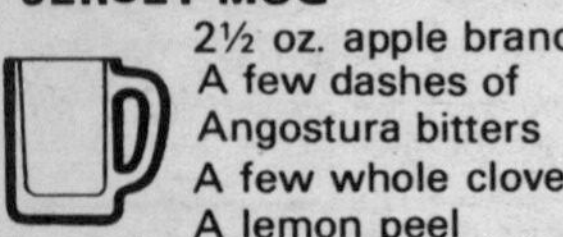

2½ oz. apple brandy
A few dashes of Angostura bitters
A few whole cloves
A lemon peel

*Combine with boiling water. Add a dash of the brandy and ignite and serve.*

**JERSEY SOUR**

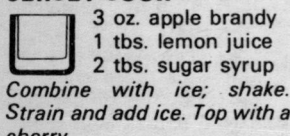

3 oz. apple brandy
1 tbs. lemon juice
2 tbs. sugar syrup

*Combine with ice; shake. Strain and add ice. Top with a cherry.*

---

**JEWEL**

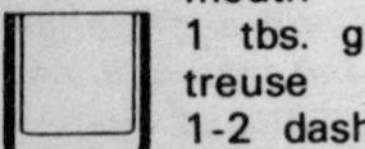

1 oz. gin
1 oz. sweet vermouth
1 tbs. green chartreuse
1-2 dashes orange bitters

*Combine with ice; shake. Strain and add ice and a twist of lemon plus the peel.*

---

**JOBURG**

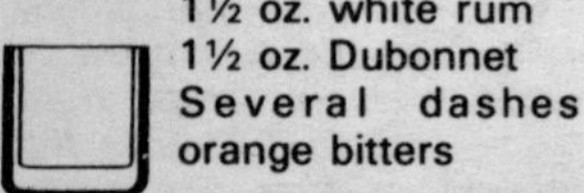

1½ oz. white rum
1½ oz. Dubonnet
Several dashes orange bitters

*Combine with ice; shake. Strain and add ice.*

**JOCKEY CLUB**

2 oz. gin
A few drops creme de noyeaux
A few drops lemon juice
A few dashes of Angostura and orange bitters

*Combine with ice; shake. Strain and add ice.*

---

**JOCOSE JULEP**

2½ oz. bourbon
1 oz. lime juice
2 tsp. green creme de menthe
1½ tsp. sugar syrup
Club soda
½ doz. mint leaves, finely chopped
Mint sprigs

*Combine (except the soda and mint sprigs) with ice; shake. Strain and add ice and club soda. Top with mint sprigs.*

---

**JOHN ALDEN**

1 oz. gold rum
1 oz. coffee liqueur
1 oz. orange curacao

*Combine with ice; shake well. Strain straight up.*

**JOHN McCLAIN**

1¼ oz. Scotch
1 tsp. sugar syrup
A few dashes of Angostura bitters

*Combine with ice; shake. Strain and add ice.*

**JOHNNY COCKTAIL**

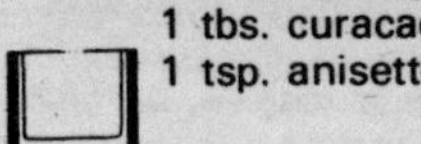

1½ oz. sloe gin
1 tbs. curacao
1 tsp. anisette

*Combine with ice; shake. Strain and add ice.*

**JOHNSON DELIGHT**

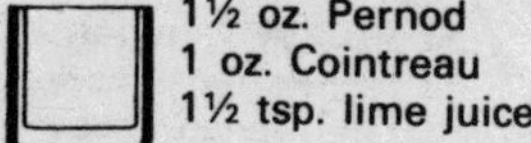

1½ oz. Pernod
1 oz. Cointreau
1½ tsp. lime juice

*Combine with ice; shake. Strain and add ice.*

**JOULOUVILLE**

1 oz. gin
2 tsp. apple brandy
2 tsp. lemon juice
1 tsp. sweet vermouth
A few drops grenadine

*Combine with ice; shake. Strain and add ice.*

**JOURNALIST**

1½ oz. dry gin
1 tsp. dry vermouth
A few drops curacao
A few drops of lemon juice
A few dashes of Angostura bitters

*Combine with ice; shake well. Strain and add ice.*

**JUBAL EARLY PUNCH**

1 pint Jamaican rum
3 pints brandy
1½ gallons lemonade
1 lb. sugar
6 bottles champagne

*Dissolve the sugar with the lemonade; add the remaining ingredients plus chunks of ice and stir well.*

---

**JUDGE, JR.**

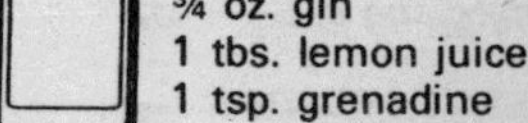

¾ oz. white rum
¾ oz. gin
1 tbs. lemon juice
1 tsp. grenadine

*Combine with ice; shake. Strain and add ice.*

---

**JUDGETTE**

¾ oz. peach brandy
¾ oz. dry gin
1 tbs. dry vermouth
1 tsp. lime juice

*Combine with ice; shake. Strain and add ice. Top with a cherry.*

**JUJUBE CORDIAL**

1 quart jujube fruit
Brown sugar
Whiskey

*Combine the jujube fruit with a brown sugar syrup (three parts sugar to one part water) in a large pot and allow to stand at room temperature for several days. Double the amount of fruit and syrup with whiskey; stir, strain, and bottle for future use.*

### JULEP

3 oz. bourbon
1 cube sugar
Mint sprigs

*Dissolve the sugar with a few drops of water. Add a few sprigs of mint; fill the glass with ice and add the bourbon. Stir and add more mint (cut and bled) into the julep. Allow to stand a few minutes before serving.*

### JUNIOR

1½ oz. rye
2 tsp. lime juice
2 tsp. Benedictine
A few dashes of Angostura bitters

*Combine with ice; shake. Strain and add ice.*

### JUPITER MARTINI

1½ oz. gin
1 tbs. dry vermouth
1 tsp. Parfait Amour
1 tsp. orange juice

*Combine with ice; shake well. Strain straight up.*

### JULGLOGG

1 bottle Burgundy
½ bottle aquavit
8 oz. sugar
Orange and lemon peels
Blanched almonds
Seedless raisins
Cinnamon
Whole cardamom seeds

*Combine in a large saucepan; heat throughly but do not bring to a boil. Serve at once. Ignite when serving, scooping a bit of the fire as well as a few of the nuts and whole spices into each mug.*

# YOUR OWN RECIPE

# YOUR OWN RECIPE

Use a bartender's mixing glass whenever the instructions state "combine" ingredients. Strain the drink from the mixing glass into the drinking glass suggested by the illustration alongside the ingredients.

The glass pictured for each drink is our suggestion; other drinking cups may be used as well.

# K

---

## KAHLUA JAVA

2 pints fresh, hot coffee
2 pints hot cocoa
3 tbs. Kahlua
Marshmallows

*Combine the coffee, cocoa, and Kahlua in a chafing dish; stir gently to blend. Serve piping hot in mugs; garnish with a marshmallow.*

## KAHLUA TOREADOR

2 oz. brandy
1 oz. Kahlua
1 egg white

*Combine with ice; shake. Strain and add ice.*

## KAISER SOUR PUNCH

1 bottle chilled Rhine wine
3 cups lemon juice
4 oz. powdered sugar

*Combine the sugar with the lemon juice in a pitcher and stir until the sugar is completely dissolved. Add the wine, plenty of ice and stir well.*

## KAMEHAMEHA RUM PUNCH

1 oz. white rum
1 oz. Jamaican rum
2 oz. pineapple juice
1 tbs. lemon juice
1 tsp. blackberry brandy
1 tsp. lemon juice
1 tsp. powdered sugar
1 pineapple stick

*Combine (except the Jamaican rum and pineapple stick) with ice; shake. Strain; add ice and float the Jamaican rum on top. Top with the pineapple stick and a cherry.*

## KANGAROO

1½ oz. vodka
¾ oz. dry vermouth

*Combine with ice; shake. Strain; add ice and a twist of lemon.*

**KCB**

1½ oz. gin
2 tsp. kirsch
A few drops apricot brandy
A few drops lemon juice

*Combine with ice; shake. Strain. Add ice and a twist of lemon with its peel.*

---

**KE KALI NEI AU**

1½ oz. white rum
1½ oz. passion fruit juice
1 oz. Jamaican rum
2 tbs. lemon juice
1½ tbs. sugar syrup
2 tsp. kirsch
1 green coconut
Red hibiscus

*Slice off the top of the coconut and drain. Combine all the liquors and juices (except the Jamaican rum) with ice; shake. Strain into the coconut; float the Jamaican rum and the red hibiscus or fruit slices.*

---

**KENNY**

2 oz. apple brandy
1 tbs. sweet vermouth
1½ tsp. lemon juice
A few dashes of Angostura bitters
A few drops of grenadine

*Combine with ice; shake. Strain and add ice.*

**KENTUCKY**

1½ oz. pineapple juice
1 tbs. bourbon

*Combine with ice; shake. Strain and add ice.*

**KENTUCKY COLONEL**

1½ oz. bourbon
2 tsp. Benedictine

*Combine with ice; shake. Strain. Add ice and a twist of lemon; add the peel.*

**KENTUCKY TODDY**

1½ oz. bourbon
1 tsp. sugar

*Dissolve the sugar with a little water. Add the bourbon and ice; stir briskly. To make a* **HOT KENTUCKY TODDY,** *add 3 ozs. of boiling water to the mug.*

**KERRY COOLER**

2 oz. Irish whiskey
1½ oz. sherry
1¼ tbs. almond extract
1¼ tbs. lemon juice
Club soda

*Combine (except the soda) with ice; shake well. Strain; add ice and soda. Top with a lemon slice.*

## KEUKA CUP

1 bottle champagne
1½ tsp. lemon juice
1 orange, sliced
1 cup pineapple cubes
1 tbs. sugar syrup

*Combine and chill. Add ice before serving.*

---

## KEY COCKTAIL

1½ oz. gin
2 tsp. lime juice
1 tsp. Jamaican rum
1 tsp. Falernum
1 pineapple stick

*Combine (except the pineapple stick) with ice; shake. Strain and add ice. Top with the pineapple stick.*

---

## KIDDIE CAR

2 oz. apple brandy
2 tsp. lime juice
1 tsp. Triple Sec

*Combine with ice; shake. Strain and add ice.*

## KING COLE

2 oz. bourbon
½ tsp. sugar syrup
A few drops Fernet Branca
1 orange slice
1 pineapple slice

*Muddle the fruit with the sugar and Fernet Branca; add the bourbon and stir.*

## KING'S PEG

6 oz. chilled champagne
2 oz. brandy

*Combine with two cubes ice and stir. For a* **QUEEN'S PEG**, *use a tablespoon of dry gin instead of the brandy.*

## KINGSTON

1 oz. Jamaican rum
2 tsp. kummel
2 tsp. orange juice
1-2 dashes Pimento Dram

*Combine with ice; shake and strain. Serve over ice.*

## KIPINSKI

1 oz. white rum
1 oz. Triple Sec
1 oz. grapefruit juice

*Combine with ice; shake well. Strain and add ice.*

## KIRSCH AND CASSIS

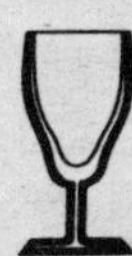

2 oz. creme de cassis
1 oz. kirsch
Club soda

*Combine the cassis and the kirsch with ice; shake. Strain. Add ice and fill with soda.*

**KIRSCH CUBA LIBRE**

1½ oz. Kirschwasser
2 tsp. lime juice
Cola

*Combine the kirschwasser and lime juice; add ice and cola. Stir.*

**KIRSCH RICKEY**

1½ oz. Kirschwasser
2 tsp. lime juice
Club soda
2 black cherries

*Combine kirschwasser and the lime juice; add ice and club soda. Stir. Top with cherries, pitted and speared.*

---

**KISS IN THE DARK**

¾ oz. dry gin
¾ oz. cherry brandy
1 tbs. dry vermouth

*Combine with ice; shake. Strain and add ice.*

---

**KISS ME QUICK**

1½ oz. Pernod
Several drops curacao
A few dashes of Angostura bitters
Soda water

*Combine (except the soda) with ice; shake. Strain; add ice and soda.*

**KISS THE BOYS GOODBYE**

1 oz. sloe gin
1 oz. brandy
1½ tsp. lemon juice
½ egg white

*Combine with ice. Shake. Strain and add ice.*

**KNICKERBOCKER**

2 oz. gin
2 tsp. dry vermouth
1 tsp. sweet vermouth

*Combine with ice; shake. Strain straight up.*

**KNOCK-OUT**

¾ oz. dry gin
¾ oz. dry vermouth
2 tsp. Pernod
1 tsp. white creme de menthe

*Combine with ice; shake. Strain and add ice.*

**KRAMBAMBULI PUNCH**

2 bottles red wine
1 pint arrack
1 pint dark rum
8 oz. sugar
A pair of oranges and lemons

*Pour the wine into a large pot; heat thoroughly but do not allow to boil. Peel the fruit; squeeze in all the juice and grate a bit of the rind. Put the sugar into a king-sized ladle; soak in a little rum and arak. Ignite and infuse the punch; stir to dissolve the sugar. Add the rest of the rum and arak; stir. Serve hot.*

**KREMLIN COLONEL**

2 oz. vodka
2 tsp. lime juice
1½ tsp. sugar syrup
Mint leaves, partially torn

*Combine (except the mint leaves) with ice; shake. Strain and add ice. Top with mint.*

**KRETCHMA**

1 oz. vodka
1 oz. white creme de cacao
2 tsp. lemon juice
A few drops of grenadine

*Combine with ice; shake well. Strain and add ice.*

**KRUPNIK**

3 cups cooking alcohol
2 cups honey
1 tsp. vanilla extract
Whole cloves, grated lemon rinds, cinnamon, whole peppercorns and vanilla

*Combine the honey with the spices and vanilla in a large saucepan; warm through. Add 2 cups of water and bring to a boil; stirring constantly. Remove from heat; add the alcohol and serve.*

**KUALA LAMPUR COOLER**

2 oz. gin
1 oz. pineapple juice
2 tsp. lime juice
Club soda
A chunk of fresh pineapple

*Combine the gin and juices; stir. Add ice and soda. Decorate with the pineapple chunk.*

**KUMMEL**

1 oz. kummel oil
1 quart cooking alcohol
4 cups of sugar

*Combine the sugar with 1 qt. of water; boil for at least twenty minutes. Remove from heat. When lukewarm, add the oil and the alcohol; stir. Bottle and store in a cool place for several months before using.*

**KUMMEL BLACKBERRY FRAPPE**

½ oz. kummel
2 tsp. blackberry brandy
1 tsp. lemon juice

*Combine without ice; stir well. Strain over crushed ice.*

---

**KVASS**

1 oz. malt
3 tbs. honey
1 doz. slices sour pumpernickel bread

*Tear the bread into tiny pieces and put it in a large crock pot. Add 5 cups of boiling water and the malt; seal and allow to stand at room temperature for a day or until fermented. Sweeten with the honey; bottle and store in your refrigerator.*

# YOUR OWN RECIPE

## YOUR OWN RECIPE

# YOUR OWN RECIPE

Use a bartender's mixing glass whenever the instructions state "combine" ingredients. Strain the drink from the mixing glass into the drinking glass suggested by the illustration alongside the ingredients.

The glass pictured for each drink is our suggestion; other drinking cups may be used as well.

# L

---

### LA BELLE CREME

1 oz. vodka
1 oz. heavy cream
2 tsp. white creme de cacao
2 tsp. Cointreau

*Combine with ice; shake well. Strain straight up.*

### LA JOLLA

1½ oz. brandy
2 tsp. banana liqueur
2 tsp. lemon juice
1 tsp. orange juice

*Combine with ice; shake. Strain and add ice.*

### LADDIES SUB-BOURBON

2 oz. bourbon
A few drops orange curacao
A few dashes of Angostura bitters
Soda water

*Combine (except the soda) with ice; shake well. Strain. Add ice and soda.*

### LADIES' COCKTAIL

1½ oz. whiskey
Several drops anisette
A few drops Pernod
A few dashes of Angostura bitters
1 pineapple stick

*Combine (except the pineapple stick) with ice; shake. Strain and add ice. Top with the pineapple.*

### LADYFINGER

1 oz. gin
2 tsp. kirsch
2 tsp. cherry brandy

*Combine with ice; shake. Strain and add ice.*

### LAFAYETTE

3 oz. rye
2 tsp. dry vermouth
2 tsp. Dubonnet
A few dashes of Angostura bitters

*Combine with ice; shake well. Strain and add ice.*

## LAFAYETTE PUNCH

1 bottle chilled Moselle
4 bottles champagne
8 oz. powdered sugar
½ doz. oranges

*Peel the oranges and cut into thin slices. Combine with the sugar, add the wine, stir, and refrigerate. Before serving, combine the sweetened wine and the champagne and add chunks of ice.*

## LAKE KEUKA PUNCH

1 bottle dry champagne
1 bottle Burgundy
1 bottle Sauterne
1 pint strawberries
4 tsp. lime juice
Grated lemon rinds

*Combine the strawberries, juice, and the rinds in a saucepan; simmer for serveral minutes. Strain and allow to cool. Before serving, combine the wines and fruit syrup. Stir and add chunks of ice.*

---

## LALLAH ROOKH COCKTAIL

1¼ oz. chilled cognac
1 tbs. Jamaican rum
2 tsp. sugar syrup
2 tsp. vanilla extract
1 tsp. heavy cream

*Combine with ice; shake. Strain and add ice.*

## LAMB'S WOOL

1 quart hot ale
6 baked apples
Sugar

*Pour the ale over the apples. Sugar to taste and dust with ginger and nutmeg. Serve piping hot.*

## LAS VEGAS JULEP

1 oz. bourbon
1 oz. lemon juice
2 tsp. Galliano
1 tsp. sugar syrup

*Combine with ice; shake well. Strain over crushed ice. Decorate with mint.*

## LASKY

¾ oz. Swedish Punch
¾ oz. dry gin
1 tbs. grape juice

*Combine with ice; shake. Strain and add ice.*

---

## LATIN BITTERS

1½ oz. Campari
1 tbs. sweet vermouth
Club soda

*Combine the Campari and the vermouth; add ice and soda. Stir well. Touch it up with a twist of lemon and drop in the peel.*

**LATIN LOVER**

1½ oz. Valentino
1 oz. tequila
2 tsp. lemon juice
A few dashes grenadine

*Combine with ice; shake well. Strain and add ice.*

**LAWHILL**

1½ oz. whiskey
1 tbs. dry vermouth
2 tsp. orange juice
A few drops Pernod
A few drops maraschino
A few dashes of Angostura bitters

*Combine with ice; shake. Strain and add ice.*

**LAYER CAKE**

1 tbs. dark creme de cacao
1 tbs. apricot brandy
1 tbs. heavy cream

*Carefully pour, floating the above in order shown. Top with a cherry and chill before serving.*

**LE COQ HARDY**

Fernet Branca
Grand Marnier
Champagne
Cognac
Angostura bitters
1 sugar cube

*Place the sugar cube on the bottom of a wide champagne glass; top it with a drop of Fernet Branca, Grand Marnier, Cognac, and bitters. Fill the glass with champagne; stir gently until the sugar has dissolved. Decorate with a slice of orange and a cherry.*

**LEAMINGTON BRANDY PUNCH**

2 bottles Sauterne
1 small bottle Cognac
1 quart lemon juice
12 oz. powdered sugar

*Dissolve the sugar with the lemon juice in a large punch bowl. Add the cognac and the wine and stir to blend. Keep refrigerated until ready to serve. Add chunks of ice. Garnish with mint.*

**LEAP YEAR**

1½ oz. gin
1 tsp. sweet vermouth
1 tsp. Grand Marnier
A few drops lemon juice

*Combine with ice; shake well. Strain. Add ice and a twist of lemon with its peel.*

**LEAPFROG**

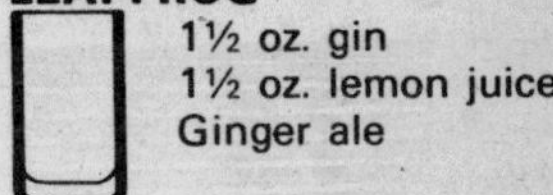

1½ oz. gin
1½ oz. lemon juice
Ginger ale

*Combine the gin and lemon juice with ice; shake well. Strain; add ice and fill with ginger ale.*

**LEAVE IT TO ME**

2 oz. gin
¼ oz. lemon juice
1 tsp. raspberry syrup
A few drops maraschino

*Combine with ice; shake. Strain and add ice.*

**LEEWARD**

1½ oz. white rum
2 tsp. calvados
2 tsp. sweet vermouth

*Combine with ice; shake. Strain. Add ice and a twist of lemon with its peel.*

---

**LEMON BISHOP**

*Follow the recipe for* **ARCHBISHOP'S PUNCH,** *using a lemon instead of an orange, and adding to the claret cinnamon, mace, allspice, and ginger before cooking.*

---

**LEMON RUM COOLER**

2 oz. white rum
2 oz. pineapple juice
2 tsp. lemon juice
2 fsp. Falernum
1 tsp. 151-proof rum
Lemon soda

*Combine (except the soda) with ice; shake. Strain. Add ice and fill with soda. Top with a lemon slice.*

**LEMON WINE**

2 tsp. citric acid
1 doz. drops of lemon essence
Several drops of cooking alcohol
1 lb. sugar
Saffron

*Boil the sugar in a quart of water until the sugar has dissolved; add the citric acid and allow to cool. Stir in the lemon essence and alcohol; add saffron for color.*

**LEONINE EGG NOG**

4 doz. eggs, separated
3 pints bourbon
1 quart milk
1 pint heavy cream
1 cup sugar

*Combine the sugar with the egg yolks; stir until the sugar is dissolved. Pour in the whiskey; add the milk and cream, and stir. (Cream can be whipped.) Beat the egg whites until stiff and gently fold them into the nog. Top with nutmeg.*

**LEPRECHAUN**

2 oz. Irish whiskey
Tonic Water

*Pour the Irish whiskey into a glass; add ice and fill with tonic water. Touch up with a twist of lemon with its peel.*

**LIBERAL**

1 oz. whiskey
1 oz. sweet vermouth
Several dashes Amer Picon
1-2 dashes orange bitters

*Combine with ice; shake. Strain and add ice.*

**LIBERTY**

1½ oz. apple brandy
1 tbs. white rum
A few drops sugar syrup

*Combine with ice; shake. Strain and add ice.*

**LIEBFRAUMILCH**

1¼ oz. white creme de cacao
1¼ oz. heavy cream
3 tsp. lime juice

*Combine with ice; shake well. Strain straight up.*

**LIL NAUE**

¾ oz. cognac
¾ oz. port
¾ oz. apricot brandy
1 egg yolk
1½ tsp. sugar syrup

*Combine with ice; shake. Strain. Add ice and a twist of lemon with its peel. Top with cinnamon.*

---

**LILLET COCKTAIL**

1½ oz. Lillet
1 tbs. gin

*Combine with ice; shake. Strain. Add ice and a twist of lemon with its peel. For a* **LILLET NOYAUX,** *follow the recipe for a* **LILLET COCKTAIL** *and add a teaspon of creme de noyaux before shaking.*

---

**LIME DAIQUIRI**

1½ oz. white rum
2 tsp. lime liqueur
2 tsp. lime juice

*Combine with ice; shake well. Strain. Add ice and a twist of lime with its peel.*

**LIME RUM PUNCH**

1 bottle white rum
8 o z. lime juice
8 oz. sugar
8 oz. water

*Combine the sugar with the water in a saucepan and heat until blended. Allow to cool before combining with the rum and juice. Add ice.*

**LIME RUM SHRUB**

1 quart Jamaican rum
8 oz. lime juice
1½ cups of sugar dissolved in 2½ cups of water

*Combine in a large bottle; mix, seal tightly, and allow to stand for a week. Serve straight up or over ice.*

**LIMEY**

1 oz. white rum
1½ tbs. lime liqueur
2 tsp. Triple Sec
2 tsp. lime juice
3 oz. crushed ice

*Combine in a blender at low speed for 15 seconds. Strain straight up. Add a twist of lime with its peel.*

**LINSTEAD**

1½ oz. whiskey
1½ oz. pineapple juice
A few drops Pernod
Several drops lemon juice
½ tsp. sugar syrup
A few dashes of Angostura bitters

*Combine with ice; shake. Strain. Add ice and a twist of lemon.*

**LITTLE DEVIL**

¾ oz. dry gin
¾ oz. gold rum
1 tsp. Triple Sec
Several drops lemon juice

*Combine with ice; shake. Strain and add ice.*

**LITTLE PRINCESS**

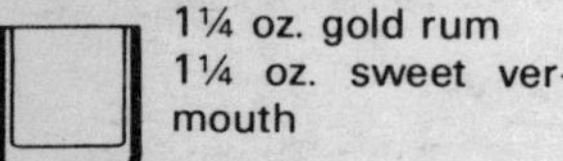

1¼ oz. gold rum
1¼ oz. sweet vermouth

*Combine with ice; shake. Strain and add ice.*

**LOCH LOMOND**

1½ oz. Scotch
1½ tsp. sugar syrup
A few dashes Angostura bitters

*Combine with ice; shake. Strain and add ice.*

**LOCOMOTIVE**

1 quart hard cider
3 eggs
Sugar
Cinnamon sticks

*Bring the cider almost to a boil. Beat the eggs in a large bowl; slowly pour the cider over the eggs, an oz. at a time. Stir constantly. Add sugar; stir until the sugar dissolves. Serve warm in mugs, using cinnamon sticks as swizzlers.*

**LOLITA**

1½ oz. tequila
3 tsp. lime juice
1 tsp. honey
A few dashes of Angostura bitters

*Combine with ice; shake. Strain and add ice.*

**LOLLIPOP**

¾ oz. Cointreau
¾ oz. kirsch
1 tbs. green chartreuse
A few drops maraschino

*Combine with ice; shake. Strain and add ice.*

**LOMA BONITA**

1½ oz. tequila
3 oz. pineapple juice

*Combine with ice; shake. Strain and add ice. Top with a cherry.*

**LONDON**

1½ oz. dry gin
½ tsp. sugar syrup
1-2 dashes orange bitters
A few drops maraschino

*Combine with ice; shake well. Strain, add ice and a twist of lemon plus peel.*

**LONDON DOCK**

1½ oz. Burgundy
2 tbs. dark rum
2 tsp. sugar
A cinnamon stick, lemon peel, and nutmeg

*Dissolve the sugar with a few drops of hot water in a mug; add everything else except the nutmeg. Fill with boiling water and stir. Garnish with nutmeg. Bordeaux wine can be used instead of the Burgundy.*

**LONDON FOG**

1 tbs. white creme de menthe
1 tbs. anisette
A few dashes of Angostura bitters

*Combine with ice; stir briskly to chill. Strain straight up.*

**LONDON SPECIAL**

Champagne
1 cube sugar
A few dashes of Peychaud's bitters

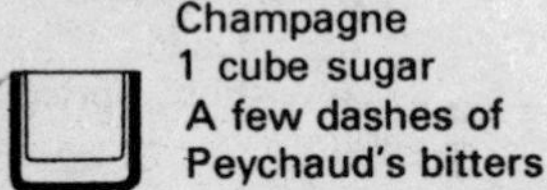

*Drop the sugar cube into a small goblet; add the bitters plus ice and fill with champagne. Top with a twist of orange; add the peel.*

**LONE TREE MARTINI**

1½ oz. dry gin
1 tbs. sweet vermouth

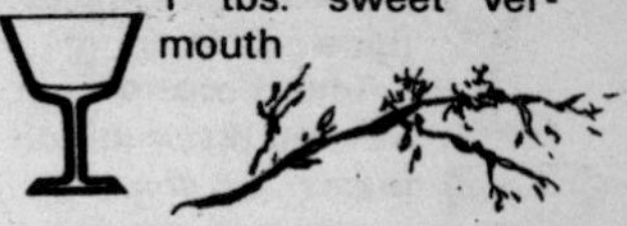

*Combine with ice; shake well. Strain straight up and top with an olive.*

**LOS ANGELES**

1½ oz. whiskey
1½ tsp. lemon juice
1½ tsp. sugar syrup
A few drops sweet vermouth
1 egg

*Combine with ice; shake. Strain and add ice.*

**LOS ANGELES LUV**

1 oz. bourbon
1 oz. creme de banana
2 tsp. Triple Sec
2 tsp. lemon juice
2 oz. pineapple juice
3 oz. crushed ice

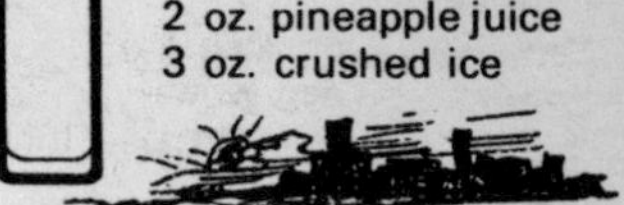

*Combine in a blender at low speed for 15 seconds. Strain. Add ice. Decorate with pineapple.*

**LOUDSPEAKER**

1 oz. brandy
1 tbs. gin
1 tsp. lime juice

*Combine with ice; shake well. Strain and add ice.*

**LOUISIANA LULLABY**

1½ ozs. Jamaican rum
2 tsp. Dubonnet
A few drops of Grand Marnier

*Combine with ice; shake well. Strain straight up. Touch it up with a twist of lemon.*

**LOUISIANA PUNCH**

2 bottles white Burgundy
1 pint apiece brandy, cognac, and curacao
1 pint lemon juice
1 lb. sugar
Cherries, whole strawberries, sliced pineapple
2 bottles club soda

*Dissolve the sugar with the lemon juice; add the wine and liquors and stir. Add the soda plus chunks of ice; garnish with fruit.*

---

**LOVE**

2 oz. sloe gin
1 egg white
Several drops lemon juice
Several drops raspberry syrup

*Combine with ice; shake. Strain and add ice.*

**LOVER'S BALM**

1 quart hard cider
3 oz. cognac
2 oz. curacao
1½ oz. sugar
3 tsp. lemon juice
Grated lemon rind
Club soda

*Dissolve the sugar with the lemon juice in a large pot; add the rinds, brandy, curacao, and cider. Stir until foamy and well-blended. Store in the refrigerator until ready to use. Serve with ice and soda.*

**LOVER'S DELIGHT**

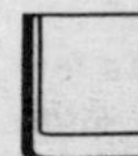

¾ oz. Cointreau
¾ oz. cognac
¾ oz. Forbidden Fruit

*Combine with ice; shake well. Strain and add ice.*

**LUCHOW'S GRAND PRIZE**

1 oz. bourbon
1 oz. cherry liqueur
1 oz. lime juice

*Combine with ice; shake. Strain and add ice.*

**LUGGER**

1 oz. brandy
1 oz. calvados
A few drops apricot brandy

*Combine with ice; shake well. Strain; add ice and a twist of orange.*

# YOUR OWN RECIPE

# YOUR OWN RECIPE

Use a bartender's mixing glass whenever the instructions state "combine" ingredients. Strain the drink from the mixing glass into the drinking glass suggested by the illustration alongside the ingredients.

The glass pictured for each drink is our suggestion; other drinking cups may be used as well.

---

### MABI PUNCH

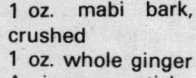

1 oz. mabi bark, crushed
1 oz. whole ginger
A cinnamon stick
5 cups brown sugar

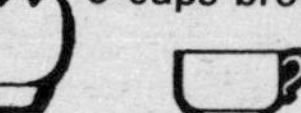

*Clean the bark, slice the ginger and boil with the cinnamon stick in 1½ cups of water for 5 minutes; strain, cool and chill. Boil the brown sugar in 3 qts. of water; add mabi brew and stir to blend. Strain into a large pot; strain and ladle until foamy. Loosely top the pot or cap lightly in a bottle. Allow to ferment for several days. Store uncovered in the refrigerator until ready to use.*

---

### MACARONI

1½ oz. Pernod
2 tsp. sweet vermouth

*Combine with ice; shake well. Strain and add ice.*

---

### MACKINNON

1½ oz. Drambuie
1½ tsp. white rum
1½ tsp. lime juice
Several drops lemon juice
Club soda

*Combine everything except the soda with ice; shake well. Strain; add ice and fill the glass with club soda.*

### MADEIRA MINT FLIP

1½ oz. Madeira
1 tbs. chocolate mint liqueur
1½ tsp. sugar syrup
1 egg

*Combine with ice; shake extremely well. Strain and add ice with nutmeg.*

### MADEIRA PUNCH

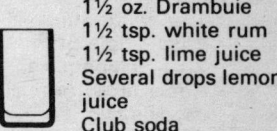

1 bottle Madeira
1 quart club soda
4 oz. brandy
Powdered sugar
Sliced peaches, strawberries, lemons and oranges

*Combine the Madeira and the brandy and sugar to taste. Decorate with fruit. Add the club soda plus chunks of ice.*

**MADISON AVENUE**

2 oz. vodka
2 oz. clam juice
2 oz. tomato juice
A few drops of lemon juice
1-2 dashes Worchestershire sauce
A pinch of salt

*Combine with ice; shake. Strain straight up.*

**MAHUKONA**

1 oz. white rum
2 tsp. Triple Sec
2 tsp. lemon juice
A few drops of rock candy syrup
A few dashes of Angostura bitters
A pineapple slice
Mint sprigs

*Combine everything except the pineapple slice with ice; shake. Strain over crushed ice. Garnish with the pineapple slice and mint.*

**MAI KAI NO**

1 oz. white rum
1 oz. 151-proof rum
2 tsp. Jamaican rum
2 tsp. passion fruit juice
2 tsps. honey
1 shot lime juice
A few dashes of Angostura bitters
Club soda
Mint sprigs
1 pineapple stick

*Combine (except soda and garnishes) over crushed ice. Touch up with a spritz of soda and top with pineapple stick and a few mint sprigs.*

**MAIDEN'S BLUSH**

1½ oz. dry gin
1 tsp. curacao
Several drops grenadine
A few drops lemon juice

*Combine with ice; shake well. Strain and add ice.*

**MAIDEN'S KISS**

*Combine equal parts curacao, maraschino, Benedictine, yellow chartreuse and Creme de Roses in a pony glass and stir gently.*

**MAIDEN'S PRAYER**

¾ oz. gin
¾ oz. Cointreau
1 tsp. lemon juice
1 tsp. orange juice

*Combine with ice; shake well. Strain and add ice. Lillet can be used in instead of the Cointreau, with 2 teaspoons each of calvados and apricot brandy instead of the juices.*

---

**MAINBRACE**

¾ oz. gin
¾ oz. Triple Sec
1 tbs. grape juice

*Combine with ice; shake well. Strain and add ice.*

**MAI-TAI**

3 oz. white rum
2 tsp. lime juice
1 tsp. Triple Sec
1 tsp. almond extract
1 tsp. sugar syrup
1 mint sprig
1 pineapple stick

*Combine (except the mint and the pineapple stick) with ice; shake. Strain and add lots of ice. Top with the mint, pineapple stick and a lime slice.*

**MAI-TAI NO. 2**

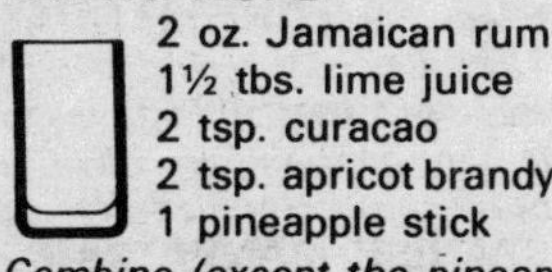

2 oz. Jamaican rum
1½ tbs. lime juice
2 tsp. curacao
2 tsp. apricot brandy
1 pineapple stick

*Combine (except the pineapple stick) with ice; shake well. Strain and add ice. Top with pineapple stick.*

**MAJOR BAILEY**

2 oz. gin
1 tsp. powdered sugar
Several drops of lime juice
Several mint leaves

*Muddle the sugar, juice and leaves on the bottom of a julep glass. Fill with crushed ice; pour in the gin and stir briskly until the glass begins to frost.*

**MAMIE TAYLOR**

3 oz. Scotch
1 tbs. lime juice
Ginger ale

*Combine the Scotch and the lime juice; add ice and fill with ginger ale. Stir gently and decorate with a lemon slice.*

**MANANA**

1½ oz. white rum
2 tsp. apricot brandy
1 tsp. lemon juice
1 tsp. grenadine

*Combine with ice; shake. Strain and add ice.*

**MANDARIN FIZZ**

1½ oz. gin
1½ oz. mandarin juice
2 tsp. sugar syrup
Club soda

*Combine everything except the soda with ice; shake. Strain. Add ice and fill with soda. Decorate with a mandarin slice.*

**MANDEVILLE**

1½ oz. white rum
1 oz. Jamaican rum
1 tbs. lemon juice
2 tsp. cola
1 tsp. Pernod

*Combine with ice; shake. Strain and add ice. Top with an orange slice.*

## MANGO COOLER

1½ oz. vodka
3 oz. mango nectar
2 tbs. orange juice
2 tsp. lemon juice
2 tsp. Cointreau
Mango slices

*Combine (except the fruit slices) with ice; shake. Strain; add lots of ice. Top with mango or orange slices.*

## MANGO DAIQUIRI

2 oz. white rum
1½ oz. lime juice
1 oz. curacao
1 tbs. powdered sugar
4 oz. pureed mango
8 oz. crushed ice

*Combine in a blender at a low speed for 15 seconds. Strain straight up. Serve with straws. Serves two.*

## MANGO MINT

1 oz. rum
1½ oz. mango nectar
2 tsp. white creme de menthe
3 oz. crushed ice

*Combine in a blender at low speed for 15 seconds. Strain and add ice.*

## MANHASSET

1½ oz. whiskey
2 tsp. lemon juice
1 tsp. dry vermouth
1 tsp. sweet vermouth

*Combine with ice; shake. Strain. Add ice and a twist of lemon with its peel.*

## MANHATTAN

2½ oz. rye
1 oz. sweet vermouth

*Combine and stir. Top with a cherry. There are many variations to the* **MANHATTAN.** *Some people prefer less vermouth and a dash of bitters. Others use a different kind of whiskey rather than rye, still others like a dash of Benedictine tossed in for effect. For a* **DRY MANHATTAN** *use dry vermouth instead of sweet, with a twist of lemon peel or an olive in place of the cherry;* **A SPANISH MANHATTAN** *is made with dry sherry instead of vermouth.*

---

## MANHATTAN COOLER

4 oz. claret
2½ oz. lemon juice
A few drops gold rum
2 tsp. sugar syrup

*Combine; add ice and stir well. Top with fruit slices*

## MANHATTAN MANEATER

1½ oz. whiskey
2 tbs. Southern Comfort
1-2 dashes orange bitters

*Combine with ice; shake. Strain and add ice; garnish with a cherry.*

## MANHATTAN VIEUX CARRE

2 oz. bourbon
1 oz. sweet vermouth
a few drops of sugar syrup

*Combine without ice; stir to blend and refrigerate in a small sealed jar for a day or two. Serve straight up with a cherry.*

## MARASCHINO PUNCH

1 bottle sweet wine
2 pints brandy
1½ oz. maraschino
Red and green cherries

*Combine the wine, brandy and maraschino stir. Add chunks of ice. Decorate with cherries.*

## MARCIA DELANO

2 oz. Puerto Rican rum
1 oz. brandy
1 egg
1 tbs. sugar

*Beat the egg with the sugar until foamy; combine it with the brandy and the rum; add boiling water and stir. Top with nutmeg.*

## MARCONI WIRELESS

1½ oz. apple brandy
1 tbs. sweet vermouth
1-2 dashes orange bitters

*Combine with ice; shake. Strain and add ice.*

## MARGARET DUFFY

1½ oz. Swedish Punch
2 tsp. brandy
A few dashes of Angostura bitters

*Combine with ice; shake. Strain and add ice.*

## MARGUERITA

2 oz. tequila
2 tsp. Cointreau
1 tbs. lime juice
½ lime

*Combine (except the lime) with ice; shake well. Rub the lime around the rim of glass and press it in salt. Strain straight up.*

## MARIA THERESA

2 oz. tequila
2 tbs. cranberry juice
1½ tsp. lime juice

*Combine with ice; shake. Strain and add ice.*

## MARQUISE PUNCH

1 quart sauterne
1 pint cognac
8 oz. sugar
The rinds of 3 lemons
A few whole cloves
Cinnamon sticks

*Combine in a large saucepan; heat and stir but do not boil. Serve hot and spicy.*

## MARSALA MARTINI

¾ oz. dry Marsala
¾ oz. gin
1 tbs. dry vermouth

*Combine with ice; shake. Strain straight up; add a twist of lemon plus the peel.*

## MARTINEZ COCKTAIL

2 oz. Old Tom gin
3 oz. dry vermouth
A few drops maraschino
A few dashes of Angostura bitters

*Combine with ice; shake. Strain and add ice.*

## MARTINI

2 oz. gin
1 tsp. dry vermouth

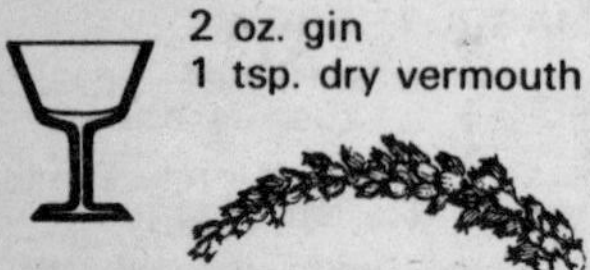

*Combine straight up and stir with an olive.* **MARTINIS** *can be made stronger and dryer (less vermouth) or weaker and dryer (more vermouth) or sweeter (half sweet, half dry vermouth). They can also be made with vodka instead of gin. Can be served on the rocks too. A twist of lemon or orange can be used instead of the olive. For a* **MARTINI, HOLLAND STYLE,** *use Dutch genever gin. For a* **MARTINI MAJADOR,** *use tequila instead of gin.*

## MARTINIQUE MILK PUNCH

1 quart milk
3 beaten egg yolks
3 oz. sugar
4 oz. rum
Nutmeg
Vanilla extract

*Bring the milk almost to a boil. Remove from heat; add the yolks and sugar, plus nutmeg and vanilla to taste. Stir until the sugar is dissolved. Pour in the rum; stir and serve piping hot. Touch up with a twist of lemon plus the peel.*

## MARY GARDEN

1½ oz. Dubonnet
1 tbs. dry vermouth

*Combine with ice; shake. Strain and add ice. Equal parts Dubonnet and vermouth can be used if you like.*

## MARY PICKFORD

1½ oz. white rum
1½ oz. pineapple juice
Several drops grenadine
Several drops maraschino

*Combine with ice; shake. Strain and add ice.*

## MATADOR

1 oz. tequila
2 oz. pineapple juice
1 tbs. lime juice

*Combine with ice; shake. Strain and add ice.*

**MATINEE**

1 oz. gin
2 tsp. sambuca
2 tsp. lime juice
½ egg white
1 tsp. heavy cream

*Combine with ice; shake extremely well. Strain and add ice.*

**MAUI COCKTAIL**

1 oz. vodka
½ oz. banana liqueur
2 tsp. pineapple juice concentrate
1 tsp. lemon juice

*Combine with ice; shake well. Strain over crushed ice.*

**MAURICE**

1½ oz. dry gin
1 tbs. sweet vermouth
1 tbs. dry vermouth
A few dashes of Angostura bitters

*Combine with ice; shake. Strain and add ice.*

**MAXIM**

1½ oz. dry gin
1 tbs. dry vermouth
A few drops white creme de cacao

*Combine with ice; shake. Strain and add ice.*

**MAY BLOSSOM FIZZ**

1½ oz. Swedish Punch
1½ oz. lemon juice
1 tsp. grenadine
Club soda

*Combine (except the soda) with ice; shake. Strain, add ice and fill with soda.*

**MAY COCKTAIL**

1½ oz. whiskey
1 tsp. kirschwasser
1 tsp. strawberry liqueur
May wine

*Combine (except the wine) with ice; shake well. Strain, add ice and wine. Top with a lemon slice.*

**MAY WINE BOWL**

2 bottles white wine
4 oz. sugar
8 oz. clean, whole small strawberries
Fresh woodruff

*Cover the woodruff with the sugar in a small glass and allow to stand for several hours. Add 2 cups of wine to the sugar and woodruff and allow to stand again, overnight. Turn out the sweetened wine into a large punch bowl; add the remaining wine plus chunks of ice immediately before serving. Decorate with the strawberries.*

**McBRANDY**

1½ oz. brandy
1 tbs. apple juice
1 tsp. lemon juice

*Combine with ice; shake well. Strain and add ice. Top with a lemon slice.*

**McCLELLAND**

1½ oz. sloe gin
1 tbs. curacao
1-2 dashes orange bitters

*Combine with ice; shake. Strain and add ice.*

**McCRORY**

1 oz. whiskey
A few dashes of Angostura bitters
Powdered sugar
Club soda

*Combine the whiskey and the bitters; add sugar to taste and stir until it is dissolved. Add soda and ice.*

**McKINLEY'S DELIGHT**

1½ oz. whiskey
1 tbs. sweet vermouth
A few drops Pernod
Several drops cherry brandy

*Combine with ice; shake well. Strain and add ice.*

**MEAD**

4 cups honey
8 oz. brown sugar
4 egg whites
A package of dry, active yeast
1½ oz. lemon juice
Grated lemon rind
Several pinches of mace
Ground cloves, nutmeg, ginger, cinnamon, pepper and rosemary

*Combine everything except the yeast in a large pot and simmer for at least one hour in 2 gals. of water. Remove from heat and strain; add the yeast when lukewarm. Turn out the brew into a crock pot; seal tightly and allow to ferment for several months. Strain and bottle for future use. Serve ice cold.*

---

**MEDIEVAL PUNCH**

5 cups port
6 oz. sugar
2 tsp. orange liqueur
Grated nutmeg, whole cloves, cinnamon
2 oz. brandy
2 large oranges, sliced

*Combine the wine with the fruit slices and spices in a saucepan; add the sugar, stir and simmer until the sugar has dissolved. Add 2 cups of boiling water, the orange liqueur, and the brandy; heat thoroughly but do not allow to boil. Serve warm and unstrained.*

## MEETINGHOUSE PUNCH

*Serves hundreds. You'd better have a good reason to use it, or you risk arrest.*

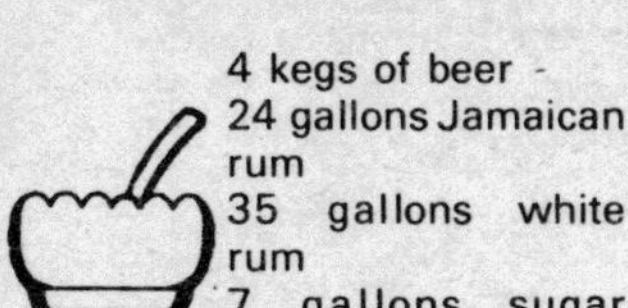

4 kegs of beer
24 gallons Jamaican rum
35 gallons white rum
7 gallons sugar syrup
25 lbs. brown sugar
Enough lemons to fill a wheelbarrow

*Combine in a large punch bowl a little at a time, i.e. a tenth of everything, and keep replenishing it — or prepare a dozen or so punch bowls at the same time. Make sure you have plenty of volunteers and a mixing system well beforehand.*

## MELON COCKTAIL

2 oz. dry gin
A few drops lemon juice
A few drops maraschino

*Combine with ice; shake. Strain and add ice. Top with a cherry.*

## MELON PRESERVE

1 large melon cantalope, cranshaw or honeydew
3 cups sugar
1½ oz. brandy
1½ tsp. lemon juice

*Slice and dice the melon meat; cook in enough water to cover until soft. Combine in a bowl with the lemon juice and brandy; allow to stand several hours. Boil the sugar in enough water to make a syrup; add the melon meat and cook a few more mins. Allow to stand overnight, then cook again until clear. Allow to cool before bottling for future use.*

---

## MERRY WIDOW

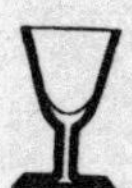

1½ oz. sherry
2 tbs. sweet vermouth

*Combine with ice; shake. Strain. Add ice and a twist of lemon; plus the peel.*

## MERRY WIDOW No. 2

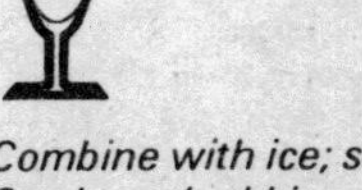

1½ oz. cherry brandy
1½ oz. maraschino

*Combine with ice; shake well. Strain and add ice. Top with a cherry.*

**MERRY WIDOWER**

1 oz. dry gin
1 oz. dry vermouth
Several drops Pernod
A few drops Benedictine
1-2 dashes Peychaud's bitters

*Combine with ice; shake well. Strain add ice and a twist of lemon.*

**METROPOLITAN**

1½ oz. brandy
1½ oz. sweet vermouth
½ tsp. sugar syrup
A few dashes of Angostura bitters

*Combine with ice; shake well. Strain. Add ice.*

**MEURICE COCKTAIL**

1 oz. vodka
1 oz. creme de banana
1 oz. heavy cream

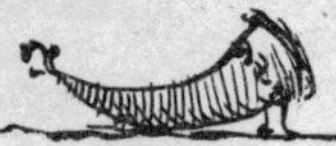

*Combine with ice; shake. Strain straight up.*

**MEXICAN FLAG**

2 oz. tequila
1 tbs. sugar syrup
2 tsp. lime juice
1 green grape
1 small scoop vanilla ice cream

*Combine the tequila, sugar and juice with ice; shake. Strain and add plenty of ice. Top with the grape, vanilla ice cream and a cherry.*

**MEXICANO**

2 oz. white rum
2 tsp. kummel
2 tsp. orange juice
A few dashes of Angostura bitters

*Combine with ice; shake. Strain and add ice.*

**MEXICO MARTINI**

1½ oz. tequila
1 tbs. dry vermouth
A few drops vanilla extract

*Combine with ice; shake well. Strain and add ice.*

**MEXICO PACIFICO**

1½ oz. tequila
1 oz. passion fruit juice
2 tsp. lime juice
3 oz. crushed ice

*Combine in blender at a low speed for 15 seconds. Strain straight up and top with a lime slice.*

**MEXITINI**

1½ oz. dry vermouth
1 tbs. tequila
1 chili bean

*Combine the vermouth and the tequila and stir. Top with the bean.*

**MIAMI BEACH**

¾ oz. Scotch
¾ oz. dry vermouth
1 tbs. grapefruit juice

*Combine with ice; shake. Strain and add ice.*

## MIAMI SUNSET

2 oz. bourbon
1 oz. Triple Sec
1 tsp. grenadine
Orange juice

*Combine the bourbon and the Triple Sec with ice; shake. Strain; add ice and the orange juice. Stir and float the grenadine.*

## MIDNIGHT COCKTAIL

1 oz. apricot brandy
2 tsp. curacao
2 tsp. lemon juice

*Combine with ice; shake. Strain and add ice.*

## MIDNIGHT SUN

1½ oz. aquavit
2 tsp. unsweetened grapefruit juice
1½ tsp. sugar syrup
A few drops grenadine

*Combine with ice; shake well. Strain straight up and with an orange slice.*

## MIKADO

1¼ oz. brandy
A few drops curacao
A few drops almond extract
1-2 dashes creme de noyaux
A few dashes of Angostura bitters

*Combine with ice; shake well. Strain and add ice.*

## MILITARY CUP

1 bottle claret
3 oz. Benedictine
3 oz. cherry bounce
2 oz. lemon juice
Mint sprigs
A few drops of cognac
4 oz. sugar
Grated lemon rind
Whole strawberries
1 bottle club soda

*Dilute the claret with 2 quarts of water in a large punch bowl; add the sugar, juice and rind. Stir well until the sugar has dissolved. Add the Benedictine, cherry bounce, and cognac. Add the soda plus chunks. Garnish with strawberries and mint.*

## MILK LEMONADE

12 oz. milk
6 oz. sugar
4 oz. lemon juice
4 oz. sherry

*Dissolve the sugar with a pint of boiling water; remove from heat and add the lemon juice and sherry. Allow to cool. Add the milk and strain through cloth until clear.*

## MILK PUNCH

2½ oz. rum
1 tsp. sugar
Milk

*Combine the rum and the sugar with ice; shake well. Strain; add ice and fill with milk. Brandy or whiskey can be used instead of rum.*

**MILLIONAIRE**

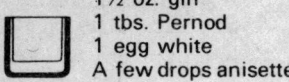

1½ oz. gin
1 tbs. Pernod
1 egg white
A few drops anisette

*Combine with ice; shake. Strain and add ice.*

**MILLIONAIRE NO. 2**

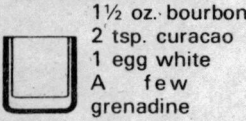

1½ oz. bourbon
2 tsp. curacao
1 egg white
A few
grenadine

*Combine with ice; shake. Strain and add ice.*

**MILLIONS COCKTAIL**

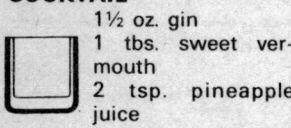

1½ oz. gin
1 tbs. sweet vermouth
2 tsp. pineapple juice
1 egg white
Several drops grenadine

*Combine with ice; shake. Strain and add ice.*

**MINT CORDIAL**

2 bottles brandy
2 large bunches fresh mint
Sugar

*Combine half the mint (whole) and half the brandy in a crock pot and allow to stand for several days. Add the remaining mint and brandy, plus at least a pint of water and sugar to taste. Strain and bottle to use as a cordial.*

**MINT DELIGHT**

4 oz. white creme de menthe
6 oz. vanilla ice cream
4 oz. light cream

*Combine in a blender at high speed until smooth. Serve straight up.*

**MINT JULEP PUNCH**

8 oz. rum
8 oz. cold water
4 oz. powdered sugar
4 doz. mint sprigs
2 bottles bourbon

*Muddle the mint leaves with the water, rum and sugar; strain carefully into a punch bowl filled with ice. Pour in the bourbon and stir.*

**MINT TEQUILA**

1½ oz. tequila
2 tsp. lemon juice
1½ tsp. sugar syrup
½ doz. mint leaves, torn
4 oz. crushed ice

*Combine in a blender at a low speed for 15 seconds. Strain into an old-fashioned glass and add ice.*

**MISSISSIPPI MULE**

1½ oz. gin
1 tsp. creme de cassis
1 tsp. lemon juice

*Combine with ice; shake. Strain and add ice.*

## MISSISSIPPI PUNCH

1½ oz. rum
1 oz. whiskey
1 oz. brandy
1½ tsp. sugar syrup
Several drops lemon juice
A few dashes of Angostura bitters

*Combine with ice; shake. Strain and add plenty of ice. Top with fruit.*

## MISTS

**MISTS** *are frappes served up in old-fashioned glasses. Straight* **MISTS** *are the most simple — 2 oz. of Scotch, bourbon or brandy over 4 oz. of well-packed crushed ice; add a twist of lemon plus the peel.*

## MISTY MANHATTAN

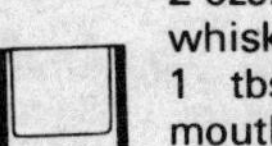

2 ozs. Canadian Mist whiskey
1 tbs. sweet vermouth
A few dashes of Angostura bitters

*Combine with ice; shake. Strain and decorate with a cherry.*

## MIXED BLESSING

4 oz. pineapple juice
2 tbs. gold rum
2 tbs. crushed pineapple
2 tsp. 151-proof rum
1 tbs. Falernum
A few drops lime juice
2 oz. crushed ice

*Combine in a blender at high speed until smooth.*

## MIXED MOCHA FRAPPE

¾ oz. Kahlua
1 tsp. white creme de menthe
1 tsp. white creme de cacao
1 tsp. Triple Sec

*Combine without ice and stir. "Sugarfrost" the rim with water. Pour over crushed ice.*

## MOBILE MULE

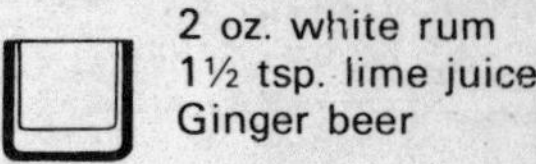

2 oz. white rum
1½ tsp. lime juice
Ginger beer

*Combine the rum and the lime juice with ginger beer, and stir. Add ice; touch up with a twist of lime plus the peel.*

## MOCHA MINT

¾ oz. Kahlua
¾ oz. white creme de menthe
¾ oz. white creme de cacao

*Combine with ice; shake. Strain and add ice.*

## MOCKINGBIRD

1½ oz. tequila
1 oz. lime juice
1 tbs. white creme de menthe

*Combine with ice; shake. Strain straight up. Top with a lime slice.*

**MODERN**

1½ oz. sloe gin
1 tbs. Scotch
A few drops Pernod
A few drops grenadine
1-2 dashes orange bitters

*Combine with ice; shake well. Strain into an old-fashioned glass and add ice.*

**MODERN NO. 2**

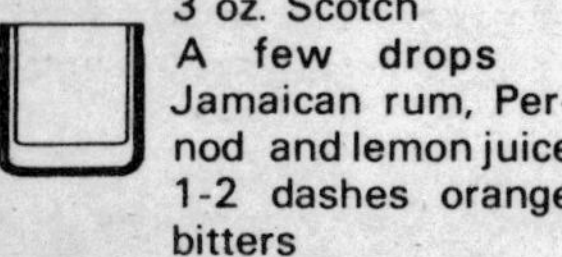

3 oz. Scotch
A few drops Jamaican rum, Pernod and lemon juice
1-2 dashes orange bitters

*Combine with ice; shake. Strain and add ice. Top with a cherry.*

**MODERN LEMONADE**

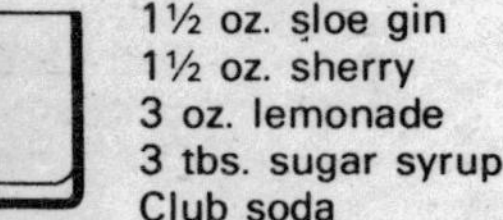

1½ oz. sloe gin
1½ oz. sherry
3 oz. lemonade
3 tbs. sugar syrup
Club soda

*Combine (except the soda) with ice; shake well. Strain; add ice and soda. Touch up with a twist of lemon plus the peel.*

**MOJITO**

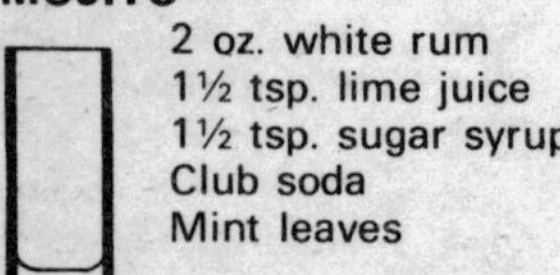

2 oz. white rum
1½ tsp. lime juice
1½ tsp. sugar syrup
Club soda
Mint leaves

*Combine the rum, lime juice and sugar with equal parts crushed ice and club soda; stir. Top with mint leaves.*

**MOLDAU**

1½ oz. gin
2 tsp. plum brandy
1 tsp. orange juice
1 tsp. lemon juice
1 brandied cherry

*Combined with ice; shake. Strain and add ice. Top with the cherry.*

**MONAHAN**

1½ oz. whiskey
1 tbs. sweet vermouth
1-2 dashes Amer Picon

*Combine; add ice and stir.*

**MONKEY GLAND**

1½ oz. gin
1 tbs. orange juice
A few drops Benedictine
A few drops grenadine

*Combine with ice; shake. Strain and add ice.*

**MONTANA**

2 oz. cognac
2 tsp. dry vermouth
2 tsp. port

*Combine; add ice and stir.*

**MONTE CARLO**

1¼ oz. rye
½ tbs. Benedictine
A few dashes of Angostura bitters

*Combine with ice; shake. Strain and add ice.*

**MONTMARTRE**

1½ oz. gin
2 tsp. Triple Sec
2 tsp. sweet vermouth

*Combine with ice; shake. Strain and add ice. Top with a cherry.*

**MONTREAL CLUB BOUNCER**

1½ oz. gin
1½ oz. Pernod

*Combine, add ice and stir.*

**MONTREAL GIN SOUR**

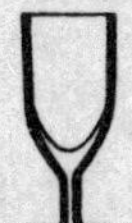

2 oz. gin
2 tsp. lemon juice
1 tsp. sugar syrup
1 egg white

*Combine with ice; shake. Strain and add ice.*

**MOOD INDIGO**

3 ozs. peppermint schnapps
3 ozs. milk
1 tbs. unflavored gelatin
3 ozs. crushed ice

*Heat the milk and combine it with the gelatin in a blender at a high speed for 30 seconds. Add the schnapps, chips, and ice, and blend another 30 seconds. Refrigerate until set.*

**MOONGLOW**

1½ oz. brandy
1½ oz. white creme de menthe

*Combine without ice; stir until blended. Keep chilled. Serve straight up.*

**MOONLIGHT**

3 oz. calvados
3 tsp. lemon juice
2 tsp. sugar syrup
Club soda

*Combine (except the soda) with ice; shake. Strain; add ice and soda. Top with fruit slices.*

**MORNING**

1 oz. brandy
1 oz. dry vermouth
A few drops Pernod, maraschino and curacao
1-2 dashes orange bitters

*Combine with ice; shake. Strain and add ice. Top with a cherry.*

**MORNING AFTER**

3 oz. Pernod
1 tsp. anisette
1 egg white
Club soda

*Combine (except the soda) with ice; shake. Strain and add ice. Touch it up with a spritz of soda.*

**MORNING GLORY**

1 oz. Scotch
1 oz. brandy
A few drops curacao
1 dash Pernod
1-2 dashes Angostura bitters
½ tsp. sugar syrup
Club soda
Powdered sugar

*Combine (except the soda and powdered sugar) with ice; shake well. Strain, add ice and soda. Stir with a wet spoon coated with powdered sugar.*

**MORNING GLORY FIZZ**

2 oz. Scotch
2 tsp. lemon juice
1½ tsp. sugar syrup
1 tsp. Pernod
½ egg white
1-2 dashes Peychaud's bitters
Club soda

*Combine (except the soda) with ice; shake. Strain; add ice and soda. Top with a lemon slice.*

**MORNING SUN**

1½ oz. gin
2 tbs. grapefruit juice
2 tbs. orange juice
1-2 dashes Angostura bitters
A few drops cherry juice

*Combine with ice; shake. Strain and add ice.*

**MOROCCAN COCKTAIL**

1 oz. gin
1 oz. Cointreau
1 oz. mandarin liqueur

*Combine with ice; shake well. Strain straight up.*

**MORRO**

1 oz. gin
2 tsp. gold rum
2 tsp. lime juice
2 tsp. pineapple juice
1 tsp. sugar syrup
Falernum
Sugar

*Combine everything except the Falernum and sugar in a mixing glass filled with ice; shake well. "Sugarfrost" the rim of a glass with Falernum. Strain in the drink; add ice if desired.*

**MOSCOW MULE**

1½ oz. vodka
1½ tsp. lime juice
Ginger beer
1 cucumber peel

*Combine the vodka and the lime juice with ice; shake. Strain add ice and top with the peel or lime slice. Ginger ale can be used instead of ginger beer. Decorate with the peel or a slice of lime.*

**MOSELLE PUNCH**

1 bottle Moselle wine
½ gallon frozen lemon sherbet

*Combine stir until smooth. Serve while ice cold.*

## MOSELLE SUPPER

1 bottle chilled Moselle
1 bottle chilled sparkling Moselle
3 ripe peaches, peeled, pitted and quartered
1½ oz. Benedictine
1 doz. cherries

*Combine the plain Moselle and the Benedictine; add the fruit plus plenty of ice. Add the sparkling Moselle immediately before serving.*

## MOTHER SHERMAN

1½ oz. apricot brandy
1 tbs. orange juice
Several dashes orange bitters

*Combine with ice; shake. Strain and add ice.*

## MOULIN ROUGE

1½ oz. sloe gin
1 tbs. sweet vermouth
A few dashes of Angostura bitters

*Combine with ice; shake. Strain and add ice.*

## MOUNT FUJI

1½ oz. gin
3 tsp. lemon juice
2 tsp. heavy cream
1 tsp. pineapple juice
1 egg white
A few drops maraschino

*Combine with ice; shake. Strain straight up; garnish with cherry.*

## MOUNTAIN

1½ oz. whiskey
A few drops lemon juice
A few drops of dry and sweet vermouths
1 egg white

*Combine with ice; shake. Strain and add ice.*

## MS. MANHATTAN

2½ oz. dry gin
1 tsp. orange juice
1 tsp. sugar syrup
A few drops lemon juice
A few mint leaves, crushed

*Combine with ice; shake. Strain and add ice.*

## MULBERRY WINE

3 quarts ripe mulberries
3 lbs. brown sugar
1½ lbs. raisins
2 tsp. gelatin dissolved in a few drops of hard cider

*Crush the mulberries. Boil the sugar in 1½ gals. of water for 15 minutes, skimming constantly until clear. Add the crushed berries, allow to cool and strain. Combine the sweetened juice with the raisins and dissolved gelatin in a large cask or jar. Store until fermentation has stopped; strain and bottle for future use.*

## MULE'S HIND LEG

½ oz. gin
½ oz. apple brandy
2 tsp. Benedictine
2 tsp. apricot brandy
2 tsp. maple syrup

*Combine with ice; shake. Strain and add ice.*

## MULLED CIDER

3 pints hard cider
4 oz. rum
3 oz. sugar
Cinnamon sticks
Allspice

*Combine in a large pot; heat but do not allow to boil; stir constantly. Strain clean and serve hot.*

## MULLED CLARET

5 oz. claret
1½ tsp. lemon juice
1 cube sugar
1-2 dashes orange bitters
Ground cinnamon

*Dissolve the sugar with 2 oz. of boiling water. Stir in the remaining ingredients and mull with a red-hot poker before serving.*

## MULLED WINE WITH EGGS

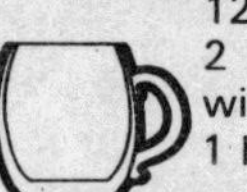

12 eggs, separated
2 bottles dry red wine
1 bottle spring water

*Heat the wine with the water in a large saucepan. Scramble the yolks and beat the egg whites until dry but not stiff; combine them and slowly stir into the wine just before the wine reaches the boiling point. Serve piping hot. Top with nutmeg.*

## MURPHY'S DREAM (for three)

3 oz. Irish Mist
3 oz. gin
3 oz. lemon juice
Several dashes orange bitters
1 egg white

*Combine with ice; shake. Strain; add ice.*

## MULLED VERMONT CIDER

2 quarts sweet cider
8 oz. apple brandy
Cinnamon sticks, ground cloves, allspice
1 tbs. brown sugar

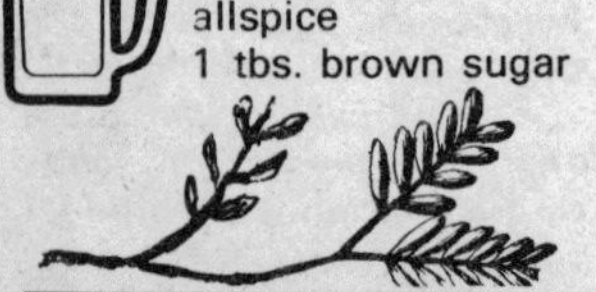

*Dissolve the sugar with the cider in a large saucepan; bring to a boil. Wrap spices in a cloth bag and infuse in the boiling cider for 15 minutes, stirring constantly. In a separate pot, warm the brandy. When the spices have saturated, remove them; add the warm brandy and stir. Serve piping hot in mugs.*

## MUSCADINE WINE

2 quarts muscadine juice
3 cups sugar
4 oz. hop yeast

*Combine the juice with the sugar in a large pot; add 2 pints of water. Heat and stir until the sugar has dissolved. Remove from heat. Add the yeast when lukewarm; cover tightly and allow to ferment for a week and a half. Re-cook until smooth; strain and re-bottle. Store for several months; re-strain and bottle for use.*

## MUSCATEL FLIP

2 oz. brandy
2 oz. muscatel
1 tbs. heavy cream
1½ tsp. sugar syrup
1 egg
4 oz. crushed ice

*Combine in blender at a high speed for a half minute. Strain; top with nutmeg.*

## MUSKMELON

1½ oz. white rum
2 oz. sliced ripe cantalope
2 tsp. lime juice
2 tsp. orange juice
1 tsp. sugar syrup
3 oz. crushed ice
1 small cantalope ball

*Combine (except the cantalope ball) in blender at a low speed for 15 seconds. Strain straight up and top with the cantalope ball, speared and bridged across the glass.*

## MYRTLE BANK PUNCH

1½ oz. 151-proof rum
1½ tbs. lime juice
1½ tsp. sugar syrup
1 tsp. maraschino

*Combine (except the maraschino) with ice; shake. Strain over crushed ice and float the maraschino on top.*

# YOUR OWN RECIPE

# YOUR OWN RECIPE

## YOUR OWN RECIPE

Use a bartender's mixing glass whenever the instructions state "combine" ingredients. Strain the drink from the mixing glass into the drinking glass suggested by the illustration alongside the ingredients.

The glass pictured for each drink is our suggestion; other drinking cups may be used as well.

### NAPOLEON

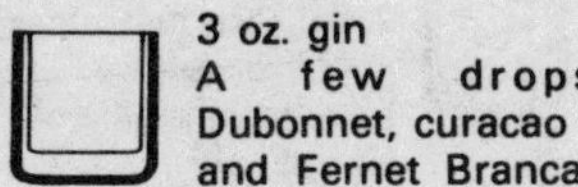

3 oz. gin
A few drops Dubonnet, curacao and Fernet Branca

*Combine with ice; shake and strain. Serve over ice.*

### NARRAGANSETT

1½ oz. whiskey
1 tbs. sweet vermouth
A few drops anisette

*Combine; add ice and stir.*

### NAVY GROG

1 oz. Jamaican rum
2 tsp. white rum, lime juice, orange juice, pineapple juice and guava nectar
1 tsp. Falernum
A few large mint leaves
4 oz. crushed ice

*Combine (except the mint leaves) in a blender at a low speed for 15 seconds. Strain; add ice and top with the mint leaves, partially torn.*

### NAVY PUNCH

1 pint dark rum
1 pint cognac
1 pint Southern Comfort
4 bottles champagne
2 cups pineapple chunks
3 oz. lemon juice
Sugar

*Combine everything except the champagne stir. Add the champagne plus chunks of ice before serving.*

### NECTARINE COOLER

2 oz. vodka
3 oz. orange juice
2 oz. sliced ripe nectarines
1 tsp. sugar
3 oz. crushed ice
Club soda

*Combine everything (except the soda and a slice of nectarine) in an electric blender at a low speed for 20 seconds. Strain; add ice and a spritz of soda. Top with the nectarine and a slice of lemon.*

## NEGRONI

¾ oz. Campari
¾ oz. sweet vermouth
1 tbs. gin

*Combine with ice; shake. Strain and add ice. Top with a twist of lemon plus the peel.*

## NEGRONI COOLER

1½ oz. Campari
1½ oz. sweet vermouth
2 tbs. gin
Club soda

*Combine (except the soda and orange slice) with ice; shake. Strain; add ice and club soda. Top with the orange slice.*

## NEGUS

1 pint port
10 cubes sugar
3 tsp. lemon juice
1 lemon twist

*Rub the cubes of sugar with the lemon twist and add them with the lemon juice to the port. Pour in a quart of boiling water and stir. Top with nutmeg and serve piping hot.*

## NEVINS

1½ oz. bourbon
2 tsp. grapefruit juice
1 tsp. lemon juice
1 tsp. apricot liqueur
A few dashes of Angostura bitters

*Combine with ice; shake. Strain and add ice.*

## NEW ORLEANS

1½ oz. white rum
2 tsp. lime juice
2 tsp. orange juice
1-2 dashes Peychaud's bitters
Ginger ale

*Combine (except the ginger ale) with ice; shake. Strain; add ice and ginger ale. Stir and top with a lime slice.*

## NEW ORLEANS GIN FIZZ

2½ oz. gin
1 oz. lemon juice
2½ tsp. sugar syrup
1 tsp. heavy cream
A few drops of orange-flower water
½ egg white
Club soda

*Combine (except the soda) with ice; shake. Strain; add ice and soda. Top with a lemon slice.*

**NEW WORLD**

1¾ oz. whiskey
2 tsp. lime juice
1 tsp. grenadine

*Combine with ice; shake. Strain. Add ice and a twist of lime plus the peel.*

**NEW YORK**

2 oz. rye
1½ tbs. lime juice
1 tsp. sugar syrup
A few drops of grenadine

*Combine with ice; shake. Strain. Add ice and a twist of orange plus the peel.*

**NEW YORK SOUR**

2 oz. whiskey
1½ oz. lemon juice
1 tbs. claret
1½ tsp. sugar syrup

*Combine (except the claret) with ice; shake. Strain straight up. Top with a slice of lemon or a cherry and float the claret on top.*

**NEWBURY**

1½ oz. gin
1½ oz. sweet vermouth
A few dashes curacao

*Combine with ice; shake. Strain and add ice. Top with an orange or lemon slice.*

**NEWTON'S APPLE COCKTAIL**

1½ oz. apple brandy
2 tsp. curacao
A few dashes of Angostura bitters

*Combine with ice; shake. Strain and add ice.*

**NICOLOSCAR**

1 square slice of lemon peel
Coarse-ground coffee
Sugar
1½ oz. brandy

*Place the coffee and the sugar on the lemon peel waferlike and chew it. Wash it down with the brandy.*

**NIGHTCAP**

1 oz. brandy
1 oz. orange curacao
1 oz. anisette
1 egg yolk

*Combine without ice; stir. Pour; add hot water and allow to stand a few minutes before drinking.*

**NIGHTMARE**

¾ oz. gin
¾ oz. Dubonnet
2 tsp. cherry brandy
2 tsp. orange juice

*Combine with ice; shake. Strain and add ice.*

**NIGHTSHADE**

1½ oz. bourbon
2 tsp. sweet vermouth
2 tsp. orange juice
A few drops yellow chartreuse

*Combine with ice; shake. Strain and add ice. Top with a slice of orange and lemon.*

**NINE-PICK**

1 oz. Pernod
1 oz. brandy
1 tbs. curacao
1 egg yolk

*Combine with ice; shake and strain. Serve over ice.*

**NINETEEN**

3 oz. dry vermouth
2 tsp. gin
2 tsp. kirsch
A few drops sugar syrup
A few drops Pernod

*Combine with ice; shake. Strain and add ice.*

**NINETEEN PICK-ME-UP**

1½ oz. Pernod
1 tbs. gin
A few drops sugar syrup
1-2 dashes Angostura and orange bitters
Club soda

*Combine (except the club soda) with ice; shake. Strain; add ice and a spritz of soda.*

**NINOTCHKA**

1½ oz. vodka
2 tsp. white creme de cacao
2 tsp. lemon juice

*Combine with ice; shake. Strain and add ice.*

**NONE BUT THE BRAVE**

1½ oz. brandy
1 tbs. Pimento Dram
1½ tsp. sugar syrup
A few drops lemon juice
1 pinch ginger

*Combine with ice; shake. Strain and add ice.*

**NORTH EXPRESS**

1 oz. Canadian whiskey
1 oz. dry vermouth
1 oz. Cordial Medoc

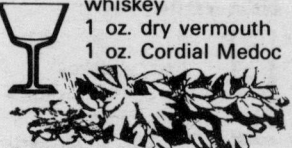

*Combine without ice; stir until well-blended. Pour out over ice. Decorate with a cherry.*

**NUPCIAL**

1 oz. tequila
1 tbs. white creme de cacao
1 tbs. white syrup
1¼ oz. evaporated milk
4 oz. crushed ice

*Combine in a blender at a low speed for a minute and a half. Strain straight up and top with a cherry.*

# YOUR OWN RECIPE

# YOUR OWN RECIPE

Use a bartender's mixing glass whenever the instructions state "combine" ingredients. Strain the drink from the mixing glass into the drinking glass suggested by the illustration alongside the ingredients.

NOTE: The number of glasses or cups shown alongside a recipe do not necessarily indicate the quantity of drinks the recipe will produce.

---

**OCHO RIOS**

1½ oz. Jamaican rum
1 oz. guava nectar
2 tsp. lime juice
2 tsp. heavy cream
1 tsp. sugar syrup
3 oz. crushed ice

*Combine in a blender at a low speed for 15 seconds. Strain straight up.*

**OGGE**

1 quart beer
4 egg yolks
1½ oz. sugar

*Add sugar to yolks; beat until sugar is dissolved. Heat beer in a saucepan until ready to boil. Slowly add the yolk mixture, stirring constantly. Serve immediately. Top it with nutmeg.*

**O'HEARN SPECIAL**

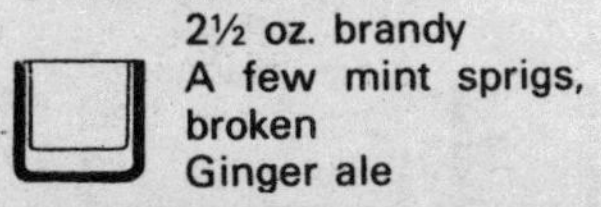

2½ oz. brandy
A few mint sprigs, broken
Ginger ale

*Pour the brandy; add ice, mint and ginger ale. Touch it up with a twist of lemon.*

**OLD BOURBON COOLER**

3 oz. bourbon
2 tsp. grenadine
1 tsp. powdered sugar
A few drops white creme de menthe
A few dashes orange bitters
Club soda
1 pineapple stick

*Combine (except the soda and the pineapple stick) with ice; shake. Strain; add ice and soda. Top with a slice of orange, a cherry and the pineapple stick.*

**OLD CASTLE PUNCH**

2 bottles Rhine wine
1 pint rum
2 cups sugar

*Dissolve the sugar in a quart of boiling water; reduce heat and slowly add the wine and the rum, stirring constantly. Do not boil. Serve piping hot.*

**OLD-FASHIONED**

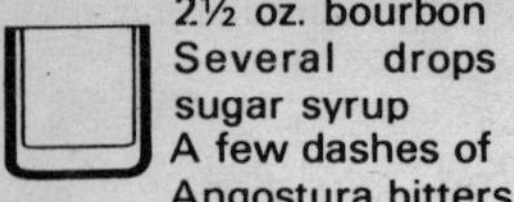

2½ oz. bourbon
Several drops of sugar syrup
A few dashes of Angostura bitters

*Combine and stir. Top with orange slice, a cherry or a twist of lemon. Any whiskey can be used.*

**OLD-FASHIONED PUNCH**

1 quart bourbon
1 doz. sugar cubes dipped in Angostura bitters
1½ oz. Maraschino cherry juice
A whole orange rind

*Combine in a large jar; seal tightly and allow to stand for at least 36 hours. Remove the orange peel; re-cover and store in a cool place for at least three weeks. Serve over fruit slices and ice.*

**OLD MAN'S MILK**

2 oz. Scotch
2 tsp. Drambuie
2 tsp. sugar syrup
1 egg beaten
8 oz. milk

*Combine in a saucepan; heat but do not allow to boil, stirring constantly to prevent the milk from scalding.*

**OLD PAL**

1¼ oz. whiskey
2 tsp. sweet vermouth
2 tsp. grenadine

*Combine with ice; shake. Strain and add ice.*

**OLE**

1½ oz tequila
1 oz. Kahlua
1 tbs. sugar syrup
Heavy cream

*Combine everything except the cream without ice; stir until well blended. Pour over crushed ice; float a little cream.*

**OLYMPIC**

¾ oz. brandy
¾ oz. curacao
1 tbs. orange juice

*Combine with ice; shake. Strain and add ice.*

**ONE IRELAND**

1 oz. Irish whiskey
1 tbs. green creme de menthe
2 oz. vanilla ice cream

*Combine in a blender at a high speed until smooth. Serve straight up.*

**OOM PAUL**

1 oz. calvados
1 oz. Dubonnet
A few dashes of Angostura bitters

*Combine with ice; shake. Strain and add ice.*

**OPAL**

1 oz. gin
2 tsp. orange juice
2 tsp. Triple Sec
½ tsp. sugar syrup
A few drops orange flower water

*Combine with ice; shake. Strain and add ice.*

**OPEN HOUSE PUNCH**

1 fifth Southern Comfort
3 quarts 7-UP
6 oz. lemon juice
6 oz. frozen lemonade concentrate
6 oz. frozen orange juice concentrate

*Combine (except the 7-UP); stir until blended. Top with slices of fruit. Add 7-UP and chunks of ice before serving.*

**OPENING**

1 oz. rye
2 tsp. sweet vermouth
2 tsp. grenadine

*Combine with ice; shake. Strain and add ice.*

**OPERA**

1½ oz. gin
1 tsp. Dubonnet
1 tsp. maraschino

*Combine with ice; shake. Strain. Add ice and a twist of orange, plus the peel.*

**ORANGE BLOOM**

1 oz. gin
2 tsp. Cointreau
2 tsp. sweet vermouth

*Combine with ice; shake. Strain and add ice. Top with a cherry.*

**ORANGE BLOSSOM**

1 oz. orange juice
2 tbs. gin

*Combine with ice; shake. Strain and add ice. Top with orange slice.*

**ORANGE BLOSSOM BLENDER**

2 oz. orange juice
2 tbs. gin
2 tsp. lemon juice
2 tsp. curacao
A few drops orange flower water
2 oz. crushed ice

*Combine in a blender at a low speed for 10 seconds. Strain straight up and top with an orange slice.*

**ORANGE BUCK**

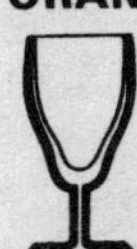

1 oz. orange juice
2 tbs. gin
2 tsp. lemon juice
Ginger ale

*Combine (except the ginger ale) with ice; shake. Strain; add ice and ginger ale. Top with orange slice.*

**ORANGE COMFORT**

½ oz. Southern Comfort
½ oz. anisette
1 tbs. orange juice
2 tsp. lemon juice

*Combine, with ice; shake. Strain and add ice. Top with orange slice.*

## ORANGE COOLER IN A SHELL

1 oz. 151-proof rum
2 tsp. curacao
2 tsp. lime juice
1½ tsp. sugar syrup
1 large California orange

*Slice off the top eighth of the orange and carefully cut out the fruit, leaving the skin intact; save 1½ oz. of the juice. Combine everything with the orange juice and with ice and shake. Strain into the orange shell. Serve with a straw in a bed of crushed ice.*

## ORANGE FIZZ

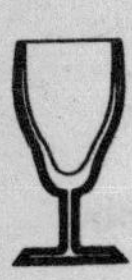

2 oz. gin
2 tbs. orange juice
2 tsp. lemon juice
2 tsp. Triple Sec
1½ tsp. sugar syrup
1-2 dashes orange bitters
Club soda

*Combine all but the soda with ice; shake. Strain; add ice and the soda. Top with orange slice.*

---

## ORANGE FLOWER

1 oz. curacao
2 tsp. orange juice
2 tsp. cherry liqueur
1 tsp. lemon juice
A few drops orange flower water
3 oz. crushed ice.

*Combine in a blender at a low speed for 15 seconds. Strain straight up.*

## ORANGE FLOWER RATAFIA

8 oz. orange blossoms
5 cups brandy
2 cups sugar

*Pound the orange blossoms into a loose powder and soak them with the brandy in a pot for at least two weeks. Combine the sugar with 6 oz. of water; stir until syrupy. Add to the orange blossoms when ready. Strain and bottle for future use.*

## ORANGE MILK CORDIAL

1 doz. small oranges
8 oz. sugar
2 quarts milk
1 pint brandy
Grated lemon rind

*Peel and separate the oranges; combine them with the milk in a large saucepan. Add lemon rind to taste; bring to a boil, stirring constantly. Boil for several minutes. Allow to cool; add the sugar and the brandy and stir until well-blended. Strain clean and bottle for future use.*

## ORANGE OASIS

1½ oz. gin
4 oz. orange juice
2 tsp. cherry liqueur
Ginger ale

*Combine (except the ginger ale) ice; shake. Strain add ice and ginger ale. Top with orange slice.*

## ORANGE POSSET

1 pint white wine
8 oz. sugar
1 tsp. grated lemon rind
1 tsp. white bread, grated
2 tsp. almond paste
4 oz. brandy

*Simmer the grated bread and rinds with a cup of water in a saucepan; add the sugar and allow to cool. Add the almond paste, wine and brandy. Beat until foamy and serve over ice.*

## ORANGE SANGAREE

4 oz. claret or Bordeaux
2 oz. orange juice
1½ oz. sugar
Club soda
2 tbs. lemon juice
A whole clove
Allspice

*Combine everything except the soda with ice; shake. Chill for one hour. Strain and add ice. Fill with club soda*

## ORANGE VODKA

4 cups cooking alcohol
1 lb. sugar
The rinds of 2 large oranges, in pieces

*Combine the fruit rinds with the alcohol in a jar or bottle; seal and allow to stand for several days in a warm place. Boil the sugar in enough water to make a syrup; combine with the rinds and alcohol when ready. Strain and bottle for future use.*

## ORANGE WARMER

8 oz. Grand Marnier
6 cups orange juice
6 tsp. tea leaves steeped in 6 cups of boiling water
4 oz. sugar
Whole orange slices stuck with cloves

*Strain the brewed tea into a large chafing dish. Dissolve sugar in hot orange juice and combine with tea. Add the Grand Marnier and top with orange slices and cloves. Serve warm.*

---

## ORANGE WATER

½ doz. large oranges
3 oz. orange blossoms
7 pints brandy
4 pints sugar

*Peel the oranges and squeeze out the juice; combine the peels and the juice with the brandy in a jar; seal and allow to stand for at least one week. Boil the sugar in enough water to make a syrup; add to the brandy when ready. Strain and bottle for future use.*

## ORANGE WINE

1 peck oranges
3 lbs. sugar

*Squeeze the juice from the oranges and mince enough rinds to make approx. 3 ozs. of rinds. Combine the juice, minced rinds and sugar in a large kettle and bring to a boil. Allow to cool; strain clear and add another cup of fresh juice. Pour into a crock pot; seal and allow to ferment, skimming often. Bottle and store for future use.*

## ORCHID

2 oz. gin
1 egg white
A few drops Creme Yvette

*Combine with ice; shake. Strain and add ice.*

## ORDINARY HIGHBALL

½ oz. rye
Club soda

*Pour rye over ice; add club soda.*

---

## ORIENTAL COCKTAIL

1 oz. whiskey
2 tsp. curacao
2 tsp. sweet vermouth
1½ tsp. lime juice

*Combine with ice; shake well. Strain and add ice.*

## OSTEND FIZZ

1½ oz. kirschwasser
2 tsp. lemon juice
2 tsp. creme de cassis
1½ tsp. sugar syrup
Club soda

*Combine everything except the club soda with ice; shake well. Strain; add ice and fill the glass with soda. Decorate with a slice of lemon.*

---

## OVER HILL 'N' DALE

1½ oz. apple brandy
2 tbs. white creme de menthe
Several drops Pernod

*Combine with ice; shake. Strain and add ice.*

---

## YOUR OWN RECIPE

# YOUR OWN RECIPE

Use a bartender's mixing glass whenever the instructions state "combine" ingredients. Strain the drink from the mixing glass into the drinking glass suggested by the illustration alongside the ingredients.

NOTE: The number of glasses or cups shown alongside a recipe do not necessarily indicate the quantity of drinks the recipe will produce.

The glass pictured for each drink is our suggestion; other drinking cups may be used as well.

---

**PACIFIC PACIFIER**

1 oz. Cointreau
1 tbs. banana liqueur
1 tbs. light cream

*Combine with ice; shake. Strain over crushed ice.*

**PADDY COCKTAIL**

1½ oz. Irish whiskey
1½ oz. sweet vermmuth
1-2 dashes Angostura bitters

*Combine with ice; shake. Strain and add ice.*

**PAGO PAGO**

1½ oz. gold rum
2 tsp. lime juice
2 tsp. pineapple juice
A few drops green chartreuse
A few drops white creme de cacao

*Combine with ice; shake. Strain and add ice.*

**PAISLEY MARTINI**

2½ oz. gin
2 tsp. dry vermouth
1 tsp. Scotch

*Combine shake well. Strain and add ice.*

**PALACE MARTINI**

3 oz. dry gin
1 tbs. dry vermouth
1 tbs. Cordial Medoc

*Combine with ice; shake. Strain straight up.*

---

**PALM BEACH**

1½ oz. gin
1 tsp. sweet vermouth
½ tbs. grapefruit juice

*Combine with ice; shake. Strain and add ice.*

## PALMETTO

1½ oz. white rum
2 tbs. sweet vermouth
1-2 dashes orange bitters

*Combine with ice; shake. Strain into glass. Add ice and a twist of lemon; drop in the peel.*

## PANAMA

1½ oz. Jamaican rum
1 tbs. dark creme de cacao
1 tbs. heavy cream

*Combine with ice; shake well. Strain into glass and add ice.*

## PANAMA COOLER

2 oz. Rhine wine
2 oz. dry sherry
1 oz. orange juice
1-2 dashes Angostura bitters
Club soda
2 tsp. maraschino
1 tsp. lime juice

*Combine all but the soda with ice; shake. Strain into glass; add ice and soda. Top with a lemon slice.*

## PAN-AMERICAN

1¼ oz. rye
½ lemon
A few drops sugar syrup

*Muddle the lemon with the sugar in a serving glass; add ice and the rye, and stir.*

## PANCHO VILLA

1 oz. white rum
1 oz. gin
1 tbs. apricot brandy
1 tsp. cherry brandy
1 tsp. pineapple juice

*Combine with ice; shake. Strain into glass straight up.*

---

## PANDEMONIUM PUNCH

3 quarts pineapple juice
1½ quarts orange juice
4½ oz. lemon juice
6 oz. citric acid
8 lb. sugar
8 bottles ginger ale
Mint sprigs, crushed
Grated orange rind

*Dilute the citric acid in a gallon and a half of boiling water; allow to cool. Combine in a large punch bowl with the fruit juices and sugar; stir until the sugar has dissolved. Garnish with the grated rind and mint. Add the ginger ale and ice before serving.*

---

## PANTOMIME

1½ oz. dry vermouth
A few drops almond extract
A few drops grenadine
1 egg white

*Combine with ice; shake well. Strain and add ice.*

**PANZERWAGEN**

1 oz. vodka
1 oz. gin
1 oz. Cointreau

*Combine with ice; shake. Strain and add ice.*

**PAPAYA SLING**

1½ oz. gin
3 tsp. lime juice
1 tbs. papaya syrup
Several dashes Angostura bitters
Club soda

*Combine everything except the soda with ice; shake well. Strain add ice and fill the glass with soda.*

**PARADISE**

1 oz. gin
1 oz. apricot brandy
1½ oz. orange juice

*Combine with ice; shake well. Strain and add ice.*

**PARADISE COOLER**

1 oz. white rum
1 oz. orange juice
2 tsp. Falernum
1 tsp. cherry brandy
1½ tsp. lime juice
Mint sprigs dipped in powdered sugar

*Combine everything except the sprigs with ice; shake. Strain; add ice. Garnish with the powdered mint and a cherry. Serve with a straw.*

**PARFAIT D'ARMOUR**

3 oz. lime rinds
1½ oz. lemon rinds
Rosemary sprigs
Ground cloves
Orange blossoms
2½ gallons cooking alcohol
20 cups sugar
caramel

*Grate the fruit rinds, pound the rosemary sprigs, and combine them with the alcohol in a pot. Seal the pot tightly and store for at least two weeks. Soak the sugar in 5 quarts of water, add to the fruit and rosemary when ready. Add a little caramel for coloring; bottle and store for future use.*

**PARISIAN**

1 tbs. dry gin
1 tbs. dry vermouth
1 tbs. creme de cassis

*Combine with ice; shake well. Strain and add ice.*

**PARISIAN BLONDE**

1 tbs. Jamaican rum
1 tbs. curacao
1 tbs. heavy cream

*Combine with ice; shake very well. Strain and add ice.*

**PARK AVENUE**

2 oz. gin
1 oz. pineapple juice
2 tsp. sweet vermouth
A few drops curacao

*Combine with ice; shake well. Strain and add ice.*

## PARK AVENUE ORANGE BLOSSOM

3 bottles champagne, iced
2 quarts orange juice, as freshly squeezed as possible
A small bottle maraschino cherries

*Combine the orange juice and the cherries in a large punch bowl; add the champagne immediately before use.*

## PARLOR PUNCH

8 oz. Jamaican rum
8 oz. raspberry syrup
2 tbs. tea steeped in
1 pint boiling water
2 lb. sugar
Club soda

*Peel and grate the rinds of three of the lemons; combine with the sugar and 1 quart of boiling water in a large saucepan. Stir and continue to boil for 10-15 minutes. Cool and add the juice of all the lemons; strain in the tea. Stir well and refrigerate. Strain in the rum and the raspberry syrup immediately before using. Serve over ice. Touch up each glass with a spritz of soda.*

## PARSNIP WINE

3 lb. parsnips
3 lb. sugar
1 package dry, activated yeast

*Slice the parsnips and boil them in a gallon of water until soft; carefully strain out all the juice. Add enough water to balance out at a gallon again and dissolve the sugar in it. Cool to lukewarm and add the yeast; turn out into a crock pot and ferment several weeks, stirring daily the first week. Strain, allow to stand a few days, then seal and store for half a year. Store in wooden casks, not glass.*

## PARTY JULEP

2 bottles bourbon
Sugar
Mint sprigs

*Reserve two large punch bowls of different sizes; fill the larger of the two with ice, then comfortably hammer home the smaller one inside it. In this bowl, muddle plenty of mint with plenty of sugar. Fill this bowl with crushed ice and pour in the bourbon. Garnish with more mint. Serve in tall glasses, catching up a bit of mint, sugar, ice, and bourbon in each.*

## PARTY PUNCH

3 cups grape juice
2 cups sugar
6 cups orange juice
2 oz. lime juice
5 cups of beer
1 bottle club soda

*Combine everything except the beer and the soda; stir to blend. Add the beer and the soda plus chunks of ice before serving.*

## PASSION DAIQUIRI

1½ oz. white rum
2 tbs. lime juice
2 tsp. passion fruit juice
1½ tsp. sugar syrup

*Combine with ice; shake well. Strain and add ice.*

## PASSION FRUIT COOLER

2½ oz. white rum
4 oz. passion fruit nectar
1 oz. gin
1 oz. orange juice
2 tsp. lemon juice
A few mint sprigs, broken

*Combine in a mixing glass; fill with ice; shake well. Strain over plenty of ice. Decorate with mint.*

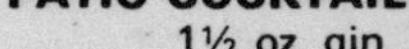

## PATIO COCKTAIL

1½ oz. gin
1 tbs. dry vermouth
1 tbs. sweet vermouth, clear
A few drops of Cointreau

*Combine with ice; shake well. Strain and add ice.*

## PEACH BRANDY

10 large peaches
8 oz. sugar
1 pint brandy

*Slice the fruit; remove the pit. Crush the kernels from the center of the pit and combine with the sliced fruit, brandy, and sugar in a large jar or bottles. Store at room temperature for a month, shaking daily. When ready, strain, bottle, and store for half a year before using.*

## PEACH BUCK

1¼ oz. vodka
2 tsp. lemon juice
2 tsp. peach brandy
Ginger ale
1 peach slice

*Combine everything except the ginger ale and the peach slice with ice. Shake. Strain over ice.*

**PEACH DAIQUIRI**

2 oz. white rum
½ ripe peach, peeled
1 tbs. lime juice
1½ tsp. sugar syrup
6 oz. crushed ice

*Combine in a blender at a low speed for 15 seconds. Strain straight up.*

**PEACH EGGNOG**

1 pint peach brandy
1 pint heavy cream
8 oz. milk
8 oz. powdered sugar
½ doz. egg yolks
Grated nutmeg

*Combine the egg yolks and the sugar in a large bowl; beat together until creamy. Slowly add the brandy. Allow to stand; add the milk and refrigerate several hours. Before serving, whip the cream and fold it into the nog. Whole eggs, separated, can be used. Beat the whites until stiff and fold into the nog after the whipped cream.*

**PEACH FLIP**

2 oz. vodka
1 oz. almond extract
3 tsp. lemon juice
2 ripe peaches
3 oz. crushed ice

*Peel and dice the peaches. Combine with the remaining ingredients in a blender at high speed until smooth. Serve straight up.*

**PEACH SANGAREE**

4 oz. claret
1½ oz. lemon juice
2 tbs. sugar
Cinnamon, allspice, and salt
4 oz. sliced peaches
Club soda

*Combine everything except the soda and the sliced peaches with ice; shake well. Add the peaches to the mixing glass; stir well and chill for one hour. When ready, strain and add ice. Fill the glass with soda and decorate with a slice of peach.*

**PEACH VELVET**

1½ oz. peach brandy
2 tbs. white creme de cacao
2 tbs. heavy cream
2 oz. crushed ice

*Combine in a blender at a high speed for 10 seconds. Serve straight up.*

**PEACH WEST INDIES**

1½ oz. white rum
½ peach, peeled
A few drops of lime juice
A few drops of maraschino
3 oz. crushed ice

*Combine in a blender at a high speed for 15 seconds. Strain. To make a* **BANANA WEST INDIES,** *substitute 1½ oz. of banana liqueur for the peach.*

## PEACHBLOW FIZZ

2 oz. gin
2 tsp. lemon juice
2 tsp. strawberry liqueur
1 tsp. sugar syrup
1 tsp. heavy cream
Club soda
1 strawberry

*Combine everything except the soda and the strawberry with ice; shake extremely well. Strain. Add ice and fill the glass with soda. Decorate with the strawberry.*

## PEAR RICKEY

1½ oz. pear brandy
1 tsp. lime juice
Club soda
Pear slices

*Pour the brandy into a highball glass. Add the lime juice plus ice; fill the glass with club soda and stir. Touch it up with a twist of lime. Decorate with pear slices.*

## PEACHED WINE

1 bottle Burgundy
1 cup peaches, peeled and sliced
3 oz. sugar
Lemon slices

*Combine; dilute with a pint of water and stir until the sugar has dissolved. Allow to stand at room temperature for at least one hour. Add ice.*

## PEAR LIQUEUR

1 quart pears peeled
Whiskey
Sugar

*Combine enough water and sugar to make enough syrup to cover the pears on the bottom of a crock pot. Seal the pot and allow to stand for a few days. Open the pot; strain and double with whiskey. Rebottle and use as a liqueur.*

### PEGGY COCKTAIL

1½ oz. dry gin
1 tbs. dry vermouth
A few drops Pernod
A few drops Dubonnet

*Combine with ice; shake well. Strain and add ice.*

### PEGU CLUB

1½ oz. gin
1 tbs. orange curacao
1 tsp. lime juice
1-2 dashes Angostura and orange bitters

*Combine with ice; shake. Strain straight up.*

### PENDENNIS COCKTAIL

1½ oz. gin
1 tbs. apricot brandy
3 tsp. lime juice
1-2 dashes Peychaud's bitters

*Combine with ice; shake well. Strain and add ice.*

### PENSACOLA

1½ oz. white rum
2 tsp. guava nectar
2 tsp. lemon juice
2 tsp. orange juice
3 oz. crushed ice

*Combine in a blender at a low speed for 15 seconds. Strain straight up.*

### PEPPER TREE PUNCH

1½ oz. white rum
1 tbs. dark rum
1 tbs. lime juice
2 tsp. sugar
1-2 dashes Angostura bitters
A pinch cinnamon
A pinch cayenne pepper

*Combine with ice; shake well. Strain and add ice.*

### PERFECT MARTINI

1½ oz. gin
2 tsp. dry vermouth
2 tsp. sweet vermmuth

*Combine with ice; shake well. Strain straight up. Decorate with an olive.*

### PENDENNIS EGGNOG

1 bottle bourbon
1 dozen eggs, separated
2 quarts heavy cream
1 lb. sugar

*Combine the sugar with the bourbon in a punch bowl; stir until the sugar is dissolved and allow to stand at room temperature a few hours. Beat the egg yolks into the bourbon mixture and let stand for a few hours. Just before serving, beat the egg whites until stiff, whip the cream, and fold both into the bourbon mixture. Garnish with nutmeg and serve in punch glasses.*

**PERNOD COCKTAIL**

2 oz. Pernod
2 tsp. water
A few drops sugar syrup
A few dashes of Angostura bitters

*Combine with ice; shake well. Strain and add ice.*

**PERNOD CURACAO FRAPPE**

2 tsp. Pernod
2 tsp. curacao
2 tsp. orange juice
1 tsp. lemon juice

*Combine without ice; stir well. Pour over crushed ice. Decorate with a slice of orange.*

**PERNOD DRIP**

1½ oz. Pernod
1 cube sugar

*Pour the Pernod into a small glass. Place the sugar cube in a tea strainer above the glass; pack the strainer with crushed ice and wait until the ice melts, dissolves the sugar, and drips into the Pernod before drinking. Stir gently; add ice if you like.*

**PERNOD FLIP**

1 oz. Pernod
2 tsp. Cointreau
2 tsp. lemon juice
1½ tsp. sugar syrup
1 egg

*Combine with ice; shake well. Strain straight up.*

**PERNOD FLIP II**

1½ oz. Pernod
1 oz. heavy cream
1 egg white
2 tsp. almond extract
4 oz. crushed ice

*Combine in a blender; at high speed for five seconds. Pour straight up.*

**PERNOD FRAPPE**

1½ oz. Pernod
2 tsp. anisette
A few dashes of Angostura bitters

*Combine with ice; shake well. Strain over crushed ice.*

**PERNOD MARTINI**

2 oz. gin
2 tsp. dry vermouth
A few drops Pernod

*Combine with ice; shake well. Strain straight up. Decorate with an olive. The Pernod can be used as a garnish for a regular martini if you like.*

**PERPETUAL**

1½ oz. sweet vermouth
1½ oz. dry vermouth
Several dashes Creme Yvette
A few drops white creme de cacao

*Combine with ice; shake well. Strain and add ice.*

## PERSIMMON BEER

Several bunches of wild persimmon
1 quart slightly sugared water
8 oz. yeast

*Mash the persimmon and simmer it in the boiling, sweet water at least a half hour. Allow to cool; add the yeast and allow to ferment for several weeks. Strain clean and bottle for future use.*

## PHILADELPHIA SCOTCHMAN

1 oz. apple brandy
1 oz. port
1 oz. orange juice
Club soda

*Combine everything except the soda with ice; shake well. Strain; add ice and fill with soda.*

## PHILLY SPECIAL

1 oz. bourbon
1 oz. heavy cream
1 oz. dark creme de cacao

*Combine with ice; shake. Strain straight up.*

## PHILOMEL

2 oz. sherry
1½ oz. Quinquina
2 tbs. orange juice
1 tbs. rum
1 pinch pepper

*Combine with ice; shake well. Strain and add ice.*

## PHOEBE SNOW

1½ oz. brandy
1½ oz. Dubonnet
A few drops Pernod

*Combine with ice; shake well. Strain and add ice.*

## PHILIP BROWN'S PUNCH

4 bottles dry white wine
1 quart brandy
1 quart gold rum
3 ounces frozen lemonade concentrate
2 quarts club soda

*Combine everything except the soda in a punch bowl and allow to stand at room temperature for one hour. Immediately before serving add the soda plus chunks of ice and stir.*

**PICADILLY PUNCH**

1 bottle cognac
1½ tbs. sugar
2 large lemons
Whole cloves
Cinnamon sticks
Ground nutmeg

*Cut the peel off the lemons; stud the peels with cloves and combine in a pot with cinnamon sticks, sugar, nutmeg, and 1 pint of warm water. Squeeze in the juice of the lemons; simmer and stir until the sugar has dissolved. Pour an oz. or so of the cognac into a ladle; ignite and infuse the punch. Add the remaining cognac; stir well and serve hot in mugs, unstrained.*

---

**PICADOR**

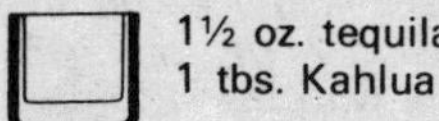

1½ oz. tequila
1 tbs. Kahlua

*Combine with ice; shake well. Strain. Add ice and a twist of lemon.*

**PICASSO**

1½ oz. cognac
2 tsp. lime juice
2 tsp. Dubonnet
1½ tsp. sugar syrup

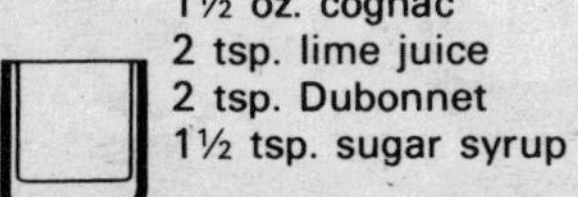

*Combine with ice; shake well. Strain; add ice and a twist of orange.*

**PICK-ME-UP**

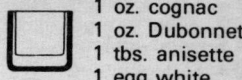

1 oz. cognac
1 oz. Dubonnet
1 tbs. anisette
1 egg white

*Combine with ice; shake well. Strain; add ice and a twist of lemon.*

**PICKENS' PUNCH**

1 oz. peach brandy
1 oz. white creme de menthe
1 oz. cherry liqueur

*Combine with ice; shake well and allow to stand for a few minutes. Strain straight up.*

**PICON**

2 tbs. Amer Picon
2 tbs. dry vermouth

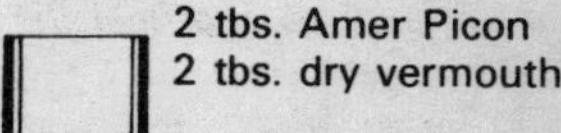

*Combine with ice; shake well. Strain and add ice.*

**PICON GRENADINE**

1½ oz. Amer Picon
1 tbs. grenadine
Club soda

*Combine the Amer Picon and the grenadine; stir well and add ice. Fill the glass with club soda.*

**PICON ON THE ROCKS**

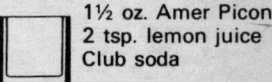

1½ oz. Amer Picon
2 tsp. lemon juice
Club soda

*Combine the Amer Picon and the lemon juice; add ice and stir. Touch it up with a spritz of soda and decorate with lemon.*

## PICON PICON

1½ oz. Amer Picon
2 tbs. orange juice
Club soda.

*Combine the Amer Picon and the orange juice; stir well and touch it up with a spritz of soda. Serve straight up.*

## PICON PUNCH

1½ oz. Amer Picon
1 tbs. cognac
A few drops grenadine
Club soda

*Combine the Amer Picon and the grenadine; touch it up with a dash of soda and stir gently. Add ice and float the cognac.*

---

## PIED PIPER PUNCH

2 bottles Piper-Heidsieck champagne
1 pint cognac
1 pint cream sherry
3 oz. Contreau
3 oz. cherry liqueur

*Combine everything except the champagne; stir well. Add a large block of ice. Pour in the champagne before serving.*

## PIMENTO DRAM

1½ quarts pimento berries
1 quart white rum
4 lb. sugar
1 pint lime juice
Cinnamon sticks

*Soak the berries with the rum and the lime juice in a crock pot for several days. Break the cinnamon sticks and boil them in ½ gal. of water. Strain and re-boil the water with the sugar until the sugar has dissolved. Squeeze the liquid out of the pimento mixture; add to the sugar water when cool. Strain and bottle for future use.*

## PIMM'S CUP COCKTAIL

1½ oz. Pimm's Cup (gin sling)
7-UP
1 cucumber peel

*Pour the Pimm's Cup into a tall glass; add ice, fill the glass with 7-UP, and stir. Decorate with the cucumber peel and a slice of lemon.*

## PINA BORRACHA

1 bottle tequila
3 cups crushed pineapple

*Combine in a large jar; seal tightly and refrigerate at least 24 hours. Strain into a bottle which can be capped. Savor as a liqueur.*

## PINA COLADA

2 oz. gold rum
2 oz. cream of coconut
4 oz. pineapple juice
1 pineapple stick

*Combine everything except the pineapple with ice; shake well. Strain. Decorate with the pineapple and a cherry. A PINA COLADA can also be mixed with a little crushed ice in a blender.*

## PINA FRIA

1 oz. white rum
2 oz. pineapple juice
1 oz. lemon juice
2 pineapple rings, torn in pieces
3 oz. crushed ice
Sprigs of mint

*Combine everything except the mint in a blender at high speed for 15 seconds. Strain; garnish with mint and serve with a straw.*

## PINATA

1 oz. tequila
1 tbs. banana liqueur
1 oz. lime juice

*Combine with ice; shake well. Strain straight up.*

## PINEAPPLE BEER

1 large pineapple
Sugar to taste

*Slice the pineapple into small chunks, skin and all. Place the chunks in a deep saucepan and cover with boiling water; add sugar to taste and stir. Store in a warm place for 12 to 18 hours; strain and bottle the juice. Allow to stand for several days before using. Serve ice cold.*

## PINEAPPLE COCKTAIL PUNCH

3 oz. pineapple juice
6 oz. dry white wine
8 oz. crushed pineapple
9 oz. sherry
1 tbs. lemon juice
Pineapple wedges

*Soak the crushed pineapple in the wine for 2-3 hours; combine both with the juices and the sherry and stir well. Strain and refrigerate. Serve over ice; decorate each glass with a pineapple wedge.*

## PINEAPPLE DAIQUIRI

1 oz. white rum
2 oz. pineapple juice
1 tsp. Cointreau
½ tsp. lime juice
4 oz. crushed ice

*Combine in blender at a high speed for 15 seconds. Strain; serve straight up.*

## PINEAPPLE DELIGHT

1½ oz. Chablis
1½ oz. sherry
2 oz. crushed pineapple
1 tbs. white rum
2 tsp. lime juice
2 tsp. Cointreau

*Combine without ice; refrigerate for several hours. Serve unstrained; add ice. Decorate with pineapple chunks.*

## PINEAPPLE LEMONADE

1½ oz. brandy
2 oz. crushed pineapple
2 tsp. sugar syrup
A few drops raspberry syrup
Club soda
1 pineapple stick

*Muddle the crushed pineapple with the sugar syrup in a mixing glass. Add the brandy and raspberry syrup plus ice and shake well. Strain;add ice and fill with soda. Decorate with the pineapple stick and a twist of lemon.*

## PINEAPPLE MAUBY

1 large, ripe pineapple
2 tbs. ginger

*Slice the pineapple into rings. Place the slices in a crock pot; add enough water to cover them and stir in the ginger. Seal and allow to stand for several days. When ready, crush the fruit, strain out the juice, and sweeten to taste. Serve over ice, garnished with ginger or mint.*

## PINEAPPLE MINT COOLER

2 oz. gin
2 tsp. white creme de menthe
1 oz. lemon juice
3 oz. pineapple juice
Club soda
1 pineapple stick and a green cherry

*Combine everything except the soda and the garnishes in with ice; shake well. Strain; add plenty of ice and touch the drink up with a spritz of soda. Decorate with the pineapple stick and the cherry.*

## PINEAPPLE MIST

1½ oz. white rum
2 oz. crushed pineapple

*Blend the pineapple with crushed ice. Pour in the rum and decorate with a cherry.*

## PINEAPPLE OKOLEHAO PUNCH

4 bottles okolehao
3 quarts pineapple juice
2 cups lemon juice
1 bottle club soda
Strawberries

*Combine the okolehao and the juices. Add the club soda plus chunks of ice before serving. Garnish with strawberries.*

**PINEAPPLE PUNCH**

1 quart pineapple juice
1 cup curacao
1 cup rum
1 quart lemonade

*Combine; stir well. Serve over ice.*

**PINEAPPLE RUM PUNCH**

5 cups white rum
4 oz. lime juice
6 cups pineapple juice
16 oz. sugar syrup

*Combine; add ice and stir.*

**PINEAPPLE SANGAREE**

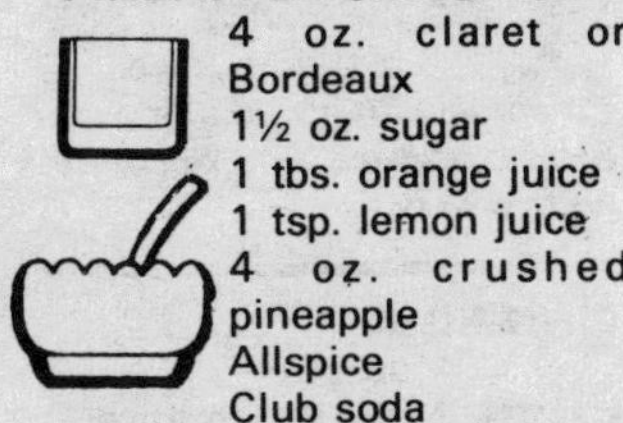

4 oz. claret or Bordeaux
1½ oz. sugar
1 tbs. orange juice
1 tsp. lemon juice
4 oz. crushed pineapple
Allspice
Club soda

*Combine everything except the allspice and the soda in with ice; shake. Chill for one hour. Strain and add ice. Fill glass with soda and garnish with allspice.*

**PINEAPPLE SUNRISE**

1½ oz. tequila
1½ oz. pineapple juice
1 tbs. grenadine
1½ tbs. lime juice

*Combine with ice; shake well. Strain straight up. Decorate with a cherry and a slice of pineapple.*

**PINEAPPLE WINE**

5 lb. pineapple, sliced
4 lb. sugar
2 tsp. isinglass gelatin
Grated lemon rinds

*Soak the pineapple slices in a gal. of water for several days; mixing well two times a day. Strain the liquid into a large pot; add the sugar and stir to dissolve. Add the rinds and gelatin; close tightly and allow to ferment for several days to a week. Strain clean, store for two weeks, then bottle and store for use.*

**PING-PONG**

1¼ oz. sloe gin
1¼ oz. creme yvette
1 oz. lemon juice

*Combine with ice; shake well. Strain and add ice.*

**PINK ALMOND**

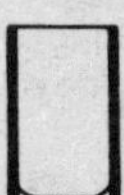

1 oz. whiskey
2 tsp. creme de noyaux, almond extract, kirsch, and lemon juice

*Combine with ice; shake well. Strain and add ice. Decorate with slices of lemon.*

**PINK CALIFORNIA SUNSHINE**

4 oz. pink champagne
4 oz. orange juice
1-2 dashes creme de cassis

*Combine; pour straight up; stir gently.*

**PINK CREOLE**

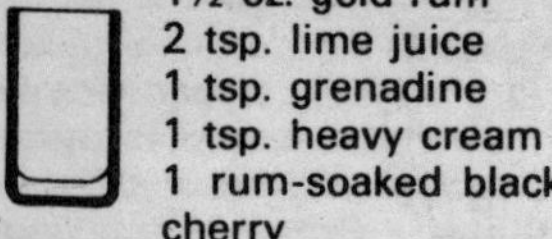

1½ oz. gold rum
2 tsp. lime juice
1 tsp. grenadine
1 tsp. heavy cream
1 rum-soaked black cherry

*Combine everything except the cherry with ice; shake very well. Strain and add ice. Drop in the cherry.*

**PINK GIN**

2 oz. gin
1-2 dashes Angostura bitters

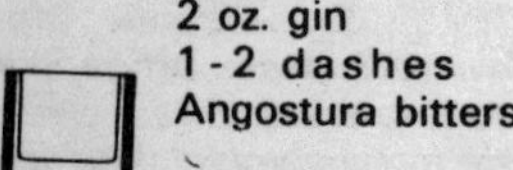

*Pour the bitters into an old-fashioned glass and tip the glass until its sides have been completely coated. Pour in the gin and add ice.*

**PINK LADY**

2 oz. gin
1 oz. lemon juice
1 oz. sugar syrup
½ oz. heavy cream
Several drops grenadine

*Combine with ice; shake very well. Strain and add ice.*

**PINK LEMONADE**

5 oz. rose wine
2 oz. lemon juice
2 oz. orange juice
3 tsp. sugar syrup
2 tsp. kirschwasser

*Combine; stir well and add ice. Decorate with a slice of lemon.*

**PINK PARADISE PUNCH**

1 bottle bourbon
12 oz. apple brandy
8 oz. lemon juice
4 oz. white de cacao
2 tsp. grenadine
4 bottles 7-UP

*Combine everything except the 7-UP;stir well. Add the 7-UP plus chunks of ice before serving.*

**PINK PEARL**

4 oz. grapefruit juice
1 oz. cherry juice
3 tbs. vodka
2 tbs. lime juice

*Combine with ice; shake well. Strain; add ice and decorate with cherry.*

**PINK ROSE**

1 oz. gin
1 tsp. lemon juice
1 tsp. heavy cream
1 egg white
Several drops grenadine

*Combine with ice; shake well. Strain; and add ice.*

**PINK RUM AND TONIC**

2½ oz. white rum
2 tsp. lime juice
1 tsp. grenadine
Tonic water

*Combine everything except the tonic water with ice; shake well. Strain; add ice and fill with tonic. Decorate with lemon.*

## PINK VERANDA

1 oz. gold rum
1½ oz. cranberry juice
2 tsp. Jamaican rum
2 tsp. lime juice
1½ tsp. sugar syrup
½ egg white

*Combine with ice; shake well. Strain and add ice.*

## PINK WHISKERS

1 tbs. apricot brandy
1 tbs. dry vermouth
2 tbs. orange juice
1 tsp. grenadine
A few drops white creme de menthe
1 oz. port

*Combine everything except the port with ice; shake well. Strain; add ice and float the port.*

## PIONEER

2 oz. Jamaican rum
2 tsp. lime juice
A few drops orange curacao
A few drops grenadine

*Combine with ice; shake. Strain and add ice.*

## PIRATES' COCKTAIL

1½ oz. Jamaican rum
1 tbs. sweet vermouth
1-2 dashes Angostura bitters

*Combine with ice; shake well. Strain and add ice.*

## PIROUETTER

1 oz. gin
1 oz. orange juice
2 tsp. Grand Marnier
1 tsp. lemon juice

*Combine with ice; shake well. Strain. Add ice plus a twist of orange.*

## PISCO PUNCH

3 oz. Pisco brandy
1 tsp. lime juice
1 tsp. pineapple juice
A few pineapple cubes

*Combine in a goblet. Add ice and fill with cold water; stir well.*

## PISCO SOUR

2 oz. Pisco brandy
1½ tsp. sugar syrup
1 tsp. lime juice
1 egg white
1-2 dashes Angostura bitters

*Combine everything except the bitters with ice; shake well. Strain; pour straight up and add the bitters.*

---

## PLANTATION COFFEE

1 cup iced coffee
4 oz. brandy
1 small banana, sliced

*Combine in blender at high speed until smooth. Serve straight up.*

## PLANTATION PUNCH

4 oz. dark rum
3 tsp. lemon juice
1 tsp. brown sugar
1 oz. sweet wine
Sprigs of mint
Slices of fruit

*Dissolve the brown sugar with a few drops of water on the bottom of a large tumbler. Fill the tumbler with crushed ice; add the rum and the juice. Stir until the glass begins to frost. Float the wine. Garnish with mint and fruit slices.*

## PLANTER'S PUNCH

1½ oz. Myer's rum
1 oz. lemon juice
1 oz. sugar syrup
1 oz. orange juice
Several drops grenadine

*Combine with ice; shake well. Strain onto crushed ice. Decorate with a cherry plus slices of fruit. Lime juice can be used instead of lemon juice; Angostura bitters instead of the grenadine. You can use two kinds of rum if you'd like. A bittered punch should be touched up with club soda.*

## PLANTER'S PUNCH II

2 oz. Puerto Rican rum
1 oz. Jamaican rum
2 tsp. sugar syrup
1 oz. lime juice
Several drops of Angostura bitters
Club soda

*Combine everything except the soda with ice; shake well. Strain; add ice and fill with soda. Stir. Garnish with fruit.*

## PLAYBOY COOLER

1½ oz. gold rum
1½ oz. coffee liqueur
3 oz. pineapple juice
2 tsp. lemon juice
Cola
1 pineapple slice

*Combine everything except the cola with ice; shake well. Strain; add plenty of ice and fill the glass with cola. Decorate with the pineapple slice.*

## PLAZA MARTINI

1 tbs. dry gin
1 tbs. dry vermouth
1 tbs. sweet vermouth
A few drops pineapple juice

*Combine with ice; shake well. Strain; serve straight up.*

## PLUM APERITIF

1½ oz. dry vermouth
2 tsp. cognac
1 tsp. prunelle

*Combine with ice; shake well. Strain and add ice. Decorate with a slice of lemon.*

## PLUM RICKEY

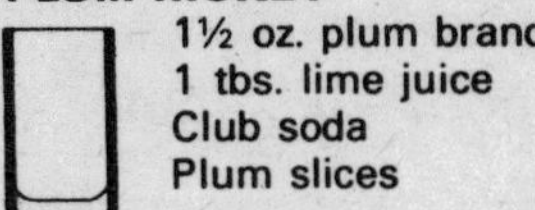

1½ oz. plum brandy
1 tbs. lime juice
Club soda
Plum slices

*Combine the brandy and lime juice. Fill the glass with club soda; stir and add ice. Add a twist of lime. Decorate with plum slices.*

## PLUM WINE

6 lb. plums
3½ lb. sugar
1 oz. yeast, spread on a piece of toast

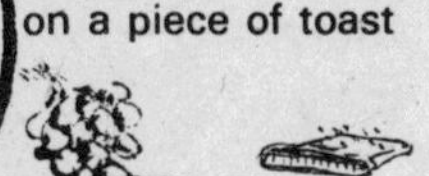

*Slice the plums and place them in a pot with a gal. of boiling water. Stand several days, stirring occasionally. Strain out the juice into another pot; add the sugar and yeast on toast. Store several weeks, until bubbles begin to appear. Transfer to another jar and allow to ferment (the bubbles will stop rising). Strain out into another jar; seal and store in a cool place for at least half a year before bottling for serving.*

## POKER

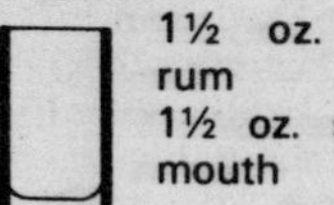

1½ oz. Jamaican rum
1½ oz. sweet vermouth

*Combine with ice; shake well. Strain and add ice.*

## POLISH SIDECAR

¾ oz. gin
¾ oz. lemon juice
1 tbs. blackberry liqueur
Fresh blackberries

*Combine everything except the blackberries with ice; shake well. Strain; and add ice. Float the blackberries.*

## POLLY'S SPECIAL

1 oz. Scotch
2 tsp. Cointreau
2 tsp. grapefruit juice

*Combine with ice; shake well. Strain and add ice.*

## POLLYANNA

2 oz. gin
2 tsp. sweet vermouth
2 tsp. grenadine
Pineapple and orange slices

*Combine everything except the fruit slices with ice; shake well. Strain and add ice. Decorate with the fruit slices.*

## POLO

1 oz. dry gin
2 tsp. lemon juice
2 tsp. orange juice

*Combine with ice; shake well. Strain and add ice.*

## POLONAISE

1½ oz. brandy
2 tsp. dry sherry
2 tsp. blackberry liqueur
1 tsp. lemon juice
1-2 dashes orange bitters

*Combine in a mixing glass filled with ice; shake well. Strain into an old-fashioned glass and add ice.*

## POLYNESIA

1½ oz. white rum
1 oz. passion fruit syrup
1 tsp. lime juice
½ egg white
3 oz. crushed ice

*Combine in blender at a low speed for 15 seconds. Strain; serve straight up.*

## POLYNESIAN APPLE

1¼ oz. apple brandy
1 tbs. pineapple juice
2 tsp. Californian brandy
1 pineapple stick

*Combine everything except the pineapple stick with ice; shake well. Strain and add ice. Decorate with the pineapple.*

## POLYNESIAN COCKTAIL

1½ oz. gin
1 tbs. cherry brandy
3 tsp. lime juice

*Combine with ice; shake well. Line the rim of glass with lime juice and press it in sugar. Strain in the drink and add ice.*

## POLYNESIAN PARADISE

1½ oz. gold rum
1 tbs. lime juice
2 tsp. sweet vermouth
1 tsp. Triple Sec
1 tsp. brown sugar
3 oz. crushed ice

*Combine in blender at a low speed for 15 seconds. Strain; serve straight up.*

## POLYNESIAN SOUR

2 oz. white rum
1 oz. orange juice
1½ tsp. lemon juice
A few drops almond extract
A few drops rock candy syrup
Sprigs of mint

*Combine everything except the mint with ice; shake. Strain over crushed ice; garnish with mint.*

## POMPANO

1 oz. gin
1 oz. grapefruit juice
2 tsp. dry vermouth
Several dashes orange bitters

*Combine with ice; shake well. Strain and add ice. Decorate with a slice of orange.*

## PONCE DE LEON

1½ oz. white rum
2 tsp. mango nectar
2 tsp. grapefruit juice
1 tsp. lemon juice

*Combine with ice; shake well. Strain and add ice.*

## POOP DECK

1 oz. brandy
2 tsp. port
2 tsp. blackberry brandy

*Combine with ice; shake well. Strain; and add ice.*

## POPO E IXTA

1 tbs. Kahlua
1 tsp. tequila

*Combine. Serve straight up; stir well.*

## POPPY

1½ oz. gin
1 tbs. dark creme de cacao

*Combine with ice; shake well. Strain and add ice.*

---

## POR MI AMANTE

*Combine 4 cups of strawberries with a bottle of tequila in a large, tightly capped jar and refrigerate for a month. Strain into another bottle and keep capped. Savor as a liqueur.*

---

## PORT ANTONIO

1 oz. gold rum
2 tsp. Jamaican rum
2 tsp. lime juice
2 tsp. Tia Maria
1 tsp. Falernum

*Combine with ice; shake well. Strain and add ice. Decorate with lime.*

## PORT COBBLER

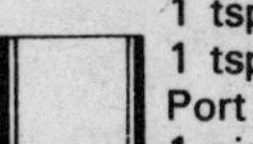

1 tsp. curacao
1 tsp. orange juice
Port
1 pineapple stick

*Fill a tumbler part-way with crushed ice; pour in the orange juice and the curacao and stir well. Fill the glass with port and decorate with the pineapple stick and a slice of orange.*

## PORT LIGHT

2 oz. bourbon
1 oz. lemon juice
2 tsp. passion fruit juice
2 tsp. honey
1 egg white
Mint sprigs
Grenadine

*Combine everything except the mint and the grenadine with ice; shake. Coat the sides of a tumbler with grenadine; add ice and strain in the drink. Garnish with mint.*

## PORT MARIA

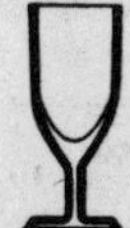

1½ oz. white rum
1 tbs. pineapple juice
2 tsp. lemon juice
1 tsp. Falernum

*Combine with ice; shake well. Strain and add ice. Garnish with nutmeg.*

**PORT SANGAREE**

2 oz. port
½ tsp. powdered sugar
1 tbs. brandy
Club soda

*Dissolve the sugar with a few drops of water; add the port plus ice and fill the glass with club soda. Garnish with nutmeg and float the brandy.*

**PORTALIA**

1½ oz. vodka
1½ oz. dry white port
2 tsp. Campari
Several drops of grenadine

*Combine without ice; stir. Strain straight up.*

**POTTED PARROT**

2 oz. white rum
2 oz. orange juice
1 oz. lemon juice
2 tsp. orange curacao
1 tsp. almond extract
1 tsp. rock candy syrup
Mint sprigs

*Combine everything except the mint with ice; shake. Strain; add ice. Garnish with mint.*

**POULET PUNCH**

1 bottle orange wine
½ bottle sauterne
1 bottle gin
several dashes of Angostura bitters

*Combine; add chunks of ice before serving.*

**POUSSE-CAFES**

POUSSE-CAFES *are usually liqueur drinks, served in many layers without ice in a pousse-cafe glass — tall and narrow. Here is one suggestion: Combine a few drops of maraschino, raspberry syrup, white creme de cacao, curacao, yellow Chartreuse, and brandy in a pousse-cafe glass; carefully and consecutively pouring each ingredient on top of the other so that they do not mix. If you haven't got the patience for so many layers, try simple twos, i.e.: coffee liqueur and sweet cream, dark creme de cacao and sweet cream. Pousse-cafe glasses are sometimes used interchangeably with their smaller cousins, pony glasses, for any liqueur straight up or over crushed ice like a frappe.*

**POWERHOUSE PUNCH**

1 bottle white rum
1 bottle brandy
3 oz. apricot brandy
1 quart lemon juice
8 oz. sugar

*Dissolve the sugar in a quart of water; add the remaining ingredients and stir well until blended. Allow to stand for at least one hour. Add chunks of ice before serving.*

**PRADO**

1½ oz. tequila
1 tbs. lime juice
2 tsp. maraschino
1 tsp. grenadine
½ egg white

*Combine with ice; shake well. Strain; serve straight up. Decorate with a slice of lemon.*

**PREAKNESS**

1½ oz. whiskey
1 tbs. sweet vermouth
Several drops Benedictine
1-2 dashes Angostura bitters

*Combine with ice; shake well. Strain. Add ice plus a twist of lemon.*

**PRESBYTERIAN**

*Pour 2½ ozs. of bourbon into a highball glass; add ice and fill the glass with equal parts ginger ale and club soda.*

**PRESIDENTE**

1½ oz. white rum
1 tbs. dry vermouth
1-2 dashes grenadine
1-2 dashes orange curacao

*Combine with ice; shake well. Strain and add ice.*

**PRESTO**

1½ oz. brandy
1 tbs. sweet vermouth
A few drops orange juice
1-2 dashes Pernod

*Combine with ice; shake well. Strain and add ice.*

**PRIMAVERA**

4 oz. pineapple juice
2 tbs. white rum
½ doz. watercress sprigs

*Slice off and save the leaves of the watercress sprigs; combine them with the juice in a blender at a high speed until the leaves are finely chopped. Pour unstrained; add the rum and fill the glass with ice. Stir well until the glass begins to frost.*

---

**PRINCE**

1¼ oz. whiskey
1-2 dashes orange bitters
A few drops white creme de menthe

*Combine the whiskey and bitters with ice; shake well. Strain and add ice. Float the white creme de menthe.*

**PRINCE EDWARD**

1¾ oz. Scotch
2 tsp. Lillet
1 tsp. Drambuie

*Combine with ice; shake well. Strain and add ice. Decorate with a slice of orange.*

**PRINCE GEORGE'S COCKTAIL**

1½ oz. Bacardi rum
1 tbs. Grand Marnier
2 tsp. lime juice

*Combine with ice; shake well. Strain and add ice; touch it up with a twist of lemon.*

## PRINCE OF WALES

1 oz. Madeira
1 oz. brandy
6 oz. champagne
Several drops curacao
1-2 dashes Angostura bitters

*Combine everything except the champagne with ice; shake well. Strain; and add the champagne. Garnish with a slice of orange.*

## PRINCE REGENCE AU VICTOR'S PUNCH

4 gallons curacao
4 gallons maraschino
1 quart white wine
½ quart kirschwasser
½ quart brandy
Slices of pineapple, oranges, and lemons
Club soda

*Combine all the beverages except the soda. Stir until well-blended. Add the fruit slices plus chunks of ice. Before serving, add an equal amount of club soda as there is existing punch.*

## PRINCE'S SMILE

2 oz. gin
1 oz. calvados
1 oz. apricot brandy
A few drops lemon juice

*Combine with ice; shake well. Strain and add ice.*

## PRINCESS MARY

1 oz. gin
1 oz. white creme de cacao
1 oz. heavy cream

*Combine with ice; shake very well. Strain straight up.*

## PRINCESS MARY'S PRIDE

1½ oz. calvados
1 tbs. Dubonnet
1 tbs. dry vermouth

*Combine with ice; shake well. Strain and add ice.*

## PRINCETON

1½ oz. gin
2 tsp. port
1-2 dashes orange bitters

*Combine with ice; shake well. Strain; add ice and a twist of lemon.*

## PUERTO APPLE

1¼ oz. apple brandy
1 tbs. Puerto Rican Rum
2 tsp. lime juice
1½ tsp. almond extract

*Combine with ice; shake well. Strain and add ice. Decorate with a slice of lime.*

**PUERTO RICAN PINK LADY**

1½ oz. gold rum
1 tbs. lemon juice
1 tsp. grenadine
½ egg white
3 oz. crushed ice

*Combine in blender at a low speed for 15 seconds. Line the rim of a glass with lemon juice and press it in sugar. Strain in the drink straight up.*

**PUMPKIN COACH COCKTAIL**

1 oz. Cesoriac
2 tsp. sweet vermouth
2 tsp. cherry juice

*Combine without ice; stir well. Pour over crushed ice into a small glass. Add a twist of lime.*

**PUNCH ROMAINE**

1 oz. rye
1 oz. Jamaican rum
3 tsp. lemon juice
2 tsp. sugar syrup

*Combine with ice; shake well. Strain and add ice.*

**PUNT E MES NEGRONI**

1 tbs. Punt e Mes
1 tbs. gin
1 tbs. sweet vermouth

*Combine with ice; shake well. Strain; add ice and a twist of lemon.*

**PURPLE COW**

1 oz. blackberry brandy
1 oz. light cream
1 tsp. Almond extract

*Combine with ice; shake. Strain and add plenty of ice.*

**PURPLE PEOPLE EATER**

1½ oz. parfait amour
1½ oz. gin
A few drops of lemon juice

*Combine with ice; shake well. Strain straight up.*

# YOUR OWN RECIPE

# YOUR OWN RECIPE

# YOUR OWN RECIPE

Use a bartender's mixing glass whenever the instructions state "combine" ingredients. Strain the drink from the mixing glass into the drinking glass suggested by the illustration alongside the ingredients.

NOTE: The number of glasses or cups shown alongside a recipe do not necessarily indicate the quantity of drinks the recipe will produce.

---

**QUADRUPLE PINEAPPLE**

6 oz. white rum
3 oz. orange juice
2 tbs. lime juice
2 tsp. maraschino
4 oz. pineapple sherbet
1 large pineapple

*Slice off the top eighth or so of the pineapple with a sharp knife and carefully carve out the meat, leaving the shell intact. Save 4 oz. of the fruit and crush. Combine the crushed fruit with the remaining ingredients in a blender at a low speed for a few seconds.*

**QUARTER DECK**

1½ oz. Jamaican rum
1 tbs. sherry
1 tsp. lime juice

*Combine with ice; shake well. Strain and add ice.*

**QUEBEC**

1½ oz. Canadian whiskey
2 tsp. dry vermouth
1 tsp. Amer Picon
1 tsp. maraschino

*Combine with ice; shake well. Strain and add ice.*

**QUEEN ELIZABETH WINE**

1 oz. dry vermouth
2 tbs. Benedictine
1 tbs. lemon juice

*Combine with ice; shake well. Strain and add ice. Lime juice can be used instead of lemon juice.*

## YOUR OWN RECIPE

Use a bartender's mixing glass whenever the instructions state "combine" ingredients. Strain the drink from the mixing glass into the drinking glass suggested by the illustration alongside the ingredients.

NOTE: The number of glasses or cups shown alongside a recipe do not necessarily indicate the quantity of drinks the recipe will produce.

The glass pictured for each drink is our suggestion; other drinking cups may be used as well.

# R

---

**RACQUET CLUB**

1½ oz. gin
1 tbs. dry vermouth
1-2 dashes orange bitters

*Combine with ice; shake well. Strain and add ice.*

**RAINBOW OLD-FASHIONED**

2 oz. rye
1¼ oz. sugar syrup
1 tsp. cherry juice
A few dashes of Angostura bitters
1 strawberry

*Combine everything except the strawberry; add ice and stir gently. Decorate with the strawberry, a slice of orange, and a cherry. Touch it up with a twist of lemon.*

**RAISIN WINE**

2 lbs. raisins
4 oz. sugar
Cinnamon sticks
A whole ginger chunk

*Combine in a large pot with a gal. of water; boil for several hours. Strain through cheesecloth and allow to stand until cold. Bottle unstrained. This wine can be drunk freshly made (when it will be mild) or stored to ferment longer (when it will be stronger and less sweet).*

**RAMOS GIN FIZZ**

2 oz. gin
2 tsp. lemon juice
2 tsp. sugar
2 tsp. heavy cream
1 tsp. lime juice
1 egg white
A few drops orange flower water
6 oz. crushed ice
Club soda

*Combine everything except the soda in a blender at a high speed for a few seconds. Strain, and fill the glass with soda.*

**RANGIRORA MADNESS**

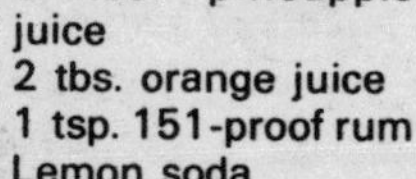

1½ oz. Jamaican rum
2 tbs. pineapple juice
2 tbs. orange juice
1 tsp. 151-proof rum
Lemon soda

*Combine everything (except the 151-proof rum) with ice. Shake. Strain, add plenty of ice and fill with lemon soda. Float the 151-proof rum; decorate with a cherry.*

**RANGOON RUBY**

2 oz. vodka
2 tbs. cranberry juice
½ lime
Club soda

*Combine the vodka and the cranberry juice stir. Squeeze in the juice of the lime and drop in the peel. Add ice and fill with soda. Stir.*

**RASPBERRY CLARET CUP**

4 oz. dry red wine
1 oz. brandy
1 oz. white raspberry brandy
1 oz. lemon juice
1 tbs. raspberry syrup
Club soda
Raspberries

*Thoroughly chill the wine and the brandies before combining them with the raspberry syrup and lemon juice in a tall glass. Stir well and add ice. Fill the glass with soda and float a few raspberries.*

**RASPBERRY COCKTAIL**

8 oz. raspberries, one raspberry left aside
4 oz. gin
4 oz. dry white wine
2 oz. kirsch

*Mash the raspberries in a bowl; pour the gin over them and allow to stand for several hours. Strain the juice and gin with ice; add the wine and kirsch. Shake well. Garnish with a raspberry.*

**RASPBERRY RICKEY**

1½ oz. white raspberry brandy
1 tsp. lime juice
Club soda
Raspberries

*Pour the brandy into a glass; add the lime juice plus ice. Fill the glass with club soda and stir well. Touch it up with a twist of lime; float a few raspberries.*

**RATTLESNAKE**

1½ oz. whiskey
1 tsp. lemon juice
1 tsp. sugar syrup
1 egg white
A few drops Pernod

*Combine with ice; shake extremely well. Strain and add ice.*

**RAYMOND HITCHCOCKTAIL**

3 oz. sweet vermouth
2 oz. orange juice
1-2 dashes orange bitters
1 pineapple slice

*Combine everything except the pineapple slice with ice; shake well. Strain and add ice. Decorate with the pineapple slice.*

**RED APPLE**

1 oz. 100-proof vodka
1 oz. apple juice
2 tsp. lemon juice
2 tsp. grenadine
1-2 dashes orange bitters

*Combine with ice; shake well. Strain and add ice.*

**RED CLOUD**

1½ oz. gin
2 tsp. apricot liqueur
2 tsp. lemon juice
1 tsp. grenadine
1-2 dashes Angostura bitters

*Combine with ice; shake well. Strain into glass and add ice.*

**RED DEVIL**

2 oz. Irish whiskey
1½ oz. clam juice
1½ oz. tomator juice
1 tsp. lime juice
A few drops Worchestershire sauce
A pinch pepper

*Combine with ice; shake gently. Strain straight up.*

**RED GAVILAN**

1 oz. Gavilan tequila
4 oz. tomato juice
A few dashes of Angostura bitters

*Combine with ice; shake well. Strain add ice to fill. Decorate with a lime.*

**RED CIDER WINE**

8 gallon cider
5 lb. honey
2 bottles dark rum
2 lb. sugar
2 lb. beet root
3 oz. red tartar
Sweet marjoran, sweet-briar

*Combine the cider and honey with a gallon and a half of cold water; stir until blended. Seal in a crock pot and allow to ferment. When ready, add the remaining ingredients; stir very well. Strain and bottle for future use.*

**RED LION**

1½ oz. Grand Marnier
1 tbs. gin
2 tsp. orange juice
2 tsp. lemon juice

*Combine with ice; shake well. Strain. Add ice and a twist of lemon.*

**RED WINE COOLER**

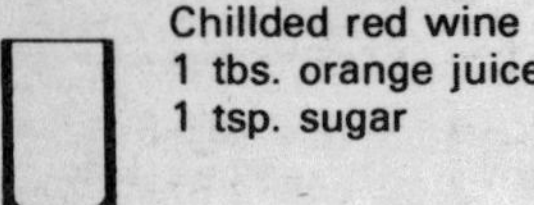

Chillded red wine
1 tbs. orange juice
1 tsp. sugar

*Dissolve the sugar with a teaspoon of water; stir until the sugar is dissolved. Add the orange juice plus ice and fill the glass with wine. Decorate with a slice of lemon.*

**REGENT'S PUNCH**

3 oz. Sauterne
2 tbs. Madeira
1 tbs. Jamaican rum
1 tsp. honey
Hot tea

*Dissolve the honey with a few drops of the hot tea in a large mug; add the Sauterne, rum, and Madeira. Fill the mug with tea and stir very well.*

**REGENT'S PUNCH**

8 oz. white wine
4 oz. Madeira
2 oz. rum
1 pint hot tea

*Combine the wine, Madeira. and rum; and stir well. Pour in the tea ana serve while hot.*

**REMSEN COOLER**

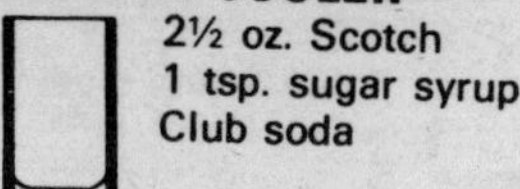

2½ oz. Scotch
1 tsp. sugar syrup
Club soda

*Combine the Scotch and sugar syrup in a tall glass. Add ice and fill the glass with club soda; stir well. Touch it up with a twist of lemon. Gin and ginger ale can be used instead of Scotch and club soda.*

---

**RENAISSANCE**

1½ oz. gin
2 tsp. dry sherry
2 tsp. heavy cream

*Combine with ice; shake very well. Strain and add ice. Garnish with nutmeg.*

**RENDEZVOUS**

1½ oz. gin
2 tsp. kirschwasser
1 tsp. Campari

*Combine with ice; shake well. Strain and add ice. Touch it up with a twist of lemon.*

## REPUBLIC CIDER PUNCH

1 quart hard cider
12 oz. sherry
8 oz. apple brandy
12 tbs. brown sugar
3 tsp. lemon juice
Lemon slices
Grated nutmeg
A slice of toast
1 bottle club soda

*Dust the toast with nutmeg and place it on the bottom of a punch bowl; pile the sugar and lemon slices upon it. Fill the bottom of the bowl with ice, building it around the toast. Carefully add the remaining ingredients, soda last. Stir gently.*

## RESOLUTE

1½ oz. gin
1 tbs. apricot brandy
2 tsp. lemon juice

*Combine with ice; shake well. Strain and add ice.*

## RHETT BUTLER

1½ oz. Southern Comfort
1 tbs. lemon juice
1 tsp. lime juice
1 tsp. curacao
1 tsp. sugar syrup

*Combine with ice; shake well. Strain and add ice.*

## RHINE WINE CUP

1 bottle Rhine wine
2 tsp. Triple Sec
2 tsp. curacao
6 oz. club soda
Fruit slices
1 cucumber peel
A few mint sprigs

*Combine the wine and the liquors; add the club soda plus ice and serve immediately, garnished with the fruit, peel, and mint.*

## RHINE WINE PUNCH

3 quarts Rhine wine
1 pint lemon juice
1 pint dry sherry
8 oz. brandy
8 oz. cold dark tea
8 oz. sugar syrup
1 quart club soda
Cucumber peels

*Combine everything except the club soda and the peels; stir and add chunks of ice. Garnish with the peels and allow to stand at least 15 minutes before removing the peels and adding the soda.*

## RHUBARB WINE

2 gallon bottles white wine
3 oz. rhubarb, sliced
1 oz. ground cardamom seeds
2 tsp ground ginger
1½ pints cooking alcohol

*Combine the rhubarb slices, cardamom, and ginger with the alcohol in a pot; close tightly and allow to stand for several days. Add the wine and bottle for future use.*

**RICHELIEU**

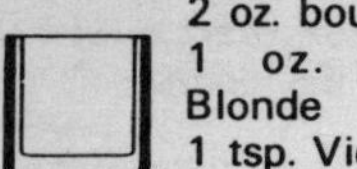

2 oz. bourbon
1 oz. Dubonnet Blonde
1 tsp. Vieille Cure

*Combine with ice; shake well. Strain and add ice. Touch it up: add a twist of orange and drop in the peel.*

**RICKEY**

1½ oz. whiskey
1½ oz. lime juice
Club soda

*Combine the whiskey and the lime juice. Add ice; fill the glass with soda and stir. Touch it up with a twist of lime.*

**RIVER PUNCH**

1 bottle sweet wine
½ doz grapefruit
2 tbs. sugar
Powdered sugar

*Line the rim of a large glass bowl or pitcher with water and press it in the powdered sugar. Squeeze in the juice of the grapefruit; add the tablespoon of sugar plus the wine and stir until the sugar is dissolved.*

**ROBBER COCKTAIL**

1½ oz. Scotch
1 tbs. sweet vermouth
1-2 dashes Angostura bitters

*Combine with ice; shake well. Strain and add ice. Decorate with a cherry. For a* **ROB ROY**, *add an extra oz. of Scotch and a lemon peel.*

**ROBSON**

1 oz. Jamaican rum
2 tsp. grenadine
1 tsp. orange juice
1 tsp. lemon juice

*Combine with ice; shake well. Strain and add ice.*

**ROCK AND RYE COOLER**

1½ oz. vodka
1 oz. rock and rye
2 tsp. lime juice
Lemon soda

*Combine everything except the soda in with ice; shake well. Strain; add ice and fill the glass with soda. Decorate with a slice of lime.*

**ROCK AND RYE TODDY**

2 oz. rock and rye
3 oz. boiling water
1-2 dashes Angostura bitters
Lemon slice

*Combine the rock and rye with the bitters add the lemon slice and pour in the boiling water. Garnish with the cinnamon stick and nutmeg.*

**ROCKY DANE**

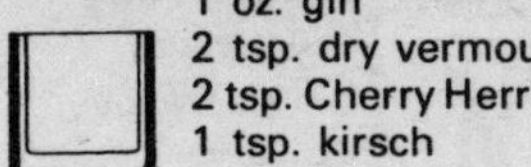

1 oz. gin
2 tsp. dry vermouth
2 tsp. Cherry Herring
1 tsp. kirsch

*Combine with ice; shake well. Strain; add ice and a twist of lemon.*

**ROCKY GREEN DRAGON**

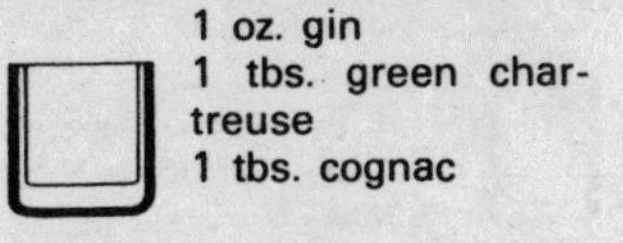

1 oz. gin
1 tbs. green chartreuse
1 tbs. cognac

*Combine with ice; shake well. Strain and add ice.*

**ROFFIGNAC**

3 oz. whiskey
1 tbs. raspberry syrup
Club soda

*Combine the whiskey and the raspberry syrup; stir well. Add ice and fill with soda.*

**ROLLS-ROYCE**

1¼ oz. gin
2 tsp. dry vermouth
2 tsp. sweet vermouth
A few drops Benedictine

*Combine with ice; shake well. Strain and add ice.*

**ROLLS ROYCE A PARIS**

1 oz. Cointreau
1 oz. orange juice
1 tbs. cognac

*Combine with ice; shake and strain. Serve over ice.*

**ROMA**

2½ oz. dry gin
1 tbs. Strega
1 tbs. Amaro

*Combine without ice; stir until well-blended. Pour straight up. Garnish with a slice of orange.*

---

**ROMAN COOLER**

1½ oz. gin
2 tsp. Punt e Mes
2 tsp. lemon juice
1½ tsp. sugar syrup
Club soda

*Combine everything except the soda in with ice; shake well. Strain; add ice and fill the glass with soda. Touch it up with a twist of lime.*

**ROMAN FRULLATI**

3 oz. gin
2 oz. diced apples
2 oz. diced pears
2 oz. sliced peaches
1 oz. maraschino
1 oz. almond extract
4 oz. crushed ice

*Combine in blender at a high speed for 20 seconds. Strain and add ice to the rim.*

**ROMAN PUNCH**

1 quart lemon sherbert
8 oz. Jamican rum

*Combine stir until smooth. Serve immediately.*

**ROMAN SNOWBALL**

2 oz. Sambuca
A few coffee beans

*Pour the Sambuca into a glass filled part-way with crushed ice; garnish with the beans. Chew the beans after they have absorbed the liqueur.*

---

**ROMPOPE**

1 pint white rum
1 dozen egg yolks
1 quart milk
8 oz. sugar
1 vanilla bean

*Combine the milk with the sugar and the bean in a saucepan; heat and stir until well-blended. Remove the bean and allow the sweetened milk to cool. Beat the yolks; add to the milk and reheat until the eggs are cooked. Cool and add the rum. Strain into a bottle; seal well and refrigerate for a few days before serving.*

---

**ROOSEVELT**

2 oz. Haitian rum
1 oz. dry vermouth
2 tsp. orange juice
A few drops sugar syrup

*Combine with ice; shake well. Strain and add ice.*

**ROOT BEER**

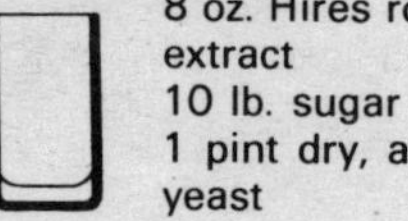

8 oz. Hires root beer extract
10 lb. sugar
1 pint dry, activated yeast

*Dissolve the sugar in 10 gallons of warm water; add the root beer extract and the yeast. Stir until mixed; strain and seal in corked bottles. Store at room temperature for a few days before using. Ice before opening.*

**ROSE**

1 oz. gin
2 tsp. lemon juice
2 tsp. apricot brandy
2 tsp. dry vermouth
1 tsp. grenadine

*Combine with ice; shake well. Strain. Add ice and a twist of lemon.*

**ROSE HALL**

1 oz. Jamaican rum
1 oz. orange juice
2 tsp. banana liqueur
1 tsp. lime juice

*Combine with ice; shake well. Strain and add ice. Decorate with a slice of lime.*

## ROSE LEMONADE

2 bottles chilled rose wine
12 oz. frozen lemonade concentrate
1 quart club soda

*Combine the wine and the lemonade concentrate in a large pitcher; stir until well-blended. Add the club soda plus ice before serving and stir.*

## ROSE OF PICARDY

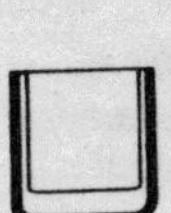

1½ oz. gin
2 tsp. Cherry Kijafa
2 tsp. Dubonnet
1 tsp. dry vermouth

*Combine with ice; shake well. Strain and add ice.*

## ROSEMARY

1½ oz. whiskey
1½ oz. dry vermouth

*Combine with ice; shake well. Strain and add ice.*

---

## ROSY DEACON

2 oz. grapefruit juice
1 oz. sloe gin
1 oz. dry gin
1 pinch powdered sugar

*Combine with ice; shake well. Line the rim of glass with water and press it in powdered sugar. Strain in the drink and add ice.*

## ROTATING PEACHES

1 large peach
Champagne

*Rub the peach with a napkin or paper towel to remove the fuzz; pierce it several times with a fork. Place the peach in a glass goblet; fill the glass with champagne. The peach should float and spin in the glass.*

---

## ROY HOWARD LILLET

1½ oz. Lillet
1 tbs. orange juice
1 tbs. brandy
A few drops grenadine

*Combine with ice; shake well. Strain and add ice.*

## ROYAL CLUB CLOVER

2½ oz. gin
1½ oz. lemon juice
1 tbs. grenadine
1 egg yolk

*Combine with ice; shake extremely well. Strain and add ice.*

## ROYAL COCKTAIL

1½ oz. gin
1½ oz. lemon juice
1½ tsp. sugar syrup
1 egg

*Combine with ice; shake extremely well. Strain and add ice.*

**ROYAL FIZZ**

1¼ oz. gin
1½ tsp. sugar syrup
1½ tsp. lemon juice
1 egg
Club soda

*Combine everything except the soda with ice; shake extremely well. Strain; add ice and fill the glass with soda.*

**ROYAL GIN FIZZ**

2½ oz. gin
2 tbs. lemon juice
2½ tsp. sugar syrup
1 egg
Club soda

*Combine everything except the soda with ice; shake extremely well. Strain; add ice and fill the glass with soda. Decorate with a slice of lemon.*

**ROYAL SMILE**

1½ oz. gin
1½ oz. grenadine
A few drops lemon juice

*Combine with ice; shake well. Strain and add ice.*

**RUBY FIZZ**

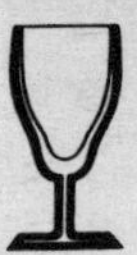

2 oz. sloe gin
1½ tsp. lemon juice
1 tsp. powdered sugar
1 tsp. grenadine
1 egg white
Club soda

*Combine everything except the soda with ice; shake extremely well. Strain; add ice and fill the glass with soda.*

**RUM AND BUTTER**

1 quart Jamaican rum
5 quarts sweet cider
8 oz. brown sugar
8 oz. boiling water
Butter

*Dissolve the brown sugar with the water in a large saucepan; stir until smooth. Add the cider; boil and add the rum. Serve piping hot in mugs. Garnish with cinnamon and top with butter.*

**RUM APERITIF**

1 oz. white rum
1 oz. dry vermouth
2 tsp. lemon juice
1 tsp. Jamaican rum
1 tsp. raspberry syrup

*Combine with ice; shake well. Strain. Add ice and a twist of lemon.*

## RUM BLOODY MARY

1½ oz. Puerto Rican rum
4 oz. tomato juice
1 tbs. lime juice
Several drops of Worchetershire sauce
Several drops of Tabasco sauce
A pinch of salt

*Combine with ice; shake well. Strain straight up.*

---

## RUM BUCK

1½ oz. white rum
2 tsp. lime juice
Roasted almonds
Ginger ale

*Combine the rum and the lime juice with ice; shake well. Strain. Add ice; fill the glass with ginger ale and stir well. Garnish with roasted almonds.*

## RUM CITRUS COOLER

2 oz. white rum
1 oz. orange juice
2 tsp. Cointreau
2 tsp. lime juice
1½ tsp. sugar syrup
7 UP

*Combine everything except the 7-UP in with ice; shake well. Strain; add ice and fill the glass with 7-UP. Decorate with slices of lemon and lime.*

## RUM COCONUT COOLER

2½ oz. white rum
1 oz. cream of coconut
2 tsp. lemon juice
Club soda

*Combine everything except the soda with ice; shake well. Strain and add ice; fill the glass with soda and stir. Decorate with a slice of lemon and a cherry.*

## RUM COCONUT FIZZ

2¼ oz. white rum
2 tsp. cream of coconut
2 tsp. lime juice
Club soda

*Combine everything except the soda with ice; shake well. Strain and add ice; fill the glass with soda and stir. Decorate with a slice of lime.*

## RUM COLLINS

2 oz. white rum
1 tsp. sugar syrup
½ lime
club soda

*Combine the rum and the syrup stir. Squeeze in the juice of the lime,drop in the peel. Add ice and fill with soda; stir. A* **RUM RICKEY** *is a* **RUM COLLINS** *without the sugar.*

## RUM CUIT

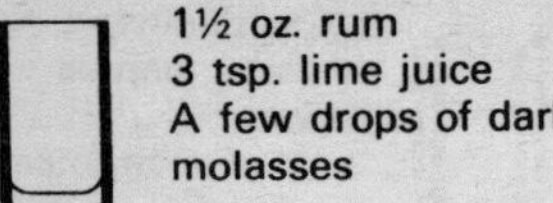

1½ oz. rum
3 tsp. lime juice
A few drops of dark molasses

*Combine with ice; shake very well. Strain into bamboo shoot cups, if you have them — or make them by cutting bamboo tubes just above the joint and fitting them around an appropriate glass.*

## RUM CURACAO COOLER

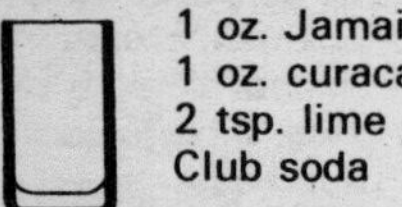

1 oz. Jamaican rum
1 oz. curacao
2 tsp. lime juice
Club soda

*Combine all but the club soda with ice; shake well. Strain and add plenty of ice. Touch it up with club soda and decorate with orange and lime slices.*

## RUM CURE

1 oz. apiece Jamaican, white, and 151-proof rums
1 oz. apiece pineapple, lemon, and orange juice
2 tsp. brandy
2 tbs. grenadine
A few drops of curacao

*Combine everything except the curacao with ice; shake well. Strain over crushed ice. Decorate with slices of fruit and float the curacao.*

## RUM DOUBLOON

1 oz. apiece Jamaican rum, white rum, and 151-proof rum
1 oz. grapefruit juice
1 oz. orange juice
A few drops of orange curacao
A few drops of Pernod

*Combine with ice; shake. Strain with crushed ice. Decorate with an orange slice and a cherry.*

## RUM DUBONNET

1½ oz. white rum
1 tbs. Dubonnet
1 tsp. lime juice

*Combine with ice; shake well. Strain. Add ice and a twist of lemon.*

## RUM FLIP

4 oz. rum
½ tbs. powdered sugar
1 egg

*Combine in a saucepan; heat well and stir. Serve piping hot. Heavy brandies or port can be used instead of the rum.*

## RUM FRAPPE

2 oz. white rum
2 tbs. lemon sherbet

*Combine and stir gently until smooth.*

## RUM FUSTIAN

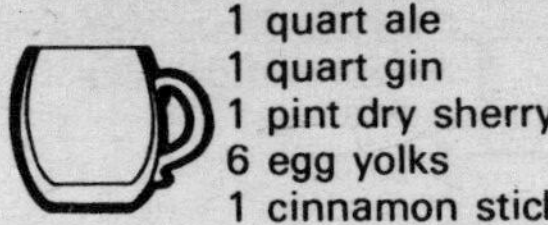

1 quart ale
1 quart gin
1 pint dry sherry
6 egg yolks
1 cinnamon stick

*Combine the yolks, ale, and gin in a large bowl and beat well. Set aside. Pour the sherry into a saucepan; add the cinnamon stick plus nutmeg and a twist of lemon and bring to a boil. Remove from heat; strain clean and combine with egg mixture. Serve piping hot in mugs.*

## RUM MARTINI

2 oz. white rum
A few drops dry vermouth

*Pour the rum with vermouth and stir gently. Touch it up with a twist of lime. Decorate with an olive or a cocktail onion.*

## RUM MINT SQUASH

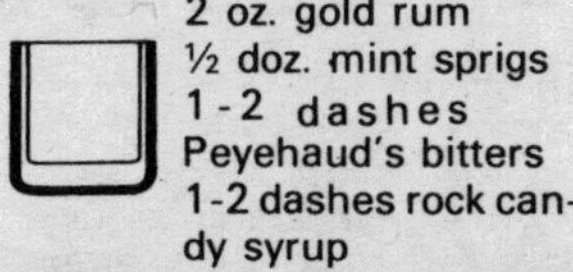

2 oz. gold rum
½ doz. mint sprigs
1-2 dashes Peyehaud's bitters
1-2 dashes rock candy syrup

*Muddle the mint with the bitters and candy syrup in an oz. of cold water; turn out into an old-fashioned glass. Add ice and rum; stir briskly. Touch it up with a twist of lemon.*

## RUM MOCHA

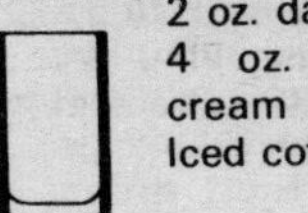

2 oz. dark rum
4 oz. vanilla ice cream
Iced coffee

*Combine the rum and the ice cream, stir until smooth. Add crushed ice and fill with iced coffee.*

## RUM PINEAPPLE FIZZ

2 oz. gold rum
3 oz. diced pineapple
2 tsp. 151-proof rum
2 tsp. lemon juice and lime juice
1½ tsp. sugar syrup
½ egg white
4 oz. crushed ice
Club soda

*Combine everything except the soda in a blender at a low speed for 15 seconds. Strain; fill the glass with ice and touch it up with a spritz of soda. Decorate with a slice of lime.*

## RUM PUNCH

1 bottle Jamaican rum
8 oz. lime juice
4 cups cold strng tea
Vanilla beans

*Steep a few vanilla beans in the bottle of rum for several hours, then combine the rum with the remaining ingredients in a large punch bowl and stir. Add ice before serving. (The ice should be made out of tea.)*

## RUM PUNCH FOR ONE

2 oz. dark rum
2 tsp. lime juice
2 tsp. sugar syrup
1 tsp. grenadine
A few drops of curacao

*Combine with ice; shake well. Strain over crushed ice. Decorate with slices of fruit.*

## RUM ROYALE

1 oz. white rum
2 oz. sauterne
2 oz. pineapple juice
2 tbs. lemon juice
1½ tsp. sugar syrup
1-2 dashes Peychaud's bitters
1 pineapple chunk

*Combine everything except the pineapple chunk with ice; shake well. Strain and add plenty of ice. Decorate with the pineapple chunk.*

## RUM SANGRIA PUNCH

1 bottle dry red wine
8 oz. Puerto Rican rum
8 oz. sugar
A large can of slices peaches
Slices of orange and lime

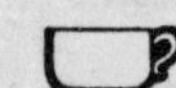

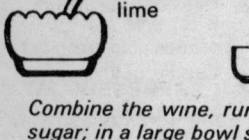

*Combine the wine, rum, and sugar; in a large bowl stil until the sugar has completely dissolved. Add the fruit slices, squeezing out a little of the juice as you go along. Add the peach slices syrup; stir well. Add ice.*

## RUM SCREWDRIVER

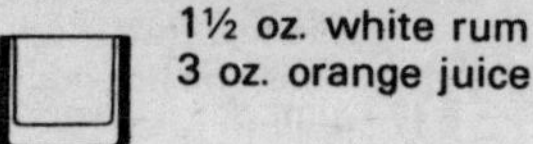

1½ oz. white rum
3 oz. orange juice

*Combine with ice; shake well. Strain and add ice. Decorate with a slice of orange.*

## RUM SHAKE

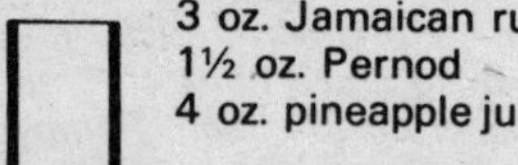

3 oz. Jamaican rum
1½ oz. Pernod
4 oz. pineapple juice

*Combine with ice; shake well. Strain, add ice.*

## RUM SHRUB

4 quarts Jamaican rum
3 pints orange juice
1 lb. sugar cubes

*Combine in a large pot; seal tightly and steep for several weeks. Strain and store well-capped.*

## RUM SOUR

2 oz. gold rum
2 tsp. lemon juice
1 tsp. orange juice
1 tsp. sugar syrup

*Combine with ice; shake well. Strain straight up. Decorate with a slice of lemon. A teaspoon of 151-proof rum may be used to top it off.*

**RUM SWIRL**

1 oz. white rum
2 oz. banana liqueur
1 tsp. lime juice

*Combine with ice; shake well. Strain and add ice.*

**RUM SWIZZLE**

3 oz. dark rum
2 tsp. water
1-2 dashes Angostura bitters

*Combine with ice; shake well. Strain with crushed ice; stir until the glass begins to frost. Drink in one gulp.*

**RUM TEA**

3-4 oz. Jamaican rum
1 pot of hot tea
Whole cinnamon sticks, whole cloves, and nutmeg
Sprigs of mint

*Steep the spices in the tea for several minutes; add the rum when ready to serve.*

**RUMRUNNER**

1½ oz. white rum
1 tbs. orange juice
2 tsp. lime juice
1½ tsp. sugar syrup
1-2 dashes orange bitters

*Combine with ice; shake well. Strain. Add ice and a twist of orange.*

**RUSSIAN BEAR**

1 oz. vodka
2 tsp. white creme de cacao
2 tsp. heavy cream

*Combine with ice; shake very well. Strain and add ice.*

**RUSSIAN COCKTAIL**

¾ oz. gin
¾ oz. vodka
1 tbs. white creme de cacao

*Combine with ice; shake well. Strain and add ice.*

**RUSSIAN COFFEE**

¾ oz. vodka
¾ oz. coffee liqueur
¾ oz. heavy cream
3 oz. crushed ice

*Combine in blender at a low speed for 15 seconds. Strain straight up.*

**RUSSIAN ESPRESSO**

1½ oz. vodka
2 tsp. espresso coffee liqueur
Several drops lemon juice

*Combine with ice; shake well. Strain. Add ice and a twist of lemon.*

## RUSTY NAIL

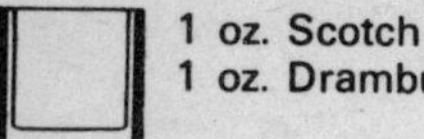

1 oz. Scotch
1 oz. Drambuie

*Combine; add ice and stir.*

---

## RYE AND DRY

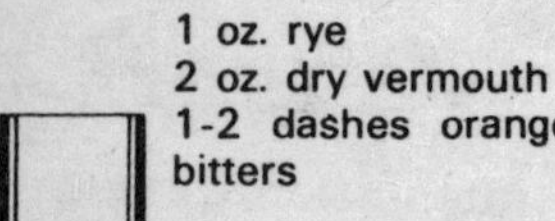

1 oz. rye
2 oz. dry vermouth
1-2 dashes orange bitters

*Combine with ice; shake well. Strain and add ice.*

## RYE COCKTAIL

2 oz. rye
1 tsp. sugar syrup
1-2 dashes Angostura bitters

*Combine with ice; shake well. Strain and add ice.*

## RYE FLIP

1¼ oz. rye
1 egg
1 tsp. sugar syrup

*Combine with ice; shake extremely well. Strain straight up. Garnish with nutmeg.*

# YOUR OWN RECIPE

## YOUR OWN RECIPE

Use a bartender's mixing glass whenever the instructions state "combine" ingredients. Strain the drink from the mixing glass into the drinking glass suggested by the illustration alongside the ingredients.

# S

NOTE: The number of glasses or cups shown alongside a recipe do not necessarily indicate the quantity of drinks the recipe will produce.

The glass pictured for each drink is our suggestion; other drinking cups may be used as well.

---

## SACK POSSET

½ pint sherry
½ pint ale
1 quart milk

*Combine the ale and the sherry in a saucepan and bring to a boil. Heat the milk in a separate saucepan and then combine it with the sherry and the ale. Sweeten to taste; add nutmeg and warm over low heat for a few hours. Serve while still warm in large mugs.*

## ST. AUGUSTINE

1½ oz. white rum
1 oz. grapefruit juice
1 tsp. Cointreau

*Combine with ice; shake well. Line the rim of glass with water and press it in sugar. Strain in the drink. Add ice and a twist of lemon.*

## ST. CROIX MILK PUNCH

1 oz. Jamaican rum
1 oz. cognac
1 oz. gin
Sugar
Milk
Nutmeg
1-2 dashes Angostura bitters

*Combine the rum, cognac, and gin. Warm enough milk to balance out the mug; combine with the liquors and sweeten to taste. Add the bitters and stir very well. Serve warm, garnished with nutmeg.*

## ST. LOU

1½ oz. gin
2 tsp. lemon juice
2 tsp. calvados
1½ tsp. sugar syrup

*Combine with ice; shake well.*

## ST. RAPHAEL AND VODKA

3 oz. St. Raphael
2 tbs. vodka
Club soda

*Combine the St. Raphael and vodka in a small goblet; add ice and stir gently. Touch it up with a spritz of soda and a twist of lemon.*

## SAKETINI

2 oz. gin
2 tsp. saki

*Combine with ice; shake well. Strain straight up and decorate with an olive.*

## SALTY DOG

*Line the rim of an old-fashioned glass with water and press it in salt. Pour in 2 oz. of vodka; add ice and fill the glass with grapefruit juice. Stir well. Serve with a salt shaker on the side.*

---

## SAMBUCA COFFEE FRAPPE

1 oz. sambuca
2 tsp. coffee liqueur
Roasted coffee beans

*Combine the sambuca and the liqueur without ice; stir well. Pour over crushed ice. Serve with a few coffee beans on a saucer.*

## SAN FRANCISCO

¾ oz. sloe gin
1 tbs. dry vermouth
1 tbs. sweet vermouth
1-2 dashes Angostura bitters and orange bitters

*Combine with ice; shake well. Strain and add ice. Decorate with a cherry.*

## SAN JUAN

1½ oz. Puerto Rican rum
1 oz. grapefruit juice
2 tsp. lime juice
2 tsp. 151-proof rum
1 tsp. cream of coconut
3 oz. crushed ice

*Combine everything except the high-proofed rum in a blender at a low speed for 15 seconds. Strain straight up; float the rum.*

---

## SAN MARTIN

1 tbs. dry gin
1 tbs. dry vermouth
1 tbs. sweet vermouth
1 tsp. anisette
1-2 dashes Angostura bitters

*Combine with ice; shake well. Line the rim of glass with water and press it in sugar. Strain in the drink and add ice.*

**SAN SEBASTIAN**

1 oz. gin
2 tsp. grapefruit juice
2 tsp. lemon juice
1 tsp. 151-proof rum
1 tsp. curacao

*Combine with ice; shake well. Strain and add ice.*

**SANCTUARY**

1½ oz. Dubonnet
1 tbs. Cointreau
1 tbs. Amer Picon

*Combine with ice; shake well. Strain and add ice.*

---

**SANGAREE COMFORT**

1 oz. Southern Comfort
1 oz. bourbon
1 tsp. peach brandy
1 tsp. lemon juice
1 tsp. sugar syrup
Club soda

*Combine everything except the soda with ice; shake well. Strain, add ice and touch it up with a spritz of soda. Garnish with nutmeg.*

**SAN'GRIA CALIFORNIA STYLE**

2 gallons zinfandel
2 cups lemon juice
8 oz. brandy
8 oz. sugar
4 oz. Strega
2 quarts orange juice
2 quarts club soda
Orange and lemon slices

*Dissolve the sugar with the orange and lemon juices and stir until the sugar is dissolved. Add everything else except the soda and the fruit slices; stir well. Add the soda and fruit plus chunks of ice before serving.*

**SAN'GRIA PUNCH**

1 bottle Spanish red wine
4 oz. sugar syrup, fresh and still hot
1 orange and 1 lime, thinly sliced

*Place the sliced fruit in a punch bowl and pour the sugar syrup over it; allow to stand for several hours. Combine the steeped fruit and sugar with the wine in a pitcher; add ice and stir.*

**SANGUENAY**

1 oz. white rum
1 oz. dry vermouth
2 tsp. creme de cassis
1 tsp. lemon juice

*Combine with ice; shake well. Strain and add ice.*

**SANO GROG**

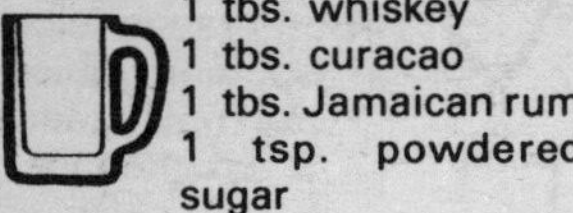

1 tbs. whiskey
1 tbs. curacao
1 tbs. Jamaican rum
1 tsp. powdered sugar

*Combine in a mug. Fill with boiling water.*

**SANTA FE**

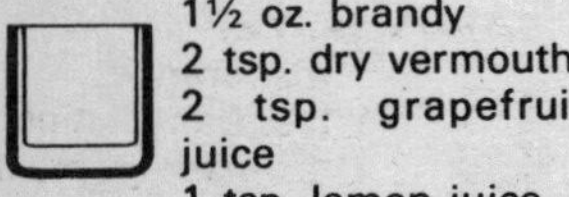

1½ oz. brandy
2 tsp. dry vermouth
2 tsp. grapefruit juice
1 tsp. lemon juice

*Combine with ice; shake well. Strain and add ice.*

**SANTIAGO**

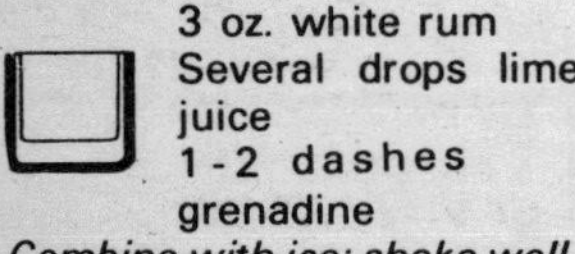

3 oz. white rum
Several drops lime juice
1-2 dashes grenadine

*Combine with ice; shake well. Strain and add ice.*

**SAP BUCKET SPECIAL**

2 oz. dark rum
1 oz. lemon juice
2 tsp. maple syrup

*Warm the maple syrup in a ladle over a low flame; combine it with the rum and juice in a warmed wine glass straight up. Stir gently until well-blended.*

**SARATOGA**

2½ oz. brandy
1 tsp. crushed pineapple
1-2 dashes maraschino
1-2 dashes Angostura bitters

*Combine with ice; shake well. Strain and add ice. A half-teaspoon of pineapple syrup can be used instead of the crushed pineapple.*

**SARA'S SPECIAL**

1½ oz. Amontillado
2 tbs. sweet vermouth

*Combine, stir gently. Touch it up with a twist of lemon and add ice.*

**SASSAFRAS MEAD**

4 large bunches sassafras roots
3½ pints molasses
3 cups honey
1 tbs. cream of tartar
Baking soda

*Boil the sassafras roots in 2 quarts of water; strain clean. Boil the tea in a separate pot; add the molasses,honey, and tartar. Stir well. Allow to cool and strain. Bottle and store for 24 hours before use. To serve: Combine 1 tbs. mead with a tall glass of cold water; add ½ tsp. soda and stir.*

### SAUCY SUE

2 oz. apple brandy
Several drops apricot brandy
Several drops Pernod

*Combine with ice; shake well. Strain and add ice. A* **SAUCY SUE** *can also be made with equal parts plain and apple brandies, with less apricot brandy and Pernod and a twist of orange.*

### SAUTERNE CUP

2 bottles sauterne
2 tbs. brandy, curacao, and maraschino
½ pint club soda

*Combine; stir gently and serve in a bed of crushed ice. Garnish with fruit slices.*

---

### SAUTERNE PUNCH

1 bottle Sauterne
1 quart orange juice
1 pint pineapple juice
8 oz. lemon juice
1 bottle club soda

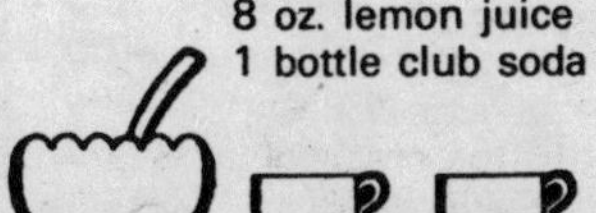

*Combine everything except the soda; stir. Add the soda plus chunks of ice before serving.*

---

### SAUZALIKY

2 oz. tequila
4 oz. orange juice
1 tsp. lemon juice
1 very ripe banana
3 oz. crushed ice

*Combine in blender at a high speed for 15 seconds. Strain straight up. Serves two.*

### SAVOY HOTEL

1 tbs. brandy
1 tbs. Benedictine
1 tbs. dark creme de cacao

*Pour each ingredient into a pony or pousse cafe glass, carefully and one at a time, floating each upon the one beneath it.*

### SAVOY TANGO

1½ oz. apple brandy
2 tbs. sloe gin

*Combine with a few ice cubes; stir to chill. Strain straight up.*

### SAZ

2 oz. bourbon
Several dashes Peychaud's bitters
A few drops Pernod

*Combine the bourbon and the bitters with ice; shake well. Pour the Pernod into a freezing cold glass and tilt the glass around until the Pernod has coated its sides. Strain in the drink straight up and touch it up with a twist of lemon.*

## SAZERAC

2 oz. whiskey
1 tsp. sugar syrup
A few drops Pernod
1-2 dashes Peychaud's bitters

*Combine the whiskey, sugar and bitters with ice; shake well. Pour the Pernod into a freezing-cold glass and tilt the glass until the Pernod has coated its sides. Strain in the drink. Add ice and a twist of lemon.*

## SCAFFAS

*A* **SCAFFA** *is a combination of Benedictine and gin, rum, or whiskey — equal parts served straight up in a small glass with a dash or two of Angostura bitters.* **BRANDY SCAFFAS** *are made with maraschino instead of Benedictine.*

## SCANDIA

2 oz. aquavit
1 oz. lime juice
2 tsp. grenadine

*Combine with ice; shake well. Strain straight up.*

## SCARLETT O'HARA

1½ oz. Southern Comfort
½ peach, soaked in brandy
3 tsp. lime juice
Several marashino cherries
3 oz. crushed ice

*Combine in blender at a high speed for 15 seconds. Strain straight up.*

## SCANDANAVIAN GLOGG

1 bottle vodka
1 bottle red wine
1 cup sugar cubes
1 cup blanched almonds
1 cup raisins
Grated orange peels
Dried figs
Cardamon seeds
Cinnamon sticks
Whole cloves

*Combine everything except the sugar cubes in a large saucepan; heat thoroughly but do not allow to boil. Lower heat and simmer for several minutes. Pile the sugar cubes on a large ladle; dip quickly in the glogg and ignite. Pour the burning sugar into the glog; stir well. Serve at once in mugs.*

## SCANDANAVIAN GLOGG II

2 quarts red wine
1 pint apiece port, vodka, rye, and cognac
4 oz. dry vermouth
1 cup blanched almonds
1 cup raisins
Cloves, anise, and fennel seeds
Sugar
Grated orange peels, cinnamon sticks, cardamom seeds

*Tie the spices into a cloth sack; soak in a bowl with the wine, port, vermouth, raisins, and nuts overnight. When ready, heat, add sugar to taste, and stir until the sugar has dissolved. Simmer a few minutes, remove from heat; add the vodka, rye, and cognac. Re-heat but do not allow to boil. Remove spices and ignite. Serve hot.*

## SCARLETT O'HARA NO. 2

1½ oz. Southern Comfort
1½ oz. cranberry juice
½ tsp. lime juice

*Combine with ice; shake well. Strain and add ice.*

## SCHUSSBOOMER'S DELIGHT

1½ oz. cognac
1 tbs. lemon juice
Champagne

*Combine the cognac and the lemon juice and add ice. Fill the glass with champagne and stir.*

## SCORPION

2 oz. white rum
2 oz. orange juice
1 oz. California brandy
2 tbs. lemon juice
2 tsp. almond extract
3 oz. crushed ice

*Combine in blender at a low speed for 15 seconds. Strain and add ice. Decorate with a slice of orange.*

## SCOTCH AND VODKA

2½ oz. vodka
2 tsp. dry vermouth
A few drops of Scotch

*Combine without ice; stir until well-blended. Pour straight up. Touch it up with a twist of lemon.*

**SCOTCH COBBLER**

2 oz. Scotch
½ tsp. curacao
½ tsp. brandy

*Combine over ice. Decorate with a slice of lemon and/or mint.*

**SCOTCH COOLER**

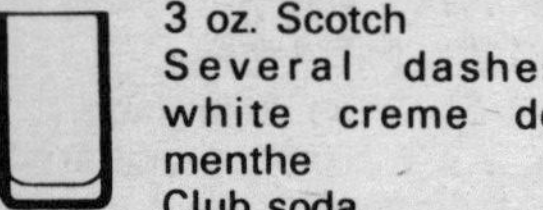

3 oz. Scotch
Several dashes white creme de menthe
Club soda

*Combine the Scotch and the creme de menthe and stir; add ice and fill the glass with soda.*

---

**SCOTCH EGGNOG**

1 bottle Scotch
3 cups milk
1 doz. egg yolks
1 pint heavy cream
8 oz. powdered sugar
Grated nutmeg

*Combine the egg yolks and the sugar in a bowl, beat together until creamy. Slowly add the Scotch, stirring constantly. Allow to stand several minutes; add the milk and refrigerate several hours. Just before serving, whip the cream and fold it into the nog. Garnish with nutmeg. Whole eggs, separated, can be used. Beat the whites until stiff and fold in after the whipped cream.*

**SCOTCH FLING**

2 oz. Scotch
1 tsp. lime juice
Ginger ale

*Combine the Scotch and the juice with ice; shake well. Strain, add ice and fill the glass with ginger ale.*

**SCOTCH FLIP**

2 oz. Scotch
1 egg white
2 tsp. sugar syrup
Club soda

*Combine the Scotch, egg white, and syrup with ice; shake well. Strain and add ice. Fill with soda.*

**SCOTCH HOLIDAY SOUR**

2 oz. Scotch
1 oz. cherry liqueur
1 oz. lemon juice
2 tsp. sweet vermouth
½ egg white

*Combine with ice; shake well. Strain, serve straight up. Decorate with a slice of lemon.*

**SCOTCH MILK PUNCH**

*Pour 2 oz. of Scotch into a highball glass; fill with milk. Add sugar to taste plus ice and stir very well. Garnish with nutmeg.*

**SCOTCH MIST**

*Pour 1½ oz. of Scotch into an old-fashioned glass packed with crushed ice. Touch it up with a twist of lemon. Other whiskeys can be used instead of Scotch.*

**SCOTCH ORANGE FIX**

2 oz. Scotch
2 tsp. lemon juice
1 tsp. sugar
1 tsp. curacao
1 spiraled orange peel

*Dissolve the sugar with 2 teaspoons of water. Drop in the peel; add the Scotch and the lemon juice and stir. Fill the glass with crushed ice and float the curacao on top.*

**SCOTCH SANGAREE**

2 oz. Scotch
A few drops honey
Club soda

*Combine the honey with the Scotch and stir until the honey is dissolved; add plenty of ice. Touch up with a spritz of soda and a twist of lemon. Garnish with nutmeg.*

**SCOTCH SAZ**

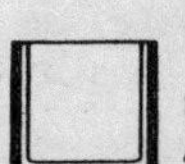

1½ oz. Scotch
1 tsp. sweet vermouth
A few drops Pernod

*Combine with ice; shake well. Strain, add ice.*

**SCOTCH SMASH**

1½ oz. Scotch
1 tsp. sugar syrup
Club soda
A few mint sprigs

*Muddle the mint with the sugar syrup; pour in the Scotch. Add ice; fill the glass with soda and stir. Decorate with slices of fruit.*

**SCOTCH SOUR**

2 oz. Scotch
2 tsp. lime juice
1 tsp. powdered sugar
Club soda

*Combine everything except the soda in with ice; shake well. Strain straight up; add a spritz of soda and decorate with a slice of orange and a cherry.*

**SCOTS GUARD**

2 oz. Canadian whiskey
2 tbs. orange juice
1 tbs. lemon juice
1 tsp. grenadine

*Combine with ice; shake well. Strain and add ice.*

**SCUPPERNONG WINE**

*Follow the recipe for* **MUSCADINE WINE,** *substituting scuppernong juice for the muscadine juice.*

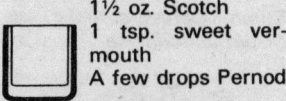

## SEA CAPTAIN'S SPECIAL

1½ oz. rye
1 cube sugar
Several dashes Angostura bitters
A few drops Pernod
Champagne

*Dissolve the sugar with the bitters. Add the rye plus ice and fill the glass with champagne; stir. Float the Pernod.*

## SEABOARD

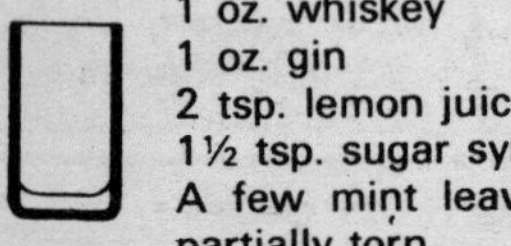

1 oz. whiskey
1 oz. gin
2 tsp. lemon juice
1½ tsp. sugar syrup
A few mint leaves, partially torn

*Combine everything except the mint with ice; shake well. Strain and add ice. Decorate with mint.*

---

## SECRET

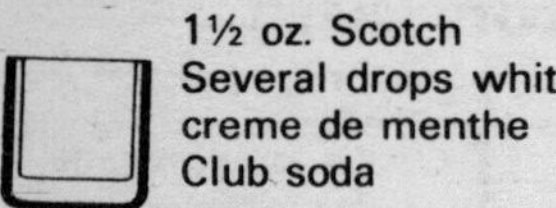

1½ oz. Scotch
Several drops white creme de menthe
Club soda

*Combine the Scotch and the creme de menthe with ice; shake well. Strain, add ice and fill the glass with soda.*

---

## SELF-STARTER

1 oz. gin
2 tsp. Lillet
1 tsp. apricot brandy
A few drops Pernod

*Combine with ice; shake well. Strain and add ice.*

## SEPTEMBER MORN

1½ oz. white rum
2 tsp. lime juice
1 tsp. grenadine
½ egg white

*Combine with ice; shake well. Line the rim of a glass with grenadine and press it in sugar. Strain in the drink and add ice.*

## SERPENT'S TOOTH

1½ oz. sweet vermouth
2 tbs. lemon juice
1 tbs. Irish whiskey
2 tsp. kummel
1-2 dashes Angostura bitters

*Combine with ice; shake well. Strain and add ice.*

## SESAME

1½ oz. white rum
2 tsp. lime juice
2 tsp. sesame syrup

*Combine with ice; shake well. Strain and add ice.*

## SEVILLA

1 oz. Jamaican rum
1 oz. sweet vermouth

*Combine with ice; shake well. Strain and add ice.*

**SEVILLA FLIP**

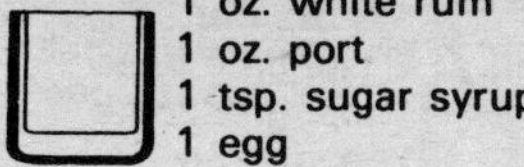

1 oz. white rum
1 oz. port
1 tsp. sugar syrup
1 egg

*Combine with ice; shake well. Strain and add ice.*

**SEVILLE**

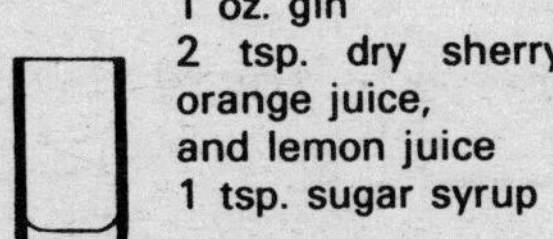

1 oz. gin
2 tsp. dry sherry, orange juice, and lemon juice
1 tsp. sugar syrup

*Combine with ice; shake well. Line the rim of a glass with water and press it in sugar. Strain in the drink and add ice.*

**SHAMROCK**

1 oz. Irish whiskey
1 oz. dry vermouth
Several drops of green creme de menthe
Several dashes of green chartreuse

*Combine with ice; shake well. Strain and decorate with an olive. The Irish whiskey can be augmented at the expense of the green Chartreuse.*

**SHANGHAI**

1½ oz. Jamaican rum
1 tbs. lemon juice
2 tsp. anisette
A few drops grenadine

*Combine with ice; shake well. Strain and add ice.*

**SHANGHAI PUNCH**

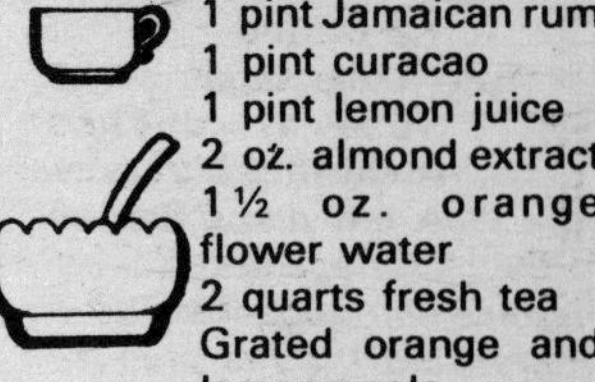

1 bottle cognac
1 pint Jamaican rum
1 pint curacao
1 pint lemon juice
2 oz. almond extract
1½ oz. orange flower water
2 quarts fresh tea
Grated orange and lemon peels
Cinnamon sticks

*Make sure the tea is boiling hot before combining it with the other ingredients in a large punch bowl. Stir serve while still hot.*

---

**SHARK'S TOOTH**

2½ oz. gold rum
2 tsp. lemon juice
½ lime
1-2 dashes grenadine
A few drops rock candy syrup
Club soda
Mint sprigs

*Combine everything except the lime and the mint with ice; shake well. Strain; add ice and fill with soda. Squeeze in the juice of the lime; stir gently. Garnish with mint.*

**SHARK'S TOOTH**

1½ oz. gold rum
1 tsp. lemon juice, passion fruit syrup, sweet vermouth, and sloe gin
1-2 dashes Angostura bitters

*Combine with ice; shake well. Line the rim of glass with water and press it in sugar; strain in the drink.*

**SHARKY PUNCH**

1½ oz. calvados
2 tsp. rye
1 tsp. sugar syrup
Club soda

*Combine everything except the soda with ice; shake well. Strain and add ice. Touch it up with a spritz of soda.*

**SHERMAN**

1 oz. sweet vermouth
2 tsp. whiskey
Several drops Pernod
1-2 dashes Angostura and orange bitters

*Combine and stir well; add ice.*

**SHERRIED COFFEE**

1½ oz. cream sherry
1½ oz. coffee liqueur
2 tsp. light cream

*Combine the sherry and the coffee liqueur with ice; shake well. Strain and add ice. Float the cream.*

**SHERRIED CORDIAL MEDOC FRAPPE**

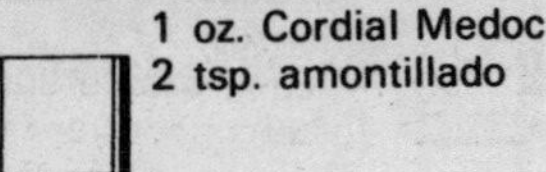

1 oz. Cordial Medoc
2 tsp. amontillado

*Combine without ice; stir well. Pour over crushed ice.*

**SHERRY COBBLER**

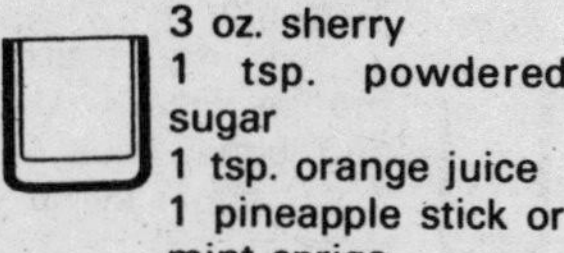

3 oz. sherry
1 tsp. powdered sugar
1 tsp. orange juice
1 pineapple stick or mint sprigs

*Stir the sherry, sugar, and juice together without ice; pour over crushed ice in a small goblet. Decorate with the pineapple stick or mint — and a slice of orange.*

**SHERRY COBBLER**

16 oz. sherry
1 quart lemonade

*Combine in a large pitcher; stir well. Pour over crushed ice. Garnish each with a twist of lemon.*

**SHERRIED SCOTCH**

1½ oz. Scotch
1 oz. orange juice
2 tbs. cream sherry
1 tsp. honey
A few dashes of Angostura bitters
1 cinnamon stick

*Combine everything except the cinnamon stick and the bitters into a saucepan; heat and stir until the honey is dissolved and the drink is ready to boil. Add the bitters and pour into a large mug. Garnish with the cinnamon and a slice of orange. Serve piping hot.*

## SHERRY SURPRISE

1 bottle cream sherry
¾ cup frozen orange juice concentrate

*Dilute the orange juice concentrate in 6 oz. of water; combine with the sherry in a large pitcher and refrigerate; stir gently.*

## SHERRY TWIST

1½ oz. sherry
2 tsp. dry vermouth
2 tsp. brandy
Several drops Cointreau
A few drops lemon juice
1 cinnamon stick

*Combine everything except the cinnamon stick with ice; shake well. Strain and add ice. Garnish with cinnamon.*

## SHERRY TWIST PUNCH

8 oz. sherry
6 oz. whiskey
4 oz. orange juice
2 tbs. Cointreau
1 tbs. lemon juice
2 cloves
1 pinch cayenne pepper

*Combine; shake well. Strain over ice. Serves 4-6.*

## SIDECAR

2 oz. brandy
2 tsp. Cointreau
2 tsp. lemon juice

*Combine with ice; shake well. Strain and add ice.*

## SILVER DOLLAR

1 oz. creme de banana
1 oz. white creme de menthe
1 oz. light cream

*Combine with ice. Strain straight up.*

## SILVER KING

1½ oz. gin
1½ oz. lemon juice
1 egg white
A few drops sugar syrup
1-2 dashes orange bitters

*Combine with ice; shake well. Strain and add ice.*

## SILVER KIRSCH

1 oz. kirsch
2 tbs. Positano
2 tsp. lemon juice
1½ tsp. sugar syrup
½ egg white
3 oz. crushed ice

*Combine in a blender at a high speed for 10 seconds. Strain straight up.*

## SILVER STALLION

1 oz. gin
1 oz. vanilla ice cream
2 tbs. lemon juice
Club soda

*Combine everything except the soda; stir until the ice cream has melted. Add ice and shake very well. Strain; add ice and fill the glass with soda.*

## SINGAPORE

1½ oz. Canadian whiskey
2 tsp. lemon juice
1 tsp. Rose's lime juice
1 tsp. sloe gin
1 cucumber peel

*Combine everything except the peel with ice; shake well. Strain and add ice. Decorate with the peel.*

---

## SINGAPORE SLING

2 oz. gin
1 oz. Cherry Herring
½ lime
1-2 dashes Angostura bitters
A few drops of Benedictine
Ginger beer

*Combine the gin, Cherry Herring, and bitters with ice; shake well. Strain; add ice. Squeeze on the juice of lime; drop in the peels; stir gently; add beer to fill the glass and float the Benedictine.*

## SINK OR SWIM

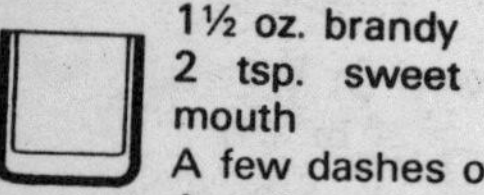

1½ oz. brandy
2 tsp. sweet vermouth
A few dashes of Angostura bitters

*Combine with ice; shake well. Strain and add ice.*

## SIR WALTER

1½ oz. brandy
1 tbs. white rum
1 tsp. curacao, lime juice, and grenadine

*Combine with ice; shake well. Strain and add ice.*

## 61

3 oz. gin
1 oz. dry vermouth
1 oz. Strega

*Combine with ice; shake well. Strain straight up.*

## SKEET SHOOTER'S SPECIAL

1½ oz. dark rum
2 tbs. apiece pineapple, grapefruit, and orange juices
1 oz. lemon soda
1 tbs. white rum
A pinch cinnamon

*Combine with ice; shake. Strain, add ice and decorate with cherries.*

## SKI JUMPER'S PUNCH

1 bottle rum
4 oz. curacao
4 oz. orange juice
3 oz. lemon juice
8 oz. sugar
1 pint hot green tea

*Dissolve the sugar with the juices in a large suacepan; add the tea. At the same time — in a separate pan — heat the curacao and the rum and then combine with the punch. Stir well and serve in a chafing dash piping hot.*

## SKIDMORE TIPPLE

2 oz. cognac
2 oz. kummel

*Combine without ice; stir until blended. Serve straight up.*

## SKIPPER'S PARTICULAR

2 pints Jamaican rum
1 pint cognac
4 oz. Benedictine
4 oz. kummel
Lemon and orange peels

*Combine in a punch bowl. Pour in 3 qts of boiling water; stir well and allow it to simmer a few minutes. Sugar to taste and serve hot.*

## SKY CLUB

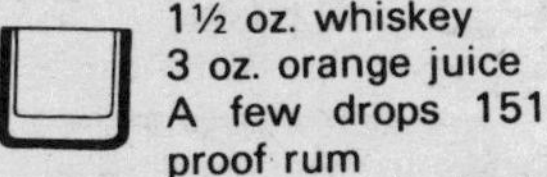

1½ oz. whiskey
3 oz. orange juice
A few drops 151-proof rum

*Combine, add ice and stir well.*

## SLEDGE HAMMER

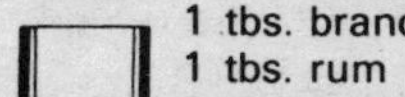

1 tbs. brandy
1 tbs. rum
1 tbs. apple brandy
1-2 dashes Pernod

*Combine with ice; shake well. Strain and add ice.*

## SLEEPER'S CIDER

1 quart hard cider
Whole cloves, allspice, cinnamon sticks
Lemon slices

*Combine the cider with spices in a large saucepan; cover and simmer for 20 minutes to a half hour. Strain and serve hot; garnish with a lemon slice.*

## SLEEPYHEAD

2½ oz. brandy
A few mint leaves, partially torn
Ginger ale

*Pour the brandy into glass; add the mint leaves plus ice and a twist of orange. Fill the glass with ginger ale.*

## SLINGS

**SLINGS** *are* **RICKEYS** *made with water: Combine 2 oz. of whiskey, brandy, gin, or vodka with 2 tablespoon of lemon juice in a highball glass. Add 1½ teaspoons sugar syrup plus ice and stir. Fill the glass with cold water.*

## SLOE BRANDY

2 oz. brandy
2 tsp. sloe gin
1 tsp. lemon juice

*Combine with ice; shake well. Strain. Add ice and a twist of lemon.*

## SLOE GIN

1 pint sloes
2 oz. sugar
2 oz. rock candy
Gin

*Place the sloes in a quart mason jar, poking each sloe through with a fork before hand. Add the sugar and candy, fill the jar with gin and seal. Shake the bottle every day for three weeks, then store in a cool dark place to ferment for at least one year.*

## SLOE GIN FIZZ

1 oz. sloe gin
1 oz. gin
1 tbs. lemon juice
Club soda

*Combine everything except the soda with ice; shake well. Strain, add ice, and fill the glass with soda. Decorate with a slice of lemon.*

## SLOE LIME FRAPPE

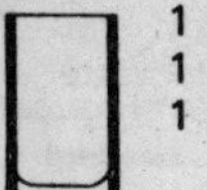

1 tbs. sloe gin
1 tbs. white rum
1 tbs. lime liqueur

*Combine without ice; stir well. Pour over crushed ice. Decorate with a slice of lime.*

## SLOE SCREW

1½ oz. sloe gin
Orange juice

*Pour the sloe gin over ice. Fill the glass with orange juice and stir.*

## SLOE TEQUILA

1 oz. tequila
2 tsp. sloe gin
2 tsp. lime juice
4 oz. crushed ice
1 cucumber peel

*Combine everything except the peel in blender at a low speed for 15 seconds. Strain; add ice to fill the glass. Decorate with the peel.*

## SLOE VERMOUTH

1 oz. sloe gin
1 oz. dry vermouth
2 tsp. lemon juice

*Combine with ice; shake well. Strain and add ice.*

## SLOPPY JOE

1 tbs. white rum
1 tbs. dry vermouth
3 tbs. lime juice
A few drops curacao and grenadine

*Combine with ice; shake well. Strain and add ice.*

## SNICKER

1½ oz. gin
1 tbs. dry vermouth
1 tsp. sugar syrup
1 egg white
A few drops maraschino
1-2 dashes orange bitters

*Combine with ice; shake well. Strain and add ice.*

## SNOWBALL

1 oz. gin
1 tsp. white creme de menthe, heavy cream, anisette, and creme de violette

*Combine with ice; shake well. Strain and add ice.*

## SOLDIER'S CAMPING PUNCH

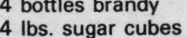

2 bottles Jamaican rum
4 bottles brandy
4 lbs. sugar cubes
4 gallons strong hot coffee

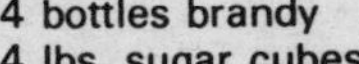

*Pour the rum and the brandy into a large saucepan. Add the sugar; heat and stir until the sugar is dissolved. Combine with the coffee in a large kettle; stir well and serve immediately.*

## SORGHUM BEER

3 lb. sorghum
4 lb. sugar
8 oz. hops
3 tbs. yeast

*Boil the sorghum in 3 quarts of water until it becomes syrupy; strain back into the pot and boil the hops in the syrup for several minutes. Add 15 quarts of water and all but one lb. of the sugar; stir until the sugar has dissolved. Remove from heat. When lukewarm, add the yeast and stand at room temperature for 24 hours. Dilute the remaining sugar in a little hot water; add to the beer. Strain and bottle; store several days before serving.*

## SORREL BEER

2 large bunches wood sorrel
1 pint Jamaican rum
Crushed ginger

*Combine the red sorrel blossom with the ginger in a crock pot; pour in 1 gallon of boiling water and allow to steep, sealed, for several days. When ready, add the rum and sugar to taste. Refrigerate until ready to use.*

## SOUL KISS

1 oz. Dubonnet
1 oz. orange juice
2 tbs. sweet vermouth
2 tbs. dry vermouth

*Combine with ice; shake well. Strain and add ice.*

## SOUPED-UP GIBSON

2 oz. gin
2 tsp. dry vermouth
Pearl onions

*Combine the gin and vermouth in a martini glass and stir well. Drop in several onions.*

## SOURS

*Almost any liquor can be turned into a sour. Simply take 2½ oz. of any liquor of your choice and combine it with 2 tablespoons of lemon. juice and 1 teaspoon of sugar syrup in a mixing glass filled with ice. Strain into a sour glass straight up. Decorate with fruit slices and a cherry.*

## SOUR APPLE WINE

1 gallon apple juice
2 lb. sugar
2 oz. isinglass gelatin
1 tbs. sourdough yeast
Wine vinegar

*Combine the apple juice and the sugar in a large saucepan; boil until clear. Allow to cool. Add the yeast; stir well. Seal and store in a warm place several weeks. Strain and reseal in a wooden barrel. Store for at least one year. Re-strain; add the isinglass and an oz. of wine vinegar per gallon of cider. Bottle for use.*

## SOUR CITRUS WINE

1 doz. oranges
1 doz. lemons
1 lb. sugar
1½ oz. dry active yeast

*Peel the fruit; boil the rinds in a gallon of water and then simmer for several hours. Squeeze in the fruit juices; add the sugar plus the yeast and stir until mixed. Turn out into a crock pot and seal tightly. Allow to ferment. After fermentation, allow the wine to stand until clear. Strain clean and bottle for future use.*

## SOUTH CAMP SPECIAL

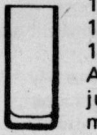

1 tbs. Jamaican rum
1 tbs. dry gin
1 tbs. Scotch
A few drops lime juice, sweet vermouth, and cherry brandy

*Combine with ice; shake well. Strain and add ice. Decorate with a cherry.*

## SOUTH PACIFIC

1½ oz. brandy
2 tsp. lemon juice
1½ oz. dry gin
1 tbs. grapefruit juice
A few drops maraschino

*Combine with ice; shake well. Strain and add ice.*

## SOUTHERN BELLE

1 oz. bourbon
1 oz. heavy cream
1 tbs. green creme de menthe
1 tbs. white creme de cacao

*Combine with ice; shake. Strain, serve straight up.*

## SOUTHERN COMFORT STRAWBERRY FRAPPE

1 tbs. Southern Comfort
1 tbs. strawberry liqueur

*Combine without ice; stir well. Pour over crushed ice. Touch it up with a twist of orange. Decorate with a slice of lemon.*

**SOUTHERN CROSS**

1 bottle port
4 oz. grapefruit juice
2 oz. sugar syrup
3 tsp. lemon juice
½ tsp. allspice
2 oz. raisins

*Combine everything except the raisins in a saucepan and heat thoroughly. Boil the raisins in a cup of water and add the raisins and the water to the wine mixture. Serve hot.*

**SOUTHERN GIN**

2½ oz. gin
1-2 dashes orange bitters
A few drops curacao

*Combine with ice; shake well. Strain; add ice and a twist of lemon.*

**SOUTHERN GINGER**

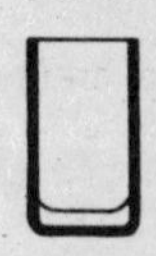

1½ oz. 100-proof bourbon
1 oz. ginger ale
1 tsp. lemon juice
A few drops ginger brandy

*Combine with ice; shake well. Strain. Add ice and a twist of lemon.*

**SOUTHERN PUNCH**

1½ oz. bourbon
1 oz. lemon juice
1 tbs. rum
2 tsp. brandy
2 tsp. sugar syrup
Club soda

*Combine everything except the rum and the soda with ice; shake. Strain into glass filled partly with crushed ice. Almost fill glass with soda and float the rum on top.*

**SOUTHGATE**

1¼ oz. whiskey
½ tsp. sugar syrup
A few dashes of Angostura bitters

*Combine with ice; shake well. Strain and add ice. Touch it up with a twist of lemon.*

**SOVIET COCKTAIL**

1½ oz. vodka
2 tsp. dry vermouth
2 tsp. amontillado

*Combine with ice; shake well. Strain and add ice. Touch it up with a twist of lemon.*

**SOYER AU CHAMPAGNE**

1 oz. vanilla ice cream
A few drops of brandy, maraschino, and curacao
4 oz. champagne

*Combine the ice cream with the brandy, maraschino, and curacao; stir until blended and add the champagne. Decorate with a slice of orange and a cherry.*

**SPANISH MOSS**

1½ oz. tequila
2 tbs. Kahlua
Several drops of green creme de menthe

*Combine with ice; shake well. Strain over one cube of ice.*

**SPANISH TOWN**

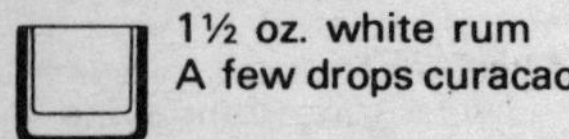

1½ oz. white rum
A few drops curacao

*Combine with ice; shake well. Strain and add ice. Garnish with nutmeg.*

**SPANISH VODKA MARTINI**

2½ oz. vodka
1 tbs. dry sherry

*Combine with ice; shake well. Strain straight up; add a twist of lemon.*

**SPECIAL ROUGH**

1½ oz. apple brandy
1½ oz. brandy
A few drops Pernod

*Combine with ice; shake well. Strain and add ice.*

**SPENCER**

1½ oz. gin
1 tbs. apricot brandy
A few dashes of Angostura bitters
A few drops orange juice

*Combine with ice; shake well. Strain and add ice.*

**SPICED COFFEE**

1 oz. brandy, rum, or bourbon
1 cup of hot coffee
Cinnamon, ground cloves, and nutmeg

*Wrap the spices in cheesecloth or any other material for infusing; soak them in the coffee for several minutes. Add the brandy, rum, or bourbon when ready to drink.*

**SPICED ORANGE BLOSSOM**

4 oz. orange juice
2 oz. gin
A few drops lemon juice
A few maraschino cherries
A few dashes of Angostura bitters
Several pinches cinnamon
A few drops cherry juice

*Combine in a blender at a high speed until foamy. Serve unstrained.*

**SPIKED ALE**

1 quart ale
4 oz. brandy
1 tbs. sugar
Cloves, nutmeg, and ginger

*Combine in a large saucepan; heat but do not bring to a boil, stirring constantly. Strain clean and serve piping hot.*

## SPIKED PINEAPPLE PUNCH

2 quarts unsweetened pineapple juice
1 pint vodka
8 oz. Grand Marnier
8 oz. Maraschino
6 oz. Orange juice
1½ lemon juice
1 bottle club soda

*Combine everything except the soda; stir well. Add the soda plus chunks of ice before serving.*

## SPINSTER'S NIGHT CAP

9 gallons hard cider
8 lb. honey
2 oz. baking soda
2 bottles Jamaican rum
Ground cinnamon, cloves, and mace

*Combine the cider, rum, and 2 quarts of cold water in a large crock pot; add the honey, baking soda, and spices to taste. Stir well until blended. Seal and allow to ferment. Stir, strain, and bottle for future use.*

## SPRING PUNCH

1 quart gin
2 6-oz. cans frozen lemonade concentrate
1½ bottles club soda
Cucumber peels

*Combine the gin and defrosted lemonade concentrate; stir well to blend. Garnish with cucumber peels. Add the soda plus chunks of ice.*

## SPINGTIME VERMOUTH

1 oz. dry vermouth
2 oz. cranberry juice
6 strawberries

*Combine the vermouth and the juice with ice; shake well. Strain and add ice. Fill with strawberries.*

## SPRITZER

5 oz. Rhine wine
Club soda

*Thoroughly chill the wine and soda. Pour the wine into a large goblet; add ice and fill with soda. Stir. Decorate with spiral lemon peel or slices of fruit.*

---

## SPRUCE BEER

A bundle of spruce sprigs
1 pint molasses
3 oz. yeast
1 oz. hops
1 tsp. ginger

*Boil the sprigs in just enough water to produce a tablespoon of strong juice. Boil the hops and the ginger in a gallon of water; strain out the spices. Add the molasses and the spruce juices. Allow to cool; add the yeast. Turn out into a crock pot; seal tightly and allow to ferment for a few days. Bottle for future use.*

**STAR**

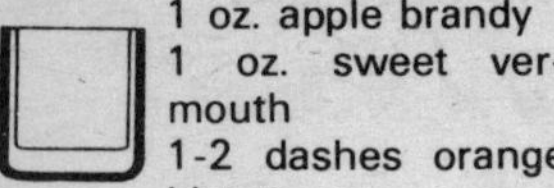

1 oz. apple brandy
1 oz. sweet vermouth
1-2 dashes orange bitters

*Combine. Shake. Strain.*

**STAR DAISY**

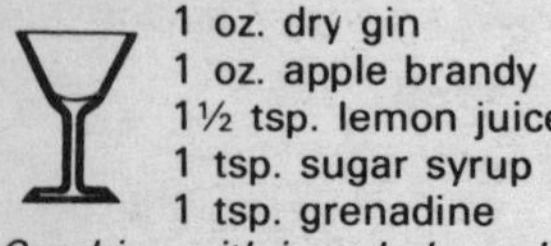

1 oz. dry gin
1 oz. apple brandy
1½ tsp. lemon juice
1 tsp. sugar syrup
1 tsp. grenadine

*Combine with ice; shake well. Strain and add ice.*

**STARBOARD**

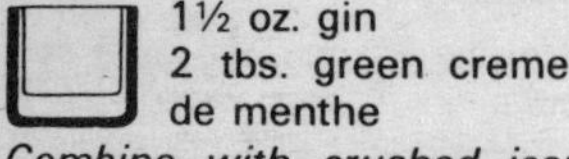

1½ oz. gin
2 tbs. green creme de menthe

*Combine with crushed ice; shake. Strain and add ice.*

**STARS AND STRIPES**

1 tbs. green chartreuse
1 tbs. maraschino
1 tbs. creme de cassis

*Slightly tip a pony glass and carefully pour in each ingredient. Do not mix.*

**STARS FELL ON ALABAMA**

1¼ oz. corn whiskey
1 tsp. sugar syrup
Several drops Pernod
A few drops orange flower water
A few dashes of Peychaud's and Angostura bitters

*Combine with ice; shake well. Strain and add ice.*

**STINGERS** *are simple, minted drinks which can be made with many kinds of liquors: Take 1½ oz. of your favorite brandy, Jamaican rum, gin, tequila, or vodka and combine it with 1 oz. of white creme de menthe. Shake them in a mixing glass filled with ice and strain into an old-fashioned glass.*

**STIRRUP CUP**

1½ oz. Southern Comfort
1½ oz. cranberry juice
1 tbs. lemon juice
Grapefruit juice
Club soda
Mint sprigs

*Combine the Southern Comfort plus the cranberry and lemon juices with ice; shake well. Strain; add ice and fill the glass with equal parts grapefruit juice and soda. Stir gently; decorate with mint.*

**STONE FENCE**

2½ oz. apple brandy
1-2 dashes Angostura bitters
Sweet cider

*Pour the brandy into a glass; add the bitters plus ice and fill with cider. Stir well.*

**STONE SOUR**

1½ oz. bourbon
1 tbs. lemon juice
1 tsp. white creme de menthe
Club soda
Mint sprigs a few

*Pour the bourbon, juice, and creme de menthe over crushed ice; stir well and fill the glass with club soda. Sweeten to taste. Decorate with sprigs of mint and a cherry.*

**STONEHENGE COLLINS**

3 oz. gin
3 tsp. lemon juice
2 tsp. sugar syrup
1 tsp. white creme de menthe

*Combine with ice; shake well. Strain over crushed ice. Garnish with fruit slices or mint.*

**STONEWALL**

2 oz. cider
1 oz. Jamaican rum

*Combine with ice; shake well. Strain and add ice.*

**STONYBROOK**

1½ oz. whiskey
2 tsp. Triple Sec
½ egg white
A few drops almond extract

*Combine with ice; shake well. Strain and add ice. Touch it up with a twist of orange and a twist of lemon.*

**STRAIGHT LAW**

2½ oz. dry sherry
1 tbs. dry gin

*Combine with ice; shake well. Strain and add ice. Touch it up with a twist of lemon.*

**STRATOSPHERE**

1 oz. rum
2 tsp. California brandy
2 tsp. lemon juice
1½ tsp. sugar syrup
1 tsp. cherry liqueur

*Combine filled with ice; shake well. Strain and add ice.*

**STRAWBERRY BOWL**

2 bottles champagne, chilled
1 pint claret
2 quarts strawberries, sliced
8 oz. sugar

*Combine the strawberries with the claret and sugar in a punch bowl; stir gently to blend and cool for at least one hour. Add the champagne before serving.*

## STRAWBERRY CORDIAL

1 peck strawberries
1 gallon brandy
16 oz. sugar
Ground cardamon, cinnamon, and cloves

*Slice and simmer half the strawberries in a saucepan with just enough water to cover them, plus a few pinches of assorted spices. Strain the liquids out; add the sugar plus the remaining berries and allow to stand for several hours. Mash the berries through cheesecloth, combine the juice with the brandy, stir and bottle for future use.*

## STRAWBERRY CREOLE PUNCH

1½ quarts claret
1 quart strawberry juice
1 pint pineapple juice
2 cups sugar
2 bottles club soda
Whole strawberries

*Dissolve the sugar with the fruit juices; add the wine and soda plus ice, and stir well. Garnish with strawberries and store in a freezer until semi-frozen.*

## STRAWBERRY PUNCH

½ peck strawberries
1 bottle white rum
1 lb. sugar
1½ gallons freshly brewed tea

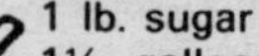

*Combine the berries with the sugar in a large bowl and refrigerate for at least two days. Strain clean and combine with the rum. Add chunks of ice plus the tea before serving.*

## STRAWBERRY RITA

1 oz. tequila
2 oz. whole strawberries
3 tsp. sugar syrup
3 oz. crushed ice
Sliced strawberries
Whipped cream

*Combine everything except the sliced strawberries and the whipped cream in blender at a high speed for 15 seconds. Line the rim of a glass with water and press it in sugar; strain in the drink. Garnish with the sliced strawberries and whipped cream plus a slice of lime.*

## STRAWBERRY RUM FLIP

1½ oz. white rum
1 oz. strawberry liqueur
1½ tsp. sugar syrup
1 tsp. lemon juice
1 egg

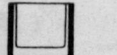

*Combine with ice; shake well. Strain straight up; garnish with nutmeg.*

## STRAWBERRY SANGAREE

4 oz. claret or Bordeaux
1½ oz. sugar
1 tsp. lemon juice
4 oz. strawberries, cleaned and crushed
Club soda

*Combine everything except the soda with ice; shake well. Leave in glass and chill for at least one hour. Strain and add ice. Fill the glass wth soda and decorate with slices of fruit.*

## STRAWBERRY SWIG

1½ oz. gin
2 tsp. strawberry liqueur
1 tsp. lime juice
1-2 dashes orange bitters

*Combine with ice; shake well. Strain and add ice. Decorate with a slice of lime.*

## STREGA FLIP

1 oz. Strega
1 oz. brandy
2 tsp. orange juice
1½ tsp. sugar syrup
1 tsp. lemon juice
1 egg

*Combine with ice; shake extremely well. Strain straight up; garnish with nutmeg.*

## STREGA SOUR

1½ oz. gin
2 tsp. lemon juice
1 tsp. Strega

*Combine with ice; shake well. Line the rim of glass with Strega and press it in sugar. Strain in the drink; add ice and decorate with a slice of lemon.*

## SUBURBAN

1 oz. whiskey
2 tsp. port
2 tsp. Jamaican rum
A few dashes of Angostura and orange bitters

*Combine with ice; shake well. Strain and add ice.*

## STRAWBERRY WINE

2 quarts strawberries
1 quart sugar
1 quart potatoes, peeled and sliced

*Slice the strawberries and put them in a crock pot. Pour the sugar on top of them and add the potatoes. Seal the pot and allow to stand for several months* **undisturbed.** *Strain and bottle the wine when ready for use.*

**SUGAR LOAF CORDIAL**

8 oz. Puerto Rican rum
1 tbs. high-proof rum
8 oz. sugar
1 large orange

*Carefully peel the orange, leaving the skin as intact as possible. Place the peel in the center of a wide, heat proof dish and fill it with sugar. Pour the high-proof rum over the sugar; the Puerto Rican rum around it like a lagoon. Ignite the sugar loaf and serve while blazing. Place a spot of sugar in each cup of rum if you wish. Another alternative — lift the orange peel after igniting the sugar and let the flames and the sweetness disperse itself around the rum until dissolved, but not cool.*

**SUISSESSE**

1½ oz. Pernod
Several drops anisette
1 egg white

*Combine with ice; shake extremely well. Strain and add ice. A few drops of heavy cream can be added before mixing.*

**SUMMER BOURBON**

1 oz. bourbon
2 oz. orange juice
1 pinch salt

*Combine without ice; stir well. Pour over crushed ice.*

**SUMMER PUNCH**

3 bottles dry white wine
12 oz. creme de cassis
1 pint strawberries
Orange slices

*Combine the wine and the cassis and stir; float the strawberries and orange slices. Add chunks of ice before serving.*

**SUMMER WINE CUP**

1 bottle white wine
4 oz. brandy
2 oz. sugar
Sliced strawberries, lemons, and oranges
Cucumber peels, sprigs of mint
1 pint club soda

*Combine the brandy with the sugar; stir until the sugar has dissolved. Add the fruit slices and allow to stand for one hour. When ready add the wine, cucumber peels, and mint; stir. Pour in the soda plus chunks of ice.*

**SUN VALLEY**

4 oz. Jamaican rum
1 quart heavy cream
4 egg yolks
2 tbs. powdered sugar
Milk

*Pour the cream into a saucepan and almost bring to a boil; remove from heat. Beat the yolks with a little milk; add them plus the sugar to the cream. Pour in the rum and stir well. Serve piping hot in small mugs.*

## SUNDOWNER

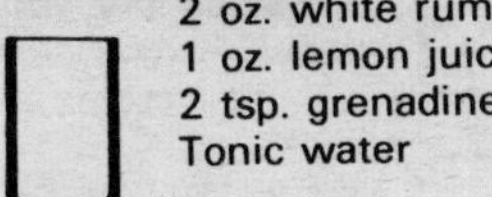

2 oz. white rum
1 oz. lemon juice
2 tsp. grenadine
Tonic water

*Combine the rum, juice, and grenadine with ice; shake. Strain, add ice and fill with tonic. Stir.*

## SUNSET

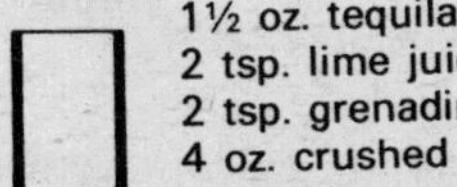

1½ oz. tequila
2 tsp. lime juice
2 tsp. grenadine
4 oz. crushed ice

*Combine in a blender at a low speed for 15 seconds. Strain and add ice. Decorate with a slice of lime.*

## SUNSHINE PUNCH

1 bottle white wine
4 oz. brandy
2 oz. sugar
1 pint club soda
Sliced pears, apples, and oranges

*Combine the wine, sugar, and fruit slices allow to stand for a few hours. Add the bran dy and soda plus chunks of ice.*

## SUPERIOR COCKTAIL

2 oz. gin
1 oz. lemon juice
A few drops dry vermouth
1-2 dashes kirschwasser
1 tsp. sugar syrup
Button mushrooms

*Combine everything except the mushrooms with ice; shake well. Strain straight up; drop in button mushrooms.*

## SUTTON PLACE SLING

1½ oz. Jamaican rum
2 tbs. orange juice
1 tsp. 151-proof rum
A few dashes of Angostura bitters
A few drops lime juice
A few drops cherry juice
Lemon soda

*Combine everything except the soda and the 151-proof rum with ice; shake well. Strain; add ice and fill with lemon soda. Float the 151-proof rum.*

## SWEDISH SNOWBALL

1½ oz. Advockaat
lemon soda

*Pour the Advockaat over ice. Fill the glass and stir. Decorate with lemon slice.*

## SWEET GRAPE WINE

10 lbs. grapes
2 lbs. sugar

*Crush the grapes with the sugar in a large pot; seal and allow to ferment. When ready, strain into bottles and store for future use.*

## SWEET LILT

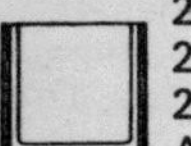

2 oz. Cognac
2 tbs. anisette
2 tbs. curacao
A chunk of fresh pineapple

*Combine everything except the pineapple with ice; shake well. Strain straight up; garnish with pineapple.*

## SWISS COCKTAIL

2 oz. Dubonnet
1 tbs. kirschwasser

*Combine with ice; shake well. Strain straight up; add a twist of lemon.*

## SW1

1 tbs. vodka
1 tbs. orange juice
1 tbs. Campari bitters

*Combine with ice; shake well. Strain and add ice.*

## SWORE

1½ oz. 100-proof vodka
2 tsp. sweet vermouth
1 tsp. kirsch
1 tsp. orange juice

*Combine with ice; shake well. Strain and add ice. Touch it up with a twist of orange.*

## SYLLABUB

16 oz. white wine
16 oz. light cream
3 cups milk
10 oz. sugar
4 egg whites
3 oz. lemon juice
Grated lemon rind
Nutmeg

*Combine the wine, rinds (to taste), and juice. Add 1 cup of the sugar and stir until it dissolved. Combine the milk with the cream in a separate bowl; add it to the wine and beat until foamy. Beat the egg whites in another bowl, adding the remaining sugar slowly. When the whites hold peaks, add them in small puffs to the wine punch and garnish the tufts with nutmeg. Serve in punch glasses, a puff in each.*

# YOUR OWN RECIPE

# YOUR OWN RECIPE

Use a bartender's mixing glass whenever the instructions state "combine" ingredients. Strain the drink from the mixing glass into the drinking glass suggested by the illustration alongside the ingredients.

The glass pictured for each drink is our suggestion; other drinking cups may be used as well.

# T

---

### TABOO

1 oz. vodka
1 oz. white rum
2 tbs. pineapple juice
2 tsp. lemon juice
A few drops rock candy syrup
2 oz. crushed ice
Mint sprigs

*Combine in a blender at a high speed for 15 seconds. Garnish with slices of fruit and sprigs of mint.*

### TAHITI CLUB

2 oz. gold rum
2 tsp. lime juice, lemon juice, pineapple juice, and maraschino

*Combine with ice; shake well. Strain and add ice. Decorate with a slice of orange.*

### TAHITI TANTALIZER

1½ oz. vodka
1 tbs. pineapple juice concentrate
2 tsp. guava nectar
2 tsp. lemon juice

*Combine with ice; shake well. Strain and add ice.*

### TAHITIAN WEDDING PUNCH

2 bottles white wine
1 bottle gold rum
2 cups crushed pineapple
8 oz. sugar
8 oz. lemon juice
Grated lemon rinds
Gardenia or other flower blossoms

*Dissolve the sugar with the lemon juice in a large pot; stir until syrupy. Add the wine, rum, pineapple, and rinds; stir until blended. Seal, and allow to stand for several hours in a cool dark place. Add large chunks of ice plus the flower blossoms and rinds.*

---

### TAILSPIN

¾ oz. gin
¾ oz. sweet vermouth
1 tbs. green chartreuse
1-2 dashes orange bitters

*Combine with ice; shake well. Strain and add ice. Touch it up with a twist of lemon and an olive.*

## TALL DUTCH EGG NOG

1½ oz. white rum
1 oz. orange juice
2 tbs. advocaat liqueur
2 tsp. 151-proof rum
1½ tsp. sugar syrup
6 oz. milk
4 oz. crushed ice

*Combine in a blender at a high speed for 10 seconds. Strain and garnish with cinnamon.*

## TALL ISLANDER

2 oz. white rum
3 oz. pineapple juice
3 tsp. lime juice
1 tsp. Jamaican rum
1 tsp. sugar syrup
Club soda

*Combine all but the soda with ice; shake well. Strain add plenty of ice and a spritz of soda. Stir well and decorate with a lime slice.*

## TANGO

1 oz. gin
2 tsp. sweet vermouth, dry vermouth, and orange juice
Several drops curacao

*Combine with ice; shake well. Strain and add ice.*

## TANTALUS

¾ oz. brandy
¾ oz. lemon juice
1 tbs. Forbidden Fruit

*Combine with ice; shake well. Strain and add ice.*

## TANGERINE MORNING PUNCH

1 quart brandy
1 doz. tangerines
1 lb. sugar
1 quart milk
1 quart light cream
Whipped cream

*Slice the tangerines and place them in a deep saucepan. Add the milk and cream; stir gently while simmering for five to ten minutes. Strain into a large punch bowl; add the sugar while the punch is warm. Stir until the sugar is dissolved. Allow to cool and add the brandy. Top each cup with whipped cream.*

**TARPON**

3 oz. orange juice
2 tbs. bourbon
2 tsp. Triple Sec
1 tsp. sugar
Club soda

*Combine everything except the soda with ice; shake. Strain add ice and fill with soda. Decorate with pineapple.*

**TEA PUNCH**

1 bottle vodka
1½ quarts strong hot tea
12 oz. frozen lemonade concentrate
8 oz. frozen orange juice concentrate
Fruit slices
Whole strawberries

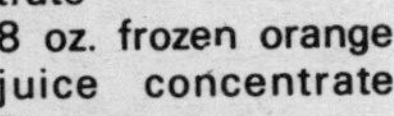

*Combine the frozen fruit juices with the tea and allow to cool. Add the vodka plus the fresh fruit slices and stir until well-blended. Add chunks of ice before serving.*

**TEMPERANCE PUNCH**

1 quart sweet cider
3 oz. cognac
2 oz. sugar
Lemon slices
Club soda

*Combine the cider, cognac, and sugar in a large pitcher; stir until the sugar has dissolved. Add ice. Serve in tall glasses over ice, 4 oz. of cider per glass. The rest is soda. Garnish each glass with lemon.*

**TEMPTATION COCKTAIL**

1½ oz. whiskey
Several drops Pernod, Dubonnet, and curacao

*Combine with ice; shake well. Strain and add ice. Touch it up with a twist of orange and of lemon.*

**TEMPTER**

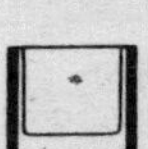

1½ oz. port
1½ oz. apricot brandy

*Combine with ice; shake well. Strain and add ice.*

**TEN TON COCKTAIL**

1½ oz. rye
1 tbs. dry vermouth
1 tbs. grapefruit juice

*Combine with ice; shake well. Strain and add ice. Decorate with a cherry.*

**TENDER**

1½ oz. gin
1 tbs. apple brandy
1 tbs. apricot brandy
A few drops lemon juice

*Combine with ice; shake well. Strain and add ice.*

**TENNESSEE**

3 oz. rye
2 tbs. maraschino
2 tsp. lemon juice

*Combine with ice; shake well. Strain add ice.*

**TEQUILA A LA CANELA**

1 oz. tequila liqueur
2 tbs. condensed milk
A few pinches cinnamon

*Combine the liqueur and the milk; stir well. Add ice and cinnamon to taste.*

**TEQUILA COCKTAIL**

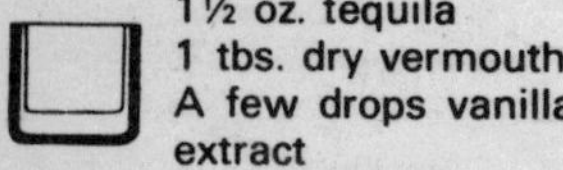

1½ oz. tequila
1 tbs. dry vermouth
A few drops vanilla extract

*Combine with ice; shake well. Strain and add ice.*

**TEQUILA COCKTAIL NO. 2**

2½ oz. tequila
1 tbs. grenadine
2 tsp. lime juice
1-2 dashes orange bitters
Grapefruit juice

*Combine everything except the grapefruit juice with ice; shake well. Strain; add ice and fill with grapefruit juice.*

**TEQUILA DAIQUIRI**

1½ oz. tequila
1½ tsp. lime juice
1½ tsp. sugar syrup

*Combine with ice; shake well. Strain.*

**TEQUILA DUBONNET**

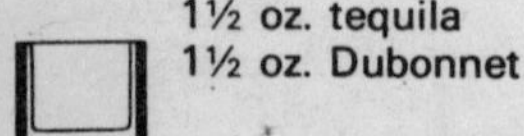

1½ oz. tequila
1½ oz. Dubonnet

*Combine; stir well and add ice. Decorate with a slice of lemon.*

**TEQUILA FIZZ**

1½ oz. tequila
1 tbs. grenadine
1 egg white
3 oz. ginger ale
3 oz. crushed ice

*Combine in a blender at a low speed for a few seconds. Strain.*

**TEQUILA FRESA**

1½ oz. tequila
1 tbs. strawberry liqueur
2 tsp. lime juice
A few drops orange bitters
1 slice of lime and a strawberry

*Combine everything except the fruit with ice; shake well. Strain and add ice. Decorate with the fruit.*

**TEQUILA FROZEN SCREWDRIVER**

1½ oz. tequila
3 oz. orange juice
3 oz. crushed ice

*Combine in a blender at a low speed for 15 seconds. Strain and add ice. Decorate with a slice of orange.*

**TEQUILA GHOST**

2 oz. tequila
1 oz. Pernod
2 tsp. lemon juice

*Combine with ice; shake well. Strain and add ice.*

**TEQUILA GUAYABA**

1½ oz. tequila
2 tsp. guava syrup, orange juice, and lime juice

*Combine with ice; shake well. Strain and add ice. Touch it up with a twist of orange.*

**TEQUILA MANHATTAN**

1½ oz. gold tequila
1 tbs. sweet vermouth

*Combine with ice; shake well. Strain. Add ice and a twist of lime; stir. Decorate with a slice of orange.*

**TEQUILA OLD-FASHIONED**

1½ oz. tequila
1 tbs. sugar syrup
1-2 dashes Angostura bitters
Club soda
1 pineapple stick

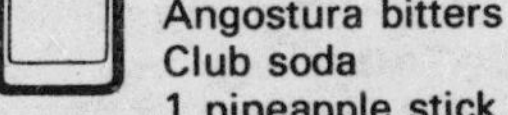

*Combine everything except the soda and the pineapple stick; add ice and stir. Touch it up with a spritz of soda and a twist of lemon; decorate with the pineapple.*

**TEQUILA PUP**

1½ oz. tequila
3 tsp. lime juice
1 tsp. honey
1-2 dashes Angostura bitters

*Combine with ice; shake very well. Strain and add ice.*

**TEQUILA RICKEY**

1½ oz. tequila
1 tsp. lime juice
Club soda
Lime and orange slices
Salt

*Pour the tequila and the lime juice into a highball glass; add ice and stir well. Fill the glass with soda. Twist in the slice of lime. Sprinkle a little salt over the drink. Decorate with the orange slice.*

**TEQUILA SOUR**

1½ oz. tequila
2 tsp. lemon juice
1½ tsp. sugar syrup

*Combine with ice; shake well. Strain straight up. Decorate with a slice of lemon.*

**TEQUILA SUNRISE**

*Pour 2 oz. of tequila into a highball glass. Add ice and 2 teaspoons of grenadine; fill the glass with orange juice and stir. A* **TIJUANA SUNRISE** *is a* **TEQUILA SUNRISE** *with a dash or two of Angostura bitters instead of the grenadine.*

**TEQUINI**

2½ oz. tequila
1 tbs. dry vermouth

*Combine straight up and sitr gently. Touch it up with a twist of lemon.*

## TEXAN

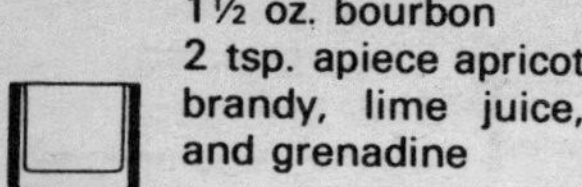

1½ oz. bourbon
2 tsp. apiece apricot brandy, lime juice, and grenadine

*Combine with ice; shake. Strain over plenty of ice; decorate with a slice of lime and a green cherry.*

## THANKSGIVING COCKTAIL

1 oz. dry gin
1 oz. dry vermouth
1 oz. apricot brandy
Several drops lemon juice

*Combine with ice; shake well. Strain and add ice. Decorate with a cherry.*

---

## THIRD DEGREE

1½ oz. gin
1 tbs. dry vermouth
1 tsp. Pernod

*Combine with ice; shake well. Strain and add ice.*

## THIRD RAIL

2 oz. dry vermouth
A few drops of curacao
Several drops white creme de menthe

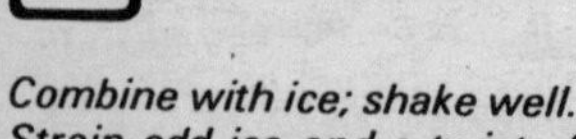

*Combine with ice; shake well. Strain add ice and a twist of lemon.*

## THREE KINGS' PUNCH

8 oz. white rum
8 oz. anisette
4 egg yolks
A cinnamon stick
8 oz. sugar
8 oz. water
14 oz. undiluted evaporated milk

*Combine the sugar, water, and cinnamon stick in a saucepan and heat until boiling. Remove from the heat and take out the stick. Slowly add the milk, rum, and anisette. Fold in the yolks, stir gently, and refrigerate. Turn out into cups garnished with cinnamon.*

---

## THREE MILLER

1½ oz. white rum
1 tbs. brandy
1 tsp. grenadine
A few drops lemon juice

*Combine with ice; shake well. Strain and add ice.*

## THREE STRIPES COCKTAIL

1 oz. dry gin
2 tsp. dry vermouth
2 tsp. orange juice

*Combine with ice; shake well. Strain and add ice.*

## THUMPER

1¾ oz. brandy
1 tbs. Tuaca

*Combine with ice; shake well. Strain and add ice. Touch it up with a touch of lemon.*

**THUNDER**

2½ oz. brandy
1 tsp. sugar syrup
1 egg yolk
1 pinch cayenne pepper

*Combine with ice; shake well. Strain and add ice.*

**THUNDERBIRD SPECIAL**

1 oz. bourbon
1 oz. heavy cream
2 tsp. creme de banana
2 tsp. Cointreau

*Combine with ice; shake. Strain with one ice cube.*

**TIDBIT**

1½ oz. dry gin
1½ oz. vanilla ice cream
A few drops cream sherry

*Combine without ice; stir until well-blended. Pour, and add ice to fill glass. Decorate with a cherry.*

**TIGER'S MILK**

1 oz. Jamaican rum
1 oz. brandy
4 oz. heavy cream
3 tsp. sugar syrup

*Combine with ice; shake very well. Strain and add ice.*

**TIGER'S TAIL**

1½ oz. Pernod
6 oz. orange juice

*Combine, stir well and add ice to fill the glass. Decorate with a slice of lime.*

**TIKI PUNCH**

1 cup gin
1 cup Triple Sec
3 oz. lime juice
2 bottles champagne

*Combine the gin, Triple Sec, and juice; add some ice and allow to stand until the ice melts. Add the champagne plus more ice.*

**TIPPERARY**

¾ oz. Irish whiskey
¾ oz. sweet vermouth
1 tbs. green chartreuse

*Combine with ice; shake well. Strain and add ice.*

**TNT**

1½ oz. rye
1½ oz. Pernod

*Combine with ice; shake well. Strain and add ice.*

**TOM AND JERRY**

1½ oz. brandy
1½ oz. rum
Hot milk
2 tsp. sugar
2 eggs
A pinch of baking soda

*Separate the eggs. Beat the whites until frothy; add the sugar and continue to beat the eggs until they form peaks. Beat the yolks in a separate bowl until creamy. Combine the yolks and the whites, and add the baking soda. Divide the egg mixture between two mugs; add half the brandy and rum to each and fill the mugs with hot milk.*

**TOM COLLINS**

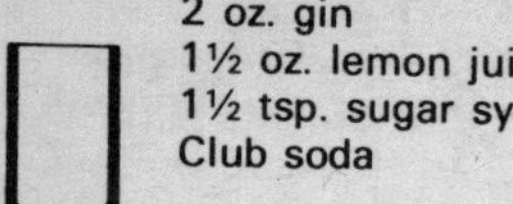

2 oz. gin
1½ oz. lemon juice
1½ tsp. sugar syrup
Club soda

*Combine everything except the soda;stir well and add ice. Fill the glass with soda and decorate with a cherry. A* **JOHN COLLINS** *is a* **TOM COLLINS** *using ginger ale instead of club soda.*

**TOM MOORE**

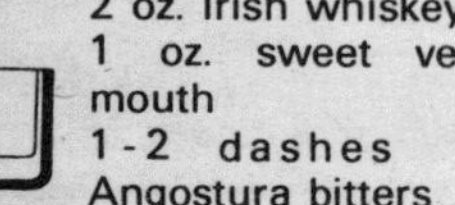

2 oz. Irish whiskey
1 oz. sweet vermouth
1-2 dashes Angostura bitters

*Combine with ice; shake well. Strain and add ice.*

**TONGA PUNCH**

1 quart white rum
1 quart orange juice
1 pint lemon juice
10 oz. orange curacao
6 oz. lime juice
4 oz. grenadine

*Combine stir. Add chunks of ice plus slices of fruit.*

**TOREADOR**

1½ oz. tequila
2 tsp. white creme de cacao
Whipped cream
Cocoa powder

*Combine the tequila and the creme de cacao with ice; shake well. Strain and add ice. Top with whipped cream and sprinkle with cocoa.*

**TORPEDO**

1½ oz. calvados
1 tbs. brandy
A few drops gin

*Combine with ice; shake well. Strain and add ice.*

---

**TORRIDORA COCKTAIL**

1½ oz. white rum
2 tsp. Tia Maria
1 tsp. heavy cream
1 tsp. 151-proof rum

*Combine everything except the high-proof rum with ice; shake very well. Strain and add ice. Float the high-proof rum.*

---

**TRADE WINDS**

2 oz. gold rum
2 tsp. lime juice
2 tsp. plum brandy
2 tsp. sugar syrup
3 oz. crushed ice

*Combine in a blender at a low speed for 15 seconds. Strain straight up.*

**TRILBY**

1½ oz. gin
2 tbs. sweet vermouth
2 tsp. Creme Yvette
1-2 dashes orange bitters

*Combine everything except the Creme Yvette with ice; shake well. Strain and add ice. Float the Creme Yvette.*

## TRILBY NO. 2

¾ oz. Scotch
¾ oz. sweet vermouth
1 tbs. Parfait Amour
A few drops Pernod
A few dashes of Angostura bitters

*Combine with ice; shake well. Strain and add ice.*

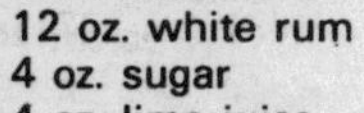

## TRINIDAD PUNCH

12 oz. white rum
4 oz. sugar
4 oz. lime juice
½ oz. Angostura bitters

*Boil the sugar in 4 oz. of water; after the sugar has dissolved, simmer another 5 minutes. Allow to cool. Combine the cool sugar syrup with the rum, juice, and bitters in a punch bowl; stir well. Refrigerate until ready to use. Add plenty of ice before serving.*

## TRIPLE C

1 oz. cognac
2 whole cardamom seeds
Hot coffee

*Drop the seeds into a coffee mug; break them open with a muddler. Add the cognac and the coffee; sugar to taste. Stir well.*

## TRIPLICE

1 oz. gin
1 oz. Benedictine
1 oz. dry vermouth

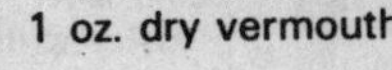

*Combine with ice; shake well. Strain and add ice.*

## TRIPLE DESIRE (For Three)

1 oz. cognac, dry vermouth, coffee brandy, creme de noyaux, blackberry brandy, and lemon juice
2 tsp sugar syrup

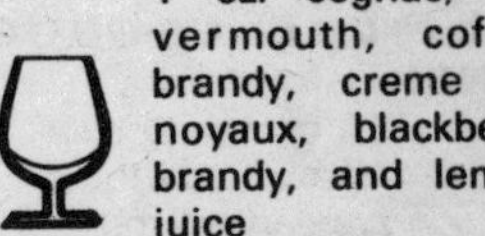

*Combine with ice; shake well. Strain and add ice.*

## TROIS RIVERES

1½ oz. Canadian whiskey
2 tsp. Dubonnet
1 tsp. Cointreau

*Combine with ice; shake well. Strain and add ice. Touch it up with a twist of lemon.*

## TROLLEY

2 oz. bourbon
Pineapple juice
Cranberry juice

*Pour the bourbon over ice. Fill the glass with equal parts pineapple and cranberry juices and stir gently. Decorate with a slice of orange.*

## TROPICAL COCKTAIL

2½ oz. gin
1 oz. frozen pineapple concentrate
1 oz. guava nectar

*Combine with ice; shake well. Strain and add ice. Touch it up with a twist of orange.*

## TROPICAL EGGNOG PUNCH

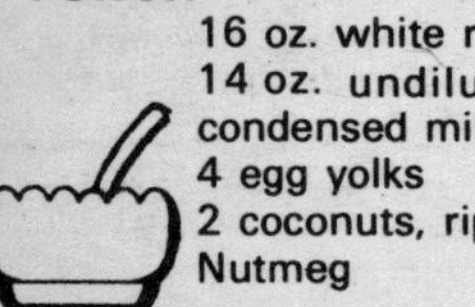

16 oz. white rum
14 oz. undiluted condensed milk
4 egg yolks
2 coconuts, ripe
Nutmeg

*Crack the coconuts into several large pieces, heat at 350 for approx. 5 minutes; remove and separate the meat from the shells. Grate the meat. Combine half the rum and a third of the coconut meat in an electric blender and blend thoroughly. Stir out all liquid. Add this liquid plus more meat to the blender and repeat the process until you have 2 cups of juice. Add the juice plus the yolks to the blender. Blend several seconds; add the milk and blend some more. Combine with the remaining rum. Refrigerate until ready to serve. Garnish with nutmeg.*

## TROPICAL SPECIAL

1½ oz. gin
1 oz. apiece orange and lime juice
2 tbs. grapefruit juice
2 tsp. sugar syrup

*Combine with ice; shake. Strain into ice; decorate with fruit slices and a cherry.*

## TROPICALA

1½ oz. dry vermouth
2 tbs. white creme de cacao
2 tbs. maraschino
1-2 dashes Angostura and orange bitters

*Combine with ice; shake well. Strain and add plenty of ice.*

## TRYST COCKTAIL

1 oz. Scotch
1 oz. sweet vermouth
1 oz. Parfait Amour
A few drops Pernod
1-2 dashes orange bitters

*Combine with ice; shake well. Strain and add ice.*

## TULIP

1 tbs. apple brandy
1 tbs. sweet vermouth
1 tbs. lemon juice
2 tsp. apricot brandy

*Combine with ice; shake well. Strain into an old-fashioned glass and add ice.*

## TURF

1 oz. gin
1 oz. dry vermouth
1 tsp. lemon juice
1 tsp. Pernod

*Combine with ice; shake well. Strain and add ice. Decorate with a slice of lemon.*

## TURF COCKTAIL

1½ oz. gin
2 tbs. dry vermouth
A few drops maraschino and Pernod
1-2 dashes orange bitters

*Combine with ice; shake well. Strain and add ice.*

## TURKISH COFFEE

1 cup coffee, hot and black
2 tsp. cognac
Sugar to taste

*Combine; stir well and sip while still piping hot.*

## TUXEDO

3 oz. sherry
1 tbs. anisette
A few drops of maraschino
1-2 dashes Peychaud's bitters

*Combine with ice; shake well. Strain and add ice.*

## TWELVE GAUGE GROG

1½ oz. Jamaican rum
1 tbs. 151-proof rum
2 oz. orange juice
1 oz. lemon juice
A few dashes of Angostura bitters
Sugar to taste
Grapefruit soda

*Combine everything except the soda with ice; shake well. Strain; add ice and fill with grapefruit soda. Decorate with an orange slice and a cherry.*

## TWENTY-FOUR HOUR COCKTAIL

1 quart corn whiskey
1 doz lemons
1 doz. oranges
1 pint pineapple juice
8 oz. sugar
Cherries

*Slice the lemons, saving the rinds. Squeeze the juice into a crock pot; add the sugar, corn whiskey, and a pint of boiling water. Drop in the rinds; close the crock and store overnight. The next afternoon, strain, squeeze in the juice of the oranges, and pour over chunks of ice. Garnish with cherries.*

### TWIN HILLS

2 oz. whiskey
2 tsp. Benedictine
1½ tsp. sugar syrup
1 tsp. lemon juice
1 tsp. lime juice

*Combine with ice; shake well. Strain straight up. Decorate with slices of lemon and lime.*

### TWIN SIN COCKTAIL

1 oz. gin
2 tsp. sweet vermouth
2 tsp. orange juice
A few drops of grenadine
1 egg white

*Combine with ice; shake well. Strain and add ice.*

### TWO-PART GLOGG

1 cup white rum
1 cup dry sherry
2 oz. sugar
Whole cloves, cinnamon sticks, raisins, whole shelled almonds.

*Combine in a large saucepan; heat thoroughly but do not allow to boil. Immediately before serving, ignite. Stir with a long-handled spoon until the flame dies out. Serve in mugs; make sure each one gets a little bit of every spice.*

## YOUR OWN RECIPE

# YOUR OWN RECIPE

Use a bartender's mixing glass whenever the instructions state "combine" ingredients. Strain the drink from the mixing glass into the drinking glass suggested by the illustration alongside the ingredients.

NOTE: The number of glasses or cups shown alongside a recipe do not necessarily indicate the quantity of drinks the recipe will produce.

---

**ULANDA**

1½ oz. gin
1 tbs. Cointreau
A few drops Pernod

*Combine with ice; shake well. Strain and add ice.*

**ULYSSES**

1 oz. brandy
1 oz. dry vermouth
1 oz. cherry brandy

*Combine with ice; shake well. Strain and add ice. Touch it up with a twist of orange.*

**UNION JACK**

1½ oz. gin
1 tbs. Creme Yvette

*Combine with ice; shake well. Strain and add ice.*

**UNION LEAGUE**

2 oz. Old Tom gin
1 oz. port
1-2 dashes orange bitters

*Combine and stir gently. Add ice to fill the glass.*

---

**UNCLE HARRY'S PUNCH**

2 bottles Rhine wine
2 bottles champagne
6 oz. curacao
6 oz. gold rum
4 oz. orange juice
4 oz. lemon juice
2 quarts club soda
Mint leaves
Fruit slices

*Chill all the bottles well before using. Combine the wine, curacao, rum, and juices; add the mint and fruit slices and stir. Add the soda and champagne plus chunks of ice before serving.*

**UNISPHERE**

1½ oz. gold rum
2 tsp. lime juice
1 tsp. grenadine
Several drops Benedictine and Pernod

*Combine with ice; shake well. Strain and add ice.*

**UPSTAIRS**

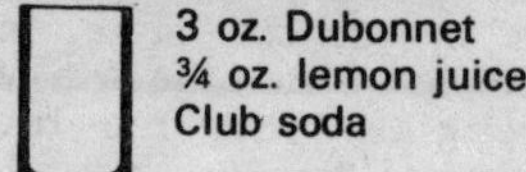

3 oz. Dubonnet
¾ oz. lemon juice
Club soda

*Combine the Dubonnet and the lemon juice with ice; shake well. Strain and add ice. Fill the tumbler with club soda.*

# YOUR OWN RECIPE

# YOUR OWN RECIPE

Use a bartender's mixing glass whenever the instructions state "combine" ingredients. Strain the drink from the mixing glass into the drinking glass suggested by the illustration alongside the ingredients.

The glass pictured for each drink is our suggestion; other drinking cups may be used as well.

---

## VALENCIA

2 oz. apricot brandy
1 oz. orange juice
1-2 dashes orange bitters

*Combine with ice; shake well. Strain and add ice.*

## VAN DER HUM

5 bottles brandy
7½ oz. tangerine peel, clean and finely chopped
2½ oz. cinnamon
4 doz. cloves
Nutmeg, cardamon seeds, and orange blossoms
Rum

*Combine the brandy with the peels and spices in an airtight cask; store at room temperature for at least a month, shaking once every day. When ready, strain out the spices and mix the brandy with rum — a few oz. of rum for every bottle of brandy. Store the finished* **VAN DER HUM** *in air-tight bottles; shake at least once a day for a week before serving.*

## VARIATION COCKTAILS

### BRANDY VARIATION

1 oz. brandy
1 oz. gin
1 oz. dry vermouth
Club soda

*Combine everything except the soda stir well and add ice. Fill the glass with soda.*

### FRENCH VARIATION

2½ oz. gin
Several drops Cointreau
Several drops dry vermouth
Ginger ale

*Combine everything except the ginger ale stir well and add ice. Fill the glass with ginger ale.*

### GIN VARIATION

2 oz. dry gin
2 tsp. sugar syrup
Club soda

*Combine everything except the soda stir well and add ice. Fill the glass with soda; touch it up with a twist of lemon.*

**VELVET HAMMER**

1½ oz. evaporated milk
1 oz. Cointreau
1 oz. white creme de cacao

*Combine with ice; shake very well. Strain. Serve straight up.*

---

**VELVET ORCHID**

1 oz. dry vermouth
1 oz. white creme de cacao
Several drops of black raspberry syrup

*Combine with ice; shake. Strain. Serve straight up.*

**VERACRUZ COCKTAIL**

1½ oz. Jamaican rum
2 oz. lime juice
1½ oz. dry vermouth
1-2 dashes pineapple juice

*Combine with ice; shake well. Strain and add ice.*

**VERBOTEN**

1 oz. gin
2 tsp. Forbidden Fruit, lemon juice and orange juice

*Combine with ice; shake well. Strain and add ice. Decorate with a cherry.*

**VERMONT PUNCH**

2 bottles whiskey
2 quarts lemon juice
1 quart maple syrup

*Combine in a large saucepan; stir well. Heat but do not allow to boil; stirring occasionally to keep smooth. Serve hot in mugs.*

**VERMOUTH**

1 pint dry white wine
1 tsp. wormwood extract

*Combine in a bottle; seal, shake, and allow to stand until the wormwood ferments in the wine.*

---

**VERMOUTH CASSIS**

1½ oz. dry vermouth
1 tbs. creme de cassis
Club soda

*Combine the vermouth and the cassis stir well and add plenty of ice. Fill the glass with club soda; decorate with a slice of lemon.*

## VERMOUTH COOLER

1½ oz. sweet vermouth
1 tbs. vodka
1½ tsp. lemon juice
1½ tsp. sugar syrup
Club soda

*Combine everything except the soda with ice; shake well. Strain add ice and fill the glass with soda. Stir gently.*

## VERMOUTH FLIP

3 oz. dry vermouth
1 egg white
1 oz. cognac
1½ tsp. lemon juice
1 tsp. powdered sugar
Club soda

*Combine everything, except the soda with ice; shake well. Strain over ice. Fill with soda and stir gently.*

## VERMOUTH FRAPPE

2 tsp. dry vermouth
A few drops orange bitters
A few drops sugar syrup

*Combine with a few cubes of ice; stir briskly. Strain. Serve straight up; add a twist of lemon.*

## VERMOUTH MARASCHINO

2 oz. dry vermouth
2 tsp. maraschino
2 tsp. lemon juice
1-2 dashes orange bitters

*Combine with ice; shake well. Strain and add ice. Decorate with a cherry.*

## VERMOUTH TRIPLE SEC

1 oz. dry vermouth
1 oz. gin
2 tsp. Triple Sec
1-2 dashes orange bitters

*Combine with ice; shake well. Strain; add ice and a twist of lemon.*

---

## VIA VENETO

1¾ oz. brandy
2 tsp. sambuca
2 tsp. lemon juice
1½ tsp. sugar syrup
½ egg white

*Combine with ice; shake well. Strain and add ice.*

## VICTOR

1 oz. sweet vermouth
2 tsp. gin
2 tsp. brandy

*Combine with ice; shake well. Strain and add ice.*

## VICTORY

1½ oz. Pernod
2 tbs. grenadine
Club soda

*Combine everything except the soda with ice; shake well. Strain and add ice. Fill the glass with soda.*

## VIENNESE ICED TEA

*Fill a tall glass part-way with crushed ice; pour in 1½ oz. of rum and fill the glass with dark, freshly brewed tea. Add sugar to taste and stir well.*

**VIKING**

1½ oz. Swedish Punch
2 tbs. aquavit
2 tbs. lime juice

*Combine with ice; shake. Strain and add ice.*

**VILLA IGIEA**

1 oz. gin
1 oz. sweet vermouth
1 oz. Amaro

*Combine with ice; shake and strain. Serve over ice.*

---

**VIN CHAUD**

1 bottle red wine
4 oz. brandy
6-8 cubes sugar
Cinnamon sticks, whole cloves
Lemon slices and a spiral lemon peel

*Place the sugar cubes in a large saucepan and dissolve them in a couple of tablespoons of hot water. Pour in the wine; heat but do not boil. Add the spices, the slices and the peel, and the brandy. Simmer a few minutes but do not allow to boil. Serve in a large chafing dish; keep warm.*

**VIN CRIOLLO**

½ peck wild grapes
1 lb. sugar
Honey

*Place the grapes in a large crock pot and add enough honey to cover them. Allow to stand for at least one week; then strain through cheesecloth. Put the sugar in the crock pot and pour the juice over it. Stir, then allow to ferment. Strain, bottle, and store in a cool place until ready to use.*

---

**VIRGIN**

¾ oz. gin
¾ oz. white creme de menthe
1 tbs. Forbidden Fruit

*Combine with ice; shake well. Strain and add ice.*

**VIRGINIA JULEP**

2 oz. bourbon
1½ tsp. sugar syrup
Mint sprigs

*Soak a few sprigs of mint in the bourbon for one hour. When ready, combine the minted bourbon with the sugar syrup and with ice and shake well. Strain over crushed ice. Stir and decorate with fresh mint.*

**VIRGINIA NIGHTCAP**

2 doz. whole cloves
6 oz. cognac
1 oz. sugar
1 pint hard cider

*Crush the cloves into a fine powder; combine with the sugar in a saucepan. Add the cognac and the cider; heat thoroughly but do not allow to boil. Serve hot in mugs.*

**VODKA CHAMPAGNE PUNCH**

¾ oz. vodka
1 tbs. white rum
2 tsp. lime juice
2 tsp. strawberry liqueur
A few drops of grenadine
1 strawberry

*Combine everything except the strawberry with ice; shake well. Line the rim of glass with water and press it in sugar; strain in the drink and decorate with the strawberry.*

**VODKA COCKTAIL**

1½ oz. vodka
1 tbs. cherry brandy
1½ tsp. lemon juice

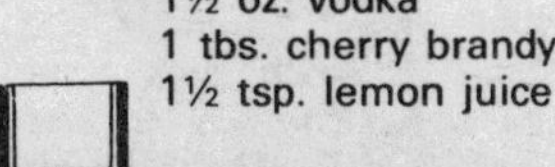

*Combine with ice; shake well. Strain and add ice.*

**VODKA FRAISE**

¾ oz. vodka
1 tbs. white rum
2 tsp. lime juice
2 tsp. strawberry liqueur
A few drops of grenadine
1 strawberry

*Combine everything except the strawberry with ice; shake well. Line the rim of glass with water and press it in sugar; strain in the drink and decorate with the strawberry.*

---

**VODKA GIBSON**

2½ oz. vodka
1 tbs. dry vermouth
1 pearl onion

*Combine the vodka with the vermouth with ice; shake well. Strain straight up. Drop in the onion.*

**VODKA GIMLET**

1½ oz. vodka
1 oz. lime juice
1½ tsp. sugar syrup

*Combine with ice; shake well. Strain and add ice.*

**VODKA GRAND MARNIER**

1½ oz. vodka
2 tsp. lime juice
2 tsp. Grand Marnier

*Combine with ice; shake well. Strain and add ice. Decorate with a slice of orange.*

## VODKA GRASSHOPPER

¾ oz. white creme de cacao
¾ oz. green creme de menthe
1 tbs. vodka

*Combine with ice; shake very well. Strain straight up.*

## VODKA GYPSY

1½ oz. vodka
1 tbs. Benedictine
1-2 dashes orange bitters

*Combine with ice; shake well. Strain and add ice.*

## VODKA ORANGE PUNCH

3 bottles vodka
18 oz. frozen orange juice concentrate
8 oz. Cointreau

*Combine; stir until well-blended and add ice. Touch it up with several drops of lemon juice and slices of orange.*

## VODKA SLING

2 oz. vodka
1½ tsp. Benedictine
1½ tsp. cherry brandy
1 tsp. lemon juice
A few dashes of Angostura and orange bitters
Club soda

*Combine everything except the soda with ice; shake well. Strain; add ice and fill the glass with soda.*

## VODKA STINGER

1½ oz. vodka
2 tbs. white creme de menthe

*Combine with ice; shake very well. Strain and add ice.*

## VOLGA BOATMAN

1½ oz. vodka
2 tbs. cherry brandy
2 tbs. orange juice

*Combine with ice; shake and strain. Serve over ice.*

## VOLSTEAD

1½ oz. Swedish Punch
2 tbs. rye
1 tbs. orange juice
1 tbs. raspberry syrup
A few drops anisette

*Combine with ice; shake well. Strain and add ice.*

# YOUR OWN RECIPE

# YOUR OWN RECIPE

Use a bartender's mixing glass whenever the instructions state "combine" ingredients. Strain the drink from the mixing glass into the drinking glass suggested by the illustration alongside the ingredients.

The glass pictured for each drink is our suggestion; other drinking cups may be used as well.

---

**WAGON WHEEL**

2½ oz. Southern Comfort
2 tbs. cognac
1 tbs. lemon juice
Several drops grenadine

*Combine with ice; shake well. Strain and add ice.*

**WALDORF**

2 oz. Swedish Punch
2 tsp. dry gin
2 tsp. lemon juice

*Combine with ice; shake. Strain and add ice.*

**WALTERS**

2 oz. Scotch
1 oz. orange juice
1 oz. lemon juice

*Combine with ice; shake well. Strain and add ice.*

**WARDAY'S COCKTAIL**

1 oz. gin
1 oz. sweet vermouth
1 oz. apple brandy
1 tsp. yellow chartreuse

*Combine with ice; shake well. Strain and add ice.*

**WARSAW**

1½ oz. vodka
2 tsp. dry vermouth
2 tsp. blackberry brandy
1 tsp. lemon juice

*Combine with ice; shake well. Strain and add ice. Touch it up with a twist of lemon.*

**WASHINGTON**

1½ oz. dry vermouth
1 tbs. brandy
Several drops sugar syrup
1-2 dashes Angostura bitters

*Combine with ice; shake well. Strain and add ice.*

## WASSAIL PUNCH

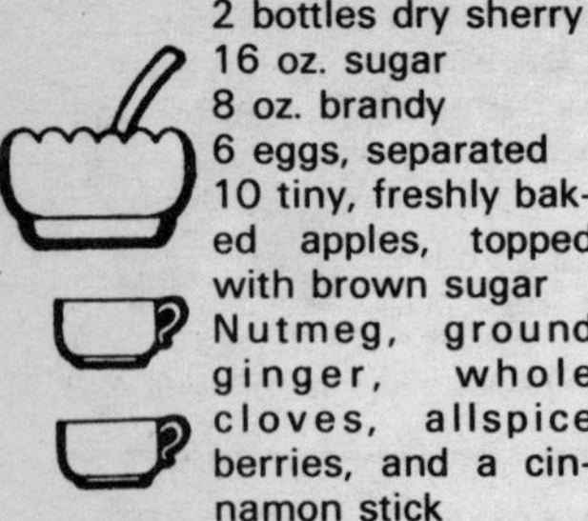

2 bottles dry sherry
16 oz. sugar
8 oz. brandy
6 eggs, separated
10 tiny, freshly baked apples, topped with brown sugar
Nutmeg, ground ginger, whole cloves, allspice berries, and a cinnamon stick

*Combine the sherry and the spices with ½ cup of water in a large saucepan; heat but do not allow to boil. In separate bowls, beat the yolks until creamy and the whites until stiff; fold them together. Strain the spices out of the wine and gently fold in the egg mixture. Pour in the brandy and stir. Serve steaming hot in a large punch bowl; float the baked apples on top.*

## WATERBURY

2½ oz. brandy
1 tbs. lemon juice
1 tsp. sugar syrup
1 egg white
A few drops of grenadine

*Combine with ice; shake extremely well. Strain and add ice.*

## WATERMELON CASSIS

2 oz. gin
1 tbs. lemon juice
2 tsp. creme de cassis
4 oz. diced seeded watermelon
4 oz. crushed ice
Club soda

*Combine everything except the soda in a blender at a low speed for 15 seconds. Strain; add ice and touch it up with a spritz of soda. Decorate with a slice of lemon.*

## WATERMELON COOLER

2¼ oz. white rum
2 tsp. lime juice
1½ tsp. sugar syrup
4 oz. diced seeded watermelon
4 oz. crushed ice

*Combine in a blender at a low speed for 15 seconds. Strain; add ice to fill the glass. Decorate with a slice of lime.*

## WEDDING BELLE

1 tbs. gin
1 tbs. Dubonnet
1 tsp. cherry brandy
1 tsp. orange juice

*Combine with ice; shake well. Strain and add ice.*

## WEEP NO MORE

1½ oz. Dubonnet
1¼ oz. brandy
2 tbs. lime juice
A few drops of maraschino

*Combine with ice; shake well. Strain and add ice.*

**WESTERN ROSE**

1 oz. gin
2 tsp. dry vermouth
2 tsp. apricot brandy
A few drops lemon juice

*Combine with ice; shake well. Strain and add ice. To make an* **ENGLISH ROSE**, *add a few drops of grenadine before shaking. A* **FRENCH ROSE** *uses cherry brandy instead of the apricot brandy. For a* **WEBSTER**, *replace half the apricot brandy with lime juice and leave out the lemon juice.*

**WHALER'S TODDY**

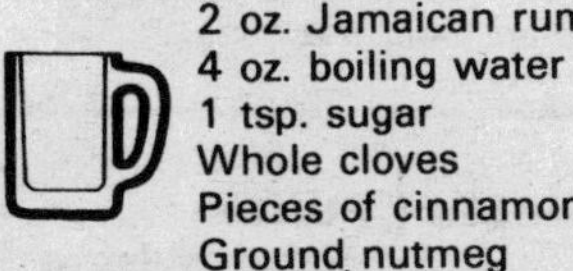

2 oz. Jamaican rum
4 oz. boiling water
1 tsp. sugar
Whole cloves
Pieces of cinnamon
Ground nutmeg

*Pour the boiling water into a mug; add the sugar and stir until dissolved. Add the rum cloves, and cinnamon pieces and stir gently. Serve piping hot, garnished with nutmeg and decorated with a slice of lemon.*

---

**WHIP**

1½ oz. brandy
1 tbs. sweet vermouth
1 tbs. dry vermouth
Several drops curacao
A few drops Pernod

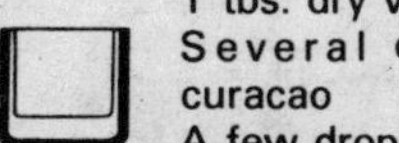

*Combine with ice; shake well. Strain and add ice.*

**WHISKEY COBBLER**

2½ oz. whiskey
1 tbs. lemon juice
2 tsp. grapefruit juice

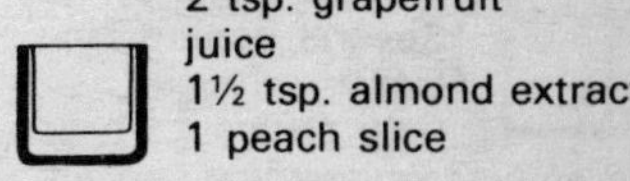

1½ tsp. almond extract
1 peach slice

*Combine everything except the peach slice; stir well and add ice to fill the glass. Decorate with the slice of peach.*

**WHISKEY COCKTAIL**

*A* **WHISKEY COCKTAIL** *is an* **OLD-FASHIONED** *made with rye instead of bourbon.*

**WHISKEY CURACAO FIZZ**

2 oz. whiskey
1 oz. lemon juice
2 tsp. curacao
1½ tsp. sugar syrup
Club soda

*Combine everything except the soda with ice; shake well. Strain; add ice and fill the glass with soda. Decorate with a slice of orange.*

## WHISKEY DAISY

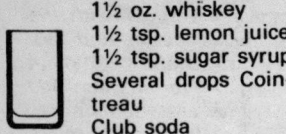

1½ oz. whiskey
1½ tsp. lemon juice
1½ tsp. sugar syrup
Several drops Cointreau
Club soda

*Combine everything except the soda with ice; shake well. Strain; add ice and fill the glass with soda. Decorate with slices of fruit. A few drops of curacao or an oz. of raspberry syrup can be used instead of the Cointreau (in the latter case, half the sugar), or a teaspoon of yellow chartreause can be floated on top and the sugar eliminated altogether.*

## WHISKEY HOUND

1½ oz. 100-proof bourbon
2 tsp. 151-proof rum
2 tsp. grapefruit juice
2 tsp. orange juice
1 oz. lemon juice
1 tbs. sugar syrup
A few drops maraschino cherry juice

*Combine with ice; shake. Strain and add ice.*

## WHISKEY KUMQUAT

3 oz. bourbon
A few drops of kumquat juice
A whole kumquat

*Pour the bourbon into glass; add the juice plus the kumquat and stir gently. Add ice.*

## WHISKEY MAC

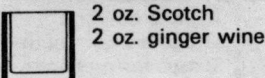

2 oz. Scotch
2 oz. ginger wine

*Combine with ice; shake well. Strain and add ice.*

## WHISKEY OUZO FIX

2 oz. whiskey
2 tsp. lemon juice
1½ tsp. sugar syrup
1 tsp. ouzo

*Combine everything except the ouzo; fill the glass with crushed ice and sir well. Touch it up with a twist of lemon; float the ouzo.*

## WHISKEY PUNCH

1½ bottles whiskey
4 cups orange juice
12 oz. lemon juice
3 oz. curacao
3 tbs. sugar syrup
2 quarts club soda

*Combine the juices with the sugar syrup; pour in all the remaining ingredients except for the soda and stir. Decorate with slices of fruit. Add the soda plus chunks of ice before serving. Half the club soda can be replaced by iced tea.*

## WHISKEY PUNCH

1 bottle bourbon
1 pint brandy
3 cups hot green tea
2 cups sugar
6 oz. orange juice
2½ lemon juice
Grated orange and lemon peels

*Dissolve the sugar with the fruit juices peels, and tea. Allow to stand at room temperature for an hour. Add the brandy and the bourbon; strain out the rinds and store in the refrigerator until cold. Add ice.*

## WHISKEY SHAKE

2 oz. whiskey
2 tbs. lime juice
1 tsp. sugar syrup

*Combine with ice; shake well. Strain and add ice.*

## WHISKEY SOUR

2 oz. whiskey
1 oz. lemon juice
1 tbs. sugar syrup

*Combine with ice; shake well. Strain straight up. Decorate with a slice of lemon. For a* **WARD EIGHT,** *add a few drops of grenadine before mixing.*

## WHISKEY SOUR IN THE ROUGH

2 oz. whiskey
1 tsp. sugar
Orange and lemon slices

*Muddle the sugar with the fruit slices in a mixing glass; add the whiskey plus plenty of ice and shake well. Pour the entire contents of the mixing glass into an old-fashioned glass and allow to settle before drinking.*

## WHISKEY SOUR PUNCH

2 pints rye
2 pints bourbon
12 oz. sugar
6 oz. lemon juice
1-2 tsp. Angostura bitters
1 pint club soda

*Boil the sugar with enough water to make a syrup allow to cool. Combine with all the remaining ingrediens except the soda; Stir well. Add the soda plus chunks of ice.*

**WHITE COCKTAIL**

3 oz. gin
1 tsp. anisette
A few drops orange bitters

*Combine; stir gently.*

**WHITE DOVE**

2 oz. white rum
2 oz. anisette

*Combine with ice; shake. Strain over crushed ice. This drink can be touched up with a little club soda.*

**WHITE HORSE**

1 oz. gin
1 oz. heavy cream
1 oz. Cointreau

*Combine with ice; shake very well. Strain straight up.*

**WHITE LADY**

2 oz. Cointreau
2 tsp. white creme de menthe
2 tsp. brandy

*Combine with ice; shake well. Strain and add ice.*

**WHITE LILY**

1 oz. gin
1 oz. white rum
1 oz. Cointreau
A few drops Pernod

*Combine with ice; shake well. Strain and add ice.*

**WHITE LION**

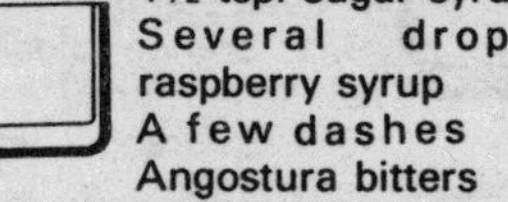

1½ oz. Jamaican rum
1½ oz. lemon juice
1½ tsp. sugar syrup
Several drops raspberry syrup
A few dashes Angostura bitters

*Combine with ice; shake well. Strain and add ice.*

**WHITE ROSE**

1¼ oz. gin
Orange juice
2 tsp lime juice
1½ tsp. sugar syrup
½ egg white

*Combine with ice, shake extremely well. Strain and add ice.*

**WHITE WAY**

1 oz. brandy
1 oz. Pernod
1 oz. anisette

*Combine with ice; shake well. Strain and add ice.*

**WHITE WINE CUP**

1 bottle white Burgundy
4 oz. sherry
2½ tbs. anisette
2½ tbs. brandy
1 bottle club soda
Lemon peels, pineapple slices, mint leaves
Sugar to taste

*Combine everything except the soda. Add ice and the soda before serving.*

## WHITE WITCH

1 oz. white rum
2 tsp. white creme de cacao
2 tsp. Cointreau
½ lime
Club soda
Sprigs of mint coated with powdered sugar

*Combine the rum, creme de cacao, and Cointreau with ice; shake well. Strain. Squeeze in the juice of the lime. Add ice and fill with soda; garnish with the mint.*

## WIDOW'S DREAM

3 oz. Benedictine
2 tbs. heavy cream
1 egg

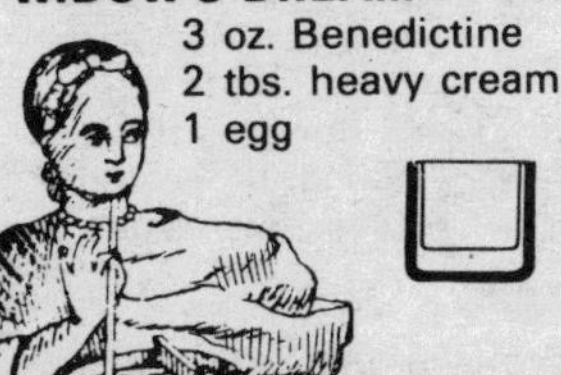

*Combine with ice; shake extremely well. Strain and add ice.*

## WIDOW'S KISS

1 oz. apple brandy
2 tsp. Benedictine
2 tsp. yellow chartreuse
1-2 dashes Angostura bitters
1 strawberry

*Combine everything except the strawberry in a mixing glass filled with ice; shake well. Strain into an old-fashioned glass and add ice. Decorate with the strawberry.*

## WILD COW

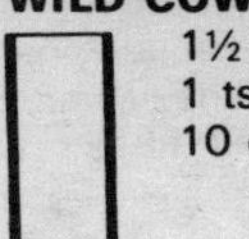

1½ oz. bourbon
1 tsp. sugar
10 oz. milk

*Dissolve the sugar in the bourbon on the bottom of a glass; add the milk plus ice to fill the glass and gently stir. Garnish with nutmeg.*

## WINDJAMMER

2 oz. white rum
2 tbs. rock and rye
2 tbs. orange curacao
An orange peel, cut in a long strip
Brown sugar

*Coat the orange peel with brown sugar; place it on the bottom of a mug. Heat the mug over a low flame until the sugar melts on the peel; add the remaining ingredients. Fill the mug with boiling water and stir well. Touch it up with a twist of lemon.*

## WINE BOWL

2 bottles champagne
Grenadine
Sliced strawberries

*Pour the champagne over chunks of ice; add enough grenadine to color the wine a light pink. Garnish with strawberries.*

**WINE REFRESHER**

1 gallon rose wine
3 cups unsweetened grapefruit juice

*Chill well before combining. Serve over plenty of ice.*

**WITCH'S BREW**

3 oz. Strega
2 tbs. orange juice
2 tbs. lemon juice
1 tbs. white creme de menthe
A few drops of Pernod

*Combine everything except the Pernod with ice; shake very well. Strain over crushed ice; stir gently until the glass begins to frost. Float the Pernod. Decorate with slices of fruit.*

**WITCH'S STEW**

1 quart cider
1 pint apiece orange and lemon sherbert
8 oz. curacao
1 large orange
2 doz. whole cloves
Nutmeg, cinnamon, allspice
1 bottle champagne

*Stick the orange with the cloves; combine with the curacao in a saucepan and simmer several minutes, turning occasionally. Add the cider and spices and heat thoroughly. Allow to cool; turn out unstrained into a large punch bowl; add the sherbert in scoops. Before serving, add the champagne.*

**WIVES' NOG**

1 quart hard cider
4 oz. sherry
2 oz. brandy
2 oz. curacao
½ oz. maple syrup
Grated nutmeg
Orange slices
Cucumber slices
Lemon peels

*Combine the cider, sherry, brandy, curacao, and maple syrup; stir until the syrup has dissolved. Garnish with the nutmeg, fruit and vegetable slices, and peels.*

**WOODRUFF WINE BOWL**

3 pints May wine
4 oz. sugar
2 bunches fresh woodruff, a few blossoms aside

*Combine the woodruff, uncut, with the wine and sugar. Allow to stand, covered, at room temperature for half an hour. Strain; add ice and reserved woodruff blossoms just before serving. Stay light on the ice to keep the fragrance of the woodruff intact.*

**WOODSTOCK**

1½ oz. gin
1 oz. lemon juice
1 tsp. maple syrup
1-2 dashes orange bitters

*Combine with ice; shake very well. Line the rim of glass with water or maple syrup and press it in sugar. Strain in the drink and add ice.*

**WOODWARD**

1 oz. Scotch
1 oz. grapefruit juice
1 oz. dry vermouth

*Combine with ice; shake well. Strain and add ice.*

**WRIGHT SPECIAL**

2½ oz. rye
2½ oz. port
3 tsp. lemon juice
2 tsp. sugar syrup
1½ egg whites

*Combine with ice; shake extremely well. Strain into a tall glass and fill the glass with ice.*

**WORLD OF TOMORROW PUNCH**

3 bottles champagne
2 bottles Tokay wine
1 bottle Madeira
2 pints brandy
1 oz. maraschino, curacao, Benedictine, and rum
2 bottles club soda
12 oz. sugar
Pineapple and orange slices
Whole strawberries

*Pound the sugar with a few of the fruit rinds until the fruit color starts to bleed in. Add the fruit slices and pour the remaining ingredients over them; club soda last. Stir very well. This punch may be strained clean if you'd like.*

# YOUR OWN RECIPE

# YOUR OWN RECIPE

# YOUR OWN RECIPE

Use a bartender's mixing glass whenever the instructions state "combine" ingredients. Strain the drink from the mixing glass into the drinking glass suggested by the illustration alongside the ingredients.

# XYZ

### XANTHIA

¾ oz. gin
¾ oz. cherry brandy
1 tbs. yellow chartreuse

*Combine with ice; shake well. Strain and add ice.*

### XERES

3 oz. sherry
1-2 dashes orange bitters
1-2 dashes peach bitters

*Combine with ice; shake well. Strain and add ice. To make a* **SHERRY COCKTAIL**, *double the orange bitters and use and equal amount of dry vermouth instead of the peach bitters.*

### XYZ

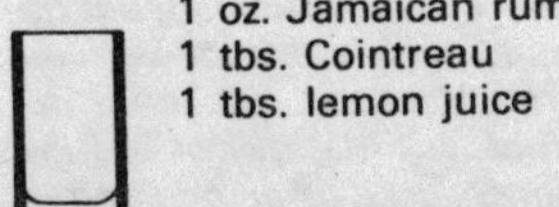

1 oz. Jamaican rum
1 tbs. Cointreau
1 tbs. lemon juice

*Combine with ice; shake well. Strain and add ice.*

### YANKEE PUNCH

2 quarts rye
1 pint rum
Pineapple and lemon slices
4 quarts water
Sugar

*Combine stir well. Add ice before serving.*

### YARD OF FLANNEL

1 quart ale
4 oz. rum
3 oz. sugar
4 eggs
Nutmeg, ground ginger

*In a wide pitcher, beat the eggs with the sugar until the sugar has dissolved and the eggs are creamy-colored. Add the rum and spices; stir. Heat the ale in a saucepan; do not boil. Remove from heat and slowly add to the egg mixture, stirring constantly. Serve hot in mugs.*

### YASHMAK

¾ oz. rye
¾ oz. dry vermouth
1 tbs. Pernod
1-2 dashes Angostura bitters
A few drops sugar syrup

*Combine with ice; shake well. Strain and add ice. Campari can be used instead of the Pernod, omitting the bitters and the sugar.*

### YELLOW PARROT

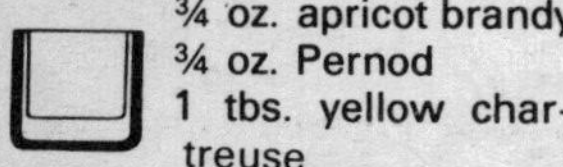

¾ oz. apricot brandy
¾ oz. Pernod
1 tbs. yellow chartreuse

*Combine with ice; shake well. Strain and add ice.*

### YELLOW PLUM

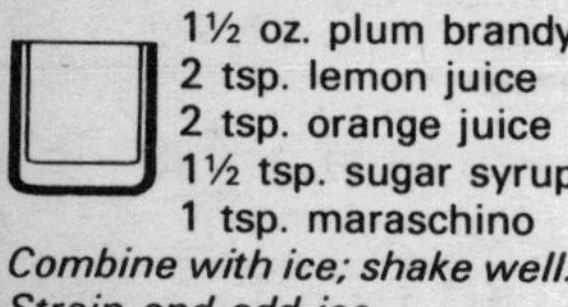

1½ oz. plum brandy
2 tsp. lemon juice
2 tsp. orange juice
1½ tsp. sugar syrup
1 tsp. maraschino

*Combine with ice; shake well. Strain and add ice.*

### YODEL

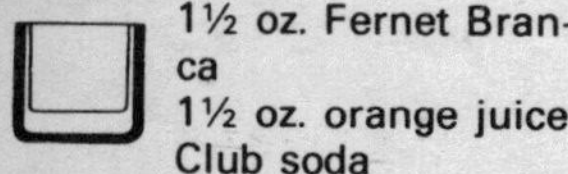

1½ oz. Fernet Branca
1½ oz. orange juice
Club soda

*Combine the Fernet Branca and the orange juice. Add ice and fill the glass with soda; stir gently.*

### YORK SPECIAL

2½ oz. dry vermouth
1 tbs. maraschino
Several dashes orange bitters

*Combine with ice; shake well. Strain and add ice. The bitters can be omitted.*

### ZENITH

2½ oz. gin
1 tbs. pineapple juice
Club soda
1 pineapple stick

*Combine the gin and the juice stir well. Add ice and fill the glass with soda. Decorate with the pineapple stick.*

### ZOMBIE

1½ oz. gold rum
3 tsp. lime juice
1 tbs. Jamaican rum
1 tbs. white rum
1 tbs. pineapple and papaya juice
1½ tsp. sugar syrup
1 tsp. 151-proof rum
1 pineapple stick
Granulated sugar

*Combine everything except the high-proof rum, pineapple stick, and granulated sugar with ice; shake well. Strain and add ice. Decorate with the pineapple stick and a cherry; float the high-proof rum and sprinkle a little sugar over it.* **ZOMBIES** *should be made with rums of various strengths, i.e. 90 and 86 proof. A little apricot brandy can be used as an addition to the fruit juices; sprigs of mint can be added to the garnishes.*

# YOUR OWN RECIPE

# NON-ALCOHOLIC DRINKS

### AGUA LOJA

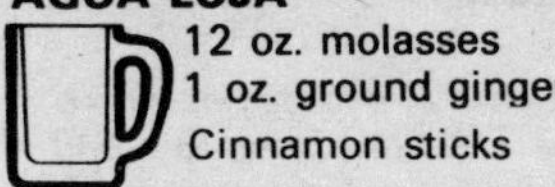

12 oz. molasses
1 oz. ground ginger
Cinnamon sticks

*Boil the ginger and several cinnamon sticks in 5 cups of water for 15 minutes. Strain clean and allow to cool. Turn out into a bowl; add the molasses and stir until blended. Refrigerate until ready to serve.*

### ALMOND PUNCH

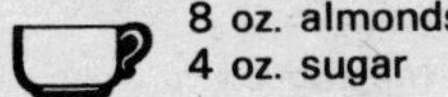

8 oz. almonds
4 oz. sugar

*Boil the almonds in 2 cups of water for several minutes; remove from heat, cool, and peel the nuts. Pound the almonds into a pulp and combine with 1 quart of water in a pot. Strain clean into a separate bowl; add the sugar and stir until the sugar is dissolved. Refrigerate until ready to serve.*

---

### ANGEL PUNCH

2 quarts white grape juice
1 quart green tea
1 pint lemon juice
8 oz. sugar syrup
2 bottles club soda

*Combine everything except the soda; stir well and refrigerate several hours. Chill the soda. Serve on ice with soda.*

### APPLE COCKTAIL

8 oz. sliced, peeled apple
8 oz. orange juice
3 oz. lemon juice
Pineapple chunks
Sugar to taste
Maraschino cherries

*Combine the fruit juices in a bowl; add sugar to taste and stir until the sugar is dissolved. Add the sliced apple and pineapple slices and refrigerate for at least an hour. Serve in large tumblers; garnish with a cherry.*

---

### APPLE JUICE

1 doz. baking apples
Sugar
Lemon juice

*Slice the apples in their peels; boil in enough water to cover until soft. Strain the juice into a large bowl; add sugar to taste. Stir until the sugar has dissolved. Allow to cool. Add 2 teaspoons lemon juice for every pint of apple juice and stir. Dilute with ice-cold water before serving.*

### BANANA MILK SHAKE

1 large banana, sliced
8 oz. milk
1½ oz. orange juice
1 tbs. honey
A few drops almond extract
Whipped cream

*Combine everything except the whipped cream; shake. Serve with whipped cream.*

## BARLEY PUNCH

2 oz. ground barley
2 oz. sugar
The peels of 1 large lime

*Combine in a large pot with 6 cups of water; bring to a boil and stir constantly until the barley is cooked. Strain out the punch and refrigerate until ready to serve.*

---

## BLACK AND WHITE MILK SHAKE

1 pint milk
2 oz. apiece vanilla and chocolate ice cream

*Combine in a blender for a few seconds at a high speed.*

## BLACK COW

8 oz. sarsaparilla
2 oz. vanilla ice cream

*Pour the sarsaparilla into a tall glass; add the ice cream and stir until well-blended.*

## BOSTON CREAM

2½ lb. sugar
2 oz. citric acid
1 tbs. concentrated lemon juice
Baking soda

*Combine the sugar and citric acid in 3 pints of boiling water; stir well until the sugar has dissolved and allow to cool. Add the lemon juice and stir. Chill in the refrigerator; bottle and store. Serve as a tonic, with a pinch of baking soda and a teaspoon of* **BOSTON CREAM** *for each glass of water.*

## BOG PUNCH

1 pint cranberries
1 pint apple juice
8 oz. sugar
8 oz. cranberry juice
4 oz. lemon juice
8 oz. pineapple chunks, from the can and packed in their own sauce
1 bottle ginger ale

*Boil the whole cranberries with the sugar in a pint of water; remove from heat and simmer until the berries are soft and the sugar has dissolved. Strain out the juice; allow to cool. Combine the fresh, warm juice with the remaining ingredients; refrigerate until ready to serve.*

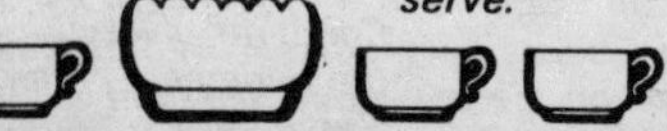

## CARRY NATION PUNCH

1 quart orange juice
3 cups lemon juice
8 oz. pineapple juice
8 oz. sugar syrup
2 bottles ginger ale
Slices of fruit

*Combine the juices and the sugar syrup, stir well and refrigerate several hours. Chill the ginger ale. Add the ginger ale and ice before serving. Decorate with fruit.*

## CHERRY BING

1 pint cherry juice
4 oz. orange juice

*Dilute the cherry juice and orange juice with 10 oz. water; stir to blend. Add chunks of ice before serving.*

## CHERRY WATER

2 lb. cherries
8 oz. sugar
1 large lemon

*Crush the cherries; strain the juice into a bowl. Squeeze in the juice of the lemon plus a few tsp. water; stir well and allow to stand for several hours. Strain into a pitcher when ready. Serve over crushed ice.*

## CHRISTMAS JUICE PUNCH

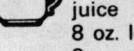

2 quarts apple juice
2 quarts cranberry juice
8 oz. lemon juice
8 oz. sugar
2 bottles ginger ale

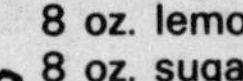

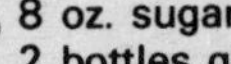

*Combine everything except the ginger ale. Stir well. Add the ginger ale plus chunks of ice before serving.*

## CIDER CUP

1 quart cider
3 oz. sugar
Whole cloves, cinnamon sticks

*Combine in a large saucepan; heat until boiling, stirring constantly. Remove from heat and allow to cool. When cool enough, strain and refrigerate for several hours. Re-heat approx. one hour before serving.*

## CIDER EGGNOG FOR TWO

4 oz. light cream
1 egg
1 tsp. powdered sugar
Sweet cider
Ground nutmeg

*Combine the cream, sugar, and egg with ice; shake well. Strain into two tall glasses; add ice and fill with cider. Dust with nutmeg.*

## CLAM JUICE COCKTAIL

5 oz. clam juice
1 tsp. catsup
1-2 dashes Tabasco sauce
A pinch of celery salt

*Combine with ice; shake well. Strain into a tumbler and add ice. A* **CLAMATO COCKTAIL** *uses half clam juice and half tomato juice, omitting the catsup.*

## CONCORD GRAPE PUNCH

1 pint Concord grape juice
1 pint cold water
4 oz. sugar
4 oz. orange juice
3 oz. lemon juice

*Combine; stir gently to blend and allow to stand until the sugar has dissolved. Add chunks of ice before serving.*

---

## CRANBERRY JUICE COCKTAIL

1 quart cranberries
4 oz. apiece lemon, orange, and pineapple juice
8 oz. sugar

*Boil the cranberries in a quart of water until soft; allow to cool. Strain the juice; add the sugar and stir until it has dissolved. Add the fruit juices plus chunks of ice when ready to serve.*

## CRANBERRY PUNCH

1 quart pineapple juice
2 16 oz. cans cranberry juice
6 oz. brown sugar
Ground cloves cinnamon, allspice, nutmeg, salt, and cinnamon sticks
A spot of butter

*Boil the brown sugar and spices (except for the cinnamon sticks) with a cup of water in a saucepan; add the pineapple juice and 3 more cups of water. Add the cranberry juice and bring to another boil; turn down the heat and simmer for several minutes. Stir and turn out into a deep chafing dish. Top with the butter. Serve in mugs, using the cinnamon sticks as swizzlers.*

---

## CRANBERRY TEA PUNCH

2 quarts cranberries
1 quart tea
2 cups sugar
Cinnamon sticks
Lemon slices
Ground nutmeg

*Boil the cranberries in 2 quarts of water; when soft, strain. Pour the juice back into the pot; add the sugar and cinnamon sticks and simmer for several minutes. Allow to cool; add the tea and lemon slices. Re-heat. Serve hot in mugs garnished with nutmeg.*

## CRANBERRY WASSAIL

2 oz. ground orange pekoe tea
8 oz. orange juice
4 oz. lemon juice
2 small bottle cranberry juice
1 cup sugar
Ground nutmeg, cinnamon, and allspice

*Combine the spices and ground tea in a cloth sack; infuse it in 2 quarts of boiling water. Immediately remove from heat; allow to steep for 15 minutes. Strain. Add sugar and juices; re-heat and stir until sugar has dissolved. Serve piping hot.*

## CREOLE COOLER

1 pint milk
8 oz. crushed pineapple, chilled
2 oz. orange juice
3 tsp. lime juice
Sugar

*Combine the pineapple with the juices in a pitcher; add sugar to taste. Add the milk and mix well. Serve straight up.*

## EGG TISANA

2 egg whites
The grated peels of 1 lime
8 oz. sugar

*Beat the egg whites until foamy; add the grated peel and continue beating until the whites hold peaks. Slowly add the sugar and continue beating the whites until stiff. Gradually combine the whites with 5 cups of water in a large bowl; beating carefully and constantly. Serve immediately.*

## EMERALD FROSTS

4 oz. mint jelly
3 tsp. lime juice
Lemon-lime soda
Lemon sherbert
Lime slices

*Melt the jelly with 4 oz. water in a saucepan; cool and add the lime juice. Drop scoops of sherbert in several tall glasses; add 2 tsps. mint syrup to each glass. Fill the glasses with soda; stir very well. Add ice if you wish; garnish with lime slices.*

---

## ENRICHED COFFEE

12 oz. ground coffee
1 egg

*Combine the coffee with the egg, well-beaten, and 4 oz. cold water. Stir to blend; tie up the soaked coffee in a cloth sack. Boil a gallon and a half of water; remove from heat and infuse with the coffee sack. Shake the sack in the water a few times, then drop it in, cover the pot, and allow it to brew for at least 12 minutes. When ready, remove sack, strain the coffee, add 4 oz. of cold water and serve immediately.*

## FLORIDA COCKTAIL

3½ oz. grapefruit juice
1½ oz. orange juice
1 tbs. lemon juice
2 oz. sugar syrup
Club soda
Mint sprigs
A pinch of salt

*Combine everything except the soda and mint with ice; shake well. Strain over crushed ice. Add an oz. of soda to each glass and decorate with mint.*

## FLORIDA PUNCH

1½ quart orange juice
1½ quart grapefruit juice
16 oz. powdered sugar
12 oz. lime juice
3 cups water
1½ quart ginger ale

*Combine the sugar and the water in a saucepan; heat and stir until the sugar is dissolved. Allow to cool. Combine the sugar syrup and the juices; stir well. Add the ginger ale plus chunks of ice before serving.*

## FRESH FRUIT PUNCH

8 oz. apiece of orange juice, pineapple juice, and grapefruit juice
1 bottle ginger ale
Sugar to taste

*Combine the juices with the sugar. Stir until the sugar is dissolved and refrigerate. Add the ginger ale plus chunks of ice before serving.*

## FRESNO APRICOT COOLER

1 pint apricot nectar
6 oz. orange juice
3 tbs. lemon juice
1½ oz. sugar
1 pint ginger ale

*Dissolve the sugar with the fruit juices. Add the nectar and stir to blend. Refrigerate until ready to serve. Add the ginger ale plus chunks of ice before serving.*

## FROSTED APRICOT SPECIAL

1 cup apricots
3 cups milk
8 oz. vanilla ice cream

*Cook the apricots until soft; remove the skins and pits. Crush the pulp in a mixing bowl; add the milk and stir to blend. Place the ice cream on the bottom of a glass pitcher; pour the fruit and milk mixture over it and stir gently until smooth. Serve in punch glasses.*

## FROSTED CHOCOLATE SHAKE

3 pints hot chocolate, chilled
1½ pints vanilla ice cream

*Combine in blender for a few seconds until smooth. Serve in a tall glass with a straw.*

## FROZEN CIDER

8 oz. sweet cider
4 oz. orange juice
1 tbs. applesauce
A few drops lemon juice
3 oz. crushed ice

*Combine in blender at a high speed or until thick. Store in the freezer until thick enough to eat with a spoon. Serve in tall glasses.*

## FROZEN PINEAPPLE AND BANANA COOLER

8 oz. pineapple juice; frozen and chopped up
½ small banana, sliced
Several drops of lemon juice

*Combine in a blender for several seconds, or until snowy.*

## FRUIT COCKTAIL PUNCH

2 cups white grape juice
12 oz. lime juice
8 oz. pineapple juice
1 bottle ginger ale
Mint sprigs

*Combine the fruit juices; chill in the refrigerator until ready to use. Before serving, add the soda plus chunks of ice. Garnish with mint.*

## FRUIT CUP

1 pineapple
½ doz. oranges
½ doz. grenadillas
Grated orange rind
Sugar syrup
Club soda

*Peel and slice the fruit meats; combine and pound into a pulp. Add sugar syrup to taste and stir to blend. Dilute with club soda and ice before serving.*

## FRUIT JUICE PUNCH

1¼ quarts pineapple juice
3 quarts grape juice
Sugar
3 bottles ginger ale

*Combine the fruit juices with a quart of water; add sugar to taste and stir until the sugar is dissolved. Add sugar, ginger ale, and ice chunks before serving; garnish with fruit slices.*

## FRUIT MILK SHAKE

1 pint apiece orange juice and grapefruit juice
1 pint milk
2 oz. sugar
A few drops vanilla extract, a few pinches of salt
8 oz. crushed ice

*Combine the ingredients in a blender in four parts (i.e. 4 oz. milk, juices, ½ oz. sugar, etc.) Blend at a high speed until smooth. Serve with a straw.*

## GARDEN PARTY PUNCH

8 oz. orange juice
8 oz. pineapple juice
4 oz. lemon juice
8 oz. sugar
1 pint ginger ale
1 pint club soda
3 cups hot tea
Orange slices
Mint leaves

*Combine the sugar with the hot tea; stir until the sugar has dissolved. Allow to cool. Combine the sweetened tea with the fruit juices; stir to blend. Add the ginger ale and soda plus chunks of ice before serving. Garnish with fruit slices and mint.*

## GENERAL HARRISON'S EGGNOG

sweet cider
1 egg
1 tsp. powdered sugar

*Combine the egg and sugar and crushed ice; stir until well-blended. Strain; add ice and fill the glass with cider. Garnish with nutmeg.*

## GINGER ALE FLOAT

Ginger ale
Fruit sherbert
Sprigs of mint

*Fill a tall glass half-way with ale; add ice and float a scoop of sherbet on top. Garnish with sprigs of mint.*

## GINGER GRAPE JUICE

1 quart grape juice
2 oz. sugar
3 tbs. lemon juice
1 pint ginger ale
Whole cloves, a cinnamon stick

*Combine the grape juice, lemon juice, and sugar; tie cloves and cinnamon into a cloth sack. Heat the juices and infuse with the spices; stir until the sugar is completely dissolved and simmer for 15 minutes. Allow to cool; then refrigerate until ready to use. Add the ginger ale plus chunks of ice before serving.*

---

## GINGER MINT JULEP

Ginger ale
Sprigs of mint
Powdered sugar

*Muddle the mint sprigs in plenty of sugar. Line the rims of several tall glasses with water and press them in fresh powdered sugar; divide out the minted sugar among them and fill each glass with crushed ice and ginger ale. Stir gently and serve garnished with mint.*

## GINGER PEACH COCKTAIL

8 oz. peach juice
8 oz. orange juice
4 oz. lemon juice
Whole ginger chunks
1 pint ginger ale

*Combine the fruit juices; stir well. When ready to serve; add the ginger ale to the pitcher. Place a chunk of ginger in each serving.*

## GINGER PUNCH

8 oz. ginger, in chunks
8 oz. sugar
4 oz. orange juice
4 oz. lemon juice
1 bottle club soda

*Boil the ginger and sugar in a cup of water for 15 minutes; allow to cool. Turn out into a large punch bowl; add the fruit juices and stir to blend. Add the soda plus chunks of ice before serving.*

## GOLDEN NECTAR

1½ pints grapefruit juice
8 oz. orange juice
2 oz. honey
4 eggs
A pinch of salt

*Combine the egg yolks, well-beaten, with the fruit juices; stir briskly until well blended. Add the honey and salt; stir until the honey has dissolved. In a separate bowl, beat the egg whites until stiff; fold carefully into the nectar. Serve at once in pre-chilled wine glasses.*

## GOLDEN PUNCH

12 oz. orange juice
12 oz. lemon juice
4 oz. pineapple juice
2 cups sugar
1 bottle ginger ale

*Boil the sugar in a cup of water for several minutes; allow to cool. In a large punch bowl, combine thefruit juices with the cool sugar syrup and another pint and a half of water; stir well. Add the ginger plus ice before serving.*

## GRANADILLA ADE

2 cups granadilla pulp
8 oz. orange juice
8 oz. sugar syrup
3 tsp. lemon juice

*Combine with 2 cups of water; stir briskly until well blended. Add plenty of ice before serving.*

## GRAPE JUICE PUNCH

2 quarts grape juice
1 bottle ginger ale
Orange slices

*Combine in a punch bowl. Add chunks of ice and oranges before serving. Garnish with mint.*

## GRAPE SODA

2 quarts white muscat grapes
1 bottle club soda

*Squeeze the juice out of the grapes; combine with club soda and stir gently. Bottle well, if not for immediate use.*

## GRAPEFRUIT ADE

Several large grapefruit
Ginger ale
Mint leaves

*Squeeze out the juice of the grapefruit; dilute with an equal amount of ginger ale and stir gently. Serve over ice garnished with mint.*

## HAWAIIAN PUNCH

8 oz. grated pineapple
4 oz. orange juice
2 oz. lemon juice
8 oz. strong iced tea
2 cups sugar
1½ bottles ginger ale

*Boil the sugar in enough water to make a syrup; allow to cool. Combine with the grated pineapple and fruit juices in a large punch bowl; add the tea, stir well, and allow to stand for several hours. Add the ginger ale plus ice before serving.*

## HOLIDAY APPLE PUNCH

1½ quarts apple juice
2 bottles ginger ale
Lemon slices
Red and green cherries

*Make this punch immediately before serving. Combine the apple juice and the ginger ale; stir gently to blend. Garnish with the fruit slices and cherries.*

## HONEY MILK SHAKE

8 oz. milk
1½ oz. vanilla ice cream
1 tbs. honey

*Combine in a blender at a high speed until smooth. Serve with a straw.*

## HOT CHOCOLATE

½ lb. unsweetened chocolate
2 quarts milk
1½ cups sugar
Whipped cream

*Cut the chocolate into small pieces; combine with the sugar over a double boiler and melt until the sugar has dissolved with the chocolate and they are well-blended. Add the milk and continue cooking until smooth. Serve immediately in mugs; top with whipped cream or a marshmallow.*

## HOT CRANBERRY-PINEAPPLE PUNCH

2 quarts cranberries
1 quart pineapple juice
8 oz. brown sugar
Cinnamon sticks, ground cloves, ground cinnamon, salt, and nutmeg
Butter

*Boil the cranberries in a quart of water until soft; strain out the juice. Combine the warm juice with the sugar, ground spices, and another cup of water in a saucepan; add the pineapple juice and bring to a boil. Serve piping hot in mugs. Garnish with cinnamon sticks and a pat of butter.*

## HOT SPICED NOGGIN

2 quarts cider
6 oz. brown sugar
1 orange sliced
1 lemon, sliced
Cinnamon sticks
Whole cloves
Allspice
A pinch salt

*Combine the sugar and spices in a saucepan; pound together into a fine powder. Add a quart of warm water; stir well and bring to a boil. In a separate saucepan, heat the cider with the fruit slices; do not allow to boil. Strain clean. Serve warm.*

## HOT SPICED PINEAPPLE JUICE

14 oz. pineapple juice
1 oz. lemon juice
A cinnamon stick
Sugar

*Combine the juices with the cinnamon stick in a saucepan; heat but do not boil. Allow to simmer for 15 minutes. Strain; add sugar to taste. Stir well until the sugar is dissolved. Serve hot in mugs.*

## ICED CIDER PUNCH

Sweet cider
Mint leaves

*Make a tray of ice cubes out of cider; use them in tall glasses filled with cider and garnished with mint.*

## ICED MINT TEA

1 doz. sprigs fresh mint
2 cups boiling water
1 quart cold water
Granulated sugar
Powdered sugar
Sprigs of mint
Spiral lemon peels

*Combine the fresh mint with the boiling water in a saucepan and steep over hot water in a double boiler for at least ½ hour. Strain the minted water clean and allow to cool. Combine with the cold water in a large pitcher; add granulated sugar to taste and stir until the sugar is completely dissolved. Serve with ice. Garnish with spiral lemon peels and sprigs of mint dusted with*

## INDEPENDENCE DAY LEMONADE

1 doz. lemons
2 cups sugar

*Boil the sugar in 2 cups of water. Allow to cool. Squeeze out the juice of the lemons into a large punch bowl; add the sugar syrup plus 3 quarts ice water. Stir well. Float the leftover rinds in the punch. Add chunks of ice before serving.*

## LEMONADE

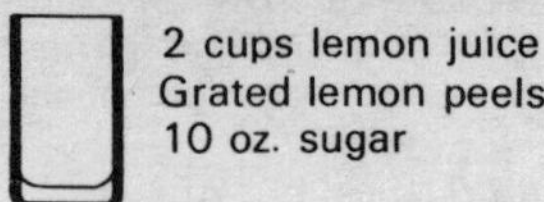

2 cups lemon juice
Grated lemon peels
10 oz. sugar

*Combine the sugar and lemon rinds with 1 cup of water in a saucepan; simmer for several minutes until syrupy. Allow to cool. Add the lemon juice and strain. Dilute the lemonade with water for each glass (for an average strength lemonade, use four times as much water as ade per serving).*

## LIME AND GINGER ALE

2 large limes
2 tbs. sugar
1 tbs. mint sprigs, cut finely
1 bottle ginger ale

*Peel the limes, slice them and combine with the sugar and chopped mint with 1½ cups boiling water. Allow to stand until cool, pressing the lime slices occasionally. Strain; add the ginger ale. Stir gently. Decorate with fresh lime slices.*

## LIME COOLER

4½ oz. lime juice
6 oz. orange juice
2 tbs. lemon juice
Mint sprigs, crushed
Sugar
16 oz. club soda

*Combine the fruit juices with the crushed mint in a punch bowl; allow to stand at least one hour. Strain and add sugar to taste; stir well until the sugar is dissolved. Add the soda plus chunks of ice before serving.*

---

## LIMEADE

9 oz. lime juice
9 oz. sugar
3 cups of water

*Boil the sugar with the water to make a syrup; combine the syrup with the lime juice in a large pitcher and stir until well-blended.*

## MAPLE NOG

1 pint milk
4 oz. whipped cream
3 oz. maple syrup
3 egg yolks, beaten
A pinch of salt
Ground ginger

*Combine the maple syrup, beaten egg yolks, and milk; stir briskly until well-blended. In a separate bowl, dust the whipped cream with the ginger. Turn out the nog into several tall glasses; top each glass with a dab of the dusted cream.*

## MAPLE SHAKE

8 oz. milk
3 tbs. maple syrup
1 oz. vanilla ice cream
Slices of banana

*Combine the maple syrup and the milk with ice; shake well. Strain into a tall glass; decorate with slices of banana and float the ice cream.*

---

## MINT AND FRUIT COCKTAIL

2 large bunches of mint leaves
9 oz. orange juice
6 oz. grapefruit juice
4 tbs. sugar

*Boil one of the mint bunches in 3 oz. of water until the water is infused. Strain out the leaves. Combine the mint water with the juices, sugar, and 4-6 oz. of crushed ice in blender at a low speed for 15 seconds. Strain into several wine glasses straight up. Garnish with the remaining mint.*

## MINT COOLER

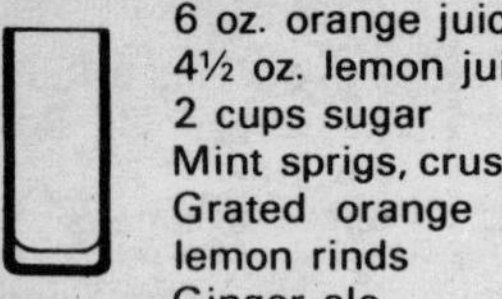

6 oz. orange juice
4½ oz. lemon juice
2 cups sugar
Mint sprigs, crushed
Grated orange and lemon rinds
Ginger ale

*Boil the sugar in enough water to make a syrup; combine the hot sugar syrup with the mint and fruit juices in a punch bowl. Add the grated rinds and allow to cool. Strain clean, bottle, and store in the refrigerator until ready to use. Serve over crushed ice diluted with ginger ale.*

## MINT TEA PUNCH

3 cups orange juice
6 cups grape juice
2 cups lemon juice
8 oz. grapefruit juice
2 oz. lime juice
2 cups sugar syrup
Cucumber slices
Mint sprigs, in pieces
1½ bottles club soda
3 bottles ginger ale
1 quart hot tea

*Infuse the mint in the tea; add the fruit juices and syrup (except grape) and stir well. Allow to cool; garnish with cucumber slices. Add the grape juice, ginger ale, and chunks of ice before serving.*

## MOCHA

2 oz. unsweetened chocolate
2 cups hot coffee
3 cups milk, scalded
6 oz. sugar
Ground cinnamon
A few drops of vanilla extract
A pinch of salt

*Combine the chocolate with 1½ oz. hot water in a double boiler; heat and stir until the chocolate has melted. Add the sugar, salt, cinnamon, and coffee; stir to blend and simmer several minutes before adding the milk and vanilla extract. Simmer at least ½ hour; whip and serve hot.*

## MOCK CHAMPAGNE

4 oz. white grape juice
4 oz. grapefruit juice
1 pint club soda
A few drops concentrated lime juice
Angostura bitters

*Chill all the ingredients extremely well. Combine the juices, stir well, and before serving add the soda; stir gently. Touch each serving up with a dash or two of bitters.*

**MOCK MANHATTAN**

2 oz. orange juice
2 oz. cranberry juice
A few drops lemon juice
A few drops of maraschino cherry juice
1-2 dashes orange bitters

*Combine with ice; shake well. Strain and add ice; decorate with a cherry.*

---

**MULTI-FRUIT PUNCH**

1 quart orange juice
1 quart grapefruit juice
9 oz. lemon juice
1 pint apiece strawberry, pineapple, and raspberry syrup
1 bottle ginger ale
Banana slices

*Combine everything except the ginger ale and banana slices; dilute with three quarts of water and stir well to blend. Add the sugar, ale plus chunks of ice before serving; garnish with banana slices.*

**OATMEAL PUNCH**

4 oz. oatmeal
The peels of one large lime

*Soak the oatmeal in 1 qt. of water and the lime peels for ½ hour. Strain out the liquid; add the sugar and stir until the sugar is dissolved. Refrigerate until ready to serve.*

---

**ORANGE MILK SHAKE**

4 oz. orange juice
2 oz. pineapple juice
1½ oz. honey
1 tbs. lemon juice
A pinch salt
2 cups milk

*Combine with ice; shake very well. Strain straight up; serve with a straw.*

**ORANGE NOG**

2 cups milk
4 eggs
10 oz. orange juice
2 oz. sugar
Ground nutmeg

*Combine the eggs, sugar, and milk; stir until well-blended. Split among four glasses; add 4 oz. milk to each glass. Add ice and garnish each with nutmeg.*

---

**NECTAR PUNCH**

3 cups apricot nectar
6 oz. lime juice
4 oz. current jelly
6 oz. white corn syrup
4 oz. sugar
Ground cinnamon
Lemon slices

*Boil the sugar, corn syrup, cinnamon, and fruit slices in a cup of water for several minutes; remove from heat. Take out the fruit slices and beat in the jelly; add the nectar and lime juice. Stir well. Refrigerate until ready to serve.*

## ORANGEADE

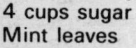

3 large oranges
3 tsp. lemon juice
4 oz. sugar

*Peel and slice one of the oranges; combine it with the sugar in a cup and a half of water; stir gently until the sugar has dissolved. In a separate bowl; combine the juice of the remaining oranges with the lemon juice. Pour it over the sliced orange; allow to settle for a few minutes before using.*

## PARTY TEA

4 tbs. ground tea
2 cups orange juice
8 oz. lemon juice
4 cups sugar
Mint leaves

*Combine the tea, sugar, and mint leaves with a quart of boiling water; allow to steep several minutes. Strain clean; add the juices plus 2 more quarts of water. Stir well. Add chunks of ice before serving.*

## PILGRIM'S PUNCH

12 oz. orange juice
3 oz. lemon juice
2 cups sugar
1 quart whole strawberries
1 bottle club soda
Mint leaves
1 cup iced tea, dark
2 cups pineapple juice
1 quart lemon sherbet

*Boil the sugar with a cup of water for several minutes (longer than it takes to dissolve the sugar). Strain out the juice of the strawberries; add it to the sugar syrup with the tea, and all the fruit juices. Allow to cool.*

## PASSION FRUIT PUNCH

1 doz. large passion fruit
2 quarts grapefruit juice
1 quart orange juice
1 quart pineapple juice
4 oz. lemon juice
6 quarts lemonade
6 bottles ginger ale
Fruit slices

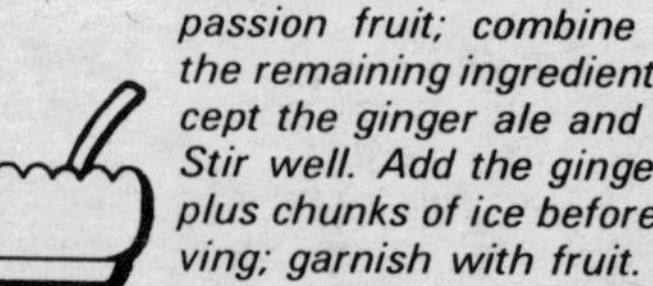

*Squeeze the juice out of the passion fruit; combine with the remaining ingredients, except the ginger ale and fruit. Stir well. Add the ginger ale plus chunks of ice before serving; garnish with fruit.*

## PINEAPPLE ADE

1 large pineapple
1 cup orange juice
Grated orange rind
Sugar

*Peel the pineapple and grate the meat; combine with the orange juice in a large bowl and set aside. Boil the pineapple skin and core with the orange rinds in 4 cups of water for 20 minutes. Strain and allow to cool. Combine with the grated pineapple; sweeten to taste and serve over ice.*

## PINEAPPLE EGG COCKTAIL

1 pint pineapple juice
5 oz. lemon juice
2 oz. sugar
2 egg whites
12 oz. crushed ice

*Combine in a blender with 4 oz. cold water; blend at a high speed until foamy. Divide out among several glasses filled with ice; decorate each glass with a cherry.*

## PINEAPPLE MINT PUNCH

2 cups pineapple juice
3 cups milk
6 oz. light cream
2 oz. sugar
1 doz. mint leaves
2 teasps. lemon juice
A pinch of salt

*Muddle the mint in a large punch bowl; remove the leaves, leaving the oils. Pour in all the ingredients and beat until frothy. Serve over ice in glasses garnished with fresh sprigs of mint.*

## PINEAPPLE PUNCH

1 large pineapple
1 cup sugar
1 bottle rose wine
3 bottles club soda

*Peel the pineapple; dice the meat and combine with the sugar. Pour in the wine; stir to dissolve the sugar and allow to stand for a couple of hours. Add the club soda plus ice.*

## PINEAPPLE SHERBERT PUNCH

8 oz. apiece of orange juice, pineapple juice, and raspberry juice
8 oz. crushed pineapple
1 cup tea
1 quart pineapple sherbet
1 bottle club soda
A few drops of concentrated lime juice

*Combine the fruit juices, crushed pineapple, and tea; stir well. Before serving, add the sherbet in small scoops, plus the soda.*

## PINEAPPLE TEA PUNCH

5 pints pineapple juice
1 pint lemon juice
4 cups powdered sugar
4 oz. tea, in leaf form

*Infuse the tea in a gallon of boiling water several minutes; strain. Add the sugar and stir until the sugar has dissolved. Add the fruit juices and a quart of cold water; refrigerate until ready to serve. Turn out over chunks of ice.*

## PRAIRIE OYSTER

1 egg yolk
1 tsp. Worchestershire sauce
Several drops of vinegar
A few drops of Tabasco sauce
A pinch of salt and pepper

*Slide the whole yolk into a wide champagne glass; add the remaining ingredients. Do not stir. A whole egg can be used if you'd like.*

## RASPBERRY DELIGHT

3 oz. raspberry sherbet
Ginger ale
Fresh raspberries

*Scoop the sherbet into glass; add ice and fill the glass with ginger ale. Float a few raspberries and serve with a straw.*

## RASPBERRY REFRESHER

12 oz. of red raspberries
2 cups sugar
1 pint orange juice

*Boil the sugar in enough water to make syrup. Add raspberries; macerate until smooth. Add the orange juice; stir and refrigerate for several hours. Strain before using. Serve wih ice.*

## RASPBERRY SHRUB

2 pints raspberries
Cider vinegar
Sugar

*Combine the raspberries with the vinegar; allow to stand for 24 hours. When ready, strain out the berries; add sugar. Boil several minutes until the sugar has dissolved. Allow to cool. Bottle for future use. Serve diluted in water.*

## RECEPTION CHOCOLATE

8 oz. cocoa
8 oz. sugar
1 quart heavy cream
2 quarts milk
1 tsp. vanilla extract
A pinch of salt

*Combine the sugar and the cocoa with a cup of boiling water; stir to blend. Heat in a saucepan; turn out into a double boiler; simmer at least ½ hour and allow to cool. Whip the heavy cream and fold it into the cocoa. Warm the milk with the vanilla and salt. Serve in tall glasses, a tablespoon of cocoa per glass of warm milk.*

## RHUBARB COCKTAIL

1 small rhubarb
4 oz. pineapple juice
1 tbs. orange juice and lemon juice

*Break the rhubarb into pieces and boil it in just enough water to cover; strain out the juice and add sugar to taste. Stir until the sugar is dissolved; allow to cool. Combine the rhubarb juice with the remaining juices; shake very well. Serve over crushed ice.*

## RUSSIAN TEA

4 tsp. ground tea
6 oz. orange juice
3 tsp. lemon juice
A cinnamon stick
Whole cloves
Sugar

*Boil the cinnamon sticks and cloves in 6 cups of water for a few minutes; add the tea, remove from heat and allow to simmer a few minutes more. Strain into a large bowl. Combine the juices; Serve hot in mugs.*

## SARATOGA

1½ oz. lemon juice
1 tsp. sugar syrup
A few dashes of Angostura bitters
Ginger ale

*Combine everything except the ginger ale with ice; shake well. Strain into a tall glass; add ice and fill the glass with ginger ale. Club soda can be used instead of ginger ale.*

---

## SESAME SEED PUNCH

1 cup sesame seeds
4 ozs. sugar

*Soak the seeds in 1 qt. of water for several hours; dry the seeds and crush them into a pulp. Combine the seed pulp with 2 cups of warm water; stir to blend and strain out the liquid into a separate bowl. Add the sugar to the sesame seed liquid; stir until the sugar has dissolved and refrigerate until ready to serve.*

## SHIRLEY TEMPLE

*Fill a champagne glass with ginger ale and add several drops of grenadine; stir gently and decorate with a couple of cherries.*

## SODA FOUNTAIN CIDER

1 quart cider
1 pint orange juice
10 oz. sugar
4 oz. lemon juice

*Boil the sugar in a pint of water stir until the sugar has dissolved. Combine the sugar syrup with the remaining ingredients in a large pot; allow to cool and strain clean. Freeze until thick before serving.*

## SOFT PUNCH

8 oz. pineapple juice
6 oz. orange juice
1½ oz. lemon juice
1 oz. sugar syrup
2 tbs. passion fruit juice

*Combine; stir well. Add ice before serving.*

## SOUR ORANGE TEA

2 fresh, sour orange sprigs
1 tsp. sugar

*Crush the sprigs and boil them in a cup of water. Strain out the infused water; add the sugar and stir until the sugar has dissolved. Serve hot in mugs.*

## SOURSOP PUNCH

2 lbs. ripe soursop fruit
6 oz. sugar

*Slice the fruit; cut out the pulp and seeds with a paring knife. Combine the pulp and seeds with a cup of water; mash and strain out the liquid. Keep repeating this process with more water until the pulp is strained out. Add the sugar to the final straining; stir until the sugar has dissolved. Refrigerate until ready to serve.*

## SOUTHERN PUNCH

5 cups sweet cider
1 quart grape juice
Cinnamon sticks
Grated orange and lemon peels
4 oz. lemon juice
2 bottles ginger ale
Orange slices
Whole cloves

*Simmer the cinnamon sticks and cloves with half the cider in a large saucepan for several minutes. Allow to cool; strain. Pour the remaining cider back into the empty pot; add the fruit juices and peels. Refrigerate. Combine the spiced and fruit cider; add the ginger ale, orange slices, and ice.*

## SPANISH HOT CHOCOLATE

8 oz. semi-sweet chocolate
8 oz. hot coffee
3 pints milk, warm
2 egg yolks
2 tsp. vanilla extract

*Combine the chocolate with the coffee in a double boiler; heat unil the chocolate has dissolved and stir well to blend. Add the milk and warm over a low flame. When ready to serve; beat the yolks; add them to the chocolate. Add the vanilla and stir well. Serve in mugs. Add sugar to taste and top with whipped cream.*

---

## SPICE PUNCH

2 quarts ginger ale
3 8-oz. cans grape juice concentrate
4 oz. lime juice
Cinnamon sticks
Whole cloves

*Combine the cinnamon sticks and cloves with a cup of water in a saucepan; bring to a boil. Let stand several minutes cooling, then strain. Combine this spiced water with the grape juice concentrate and the lime juice. Stir until well-blended. Add ice and ginger ale.*

## SPICED APPLE JUICE

½ doz. apples
8 oz. sugar
Cinnamon sticks, allspice berries,
Whole cloves

*Boil the apples in their peels with enough water to cover them; when soft, strain out all the juice. Tie up the spices in a cloth bag and infuse in boiling juice for several minutes; add the sugar and stir until the sugar is dissolved. Strain clean and serve piping hot.*

## SPICED LEMONADE

12 oz. lemon juice
8 oz. sugar syrup
1 doz. whole cloves
1 quart cold water
Cinnamon sticks

*Simmer the sugar, cinnamon, and cloves in a saucepan for a few minutes; add the lemon juice and remove from heat. Allow to stand for at least one hour. Strain and combine with the water; stir well. Serve over crushed ice.*

## STRAWBERRY WATER

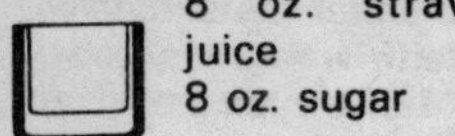

8 oz. strawberry juice
8 oz. sugar

*Dilute the juice with a quart of water in a large bowl; add the sugar and stir well until the sugar is completely dissolved. Serve over ice. If you are using fresh strawberries, allow approx. twice as much volume for the fruit meat.* **RASPBERRY** *and* **PINEAPPLE WATER** *can be made with this recipe; merely change the fruits.*

## TAMARIND PUNCH

1 lb. whole tamarind seeds
1 cup sugar

*Combine the seeds with a cup of water in a mixing bowl; mash to a pulp and strain out the juice with the water. Save the mashed seeds. Repeat this process until the seeds emit no more juice. Add the sugar to the punch; stir until the sugar is dissolved and refrigerate until ready to serve.*

## TEA PUNCH

3 cups strong, iced tea
16 oz. raspberry syrup
8 oz. lime juice
8 oz. crushed pineapple
1 quart orange juice
2 bottles club soda

*Combine everything except the soda; add the soda plus chunks of ice.*

## TOMATO COCKTAILS

*These are the most popular of non-alcoholic drinks. There are dozens of variations to a* **TOMATO COCKTAIL;** *all are made with 8 oz. of tomato juice and are mixed in an electric blender. Here a few suggestions.*

## TOMATO COCKTAIL WITH CARROTS

*Combine the juice with 4 oz. of thinly sliced carrots, a pinch of salt, and a dash of Tabasco. Blend until smooth; serve over ice.*

## TOMATO COCKTAIL WITH HOT CHILI PEPPERS

*Combine the juice with a can of peeled, green chili peppers and a few drops of lemon juice. Blend until smooth; serve over ice.*

## TOMATO COCKTAIL PROVENCALE

*Combine the juice with a whole clove garlic (slightly chopped), several fresh basil leaves, a dash of salt, and a few drops of lemon juice. Blend until the garlic is finely distributed. Serve over ice.*

## TOMATO COCKTAIL CALIFORNIAN

*Combine the juice with 4 oz. of thinly sliced raw carrots, ¾ oz. lemon juice, a few drops of Worchestershire sauce, a pinch of salt, and a few sprigs of parsley, finely chopped. Blend for at least 30 seconds or until the parsley is evenly distributed. Serve over ice; decorate with a scoop of sour cream and a dash of paprika.*

## TOMATO AND YOGURT COCKTAIL

*Use only 4 oz. of tomato juice. Combine the juice with 4 oz. of plain yogurt, 1 oz. small, diced onion, and a few sprigs of chopped watercress. Blend until the watercress is evenly distributed. Serve over ice. Slices of cucumber can be used instead of the watercress.*

## YOGURT FRUIT COCKTAIL

8 oz. plain yogurt
2½ oz. frozen orange juice concentrate

*Combine in blender at a high speed for a few seconds. Serve over ice. Pineapple juice (4 oz.) can be used instead of the orange juice concentrate.*

## TROPICAL AMBROSIA

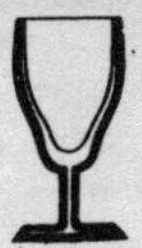

2 small cans mandarin oranges, sliced
3 large apples
8 oz. grated coconut meat
A few drops lemon juice

*Peel and slice the apples; arrange in a deep bowl with the orange slices. Dab with lemon juice and garnish with the grated coconut.*

## VISHNADA

1 lb. sour cherries
12 oz. sugar
2 tbs. lemon juice

*Clean and stem the cherries; combine them with the sugar and lemon juice in a cup of water. Bring to a boil; lower the heat and simmer several minutes until the cherries soften, break, and blend with the rest. Cool, strain, and refrigerate. Use as a concentrate, one tablespoon per glass of water.*

## YULETIDE PUNCH

1 quart cider
2 cups cranberry juice
8 oz. orange juice
8 oz. cold tea
1 oz. lemon juice, grated lemon rinds, fruit slices

*Combine the cider, juices, and tea; add grated rinds and fruit slices. Slide in chunks of ice before serving.*

# YOUR OWN RECIPE

## YOUR OWN RECIPE

## YOUR OWN RECIPE

## Low Calorie Drinks

This section of the Bartender's Guide is intended for people who are interested in a good drink which is also low in calories.

**CALORIES**

One gram of alcohol metabolized in the body yields seven calories which adds up to approximately 200 calories per fluid ounce (approx. 30 milliliters) of absolute alcohol, or 100 calories per fluid ounce of 100-U.S.-proof distilled spirits. Rums, whiskies, and vodkas are equal in calories, per oz., to their proof and most range between 80-100 calories per oz. In beer, some additional calories, about four per ounce, remain from the surviving cereal content of the original grain. (These non-alcoholic calories, however, are now being eliminated by some manufacturers catering to the weight conscious.)

**DIETERS' DRINKS:**

Since liquor has as many calories per ounce as its proof, i.e. one ounce of 86-proof rum contains 86 calories—no alcoholic drink will help you lose weight. But there are lesser evils to choose from and these are among them:

Sprittzers: White wines mixed with club soda (50/50 ratio) makes a low calorie refreshment that can be touched up with a twist of lemon and ice.

Wines in general are better for the weight conscious than mixed drinks because many of the vitamins and minerals stick with the wine through fermentation. Distillation causes spirits to lose almost everything except potency and calories.

Highballs: Mix down the usual amount of liquor (say 2 tsps.) of Scotch, vodka, or gin per glass of soda.

Tomato Vermouth: Tomato juice is the least fattening juice mixer. Combine 4 oz. of tomato juice with 2 oz. of dry vermouth in a glass with ice; shake well. Strain into an old-fashioned glass and add ice.

Bitters and Mixers: Campari and soda, lemon juice and soda with a dash or two of Angostura bitters or Perrier water with a touch of lemon and a dash of creme de cassis all make good, non-alcoholic, low-calorie drinks.

## ALFONSO COCKTAIL
(80 Calories)

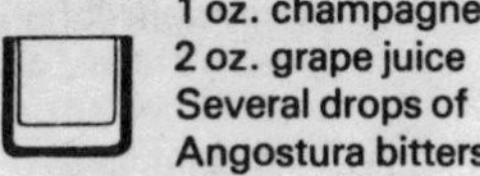

1 oz. champagne
2 oz. grape juice
Several drops of
Angostura bitters

*Combine; serve over ice.*

## APPLEJACK DAISY
(99 Calories)

½ oz. gin
½ oz. apple brandy
1 tbs. lemonade

*Combine and serve over crushed ice.*

## APPLE PIE
(60 Calories)

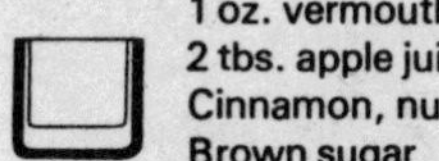

1 oz. vermouth (dry)
2 tbs. apple juice
Cinnamon, nutmeg
Brown sugar

*Combine the juice and vermouth over ice. Add dashes of the spices and sugar.*

## BARBIE'S SPECIAL
(75 Calories)

1 ½ tbs. apricot nectar
1 oz. defrosted vanilla ice milk
A few drops of gin

*Combine and shake with ice. Serve straight up*

## BIFFY
(75 Calories)

½ oz. gin
2 tbs. pineapple juice
1 tbs. lemon juice

*Combine and shake with ice. Serve over crushed ice.*

## BLOODY PICK-ME-UP
(50 Calories)

½ oz. gin
1 tbs. catsup
1 tbs. lemon juice
A few drops of
Worchestershire
sauce

*Combine in a blender at high speed for 15 seconds. Serve over crushed ice.*

## CAMPARI SPECIAL
(70 Calories)

1 ½ oz. Campari
Ginger ale
A few drops of
orange bitters

*Combine over ice. Touch up with a slice of orange.*

## CARDINAL
(45 Calories)

¾ oz. dry vermouth
1 tbs. orange juice
1 tbs. tomato juice
Ripe olive

*Combine. Serve chilled.*

## CARTHUSIAN COOLER
(60 Calories)

1 oz. port
Club soda
½ honeydew melon

*Hollow out ½ honeydew melon. Blend fruit with port; pour into shell and fill with club soda.*

**CHAMPAGNE COBBLER**
(82 Calories)

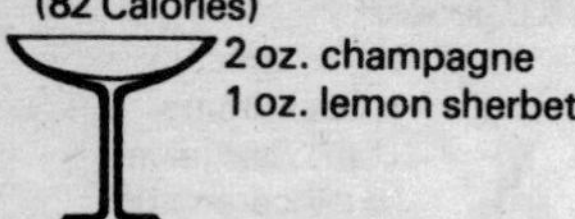

2 oz. champagne
1 oz. lemon sherbet

*Combine over crushed ice. Decorate with a cherry.*

**CHERRY RUM**
(106 Calories)

½ oz. rum
2 oz. canned sour cherries in syrup
1 tbs. light cream
3 oz. crushed ice

*Blend at low speed; strain and serve straight up.*

**CITY STREET**
(100 Calories)

2 oz. dry vermouth
2 tbs. cranberry juice
Several dashes orange bitters

*Combine and touch up with an orange slice.*

**CLARE'S CUP**
(62 Calories)

2 oz. dry white wine
1 cucumber
Mint leaves
Lemon slices
Grated lime rinds
Club soda

*Hollow out the cucumber, flatten one end. Pour in the wine, add soda to fill and garnish with mint and fruit.*

**COFFEE NOG**
(95 Calories)

½ cup dark coffee (freshly brewed and partially cooled)
1 cup light cream
1 egg, separated
1 tbs. brown sugar
A pinch of salt

*Combine the coffee, egg yolk, sugar, and salt in the top of a double boiler; cook until thick. Remove from heat and allow to cool. In a separate bowl, beat the egg whites with the cream until foamy but not stiff; fold into the coffee mixture and serve immediately.*

**CORONATION**
(80 Calories)

2 tbs. apricot nectar
½ oz. creme de menthe

*Combine; serve over crushed ice.*

**CORONET COCKTAIL**
(90 Calories)

1 oz. port
½ oz. gin
Several dashes orange bitters

*Combine. Serve straight up.*

**COUNT CURREY**
(95 Calories)

2 oz. champagne
½ oz. gin
1 tsp. maple syrup

*Combine and serve with mint sprig.*

## COUNTRY CLUB COOLER
(50 Calories)

1 ½ oz. dry vermouth
¼ oz. grenadine
2 oz. club soda

*Combine and garnish with a lime slice.*

## COWBOY
(78 Calories)

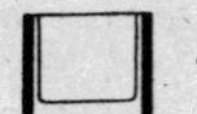

½ oz. whiskey
1 oz. flavored yogurt

*Combine with ice, shake very well. Serve over ice.*

## CREOLE PUNCH
(60 Calories)

1 ½ oz. canned pineapple juice
½ oz. 86-proof rum
½ oz. lemon juice

*Combine and serve chilled.*

## CREME DE CACAO FLOAT
(95 Calories)

½ oz. creme de cacao
1 tsp. chocolate
Ice milk

*Float the ice milk on top of the liqueur.*

## CUBA LIBRE
(70 Calories)

2 tsp. lime juice
½ oz. 86-proof rum
½ oz. grenadine

*Combine and serve over ice.*

## CURRIER
(78 Calories)

½ oz. whiskey
1 tsp. kummel
1 tsp. lime juice (unsweetened)

*Combine and shake well. Serve straight up.*

## CYNTHIA
(60 Calories)

1 oz. dry vermouth
½ oz. sweet vermouth
1 tsp. gin
Mint sprigs

*Combine over ice. Decorate with mint.*

## DILL MARY
(65 Calories)

3 oz. tomato juice
1 tbs. vodka
½ tsp. crushed dill
A pinch of salt and pepper
A few dashes of tobasco sauce

*Place the dill on the bottom of a mixing glass; add the vodka and tomato juice and allow to stand for several minutes. Add the salt, tobasco sauce plus ice; shake well. Strain over ice. Garnish with pepper.*

**DRY PUNCH**
(30 Calories)

⅔ oz. dried mint
2 cups boiling water
16 oz. cold water
3 oz. grenadine
Mint sprigs
Lime peels

*Steep mint in boiling water for 40 minutes. Combine with cold water and add grenadine. Float the lime peels and garnish with mint.*

**ENGLISH POSSET**
(61 Calories)

1 oz. dry sherry
½ oz. light cream
Nutmeg

*Combine and serve chilled. Garnish with nutmeg.*

**FIG LEAF FLIP**
(90 Calories)

1 oz. creme de menthe
1 tsp. gelatin
1 oz. water
3 oz. crushed ice

*Boil water and combine with the gelatin in a blender at high speed for 30 seconds. Add the creme de menthe and blend again. Add ice and blend one final time. Serve as a dessert.*

**FIRE AND ICE**
(100 Calories)

½ oz. Cherry Herring
1 tbs. Kirsch

*Combine with an ice cube. Stir until the ice begins to melt. Decorate with an orange slice.*

**FULL IN BED COCKTAIL**
(65 Calories)

½ oz. port
⅓ cup apple juice

*Combine and serve on ice.*

**GIN COCKTAIL**
(65 Calories)

¾ oz. gin
A few drops of orange bitters

*Serve over ice. Add a twist of lime.*

**GEORGE'S BEAUTY**
(95 Calories)

½ oz. brandy
2 tsp. lemon juice
1 tsp. grenadine
1 egg white

*Combine with ice; shake well. Strain and add ice.*

**HONOLULU SLING**
(95 Calories)

1 tbs. vodka
1 oz. sherry
1 oz. Hawaiian Punch

*Combine with ice; shake. Strain over crushed ice.*

**HONOLULU SPECIAL**
(75 Calories)

1 oz. low proof rum
1 tbs. lemon juice
1 tsp. grenadine
1 tsp. pineapple juice

*Combine with ice. Garnish with pineapple.*

**ISLAND TEA**
(40 Calories)

3 oz. freshly brewed green tea
1 oz. grenadine
Fresh mint
1 tsp. lemon juice

*Combine and decorate with mint.*

**LORENZO**
(85 Calories)

½ oz. vodka
1 tbs. Tuaca
2 tsp. lime juice
1 tsp. grenadine

*Combine; serve over ice.*

**LOW-CAL EGG NOG**
(80 Calories)

3 oz. evaporated Skim milk
8 oz. water
1 egg
Several drops of low-proof rum
1 tsp. grenadine

*Combine with ice. Shake and serve straight up. Garnish with nutmeg. (Serves two).*

**LUMBERJACK**
(75 Calories)

½ oz. whiskey
1 oz. apple juice (unsweetened)
1 tsp. brown sugar
Cinnamon and nutmeg

*Add the sugar to the juice and whiskey. Garnish with spices.*

**MASS TEA PUNCH**
(70 Calories)

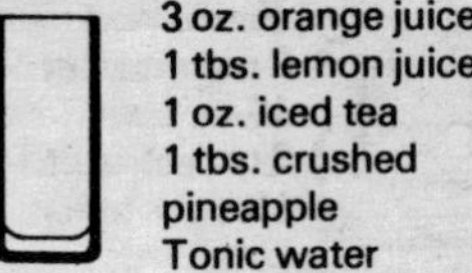

3 oz. orange juice
1 tbs. lemon juice
1 oz. iced tea
1 tbs. crushed pineapple
Tonic water

*Combine and shake. Strain over ice. Add a twist of lime.*

**NETHERLAND**
(90 Calories)

½ oz. brandy
A few drops of Curacao
1 tsp. cranberry juice
Several drops of Angostura bitters
1 cucumber shell

*Combine and add ice. Serve in the cucumber. Add a twist of orange and lemon.*

**NORTHERN HONEY BEE**
(103 Calories)

1 oz. brandy
½ oz. lemon juice
1 tsp. honey

*Warm the honey in a ladle over a low flame. Combine with the juice and brandy. Serve warmed.*

**OUZO RICKEY**
(80 Calories)

¾ oz. Ouzo
½ oz. cognac
1 tsp. lime juice
Club soda

*Combine and stir. Add soda to fill glass.*

**PANSY**
(75 Calories)

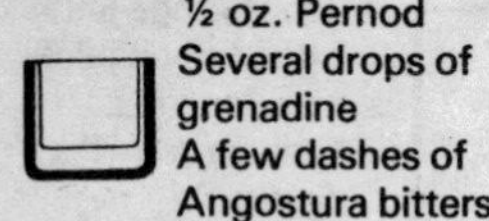

½ oz. Pernod
Several drops of grenadine
A few dashes of Angostura bitters

*Combine with ice; twist in a lemon.*

---

**PINK SQUIRREL**
(75 Calories)

½ oz. gin
1 tsp. creme de noyaux
1 oz. lemon juice

*Combine with ice. Shake and serve over ice.*

---

**PLANTER'S COCKTAIL**
(60 Calories)

½ oz. rum
1 tbs. orange juice
1 tsp. lemon juice

*Serve over crushed ice. Decorate with mint.*

**SHOOT**
(85 Calories)

½ oz. Scotch
½ oz. dry sherry
1 tsp. lemon juice
1 tsp. maple syrup

*Combine with ice. Shake and add ice.*

**SHRINER**
(90 Calories)

½ oz. brandy
½ oz. sloe gin
A few drops of Peychaud's bitters
1 tsp. grenadine

*Combine and serve straight up.*

**TOBAGO**
(90 Calories)

½ oz. low-proof rum
½ oz. gin
1 tsp. lime juice
1 tsp. guava syrup
1 oz. crushed ice

*Combine and blend. Serve over crushed ice.*

**TROPICAL SLING**
(70 Calories)

½ oz. gin
1 ½ tsp. lime juice
1 tsp. grenadine
½ tsp. maraschino
club soda
Sprigs of mint

*Combine everything except the soda and mint. Shake. Add ice and fill with soda.*

**WAVERLY**
(90 Calories)

½ oz. gin
1 tsp. creme de cassis
1 tbs. orange juice
Crushed ice

*Combine and touch up with an orange slice.*

---

**WEST INDIAN PUNCH**
(70 Calories)

1 oz. dry sherry
1 tsp. limeade
1 tsp. guave nectar
2 oz. dark, cold tea

*Combine and twist in a lime. Shake.*

# YOUR OWN RECIPE

## YOUR OWN RECIPE

# *INDEX*

## ADES



## ADVOCKAAT DRINKS



## ALES, PORTER, STOUT, LAGER, BOCK BEER, BEER



## AMER PICON DRINKS



## AMONTILLADO DRINKS



## ANISETTE DRINKS

AQUAVIT DRINKS



ARRACK DRINKS



BENEDICTINE DRINKS



BOURBON DRINKS

## BRANDY DRINKS

## BREWS



## CAMPARI DRINKS

## CANADIAN WHISKEY DRINKS



## CHAMPAGNE DRINKS

### CHARTREUSE DRINKS



### CHERRY HEERING DRINKS



### CIDER DRINKS



### CLARET DRINKS

## COBBLERS



## COFFEE DRINKS



## COINTREAU DRINKS

## COLLINS



## COOLERS

## CORDIAL MEDOC DRINKS



## CREME DE CACAO DRINKS



## CREME DE CASSIS DRINKS



## CREME DE MENTHE DRINKS

## CREME DE YVETTE DRINKS



## CREME NOYAUX DRINKS



## CUPS

## CURACAO DRINKS

## DAIQUIRIS



## DAISIES



## DRAMBUIE DRINKS

**DUBONNET DRINKS**



**EGG NOGS**



**FALERNUM DRINKS**

## FERNET BRANCA DRINKS



## FIXES



## FIZZES



## FLAMBEES



## FLIPS

## FORBIDDEN FRUIT DRINKS



## FRAPPES



## FROZEN DRINKS



## FRUIT LIQUEURS

## GIN DRINKS

## GRAND MARNIER DRINKS



## HOT DRINKS

## ICE CREAM, MILK, AND YOGURT BASED DRINKS

### IRISH MIST DRINKS



### IRISH WHISKEY DRINKS



### ITALIAN LIQUEURS



### JULEPS



### KAHLUA DRINKS



### KIRSCH DRINKS

## KUMMEL DRINKS



## LILLET DRINKS



## MADEIRA AND MUSCATEL DRINKS



## MARASCHINO DRINKS

## MARTINIS



## PERNOD DRINKS

## PORT WINE DRINKS

## PUNCHES

**PUNT E MES DRINKS**

## RYE DRINKS



## SAKI DRINKS



## SAMBUCA DRINKS



## SANGAREES AND SANGRIAS



## SAUTERNE DRINKS



## SCOTCH DRINKS

## SHERRY DRINKS

## SHRUBS



## SLINGS



## SLOE GIN DRINKS



## SMASHES



## SOURS

## TIA MARIA DRINKS



## TODDIES



## TRIPLE SEC DRINKS

## VERMOUTH DRINKS

## VODKA DRINKS

## WHISKEY DRINKS

**WHITE WINE DRINKS**

# SPECIAL MONEY SAVING OFFER

*Now you can have an up-to-date listing of Bantam's hundreds of titles plus take advantage of our unique and exciting bonus book offer. A special offer which gives you the opportunity to purchase a Bantam book for only 50¢. Here's how!*

*By ordering any five books at the regular price per order, you can also choose any other single book listed (up to a $4.95 value) for just 50¢. Some restrictions do apply, but for further details why not send for Bantam's listing of titles today!*

*Just send us your name and address plus 50¢ to defray the postage and handling costs.*

---

BANTAM BOOKS, INC.
Dept. FC, 414 East Golf Road, Des Plaines, Ill 60016

Mr./Mrs./Miss/Ms. ____________________
(please print)

Address ____________________

City__________ State________ Zip________

FC—3/84

# HARRAP'S

# MINI PLUS
# DICTIONARY • DICTIONNAIRE

English-French • Français-Anglais

HARRAP

21, rue du Montparnasse
75283 Paris Cedex 06
France

ISBN 978 0245 51003 8

HARRAP est une marque de Larousse SAS.
Harrap® est une marque déposée.
www.harrap.com



Maquette et mise en page : Chambers Harrap Publishers Ltd, Edinburgh

*Project Manager/Coordination éditoriale*
Kate Nicholson

*Editors/Rédaction*
Isabelle Elkaim
Stuart Fortey
Rachel Skeet

*Publishing Manager/Direction éditoriale*
Anna Stevenson

*Prepress/Prépresse*
Becky Pickard

**Trademarks**

Words considered to be trademarks have been designated in this dictionary by the symbol ®. However, no judgement is implied concerning the legal status of any trademark by the presence or absence of such a symbol.

**Marques déposées**

Les termes considérés comme des marques déposées sont signalés dans ce dictionnaire par le symbole ®. Cependant, la présence ou l'absence de ce symbole ne constitue nullement une indication quant à la valeur juridique de ces termes.

# Contents

# Table des matières

# Preface

This new English-French *Mini Plus Dictionary* from Harrap aims to provide students of French at beginner and intermediate level with a reliable and user-friendly dictionary in a compact form. The clear, systematic presentation makes the dictionary an easy-to-use tool and its broad coverage should ensure that it becomes an invaluable resource.

With over 40,000 references, the *Mini Plus* covers all the words and phrases needed for everyday situations and travels in French-speaking countries. It includes colloquial and idiomatic expressions as well as vocabulary from a range of specialized fields, such as IT, sport and finance.

The middle supplement provides extra help with both English and French irregular verbs, plus sections on numbers, days, months and time, while pronunciation tips can be found at the start of the book. In addition, a brand-new communication guide provides essential phrases for travel and holidays in French-speaking countries, making this an essential pocket resource.

# Préface

Ce nouveau dictionnaire français-anglais *Mini Plus* de Harrap's a pour but de fournir aux apprenants d'anglais de niveau débutant ou intermédiaire un dictionnaire fiable et pratique sous forme compacte. La présentation claire et systématique en fait un outil d'usage facile, et grâce à son traitement du vocabulaire, il devrait s'avérer une aide précieuse pour l'utilisateur.

Avec plus de 40,000 références, le *Mini Plus* traite tous les mots et expressions utiles pour les situations courantes et les voyages aux pays anglo-saxons. Il contient des expressions familiers et idiomatiques, ainsi que des termes issus de domaines spécialisés variés tels que l'informatique, le sport ou la finance.

Des tableaux de prononciation se trouvent au début de livre, et le supplément central contient des informations sur les verbes irréguliers anglais et français ainsi que sur les nombres, les jours, les mois de l'année et l'heure. De plus, un tout nouveau guide de conversation propose des phrases essentielles pour les voyages et les vacances aux pays anglophones, faisant de l'ouvrage une ressource de poche essentielle.

| Abbreviations | | Abréviations |
|---|---|---|
| gloss | = | glose |
| [introduces an explanation] | | [introduit une explication] |
| cultural equivalent | ≃ | équivalent culturel |
| [introduces a translation which has a roughly equivalent status in the target language] | | [introduit une traduction dont les connotations dans la langue cible sont comparables] |
| abbreviation | *abbr, abrév* | abréviation |
| adjective | *adj* | adjectif |
| adverb | *adv* | adverbe |
| agriculture | *Agr* | agriculture |
| American English | *Am* | anglais américain |
| anatomy | *Anat* | anatomie |
| architecture | *Archit* | architecture |
| slang | *Arg* | argot |
| astrology | *Astrol* | astrologie |
| cars | *Aut* | automobile |
| auxiliary | *aux* | auxiliaire |
| aviation | *Aviat* | aviation |
| Belgian French | *Belg* | belgicisme |
| biology | *Biol* | biologie |
| botany | *Bot* | botanique |
| British English | *Br* | anglais britannique |
| Canadian French | *Can* | canadianisme |
| chemistry | *Chem, Chim* | chimie |
| cinema | *Cin* | cinéma |
| commerce | *Com* | commerce |
| computing | *Comptr* | informatique |
| conjunction | *conj* | conjonction |
| cooking | *Culin* | cuisine |
| economics | *Econ, Écon* | économie |
| electricity, electronics | *El, Él* | électricité, électronique |
| exclamation | *exclam* | exclamation |
| feminine | *f* | féminin |
| familiar | *Fam* | familier |
| figurative | *Fig* | figuré |
| finance | *Fin* | finance |
| geography | *Geog, Géog* | géographie |
| geology | *Geol, Géol* | géologie |
| grammar | *Gram* | grammaire |
| gymnastics | *Gym* | gymnastique |
| history | *Hist* | histoire |

| | | |
|---|---|---|
| humorous | *Hum* | humoristique |
| invariable | *inv* | invariable |
| journalism | *Journ* | journalisme |
| law | *Jur* | droit |
| linguistics | *Ling* | linguistique |
| masculine | *m* | masculin |
| mathematics | *Math* | mathématique |
| medicine | *Med, Méd* | médecine |
| military | *Mil* | militaire |
| music | *Mus* | musique |
| noun | *n* | nom |
| shipping | *Naut* | nautisme |
| feminine noun | *nf* | nom féminin |
| feminine plural noun | *nfpl* | nom féminin pluriel |
| masculine noun | *nm* | nom masculin |
| masculine and feminine noun | *nmf* | nom masculin et féminin |
| masculine plural noun | *nmpl* | nom masculin pluriel |
| plural noun | *npl* | nom pluriel |
| computing | *Ordinat* | ordinateurs, informatique |
| pejorative | *Pej, Péj* | péjoratif |
| philosophy | *Phil* | philosophie |
| photography | *Phot* | photographie |
| physics | *Phys* | physique |
| plural | *pl* | pluriel |
| politics | *Pol* | politique |
| past participle | *pp* | participe passé |
| prefix | *pref, préf* | préfixe |
| preposition | *prep, prép* | préposition |
| pronoun | *pron* | pronom |
| past tense | *pt* | prétérit |
| something | *qch* | quelque chose |
| registered trademark | ® | marque déposée |
| rail | *Rail* | chemin de fer |
| religion | *Rel* | religion |
| somebody | *sb* | quelqu'un |
| school | *Sch, Scol* | domaine scolaire |
| Scottish English | *Scot* | anglais d'Écosse |
| singular | *sing* | singulier |
| something | *sth* | quelque chose |
| suffixe | *suff* | suffixe |
| technology | *Tech* | technologie |
| telecommunications | *Tel, Tél* | télécommunications |
| theatre | *Theat, Théât* | théâtre |
| television | *TV* | télévision |

| | | |
|---|---|---|
| typography, printing | *Typ* | typographie, imprimerie |
| university | *Univ* | domaine universitaire |
| verb | *v* | verbe |
| intransitive verb | *vi* | verbe intransitif |
| reflexive verb | *vpr* | verbe pronominal |
| transitive verb | *vt* | verbe transitif |
| inseparable transitive verb | *vt insep* | verbe transitif à particule inséparable [par ex.: **he looks after the children** il s'occupe des enfants] |
| separable transitive verb | *vt sep* | verbe transitif à particule séparable [par ex.: **she sent the present back** *or* **she sent back the present** elle a rendu le cadeau] |

All other labels are written in full.
Toutes les autres indications d'usage sont données en entier.

# Prononciation de l'anglais

Pour indiquer la prononciation anglaise, nous avons utilisé dans ce dictionnaire les symboles de l'API (Alphabet phonétique international). Pour chaque son anglais, vous trouverez dans le tableau ci-dessous des exemples de mots anglais, suivis de mots français présentant un son similaire. Une explication est donnée lorsqu'il n'y a pas d'équivalent en français.

| *Caractère API* | *Exemple en anglais* | *Exemple en français* |
|---|---|---|
| **Consonnes** | | |
| [b] | **b**a**bb**le | **b**é**b**é |
| [d] | **d**ig | **d**ent |
| [dʒ] | **g**iant, **j**ig | **j**ean |
| [f] | **f**it, **ph**ysics | **f**ace |
| [g] | **g**rey, bi**g** | **g**a**g** |
| [h] | **h**appy | h aspiré : à quelques rares exceptions près, il est toujours prononcé en anglais |
| [j] | **y**ellow | **y**aourt |
| [k] | **c**lay, **k**i**ck** | **c**ar |
| [l] | **l**ip, pi**ll** | **l**i**l**as |
| [m] | **m**u**mm**y | **m**a**m**an |
| [n] | **n**ip, pi**n** | **n**é |
| [ŋ] | si**ng** | parki**ng** |
| [p] | **p**i**p** | **p**a**p**a |
| [r] | **r**ig, **wr**ite | Pas d'équivalent français : se prononce en plaçant le bout de la langue au milieu du palais |
| [(r)] | | Seulement prononcé en cas de liaison avec la voyelle qui suit comme dans : fa**r** away; the ca**r** is blue |
| [s] | **s**ick, **sc**ience | **s**ilen**ce** |
| [ʃ] | **sh**ip, na**t**ion | **ch**èvre |
| [t] | **t**ip, bu**tt** | **t**ar**t**ine |
| [tʃ] | **ch**ip, ba**tch** | a**tch**oum |
| [θ] | **th**ick | Son proche du /s/ français, il se prononce en plaçant le bout de la langue entre les dents du haut et celles du bas |

| *Caractère API* | *Exemple en anglais* | *Exemple en français* |
|---|---|---|
| [ð] | **th**is | Son proche du /z/ français, il se prononce en plaçant le bout de la langue entre les dents du haut et celles du bas |
| [v] | **v**ague, gi**ve** | **v**ie |
| [w] | **w**it, **wh**y | **w**hisky |
| [z] | **z**ip, phy**s**ics | ro**s**e |
| [ʒ] | plea**s**ure | **j**e |
| [χ] | lo**ch** | Existe seulement dans certains mots écossais. Pas d'équivalent français : se prononce du fond de la gorge, comme Ba**ch** en allemand ou la '**j**ota' espagnole. |

**Voyelles**

| | | |
|---|---|---|
| [æ] | r**a**g | n**a**tte |
| [ɑː] | l**ar**ge, h**al**f | p**â**te |
| [e] | s**e**t | /e/ moins ouvert que le [ε] français |
| [ɜː] | c**ur**tain, w**ere** | h**eu**re |
| [ə] | utt**er** | **che**val |
| [ɪ] | b**i**g, w**o**m**e**n | /i/ bref, à mi-chemin entre les sons [ε] et [i] français (plus proche de 'n**e**t' que de 'v**i**te') |
| [iː] | l**ea**k, w**ee** | /i/ plus long que le [i] français |
| [ɒ] | l**o**ck | b**o**nne – mais plus ouvert et prononcé au fond du palais |
| [ɔː] | w**a**ll, c**or**k | b**au**me – mais plus ouvert et prononcé au fond du palais |
| [ʊ] | p**u**t, l**oo**k | Son à mi-chemin entre un /ou/ bref et un /o/ ouvert |
| [uː] | m**oo**n | Son /ou/ prolongé |
| [ʌ] | c**u**p | À mi-chemin entre un /a/ et un /e/ ouverts |

**Diphtongues**

Elles sont rares en français et sont la combinaison de deux sons.

| | | |
|---|---|---|
| [aɪ] | wh**y**, h**igh**, l**ie** | **aïe** |
| [aʊ] | h**ow** | mi**aou**, **aoû**tat – mais se prononce comme un seul son |

| | | |
|---|---|---|
| [eə] | b**ear**, sh**are**, wh**ere** | fl**air** |
| [eɪ] | d**ay**, m**a**ke, m**ai**n | merv**eille** |
| [əʊ] | sh**ow**, g**o** | Combinaison d'un /o/ fermé et d'un /ou/ |
| [ɪə] | h**ere**, g**ear** | Combinaison d'un /i/ long suivi d'un /e/ ouvert bref |
| [ɔɪ] | b**oy**, s**oi**l | langue d'**oïl** |
| [ʊə] | **sure** | Combinaison d'un son /ou/ suivi d'un /e/ ouvert bref |

# Prononciation de l'anglais américain

L'accent américain est différent de l'accent anglais : il est facile de le constater dans la prononciation du mot **tomato** qui se dit [tə'meɪtəʊ] en anglais américain et [tə'mɑːtəʊ] en anglais britannique. Le r, qui disparaît souvent en anglais, est toujours prononcé en américain : **mother** se dit ['mʌðər] aux États-Unis et ['mʌðə] en Grande-Bretagne.

Quelques exemples :

| | *Prononciation américaine* | *Prononciation anglaise* |
|---|---|---|
| advertisement | [ædvə'taɪzmənt] | [əd'vɜːtɪsmənt] |
| clerk | [klɜːk] | [klɑːk] |
| derby | ['dɜːbɪ] | ['dɑːbɪ] |
| leisure | ['liːʒər] | ['leʒə] |
| privacy | ['praɪvəsɪ] | ['prɪvəsɪ] |
| schedule | ['skedjʊl] | ['ʃedjuːl] |
| tube | [tuːb] | [tjuːb] |
| vase | [veɪz] | [vɑːz] |
| z | [ziː] | [zed] |

L'accent tonique est souvent différent : **distribute** se prononce [dɪs'trɪbjuːt] aux États-Unis et ['dɪstrɪbjuːt] en Grande-Bretagne ; **ballet** se dit [bæ'leɪ] en américain et ['bæleɪ] en anglais britannique.

Autres exemples :

| | *Prononciation américaine* | *Prononciation anglaise* |
|---|---|---|
| Birmingham | [bɜːmɪŋ'hæm] | ['bɜːmɪŋəm] |
| laboratory | ['læbrətərɪ] | [lə'bɒrətərɪ] |
| fillet | [fɪ'leɪ] | ['fɪlɪt] |
| garage | [gə'rɑːʒ] | ['gærɪdʒ] |
| pecan | [pɪ'kæn] | ['piːkæn] |

# French Pronunciation

French pronunciation is shown in this dictionary using the symbols of the IPA (International Phonetic Alphabet). In the table below, examples of French words using these sounds are given, followed by English words which have a similar sound. Where there is no equivalent in English, an explanation is given.

| *IPA symbol* | *French example* | *English example* |
|---|---|---|
| Consonants | | |
| [b] | **b**é**b**é | **b**ut |
| [d] | **d**onner | **d**oor |
| [f] | **f**orêt | **f**ire |
| [g] | **g**are | **g**et |
| [ʒ] | **j**our | plea**s**ure |
| [k] | **c**arte | **k**itten |
| [l] | **l**ire | **l**one**l**y |
| [m] | **m**a**m**an | **m**at |
| [n] | **n**i | **n**ow |
| [ŋ] | parki**ng** | si**ng**i**ng** |
| [ɲ] | campa**gn**e | ca**ny**on |
| [p] | **p**atte | **p**at |
| [r] | **r**a**r**e | Like an English /r/ but pronounced at the back of the throat |
| [s] | **s**oir | **s**it |
| [ʃ] | **ch**ose | **sh**am |
| [t] | **t**able | **t**ap |
| [v] | **v**aleur | **v**alue |
| [z] | **z**éro | **z**ero |
| | | |
| **Vowels** | | |
| [a] | ch**a**t | c**a**t |
| [ɑ] | **â**ge | g**a**sp |
| [e] | **é**t**é** | b**ay** |
| [ɛ] | p**è**re | b**e**d |
| [ə] | l**e** | **a**mend |
| [ø] | d**eu**x | Does not exist in English: [e] pronounced with the lips rounded |

| | | |
|---|---|---|
| [œ] | seul | curtain |
| [i] | vite | bee – not quite as long as the English [iː] |
| [ɔ] | donner | cot – slightly more open than the English/o/ |
| [o] | chaud | daughter – but higher than its English equivalent |
| [u] | tout | you – but shorter than its English equivalent |
| [y] | voiture | Does not exist in English: [i] with lips rounded |
| [ɑ̃] | enfant | Nasal sound pronounced lower and further back in the mouth than [ɔ̃] |

**Vowels**

| | | |
|---|---|---|
| [ɛ̃] | vin | Nasal sound: /a/ sound pronounced letting air pass through the nose |
| [ɔ̃] | bonjour | Nasal sound: closed /o/ sound pronounced letting air pass through the nose |
| [œ̃] | **un** | Nasal sound: like [ɛ̃] but with lips more rounded |

**Semi-vowels**

| | | |
|---|---|---|
| [w] | voir | week |
| [j] | yoyo, paille | yard |
| [ɥ] | nuit | Does not exist in English: the vowel [y] elided with the following vowel |

# ENGLISH-FRENCH

# Aa

**A, a**[1] [eɪ] *n* (**a**) A, a *m inv*; **5A** *(in address, street number)* 5 bis; **to go from A to B** aller du point A au point B (**b**) *Sch (grade)* **to get an A in French** = avoir une très bonne note en français, ≃ avoir entre 16 et 20 en français (**c**) *(street atlas)* **an A to Z of London** un plan de Londres

**A**[2] [ə, *stressed* eɪ]

a devient **an** [ən, *stressed* æn] devant voyelle ou h muet.

*indefinite article* (**a**) *(in general)* un, une; **a man** un homme; **an apple** une pomme; **an hour** une heure

(**b**) *(definite article in French)* **60 pence a kilo** 60 pence le kilo; **50 km an hour** 50 km à l'heure; **I have a broken arm** j'ai le bras cassé

(**c**) *(article omitted in French)* **he's a doctor/a father** il est médecin/père; **Caen, a town in Normandy** Caen, ville de Normandie; **what a man!** quel homme!; **a hundred** cent

(**d**) *(a certain)* **a Mr Smith** un certain M. Smith

(**e**) *(time)* **twice a month** deux fois par mois

**aback** [ə'bæk] *adv* **taken a. (by)** déconcerté (par)

**abandon** [ə'bændən] **1** *n* abandon *m* **2** *vt* abandonner; **to a. ship** abandonner le navire

**abbey** ['æbɪ] (*pl* **-eys**) *n* abbaye *f*

**abbreviate** [ə'bri:vɪeɪt] *vt* abréger ▪ **abbreviation** *n* abréviation *f*

**abdicate** ['æbdɪkeɪt] *vt & vi* abdiquer

**abdomen** ['æbdəmən] *n* abdomen *m*

**abduct** [æb'dʌkt] *vt (kidnap)* enlever ▪ **abduction** *n* enlèvement *m*, rapt *m*

**ability** [ə'bɪlətɪ] (*pl* **-ies**) *n* capacité *f* (**to do** de faire); **to the best of my a.** de mon mieux

**ablaze** [ə'bleɪz] *adj* en feu; *Fig* **a. with** *(light)* resplendissant de

**able** ['eɪbəl] *adj* capable; **to be a. to do sth** être capable de faire qch, pouvoir faire qch; **to be a. to swim/drive** savoir nager/conduire ▪ **able-bodied** *adj* robuste

**abnormal** [æb'nɔ:məl] *adj* anormal

**aboard** [ə'bɔ:d] **1** *adv (on ship, plane)* à bord; **to go a.** monter à bord **2** *prep* **a. the ship/plane** à bord du navire/de l'avion; **a. the train** dans le train

**abolish** [ə'bɒlɪʃ] *vt* abolir ▪ **abolition** [æbə'lɪʃən] *n* abolition *f*

**abominable** [ə'bɒmɪnəbəl] *adj* abominable

**Aborigine** [æbə'rɪdʒɪnɪ] *n* Aborigène *mf* (d'Australie)

**abort** [ə'bɔ:t] **1** *vt (space flight, computer program)* avorter **2** *vi Med* faire une fausse couche ▪ **abortion** *n* avortement *m*; **to have an a.** se faire avorter

**ABOUT** [ə'baʊt] **1** *adv* (**a**) *(approximately)* à peu près, environ; **at a. two o'clock**

(**b**) *(here and there)* çà et là, ici et là; *Fig* **there's a lot of flu a. at the moment** il y a beaucoup de cas de grippe en ce moment; **there's a rumour a. (that...)** il y a une rumeur qui circule (selon laquelle...); **to look a.** regarder autour de soi; **to follow someone a.** suivre quelqu'un partout

**2** *prep* (**a**) *(around)* **a. the garden** autour du jardin

(**b**) *(near to)* **a. here** par ici

(**c**) *(concerning)* au sujet de; **to talk a. sth** parler de qch; **a book a. sth** un livre sur qch; **what's it (all) a.?** de quoi s'agit-il?
(**d**) *(+ infinitive)* **a. to do** sur le point de faire; **I was a. to say...** j'étais sur le point de dire...

**above** [əˈbʌv] **1** *adv* au-dessus; *(in book)* ci-dessus; **from a.** d'en haut; **the floor a.** l'étage *m* du dessus
**2** *prep* (**a**) *(in height, hierarchy)* au-dessus de; **he's a. me** *(in rank)* c'est mon supérieur; **she's not a. lying** elle n'est pas incapable de mentir; **he's not a. asking** il n'est pas trop fier pour demander; **a. all** surtout
(**b**) *(with numbers)* plus de ■ **above-board 1** *adj* honnête **2** *adv* sans tricherie ■ **above-mentioned** *adj* susmentionné

**abreast** [əˈbrest] *adv* côte à côte, de front; **four a.** par rangs de quatre; **to keep a. of sth** se tenir au courant de qch

**abroad** [əˈbrɔːd] *adv* à l'étranger; **from a.** de l'étranger

**abrupt** [əˈbrʌpt] *adj (sudden)* brusque, soudain; *(rude)* brusque, abrupt; *(slope, style)* abrupt

**abscess** [ˈæbses] *n* abcès *m*

**absence** [ˈæbsəns] *n* absence *f*; **in the a. of** *(person)* en l'absence de; *(thing)* faute de

**absent 1** [ˈæbsənt] *adj* absent (**from** de) **2** [æbˈsent] *vt* **to a. oneself (from)** s'absenter (de) ■ **absent-minded** *adj* distrait

**absentee** [æbsənˈtiː] *n* absent, -e *mf*

**absolute** [ˈæbsəluːt] *adj* absolu; *(proof)* indiscutable; **he's an a. fool!** il est complètement idiot!; **it's an a. disgrace!** c'est une honte! ■ **absolutely** *adv* absolument; **you're a. right** tu as tout à fait raison

**absorb** [əbˈzɔːb] *vt (liquid)* absorber; *(shock)* amortir; **to be absorbed in sth** être plongé dans qch ■ **absorbent** *adj* absorbant

**abstain** [əbˈsteɪn] *vi Pol* s'abstenir; **to a. from sth/from doing sth** s'abstenir de qch/de faire qch

**abstract** [ˈæbstrækt] **1** *adj* abstrait **2** *n* (**a**) *(notion)* **the a.** l'abstrait *m* (**b**) *(summary)* résumé *m*

**absurd** [əbˈsɜːd] *adj* absurde, ridicule

**abundant** [əˈbʌndənt] *adj* abondant ■ **abundantly** *adv* **a. clear** parfaitement clair

**abuse 1** [əˈbjuːs] *n (of power)* abus *m* (**of** de); *(of child)* mauvais traitements *mpl*; *(insults)* injures *fpl* **2** [əˈbjuːz] *vt (misuse)* abuser de; *(ill-treat)* maltraiter; *(insult)* injurier ■ **abusive** [əˈbjuːsɪv] *adj (person, language)* grossier, -ère

**abysmal** [əˈbɪzməl] *adj Fam (bad)* exécrable

**academic** [ækəˈdemɪk] **1** *adj* (**a**) *(year, diploma) (of school)* scolaire; *(of university)* universitaire (**b**) *(scholarly)* intellectuel, -elle (**c**) *(theoretical)* **the issue is of purely a. interest** cette question n'a d'intérêt que d'un point de vue théorique; **this is a. now** cela n'a plus d'importance **2** *n (teacher)* universitaire *mf*

**academy** [əˈkædəmɪ] (*pl* **-ies**) *n (society)* académie *f*; *(military)* école *f*

**accelerate** [əkˈseləreɪt] **1** *vt* accélérer **2** *vi (of pace)* s'accélérer; *(of vehicle, driver)* accélérer ■ **accelerator** *n* accélérateur *m*

**accent** [ˈæksənt] *n* accent *m*

**accept** [əkˈsept] *vt* accepter ■ **acceptable** *adj (worth accepting, tolerable)* acceptable; **to be a. to sb** convenir à qn

**access** [ˈækses] **1** *n* accès *m* (**to sth** à qch; **to sb** auprès de qn); *Comptr* **a. provider** fournisseur *m* d'accès; **a. road** route *f* d'accès **2** *vt Comptr* accéder à ■ **accessible** *adj* accessible

**accessories** [əkˈsesərɪz] *npl (objects)* accessoires *mpl*

**accessory** [əkˈsesərɪ] (*pl* **-ies**) *n Law (accomplice)* complice *mf* (**to** de)

**accident** [ˈæksɪdənt] *n* accident *m*; **by a.** accidentellement; *(by chance)* par hasard ▪ **accidental** *adj* accidentel, -elle ▪ **accidentally** *adv* accidentellement; *(by chance)* par hasard

**acclaim** [ə'kleɪm] **1** *n* **(critical) a.** éloges *mpl* **2** *vt (cheer)* acclamer; *(praise)* faire l'éloge de

**acclimatize** [ə'klaɪmətaɪz] (*Am* **acclimate** ['ækləmeɪt]) *vi* s'acclimater

**accommodate** [ə'kɒmədeɪt] *vt* (**a**) *(of house)* loger (**b**) *(oblige)* rendre service à ▪ **accommodating** *adj* accommodant, obligeant

**accommodation** [əkɒmə'deɪʃən] *n* (*Am* **accommodations**) *(lodging)* logement *m*; *(rented room(s))* chambre(s) *f(pl)*

**accompany** [ə'kʌmpənɪ] (*pt & pp* **-ied**) *vt* accompagner

**accomplice** [ə'kʌmplɪs] *n* complice *mf*

**accomplish** [ə'kʌmplɪʃ] *vt (task, duty)* accomplir; *(aim)* atteindre ▪ **accomplishment** *n (of task, duty)* accomplissement *m*; *(thing achieved)* réalisation *f*

**accord** [ə'kɔ:d] **1** *n* accord *m*; **of my own a.** de mon plein gré **2** *vt (grant)* accorder ▪ **accordance** *n* **in a. with** conformément à

**according** [ə'kɔ:dɪŋ] **according to** *prep* selon, d'après ▪ **accordingly** *adv* en conséquence

**accordion** [ə'kɔ:dɪən] *n* accordéon *m*

**accost** [ə'kɒst] *vt* accoster, aborder

**account** [ə'kaʊnt] **1** *n* (**a**) *(with bank or company)* compte *m* (**b**) *(report)* compte rendu *m*; *(explanation)* explication *f* (**c**) *(expressions)* **by all accounts** au dire de tous; **on a. of** à cause de; **on no a.** en aucun cas; **to take sth into a.** tenir compte de qch **2** *vi* **to a. for** *(explain)* expliquer; *(give reckoning of)* rendre compte de; *(represent)* représenter ▪ **accountable** *adj* responsable (**for/to** de/devant)

**accountant** [ə'kaʊntənt] *n* comptable *mf*

**accounting** [ə'kaʊntɪŋ] *n* comptabilité *f*

**accumulate** [ə'kju:mjʊleɪt] **1** *vt* accumuler **2** *vi* s'accumuler

**accuracy** ['ækjʊrəsɪ] *n* exactitude *f*, précision *f*

**accurate** ['ækjʊrət] *adj* exact, précis

**accuse** [ə'kju:z] *vt* **to a. sb (of sth/of doing sth)** accuser qn (de qch/de faire qch) ▪ **accusation** *n* accusation *f*; **to make an a. against sb** lancer une accusation contre qn ▪ **accused** *n Law* **the a.** l'accusé, -e *mf*

**accustom** [ə'kʌstəm] *vt* habituer, accoutumer ▪ **accustomed** *adj* **to be a. to sth/to doing sth** être habitué à qch/à faire qch; **to get a. to sth/to doing sth** s'habituer à qch/à faire qch

**ace** [eɪs] *n* (**a**) *(card, person)* as *m* (**b**) *(at tennis)* ace *m*

**ache** [eɪk] **1** *n* douleur *f* **2** *vi* faire mal; **my head aches** j'ai mal à la tête

**achieve** [ə'tʃi:v] *vt (result)* obtenir; *(aim)* atteindre; *(ambition)* réaliser; *(victory)* remporter; **to a. success** réussir ▪ **achievement** *n (success)* réussite *f*; *(of ambition)* réalisation *f*

**aching** [eɪkɪŋ] *adj* douloureux, -euse

**acid** ['æsɪd] *adj & n* acide *(m)*; **a. rain** pluies *fpl* acides

**acknowledge** [ək'nɒlɪdʒ] *vt* reconnaître (**as** pour); *(greeting)* répondre à ▪ **acknowledg(e)ment** *n (of letter)* accusé *m* de réception; *(receipt)* reçu *m*; *(confession)* aveu *m* (**of** de)

**acne** ['æknɪ] *n* acné *f*

**acoustics** [ə'ku:stɪks] *npl* acoustique *f*

**acquaint** [ə'kweɪnt] *vt* **to be acquainted with** *(person)* connaître; *(fact)* savoir ▪ **acquaintance** *n (person, knowledge)* connaissance *f*

**acquire** [ə'kwaɪə(r)] *vt* acquérir; *(taste)* prendre (**for** à); *(friends)* se faire

**acquit** [ə'kwɪt] (*pt & pp* **-tt-**) *vt* (**a**) *Law* **to a. sb (of a crime)** acquitter qn (**b**) **to a. oneself badly/well** mal/bien s'en tirer

**acre** ['eɪkə(r)] *n* ≃ demi-hectare *m*, acre *f*; *Fam* **acres of space** plein de place

**acrimonious** [ækrɪ'məʊnɪəs] *adj (person, remark)* acrimonieux, -euse, hargneux, -euse; *(attack, dispute)* virulent

**acrobat** ['ækrəbæt] *n* acrobate *mf* ▪ **acrobatics** *npl* acrobaties *fpl*

**acronym** ['ækrənɪm] *n* sigle *m*

**across** [ə'krɒs] **1** *prep (from side to side of)* d'un côté à l'autre de; *(on the other side of)* de l'autre côté de; *(crossways)* en travers de; **a bridge a. the river** un pont sur la rivière; **to walk** *or* **go a.** *(street, lawn)* traverser; **to run/swim a.** traverser en courant/à la nage **2** *adv* **to be a kilometre a.** *(wide)* avoir un kilomètre de large; **to get sth a. to sb** faire comprendre qch à qn

**acrylic** [ə'krɪlɪk] *adj (paint, fibre)* acrylique; *(garment)* en acrylique

**act** [ækt] **1** *n* (**a**) *(deed)* acte *m*; **a. (of parliament)** loi *f*; **caught in the a.** pris sur le fait

(**b**) *Theatre (part of play)* acte *m*; *(in circus, cabaret)* numéro *m*; *Fig* **to get one's a. together** se secouer; *Fam* **in on the a.** dans le coup

**2** *vt (part)* jouer; **to a. the fool** faire l'idiot

**3** *vi* (**a**) *(take action, behave)* agir; **it's time to a.** il est temps d'agir; **to a. as secretary/***etc* faire office de secrétaire/*etc*; **to a. (up)on** *(affect)* agir sur; *(advice)* suivre; **to a. on behalf of sb** représenter qn; *Fam* **to a. up** *(of person, machine)* faire des siennes

(**b**) *(in play, film)* jouer; *(pretend)* jouer la comédie ▪ **acting 1** *adj (temporary)* intérimaire **2** *n (of play)* représentation *f*; *(art)* jeu *m*; *(career)* théâtre *m*

**action** ['ækʃən] *n* action *f*; *(military)* combats *mpl*; *(legal)* procès *m*, action *f*; **to take a.** prendre des mesures; **to put into a.** *(plan)* exécuter; **out of a.** *(machine)* hors service; *(person)* hors de combat

**active** ['æktɪv] **1** *adj* actif, -ive; *(interest, dislike)* vif (*f* vive); *(volcano)* en activité **2** *n Gram* actif *m* ▪ **activity** (*pl* **-ies**) *n* activité *f*; *(in street)* animation *f*

**actor** ['æktə(r)] *n* acteur *m* ▪ **actress** *n* actrice *f*

**actual** ['æktʃʊəl] *adj* réel (*f* réelle); *(example)* concret, -ète; **the a. book** le livre même; **in a. fact** en réalité ▪ **actually** *adv (truly)* réellement; *(in fact)* en réalité, en fait

**acupuncture** ['ækjʊpʌŋktʃə(r)] *n* acuponcture *f*

**acute** [ə'kjuːt] *adj (pain, angle)* aigu (*f* aiguë); *(anxiety, emotion)* vif (*f* vive); *(mind, observer)* perspicace; *(shortage)* grave ▪ **acutely** *adv (suffer, feel)* profondément; *(painful)* extrêmement

**AD** [eɪ'diː] (*abbr* **anno Domini**) apr. J.-C.

**ad** [æd] *n Fam (on radio, TV)* pub *f*; *(private, in newspaper)* annonce *f*; *Br* **small ad,** *Am* **want ad** petite annonce *f*

**adapt** [ə'dæpt] **1** *vt* adapter (**to** à); **to a. oneself to sth** s'adapter à qch **2** *vi* s'adapter ▪ **adaptable** *adj (person)* souple; *(instrument)* adaptable ▪ **adapter, adaptor** *n (for use abroad)* adaptateur *m*; *(for several plugs)* prise *f* multiple

**add** [æd] **1** *vt* ajouter (**to/that** à/que); **to a. (up** *or* **together)** *(numbers)* additionner; **to a. in** inclure **2** *vi* **to a. to** *(increase)* augmenter; **to a. up to** *(total)* s'élever à; *(mean)* signifier; *(represent)* constituer

**adder** ['ædə(r)] *n* vipère *f*

**addict** ['ædɪkt] *n* **drug a.** toxicomane *mf*, drogué, -e *mf*; **TV a.** fana(tique) *mf* de la télé ▪ **addicted** *adj* **to be a. to drugs** être toxicomane; **to be a. to alcohol** être alcoolique; **to be a. to cigarettes** ne pas pouvoir se passer de tabac ▪ **addictive** *adj (drug, TV)* qui crée une dépendance

**addition** [ə'dɪʃən] *n* addition *f*; *(increase)* augmentation *f*; **in a.** de plus; **in a. to** en plus de ▪ **additional** *adj* supplémentaire

**additive** ['ædɪtɪv] *n* additif *m*

**address** [*Br* ə'dres, *Am* 'ædres] **1** *n (on letter, parcel)* adresse *f*; *(speech)* allocution *f* **2** [ə'dres] *vt (person, audience)* s'adresser à; *(words, speech)* adresser (**to** à); *(letter)* mettre l'adresse sur

**adept** [ə'dept] *adj* expert (**in** *or* **at** à)

**adequate** ['ædɪkwət] *adj (enough)* suffisant; *(acceptable)* convenable; *(performance)* acceptable ▪ **adequately** *adv (sufficiently)* suffisamment; *(acceptably)* convenablement

**adhere** [əd'hɪə(r)] *vi* **to a. to** adhérer à; *(decision, rule)* s'en tenir à ▪ **adhesive** [-'hi:sɪv] *adj & n* adhésif *(m)*

**adjacent** [ə'dʒeɪsənt] *adj (house, angle)* adjacent (**to** à)

**adjective** ['ædʒɪktɪv] *n* adjectif *m*

**adjoin** [ə'dʒɔɪn] *vt* être attenant à ▪ **adjoining** *adj* attenant

**adjourn** [ə'dʒɜ:n] **1** *vt (postpone)* ajourner; *(session)* suspendre **2** *vi* suspendre la séance

**adjust** [ə'dʒʌst] *vt (machine)* régler; *(machine part)* ajuster, régler; *(salaries, prices)* (r)ajuster; *(clothes)* rajuster; **to a. to sth** s'adapter à qch ▪ **adjustable** *adj (seat)* réglable

**ad-lib** [æd'lɪb] *vi (pt & pp* **-bb-**) improviser

**administer** [əd'mɪnɪstə(r)] *vt* administrer (**to** à) ▪ **administration** *n* administration *f*; *(government)* gouvernement *m* ▪ **administrator** *n* administrateur, -trice *mf*

**admiral** ['ædmərəl] *n* amiral *m*

**admire** [əd'maɪə(r)] *vt* admirer (**for sth** pour qch; **for doing sth** de faire qch) ▪ **admirable** *adj* admirable

**admit** [əd'mɪt] *(pt & pp* **-tt-**) **1** *vt (let in)* laisser entrer; *(to hospital, college)* admettre; *(acknowledge)* reconnaître, admettre (**that** que) **2** *vi* **to a. to sth** avouer qch; *(mistake)* reconnaître qch ▪ **admission** *n (to theatre)* entrée *f* (**to** à *ou* de); *(to club, school)* admission *f*; *(acknowledgement)* aveu *m*; **a. (charge)** (prix *m* d')entrée *f* ▪ **admittance** *n* entrée *f*; **'no a.'** 'entrée interdite' ▪ **admittedly** [-ɪdlɪ] *adv* de l'aveu général

**adolescent** [ædə'lesənt] *n* adolescent, -e *mf*

**adopt** [ə'dɒpt] *vt* adopter; *Pol (candidate)* choisir ▪ **adopted** *adj (child)* adopté; *(son, daughter)* adoptif, -ive; *(country)* d'adoption ▪ **adoptive** *adj (parent)* adoptif, -ive

**adore** [ə'dɔ:(r)] *vt* adorer (**doing** faire) ▪ **adorable** *adj* adorable

**Adriatic** [eɪdrɪ'ætɪk] *n* **the A.** l'Adriatique *f*

**adult** ['ædʌlt, ə'dʌlt] **1** *n* adulte *mf* **2** *adj (animal)* adulte; **a. class/film** classe *f*/film *m* pour adultes

**adultery** [ə'dʌltərɪ] *n* adultère *m*; **to commit a.** commettre l'adultère

**advance** [əd'vɑ:ns] **1** *n (movement, money)* avance *f*; *(of science)* progrès *mpl*; **advances** *(sexual)* avances *fpl*; **in a.** *(book, inform, apply)* à l'avance; *(pay)* d'avance; *(arrive)* en avance

**2** *adj (payment)* anticipé; **a. booking** réservation *f*

**3** *vt* (**a**) *(put forward)* faire avancer (**b**) *(science, one's work)* faire progresser; *(opinion)* avancer

**4** *vi (go forward, progress)* avancer; **to a. towards sb** s'avancer *ou* avancer vers qn ▪ **advanced** *adj* avancé; *(studies, level)* supérieur; *(course)* de niveau supérieur; **a. in years** âgé

**advantage** [əd'vɑ:ntɪdʒ] *n* avantage *m* (**over** sur); **to take a. of** *(situation)* profiter de; *(person)* exploiter; *(woman)* séduire; **a. Hewitt** *(in tennis)* avantage Hewitt

**advent** ['ædvent] *n* arrivée *f*, avènement *m*; *Rel* **A.** l'Avent *m*

**adventure** [əd'ventʃə(r)] **1** *n* aventure *f* **2** *adj (film, story)* d'aventures ▪ **adventurous** *adj* aventureux, -euse

**adverb** ['ædvɜ:b] *n* adverbe *m*

**adverse** ['ædvɜ:s] *adj* défavorable; *(effect)* négatif, -ive

**advert** ['ædvɜ:t] *n Br* pub *f*; *(private, in newspaper)* annonce *f*

**advertise** ['ædvətaɪz] **1** *vt (commercially)* faire de la publicité pour; *(privately)* passer une annonce pour vendre **2** *vi* faire de la publicité; *(privately)* passer une annonce (**for** pour trouver) ▪ **advertising** *n* publicité *f*; **a. agency** agence *f* de publicité; **a. campaign** campagne *f* de publicité

**advertisement** [*Br* əd'vɜ:tɪsmənt, *Am* ædvər'taɪzmənt] *n* publicité *f*; *(private or in newspaper)* annonce *f*; *(poster)* affiche *f*; *TV* **the advertisements** la publicité

**advice** [əd'vaɪs] *n* conseil(s) *m(pl)*; *Com (notification)* avis *m*; **a piece of a.** un conseil; **to ask sb's a.** demander conseil à qn; **to take sb's a.** suivre les conseils de qn

**advise** [əd'vaɪz] *vt* (**a**) *(counsel)* conseiller; *(recommend)* recommander; **to a. sb to do sth** conseiller à qn de faire qch; **to a. sb against doing sth** déconseiller à qn de faire qch (**b**) *(inform)* **to a. sb that...** aviser qn que... ▪ **advisable** *adj (action)* à conseiller; **it's a. to wait**/*etc* il est plus prudent d'attendre/*etc* ▪ **adviser, advisor** *n* conseiller, -ère *mf*

**advocate 1** ['ædvəkət] *n (of cause)* défenseur *m*; *(lawyer)* avocat, -e *mf* **2** ['ædvəkeɪt] *vt* préconiser

**aerial** ['eərɪəl] **1** *n Br* antenne *f* **2** *adj (photo)* aérien, -enne

**aerobics** [eə'rəʊbɪks] *npl* aérobic *m*

**aeroplane** ['eərəpleɪn] *n Br* avion *m*

**aerosol** ['eərəsɒl] *n* aérosol *m*

**aesthetic** [*Br* i:s'θetɪk, *Am* es'θetɪk] *adj* esthétique

**affair** ['əfeə(r)] *n (matter, concern)* affaire *f*; **(love) a.** liaison *f*; **state of affairs** situation *f*

**affect** [ə'fekt] *vt (concern)* concerner; *(move, pretend to have)* affecter; *(harm)* nuire à; *(influence)* influer sur; **to be deeply affected by sth** être très affecté par qch ▪ **affected** *adj (manner)* affecté

**affection** [ə'fekʃən] *n* affection *f* (**for** pour) ▪ **affectionate** *adj* affectueux, -euse

**affinity** [ə'fɪnɪtɪ] (*pl* **-ies**) *n* affinité *f*

**affirm** [ə'fɜ:m] *vt* affirmer ▪ **affirmative 1** *adj* affirmatif, -ive **2** *n* affirmative *f*; **to answer in the a.** répondre par l'affirmative

**affix** [ə'fɪks] *vt (stamp, signature)* apposer

**afflict** [ə'flɪkt] *vt* affliger (**with** de) ▪ **affliction** *n (misery)* affliction *f*; *(disability)* infirmité *f*

**affluent** ['æflʊənt] *adj* riche; **a. society** société *f* d'abondance

**afford** [ə'fɔ:d] *vt (pay for)* **I can't a. it/a new car** je n'ai pas les moyens de l'acheter/d'acheter une nouvelle voiture; **he can't a. the time (to read it)** il n'a pas le temps (de le lire); **I can a. to wait** je peux me permettre d'attendre ▪ **affordable** *adj (price)* abordable

**Afghanistan** [æf'gænɪstɑ:n] *n* l'Afghanistan *m*

**afield** [ə'fi:ld] *adv* **further a.** plus loin

**afloat** [ə'fləʊt] *adv (ship, swimmer, business)* à flot; *(awash)* submergé; **to stay a.** *(of ship)* rester à flot; *(of business)* se maintenir à flot

**afraid** [ə'freɪd] *adj* **to be a.** avoir peur (**of** de); **to be a. to do** *or* **of doing sth** avoir peur de faire qch; **I'm a. (that) he'll fall** j'ai peur qu'il (ne) tombe; **I'm a. he's out** je regrette, il est sorti

**afresh** [ə'freʃ] *adv* de nouveau; **to start a.** recommencer

**Africa** ['æfrɪkə] *n* l'Afrique *f* ▪ **African 1** *adj* africain **2** *n* Africain, -e *mf*

**after** ['ɑ:ftə(r)] **1** *adv* après; **soon/long a.** peu/longtemps après; **the month a.** le mois d'après; **the day a.** le lendemain

**2** *prep* après; **a. three days** au bout de trois jours; **the day a. the battle** le lendemain de la bataille; **a. eating** après avoir mangé; **day a. day** jour après jour; **a. all** après tout; **it's a. five** il est cinq heures passées; *Am* **ten a. four** quatre heures dix; **to be a. sb/sth** *(seek)* chercher qn/qch

**3** *conj* après que; **a. he saw you** après qu'il t'a vu ▪ **after-effects** *npl* suites *fpl*, séquelles *fpl* ▪ **afterlife** *n* vie *f* après la mort ▪ **aftermath** *n* suites *fpl* ▪ **after-sales service** *n* service *m* après-vente ▪ **aftershave** *n* (lotion *f*) après-rasage *m*, after-shave *m inv* ▪ **afterthought** *n* réflexion *f* après coup; **to add/say sth as an a.** ajouter/dire qch après coup ▪ **afterward(s)** *adv* après, plus tard

**afternoon** [ɑːftəˈnuːn] *n* après-midi *m ou f inv*; **in the a.** l'après-midi; **at three in the a.** à trois heures de l'après-midi; **every Monday a.** tous les lundis après-midi; **good a.!** bonjour!

**again** [əˈgen] *adv* de nouveau, encore une fois; *(furthermore)* en outre; **to go down/up a.** redescendre/remonter; **she won't do it a.** elle ne le fera plus; **never a.** plus jamais; **a. and a.** bien des fois; **what's his name a.?** comment s'appelle-t-il déjà?

**against** [əˈgenst, əˈgeɪnst] *prep* contre; **to lean a. sth** s'appuyer contre qch; **to go** *or* **be a. sth** s'opposer à qch; **a. the law** illégal; *Br* **a. the rules,** *Am* **a. the rule** interdit, contraire aux règlements; **the pound rose a. the dollar** la livre est en hausse par rapport au dollar

**age** [eɪdʒ] **1** *n* âge *m*; **(old) a.** vieillesse *f*; **what a. are you?, what's your a.?** quel âge as-tu?; **five years of a.** âgé de cinq ans; **under a.** trop jeune, mineur; *Fam* **to wait (for) ages** attendre une éternité; **a. gap** différence *f* d'âge; **a. limit** limite *f* d'âge

**2** *vt & vi* (*pres p* **ag(e)ing**) vieillir ▪ **aged** *adj* (**a**) [eɪdʒd] **a. ten** âgé de dix ans (**b**) [ˈeɪdʒɪd] vieux (*f* vieille), âgé; **the a.** les personnes *fpl* âgées

**agenda** [əˈdʒendə] *n* ordre *m* du jour

**agent** [ˈeɪdʒənt] *n* agent *m*; *(car dealer)* concessionnaire *mf* ▪ **agency** *n* agence *f*

**aggravate** [ˈægrəveɪt] *vt (make worse)* aggraver; *Fam (annoy)* exaspérer

**aggregate** [ˈægrɪgət] **1** *adj* global **2** *n (total)* ensemble *m*; **on a.** au total

**aggressive** [əˈgresɪv] *adj* agressif, -ive

**aggrieved** [əˈgriːvd] *adj (offended)* blessé, froissé; *(tone)* peiné

**aghast** [əˈgɑːst] *adj* horrifié (**at** par)

**agile** [*Br* ˈædʒaɪl, *Am* ˈædʒəl] *adj* agile

**agitated** [ˈædʒɪteɪtɪd] *adj* agité

**agnostic** [ægˈnɒstɪk] *adj & n* agnostique *(mf)*

**ago** [əˈgəʊ] *adv* **a year a.** il y a un an; **how long a.?** il y a combien de temps (de cela)?; **long a.** il y a longtemps; **a short time a.** il y a peu de temps

**agonizing** [ˈægənaɪzɪŋ] *adj (pain)* atroce; *(situation)* angoissant

**agony** [ˈægənɪ] (*pl* **-ies**) *n (pain)* douleur *f* atroce; *(anguish)* angoisse *f*; **to be in a.** être au supplice; **a. column** *(in newspaper)* courrier *m* du cœur

**agree** [əˈgriː] **1** *vi (come to an agreement)* se mettre d'accord; *(be in agreement)* être d'accord (**with** avec); *(of facts, dates)* concorder; *(of verb)* s'accorder; **to a. (up)on** *(decide)* convenir de; **to a. to sth/to doing sth** consentir à qch/à faire qch

**2** *vt (plan)* se mettre d'accord sur; *(date, price)* convenir de; *(approve)* approuver; **to a. to do sth** accepter de faire qch; **to a. that...** admettre que... ▪ **agreed** *adj (time, place)* convenu ▪ **agreement** *n (contract, assent) & Gram* accord *m* (**with** avec); **to be in a. with sb** être d'accord avec qn; **to come to an a.** se mettre d'accord

**agreeable** [əˈgriːəbəl] *adj (pleasant)* agréable; **to be a.** *(agree)* être d'accord; **to be a. to sth** consentir à qch

**agriculture** [ˈægrɪkʌltʃə(r)] *n* agriculture *f* ▪ **agricultural** *adj* agricole

**aground** [əˈgraʊnd] *adv* **to run a.** *(of ship)* (s')échouer

**ahead** [əˈhed] *adv (in space)* en avant; *(leading)* en tête; *(in the future)* à l'avenir; **a. of** *(in space)* devant; *(in time)* avant; **one hour/*etc* a. (of)** une heure/*etc* d'avance (sur); **to be a. of schedule** être en avance; **to go on a.**

partir devant; **to go a.** *(advance)* avancer; *(continue)* continuer; *(start)* commencer; **go a.!** allez-y!; **to think a.** prévoir

**aid** [eɪd] **1** *n (help)* aide *f*; *(device)* accessoire *m*; **with the a. of sb** avec l'aide de qn; **with the a. of sth** à l'aide de qch; **in a. of** *(charity)* au profit de **2** *vt* aider (**sb to do** qn à faire)

**aide** [eɪd] *n* collaborateur, -trice *mf*

**AIDS** [eɪdz] *(abbr* **Acquired Immune Deficiency Syndrome***)* *n* SIDA *m*

**ailing** ['eɪlɪŋ] *adj (ill)* souffrant; *(company)* en difficulté ▪ **ailment** *n* affection *f*

**aim** [eɪm] **1** *n* but *m*; **to take a. (at)** viser; **with the a. of** dans le but de **2** *vt (gun)* braquer (**at** sur); *(stone)* lancer (**at** à *ou* vers); *(blow, remark)* décocher (**at** à) **3** *vi* viser; **to a. at sb** viser qn; **to a. to do sth** avoir l'intention de faire qch ▪ **aimless** *adj (existence)* sans but

**air** [eə(r)] **1** *n* (**a**) *(atmosphère)* air *m*; **in the open a.** en plein air; **by a.** *(travel)* en *ou* par avion; *(send letter, goods)* par avion; **to be** *or* **go on (the) a.** *(of person)* passer à l'antenne; *(of programme)* être diffusé; **to throw sth in(to) the a.** jeter qch en l'air; *Fig* **there's something in the a.** il se prépare quelque chose; *Aut* **a. bag** airbag *m*; **a. base** base *f* aérienne; **a. bed** matelas *m* pneumatique; **a. fare** prix *m* du billet d'avion; **a. force** armée *f* de l'air; **a. freshener** désodorisant *m* *(pour la maison)*

(**b**) *(appearance, tune)* air *m*; **to put on airs** se donner des airs; **with an a. of sadness** d'un air triste

**2** *vt (room)* aérer; *(views)* exposer ▪ **air-conditioning** *n* climatisation *f* ▪ **aircraft** *n inv* avion *m*; **a. carrier** porte-avions *m inv* ▪ **airfield** *n* terrain *m* d'aviation ▪ **airgun** *n* carabine *f* à air comprimé ▪ **airlift** *vt* transporter par avion ▪ **airline** *n* compagnie *f* aérienne; **a. ticket** billet *m* d'avion ▪ **airmail** *n* poste *f* aérienne; **by a.** par avion ▪ **airplane** *n Am* avion *m* ▪ **airport** *n* aéroport *m* ▪ **air-raid shelter** *n* abri *m* antiaérien ▪ **airship** *n* dirigeable *m* ▪ **airtight** *adj* hermétique ▪ **air-traffic controller** *n* contrôleur *m* aérien, aiguilleur *m* du ciel

**airy** ['eərɪ] (**-ier, -iest**) *adj (room)* clair et spacieux, -euse; *Fig (manner)* désinvolte

**aisle** [aɪl] *n (in supermarket, cinema)* allée *f*; *(in plane)* couloir *m*; *(in church)* *(on side)* nef *f* latérale; *(central)* allée *f* centrale

**ajar** [ə'dʒɑː(r)] *adj & adv (door)* entrouvert

**alarm** [ə'lɑːm] **1** *n (warning, fear, device)* alarme *f*; *(mechanism)* sonnerie *f* (d'alarme); **false a.** fausse alerte *f*; **a. clock** réveil *m* **2** *vt (frighten)* alarmer; *(worry)* inquiéter; **they were alarmed at the news** la nouvelle les a beaucoup inquiétés

**alas** [ə'læs] *exclam* hélas!

**Albania** [æl'beɪnɪə] *n* l'Albanie *f* ▪ **Albanian 1** *adj* albanais **2** *n* Albanais, -e *mf*

**album** ['ælbəm] *n (book, record)* album *m*

**alcohol** ['ælkəhɒl] *n* alcool *m* ▪ **alcoholic 1** *adj (person)* alcoolique; **a. drink** boisson *f* alcoolisée **2** *n (person)* alcoolique *mf*

**alcove** ['ælkəʊv] *n* alcôve *f*

**ale** [eɪl] *n* bière *f*

**alert** [ə'lɜːt] **1** *adj (watchful)* vigilant; *(lively) (mind, baby)* éveillé **2** *n* alerte *f*; **on the a.** sur le qui-vive **3** *vt* alerter

**A level** ['eɪlevəl] *n Br (exam)* ≃ épreuve *f* de baccalauréat

**algebra** ['ældʒɪbrə] *n* algèbre *f*

**Algeria** [æl'dʒɪərɪə] *n* l'Algérie *f* ▪ **Algerian 1** *adj* algérien, -enne **2** *n* Algérien, -enne *mf*

**alias** ['eɪlɪəs] **1** *adv* alias **2** (*pl* **aliases**) *n* nom *m* d'emprunt

**alibi** ['ælɪbaɪ] *n* alibi *m*

**alien** ['eɪlɪən] **1** *adj* étranger, -ère (**to** à) **2** *n (from outer space)* extraterrestre *mf*; *Formal (foreigner)* étranger, -ère *mf*

▪ **alienate** *vt (friend, supporters, readers)* s'aliéner; **to feel alienated** se sentir exclu

**alight¹** [ə'laɪt] *adj (fire)* allumé; *(building)* en feu; *(face)* éclairé; **to set sth a.** mettre le feu à qch

**alight²** [ə'laɪt] *(pt & pp* **alighted** *or* **alit**) *vi* (**a**) *Formal (from bus, train)* descendre (**from** de) (**b**) *(of bird)* se poser (**on** sur)

**align** [ə'laɪn] *vt* aligner

**alike** [ə'laɪk] **1** *adj (people, things)* semblables, pareils, -eilles; **to look** *or* **be a.** se ressembler **2** *adv* de la même manière; **summer and winter a.** été comme hiver

**alimony** [*Br* 'ælɪmənɪ, *Am* 'ælɪməʊnɪ] *n Law* pension *f* alimentaire

**alit** [ə'lɪt] *pt & pp of* **alight²**

**alive** [ə'laɪv] *adj* vivant, en vie; **to stay a.** survivre; **a. and well** bien portant; *Fam* **a. and kicking** plein de vie

---

**ALL** [ɔ:l] **1** *adj* tout, toute, *pl* tous, toutes; **a. day** toute la journée; **a. men** tous les hommes; **a. the girls** toutes les filles; **a. four of them** tous les quatre; **for a. his wealth** malgré toute sa fortune

**2** *pron (everyone)* tous *mpl*, toutes *fpl*; *(everything)* tout; **my sisters are a. here** toutes mes sœurs sont ici; **he ate it a., he ate a. of it** il a tout mangé; **take a. of it** prends (le) tout; **a. of us** nous tous; **a. together** tous ensemble; **a. (that) he has** tout ce qu'il a; **a. in a.** à tout prendre; **anything at a.** quoi que ce soit; **if there's any wind at a.** s'il y a le moindre vent; **nothing at a.** rien du tout; **not at a.** pas du tout; *(after 'thank you')* il n'y a pas de quoi

**3** *adv* tout; **a. alone** tout seul; **a. bad** entièrement mauvais; **a. over** *(everywhere)* partout; *(finished)* fini; **a. too soon** bien trop tôt; *Sport* **six a.** six partout; *Fam* **not a. there** un peu fêlé ▪ **all-night** *adj (party)* qui dure toute la nuit; *(shop)* ouvert toute la nuit ▪ **all-out** *adj (effort)* acharné; *(war, strike)* tous azimuts ▪ **all-purpose** *adj (tool)* universel, -elle ▪ **all-round** *adj (knowledge)* approfondi; *(athlete)* complet, -ète ▪ **all-time** *adj (record)* jamais battu; **to reach an a. low/high** arriver à son point le plus bas/le plus haut

---

**allegation** [ælɪ'geɪʃən] *n* accusation *f*

**allege** [ə'ledʒ] *vt* prétendre (**that** que) ▪ **alleged** *adj (so-called) (crime, fact)* prétendu; *(author, culprit)* présumé; **he is a. to be...** on prétend qu'il est...

**allegiance** [ə'li:dʒəns] *n (to party, cause)* fidélité *f* (**to** à)

**allergy** ['ælədʒɪ] *(pl* **-ies**) *n* allergie *f* (**to** à) ▪ **allergic** [ə'lɜ:dʒɪk] *adj* allergique (**to** à)

**alleviate** [ə'li:vɪeɪt] *vt (pain, suffering)* soulager; *(burden, task)* alléger; *(problem)* remédier à

**alley** ['ælɪ] *(pl* **-eys**) *n* ruelle *f*; *Fam* **that's (right) up my a.** c'est mon rayon

**alliance** [ə'laɪəns] *n* alliance *f*

**allied** ['ælaɪd] *adj (country)* allié; *(matters)* lié

**alligator** ['ælɪgeɪtə(r)] *n* alligator *m*

**allocate** ['æləkeɪt] *vt (assign)* affecter (**to** à); *(distribute)* répartir

**allot** [ə'lɒt] *(pt & pp* **-tt-**) *vt (assign)* attribuer (**to** à); *(distribute)* répartir; **in the allotted time** dans le temps imparti ▪ **allotment** *n Br (land)* jardin *m* ouvrier

**allow** [ə'laʊ] **1** *vt* permettre (**sb sth** qch à qn); *(give, grant)* accorder (**sb sth** qch à qn); *(request)* accéder à; **to a. sb to do** permettre à qn de faire; **to a. an hour/a metre/***etc* prévoir une heure/un mètre/*etc*; **it's not allowed** c'est interdit; **you're not allowed to go** on vous interdit de partir **2** *vi* **to a. for sth** tenir compte de qch ▪ **allowable** *adj (acceptable)* admissible; *(expense)* déductible

**allowance** [ə'laʊəns] *n* allocation *f*; *(for travel, housing, food)* indemnité *f*; *(tax-free amount)* abattement *m*; **to make allowances for** *(person)* être indulgent envers; *(thing)* tenir compte de

**alloy** ['ælɔɪ] *n* alliage *m*

**all right** [ɔːl'raɪt] **1** *adj (satisfactory)* bien *inv*; *(unharmed)* sain et sauf; *(undamaged)* intact; *(without worries)* tranquille; **it's a.** ça va; **are you a.?** ça va?; **I'm a.** *(healthy)* je vais bien; *(financially)* je m'en sors; **to be a. at maths** se débrouiller en maths; **the TV is a. now** *(fixed)* la télé marche maintenant **2** *adv (well)* bien; **a.!** *(in agreement)* d'accord!; **is it a. if I smoke?** ça ne vous dérange pas si je fume?

**allude** [ə'luːd] *vi* **to a. to** faire allusion à ▪ **allusion** *n* allusion *f*

**ally 1** ['ælaɪ] *(pl* **-ies***)* *n* allié, -e *mf* **2** [ə'laɪ] *(pt & pp* **-ied***)* *vt* **to a. oneself with** s'allier à *ou* avec

**almighty** [ɔːl'maɪtɪ] **1** *adj* (**a**) *(powerful)* tout-puissant (*f* toute-puissante) (**b**) *Fam (enormous)* terrible, formidable **2** *n* **the A.** le Tout-Puissant

**almond** ['ɑːmənd] *n* amande *f*

**almost** ['ɔːlməʊst] *adv* presque; **he a. fell** il a failli tomber

**alone** [ə'ləʊn] *adj & adv* seul; **an expert a. can...** seul un expert peut...; **I did it (all) a.** je l'ai fait (tout) seul; **to leave** *or* **let a.** *(person)* laisser tranquille; *(thing)* ne pas toucher à; **I can't afford a bike, let a. a car!** je n'ai pas les moyens de m'acheter un vélo, encore moins une voiture

**along** [ə'lɒŋ] **1** *prep* **(all) a.** (tout) le long de; **to walk a. the shore** marcher le long du rivage; **to walk a. the street** marcher dans la rue; **a. here** par ici; *Fig* **somewhere a. the way** à un moment donné

**2** *adv* **to move a.** avancer; **I'll be** *or* **come a. shortly** je viendrai tout à l'heure; **come a.!** venez donc!; **to bring sth a.** apporter qch; **to bring sb a.** amener qn; **all a.** *(all the time)* dès le début; *(all the way)* d'un bout à l'autre; **a. with** ainsi que

**alongside** [əlɒŋ'saɪd] *prep & adv* à côté (de); **a. the kerb** le long du trottoir

**aloof** [ə'luːf] **1** *adj* distant **2** *adv* à distance

**aloud** [ə'laʊd] *adv* à haute voix

**alphabet** ['ælfəbet] *n* alphabet *m* ▪ **alphabetical** *adj* alphabétique

**Alps** [ælps] *npl* **the A.** les Alpes *fpl* ▪ **Alpine** *adj (club, range)* alpin; *(scenery)* alpestre

**already** [ɔːl'redɪ] *adv* déjà

**alright** [ɔːl'raɪt] *adv Fam* = **all right**

**Alsatian** [æl'seɪʃən] *n (dog)* berger *m* allemand

**also** ['ɔːlsəʊ] *adv* aussi, également; *(moreover)* de plus

**altar** ['ɔːltə(r)] *n* autel *m*

**alter** ['ɔːltə(r)] **1** *vt* changer; *(clothing)* retoucher **2** *vi* changer ▪ **alteration** *n* changement *m* (**in** de); *(of clothing)* retouche *f*; **alterations** *(to building)* travaux *mpl*

**alternate 1** [ɔːl'tɜːnət] *adj* alterné; **on a. days** tous les deux jours **2** ['ɔːltəneɪt] *vt* faire alterner **3** ['ɔːltəneɪt] *vi* alterner (**with** avec); *El* **alternating current** courant *m* alternatif

**alternative** [ɔːl'tɜːnətɪv] **1** *adj (other)* de remplacement; **an a. way** une autre façon; **a. medicine** médecine *f* douce **2** *n (choice)* alternative *f*; **she had no a. but to obey** elle n'a pas pu faire autrement que d'obéir ▪ **alternatively** *adv* **(or) a.** ou alors, ou bien

**although** [ɔːl'ðəʊ] *adv* bien que *(+ subjunctive)*

**altitude** ['æltɪtjuːd] *n* altitude *f*

**altogether** [ɔːltə'geðə(r)] *adv (completely)* tout à fait; *(on the whole)* somme toute; **how much a.?** combien en tout?

**aluminium** [*Br* æljʊ'mɪnɪəm] (*Am* **aluminum** [ə'luːmɪnəm]) *n* aluminium *m*

**always** ['ɔːlweɪz] *adv* toujours; **he's a. criticizing** il est toujours à critiquer; **as a.** comme toujours

**am** [æm, *unstressed* əm] *see* **be**

**a.m.** [eɪ'em] *adv* du matin

**amalgamate** [ə'mælgəmeɪt] *vt & vi* fusionner

**amateur** ['æmətə(r)] **1** *n* amateur *m* **2** *adj (interest, sports, performance)* d'amateur; **a. painter/actress** peintre *m*/actrice *f* amateur

**amaze** [ə'meɪz] *vt* stupéfier ■ **amazed** *adj* stupéfait (**at sth** de qch); *(filled with wonder)* émerveillé; **I was a. by his courage** son courage m'a stupéfié ■ **amazing** *adj (surprising)* stupéfiant; *(incredible)* extraordinaire

**ambassador** [æm'bæsədə(r)] *n* ambassadeur, -drice *mf*

**amber** ['æmbə(r)] *n* ambre *m*; **a. (light)** *(of traffic signal)* (feu *m*) orange *m*

**ambiguous** [æm'bɪgjʊəs] *adj* ambigu (*f* ambiguë)

**ambition** [æm'bɪʃən] *n* ambition *f* ■ **ambitious** *adj* ambitieux, -euse

**ambivalent** [æm'bɪvələnt] *adj* ambivalent

**ambulance** ['æmbjʊləns] *n* ambulance *f*; **a. driver** ambulancier, -ère *mf*

**ambush** ['æmbʊʃ] **1** *n* embuscade *f* **2** *vt* tendre une embuscade à; **to be ambushed** tomber dans une embuscade

**amend** [ə'mend] *vt (text)* modifier; *Pol (law)* amender

**amends** [ə'mendz] *npl* **to make a.** se racheter; **to make a. for sth** réparer qch

**amenities** [*Br* ə'mi:nɪtɪz, *Am* ə'menɪtɪz] *npl (of town)* aménagements *mpl*; *(shops)* commerces *mpl*

**America** [ə'merɪkə] *n* l'Amérique *f*; **North/South A.** l'Amérique *f* du Nord/du Sud ■ **American 1** *adj* américain **2** *n* Américain, -e *mf*

**amiable** ['eɪmɪəbəl] *adj* aimable

**amicable** ['æmɪkəbəl] *adj* amical

**amid(st)** [ə'mɪd(st)] *prep* au milieu de, parmi

**amiss** [ə'mɪs] *adv & adj* **something is a.** *(wrong)* quelque chose ne va pas; **that wouldn't go a.** ça ne ferait pas de mal

**ammunition** [æmjʊ'nɪʃən] *n* munitions *fpl*

**among(st)** [ə'mʌŋ(st)] *prep (amidst)* parmi; *(between)* entre; **a. the crowd/books/others/***etc* parmi la foule/les livres/les autres/*etc*; **a. friends** entre amis; **a. other things** entre autres (choses)

**amoral** [eɪ'mɒrəl] *adj* amoral

**amount** [ə'maʊnt] **1** *n* quantité *f*; *(sum of money)* somme *f*; *(total figure of invoice, debt)* montant *m*; *(scope, size)* importance *f* **2** *vi* **to a. to** *(bill)* s'élever à; *Fig* **it amounts to blackmail** ce n'est rien d'autre que du chantage; **it amounts to the same thing** ça revient au même

**amp** [æmp] *n (unit of electricity)* ampère *m*; *Br* **3-a. plug** prise *f* avec fusible de 3 ampères

**ample** ['æmpəl] *adj* (**a**) *(plentiful)* abondant (**b**) *(large) (woman, bosom)* fort (**c**) *(roomy) (garment)* large

**amplify** ['æmplɪfaɪ] (*pt & pp* **-ied**) *vt (essay, remarks)* développer; *(sound)* amplifier ■ **amplifier** *n* amplificateur *m*

**amputate** ['æmpjʊteɪt] *vt* amputer; **to a. sb's hand/***etc* amputer qn de la main/*etc*

**amuse** [ə'mju:z] *vt* amuser; **to keep sb amused** distraire qn ■ **amusement** *n* amusement *m*, divertissement *m*; *(pastime)* distraction *f*; **amusements** *(at fairground)* attractions *fpl*; *(gambling machines)* machines *fpl* à sous; **a. arcade** salle *f* de jeux; **a. park** parc *m* d'attractions

**an** [æn, *unstressed* ən] *see* **a**

**an(a)emic** [ə'ni:mɪk] *adj* anémique; **to become a.** faire de l'anémie

**an(a)esthetic** [ænəsθetɪk] *n (process)* anesthésie *f*; *(substance)* anesthésique *m*; **under a.** sous anesthésie; **general/local a.** anesthésie *f* générale/locale

**analogy** [ə'nælədʒɪ] (*pl* **-ies**) *n* analogie *f* (**with** avec)

**analyse** ['ænəlaɪz] *vt* analyser ■ **analysis** (*pl* **-yses** [-əsi:z]) *n* analyse *f* ■ **analyst** *n* analyste *mf*

**anarchy** ['ænəkɪ] *n* anarchie *f* ■ **anarchist** *n* anarchiste *mf*

**anatomy** [ə'nætəmɪ] *n* anatomie *f*
**ancestor** ['ænsestə(r)] *n* ancêtre *m*
**anchor** ['æŋkə(r)] **1** *n* ancre *f* **2** *vt (ship)* mettre à l'ancre **3** *vi* jeter l'ancre, mouiller
**anchovy** [*Br* 'æntʃəvɪ, *Am* æn'tʃəʊvɪ] (*pl* **-ies**) *n* anchois *m*
**ancient** ['eɪnʃənt] *adj* ancien, -enne; *(pre-medieval)* antique
**and** [ænd, *unstressed* ən(d)] *conj* et; **a knife a. fork** un couteau et une fourchette; **my mother a. father** mon père et ma mère; **two hundred a. two** deux cent deux; **four a. three quarters** quatre trois quarts; **nice a. warm** bien chaud; **better a. better** de mieux en mieux; **she can read a. write** elle sait lire et écrire; **go a. see** va voir; **I knocked a. knocked** j'ai frappé pendant un bon moment
**anemic** [ə'ni:mɪk] *adj* = **anaemic**
**anesthetic** [ænɪs'θetɪk] *n* = **anaesthetic**
**angel** ['eɪndʒəl] *n* ange *m* ▪ **angelic** *adj* angélique
**anger** ['æŋgə(r)] **1** *n* colère *f*; **in a., out of a.** sous le coup de la colère **2** *vt* mettre en colère
**angina** [æn'dʒaɪnə] *n* angine *f* de poitrine
**angle**[1] ['æŋgəl] *n* angle *m*; **at an a.** en biais
**angle**[2] ['æŋgəl] *vi (fish)* pêcher à la ligne; *Fig* **to a. for** *(compliments)* quêter ▪ **angler** *n* pêcheur, -euse *mf* à la ligne
**Anglican** ['æŋglɪkən] *adj & n* anglican, -e *(mf)*
**Anglo-** ['æŋgləʊ] *pref* anglo- ▪ **Anglo-Saxon** *adj & n* anglo-saxon, -onne *(mf)*
**angry** ['æŋgrɪ] (**-ier, -iest**) *adj (person)* en colère, fâché; *(look)* furieux, -euse; **an a. letter** une lettre indignée; **a. words** des paroles indignées; **to get a. (with)** se fâcher (contre)
**anguish** ['æŋgwɪʃ] *n* angoisse *f*
**animal** ['ænɪməl] *n* animal *m*
**animated** ['ænɪmeɪtɪd] *adj (lively)* animé; **to become a.** s'animer
**animation** [ænɪ'meɪʃən] *n (liveliness) & Cin* animation *f*
**aniseed** ['ænɪsi:d] *n (as flavouring)* anis *m*
**ankle** ['æŋkəl] *n* cheville *f*; **a. sock** socquette *f*
**annex**[1] [ə'neks] *vt* annexer
**annex**[2], *Br* **annexe** ['æneks] *n (building)* annexe *f*
**anniversary** [ænɪ'vɜ:sərɪ] (*pl* **-ies**) *n (of event)* anniversaire *m*
**announce** [ə'naʊns] *vt* annoncer; *(birth, marriage)* faire part de ▪ **announcement** *n (statement)* annonce *f*; *(notice of birth, marriage, death) (in newspaper)* avis *m*; *(private letter)* faire-part *m inv* ▪ **announcer** *n (on TV)* speaker, -ine *mf*
**annoy** [ə'nɔɪ] *vt (inconvenience)* ennuyer; *(irritate)* agacer ▪ **annoyed** *adj* fâché; **to get a. (with)** se fâcher (contre) ▪ **annoying** *adj* ennuyeux, -euse
**annual** ['ænjʊəl] **1** *adj* annuel, -elle **2** *n (yearbook)* annuaire *m*; *(children's)* album *m*; *(plant)* plante *f* annuelle ▪ **annually** *adv (every year)* tous les ans; *(per year)* par an
**annul** [ə'nʌl] (*pt & pp* **-ll-**) *vt (contract, marriage)* annuler
**anoint** [ə'nɔɪnt] *vt* oindre (**with** de)
**anomalous** [ə'nɒmələs] *adj* anormal ▪ **anomaly** (*pl* **-ies**) *n* anomalie *f*
**anonymous** [ə'nɒnɪməs] *adj* anonyme
**anorak** ['ænəræk] *n* anorak *m*
**anorexia** [ænə'reksɪə] *n* anorexie *f* ▪ **anorexic** *adj & n* anorexique *(mf)*
**another** [ə'nʌðə(r)] *adj & pron* un(e) autre; **a. man** *(different)* un autre homme; **a. month** *(additional)* encore un mois; **a. ten** encore dix; **one a.** l'un(e) l'autre, *pl* les un(e)s les autres; **they love one a.** ils s'aiment
**answer** ['ɑ:nsə(r)] **1** *n* réponse *f*; *(to problem, riddle) & Math* solution *f* (**to** de); *(reason)* explication *f*; **in a. to your letter** en réponse à votre lettre

**2** *vt (person, question, letter)* répondre à; *(prayer, wish)* exaucer; **he answered yes** il a répondu oui; **to a. the door** ouvrir la porte; **to a. the phone** répondre au téléphone

**3** *vi* répondre ▪ **answering machine** *n* répondeur *m*

**ant** [ænt] *n* fourmi *f*

**antagonize** [æn'tægənaɪz] *vt* provoquer (l'hostilité de)

**Antarctic** [æn'tɑːktɪk] **1** *adj* antarctique **2** *n* **the A.** l'Antarctique *m*

**antenatal** [æntɪ'neɪtəl] *adj Br* prénatal; **a. classes** préparation *f* à l'accouchement

**antenna**[1] [æn'tenə] (*pl* **-ae** [-iː]) *n (of insect)* antenne *f*

**antenna**[2] [æn'tenə] (*pl* **-as**) *n Am (for TV, radio)* antenne *f*

**anthem** ['ænθəm] *n* **national a.** hymne *m* national

**anthology** [æn'θɒlədʒɪ] (*pl* **-ies**) *n* anthologie *f*

**anti-** [*Br* 'æntɪ, *Am* 'æntaɪ] *pref* anti- ▪ **antibiotic** *adj & n* antibiotique *(m)* ▪ **anticlimax** *n* déception *f* ▪ **anticlockwise** *adv Br* dans le sens inverse des aiguilles d'une montre ▪ **antidote** *n* antidote *m* ▪ **antifreeze** *n (for vehicle)* antigel *m* ▪ **antihistamine** *n (drug)* antihistaminique *m* ▪ **antiperspirant** *n* déodorant *m* ▪ **anti-Semitic** *adj* antisémite ▪ **antiseptic** *adj & n* antiseptique *(m)* ▪ **antisocial** *adj (unsociable)* peu sociable

**anticipate** [æn'tɪsɪpeɪt] *vt (foresee)* anticiper; *(expect)* s'attendre à, prévoir; *(forestall)* devancer ▪ **anticipation** *n (expectation)* attente *f*; *(foresight)* prévision *f*; **in a. of** en prévision de; **in a.** *(thank, pay)* d'avance

**antics** ['æntɪks] *npl* singeries *fpl*; **he's up to his a. again** il a encore fait des siennes

**antiquated** ['æntɪkweɪtɪd] *adj (expression, custom)* vieillot, -otte; *(person)* vieux jeu *inv*; *(object, machine)* antédiluvien, -enne

**antique** [æn'tiːk] **1** *adj (furniture)* ancien, -enne; *(of Greek or Roman antiquity)* antique; **a. dealer** antiquaire *mf*; **a. shop** magasin *m* d'antiquités **2** *n* antiquité *f*, objet *m* d'époque

**Antwerp** ['æntwɜːp] *n* Anvers *m ou f*

**anxiety** [æŋ'zaɪətɪ] (*pl* **-ies**) *n (worry)* inquiétude *f* (**about** au sujet de); *(fear)* anxiété *f*; *(eagerness)* désir *m* (**to do** de faire; **for sth** de qch)

**anxious** ['æŋkʃəs] *adj (worried)* inquiet, -ète (**about** pour); *(troubled)* anxieux, -euse; *(causing worry)* angoissant; *(eager)* impatient (**to do** de faire)

---

**ANY** ['enɪ] **1** *adj* (**a**) *(in questions)* du, de la, des; **have you a. milk/tickets?** avez-vous du lait/des billets?

(**b**) *(in negatives)* de; *(the slightest)* aucun; **he hasn't got a. milk/tickets** il n'a pas de lait/de billets; **there isn't a. doubt/problem** il n'y a aucun doute/problème

(**c**) *(no matter which)* n'importe quel; **ask a. doctor** demande à n'importe quel médecin

(**d**) *(every)* tout; **at a. moment** à tout moment; **in a. case, at a. rate** de toute façon

**2** *pron* (**a**) *(no matter which one)* n'importe lequel; *(somebody)* quelqu'un; **if a. of you...** si l'un d'entre vous..., si quelqu'un parmi vous...

(**b**) *(quantity)* en; **have you got a.?** en as-tu?; **I don't see a.** je n'en vois pas

**3** *adv* **not a. further/happier** pas plus loin/plus heureux, -euse; **I don't see him a. more** je ne le vois plus; **a. more tea?** encore un peu de thé?; **I'm not a. better** je ne vais pas mieux

---

**anybody** ['enɪbɒdɪ] *pron* (**a**) *(somebody)* quelqu'un; **do you see a.?** tu vois quelqu'un?; **more than a.** plus que tout autre (**b**) *(in negatives)* personne; **he doesn't know a.** il ne connaît personne (**c**) *(no matter who)* n'importe qui; **a. would think that...** on croirait que...

**anyhow** ['enɪhaʊ] *adv (at any rate)* de

toute façon; *Fam (badly)* n'importe comment

**anyone** ['enɪwʌn] *pron* = **anybody**

**anyplace** ['enɪpleɪs] *adv Am* = **anywhere**

**anything** ['enɪθɪŋ] *pron* (**a**) *(something)* quelque chose; **can you see a.?** tu vois quelque chose?

(**b**) *(in negatives)* rien; **he doesn't do a.** il ne fait rien; **without a.** sans rien

(**c**) *(everything)* tout; **a. you like** tout ce que tu veux; *Fam* **like a.** *(work)* comme un fou

(**d**) *(no matter what)* **a. (at all)** n'importe quoi

**anyway** ['enɪweɪ] *adv (at any rate)* de toute façon

**anywhere** ['enɪweə(r)] *adv* (**a**) *(no matter where)* n'importe où

(**b**) *(everywhere)* partout; **a. you go** où que vous alliez, partout où vous allez; **a. you like** (là) où tu veux

(**c**) *(somewhere)* quelque part; **is he going a.?** va-t-il quelque part?

(**d**) *(in negatives)* nulle part; **he doesn't go a.** il ne va nulle part; **without a. to put it** sans un endroit où le/la mettre

**apart** [ə'pɑːt] *adv* (**a**) *(separated)* **we kept them a.** nous les tenions séparés; **two years a.** à deux ans d'intervalle; **they are a metre a.** ils se trouvent à un mètre l'un de l'autre; **to come a.** *(of two objects)* se séparer; **to tell two things/people a.** distinguer deux choses/personnes (l'une de l'autre)

(**b**) *(to pieces)* **to tear a.** mettre en pièces; **to take a.** démonter

(**c**) *(to one side)* à part; **joking a.** sans blague; **a. from** *(except for)* à part

**apartment** [ə'pɑːtmənt] *n* appartement *m*; *Am* **a. building, a. house** immeuble *m* (d'habitation)

**apathy** ['æpəθɪ] *n* apathie *f*

**ape** [eɪp] **1** *n* grand singe *m* **2** *vt (imitate)* singer

**aperitif** [əperɪ'tiːf] *n* apéritif *m*

**aperture** ['æpətʃʊə(r)] *n* ouverture *f*

**apiece** [ə'piːs] *adv* chacun; **£2 a.** 2 livres pièce *ou* chacun

**apologetic** [əpɒlə'dʒetɪk] *adj (letter)* plein d'excuses; *(smile)* d'excuse; **to be a. (about)** s'excuser (de)

**apology** [ə'pɒlədʒɪ] (*pl* **-ies**) *n* excuses *fpl* ■ **apologize** *vi* s'excuser (**for** de); **he apologized for being late** il s'est excusé de son retard; **to a. to sb (for)** faire ses excuses à qn (pour)

**apostle** [ə'pɒsəl] *n* apôtre *m*

**apostrophe** [ə'pɒstrəfɪ] *n* apostrophe *f*

**appal** [ə'pɔːl] (*Am* **appall**) (*pt & pp* **-ll-**) *vt* consterner; **to be appalled (at)** être horrifié (par) ■ **appalling** *adj* épouvantable

**apparatus** [æpə'reɪtəs] *n (equipment, organization)* appareil *m*; *Br (in gym)* agrès *mpl*

**apparent** [ə'pærənt] *adj (seeming)* apparent; *(obvious)* évident; **it's a. that...** il est clair que... ■ **apparently** *adv* apparemment; **a. she's going to Venice** il paraît qu'elle va à Venise

**appeal** [ə'piːl] **1** *n (charm)* attrait *m*; *(interest)* intérêt *m*; *(call)* appel *m*; *(pleading)* supplication *f*; *(to a court)* appel *m* **2** *vt* (**a**) *(in court)* faire appel (**b**) **to a. to sb** *(attract)* plaire à qn; *(interest)* intéresser qn; *(ask for help)* faire appel à qn; **to a. to sb's generosity** faire appel à la générosité de qn; **to a. to sb for sth** demander qch à qn; **to a. to sb to do sth** supplier qn de faire qch ■ **appealing** *adj (attractive) (offer, idea)* séduisant; *(begging) (look)* suppliant

**appear** [ə'pɪə(r)] *vi (become visible)* apparaître; *(seem, be published)* paraître; *(on stage, in film)* jouer; *(in court)* comparaître; **it appears that...** *(it seems that)* il semble que... *(+ subjunctive or indicative)*; *(it is rumoured that)* il paraît que... *(+ indicative)* ■ **appearance** *n (act)* apparition *f*; *(look)* apparence *f*; *(of book)* parution *f*; **to put in an a.** faire acte de présence; **to keep up appearances** sauver les apparences

**appendix** [ə'pendɪks] (*pl* **-ixes** [-ɪksɪz] *or* **-ices** [-ɪsiːz]) *n (in book, body)* appendice *m*; **to have one's a. out** se faire opérer de l'appendicite ▪ **appendicitis** *n* appendicite *f*

**appetite** ['æpɪtaɪt] *n* appétit *m* ▪ **appetizer** *n (drink)* apéritif *m*; *(food)* amuse-gueule *m inv* ▪ **appetizing** *adj* appétissant

**applaud** [ə'plɔːd] **1** *vt (clap)* applaudir; *(approve of)* approuver, applaudir à **2** *vi* applaudir ▪ **applause** *n* applaudissements *mpl*

**apple** ['æpəl] *n* pomme *f*; *Br* **stewed apples** compote *f* de pommes; **cooking a.** pomme *f* à cuire; **eating a.** pomme *f* de dessert; **a. core** trognon *m* de pomme; **a. pie** tarte *f* aux pommes; **a. sauce** compote *f* de pommes; **a. tree** pommier *m*

**appliance** [ə'plaɪəns] *n* appareil *m*

**applicable** [ə'plɪkəbəl] *adj (rule)* applicable (**to** à); *(relevant)* pertinent (**to** à)

**applicant** ['æplɪkənt] *n* candidat, -e *mf* (**for** à)

**application** [æplɪ'keɪʃən] *n* (**a**) *(request)* demande *f* (**for** de); *(for job)* candidature *f* (**for** de); *(for membership)* demande *f* d'inscription; **a. (form)** *(for job)* formulaire *m* de candidature; *(for club)* formulaire *m* d'inscription (**b**) *(diligence)* application *f*

**apply** [ə'plaɪ] (*pt & pp* **-ied**) **1** *vt (put on, carry out)* appliquer; *(brake)* appuyer sur; **to a. oneself (to)** s'appliquer (à) **2** *vi (be relevant)* s'appliquer (**to** à); **to a. for** *(job)* poser sa candidature à; **to a. to sb (for)** *(ask)* s'adresser à qn (pour) ▪ **applied** *adj (maths, linguistics)* appliqué

**appoint** [ə'pɔɪnt] *vt (person)* nommer (**to a post** à un poste; **to do** pour faire); *(director, minister)* nommer; *(secretary, clerk)* engager; *(time, place)* fixer; **at the appointed time** à l'heure dite ▪ **appointment** *n* nomination *f*; *(meeting)* rendez-vous *m inv*; *(post)* situation *f*; **to make an a. with** prendre rendez-vous avec

**appraise** [ə'preɪz] *vt* évaluer ▪ **appraisal** *n* évaluation *f*

**appreciate** [ə'priːʃɪeɪt] **1** *vt (enjoy, value, assess)* apprécier; *(understand)* comprendre; *(be grateful for)* être reconnaissant de **2** *vi (of goods)* prendre de la valeur ▪ **appreciation** *n* (**a**) *(gratitude)* reconnaissance *f*; *(judgement)* appréciation *f* (**b**) *(rise in value)* augmentation *f* (de la valeur) ▪ **appreciative** *adj (grateful)* reconnaissant (**of** de); *(favourable)* élogieux, -euse; **to be a. of** *(enjoy)* apprécier

**apprehend** [æprɪ'hend] *vt (seize, arrest)* appréhender

**apprehensive** [æprɪ'hensɪv] *adj* inquiet, -ète (**about** de *ou* au sujet de); **to be a. of** appréhender

**apprentice** [ə'prentɪs] *n* apprenti, -e *mf* ▪ **apprenticeship** *n* apprentissage *m*

**approach** [ə'prəʊtʃ] **1** *n (method)* façon *f* de s'y prendre; *(path, route)* voie *f* d'accès; *(of winter, vehicle)* approche *f* **2** *vt (draw near to)* s'approcher de; *(go up to, tackle)* aborder; **to a. sb about sth** parler à qn de qch; **he's approaching forty** il va sur ses quarante ans **3** *vi (of person, vehicle)* s'approcher; *(of date)* approcher ▪ **approachable** *adj (person)* d'un abord facile

**appropriate 1** [ə'prəʊprɪət] *adj (place, clothes, means)* approprié (**to** à); *(remark, time)* opportun; **a. to** *or* **for** qui convient à **2** [ə'prəʊprɪeɪt] *vt (steal)* s'approprier; *(set aside)* affecter (**for** à)

**approve** [ə'pruːv] *vt* approuver; **to a. of** *(conduct, decision, idea)* approuver; **I don't a. of him** il ne me plaît pas ▪ **approval** *n* approbation *f*; **on a.** *(goods)* à l'essai

**approving** [ə'pruːvɪŋ] *adj (look)* approbateur, -trice

**approximate 1** [ə'prɒksɪmət] *adj* approximatif, -ive **2** [ə'prɒksɪmeɪt] *vi* **to**

**a. to sth** se rapprocher de qch
**apricot** ['eɪprɪkɒt] *n* abricot *m*
**April** ['eɪprəl] *n* avril *m*; **A. fool!** poisson d'avril!
**apron** ['eɪprən] *n (garment)* tablier *m*
**apt** [æpt] *adj (remark, reply, means)* qui convient; *(word, name)* bien choisi; **to be a. to do sth** avoir tendance à faire qch ▪ **aptly** *adv (described)* justement; *(chosen)* bien
**aptitude** ['æptɪtju:d] *n* aptitude *f* (**for** pour); *(of student)* don *m* (**for** pour)
**aquarium** [ə'kweərɪəm] *n* aquarium *m*
**Aquarius** [ə'kweərɪəs] *n (sign)* le Verseau
**aquatic** [ə'kwætɪk] *adj (plant)* aquatique; *(sport)* nautique
**Arab** ['ærəb] **1** *adj* arabe **2** *n* Arabe *mf* ▪ **Arabian** *adj* arabe ▪ **Arabic** *adj & n (language)* arabe *(m)*; **A. numerals** chiffres *mpl* arabes
**arbitrary** ['ɑ:bɪtrərɪ] *adj* arbitraire
**arbitration** [ɑ:bɪ'treɪʃən] *n* arbitrage *m*
**arc** [ɑ:k] *n (of circle)* arc *m*
**arcade** [ɑ:'keɪd] *n (for shops) (small)* passage *m* couvert; *(large)* galerie *f* marchande
**arch** [ɑ:tʃ] **1** *n (of bridge)* arche *f*; *(of building)* voûte *f*, arc *m*; *(of foot)* cambrure *f* **2** *vt* **to a. one's back** *(inwards)* se cambrer; *(outwards)* se voûter
**arch-** [ɑ:tʃ] *pref* **a.-enemy** ennemi *m* juré; **a.-rival** grand rival *m*
**archaeology** [ɑ:kɪ'ɒlədʒɪ] *n* archéologie *f* ▪ **archaeologist** *n* archéologue *mf*
**archaic** [ɑ:'keɪɪk] *adj* archaïque
**archbishop** [ɑ:tʃ'bɪʃəp] *n* archevêque *m*
**archeologist** [ɑ:kɪ'ɒlədʒɪst] *n* = **archaeologist**
**archeology** [ɑ:kɪ'ɒlədʒɪ] *n* = **archaeology**
**archer** ['ɑ:tʃə(r)] *n* archer *m*
**archetype** ['ɑ:kɪtaɪp] *n* archétype *m*
**architect** ['ɑ:kɪtekt] *n* architecte *mf* ▪ **architecture** *n* architecture *f*
**archives** ['ɑ:kaɪvz] *npl* archives *fpl*
**archway** ['ɑ:tʃweɪ] *n* voûte *f*
**arctic** ['ɑ:ktɪk] **1** *adj* arctique; *(weather)* polaire, glacial **2** *n* **the A.** l'Arctique *m*
**ardent** ['ɑ:dənt] *adj (supporter)* ardent, chaud
**ardour** ['ɑ:də(r)] *n* ardeur *f*
**arduous** ['ɑ:djʊəs] *adj* pénible, ardu
**are** [ɑ:(r)] *see* **be**
**area** ['eərɪə] *n (of country)* région *f*; *(of town)* quartier *m*; *Mil* zone *f*; *(surface)* superficie *f*; *Fig (of knowledge)* domaine *m*; **kitchen a.** coin-cuisine *m*; **play a.** aire *f* de jeux; *Am* **a. code** *(in phone number)* indicatif *m*
**arena** [ə'ri:nə] *n (for sports) & Fig* arène *f*
**aren't** [ɑ:nt] = **are not**
**Argentina** [ɑ:dʒən'ti:nə] *n* l'Argentine *f*
**arguable** ['ɑ:gjʊəbəl] *adj* discutable
**argue** ['ɑ:gju:] **1** *vt (matter)* discuter (de); *(position)* défendre; **to a. that...** soutenir que... **2** *vi (quarrel)* se disputer (**with/about** avec/au sujet de); *(reason)* raisonner (**with/about** avec/sur)
**argument** ['ɑ:gjʊmənt] *n (quarrel)* dispute *f*; *(debate)* discussion *f*; *(point)* argument *m*; **to have an a. with sb** *(quarrel)* se disputer avec qn ▪ **argumentative** *adj (person)* querelleur, -euse
**Aries** ['eəri:z] *n (sign)* le Bélier; **to be A.** être Bélier
**arise** [ə'raɪz] (*pt* **arose**, *pp* **arisen** [ə'rɪzən]) *vi (of problem, opportunity)* se présenter; *(of cry, objection)* s'élever; *(result)* provenir (**from** de)
**aristocracy** [ærɪ'stɒkrəsɪ] *n* aristocratie *f* ▪ **aristocrat** [*Br* 'ærɪstəkræt, *Am* ə'rɪstəkræt] *n* aristocrate *mf*
**arithmetic** [ə'rɪθmətɪk] *n* arithmétique *f*
**ark** [ɑ:k] *n* **Noah's a.** l'arche *f* de Noé
**arm**[1] [ɑ:m] *n* bras *m*; **a. in a.** bras dessus bras dessous; **with open arms** à bras ouverts ▪ **armband** *n* brassard

*m* ▪ **armchair** *n* fauteuil *m* ▪ **armpit** *n* aisselle *f*

**arm²** [ɑːm] *vt (with weapon)* armer (**with** de) ▪ **armaments** *npl* armements *mpl*

**armistice** [ˈɑːmɪstɪs] *n* armistice *m*

**armour** [ˈɑːmə(r)] *n (of knight)* armure *f*; *(of tank)* blindage *m* ▪ **armoured, armour-plated** [ˈɑːməpleɪtɪd] *adj (car)* blindé

**arms** [ɑːmz] *npl (weapons)* armes *fpl*; **the a. race** la course aux armements

**army** [ˈɑːmɪ] **1** (*pl* **-ies**) *n* armée *f*; **to join the a.** s'engager **2** *adj (uniform)* militaire

**A road** [ˈeɪrəʊd] *n Br* ≃ route *f* nationale

**aroma** [əˈrəʊmə] *n* arôme *m* ▪ **aromatherapy** *n* aromathérapie *f* ▪ **aromatic** [ærəʊˈmætɪk] *adj* aromatique

**arose** [əˈrəʊz] *pp of* **arise**

**around** [əˈraʊnd] **1** *prep* autour de; *(approximately)* environ; **to travel a. the world** faire le tour du monde **2** *adv* autour; **all a.** tout autour; **a. here** par ici; **to follow sb a.** suivre qn partout; **to rush a.** courir dans tous les sens; **is Jack a.?** est-ce que Jack est dans le coin?; **he's still a.** il est encore là; **there's a lot of flu a.** beaucoup de gens ont la grippe en ce moment

**arouse** [əˈraʊz] *vt (suspicion, anger, curiosity)* éveiller

**arrange** [əˈreɪndʒ] *vt* arranger; *(time, meeting)* fixer; **to a. to do sth** s'arranger pour faire qch ▪ **arrangement** *n (layout, agreement, for music)* arrangement *m*; **arrangements** *(preparations)* préparatifs *mpl*; *(plans)* projets *mpl*; **to make arrangements to do sth** prendre des dispositions pour faire qch

**arrears** [əˈrɪəz] *npl (payment)* arriéré *m*; **to be in a.** avoir du retard dans ses paiements

**arrest** [əˈrest] **1** *vt (criminal, progress)* arrêter **2** *n (of criminal)* arrestation *f*; **under a.** en état d'arrestation

**arrive** [əˈraɪv] *vi* arriver; **to a. at** *(conclusion, decision)* arriver à, parvenir à ▪ **arrival** *n* arrivée *f*; **on my a.** à mon arrivée; **new a.** nouveau venu *m*, nouvelle venue *f*; *(baby)* nouveau-né, -e *mf*

**arrogant** [ˈærəgənt] *adj* arrogant ▪ **arrogance** *n* arrogance *f*

**arrow** [ˈærəʊ] *n* flèche *f*

**arson** [ˈɑːsən] *n* incendie *m* criminel

**art** [ɑːt] *n* art *m*; **faculty of arts, arts faculty** faculté *f* des lettres; **arts degree** ≃ licence *f* ès lettres; **a. exhibition** exposition *f* d'œuvres d'art; **a. gallery** *(museum)* musée *m* d'art; *(shop)* galerie *f* d'art; **a. school** école *f* des beaux-arts

**artery** [ˈɑːtərɪ] (*pl* **-ies**) *n* artère *f*

**arthritis** [ɑːˈθraɪtɪs] *n* arthrite *f*

**artichoke** [ˈɑːtɪtʃəʊk] *n* **(globe) a.** artichaut *m*; **Jerusalem a.** topinambour *m*

**article** [ˈɑːtɪkəl] *n* article *m*; **a. of clothing** vêtement *m*; *Br* **articles** *(of lawyer)* contrat *m* de stage

**articulate 1** [ɑːˈtɪkjʊlət] *adj (person)* qui s'exprime clairement; *(speech)* clair **2** [ɑːˈtɪkjʊleɪt] *vt & vi (speak)* articuler ▪ **articulation** [-ˈleɪʃən] *n* articulation *f*

**artificial** [ɑːtɪˈfɪʃəl] *adj* artificiel, -elle

**artillery** [ɑːˈtɪlərɪ] *n* artillerie *f*

**artist** [ˈɑːtɪst] *n* artiste *mf* ▪ **artiste** *n (singer, dancer)* artiste *mf* ▪ **artistic** *adj (pattern, treasure)* artistique; *(person)* artiste

**artless** [ˈɑːtləs] *adj* naturel, -elle

**arty** [ˈɑːtɪ] *adj Pej* du genre artiste

**AS** [æz, *unstressed* əz] **1** *adv* (**a**) *(with manner)* comme; **as promised/planned** comme promis/prévu; **as you like** comme tu veux; **such as** comme, tel que; **as much as I can** (au)tant que je peux; **as it is** *(this being the case)* les choses étant ainsi; **to leave sth as it is** laisser qch comme ça *ou* tel quel; **it's late as it is** il est déjà tard; **as if, as though** comme si; **you look as if** *or* **as though you're tired** tu as l'air fatigué (**b**) *(comparison)* **as tall as you** aussi grand que vous; **as white as a sheet** blanc (*f* blanche) comme un linge; **as much as you** autant que vous; **as much money as** autant d'argent que; **as many people as** autant de gens que; **twice as big as** deux fois plus grand que; **the same as** le même que

**2** *conj* (**a**) *(expressing time)* **as always** comme toujours; **as I was leaving, as I left** comme je partais; **as one grows older** à mesure que l'on vieillit; **as he slept** pendant qu'il dormait; **one day as...** un jour que...; **as from, as of** *(time)* à partir de

(**b**) *(expressing reason)* puisque, comme; **as it's late...** puisqu'il est tard..., comme il est tard...

(**c**) *(though)* **(as) clever as he is...** si intelligent qu'il soit...

(**d**) *(concerning)* **as for that** quant à cela

(**e**) *(+ infinitive)* **so as to...** de manière à...; **so stupid as to...** assez bête pour...

**3** *prep* comme; **she works as a cashier** elle est caissière, elle travaille comme caissière; **dressed up as a clown** déguisé en clown; **as a teacher** en tant que professeur

---

**asap** [eɪeseɪ'piː] (*abbr* **as soon as possible**) dès que possible

**ascend** [ə'send] **1** *vt (throne)* accéder à; *(stairs, mountain)* gravir **2** *vi* monter ▪ **ascent** *n* ascension *f* (**of** de); *(slope)* côte *f*

**ascertain** [æsə'teɪn] *vt (discover)* établir; *(check)* s'assurer de; **to a. that...** s'assurer que...

**ash** [æʃ] *n* (**a**) *(of cigarette, fire)* cendre *f*; **A. Wednesday** mercredi *m* des Cendres (**b**) *(tree)* frêne *m* ▪ **ashtray** *n* cendrier *m*

**ashamed** [ə'ʃeɪmd] *adj* **to be/feel a. (of sb/sth)** avoir honte (de qn/qch); **to be a. of oneself** avoir honte; **to make sb a.** faire honte à qn

**ashore** [ə'ʃɔː(r)] *adv* à terre; **to go a.** débarquer

**Asia** ['eɪʃə, 'eɪʒə] *n* l'Asie *f* ▪ **Asian 1** *adj* asiatique; *Br (from Indian sub-continent)* = du sous-continent indien **2** *n* Asiatique *mf*; *Br (from Indian sub-continent)* = personne originaire du sous-continent indien

**aside** [ə'saɪd] **1** *adv* de côté; **to take** *or* **draw sb a.** prendre qn à part; **to step a.** s'écarter; *Am* **a. from** en dehors de **2** *n (in play, film)* aparté *m*

**ask** [ɑːsk] **1** *vt (request, inquire about)* demander; *(invite)* inviter (**to sth** à qch); **to a. sb sth** demander qch à qn; **to a. sb about sb/sth** interroger qn sur qn/qch; **to a. (sb) a question** poser une question (à qn); **to a. sb the time/way** demander l'heure/son chemin à qn; **to a. sb for sth** demander qch à qn; **to a. sb to do** *(request)* demander à qn de faire; *(invite)* inviter qn à faire; **to a. to leave**/*etc* demander à partir/*etc*

**2** *vi (inquire)* se renseigner (**about** sur); *(request)* demander; **to a. for sb/sth** demander qn/qch; **to a. after** *or* **about sb** demander des nouvelles de qn; **the asking price** le prix demandé

**askew** [ə'skjuː] *adv* de travers

**asleep** [ə'sliːp] *adj* endormi; *(arm, leg)* engourdi; **to be a.** dormir; **to fall a.** s'endormir

**asparagus** [ə'spærəgəs] *n (plant)* asperge *f*; *(food)* asperges *fpl*

**aspect** ['æspekt] *n* aspect *m*; *(of house)* orientation *f*

**asphyxiate** [æs'fɪksɪeɪt] *vt* asphyxier

**aspire** [ə'spaɪə(r)] *vi* **to a. to** aspirer à ▪ **aspiration** [æspɪ'reɪʃən] *n* aspiration *f*

**aspirin** ['æsprɪn] *n* aspirine *f*

**ass** [æs] *n* âne *m*

**assailant** [ə'seɪlənt] *n* agresseur *m*

**assassin** [ə'sæsɪn] *n* assassin *m* ▪ **assassinate** *vt* assassiner ▪ **assassination** *n* assassinat *m*

**assault** [ə'sɔːlt] **1** *n (military)* assaut *m*; *(crime)* agression *f* **2** *vt (attack)* agresser; **to be sexually assaulted**

être victime d'une agression sexuelle
**assemble** [ə'sembəl] **1** *vt (objects, ideas)* assembler; *(people)* rassembler; *(machine)* monter **2** *vi* se rassembler ▪ **assembly** *n (meeting)* assemblée *f*; *(of machine)* montage *m*, assemblage *m*; *(in school)* rassemblement *m (avant les cours)*; **a. line** *(in factory)* chaîne *f* de montage
**assent** [ə'sent] **1** *n* assentiment *m* **2** *vi* consentir (**to** à)
**assert** [ə'sɜːt] *vt* affirmer (**that** que); *(rights)* faire valoir; **to a. oneself** s'affirmer ▪ **assertion** *n (statement)* affirmation *f*; *(of rights)* revendication *f* ▪ **assertive** *adj (forceful) (tone, person)* affirmatif, -ive; *(authoritarian)* autoritaire
**assess** [ə'ses] *vt (value, damage)* évaluer; *(situation)* analyser; *(decide amount of)* fixer le montant de; *(person)* juger ▪ **assessment** *n (of value, damage)* évaluation *f*; *(of situation)* analyse *f*; *(of person)* jugement *m*
**asset** ['æset] *n (advantage)* atout *m*; **assets** *(of business)* avoir *m*
**assign** [ə'saɪn] *vt (give)* attribuer; *(day, time)* fixer; *(appoint)* nommer; *(send, move)* affecter (**to** à) ▪ **assignment** *n (task)* mission *f*; *(for student)* devoir *m*
**assimilate** [ə'sɪmɪleɪt] **1** *vt (absorb)* assimiler **2** *vi (of immigrants)* s'assimiler
**assist** [ə'sɪst] *vt & vi* aider (**in doing** *or* **to do** à faire) ▪ **assistance** *n* aide *f*; **to be of a. to sb** aider qn ▪ **assistant 1** *n* assistant, -e *mf*; *Br (in shop)* vendeur, -euse *mf* **2** *adj* adjoint
**associate 1** [ə'səʊʃɪeɪt] *vt* associer (**with sth** à *ou* avec qch; **with sb** à qn) **2** [ə'səʊʃɪeɪt] *vi* **to a. with sb** *(mix socially)* fréquenter qn **3** [ə'səʊʃɪət] *n & adj* associé, -e *(mf)* ▪ **association** [-'eɪʃən] *n* association *f*
**assorted** [ə'sɔːtɪd] *adj (different)* variés; *(foods)* assortis ▪ **assortment** *n* assortiment *m*; **an a. of people** des gens de toutes sortes
**assume** [ə'sjuːm] *vt* (**a**) *(suppose)* supposer (**that** que); **let us a. that...** supposons que... *(+ subjunctive)* (**b**) *(take on) (power, control)* prendre; *(responsibility, role)* assumer; *(attitude, name)* adopter ▪ **assumed** *adj (feigned)* faux (*f* fausse); **a. name** nom *m* d'emprunt ▪ **assumption** [ə'sʌmpʃən] *n (supposition)* supposition *f*; **on the a. that...** en supposant que... *(+ subjunctive)*
**assure** [ə'ʃʊə(r)] *vt* assurer ▪ **assurance** *n* (**a**) *(confidence, promise)* assurance *f* (**b**) *Br (insurance)* assurance *f*
**asterisk** ['æstərɪsk] *n* astérisque *m*
**asthma** [*Br* 'æsmə, *Am* 'æzmə] *n* asthme *m*
**astonish** [ə'stɒnɪʃ] *vt* étonner; **to be astonished (at sth)** s'étonner (de qch) ▪ **astonishing** *adj* étonnant ▪ **astonishment** *n* étonnement *m*
**astound** [ə'staʊnd] *vt* stupéfier ▪ **astounding** *adj* stupéfiant
**astray** [ə'streɪ] *adv* **to go a.** s'égarer; **to lead a.** détourner du droit chemin
**astride** [ə'straɪd] **1** *adv* à califourchon **2** *prep* à cheval sur
**astrology** [ə'strɒlədʒɪ] *n* astrologie *f*
**astronaut** ['æstrənɔːt] *n* astronaute *mf*
**astronomy** [ə'strɒnəmɪ] *n* astronomie *f* ▪ **astronomer** *n* astronome *mf*
**astute** [ə'stjuːt] *adj (crafty)* rusé; *(clever)* astucieux, -euse
**asylum** [ə'saɪləm] *n* asile *m*

**AT** [æt, *unstressed* ət] *prep* (**a**) à; **at the end** à la fin; **at school** à l'école; **at work** au travail; **at six (o'clock)** à six heures; **at Easter** à Pâques; **to drive at 10 mph** rouler à ≃ 15 km; **to buy/sell at 10 euros a kilo** acheter/vendre (à) 10 euros le kilo
(**b**) chez; **at the doctor's** chez le médecin; **at home** chez soi, à la maison
(**c**) en; **at sea** en mer; **at war** en guerre; **good at maths** fort en maths
(**d**) contre; **angry at** fâché contre
(**e**) sur; **to shoot at** tirer sur; **at my request** sur ma demande
(**f**) de; **to laugh at sb/sth** rire de qn/

qch; **surprised at sth** surpris de qch
(**g**) (au)près de; **at the window** près de la fenêtre
(**h**) par; **six at a time** six par six
(**i**) *(phrases)* **at night** la nuit; **to look at** regarder; **while you're at it** tant que tu y es

---

**ate** [eɪt] *pt of* **eat**
**atheist** ['eɪθɪɪst] *n* athée *mf*
**Athens** ['æθənz] *n* Athènes *m ou f*
**athlete** ['æθli:t] *n* athlète *mf*; **a.'s foot** *(disease)* mycose *f* ▪ **athletic** *adj* athlétique ▪ **athletics** *npl Br* athlétisme *m*; *Am* sport *m*
**Atlantic** [ət'læntɪk] **1** *adj (coast, ocean)* atlantique **2** *n* **the A.** l'Atlantique *m*
**atlas** ['ætləs] *n* atlas *m*
**atmosphere** ['ætməsfɪə(r)] *n* atmosphère *f* ▪ **atmospheric** [-'ferɪk] *adj* atmosphérique
**atom** ['ætəm] *n* atome *m*; **a. bomb** bombe *f* atomique ▪ **atomic** *adj* atomique
**atrocious** [ə'trəʊʃəs] *adj* atroce ▪ **atrocity** *n (cruel action)* atrocité *f*
**attach** [ə'tætʃ] *vt* attacher (**to** à); *(document)* joindre (**to** à); **attached to sb** *(fond of)* attaché à qn ▪ **attachment** *n* (**a**) *(affection)* attachement *m* (**to sb** à qn) (**b**) *(tool)* accessoire *m* (**c**) *(to e-mail)* fichier *m* joint
**attack** [ə'tæk] **1** *n* *(military)* attaque *f* (**on** contre); *(on someone's life)* attentat *m*; *(of illness)* crise *f*; *(of fever)* accès *m* **2** *vt* attaquer; *(problem, plan)* s'attaquer à **3** *vi* attaquer ▪ **attacker** *n* agresseur *m*
**attain** [ə'teɪn] *vt (aim)* atteindre; *(goal, ambition)* réaliser; *(rank)* parvenir à
**attempt** [ə'tempt] **1** *n* tentative *f*; **to make an a. to do** tenter de faire **2** *vt* tenter; *(task)* entreprendre; **to a. to do** tenter de faire; **attempted murder** tentative *f* d'assassinat
**attend** [ə'tend] **1** *vt (meeting)* assister à; *(course)* suivre; *(school, church)* aller à **2** *vi* assister; **to a. to** *(take care of)* s'occuper de
**attendance** [ə'tendəns] *n* présence *f* (**at** à); *(people)* assistance *f*; **(school) a.** scolarité *f*; **in a.** de service ▪ **attendant** *n* employé, -e *mf*; *(in service station)* pompiste *mf*; *Br (in museum)* gardien, -enne *mf*
**attention** [ə'tenʃən] *n* attention *f*; **to pay a.** faire *ou* prêter attention (**to** à); **for the a. of** à l'attention de ▪ **attentive** *adj (heedful)* attentif, -ive (**to** à); *(thoughtful)* attentionné (**to** pour)
**attest** [ə'test] **1** *vt (certify, confirm)* confirmer **2** *vi* **to a. to** témoigner de
**attic** ['ætɪk] *n* grenier *m*
**attitude** ['ætɪtju:d] *n* attitude *f*
**attorney** [ə'tɜ:nɪ] (*pl* **-eys**) *n Am (lawyer)* avocat *m*
**attract** [ə'trækt] *vt* attirer ▪ **attraction** *n (charm, appeal)* attrait *m*; *(place, person)* attraction *f*; *(between people)* attirance *f*; *Phys* attraction *f* terrestre
**attractive** [ə'træktɪv] *adj (house, room, person, car)* beau (*f* belle); *(price, offer)* intéressant; *(landscape)* attrayant
**attribute 1** ['ætrɪbju:t] *n (quality)* attribut *m* **2** [ə'trɪbju:t] *vt (ascribe)* attribuer (**to** à)
**aubergine** ['əʊbəʒi:n] *n Br* aubergine *f*
**auburn** ['ɔ:bən] *adj (hair)* auburn *inv*
**auction** ['ɔ:kʃən] **1** *n* vente *f* aux enchères **2** *vt* **to a. (off)** vendre aux enchères ▪ **auctioneer** *n* commissaire-priseur *m*
**audacity** [ɔ:'dæsɪtɪ] *n* audace *f*
**audible** ['ɔ:dɪbəl] *adj (sound, words)* audible
**audience** ['ɔ:dɪəns] *n* (**a**) *(of speaker, musician, actor)* public *m*; *(of radio broadcast)* auditeurs *mpl*; **TV a.** téléspectateurs *mpl* (**b**) *(interview)* audience *f* (**with sb** avec qn)
**audio** ['ɔ:dɪəʊ] *adj (cassette, system)* audio *inv*; **a. tape** cassette *f* audio ▪ **audiotypist** *n* audiotypiste *mf* ▪ **audiovisual** *adj* audiovisuel, -elle
**audit** ['ɔ:dɪt] **1** *n* audit *m* **2** *vt (accounts)* vérifier

**audition** [ɔːˈdɪʃən] **1** *n* audition *f* **2** *vt & vi* auditionner
**auditorium** [ɔːdɪˈtɔːrɪəm] *n (of theatre, concert hall)* salle *f*
**August** [ˈɔːgəst] *n* août *m*
**aunt** [ɑːnt] *n* tante *f* ▪ **auntie, aunty** (*pl* **-ies**) *n Fam* tata *f*
**au pair** [əʊˈpeə(r)] *n* **a. (girl)** jeune fille *f* au pair
**aura** [ˈɔːrə] *n (of place)* atmosphère *f*; *(of person)* aura *f*
**austere** [ɔːˈstɪə(r)] *adj* austère ▪ **austerity** *n* austérité *f*
**Australia** [ɒˈstreɪlɪə] *n* l'Australie *f* ▪ **Australian 1** *adj* australien, -enne **2** *n* Australien, -enne *mf*
**Austria** [ˈɒstrɪə] *n* l'Autriche *f* ▪ **Austrian 1** *adj* autrichien, -enne **2** *n* Autrichien, -enne *mf*
**authentic** [ɔːˈθentɪk] *adj* authentique ▪ **authenticate** *vt* authentifier
**author** [ˈɔːθə(r)] *n* auteur *m*
**authority** [ɔːˈθɒrɪtɪ] (*pl* **-ies**) *n* autorité *f*; *(permission)* autorisation *f* (**to do** de faire); **to be in a.** *(in charge)* être responsable ▪ **authoritarian** *adj & n* autoritaire *(mf)* ▪ **authoritative** *adj (report, book)* qui fait autorité; *(tone, person)* autoritaire
**authorize** [ˈɔːθəraɪz] *vt* autoriser (**to do** à faire) ▪ **authorization** [-ˈzeɪʃən] *n* autorisation *f* (**to do** de faire)
**autistic** [ɔːˈtɪstɪk] *adj* autiste
**auto** [ˈɔːtəʊ] (*pl* **-os**) *n Am* auto *f*
**autobiography** [ɔːtəʊbaɪˈɒgrəfɪ] (*pl* **-ies**) *n* autobiographie *f*
**autograph** [ˈɔːtəgrɑːf] **1** *n* autographe *m*; **a. book** album *m* d'autographes **2** *vt* dédicacer (**for sb** à qn)
**automatic** [ɔːtəˈmætɪk] *adj* automatique
**automobile** [ˈɔːtəməbiːl] *n Am* automobile *f*
**autonomous** [ɔːˈtɒnəməs] *adj* autonome ▪ **autonomy** *n* autonomie *f*
**autopsy** [ˈɔːtɒpsɪ] (*pl* **-ies**) *n* autopsie *f*
**autumn** [ˈɔːtəm] *n* automne *m*; **in a.** en automne
**auxiliary** [ɔːgˈzɪljərɪ] (*pl* **-ies**) *adj & n* auxiliaire *(mf)*; **a. (verb)** (verbe *m*) auxiliaire *m*
**avail** [əˈveɪl] **1** *n* **to no a.** en vain **2** *vt* **to a. oneself of** profiter de ▪ **availability** *n (of object)* disponibilité *f*; *(of education)* accessibilité *f*
**available** [əˈveɪləbəl] *adj* disponible; **tickets are still a.** il reste des tickets; **this model is a. in black or green** ce modèle existe en noir et en vert
**avalanche** [ˈævəlɑːnʃ] *n* avalanche *f*
**Ave** (*abbr* **Avenue**) av.
**avenge** [əˈvendʒ] *vt* venger; **to a. oneself (on)** se venger (de)
**avenue** [ˈævənjuː] *n* avenue *f*; *Fig (possibility)* possibilité *f*
**average** [ˈævərɪdʒ] **1** *n* moyenne *f*; **on a.** en moyenne; **above/below a.** au-dessus/au-dessous de la moyenne **2** *adj* moyen, -enne **3** *vt (do)* faire en moyenne; *(reach)* atteindre la moyenne de; *(figures)* faire la moyenne de
**averse** [əˈvɜːs] *adj* **to be a. to doing** répugner à faire
**aversion** [əˈvɜːʃən] *n (dislike)* aversion *f*; **to have an a. to sth/to doing sth** avoir de la répugnance pour qch/à faire qch
**avert** [əˈvɜːt] *vt (prevent)* éviter; **to a. one's eyes (from)** *(turn away)* détourner les yeux (de)
**aviation** [eɪvɪˈeɪʃən] *n* aviation *f*
**avid** [ˈævɪd] *adj* avide (**for** de)
**avocado** [ævəˈkɑːdəʊ] (*pl* **-os**) *n* avocat *m*
**avoid** [əˈvɔɪd] *vt* éviter; **to a. doing** éviter de faire ▪ **avoidable** *adj* évitable
**await** [əˈweɪt] *vt* attendre
**awake** [əˈweɪk] **1** *adj* réveillé, éveillé; **he's still a.** il ne dort pas encore **2** (*pt* **awoke**, *pp* **awoken**) *vi* se réveiller **3** *vt* réveiller ▪ **awaken 1** *vi* se réveiller **2** *vt* réveiller
**award** [əˈwɔːd] **1** *n (prize)* prix *m*, récompense *f*; *(scholarship)* bourse *f* **2** *vt (money)* attribuer; *(prize)* décerner; **to a. damages** *(of judge)* accorder

des dommages-intérêts

**aware** [ə'weə(r)] *adj* **to be a. of** *(conscious)* être conscient de; *(informed)* être au courant de; *(realize)* se rendre compte de; **to become a. of/that** se rendre compte de/que ▪ **awareness** *n* conscience *f*

**AWAY** [ə'weɪ] *adv* (**a**) *(distant)* loin; **5 km a.** à 5 km (de distance)

(**b**) *(in time)* **ten days a.** dans dix jours

(**c**) *(absent, gone)* absent; **to drive a.** partir (en voiture); **to fade/melt a.** disparaître/fondre complètement

(**d**) *(to one side)* **to look** *or* **turn a.** détourner les yeux

(**e**) *(continuously)* **to work/talk a.** travailler/parler sans arrêt

(**f**) *Br* **to play a.** *(of team)* jouer à l'extérieur

**awe** [ɔː] *n* crainte *f* (mêlée de respect); **to be in a. of sb** éprouver pour qn une crainte mêlée de respect ▪ **awesome** *adj* *(impressive)* impressionnant; *(frightening)* effrayant; *Am Fam (excellent)* super *inv*

**awful** ['ɔːfəl] *adj* affreux, -euse; *(terrifying)* effroyable; *Fam* **an a. lot (of)** énormément (de); **I feel a. (about it)** j'ai vraiment honte ▪ **awfully** *adv* *(suffer)* affreusement; *(very) (good, pretty)* extrêmement; *(bad, late)* affreusement

**awkward** ['ɔːkwəd] *adj* (**a**) *(clumsy) (person, gesture)* maladroit (**b**) *(difficult)* difficile; *(cumbersome)* gênant; *(tool)* peu commode; *(time)* mal choisi; *(silence)* gêné ▪ **awkwardly** *adv* *(walk)* maladroitement; *(speak)* d'un ton gêné; *(placed, situated)* à un endroit peu pratique

**awning** ['ɔːnɪŋ] *n (of tent)* auvent *m*; *(over shop, window)* store *m*; *(canvas or glass canopy)* marquise *f*

**awoke** [ə'wəʊk] *pt of* **awake**

**awoken** [ə'wəʊkən] *pp of* **awake**

**axe** [æks] *(Am* **ax**) **1** *n* hache *f*; *Fig (reduction)* coupe *f* sombre; **to get the a.** *(of project)* être abandonné; *(of worker)* être mis à la porte; *Fig* **to have an a. to grind** agir dans un but intéressé **2** *vt (costs)* réduire; *(job)* supprimer; *(project)* abandonner

**axis** ['æksɪs] *(pl* **axes** ['æksiːz]) *n* axe *m*

**axle** ['æksəl] *n* essieu *m*

# Bb

**B, b** [biː] *n* B, b *m inv*; **2B** *(number)* 2 ter

**BA** [biːˈeɪ] *n (abbr* **Bachelor of Arts**) **to have a BA in history** ≃ avoir une licence en histoire

**babble** [ˈbæbəl] **1** *vi (mumble)* bredouiller; *(of baby, stream)* gazouiller **2** *n inv (of voices)* rumeur *f*; *(of baby, stream)* gazouillis *m*

**baboon** [bəˈbuːn] *n* babouin *m*

**baby** [ˈbeɪbɪ] (*pl* **-ies**) *n* bébé *m*; **b. boy** petit garçon *m*; **b. girl** petite fille *f*; **b. tiger/***etc* bébé-tigre/*etc m*; **b. clothes/ toys/***etc* vêtements *mpl*/jouets *mpl*/ *etc* de bébé; *Am* **b. carriage** landau *m*; **b. sling** kangourou *m*, porte-bébé *m* ▪ **baby-sit** (*pt & pp* **-sat,** *pres p* **-sitting**) *vi* faire du baby-sitting ▪ **baby-sitter** *n* baby-sitter *mf*

**bachelor** [ˈbætʃələ(r)] *n* (**a**) *(not married)* célibataire *m* (**b**) *Univ* **B. of Arts/of Science** *(person)* ≃ licencié, -e *mf* ès lettres/ès sciences; *(qualification)* ≃ licence *f* de lettres/de sciences

**back** [bæk] **1** *n (of person, animal, hand)* dos *m*; *(of chair)* dossier *m*; *(of house, vehicle, train, head)* arrière *m*; *(of room)* fond *m*; *(of page)* verso *m*; *(of fabric)* envers *m*; *(in sport)* arrière *m*; **at the b. of the book** à la fin du livre; **at the b. of the car** à l'arrière de la voiture; **at the b. of one's mind** derrière la tête; **b. to front** devant derrière, à l'envers; *Fam* **to get off sb's b.** ficher la paix à qn; *Fam* **to get sb's b. up** braquer qn

**2** *adj (wheel, seat)* arrière *inv*; **b. door** porte *f* de derrière; **b. room** pièce *f* du fond; **b. street** rue *f* écartée; **b. tooth** molaire *f*

**3** *adv (behind)* en arrière; **far b., a long way b.** loin derrière; **a month b.** il y a un mois; **to go b. and forth** aller et venir; **to come b.** revenir; **he's b.** il est de retour, il est revenu; **the journey there and b.** le voyage aller et retour

**4** *vt (with money)* financer; *(horse)* parier sur; *(vehicle)* faire reculer; **to be backed with** *(of curtain, picture)* être renforcé de; **to b. sb (up)** *(support)* appuyer qn; *Comptr* **to b. up** sauvegarder

**5** *vi (move backwards)* reculer; **to b. down** faire marche arrière; **to b. out** *(withdraw)* se retirer; *(of vehicle)* sortir en marche arrière; **to b. on to** *(of house)* donner par derrière sur; **to b. up** *(of vehicle)* faire marche arrière ▪ **backache** *n* mal *m* de dos ▪ **backbencher** *n Br Pol* député *m* de base ▪ **backbone** *n* colonne *f* vertébrale; *(of fish)* grande arête *f*; *Fig (main support)* pivot *m* ▪ **backpack** *n* sac *m* à dos ▪ **backside** *n Fam (buttocks)* derrière *m* ▪ **backstage** *adv* dans les coulisses ▪ **backstroke** *n (in swimming)* dos *m* crawlé ▪ **backup** *n* appui *m*; *Am (tailback)* embouteillage *m*; *Comptr* sauvegarde *f* ▪ **backyard** *n Br (enclosed area)* arrière-cour *f*; *Am (garden)* jardin *m* de derrière

**backer** [ˈbækə(r)] *n (supporter)* partisan *m*; *(on horses)* parieur, -euse *mf*; *(financial)* commanditaire *m*

**backfire** [bækˈfaɪə(r)] *vi* (**a**) *(of vehicle)*

pétarader (**b**) *Fig* **to b. on sb** *(of plot)* se retourner contre qn

**backgammon** ['bækgæmən] *n* backgammon *m*

**background** ['bækgraʊnd] *n* fond *m*, arrière-plan *m*; *(educational)* formation *f*; *(professional)* expérience *f*; *(environment)* milieu *m*; *(circumstances)* contexte *m*; **b. music/noise** musique *f*/bruit *m* de fond

**backlash** ['bæklæʃ] *n* retour *m* de bâton

**backlog** ['bæklɒg] *n* **a b. of work** du travail en retard

**backward** ['bækwəd] **1** *adj (person, country)* arriéré; *(glance)* en arrière **2** *adv* = **backwards** ▪ **backwards** *adv* en arrière; *(walk)* à reculons; *(fall)* à la renverse; **to go** *or* **move b.** reculer

**bacon** ['beɪkən] *n* bacon *m*; **b. and eggs** œufs *mpl* au bacon

**bacteria** [bæk'tɪərɪə] *npl* bactéries *fpl*

**bad** [bæd] (**worse, worst**) *adj* mauvais; *(wicked)* méchant; *(sad)* triste; *(accident, wound)* grave; *(tooth)* carié; *(arm, leg)* malade; *(pain)* violent; **b. language** gros mots *mpl*; **b. cheque** chèque *m* sans provision; **to feel b.** *(ill)* se sentir mal; **to be b. at maths** être mauvais en maths; **things are b.** ça va mal; **it's not b.** ce n'est pas mal; **to go b.** *(of fruit, meat)* se gâter; *(of milk)* tourner; **too b.!** tant pis! ▪ **bad-mannered** *adj* mal élevé ▪ **bad-tempered** *adj* grincheux, -euse

**bade** [bæd] *pt of* **bid**

**badge** [bædʒ] *n (of plastic, bearing slogan or joke)* badge *m*; *(of metal, bearing logo)* pin's *m*; *(of postman, policeman)* plaque *f*; *(on school uniform)* insigne *m*

**badger** ['bædʒə(r)] **1** *n (animal)* blaireau *m* **2** *vt* importuner

**badly** ['bædlɪ] *adv* mal; *(hurt)* grièvement; **to be b. mistaken** se tromper lourdement; **b. off** dans la gêne; **to want sth b.** avoir grande envie de qch

**badminton** ['bædmɪntən] *n* badminton *m*

**baffle** ['bæfəl] *vt (person)* laisser perplexe

**bag** [bæg] *n* sac *m*; **bags** *(luggage)* bagages *mpl*; *(under eyes)* poches *fpl*; *Fam Pej* **an old b.** une vieille taupe; *Fam* **in the b.** dans la poche

**baggage** ['bægɪdʒ] *n* bagages *mpl*; *Am* **b. car** fourgon *m*; **b. handler** *(in airport)* bagagiste *mf*; *Am* **b. room** consigne *f*

**baggy** ['bægɪ] (**-ier, -iest**) *adj (garment) (out of shape)* déformé; *(by design)* large

**bagpipes** ['bægpaɪps] *npl* cornemuse *f*

**Bahamas** [bə'hɑːməz] *npl* **the B.** les Bahamas *fpl*

**bail** [beɪl] **1** *n Law* caution *f*; **on b.** sous caution; **to grant sb b.** libérer qn sous caution **2** *vt* **to b. sb out** *Law* se porter garant de qn; *Fig* tirer qn d'affaire **3** *vi* **to b. out** *(from aircraft)* s'éjecter

**bailiff** ['beɪlɪf] *n (law officer)* huissier *m*; *Br (of landowner)* régisseur *m*

**bait** [beɪt] **1** *n* appât *m* **2** *vt* (**a**) *(fishing hook)* amorcer (**b**) *(annoy)* tourmenter

**bake** [beɪk] **1** *vt* (faire) cuire au four **2** *vi (of person) (make cakes)* faire de la pâtisserie; *(make bread)* faire du pain; *(of food)* cuire (au four); *Fam* **it's baking (hot)** on crève de chaleur ▪ **baked** *adj (potatoes, apples)* au four; **b. beans** haricots *mpl* blancs à la tomate

**baker** ['beɪkə(r)] *n* boulanger, -ère *mf* ▪ **bakery** *n* boulangerie *f*

**baking** ['beɪkɪŋ] *n* cuisson *f*; **b. powder** levure *f* chimique; **b. tin** moule *m* à pâtisserie

**balaclava** [bælə'klɑːvə] *n Br* passe-montagne *m*

**balance** ['bæləns] **1** *n (equilibrium)* équilibre *m*; *(of account)* solde *m*; *(remainder)* reste *m*; *(in accounting)* bilan *m*; *(for weighing)* balance *f*; **to lose one's b.** perdre l'équilibre; **to strike a b.** trouver le juste milieu; **on b.** à tout prendre; **b. of payments** balance *f* des paiements; **b. sheet** bilan *m*

**2** *vt* maintenir en équilibre (**on** sur); *(budget, account)* équilibrer; *(compare)* mettre en balance; **to b. (out)** *(compensate for)* compenser

**3** *vi (of person)* se tenir en équilibre; *(of accounts)* être en équilibre, s'équilibrer; **to b. (out)** *(even out)* s'équilibrer

**balcony** ['bælkənɪ] (*pl* **-ies**) *n* balcon *m*

**bald** [bɔːld] (**-er, -est**) *adj* chauve; *(statement)* brutal; *(tyre)* lisse; **b. patch** *or* **spot** tonsure *f*

**balk** [bɔːk] *vi* reculer (**at** devant)

**Balkans** ['bɔːlkənz] *npl* **the B.** les Balkans *fpl*

**ball[1]** [bɔːl] *n* balle *f*; *(inflated, for football, rugby)* ballon *m*; *(for snooker, pool)* bille *f*; *(of string, wool)* pelote *f*; *(sphere)* boule *f*; *(of meat, fish)* boulette *f*; *Fam* **to be on the b.** *(alert)* avoir de la présence d'esprit; *(knowledgeable)* connaître son affaire; **b. bearing** roulement *m* à billes; *Am* **b. game** match *m* de base-ball; *Fig* **it's a whole new b. game** c'est une tout autre affaire

**ball[2]** [bɔːl] *n (dance)* bal *m* (*pl* bals)

**ballad** ['bæləd] *n (poem)* ballade *f*; *(song)* romance *f*

**ballast** ['bæləst] **1** *n* lest *m* **2** *vt* lester

**ballet** ['bæleɪ] *n* ballet *m* ■ **ballerina** *n* ballerine *f*

**balloon** [bə'luːn] *n (toy, airship)* ballon *m*; *(in cartoon)* bulle *f*

**ballot** ['bælət] **1** *n (voting)* scrutin *m*; **b. paper** bulletin *m* de vote; **b. box** urne *f* **2** *vt (members)* consulter (par un scrutin)

**ballpoint (pen)** ['bɔːlpɔɪnt(pen)] *n* stylo *m* à bille

**ballroom** ['bɔːlruːm] *n* salle *f* de danse

**Baltic** ['bɔːltɪk] *n* **the B.** la Baltique

**bamboo** [bæm'buː] *n* bambou *m*; **b. shoots** pousses *fpl* de bambou

**ban** [bæn] **1** *n* interdiction *f*; **to impose a b. on sth** interdire qch **2** (*pt & pp* **-nn-**) *vt* interdire; **to b. sb from doing sth** interdire à qn de faire qch; **to b. sb from** *(club)* exclure qn de

**banal** [bə'næl] *adj* banal (*mpl* -als)

**banana** [bə'nɑːnə] *n* banane *f*

**band** [bænd] **1** *n* (**a**) *(strip)* bande *f*; *(of hat)* ruban *m*; **rubber** *or* **elastic b.** élastique *m* (**b**) *(group of people)* bande *f*; *(of musicians)* (petit) orchestre *m*; *(pop group)* groupe *m* **2** *vi* **to b. together** se (re)grouper

**bandage** ['bændɪdʒ] **1** *n (strip)* bande *f*; *(dressing)* bandage *m* **2** *vt* **to b. (up)** *(arm, leg)* bander; *(wound)* mettre un bandage sur; **to b. sb's arm** bander le bras à qn

**Band-aid**® ['bændeɪd] *n Am* pansement *m* adhésif

**B and B, B & B** [biːənd'biː] *n* (*abbr* **bed and breakfast**) *(service)* ≃ chambre *f* avec petit déjeuner; **to stay at a B and B** ≃ prendre une chambre d'hôte

**bandit** ['bændɪt] *n* bandit *m*

**bandwagon** ['bændwægən] *n Fig* **to jump on the b.** prendre le train en marche

**bandy[1]** ['bændɪ] (**-ier, -iest**) *adj* **to have b. legs** avoir les jambes arquées

**bandy[2]** ['bændɪ] (*pt & pp* **-ied**) *vt* **to b. about** *(story, rumour)* faire circuler

**bang[1]** [bæŋ] **1** *n (blow, noise)* coup *m* (violent); *(of gun)* détonation *f*; *(of door)* claquement *m*

**2** *vt (hit)* cogner, frapper; *(door)* (faire) claquer; **to b. one's head** se cogner la tête

**3** *vi* cogner, frapper; *(of door)* claquer; **to b. into sb/sth** heurter qn/qch

**4** *exclam* vlan!, pan!; **to go b.** éclater

**bang[2]** [bæŋ] *adv Br Fam (exactly)* exactement; **b. in the middle** en plein milieu; **b. on six** à six heures tapantes

**banger** ['bæŋə(r)] *n Br* (**a**) *Fam (sausage)* saucisse *f* (**b**) *(firecracker)* pétard *m* (**c**) *Fam* **old b.** *(car)* vieille guimbarde *f*

**bangle** ['bæŋgəl] *n* bracelet *m*

**bangs** [bæŋz] *npl Am (of hair)* frange *f*

**banish** ['bænɪʃ] *vt* bannir

**banister** ['bænɪstə(r)] *n* **banister(s)** rampe *f* (d'escalier)

**banjo** ['bændʒəʊ] (*pl* **-os** *or* **-oes**) *n* banjo *m*

**bank**[1] [bæŋk] **1** *n (of river)* bord *m*, rive *f*; *(raised)* berge *f*; *(of earth)* talus *m*; *(of sand)* banc *m*; **the Left B.** *(in Paris)* la Rive gauche **2** *vt* **to b. (up)** *(earth)* amonceler; *(fire)* couvrir **3** *vi (of aircraft)* virer

**bank**[2] [bæŋk] **1** *n (for money)* banque *f*; **b. account** compte *m* en banque; **b. card** carte *f* d'identité bancaire; *Br* **b. holiday** jour *m* férié; *Br* **b. note** billet *m* de banque **2** *vt (money)* mettre à la banque **3** *vi* avoir un compte en banque (**with** à) ▪ **banker** *n* banquier, -ère *mf*; *Br* **b.'s card** carte *f* d'identité bancaire ▪ **banking 1** *adj (transaction)* bancaire **2** *n (activity, profession)* la banque

**bank**[3] [bæŋk] *vi* **to b. on sb/sth** *(rely on)* compter sur qn/qch

**bankrupt** ['bæŋkrʌpt] **1** *adj* **to go b.** faire faillite **2** *vt* mettre en faillite

**banner** ['bænə(r)] *n* banderole *f*; *(military flag) & Fig* bannière *f*

**banns** [bænz] *npl* bans *mpl*; **to put up the b.** publier les bans

**banquet** ['bæŋkwɪt] *n* banquet *m*

**banter** ['bæntə(r)] **1** *n* plaisanteries *fpl* **2** *vi* plaisanter

**baptism** ['bæptɪzəm] *n* baptême *m* ▪ **Baptist** *n & adj* baptiste *(mf)*

**baptize** [bæp'taɪz] *vt* baptiser

**bar** [bɑː(r)] **1** *n* (**a**) *(of metal)* barre *f*; *(of gold)* lingot *m*; *(of chocolate)* tablette *f*; *(on window)* barreau *m*; **b. of soap** savonnette *f*; **behind bars** *(criminal)* sous les verrous; *Law* **the B.** le barreau; **b. code** *(on product)* code-barres *m*

(**b**) *(pub)* bar *m*; *(counter)* bar *m*, comptoir *m*

(**c**) *(group of musical notes)* mesure *f*

**2** (*pt & pp* **-rr-**) *vt* (**a**) **to b. sb's way** barrer le passage à qn; **barred window** fenêtre *f* munie de barreaux

(**b**) *(prohibit)* interdire (**sb from doing** à qn de faire); *(exclude)* exclure (**from** à)

**3** *prep (except)* sauf; **b. none** sans exception ▪ **barmaid** *n Br* serveuse *f* (de bar) ▪ **barman** (*pl* **-men**) *n Br* barman *m* ▪ **bartender** *n Am* barman *m*

**Barbados** [bɑː'beɪdɒs] *n* la Barbade

**barbaric** [bɑː'bærɪk] *adj* barbare

**barbecue** ['bɑːbɪkjuː] **1** *n* barbecue *m* **2** *vt* cuire au barbecue

**barbed wire** [bɑːbd'waɪə(r)] *n* fil *m* de fer barbelé; *(fence)* barbelés *mpl*

**barber** ['bɑːbə(r)] *n* coiffeur *m* pour hommes

**bare** [beə(r)] **1** (**-er, -est**) *adj* nu; *(tree, hill)* dénudé; *(room, cupboard)* vide; *(mere)* simple; **the b. necessities** le strict nécessaire; **with his b. hands** à mains nues **2** *vt (arm, wire)* dénuder ▪ **barefoot 1** *adv* nu-pieds **2** *adj* aux pieds nus

**barely** ['beəlɪ] *adv (scarcely)* à peine; **b. enough** tout juste assez

**bargain** ['bɑːgɪn] **1** *n (deal)* marché *m*, affaire *f*; **a b.** *(good buy)* une occasion, une bonne affaire; **to make a b. (with sb)** faire un marché (avec qn); **into the b.** *(in addition)* par-dessus le marché; **b. price** prix *m* exceptionnel **2** *vi (negotiate)* négocier; *(haggle)* marchander; **to b. for** *or* **on sth** *(expect)* s'attendre à qch

**barge** [bɑːdʒ] **1** *n* péniche *f* **2** *vi* **to b. in** *(enter room)* faire irruption; *(interrupt)* interrompre

**bark**[1] [bɑːk] *n (of tree)* écorce *f*

**bark**[2] [bɑːk] **1** *n* aboiement *m* **2** *vi* aboyer

**barley** ['bɑːlɪ] *n* orge *f*; **b. sugar** sucre *m* d'orge

**barn** [bɑːn] *n (for crops)* grange *f*; *(for horses)* écurie *f*; *(for cattle)* étable *f* ▪ **barnyard** *n* cour *f* de ferme

**barometer** [bə'rɒmɪtə(r)] *n* baromètre *m*

**baron** ['bærən] *n* baron *m*; *Fig (industrialist)* magnat *m*; **press/oil b.** magnat de la presse/du pétrole ▪ **baroness** *n* baronne *f*

**barracks** ['bærəks] *npl* caserne *f*

**barrage** [*Br* 'bærɑːʒ, *Am* bə'rɑːʒ] *n*

*(across river)* barrage *m*; *Fig* **a b. of questions** un feu roulant de questions

**barrel** ['bærəl] *n* (**a**) *(cask)* tonneau *m*; *(of oil)* baril *m* (**b**) *(of gun)* canon *m* (**c**) **b. organ** orgue *m* de Barbarie

**barren** ['bærən] *adj (land, woman, ideas)* stérile; *(style)* aride

**barricade** ['bærɪkeɪd] **1** *n* barricade *f* **2** *vt* barricader; **to b. oneself (in)** se barricader (dans)

**barrier** ['bærɪə(r)] *n also Fig* barrière *f*; *Br* **(ticket) b.** *(of station)* portillon *m*; **sound b.** mur *m* du son

**barring** ['bɑːrɪŋ] *prep* sauf

**barrister** ['bærɪstə(r)] *n Br* ≃ avocat *m*

**barrow** ['bærəʊ] *n (wheelbarrow)* brouette *f*; *(cart)* charrette *f ou* voiture *f* à bras

**barter** ['bɑːtə(r)] **1** *n* troc *m* **2** *vt* troquer (**for** contre)

**base** [beɪs] **1** *n* (**a**) *(bottom, main ingredient)* base *f*; *(of tree, lamp)* pied *m*; **b. rate** *(of bank)* taux *m* de base (**b**) *(military)* base *f* **2** *adj (dishonourable)* bas (*f* basse) **3** *vt* baser, fonder (**on** sur); **based in London** *(person, company)* basé à Londres

**baseball** ['beɪsbɔːl] *n* base-ball *m*

**basement** ['beɪsmənt] *n* sous-sol *m*

**bash** [bæʃ] **1** *n (bang)* coup *m*; *Br Fam* **to have a b.** *(try)* essayer un coup **2** *vt (hit)* cogner; **to b. (about)** *(ill-treat)* malmener; **to b. in** *or* **down** *(door, fence)* défoncer

**bashful** ['bæʃfəl] *adj* timide

**basic** ['beɪsɪk] **1** *adj* essentiel, -elle, de base; *(elementary)* élémentaire; *(pay, food)* de base; *(room, house, meal)* tout simple **2** *n* **the basics** l'essentiel *m* ▪ **basically** *adv (on the whole)* en gros; *(in fact)* en fait; *(fundamentally)* au fond

**basil** [*Br* 'bæzəl, *Am* 'beɪzəl] *n* basilic *m*

**basin** [*Br* 'beɪsən, *Am* 'beɪzən] *n* (**a**) *(made of plastic)* bassine *f*; *(for soup, food)* (grand) bol *m*; *(portable washbasin)* cuvette *f*; *(sink)* lavabo *m* (**b**) *(of river)* bassin *m*

**basis** ['beɪsɪs] (*pl* **-ses** [-siːz]) *n (for discussion)* base *f*; *(for opinion, accusation)* fondement *m*; *(of agreement)* bases *fpl*; **on the b. of** d'après; **on a weekly b.** chaque semaine

**basket** ['bɑːskɪt] *n* panier *m*; *(for bread, laundry, litter)* corbeille *f* ▪ **basketball** *n* basket(-ball) *m*

**Basque** [bæsk] **1** *adj* basque **2** *n* Basque *mf*

**bass**[1] [beɪs] **1** *n Mus* basse *f* **2** *adj (note, voice, instrument)* bas (*f* basse)

**bass**[2] [bæs] *n (sea fish)* bar *m*; *(freshwater fish)* perche *f*

**bassoon** [bə'suːn] *n* basson *m*

**bat**[1] [bæt] *n (animal)* chauve-souris *f*

**bat**[2] [bæt] **1** *n (for cricket, baseball)* batte *f*; *(for table-tennis)* raquette *f*; **off my own b.** de ma propre initiative **2** (*pt & pp* **-tt-**) *vt* (**a**) *(ball)* frapper (**b**) **she didn't b. an eyelid** elle n'a pas sourcillé

**batch** [bætʃ] *n (of people)* groupe *m*; *(of letters)* paquet *m*; *(of books)* lot *m*; *(of loaves)* fournée *f*; *(of papers)* liasse *f*

**bath** [bɑːθ] **1** (*pl* **baths** [bɑːðz]) *n* bain *m*; *(tub)* baignoire *f*; **to have** *or* **take a b.** prendre un bain; **b. towel** drap *m* de bain; *Br* **swimming baths** piscine *f* **2** *vt Br* baigner ▪ **bathrobe** *n Br* peignoir *m* de bain; *Am* robe *f* de chambre ▪ **bathroom** *n* salle *f* de bain(s); *Am (toilet)* toilettes *fpl* ▪ **bathtub** *n* baignoire *f*

**bathe** [beɪð] **1** *vt* baigner; *(wound)* laver **2** *vi (swim)* se baigner; *Am (have bath)* prendre un bain ▪ **bathing** *n* baignades *fpl*; **b. suit,** *Br* **b. costume** maillot *m* de bain

**baton** [*Br* 'bætən, *Am* bə'tɒn] *n (of conductor)* baguette *f*; *(of policeman)* matraque *f*; *(of soldier, drum majorette)* bâton *m*; *(in relay race)* témoin *m*

**battalion** [bə'tæljən] *n* bataillon *m*

**batter** ['bætə(r)] **1** *n* pâte *f* à frire **2** *vt (strike)* cogner sur; *(person)* frapper; *(town)* pilonner; **to b. down** *(door)* défoncer ▪ **battered** *adj (car, hat)* cabossé; *(house)* délabré; *(face)* meurtri; **b. child** enfant *m* martyr; **b. wife** femme *f* battue

**battery** ['bætərɪ] (*pl* **-ies**) *n (in vehicle, of guns, for hens)* batterie *f*; *(in radio, appliance)* pile *f*; **b. hen** poule *f* de batterie

**battle** ['bætəl] **1** *n* bataille *f*; *(struggle)* lutte *f*; *Fam* **that's half the b.** la partie est à moitié gagnée **2** *vi* se battre, lutter ■ **battlefield** *n* champ *m* de bataille ■ **battleship** *n* cuirassé *m*

**bawl** [bɔːl] *vt & vi* **to b. (out)** brailler; *Fam* **to b. sb out** engueuler qn

**bay**[1] [beɪ] **1** *n* (**a**) *(part of coastline)* baie *f* (**b**) *(in room)* renfoncement *m*; **b. window** bow-window *m*, oriel *m* (**c**) *Br (for loading)* aire *f* de chargement (**d**) **at b.** *(animal, criminal)* aux abois; **to keep** *or* **hold at b.** *(enemy, wild dog)* tenir en respect; *(disease)* juguler **2** *vi* aboyer **3** *adj (horse)* bai

**bay**[2] [beɪ] *n (tree)* laurier *m*; **b. leaf** feuille *f* de laurier

**bayonet** ['beɪənɪt] *n* baïonnette *f*

**bazaar** [bə'zɑː(r)] *n (market, shop)* bazar *m*; *(charity sale)* vente *f* de charité

**BC** [biː'siː] (*abbr* **before Christ**) av. J.-C.

---

**BE** [biː] (*present tense* **am, are, is;** *past tense* **was, were;** *pp* **been;** *pres p* **being**) **1** *vi* (**a**) *(gen)* être; **it is green/small/***etc* c'est vert/petit/*etc*; **he's a doctor** il est médecin; **he's an Englishman** c'est un Anglais; **it's him** c'est lui; **it's them** ce sont eux; **it's three (o'clock)** il est trois heures; **it's the sixth of May,** *Am* **it's May sixth** nous sommes le six mai; **to be hot/right/lucky** avoir chaud/raison/de la chance; **my feet are cold** j'ai froid aux pieds

(**b**) *(with age, height)* avoir; **to be twenty** *(age)* avoir vingt ans; **to be 2 metres high** avoir 2 m de haut; **to be 6 feet tall** ≃ mesurer 1,80 m

(**c**) *(with health)* aller; **how are you?** comment vas-tu?; **I'm well/not well** je vais bien/mal

(**d**) *(with place, situation)* se trouver, être; **she's in York** elle se trouve *ou* elle est à York

(**e**) *(exist)* être; **the best painter there is** le meilleur peintre qui soit

(**f**) *(go, come)* **I've been to see her** je suis allé la voir; **he's (already) been** il est (déjà) venu

(**g**) *(with weather, calculations)* faire; **it's nice** il fait beau; **it's foggy** il y a du brouillard; **2 and 2 are 4** 2 et 2 font 4

(**h**) *(cost)* coûter, faire; **it's 20 pence** ça coûte 20 pence; **how much is it?** ça fait combien?, c'est combien?

**2** *v aux* (**a**) **I am going** je vais; **I was going** j'allais; **I'll be staying** je vais rester; **I'm listening to the radio** je suis en train d'écouter la radio; **what has she been doing?** qu'est-ce qu'elle a fait?; **she's been there some time** elle est là depuis un moment; **he was killed** il a été tué; **I've been waiting (for) two hours** j'attends depuis deux heures; **it is said** on dit

(**b**) *(in questions and answers)* **isn't it?/aren't you?/***etc* n'est-ce pas?, non?; **she's ill, is she?** *(in surprise)* alors, comme ça, elle est malade?; **he isn't English, is he?** il n'est pas anglais, si?

(**c**) *(+ infinitive)* **he is to come at once** *(must)* il doit venir tout de suite

(**d**) **there is/are** il y a; *(pointing)* voilà; **here is/are** voici; **there she is** la voilà; **here they are** les voici

---

**beach** [biːtʃ] *n* plage *f*

**beacon** ['biːkən] *n (for ship, aircraft)* balise *f*; *(lighthouse)* phare *m*

**bead** [biːd] *n (small sphere)* perle *f*; *(of rosary)* grain *m*; *(of sweat)* goutte *f*, gouttelette *f*; **(string of) beads** collier *m*

**beak** [biːk] *n* bec *m*

**beaker** ['biːkə(r)] *n* gobelet *m*

**beam** [biːm] **1** *n* (**a**) *(of wood)* poutre *f* (**b**) *(of light, sunlight)* rayon *m*; *(of headlight, flashlight)* faisceau *m* (lumineux) **2** *vi (of light)* rayonner; *(of sun, moon)* briller; *(smile broadly)* sourire largement; **to b. with pride/joy** rayonner de fierté/joie **3** *vt (signals, programme)* transmettre (**to** à)

**bean** [bi:n] *n* haricot *m*; *(of coffee)* grain *m*; *Fam* **to be full of beans** être plein d'énergie

**bear¹** [beə(r)] *n (animal)* ours *m*; **b. cub** ourson *m*

**bear²** [beə(r)] **1** (*pt* **bore,** *pp* **borne**) *vt (carry, show)* porter; *(endure)* supporter; *(resemblance)* offrir; **I can't b. him/it** je ne peux pas le supporter/supporter ça; **to b. sth in mind** *(remember)* se souvenir de qch; *(take into account)* tenir compte de qch **2** *vi* **to b. left/right** *(turn)* tourner à gauche/droite; **to b. up** tenir le coup; **b. up!** courage!

**bearable** ['beərəbəl] *adj* supportable

**beard** [bɪəd] *n* barbe *f*; **to have a b.** porter la barbe

**bearing** ['beərɪŋ] *n (relevance)* rapport *m* (**on** avec); *(posture, conduct)* port *m*; *(of ship, aircraft)* position *f*; **to get one's bearings** s'orienter

**beast** [bi:st] *n* bête *f*; *Fam (person)* brute *f*

**beat** [bi:t] **1** *n (of heart, drum)* battement *m*; *(of policeman)* ronde *f*; *(in music)* rythme *m* **2** (*pt* **beat,** *pp* **beaten** [bi:tən]) *vt* battre; *Fam* **it beats me** ça me dépasse; *Fam* **b. it!** fiche le camp!; **to b. sb to it** devancer qn; **to b. down** *or* **in** *(door)* défoncer; **to b. sb up** tabasser qn **3** *vi* battre; *(at door)* frapper (**at** à); *Fam* **to b. about** *or* **around the bush** tourner autour du pot ▪ **beating** *n (blows, defeat)* raclée *f*; *(of heart, drums)* battement *m*

**beater** ['bi:tə(r)] *n (whisk)* fouet *m*

**beautician** [bju:'tɪʃən] *n* esthéticienne *f*

**beautiful** ['bju:tɪfəl] *adj* (très) beau (*f* belle); *(superb)* merveilleux, -euse

**beauty** ['bju:tɪ] (*pl* **-ies**) *n (quality, woman)* beauté *f*; **it's a b.!** *(car, house)* c'est une merveille!; **b. parlour** *or* **salon** institut *m* de beauté; **b. spot** *(on skin)* grain *m* de beauté; *Br (in countryside)* endroit *m* pittoresque

**beaver** ['bi:və(r)] **1** *n* castor *m* **2** *vi* **to b. away (at sth)** travailler dur (à qch)

**became** [bɪ'keɪm] *pt of* **become**

**because** [bɪ'kɒz] *conj* parce que; **b. of** à cause de

**beckon** ['bekən] *vt & vi* **to b. (to) sb (to do sth)** faire signe à qn (de faire qch)

**become** [bɪ'kʌm] (*pt* **became,** *pp* **become**) *vi* devenir; **to b. a painter** devenir peintre; **to b. thin** maigrir; **what has b. of her?** qu'est-elle devenue?

**becoming** [bɪ'kʌmɪŋ] *adj (clothes)* seyant; *(modesty)* bienséant

**bed** [bed] *n* lit *m*; *(flowerbed)* parterre *m*; *(of vegetables)* carré *m*; *(of sea)* fond *m*; *(of river)* lit *m*; *(of rock)* couche *f*; **to go to b.** (aller) se coucher; **to put sb to b.** coucher qn; **in b.** couché; **to get out of b.** se lever; **to make the b.** faire le lit; **b. and breakfast** *(in hotel)* chambre *f* avec petit déjeuner; **to stay in a b. and breakfast** ≃ prendre une chambre d'hôte; *Br* **b. settee** (canapé *m*) convertible *m* ▪ **bedclothes** *npl*, **bedding** *n* couvertures *fpl* et draps *mpl* ▪ **bedridden** *adj* alité ▪ **bedroom** *n* chambre *f* à coucher ▪ **bedside** *n* chevet *m*; **b. lamp/book/table** lampe *f*/livre *m*/table *f* de chevet ▪ **bedsit, bedsitter** ['bedsɪtə(r)] *n Br* chambre *f* meublée ▪ **bedspread** *n* dessus-de-lit *m inv* ▪ **bedtime** *n* heure *f* du coucher; **b. story** histoire *f (pour endormir les enfants)*

**bedraggled** [bɪ'drægəld] *adj (clothes, person)* débraillé et tout trempé

**bee** [bi:] *n* abeille *f* ▪ **beehive** *n* ruche *f*

**beech** [bi:tʃ] *n (tree, wood)* hêtre *m*

**beef** [bi:f] *n* bœuf *m* ▪ **beefburger** *n* hamburger *m*

**been** [bi:n] *pp of* **be**

**beer** [bɪə(r)] *n* bière *f*; **b. glass** chope *f*

**beet** [bi:t] *n Am* betterave *f*

**beetle** ['bi:təl] *n* scarabée *m*

**beetroot** ['bi:tru:t] *n Br* betterave *f*

**before** [bɪ'fɔ:(r)] **1** *adv* avant; *(already)* déjà; *(in front)* devant; **the month b.** le mois d'avant *ou* précédent; **the day b.** la veille; **I've seen it b.** je l'ai déjà vu; **I've never done it b.** je ne l'ai (encore) jamais fait

2 *prep (time)* avant; *(place)* devant; **the year b. last** il y a deux ans; **b. my very eyes** sous mes yeux

3 *conj* avant que (ne) *(+ subjunctive)*, avant de *(+ infinitive)*; **b. he goes** avant qu'il (ne) parte; **b. going** avant de partir

**befriend** [bɪ'frend] *vt* **to b. sb** se prendre d'amitié pour qn

**beg** [beg] **1** *(pt & pp* **-gg-**) *vt* **to b. (for)** *(favour, help)* demander; *(bread, money)* mendier; **to b. sb to do sth** supplier qn de faire qch **2** *vi (in street)* mendier; *(ask earnestly)* supplier

**began** [bɪ'gæn] *pt of* **begin**

**beggar** ['begə(r)] *n* mendiant, -e *mf*; *Br Fam (person)* type *m*; **lucky b.** veinard, -e *mf*

**begin** [bɪ'gɪn] **1** *(pt* **began,** *pp* **begun,** *pres p* **beginning**) *vt* commencer; *(fashion, campaign)* lancer; *(bottle, sandwich)* entamer; *(conversation)* engager; **to b. doing** *or* **to do sth** commencer *ou* se mettre à faire qch; **he began laughing** il s'est mis à rire

**2** *vi* commencer (**with** par; **by doing** par faire); **beginning from** à partir de; **to b. with** *(first of all)* d'abord ▪ **beginner** *n* débutant, -e *mf* ▪ **beginning** *n* commencement *m*, début *m*; **in** *or* **at the b.** au début, au commencement

**begrudge** [bɪ'grʌdʒ] *vt (envy)* envier (**sb sth** qch à qn); *(reproach)* reprocher (**sb sth** qch à qn); *(give unwillingly)* donner à contrecœur; **to b. doing sth** faire qch à contrecœur

**begun** [bɪ'gʌn] *pp of* **begin**

**behalf** [bɪ'hɑːf] *n* **on b. of sb, on sb's b.** *(representing)* au nom de qn, de la part de qn; *(in the interests of)* en faveur de qn

**behave** [bɪ'heɪv] *vi* se conduire; **to b. (oneself)** se tenir bien; *(of child)* être sage ▪ **behaviour** (*Am* **behavior**) *n* conduite *f*, comportement *m*; **to be on one's best b.** se tenir particulièrement bien

**behind** [bɪ'haɪnd] **1** *prep* derrière; *(in terms of progress)* en retard sur **2** *adv* derrière; *(late)* en retard; **to be b. with one's work** avoir du travail en retard **3** *n Fam (buttocks)* derrière *m*

**beige** [beɪʒ] *adj & n* beige *(m)*

**Beijing** [beɪ'dʒɪŋ] *n* Beijing *m ou f*

**being** ['biːɪŋ] *n (person, soul)* être *m*; **to come into b.** naître

**belated** [bɪ'leɪtɪd] *adj* tardif, -ive

**belch** [beltʃ] **1** *n* renvoi *m* **2** *vi (of person)* roter **3** *vt* **to b. (out)** *(smoke)* vomir

**Belgium** ['beldʒəm] *n* la Belgique ▪ **Belgian 1** *adj* belge **2** *n* Belge *mf*

**belief** [bɪ'liːf] *n (believing, thing believed)* croyance *f* (**in sb** en qn; **in sth** à *ou* en qch); *(trust)* confiance *f*, foi *f* (**in** en); *(religious faith)* foi *f*

**believe** [bɪ'liːv] **1** *vt* croire; **I don't b. it** c'est pas possible; **I b. I'm right** je crois avoir raison, je crois que j'ai raison

**2** *vi* croire (**in sth** à qch); **to believe in God** croire en Dieu; **I b. so/not** je crois que oui/que non; **to b. in doing sth** croire qu'il faut faire qch ▪ **believable** *adj* crédible ▪ **believer** *n (religious)* croyant, -e *mf*; **to be a b. in sth** croire à qch

**belittle** [bɪ'lɪtəl] *vt* dénigrer

**bell** [bel] *n (large) (of church)* cloche *f*; *(small)* clochette *f*; *(in phone, mechanism, alarm)* sonnerie *f*; *(on door, bicycle)* sonnette *f*; **b. tower** clocher *m* ▪ **bellboy, bellhop** *n Am* groom *m*

**bellow** ['beləʊ] *vi* beugler, mugir

**belly** ['belɪ] *(pl* **-ies**) *n* ventre *m*; *Fam* **b. button** nombril *m*; **b. dancing** danse *f* du ventre

**belong** [bɪ'lɒŋ] *vi* appartenir (**to** à); **to b. to a club** être membre d'un club; **that book belongs to me** ce livre m'appartient *ou* est à moi; **the cup belongs here** cette tasse se range ici ▪ **belongings** *npl* affaires *fpl*

**beloved** [bɪ'lʌvɪd] *adj & n Literary* bien-aimé, -e *(mf)*

**below** [bɪ'ləʊ] **1** *prep (lower than)* au-dessous de; *(under)* sous; *(with numbers)* moins de; *Fig (unworthy of)* indigne de **2** *adv* en dessous; *(in text)* ci-dessous; **on the floor b.** à l'étage du dessous; **it's 10 degrees b.** il fait moins 10

**belt** [belt] **1** *n* ceinture *f*; *(in machine)* courroie *f*; *(area)* zone *f*, région *f* **2** *vi* **to b. up** *(fasten seat belt)* attacher sa ceinture; *Br Fam* **b. up!** *(shut up)* boucle-la! **3** *vt Fam (hit) (ball)* cogner dans; *(person)* flanquer un gnon à

**bemused** [bɪ'mju:zd] *adj* perplexe

**bench** [bentʃ] *n (seat)* banc *m*; *(work table)* établi *m*; *Law* **the B.** *(magistrates)* la magistrature (assise); *(court)* le tribunal; *Sport* **to be on the b.** être remplaçant, -e

**bend** [bend] **1** *n* courbe *f*; *(in river, pipe)* coude *m*; *(in road)* virage *m*; *Fam* **round the b.** *(mad)* cinglé **2** (*pt & pp* **bent**) *vt* courber; *(leg, arm)* plier; **to b. one's head** baisser la tête; **to b. the rules** faire une entorse au règlement **3** *vi (of branch)* plier; *(of road)* tourner; *(of river)* faire un coude; **to b. (down)** *(stoop)* se courber; **to b. (over** *or* **forward)** se pencher

**beneath** [bɪ'ni:θ] **1** *prep* sous; *(unworthy of)* indigne de **2** *adv* (au-)dessous

**benefactor** ['benɪfæktə(r)] *n* bienfaiteur *m* ▪ **benefactress** *n* bienfaitrice *f*

**beneficial** [benɪ'fɪʃəl] *adj* bénéfique

**benefit** ['benɪfɪt] **1** *n (advantage)* avantage *m*; *(money)* allocation *f*; **benefits** *(of science, education)* bienfaits *mpl*; **to sb's b.** dans l'intérêt de qn; **for your (own) b.** pour vous, pour votre bien; **to be of b. (to sb)** faire du bien (à qn); **b. concert** concert *m* de bienfaisance **2** *vt* faire du bien à; *(be useful to)* profiter à **3** *vi* **to b. from doing sth** gagner à faire qch

**Benelux** ['benɪlʌks] *n* Benelux *m*

**benevolent** [bɪ'nevələnt] *adj* bienveillant

**benign** [bɪ'naɪn] *adj (kind)* bienveillant; *(climate)* doux (*f* douce); **b. tumour** tumeur *f* bénigne

**bent** [bent] **1** *adj (nail, mind)* tordu; *Fam (dishonest)* pourri; **b. on doing sth** résolu à faire qch **2** *n (talent)* aptitude *f* (**for** pour); *(inclination, liking)* penchant *m*, goût *m* (**for** pour) **3** *pt & pp of* **bend**

**bequeath** [bɪ'kwi:ð] *vt Formal* léguer (**to** à)

**bereaved** [bɪ'ri:vd] **1** *adj* endeuillé **2** *npl* **the b.** la famille du défunt/de la défunte ▪ **bereavement** *n* deuil *m*

**beret** [*Br* 'bereɪ, *Am* bə'reɪ] *n* béret *m*

**Berlin** [bɜ:'lɪn] *n* Berlin *m ou f*

**Bermuda** [bə'mju:də] *n* les Bermudes *fpl*

**berry** ['berɪ] (*pl* **-ies**) *n* baie *f*

**berserk** [bə'zɜ:k] *adj* **to go b.** devenir fou furieux (*f* folle furieuse)

**berth** [bɜ:θ] **1** *n* (**a**) *(in ship, train)* couchette *f* (**b**) *(anchorage)* poste *m* à quai; *Fig* **to give sb a wide b.** éviter qn comme la peste **2** *vi (of ship)* aborder à quai

**beset** [bɪ'set] (*pt & pp* **beset,** *pres p* **besetting**) *vt* assaillir

**beside** [bɪ'saɪd] *prep* à côté de; **that's b. the point** ça n'a rien à voir

**besides** [bɪ'saɪdz] **1** *prep (in addition to)* en plus de; *(except)* excepté; **there are ten of us b. Paul** nous sommes dix sans compter Paul; **what else can you do b. singing?** que savez-vous faire à part chanter? **2** *adv (in addition)* en plus; *(moreover)* d'ailleurs

**besiege** [bɪ'si:dʒ] *vt (of soldiers, crowd)* assiéger; *Fig (annoy)* assaillir (**with** de)

**besought** [bɪ'sɔ:t] *pt & pp of* **beseech**

**best** [best] **1** *adj* meilleur; **my b. dress** ma plus belle robe; **the b. part of** *(most)* la plus grande partie de; **the b. thing is to accept** le mieux c'est d'accepter; **'b. before...'** *(on product)* 'à consommer avant...'; **b. man** *(at wedding)* témoin *m*

**2** *n* **the b. (one)** le meilleur, la meilleure; **it's for the b.** c'est pour le mieux; **at b.** au mieux; **to do one's b.** faire de son mieux; **to look one's b., to be at one's b.** être à son avantage; **to the b. of my knowledge** autant que je sache; **to make the b. of sth** *(accept)* s'accommoder de qch; **to get the b. out of sth** tirer le meilleur parti de qch; **in one's Sunday b.** endimanché; **all the b.!** *(when leaving)* prends bien soin de toi!; *(good luck)* bonne chance!; *(in letter)* amicalement

**3** *adv* **(the) b.** *(play, sing)* le mieux; **to like sb/sth (the) b.** aimer qn/qch le plus; **I think it b. to wait** je juge prudent d'attendre ▪ **best-seller** *n (book)* best-seller *m*

**bet** [bet] **1** *n* pari *m* **2** *(pt & pp* **bet** *or* **betted,** *pres p* **betting**) *vt* parier (**on** sur; **that** que); *Fam* **you b.!** tu parles! ▪ **betting** *n* paris *mpl*; *Br* **b. shop** ≃ PMU *m*

**betray** [bɪ'treɪ] *vt (person, secret)* trahir ▪ **betrayal** *n (disloyalty)* trahison *f*; *(disclosure) (of secret)* révélation *f*

**better** ['betə(r)] **1** *adj* meilleur (**than** que); **I need a b. car** j'ai besoin d'une meilleure voiture; **that's b.** c'est mieux; **she's (much) b.** *(in health)* elle va (beaucoup) mieux; **to get b.** *(recover)* se remettre; *(improve)* s'améliorer; **it's b. to go** il vaut mieux partir; **the b. part of** *(most)* la plus grande partie de

**2** *adv* mieux (**than** que); **b. dressed/known/***etc* mieux habillé/connu/*etc*; **to look b.** *(of ill person)* avoir meilleure mine; **b. and b.** de mieux en mieux; **so much the b., all the b.** tant mieux (**for** pour); **I'd b. go** il vaut mieux que je parte; **to be b. off** *(financially)* être plus à l'aise

**3** *n* **to get the b. of sb** l'emporter sur qn; **to change for the b.** *(of person)* changer en bien; *(of situation)* s'améliorer; **one's betters** ses supérieurs *mpl*

**4** *vt (improve)* améliorer; *(do better than)* dépasser; **to b. oneself** améliorer sa condition; **to b. sb's results/***etc* dépasser les résultats/*etc* de qn

**between** [bɪ'twi:n] **1** *prep* entre; **in b.** entre **2** *adv* **in b.** *(space)* au milieu; *(time)* dans l'intervalle

**beware** [bɪ'weə(r)] *vi* se méfier (**of** de); **b.!** attention!; **'b. of the dog!'** 'attention, chien méchant!'

**bewilder** [bɪ'wɪldə(r)] *vt* dérouter, laisser perplexe

**beyond** [bɪ'jɒnd] **1** *prep* (**a**) *(further than)* au-delà de; **b. reach/doubt** hors de portée/de doute; **b. belief** incroyable; **b. my/our/***etc* **means** au-dessus de mes/nos/*etc* moyens; **it's b. me** ça me dépasse (**b**) *(except)* sauf **2** *adv (further)* au-delà

**bias** ['baɪəs] **1** *n* (**a**) *(inclination)* penchant *m* (**towards** pour); *(prejudice)* préjugé *m*, parti pris *m* (**towards/against** en faveur de/contre) (**b**) **cut on the b.** *(fabric)* coupé dans le biais **2** *(pt & pp* **-ss-** *or* **-s-**) *vt* influencer (**towards/against** en faveur de/contre) ▪ **bias(s)ed** *adj* partial; **to be b. against** avoir des préjugés contre

**bib** [bɪb] *n (for baby)* bavoir *m*

**bible** ['baɪbəl] *n* bible *f*; **the B.** la Bible ▪ **biblical** *adj* biblique

**bibliography** [bɪblɪ'ɒgrəfɪ] *(pl* **-ies**) *n* bibliographie *f*

**biceps** ['baɪseps] *n inv (muscle)* biceps *m*

**bicker** ['bɪkə(r)] *vi* se chamailler

**bicycle** ['baɪsɪkəl] *n* bicyclette *f*; **by b.** à bicyclette

**bid¹** [bɪd] **1** *n* (**a**) *(offer)* offre *f*; *(at auction)* enchère *f* (**for** pour) (**b**) *(attempt)* tentative *f* **2** *(pt & pp* **bid,** *pres p* **bidding**) *vt (sum of money)* offrir; *(at auction)* faire une enchère de **3** *vi* faire une offre (**for** pour); *(at auction)* faire une enchère (**for** sur) ▪ **bidder** *n (at auction)* enchérisseur, -euse *mf*; **to the highest b.** au plus offrant

**bid²** [bɪd] *(pt* **bade,** *pp* **bidden** ['bɪdən] *or* **bid,** *pres p* **bidding**) *vt Literary (command)* commander (**sb to do** à qn de faire); *(say, wish)* dire, souhaiter

**bide** [baɪd] *vt* **to b. one's time** attendre le bon moment

**big** [bɪg] (**bigger, biggest**) *adj (tall, large)* grand; *(fat)* gros (*f* grosse); *(drop, increase)* fort; **to get big(ger)**

*(taller)* grandir; *(fatter)* grossir; **my b. brother** mon grand frère; *Fam* **b. mouth** grande gueule *f*; **b. toe** gros orteil *m* ■ **bighead** *n Fam* crâneur, -euse *mf* ■ **bigshot, bigwig** *n Fam* gros bonnet *m*

**bigot** ['bɪgət] *n* sectaire *mf*; *(religious)* bigot, -e *mf* ■ **bigoted** *adj* sectaire; *(religious)* bigot

**bike** [baɪk] *n Fam* vélo *m*; *(motorbike)* moto *f*

**bikini** [bɪ'kiːnɪ] *n* Bikini® *m*; **b. briefs** mini-slip *m*

**bilberry** ['bɪlbərɪ] (*pl* **-ies**) *n* myrtille *f*

**bilingual** [baɪ'lɪŋgwəl] *adj* bilingue

**bill**[1] [bɪl] **1** *n* (**a**) *(invoice)* facture *f*; *(in restaurant)* addition *f*; *(in hotel)* note *f* (**b**) *Am (banknote)* billet *m* (**c**) *(bank draft)* effet *m* (**d**) *(notice)* affiche *f* (**e**) *Pol* projet *m* de loi; **B. of Rights** = les dix premiers amendements de la Constitution américaine
**2** *vt* (**a**) **to b. sb** envoyer la facture à qn (**b**) *(publicize)* annoncer ■ **billboard** *n* panneau *m* d'affichage

**bill**[2] [bɪl] *n (of bird)* bec *m*

**billiards** ['bɪljədz] *n* billard *m*

**billion** ['bɪljən] *n* milliard *m* ■ **billionaire** *n* milliardaire *mf*

**billow** ['bɪləʊ] **1** *n (of smoke)* volute *f* **2** *vi (of smoke)* tourbillonner; *(of sea)* se soulever; *(of sail)* se gonfler

**bimonthly** [baɪ'mʌnθlɪ] *adj (every two weeks)* bimensuel, -elle; *(every two months)* bimestriel, -elle

**bin** [bɪn] **1** *n* boîte *f*; *(for litter)* poubelle *f* **2** (*pt & pp* **-nn-**) *vt Fam* mettre à la poubelle

**binary** ['baɪnərɪ] *adj* binaire

**bind** [baɪnd] **1** (*pt & pp* **bound**) *vt (fasten)* attacher; *(book)* relier; *(fabric, hem)* border; *(unite)* lier; **to b. sb hand and foot** ligoter qn; **to be bound by sth** être lié par qch **2** *n Fam (bore)* plaie *f* ■ **binding 1** *n (of book)* reliure *f* **2** *adj (contract)* qui lie; **to be b. on sb** *(legally)* lier qn

**binder** ['baɪndə(r)] *n (for papers)* classeur *m*

**binge** [bɪndʒ] *n Fam* **to go on a b.** *(drinking)* faire la bringue; *(eating)* se gaver

**bingo** ['bɪŋgəʊ] *n* ≃ loto *m*

**binoculars** [bɪ'nɒkjʊləz] *npl* jumelles *fpl*

**biochemistry** [baɪəʊ'kemɪstrɪ] *n* biochimie *f*

**biodegradable** [baɪəʊdɪ'greɪdəbəl] *adj* biodégradable

**biography** [baɪ'ɒgrəfɪ] (*pl* **-ies**) *n* biographie *f*

**biology** [baɪ'ɒlədʒɪ] *n* biologie *f* ■ **biological** *adj* biologique; **b. warfare** guerre *f* bactériologique

**bird** [bɜːd] *n* (**a**) *(animal)* oiseau *m*; *(fowl)* volaille *f*; **b. of prey** oiseau *m* de proie; **b.'s-eye view** perspective *f* à vol d'oiseau; *Fig* vue *f* d'ensemble (**b**) *Br Fam (girl)* nana *f* ■ **birdseed** *n* graines *fpl* pour oiseaux

**birth** [bɜːθ] *n* naissance *f*; **to give b. to** donner naissance à; **from b.** *(blind, deaf)* de naissance; **b. certificate** acte *m* de naissance; **b. control** limitation *f* des naissances; **b. rate** (taux *m* de) natalité *f* ■ **birthday** *n* anniversaire *m*; **happy b.!** joyeux anniversaire!; **b. party** fête *f* d'anniversaire; *Fig* **in one's b. suit** *(man)* en costume d'Adam; *(woman)* en costume d'Ève ■ **birthmark** *n* tache *f* de naissance ■ **birthplace** *n* lieu *m* de naissance; *(house)* maison *f* natale

**biscuit** ['bɪskɪt] *n Br* biscuit *m*, petit gâteau *m*; *Am* petit pain *m* au lait

**bishop** ['bɪʃəp] *n* évêque *m*; *(in chess)* fou *m*

**bit**[1] [bɪt] *n* (**a**) *(of string, time)* bout *m*; **a b.** *(a little)* un peu; **not a b.** pas du tout; **a b. of luck** une chance; **b. by b.** petit à petit; **in bits (and pieces)** en morceaux (**b**) *(coin)* pièce *f* (**c**) *(of horse)* mors *m* (**d**) *(of drill)* mèche *f* (**e**) *Comptr* bit *m*

**bit**[2] [bɪt] *pt of* **bite**

**bitch** [bɪtʃ] **1** *n (dog)* chienne *f*; *very Fam Pej (woman)* garce *f* **2** *vi Fam (complain)* râler (**about** après)

**bite** [baɪt] **1** *n* (**a**) *(wound)* morsure *f*; *(from insect)* piqûre *f*; *Fishing* touche *f* (**b**) *(mouthful)* bouchée *f*; **to have a b. to eat** manger un morceau **2** (*pt* **bit,** *pp* **bitten** ['bɪtən]) *vt* mordre; *(of insect)* piquer; **to b. one's nails** se ronger les ongles; **to b. sth off** arracher qch d'un coup de dents **3** *vi* mordre; *(of insect)* piquer; **to b. into sth** mordre dans qch ▪ **biting** *adj (cold)* mordant; *(wind)* cinglant

**bitter** ['bɪtə(r)] **1** *n Br (beer)* = bière anglaise brune **2** *adj (person, taste, irony)* amer, -ère; *(cold, wind)* glacial; *(criticism)* acerbe; *(shock, fate)* cruel (*f* cruelle); *(conflict)* violent; **to feel b. (about sth)** être plein d'amertume (à cause de qch) ▪ **bitterly** *adv* **to cry/regret b.** pleurer/regretter amèrement; **b. disappointed** cruellement déçu; **it's b. cold** il fait un froid de canard ▪ **bittersweet** *adj* doux-amer (*f* douce-amère); *Am* **b. chocolate** chocolat *m* noir

**bizarre** [bɪ'zɑ:(r)] *adj* bizarre

**blab** [blæb] (*pt & pp* **-bb-**) *vi* jaser

**black** [blæk] **1** (**-er, -est**) *adj* noir; **b. eye** œil *m* au beurre noir; **b. and blue** *(bruised)* couvert de bleus; *Aviat* **b. box** boîte *f* noire; *Br* **b. ice** verglas *m*; *Br* **b. pudding** boudin *m* noir; *Fig* **b. sheep** brebis *f* galeuse **2** *n (colour)* noir *m*; *(person)* Noir, -e *mf* ▪ **blackberry** (*pl* **-ies**) *n* mûre *f* ▪ **blackbird** *n* merle *m* (noir) ▪ **blackboard** *n* tableau *m* (noir) ▪ **blackcurrant** *n* cassis *m* ▪ **blacken** *vt & vi* noircir ▪ **blacklist 1** *n* liste *f* noire **2** *vt* mettre sur la liste noire ▪ **blackmail 1** *n* chantage *m* **2** *vt* faire chanter; **to b. sb into doing sth** faire chanter qn pour qu'il/elle fasse qch ▪ **blackout** *n* panne *f* d'électricité; *(during war)* black-out *m inv*; *(fainting fit)* évanouissement *m*; **(news) b.** black-out *m inv* ▪ **blacksmith** *n* forgeron *m*; *(working with horses)* maréchal-ferrant *m*

▸ **black out** *vi (faint)* s'évanouir

**bladder** ['blædə(r)] *n* vessie *f*

**blade** [bleɪd] *n* lame *f*; **b. of grass** brin *m* d'herbe

**blame** [bleɪm] **1** *n* responsabilité *f*; *(criticism)* blâme *m*; **to lay the b. (for sth) on sb** faire porter à qn la responsabilité (de qch); **to take the b. for sth** endosser la responsabilité de qch **2** *vt* rendre responsable, faire porter la responsabilité à (**for** de); **to b. sb for doing sth** reprocher à qn d'avoir fait qch; **you're to b.** c'est de ta faute ▪ **blameless** *adj* irréprochable

**blanch** [blɑ:ntʃ] **1** *vt (vegetables)* blanchir **2** *vi (turn pale)* blêmir

**bland** [blænd] (**-er, -est**) *adj (person)* terne; *(food)* insipide; *(remark, joke)* quelconque

**blank** [blæŋk] **1** *adj (paper, page)* blanc (*f* blanche), vierge; *(cheque)* en blanc; *(look, mind)* vide; **b. tape** cassette *f* vierge **2** *n (space)* blanc *m*; *(cartridge)* cartouche *f* à blanc; **to fire blanks** tirer à blanc; **my mind's a b.** j'ai un trou

**blanket** ['blæŋkɪt] **1** *n (on bed)* couverture *f*; *(of snow, leaves)* couche *f* **2** *adj (term, remark)* général

**blankly** ['blæŋklɪ] *adv* **to look b. at sb/sth** *(without expression)* regarder qn/qch, le visage inexpressif; *(without understanding)* regarder qn/qch sans comprendre

**blare** [bleə(r)] **1** *n (noise)* beuglements *mpl*; *(of trumpet)* sonnerie *f* **2** *vi* **to b. (out)** *(of radio)* beugler; *(of music, car horn)* retentir

**blasé** ['blɑ:zeɪ] *adj* blasé

**blasphemous** ['blæsfəməs] *adj (text)* blasphématoire; *(person)* blasphémateur, -trice

**blast** [blɑ:st] **1** *n* explosion *f*; *(air from explosion)* souffle *m*; *(of wind)* rafale *f*; *(of trumpet)* sonnerie *f*; **(at) full b.** *(loud)* à fond **2** *vt (hole, tunnel)* creuser *(en dynamitant)*; *Fam (criticize)* démolir **3** *exclam Br Fam* zut! ▪ **blasted** *adj Br Fam* fichu ▪ **blast-off** *n (of spacecraft)* mise *f* à feu

**blatant** ['bleɪtənt] *adj (obvious)* flagrant; *(shameless)* éhonté

**blaze** [bleɪz] **1** *n (fire)* feu *m*; *(large)* incendie *m*; *Fig (splendour)* éclat *m*; **a b. of colour** une explosion de couleurs; **b. of light** torrent *m* de lumière **2** *vi (of fire, sun)* flamboyer; *(of light, eyes)* être éclatant **3** *vt Fig* **to b. a trail** ouvrir la voie ▪ **blazing** *adj (burning)* en feu; *(sun)* brûlant; *Fig (argument)* violent

**blazer** ['bleɪzə(r)] *n* blazer *m*

**bleach** [bliːtʃ] **1** *n (household)* (eau *f* de) Javel *f*; *(for hair)* décolorant *m* **2** *vt (clothes)* passer à l'eau de Javel; *(hair)* décolorer

**bleak** [bliːk] (**-er, -est**) *adj (appearance, countryside, weather)* morne; *(outlook)* lugubre; *(prospect)* peu encourageant

**bleat** [bliːt] *vi* bêler

**bleed** [bliːd] *(pt & pp* **bled** [bled]) **1** *vi* saigner; **to b. to death** saigner à mort; **her nose is bleeding** elle saigne du nez **2** *vt (radiator)* purger

**bleep** [bliːp] **1** *n* bip *m* **2** *vt* appeler au bip **3** *vi* faire bip ▪ **bleeper** *n (pager)* bip *m*

**blemish** ['blemɪʃ] **1** *n (fault)* défaut *m*; *(mark)* marque *f* **2** *vt Fig (reputation)* entacher

**blend** [blend] **1** *n* mélange *m* **2** *vt* mélanger (**with** à *ou* avec) **3** *vi* se mélanger; *(of styles, colours)* se marier (**with** avec) ▪ **blender** *n* mixer *m*

**bless** [bles] *vt* bénir; **to be blessed with sth** être doté de qch; **b. you!** *(when sneezing)* à vos souhaits! ▪ **blessed** *adj* (**a**) *(holy)* béni (**b**) *Fam (blasted)* fichu ▪ **blessing** *n Rel* bénédiction *f*; *(benefit)* bienfait *m*; **it was a b. in disguise** finalement, ça a été une bonne chose

**blew** [bluː] *pt of* **blow²**

**blind¹** [blaɪnd] **1** *adj* aveugle; **b. person** aveugle *mf*; **b. in one eye** borgne; *Fig* **to be b. to sth** ne pas voir qch; **b. alley** impasse *f*; **b. date** = rencontre arrangée avec quelqu'un qu'on ne connaît pas **2** *npl* **the b.** les aveugles *mpl* **3** *adv* **b. drunk** ivre mort **4** *vt (dazzle, make blind)* aveugler

**blind²** [blaɪnd] *n Br (on window)* store *m*

**blindfold** ['blaɪndfəʊld] **1** *n* bandeau *m* **2** *vt* bander les yeux à **3** *adv* les yeux bandés

**blindly** ['blaɪndlɪ] *adv Fig* aveuglément

**blink** [blɪŋk] **1** *n* clignement *m*; *Br Fam* **on the b.** *(machine)* détraqué **2** *vt* **to b. one's eyes** cligner des yeux **3** *vi (of person)* cligner des yeux; *(of eyes)* cligner; *(of light)* clignoter

**blissful** ['blɪsfʊl] *adj (wonderful)* merveilleux, -euse; *(very happy) (person)* aux anges ▪ **blissfully** *adv (happy)* merveilleusement; **to be b. unaware that…** ne pas se douter le moins du monde que…

**blister** ['blɪstə(r)] **1** *n (on skin)* ampoule *f* **2** *vi* se couvrir d'ampoules

**blitz** [blɪts] **1** *n (air attack)* raid *m* éclair; *(bombing)* bombardement *m* aérien; *Fam (onslaught)* offensive *f* **2** *vt* bombarder

**blizzard** ['blɪzəd] *n* tempête *f* de neige

**bloated** ['bləʊtɪd] *adj (swollen)* gonflé

**blob** [blɒb] *n (of ink, colour)* tache *f*

**block** [blɒk] **1** *n (of stone)* bloc *m*; *(of buildings)* pâté *m* de maisons; *(in pipe)* obstruction *f*; **b. of flats** immeuble *m*; *Am* **a b. away** une rue plus loin; **b. booking** réservation *f* de groupe; **b. capitals** *or* **letters** majuscules *fpl* **2** *vt (obstruct)* bloquer; *(pipe)* boucher; *(view)* cacher; **to b. up** *(pipe, hole)* boucher ▪ **blockage** *n* obstruction *f* ▪ **blockbuster** *n (film)* film *m* à grand spectacle

**bloke** [bləʊk] *n Br Fam* type *m*

**blond** [blɒnd] *adj & n* blond *(m)* ▪ **blonde** *adj & n* blonde *(f)*

**blood** [blʌd] *n* sang *m*; **b. bank** banque *f* du sang; **b. bath** bain *m* de sang; **b. donor** donneur, -euse *mf* de sang; **b. group** groupe *m* sanguin; **b. poisoning** empoisonnement *m* du sang; **b. pressure** tension *f* artérielle; **high b. pressure** hypertension *f*; **to**

**have high b. pressure** avoir de la tension; *Am* **b. sausage** boudin *m*; **b. test** prise *f* de sang ▪ **bloodshed** *n* effusion *f* de sang ▪ **bloodshot** *adj (eye)* injecté de sang ▪ **bloodstream** *n* sang *m* ▪ **bloodthirsty** *adj* sanguinaire

**bloody** ['blʌdɪ] **1** (**-ier, -iest**) *adj* (**a**) *(covered in blood)* ensanglanté (**b**) *Br very Fam* foutu; **a b. liar** un sale menteur; **you b. fool!** espèce de connard! **2** *adv Br Fam (very)* vachement; **it's b. hot!** il fait une putain de chaleur! ▪ **bloody-minded** *adj* pas commode

**bloom** [blu:m] **1** *n* fleur *f*; **in b.** *(tree)* en fleur(s); *(flower)* éclos **2** *vi (of tree, flower)* fleurir; *Fig (of person)* s'épanouir ▪ **blooming** *adj* (**a**) *(in bloom)* en fleur(s); *(person)* resplendissant; *(thriving)* florissant (**b**) *Br Fam (for emphasis)* sacré; **you b. idiot!** espèce d'idiot!

**blossom** ['blɒsəm] **1** *n* fleurs *fpl* **2** *vi* fleurir; **to b. (out)** *(of person)* s'épanouir

**blot** [blɒt] **1** *n* tache *f* **2** (*pt & pp* **-tt-**) *vt (stain)* tacher; *(dry)* sécher; **to b. sth out** *(obliterate)* effacer qch ▪ **blotting paper** *n* (papier *m*) buvard *m*

**blotch** [blɒtʃ] *n* tache *f* ▪ **blotchy** (**-ier, -iest**) *adj* couvert de taches; *(face, skin)* marbré

**blouse** [blaʊz] *n* chemisier *m*

**blow¹** [bləʊ] *n (hit, setback)* coup *m*; **to come to blows** en venir aux mains

**blow²** [bləʊ] **1** (*pt* **blew**, *pp* **blown**) *vt (of wind)* pousser; *(of person) (smoke, glass)* souffler; *(bubbles)* faire; *(trumpet)* souffler dans; *(kiss)* envoyer (**to** à); *Br Fam (money)* claquer (**on sth** pour s'acheter qch); **to b. a fuse** faire sauter un plomb; **to b. one's nose** se moucher; **to b. a whistle** donner un coup de sifflet **2** *vi (of wind, person)* souffler; *(of fuse)* sauter; *(of papers) (in wind)* s'éparpiller

▸ **blow away 1** *vt sep (of wind)* emporter **2** *vi (of hat, paper)* s'envoler

▸ **blow down 1** *vt sep (chimney, fence)* faire tomber **2** *vi (fall)* tomber

▸ **blow off** *vt sep (hat)* emporter; *(arm)* arracher

▸ **blow out 1** *vt sep (candle)* souffler; *(cheeks)* gonfler **2** *vi (of light)* s'éteindre

▸ **blow over 1** *vt & vi* = **blow down 2** *vi (of quarrel)* se tasser

▸ **blow up 1** *vt sep (building)* faire sauter; *(pump up)* gonfler; *(photo)* agrandir **2** *vi (explode)* exploser

**blow-dry** ['bləʊdraɪ] **1** *n* brushing® *m* **2** *vt* **to b. sb's hair** faire un brushing® à qn

**blown** [bləʊn] *pp of* **blow**

**blowout** ['bləʊaʊt] *n* (**a**) *(tyre)* éclatement *m* (**b**) *Br Fam (meal)* gueuleton *m*

**blowtorch** ['bləʊtɔ:tʃ] *n* chalumeau *m*

**bludgeon** ['blʌdʒən] **1** *n* gourdin *m* **2** *vt* matraquer

**blue** [blu:] **1** (**-er, -est**) *adj* bleu; *Fam* **to feel b.** avoir le cafard; *Fam* **b. movie** film *m* porno **2** *n* bleu *m*; **blues** *(music)* le blues; *Fam* **the blues** *(depression)* le cafard; **out of the b.** *(unexpectedly)* sans crier gare ▪ **bluebell** *n* jacinthe *f* des bois ▪ **blueberry** (*pl* **-ies**) *n* airelle *f* ▪ **bluebottle** *n* mouche *f* de la viande ▪ **blueprint** *n Fig* plan *m*

**bluff** [blʌf] **1** *n* bluff *m* **2** *vt & vi* bluffer

**blunder** ['blʌndə(r)] **1** *n (mistake)* gaffe *f* **2** *vi* faire une gaffe

**blunt** [blʌnt] **1** (**-er, -est**) *adj (edge)* émoussé; *(pencil)* mal taillé; *(question, statement)* direct; *(person)* brusque **2** *vt (blade)* émousser; *(pencil)* épointer

**blur** [blɜ:(r)] **1** *n* tache *f* floue **2** (*pt & pp* **-rr-**) *vt (outline)* brouiller ▪ **blurred** *adj (image, outline)* flou

**blurb** [blɜ:b] *n* notice *f* publicitaire

**blurt** [blɜ:t] *vt* **to b. (out)** *(secret)* laisser échapper; *(excuse)* bredouiller

**blush** [blʌʃ] **1** *n* rougeur *f* **2** *vi* rougir (**with** de)

**blustery** ['blʌstərɪ] *adj (weather)* de grand vent; *(wind)* violent

**boar** [bɔ:(r)] *n* **(wild) b.** sanglier *m*

**board[1]** [bɔːd] **1** *n (piece of wood)* planche *f*; *(for notices)* panneau *m*; *(for games)* tableau *m*; *(cardboard)* carton *m*; **on b. (a ship/plane)** à bord (d'un navire/avion) **2** *vt (ship, plane)* monter à bord de; *(bus, train)* monter dans; **to b. up** *(door)* condamner **3** *vi* **flight Z001 is now boarding** vol Z001, embarquement immédiat ▪ **boarding** *n (of passengers)* embarquement *m*; **b. pass** carte *f* d'embarquement ▪ **boardwalk** *n Am (on beach)* promenade *f*

**board[2]** [bɔːd] *n (committee)* conseil *m*; **b. (of directors)** conseil *m* d'administration; **b. (of examiners)** jury *m* (d'examen); **across the b.** *(pay increase)* global; *(apply)* globalement; **b. room** salle *f* du conseil

**board[3]** [bɔːd] **1** *n (food)* pension *f*; **b. and lodging,** *Br* **full b.** pension *f* complète; *Br* **half b.** demi-pension *f* **2** *vi (lodge)* être en pension (**with** chez); **boarding house** pension *f* de famille; **boarding school** pensionnat *m* ▪ **boarder** *n* pensionnaire *mf*

**boast** [bəʊst] **1** *n* vantardise *f* **2** *vt* se glorifier de **3** *vi* se vanter (**about** *or* **of** de) ▪ **boastful** *adj* vantard

**boat** [bəʊt] *n* bateau *m*; *(small)* canot *m*; *(liner)* paquebot *m*; **by b.** en bateau; *Fig* **in the same b.** logé à la même enseigne; **b. race** course *f* d'aviron

**bode** [bəʊd] *vi* **to b. well/ill (for)** être de bon/mauvais augure (pour)

**bodily** ['bɒdɪlɪ] **1** *adj (need)* physique **2** *adv (lift, seize)* à bras-le-corps; *(carry)* dans ses bras

**body** ['bɒdɪ] (*pl* **-ies**) *n* corps *m*; *(of car)* carrosserie *f*; *(quantity)* masse *f*; *(institution)* organisme *m*; **(dead) b.** cadavre *m*; **b. building** culturisme *m*; **b. warmer** gilet *m* matelassé ▪ **bodyguard** *n* garde *m* du corps ▪ **bodywork** *n* carrosserie *f*

**bog** [bɒg] **1** *n (swamp)* marécage *m* **2** *vt* **to get bogged down in** *(mud, work)* s'enliser (dans); *(details)* se perdre (dans)

**bogus** ['bəʊgəs] *adj* faux (*f* fausse)

**boil[1]** [bɔɪl] *n (pimple)* furoncle *m*

**boil[2]** [bɔɪl] **1** *n* **to come to the b.** bouillir; **to bring sth to the b.** amener qch à ébullition **2** *vt* **to b. (up)** faire bouillir; **to b. the kettle** mettre de l'eau à chauffer **3** *vi* bouillir; *Fig* **to b. down to** *(of situation, question)* revenir à; **to b. over** *(of milk)* déborder; *Fig (of situation)* empirer ▪ **boiled** *adj* bouilli; **b. egg** œuf *m* à la coque ▪ **boiling 1** *n* ébullition *f*; **to be at b. point** *(of liquid)* bouillir **2** *adj* **b. (hot)** bouillant; **it's b. (hot)** *(weather)* il fait une chaleur infernale

**boiler** ['bɔɪlə(r)] *n* chaudière *f*; *Br* **b. suit** bleus *mpl* de chauffe

**boisterous** ['bɔɪstərəs] *adj (noisy)* bruyant; *(child)* turbulent; *(meeting)* houleux, -euse

**bold** [bəʊld] (**-er, -est**) *adj* hardi

**bolster** ['bəʊlstə(r)] **1** *n (pillow)* traversin *m* **2** *vt (confidence, pride)* renforcer, consolider

**bolt** [bəʊlt] **1** *n* (**a**) *(on door)* verrou *m*; *(for nut)* boulon *m* (**b**) *(dash)* **to make a b. for the door** se précipiter vers la porte (**c**) **b. of lightning** éclair *m* **2** *adv* **b. upright** tout droit **3** *vt* (**a**) *(door)* verrouiller (**b**) *(food)* engloutir **4** *vi (dash)* se précipiter; *(run away)* détaler; *(of horse)* s'emballer

**bomb** [bɒm] **1** *n* bombe *f*; **b. scare** alerte *f* à la bombe **2** *vt (from the air)* bombarder; *(of terrorist)* faire sauter une bombe dans *ou* à ▪ **bombshell** *n* **to come as a b.** faire l'effet d'une bombe ▪ **bombsite** *n* zone *f* bombardée

**bombard** [bɒm'bɑːd] *vt (with bombs, questions)* bombarder (**with** de)

**bona fide** [bəʊnə'faɪdɪ] *adj* véritable

**bond** [bɒnd] **1** *n (link)* lien *m*; *(agreement)* engagement *m*; *Fin* obligation *f* **2** *vt (of glue)* coller (**to** à) **3** *vi (form attachment)* créer des liens affectifs (**with** avec)

**bone** [bəʊn] **1** *n* os *m*; *(of fish)* arête *f*; **b. china** porcelaine *f* tendre **2** *vt (meat)* désosser; *(fish)* ôter les arêtes de **3** *vi*

*Fam* **to b. up on** *(subject)* bûcher ▪ **bone-dry** *adj* complètement sec (*f* sèche) ▪ **bone-idle** *adj Br* paresseux, -euse

**bonfire** ['bɒnfaɪə(r)] *n (for celebration)* feu *m* de joie; *Br (for dead leaves)* feu *m* (de jardin)

**bonkers** ['bɒŋkəz] *adj Br Fam* dingue

**bonnet** ['bɒnɪt] *n (hat)* bonnet *m*; *Br (of vehicle)* capot *m*

**bonus** ['bəʊnəs] (*pl* **-uses** [-əsɪz]) *n* prime *f*; **no-claims b.** *(in motor insurance)* bonus *m*

**boo** [bu:] **1** *exclam (to frighten)* hou! **2** *n* **boos** huées *fpl* **3** (*pt & pp* **booed**) *vt & vi* huer

**boob** [bu:b] *Br Fam* **1** *n* (**a**) *(mistake)* gaffe *f* (**b**) **boobs** *(breasts)* nénés *mpl* **2** *vi* gaffer

**booby-trap** ['bu:bɪtræp] **1** *n* engin *m* piégé **2** (*pt & pp* **-pp-**) *vt* piéger

**book** [bʊk] **1** *n* livre *m*; *(record)* registre *m*; *(of tickets)* carnet *m*; *(for exercises and notes)* cahier *m*; **books** *(accounts)* comptes *mpl*; **b. club** club *m* du livre

**2** *vt (seat)* réserver; *Br* **to b. sb** *(for traffic offence)* dresser une contravention à qn; **fully booked** *(hotel)* complet, -ète; *(person)* pris

**3** *vi* **to b. (up)** réserver des places; **to b. in** *(to hotel)* signer le registre; **to b. into a hotel** prendre une chambre dans un hôtel ▪ **bookcase** *n* bibliothèque *f* ▪ **bookend** *n* serre-livres *m inv* ▪ **bookie** *n Fam* bookmaker *m* ▪ **booking** *n* réservation *f*; **b. office** bureau *m* de location ▪ **bookkeeping** *n* comptabilité *f* ▪ **booklet** *n* brochure *f* ▪ **bookmaker** *n* bookmaker *m* ▪ **bookmark** *n* marque-page *m* ▪ **bookseller** *n* libraire *mf* ▪ **bookshelf** *n* étagère *f* ▪ **bookshop** (*Am* **bookstore**) *n* librairie *f* ▪ **bookstall** *n* kiosque *m* à journaux ▪ **bookworm** *n* passionné, -e *mf* de lecture

**boom** [bu:m] **1** *n* (**a**) *(noise)* grondement *m* (**b**) *(economic)* boom *m* **2** *vi* (**a**) *(of thunder, gun)* gronder (**b**) *(of business, trade)* être florissant

**boor** [bʊə(r)] *n* rustre *m*

**boost** [bu:st] **1** *n* **to give sb a b.** remonter le moral à qn **2** *vt (increase)* augmenter; *(economy)* stimuler; **to b. sb's morale** remonter le moral à qn ▪ **booster** *n* **b. (injection)** rappel *m*

**boot[1]** [bu:t] **1** *n* (**a**) *(footwear)* botte *f*; **(ankle) b.** bottillon *m*; **(knee) b.** bottine *f*; *Fam* **to get the b.** être mis à la porte (**b**) *Br (of vehicle)* coffre *m* (**c**) **to b.** *(in addition)* en plus **2** *vt Fam (kick)* donner un coup/des coups de pied à; **to b. sb out** mettre qn à la porte

**boot[2]** [bu:t] *Comptr* **1** *vt* amorcer **2** *vi* s'amorcer

**booth** [bu:θ, bu:ð] *n (for phone, in language lab)* cabine *f*; *(at fair)* stand *m*; *(for voting)* isoloir *m*

**booze** [bu:z] *Fam* **1** *n* alcool *m* **2** *vi* picoler ▪ **boozer** *n Fam (person)* poivrot, -e *mf*; *Br (pub)* pub *m*

**border** ['bɔ:də(r)] **1** *n (of country) & Fig* frontière *f*; *(edge)* bord *m*; *(of garden)* bordure *f* **2** *adj (town)* frontière *inv* **3** *vt (street)* border; **to b. (on)** *(country)* avoir une frontière commune avec; *(resemble, verge on)* être voisin de

**bore[1]** [bɔ:(r)] **1** *vt (weary)* ennuyer; **to be bored** s'ennuyer **2** *n (person)* raseur, -euse *mf*; **it's a b.** c'est ennuyeux *ou* rasoir ▪ **boredom** *n* ennui *m* ▪ **boring** *adj* ennuyeux, -euse

**bore[2]** [bɔ:(r)] **1** *n (of gun)* calibre *m* **2** *vt (hole)* percer; *(rock, well)* forer, creuser **3** *vi* forer

**bore[3]** [bɔ:(r)] *pt of* **bear[2]**

**born** [bɔ:n] *adj* né; **to be b.** naître; **he was b. in Paris/in 1980** il est né à Paris/en 1980

**borne** [bɔ:n] *pp of* **bear[2]**

**borough** ['bʌrə] *n* circonscription *f* électorale urbaine

**borrow** ['bɒrəʊ] *vt* emprunter (**from** à)

**Bosnia** ['bɒznɪə] *n* la Bosnie

**bosom** ['bʊzəm] *n (chest, breasts)* poitrine *f*; *(breast)* sein *m*; *Fig (heart, soul)* sein *m*

**boss** [bɒs] **1** *n* patron, -onne *mf* **2** *vt* **to b. sb around** *or* **about** donner des ordres à qn ▪ **bossy** (**-ier, -iest**) *adj Fam* autoritaire

**botany** ['bɒtənɪ] *n* botanique *f*

**botch** [bɒtʃ] *vt Fam* **to b. (up)** *(spoil)* bâcler; *(repair badly)* rafistoler

**both** [bəʊθ] **1** *adj* les deux; **b. brothers** les deux frères

**2** *pron* tous/toutes (les) deux; **b. of the boys** les deux garçons; **b. of us** tous les deux; **b. of them died** ils sont morts tous les deux

**3** *adv (at the same time)* à la fois; **b. in England and in France** en Angleterre comme en France; **b. you and I know that...** vous et moi, nous savons que...

**bother** ['bɒðə(r)] **1** *n (trouble)* ennui *m*; *(effort)* peine *f*; *(inconvenience)* dérangement *m* **2** *vt (annoy, worry)* ennuyer; *(disturb)* déranger; *(pester)* importuner; *(hurt, itch) (of foot, eye)* gêner; **to b. doing** *or* **to do sth** se donner la peine de faire qch; **I can't be bothered** ça ne me dit rien **3** *vi* **to b. about** *(worry about)* se préoccuper de; *(deal with)* s'occuper de; **don't b.!** ce n'est pas la peine!

**bottle** ['bɒtəl] **1** *n* bouteille *f*; *(for perfume)* flacon *m*; *(for baby)* biberon *m*; **b. bank** conteneur *m* pour verre usagé; **b. opener** ouvre-bouteilles *m inv* **2** *vt (milk, wine)* mettre en bouteilles; **to b. up** *(feeling)* refouler ▪ **bottle-feed** (*pt & pp* **-fed**) *vt* nourrir au biberon ▪ **bottleneck** *n (in road)* goulot *m* d'étranglement; *(in traffic)* bouchon *m*

**bottom** ['bɒtəm] **1** *n (of sea, box)* fond *m*; *(of page, hill)* bas *m*; *(of table)* bout *m*; *(buttocks)* derrière *m*; **to be (at the) b. of the class** être le dernier/la dernière de la classe

**2** *adj (shelf)* inférieur, du bas; **b. floor** rez-de-chaussée *m*; **b. gear** première vitesse *f*; **b. part** *or* **half** partie *f* inférieure; *Fig* **the b. line is that...** le fait est que... ▪ **bottomless** *adj (funds)* inépuisable; **b. pit** gouffre *m*

**bought** [bɔːt] *pt & pp of* **buy**

**boulder** ['bəʊldə(r)] *n* rocher *m*

**bounce** [baʊns] **1** *n* rebond *m* **2** *vt (ball)* faire rebondir **3** *vi (of ball)* rebondir (**off** contre); *(of person)* faire des bonds; *Fam (of cheque)* être sans provision

**bouncer** ['baʊnsə(r)] *n Fam (doorman)* videur *m*

**bound**[1] [baʊnd] *adj* (**a**) **b. to do** *(obliged)* obligé de faire; *(certain)* sûr de faire; **it's b. to snow** il va sûrement neiger; **to be b. for** *(of person, ship)* être en route pour; *(of train, plane)* être à destination de (**b**) **b. up with** *(connected)* lié à

**bound**[2] [baʊnd] **1** *n (leap)* bond *m* **2** *vi* bondir

**bound**[3] [bæʊnd] *pt & pp of* **bind**

**boundary** ['baʊndərɪ] (*pl* **-ies**) *n* limite *f*

**bounds** [baʊndz] *npl* limites *fpl*; **out of b.** *(place)* interdit

**bouquet** [bəʊ'keɪ] *n (of flowers, wine)* bouquet *m*

**bout** [baʊt] *n (of fever, coughing, violence)* accès *m*; *(of asthma, malaria)* crise *f*; *(session)* séance *f*; *(period)* période *f*; *(in boxing)* combat *m*; **a b. of flu** une grippe

**boutique** [buː'tiːk] *n* boutique *f* (de mode)

**bow**[1] [bəʊ] *n (weapon)* arc *m*; *(of violin)* archet *m*; *(knot)* nœud *m*; **b. tie** nœud *m* papillon ▪ **bow-legged** *adj* aux jambes arquées

**bow**[2] [baʊ] **1** *n (with knees bent)* révérence *f*; *(nod)* salut *m* **2** *vt* **to b. one's head** incliner la tête **3** *vi* s'incliner (**to** devant); *(nod)* incliner la tête (**to** devant); **to b. down (to)** *(submit)* s'incliner (devant)

**bow**[3] [baʊ] *n (of ship)* proue *f*

**bowels** ['baʊəlz] *npl* intestins *mpl*

**bowl**[1] [bəʊl] *n (small dish)* bol *m*; *(for salad)* saladier *m*; *(for soup)* assiette *f* creuse; *(of toilet)* cuvette *f*

**bowl**[2] [bəʊl] **1** *n* **bowls** *(game)* boules

*fpl* **2** *vi (in cricket)* lancer la balle ▪ **bowling** *n* **(tenpin) b.** bowling *m*; **b. alley** bowling *m*; **b. ball** boule *f* de bowling; **b. green** terrain *m* de boules

▸**bowl over** *vt sep (knock down)* renverser; *Fig (astound)* **to be bowled over by sth** être stupéfié par qch

**box** [bɒks] **1** *n* boîte *f*; *(larger)* caisse *f*; *(made of cardboard)* carton *m*; *(in theatre)* loge *f*; *(for horse, in stable)* box *m*; *Br Fam (television)* télé *f*; **b. office** bureau *m* de location; *Br* **b. room** *(for storage)* débarras *m*; *(bedroom)* petite chambre *f*

**2** *vt* (**a**) **to b. (up)** mettre en boîte/caisse; **to b. in** *(enclose)* enfermer (**b**) **to b. sb's ears** gifler qn

**3** *vi* boxer ▪ **boxing** *n* (**a**) *(sport)* boxe *f*; **b. gloves/match** gants *mpl*/combat *m* de boxe; **b. ring** ring *m* (**b**) *Br* **B. Day** le lendemain de Noël

**boxer** ['bɒksə(r)] *n (fighter)* boxeur *m*; *(dog)* boxer *m*

**boy** [bɔɪ] *n* garçon *m* ▪ **boyfriend** *n* petit ami *m*

**boycott** ['bɔɪkɒt] **1** *n* boycottage *m* **2** *vt* boycotter

**bra** [brɑː] *n* soutien-gorge *m*

**brace** [breɪs] **1** *n (dental)* appareil *m* dentaire; *(on leg, arm)* appareil *m* orthopédique; *(for fastening)* attache *f*; *Br* **braces** *(for trousers)* bretelles *fpl* **2** *vt* **to b. oneself for sth** *(news, shock)* se préparer à qch ▪ **bracing** *adj (air)* vivifiant

**bracelet** ['breɪslɪt] *n* bracelet *m*

**bracket** ['brækɪt] **1** *n (for shelves)* équerre *f*; *(in writing)* parenthèse *f*; *(group)* groupe *m*; *(for tax)* tranche *f*; **in brackets** entre parenthèses **2** *vt* mettre entre parenthèses

**brag** [bræg] *(pt & pp* **-gg-**) *vi* se vanter (**about** *or* **of sth** de qch; **about doing sth** de faire qch)

**braid** [breɪd] **1** *n (of hair)* tresse *f*; *(trimming)* galon *m* **2** *vt (hair)* tresser; *(trim)* galonner

**Braille** [breɪl] *n* braille *m*; **in B.** en braille

**brain** [breɪn] **1** *n* cerveau *m*; *(of animal, bird)* cervelle *f*; *Fam* **to have brains** être intelligent; *Fam* **to have sth on the b.** être obsédé par qch; **b. death** mort *f* cérébrale; **b. drain** fuite *f* des cerveaux **2** *vt Fam (hit)* assommer ▪ **brainchild** *n* trouvaille *f* ▪ **brainstorm** *n Am (brilliant idea)* idée *f* géniale; *Br (mental confusion)* aberration *f* ▪ **brainwash** *vt* faire un lavage de cerveau à ▪ **brainwave** *n* idée *f* géniale

**brainy** ['breɪnɪ] (**-ier, -iest**) *adj Fam* intelligent

**brake** [breɪk] **1** *n* frein *m*; **b. light** stop *m* **2** *vi* freiner

**bran** [bræn] *n* son *m*

**branch** [brɑːntʃ] **1** *n* branche *f*; *(of road)* embranchement *m*; *(of river)* bras *m*; *(of shop)* succursale *f*; *(of bank)* agence *f*; **b. office** succursale *f* **2** *vi* **to b. off** *(of road)* bifurquer; **to b. out** *(of company, person)* étendre ses activités; *(of family, tree)* se ramifier

**brand** [brænd] **1** *n (on product, on cattle)* marque *f*; *(type)* type *m*, style *m*; **b. name** marque *f* **2** *vt (mark)* marquer; *Fig* **to be branded as a liar/coward** avoir une réputation de menteur/lâche

**brandish** ['brændɪʃ] *vt* brandir

**brand-new** [brænd'njuː] *adj* tout neuf (*f* toute neuve)

**brandy** ['brændɪ] (*pl* **-ies**) *n* cognac *m*; *(made with fruit)* eau-de-vie *f*

**brash** [bræʃ] *adj* exubérant

**brass** [brɑːs] *n* cuivre *m*; *(instruments in orchestra)* cuivres *mpl*; *Fam* **b. band** fanfare *f*

**brat** [bræt] *n Pej (child)* morveux, -euse *mf*; *(badly behaved)* sale gosse *mf*

**brave** [breɪv] **1** (**-er, -est**) *adj* courageux, -euse **2** *n (native American)* brave *m* **3** *vt (danger)* braver ▪ **bravery** *n* courage *m*

**brawl** [brɔːl] **1** *n (fight)* bagarre *f* **2** *vi* se bagarrer

**Brazil** [brə'zɪl] *n* le Brésil ▪ **Brazilian 1**

*adj* brésilien, -enne **2** *n* Brésilien, -enne *mf*

**breach** [bri:tʃ] **1** *n (of rule)* violation *f* (**of** de); **b. of contract** rupture *f* de contrat; **b. of trust** abus *m* de confiance **2** *vt (law, code)* enfreindre à; *(contract)* rompre

**bread** [bred] *n* pain *m*; *Fam (money)* blé *m*; **loaf of b.** pain *m*; **brown b.** pain *m* bis; **(slice** *or* **piece of) b. and butter** pain *m* beurré; **b. knife** couteau *m* à pain ▪ **breadbin** (*Am* **breadbox**) *n* boîte *f* à pain ▪ **breadboard** *n* planche *f* à pain ▪ **breadcrumb** *n* miette *f* de pain; **breadcrumbs** *(in cooking)* chapelure *f* ▪ **breaded** *adj* pané ▪ **breadline** *n* **on the b.** indigent ▪ **breadwinner** *n* **to be the b.** faire bouillir la marmite

**breadth** [bretθ] *n* largeur *f*

**break** [breɪk] **1** *n* cassure *f*; *(in bone)* fracture *f*; *(with person, group)* rupture *f*; *(in journey)* interruption *f*; *(rest)* repos *m*; *(in activity)* pause *f*; *(at school)* récréation *f*; *(holidays)* vacances *fpl*

**2** (*pt* **broke**, *pp* **broken**) *vt* casser; *(into pieces, with force)* briser; *(silence, spell, vow)* rompre; *(strike, will, ice)* briser; *(agreement, promise)* manquer à; *(law)* violer; *(record)* battre; *(journey)* interrompre; *(news)* annoncer (**to** à); *(habit)* se débarrasser de; **to b. one's arm** se casser le bras; **to b. sb's heart** briser le cœur à qn; *Fam* **to b. the sound barrier** franchir le mur du son; **to b. a fall** amortir une chute

**3** *vi* se casser; *(into pieces, of heart, of voice)* se briser; *(of boy's voice)* muer; *(of spell)* se rompre; *(of weather)* changer; *(of news)* éclater; *(of day)* se lever; *(stop work)* faire la pause; **to b. in two** se casser en deux; **to b. free** se libérer; **to b. loose** se détacher ▪ **breakable** *adj* fragile ▪ **breakage** *n* **were there any breakages?** est-ce qu'il y a eu de la casse? ▪ **breakdown** *n (of machine)* panne *f*; *(of argument, figures)* analyse *f*; *(of talks, negotiations)* échec *m*; *(of person)* dépression *f*; *Br* **b. lorry** *or* **van** dépanneuse *f*

▸ **break away 1** *vi* se détacher **2** *vt sep* détacher

▸ **break down 1** *vt sep (door)* enfoncer; *(resistance)* briser; *(argument, figures)* analyser **2** *vi (of machine)* tomber en panne; *(of talks, negotiations)* échouer; *(of person) (have nervous breakdown)* craquer; *(start crying)* éclater en sanglots

▸ **break in 1** *vi (of burglar)* entrer par effraction; *(interrupt)* interrompre **2** *vt sep (door)* enfoncer; *(horse)* dresser

▸ **break into** *vt insep (house)* entrer par effraction; *(safe)* forcer; **to b. into song/a run** se mettre à chanter/courir

▸ **break off 1** *vt sep (detach) (twig, handle)* détacher; *(relations)* rompre **2** *vi (become detached)* se casser; *(stop)* s'arrêter; **to b. off with sb** rompre avec qn

▸ **break out** *vi (of war, fire)* éclater; *(escape)* s'échapper (**of** de); **to b. out in a rash** se couvrir de boutons

▸ **break through 1** *vi (of sun, army)* percer **2** *vt insep (defences)* percer; *(barrier)* forcer; *(wall)* faire une brèche dans

▸ **break up 1** *vt sep (reduce to pieces)* mettre en morceaux; *(marriage)* briser; *(fight)* mettre fin à **2** *vi (end)* prendre fin; *(of group)* se disperser; *(of marriage)* se briser; *(from school)* partir en vacances

**breakfast** ['brekfəst] *n* petit déjeuner *m*; **to have b.** prendre le petit déjeuner; **b. TV** émissions *fpl* (télévisées) du matin

**break-in** ['breɪkɪn] *n* cambriolage *m*

**breaking-point** ['breɪkɪŋpɔɪnt] *n* **at b.** *(person, patience)* à bout; *(marriage)* au bord de la rupture

**breakthrough** ['breɪkθru:] *n (discovery)* découverte *f* fondamentale

**breast** [brest] *n (of woman)* sein *m*; *(chest)* poitrine *f*; *(of chicken)* blanc *m* ▪ **breastfeed** (*pt & pp* **-fed**) *vt* allaiter ▪ **breaststroke** *n (in swimming)* brasse *f*

**breath** [breθ] *n* souffle *m*; **bad b.** mauvaise haleine *f*; **out of b.** à bout de souffle; **to hold one's b.** retenir son souffle; **under one's b.** tout bas ▪ **breathalyser®** *n* Alcotest® *m* ▪ **breathless** *adj* hors d'haleine ▪ **breathtaking** *adj* à couper le souffle

**breathe** [bri:ð] **1** *vi (of person, animal)* respirer; **to b. in** inhaler; **to b. out** expirer **2** *vt* respirer; **to b. a sigh of relief** pousser un soupir de soulagement ▪ **breathing** *n* respiration *f*; *Fig* **b. space** moment *m* de repos

**bred** [bred] **1** *pt & pp of* **breed 2** *adj* **well-b.** bien élevé

**breed** [bri:d] **1** *n* race *f* **2** (*pt & pp* **bred**) *vt (animals)* élever; *Fig (hatred, violence)* engendrer **3** *vi (of animals)* se reproduire ▪ **breeding** *n (of animals)* élevage *m*; *Fig (manners)* éducation *f*

**breeze** [bri:z] *n* brise *f* ▪ **breezy** (**-ier, -iest**) *adj* (**a**) *(weather, day)* frais (*f* fraîche), venteux, -euse (**b**) *(cheerful)* jovial; *(relaxed)* décontracté

**brew** [bru:] **1** *n (drink)* breuvage *m*; *(of tea)* infusion *f* **2** *vt (beer)* brasser; *Fig (trouble, plot)* préparer **3** *vi (of beer)* fermenter; *(of tea)* infuser; *Fig (of storm)* se préparer ▪ **brewery** (*pl* **-ies**) *n* brasserie *f*

**bribe** [braɪb] **1** *n* pot-de-vin *m* **2** *vt* acheter, soudoyer; **to b. sb into doing sth** soudoyer qn pour qu'il fasse qch ▪ **bribery** *n* corruption *f*

**brick** [brɪk] *n* brique *f*; **b. wall** mur en briques ▪ **bricklayer** *n* maçon *m*

**bridal** ['braɪdəl] *adj (ceremony, bed)* nuptial; **b. suite** *(in hotel)* suite *f* nuptiale

**bride** [braɪd] *n* mariée *f*; **the b. and groom** les mariés *mpl* ▪ **bridegroom** *n* marié *m* ▪ **bridesmaid** *n* demoiselle *f* d'honneur

**bridge¹** [brɪdʒ] **1** *n* pont *m*; *(on ship)* passerelle *f*; *(of nose)* arête *f*; *(on teeth)* bridge *m* **2** *vt* **to b. a gap** combler une lacune

**bridge²** [brɪdʒ] *n (game)* bridge *m*

**brief¹** [bri:f] (**-er, -est**) *adj* bref (*f* brève); **in b.** en résumé ▪ **briefly** *adv (say)* brièvement; *(hesitate, smile)* un court instant

**brief²** [bri:f] **1** *n (instructions)* instructions *fpl*; *(legal)* dossier *m*; *Fig (task)* tâche *f* **2** *vt* donner des instructions à; *(inform)* mettre au courant (**on** de) ▪ **briefing** *n (information)* instructions *fpl*; *(meeting)* briefing *m*

**briefcase** ['bri:fkeɪs] *n* serviette *f*

**briefs** [bri:fs] *npl (underwear)* slip *m*

**brigade** [brɪ'geɪd] *n* brigade *f*

**bright** [braɪt] **1** (**-er, -est**) *adj (star, eyes, situation)* brillant; *(light, colour)* vif (*f* vive); *(weather, room)* clair; *(clever)* intelligent; *(happy)* joyeux, -euse; *(future)* prometteur, -euse; *(idea)* génial **2** *adv* **b. and early** de bon matin ▪ **brightly** *adv (shine)* avec éclat

**brighten** ['braɪtən] **1** *vt* **to b. (up)** *(room)* égayer **2** *vi* **to b. (up)** *(of weather)* s'éclaircir; *(of face)* s'éclairer; *(of person)* s'égayer

**brilliant** ['brɪljənt] *adj (light)* éclatant; *(person, idea, career)* brillant; *Br Fam (fantastic)* super *inv*

**brim** [brɪm] **1** *n (of hat, cup)* bord *m* **2** (*pt & pp* **-mm-**) *vi* **to b. over (with)** déborder (de)

**bring** [brɪŋ] (*pt & pp* **brought**) *vt (person, animal, car)* amener; *(object)* apporter; *(cause)* provoquer; **it has brought me great happiness** cela m'a procuré un grand bonheur; **to b. sth to sb's attention** attirer l'attention de qn sur qch; **to b. sth to an end** mettre fin à qch

▸ **bring about** *vt sep* provoquer

▸ **bring along** *vt sep (object)* apporter; *(person)* amener

▸ **bring back** *vt sep (person)* ramener; *(object)* rapporter; *(memories)* rappeler

▸ **bring down** *vt sep (object)* descendre; *(overthrow)* faire tomber; *(reduce)* réduire; *(shoot down) (plane)* abattre

▸ **bring forward** *vt sep (in time or space)* avancer; *(witness)* produire

▸ **bring in** *vt sep (object)* rentrer;

*(person)* faire entrer; *(introduce)* introduire; *(income)* rapporter

▸**bring off** *vt sep (task)* mener à bien

▸**bring out** *vt sep (object)* sortir; *(person)* faire sortir; *(meaning)* faire ressortir; *(book)* publier; *(product)* lancer

▸**bring round** *vt sep (revive)* ranimer; *(convert)* convaincre; **she brought him round to her point of view** elle a su le convaincre

▸**bring to** *vt sep* **to b. sb to** ranimer qn

▸**bring together** *vt sep (friends, members)* réunir; *(reconcile)* réconcilier; *(put in touch)* mettre en contact

▸**bring up** *vt sep (object)* monter; *(child)* élever; *(question)* soulever; *(subject)* mentionner; *(food)* rendre

**brink** [brɪŋk] *n* bord *m*; **on the b. of sth** au bord de qch

**brisk** [brɪsk] (**-er, -est**) *adj (lively)* vif (*f* vive); **at a b. pace** vite; **business is b.** les affaires marchent bien

**bristle** ['brɪsəl] **1** *n* poil *m* **2** *vi* se hérisser

**Britain** ['brɪtən] *n* la Grande-Bretagne ▪ **British 1** *adj* britannique; **the B. Isles** les îles *fpl* Britanniques; **B. Summer Time** heure *f* d'été *(en Grande-Bretagne)* **2** *npl* **the B.** les Britanniques *mpl* ▪ **Briton** *n* Britannique *mf*

**Brittany** ['brɪtənɪ] *n* la Bretagne

**brittle** ['brɪtəl] *adj* cassant

**broad** [brɔːd] (**-er, -est**) *adj (wide)* large; *(accent)* prononcé; **in b. daylight** en plein jour; **the b. outline of** *(plan)* les grandes lignes de; **b. bean** fève *f*; *Am Sport* **b. jump** saut *m* en longueur ▪ **broad-minded** *adj (person)* à l'esprit large; ▪ **broad-shouldered** *adj* large d'épaules ▪ **broaden 1** *vt* élargir **2** *vi* s'élargir ▪ **broadly** *adv* **b. (speaking)** en gros

**broadcast** ['brɔːdkɑːst] **1** *n* émission *f* **2** (*pt & pp* **broadcast**) *vt* diffuser **3** *vi (of station)* émettre; *(of person)* parler à la radio/à la télévision

**broccoli** ['brɒkəlɪ] *n inv (plant)* brocoli *m*; *(food)* brocolis *mpl*

**brochure** ['brəʊʃə(r)] *n* brochure *f*

**broil** [brɔɪl] *vt & vi Am* griller

**broke** [brəʊk] **1** *pt of* **break 2** *adj Fam (penniless)* fauché ▪ **broken 1** *pp of* **break 2** *adj (man, voice, line)* brisé; *(ground)* accidenté; *(spirit)* abattu; **in b. English** en mauvais anglais; **b. home** famille *f* désunie

**broker** ['brəʊkə(r)] *n (for shares, currency)* agent *m* de change; *(for goods, insurance)* courtier, -ère *mf*

**bronchitis** [brɒŋ'kaɪtɪs] *n* bronchite *f*

**bronze** [brɒnz] *n* bronze *m*; **b. statue** statue *f* en bronze

**brooch** [brəʊtʃ] *n (ornament)* broche *f*

**brood** [bruːd] **1** *n* couvée *f* **2** *vi (of bird)* couver; *Fig* **to b. over sth** *(of person)* ruminer qch ▪ **broody** (**-ier, -iest**) *adj (person) (sulky)* maussade; *(dreamy)* rêveur, -euse; *Br Fam (woman)* en mal d'enfant

**broom** [bruːm] *n* (**a**) *(for sweeping)* balai *m* (**b**) *(plant)* genêt *m*

**broth** [brɒθ] *n (thin)* bouillon *m*; *(thick)* potage *m*

**brothel** ['brɒθəl] *n* maison *f* close

**brother** ['brʌðə(r)] *n* frère *m* ▪ **brother-in-law** (*pl* **brothers-in-law**) *n* beau-frère *m*

**brought** [brɔːt] *pt & pp of* **bring**

**brow** [braʊ] *n* (**a**) *(forehead)* front *m* (**b**) *(of hill)* sommet *m*

**brown** [braʊn] **1** (**-er, -est**) *adj* marron *inv*; *(hair)* châtain; *(tanned)* bronzé **2** *n* marron *m* **3** *vt (food)* faire dorer **4** *vi (of food)* dorer

**Brownie** ['braʊnɪ] *n (girl scout)* ≃ jeannette *f*

**brownie** ['braʊnɪ] *n (cake)* brownie *m*

**browse** [braʊz] **1** *vt Comptr* **to b. the Web** naviguer sur le Web **2** *vi (in bookshop)* feuilleter des livres; *(in shop, supermarket)* regarder; **to b. through** *(book)* feuilleter

**bruise** [bruːz] **1** *n* bleu *m*; *(on fruit)* meurtrissure *f* **2** *vt* **to b. one's knee/hand** se faire un bleu au genou/à la main ▪ **bruised** *adj (covered in bruises)* couvert de bleus

**brunch** [brʌntʃ] *n* brunch *m*

**brunette** [bruːˈnet] *n* brunette *f*

**brunt** [brʌnt] *n* **to bear the b. of** *(attack, anger)* subir le plus gros de; *(expense)* assumer la plus grosse part de

**brush** [brʌʃ] **1** *n (tool)* brosse *f*; *(for shaving)* blaireau *m*; *(for sweeping)* balayette *f*; **to give sth a b.** donner un coup de brosse à qch
**2** *vt (teeth, hair)* brosser; *(clothes)* donner un coup de brosse à; **to b. sb/sth aside** écarter qn/qch; **to b. sth away** *or* **off** enlever qch; **to b. up (on) one's French** se remettre au français **3** *vi* **to b. against sb/sth** effleurer qn/qch ▪ **brush-off** *n Fam* **to give sb the b.** envoyer promener qn

**brusque** [bruːsk] *adj* brusque

**Brussels** [ˈbrʌsəlz] *n* Bruxelles *m ou f*; **B. sprouts** choux *mpl* de Bruxelles

**brutal** [ˈbruːtəl] *adj* brutal; *(attack)* sauvage

**brute** [bruːt] **1** *n (animal)* bête *f*; *(person)* brute *f* **2** *adj* **by b. force** par la force

**BSc** [biːesˈsiː] (*Am* **BS** [biːˈes]) (*abbr* **Bachelor of Science**) *(person)* ≃ licencié, -e *mf* ès sciences; *(qualification)* ≃ licence *f* de sciences

**BSE** [biːesˈiː] (*abbr* **bovine spongiform encephalopathy**) *n* EBS *f*, maladie *f* de la vache folle

**bubble** [ˈbʌbəl] **1** *n (of air, soap)* bulle *f*; **b. bath** bain *m* moussant; **b. gum** chewing-gum *m* **2** *vi (of liquid)* bouillonner; **to b. over (with)** déborder (de)

**bubbly** [ˈbʌblɪ] **1** *adj (liquid)* plein de bulles; *(person, personality)* débordant de vitalité **2** *n Fam* champ *m*

**buck** [bʌk] **1** *n* (**a**) *Am Fam* dollar *m* (**b**) *(of rabbit)* mâle *m* **2** *vt Fam* **to b. sb up** remonter le moral à qn **3** *vi Fam* **to b. up** *(become livelier)* reprendre du poil de la bête; *(hurry)* se grouiller

**bucket** [ˈbʌkɪt] *n* seau *m*

**buckle** [ˈbʌkəl] **1** *n* boucle *f* **2** *vt* (**a**) *(fasten)* boucler (**b**) *(deform)* déformer **3** *vi (deform)* se déformer

**bud** [bʌd] **1** *n (on tree)* bourgeon *m*; *(on flower)* bouton *m* **2** *(pt & pp* **-dd-***) vi* bourgeonner; *(of flower)* pousser des boutons ▪ **budding** *adj (talent)* naissant; *(doctor)* en herbe

**Buddhist** [ˈbʊdɪst] *adj & n* bouddhiste *(mf)*

**buddy** [ˈbʌdɪ] *(pl* **-ies***) n Am Fam* pote *m*

**budge** [bʌdʒ] **1** *vi* bouger **2** *vt* faire bouger

**budgerigar** [ˈbʌdʒərɪgɑː(r)] *n Br* perruche *f*

**budget** [ˈbʌdʒɪt] **1** *n* budget *m* **2** *vi* dresser un budget; **to b. for sth** inscrire qch au budget

**budgie** [ˈbʌdʒɪ] *n Br Fam* perruche *f*

**buff** [bʌf] **1** *adj* **b.(-coloured)** chamois *inv* **2** *n Fam* **jazz/film b.** fanatique *mf* de jazz/de cinéma

**buffalo** [ˈbʌfələʊ] *(pl* **-oes** *or* **-o***) n* buffle *m*; **(American) b.** bison *m*

**buffer** [ˈbʌfə(r)] *n (on train)* tampon *m*; *(at end of track)* butoir *m*; *Fig (safeguard)* protection *f* (**against** contre)

**buffet**[1] [ˈbʊfeɪ] *n (meal, café)* buffet *m*; **cold b.** viandes *fpl* froides; *Br* **b. car** *(on train)* wagon-restaurant *m*

**buffet**[2] [ˈbʌfɪt] *vt (of waves)* secouer; *(of wind, rain)* cingler

**bug**[1] [bʌg] **1** *n* (**a**) *(insect)* bestiole *f*; *(bedbug)* punaise *f*; *Fam (germ)* microbe *m* (**b**) *(in machine)* défaut *m*; *Comptr* bogue *m* (**c**) *(listening device)* micro *m* **2** *(pt & pp* **-gg-***) vt (room)* installer des micros dans

**bug**[2] [bʌg] *(pt & pp* **-gg-***) vt Fam (nag)* embêter

**buggy** [ˈbʌgɪ] *(pl* **-ies***) n Br* **(baby) b.** *(pushchair)* poussette *f*; *Am (pram)* landau *m*

**build** [bɪld] **1** *n (of person)* carrure *f* **2** *(pt & pp* **built** [bɪlt]*) vt* construire; **to b. sth up** *(increase)* augmenter qch; *(business)* monter qch **3** *vi* **to b. up** *(of tension, pressure)* augmenter; *(of dust, snow, interest)* s'accumuler; *(of traffic)* devenir dense ▪ **builder** *n (skilled)* maçon *m*; *(unskilled)* ouvrier *m*; *(contractor)* entrepreneur *m* ▪ **building** *n* bâtiment *m*; *(flats, offices)* immeuble *m*; *(action)* construction *f*; **b. site** chantier *m*; *Br* **b. society** ≃ société *f* de crédit immobilier ▪ **build-up** *n (increase)* augmentation *f*; *(of dust)* accumulation *f*; *(for author, book)* publicité *f*

**built-in** [bɪlt'ɪn] *adj (cupboard)* encastré; *(part of machine)* incorporé; *Fig (innate)* inné

**built-up** ['bɪltʌp] *adj* urbanisé; **b. area** agglomération *f*

**bulb** [bʌlb] *n (of plant)* bulbe *m*; *(of lamp)* ampoule *f*

**bulge** [bʌldʒ] **1** *n* renflement *m* **2** *vi* **to b. (out)** bomber; *(of eyes)* sortir de la tête ▪ **bulging** *adj* bombé; *(eyes)* protubérant; **to be b. (with)** *(of bag, pocket)* être bourré (de)

**bulimia** [bʊ'lɪmɪə] *n* boulimie *f*

**bulk** [bʌlk] *n inv (of building, parcel)* volume *m*; *(of person)* grosseur *f*; **the b. of sth** la majeure partie de qch; **in b.** *(buy, sell)* en gros ▪ **bulky** (**-ier, -iest**) *adj* volumineux, -euse

**bull** [bʊl] *n* (**a**) *(animal)* taureau *m* (**b**) *very Fam (nonsense)* conneries *fpl* ▪ **bullfight** *n* corrida *f*

**bulldozer** ['bʊldəʊzə(r)] *n* bulldozer *m*

**bullet** ['bʊlɪt] *n* balle *f* ▪ **bulletproof** *adj (car)* blindé; **b. glass** vitre *f* blindée; *Br* **b. jacket,** *Am* **b. vest** gilet *m* pare-balles *inv*

**bulletin** ['bʊlətɪn] *n* bulletin *m*; *Am* **b. board** panneau *m* d'affichage

**bullion** ['bʊljən] *n* **gold b.** lingots *mpl* d'or

**bull's-eye** ['bʊlzaɪ] *n (of target)* centre *m*; **to hit the b.** mettre dans le mille

**bully** ['bʊlɪ] **1** (*pl* **-ies**) *n* terreur *f* **2** (*pt & pp* **-ied**) *vt (ill-treat)* maltraiter

**bum** [bʌm] *Fam* **1** *n* (**a**) *(loafer)* clochard, -e *mf*; *(good-for-nothing)* bon *m* à rien, bonne *f* à rien (**b**) *Br (buttocks)* derrière *m*; **b. bag** banane *f* **2** (*pt & pp* **-mm-**) *vi* **to b. (around)** *(be idle)* glander; *(travel)* vadrouiller **3** *vt* **to b. sth off sb** taxer qch à qn

**bump** [bʌmp] **1** *n (impact)* choc *m*; *(jerk)* secousse *f*; *(on road, body)* bosse *f* **2** *vt (of car)* heurter; **to b. one's head/knee** se cogner la tête/le genou; **to b. into** *(of person)* se cogner contre; *(of car)* rentrer dans; *(meet)* tomber sur ▪ **bumper 1** *n (of car)* pare-chocs *m inv* **2** *adj (crop, year)* exceptionnel, -elle

**bumpy** ['bʌmpɪ] (**-ier, -iest**) *adj (road, ride)* cahoteux, -euse

**bun** [bʌn] *n* (**a**) *(cake)* petit pain *m* au lait (**b**) *(of hair)* chignon *m*

**bunch** [bʌntʃ] *n (of flowers)* bouquet *m*; *(of keys)* trousseau *m*; *(of bananas)* régime *m*; *(of grapes)* grappe *f*; *(of people)* bande *f*

**bundle** ['bʌndəl] **1** *n* paquet *m*; *(of papers)* liasse *f*; *(of firewood)* fagot *m* **2** *vt (put)* fourrer (**into** dans); *(push)* pousser (**into** dans); **to b. up** *(newspapers, letters)* mettre en paquet **3** *vi* **to b. (oneself) up** (bien) se couvrir

**bungalow** ['bʌŋgələʊ] *n* pavillon *m* de plain-pied

**bungle** ['bʌŋgəl] **1** *vt* gâcher **2** *vi* se tromper

**bunk** [bʌŋk] *n (in ship, train)* couchette *f*; **b. beds** lits *mpl* superposés

**bunker** ['bʌŋkə(r)] *n Mil & Golf* bunker *m*; *(for coal)* coffre *m* à charbon

**bunny** ['bʌnɪ] (*pl* **-ies**) *n Fam* **b. (rabbit)** petit lapin *m*

**buoy** [bɔɪ] **1** *n* bouée *f* **2** *vt Fig* **to b. up** *(support)* soutenir

**buoyant** ['bɔɪənt] *adj (in water)* qui flotte; *Fig (economy, prices)* stable; *Fig (person, mood)* plein d'allant

**burden** ['bɜːdən] **1** *n* fardeau *m* **2** *vt* charger (**with** de); *Fig* accabler (**with** de)

**bureau** ['bjʊərəʊ] (*pl* **-eaux** [-əʊz]) *n (office)* bureau *m*; *Br (desk)* secrétaire *m*; *Am (chest of drawers)* commode *f*

**bureaucracy** [bjʊə'rɒkrəsɪ] *n* bureaucratie *f* ▪ **bureaucrat** *n* bureaucrate *mf*

**burger** ['bɜːgə(r)] *n* hamburger *m*

**burglar** ['bɜːɡlə(r)] *n* cambrioleur, -euse *mf*; **b. alarm** alarme *f* antivol ▪ **burglarize** *vt Am* cambrioler ▪ **burgle** *vt Br* cambrioler

**burial** ['berɪəl] **1** *n* enterrement *m* **2** *adj (service)* funèbre; **b. ground** cimetière *m*

**burn** [bɜːn] **1** *n* brûlure *f* **2** (*pt & pp* **burned** *or* **burnt**) *vt* brûler; **to b. sth down** incendier qch **3** *vi* brûler; **to b. down** *(of house)* être détruit par les flammes; *(of fuse)* sauter ▪ **burning 1** *adj* en feu; *(fire)* allumé; *Fig (fever)* dévorant **2** *n* **a smell of b.** une odeur de brûlé

**burner** ['bɜːnə(r)] *n (on stove)* brûleur *m*; *Fig* **to put sth on the back b.** remettre qch à plus tard

**burp** [bɜːp] *Fam* **1** *n* rot *m* **2** *vi* roter

**burrow** ['bʌrəʊ] **1** *n (hole)* terrier *m* **2** *vt & vi* creuser

**burst** [bɜːst] **1** *n (of shell)* éclatement *m*, explosion *f*; *(of laughter)* éclat *m*; *(of applause)* salve *f*; *(of thunder)* coup *m*; *(surge)* élan *m*

**2** (*pt & pp* **burst**) *vt (bubble, balloon, boil)* crever; *(tyre)* faire éclater; **to b. open** *(door)* ouvrir brusquement

**3** *vi (of bubble, balloon, boil, tyre, cloud)* crever; *(with force) (of shell, boiler, tyre)* éclater; **to b. into a room** faire irruption dans une pièce; **to b. into flames** prendre feu; **to b. into tears** fondre en larmes; **to b. out laughing** éclater de rire; **to b. open** *(of door)* s'ouvrir brusquement

**bury** ['berɪ] (*pt & pp* **-ied**) *vt (body)* enterrer; *(hide)* enfouir; *(plunge)* plonger (**in** dans); **buried in one's work** plongé dans son travail

**bus** [bʌs] (*pl* **buses** *or* **busses**) *n* autobus *m*, bus *m*; *(long-distance)* autocar *m*, car *m*; **by b.** en bus/en car; **b. driver** chauffeur *m* de bus/car; **b. shelter** Abribus® *m*; **b. station** gare *f* routière; **b. stop** arrêt *m* de bus

**bush** [bʊʃ] *n* buisson *m*; **the b.** *(land)* la brousse ▪ **bushy** (**-ier, -iest**) *adj (hair, tail)* touffu

**bushed** [bʊʃt] *adj Fam (tired)* crevé

**business** ['bɪznɪs] **1** *n* affaires *fpl*, commerce *m*; *(shop)* commerce *m*; *(company, task, concern, matter)* affaire *f*; **the textile/construction b.** l'industrie *f* du textile/de la construction; **big b.** les grosses entreprises *fpl*; **to go out of b.** *(stop trading)* fermer; **that's none of your b.!, mind your own b.!** ça ne vous regarde pas!

**2** *adj* commercial; *(meeting, trip, lunch)* d'affaires; **b. card** carte *f* de visite; **b. hours** *(office)* heures *fpl* de bureau; *(shop)* heures *fpl* d'ouverture; **b. school** école *f* de commerce ▪ **businessman** (*pl* **-men**) *n* homme *m* d'affaires ▪ **businesswoman** (*pl* **-women**) *n* femme *f* d'affaires

**bust** [bʌst] **1** *n (statue)* buste *m*; *(of woman)* poitrine *f* **2** *adj Fam (broken)* fichu; **to go b.** *(bankrupt)* faire faillite **3** (*pt & pp* **bust** *or* **busted**) *vt Fam (break)* bousiller; *(arrest)* coffrer ▪ **bust-up** *n Fam (quarrel)* engueulade *f*; *(break-up)* rupture *f*

**bustle** ['bʌsəl] **1** *n* animation *f* **2** *vi* **to b. (about)** s'affairer

**busy** ['bɪzɪ] **1** (**-ier, -iest**) *adj* occupé; *(active)* actif, -ive; *(day)* chargé; *(street)* animé; *Am (phone, line)* occupé; **to be b. doing** *(in the process of)* être occupé à faire; **to keep oneself b.** s'occuper; **the shops were very b.** il y avait plein de monde dans les magasins; *Am* **b. signal** sonnerie *f* occupé **2** *vt* **to b. oneself** s'occuper (**with sth** à qch; **doing sth** à faire qch) ▪ **busybody** (*pl* **-ies**) *n Fam* fouineur, -euse *mf*

**but** [bʌt, *unstressed* bət] **1** *conj* mais **2** *prep (except)* sauf; **b. for him** sans lui; **no one b. you** personne d'autre que toi; **the last b. one** l'avant-dernier, -ère *mf*

**butcher** ['bʊtʃə(r)] **1** *n* boucher *m*; **b.'s (shop)** boucherie *f* **2** *vt (people)* massacrer; *(animal)* abattre

**butler** ['bʌtlə(r)] *n* maître *m* d'hôtel

**butt** [bʌt] **1** *n (of cigarette)* mégot *m*; *(of*

*gun)* crosse *f*; *Am Fam (buttocks)* derrière *m* **2** *vt (with head)* donner un coup de tête à **3** *vi* **to b. in** intervenir

**butter** ['bʌtə(r)] **1** *n* beurre *m*; *Br* **b. bean** = gros haricot blanc; **b. dish** beurrier *m* **2** *vt* beurrer; *Fam* **to b. sb up** passer de la pommade à qn ▪ **butterscotch** *n* caramel *m* dur au beurre

**butterfly** ['bʌtəflaɪ] *(pl* **-ies***) n* papillon *m*; *Fam* **to have butterflies** avoir l'estomac noué; **b. stroke** *(in swimming)* brasse *f* papillon

**buttock** ['bʌtək] *n* fesse *f*

**button** ['bʌtən] **1** *n* bouton *m*; *(of phone)* touche *f*; *Am (badge)* badge *m* **2** *vt* **to b. (up)** boutonner **3** *vi* **to b. (up)** *(of garment)* se boutonner ▪ **buttonhole 1** *n* boutonnière *f* **2** *vt Fam (person)* coincer

**buy** [baɪ] **1** *n* **a good b.** une bonne affaire **2** *(pt & pp* **bought***) vt* (**a**) *(purchase)* acheter (**from sb** à qn; **for sb** à *ou* pour qn) (**b**) *Am Fam (believe)* avaler; **I'll b. that!** je veux bien le croire! ▪ **buyer** *n* acheteur, -euse *mf*

**buzz** [bʌz] **1** *n* (**a**) *(noise)* bourdonnement *m* (**b**) *Fam (phone call)* **to give sb a b.** passer un coup de fil à qn **2** *vt* **to b. sb** *(using buzzer)* appeler qn **3** *vi* bourdonner; *Fam* **to b. off** se tirer ▪ **buzzer** *n (internal phone)* Interphone® *m*; *(of bell, clock)* sonnerie *f*

**BY** [baɪ] **1** *prep* (**a**) *(agent)* par; de; **hit/chosen by** frappé/choisi par; **surrounded/followed by** entouré/suivi de; **a book/painting by...** un livre/tableau de...

(**b**) *(manner, means)* par; en; à; de; **by sea** par mer; **by mistake** par erreur; **by car/train** en voiture/train; **by bicycle** à bicyclette; **by moonlight** au clair de lune; **by doing** en faisant; **one by one** un à un; **day by day** de jour en jour; **by sight/day** de vue/jour; **(all) by oneself** tout seul

(**c**) *(next to)* à côté de; *(near)* près de; **by the lake/sea** au bord du lac/de la mer; **to go** *or* **pass by the bank/school** passer devant la banque/l'école

(**d**) *(before in time)* avant; **by Monday** avant lundi, d'ici lundi; **by now** à cette heure-ci; **by yesterday** (dès) hier

(**e**) *(amount, measurement)* à; **by the kilo** au kilo; **taller by a metre** plus grand d'un mètre; **paid by the hour** payé à l'heure

(**f**) *(according to)* à, d'après; **by my watch** à ma montre; **it's fine** *or* **OK** *or* **all right by me** je n'y vois pas d'objection

**2** *adv* **close by** tout près; **to go** *or* **pass by** passer; **by and large** en gros

**bye(-bye)** ['baɪ('baɪ)] *exclam Fam* salut!, au revoir!

**by-law** ['baɪlɔː] *n* arrêté *m* (municipal)

**bypass** ['baɪpɑːs] **1** *n* rocade *f*; **(heart) b. operation** pontage *m* **2** *vt (town)* contourner; *Fig (ignore)* court-circuiter

**bystander** ['baɪstændə(r)] *n* passant, -e *mf*

**byte** [baɪt] *n Comptr* octet *m*

# Cc

**C, c**[1] [siː] *n* C, c *m inv*

**c**[2] (*abbr* **cent(s)**) ct

**cab** [kæb] *n* taxi *m*; *(of lorry)* cabine *f*

**cabaret** ['kæbəreɪ] *n* cabaret *m*

**cabbage** ['kæbɪdʒ] *n* chou *m* (*pl* choux)

**cabin** ['kæbɪn] *n (on ship)* cabine *f*; *(hut)* cabane *f*; *Aviat* **c. crew** équipage *m*

**cabinet**[1] ['kæbɪnɪt] *n (cupboard)* armoire *f*; *(for display)* vitrine *f*; **(filing) c.** classeur *m (meuble)*

**cabinet**[2] ['kæbɪnɪt] *n (government ministers)* gouvernement *m*; **c. minister** ministre *m*

**cable** ['keɪbəl] **1** *n* câble *m*; **c. car** *(with overhead cable)* téléphérique *m*; **c. television** la télévision par câble **2** *vt (message)* câbler (**to** à)

**cactus** ['kæktəs] (*pl* **-ti** [-taɪ] *or* **-tuses** [-təsɪz]) *n* cactus *m*

**caddie** ['kædɪ] *n Golf* caddie *m*

**cadet** [kə'det] *n* élève *m* officier

**cadge** [kædʒ] *vt Fam* **to c. money from** *or* **off sb** taper qn

**café** ['kæfeɪ] *n* café *m*

**caffeine** ['kæfiːn] *n* caféine *f*

**cage** [keɪdʒ] **1** *n* cage *f* **2** *vt* **to c. (up)** mettre en cage

**cajole** [kə'dʒəʊl] *vt* enjôler

**cake** [keɪk] *n* gâteau *m*; *(small)* pâtisserie *f*

**calamity** [kə'læmɪtɪ] (*pl* **-ies**) *n* calamité *f*

**calculate** ['kælkjʊleɪt] *vti* calculer; **to c. that...** *(estimate)* calculer que... ▪ **calculated** *adj (deliberate)* délibéré; **a c. risk** un risque calculé ▪ **calculation** [-'leɪʃən] *n* calcul *m* ▪ **calculator** *n* calculatrice *f*

**calendar** ['kælɪndə(r)] *n* calendrier *m*; *Am (for engagements)* agenda *m*; **c. month** mois *m* civil

**calf** [kɑːf] (*pl* **calves**) *n* (**a**) *(animal)* veau *m* (**b**) *(part of leg)* mollet *m*

**calibre** ['kælɪbə(r)] (*Am* **caliber**) *n* calibre *m*

**call** [kɔːl] **1** *n (shout)* cri *m*; *(visit)* visite *f*; **(telephone) c.** appel *m* (téléphonique); **to make a c.** téléphoner (**to** à); **to give sb a c.** téléphoner à qn; *Br* **c. box** cabine *f* téléphonique; **c. centre** centre *m* d'appels

**2** *vt (phone)* appeler; *(shout to)* crier; **he's called David** il s'appelle David; **to c. sb a liar** traiter qn de menteur

**3** *vi* appeler; *(cry out)* crier; *(visit)* passer

▸ **call back 1** *vt sep* rappeler **2** *vi* rappeler

▸ **call by** *vi (visit)* passer

▸ **call for** *vt insep (require)* demander; *(collect)* passer prendre

▸ **call in 1** *vt sep (into room)* faire entrer; *(police)* appeler **2** *vi* **to c. in (on sb)** *(visit)* passer (chez qn)

▸ **call off** *vt sep (cancel)* annuler; *(strike)* mettre fin à

▸ **call on** *vt insep (visit)* passer voir; **to c. on sb to do** *(urge)* sommer qn de faire

▸ **call out 1** *vt sep (shout)* crier; *(doctor)* appeler; *(workers)* donner une consigne de grève à **2** *vi (shout)* crier; **to c. out to sb** interpeller qn

▸ **call round** *vi (visit)* passer

▸**call up** *vt sep (phone)* appeler; *Mil (recruits)* appeler (sous les drapeaux)

**caller** ['kɔːlə(r)] *n* visiteur, -euse *mf*; *(on phone)* correspondant, -e *mf*

**callous** ['kæləs] *adj (cruel)* insensible

**calm** [kɑːm] **1** (**-er, -est**) *adj* calme, tranquille; **keep c.!** restez calme! **2** *n* calme *m* **3** *vt* **to c. (down)** calmer **4** *vi* **to c. down** se calmer ▪ **calmly** *adv* calmement

**calorie** ['kælərɪ] *n* calorie *f*

**calves** [kɑːvz] *pl of* **calf**

**camcorder** ['kæmkɔːdə(r)] *n* caméscope® *m*

**came** [keɪm] *pt of* **come**

**camel** ['kæməl] *n* chameau *m*

**camera** ['kæmrə] *n* appareil photo *m*; *(for film, video)* caméra *f*

**camouflage** ['kæməflɑːʒ] **1** *n* camouflage *m* **2** *vt also Fig* camoufler

**camp**[1] [kæmp] **1** *n* camp *m*, campement *m*; **c. bed** lit *m* de camp **2** *vi* **to c. (out)** camper ▪ **camper** *n (person)* campeur, -euse *mf*; *(vehicle)* camping-car *m* ▪ **camping** *n* camping *m*; **c. site** (terrain *m* de) camping *m* ▪ **campsite** *n* camping *m*

**camp**[2] [kæmp] *adj (effeminate)* efféminé

**campaign** [kæm'peɪn] **1** *n (political, military)* campagne *f*; **press/publicity c.** campagne *f* de presse/publicité **2** *vi* faire campagne (**for/against** pour/contre) ▪ **campaigner** *n* militant, -e *mf* (**for** pour)

**campus** ['kæmpəs] *n (of university)* campus *m*

**CAN**[1] [kæn, *unstressed* kən] (*pt* **could**)

> Le verbe **can** n'a ni infinitif, ni gérondif, ni participe. Pour exprimer l'infinitif ou le participe, on aura recours à la forme correspondante de **be able to** (he wanted to be able to speak English; she has always been able to swim). La forme négative est **can't**, qui s'écrit **cannot** dans la langue soutenue.

*v aux (be able to)* pouvoir; *(know how to)* savoir; **he couldn't help me** il ne pouvait pas m'aider; **she c. swim** elle sait nager; **he could do it tomorrow** il pourrait le faire demain; **he could have done it** il aurait pu le faire; **you could be wrong** *(possibility)* tu as peut-être tort; **he can't be dead** *(probability)* il ne peut pas être mort; **c. I come in?** *(permission)* puis-je entrer?; **yes, you c.!** oui!

---

**can**[2] [kæn] **1** *n (for food)* boîte *f*; *(for beer)* can(n)ette *f* **2** (*pt & pp* **-nn-**) *vt* mettre en boîte ▪ **canned** *adj* en boîte, en conserve; **c. beer** bière *f* en can(n)ette; **c. food** conserves *fpl* ▪ **can-opener** *n* ouvre-boîtes *m inv*

**Canada** ['kænədə] *n* le Canada ▪ **Canadian 1** *adj* canadien, -enne **2** *n* Canadien, -enne *mf*

**canal** [kə'næl] *n* canal *m*

**canary** [kə'neərɪ] (*pl* **-ies**) *n* canari *m*

**cancel** ['kænsəl] **1** (*Br* **-ll-**, *Am* **-l-**) *vt (flight, appointment)* annuler; *(goods, taxi)* décommander; *(train)* supprimer **2** *vi* se décommander ▪ **cancellation** [-'leɪʃən] *n* annulation *f*; *(of train)* suppression *f*

**cancer** ['kænsə(r)] *n* cancer *m*; **stomach/skin c.** cancer *m* de l'estomac/la peau

**candid** ['kændɪd] *adj* franc (*f* franche)

**candidate** ['kændɪdeɪt] *n* candidat, -e *mf* (**for** à)

**candle** ['kændəl] *n (made of wax)* bougie *f*; *(in church)* cierge *m* ▪ **candlelight** *n* **to have dinner by c.** dîner aux chandelles ▪ **candlestick** *n* bougeoir *m*; *(taller)* chandelier *m*

**candy** ['kændɪ] (*pl* **-ies**) *n Am* bonbon *m*; *(sweets)* bonbons *mpl*; **c. store** confiserie *f* ▪ **candyfloss** *n Br* barbe *f* à papa

**cane** [keɪn] **1** *n (stick)* canne *f*; *(for punishment)* baguette *f* **2** *vt (punish)* frapper avec une baguette

**canine** ['keɪnaɪn] *adj (tooth, race)* canin

**canister** ['kænɪstə(r)] *n* boîte *f* (en métal)

**cannabis** ['kænəbɪs] *n (drug)* cannabis *m*

**cannon** ['kænən] *(pl* **-s** *or* **cannon)** *n* canon *m*
**cannot** ['kænɒt] = **can not**
**canoe** [kə'nu:] *n* canoë *m*; *(dugout)* pirogue *f* ▪ **canoeing** *n* **to go c.** faire du canoë-kayak
**canopy** ['kænəpɪ] *(pl* **-ies)** *n (awning)* auvent *m*; *(made of glass)* marquise *f*
**can't** [kɑ:nt] = **can not**
**canteen** [kæn'ti:n] *n (in school, factory)* cantine *f*; *Br* **c. of cutlery** ménagère *f*
**canvas** ['kænvəs] *n* (**a**) *(cloth)* (grosse) toile *f*; *(for embroidery)* canevas *m* (**b**) *(painting)* toile *f*
**canvass** ['kænvəs] *vt (opinions)* sonder; **to c. sb** *(seek votes)* solliciter le suffrage de qn; *(seek orders)* solliciter des commandes de qn ▪ **canvassing** *n (for orders)* démarchage *m*; *(for votes)* démarchage *m* électoral
**canyon** ['kænjən] *n* cañon *m*, canyon *m*
**cap¹** [kæp] *n* (**a**) *(hat)* casquette *f*; *(for shower, of sailor)* bonnet *m*; *(of soldier)* képi *m* (**b**) *(of tube, valve)* bouchon *m*; *(of bottle)* capsule *f*; *(of pen)* capuchon *m* (**c**) *(of child's gun)* amorce *f*
**cap²** [kæp] *(pt & pp* **-pp-**) *vt* (**a**) *(outdo)* surpasser (**b**) *Br (spending)* limiter
**capable** ['keɪpəbəl] *adj (person)* capable (**of sth** de qch; **of doing sth** de faire qch) ▪ **capability** *n* capacité *f*
**capacity** [kə'pæsətɪ] *(pl* **-ies)** *n (of container)* capacité *f*; *(ability)* aptitude *f*, capacité *f* (**for sth** pour qch; **for doing sth** à faire qch); *(output)* rendement *m*; **in my c. as a doctor** en ma qualité de médecin
**cape** [keɪp] *n (cloak)* cape *f*; *(of cyclist)* pèlerine *f*
**capital** ['kæpɪtəl] **1** *adj (letter, importance)* capital; **c. punishment** peine *f* capitale **2** *n* (**a**) **c. (city)** capitale *f*; **c. (letter)** majuscule *f* (**b**) *(money)* capital *m* ▪ **capitalism** *n* capitalisme *m* ▪ **capitalist** *adj & n* capitaliste *(mf)* ▪ **capitalize** *vi* **to c. on** tirer parti de
**capsize** [kæp'saɪz] **1** *vt* faire chavirer **2** *vi* chavirer
**capsule** [*Br* 'kæpsju:l, *Am* 'kæpsəl] *n (of medicine)* gélule *f*; **(space) c.** capsule *f* spatiale
**captain** ['kæptɪn] **1** *n* capitaine *m* **2** *vt (ship)* commander; *(team)* être le capitaine de
**caption** ['kæpʃən] *n (of illustration)* légende *f*; *(of film, article)* sous-titre *m*
**captivate** ['kæptɪveɪt] *vt* captiver
**captive** ['kæptɪv] *n* captif, -ive *mf* ▪ **captivity** *n* **in c.** en captivité
**capture** ['kæptʃə(r)] **1** *n* capture *f*; *(of town)* prise *f* **2** *vt (person, animal)* capturer; *(escaped prisoner or animal)* reprendre; *(town)* prendre; *Fig (mood)* rendre
**car** [kɑ:(r)] *n* voiture *f*, automobile *f*; *(train carriage)* wagon *m*, voiture *f*; **c. insurance/industry** assurance *f*/industrie *f* automobile; **the c. door** la portière de la voiture; **c. crash** accident *m* de voiture; **c. ferry** ferry *m*; *Br* **c. hire** location *f* de voitures; *Br* **c. park** parking *m*; **c. phone** téléphone *m* de voiture; **c. radio** autoradio *m*; **c. rental** location *f* de voitures; **c. wash** *(machine)* = station de lavage automatique pour voitures ▪ **carport** *n* abri *m* pour voiture
**carafe** [kə'ræf] *n* carafe *f*
**caramel** ['kærəməl] *n* caramel *m*
**carat** ['kærət] *n* carat *m*; **18-c. gold** or *m* (à) 18 carats
**caravan** ['kærəvæn] *n* caravane *f*; *(horse-drawn)* roulotte *f*; **c. site** camping *m* pour caravanes
**carbohydrates** [kɑ:bəʊ'haɪdreɪts] *npl* hydrates *mpl* de carbone; *(in food)* glucides *mpl*
**carbon** ['kɑ:bən] *n* carbone *m*; **c. dioxide** dioxyde *m* de carbone, gaz *m* carbonique
**card** [kɑ:d] *n* carte *f*; *(cardboard)* carton *m*; **(index) c.** fiche *f*; **to play cards** jouer aux cartes ▪ **cardboard** *n* carton *m*; **c. box** boîte *f* en carton, carton *m* ▪ **cardphone** *n* téléphone *m* à carte
**cardigan** ['kɑ:dɪgən] *n* cardigan *m*
**cardinal** ['kɑ:dɪnəl] *n Rel* cardinal *m*

**care** [keə(r)] **1** *n (attention)* soin *m*; *(protection)* soins *mpl*; *(worry)* souci *m*; **to take c. to do** veiller à faire; **to take c. not to do** faire attention à ne pas faire; **to take c. of sb/sth** s'occuper de qn/qch; **to take c. of oneself** *(manage)* savoir se débrouiller tout seul; *(keep healthy)* faire bien attention à soi; **take c.!** *(goodbye)* au revoir!; **'c. of'** *(on envelope)* 'chez'

**2** *vt* **I don't c. what he says** peu m'importe ce qu'il en dit

**3** *vi* **I don't c.** ça m'est égal; **who cares?** qu'est-ce que ça peut faire?; **to c. about** *(feel concern about)* se soucier de; **to c. about** *or* **for sb** *(be fond of)* avoir de la sympathie pour qn; **to c. for sb** *(look after)* soigner qn

**career** [kə'rɪə(r)] **1** *n* carrière *f* **2** *vi* **to c. along** aller à vive allure

**carefree** ['keəfriː] *adj* insouciant

**careful** ['keəfəl] *adj (exact, thorough)* soigneux, -euse (**about** de); *(cautious)* prudent; **to be c. of** *or* **with sth** faire attention à qch; **be c.!** (fais) attention! ▪ **carefully** *adv (thoroughly)* avec soin; *(cautiously)* prudemment

**careless** ['keələs] *adj* négligent; *(work)* peu soigné; **c. mistake** faute *f* d'étourderie ▪ **carelessness** *n* négligence *f*

**carer** ['keərə(r)] *n (relative)* = personne s'occupant d'un parent malade ou âgé

**caress** [kə'res] **1** *n* caresse *f* **2** *vt* caresser

**caretaker** ['keəteɪkə(r)] *n* gardien, -enne *mf*, concierge *mf*

**cargo** ['kɑːgəʊ] (*pl* **-oes** *or* **-os**) *n* cargaison *f*; **c. ship** cargo *m*

**Caribbean** [*Br* kærɪ'biːən, *Am* kə'rɪbɪən] **1** *adj* caraïbe **2** *n* **the C. (islands)** les Antilles *fpl*

**caricature** ['kærɪkətʃʊə(r)] **1** *n* caricature *f* **2** *vt* caricaturer

**caring** ['keərɪŋ] *adj (loving)* aimant; *(understanding)* très humain

**carnation** [kɑː'neɪʃən] *n* œillet *m*

**carnival** ['kɑːnɪvəl] *n* carnaval *m* (*pl* -als)

**carol** ['kærəl] *n* chant *m* de Noël

**carp** [kɑːp] **1** *n inv (fish)* carpe *f* **2** *vi* se plaindre (**at** de)

**carpenter** ['kɑːpɪntə(r)] *n (for house building)* charpentier *m*; *(for light woodwork)* menuisier *m* ▪ **carpentry** *n* charpenterie *f*; *(light woodwork)* menuiserie *f*

**carpet** ['kɑːpɪt] **1** *n (rug)* tapis *m*; *(fitted)* moquette *f* **2** *vt* recouvrir d'un tapis/d'une moquette

**carriage** ['kærɪdʒ] *n Br (of train)* voiture *f*; *(horse-drawn)* voiture *f*, équipage *m*; *Br (transport of goods)* transport *m*; *(cost)* frais *mpl*; *(of typewriter)* chariot *m* ▪ **carriageway** *n Br* chaussée *f*

**carrier** ['kærɪə(r)] *n (company, airline)* transporteur *m*; *Br* **c. (bag)** sac *m* en plastique

**carrot** ['kærət] *n* carotte *f*

**carry** ['kærɪ] (*pt & pp* **-ied**) **1** *vt* porter; *(goods, passengers)* transporter; *(gun, money)* avoir sur soi; *Math (in calculation)* retenir **2** *vi (of sound)* porter

▸ **carry away** *vt sep* emporter; **to be** *or* **get carried away** *(excited)* s'emballer

▸ **carry back** *vt sep (thing)* rapporter; *(person)* ramener

▸ **carry forward** *vt sep (in bookkeeping)* reporter

▸ **carry off** *vt sep (take away)* emporter

▸ **carry on 1** *vt sep (continue)* continuer (**doing** à faire); *(negotiations)* mener; *(conversation)* poursuivre **2** *vi (continue)* continuer; *Pej (behave badly)* se conduire mal; **to c. on with sth** continuer qch

▸ **carry out** *vt sep (plan, promise)* mettre à exécution; *(order)* exécuter; *(repair, reform)* effectuer; *(duty)* accomplir; *Am (meal)* emporter

▸ **carry through** *vt sep (plan)* mener à bien

**carrycot** ['kærɪkɒt] *n Br* porte-bébé *m inv*

**cart** [kɑːt] **1** *n (horse-drawn)* charrette

*f*; *(handcart)* voiture *f* à bras; *Am (in supermarket)* Caddie® *m* **2** *vt Fam* **to c. (around)** trimbaler

**carton** ['kɑːtən] *n (box)* carton *m*; *(of milk, fruit juice)* brique *f*; *(of cigarettes)* cartouche *f*; *(of cream)* pot *m*

**cartoon** [kɑː'tuːn] *n (in newspaper)* dessin *m* humoristique; *(film)* dessin *m* animé; **c. (strip)** bande *f* dessinée

**cartridge** ['kɑːtrɪdʒ] *n* cartouche *f*

**carve** [kɑːv] *vt (cut)* tailler (**out of** dans); *(name)* graver; *(sculpt)* sculpter; **to c. (up)** *(meat)* découper ■ **carving 1** *adj* **c. knife** couteau *m* à découper **2** *n* **(wood) c.** sculpture *f* sur bois

**cascade** [kæs'keɪd] *vi* tomber en cascade

**case**[1] [keɪs] *n (instance, situation) & Med* cas *m*; *Law* affaire *f*; *Fig (arguments)* arguments *mpl*; **in any c.** en tout cas; **in c. it rains** au cas où il pleuvrait; **in c. of** en cas de

**case**[2] [keɪs] *n (bag)* valise *f*; *(crate)* caisse *f*; *(for pen, glasses, camera, violin, cigarettes)* étui *m*; *(for jewels)* écrin *m*

**cash** [kæʃ] **1** *n (coins, banknotes)* liquide *m*; *Fam (money)* sous *mpl*; **to pay (in) c.** payer en liquide; **c. box** caisse *f*; *Br* **c. desk** caisse *f*; **c. dispenser** *or* **machine** distributeur *m* de billets; **c. price** prix *m* (au) comptant; **c. register** caisse *f* enregistreuse **2** *vt* **to c. a cheque** *or Am* **check** *(of person)* encaisser un chèque; *(of bank)* payer un chèque

**cashew** ['kæʃuː] *n* **c. (nut)** noix *f* de cajou

**cashier** [kæ'ʃɪə(r)] *n* caissier, -ère *mf*

**casino** [kə'siːnəʊ] (*pl* **-os**) *n* casino *m*

**casket** ['kɑːskɪt] *n (box)* coffret *m*; *(coffin)* cercueil *m*

**casserole** ['kæsərəʊl] *n (covered dish)* cocotte *f*; *(stew)* ragoût *m*

**cassette** [kə'set] *n (audio, video)* cassette *f*; *(for camera)* cartouche *f*; **c. player** lecteur *m* de cassettes; **c. recorder** magnétophone *m* à cassettes

**cast** [kɑːst] **1** *n (actors)* acteurs *mpl*; *(list of actors)* distribution *f*; *Med* **in a c.** dans le plâtre **2** (*pt & pp* **cast**) *vt (throw)* jeter; *(light, shadow)* projeter; *(glance)* jeter (**at** à *ou* sur); **to c. doubt on sth** jeter le doute sur qch; **c. iron** fonte *f* ■ **cast-iron** *adj (pan)* en fonte; *Fig (alibi, excuse)* en béton

**caster** ['kɑːstə(r)] *n (wheel)* roulette *f*; *Br* **c. sugar** sucre *m* en poudre

**castle** ['kɑːsəl] *n* château *m*; *(in chess)* tour *f*

**castoffs** ['kɑːstɒfs] *npl* vieux vêtements *mpl*

**castrate** [kæ'streɪt] *vt* châtrer

**casual** ['kæʒjʊəl] *adj (offhand) (remark, glance)* en passant; *(relaxed, informal)* décontracté; *(conversation)* à bâtons rompus; *(clothes)* sport *inv*; *(careless)* désinvolte; *(employment, worker)* temporaire ■ **casually** *adv (remark, glance)* en passant; *(informally)* avec décontraction; *(dress)* sport; *(carelessly)* avec désinvolture

**casualty** ['kæʒjʊəltɪ] (*pl* **-ies**) *n* victime *f*; *Br* **c. (department)** *(in hospital)* (service *m* des) urgences *fpl*

**cat** [kæt] *n* chat *m*; *(female)* chatte *f*

**catalogue** ['kætəlɒg] (*Am* **catalog**) **1** *n* catalogue *m* **2** *vt* cataloguer

**catalyst** ['kætəlɪst] *n Chem & Fig* catalyseur *m*

**catapult** ['kætəpʌlt] **1** *n (toy)* lance-pierres *m inv* **2** *vt* catapulter

**catastrophe** [kə'tæstrəfɪ] *n* catastrophe *f*

**catch** [kætʃ] **1** *n (in fishing)* prise *f*; *(of a whole day)* pêche *f*; *(difficulty)* piège *m*; *(on door)* loquet *m*

**2** (*pt & pp* **caught**) *vt (ball, thief, illness)* attraper; *(fish, train, bus)* prendre; *(grab)* prendre, saisir; *(surprise)* surprendre; *(understand)* saisir; *(garment)* accrocher (**on** à); **to c. sb's eye** *or* **attention** attirer l'attention de qn; **to c. sight of sb/sth** apercevoir qn/qch; **to c. fire** prendre feu; **to c. sb doing** surprendre qn à faire; **to c. sb out** prendre qn en défaut; **to c. sb up** rattraper qn

**3** *vi* **her skirt (got) caught in the door** sa jupe s'est prise dans la porte; **to c. up with sb** rattraper qn ▪ **catching** *adj (illness)* contagieux, -euse

**catchy** ['kætʃɪ] (**-ier, -iest**) *adj (tune, slogan)* facile à retenir

**category** ['kætɪgərɪ] (*pl* **-ies**) *n* catégorie *f* ▪ **categorical** *adj* catégorique

**cater** ['keɪtə(r)] *vi (provide food)* s'occuper des repas (**for** pour); **to c. to,** *Br* **to c. for** *(need, taste)* satisfaire ▪ **caterer** *n* traiteur *m* ▪ **catering** *n* restauration *f*; **to do the c.** s'occuper des repas

**caterpillar** ['kætəpɪlə(r)] *n* chenille *f*

**cathedral** [kə'θiːdrəl] *n* cathédrale *f*

**Catholic** ['kæθlɪk] *adj & n* catholique *(mf)*

**cattle** ['kætəl] *npl* bétail *m*

**caught** [kɔːt] *pt & pp of* **catch**

**cauliflower** ['kɒlɪflaʊə(r)] *n* chou-fleur *m*

**cause** [kɔːz] **1** *n (origin, ideal) & Law* cause *f*; *(reason)* raison *f*, motif *m* (**of** de) **2** *vt* causer, occasionner; **to c. trouble for sb** créer *ou* causer des ennuis à qn

**caution** ['kɔːʃən] **1** *n (care)* prudence *f*; *(warning)* avertissement *m* **2** *vt (warn)* avertir; *Sport* donner un avertissement à ▪ **cautious** *adj* prudent

**cavalry** ['kævəlrɪ] *n* cavalerie *f*

**cave** [keɪv] **1** *n* grotte *f* **2** *vi* **to c. in** *(of ceiling)* s'effondrer; *(of floor)* s'affaisser

**cavern** ['kævən] *n* caverne *f*

**cavity** ['kævɪtɪ] (*pl* **-ies**) *n* cavité *f*

**CD** [siː'diː] (*abbr* **compact disc**) *n* CD *m*; **CD player** lecteur *m* de CD

**CD-ROM** [siːdiː'rɒm] (*abbr* **compact disc read-only memory**) *n Comptr* CD-ROM *m inv*

**cease** [siːs] **1** *vt* cesser (**doing** de faire) **2** *vi* cesser ▪ **cease-fire** *n* cessez-le-feu *m inv* ▪ **ceaseless** *adj* incessant

**cedar** ['siːdə(r)] *n (tree, wood)* cèdre *m*

**ceiling** ['siːlɪŋ] *n (of room) & Fig (limit)* plafond *m*

**celebrate** ['selɪbreɪt] **1** *vt (event)* célébrer, fêter; *(mass)* célébrer **2** *vi* faire la fête ▪ **celebration** [-'breɪʃən] *n (event)* fête *f*; **the celebrations** les festivités *fpl*

**celebrity** [sə'lebrətɪ] (*pl* **-ies**) *n* célébrité *f*

**celery** ['selərɪ] *n* céleri *m*

**celibate** ['selɪbət] *adj* **to be c.** ne pas avoir de rapports sexuels; *(by choice)* être chaste

**cell** [sel] *n* cellule *f*; *El* élément *m*

**cellar** ['selə(r)] *n* cave *f*

**cello** ['tʃeləʊ] (*pl* **-os**) *n* violoncelle *m*

**cellophane®** ['seləfeɪn] *n* Cellophane®*f*

**cellphone** ['selfəʊn] *n Am* (téléphone *m*) portable *m*

**cellular** ['seljʊlə(r)] *adj* cellulaire; **c. phone** téléphone *m* cellulaire

**Celsius** ['selsɪəs] *adj* Celsius *inv*

**cement** [sɪ'ment] **1** *n* ciment *m*; **c. mixer** bétonnière *f* **2** *vt also Fig* cimenter

**cemetery** ['semətrɪ] (*pl* **-ies**) *n* cimetière *m*

**censor** ['sensə(r)] **1** *n* censeur *m* **2** *vt* censurer ▪ **censorship** *n* censure *f*

**census** ['sensəs] *n* recensement *m*

**cent** [sent] *n (coin)* cent *m*

**centenary** [*Br* sen'tiːnərɪ, *Am* sen'tenərɪ] (*pl* **-ies**) *n* centenaire *m*

**center** ['sentə(r)] *n Am* = **centre**

**centigrade** ['sentɪgreɪd] *adj* centigrade

**centimetre** ['sentɪmiːtə(r)] *n* centimètre *m*

**central** ['sentrəl] *adj* central; **C. London** le centre de Londres; **c. heating** chauffage *m* central ▪ **centralize** *vt* centraliser

**centre** ['sentə(r)] (*Am* **center**) **1** *n* centre *m*; *Football* **c. forward** avant-centre *m* **2** *vt (attention, interest)* concentrer (**on** sur)

**century** ['sentʃərɪ] (*pl* **-ies**) *n* siècle *m*; **in the twenty-first c.** au vingt et unième siècle

**ceramic** [sə'ræmɪk] *adj (tile)* en céramique

**cereal** ['sɪərɪəl] *n* céréale *f*; **(breakfast) c.** céréales *fpl (pour le petit déjeuner)*

**ceremony** ['serɪmənɪ] (*pl* **-ies**) *n (event)* cérémonie *f*

**certain** ['sɜːtən] *adj* (**a**) *(sure)* certain (**that** que); **she's c. to come, she'll come for c.** c'est certain qu'elle viendra; **to be c. of sth** être certain *ou* sûr de qch; **for c.** *(say, know)* avec certitude (**b**) *(particular, some)* certain; **c. people** certaines personnes ▪ **certainly** *adv (undoubtedly)* certainement; *(yes)* bien sûr ▪ **certainty** (*pl* **-ies**) *n* certitude *f*

**certificate** [sə'tɪfɪkɪt] *n* certificat *m*; *(from university)* diplôme *m*

**certify** ['sɜːtɪfaɪ] (*pt & pp* **-ied**) *vt (document, signature)* certifier; *Am* **certified letter** ≃ lettre *f* recommandée; *Am* **certified public accountant** expert-comptable *m*

**chain** [tʃeɪn] **1** *n (of rings, mountains)* chaîne *f*; *(of events)* suite *f*; *(of lavatory)* chasse *f* d'eau; **c. reaction** réaction *f* en chaîne; **c. saw** tronçonneuse *f*; **c. store** magasin *m* à succursales multiples **2** *vt* **to c. (up)** *(dog)* mettre à l'attache ▪ **chain-smoker** *n* **to be a c.** fumer cigarette sur cigarette

**chair** [tʃeə(r)] **1** *n* chaise *f*; *(armchair)* fauteuil *m*; *Univ (of professor)* chaire *f*; **the c.** *(office of chairperson)* la présidence; **c. lift** télésiège *m* **2** *vt (meeting)* présider ▪ **chairman** (*pl* **-men**), ▪ **chairperson** *n* président, -e *mf*

**chalet** ['ʃæleɪ] *n* chalet *m*

**chalk** [tʃɔːk] **1** *n* craie *f* **2** *vt* marquer à la craie

**challenge** ['tʃælɪndʒ] **1** *n* défi *m*; *(task)* challenge *m*, gageure *f* **2** *vt* défier (**sb to do** qn de faire); *(question, dispute)* contester ▪ **challenger** *n Sport* challenger *m*

**chamber** ['tʃeɪmbə(r)] *n (room, assembly, of gun)* chambre *f*; **c. music/orchestra** musique *f*/orchestre *m* de chambre ▪ **chambermaid** *n* femme *f* de chambre

**champagne** [ʃæm'peɪn] *n* champagne *m*

**champion** ['tʃæmpɪən] **1** *n* champion, -onne *mf*; **c. skier, skiing c.** champion, -onne *mf* de ski **2** *vt (support)* se faire le champion de ▪ **championship** *n* championnat *m*

**chance** [tʃɑːns] **1** *n (luck)* hasard *m*; *(possibility)* chance *f*; *(opportunity)* occasion *f*; *(risk)* risque *m*; **by c.** par hasard; **to have the c. to do sth** *or* **of doing sth** avoir l'occasion de faire qch; **to give sb a c.** donner une chance à qn; **to take a c.** tenter le coup **2** *adj (remark)* fait au hasard **3** *vt* **to c. it** risquer le coup

**chancellor** ['tʃɑːnsələ(r)] *n Pol* chancelier *m*

**chandelier** [ʃændə'lɪə(r)] *n* lustre *m*

**change** [tʃeɪndʒ] **1** *n* changement *m*; *(money)* monnaie *f*; **for a c.** pour changer; **a c. of clothes** des vêtements de rechange

**2** *vt (modify)* changer; *(exchange)* échanger (**for** pour *ou* contre); *(money)* changer (**into** en); *(transform)* changer, transformer (**into** en); **to c. trains/colour/one's skirt** changer de train/de couleur/de jupe; **to c. gear** *(in vehicle)* changer de vitesse; **to c. the subject** changer de sujet; **to get changed** *(put on other clothes)* se changer

**3** *vi (alter)* changer; *(change clothes)* se changer; **to c. into sth** *(be transformed)* se changer *ou* se transformer en qch; **she changed into a dress** elle a mis une robe; **to c. over** passer (**from** de; **to** à) ▪ **changeable** *adj (weather, mood)* changeant ▪ **changeover** *n* passage *m* (**from** de; **to** à)

**changing** ['tʃeɪndʒɪŋ] *n* **c. room** vestiaire *m*; *(in shop)* cabine *f* d'essayage

**channel** ['tʃænəl] **1** *n (on television)* chaîne *f*; *(for boats)* chenal *m*; *(groove)* rainure *f*; *(of communication, distribution)* canal *m*; *Geog* **the C.** la Manche; **the C. Islands** les îles Anglo-Normandes; **the C. Tunnel** le tunnel sous la Manche **2** (*Br* **-ll-**, *Am* **-l-**) *vt (energies, crowd, money)* canaliser (**into** vers)

**chant** [tʃɑːnt] **1** *vt (slogan)* scander **2** *vi (of demonstrators)* scander des slogans

**chaos** ['keɪɒs] *n* chaos *m* ▪ **chaotic** *adj (situation, scene)* chaotique

**chapel** ['tʃæpəl] *n* chapelle *f*; *(nonconformist church)* temple *m*

**chaplain** ['tʃæplɪn] *n* aumônier *m*

**chapped** ['tʃæpt] *adj (hands, lips)* gercé

**chapter** ['tʃæptə(r)] *n* chapitre *m*

**character** ['kærɪktə(r)] *n* (**a**) *(of person, place)* caractère *m*; *(in book, film)* personnage *m*; *(person)* individu *m*; *(unusual person)* personnage *m* (**b**) *(letter)* caractère *m* ▪ **characteristic** *adj & n* caractéristique *(f)*

**charcoal** ['tʃɑːkəʊl] *n Art* fusain *m*

**charge**[1] [tʃɑːdʒ] **1** *n (in battle)* charge *f*; *Law* chef *m* d'accusation; *(care)* garde *f*; **to take c. of sth** prendre qch en charge; **to be in c. of** être responsable de **2** *vt (battery, soldiers)* charger; *Law (accuse)* inculper (**with** de) **3** *vi (rush)* se précipiter; *(soldiers)* charger ▪ **charger** *n (for battery)* chargeur *m*

**charge**[2] [tʃɑːdʒ] **1** *n (cost)* prix *m*; **charges** *(expenses)* frais *mpl* **2** *vt (amount)* demander (**for** pour); **to c. sb** faire payer qn

**charity** ['tʃærɪtɪ] (*pl* **-ies**) *n (kindness, alms)* charité *f*; *(society)* œuvre *f* de charité

**charm** [tʃɑːm] **1** *n (attractiveness)* charme *m*; *(trinket)* breloque *f* **2** *vt* charmer ▪ **charming** *adj* charmant

**chart** [tʃɑːt] *n (map)* carte *f*; *(table)* tableau *m*; *(graph)* graphique *m*; **(pop) charts** hit-parade *m*

**charter** ['tʃɑːtə(r)] *n (aircraft)* charter *m*; **c. flight** vol *m* charter ▪ **chartered accountant** *n Br* expert-comptable *m*

**chase** [tʃeɪs] **1** *n* poursuite *f* **2** *vt* poursuivre; **to c. sb away** *or* **off** chasser qn **3** *vi* **to c. after sb/sth** courir après qn/qch

**chasm** ['kæzəm] *n also Fig* abîme *m*, gouffre *m*

**chassis** ['ʃæsɪ] *n (of vehicle)* châssis *m*

**chaste** [tʃeɪst] *adj* chaste

**chat** [tʃæt] **1** *n* petite conversation *f*; *Comptr* bavardage *m*; **to have a c.** causer (**with** avec); *Comptr* **c. room** site *m* de bavardage **2** (*pt & pp* **-tt-**) *vi* causer (**with** avec); *Comptr* bavarder **3** *vt Br Fam* **to c. sb up** draguer qn

**chatter** ['tʃætə(r)] **1** *n* bavardage *m* **2** *vi (of person)* bavarder; **his teeth were chattering** il claquait des dents

**chatty** ['tʃætɪ] (**-ier, -iest**) *adj (person)* bavard; *(letter)* plein de détails

**chauffeur** ['ʃəʊfə(r)] *n* chauffeur *m*

**chauvinist** ['ʃəʊvɪnɪst] *n Pej* **(male) c.** macho *m*, phallocrate *m*

**cheap** [tʃiːp] **1** (**-er, -est**) *adj* bon marché *inv*, pas cher (*f* pas chère); *(rate, fare)* réduit; *(worthless)* sans valeur; *(vulgar)* de mauvais goût; **cheaper** meilleur marché *inv*, moins cher (*f* moins chère) **2** *adv (buy)* (à) bon marché, au rabais ▪ **cheaply** *adv* (à) bon marché

**cheat** [tʃiːt] **1** *n (at games)* tricheur, -euse *mf*; *(crook)* escroc *m* **2** *vt (deceive)* tromper; *(defraud)* frauder; **to c. sb out of sth** escroquer qch à qn **3** *vi (at games)* tricher

**check**[1] [tʃek] *n* **c. (pattern)** carreaux *mpl* ▪ **checked** *adj (patterned)* à carreaux

**check**[2] [tʃek] **1** *n* vérification *f* (**on** de); *(inspection)* contrôle *m*; *(in chess)* échec *m*; *Am (tick)* ≃ croix *f*; *Am (receipt)* reçu *m*; *Am (restaurant bill)* addition *f*; *Am (cheque)* chèque *m*; **to keep a c. on sth** contrôler qch

**2** *vt (examine)* vérifier; *(inspect)* contrôler; *(mark off)* cocher; *Am (baggage)* mettre à la consigne

**3** *vi* vérifier; **to c. on sth** vérifier qch; **to c. on sb** surveiller qn ▪ **checkbook** *n Am* carnet *m* de chèques ▪ **check-in** *n (at airport)* enregistrement *m* (des bagages) ▪ **checklist** *n* liste *f* de contrôle; *Aviat* check-list *f* ▪ **checkout** *n (in supermarket)* caisse *f* ▪ **checkpoint** *n* poste *m* de contrôle ▪ **checkroom** *n Am* vestiaire *m*; *Am (left-luggage office)* consigne *f* ▪ **checkup** *n (medical)* bilan *m* de santé; **to have a c.** faire un bilan de santé

▸**check in 1** *vt sep (luggage)* enregistrer **2** *vi (arrive)* arriver; *(sign in)* signer le registre; *(at airport)* se présenter à l'enregistrement

▸**check out 1** *vt sep (confirm)* confirmer **2** *vi (at hotel)* régler sa note

▸**check up** *vi* vérifier

**checkers** ['tʃekərz] *npl Am* jeu *m* de dames

**cheddar** ['tʃedə(r)] *n* cheddar *m (fromage)*

**cheek** [tʃi:k] *n* joue *f*; *Br (impudence)* culot *m* ▪ **cheeky** (**-ier, -iest**) *adj Br (person, reply)* insolent

**cheer** [tʃɪə(r)] **1** *n* **cheers** *(shouts)* acclamations *fpl*; *Fam* **cheers!** *(when drinking)* à votre santé!; *(thanks)* merci! **2** *vt (applaud)* acclamer; **to c. sb up** *(comfort)* remonter le moral à qn; *(amuse)* faire sourire qn **3** *vi* applaudir; **to c. up** reprendre courage; **c. up!** (du) courage! ▪ **cheering** *n (shouts)* acclamations *fpl*

**cheerful** ['tʃɪəfəl] *adj* gai

**cheerio** [tʃɪərɪ'əʊ] *exclam Br* salut!, au revoir!

**cheese** [tʃi:z] *n* fromage *m* ▪ **cheeseburger** *n* cheeseburger *m* ▪ **cheesecake** *n* cheesecake *m*, tarte *f* au fromage blanc

**chef** [ʃef] *n* chef *m* (cuisinier)

**chemical 1** *adj* chimique **2** *n* produit *m* chimique

**chemist** ['kemɪst] *n Br (pharmacist)* pharmacien, -enne *mf*; *(scientist)* chimiste *mf*; *Br* **c.'s (shop)** pharmacie *f* ▪ **chemistry** *n* chimie *f*

**cheque** [tʃek] *n Br* chèque *m*; **c. card** carte *f* d'identité bancaire *(sans laquelle un chéquier n'est pas valable)* ▪ **chequebook** *n Br* carnet *m* de chèques

**cherry** ['tʃerɪ] *(pl* **-ies***) n* cerise *f*

**chess** [tʃes] *n* échecs *mpl* ▪ **chessboard** *n* échiquier *m*

**chest** [tʃest] *n* (**a**) *(part of body)* poitrine *f*; *Fig* **to get it off one's c.** dire ce qu'on a sur le cœur (**b**) *(box)* coffre *m*; **c. of drawers** commode *f*

**chestnut** ['tʃestnʌt] **1** *n (nut)* châtaigne *f*; *(cooked)* marron *m* **2** *adj (hair)* châtain

**chew** [tʃu:] **1** *vt* **to c. (up)** mâcher **2** *vi* mastiquer; **chewing gum** chewing-gum *m*

**chewy** ['tʃu:ɪ] *adj (meat)* caoutchouteux, -euse; *(sweet)* mou (*f* molle)

**chick** [tʃɪk] *n (chicken)* poussin *m*

**chicken** ['tʃɪkɪn] **1** *n* poulet *m* **2** *vi Fam* **to c. out** se dégonfler ▪ **chickenpox** *n* varicelle *f*

**chickpea** ['tʃɪkpi:] *n* pois *m* chiche

**chief** [tʃi:f] **1** *n* chef *m*; *Fam (boss)* patron *m* **2** *adj (most important)* principal; *Com* **c. executive** directeur *m* général ▪ **chiefly** *adv* principalement, surtout

**chilblain** ['tʃɪlbleɪn] *n* engelure *f*

**child** [tʃaɪld] *(pl* **children***) n* enfant *mf*; **c. abuse** mauvais traitements *mpl* à enfant, maltraitance *f*; **c. care** *(for working parents)* crèches *fpl* et garderies *fpl*; *Br* **c. minder** assistante *f* maternelle ▪ **childhood** *n* enfance *f* ▪ **childish** *adj* puéril ▪ **childlike** *adj* enfantin ▪ **childproof** *adj (lock, bottle)* que les enfants ne peuvent pas ouvrir

**children** ['tʃɪldrən] *pl of* **child**

**chill** [tʃɪl] **1** *n* froid *m*; *(illness)* refroidissement *m*; **to catch a c.** prendre froid **2** *vt (wine, melon)* mettre au frais; *(meat)* réfrigérer

**chilli** ['tʃɪlɪ] *(pl* **-is** *or* **-ies***) n (vegetable)* piment *m*; *(dish)* chili *m* con carne; **c. powder** ≃ chili *m*

**chilly** ['tʃɪlɪ] (**-ier, -iest**) *adj* froid; **it's c.** il fait (un peu) froid

**chime** [tʃaɪm] *vi (of bell)* carillonner; *(of clock)* sonner

**chimney** ['tʃɪmnɪ] *(pl* **-eys***) n* cheminée *f*

**chimpanzee** [tʃɪmpæn'zi:] *n* chimpanzé *m*
**chin** [tʃɪn] *n* menton *m*
**China** ['tʃaɪnə] *n* la Chine ■ **Chinese 1** *adj* chinois **2** *n inv (person)* Chinois, -e *mf*; *(language)* chinois *m*
**china** ['tʃaɪnə] **1** *n inv* porcelaine *f* **2** *adj* en porcelaine
**chink** [tʃɪŋk] **1** *n (slit)* fente *f* **2** *vt* faire tinter
**chip** [tʃɪp] **1** *n (splinter)* éclat *m*; *(break)* ébréchure *f*; *(counter)* jeton *m*; *Comptr* puce *f*; **chips** *Br (French fries)* frites *fpl*; *Am (crisps)* chips *fpl*; *Br* **c. shop** = boutique où l'on vend du poisson pané et des frites **2** *(pt & pp* **-pp-**) *vt (cup)* ébrécher; *(paint)* écailler
**chiropodist** [kɪ'rɒpədɪst] *n Br* pédicure *mf*
**chirp** [tʃɜ:p] *vi (of bird)* pépier
**chisel** ['tʃɪzəl] **1** *n* ciseau *m* **2** (*Br* **-ll-**, *Am* **-l-**) *vt* ciseler
**chives** [tʃaɪvz] *npl* ciboulette *f*
**chlorine** ['klɒri:n] *n Chem* chlore *m*
**choc-ice** ['tʃɒkaɪs] *n Br* = glace individuelle enrobée de chocolat
**chocolate** ['tʃɒklɪt] **1** *n* chocolat *m*; **hot c.** chocolat *m* chaud; **plain c.** chocolat *m* à croquer **2** *adj (made of chocolate)* en chocolat; *(chocolate-flavoured)* au chocolat
**choice** [tʃɔɪs] *n* choix *m*; **to make a c.** choisir
**choir** ['kwaɪə(r)] *n* chœur *m* ■ **choirboy** *n* jeune choriste *m*
**choke** [tʃəʊk] **1** *n (of car)* starter *m* **2** *vt (strangle)* étrangler; *(clog)* boucher **3** *vi* **she choked on a fishbone** elle a failli s'étouffer avec une arête
**cholesterol** [kə'lestərɒl] *n* cholestérol *m*
**choose** [tʃu:z] **1** (*pt* **chose**, *pp* **chosen**) *vt* choisir; **to c. to do sth** choisir de faire qch **2** *vi* choisir ■ **choos(e)y** (**choosier, choosiest**) *adj Fam* difficile (**about** sur)
**chop** [tʃɒp] **1** *n (of lamb, pork)* côtelette *f* **2** *(pt & pp* **-pp-**) *vt (wood)* couper (à la hache); *(food)* couper en morceaux; *(finely)* hacher; **to c. down** *(tree)* abattre; **to c. off** *(branch, finger)* couper; **to c. up** couper en morceaux
**choppy** ['tʃɒpɪ] (**-ier, -iest**) *adj (sea)* agité
**chopsticks** ['tʃɒpstɪks] *npl* baguettes *fpl (pour manger)*
**choral** ['kɔ:rəl] *adj* choral
**chord** [kɔ:d] *n Mus* accord *m*
**chore** [tʃɔ:(r)] *n* corvée *f*; **(household) chores** travaux *mpl* du ménage
**chorus** ['kɔ:rəs] *n (of song)* refrain *m*; *(singers)* chœur *m*; *(dancers)* troupe *f*
**chose** [tʃəʊz] *pt of* **choose**
**chosen** ['tʃəʊzən] *pp of* **choose**
**Christ** [kraɪst] *n* le Christ ■ **Christian** *adj & n* chrétien, -enne *(mf)*; **C. name** prénom *m* ■ **Christianity** *n* christianisme *m*
**christen** ['krɪsən] *vt (person, ship)* baptiser ■ **christening** *n* baptême *m*
**Christmas** ['krɪsməs] **1** *n* Noël *m*; **at C.** **(time)** à Noël; **Merry** *or* **Happy C.!** Joyeux Noël! **2** *adj (tree, card, Day, party)* de Noël; **C. Eve** la veille de Noël
**chrome** [krəʊm], **chromium** ['krəʊmɪəm] *n* chrome *m*
**chronic** ['krɒnɪk] *adj (disease, state)* chronique
**chronological** [krɒnə'lɒdʒɪkəl] *adj* chronologique; **in c. order** par ordre chronologique
**chubby** ['tʃʌbɪ] (**-ier, -iest**) *adj (person, hands)* potelé; *(cheeks)* rebondi
**chuck** [tʃʌk] *vt Fam (throw)* lancer; *(boyfriend, girlfriend)* plaquer; *Br* **to c. (in** *or* **up)** *(give up)* laisser tomber; **to c. out** *(throw away)* balancer; *(from house, school, club)* vider
**chuckle** ['tʃʌkəl] *vi* rire tout bas
**chug** [tʃʌg] *(pt & pp* **-gg-**) *vi* **to c. along** *(of vehicle)* avancer lentement; *(of train)* haleter
**chum** [tʃʌm] *n Fam* copain *m*, copine *f*
**chunk** [tʃʌŋk] *n* (gros) morceau *m*
**church** [tʃɜ:tʃ] *n* église *f*; **to go to c.** aller à l'église; **c. hall** salle *f* paroissiale ■ **churchyard** *n* cimetière *m*
**churn** [tʃɜ:n] *vt Pej* **to c. out** *(books)*

pondre (en série); *(goods)* produire en série

**chute** [ʃuːt] *n Br (in pool, playground)* toboggan *m*; *(for rubbish)* vide-ordures *m inv*

**CID** [siːaɪˈdiː] (*abbr* **Criminal Investigation Department**) *n Br* ≃ PJ *f*

**cider** [ˈsaɪdə(r)] *n* cidre *m*

**cigar** [sɪˈgɑː(r)] *n* cigare *m*

**cigarette** [sɪgəˈret] *n* cigarette *f*; **c. end** mégot *m*

**cinder** [ˈsɪndə(r)] *n* cendre *f*

**cinema** [ˈsɪnəmə] *n (art)* cinéma *m*; *Br (place)* cinéma; *Br* **to go to the c.** aller au cinéma ▪ **cinemagoer** *n Br* cinéphile *mf*

**cinnamon** [ˈsɪnəmən] *n* cannelle *f*

**circle** [ˈsɜːkəl] **1** *n (shape, group, range)* cercle *m*; *Theatre* balcon *m* **2** *vt (move round)* tourner autour de; *(surround)* entourer (**with** de) **3** *vi (of aircraft, bird)* décrire des cercles

**circuit** [ˈsɜːkɪt] *n (electrical path, journey, for motor racing)* circuit *m*; *El* **c. breaker** disjoncteur *m*

**circular** [ˈsɜːkjʊlə(r)] **1** *adj* circulaire **2** *n (letter)* circulaire *f*; *(advertisement)* prospectus *m*

**circulate** [ˈsɜːkjʊleɪt] **1** *vt* faire circuler **2** *vi* circuler ▪ **circulation** [-ˈleɪʃən] *n (of air, blood, money)* circulation *f*; *(of newspaper)* tirage *m*

**circumcised** [ˈsɜːkəmsaɪzd] *adj* circoncis

**circumference** [sɜːˈkʌmfərəns] *n* circonférence *f*

**circumstance** [ˈsɜːkəmstæns] *n* circonstance *f*; **circumstances** *(financial)* situation *f* financière; **in** *or* **under the circumstances** étant donné les circonstances; **in** *or* **under no circumstances** en aucun cas

**circus** [ˈsɜːkəs] *n* cirque *m*

**citizen** [ˈsɪtɪzən] *n* citoyen, -enne *mf*; *(of city)* habitant, -e *mf*

**citrus** [ˈsɪtrəs] *adj* **c. fruit(s)** agrumes *mpl*

**city** [ˈsɪtɪ] (*pl* **-ies**) *n* (grande) ville *f*, cité *f*; *Br* **the C.** la City *(quartier des affaires de Londres)*; **c. centre** centre-ville *m*; *Am* **c. hall** hôtel *m* de ville

**civil** [ˈsɪvəl] *adj* (**a**) *(rights, war, marriage)* civil; **c. servant** fonctionnaire *mf*; **c. service** fonction *f* publique (**b**) *(polite)* civil

**civilian** [sɪˈvɪljən] *adj & n* civil, -e *(mf)*

**civilize** [ˈsɪvɪlaɪz] *vt* civiliser ▪ **civilization** [-ˈzeɪʃən] *n* civilisation *f*

**claim** [kleɪm] **1** *n (demand) (for damages, compensation)* demande *f* d'indemnisation; *(as a right)* revendication *f*; *(statement)* affirmation *f*; *(right)* droit *m* (**to** à); **(insurance) c.** demande *f* d'indemnité

**2** *vt (as a right)* réclamer, revendiquer; *(payment, benefit, reduction)* demander à bénéficier de; **to c. damages (from sb)** réclamer des dommages et intérêts (à qn); **to c. that...** *(assert)* prétendre que... ▪ **claimant** *n Br (for social benefits, insurance)* demandeur, -euse *mf*

**clam** [klæm] *n* palourde *f*

**clamber** [ˈklæmbə(r)] *vi* **to c. up** grimper

**clamour** [ˈklæmə(r)] (*Am* **clamor**) **1** *n* clameur *f* **2** *vi* **to c. for sth** demander qch à grands cris

**clamp** [klæmp] **1** *n (clip-like)* pince *f*; **(wheel) c.** *(for vehicle)* sabot *m* (de Denver) **2** *vt* serrer; *(vehicle)* mettre un sabot à **3** *vi* **to c. down on** sévir contre ▪ **clampdown** *n* coup *m* d'arrêt (**on** à)

**clan** [klæn] *n also Fig* clan *m*

**clang** [klæŋ] *n* son *m* métallique

**clap** [klæp] (*pt & pp* **-pp-**) *vti (applaud)* applaudir; **to c. (one's hands)** applaudir; *(once)* frapper dans ses mains ▪ **clapping** *n* applaudissements *mpl*

**claret** [ˈklærət] *n (wine)* bordeaux *m* rouge

**clarify** [ˈklærɪfaɪ] (*pt & pp* **-ied**) *vt* clarifier ▪ **clarification** [-ɪˈkeɪʃən] *n* clarification *f*

**clarinet** [klærɪˈnet] *n* clarinette *f*

**clarity** [ˈklærətɪ] *n (of expression, argument)* clarté *f*; *(of sound)* pureté *f*

**clash** [klæʃ] **1** *n (of interests)* conflit *m*; *(of events)* coïncidence *f* **2** *vi (of objects)* s'entrechoquer; *(of interests, armies)* s'affronter; *(of colours)* jurer (**with** avec); *(coincide)* tomber en même temps (**with** que)

**clasp** [klɑːsp] **1** *n (fastener)* fermoir *m*; *(of belt)* boucle *f* **2** *vt (hold)* serrer; **to c. one's hands** joindre les mains

**class** [klɑːs] **1** *n* classe *f*; *(lesson)* cours *m* **2** *vt* classer (**as** comme) ■ **classmate** *n* camarade *mf* de classe ■ **classroom** *n* (salle *f* de) classe *f*

**classic** ['klæsɪk] **1** *adj* classique **2** *n (writer, work)* classique *m* ■ **classical** *adj* classique

**classify** ['klæsɪfaɪ] (*pt & pp* **-ied**) *vt* classer ■ **classification** *n* classification *f* ■ **classified** *adj (information, document)* confidentiel, -elle; **c. advertisement** petite annonce *f*

**classy** ['klɑːsɪ] (**-ier, -iest**) *adj Fam* chic *inv*

**clatter** ['klætə(r)] *n* fracas *m*

**clause** [klɔːz] *n (in sentence)* proposition *f*; *(in legal document)* clause *f*

**claustrophobic** [klɔːstrə'fəʊbɪk] *adj (person)* claustrophobe; *(room, atmosphere)* oppressant

**claw** [klɔː] **1** *n (of lobster)* pince *f*; *(of cat, sparrow)* griffe *f*; *(of eagle)* serre *f* **2** *vt (scratch)* griffer

**clay** [kleɪ] *n* argile *f*

**clean** [kliːn] **1** (**-er, -est**) *adj* propre; *(clear-cut)* net (*f* nette); *(joke)* pour toutes les oreilles; *(game, fight)* dans les règles; **to come c.** tout avouer

**2** *adv (utterly)* complètement

**3** *n* **to give sth a c.** nettoyer qch

**4** *vt* nettoyer; *(wash)* laver; **to c. one's teeth** se brosser *ou* se laver les dents; **to c. out** *(room)* nettoyer à fond; *(empty)* vider; **to c. up** *(room)* nettoyer; *Fig (reform)* épurer

**5** *vi* **to c. (up)** faire le nettoyage ■ **cleaner** *n (in home)* femme *f* de ménage; **(dry) c.** teinturier, -ère *mf* ■ **cleaning** *n* nettoyage *m*; *(housework)* ménage *m*; **c. woman** femme *f* de ménage ■ **cleanly** *adv (break, cut)* net ■ **clean-shaven** *adj (with no beard or moustache)* glabre; *(closely shaven)* rasé de près

**cleanse** [klenz] *vt (wound)* nettoyer; **cleansing cream** crème *f* démaquillante

**clear** [klɪə(r)] **1** (**-er, -est**) *adj (sky, water, sound, thought)* clair; *(glass)* transparent; *(outline, photo, skin, majority)* net (*f* nette); *(road)* libre; *(winner)* incontesté; *(obvious)* évident, clair; *(certain)* certain; **to make oneself c.** se faire comprendre; **it is c. that...** il est évident *ou* clair que...

**2** *adv* **to keep** *or* **steer c. of** se tenir à l'écart de; **to get c. of** *(away from)* s'éloigner de

**3** *vt (table)* débarrasser; *(road, area)* dégager; *(accused person)* disculper; *(cheque)* compenser; *(debts)* liquider; *(through customs)* dédouaner; *(for security)* autoriser; **to c. one's throat** s'éclaircir la gorge

**4** *vi (of weather)* s'éclaircir; *(of fog)* se dissiper ■ **clearing** *n (in woods)* clairière *f* ■ **clearly** *adv (explain, write)* clairement; *(see, understand)* bien; *(obviously)* évidemment

▸ **clear away** *vt sep (remove)* enlever

▸ **clear off** *vi Fam (leave)* filer

▸ **clear out** *vt sep (empty)* vider; *(remove)* enlever

▸ **clear up 1** *vt sep (mystery)* éclaircir; *(room)* ranger **2** *vi (of weather)* s'éclaircir; *(tidy)* ranger

**clearance** ['klɪərəns] *n (sale)* liquidation *f*; *(space)* dégagement *m*; *(permission)* autorisation *f*

**clear-cut** [klɪə'kʌt] *adj* net (*f* nette)

**clef** [klef] *n Mus* clef *f*

**clench** [klentʃ] *vt* **to c. one's fist/teeth** serrer le poing/les dents

**clergy** ['klɜːdʒɪ] *n* clergé *m* ■ **clergyman** (*pl* **-men**) *n* ecclésiastique *m*

**clerical** ['klerɪkəl] *adj (job)* d'employé; *(work)* de bureau

**clerk** [*Br* klɑːk, *Am* klɜːk] *n* employé, -e

*mf* de bureau; *Am (in store)* vendeur, -euse *mf*

**clever** ['klevə(r)] (**-er, -est**) *adj* intelligent; *(smart, shrewd)* astucieux, -euse; *(skilful)* habile (**at sth** à qch; **at doing** à faire); *(ingenious) (machine, plan)* ingénieux, -euse; *(gifted)* doué; **c. with one's hands** adroit de ses mains ▪ **cleverly** *adv* intelligemment; *(ingeniously)* astucieusement; *(skilfully)* habilement

**cliché** ['kli:ʃeɪ] *n* cliché *m*

**click** [klɪk] **1** *n* bruit *m* sec **2** *vi* faire un bruit sec; *Fam* **it suddenly clicked** ça a fait tilt

**client** ['klaɪənt] *n* client, -e *mf* ▪ **clientele** *n* clientèle *f*

**cliff** [klɪf] *n* falaise *f*

**climate** ['klaɪmɪt] *n (weather) & Fig (conditions)* climat *m*

**climax** ['klaɪmæks] *n* point *m* culminant; *(sexual)* orgasme *m*

**climb** [klaɪm] **1** *n* montée *f* **2** *vt* **to c. (up)** *(steps, hill)* gravir; *(mountain)* faire l'ascension de; *(tree, ladder)* grimper à; **to c. (over)** *(wall)* escalader; **to c. down (from)** *(wall, tree)* descendre de; *(hill)* descendre **3** *vi (of plant)* grimper; **to c. (up)** *(steps, tree, hill)* monter; **to c. down** descendre; *Fig (back down)* revenir sur sa décision ▪ **climber** *n (mountaineer)* alpiniste *mf*; *(on rocks)* varappeur, -euse *mf*; *(plant)* plante *f* grimpante ▪ **climbing** *n* **(mountain) c.** alpinisme *m*; **(rock-)c.** varappe *f*

**climb-down** ['klaɪmdaʊn] *n* reculade *f*

**clinch** [klɪntʃ] *vt (deal)* conclure

**cling** [klɪŋ] (*pt & pp* **clung**) *vi* s'accrocher (**to** à); *(stick)* adhérer (**to** à)

**clinic** ['klɪnɪk] *n Br (private)* clinique *f*; *(part of hospital)* service *m* ▪ **clinical** *adj Med* clinique

**clink** [klɪŋk] **1** *vt* faire tinter **2** *vi* tinter

**clip** [klɪp] **1** *n* (**a**) *(for paper)* trombone *m*; *(fastener)* attache *f*; *(of brooch, of cyclist, for hair)* pince *f* (**b**) *(of film)* extrait *m* **2** (*pt & pp* **-pp-**) *vt (paper)* attacher *(avec un trombone)*; *(cut)* couper; *(hedge)* tailler; *(ticket)* poinçonner; **to c. (on)** *(attach)* attacher (**to** à) **3** *vi* **to c. together** s'emboîter ▪ **clippers** *npl (for hair)* tondeuse *f*; *(for fingernails)* coupe-ongles *m inv* ▪ **clipping** *n Am (from newspaper)* coupure *f*

**clique** [kli:k] *n Pej* clique *f*

**cloak** [kləʊk] *n* cape *f* ▪ **cloakroom** *n* vestiaire *m*; *Br (lavatory)* toilettes *fpl*

**clock** [klɒk] *n (large)* horloge *f*; *(small)* pendule *f*; *Br Fam (mileometer)* compteur *m*; **round the c.** vingt-quatre heures sur vingt-quatre; **to put the clocks forward/back** *(in spring, autumn)* avancer/retarder les pendules; **c. radio** radioréveil *m*; **c. tower** clocher *m* ▪ **clockwise** *adv* dans le sens des aiguilles d'une montre ▪ **clockwork 1** *adj (toy)* mécanique **2** *n* **to go like c.** marcher comme sur des roulettes

**clog** [klɒg] **1** *n (shoe)* sabot *m* **2** (*pt & pp* **-gg-**) *vt* **to c. (up)** *(obstruct)* boucher

**cloister** ['klɔɪstə(r)] *n* cloître *m*

**close¹** [kləʊs] **1** (**-er, -est**) *adj (in distance, time, relationship)* proche; *(collaboration, resemblance, connection)* étroit; *(friend)* intime; *(contest)* serré; *(study)* rigoureux, -euse; *Br* **it's c.** *(of weather)* il fait lourd; **c. to** *(near)* près de, proche de; **that was a c. shave** *or* **call** il s'en est fallu de peu

**2** *adv* **c. (by), c. at hand** tout près; **we stood/sat c. together** nous étions debout/assis serrés les uns contre les autres; **to follow c. behind** suivre de près ▪ **close-fitting** *adj (clothes)* ajusté ▪ **closing 1** *n* fermeture *f* **2** *adj (remarks)* dernier, -ère; **c. date** *(for application)* date *f* limite; **c. time** heure *f* de fermeture ▪ **close-up** *n* gros plan *m*

**close²** [kləʊz] **1** *n (end)* fin *f* **2** *vt (door, shop, account, book, eye)* fermer; *(road)* barrer; *(gap)* réduire; *(deal)* conclure **3** *vi (of door)* se fermer; *(of shop)* fermer ▪ **closed** *adj (door, shop)* fermé; **c.-circuit television** télévision *f* en circuit fermé ■ **closure** *n (of business, factory)* fermeture *f* (définitive)

▸**close down** **1** *vt sep (business, factory)* fermer (définitivement) **2** *vi (of TV channel)* terminer les émissions; *(of business, factory)* fermer (définitivement)

▸**close in** *vi (approach)* approcher; **to c. in on sb** se rapprocher de qn

▸**close up** **1** *vt sep* fermer **2** *vi (of shopkeeper)* fermer; *(of wound)* se refermer; *(of line of people)* se resserrer

**closet** ['klɒzɪt] *n Am (cupboard)* placard *m*; *(wardrobe)* penderie *f*

**clot** [klɒt] **1** *n (of blood)* caillot *m* **2** (*pt & pp* **-tt-**) *vi (of blood)* (se) coaguler

**cloth** [klɒθ] *n* tissu *m*; *(for dusting)* chiffon *m*; *(for dishes)* torchon *m*; *(tablecloth)* nappe *f* ■ **clothing** *n (clothes)* vêtements *mpl*

**clothes** [kləʊðz] *npl* vêtements *mpl*; **to put one's c. on** s'habiller; **to take one's c. off** se déshabiller; **c. line** corde *f* à linge; *Br* **c. peg**, *Am* **c. pin** pince *f* à linge; **c. shop** magasin *m* de vêtements

**cloud** [klaʊd] **1** *n* nuage *m* **2** *vi* **to c. over** *(of sky)* se couvrir ■ **cloudy** (**-ier, -iest**) *adj (weather, sky)* nuageux, -euse; *(liquid)* trouble

**clove** [kləʊv] *n (spice)* clou *m* de girofle; **c. of garlic** gousse *f* d'ail

**clover** ['kləʊvə(r)] *n* trèfle *m*

**clown** [klaʊn] **1** *n* clown *m* **2** *vi* **to c. around** *or* **about** faire le clown

**club** [klʌb] **1** *n* (**a**) *(society)* club *m* (**b**) *(nightclub)* boîte *f* de nuit (**c**) *(weapon)* massue *f*; *(in golf)* club *m* (**d**) **clubs** *(in cards)* trèfle *m* **2** (*pt & pp* **-bb-**) *vi Br* **to c. together** se cotiser (**to buy sth** pour acheter qch)

**clue** [klu:] *n* indice *m*; *(of crossword)* définition *f*; *Fam* **I don't have a c.** je n'en ai pas la moindre idée

**clump** [klʌmp] *n (of flowers, trees)* massif *m*

**clumsy** ['klʌmzɪ] (**-ier, -iest**) *adj* maladroit

**clung** [klʌŋ] *pt & pp of* **cling**

**cluster** ['klʌstə(r)] **1** *n* groupe *m* **2** *vi* se grouper

**clutch** [klʌtʃ] **1** *n (in car)* embrayage *m*; *(pedal)* pédale *f* d'embrayage **2** *vt* tenir fermement **3** *vi* **to c. at** essayer de saisir

**clutter** ['klʌtə(r)] **1** *n (objects)* désordre *m* **2** *vt* **to c. (up)** *(room, table)* encombrer (**with** de)

**cm** (*abbr* **centimetre(s)**) cm

**Co** (*abbr* **company**) Cie

**co-** [kəʊ] *pref* co-

**c/o** (*abbr* **care of**) *(on envelope)* chez

**coach** [kəʊtʃ] **1** *n* (**a**) *Br (train carriage)* voiture *f*, wagon *m*; *Br (bus)* car *m*; *(horse-drawn)* carrosse *m* (**b**) *(for sports)* entraîneur, -euse *mf* **2** *vt (sportsman, team)* entraîner

**coal** [kəʊl] **1** *n* charbon *m* **2** *adj (fire)* de charbon; **c. industry** industrie *f* houillère ■ **coalmine** *n* mine *f* de charbon

**coalition** [kəʊə'lɪʃən] *n* coalition *f*

**coarse** [kɔ:s] (**-er, -est**) *adj (person, manners)* grossier, -ère, vulgaire; *(surface, fabric)* grossier, -ère

**coast** [kəʊst] *n* côte *f*

**coaster** ['kəʊstə(r)] *n (for glass)* dessous-de-verre *m inv*

**coat** [kəʊt] **1** *n* manteau *m*; *(overcoat)* pardessus *m*; *(jacket)* veste *f*; *(of animal)* pelage *m*; *(of paint)* couche *f*; **c. hanger** cintre *m* **2** *vt* couvrir (**with** de); *(with chocolate, sugar)* enrober (**with** de) ■ **coating** *n* couche *f*

**coax** [kəʊks] *vt* **to c. sb to do** *or* **into doing sth** amener qn à faire qch par des cajoleries

**cob** [kɒb] *n (of corn)* épi *m*

**cobbled** ['kɒbəld] *adj (street)* pavé

**cobweb** ['kɒbweb] *n* toile *f* d'araignée

**Coca-Cola®** [kəʊkə'kəʊlə] *n* Coca-Cola® *m*

**cocaine** [kəʊ'keɪn] *n* cocaïne *f*

**cock** [kɒk] *n (rooster)* coq *m*

**cockerel** ['kɒkərəl] *n* jeune coq *m*

**cockney** ['kɒknɪ] *adj & n* cockney *(mf) (natif des quartiers est de Londres)*

**cockpit** ['kɒkpɪt] *n (of aircraft)* poste *m* de pilotage

**cockroach** ['kɒkrəʊtʃ] *n* cafard *m*
**cocktail** ['kɒkteɪl] *n* cocktail *m*; **fruit c.** macédoine *f* de fruits; **c. party** cocktail *m*
**cocky** ['kɒkɪ] (**-ier, -iest**) *adj Fam* culotté
**cocoa** ['kəʊkəʊ] *n* cacao *m*
**coconut** ['kəʊkənʌt] *n* noix *f* de coco
**COD** [si:əʊ'di:] (*abbr* **cash on delivery**) *n Br Com* paiement *m* à la livraison
**cod** [kɒd] *n* morue *f*; *(as food)* cabillaud *m*
**code** [kəʊd] *n* code *m*; **in c.** *(letter, message)* codé; **c. word** code
**co-educational** [kəʊedjʊ'keɪʃənəl] *adj (school, teaching)* mixte
**coerce** [kəʊ'ɜ:s] *vt* contraindre (**sb into doing** qn à faire)
**coexist** [kəʊɪg'zɪst] *vi* coexister
**coffee** ['kɒfɪ] *n* café *m*; **c. with milk,** *Br* **white c.** café *m* au lait; **black c.** café *m* noir; *Br* **c. bar, c. house** café *m*; **c. break** pause-café *f*; **c. pot** cafetière *f*; **c. table** table *f* basse
**coffin** ['kɒfɪn] *n* cercueil *m*
**cog** [kɒg] *n* dent *f*
**cognac** ['kɒnjæk] *n* cognac *m*
**cohabit** [kəʊ'hæbɪt] *vi* vivre en concubinage (**with** avec)
**coherent** [kəʊ'hɪərənt] *adj (logical)* cohérent; *(way of speaking)* compréhensible, intelligible
**coil** [kɔɪl] *n (of wire, rope)* rouleau *m*; *(contraceptive)* stérilet *m*
**coin** [kɔɪn] *n* pièce *f* (de monnaie)
**coincide** [kəʊɪn'saɪd] *vi* coïncider (**with** avec) ▪ **coincidence** *n* coïncidence *f*
**coke** [kəʊk] *n (fuel)* coke *m*; *(Coca-Cola®)* Coca® *m inv*
**colander** ['kʌləndə(r)] *n (for vegetables)* passoire *f*
**cold** [kəʊld] **1** (**-er, -est**) *adj* froid; **to be** *or* **feel c.** *(of person)* avoir froid; **my hands are c.** j'ai froid aux mains; **it's c.** *(of weather)* il fait froid; **to get c.** *(of weather)* se refroidir; *(of food)* refroidir; *Fam* **to get c. feet** se dégonfler; *Br* **c. meats,** *Am* **c. cuts** viandes *fpl* froides **2** *n* (**a**) *(temperature)* froid *m* (**b**) *(illness)* rhume *m*; **to have a c.** être enrhumé; **to catch a c.** attraper un rhume; **to get a c.** s'enrhumer ▪ **coldness** *n* froideur *f*
**coleslaw** ['kəʊlslɔ:] *n* = salade de chou cru à la mayonnaise
**collaborate** [kə'læbəreɪt] *vi* collaborer (**on** à) ▪ **collaboration** [-'reɪʃən] *n* collaboration *f*
**collage** ['kɒlɑ:ʒ] *n (picture)* collage *m*
**collapse** [kə'læps] **1** *n* effondrement *m*; *(of government)* chute *f* **2** *vi (of person, building)* s'effondrer; *(faint)* se trouver mal; *(of government)* tomber
**collar** ['kɒlə(r)] *n (on garment)* col *m*; *(of dog)* collier *m*
**colleague** ['kɒli:g] *n* collègue *mf*
**collect** [kə'lekt] **1** *vt (pick up)* ramasser; *(gather)* rassembler; *(information)* recueillir; *(stamps)* collectionner; **to c. money** *(in street, church)* quêter; **to c. sb** *(pick up)* passer prendre qn **2** *vi (in street, church)* quêter (**for** pour) **3** *adv Am* **to call** *or* **phone sb c.** téléphoner à qn en PCV
**collection** [kə'lekʃən] *n (of objects, stamps)* collection *f*; *(of poems)* recueil *m*; *(of money for church)* quête *f*; *(of mail)* levée *f*
**collector** [kə'lektə(r)] *n (of stamps)* collectionneur, -euse *mf*
**college** ['kɒlɪdʒ] *n Br (of further education)* établissement *m* d'enseignement supérieur; *Am (university)* université *f*; **to be at c.** être étudiant
**collide** [kə'laɪd] *vi* entrer en collision (**with** avec) ▪ **collision** *n* collision *f*
**colloquial** [kə'ləʊkwɪəl] *adj* familier, -ère
**colon** ['kəʊlən] *n* (**a**) *(punctuation mark)* deux-points *m* (**b**) *Anat* côlon *m*
**colonel** ['kɜ:nəl] *n* colonel *m*
**colonial** [kə'ləʊnɪəl] *adj* colonial
**colony** ['kɒlənɪ] (*pl* **-ies**) *n* colonie *f*
**colossal** [kə'lɒsəl] *adj* colosse
**colour** ['kʌlə(r)] (*Am* **color**) **1** *n* couleur *f* **2** *adj (photo, television)* en couleurs; *(television set)* couleur *inv* **3** *vt*

colorer; **to c. (in)** *(drawing)* colorier ■ **coloured** *adj (person, pencil)* de couleur; *(glass)* coloré ■ **colouring** *n (in food)* colorant *m*; *(shade, effect)* coloris *m*; **c. book** album *m* de coloriages

**colour-blind** ['kʌləblaɪnd] *adj* daltonien, -enne

**colourful** ['kʌləfəl] *adj (crowd, story)* coloré; *(person)* pittoresque

**column** ['kɒləm] *n* colonne *f*; *(newspaper feature)* rubrique *f*

**coma** ['kəʊmə] *n* **in a c.** dans le coma

**comb** [kəʊm] **1** *n* peigne *m* **2** *vt Fig (search)* ratisser, passer au peigne fin; **to c. one's hair** se peigner

**combat** ['kɒmbæt] *n* combat *m*

**combination** [kɒmbɪ'neɪʃən] *n* combinaison *f*; **in c. with** en association avec; **c. lock** serrure *f* à combinaison

**combine** [kəm'baɪn] *vt (activities, qualities, elements, sounds)* combiner; *(efforts)* joindre, unir

**combustion** [kəm'bʌstʃən] *n* combustion *f*

**COME** [kʌm] (*pt* **came**, *pp* **come**) *vi* venir (**from** de; **to** à); **to c. home** rentrer (à la maison); **to c. first** *(in race, exam)* se classer premier; **c. and see me** viens me voir; **to c. near** *or* **close to doing sth** faillir faire qch; **in the years to c.** dans les années à venir

▸**come about** *vi (happen)* arriver

▸**come across 1** *vi* **to c. across well/badly** bien/mal passer **2** *vt insep (find)* tomber sur

▸**come along** *vi* venir (**with** avec); *(progress) (of work)* avancer; *(of student)* progresser

▸**come away** *vi (leave, come off)* partir (**from** de); **to c. away from sb/sth** *(step or move back from)* s'écarter de qn/qch

▸**come back** *vi* revenir; *(return home)* rentrer

▸**come by** *vt insep (obtain)* obtenir; *(find)* trouver

▸**come down 1** *vi* descendre; *(of rain, temperature, price)* tomber; *(of building)* être démoli **2** *vt insep (stairs, hill)* descendre

▸**come down with** *vt insep (illness)* attraper

▸**come for** *vt insep* venir chercher

▸**come forward** *vi (make oneself known, volunteer)* se présenter

▸**come in** *vi (enter)* entrer; *(of train)* arriver; *(of money)* rentrer; **to c. in useful** être bien utile

▸**come in for** *vt insep* **to c. in for criticism** faire l'objet de critiques

▸**come into** *vt insep (room)* entrer dans; *(money)* hériter de

▸**come off 1** *vi (of button)* se détacher; *(succeed)* réussir **2** *vt insep (fall from)* tomber de; *(get down from)* descendre de

▸**come on** *vi (make progress) (of work)* avancer; *(of student)* progresser; **c. on!** allez!

▸**come out** *vi* sortir; *(of sun, book)* paraître; *(of stain)* s'enlever, partir; *(of photo)* réussir; *(of homosexual)* révéler son homosexualité; **to c. out (on strike)** se mettre en grève

▸**come over** *vi (visit)* passer (**to** chez); **to c. over to** *(approach)* s'approcher de

▸**come round** *vi (visit)* passer (**to** chez); *(regain consciousness)* revenir à soi

▸**come through 1** *vi (survive)* s'en tirer **2** *vt insep (crisis)* sortir indemne de

▸**come to 1** *vi (regain consciousness)* revenir à soi **2** *vt insep (amount to)* revenir à; **to c. to a conclusion** arriver à une conclusion; **to c. to a decision** se décider

▸**come under** *vt insep (heading)* être classé sous

▸**come up 1** *vi (rise)* monter; *(of question, job)* se présenter **2** *vt insep (stairs)* monter

▸**come up against** *vt insep (problem)* se heurter à

▸**come upon** *vt insep (book, reference)* tomber sur

▸**come up to** *vt insep (reach)* arriver jusqu'à; *(approach)* s'approcher de
▸**come up with** *vt insep (idea, money)* trouver

---

**comeback** ['kʌmbæk] *n* **to make a c.** *(of actor, athlete)* faire un come-back
**comedy** ['kɒmɪdɪ] (*pl* **-ies**) *n* comédie *f* ▪ **comedian** *n* comique *mf*
**comet** ['kɒmɪt] *n* comète *f*
**comfort** ['kʌmfət] **1** *n (ease)* confort *m*; *(consolation)* réconfort *m*, consolation *f* **2** *vt* consoler ▪ **comfortable** *adj (chair, house)* confortable; *(rich)* aisé
**comfortably** ['kʌmftəblɪ] *adv (sit)* confortablement; *(win)* facilement; **c. off** *(rich)* à l'aise financièrement
**comic** ['kɒmɪk] **1** *adj* comique **2** *n Br (magazine)* bande *f* dessinée, BD *f*; **c. strip** bande *f* dessinée ▪ **comical** *adj* comique
**coming** ['kʌmɪŋ] **1** *adj (future) (years, election)* à venir; **the c. days** les prochains jours **2** *n* **comings and goings** allées *fpl* et venues *fpl*
**comma** ['kɒmə] *n* virgule *f*
**command** [kə'mɑːnd] **1** *n (order)* ordre *m*; *(authority)* commandement *m*; *(mastery)* maîtrise *f* (**of** de); *Comptr* commande *f* **2** *vt (order)* commander (**sb to do** à qn de faire) ▪ **commander** *n Mil* commandant *m* ▪ **commanding** *adj (authoritative)* imposant; *(position)* dominant; **c. officer** commandant *m*
**commandment** [kə'mɑːndmənt] *n Rel* commandement *m*
**commemorate** [kə'meməreɪt] *vt* commémorer ▪ **commemoration** [-'reɪʃən] *n* commémoration *f*
**commence** [kə'mens] *vti Formal* commencer (**doing** à faire)
**commend** [kə'mend] *vt (praise)* louer ▪ **commendable** *adj* louable
**comment** ['kɒment] **1** *n* commentaire *m* (**on** sur) **2** *vi* faire des commentaires (**on** sur); **to c. on** *(text, event, news item)* commenter; **to c. that...** remarquer que... ▪ **commentary** (*pl* **-ies**) *n* commentaire *m*; **live c.** *(on TV or radio)* reportage *m* en direct ▪ **commentator** *n* commentateur, -trice *mf* (**on** de)
**commerce** ['kɒmɜːs] *n* commerce *m* ▪ **commercial** [kə'mɜːʃəl] **1** *adj* commercial **2** *n (advertisement)* publicité *f*; **the commercials** la publicité
**commercialize** [kə'mɜːʃəlaɪz] *vt Pej (event)* transformer en une affaire de gros sous
**commiserate** [kə'mɪzəreɪt] *vi* **to c. with sb** être désolé pour qn
**commission** [kə'mɪʃən] **1** *n (fee, group)* commission *f*; *(order for work)* commande *f* **2** *vt (artist)* passer une commande à; *(book)* commander; **to c. sb to do sth** charger qn de faire qch ▪ **commissioner** *n Br* **(police) c.** commissaire *m* de police
**commit** [kə'mɪt] (*pt & pp* **-tt-**) *vt (crime)* commettre; *(bind)* engager; *(devote)* consacrer; **to c. suicide** se suicider; **to c. oneself** *(make a promise)* s'engager (**to** à) ▪ **commitment** *n (duty, responsibility)* obligation *f*; *(promise)* engagement *m*; *(devotion)* dévouement *m* (**to** à)
**committee** [kə'mɪtɪ] *n* comité *m*
**commodity** [kə'mɒdɪtɪ] (*pl* **-ies**) *n Econ* marchandise *f*, produit *m*
**common** ['kɒmən] (**-er, -est**) *adj (shared, vulgar)* commun; *(frequent)* courant, commun; **in c.** *(shared)* en commun (**with** avec); **to have nothing in c.** n'avoir rien de commun (**with** avec); **c. room** *(for students)* salle *f* commune; *(for teachers)* salle *f* des professeurs; **c. sense** sens *m* commun, bon sens *m* ▪ **commonly** *adv* communément
**commonplace** ['kɒmənpleɪs] *adj* courant
**Commonwealth** ['kɒmənwelθ] *n Br* **the C.** le Commonwealth
**commotion** [kə'məʊʃən] *n (disruption)* agitation *f*
**communal** [kə'mjuːnəl] *adj (shared) (bathroom, kitchen)* commun; *(of the community)* communautaire
**commune** ['kɒmjuːn] *n (district)*

commune *f*; *(group)* communauté *f*
**communicate** [kə'mju:nɪkeɪt] **1** *vt* communiquer **2** *vi (of person)* communiquer (**with** avec) ▪ **communication** [-'keɪʃən] *n* communication *f*; *Br* **c. cord** *(on train)* signal *m* d'alarme
**Communion** [kə'mju:njən] *n* **(Holy) C.** communion; **to take C.** communier
**communism** ['kɒmjʊnɪzəm] *n* communisme *m* ▪ **communist** *adj & n* communiste *(mf)*
**community** [kə'mju:nɪtɪ] **1** *(pl* **-ies**) *n* communauté *f*; **the student c.** les étudiants *mpl* **2** *adj (life, spirit)* communautaire; **c. centre** centre *m* socioculturel
**commute** [kə'mju:t] *vi* **to c. (to work)** faire la navette entre son domicile et son travail ▪ **commuter** *n* banlieusard, -e *mf*; **c. train** train *m* de banlieue
**compact**[1] [kəm'pækt] *adj (car, crowd, substance)* compact; **c. disc** ['kɒmpækt] disque *m* compact
**compact**[2] ['kɒmpækt] *n (for face powder)* poudrier *m*
**companion** [kəm'pænjən] *n (person)* compagnon *m*, compagne *f*
**company** ['kʌmpənɪ] *(pl* **-ies**) *n (companionship)* compagnie *f*; *(guests)* invités *mpl*, -es *fpl*; *(business)* société *f*, compagnie *f*; **(theatre) c.** compagnie *f* (théâtrale); **to keep sb c.** tenir compagnie à qn; **c. car** voiture *f* de société
**comparable** ['kɒmpərəbəl] *adj* comparable (**with** *or* **to** à)
**comparative** [kəm'pærətɪv] *adj (relative) (costs, comfort)* relatif, -ive ▪ **comparatively** *adv* relativement
**compare** [kəm'peə(r)] **1** *vt* comparer (**with** *or* **to** à); **compared to** *or* **with** en comparaison de **2** *vi* être comparable (**with** à) ▪ **comparison** [kəm'pærɪsən] *n* comparaison *f* (**between** entre; **with** avec); **by** *or* **in c.** en comparaison
**compartment** [kəm'pɑ:tmənt] *n* compartiment *m*
**compass** ['kʌmpəs] *n* (**a**) *(for finding direction)* boussole *f* (**b**) **(pair of) compasses** compas *m*
**compassion** [kəm'pæʃən] *n* compassion *f*
**compatible** [kəm'pætɪbəl] *adj* compatible
**compatriot** [kəm'pætrɪət, kəm'peɪtrɪət] *n* compatriote *mf*
**compel** [kəm'pel] *(pt & pp* **-ll-**) *vt* forcer, obliger; **to c. sb to do sth** forcer qn à faire qch ▪ **compelling** *adj (argument)* convaincant
**compensate** ['kɒmpənseɪt] **1** *vt* **to c. sb** *(with payment, reward)* dédommager qn (**for** de) **2** *vi* compenser; **to c. for sth** *(make up for)* compenser qch ▪ **compensation** [-'seɪʃən] *n (financial)* dédommagement *m*; *(consolation)* compensation *f*
**compère** ['kɒmpeə(r)] *n* animateur, -trice *mf*
**compete** [kəm'pi:t] *vi (take part in race)* concourir (**in** à); **to c. (with sb)** rivaliser (avec qn); *(in business)* faire concurrence (à qn); **to c. for sth** se disputer qch
**competent** ['kɒmpɪtənt] *adj (capable)* compétent (**to do** pour faire) ▪ **competently** *adv* avec compétence
**competition** [kɒmpə'tɪʃən] *n* (**a**) *(rivalry)* rivalité *f*; *(between companies)* concurrence *f* (**b**) *(contest)* concours *m*; *(in sport)* compétition *f*
**competitive** [kəm'petɪtɪv] *adj (price, market)* compétitif, -ive; *(person)* qui a l'esprit de compétition ▪ **competitor** *n* concurrent, -e *mf*
**compile** [kəm'paɪl] *vt (list, catalogue)* dresser; *(documents)* compiler
**complacent** [kəm'pleɪsənt] *adj* content de soi
**complain** [kəm'pleɪn] *vi* se plaindre (**to sb** à qn; **of** *or* **about sb/sth** de qn/qch; **that** que) ▪ **complaint** *n* plainte *f*; *(in shop)* réclamation *f*; *(illness)* maladie *f*
**complement** ['kɒmplɪment] *vt* compléter

**complete** [kəm'pliːt] **1** *adj (whole)* complet, -ète; *(utter)* total; *(finished)* achevé **2** *vt (finish)* achever; *(form)* compléter ▪ **completely** *adv* complètement

**complex** ['kɒmpleks] **1** *adj* complexe **2** *n (feeling, buildings)* complexe *m* ▪ **complexion** [kəm'plekʃən] *n (of face)* teint *m*

**complicate** ['kɒmplɪkeɪt] *vt* compliquer ▪ **complication** *n* complication *f*

**compliment 1** ['kɒmplɪmənt] *n* compliment *m*; **to pay sb a c.** faire un compliment à qn **2** ['kɒmplɪment] *vt* **to c. sb on sth** *(bravery)* féliciter qn de qch; *(dress, haircut)* faire des compliments à qn sur qch ▪ **complimentary** [-'mentərɪ] *adj* (**a**) *(praising)* élogieux, -euse (**b**) *(free)* gratuit; **c. ticket** billet *m* de faveur

**comply** [kəm'plaɪ] *(pt & pp* **-ied***) vi* **to c. with** *(order)* obéir à; *(request)* accéder à

**component** [kəm'pəʊnənt] *n (of structure, furniture)* élément *m*; *(of machine)* pièce *f*

**compose** [kəm'pəʊz] *vt* composer; **to c. oneself** se calmer ▪ **composed** *adj* calme ▪ **composer** *n (of music)* compositeur, -trice *mf* ▪ **composition** [kɒmpə'zɪʃən] *n (in music, art, chemistry)* composition *f*

**compost** ['kɒmpɒst] *n* compost *m*

**composure** [kəm'pəʊʒə(r)] *n* sang-froid *m*

**compound** ['kɒmpaʊnd] **1** *n (word) & Chem (substance)* composé *m*; *(area)* enclos *m* **2** *adj (word, substance) & Fin (interest)* composé

**comprehend** [kɒmprɪ'hend] *vt* comprendre

**comprehensive** [kɒmprɪ'hensɪv] **1** *adj* complet, -ète; *(study)* exhaustif, -ive; *(knowledge)* étendu; *(insurance)* tous risques *inv* **2** *adj & n Br* **c. (school)** ≃ établissement *m* d'enseignement secondaire *(n'opérant pas de sélection à l'entrée)*

**compress** [kəm'pres] *vt (gas, air)* comprimer

**comprise** [kəm'praɪz] *vt (consist of)* comprendre; *(make up)* constituer

**compromise** ['kɒmprəmaɪz] **1** *n* compromis *m* **2** *vt (person, security)* compromettre **3** *vi* transiger (**on** sur)

**compulsion** [kəm'pʌlʃən] *n (urge)* besoin *m*; *(obligation)* contrainte *f* ▪ **compulsive** *adj (smoker, gambler, liar)* invétéré

**compulsory** [kəm'pʌlsərɪ] *adj* obligatoire

**computer** [kəm'pjuːtə(r)] **1** *n* ordinateur *m* **2** *adj (program, system, network)* informatique; *(course, firm)* d'informatique; **c. game** jeu *m* électronique; **c. science** informatique *f* ▪ **computerized** *adj* informatisé

**computing** [kəm'pjuːtɪŋ] *n* informatique *f*

**con** [kɒn] *Fam* **1** *n* arnaque *f*; **c. man** arnaqueur *m* **2** *(pt & pp* **-nn-***) vt* arnaquer; **to be conned** se faire arnaquer

**conceal** [kən'siːl] *vt (hide) (object)* dissimuler (**from sb** à qn); *(plan, news)* cacher (**from sb** à qn)

**concede** [kən'siːd] **1** *vt* concéder (**to** à; **that** que) **2** *vi* s'incliner

**conceited** [kən'siːtɪd] *adj* vaniteux, -euse

**conceive** [kən'siːv] **1** *vt (idea, child)* concevoir **2** *vi (of woman)* concevoir; **to c. of sth** concevoir qch ▪ **conceivable** *adj* concevable; **it's c. that...** il est concevable que... (*+ subjunctive*)

**concentrate** ['kɒnsəntreɪt] **1** *vt* concentrer (**on** sur) **2** *vi* se concentrer (**on** sur); **to c. on doing sth** s'appliquer à faire qch ▪ **concentration** [-'treɪʃən] *n* concentration *f*; **c. camp** camp *m* de concentration

**concept** ['kɒnsept] *n* concept *m*

**concern** [kən'sɜːn] **1** *n (matter)* affaire *f*; *(worry)* inquiétude *f*; **his c. for** son souci de; **(business) c.** entreprise *f* **2** *vt* concerner; **to be concerned about** *(be worried)* s'inquiéter de; **as far as I'm concerned...** en ce qui me concerne... ▪ **concerned** *adj (anxious)* inquiet, -ète (**about/at** au sujet de); **the person c.** *(in question)* la personne dont il s'agit; *(involved)* la personne concernée ▪ **concerning** *prep* en ce qui concerne

**concert** ['kɒnsət] *n* concert *m*; **c. hall** salle *f* de concert

**concerto** [kən'tʃɜːtəʊ] *(pl* **-os***) n* concerto *m*; **piano c.** concerto *m* pour piano

**concession** [kən'seʃən] *n* concession *f* (**to** à)

**conciliatory** [kən'sɪlɪətərɪ, *Am* -tɔːrɪ] *adj (tone, person)* conciliant

**concise** [kən'saɪs] *adj* concis

**conclude** [kən'kluːd] **1** *vt (end, settle)* conclure; **to c. that...** *(infer)* conclure que... **2** *vi (of event)* se terminer (**with** par); *(of speaker)* conclure ▪ **conclusion** *n* conclusion *f* ▪ **conclusive** *adj* concluant

**concoct** [kən'kɒkt] *vt (dish, scheme)* concocter ▪ **concoction** *n (dish, drink)* mixture *f*

**concourse** ['kɒŋkɔːs] *n (in airport, train station)* hall *m*

**concrete** ['kɒŋkriːt] **1** *n* béton *m*; **c. wall** mur *m* en béton **2** *adj (ideas, example)* concret, -ète

**concur** [kən'kɜː(r)] *(pt & pp* **-rr-***) vi (agree)* être d'accord (**with** avec)

**concurrently** [kən'kʌrəntlɪ] *adv* simultanément

**concussion** [kən'kʌʃən] *n (injury)* commotion *f* cérébrale

**condemn** [kən'dem] *vt* condamner (**to** à); *(building)* déclarer inhabitable

**condense** [kən'dens] *vt* condenser ▪ **condensation** [kɒnden'seɪʃən] *n (mist)* buée *f*

**condescend** [kɒndɪ'send] *vi* condescendre (**to do** à faire)

**condition** [kən'dɪʃən] *n (stipulation, circumstance)* condition *f*; *(state)* état *m*, condition *f*; *(disease)* maladie *f*; **on the c. that...** à la condition que... *(+ subjunctive)*; **in good c.** en bon état; **in/out of c.** en bonne/mauvaise forme ▪ **conditional** *adj* conditionnel, -elle

**conditioner** [kən'dɪʃənə(r)] *n* **(hair) c.** après-shampooing *m*

**condo** ['kɒndəʊ] *(pl* **-os***) n Am* = **condominium**

**condolences** [kən'dəʊlənsɪz] *npl* condoléances *fpl*

**condom** ['kɒndɒm] *n* préservatif *m*

**condominium** [kɒndə'mɪnɪəm] *n Am (building)* immeuble *m* en copropriété; *(apartment)* appartement *m* en copropriété

**condone** [kən'dəʊn] *vt (overlook)* fermer les yeux sur; *(forgive)* excuser

**conducive** [kən'djuːsɪv] *adj* **to be c. to** être favorable à

**conduct 1** ['kɒndʌkt] *n (behaviour, directing)* conduite *f* **2** [kən'dʌkt] *vt (campaign, inquiry, experiment)* mener; *(orchestra)* diriger; *(electricity, heat)* conduire; **to c. oneself** se conduire; **conducted tour** *(of building, region)* visite *f* guidée

**conductor** [kən'dʌktə(r)] *n (of orchestra)* chef *m* d'orchestre; *Br (on bus)* receveur *m*; *Am (on train)* chef *m* de train

**cone** [kəʊn] *n* cône *m*; *(for ice cream)* cornet *m*; **pine** *or* **fir c.** pomme *f* de pin; *Br* **traffic c.** cône de chantier

**confectionery** [kən'fekʃənərɪ] *n (sweets)* confiserie *f*; *(cakes)* pâtisserie *f*

**confederation** [kənfedə'reɪʃən] *n* confédération *f*

**confer** [kən'fɜː(r)] *(pt & pp* **-rr-***)* **1** *vt (grant)* octroyer (**on** à) **2** *vi (talk together)* se consulter (**on** *or* **about** sur); **to c. with sb** consulter qn

**conference** ['kɒnfərəns] *n* conférence *f*; *(scientific, academic)* congrès *m*; **press** *or* **news c.** conférence *f* de presse

**confess** [kən'fes] **1** *vt* avouer, confesser (**that** que; **to sb** à qn); *Rel* confesser **2** *vi* avouer; *Rel* se confesser; **to c. to sth** *(crime)* avouer *ou* confesser qch ▪ **confession** *n* aveu *m*, confession *f*; *Rel* confession *f*; **to go to c.** aller à confesse

**confetti** [kən'fetɪ] *n* confettis *mpl*

**confide** [kən'faɪd] **1** *vt* confier (**to** à; **that** que) **2** *vi* **to c. in sb** se confier à qn

**confidence** ['kɒnfɪdəns] *n (trust)* confiance *f* (**in** en); **(self-)c.** confiance *f* en soi; **in c.** en confidence; **c. trick** escroquerie *f* ▪ **confident** *adj (smile, exterior)* confiant; **(self-)c.** sûr de soi ▪ **confidently** *adv* avec confiance

**confidential** [kɒnfɪ'denʃəl] *adj* confidentiel, -elle ▪ **confidentially** *adv* en confidence

**confine** [kən'faɪn] *vt* (**a**) *(limit)* limiter (**to** à); **to c. oneself to doing sth** se limiter à faire qch (**b**) *(keep prisoner)* enfermer (**to/in** dans) ▪ **confined** *adj (space)* réduit; **c. to bed** alité; **c. to one's room** obligé de garder la chambre

**confirm** [kən'fɜːm] *vt* confirmer (**that** que) ▪ **confirmation** [kɒnfə'meɪʃən] *n also Rel* confirmation *f* ▪ **confirmed** *adj (bachelor)* endurci; *(smoker)* invétéré

**confiscate** ['kɒnfɪskeɪt] *vt* confisquer (**from** à)

**conflict 1** ['kɒnflɪkt] *n* conflit *m* **2** [kən'flɪkt] *vi (of statement)* être en contradiction (**with** avec); *(of dates, events, programmes)* tomber en même temps (**with** que) ▪ **conflicting** *adj (views, theories, evidence)* contradictoire; *(dates)* incompatible

**conform** [kən'fɔːm] *vi (of person)* se conformer (**to** *or* **with** à); *(of ideas, actions)* être en conformité (**to** with); *(of product)* être conforme (**to** *or* **with** à)

**confront** [kən'frʌnt] *vt (danger)* affronter; *(problem)* faire face à; **to c. sb** *(be face to face with)* se trouver en face de qn; *(oppose)* s'opposer à qn; **to c. sb with sth** mettre qn en face de qch ▪ **confrontation** [kɒnfrʌn'teɪʃən] *n* confrontation *f*

**confuse** [kən'fjuːz] *vt (make unsure)* embrouiller; **to c. sb/sth with** *(mistake for)* confondre qn/qch avec; **to c. matters** *or* **the issue** embrouiller la question ▪ **confused** *adj (situation, noises, idea)* confus; **to get c.** s'embrouiller ▪ **confusing** *adj* déroutant ▪ **confusion** [-ʒən] *n (bewilderment)* perplexité *f*; *(disorder, lack of clarity)* confusion *f*

**congested** [kən'dʒestɪd] *adj (street, town, lungs)* congestionné; *(nose)* bouché ▪ **congestion** [-tʃən] *n (traffic)* encombrements *mpl*; *(overcrowding)* surpeuplement *m*

**congratulate** [kən'grætʃʊleɪt] *vt* féliciter (**sb on sth** qn de qch; **sb on doing sth** qn d'avoir fait qch) ▪ **congratulations** [-'leɪʃənz] *npl* félicitations *fpl* (**on** pour)

**congregate** ['kɒŋgrɪgeɪt] *vi* se rassembler ▪ **congregation** [-'geɪʃən] *n (worshippers)* fidèles *mpl*

**Congress** ['kɒŋgres] *n Am Pol* le Congrès *(assemblée législative américaine)*

**conifer** ['kɒnɪfə(r)] *n* conifère *m*

**conjunction** [kən'dʒʌŋkʃən] *n* **in c. with** conjointement avec

**connect** [kə'nekt] **1** *vt* relier (**with** *or* **to** à); *(telephone, washing machine)* brancher; **to c. sb with sb** *(on phone)* mettre qn en communication avec qn; **to c. sb/sth with sb/sth** établir un lien entre qn/qch et qn/qch **2** *vi* **to c. with** *(of train, bus)* assurer la correspondance avec ▪ **connected** *adj (facts, events)* lié; **to be c. with** *(have to do with, relate to)* avoir un lien avec

**connection** [kə'nekʃən] *n (link)* rapport *m*, lien *m* (**with** avec); *(train, bus)* correspondance *f*; *(phone call)* communication *f*; *(between electrical wires)* contact *m*; **connections** *(contacts)* relations *fpl*; **to have no c. with** n'avoir aucun rapport avec; **in c. with** à propos de

**connive** [kə'naɪv] *vi* **to c. with sb** être de connivence avec qn

**connoisseur** [kɒnə'sɜː(r)] *n* connaisseur *m*

**connotation** [kɒnə'teɪʃən] *n* connotation *f*

**conquer** ['kɒŋkə(r)] *vt (country)* conquérir; *(enemy, habit, difficulty)* vaincre ■ **conquest** *n* conquête *f*

**cons** [kɒnz] *npl* **the pros and (the) c.** le pour et le contre

**conscience** ['kɒnʃəns] *n* conscience *f*; **to have sth on one's c.** avoir qch sur la conscience

**conscientious** [kɒnʃɪ'enʃəs] *adj* consciencieux, -euse; **c. objector** objecteur *m* de conscience

**conscious** ['kɒnʃəs] *adj (awake)* conscient; **to make a c. effort to do sth** faire un effort particulier pour faire qch; **c. of sth** *(aware)* conscient de qch ■ **consciously** *adv (knowingly)* consciemment ■ **consciousness** *n* **to lose/regain c.** perdre/reprendre connaissance

**conscript 1** ['kɒnskrɪpt] *n (soldier)* conscrit *m* **2** [kən'skrɪpt] *vt* enrôler ■ **conscription** [kən'skrɪpʃən] *n* conscription *f*

**consecutive** [kən'sekjʊtɪv] *adj* consécutif, -ive

**consensus** [kən'sensəs] *n* consensus *m*

**consent** [kən'sent] **1** *n* consentement *m* **2** *vi* consentir (**to** à)

**consequence** ['kɒnsɪkwəns] *n (result)* conséquence *f* ■ **consequently** *adv* par conséquent

**conservative** [kən'sɜːvətɪv] **1** *adj (estimate)* modeste; *(view, attitude)* traditionnel, -elle; *(person)* traditionaliste; *Br Pol* conservateur, -trice **2** *n Br Pol* conservateur, -trice *mf*

**conservatory** [kən'sɜːvətrɪ] (*pl* **-ies**) *n Br (room)* véranda *f*

**conserve** [kən'sɜːv] *vt (energy, water, electricity)* faire des économies de ■ **conservation** [kɒnsə'veɪʃən] *n (of energy)* économies *fpl*; *(of nature)* protection *f* de l'environnement

**consider** [kən'sɪdə(r)] *vt (think over)* considérer; *(take into account)* tenir compte de; *(an offer)* étudier; **to c. doing sth** envisager de faire qch; **to c. that...** considérer que...; **I c. her (as) a friend** je la considère comme une amie; **all things considered** tout bien considéré

**considerable** [kən'sɪdərəbəl] *adj (large)* considérable; *(much)* beaucoup de ■ **considerably** *adv* considérablement

**considerate** [kən'sɪdərət] *adj* attentionné (**to** à l'égard de)

**consideration** [kənsɪdə'reɪʃən] *n* considération *f*; **to take sth into c.** prendre qch en considération

**considering** [kən'sɪdərɪŋ] **1** *prep* étant donné **2** *conj* **c. (that)** étant donné que

**consignment** [kən'saɪnmənt] *n (goods)* envoi *m*

**consist** [kən'sɪst] *vi* consister (**of** en; **in** en; **in doing** à faire)

**consistent** [kən'sɪstənt] *adj (unchanging) (quality, results)* constant ■ **consistency** *n (of substance, liquid)* consistance *f* ■ **consistently** *adv (always)* constamment; *(regularly)* régulièrement

**console¹** [kən'səʊl] *vt* consoler ■ **consolation** *n* consolation *f*; **c. prize** lot *m* de consolation

**console²** ['kɒnsəʊl] *n (control desk)* console *f*

**consolidate** [kən'sɒlɪdeɪt] *vt* consolider

**consonant** ['kɒnsənənt] *n* consonne *f*

**conspicuous** [kən'spɪkjʊəs] *adj (noticeable)* bien visible; *(striking)* manifeste; *(showy)* voyant

**conspiracy** [kən'spɪrəsɪ] (*pl* **-ies**) *n* conspiration *f*

**conspire** [kən'spaɪə(r)] *vi* conspirer (**against** contre); **to c. to do sth** comploter de faire qch

**constable** ['kɒnstəbəl] *n Br* **(police) c.** agent *m* de police

**constant** ['kɒnstənt] *adj (frequent)* incessant; *(unchanging)* constant ■ **constantly** *adv* constamment, sans cesse

**constellation** [kɒnstə'leɪʃən] *n* constellation *f*

**constipated** ['kɒnstɪpeɪtɪd] *adj* constipé

**constituent** [kən'stɪtjʊənt] *n Pol (voter)* électeur, -trice *mf* ▪ **constituency** (*pl* **-ies**) *n* circonscription *f* électorale; *(voters)* électeurs *mpl*

**constitute** ['kɒnstɪtju:t] *vt* constituer ▪ **constitution** *n* constitution *f*

**constraint** [kən'streɪnt] *n* contrainte *f*

**construct** [kən'strʌkt] *vt* construire ▪ **construction** *n (building, structure, in grammar)* construction *f*; **under c.** en construction; **c. site** chantier *m* ▪ **constructive** *adj* constructif, -ive

**consul** ['kɒnsəl] *n* consul *m* ▪ **consulate** [-sjʊlət] *n* consulat *m*

**consult** [kən'sʌlt] **1** *vt* consulter **2** *vi* **to c. with sb** discuter avec qn; *Br* **consulting room** *(of doctor)* cabinet *m* de consultation ▪ **consultation** [kɒnsəl'teɪʃən] *n* consultation *f*

**consultancy** [kən'sʌltənsɪ] (*pl* **-ies**) *n* **c. (firm)** cabinet-conseil *m* ▪ **consultant** *n Br (doctor)* spécialiste *mf*; *(adviser)* consultant *m*

**consume** [kən'sju:m] *vt (food, supplies)* consommer; *(of fire)* consumer; *(of grief, hate)* dévorer ▪ **consumer** *n* consommateur, -trice *mf* ▪ **consumption** [-'sʌmpʃən] *n* consommation *f*

**contact** ['kɒntækt] **1** *n (act of touching)* contact *m*; *(person)* relation *f*; **in c. with** en contact avec; **c. lenses** lentilles *fpl* de contact **2** *vt* contacter

**contagious** [kən'teɪdʒəs] *adj (disease)* contagieux, -euse

**contain** [kən'teɪn] *vt (enclose, hold back)* contenir ▪ **container** *n (box, jar)* récipient *m*; *(for transporting goods)* conteneur *m*

**contaminate** [kən'tæmɪneɪt] *vt* contaminer

**contemplate** ['kɒntəmpleɪt] *vt (look at)* contempler; *(consider)* envisager (**doing** de faire)

**contemporary** [kən'tempərərɪ] **1** *adj* contemporain (**with** de); *(style)* moderne **2** (*pl* **-ies**) *n (person)* contemporain, -e *mf*

**contempt** [kən'tempt] *n* mépris *m*; **to hold sb/sth in c.** mépriser qn/qch ▪ **contemptible** *adj* méprisable ▪ **contemptuous** *adj* méprisant; **to be c. of sth** mépriser qch

**contend** [kən'tend] *vi* **to c. with** *(problem)* faire face à ▪ **contender** *n (in sport)* concurrent, -e *mf*; *(in election, for job)* candidat, -e *mf*

**content**[1] [kən'tent] *adj (happy)* satisfait (**with** de) ▪ **contented** *adj* satisfait ▪ **contentment** *n* contentement *m*

**content**[2] ['kɒntent] *n (of book, text, film) (subject matter)* contenu *m*; **contents** contenu *m*; *(in book)* table *f* des matières; **alcoholic/iron c.** teneur *f* en alcool/fer

**contest 1** ['kɒntest] *n (competition)* concours *m*; *(fight)* lutte *f*; *(in boxing)* combat *m* **2** [kən'test] *vt (dispute)* contester ▪ **contestant** [kən'testənt] *n* concurrent, -e *mf*; *(in fight)* adversaire *mf*

**context** ['kɒntekst] *n* contexte *m*; **in/out of c.** en/hors contexte

**continent** ['kɒntɪnənt] *n* continent *m*; **the C.** l'Europe *f* continentale; **on the C.** en Europe ▪ **continental** [-'nentəl] *adj (of Europe)* européen, -enne; **c. breakfast** petit déjeuner *m* à la française

**contingent** [kən'tɪndʒənt] *n (group)* contingent *m* ▪ **contingency** (*pl* **-ies**) *n* éventualité *f*; **c. plan** plan *m* d'urgence

**continual** [kən'tɪnjʊəl] *adj* continuel, -elle

**continue** [kən'tɪnju:] **1** *vt* continuer (**to do** *or* **doing** à *ou* de faire); **to c. (with)** *(work, speech)* poursuivre; *(resume)* reprendre **2** *vi* continuer; *(resume)* reprendre

**continuous** [kən'tɪnjʊəs] *adj* continu; *Sch & Univ* **c. assessment** contrôle *m* continu des connaissances ▪ **continuously** *adv* sans interruption

**contour** ['kɒntʊə(r)] *n* contour *m*

**contraception** [kɒntrə'sepʃən] *n*

contraception *f* ▪ **contraceptive** *n* contraceptif *m*

**contract¹** ['kɒntrækt] **1** *n* contrat *m*; **to be under c.** être sous contrat; **c. work** travail *m* en sous-traitance **2** *vt* **to c. work out** sous-traiter du travail ▪ **contractor** *n* entrepreneur *m*

**contract²** [kən'trækt] **1** *vt (illness)* contracter **2** *vi (shrink)* se contracter

**contradict** [kɒntrə'dɪkt] *vt (person, statement)* contredire; *(deny)* démentir; **to c. oneself** se contredire ▪ **contradictory** *adj* contradictoire

**contraption** [kən'træpʃən] *n Fam* machin *m*

**contrary** ['kɒntrərɪ] **1** *adj (opposite)* contraire (**to** à) **2** *adv* **c. to** contrairement à **3** *n* contraire *m*; **on the c.** au contraire; **unless you/I/***etc* **hear to the c.** sauf avis contraire

**contrast 1** ['kɒntrɑːst] *n* contraste *m*; **in c. to** par opposition à **2** [kən'trɑːst] *vt* mettre en contraste **3** [kən'trɑːst] *vi* contraster (**with** avec)

**contravention** [kɒntrə'venʃən] *n* **in c. of a treaty** en violation d'un traité

**contribute** [kən'trɪbjuːt] **1** *vt (time, clothes)* donner (**to** à); *(article)* écrire (**to** pour); **to c. money to** verser de l'argent à **2** *vi* **to c. to** contribuer à; *(publication)* collaborer à; *(discussion)* prendre part à; *(charity)* donner à ▪ **contribution** [kɒntrɪ'bjuːʃən] *n* contribution *f* ▪ **contributor** *n (to newspaper)* collaborateur, -trice *mf*; *(of money)* donateur, -trice *mf*

**contrive** [kən'traɪv] *vt* **to c. to do sth** trouver moyen de faire qch

**contrived** [kən'traɪvd] *adj* qui manque de naturel

**control** [kən'trəʊl] **1** *n* contrôle *m*; *(authority)* autorité *f* (**over** sur); **(self-)c.** la maîtrise (de soi); **the situation** *or* **everything is under c.** je/il/*etc* contrôle la situation; **to lose c. of** *(situation, vehicle)* perdre le contrôle de; **out of c.** *(situation, crowd)* difficilement maîtrisable; *Comptr* **c. key** touche *f* de contrôle; **c. panel** tableau *m* de bord **2** *(pt & pp* **-ll-***) vt (business, organization)* diriger; *(prices, quality)* contrôler; *(emotion, reaction)* maîtriser; *(disease)* enrayer; **to c. oneself** se contrôler

**controversy** ['kɒntrəvɜːsɪ] *(pl* **-ies***) n* controverse *f* ▪ **controversial** [-'vɜːʃəl] *adj* controversé

**convalesce** [kɒnvə'les] *vi (rest)* être en convalescence

**convenience** [kən'viːnɪəns] *n* commodité *f*; *Br* **(public) conveniences** toilettes *fpl*; **c. food(s)** plats *mpl* tout préparés; **c. store** magasin *m* de proximité

**convenient** [kən'viːnɪənt] *adj* commode, pratique; **to be c. (for)** *(suit)* convenir (à) ▪ **conveniently** *adv* **c. situated** bien situé

**convention** [kən'venʃən] *n (custom)* usage *m*; *(agreement)* convention *f*; *(conference)* convention *f*, congrès *m* ▪ **conventional** *adj* conventionnel, -elle

**converge** [kən'vɜːdʒ] *vi* converger (**on** sur)

**conversation** [kɒnvə'seɪʃən] *n* conversation *f* (**with** avec)

**convert** [kən'vɜːt] **1** ['kɒnvɜːt] *n* converti, -e *mf* **2** *vt (change)* convertir (**into** *or* **to** en); *(building)* aménager (**into, to** en); *Rel* **to c. sb** convertir qn (**to** à) **3** *vi (change religion)* se convertir (**to** à) ▪ **conversion** *n* conversion *f*; *(of building)* aménagement *m*

**convertible** [kən'vɜːtəbəl] **1** *adj (sofa)* convertible **2** *n (car)* décapotable *f*

**convey** [kən'veɪ] *vt (transport)* transporter; *(communicate)* transmettre ▪ **conveyor belt** *n* tapis *m* roulant

**convict 1** ['kɒnvɪkt] *n* détenu *m* **2** [kən'vɪkt] *vt* déclarer coupable (**of** de) ▪ **conviction** [kən'vɪkʃən] *n (for crime)* condamnation *f*; *(belief)* conviction *f* (**that** que)

**convince** [kən'vɪns] *vt* convaincre (**of sth** de qch; **sb to do sth** qn de faire qch) ▪ **convincing** *adj (argument,* *person)* convaincant

**convoy** ['kɒnvɔɪ] *n* convoi *m*

**cook** [kʊk] **1** *n (person)* cuisinier, -ère *mf* **2** *vt (meal)* préparer; *(food)* (faire) cuire **3** *vi (of food)* cuire; *(of person)* faire la cuisine ▪ **cookbook** *n* livre *m* de cuisine ▪ **cooker** *n Br (stove)* cuisinière *f* ▪ **cookery** *n* cuisine *f*; *Br* **c. book** livre *m* de cuisine ▪ **cooking** *n (activity, food)* cuisine *f*; *(process)* cuisson *f*; **to do the c.** faire la cuisine; **c. apple** pomme *f* à cuire

**cookie** ['kʊkɪ] *n Am* gâteau *m* sec

**cool** [ku:l] **1** (**-er, -est**) *adj (weather, place, wind)* frais (*f* fraîche); *(tea, soup)* tiède; *(calm)* calme; *(unfriendly)* froid; *Fam (good)* cool *inv*; *Fam (fashionable)* branché; **a (nice) c. drink** une boisson (bien) fraîche; **the weather is c., it's c.** il fait frais; **to keep sth c.** tenir qch au frais

**2** *n* **to keep/lose one's c.** garder/perdre son sang-froid

**3** *vt* **to c. (down)** refroidir, rafraîchir

**4** *vi* **to c. (down** *or* **off)** *(of hot liquid)* refroidir; *(of enthusiasm)* se refroidir; *(of angry person)* se calmer; **to c. off** *(by drinking, swimming)* se rafraîchir ▪ **cooler** *n (for food)* glacière *f*

**coop** [ku:p] *vt* **to c. up** *(person, animal)* enfermer

**co-op** ['kəʊɒp] *n* coopérative *f*

**cooperate** [kəʊ'ɒpəreɪt] *vi* coopérer (**in** à; **with** avec) ▪ **cooperation** *n* coopération *f*

**coordinate** [kəʊ'ɔ:dɪneɪt] *vt* coordonner ▪ **coordination** [-'neɪʃən] *n* coordination *f*

**cop** [kɒp] *n Fam (policeman)* flic *m*

**cope** [kəʊp] *vi* **to c. with** *(problem, demand)* faire face à

**copier** ['kɒpɪə(r)] *n (photocopier)* photocopieuse *f*

**copper** ['kɒpə(r)] *n (metal)* cuivre *m*; *Br* **coppers** *(coins)* petite monnaie *f*

**copy** ['kɒpɪ] **1** (*pl* **-ies**) *n (of letter, document)* copie *f*; *(of book, magazine)* exemplaire *m*; *(of photo)* épreuve *f* **2** (*pt & pp* **-ied**) *vt* copier; **to c. out** *or* **down** *(text, letter)* copier **3** *vi* copier

**coral** ['kɒrəl] *n* corail *m*

**cord** [kɔ:d] *n* (**a**) *(of curtain, bell, pyjamas)* cordon *m*; *(electrical)* cordon électrique (**b**) **cords** *(trousers)* pantalon *m* en velours côtelé

**cordial** ['kɔ:dɪəl] **1** *adj (friendly)* cordial **2** *n Br* **(fruit) c.** sirop *m*

**cordless** ['kɔ:dləs] *adj* **c. phone** téléphone *m* sans fil

**cordon** ['kɔ:dən] **1** *n* cordon *m* **2** *vt* **to c. off** *(road)* barrer; *(area)* boucler

**corduroy** ['kɔ:dərɔɪ] *n* velours *m* côtelé

**core** [kɔ:(r)] *n (of apple)* trognon *m*; *(of problem)* cœur *m*; *(group of people)* noyau *m*

**cork** [kɔ:k] **1** *n (material)* liège *m*; *(stopper)* bouchon *m* **2** *vt (bottle)* boucher ▪ **corkscrew** *n* tire-bouchon *m*

**corn**[1] [kɔ:n] *n Br (wheat)* blé *m*; *Am (maize)* maïs *m*; **c. on the cob** maïs *m* en épi, *Can* blé *m* en Inde

**corn**[2] [kɔ:n] *n (on foot)* cor *m*

**corner** ['kɔ:nə(r)] **1** *n (of street, room, page, screen)* coin *m*; *(bend in road)* virage *m*; *(in football)* corner *m*; **it's just round the c.** c'est juste au coin; **c. shop** épicerie *f* du coin **2** *vt (person, animal)* acculer

**cornet** ['kɔ:nɪt] *n Br (of ice cream)* cornet *m*

**cornflakes** ['kɔ:nfleɪks] *npl* corn flakes *mpl*

**corny** ['kɔ:nɪ] (**-ier, -iest**) *adj Fam (joke)* nul (*f* nulle); *(film)* tarte

**coronary** ['kɒrənərɪ] (*pl* **-ies**) *n Med* infarctus *m*

**coronation** [kɒrə'neɪʃən] *n* couronnement *m*

**corporal**[1] ['kɔ:pərəl] *n (in army)* caporal-chef *m*

**corporal**[2] ['kɔ:pərəl] *adj* **c. punishment** châtiment *m* corporel

**corporate** ['kɔ:pərət] *adj (decision)* collectif, -ive

**corporation** [kɔ:pə'reɪʃən] *n (business)* société *f*

**corps** [kɔ:(r), *pl* kɔ:z] *n inv Mil & Pol*

corps *m*; **the press c.** les journalistes *mpl*

**corpse** [kɔ:ps] *n* cadavre *m*

**correct** [kə'rekt] **1** *adj (accurate)* exact; *(proper)* correct; **he's c.** il a raison; **the c. time** l'heure exacte **2** *vt* corriger ▪ **correction** *n* correction *f*

**correspond** [kɒrɪ'spɒnd] *vi* correspondre ▪ **corresponding** *adj (matching)* correspondant; *(similar)* semblable

**correspondence** [kɒrɪ'spɒndəns] *n* correspondance *f*; **c. course** cours *m* par correspondance

**corridor** ['kɒrɪdɔ:(r)] *n* couloir *m*, corridor *m*

**corrosion** [kə'rəʊʒən] *n* corrosion *f*

**corrugated** ['kɒrəgeɪtɪd] *adj* ondulé

**corrupt** [kə'rʌpt] **1** *adj* corrompu **2** *vt* corrompre ▪ **corruption** *n* corruption *f*

**Corsica** ['kɔ:sɪkə] *n* la Corse

**cosmetic** [kɒz'metɪk] **1** *adj* **c. surgery** chirurgie *f* esthétique **2** *n* produit *m* de beauté

**cosmopolitan** [kɒzmə'pɒlɪtən] *adj* cosmopolite

**cost** [kɒst] **1** *n* coût *m*; **the c. of living** le coût de la vie; **at any c., at all costs** à tout prix

**2** (*pt & pp* **cost**) *vti* coûter; **how much does it c.?** ça coûte combien? ▪ **costly** (**-ier, -iest**) *adj (expensive) (car, trip)* coûteux, -euse

**costume** ['kɒstju:m] *n* costume *m*; *Br* **(swimming) c.** maillot *m* de bain

**cosy** ['kəʊzɪ] **1** (**-ier, -iest**) *adj Br (house)* douillet, -ette; *(atmosphere)* intime **2** *n* **(tea) c.** couvre-théière *m*

**cot** [kɒt] *n Br (for child)* lit *m* d'enfant; *Am (camp bed)* lit *m* de camp

**cottage** ['kɒtɪdʒ] *n* petite maison *f* de campagne; **(thatched) c.** chaumière *f*; **c. cheese** fromage *m* blanc (maigre)

**cotton** ['kɒtən] *n* coton *m*; *(yarn)* fil *m* de coton; *Br* **c. wool,** *Am* **absorbent c.** coton *m* hydrophile, ouate *f*; **c. shirt** chemise *f* en coton; *Am* **c. candy** barbe *f* à papa

**couch** [kaʊtʃ] *n (sofa)* canapé *m*; *(for doctor's patient)* lit *m*

**couchette** [ku:'ʃet] *n Br (on train)* couchette *f*

**cough** [kɒf] **1** *n* toux *f*; **c. syrup** *or* **medicine,** *Br* **c. mixture** sirop *m* pour la toux **2** *vt* **to c. up** *(blood)* cracher **3** *vi* tousser

**could** [kʊd, *unstressed* kəd] *pt of* **can**[1]

**couldn't** ['kʊdənt] = **could not**

**council** ['kaʊnsəl] *n* **(town/city) c.** conseil *m* municipal; *Br* **c. flat/house** ≃ HLM *f*; *Br* **c. tax** = impôt regroupant taxe d'habitation et impôts locaux ▪ **councillor** *n* **(town) c.** conseiller *m* municipal

**counselling** ['kaʊnsəlɪŋ] (*Am* **counseling**) *n* assistance *f* psychosociale

**count**[1] [kaʊnt] **1** *n (calculation)* compte *m*; **to keep c. of sth** tenir le compte de qch

**2** *vt (find number of, include)* compter; *(consider)* considérer; **c. me in!** j'en suis!; **c. me out!** ne compte pas sur moi!

**3** *vi* compter; **to c. against sb** jouer contre qn; **to c. on sb/sth** *(rely on)* compter sur qn/qch; **to c. on doing sth** compter faire qch ▪ **countdown** *n* compte *m* à rebours

**count**[2] [kaʊnt] *n (title)* comte *m*

**counter** ['kaʊntə(r)] **1** *n* (**a**) *(in shop, bar)* comptoir *m*; *(in bank)* guichet *m* (**b**) *(in games)* jeton *m* (**c**) *(counting device)* compteur *m* **2** *adv* **c. to** contrairement à **3** *vt (threat)* répondre à; *(effects)* neutraliser **4** *vi* riposter (**with** par)

**counter-** ['kaʊntə(r)] *pref* contre-

**counterattack** ['kaʊntərətæk] **1** *n* contre-attaque *f* **2** *vti* contre-attaquer

**counterclockwise** [kaʊntə'klɒkwaɪz] *adj & adv Am* dans le sens inverse des aiguilles d'une montre

**counterfeit** ['kaʊntəfɪt] **1** *adj* faux (*f* fausse) **2** *vt* contrefaire

**counterpart** ['kaʊntəpɑ:t] *n (thing)* équivalent *m*; *(person)* homologue *mf*

**countless** ['kaʊntlɪs] *adj* innombrable

**country** ['kʌntrɪ] (*pl* **-ies**) **1** *n* pays *m*; *(opposed to town)* campagne *f*; **in the c.** à la campagne **2** *adj (house, road)* de campagne; **c. and western music** country *f* ▪ **countryman** (*pl* **-men**) *n* **(fellow) c.** compatriote *m* ▪ **countryside** *n* campagne *f*; **in the c.** à la campagne

**county** ['kaʊntɪ] (*pl* **-ies**) *n* comté *m*

**coup** [ku:, *pl* ku:z] *n Pol* coup *m* d'État

**couple** ['kʌpəl] **1** *n (of people)* couple *m*; **a c. of** deux ou trois; *(a few)* quelques **2** *vt (connect)* accoupler

**coupon** ['ku:pɒn] *n (for discount)* bon *m*; *(form)* coupon *m*

**courage** ['kʌrɪdʒ] *n* courage *m* ▪ **courageous** [kə'reɪdʒəs] *adj* courageux, -euse

**courgette** [kʊə'ʒet] *n Br* courgette *f*

**courier** ['kʊrɪə(r)] *n (for tourists)* guide *mf*; *(messenger)* messager *m*

**course** [kɔ:s] **1** *n* (**a**) *(of river, time, events)* cours *m*; *(of ship)* route *f*; **c. of action** ligne *f* de conduite; **in the c. of** au cours de; **in due c.** en temps utile (**b**) *(lessons)* cours *m* (**c**) *Med* **c. of treatment** traitement *m* (**d**) *(of meal)* plat *m*; **first c.** entrée *f* (**e**) *(for race)* parcours *m*; *(for horseracing)* champ *m* de courses; *(for golf)* terrain *m* **2** *adv* **of c.!** bien sûr!; **of c. not!** bien sûr que non!

**court¹** [kɔ:t] *n (of king)* cour *f*; *(for trials)* cour *f*, tribunal *m*; *(for tennis)* court *m*; **to go to c.** aller en justice; **to take sb to c.** poursuivre qn en justice ▪ **courthouse** *n Am* palais *m* de justice ▪ **courtroom** *n Law* salle *f* d'audience ▪ **courtyard** *n* cour *f*

**court²** [kɔ:t] **1** *vt (woman)* faire la cour à; *(danger)* aller au-devant de **2** *vi* **to be courting** *(of couple)* se fréquenter

**courteous** ['kɜ:tɪəs] *adj* poli, courtois ▪ **courtesy** [-təsɪ] (*pl* **-ies**) *n* politesse *f*, courtoisie *f*; **c. car** = voiture mise à la disposition d'un client par un hôtel, un garage etc

**cousin** ['kʌzən] *n* cousin, -e *mf*

**cover** ['kʌvə(r)] **1** *n (lid)* couvercle *m*; *(of book)* couverture *f*; *(for furniture, typewriter)* housse *f*; **to take c.** se mettre à l'abri; **under c.** *(sheltered)* à l'abri; **c. charge** *(in restaurant)* couvert *m* **2** *vt* couvrir (**with** *or* **in** de); *(include)* englober; *(treat)* traiter; *(distance)* parcourir; *(event) (in newspaper, on TV)* couvrir; *(insure)* assurer (**against** contre); **to c. up** recouvrir; *(truth, tracks)* dissimuler; *(scandal)* étouffer **3** *vi* **to c. for sb** *(of colleague)* remplacer qn; **to c. up for sb** cacher la vérité pour protéger qn ▪ **cover-up** *n* **there was a c.** on a étouffé l'affaire

**coverage** ['kʌvərɪdʒ] *n (on TV, in newspaper)* couverture *f* médiatique

**covering** ['kʌvərɪŋ] *n (wrapping)* enveloppe *f*; *(layer)* couche *f*; **c. letter** lettre *f* jointe

**cow** [kaʊ] *n* vache *f*; *very Fam (nasty woman)* peau *f* de vache ▪ **cowboy** *n* cow-boy *m*; *Br Fam Pej (workman)* rigolo *m*

**coward** ['kaʊəd] *n* lâche *mf*

**cower** ['kaʊə(r)] *vi (with fear)* trembler

**cozy** ['kəʊzɪ] *adj Am* = **cosy**

**crab** [kræb] *n (crustacean)* crabe *m*

**crack¹** [kræk] **1** *n (split)* fente *f*; *(in glass, china, bone)* fêlure *f*; *(noise)* craquement *m* **2** *vt (glass, ice)* fêler; *(nut)* casser; *(whip)* faire claquer; *(problem)* résoudre; *(code)* déchiffrer; *Fam (joke)* raconter **3** *vi* se fêler; *(of branch, wood)* craquer; **to c. down on** prendre des mesures énergiques en matière de

**crack²** [kræk] *adj (first-rate) (driver, skier)* d'élite; **c. shot** fin tireur *m*

**crack³** [kræk] *n (drug)* crack *m*

**cracker** ['krækə(r)] *n* (**a**) *(biscuit)* biscuit *m* salé (**b**) *(firework)* pétard *m*; **Christmas c.** diablotin *m*

**crackle** ['krækəl] *vi (of fire)* crépiter; *(of frying)* grésiller; *(of radio)* crachoter

**cradle** ['kreɪdəl] **1** *n* berceau *m* **2** *vt* bercer

**craft** [krɑ:ft] **1** *n (skill)* art *m*; *(job)* métier *m* **2** *vt* façonner ▪ **craftsman** (*pl*

**-men**) *n* artisan *m* ▪ **craftsmanship** *n* *(skill)* art *m*

**crafty** ['krɑːftɪ] (**-ier, -iest**) *adj* astucieux, -euse; *Pej* rusé

**cram** [kræm] (*pt & pp* **-mm-**) **1** *vt* **to c. sth into** *(force)* fourrer qch dans; **to c. with** *(fill)* bourrer de **2** *vi* **to c. into** *(of people)* s'entasser dans; **to c. (for an exam)** bûcher

**cramp** [kræmp] *n (pain)* crampe *f* (**in** à)

**cramped** [kræmpt] *adj (surroundings)* exigu (*f* exiguë)

**crane** [kreɪn] **1** *n (machine, bird)* grue *f* **2** *vt* **to c. one's neck** tendre le cou

**crank¹** [kræŋk] *n (handle)* manivelle *f*

**crank²** [kræŋk] *n Fam (person)* excentrique *mf*; *(fanatic)* fanatique *mf*

**crash** [kræʃ] **1** *n (accident)* accident *m*; *(collapse of firm)* faillite *f*; *(noise)* fracas *m*; **c. course/diet** cours *m*/régime *m* intensif; **c. barrier** *(on road)* glissière *f* de sécurité; **c. helmet** casque *m*; **c. landing** atterrissage *m* en catastrophe **2** *exclam (of fallen object)* patatras! **3** *vt (car)* avoir un accident avec; **to c. one's car into sth** rentrer dans qch (avec sa voiture) **4** *vi (of car, plane)* s'écraser; **to c. into** rentrer dans

**crate** [kreɪt] *n (large)* caisse *f*; *(small)* cageot *m*; *(for bottles)* casier *m*

**crater** ['kreɪtə(r)] *n* cratère *m*; **(bomb) c.** entonnoir *m*

**craving** ['kreɪvɪŋ] *n* envie *f* (**for** de)

**crawl** [krɔːl] **1** *n (swimming stroke)* crawl *m* **2** *vi (of snake, animal)* ramper; *(of child)* marcher à quatre pattes; *(of vehicle)* avancer au pas; **to be crawling with** grouiller de

**crayon** ['kreɪən] *n (wax)* crayon *m* gras

**craze** [kreɪz] *n* engouement *m* (**for** pour)

**crazy** ['kreɪzɪ] (**-ier, -iest**) *adj* fou (*f* folle) (**about** de); **to drive sb c.** rendre qn fou; **to run/work like c.** courir/travailler comme un fou

**creak** [kriːk] *vi (of hinge)* grincer; *(of floor, timber)* craquer

**cream** [kriːm] *n (of milk, lotion)* crème *f*; **c. of tomato soup** crème *f* de tomates; **c. cake** gâteau *m* à la crème; **c. cheese** fromage *m* à tartiner

**creamy** ['kriːmɪ] (**-ier, -iest**) *adj* crémeux, -euse

**crease** [kriːs] **1** *n* pli *m* **2** *vt* froisser **3** *vi* se froisser

**create** [kriː'eɪt] *vt* créer ▪ **creation** *n* création *f* ▪ **creative** *adj (person, activity)* créatif, -ive ▪ **creator** *n* créateur, -trice *mf*

**creature** ['kriːtʃə(r)] *n (animal)* bête *f*; *(person)* créature *f*

**crèche** [kreʃ] *n Br (nursery)* crèche *f*

**credentials** [krɪ'denʃəlz] *npl (proof of ability)* références *fpl*

**credible** ['kredɪbəl] *adj* crédible ▪ **credibility** *n* crédibilité *f*

**credit** ['kredɪt] **1** *n (financial)* crédit *m*; *(merit)* mérite *m*; *(from university)* unité *f* de valeur; **credits** *(of film)* générique *m*; **to buy sth on c.** acheter qch à crédit; **to be in c.** *(of account)* être créditeur; *(of person)* avoir un solde positif; **to her c., she refused** c'est tout à son honneur d'avoir refusé; **c. card** carte *f* de crédit **2** *vt (of bank)* créditer (**sb with sth** qn de qch); *(believe)* croire

**credulous** ['kredjʊləs] *adj* crédule

**creek** [kriːk] *n (bay)* crique *f*; *Am (stream)* ruisseau *m*

**creep** [kriːp] **1** *n Fam* **it gives me the creeps** ça me fait froid dans le dos **2** (*pt & pp* **crept**) *vi* ramper; *(silently)* se glisser (furtivement); *(slowly)* avancer lentement ▪ **creepy** (**-ier, -iest**) *adj Fam* sinistre

**cremate** [krɪ'meɪt] *vt* incinérer ▪ **cremation** *n* crémation *f*

**crematorium** [kremə'tɔːrɪəm] (*pl* **-ia** [-ɪə]) (*Am* **crematory** ['kriːmətɔːrɪ]) *n* crématorium *m*

**crept** [krept] *pt & pp of* **creep**

**crescent** ['kresənt] *n (shape)* croissant *m*; *Br Fig (street)* rue *f* en demi-lune

**crest** [krest] *n (of wave, mountain, bird)* crête *f*; *(of hill)* sommet *m*; *(on seal, letters)* armoiries *fpl*

**Crete** [kri:t] *n* la Crète
**crevice** ['krevɪs] *n (crack)* fente *f*
**crew** [kru:] *n (of ship, plane)* équipage *m*; *Fam (gang)* équipe *f*; **c. cut** coupe *f* en brosse
**crib** [krɪb] **1** *n Am (cot)* lit *m* d'enfant; *(cradle)* berceau *m* **2** *(pt & pp* **-bb-***) vti Fam* pomper
**cricket**[1] ['krɪkɪt] *n (game)* cricket *m*
**cricket**[2] ['krɪkɪt] *n (insect)* grillon *m*
**crime** [kraɪm] *n* crime *m*; *Law* délit *m*; *(criminal activity)* criminalité *f*
**criminal** ['krɪmɪnəl] *adj & n* criminel, -elle *(mf)*; **c. offence** *(minor)* délit *m*; *(serious)* crime *m*; **c. record** casier *m* judiciaire
**crimson** ['krɪmzən] *adj & n* cramoisi *(m)*
**cringe** [krɪndʒ] *vi (show fear)* avoir un mouvement de recul; *(be embarrassed)* avoir envie de rentrer sous terre
**crinkle** ['krɪŋkəl] **1** *n (in paper, fabric)* pli *m* **2** *vt (paper, fabric)* froisser
**cripple** ['krɪpəl] **1** *n (lame)* estropié, -e *mf*; *(disabled)* infirme *mf* **2** *vt (disable)* rendre infirme; *Fig (nation, system)* paralyser
**crisis** ['kraɪsɪs] *(pl* **crises** ['kraɪsi:z]) *n* crise *f*
**crisp** [krɪsp] **1** (**-er, -est**) *adj (biscuit)* croustillant; *(apple, vegetables)* croquant **2** *npl Br* **(potato) crisps** chips *fpl* ▪ **crispbread** *n* pain *m* suédois
**criterion** [kraɪ'tɪərɪən] *(pl* **-ia** [-ɪə]) *n* critère *m*
**critic** ['krɪtɪk] *n (reviewer)* critique *mf*; *(opponent)* détracteur, -trice *mf* ▪ **critical** *adj* critique ▪ **critically** *adv (examine)* en critique; **to be c. ill** être dans un état critique ▪ **criticism** [-sɪzəm] *n* critique *f* ▪ **criticize** [-saɪz] *vti* critiquer
**croak** [krəʊk] *vi (of frog)* croasser
**Croatia** [krəʊ'eɪʃə] *n* la Croatie
**crockery** ['krɒkərɪ] *n* vaisselle *f*
**crocodile** ['krɒkədaɪl] *n* crocodile *m*
**crocus** ['krəʊkəs] *(pl* **-uses** [-əsɪz]) *n* crocus *m*
**crook** [krʊk] *n (thief)* escroc *m*
**crooked** ['krʊkɪd] *adj (hat, picture)* de travers; *(deal, person)* malhonnête
**crop** [krɒp] **1** *n (harvest)* récolte *f*; *(produce)* culture *f* **2** *(pt & pp* **-pp-***) vt (hair)* couper ras **3** *vi* **to c. up** *(of issue)* survenir; *(of opportunity)* se présenter; *(of name)* être mentionné
**cross**[1] [krɒs] **1** *n* croix *f*; **a c. between** *(animal)* un croisement entre; *Fig* **it's a c. between a car and a van** c'est un compromis entre une voiture et une camionnette **2** *vt (street, room)* traverser; *(barrier, threshold)* franchir; *(legs, animals)* croiser; *(cheque)* barrer; **to c. off** *or* **out** *(word, name)* rayer; **to c. over** *(road)* traverser **3** *vi (of paths)* se croiser; **to c. over** traverser
**cross**[2] [krɒs] *adj (angry)* fâché (**with** contre); **to get c.** se fâcher (**with** contre) ▪ **cross-country** *adj* **c. race** cross *m*; **c. runner** coureur, -euse *mf* de fond ▪ **cross-legged** *adj & adv* **to sit c.** être assis en tailleur ▪ **crossroads** *n* carrefour *m* ▪ **cross-section** *n* coupe *f* transversale; *(sample)* échantillon *m* représentatif ▪ **crossword (puzzle)** *n* mots *mpl* croisés
**crossing** ['krɒsɪŋ] *n (of sea, river)* traversée *f*; *Br* **(pedestrian) c.** passage *m* clouté
**crotch** [krɒtʃ] *n (of garment, person)* entrejambe *m*
**crouch** [kraʊtʃ] *vi* **to c. (down)** *(of person)* s'accroupir; *(of animal)* se tapir
**crow** [krəʊ] **1** *n* corbeau *m*; **as the c. flies** à vol d'oiseau **2** *vi (of cock)* chanter; *Fig (boast)* se vanter (**about** de)
**crowbar** ['krəʊbɑ:(r)] *n* levier *m*
**crowd** [kraʊd] **1** *n* foule *f*; *Fam (group of people)* bande *f*; **there was quite a c.** il y avait beaucoup de monde **2** *vt (street)* envahir; **to c. people/objects into** entasser des gens/des objets dans **3** *vi* **to c. into** *(of people)* s'entasser dans; **to c. round sb/sth** se presser autour de qn/qch; **to c. together** se serrer ▪ **crowded** *adj* plein (**with**

de); *(train, room)* bondé; *(city)* surpeuplé; **it's very c.** il y a beaucoup de monde

**crown** [kraʊn] **1** *n (of king)* couronne *f*; *(of head, hill)* sommet *m*; **the C.** *(monarchy)* la Couronne **2** *vt* couronner

**crucial** ['kruːʃəl] *adj* crucial

**crucify** ['kruːsɪfaɪ] (*pt & pp* **-ied**) *vt* crucifier ▪ **crucifix** [-fɪks] *n* crucifix *m*

**crude** [kruːd] (**-er, -est**) *adj (manners, person, language)* grossier, -ère; *(painting, work)* rudimentaire; **c. oil** pétrole *m* brut

**cruel** [krʊəl] (**crueller, cruellest**) *adj* cruel, -elle ▪ **cruelty** *n* cruauté *f*

**cruise** [kruːz] **1** *n* croisière *f*; **to go on a c.** partir en croisière; **c. ship** bateau *m* de croisière **2** *vi (of ship)* croiser; *(of vehicle)* rouler; *(of taxi)* marauder; *(of tourists)* faire une croisière

**crumb** [krʌm] *n* miette *f*

**crumble** ['krʌmbəl] **1** *vt (bread)* émietter **2** *vi (of bread)* s'émietter; *(collapse) (of resistance)* s'effondrer; **to c. (away)** *(in small pieces)* s'effriter

**crumpet** ['krʌmpɪt] *n Br* = petite crêpe grillée servie beurrée

**crumple** ['krʌmpəl] **1** *vt* froisser **2** *vi* se froisser

**crunch** [krʌntʃ] *vt (food)* croquer

**crusade** [kruː'seɪd] *n Hist & Fig* croisade *f*

**crush** [krʌʃ] **1** *n (crowd)* foule *f*; *(rush)* bousculade *f*; *Fam* **to have a c. on sb** en pincer pour qn **2** *vt* écraser; *(clothes)* froisser; *(cram)* entasser (**into** dans)

**crust** [krʌst] *n* croûte *f* ▪ **crusty** (**-ier, -iest**) *n (bread)* croustillant

**crutch** [krʌtʃ] *n* (**a**) *(of invalid)* béquille *f* (**b**) *(crotch)* entrejambe *m*

**cry** [kraɪ] **1** (*pl* **cries**) *n (shout)* cri *m* **2** (*pt & pp* **cried**) *vt* **to c. (out)** *(shout)* crier **3** *vi (weep)* pleurer; **to c. (out)** pousser un cri; **to c. for help** appeler au secours; **to c. over sb/sth** pleurer qn/qch ▪ **crying** *n (weeping)* pleurs *mpl*

**crypt** [krɪpt] *n* crypte *f*

**crystal** ['krɪstəl] *n* cristal *m*; **c. vase** vase *m* en cristal

**cub** [kʌb] *n* (**a**) *(of animal)* petit *m* (**b**) *(scout)* louveteau *m*

**Cuba** ['kjuːbə] *n* Cuba *f*

**cube** [kjuːb] *n* cube *m*; *(of meat, vegetables)* dé *m*; *(of sugar)* morceau *m* ▪ **cubic** *adj* **c. capacity** volume *m*; *(of engine)* cylindrée *f*; **c. metre** mètre *m* cube

**cubicle** ['kjuːbɪkəl] *n (for changing clothes)* cabine *f*

**cuckoo** ['kʊkuː] (*pl* **-oos**) *n (bird)* coucou *m*

**cucumber** ['kjuːkʌmbə(r)] *n* concombre *m*

**cuddle** ['kʌdəl] **1** *n* câlin *m*; **to give sb a c.** faire un câlin à qn **2** *vt (hug)* serrer dans ses bras; *(caress)* câliner **3** *vi (of lovers)* se faire des câlins ▪ **cuddly** (**-ier, -iest**) *adj (person)* mignon, -onne à croquer; **c. toy** peluche *f*

**cue**[1] [kjuː] *n (in theatre)* réplique *f*; *(signal)* signal *m*

**cue**[2] [kjuː] *n* **(billiard) c.** queue *f* de billard

**cuff** [kʌf] *n (of shirt)* poignet *m*; *Am (of trousers)* revers *m*; **off the c.** *(remark)* impromptu; **c. link** bouton *m* de manchette

**cul-de-sac** ['kʌldəsæk] *n Br* impasse *f*

**culinary** ['kʌlɪnərɪ] *adj* culinaire

**culminate** ['kʌlmɪneɪt] *vi* **to c. in** aboutir à

**culprit** ['kʌlprɪt] *n* coupable *mf*

**cult** [kʌlt] *n* culte *m*; **c. film** film *m* culte

**cultivate** ['kʌltɪveɪt] *vt (land, mind)* cultiver ▪ **cultivated** *adj* cultivé

**culture** ['kʌltʃə(r)] *n* culture *f* ▪ **cultural** *adj* culturel, -elle ▪ **cultured** *adj (person, mind)* cultivé

**cumbersome** ['kʌmbəsəm] *adj* encombrant

**cunning** ['kʌnɪŋ] **1** *adj (ingenious)* astucieux, -euse; *(devious)* rusé **2** *n* astuce *f*; *Pej* ruse *f*

**cup** [kʌp] *n* tasse *f*; *(prize)* coupe *f*; **c. final** *(in football)* finale *f* de la coupe

**cupboard** ['kʌbəd] *n Br* armoire *f*;

*(built into wall)* placard *m*
**curable** ['kjʊərəbəl] *adj* guérissable
**curate** ['kjʊərɪt] *n* vicaire *m*
**curb** [kɜ:b] **1** *n* (**a**) *(limit)* **to put a c. on** mettre un frein à (**b**) *Am (kerb)* bord *m* du trottoir **2** *vt (feelings)* refréner; *(ambitions)* modérer; *(expenses)* réduire
**cure** ['kjʊə(r)] **1** *n* remède *m* (**for** contre) **2** *vt* (**a**) *(person, illness)* guérir; **to c. sb of** guérir qn de (**b**) *(meat, fish) (smoke)* fumer; *(salt)* saler; *(dry)* sécher
**curious** ['kjʊərɪəs] *adj* curieux, -euse (**about** de); **to be c. to know/see** être curieux de savoir/voir ▪ **curiosity** (*pl* **-ies**) *n* curiosité *f* (**about** de)
**curl** [kɜ:l] **1** *n (in hair)* boucle *f* **2** *vti (hair)* boucler; *(with small, tight curls)* friser **3** *vi* **to c. up** *(shrivel)* se racornir ▪ **curler** *n* bigoudi *m* ▪ **curly** (**-ier, -iest**) *adj (hair)* bouclé; *(having many tight curls)* frisé
**currant** ['kʌrənt] *n (dried grape)* raisin *m* de Corinthe
**currency** ['kʌrənsɪ] (*pl* **-ies**) *n (money)* monnaie *f*; **(foreign) c.** devises *fpl* (étrangères)
**current** ['kʌrənt] **1** *adj (fashion, trend)* actuel, -elle; *(opinion, use)* courant; *(year, month)* en cours; **c. account** *(in bank)* compte *m* courant; **c. affairs** questions *fpl* d'actualité **2** *n (of river, air, electricity)* courant *m* ▪ **currently** *adv* actuellement
**curriculum** [kə'rɪkjʊləm] (*pl* **-la** [-lə]) *n* programme *m* scolaire; *Br* **c. vitae** curriculum vitae *m inv*
**curry** ['kʌrɪ] (*pl* **-ies**) *n (dish)* curry *m*, cari *m*
**curse** [kɜ:s] **1** *n* malédiction *f*; *(swearword)* juron *m*; *(scourge)* fléau *m* **2** *vt* maudire; **cursed with sth** affligé de qch **3** *vi (swear)* jurer
**cursor** ['kɜ:sə(r)] *n Comptr* curseur *m*
**cursory** ['kɜ:sərɪ] *adj* superficiel, -elle
**curt** [kɜ:t] *adj* brusque
**curtail** [kɜ:'teɪl] *vt (visit)* écourter
**curtain** ['kɜ:tən] *n* rideau *m*; **to draw the curtains** *(close)* tirer les rideaux
**curts(e)y** ['kɜ:tsɪ] **1** (*pl* **-ies** *or* **-eys**) *n* révérence *f* **2** (*pt & pp* **-ied**) *vi* faire une révérence (**to** à)
**curve** [kɜ:v] **1** *n* courbe *f*; *(in road)* virage *m* **2** *vt* courber **3** *vi* se courber; *(of road)* faire une courbe ▪ **curved** *adj (line)* courbe
**cushion** ['kʊʃən] **1** *n* coussin *m* **2** *vt (shock)* amortir
**cushy** ['kʊʃɪ] (**-ier, -iest**) *adj Fam (job, life)* pépère
**custard** ['kʌstəd] *n* crème *f* anglaise; *(when set)* crème *f* renversée
**custody** ['kʌstədɪ] *n (of child, important papers)* garde *f*
**custom** ['kʌstəm] *n* coutume *f*; *(of individual)* habitude *f*; *(customers)* clientèle *f* ▪ **customary** *adj* habituel, -elle; **it is c. to...** il est d'usage de...
**customer** ['kʌstəmə(r)] *n* client, -e *mf*; *Pej (individual)* individu *m*
**customs** ['kʌstəmz] *npl* **(the) c.** la douane; **to go through c.** passer la douane; **c. officer** douanier *m*
**cut** [kʌt] **1** *n (mark)* coupure *f*; *(stroke)* coup *m*; *(of clothes, hair)* coupe *f*; *(in salary, prices)* réduction *f*; *(of meat)* morceau *m*

**2** (*pt & pp* **cut**, *pres p* **cutting**) *vt* couper; *(meat, chicken)* découper; *(glass, diamond, tree)* tailler; *(salary, prices, profits)* réduire; **to c. sb's hair** couper les cheveux à qn; **to c. sth open** ouvrir qch avec un couteau/des ciseaux/*etc*; **to c. sth short** *(visit)* écourter qch

**3** *vi (of knife, scissors)* couper
▸ **cut back** *vt sep & vi* réduire ▪ **cutback** *n* réduction *f*
▸ **cut down 1** *vt sep* (**a**) *(tree)* abattre (**b**) *(reduce)* réduire **2** *vi* réduire
▸ **cut in** *vi (interrupt)* interrompre; *(in vehicle)* faire une queue de poisson (**on sb** à qn)
▸ **cut off** *vt sep (piece, limb, hair)* couper; *(isolate)* isoler
▸ **cut out 1** *vt sep (article)* découper; *(remove)* enlever; *(eliminate)* supprimer; **to c. out drinking** s'arrêter de

boire; *Fam* **c. it out!** ça suffit!; **c. out to be a doctor** fait pour être médecin **2** *vi (of car engine)* caler

▸**cut up** *vt sep* couper en morceaux; *(meat, chicken)* découper; **to be very c. up about sth** *(upset)* être complètement chamboulé par qch

**cute** [kju:t] (**-er, -est**) *adj Fam (pretty)* mignon, -onne

**cutlery** ['kʌtləri] *n* couverts *mpl*

**cutlet** ['kʌtlɪt] *n* côtelette *f*

**cut-price** [kʌt'praɪs] *adj* à prix réduit

**cutting** ['kʌtɪŋ] **1** *n (from newspaper)* coupure *f*; *(plant)* bouture *f* **2** *adj (wind, remark)* cinglant

**CV** [si:'vi:] (*abbr* **curriculum vitae**) *n Br* CV *m*

**cybercafé** [saɪbə'kæfeɪ] *n* cybercafé *m*

**cyberspace** ['saɪbəspeɪs] *n Comptr* cyberespace *m*

**cycle**[1] ['saɪkəl] **1** *n (bicycle)* bicyclette *f*; **c. lane** voie *f* réservée aux vélos; **c. path** piste *f* cyclable **2** *vi* aller à bicyclette (**to** à); *(as activity)* faire de la bicyclette ▪ **cycling** *n* cyclisme *m* ▪ **cyclist** *n* cycliste *mf*

**cycle**[2] ['saɪkəl] *n (series, period)* cycle *m*

**cylinder** ['sɪlɪndə(r)] *n* cylindre *m*

**cymbal** ['sɪmbəl] *n* cymbale *f*

**cynical** ['sɪnɪkəl] *adj* cynique

**Cyprus** ['saɪprəs] *n* Chypre *f*

**cyst** [sɪst] *n Med* kyste *m*

**Czech** [tʃek] **1** *adj* tchèque; **the C. Republic** la République tchèque **2** *n (person)* Tchèque *mf*; *(language)* tchèque *m*

# Dd

**D, d** [diː] *n* D, d *m inv*

**dab** [dæb] **1** *n* **a d. of** un petit peu de **2** (*pt & pp* **-bb-**) *vt (wound, brow)* tamponner; **to d. sth on sth** appliquer qch (à petits coups) sur qch

**dabble** ['dæbəl] *vi* **to d. in politics/journalism** faire vaguement de la politique/du journalisme

**dad** [dæd] *n Fam* papa *m* ■ **daddy** (*pl* **-ies**) *n Fam* papa *m*

**daffodil** ['dæfədɪl] *n* jonquille *f*

**daft** [dɑːft] (**-er, -est**) *adj Fam* bête

**dagger** ['dægə(r)] *n* dague *f*

**daily** ['deɪlɪ] **1** *adj* quotidien, -enne; *(wage)* journalier, -ère; **d. paper** quotidien *m* **2** *adv* chaque jour, quotidiennement; **twice d.** deux fois par jour **3** (*pl* **-ies**) *n (newspaper)* quotidien *m*

**dainty** ['deɪntɪ] (**-ier, -iest**) *adj* délicat

**dairy** ['deərɪ] **1** (*pl* **-ies**) *n (factory)* laiterie *f*; *(shop)* crémerie *f* **2** *adj* laitier, -ère; **d. produce** produits *mpl* laitiers

**daisy** ['deɪzɪ] (*pl* **-ies**) *n* pâquerette *f*; *(bigger)* marguerite *f*

**dam** [dæm] *n (wall)* barrage *m*

**damage** ['dæmɪdʒ] **1** *n* dégâts *mpl*; *(harm)* préjudice *m*; **damages** *(in court)* dommages-intérêts *mpl* **2** *vt (object)* endommager, abîmer; *(health)* nuire à; *(eyesight)* abîmer; *(plans, reputation)* compromettre ■ **damaging** *adj (harmful)* préjudiciable (**to** à)

**damn** [dæm] **1** *n Fam* **he doesn't care** *or* **give a d.** il s'en fiche pas mal **2** *adj Fam* fichu **3** *adv Fam (very)* vachement **4** *vt (condemn, doom)* condamner; *(curse)* maudire; *Fam* **d. him!** qu'il aille se faire voir! **5** *exclam Fam* **d. (it)!** mince! ■ **damned** *Fam* **1** *adj (awful)* fichu **2** *adv* vachement

**damp** [dæmp] **1** (**-er, -est**) *adj* humide; *(skin)* moite **2** *n* humidité *f* ■ **damp(en)** *vt* humecter; **to d. (down)** *(enthusiasm, zeal)* refroidir

**damson** ['dæmzən] *n* prune *f* de Damas

**dance** [dɑːns] **1** *n* danse *f*; *(social event)* bal *m* (*pl* bals); **d. hall** dancing *m* **2** *vt (waltz, tango)* danser **3** *vi* danser ■ **dancing** *n* danse *f*

**dandelion** ['dændɪlaɪən] *n* pissenlit *m*

**dandruff** ['dændrʌf] *n* pellicules *fpl*

**Dane** [deɪn] *n* Danois, -e *mf*

**danger** ['deɪndʒə(r)] *n* danger *m* (**to** pour); **in d.** en danger; **out of d.** hors de danger; **to be in d. of doing sth** risquer de faire qch ■ **dangerous** *adj* dangereux, -euse (**to** pour)

**dangle** ['dæŋgəl] **1** *vt* balancer **2** *vi (hang)* pendre; *(swing)* se balancer

**Danish** ['deɪnɪʃ] **1** *adj* danois **2** *n (language)* danois *m*

**dare** [deə(r)] *vt* **to d. (to) do sth** oser faire qch; **I d. say he tried** il a essayé, c'est bien possible; **to d. sb to do sth** défier qn de faire qch ■ **daring 1** *adj* audacieux, -euse **2** *n* audace *f*

**dark** [dɑːk] **1** (**-er, -est**) *adj (room, night) & Fig* sombre; *(colour, skin, hair, eyes)* foncé; **it's d. at six** il fait nuit à six heures; **d. glasses** lunettes *fpl* noires **2** *n* obscurité *f*; **after d.** une fois la nuit tombée; *Fig* **to keep sb in the d.** laisser qn dans l'ignorance (**about** de)

▪ **dark-haired** *adj* aux cheveux bruns ▪ **dark-skinned** *adj (person)* à peau brune

**darken** ['dɑːkən] **1** *vt* assombrir; *(colour)* foncer **2** *vi* s'assombrir; *(of colour)* foncer

**darkness** ['dɑːknəs] *n* obscurité *f*

**darkroom** ['dɑːkruːm] *n (for photography)* chambre *f* noire

**darling** ['dɑːlɪŋ] *n (favourite)* chouchou, -oute *mf*; **(my) d.** (mon) chéri/(ma) chérie

**darn** [dɑːn] *vt (mend)* repriser

**dart** [dɑːt] **1** *n (in game)* fléchette *f*; **darts** *(game)* fléchettes *fpl* **2** *vi (dash)* se précipiter (**for** vers)

**dash** [dæʃ] **1** *n* (**a**) *(run, rush)* ruée *f*; **to make a d. for sth** se ruer vers qch (**b**) **a d. of sth** un petit peu de qch (**c**) *(handwritten stroke)* trait *m*; *(punctuation sign)* tiret *m* **2** *vt (throw)* jeter; **to d. off** *(letter)* écrire en vitesse **3** *vi (rush)* se précipiter; **to d. in/out** entrer/sortir en vitesse; **to d. off** *or* **away** filer ▪ **dashboard** *n (of vehicle)* tableau *m* de bord

**data** ['deɪtə] *npl* informations *fpl*; *Comptr* données *fpl*; **d. base** base *f* de données; **d. processing** informatique *f*

**date**[1] [deɪt] **1** *n (day)* date *f*; *Fam (meeting)* rendez-vous *m inv*; *Fam (person)* ami, -e *mf*; **d. of birth** date *f* de naissance; **up to d.** *(in fashion)* à la mode; *(information)* à jour; *(well-informed)* au courant (**on** de); **out of d.** *(old-fashioned)* démodé; *(expired)* périmé **2** *vt (letter)* dater; *Fam (girl, boy)* sortir avec **3** *vi (go out of fashion)* dater; **to d. back to, to d. from** dater de

**date**[2] [deɪt] *n (fruit)* datte *f*

**dated** ['deɪtɪd] *adj* démodé

**daughter** ['dɔːtə(r)] *n* fille *f* ▪ **daughter-in-law** (*pl* **daughters-in-law**) *n* belle-fille *f*

**dawdle** ['dɔːdəl] *vi* traînasser

**dawn** [dɔːn] **1** *n* aube *f*; **at d.** à l'aube **2** *vi (of day)* se lever; **it dawned on him that...** il s'est rendu compte que...

**day** [deɪ] *n (period of daylight, 24 hours)* jour *m*; *(referring to duration)* journée *f*; **all d. (long)** toute la journée; **what d. is it?** quel jour sommes-nous?; **the following** *or* **next d.** le lendemain; **the d. before** la veille; **the d. before yesterday** *or* **before last** avant-hier; **the d. after tomorrow** après-demain; **in those days** en ce temps-là; **these days** de nos jours ▪ **daybreak** *n* point *m* du jour ▪ **daydream 1** *n* rêverie *f* **2** *vi* rêvasser ▪ **daylight** *n* (lumière *f* du) jour *m* ▪ **daytime** *n* journée *f*, jour *m*

**daze** [deɪz] **1** *n* **in a d.** étourdi; *(because of drugs)* hébété; *(astonished)* ahuri **2** *vt (by blow)* étourdir

**dazzle** ['dæzəl] *vt* éblouir

**dead** [ded] **1** *adj* mort; *(numb) (limb)* engourdi; **the phone's d.** il n'y a pas de tonalité; **d. end** *(street) & Fig* impasse *f*; **a d. stop** un arrêt complet **2** *npl* **the d.** les morts *mpl* **3** *adv (completely)* totalement; *Fam (very)* très; **to stop d.** s'arrêter net

**deaden** ['dedən] *vt (shock)* amortir; *(pain)* calmer

**deadline** ['dedlaɪn] *n* date *f* limite; *(hour)* heure *f* limite

**deadlock** ['dedlɒk] *n Fig* impasse *f*

**deadly** ['dedlɪ] **1** (**-ier, -iest**) *adj (poison, blow, enemy)* mortel, -elle; **d. weapon** arme *f* meurtrière **2** *adv (pale, boring)* mortellement

**deaf** [def] **1** *adj* sourd; **d. and dumb** sourd-muet (*f* sourde-muette) **2** *npl* **the d.** les sourds *mpl* ▪ **deafen** *vt* assourdir

**deal**[1] [diːl] *n* **a good** *or* **great d. (of)** *(a lot)* beaucoup (de)

**deal**[2] [diːl] *n* **1** *(in business)* marché *m*, affaire *f*; *(in card games)* donne *f*; **to make** *or* **do a d. (with sb)** conclure un marché (avec qn); **it's a d.!** d'accord!; *Ironic* **big d.!** la belle affaire! **2** (*pt & pp* **dealt**) *vt* **to d. (out)** *(cards, money)* distribuer **3** *vi (trade)* traiter (**with sb** avec qn); **to d. in** faire le commerce de; **to d. with** *(take care* *of)* s'occuper de; *(concern) (of book)* traiter de, parler de ▪ **dealer** *n* marchand, -e *mf* (**in** de); *(for cars)* concessionnaire *mf*; *(in drugs)* revendeur, -euse *mf*; *(in card games)* donneur, -euse *mf* ▪ **dealings** *npl* relations *fpl* (**with** avec); *(in business)* transactions *fpl*

**dealt** [delt] *pt & pp of* **deal**

**dear** [dɪə(r)] **1** (**-er, -est**) *adj (loved, precious, expensive)* cher (*f* chère); **D. Madam** *(in letter)* Madame; **D. Sir** Monsieur; **D. Jane** chère Jane; **oh d.!** oh là là! **2** *n* **(my) d.** *(darling)* (mon) chéri/(ma) chérie; *(friend)* mon cher/ma chère **3** *adv (cost, pay)* cher

**dearly** ['dɪəlɪ] *adv (love)* tendrement; *(very much)* beaucoup; **to pay d. for sth** payer qch cher

**death** [deθ] *n* mort *f*; **to be bored to d.** s'ennuyer à mourir; **to be scared to d.** être mort de peur; **to be sick to d.** en avoir vraiment marre (**of** de); **d. certificate** acte *m* de décès; **d. penalty** peine *f* de mort; **d. sentence** condamnation *f* à mort ▪ **deathly** *adj (silence, paleness)* de mort

**debate** [dɪ'beɪt] **1** *n* débat *m* **2** *vti* discuter ▪ **debatable** *adj* **it's d. whether she will succeed** il est difficile de dire si elle réussira

**debit** ['debɪt] **1** *n* débit *m*; **in d.** *(account)* débiteur **2** *vt* débiter (**sb with sth** qn de qch)

**debris** ['debri:] *n (of building)* décombres *mpl*; *(of plane, car)* débris *mpl*

**debt** [det] *n* dette *f*; **to be in d.** avoir des dettes; **to run** *or* **get into d.** faire des dettes ▪ **debtor** *n* débiteur, -trice *mf*

**debut** ['debju:] *n (on stage)* début *m*; **to make one's d.** faire ses débuts

**decade** ['dekeɪd] *n* décennie *f*

**decadent** ['dekədənt] *adj* décadent

**decaffeinated** [di:'kæfɪneɪtɪd] *adj* décaféiné

**decanter** [dɪ'kæntə(r)] *n* carafe *f*

**decay** [dɪ'keɪ] **1** *n (rot)* pourriture *f*; *(of tooth)* carie *f*; **to fall into d.** *(of building)* tomber en ruine **2** *vi (go bad)* se gâter; *(rot)* pourrir; *(of tooth)* se carier

**deceased** [dɪ'si:st] **1** *adj* décédé **2** *n* **the d.** le défunt/la défunte

**deceit** [dɪ'si:t] *n* tromperie *f* ▪ **deceitful** *adj (person)* fourbe; *(behaviour)* malhonnête

**deceive** [dɪ'si:v] *vti* tromper; **to d. oneself** se faire des illusions

**December** [dɪ'sembə(r)] *n* décembre *m*

**decent** ['di:sənt] *adj (respectable)* convenable; *(good)* bon (*f* bonne); *(kind)* gentil, -ille ▪ **decency** *n* décence *f*; *(kindness)* gentillesse *f*

**deception** [dɪ'sepʃən] *n* tromperie *f* ▪ **deceptive** *adj* trompeur, -euse

**decide** [dɪ'saɪd] **1** *vt (outcome, future)* décider de; *(question, matter)* régler; **to d. to do sth** décider de faire qch; **to d. that...** décider que... **2** *vi (make decisions)* décider; *(make up one's mind)* se décider (**on doing** à faire); **to d. on sth** décider de qch; *(choose)* choisir qch

**decimal** ['desɪməl] **1** *adj* décimal; **d. point** virgule *f* **2** *n* décimale *f*

**decipher** [dɪ'saɪfə(r)] *vt* déchiffrer

**decision** [dɪ'sɪʒən] *n* décision *f*

**decisive** [dɪ'saɪsɪv] *adj (action, event, tone)* décisif, -ive; *(person)* résolu

**deck** [dek] **1** *n* (**a**) *(of ship)* pont *m*; **top d.** *(of bus)* impériale *f* (**b**) **d. of cards** jeu *m* de cartes (**c**) *(of record player)* platine *f* **2** *vt* **to d. (out)** *(adorn)* orner ▪ **deckchair** *n* chaise *f* longue

**declare** [dɪ'kleə(r)] *vt* déclarer (**that** que); *(result)* proclamer ▪ **declaration** *n* déclaration *f*

**decline** [dɪ'klaɪn] **1** *n* déclin *m*; *(fall)* baisse *f* **2** *vt (offer)* décliner; **to d. to do sth** refuser de faire qch **3** *vi (become less) (of popularity, birthrate)* être en baisse; *(deteriorate) (of health, strength)* décliner; *(refuse)* refuser

**decode** [di:'kəʊd] *vt (message)* décoder ▪ **decoder** *n Comptr & TV* décodeur *m*

**decompose** [di:kəm'pəʊz] *vi (rot)* se décomposer

**decor** ['deɪkɔ:(r)] *n* décor *m*

**decorate** ['dekəreɪt] *vt (cake, house, soldier)* décorer (**with** de); *(hat, skirt)* orner (**with** de); *(paint)* peindre; *(wallpaper)* tapisser ▪ **decoration** *n* décoration *f* ▪ **decorative** *adj* décoratif, -ive ▪ **decorator** *n Br (house painter)* peintre *m* décorateur; **(interior) d.** décorateur, -trice *mf*

**decrease 1** ['di:kri:s] *n* diminution *f* (**in** de) **2** [dɪ'kri:s] *vti* diminuer

**decree** [dɪ'kri:] **1** *n (by court)* jugement *m*; *(municipal)* arrêté *m* **2** *(pt & pp* **-eed**) *vt* décréter (**that** que)

**decrepit** [dɪ'krepɪt] *adj (building)* en ruine; *(person)* décrépit

**dedicate** ['dedɪkeɪt] *vt (devote)* consacrer (**to** à); *(book)* dédier (**to** à); **to d. oneself to sth** se consacrer à qch ▪ **dedicated** *adj (teacher)* consciencieux, -euse ▪ **dedication** *n (in book)* dédicace *f*; *(devotion)* dévouement *m*

**deduce** [dɪ'dju:s] *vt (conclude)* déduire (**from** de; **that** que)

**deduct** [dɪ'dʌkt] *vt* déduire (**from** de) ▪ **deductible** *adj (from income) (expenses)* déductible ▪ **deduction** *n (subtraction, conclusion)* déduction *f*

**deed** [di:d] *n* action *f*, acte *m*; *(feat)* exploit *m*; *(legal document)* acte *m* notarié

**deep** [di:p] **1** (**-er, -est**) *adj* profond; *(snow)* épais (*f* épaisse); *(voice)* grave; *(musical note)* bas (*f* basse); **to be 6 metres d.** avoir 6 mètres de profondeur; **d. in thought** plongé dans ses pensées; **d. red** rouge foncé **2** *adv* profondément ▪ **deeply** *adv* profondément

**deepen** ['di:pən] **1** *vt (increase)* augmenter; *(canal, knowledge)* approfondir **2** *vi (of river)* devenir plus profond; *(of mystery)* s'épaissir; *(of voice)* devenir plus grave

**deep-freeze** [di:p'fri:z] **1** *n* congélateur *m* **2** *vt* surgeler

**deer** [dɪə(r)] *n inv* cerf *m*

**deface** [dɪ'feɪs] *vt (damage)* dégrader; *(daub)* barbouiller

**default** [dɪ'fɔ:lt] *n* **by d.** par défaut; **to win by d.** gagner par forfait

**defeat** [dɪ'fi:t] **1** *n* défaite *f* **2** *vt (opponent, army)* vaincre; **that defeats the purpose** *or* **object** ça va à l'encontre du but recherché

**defect**[1] ['di:fekt] *n* défaut *m*

**defect**[2] [dɪ'fekt] *vi (of party member, soldier)* déserter

**defective** [dɪ'fektɪv] *adj (machine)* défectueux, -euse

**defence** [dɪ'fens] (*Am* **defense**) *n* défense *f* (**against** contre); **in his d.** à sa décharge

**defend** [dɪ'fend] *vti* défendre ▪ **defendant** *n (accused)* prévenu, -e *mf* ▪ **defender** *n* défenseur *m*; *(of sports title)* tenant, -e *mf*

**defense** [dɪ'fens] *n Am* = **defence**

**defensive** [dɪ'fensɪv] **1** *adj* défensif, -ive; **to be d.** être sur la défensive **2** *n* **on the d.** sur la défensive

**defer** [dɪ'fɜ:(r)] (*pt & pp* **-rr-**) *vt (postpone)* différer

**defiant** [dɪ'faɪənt] *adj (person)* provocant ▪ **defiance** *n (resistance)* défi *m* (**of** à)

**deficient** [dɪ'fɪʃənt] *adj (not adequate)* insuffisant; *(faulty)* défectueux, -euse; **to be d. in** manquer de ▪ **deficiency** (*pl* **-ies**) *n (shortage)* manque *m*; *(in vitamins, minerals)* carence *f* (**in** de); *(flaw)* défaut *m*

**deficit** ['defɪsɪt] *n* déficit *m*

**define** [dɪ'faɪn] *vt* définir

**definite** ['defɪnɪt] *adj (exact) (date, plan, answer)* précis; *(clear) (improvement, advantage)* net (*f* nette); *(firm) (offer, order)* ferme; *(certain)* certain; **he was quite d.** il a été tout à fait formel; **d. article** *(in grammar)* article *m* défini ▪ **definitely** *adv* certainement; *(improved, superior)* nettement; *(say)* catégoriquement

**definition** [defɪ'nɪʃən] *n* définition *f*

**deflect** [dɪ'flekt] *vt (bullet)* faire dévier

**deformed** [dɪ'fɔːmd] *adj (body)* difforme

**defraud** [dɪ'frɔːd] *vt (customs, State)* frauder; **to d. sb of sth** escroquer qch à qn

**defrost** [diː'frɒst] *vt (fridge)* dégivrer; *(food)* décongeler

**defuse** [diː'fjuːz] *vt (bomb, conflict)* désamorcer

**defy** [dɪ'faɪ] *(pt & pp* **-ied**) *vt (person, death, logic)* défier; *(efforts)* résister à; **to d. sb to do sth** défier qn de faire qch

**degenerate 1** [dɪ'dʒenerət] *adj & n* dégénéré, -e *(mf)* **2** [dɪ'dʒenəreɪt] *vi* dégénérer (**into** en)

**degrading** [dɪ'greɪdɪŋ] *adj* dégradant

**degree** [dɪ'griː] *n* (**a**) *(of angle, temperature, extent)* degré *m*; **it's 20 degrees** *(temperature)* il fait 20 degrés; **to some d., to a certain d.** jusqu'à un certain point; **to such a d.** à tel point (**that** que) (**b**) *(from university)* diplôme *m*; *(Bachelor's)* ≃ licence *f*; *(Master's)* ≃ maîtrise *f*; *(PhD)* ≃ doctorat *m*

**dehydrated** [diːhaɪ'dreɪtɪd] *adj* déshydraté; **to get d.** se déshydrater

**de-ice** [diː'aɪs] *vt (car window)* dégivrer

**dejected** [dɪ'dʒektɪd] *adj* abattu

**delay** [dɪ'leɪ] **1** *n (lateness)* retard *m*; *(waiting period)* délai *m*; **without d.** sans tarder **2** *vt* retarder; *(payment)* différer; **to d. doing sth** tarder à faire qch; **to be delayed** avoir du retard **3** *vi (be slow)* tarder (**in doing** à faire)

**delegate 1** ['delɪgət] *n* délégué, -e *mf* **2** ['delɪgeɪt] *vt* déléguer (**to** à) ▪ **delegation** *n* délégation *f*

**delete** [dɪ'liːt] *vt* supprimer

**deliberate** [dɪ'lɪbərət] *adj (intentional)* délibéré; *(slow)* mesuré ▪ **deliberately** *adv (intentionally)* délibérément

**delicate** ['delɪkət] *adj* délicat ▪ **delicacy** *(pl* **-ies**) *n (quality)* délicatesse *f*; *(food)* mets *m* délicat

**delicatessen** [delɪkə'tesən] *n (shop)* épicerie *f* fine

**delicious** [dɪ'lɪʃəs] *adj* délicieux, -euse

**delight** [dɪ'laɪt] **1** *n (pleasure)* plaisir *m*, joie *f* **2** *vt* ravir **3** *vi* **to d. in doing sth** prendre plaisir à faire qch ▪ **delighted** *adj* ravi (**with sth** de qch; **to do** de faire; **that** que)

**delightful** [dɪ'laɪtfəl] *adj* charmant; *(meal, perfume, sensation)* délicieux, -euse

**delinquent** [dɪ'lɪŋkwənt] *adj & n* délinquant, -e *(mf)*

**delirious** [dɪ'lɪrɪəs] *adj* délirant; **to be d.** délirer

**deliver** [dɪ'lɪvə(r)] *vt* (**a**) *(goods)* livrer; *(letters)* distribuer; *(hand over)* remettre (**to** à) (**b**) *(rescue)* délivrer (**from** de) (**c**) **to d. a woman's baby** accoucher une femme (**d**) *(speech)* prononcer; *(warning, ultimatum)* lancer

**delivery** [dɪ'lɪvərɪ] *(pl* **-ies**) *n* (**a**) *(of goods)* livraison *f*; *(of letters)* distribution *f* (**b**) *(birth)* accouchement *m* (**c**) *(speaking)* débit *m*

**delude** [dɪ'luːd] *vt* tromper; **to d. oneself** se faire des illusions ▪ **delusion** *n* illusion *f*; *(in mental illness)* aberration *f* mentale

**de luxe** [dɪ'lʌks] *adj* de luxe

**demand** [dɪ'mɑːnd] **1** *n* exigence *f*; *(claim)* revendication *f*; *(for goods)* demande *f* (**for** pour); **to be in (great) d.** être très demandé; **to make demands on sb** exiger beaucoup de qn **2** *vt* exiger (**sth from sb** qch de qn); *(rights, more pay)* revendiquer; **to d. that...** exiger que... ▪ **demanding** *adj* exigeant

**demeaning** [dɪ'miːnɪŋ] *adj* dégradant

**demeanour** [dɪ'miːnə(r)] (*Am* **demeanor**) *n (behaviour)* comportement *m*

**demo** ['deməʊ] *(pl* **-os**) *n Fam (demonstration)* manif *f*

**democracy** [dɪ'mɒkrəsɪ] *(pl* **-ies**) *n*

démocratie *f* ■ **democratic** *adj (institution)* démocratique; *(person)* démocrate

**demolish** [dɪˈmɒlɪʃ] *vt* démolir

**demon** [ˈdiːmən] *n* démon *m*

**demonstrate** [ˈdemənstreɪt] **1** *vt* démontrer; *(machine)* faire une démonstration de; **to d. how to do sth** montrer comment faire qch **2** *vi (protest)* manifester ■ **demonstration** [-ˈstreɪʃən] *n* démonstration *f*; *(protest)* manifestation *f* ■ **demonstrator** *n (protester)* manifestant, -e *mf*

**demoralize** [dɪˈmɒrəlaɪz] *vt* démoraliser

**demote** [dɪˈməʊt] *vt* rétrograder

**den** [den] *n (of lion, person)* antre *m*

**denial** [dɪˈnaɪəl] *n (of rumour, allegation)* démenti *m*

**denigrate** [ˈdenɪgreɪt] *vt* dénigrer

**denim** [ˈdenɪm] *n* denim *m*; **denims** *(jeans)* jean *m*

**Denmark** [ˈdenmɑːk] *n* le Danemark

**denomination** [dɪnɒmɪˈneɪʃən] *n (religion)* confession *f*; *(of coin, banknote)* valeur *f*

**denote** [dɪˈnəʊt] *vt* dénoter

**denounce** [dɪˈnaʊns] *vt (person, injustice)* dénoncer (**to** à)

**dense** [dens] (**-er, -est**) *adj* dense; *Fam (stupid)* lourd ■ **densely** *adv* **d. populated** très peuplé

**dent** [dent] **1** *n (in car, metal)* bosse *f* **2** *vt* cabosser

**dental** [ˈdentəl] *adj* dentaire; **d. appointment** rendez-vous *m inv* chez le dentiste

**dentist** [ˈdentɪst] *n* dentiste *mf*; **to go to the d.** aller chez le dentiste

**dentures** [ˈdentʃəz] *npl* dentier *m*

**deny** [dɪˈnaɪ] (*pt & pp* **-ied**) *vt* nier (**doing** avoir fait; **that** que); *(rumour)* démentir; **to d. sb sth** refuser qch à qn

**deodorant** [diːˈəʊdərənt] *n* déodorant *m*

**depart** [dɪˈpɑːt] *vi* partir; *(deviate)* s'écarter (**from** de)

**department** [dɪˈpɑːtmənt] *n* département *m*; *(in office)* service *m*; *(in shop)* rayon *m*; *(of government)* ministère *m*; **d. store** grand magasin *m*

**departure** [dɪˈpɑːtʃə(r)] *n* départ *m*; **d. lounge** *(in airport)* salle *f* d'embarquement

**depend** [dɪˈpend] *vi* dépendre (**on** *or* **upon** de); **to d. (up)on** *(rely on)* compter sur (**for sth** pour qch) ■ **dependant** *n* personne *f* à charge ■ **dependent** *adj (relative, child)* à charge; **to be d. (up)on** dépendre de; **to be d. on sb** *(financially)* être à la charge de qn

**depict** [dɪˈpɪkt] *vt (describe)* décrire; *(in pictures)* représenter

**deplorable** [dɪˈplɔːrəbəl] *adj* déplorable

**deploy** [dɪˈplɔɪ] *vt (troops)* déployer

**deport** [dɪˈpɔːt] *vt (foreigner, criminal)* expulser

**deposit** [dɪˈpɒzɪt] **1** *n* (**a**) *(in bank)* dépôt *m*; *(part payment)* acompte *m*; *(returnable)* caution *f* (**b**) *(sediment)* dépôt *m*; *(of gold, oil)* gisement *m* **2** *vt (object, money)* déposer

**depot** [*Br* ˈdepəʊ, *Am* ˈdiːpəʊ] *n (for goods)* dépôt *m*; *Am (railroad station)* gare *f*; *Am* **(bus) d.** gare *f* routière

**depraved** [dɪˈpreɪvd] *adj* dépravé

**depreciate** [dɪˈpriːʃɪeɪt] *vi (fall in value)* se déprécier

**depress** [dɪˈpres] *vt (discourage)* déprimer ■ **depressed** *adj (person, market)* déprimé; **to get d.** se décourager ■ **depression** *n* dépression *f*

**deprive** [dɪˈpraɪv] *vt* priver (**of** de) ■ **deprived** *adj (child)* défavorisé

**depth** [depθ] *n* profondeur *f*; **in the depths of** *(forest, despair)* au plus profond de; *(winter)* au cœur de; **in d.** en profondeur

**deputy** [ˈdepjʊtɪ] (*pl* **-ies**) *n (replacement)* remplaçant, -e *mf*; *(assistant)* adjoint, -e *mf*

**derailed** [dɪˈreɪld] *adj* **to be d.** *(of train)* dérailler

**derelict** [ˈderɪlɪkt] *adj (building)* abandonné

**derision** [dɪˈrɪʒən] *n* dérision *f*
**derisory** [dɪˈraɪsərɪ] *adj (amount)* dérisoire
**derive** [dɪˈraɪv] **1** *vt* provenir (**from** de); **to be derived from** provenir de **2** *vi* **to d. from** provenir de ▪ **derivation** *n Ling* dérivation *f*
**descend** [dɪˈsend] **1** *vt (stairs, hill)* descendre; **to be descended from** descendre de **2** *vi* descendre (**from** de); **to d. upon** *(of tourists)* envahir; *(attack)* faire une descente sur; **in descending order** en ordre décroissant ▪ **descendant** *n* descendant, -e *mf*
**descent** [dɪˈsent] *n* (**a**) *(of aircraft)* descente *f* (**b**) *(ancestry)* origine *f*; **to be of Norman d.** être d'origine normande
**describe** [dɪˈskraɪb] *vt* décrire ▪ **description** *n* description *f*
**desert**[1] [ˈdezət] *n* désert *m*; **d. island** île *f* déserte
**desert**[2] [dɪˈzɜːt] **1** *vt (person)* abandonner; *(place, cause)* déserter **2** *vi (of soldier)* déserter ▪ **deserted** *adj* désert
**deserve** [dɪˈzɜːv] *vt* mériter (**to do** de faire) ▪ **deserving** *adj (person)* méritant; *(action, cause)* méritoire
**design** [dɪˈzaɪn] **1** *n* (**a**) *(pattern)* motif *m*; *(sketch)* plan *m*; *(of dress, car, furniture)* modèle *m* (**b**) *(aim)* dessein *m*; **to have designs on** avoir des vues sur **2** *vt (car, building)* concevoir; *(dress)* créer; **designed to do sth/for sth** conçu pour faire qch/pour qch ▪ **designer** *n (artistic)* dessinateur, -trice *mf*; *(industrial)* concepteur-dessinateur *m*; *(of clothes)* styliste *mf*; *(well-known)* couturier *m*; **d. clothes** vêtements *mpl* de marque
**designate** [ˈdezɪgneɪt] *vt* désigner
**desire** [dɪˈzaɪə(r)] **1** *n* désir *m* **2** *vt* désirer (**to do** faire) ▪ **desirable** *adj* désirable
**desk** [desk] *n (in school)* table *f*; *(in office)* bureau *m*; *Br (in shop)* caisse *f*; **(reception) d.** *(in hotel)* réception *f*; *Am* **d. clerk** *(in hotel)* réceptionniste *mf*
**desktop** [ˈdesktɒp] *n Comptr* bureau *m*; **d. computer** ordinateur *m* de bureau; **d. publishing** publication *f* assistée par ordinateur
**desolate** [ˈdesələt] *adj (deserted)* désolé; *(dreary, bleak)* morne, triste
**despair** [dɪˈspeə(r)] **1** *n* désespoir *m*; **to be in d.** être au désespoir **2** *vi* désespérer (**of sb** de qn; **of doing** de faire)
**despatch** [dɪˈspætʃ] *n & vt* = **dispatch**
**desperate** [ˈdespərət] *adj* désespéré; **to be d. for** *(money, love)* avoir désespérément besoin de; *(cigarette, baby)* mourir d'envie d'avoir ▪ **desperately** *adv (ill)* gravement
**despicable** [dɪˈspɪkəbəl] *adj* méprisable
**despise** [dɪˈspaɪz] *vt* mépriser
**despite** [dɪˈspaɪt] *prep* malgré
**despondent** [dɪˈspɒndənt] *adj* abattu
**dessert** [dɪˈzɜːt] *n* dessert *m* ▪ **dessertspoon** *n Br* cuillère *f* à dessert
**destination** [destɪˈneɪʃən] *n* destination *f*
**destine** [ˈdestɪn] *vt* destiner (**for** à; **to do** à faire)
**destiny** [ˈdestɪnɪ] (*pl* **-ies**) *n* destin *m*, destinée *f*
**destitute** [ˈdestɪtjuːt] *adj (poor)* indigent
**destroy** [dɪˈstrɔɪ] *vt* détruire; *(cat, dog)* faire piquer
**destruction** [dɪˈstrʌkʃən] *n* destruction *f* ▪ **destructive** *adj (person, war)* destructeur, -trice
**detach** [dɪˈtætʃ] *vt* détacher (**from** de) ▪ **detached** *adj Br* **d. house** maison *f* individuelle
**detachable** [dɪˈtætʃəbəl] *adj* amovible
**detail** [ˈdiːteɪl] *n (item of information)* détail *m*; **in d.** en détail; **to go into d.** entrer dans les détails ▪ **detailed** *adj (account)* détaillé
**detain** [dɪˈteɪn] *vt (delay)* retenir; *(prisoner)* placer en détention; *(in hospital)* garder ▪ **detention** *n (at school)* retenue *f*

**detect** [dɪˈtekt] *vt* détecter

**detective** [dɪˈtektɪv] *n (police officer)* ≃ inspecteur *m* de police; *(private)* détective *m* privé; **d. film/novel** film *m*/roman *m* policier

**detector** [dɪˈtektə(r)] *n* détecteur *m*

**deter** [dɪˈtɜː(r)] *(pt & pp* **-rr-***) vt* **to d. sb** dissuader qn (**from doing** de faire)

**detergent** [dɪˈtɜːdʒənt] *n* détergent *m*

**deteriorate** [dɪˈtɪərɪəreɪt] *vi* se détériorer

**determine** [dɪˈtɜːmɪn] *vt (cause, date)* déterminer; **to d. to do sth** décider de faire qch ▪ **determined** *adj (look, person)* déterminé; **to be d. to do sth** être décidé à faire qch

**deterrent** [dɪˈterənt] *n* **to be a d., to act as a d.** être dissuasif, -ive

**detest** [dɪˈtest] *vt* détester (**doing** faire)

**detonate** [ˈdetəneɪt] **1** *vt* faire exploser **2** *vi* exploser

**detour** [ˈdiːtʊə(r)] *n* détour *m*; **to make a d.** faire un détour

**detract** [dɪˈtrækt] *vi* **to d. from** *(make less)* diminuer

**detriment** [ˈdetrɪmənt] *n* **to the d. of** au détriment de ▪ **detrimental** *adj* préjudiciable (**to** à)

**devaluation** [diːvæljʊˈeɪʃən] *n (of money)* dévaluation *f*

**devastate** [ˈdevəsteɪt] *vt (crop, village)* dévaster; *(person)* anéantir ▪ **devastating** *adj (news, results)* accablant

**develop** [dɪˈveləp] **1** *vt (theory, argument)* développer; *(area, land)* mettre en valeur; *(habit)* contracter; *(photo)* développer **2** *vi (grow)* se développer; *(of event, crisis)* se produire; *(of talent, illness)* se manifester; **to d. into** devenir ▪ **developing** *adj* **d. country** pays *m* en voie de développement

**developer** [dɪˈveləpə(r)] *n* **(property) d.** promoteur *m*

**development** [dɪˈveləpmənt] *n (growth, progress)* développement *m*; **(housing) d.** lotissement *m*; *(large)* grand ensemble *m*; **a (new) d.** *(in situation)* un fait nouveau

**deviate** [ˈdiːvɪeɪt] *vi* dévier (**from** de)

**device** [dɪˈvaɪs] *n (instrument, gadget)* dispositif *m*; *(scheme)* procédé *m*; **explosive d.** engin *m* explosif; **left to one's own devices** livré à soi-même

**devil** [ˈdevəl] *n* diable *m*; *Fam* **what/where/why the d....?** que/où/pourquoi diable...?

**devious** [ˈdiːvɪəs] *adj (mind, behaviour)* tortueux, -euse

**devise** [dɪˈvaɪz] *vt* imaginer; *(plot)* ourdir

**devoid** [dɪˈvɔɪd] *adj* **d. of** dénué *ou* dépourvu de

**devote** [dɪˈvəʊt] *vt* consacrer (**to** à) ▪ **devoted** *adj* dévoué; *(admirer)* fervent

**devotion** [dɪˈvəʊʃən] *n (to friend, family, cause)* dévouement *m* (**to sb** à qn); *(religious)* dévotion *f*

**devour** [dɪˈvaʊə(r)] *vt (eat, engulf, read)* dévorer

**devout** [dɪˈvaʊt] *adj (person)* dévot

**dew** [djuː] *n* rosée *f*

**diabetes** [daɪəˈbiːtiːz] *n* diabète *m* ▪ **diabetic** [-ˈbetɪk] **1** *adj* diabétique **2** *n* diabétique *mf*

**diagnose** [daɪəgˈnəʊz] *vt* diagnostiquer ▪ **diagnosis** [-ˈnəʊsɪs] *(pl* **-oses** [-əʊsiːz]) *n* diagnostic *m*

**diagonal** [daɪˈægənəl] **1** *adj* diagonal **2** *n* diagonale *f* ▪ **diagonally** *adv* en diagonale

**diagram** [ˈdaɪəgræm] *n* schéma *m*

**dial** [ˈdaɪəl] **1** *n* cadran *m*; *Am* **d. tone** tonalité *f* **2** *(Br* **-ll-**, *Am* **-l-***) vt (phone number)* composer; *(person)* appeler ▪ **dialling** *n Br* **d. code** indicatif *m*; *Br* **d. tone** tonalité *f*

**dialect** [ˈdaɪəlekt] *n* dialecte *m*

**dialogue** [ˈdaɪəlɒg] *(Am* **dialog***) n* dialogue *m*

**diameter** [daɪˈæmɪtə(r)] *n* diamètre *m*

**diamond** [ˈdaɪəmənd] *n* (**a**) *(stone)* diamant *m*; *(shape)* losange *m*; **d. necklace** rivière *f* de diamants (**b**) **diamond(s)** *(in card games)* carreau *m*

**diaper** [ˈdaɪpər] *n Am* couche *f*

**diarrh(o)ea** [daɪəˈriːə] *n* diarrhée *f*;

**to have d.** avoir la diarrhée

**diary** ['daɪərɪ] (*pl* **-ies**) *n Br (for appointments)* agenda *m*; *(private)* journal *m* (intime)

**dice** [daɪs] *n inv* dé *m*

**dictate** [dɪk'teɪt] **1** *vt (letter, conditions)* dicter (**to** à) **2** *vi* dicter qn ▪ **dictation** *n* dictée *f*

**dictator** [dɪk'teɪtə(r)] *n* dictateur *m*

**dictionary** ['dɪkʃənərɪ] (*pl* **-ies**) *n* dictionnaire *m*

**did** [dɪd] *pt of* **do**

**die** [daɪ] (*pt & pp* **died**, *pres p* **dying**) *vi* mourir (**of** *or* **from** de); *Fig* **to be dying to do sth** mourir d'envie de faire qch; **to be dying for sth** avoir une envie folle de qch; **to d. away** *(of noise)* mourir; **to d. down** *(of storm)* se calmer; **to d. out** *(of custom)* mourir

**diesel** ['diːzəl] *adj & n* **d. (engine)** (moteur *m*) diesel *m*; **d. (oil)** gazole *m*

**diet** ['daɪət] **1** *n (usual food)* alimentation *f*; *(restricted food)* régime *m*; **to go on a d.** faire un régime **2** *vi* être au régime

**differ** ['dɪfə(r)] *vi* différer (**from** de); *(disagree)* ne pas être d'accord (**from** avec)

**difference** ['dɪfərəns] *n* différence *f* (**in** de); **d. of opinion** différend *m*; **it makes no d.** ça n'a pas d'importance

**different** ['dɪfərənt] *adj* différent (**from** de); *(another)* autre; *(various)* divers

**differentiate** [dɪfə'renʃɪeɪt] **1** *vt* différencier (**from** de) **2** *vi* faire la différence (**between** entre) ▪ **differently** *adv* différemment (**from** de)

**difficult** ['dɪfɪkəlt] *adj* difficile (**to do** à faire)

**difficulty** ['dɪfɪkəltɪ] (*pl* **-ies**) *n* difficulté *f*; **to have d. doing sth** avoir du mal à faire qch;

**dig** [dɪg] **1** *n (with elbow)* coup de coude; *Fam (remark)* pique *f* **2** (*pt & pp* **dug**, *pres p* **digging**) *vt (ground, garden)* bêcher; *(hole, grave)* creuser; **to d. sth into sth** *(push)* planter qch dans qch; **to d. out** *(from ground)* déterrer; *Fam (find)* dénicher; **to d. up** *(from ground)* déterrer; *(road)* excaver **3** *vi (dig a hole)* creuser

**digest** [daɪ'dʒest] *vti* digérer ▪ **digestion** *n* digestion *f*

**digit** ['dɪdʒɪt] *n (number)* chiffre *m* ▪ **digital** *adj* numérique; *(tape, recording)* audionumérique

**dignified** ['dɪgnɪfaɪd] *adj* digne ▪ **dignity** *n* dignité *f*

**digress** [daɪ'gres] *vi* faire une digression

**dilapidated** [dɪ'læpɪdeɪtɪd] *adj (house)* délabré

**dilemma** [daɪ'lemə] *n* dilemme *m*

**diligent** ['dɪlɪdʒənt] *adj* appliqué

**dilute** [daɪ'luːt] *vt* diluer

**dim** [dɪm] **1** (**dimmer, dimmest**) *adj (light)* faible; *(room)* sombre; *(memory)* vague; *(person)* stupide **2** (*pt & pp* **-mm-**) *vt (light)* baisser; *Am* **to d. one's headlights** se mettre en code

**dime** [daɪm] *n Am* (pièce *f* de) dix cents *mpl*

**dimension** [daɪ'menʃən] *n* dimension *f*

**diminish** [dɪ'mɪnɪʃ] *vti* diminuer

**dimple** ['dɪmpəl] *n* fossette *f*

**din** [dɪn] *n (noise)* vacarme *m*

**dine** [daɪn] *vi* dîner (**on** *or* **off** de); **to d. out** aller dîner au restaurant ▪ **diner** *n (person)* dîneur, -euse *mf*; *Am (restaurant)* petit restaurant *m* ▪ **dining** *n* **d. car** *(on train)* wagon-restaurant *m*; **d. room** salle *f* à manger

**dinghy** ['dɪŋgɪ] (*pl* **-ies**) *n* petit canot *m*; **(rubber) d.** canot *m* pneumatique

**dingy** ['dɪndʒɪ] (**-ier, -iest**) *adj (room)* minable; *(colour)* terne

**dinner** ['dɪnə(r)] *n (evening meal)* dîner *m*; *(lunch)* déjeuner *m*; **to have d.** dîner; **d. jacket** smoking *m*; **d. party** dîner *m*; **d. plate** grande assiette *f*; **d. service, d. set** service *m* de table

**dinosaur** ['daɪnəsɔː(r)] *n* dinosaure *m*

**dip** [dɪp] **1** *n (in road)* petit creux *m*; **to go for a d.** *(swim)* faire trempette **2** (*pt & pp* **-pp-**) *vt* plonger; *Br* **to d. one's headlights** se mettre en code **3** *vi (of*

*road)* plonger; **to d. into** *(pocket, savings)* puiser dans; *(book)* feuilleter
**diploma** [dɪ'pləʊmə] *n* diplôme *m*
**diplomat** ['dɪpləmæt] *n* diplomate *mf*
▪ **diplomatic** *adj* diplomatique
**dire** ['daɪə(r)] *adj (situation)* affreux, -euse; *(consequences)* tragique; *(poverty, need)* extrême; **to be in d. straits** être dans une mauvaise passe
**direct** [daɪ'rekt] **1** *adj (result, flight, person)* direct; *Br* **d. debit** prélèvement *m* automatique
**2** *adv* directement
**3** *vt (gaze, light, attention)* diriger (**at** sur); *(traffic)* régler; *(letter, remark)* adresser (**to** à); *(film)* réaliser; *(play)* mettre en scène; **to d. sb to** *(place)* indiquer à qn le chemin de; **to d. sb to do sth** charger qn de faire qch
**direction** [daɪ'rekʃən] *n* direction *f*, sens *m*; **directions** *(orders)* indications *fpl*; **directions (for use)** mode *m* d'emploi
**directly** [daɪ'rektlɪ] *adv (without detour)* directement; *(exactly)* juste; *(at once)* tout de suite; **d. in front** juste devant
**director** [daɪ'rektə(r)] *n* directeur, -trice *mf*; *(board member)* administrateur, -trice *mf*; *(of film)* réalisateur, -trice *mf*; *(of play)* metteur *m* en scène
**directory** [daɪ'rektərɪ] (*pl* **-ies**) *n (phone book)* annuaire *m*; *(of addresses) & Comptr* répertoire *m*; **telephone d.** annuaire *m* du téléphone; *Br* **d. enquiries** renseignements *mpl* téléphoniques
**dirt** [dɜːt] *n* saleté *f*; *(mud)* boue *f*; *(earth)* terre *f*; *Fam* **d. cheap** très bon marché
**dirty** ['dɜːtɪ] **1** (**-ier, -iest**) *adj* sale; *(job)* salissant; *(word)* grossier, -ère; **to get d.** se salir; **to get sth d.** salir qch; **a d. joke** une histoire cochonne; **a d. trick** un sale tour **2** *vt* salir
**disability** [dɪsə'bɪlɪtɪ] (*pl* **-ies**) *n (injury)* infirmité *f*; *(condition)* invalidité *f*; *Fig* désavantage *m*
**disabled** [dɪ'seɪbəld] **1** *adj* handicapé **2** *npl* **the d.** les handicapés *mpl*
**disadvantage** [dɪsəd'vɑːntɪdʒ] **1** *n* désavantage *m* **2** *vt* désavantager
**disagree** [dɪsə'griː] *vi* ne pas être d'accord (**with** avec); **to d. with sb** *(of food, climate, medicine)* ne pas réussir à qn ▪ **disagreement** *n* désaccord *m*; *(quarrel)* différend *m*
**disagreeable** [dɪsə'griːəbəl] *adj* désagréable
**disappear** [dɪsə'pɪə(r)] *vi* disparaître
▪ **disappearance** *n* disparition *f*
**disappoint** [dɪsə'pɔɪnt] *vt* décevoir
▪ **disappointing** *adj* décevant ▪ **disappointment** *n* déception *f*
**disapproval** [dɪsə'pruːvəl] *n* désapprobation *f*
**disapprove** [dɪsə'pruːv] *vi* **to d. of sb/sth** désapprouver qn/qch
**disarray** [dɪsə'reɪ] *n* **in d.** *(army, political party)* en plein désarroi; *(clothes, hair)* en désordre
**disaster** [dɪ'zɑːstə(r)] *n* désastre *m*, catastrophe *f*; **d. area** région *f* sinistrée ▪ **disastrous** *adj* désastreux, -euse
**disband** [dɪs'bænd] **1** *vt* dissoudre **2** *vi* se dissoudre
**disbelief** [dɪsbə'liːf] *n* incrédulité *f*
**disc** [dɪsk] (*Am* **disk**) *n* disque *m*; **d. jockey** disc-jockey *m*
**discard** [dɪs'kɑːd] *vt (get rid of)* se débarrasser de; *(plan)* abandonner
**discern** [dɪ'sɜːn] *vt* discerner ▪ **discerning** *adj (person)* averti
**discernible** [dɪ'sɜːnəbəl] *adj* perceptible
**discharge** **1** ['dɪstʃɑːdʒ] *n (of gun, electricity)* décharge *f*; *(dismissal)* renvoi *m*; *(freeing)* libération *f* **2** [dɪs'tʃɑːdʒ] *vt (patient)* laisser sortir; *(employee)* renvoyer; *(soldier, prisoner)* libérer; *(gun)* décharger
**disciple** [dɪ'saɪpəl] *n* disciple *m*
**discipline** ['dɪsɪplɪn] **1** *n (behaviour, subject)* discipline *f* **2** *vt (control)* discipliner; *(punish)* punir
**disclose** [dɪs'kləʊz] *vt* révéler ▪ **disclosure** [-ʒə(r)] *n* révélation *f*

**disco** ['dɪskəʊ] *(pl* **-os***)* *n* discothèque *f*

**discolour** [dɪs'kʌlə(r)] *(Am* **discolor***)* *vt* décolorer; *(teeth)* jaunir

**discomfort** [dɪs'kʌmfət] *n (physical)* petite douleur *f*; *(mental)* malaise *m*

**disconcerting** [dɪskən'sɜːtɪŋ] *adj* déconcertant

**disconnect** [dɪskə'nekt] *vt (unfasten)* détacher; *(unplug)* débrancher; *(gas, telephone, electricity)* couper

**discontented** [dɪskən'tentɪd] *adj* mécontent (**with** de)

**discord** ['dɪskɔːd] *n (disagreement)* discorde *f*

**discotheque** ['dɪskətek] *n (club)* discothèque *f*

**discount 1** ['dɪskaʊnt] *n (on article)* réduction *f*; *(on account paid early)* escompte *m*; **d. store** solderie *f* **2** [dɪs'kaʊnt] *vt (story)* ne pas tenir compte de

**discourage** [dɪs'kʌrɪdʒ] *vt* décourager (**sb from doing** qn de faire)

**discover** [dɪs'kʌvə(r)] *vt* découvrir (**that** que) ▪ **discovery** *(pl* **-ies***)* *n* découverte *f*

**discredit** [dɪs'kredɪt] *vt (cast slur on)* discréditer

**discreet** [dɪ'skriːt] *adj* discret, -ète

**discrepancy** [dɪ'skrepənsɪ] *(pl* **-ies***)* *n* décalage *m* (**between** entre)

**discretion** [dɪ'skreʃən] *n (tact)* discrétion *f*

**discriminate** [dɪ'skrɪmɪneɪt] *vi* **to d. against** faire de la discrimination envers; **to d. between** distinguer entre ▪ **discrimination** [-'neɪʃən] *n (bias)* discrimination *f*

**discus** ['dɪskəs] *n Sport* disque *m*

**discuss** [dɪ'skʌs] *vt* discuter de ▪ **discussion** *n* discussion *f*

**disdain** [dɪs'deɪn] *n* dédain *m*

**disease** [dɪ'ziːz] *n* maladie *f*

**disembark** [dɪsɪm'bɑːk] *vti* débarquer

**disenchanted** [dɪsɪn'tʃɑːntɪd] *adj* désenchanté

**disfigured** [dɪs'fɪgə(r)] *adj* défiguré

**disgrace** [dɪs'greɪs] **1** *n (shame)* honte *f* (**to** à) **2** *vt* déshonorer ▪ **disgraceful** *adj* honteux, -euse

**disgruntled** [dɪs'grʌntəld] *adj* mécontent

**disguise** [dɪs'gaɪz] **1** *n* déguisement *m*; **in d.** déguisé **2** *vt* déguiser (**as** en)

**disgust** [dɪs'gʌst] **1** *n* dégoût *m* (**for** *or* **at** *or* **with** de) **2** *vt* dégoûter ▪ **disgusted** *adj* dégoûté (**at** *or* **by** *or* **with** de); **to be d. with sb** *(annoyed)* être fâché contre qn ▪ **disgusting** *adj* dégoûtant

**dish** [dɪʃ] **1** *n (container, food)* plat *m*; **to do the dishes** faire la vaisselle **2** *vt* **to d. out** *or* **up** *(food)* servir ▪ **dishcloth** *n (for washing)* lavette *f*; *(for drying)* torchon *m* ▪ **dishtowel** *n* torchon *m* (à vaisselle) ▪ **dishwasher** *n (machine)* lave-vaisselle *m inv*

**dishevelled** [dɪ'ʃevəld] *(Am* **disheveled***)* *adj (person, hair)* ébouriffé

**dishonest** [dɪs'ɒnɪst] *adj* malhonnête ▪ **dishonesty** *n* malhonnêteté *f*

**dishonourable** [dɪs'ɒnərəbəl] *(Am* **dishonorable***)* *adj* déshonorant

**disillusion** [dɪsɪ'luːʒən] *vt* décevoir; **to be disillusioned** être déçu (**with** de)

**disinclined** [dɪsɪŋ'klaɪnd] *adj* peu disposé (**to do** à faire)

**disinfect** [dɪsɪn'fekt] *vt* désinfecter ▪ **disinfectant** *n* désinfectant *m*

**disinherit** [dɪsɪn'herɪt] *vt* déshériter

**disintegrate** [dɪs'ɪntɪgreɪt] *vi* se désintégrer

**disinterested** [dɪs'ɪntrɪstɪd] *adj (impartial)* désintéressé

**disjointed** [dɪs'dʒɔɪntɪd] *adj (words, style)* décousu

**disk** [dɪsk] *n* (**a**) *Am* = **disc** (**b**) *Comptr* disque *m*; *(floppy)* disquette *f*; **on d.** sur disque; **d. drive** unité *f* de disques ▪ **diskette** *n Comptr* disquette *f*

**dislike** [dɪs'laɪk] **1** *n* aversion *f* (**for** *or* **of** pour); **to take a d. to sb/sth** prendre qn/qch en grippe **2** *vt* ne pas aimer (**doing** faire)

**dislocate** ['dɪsləkeɪt] *vt (limb)* démettre; **to d. one's shoulder** se démettre l'épaule

**dislodge** [dɪs'lɒdʒ] *vt* faire bouger, déplacer; *(enemy)* déloger
**disloyal** [dɪs'lɔɪəl] *adj* déloyal
**dismal** ['dɪzməl] *adj* lugubre ▪ **dismally** *adv (fail, behave)* lamentablement
**dismantle** [dɪs'mæntəl] *vt (machine)* démonter; *(organization)* démanteler
**dismay** [dɪs'meɪ] **1** *n* consternation *f* **2** *vt* consterner
**dismiss** [dɪs'mɪs] *vt (from job)* renvoyer (**from** de); *(official)* destituer; *(thought, suggestion)* écarter; **to d. a case** *(of judge)* classer une affaire ▪ **dismissal** *n* renvoi *m*; *(of official)* destitution *f*
**dismount** [dɪs'maʊnt] *vi (of person)* descendre (**from** de)
**disobedient** [dɪsə'bi:dɪənt] *adj* désobéissant
**disobey** [dɪsə'beɪ] **1** *vt* désobéir à **2** *vi* désobéir
**disorder** [dɪs'ɔ:də(r)] *n (confusion)* désordre *m*; *(illness, riots)* troubles *mpl* ▪ **disorderly** *adj (behaviour)* désordonné; *(meeting, crowd)* houleux, -euse
**disorganized** [dɪs'ɔ:gənaɪzd] *adj* désorganisé
**disorientate** [dɪs'ɔ:rɪənteɪt] (*Am* **disorient** [dɪs'ɔ:rɪənt]) *vt* désorienter
**disown** [dɪs'əʊn] *vt* renier
**disparaging** [dɪs'pærɪdʒɪŋ] *adj (remark)* désobligeant
**dispatch** [dɪ'spætʃ] **1** *n (sending)* expédition *f* (**of** de); *(message)* dépêche *f* **2** *vt (send, finish off)* expédier; *(troops, messenger)* envoyer
**dispel** [dɪ'spel] (*pt & pp* **-ll-**) *vt* dissiper
**dispensary** [dɪ'spensərɪ] (*pl* **-ies**) *n (in chemist's shop)* officine *f*
**dispense** [dɪ'spens] **1** *vt (give out)* distribuer; *(medicine)* préparer **2** *vi* **to d. with** *(do without)* se passer de ▪ **dispenser** *n (device)* distributeur *m*
**disperse** [dɪ'spɜ:s] **1** *vt* disperser **2** *vi* se disperser
**displace** [dɪs'pleɪs] *vt (shift)* déplacer; *(replace)* supplanter
**display** [dɪ'spleɪ] **1** *n (in shop)* étalage *m*; *(of paintings, handicrafts)* exposition *f*; **d. (unit)** *(of computer)* moniteur *m*; **on d.** exposé **2** *vt (goods)* exposer; *(sign, notice)* afficher; *(emotion)* manifester; *(talent, concern, ignorance)* faire preuve de
**displeased** [dɪs'pli:zd] *adj* mécontent (**with** de)
**disposable** [dɪ'spəʊzəbəl] *adj Br (plate, nappy)* jetable; *(income)* disponible
**disposal** [dɪ'spəʊzəl] *n (of waste)* évacuation *f*; **at sb's d.** à la disposition de qn
**dispose**[1] [dɪ'spəʊz] *vi* **to d. of** *(get rid of)* se débarrasser de; *(throw away)* jeter; *(matter, problem)* régler
**dispose**[2] [dɪ'spəʊz] *vt* **to be disposed to do** être disposé à faire; **well-disposed towards** bien disposé envers
**disposition** [dɪspə'zɪʃən] *n (character)* tempérament *m*
**dispossess** [dɪspə'zes] *vt* déposséder (**of** de)
**disproportionate** [dɪsprə'pɔ:ʃənət] *adj* disproportionné
**disprove** [dɪs'pru:v] (*pp* **disproved,** *Law* **disproven** [-'prəʊvən]) *vt* réfuter
**dispute** [dɪ'spju:t] **1** *n (quarrel)* dispute *f*; *(legal)* litige *m*; **(industrial) d.** conflit *m* social **2** *vt (claim, will)* contester
**disqualify** [dɪs'kwɒlɪfaɪ] (*pt & pp* **-ied**) *vt (make unfit)* rendre inapte (**from** à); *Sport* disqualifier; **to d. sb from driving** retirer son permis à qn ▪ **disqualification** *n Sport* disqualification *f*
**disregard** [dɪsrɪ'gɑ:d] **1** *n* mépris *m* (**for** de) **2** *vt* ne tenir aucun compte de
**disrepair** [dɪsrɪ'peə(r)] *n* **in (a state of) d.** délabré
**disreputable** [dɪs'repjʊtəbəl] *adj* peu recommandable; *(behaviour)* honteux, -euse
**disrepute** [dɪsrɪ'pju:t] *n* **to bring sb/sth into d.** discréditer qn/qch
**disrespectful** [dɪsrɪ'spektfʊl] *adj*

irrespectueux, -euse (**to** envers)
**disrupt** [dɪs'rʌpt] *vt (traffic, class)* perturber; *(communications)* interrompre; *(plan)* déranger ▪ **disruption** *n* perturbation *f*
**disruptive** [dɪs'rʌptɪv] *adj* perturbateur, -trice
**dissatisfied** [dɪ'sætɪsfaɪd] *adj* mécontent (**with** de) ▪ **dissatisfaction** [-'fækʃən] *n* mécontentement *m* (**with** devant)
**dissent** [dɪ'sent] **1** *n* désaccord *m* **2** *vi* être en désaccord (**from** avec)
**dissertation** [dɪsə'teɪʃən] *n* mémoire *m*
**dissident** ['dɪsɪdənt] *adj & n* dissident, -e *(mf)*
**dissimilar** [dɪ'sɪmɪlə(r)] *adj* différent (**to** de)
**dissipate** ['dɪsɪpeɪt] *vt (fog, fears)* dissiper; *(energy, fortune)* gaspiller
**dissociate** [dɪ'səʊʃɪeɪt] *vt* dissocier (**from** de)
**dissolute** ['dɪsəlu:t] *adj* dissolu
**dissolve** [dɪ'zɒlv] **1** *vt* dissoudre **2** *vi* se dissoudre
**dissuade** [dɪ'sweɪd] *vt* dissuader (**from doing** de faire)
**distance** ['dɪstəns] *n* distance *f*; **in the d.** au loin; **from a d.** de loin; **to keep one's d.** garder ses distances
**distant** ['dɪstənt] *adj* lointain; *(relative)* éloigné; *(reserved)* distant
**distasteful** [dɪs'teɪstfʊl] *adj* déplaisant
**distil** [dɪ'stɪl] *(pt & pp* **-ll-**) *vt* distiller; **distilled water** eau *f* déminéralisée
**distinct** [dɪ'stɪŋkt] *adj* (**a**) *(clear)* clair; *(preference, improvement, difference)* net (*f* nette) (**b**) *(different)* distinct (**from** de) ▪ **distinctly** *adv (see, hear)* distinctement; *(remember)* très bien; *(better, easier)* nettement
**distinction** [dɪ'stɪŋkʃən] *n* distinction *f*; *(in exam)* mention *f* bien
**distinctive** [dɪ'stɪŋktɪv] *adj* distinctif, -ive
**distinguish** [dɪ'stɪŋgwɪʃ] *vti* distinguer (**from** de; **between** entre); **to d. oneself** se distinguer (**as** en tant que)
**distinguished** [dɪs'tɪŋgwɪʃd] *adj* distingué
**distort** [dɪ'stɔ:t] *vt* déformer ▪ **distortion** *n (of features, sound)* distorsion *f*; *(of truth)* déformation *f*
**distract** [dɪ'strækt] *vt* distraire (**from** de) ▪ **distracted** *adj* préoccupé
**distraction** [dɪ'strækʃən] *n* distraction *f*
**distraught** [dɪ'strɔ:t] *adj* éperdu
**distress** [dɪ'stres] **1** *n (mental)* détresse *f*; *(physical)* douleur *f* **2** *vt* bouleverser ▪ **distressing** *adj* bouleversant
**distribute** [dɪ'strɪbju:t] *vt (give out) & Com (supply)* distribuer; *(spread evenly)* répartir ▪ **distribution** [-'bju:ʃən] *n* distribution *f*
**distributor** [dɪs'trɪbjʊtə(r)] *n (in car, of films)* distributeur *m*
**district** ['dɪstrɪkt] *n* région *f*; *(of town)* quartier *m*; *(administrative)* district *m*
**distrust** [dɪs'trʌst] **1** *n* méfiance *f* (**of** à l'égard de) **2** *vt* se méfier de
**disturb** [dɪ'stɜ:b] *vt (sleep, water)* troubler; *(papers, belongings)* déranger; **to d. sb** *(bother)* déranger qn; *(worry, alarm)* troubler qn ▪ **disturbing** *adj (worrying)* inquiétant; *(annoying, irksome)* gênant
**disturbance** [dɪ'stɜ:bəns] *n (noise)* tapage *m*; **disturbances** *(riots)* troubles *mpl*
**disunity** [dɪs'ju:nɪtɪ] *n* désunion *f*
**disuse** [dɪs'ju:s] *n* **to fall into d.** tomber en désuétude ▪ **disused** *adj (building)* désaffecté
**ditch** [dɪtʃ] **1** *n* fossé *m* **2** *vt Fam (get rid of)* se débarrasser de; *(plan)* laisser tomber
**ditto** ['dɪtəʊ] *adv* idem
**dive** [daɪv] **1** *n (of swimmer, goalkeeper)* plongeon *m*; *(of aircraft)* piqué *m* **2** (*pt* **dived,** *Am* **dove**) *vi* plonger; *(of plane)* piquer ▪ **diver** *n* plongeur, -euse *mf*; *(deep-sea)* scaphandrier *m*
**diverge** [daɪ'vɜ:dʒ] *vi* diverger (**from** de)

**diverse** [daɪ'vɜːs] *adj* divers ▪ **diversity** *n* diversité *f* ▪ **diversify** *(pt & pp* **-ied***)* *vi (of firm)* se diversifier

**diversion** [daɪ'vɜːʃən] *n Br (on road)* déviation *f*; *(amusement)* distraction *f*; **to create a d.** faire diversion

**divert** [daɪ'vɜːt] *vt (attention, suspicions, river, plane)* détourner; *Br (traffic)* dévier; *(amuse)* divertir

**divide** [dɪ'vaɪd] *vt Math* diviser (**into** en; **by** par); *(food, money, time)* partager (**between** *or* **among** entre); **to d. sth (off) (from sth)** séparer qch (de qch); **to d. sth up** *(share out)* partager qch

**divine** [dɪ'vaɪn] *adj* divin

**diving** ['daɪvɪŋ] *n (underwater)* plongée *f* sous-marine; **d. board** plongeoir *m*

**division** [dɪ'vɪʒən] *n* division *f*; *(distribution)* partage *m*; *Sport* **first d.** première division

**divorce** [dɪ'vɔːs] **1** *n* divorce *m* **2** *vt (husband, wife)* divorcer de; *Fig (idea)* séparer (**from** de) **3** *vi* divorcer ▪ **divorced** *adj* divorcé (**from** de); **to get d.** divorcer ▪ **divorcee** [dɪvɔː'siː, *Am* dɪvɔːr'seɪ] *n* divorcé, -e *mf*

**divulge** [dɪ'vʌldʒ] *vt* divulguer

**DIY** [diːaɪ'waɪ] *(abbr* **do-it-yourself***)* *n Br* bricolage *m*

**dizzy** ['dɪzɪ] (**-ier, -iest**) *adj* **to be** *or* **feel d.** avoir le vertige; **to make sb (feel) d.** donner le vertige à qn

**DJ** ['diːdʒeɪ] *(abbr* **disc-jockey***)* *n* disc-jockey *m*

**DO** [duː]

Les formes négatives sont **don't/doesn't** et **didn't**, qui deviennent **do not/does not** et **did not** dans un style plus soutenu.

**1** *(3rd person sing present tense* **does,** *pt* **did,** *pp* **done,** *pres p* **doing***)* *v aux* **do you know?** savez-vous?, est-ce que vous savez?; **I do not** *or* **don't see** je ne vois pas; **he did say so** *(emphasis)* il l'a bien dit; **do stay** reste donc; **you know him, don't you?** tu le connais, n'est-ce pas?; **better than I do** mieux que je ne le fais; **so do I** moi aussi; **don't!** non!

**2** *vt* faire; **what does she do?** *(in general)* qu'est-ce qu'elle fait?, que fait-elle?; **what is she doing?** *(now)* qu'est-ce qu'elle fait?, que fait-elle?; **what have you done (with...)?** qu'as-tu fait (de...)?; **well done** *(congratulations)* bravo!; *(steak)* bien cuit; **it's over and done (with)** c'est fini; **that'll do me** *(suit)* ça m'ira; *Br Fam* **I've been done** *(cheated)* je me suis fait avoir; **to do sb out of sth** escroquer qch à qn; *Fam* **I'm done (in)** *(tired)* je suis claqué; **to do out** *(clean)* nettoyer; **to do over** *(redecorate)* refaire; **to do up** *(coat, buttons)* boutonner; *(zip)* fermer; *(house)* refaire; *(goods)* emballer

**3** *vi* **do as you're told** fais ce qu'on te dit; **that will do** *(be OK)* ça ira; *(be enough)* ça suffit; **have you done?** vous avez fini?; **to do well/badly** *(of person)* bien/mal se débrouiller; **business is doing well** les affaires marchent bien; **how are you doing?** (comment) ça va?; **how do you do** *(introduction)* enchanté; *(greeting)* bonjour; **to make do** se débrouiller; **to do away with sb/sth** supprimer qn/qch; **I could do with a coffee** *(need, want)* je prendrais bien un café; **it has to do with...** *(relates to)* cela a à voir avec...; *(concerns)* cela concerne...

**4** *n (pl* **dos***)* *Br Fam (party)* fête *f*

**docile** ['dəʊsaɪl] *adj* docile

**dock** [dɒk] **1** *n* (**a**) *(for ship)* dock *m* (**b**) *(in court)* banc *m* des accusés **2** *vi (of ship) (at quayside)* accoster; *(in port)* relâcher

**doctor** ['dɒktə(r)] **1** *n (medical)* médecin *m*, docteur *m*; *(having doctor's degree)* docteur *m* **2** *vt (text, food)* altérer; *Br (cat)* châtrer ▪ **doctorate** *n* doctorat *m* (**in** ès/en)

**document** ['dɒkjʊmənt] *n* document *m* ▪ **documentary** [-'mentərɪ] *(pl* **-ies***)* *n (film)* documentaire *m*

**dodge** [dɒdʒ] **1** *n (trick)* truc *m* **2** *vt (question)* esquiver; *(person)* éviter;

*(pursuer)* échapper à; *(tax)* éviter de payer **3** *vi (to one side)* faire un saut de côté; **to d. through** *(crowd)* se faufiler dans

**Dodgems®** ['dɒdʒəmz] *npl* autos *fpl* tamponneuses

**dodgy** ['dɒdʒɪ] (**-ier, -iest**) *adj Fam (suspect)* louche; *(not working properly)* en mauvais état; *(risky)* risqué

**does** [dʌz] *see* **do**

**doesn't** ['dʌzənt] = **does not**

**dog¹** [dɒg] *n* chien *m*; *(female)* chienne *f*

**dog²** [dɒg] (*pt & pp* **-gg-**) *vt (follow)* suivre de près

**doggedly** ['dɒgɪdlɪ] *adv* obstinément

**doing** ['du:ɪŋ] *n* **that's your d.** c'est toi qui as fait ça

**do-it-yourself** [du:ɪtjə'self] *n Br* bricolage *m*; **d. store/book** magasin *m*/livre *m* de bricolage

**dole** [dəʊl] *n Br* **d. (money)** allocation *f* de chômage; **to go on the d.** s'inscrire au chômage

**doll** [dɒl] *n* poupée *f*; *Br* **doll's house,** *Am* **dollhouse** maison *f* de poupée

**dollar** ['dɒlə(r)] *n* dollar *m*

**dollop** ['dɒləp] *n (of cream, purée)* grosse cuillerée *f*

**dolphin** ['dɒlfɪn] *n* dauphin *m*

**domain** [dəʊ'meɪn] *n (land, sphere)* domaine *m*

**dome** [dəʊm] *n* dôme *m*

**domestic** [də'mestɪk] *adj (appliance, use, tasks)* ménager, -ère; *(animal)* domestique; *(policy, flight, affairs)* intérieur

**dominant** ['dɒmɪnənt] *adj* dominant; *(person)* dominateur, -trice

**dominate** ['dɒmɪneɪt] *vti* dominer

**domineering** [dɒmɪ'nɪərɪŋ] *adj (person, character)* dominateur, -trice

**domino** ['dɒmɪnəʊ] (*pl* **-oes**) *n* domino *m*; **dominoes** *(game)* dominos *mpl*

**donate** [dəʊ'neɪt] **1** *vt* faire don de; *(blood)* donner **2** *vi* donner ▪ **donation** *n* don *m*

**done** [dʌn] *pp of* **do**

**donkey** ['dɒŋkɪ] (*pl* **-eys**) *n* âne *m*

**donor** ['dəʊnə(r)] *n* donneur, -euse *mf*

**don't** [dəʊnt] = **do not**

**donut** ['dəʊnʌt] *n Am* beignet *m*

**doom** [du:m] **1** *n (fate)* destin *m* **2** *vt* condamner (**to** à); **to be doomed (to failure)** *(of project)* être voué à l'échec

**door** [dɔ:(r)] *n* porte *f*; *(of vehicle, train)* portière *f*; **d. handle** poignée *f* de porte ▪ **doorbell** *n* sonnette *f* ▪ **doorknob** *n* bouton *m* de porte ▪ **doorman** (*pl* **-men**) *n (of hotel)* portier *m* ▪ **doormat** *n* paillasson *m* ▪ **doorstep** *n* seuil *m* ▪ **door-to-door** *adj* **d. salesman** démarcheur *m* ▪ **doorway** *n* **in the d.** dans l'embrasure de la porte

**dope** [dəʊp] *n Fam* (**a**) *(drugs)* drogue *f* (**b**) *(idiot)* andouille *f*

**dormitory** [*Br* 'dɔ:mɪtrɪ, *Am* 'dɔ:rmɪtɔ:rɪ] (*pl* **-ies**) *n* dortoir *m*; *Am (university residence)* résidence *f* universitaire

**dosage** ['dəʊsɪdʒ] *n (amount)* dose *f*

**dose** [dəʊs] *n* dose *f*; **a d. of flu** une grippe

**dossier** ['dɒsɪeɪ] *n (papers)* dossier *m*

**dot** [dɒt] **1** *n* point *m*; *Fam* **on the d.** à l'heure pile **2** (*pt & pp* **-tt-**) *vt (letter)* mettre un point sur; **dotted with** parsemé de; **dotted line** pointillé *m*

**dote** [dəʊt] *vt* **to d. on** adorer

**dot-matrix** [dɒt'meɪtrɪks] *n Comptr* **d. printer** imprimante *f* matricielle

**double** ['dʌbəl] **1** *adj* double; **a d. bed** un grand lit; **a d. room** une chambre pour deux personnes; **d. 's'** deux 's'; **d. three four two** *(phone number)* trente-trois quarante-deux

**2** *adv (twice)* deux fois; *(fold)* en deux; **he earns d. what I do** il gagne le double de moi

**3** *n* double *m*; *(person)* double *m*, sosie *m*; *(stand-in in film)* doublure *f*

**4** *vt* doubler; **to d. sth back** *or* **over** *(fold)* replier qch; **to be doubled up with pain/laughter** être plié (en deux) de douleur/rire

**5** *vi* doubler; **to d. back** *(of person)* revenir en arrière ▪ **double-bass** *n Br (instrument)* contrebasse *f* ▪ **double-check** *vti* revérifier ▪ **double-cross** *vt* doubler ▪ **double-decker** *n* **d. (bus)** autobus *m* à impériale ▪ **double-glazing** *n (window)* double vitrage *m*

**doubt** [daʊt] **1** *n* doute *m*; **I have no d. about it** je n'en doute pas; **no d.** *(probably)* sans doute; **in d.** *(result, career)* dans la balance **2** *vt* douter de; **to d. whether** *or* **that** *or* **if…** douter que… *(+ subjunctive)*

**doubtful** ['daʊtfəl] *adj (person, future, success)* incertain; **to be d. (about sth)** avoir des doutes (sur qch); **it's d. whether** *or* **that** *or* **if…** il n'est pas certain que… *(+ subjunctive)* ▪ **doubtless** *adv* sans doute

**dough** [dəʊ] *n* pâte *f*; *Fam (money)* blé *m*

**doughnut** ['dəʊnʌt] *n* beignet *m*

**dove**[1] [dʌv] *n* colombe *f*

**dove**[2] [dəʊv] *Am pt of* **dive**

**Dover** ['dəʊvə(r)] *n* Douvres *m ou f*

**dowdy** ['daʊdɪ] (**-ier, -iest**) *adj* peu élégant

**DOWN** [daʊn] **1** *adj* **d. payment** acompte *m*

**2** *adv* en bas; *(to the ground)* à terre; **d. there** *or* **here** en bas; *Fam* **to feel d.** *(depressed)* avoir le cafard; **d. to** *(in series, numbers, dates)* jusqu'à; **d. under** aux antipodes, en Australie

**3** *prep (at bottom of)* en bas de; *(from top to bottom of)* du haut en bas de; *(along)* le long de; **to go d.** *(hill, street, stairs)* descendre; **to live d. the street** habiter plus loin dans la rue

**4** *vt* **to d. a drink** vider un verre ▪ **down-and-out 1** *adj* sur le pavé **2** *n* clochard, -e *mf* ▪ **downcast** *adj* découragé ▪ **downfall** *n* chute *f* ▪ **down-hearted** *adj* découragé ▪ **downhill** *adv* en pente; **to go d.** descendre; *(of sick person, business)* aller de plus en plus mal ▪ **downmarket** *adj Br (car, furniture)* bas de gamme *inv*; *(neighbourhood)* populaire ▪ **downpour** *n* averse *f* ▪ **downright 1** *adj (rogue)* véritable; *(refusal)* catégorique **2** *adv (rude, disagreeable)* franchement ▪ **downstairs 1** ['daʊnsteəz] *adj (room, neighbours) (below)* d'en bas; *(on the ground floor)* du rez-de-chaussée **2** [daʊn'steəz] *adv* en bas; *(to the ground floor)* au rez-de-chaussée; **to come** *or* **go d.** descendre l'escalier ▪ **down-to-earth** *adj* terre-à-terre *inv* ▪ **downtown** *adv Am* en ville; **d. Chicago** le centre de Chicago ▪ **downward** *adj* vers le bas; *(path)* qui descend; *(trend)* à la baisse ▪ **downward(s)** *adv* vers le bas

**doze** [dəʊz] **1** *n* petit somme *m* **2** *vi* sommeiller; **to d. off** s'assoupir

**dozen** ['dʌzən] *n* douzaine *f*; **a d. books/eggs** une douzaine de livres/d'œufs; *Fig* **dozens of** des dizaines de

**Dr** *(abbr* **Doctor**) Docteur

**drab** [dræb] *adj* terne; *(weather)* gris

**draft**[1] [drɑːft] **1** *n* (**a**) *(outline)* ébauche *f*; *(of letter)* brouillon *m* (**b**) *Am (military)* conscription *f* **2** *vt* (**a**) **to d. (out)** *(sketch out)* faire le brouillon de; *(write out)* rédiger (**b**) *Am (conscript)* appeler sous les drapeaux

**draft**[2] [drɑːft] *n Am* = **draught**

**drafty** ['drɑːftɪ] (**-ier, -iest**) *adj Am* = **draughty**

**drag** [dræg] **1** *n Fam* **it's a d.!** *(boring)* c'est la barbe! **2** (*pt & pp* **-gg-**) *vt* traîner; **to d. sb/sth along** (en)traîner qn/qch; **to d. sb away from** arracher qn à; **to d. sb into** entraîner qn dans **3** *vi* traîner; **to d. on** *or* **out** *(of film, day)* traîner en longueur

**dragon** ['drægən] *n* dragon *m*

**dragonfly** ['drægənflaɪ] (*pl* **-ies**) *n* libellule *f*

**drain** [dreɪn] **1** *n (sewer)* égout *m*; *(in street)* bouche *f* d'égout **2** *vt (glass, tank)* vider; *(vegetables)* égoutter; **to d. (off)** *(liquid)* faire écouler; **to feel drained** être épuisé **3** *vi* **to d. (off)** *(of liquid)* s'écouler ▪ **draining** *n* **d. board** paillasse *f*

**drainpipe** ['dreɪnpaɪp] *n* tuyau *m*

d'évacuation
**drama** ['drɑ:mə] *n (event)* drame *m*; *(dramatic art)* théâtre *m*
**dramatic** [drə'mætɪk] *adj* dramatique; *(very great, striking)* spectaculaire
**dramatize** ['dræmətaɪz] *vt (exaggerate)* dramatiser; *(novel)* adapter pour la scène/l'écran
**drank** [dræŋk] *pt of* **drink**
**drape** [dreɪp] *vt (person, shoulders)* draper (**with** de) ▪ **drapes** *npl Am (curtains)* rideaux *mpl*
**drastic** ['dræstɪk] *adj (change, measure)* radical; *(remedy)* puissant
**draught** [drɑ:ft] (*Am* **draft**) *n* (**a**) *(wind)* courant *m* d'air (**b**) *Br* **draughts** *(game)* dames *fpl* (**c**) **d. beer** bière *f* (à la) pression
**draughty** ['drɑ:ftɪ] (*Am* **drafty**) (**-ier, -iest**) *adj (room)* plein de courants d'air
**draw¹** [drɔ:] **1** *n Sport* match *m* nul; *(of lottery)* tirage *m* au sort; *(attraction)* attraction *f*
**2** (*pt* **drew**, *pp* **drawn**) *vt* (**a**) *(pull)* tirer; *(pass, move)* passer (**over** sur; **into** dans); **to d. up** *(chair)* approcher; *(contract, list, plan)* dresser, rédiger
(**b**) *(extract)* retirer; *(pistol, sword)* dégainer; *Fig (strength, comfort)* retirer, puiser (**from** de)
(**c**) *(attract)* attirer
**3** *vi Sport* faire match nul; **to d. near (to)** s'approcher (de); *(of time)* approcher (de); **to d. back** *(go backwards)* reculer; **to d. up** *(of vehicle)* s'arrêter
**draw²** [drɔ:] **1** (*pt* **drew**, *pp* **drawn**) *vt (picture)* dessiner; *(circle)* tracer; *Fig (parallel, distinction)* faire (**between** entre) **2** *vi (as artist)* dessiner
**drawback** ['drɔ:bæk] *n* inconvénient *m*
**drawer** [drɔ:(r)] *n (in furniture)* tiroir *m*
**drawing** ['drɔ:ɪŋ] *n* dessin *m*; *Br* **d. pin** punaise *f*; **d. room** salon *m*
**drawl** [drɔ:l] *n* voix *f* traînante
**drawn** [drɔ:n] **1** *pp of* **draw¹˒²** **2** *adj* **d. match** *or* **game** match *m* nul
**dread** [dred] **1** *n* terreur *f* **2** *vt (exam)* appréhender; **to d. doing sth** appréhender de faire qch
**dreadful** ['dredfəl] *adj* épouvantable; *(child)* insupportable; **I feel d.** *(ill)* je ne me sens vraiment pas bien; **I feel d. about it** j'ai vraiment honte ▪ **dreadfully** *adv* terriblement; **to be d. sorry** regretter infiniment
**dream** [dri:m] **1** *n* rêve *m*; **to have a d.** faire un rêve (**about** de); **a d. world** un monde imaginaire **2** (*pt & pp* **dreamed** *or* **dreamt** [dremt]) *vt* rêver (**that** que); **I never dreamt that...** *(imagined)* je n'aurais jamais songé que...; **to d. sth up** imaginer qch **3** *vi* rêver (**of** *or* **about sb/sth** de qn/qch; **of** *or* **about doing** de faire)
**dreary** ['drɪərɪ] (**-ier, -iest**) *adj* morne
**drench** [drentʃ] *vt* tremper; **to get drenched** se faire tremper (jusqu'aux os)
**dress** [dres] **1** *n (garment)* robe *f*; *(style of dressing)* tenue *f*; *Br* **d. circle** *(in theatre)* premier balcon *m*; **d. rehearsal** *(in theatre)* (répétition *f*) générale *f*
**2** *vt (person)* habiller; *(wound)* panser; *(salad)* assaisonner; **to get dressed** s'habiller
**3** *vi* s'habiller; **to d. up** *(smartly)* bien s'habiller; *(in disguise)* se déguiser (**as** en)
**dressing** ['dresɪŋ] *n (for wound)* pansement *m*; *(seasoning)* assaisonnement *m*; *Br* **d. gown** robe *f* de chambre; **d. room** *(in theatre)* loge *f*; *(in shop)* cabine *f* d'essayage; **d. table** coiffeuse *f*
**drew** [dru:] *pt of* **draw¹˒²**
**dribble** ['drɪbəl] *vi* (**a**) *(of baby)* baver; *(of liquid)* tomber goutte à goutte (**b**) *(of footballer)* dribbler
**dribs** [drɪbz] *npl* **in d. and drabs** par petites quantités; *(arrive)* par petits groupes
**dried** [draɪd] *adj (fruit)* sec (*f* sèche); *(milk, eggs)* en poudre; *(flowers)* séché
**drier** ['draɪə(r)] *n* = **dryer**
**drift** [drɪft] **1** *n (movement)* mouve-

ment *m*; *(of snow)* congère *f*; *(meaning)* sens *m* général **2** *vi (through air)* être emporté par le vent; *(on water)* être emporté par le courant; *(of ship)* dériver; *Fig (of person, nation)* aller à la dérive

**drill** [drɪl] **1** *n* (**a**) *(tool)* perceuse *f*; *(bit)* mèche *f*; *(pneumatic)* marteau *m* piqueur; *(dentist's)* roulette *f* (**b**) *(exercise)* exercice *m*; *(correct procedure)* marche *f* à suivre **2** *vt (wood)* percer; *(tooth)* fraiser **3** *vi* **to d. for oil** faire de la recherche pétrolière

**drily** ['draɪlɪ] *adv (remark)* sèchement, d'un ton sec

**drink** [drɪŋk] **1** *n* boisson *f*; **to have a d.** boire quelque chose; *(alcoholic)* prendre un verre

**2** (*pt* **drank,** *pp* **drunk**) *vt* boire **3** *vi* boire (**out of** dans); **to d. up** finir son verre ▪ **drink-driving** *n Br* conduite *f* en état d'ivresse ▪ **drinking** *n* **d. chocolate** chocolat *m* en poudre; **d. water** eau *f* potable

**drinkable** ['drɪŋkəbəl] *adj (fit for drinking)* potable; *(not unpleasant)* buvable

**drip** [drɪp] **1** *n (drop)* goutte *f*; *(sound)* bruit *m* de l'eau qui goutte; *Med* **to be on a d.** être sous perfusion **2** (*pt & pp* **-pp-**) *vt (paint)* laisser tomber goutte à goutte; **you're dripping water everywhere!** tu mets de l'eau partout! **3** *vi (of water, rain)* goutter; *(of tap)* fuir

**drive** [draɪv] **1** *n (in car)* promenade *f* en voiture; *(road to private house)* allée *f*; *(energy)* énergie *f*; *(campaign)* campagne *f*; *Comptr* lecteur *m*; **an hour's d.** une heure de voiture

**2** (*pt* **drove,** *pp* **driven**) *vt (vehicle, train, passenger)* conduire (**to** à); *(machine)* actionner; **to d. sb to do sth** pousser qn à faire qch; **to d. sb mad** *or* **crazy** rendre qn fou/folle; **he drives a Ford** il a une Ford

**3** *vi (drive a car)* conduire; *(go by car)* rouler; **to d. on the left** rouler à gauche; **to d. to Paris** aller en voiture à Paris; **to d. to work** aller au travail en voiture; *Fig* **what are you driving at?** où veux-tu en venir?

▸**drive along** *vi (in car)* rouler

▸**drive away 1** *vt sep (chase away)* chasser **2** *vi (in car)* partir en voiture

▸**drive back 1** *vt sep (passenger)* ramener (en voiture); *(enemy)* repousser **2** *vi (in car)* revenir (en voiture)

▸**drive in** *vt sep (nail)* enfoncer

▸**drive off** *vi (in car)* partir (en voiture)

▸**drive on** *vi (in car)* continuer sa route

▸**drive out** *vt sep (chase away)* chasser

▸**drive up** *vi (in car)* arriver (en voiture)

**drive-in** ['draɪvɪn] *adj Am* **d. (movie theater)** drive-in *m inv*; **d. (restaurant)** = restaurant où l'on est servi dans sa voiture

**drivel** ['drɪvəl] *n* idioties *fpl*

**driven** ['drɪvən] *pp of* **drive**

**driver** ['draɪvə(r)] *n (of car)* conducteur, -trice *mf*; *(of taxi, truck)* chauffeur *m*; **(train** *or* **engine) d.** mécanicien *m*; **she's a good d.** elle conduit bien; *Am* **d.'s license** permis *m* de conduire

**driveway** ['draɪvweɪ] *n (road to house)* allée *f*

**driving** ['draɪvɪŋ] *n (in car)* conduite *f*; **d. lesson** leçon *f* de conduite; *Br* **d. licence** permis *m* de conduire; **d. school** auto-école *f*; **d. test** examen *m* du permis de conduire

**drizzle** ['drɪzəl] *vi* bruiner

**droop** [dru:p] *vi (of flower)* se faner; *(of head)* pencher; *(of eyelids, shoulders)* tomber

**drop** [drɒp] **1** *n* (**a**) *(of liquid)* goutte *f*; **eye/nose drops** gouttes *fpl* pour les yeux/le nez

(**b**) *(fall)* baisse *f*, chute *f* (**in** de); *(distance of fall)* hauteur *f* de chute; *(slope)* descente *f*

**2** (*pt & pp* **-pp-**) *vt* laisser tomber; *(price, voice)* baisser; *(bomb)* larguer; *(passenger, goods from vehicle)* déposer; *(leave out)* faire sauter, omettre;

*(get rid of)* supprimer; *(team member)* écarter; **to d. sb off** *(from vehicle)* déposer qn; **to d. sb a line** écrire un petit mot à qn; **to d. a hint that...** laisser entendre que...

**3** *vi (fall)* tomber; *(of person)* se laisser tomber; *(of price)* baisser; **to d. back** *or* **behind** rester en arrière; **to d. by** *or* **in** *(visit sb)* passer; **to d. off** *(fall asleep)* s'endormir; *(fall off)* tomber; *(of interest, sales)* diminuer; **to d. out** *(fall out)* tomber; *(withdraw)* se retirer; *(of student)* laisser tomber ses études; **to d. round** *(visit sb)* passer

**dropout** ['drɒpaʊt] *n* marginal, -e *mf*; *(student)* étudiant, -e *mf* qui abandonne ses études

**droppings** ['drɒpɪŋz] *npl (of animal)* crottes *fpl*; *(of bird)* fiente *f*

**drought** [draʊt] *n* sécheresse *f*

**drove** [drəʊv] *pt of* **drive**

**drown** [draʊn] **1** *vt* noyer; **to d. oneself, to be drowned** se noyer **2** *vi* se noyer

**drowsy** ['draʊzɪ] (**-ier, -iest**) *adj* **to be** *or* **feel d.** avoir sommeil

**drudgery** ['drʌdʒərɪ] *n* corvée *f*

**drug** [drʌg] **1** *n (against illness)* médicament *m*; *(narcotic)* drogue *f*; **drugs** *(narcotics in general)* la drogue; **to be on drugs, to take drugs** se droguer; **d. addict** drogué, -e *mf*; **d. dealer** *(large-scale)* trafiquant *m* de drogue; *(small-scale)* petit trafiquant *m* de drogue, dealer *m* **2** (*pt & pp* **-gg-**) *vt* droguer

**druggist** ['drʌgɪst] *n Am* pharmacien, -enne *mf*

**drugstore** ['drʌgstɔ:r] *n Am* drugstore *m*

**drum** [drʌm] **1** *n Mus* tambour *m*; *(for oil)* bidon *m*; **the drums** *(of rock group)* la batterie **2** (*pt & pp* **-mm-**) *vt* **to d. sth into sb** enfoncer qch dans la tête de qn; **to d. up** *(support, interest)* rechercher ▪ **drummer** *n* tambour *m*; *(in rock group)* batteur *m* ▪ **drumstick** *n (for drum)* baguette *f* de tambour; *(of chicken)* pilon *m*

**drunk** [drʌŋk] **1** *pp of* **drink 2** *adj* ivre; **to get d.** s'enivrer **3** *n* ivrogne *mf* ▪ **drunkard** *n* ivrogne *mf* ▪ **drunken** *adj (person) (regularly)* ivrogne; *(driver)* ivre; *(quarrel, brawl)* d'ivrogne

**dry** [draɪ] **1** (**drier, driest**) *adj* sec (*f* sèche); *(well, river)* à sec; *(day)* sans pluie; *(subject, book)* aride; **to wipe sth d.** essuyer qch

**2** *vt* sécher; *(by wiping)* essuyer; *(clothes)* faire sécher; **to d. the dishes** essuyer la vaisselle; **to d. sth off** *or* **up** sécher qch

**3** *vi* sécher; **to d. off** sécher; **to d. up** sécher; *(dry the dishes)* essuyer la vaisselle; *(of stream)* se tarir ▪ **dryer** *n (for hair, clothes)* séchoir *m*

**dry-clean** [draɪ'kli:n] *vt* nettoyer à sec ▪ **dry-cleaner** *n* **the d.'s** *(shop)* le pressing, la teinturerie

**dual** ['dju:əl] *adj* double; *Br* **d. carriageway** route *f* à deux voies

**dub** [dʌb] (*pt & pp* **-bb-**) *vt (film)* doubler (**into** en)

**dubious** ['dju:bɪəs] *adj (offer, person)* douteux, -euse; **I'm d. about going** *or* **about whether to go** je me demande si je dois y aller

**duchess** ['dʌtʃɪs] *n* duchesse *f*

**duck** [dʌk] **1** *n* canard *m* **2** *vt (head)* baisser subitement **3** *vi* se baisser ▪ **duckling** *n* caneton *m*

**due** [dju:] *adj (money, sum)* dû (*f* due) (**to** à); *(rent, bill)* à payer; *(fitting, proper)* qui convient; **he's d. (to arrive)** il doit arriver d'un moment à l'autre; **in d. course** *(when appropriate)* en temps voulu; *(eventually)* le moment venu; **d. to** par suite de, en raison de

**duel** ['dju:əl] **1** *n* duel *m* **2** (*Br* **-ll-**, *Am* **-l-**) *vi* se battre en duel

**duet** [dju:'et] *n* duo *m*

**duffel, duffle** ['dʌfəl] *adj* **d. coat** duffel-coat *m*

**dug** [dʌg] *pt & pp of* **dig**

**duke** [dju:k] *n* duc *m*

**dull** [dʌl] **1** (**-er, -est**) *adj (boring)* ennuyeux, -euse; *(colour, character)* terne; *(weather)* maussade; *(sound,* *ache)* sourd; *(edge, blade)* émoussé **2** *vt (pain)* endormir

**duly** ['dju:lɪ] *adv (properly)* dûment; *(as expected)* comme prévu

**dumb** [dʌm] (**-er, -est**) *adj* muet (*f* muette); *Fam (stupid)* bête

**dumbfound** [dʌm'faʊnd] *vt* sidérer

**dummy** ['dʌmɪ] **1** (*pl* **-ies**) *n Br (of baby)* tétine *f*; *(for displaying clothes)* mannequin *m*; *(of ventriloquist)* pantin *m* **2** *adj* factice

**dump** [dʌmp] **1** *n (for refuse)* décharge *f*; *Fam Pej (town)* trou *m*; *Fam Pej (house)* baraque *f* **2** *vt (rubbish)* déposer; *Fam* **to d. sb** plaquer qn

**dumpling** ['dʌmplɪŋ] *n (in stew)* boulette *f* de pâte

**dune** [dju:n] *n* **(sand) d.** dune *f*

**dung** [dʌŋ] *n (of horse)* crottin *m*; *(of cattle)* bouse *f*; *(manure)* fumier *m*

**dungarees** [dʌŋgə'ri:z] *npl (of child, workman)* salopette *f*; *Am (jeans)* jean *m*

**dunk** [dʌŋk] *vt* tremper

**dupe** [dju:p] *vt* duper

**duplex** ['du:pleks] *n Am (apartment)* duplex *m*

**duplicate 1** ['dju:plɪkət] *n* double *m*; **in d.** en deux exemplaires **2** ['dju:plɪkeɪt] *vt (key, map)* faire un double de; *(on machine)* photocopier

**durable** ['djʊərəbəl] *adj (material, shoes)* résistant

**duration** [djʊə'reɪʃən] *n* durée *f*

**duress** [djʊ'res] *n* **under d.** sous la contrainte

**during** ['djʊərɪŋ] *prep* pendant, durant

**dusk** [dʌsk] *n (twilight)* crépuscule *m*

**dust** [dʌst] **1** *n* poussière *f*; **d. cover** *or* **sheet** *(for furniture)* housse *f*; **d. cover** *or* **jacket** *(for book)* jaquette *f* **2** *vt (furniture)* dépoussiérer **3** *vi* faire la poussière ▪ **dustbin** *n Br* poubelle *f* ▪ **dustman** (*pl* **-men**) *n Br* éboueur *m* ▪ **dustpan** *n* pelle *f* (à poussière) ▪ **dusty** (**-ier, -iest**) *adj* poussiéreux, -euse

**duster** ['dʌstə(r)] *n* chiffon *m*

**Dutch** [dʌtʃ] **1** *adj* hollandais **2** *n* (**a**) **the D.** *(people)* les Hollandais *mpl* (**b**) *(language)* hollandais *m*

**duty** ['dju:tɪ] (*pl* **-ies**) *n* devoir *m*; *(tax)* droit *m*; **duties** *(responsibilities)* fonctions *fpl*; **to be on/off d.** être/ne pas être de service

**duty-free** ['dju:tɪ'fri:] *adj (goods, shop)* hors taxe *inv*

**duvet** ['du:veɪ] *n Br* couette *f*

**DVD** [di:vi:'di:] (*abbr* **Digital Versatile Disk, Digital Video Disk**) *n Comptr* DVD *m inv*, disque *m* vidéo numérique

**dwarf** [dwɔ:f] *n* nain, -e *mf*

**dwell** [dwel] (*pt & pp* **dwelt** [dwelt]) *vi* demeurer; **to d. (up)on** *(think about)* penser sans cesse à; *(speak about)* parler sans cesse de

**dwindle** ['dwɪndəl] *vi* diminuer (peu à peu)

**dye** [daɪ] **1** *n* teinture *f* **2** *vt* teindre; **to d. sth green** teindre qch en vert

**dying** ['daɪɪŋ] **1** *pres p of* **die**[1] **2** *adj (person, animal)* mourant; *(wish, words)* dernier, -ère **3** *n (death)* mort *f*

**dynamic** [daɪ'næmɪk] *adj* dynamique

**dynamite** ['daɪnəmaɪt] *n* dynamite *f*

**dynamo** ['daɪnəməʊ] (*pl* **-os**) *n* dynamo *f*

**dyslexic** [dɪs'leksɪk] *adj & n* dyslexique *(mf)*

# Ee

**E, e** [iː] *n (letter)* E, e *m inv*

**each** [iːtʃ] **1** *adj* chaque; **e. one** chacun, -e; **e. one of us** chacun d'entre nous

**2** *pron* chacun, -e; **e. other** l'un(e) l'autre, *pl* les un(e)s les autres; **to see/greet e. other** se voir/se saluer; **e. of us** chacun, -e d'entre nous

**eager** ['iːgə(r)] *adj (impatient)* impatient (**to do** de faire); *(enthusiastic)* plein d'enthousiasme ▪ **eagerly** *adv (work)* avec enthousiasme; *(await)* avec impatience

**eagle** ['iːgəl] *n* aigle *m*

**ear** [ɪə(r)] *n* oreille *f*; **to play it by e.** improviser ▪ **earache** *n* mal *m* d'oreille ▪ **earphones** *npl* écouteurs *mpl* ▪ **earplug** *n* boule *f* Quiès® ▪ **earring** *n* boucle *f* d'oreille ▪ **earshot** *n* **within e.** à portée de voix

**early** ['ɜːlɪ] **1** (**-ier, -iest**) *adj (first)* premier, -ère; *(death)* prématuré; *(age)* jeune; *(painting, work)* de jeunesse; *(retirement)* anticipé; **it's e.** *(on clock)* il est tôt; *(referring to meeting, appointment)* c'est tôt; **to be e.** *(ahead of time)* être en avance; **in the e. 1990s** au début des années 90; **to be in one's e. fifties** avoir à peine plus de cinquante ans

**2** *adv* tôt, de bonne heure; *(ahead of time)* en avance; *(die)* prématurément; **earlier (on)** plus tôt; **at the earliest** au plus tôt

**earmark** ['ɪəmɑːk] *vt (funds)* assigner (**for** à)

**earn** [ɜːn] *vt* gagner; *(interest)* rapporter; **to e. one's living** gagner sa vie ▪ **earnings** *npl (wages)* salaire *m*; *(profits)* bénéfices *mpl*

**earnest** ['ɜːnɪst] **1** *adj (serious)* sérieux, -euse **2** *n* **in e.** sérieusement

**earth** [ɜːθ] *n (ground)* sol *m*; *(soil)* terre *f*; *Br (electrical wire)* terre *f*, masse *f*; **the E.** *(planet)* la Terre; **where/what on e....?** où/que diable...? ▪ **earthquake** *n* tremblement *m* de terre

**ease** [iːz] **1** *n (facility)* facilité *f*; **with e.** facilement; **to be at e./ill at e.** être à l'aise/mal à l'aise **2** *vt (pain)* soulager; *(mind)* calmer; *(tension)* réduire; *(restrictions)* assouplir **3** *vi* **to e. (off** *or* **up)** *(of pressure)* diminuer; *(of demand)* baisser; *(of pain)* se calmer

**easily** ['iːzɪlɪ] *adv* facilement; **e. the best** de loin le meilleur/la meilleure

**east** [iːst] **1** *n* est *m*; **(to the) e. of** à l'est de; **the E.** *(Eastern Europe)* l'Est *m*; *(the Orient)* l'Orient *m*

**2** *adj (coast)* est *inv*; *(wind)* d'est; **E. Africa** l'Afrique *f* orientale

**3** *adv* à l'est; *(travel)* vers l'est ▪ **eastbound** *adj (traffic)* en direction de l'est; *Br (carriageway)* est *inv* ▪ **easterly** *adj (direction)* de l'est ▪ **eastern** *adj (coast)* est *inv*; **E. France** l'est *m* de la France; **E. Europe** l'Europe *f* de l'Est ▪ **eastward(s)** *adj & adv* vers l'est

**Easter** ['iːstə(r)] *n* Pâques *fpl*; **Happy E.!** joyeuses Pâques!; **E. egg** œuf *m* de Pâques

**easy** ['iːzɪ] **1** (**-ier, -iest**) *adj (not difficult)* facile; *(solution)* simple; *(pace)* modéré; **e. chair** fauteuil *m* **2** *adv* doucement; **go e. on the salt** vas-y mollo avec le sel; **go e. on him** ne sois pas trop dur avec lui; **take it e.** *(rest)* repose-toi; *(work less)* ne te fatigue pas; *(calm down)* calme-toi; *(go slow)* ne te presse pas ▪ **easygoing** *adj (carefree)* insouciant; *(easy to get along with)* facile à vivre

**eat** [iːt] (*pt* **ate** [*Br* et, eɪt, *Am* eɪt], *pp* **eaten** [ˈiːtən]) **1** *vt* manger; *(meal)* prendre; **to e. sth up** *(finish)* finir qch **2** *vi* manger; **to e. into one's savings** entamer ses économies; **to e. out** manger dehors ▪ **eater** *n* **big e.** gros mangeur *m*, grosse mangeuse *f*

**eaves** [iːvz] *npl* avant-toit *m* ▪ **eavesdrop** (*pt & pp* **-pp-**) *vti* **to e. (on)** écouter avec indiscrétion

**ebb** [eb] **1** *n* **the e. and flow** le flux et le reflux; *Fig* **to be at a low e.** *(of patient, spirits)* être déprimé **2** *vi Fig* **to e. (away)** *(of strength)* décliner

**EC** [iːˈsiː] (*abbr* **European Community**) *n* CE *f*

**eccentric** [ɪkˈsentrɪk] *adj & n* excentrique *(mf)*

**ecclesiastical** [ɪkliːzɪˈæstɪkəl] *adj* ecclésiastique

**echo** [ˈekəʊ] **1** (*pl* **-oes**) *n* écho *m* **2** (*pt & pp* **echoed**) *vt Fig (repeat)* répéter **3** *vi* résonner (**with** de)

**eclipse** [ɪˈklɪps] *n (of sun, moon)* éclipse *f*

**ecological** [iːkəˈlɒdʒɪkəl] *adj* écologique

**economic** [iːkəˈnɒmɪk] *adj* économique; *(profitable)* rentable ▪ **economical** *adj* économique ▪ **economics 1** *n* économie *f* **2** *npl (profitability)* aspect *m* financier

**economize** [ɪˈkɒnəmaɪz] *vti* économiser (**on** sur)

**economy** [ɪˈkɒnəmɪ] (*pl* **-ies**) *n* économie *f*; *Av* **e. class** classe *f* économique

**ecstasy** [ˈekstəsɪ] (*pl* **-ies**) *n (state)* extase *f*; *(drug)* ecstasy *f* ▪ **ecstatic** [ekˈstætɪk] *adj* fou (*f* folle) de joie; **to be e. about** s'extasier sur

**edge** [edʒ] **1** *n* bord *m*; *(of forest)* lisière *f*; *(of town)* abords *mpl*; *(of page)* marge *f*; *(of knife, blade)* tranchant *m* **2** *vt (clothing)* border (**with** de) **3** *vi* **to e. forward** avancer doucement

**edgeways** [ˈedʒweɪz] (*Am* **edgewise** [ˈedʒwaɪz]) *adv* de côté; *Fam* **I can't get a word in e.** je ne peux pas en placer une

**edgy** [ˈedʒɪ] (**-ier, -iest**) *adj* énervé

**edible** [ˈedɪbəl] *adj (safe to eat)* comestible; *(fit to eat)* mangeable

**edifice** [ˈedɪfɪs] *n (building)* édifice *m*

**Edinburgh** [ˈedɪnbərə] *n* Édimbourg *m ou f*

**edit** [ˈedɪt] *vt (newspaper)* diriger; *(article)* corriger; *(prepare for publication)* préparer pour la publication; *(film)* monter

**edition** [ɪˈdɪʃən] *n* édition *f*

**editor** [ˈedɪtə(r)] *n (of newspaper)* rédacteur, -trice *mf* en chef; *(of film)* monteur, -euse *mf*; *Comptr (software)* éditeur *m*

**educate** [ˈedjʊkeɪt] *vt (bring up)* éduquer; *(in school)* instruire ▪ **educated** *adj* **(well-)e.** *(person)* instruit

**education** [edjʊˈkeɪʃən] *n* éducation *f*; *(teaching)* enseignement *m*; *(training)* formation *f*; *(university subject)* pédagogie *f* ▪ **educational** *adj (qualification)* d'enseignement; *(method, theory, content)* pédagogique; *(game, film, system)* éducatif, -ive; *(establishment)* scolaire

**eel** [iːl] *n* anguille *f*

**eerie** [ˈɪərɪ] (**-ier, -iest**) *adj* sinistre

**effect** [ɪˈfekt] **1** *n (result, impression)* effet *m* (**on** sur); **in e.** en fait; **to come into e., to take e.** *(of law)* entrer en vigueur **2** *vt (change, rescue)* effectuer

**effective** [ɪˈfektɪv] *adj (efficient)* efficace; *(actual)* réel (*f* réelle); **to become e.** *(of law)* prendre effet ▪ **effectively** *adv (efficiently)* efficacement; *(in fact)* effectivement

**efficient** [ɪˈfɪʃənt] *adj* efficace; *(productive)* performant ▪ **efficiently** *adv* efficacement

**effort** [ˈefət] *n* effort *m*; **to make an e.**

faire un effort (**to** pour) ▪ **effortlessly** *adv* sans effort

**e.g.** [iː'dʒiː] (*abbr* **exempli gratia**) p. ex.

**egg**[1] [eg] *n* œuf *m*; **e. timer** sablier *m* ▪ **eggplant** *n Am* aubergine *f*

**egg**[2] [eg] *vt* **to e. sb on** encourager qn (**to do** à faire)

**ego** ['iːgəʊ] (*pl* **-os**) *n* **to have an enormous e.** avoir une très haute opinion de soi-même

**egoistic(al)** [iːgəʊ'ɪstɪk(əl)] *adj* égoïste

**Egypt** ['iːdʒɪpt] *n* l'Égypte *f* ▪ **Egyptian** [ɪ'dʒɪpʃən] **1** *adj* égyptien, -enne **2** *n* Égyptien, -enne *mf*

**eight** [eɪt] *adj & n* huit *(m)* ▪ **eighth** *adj & n* huitième *(mf)*; **an e.** *(fraction)* un huitième

**eighteen** [eɪ'tiːn] *adj & n* dix-huit *(m)* ▪ **eighteenth** *adj & n* dix-huitième *(mf)*

**eighty** ['eɪtɪ] *adj & n* quatre-vingts *(m)*; **e.-one** quatre-vingt-un; **in the eighties** dans les années 80 ▪ **eightieth** *adj & n* quatre-vingtième *(mf)*

**Eire** ['eərə] *n* l'Eire *f*

**either** ['aɪðə(r), iːðə(r)] **1** *adj & pron (one or other)* l'un(e) ou l'autre; *(with negative)* ni l'un(e) ni l'autre; *(each)* chaque; **on e. side** des deux côtés **2** *adv* **she can't swim e.** elle ne sait pas nager non plus; **I don't e.** (ni) moi non plus **3** *conj* **e.... or...** ou... ou..., soit... soit...; *(with negative)* ni... ni...

**eject** [ɪ'dʒekt] **1** *vt (troublemaker)* expulser (**from** de); *(from machine)* éjecter **2** *vi (of pilot)* s'éjecter

**elaborate**[1] [ɪ'læbərət] *adj (meal)* élaboré; *(scheme)* compliqué; *(description)* détaillé; *(style)* recherché

**elaborate**[2] [ɪ'læbəreɪt] **1** *vt (theory)* élaborer **2** *vi* entrer dans les détails (**on** de)

**elapse** [ɪ'læps] *vi* s'écouler

**elastic** [ɪ'læstɪk] **1** *adj* élastique; *Br* **e. band** élastique *m* **2** *n (fabric)* élastique *m*

**elated** [ɪ'leɪtɪd] *adj* transporté de joie

**elbow** ['elbəʊ] **1** *n* coude *m* **2** *vt* **to e. one's way** se frayer un chemin en jouant des coudes (**through** à travers)

**elder** ['eldə(r)] *adj & n (of two people)* aîné, -e *(mf)* ▪ **eldest** *adj & n* aîné, -e *(mf)*; **his/her e. brother** l'aîné de ses frères

**elderly** ['eldəlɪ] **1** *adj* âgé **2** *npl* **the e.** les personnes *fpl* âgées

**elect** [ɪ'lekt] *vt (by voting)* élire (**to** à)

**election** [ɪ'lekʃən] **1** *n* élection *f*; **general e.** élections *fpl* législatives **2** *adj (campaign)* électoral; *(day, results)* des élections

**electoral** [ɪ'lektərəl] *adj* électoral ▪ **electorate** *n* électorat *m*

**electric** [ɪ'lektrɪk] *adj* électrique; **e. blanket** couverture *f* chauffante; *Br* **e. fire** radiateur *m* électrique; **e. shock** décharge *f* électrique ▪ **electrical** *adj* électrique

**electrician** [ɪlek'trɪʃən] *n* électricien *m*

**electricity** [ɪlek'trɪsɪtɪ] *n* électricité *f*

**electrify** [ɪ'lektrɪfaɪ] (*pt & pp* **-ied**) *vt (excite)* électriser

**electronic** [ɪlek'trɒnɪk] *adj* électronique ▪ **electronics** *n (subject)* électronique *f*

**elegant** ['elɪgənt] *adj* élégant ▪ **elegantly** *adv* avec élégance

**element** ['eləmənt] *n (component, chemical, person)* élément *m*; *(of heater, kettle)* résistance *f*; **the elements** *(bad weather)* les éléments *mpl*; **to be in one's e.** être dans son élément

**elementary** [elɪ'mentərɪ] *adj* élémentaire; *Am (school)* primaire

**elephant** ['elɪfənt] *n* éléphant *m*

**elevate** ['elɪveɪt] *vt* élever (**to** à)

**elevator** ['elɪveɪtə(r)] *n Am* ascenseur *m*

**eleven** [ɪ'levən] *adj & n* onze *(m)* ▪ **eleventh** *adj & n* onzième *(mf)*

**elicit** [ɪ'lɪsɪt] *vt* tirer (**from** de)

**eligible** ['elɪdʒəbəl] *adj (for post)* admissible (**for** à); **to be e. for sth** *(entitled to)* avoir droit à qch

**eliminate** [ɪ'lɪmɪneɪt] *vt* éliminer
**elite** [eɪ'li:t] *n* élite *f* (**of** de)
**elongated** ['i:lɒŋgeɪtɪd] *adj* allongé
**elope** [ɪ'ləʊp] *vi (of lovers)* s'enfuir (**with** avec)
**eloquent** ['eləkwənt] *adj* éloquent
**else** [els] *adv* d'autre; **somebody/anybody e.** quelqu'un/n'importe qui d'autre; **everybody e.** tous les autres; **something e.** autre chose; **anything e.?** *(in shop)* est-ce qu'il vous faut autre chose?; **somewhere e.,** *Am* **someplace e.** ailleurs, autre part; **nowhere e.** nulle part ailleurs; **who e.?** qui d'autre?; **or e.** ou bien, sinon ▪ **elsewhere** *adv* ailleurs
**elude** [ɪ'lu:d] *vt* échapper à ▪ **elusive** *adj (person)* insaisissable
**emaciated** [ɪ'meɪsɪeɪtɪd] *adj* émacié
**e-mail** ['i:meɪl] **1** *n* courrier *m* électronique, mél *m*; **e. address** adresse *f* électronique **2** *vt* envoyer un courrier électronique *ou* un mél à
**emanate** ['eməneɪt] *vi* émaner (**from** de)
**emancipation** [ɪmænsɪ'peɪʃən] *n* émancipation *f*
**embankment** [ɪm'bæŋkmənt] *n (of path)* talus *m*; *(of river)* berge *f*
**embargo** [ɪm'bɑ:gəʊ] (*pl* **-oes**) *n* embargo *m*
**embark** [ɪm'bɑ:k] *vi* (s')embarquer; **to e. on sth** s'embarquer dans qch
**embarrass** [ɪm'bærəs] *vt* embarrasser ▪ **embarrassing** *adj* embarrassant
**embassy** ['embəsɪ] (*pl* **-ies**) *n* ambassade *f*
**embellish** [ɪm'belɪʃ] *vt* embellir
**embers** ['embəz] *npl* braises *fpl*
**embezzle** [ɪm'bezəl] *vt (money)* détourner
**emblem** ['embləm] *n* emblème *m*
**embody** [ɪm'bɒdɪ] (*pt & pp* **-ied**) *vt (express)* exprimer; *(represent)* incarner
**embrace** [ɪm'breɪs] **1** *n* étreinte *f* **2** *vt (person)* étreindre; *Fig (belief)* embrasser **3** *vi* s'étreindre
**embroider** [ɪm'brɔɪdə(r)] *vt (cloth)* broder; *Fig (story, facts)* enjoliver ▪ **embroidery** *n* broderie *f*
**embryo** ['embrɪəʊ] (*pl* **-os**) *n* embryon *m*
**emerald** ['emərəld] *n* émeraude *f*
**emerge** [ɪ'mɜ:dʒ] *vi* apparaître (**from** de); *(from hole)* sortir; *(from water)* émerger
**emergency** [ɪ'mɜ:dʒənsɪ] **1** (*pl* **-ies**) *n (situation, case)* urgence *f*; **in an e.** en cas d'urgence **2** *adj (measure, operation, services)* d'urgence; **e. exit** sortie *f* de secours; **e. landing** atterrissage *m* forcé
**emigrant** ['emɪgrənt] *n* émigrant, -e *mf* ▪ **emigrate** [-greɪt] *vi* émigrer
**eminent** ['emɪnənt] *adj* éminent
**emission** [ɪ'mɪʃən] *n (of gas, light)* émission *f*
**emit** [ɪ'mɪt] (*pt & pp* **-tt-**) *vt (light, heat)* émettre
**emotion** [ɪ'məʊʃən] *n (strength of feeling)* émotion *f*; *(individual feeling)* sentiment *m*
**emotional** [ɪ'məʊʃənəl] *adj (person, reaction)* émotif, -ive; *(speech, plea)* émouvant
**emotive** [ɪ'məʊtɪv] *adj (word)* affectif, -ive
**empathy** ['empəθɪ] *n* compassion *f*
**emperor** ['empərə(r)] *n* empereur *m*
**emphasis** ['emfəsɪs] (*pl* **-ases** [-əsi:z]) *n (in word or phrase)* accent *m*; *(insistence)* insistance *f*
**emphasize** ['emfəsaɪz] *vt (importance)* souligner; *(word, fact)* insister sur, souligner; *(syllable)* appuyer sur; **to e. that...** souligner que...
**emphatic** [em'fætɪk] *adj (denial, refusal) (clear)* catégorique; *(forceful)* énergique
**empire** ['empaɪə(r)] *n* empire *m*
**employ** [ɪm'plɔɪ] *vt (person, means)* employer ▪ **employee** [em'plɔɪi:] *n* employé, -e *mf* ▪ **employer** *n* patron, -onne *mf* ▪ **employment** *n* emploi *m*; **e. agency** bureau *m* de placement
**emptiness** ['emptɪnɪs] *n* vide *m*
**empty** ['emptɪ] **1** (**-ier, -iest**) *adj* vide;

*(threat, promise)* vain; **on an e. stomach** à jeun **2** *npl* **empties** *(bottles)* bouteilles *fpl* vides **3** *(pt & pp* **-ied***)* *vt* **to e. (out)** *(box, pocket, liquid)* vider; *(objects from box)* sortir (**from** *or* **out of** de) **4** *vi (of building, tank)* se vider ▪ **empty-handed** *adv* **to return e.** revenir les mains vides

**emulate** ['emjʊleɪt] *vt* imiter

**enable** [ɪ'neɪbəl] *vt* **to e. sb to do sth** permettre à qn de faire qch

**enamel** [ɪ'næməl] **1** *n* émail *m (pl* émaux) **2** *adj* en émail

**enamoured** [ɪ'næməd] *adj* **e. of** *(thing)* séduit par; *(person)* amoureux, -euse de

**encapsulate** [ɪn'kæpsjʊleɪt] *vt (ideas, views)* résumer

**encase** [ɪn'keɪs] *vt (cover)* envelopper (**in** dans)

**enchanting** [ɪn'tʃɑːntɪŋ] *adj* enchanteur, -eresse

**encircle** [ɪn'sɜːkəl] *vt* entourer; *(of army, police)* encercler

**encl** *(abbr* **enclosure(s)**) PJ

**enclose** [ɪn'kləʊz] *vt (send with letter)* joindre (**in** *or* **with** à); *(fence off)* clôturer ▪ **enclosed** *adj (receipt, document)* ci-joint; **please find e....** veuillez trouver ci-joint…

**enclosure** [ɪn'kləʊʒə(r)] *n (in letter)* pièce *f* jointe; *(place)* enceinte *f*

**encompass** [ɪn'kʌmpəs] *vt (include)* inclure

**encore** ['ɒŋkɔː(r)] *exclam & n* bis *(m)*

**encounter** [ɪn'kaʊntə(r)] **1** *n* rencontre *f* **2** *vt (person, resistance)* rencontrer

**encourage** [ɪn'kʌrɪdʒ] *vt* encourager (**to do** à faire) ▪ **encouragement** *n* encouragement *m*

**encroach** [ɪn'krəʊtʃ] *vi* empiéter (**on** *or* **upon** sur)

**encyclop(a)edia** [ɪnsaɪklə'piːdɪə] *n* encyclopédie *f*

**end** [end] **1** *n (extremity)* bout *m*, extrémité *f*; *(of month, meeting, book)* fin *f*; *(purpose)* but *m*; **at an e.** *(discussion, war)* fini; *(period of time)* écoulé; **in the e.** à la fin; **to come to an e.** prendre fin; **for days on e.** pendant des jours et des jours; **to stand sth on e.** mettre qch debout
**2** *adj (row, house)* dernier, -ère
**3** *vt* finir, terminer (**with** par); *(rumour, speculation)* mettre fin à
**4** *vi* finir, se terminer; **to e. up doing sth** finir par faire qch; **he ended up in prison/a doctor** il a fini en prison/médecin

**endanger** [ɪn'deɪndʒə(r)] *vt* mettre en danger; **endangered species** espèce *f* menacée

**endearing** [ɪn'dɪərɪŋ] *adj (quality)* qui inspire la sympathie

**endeavour** [ɪn'devə(r)] (*Am* **endeavor**) **1** *n* effort *m* (**to do** pour faire) **2** *vi* s'efforcer (**to do** de faire)

**ending** ['endɪŋ] *n* fin *f*; *(of word)* terminaison *f*

**endless** ['endləs] *adj (speech, series, list)* interminable; *(countless)* innombrable

**endorse** [ɪn'dɔːs] *vt (cheque)* endosser; *(action, plan)* approuver ▪ **endorsement** *n Br (on driving licence)* = contravention inscrite sur le permis de conduire

**endow** [ɪn'daʊ] *vt* **to be endowed with** *(of person)* être doté de ▪ **endowment** *n* dotation *f*

**endurance** [ɪn'djʊərəns] *n* endurance *f*

**endure** [ɪn'djʊə(r)] **1** *vt (violence)* endurer; *(person, insult)* supporter **2** *vi (last)* survivre

**enemy** ['enəmɪ] **1** *(pl* **-ies***)* *n* ennemi, -e *mf* **2** *adj (army, tank)* ennemi

**energetic** [enə'dʒetɪk] *adj* énergique

**energy** ['enədʒɪ] **1** *(pl* **-ies***)* *n* énergie *f* **2** *adj (resources)* énergétique; **e. crisis** crise *f* de l'énergie

**enforce** [ɪn'fɔːs] *vt (law)* faire respecter; *(discipline)* imposer (**on** à)

**engage** [ɪn'geɪdʒ] *vt (take on)* engager ▪ **engaged** *adj* (**a**) *(occupied) (person, toilet, phone)* occupé (**b**) **e. (to be married)** fiancé; **to get e.** se fiancer

**engagement** [ɪn'geɪdʒmənt] *n (to

*marry)* fiançailles *fpl*; *(meeting)* rendez-vous *m inv*; **e. ring** bague *f* de fiançailles

**engine** ['endʒɪn] *n (of vehicle, aircraft)* moteur *m*; *(of train)* locomotive *f*; *(of ship)* machine *f*

**engineer** [endʒɪ'nɪə(r)] **1** *n* ingénieur *m*; *Br (repairer)* dépanneur *m*; **civil e.** ingénieur *m* des travaux publics **2** *vt (arrange secretly)* manigancer ▪ **engineering** *n* ingénierie *f*; **(civil) e.** génie *m* civil

**England** ['ɪŋglənd] *n* l'Angleterre *f*

**English** ['ɪŋglɪʃ] **1** *adj* anglais; **E. teacher** professeur *m* d'anglais; **the E. Channel** la Manche **2** *n (language)* anglais *m*; **the E.** *(people)* les Anglais *mpl* ▪ **Englishman** (*pl* **-men**) *n* Anglais *m* ▪ **English-speaking** *adj* anglophone ▪ **Englishwoman** (*pl* **-women**) *n* Anglaise *f*

**engraving** [ɪn'greɪvɪŋ] *n* gravure *f*

**engrossed** [ɪn'grəʊst] *adj* **e. in one's work/book** absorbé par son travail/dans sa lecture

**engulf** [ɪn'gʌlf] *vt* engloutir

**enhance** [ɪn'hɑːns] *vt (beauty, prestige)* rehausser; *(value)* augmenter

**enigma** [ɪ'nɪgmə] *n* énigme *f*

**enjoy** [ɪn'dʒɔɪ] *vt (like)* aimer (**doing** faire); *(meal)* savourer; *(benefit from)* jouir de; **to e. oneself** s'amuser ▪ **enjoyable** *adj* agréable; *(meal)* excellent ▪ **enjoyment** *n* plaisir *m*

**enlarge** [ɪn'lɑːdʒ] **1** *vt* agrandir **2** *vi* **to e. (up)on sth** s'étendre sur qch ▪ **enlargement** *n (increase) & Phot* agrandissement *m*

**enlighten** [ɪn'laɪtən] *vt* éclairer (**sb on** *or* **about sth** qn sur qch) ▪ **enlightening** *adj* instructif, -ive

**enlist** [ɪn'lɪst] **1** *vt (recruit)* engager; *(supporter)* recruter; *(support)* s'assurer **2** *vi (in the army)* s'engager

**enormous** [ɪ'nɔːməs] *adj* énorme; *(explosion, blow)* terrible; *(patience, gratitude, success)* immense ▪ **enormously** *adv (very much)* énormément; *(very)* extrêmement

**enough** [ɪ'nʌf] **1** *adj* assez de; **e. time/cups** assez de temps/de tasses **2** *pron* assez; **to have e. to live on** avoir de quoi vivre; **to have had e. of sb/sth** en avoir assez de qn/qch; **that's e.** ça suffit **3** *adv (work, sleep)* assez; **big/good e.** assez grand/bon (**to** pour)

**enquire** [ɪn'kwaɪə(r)] *vti* = **inquire**

**enquiry** [ɪn'kwaɪərɪ] *n* = **inquiry**

**enrage** [ɪn'reɪdʒ] *vt* mettre en rage

**enrich** [ɪn'rɪtʃ] *vt* enrichir; *(soil)* fertiliser

**enrol** [ɪn'rəʊl] (*Am* **enroll**) (*pt & pp* **-ll-**) **1** *vt* inscrire **2** *vi* s'inscrire (**on** *or* **for** à) ▪ **enrolment** (*Am* **enrollment**) *n* inscription *f*

**ensemble** [ɒn'sɒmbəl] *n (musicians, clothes)* ensemble *m*

**ensue** [ɪn'sjuː] *vi* s'ensuivre ▪ **ensuing** *adj (in the past)* qui a suivi; *(in the future)* qui suivra

**ensure** [ɪn'ʃʊə(r)] *vt* assurer; **to e. that...** s'assurer que…

**entail** [ɪn'teɪl] *vt (involve)* occasionner; **what does the job e.?** en quoi le travail consiste-t-il?

**entangle** [ɪn'tæŋgəl] *vt* **to get entangled in sth** *(of person, animal)* s'empêtrer dans qch

**enter** ['entə(r)] **1** *vt (room, army)* entrer dans; *(race, competition)* participer à; *(write down) (on list)* inscrire (**in** dans; **on** sur); *(in accounts book)* porter (**in** sur); *Comptr (data)* entrer; **it didn't e. my head** *or* **mind** ça ne m'est pas venu à l'esprit (**that** que) **2** *vi* entrer; **to e. for** *(exam)* se présenter à; *(race)* se faire inscrire à; **to e. into** *(relations)* entrer en; *(negotiations)* entamer; *(agreement)* conclure; *(contract)* passer (**with** avec)

**enterprise** ['entəpraɪz] *n (undertaking, firm)* entreprise *f*; *(spirit, initiative)* initiative *f* ▪ **enterprising** *adj (person)* entreprenant

**entertain** [entə'teɪn] **1** *vt* amuser, distraire; *(guest)* recevoir; *(idea, possibility)* envisager **2** *vi (receive guests)* recevoir ▪ **entertainer** *n (comedian)* comique *mf*; *(singer, dancer)* artiste *mf* de music-hall ▪ **entertainment** *n* amusement *m*; *(show)* spectacle *m*

**enthusiasm** [ɪn'θjuːzɪæzəm] *n* enthousiasme *m* ▪ **enthusiast** *n* enthousiaste *mf*; **jazz e.** passionné, -e *mf* de jazz

**enthusiastic** [ɪnθjuːzɪ'æstɪk] *adj* enthousiaste; *(golfer, photographer)* passionné; **to get e.** s'emballer (**about** pour)

**entice** [ɪn'taɪs] *vt* attirer (**into** dans); **to e. sb to do sth** inciter qn à faire qch ▪ **enticing** *adj* séduisant

**entire** [ɪn'taɪə(r)] *adj* entier, -ère ▪ **entirely** *adv* entièrement

**entirety** [ɪn'taɪərətɪ] *n* intégralité *f*; **in its e.** dans son intégralité

**entitle** [ɪn'taɪtəl] *vt* **to e. sb to sth/to do sth** donner à qn le droit à qch/de faire qch ▪ **entitled** *adj* **to be e. to do sth** avoir le droit de faire qch; **to be e. to sth** avoir droit à qch

**entrance** ['entrəns] *n* entrée *f* (**to** de); *(to university, school)* admission *f* (**to** à); **e. fee** droit *m* d'entrée

**entrant** ['entrənt] *n (in race)* concurrent, -e *mf*; *(for exam)* candidat, -e *mf*

**entrée** ['ɒntreɪ] *n Culin (course before main dish)* entrée *f*; *Am (main dish)* plat *m* principal

**entrepreneur** [ɒntrəprə'nɜː(r)] *n* entrepreneur *m*

**entrust** [ɪn'trʌst] *vt* confier (**to** à); **to e. sb with sth** confier qch à qn

**entry** ['entrɪ] *n* entrée *f*; *(in race)* concurrent, -e *mf*; *(to be judged in competition)* objet *m*/œuvre *f*/projet *m* soumis au jury; **e. form** feuille *f* d'inscription; **'no e.'** *(on door)* 'entrée interdite'; *(road sign)* 'sens interdit'

**envelope** ['envələʊp] *n* enveloppe *f*

**enviable** ['envɪəbəl] *adj* enviable

**envious** ['envɪəs] *adj* envieux, -euse (**of** de); **to be e. of sb** envier qn

**environment** [ɪn'vaɪərənmənt] *n (social, moral)* milieu *m*; **the e.** *(natural)* l'environnement *m* ▪ **environmental** [-'mentəl] *adj (policy)* de l'environnement; **e. disaster** catastrophe *f* écologique ▪ **environmentally** *adv* **e. friendly product** produit *m* qui ne nuit pas à l'environnement

**envisage** [ɪn'vɪzɪdʒ] (*Am* **envision** [ɪn'vɪʒən]) *vt (imagine)* envisager; *(foresee)* prévoir; **to e. doing sth** envisager de faire qch

**envoy** ['envɔɪ] *n (messenger)* envoyé, -e *mf*; *(diplomat)* ministre *m* plénipotentiaire

**envy** ['envɪ] **1** *n* envie *f* **2** (*pt & pp* **-ied**) *vt* envier; **to e. sb sth** envier qch à qn

**ephemeral** [ɪ'femərəl] *adj* éphémère

**epic** ['epɪk] **1** *adj* épique **2** *n (poem, novel)* épopée *f*; *(film)* film *m* à grand spectacle

**epidemic** [epɪ'demɪk] *n* épidémie *f*

**epileptic** [epɪ'leptɪk] *adj & n* épileptique *(mf)*

**epilogue** ['epɪlɒg] *n* épilogue *m*

**episode** ['epɪsəʊd] *n (part of story)* épisode *m*; *(incident)* incident *m*

**epitaph** ['epɪtɑːf] *n* épitaphe *f*

**epitome** [ɪ'pɪtəmɪ] *n* **to be the e. of sth** être l'exemple même de qch ▪ **epitomize** *vt* incarner

**epoch** ['iːpɒk] *n* époque *f*

**equal** ['iːkwəl] **1** *adj* égal (**to** à); **to be e. to sth** *(in quantity)* égaler qch; *(good enough)* être à la hauteur de qch **2** *n (person)* égal, -e *mf* **3** (*Br* **-ll-**, *Am* **-l-**) *vt* égaler (**in** en)

**equality** [ɪ'kwɒlətɪ] *n* égalité *f*

**equalize** ['iːkwəlaɪz] *vi (in sport)* égaliser

**equally** ['iːkwəlɪ] *adv (to an equal degree, also)* également; *(divide)* en parts égales

**equals** ['iːkwəlz] *n* **e. sign** signe *m* d'égalité

**equation** [ɪ'kweɪʒən] *n Math* équation *f*

**equator** [ɪ'kweɪtə(r)] *n* équateur *m*; **at** *or* **on the e.** sous l'équateur

**equilibrium** [iːkwɪ'lɪbrɪəm] *n* équilibre *m*

**equip** [ɪ'kwɪp] *(pt & pp* **-pp-**) *vt (provide with equipment)* équiper (**with** de); *(prepare)* préparer (**for** pour); **to be (well-)equipped to do sth** être compétent pour faire qch ▪ **equipment** *n* équipement *m*; *(in factory)* matériel *m*

**equivalent** [ɪ'kwɪvələnt] *adj & n* équivalent *(m)*

**era** [*Br* 'ɪərə, *Am* 'erə] *n* époque *f*; *(historical, geological)* ère *f*

**eradicate** [ɪ'rædɪkeɪt] *vt* éradiquer

**erase** [*Br* ɪ'reɪz, *Am* ɪ'reɪs] *vt* effacer; *(with eraser)* gommer ▪ **eraser** *n* gomme *f*

**erect** [ɪ'rekt] **1** *adj (upright)* droit **2** *vt (building)* construire; *(statue, monument)* ériger; *(scaffolding)* monter; *(tent)* dresser

**erode** [ɪ'rəʊd] *vt (of sea)* éroder; *Fig (confidence)* miner ▪ **erosion** [-ʒən] *n* érosion *f*

**erotic** [ɪ'rɒtɪk] *adj* érotique

**errand** ['erənd] *n* commission *f*, course *f*; **to run errands for sb** faire des courses pour qn

**erratic** [ɪ'rætɪk] *adj (unpredictable) (behaviour)* imprévisible; *(service, machine)* fantaisiste; *(person)* lunatique; *(irregular) (performance, results)* irrégulier, -ère

**error** ['erə(r)] *n (mistake)* erreur *f*; **typing/printing e.** faute *f* de frappe/d'impression

**erupt** [ɪ'rʌpt] *vi (of volcano)* entrer en éruption; *(of war, violence)* éclater ▪ **eruption** *n (of volcano)* éruption *f*; *(of violence)* flambée *f*

**escalate** ['eskəleɪt] *vi (of war, violence)* s'intensifier; *(of prices)* monter en flèche

**escalator** ['eskəleɪtə(r)] *n* escalier *m* roulant

**escapade** ['eskəpeɪd] *n* frasque *f*

**escape** [ɪ'skeɪp] **1** *n (of gas, liquid)* fuite *f*; *(of person)* évasion *f*; **he had a lucky** *or* **narrow e.** il l'a échappé belle **2** *vt (death, punishment)* échapper à **3** *vi (of gas, animal)* s'échapper (**from** de); *(of prisoner)* s'évader (**from** de)

**escort 1** ['eskɔːt] *n (for convoy)* escorte *f*; *(of woman)* cavalier *m* **2** [ɪ'skɔːt] *vt* escorter; *(prisoner)* conduire sous escorte

**Eskimo** ['eskɪməʊ] *(pl* **-os**) *n* Esquimau, -aude *mf*

**especially** [ɪs'peʃəlɪ] *adv (in particular)* surtout; *(more than normally)* particulièrement; *(for a purpose)* (tout) spécialement; **e. as** d'autant plus que

**espresso** [e'spresəʊ] *(pl* **-os**) *n* express *m*

**Esq** *(abbr* **Esquire**) *Br* **John Smith Esq** = Monsieur John Smith

**essay** ['eseɪ] *n (at school)* rédaction *f*; *(at university)* dissertation *f* (**on** sur)

**essence** ['esəns] *n (distinctive quality)* essence *f*; *Culin (extract)* extrait *m*; **the e. of sth** *(main point)* l'essentiel *m* de qch; **in e.** essentiellement

**essential** [ɪ'senʃəl] **1** *adj (principal)* essentiel, -elle; *(necessary)* indispensable, essentiel, -elle; **it's e. that...** il est indispensable que... *(+ subjunctive)* **2** *npl* **the essentials** l'essentiel *m* (**of** de)

**establish** [ɪ'stæblɪʃ] *vt* établir; *(state, society, company)* fonder; *(post)* créer ▪ **established** *adj* **(well-)e.** *(company)* solide; *(fact)* reconnu; *(reputation)* établi ▪ **establishment** *n (institution, company)* établissement *m*; **the E.** *(dominant group)* les classes *fpl* dirigeantes

**estate** [ɪ'steɪt] *n (land)* terres *fpl*, propriété *f*; *(possessions)* biens *mpl*; *(property after death)* succession *f*; *Br* **e. agent** agent *m* immobilier; *Br* **e. car** break *m*

**esteem** [ɪ'stiːm] **1** *n* estime *f*; **to hold sb in high e.** avoir qn en haute estime **2** *vt* estimer

**esthetic** [es'θetɪk] *adj Am* esthétique

**estimate 1** ['estɪmət] *n* évaluation *f*; *Com* devis *m* **2** ['estɪmeɪt] *vt (value)* estimer, évaluer; *(consider)* estimer (**that** que)

**estranged** [ɪ'streɪndʒd] *adj* **her e.**

**husband** son mari, dont elle vit séparée

**estuary** ['estjʊərɪ] (*pl* **-ies**) *n* estuaire *m*

**etc** [et'setərə] (*abbr* **et cetera**) *adv* etc

**etching** ['etʃɪŋ] *n (picture)* eau-forte *f*

**eternal** [ɪ'tɜːnəl] *adj* éternel, -elle ▪ **eternity** *n* éternité *f*

**ethical** ['eθɪkəl] *adj* moral, éthique

**ethics** ['eθɪks] *n* éthique *f*, morale *f*; *(of profession)* déontologie *f*

**ethnic** ['eθnɪk] *adj* ethnique

**etiquette** ['etɪket] *n* étiquette *f*

**etymology** [etɪ'mɒlədʒɪ] *n* étymologie *f*

**EU** [iː'juː] (*abbr* **European Union**) *n* UE *f*

**euphemism** ['juːfəmɪzəm] *n* euphémisme *m*

**euphoria** [juː'fɔːrɪə] *n* euphorie *f*

**euro** ['jʊərəʊ] (*pl* **-os**) *n (currency)* euro *m*

**Euro-** ['jʊərəʊ] *pref* euro-; **E.-MP** député *m* européen

**Europe** ['jʊərəp] *n* l'Europe *f* ▪ **European** [-'piːən] **1** *adj* européen, -enne; **E. Union** Union *f* européenne **2** *n* Européen, -enne *mf*

**evacuate** [ɪ'vækjʊeɪt] *vt* évacuer

**evade** [ɪ'veɪd] *vt* éviter, esquiver; *(pursuer)* échapper à; *(law, question)* éluder; **to e. tax** frauder le fisc

**evaluate** [ɪ'væljʊeɪt] *vt* évaluer (**at** à)

**evangelical** [iːvæn'dʒelɪkəl] *adj* évangélique

**evaporate** [ɪ'væpəreɪt] *vi (of liquid)* s'évaporer; **evaporated milk** lait *m* condensé

**evasion** [ɪ'veɪʒən] *n (of pursuer, responsibilities, question)* dérobade *f* (**of** devant); **tax e.** évasion *f* fiscale

**evasive** [ɪ'veɪsɪv] *adj* évasif, -ive

**eve** [iːv] *n* **on the e. of** à la veille de

**even** ['iːvən] **1** *adj (equal, flat)* égal; *(smooth)* uni; *(regular)* régulier, -ère; *(temperature)* constant; *(number)* pair; *Fig* **to get e. with sb** prendre sa revanche sur qn; **to break e.** *(financially)* s'y retrouver

**2** *adv* même; **e. better/more** encore mieux/plus; **e. if** *or* **though...** bien que... *(+ subjunctive)*; **e. so** quand même

**3** *vt* **to e. sth (out** *or* **up)** égaliser qch ▪ **evenly** *adv (equally)* de manière égale; *(regularly)* régulièrement

**evening** ['iːvnɪŋ] *n* soir *m*; *(referring to duration, event)* soirée *f*; **tomorrow/yesterday e.** demain/hier soir; **in the e.**, *Am* **evenings** le soir; **at seven in the e.** à sept heures du soir; **every Tuesday e.** tous les mardis soir; **e. meal/paper** repas *m*/journal *m* du soir; **e. class** cours *m* du soir; **e. dress** *(of man)* tenue *f* de soirée; *(of woman)* robe *f* du soir

**event** [ɪ'vent] *n* événement *m*; *(in sport)* épreuve *f* ▪ **eventful** *adj (day, journey, life)* mouvementé; *(occasion)* mémorable

**eventual** [ɪ'ventʃʊəl] *adj (final)* final, définitif, -ive ▪ **eventuality** [-tjʊ'ælətɪ] (*pl* **-ies**) *n* éventualité *f* ▪ **eventually** *adv* finalement; *(some day)* par la suite

**ever** ['evə(r)] *adv* jamais; **have you e. been to Spain?** es-tu déjà allé en Espagne?; **the first e.** le tout premier; **e. since (1990)** depuis (1990); **for e.** pour toujours; **e. so sorry** vraiment désolé; **she's e. so nice** elle est tellement gentille; **all she e. does is criticize** elle ne fait que critiquer

**evergreen** ['evəgriːn] *n* arbre *m* à feuilles persistantes

**everlasting** [evə'lɑːstɪŋ] *adj* éternel, -elle

**every** ['evrɪ] *adj* chaque; **e. time** chaque fois (**that** que); **e. one** chacun; **e. second** *or* **other day** tous les deux jours; **e. so often, e. now and then** de temps en temps

**everybody** ['evrɪbɒdɪ] *pron* tout le monde ▪ **everyday** *adj (happening, life)* de tous les jours; *(ordinary)* banal (*mpl* -als); **in e. use** d'usage courant ▪ **everyone** *pron* = **everybody** ▪ **everyplace** *adv Am* = **everywhere** ▪ **everything** *pron* tout; **e. (that) I**

**have** tout ce que j'ai ▪ **everywhere** *adv* partout; **e. she goes** où qu'elle aille

**evict** [ɪ'vɪkt] *vt* expulser (**from** de)

**evidence** ['evɪdəns] *n (proof)* preuve(s) *f(pl)*; *(testimony)* témoignage *m*; **to give e.** témoigner (**against** contre)

**evident** ['evɪdənt] *adj* évident (**that** que); **it is e. from...** il apparaît de... (**that** que) ▪ **evidently** *adv (clearly)* manifestement; *(apparently)* apparemment

**evil** ['i:vəl] **1** *adj (spell, influence, person)* malfaisant; *(deed, system)* mauvais **2** *n* mal *m*

**evoke** [ɪ'vəʊk] *vt (conjure up)* évoquer ▪ **evocative** [ɪ'vɒkətɪv] *adj* évocateur, -trice (**of** de)

**evolution** [i:və'lu:ʃən] *n* évolution *f*

**evolve** [ɪ'vɒlv] **1** *vt (system)* mettre au point **2** *vi (of society, idea)* évoluer; *(of plan)* se développer

**ewe** [ju:] *n* brebis *f*

**ex** [eks] *n Fam (former spouse)* ex *mf*

**ex-** [eks] *pref* ex-; **ex-minister** ancien ministre *m*

**exact** [ɪg'zækt] **1** *adj* exact **2** *vt (demand)* exiger (**from** de); *(money, promise)* extorquer (**from** à) ▪ **exactly** *adv* exactement

**exaggerate** [ɪg'zædʒəreɪt] *vti* exagérer

**exam** [ɪg'zæm] (*abbr* **examination**) *n* examen *m*

**examine** [ɪg'zæmɪn] *vt (evidence, patient, question)* examiner; *(accounts, luggage)* vérifier; *(passport)* contrôler; *(student)* interroger ▪ **examination** *n* examen *m*; *(of accounts)* vérification *f*; *(of passport)* contrôle *m*

**example** [ɪg'zɑ:mpəl] *n* exemple *m*; **for e.** par exemple; **to set an e.** *or* **a good e.** donner l'exemple (**to** à); **to set a bad e.** donner le mauvais exemple (**to** à)

**exasperate** [ɪg'zɑ:spəreɪt] *vt* exaspérer

**excavate** ['ekskəveɪt] *vt (dig)* creuser; *(archaeological site)* faire des fouilles dans ▪ **excavation** [-'veɪʃən] *n (archaeological)* fouilles *fpl*

**exceed** [ɪk'si:d] *vt* dépasser; *(one's powers)* excéder

**exceedingly** [ɪk'si:dɪŋlɪ] *adv* extrêmement

**excel** [ɪk'sel] (*pt & pp* **-ll-**) **1** *vt (be better than)* surpasser **2** *vi* **to e. in** *or* **at sth** exceller en qch

**excellent** ['eksələnt] *adj* excellent

**except** [ɪk'sept] **1** *prep* sauf, excepté; **e. for** à part; **e. that...** sauf que... **2** *vt* excepter (**de** from)

**exception** [ɪk'sepʃən] *n* exception *f*; **with the e. of...** à l'exception de...

**exceptional** [ɪk'sepʃənəl] *adj* exceptionnel, -elle

**excerpt** ['eksɜ:pt] *n (from film, book)* extrait *m*

**excess** ['ekses] *n* excès *m*; *(surplus)* excédent *m*; **a sum in e. of...** une somme qui dépasse...; **e. luggage** excédent *m* de bagages

**excessive** [ɪk'sesɪv] *adj* excessif, -ive ▪ **excessively** *adv (too much)* excessivement; *(very)* extrêmement

**exchange** [ɪks'tʃeɪndʒ] **1** *n* échange *m*; *Fin (of currency)* change *m*; **(telephone) e.** central *m* téléphonique; **in e.** en échange (**for** de); **e. rate** taux *m* de change **2** *vt* échanger (**for** contre)

**Exchequer** [ɪks'tʃekə(r)] *n Br* **Chancellor of the E.** ≃ ministre *m* des Finances

**excitable** [ɪk'saɪtəbəl] *adj* nerveux, -euse

**excite** [ɪk'saɪt] *vt (get worked up)* surexciter; *(enthuse)* passionner; *(provoke, stimulate)* exciter ▪ **excited** *adj (happy)* surexcité; *(nervous)* énervé; *(enthusiastic)* enthousiaste; **to get e. (about)** s'exciter (pour); *(angry)* s'énerver (contre) ▪ **exciting** *adj (book, adventure)* passionnant

**excitement** [ɪk'saɪtmənt] *n* agitation *f*; *(enthusiasm)* enthousiasme *m*

**exclaim** [ɪk'skleɪm] *vti* s'écrier (**that** que) ▪ **exclamation** *n* exclamation *f*;

*Br* **e. mark,** *Am* **e. point** point *m* d'exclamation
**exclude** [ɪk'skluːd] *vt* exclure (**from** de); **excluding...** à l'exclusion de...
**exclusive** [ɪk'skluːsɪv] *adj (right, interview, design)* exclusif, -ive; *(club, group)* fermé ▪ **exclusively** *adv* exclusivement
**excruciating** [ɪk'skruːʃɪeɪtɪŋ] *adj* atroce
**excursion** [ɪk'skɜːʃən] *n* excursion *f*
**excuse 1** [ɪk'skjuːs] *n* excuse *f*; **to make an e., to make excuses** se trouver une excuse **2** [ɪk'skjuːz] *vt (forgive, justify)* excuser; *(exempt)* dispenser (**from** de); **e. me!** excusez-moi!, pardon!
**ex-directory** [eksdaɪ'rektərɪ] *adj Br* **to be e.** être sur la liste rouge
**execute** ['eksɪkjuːt] *vt (prisoner, order)* exécuter; *(plan)* mettre à exécution
**execution** [eksɪ'kjuːʃən] *n* exécution *f*
**executive** [ɪg'zekjʊtɪv] **1** *adj (job)* de cadre; *(car)* de luxe **2** *n (person)* cadre *m*
**exemplary** [ɪg'zemplərɪ] *adj* exemplaire
**exemplify** [ɪg'zemplɪfaɪ] *(pt & pp* **-ied**) *vt* illustrer
**exempt** [ɪg'zempt] **1** *adj (person)* dispensé (**from** de) **2** *vt* dispenser (**from** de; **from doing** de faire)
**exemption** [ɪg'zem(p)ʃən] *n* dispense *f* (**from** de)
**exercise** ['eksəsaɪz] **1** *n* exercice *m*; **e. book** cahier *m* **2** *vt* exercer; *(dog, horse)* promener; *(caution, restraint)* user de **3** *vi* faire de l'exercice
**exert** [ɪg'zɜːt] *vt* exercer; *(force)* employer; **to e. oneself** se donner du mal ▪ **exertion** *n* effort *m*
**exhale** [eks'heɪl] *vi* expirer
**exhaust** [ɪg'zɔːst] **1** *n* **e. (fumes)** gaz *mpl* d'échappement; **e. (pipe)** tuyau *m* d'échappement **2** *vt (person, resources)* épuiser ▪ **exhausted** *adj (person, resources)* épuisé ▪ **exhausting** *adj* épuisant
**exhaustive** [ɪg'zɔːstɪv] *adj (list)* exhaustif, -ive; *(analysis)* détaillé; *(inquiry)* approfondi
**exhibit** [ɪg'zɪbɪt] **1** *n* objet *m* exposé; *(in court)* pièce *f* à conviction **2** *vt (put on display)* exposer ▪ **exhibition** [eksɪ'bɪʃən] *n* exposition *f*
**exhilarating** [ɪg'zɪləreɪtɪŋ] *adj (experience)* grisant
**exile** ['egzaɪl] **1** *n (banishment)* exil *m*; *(person)* exilé, -e *mf* **2** *vt* exiler
**exist** [ɪg'zɪst] *vi* exister; *(live)* survivre (**on** avec) ▪ **existing** *adj (situation, circumstances)* actuel, -elle; *(law)* existant
**existence** [ɪg'zɪstəns] *n* existence *f*; **to come into e.** être créé; **to be in e.** exister
**exit** ['eksɪt, 'egzɪt] **1** *n* sortie *f* **2** *vi (leave) & Comptr* sortir
**exodus** ['eksədəs] *n inv* exode *m*
**exorbitant** [ɪg'zɔːbɪtənt] *adj* exorbitant
**exotic** [ɪg'zɒtɪk] *adj* exotique
**expand** [ɪk'spænd] **1** *vt (production, influence)* accroître; *(knowledge)* étendre; *(trade, range, idea)* développer **2** *vi (of knowledge)* s'étendre; *(of trade)* se développer; *(of production)* augmenter; *(of gas)* se dilater; **to e. on** développer
**expanse** [ɪk'spæns] *n* étendue *f*
**expatriate** [ *Br* eks'pætrɪət, *Am* eks'peɪtrɪət] *adj & n* expatrié, -e *(mf)*
**expect** [ɪk'spekt] *vt (anticipate)* s'attendre à; *(think)* penser (**that** que); *(await)* attendre; **to e. to do sth** compter faire qch; **to e. that...** *(anticipate)* s'attendre à ce que... *(+ subjunctive)*; **to be expecting a baby** attendre un enfant; **as expected** comme prévu
**expectation** [ekspek'teɪʃən] *n* **to come up to expectations** se montrer à la hauteur
**expedient** [ɪks'piːdɪənt] **1** *adj* opportun **2** *n* expédient *m*
**expedition** [ekspɪ'dɪʃən] *n* expédition *f*

**expel** [ɪk'spel] *(pt & pp* **-ll-***)* *vt* expulser (**from** de); *(from school)* renvoyer

**expend** [ɪk'spend] *vt (energy, money)* dépenser ▪ **expendable** *adj (person)* qui n'est pas irremplaçable

**expenditure** [ɪk'spendɪtʃə(r)] *n (of money, energy)* dépense *f*

**expense** [ɪk'spens] *n* frais *mpl*, dépense *f*; *Com* **expenses** frais *mpl*; **at the e. of sb/sth** aux dépens de qn/qch

**expensive** [ɪk'spensɪv] *adj (goods, hotel, shop)* cher (*f* chère) ▪ **expensively** *adv* **e. dressed/furnished** habillé/meublé luxueusement

**experience** [ɪk'spɪərɪəns] **1** *n* expérience *f*; **from** *or* **by e.** par expérience **2** *vt (emotion)* ressentir; *(hunger, success)* connaître; *(difficulty)* éprouver ▪ **experienced** *adj (person)* expérimenté; **to be e. in sth** s'y connaître en qch

**experiment 1** [ɪk'sperɪmənt] *n* expérience *f* **2** [ɪk'sperɪment] *vi* expérimenter (**on** sur); **to e. with sth** *(technique, drugs)* essayer qch

**expert** ['ekspɜːt] **1** *n* expert *m* (**on** *or* **in** en) **2** *adj* expert (**in sth** en qch; **in** *or* **at doing** à faire) ▪ **expertise** [-tiːz] *n* compétence *f* (**in** en)

**expiration** [ekspə'reɪʃən] *n Am* = **expiry**

**expire** [ɪk'spaɪə(r)] *vi* expirer ▪ **expired** *adj (ticket, passport)* périmé

**expiry** [ɪk'spaɪərɪ] (*Am* **expiration** [ekspə'reɪʃən]) *n* expiration *f*; **e. date** *(on ticket)* date *f* d'expiration; *(on product)* date *f* limite d'utilisation

**explain** [ɪk'spleɪn] *vt* expliquer (**to** à; **that** que); *(reasons)* exposer; *(mystery)* éclaircir

**explanation** [eksplə'neɪʃən] *n* explication *f*

**explanatory** [ɪk'splænətərɪ] *adj* explicatif, -ive

**expletive** [ɪk'spliːtɪv] *n* juron *m*

**explicit** [ɪk'splɪsɪt] *adj* explicite ▪ **explicitly** *adv* explicitement

**explode** [ɪk'spləʊd] **1** *vt (bomb)* faire exploser **2** *vi (of bomb)* exploser

**exploit 1** ['eksplɔɪt] *n* exploit *m* **2** [ɪk'splɔɪt] *vt (person, land)* exploiter ▪ **exploitation** [eksplɔɪ'teɪʃən] *n* exploitation *f*

**exploratory** [ɪk'splɒrətərɪ] *adj (talks, surgery)* exploratoire

**explore** [ɪk'splɔː(r)] *vt* explorer; *(causes, possibilities)* examiner

**explosion** [ɪk'spləʊʒən] *n* explosion *f*

**explosive** [ɪk'spləʊsɪv] **1** *adj (weapon, situation)* explosif, -ive **2** *n* explosif *m*

**export 1** ['ekspɔːt] *n (activity, product)* exportation *f* **2** [ɪk'spɔːt] *vt* exporter (**to** vers; **from** de) ▪ **exporter** *n* exportateur, -trice *mf*; *(country)* pays *m* exportateur

**expose** [ɪk'spəʊz] *vt (to air, cold, danger) & Phot* exposer (**to** à); *(plot, scandal)* révéler; *(criminal)* démasquer

**exposure** [ɪk'spəʊʒə(r)] *n* exposition *f* (**to** à); *Phot* pose *f*; **to get a lot of e.** *(in the media)* faire l'objet d'une importante couverture médiatique

**express**[1] [ɪk'spres] *vt* exprimer; **to e. oneself** s'exprimer

**express**[2] [ɪk'spres] **1** *adj (letter, delivery)* exprès *inv*; *(train)* rapide, express *inv* **2** *adv (send)* en exprès **3** *n (train)* rapide *m*, express *m inv*

**expression** [ɪk'spreʃən] *n* expression *f*

**expressive** [ɪk'spresɪv] *adj* expressif, -ive

**expressly** [ɪks'preslɪ] *adv (forbid)* expressément

**expressway** [ɪk'spresweɪ] *n Am* autoroute *f*

**expulsion** [ɪk'spʌlʃən] *n* expulsion *f*; *(from school)* renvoi *m*

**exquisite** [ɪk'skwɪzɪt] *adj* exquis

**extend** [ɪk'stend] **1** *vt (in space)* étendre; *(in time)* prolonger (**by** de); *(hand)* tendre (**to sb** à qn); *(house)* agrandir; *(knowledge)* accroître; *(thanks)* offrir (**to** à) **2** *vi (in space)* s'étendre (**to** jusqu'à); *(in time)* se prolonger

**extension** [ɪk'stenʃən] *n (for table)* rallonge *f*; *(to building)* annexe *f*; *(for telephone)* poste *m*; *(for essay)* délai *m* supplémentaire

**extensive** [ɪk'stensɪv] *adj (powers, forests)* vaste; *(repairs, damage)* important ▪ **extensively** *adv (very much)* énormément

**extent** [ɪk'stent] *n (scope)* étendue *f*; *(size)* importance *f*; **to a large** *or* **great e.** dans une large mesure; **to some e.** *or* **a certain e.** dans une certaine mesure; **to such an e. that...** à tel point que...

**exterior** [ɪk'stɪərɪə(r)] *adj & n* extérieur *(m)*

**exterminate** [ɪk'stɜːmɪneɪt] *vt* exterminer

**external** [ɪk'stɜːnəl] *adj (trade, event)* extérieur; *(wall)* externe

**extinct** [ɪk'stɪŋkt] *adj (volcano)* éteint; *(species, animal)* disparu

**extinguish** [ɪk'stɪŋgwɪʃ] *vt* éteindre ▪ **extinguisher** *n* **(fire) e.** extincteur *m*

**extortionate** [ɪk'stɔːʃənət] *adj* exorbitant

**extra** ['ekstrə] **1** *adj (additional)* supplémentaire; **to be e.** *(spare)* être en trop; *(cost more)* être en supplément; **e. charge** supplément *m*; **e. time** *(in sport)* prolongation *f* **2** *adv (more than usual)* extrêmement; **to pay e.** payer un supplément; **wine costs** *or* **is £10 e.** il y a un supplément de 10 livres pour le vin **3** *n (perk)* à-côté *m*; *(actor in film)* figurant, -e *mf*; *(on bill)* supplément *m*

**extra-** ['ekstrə] *pref* extra-

**extract 1** ['ekstrækt] *n* extrait *m* **2** [ɪk'strækt] *vt* extraire (**from** de); *(information, money)* soutirer (**from** à)

**extra-curricular** [ekstrəkə'rɪkjʊlə(r)] *adj Sch* extrascolaire

**extraordinary** [ɪk'strɔːdənərɪ] *adj* extraordinaire

**extravagant** [ɪk'strævəgənt] *adj (behaviour, idea)* extravagant; *(wasteful)* dépensier, -ère; *(tastes)* dispendieux, -euse ▪ **extravagance** *n (of behaviour)* extravagance *f*; *(wastefulness)* gaspillage *m*; *(thing bought)* folie *f*

**extreme** [ɪk'striːm] **1** *adj* extrême **2** *n* extrême *m*; **to carry** *or* **take sth to extremes** pousser qch à l'extrême ▪ **extremely** *adv* extrêmement

**extremist** [ɪk'striːmɪst] *adj & n* extrémiste *(mf)*

**extremity** [ɪk'stremətɪ] *(pl* **-ies***) n* extrémité *f*

**extrovert** ['ekstrəvɜːt] *n* extraverti, -e *mf*

**exuberant** [ɪg'zjuːbərənt] *adj* exubérant

**exude** [ɪg'zjuːd] *vt (health, honesty)* respirer

**eye** [aɪ] **1** *n* œil *m* *(pl* yeux); **to have one's e. on sth** avoir qch en vue; **to keep an e. on sb/sth** surveiller qn/qch; *Am* **e. doctor** opticien, -enne *mf* **2** *vt* regarder ▪ **eyebrow** *n* sourcil *m* ▪ **eyelash** *n* cil *m* ▪ **eyelid** *n* paupière *f* ▪ **eyeliner** *n* eye-liner *m* ▪ **eyeshadow** *n* fard *m* à paupières ▪ **eyesight** *n* vue *f* ▪ **eyesore** *n* horreur *f* ▪ **eyewitness** *n* témoin *m* oculaire

▸**eye up** *vt sep* reluquer

# Ff

**F, f** [ef] *n (letter)* F, f *m inv*
**fable** ['feɪbəl] *n* fable *f*
**fabric** ['fæbrɪk] *n (cloth)* tissu *m*, étoffe *f*
**fabricate** ['fæbrɪkeɪt] *vt* fabriquer
**fabulous** ['fæbjʊləs] *adj (legendary, incredible)* fabuleux, -euse
**face** [feɪs] **1** *n (of person)* visage *m*, figure *f*; *(expression)* mine *f*; *(of clock)* cadran *m*; *(of building)* façade *f*; *(of cube)* face *f*; *(of cliff)* paroi *f*; **f. down (wards)** *(person)* face contre terre; *(thing)* à l'envers; **f. to f.** face à face; **to save/lose f.** sauver/perdre la face; *Br* **f. cloth** gant *m* de toilette
**2** *vt (danger, enemy, problem)* faire face à; **to f., to be facing** *(be opposite)* être en face de; *(of window, door, room)* donner sur; **faced with** *(prospect, problem)* confronté à; *(defeat)* menacé par
**3** *vi* **to f. north** *(of building)* être orienté au nord; **to f. up to** *(danger, problem)* faire face à; *(fact)* accepter
**faceless** ['feɪsləs] *adj* anonyme
**face-lift** ['feɪslɪft] *n (by surgeon)* lifting *m*; *(of building)* ravalement *m*
**facetious** [fə'siːʃəs] *adj (person)* facétieux, -euse
**facial** ['feɪʃəl] **1** *adj (expression)* du visage **2** *n* soin *m* du visage
**facilitate** [fə'sɪlɪteɪt] *vt* faciliter ▪ **facilities** *npl (for sports, cooking)* équipements *mpl*; *(in harbour, airport)* installations *fpl*
**fact** [fækt] *n* fait *m*; **as a matter of f., in f.** en fait
**faction** ['fækʃən] *n* faction *f*
**factor** ['fæktə(r)] *n* facteur *m*
**factory** ['fæktərɪ] (*pl* **-ies**) *n (large)* usine *f*; *(small)* fabrique *f*
**factual** ['fæktʃʊəl] *adj* basé sur les faits
**faculty** ['fækəltɪ] (*pl* **-ies**) *n (of mind, in university)* faculté *f*
**fad** [fæd] *n (fashion)* mode *f* (**for** de); *(personal habit)* marotte *f*
**fade** [feɪd] *vi (of flower, material, colour)* se faner; *(of light)* baisser; **to f. (away)** *(of memory, smile)* s'effacer; *(of sound)* s'affaiblir; *(of person)* dépérir
**fag** [fæg] *n Br Fam (cigarette)* clope *m ou f*
**fail** [feɪl] **1** *n* **without f.** sans faute **2** *vt (exam)* échouer à; *(candidate)* recaler; **to f. to do** *(forget)* manquer de faire; *(not be able)* ne pas arriver à faire **3** *vi (of person, plan)* échouer; *(of business)* faire faillite; *(of health, sight)* baisser; *(of memory, strength)* défaillir; *(of brakes)* lâcher ▪ **failed** *adj (attempt, poet)* raté ▪ **failing 1** *n (fault)* défaut *m* **2** *prep* à défaut de; **f. this, f. that** à défaut
**failure** ['feɪljə(r)] *n* échec *m*; *(of business)* faillite *f*; *(person)* raté, -e *mf*
**faint** [feɪnt] **1** (**-er, -est**) *adj (weak) (voice, trace, breeze, hope)* faible; *(colour)* pâle; **to feel f.** se sentir mal **2** *vi* s'évanouir (**with** *or* **from** de)
**fair**[1] [feə(r)] *n (trade fair)* foire *f*; *Br (funfair)* fête *f* foraine ▪ **fairground** *n* parc *m* d'attractions
**fair**[2] [feə(r)] **1** (**-er, -est**) *adj* (**a**) *(just)* juste; *(game, fight)* loyal; **f. play** fair-play *m inv* (**b**) *(rather good)* assez

bon (*f* bonne); *(price)* raisonnable; **a f. amount (of)** *(a lot)* pas mal (de) (**c**) *(wind)* favorable; *(weather)* beau (*f* belle) **2** *adv (fight)* loyalement; **to play f.** jouer franc jeu ▪ **fairly** *adv* (**a**) *(treat)* équitablement; *(act, fight, get)* loyalement (**b**) *(rather)* assez

**fair³** [feə(r)] *adj (hair, person)* blond; *(complexion, skin)* clair ▪ **fair-haired** *adj* blond

**fairy** ['feərɪ] (*pl* **-ies**) *n* fée *f* ▪ **fairytale** *n* conte *m* de fées

**faith** [feɪθ] *n* foi *f*; **to have f. in sb** avoir foi en qn; **in good/bad f.** *(act)* de bonne/mauvaise foi

**faithful** ['feɪθfəl] *adj* fidèle ▪ **faithfully** *adv* fidèlement; *Br* **yours f.** *(in letter)* veuillez agréer l'expression de mes sentiments distingués

**fake** [feɪk] **1** *adj* faux (*f* fausse) **2** *n (object)* faux *m*; *(person)* imposteur *m* **3** *vt (signature)* contrefaire **4** *vi (pretend)* faire semblant

**fall** [fɔ:l] **1** *n (of person, snow, city)* chute *f*; *(in price, demand)* baisse *f*; *Am (season)* automne *m* **2** (*pt* **fell**, *pp* **fallen**) *vi* tomber; *(of price, temperature)* baisser; **the dollar is falling** le dollar est en baisse; **to f. into** *(hole, trap)* tomber dans; *(habit)* prendre; **to f. off a bicycle/ladder** tomber d'une bicyclette/échelle; **to f. out of a window** tomber d'une fenêtre; **to f. over sth** tomber en butant contre qch; **to f. asleep** s'endormir; **to f. ill** tomber malade

▸ **fall apart** *vi (of book, machine)* tomber en morceaux; *(of person)* s'effondrer

▸ **fall back on** *vt insep (resort to)* se rabattre sur

▸ **fall behind** *vi (in work, payments)* prendre du retard

▸ **fall down** *vi* tomber; *(of building)* s'effondrer

▸ **fall for** *vt insep (person)* tomber amoureux, -euse de; *(trick)* se laisser prendre à

▸ **fall in** *vi (collapse)* s'écrouler

▸ **fall off** *vi (come off)* tomber; *(of numbers)* diminuer

▸ **fall out** *vi (quarrel)* se brouiller (**with** avec)

▸ **fall over** *vi* tomber; *(of table, vase)* se renverser

▸ **fall through** *vi (of plan)* tomber à l'eau, échouer

**fallacy** ['fæləsɪ] (*pl* **-ies**) *n* erreur *f*

**fallen** ['fɔ:lən] **1** *pp of* **fall 2** *adj* tombé; **f. leaves** feuilles *fpl* mortes

**fallible** ['fæləbəl] *adj* faillible

**false** [fɔ:ls] *adj* faux (*f* fausse); **f. teeth** dentier *m*

**falsify** ['fɔ:lsɪfaɪ] (*pt & pp* **-ied**) *vt (forge)* falsifier

**falter** ['fɔ:ltə(r)] *vi (of voice, speaker)* hésiter

**fame** [feɪm] *n* renommée *f* ▪ **famed** *adj* renommé (**for** pour)

**familiar** [fə'mɪljə(r)] *adj (well-known)* familier, -ère (**to** à); **to be f. with sb/sth** bien connaître qn/qch; **he looks f.** je l'ai déjà vu (quelque part)

**familiarize** [fə'mɪljəraɪz] *vt* **to f. oneself with sth** se familiariser avec qch

**family** ['fæmɪlɪ] **1** (*pl* **-ies**) *n* famille *f* **2** *adj (name, doctor, jewels)* de famille; *(planning, problems, business)* familial; **f. man** homme *m* attaché à sa famille

**famine** ['fæmɪn] *n* famine *f*

**famished** ['fæmɪʃt] *adj* affamé

**famous** ['feɪməs] *adj* célèbre (**for** pour)

**fan¹** [fæn] **1** *n (held in hand)* éventail *m* (*pl* -ails); *(mechanical)* ventilateur *m* **2** (*pt & pp* **-nn-**) *vt (person)* éventer

**fan²** [fæn] *n (of person)* fan *mf*; *(of team)* supporter *m*; **to be a jazz/sports f.** être passionné de jazz/de sport

**fanatic** [fə'nætɪk] *n* fanatique *mf* ▪ **fanatical** *adj* fanatique

**fanciful** ['fænsɪfəl] *adj* fantaisiste

**fancy** ['fænsɪ] **1** *n* **I took a f. to it, it took my f.** j'en ai eu envie **2** *adj (jewels, hat, button)* fantaisie *inv*; *(car)* de luxe; *(house, restaurant)* chic *inv*; *Br* **f. dress** déguisement *m*; *Br* **f. dress**

**party** soirée *f* déguisée **3** (*pt & pp* **-ied**) *vt* (**a**) *Br Fam (want)* avoir envie de; **he fancies her** elle lui plaît (**b**) **to f. that...** *(imagine)* se figurer que...; *(think)* croire que...

**fanfare** ['fænfeə(r)] *n* fanfare *f*

**fantastic** [fæn'tæstɪk] *adj* fantastique; *(wealth, size)* prodigieux, -euse; *Fam (excellent)* formidable

**fantasy** ['fæntəsɪ] (*pl* **-ies**) *n (imagination)* fantaisie *f*; *(dream)* chimère *f*; *(fanciful, sexual)* fantasme *m* ▪ **fantasize** *vi* fantasmer (**about** sur)

**FAR** [fɑː(r)] **1** (**farther** *or* **further, farthest** *or* **furthest**) *adj* **the f. side/end** l'autre côté/bout; **the F. East** l'Extrême-Orient *m*; *Pol* **the f. left/right** l'extrême gauche *f*/droite *f*

**2** *adv* (**a**) *(in distance)* loin (**from** de); **how f. is it to Toulouse?** combien y a-t-il d'ici à Toulouse?; **is it f. to...?** sommes-nous/suis-je/*etc* loin de...?; **how f. has he got with his work?** où en est-il dans son travail?; **as f. as** jusqu'à; **as f.** *or* **so f. as I know** autant que je sache; **as f.** *or* **so f. as I'm concerned** en ce qui me concerne; **f. from doing sth** loin de faire qch; **f. away** *or* **off** au loin; **to be f. away** être loin (**from** de)

(**b**) *(in time)* **as f. back as 1820** dès 1820; **so f.** jusqu'ici

(**c**) *(much)* **f. bigger/more expensive** beaucoup plus grand/plus cher (*f* chère) (**than** que); **f. more/better** beaucoup plus/mieux (**than** que); **by f.** de loin ▪ **far-away** *adj (country)* lointain; *(look)* perdu dans le vague ▪ **far-fetched** *adj* tiré par les cheveux ▪ **far-reaching** *adj* de grande portée ▪ **far-sighted** *adj* clairvoyant

**farce** [fɑːs] *n* farce *f* ▪ **farcical** *adj* grotesque

**fare** [feə(r)] **1** *n (for journey) (in train, bus)* prix *m* du billet; *(in taxi)* prix *m* de la course **2** *vi (manage)* se débrouiller

**farewell** [feə'wel] **1** *n & exclam* adieu *(m)* **2** *adj (party, speech)* d'adieu

**farm** [fɑːm] **1** *n* ferme *f* **2** *adj (worker, produce)* agricole **3** *vt* cultiver **4** *vi* être agriculteur, -trice ▪ **farmer** *n* fermier, -ère *mf*, agriculteur, -trice *mf* ▪ **farmhouse** *n* ferme *f* ▪ **farming** *n* agriculture *f*; *(breeding)* élevage *m* ▪ **farmyard** *n* cour *f* de ferme

**fart** [fɑːt] *Fam* **1** *n* pet *m* **2** *vi* péter

**farther** ['fɑːðə(r)] **1** *comparative of* **far 2** *adv* plus loin; **f. forward** plus avancé; **to get f. away** s'éloigner ▪ **farthest 1** *superlative of* **far 2** *adj* le plus éloigné **3** *adv* le plus loin

**fascinate** ['fæsɪneɪt] *vt* fasciner ▪ **fascinating** *adj* fascinant

**fascist** ['fæʃɪst] *adj & n* fasciste *(mf)*

**fashion** ['fæʃən] **1** *n* (**a**) *(in clothes)* mode *f*; **in f.** à la mode; **out of f.** démodé; **f. show** défilé *m* de mode (**b**) *(manner)* façon *f*; **after a f.** tant bien que mal **2** *vt (form)* façonner; *(make)* confectionner ▪ **fashionable** *adj* à la mode ▪ **fashionably** *adv (dressed)* à la mode

**fast**[1] [fɑːst] **1** (**-er, -est**) *adj* rapide; **to be f.** *(of clock)* avancer (**by** de); **f. food** restauration *f* rapide; **f. food restaurant** fast-food *m* **2** *adv* (**a**) *(quickly)* vite; **how f.?** à quelle vitesse? (**b**) **f. asleep** profondément endormi

**fast**[2] [fɑːst] **1** *n* jeûne *m* **2** *vi* jeûner

**fasten** ['fɑːsən] **1** *vt* attacher (**to** à); *(door, window)* fermer; **to f. sth down** attacher qch **2** *vi (of dress)* s'attacher; *(of door, window)* se fermer ▪ **fastener, fastening** *n (clip)* attache *f*; *(hook)* agrafe *f*; *(press stud)* bouton-pression *m*; *(of bag)* fermoir *m*

**fat** [fæt] **1** (**fatter, fattest**) *adj* gras (*f* grasse); *(cheeks, salary, book)* gros (*f* grosse); **to get f.** grossir **2** *n* graisse *f*; *(on meat)* gras *m*

**fatal** ['feɪtəl] *adj* mortel, -elle ▪ **fatally** *adv* **f. wounded** mortellement blessé

**fatality** [fə'tælətɪ] (*pl* **-ies**) *n (person)* victime *f*

**fate** [feɪt] *n* destin *m*, sort *m* ▪ **fateful** *adj (words, day)* fatidique

**father** ['fɑːðə(r)] **1** *n* père *m*; **F. Christmas** le père Noël **2** *vt (child)* engendrer ▪ **father-in-law** (*pl* **fathers-in-law**) *n* beau-père *m*

**fatherhood** ['fɑːðəhʊd] *n* paternité *f*

**fatherly** ['fɑːðəlɪ] *adj* paternel, -elle

**fatigue** [fə'tiːg] *n (tiredness)* fatigue *f*

**fatten** ['fætən] *vt* **to f. (up)** engraisser ▪ **fattening** *adj (food)* qui fait grossir

**fatty** ['fætɪ] (**-ier, -iest**) *adj (food)* gras (*f* grasse)

**faucet** ['fɔːsɪt] *n Am (tap)* robinet *m*

**fault** [fɔːlt] **1** *n (blame)* faute *f*; *(defect, failing)* défaut *m*; *Geol* faille *f*; **to find f. (with)** trouver à redire (à); **it's your f.** c'est (de) ta faute **2** *vt* **to f. sb/sth** trouver des défauts chez qn/à qch

**faultless** ['fɔːltləs] *adj* irréprochable

**faulty** ['fɔːltɪ] (**-ier, -iest**) *adj* défectueux, -euse

**favour** ['feɪvə(r)] (*Am* **favor**) **1** *n (act of kindness)* service *m*; *(approval)* faveur *f*; **to do sb a f.** rendre service à qn; **in f. (with sb)** bien vu (de qn); **to be in f. of sth** être partisan de qch **2** *vt (encourage)* favoriser; *(support)* être partisan de ▪ **favourable** (*Am* **favorable**) *adj* favorable (**to** à)

**favourite** ['feɪvərɪt] (*Am* **favorite**) **1** *adj* favori, -ite, préféré **2** *n* favori, -ite *mf* ▪ **favouritism** (*Am* **favoritism**) *n* favoritisme *m*

**fawn** [fɔːn] **1** *n (deer)* faon *m* **2** *adj & n (colour)* fauve *(m)*

**fax** [fæks] **1** *n (message)* télécopie *f*, fax *m*; **f. (machine)** télécopieur *m*, fax *m* **2** *vt (message)* faxer; **to f. sb** envoyer un fax à qn

**fear** [fɪə(r)] **1** *n* peur *f*; *(worry)* crainte *f*; **for f. of doing sth** de peur de faire qch; **for f. that...** de peur que... *(+ ne + subjunctive)* **2** *vt* craindre; **I f. that he might leave** je crains qu'il ne parte **3** *vi* **to f. for one's life** craindre pour sa vie ▪ **fearful** *adj (person)* apeuré; *(noise, pain, consequence)* épouvantable ▪ **fearless** *adj* intrépide

**feasible** ['fiːzəbəl] *adj* faisable

**feast** [fiːst] **1** *n* festin *m*; *(religious)* fête *f* **2** *vi* **to f. on sth** se régaler de qch

**feat** [fiːt] *n* exploit *m*

**feather** ['feðə(r)] *n* plume *f*

**feature** ['fiːtʃə(r)] **1** *n (of face, person)* trait *m*; *(of thing, place, machine)* caractéristique *f*; **f. (article)** article *m* de fond; **f. (film)** long métrage *m* **2** *vt (of newspaper, exhibition, film) (present)* présenter; *(portray)* représenter; **a film featuring Nicole Kidman** un film ayant pour vedette Nicole Kidman **3** *vi (appear)* figurer (**in** dans)

**February** ['febrʊərɪ] *n* février *m*

**fed** [fed] **1** *pt & pp of* **feed 2** *adj Fam* **to be f. up** en avoir marre *ou* ras le bol (**with** de)

**federal** ['fedərəl] *adj* fédéral ▪ **federation** [-'reɪʃən] *n* fédération *f*

**fee** [fiː] *n* **fee(s)** *(of doctor, lawyer)* honoraires *mpl*; *(of artist)* cachet *m*; *(for registration, examination)* droits *mpl*; *(for membership)* cotisation *f*; **school** *or* **tuition fees** frais *mpl* d'inscription

**feeble** ['fiːbəl] (**-er, -est**) *adj* faible; *(excuse, smile)* pauvre; *(attempt)* peu convaincant

**feed** [fiːd] **1** *n (animal food)* nourriture *f*; *(for baby) (from breast)* tétée *f*; *(from bottle)* biberon *m* **2** (*pt & pp* **fed**) *vt* donner à manger à; *(baby) (from breast)* donner la tétée à; *(from bottle)* donner son biberon à; **to f. sb sth** faire manger qch à qn **3** *vi (eat)* manger; **to f. on sth** se nourrir de qch

**feedback** ['fiːdbæk] *n (response)* réactions *fpl*

**feel** [fiːl] **1** *n (touch)* toucher *m*; **to have a f. for sth** avoir qch dans la peau

**2** (*pt & pp* **felt**) *vt (be aware of)* sentir; *(experience)* éprouver, ressentir; *(touch)* tâter; **to f. that...** penser que...; **to f. one's way** avancer à tâtons

**3** *vi* **to f. (about)** *(grope)* tâtonner; *(in pocket)* fouiller (**for sth** pour trouver qch); **it feels hard** c'est dur au toucher; **to f. tired/old** se sentir fatigué/vieux (*f* vieille); **I f. hot/sleepy/hungry** j'ai chaud/sommeil/faim; **she**

**feels better** elle va mieux; **to f. like sth** *(want)* avoir envie de qch; **it feels like cotton** on dirait du coton; **what do you f. about...?** que pensez-vous de...?; **I f. bad about it** ça m'ennuie

**feeling** ['fi:lɪŋ] *n (emotion, impression)* sentiment *m*; *(physical)* sensation *f*; **to have a f. for** *(music, painting)* être sensible à

**feet** [fi:t] *pl of* **foot**[1]

**feign** [feɪn] *vt* feindre

**feline** ['fi:laɪn] *adj* félin

**fell** [fel] **1** *pt of* **fall 2** *vt (tree)* abattre; *(opponent)* terrasser

**fellow** ['feləʊ] *n* (**a**) *(man, boy)* gars *m* (**b**) *(companion)* **f. countryman/f. countrywoman** compatriote *mf*; **f. worker** collègue *mf* (**c**) *(of society)* membre *m*

**fellowship** ['feləʊʃɪp] *n (scholarship)* bourse *f* de recherche

**felt**[1] [felt] *pt & pp of* **feel**

**felt**[2] [felt] *n* feutre *m* ▪ **felt-tip** *n* **f. (pen)** crayon-feutre *m*

**female** ['fi:meɪl] **1** *adj (person, name, voice)* féminin; *(animal)* femelle **2** *n (woman)* femme *f*; *(girl)* fille *f*; *(animal, plant)* femelle *f*

**feminine** ['femɪnɪn] **1** *adj* féminin **2** *n (in grammar)* féminin *m* ▪ **feminist** *adj & n* féministe *(mf)*

**fence** [fens] **1** *n (barrier)* clôture *f*; *(more solid)* barrière *f*; *(in race)* obstacle *m* **2** *vt* **to f. (in)** *(land)* clôturer **3** *vi (as sport)* faire de l'escrime ▪ **fencing** *n (sport)* escrime *f*

**fend** [fend] **1** *vi* **to f. for oneself** se débrouiller **2** *vt* **to f. off** *(blow)* parer

**fender** ['fendə(r)] *n Am (of car)* aile *f*

**ferment** [fə'ment] *vi* fermenter

**ferocious** [fə'rəʊʃəs] *adj* féroce

**ferret** ['ferɪt] **1** *n (animal)* furet *m* **2** *vt* **to f. out** *(object, information)* dénicher

**ferry** ['ferɪ] **1** (*pl* **-ies**) *n* ferry-boat *m*; *(small, for river)* bac *m* **2** (*pt & pp* **-ied**) *vt* transporter

**fertile** [*Br* 'fɜ:taɪl, *Am* 'fɜ:rtəl] *adj (land, imagination)* fertile; *(person, animal)* fécond ▪ **fertilizer** *n* engrais *m*

**fervent** ['fɜ:vənt] *adj* fervent

**festival** ['festɪvəl] *n (of music, film)* festival *m* (*pl* -als); *(religious)* fête *f*

**festive** ['festɪv] *adj* de fête; *(mood)* festif, -ive; **the f. season** les fêtes *fpl* de fin d'année ▪ **festivities** *npl* festivités *fpl*

**fetch** [fetʃ] *vt* (**a**) *(bring)* aller chercher (**b**) *(be sold for)* rapporter

**fête** [feɪt] **1** *n Br* fête *f* **2** *vt* fêter

**fetus** ['fi:təs] *n Am* = **foetus**

**feud** [fju:d] *n* querelle *f*

**fever** ['fi:və(r)] *n* fièvre *f*; **to have a f.** *(temperature)* avoir de la fièvre ▪ **feverish** *adj (person, activity)* fiévreux, -euse

---

**FEW** [fju:] **1** *adj* (**a**) *(not many)* peu de; **f. towns** peu de villes; **every f. days** tous les trois ou quatre jours; **one of the f. books** l'un des rares livres; **f. and far between** rarissime

(**b**) *(some)* **a f. towns** quelques villes; **a f. more books** encore quelques livres; **quite a f...., a good f....** bon nombre de...

**2** *pron* peu; **f. came** peu sont venus; **f. of them** un petit nombre d'entre eux; **a f.** quelques-un(e)s (**of** de); **a f. of us** quelques-uns d'entre nous

---

**fewer** ['fju:ə(r)] **1** *adj* moins de; **f. houses** moins de maisons (**than** que); **to be f. (than)** être moins nombreux (que) **2** *pron* moins ▪ **fewest 1** *adj* le moins de **2** *pron* le moins

**fiancé** [fɪ'ɒnseɪ] *n* fiancé *m*

**fiancée** [fɪ'ɒnseɪ] *n* fiancée *f*

**fiasco** [fɪ'æskəʊ] (*pl* **-os**, *Am* **-oes**) *n* fiasco *m*

**fib** [fɪb] *Fam* **1** *n* bobard *m* **2** (*pt & pp* **-bb-**) *vi* raconter des bobards

**fibre** ['faɪbə(r)] (*Am* **fiber**) *n* fibre *f*; *(in diet)* fibres *fpl*

**fickle** ['fɪkəl] *adj* inconstant

**fiction** ['fɪkʃən] *n (invention)* fiction *f*; **(works of) f.** livres *mpl* de fiction ▪ **fictional** *adj (character)* fictif, -ive

**fictitious** [fɪk'tɪʃəs] *adj* fictif, -ive

**fiddle** ['fɪdəl] **1** *n* (**a**) *(violin)* violon *m*

(**b**) *Br Fam (dishonest act)* combine *f* **2** *vt Br Fam (accounts)* truquer **3** *vi* **to f. about** *(waste time)* traînailler; **to f. (about) with sth** tripoter qch

**fiddly** ['fɪdlɪ] (**-ier, -iest**) *adj Fam (task)* minutieux, -euse

**fidget** ['fɪdʒɪt] **1** *n* **to be a f.** ne pas tenir en place **2** *vi* **to f. (about)** gigoter ▪ **fidgety** *adj* agité

**field** [fiːld] *n* champ *m*; *(for sports)* terrain *m*; *(sphere)* domaine *m*

**fierce** [fɪəs] (**-er, -est**) *adj (animal, warrior, tone)* féroce; *(attack, wind)* violent

**fiery** ['faɪərɪ] (**-ier, -iest**) *adj (person, speech)* fougueux, -euse

**fifteen** [fɪf'tiːn] *adj & n* quinze *(m)* ▪ **fifteenth** *adj & n* quinzième *(mf)*

**fifth** [fɪfθ] *adj & n* cinquième *(mf)*; **a f.** *(fraction)* un cinquième

**fifty** ['fɪftɪ] *adj & n* cinquante *(m)* ▪ **fifty-fifty** *adj & adv* **a f. chance** une chance sur deux; **to split the profits f.** partager les bénéfices moitié-moitié ▪ **fiftieth** *adj & n* cinquantième *(mf)*

**fig** [fɪg] *n* figue *f*

**fight** [faɪt] **1** *n (between people)* bagarre *f*; *(between boxers, soldiers)* combat *m*; *(struggle)* lutte *f* (**against/for** contre/pour); *(quarrel)* dispute *f*

**2** (*pt & pp* **fought**) *vt (person)* se battre contre; *(decision, enemy)* combattre; *(fire, temptation)* lutter contre; **to f. a battle** livrer bataille; *Pol* **to f. an election** se présenter à une élection; **to f. off** *(attacker, attack)* repousser

**3** *vi* se battre (**against** contre); *(of soldiers)* combattre; *(struggle)* lutter (**against/for** contre/pour); *(quarrel)* se disputer; **to f. back** *(retaliate)* se défendre; **to f. over sth** se disputer qch

**fighter** ['faɪtə(r)] *n (determined person)* battant, -e *mf*; *(in brawl, battle)* combattant, -e *mf*; *(boxer)* boxeur *m*; *(aircraft)* avion *m* de chasse

**fighting** ['faɪtɪŋ] *n (brawling)* bagarres *fpl*; *Mil* combat *m*

**figment** ['fɪgmənt] *n* **it's a f. of your imagination** c'est le fruit de ton imagination

**figurative** ['fɪgjʊrətɪv] *adj (meaning)* figuré; *(art)* figuratif, -ive

**figure**[1] [*Br* 'fɪgə(r), *Am* 'fɪgjə(r)] *n* (**a**) *(numeral)* chiffre *m* (**b**) *(shape)* forme *f*; *(outline)* silhouette *f*; **she has a nice f.** elle est bien faite (**c**) *(diagram)* figure *f*; **f. skating** patinage *m* artistique (**d**) *(expression, word)* **a f. of speech** une figure de rhétorique (**e**) *(important person)* personnage *m*

**figure**[2] [*Br* 'fɪgə(r), *Am* 'fɪgjə(r)] **1** *vt* **to f. that...** *(think)* penser que...; *(estimate)* supposer que...; **to f. out** *(person, motive)* arriver à comprendre; *(answer)* trouver; *(amount)* calculer **2** *vi (appear)* figurer (**on** sur); **to f. on doing sth** compter faire qch

**file**[1] [faɪl] **1** *n (tool)* lime *f* **2** *vt* **to f. (down)** limer

**file**[2] [faɪl] **1** *n (folder)* chemise *f*; *(documents)* dossier *m* (**on** sur); *Comptr* fichier *m*; **to be on f.** figurer au dossier **2** *vt (document)* classer; *(complaint, claim)* déposer

**file**[3] [faɪl] **1** *n (line)* file *f*; **in single f.** en file indienne **2** *vi* **to f. in/out** entrer/sortir à la queue leu leu; **to f. past sb/sth** défiler devant qn/qch ▪ **filing** *adj* **f. cabinet** classeur *m (meuble)*

**fill** [fɪl] **1** *n* **to eat one's f.** manger à sa faim

**2** *vt* remplir (**with** de); *(tooth)* plomber; *(time)* occuper; **to f. in** *(form)* remplir; *(hole)* combler; **to f. sb in on sth** mettre qn au courant de qch; **to f. out** *(form)* remplir; **to f. up** *(container)* remplir

**3** *vi* **to f. (up)** se remplir (**with** de); **to f. in for sb** remplacer qn; **to f. up** *(with petrol)* faire le plein

**fillet** [*Br* 'fɪlɪt, *Am* fɪ'leɪ] **1** *n (of fish, meat)* filet *m* **2** (*Am pt & pp* [fɪ'leɪd]) *vt (fish)* découper en filets; *(meat)* désosser

**filling** ['fɪlɪŋ] **1** *adj (meal)* nourrissant **2** *n (in tooth)* plombage *m*; *(in food)* garniture *f*; **f. station** station-service *f*

**film** [fɪlm] **1** *n* film *m*; *(for camera, layer)* pellicule *f*; *(for food)* film *m* plastique **2** *adj (studio, technician, critic)* de cinéma; **f. star** vedette *f* de cinéma **3** *vt* filmer **4** *vi (of film maker, actor)* tourner

**Filofax®** ['faɪləfæks] *n* organiseur *m*

**filter** ['fɪltə(r)] **1** *n* filtre *m*; *Br (traffic sign)* flèche *f* de dégagement; **f. coffee** café *m* filtre **2** *vt* filtrer **3** *vi* **to f. through** filtrer ▪ **filter-tipped** *adj (cigarette)* bout filtre *inv*

**filth** [fɪlθ] *n* saleté *f*; *Fig (obscenities)* saletés *fpl* ▪ **filthy** (**-ier, -iest**) *adj (hands, shoes)* sale; *(language)* obscène; *(habit)* dégoûtant

**fin** [fɪn] *n (of fish)* nageoire *f*; *(of shark)* aileron *m*

**final** ['faɪnəl] **1** *adj (last)* dernier, -ère; *(definite)* définitif, -ive **2** *n (in sport)* finale *f*; *Univ* **finals** examens *mpl* de dernière année ▪ **finalist** *n* finaliste *mf* ▪ **finalize** *vt (plan)* mettre au point; *(date)* fixer définitivement; *(deal)* conclure ▪ **finally** *adv (lastly)* enfin; *(eventually)* finalement; *(irrevocably)* définitivement

**finale** [fɪ'nɑːlɪ] *n (musical)* finale *m*

**finance** ['faɪnæns] **1** *n* finance *f*; **finances** *(of person)* finances *fpl*; *(of company)* situation *f* financière **2** *vt* financer

**financial** [faɪ'nænʃəl] *adj* financier, -ère; *Br* **f. year** exercice *m* comptable

**financier** [faɪ'nænsɪə(r)] *n* financier *m*

**find** [faɪnd] **1** *n (discovery)* découverte *f* **2** (*pt & pp* **found**) *vt* trouver; **I f. that...** je trouve que...

▸ **find out 1** *vt (secret, information)* découvrir; *(person)* prendre en défaut **2** *vi (inquire)* se renseigner (**about** sur); **to f. out about sth** *(discover)* apprendre qch

**findings** ['faɪndɪŋz] *npl* conclusions *fpl*

**fine¹** [faɪn] **1** *n (money)* amende *f*; *(for driving offence)* contravention *f* **2** *vt* **to f. sb £100** infliger une amende de 100 livres à qn

**fine²** [faɪn] **1** (**-er, -est**) *adj* (**a**) *(thin, not coarse) (hair, needle)* fin; *(gold, metal)* pur; *(distinction)* subtil (**b**) *(very good)* excellent; *(beautiful) (weather, statue)* beau (*f* belle); **it's f.** *(weather)* il fait beau; **he's f.** *(healthy)* il va bien **2** *adv (very well)* très bien ▪ **finely** *adv (dressed)* magnifiquement; *(embroidered, ground)* finement; **f. chopped** haché menu

**finger** ['fɪŋgə(r)] **1** *n* doigt *m*; **little f.** petit doigt *m*, auriculaire *m* **2** *vt* tâter ▪ **fingernail** *n* ongle *m* ▪ **fingertip** *n* bout *m* du doigt

**finish** ['fɪnɪʃ] **1** *n (end)* fin *f*; *(of race)* arrivée *f*; *(of article, car)* finition *f* **2** *vt* **to f. sth (off** *or* **up)** finir qch; **to f. doing sth** finir de faire qch **3** *vi (of meeting, event)* finir, se terminer; *(of person)* finir, terminer; **to have finished with** *(object)* ne plus avoir besoin de; *(activity, person)* en avoir fini avec; **to f. off** *(of person)* finir, terminer ▪ **finishing** *adj* **f. line** *(of race)* ligne *f* d'arrivée; **to put the f. touches to sth** mettre la dernière main à qch ▪ **finished** *adj (ended, complete, ruined)* fini

**finite** ['faɪnaɪt] *adj* fini

**Finland** ['fɪnlənd] *n* la Finlande ▪ **Finn** *n* Finlandais, -e *mf*, Finnois, -e *mf* ▪ **Finnish 1** *adj* finlandais, finnois **2** *n (language)* finnois *m*

**fir** [fɜː(r)] *n* sapin *m*

**fire** ['faɪə(r)] **1** *n* feu *m*; *(accidental)* incendie *m*; *Br (electric heater)* radiateur *m*; **to light** *or* **make a f.** faire du feu; **to set f. to sth** mettre le feu à qch; **on f.** en feu; **f.!** *(alarm)* au feu!; **to open f.** ouvrir le feu; **f. alarm** sirène *f* d'incendie; *Br* **f. brigade**, *Am* **f. department** pompiers *mpl*; **f. engine** voiture *f* des pompiers; **f. escape** escalier *m* de secours; **f. station** caserne *f* des pompiers **2** *vt (cannon)* tirer; *(pottery)* cuire; **to f. a gun** tirer un coup de fusil/de pistolet; **to f. questions at sb** bombarder qn de questions; **to f. sb** *(dismiss)* renvoyer qn

**3** *vi* tirer (**at** sur); **f.!** feu! ▪ **firearm** *n* arme *f* à feu ▪ **fireguard** *n* garde-feu *m inv* ▪ **fireman** (*pl* **-men**) *n* sapeur-pompier *m* ▪ **fireplace** *n* cheminée *f* ▪ **fireproof** *adj (door)* ignifugé ▪ **fireside** *n* **by the f.** au coin du feu ▪ **firewood** *n* bois *m* de chauffage ▪ **firework** *n* fusée *f*; *(firecracker)* pétard *m*; **fireworks,** *Br* **f. display** feu *m* d'artifice

**firm¹** [fɜːm] *n (company)* entreprise *f*, firme *f*

**firm²** [fɜːm] **1** (**-er, -est**) *adj (earth, decision)* ferme; *(foundations)* solide **2** *adv* **to stand f.** tenir bon *ou* ferme ▪ **firmly** *adv (believe)* fermement; *(shut)* bien

**first** [fɜːst] **1** *adj* premier, -ère; **f. aid** premiers secours *mpl*

**2** *adv* d'abord; *(for the first time)* pour la première fois; **f. of all, f. and foremost** tout d'abord; **at f.** d'abord; **to come f.** *(in race)* arriver premier; *(in exam)* être reçu premier

**3** *n (person, thing)* premier, -ère *mf*; **f. (gear)** *(of vehicle)* première *f* ▪ **first-class 1** *adj* excellent; *(ticket)* de première classe; *(mail)* ordinaire **2** *adv (travel)* en première ▪ **first-hand** *adj* **to have (had) f. experience of sth** avoir fait l'expérience personnelle de qch ▪ **first-rate** *adj* excellent

**firstly** [ˈfɜːstlɪ] *adv* premièrement

**fish** [fɪʃ] **1** (*pl inv or* **-es** [-ɪz]) *n* poisson *m*; **f. bone** arête *f*; *Br* **f. fingers,** *Am* **f. sticks** bâtonnets *mpl* de poisson; **f. shop** poissonnerie *f*; **f. tank** aquarium *m*

**2** *vt* **to f. sth out** *(from water)* repêcher qch

**3** *vi* pêcher ▪ **fish-and-chip** *adj Br* **f. shop** = magasin où on vend du poisson frit et des frites ▪ **fishing** *n* pêche *f*; **to go f.** aller à la pêche; **f. boat** bateau *m* de pêche; **f. net** filet *m* (de pêche); **f. rod** canne à pêche

**fisherman** [ˈfɪʃəmən] (*pl* **-men**) *n* pêcheur *m*

**fishmonger** [ˈfɪʃmʌŋgə(r)] *n* poissonnier, -ère *mf*

**fishy** [ˈfɪʃɪ] (**-ier, -iest**) *adj (smell, taste)* de poisson; *Fig (suspicious)* louche

**fist** [fɪst] *n* poing *m* ▪ **fistful** *n* poignée *f* (**of** de)

**fit¹** [fɪt] **1** (**fitter, fittest**) *adj* (**a**) *(healthy)* en forme; **to keep f.** se maintenir en forme

(**b**) *(suitable)* propre (**for** à; **to do** à faire); *(worthy)* digne (**for** de; **to do** de faire); *(able)* apte (**for** à; **to do** à faire)

**2** *n* **a good f.** *(clothes)* à la bonne taille; **a tight f.** *(clothes)* ajusté

**3** (*pt & pp* **-tt-**) *vt (be the right size for)* aller bien à; *(match)* correspondre à; *(put in)* poser; *(go in)* aller dans; *(go on)* aller sur; **to f. sth (on) to sth** *(put)* poser qch sur qch; *(adjust)* adapter qch à qch; *(fix)* fixer qch à qch; **to f. sth in** *(install)* poser qch; *(insert)* faire entrer qch

**4** *vi (of clothes, lid, key, plug)* aller; **this shirt fits** *(fits me)* cette chemise me va; **to f. (in)** *(go in)* aller; *(of facts, plans)* cadrer (**with** avec); **he doesn't f. in** il n'est pas à sa place

**fit²** [fɪt] *n (seizure)* attaque *f*; **a f. of coughing** une quinte de toux; **in fits and starts** par à-coups

**fitness** [ˈfɪtnɪs] *n (health)* santé *f*; *(for job)* aptitude *f* (**for** à)

**fitted** [ˈfɪtɪd] *adj Br (cupboard)* encastré; *(garment)* ajusté; **f. carpet** moquette *f*; **f. kitchen** cuisine *f* intégrée

**fitting** [ˈfɪtɪŋ] **1** *adj (suitable)* approprié (**to** à) **2** *n* **f. room** cabine *f* d'essayage; **fittings** *(in house)* installations *fpl*

**five** [faɪv] *adj & n* cinq *(m)* ▪ **fiver** *n Br Fam* billet *m* de cinq livres

**fix** [fɪks] **1** *vt (make firm, decide)* fixer (**to** à); *(mend)* réparer; *(deal with)* arranger; *(prepare)* préparer; *Fam (election)* truquer; **to f. sth on** *(lid)* mettre qch en place; **to f. sth up** *(trip, meeting)* arranger qch **2** *n Fam* **in a f.** dans le pétrin

**fixed** [fɪkst] *adj (price)* fixe; *(idea)* bien arrêté

**fixture** ['fɪkstʃə(r)] *n* (**a**) *(in sport)* rencontre *f* (**b**) **fixtures** *(in house)* installations *fpl*

**fizz** [fɪz] *vi (of champagne)* pétiller ▪ **fizzy** (**-ier, -iest**) *adj* gazeux, -euse

▸ **fizzle out** ['fɪzəl] *vi (of firework)* rater; *Fam (of plan)* tomber à l'eau

**flabbergasted** ['flæbəgɑ:stɪd] *adj Fam* sidéré

**flabby** ['flæbɪ] (**-ier, -iest**) *adj (person)* bouffi; *(skin)* mou (*f* molle)

**flag** [flæg] **1** *n* drapeau *m*; *Naut* pavillon *m*; *(for charity)* insigne *m* **2** (*pt & pp* **-gg-**) *vt* marquer; **to f. down a taxi** héler un taxi **3** *vi (of person, conversation)* faiblir ▪ **flagpole** *n* mât *m*

**flagrant** ['fleɪgrənt] *adj* flagrant

**flagstone** ['flægstəʊn] *n* dalle *f*

**flair** [fleə(r)] *n (intuition)* don *m* (**for** pour); **to have a f. for business** avoir le sens des affaires

**flake** [fleɪk] **1** *n (of snow)* flocon *m*; *(of paint)* écaille *f*; *(of soap)* paillette *f* **2** *vi* **to f. (off)** *(of paint)* s'écailler ▪ **flaky** *adj Br* **f. pastry** pâte *f* feuilletée

**flamboyant** [flæm'bɔɪənt] *adj (person)* extraverti

**flame** [fleɪm] *n* flamme *f*; **to go up in flames** prendre feu

**flamingo** [flə'mɪŋgəʊ] (*pl* **-os** *or* **-oes**) *n* flamant *m*

**flammable** ['flæməbəl] *adj* inflammable

**flan** [flæn] *n* tarte *f*

**flank** [flæŋk] **1** *n* flanc *m* **2** *vt* flanquer (**with** *or* **by** de)

**flannel** ['flænəl] *n Br (face cloth)* gant *m* de toilette

**flap** [flæp] **1** *n (of pocket, envelope)* rabat *m*; *(of table)* abattant *m* **2** (*pt & pp* **-pp-**) *vt* **to f. its wings** *(of bird)* battre des ailes **3** *vi (of wings, sail, shutter)* battre

**flare** [fleə(r)] **1** *n* (**a**) *(rocket)* fusée *f* éclairante (**b**) **(pair of) flares** *(trousers)* pantalon *m* pattes d'éléphant **2** *vi* **to f. up** *(of fire)* s'embraser; *(of violence, trouble)* éclater

**flared** [fleəd] *adj (skirt)* évasé; *(trousers)* (à) pattes d'éléphant

**flash** [flæʃ] **1** *n (of light)* éclair *m*; *(for camera)* flash *m*; **f. of lightning** éclair *m* **2** *vt (light)* projeter; *(aim)* diriger (**on** *or* **at** sur); *(show)* montrer rapidement; **to f. one's headlights** faire un appel de phares **3** *vi (shine)* briller; *(on and off)* clignoter; **to f. past** *or* **by** *(rush)* passer comme un éclair ▪ **flashback** *n* retour *m* en arrière ▪ **flashlight** *n Am (torch)* lampe *f* électrique; *(for camera)* flash *m*

**flashy** ['flæʃɪ] (**-ier, -iest**) *adj Fam (clothes, car)* tape-à-l'œil *inv*

**flask** [flɑ:sk] *n (Thermos®)* Thermos® *f inv*; *(for alcohol)* flasque *f*

**flat**[1] [flæt] **1** (**flatter, flattest**) *adj* plat; *(tyre, battery)* à plat; *(drink)* éventé; *(refusal)* net (*f* nette); **f. rate** tarif *m* unique; **to put** *or* **lay sth (down) f.** mettre qch à plat **2** *n (puncture)* crevaison *f*; *(of hand)* plat *m*; *(in music)* bémol *m* **3** *adv* **to sing f.** chanter trop bas; **to fall f. on one's face** tomber à plat ventre; **to fall f.** *(of joke, play)* tomber à plat; **f. out** *(work)* d'arrache-pied; *(run)* à toute vitesse ▪ **flatly** *adv (deny, refuse)* catégoriquement

**flat**[2] [flæt] *n Br (in building)* appartement *m*

**flatmate** ['flætmeɪt] *n Br* colocataire *mf*

**flatten** ['flætən] *vt* aplatir; *(crops)* coucher; *(town, buildings)* raser

**flatter** ['flætə(r)] *vt* flatter ▪ **flattering** *adj (remark, words)* flatteur, -euse

**flattery** ['flætərɪ] *n* flatterie *f*

**flaunt** [flɔ:nt] *vt (show off)* faire étalage de

**flavour** ['fleɪvə(r)] (*Am* **flavor**) **1** *n (taste)* goût *m*; *(of ice cream)* parfum *m* **2** *vt (food)* relever (**with** de); **lemon-flavoured** (parfumé) au citron

■ **flavouring** (*Am* **flavoring**) *n (seasoning)* assaisonnement *m*; *(in cake, ice cream)* parfum *m*

**flaw** [flɔ:] *n* défaut *m* ■ **flawed** *adj* qui a un défaut/des défauts ■ **flawless** *adj* parfait

**flea** [fli:] *n* puce *f*; **f. market** marché *m* aux puces

**fleck** [flek] *n (mark)* petite tache *f*

**fled** [fled] *pt & pp of* **flee**

**flee** [fli:] **1** (*pt & pp* **fled**) *vt (place)* s'enfuir de; *(danger)* fuir **2** *vi* s'enfuir, fuir

**fleece** [fli:s] **1** *n (of sheep)* toison *f*; *(garment)* fourrure *f* polaire **2** *vt Fam (overcharge)* écorcher ■ **fleecy** (**-ier, -iest**) *adj (gloves)* molletonné

**fleet** [fli:t] *n (of ships)* flotte *f*; *(of taxis, buses)* parc *m* ■ **fleeting** *adj (visit, moment)* bref (*f* brève)

**Flemish** ['flemɪʃ] **1** *adj* flamand **2** *n (language)* flamand *m*

**flesh** [fleʃ] *n* chair *f*; **in the f.** en chair et en os

**flew** [flu:] *pt of* **fly**[2]

**flex** [fleks] **1** *n (wire)* fil *m*; *(for telephone)* cordon *m* **2** *vt (limb)* fléchir; *(muscle)* faire jouer

**flexible** ['fleksɪbəl] *adj* flexible

**flexitime** ['fleksɪtaɪm] *n* horaires *mpl* flexibles *ou* à la carte

**flick** [flɪk] **1** *n (with finger)* chiquenaude *f*; *Br* **f. knife** couteau *m* à cran d'arrêt **2** *vt (with finger)* donner une chiquenaude à; **to f. sth off** *(remove)* enlever qch d'une chiquenaude; **to f. a switch** pousser un bouton **3** *vi* **to f. through** *(book, magazine)* feuilleter

**flicker** ['flɪkə(r)] *vi (of flame, light)* vaciller

**flier** ['flaɪə(r)] *n (leaflet)* prospectus *m*

**flies** [flaɪz] *npl (of trousers)* braguette *f*

**flight** [flaɪt] *n* (**a**) *(of bird, aircraft)* vol *m*; **f. attendant** *(man)* steward *m*; *(woman)* hôtesse *f* de l'air (**b**) *(floor)* étage *m*; **f. of stairs** escalier *m* (**c**) *(escape)* fuite *f* (**from** de); **to take f.** prendre la fuite

**flimsy** ['flɪmzɪ] (**-ier, -iest**) *adj (cloth, structure) (light)* (trop) léger, -ère; *(thin)* (trop) mince; *(excuse)* piètre

**flinch** [flɪntʃ] *vi (with pain)* tressaillir

**fling** [flɪŋ] **1** *n (affair)* aventure *f* **2** (*pt & pp* **flung**) *vt* jeter

**flint** [flɪnt] *n (of lighter)* pierre *f*

**flip** [flɪp] **1** (*pt & pp* **-pp-**) *vt (with finger)* donner une chiquenaude à; **to f. a coin** jouer à pile ou face; **to f. sth over** retourner qch **2** *vi* **to f. through a book** feuilleter un livre

**flip-flops** ['flɪpflɒps] *npl* tongs *fpl*

**flippant** ['flɪpənt] *adj* désinvolte

**flipper** ['flɪpə(r)] *n (of swimmer)* palme *f*; *(of animal)* nageoire *f*

**flirt** [flɜ:t] **1** *n* charmeur, -euse *mf* **2** *vi* flirter (**with** avec)

**flit** [flɪt] (*pt & pp* **-tt-**) *vi (fly)* voltiger; *Fig* **to f. in and out** *(of person)* entrer et sortir rapidement

**float** [fləʊt] **1** *n (for fishing line)* bouchon *m*; *(for swimming)* flotteur *m*; *(in procession)* char *m* **2** *vt (idea)* lancer; *(company)* introduire en Bourse **3** *vi* flotter (**on** sur); **to f. down the river** descendre la rivière ■ **floating** *adj (wood)* flottant; **f. voters** électeurs *mpl* indécis

**flock** [flɒk] **1** *n (of sheep)* troupeau *m*; *(of birds)* volée *f*; *(of people)* foule *f* **2** *vi* **people are flocking to the exhibition** les gens vont en foule voir l'exposition

**flood** [flʌd] **1** *n* inondation *f* **2** *vt (land, bathroom, market)* inonder (**with** de); **to f. (out)** *(house)* inonder **3** *vi (of river)* déborder; **to f. in** *(of people, money)* affluer ■ **flooding** *n* inondation(s) *f(pl)*

**floodlight** ['flʌdlaɪt] **1** *n* projecteur *m* **2** (*pt & pp* **-lit**) *vt* illuminer

**floor** [flɔ:(r)] **1** *n (of room)* sol *m*; *(wooden)* plancher *m*; *(storey)* étage *m*; **on the f.** par terre; **on the first f.** *Br* au premier étage; *Am (ground floor)* au rez-de-chaussée **2** *vt (knock down)* envoyer au tapis; *(puzzle)* stupéfier

**floorboard** ['flɔ:bɔ:d] *n* latte *f (de plancher)*

**flop** [flɒp] *Fam* **1** *n* fiasco *m*; *(play)* four *m* **2** (*pt & pp* **-pp-**) *vi (fail) (of business)* échouer; *(of play, film)* faire un four; **to f. down** s'effondrer

**floppy** ['flɒpɪ] (**-ier, -iest**) *adj (soft)* mou (*f* molle); *(clothes)* (trop) large; *Comptr* **f. disk** disquette *f*

**floral** ['flɔ:rəl] *adj (material, pattern)* à fleurs

**florist** ['flɒrɪst] *n* fleuriste *mf*

**floss** [flɒs] *n* **(dental) f.** fil *m* dentaire

**flour** ['flaʊə(r)] *n* farine *f*

**flourish** ['flʌrɪʃ] **1** *n (gesture)* grand geste *m*; *(decoration)* fioriture *f* **2** *vt (wave)* brandir **3** *vi (of person, plant)* prospérer; *(of arts, business)* être florissant ▪ **flourishing** *adj (plant)* qui prospère; *(business)* florissant

**flow** [fləʊ] **1** *n (of river)* courant *m*; *(of tide)* flux *m*; *(of current, information, blood)* circulation *f*; *(of liquid)* écoulement *m*; **f. of traffic** circulation *f*; **f. chart** organigramme *m* **2** *vi* couler; *(of electric current)* circuler; *(of hair, clothes)* flotter; *(of traffic)* s'écouler; **to f. in** *(of money)* affluer ▪ **flowing** *adj (movement, style)* fluide; *(hair, beard)* flottant

**flower** ['flaʊə(r)] **1** *n* fleur *f*; **in f.** en fleur(s); **f. bed** parterre *m*; **f. pot** pot *m* de fleurs; **f. shop** fleuriste *mf* **2** *vi* fleurir ▪ **flowering** *adj (in bloom)* en fleurs; *(producing flowers) (shrub)* à fleurs

**flowery** ['flaʊərɪ] *adj (style)* fleuri; *(material)* à fleurs

**flown** [fləʊn] *pp of* **fly**[2]

**flu** [flu:] *n (influenza)* grippe *f*

**fluctuate** ['flʌktʃʊeɪt] *vi* varier ▪ **fluctuation** [-'eɪʃən] *n* variation *f* (**in** de)

**fluent** ['flu:ənt] *adj* **he's f. in Russian, his Russian is f.** il parle couramment le russe; **to be a f. speaker** s'exprimer avec facilité ▪ **fluently** *adv (write, express oneself)* avec facilité; *(speak language)* couramment

**fluff** [flʌf] *n* peluche *f* ▪ **fluffy** (**-ier, -iest**) *adj (toy)* en peluche

**fluid** ['flu:ɪd] **1** *adj* fluide; *(plans)* mal défini; **f. ounce** = 0,03 l **2** *n* fluide *m*, liquide *m*

**fluke** [flu:k] *n Fam* coup *m* de chance; **by a f.** par hasard

**flung** [flʌŋ] *pt & pp of* **fling**

**flunk** [flʌŋk] *Am Fam* **1** *vt (exam)* être collé à; *(pupil)* coller **2** *vi (in exam)* être collé

**fluorescent** [flʊə'resənt] *adj* fluorescent

**fluoride** ['flʊəraɪd] *n* fluorure *m*; **f. toothpaste** dentifrice *m* au fluor

**flurry** ['flʌrɪ] (*pl* **-ies**) *n (of snow)* bourrasque *f*; **a f. of activity** une soudaine activité

**flush** [flʌʃ] **1** *adj (level)* de niveau (**with** de) **2** *n* (**a**) *(blush)* rougeur *f* (**b**) *(in toilet)* chasse *f* d'eau **3** *vt* **to f. sth (out)** *(clean)* nettoyer qch à grande eau; **to f. the toilet** tirer la chasse d'eau **4** *vi (blush)* rougir (**with** de)

**fluster** ['flʌstə(r)] *vt* démonter; **to get flustered** se démonter

**flute** [flu:t] *n* flûte *f*

**flutter** ['flʌtə(r)] **1** *vt* **to f. its wings** *(of bird)* battre des ailes **2** *vi (of bird, butterfly)* voleter; *(of flag)* flotter

**fly**[1] [flaɪ] (*pl* **-ies**) *n (insect)* mouche *f*

**fly**[2] [flaɪ] **1** (*pt* **flew**, *pp* **flown**) *vt (aircraft)* piloter; *(passengers)* transporter; *(flag)* arborer; *(kite)* faire voler; **to f. the Atlantic** traverser l'Atlantique en avion

**2** *vi (of bird, aircraft)* voler; *(of passenger)* aller en avion; *(of time)* passer vite; *(of flag)* flotter; **to f. away** *or* **off** s'envoler; **to f. across** *or* **over** *(country, city)* survoler; **I must f.!** il faut que je file! ▪ **flyer** *n* = **flier** ▪ **flying 1** *n (as passenger)* voyage *m* en avion **2** *adj* **to pass with f. colours** réussir haut la main; **to get off to a f. start** prendre un très bon départ; **f. saucer** soucoupe *f* volante; **f. visit** visite *f* éclair *inv* ▪ **flyover** *n Br (bridge)* pont-route *m*

**fly**[3] [flaɪ] *n Br (on trousers)* braguette *f*

**foal** [fəʊl] *n* poulain *m*

**foam** [fəʊm] **1** *n (on sea, mouth)* écume *f*; *(on beer)* mousse *f*; **f. bath**

bain *m* moussant; **f. rubber** caoutchouc *m* Mousse® **2** *vi (of beer, soap)* mousser

**focal** ['fəʊkəl] *adj* focal

**focus** ['fəʊkəs] **1** (*pl* **focuses** ['fəʊkəsəz] *or* **foci** ['fəʊkaɪ]) *n (of attention, interest)* centre *m*; *(optical)* foyer *m*; **the photo is in f./out of f.** la photo est nette/floue

**2** *vt (image, camera)* mettre au point; *(attention, efforts)* concentrer (**on** sur)

**3** *vi* **to f. on sb/sth** *(with camera)* faire la mise au point sur qn/qch

**4** *vti* **to f. (one's eyes) on sb/sth** fixer les yeux sur qn/qch; **to f. (one's attention) on sb/sth** se tourner vers qn/qch

**fodder** ['fɒdə(r)] *n* fourrage *m*

**foe** [fəʊ] *n* ennemi, -e *mf*

**foetus** ['fi:təs] (*Am* **fetus**) *n* fœtus *m*

**fog** [fɒg] *n* brouillard *m* ▪ **foglamp, foglight** *n (on vehicle)* phare *m* antibrouillard

**fogey** ['fəʊgɪ] *n* = **fogy**

**foggy** ['fɒgɪ] (**-ier, -iest**) *adj* brumeux, -euse; **it's f.** il y a du brouillard; *Fam* **I haven't got the foggiest (idea)** je n'en ai pas la moindre idée

**fogy** ['fəʊgɪ] *n* **old f.** vieux schnock *m*

**foil** [fɔɪl] **1** *n* (**a**) *(for cooking)* papier *m* alu (**b**) *(sword)* fleuret *m* **2** *vt (plans)* contrecarrer

**fold** [fəʊld] **1** *n (in paper, cloth)* pli *m* **2** *vt* plier; **to f. away** *or* **down** *or* **up** *(chair)* plier; **to f. back** *or* **over** *(blanket)* replier; **to f. one's arms** croiser les bras **3** *vi Fam (of business)* fermer ses portes; **to f. (away** *or* **down** *or* **up)** *(of chair)* se plier ▪ **folding** *adj (chair, bed)* pliant

**-fold** [fəʊld] *suff* **1** *adj* **tenfold** par dix **2** *adv* **tenfold** dix fois

**folder** ['fəʊldə(r)] *n (file holder)* chemise *f*; *Comptr* répertoire *m*

**foliage** ['fəʊlɪɪdʒ] *n* feuillage *m*

**folk** [fəʊk] **1** (*Am* **folks**) *npl* gens *mpl*; *Fam* **my folks** *(parents)* mes parents *mpl* **2** *adj (dance, costume)* folklorique; **f. music** *(contemporary)* folk *m*

**follow** ['fɒləʊ] **1** *vt* suivre; *(career)* poursuivre; **to f. through** *(plan, idea)* mener à son terme; **to f. up** *(idea, story)* creuser; *(clue, case)* suivre; *(letter)* donner suite à; *(remark)* faire suivre (**with** de); *(advantage)* exploiter **2** *vi (of person, event)* suivre; **it follows that...** il s'ensuit que...; **to f. on** *(come after)* suivre

**follower** ['fɒləʊə(r)] *n (of ideas, politician)* partisan *m*

**following** ['fɒləʊɪŋ] **1** *adj* suivant **2** *n (of politician)* partisans *mpl* **3** *prep* à la suite de

**folly** ['fɒlɪ] (*pl* **-ies**) *n* folie *f*

**fond** [fɒnd] (**-er, -est**) *adj (loving)* affectueux, -euse; *(memory, thought)* doux (*f* douce); **to be (very) f. of sb/sth** aimer beaucoup qn/qch ▪ **fondly** *adv* tendrement

**fondle** ['fɒndəl] *vt* caresser

**font** [fɒnt] *n* (**a**) *Rel* fonts *mpl* baptismaux (**b**) *Typ & Comptr* police *f* de caractères

**food** [fu:d] **1** *n* nourriture *f*; *(particular substance)* aliment *m*; *(cooking)* cuisine *f*; *(for cats, dogs, pigs)* pâtée *f*; *(for plants)* engrais *m* **2** *adj (industry)* alimentaire; **f. poisoning** intoxication *f* alimentaire

**foodstuffs** ['fu:dstʌfs] *npl* denrées *fpl* alimentaires

**fool** [fu:l] **1** *n* imbécile *mf*; **to make a f. of sb** *(ridicule)* ridiculiser qn; *(trick)* rouler qn; **to make a f. of oneself** se couvrir de ridicule **2** *vt (trick)* duper **3** *vi* **to f. about** *or* **around** faire l'imbécile; *(waste time)* perdre son temps

**foolish** ['fu:lɪʃ] *adj* bête ▪ **foolishly** *adv* bêtement

**foolproof** ['fu:lpru:f] *adj (scheme)* infaillible

**foot**[1] [fʊt] (*pl* **feet**) *n* pied *m*; *(of animal)* patte *f*; *(unit of measurement)* = 30,48 cm, pied *m*; **at the f. of** *(page, stairs)* au bas de; **on f.** à pied ▪ **football** *n (soccer)* football *m*; *(American game)* football *m* américain; *(ball)* ballon *m* ▪ **footballer** *n Br* joueur,

-euse *mf* de football ▪ **footbridge** *n* passerelle *f* ▪ **foothold** *n* prise *f* (de pied); *Fig* position *f*; **to gain a f.** *(of person)* prendre pied (**in** dans) ▪ **footnote** *n* note *f* de bas de page; *Fig (extra comment)* post-scriptum *m inv* ▪ **footpath** *n* sentier *m* ▪ **footstep** *n* pas *m*; **to follow in sb's footsteps** suivre les traces de qn ▪ **footstool** *n* petit tabouret *m* ▪ **footwear** *n* chaussures *fpl*

**foot²** [fʊt] *vt (bill)* payer

**footage** ['fʊtɪdʒ] *n Cin* séquences *fpl*

**footing** ['fʊtɪŋ] *n* (**a**) *(balance)* **to lose one's f.** perdre l'équilibre (**b**) *(level)* **to be on an equal f.** être sur un pied d'égalité (**with** avec)

---

**FOR** [fɔ:(r), *unstressed* fə(r)] **1** *prep* pour; *(for a distance or period of)* pendant; *(in spite of)* malgré; **what's it f.?** ça sert à quoi?; **I did it f. love/pleasure** je l'ai fait par amour/par plaisir; **to swim/rush f.** *(towards)* nager/se précipiter vers; **a train f.** un train à destination de; **the road f. London** la route de Londres; **it's time f. breakfast** c'est l'heure du petit déjeuner; **to come f. dinner** venir dîner; **to sell sth f. 7 dollars** vendre qch 7 dollars; **what's the French f. 'book'?** comment dit-on 'book' en français?; **she walked f. a kilometre** elle a marché pendant un kilomètre; **he was away f. a month** il a été absent pendant un mois; **he's been here f. a month** il est ici depuis un mois; **I haven't seen him f. ten years** ça fait dix ans que je ne l'ai pas vu, je ne l'ai pas vu depuis dix ans; **it's easy f. her to do it** il lui est facile de le faire; **f. that to be done** pour que ça soit fait **2** *conj (because)* car

---

**forbad** [fə'bæd] *pt of* **forbid**

**forbade** [fə'bæd, fə'beɪd] *pt of* **forbid**

**forbid** [fə'bɪd] (*pt* **forbad(e)**, *pp* **forbidden** [fə'bɪdən], *pres p* **forbidding**) *vt* interdire, défendre (**sb to do** à qn de faire); **to f. sb sth** interdire qch à qn; **she is f. to leave** il lui est interdit de partir ▪ **forbidden 1** *pp of* **forbid 2** *adj (fruit, region)* défendu

**force** [fɔ:s] **1** *n* force *f*; **the (armed) forces** les forces *fpl* armées; **by f.** de force; **in f.** *(rule)* en vigueur; *(in great numbers)* en force **2** *vt* forcer (**to do** à faire); *(impose)* imposer (**on** à); *(door, lock)* forcer; *(confession)* arracher (**from** à); **to f. sth into sth** faire entrer qch de force dans qch ▪ **forced** *adj* **f. to do** obligé *ou* forcé de faire; **a f. smile** un sourire forcé

**forceful** ['fɔ:sfəl] *adj* énergique

**ford** [fɔ:d] **1** *n* gué *m* **2** *vt (river)* passer à gué

**fore** [fɔ:(r)] *n* **to come to the f.** *(of issue)* passer au premier plan

**forearm** ['fɔ:rɑ:m] *n* avant-bras *m inv*

**foreboding** [fɔ:'bəʊdɪŋ] *n (feeling)* pressentiment *m*

**forecast** ['fɔ:kɑ:st] **1** *n (of weather)* prévisions *fpl*; *(in racing)* pronostic *m* **2** (*pt & pp* **forecast(ed)**) *vt* prévoir; *(in racing)* pronostiquer

**forecourt** ['fɔ:kɔ:t] *n (of hotel)* avant-cour *f*; *(of petrol station)* devant *m*

**forefinger** ['fɔ:fɪŋgə(r)] *n* index *m*

**forefront** ['fɔ:frʌnt] *n* **in the f. of** au premier plan de

**forego** [fɔ:'gəʊ] (*pp* **-gone**) *vt* renoncer à

**foreground** ['fɔ:graʊnd] *n* premier plan *m*

**forehead** ['fɒrɪd, 'fɔ:hed] *n* front *m*

**foreign** ['fɒrɪn] *adj (language, person, country)* étranger, -ère; *(trade)* extérieur; *(travel, correspondent)* à l'étranger; **F. Minister,** *Br* **F. Secretary** ministre *m* des Affaires étrangères; *Br* **F. Office** ministère *m* des Affaires étrangères ▪ **foreigner** *n* étranger, -ère *mf*

**foreman** ['fɔ:mən] (*pl* **-men**) *n (worker)* contremaître *m*

**foremost** ['fɔ:məʊst] *adj* principal

**forerunner** ['fɔ:rʌnə(r)] *n (person)* précurseur *m*

**foresee** [fɔ:'si:] (*pt* **-saw**, *pp* **-seen**) *vt* prévoir

**foreshadow** [fɔː'ʃædəʊ] *vt* annoncer

**foresight** ['fɔːsaɪt] *n* prévoyance *f*

**forest** ['fɒrɪst] *n* forêt *f*

**forestall** [fɔː'stɔːl] *vt* devancer

**foretell** [fɔː'tel] (*pt & pp* **-told**) *vt* prédire

**forever** [fə'revə(r)] *adv (for always)* pour toujours; *(continually)* sans cesse

**foreword** ['fɔːwɜːd] *n* avant-propos *m inv*

**forfeit** ['fɔːfɪt] **1** *n (in game)* gage *m* **2** *vt (lose)* perdre

**forge** [fɔːdʒ] **1** *vt (signature, money)* contrefaire; **to f. a passport** faire un faux passeport **2** *vi* **to f. ahead** *(progress)* aller de l'avant ▪ **forged** *adj* faux (*f* fausse)

**forgery** ['fɔːdʒərɪ] (*pl* **-ies**) *n* contrefaçon *f*

**forget** [fə'get] **1** (*pt* **forgot**, *pp* **forgotten**, *pres p* **forgetting**) *vt* oublier (**to do** de faire); *Fam* **f. it!** *(when thanked)* pas de quoi!; *(it doesn't matter)* laisse tomber! **2** *vi* oublier; **to f. about sb/sth** oublier qn/qch ▪ **forgetful** *adj* **to be f.** avoir une mauvaise mémoire

**forgive** [fə'gɪv] (*pt* **-gave**, *pp* **-given**) *vt* pardonner (**sb sth** qch à qn) ▪ **forgiveness** *n* pardon *m*

**forgo** [fɔː'gəʊ] (*pp* **-gone**) *vt* renoncer à

**forgot** [fə'gɒt] *pt of* **forget**

**forgotten** [fə'gɒtən] *pp of* **forget**

**fork** [fɔːk] **1** *n (for eating)* fourchette *f*; *(for gardening, in road)* fourche *f* **2** *vt Fam* **to f. out** *(money)* allonger **3** *vi (of road)* bifurquer; *Fam* **to f. out** *(pay)* casquer (**for** *or* **on** pour) ▪ **forklift** *n* **f. (truck)** chariot *m* élévateur

**forlorn** [fə'lɔːn] *adj (forsaken)* abandonné; *(unhappy)* triste

**form** [fɔːm] **1** *n (shape, type, style)* forme *f*; *(document)* formulaire *m*; *Br Sch* classe *f*; **in the f. of** sous forme de; **on f., in good** *or* **top f.** en (pleine) forme **2** *vt (group, basis, character)* former; *(clay)* façonner; *(habit)* contracter; *(obstacle)* constituer; **to f. part of sth** faire partie de qch **3** *vi (appear)* se former

**formal** ['fɔːməl] *adj (person, tone)* cérémonieux, -euse; *(announcement, dinner, invitation)* officiel, -elle; *(agreement)* en bonne et due forme; *(language)* soutenu; **f. dress** tenue *f* de soirée ▪ **formality** [-'mælɪtɪ] (*pl* **-ies**) *n (procedure)* formalité *f* ▪ **formally** *adv (declare)* officiellement; **f. dressed** en tenue de soirée

**format** ['fɔːmæt] **1** *n* format *m* **2** (*pt & pp* **-tt-**) *vt Comptr* formater

**formation** [fɔː'meɪʃən] *n* formation *f*

**former** ['fɔːmə(r)] **1** *adj (previous) (president, teacher, job, house)* ancien, -enne *(before noun)* **2** *pron* **the f.** celui-là, celle-là ▪ **formerly** *adv* autrefois

**formidable** ['fɔːmɪdəbəl] *adj* effroyable

**formula** ['fɔːmjʊlə] *n* (**a**) (*pl* **-as** *or* **-ae** [-iː]) *(rule, symbols)* formule *f* (**b**) (*pl* **-as**) *(baby food)* lait *m* en poudre ▪ **formulate** [-leɪt] *vt* formuler

**fort** [fɔːt] *n Mil* fort *m*

**forth** [fɔːθ] *adv* en avant; **and so f.** et ainsi de suite

**forthcoming** [fɔːθ'kʌmɪŋ] *adj* (**a**) *(event)* à venir (**b**) *(available)* disponible (**c**) *(informative)* expansif, -ive (**about** sur)

**forthright** ['fɔːθraɪt] *adj* franc (*f* franche)

**fortieth** ['fɔːtɪəθ] *adj & n* quarantième *(mf)*

**fortify** ['fɔːtɪfaɪ] (*pt & pp* **-ied**) *vt (strengthen)* fortifier; **to f. sb** *(of food, drink)* réconforter qn, remonter qn ▪ **fortification** [-fɪ'keɪʃən] *n* fortification *f*

**fortnight** ['fɔːtnaɪt] *n Br* quinzaine *f* de jours

**fortress** ['fɔːtrɪs] *n* forteresse *f*

**fortunate** ['fɔːtʃənət] *adj* heureux, -euse; **to be f.** *(of person)* avoir de la chance; **it's f. (for her) that...** c'est heureux (pour elle) que... *(+ subjunctive)* ▪ **fortunately** *adv* heureusement

**fortune** ['fɔːtʃuːn] *n (wealth)* fortune *f*; *(luck)* chance *f* ▪ **fortune-teller** *n* diseur, -euse *mf* de bonne aventure
**forty** ['fɔːtɪ] *adj & n* quarante *(m)*
**forum** ['fɔːrəm] *n* forum *m*
**forward** ['fɔːwəd] **1** *adj (position)* avant *inv*; *(movement)* en avant; *Fig (impudent)* effronté **2** *n (in sport)* avant *m* **3** *adv* en avant; **to go f.** avancer **4** *vt (letter)* faire suivre; *(goods)* expédier
**forwards** ['fɔːwədz] *adv* = **forward**
**fossil** ['fɒsəl] *n* fossile *m*
**foster** ['fɒstə(r)] *adj* **f. child** = enfant placé dans une famille d'accueil; **f. parents** parents *mpl* nourriciers
**fought** [fɔːt] *pt & pp of* **fight**
**foul** [faʊl] **1** (**-er, -est**) *adj* (**a**) *(smell, taste, weather, person)* infect; *(breath)* fétide; *(language)* grossier, -ère; *(place)* immonde (**b**) **f. play** *(in sport)* jeu *m* irrégulier; *(in law)* acte *m* criminel **2** *n (in sport)* faute *f* **3** *vt Fam* **to f. up** *(ruin)* gâcher
**found**[1] [faʊnd] *pt & pp of* **find**
**found**[2] [faʊnd] *vt (town, party)* fonder; *(opinion, suspicions)* fonder, baser (**on** sur) ▪ **founder** *n* fondateur, -trice *mf*
**foundation** [faʊn'deɪʃən] *n (basis)* fondement *m*; **the foundations** *(of building)* les fondations *fpl*
**fountain** ['faʊntɪn] *n* fontaine *f*; **f. pen** stylo-plume *m*
**four** [fɔː(r)] *adj & n* quatre *(m)*; **on all fours** à quatre pattes ▪ **fourth** *adj & n* quatrième *(mf)* ▪ **four-letter** *adj* **f. word** gros mot *m*
**foursome** ['fɔːsəm] *n* groupe *m* de quatre personnes
**fourteen** [fɔː'tiːn] *adj & n* quatorze *(m)* ▪ **fourteenth** *adj & n* quatorzième *(mf)*
**fowl** [faʊl] *n inv* volaille *f*
**fox** [fɒks] **1** *n* renard *m* **2** *vt (puzzle)* laisser perplexe; *(deceive)* duper
**foyer** ['fɔɪeɪ] *n (in theatre)* foyer *m*; *(in hotel)* hall *m*
**fraction** ['frækʃən] *n* fraction *f*
**fracture** ['fræktʃə(r)] **1** *n* fracture *f* **2** *vt* fracturer; **to f. one's leg** se fracturer la jambe
**fragile** [*Br* 'frædʒaɪl, *Am* 'frædʒəl] *adj* fragile
**fragment** ['frægmənt] *n* fragment *m*
**fragrant** ['freɪgrənt] *adj* parfumé ▪ **fragrance** *n* parfum *m*
**frail** [freɪl] (**-er, -est**) *adj (person)* frêle; *(health)* fragile
**frame** [freɪm] **1** *n (of picture, bicycle)* cadre *m*; *(of door, window)* encadrement *m*; *(of spectacles)* monture *f*; **f. of mind** état *m* d'esprit **2** *vt (picture)* encadrer; *Fig (proposals, ideas)* formuler ▪ **framework** *n* structure *f*; **(with)in the f. of** *(context)* dans le cadre de
**franc** [fræŋk] *n* franc *m*
**France** [frɑːns] *n* la France
**franchise** ['fræntʃaɪz] *n (right to vote)* droit *m* de vote; *(right to sell product)* franchise *f*
**Franco-** ['fræŋkəʊ] *pref* franco-
**frank**[1] [fræŋk] (**-er, -est**) *adj (honest)* franc (*f* franche) ▪ **frankly** *adv* franchement
**frank**[2] [fræŋk] *vt (letter)* affranchir
**frantic** ['fræntɪk] *adj (activity, shouts, pace)* frénétique; *(attempt, efforts)* désespéré ▪ **frantically** *adv* frénétiquement; *(run, search)* comme un fou/une folle; *(work)* avec frénésie
**fraternize** ['frætənaɪz] *vi* fraterniser (**with** avec)
**fraud** [frɔːd] *n* (**a**) *(crime)* fraude *f* (**b**) *(person)* imposteur *m* ▪ **fraudulent** *adj* frauduleux, -euse
**fraught** [frɔːt] *adj (situation)* tendu; **f. with** plein de
**fray** [freɪ] *vi (of garment)* s'effilocher; *(of rope)* s'user ▪ **frayed** *adj (garment)* élimé
**freak** [friːk] **1** *n (person)* monstre *m*; *Fam* **jazz f.** fana *mf* de jazz **2** *adj (result, weather)* anormal
▸ **freak out** *Fam* **1** *vt sep (shock, scare)* faire flipper **2** *vi (panic)* paniquer; *(get angry)* piquer une crise
**freckle** ['frekəl] *n* tache *f* de rousseur

▪ **freckled** *adj* couvert de taches de rousseur

**free** [fri:] **1** (**freer, freest**) *adj (at liberty, not occupied)* libre; *(without cost)* gratuit; *(lavish)* généreux, -euse (**with** de); **to get f.** se libérer; **to be f. to do sth** être libre de faire qch; **f. of charge** gratuit; **f. gift** cadeau *m*; **f. kick** *(in football)* coup *m* franc; **f. trade** libre-échange *m*
**2** *adv* **f. (of charge)** gratuitement
**3** (*pt & pp* **freed**) *vt (prisoner, country)* libérer; *(trapped person)* dégager; *(untie)* détacher ▪ **Freefone®** *n Br (phone number)* ≃ numéro *m* vert ▪ **freelance 1** *adj* indépendant **2** *n* travailleur, -euse *mf* indépendant(e) **3** *adv* **to work f.** travailler en indépendant ▪ **Freepost®** *n Br* ≃ correspondance-réponse *f* ▪ **free-range** *adj Br* **f. egg** œuf *m* de ferme ▪ **freestyle** *n (in swimming)* nage *f* libre ▪ **freeway** *n Am* autoroute *f*

**freedom** ['fri:dəm] *n* liberté *f*

**freely** ['fri:lɪ] *adv (speak, act, circulate)* librement; *(give)* sans compter

**freeze** [fri:z] **1** *n (in weather)* gel *m*; *(of prices, salaries)* blocage *m* **2** (*pt* **froze,** *pp* **frozen**) *vt (food)* congeler; *(credits, river)* geler; *(prices, wages)* bloquer; **frozen food** surgelés *mpl* **3** *vi* geler; **to f. to death** mourir de froid; **to f. up** *or* **over** *(of lake)* geler ▪ **freezer** *n (deep-freeze)* congélateur *m*; *(ice-box)* freezer *m* ▪ **freezing 1** *adj (weather)* glacial; *(hands, feet)* gelée; **it's f.** il gèle **2** *n* **it's 5 degrees below f.** il fait 5 degrés au-dessous de zéro **3** *adv* **f. cold** très froid

**freight** [freɪt] *n Com (goods)* cargaison *f*; **f. train** train *m* de marchandises ▪ **freighter** *n (ship)* cargo *m*

**French** [frentʃ] **1** *adj* français; *(teacher)* de français; *(embassy)* de France; **F. fries** frites *fpl* **2** *n (language)* français *m*; **the F.** *(people)* les Français *mpl* ▪ **Frenchman** (*pl* **-men**) *n* Français *m* ▪ **French-speaking** *adj* francophone ▪ **Frenchwoman** (*pl* **-women**) *n* Française *f*

**frenzy** ['frenzɪ] (*pl* **-ies**) *n* frénésie *f* ▪ **frenzied** *adj (activity)* frénétique; *(attack)* violent

**frequency** ['fri:kwənsɪ] (*pl* **-ies**) *n* fréquence *f*

**frequent 1** ['fri:kwənt] *adj* fréquent **2** [frɪ'kwent] *vt* fréquenter ▪ **frequently** *adv* fréquemment

**fresh** [freʃ] **1** (**-er, -est**) *adj* frais (*f* fraîche); *(new)* nouveau (*f* nouvelle); *Am Fam (cheeky)* insolent; **to get some f. air** prendre l'air **2** *adv* **to be f. from** *(school, university)* sortir tout juste de ▪ **freshly** *adv (arrived, picked)* fraîchement

▸**freshen up** ['freʃən] **1** *vi (have a wash)* faire un brin de toilette **2** *vt sep (house)* retaper

**fret** [fret] (*pt & pp* **-tt-**) *vi (worry)* se faire du souci

**friction** ['frɪkʃən] *n* friction *f*

**Friday** ['fraɪdeɪ] *n* vendredi *m*; **Good F.** le vendredi saint

**fridge** [frɪdʒ] *n* frigo *m*

**fried** [fraɪd] **1** *pt & pp of* **fry 2** *adj* frit; **f. egg** œuf *m* sur le plat

**friend** [frend] *n* ami, -e *mf* ▪ **friendly 1** (**-ier, -iest**) *adj* amical **2** *n (match)* match *m* amical ▪ **friendship** *n* amitié *f*

**fright** [fraɪt] *n* peur *f*; **to give sb a f.** faire peur à qn

**frighten** ['fraɪtən] *vt* effrayer, faire peur à; **to f. sb away** *or* **off** faire fuir qn ▪ **frightened** *adj* effrayé; **to be f.** avoir peur (**of** de) ▪ **frightening** *adj* effrayant

**frightful** ['fraɪtfəl] *adj* affreux, -euse

**frill** [frɪl] *n* volant *m*

**fringe** [frɪndʒ] *n* (**a**) *(of hair, on clothes)* frange *f* (**b**) *(margin)* **on the fringes of society** en marge de la société

**frisk** [frɪsk] *vt (search)* fouiller

**frisky** ['frɪskɪ] (**-ier, -iest**) *adj (lively)* vif (*f* vive)

**fritter** ['frɪtə(r)] **1** *n Culin* beignet *m* **2** *vt* **to f. away** gaspiller

**frivolous** ['frɪvələs] *adj* frivole

**frizzy** ['frɪzɪ] *adj* crépu

**fro** [frəʊ] *adv* **to go to and f.** aller et venir

**frock** [frɒk] *n (dress)* robe *f*

**frog** [frɒg] *n* grenouille *f*

**frolic** ['frɒlɪk] (*pt & pp* **-ck-**) *vi* **to f. (about)** gambader

**FROM** [frɒm, *unstressed* frəm] *prep*
(**a**) *(expressing origin)* de; **a letter f. sb** une lettre de qn; **to suffer f. sth** souffrir de qch; **where are you f.?** d'où êtes-vous?; **a train f. Paris** un train en provenance de Paris; **to be 10 m (away) f. the house** être à 10 m de la maison
(**b**) *(expressing time)* à partir de; **f. today (on), as f. today** à partir d'aujourd'hui; **f. the beginning** dès le début
(**c**) *(expressing range)* **f.... to...** de... à...; **f. morning till night** du matin au soir; **they take children f. the age of five** ils acceptent les enfants à partir de cinq ans
(**d**) *(expressing source)* de; **to take/borrow sth f. sb** prendre/emprunter qch à qn; **to drink f. a cup** boire dans une tasse
(**e**) *(expressing removal)* de; **to take sth f. sb** prendre qch à qn; **to take sth f. a box/f. the table** prendre qch dans une boîte/sur la table
(**f**) *(according to)* d'après; **f. what I saw...** d'après ce que j'ai vu...
(**g**) *(on behalf of)* de la part de; **tell her f. me** dis-lui de ma part

**front** [frʌnt] **1** *n* devant *m*; *(of boat, car)* avant *m*; *(of building)* façade *f*; *(of crowd)* premier rang *m*; *Mil, Pol & Met* front *m*; **in f. of sb/sth** devant qn/qch; **in f.** devant; *(further ahead)* en avant; *(in race)* en tête **2** *adj (tooth, garden)* de devant; *(car seat)* avant *inv*; *(row, page)* premier, -ère; **f. door** porte *f* d'entrée **3** *vt (organization)* être à la tête de; *(TV programme)* présenter ▪ **frontrunner** *n Fig* favori, -ite *mf* ▪ **front-wheel** *adj Aut* **f. drive** traction *f* avant

**frontier** ['frʌntɪə(r)] *n* frontière *f*

**frost** [frɒst] **1** *n* gel *m* **2** *vi* **to f. up** *(of window)* se couvrir de givre

**frostbite** ['frɒstbaɪt] *n* gelure *f* ▪ **frostbitten** *adj* gelé

**frosting** ['frɒstɪŋ] *n Am (on cake)* glaçage *m*

**frosty** ['frɒstɪ] (**-ier, -iest**) *adj (air, night)* glacé; *Fig (welcome)* glacial; **it's f.** il gèle

**froth** [frɒθ] **1** *n (on beer)* mousse *f*; *(on waves)* écume *f* **2** *vi (liquid)* mousser ▪ **frothy** (**-ier, -iest**) *adj (beer)* mousseux, -euse

**frown** [fraʊn] **1** *n* froncement *m* de sourcils **2** *vi* froncer les sourcils; *Fig* **to f. (up)on** désapprouver

**froze** [frəʊz] *pt of* **freeze**

**frozen** ['frəʊzən] *pp of* **freeze**

**frugal** ['fru:gəl] *adj* frugal

**fruit** [fru:t] *n* fruit *m*; **some f.** *(one item)* un fruit; *(more than one)* des fruits; **f. juice** jus *m* de fruits; **f. salad** salade *f* de fruits; *Br* **f. machine** *(for gambling)* machine *f* à sous ▪ **fruitcake** *n* cake *m*

**fruitful** ['fru:tfəl] *adj (meeting, discussion)* fructueux, -euse ▪ **fruitless** *adj (attempt, search)* infructueux, -euse

**frustrate** [frʌ'streɪt] *vt (person)* frustrer; *(plans)* contrarier ▪ **frustrating** *adj* frustrant ▪ **frustration** *n* frustration *f*

**fry** [fraɪ] (*pt & pp* **fried**) **1** *vt* faire frire **2** *vi* frire ▪ **frying** *n* **f. pan** poêle *f* (à frire)

**ft** (*abbr* **foot, feet**) pied(s) *m(pl)*

**fudge** [fʌdʒ] **1** *n (sweet)* caramel *m* mou **2** *vt* **to f. the issue** éluder une question

**fuel** [fjʊəl] *n* combustible *m*; *(for engine)* carburant *m*; **f. oil** mazout *m*; **f. tank** *(in vehicle)* réservoir *m*

**fugitive** ['fju:dʒɪtɪv] *n* fugitif, -ive *mf*

**fulfil** [fʊl'fɪl] (*Am* **fulfill**) (*pt & pp* **-ll-**) *vt (ambition, dream)* réaliser; *(condition, duty)* remplir; *(desire, need)* satisfaire ▪ **fulfilling** *adj* satisfaisant ▪ **fulfilment** (*Am* **fulfillment**) *n (of* *ambition)* réalisation *f* (**of** de); *(satisfaction)* épanouissement *m*

**full** [fʊl] **1** (**-er, -est**) *adj* plein (**of** de); *(bus, theatre, hotel, examination)* complet, -ète; *(amount)* intégral; *(day, programme)* chargé; *(skirt)* bouffant; **to be f. (up)** *(of person)* n'avoir plus faim; *(of hotel)* être complet; **at f. speed** à toute vitesse; **f. name** nom et prénom; *Br* **f. stop** point *m*
**2** *n* **in f.** *(pay)* intégralement; *(write)* en toutes lettres
**3** *adv* **to know f. well** savoir fort bien ▪ **full-length** *adj (portrait)* en pied; *(dress)* long (*f* longue); **f. film** long métrage *m* ▪ **full-scale** *adj (model)* grandeur nature *inv*; *(operation)* de grande envergure ▪ **full-time** *adj & adv (work)* à plein temps

**fully** ['fʊlɪ] *adv (completely)* entièrement; *(understand)* parfaitement; *(at least)* au moins ▪ **fully-fledged** (*Am* **full-fledged**) *adj (engineer, teacher)* diplômé; *(member)* à part entière ▪ **fully-grown** *adj* adulte

**fumble** ['fʌmbəl] *vi* **to f. (about)** *(grope)* tâtonner; *(search)* fouiller (**for** pour trouver)

**fume** [fjuːm] *vi* **to be fuming** *(of person)* rager ▪ **fumes** *npl* émanations *fpl*; *(from car)* gaz *mpl* d'échappement

**fun** [fʌn] *n* plaisir *m*; **for f., for the f. of it** pour le plaisir; **to be (good** *or* **great) f.** être (très) amusant; **to have (some) f.** s'amuser; **to make f. of sb/sth** se moquer de qn/qch

**function** ['fʌŋkʃən] **1** *n (role, duty) & Comptr* fonction *f*; *(party)* réception *f* **2** *vi* fonctionner; **to f. as** faire fonction de ▪ **functional** *adj* fonctionnel, -elle

**fund** [fʌnd] **1** *n (of money)* fonds *m*; **funds** fonds *mpl* **2** *vt* financer

**fundamental** [fʌndə'mentəl] *adj* fondamental

**funeral** ['fjuːnərəl] *n* enterrement *m*; *(grandiose)* funérailles *fpl*; **f. service** service *m* funèbre; *Br* **f. parlour**, *Am* **f. home** entreprise *f* de pompes funèbres

**funfair** ['fʌnfeə(r)] *n Br* fête *f* foraine

**fungus** ['fʌŋgəs] (*pl* **-gi** [-gaɪ]) *n (plant)* champignon *m*; *(on walls)* moisissure *f*

**funnel** ['fʌnəl] *n* (**a**) *(of ship)* cheminée *f* (**b**) *(for filling)* entonnoir *m*

**funny** ['fʌnɪ] (**-ier, -iest**) *adj (amusing)* drôle; *(strange)* bizarre; **a f. idea** une drôle d'idée ▪ **funnily** *adv* **f. enough, I was just about to...** bizarrement, j'étais sur le point de...

**fur** [fɜː(r)] **1** *n (of animal, for wearing)* fourrure *f*; *(of dog, cat)* poil *m*; **f. coat** manteau *m* de fourrure **2** (*pt & pp* **-rr-**) *vi Br* **to f. (up)** *(of kettle)* s'entartrer

**furious** ['fjʊərɪəs] *adj (violent, angry)* furieux, -euse (**with** *or* **at** contre); *(efforts, struggle)* violent

**furnace** ['fɜːnɪs] *n (forge)* fourneau *m*

**furnish** ['fɜːnɪʃ] *vt* (**a**) *(room, house)* meubler (**b**) *(supply)* fournir (**sb with sth** qch à qn) ▪ **furnishings** *npl* ameublement *m*

**furniture** ['fɜːnɪtʃə(r)] *n* meubles *mpl*; **a piece of f.** un meuble

**furrow** ['fʌrəʊ] *n (in earth, on brow)* sillon *m*

**furry** ['fɜːrɪ] *adj (animal)* à poil; *(toy)* en peluche

**further** ['fɜːðə(r)] **1** *adv & adj* = **farther 2** *adj (additional)* supplémentaire; *Br* **f. education** = enseignement supérieur dispensé par un établissement autre qu'une université **3** *adv (more)* davantage **4** *vt (cause, research, career)* promouvoir ▪ **furthermore** *adv* en outre ▪ **furthest** *adj & adv* = **farthest**

**furtive** ['fɜːtɪv] *adj* sournois

**fury** ['fjʊərɪ] *n (violence, anger)* fureur *f*

**fuse** [fjuːz] **1** *n (wire)* fusible *m*; *(of bomb)* amorce *f* **2** *vt (join)* fusionner; *Br* **to f. the lights** faire sauter les plombs **3** *vi Br* **the lights have fused** les plombs ont sauté

**fusion** ['fjuːʒən] *n* fusion *f*

**fuss** [fʌs] **1** *n* histoires *fpl*; **to kick up** *or* **make a f.** faire des histoires; **to make**

**a f. of sb** être aux petits soins pour qn **2** *vi* faire des histoires; **to f. over sb** être aux petits soins pour qn ▪ **fussy** (**-ier, -iest**) *adj* exigeant (**about** sur); **I'm not f.** *(I don't mind)* ça m'est égal

**futile** [*Br* 'fju:taɪl, *Am* 'fju:təl] *adj (remark)* futile; *(attempt)* vain

**futon** ['fu:tɒn] *n* futon *m*

**future** ['fju:tʃə(r)] **1** *n* avenir *m*; *(in grammar)* futur *m*; **in (the) f.** à l'avenir **2** *adj* futur; **my f. wife** ma future épouse; **the f. tense** le futur

**fuze** [fju:z] *n & vti Am* = **fuse**

**fuzzy** ['fʌzɪ] (**-ier, -iest**) *adj* (**a**) *(unclear) (picture, idea)* flou (**b**) *(hair)* crépu

# Gg

**G, g** [dʒiː] *n (letter)* G, g *m inv*
**gabble** ['gæbəl] *vi (chatter)* jacasser; *(indistinctly)* bredouiller
**gable** ['geɪbəl] *n* pignon *m*
**gadget** ['gædʒɪt] *n* gadget *m*
**gaffe** [gæf] *n (blunder)* gaffe *f*
**gag** [gæg] **1** *n* (**a**) *(on mouth)* bâillon *m* (**b**) *Fam (joke)* blague *f* **2** *(pt & pp* **-gg-**) *vt (person)* bâillonner; *Fig (press)* museler **3** *vi (choke)* s'étouffer (**on** avec)
**gaily** ['geɪlɪ] *adv* gaiement
**gain** [geɪn] **1** *n (increase)* augmentation *f* (**in** de); *(profit)* gain *m*; *Fig (advantage)* avantage *m* **2** *vt (obtain, win)* gagner; *(experience, reputation)* acquérir; **to g. speed/weight** prendre de la vitesse/du poids **3** *vi (of clock)* avancer; **to g. on sb** gagner du terrain sur qn; **to g. by sth** bénéficier de qch
**gala** [*Br* 'gɑːlə, *Am* 'geɪlə] *n* gala *m*; *Br* **swimming g.** concours *m* de natation
**galaxy** ['gæləksɪ] *(pl* **-ies**) *n* galaxie *f*
**gale** [geɪl] *n* grand vent *m*
**gallant** ['gælənt] *adj (brave)* brave; *(polite)* galant
**gallery** ['gælərɪ] *(pl* **-ies**) *n (room)* galerie *f*; *(museum)* musée *m*; *(for public, press)* tribune *f*
**Gallic** ['gælɪk] *adj (French)* français
**gallon** ['gælən] *n* gallon *m (Br = 4,5 l, Am = 3,8 l)*
**gallop** ['gæləp] **1** *n* galop *m* **2** *vi* galoper
**gamble** ['gæmbəl] **1** *n (risk)* coup *m* risqué **2** *vt (bet)* parier, jouer **3** *vi* jouer (**on** sur; **with** avec); **to g. on sth** *(count on)* miser sur qch ▪ **gambler** *n* joueur, -euse *mf* ▪ **gambling** *n* jeu *m*
**game¹** [geɪm] *n* (**a**) *(activity)* jeu *m*; *(of football, cricket)* match *m*; *(of tennis, chess, cards)* partie *f*; **to have a g. of football/tennis** faire un match de football/une partie de tennis; *Br* **games** *(in school)* le sport; **g. show** *(on television)* jeu *m* télévisé; *(on radio)* jeu *m* radiophonique (**b**) *(animals, birds)* gibier *m*
**game²** [geɪm] *adj (brave)* courageux, -euse; **to be g. (to do sth)** être partant (pour faire qch)
**gammon** ['gæmən] *n Br* jambon *m*
**gang** [gæŋ] **1** *n (of children, friends)* bande *f*; *(of workers)* équipe *f*; *(of criminals)* gang *m* **2** *vi* **to g. up on** *or* **against** se mettre à plusieurs contre
**gangster** ['gæŋstə(r)] *n* gangster *m*
**gangway** ['gæŋweɪ] *n Br* passage *m*; *(in train, plane)* couloir *m*; *(on ship)* passerelle *f*; *(in bus, cinema, theatre)* allée *f*
**gaol** [dʒeɪl] *n & vt Br* = **jail**
**gap** [gæp] *n (space)* espace *m* (**between** entre); *(in wall, fence)* trou *m*; *(in time)* intervalle *m*; *(in knowledge)* lacune *f*
**gape** [geɪp] *vi (stare)* rester bouche bée; **to g. at sb/sth** regarder qn/qch bouche bée ▪ **gaping** *adj* béant
**garage** [*Br* 'gærɑː(d)ʒ, 'gærɪdʒ, *Am* gə'rɑːʒ] *n* garage *m*
**garbage** ['gɑːbɪdʒ] *n Am* ordures *fpl*; **g. can** poubelle *f*; **g. man** *or* **collector** éboueur *m*
**garbled** ['gɑːbəld] *adj* confus
**garden** ['gɑːdən] **1** *n* jardin *m*; **gardens**

*(park)* parc *m*; **g. centre** jardinerie *f*; **g. party** garden-party *f* **2** *vi* jardiner, faire du jardinage ■ **gardener** *n* jardinier, -ère *mf* ■ **gardening** *n* jardinage *m*

**gargle** ['gɑ:gəl] *vi* se gargariser

**garish** [*Br* 'geərɪʃ, *Am* 'gærɪʃ] *adj (clothes)* voyant; *(colour)* criard; *(light)* cru

**garland** ['gɑ:lənd] *n* guirlande *f*

**garlic** ['gɑ:lɪk] *n* ail *m*; **g. bread** = pain chaud au beurre d'ail

**garment** ['gɑ:mənt] *n* vêtement *m*

**garnish** ['gɑ:nɪʃ] **1** *n* garniture *f* **2** *vt* garnir (**with** de)

**garter** ['gɑ:tə(r)] *n (round leg)* jarretière *f*; *(for socks)* fixe-chaussette *m*; *Am (attached to belt)* jarretelle *f*

**gas** [gæs] **1** *n* gaz *m inv*; *Am (gasoline)* essence *f*; *Br* **g. cooker** cuisinière *f* à gaz; *Br* **g. heater, g. fire** radiateur *m* à gaz; *Am* **g. station** station-service *f*; **g. stove** *(large)* cuisinière *f* à gaz; *(portable)* réchaud *m* à gaz; *Am* **g. tank** réservoir *m* à essence **2** (*pt & pp* **-ss-**) *vt (person)* asphyxier; *(deliberately)* gazer

**gash** [gæʃ] **1** *n* entaille *f* **2** *vt* **to g. one's knee** se faire une blessure profonde au genou

**gasoline** ['gæsəli:n] *n Am* essence *f*

**gasp** [gɑ:sp] **1** *n* halètement *m*; *(of surprise)* sursaut *m* **2** *vi* avoir le souffle coupé (**with** *or* **in** de); **to g. for breath** haleter

**gassy** ['gæsɪ] (**-ier, -iest**) *adj* gazeux, -euse

**gastric** ['gæstrɪk] *adj* gastrique

**gate** [geɪt] *n (in garden, field)* barrière *f*; *(made of metal)* grille *f*; *(of castle, at airport)* porte *f*; *(at stadium)* entrée *f*

**gâteau** ['gætəʊ] (*pl* **-eaux** [-əʊz]) *n Br (cake)* gros gâteau *m* à la crème

**gatecrash** ['geɪtkræʃ] *vt* **to g. a party** s'inviter à une réception

**gateway** ['geɪtweɪ] *n* entrée *f*

**gather** ['gæðə(r)] **1** *vt* (**a**) *(people, objects)* rassembler; *(pick up)* ramasser; *(flowers, fruit)* cueillir; *(information)* recueillir; **to g. speed** prendre de la vitesse; **to g. in** *(crops, harvest)* rentrer; **to g. one's strength** rassembler ses forces (**b**) *(understand)* **I g. that...** je crois comprendre que... (**c**) *(sew pleats in)* froncer

**2** *vi (of people)* se rassembler; *(of clouds)* se former; *(of dust)* s'accumuler; **to g. round** *(come closer)* s'approcher; **to g. round sb** entourer qn

**gathering** ['gæðərɪŋ] *n (group)* rassemblement *m*

**gauge** [geɪdʒ] **1** *n (instrument)* jauge *f*; *Fig* **to be a g. of sth** permettre de jauger qch **2** *vt* évaluer

**gaunt** [gɔ:nt] *adj* décharné

**gauze** [gɔ:z] *n* gaze *f*

**gave** [geɪv] *pt of* **give**

**gawk** [gɔ:k], **gawp** [gɔ:p] *vi* **to g. at sb/sth** regarder qn/qch bouche bée

**gay** [geɪ] (**-er, -est**) **1** *adj* (**a**) *(homosexual)* homosexuel, -elle (**b**) *Old-fashioned (cheerful)* gai **2** *n* homosexuel, -elle *mf*

**gaze** [geɪz] **1** *n* regard *m* **2** *vi* **to g. at sb/sth** regarder fixement qn/qch

**GB** [dʒi:'bi:] (*abbr* **Great Britain**) *n* GB

**GCSE** [dʒi:si:es'i:] (*abbr* **General Certificate of Secondary Education**) *n Br* = diplôme de fin de premier cycle de l'enseignement secondaire, sanctionnant une matière déterminée

**gear** [gɪə(r)] **1** *n* (**a**) *Fam (equipment)* attirail *m*; *(belongings)* affaires *fpl*; *(clothes)* fringues *fpl* (**b**) *(on car, bicycle)* vitesse *f*; **in g.** *(vehicle)* en prise; *Br* **g. lever**, *Am* **g. shift** levier *m* de (changement de) vitesse **2** *vt* **to g. sth to sth** adapter qch à qch; **to be geared up to do sth** être prêt à faire qch ■ **gearbox** *n* boîte *f* de vitesses

**geese** [gi:s] *pl of* **goose**

**gel** [dʒel] *n* gel *m*

**gelatin(e)** [*Br* 'dʒeləti:n, *Am* -tən] *n* gélatine *f*

**gem** [dʒem] *n (stone)* pierre *f* précieuse; *Fig (person)* perle *f*; *Fig (thing)* bijou *m* (*pl* -oux)

**gen** [dʒen] *Br Fam* **1** *n (information)*

tuyaux *mpl* **2** (*pt & pp* **-nn-**) *vi* **to g. up on sb/sth** se rancarder sur qn/qch

**gender** ['dʒendə(r)] *n (in grammar)* genre *m*; *(of person)* sexe *m*

**gene** [dʒiːn] *n Biol* gène *m*

**general** ['dʒenərəl] **1** *adj* général; **in g.** en général; **the g. public** le grand public; *Am* **g. delivery** poste *f* restante **2** *n Mil* général *m*

**generalize** ['dʒenərəlaɪz] *vi* généraliser ▪ **generalization** [-'zeɪʃən] *n* généralisation *f*

**generally** ['dʒenərəlɪ] *adv* généralement; **g. speaking** de manière générale

**generate** ['dʒenəreɪt] *vt (fear, hope, unemployment)* engendrer; *(heat, electricity)* produire; *(interest, ideas)* faire naître; *(jobs)* créer

**generation** [dʒenə'reɪʃən] *n (of people, products)* génération *f*; *(of electricity)* production *f*; **g. gap** conflit *m* des générations

**generator** ['dʒenəreɪtə(r)] *n* générateur *m*

**generosity** ['dʒenə'rɒsɪtɪ] *n* générosité *f*

**generously** ['dʒenərəslɪ] *adv* généreusement

**genesis** ['dʒenəsɪs] *n* genèse *f*

**genetic** [dʒɪ'netɪk] *adj* génétique; **g. engineering** génie *m* génétique ▪ **genetically** *adv* **g. modified** génétiquement modifié ▪ **genetics** *n* génétique *f*

**Geneva** [dʒɪ'niːvə] *n* Genève *m ou f*

**genitals** ['dʒenɪtəlz] *npl* organes *mpl* génitaux

**genius** ['dʒiːnɪəs] *n (ability, person)* génie *m*

**gent** [dʒent] *n Br Fam* monsieur *m*; **gents' shoes** chaussures *fpl* pour hommes; **the gents** *(toilet)* les toilettes *fpl* des hommes

**gentle** ['dʒentəl] (**-er, -est**) *adj (person, sound, slope)* doux (*f* douce); *(hint)* discret, -ète; *(exercise, speed)* modéré ▪ **gently** *adv* doucement; *(land)* en douceur

**gentleman** ['dʒentəlmən] (*pl* **-men**) *n* monsieur *m*; *(well-bred)* gentleman *m*

**genuine** ['dʒenjʊɪn] *adj (leather, diamond)* véritable; *(signature, work of art)* authentique; *(sincere)* sincère ▪ **genuinely** *adv (sincerely)* sincèrement

**geography** [dʒɪ'ɒgrəfɪ] *n* géographie *f* ▪ **geographical** [dʒɪə'græfɪkəl] *adj* géographique

**geology** [dʒɪ'ɒlədʒɪ] *n* géologie *f* ▪ **geological** [dʒɪə'lɒdʒɪkəl] *adj* géologique

**geometry** [dʒɪ'ɒmɪtrɪ] *n* géométrie *f* ▪ **geometric(al)** [dʒɪə'metrɪk(əl)] *adj* géométrique

**geriatric** [dʒerɪ'ætrɪk] *adj (hospital)* gériatrique

**germ** [dʒɜːm] *n (causing disease)* microbe *m*

**German** ['dʒɜːmən] **1** *adj* allemand; **G. teacher** professeur *m* d'allemand; **G. measles** rubéole *f* **2** *n (person)* Allemand, -e *mf*; *(language)* allemand *m*

**Germany** ['dʒɜːmənɪ] *n* l'Allemagne *f*

**germinate** ['dʒɜːmɪneɪt] *vi (of seed, idea)* germer

**gesticulate** [dʒe'stɪkjʊleɪt] *vi* gesticuler

**gesture** ['dʒestʃə(r)] **1** *n* geste *m* **2** *vi* **to g. to sb to do sth** faire signe à qn de faire qch

**GET** [get] (*pt & Br pp* **got**, *Am pp* **gotten**, *pres p* **getting**) **1** *vt (obtain)* obtenir, avoir; *(find)* trouver; *(buy)* acheter; *(receive)* recevoir; *(catch)* attraper; *(bus, train)* prendre; *(seize)* prendre, saisir; *(fetch)* aller chercher; *(put)* mettre; *(derive)* tirer (**from** de); *(prepare)* préparer; *(lead)* mener; *(hit with fist, stick)* atteindre; *(reputation)* se faire; *Fam (understand)* piger; *Fam (annoy)* énerver; **to g. sb to do sth** faire faire qch à qn; **to g. sth done** faire faire qch; **to g. sth clean/dirty** nettoyer/salir qch; **to g. sth to sb** *(send)* faire parvenir qch à qn; **to g. sb to the station** amener qn à la gare;

**can I g. you anything?** je te rapporte quelque chose?
2 *vi (go)* aller (**to** à); *(arrive)* arriver (**to** à); *(become)* devenir; **to g. old** vieillir; **to g. caught/run over** se faire prendre/écraser; **to g. dressed/washed** s'habiller/se laver; **to g. paid** être payé; **where have you got** *or Am* **gotten to?** où en es-tu?; **you've got to stay** *(must)* tu dois rester; **to g. to do sth** *(succeed in doing)* parvenir à faire qch; **to g. going** *(leave)* se mettre en route; *(start working)* se mettre au travail ■ **getaway** *n (escape)* fuite *f* ■ **get-together** *n Fam* réunion *f* ■ **get-up** *n Fam (clothes)* accoutrement *m*

▸**get about** *vi* se déplacer; *(of news)* circuler

▸**get across 1** *vt sep (message)* faire passer **2** *vi (succeed in crossing)* traverser; **to g. across to sb that...** faire comprendre à qn que...

▸**get along** *vi (manage)* se débrouiller; *(progress)* avancer; *(be on good terms)* s'entendre (**with** avec); *(leave)* s'en aller

▸**get around** *vi* = **get about**

▸**get at** *vt insep (reach)* atteindre; **what is he getting at?** où veut-il en venir?

▸**get away** *vi (leave)* s'en aller; *(escape)* se sauver; **to g. away with a fine** s'en tirer avec une amende; **he got away with that crime** il n'a pas été inquiété pour ce crime

▸**get back 1** *vt sep (recover)* récupérer; **to g. one's own back on sb** se venger de qn **2** *vi (return)* revenir; **to g. back at sb** se venger de qn

▸**get by** *vi (manage)* se débrouiller

▸**get down 1** *vi (go down)* descendre (**from** de); **to g. down to** *(work)* se mettre à **2** *vt sep (bring down)* descendre (**from** de); *Fam* **to g. sb down** *(depress)* déprimer qn **3** *vt insep* **to g. down the stairs/a ladder** descendre l'escalier/d'une échelle

▸**get in 1** *vt sep (stock up with)* faire provision de; **to g. sb in** *(call for)* faire venir qn **2** *vi (enter)* entrer; *(come home)* rentrer; *(enter vehicle or train)* monter; *(arrive)* arriver; *(be elected)* être élu

▸**get into** *vt insep* entrer dans; *(vehicle, train)* monter dans; *(habit)* prendre; **to g. into bed/a rage** se mettre au lit/en colère

▸**get off 1** *vt sep (remove)* enlever; *(send)* expédier; *(in court)* faire acquitter; *Fam* **to g. off doing sth** se dispenser de faire qch **2** *vt insep* **to g. off a chair** se lever d'une chaise; **to g. off a bus** descendre d'un bus **3** *vi (leave)* partir; *(from vehicle or train)* descendre (**from** de); *(escape punishment)* s'en tirer

▸**get on 1** *vt sep (shoes, clothes)* mettre **2** *vt insep (bus, train)* monter dans **3** *vi (enter bus or train)* monter; *(manage)* se débrouiller; *(succeed)* réussir; *(be on good terms)* s'entendre (**with** avec); **how are you getting on?** comment ça va?; **how did you g. on?** *(in exam)* comment ça s'est passé?; **to be getting on (in years)** se faire vieux (*f* vieille); **to g. onto sb** *(on phone)* contacter qn; **to g. on with** *(task)* continuer

▸**get out 1** *vt sep (remove)* enlever; *(bring out)* sortir **2** *vi* sortir; *(from vehicle or train)* descendre (**of** *or* **from** de); **to g. out of** *(obligation)* échapper à; *(danger)* se tirer de; *(habit)* perdre

▸**get over 1** *vt sep (ideas)* faire passer; **let's g. it over with** finissons-en **2** *vt insep (illness)* se remettre de; *(shock)* revenir de

▸**get round 1** *vt insep (obstacle)* contourner **2** *vi (visit)* passer; **to g. round to doing sth** trouver le temps de faire qch

▸**get through 1** *vt sep (communicate)* **to g. sth through to sb** faire comprendre qch à qn **2** *vt insep (hole)* passer par; *(task)* venir à bout de; *(exam, interview)* survivre à; *(food)* consommer **3** *vi (pass)* passer; *(pass exam)* être reçu; **to g. through to sb** *(communicate with)* se faire comprendre de qn; *(on the phone)* obtenir la communication avec qn

▸ **get together** *vi (of people)* se réunir

▸ **get up 1** *vt sep* **to g. sb up** *(out of bed)* faire lever qn; **to g. sth up** *(bring up)* monter qch **2** *vt insep (ladder, stairs)* monter **3** *vi (rise, stand up)* se lever (**from** de); **to g. up to something** *or* **to mischief** faire des bêtises; **where have you got up to?** *(in book)* où en es-tu?

---

**ghastly** ['gɑ:stlɪ] (**-ier, -iest**) *adj (horrible)* épouvantable

**gherkin** ['gɜ:kɪn] *n* cornichon *m*

**ghetto** ['getəʊ] (*pl* **-oes** *or* **-os**) *n* ghetto *m*; *Fam* **g. blaster** radiocassette *f*

**ghost** [gəʊst] *n* fantôme *m*; **g. story** histoire *f* de fantômes ▪ **ghostly** *adj* spectral

**giant** ['dʒaɪənt] **1** *adj (tree, packet)* géant **2** *n* géant *m*

**gibe** [dʒaɪb] **1** *n* moquerie *f* **2** *vi* **to g. at sb** se moquer de qn

**giddy** ['gɪdɪ] (**-ier, -iest**) *adj* **to be** *or* **feel g.** avoir le vertige; **to make sb g.** donner le vertige à qn

**gift** [gɪft] *n* cadeau *m*; *(talent, donation)* don *m*; *Br* **g. voucher** *or* **token** chèque-cadeau *m* ▪ **gifted** *adj* doué (**with** de; **for** pour)

**gift-wrapped** ['gɪftræpt] *adj* sous paquet-cadeau

**gig** [gɪg] *n Fam (pop concert)* concert *m*

**gigantic** [dʒaɪ'gæntɪk] *adj* gigantesque

**giggle** ['gɪgəl] **1** *n* petit rire *m* bête **2** *vi* rire (bêtement)

**gilt** [gɪlt] **1** *adj* doré **2** *n* dorure *f*

**gimmick** ['gɪmɪk] *n (trick, object)* truc *m*

**gin** [dʒɪn] *n (drink)* gin *m*

**ginger** ['dʒɪndʒə(r)] **1** *adj (hair)* roux (*f* rousse) **2** *n (spice)* gingembre *m*; **g. beer** limonade *f* au gingembre ▪ **gingerbread** *n* pain *m* d'épice

**gipsy** ['dʒɪpsɪ] (*pl* **-ies**) *n* bohémien, -enne *mf*; *(Eastern European)* tsigane *mf*; *(Spanish)* gitan, -e *mf*

**giraffe** [dʒɪ'ræf, *Br* dʒɪ'rɑ:f] *n* girafe *f*

**girl** [gɜ:l] *n (child)* (petite) fille *f*, fillette *f*; *(young woman)* jeune fille *f*; **English g.** jeune Anglaise *f*; **G. Guide** éclaireuse *f* ▪ **girlfriend** *n (of girl)* amie *f*; *(of boy)* petite amie *f* ▪ **girlish** *adj* de (jeune) fille

**giro** ['dʒaɪrəʊ] (*pl* **-os**) *n Br* **bank g.** virement *m* bancaire; **g. account** compte *m* courant postal, CCP *m*

**gist** [dʒɪst] *n* **to get the g. of sth** saisir l'essentiel de qch

---

**GIVE** [gɪv] **1** *n (of fabric)* élasticité *f*
**2** (*pt* **gave**, *pp* **given**) *vt* donner; *(as present)* offrir; *(support)* apporter; *(smile, gesture, pleasure)* faire; *(sigh)* pousser; *(look)* jeter; *(blow)* porter; **to g. sth to sb, to g. sb sth** donner *ou* offrir qch à qn; **to g. way** *(of branch, person)* céder; *(of roof)* s'effondrer; *(in vehicle)* céder la priorité (**to** à)
**3** *vi* (**a**) *(donate)* donner (**b**) *(of shoes)* se faire; *(of support)* céder

▸ **give away** *vt sep (prize)* distribuer; *(money)* donner; *(betray)* trahir

▸ **give back** *vt sep (return)* rendre

▸ **give in 1** *vt sep (hand in)* remettre **2** *vi (surrender)* céder (**to** à)

▸ **give off** *vt sep (smell, heat)* dégager

▸ **give out** *vt sep (hand out)* distribuer; *(make known)* annoncer

▸ **give over** *vi Br Fam* **g. over!** arrête!

▸ **give up 1** *vt sep (possessions)* abandonner; *(activity)* renoncer à; *(seat)* céder (**to** à); **to g. up smoking** cesser de fumer **2** *vi* abandonner

---

**given** ['gɪvən] **1** *pp of* **give 2** *adj (fixed)* donné **3** *conj (considering)* étant donné; **g. that...** étant donné que...

**glacier** [*Br* 'glæsɪə(r), *Am* 'gleɪʃər] *n* glacier *m*

**glad** [glæd] *adj (person)* content (**of/about** de; **that** que + *subjunctive*) ▪ **gladly** *adv* volontiers

**glamorous** ['glæmərəs] *adj (person,*

*dress)* élégant; *(job)* prestigieux, -euse

**glance** [glɑ:ns] **1** *n* coup *m* d'œil **2** *vi* **to g. at sb/sth** jeter un coup d'œil à qn/qch

**gland** [glænd] *n* glande *f*

**glare** [gleə(r)] **1** *n (look)* regard *m* furieux **2** *vi* **to g. at sb** foudroyer qn (du regard) ▪ **glaring** *adj (light)* éblouissant; *(eyes)* furieux, -euse; **a g. mistake** une faute grossière

**glass** [glɑ:s] **1** *n* verre *m* **2** *adj (bottle)* de verre; **g. door** porte *f* vitrée ▪ **glassful** *n* (plein) verre *m*

**glasses** ['glɑ:sɪz] *npl (spectacles)* lunettes *fpl*

**glaze** [gleɪz] **1** *n (on pottery)* vernis *m* **2** *vt (window)* vitrer; *(pottery)* vernisser

**gleam** [gli:m] **1** *n* lueur *f* **2** *vi* luire

**glean** [gli:n] *vt (information)* glaner

**glee** [gli:] *n* joie *f*

**glen** [glen] *n Scot* vallon *m*

**glide** [glaɪd] *vi* glisser; *(of aircraft, bird)* planer ▪ **glider** *n (aircraft)* planeur *m* ▪ **gliding** *n (sport)* vol *m* à voile

**glimmer** ['glɪmə(r)] **1** *n (light, of hope)* faible lueur *f* **2** *vi* luire (faiblement)

**glimpse** [glɪmps] **1** *n* aperçu *m*; **to catch** *or* **get a g. of sth** entrevoir qch **2** *vt* entrevoir

**glint** [glɪnt] *vi (of light, eye)* briller

**glisten** ['glɪsən] *vi (of wet surface)* briller; *(of water)* miroiter

**glitter** ['glɪtə(r)] *vi* scintiller

**gloat** [gləʊt] *vi* jubiler (**over** à l'idée de)

**global** ['gləʊbəl] *adj (universal)* mondial; *(comprehensive)* global; **g. warming** réchauffement *m* de la planète ▪ **globalization** *n Econ* mondialisation *f*

**globe** [gləʊb] *n* globe *m*

**gloom** [glu:m] *n (sadness)* morosité *f*; *(darkness)* obscurité *f* ▪ **gloomy** (**-ier, -iest**) *adj (sad)* morose; *(dark, dismal)* sombre

**glorious** ['glɔ:rɪəs] *adj (splendid)* magnifique; *(full of glory)* glorieux, -euse

**glory** ['glɔ:rɪ] **1** *n* gloire *f*; *(great beauty)* splendeur *f* **2** *vi* **to g. in sth** se glorifier de qch

**gloss** [glɒs] **1** *n (shine)* lustre *m*; **g. paint** peinture *f* brillante **2** *vt* **to g. over sth** glisser sur qch ▪ **glossy** (**-ier, -iest**) *adj* brillant; *(photo)* glacé; *(magazine)* de luxe

**glossary** ['glɒsərɪ] (*pl* **-ies**) *n* glossaire *m*

**glove** [glʌv] *n* gant *m*; **g. compartment** *(in car)* boîte *f* à gants

**glow** [gləʊ] **1** *n (light)* lueur *f* **2** *vi (of sky, fire)* rougeoyer; *Fig (of eyes, person)* rayonner (**with** de) ▪ **glowing** *adj (account, terms, reference)* enthousiaste

**glue** [glu:] **1** *n* colle *f* **2** *vt* coller (**to/on** à)

**glum** [glʌm] (**glummer, glummest**) *adj* triste

**glutton** ['glʌtən] *n* goinfre *mf*

**GM** [dʒi:'em] (*abbr* **genetically modified**) *adj* génétiquement modifié

**GMT** [dʒi:em'ti:] (*abbr* **Greenwich Mean Time**) *n* GMT *m*

**gnat** [næt] *n* moucheron *m*

**gnaw** [nɔ:] *vti* **to g. (at) sth** ronger qch

**gnome** [nəʊm] *n* gnome *m*

---

**GO** [gəʊ] **1** (*pl* **goes**) *n (turn)* tour *m*; *(energy)* dynamisme *m*; **to have a go at (doing) sth** essayer (de faire) qch; **at** *or* **in one go** d'un seul coup; **on the go** en mouvement; **to make a go of sth** réussir qch

**2** (*3rd person sing present tense* **goes**; *pt* **went**; *pp* **gone**; *pres p* **going**) *vt (make sound)* faire; **to go it alone** se lancer en solo

**3** *vi* aller (**to** à; **from** de); *(depart)* partir, s'en aller; *(disappear)* disparaître; *(be sold)* se vendre; *(function)* marcher; *(progress)* aller; *(become)* devenir; *(of time)* passer; *(of hearing, strength)* baisser; *(of fuse)* sauter; *(of light bulb)* griller; **to go well/badly** *(of event)* se passer bien/mal; **she's going to do sth** *(is about to, intends to)* elle va faire qch; **it's going to rain** il va pleuvoir; **it's all gone**

*(finished)* il n'y en a plus; **to go and get sb/sth** *(fetch)* aller chercher qn/ qch; **to go and see** aller voir; **to go riding/on a trip** faire du cheval/un voyage; **to go to a doctor/lawyer** aller voir un médecin/un avocat; **is there any beer going?** y a-t-il de la bière?; **two hours to go** encore deux heures

▸ **go about 1** *vi (of person)* se promener; *(of rumour)* circuler **2** *(get on with)* s'occuper de; *(set about)* se mettre à; **how do you go about it?** comment est-ce qu'on procède?

▸ **go across 1** *vt insep* traverser **2** *vi (cross)* traverser; *(go)* aller (**to** à); **to go across to sb('s)** faire un saut chez qn

▸ **go after** *vt insep (chase)* poursuivre; *(job)* essayer d'obtenir

▸ **go against** *vt insep (contradict)* aller à l'encontre de; *(be unfavourable to)* être défavorable à

▸ **go ahead** *vi (take place)* avoir lieu; *(go in front)* passer devant; **to go ahead with sth** entreprendre qch; **go ahead!** allez-y!

▸ **go along** *vi (proceed)* se dérouler; **to go along with sb/sth** être d'accord avec qn/qch; **we'll see as we go along** nous verrons au fur et à mesure

▸ **go around** *vi* = **go about**

▸ **go away** *vi* partir, s'en aller

▸ **go back** *vi (return)* revenir; *(step back, retreat)* reculer; **to go back to sleep** se rendormir; **to go back to doing sth** se remettre à faire qch; **to go back to** *(in time)* remonter à; **to go back on one's promise** *or* **word** revenir sur sa promesse

▸ **go by 1** *vt insep (act according to)* se fonder sur; *(judge from)* juger d'après; **to go by the name of...** être connu sous le nom de... **2** *vi* passer

▸ **go down 1** *vt insep (stairs, street)* descendre **2** *vi* descendre; *(fall down)* tomber; *(of ship)* sombrer; *(of sun)* se coucher; *(of temperature, price)* baisser; *(of tyre, balloon)* se dégonfler; **to go down well/badly** être bien/mal reçu

▸ **go for** *vt insep (fetch)* aller chercher; *(attack)* attaquer; **the same goes for you** ça vaut aussi pour toi

▸ **go forward(s)** *vi* avancer

▸ **go in** *vi* (r)entrer; *(of sun)* se cacher; *Br* **to go in for** *(exam)* s'inscrire à; **she doesn't go in for cooking** elle n'est pas très portée sur la cuisine

▸ **go into** *vt insep (enter)* entrer dans; *(examine)* examiner

▸ **go off 1** *vt insep (lose liking for)* se lasser de **2** *vi (leave)* partir; *(go bad)* se gâter; *(of alarm)* se déclencher; *(of bomb)* exploser

▸ **go on** *vi* continuer (**doing** à faire); *(travel)* poursuivre sa route; *(happen)* se passer; *(last)* durer; **to go on to sth** passer à qch; *Fam* **to go on at sb** *(nag)* s'en prendre à qn; *Fam* **to go on about sb/sth** parler sans cesse de qn/qch

▸ **go out** *vi* sortir; *(of light, fire)* s'éteindre; *(of tide)* descendre; *(depart)* partir; *(date)* sortir ensemble; **to go out for a meal** aller au restaurant; **to go out with sb** sortir avec qn; **to go out to work** travailler (hors de chez soi)

▸ **go over 1** *vt insep* (**a**) *(cross over)* traverser; **the ball went over the wall** la balle est passée par-dessus le mur (**b**) *(examine)* passer en revue; *(speech)* revoir **2** *vi (go)* aller (**to** à); *(to enemy)* passer (**to** à); **to go over to sb** aller vers qn; **to go over to sb's** *(visit)* faire un saut chez qn

▸ **go round 1** *vt insep* **to go round a corner** tourner au coin; **to go round the shops** faire les magasins; **to go round the world** faire le tour du monde **2** *vi (turn)* tourner; *(make a detour)* faire le tour; *(of rumour)* circuler; **to go round to sb's** faire un saut chez qn; **there is enough to go round** il y en a assez pour tout le monde

▸ **go through 1** *vt insep (suffer, undergo)* subir; *(examine)* passer en revue; *(search)* fouiller; *(spend)* dépenser; *(wear out)* user; *(perform)* accomplir;

**to go through with sth** aller jusqu'au bout de qch **2** *vi* passer; *(of deal)* être conclu

▸**go under** *vi (of ship)* couler; *Fig (of firm)* faire faillite

▸**go up 1** *vt insep* monter **2** *vi* monter; *(explode)* sauter; **to go up to sth** *(approach)* se diriger vers qch; *(reach)* aller jusqu'à qch

▸**go with** *vt insep* aller de pair avec; **the company car goes with the job** le poste donne droit à une voiture de fonction

▸**go without** *vt insep* se passer de

---

**goad** [gəʊd] *vt* **to g. sb (on)** aiguillonner qn

**go-ahead** ['gəʊəhed] **1** *adj* dynamique **2** *n* **to get the g.** avoir le feu vert; **to give sb the g.** donner le feu vert à qn

**goal** [gəʊl] *n* but *m* ▪ **goalkeeper** *n* gardien *m* de but, goal *m* ▪ **goalpost** *n* poteau *m* de but

**goat** [gəʊt] *n* chèvre *f*

**gobble** ['gɒbəl] *vt* **to g. (up** *or* **down)** *(food)* engloutir

**go-between** ['gəʊbɪtwiːn] *n* intermédiaire *mf*

**goblet** ['gɒblɪt] *n* verre *m* à pied

**god** [gɒd] *n* dieu *m*; **G.** Dieu; *Fam* **oh G.!, my G.!** mon Dieu! ▪ **goddaughter** *n* filleule *f* ▪ **godfather** *n* parrain *m* ▪ **godforsaken** *adj (place)* perdu ▪ **godmother** *n* marraine *f* ▪ **godson** *n* filleul *m*

**goddam(n)** ['gɒdæm] *adj Am Fam* foutu

**goddess** ['gɒdɪs] *n* déesse *f*

**godsend** ['gɒdsend] *n* **to be a g.** être un don du ciel

**goes** [gəʊz] *3rd person sing present tense & npl of* **go**

**goggles** ['gɒgəlz] *npl* lunettes *fpl (de protection, de plongée)*

**going** ['gəʊɪŋ] **1** *n* **it's hard** *or* **heavy g.** c'est difficile **2** *adj* **the g. rate** le tarif en vigueur; **a g. concern** une affaire qui tourne ▪ **goings-on** *npl Pej* activités *fpl*

**go-kart** ['gəʊkɑːt] *n (for racing)* kart *m*

**gold** [gəʊld] **1** *n* or *m* **2** *adj (watch)* en or; *(coin, dust)* d'or; **g. medal** *(in sport)* médaille *f* d'or ▪ **golden** *adj (of gold colour)* doré; **g. rule** règle *f* d'or ▪ **goldmine** *n* mine *f* d'or ▪ **gold-plated** *adj* plaqué or ▪ **goldsmith** *n* orfèvre *m*

**goldfish** ['gəʊldfɪʃ] *n* poisson *m* rouge

**golf** [gɒlf] *n* golf *m*; **g. club** *(stick, association)* club *m* de golf; **g. course** parcours *m* de golf ▪ **golfer** *n* golfeur, -euse *mf*

**gone** [gɒn] **1** *pp of* **go 2** *adj Br Fam* **it's g. two** il est plus de deux heures

**gong** [gɒŋ] *n* gong *m*

---

**GOOD** [gʊd] **1** (**better, best**) *adj* bon (*f* bonne); *(kind)* gentil, -ille; *(well-behaved)* sage; **my g. friend** mon cher ami; **g.!** bon!, bien!; **very g.!** *(all right)* très bien!; **that isn't g. enough** *(bad)* ça ne va pas; *(not sufficient)* ça ne suffit pas; **that's g. of you** c'est gentil de ta part; **to taste g.** avoir bon goût; **to feel g.** se sentir bien; **to have g. weather** avoir beau temps; **to be g. at French** être bon en français; **to be g. at swimming/telling jokes** savoir bien nager/raconter des blagues; **to be g. with children** savoir s'y prendre avec les enfants; **a g. many, a g. deal (of)** beaucoup (de); **as g. as** *(almost)* pratiquement; **g. afternoon, g. morning** bonjour; *(on leaving someone)* au revoir; **g. evening** bonsoir; **g. night** bonsoir; *(before going to bed)* bonne nuit

**2** *n (advantage, virtue)* bien *m*; **for her (own) g.** pour son bien; **for the g. of your family/career** pour ta famille/carrière; **it will do you (some) g.** ça te fera du bien; **it's no g. crying/shouting** ça ne sert à rien de pleurer/crier; **that's no g.** *(worthless)* ça ne vaut rien; *(bad)* ça ne va pas; **for g.** *(leave, give up)* pour de bon ▪ **good-for-nothing** *n* propre-à-rien *mf* ▪ **good-looking** *adj* beau (*f* belle)

**goodbye** [gʊd'baɪ] *exclam & n* au revoir *(m inv)*

**goodness** ['gʊdnɪs] *n* bonté *f*; **my g.!** mon Dieu!

**goods** [gʊdz] *npl* marchandises *fpl*; **g. train** train *m* de marchandises

**goodwill** [gʊd'wɪl] *n (willingness)* bonne volonté *f*; *(benevolence)* bienveillance *f*

**goose** [gu:s] *(pl* **geese**) *n* oie *f*; **g.** *Br* **pimples** *or Am* **bumps** chair *f* de poule ▪ **gooseflesh** *n* chair *f* de poule

**gooseberry** ['gʊzbərɪ] *(pl* **-ies**) *n* groseille *f* à maquereau

**gorge** [gɔ:dʒ] **1** *n (ravine)* gorge *f* **2** *vt* **to g. oneself** se gaver (**on** de)

**gorgeous** ['gɔ:dʒəs] *adj* magnifique

**gorilla** [gə'rɪlə] *n* gorille *m*

**gormless** ['gɔ:mləs] *adj Br Fam* balourd

**gory** ['gɔ:rɪ] (**-ier, -iest**) *adj (bloody)* sanglant

**gosh** [gɒʃ] *exclam Fam* mince (alors)!

**go-slow** [gəʊ'sləʊ] *n Br (strike)* grève *f* du zèle

**gospel** ['gɒspəl] *n* évangile *m*

**gossip** ['gɒsɪp] **1** *n (talk)* bavardages *mpl*; *(malicious)* cancans *mpl*; *(person)* commère *f*; **g. column** *(in newspaper)* échos *mpl* **2** *vi* bavarder; *(maliciously)* colporter des commérages

**got** [gɒt] *pt & Br pp of* **get**

**Gothic** ['gɒθɪk] *adj & n* gothique *(m)*

**gotten** ['gɒtən] *Am pp of* **get**

**gourmet** ['gʊəmeɪ] *n* gourmet *m*

**govern** ['gʌvən] **1** *vt (rule)* gouverner; *(city, province)* administrer; *(influence)* déterminer **2** *vi (rule)* gouverner

**government** ['gʌvənmənt] **1** *n* gouvernement *m*; **local g.** administration *f* locale **2** *adj (decision, policy)* gouvernemental

**governor** ['gʌvənə(r)] *n* gouverneur *m*; *(of school)* administrateur, -trice *mf*; *(of prison)* directeur, -trice *mf*

**gown** [gaʊn] *n (of woman)* robe *f*; *Br (of judge, lecturer)* toge *f*

**GP** [dʒi:'pi:] *(abbr* **general practitioner**) *n* généraliste *mf*

**grab** [græb] *(pt & pp* **-bb-**) *vt* **to g. (hold of) sb/sth** saisir qn/qch; **to g. sth from sb** arracher qch à qn

**grace** [greɪs] **1** *n (charm, goodwill, religious mercy)* grâce *f*; *Rel* **to say g.** dire le bénédicité; **ten days' g.** dix jours de grâce **2** *vt (adorn)* orner; *(honour)* honorer (**with** de) ▪ **graceful** *adj (movement, person)* gracieux, -euse

**gracious** ['greɪʃəs] *adj (kind)* aimable (**to** envers); *Fam* **good g.!** bonté divine!

**grade** [greɪd] **1** *n* (**a**) *(rank)* grade *m*; *(in profession)* échelon *m*; *(quality)* qualité *f*; *Am* **g. crossing** passage *m* à niveau (**b**) *Am Sch (mark)* note *f*; *(year)* classe *f*; **g. school** école *f* primaire **2** *vt (classify)* classer; *Am (exam)* noter

**gradient** ['greɪdɪənt] *n (slope)* dénivellation *f*

**gradual** ['grædʒʊəl] *adj* progressif, -ive; *(slope)* doux *(f* douce) ▪ **gradually** *adv* progressivement

**graduate 1** ['grædʒʊət] *n Br (from university)* ≃ licencié, -e *mf*; *Am (from high school)* ≃ bachelier, -ère *mf* **2** ['grædʒʊeɪt] *vi Br (from university)* ≃ obtenir sa licence; *Am (from high school)* ≃ obtenir son baccalauréat; **to g. from sth to sth** passer de qch à qch ▪ **graduation** *n Univ* remise *f* des diplômes

**graffiti** [grə'fi:tɪ] *npl* graffiti *mpl*

**grain** [greɪn] *n* (**a**) *(seed, particle)* grain *m*; *(cereals)* céréales *fpl* (**b**) *(in wood, leather)* grain *m*

**gram** [græm] *n* gramme *m*

**grammar** ['græmə(r)] *n* grammaire *f*; *Br* **g. school** ≃ lycée *m* ▪ **grammatical** *adj* grammatical

**gramme** [græm] *n* gramme *m*

**grand** [grænd] **1** (**-er, -est**) *adj (splendid)* grandiose; *Fam (excellent)* excellent; **g. piano** piano *m* à queue; **g. total** somme *f* totale **2** *n inv Br Fam* mille livres *fpl*; *Am Fam* mille dollars *mpl* ▪ **grandchild** *(pl* **-children**) *n* petit-fils *m*, petite-fille *f*; **grandchildren** petits-enfants *mpl* ▪ **grand(d)ad** *n*

*Fam* papi *m* ▪ **granddaughter** *n* petite-fille *f* ▪ **grandfather** *n* grand-père *m* ▪ **grandma** *n Fam* mamie *f* ▪ **grandmother** *n* grand-mère *f* ▪ **grandpa** *n Fam* papi *m* ▪ **grandparents** *npl* grands-parents *mpl* ▪ **grandson** *n* petit-fils *m*

**grandstand** ['grændstænd] *n* tribune *f*

**granite** ['grænɪt] *n* granit *m*

**granny** ['grænɪ] (*pl* **-ies**) *n Fam* mamie *f*

**grant** [grɑ:nt] **1** *n* subvention *f*; *(for student)* bourse *f* **2** *vt* accorder (**to** à); *(request)* accéder à; *(prayer, wish)* exaucer; *(admit)* admettre (**that** que); **to take sth for granted** considérer qch comme allant de soi; **to take sb for granted** ne pas avoir d'égard pour qn

**granule** ['grænju:l] *n* granule *m*

**grape** [greɪp] *n* grain *m* de raisin; **some grapes** du raisin; **g. juice** jus *m* de raisin

**grapefruit** ['greɪpfru:t] *n* pamplemousse *m*

**graph** [græf, grɑ:f] *n* graphique *m*; **g. paper** papier *m* millimétré

**graphic** ['græfɪk] *adj (description)* très détaillé; **g. artist** graphiste *mf* ▪ **graphics** *npl* **(computer) g.** graphiques *mpl*

**grapple** ['græpəl] *vi* **to g. with** *(problem)* se débattre avec

**grasp** [grɑ:sp] **1** *n (hold)* prise *f*; *(understanding)* compréhension *f*; **within sb's g.** à la portée de qn **2** *vt (seize, understand)* saisir ▪ **grasping** *adj (mean)* avide

**grass** [grɑ:s] *n* herbe *f*; *(lawn)* gazon *m* ▪ **grasshopper** *n* sauterelle *f* ▪ **grassy** *adj* herbeux, -euse

**grate** [greɪt] **1** *n (for fireplace)* grille *f* **2** *vt (cheese, carrot)* râper **3** *vi (of sound)* grincer ▪ **grater** *n* râpe *f* ▪ **grating 1** *adj (sound)* grinçant **2** *n (bars)* grille *f*

**grateful** ['greɪtfəl] *adj* reconnaissant (**to** à; **for** de); *(words, letter)* de remerciement ▪ **gratefully** *adv* avec reconnaissance

**gratified** ['grætɪfaɪd] *adj (pleased)* satisfait (**by** *or* **with** de; **to do** de faire) ▪ **gratifying** *adj* très satisfaisant

**gratis** ['grætɪs, 'greɪtɪs] *adv* gratis

**gratitude** ['grætɪtju:d] *n* gratitude *f* (**for** de)

**gratuitous** [grə'tju:ɪtəs] *adj (act)* gratuit

**grave**[1] [greɪv] *n* tombe *f* ▪ **gravestone** *n* pierre *f* tombale ▪ **graveyard** *n* cimetière *m*

**grave**[2] [greɪv] (**-er, -est**) *adj (serious)* grave; *(manner, voice)* solennel, -elle

**gravel** ['grævəl] *n* gravier *m*; **g. path** allée *f* de gravier

**gravitate** ['grævɪteɪt] *vi* **to g. towards sth** *(be drawn to)* être attiré par qch; *(move towards)* se diriger vers qch

**gravity** ['grævɪtɪ] *n* (**a**) *Phys (force)* pesanteur *f* (**b**) *(seriousness)* gravité *f*

**gravy** ['greɪvɪ] *n* = sauce à base de jus de viande

**gray** [greɪ] *adj, n & vi Am* = **grey**

**graze**[1] [greɪz] **1** *n (wound)* écorchure *f* **2** *vt (scrape)* écorcher

**graze**[2] [greɪz] *vi (of cattle)* paître

**grease** [gri:s] **1** *n* graisse *f* **2** *vt* graisser ▪ **greasy** (**-ier, -iest**) *adj* graisseux, -euse; *(hair, skin, food)* gras (*f* grasse)

**great** [greɪt] (**-er, -est**) *adj* grand; *(effort, heat)* gros (*f* grosse), grand; *Fam (very good)* génial; *Fam* **to be g. at tennis** être très doué pour le tennis; **a g. deal** *or* **number (of), a g. many** beaucoup (de); **G. Britain** la Grande-Bretagne; **Greater London** le grand Londres ▪ **great-grandfather** *n* arrière-grand-père *m* ▪ **great-grandmother** *n* arrière-grand-mère *f*

**greatly** ['greɪtlɪ] *adv* très; *(much)* beaucoup

**Greece** [gri:s] *n* la Grèce

**greed** [gri:d] *n* avidité *f* (**for** de); *(for food)* gourmandise *f* ▪ **greedy** (**-ier, -iest**) *adj* avide (**for** de); *(for food)* gourmand

**Greek** [gri:k] **1** *adj* grec (*f* grecque) **2** *n (person)* Grec *m*, Grecque *f*; *(language)* grec *m*

**green** [gri:n] **1** (**-er, -est**) *adj* vert; *Fig (immature)* inexpérimenté; *Pol* écologiste; **to turn** *or* **go g.** *(of traffic lights)* passer au vert; *(of person, garden, tree)* verdir; *Am* **g. card** ≃ permis *m* de travail **2** *n (colour)* vert *m*; *(grassy area)* pelouse *f*; **greens** *(vegetables)* légumes *mpl* verts; *Pol* **the Greens** les Verts *mpl* ▪ **greenery** *n* verdure *f* ▪ **greengrocer** *n Br* marchand, -e *mf* de fruits et légumes ▪ **greenhouse** *n* serre *f*; **the g. effect** l'effet *m* de serre

**greet** [gri:t] *vt (say hello to)* saluer; *(welcome)* accueillir ▪ **greeting** *n* accueil *m*; **greetings** *(for birthday, festival)* vœux *mpl*

**gregarious** [grɪ'geərɪəs] *adj* sociable

**grenade** [grə'neɪd] *n (bomb)* grenade *f*

**grew** [gru:] *pt of* **grow**

**grey** [greɪ] **1** *adj* (**-er, -est**) gris; **to be going g.** grisonner **2** *n* gris *m* **3** *vi (of hair)* grisonner ▪ **grey-haired** *adj* aux cheveux gris ▪ **greyhound** *n* lévrier *m*

**grid** [grɪd] *n (bars)* grille *f*; *(on map)* quadrillage *m*

**griddle** ['grɪdəl] *n (for cooking)* tôle *f*

**gridlock** ['grɪdlɒk] *n (traffic jam)* embouteillage *m*

**grief** [gri:f] *n* chagrin *m*; **to come to g.** échouer

**grievance** ['gri:vəns] *n* grief *m*; **grievances** *(complaints)* doléances *fpl*

**grieve** [gri:v] **1** *vt* affliger **2** *vi* **to g. for sb/over sth** pleurer qn/qch

**grill** [grɪl] **1** *n (utensil)* gril *m*; *(dish)* grillade *f* **2** *vt* griller

**grille** [grɪl] *n (bars)* grille *f*

**grim** [grɪm] (**grimmer, grimmest**) *adj (stern)* sinistre; *Fam (bad)* lamentable

**grimace** ['grɪməs] **1** *n* grimace *f* **2** *vi* grimacer

**grime** [graɪm] *n* crasse *f* ▪ **grimy** (**-ier, -iest**) *adj* crasseux, -euse

**grin** [grɪn] **1** *n* large sourire *m* **2** (*pt & pp* **-nn-**) *vi* avoir un large sourire

**grind** [graɪnd] **1** *n Fam (work)* corvée *f* **2** (*pt & pp* **ground**) *vt (coffee, pepper)* moudre; *Am (meat)* hacher **3** *vi* **to g. to a halt** s'immobiliser ▪ **grinder** *n* **coffee g.** moulin *m* à café

**grip** [grɪp] **1** *n (hold)* prise *f*; *(handle)* poignée *f*; *Fig* **to get to grips with sth** s'attaquer à qch **2** (*pt & pp* **-pp-**) *vt (seize)* saisir; *(hold)* empoigner; **the audience was gripped by the play** la pièce a captivé les spectateurs ▪ **gripping** *adj* passionnant

**grisly** ['grɪzlɪ] *adj (gruesome)* horrible

**gristle** ['grɪsəl] *n (in meat)* nerfs *mpl*

**grit** [grɪt] **1** *n (sand)* sable *m*; *(gravel)* gravillons *mpl* **2** (*pt & pp* **-tt-**) *vt* (**a**) *(road)* sabler (**b**) **to g. one's teeth** serrer les dents

**groan** [grəʊn] **1** *n (of pain)* gémissement *m*; *(of dissatisfaction)* grognement *m* **2** *vi (with pain)* gémir; *(complain)* grogner

**grocer** ['grəʊsə(r)] *n* épicier, -ère *mf*; **g.'s (shop)** épicerie *f* ▪ **groceries** *npl (food)* provisions *fpl* ▪ **grocery** (*pl* **-ies**) *n Am (shop)* épicerie *f*

**groin** [grɔɪn] *n* aine *f*

**groom** [gru:m] **1** *n* (**a**) *(bridegroom)* marié *m* (**b**) *(for horses)* lad *m* **2** *vt (horse)* panser; **to g. sb for sth** préparer qn pour qch

**groove** [gru:v] *n (in wood, metal)* rainure *f*; *(in record)* sillon *m*

**grope** [grəʊp] *vi* **to g. (about) for sth** chercher qch à tâtons

**gross** [grəʊs] **1** *adj* (**a**) *(total) (weight, income, profit)* brut (**b**) (**-er, -est**) *(coarse)* grossier, -ère; *(injustice)* flagrant **2** *n inv* grosse *f* **3** *vt* gagner brut ▪ **grossly** *adv (negligent)* extrêmement; *(exaggerated)* grossièrement; *(unfair)* vraiment

**grotesque** [grəʊ'tesk] *adj* grotesque

**grotto** ['grɒtəʊ] (*pl* **-oes** *or* **-os**) *n* grotte *f*

**grotty** ['grɒtɪ] (**-ier, -iest**) *adj Br Fam* minable

**ground**[1] [graʊnd] **1** *n (earth)* terre *f*, sol *m*; *(land)* terrain *m*; *(estate)* terres *fpl*; **grounds** *(gardens)* parc *m*; *Fig (reasons)* motifs *mpl*; **on the g.** *(lying, sitting)* par terre; **to gain/lose g.**

gagner/perdre du terrain; *Br* **g. floor** rez-de-chaussée *m inv*
**2** *vt (aircraft)* interdire de vol ■ **grounding** *n (basic knowledge)* bases *fpl* (**in** de) ■ **groundless** *adj* sans fondement ■ **groundsheet** *n* tapis *m* de sol ■ **groundwork** *n* travail *m* préparatoire

**ground²** [graʊnd] **1** *pt & pp of* **grind 2** *adj (coffee)* moulu; *Am* **g. meat** viande *f* hachée **3** *npl* **(coffee) grounds** marc *m* (de café)

**group** [gru:p] **1** *n* groupe *m* **2** *vt* **to g. (together)** grouper **3** *vi* se grouper ■ **grouping** *n (group)* groupe *m*

**grovel** ['grɒvəl] (*Br* **-ll-**, *Am* **-l-**) *vi (be humble)* ramper, s'aplatir (**to** devant)

**grow** [grəʊ] **1** (*pt* **grew**, *pp* **grown**) *vt (vegetables)* cultiver; **to g. a beard** se laisser pousser la barbe **2** *vi (of person)* grandir; *(of plant, hair)* pousser; *(of economy, feeling)* croître; *(of firm, town)* se développer; *(of gap, family)* s'agrandir; **to g. to like sth** finir par aimer qch; **when I g. up** quand je serai grand; **it'll g. on you** *(of music, book)* tu finiras par t'y intéresser ■ **grower** *n (person)* cultivateur, -trice *mf* (**of** de) ■ **growing** *adj (child)* en pleine croissance; *(number, discontent)* grandissant

**growl** [graʊl] **1** *n* grognement *m* **2** *vi* grogner (**at** contre)

**grown** [grəʊn] **1** *pp of* **grow 2** *adj (man, woman)* adulte

**grown-up** ['grəʊnʌp] **1** *n* grande personne *f* **2** *adj (ideas, behaviour)* d'adulte

**growth** [grəʊθ] *n* croissance *f*; *(increase)* augmentation *f* (**in** de); *(lump)* grosseur *f* (**on** à)

**grub** [grʌb] *n* (**a**) *Fam (food)* bouffe *f* (**b**) *(insect)* larve *f*

**grubby** ['grʌbɪ] (**-ier, -iest**) *adj* sale

**grudge** [grʌdʒ] **1** *n* rancune *f*; **to have a g. against sb** garder rancune à qn **2** *vt* **to g. sb sth** *(give)* donner qch à qn à contrecœur ■ **grudgingly** *adv* à contrecœur

**gruelling** ['grʊəlɪŋ] (*Am* **grueling**) *adj (journey, experience)* épuisant

**gruesome** ['gru:səm] *adj* horrible

**gruff** [grʌf] (**-er, -est**) *adj* bourru

**grumble** ['grʌmbəl] *vi (complain)* grommeler; **to g. about sth** rouspéter contre qch

**grumpy** ['grʌmpɪ] (**-ier, -iest**) *adj* grincheux, -euse

**grunt** [grʌnt] **1** *n* grognement *m* **2** *vti* grogner

**guarantee** [gærən'ti:] **1** *n* garantie *f* **2** *vt* garantir (**against** contre); *(vouch for)* se porter garant de; **to g. sb that...** garantir à qn que...

**guard** [gɑ:d] **1** *n (supervision)* garde *f*; *(sentry)* garde *m*; *(on train)* chef *m* de train; **under g.** sous surveillance; **on one's g.** sur ses gardes; **on g. (duty)** de garde; **to catch sb off (his/her) g.** prendre qn au dépourvu **2** *vt (protect)* garder **3** *vt insep* **to g. against** *(protect oneself)* se prémunir contre; *(prevent)* empêcher; **to g. against doing sth** se garder de faire qch

**guardian** ['gɑ:dɪən] *n (of child)* tuteur, -trice *mf*; *(protector)* gardien, -enne *mf*

**guerilla, guerrilla** [gə'rɪlə] *n (person)* guérillero *m*

**guess** [ges] **1** *n (estimate)* estimation *f*; **to make** *or* **take a g.** deviner; **at a g.** à vue de nez **2** *vt* deviner (**that** que); *(suppose)* supposer, croire **3** *vi* deviner; **I g. (so)** je crois ■ **guesswork** *n* conjecture *f*; **by g.** au jugé

**guest** [gest] *n* invité, -e *mf*; *(in hotel)* client, -e *mf*; *(at meal)* convive *mf*; **g. room** chambre *f* d'amis; **g. speaker** conférencier, -ère *mf* ■ **guesthouse** *n* pension *f* de famille

**guidance** ['gaɪdəns] *n (advice)* conseils *mpl*

**guide** [gaɪd] **1** *n (person)* guide *m*; *(indication)* indication *f*; **g. (book)** guide *m*; *Br* **(Girl) G.** éclaireuse *f*; **g. dog** chien *m* d'aveugle **2** *vt (lead)* guider ■ **guided** *adj (missile)* guidé; **g. tour** visite *f* guidée ■ **guidelines** *npl* directives *fpl*

**guild** [gɪld] *n* association *f*
**guilt** [gɪlt] *n* culpabilité *f* ■ **guilty** (**-ier, -iest**) *adj* coupable; **to find sb g./not g.** déclarer qn coupable/non coupable
**guinea** ['gɪnɪ] *n* **g. pig** *(animal) & Fig* cobaye *m*
**guise** [gaɪz] *n* **under the g. of** sous l'apparence de
**guitar** [gɪ'tɑː(r)] *n* guitare *f* ■ **guitarist** *n* guitariste *mf*
**gulf** [gʌlf] *n (in sea)* golfe *m*; *(chasm)* gouffre *m* (**between** entre)
**gull** [gʌl] *n* mouette *f*
**gullible** ['gʌlɪbəl] *adj* crédule
**gulp** [gʌlp] **1** *n (of drink)* gorgée *f*; **in** *or* **at one g.** d'un coup **2** *vt* **to g. (down)** engloutir **3** *vi (with surprise)* avoir la gorge serrée
**gum**[1] [gʌm] *n (in mouth)* gencive *f*
**gum**[2] [gʌm] **1** *n* (**a**) *(glue)* colle *f* (**b**) *(for chewing)* chewing-gum *m* **2** *(pt & pp* **-mm-**) *vt* coller
**gun** [gʌn] **1** *n* pistolet *m*; *(rifle)* fusil *m*; *(firing shells)* canon *m* **2** *(pt & pp* **-nn-**) *vt sep* **to g. down** abattre ■ **gunfire** *n* coups *mpl* de feu; *(in battle)* tir *m* d'artillerie ■ **gunpowder** *n* poudre *f* à canon ■ **gunshot** *n* coup *m* de feu
**gurgle** ['gɜːgəl] *vi (of water)* gargouiller; *(of baby)* gazouiller
**gush** [gʌʃ] *vi* **to g. (out)** jaillir (**of** de)
**gust** [gʌst] **1** *n (of wind)* rafale *f* **2** *vi (of wind)* souffler par rafales
**gusto** ['gʌstəʊ] *n* **with g.** avec entrain
**gut** [gʌt] **1** *n (inside body)* intestin *m*; *Fam* **guts** *(insides)* entrailles *fpl*; *(courage)* cran *m* **2** *(pt & pp* **-tt-**) *vt (of fire)* ravager
**gutter** ['gʌtə(r)] *n (on roof)* gouttière *f*; *(in street)* caniveau *m* ■ **guttering** *n* gouttières *fpl*
**guy** [gaɪ] *n Fam (man)* type *m*
**guzzle** ['gʌzəl] *vt (eat)* engloutir; *(drink)* siffler
**gym** [dʒɪm] *n (activity)* gym *f*; *(gymnasium)* gymnase *m*; **g. shoes** chaussures *fpl* de gym ■ **gymnasium** [-'neɪzɪəm] *n* gymnase *m* ■ **gymnastics** *n* gymnastique *f*
**gynaecologist** [gaɪnɪ'kɒlədʒɪst] (*Am* **gynecologist**) *n* gynécologue *mf*
**gypsy** ['dʒɪpsɪ] *n* = **gipsy**
**gyrate** [dʒaɪ'reɪt] *vi* tournoyer

# Hh

**H, h** [eɪtʃ] *n (letter)* H, h *m inv*; **H bomb** bombe *f* H

**habit** ['hæbɪt] *n* (**a**) *(custom, practice)* habitude *f*; **to be in/get into the h. of doing sth** avoir/prendre l'habitude de faire qch; **to make a h. of doing sth** avoir pour habitude de faire qch (**b**) *Fam (addiction)* accoutumance *f* (**c**) *(of monk, nun)* habit *m*

**habitat** ['hæbɪtæt] *n (of animal, plant)* habitat *m*

**habitual** [hə'bɪtʃʊəl] *adj* habituel, -elle; *(smoker, drunk)* invétéré

**hack** [hæk] *vt (cut)* tailler

**hacker** ['hækə(r)] *n Comptr* pirate *m* informatique

**hackneyed** ['hæknɪd] *adj (saying)* rebattu

**had** [hæd] *pt & pp of* **have**

**haemorrhage** ['hemərɪdʒ] (*Am* **hemorrhage**) *n* hémorragie *f*

**haemorrhoids** ['hemərɔɪdz] (*Am* **hemorrhoids**) *npl Med* hémorroïdes *fpl*

**hag** [hæg] *n Pej* **(old) h.** vieille taupe *f*

**haggard** ['hægəd] *adj* hâve

**haggle** ['hægəl] *vi* marchander; **to h. over the price of sth** chicaner sur le prix de qch ▪ **haggling** *n* marchandage *m*

**Hague** [heɪg] *n* **The H.** La Haye

**hail¹** [heɪl] **1** *n* grêle *f* **2** *vi* **it's hailing** il grêle

**hail²** [heɪl] **1** *vt (greet)* saluer (**as** comme); *(taxi)* héler **2** *vt insep* **to h. from** *(of person)* être originaire de

**hair** [heə(r)] *n (on head)* cheveux *mpl*; *(on body, of animal)* poils *mpl*; **a h.** *(on head)* un cheveu; *(on body, of animal)* un poil; **by a h.'s breadth** de justesse ▪ **hairbrush** *n* brosse *f* à cheveux ▪ **haircut** *n* coupe *f* de cheveux; **to have a h.** se faire couper les cheveux ▪ **hairdo** (*pl* **-dos**) *n Fam* coiffure *f* ▪ **hairdresser** *n* coiffeur, -euse *mf* ▪ **hairdryer** *n* sèche-cheveux *m inv* ▪ **hairgrip** *n* pince *f* à cheveux ▪ **hairnet** *n* résille *f* ▪ **hairpin** *n* épingle *f* à cheveux; **h. bend** *(in road)* virage *m* en épingle à cheveux ▪ **hairspray** *n* laque *f* ▪ **hairstyle** *n* coiffure *f*

**-haired** [heəd] *suff* **long-/red-h.** aux cheveux longs/roux

**hairy** ['heərɪ] (**-ier, -iest**) *adj (person, animal, body)* poilu

**half** [hɑːf] **1** (*pl* **halves**) *n* moitié *f*; *(part of match)* mi-temps *f*; *Br (half fare)* demi-tarif *m*; *Br (beer)* demi *m*; **h. (of) the apple** la moitié de la pomme; **h. past one** une heure et demie; **ten and a h.** dix et demi; **h. a dozen** une demi-douzaine; **to cut in h.** couper en deux

**2** *adj* demi; **h. board** demi-pension *f*; **h. fare** demi-tarif *m*; **at h. price** à moitié prix

**3** *adv (dressed, full, asleep)* à moitié; **h. as much as** moitié moins que ▪ **half-caste** *n* métis, -isse *mf* ▪ **half-day** *n* demi-journée *f* ▪ **half-hearted** *adj (person, manner)* peu enthousiaste ▪ **half-hour** *n* demi-heure *f* ▪ **half-light** *n* demi-jour *m* ▪ **half-open** *adj* entrouvert ▪ **half-price** *adj & adv* à moitié prix ▪ **half-term** *n Br Sch* congé *m* de milieu de trimestre

▪ **half-time** *n (in game)* mi-temps *f* ▪ **halfway** *adv (between places)* à mi-chemin (**between** entre)

**hall** [hɔːl] *n (room)* salle *f*; *(entrance room)* entrée *f*; *(of hotel)* hall *m*; *(mansion)* manoir *m*; *Br Univ* **h. of residence** résidence *f* universitaire

**hallelujah** [hælɪ'luːjə] *n & exclam* alléluia *(m)*

**hallo** [hə'ləʊ] *exclam* = **hello**

**Hallowe'en** [hæləʊ'iːn] *n* = veille de la Toussaint durant laquelle les enfants se déguisent en fantôme ou en sorcière

**hallucination** [həluːsɪ'neɪʃən] *n* hallucination *f*

**hallway** ['hɔːlweɪ] *n* entrée *f*

**halo** ['heɪləʊ] (*pl* **-oes** *or* **-os**) *n* auréole *f*

**halt** [hɔːlt] **1** *n* halte *f*; **to come to a h.** s'arrêter **2** *exclam* halte! **3** *vt* arrêter **4** *vi (of soldiers)* faire halte; *(of production)* s'arrêter

**halve** [hɑːv] *vt (reduce by half)* réduire de moitié; *(divide in two)* diviser en deux

**ham** [hæm] *n (meat)* jambon *m*; **h. and eggs** œufs *mpl* au jambon

**hamburger** ['hæmbɜːgə(r)] *n* hamburger *m*

**hammer** ['hæmə(r)] **1** *n* marteau *m* **2** *vt (nail)* enfoncer (**into** dans); *(metal)* marteler; *Fam (defeat)* écraser; **to h. sth out** *(agreement, plan)* mettre au point qch

**hammock** ['hæmək] *n* hamac *m*

**hamper** ['hæmpə(r)] **1** *n Br (for food)* panier *m*; *Am (laundry basket)* panier *m* à linge **2** *vt (hinder)* gêner

**hamster** ['hæmstə(r)] *n* hamster *m*

**hand¹** [hænd] **1** *n* (**a**) *(part of the body)* main *f*; **to hold sth in one's h.** tenir qch à la main; **to hold hands** se tenir par la main; **by h.** *(make, sew)* à la main; **on the one h....** d'une part...; **on the other h....** d'autre part...; **to lend sb a (helping) h.** donner un coup de main à qn; **to get out of h.** *(of child)* devenir impossible; *(of situation)* devenir incontrôlable; **h. in h.** la main dans la main (**b**) *(of clock)* aiguille *f*; *(in card game)* jeu *m*; *(style of writing)* écriture *f*

**2** *adj (luggage, grenade)* à main; *(cream, lotion)* pour les mains ▪ **handbag** *n* sac *m* à main ▪ **handball** *n* handball *m* ▪ **handbook** *n (manual)* manuel *m*; *(guide)* guide *m* ▪ **handbrake** *n* frein *m* à main ▪ **handmade** *adj* fait à la main ▪ **handshake** *n* poignée *f* de main ▪ **hands-on** *adj (experience)* pratique ▪ **handwriting** *n* écriture *f* ▪ **handwritten** *adj* écrit à la main

**hand²** [hænd] *vt (give)* donner (**to** à); **to h. sth in** remettre qch; **to h. sth out** distribuer qch; **to h. sth over** remettre qch; **to h. sth round** faire circuler qch

**handful** ['hændfʊl] *n (bunch, group)* poignée *f*

**handicap** ['hændɪkæp] **1** *n (disadvantage, in sport)* handicap *m* **2** (*pt & pp* **-pp-**) *vt* handicaper ▪ **handicapped** *adj (disabled)* handicapé

**handicraft** ['hændɪkrɑːft] *n (skill)* artisanat *m*

**handkerchief** ['hæŋkətʃɪf] (*pl* **-chiefs**) *n* mouchoir *m*

**handle** ['hændəl] **1** *n (of door)* poignée *f*; *(of knife)* manche *m*; *(of cup)* anse *f*; *(of saucepan)* queue *f* **2** *vt (manipulate)* manier; *(touch)* toucher à; *(deal with)* s'occuper de; *(vehicle)* manœuvrer; *(difficult child)* s'y prendre avec

**handout** ['hændaʊt] *n (leaflet)* prospectus *m*; *(money)* aumône *f*

**handsome** ['hænsəm] *adj (person, building)* beau (*f* belle); *(profit, sum)* considérable ▪ **handsomely** *adv (generously)* généreusement

**handy** ['hændɪ] (**-ier, -iest**) *adj (convenient)* commode; *(useful)* pratique; *(skilful)* habile (**at doing** à faire); **to come in h.** être utile; **the flat is h. for the shops** l'appartement est près des commerces ▪ **handyman** (*pl* **-men**) *n* homme *m* à tout faire

**hang[1]** [hæŋ] **1** *n Fam* **to get the h. of sth** piger qch **2** (*pt & pp* **hung**) *vt* suspendre (**on/from** à); *(on hook)* accrocher (**on** *or* **from** à); *(wallpaper)* poser **3** *vi (dangle)* pendre ▪ **hanging** *adj* suspendu (**from** à); **h. on the wall** accroché au mur ▪ **hang-up** *n Fam* complexe *m*

▸**hang about, hang around** *vi (loiter)* traîner; *Fam (wait)* poireauter

▸**hang down** *vi (dangle)* pendre

▸**hang on** *vi (hold out)* tenir le coup; *Fam (wait)* patienter; **to h. on to sth** garder qch

▸**hang out 1** *vt sep (washing)* étendre **2** *vi (from pocket, box)* dépasser; *Fam (spend time)* traîner

▸**hang together** *vi (of facts)* se tenir

▸**hang up 1** *vt sep (picture)* accrocher **2** *vi (on phone)* raccrocher

**hang[2]** [hæŋ] (*pt & pp* **hanged**) *vt (criminal)* pendre (**for** pour)

**hanger** ['hæŋə(r)] *n* **(coat) h.** cintre *m*

**hang-glider** ['hæŋglaɪdə(r)] *n* Deltaplane *m* ▪ **hang-gliding** *n* vol *m* libre

**hangover** ['hæŋəʊvə(r)] *n Fam* gueule *f* de bois

**hankie, hanky** ['hæŋkɪ] (*pl* **-ies**) *n Fam* mouchoir *m*

**haphazard** [hæp'hæzəd] *adj (choice, decision)* pris au hasard

**happen** ['hæpən] *vi* arriver, se produire; **to h. to sb** arriver à qn; **do you h. to have…?** est-ce que par hasard vous avez…?

**happily** ['hæpɪlɪ] *adv* joyeusement; *(contentedly)* tranquillement; *(fortunately)* heureusement

**happiness** ['hæpɪnəs] *n* bonheur *m*

**happy** ['hæpɪ] (**-ier, -iest**) *adj* heureux, -euse (**to do** de faire; **about** de); **H. New Year!** bonne année!; **H. Christmas!** joyeux Noël!; **h. birthday!** joyeux anniversaire! ▪ **happy-go-lucky** *adj* insouciant

**harass** [*Br* 'hærəs, *Am* hə'ræs] *vt* harceler ▪ **harassment** *n* harcèlement *m*

**harbour** ['hɑːbə(r)] (*Am* **harbor**) **1** *n* port *m* **2** *vt (fugitive)* cacher; *(hope, suspicion)* nourrir

**hard** [hɑːd] (**-er, -est**) **1** *adj (not soft, severe)* dur; *(difficult)* difficile, dur; *(water)* calcaire; **to be h. on sb** être dur avec qn; **to be h. of hearing** être dur d'oreille; *Fam* **h. up** *(broke)* fauché; *Comptr* **h. disk** disque *m* dur; **h. drugs** drogues *fpl* dures; **h. shoulder** *(on motorway)* bande *f* d'arrêt d'urgence

**2** *adv (work)* dur; *(pull, push, hit)* fort; *(study)* assidûment; *(rain)* à verse; **to think h.** réfléchir bien; **to try h.** faire de son mieux; **h. at work** en plein travail ▪ **hardback** *n* livre *m* relié ▪ **hardboard** *n* aggloméré *m* ▪ **hard-boiled** *adj (egg)* dur ▪ **hard-earned** *adj (money)* durement gagné; *(rest)* bien mérité ▪ **hard-wearing** *adj* résistant ▪ **hard-working** *adj* travailleur, -euse

**harden** ['hɑːdən] **1** *vt* endurcir; **to become hardened to sth** s'endurcir à qch **2** *vi (of substance, attitude)* durcir

**hardly** ['hɑːdlɪ] *adv* à peine; **I had h. arrived when…** j'étais à peine arrivé que…; **h. anyone/anything** presque personne/rien; **h. ever** presque jamais

**hardware** ['hɑːdweə(r)] *n inv* quincaillerie *f*; *Comptr & Mil* matériel *m*

**hardy** ['hɑːdɪ] (**-ier, -iest**) *adj* résistant

**hare** [heə(r)] *n* lièvre *m*

**harm** [hɑːm] **1** *n (hurt)* mal *m*; *(wrong)* tort *m*; **to do sb h.** faire du mal à qn **2** *vt (physically)* faire du mal à; *(health, interests, cause)* nuire à; *(object)* abîmer ▪ **harmful** *adj (influence)* néfaste; *(substance)* nocif, -ive ▪ **harmless** *adj (person)* inoffensif, -ive; *(hobby, joke)* innocent

**harmonica** [hɑː'mɒnɪkə] *n* harmonica *m*

**harmonious** [hɑː'məʊnɪəs] *adj* harmonieux, -euse

**harmonize** ['hɑːmənaɪz] **1** *vt* harmoniser **2** *vi* s'harmoniser

**harmony** ['hɑːmənɪ] (*pl* **-ies**) *n* harmonie *f*

**harness** ['hɑːnɪs] **1** *n (for horse, baby)* harnais *m* **2** *vt (horse)* harnacher; *Fig (resources)* exploiter

**harp** [hɑːp] **1** *n* harpe *f* **2** *vi Fam* **to h. on about sth** revenir sans arrêt sur qch

**harrowing** ['hærəʊɪŋ] *adj (story)* poignant; *(experience)* très éprouvant

**harsh** [hɑːʃ] (**-er, -est**) *adj (person, treatment)* dur; *(winter, climate)* rude; *(sound, voice)* strident; *(light)* cru; **to be h. with sb** être dur envers qn

**harvest** ['hɑːvɪst] **1** *n* moisson *f*; *(of fruit)* récolte *f* **2** *vt* moissonner; *(fruit)* récolter

**has** [hæz] *see* **have**

**has-been** ['hæzbiːn] *n Fam Pej* has been *mf inv*

**hashish** ['hæʃiːʃ] *n* haschisch *m*

**hassle** ['hæsəl] *n Fam* embêtements *mpl*

**haste** [heɪst] *n* hâte *f*; **in h.** à la hâte; **to make h.** se hâter

**hasten** ['heɪsən] **1** *vt* hâter **2** *vi* se hâter (**to do** de faire)

**hasty** ['heɪstɪ] (**-ier, -iest**) *adj (departure)* précipité; *(visit)* rapide; *(decision)* hâtif, -ive ■ **hastily** *adv (write, prepare)* hâtivement; *(say)* précipitamment

**hat** [hæt] *n* chapeau *m*; *(of child)* bonnet *m*

**hatch** [hætʃ] **1** *n Br (in kitchen)* passe-plat *m* **2** *vt* faire éclore; *Fig (plot)* tramer **3** *vi (of chick, egg)* éclore

**hatchback** ['hætʃbæk] *n (car) (three-door)* trois-portes *f inv*; *(five-door)* cinq-portes *f inv*

**hate** [heɪt] **1** *n* haine *f* **2** *vt* haïr, détester; **to h. doing** *or* **to do sth** détester faire qch ■ **hateful** *adj* odieux, -euse

**hatred** ['heɪtrɪd] *n* haine *f*

**haughty** ['hɔːtɪ] (**-ier, -iest**) *adj* hautain

**haul** [hɔːl] **1** *n (fish caught)* prise *f*; *(of thief)* butin *m*; **a long h.** *(trip)* un long voyage **2** *vt (pull)* tirer

**haunt** [hɔːnt] **1** *n (place)* lieu *m* de rendez-vous; *(of criminal)* repaire *m* **2** *vt* hanter ■ **haunted** *adj (house)* hanté

**HAVE** [hæv] **1** (*3rd person sing present tense* **has,** *pt & pp* **had,** *pres p* **having**) *vt* avoir; *(meal, bath, lesson)* prendre; **he has (got) a big house** il a une grande maison; **she doesn't h.** *or* **hasn't got a car** elle n'a pas de voiture; **to h. a drink** prendre un verre; **to h. a walk/dream** faire une promenade/un rêve; **to h. a wash** se laver; **to h. a pleasant holiday** passer d'agréables vacances; **to h. flu** avoir la grippe; **will you h. some tea?** est-ce que tu veux du thé?; **to let sb h. sth** donner qch à qn; *Fam* **you've had it!** tu es fichu!; *Fam* **I've been had** *(cheated)* je me suis fait avoir; **to h. gloves/a dress on** porter des gants/une robe; **to h. sb over** *or* **round** inviter qn chez soi

**2** *v aux* avoir; *(with entrer, monter, sortir etc & pronominal verbs)* être; **to h. decided** avoir décidé; **to h. gone** être allé; **to h. cut oneself** s'être coupé; **she has been punished** elle a été punie, on l'a punie; **I've got to go, I h. to go** je dois partir, il faut que je parte; **I don't h. to go** je ne suis pas obligé de partir; **to h. sb do sth** faire faire qch à qn; **to h. one's hair cut** se faire couper les cheveux; **he's had his suitcase brought up** il a fait monter sa valise; **I've had my car stolen** on m'a volé mon auto; **I've been doing it for months** je le fais depuis des mois; **you h. told him, haven't you?** tu le lui as dit, n'est-ce pas?; **you've seen this film before – no I haven't!** tu as déjà vu ce film – mais non!; **you haven't done the dishes – yes I h.!** tu n'as pas fait la vaisselle – mais si, je l'ai faite!; **after he had eaten** *or* **after having eaten, he left** après avoir mangé, il partit

▸ **have on** *vt sep* (**a**) *(be wearing)* porter (**b**) *Br Fam (fool)* **to h. sb on** faire marcher qn (**c**) *(have arranged)* **to h. a lot on** avoir beaucoup à faire; **to h. nothing on** n'avoir rien de prévu

▸ **have out** *vt sep* (**a**) *(have removed)* **to h. a tooth out** se faire arracher une dent (**b**) *(resolve)* **to h. it out with sb** s'expliquer avec qn

---

**haven** ['heɪvən] *n* refuge *m*
**haven't** ['hævənt] = **have not**
**havoc** ['hævək] *n* ravages *mpl*; **to wreak** *or* **cause h.** faire des ravages
**hawk** [hɔ:k] *n* faucon *m*
**hay** [heɪ] *n* foin *m* ▪ **hayfever** *n* rhume *m* des foins ▪ **haystack** *n* meule *f* de foin
**haywire** ['heɪwaɪə(r)] *adj* **to go h.** *(of machine)* se détraquer; *(of plan)* mal tourner
**hazard** ['hæzəd] **1** *n* risque *m*; *Br Aut* **h. (warning) lights** feux *mpl* de détresse **2** *vt (remark)* risquer ▪ **hazardous** *adj* dangereux, -euse
**haze** [heɪz] *n* brume *f*
**hazelnut** ['heɪzəlnʌt] *n* noisette *f*
**hazy** ['heɪzɪ] (**-ier, -iest**) *adj (weather)* brumeux, -euse; *(photo, idea)* flou
**he** [hi:] **1** *pron* il; *(stressed)* lui; **he's a happy man** c'est un homme heureux; **he and I** lui et moi **2** *n Fam* **it's a he** *(baby)* c'est un garçon
**head** [hed] **1** *n (of person, hammer)* tête *f*; *(leader)* chef *m*; *Br (of school)* directeur, -trice *mf*; *(of bed)* chevet *m*, tête *f*; **h. of hair** chevelure *f*; **h. of state** chef *m* d'État; **h. first** la tête la première; **at the h. of** *(in charge of)* à la tête de; **it didn't enter my h.** ça ne m'est pas venu à l'esprit (**that** que); **heads or tails?** pile ou face?; **per h., a h.** *(each)* par personne
**2** *adj* **h. office** siège *m* social; **h. waiter** maître *m* d'hôtel
**3** *vt (group, firm)* être à la tête de; *(list, poll)* être en tête de; **to h. sb off** détourner qn de son chemin; **to h. sth off** éviter qch
**4** *vi* **to h. for, to be heading for** *(place)* se diriger vers ▪ **headache** *n* mal *m* de tête; *Fig (problem)* casse-tête *m inv*; **to have a h.** avoir mal à la tête ▪ **headlamp, headlight** *n (of vehicle)* phare *m* ▪ **headline** *n (of newspaper, TV news)* titre *m* ▪ **headlong** *adv (fall)* la tête la première; *(rush)* tête baissée ▪ **headmaster** *n Br (of school)* directeur *m* ▪ **headmistress** *n Br (of school)* directrice *f* ▪ **head-on** *adv & adj* de front ▪ **headphones** *npl* écouteurs *mpl* ▪ **headquarters** *npl (of company, political party)* siège *m* (social); *(of army, police)* quartier *m* général, QG *m* ▪ **headrest** *n* appuie-tête *m inv* ▪ **headscarf** (*pl* **-scarves**) *n* foulard *m* ▪ **headstrong** *adj* têtu
**headed** ['hedɪd] *adj Br* **h. (note)paper** papier *m* à en-tête
**header** ['hedə(r)] *n (in football)* (coup *m* de) tête *f*
**heading** ['hedɪŋ] *n (of chapter, page)* titre *m*; *(of subject)* rubrique *f*; *(printed on letter)* en-tête *m*
**heady** ['hedɪ] (**-ier, -iest**) *adj (wine, perfume)* capiteux, -euse; *(atmosphere)* enivrant
**heal** [hi:l] **1** *vt (wound)* cicatriser **2** *vi* **to h. (up)** *(of wound)* cicatriser
**health** [helθ] *n* santé *f*; **in good/bad h.** en bonne/mauvaise santé; **h. food shop** *or Am* **store** magasin *m* de produits biologiques; **h. resort** station *f* climatique; *Br* **the (National) H. Service** ≃ la Sécurité sociale
**healthy** ['helθɪ] (**-ier, -iest**) *adj (person)* en bonne santé; *(food, attitude)* sain; *(appetite)* robuste
**heap** [hi:p] **1** *n* tas *m*; *Fam* **heaps of** *(money, people)* des tas de **2** *vt* entasser; **to h. sth on sb** *(praise, gifts)* couvrir qn de qch; *(insults, work)* accabler qn de qch
**hear** [hɪə(r)] (*pt & pp* **heard** [hɜ:d]) **1** *vt* entendre; *(listen to)* écouter; *(learn)* apprendre (**that** que); **I heard him come** *or* **coming** je l'ai entendu venir; **have you heard the news?** connais-tu la nouvelle?; **h., h.!** bravo!
**2** *vi* entendre; **to h. from sb** avoir des nouvelles de qn; **I've heard of him** j'ai entendu parler de lui
**hearing** ['hɪərɪŋ] *n* (**a**) *(sense)* ouïe *f*; **h. aid** audiophone *m* (**b**) *(of committee)* séance *f*; *(inquiry)* audition *f*
**hearse** [hɜ:s] *n* corbillard *m*

**heart** [hɑːt] *n* cœur *m*; **hearts** *(in card games)* cœur *m*; **(off) by h.** *(know)* par cœur; **at h.** au fond; **h. attack** crise *f* cardiaque ■ **heartache** *n* chagrin *m* ■ **heartbeat** *n* battement *m* de cœur ■ **heartbreaking** *adj* navrant ■ **heartbroken** *adj* inconsolable

**heartening** ['hɑːtənɪŋ] *adj* encourageant

**hearth** [hɑːθ] *n* foyer *m*

**hearty** ['hɑːtɪ] (**-ier, -iest**) *adj (appetite, meal)* gros (*f* grosse)

**heat** [hiːt] **1** *n* (**a**) chaleur *f*; *(heating)* chauffage *m*; *(of oven)* température *f*; **on a low h.** *(cook)* à feu doux; **h. wave** vague *f* de chaleur (**b**) *(in competition)* éliminatoire *f* **2** *vti* **to h. (up)** chauffer ■ **heated** *adj (swimming pool)* chauffé; *(argument)* animé ■ **heating** *n* chauffage *m*

**heater** ['hiːtə(r)] *n* radiateur *m*

**heath** [hiːθ] *n (land)* lande *f*

**heather** ['heðə(r)] *n* bruyère *f*

**heave** [hiːv] *vt (lift)* soulever avec effort; *(pull)* tirer fort; *Fam (throw)* balancer

**heaven** ['hevən] *n* paradis *m*, ciel *m*; *Fam* **good heavens!** mon Dieu!

**heavily** ['hevɪlɪ] *adv (walk, tax)* lourdement; *(breathe)* bruyamment; *(smoke, drink)* beaucoup; **h. in debt** lourdement endetté; **to rain h.** pleuvoir à verse; **to be h. defeated** subir une lourde défaite

**heavy** ['hevɪ] (**-ier, -iest**) *adj* lourd; *(work, cold)* gros (*f* grosse); *(blow)* violent; *(rain)* fort; *(traffic)* dense; *(timetable, schedule)* chargé; **to be a h. drinker/smoker** boire/fumer beaucoup ■ **heavyweight** *n (in boxing)* poids *m* lourd; *Fig* personnage *m* important

**Hebrew** ['hiːbruː] *n (language)* hébreu *m*

**heck** [hek] *n Fam* zut!; **a h. of a lot** des masses (**of** de)

**heckle** ['hekəl] *vt* interpeller ■ **heckling** *n* chahut *m*

**hectic** ['hektɪk] *adj (busy)* agité; *(eventful)* mouvementé

**he'd** [hiːd] = **he had, he would**

**hedge** [hedʒ] **1** *n (in garden, field)* haie *f* **2** *vi (answer evasively)* ne pas se mouiller

**hedgehog** ['hedʒhɒg] *n* hérisson *m*

**hedgerow** ['hedʒrəʊ] *n Br* haie *f*

**heed** [hiːd] **1** *n* **to pay h. to sth, to take h. of sth** tenir compte de qch **2** *vt* tenir compte de

**heel** [hiːl] *n (of foot, shoe)* talon *m*

**hefty** ['heftɪ] (**-ier, -iest**) *adj (large, heavy)* gros (*f* grosse); *(person)* costaud

**height** [haɪt] *n* hauteur *f*; *(of person)* taille *f*; *(of mountain, aircraft)* altitude *f*; **the h. of** *(success, fame, glory)* l'apogée *m* de; *(folly)* le comble de; **at the h. of** *(summer, storm)* au cœur de

**heighten** ['haɪtən] *vt (tension, interest)* augmenter

**heir** [eə(r)] *n* héritier *m*; **to be h. to sth** être l'héritier de qch ■ **heiress** *n* héritière *f* ■ **heirloom** *n* **a family h.** un objet de famille

**held** [held] *pt & pp of* **hold**

**helicopter** ['helɪkɒptə(r)] *n* hélicoptère *m* ■ **heliport** *n* héliport *m*

**hell** [hel] *n* enfer *m*; *Fam* **a h. of a lot (of)** énormément (de); *Fam* **what the h. are you doing?** qu'est-ce que tu fous?

**he'll** [hiːl] = **he will**

**hello** [hə'ləʊ] *exclam* bonjour!; *(answering phone)* allô!

**helm** [helm] *n (of ship)* barre *f*

**helmet** ['helmɪt] *n* casque *m*

**help** [help] **1** *n* aide *f*; *Br (cleaning woman)* femme *f* de ménage; *(office or shop workers)* employés, -es *mfpl*; **with the h. of sth** à l'aide de qch; **h.!** au secours!

**2** *vt* aider; **to h. sb do** *or* **to do sth** aider qn à faire qch; **to h. oneself (to sth)** se servir (de qch); **to h. sb out** aider qn; **I can't h. laughing** je ne peux pas m'empêcher de rire

**3** *vi* aider ■ **helper** *n* assistant, -e *mf* ■ **helping** *n (serving)* portion *f*

**helpful** ['helpfəl] *adj (person)* serviable; *(useful)* utile

**helpless** ['helpləs] *adj (powerless)* impuissant

**helpline** ['helplaɪn] *n* service *m* d'assistance téléphonique

**hem** [hem] **1** *n* ourlet *m* **2** *(pt & pp* **-mm-**) *vt (garment)* ourler; **to be hemmed in** *(surrounded)* être cerné (**by** de)

**hemisphere** ['hemɪsfɪə(r)] *n* hémisphère *m*

**hemorrhage** ['hemərɪdʒ] *n Am* = **haemorrhage**

**hemorrhoids** ['hemərɔɪdz] *npl Am* = **haemorrhoids**

**hen** [hen] *n* poule *f*

**hence** [hens] *adv* (**a**) *(thus)* d'où (**b**) *(from now)* **ten years h.** d'ici dix ans

**her** [hɜ:(r)] **1** *pron* la, l'; *(after prep, 'than', 'it is')* elle; **(to) h.** *(indirect)* lui; **I saw h.** je l'ai vue; **I gave it (to) h.** je le lui ai donné **2** *possessive adj* son, sa, *pl* ses

**herb** [*Br* hɜ:b, *Am* ɜ:b] *n* herbe *f* aromatique ▪ **herbal** *adj* **h. tea** tisane *f*

**herd** [hɜ:d] **1** *n* troupeau *m* **2** *vt (cattle, people)* rassembler

**here** [hɪə(r)] **1** *adv* ici; **h. it/he is** le voici; **h. she comes!** la voilà!; **h. is a good example** voici un bon exemple; **I won't be h. tomorrow** je ne serai pas là demain; **h. and there** çà et là; **h. you are!** *(take this)* tenez! **2** *exclam* **h.!** *(giving sb sth)* tenez! ▪ **hereabouts** *adv* par ici

**hereditary** [hɪ'redɪtərɪ] *adj* héréditaire

**heritage** ['herɪtɪdʒ] *n* patrimoine *m*

**hero** ['hɪərəʊ] (*pl* **-oes**) *n* héros *m* ▪ **heroic** *adj* héroïque ▪ **heroine** *n* héroïne *f*

**heroin** ['herəʊɪn] *n (drug)* héroïne *f*

**heron** ['herən] *n* héron *m*

**herring** ['herɪŋ] *n* hareng *m*

**hers** [hɜ:z] *possessive pron* le sien, la sienne, *pl* les sien(ne)s; **this hat is h.** ce chapeau est à elle *ou* est le sien; **a friend of h.** un ami à elle

**herself** [hɜ:'self] *pron* elle-même; *(reflexive)* se, s'; *(after prep)* elle; **she cut h.** elle s'est coupée

**hesitant** ['hezɪtənt] *adj* hésitant

**hesitate** ['hezɪteɪt] **1** *vt* **to h. to do sth** hésiter à faire qch **2** *vi* hésiter (**over** *or* **about** sur) ▪ **hesitation** *n* hésitation *f*

**heterosexual** [hetərə'sekʃʊəl] *adj & n* hétérosexuel, -elle *(mf)*

**hexagon** ['heksəgən] *n* hexagone *m*

**hey** [heɪ] *exclam (calling sb)* hé!, ohé!; *(expressing surprise, annoyance)* ho!

**hi** [haɪ] *exclam Fam* salut!

**hibernate** ['haɪbəneɪt] *vi* hiberner

**hiccup, hiccough** ['hɪkʌp] **1** *n* hoquet *m*; *Fig (in plan)* accroc *m*; **to have (the) hiccups** *or* **(the) hiccoughs** avoir le hoquet **2** *vi* hoqueter

**hide**[1] [haɪd] (*pt* **hid** [hɪd], *pp* **hidden** [hɪdən]) **1** *vt* cacher (**from** à) **2** *vi* **to h. (away** *or* **out)** se cacher (**from** de)

**hide**[2] [haɪd] *n (skin)* peau *f* ▪ **hide-and-seek** *n* **to play h.** jouer à cache-cache

**hideaway** ['haɪdəweɪ] *n* cachette *f*

**hideous** ['hɪdɪəs] *adj (ugly)* hideux, -euse; *(horrific)* horrible

**hide-out** ['haɪdaʊt] *n* cachette *f*

**hiding**[1] ['haɪdɪŋ] *n* **to go into h.** se cacher; **h. place** cachette *f*

**hiding**[2] ['haɪdɪŋ] *n Fam* **a good h.** *(thrashing)* une bonne raclée

**hierarchy** ['haɪərɑ:kɪ] (*pl* **-ies**) *n* hiérarchie *f*

**hi-fi** ['haɪfaɪ] **1** *n (system, equipment)* chaîne *f* hi-fi **2** *adj* hi-fi *inv*

**high** [haɪ] **1** (**-er, -est**) *adj* haut; *(speed)* grand; *(price, standards)* élevé; *(number, ideal)* grand, élevé; *(voice, tone)* aigu (*f* aiguë); *Fam (on drugs)* défoncé; **to be 5 metres h.** avoir 5 mètres de haut; **it is h. time that you went** il est grand temps que tu y ailles; **h. jump** *(sporting event)* saut *m* en hauteur; **h. school** ≃ lycée *m*; *Br* **h. street** grand-rue *f*; **h. tide** marée *f* haute
**2** *adv* **h. (up)** *(fly, throw, aim)* haut
**3** *n* **a new h., an all-time h.** *(peak)* un nouveau record ▪ **highchair** *n* chaise *f* haute ▪ **high-class** *adj (service)* de

premier ordre; *(person)* raffiné ▪ **high-powered** *adj (engine, car)* très puissant; *(job)* à hautes responsabilités ▪ **high-profile** *adj (person)* très en vue; *(campaign)* de grande envergure ▪ **high-rise** *adj Br* **h. building** tour *f* ▪ **high-speed** *adj* ultrarapide; **h. train** train *m* à grande vitesse ▪ **high-tech** *adj (appliance)* perfectionné; *(industry)* de pointe

**highbrow** ['haɪbraʊ] *adj & n* intellectuel, -elle *(mf)*

**higher** ['haɪə(r)] **1** *adj (number, speed, quality)* supérieur (**than** à); **h. education** enseignement *m* supérieur **2** *adv (fly, aim)* plus haut (**than** que)

**highlands** ['haɪləndz] *npl* régions *fpl* montagneuses

**highlight** ['haɪlaɪt] **1** *n (of visit, day)* point *m* culminant; *(of show)* clou *m*; *(in hair)* reflet *m* **2** *vt* souligner; *(with marker)* surligner

**highly** ['haɪlɪ] *adv (very)* très; *(recommend)* chaudement; **h. paid** très bien payé; **to speak h. of sb** dire beaucoup de bien de qn; *Br* **h. strung** hypersensible

**Highness** ['haɪnɪs] *n* **His/Her Royal H.** Son Altesse *f*

**highway** ['haɪweɪ] *n Am (motorway)* autoroute *f*; *Br* **H. Code** code *m* de la route

**hijack** ['haɪdʒæk] **1** *n* détournement *m* **2** *vt (plane)* détourner ▪ **hijacker** *n (of plane)* pirate *m* de l'air

**hike** [haɪk] **1** *n (walk)* randonnée *f* **2** *vi* faire de la randonnée ▪ **hiker** *n* randonneur, -euse *mf*

**hilarious** [hɪ'leərɪəs] *adj* hilarant

**hill** [hɪl] *n* colline *f*; *(slope)* pente *f* ▪ **hillside** *n* **on the h.** à flanc de coteau ▪ **hilly** (**-ier, -iest**) *adj* vallonné

**him** [hɪm] *pron* le, l'; *(after prep, 'than', 'it is')* lui; **(to) h.** *(indirect)* lui; **I saw h.** je l'ai vu; **I gave it (to) h.** je le lui ai donné

**himself** [hɪm'self] *pron* lui-même; *(reflexive)* se, s'; *(after prep)* lui; **he cut h.** il s'est coupé

**hind** [haɪnd] *adj* **h. legs** pattes *fpl* de derrière

**hinder** ['hɪndə(r)] *vt (obstruct)* gêner; *(delay)* retarder; **to h. sb from doing sth** empêcher qn de faire qch ▪ **hindrance** *n* obstacle *m*

**hindsight** ['haɪndsaɪt] *n* **with h.** avec le recul

**Hindu** ['hɪndu:] **1** *adj* hindou **2** *n* Hindou, -e *mf*

**hinge** [hɪndʒ] **1** *n* gond *m*, charnière *f* **2** *vt insep* **to h. on** *(depend on)* dépendre de

**hint** [hɪnt] **1** *n (insinuation)* allusion *f*; *(sign)* signe *m*; *(clue)* indice *m* **2** *vt* laisser entendre (**that** que) **3** *vt insep* **to h. at sb/sth** faire allusion à qn/qch

**hip** [hɪp] *n* hanche *f*

**hippie** ['hɪpɪ] *n* hippie *mf*

**hippopotamus** [hɪpə'pɒtəməs] *n* hippopotame *m*

**hire** ['haɪə(r)] **1** *n* location *f*; **for h.** à louer; *Br (sign on taxi)* 'libre'; **on h.** en location; *Br* **on h. purchase** à crédit **2** *vt (vehicle)* louer; *(worker)* engager; **to h. sth out** louer qch

**his** [hɪz] **1** *possessive pron* le sien, la sienne, *pl* les sien(ne)s; **this hat is h.** ce chapeau est à lui *ou* est le sien; **a friend of h.** un ami à lui **2** *possessive adj* son, sa, *pl* ses

**Hispanic** [hɪ'spænɪk] *Am* **1** *adj* hispano-américain **2** *n* Hispano-Américain, -e *mf*

**hiss** [hɪs] **1** *n* sifflement *m*; **hisses** *(booing)* sifflets *mpl* **2** *vti* siffler

**history** ['hɪstərɪ] (*pl* **-ies**) *n (study, events)* histoire *f*; **medical h.** antécédents *mpl* médicaux ▪ **historian** *n* historien, -enne *mf* ▪ **historic(al)** [hɪ'stɒrɪk(əl)] *adj* historique

**hit** [hɪt] **1** *n (blow)* coup *m*; *(in shooting)* tir *m* réussi; *(success)* succès *m*; *Comptr (visit to website)* hit *m*, contact *m*; **h. (song)** hit *m*

**2** (*pt & pp* **hit**, *pres p* **hitting**) *vt (beat)* frapper; *(bump into)* heurter; *(reach)* atteindre; *(affect)* toucher; *(problem, difficulty)* rencontrer; *Fam* **to h. it off**

s'entendre bien (**with sb** avec qn)

**3** *vi* frapper; **to h. back** riposter (**at** à); **to h. out at sb** *(physically)* frapper qn; *(verbally)* s'en prendre à qn; **to h. (up)on sth** *(solution, idea)* trouver qch ▪ **hit-and-run** *n* **h. driver** chauffard *m* (qui prend la fuite) ▪ **hit-or-miss** *adj (chancy, random)* aléatoire

**hitch** [hɪtʃ] **1** *n (difficulty)* problème *m* **2** *vt (fasten)* accrocher (**to** à)

**3** *vti* **to h. (a ride),** *Br* **to h. a lift** faire du stop (**to** jusqu'à) ▪ **hitchhike** *vi* faire du stop (**to** jusqu'à) ▪ **hitchhiker** *n* auto-stoppeur, -euse *mf* ▪ **hitchhiking** *n* auto-stop *m*

**HIV** [eɪtʃaɪ'viː] (*abbr* **human immunodeficiency virus**) *n (virus)* VIH *m*; **HIV positive** séropositif, -ive; **HIV negative** séronégatif, -ive

**hive** [haɪv] **1** *n* ruche *f* **2** *vt* **to h. off** *(separate)* séparer

**hoard** [hɔːd] **1** *n* réserve *f*; *(of money)* trésor *m* **2** *vt* amasser

**hoarding** ['hɔːdɪŋ] *n Br (for advertising)* panneau *m* d'affichage

**hoarse** [hɔːs] (**-er, -est**) *adj* enroué

**hoax** [həʊks] *n* canular *m*

**hob** [hɒb] *n (on stove)* plaque *f* chauffante

**hobby** ['hɒbɪ] (*pl* **-ies**) *n* passe-temps *m inv*

**hockey** ['hɒkɪ] *n* hockey *m*; *Br (field hockey)* hockey *m* sur gazon; *Am (ice hockey)* hockey *m* sur glace; **h. stick** crosse *f* de hockey

**hog** [hɒg] **1** *n (pig)* porc *m* châtré **2** (*pt & pp* **-gg-**) *vt Fam* monopoliser

**hoist** [hɔɪst] **1** *n (machine)* palan *m* **2** *vt* hisser

**HOLD** [həʊld] **1** *n (grip)* prise *f*; *(of ship)* cale *f*; *(of plane)* soute *f*; **to get h. of** *(grab)* saisir; *(contact)* joindre; *(find)* trouver; **to be on h.** *(of project)* être en suspens; **to put sb on h.** *(on phone)* mettre qn en attente

**2** (*pt & pp* **held**) *vt* tenir; *(heat, attention)* retenir; *(post)* occuper; *(record)* détenir; *(title, opinion)* avoir; *(party, exhibition)* organiser; *(ceremony)* célébrer; *(contain)* contenir; *(keep)* garder; **to h. sb prisoner** retenir qn prisonnier; **to h. one's breath** retenir son souffle; **h. the line!** *(on phone)* ne quittez pas!; **h. it!** *(stay still)* ne bouge pas!; **to be held** *(of event)* avoir lieu

**3** *vi (of nail, rope)* tenir; *(of weather)* se maintenir ▪ **hold-up** *n (attack)* hold-up *m inv*; *Br (traffic jam)* ralentissement *m*; *(delay)* retard *m*

▸ **hold back** *vt sep (restrain)* retenir; *(hide)* cacher (**from sb** à qn)

▸ **hold down** *vt sep (person on ground)* maintenir au sol; **to h. down a job** *(keep)* garder un emploi; *(occupy)* avoir un emploi

▸ **hold forth** *vi Pej (talk)* disserter

▸ **hold off 1** *vt sep (enemy)* tenir à distance **2** *vi* **if the rain holds off** s'il ne pleut pas

▸ **hold on 1** *vt sep (keep in place)* tenir en place **2** *vi (wait)* patienter; *(stand firm)* tenir bon; **h. on!** *(on phone)* ne quittez pas!; **h. on (tight)!** tenez bon!

▸ **hold on to** *vt insep (cling to)* tenir bien; *(keep)* garder

▸ **hold out 1** *vt sep (offer)* offrir; *(hand)* tendre **2** *vi (resist)* résister; *(last)* durer

▸ **hold over** *vt sep (postpone)* remettre

▸ **hold together** *vt sep (nation, group)* assurer l'union de

▸ **hold up** *vt sep (raise)* lever; *(support)* soutenir; *(delay)* retarder; *(rob)* attaquer

**holdall** ['həʊldɔːl] *n Br* fourre-tout *m inv*

**holder** ['həʊldə(r)] *n* (**a**) *(of passport, degree, post)* titulaire *mf*; *(of record, card, ticket)* détenteur, -trice *mf* (**b**) *(container)* support *m*

**hole** [həʊl] *n* trou *m*

**holiday** ['hɒlɪdeɪ] **1** *n Br* **holiday(s)** *(from work, school)* vacances *fpl*; **a h.** *(day off)* un congé; **a (public** *or* **bank) h.,** *Am* **a legal h.** un jour férié; **to be/go on h.** être/partir en vacances **2** *adj (camp, clothes)* de vacances ▪ **holidaymaker** *n Br* vacancier, -ère *mf*

**Holland** ['hɒlənd] *n* la Hollande
**hollow** ['hɒləʊ] **1** *adj* creux (*f* creuse); *(promise)* vain **2** *n* creux *m* **3** *vt* **to h. sth out** évider qch
**holly** ['hɒlɪ] *n* houx *m*
**holy** ['həʊlɪ] (**-ier, -iest**) *adj* saint; *(bread, water)* bénit; *(ground)* sacré
**homage** ['hɒmɪdʒ] *n* hommage *m*; **to pay h. to sb** rendre hommage à qn
**home**[1] [həʊm] **1** *n* maison *f*; *(country)* patrie *f*; **at h.** à la maison, chez soi; **to feel at h.** se sentir chez soi; **make yourself at h.** faites comme chez vous
**2** *adv* à la maison, chez soi; **to go** *or* **come (back) h.** rentrer chez soi
**3** *adj (cooking)* familial; *(visit, match)* à domicile; **h. address** adresse *f* personnelle; *Br* **h. help** aide *f* ménagère; *Br* **H. Office** ≃ ministère *m* de l'Intérieur; **h. owner** propriétaire *mf*; *Comptr* **h. page** page *f* d'accueil; *Br* **H. Secretary** ≃ ministre *m* de l'Intérieur; **h. team** équipe *f* qui reçoit; **h. town** ville *f* natale ▪ **homegrown** *adj (fruit, vegetables)* du jardin; *(not grown abroad)* du pays ▪ **homeland** *n* patrie *f* ▪ **homemade** *adj* (fait) maison *inv* ▪ **homesick** *adj* **to be h.** avoir le mal du pays
**home**[2] [həʊm] *vi* **to h. in on sth** se diriger automatiquement sur qch
**homeless** ['həʊmlɪs] **1** *adj* sans abri **2** *npl* **the h.** les sans-abri *mpl*
**homely** ['həʊmlɪ] (**-ier, -iest**) *adj (comfortable)* agréable et sans prétention; *Am (ugly)* sans charme
**homeward** ['həʊmwəd] **1** *adj (trip)* de retour **2** *adv* **h. bound** sur le chemin de retour
**homework** ['həʊmwɜːk] *n Sch* devoirs *mpl*
**homicide** ['hɒmɪsaɪd] *n* homicide *m*
**homosexual** [həʊmə'sekʃʊəl] *adj & n* homosexuel, -elle *(mf)*
**honest** ['ɒnɪst] *adj* honnête (**with** avec) ▪ **honestly** *adv* honnêtement ▪ **honesty** *n* honnêteté *f*
**honey** ['hʌnɪ] *n* miel *m* ▪ **honeymoon** *n* voyage *m* de noces
**honk** [hɒŋk] *vi (of driver)* klaxonner
**honorary** ['ɒnərərɪ] *adj (member)* honoraire; *(title)* honorifique
**honour** ['ɒnə(r)] (*Am* **honor**) **1** *n* honneur *m*; **in h. of** en l'honneur de; *Br Univ* **honours degree** diplôme *m* universitaire **2** *vt* honorer (**with** de)
**honourable** ['ɒnərəbəl] (*Am* **honorable**) *adj* honorable
**hood** [hʊd] *n (of coat)* capuche *f*; *(with eye-holes)* cagoule *f*; *Br (of car, pram)* capote *f*; *Am (car bonnet)* capot *m*
**hoof** [huːf] (*pl* **hoofs** [huːfs] *or* **hooves** [huːvz]) *n* sabot *m*
**hook** [hʊk] **1** *n* crochet *m*; *(on clothes)* agrafe *f*; *(for fishing)* hameçon *m*; **off the h.** *(phone)* décroché **2** *vt* **to h. (on** *or* **up)** accrocher (**to** à) ▪ **hooked** *adj (nose)* crochu; *Fam* **to be h. on sth** être accro à qch
**hook(e)y** ['hʊkɪ] *n Am Fam* **to play h.** sécher (les cours)
**hooligan** ['huːlɪgən] *n* hooligan *m*
**hoot** [huːt] *vi Br (of vehicle)* klaxonner; *(of owl)* hululer ▪ **hooter** *n Br (of vehicle)* Klaxon® *m*
**hoover**® ['huːvə(r)] *Br* **1** *n* aspirateur *m* **2** *vt (room)* passer l'aspirateur dans; *(carpet)* passer l'aspirateur sur; **to h. sth up** *(dust, crumbs)* enlever qch à l'aspirateur
**hop** [hɒp] **1** *n (leap)* saut *m* **2** (*pt & pp* **-pp-**) *vi (jump)* sautiller; *(on one leg)* sauter à cloche-pied **3** *vt Fam* **h. it!** fiche le camp!
**hope** [həʊp] **1** *n* espoir *m*
**2** *vt* **to h. to do sth** espérer faire qch; **to h. that...** espérer que...
**3** *vi* espérer; **to h. for sth** espérer qch; **I h. so/not** j'espère que oui/non ▪ **hopeful** *adj (person)* optimiste; *(situation)* encourageant; **to be h. that...** avoir bon espoir que... ▪ **hopefully** *adv (with luck)* avec un peu de chance ▪ **hopeless** ['həʊplɪs] *adj* désespéré; *Fam (useless, bad)* nul (*f* nulle) ▪ **hopelessly** *adv (lost)* complètement; *(in love)* éperdument
**horde** [hɔːd] *n* horde *f*

**horizon** [həˈraɪzən] *n* horizon *m*; **on the h.** à l'horizon ▪ **horizontal** *adj* horizontal

**hormone** [ˈhɔːməʊn] *n* hormone *f*

**horn** [hɔːn] *n (of animal)* corne *f*; *(on vehicle)* Klaxon® *m*; *(musical instrument)* cor *m*

**hornet** [ˈhɔːnɪt] *n* frelon *m*

**horoscope** [ˈhɒrəskəʊp] *n* horoscope *m*

**horrendous** [hɒˈrendəs] *adj* horrible

**horrible** [ˈhɒrəbəl] *adj* horrible

**horrid** [ˈhɒrɪd] *adj (unpleasant)* affreux, -euse; *(unkind)* méchant

**horrific** [həˈrɪfɪk] *adj* horrible

**horrify** [ˈhɒrɪfaɪ] (*pt & pp* **-ied**) *vt* horrifier

**horror** [ˈhɒrə(r)] *n* horreur *f*; **h. film** film *m* d'horreur; **h. story** histoire *f* épouvantable

**hors d'œuvre** [ɔːˈdɜːv] (*pl inv or* **hors d'œuvres**) *n* hors-d'œuvre *m inv*

**horse** [hɔːs] *n* (**a**) *(animal)* cheval *m*; **to go h. riding** faire du cheval; **h. racing** courses *fpl* (**b**) **h. chestnut** *(fruit)* marron *m* ▪ **horseback** *n* **on h.** à cheval; *Am* **to go h. riding** faire du cheval ▪ **horsepower** *n (unit)* cheval-vapeur *m* ▪ **horseradish** *n* raifort *m*

**horticulture** [ˈhɔːtɪkʌltʃə(r)] *n* horticulture *f*

**hose** [həʊz] **1** *n (pipe)* tuyau *m* **2** *vt* arroser (au jet d'eau); **to h. sth down** *(car)* laver qch au jet ▪ **hosepipe** *n Br* tuyau *m* d'arrosage

**hospitable** [hɒˈspɪtəbəl] *adj* hospitalier, -ère (**to** envers) ▪ **hospitality** [-ˈtælɪtɪ] *n* hospitalité *f*

**hospital** [ˈhɒspɪtəl] *n* hôpital *m*; **in h.**, *Am* **in the h.** à l'hôpital; **h. bed** lit *m* d'hôpital; **h. staff** personnel *m* hospitalier ▪ **hospitalize** *vt* hospitaliser

**host**[1] [həʊst] **1** *n (of guests)* hôte *m*; *(on TV or radio show)* présentateur, -trice *mf*; **h. country** pays *m* d'accueil **2** *vt (programme)* présenter

**host**[2] [həʊst] *n* **a h. of** *(many)* une foule de

**host**[3] [həʊst] *n Rel* hostie *f*

**hostage** [ˈhɒstɪdʒ] *n* otage *m*; **to take sb h.** prendre qn en otage; **to be held h.** être retenu en otage

**hostel** [ˈhɒstəl] *n* foyer *m*; **(youth) h.** auberge *f* de jeunesse

**hostess** [ˈhəʊstɪs] *n (in house, nightclub)* hôtesse *f*; **(air) h.** hôtesse *f* (de l'air)

**hostile** [*Br* ˈhɒstaɪl, *Am* ˈhɒstəl] *adj* hostile (**to** *or* **towards** à)

**hostility** [hɒsˈtɪlɪtɪ] *n* hostilité *f* (**to** *or* **towards** envers); **hostilities** *(in battle)* hostilités *fpl*

**hot**[1] [hɒt] (**hotter, hottest**) *adj* chaud; *(spice)* fort; **to be** *or* **feel h.** avoir chaud; **it's h.** il fait chaud ▪ **hotdog** *n* hot dog *m* ▪ **hotheaded** *adj* exalté ▪ **hotly** *adv* passionnément ▪ **hotplate** *n* chauffe-plat *m*; *(on stove)* plaque *f* chauffante ▪ **hot-water** *n* **h. bottle** bouillotte *f*

**hot**[2] [hɒt] (*pt & pp* **-tt-**) *vi Fam* **to h. up** *(increase)* s'intensifier; *(become dangerous or excited)* s'envenimer

**hotchpotch** [ˈhɒtʃpɒtʃ] *n Fam* fatras *m*

**hotel** [həʊˈtel] *n* hôtel *m*; **h. room/bed** chambre *f*/lit *m* d'hôtel

**hound** [haʊnd] **1** *n (dog)* chien *m* de chasse **2** *vt (pursue)* traquer; *(bother, worry)* harceler

**hour** [ˈaʊə(r)] *n* heure *f*; **half an h.** une demi-heure; **a quarter of an h.** un quart d'heure; **paid £10 an h.** payé 10 livres (de) l'heure; **10 miles an h.** 10 miles à l'heure; **h. hand** *(of watch, clock)* petite aiguille *f*

**hourly** [ˈaʊəlɪ] **1** *adj (rate, pay)* horaire **2** *adv* toutes les heures; **h. paid, paid h.** payé à l'heure

**house 1** [haʊs] (*pl* **-ses** [-zɪz]) *n* maison *f*; *Pol* **the H. of Commons/Lords** la Chambre des communes/lords; **the Houses of Parliament** le Parlement; **the H. of Representatives** la Chambre des représentants; **at/to my h.** chez moi; **on the h.** *(free of charge)* aux frais de la maison; **h. plant** plante *f* d'intérieur; **h. prices**

prix *mpl* de l'immobilier; **h. wine** vin *m* maison
2 [haʊz] *vt* loger; *(of building)* abriter ■ **houseboat** *n* péniche *f* aménagée ■ **housebound** *adj* confiné chez soi ■ **household** *n* ménage *m*; **h. chores** tâches *fpl* ménagères ■ **householder** *n (owner)* propriétaire *mf* ■ **housekeeper** *n (employee)* gouvernante *f* ■ **housekeeping** *n* ménage *m* ■ **houseproud** *adj* qui s'occupe méticuleusement de sa maison ■ **housetrained** *adj Br (dog)* propre ■ **housewarming** *n & adj* **to have a h. (party)** pendre la crémaillère ■ **housewife** *(pl* **-wives***)* *n* ménagère *f* ■ **housework** *n* ménage *m*

**housing** [haʊzɪŋ] *n* logement *m*; *(houses)* logements *mpl*; *Br* **h. estate** lotissement *m*; *(council-owned)* cité *f*

**hovel** ['hɒvəl] *n* taudis *m*

**hover** ['hɒvə(r)] *vi (of bird, aircraft)* planer; **to h. (around)** *(of person)* rôder

**hovercraft** ['hɒvəkrɑːft] *n* aéroglisseur *m*

**how** [haʊ] *adv* comment; **h. kind!** comme c'est gentil!; **h. long/high is...?** quelle est la longueur/hauteur de...?; **h. much?, h. many?** combien?; **h. much time?** combien de temps?; **h. many apples?** combien de pommes?; **h. about some coffee?** (si on prenait) du café?; **h. do you do?** *(greeting)* enchanté; *Fam* **h.'s that?, h. so?, h. come?** comment ça?

**however** [haʊ'evə(r)] **1** *adv* **h. big he may be** si grand soit-il; **h. she may do it, h. she does it** de quelque manière qu'elle le fasse; **h. did she find out?** comment a-t-elle bien pu l'apprendre? **2** *conj* cependant

**howl** [haʊl] **1** *n* hurlement *m*; **h. of laughter** éclat *m* de rire **2** *vi* hurler; *(of wind)* mugir

**HP** [eɪtʃ'piː] *(abbr* **hire purchase***)* *n Br* achat *m* à crédit

**hp** *(abbr* **horsepower***)* CV

**HQ** [eɪtʃ'kjuː] *(abbr* **headquarters***)* *n* QG *m*

**hub** [hʌb] *n (of wheel)* moyeu *m*; *Fig* centre *m* ■ **hubcap** *n (of wheel)* enjoliveur *m*

**huddle** ['hʌdəl] *vi* **to h. (together)** se blottir (les uns contre les autres)

**huff** [hʌf] *n Fam* **in a h.** *(offended)* fâché

**hug** [hʌg] **1** *n* **to give sb a h.** serrer qn (dans ses bras) **2** *(pt & pp* **-gg-***)* *vt (person)* serrer dans ses bras

**huge** [hjuːdʒ] *adj* énorme

**hull** [hʌl] *n (of ship)* coque *f*

**hullo** [hʌ'ləʊ] *exclam Br* bonjour!; *(answering phone)* allô!

**hum** [hʌm] **1** *n (of insect)* bourdonnement *m* **2** *(pt & pp* **-mm-***)* *vt (tune)* fredonner **3** *vi (of insect)* bourdonner; *(of person)* fredonner; *(of engine)* ronronner

**human** ['hjuːmən] **1** *adj* humain; **h. being** être *m* humain; **h. rights** droits *mpl* de l'homme **2** *n* être *m* humain

**humane** [hjuː'meɪn] *adj (kind)* humain

**humanity** [hjuː'mænətɪ] *n (human beings, kindness)* humanité *f*

**humble** ['hʌmbəl] **1** *adj* humble **2** *vt* humilier

**humid** ['hjuːmɪd] *adj* humide ■ **humidity** *n* humidité *f*

**humiliate** [hjuː'mɪlɪeɪt] *vt* humilier ■ **humiliation** [-'eɪʃən] *n* humiliation *f*

**humility** [hjuː'mɪlətɪ] *n* humilité *f*

**humorous** ['hjuːmərəs] *adj (book, writer)* humoristique; *(person, situation)* drôle

**humour** ['hjuːmə(r)] *(Am* **humor***)* **1** *n (fun)* humour *m* **2** *vt* **to h. sb** faire plaisir à qn

**hump** [hʌmp] *n (lump, mound in road)* bosse *f*

**hunch** [hʌntʃ] **1** *n Fam (intuition)* intuition *f* **2** *vt* **to h. one's shoulders** rentrer les épaules ■ **hunchback** *n* bossu, -e *mf*

**hundred** ['hʌndrəd] *adj & n* cent *(m)*; **a h. pages** cent pages; **two h. pages** deux cents pages; **hundreds of** des centaines de ■ **hundredth** *adj & n* centième *(mf)* ▪ **hundredweight** *n Br* = 50,8 kg, 112 livres; *Am* = 45,3 kg, 100 livres

**hung** [hʌŋ] *pt & pp of* **hang**[1]

**Hungary** ['hʌŋgərɪ] *n* la Hongrie ▪ **Hungarian** [-'geərɪən] **1** *adj* hongrois **2** *n (person)* Hongrois, -e *mf*; *(language)* hongrois *m*

**hunger** ['hʌŋgə(r)] *n* faim *f* ▪ **hungry** (**-ier, -iest**) *adj* **to be** *or* **feel h.** avoir faim; **h. for sth** avide de qch

**hunk** [hʌŋk] *n (piece)* gros morceau *m*

**hunt** [hʌnt] **1** *n (search)* recherche *f* (**for** de); *(for animals)* chasse *f* **2** *vt (animals)* chasser; *(pursue)* poursuivre; **to h. down** *(animal, fugitive)* traquer **3** *vi (kill animals)* chasser; **to h. for sth** rechercher qch ▪ **hunter** *n* chasseur *m* ▪ **hunting** *n* chasse *f*

**hurdle** ['hɜːdəl] *n (fence in race)* haie *f*; *Fig (problem)* obstacle *m*

**hurl** [hɜːl] *vt (throw)* jeter, lancer (**at** à); **to h. insults** *or* **abuse at sb** lancer des insultes à qn

**hurray** [hʊ'reɪ] *exclam* hourra!

**hurricane** [*Br* 'hʌrɪkən, *Am* 'hʌrɪkeɪn] *n* ouragan *m*

**hurried** ['hʌrɪd] *adj (decision)* précipité; *(work)* fait à la hâte; *(visit)* éclair *inv*

**hurry** ['hʌrɪ] **1** *n* hâte *f*; **in a h.** à la hâte; **to be in a h.** être pressé; **to be in a h. to do sth** avoir hâte de faire qch; **there's no h.** rien ne presse **2** (*pt & pp* **-ied**) *vt (person)* presser; *(work)* hâter **3** *vi* se dépêcher, se presser (**to do** de faire); **to h. up** se dépêcher; **to h. out** sortir à la hâte; **to h. towards sb/sth** se précipiter vers qn/qch

**hurt** [hɜːt] **1** *adj (wounded, offended)* blessé **2** *n (emotional)* blessure *f* **3** (*pt & pp* **hurt**) *vt (physically)* faire du mal à; *(causing a wound)* blesser; *(emotionally)* faire de la peine à; *(reputation, chances)* nuire à; **to h. sb's feelings** blesser qn **4** *vi* faire mal; **his arm hurts** son bras lui fait mal ▪ **hurtful** *adj (remark)* blessant

**hurtle** ['hɜːtəl] *vi* **to h. along** aller à toute vitesse

**husband** ['hʌzbənd] *n* mari *m*

**hush** [hʌʃ] **1** *n* silence *m* **2** *exclam* chut! **3** *vt (person)* faire taire; *(baby)* calmer; **to h. up** *(scandal)* étouffer ▪ **hushed** *adj (voice)* étouffé; *(silence)* profond

**husky** ['hʌskɪ] (**-ier, -iest**) *adj (voice)* rauque

**hustle** ['hʌsəl] **1** *n* **h. and bustle** effervescence *f* **2** *vt (shove, push)* **to h. sb away** emmener qn de force

**hut** [hʌt] *n* cabane *f*; *(dwelling)* hutte *f*

**hybrid** ['haɪbrɪd] *adj & n* hybride *(m)*

**hydrogen** ['haɪdrədʒən] *n Chem* hydrogène *m*

**hygiene** ['haɪdʒiːn] *n* hygiène *f* ▪ **hygienic** *adj* hygiénique

**hymn** [hɪm] *n* cantique *m*

**hype** [haɪp] *n Fam (publicity)* battage *m* publicitaire

**hyper-** ['haɪpə(r)] *pref* hyper-

**hypermarket** ['haɪpəmɑːkɪt] *n* hypermarché *m*

**hyphen** ['haɪfən] *n* trait *m* d'union ▪ **hyphenated** *adj (word)* à trait d'union

**hypnotize** ['hɪpnətaɪz] *vt* hypnotiser

**hypochondriac** [haɪpə'kɒndrɪæk] *n* hypocondriaque *mf*

**hypocrisy** [hɪ'pɒkrɪsɪ] *n* hypocrisie *f* ▪ **hypocrite** ['hɪpəkrɪt] *n* hypocrite *mf* ▪ **hypocritical** [hɪpə'krɪtɪkəl] *adj* hypocrite

**hypothesis** [haɪ'pɒθɪsɪs] (*pl* **-theses** [-θɪsiːz]) *n* hypothèse *f* ▪ **hypothetical** [haɪpə'θetɪkəl] *adj* hypothétique

**hysterical** [hɪs'terɪkəl] *adj (very upset)* qui a une crise de nerfs; *Fam (funny)* tordant ▪ **hysterics** *npl (tears)* crise *f* de nerfs; **to be in h.** avoir une crise de nerfs; *(with laughter)* être écroulé de rire

# Ii

**I**[1], **i** [aɪ] *n (letter)* I, i *m inv*
**I**[2] [aɪ] *pron* je, j'; *(stressed)* moi
**ice**[1] [aɪs] **1** *n* glace *f*; *(on road)* verglas *m*; **i. cream** glace *f*; **i. cube** glaçon *m*; **i. hockey** hockey *m* sur glace **2** *vi* **to i. over** *or* **up** *(of lake)* geler; *(of window)* se givrer ▪ **iceberg** *n* iceberg *m* ▪ **icebox** *n Am (fridge)* réfrigérateur *m*; *Br (in fridge)* freezer *m* ▪ **iced** *adj (tea, coffee)* glacé ▪ **ice-skating** *n* patinage *m* (sur glace)
**ice**[2] [aɪs] *vt Br (cake)* glacer ▪ **icing** *n Br (on cake)* glaçage *m*
**Iceland** ['aɪslənd] *n* l'Islande *f* ▪ **Icelandic** [-'lændɪk] *adj* islandais
**icicle** ['aɪsɪkəl] *n* glaçon *m (de gouttière etc)*
**icon** ['aɪkɒn] *n* icône *f*
**icy** ['aɪsɪ] (**-ier, -iest**) *adj (road)* verglacé; *(water, hands)* glacé
**ID** [aɪ'diː] *n* pièce *f* d'identité
**I'd** [aɪd] = **I had, I would**
**idea** [aɪ'dɪə] *n* idée *f*; **I have an i. that...** j'ai l'impression que...
**ideal** [aɪ'dɪəl] *adj & n* idéal *(m)*
**idealistic** [aɪdɪə'lɪstɪk] *adj* idéaliste
**ideally** [aɪ'dɪəlɪ] *adv* idéalement; **i., we should stay** l'idéal, ce serait que nous restions
**identical** [aɪ'dentɪkəl] *adj* identique (**to** *or* **with** à)
**identify** [aɪ'dentɪfaɪ] *(pt & pp* **-ied***) vt* identifier; **to i. (oneself) with** s'identifier avec ▪ **identification** [-fɪ'keɪʃən] *n* identification *f*; **to have (some) i.** *(document)* avoir une pièce d'identité
**identity** [aɪ'dentɪtɪ] *(pl* **-ies***) n* identité *f*; **i. card** carte *f* d'identité
**ideology** [aɪdɪ'ɒlədʒɪ] *(pl* **-ies***) n* idéologie *f*
**idiom** ['ɪdɪəm] *n (phrase)* expression *f* idiomatique
**idiosyncrasy** [ɪdɪə'sɪŋkrəsɪ] *(pl* **-ies***) n* particularité *f*
**idiot** ['ɪdɪət] *n* idiot, -e *mf* ▪ **idiotic** [-'ɒtɪk] *adj* idiot, bête
**idle** ['aɪdəl] **1** *adj (unoccupied)* désœuvré; *(lazy)* oisif, -ive; *(rumour)* sans fondement; **to lie i.** *(of machine)* être au repos **2** *vt* **to i. away the** *or* **one's time** passer son temps à ne rien faire **3** *vi (of engine, machine)* tourner au ralenti
**idol** ['aɪdəl] *n* idole *f* ▪ **idolize** *vt (adore)* idolâtrer
**idyllic** [aɪ'dɪlɪk] *adj* idyllique
**i.e.** [aɪ'iː] *(abbr* **id est***)* c'est-à-dire
**if** [ɪf] *conj* si; **if he comes** s'il vient; **if so** si c'est le cas; **if not** sinon; **as if** comme si; **if necessary** s'il le faut
**ignite** [ɪg'naɪt] **1** *vt* mettre le feu à **2** *vi* prendre feu ▪ **ignition** [-'nɪʃən] *n (in vehicle)* allumage *m*; **to switch on/off the i.** mettre/couper le contact; **i. key** clef *f* de contact
**ignorance** ['ɪgnərəns] *n* ignorance *f* (**of** de) ▪ **ignorant** *adj* ignorant (**of** de)
**ignore** [ɪg'nɔː(r)] *vt* ignorer
**I'll** [aɪl] = **I will, I shall**
**ill** [ɪl] **1** *adj (sick)* malade; *(bad)* mauvais; **i. will** malveillance *f* **2** *npl* **ills** maux *mpl* **3** *adv* mal ▪ **ill-advised** *adj (person)* malavisé ▪ **ill-informed** *adj* mal renseigné ▪ **ill-mannered** *adj* mal élevé

**illegal** [ɪ'li:gəl] *adj* illégal
**illegible** [ɪ'ledʒəbəl] *adj* illisible
**illegitimate** [ɪlɪ'dʒɪtɪmət] *adj* illégitime
**illicit** [ɪ'lɪsɪt] *adj* illicite
**illiterate** [ɪ'lɪtərət] *adj & n* analphabète *(mf)*
**illness** ['ɪlnɪs] *n* maladie *f*
**illogical** [ɪ'lɒdʒɪkəl] *adj* illogique
**illuminate** [ɪ'lu:mɪneɪt] *vt (monument)* illuminer; *(street, question)* éclairer
**illusion** [ɪ'lu:ʒən] *n* illusion *f* (**about** sur)
**illustrate** ['ɪləstreɪt] *vt (with pictures, examples)* illustrer (**with** de) ▪ **illustration** *n* illustration *f*
**image** ['ɪmɪdʒ] *n* image *f*; **(public) i.** *(of company)* image *f* de marque; **he's the (living** *or* **spitting** *or* **very) i. of his brother** c'est tout le portrait de son frère ▪ **imagery** *n* imagerie *f*
**imaginary** [ɪ'mædʒɪnərɪ] *adj* imaginaire
**imagination** [ɪmædʒɪ'neɪʃən] *n* imagination *f*
**imaginative** [ɪ'mædʒɪnətɪv] *adj (plan, novel)* original; *(person)* imaginatif, -ive
**imagine** [ɪ'mædʒɪn] *vt* imaginer (**that** que) ▪ **imaginable** *adj* imaginable
**imitate** ['ɪmɪteɪt] *vt* imiter ▪ **imitation** *n* imitation *f*; *Br* **i. jewellery,** *Am* **i. jewelry** faux bijoux *mpl*
**immaculate** [ɪ'mækjʊlət] *adj* impeccable
**immaterial** [ɪmə'tɪərɪəl] *adj* sans importance (**to** pour)
**immature** [ɪmə'tʃʊə(r)] *adj (person)* immature
**immediate** [ɪ'mi:dɪət] *adj* immédiat ▪ **immediately 1** *adv (at once)* tout de suite, immédiatement; **it's i. above/below** c'est juste au-dessus/en dessous **2** *conj Br (as soon as)* dès que
**immense** [ɪ'mens] *adj* immense ▪ **immensely** *adv (rich)* immensément; **to enjoy oneself i.** s'amuser énormément
**immerse** [ɪ'mɜ:s] *vt (in liquid)* plonger; *Fig* **to i. oneself in sth** se plonger dans qch ▪ **immersion** *n Br* **i. heater** chauffe-eau *m inv* électrique
**immigrate** ['ɪmɪgreɪt] *vi* immigrer ▪ **immigrant** *adj & n* immigré, -e *(mf)* ▪ **immigration** *n* immigration *f*
**imminent** ['ɪmɪnənt] *adj* imminent
**immobile** [*Br* ɪ'məʊbaɪl, *Am* ɪ'məʊbəl] *adj* immobile ▪ **immobilize** *vt* immobiliser
**immoral** [ɪ'mɒrəl] *adj* immoral
**immortal** [ɪ'mɔ:təl] *adj* immortel, -elle
**immune** [ɪ'mju:n] *adj Med (to disease)* immunisé (**to** contre); *Fig* **i. to criticism** imperméable à la critique ▪ **immunize** ['ɪmjʊnaɪz] *vt* immuniser (**against** contre)
**impact** ['ɪmpækt] *n* impact *m*; **to make an i. on sb/sth** avoir un impact sur qn/qch
**impair** [ɪm'peə(r)] *vt (sight, hearing)* diminuer, affaiblir
**impartial** [ɪm'pɑ:ʃəl] *adj* impartial
**impassable** [ɪm'pɑ:səbəl] *adj (road)* impraticable; *(river)* infranchissable
**impasse** [*Br* æm'pɑ:s, *Am* 'ɪmpæs] *n (situation)* impasse *f*
**impassive** [ɪm'pæsɪv] *adj* impassible
**impatient** [ɪm'peɪʃənt] *adj* impatient (**to do** de faire); **to get i. (with sb)** s'impatienter (contre qn)
**impeccable** [ɪm'pekəbəl] *adj (manners, person)* impeccable
**impede** [ɪm'pi:d] *vt* gêner; **to i. sb from doing** *(prevent)* empêcher qn de faire
**impediment** [ɪm'pedɪmənt] *n* obstacle *m*; **speech i.** défaut *m* d'élocution
**impending** [ɪm'pendɪŋ] *adj* imminent
**impenetrable** [ɪm'penɪtrəbəl] *adj (forest, mystery)* impénétrable
**imperative** [ɪm'perətɪv] **1** *adj* **it is i. that he should come** il faut impérativement qu'il vienne **2** *n (in grammar)* impératif *m*
**imperceptible** [ɪmpə'septəbəl] *adj* imperceptible (**to** à)

**imperfect** [ɪm'pɜːfɪkt] **1** *adj* imparfait; *(goods)* défectueux, -euse **2** *adj & n* **i. (tense)** *(in grammar)* imparfait *(m)* ▪ **imperfection** [-pə'fekʃən] *n* imperfection *f*

**imperial** [ɪm'pɪərɪəl] *adj* impérial; *Br* **i. measure** = système de mesure anglo-saxon utilisant les miles, les pints etc

**impersonal** [ɪm'pɜːsənəl] *adj* impersonnel, -elle

**impersonate** [ɪm'pɜːsəneɪt] *vt (pretend to be)* se faire passer pour; *(imitate)* imiter

**impertinent** [ɪm'pɜːtɪnənt] *adj* impertinent (**to** envers)

**impervious** [ɪm'pɜːvɪəs] *adj also Fig* imperméable (**to** à)

**impetuous** [ɪm'petjʊəs] *adj* impétueux, -euse

**impetus** ['ɪmpɪtəs] *n* impulsion *f*

**impinge** [ɪm'pɪndʒ] *vi* **to i. on sth** *(affect)* affecter qch; *(encroach on)* empiéter sur qch

**implant 1** ['ɪmplɑːnt] *n Med* implant *m* **2** [ɪm'plɑːnt] *vt Med* implanter (**in** dans); *(ideas)* inculquer (**in** à)

**implement**[1] ['ɪmplɪmənt] *n (tool)* instrument *m*; *(utensil)* ustensile *m*

**implement**[2] ['ɪmplɪment] *vt (carry out)* mettre en œuvre

**implicate** ['ɪmplɪkeɪt] *vt* impliquer (**in** dans) ▪ **implication** *n (consequence)* conséquence *f*; *(innuendo)* insinuation *f*; *(impact)* portée *f*; **by i.** implicitement

**implicit** [ɪm'plɪsɪt] *adj (implied)* implicite; *(absolute)* absolu

**implore** [ɪm'plɔː(r)] *vt* implorer (**sb to do** qn de faire)

**imply** [ɪm'plaɪ] (*pt & pp* **-ied**) *vt (insinuate)* insinuer (**that** que); *(presuppose)* supposer (**that** que); *(involve)* impliquer (**that** que) ▪ **implied** *adj* implicite

**impolite** [ɪmpə'laɪt] *adj* impoli

**import 1** ['ɪmpɔːt] *n (item, activity)* importation *f* **2** [ɪm'pɔːt] *vt (goods) & Comptr* importer (**from** de) ▪ **importer** *n* importateur, -trice *mf*

**importance** [ɪm'pɔːtəns] *n* importance *f*; **to be of i.** avoir de l'importance

**important** [ɪm'pɔːtənt] *adj* important (**to/for** pour); **it's i. that...** il est important que... *(+ subjunctive)*

**impose** [ɪm'pəʊz] **1** *vt (conditions, silence)* imposer (**on** à); *(fine, punishment)* infliger (**on sb** à qn) **2** *vi (take advantage)* s'imposer; **to i. on sb** abuser de la gentillesse de qn ▪ **imposition** [-pə'zɪʃən] *n (inconvenience)* dérangement *m*

**imposing** [ɪm'pəʊzɪŋ] *adj* imposant

**impossible** [ɪm'pɒsəbəl] **1** *adj* impossible (**to do** à faire); **it is i. (for us) to do it** il (nous) est impossible de le faire **2** *n* **to do the i.** faire l'impossible ▪ **impossibility** (*pl* **-ies**) *n* impossibilité *f*

**impostor** [ɪm'pɒstə(r)] *n* imposteur *m*

**impotent** ['ɪmpətənt] *adj* impuissant

**impound** [ɪm'paʊnd] *vt (of police)* saisir; *(vehicle)* mettre à la fourrière

**impoverished** [ɪm'pɒvərɪʃd] *adj* appauvri

**impractical** [ɪm'præktɪkəl] *adj* peu réaliste

**imprecise** [ɪmprɪ'saɪs] *adj* imprécis

**impregnate** ['ɪmpregneɪt] *vt (soak)* imprégner (**with** de)

**impress** [ɪm'pres] *vt (person)* impressionner; **to be impressed with** *or* **by sb/sth** être impressionné par qn/qch

**impression** [ɪm'preʃən] *n* impression *f*; **to be under** *or* **have the i. that...** avoir l'impression que...; **to make a good/bad i. on sb** faire une bonne/mauvaise impression à qn ▪ **impressionable** *adj (person)* impressionnable

**impressionist** [ɪm'preʃənɪst] *n (mimic)* imitateur, -trice *mf*

**impressive** [ɪm'presɪv] *adj* impressionnant

**imprint 1** ['ɪmprɪnt] *n* empreinte *f* **2** [ɪm'prɪnt] *vt* imprimer

**imprison** [ɪm'prɪzən] *vt* emprisonner

▪ **imprisonment** *n* emprisonnement *m*; **life i.** la prison à vie

**improbable** [ɪm'prɒbəbəl] *adj (unlikely)* improbable; *(unbelievable)* invraisemblable

**impromptu** [ɪm'prɒmptju:] *adj (speech, party)* improvisé

**improper** [ɪm'prɒpə(r)] *adj* (**a**) *(indecent)* indécent (**b**) *(use, purpose)* mauvais; *(behaviour)* déplacé

**improve** [ɪm'pru:v] **1** *vt* améliorer; *(technique, invention)* perfectionner; **to i. one's English** se perfectionner en anglais **2** *vi* s'améliorer; *(of business)* reprendre ▪ **improvement** *n* amélioration *f* (**in** de); *(progress)* progrès *mpl*; **to be an i. on sth** *(be better than)* être meilleur que qch

**improvise** ['ɪmprəvaɪz] *vti* improviser ▪ **improvisation** *n* improvisation *f*

**impudent** ['ɪmpjʊdənt] *adj* impudent

**impulse** ['ɪmpʌls] *n* impulsion *f*; **on i.** sur un coup de tête ▪ **impulsive** *adj (person)* impulsif, -ive

**impunity** [ɪm'pju:nɪtɪ] *n* **with i.** impunément

**impurity** [ɪm'pjʊərətɪ] (*pl* **-ies**) *n* impureté *f*

**IN** [ɪn] **1** *prep* (**a**) dans; **in the box/the school** dans la boîte/l'école; **in an hour('s time)** dans une heure; **in so far as** dans la mesure où

(**b**) à; **in school** à l'école; **in Paris** à Paris; **in the USA** aux USA; **in pencil** au crayon; **in spring** au printemps; **the woman in the red dress** la femme à la robe rouge

(**c**) en; **in summer/French** en été/français; **in Spain** en Espagne; **in May** en mai; **in 2001** en 2001; **in an hour** *(during an hour)* en une heure; **in doing sth** en faisant qch; **dressed in black** habillé en noir

(**d**) de; **in a soft voice** d'une voix douce; **the best in the class** le meilleur/la meilleure de la classe; **an increase in salary** une augmentation de salaire; **at six in the evening** à six heures du soir

(**e**) chez; **in children/animals** chez les enfants/les animaux; **in Shakespeare** chez Shakespeare

(**f**) **in the morning** le matin; **he hasn't done it in months** ça fait des mois qu'il ne l'a pas fait; **one in ten** un sur dix; **in tens** dix par dix; **in hundreds/thousands** par centaines/milliers; **in here** ici; **in there** là-dedans

**2** *adv* **to be in** *(home)* être là; *(of train)* être arrivé; *(in fashion)* être en vogue; *(in power)* être au pouvoir; **day in, day out** jour après jour; **in on a secret** au courant d'un secret; **we're in for some rain/trouble** on va avoir de la pluie/des ennuis

**3** *npl* **the ins and outs of** les moindres détails de

**in-** [ɪn] *pref* in-

**inability** [ɪnə'bɪlɪtɪ] (*pl* **-ies**) *n* incapacité *f* (**to do** de faire)

**inaccessible** [ɪnək'sesəbəl] *adj* inaccessible

**inaccurate** [ɪn'ækjʊrət] *adj* inexact

**inadequate** [ɪn'ædɪkwət] *adj (quantity)* insuffisant; *(person)* pas à la hauteur; *(work)* médiocre

**inadmissible** [ɪnəd'mɪsəbəl] *adj* inadmissible

**inadvertently** [ɪnəd'vɜ:təntlɪ] *adv* par inadvertance

**inadvisable** [ɪnəd'vaɪzəbəl] *adj* **it is i. to go out alone** il est déconseillé de sortir seul

**inanimate** [ɪn'ænɪmət] *adj* inanimé

**inappropriate** [ɪnə'prəʊprɪət] *adj (unsuitable) (place, clothes)* peu approprié; *(remark, moment)* inopportun

**inarticulate** [ɪnɑ:'tɪkjʊlət] *adj (person)* incapable de s'exprimer

**inasmuch as** [ɪnəz'mʌtʃəz] *conj (because)* dans la mesure où; *(to the extent that)* en ce sens que

**inattentive** [ɪnə'tentɪv] *adj* inattentif, -ive (**to** à)

**inaudible** [ɪn'ɔ:dɪbəl] *adj* inaudible

**inauguration** [ɪnɔ:gjʊ'reɪʃən] *n* inauguration *f*; *(of official)* investiture *f*

**inborn** [ɪn'bɔ:n] *adj* inné

**Inc** (*abbr* **Incorporated**) *Am Com* ≃ SARL

**incalculable** [ɪn'kælkjʊləbəl] *adj* incalculable

**incapable** [ɪn'keɪpəbəl] *adj* incapable (**of doing** de faire)

**incapacitate** [ɪnkə'pæsɪteɪt] *vt* rendre infirme

**incense**[1] ['ɪnsens] *n (substance)* encens *m*

**incense**[2] [ɪn'sens] *vt* rendre furieux, -euse

**incentive** [ɪn'sentɪv] *n* motivation *f*; *(payment)* prime *f*; **to give sb an i. to work** encourager qn à travailler

**incessant** [ɪn'sesənt] *adj* incessant

**incestuous** [ɪn'sestjʊəs] *adj* incestueux, -euse

**inch** [ɪntʃ] **1** *n* pouce *m (2,54 cm)*; **i. by i.** petit à petit **2** *vti* **to i. (one's way) forward** avancer tout doucement

**incident** ['ɪnsɪdənt] *n* incident *m*; *(in book, film)* épisode *m*

**incidental** [ɪnsɪ'dentəl] *adj (additional)* accessoire; **i. music** *(in film)* musique *f* ▪ **incidentally** *adv (by the way)* au fait

**incinerator** [ɪn'sɪnəreɪtə(r)] *n* incinérateur *m*

**incision** [ɪn'sɪʒən] *n* incision *f*

**incisive** [ɪn'saɪsɪv] *adj* incisif, -ive

**incite** [ɪn'saɪt] *vt* inciter (**to do** à faire)

**inclination** [ɪnklɪ'neɪʃən] *n (liking)* inclination *f*; *(desire)* envie *f* (**to do** de faire)

**incline** **1** ['ɪnklaɪn] *n (slope)* pente *f* **2** [ɪn'klaɪn] *vt (bend, tilt)* incliner; **to be inclined to do sth** *(feel desire to)* avoir bien envie de faire qch; *(tend to)* avoir tendance à faire qch **3** [in'klaɪn] *vi* **to i. to** *or* **towards sth** pencher pour qch

**include** [ɪn'klu:d] *vt (contain)* comprendre, inclure; *(in letter)* joindre; **to be included** être compris; *(on list)* être inclus ▪ **including** *prep* y compris; **not i.** sans compter; **i. service** service compris

**inclusive** [ɪn'klu:sɪv] *adj* inclus; **from the fourth to the tenth of May i.** du quatre au dix mai inclus; **to be i. of** comprendre; **i. of tax** toutes taxes comprises

**incoherent** [ɪnkəʊ'hɪərənt] *adj* incohérent

**income** ['ɪŋkʌm] *n* revenu *m* (**from** de); **private i.** rentes *fpl*; **i. tax** impôt *m* sur le revenu

**incoming** ['ɪnkʌmɪŋ] *adj (president)* nouveau (*f* nouvelle); **i. calls** *(on telephone)* appels *mpl* de l'extérieur; **i. tide** marée *f* montante

**incomparable** [ɪn'kɒmpərəbəl] *adj* incomparable

**incompatible** [ɪnkəm'pætəbəl] *adj* incompatible (**with** avec)

**incompetent** [ɪn'kɒmpɪtənt] *adj* incompétent

**incomplete** [ɪnkəm'pli:t] *adj* incomplet, -ète

**incomprehensible** [ɪnkɒmprɪ'hensəbəl] *adj* incompréhensible

**inconceivable** [ɪnkən'si:vəbəl] *adj* inconcevable

**inconclusive** [ɪnkən'klu:sɪv] *adj* peu concluant

**inconsiderate** [ɪnkən'sɪdərət] *adj (action, remark)* inconsidéré; *(person)* sans égards pour les autres

**inconsistent** [ɪnkən'sɪstənt] *adj (person)* incohérent; *(uneven)* irrégulier, -ère

**inconspicuous** [ɪnkən'spɪkjʊəs] *adj* qui passe inaperçu

**inconvenient** [ɪnkən'vi:nɪənt] *adj (moment)* mauvais; *(arrangement)* peu commode; **it's i. (for me) to...** ça me dérange de... ▪ **inconvenience** **1** *n (bother)* dérangement *m*; *(disadvantage)* inconvénient *m* **2** *vt* déranger

**incorporate** [ɪn'kɔ:pəreɪt] *vt (contain)* contenir; *(introduce)* incorporer (**into** dans)

**incorrect** [ɪnkə'rekt] *adj* incorrect

**increase** [ɪn'kri:s] **1** ['ɪnkri:s] *n* augmentation *f* (**in** *or* **of** de); **on the i.** en hausse **2** *vt* augmenter **3** *vi* augmenter; **to i. in price** augmenter ▪ **increasing** *adj* croissant ▪ **increasingly** *adv* de plus en plus

**incredible** [ɪn'kredəbəl] *adj* incroyable

**incredulous** [ɪn'kredjʊləs] *adj* incrédule

**increment** ['ɪŋkrəmənt] *n* augmentation *f*

**incriminate** [ɪn'krɪmɪneɪt] *vt* incriminer ▪ **incriminating** *adj* compromettant

**incubate** ['ɪŋkjʊbeɪt] *vt (eggs)* couver ▪ **incubator** *n (for baby)* couveuse *f*

**incur** [ɪn'kɜ:(r)] *(pt & pp* **-rr-***) vt (expenses)* encourir; *(debt)* contracter; *(criticism, anger)* s'attirer

**incurable** [ɪn'kjʊərəbəl] *adj* incurable

**indebted** [ɪn'detɪd] *adj* **i. to sb for sth/for doing sth** redevable à qn de qch/d'avoir fait qch

**indecent** [ɪn'di:sənt] *adj (obscene)* indécent

**indecisive** [ɪndɪ'saɪsɪv] *adj (person)* indécis

**indeed** [ɪn'di:d] *adv* en effet; **very good i.** vraiment très bon; **thank you very much i.!** merci infiniment!

**indefensible** [ɪndɪ'fensəbəl] *adj* indéfendable

**indefinite** [ɪn'defɪnət] *adj (duration, number)* indéterminé; *(plan)* mal défini ▪ **indefinitely** *adv* indéfiniment

**indented** [ɪn'dentɪd] *adj (edge, coastline)* découpé

**independence** [ɪndɪ'pendəns] *n* indépendance *f*

**independent** [ɪndɪ'pendənt] *adj* indépendant (**of** de); *(opinions, reports)* de sources différentes ▪ **independently** *adv* de façon indépendante; **i. of** indépendamment de

**indescribable** [ɪndɪ'skraɪbəbəl] *adj* indescriptible

**indestructible** [ɪndɪ'strʌktəbəl] *adj* indestructible

**indeterminate** [ɪndɪ'tɜ:mɪnət] *adj* indéterminé

**index** ['ɪndeks] **1** *n (in book)* index *m*; *(in library)* fichier *m*; *(number, sign)* indice *m*; **i. card** fiche *f*; **i. finger** index *m* **2** *vt (classify)* classer

**India** ['ɪndɪə] *n* l'Inde *f* ▪ **Indian 1** *adj* indien, -enne **2** *n* Indien, -enne *mf*

**indicate** ['ɪndɪkeɪt] *vt* indiquer (**that** que); **I was indicating right** *(in vehicle)* j'avais mis mon clignotant droit ▪ **indication** *n (sign)* signe *m*; *(information)* indication *f*

**indicative** [ɪn'dɪkətɪv] *adj* **to be i. of** *(symptomatic)* être symptomatique de

**indicator** ['ɪndɪkeɪtə(r)] *n (sign)* indication *f* (**of** de); *Br (in vehicle)* clignotant *m*

**indifferent** [ɪn'dɪfərənt] *adj* indifférent (**to** à); *(mediocre)* médiocre

**indigestion** [ɪndɪ'dʒestʃən] *n* troubles *mpl* digestifs; **(an attack of) i.** une indigestion

**indignant** [ɪn'dɪgnənt] *adj* indigné (**at** *or* **about** de)

**indirect** [ɪndaɪ'rekt] *adj* indirect

**indiscreet** [ɪndɪ'skri:t] *adj* indiscret, -ète

**indiscriminately** [ɪndɪ'skrɪmɪnətlɪ] *adv (at random)* au hasard; *(without discrimination)* sans discernement

**indispensable** [ɪndɪ'spensəbəl] *adj* indispensable (**to** à)

**indisputable** [ɪndɪ'spju:təbəl] *adj* incontestable

**indistinct** [ɪndɪ'stɪŋkt] *adj* indistinct

**indistinguishable** [ɪndɪ'stɪŋgwɪʃəbəl] *adj* indifférenciable (**from** de)

**individual** [ɪndɪ'vɪdʒʊəl] **1** *adj (separate, personal)* individuel, -elle; *(specific)* particulier, -ère **2** *n (person)* individu *m* ▪ **individually** *adv (separately)* individuellement

**indivisible** [ɪndɪ'vɪzəbəl] *adj* indivisible

**indoctrinate** [ɪn'dɒktrɪneɪt] *vt* endoctriner

**Indonesia** [ɪndəʊ'ni:zɪə] *n* l'Indonésie *f*

**indoor** ['ɪndɔ:(r)] *adj (games, shoes)* d'intérieur; *(swimming pool)* couvert ▪ **indoors** *adv* à l'intérieur; **to go/come i.** rentrer

**induce** [ɪn'dju:s] *vt (persuade)* persuader (**to do** de faire); *(cause)* provoquer

**indulge** [ɪn'dʌldʒ] **1** *vt (sb's wishes)* satisfaire; *(child)* gâter **2** *vi* **to i. in sth** *(ice cream, cigar)* s'offrir qch; *(hobby, vice)* s'adonner à qch ▪ **indulgent** *adj* indulgent (**to** envers)

**industrial** [ɪn'dʌstrɪəl] *adj* industriel, -elle; *Br* **to take i. action** se mettre en grève; *Br* **i. estate,** *Am* **i. park** zone *f* industrielle ▪ **industrialist** *n* industriel *m* ▪ **industrialized** *adj* industrialisé

**industrious** [ɪn'dʌstrɪəs] *adj* travailleur, -euse

**industry** ['ɪndəstrɪ] *(pl* **-ies***) n (economic sector)* industrie *f*; *(hard work)* application *f*

**inedible** [ɪn'edəbəl] *adj* immangeable

**ineffective** [ɪnɪ'fektɪv] *adj (measure)* inefficace; *(person)* incapable

**ineffectual** [ɪnɪ'fektʃʊəl] *adj (measure)* inefficace; *(person)* incompétent

**inefficient** [ɪnɪ'fɪʃənt] *adj (person, measure)* inefficace; *(machine)* peu performant

**ineligible** [ɪn'elɪdʒəbəl] *adj (candidate)* inéligible; **to be i. for sth** *(scholarship)* ne pas avoir droit à qch

**inept** [ɪ'nept] *adj (incompetent)* incompétent; *(foolish)* inepte

**inequality** [ɪnɪ'kwɒlətɪ] *(pl* **-ies***) n* inégalité *f*

**inert** [ɪ'nɜːt] *adj* inerte

**inescapable** [ɪnɪ'skeɪpəbəl] *adj (outcome)* inéluctable; *(conclusion)* incontournable

**inevitable** [ɪn'evɪtəbəl] *adj* inévitable

**inexcusable** [ɪnɪk'skjuːzəbəl] *adj* inexcusable

**inexpensive** [ɪnɪk'spensɪv] *adj* bon marché *inv*

**inexperienced** [ɪnɪks'pɪərɪənst] *adj* inexpérimenté

**inexplicable** [ɪnɪk'splɪkəbəl] *adj* inexplicable

**infallible** [ɪn'fæləbəl] *adj* infaillible

**infamous** ['ɪnfəməs] *adj (well-known)* tristement célèbre; *(crime)* infâme

**infant** ['ɪnfənt] *n* bébé *m*; *Br* **i. school** = école primaire pour enfants de cinq à sept ans

**infantry** ['ɪnfəntrɪ] *n* infanterie *f*

**infatuated** [ɪn'fætʃʊeɪtɪd] *adj* entiché (**with** de)

**infect** [ɪn'fekt] *vt (wound, person)* infecter; *(water, food)* contaminer; **to get** *or* **become infected** s'infecter ▪ **infection** *n* infection *f* ▪ **infectious** [-ʃəs] *adj (disease)* infectieux, -euse

**infer** [ɪn'fɜː(r)] *(pt & pp* **-rr-***) vt* déduire (**from** de; **that** que)

**inferior** [ɪn'fɪərɪə(r)] **1** *adj* inférieur (**to** à); *(goods, work)* de qualité inférieure **2** *n (person)* inférieur, -e *mf* ▪ **inferiority** [-rɪ'ɒrɪtɪ] *n* infériorité *f*

**infernal** [ɪn'fɜːnəl] *adj* infernal

**inferno** [ɪn'fɜːnəʊ] *(pl* **-os***) n (blaze)* brasier *m*

**infertile** [*Br* ɪn'fɜːtaɪl, *Am* ɪn'fɜːrtəl] *adj (person, land)* stérile

**infest** [ɪn'fest] *vt* infester (**with** de)

**infidelity** [ɪnfɪ'delɪtɪ] *(pl* **-ies***) n* infidélité *f*

**infiltrate** ['ɪnfɪltreɪt] **1** *vt* infiltrer **2** *vi* s'infiltrer (**into** dans)

**infinite** ['ɪnfɪnɪt] *adj* infini ▪ **infinitely** *adv* infiniment

**infinitive** [ɪn'fɪnɪtɪv] *n (in grammar)* infinitif *m*

**infinity** [ɪn'fɪnɪtɪ] *n Math & Phot* infini *m*

**infirmary** [ɪn'fɜːmərɪ] *(pl* **-ies***) n (hospital)* hôpital *m*

**inflamed** [ɪn'fleɪmd] *adj (throat, wound)* enflammé; **to become i.** s'enflammer

**inflammable** [ɪn'flæməbəl] *adj* inflammable ▪ **inflammation** [-flə'meɪʃən] *n* inflammation *f*

**inflate** [ɪn'fleɪt] *vt (balloon, prices)* gonfler ▪ **inflatable** *adj* gonflable

**inflation** [ɪn'fleɪʃən] *n Econ* inflation *f*

**inflexible** [ɪn'fleksəbəl] *adj* inflexible

**inflict** [ɪn'flɪkt] *vt (punishment, defeat)*

infliger (**on** à); *(wound, damage)* occasionner (**on** à)

**influence** ['ɪnflʊəns] **1** *n* influence *f* (**on** sur) **2** *vt* influencer ▪ **influential** [-'enʃəl] *adj* influent

**influenza** [ɪnflʊ'enzə] *n* grippe *f*

**influx** ['ɪnflʌks] *n* afflux *m* (**of** de)

**info** ['ɪnfəʊ] *n Fam* renseignements *mpl* (**on** sur)

**inform** [ɪn'fɔːm] **1** *vt* informer (**of** *or* **about** de; **that** que) **2** *vi* **to i. on sb** dénoncer qn ▪ **informed** *adj* **to keep sb i. of sth** tenir qn au courant de qch

**informal** [ɪn'fɔːməl] *adj (unaffected)* simple; *(casual)* décontracté; *(tone, language)* familier, -ère; *(unofficial)* officieux, -euse ▪ **informally** *adv (unaffectedly)* avec simplicité; *(casually)* avec décontraction; *(meet, discuss)* officieusement

**information** [ɪnfə'meɪʃən] *n (facts, news)* renseignements *mpl* (**about** *or* **on** sur); *Comptr* information *f*; **a piece of i.** un renseignement, une information; **to get some i.** se renseigner; **i. technology** informatique *f*

**informative** [ɪn'fɔːmətɪv] *adj* instructif, -ive

**infrequent** [ɪn'friːkwənt] *adj* peu fréquent

**infringe** [ɪn'frɪndʒ] **1** *vt (rule, law)* enfreindre à **2** *vt insep* **to i. upon sth** empiéter sur qch

**infuriating** [ɪn'fjʊːrɪeɪtɪŋ] *adj* exaspérant

**infusion** [ɪn'fjuːʒən] *n (drink)* infusion *f*

**ingenious** [ɪn'dʒiːnɪəs] *adj* ingénieux, -euse

**ingrained** [ɪn'greɪnd] *adj (prejudice, attitude)* enraciné; **i. dirt** crasse *f*

**ingredient** [ɪn'griːdɪənt] *n* ingrédient *m*

**inhabit** [ɪn'hæbɪt] *vt* habiter ▪ **inhabitant** *n* habitant, -e *mf*

**inhale** [ɪn'heɪl] *vt (gas, fumes)* inhaler; *(cigarette smoke)* avaler

**inherent** [ɪn'hɪərənt] *adj* inhérent (**in** à)

**inherit** [ɪn'herɪt] *vt* hériter (**from** de); *(title)* accéder à ▪ **inheritance** *n (legacy)* héritage *m*

**inhibit** [ɪn'hɪbɪt] *vt (progress, growth)* entraver; *(of person)* inhiber; **to i. sb from doing sth** empêcher qn de faire qch ▪ **inhibited** *adj (person)* inhibé ▪ **inhibition** *n* inhibition *f*

**inhospitable** [ɪnhɒ'spɪtəbəl] *adj* inhospitalier, -ère

**inhuman** [ɪn'hjuːmən] *adj* inhumain ▪ **inhumane** [-'meɪn] *adj* inhumain

**initial** [ɪ'nɪʃəl] **1** *adj* initial **2** *npl* **initials** *(letters)* initiales *fpl*; *(signature)* paraphe *m* **3** (*Br* **-ll-**, *Am* **-l-**) *vt* parapher ▪ **initially** *adv* au début, initialement

**initiate** [ɪ'nɪʃɪeɪt] *vt (reform, negotiations)* amorcer; *(attack, rumour, project)* lancer

**initiative** [ɪ'nɪʃətɪv] *n* initiative *f*

**inject** [ɪn'dʒekt] *vt* injecter (**into** dans); **to i. sth into sb, to i. sb with sth** faire une piqûre de qch à qn ▪ **injection** *n* injection *f*, piqûre *f*; **to give sb an i.** faire une piqûre à qn

**injure** ['ɪndʒə(r)] *vt (physically)* blesser; *(reputation)* nuire à; **to i. one's foot** se blesser au pied ▪ **injured 1** *adj* blessé **2** *npl* **the i.** les blessés *mpl*

**injury** ['ɪndʒərɪ] (*pl* **-ies**) *n (physical)* blessure *f*; **i. time** *(in sport)* arrêts *mpl* de jeu

**injustice** [ɪn'dʒʌstɪs] *n* injustice *f*

**ink** [ɪŋk] *n* encre *f*

**inlaid** [ɪn'leɪd] *adj (with jewels)* incrusté (**with** de); *(with wood)* marqueté

**inland 1** ['ɪnlənd, 'ɪnlænd] *adj* intérieur; *Br* **the I. Revenue** ≃ le fisc **2** [ɪn'lænd] *adv (travel)* vers l'intérieur

**in-laws** ['ɪnlɔːz] *npl* belle-famille *f*

**inlet** ['ɪnlet] *n (of sea)* crique *f*

**inmate** ['ɪnmeɪt] *n (of prison)* détenu, -e *mf*; *(of asylum)* interné, -e *mf*

**inn** [ɪn] *n* auberge *f*

**innate** [ɪ'neɪt] *adj* inné

**inner** ['ɪnə(r)] *adj* intérieur; *(feelings)* intime; **i. circle** *(of society)* initiés *mpl*; **i. city** quartiers *mpl* déshérités du centre-ville; **i. tube** chambre *f* à air ▪ **innermost** *adj* le plus profond (*f* la plus profonde); *(thoughts)* le plus secret (*f* la plus secrète)

**inning** ['ɪnɪŋ] *n (in baseball)* tour *m* de batte ▪ **innings** *n inv (in cricket)* tour *m* de batte

**innocent** ['ɪnəsənt] *adj* innocent

**innovation** [ɪnə'veɪʃən] *n* innovation *f*

**innumerable** [ɪ'nju:mərəbəl] *adj* innombrable

**inoculate** [ɪ'nɒkjʊleɪt] *vt* vacciner (**against** contre) ▪ **inoculation** *n* inoculation *f*

**inoffensive** [ɪnə'fensɪv] *adj* inoffensif, -ive

**inopportune** [ɪn'ɒpətju:n] *adj* inopportun

**in-patient** ['ɪnpeɪʃənt] *n Br* malade *mf* hospitalisé(e)

**input** ['ɪnpʊt] **1** *n (contribution)* contribution *f*; *Comptr (operation)* entrée *f*; *(data)* données *fpl* **2** (*pt & pp* **-put**) *vt Comptr (data)* entrer

**inquest** ['ɪnkwest] *n (legal investigation)* enquête *f*

**inquire** [ɪn'kwaɪə(r)] **1** *vt* demander; **to i. how to get to...** demander le chemin de... **2** *vi* se renseigner (**about** sur); **to i. after sb** demander des nouvelles de qn; **to i. into sth** faire des recherches sur qch

**inquiry** [ɪn'kwaɪərɪ] (*pl* **-ies**) *n (request for information)* demande *f* de renseignements; *(official investigation)* enquête *f*; **to make inquiries** demander des renseignements; *(of police)* enquêter

**inquisitive** [ɪn'kwɪzɪtɪv] *adj* curieux, -euse

**insane** [ɪn'seɪn] *adj* dément, fou (*f* folle); **to go i.** perdre la raison

**insatiable** [ɪn'seɪʃəbəl] *adj* insatiable

**inscribe** [ɪn'skraɪb] *vt* inscrire; *(book)* dédicacer (**to** à) ▪ **inscription** [-'skrɪpʃən] *n* inscription *f*; *(in book)* dédicace *f*

**insect** ['ɪnsekt] *n* insecte *m*; **i. repellent** anti-moustiques *m inv*

**insecure** [ɪnsɪ'kjʊə(r)] *adj (unsafe)* peu sûr; *(job, future)* précaire; *(person)* angoissé

**insemination** [ɪnsemɪ'neɪʃən] *n* **artificial i.** insémination *f* artificielle

**insensitive** [ɪn'sensɪtɪv] *adj (person)* insensible (**to** à); *(remark)* indélicat

**inseparable** [ɪn'sepərəbəl] *adj* inséparable (**from** de)

**insert** [ɪn'sɜ:t] *vt* insérer (**in** *or* **into** dans) ▪ **insertion** *n* insertion *f*

**inside 1** ['ɪnsaɪd] *adj* intérieur; *(information)* obtenu à la source; *Aut* **the i. lane** *Br* la voie de gauche, *Am* la voie de droite

**2** ['ɪn'saɪd] *n* intérieur *m*; *Fam* **insides** *(stomach)* entrailles *fpl*; **on the i.** à l'intérieur (**of** de); **i. out** *(clothes)* à l'envers; *(know, study)* à fond

**3** [ɪn'saɪd] *adv* à l'intérieur

**4** [ɪn'saɪd] *prep* à l'intérieur de, dans; *(time)* en moins de

**insider** [ɪn'saɪdə(r)] *n* initié, -e *mf*

**insidious** [ɪn'sɪdɪəs] *adj* insidieux, -euse

**insight** ['ɪnsaɪt] *n* perspicacité *f*; *(into question)* aperçu *m*

**insignificant** [ɪnsɪg'nɪfɪkənt] *adj* insignifiant

**insincere** [ɪnsɪn'sɪə(r)] *adj* peu sincère

**insinuate** [ɪn'sɪnjʊeɪt] *vt (suggest)* insinuer (**that** que)

**insipid** [ɪn'sɪpɪd] *adj* insipide

**insist** [ɪn'sɪst] **1** *vt (maintain)* soutenir (**that** que); **I i. that you come** *or* **on your coming** *(I demand it)* j'insiste pour que tu viennes **2** *vi* insister; **to i. on sth** *(demand)* exiger qch; *(assert)* affirmer qch; **to i. on doing sth** tenir à faire qch

**insistence** [ɪn'sɪstəns] *n* insistance *f* ▪ **insistent** *adj (person)* pressant; **to be i. (that)** insister (pour que + *subjunctive*)

**insolent** ['ɪnsələnt] *adj* insolent

**insoluble** [ɪn'sɒljʊbəl] *adj* insoluble

**insolvent** [ɪn'sɒlvənt] *adj (financially)* insolvable

**insomnia** [ɪn'sɒmnɪə] *n* insomnie *f*
**insomuch as** [ɪnsəʊ'mʌtʃəz] *adv* = **inasmuch as**
**inspect** [ɪn'spekt] *vt* inspecter; *(tickets)* contrôler; *(troops)* passer en revue ▪ **inspector** *n* inspecteur, -trice *mf*; *(on train)* contrôleur, -euse *mf*
**inspire** [ɪn'spaɪə(r)] *vt* inspirer; **to i. sb to do sth** pousser qn à faire qch ▪ **inspiration** [-spə'reɪʃən] *n* inspiration *f*; *(person)* source *f* d'inspiration
**instability** [ɪnstə'bɪlɪtɪ] *n* instabilité *f*
**install** [ɪn'stɔːl] (*Am* **instal**) *vt* installer
**instalment** [ɪn'stɔːlmənt] (*Am* **installment**) *n (part payment)* versement *m*; *(of serial, story)* épisode *m*; *(of publication)* fascicule *m*; **to pay by instalments** payer par versements échelonnés; *Am* **to buy on the i. plan** acheter à crédit
**instance** ['ɪnstəns] *n (example)* exemple *m*; *(case)* cas *m*; **for i.** par exemple; **in this i.** dans le cas présent
**instant** ['ɪnstənt] **1** *adj* immédiat; **i. coffee** café *m* instantané **2** *n (moment)* instant *m*; **this (very) i.** *(at once)* à l'instant; **the i. that I saw her** dès que je l'ai vue ▪ **instantly** *adv* immédiatement
**instantaneous** [ɪnstən'teɪnɪəs] *adj* instantané
**instead** [ɪn'sted] *adv (in place of sth)* à la place; *(in place of sb)* à ma/ta/*etc* place; **i. of sth** au lieu de qch; **i. of doing sth** au lieu de faire qch; **i. of him/her** à sa place
**instigate** ['ɪnstɪgeɪt] *vt* provoquer ▪ **instigator** *n* instigateur, -trice *mf*
**instil** [ɪn'stɪl] (*Am* **instill**) *(pt & pp* **-ll-***)* *vt (idea)* inculquer (**into** à); *(doubt)* instiller (**in** à)
**instinct** ['ɪnstɪŋkt] *n* instinct *m*; **by i.** d'instinct ▪ **instinctive** *adj* instinctif, -ive
**institute** ['ɪnstɪtjuːt] **1** *n* institut *m* **2** *vt (rule, practice)* instituer; *(legal inquiry)* ordonner
**institution** [ɪnstɪ'tjuːʃən] *n (organization, custom)* institution *f*; *(public, financial, religious, psychiatric)* établissement *m*
**instruct** [ɪn'strʌkt] *vt (teach)* enseigner (**sb in sth** qch à qn); **to i. sb about sth** *(inform)* instruire qn de qch; **to i. sb to do** *(order)* charger qn de faire ▪ **instruction** [-ʃən] *n (teaching, order)* instruction *f*; **instructions (for use)** mode *m* d'emploi ▪ **instructor** *n (for judo, dance)* professeur *m*; *(for skiing, swimming)* moniteur, -trice *mf*; **driving i.** moniteur, -trice *mf* d'auto-école
**instrument** ['ɪnstrəmənt] *n* instrument *m*
**instrumental** [ɪnstrə'mentəl] *adj (music)* instrumental; **to be i. in sth/in doing sth** contribuer à qch/à faire qch
**insubordinate** [ɪnsə'bɔːdɪnət] *adj* insubordonné
**insufferable** [ɪn'sʌfərəbəl] *adj* intolérable
**insufficient** [ɪnsə'fɪʃənt] *adj* insuffisant ▪ **insufficiently** *adv* insuffisamment
**insulate** ['ɪnsjʊleɪt] *vt (against cold) & El* isoler; *(against sound)* insonoriser ▪ **insulation** *n* isolation *f*; *(against sound)* insonorisation *f*; *(material)* isolant *m*
**insulin** ['ɪnsjʊlɪn] *n* insuline *f*
**insult 1** ['ɪnsʌlt] *n* insulte *f* (**to** à) **2** [ɪn'sʌlt] *vt* insulter
**insure** [ɪn'ʃʊə(r)] *vt* (**a**) *(house, car, goods)* assurer (**against** contre) (**b**) *Am* = **ensure** ▪ **insurance** *n* assurance *f*; **i. policy** police *f* d'assurance
**insurmountable** [ɪnsə'maʊntəbəl] *adj* insurmontable
**intact** [ɪn'tækt] *adj* intact
**intake** ['ɪnteɪk] *n (of food)* consommation *f*; *(of students, schoolchildren)* admissions *fpl*
**intangible** [ɪn'tændʒəbəl] *adj* intangible
**integral** ['ɪntɪgrəl] *adj* intégral; **to be**

**an i. part of sth** faire partie intégrante de qch

**integrate** ['ɪntɪgreɪt] **1** *vt* intégrer (**into** dans) **2** *vi* s'intégrer (**into** dans) ■ **integration** *n* intégration *f*; **(racial) i.** déségrégation *f* raciale

**integrity** [ɪn'tegrətɪ] *n* intégrité *f*

**intellect** ['ɪntɪlekt] *n* intelligence *f*, intellect *m* ■ **intellectual** *adj & n* intellectuel, -elle *(mf)*

**intelligence** [ɪn'telɪdʒəns] *n* intelligence *f*

**intelligent** [ɪn'telɪdʒənt] *adj* intelligent

**intelligible** [ɪn'telɪdʒəbəl] *adj* intelligible

**intend** [ɪn'tend] *vt (gift, remark)* destiner (**for** à); **to be intended to do sth** être destiné à faire qch; **to i. to do sth** avoir l'intention de faire qch ■ **intended** *adj (deliberate)* voulu; *(planned)* prévu

**intense** [ɪn'tens] *adj* intense; *(interest)* vif (*f* vive); *(person)* passionné ■ **intensely** *adv (look at)* intensément; *Fig (very)* extrêmement

**intensify** [ɪn'tensɪfaɪ] (*pt & pp* **-ied**) **1** *vt* intensifier **2** *vi* s'intensifier

**intensity** [ɪn'tensətɪ] *n* intensité *f*

**intensive** [ɪn'tensɪv] *adj* intensif, -ive; **in i. care** en réanimation

**intent** [ɪn'tent] **1** *adj (look)* intense; **to be i. on doing** être résolu à faire **2** *n* intention *f*; **to all intents and purposes** quasiment

**intention** [ɪn'tenʃən] *n* intention *f* (**of doing** de faire)

**intentional** [ɪn'tenʃənəl] *adj* intentionnel, -elle; **it wasn't i.** ce n'était pas fait exprès ■ **intentionally** *adv* intentionnellement, exprès

**inter** [ɪn'tɜː(r)] (*pt & pp* **-rr-**) *vt* enterrer

**inter-** ['ɪntə(r)] *pref* inter-

**interact** [ɪntər'ækt] *vi (of person)* communiquer (**with** avec); *(of several people)* communiquer entre eux/elles; *(of chemicals)* réagir (**with** avec)

**interactive** [ɪntə'ræktɪv] *adj Comptr* interactif, -ive

**intercept** [ɪntə'sept] *vt* intercepter

**interchange** ['ɪntətʃeɪndʒ] *n Br (on road)* échangeur *m*

**interchangeable** [ɪntə'tʃeɪndʒəbəl] *adj* interchangeable

**inter-city** [ɪntə'sɪtɪ] *adj Br* **i. train** train *m* de grandes lignes

**intercom** ['ɪntəkɒm] *n* Interphone® *m*

**interconnected** [ɪntəkə'nektɪd] *adj (facts)* lié(e)s

**intercourse** ['ɪntəkɔːs] *n (sexual)* rapports *mpl* sexuels

**interdependent** [ɪntədɪ'pendənt] *adj* interdépendant; *(parts of machine)* solidaire

**interest** ['ɪntərest, 'ɪntrɪst] **1** *n* intérêt *m*; *(hobby)* centre *m* d'intérêt; *(money)* intérêts *mpl*; **to take an i. in sb/sth** s'intéresser à qn/qch; **to lose i. in sb/sth** se désintéresser de qn/qch; **to be of i. to sb** intéresser qn **2** *vt* intéresser ■ **interested** *adj* intéressé; **to be i. in sb/sth** s'intéresser à qn/qch; **are you i.?** ça vous intéresse? ■ **interest-free** *adj (loan)* sans intérêts; *(credit)* gratuit ■ **interesting** *adj* intéressant

**interfere** [ɪntə'fɪə(r)] *vi (meddle)* se mêler (**in** de); **to i. with sth** *(hinder)* gêner qch; *(touch)* toucher à qch

**interference** [ɪntə'fɪərəns] *n* ingérence *f*; *(on television, radio)* parasites *mpl*

**interim** ['ɪntərɪm] **1** *n* **in the i.** entretemps **2** *adj (measure)* provisoire

**interior** [ɪn'tɪərɪə(r)] *adj & n* intérieur *(m)*

**interlock** [ɪntə'lɒk] *vi (of machine parts)* s'emboîter

**interlude** ['ɪntəluːd] *n (on TV)* interlude *m*; *(in theatre)* intermède *m*; *(period of time)* intervalle *m*

**intermediary** [ɪntə'miːdɪərɪ] (*pl* **-ies**) *n* intermédiaire *mf*

**intermediate** [ɪntə'miːdɪət] *adj* intermédiaire; *(course, student)* de niveau moyen

**intermission** [ɪntə'mɪʃən] *n* entracte *m*

**intermittent** [ɪntə'mɪtənt] *adj* intermittent

**intern 1** ['ɪntɜːn] *n Am Med* interne *mf* **2** [ɪn'tɜːn] *vt (imprison)* interner

**internal** [ɪn'tɜːnəl] *adj* interne; *(flight, policy)* intérieur; *Am* **the I. Revenue Service** ≃ le fisc ▪ **internally** *adv* intérieurement

**international** [ɪntə'næʃənəl] **1** *adj* international **2** *n (match)* rencontre *f* internationale; *(player)* international *m*

**Internet** ['ɪntənet] *n Comptr* **the I.** l'Internet *m*; **I. access** accès *m* (à l')Internet; **I. service provider** fournisseur *m* d'accès Internet

**interpret** [ɪn'tɜːprɪt] **1** *vt* interpréter **2** *vi (translate for people)* faire l'interprète ▪ **interpretation** *n* interprétation *f* ▪ **interpreter** *n* interprète *mf*

**interrelated** [ɪntərɪ'leɪtɪd] *adj* lié

**interrogate** [ɪn'terəgeɪt] *vt* interroger ▪ **interrogation** [-'geɪʃən] *n* interrogation *f*; *(by police)* interrogatoire *m*

**interrupt** [ɪntə'rʌpt] **1** *vt* interrompre **2** *vi* **I'm sorry to i.** je suis désolé de vous interrompre ▪ **interruption** *n* interruption *f*

**intersect** [ɪntə'sekt] **1** *vt* couper **2** *vi* se couper ▪ **intersection** *n* intersection *f*; *(of roads)* croisement *m*

**interval** ['ɪntəvəl] *n* intervalle *m*; *Br (in theatre, cinema)* entracte *m*; **at intervals** *(in time)* de temps à autre; *(in space)* par intervalles; **at five-minute intervals** toutes les cinq minutes

**intervene** [ɪntə'viːn] *vi (of person)* intervenir (**in** dans); *(of event)* survenir ▪ **intervention** [-'venʃən] *n* intervention *f*

**interview** ['ɪntəvjuː] **1** *n* entretien *m* (**with** avec); *TV & Journ* interview *m ou f* **2** *vt (for job)* faire passer un entretien à; *TV & Journ* interviewer ▪ **interviewer** *n TV* intervieweur, -euse *mf*; *(for research, in canvassing)* enquêteur, -euse *mf*

**intestine** [ɪn'testɪn] *n* intestin *m*

**intimate** ['ɪntɪmət] *adj* intime; *(friendship)* profond; *(knowledge)* approfondi ▪ **intimately** *adv* intimement

**intimidate** [ɪn'tɪmɪdeɪt] *vt* intimider

**into** ['ɪntuː, *unstressed* 'ɪntə] *prep* (**a**) dans; **to put sth i. sth** mettre qch dans qch; **to go i. a room** entrer dans une pièce

(**b**) en; **to translate i. French** traduire en français; **to change sb i. sth** changer qn en qch; **to break sth i. pieces** briser qch en morceaux; **to go i. town** aller en ville

(**c**) *Math* **three i. six goes two** six divisé par trois fait deux

(**d**) *Fam* **to be i. jazz** être branché jazz

**intolerable** [ɪn'tɒlərəbəl] *adj* intolérable (**that** que + *subjunctive*)

**intolerance** [ɪn'tɒlərəns] *n* intolérance *f* ▪ **intolerant** *adj* intolérant

**intonation** [ɪntə'neɪʃən] *n* intonation *f*

**intoxicated** [ɪn'tɒksɪkeɪtɪd] *adj* ivre

**intransigent** [ɪn'trænsɪdʒənt] *adj* intransigeant

**intransitive** [ɪn'trænsɪtɪv] *adj (in grammar)* intransitif, -ive

**intricate** ['ɪntrɪkət] *adj* compliqué

**intrigue 1** ['ɪntriːg] *n (plot)* intrigue *f* **2** [ɪn'triːg] *vt (interest)* intriguer ▪ **intriguing** *adj (news, attitude)* curieux, -euse

**introduce** [ɪntrə'djuːs] *vt (bring in, insert)* introduire (**into** dans); *(programme, subject)* présenter; **to i. sb (to sb)** présenter qn (à qn)

**introduction** [ɪntrə'dʌkʃən] *n* introduction *f*; *(of person to person)* présentation *f* ▪ **introductory** *adj (words, speech)* d'introduction; *(course)* d'initiation

**introvert** ['ɪntrəvɜːt] *n* introverti, -e *mf*

**intrude** [ɪn'truːd] *vi (of person)* déranger (**on sb** qn) ▪ **intruder** *n* intrus, -e *mf* ▪ **intrusion** *n (bother)* dérangement *m*; *(interference)* intrusion *f* (**into** dans)

**intuition** [ɪntjuː'ɪʃən] *n* intuition *f*

**inundate** ['ɪnʌndeɪt] *vt* inonder (**with** de); **inundated with work/letters** submergé de travail/lettres

**invade** [ɪn'veɪd] *vt* envahir ▪ **invader** *n* envahisseur, -euse *mf*

**invalid**[1] ['ɪnvəlɪd] *adj & n* malade *(mf)*; *(disabled person)* infirme *(mf)*

**invalid**[2] [ɪn'vælɪd] *adj (ticket, passport)* non valable ▪ **invalidate** *vt (ticket)* annuler; *(election, law)* invalider; *(theory)* infirmer

**invaluable** [ɪn'væljʊəbəl] *adj* inestimable

**invariably** [ɪn'veərɪəblɪ] *adv* invariablement

**invasion** [ɪn'veɪʒən] *n* invasion *f*

**invent** [ɪn'vent] *vt* inventer ▪ **invention** *n* invention *f* ▪ **inventor** *n* inventeur, -trice *mf*

**inventory** ['ɪnvəntərɪ] (*pl* **-ies**) *n* inventaire *m*

**invert** [ɪn'vɜːt] *vt (order)* intervertir; *(turn upside down)* renverser; *Br* **inverted commas** guillemets *mpl*

**invest** [ɪn'vest] **1** *vt (money)* investir (**in** dans); *(time, effort)* consacrer (**in** à) **2** *vi* **to i. in** *(company)* investir dans; *Fig (car)* se payer ▪ **investment** *n* investissement *m* ▪ **investor** *n (in shares)* investisseur *m*

**investigate** [ɪn'vestɪgeɪt] *vt (examine)* examiner; *(crime)* enquêter sur ▪ **investigation** *n* examen *m*, étude *f*; *(inquiry by journalist, police)* enquête *f* (**of** *or* **into** sur) ▪ **investigator** *n (detective)* enquêteur, -euse *mf*; *(private)* détective *m*

**invigilator** [ɪn'vɪdʒɪleɪtə(r)] *n Br* surveillant, -e *mf (à un examen)*

**invigorating** [ɪn'vɪgəreɪtɪŋ] *adj* vivifiant

**invincible** [ɪn'vɪnsəbəl] *adj* invincible

**invisible** [ɪn'vɪzəbəl] *adj* invisible

**invite 1** [ɪn'vaɪt] *vt* inviter (**to do** à faire); *(ask for)* demander; **to i. sb out** inviter qn (à sortir) **2** ['ɪnvaɪt] *n Fam* invit' *f* ▪ **invitation** [-vɪ'teɪʃən] *n* invitation *f*

**invoice** ['ɪnvɔɪs] **1** *n* facture *f* **2** *vt (goods)* facturer; *(person)* envoyer la facture à

**invoke** [ɪn'vəʊk] *vt* invoquer

**involuntary** [ɪn'vɒləntərɪ] *adj* involontaire

**involve** [ɪn'vɒlv] *vt (entail)* entraîner; **to i. sb in sth** impliquer qn dans qch; *(in project)* associer qn à qch; **the job involves going abroad** le poste nécessite des déplacements à l'étranger

**involved** [ɪn'vɒlvd] *adj* (**a**) **to be i. in an accident** avoir un accident; **fifty people were i. in the project** cinquante personnes ont pris part au projet; **to be i. with sb** *(emotionally)* avoir une liaison avec qn; **the factors i.** *(at stake)* les facteurs en jeu; **the person i.** *(concerned)* la personne en question (**b**) *(complicated)* compliqué

**involvement** [ɪn'vɒlvmənt] *n* participation *f* (**in** à); *(commitment)* engagement *m* (**in** dans)

**invulnerable** [ɪn'vʌlnərəbəl] *adj* invulnérable

**inward** ['ɪnwəd] **1** *adj & adv (movement, move)* vers l'intérieur **2** *adj (inner) (happiness)* intérieur; *(thoughts)* intime ▪ **inwardly** *adv (laugh, curse)* intérieurement ▪ **inwards** *adv* vers l'intérieur

**iodine** [*Br* 'aɪədiːn, *Am* 'aɪədaɪn] *n (antiseptic)* teinture *f* d'iode

**IOU** [aɪəʊ'juː] (*abbr* **I owe you**) *n* reconnaissance *f* de dette

**IQ** [aɪ'kjuː] (*abbr* **intelligence quotient**) *n* QI *m inv*

**Iran** [ɪ'rɑːn, ɪ'ræn] *n* l'Iran *m* ▪ **Iranian** [ɪ'reɪnɪən, *Am* ɪ'rɑːnɪən] **1** *adj* iranien, -enne **2** *n* Iranien, -enne *mf*

**Iraq** [ɪ'rɑːk] *n* l'Irak *m* ▪ **Iraqi 1** *adj* irakien, -enne **2** *n* Irakien, -enne *mf*

**irate** [aɪ'reɪt] *adj* furieux, -euse

**Ireland** ['aɪələnd] *n* l'Irlande *f* ▪ **Irish** ['aɪrɪʃ] **1** *adj* irlandais **2** *n (language)* irlandais *m*; **the I.** *(people)* les Irlandais *mpl* ▪ **Irishman** (*pl* **-men**) *n* Irlandais *m* ▪ **Irishwoman** (*pl* **-women**) *n* Irlandaise *f*

**iris** ['aɪərɪs] *n (plant, of eye)* iris *m*
**iron** ['aɪən] **1** *n* fer *m*; *(for clothes)* fer *m* à repasser **2** *vt (clothes)* repasser; *Fig* **to i. out difficulties** aplanir les difficultés ▪ **ironing** *n* repassage *m*; **i. board** planche *f* à repasser
**ironmonger** ['aɪənmʌŋgə(r)] *n* quincaillier, -ère *mf*; **i.'s (shop)** quincaillerie *f*
**irony** ['aɪərənɪ] *n* ironie *f* ▪ **ironic(al)** [aɪ'rɒnɪk(əl)] *adj* ironique
**irrational** [ɪ'ræʃənəl] *adj* irrationnel, -elle
**irrefutable** [ɪrɪ'fju:təbəl] *adj (evidence)* irréfutable
**irregular** [ɪ'regjʊlə(r)] *adj* irrégulier, -ère ▪ **irregularity** [-'lærɪtɪ] (*pl* **-ies**) *n* irrégularité *f*
**irrelevant** [ɪ'reləvənt] *adj* sans rapport (**to** avec); *(remark)* hors de propos; **that's i.** ça n'a rien à voir (avec la question)
**irreparable** [ɪ'repərəbəl] *adj (harm, loss)* irréparable
**irreplaceable** [ɪrɪ'pleɪsəbəl] *adj* irremplaçable
**irresistible** [ɪrɪ'zɪstəbəl] *adj (person, charm)* irrésistible
**irrespective** [ɪrɪ'spektɪv] *prep* **i. of** indépendamment de
**irresponsible** [ɪrɪ'spɒnsəbəl] *adj (act)* irréfléchi; *(person)* irresponsable
**irreverent** [ɪ'revərənt] *adj* irrévérencieux, -euse
**irreversible** [ɪrɪ'vɜ:səbəl] *adj (process)* irréversible; *(decision)* irrévocable
**irrigate** ['ɪrɪgeɪt] *vt* irriguer
**irritable** ['ɪrɪtəbəl] *adj (easily annoyed)* irritable
**irritant** ['ɪrɪtənt] *n (to eyes, skin)* irritant *m*
**irritate** ['ɪrɪteɪt] *vt (annoy, inflame)* irriter ▪ **irritating** *adj* irritant
**is** [ɪz] *see* **be**
**Islam** ['ɪzlɑ:m] *n* l'Islam *m* ▪ **Islamic** [ɪz'læmɪk] *adj* islamique
**island** ['aɪlənd] *n* île *f*; **(traffic) i.** refuge *m* (pour piétons) ▪ **islander** *n* insulaire *mf*
**isle** [aɪl] *n* île *f*
**isn't** ['ɪzənt] = **is not**
**isolate** ['aɪsəleɪt] *vt* isoler (**from** de) ▪ **isolated** *adj (remote, unique)* isolé ▪ **isolation** *n* isolement *m*; **in i.** isolément
**ISP** [aɪes'pi:] *(abbr* **Internet Service Provider**) *n Comptr* fournisseur *m* d'accès Internet
**Israel** ['ɪzreɪl] *n* Israël *m* ▪ **Israeli 1** *adj* israélien, -enne **2** *n* Israélien, -enne *mf*
**issue** ['ɪʃu:] **1** *n (of newspaper, magazine)* numéro *m*; *(matter)* question *f*; **at i.** *(at stake)* en cause; **to make an i.** *or* **a big i. of sth** faire toute une affaire de qch **2** *vt (book)* publier; *(tickets)* distribuer; *(passport)* délivrer; *(order)* donner; *(warning)* lancer; *(stamps, banknotes)* émettre; *(supply)* fournir (**with** de; **to** à); **to i. a statement** faire une déclaration

---

**IT** [ɪt] *pron* (**a**) *(subject)* il, elle; *(object)* le, la, l'; **(to) it** *(indirect object)* lui; **it bites** *(dog)* il mord; **I've done it** je l'ai fait
(**b**) *(impersonal)* il; **it's snowing** il neige; **it's hot** il fait chaud
(**c**) *(non-specific)* ce, cela, ça; **it's good** c'est bon; **who is it?** qui est-ce?; **to consider it wise to do sth** juger prudent de faire qch; **it was Paul who...** c'est Paul qui... **to have it in for sb** en vouloir à qn
(**d**) **of it, from it, about it** en; **in it, to it, at it** y; **on it** dessus; **under it** dessous

---

**italics** [ɪ'tælɪks] *npl* italique *m*; **in i.** en italique
**Italy** ['ɪtəlɪ] *n* l'Italie *f* ▪ **Italian** [ɪ'tælɪən] **1** *adj* italien, -enne **2** *n (person)* Italien, -enne *mf*; *(language)* italien *m*
**itch** [ɪtʃ] **1** *n* démangeaison *f* **2** *vi (of person)* avoir des démangeaisons; **his arm itches** son bras le *ou* lui démange; *Fig* **to be itching to do sth** brûler d'envie de faire qch

**item** ['aɪtəm] *n (in collection, on list, in newspaper)* article *m*; *(matter)* question *f*; **i. of clothing** vêtement *m*; **news i.** information *f* ▪ **itemize** *vt (invoice)* détailler

**itinerary** [aɪ'tɪnərərɪ] (*pl* **-ies**) *n* itinéraire *m*

**its** [ɪts] *possessive adj* son, sa, *pl* ses ▪ **itself** *pron* lui-même, elle-même; *(reflexive)* se, s'; **by i.** tout seul

**I've** [aɪv] = **I have**

**ivory** ['aɪvərɪ] *n* ivoire *m*

**ivy** ['aɪvɪ] *n* lierre *m*

# Jj

**J, j** [dʒeɪ] *n (letter)* J, j *m inv*

**jab** [dʒæb] **1** *n* coup *m*; *Br Fam (injection)* piqûre *f* **2** *(pt & pp* **-bb-***) vt (knife, stick)* enfoncer (**into** dans); *(prick)* piquer (**with** du bout de)

**jack** [dʒæk] **1** *n* (**a**) *(for vehicle)* cric *m* (**b**) *(card)* valet *m* **2** *vt* **to j. up** *(vehicle)* soulever *(avec un cric)*

**jacket** ['dʒækɪt] *n (coat)* veste *f*; *(of book)* jaquette *f*; *Br* **j. potato** pomme *f* de terre en robe des champs

**jackknife** ['dʒæknaɪf] **1** *(pl* **-knives***) n* couteau *m* de poche **2** *vi Br (of truck)* se mettre en travers de la route

**jackpot** ['dʒækpɒt] *n* gros lot *m*

**Jacuzzi**® [dʒə'ku:zɪ] *n* Jacuzzi® *m*

**jagged** ['dʒægɪd] *adj* déchiqueté

**jail** [dʒeɪl] **1** *n* prison *f* **2** *vt* emprisonner (**for** pour)

**jam¹** [dʒæm] *n (preserve)* confiture *f*; **strawberry j.** confiture *f* de fraises ▪ **jamjar** *n* pot *m* à confiture

**jam²** [dʒæm] **1** *n* **(traffic) j.** embouteillage *m* **2** *(pt & pp* **-mm-***) vt (squeeze, make stuck)* coincer; *(street, corridor)* encombrer; **to j. sth into sth** entasser qch dans qch; **to j. on the brakes** écraser la pédale de frein **3** *vi (get stuck)* se coincer ▪ **jammed** *adj (machine)* coincé; *(street)* encombré ▪ **jam-packed** *adj (hall, train)* bourré

**Jamaica** [dʒə'meɪkə] *n* la Jamaïque

**jangle** ['dʒæŋgəl] *vi* cliqueter

**janitor** ['dʒænɪtə(r)] *n Am & Scot (caretaker)* concierge *m*

**January** ['dʒænjʊərɪ] *n* janvier *m*

**Japan** [dʒə'pæn] *n* le Japon ▪ **Japanese** [dʒæpə'ni:z] **1** *adj* japonais **2** *n (person)* Japonais, -e *mf*; *(language)* japonais *m*

**jar¹** [dʒɑ:(r)] *n (container)* pot *m*; *(large, glass)* bocal *m*

**jar²** [dʒɑ:(r)] **1** *n (jolt)* choc *m* **2** *(pt & pp* **-rr-***) vt (shake)* ébranler **3** *vi (of noise)* grincer; *(of colours, words)* jurer (**with** avec) ▪ **jarring** *adj (noise, voice)* discordant

**jargon** ['dʒɑ:gən] *n* jargon *m*

**jaunt** [dʒɔ:nt] *n (journey)* balade *f*

**javelin** ['dʒævlɪn] *n* javelot *m*

**jaw** [dʒɔ:] *n Anat* mâchoire *f*

**jazz** [dʒæz] **1** *n* jazz *m* **2** *vt Fam* **to j. sth up** *(clothes, room, style)* égayer qch; *(music)* jazzifier qch

**jealous** ['dʒeləs] *adj* jaloux, -ouse (**of** de) ▪ **jealousy** *n* jalousie *f*

**jeans** [dʒi:nz] *npl* **(pair of) j.** jean *m*

**Jeep**® [dʒi:p] *n* Jeep® *f*

**jeer** [dʒɪə(r)] **1** *n* **jeers** *(boos)* huées *fpl* **2** *vt (boo)* huer; *(mock)* se moquer de **3** *vi* **to j. at sb/sth** *(boo)* huer qn/qch; *(mock)* se moquer de qn/qch ▪ **jeering 1** *adj* railleur, -euse **2** *n (mocking)* railleries *fpl*; *(of crowd)* huées *fpl*

**jell** [dʒel] *vi Fam (of ideas)* prendre tournure

**jello**® ['dʒeləʊ] *n Am (dessert)* gelée *f*

**jelly** ['dʒelɪ] *(pl* **-ies***) n (preserve, dessert)* gelée *f* ▪ **jellyfish** *n* méduse *f*

**jeopardy** ['dʒepədɪ] *n* **in j.** en péril ▪ **jeopardize** *vt* mettre en danger

**jerk** [dʒɜ:k] **1** *n* secousse *f* **2** *vt (pull)* tirer brusquement

**jerky** ['dʒɜ:kɪ] (**-ier, -iest**) *adj (movement, voice)* saccadé

**Jersey** ['dʒɜ:zɪ] *n* Jersey *m ou f*

**jersey** ['dʒɜːzɪ] (*pl* **-eys**) *n (garment)* tricot *m*; *(of footballer)* maillot *m*

**jest** [dʒest] **1** *n* plaisanterie *f*; **in j.** pour rire **2** *vi* plaisanter

**Jesus** ['dʒiːzəs] *n* Jésus *m*; **J. Christ** Jésus-Christ *m*

**jet** [dʒet] **1** *n* (**a**) *(plane)* avion *m* à réaction; **j. engine** réacteur *m*, moteur *m* à réaction; **j. lag** fatigue *f* due au décalage horaire (**b**) *(steam, liquid)* jet *m* **2** *vi Fam* **to j. off** s'envoler (**to** pour)

**jet-black** [dʒet'blæk] *adj* (noir) de jais

**jetfoil** ['dʒetfɔɪl] *n* hydroglisseur *m*

**jet-lagged** ['dʒetlægd] *adj* qui souffre du décalage horaire

**jetty** ['dʒetɪ] (*pl* **-ies**) *n* jetée *f*; *(landing place)* embarcadère *m*

**Jew** [dʒuː] *n (man)* Juif *m*; *(woman)* Juive *f* ▪ **Jewish** *adj* juif (*f* juive)

**jewel** ['dʒuːəl] *n* bijou *m* (*pl* -oux); *(in watch)* rubis *m* ▪ **jeweller** (*Am* **jeweler**) *n* bijoutier, -ère *mf* ▪ **jewellery** (*Am* **jewelry**) *n* bijoux *mpl*

**jibe** [dʒaɪb] *n & vi* = **gibe**

**Jiffy** ['dʒɪfɪ] *n* **J. bag®** enveloppe *f* matelassée

**jiffy** ['dʒɪfɪ] *n Fam* instant *m*

**jig** [dʒɪg] *n (dance, music)* gigue *f*

**jigsaw** ['dʒɪgsɔː] *n* **j. (puzzle)** puzzle *m*

**jilt** [dʒɪlt] *vt (lover)* laisser tomber

**jingle** ['dʒɪŋgəl] **1** *vt* faire tinter **2** *vi (of keys, bell)* tinter

**jinx** [dʒɪŋks] *n (spell, curse)* mauvais sort *m*

**jittery** ['dʒɪtərɪ] *adj Fam* **to be j.** être à cran

**job** [dʒɒb] *n (employment, post)* travail *m*, emploi *m*; *(task)* tâche *f*; **to have a (hard) j. doing** *or* **to do sth** avoir du mal à faire qch; **j. offer** offre *f* d'emploi

**Jobcentre** ['dʒɒbsentə(r)] *n Br* ≃ agence *f* nationale pour l'emploi

**jobless** ['dʒɒbləs] *adj* au chômage

**jockey** ['dʒɒkɪ] (*pl* **-eys**) *n* jockey *m*

**jocular** ['dʒɒkjʊlə(r)] *adj* jovial

**jog** [dʒɒg] (*pt & pp* **-gg-**) **1** *vt (shake)* secouer; *(push)* pousser; *Fig (memory)* rafraîchir **2** *vi (for fitness)* faire du jogging ▪ **jogging** *n (for fitness)* jogging *m*; **to go jogging** aller faire un jogging

**john** [dʒɒn] *n Am Fam* **the j.** *(lavatory)* le petit coin

**join** [dʒɔɪn] **1** *n* raccord *m*

**2** *vt* (**a**) *(put together)* joindre; *(wires, pipes)* raccorder; *(words, towns)* relier; **to j. two things together** relier une chose à une autre; **to j. sb** *(catch up with, meet)* rejoindre qn; *(associate oneself with, go with)* se joindre à qn (**in doing** pour faire)

(**b**) *(become a member of)* s'inscrire à; *(army, police, company)* entrer dans; **to j. the queue** *or Am* **line** prendre la queue

**3** *vi* (**a**) *(of roads, rivers)* se rejoindre; **to j. (together** *or* **up)** *(of objects)* se joindre (**with** à); **to j. in sth** prendre part à qch

(**b**) *(become a member)* devenir membre; *Mil* **to j. up** s'engager

**joiner** ['dʒɔɪnə(r)] *n Br* menuisier *m*

**joint** [dʒɔɪnt] **1** *n* (**a**) *(in body)* articulation *f*; *Br (meat)* rôti *m*; *Tech* joint *m*; *(in carpentry)* assemblage *m* (**b**) *Fam (nightclub)* boîte *f* (**c**) *Fam (cannabis cigarette)* joint *m* **2** *adj (decision)* commun; **j. account** compte *m* joint; **j. efforts** efforts *mpl* conjugués ▪ **jointly** *adv* conjointement

**joke** [dʒəʊk] **1** *n* plaisanterie *f*; *(trick)* tour *m* **2** *vi* plaisanter (**about** sur) ▪ **joker** *n* plaisantin *m*; *(card)* joker *m* ▪ **jokingly** *adv (say)* en plaisantant

**jolly** ['dʒɒlɪ] (**-ier, -iest**) *adj (happy)* gai

**jolt** [dʒɒlt] **1** *n* secousse *f* **2** *vt (shake)* secouer

**jostle** ['dʒɒsəl] **1** *vt (push)* bousculer **2** *vi (push each other)* se bousculer (**for sth** pour obtenir qch)

**jot** [dʒɒt] (*pt & pp* **-tt-**) *vt* **to j. sth down** noter qch ▪ **jotter** *n (notepad)* bloc-notes *m*

**journal** ['dʒɜːnəl] *n (periodical)* revue *f*

**journalism** ['dʒɜːnəlɪzəm] *n* journalisme *m* ▪ **journalist** *n* journaliste *mf*

**journey** ['dʒɜːnɪ] **1** (*pl* **-eys**) *n (trip)*

voyage *m*; *(distance)* trajet *m*; **to go on a j.** partir en voyage **2** *vi* voyager

**jovial** ['dʒəʊvɪəl] *adj* jovial

**joy** [dʒɔɪ] *n* joie *f*; **the joys of** *(countryside, motherhood)* les plaisirs *mpl* de ▪ **joyful** *adj* joyeux, -euse

**joyrider** ['dʒɔɪraɪdə(r)] *n* = chauffard qui conduit une voiture volée

**joystick** ['dʒɔɪstɪk] *n (of aircraft, computer)* manche *m* à balai

**jubilant** ['dʒu:bɪlənt] *adj* **to be j.** jubiler

**jubilee** ['dʒu:bɪli:] *n* **(golden) j.** jubilé *m*

**judder** ['dʒʌdə(r)] **1** *n* vibration *f* **2** *vi (shake)* vibrer

**judge** [dʒʌdʒ] **1** *n* juge *m* **2** *vti* juger; **to j. sb by** *or* **on sth** juger qn sur *ou* d'après qch; **judging by...** à en juger par... ▪ **judg(e)ment** *n* jugement *m*

**judicial** [dʒu:'dɪʃəl] *adj* judiciaire

**judo** ['dʒu:dəʊ] *n* judo *m*

**jug** [dʒʌg] *n* cruche *f*; *(for milk)* pot *m*

**juggle** ['dʒʌgəl] **1** *vt* jongler avec **2** *vi* jongler (**with** avec) ▪ **juggler** *n* jongleur, -euse *mf*

**juice** [dʒu:s] *n* jus *m* ▪ **juicy** (**-ier, -iest**) *adj (fruit)* juteux, -euse; *(meat)* succulent; *Fig (story)* savoureux, -euse

**jukebox** ['dʒu:kbɒks] *n* juke-box *m*

**July** [dʒu:'laɪ] *n* juillet *m*

**jumble** ['dʒʌmbəl] **1** *n (disorder)* fouillis *m*; *Br (unwanted articles)* bric-à-brac *m inv*; *Br* **j. sale** vente *f* de charité *(articles d'occasion uniquement)* **2** *vt* **to j. (up)** *(objects, facts)* mélanger

**jumbo** ['dʒʌmbəʊ] **1** *adj (packet)* géant **2** (*pl* **-os**) *adj & n* **j. (jet)** jumbo-jet *(m)*

**jump** [dʒʌmp] **1** *n (leap)* saut *m*; *(start)* sursaut *m*; *(increase)* hausse *f* soudaine; *Am* **j. rope** corde *f* à sauter

**2** *vt (ditch)* sauter; *Br* **to j. the queue** passer avant son tour, resquiller

**3** *vi* sauter (**at** sur); *(start)* sursauter; *(of price)* faire un bond; **to j. across sth** traverser qch d'un bond; **to j. in** *or* **on** *(train, vehicle, bus)* sauter dans; **to j. off** *or* **out** sauter; *(from bus)* descendre; **to j. off sth, to j. out of sth** sauter de qch; **to j. out of the window** sauter par la fenêtre; **to j. up** se lever d'un bond ▪ **jumpy** ['dʒʌmpɪ] (**-ier, -iest**) *adj* nerveux, -euse

**jumper** ['dʒʌmpə(r)] *n Br* pull(-over) *m*; *Am (dress)* robe *f* chasuble

**junction** ['dʒʌŋkʃən] *n (crossroads)* carrefour *m*; *Br* **j. 23** *(on motorway) (exit)* la sortie 23; *(entrance)* l'entrée *f* 23

**June** [dʒu:n] *n* juin *m*

**jungle** ['dʒʌŋgəl] *n* jungle *f*

**junior** ['dʒu:nɪə(r)] **1** *adj (younger)* plus jeune; *(in rank, status)* subalterne; *(teacher, doctor)* jeune; **to be sb's j.** être plus jeune que qn; *(in rank, status)* être au-dessous de qn; *Br* **j. school** école *f* primaire *(entre 7 et 11 ans)*; *Am* **j. high school** ≃ collège *m* d'enseignement secondaire

**2** *n* cadet, -ette *mf*; *(in school)* petit, -e *mf*; *(in sports)* junior *mf*, cadet, -ette *mf*

**junk** [dʒʌŋk] **1** *n (unwanted objects)* bric-à-brac *m inv*; *(inferior goods)* camelote *f*; *(bad film, book)* navet *m*; **j. food** cochonneries *fpl*; **j. mail** prospectus *mpl*; **j. shop** boutique *f* de brocanteur **2** *vt Fam (get rid of)* balancer

**junkie** ['dʒʌŋkɪ] *n Fam* drogué, -e *mf*

**jury** ['dʒʊərɪ] (*pl* **-ies**) *n (in competition, court)* jury *m*

**just** [dʒʌst] **1** *adv (exactly, slightly)* juste; *(only)* juste, seulement; *(simply)* (tout) simplement; **it's j. as I thought** c'est bien ce que je pensais; **she has/had j. left** elle vient/venait de partir; **he j. missed it** il l'a manqué de peu; **j. as big/light** tout aussi grand/léger (**as** que); **j. a moment!** un instant!; **j. one** un(e) seul(e) (**of** de); **j. about** *(approximately)* à peu près; *(almost)* presque; **to be j. about to do sth** être sur le point de faire qch **2** *adj (fair)* juste (**to** envers)

**justice** ['dʒʌstɪs] *n* justice *f*; **it doesn't do you j.** *(hat, photo)* cela ne vous avantage pas

**justify** ['dʒʌstɪfaɪ] (*pt & pp* **-ied**) *vt*

justifier; **to be justified in doing sth** *(have reason)* être fondé à faire qch ▪ **justifiable** *adj* justifiable ▪ **justification** [-fɪ'keɪʃən] *n* justification *f*

**jut** [dʒʌt] *(pt & pp* **-tt-***)* *vi* **to j. out** faire saillie

**juvenile** ['dʒu:vənaɪl, *Am* -ənəl] **1** *n (in law)* mineur, -e *mf* **2** *adj (court)* pour enfants; *Pej (behaviour)* puéril; **j. delinquent** jeune délinquant, -e *mf*

**juxtapose** [dʒʌkstə'pəʊz] *vt* juxtaposer

# Kk

**K, k** [keɪ] *n (letter)* K, k *m inv*
**kangaroo** [kæŋgəˈruː] *n* kangourou *m*
**karate** [kəˈrɑːtɪ] *n* karaté *m*
**kebab** [kəˈbæb] *n* brochette *f*
**keel** [kiːl] **1** *n (of boat)* quille *f* **2** *vi* **to k. over** *(of boat)* chavirer
**keen** [kiːn] *adj* (**a**) *Br (eager, enthusiastic)* plein d'enthousiasme; **to be k. on sth** *(music, sport)* être passionné de qch; **he is k. on her/the idea** elle/ l'idée lui plaît beaucoup (**b**) *(edge, appetite)* aiguisé; *(interest)* vif (*f* vive); *(mind)* pénétrant; *(wind)* glacial

---

**KEEP** [kiːp] **1** (*pt & pp* **kept**) *vt* garder; *(shop, car)* avoir; *(diary, promise)* tenir; *(family)* entretenir; *(rule)* respecter; *(delay, detain)* retenir; *(put)* mettre; **to k. doing sth** continuer à faire qch; **to k. sth clean** garder qch propre; **to k. sth from sb** dissimuler qch à qn; **to k. sb from doing sth** empêcher qn de faire qch; **to k. sb waiting/working** faire attendre/travailler qn; **to k. an appointment** se rendre à un rendez-vous

**2** *vi (remain)* rester; *(continue)* continuer; *(of food)* se conserver; **how is he keeping?** comment va-t-il?; **to k. still** rester immobile; **to k. left** tenir sa gauche; **to k. going** continuer; **to k. at it** *(keep doing it)* persévérer

**3** *n (food)* subsistance *f*; *Fam* **for keeps** pour toujours

▸**keep away 1** *vt (person)* éloigner (**from** de) **2** *vi* ne pas s'approcher (**from** de)

▸**keep back 1** *vt sep (crowd)* contenir; *(delay, withhold)* retarder; *(hide)* cacher (**from** à) **2** *vi* ne pas s'approcher (**from** de)

▸**keep down** *vt sep (restrict)* limiter; *(price, costs)* maintenir bas

▸**keep in** *vt sep (not allow out)* empêcher de sortir; *(as punishment in school)* garder en retenue

▸**keep off 1** *vt sep (person)* éloigner; **k. your hands off!** n'y touche pas! **2** *vt insep* **'k. off the grass'** 'défense de marcher sur les pelouses' **3** *vi (not go near)* ne pas s'approcher

▸**keep on 1** *vt sep (hat, employee)* garder; **to k. on doing sth** continuer à faire qch **2** *vi* **to k. on at sb** harceler qn

▸**keep out 1** *vt sep* empêcher d'entrer **2** *vi* rester en dehors (**of** de)

▸**keep to 1** *vt insep (subject, path)* ne pas s'écarter de; *(room)* garder **2** *vi* **to k. to the left** tenir la gauche; **to k. to oneself** rester à l'écart

▸**keep up 1** *vt sep (continue, maintain)* continuer; *(keep awake)* empêcher de dormir; **to k. up appearances** sauver les apparences **2** *vi (continue)* continuer; *(follow)* suivre; **to k. up with sb** *(follow)* aller à la même allure que qn; *(in quality of work)* se maintenir à la hauteur de qn

---

**keeper** [ˈkiːpə(r)] *n (in park, in zoo, goalkeeper)* gardien, -enne *mf*
**keeping** [ˈkiːpɪŋ] *n* **in k. with** conformément à
**kennel** [ˈkenəl] *n Br* niche *f*
**Kenya** [ˈkiːnjə, ˈkenjə] *n* le Kenya
**kept** [kept] **1** *pt & pp of* **keep 2** *adj* **well** *or* **nicely k.** *(house)* bien tenu

**kerb** [kɜːb] *n Br* bord *m* du trottoir

**kernel** ['kɜːnəl] *n (of nut)* amande *f*

**kerosene** ['kerəsiːn] *n Am (paraffin)* pétrole *m* (lampant)

**ketchup** ['ketʃəp] *n* ketchup *m*

**kettle** ['ketəl] *n* bouilloire *f*; **the k. is boiling** l'eau bout; **to put the k. on** mettre l'eau à chauffer

**key** [kiː] **1** *n* clef *f*, clé *f*; *(of piano, typewriter, computer)* touche *f* **2** *adj (industry, post)* clef, clé **3** *vt* **to k. in** *(data)* saisir ▪ **keyboard** *n (of piano, computer)* clavier *m* ▪ **keyhole** *n* trou *m* de serrure ▪ **keynote** *n (of speech)* point *m* essentiel ▪ **keyring** *n* porte-clefs *m inv*

**keyed** [kiːd] *adj* **to be k. up** être surexcité

**khaki** ['kɑːkɪ] *adj & n* kaki *(m) inv*

**kick** [kɪk] **1** *n* coup *m* de pied; *(of horse)* ruade *f* **2** *vt* donner un coup de pied/des coups de pied à; *(of horse)* lancer une ruade à **3** *vi* donner des coups de pied; *(of horse)* ruer ▪ **kick-off** *n (in football)* coup *m* d'envoi

▸ **kick down, kick in** *vt sep (door)* démolir à coups de pied

▸ **kick off** *vi (of footballer)* donner le coup d'envoi; *Fam (start)* démarrer

▸ **kick out** *vt sep Fam (throw out)* flanquer dehors

▸ **kick up** *vt sep Br Fam* **to k. up a fuss** faire des histoires

**kid** [kɪd] **1** *n* (**a**) *Fam (child)* gosse *mf*; *Am Fam* **my k. brother** mon petit frère (**b**) *(goat)* chevreau *m* **2** *(pt & pp* **-dd-**) *vti Fam (joke, tease)* faire marcher; **to be kidding** plaisanter; **no kidding!** sans blague!

**kidnap** ['kɪdnæp] *(pt & pp* **-pp-**) *vt* kidnapper ▪ **kidnapper** *n* ravisseur, -euse *mf* ▪ **kidnapping** *n* enlèvement *m*

**kidney** ['kɪdnɪ] *(pl* **-eys**) *n* rein *m*; *(as food)* rognon *m*; **k. bean** haricot *m* rouge

**kill** [kɪl] **1** *vt (person, animal, plant)* tuer; **to k. oneself** se tuer; *Fam* **my feet are killing me** j'ai les pieds en compote; **to k. time** tuer le temps **2** *vi* tuer ▪ **killer** *n* tueur, -euse *mf* ▪ **killing** *n (of person)* meurtre *m*; *(of group)* massacre *m*; *(of animal)* mise *f* à mort

**killjoy** ['kɪldʒɔɪ] *n* rabat-joie *mf inv*

**kilo** ['kiːləʊ] *(pl* **-os**) *n* kilo *m* ▪ **kilogram(me)** ['kɪləgræm] *n* kilogramme *m*

**kilobyte** ['kɪləbaɪt] *n Comptr* kilo-octet *m*

**kilometre** [kɪ'lɒmɪtə(r)] (*Am* **kilometer**) *n* kilomètre *m*

**kilt** [kɪlt] *n* kilt *m*

**kin** [kɪn] *n* **one's next of k.** son plus proche parent

**kind**[1] [kaɪnd] *n (sort, type)* genre *m*, espèce *f* (**of** de); **what k. of drink is it?** qu'est-ce que c'est comme boisson?; *Fam* **k. of worried/sad** plutôt inquiet/triste

**kind**[2] [kaɪnd] (**-er, -est**) *adj (helpful, pleasant)* gentil, -ille (**to** avec); **that's k. of you** c'est gentil de votre part

**kindergarten** ['kɪndəgɑːtən] *n* jardin *m* d'enfants

**kindly** ['kaɪndlɪ] **1** *adv* gentiment; **k. wait** ayez la bonté d'attendre **2** *adj (person)* bienveillant

**kindness** ['kaɪndnɪs] *n* gentillesse *f*

**king** [kɪŋ] *n* roi *m* ▪ **kingdom** *n* royaume *m*; **animal/plant k.** règne *m* animal/végétal ▪ **king-size(d)** *adj* géant

**kiosk** ['kiːɒsk] *n* kiosque *m*; *Br* **(telephone) k.** cabine *f* téléphonique

**kip** [kɪp] *(pt & pp* **-pp-**) *vi Br Fam (sleep)* roupiller

**kipper** ['kɪpə(r)] *n* hareng *m* salé et fumé

**kiss** [kɪs] **1** *n* baiser *m*; **the k. of life** *(in first aid)* le bouche-à-bouche **2** *vt (person)* embrasser **3** *vi* s'embrasser

**kit** [kɪt] **1** *n* équipement *m*, matériel *m*; *(set of articles)* trousse *f*; *Br (belongings)* affaires *fpl*; *Br (sports clothes)* tenue *f*; **first-aid k.** trousse *f* de pharmacie; **(do-it-yourself) k.** kit *m* **2** *(pt & pp* **-tt-**) *vt Br* **to k. sb out** équiper qn (**with** de)

**kitchen** ['kɪtʃɪn] *n* cuisine *f*; **k. sink**

évier *m*; **k. units** éléments *mpl* de cuisine ▪ **kitchenette** *n* coin-cuisine *m*

**kite** [kaɪt] *n (toy)* cerf-volant *m*

**kitten** ['kɪtən] *n* chaton *m*

**kitty** ['kɪtɪ] *(pl* **-ies***) n (fund)* cagnotte *f*

**kiwi** ['ki:wi:] *n (bird, fruit)* kiwi *m*

**km** *(abbr* **kilometre(s)***)* km

**knack** [næk] *n (skill)* talent *m*; **to have the k. of doing sth** avoir le don de faire qch

**knackered** ['nækəd] *adj Br Fam (tired)* vanné

**knapsack** ['næpsæk] *n* sac *m* à dos

**knead** [ni:d] *vt (dough)* pétrir

**knee** [ni:] *n* genou *m*; **to go down on one's knees** s'agenouiller ▪ **kneecap** *n* rotule *f*

**kneel** [ni:l] *(pt & pp* **knelt** *or* **kneeled***) vi* **to k. (down)** s'agenouiller (**before** devant); **to be kneeling (down)** être à genoux

**knelt** [nelt] *pt & pp of* **kneel**

**knew** [nju:] *pt of* **know**

**knickers** ['nɪkəz] *npl Br (underwear)* culotte *f*

**knick-knack** ['nɪknæk] *n Fam* babiole *f*

**knife** [naɪf] **1** *(pl* **knives***) n* couteau *m*; *(penknife)* canif *m* **2** *vt* poignarder

**knight** [naɪt] **1** *n* chevalier *m*; *(chess piece)* cavalier *m* **2** *vt Br* **to be knighted** être fait chevalier ▪ **knighthood** *n Br* titre *m* de chevalier

**knit** [nɪt] *(pt & pp* **-tt-***)* **1** *vt* tricoter **2** *vi* tricoter; **to k. (together)** *(of bones)* se ressouder ▪ **knitting** *n (activity, material)* tricot *m*; **k. needle** aiguille *f* à tricoter

**knob** [nɒb] *n (on door)* poignée *f*; *(on radio)* bouton *m*

**knock** [nɒk] **1** *n (blow)* coup *m*; **there's a k. at the door** on frappe à la porte **2** *vt (strike)* frapper; *(collide with)* heurter; **to k. one's head on sth** se cogner la tête contre qch **3** *vi (strike)* frapper; **to k. against** *or* **into sth** heurter qch ▪ **knocker** *n (for door)* marteau *m* ▪ **knockout** *n (in boxing)* knock-out *m inv*

▸**knock about** *vt sep (ill-treat)* malmener

▸**knock back** *vt sep Br Fam (drink, glass)* s'envoyer (derrière la cravate)

▸**knock down** *vt sep (object, pedestrian)* renverser; *(house, tree, wall)* abattre; *(price)* baisser

▸**knock in** *vt sep (nail)* enfoncer

▸**knock off 1** *vt sep (person, object)* faire tomber (**from** de); *Fam (do quickly)* expédier; **to k. £5 off (the price)** baisser le prix de 5 livres **2** *vi Fam (stop work)* s'arrêter de travailler

▸**knock out** *vt sep (make unconscious)* assommer; *(boxer)* mettre K.-O.; *(beat in competition)* éliminer

▸**knock over** *vt sep (pedestrian, object)* renverser

**knot** [nɒt] **1** *n* (**a**) *(in rope)* nœud *m*; *Fig* **to tie the k.** se marier (**b**) *Naut (unit of speed)* nœud *m* **2** *(pt & pp* **-tt-***) vt* nouer

**KNOW** [nəʊ] **1** *n Fam* **to be in the k.** être au courant

**2** *(pt* **knew**, *pp* **known***) vt (facts, language)* savoir; *(person, place)* connaître; *(recognize)* reconnaître (**by** à); **to k. that...** savoir que...; **to k. how to do sth** savoir faire qch; **for all I k.** que je sache; **I'll let you k.** je vous le ferai savoir; **to k. (a lot) about cars/sewing** s'y connaître en voitures/couture; **to get to k. sb** apprendre à connaître qn

**3** *vi* savoir; **I k.** je (le) sais; **I wouldn't k., I k. nothing about it** je n'en sais rien; **to k. about sth** être au courant de qch; **do you k. of a good dentist?** connais-tu un bon dentiste? ▪ **know-all** *n Fam Pej* je-sais-tout *mf* ▪ **know-how** *n Fam* savoir-faire *m inv* ▪ **knowingly** *adv (consciously)* sciemment ▪ **know-it-all** *n Fam Pej* je-sais-tout *mf*

**knowledge** ['nɒlɪdʒ] *n (of fact)* connaissance *f*; *(learning)* connaissances *fpl*, savoir *m*; **general k.** culture *f* générale ▪ **knowledgeable** *adj* savant; **to be k. about sth** bien s'y connaître en qch

**known** [nəʊn] **1** *pp of* **know 2** *adj* connu; **she is k. to be…** on sait qu'elle est…

**knuckle** ['nʌkəl] *n* articulation *f* (du doigt)

▸ **knuckle down** *vi Fam* se mettre au boulot; **to k. down to sth** se mettre à qch

**Koran** [kə'rɑːn] *n* **the K.** le Coran

**Korea** [kə'rɪə] *n* la Corée

**kosher** ['kəʊʃə(r)] *adj Rel (food)* kasher *inv*

**kudos** ['kjuːdɒs] *n (glory)* gloire *f*; *(prestige)* prestige *m*

**Kuwait** [kʊ'weɪt] *n* le Koweït

# Ll

**L, l** [el] *n (letter)* L, l *m inv*

**lab** [læb] *n Fam* labo *m* ▪ **laboratory** [lə'bɒrətrɪ, *Am* 'læbrətɔːrɪ] *n* laboratoire *m*

**label** ['leɪbəl] **1** *n* étiquette *f*; *(of record company)* label *m* **2** *(Br* **-ll-**, *Am* **-l-***) vt* étiqueter; *Fig* **to l. sb (as) a liar** qualifier qn de menteur

**laborious** [lə'bɔːrɪəs] *adj* laborieux, -euse

**labour** ['leɪbə(r)] *(Am* **labor***)* **1** *n (work)* travail *m*; *(workers)* main-d'œuvre *f*; *Br* **L.** *(political party)* le parti travailliste; **in l.** *(woman)* en train d'accoucher **2** *adj (market)* du travail; **l. force** effectifs *mpl*; *Am* **l. union** syndicat *m* **3** *vi (toil)* peiner (**over** sur) ▪ **labourer** *(Am* **laborer***) n (on roads)* manœuvre *m*; *(on farm)* ouvrier *m* agricole

**labyrinth** ['læbərɪnθ] *n* labyrinthe *m*

**lace** [leɪs] **1** *n* (**a**) *(cloth)* dentelle *f* (**b**) *(of shoe)* lacet *m* **2** *vt* **to l. (up)** *(tie up)* lacer

**lack** [læk] **1** *n* manque *m* (**of** de); **for l. of sth** à défaut de qch **2** *vt* manquer de **3** *vi* **to be lacking** manquer (**in** de)

**lad** [læd] *n Fam (young man)* jeune gars *m*; *(child)* garçon *m*

**ladder** ['lædə(r)] **1** *n* échelle *f*; *Br (in tights)* maille *f* filée **2** *vti Br* filer

**laden** ['leɪdən] *adj* chargé (**with** de)

**lady** ['leɪdɪ] *(pl* **-ies***) n* dame *f*; **a young l.** une jeune fille; *(married)* une jeune dame; **Ladies and Gentlemen!** Mesdames, Mesdemoiselles, Messieurs!; **the ladies' room**, *Br* **the ladies** les toilettes *fpl* pour dames

**ladybird** ['leɪdɪbɜːd] *(Am* **ladybug** ['leɪdɪbʌg]*) n* coccinelle *f*

**lag** [læg] **1** *n* **time l.** *(between events)* décalage *m*; *(between countries)* décalage *m* horaire **2** *(pt & pp* **-gg-***) vt (pipe)* isoler **3** *vi* **to l. behind** *(in progress, work)* avoir du retard; *(dawdle)* être à la traîne

**lager** ['lɑːgə(r)] *n Br* bière *f* blonde

**lagoon** [lə'guːn] *n* lagune *f*; *(of atoll)* lagon *m*

**laid** [leɪd] *pt & pp of* **lay**[3] ▪ **laid-back** *adj Fam* cool *inv*

**lain** [leɪn] *pp of* **lie**[2]

**lair** [leə(r)] *n* tanière *f*

**lake** [leɪk] *n* lac *m*

**lamb** [læm] *n* agneau *m*

**lame** [leɪm] (**-er, -est**) *adj (person, argument)* boiteux, -euse; *(excuse)* piètre; **to be l.** *(of person)* boiter

**lament** [lə'ment] *vt* **to l. (over)** se lamenter sur

**laminated** ['læmɪneɪtɪd] *adj (glass)* feuilleté; *(wood, plastic)* stratifié

**lamp** [læmp] *n* lampe *f* ▪ **lamppost** *n* réverbère *m* ▪ **lampshade** *n* abat-jour *m inv*

**lance** [lɑːns] **1** *n (weapon)* lance *f* **2** *vt (abscess)* inciser

**land** [lænd] **1** *n* terre *f*; *(country)* pays *m*; **(plot of) l.** terrain *m*

**2** *adj (reform)* agraire

**3** *vt (passengers, cargo)* débarquer; *(aircraft)* poser; *(blow)* flanquer (**on** à); *Fam (job, prize)* décrocher

**4** *vi (of aircraft)* atterrir; *(of passengers)* débarquer; *(of bomb, missile)* tomber; **to l. up in a ditch/in jail** se retrouver dans un fossé/en prison ▪ **landing** *n* (**a**) *(of aircraft)* atterrissage *m*; *(of cargo, troops)* débarquement *m* (**b**) *(of staircase)* palier *m* ▪ **landlady** (*pl* **-ies**) *n* propriétaire *f*; *(of pub)* patronne *f* ▪ **landlord** *n* propriétaire *m*; *(of pub)* patron *m* ▪ **landmark** *n* point *m* de repère ▪ **landowner** *n* propriétaire *m* foncier ▪ **landslide** *n* *(falling rocks)* glissement *m* de terrain; *(election victory)* raz de marée *m inv* électoral

**landscape** ['lændskeɪp] *n* paysage *m*

**lane** [leɪn] *n (in country)* chemin *m*; *(in town)* ruelle *f*; *(division of road)* voie *f*; *(line of traffic)* file *f*; *(for shipping, swimming)* couloir *m*

**language** ['læŋgwɪdʒ] **1** *n (of a people)* langue *f*; *(faculty, style)* langage *m* **2** *adj (laboratory)* de langues; *(teacher, studies)* de langue(s)

**languish** ['læŋgwɪʃ] *vi* languir (**for** *or* **after** après)

**lanky** ['læŋkɪ] (**-ier, -iest**) *adj* dégingandé

**lantern** ['læntən] *n* lanterne *f*

**lap** [læp] **1** *n* (**a**) *(of person)* genoux *mpl* (**b**) *(in race)* tour *m* de piste **2** (*pt & pp* **-pp-**) *vt* **to l. up** *(drink)* laper **3** *vi (of waves)* clapoter

**lapel** [lə'pel] *n* revers *m*

**lapse** [læps] **1** *n* (**a**) *(in concentration, standards)* baisse *f*; **a l. of memory** un trou de mémoire (**b**) *(interval)* laps *m* de temps; **a l. of time** un intervalle (**between** entre) **2** *vi* (**a**) *(of concentration, standards)* baisser (**b**) *(expire)* *(of subscription)* expirer

**laptop** ['læptɒp] *adj & n* **l. (computer)** ordinateur *m* portable

**lard** [lɑːd] *n* saindoux *m*

**larder** ['lɑːdə(r)] *n* garde-manger *m inv*

**large** [lɑːdʒ] (**-er, -est**) *adj (big)* grand; *(fat, bulky)* gros (*f* grosse); *(quantity)* grand, important; **to become** *or* **grow** *or* **get l.** s'agrandir; *(of person)* grossir; **at l.** *(of prisoner, animal)* en liberté; *(as a whole)* en général ▪ **large-scale** *adj (operation, reform)* de grande envergure

**largely** ['lɑːdʒlɪ] *adv* en grande partie

**lark**[1] [lɑːk] *n (bird)* alouette *f*

**lark**[2] [lɑːk] *Fam* **1** *n (joke)* rigolade *f* **2** *vi Br* **to l. about** faire le fou/la folle

**larva** ['lɑːvə] (*pl* **-vae** [-viː]) *n* larve *f*

**laryngitis** [lærɪn'dʒaɪtɪs] *n Med* laryngite *f*

**lasagne, lasagna** [lə'zænjə] *n* lasagnes *fpl*

**laser** ['leɪzə(r)] *n* laser *m*; **l. beam/printer** rayon *m*/imprimante *f* laser

**lash**[1] [læʃ] **1** *n (with whip)* coup *m* de fouet **2** *vt (strike)* fouetter; *(tie)* attacher (**to** à) **3** *vi* **to l. out at sb** *(hit)* donner des coups à qn; *(criticize)* fustiger qn

**lash**[2] [læʃ] *n (eyelash)* cil *m*

**lass** [læs] *n Br* jeune fille *f*

**last**[1] [lɑːst] **1** *adj* dernier, -ère; **the l. ten lines** les dix dernières lignes; **l. night** *(evening)* hier soir; *(night)* la nuit dernière; **l. name** nom *m* de famille

**2** *adv (lastly)* en dernier lieu; *(on the last occasion)* (pour) la dernière fois; **to leave l.** sortir le dernier

**3** *n (person, object)* dernier, -ère *mf*; **l. but one** avant-dernier *m* (*f* avant-dernière); **at (long) l.** enfin ▪ **last-minute** *adj (decision)* de dernière minute

**last**[2] [lɑːst] *vi* durer; **to l. (out)** *(endure, resist)* tenir (le coup); *(of money, supplies)* suffire; **it lasted me ten years** ça m'a fait dix ans

**lasting** ['lɑːstɪŋ] *adj (impression, peace)* durable

**lastly** ['lɑːstlɪ] *adv* en dernier lieu

**latch** [lætʃ] **1** *n* loquet *m*; **the door is on the l.** la porte n'est pas fermée à clef **2** *vt insep Fam* **to l. onto** *(understand)* piger; *(adopt)* adopter

**late**[1] [leɪt] **1** (**-er, -est**) *adj (meal, season, hour)* tardif, -ive; *(stage)* avancé; *(edition)* dernier, -ère; **to be l. (for sth)** être en retard (pour qch); **he's an hour l.** il a une heure de retard; **it's l.** il est tard; **in the l. nineties** à la

fin des années 90; **to be in one's l. forties** approcher de la cinquantaine; **at a later date** à une date ultérieure; **at the latest** au plus tard
**2** *adv (in the day, season)* tard; *(not on time)* en retard; **it's getting l.** il se fait tard; **later (on)** plus tard; **of l.** récemment

**late²** [leɪt] *adj* **the l. Mr Smith** feu Monsieur Smith

**latecomer** ['leɪtkʌmə(r)] *n* retardataire *mf*

**lately** ['leɪtlɪ] *adv* dernièrement

**latent** ['leɪtənt] *adj (disease, tendency)* latent

**lateral** ['lætərəl] *adj* latéral

**lather** ['lɑːðə(r)] **1** *n* mousse *f* **2** *vt* savonner

**Latin** ['lætɪn] **1** *adj* latin; **L. America** l'Amérique *f* latine ▪ **L. American 1** *adj* d'Amérique latine **2** *n* Latino-Américain, -e *mf* **2** *n (language)* latin *m*

**latitude** ['lætɪtjuːd] *n (on map, freedom)* latitude *f*

**latter** ['lætə(r)] **1** *adj (later, last-named)* dernier, -ère; *(second)* deuxième **2** *n* **the l.** le dernier (*f* la dernière); *(of two)* le second (*f* la seconde)

**lattice** ['lætɪs] *n* treillis *m*

**laudable** ['lɔːdəbəl] *adj* louable

**laugh** [lɑːf] **1** *n* rire *m*; **to have a good l.** bien rire **2** *vt* **to l. sth off** tourner qch en plaisanterie **3** *vi* rire (**at/about** de) ▪ **laughing** *adj* riant; **it's no l. matter** il n'y a pas de quoi rire; **to be the l. stock of** être la risée de

**laughable** ['lɑːfəbəl] *adj* ridicule

**laughter** ['lɑːftə(r)] *n* rire(s) *m(pl)*

**launch** [lɔːntʃ] **1** *n* (**a**) *(motorboat)* vedette *f*; *(pleasure boat)* bateau *m* de plaisance (**b**) *(of ship, rocket, product)* lancement *m* **2** *vt (ship, rocket, product)* lancer **3** *vi* **to l. (out) into** *(begin)* se lancer dans

**launder** ['lɔːndə(r)] *vt (clothes, money)* blanchir

**launderette** [lɔːndə'ret] (*Am* **Laundromat**® ['lɔːndrəmæt]) *n* laverie *f* automatique

**laundry** ['lɔːndrɪ] *n (place)* blanchisserie *f*; *(clothes)* linge *m*; **to do the l.** faire la lessive

**lava** ['lɑːvə] *n* lave *f*

**lavatory** ['lævətərɪ] (*pl* **-ies**) *n* toilettes *fpl*

**lavender** ['lævɪndə(r)] *n* lavande *f*

**lavish** ['lævɪʃ] **1** *adj* prodigue (**with** de); *(meal, décor, gift)* somptueux, -euse; *(expenditure)* excessif, -ive **2** *vt* **to l. sth on sb** couvrir qn de qch

**law** [lɔː] *n (rule, rules)* loi *f*; *(study, profession, system)* droit *m*; **against the l.** illégal; **court of l., l. court** cour *f* de justice; **l. and order** l'ordre *m* public

**lawful** ['lɔːfəl] *adj (action)* légal; *(claim)* légitime

**lawless** ['lɔːləs] *adj (country)* anarchique

**lawn** [lɔːn] *n* pelouse *f*, gazon *m*; **l. mower** tondeuse *f* à gazon

**lawsuit** ['lɔːsuːt] *n* procès *m*

**lawyer** ['lɔːjə(r)] *n (in court)* avocat, -e *mf*; *(for wills, sales)* notaire *m*; *(legal expert)* juriste *mf*

**lax** [læks] *adj (person)* laxiste; *(discipline, behaviour)* relâché

**laxative** ['læksətɪv] *n* laxatif *m*

**lay¹** [leɪ] *pt of* **lie²**

**lay²** [leɪ] *adj (non-religious)* laïque; **l. person** profane *mf* ▪ **layman** (*pl* **-men**) *n (nonspecialist)* profane *mf*

**lay³** [leɪ] (*pt & pp* **laid**) **1** *vt (put down, place)* poser; *(blanket)* étendre (**over** sur); *(trap)* tendre; *(egg)* pondre; *Br* **to l. the table** mettre la table **2** *vi (of bird)* pondre ▪ **layabout** *n Fam* fainéant, -e *mf* ▪ **lay-by** (*pl* **-bys**) *n Br (for vehicles)* aire *f* de stationnement ▪ **layout** *n* disposition *f*; *(of text)* mise *f* en page

▸ **lay down** *vt sep (put down)* poser; *(arms)* déposer; *(principle, condition)* établir; **to l. down the law** dicter sa loi (**to** à)

▸ **lay into** *vt insep Fam (physically)* rosser; *(verbally)* voler dans les plumes à

▸ **lay off** *vt sep* **to l. sb off** *(worker)* licencier qn

▸**lay on** *vt sep Br (install)* installer; *(supply)* fournir

▸**lay out** *vt sep (garden)* dessiner; *(house)* concevoir; *(display)* disposer; *Fam (money)* mettre (**on** dans)

**layer** ['leɪə(r)] *n* couche *f*

**laze** [leɪz] *vi* **to l. (about** *or* **around)** paresser

**lazy** ['leɪzɪ] (**-ier, -iest**) *adj (person)* paresseux, -euse ▪ **lazybones** *n Fam* flemmard, -e *mf*

**lb** (*abbr* **libra**) **3lb** 3 livres *(unité de poids)*

**lead**[1] [led] *n (metal)* plomb *m*; *(of pencil)* mine *f* ▪ **leaded** *adj (petrol)* au plomb ▪ **lead-free** *adj (paint)* sans plomb

**lead**[2] [li:d] **1** *n (distance or time ahead)* avance *f* (**over** sur); *(example)* exemple *m*; *(clue)* indice *m*; *(in film)* rôle *m* principal; *Br (for dog)* laisse *f*; *(electric wire)* fil *m* électrique; **to take the l.** *(in race)* prendre la tête; **to be in the l.** *(in race)* être en tête; *(in match)* mener (à la marque)

**2** (*pt & pp* **led**) *vt (guide, conduct, take)* mener, conduire (**to** à); *(team, government)* diriger; *(expedition, attack)* commander; *(procession)* être en tête de; **to l. a happy life** mener une vie heureuse; **to l. sb in/out** faire entrer/sortir qn; **to l. sb to do sth** *(cause, induce)* amener qn à faire qch

**3** *vi (of street, door)* mener, conduire (**to** à); *(in race)* être en tête; *(in match)* mener (à la marque); *(go ahead)* aller devant; **to l. to sth** *(result in)* aboutir à qch; *(cause)* mener à qch; **to l. up to** *(precede)* précéder

▸**lead away** *vt sep* emmener

▸**lead off** *vt sep* emmener

▸**lead on** *vt sep (deceive)* tromper, duper

**leader** ['li:də(r)] *n* (**a**) *(person)* chef *m*; *(of country, party)* dirigeant, -e *mf*; *(of strike, riot)* meneur, -euse *mf*; *(guide)* guide *m*; **to be the l.** *(in race)* être en tête (**b**) *Br (newspaper article)* éditorial *m* ▪ **leadership** *n* direction *f*; *(qualities)* qualités *fpl* de chef; *(leaders) (of country, party)* dirigeants *mpl*

**leading** ['li:dɪŋ] *adj (best, most important)* principal; **a l. figure, a l. light** un personnage marquant

**leaf** [li:f] **1** (*pl* **leaves**) *n* feuille *f*; *(of book)* feuillet *m*; *(of table)* rallonge *f* **2** *vi* **to l. through** *(book)* feuilleter

**leaflet** ['li:flɪt] *n* prospectus *m*; *(containing instructions)* notice *f*

**league** [li:g] *n (alliance)* ligue *f*; *(in sport)* championnat *m*; *Pej* **in l. with** de connivence avec

**leak** [li:k] **1** *n (in pipe, information)* fuite *f*; *(in boat)* voie *f* d'eau **2** *vt Fig (information)* divulguer; **the pipe was leaking gas** du gaz fuyait du tuyau **3** *vi (of liquid, pipe, tap)* fuir; *(of ship)* faire eau; *Fig* **to l. out** *(of information)* être divulgué

**leaky** ['li:kɪ] (**-ier, -iest**) *adj (kettle, pipe, tap)* qui fuit; *(roof)* qui a une fuite

**lean**[1] [li:n] (**-er, -est**) *adj (meat)* maigre; *(person)* mince

**lean**[2] [li:n] (*pt & pp* **leaned** *or* **leant** [lent]) **1** *vt* **to l. sth on/against sth** appuyer qch sur/contre qch **2** *vi (of object)* pencher; *(of person)* se pencher; **to l. against/on sth** *(of person)* s'appuyer contre/sur qch; **to l. forward** *(of person)* se pencher (en avant); **to l. over** *(of person)* se pencher; *(of object)* pencher ▪ **leaning** *adj* penché; **l. against** *(resting)* appuyé contre ▪ **leanings** *npl* tendances *fpl* (**towards** à)

**leap** [li:p] **1** *n (jump)* bond *m*, saut *m*; *Fig (change, increase)* bond *m*; **l. year** année *f* bissextile **2** (*pt & pp* **leaped** *or* **leapt**) *vi* bondir, sauter; **to l. to one's feet, to l. up** se lever d'un bond

**leapt** [lept] *pt & pp of* **leap**

**learn** [lɜ:n] (*pt & pp* **learned** *or* **learnt** [lɜ:nt]) **1** *vt* apprendre (**that** que); **to l. (how) to do sth** apprendre à faire qch **2** *vi* apprendre; **to l. about sth** *(study)* étudier qch; *(hear about)* apprendre qch ▪ **learned** [-ɪd] *adj* savant ▪ **learner** *n (beginner)* débutant,

-e *mf*; *(student)* étudiant, -e *mf* ▪ **learning** *n (of language)* apprentissage *m* (**of** de); *(knowledge)* savoir *m*

**lease** [li:s] **1** *n* bail *m* (*pl* baux) **2** *vt (house)* louer à bail (**from/to** à)

**leash** [li:ʃ] *n (of dog)* laisse *f*; **on a l.** en laisse

**least** [li:st] **1** *adj* **the l.** *(smallest amount of)* le moins de; **he has (the) l. talent** il a le moins de talent (**of all** de tous); **the l. effort/noise** le moindre effort/bruit **2** *n* **the l.** le moins; **at l.** du moins; *(with quantity)* au moins; **not in the l.** pas du tout **3** *adv (work, eat)* le moins; **the l. difficult** le/la moins difficile; **l. of all** *(especially not)* surtout pas

**leather** ['leðə(r)] *n* cuir *m*

**leave** [li:v] **1** *n (holiday)* congé *m*; *(of soldier, permission)* permission *f*; **to be on l.** être en congé; *(of soldier)* être en permission; **to take (one's) l. of sb** prendre congé de qn

**2** (*pt & pp* **left**) *vt (allow to remain, forget)* laisser; *(depart from)* quitter; **to l. sth with sb** *(entrust, give)* laisser qch à qn; **to be left (over)** rester; **there's no bread left** il ne reste plus de pain; **I'll l. it (up) to you** je m'en remets à toi

**3** *vi (go away)* partir (**from** de; **for** pour)

▸ **leave behind** *vt sep* **to l. sth behind** *(on purpose)* laisser qch; *(accidentally)* oublier qch; **to l. sb behind** *(not take)* partir sans qn; *(surpass)* dépasser qn; *(in race, at school)* distancer qn

▸ **leave off** *vt sep (lid)* ne pas remettre; *Fam* **to l. off doing sth** *(stop)* arrêter de faire qch

▸ **leave on** *vt sep (clothes)* garder

▸ **leave out** *vt sep (forget to put)* oublier de mettre; *(deliberately omit)* décider de ne pas inclure; *(when reading) (word, line)* sauter; *(exclude)* exclure

**Lebanon** ['lebənən] *n* le Liban

**lecherous** ['letʃərəs] *adj* lubrique

**lecture** ['lektʃə(r)] **1** *n (public speech)* conférence *f*; *(as part of series at university)* cours *m* magistral; *(scolding)* sermon *m*; **l. hall** amphithéâtre *m* **2** *vt Fam (scold)* faire la morale à **3** *vi* faire une conférence/un cours ▪ **lecturer** *n* conférencier, -ère *mf*; *(at university)* enseignant, -e *mf*

**led** [led] *pt & pp of* **lead**[2]

**ledge** [ledʒ] *n (on wall, window)* rebord *m*

**ledger** ['ledʒə(r)] *n* grand livre *m*

**leek** [li:k] *n* poireau *m*

**leer** [lɪə(r)] *vi* **to l. at sb** *(lustfully)* regarder qn d'un air lubrique

**leeway** ['li:weɪ] *n* marge *f* (de manœuvre)

**left**[1] [left] *pt & pp of* **leave** ▪ **left-luggage** *n Br* **l. office** consigne *f*

**left**[2] [left] **1** *adj (side, hand)* gauche **2** *n* gauche *f*; **on** *or* **to the l.** à gauche (**of** de) **3** *adv* à gauche ▪ **left-hand** *adj* de gauche; **on the l. side** à gauche (**of** de); **l. drive** conduite *f* à gauche ▪ **left-handed** *adj (person)* gaucher, -ère ▪ **left-wing** *adj (views, government)* de gauche

**leftovers** ['leftəʊvəz] *npl* restes *mpl*

**leg** [leg] *n* jambe *f*; *(of dog, bird)* patte *f*; *(of table)* pied *m*; *(of journey)* étape *f*; **l. of chicken, chicken l.** cuisse *f* de poulet; **to pull sb's l.** *(make fun of)* mettre qn en boîte

**legacy** ['legəsɪ] (*pl* **-ies**) *n (in a will)* & *Fig* legs *m*

**legal** ['li:gəl] *adj (lawful)* légal; *(affairs, adviser)* juridique ▪ **legalize** *vt* légaliser ▪ **legally** *adv* légalement

**legend** ['ledʒənd] *n (story, inscription)* légende *f* ▪ **legendary** *adj* légendaire

**leggings** ['legɪŋz] *npl (of woman)* caleçon *m*

**legible** ['ledʒɪbəl] *adj* lisible

**legislation** [ledʒɪs'leɪʃən] *n (laws)* législation *f*; **(piece of) l.** loi *f*

**legislative** ['ledʒɪslətɪv] *adj* législatif, -ive

**legitimate** [lɪ'dʒɪtɪmət] *adj* légitime

**legroom** ['legru:m] *n* place *f* pour les jambes

**leisure** [*Br* 'leʒə(r), *Am* 'li:ʒər] *n* **l.**

**(time)** loisirs *mpl*; **l. centre** *or* **complex** centre *m* de loisirs; **at (one's) l.** à tête reposée ▪ **leisurely** [*Br* 'leʒəlɪ, *Am* 'liːʒərlɪ] *adj (walk, occupation)* peu fatigant; *(meal, life)* tranquille; **at a l. pace, in a l. way** sans se presser

**lemon** ['lemən] *n* citron *m*; *Br* **l. drink, l. squash** citronnade *f*; **l. tea** thé *m* au citron ▪ **lemonade** *n (still)* citronnade *f*; *Br (fizzy)* limonade *f*

**lend** [lend] *(pt & pp* **lent***) vt* prêter (**to** à); *(support)* apporter (**to** à); *Fig (charm, colour)* donner (**to** à) ▪ **lender** *n* prêteur, -euse *mf*

**length** [leŋθ] *n (in space)* longueur *f*; *(section of road, string)* tronçon *m*; *(of cloth)* métrage *m*; *(duration)* durée *f*; **at l.** *(at last)* enfin; **at (great) l.** *(in detail)* dans le détail; **to go to great lengths** se donner beaucoup de mal (**to do** pour faire)

**lengthen** ['leŋθən] *vt (garment)* allonger; *(holiday, visit)* prolonger ▪ **lengthwise** *adv* dans le sens de la longueur ▪ **lengthy** (**-ier, -iest**) *adj* long (*f* longue)

**lenient** ['liːnɪənt] *adj* indulgent (**to** envers) ▪ **leniently** *adv* avec indulgence

**lens** [lenz] *(pl* **lenses** [-zəz]*) n* lentille *f*; *(in spectacles)* verre *m*; *(of camera)* objectif *m*

**Lent** [lent] *n Rel* carême *m*

**lent** [lent] *pt & pp of* **lend**

**lentil** ['lentəl] *n* lentille *f*

**leopard** ['lepəd] *n* léopard *m*

**leotard** ['liːətɑːd] *n* justaucorps *m*

**lesbian** ['lezbɪən] **1** *adj* lesbien, -enne **2** *n* lesbienne *f*

**less** [les] **1** *adj & pron* moins (de) (**than** que); **l. time** moins de temps; **she has l. (than you)** elle en a moins (que toi); **l. than a kilo** moins d'un kilo **2** *adv* moins (**than** que); **l. (often)** moins souvent; **one l.** un(e) de moins **3** *prep* moins

**-less** [ləs] *suff* sans; **childless** sans enfants

**lessen** ['lesən] *vti* diminuer

**lesser** ['lesə(r)] **1** *adj* moindre **2** *n* **the l. of** le/la moindre de

**lesson** ['lesən] *n* leçon *f*; **an English l.** une leçon d'anglais; *Fig* **he has learnt his l.** ça lui a servi de leçon

**lest** [lest] *conj* de peur que… *(+ ne + subjunctive)*

---

**LET[1]** [let] **1** *(pt & pp* **let**, *pres p* **letting***) vt (allow)* **to l. sb do sth** laisser qn faire qch; **to l. sb have sth** donner qch à qn; **to l. go of sb/sth** lâcher qn/qch **2** *v aux* **l.'s eat/go** mangeons/partons; **l.'s go for a stroll** allons nous promener; **l. him come** qu'il vienne ▪ **letdown** *n* déception *f*

▸ **let down** *vt sep (lower)* baisser; *(hair)* dénouer; *(tyre)* dégonfler; **to l. sb down** *(disappoint)* décevoir qn; **don't l. me down** je compte sur toi

▸ **let in** *vt sep (person, dog)* faire entrer; *(light)* laisser entrer; **to l. sb in on sth** mettre qn au courant de qch; **to l. oneself in for trouble** s'attirer des ennuis

▸ **let off** *vt sep (firework)* tirer; *(bomb)* faire exploser; *(gun)* faire partir; **to l. sb off** *(allow to leave)* laisser partir qn; *(not punish)* ne pas punir qn; **to be l. off with a fine** s'en tirer avec une amende; **to l. sb off doing sth** dispenser qn de faire qch

▸ **let on** *vi Fam* **to l. on that…** *(reveal)* dire que…

▸ **let out** *vt sep (allow to leave)* laisser sortir; *(prisoner)* relâcher; *(cry, secret)* laisser échapper; *(skirt)* élargir

▸ **let up** *vi (of rain, person)* s'arrêter

---

**let[2]** [let] *(pt & pp* **let**, *pres p* **letting***) vt* **to l. (out)** *(house, room)* louer

**lethal** ['liːθəl] *adj (blow, dose)* mortel, -elle; *(weapon)* meurtrier, -ère

**lethargic** [lɪ'θɑːdʒɪk] *adj* léthargique

**letter** ['letə(r)] *n (message, part of word)* lettre *f*; **l. opener** coupe-papier *m inv* ▪ **letterbox** *n Br* boîte *f* aux lettres ▪ **letterheaded** *adj* **l. paper** papier *m* à en-tête ▪ **lettering** *n (letters)* lettres *fpl*

**lettuce** ['letɪs] *n* laitue *f*
**letup** ['letʌp] *n* répit *m*
**level** ['levəl] **1** *n* niveau *m*; **at eye l.** à hauteur des yeux **2** *adj (surface)* plat; *(equal in score)* à égalité (**with** avec); *(in height)* à la même hauteur (**with** que); *Br* **l. crossing** *(for train)* passage *m* à niveau **3** (*Br* **-ll-**, *Am* **-l-**) *vt (surface, differences)* aplanir; *(building)* raser; *(gun)* braquer (**at** sur); *(accusation)* lancer (**at** contre) **4** *vi* **to l. off** *or* **out** *(of prices)* se stabiliser ▪ **level-headed** *adj* équilibré
**lever** [ *Br* 'li:və(r), *Am* 'levər] *n* levier *m*
**levy** ['levɪ] **1** (*pl* **-ies**) *n (tax)* impôt *m* (**on** sur) **2** (*pt & pp* **-ied**) *vt (tax)* lever
**lewd** [lu:d] (**-er, -est**) *adj* obscène
**liability** [laɪə'bɪlətɪ] *n (legal responsibility)* responsabilité *f* (**for** de); *(disadvantage)* handicap *m*; *Fin* **liabilities** *(debts)* passif *m*
**liable** ['laɪəbəl] *adj* **l. to** *(dizziness)* sujet, -ette à; *(fine, tax)* passible de; **to be l. to do sth** risquer de faire qch; **l. for sth** *(responsible)* responsable de qch
**liaise** [li:'eɪz] *vi* travailler en liaison (**with** avec) ▪ **liaison** [li:'eɪzɒn] *n (contact, love affair)* liaison *f*
**liar** ['laɪə(r)] *n* menteur, -euse *mf*
**libel** ['laɪbəl] **1** *n (in law)* diffamation *f* **2** (*Br* **-ll-**, *Am* **-l-**) *vt* diffamer (par écrit)
**liberal** ['lɪbərəl] **1** *adj (open-minded)* & *Pol* libéral; *(generous)* généreux, -euse (**with** de) **2** *n Pol* libéral, -e *mf*
**liberate** ['lɪbəreɪt] *vt* libérer ▪ **liberation** *n* libération *f*
**liberty** ['lɪbətɪ] (*pl* **-ies**) *n* liberté *f*; **to be at l. to do sth** être libre de faire qch; **to take liberties with sb/sth** prendre des libertés avec qn/qch
**library** ['laɪbrərɪ] (*pl* **-ies**) *n* bibliothèque *f* ▪ **librarian** [-'breərɪən] *n* bibliothécaire *mf*
**libretto** [lɪ'bretəʊ] (*pl* **-os**) *n Mus* livret *m*
**Libya** ['lɪbɪə] *n* la Libye
**lice** [laɪs] *pl of* **louse**
**licence** ['laɪsəns] (*Am* **license**) *n* *(permit)* permis *m*; *(for trading)* licence *f*; **(TV) l.** redevance *f*; **l. plate/number** *(of vehicle)* plaque *f*/numéro *m* d'immatriculation
**license** ['laɪsəns] **1** *n Am* = **licence 2** *vt* accorder un permis/une licence à
**lick** [lɪk] *vt* lécher
**licorice** ['lɪkərɪʃ, 'lɪkərɪs] *n* réglisse *f*
**lid** [lɪd] *n (of box, pan)* couvercle *m*
**lie**[1] [laɪ] **1** *n* mensonge *m* **2** (*pt & pp* **lied**, *pres p* **lying**) *vi (tell lies)* mentir
**lie**[2] [laɪ] (*pt* **lay**, *pp* **lain**, *pres p* **lying**) *vi* (**a**) *(of person, animal) (be in a flat position)* être allongé; *(get down)* s'allonger; **to be lying on the grass** être allongé sur l'herbe; **he lay asleep** il dormait; **here lies...** *(on tomb)* ci-gît... (**b**) *(of object)* être, se trouver; **the problem lies in the fact that...** le problème réside dans le fait que... ▪ **lie-down** *n Br* **to have a l.** faire une sieste ▪ **lie-in** *n Br* **to have a l.** faire la grasse matinée
▸**lie about, lie around** *vi (of objects, person)* traîner
▸**lie down** *vi* s'allonger; **to be lying down** être allongé
▸**lie in** *vi Br* faire la grasse matinée
**lieu** [lu:] *n* **in l. of sth** au lieu de qch
**lieutenant** [lu:'tenənt, *Br* lef'tenənt] *n* lieutenant *m*
**life** [laɪf] (*pl* **lives**) *n* vie *f*; *(of battery, machine)* durée *f* de vie; **to come to l.** *(of party, street)* s'animer; **to take one's (own) l.** se donner la mort; **l. expectancy** espérance *f* de vie; **l. insurance** assurance-vie *f*; **l. jacket** gilet *m* de sauvetage ▪ **lifebelt** *n* ceinture *f* de sauvetage ▪ **lifeboat** *n* canot *m* de sauvetage ▪ **lifebuoy** *n* bouée *f* de sauvetage ▪ **lifeguard** *n* maître nageur *m* ▪ **lifeless** *adj* sans vie ▪ **lifelike** *adj* très ressemblant ▪ **lifelong** *adj* de toute sa vie; *(friend)* de toujours ▪ **lifesize(d)** *adj* grandeur nature *inv* ▪ **lifestyle** *n* style *m* de vie ▪ **lifetime** *n* vie *f*; *Fig* éternité *f*
**lift** [lɪft] **1** *n Br (elevator)* ascenseur *m*; **to give sb a l.** emmener qn en voiture

(**to** à) **2** *vt* lever; *(heavy object)* soulever; *Fig (ban)* lever; *Fig (steal)* piquer (**from** à) **3** *vi (of fog)* se lever ■ **lift-off** *n (of space vehicle)* décollage *m*

▸ **lift down** *vt sep (take down)* descendre (**from** de)

▸ **lift off 1** *vt sep (take down)* descendre (**from** de) **2** *vi (of spacecraft)* décoller

▸ **lift out** *vt sep (take out)* sortir

▸ **lift up** *vt sep (arm, object, eyes)* lever; *(heavy object)* soulever

**ligament** ['lɪgəmənt] *n* ligament *m*

**light**[1] [laɪt] **1** *n* lumière *f*; *(on vehicle)* feu *m*; *(vehicle headlight)* phare *m*; **by the l. of sth** à la clarté de qch; **in the l. of...** *(considering)* à la lumière de...; **to bring sth to l.** mettre qch en lumière; **to come to l.** être découvert; **do you have a l.?** *(for cigarette)* est-ce que vous avez du feu?; **to set l. to sth** mettre le feu à qch; **turn right at the lights** tournez à droite après les feux; **l. bulb** ampoule *f*; **l. switch** interrupteur *m*

**2** *adj* **it will soon be l.** il fera bientôt jour

**3** (*pt & pp* **lit** *or* **lighted**) *vt (fire, candle, gas)* allumer; *(match)* allumer, gratter; **to l. (up)** *(room)* éclairer; *(cigarette)* allumer

**4** *vi* **to l. up** *(of smoker)* allumer une cigarette/un cigare/sa pipe ■ **lighting** *n (act, system)* éclairage *m*

**light**[2] [laɪt] *adj (bright, not dark)* clair; **a l. green jacket** une veste vert clair

**light**[3] [laɪt] *adj (in weight, quantity, strength)* léger, -ère; *(task)* facile; **l. rain** pluie *f* fine; **to travel l.** voyager avec peu de bagages ■ **light-hearted** *adj* enjoué

**lighten** ['laɪtən] *vt (make less heavy)* alléger

**lighter** ['laɪtə(r)] *n* briquet *m*; *(for cooker)* allume-gaz *m inv*

**lighthouse** ['laɪthaʊs] *n* phare *m*

**lightly** ['laɪtlɪ] *adv* légèrement; **to get off l.** s'en tirer à bon compte

**lightning** ['laɪtnɪŋ] **1** *n* éclairs *mpl*; **(flash of) l.** éclair *m* **2** *adj (speed)* foudroyant; *(visit)* éclair *inv*

**lightweight** ['laɪtweɪt] **1** *adj (shoes, fabric)* léger, -ère; *Fig & Pej (person)* pas sérieux, -euse **2** *n (in boxing)* poids *m* léger

**like**[1] [laɪk] **1** *prep* comme; **l. this** comme ça; **what's he l.?** comment est-il?; **to be** *or* **look l. sb/sth** ressembler à qn/qch; **what was the book l.?** comment as-tu trouvé le livre?

**2** *adv* **nothing l. as big** loin d'être aussi grand

**3** *conj Fam (as)* comme; **do l. I do** fais comme moi

**4** *n* **...and the l.** ...et ainsi de suite; **the likes of you** des gens de ton acabit

**like**[2] [laɪk] **1** *vt* aimer (bien) (**to do** *or* **doing** faire); **I l. him** je l'aime bien; **I'd l. to come** j'aimerais bien venir; **I'd l. a kilo of apples** je voudrais un kilo de pommes; **would you l. an apple?** voulez-vous une pomme?; **if you l.** si vous voulez

**2** *npl* **one's likes and dislikes** nos préférences *fpl* ■ **liking** *n* **a l. for** *(person)* de la sympathie pour; *(thing)* du goût pour; **to my l.** à mon goût

**likeable** ['laɪkəbəl] *adj* sympathique

**likely** ['laɪklɪ] **1** (**-ier, -iest**) *adj (result, event)* probable; *(excuse)* vraisemblable; **it's l. (that) she'll come** il est probable qu'elle viendra **2** *adv* **very l.** très probablement ■ **likelihood** *n* probabilité *f*; **there isn't much l. that...** il y a peu de chances que... *(+ subjunctive)*

**liken** ['laɪkən] *vt* comparer (**to** à)

**likeness** ['laɪknɪs] *n (similarity)* ressemblance *f*; **it's a good l.** c'est très ressemblant

**likewise** ['laɪkwaɪz] *adv (similarly)* de même

**lilac** ['laɪlək] **1** *n* lilas *m* **2** *adj (colour)* lilas *inv*

**Lilo®** ['laɪləʊ] (*pl* **-os**) *n Br* matelas *m* pneumatique

**lily** ['lɪlɪ] (*pl* **-ies**) *n* lis *m*

**limb** [lɪm] *n (of body)* membre *m*

**limber** ['lɪmbə(r)] *vi* **to l. up** s'échauffer

**lime** [laɪm] *n (fruit)* citron *m* vert

**limelight** ['laɪmlaɪt] *n* **to be in the l.** occuper le devant de la scène

**limit** ['lɪmɪt] **1** *n* limite *f*; *(restriction)* limitation *f* (**on** de); *Fam* **that's the l.!** c'est le comble!; **within limits** jusqu'à un certain point **2** *vt* limiter (**to** à); **to l. oneself to sth/doing sth** se borner à qch/faire qch ▪ **limitation** *n* limitation *f*

**limited** ['lɪmɪtɪd] *adj (restricted)* limité; *(edition)* à tirage limité; *Br* **l. company** société *f* à responsabilité limitée; *Br* **(public) l. company** *(with shareholders)* société *f* anonyme

**limousine** [lɪmə'ziːn] *n (car)* limousine *f*

**limp¹** [lɪmp] **1** *n* **to have a l.** boiter **2** *vi (of person)* boiter

**limp²** [lɪmp] (**-er, -est**) *adj (soft)* mou (*f* molle); *(flabby) (skin)* flasque; *(person, hat)* avachi

**line¹** [laɪn] **1** *n* ligne *f*; *(stroke)* trait *m*; *(of poem)* vers *m*; *(wrinkle)* ride *f*; *(track)* voie *f*; *(rope)* corde *f*; *(row)* rangée *f*; *(of vehicles)* file *f*; *(queue of people)* file *f*, queue *f*; *(of goods)* ligne *f* (de produits); **to learn one's lines** *(of actor)* apprendre son texte; **to be on the l.** *(at other end of phone line)* être au bout du fil; *(at risk) (of job)* être menacé; *Am* **to stand in l.** faire la queue; **in l. with sth** conforme à qch; **along the same lines** *(work, think, act)* de la même façon; *Fam* **to drop sb a l.** *(send a letter)* envoyer un mot à qn; **l. dancing** = danse de style country effectuée en rangs

**2** *vt* **to l. the street** *(of trees)* border la rue; *(of people)* s'aligner le long du trottoir; **to l. up** *(children, objects)* aligner; *(arrange)* organiser; **lined paper** papier *m* réglé

**3** *vi* **to l. up** s'aligner; *Am (queue up)* faire la queue ▪ **line-up** *n (row of people)* file *f*; *TV (of guests)* plateau *m*

**line²** [laɪn] *vt (clothes)* doubler

**linen** ['lɪnɪn] *n (sheets)* linge *m*; *(material)* (toile *f* de) lin *m*

**liner** ['laɪnə(r)] *n* (**a**) **(ocean) l.** paquebot *m* (**b**) *Br* **(dust)bin l.**, *Am* **garbage can l.** sac-poubelle *m*

**linesman** ['laɪnzmən] (*pl* **-men**) *n (in football)* juge *m* de touche

**linger** ['lɪŋgə(r)] *vi* **to l. (on)** *(of person)* s'attarder; *(of smell, memory)* persister; *(of doubt)* subsister

**linguist** ['lɪŋgwɪst] *n (specialist)* linguiste *mf* ▪ **linguistic** *adj* linguistique ▪ **linguistics** *n* linguistique *f*

**lining** ['laɪnɪŋ] *n (of clothes)* doublure *f*

**link** [lɪŋk] **1** *n (connection) & Comptr* lien *m*; *(of chain)* maillon *m*; *(by road, rail)* liaison *f* **2** *vt (connect)* relier (**to** à); *(relate, associate)* lier (**to** à); **to l. up** relier; *(computer)* connecter **3** *vi* **to l. up** *(of companies, countries)* s'associer; *(of roads)* se rejoindre

**lino** ['laɪnəʊ] (*pl* **-os**) *n Br* lino *m*

**lint** [lɪnt] *n (bandage)* tissu *m* ouaté; *(fluff)* peluches *fpl*

**lion** ['laɪən] *n* lion *m*; **l. cub** lionceau *m*

**lip** [lɪp] *n (of person)* lèvre *f*; *(of cup)* bord *m* ▪ **lip-read** (*pt & pp* **-read** [-red]) *vi* lire sur les lèvres ▪ **lipstick** *n* rouge *m* à lèvres

**liqueur** [*Br* lɪ'kjʊə(r), *Am* lɪ'kɜːr] *n* liqueur *f*

**liquid** ['lɪkwɪd] *n & adj* liquide *(m)*

**liquidate** ['lɪkwɪdeɪt] *vt (debt) & Fam (kill)* liquider

**liquidizer** ['lɪkwɪdaɪzə(r)] *n Br (for fruit juices, purées)* mixeur *m* ▪ **liquidize** *vt Br* passer au mixeur

**liquor** ['lɪkə(r)] *n Am* alcool *m*; **l. store** magasin *m* de vins et de spiritueux

**liquorice** ['lɪkərɪʃ, 'lɪkərɪs] *n Br* réglisse *f*

**lira** ['lɪərə] (*pl* **lire** ['lɪəreɪ]) *n* lire *f*

**lisp** [lɪsp] **1** *n* **to have a l.** zézayer **2** *vi* zézayer

**list** [lɪst] **1** *n* liste *f* **2** *vt (things)* faire la liste de; *(names)* mettre sur la liste; *(name one by one)* énumérer; *Br* **listed**

**building** monument *m* classé

**listen** ['lɪsən] *vi* écouter; **to l. to sb/sth** écouter qn/qch; **to l. (out) for** *(telephone, person)* guetter ▪ **listener** *n (to radio)* auditeur, -trice *mf*

**listless** ['lɪstləs] *adj* apathique

**lit** [lɪt] *pt & pp of* **light**[1]

**liter** ['li:tə(r)] *n Am* litre *m*

**literal** ['lɪtərəl] *adj* littéral; *(not exaggerated)* réel (*f* réelle)

**literally** ['lɪtərəlɪ] *adv* littéralement; *(really)* réellement ▪ **literary** *adj* littéraire

**literate** ['lɪtərət] *adj* qui sait lire et écrire

**literature** ['lɪtərətʃə(r)] *n* littérature *f*; *(pamphlets)* documentation *f*

**lithe** [laɪð] *adj* agile

**litigation** [lɪtɪ'geɪʃən] *n* litige *m*

**litre** ['li:tə(r)] (*Am* **liter**) *n* litre *m*

**litter** ['lɪtə(r)] **1** *n* (**a**) *(rubbish)* détritus *mpl*; *(papers)* papiers *mpl* (**b**) *Br* **l. bin** boîte *f* à ordures; *(young animals)* portée *f*; *(for cat)* litière *f* **2** *vt Br* **to be littered with sth** être jonché de qch

---

**LITTLE** ['lɪtəl] **1** *n* peu *m*; **I've l. left** il m'en reste peu; **she eats l.** elle mange peu; **I have a l.** j'en ai un peu

**2** *adj* (**a**) *(small)* petit; **a l. bit** un (petit) peu (**b**) *(not much)* peu de; **l. time/money** peu de temps/d'argent; **a l. time/money** un peu de temps/d'argent

**3** *adv (somewhat, rather)* peu; **l. by l.** peu à peu; **as l. as possible** le moins possible; **a l. heavy/better** un peu lourd/mieux; **to work a l.** travailler un peu

---

**live**[1] [laɪv] **1** *adj* (**a**) *(electric wire)* sous tension; *(plugged in) (appliance)* branché; *(ammunition)* réel (*f* réelle), de combat (**b**) *(alive)* vivant **2** *adj & adv (on radio, television)* en direct; **a l. broadcast** une émission en direct; **a l. recording** un enregistrement public

**live**[2] [lɪv] **1** *vt (life)* mener, vivre **2** *vi* vivre; **where do you l.?** où habitez-vous?; **to l. in Paris** habiter (à) Paris

▸ **live down** *vt sep* faire oublier

▸ **live off** *vt insep (eat)* vivre de; *(sponge off)* vivre aux crochets de

▸ **live on 1** *vt sep* = **live off 2** *vi (of memory)* survivre

▸ **live through** *vt insep (experience)* vivre

▸ **live up to** *vt insep (sb's expectations)* se montrer à la hauteur de

**livelihood** ['laɪvlɪhʊd] *n* **my l.** mon gagne-pain; **to earn one's** *or* **a l.** gagner sa vie

**lively** ['laɪvlɪ] (**-ier, -iest**) *adj (person, style)* plein de vie; *(story)* vivant; *(mind)* vif (*f* vive); *(discussion, conversation)* animé

▸ **liven up** ['laɪvən] **1** *vt sep (person)* égayer; *(party)* animer **2** *vi (of person, party)* s'animer

**liver** ['lɪvə(r)] *n* foie *m*

**livestock** ['laɪvstɒk] *n* bétail *m*

**livid** ['lɪvɪd] *adj (angry)* furieux, -euse

**living** ['lɪvɪŋ] **1** *adj (alive)* vivant; **within l. memory** de mémoire d'homme; **the l.** les vivants *mpl* **2** *n (livelihood)* vie *f*; **to make** *or* **earn a** *or* **one's l.** gagner sa vie; **l. room** salle *f* de séjour

**lizard** ['lɪzəd] *n* lézard *m*

**load** [ləʊd] **1** *n (object carried, burden)* charge *f*; *(freight)* chargement *m*; *(strain, weight)* poids *m*; *Fam* **a l. of, loads of** *(people, money)* un tas de **2** *vt (truck, gun)* charger (**with** de); **to l. up** *(car, ship)* charger (**with** de) **3** *vi* **to l. (up)** prendre un chargement

**loaded** ['ləʊdɪd] *adj (gun, vehicle)* chargé; *Fam (rich)* plein aux as

**loaf** [ləʊf] **1** (*pl* **loaves**) *n* pain *m* **2** *vi* **to l. (about)** fainéanter

**loan** [ləʊn] **1** *n (money lent)* prêt *m*; *(money borrowed)* emprunt *m*; **on l. from** prêté par **2** *vt (lend)* prêter (**to** à)

**loathe** [ləʊð] *vt* détester (**doing** faire)

**lobby** ['lɒbɪ] **1** (*pl* **-ies**) *n* (**a**) *(of hotel)* hall *m*; *(of theatre)* foyer *m* (**b**) *(in politics)* groupe *m* de pression **2** (*pt & pp* **-ied**) *vt* faire pression sur **3** *vi* **to l. for sth** faire pression pour obtenir qch

**lobster** ['lɒbstə(r)] *n* homard *m*; *(spiny)* langouste *f*

**local** ['ləʊkəl] **1** *adj* local; *(regional)* régional; *(of the neighbourhood)* du quartier; **a l. phone call** *(within town)* une communication urbaine **2** *n Br Fam (pub)* bistrot *m* du coin; **the locals** *(people)* les gens *mpl* du coin

**locality** [ləʊ'kælətɪ] (*pl* **-ies**) *n (neighbourhood)* environs *mpl*

**locally** ['ləʊkəlɪ] *adv* dans le quartier

**locate** [ləʊ'keɪt] *vt (find)* repérer; *(pain, noise, leak)* localiser; *(situate)* situer; **to be located in Paris** être situé à Paris ▪ **location** *n (site)* emplacement *m*; **on l.** *(shoot a film)* en extérieur

**lock¹** [lɒk] *n (of hair)* mèche *f*

**lock²** [lɒk] **1** *n* (**a**) *(on door, chest)* serrure *f*; **(anti-theft) l.** *(on vehicle)* antivol *m* (**b**) *(on canal)* écluse *f* **2** *vt (door, car)* fermer à clef **3** *vi* fermer à clef

▸ **lock away** *vt sep (prisoner)* enfermer; *(jewels)* mettre sous clef

▸ **lock in** *vt sep (person)* enfermer; **to l. sb in sth** enfermer qn dans qch

▸ **lock out** *vt sep (person)* enfermer dehors

▸ **lock up 1** *vt sep (house, car)* fermer à clef; *(prisoner)* enfermer; *(jewels)* mettre sous clef, enfermer **2** *vi* fermer à clef

**locker** ['lɒkə(r)] *n (in school)* casier *m*; *(for luggage) (at station, airport)* casier *m* de consigne automatique; *(for clothes)* vestiaire *m* (métallique); *Am Sport* **l. room** vestiaire *m*

**locket** ['lɒkɪt] *n* médaillon *m*

**locksmith** ['lɒksmɪθ] *n* serrurier *m*

**locomotive** [ləʊkə'məʊtɪv] *n* locomotive *f*

**locust** ['ləʊkəst] *n* sauterelle *f*

**lodge** [lɒdʒ] **1** *n (house)* pavillon *m*; *(of porter)* loge *f* **2** *vt (person)* loger **3** *vi (of bullet)* se loger (**in** dans)

**lodger** ['lɒdʒə(r)] *n (room and meals)* pensionnaire *mf*; *(room only)* locataire *mf*

**lodgings** ['lɒdʒɪŋz] *n (flat)* logement *m*; *(room)* chambre *f*; **in l.** en meublé

**loft** [lɒft] *n* grenier *m*

**lofty** ['lɒftɪ] (**-ier, -iest**) *adj (high, noble)* élevé

**log** [lɒg] **1** *n (tree trunk)* tronc *m* d'arbre; *(for fire)* bûche *f*; **l. cabin** hutte *f* en rondin; **l. fire** feu *m* de bois **2** (*pt & pp* **-gg-**) *vt (facts)* noter **3** *vi Comptr* **to l. in/out** entrer/sortir ▪ **logbook** *n (on ship)* journal *m* de bord; *(on plane)* carnet *m* de vol

**logic** ['lɒdʒɪk] *n* logique *f* ▪ **logical** *adj* logique ▪ **logically** *adv* logiquement

**logistics** [lə'dʒɪstɪks] *n* logistique *f*

**logo** ['ləʊgəʊ] (*pl* **-os**) *n* logo *m*

**loiter** ['lɔɪtə(r)] *vi* traîner

**loll** [lɒl] *vi (in armchair)* se prélasser

**lollipop** ['lɒlɪpɒp] *n* sucette *f*; *Br* **l. man/lady** = contractuel ou contractuelle qui aide les écoliers à traverser la rue ▪ **lolly** (*pl* **-ies**) *n Fam (lollipop)* sucette *f*; **(ice) l.** glace *f* à l'eau

**London** ['lʌndən] **1** *n* Londres *m ou f* **2** *adj* londonien, -enne

**lone** [ləʊn] *adj* solitaire

**loneliness** ['ləʊnlɪnəs] *n* solitude *f* ▪ **lonely** (**-ier, -iest**) *adj (road, house, life)* solitaire; *(person)* seul

**loner** ['ləʊnə(r)] *n* solitaire *mf*

**LONG¹** [lɒŋ] **1** (**-er, -est**) *adj* long (*f* longue); **to be 10 metres l.** avoir 10 mètres de long; **to be six weeks l.** durer six semaines; **how l. is...?** quelle est la longueur de...?; *(time)* quelle est la durée de...?; **a l. time** longtemps; **l. jump** *(sport)* saut *m* en longueur

**2** *adv (a long time)* longtemps; **has he been here l.?** il y a longtemps qu'il est ici?; **how l.?** *(in time)* combien de temps?; **not l.** peu de temps; **before l.** sous peu; **no longer** ne... plus; **a bit longer** *(wait)* encore un peu; **I won't be l.** je n'en ai pas pour longtemps; **don't be l.** dépêche-toi; **all summer/winter l.** tout l'été/l'hiver; **l. live the queen!** vive la reine!; **as l. as, so l. as**

*(provided that)* pourvu que *(+ subjunctive)*; **as l. as I live** tant que je vivrai ▪ **long-distance** *adj (race)* de fond; *(phone call)* interurbain ▪ **long-haired** *adj* aux cheveux longs ▪ **long-life** *adj (battery)* longue durée *inv*; *(milk)* longue conservation *inv* ▪ **long-range** *adj (forecast)* à long terme ▪ **longsighted** *adj (person)* presbyte ▪ **longstanding** *adj* de longue date ▪ **long-term** *adj* à long terme ▪ **long-winded** *adj (speech, speaker)* verbeux, -euse

---

**long²** [lɒŋ] *vi* **to l. for sth** avoir très envie de qch; **to l. to do sth** avoir très envie de faire qch ▪ **longing** *n* désir *m*

**longitude** ['lɒndʒɪtju:d] *n* longitude *f*

**loo** [lu:] *(pl* **loos***) n Br Fam* **the l.** le petit coin

**look** [lʊk] **1** *n (glance)* regard *m*; *(appearance)* air *m*, allure *f*; **to have a l. (at sth)** jeter un coup d'œil (à qch); **to have a l. (for sth)** chercher (qch); **to have a l. (a)round** regarder; *(walk)* faire un tour; **let me have a l.** fais voir

**2** *vt* **to l. sb in the face** regarder qn dans les yeux

**3** *vi* regarder; **to l. tired/happy** *(seem)* avoir l'air fatigué/heureux; **to l. pretty/ugly** être joli/laid; **you l. like** *or* **as if** *or* **as though you're tired** tu as l'air fatigué; **to l. like an apple** avoir l'air d'une pomme; **you l. like my brother** tu ressembles à mon frère; **it looks like rain** on dirait qu'il va pleuvoir; **what does he l. like?** comment est-il?; **to l. well** *or* **good** *(of person)* avoir bonne mine; **you l. good in that hat** ce chapeau te va très bien; **that looks bad** *(action)* ça fait mauvais effet

▸**look after** *vt insep (take care of)* s'occuper de; *(keep safely)* garder (**for sb** pour qn); **to l. after oneself** *(keep healthy)* faire bien attention à soi; *(manage, cope)* se débrouiller

▸**look around 1** *vt insep (town, shops)* faire un tour dans **2** *vi (have a look)* regarder; *(walk round)* faire un tour

▸**look at** *vt insep* regarder; *(consider)* considérer

▸**look away** *vi* détourner les yeux

▸**look back** *vi* regarder derrière soi; *(in time)* regarder en arrière

▸**look down** *vi* baisser les yeux; *(from a height)* regarder en bas; **to l. down on** *(consider scornfully)* regarder de haut

▸**look for** *vt insep (seek)* chercher

▸**look forward to** *vt insep (event)* attendre avec impatience; **to l. forward to doing sth** avoir hâte de faire qch

▸**look in** *vi* regarder à l'intérieur; **to l. in on sb** passer voir qn

▸**look into** *vt insep (examine)* examiner; *(find out about)* se renseigner sur

▸**look on 1** *vt insep (consider)* considérer (**as** comme) **2** *vi (watch)* regarder; **to l. on to** *(of window, house)* donner sur

▸**look out** *vi (be careful)* faire attention; **to l. out for sb/sth** *(seek)* chercher qn/qch; *(watch)* guetter qn/qch; **to l. out on to** *(of window, house)* donner sur

▸**look over** *vt insep (examine fully)* examiner; *(briefly)* parcourir; *(region, town)* parcourir, visiter

▸**look round 1** *vt insep (visit)* visiter **2** *vi (have a look)* regarder; *(walk round)* faire un tour; *(look back)* se retourner; **to l. round for sb/sth** *(seek)* chercher qn/qch

▸**look through** *vt insep (inspect)* passer en revue

▸**look up 1** *vt sep (word)* chercher; **to l. sb up** *(visit)* passer voir qn **2** *vi (of person)* lever les yeux; *(into the air or sky)* regarder en l'air; *(improve) (of situation)* s'améliorer; *Fig* **to l. up to sb** respecter qn

**-looking** ['lʊkɪŋ] *suff* **pleasant-/tired-l.** à l'air agréable/fatigué

**lookout** ['lʊkaʊt] *n (soldier)* guetteur *m*; **l. (post)** observatoire *m*; **to be on the l. for sb/sth** guetter qn/qch

**loom** [lu:m] **1** *n (weaving machine)* métier *m* à tisser **2** *vi* **to l. (up)** *(of* *mountain)* apparaître indistinctement; *(of event)* paraître imminent

**loony** ['lu:nɪ] (*pl* **-ies**) *n & adj Fam* dingue *(mf)*

**loop** [lu:p] *n* boucle *f*

**loophole** ['lu:phəʊl] *n (in law)* vide *m* juridique

**loose** [lu:s] **1** (**-er, -est**) *adj (screw, belt, knot)* desserré; *(tooth, stone)* qui bouge; *(page)* détaché; *(clothes)* flottant; *(hair)* dénoué; *(translation)* vague; *(articles for sale)* en vrac; *Br (cheese, tea)* au poids; **there's an animal/prisoner l.** *(having escaped)* il y a un animal échappé/un prisonnier évadé; **l. change** petite monnaie *f*; **to come l.** *(of knot, screw)* se desserrer; *(of page)* se détacher; *(of tooth)* se mettre à bouger; **to get l.** *(of dog)* se détacher; **to set** *or* **turn l.** *(dog)* lâcher **2** *n* **on the l.** *(prisoner)* en cavale; *(animal)* en liberté

**loosely** ['lu:slɪ] *adv (hang)* lâchement; *(hold, tie)* sans serrer; *(translate)* de façon approximative

**loosen** ['lu:sən] *vt (knot, belt, screw)* desserrer; *(rope)* détendre; **to l. one's grip** relâcher son étreinte

**loot** [lu:t] **1** *n* butin *m*; *Fam (money)* fric *m* **2** *vt* piller ▪ **looting** *n* pillage *m*

**lop** [lɒp] (*pt & pp* **-pp-**) *vt* **to l. (off)** couper

**lop-sided** [lɒp'saɪdɪd] *adj (crooked)* de travers

**lord** [lɔ:d] *n* seigneur *m*; *(British title)* lord *m*; **the L.** *(God)* le Seigneur; *Fam* **good L.!** bon sang!

**lorry** ['lɒrɪ] (*pl* **-ies**) *n Br* camion *m*; *(heavy)* poids *m* lourd; **l. driver** camionneur *m*; **(long-distance) l. driver** routier *m*

**lose** [lu:z] (*pt & pp* **lost**) **1** *vt* perdre; **to l. one's life** trouver la mort (**in** dans); **to l. one's way, to get lost** *(of person)* se perdre; *Fam* **get lost!** fous le camp!; **that lost us the war/our jobs** cela nous a coûté la guerre/notre travail; **the clock loses six minutes a day** la pendule retarde de six minutes par jour **2** *vi* perdre; **to l. out** être perdant; **to l. to sb** *(in contest)* être battu par qn ▪ **loser** *n (in contest)* perdant, -e *mf*; *Fam (failure in life)* minable *mf* ▪ **losing** *adj (number, team, horse)* perdant

**loss** [lɒs] *n* perte *f*; **to sell sth at a l.** vendre qch à perte; **to make a l.** *(financially)* perdre de l'argent

**lost** [lɒst] **1** *pt & pp of* **lose** **2** *adj* perdu; *Br* **l. property,** *Am* **l. and found** objets *mpl* trouvés

**lot¹** [lɒt] *n (destiny)* sort *m*; *(batch)* lot *m*; **to draw lots** tirer au sort

**lot²** [lɒt] *n* **the l.** *(everything)* (le) tout; **the l. of you** vous tous; **a l. of, lots of** beaucoup de; **a l.** beaucoup; **quite a l.** pas mal (**of** de)

**lotion** ['ləʊʃən] *n* lotion *f*

**lottery** ['lɒtərɪ] (*pl* **-ies**) *n* loterie *f*; **l. ticket** billet *m* de loterie

**loud** [laʊd] **1** (**-er, -est**) *adj (voice, music)* fort; *(noise, cry)* grand; *(laugh)* gros (*f* grosse); *(gaudy)* voyant **2** *adv (shout)* fort; **out l.** tout haut ▪ **loudly** *adv (speak, laugh, shout)* fort ▪ **loudspeaker** *n* haut-parleur *m*; *(for speaking to crowd)* porte-voix *m inv*; *(of stereo system)* enceinte *f*

**lounge** [laʊndʒ] **1** *n (in house, hotel)* salon *m*; **airport l.** salle *f* d'aéroport **2** *vi (loll in armchair)* se prélasser; **to l. about** *(idle)* paresser

**louse** [laʊs] (*pl* **lice**) *n (insect)* pou *m*

**lousy** ['laʊzɪ] (**-ier, -iest**) *adj Fam (bad)* nul (*f* nulle); *(food, weather)* dégueulasse; **to feel l.** être mal fichu

**lout** [laʊt] *n* voyou *m*

**love** [lʌv] **1** *n* (**a**) *(feeling)* amour *m*; **in l.** amoureux, -euse (**with** de); **they're in l.** ils s'aiment; **give him/her my l.** *(greeting)* dis-lui bien des choses de ma part; **l. affair** liaison *f* (**b**) *(in tennis)* rien *m*; **15 l.** 15 à rien **2** *vt (person)* aimer; *(thing, activity)* adorer (**to do** *or* **doing** faire) ▪ **loving** *adj* affectueux, -euse

**lovely** ['lʌvlɪ] (**-ier, -iest**) *adj (idea, smell)* très bon (*f* bonne); *(pretty)* joli;

*(charming)* charmant; *(kind)* gentil, -ille; **the weather's l., it's l.** il fait beau; **(it's) l. to see you!** je suis ravi de te voir!

**lover** ['lʌvə(r)] *n (man)* amant *m*; *(woman)* maîtresse *f*; **a l. of music/art** un amateur de musique/d'art

**low¹** [ləʊ] **1** (**-er, -est**) *adj* bas (*f* basse); *(speed, income, intelligence)* faible; *(opinion, quality)* mauvais; **she's l. on** *(money)* elle n'a plus beaucoup de; **to feel l.** *(depressed)* être déprimé; **lower** inférieur; *Am* **l. beams** *(of vehicle)* codes *mpl*

**2** (**-er, -est**) *adv* bas; **to turn (down) l.** mettre plus bas; **to run l.** *(of supplies)* s'épuiser

**3** *n* **to reach a new l.** *or* **an all-time l.** *(of prices)* atteindre leur niveau le plus bas ▪ **low-cut** *adj* décolleté ▪ **low-down** *n Fam (facts)* tuyaux *mpl* ▪ **low-fat** *adj (milk)* écrémé; *(cheese)* allégé ▪ **low-key** *adj (discreet)* discret, -ète ▪ **low-paid** *adj* mal payé

**low²** [ləʊ] *vi (of cattle)* meugler

**lower** ['ləʊə(r)] *vt* baisser; **to l. sb/sth** *(by rope)* descendre qn/qch; *Fig* **to l. oneself** s'abaisser

**lowly** ['ləʊlɪ] (**-ier, -iest**) *adj* humble

**loyal** ['lɔɪəl] *adj* loyal (**to** envers) ▪ **loyalty** *n* loyauté *f*

**lozenge** ['lɒzɪndʒ] *n (tablet)* pastille *f*; *(shape)* losange *m*

**LP** [el'piː] (*abbr* **long-playing record**) *n* 33 tours *m inv*

**L-plate** ['elpleɪt] *n Br* = plaque apposée sur une voiture pour signaler que le conducteur est en conduite accompagnée

**Ltd** (*abbr* **Limited**) *Br Com* ≃ SARL

**lubricate** ['luːbrɪkeɪt] *vt* lubrifier; *(machine, car wheels)* graisser

**lucid** ['luːsɪd] *adj* lucide

**luck** [lʌk] *n (chance)* chance *f*; *(good fortune)* (bonne) chance *f*, bonheur *m*; **to be in l.** avoir de la chance; **to be out of l.** ne pas avoir de chance; **to wish sb l.** souhaiter bonne chance à qn; **bad l.** malchance *f*; **hard l.!, tough l.!** pas de chance!

**luckily** ['lʌkɪlɪ] *adv* heureusement

**lucky** ['lʌkɪ] (**-ier, -iest**) *adj (person)* chanceux, -euse; **to be l.** *(of person)* avoir de la chance; **it's l. that...** c'est une chance que... *(+ subjunctive)*; **l. number** chiffre *m* porte-bonheur

**lucrative** ['luːkrətɪv] *adj* lucratif, -ive

**ludicrous** ['luːdɪkrəs] *adj* ridicule

**luggage** ['lʌgɪdʒ] *n* bagages *mpl*; **a piece of l.** un bagage; **hand l.** bagages *mpl* à main; **l. compartment** compartiment *m* à bagages

**lukewarm** ['luːkwɔːm] *adj (water, soup)* tiède

**lull** [lʌl] **1** *n* arrêt *m*; *(in storm)* accalmie *f* **2** *vt* **to l. sb to sleep** endormir qn en le/la berçant

**lullaby** ['lʌləbaɪ] (*pl* **-ies**) *n* berceuse *f*

**lumber¹** ['lʌmbə(r)] *n (timber)* bois *m* de charpente; *Br (junk)* bric-à-brac *m inv*

**lumber²** ['lʌmbə(r)] *vt Br Fam* **to l. sb with sb/sth** coller qn/qch à qn

**luminous** ['luːmɪnəs] *adj (colour, paper, ink)* fluorescent; *(dial, clock)* lumineux, -euse

**lump** [lʌmp] **1** *n* morceau *m*; *(in soup)* grumeau *m*; *(bump)* bosse *f*; *(swelling)* grosseur *f*; **l. sum** somme *f* forfaitaire **2** *vt* **to l. together** réunir; *Fig & Pej* mettre dans le même sac ▪ **lumpy** (**-ier, -iest**) *adj (soup)* grumeleux, -euse; *(surface)* bosselé

**lunar** ['luːnə(r)] *adj* lunaire; **l. eclipse** éclipse *f* de lune

**lunatic** ['luːnətɪk] *n* fou *m*, folle *f*

**lunch** [lʌntʃ] **1** *n* déjeuner *m*; **to have l.** déjeuner; **l. break, l. hour, l. time** heure *f* du déjeuner **2** *vi* déjeuner (**on** *or* **off** de) ▪ **lunchbox** *n* = boîte dans laquelle on transporte son déjeuner

**luncheon** ['lʌnʃən] *n* déjeuner *m*; *Br* **l. voucher** Chèque-Restaurant *m*

**lung** [lʌŋ] *n* poumon *m*

**lunge** [lʌndʒ] *vi* **to l. at sb** se ruer sur qn

**lurch** [lɜːtʃ] **1** *n Fam* **to leave sb in the l.**

laisser qn dans le pétrin **2** *vi (of person)* tituber

**lure** [lʊə(r)] **1** *n (attraction)* attrait *m* **2** *vt* attirer (par la ruse) (**into** dans)

**lurid** ['lʊərɪd] *adj (story, description)* cru; *(gaudy)* voyant

**lurk** [lɜːk] *vi (hide)* être tapi (**in** dans); *(prowl)* rôder

**luscious** ['lʌʃəs] *adj (food)* appétissant

**lush** [lʌʃ] *adj (vegetation)* luxuriant; *(wealthy) (surroundings)* luxueux, -euse

**lust** [lʌst] **1** *n (for person)* désir *m*; *(for object)* convoitise *f* (**for** de); *(for power, knowledge)* soif *f* (**for** de) **2** *vi* **to l. after** *(object, person)* convoiter; *(power, knowledge)* avoir soif de

**lustre** ['lʌstə(r)] (*Am* **luster**) *n (gloss)* lustre *m*

**Luxembourg** ['lʌksəmbɜːg] *n* le Luxembourg

**luxury** ['lʌkʃərɪ] **1** *n* luxe *m* **2** *adj (goods, car, home)* de luxe ▪ **luxurious** [lʌg'ʒʊərɪəs] *adj* luxueux, -euse

**lying** ['laɪɪŋ] **1** *pres p of* **lie**[1,2] **2** *n* mensonges *mpl* **3** *adj (person)* menteur, -euse

**lynch** [lɪntʃ] *vt* lyncher

**lyric** ['lɪrɪk] *adj* lyrique ▪ **lyrics** *npl (of song)* paroles *fpl*

# Mm

**M, m** [em] *n (letter)* M, m *m inv*

**m** (**a**) (*abbr* **metre**) mètre *m* (**b**) (*abbr* **mile**) mile *m*

**MA** (*abbr* **Master of Arts**) *n Univ* **to have an MA in French** ≃ avoir une maîtrise de français

**mac** [mæk] *n Br Fam (raincoat)* imper *m*

**macabre** [mə'kɑːbrə] *adj* macabre

**machine** [mə'ʃiːn] *n (apparatus, car, system)* machine *f*; **m. gun** mitrailleuse *f*

**machinery** [mə'ʃiːnərɪ] *n (machines)* machines *fpl*; *(works)* mécanisme *m*

**mackerel** ['mækrəl] *n* maquereau *m*

**mackintosh** ['mækɪntɒʃ] *n Br* imperméable *m*

**macro** ['mækrəʊ] (*pl* **-os**) *n Comptr* macrocommande *f*

**mad** [mæd] (**madder, maddest**) *adj* fou (*f* folle); **to be m. at sb** être furieux, -euse contre qn ▪ **madly** *adv (insanely, desperately)* comme un fou/une folle ▪ **madman** (*pl* **-men**) *n* fou *m* ▪ **madness** *n* folie *f*

**madam** ['mædəm] *n* **yes, m.** oui, madame

**made** [meɪd] *pt & pp of* **make** ▪ **made-to-measure** *adj Br (garment)* (fait) sur mesure

**magazine** [mægə'ziːn] *n* (**a**) *(periodical, TV or radio broadcast)* magazine *m* (**b**) *(of gun, slide projector)* magasin *m*

**magic** ['mædʒɪk] **1** *adj* magique **2** *n* magie *f* ▪ **magician** [mə'dʒɪʃən] *n* magicien, -enne *mf*

**magistrate** ['mædʒɪstreɪt] *n* magistrat *m*

**magnet** ['mægnɪt] *n* aimant *m* ▪ **magnetic** [-'netɪk] *adj* magnétique

**magnificent** [mæg'nɪfɪsənt] *adj* magnifique

**magnify** ['mægnɪfaɪ] (*pt & pp* **-ied**) *vt (image)* grossir; **magnifying glass** loupe *f*

**mahogany** [mə'hɒgənɪ] *n* acajou *m*

**maid** [meɪd] *n (servant)* bonne *f*

**maiden** ['meɪdən] *adj (flight, voyage)* inaugural; **m. name** nom *m* de jeune fille

**mail** [meɪl] **1** *n (system)* poste *f*; *(letters)* courrier *m*; *(e-mails)* méls *mpl*, courrier *m* électronique **2** *adj (bag, train)* postal; **m. order** vente *f* par correspondance **3** *vt* poster; **mailing list** liste *f* d'adresses ▪ **mailbox** *n Am & Comptr* boîte *f* aux lettres

**maim** [meɪm] *vt* mutiler

**main**[1] [meɪn] *adj* principal; **m. course** plat *m* de résistance; **m. road** grande route *f*

**main**[2] [meɪn] *n* **water/gas m.** conduite *f* d'eau/de gaz; **the mains** *(electricity)* le secteur ▪ **mainland** *n* continent *m* ▪ **mainly** *adv* principalement; **they were m. Spanish** la plupart étaient espagnols

**mainstay** ['meɪnsteɪ] *n (of organization, policy)* pilier *m*

**maintain** [meɪn'teɪn] *vt (continue)* maintenir; *(machine, road)* entretenir; **to m. that...** affirmer que... ▪ **maintenance** ['meɪntənəns] *n (of vehicle, road)* entretien *m*; *(alimony)* pension *f* alimentaire

**maize** [meɪz] *n Br* maïs *m*

**majesty** ['mædʒəstɪ] *n* majesté *f*; **Your M.** Votre Majesté ■ **majestic** [mə'dʒestɪk] *adj* majestueux, -euse

**major** ['meɪdʒə(r)] **1** *adj (main, great)* & *Mus* majeur **2** *n* (**a**) *(officer)* commandant *m* (**b**) *Am Univ (subject)* dominante *f* **3** *vi Am Univ* **to m. in** se spécialiser en

**Majorca** [mə'jɔːkə] *n* Majorque *f*

**majority** [mə'dʒɒrətɪ] (*pl* **-ies**) *n* majorité *f* (**of** de); **the m. of people** la plupart des gens

**MAKE** [meɪk] **1** (*pt & pp* **made**) *vt* faire; *(tool, vehicle)* fabriquer; **to m. a decision** prendre une décision; **to m. sb happy/sad** rendre qn heureux/triste; **to m. sb do sth** faire faire qch à qn; *Fam* **to m. it** *(succeed)* réussir; **sorry I can't m. it to the meeting** désolé, je ne pourrai pas assister à la réunion; **what time do you m. it?** quelle heure avez-vous?; **what do you m. of it?** qu'en penses-tu?; **he made 10 pounds on it** ça lui a rapporté 10 livres; **to be made of wood** être en bois; **made in France** fabriqué en France

**2** *vi* **to m. do** *(manage)* se débrouiller (**with** avec); **to m. do with sb/sth** *(be satisfied with)* se contenter de qn/qch; **to m. believe that one is...** faire semblant d'être...

**3** *n (brand)* marque *f*; **of French m.** de fabrication française ■ **make-up** *n (for face)* maquillage *m*; *(of team, group)* constitution *f*

▸**make for** *vt insep (go towards)* aller vers

▸**make off** *vi Fam (leave)* filer

▸**make out 1** *vt sep (see, hear)* distinguer; *(understand)* comprendre; *(decipher)* déchiffrer; *(cheque, list)* faire; *Fam* **to m. out that...** *(claim)* prétendre que... **2** *vi Fam (manage)* se débrouiller

▸**make over** *vt sep (transfer)* céder (**to** à); *(change, convert)* transformer (**into** en)

▸**make up 1** *vt sep (story)* inventer; *(put together) (list, collection, bed)* faire; *(prepare)* préparer; *(form)* former, composer; *(loss)* compenser; *(quantity)* compléter; *(quarrel)* régler; **to m. oneself up** se maquiller

**2** *vi (of friends)* se réconcilier; **to m. up for** *(loss, damage, fault)* compenser; *(lost time, mistake)* rattraper

**makeshift** ['meɪkʃɪft] *adj (arrangement, building)* de fortune

**malaria** [mə'leərɪə] *n Med* paludisme *m*

**male** [meɪl] **1** *adj (child, animal)* mâle; *(sex)* masculin; **m. nurse** infirmier *m* **2** *n (person)* homme *m*; *(animal)* mâle *m*

**malfunction** [mæl'fʌŋkʃən] *vi* fonctionner mal

**malice** ['mælɪs] *n* méchanceté *f* ■ **malicious** [mə'lɪʃəs] *adj* malveillant

**malignant** [mə'lɪgnənt] *adj* **m. tumour** *or* **growth** tumeur *f* maligne

**mall** [mɔːl] *n Am* **(shopping) m.** centre *m* commercial

**malnutrition** [mælnjuː'trɪʃən] *n* malnutrition *f*

**malt** [mɔːlt] *n* malt *m*

**Malta** ['mɔːltə] *n* Malte *f*

**mammal** ['mæməl] *n* mammifère *m*

**man** [mæn] **1** (*pl* **men**) *n (adult male)* homme *m*; *(player in sports team)* joueur *m*; *(humanity)* l'homme *m*; *(chess piece)* pièce *f*; *Fam* **my old m.** *(father)* mon père; *(husband)* mon homme

**2** (*pt & pp* **-nn-**) *vt (be on duty at)* être de service à; *(machine)* assurer le fonctionnement de; *(plane, ship)* être membre de l'équipage de

**manage** ['mænɪdʒ] **1** *vt (company, project)* diriger; *(shop, hotel)* être le gérant de; *(economy, money, time, situation)* gérer; **to m. to do sth** *(succeed)* réussir *ou* arriver à faire qch; *(by being smart)* se débrouiller pour faire qch

**2** *vi (succeed)* y arriver; *(make do)* se débrouiller (**with** avec); **to m. without sb/sth** se passer de qn/qch; **managing director** directeur, -trice *mf* général, -e ■ **management** *n (running,* *managers)* direction *f*; *(of property, economy)* gestion *f*; *(executive staff)* cadres *mpl*

**manager** ['mænɪdʒə(r)] *n (of company)* directeur, -trice *mf*; *(of shop, café)* gérant, -e *mf*; **(business) m.** *(of singer, boxer)* manager *m* ▪ **manageress** *n* directrice *f*; *(of shop, café)* gérante *f*

**mandate** ['mændeɪt] *n* mandat *m*

**mane** [meɪn] *n* crinière *f*

**maneuver** [mə'nu:vər] *n & vti Am* = **manoeuvre**

**mangle** ['mæŋgəl] *vt (body)* mutiler

**mango** ['mæŋgəʊ] (*pl* **-oes** *or* **-os**) *n* mangue *f*

**manhunt** ['mænhʌnt] *n* chasse *f* à l'homme

**mania** ['meɪnɪə] *n (liking)* passion *f*; *(psychological)* manie *f*

**maniac** ['meɪnɪæk] *n* fou *m*, folle *f*

**manicure** ['mænɪkjʊə(r)] *n* manucure *f*

**manifesto** [mænɪ'festəʊ] (*pl* **-os** *or* **-oes**) *n Pol* manifeste *m*

**manipulate** [mə'nɪpjʊleɪt] *vt* manipuler

**mankind** [mæn'kaɪnd] *n* l'humanité *f*

**man-made** ['mænmeɪd] *adj (lake)* artificiel, -elle; *(fibre)* synthétique

**manner** ['mænə(r)] *n (way)* manière *f*; *(behaviour)* comportement *m*; **manners** *(social habits)* manières *fpl*; **in this m.** *(like this)* de cette manière; **to have good/bad manners** être bien/mal élevé

**mannerism** ['mænərɪzəm] *n Pej* tic *m*

**manoeuvre** [mə'nu:və(r)] (*Am* **maneuver**) **1** *n* manœuvre *f* **2** *vti* manœuvrer

**manpower** ['mænpaʊə(r)] *n (labour)* main-d'œuvre *f*

**mansion** ['mænʃən] *n (in town)* hôtel *m* particulier; *(in country)* manoir *m*

**manslaughter** ['mænslɔ:tə(r)] *n (in law)* homicide *m* involontaire

**mantelpiece** ['mæntəlpi:s] *n* dessus *m* de cheminée; **on the m.** sur la cheminée

**manual** ['mænjʊəl] **1** *adj (work, worker)* manuel, -elle **2** *n (book)* manuel *m*

**manufacture** [mænjʊ'fæktʃə(r)] **1** *n* fabrication *f*; *(of cars)* construction *f* **2** *vt* fabriquer; *(cars)* construire ▪ **manufacturer** *n* fabricant, -e *mf*; *(of cars)* constructeur *m*

**manure** [mə'njʊə(r)] *n* fumier *m*

**manuscript** ['mænjʊskrɪpt] *n* manuscrit *m*

**many** ['menɪ] **1** *adj* beaucoup de; **(a good** *or* **great) m. of** un (très) grand nombre de; **how m.?** combien (de)?; **too m.** trop de **2** *pron* beaucoup; **too m.** trop; **m. of them** beaucoup d'entre eux; **as m. as fifty** *(up to)* jusqu'à cinquante

**map** [mæp] **1** *n* carte *f*; *(plan of town, underground)* plan *m* **2** (*pt & pp* **-pp-**) *vt* **to m. out** *(plan, programme)* élaborer

**maple** ['meɪpəl] *n (tree, wood)* érable *m*; **m. syrup** sirop *m* d'érable

**marathon** ['mærəθən] *n* marathon *m*

**marble** ['mɑ:bəl] *n (substance)* marbre *m*; *(toy ball)* bille *f*

**March** [mɑ:tʃ] *n* mars *m*

**march** [mɑ:tʃ] **1** *n* marche *f* **2** *vi (of soldiers, demonstrators)* défiler; *(walk in step)* marcher au pas

**mare** [meə(r)] *n* jument *f*

**margarine** [mɑ:dʒə'ri:n] *n* margarine *f*

**margin** ['mɑ:dʒɪn] *n (on page)* marge *f*; **to win by a narrow m.** gagner de justesse ▪ **marginally** *adv* très légèrement

**marijuana** [mærɪ'wɑ:nə] *n* marijuana *f*

**marinate** ['mærɪneɪt] *vti Culin* (faire) mariner

**marine** [mə'ri:n] **1** *adj (life, flora)* marin **2** *n (soldier)* fusilier *m* marin; *Am* marine *m*

**marital** ['mærɪtəl] *adj* conjugal; **m. status** situation *f* de famille

**maritime** ['mærɪtaɪm] *adj* maritime

**mark** [mɑ:k] **1** *n (symbol)* marque *f*; *(stain, trace)* tache *f*, marque *f*; *(token, sign)* signe *m*; *(in test, exam)* note *f* **2** *vt* marquer; *(exam)* noter; **to m. sth off** *(separate)* délimiter qch; *(on list)* cocher qch; **to m. sb out** distinguer qn

**marked** [mɑːkt] *adj (noticeable)* marqué

**market** ['mɑːkɪt] **1** *n* marché *m*; **to put sth on the m.** mettre qch en vente; **on the black m.** au marché noir; **m. price** prix *m* courant
**2** *vt* commercialiser ▪ **marketing** *n* marketing *m*, mercatique *f* ▪ **marketplace** *n (in village, town)* place *f* du marché

**markings** ['mɑːkɪŋz] *npl (on animal)* taches *fpl*; *(on road)* signalisation *f* horizontale

**marmalade** ['mɑːməleɪd] *n* confiture *f* d'oranges

**marooned** [mə'ruːnd] *adj* abandonné

**marriage** ['mærɪdʒ] *n* mariage *m*; **m. certificate** extrait *m* d'acte de mariage

**marrow** ['mærəʊ] *n Br (vegetable)* courge *f*

**marry** ['mærɪ] **1** *(pt & pp* **-ied***) vt* épouser, se marier avec; *(of priest)* marier **2** *vi* se marier ▪ **married** *adj* marié; **m. life** vie *f* maritale; **m. name** nom *m* de femme mariée; **to get m.** se marier

**marsh** [mɑːʃ] *n* marais *m*, marécage *m*

**martial** ['mɑːʃəl] *adj* martial

**martyr** ['mɑːtə(r)] *n* martyr, -e *mf*

**marvel** ['mɑːvəl] **1** *n (wonder)* merveille *f* **2** *(Br* **-ll-**, *Am* **-l-***) vi* s'émerveiller (**at** de)

**marvellous** ['mɑːvələs] *(Am* **marvelous***) adj* merveilleux, -euse

**Marxist** ['mɑːksɪst] *adj & n* marxiste *(mf)*

**marzipan** ['mɑːzɪpæn] *n* pâte *f* d'amandes

**mascara** [mæ'skɑːrə] *n* mascara *m*

**masculine** ['mæskjʊlɪn] *adj* masculin

**mash** [mæʃ] **1** *n Br (potatoes)* purée *f* (de pommes de terre) **2** *vt* **to m. (up)** *(vegetables)* écraser (en purée); **mashed potatoes** purée *f* de pommes de terre

**mask** [mɑːsk] **1** *n* masque *m* **2** *vt (cover, hide)* masquer (**from** à)

**masochist** ['mæsəkɪst] *n* masochiste *mf*

**mason** ['meɪsən] *n (stonemason, Freemason)* maçon *m* ▪ **masonry** *n* maçonnerie *f*

**mass**[1] [mæs] **1** *n Phys & (shapeless substance)* masse *f*; **a m. of** *(many)* une multitude de; *Pol* **the masses** le peuple
**2** *adj (demonstration, culture)* de masse; *(protests)* en masse; *(unemployment, destruction)* massif, -ive; **m. media** mass media *mpl*; **m. production** production *f* en série
**3** *vi (of troops, people)* se masser ▪ **mass-produce** *vt* fabriquer en série

**mass**[2] [mæs] *n (church service)* messe *f*

**massacre** ['mæsəkə(r)] **1** *n* massacre *m* **2** *vt* massacrer

**massage** ['mæsɑːʒ] **1** *n* massage *m* **2** *vt* masser

**massive** ['mæsɪv] *adj (increase, dose, vote)* massif, -ive; *(amount, building)* énorme

**mast** [mɑːst] *n (of ship)* mât *m*; *(for TV, radio)* pylône *m*

**master** ['mɑːstə(r)] **1** *n* maître *m*; *Br (teacher)* professeur *m*; **M. of Arts/Science** *(qualification)* ≃ maîtrise *f* ès lettres/sciences; *(person)* ≃ maître *mf* ès lettres/sciences; **m. of ceremonies** *(presenter)* animateur, -trice *mf*; **m. copy** original *m*; **m. key** passe-partout *m inv*; **m. plan** plan *m* d'action **2** *vt* maîtriser; *(subject, situation)* dominer

**mastermind** ['mɑːstəmaɪnd] **1** *n (person)* cerveau *m* **2** *vt* organiser

**masterpiece** ['mɑːstəpiːs] *n* chef-d'œuvre *m*

**mastery** ['mɑːstərɪ] *n* maîtrise *f* (**of** de)

**masturbate** ['mæstəbeɪt] *vi* se masturber

**mat** [mæt] *n* tapis *m*; *(of straw)* natte *f*; *(at door)* paillasson *m*; **(table) m.** *(for plates)* set *m* de table; *(for dishes)* dessous-de-plat *m inv*

**match**[1] [mætʃ] *n (for lighting fire, cigarette)* allumette *f* ▪ **matchbox** *n* boîte *f* d'allumettes ▪ **matchstick** *n* allumette *f*

**match²** [mætʃ] *n (in sport)* match *m*

**match³** [mætʃ] **1** *n (equal)* égal, -e *mf*; *(marriage)* mariage *m*; **to be a good m.** *(of colours, people)* aller bien ensemble; **to meet one's m.** trouver son maître

**2** *vt (of clothes, colour)* être assorti à; *(coordinate)* assortir; *(equal)* égaler; **to m. up** *(colours, clothes, plates)* assortir

**3** *vi (of colours, clothes)* être assortis, -es ▪ **matching** *adj* assorti

**mate¹** [meɪt] **1** *n (of animal) (male)* mâle *m*; *(female)* femelle *f*; *Br (friend)* copain *m*, copine *f* **2** *vi (of animals)* s'accoupler (**with** avec)

**mate²** [meɪt] **1** *n (in chess)* mat *m* **2** *vt* mettre mat

**material** [mə'tɪərɪəl] **1** *adj (needs, world)* matériel, -elle; *(important)* essentiel, -elle **2** *n (substance)* matière *f*; *(cloth)* tissu *m*; *(for book)* matériaux *mpl*; **material(s)** *(equipment)* matériel *m* ▪ **materialistic** *adj* matérialiste

**materialize** [mə'tɪərɪəlaɪz] *vi* se matérialiser; *(of hope, threat)* se réaliser

**maternal** [mə'tɜ:nəl] *adj* maternel, -elle

**maternity** [mə'tɜ:nətɪ] *n* **m. dress** robe *f* de grossesse; **m. hospital, m. unit** maternité *f*; **m. leave** congé *m* de maternité

**mathematical** [mæθə'mætɪkəl] *adj* mathématique

**mathematics** [mæθə'mætɪks] *n (subject)* mathématiques *fpl* ▪ **maths** (*Am* **math**) *n Fam* maths *fpl*

**matinée** ['mætɪneɪ] *n (of play, film)* matinée *f*

**matrimony** ['mætrɪmənɪ] *n* mariage *m*

**matt** [mæt] *adj (paint, paper)* mat

**matter** ['mætə(r)] **1** *n (substance)* matière *f*; *(issue, affair)* question *f*; **as a m. of fact** en fait; **no m. what she does** quoi qu'elle fasse; **no m. who you are** qui que vous soyez; **what's the m.?** qu'est-ce qu'il y a?; **there's something the m. with my leg** j'ai quelque chose à la jambe

**2** *vi (be important)* importer (**to** à); **it doesn't m. if/when/who...** peu importe si/quand/qui...; **it doesn't m.** ça ne fait rien

**matter-of-fact** [mætərəv'fækt] *adj (person, manner)* terre à terre *inv*

**mattress** ['mætrəs] *n* matelas *m*

**mature** [mə'tʃʊə(r)] **1** *adj (person)* mûr; *(cheese)* fort **2** *vi (person)* mûrir

**maul** [mɔ:l] *vt (of animal)* mutiler

**maximize** ['mæksɪmaɪz] *vt* maximaliser

**maximum** ['mæksɪməm] **1** (*pl* **-ima** [-ɪmə] *or* **-imums**) *n* maximum *m* **2** *adj* maximal

**May** [meɪ] *n* mai *m*

**MAY** [meɪ] (*pt* **might** [maɪt])

> **May** et *m* **might** peuvent s'utiliser indifféremment ou presque dans les expressions de la catégorie (**a**).

*v aux* (**a**) *(expressing possibility)* **he m. come** il se peut qu'il vienne; **I m.** *or* **might be wrong** je me trompe peut-être; **he m.** *or* **might have lost it** il se peut qu'il l'ait perdu; **we m.** *or* **might as well go** autant y aller; **she's afraid I m.** *or* **might get lost** elle a peur que je ne me perde

(**b**) *Formal (for asking permission)* **m. I stay?** puis-je rester?; **you m. go** tu peux partir

(**c**) *Formal (expressing wish)* **m. you be happy** sois heureux; **m. the best man win!** que le meilleur gagne!

**maybe** ['meɪbi:] *adv* peut-être

**mayhem** ['meɪhem] *n (chaos)* pagaille *f*

**mayonnaise** [meɪə'neɪz] *n* mayonnaise *f*

**mayor** [meə(r)] *n* maire *m*

**maze** [meɪz] *n* labyrinthe *m*

**me** [mi:] *pron* me, m'; *(after prep, 'than', 'it is')* moi; **(to) me** *(indirect)* me, m'; **he helps me** il m'aide; **he gave it to me** il me l'a donné

**meadow** ['medəʊ] *n* pré *m*, prairie *f*

**meagre** ['mi:gə(r)] (*Am* **meager**) *adj* maigre

**meal** [mi:l] *n (food)* repas *m*

**mean¹** [mi:n] (*pt & pp* **meant**) *vt (of word, event)* signifier; *(of person)* vouloir dire; *(result in)* entraîner; *(represent)* représenter; **to m. to do sth** avoir l'intention de faire qch; **it means a lot to me** c'est très important pour moi; **I didn't m. to!** je ne l'ai pas fait exprès!

**mean²** [mi:n] (**-er, -est**) *adj (miserly)* avare; *(nasty)* méchant

**mean³** [mi:n] **1** *adj (average)* moyen, -enne **2** *n Math (average, mid-point)* moyenne *f*

**meaning** ['mi:nɪŋ] *n* sens *m*, signification *f* ▪ **meaningful** *adj* significatif, -ive ▪ **meaningless** *adj* vide de sens

**means** [mi:nz] **1** *n (method)* moyen *m* (**to do** *or* **of doing** de faire); **by m. of...** au moyen de...; **by no m.** nullement **2** *npl (wealth)* moyens *mpl*

**meant** [ment] *pt & pp of* **mean¹**

**meantime** ['mi:ntaɪm] *adv & n* **(in the) m.** *(at the same time)* pendant ce temps; *(between two events)* entre-temps

**meanwhile** ['mi:nwaɪl] *adv (at the same time)* pendant ce temps; *(between two events)* entre-temps

**measles** ['mi:zəlz] *n Med* rougeole *f*

**measure** ['meʒə(r)] **1** *n* mesure *f*; *(ruler)* règle *f* **2** *vt* mesurer; **to m. sth out** *(ingredient)* mesurer qch **3** *vi* **to m. up to** *(task)* être à la hauteur de

**measurement** ['meʒəmənt] *n* mesure *f*; **hip/waist measurement(s)** tour *m* de hanches/de taille

**meat** [mi:t] *n* viande *f*; *(of crab, lobster)* chair *f*; *Fig* substance *f*

**mechanic** [mɪ'kænɪk] *n* mécanicien, -enne *mf* ▪ **mechanical** *adj* mécanique ▪ **mechanics** *n (science)* mécanique *f*; **the m.** *(working parts)* le mécanisme

**mechanism** ['mekənɪzəm] *n* mécanisme *m*

**medal** ['medəl] *n* médaille *f*

**medallion** [mə'dæljən] *n* médaillon *m*

**meddle** ['medəl] *vi (interfere)* se mêler (**in** de); *(tamper)* toucher (**with** à)

**media** ['mi:dɪə] *npl* **1 the m.** les médias *mpl* **2** *pl of* **medium**

**mediaeval** [medɪ'i:vəl] *adj* médiéval

**mediate** ['mi:dɪeɪt] *vi* servir d'intermédiaire (**between** entre) ▪ **mediator** *n* médiateur, -trice *mf*

**medical** ['medɪkəl] **1** *adj* médical; *(school, studies)* de médecine; *(student)* en médecine; **m. insurance** assurance *f* maladie

**2** *n (in school, army)* visite *f* médicale; *(private)* examen *m* médical

**medication** [medɪ'keɪʃən] *n* médicaments *mpl*; **to be on m.** être en traitement

**medicine** ['medəsən] *n (substance)* médicament *m*; *(science)* médecine *f*; **m. cabinet, m. chest** (armoire *f* à) pharmacie *f*

**medieval** [medɪ'i:vəl] *adj* médiéval

**mediocre** [mi:dɪ'əʊkə(r)] *adj* médiocre

**meditate** ['medɪteɪt] *vi* méditer (**on** sur) ▪ **meditation** *n* méditation *f*

**Mediterranean** [medɪtə'reɪnɪən] **1** *adj* méditerranéen, -enne **2** *n* **the M.** la Méditerranée

**medium** ['mi:dɪəm] **1** *adj (average, middle)* moyen, -enne **2** *n* (**a**) (*pl* **media** ['mi:dɪə]) *(for conveying data or publicity)* support *m* (**b**) (*pl* **mediums**) *(person)* médium *m* ▪ **medium-sized** *adj* de taille moyenne

**medley** ['medlɪ] (*pl* **-eys**) *n* mélange *m*; *(of songs, tunes)* pot-pourri *m*

**meet** [mi:t] **1** *vt* (*pt & pp* **met**) *(person, team)* rencontrer; *(by arrangement)* retrouver; *(pass in street, road)* croiser; *(fetch)* aller chercher; *(wait for)* attendre; *(debt, enemy, danger)* faire face à; *(need)* combler; **have you met my husband?** connaissez-vous mon mari?

**2** *vi (of people, teams)* se rencontrer; *(by arrangement)* se retrouver; *(of club,* *society)* se réunir; *(of rivers)* se rejoindre **3** *n Am Sport* réunion *f*

▸ **meet up** *vi (by arrangement)* se retrouver; **to m. up with sb** retrouver qn

▸ **meet with** *vt insep (problem, refusal)* se heurter à; *(accident)* avoir; *Am* **to m. with sb** rencontrer qn; *(as arranged)* retrouver qn

**meeting** ['mi:tɪŋ] *n (for business)* réunion *f*; *(large)* assemblée *f*; *(by accident)* rencontre *f*; *(by arrangement)* rendez-vous *m inv*; **to be in a m.** être en réunion; **m. place** lieu *m* de rendez-vous

**megaphone** ['megəfəʊn] *n* porte-voix *m inv*

**mellow** ['meləʊ] (**-er, -est**) *adj (wine)* moelleux, -euse; *(flavour)* suave; *(colour, voice)* chaud

**melodic** [mɪ'lɒdɪk] *adj* mélodique

**melodrama** ['melədrɑ:mə] *n* mélodrame *m* ▪ **melodramatic** [-drə'mætɪk] *adj* mélodramatique

**melody** ['melədɪ] (*pl* **-ies**) *n* mélodie *f*

**melon** ['melən] *n* melon *m*

**melt** [melt] **1** *vt* faire fondre; **to m. down** *(metal object)* fondre **2** *vi* fondre

**member** ['membə(r)] *n* membre *m*; *Br* **M. of Parliament,** *Am* **M. of Congress** ≃ député *m* ▪ **membership** *n (state)* adhésion *f* (**of** à); *(members)* membres *mpl*; **m. card** carte *f* de membre; **m. fee** cotisation *f*

**memento** [mə'mentəʊ] (*pl* **-os** *or* **-oes**) *n* souvenir *m*

**memo** ['meməʊ] (*pl* **-os**) *n* note *f* de service

**memoirs** ['memwɑ:z] *npl (autobiography)* mémoires *mpl*

**memorable** ['memərəbəl] *adj* mémorable

**memorial** [mə'mɔ:rɪəl] **1** *adj* commémoratif, -ive; **m. service** commémoration *f* **2** *n* mémorial *m*

**memorize** ['meməraɪz] *vt* mémoriser

**memory** ['memərɪ] (*pl* **-ies**) *n (faculty) & Comptr* mémoire *f*; *(recollection)* souvenir *m*; **to the** *or* **in m. of...** à la mémoire de...

**men** [men] *npl see* **man**; **the men's room** les toilettes *fpl* pour hommes

**menace** ['menɪs] **1** *n (danger)* danger *m*; *(threat)* menace *f* **2** *vt* menacer

**mend** [mend] *vt (repair)* réparer; *(clothes)* raccommoder

**menial** ['mi:nɪəl] *adj (work)* subalterne

**meningitis** [menɪn'dʒaɪtɪs] *n Med* méningite *f*

**menopause** ['menəpɔ:z] *n* ménopause *f*

**menstruation** [menstrʊ'eɪʃən] *n* menstruation *f*

**menswear** ['menzweə(r)] *n* vêtements *mpl* pour hommes

**mental** ['mentəl] *adj* mental; **m. block** blocage *m*

**mentality** [men'tælətɪ] (*pl* **-ies**) *n* mentalité *f* ▪ **mentally** *adv* mentalement; **he's m. handicapped** c'est un handicapé mental; **she's m. ill** c'est une malade mentale

**mention** ['menʃən] **1** *n* mention *f* **2** *vt* mentionner; **not to m....** sans parler de...; **don't m. it!** il n'y a pas de quoi!

**menu** ['menju:] *n (in restaurant) (for set meal)* menu *m*; *(list)* carte *f*; *Comptr* menu

**MEP** [emi:'pi:] (*abbr* **Member of the European Parliament**) *n* député *m* du Parlement européen

**merchandise** ['mɜ:tʃəndaɪz] *n* marchandises *fpl*

**merchant** ['mɜ:tʃənt] *n (trader)* négociant, -e *mf*; *(retailer)* commerçant, -e *mf*

**merciless** ['mɜ:sɪləs] *adj* impitoyable

**mercury** ['mɜ:kjʊrɪ] *n (metal)* mercure *m*

**mercy** ['mɜ:sɪ] (*pl* **-ies**) *n* pitié *f*; *(of God)* miséricorde *f*; **at the m. of** à la merci de

**mere** [mɪə(r)] *adj* simple; **she's a m. child** ce n'est qu'une enfant ▪ **merely** *adv* simplement

**merge** [mɜ:dʒ] **1** *vt (companies) & Comptr* fusionner **2** *vi (blend)* se mêler (**with** à); *(of roads)* se rejoindre; *(of* *companies, banks)* fusionner ▪ **merger** *n Com* fusion *f*

**merit** ['merɪt] **1** *n* mérite *m* **2** *vt* mériter

**merry** ['merɪ] (**-ier, -iest**) *adj (happy, drunk)* gai ▪ **merry-go-round** *n* manège *m*

**mesh** [meʃ] *n (of net, sieve)* mailles *fpl*

**mesmerize** ['mezməraɪz] *vt* hypnotiser

**mess** [mes] **1** *n (confusion)* désordre *m*; *(muddle)* gâchis *m*; *(dirt)* saletés *fpl*; **in a m.** en désordre; *(in trouble)* dans le pétrin; **to make a m. of sth** *(do badly, get dirty)* saloper qch

**2** *vt Br Fam* **to m. sb about** *(bother, treat badly)* embêter qn; **to m. sth up** *(plans)* ficher qch en l'air; *(hair, room, papers)* mettre qch en désordre

**3** *vi* **to m. about** *or* **around** *(waste time)* traîner; *(play the fool)* faire l'imbécile; **to m. about** *or* **around with sth** *(fiddle with)* tripoter avec qch

**message** ['mesɪdʒ] *n* message *m*

**messenger** ['mesɪndʒə(r)] *n* messager, -ère *mf*; *(in office, hotel)* coursier, -ère *mf*

**messy** ['mesɪ] (**-ier, -iest**) *adj (untidy)* en désordre; *(dirty)* sale; *(job)* salissant

**met** [met] *pt & pp of* **meet**

**metal** ['metəl] *n* métal *m*; **m. ladder** échelle *f* métallique ▪ **metallic** [mɪ'tælɪk] *adj (sound)* métallique; *(paint)* métallisé ▪ **metalwork** *n (study, craft)* travail *m* des métaux; *(objects)* ferronnerie *f*

**metaphor** ['metəfə(r)] *n* métaphore *f* ▪ **metaphorical** [-'fɒrɪkəl] *adj* métaphorique

**meteor** ['mi:tɪə(r)] *n* météore *m*

**meteorological** [mi:tɪərə'lɒdʒɪkəl] *adj* météorologique

**meter¹** ['mi:tə(r)] *n (device)* compteur *m*; **(parking) m.** parcmètre *m*

**meter²** ['mi:tə(r)] *n Am (measurement)* mètre *m*

**method** ['meθəd] *n* méthode *f* ▪ **methodical** [mɪ'θɒdɪkəl] *adj* méthodique

**meticulous** [mɪ'tɪkjʊləs] *adj* méticuleux, -euse

**metre** ['mi:tə(r)] (*Am* **meter**) *n* mètre *m* ▪ **metric** ['metrɪk] *adj* métrique

**metropolitan** [metrə'pɒlɪtən] *adj* métropolitain

**Mexico** ['meksɪkəʊ] *n* le Mexique ▪ **Mexican 1** *adj* mexicain **2** *n* Mexicain, -e *mf*

**miaow** [mi:'aʊ] **1** *exclam* miaou! **2** *vi* miauler

**mice** [maɪs] *pl of* **mouse**

**mickey** ['mɪkɪ] *n Br Fam* **to take the m. out of sb** charrier qn

**microchip** ['maɪkrəʊtʃɪp] *n Comptr* microprocesseur *m*

**microfilm** ['maɪkrəʊfɪlm] *n* microfilm *m*

**microphone** ['maɪkrəfəʊn] *n* micro *m*

**microscope** ['maɪkrəskəʊp] *n* microscope *m*

**microwave** ['maɪkrəʊweɪv] *n* **m. (oven)** (four *m* à) micro-ondes *m inv*

**mid** [mɪd] *adj* **(in) m. June** (à) la mi-juin; **in m. air** en plein ciel; **to be in one's m.-twenties** avoir environ vingt-cinq ans

**midday** [mɪd'deɪ] **1** *n* **at m.** à midi **2** *adj (sun, meal)* de midi

**middle** ['mɪdəl] **1** *n* milieu *m*; *Fam (waist)* taille *f*; **(right) in the m. of sth** au (beau) milieu de qch

**2** *adj (central)* du milieu; **the M. Ages** le Moyen Âge; **the M. East** le Moyen-Orient; **the m. class(es)** les classes moyennes; **m. name** deuxième prénom *m* ▪ **middle-aged** *adj* d'âge mûr ▪ **middle-class** *adj* bourgeois ▪ **middle-of-the-road** *adj (politics, views)* modéré; *(music)* grand public *inv*

**midge** [mɪdʒ] *n* moucheron *m*

**midget** ['mɪdʒɪt] *n (small person)* nain, -e *mf*

**midnight** ['mɪdnaɪt] *n* minuit *m*

**midst** [mɪdst] *n* **in the m. of** *(middle)* au milieu de

**midway** [mɪd'weɪ] *adj & adv* à mi-chemin

**midweek** [mɪd'wiːk] *adv* en milieu de semaine

**midwife** ['mɪdwaɪf] (*pl* **-wives**) *n* sage-femme *f*

**might[1]** [maɪt] *v aux see* **may**

La forme **mightn't** s'écrit **might not** dans un style plus soutenu.

**might[2]** [maɪt] *n (strength)* force *f* ▪ **mighty** (**-ier, -iest**) **1** *adj* puissant; *Fam (very great)* sacré **2** *adv Am Fam (very)* rudement

**migraine** ['miːgreɪn, 'maɪgreɪn] *n* migraine *f*

**migrate** [maɪ'greɪt] *vi (of people)* émigrer; *(of birds)* migrer ▪ **migrant** ['maɪgrənt] *adj & n* **m. (worker)** (travailleur, -euse *mf*) immigré, -e

**mike** [maɪk] (*abbr* **microphone**) *n Fam* micro *m*

**mild** [maɪld] (**-er, -est**) *adj (weather, cheese, soap, person)* doux (*f* douce); *(punishment)* léger, -ère; *(curry)* peu épicé

**mile** [maɪl] *n* mile *m*; **he lives miles away** il habite très loin d'ici ▪ **mileage** *n (distance)* ≃ kilométrage *m*; *(rate of fuel consumption)* consommation *f* ▪ **mileometer** *n Br* ≃ compteur *m* kilométrique ▪ **milestone** *n (in history, career)* étape *f* importante

**militant** ['mɪlɪtənt] *adj & n* militant, -e (*mf*)

**military** ['mɪlɪtərɪ] **1** *adj* militaire **2** *n* **the m.** les militaires *mpl*

**milk** [mɪlk] **1** *n* lait *m*; **m. chocolate** chocolat *m* au lait; **m. shake** milk-shake *m* **2** *vt (cow)* traire; *Fig (exploit)* exploiter ▪ **milky** (**-ier, -iest**) *adj (coffee, tea)* au lait

**mill** [mɪl] **1** *n (for flour)* moulin *m*; *(textile factory)* filature *f* **2** *vi* **to m. around** *(of crowd)* grouiller

**millennium** [mɪ'lenɪəm] (*pl* **-nia** [-nɪə]) *n* millénaire *m*

**milligram(me)** ['mɪlɪgræm] *n* milligramme *m*

**millimetre** ['mɪlɪmiːtə(r)] (*Am* **millimeter**) *n* millimètre *m*

**million** ['mɪljən] *n* million *m*; **a m. men** un million d'hommes; **two m.** deux millions ▪ **millionaire** *n* millionnaire *mf*

**milometer** [maɪ'lɒmɪtə(r)] *n Br* ≃ compteur *m* kilométrique

**mime** [maɪm] **1** *n (art)* mime *m* **2** *vti* mimer; *(of singer)* chanter en playback

**mimic** ['mɪmɪk] **1** *n* imitateur, -trice *mf* **2** (*pt & pp* **-ck-**) *vt* imiter

**mince** [mɪns] **1** *n (meat)* viande *f* hachée; **m. pie** *(containing fruit)* = tartelette fourrée aux fruits secs et aux épices **2** *vt* hacher ▪ **mincemeat** *n (dried fruit)* = mélange de fruits secs et d'épices utilisé en pâtisserie ▪ **mincer** *n (machine)* hachoir *m*

**MIND[1]** [maɪnd] *n* esprit *m*; *(sanity)* raison *f*; *Br* **to my m.** à mon avis; **to change one's m.** changer d'avis; **to speak one's m.** dire ce que l'on pense; *Br* **to be in two minds** *(undecided)* hésiter; **to bear** *or* **keep sth in m.** garder qch à l'esprit; **to have sb/sth in m.** avoir qn/qch en vue; **to make up one's m.** se décider; *Fam* **to be out of one's m.** avoir perdu la tête; **it's on my m.** cela me préoccupe; *Br* **to have a good m. to do sth** avoir bien envie de faire qch

**MIND[2]** [maɪnd] **1** *vt Br (pay attention to)* faire attention à; *(look after)* garder; *Br* **m. you don't fall** fais attention à ne pas tomber; **I don't m. the cold/noise** le froid/bruit ne me gêne pas; **if you don't m. my asking...** si je peux me permettre...; **never m. the car** peu importe la voiture; *Br* **m. you...** remarquez...; **m. your own business!** occupe-toi de tes affaires!

**2** *vi* **I don't m.** ça m'est égal; **do you m. if I smoke?** ça vous gêne si je fume?; **never m.!** ça ne fait rien!, tant pis!; *Br* **m. (out)!** *(watch out)* attention!

**mind-boggling** ['maɪndbɒglɪŋ] *adj* stupéfiant

**minder** ['maɪndə(r)] *n Fam (bodyguard)* gorille *m*

**mindless** ['maɪndləs] *adj (job, destruction)* stupide

**mine[1]** [maɪn] *possessive pron* le mien, la mienne, *pl* les mien(ne)s; **this hat is m.** ce chapeau est à moi *ou* est le mien; **a friend of m.** un ami à moi, un de mes amis

**mine[2]** [maɪn] **1** *n* (**a**) *(for coal, gold) & Fig* mine *f* (**b**) *(explosive)* mine *f* **2** *vt (coal, gold)* extraire ▪ **mining** *n* exploitation *f* minière

**mineral** ['mɪnərəl] *adj & n* minéral *(m)*; **m. water** eau *f* minérale

**mingle** ['mɪŋgəl] *vi (of things)* se mêler (**with** à); *(of people)* parler un peu à tout le monde

**miniature** ['mɪnɪtʃə(r)] **1** *adj (train, model)* miniature *inv* **2** *n* miniature *f*; **in m.** en miniature

**minicab** ['mɪnɪkæb] *n Br* radio-taxi *m*

**minimal** ['mɪnɪməl] *adj* minimal

**minimize** ['mɪnɪmaɪz] *vt* minimiser

**minimum** ['mɪnɪməm] **1** (*pl* **-ima** *or* **-imums**) *n* minimum *m* **2** *adj* minimal; **m. wage** salaire *m* minimum

**miniskirt** ['mɪnɪskɜːt] *n* minijupe *f*

**minister** ['mɪnɪstə(r)] *n Br (politician)* ministre *m*; *(of religion)* pasteur *m* ▪ **ministry** (*pl* **-ies**) *n Br Pol* ministère *m*

**minor** ['maɪnə(r)] **1** *adj (unimportant) & Mus* mineur; *Med (operation)* bénin, -igne; *(road)* secondaire **2** *n (in age)* mineur, -e *mf*

**minority** [maɪ'nɒrətɪ] **1** (*pl* **-ies**) *n* minorité *f*; **to be in the** *or* **a m.** être minoritaire **2** *adj* minoritaire

**mint[1]** [mɪnt] **1** *n* **the (Royal) M.** ≃ l'hôtel *m* de la Monnaie **2** *vt (coins)* frapper

**mint[2]** [mɪnt] *n (herb)* menthe *f*; *(sweet)* bonbon *m* à la menthe

**minus** ['maɪnəs] **1** *adj & n* **m. (sign)** (signe *m*) moins *m* **2** *prep (with numbers)* moins; *Fam (without)* sans; **it's m. 10 (degrees)** il fait moins 10

**minute[1]** ['mɪnɪt] *n (of time)* minute *f*; **this (very) m.** *(now)* tout de suite; **any m. (now)** d'une minute à l'autre ▪ **minutes** *npl (of meeting)* procès-verbal *m*

**minute[2]** [maɪ'njuːt] *adj (tiny)* minuscule

**miracle** ['mɪrəkəl] *n* miracle *m* ▪ **miraculous** [mɪ'rækjʊləs] *adj* miraculeux, -euse

**mirror** ['mɪrə(r)] *n* miroir *m*, glace *f*; **(rearview) m.** *(of vehicle)* rétroviseur *m*

**misbehave** [mɪsbɪ'heɪv] *vi* se conduire mal

**miscalculate** [mɪs'kælkjʊleɪt] *vi* faire une erreur de calcul; *Fig* faire un mauvais calcul

**miscarriage** [mɪs'kærɪdʒ] *n Med* **to have a m.** faire une fausse couche; **m. of justice** erreur *f* judiciaire

**miscellaneous** [mɪsə'leɪnɪəs] *adj* divers

**mischief** ['mɪstʃɪf] *n* espièglerie *f*; **to get into m.** faire des bêtises ▪ **mischievous** *adj (naughty)* espiègle; *(malicious)* méchant

**misconduct** [mɪs'kɒndʌkt] *n (bad behaviour)* inconduite *f*

**misdemeanor** [mɪsdɪ'miːnə(r)] *n Am (crime)* délit *m*

**miser** ['maɪzə(r)] *n* avare *mf* ▪ **miserly** *adj* avare

**miserable** ['mɪzərəbəl] *adj (wretched)* misérable; *(unhappy)* malheureux, -euse; *(awful)* affreux, -euse

**misery** ['mɪzərɪ] (*pl* **-ies**) *n (suffering)* malheur *m*; *(sadness)* détresse *f*

**misfire** [mɪs'faɪə(r)] *vi (of plan)* rater

**misfit** ['mɪsfɪt] *n Pej* inadapté, -e *mf*

**misfortune** [mɪs'fɔːtʃuːn] *n* malheur *m*

**misgivings** [mɪs'gɪvɪŋz] *npl (doubts)* doutes *mpl* (**about** sur); *(fears)* craintes *fpl* (**about** à propos de)

**misguided** [mɪs'gaɪdɪd] *adj (attempt)* malencontreux, -euse

**mishandle** [mɪs'hændəl] *vt (situation)* mal gérer; *(person)* malmener

**mishap** ['mɪshæp] *n* incident *m*

**misinform** [mɪsɪn'fɔːm] *vt* mal renseigner

**misinterpret** [mɪsɪn'tɜ:prɪt] *vt* mal interpréter

**mislay** [mɪs'leɪ] (*pt & pp* **-laid**) *vt* égarer

**mislead** [mɪs'li:d] (*pt & pp* **-led**) *vt* tromper ▪ **misleading** *adj* trompeur, -euse

**mismanage** [mɪs'mænɪdʒ] *vt* mal gérer

**misplace** [mɪs'pleɪs] *vt (lose)* égarer

**misprint** ['mɪsprɪnt] *n* faute *f* d'impression, coquille *f*

**mispronounce** [mɪsprə'naʊns] *vt* mal prononcer

**misrepresent** [mɪsreprɪ'zent] *vt (theory)* dénaturer; *(person)* présenter sous un faux jour

**Miss** [mɪs] *n* Mademoiselle *f*

**miss** [mɪs] **1** *n* coup *m* raté; **that was** *or* **we had a near m.** on l'a échappé belle; *Fam* **I'll give it a m.** *(not go)* je n'y irai pas

**2** *vt (train, target, opportunity)* manquer, rater; *(not see)* ne pas voir; *(not understand)* ne pas comprendre; *(feel the lack of)* regretter; **to m. sth out** *(accidentally)* oublier qch; *(intentionally)* omettre qch

**3** *vi* manquer *ou* rater son coup; **to m. out on sth** rater qch

**missile** [*Br* 'mɪsaɪl, *Am* 'mɪsəl] *n (rocket)* missile *m*; *(object thrown)* projectile *m*

**missing** ['mɪsɪŋ] *adj (absent)* absent; *(in war, after disaster)* disparu; *(object)* manquant; **there are two cups/students m.** il manque deux tasses/étudiants; **to go m.** disparaître

**mission** ['mɪʃən] *n* mission *f*

**missionary** ['mɪʃənərɪ] (*pl* **-ies**) *n Rel* missionnaire *m*

**misspell** [mɪs'spel] (*pt & pp* **-ed** *or* **-spelt**) *vt* mal écrire

**mist** [mɪst] **1** *n (fog)* brume *f*; *(on glass)* buée *f* **2** *vi* **to m. over** *or* **up** s'embuer

**mistake** [mɪ'steɪk] **1** *n* erreur *f*, faute *f*; **to make a m.** faire une erreur; **by m.** par erreur **2** (*pt* **-took**, *pp* **-taken**) *vt (meaning, intention)* se tromper sur; **to m. sb for** prendre qn pour ▪ **mistaken** *adj (belief, impression)* erroné; **to be m.** *(of person)* se tromper (**about** sur) ▪ **mistakenly** *adv* par erreur

**Mister** ['mɪstə(r)] *n* Monsieur *m*

**mistreat** [mɪs'tri:t] *vt* maltraiter

**mistress** ['mɪstrɪs] *n* maîtresse *f*; *Br (in secondary school)* professeur *m*

**mistrust** [mɪs'trʌst] **1** *n* méfiance *f* **2** *vt* se méfier de

**misty** ['mɪstɪ] (**-ier, -iest**) *adj (foggy)* brumeux, -euse

**misunderstand** [mɪsʌndə'stænd] (*pt & pp* **-stood**) *vti* mal comprendre ▪ **misunderstanding** *n (disagreement)* mésentente *f*; *(misconception)* malentendu *m*

**misuse 1** [mɪs'ju:s] *n (of equipment, resources)* mauvais emploi *m*; *(of power)* abus *m* **2** [mɪs'ju:z] *vt (equipment, resources)* mal employer; *(power)* abuser de

**mitt(en)** [mɪt, 'mɪtən] *n (glove)* moufle *f*

**mix** [mɪks] **1** *n (mixture)* mélange *m* **2** *vt* mélanger; *(cement, drink, cake)* préparer; **to m. up** *(papers)* mélanger; *(mistake)* confondre (**with** avec); **to be mixed up in sth** être mêlé à qch **3** *vi (blend)* se mélanger; **to m. with sb** *(socially)* fréquenter qn

**mixed** [mɪkst] *adj (school, marriage)* mixte; *(nuts, chocolates)* assortis; **to be (all) m. up** *(of person)* être désorienté; *(of facts, account)* être confus

**mixer** ['mɪksə(r)] *n (for cooking)* mixeur *m*

**mixture** ['mɪkstʃə(r)] *n* mélange *m*

**mix-up** ['mɪksʌp] *n* confusion *f*

**mm** (*abbr* **millimetre(s)**) mm

**moan** [məʊn] **1** *n (sound)* gémissement *m* **2** *vi (make sound)* gémir; *(complain)* se plaindre (**to** à; **about** de; **that** que)

**mob** [mɒb] **1** *n (crowd)* foule *f* **2** (*pt & pp* **-bb-**) *vt* prendre d'assaut

**mobile** [*Br* 'məʊbaɪl, *Am* 'məʊbəl] **1** *adj* mobile; **m. home** mobile home *m*; *Br*

**m. phone** téléphone *m* portable **2** *n Br (phone)* portable *m*

**mobilize** ['məʊbɪlaɪz] *vti* mobiliser

**mock** [mɒk] **1** *adj (false)* simulé; *Br Sch* **m. exam** examen *m* blanc **2** *vt* se moquer de; *(mimic)* singer ▪ **mockery** *n (act)* moqueries *fpl*; *(farce, parody)* parodie *f*; **to make a m. of sth** tourner qch en ridicule

**mode** [məʊd] *n (manner, way) & Comptr* mode *m*

**model** ['mɒdəl] **1** *n (example, person)* modèle *m*; *(small version)* maquette *f*; *(in fashion show, magazine* mannequin *m*; **(scale) m.** modèle *m* réduit **2** *adj (behaviour, student)* modèle; *(car, plane)* modèle réduit *inv* **3** (*Br* **-ll-**, *Am* **-l-**) *vt (clay)* modeler; *(hats, dresses)* présenter; **to m. sth on** modeler qch sur **4** *vi (for fashion)* être mannequin; *(pose for artist)* poser

**modem** ['məʊdəm] *n Comptr* modem *m*

**moderate** ['mɒdərət] **1** *adj* modéré **2** *n Pol* modéré, -e *mf* ▪ **moderately** *adv (in moderation)* modérément; *(averagely)* moyennement

**moderation** [mɒdə'reɪʃən] *n* modération *f*; **in m.** avec modération

**modern** ['mɒdən] *adj* moderne; **m. languages** langues *fpl* vivantes

**modernize** ['mɒdənaɪz] *vt* moderniser

**modest** ['mɒdɪst] *adj (unassuming, moderate)* modeste

**modify** ['mɒdɪfaɪ] (*pt & pp* **-ied**) *vt* modifier ▪ **modification** *n* modification *f* (**to** à)

**module** ['mɒdju:l] *n* module *m*

**moist** [mɔɪst] (**-er, -est**) *adj* humide; *(skin, hand)* moite ▪ **moisten** ['mɔɪsən] *vt* humecter

**moisture** ['mɔɪstʃə(r)] *n* humidité *f*; *(on glass)* buée *f* ▪ **moisturizer** *n* crème *f* hydratante

**mold** [məʊld] *n & vt Am* = **mould**

**mole** [məʊl] *n* (**a**) *(on skin)* grain *m* de beauté (**b**) *(animal, spy)* taupe *f*

**molecule** ['mɒlɪkju:l] *n* molécule *f*

**molest** [mə'lest] *vt (child, woman)* agresser (sexuellement)

**molt** [məʊlt] *vi Am* = **moult**

**mom** [mɒm] *n Am Fam* maman *f*

**moment** ['məʊmənt] *n* moment *m*, instant *m*; **at the m.** en ce moment; **for the m.** pour le moment; **in a m.** dans un instant; **any m. (now)** d'un instant à l'autre

**momentary** ['məʊməntərɪ] *adj* momentané ▪ **momentarily** [*Br* 'məʊməntərɪlɪ, *Am* məʊmən'terɪlɪ] *adv (temporarily)* momentanément; *Am (soon)* tout de suite

**momentum** [məʊ'mentəm] *n (speed)* élan *m*; **to gather** *or* **gain m.** *(of campaign)* prendre de l'ampleur

**mommy** ['mɒmɪ] *n Am Fam* maman *f*

**monarch** ['mɒnək] *n* monarque *m* ▪ **monarchy** (*pl* **-ies**) *n* monarchie *f*

**monastery** ['mɒnəstərɪ] (*pl* **-ies**) *n* monastère *m*

**Monday** ['mʌndeɪ] *n* lundi *m*

**monetary** ['mʌnɪtərɪ] *adj* monétaire

**money** ['mʌnɪ] *n* argent *m*; **to make m.** *(of person)* gagner de l'argent; *(of business)* rapporter de l'argent ▪ **moneybox** *n* tirelire *f* ▪ **moneylender** *n* prêteur, -euse *mf*

**mongrel** ['mʌŋgrəl] *n* bâtard *m*

**monitor** ['mɒnɪtə(r)] **1** *n Comptr, TV & Tech (screen, device)* moniteur *m* **2** *vt (check)* surveiller

**monk** [mʌŋk] *n* moine *m*

**monkey** ['mʌŋkɪ] (*pl* **-eys**) *n* singe *m*

**monologue** ['mɒnəlɒg] *n* monologue *m*

**monopoly** [mə'nɒpəlɪ] *n* monopole *m* ▪ **monopolize** *vt* monopoliser

**monotonous** [mə'nɒtənəs] *adj* monotone

**monster** ['mɒnstə(r)] *n* monstre *m*

**monstrosity** [mɒn'strɒsətɪ] (*pl* **-ies**) *n* monstruosité *f*

**monstrous** ['mɒnstrəs] *adj* monstrueux, -euse

**month** [mʌnθ] *n* mois *m* ▪ **monthly** **1** *adj* mensuel, -elle; **m. payment**

mensualité *f* **2** (*pl* **-ies**) *n (periodical)* mensuel *m* **3** *adv* tous les mois

**Montreal** [mɒntrɪ'ɔ:l] *n* Montréal *m ou f*

**monument** ['mɒnjʊmənt] *n* monument *m*

**moo** [mu:] (*pt & pp* **mooed**) *vi* meugler

**mood** [mu:d] *n (of person)* humeur *f*; *(in grammar)* mode *m*; **in a good/bad m.** de bonne/mauvaise humeur; **to be in the m. to do** *or* **for doing sth** être d'humeur à faire qch

**moody** ['mu:dɪ] (**-ier, -iest**) *adj (bad-tempered)* maussade; *(changeable)* lunatique

**moon** [mu:n] *n* lune *f* ▪ **moonlight** *n* **by m.** au clair de lune

**moor** [mʊə(r)] **1** *n (heath)* lande *f* **2** *vt (ship)* amarrer **3** *vi (of ship)* mouiller

**moose** [mu:s] *n inv (animal)* élan *m*

**mop** [mɒp] **1** *n (for floor)* balai *m* à franges; *(with sponge)* balai-éponge *m* **2** (*pt & pp* **-pp-**) *vt* **to m. sth up** *(liquid)* éponger qch

**mope** [məʊp] *vi* **to m. about** broyer du noir

**moped** ['məʊped] *n* Mobylette® *f*

**moral** ['mɒrəl] **1** *adj* moral **2** *n (of story)* morale *f*; **morals** *(principles)* moralité *f* ▪ **morale** [mɒ'rɑ:l] *n* moral *m* ▪ **morality** [mə'rælətɪ] *n* moralité *f*

**morbid** ['mɔ:bɪd] *adj* morbide

**MORE** [mɔ:(r)] **1** *adj* plus de; **m. cars** plus de voitures; **he has m. books than you** il a plus de livres que toi; **a few m. months** quelques mois de plus; **(some) m. tea** encore du thé; **(some) m. details** d'autres détails; **m. than a kilo/ten** plus d'un kilo/de dix

**2** *adv (to form comparative of adjectives and adverbs)* plus (**than** que); **m. and m.** de plus en plus; **m. or less** plus ou moins

**3** *pron* plus; **have some m.** reprenez-en; **she doesn't have any m.** elle n'en a plus; **the m. he shouts, the m. hoarse he gets** plus il crie, plus il s'enroue; **what's m.** qui plus est

**moreover** [mɔ:'rəʊvə(r)] *adv* de plus

**morning** ['mɔ:nɪŋ] **1** *n* matin *m*; *(referring to duration)* matinée *f*; **in the m.** le matin; *(during the course of the morning)* pendant la matinée; *(tomorrow)* demain matin; **every Tuesday m.** tous les mardis matin **2** *adj (newspaper)* du matin ▪ **mornings** *adv Am* le matin

**Morocco** [mə'rɒkəʊ] *n* le Maroc ▪ **Moroccan 1** *adj* marocain **2** *n* Marocain, -e *mf*

**moron** ['mɔ:rɒn] *n* crétin, -e *mf*

**mortal** ['mɔ:təl] *adj & n* mortel, -elle *(mf)*

**mortgage** ['mɔ:gɪdʒ] *n (money lent)* prêt *m* immobilier; *(money borrowed)* emprunt *m* immobilier

**mortuary** ['mɔ:tʃʊərɪ] (*pl* **-ies**) *n* morgue *f*

**mosaic** [məʊ'zeɪɪk] *n* mosaïque *f*

**Moscow** [*Br* 'mɒskəʊ, *Am* 'mɒskaʊ] *n* Moscou *m ou f*

**Moslem** ['mɒzlɪm] *adj & n* musulman, -e *(mf)*

**mosque** [mɒsk] *n* mosquée *f*

**mosquito** [mɒ'ski:təʊ] (*pl* **-oes** *or* **-os**) *n* moustique *m*

**moss** [mɒs] *n* mousse *f*

**MOST** [məʊst] **1** *adj* (**a**) *(the majority of)* la plupart de; **m. women** la plupart des femmes

(**b**) *(greatest amount of)* **the m.** le plus de; **I have the m. books** j'ai le plus de livres

**2** *adv* (**a**) *(to form superlative of adjectives and adverbs)* plus; **the m. beautiful** le plus beau (*f* la plus belle) (**in/of** de); **to talk (the) m.** parler le plus; **m. of all** *(especially)* surtout

(**b**) *(very)* extrêmement

**3** *pron* (**a**) *(the majority)* la plupart; **m. of the people/the time** la plupart des gens/du temps; **m. of the cake** la plus grande partie du gâteau; **m. of them** la plupart d'entre eux

(**b**) *(greatest amount)* le plus; **he earns the m.** c'est lui qui gagne le plus; **to make the m. of sth** *(situation, talent)* tirer le meilleur parti de qch;

*(holiday)* profiter au maximum de qch; **at (the very) m.** tout au plus ▪ **mostly** *adv (in the main)* surtout; *(most often)* le plus souvent

**MOT** [emәʊ'tiː] (*abbr* **Ministry of Transport**) *n Br* = contrôle obligatoire des véhicules de plus de trois ans

**motel** [mәʊ'tel] *n* motel *m*

**moth** [mɒθ] *n* papillon *m* de nuit; *(in clothes)* mite *f*

**mother** ['mʌðә(r)] *n* mère *f*; **M.'s Day** la fête des Mères ▪ **motherhood** *n* maternité *f* ▪ **mother-in-law** (*pl* **mothers-in-law**) *n* belle-mère *f* ▪ **mother-to-be** (*pl* **mothers-to-be**) *n* future mère *f*

**motion** ['mәʊʃәn] **1** *n (of arm)* mouvement *m*; *(in meeting)* motion *f*; **to set sth in m.** mettre qch en mouvement; **m. picture** film *m* **2** *vti* **to m. (to) sb to do sth** faire signe à qn de faire qch ▪ **motionless** *adj* immobile

**motivate** ['mәʊtɪveɪt] *vt (person, decision)* motiver ▪ **motivation** *n* motivation *f*

**motive** ['mәʊtɪv] *n* motif *m* (**for** de)

**motor** ['mәʊtә(r)] **1** *n (engine)* moteur *m*; *Br Fam (car)* auto *f* **2** *adj (industry, insurance)* automobile; **m. racing** courses *fpl* automobiles ▪ **motorbike** *n* moto *f* ▪ **motorboat** *n* canot *m* à moteur ▪ **motorcycle** *n* moto *f*, motocyclette *f* ▪ **motorcyclist** *n* motocycliste *mf* ▪ **motorist** *n Br* automobiliste *mf* ▪ **motorway** *n Br* autoroute *f*

**motto** ['mɒtәʊ] (*pl* **-oes** *or* **-os**) *n* devise *f*

**mould**[1] [mәʊld] (*Am* **mold**) **1** *n (shape)* moule *m* **2** *vt (clay, person's character)* modeler

**mould**[2] [mәʊld] (*Am* **mold**) *n (fungus)* moisissure *f*

**mouldy** ['mәʊldɪ] (*Am* **moldy**) ( **-ier, -iest**) *adj* moisi; **to go m.** moisir

**moult** [mәʊlt] (*Am* **molt**) *vi* muer

**mound** [maʊnd] *n (of earth)* tertre *m*; *Fig (untidy pile)* tas *m*

**mount** [maʊnt] **1** *n (frame for photo or slide)* cadre *m* **2** *vt (horse, jewel, photo, demonstration)* monter; *(ladder)* monter à **3** *vi* (**a**) *(on horse)* se mettre en selle (**b**) *(increase, rise)* monter; **to m. up** *(add up)* monter, augmenter; *(accumulate) (of debts, bills)* s'accumuler

**mountain** ['maʊntɪn] *n* montagne *f*; **m. bike** vélo *m* tout-terrain, VTT *m* ▪ **mountaineer** *n* alpiniste *mf* ▪ **mountaineering** *n* alpinisme *m* ▪ **mountainous** *adj* montagneux, -euse

**mourn** [mɔːn] *vti* **to m. (for) sb** pleurer qn ▪ **mourner** *n* = personne assistant aux obsèques ▪ **mourning** *n* deuil *m*; **in m.** en deuil

**mouse** [maʊs] (*pl* **mice** [maɪs]) *n (animal) & Comptr* souris *f*

**mousse** [muːs] *n* mousse *f*

**moustache** [*Br* mә'stɑːʃ, *Am* 'mʌstæʃ] *n* moustache *f*

**mouth** [maʊθ] (*pl* **-s** [maʊðz]) *n (of person, horse)* bouche *f*; *(of other animals)* gueule *f*; *(of river)* embouchure *f*; *(of cave, harbour)* entrée *f* ▪ **mouthful** ['maʊθfʊl] *n (of food)* bouchée *f*; *(of liquid)* gorgée *f* ▪ **mouth-organ** *n* harmonica *m* ▪ **mouthpiece** *n (of musical instrument)* embouchure *f*; *(spokesperson)* porte-parole *m inv* ▪ **mouthwash** *n* bain *m* de bouche ▪ **mouthwatering** *adj* appétissant

**movable** ['muːvәbәl] *adj* mobile

**move** [muːv] **1** *n* mouvement *m*; *(change of house)* déménagement *m*; *(change of job)* changement *m* d'emploi; *(in game)* coup *m*; **to make a m.** *(leave)* se préparer à partir; *(act)* passer à l'action; **it's your m.** *(turn)* c'est à toi de jouer; *Fam* **to get a m. on** se grouiller

**2** *vt* déplacer; *(arm, leg)* remuer; *(employee)* muter; *(piece in game)* jouer; **to m. sb** *(emotionally)* émouvoir qn; **to m. house** déménager

**3** *vi* bouger; *(change position)* se déplacer (**to** à); *(leave)* partir; *(act)* agir; *(play)* jouer; *(change house)* déménager; **to m. to Paris** aller habiter Paris

▸ **move about** *vi* se déplacer; *(fidget)* remuer

▸ **move along** *vi* avancer
▸ **move around** *vi* = **move about**
▸ **move away** *vi (go away)* s'éloigner; *(move house)* déménager
▸ **move back 1** *vt sep (chair)* reculer; *(to its original position)* remettre en place **2** *vi (withdraw)* reculer; *(return)* retourner (**to** à)
▸ **move down** *vt sep (take down)* descendre
▸ **move forward** *vt sep & vi* avancer
▸ **move in** *vi (into house)* emménager
▸ **move off** *vi (go away)* s'éloigner; *(of vehicle)* démarrer
▸ **move out** *vi (out of house)* déménager
▸ **move over 1** *vt sep* pousser **2** *vi (make room)* se pousser
▸ **move up** *vi (on seats)* se pousser

**movement** ['mu:vmənt] *n* mouvement *m*

**movie** ['mu:vɪ] *n* film *m*; **the movies** *(cinema)* le cinéma; **m. star** vedette *f* de cinéma; *Am* **m. theater** cinéma *m*

**moving** ['mu:vɪŋ] *adj* en mouvement; *(vehicle)* en marche; *(touching)* émouvant

**mow** [məʊ] (*pp* **mown** [məʊn] *or* **mowed**) *vt* **to m. the lawn** tondre le gazon ▪ **mower** *n* **(lawn) m.** tondeuse *f* (à gazon)

**MP** [em'pi:] (*abbr* **Member of Parliament**) *n* député *m*

**mph** [empi:'eɪtʃ] (*abbr* **miles per hour**) ≃ km/h

**Mr** ['mɪstə(r)] *n* **Mr Brown** M. Brown

**Mrs** ['mɪsɪz] *n* **Mrs Brown** Mme Brown

**MS** [em'es] (*abbr* **Master of Science**) *n Am Univ* **to have an MS in chemistry** avoir une maîtrise de chimie

**Ms** [mɪz] *n* **Ms Brown** ≃ Mme Brown *(ne renseigne pas sur le statut de famille)*

**MSc** [emes'si:] (*abbr* **Master of Science**) *n Univ* **to have an M. in chemistry** avoir une maîtrise de chimie

**MUCH** [mʌtʃ] **1** *adj*

> Hormis dans la langue soutenue et dans certaines expressions, ne s'utilise que dans des structures négatives ou interrogatives.

beaucoup de; **not m. time/money** pas beaucoup de temps/d'argent; **how m. sugar do you want?** combien de sucre voulez-vous?; **twice as m. traffic** deux fois plus de circulation; **too m. work** trop de travail
**2** *adv* beaucoup; **very m.** beaucoup; **m. better** bien meilleur; **I love him so m.** je l'aime tellement; **she doesn't say very m.** elle ne dit pas grand-chose
**3** *pron* beaucoup; **there isn't m. left** il n'en reste pas beaucoup; **it's not m. of a garden** ce n'est pas terrible comme jardin; **twice as m.** deux fois plus; **as m. as you like** autant que tu veux; *Fam* **that's a bit m.!** c'est un peu fort!

**muck** [mʌk] **1** *n (manure)* fumier *m*; *Fig (filth)* saleté *f* **2** *vt Br Fam* **to m. sth up** *(task)* bâcler qch; *(plans)* chambouler qch **3** *vi Br Fam* **to m. about** *or* **around** *(waste time)* traîner; *(play the fool)* faire l'imbécile ▪ **mucky** (**-ier, -iest**) *adj Fam* sale

**mud** [mʌd] *n* boue *f* ▪ **muddy** (**-ier, -iest**) *adj (water, road)* boueux, -euse; *(hands)* couvert de boue ▪ **mudguard** *n* garde-boue *m inv*

**muddle** ['mʌdəl] **1** *n* confusion *f*; **to be in a m.** *(person)* ne plus s'y retrouver; *(of things)* être en désordre **2** *vt (facts)* mélanger; **to get muddled** *(of person)* s'embrouiller

**muesli** ['mju:zlɪ, 'mu:zlɪ] *n* muesli *m*

**muffin** ['mʌfɪn] *n (cake)* muffin *m*

**muffled** ['mʌfəld] *adj (noise)* sourd

**muffler** ['mʌflə(r)] *n Am (on vehicle)* silencieux *m*

**mug**[1] [mʌg] *n* (**a**) *(for tea, coffee)* grande tasse *f*; **(beer) m.** chope *f* (**b**) *Br Fam (fool)* poire *f*

**mug**[2] [mʌg] (*pt & pp* **-gg-**) *vt (attack in street)* agresser ▪ **mugger** *n* agresseur *m*

**mule** [mju:l] *n (male)* mulet *m*; *(female)* mule *f*

**multicoloured** ['mʌltɪkʌləd] *adj* multicolore

**multimedia** [mʌltɪ'mi:dɪə] *adj* multimédia

**multimillionaire** [mʌltɪmɪljə'neə(r)] *n* multimillionnaire *mf*

**multiple** ['mʌltɪpəl] **1** *adj* multiple **2** *n Math* multiple *m*

**multiple-choice** [mʌltɪpəl'tʃɔɪs] *adj* à choix multiple

**multiplication** [mʌltɪplɪ'keɪʃən] *n* multiplication *f*

**multiply** ['mʌltɪplaɪ] (*pt & pp* **-ied**) **1** *vt* multiplier **2** *vi (of animals, insects)* se multiplier

**multiracial** [mʌltɪ'reɪʃəl] *adj* multiracial

**multistorey** [mʌltɪ'stɔ:rɪ] (*Am* **multistoried**) *adj (car park)* à plusieurs niveaux

**multitude** ['mʌltɪtju:d] *n* multitude *f*

**mum** [mʌm] *n Br Fam* maman *f*

**mumble** ['mʌmbəl] *vti* marmotter

**mummy**[1] ['mʌmɪ] (*pl* **-ies**) *n Br Fam (mother)* maman *f*

**mummy**[2] ['mʌmɪ] (*pl* **-ies**) *n (embalmed body)* momie *f*

**mumps** [mʌmps] *n Med* oreillons *mpl*

**munch** [mʌntʃ] *vti (chew)* mâcher

**municipal** [mju:'nɪsɪpəl] *adj* municipal

**mural** ['mjʊərəl] *n* peinture *f* murale

**murder** ['mɜ:də(r)] **1** *n* meurtre *m* **2** *vt (kill)* assassiner ▪ **murderer** *n* meurtrier, -ère *mf*, assassin *m*

**murky** ['mɜ:kɪ] (**-ier, -iest**) *adj (water, business, past)* trouble

**murmur** ['mɜ:mə(r)] **1** *n* murmure *m* **2** *vti* murmurer

**muscle** ['mʌsəl] *n* muscle *m* ▪ **muscular** ['mʌskjʊlə(r)] *adj (person, arm)* musclé

**museum** [mju:'zɪəm] *n* musée *m*

**mush** [mʌʃ] *n (pulp)* bouillie *f* ▪ **mushy** (**-ier, -iest**) *adj (food)* en bouillie

**mushroom** ['mʌʃrʊm] *n* champignon *m*

**music** ['mju:zɪk] *n* musique *f* ▪ **musical 1** *adj* musical; **m. instrument** instrument *m* de musique **2** *n (film, play)* comédie *f* musicale ▪ **musician** [-'zɪʃən] *n* musicien, -enne *mf*

**Muslim** ['mʊzlɪm] *adj & n* musulman, -e *(mf)*

**mussel** ['mʌsəl] *n* moule *f*

---

**MUST** [mʌst] **1** *n* **this is a m.** c'est indispensable; **this film is a m.** il faut absolument voir ce film
**2** *v aux* (**a**) *(expressing necessity)* **you m. obey** tu dois obéir, il faut que tu obéisses (**b**) *(expressing probability)* **she m. be clever** elle doit être intelligente; **I m. have seen it** j'ai dû le voir

---

**mustache** ['mʌstæʃ] *n Am* moustache *f*

**mustard** ['mʌstəd] *n* moutarde *f*

**muster** ['mʌstə(r)] *vt (gather)* rassembler

**mustn't** ['mʌsənt] = **must not**

**musty** ['mʌstɪ] (**-ier, -iest**) *adj (smell, taste)* de moisi

**mute** [mju:t] *adj (silent) & Ling* muet (*f* muette)

**mutiny** ['mju:tɪnɪ] **1** (*pl* **-ies**) *n* mutinerie *f* **2** (*pt & pp* **-ied**) *vi* se mutiner

**mutter** ['mʌtə(r)] *vti* marmonner

**mutton** ['mʌtən] *n (meat)* mouton *m*

**mutual** ['mju:tʃʊəl] *adj (help, love)* mutuel, -elle; *(friend)* commun ▪ **mutually** *adv* mutuellement

**muzzle** ['mʌzəl] **1** *n (device for dog)* muselière *f*; *(snout)* museau *m* **2** *vt (animal, the press)* museler

**my** [maɪ] *possessive adj* mon, ma, *pl* mes

**myself** [maɪ'self] *pron* moi-même; *(reflexive)* me, m'; *(after prep)* moi; **I wash m.** je me lave

**mystery** ['mɪstərɪ] (*pl* **-ies**) *n* mystère *m* ▪ **mysterious** [mɪs'tɪərɪəs] *adj* mystérieux, -euse

**mystical** ['mɪstɪkəl] *adj* mystique

**mystify** ['mɪstɪfaɪ] (*pt & pp* **-ied**) *vt (bewilder)* déconcerter

**myth** [mɪθ] *n* mythe *m* ▪ **mythology** (*pl* **-ies**) *n* mythologie *f*

# Nn

**N, n** [en] *n (letter)* N, n *m inv*
**nab** [næb] *(pt & pp* **-bb-**) *vt Fam (catch, arrest)* coffrer
**nag** [næg] *(pt & pp* **-gg-**) *vti* **to n. (at) sb** *(of person)* être sur le dos de qn
**nail** [neɪl] **1** *n* (**a**) *(of finger, toe)* ongle *m*; **n. file** lime *f* à ongles; **n. polish,** *Br* **n. varnish** vernis *m* à ongles
(**b**) *(metal)* clou *m*
**2** *vt* clouer; **to n. sth down** *(lid)* clouer qch
**naïve** [naɪ'iːv] *adj* naïf (*f* naïve)
**naked** ['neɪkɪd] *adj (person, flame)* nu
**name** [neɪm] **1** *n* nom *m*; *(reputation)* réputation *f*; **my n. is...** je m'appelle...; **in the n. of** au nom de; **first n., given n.** prénom *m* **2** *vt* nommer; *(ship, street)* baptiser; *(date, price)* fixer
**namely** ['neɪmlɪ] *adv* à savoir
**nanny** ['nænɪ] (*pl* **-ies**) *n* nurse *f*; *Fam (grandmother)* mamie *f*
**nap** [næp] **1** *n (sleep)* **to have** *or* **take a n.** faire un petit somme **2** (*pt & pp* **-pp-**) *vi* faire un somme
**napkin** ['næpkɪn] *n (at table)* serviette *f*
**nappy** ['næpɪ] (*pl* **-ies**) *n Br (for baby)* couche *f*
**narcotic** [nɑː'kɒtɪk] *adj & n* narcotique *(m)*
**narrate** [nə'reɪt] *vt* raconter ▪ **narrative** ['nærətɪv] *n* récit *m* ▪ **narrator** *n* narrateur, -trice *mf*
**narrow** ['nærəʊ] **1** (**-er, -est**) *adj* étroit **2** *vt* **to n. (down)** *(choice, meaning)* limiter **3** *vi (of path)* se rétrécir ▪ **narrowly** *adv (only just)* de peu; **he n. escaped being killed** il a bien failli être tué
**narrow-minded** [nærəʊ'maɪndɪd] *adj* borné
**nasty** ['nɑːstɪ] (**-ier, -iest**) *adj (bad)* mauvais; *(spiteful)* méchant (**to** *or* **towards** avec)
**nation** ['neɪʃən] *n* nation *f*
**national** ['næʃənəl] **1** *adj* national; **n. anthem** hymne *m* national; *Br* **N. Health Service** ≃ Sécurité *f* sociale; *Br* **n. insurance** contributions *fpl* sociales **2** *n (citizen)* ressortissant, -e *mf*
**nationalist** ['næʃənəlɪst] *n* nationaliste *mf*
**nationality** [næʃə'nælətɪ] (*pl* **-ies**) *n* nationalité *f*
**nationalize** ['næʃənəlaɪz] *vt* nationaliser
**nationwide** ['neɪʃənwaɪd] *adj & adv* dans tout le pays
**native** ['neɪtɪv] **1** *adj (country)* natal (*mpl* -als); *(tribe, plant)* indigène; **to be an English n. speaker** avoir l'anglais comme langue maternelle **2** *n (person)* indigène *mf*; **to be a n. of** être originaire de
**NATO** ['neɪtəʊ] (*abbr* **North Atlantic Treaty Organization**) *n Mil* OTAN *f*
**natter** ['nætə(r)] *vi Br Fam* bavarder
**natural** ['nætʃərəl] *adj* naturel, -elle; *(talent)* inné ▪ **naturally** *adv (unaffectedly, of course)* naturellement; *(by nature)* de nature
**nature** ['neɪtʃə(r)] *n (world, character)* nature *f*; **by n.** de nature; **n. reserve** réserve *f* naturelle
**naughty** ['nɔːtɪ] (**-ier, -iest**) *adj (child)* vilain

**nausea** ['nɔːzɪə] *n* nausée *f* ▪ **nauseate** ['nɔːzɪeɪt] *vt* écœurer ▪ **nauseous** ['nɔːʃəs] *adj Am* **to feel n.** *(sick)* avoir envie de vomir

**nautical** ['nɔːtɪkəl] *adj* nautique

**naval** ['neɪvəl] *adj* naval (*mpl* -als); *(power)* maritime; *(officer)* de marine

**nave** [neɪv] *n (of church)* nef *f*

**navel** ['neɪvəl] *n* nombril *m*

**navigate** ['nævɪgeɪt] **1** *vt (boat)* piloter; *(river)* naviguer sur **2** *vi* naviguer

**navy** ['neɪvɪ] **1** (*pl* **-ies**) *n* marine *f* **2** *adj* **n. (blue)** bleu marine *inv*

**Nazi** ['nɑːtsɪ] *adj & n Pol & Hist* nazi, -e *(mf)*

**NB** [en'biː] (*abbr* **nota bene**) NB

**near** [nɪə(r)] **1** (**-er, -est**) *prep* **n. (to)** près de; **n. (to) the end** vers la fin

**2** (**-er, -est**) *adv* près; **n. to sth** près de qch; **n. enough** *(more or less)* plus ou moins

**3** (**-er, -est**) *adj* proche; **in the n. future** dans un avenir proche; **to the nearest euro** *(calculate)* à un euro près; *Aut* **n. side** *Br* côté *m* gauche, *Am* côté *m* droit

**4** *vt (approach)* approcher de

**nearby 1** [nɪə'baɪ] *adv* tout près **2** ['nɪəbaɪ] *adj* proche

**nearly** ['nɪəlɪ] *adv* presque; **she (very) n. fell** elle a failli tomber

**neat** [niːt] (**-er, -est**) *adj (clothes, work)* soigné; *(room)* bien rangé; *Am Fam (good)* super *inv* ▪ **neatly** *adv (carefully)* avec soin; *(skilfully)* habilement

**necessary** ['nesɪsərɪ] *adj* nécessaire ▪ **necessarily** [-'serəlɪ] *adv* **not n.** pas forcément

**necessity** [nɪ'sesətɪ] (*pl* **-ies**) *n (obligation, need)* nécessité *f*; **to be a n.** être indispensable ▪ **necessitate** *vt* nécessiter

**neck** [nek] *n* cou *m*; *(of dress)* encolure *f*; *(of bottle)* goulot *m*

**necklace** ['neklɪs] *n* collier *m* ▪ **necktie** *n* cravate *f*

**nectarine** ['nektəriːn] *n (fruit)* nectarine *f*, brugnon *m*

**need** [niːd] **1** *n* besoin *m*; **to be in n. of sth** avoir besoin de qch; **there's no n. (for you) to do that** tu n'as pas besoin de faire cela

**2** *vt* avoir besoin de; **you n. it** tu en as besoin; **her hair needs cutting** il faut qu'elle se fasse couper les cheveux

**3** *v aux* **I needn't have rushed** ce n'était pas la peine de me presser; **you needn't worry** inutile de t'inquiéter

**needle** ['niːdəl] *n* aiguille *f*; *(of record player)* saphir *m* ▪ **needlework** *n* couture *f*; *(object)* ouvrage *m*

**needlessly** ['niːdlɪslɪ] *adv* inutilement

**needy** ['niːdɪ] (**-ier, -iest**) *adj* nécessiteux, -euse

**negative** ['negətɪv] **1** *adj* négatif, -ive **2** *n (of photo)* négatif *m*

**neglect** [nɪ'glekt] **1** *n (of person)* négligence *f* **2** *vt (person, health, work)* négliger; *(garden, car)* ne pas s'occuper de; *(duty)* manquer à; **to n. to do sth** négliger de faire qch ▪ **neglected** *adj (appearance)* négligé; *(garden, house)* mal tenu; **to feel n.** se sentir abandonné

**negligent** ['neglɪdʒənt] *adj* négligent

**negligible** ['neglɪdʒəbəl] *adj* négligeable

**negotiate** [nɪ'gəʊʃɪeɪt] *vti (discuss)* négocier ▪ **negotiation** *n* négociation *f*

**neigh** [neɪ] *vi* hennir

**neighbour** ['neɪbə(r)] (*Am* **neighbor**) *n* voisin, -e *mf*

**neighbourhood** ['neɪbəhʊd] (*Am* **neighborhood**) *n (district)* quartier *m*, voisinage *m*; *(neighbours)* voisinage *m*; **in the n. of $10/10 kilos** dans les 10 dollars/10 kilos

**neighbouring** ['neɪbərɪŋ] (*Am* **neighboring**) *adj* voisin

**neither** [*Br* 'naɪðə(r), *Am* 'niːðə(r)] **1** *conj* **n.... nor...** ni... ni...; **he n. sings nor dances** il ne chante ni ne danse

**2** *adv* **n. do I/n. can I** (ni) moi non plus

**3** *adj* **n. boy came** aucun des deux garçons n'est venu

**4** *pron* **n. (of them)** aucun(e) (des deux)

**neon** ['ni:ɒn] *adj* **n. sign** enseigne *f* au néon

**nephew** ['nefju:] *n* neveu *m*

**nerve** [nɜ:v] *n* nerf *m*; *(courage)* courage *m*; *Fam (impudence)* culot *m*; *Fam* **he gets on my nerves** il me tape sur les nerfs ▪ **nerve-racking** *adj* éprouvant

**nervous** ['nɜ:vəs] *adj (apprehensive)* nerveux, -euse; **to be n. about sth/doing sth** être nerveux à l'idée de qch/de faire qch

**nest** [nest] **1** *n* nid *m*; *Fig* **n. egg** pécule *m* **2** *vi (of bird)* nicher

**nestle** ['nesəl] *vi* se pelotonner (**up to** contre)

**Net** [net] *n Comptr* **the N.** le Net

**net**[1] [net] *n* filet *m*

**net**[2] [net] **1** *adj (profit, weight)* net (*f* nette) **2** (*pt & pp* **-tt-**) *vt (of person, company)* gagner net

**Netherlands** ['neðələndz] *npl* **the N.** les Pays-Bas *mpl*

**nettle** ['netəl] *n* ortie *f*

**network** ['netwɜ:k] *n* réseau *m*

**neurotic** [njʊ'rɒtɪk] *adj & n* névrosé, -e *(mf)*

**neuter** ['nju:tə(r)] **1** *adj & n Gram* neutre *(m)* **2** *vt (cat)* châtrer

**neutral** ['nju:trəl] **1** *adj* neutre; *(policy)* de neutralité **2** *n* **in n. (gear)** *(vehicle)* au point mort ▪ **neutralize** *vt* neutraliser

**never** ['nevə(r)] *adv (not ever)* (ne...) jamais; **she n. lies** elle ne ment jamais; **n. again** plus jamais ▪ **never-ending** *adj* interminable

**nevertheless** [nevəðə'les] *adv* néanmoins

**new** [nju:] *adj* (**a**) (**-er, -est**) nouveau (*f* nouvelle); *(brand-new)* neuf (*f* neuve); **to be n. to** *(job)* être nouveau dans; *(city)* être un nouveau-venu (*f* une nouvelle-venue) dans (**b**) *(different)* **a n. glass/pen** un autre verre/stylo ▪ **newborn** *adj* **a n. baby** un nouveau-né, une nouveau-née ▪ **newcomer** [-kʌmə(r)] *n* nouveau-venu *m*, nouvelle-venue *f* (**to** dans) ▪ **newly** *adv* nouvellement ▪ **newlyweds** *n* jeunes mariés *mpl*

**news** [nju:z] *n* nouvelles *fpl*; *(in the media)* informations *fpl*; **a piece of n.** une nouvelle; **sports n.** *(newspaper column)* rubrique *f* sportive ▪ **newsagent** *n Br* marchand, -e *mf* de journaux ▪ **newsdealer** *n Am* marchand, -e *mf* de journaux ▪ **newsflash** *n* flash *m* d'informations ▪ **newsletter** *n (of club, group)* bulletin *m* ▪ **newspaper** *n* journal *m* ▪ **newsreader** *n Br* présentateur, -trice *mf* de journal

**New Zealand** [nju:'zi:lənd] *n* la Nouvelle-Zélande

**next** [nekst] **1** *adj* prochain; *(room, house)* d'à côté; *(following)* suivant; **n. month** *(in the future)* le mois prochain; **the n. day** le lendemain; **within the n. ten days** d'ici dix jours; **you're n.** c'est ton tour; **the n. size up** la taille au-dessus; **to live n. door** habiter à côté (**to** de)

**2** *n (in series)* suivant, -e *mf*

**3** *adv (afterwards)* ensuite, après; *(now)* maintenant; **when you come n.** la prochaine fois que tu viendras; **n. to** *(beside)* à côté de

**next-door** ['nekstdɔ:(r)] *adj* **n. neighbour/room** voisin *m*/pièce *f* d'à côté

**NHS** [eneɪtʃ'es] (*abbr* **National Health Service**) *n Br* ≃ Sécurité *f* sociale

**nibble** ['nɪbəl] *vti* grignoter

**nice** [naɪs] (**-er, -est**) *adj (pleasant)* agréable; *(tasty)* bon (*f* bonne); *(physically attractive)* beau (*f* belle); *(kind)* gentil, -ille (**to** avec); **n. and warm** bien chaud; **have a n. day!** bonne journée! ▪ **nicely** *adv (well)* bien

**niche** [ni:ʃ, nɪtʃ] *n (recess)* niche *f*; **(market) n.** créneau *m*

**nick** [nɪk] **1** *n (on skin, wood)* entaille *f*; *(in blade, crockery)* brèche *f*; **in the n. of time** juste à temps **2** *vt Br Fam (steal)* piquer

**nickel** ['nɪkəl] *n Am (coin)* pièce *f* de cinq cents

**nickname** ['nɪkneɪm] **1** *n (informal)* surnom *m* **2** *vt* surnommer

**niece** [ni:s] *n* nièce *f*

**night** [naɪt] **1** *n* nuit *f*; *(evening)* soir *m*; **at n.** la nuit; **last n.** *(evening)* hier soir; *(night)* cette nuit; **to have an early/a late n.** se coucher tôt/tard

**2** *adj (work, flight)* de nuit; **n. shift** *(job)* poste *m* de nuit; *(workers)* équipe *f* de nuit ■ **nightcap** *n (drink)* = boisson alcoolisée ou chaude prise avant de se coucher ■ **nightclub** *n* boîte *f* de nuit ■ **nightdress** ['naɪtdres], **nightgown** ['naɪtgəʊn], *Fam* **nightie** ['naɪtɪ] *n* chemise *f* de nuit ■ **nightfall** *n* **at n.** à la tombée de la nuit ■ **nightlife** *n* vie *f* nocturne ■ **night-time** *n* nuit *f*

**nightingale** ['naɪtɪŋgeɪl] *n* rossignol *m*

**nightly** ['naɪtlɪ] **1** *adv* chaque nuit; *(every evening)* chaque soir **2** *adj* de chaque nuit/soir

**nightmare** ['naɪtmeə(r)] *n* cauchemar *m*

**nil** [nɪl] *n (nothing) & Br (score)* zéro *m*; **two n.** deux à zéro

**Nile** [naɪl] *n* **the N.** le Nil

**nimble** ['nɪmbəl] (**-er, -est**) *adj (person)* souple

**nine** [naɪn] *adj & n* neuf *(m)*

**nineteen** [naɪn'ti:n] *adj & n* dix-neuf *(m)*

**ninety** ['naɪntɪ] *adj & n* quatre-vingt-dix *(m)*

**ninth** ['naɪnθ] *adj & n* neuvième *(mf)*; **a n.** *(fraction)* un neuvième

**nip** [nɪp] **1** *(pt & pp* **-pp-***) vt (pinch)* pincer **2** *vi Br Fam* **to n. round to sb's house** faire un saut chez qn; **to n. out** sortir un instant

**nipple** ['nɪpəl] *n* mamelon *m*; *Am (on baby's bottle)* tétine *f*

**nitrogen** ['naɪtrədʒən] *n* azote *m*

---

**NO** [nəʊ] **1** *(pl* **noes** *or* **nos***) n* non *m inv*

**2** *adj (not any)* pas de; **there's no bread** il n'y a pas de pain; **I have no idea** je n'ai aucune idée; **no child came** aucun enfant n'est venu; **of no importance** sans importance

**3** *adv (interjection)* non; **no more time** plus de temps; **no more/fewer than ten** pas plus/moins de dix

---

**noble** ['nəʊbəl] (**-er, -est**) *adj* noble ■ **nobility** *n* noblesse *f*

**nobody** ['nəʊbɒdɪ] **1** *pron* (ne…) personne; **n. came** personne n'est venu; **he knows n.** il ne connaît personne **2** *n* **a n.** une nullité

**nod** [nɒd] **1** *n* signe *m* de tête **2** *(pt & pp* **-dd-***) vti* **to n. (one's head)** faire un signe de tête **3** *vi Fam* **to n. off** s'assoupir

**noise** [nɔɪz] *n* bruit *m*; **to make a n.** faire du bruit

**noisy** ['nɔɪzɪ] (**-ier, -iest**) *adj (person, street)* bruyant ■ **noisily** *adv* bruyamment

**nominal** ['nɒmɪnəl] *adj* nominal; *(rent, salary)* symbolique

**nominate** ['nɒmɪneɪt] *vt (appoint)* nommer; *(propose)* proposer (**for** comme candidat à) ■ **nomination** *n (appointment)* nomination *f*; *(proposal)* candidature *f*

**nondescript** ['nɒndɪskrɪpt] *adj* très ordinaire

---

**NONE** [nʌn] **1** *pron* aucun, -e *mf*; *(in filling out a form)* néant; **n. of them** aucun d'eux; **she has n. (at all)** elle n'en a pas (du tout); **n. came** pas un(e) seul(e) n'est venu(e)

**2** *adv* **n. too hot** pas très chaud; **he's n. the wiser (for it)** il n'est pas plus avancé ■ **nonetheless** *adv* néanmoins

---

**nonentity** [nɒ'nentətɪ] *(pl* **-ies***) n (person)* nullité *f*

**nonexistent** [nɒnɪg'zɪstənt] *adj* inexistant

**non-fiction** [nɒn'fɪkʃən] *n* ouvrages *mpl* généraux

**nonsense** ['nɒnsəns] *n* bêtises *fpl*; **that's n.** c'est absurde

**non-smoker** [nɒn'sməʊkə(r)] *n*

*(person)* non-fumeur, -euse *mf*; *(compartment on train)* compartiment *m* non-fumeurs

**non-stop** [nɒn'stɒp] **1** *adj* sans arrêt; *(train, flight)* sans escale **2** *adv (work)* sans arrêt; *(fly)* sans escale

**noodles** ['nu:dəlz] *npl* nouilles *fpl*; *(in soup)* vermicelles *mpl*

**noon** [nu:n] *n* midi *m*

**no-one** ['nəʊwʌn] *pron* = **nobody**

**noose** [nu:s] *n* nœud *m* coulant

**nor** [nɔ:(r)] *conj* ni; **neither you n. me** ni toi ni moi; **she neither drinks n. smokes** elle ne fume ni ne boit; **n. do I/can I**/*etc* (ni) moi non plus

**norm** [nɔ:m] *n* norme *f*

**normal** ['nɔ:məl] **1** *adj* normal **2** *n* **above/below n.** au-dessus/au-dessous de la normale ▪ **normally** *adv* normalement

**north** [nɔ:θ] **1** *n* nord *m*; **(to the) n. of** au nord de

**2** *adj (coast)* nord *inv*; *(wind)* du nord; **N. America/Africa** Amérique *f*/ Afrique *f* du Nord; **N. American** *adj* nord-américain; *n* Nord-Américain, -e *mf*

**3** *adv* au nord; *(travel)* vers le nord ▪ **northbound** *adj (traffic)* en direction du nord; *Br (carriageway)* nord *inv* ▪ **north-east** *n & adj* nord-est *(m)* ▪ **northerly** ['nɔ:ðəlɪ] *adj (direction)* du nord ▪ **northern** ['nɔ:ðən] *adj (coast)* nord *inv*; *(town)* du nord; **N. France** le nord de la France; **N. Ireland** l'Irlande *f* du Nord ▪ **northerner** ['nɔ:ðənə(r)] *n* habitant, -e *mf* du Nord ▪ **northward(s)** *adj & adv* vers le nord ▪ **north-west** *n & adj* nord-ouest *(m)*

**Norway** ['nɔ:weɪ] *n* la Norvège ▪ **Norwegian** **1** *adj* norvégien, -enne **2** *n (person)* Norvégien, -enne *mf*; *(language)* norvégien *m*

**nose** [nəʊz] *n* nez *m*; **her n. is bleeding** elle saigne du nez ▪ **nosebleed** *n* saignement *m* de nez

**nosey** ['nəʊzɪ] (**-ier, -iest**) *adj Fam* indiscret, -ète

**no-smoking** [nəʊ'sməʊkɪŋ] *adj* *(carriage, area)* non-fumeurs

**nostalgic** [nɒs'tældʒɪk] *adj* nostalgique

**nostril** ['nɒstrəl] *n (of person)* narine *f*

**nosy** ['nəʊzɪ] *adj* = **nosey**

**NOT** [nɒt]

À l'oral, et à l'écrit dans un style familier, on utilise généralement **not** à la forme contractée lors qu'il suit un modal ou un auxiliaire (**don't go!**; **she wasn't there**; **he couldn't see me**).

*adv* (**a**) (ne...) pas; **he's n. there, he isn't there** il n'est pas là; **n. yet** pas encore; **n. at all** pas du tout; *(after 'thank you')* je vous en prie

(**b**) non; **I think/hope n.** je pense/ j'espère que non; **n. guilty** non coupable; **isn't she?/don't you?**/*etc* non?

**notable** ['nəʊtəbəl] *adj* notable ▪ **notably** *adv (noticeably)* notablement; *(particularly)* notamment

**notch** [nɒtʃ] **1** *n (in wood)* encoche *f*; *(in belt, wheel)* cran *m* **2** *vt* **to n. up** *(points)* marquer; *(victory)* remporter

**note** [nəʊt] **1** *n (information, reminder) & Mus* note *f*; *Br (banknote)* billet *m*; *(letter)* mot *m*; **to take (a) n. of sth, to make a n. of sth** prendre note de qch **2** *vt (notice)* remarquer, noter; **to n. sth down** *(word, remark)* noter qch ▪ **notebook** *n* carnet *m*; *(for school)* cahier *m* ▪ **notepad** *n* bloc-notes *m* ▪ **notepaper** *n* papier *m* à lettres

**noted** ['nəʊtɪd] *adj* éminent

**nothing** ['nʌθɪŋ] **1** *pron* (ne...) rien; **he knows n.** il ne sait rien; **n. at all** rien du tout; **n. much** pas grand-chose; **I've got n. to do with it** je n'y suis pour rien; **for n.** *(in vain, free of charge)* pour rien

**2** *adv* **to look n. like sb** ne ressembler nullement à qn

**3** *n* **to come to n.** être anéanti

**notice** ['nəʊtɪs] **1** *n (notification)* avis *m*; *(sign)* pancarte *f*, écriteau *m*; *(poster)* affiche *f*; **to give sb (advance) n.** *(inform)* avertir qn (**of** de); **n. (to quit), n. of dismissal** congé *m*; **to give in** *or*

**hand in one's n.** *(resign)* donner sa démission; **to take n.** faire attention (**of** à); **until further n.** jusqu'à nouvel ordre; **at short n.** au dernier moment **2** *vt* remarquer (**that** que) ▪ **noticeboard** *n Br* tableau *m* d'affichage

**noticeable** ['nəʊtɪsəbəl] *adj* perceptible

**notify** ['nəʊtɪfaɪ] (*pt & pp* **-ied**) *vt (inform)* avertir (**sb of sth** qn de qch); *(announce)* notifier (**to** à) ▪ **notification** [-fɪ'keɪʃən] *n* avis *m*

**notion** ['nəʊʃən] *n* notion *f*

**notorious** [nəʊ'tɔːrɪəs] *adj* tristement célèbre; *(criminal)* notoire

**nought** [nɔːt] *n Br Math* zéro *m*

**noun** [naʊn] *n* nom *m*

**nourish** ['nʌrɪʃ] *vt* nourrir ▪ **nourishment** *n* nourriture *f*

**novel** ['nɒvəl] **1** *n* roman *m* **2** *adj (new)* nouveau (*f* nouvelle), original ▪ **novelist** *n* romancier, -ère *mf* ▪ **novelty** *n* nouveauté *f*

**November** [nəʊ'vembə(r)] *n* novembre *m*

**novice** ['nɒvɪs] *n (beginner)* débutant, -e *mf* (**at** en)

**now** [naʊ] **1** *adv* maintenant; **for n.** pour le moment; **from n. on** désormais; **until n., up to n.** jusqu'ici, jusqu'à maintenant; **n. and then** de temps à autre; **she ought to be here by n.** elle devrait déjà être ici **2** *conj* **n. (that)...** maintenant que...

**nowadays** ['naʊədeɪz] *adv* de nos jours

**nowhere** ['nəʊweə(r)] *adv* nulle part; **n. else** nulle part ailleurs; **n. near enough** loin d'être assez

**nozzle** ['nɒzəl] *n* embout *m*; *(of hose)* jet *m*

**nuance** ['njuːɑːns] *n* nuance *f*

**nuclear** ['njuːklɪə(r)] *adj* nucléaire

**nucleus** ['njuːklɪəs] (*pl* **-clei** [-klɪaɪ]) *n* noyau *m* (*pl* -aux)

**nude** [njuːd] **1** *adj* nu **2** *n* nu *m*; **in the n.** tout nu (*f* toute nue)

**nudge** [nʌdʒ] **1** *n* coup *m* de coude **2** *vt* pousser du coude

**nudist** ['njuːdɪst] **1** *n* nudiste *mf* **2** *adj (camp)* de nudistes

**nuisance** ['njuːsəns] *n* **to be a n.** être embêtant

**null** [nʌl] *adj* **n. (and void)** nul (et non avenu) (*f* nulle (et non avenue))

**numb** [nʌm] *adj (stiff) (hand)* engourdi

**number** ['nʌmbə(r)] **1** *n* nombre *m*; *(of page, house, telephone)* numéro *m*; *(song)* chanson *f*; **a/any n. of** un certain/grand nombre de **2** *vt (assign number to)* numéroter ▪ **numberplate** *n Br* plaque *f* d'immatriculation

**numeral** ['njuːmərəl] *n* chiffre *m*

**numerical** [njuː'merɪkəl] *adj* numérique

**numerous** ['njuːmərəs] *adj* nombreux, -euse

**nun** [nʌn] *n* religieuse *f*

**nurse** [nɜːs] **1** *n* infirmière *f*; *(for children)* nurse *f* **2** *vt (look after)* soigner; *(suckle)* allaiter ▪ **nursing** *n (care)* soins *mpl*; *(job)* profession *f* d'infirmière; *Br* **n. home** *(for old people)* maison *f* de retraite

**nursery** ['nɜːsərɪ] (*pl* **-ies**) *n (children's room)* chambre *f* d'enfants; *(for plants, trees)* pépinière *f*; **(day) n.** *(school)* garderie *f*; **n. rhyme** comptine *f*; **n. school** école *f* maternelle

**nut**[1] [nʌt] *n (fruit)* = noix, noisette ou autre fruit sec de cette nature; **Brazil n.** noix *f* du Brésil ▪ **nutcrackers** *npl* casse-noix *m inv* ▪ **nutshell** *n Fig* **in a n.** en un mot

**nut**[2] [nʌt] *n (for bolt)* écrou *m*

**nut**[3] [nʌt] *n Fam (crazy person)* cinglé, -e *mf* ▪ **nutcase** *n Fam* cinglé, -e *mf*

**nutmeg** ['nʌtmeg] *n* muscade *f*

**nutritious** [njuː'trɪʃəs] *adj* nutritif, -ive ▪ **nutrition** [-ʃən] *n* nutrition *f*

**nuts** [nʌts] *adj Fam (crazy)* cinglé

**nylon** ['naɪlɒn] *n* Nylon® *m*; **n. shirt** chemise *f* en Nylon®

# Oo

**O, o** [əʊ] *n (letter)* O, o *m inv*
**oaf** [əʊf] *n* balourd *m*
**oak** [əʊk] *n (tree, wood)* chêne *m*
**OAP** [əʊeɪ'piː] *(abbr* **old-age pensioner***) n Br* retraité, -e *mf*
**oar** [ɔː(r)] *n* aviron *m*, rame *f*
**oasis** [əʊ'eɪsɪs] *(pl* **oases** [əʊ'eɪsiːz]) *n* oasis *f*
**oath** [əʊθ] *(pl* **-s** [əʊðz]) *n (promise)* serment *m*; *(profanity)* juron *m*
**oats** [əʊts] *npl* avoine *f*; **(porridge) o.** flocons *mpl* d'avoine
**obedient** [ə'biːdɪənt] *adj* obéissant ▪ **obedience** *n* obéissance *f* (**to** à)
**obese** [əʊ'biːs] *adj* obèse
**obey** [ə'beɪ] **1** *vt* obéir à **2** *vi* obéir
**obituary** [ə'bɪtʃʊərɪ] *(pl* **-ies**) *n* nécrologie *f*
**object¹** ['ɒbdʒɪkt] *n (thing)* objet *m*; *(aim)* but *m*, objet; *(in grammar)* complément *m* d'objet
**object²** [əb'dʒekt] **1** *vt* **to o. that…** objecter que… **2** *vi* émettre une objection; **to o. to sth/to doing sth** ne pas être d'accord avec qch/pour faire qch
**objection** [əb'dʒekʃən] *n* objection *f*
**objective** [əb'dʒektɪv] **1** *adj (impartial)* objectif, -ive **2** *n (aim, target)* objectif *m*
**obligation** [ɒblɪ'geɪʃən] *n* obligation *f*; **to be under an o. to do sth** être dans l'obligation de faire qch
**obligatory** [ə'blɪgətərɪ] *adj* obligatoire
**oblige** [ə'blaɪdʒ] *vt* (**a**) *(compel)* **to o. sb to do sth** obliger qn à faire qch (**b**) *(help)* rendre service à; **to be obliged to sb** être reconnaissant à qn (**for** de) ▪ **obliging** *adj* serviable
**oblique** [ə'bliːk] *adj (line, angle)* oblique; *(reference)* indirect
**oblivion** [ə'blɪvɪən] *n* oubli *m* ▪ **oblivious** *adj* inconscient (**to** *or* **of** de)
**oblong** ['ɒblɒŋ] **1** *adj (rectangular)* rectangulaire **2** *n* rectangle *m*
**obnoxious** [əb'nɒkʃəs] *adj (person, behaviour)* odieux, -euse
**oboe** ['əʊbəʊ] *n* hautbois *m*
**obscene** [əb'siːn] *adj* obscène ▪ **obscenity** [əb'senətɪ] *(pl* **-ies**) *n* obscénité *f*
**obscure** [əb'skjʊə(r)] **1** *adj* obscur **2** *vt (hide)* cacher; *(confuse)* obscurcir
**observant** [əb'zɜːvənt] *adj* observateur, -trice
**observation** [ɒbzə'veɪʃən] *n (observing, remark)* observation *f*; **under o.** *(hospital patient)* en observation
**observe** [əb'zɜːv] *vt* observer; **to o. the speed limit** respecter la limitation de vitesse ▪ **observer** *n* observateur, -trice *mf*
**obsess** [əb'ses] *vt* obséder ▪ **obsession** *n* obsession *f* ▪ **obsessive** *adj (idea)* obsédant; *(person)* obsessionnel, -elle; **to be o. about sth** être obsédé par qch
**obsolete** ['ɒbsəliːt] *adj* obsolète; *(design, model)* dépassé
**obstacle** ['ɒbstəkəl] *n* obstacle *m*
**obstinate** ['ɒbstɪnət] *adj* obstiné
**obstruct** [əb'strʌkt] *vt (block) (road, pipe)* obstruer; *(view)* cacher; *(hinder)* gêner ▪ **obstruction** *n (action, in sport), Med & Pol* obstruction *f*; *(obstacle)* obstacle *m*; *(in pipe)* bouchon *m*

**obtain** [əb'teɪn] *vt* obtenir
**obvious** ['ɒbvɪəs] *adj* évident (**that** que) ▪ **obviously** *adv (of course)* évidemment; *(conspicuously)* manifestement
**occasion** [ə'keɪʒən] *n (time, opportunity)* occasion *f*; *(event)* événement *m*; **on the o. of...** à l'occasion de...; **on several occasions** à plusieurs reprises
**occasional** [ə'keɪʒənəl] *adj* occasionnel, -elle; **she drinks the o. whisky** elle boit un whisky de temps en temps ▪ **occasionally** *adv* de temps en temps
**occupant** ['ɒkjʊpənt] *n (of house, car)* occupant, -e *mf*
**occupation** [ɒkjʊ'peɪʃən] *n* (**a**) *(pastime)* occupation *f*; *(profession)* métier *m* (**b**) *(of house, land)* occupation *f*
**occupier** ['ɒkjʊpaɪə(r)] *n (of house)* occupant, -e *mf*; *(of country)* occupant *m*
**occupy** ['ɒkjʊpaɪ] (*pt & pp* **-ied**) *vt (space, time, attention)* occuper; **to keep oneself occupied** s'occuper (**doing** à faire)
**occur** [ə'kɜː(r)] (*pt & pp* **-rr-**) *vi (happen)* avoir lieu; *(of opportunity)* se présenter; *(be found)* se trouver; **it occurs to me that...** il me vient à l'esprit que...
**occurrence** [ə'kʌrəns] *n (event)* événement *m*
**ocean** ['əʊʃən] *n* océan *m*
**o'clock** [ə'klɒk] *adv* **(it's) three o.** (il est) trois heures
**octagonal** [ɒk'tægənəl] *adj* octogonal
**October** [ɒk'təʊbə(r)] *n* octobre *m*
**octopus** ['ɒktəpəs] *n* pieuvre *f*
**odd** [ɒd] *adj* (**a**) *(strange)* bizarre, curieux, -euse
(**b**) *(number)* impair
(**c**) *(left over)* **sixty o.** soixante et quelques; **an o. glove/sock** un gant/une chaussette dépareillé(e)
(**d**) *(occasional)* **I smoke the o. cigarette** je fume une cigarette de temps en temps; **o. jobs** petits travaux *mpl* ▪ **oddly** *adv* bizarrement; **o. enough, he was elected** chose curieuse, il a été élu
**odds** [ɒdz] *npl* (**a**) *(in betting)* cote *f*; *(chances)* chances *fpl*; *Fam* **it makes no o.** ça n'a pas d'importance (**b**) *(expressions)* **to be at o. (with sb)** être en désaccord (avec qn); *Fam* **o. and ends** des bricoles *fpl*
**odious** ['əʊdɪəs] *adj* odieux, -euse
**odometer** [əʊ'dɒmɪtə(r)] *n Am* compteur *m* kilométrique
**odour** ['əʊdə(r)] (*Am* **odor**) *n* odeur *f*

**OF** [əv, *stressed* ɒv] *prep* de, d'; **of the boy** du garçon; **of the boys** des garçons; **of wood/paper** de *ou* en bois/papier; **she has a lot of it/of them** elle en a beaucoup; **there are ten of us** nous sommes dix; **a friend of his** un ami à lui, un de ses amis; **that's nice of you** c'est gentil de ta part; **of no value/interest** sans valeur/intérêt; *Br* **the fifth of June** le cinq juin

**OFF** [ɒf] **1** *adj (light, gas, radio)* éteint; *(tap)* fermé; *(switched off at mains)* coupé; *(removed)* enlevé; *(cancelled)* annulé; *(not fit to eat or drink)* mauvais; *(milk, meat)* tourné; **I'm o. today** j'ai congé aujourd'hui
**2** *adv* **to be o.** *(leave)* partir; **a day o.** *(holiday)* un jour de congé; **I have today o.** j'ai congé aujourd'hui; **five percent o.** une réduction de cinq pour cent; **on and o., o. and on** *(sometimes)* de temps à autre
**3** *prep (from)* de; *(distant)* éloigné de; **to fall o. the wall/ladder** tomber du mur/de l'échelle; **to take sth o. the table** prendre qch sur la table; **she's o. her food** elle ne mange plus rien ▪ **off-chance** *n* **on the o.** à tout hasard ▪ **off-colour** (*Am* **off-color**) *adj Br (ill)* patraque; *(indecent)* d'un goût douteux ▪ **offhand 1** *adj* désinvolte **2** *adv (immediately)* au pied levé ▪ **off-licence** *n Br* ≃ magasin *m* de vins et de spiritueux ▪ **off-line** *adj (computer)* autonome ▪ **off-peak** *adj (rate, price)* heures creuses *inv* ▪ **off-putting** *adj*

*Br Fam* peu engageant ▪ **offside** *adj* **to be o.** *(of footballer)* être hors jeu ▪ **offspring** *n* progéniture *f* ▪ **off-the-peg** (*Am* **off-the-rack**) *adj (clothes)* de confection

---

**offence** [ə'fens] (*Am* **offense**) *n (against the law)* infraction *f*; *(more serious)* délit *m*; **to take o.** s'offenser (**at** de); **to give o.** offenser

**offend** [ə'fend] *vt* offenser; **to be offended** s'offenser (**at** de) ▪ **offender** *n (criminal)* délinquant, -e *mf*

**offense** [ə'fens] *n Am* = **offence**

**offensive** [ə'fensɪv] **1** *adj* choquant **2** *n* offensive *f*; **to be on the o.** être passé à l'offensive

**offer** ['ɒfə(r)] **1** *n* offre *f*; **to make sb an o.** faire une offre à qn; **on (special) o.** en promotion **2** *vt* offrir; *(explanation)* donner; *(apologies)* présenter; **to o. sb sth, to o. sth to sb** offrir qch à qn; **to o. to do sth** proposer *ou* offrir de faire qch ▪ **offering** *n (gift)* offrande *f*

**office** ['ɒfɪs] *n* (**a**) *(room)* bureau *m*; *Am (of doctor)* cabinet *m*; **o. hours** heures *fpl* de bureau; **o. worker** employé, -e *mf* de bureau (**b**) *(position)* fonctions *fpl*; **to be in o.** être au pouvoir

**officer** ['ɒfɪsə(r)] *n (in the army, navy)* officier *m*; **(police) o.** agent *m* de police

**official** [ə'fɪʃəl] **1** *adj* officiel, -elle **2** *n* responsable *mf*; *(civil servant)* fonctionnaire *mf* ▪ **officially** *adv* officiellement

**offset** ['ɒfset, ɒf'set] (*pt & pp* **offset**, *pres p* **offsetting**) *vt (compensate for)* compenser

**often** ['ɒf(t)ən] *adv* souvent; **how o.?** combien de fois?; **every so o.** de temps en temps

**oh** [əʊ] *exclam* oh!, ah!; *(in pain)* aïe!; **oh yes!** mais oui!

**oil** [ɔɪl] **1** *n (for machine, cooking)* huile *f*; *(petroleum)* pétrole *m*; *(fuel)* mazout *m* **2** *adj (industry)* pétrolier, -ère; *(painting, paint)* à l'huile; **o. lamp** lampe *f* à pétrole **3** *vt (machine)* huiler ▪ **oilcan** *n* burette *f* ▪ **oilfield** *n* gisement *m* de pétrole ▪ **oily** (**-ier, -iest**) *adj (hands, rag)* graisseux, -euse; *(skin, hair)* gras (*f* grasse)

**ointment** ['ɔɪntmənt] *n* pommade *f*

**OK, okay** ['əʊ'keɪ] **1** *adj & adv see* **all right 2** (*pt & pp* **OKed, okayed,** *pres p* **OKing, okaying**) *vt* donner le feu vert à

**old** [əʊld] **1** (**-er, -est**) *adj* vieux (*f* vieille); *(former)* ancien, -enne; **how o. is he?** quel âge a-t-il?; **he's ten years o.** il a dix ans; **he's older than me** il est plus âgé que moi; **the oldest son** le fils aîné; **to get** *or* **grow old(er)** vieillir; **o. age** vieillesse *f*; **o. man** vieillard *m*, vieil homme *m*; **o. people** les personnes *fpl* âgées; **o. people's home** maison *f* de retraite; *Fam* **any o. how** n'importe comment
**2** *npl* **the o.** les personnes *fpl* âgées

**old-fashioned** [əʊld'fæʃənd] *adj (out-of-date)* démodé; *(person)* vieux jeu *inv*; *(traditional)* d'autrefois

**olive** ['ɒlɪv] *n (fruit)* olive *f*; **o. oil** huile *f* d'olive

**Olympic** [ə'lɪmpɪk] *adj* **the O. Games** les jeux *mpl* Olympiques

**omelet(te)** ['ɒmlɪt] *n* omelette *f*; **cheese o.** omelette *f* au fromage

**omen** ['əʊmən] *n* augure *m*

**ominous** ['ɒmɪnəs] *adj* inquiétant; *(event)* de mauvais augure

**omit** [əʊ'mɪt] (*pt & pp* **-tt-**) *vt* omettre (**to do** de faire) ▪ **omission** *n* omission *f*

---

**ON** [ɒn] **1** *prep* (**a**) *(expressing position)* sur; **on page 4** à la page 4; **on the right/left** à droite/gauche
(**b**) *(about)* sur
(**c**) *(expressing manner or means)* **on the train/plane** dans le train/l'avion; **to be on** *(a course)* suivre; *(project)* travailler à; *(salary)* toucher; *(team, committee)* faire partie de; *Fam* **it's on me!** *(I'll pay)* c'est pour moi!
(**d**) *(with time)* **on Monday** lundi; **on Mondays** le lundi; **on (the evening of) May 3rd** le 3 mai (au soir); **on my arrival** à mon arrivée

(**e**) *(+ present participle)* en; **on learning that...** en apprenant que...
**2** *adv (ahead)* en avant; *(in progress)* en cours; *(lid, brake)* mis; *(light, radio)* allumé; *(gas, tap)* ouvert; *(machine)* en marche; **she has her hat on** elle a mis son chapeau; **I've got something on** *(I'm busy)* je suis pris; **the strike is on** la grève aura lieu; **what's on?** *(on TV)* qu'est-ce qu'il y a à la télé?; *(in theatre, cinema)* qu'est-ce qu'on joue?; **he went on and on about it** il n'en finissait pas; *Fam* **that's just not on!** c'est inadmissible!; **I've been on to him** *(on phone)* je l'ai eu au bout du fil ▪ **ongoing** *adj (project, discussion)* en cours ▪ **on-line** *adj (computer)* en ligne

**once** [wʌns] **1** *adv (on one occasion)* une fois; *(formerly)* autrefois; **o. a month** une fois par mois; **o. again, o. more** encore une fois; **at o.** *(immediately)* tout de suite; **all at o.** *(suddenly)* tout à coup; *(at the same time)* à la fois **2** *conj* une fois que

**ONE** [wʌn] **1** *adj* (**a**) un, une; **page o.** la page un; **twenty-o.** vingt et un
(**b**) *(only)* seul
(**c**) *(same)* le même (*f* la même); **in the o. bus** dans le même bus
**2** *pron* (**a**) un, une; **do you want o.?** en veux-tu (un)?; **o. of them** l'un d'eux, l'une d'elles; **a big/small o.** un grand/petit; **this o.** celui-ci, celle-ci; **that o.** celui-là, celle-là; **the o. who/which...** celui/celle qui...; **another o.** un(e) autre; **I for o.** pour ma part (**b**) *(impersonal)* on; **o. knows** on sait; **it helps o.** ça vous aide; **o.'s family** sa famille ▪ **one-off, one-of-a-kind** *adj Fam* unique ▪ **one-sided** *adj (biased)* partial; *(contest)* inégal ▪ **one-time** *adj (former)* ancien, -enne ▪ **one-to-one** *adj (discussion)* en tête à tête ▪ **one-way** *adj (street)* à sens unique; **o. ticket** billet *m* simple

**oneself** [wʌn'self] *pron* soi-même; *(reflexive)* se, s'; **to cut o.** se couper

**onion** ['ʌnjən] *n* oignon *m*

**onlooker** ['ɒnlʊkə(r)] *n* spectateur, -trice *mf*

**only** ['əʊnlɪ] **1** *adj* seul; **the o. one** le seul, la seule; **an o. son** un fils unique **2** *adv* seulement, ne... que; **I o. have ten** je n'en ai que dix, j'en ai dix seulement; **if o.** si seulement; **I have o. just seen it** je viens tout juste de le voir; **o. he knows** lui seul le sait **3** *conj Fam (but)* mais

**onset** ['ɒnset] *n (of disease, winter)* début *m*

**onto** ['ɒntu:, *unstressed* 'ɒntə] *prep* = **on to**

**onward(s)** ['ɒnwəd(z)] *adv* en avant; **from that day o.** à partir de ce jour-là

**opaque** [əʊ'peɪk] *adj* opaque

**open** ['əʊpən] **1** *adj* ouvert; *(view, road)* dégagé; *(post, job)* vacant; *(airline ticket)* open *inv*; **in the o. air** au grand air; **o. to** *(criticism, attack)* exposé à; *(ideas, suggestions)* ouvert à; **to leave sth o.** *(date)* ne pas préciser qch
**2** *n* **(out) in the o.** *(outside)* dehors; **to sleep (out) in the o.** dormir à la belle étoile
**3** *vt* ouvrir; *(arms, legs)* écarter; **to o. sth out** *(paper, map)* ouvrir qch; **to o. sth up** *(bag, shop)* ouvrir qch
**4** *vi (of flower, door, eyes)* s'ouvrir; *(of shop, office)* ouvrir; *(of play)* débuter; **to o. on to sth** *(of window)* donner sur qch; **to o. out** *(widen)* s'élargir; **to o. up** *(of flower, person)* s'ouvrir; *(of shopkeeper)* ouvrir ▪ **open-air** *adj (pool)* en plein air ▪ **open-minded** *adj* à l'esprit ouvert ▪ **open-plan** *adj (office)* paysager, -ère

**opening** ['əʊpənɪŋ] **1** *n* ouverture *f*; *(job, trade outlet)* débouché *m*; *(opportunity)* occasion *f* favorable; **late-night o.** *(of shops)* nocturne *f*
**2** *adj (time, hours, speech)* d'ouverture; **o. night** *(of play, musical)* première *f*

**openly** ['əʊpənlɪ] *adv* ouvertement

**opera** ['ɒprə] *n* opéra *m*

**operate** ['ɒpəreɪt] **1** *vt (machine)* faire fonctionner; *(service)* assurer **2** *vi* (**a**) **to o. on sb (for sth)** *(of surgeon)* opérer qn (de qch) (**b**) *(of machine)* fonctionner; *(of company)* opérer ▪ **operating** *adj Br* **o. theatre,** *Am* **o. room** salle *f* d'opération; *Comptr* **o. system** système *m* d'exploitation

**operation** [ɒpə'reɪʃən] *n Med, Mil & Math* opération *f*; *(of machine)* fonctionnement *m*; **in o.** *(machine)* en service; *(plan)* en vigueur; **to have an o.** se faire opérer

**operator** ['ɒpəreɪtə(r)] *n (on phone, machine)* opérateur, -trice *mf*

**opinion** [ə'pɪnjən] *n* opinion *f*; **in my o.** à mon avis

**opponent** [ə'pəʊnənt] *n* adversaire *mf*

**opportune** ['ɒpətju:n] *adj* opportun

**opportunity** [ɒpə'tju:nətɪ] (*pl* **-ies**) *n* occasion *f* (**to do** *or* **of doing** de faire); **opportunities** *(prospects)* perspectives *fpl*; **to take the o. to do sth** profiter de l'occasion pour faire qch

**oppose** [ə'pəʊz] *vt* s'opposer à ▪ **opposed** *adj* opposé (**to** à); **as o. to...** par opposition à... ▪ **opposing** *adj (viewpoints)* opposé; *(team)* adverse

**opposite** ['ɒpəzɪt] **1** *adj (side)* opposé; *(house, page)* d'en face; **in the o. direction** en sens inverse **2** *adv* en face; **the house o.** la maison d'en face **3** *prep* **o. (to)** en face de **4** *n* **the o.** le contraire

**opposition** [ɒpə'zɪʃən] *n* opposition *f* (**to** à); **the o.** *(rival camp)* l'adversaire *m*; *(in business)* la concurrence

**oppress** [ə'pres] *vt (treat cruelly)* opprimer ▪ **oppression** *n* oppression *f* ▪ **oppressive** *adj (heat)* accablant, étouffant; *(ruler, regime)* oppressif, -ive

**opt** [ɒpt] *vi* **to o. for sth** opter pour qch; **to o. to do sth** choisir de faire qch; **to o. out** se désengager (**of** de)

**optical** ['ɒptɪkəl] *adj* optique; *(instrument, illusion)* d'optique

**optician** [ɒp'tɪʃən] *n (dispensing)* opticien, -enne *mf*

**optimism** ['ɒptɪmɪzəm] *n* optimisme *m* ▪ **optimistic** *adj* optimiste (**about** quant à)

**optimum** ['ɒptɪməm] *adj & n* optimum *(m)*

**option** ['ɒpʃən] *n (choice)* choix *m*; *(school subject)* matière *f* à option; **she has no o.** elle n'a pas le choix ▪ **optional** *adj* facultatif, -ive

**or** [ɔ:(r)] *conj* ou; **he doesn't drink or smoke** il ne boit ni ne fume; **ten or so** environ dix

**oral** ['ɔ:rəl] **1** *adj* oral **2** *n (exam)* oral *m*

**orange** ['ɒrɪndʒ] **1** *n (fruit)* orange *f*; **o. juice** jus *m* d'orange **2** *adj & n (colour)* orange *(m) inv*

**orbit** ['ɔ:bɪt] **1** *n (of planet)* orbite *f* **2** *vt* être en orbite autour de

**orchard** ['ɔ:tʃəd] *n* verger *m*

**orchestra** ['ɔ:kɪstrə] *n* orchestre *m*; *Am* **the o.** *(in theatre)* l'orchestre *m*

**orchid** ['ɔ:kɪd] *n* orchidée *f*

**ordeal** [ɔ:'di:l] *n* épreuve *f*

**order** ['ɔ:də(r)] **1** *n (instruction, arrangement) & Rel* ordre *m*; *(purchase)* commande *f*; **in o.** *(passport)* en règle; **in o. of age** par ordre d'âge; **in o. to do sth** afin de faire qch; **in o. that...** afin que... *(+ subjunctive)*; **out of o.** *(machine)* en panne; *(telephone)* en dérangement; **o. form** bon *m* de commande **2** *vt (meal, goods)* commander; *(taxi)* appeler; **to o. sb to do sth** ordonner à qn de faire qch **3** *vi (in café)* commander

**orderly** ['ɔ:dəlɪ] *adj (room, life)* ordonné; *(crowd)* discipliné

**ordinary** ['ɔ:dənrɪ] *adj* ordinaire; **it's out of the o.** ça sort de l'ordinaire; **she was just an o. tourist** c'était une touriste comme une autre

**organ** ['ɔ:gən] *n* (**a**) *(part of body)* organe *m* (**b**) *(musical instrument)* orgue *m*

**organic** [ɔ:'gænɪk] *adj* organique; *(vegetables, farming)* biologique

**organism** ['ɔ:gənɪzəm] *n* organisme *m*

**organization** [ɔ:gənaɪ'zeɪʃən] *n* organisation *f*

**organize** ['ɔːgənaɪz] *vt* organiser ▪ **organizer** *n (person)* organisateur, -trice *mf*; **(personal) o.** *(diary)* agenda *m*

**orgasm** ['ɔːgæzəm] *n* orgasme *m*

**oriental** [ɔːrɪ'entəl] *adj* oriental

**orientate** ['ɔːrɪənteɪt] (*Am* **orient** ['ɔːrɪənt]) *vt* orienter

**origin** ['ɒrɪdʒɪn] *n* origine *f*

**original** [ə'rɪdʒɪnəl] **1** *adj (novel, innovative)* original; *(first)* d'origine **2** *n (document, painting)* original *m* ▪ **originally** *adv (at first)* à l'origine

**originate** [ə'rɪdʒɪneɪt] **1** *vt* être à l'origine de **2** *vi (begin)* prendre naissance (**in** dans); **to o. from** *(of idea)* émaner de

**ornament** ['ɔːnəmənt] *n* ornement *m* ▪ **ornamental** [-'mentəl] *adj* ornemental

**ornate** [ɔː'neɪt] *adj* très orné

**orphan** ['ɔːfən] *n* orphelin, -e *mf*

**orthodox** ['ɔːθədɒks] *adj* orthodoxe

**Oscar** ['ɒskə(r)] *n Cin* oscar *m*

**ostentatious** [ɒsten'teɪʃəs] *adj* prétentieux, -euse

**ostrich** ['ɒstrɪtʃ] *n* autruche *f*

**other** ['ʌðə(r)] **1** *adj* autre; **o. doctors** d'autres médecins; **the o. one** l'autre *mf*

**2** *pron* **the o.** l'autre *mf*; **(some) others** d'autres; **none o. than, no o. than** nul autre que

**3** *adv* **o. than** autrement que ▪ **otherwise** *adv & conj* autrement

**ouch** [aʊtʃ] *exclam* aïe!

**ought** [ɔːt]

> La forme négative **ought not** s'écrit **oughtn't** en forme contractée.

*v aux* (**a**) *(expressing obligation, desirability)* **you o. to leave** tu devrais partir; **I o. to have done it** j'aurais dû le faire (**b**) *(expressing probability)* **it o. to be ready** ça devrait être prêt

**ounce** [aʊns] *n (unit of weight)* = 28,35 g, once *f*

**our** [aʊə(r)] *possessive adj* notre, *pl* nos

**ours** [aʊəz] *possessive pron* le nôtre, la nôtre, *pl* les nôtres; **this book is o.** ce livre est à nous *ou* est le nôtre; **a friend of o.** un de nos amis

**ourselves** [aʊə'selvz] *pron* nous-mêmes; *(reflexive and after prep)* nous; **we wash o.** nous nous lavons

**oust** [aʊst] *vt* évincer (**from** de)

---

**OUT** [aʊt] **1** *adv (outside)* dehors; *(not at home)* sorti; *(light, fire)* éteint; *(flower)* ouvert; *(book)* publié; **to have a day o.** sortir pour la journée; **the sun's o.** il fait soleil; **the tide's o.** la marée est basse; **you're o.** *(wrong)* tu t'es trompé; *(in game)* tu es éliminé (**of** de); **I was £10 o.** *(under)* il me manquait 10 livres; **before the week is o.** avant la fin de la semaine; **the journey o.** l'aller *m*; **o. here** ici; **o. there** là-bas

**2** *prep* **o. of** *(outside)* hors de; **to be o. of the country** être à l'étranger; **she's o. of town** elle n'est pas en ville; **to look/jump o. of the window** regarder/sauter par la fenêtre; **to drink/take/copy sth o. of sth** boire/prendre/copier qch dans qch; **made o. of wood** fait en bois; **o. of pity/love** par pitié/amour; **four o. of five** quatre sur cinq ▪ **out-of-date** *adj (expired)* périmé; *(old-fashioned)* démodé ▪ **out-of-doors** *adv* dehors ▪ **out-of-the-way** *adj (place)* isolé

---

**outbreak** ['aʊtbreɪk] *n (of war, epidemic)* début *m*; *(of violence)* flambée *f*; *(of hostilities)* déclenchement *m*

**outburst** ['aʊtbɜːst] *n (of anger, joy)* explosion *f*; *(of violence)* flambée *f*

**outcast** ['aʊtkɑːst] *n* **(social) o.** paria *m*

**outcome** ['aʊtkʌm] *n* résultat *m*, issue *f*

**outcry** ['aʊtkraɪ] (*pl* **-ies**) *n* tollé *m*

**outdated** [aʊt'deɪtɪd] *adj* démodé

**outdo** [aʊt'duː] (*pt* **-did,** *pp* **-done**) *vt* surpasser (**in** en)

**outdoor** ['aʊtdɔː(r)] *adj (pool, market)* découvert ▪ **outdoors** *adv* dehors

**outer** ['aʊtə(r)] *adj* extérieur; **o. space** l'espace *m* intersidéral

**outfit** ['aʊtfɪt] *n (clothes)* ensemble *m*; **sports/ski o.** tenue *f* de sport/de ski

**outgoing** ['aʊtgəʊɪŋ] *adj* (**a**) *(minister)* sortant; *(mail)* en partance; **o. calls** *(on phone)* appels *mpl* vers l'extérieur (**b**) *(sociable)* liant ▪ **outgoings** *npl (expenses)* dépenses *fpl*

**outgrow** [aʊt'grəʊ] *(pt* **-grew,** *pp* **-grown***) vt (habit)* passer l'âge de; **she's outgrown her jacket** sa veste est devenue trop petite pour elle

**outing** ['aʊtɪŋ] *n (excursion)* sortie *f*

**outlast** [aʊt'lɑːst] *vt (object)* durer plus longtemps que; *(person)* survivre à

**outlaw** ['aʊtlɔː] **1** *n* hors-la-loi *m inv* **2** *vt (ban)* proscrire

**outlay** ['aʊtleɪ] *n (expense)* dépenses *fpl*

**outlet** ['aʊtlet] *n (shop)* point *m* de vente; *(market for goods)* débouché *m*; *(for liquid)* sortie *f*; *(for feelings, energy)* exutoire *m*

**outline** ['aʊtlaɪn] **1** *n (shape)* contour *m*; *(of play, novel)* résumé *m*; **rough o.** *(of article, plan)* esquisse *f*; **the broad** *or* **general** *or* **main o.** *(of plan, policy)* les grandes lignes **2** *vt (plan, situation)* esquisser

**outlive** [aʊt'lɪv] *vt* survivre à

**outlook** ['aʊtlʊk] *n (for future)* perspectives *fpl*; *(point of view)* façon *f* de voir les choses; *(of weather)* prévisions *fpl*

**outmoded** [aʊt'məʊdɪd] *adj* démodé

**outnumber** [aʊt'nʌmbə(r)] *vt* l'emporter en nombre sur

**outpatient** ['aʊtpeɪʃənt] *n Br* malade *mf* en consultation externe

**output** ['aʊtpʊt] *n (of goods)* production *f*; *(computer data)* données *fpl* de sortie

**outrage** ['aʊtreɪdʒ] **1** *n (scandal)* scandale *m*; *(anger)* indignation *f* (**at** face à); *(crime)* atrocité *f* **2** *vt (make indignant)* scandaliser

**outrageous** [aʊt'reɪdʒəs] *adj (shocking)* scandaleux, -euse; *(atrocious)* atroce

**outright 1** [aʊt'raɪt] *adv (refuse)* catégoriquement; *(be killed)* sur le coup **2** ['aʊtraɪt] *adj (failure)* total; *(refusal)* catégorique; *(winner)* incontesté

**outset** ['aʊtset] *n* **at the o.** au début; **from the o.** dès le départ

**outside 1** [aʊt'saɪd] *adv* dehors, à l'extérieur; **to go o.** sortir

**2** [aʊt'saɪd] *prep* à l'extérieur de, en dehors de; *(in front of)* devant; *(apart from)* en dehors de

**3** [aʊt'saɪd] *n* extérieur *m*

**4** ['aʊtsaɪd] *adj* extérieur; **the o. lane** *(on road) Br* la voie de droite, *Am* la voie de gauche; **an o. chance** une petite chance

**outsider** [aʊt'saɪdə(r)] *n (stranger)* étranger, -ère *mf*; *(horse in race)* outsider *m*

**outskirts** ['aʊtskɜːts] *npl* banlieue *f*

**outspoken** [aʊt'spəʊkən] *adj (frank)* franc (*f* franche)

**outstanding** [aʊt'stændɪŋ] *adj* exceptionnel, -elle; *(problem, business)* en suspens; *(debt)* impayé

**outstay** [aʊt'steɪ] *vt* **to o. one's welcome** abuser de l'hospitalité de son hôte

**outstretched** [aʊt'stretʃt] *adj (arm)* tendu

**outward** ['aʊtwəd] *adj (sign, appearance)* extérieur; **o. journey** *or* **trip** aller *m* ▪ **outward(s)** *adv* vers l'extérieur

**oval** ['əʊvəl] *adj & n* ovale *(m)*

**ovary** ['əʊvərɪ] *(pl* **-ies***) n Anat* ovaire *m*

**ovation** [əʊ'veɪʃən] *n* ovation *f*; **to give sb a standing o.** se lever pour applaudir qn

**oven** ['ʌvən] *n* four *m*

**OVER** ['əʊvə(r)] **1** *prep (on)* sur; *(above)* au-dessus de; *(on the other side of)* par-dessus; **the bridge o. the river** le pont qui traverse le fleuve; **to jump/look o. sth** sauter/regarder par-dessus qch; **o. it** *(on)* dessus; *(above)* au-dessus; **to fight o. sth** se battre pour qch; **o. the phone** au téléphone; *Br* **o. the holidays** pendant les vacances; **o. ten days** *(more than)* plus de dix jours; **men o. sixty** les hommes de plus de soixante ans; **o. and above** en plus de; **he's o. his flu** il est remis de sa grippe

**2** *adv (above)* par-dessus; **o. here** ici; **o. there** là-bas; **he's o. in Italy** il est en Italie; **she's o. from Paris** elle est venue de Paris; **to ask sb o.** inviter qn; **to be (all) o.** être terminé; **to start all o. (again)** recommencer à zéro; **a kilo or o.** *(more)* un kilo ou plus; **I have ten o.** *(left)* il m'en reste dix; **o. and o. (again)** *(often)* à plusieurs reprises; **children of five and o.** les enfants de cinq ans et plus

---

**overall 1** ['əʊvərɔ:l] *adj (measurement, length)* total; *(result)* global

**2** [əʊvər'ɔ:l] *adv* dans l'ensemble

**3** ['əʊvərɔ:l] *n (protective coat)* blouse *f*; *Am (boiler suit)* bleu *m* de travail ▪ **overalls** *npl Br (boiler suit)* bleu *m* de travail; *Am (dungarees)* salopette *f*

**overbearing** [əʊvə'beərɪŋ] *adj* autoritaire

**overboard** ['əʊvəbɔ:d] *adv* par-dessus bord

**overcast** [əʊvə'kɑ:st] *adj* nuageux, -euse

**overcharge** [əʊvə'tʃɑ:dʒ] *vt* **to o. sb for sth** faire payer qch trop cher à qn

**overcoat** ['əʊvəkəʊt] *n* pardessus *m*

**overcome** [əʊvə'kʌm] (*pt* **-came,** *pp* **-come**) *vt (problem, disgust)* surmonter; *(shyness, fear, enemy)* vaincre; **to be o. by grief** être accablé de chagrin

**overcook** [əʊvə'kʊk] *vt* faire cuire trop

**overcrowded** [əʊvə'kraʊdɪd] *adj (house, country)* surpeuplé; *(bus, train)* bondé

**overdo** [əʊvə'du:] (*pt* **-did,** *pp* **-done**) *vt* exagérer; *(overcook)* faire cuire trop; **to o. it** se surmener

**overdose** ['əʊvədəʊs] *n* overdose *f*

**overdraft** ['əʊvədrɑ:ft] *n Fin* découvert *m*

**overdrawn** [əʊvə'drɔ:n] *adj Fin (account)* à découvert

**overdue** [əʊvə'dju:] *adj (train, bus)* en retard; *(bill)* impayé; *(book)* qui n'a pas été rendu

**overestimate** [əʊvər'estɪmeɪt] *vt* surestimer

**overexcited** [əʊvərɪk'saɪtɪd] *adj* surexcité

**overflow 1** ['əʊvəfləʊ] *n (outlet)* trop-plein *m* **2** [əʊvə'fləʊ] *vi (of river, bath)* déborder; **to be overflowing with sth** *(of town, shop, house)* regorger de qch

**overgrown** [əʊvə'grəʊn] *adj (garden, path)* envahi par la végétation

**overhaul 1** ['əʊvəhɔ:l] *n* révision *f* **2** [əʊvə'hɔ:l] *vt (vehicle, schedule, text)* réviser

**overhead 1** [əʊvə'hed] *adv* au-dessus **2** ['əʊvəhed] *adj (cable)* aérien, -enne **3** ['əʊvəhed] *n Am* = **overheads** ▪ **overheads** *npl Br (expenses)* frais *mpl* généraux

**overhear** [əʊvə'hɪə(r)] (*pt & pp* **-heard**) *vt (conversation)* surprendre; *(person)* entendre

**overheat** [əʊvə'hi:t] *vi (of engine)* chauffer

**overjoyed** [əʊvə'dʒɔɪd] *adj* fou (*f* folle) de joie

**overland** ['əʊvəlænd] *adj & adv* par voie de terre

**overlap** [əʊvə'læp] **1** (*pt & pp* **-pp-**) *vt* chevaucher **2** *vi* se chevaucher

**overleaf** [əʊvə'li:f] *adv* au verso

**overload** [əʊvə'ləʊd] *vt* surcharger

**overlook** [əʊvə'lʊk] *vt* (**a**) *(not notice)* ne pas remarquer; *(forget)* oublier; *(disregard)* fermer les yeux sur (**b**) *(of window, house)* donner sur

**overnight 1** [əʊvə'naɪt] *adv (during the night)* pendant la nuit; *Fig (suddenly)* du jour au lendemain; **to stay o.** passer la nuit **2** ['əʊvənaɪt] *adj (train, flight)* de nuit; *(stay)* d'une nuit; **o. bag** (petit) sac *m* de voyage

**overpopulated** [əʊvə'pɒpjʊleɪtɪd] *adj* surpeuplé

**overpower** [əʊvə'paʊə(r)] *vt* maîtriser ▪ **overpowering** *adj (heat, smell)* suffocant

**overpriced** [əʊvə'praɪst] *adj* trop cher (*f* trop chère)
**overrated** [əʊvə'reɪtɪd] *adj* surfait
**overreach** [əʊvə'riːtʃ] *vt* **to o. oneself** trop présumer de ses forces
**overreact** [əʊvərɪ'ækt] *vi* réagir excessivement
**override** [əʊvə'raɪd] (*pt* **-rode**, *pp* **-ridden**) *vt (be more important than)* l'emporter sur; *(invalidate)* annuler; *(take no notice of)* passer outre à ■ **overriding** *adj (importance)* capital; *(factor)* prédominant
**overrule** [əʊvə'ruːl] *vt (decision)* annuler; *(objection)* rejeter
**overrun** [əʊvə'rʌn] (*pt* **-ran**, *pp* **-run**, *pres p* **-running**) *vt (invade)* envahir; *(go beyond)* dépasser
**overseas 1** ['əʊvəsiːz] *adj* d'outremer; *(trade)* extérieur **2** [əʊvə'siːz] *adv* à l'étranger
**oversee** [əʊvə'siː] (*pt* **-saw**, *pp* **-seen**) *vt (work)* superviser
**overshadow** [əʊvə'ʃædəʊ] *vt (make less important)* éclipser; *(make gloomy)* assombrir
**oversight** ['əʊvəsaɪt] *n* oubli *m*, omission *f*
**oversleep** [əʊvə'sliːp] (*pt & pp* **-slept**) *vi* ne pas se réveiller à temps
**overspend** [əʊvə'spend] (*pt & pp* **-spent**) *vi* dépenser trop
**overstate** [əʊvə'steɪt] *vt* exagérer
**overstay** [əʊvə'steɪ] *vt* **to o. one's welcome** abuser de l'hospitalité de son hôte
**overstep** [əʊvə'step] (*pt & pp* **-pp-**) *vt* outrepasser; *Fig* **to o. the mark** dépasser les bornes
**overt** ['əʊvɜːt] *adj* manifeste
**overtake** [əʊvə'teɪk] (*pt* **-took**, *pp* **-taken**) **1** *vt* dépasser **2** *vi (in vehicle)* doubler, dépasser
**overthrow** [əʊvə'θrəʊ] (*pt* **-threw**, *pp* **-thrown**) *vt* renverser
**overtime** ['əʊvətaɪm] **1** *n* heures *fpl* supplémentaires **2** *adv* **to work o.** faire des heures supplémentaires
**overturn** [əʊvə'tɜːn] **1** *vt (chair, table, car)* renverser; *(boat)* faire chavirer; *Fig (decision)* annuler **2** *vi (of car)* capoter; *(of boat)* chavirer
**overweight** [əʊvə'weɪt] *adj* trop gros (*f* trop grosse)
**overwhelm** [əʊvə'welm] *vt (of feelings, heat)* accabler; *(enemy, opponent)* écraser; *(amaze)* bouleverser ■ **overwhelmed** *adj* **o. with** *(work, offers)* submergé de; **o. by** *(kindness, gift)* vivement touché par ■ **overwhelming** *adj (heat, grief)* accablant; *(majority, defeat)* écrasant; *(desire)* irrésistible
**overwork** [əʊvə'wɜːk] **1** *n* surmenage *m* **2** *vt (person)* surcharger de travail **3** *vi* se surmener
**owe** [əʊ] *vt* devoir; **to o. sb sth, to o. sth to sb** devoir qch à qn ■ **owing 1** *adj* **the money o. to me** l'argent que l'on me doit **2** *prep* **o. to** à cause de
**owl** [aʊl] *n* hibou *m* (*pl* -oux)
**own** [əʊn] **1** *adj* propre
**2** *pron* **my o.** le mien, la mienne; **a house of his o.** sa propre maison, sa maison à lui; **to do sth on one's o.** faire qch tout seul; **to be (all) on one's o.** être tout seul; **to get one's o. back (on sb)** se venger (de qn)
**3** *vt (possess)* posséder; **who owns this ball?** à qui appartient cette balle?
**4** *vi* **to o. up (to sth)** *(confess)* avouer (qch)
**owner** ['əʊnə(r)] *n* propriétaire *mf* ■ **ownership** *n* possession *f*
**ox** [ɒks] (*pl* **oxen** ['ɒksən]) *n* bœuf *m*
**oxygen** ['ɒksɪdʒən] *n* oxygène *m*; **o. mask** masque *m* à oxygène
**oyster** ['ɔɪstə(r)] *n* huître *f*
**oz** (*abbr* **ounce**) once *f*
**ozone** ['əʊzəʊn] *n Chem* ozone *m*; **o. layer** couche *f* d'ozone

# Pp

**P, p¹** [piː] *n (letter)* P, p *m inv*
**p²** [piː] *(abbr* **penny, pence***)* *Br* penny *m*/pence *mpl*
**pa** [pɑː] *n Fam (father)* papa *m*
**pace** [peɪs] **1** *n (speed)* allure *f*; *(step, measure)* pas *m*; **to keep p. with sb** *(follow)* suivre qn; *(in quality of work)* se maintenir à la hauteur de qn **2** *vi* **to p. up and down** faire les cent pas
**pacemaker** ['peɪsmeɪkə(r)] *n (for heart)* stimulateur *m* cardiaque
**Pacific** [pə'sɪfɪk] *adj* **the P. (Ocean)** le Pacifique, l'océan *m* Pacifique
**pacifier** ['pæsɪfaɪə(r)] *n Am (of baby)* tétine *f*
**pacifist** ['pæsɪfɪst] *n* pacifiste *mf*
**pacify** ['pæsɪfaɪ] *(pt & pp* **-ied***)* *vt (crowd, person)* calmer
**pack** [pæk] **1** *n* (**a**) *(of cigarettes, washing powder)* paquet *m*; *(of beer)* pack *m*; *(of cards)* jeu *m*; *(of hounds, wolves)* meute *f*; **a p. of lies** un tissu de mensonges
(**b**) *(rucksack)* sac *m* à dos
**2** *vt (fill)* remplir (**with** de); *(object into box, suitcase)* mettre; *(make into package)* empaqueter; *(crush, compress)* tasser; **to p. one's bags** faire ses valises
**3** *vi (fill one's bags)* faire sa valise/ses valises
▸**pack in** *vt sep Br Fam (stop)* arrêter; *(give up)* laisser tomber
▸**pack into 1** *vt sep (cram)* entasser dans; *(put)* mettre dans **2** *vt insep (crowd into)* s'entasser dans
▸**pack off** *vt sep Fam (person)* expédier
▸**pack up 1** *vt sep (put into box)* emballer; *Fam (give up)* laisser tomber **2** *vi Fam (of machine, vehicle)* tomber en panne
**package** ['pækɪdʒ] **1** *n* paquet *m*; *(contract)* contrat *m* global; *Br* **p. deal** *or* **holiday** forfait *m (comprenant au moins transport et logement)* **2** *vt* emballer ▪ **packaging** *n (material, action)* emballage *m*
**packed** [pækt] *adj (bus, room)* bondé
**packet** ['pækɪt] *n* paquet *m*; *Fam* **to cost a p.** coûter les yeux de la tête
**packing** ['pækɪŋ] *n (material, action)* emballage *m*; **to do one's p.** faire sa valise/ses valises
**pact** [pækt] *n* pacte *m*
**pad** [pæd] **1** *n (of cotton wool)* tampon *m*; *(for writing)* bloc *m*; **ink(ing) p.** tampon encreur **2** *(pt & pp* **-dd-***)* *vt* **to p. out** *(speech, essay)* étoffer ▪ **padded** *adj (jacket)* matelassé ▪ **padding** *n (material)* rembourrage *m*; *(in speech, essay)* remplissage *m*
**paddle** ['pædəl] **1** *n (for canoe)* pagaie *f*; **to have a p.** patauger **2** *vt* **to p. a canoe** pagayer **3** *vi (walk in water)* patauger
**paddling** ['pædlɪŋ] *n Br* **p. pool** *(inflatable)* piscine *f* gonflable; *(in park)* pataugeoire *f*
**padlock** ['pædlɒk] **1** *n* cadenas *m* **2** *vt* cadenasser
**paediatrician** [piːdɪə'trɪʃən] *(Am* **pediatrician***)* *n* pédiatre *mf*
**page¹** [peɪdʒ] *n (of book)* page *f*; **on p. 6** à la page 6
**page²** [peɪdʒ] **1** *n* **p. (boy)** *(in hotel)*

groom *m* **2** *vt* **to p. sb** faire appeler qn; *(by electronic device)* biper qn ■ **pager** *n* récepteur *m* d'appel

**paid** [peɪd] **1** *pt & pp of* **pay 2** *adj (person, work)* rémunéré

**pain** [peɪn] *n (physical)* douleur *f*; *(emotional)* peine *f*; **to have a p. in one's arm** avoir une douleur au bras; **to go to** *or* **take (great) pains to do sth** se donner du mal pour faire qch; *Fam* **to be a p. (in the neck)** être casse-pieds ■ **painful** *adj (physically)* douloureux, -euse; *(emotionally)* pénible ■ **painless** *adj (not painful)* indolore

**painkiller** ['peɪnkɪlə(r)] *n* calmant *m*

**painstaking** ['peɪnzteɪkɪŋ] *adj* minutieux, -euse

**paint** [peɪnt] **1** *n* peinture *f* **2** *vt* peindre; **to p. sth blue** peindre qch en bleu **3** *vi* peindre ■ **painter** *n* peintre *m*; *Br* **p. and decorator,** *Am* **(house) p.** peintre-tapissier *m* ■ **painting** *n (activity)* la peinture; *(picture)* tableau *m*, peinture *f*

**paintbrush** ['peɪntbrʌʃ] *n* pinceau *m*

**paintwork** ['peɪntwɜːk] *n (of building, vehicle)* peinture *f*

**pair** [peə(r)] *n* paire *f*; **a p. of shorts/trousers** un short/pantalon

**pajamas** [pə'dʒɑːməz] *npl Am* = **pyjamas**

**Pakistan** [pɑːkɪ'stɑːn] *n* le Pakistan ■ **Pakistani 1** *adj* pakistanais **2** *n* Pakistanais, -e *mf*

**pal** [pæl] *n Fam* copain *m*, copine *f*

**palace** ['pælɪs] *n* palais *m*

**pale** [peɪl] **1** (**-er, -est**) *adj* pâle **2** *vi* pâlir

**Palestine** ['pæləstaɪn] *n* la Palestine ■ **Palestinian** [-'stɪnɪən] **1** *adj* palestinien, -enne **2** *n* Palestinien, -enne *mf*

**palette** ['pælɪt] *n (of artist)* palette *f*

**palm[1]** [pɑːm] *n (of hand)* paume *f*

**palm[2]** [pɑːm] *n* **p. (tree)** palmier *m*

**pamper** ['pæmpə(r)] *vt* dorloter

**pamphlet** ['pæmflɪt] *n* brochure *f*

**pan** [pæn] *n (saucepan)* casserole *f*; *(for frying)* poêle *f*

**Panama** ['pænəmɑː] *n* **the P. Canal** le canal de Panama

**pancake** ['pænkeɪk] *n* crêpe *f*; **P. Day** mardi *m* gras

**panda** ['pændə] *n* panda *m*

**pandemonium** [pændɪ'məʊnɪəm] *n (confusion)* chaos *m*; *(uproar)* vacarme *m*

**pander** ['pændə(r)] *vi* **to p. to sb/sth** flatter qn/qch

**pane** [peɪn] *n* vitre *f*

**panel** ['pænəl] *n* (**a**) *(of door)* panneau *m*; **(instrument) p.** *(in aircraft, vehicle)* tableau *m* de bord (**b**) *(of judges)* jury *m*; *(of experts)* comité *m*; *(of TV or radio guests)* invités *mpl*

**panic** ['pænɪk] **1** *n* panique *f* **2** (*pt & pp* **-ck-**) *vi* paniquer

**panorama** [pænə'rɑːmə] *n* panorama *m*

**pansy** ['pænzɪ] (*pl* **-ies**) *n (flower)* pensée *f*

**pant** [pænt] *vi* haleter

**pantomime** ['pæntəmaɪm] *n Br (show)* = spectacle de Noël

**pantry** ['pæntrɪ] (*pl* **-ies**) *n (larder)* garde-manger *m inv*

**pants** [pænts] *npl (underwear)* slip *m*; *Am (trousers)* pantalon *m*

**pantyhose** ['pæntɪhəʊz] *n Am (tights)* collant *m*

**paper** ['peɪpə(r)] **1** *n* papier *m*; *(newspaper)* journal *m*; *(wallpaper)* papier *m* peint; *(exam)* épreuve *f* écrite; *(student's exercise)* copie *f*; *(scholarly study, report)* article *m*; **a piece of p.** un bout de papier; **to put sth down on p.** mettre qch par écrit; **papers** *(documents)* papiers

**2** *adj (bag)* en papier; *(cup, plate)* en carton; *Br* **p. shop** marchand *m* de journaux; **p. towel** essuie-tout *m inv*

**3** *vt (room, wall)* tapisser ■ **paperback** *n* livre *m* de poche ■ **paperclip** *n* trombone *m* ■ **paperweight** *n* presse-papiers *m inv* ■ **paperwork** *n (in office)* écritures *fpl*; *Pej (red tape)* paperasserie *f*

**par** [pɑː(r)] *n (in golf)* par *m*; **on a p.** au

même niveau (**with** que)

**paracetamol** [pærə'si:təmɒl] *n* paracétamol *m*

**parachute** ['pærəʃu:t] *n* parachute *m*; **p. jump** saut *m* en parachute

**parade** [pə'reɪd] **1** *n* (**a**) *(procession)* défilé *m* (**b**) *Br (street)* avenue *f* **2** *vt Fig (wealth, knowledge)* faire étalage de **3** *vi (of troops)* défiler; **to p. about** *(of person)* se pavaner

**paradise** ['pærədaɪs] *n* paradis *m*

**paradoxically** [pærə'dɒksɪklɪ] *adv* paradoxalement

**paraffin** ['pærəfɪn] *n Br* pétrole *m* lampant; *Br* **p. lamp** lampe *f* à pétrole

**paragliding** ['pærəglaɪdɪŋ] *n* parapente *m*; **to go p.** faire du parapente

**paragraph** ['pærəgrɑ:f] *n* paragraphe *m*

**parallel** ['pærəlel] **1** *adj Math* parallèle (**with** *or* **to** à); *Fig (comparable)* semblable (**with** *or* **to** à) **2** *n Math (line)* parallèle *f*; *Fig (comparison) & Geog* parallèle *m*

**paralysis** [pə'ræləsɪs] *(pl* **-yses** [-əsi:z]) *n* paralysie *f* ▪ **paralyse** ['pærəlaɪz] (*Am* **paralyze**) *vt* paralyser

**paramedic** [pærə'medɪk] *n* auxiliaire *mf* médical(e)

**paranoid** ['pærənɔɪd] *adj* paranoïaque

**paraphrase** ['pærəfreɪz] *vt* paraphraser

**parasite** ['pærəsaɪt] *n (person, organism)* parasite *m*

**parasol** ['pærəsɒl] *n (over table, on beach)* parasol *m*; *(lady's)* ombrelle *f*

**parcel** ['pɑ:səl] **1** *n* colis *m*, paquet *m* **2** (*Br* **-ll-**, *Am* **-l-**) *vt* **to p. sth up** empaqueter

**parched** [pɑ:tʃt] *adj* **to be p.** *(of person)* être assoiffé

**pardon** ['pɑ:dən] **1** *n (forgiveness)* pardon *m*; *(in law)* grâce *f*; **I beg your p.** *(apologizing)* je vous prie de m'excuser; **I beg your p.?** *(not hearing)* pardon? **2** *vt (in law)* gracier; **to p. sb (for sth)** pardonner (qch) à qn; **p. (me)!** *(sorry)* pardon!

**parent** ['peərənt] *n (father)* père *m*; *(mother)* mère *f*; **parents** parents *mpl*

**Paris** ['pærɪs] *n* Paris *m ou f* ▪ **Parisian** [pə'rɪzɪən, *Am* pə'ri:ʒən] **1** *adj* parisien, -enne **2** *n* Parisien, -enne *mf*

**parish** ['pærɪʃ] *n (religious)* paroisse *f*; *(civil)* ≃ commune *f*

**park¹** [pɑ:k] *n (garden)* parc *m*

**park²** [pɑ:k] **1** *vt (vehicle)* garer **2** *vi (of vehicle)* se garer; *(remain parked)* stationner ▪ **parking** *n* stationnement *m*; **'no p.'** 'défense de stationner'; *Am* **p. lot** parking *m*; **p. meter** parcmètre *m*; **p. place** *or* **space** place *f* de parking; **p. ticket** contravention *f*

**parliament** ['pɑ:ləmənt] *n* parlement *m*

**parody** ['pærədɪ] **1** *(pl* **-ies**) *n* parodie *f* **2** *(pt & pp* **-ied**) *vt* parodier

**parole** [pə'rəʊl] *n* **to be (out) on p.** être en liberté conditionnelle

**parrot** ['pærət] *n* perroquet *m*

**parsley** ['pɑ:slɪ] *n* persil *m*

**parsnip** ['pɑ:snɪp] *n* panais *m*

**parson** ['pɑ:sən] *n* pasteur *m*

**part¹** [pɑ:t] **1** *n* partie *f*; *(quantity in mixture)* mesure *f*; *(of machine)* pièce *f*; *(of serial)* épisode *m*; *(role in play, film)* rôle *m*; *Am (in hair)* raie *f*; **to take p.** participer (**in** à); **to be a p. of sth** faire partie de qch; **for the most p.** dans l'ensemble; **on the p. of...** de la part de...; **for my p.** pour ma part **2** *adv (partly)* en partie; **p. silk, p. cotton** soie et coton

**part²** [pɑ:t] **1** *vt (separate)* séparer; **to p. one's hair** se faire une raie **2** *vi (of friends)* se quitter; *(of married couple)* se séparer; **to p. with sth** se défaire de qch

**partial** ['pɑ:ʃəl] *adj (not total)* partiel, -elle; *(biased)* partial (**towards** envers); **to be p. to sth** avoir un faible pour qch

**participate** [pɑ:'tɪsɪpeɪt] *vi* participer (**in** à) ▪ **participant** *n* participant, -e *mf* ▪ **participation** *n* participation *f*

**particular** [pə'tɪkjʊlə(r)] **1** *adj (specific, special)* particulier, -ère; *(exacting)* méticuleux, -euse; **this p. book** ce livre en particulier; **to be p. about sth** faire très attention à qch **2** *n* **in p.** en particulier ▪ **particularly** *adv* particulièrement ▪ **particulars** *npl (details)* détails *mpl*; **to take down sb's p.** noter les coordonnées de qn

**parting** ['pɑːtɪŋ] *n Br (in hair)* raie *f*

**partition** [pɑː'tɪʃən] **1** *n (of room)* cloison *f* **2** *vt* **to p. sth off** cloisonner qch

**partly** ['pɑːtlɪ] *adv* en partie; **p. English, p. French** moitié anglais, moitié français

**partner** ['pɑːtnə(r)] *n (in game)* partenaire *mf*; *(in business)* associé, -e *mf*; *(in relationship)* compagnon *m*, compagne *f*; **(dancing) p.** cavalier, -ère *mf* ▪ **partnership** *n* association *f*; **in p. with** en association avec

**partridge** ['pɑːtrɪdʒ] *n* perdrix *f*

**part-time** ['pɑːt'taɪm] *adj & adv* à temps partiel

**party** ['pɑːtɪ] *(pl* **-ies***)* *n* (**a**) *(gathering)* fête *f*; **to have** *or* **throw a p.** donner une fête (**b**) *(group)* groupe *m*; *(political)* parti *m*; *(in contract, lawsuit)* partie *f*

**pass[1]** [pɑːs] *n (over mountains)* col *m*

**pass[2]** [pɑːs] *n (entry permit)* laissez-passer *m inv*; *(for travel)* carte *f* d'abonnement; *(in sport)* passe *f*; **p. mark** *(in exam)* moyenne *f*

**pass[3]** [pɑːs] **1** *vt (move, give)* passer (**to** à); *(go past)* passer devant; *(vehicle, runner)* dépasser; *(exam)* être reçu à; *(law)* voter; **to p. sb** *(in street)* croiser qn; **to p. the time** passer le temps; **to p. sentence** *(of judge)* prononcer le verdict

**2** *vi (go past, go away)* passer (**to** à; **through** par); *(in exam)* avoir la moyenne; *(of time)* passer

▸ **pass away** *vi* décéder

▸ **pass by 1** *vt insep (building)* passer devant; **to p. by sb** *(in street)* croiser qn **2** *vi* passer à côté

▸ **pass off** *vt sep* **to p. oneself off as sb** se faire passer pour qn

▸ **pass on** *vt sep (message, illness)* transmettre (**to** à)

▸ **pass out 1** *vt sep (hand out)* distribuer **2** *vi (faint)* s'évanouir

▸ **pass over** *vt insep (ignore)* passer sur

▸ **pass round** *vt sep (cakes, document)* faire passer; *(hand out)* distribuer

▸ **pass through** *vi* passer

▸ **pass up** *vt sep (opportunity)* laisser passer

**passable** ['pɑːsəbəl] *adj (not bad)* passable

**passage** ['pæsɪdʒ] *n* (**a**) *(way through)* passage *m*; *(corridor)* couloir *m*; **with the p. of time** avec le temps (**b**) *(of text)* passage *m*

**passbook** ['pɑːsbʊk] *n* livret *m* de caisse d'épargne

**passenger** ['pæsɪndʒə(r)] *n* passager, -ère *mf*; *(on train)* voyageur, -euse *mf*

**passer-by** [pɑːsə'baɪ] *(pl* **passers-by***)* *n* passant, -e *mf*

**passing** ['pɑːsɪŋ] **1** *adj (vehicle)* qui passe **2** *n (of time)* écoulement *m*; **in p.** en passant

**passion** ['pæʃən] *n* passion *f*; **to have a p. for sth** adorer qch ▪ **passionate** *adj* passionné

**passive** ['pæsɪv] **1** *adj* passif, -ive **2** *n (in grammar)* passif *m*; **in the p.** au passif

**passport** ['pɑːspɔːt] *n* passeport *m*; **p. photo** photo *f* d'identité

**password** ['pɑːswɜːd] *n* mot *m* de passe

**past** [pɑːst] **1** *n* passé *m*; **in the p.** autrefois

**2** *adj (gone by)* passé; *(former)* ancien, -enne; **these p. months** ces derniers mois; **in the p. tense** au passé

**3** *prep (in front of)* devant; *(after)* après; *(beyond)* au-delà de; **it's p. four o'clock** il est quatre heures passées

**4** *adv* devant; **to go p.** passer

**pasta** ['pæstə] *n* pâtes *fpl*

**paste** [peɪst] **1** *n* (**a**) *(mixture)* pâte *f*; *(of meat)* pâté *m* (**b**) *(glue)* colle *f* **2** *vt* coller; **to p. sth up** coller qch

**pastel** [*Br* 'pæstəl, *Am* pæ'stel] *n* pastel *m*
**pasteurized** ['pæstʃəraɪzd] *adj* **p. milk** lait *m* pasteurisé
**pastille** [*Br* 'pæstɪl, *Am* pæ'sti:l] *n* pastille *f*
**pastime** ['pɑ:staɪm] *n* passe-temps *m inv*
**pastor** ['pɑ:stə(r)] *n Rel* pasteur *m*
**pastry** ['peɪstrɪ] (*pl* **-ies**) *n (dough)* pâte *f*; *(cake)* pâtisserie *f*
**pasture** ['pɑ:stʃə(r)] *n* pré *m*, pâture *f*
**pasty** ['pæstɪ] (*pl* **-ies**) *n (pie)* feuilleté *m*
**pat** [pæt] (*pt & pp* **-tt-**) *vt (tap)* tapoter; *(animal)* caresser
**patch** [pætʃ] **1** *n (for clothes)* pièce *f*; *(over eye)* bandeau *m*; *(of colour)* tache *f*; *(of ice)* plaque *f*; *Fig* **to be going through a bad p.** traverser une mauvaise passe **2** *vt* **to p. (up)** *(clothing)* rapiécer; **to p. things up** *(after argument)* se raccommoder
**patchwork** ['pætʃwɜ:k] *n* patchwork *m*
**patchy** ['pætʃɪ] (**-ier, -iest**) *adj* inégal
**patent** ['peɪtənt, 'pætənt] **1** *n* brevet *m* d'invention **2** *vt* (faire) breveter ▪ **patently** *adv* manifestement
**paternal** [pə'tɜ:nəl] *adj* paternel, -elle
**path** [pɑ:θ] (*pl* **-s** [pɑ:ðz]) *n* chemin *m*; *(narrow)* sentier *m*; *(in park)* allée *f*; *(of river)* cours *m*; *(of bullet)* trajectoire *f*
**pathetic** [pə'θetɪk] *adj* pitoyable
**pathway** ['pɑ:θweɪ] *n* sentier *m*
**patience** ['peɪʃəns] *n* (**a**) *(quality)* patience *f*; **to lose p.** perdre patience (**with sb** avec qn) (**b**) *Br (card game)* **to play p.** faire une réussite
**patient** ['peɪʃənt] **1** *adj* patient **2** *n* patient, -e *mf* ▪ **patiently** *adv* patiemment
**patio** ['pætɪəʊ] (*pl* **-os**) *n* patio *m*
**patriot** ['pætrɪət, 'peɪtrɪət] *n* patriote *mf* ▪ **patriotic** [-rɪ'ɒtɪk, peɪtrɪ'ɒtɪk] *adj (views, speech)* patriotique; *(person)* patriote
**patrol** [pə'trəʊl] **1** *n* patrouille *f*; **to be on p.** être de patrouille; **p. car** voiture *f* de police **2** (*pt & pp* **-ll-**) *vt* patrouiller dans **3** *vi* patrouiller ▪ **patrolman** (*pl* **-men**) *n Am (policeman)* agent *m* de police
**patron** ['peɪtrən] *n (of arts)* protecteur, -trice *mf*; *(of charity)* patron, -onne *mf*; *(customer)* client, -e *mf*; *Rel* **p. saint** patron, -onne *mf*
**patronize** [*Br* 'pætrənaɪz, *Am* 'peɪtrənaɪz] *vt (be condescending towards)* traiter avec condescendance ▪ **patronizing** *adj* condescendant
**patter** ['pætə(r)] *n (of footsteps)* petit bruit *m*; *(of rain)* crépitement *m*
**pattern** ['pætən] *n (design)* dessin *m*, motif *m*; *(in sewing)* patron *m*; *(in knitting) & Fig (norm)* modèle *m*; *(tendency)* tendance *f*
**paunch** [pɔ:ntʃ] *n* ventre *m*
**pause** [pɔ:z] **1** *n* pause *f*; *(in conversation)* silence *m* **2** *vi (stop)* faire une pause; *(hesitate)* hésiter
**pave** [peɪv] *vt (road)* paver (**with** de); *Fig* **to p. the way for sth** ouvrir la voie à qch ▪ **paving** *n* **p. stone** pavé *m*
**pavement** ['peɪvmənt] *n Br (beside road)* trottoir *m*; *Am (roadway)* chaussée *f*
**pavilion** [pə'vɪljən] *n* pavillon *m*
**paw** [pɔ:] *n* patte *f*
**pawn**[1] [pɔ:n] *n (chess piece)* pion *m*
**pawn**[2] [pɔ:n] *vt* mettre en gage ▪ **pawnbroker** *n* prêteur, -euse *mf* sur gages ▪ **pawnshop** *n* mont-de-piété *m*
**pay** [peɪ] **1** *n* paie *f*, salaire *m*; *(of soldier)* solde *f*; **p. rise** augmentation *f* de salaire; *Br* **p. slip,** *Am* **p. stub** fiche *f* de paie
**2** (*pt & pp* **paid**) *vt (person, money, bill)* payer; *(sum, deposit)* verser; *(yield) (of investment)* rapporter; **I paid £5 for it** je l'ai payé 5 livres; **to p. sb to do sth** *or* **for doing sth** payer qn pour qu'il fasse qch; **to p. sb for sth** payer qch à qn
**3** *vi* payer ▪ **payable** *adj (due)* payable; **to make a cheque p. to sb** libeller un chèque à l'ordre de qn

▪ **payment** *n* paiement *m*; *(of deposit)* versement *m*; **on p. of 20 euros** moyennant 20 euros ▪ **payphone** *n* téléphone *m* public

▸ **pay back** *vt sep (person, loan)* rembourser; *Fig* **I'll p. you back for this!** tu me le paieras!

▸ **pay for** *vt insep* payer

▸ **pay in** *vt sep (cheque, money)* verser sur un compte

▸ **pay off** **1** *vt sep (debt)* rembourser; *(in instalments)* rembourser par acomptes **2** *vi (of work, effort)* porter ses fruits

▸ **pay out** *vt sep (spend)* dépenser

▸ **pay up** *vi* payer

**PC** [piː'siː] (**a**) (*abbr* **personal computer**) PC *m*, micro *m* (**b**) (*abbr* **politically correct**) politiquement correct

**PE** [piː'iː] (*abbr* **physical education**) *n* EPS *f*

**pea** [piː] *n* pois *m*; **peas,** *Br* **garden** *or* **green peas** petits pois *mpl*

**peace** [piːs] *n* paix *f*; **p. of mind** tranquillité *f* d'esprit; **at p.** en paix (**with** avec); **I'd like some p. and quiet** j'aimerais un peu de silence

**peaceful** ['piːsfəl] *adj (calm)* paisible; *(non-violent)* pacifique

**peach** [piːtʃ] *n (fruit)* pêche *f*

**peacock** ['piːkɒk] *n* paon *m*

**peak** [piːk] **1** *n (mountain top)* sommet *m*; *(mountain)* pic *m*; *(of cap)* visière *f*; *Fig (of fame, success)* apogée *m* **2** *adj (hours, period)* de pointe

**peal** [piːl] **1** *n (of bells)* sonnerie *f*; **peals of laughter** éclats *mpl* de rire **2** *vi* **to p. (out)** *(of bells)* sonner à toute volée

**peanut** ['piːnʌt] *n* cacah(o)uète *f*; **p. butter** beurre *m* de cacah(o)uètes

**pear** [peə(r)] *n* poire *f*

**pearl** [pɜːl] *n* perle *f*; **p. necklace** collier *m* de perles

**peasant** ['pezənt] *n & adj* paysan, -anne *(mf)*

**peat** [piːt] *n* tourbe *f*

**pebble** ['pebəl] *n (stone)* caillou *m* (*pl* -oux); *(on beach)* galet *m*

**pecan** ['piːkən] *n (nut)* noix *f* de pécan

**peck** [pek] *vti* **to p. (at)** *(grain)* picorer; *(person)* donner un coup de bec à

**peckish** ['pekɪʃ] *adj Br* **to be p.** avoir un petit creux

**peculiar** [pɪ'kjuːlɪə(r)] *adj (strange)* bizarre; *(special, characteristic)* particulier, -ère (**to** à)

**pedal** ['pedəl] **1** *n* pédale *f*; **p. bin** poubelle *f* à pédale **2** (*Br* **-ll-**, *Am* **-l-**) *vt* **to p. a bicycle** être à bicyclette **3** *vi* pédaler

**pedantic** [pɪ'dæntɪk] *adj* pédant

**peddle** ['pedəl] *vt (goods, ideas)* colporter; *(drugs)* faire du trafic de ▪ **peddler** *n (door-to-door)* colporteur, -euse *mf*; *(in street)* camelot *m*; **(drug) p.** trafiquant, -e *mf* de drogue

**pedestal** ['pedɪstəl] *n* piédestal *m*

**pedestrian** [pə'destrɪən] *n* piéton *m*; *Br* **p. crossing** passage *m* pour piétons; *Br* **p. precinct** zone *f* piétonnière

**pediatrician** [piːdɪə'trɪʃən] *n Am* = **paediatrician**

**pedigree** ['pedɪgriː] **1** *n (of animal)* pedigree *m*; *(of person)* ascendance *f* **2** *adj (animal)* de race

**pedlar** ['pedlə(r)] *n (door-to-door)* colporteur, -euse *mf*; *(in street)* camelot *m*

**pee** [piː] *Fam* **1** *n* **to go for a p.** faire pipi **2** *vi* faire pipi

**peek** [piːk] *vi* jeter un coup d'œil furtif (**at** à)

**peel** [piːl] **1** *n (of vegetable, fruit)* peau *f*; *(of orange, lemon)* écorce *f* **2** *vt (vegetable)* éplucher; *(fruit)* peler; **to p. sth off** *(label)* décoller qch **3** *vi (of skin, person)* peler; *(of paint)* s'écailler ▪ **peeler** *n* **(potato) p.** épluche-légumes *m inv* ▪ **peelings** *npl* épluchures *fpl*

**peep** [piːp] *vi* jeter un coup d'œil furtif (**at** à); **to p. out** se montrer

**peer** [pɪə(r)] **1** *n (equal) & Br (nobleman)* pair *m* **2** *vi* **to p. at sb/sth** scruter qn/qch du regard

**peeved** [piːvd] *adj* en rogne

**peevish** ['piːvɪʃ] *adj* irritable

**peg** [peg] *n (for coat, hat)* patère *f*; *(for drying clothes)* pince *f* à linge; *(for tent)* piquet *m*; *(wooden pin)* cheville *f*; *Br* **to buy sth off the p.** acheter qch en prêt-à-porter

**pejorative** [pɪ'dʒɒrətɪv] *adj* péjoratif, -ive

**pelican** ['pelɪkən] *n* pélican *m*; *Br* **p. crossing** feux *mpl* à commande manuelle

**pelt** [pelt] **1** *vt* bombarder (**with** de) **2** *vi Fam* **it's pelting down** il pleut à verse

**pelvis** ['pelvɪs] *n Anat* pelvis *m*

**pen**[1] [pen] *n (for writing)* stylo *m*; **p. friend** *or* **pal** correspondant, -e *mf*

**pen**[2] [pen] *n (for sheep, cattle)* parc *m*

**penal** ['pi:nəl] *adj (code, law)* pénal ▪ **penalize** *vt* pénaliser

**penalty** ['penəltɪ] (*pl* **-ies**) *n (prison sentence)* peine *f*; *(fine)* amende *f*; *(in football)* penalty *m*; *(in rugby)* pénalité *f*

**pence** [pens] *pl of* **penny**

**pencil** ['pensəl] **1** *n* crayon *m*; **in p.** au crayon; **p. sharpener** taille-crayon *m* **2** (*Br* **-ll-**, *Am* **-l-**) *vt Fig* **to p. sth in** fixer qch provisoirement

**pendant** ['pendənt] *n (around neck)* pendentif *m*

**pending** ['pendɪŋ] **1** *adj (matter, business)* en attente **2** *prep (until)* en attendant

**pendulum** ['pendjʊləm] *n* pendule *m*

**penetrate** ['penɪtreɪt] **1** *vt (substance)* pénétrer; *(mystery)* percer **2** *vti* **to p. (into)** *(forest)* pénétrer dans; *(group)* s'infiltrer dans ▪ **penetrating** *adj (mind, cold)* pénétrant

**penguin** ['peŋgwɪn] *n* manchot *m*

**penicillin** [penɪ'sɪlɪn] *n* pénicilline *f*

**peninsula** [pə'nɪnsjʊlə] *n* presqu'île *f*; *(larger)* péninsule *f*

**penis** ['pi:nɪs] *n* pénis *m*

**penitentiary** [penɪ'tenʃərɪ] (*pl* **-ies**) *n Am* prison *f* centrale

**penknife** ['pennaɪf] (*pl* **-knives**) *n* canif *m*

**penniless** ['penɪləs] *adj* sans le sou

**penny** ['penɪ] *n* (**a**) (*pl* **-ies**) *Br (coin)* penny *m*; *Am & Can (cent)* cent *m*; *Fig* **I don't have a p.** je n'ai pas un sou (**b**) (*pl* **pence**) *Br (value, currency)* penny *m*

**pension** ['penʃən] **1** *n* pension *f*; **(retirement) p.** retraite *f*; *Br* **old age p.** pension *f* de vieillesse **2** *vt* **to p. sb off** mettre qn à la retraite ▪ **pensioner** *n* retraité, -e *mf*; *Br* **old age p.** retraité, -e *mf*

**pent-up** ['pent'ʌp] *adj (feelings)* refoulé

**penultimate** [pɪ'nʌltɪmət] *adj* avant-dernier, -ère

**people** ['pi:pəl] **1** *n (nation)* peuple *m* **2** *npl (as group)* gens *mpl*; *(as individuals)* personnes *fpl*; **the p.** *(citizens)* le peuple; **two p.** deux personnes; **English p.** les Anglais *mpl*; **p. think that...** les gens pensent que...

**pepper** ['pepə(r)] *n* poivre *m*; *(vegetable)* poivron *m*; **p. mill** moulin *m* à poivre

**peppermint** ['pepəmɪnt] *n (flavour)* menthe *f*; *(sweet)* bonbon *m* à la menthe

**per** [pɜ:(r)] *prep* par; **p. annum** par an; **50 pence p. kilo** 50 pence le kilo; **40 km p. hour** 40 km à l'heure

**perceive** [pə'si:v] *vt (see, hear)* percevoir; *(notice)* remarquer (**that** que)

**percentage** [pə'sentɪdʒ] *n* pourcentage *m* ▪ **percent** *adv* pour cent

**perception** [pə'sepʃən] *n* perception *f* (**of** de)

**perceptive** [pə'septɪv] *adj (person)* perspicace; *(study, remark)* pertinent

**perch** [pɜ:tʃ] **1** *n (for bird)* perchoir *m* **2** *vi* se percher

**percolator** ['pɜ:kəleɪtə(r)] *n* cafetière *f* à pression; *(in café, restaurant)* percolateur *m*

**perennial** [pə'renɪəl] **1** *adj (plant)* vivace; *(worry)* perpétuel, -elle **2** *n* plante *f* vivace

**perfect** **1** ['pɜ:fɪkt] *adj* parfait; *Gram* **p. tense** parfait *m* **2** ['pɜ:fɪkt] *n Gram* parfait *m* **3** [pə'fekt] *vt* parfaire; **to p. one's French** parfaire ses connaissances en français

**perfection** [pə'fekʃən] *n (quality)* perfection *f* ▪ **perfectly** *adv* parfaitement

**perforate** ['pɜ:fəreɪt] *vt* perforer ▪ **perforation** *n* perforation *f*

**perform** [pə'fɔ:m] **1** *vt (task, miracle)* accomplir; *(duty, function)* remplir; *(play, piece of music)* jouer **2** *vi (act, play)* jouer; *(sing)* chanter; *(dance)* danser; **to p. well/badly** *(in job)* bien/mal s'en tirer ▪ **performance** *n* (**a**) *(of play)* représentation *f* (**b**) *(of actor, musician)* interprétation *f*; *(of athlete)* performance *f*; *(of company)* résultats *mpl*

**performer** [pə'fɔ:mə(r)] *n (entertainer)* artiste *mf*; *(in play, of music)* interprète *mf* (**of** de)

**perfume** ['pɜ:fju:m] *n* parfum *m*

**perhaps** [pə'hæps] *adv* peut-être; **p. not/so** peut-être que non/que oui; **p. she'll come** peut-être qu'elle viendra, elle viendra peut-être

**peril** ['perɪl] *n* péril *m*, danger *m*

**period** ['pɪərɪəd] **1** *n* (**a**) *(stretch of time)* période *f*; *(historical)* époque *f*; *(school lesson)* heure *f* de cours; **(monthly) period(s)** *(of woman)* règles *fpl* (**b**) *Am (full stop)* point *m*; **I refuse, p.!** je refuse, un point c'est tout! **2** *adj (furniture, costume)* d'époque ▪ **periodical** [-rɪ'ɒdɪkəl] *n (magazine)* périodique *m* ▪ **periodically** [-rɪ'ɒdɪklɪ] *adv* périodiquement

**peripheral** [pə'rɪfərəl] *n Comptr* périphérique *m*

**perish** ['perɪʃ] *vi (of person)* périr

**perishable** ['perɪʃəbəl] *adj (food)* périssable

**perjury** ['pɜ:dʒərɪ] *n* faux témoignage *m*

**perk** [pɜ:k] **1** *n Br Fam (in job)* avantage *m* **2** *vt* **to p. sb up** *(revive)* ragaillardir qn; *(cheer up)* remonter le moral à qn **3** *vi* **to p. up** reprendre du poil de la bête

**perm** [pɜ:m] **1** *n* permanente *f* **2** *vt* **to have one's hair permed** se faire faire une permanente

**permanent** ['pɜ:mənənt] *adj* permanent; *(address)* fixe ▪ **permanently** *adv* à titre permanent

**permissible** [pə'mɪsəbəl] *adj* permis

**permission** [pə'mɪʃən] *n* permission *f*, autorisation *f* (**to do** de faire); **to give sb p. (to do sth)** donner la permission à qn (de faire qch)

**permissive** [pə'mɪsɪv] *adj* permissif, -ive

**permit 1** ['pɜ:mɪt] *n* permis *m* **2** [pə'mɪt] *(pt & pp* **-tt-***) vt* permettre (**sb to do** à qn de faire)

**perpendicular** [pɜ:pən'dɪkjʊlə(r)] *adj & n* perpendiculaire *(f)*

**perpetrate** ['pɜ:pɪtreɪt] *vt (crime)* perpétrer ▪ **perpetrator** *n* auteur *m*

**perpetual** [pə'petʃʊəl] *adj* perpétuel, -elle ▪ **perpetuate** [-ʊeɪt] *vt* perpétuer

**perplexed** [pə'plekst] *adj* perplexe

**persecute** ['pɜ:sɪkju:t] *vt* persécuter ▪ **persecution** *n* persécution *f*

**persevere** [pɜ:sɪ'vɪə(r)] *vi* persévérer (**with** dans) ▪ **perseverance** *n* persévérance *f*

**Persian** ['pɜ:ʃən, 'pɜ:ʒən] **1** *adj (carpet, cat)* persan; **the P. Gulf** le golfe Persique **2** *n (language)* persan *m*

**persist** [pə'sɪst] *vi* persister (**in doing** à faire; **in sth** dans qch) ▪ **persistent** *adj (person)* tenace; *(smell, rumours)* persistant; *(attempts)* continuel, -elle

**person** ['pɜ:sən] *n* personne *f*; **in p.** en personne

**personal** ['pɜ:sənəl] *adj* personnel, -elle; *(friend)* intime; *(life)* privé; *(indiscreet)* indiscret, -ète; **p. computer** ordinateur *m* individuel; **p. organizer** agenda *m* électronique; **p. stereo** baladeur *m*

**personality** [pɜ:sə'nælətɪ] *(pl* **-ies***) n (character, famous person)* personnalité *f*

**personally** ['pɜ:sənəlɪ] *adv* personnellement; *(in person)* en personne

**personify** [pə'sɒnɪfaɪ] *(pt & pp* **-ied***) vt* personnifier

**personnel** [pɜ:sə'nel] *n (staff)* personnel *m*

**perspective** [pə'spektɪv] *n* perspective *f*; *Fig* **in p.** sous son vrai jour

**perspire** [pə'spaɪə(r)] *vi* transpirer

**persuade** [pə'sweɪd] *vt* persuader (**sb to do** qn de faire) ▪ **persuasion** *n* persuasion *f*; *(creed)* religion *f* ▪ **persuasive** *adj (person, argument)* persuasif, -ive

**pertain** [pə'teɪn] *vi Formal* **to p. to** *(relate)* se rapporter à

**pertinent** ['pɜ:tɪnənt] *adj* pertinent

**perturb** [pə'tɜ:b] *vt* troubler

**Peru** [pə'ru:] *n* le Pérou

**peruse** [pə'ru:z] *vt Formal (read carefully)* lire attentivement; *(skim through)* parcourir

**pervade** [pə'veɪd] *vt* imprégner ▪ **pervasive** *adj (feeling)* général; *(influence)* omniprésent

**perverse** [pə'vɜ:s] *adj (awkward)* contrariant ▪ **perversion** [-ʃən, *Am* -ʒən] *n (sexual)* perversion *f*

**pervert 1** ['pɜ:vɜ:t] *n (sexual deviant)* pervers, -e *mf* **2** [pə'vɜ:t] *vt* pervertir; *(mind)* corrompre

**pessimism** ['pesɪmɪzəm] *n* pessimisme *m* ▪ **pessimistic** *adj* pessimiste

**pest** [pest] *n (animal)* animal *m* nuisible; *(insect)* insecte *m* nuisible; *Fam (person)* plaie *f*

**pester** ['pestə(r)] *vt* tourmenter; **to p. sb to do sth** harceler qn pour qu'il fasse qch

**pesticide** ['pestɪsaɪd] *n* pesticide *m*

**pet** [pet] **1** *n* animal *m* domestique; *(favourite person)* chouchou, -oute *mf*; *(term of address)* petit chou *m* **2** *adj (dog, cat)* domestique; *(favourite)* favori, -ite; **p. shop** animalerie *f* **3** *(pt & pp* **-tt-**) *vt (fondle)* caresser **4** *vi Fam* se peloter

**petal** ['petəl] *n* pétale *m*

**peter** ['pi:tə(r)] *vi* **to p. out** *(of conversation)* tarir; *(of scheme)* n'aboutir à rien; *(of path, stream)* disparaître

**petition** [pə'tɪʃən] *n (signatures)* pétition *f*; *(request to court of law)* requête *f*

**petrify** ['petrɪfaɪ] *(pt & pp* **-ied**) *vt* pétrifier

**petrol** ['petrəl] *n Br* essence *f*; **p. station** station-service *f*; **p. tank** réservoir *m* d'essence

**petticoat** ['petɪkəʊt] *n* jupon *m*

**petty** ['petɪ] (**-ier, -iest**) *adj (trivial)* insignifiant; *(mean)* mesquin; **p. cash** petite caisse *f*

**pew** [pju:] *n* banc *m* d'église

**phantom** ['fæntəm] *n* fantôme *m*

**pharmacy** ['fɑ:məsɪ] *(pl* **-ies**) *n* pharmacie *f* ▪ **pharmacist** *n* pharmacien, -enne *mf*

**phase** [feɪz] **1** *n* phase *f* **2** *vt* **to p. sth in/out** introduire/supprimer qch progressivement

**PhD** [pi:eɪtʃ'di:] *(abbr* **Doctor of Philosophy**) *n (degree)* doctorat *m* (**in** de); *(person)* docteur *m*

**phenomenon** [fɪ'nɒmɪnən] *(pl* **-ena** [-ɪnə]) *n* phénomène *m* ▪ **phenomenal** *adj* phénoménal

**Philippines** ['fɪlɪpi:nz] *npl* **the P.** les Philippines *fpl*

**philistine** ['fɪlɪstaɪn] *n* béotien, -enne *mf*, philistin *m*

**philosopher** [fɪ'lɒsəfə(r)] *n* philosophe *mf*

**philosophical** [fɪlə'sɒfɪkəl] *adj* philosophique; *Fig (stoical, resigned)* philosophe

**philosophy** [fɪ'lɒsəfɪ] *(pl* **-ies**) *n* philosophie *f*

**phlegm** [flem] *n (in throat)* glaires *fpl*

**phobia** ['fəʊbɪə] *n* phobie *f*

**phone** [fəʊn] **1** *n* téléphone *m*; **to be on the p.** *(be talking)* être au téléphone; *(have a telephone)* avoir le téléphone; **p. call** coup *m* de téléphone; **to make a p. call** téléphoner (**to** à); **p. book** annuaire *m*; **p. box,** *Br* **p. booth** cabine *f* téléphonique; **p. number** numéro *m* de téléphone
**2** *vt* téléphoner (**to** à); **to p. sb (up)** téléphoner à qn; **to p. sb back** rappeler qn
**3** *vi* **to p. (up)** téléphoner; **to p. back** rappeler ▪ **phonecard** *n Br* carte *f* de téléphone

**phonetic** [fə'netɪk] *adj* phonétique

**phoney** ['fəʊnɪ] *Fam* **1** (**-ier, -iest**) *adj (company, excuse)* bidon *inv* **2** *n (impostor)* imposteur *m*; *(insincere person)* faux jeton *m*

**photo** ['fəʊtəʊ] (*pl* **-os**) *n* photo *f*; **to take sb's p.** prendre qn en photo; **to have one's p. taken** se faire prendre en photo; **p. album** album *m* de photos

**photocopy** ['fəʊtəʊkɒpɪ] **1** (*pl* **-ies**) *n* photocopie *f* **2** (*pt & pp* **-ied**) *vt* photocopier ▪ **photocopier** *n* photocopieuse *f*

**photograph** ['fəʊtəgrɑːf] **1** *n* photographie *f* **2** *vt* photographier ▪ **photographer** [fə'tɒgrəfə(r)] *n* photographe *mf* ▪ **photography** [fə'tɒgrəfɪ] *n (activity)* photographie *f*

**phrase** [freɪz] **1** *n (saying)* expression *f*; *(idiom, in grammar)* locution *f*; **p. book** manuel *m* de conversation **2** *vt (verbally)* exprimer; *(in writing)* rédiger

**physical** ['fɪzɪkəl] *adj* physique; **p. education** éducation *f* physique; **p. examination** visite *f* médicale

**physician** [fɪ'zɪʃən] *n* médecin *m*

**physics** ['fɪzɪks] *n (science)* physique *f*

**physiology** [fɪzɪ'ɒlədʒɪ] *n* physiologie *f*

**physiotherapy** [fɪzɪəʊ'θerəpɪ] *n* kinésithérapie *f*

**physique** [fɪ'ziːk] *n* physique *m*

**piano** [pɪ'ænəʊ] (*pl* **-os**) *n* piano *m* ▪ **pianist** ['pɪənɪst] *n* pianiste *mf*

**pick**[1] [pɪk] **1** *n (choice)* choix *m*; **to take one's p.** choisir **2** *vt (choose)* choisir; *(flower, fruit)* cueillir; *(hole)* faire (**in** dans); *(lock)* crocheter; **to p. a fight** chercher la bagarre (**with** avec)

▸**pick at** *vt insep* **to p. at one's food** picorer

▸**pick off** *vt sep (remove)* enlever

▸**pick on** *vt insep (nag, blame)* s'en prendre à

▸**pick out** *vt sep (choose)* choisir; *(identify)* repérer

▸**pick up 1** *vt sep (lift up)* ramasser; *(person into air, weight)* soulever; *(baby)* prendre dans ses bras; *(cold)* attraper; *(habit, accent, speed)* prendre; *(fetch, collect)* passer prendre; *(radio programme)* capter; *(arrest)* arrêter; *(learn)* apprendre; **to p. up the phone** décrocher le téléphone

**2** *vi (improve)* s'améliorer; *(of business)* reprendre; **let's p. up where we left off** reprenons (là où nous en étions restés)

**pick**[2] [pɪk] *n (tool)* pic *m*; **ice p.** pic *m* à glace

**pickaxe** ['pɪkæks] (*Am* **pickax**) *n* pioche *f*

**picket** ['pɪkɪt] *n (in strike)* **p. (line)** piquet *m* de grève

**pickle** ['pɪkəl] **1** *n* **pickles** *(vegetables) Br* conserves *fpl* (au vinaigre); *Am* concombres *mpl*, cornichons *mpl*; *Fam* **to be in a p.** être dans le pétrin **2** *vt* conserver dans du vinaigre; **pickled onion** oignon *m* au vinaigre

**pickpocket** ['pɪkpɒkɪt] *n* pickpocket *m*

**pick-up** ['pɪkʌp] *n* **p. (truck)** pick-up *m inv (petite camionnette à plateau)*; **p. point** *(for goods, passengers)* point *m* de ramassage

**picky** ['pɪkɪ] (**-ier, -iest**) *adj Fam (choosy)* difficile (**about** sur)

**picnic** ['pɪknɪk] **1** *n* pique-nique *m* **2** (*pt & pp* **-ck-**) *vi* pique-niquer

**picture** ['pɪktʃə(r)] **1** *n* image *f*; *(painting)* tableau *m*; *(drawing)* dessin *m*; *(photo)* photo *f*; *Fig (situation)* situation *f*; *Br Fam (film)* film *m*; *Br Fam* **the pictures** le cinéma; **p. frame** cadre *m* **2** *vt* **to p. sth (to oneself)** s'imaginer qch

**picturesque** [pɪktʃə'resk] *adj* pittoresque

**pie** [paɪ] *n (open)* tarte *f*; *(with pastry on top)* tourte *f*; **p. chart** camembert *m*

**piece** [piːs] **1** *n* morceau *m*; *(smaller)* bout *m*; *(in chess, puzzle)* pièce *f*; **to take sth to pieces** démonter qch; **a p. of news/advice/luck** une nouvelle/

un conseil/une chance; **in one p.** *(object)* intact **2** *vt* **to p. together** *(facts)* reconstituer

**pier** [pɪə(r)] *n (for walking, with entertainments)* jetée *f*

**pierce** [pɪəs] *vt* percer; *(of cold, bullet, sword)* transpercer; **to have one's ears pierced** se faire percer les oreilles ▪ **piercing** *adj (voice, look)* perçant; *(wind)* vif (*f* vive)

**pig** [pɪg] *n (animal)* cochon *m*, porc *m*; *Fam (greedy person)* goinfre *m*

**pigeon** ['pɪdʒɪn] *n* pigeon *m*

**pigeonhole** ['pɪdʒɪnhəʊl] **1** *n* casier *m* **2** *vt (classify, label)* classer; *(person)* étiqueter

**piggy** ['pɪgɪ] *n* **p. bank** tirelire *f (en forme de cochon)*

**piggyback** ['pɪgɪbæk] *n* **to give sb a p.** porter qn sur son dos

**pigment** ['pɪgmənt] *n* pigment *m*

**pigtail** ['pɪgteɪl] *n (hair)* natte *f*

**pilchard** ['pɪltʃəd] *n* pilchard *m*

**pile** [paɪl] **1** *n (heap)* tas *m*; *(neat stack)* pile *f*; *Fam* **to have piles of** *or* **a p. of things to do** avoir un tas de choses à faire **2** *vt* entasser; *(stack)* empiler

▸ **pile up 1** *vt sep* entasser; *(stack)* empiler **2** *vi (accumulate)* s'accumuler

**piles** [paɪlz] *npl (illness)* hémorroïdes *fpl*

**pile-up** ['paɪlʌp] *n Fam (on road)* carambolage *m*

**pilgrim** ['pɪlgrɪm] *n* pèlerin *m* ▪ **pilgrimage** *n* pèlerinage *m*

**pill** [pɪl] *n* pilule *f*; **to be on the p.** *(of woman)* prendre la pilule

**pillage** ['pɪlɪdʒ] **1** *n* pillage *m* **2** *vti* piller

**pillar** ['pɪlə(r)] *n* pilier *m*; *Br* **p. box** boîte *f* aux lettres

**pillow** ['pɪləʊ] *n* oreiller *m* ▪ **pillowcase** *n* taie *f* d'oreiller

**pilot** ['paɪlət] **1** *n (of plane, ship)* pilote *m* **2** *adj* **p. light** veilleuse *f*; **p. scheme** projet *m* pilote **3** *vt (plane, ship)* piloter

**pimple** ['pɪmpəl] *n* bouton *m*

**PIN** [pɪn] (*abbr* **personal identification number**) *n Br* **P. (number)** code *m* confidentiel

**pin** [pɪn] **1** *n* épingle *f*; *Br (drawing pin)* punaise *f*; *(in machine)* goupille *f* **2** (*pt & pp* **-nn-**) *vt (attach)* épingler (**to** à); *(to wall)* punaiser (**to** *or* **on** à); **to p. down** *(immobilize)* immobiliser; *(fix)* fixer; **to p. sth up** *(notice)* fixer qch au mur

**pinball** ['pɪnbɔːl] *n* flipper *m*; **p. machine** flipper *m*

**pincers** ['pɪnsəz] *npl (tool)* tenailles *fpl*

**pinch** [pɪntʃ] **1** *n (of salt)* pincée *f*; **to give sb a p.** pincer qn; *Br* **at a p.**, *Am* **in a p.** à la rigueur **2** *vt* pincer; *Br Fam (steal)* piquer (**from** à) **3** *vi (of shoes)* serrer

**pine** [paɪn] **1** *n (tree, wood)* pin *m*; **p. forest** pinède *f* **2** *vi* **to p. for sb/sth** se languir de qn/qch

**pineapple** ['paɪnæpəl] *n* ananas *m*

**pink** [pɪŋk] *adj & n (colour)* rose *(m)*

**pinnacle** ['pɪnəkəl] *n Fig (of fame, career)* apogée *m*

**pinpoint** ['pɪnpɔɪnt] *vt (locate)* repérer; *(identify)* identifier

**pint** [paɪnt] *n* pinte *f (Br = 0,57 l, Am = 0,47 l)*; **a p. of beer** ≃ un demi

**pioneer** [paɪə'nɪə(r)] **1** *n* pionnier, -ère *mf* **2** *vt* **to p. sth** être le premier/la première à mettre au point qch

**pious** ['paɪəs] *adj (person, deed)* pieux (*f* pieuse)

**pip** [pɪp] *n Br (of fruit)* pépin *m*

**pipe** [paɪp] **1** *n* tuyau *m*; *(for smoking)* pipe *f*; *(musical instrument)* pipeau *m*; **to smoke a p.** fumer la pipe **2** *vi Fam* **to p. down** *(shut up)* se taire ▪ **piping** *adv* **p. hot** très chaud

**pipeline** ['paɪplaɪn] *n (for oil)* pipeline *m*; *Fig* **to be in the p.** être en préparation

**pirate** ['paɪərət] *n* pirate *m* ▪ **pirated** *adj (book, record, CD)* pirate

**pissed** [pɪst] *adj very Fam (drunk)* bourré; *Am (angry)* en rogne

**pistachio** [pɪ'stæʃɪəʊ] (*pl* **-os**) *n (nut, flavour)* pistache *f*

**pistol** ['pɪstəl] *n* pistolet *m*

**pit¹** [pɪt] *n (hole)* fosse *f*; *(mine)* mine *f*
**pit²** [pɪt] *n Am (stone of fruit)* noyau *m* (*pl* -aux); *(smaller)* pépin *m*
**pit³** [pɪt] (*pt & pp* **-tt-**) *vt* **to p. oneself against sb** se mesurer à qn
**pitch** [pɪtʃ] **1** *n* (**a**) *(for football)* terrain *m* (**b**) *(of voice)* hauteur *f*; *(musical)* ton *m* **2** *vt (tent)* dresser; *(ball)* lancer **3** *vi Fam* **to p. in** *(cooperate)* mettre du sien ▪ **pitch-black, pitch-dark** *adj* noir comme dans un four
**pitcher** ['pɪtʃə(r)] *n* cruche *f*
**pitfall** ['pɪtfɔːl] *n (trap)* piège *m*
**pith** [pɪθ] *n (of orange)* peau *f* blanche
**pitiful** ['pɪtɪfəl] *adj* pitoyable ▪ **pitiless** *adj* impitoyable
**pittance** ['pɪtəns] *n (income)* salaire *m* de misère
**pity** ['pɪtɪ] **1** *n* pitié *f*; **to take** *or* **have p. on sb** avoir pitié de qn; **what a p.!** quel dommage!; **it's a p. that...** c'est dommage que... *(+ subjunctive)* **2** (*pt & pp* **-ied**) *vt* plaindre
**pivot** ['pɪvət] **1** *n* pivot *m* **2** *vi* pivoter (**on** sur)
**pizza** ['piːtsə] *n* pizza *f*
**placard** ['plækɑːd] *n (on wall)* affiche *f*; *(hand-held)* pancarte *f*
**place** [pleɪs] **1** *n* endroit *m*, lieu *m*; *(seat, position, rank)* place *f*; *Fam* **my p.** chez moi; **to lose one's p.** *(in queue)* perdre sa place; *(in book)* perdre sa page; **to take the p. of sb/sth** remplacer qn/qch; **to take p.** *(happen)* avoir lieu; *Br* **to set** *or* **lay three places** *(at the table)* mettre trois couverts; *Am* **some p.** *(somewhere)* quelque part; *Am* **no p.** *(nowhere)* nulle part; **all over the p.** un peu partout; **in the first p.** *(firstly)* en premier lieu; **in p. of** à la place de; **out of p.** *(remark)* déplacé; *(object)* pas à sa place; **p. of work** lieu *m* de travail
**2** *vt (put, situate, invest, in sport)* placer; **to be placed third** se classer troisième; **to p. an order with sb** passer une commande à qn
**placement** ['pleɪsmənt] *n* stage *m*
**placid** ['plæsɪd] *adj* placide
**plague** [pleɪg] **1** *n (disease)* peste *f* **2** *vt (of person)* harceler (**with** de)
**plaice** [pleɪs] *n (fish)* carrelet *m*
**plain¹** [pleɪn] **1** (**-er, -est**) *adj (clear, obvious)* clair; *(simple)* simple; *(without a pattern)* uni; *(not beautiful)* quelconque; **in p. clothes** en civil; **to make it p. to sb that...** faire comprendre à qn que...; **p. chocolate** chocolat *m* noir; **p. flour** farine *f (sans levure)* **2** *adv Fam (utterly)* complètement ▪ **plainly** *adv (clearly)* clairement; *(frankly)* franchement
**plain²** [pleɪn] *n (land)* plaine *f*
**plait** [plæt] **1** *n* tresse *f*, natte *f* **2** *vt* tresser, natter
**plan** [plæn] **1** *n (proposal, intention)* projet *m*; *(of building, town, essay)* plan *m*; **to go according to p.** se passer comme prévu **2** (*pt & pp* **-nn-**) *vt (arrange)* projeter; *(crime)* comploter; *(building, town)* faire le plan de; **to p. to do** *or* **on doing sth** *(intend)* projeter de faire qch; **as planned** comme prévu **3** *vi* faire des projets
**plane¹** [pleɪn] *n (aircraft)* avion *m*
**plane²** [pleɪn] **1** *n (tool)* rabot *m* **2** *vt* raboter
**plane³** [pleɪn] *n (level, surface) & Fig* plan *m*
**planet** ['plænɪt] *n* planète *f*
**plank** [plæŋk] *n* planche *f*
**planning** ['plænɪŋ] *n* conception *f*; **family p.** planning *m* familial
**plant** [plɑːnt] **1** *n* (**a**) *(living thing)* plante *f* (**b**) *(factory)* usine *f*; *(machinery)* matériel *m* **2** *vt (tree, flower)* planter; *(crops, seeds)* semer; *(field)* ensemencer (**with** en); *Fig (bomb)* poser
**plantation** [plæn'teɪʃən] *n (trees, land)* plantation *f*
**plaque** [plæk] *n (sign)* plaque *f*; *(on teeth)* plaque *f* dentaire
**plaster** ['plɑːstə(r)] **1** *n* (**a**) *(on wall)* plâtre *m*; **to put sb's leg in p.** mettre la jambe de qn dans le plâtre; **p. cast** *(for broken bone)* plâtre *m* (**b**) *Br* **(sticking) p.** pansement *m* adhésif **2** *vt*

*(wall)* plâtrer; **to p. sth with** *(cover)* couvrir qch de

**plastic** ['plæstɪk] **1** *adj (object)* en plastique; **p. bag** sac *m* en plastique; **p. surgery** *(cosmetic)* chirurgie *f* esthétique **2** *n* plastique *m*

**plate** [pleɪt] *n (dish)* assiette *f*; *(metal sheet)* plaque *f*; *(book illustration)* gravure *f*

**plateau** ['plætəʊ] *(pl* **-eaus** [-əʊz] *or* **-eaux**) *n (flat land)* plateau *m*

**platform** ['plætfɔːm] *n (raised surface)* plate-forme *f*; *(in train station)* quai *m*; *(for speaker)* estrade *f*

**platinum** ['plætɪnəm] *n (metal)* platine *m*

**plausible** ['plɔːzəbəl] *adj (argument, excuse)* plausible

**play** [pleɪ] **1** *n (drama)* pièce *f* (de théâtre); *(amusement)* jeu *m*; **to come into p.** entrer en jeu; **a p. on words** un jeu de mots

**2** *vt (part, tune, card)* jouer; *(game)* jouer à; *(instrument)* jouer de; *(match)* disputer (**with** avec); *(team, opponent)* jouer contre; *(record, compact disc)* passer; *(radio, tape recorder)* faire marcher; *Fig* **to p. a part in doing/in sth** contribuer à faire/à qch

**3** *vi* jouer (**with** avec; **at** à); *(of record player, tape recorder)* marcher; *Fam* **what are you playing at?** à quoi tu joues? ▪ **playboy** *n* play-boy *m* ▪ **playground** *n Br (in school)* cour *f* de récréation; *(in park)* terrain *m* de jeux ▪ **playgroup** *n* garderie *f* ▪ **playmate** *n* camarade *mf* de jeu ▪ **playschool** *n* garderie *f* ▪ **playtime** *n (in school)* récréation *f* ▪ **playwright** *n* dramaturge *mf*

▸**play about, play around** *vi* jouer, s'amuser

▸**play back** *vt sep (tape)* réécouter

▸**play down** *vt sep* minimiser

▸**play on** *vt insep (feelings, fears)* jouer sur

▸**play out** *vt sep (scene, fantasy)* jouer

▸**play up** *vi Fam (of child, machine)* faire des siennes

**player** ['pleɪə(r)] *n (in game, of instrument)* joueur *m*, joueuse *f*; **clarinet p.** joueur *m*/joueuse *f* de clarinette

**playful** ['pleɪfəl] *adj (mood, tone)* enjoué; *(child, animal)* joueur (*f* joueuse)

**playing** ['pleɪɪŋ] *n* jeu *m*; **p. card** carte *f* à jouer; **p. field** terrain *m* de jeux

**plc** [piːel'siː] (*abbr* **public limited company**) *n Br Com* ≃ SA *f*

**plea** [pliː] *n (request)* appel *m*

**plead** [pliːd] **1** *vt (argue)* plaider; *(as excuse)* alléguer **2** *vi* **to p. with sb (to do sth)** implorer qn (de faire qch); **to p. guilty** plaider coupable

**pleasant** ['plezənt] *adj* agréable (**to** avec)

**please** [pliːz] **1** *adv* s'il te/vous plaît; **p. sit down** asseyez-vous, je vous prie; **p. do!** bien sûr!, je vous en prie!

**2** *vt* **to p. sb** faire plaisir à qn; *(satisfy)* contenter qn

**3** *vi* plaire; **do as you p.** fais comme tu veux ▪ **pleased** *adj* content (**with** de); **p. to meet you!** enchanté! ▪ **pleasing** *adj* agréable, plaisant

**pleasure** ['pleʒə(r)] *n* plaisir *m*

**pleat** [pliːt] *n* pli *m* ▪ **pleated** *adj* plissé

**pledge** [pledʒ] **1** *n (promise)* promesse *f* (**to do** de faire) **2** *vt* promettre (**to do** de faire)

**plenty** ['plentɪ] *n* **p. of** beaucoup de; **that's p.** *(of food)* merci, j'en ai assez ▪ **plentiful** *adj* abondant

**pliers** ['plaɪəz] *npl* pince *f*

**plight** [plaɪt] *n (crisis)* situation *f* critique

**plimsolls** ['plɪmsəʊlz] *npl Br* tennis *mpl*

**plod** [plɒd] (*pt & pp* **-dd-**) *vi* **to p. (along)** *(walk)* avancer laborieusement; *(work)* travailler laborieusement

**plonk¹** [plɒŋk] *vt Fam* **to p. sth (down)** *(drop)* poser qch

**plonk²** [plɒŋk] *n Br Fam (wine)* pinard *m*

**plot** [plɒt] **1** *n (conspiracy)* complot *m*; *(of novel, film)* intrigue *f*; **p. (of land)** parcelle *f* de terrain **2** (*pt & pp* **-tt-**) *vti* comploter (**to do** de faire) **3** *vt* **to p. (out)** *(route)* déterminer; *(graph)* tracer

**plough** [plaʊ] (*Am* **plow**) **1** *n* charrue *f* **2** *vt (field)* labourer **3** *vi* labourer ▪ **ploughman** (*pl* **-men**) *n Br* **p.'s lunch** = assiette de fromage ou jambon avec de la salade et des condiments

**pluck** [plʌk] **1** *n* courage *m* **2** *vt (hair, feathers)* arracher; *(flower)* cueillir; *(fowl)* plumer; *(eyebrows)* épiler; *(string of guitar)* pincer; **to p. up the courage to do sth** trouver le courage de faire qch ▪ **plucky** (**-ier, -iest**) *adj* courageux, -euse

**plug** [plʌg] **1** *n* (**a**) *(of cotton wool, wood)* tampon *m*; *(for sink, bath)* bonde *f* (**b**) *(electrical) (on device)* fiche *f*; *(socket)* prise *f* (de courant); *Aut* **(spark) p.** bougie *f* **2** (*pt & pp* **-gg-**) *vt* (**a**) **to p. (up)** *(gap, hole)* boucher; **to p. sth in** *(appliance)* brancher qch (**b**) *Fam (promote)* faire de la pub pour ▪ **plughole** *n* trou *m* d'écoulement

**plum** [plʌm] *n* prune *f*

**plumb** [plʌm] *adv Am Fam (crazy)* complètement

▸**plumb in** *vt sep (washing machine)* brancher

**plumber** ['plʌmə(r)] *n* plombier *m* ▪ **plumbing** *n (job, system)* plomberie *f*

**plummet** ['plʌmɪt] *vi (of prices)* s'effondrer; *(of aircraft)* plonger

**plump** [plʌmp] **1** (**-er, -est**) *adj (person, arm)* potelé; *(chicken)* dodu; *(cheek)* rebondi **2** *vi Fam* **to p. for sth** se décider pour qch

**plunder** ['plʌndə(r)] **1** *n (goods)* butin *m* **2** *vt* piller

**plunge** [plʌndʒ] **1** *n (dive)* plongeon *m*; *Fig (decrease)* chute *f*; *Fam* **to take the p.** *(take on difficult task)* se jeter à l'eau; *(get married)* se marier **2** *vt (thrust)* plonger (**into** dans) **3** *vi (dive)* plonger (**into** dans); *Fig (decrease)* chuter

**plural** ['plʊərəl] **1** *adj (noun)* au pluriel **2** *n* pluriel *m*; **in the p.** au pluriel

**plus** [plʌs] **1** *prep* plus; *(as well as)* en plus de **2** *adj (factor) & El* positif, -ive; **twenty p.** plus de vingt **3** (*pl* **plusses** ['plʌsɪz]) *n* **p. (sign)** (signe *m*) plus *m*; **that's a p.** c'est un plus

**ply** [plaɪ] (*pt & pp* **plied**) **1** *vt (trade)* exercer; **to p. sb with questions** bombarder qn de questions **2** *vi* **to p. between** *(travel)* faire la navette entre

**p.m.** [piː'em] *adv (afternoon)* de l'après-midi; *(evening)* du soir

**pneumonia** [njuː'məʊnɪə] *n* pneumonie *f*

**poach** [pəʊtʃ] **1** *vt (egg)* pocher; *(employee)* débaucher **2** *vi (hunt)* braconner

**PO Box** [piː'əʊbɒks] (*abbr* **Post Office Box**) *n* boîte *f* postale, BP *f*

**pocket** ['pɒkɪt] **1** *n* poche *f*; **to be out of p.** en être de sa poche; **p. calculator** calculette *f*; **p. money** argent *m* de poche **2** *vt (put in pocket)* empocher; *Fam (steal)* rafler ▪ **pocketbook** *n Am (handbag)* sac *m* à main ▪ **pocketful** *n* **a p. of** une pleine poche de

**podium** ['pəʊdɪəm] *n* podium *m*

**poem** ['pəʊɪm] *n* poème *m* ▪ **poet** *n* poète *m* ▪ **poetic** [pəʊ'etɪk] *adj* poétique ▪ **poetry** *n* poésie *f*

**poignant** ['pɔɪnjənt] *adj* poignant

**point** [pɔɪnt] **1** *n* (**a**) *(of knife, needle)* pointe *f*; *Br* **points** *(for train)* aiguillage *m*

(**b**) *(dot, score, degree, argument)* point *m*; *(location)* endroit *m*; *(importance)* intérêt *m*; **to make a p. of doing sth** mettre un point d'honneur à faire qch; **you have a p.** tu as raison; **there's no p. (in) staying** ça ne sert à rien de rester; **to get to the p.** en arriver au fait; **at this p. in time** en ce moment; **to be on the p. of doing sth** être sur le point de faire qch; **his good points** ses qualités *fpl*; **p. of view** point *m* de vue

(**c**) *Math* **three p. five** trois virgule cinq

**2** *vt (aim)* diriger; *(camera, gun)* braquer (**at** sur); **to p. one's finger at sb**

montrer qn du doigt; **to p. sth out** *(show)* montrer qch; *(error, fact)* signaler qch
**3** *vi* **to p. at** *or* **to sb/sth** *(with finger)* montrer qn/qch du doigt; **to p. north** *(of arrow, compass)* indiquer le nord

**point-blank** [pɔɪnt'blæŋk] **1** *adj (refusal)* catégorique; **at p. range** à bout portant **2** *adv (refuse)* (tout) net

**pointed** ['pɔɪntɪd] *adj* pointu; *(beard)* en pointe; *Fig (remark, criticism)* pertinent

**pointer** ['pɔɪntə(r)] *n (on dial)* aiguille *f*; *(stick)* baguette *f*; *(clue)* indice *m*

**pointless** ['pɔɪntləs] *adj* inutile

**poise** [pɔɪz] *n (composure)* assurance *f*; *(grace)* grâce *f* ■ **poised** *adj (composed)* calme; *(hanging)* suspendu; *(balanced)* en équilibre; **to be p. to do sth** *(ready)* être prêt à faire qch

**poison** ['pɔɪzən] **1** *n* poison *m*; *(of snake)* venin *m* **2** *vt* empoisonner ■ **poisonous** *adj (fumes, substance)* toxique; *(snake)* venimeux, -euse; *(plant)* vénéneux, -euse

**poke** [pəʊk] **1** *vt (person)* donner un coup à; *(object)* tâter; *(fire)* attiser; **to p. sth into sth** enfoncer qch dans qch; **to p. one's finger at sb** pointer son doigt vers qn; *Fig* **to p. one's nose into sth** mettre son nez dans qch **2** *vi* **to p. at sth** *(with finger, stick)* tâter qch

**poker**[1] ['pəʊkə(r)] *n (for fire)* tisonnier *m*

**poker**[2] ['pəʊkə(r)] *n (card game)* poker *m*

**Poland** ['pəʊlənd] *n* la Pologne ■ **Pole** *n* Polonais, -e *mf* ■ **Polish** ['pəʊlɪʃ] **1** *adj* polonais **2** *n (language)* polonais *m*

**polar** ['pəʊlə(r)] *adj* polaire; **p. bear** ours *m* blanc

**Polaroid**® ['pəʊlərɔɪd] *n (camera, photo)* Polaroid® *m*

**pole**[1] [pəʊl] *n (rod)* perche *f*; *(fixed)* poteau *m*; *(for flag)* hampe *f*; **p. vault** *or* **vaulting** saut *m* à la perche

**pole**[2] [pəʊl] *n Geog* pôle *m*; **North/South P.** pôle *m* Nord/Sud

**police** [pə'li:s] **1** *n* police *f* **2** *adj (inquiry, dog)* policier, -ère; **p. car** voiture *f* de police; **p. station** poste *m* de police **3** *vt (city, area)* maintenir l'ordre dans ■ **policeman** (*pl* **-men**) *n* agent *m* de police ■ **policewoman** (*pl* **-women**) *n* agent *m* de police

**policy** ['pɒlɪsɪ] (*pl* **-ies**) *n* (**a**) *(of government, organization)* politique *f* (**b**) **(insurance) p.** police *f* (d'assurance)

**polio** ['pəʊlɪəʊ] *n* polio *f*

**polish** ['pɒlɪʃ] **1** *n (for shoes)* cirage *m*; *(for floor, furniture)* cire *f*; *(for nails)* vernis *m*; *Fig* raffinement *m*; **to give sth a p.** faire briller qch
**2** *vt (floor, table, shoes)* cirer; *(metal)* astiquer; *Fig (style)* polir; *Fam* **to p. off** *(food)* avaler; *(drink)* descendre; *(work)* expédier; **to p. up one's French** travailler son français

**polite** [pə'laɪt] (**-er, -est**) *adj* poli (**to** *or* **with** avec) ■ **politely** *adv* poliment

**political** [pə'lɪtɪkəl] *adj* politique ■ **politically** *adv* **p. correct** politiquement correct

**politician** [pɒlɪ'tɪʃən] *n* homme *m*/femme *f* politique

**politics** ['pɒlɪtɪks] *n* politique *f*

**poll** [pəʊl] **1** *n (voting)* scrutin *m*; **to go to the polls** aller aux urnes; **(opinion) p.** sondage *m* (d'opinion) **2** *vt (votes)* obtenir; *(people)* sonder

**pollen** ['pɒlən] *n* pollen *m*

**polling** ['pəʊlɪŋ] *n (election)* élections *fpl*; *Br* **p. station,** *Am* **p. place** bureau *m* de vote

**pollute** [pə'lu:t] *vt* polluer ■ **pollution** *n* pollution *f*

**polo** ['pəʊləʊ] *n (sport)* polo *m*; **p. neck** *(sweater, neckline)* col *m* roulé

**polyester** [pɒlɪ'estə(r)] *n* polyester *m*; **p. shirt** chemise *f* en polyester

**polythene** ['pɒlɪθi:n] *n Br* polyéthylène *m*; **p. bag** sac *m* en plastique

**pompous** ['pɒmpəs] *adj* pompeux, -euse

**pond** [pɒnd] *n* étang *m*; *(smaller)* mare *f*; *(artificial)* bassin *m*

**ponder** ['pɒndə(r)] **1** *vt* réfléchir à **2** *vi*

**to p. (over sth)** réfléchir (à qch)
**pong** [pɒŋ] *Br Fam* **1** *n (smell)* puanteur *f* **2** *vi* puer
**pony** ['pəʊnɪ] (*pl* **-ies**) *n* poney *m* ▪ **ponytail** *n* queue *f* de cheval
**poodle** ['puːdəl] *n* caniche *m*
**pool**[1] [puːl] *n (puddle)* flaque *f*; *(of blood)* mare *f*; *(for swimming)* piscine *f*
**pool**[2] [puːl] **1** *n (of money, helpers)* réserve *f*; *(of typists)* pool *m*; *Br* **the (football) pools** = concours de pronostics des matchs de football **2** *vt (share)* mettre en commun
**pool**[3] [puːl] *n (game)* billard *m* américain
**poor** [pʊə(r)] **1** (**-er, -est**) *adj (not rich)* pauvre; *(bad)* mauvais; *(chances)* maigre; *(harvest, reward)* faible; **to be in p. health** ne pas bien se porter **2** *npl* **the p.** les pauvres *mpl* ▪ **poorly 1** *adv* mal; *(clothed, furnished)* pauvrement **2** *adj Br Fam* malade
**pop**[1] [pɒp] **1** *exclam* pan! **2** *n (noise)* bruit *m* sec; **to go p.** faire pan **3** (*pt & pp* **-pp-**) *vt* (**a**) *(balloon)* crever; *(cork)* faire sauter (**b**) *Fam (put)* mettre **4** *vi* (**a**) *(burst)* éclater; *(of cork)* sauter (**b**) *Br Fam* **to p. in** passer; **to p. out** sortir (un instant); **to p. up** surgir
**pop**[2] [pɒp] **1** *n (music)* pop *f* **2** *adj (concert, singer, group)* pop *inv*
**pop**[3] [pɒp] *n Am Fam (father)* papa *m*
**pop**[4] [pɒp] *n Am* **(soda) p.** *(drink)* soda *m*
**popcorn** ['pɒpkɔːn] *n* pop-corn *m inv*
**pope** [pəʊp] *n* pape *m*
**poplar** ['pɒplə(r)] *n (tree, wood)* peuplier *m*
**poppy** ['pɒpɪ] (*pl* **-ies**) *n (red, wild)* coquelicot *m*; *(cultivated)* pavot *m*
**Popsicle**® ['pɒpsɪkəl] *n Am (ice lolly)* ≃ Esquimau® *m*
**popular** ['pɒpjʊlə(r)] *adj* populaire; *(fashionable)* à la mode; *(restaurant)* qui a beaucoup de succès ▪ **popularity** [-'lærətɪ] *n* popularité *f* (**with** auprès de)
**populated** ['pɒpjʊleɪtɪd] *adj* **densely/sparsely populated** très/peu peuplé
**population** [pɒpjʊ'leɪʃən] *n* population *f*
**porcelain** ['pɔːsəlɪn] *n* porcelaine *f*
**porch** [pɔːtʃ] *n* porche *m*; *Am (veranda)* véranda *f*
**pore** [pɔː(r)] **1** *n (of skin)* pore *m* **2** *vi* **to p. over sth** *(book, question)* étudier qch de près
**pork** [pɔːk] *n (meat)* porc *m*; **p. pie** ≃ pâté *m* en croûte
**pornography** [pɔː'nɒgrəfɪ] *n* pornographie *f*
**porridge** ['pɒrɪdʒ] *n* porridge *m*
**port**[1] [pɔːt] *n (harbour)* port *m*; **p. of call** escale *f*
**port**[2] [pɔːt] *n Naut (left-hand side)* bâbord *m*
**port**[3] [pɔːt] *n (wine)* porto *m*
**portable** ['pɔːtəbəl] *adj* portable
**porter** ['pɔːtə(r)] *n (for luggage)* porteur *m*; *(door attendant)* chasseur *m*
**portfolio** [pɔːt'fəʊlɪəʊ] (*pl* **-os**) *n (for documents)* porte-documents *m inv*; *(of shares, government minister)* portefeuille *m*
**porthole** ['pɔːthəʊl] *n* hublot *m*
**portion** ['pɔːʃən] *n* partie *f*; *(share, helping)* portion *f*
**portrait** ['pɔːtreɪt, 'pɔːtrɪt] *n* portrait *m*
**portray** [pɔː'treɪ] *vt (describe)* dépeindre ▪ **portrayal** *n (description)* tableau *m*
**Portugal** ['pɔːtjʊgəl] *n* le Portugal ▪ **Portuguese** [-'giːz] **1** *adj* portugais **2** *n (person)* Portugais, -e *mf*; *(language)* portugais *m*; **the P.** *(people)* les Portugais
**pose** [pəʊz] **1** *n (position)* pose *f* **2** *vt (question)* poser; *(threat)* représenter **3** *vi* poser (**for** pour); **to p. as a lawyer** se faire passer pour un avocat
**posh** [pɒʃ] *adj Fam (smart)* chic *inv*
**position** [pə'zɪʃən] **1** *n (place, posture, opinion)* position *f*; *(of building, town)* emplacement *m*; *(job, circumstances)* situation *f*; **in a p. to do sth** en mesure de faire qch; **in p.** en place **2** *vt (put)* placer; *(troops)* poster

**positive** ['pɒzɪtɪv] *adj (person, answer, test)* positif, -ive; *(progress, change)* réel (*f* réelle); *(certain)* sûr, certain (**of** de; **that** que) ▪ **positively** *adv (identify)* formellement; *(think, react)* de façon positive; *(for emphasis)* véritablement

**possess** [pə'zes] *vt* posséder ▪ **possession** *n (ownership)* possession *f*; *(thing possessed)* bien *m*; **to be in p. of sth** être en possession de qch

**possessive** [pə'zesɪv] **1** *adj* possessif, -ive **2** *adj & n (in grammar)* possessif *(m)*

**possibility** [pɒsə'bɪlətɪ] (*pl* **-ies**) *n* possibilité *f*

**possible** ['pɒsəbəl] *adj* possible; **it is p. (for us) to do it** il (nous) est possible de le faire; **it is p. that...** il est possible que... *(+ subjunctive)*; **as soon as p.** dès que possible

**possibly** ['pɒsəblɪ] *adv* (**a**) *(perhaps)* peut-être (**b**) *(for emphasis)* **to do all one p. can** faire tout son possible (**to do** pour faire); **he cannot p. stay** il ne peut absolument pas rester

**post-** [pəʊst] *pref* post-; **post-1800** après 1800

**post¹** [pəʊst] **1** *n Br (postal system)* poste *f*; *(letters)* courrier *m*; **by p.** par la poste; **p. office** (bureau *m* de) poste *f* **2** *vt (letter)* poster; **to keep sb posted** tenir qn au courant ▪ **postbox** *n Br* boîte *f* aux lettres ▪ **postcard** *n* carte *f* postale ▪ **postcode** *n Br* code *m* postal ▪ **postdate** *vt* postdater ▪ **postman** (*pl* **-men**) *n Br* facteur *m* ▪ **postmark** *n* cachet *m* de la poste

**post²** [pəʊst] **1** *n (job, place)* poste *m* **2** *vt (sentry, guard)* poster; *Br (employee)* affecter (**to** à)

**post³** [pəʊst] *n (pole)* poteau *m*; *(of door, bed)* montant *m*; **finishing** *or* **winning p.** *(in race)* poteau *m* d'arrivée

**postage** ['pəʊstɪdʒ] *n* affranchissement *m* (**to** pour); **p. paid** port *m* payé; **p. stamp** timbre-poste *m*

**postal** ['pəʊstəl] *adj (services)* postal; *(vote)* par correspondance; *Br* **p. order** mandat *m* postal

**poster** ['pəʊstə(r)] *n* affiche *f*; *(for decoration)* poster *m*

**postgraduate** [pəʊst'grædjʊət] **1** *adj* de troisième cycle **2** *n* étudiant, -e *mf* de troisième cycle

**posthumous** ['pɒstjʊməs] *adj* posthume

**postmortem** [pəʊst'mɔːtəm] *adj & n* **p. (examination)** autopsie *f* (**on** de)

**postpone** [pəʊs'pəʊn] *vt* reporter

**posture** ['pɒstʃə(r)] *n (of body)* posture *f*; *Fig* attitude *f*

**postwar** ['pəʊstwɔː(r)] *adj* d'après-guerre

**posy** ['pəʊzɪ] (*pl* **-ies**) *n* petit bouquet *m*

**pot¹** [pɒt] *n* pot *m*; *(for cooking)* casserole *f*; *Fam* **to go to p.** aller à la ruine

**pot²** [pɒt] *n Fam (drug)* hasch *m*

**potato** [pə'teɪtəʊ] (*pl* **-oes**) *n* pomme *f* de terre; *Br* **p. crisps,** *Am* **p. chips** chips *fpl*

**potent** ['pəʊtənt] *adj* puissant; *(drink)* fort

**potential** [pə'tenʃəl] **1** *adj* potentiel, -elle **2** *n* potentiel *m*; **to have p.** avoir du potentiel

**pothole** ['pɒthəʊl] *n (in road)* nid-de-poule *m*; *(cave)* caverne *f*

**potion** ['pəʊʃən] *n* potion *f*

**potter** ['pɒtə(r)] **1** *n (person)* potier, -ère *mf* **2** *vi Br* **to p. about** *(do odd jobs)* bricoler ▪ **pottery** *n (art)* poterie *f*; *(objects)* poteries *fpl*; **a piece of p.** une poterie

**potty¹** ['pɒtɪ] *n (for baby)* pot *m*

**potty²** ['pɒtɪ] (**-ier, -iest**) *adj Br Fam (mad)* dingue

**pouch** [paʊtʃ] *n* bourse *f*; *(for tobacco)* blague *f*

**poultry** ['pəʊltrɪ] *n* volaille *f*

**pounce** [paʊns] *vi (of animal)* bondir (**on** sur); *(of person)* se précipiter (**on** sur)

**pound¹** [paʊnd] *n* (**a**) *(weight)* livre *f* (*= 453,6 g*) (**b**) **p. (sterling)** livre *f* (sterling)

**pound²** [paʊnd] *n (for cars, dogs)* fourrière *f*

**pound³** [paʊnd] **1** *vt Mil (town)* pilonner **2** *vi (of heart)* battre à tout rompre

**pour** [pɔː(r)] **1** *vt* verser; **to p. sb a drink** verser à boire à qn **2** *vi* **it's pouring** il pleut à verse

▸ **pour down** *vi* **it's pouring down** il pleut à verse

▸ **pour in 1** *vt sep (liquid)* verser **2** *vi (of water, sunshine)* entrer à flots; *Fig (of people, money)* affluer

▸ **pour off** *vt sep (liquid)* vider

▸ **pour out 1** *vt sep (liquid)* verser; *Fig (anger, grief)* déverser **2** *vi (of liquid)* se déverser; *Fig (of people)* sortir en masse (**from** de)

**pout** [paʊt] *vi* faire la moue

**poverty** ['pɒvətɪ] *n* pauvreté *f*

**powder** ['paʊdə(r)] **1** *n* poudre *f*; **p. puff** houppette *f*; **p. room** toilettes *fpl* pour dames **2** *vt (body, skin)* poudrer; **to p. one's face** *or* **nose** se poudrer ▪ **powdered** *adj (milk, eggs)* en poudre

**power** ['paʊə(r)] **1** *n (ability, authority)* pouvoir *m*; *(strength, nation)* puissance *f*; *(energy)* énergie *f*; *(electric current)* courant *m*; **to be in p.** être au pouvoir; **to have sb in one's p.** tenir qn à sa merci; *Br* **p. failure** *or* **cut** coupure *f* de courant; *Br* **p. station,** *Am* **p. plant** centrale *f* électrique; *Aut* **p. steering** direction *f* assistée

**2** *vt (provide with power)* actionner

**powerful** ['paʊəfəl] *adj* puissant; *(drug)* fort ▪ **powerless** *adj* impuissant (**to do** à faire)

**PR** [piː'ɑː(r)] (*abbr* **public relations**) *n* RP *fpl*

**practical** ['præktɪkəl] *adj (tool, knowledge, solution)* pratique; **to be p.** *(of person)* avoir l'esprit pratique; **p. joke** farce *f*

**practically** ['præktɪkəlɪ] *adv (almost)* pratiquement

**practice** ['præktɪs] **1** *n (action, exercise, custom)* pratique *f*; *(in sport)* entraînement *m*; *(surgery)* centre *m* médical; **in p.** *(in reality)* dans la *ou* en pratique; **to put sth into p.** mettre qch en pratique; **to be out of p.** avoir perdu l'habitude **2** *vti Am* = **practise**

**practise** ['præktɪs] (*Am* **practice**) **1** *vt (sport, language, art, religion)* pratiquer; *(medicine, law)* exercer; *(musical instrument)* travailler

**2** *vi (of musician)* s'exercer; *(of sportsperson)* s'entraîner; *(of doctor, lawyer)* exercer ▪ **practising** *adj (doctor, lawyer)* en exercice; *Rel* pratiquant

**practitioner** [præk'tɪʃənə(r)] *n* **general p.** (médecin *m*) généraliste *m*

**pragmatic** [præg'mætɪk] *adj* pragmatique

**Prairie** ['preərɪ] *n* **the P.** *(in USA)* la (Grande) Prairie; *(in Canada)* les Prairies *fpl*

**praise** [preɪz] **1** *n* éloges *mpl* **2** *vt* faire l'éloge de; *(God)* louer; **to p. sb for doing** *or* **having done sth** louer qn d'avoir fait qch

**pram** [præm] *n Br* landau *m* (*pl* -aus)

**prank** [præŋk] *n* farce *f*

**prawn** [prɔːn] *n* crevette *f* rose

**pray** [preɪ] **1** *vt* **to p. that...** prier pour que... *(+ subjunctive)* **2** *vi* prier; *Fig* **to p. for good weather** prier pour qu'il fasse beau

**prayer** [preə(r)] *n* prière *f*

**pre-** [priː] *pref* **pre-1800** avant 1800

**preach** [priːtʃ] *vti* prêcher; **to p. to sb** prêcher qn; *Fig* faire la morale à qn ▪ **preacher** *n* prédicateur, -trice *mf*

**prearrange** [priːə'reɪndʒ] *vt* arranger à l'avance

**precarious** [prɪ'keərɪəs] *adj* précaire

**precaution** [prɪ'kɔːʃən] *n* précaution *f*; **as a p.** par précaution

**precede** [prɪ'siːd] *vti* précéder

**precedence** ['presɪdəns] *n* **to take p. over sb** avoir la préséance sur qn; **to take p. over sth** passer avant qch

**precedent** ['presɪdənt] *n* précédent *m*

**precinct** ['priːsɪŋkt] *n Br (for shopping)* zone *f* commerçante piétonnière; *Am (electoral district)* circonscription *f*; *Am (police district)* secteur *m*

**precious** ['preʃəs] **1** *adj* précieux, -euse **2** *adv* **p. little** très peu (de)
**precipice** ['presɪpɪs] *n* précipice *m*
**precipitate** [prɪ'sɪpɪteɪt] *vt (hasten, throw)* & *Chem* précipiter
**precise** [prɪ'saɪs] *adj (exact)* précis; *(meticulous)* méticuleux, -euse ▪ **precisely** *adv* précisément; **at three o'clock p.** à trois heures précises ▪ **precision** [-'sɪʒən] *n* précision *f*
**preclude** [prɪ'klu:d] *vt (prevent)* empêcher (**from doing** de faire); *(possibility)* exclure
**precocious** [prɪ'kəʊʃəs] *adj* précoce
**preconception** [pri:kən'sepʃən] *n* idée *f* préconçue
**precondition** [pri:kən'dɪʃən] *n* condition *f* préalable
**predator** ['predətə(r)] *n* prédateur *m*
**predecessor** ['pri:dɪsesə(r)] *n* prédécesseur *m*
**predicament** [prɪ'dɪkəmənt] *n* situation *f* difficile
**predict** [prɪ'dɪkt] *vt* prédire ▪ **predictable** *adj* prévisible ▪ **prediction** *n* prédiction *f*
**predispose** [pri:dɪs'pəʊz] *vt* prédisposer (**to do** à faire)
**predominant** [prɪ'dɒmɪnənt] *adj* prédominant ▪ **predominate** *vi* prédominer (**over** sur)
**pre-empt** [pri:'empt] *vt* devancer
**preface** ['prefɪs] *n (of book)* préface *f*
**prefect** ['pri:fekt] *n Br Sch* = élève chargé de la surveillance
**prefer** [prɪ'fɜ:(r)] *(pt & pp* **-rr-***) vt* préférer (**to** à); **to p. to do sth** préférer faire qch
**preferable** ['prefərəbəl] *adj* préférable (**to** à)
**preference** ['prefərəns] *n* préférence *f* (**for** pour); **in p. to** plutôt que
**prefix** ['pri:fɪks] *n (before word)* préfixe *m*
**pregnant** ['pregnənt] *adj (woman)* enceinte; *(animal)* pleine; **five months p.** enceinte de cinq mois ▪ **pregnancy** *(pl* **-ies***) n* grossesse *f*; **p. test** test *m* de grossesse
**prehistoric** [pri:hɪ'stɒrɪk] *adj* préhistorique
**prejudge** [pri:'dʒʌdʒ] *vt (question)* préjuger de; *(person)* juger sans connaître
**prejudice** ['predʒədɪs] **1** *n (bias)* préjugé *m* **2** *vt (bias)* prévenir (**against/in favour of** contre/en faveur de); *(harm)* nuire à ▪ **prejudiced** *adj* **to be p.** avoir des préjugés (**against/in favour of** contre/en faveur de)
**preliminary** [prɪ'lɪmɪnərɪ] *adj* préliminaire ▪ **preliminaries** *npl* préliminaires *mpl*
**prelude** ['prelju:d] *n* prélude *m* (**to** à)
**premature** [*Br* 'premətʃʊə(r), *Am* pri:mə'tʃʊər] *adj* prématuré
**premeditate** [pri:'medɪteɪt] *vt* préméditer
**premier** [*Br* 'premɪə(r), *Am* prɪ'mɪər] *n* Premier ministre *m*
**première** [*Br* 'premɪeə(r), *Am* prɪ'mɪər] *n (of play, film)* première *f*
**premises** ['premɪsɪz] *npl* locaux *mpl*; **on the p.** sur place
**premium** ['pri:mɪəm] *n Fin (for insurance)* prime *f*; *(additional sum)* supplément *m*
**premonition** [*Br* premə'nɪʃən, *Am* pri:mə'nɪʃən] *n* prémonition *f*
**prenatal** [pri:'neɪtəl] *adj Am* prénatal
**preoccupy** [pri:'ɒkjʊpaɪ] *(pt & pp* **-ied***) vt* préoccuper au plus haut point; **to be preoccupied** être préoccupé (**with** par) ▪ **preoccupation** *n* préoccupation *f* (**with** pour)
**prep** [prep] *adj* **p. school** *Br* école *f* primaire privée; *Am* école *f* secondaire privée
**pre-packed** [pri:'pækt] *adj (meat, vegetables)* préemballé
**prepaid** [pri:'peɪd] *adj* prépayé
**preparation** [prepə'reɪʃən] *n* préparation *f*; **preparations** préparatifs *mpl* (**for** de)
**preparatory** [prə'pærətərɪ] *adj* préparatoire; **p. school** *Br* école *f* primaire privée; *Am* école *f* secondaire privée

**prepare** [prɪˈpeə(r)] **1** *vt* préparer (**sth for** qch pour; **sb for** qn à) **2** *vi* se préparer pour; **to p. to do sth** se préparer à faire qch ▪ **prepared** *adj (ready)* prêt (**to do** à faire); **to be p. for sth** s'attendre à qch

**preposition** [prepəˈzɪʃən] *n* préposition *f*

**preposterous** [prɪˈpɒstərəs] *adj* ridicule

**prerecorded** [priːrɪˈkɔːdɪd] *adj* préenregistré

**prerequisite** [priːˈrekwɪzɪt] *n* (condition *f*) préalable *m*

**prerogative** [prɪˈrɒgətɪv] *n* prérogative *f*

**preschool** [ˈpriːskuːl] *adj* préscolaire

**prescribe** [prɪˈskraɪb] *vt (of doctor)* prescrire ▪ **prescribed** *adj (textbook)* (inscrit) au programme ▪ **prescription** *n (for medicine)* ordonnance *f*; **on p.** sur ordonnance

**presence** [ˈprezəns] *n* présence *f*; **in the p. of** en présence de; **p. of mind** présence *f* d'esprit

**present**[1] [ˈprezənt] **1** *adj* (**a**) *(in attendance)* présent (**at** à; **in** dans) (**b**) *(current)* actuel, -elle; **the p. tense** le présent **2** *n* **the p.** *(time, tense)* le présent; **for the p.** pour l'instant; **at p.** en ce moment ▪ **present-day** *adj* actuel, -elle ▪ **presently** *adv (soon)* bientôt; *Am (now)* actuellement

**present**[2] **1** [ˈprezənt] *n (gift)* cadeau *m* **2** [prɪˈzent] *vt (show, introduce)* présenter (**to** à); *(concert, film)* donner; **to p. sb with** *(gift)* offrir à qn; *(prize)* remettre à qn ▪ **presentable** [prɪˈzentəbəl] *adj (person, appearance)* présentable ▪ **presenter** [prɪˈzentə(r)] *n* présentateur, -trice *mf*

**presentation** [prezənˈteɪʃən] *n* présentation *f*; *(of prize)* remise *f*

**preservation** [prezəˈveɪʃən] *n (of building)* conservation *f*; *(of species)* protection *f*

**preservative** [prɪˈzɜːvətɪv] *n* conservateur *m*

**preserve** [prɪˈzɜːv] **1** *n (jam)* confiture *f* **2** *vt (keep, maintain)* conserver; *(fruit)* mettre en conserve

**preside** [prɪˈzaɪd] *vi* présider; **to p. over** *or* **at a meeting** présider une réunion

**presidency** [ˈprezɪdənsɪ] (*pl* **-ies**) *n* présidence *f*

**president** [ˈprezɪdənt] *n (of country)* président, -e *mf* ▪ **presidential** [-ˈdenʃəl] *adj* présidentiel, -elle

**press**[1] [pres] *n* (**a**) **the p.** *(newspapers)* la presse; **p. conference** conférence *f* de presse; **p. release** communiqué *m* de presse (**b**) *(machine)* presse *f*; *(for making wine)* pressoir *m*; **(printing) p.** presse *f*

**press**[2] [pres] **1** *n* **to give sth a p.** *(clothes)* repasser qch; **p. stud** bouton-pression *m* **2** *vt (button, doorbell)* appuyer sur; *(hand)* serrer; *(clothes)* repasser; **to p. sb to do sth** presser qn de faire qch **3** *vi (push)* appuyer (**on** sur); *(of weight)* faire pression (**on** sur) ▪ **press-up** *n (exercise)* pompe *f*

▸ **press down** *vt insep (button)* appuyer sur

▸ **press for** *vt sep (demand)* exiger

▸ **press on** *vi (carry on)* continuer

**pressed** [prest] *adj* **to be hard p.** *(in difficulties)* être en difficulté; **to be p. for time** être pressé par le temps

**pressing** [ˈpresɪŋ] *adj (urgent)* pressant

**pressure** [ˈpreʃə(r)] **1** *n* pression *f*; **to be under p.** être stressé; **to put p. on sb (to do sth)** faire pression sur qn (pour qu'il fasse qch) **2** *vt* **to p. sb to do sth** *or* **into doing sth** faire pression sur qn pour qu'il fasse qch

**pressurize** [ˈpreʃəraɪz] *vt* **to p. sb (into doing sth)** faire pression sur qn (pour qu'il fasse qch)

**prestige** [preˈstiːʒ] *n* prestige *m* ▪ **prestigious** [presˈtɪdʒəs, *Am* preˈstiːdʒəs] *adj* prestigieux, -euse

**presume** [prɪˈzjuːm] *vt (suppose)* présumer (**that** que) ▪ **presumably** *adv* sans doute ■ **presumption** [-'zʌmpʃən] *n* présomption *f*

**presumptuous** [prɪ'zʌmptʃʊəs] *adj* présomptueux, -euse

**pretence** [prɪ'tens] (*Am* **pretense**) *n* *(sham)* simulation *f*; *(claim, affectation)* prétention *f*; **to make a p. of doing sth** feindre de faire qch; **under false pretences** sous des prétextes fallacieux

**pretend** [prɪ'tend] **1** *vt (make believe)* faire semblant (**to do** de faire); *(claim, maintain)* prétendre (**to do** faire; **that** que) **2** *vi* faire semblant

**pretense** [prɪ'tens] *n Am* = **pretence**

**pretentious** [prɪ'tenʃəs] *adj* prétentieux, -euse

**pretext** ['pri:tekst] *n* prétexte *m*; **on the p. of/that** sous prétexte de/que

**pretty** ['prɪtɪ] **1** (**-ier, -iest**) *adj* joli **2** *adv Fam (rather, quite)* assez; **p. well, p. much** *(almost)* pratiquement

**prevail** [prɪ'veɪl] *vi (predominate)* prédominer; *(be successful)* l'emporter (**over** sur); **to p. (up)on sb to do sth** persuader qn de faire qch ■ **prevailing** *adj* prédominant; *(wind)* dominant

**prevalent** ['prevələnt] *adj* très répandu

**prevent** [prɪ'vent] *vt* empêcher (**from doing** de faire) ■ **prevention** *n* prévention *f*

**preview** ['pri:vju:] *n (of film, play)* avant-première *f*

**previous** ['pri:vɪəs] **1** *adj* précédent; **to have p. experience** avoir une expérience préalable **2** *adv* **p. to** avant ■ **previously** *adv* auparavant

**prewar** ['pri:'wɔ:(r)] *adj* d'avant-guerre

**prey** [preɪ] **1** *n* proie *f*; *Fig* **to be (a) p. to** être en proie à **2** *vi* **to p. on** *(person)* prendre pour cible; *(fears, doubts)* exploiter; **to p. on sb's mind** tourmenter qn

**price** [praɪs] **1** *n* prix *m*; **he wouldn't do it at any p.** il ne le ferait à aucun prix **2** *adj (control, rise)* des prix; **p. list** tarif *m* **3** *vt* **it's priced at £5** ça coûte 5 livres ■ **priceless** *adj (invaluable)* qui n'a pas de prix

**pricey** ['praɪsɪ] (**-ier, -iest**) *adj Fam* cher (*f* chère)

**prick** [prɪk] **1** *n (of needle)* piqûre *f* **2** *vt (jab)* piquer (**with** avec); *(burst)* crever ■ **prickly** (**-ier, -iest**) *adj (plant)* à épines; *(animal)* couvert de piquants; *(beard)* piquant

**pride** [praɪd] **1** *n (satisfaction)* fierté *f*; *(self-esteem)* amour-propre *m*; *Pej (vanity)* orgueil *m*; **to take p. in sth** mettre toute sa fierté dans qch **2** *vt* **to p. oneself on sth/on doing sth** s'enorgueillir de qch/de faire qch

**priest** [pri:st] *n* prêtre *m*

**prim** [prɪm] (**primmer, primmest**) *adj* **p. (and proper)** *(person)* collet monté *inv*; *(manner)* guindé

**primarily** [*Br* 'praɪmərəlɪ, *Am* praɪ'merəlɪ] *adv* essentiellement

**primary** ['praɪmərɪ] **1** *adj (main)* principal; *Br* **p. school** école *f* primaire **2** (*pl* **-ies**) *n Am (election)* primaire *f*

**prime** [praɪm] **1** *adj (principal)* principal; *(importance)* capital; *(excellent)* excellent; **P. Minister** Premier ministre *m*; *Math* **p. number** nombre *m* premier

**2** *n* **in the p. of life** dans la fleur de l'âge

**3** *vt (surface)* apprêter ■ **primer** *n* (**a**) *(book)* manuel *m* élémentaire (**b**) *(paint)* apprêt *m*

**primitive** ['prɪmɪtɪv] *adj (original)* primitif, -ive; *(basic)* de base

**prince** [prɪns] *n* prince *m* ■ **princess** *n* princesse *f*

**principal** ['prɪnsɪpəl] **1** *adj (main)* principal **2** *n (of school)* proviseur *m*; *(of university)* ≃ président, -e *mf*

**principle** ['prɪnsɪpəl] *n* principe *m*; **in p.** en principe; **on p.** par principe

**print** [prɪnt] **1** *n (of finger, foot)* empreinte *f*; *(letters)* caractères *mpl*; *(engraving)* estampe *f*; *(photo)* épreuve *f*; *(fabric)* imprimé *m*; **out of p.** *(book)* épuisé

2 *vt (book, newspaper)* imprimer; *(photo)* tirer; *(write)* écrire en script; *Comptr* **to p. out** imprimer ▪ **printed** *adj* imprimé; **p. matter** imprimés *mpl* ▪ **printing** *n (technique, industry)* imprimerie *f*; *(action)* tirage *m*; **p. error** faute *f* d'impression ▪ **printout** *n Comptr* sortie *f* papier

**printer** ['prɪntə(r)] *n (machine)* imprimante *f*

**prior** ['praɪə(r)] **1** *adj* antérieur; *(experience)* préalable **2** *adv* **p. to sth** avant qch

**priority** [praɪ'ɒrətɪ] (*pl* **-ies**) *n* priorité *f* (**over** sur)

**prison** ['prɪzən] **1** *n* prison *f*; **in p.** en prison **2** *adj (life, system)* pénitentiaire; *(camp)* de prisonniers; **p. officer** gardien, -enne *mf* de prison ▪ **prisoner** *n* prisonnier, -ère *mf*; **to take sb p.** faire qn prisonnier; **p. of war** prisonnier *m* de guerre

**privacy** ['praɪvəsɪ, *Br* 'prɪvəsɪ] *n* intimité *f*

**private** ['praɪvɪt] **1** *adj* privé; *(lesson)* particulier, -ère; *(letter)* confidentiel, -elle; *(personal)* personnel, -elle; *(dinner, wedding)* intime; **p. detective, p. investigator,** *Fam* **p. eye** détective *m* privé

**2** *n* (**a**) **in p.** *(not publicly)* en privé; *(have dinner, get married)* dans l'intimité (**b**) *(soldier)* simple soldat *m*

**privately** ['praɪvɪtlɪ] *adv (in private)* en privé; *(in one's heart of hearts)* en son for intérieur; *(personally)* à titre personnel; **p. owned** *(company)* privé

**privatize** ['praɪvətaɪz] *vt* privatiser

**privilege** ['prɪvɪlɪdʒ] *n* privilège *m* ▪ **privileged** *adj* privilégié; **to be p. to do sth** avoir le privilège de faire qch

**prize**[1] [praɪz] *n* prix *m*; *(in lottery)* lot *m* ▪ **prizegiving** *n* distribution *f* des prix ▪ **prizewinner** *n (in contest)* lauréat, -e *mf*; *(in lottery)* gagnant, -e *mf*

**prize**[2] [praɪz] *vt (value)* attacher de la valeur à

**prize**[3] [praɪz] *vt Br* = **prise**

**pro** [prəʊ] (*pl* **pros**) *n Fam (professional)* pro *mf*

**probable** ['prɒbəbəl] *adj* probable (**that** que) ▪ **probability** (*pl* **-ies**) *n* probabilité *f*; **in all p.** selon toute probabilité ▪ **probably** *adv* probablement

**probation** [prə'beɪʃən] *n* **on p.** *(criminal)* en liberté surveillée; *(in job)* en période d'essai

**probe** [prəʊb] **1** *n (device)* sonde *f*; *(inquiry)* enquête *f* (**into** dans) **2** *vt (prod)* sonder; *(inquire into)* enquêter sur **3** *vi* **to p. into sth** *(past, private life)* fouiller dans qch ▪ **probing** *adj (question)* perspicace

**problem** ['prɒbləm] *n* problème *m*; *Fam* **no p.!** pas de problème! ▪ **problematic** *adj* problématique

**procedure** [prə'siːdʒə(r)] *n* procédure *f*

**proceed** [prə'siːd] *vi (go on)* se poursuivre; **to p. with sth** poursuivre qch; **to p. to do sth** se mettre à faire qch

**proceedings** [prə'siːdɪŋz] *npl (events)* opérations *fpl*; **to take (legal) p.** intenter un procès (**against** contre)

**proceeds** ['prəʊsiːdz] *npl* recette *f*

**process** ['prəʊses] **1** *n* processus *m*; *(method)* procédé *m*; **in the p. of doing sth** en train de faire qch **2** *vt (food, data)* traiter; *(film)* développer; **processed food** aliments *mpl* conditionnés

**procession** [prə'seʃən] *n* défilé *m*

**processor** ['prəʊsesə(r)] *n Comptr* processeur *m*; **food p.** robot *m* de cuisine

**proclaim** [prə'kleɪm] *vt* proclamer (**that** que); **to p. sb king** proclamer qn roi

**prod** [prɒd] (*pt & pp* **-dd-**) *vt (poke)* donner un petit coup dans

**prodigy** ['prɒdɪdʒɪ] (*pl* **-ies**) *n* prodige *m*; **child p.** enfant *mf* prodige

**produce**[1] [prə'djuːs] *vt (create)* produire; *(machine)* fabriquer; *(passport, ticket)* présenter; *(documents)* fournir; *(from bag, pocket)* sortir; *(film, play,* *programme)* produire ▪ **producer** *n* producteur, -trice *mf*

**produce²** ['prɒdju:s] *n (products)* produits *mpl*

**product** ['prɒdʌkt] *n (article, creation) & Math* produit *m*

**production** [prə'dʌkʃən] *n* production *f*; *(of play)* mise *f* en scène; **to work on a p. line** travailler à la chaîne

**productive** [prə'dʌktɪv] *adj* productif, -ive ▪ **productivity** [prɒdʌk'tɪvətɪ] *n* productivité *f*

**profession** [prə'feʃən] *n* profession *f*; **by p.** de profession ▪ **professional 1** *adj* professionnel, -elle; *(man, woman)* qui exerce une profession libérale; *(army)* de métier; *(piece of work)* de professionnel **2** *n* professionnel, -elle *mf*

**professor** [prə'fesə(r)] *n Br* ≃ professeur *m* d'université; *Am* = enseignant d'université

**proficient** [prə'fɪʃənt] *adj* compétent (**in** en)

**profile** ['prəʊfaɪl] *n (of person, object)* profil *m*; *(description)* portrait *m*; **in p.** de profil; *Fig* **to keep a low p.** garder un profil bas

**profit** ['prɒfɪt] **1** *n* profit *m*, bénéfice *m*; **to sell at a p.** vendre à profit **2** *vi* **to p. by** *or* **from sth** tirer profit de qch ▪ **profit-making** *adj (aiming to make profit)* à but lucratif; *(profitable)* rentable

**profitable** ['prɒfɪtəbəl] *adj (commercially)* rentable; *Fig (worthwhile)* profitable

**profound** [prə'faʊnd] *adj* profond ▪ **profoundly** *adv* profondément

**profusely** [prə'fju:slɪ] *adv (bleed)* abondamment; *(thank)* avec effusion; **to apologize p.** se confondre en excuses

**programme** ['prəʊgræm] (*Am* **program**) **1** *n (for play, political party, computer)* programme *m*; *(on TV, radio)* émission *f* **2** (*pt & pp* **-mm-**) *vt (machine)* programmer ▪ **programmer** *n* **(computer) p.** programmeur, -euse *mf* ▪ **programming** *n* **(computer) p.** programmation *f*

**progress 1** ['prəʊgres] *n* progrès *m*; **to make (good) p.** faire des progrès; **in p.** en cours **2** [prə'gres] *vi (advance, improve)* progresser; *(of story, meeting)* se dérouler

**progressive** [prə'gresɪv] *adj (gradual)* progressif, -ive; *(company, ideas, political party)* progressiste

**prohibit** [prə'hɪbɪt] *vt* interdire (**sb from doing** à qn de faire)

**prohibitive** [prə'hɪbɪtɪv] *adj* prohibitif, -ive

**project 1** ['prɒdʒekt] *n (plan, undertaking)* projet *m*; *(at school)* dossier *m*; *Am* **(housing) p.** cité *f* HLM **2** [prə'dʒekt] *vt (propel, show)* projeter **3** [prə'dʒekt] *vi (protrude)* dépasser

**projector** [prə'dʒektə(r)] *n* projecteur *m*

**proliferate** [prə'lɪfəreɪt] *vi* proliférer

**prolific** [prə'lɪfɪk] *adj* prolifique

**prologue** ['prəʊlɒg] *n* prologue *m* (**to** de)

**prolong** [prə'lɒŋ] *vt* prolonger

**prom** [prɒm] (*abbr* **promenade**) *n* (**a**) *Br (at seaside)* front *m* de mer (**b**) *Am (dance)* bal *m* d'étudiants

**promenade** [prɒmə'nɑ:d] *n Br (at seaside)* front *m* de mer

**prominent** ['prɒmɪnənt] *adj (important)* important; *(nose, chin)* proéminent ▪ **prominently** *adv* bien en vue

**promiscuous** [prə'mɪskjʊəs] *adj (person)* qui a de multiples partenaires

**promise** ['prɒmɪs] **1** *n* promesse *f*; **to show p.** promettre **2** *vt* promettre (**to do** de faire); **to p. sth to sb, to p. sb sth** promettre qch à qn **3** *vi* **I p.!** je te le promets! ▪ **promising** *adj* prometteur, -euse

**promote** [prə'məʊt] *vt (raise in rank, encourage)* promouvoir; *(advertise)* faire la promotion de ▪ **promotion** *n* promotion *f*

**prompt¹** [prɒmpt] **1** *adj (speedy)* rapide; *(punctual)* ponctuel, -elle **2** *adv* **at eight o'clock p.** à huit heures précises ■ **promptly** *adv (rapidly)* rapidement; *(punctually)* ponctuellement; *(immediately)* immédiatement

**prompt²** [prɒmpt] *vt* (**a**) *(cause)* provoquer; **to p. sb to do sth** pousser qn à faire qch (**b**) *(actor)* souffler à

**prone** [prəʊn] *adj* **to be p. to sth** être sujet, -ette à qch; **to be p. to do sth** avoir tendance à faire qch

**pronoun** ['prəʊnaʊn] *n* pronom *m*

**pronounce** [prə'naʊns] *vt (say, articulate)* prononcer ■ **pronunciation** [-nʌnsɪ'eɪʃən] *n* prononciation *f*

**proof** [pru:f] *n (evidence)* preuve *f*; *(of book, photo)* épreuve *f*; **p. of identity** pièce *f* d'identité ■ **proofreader** *n* correcteur, -trice *mf*

**prop** [prɒp] **1** *n (physical support)* support *m*; *(in a play)* accessoire *m* **2** *(pt & pp* **-pp-***) vt* **to p. sth (up) against sth** appuyer qch contre qch; **to p. sth up** *(building, tunnel)* étayer qch; *Fig (economy, regime)* soutenir qch

**propaganda** [prɒpə'gændə] *n* propagande *f*

**propel** [prə'pel] *(pt & pp* **-ll-***) vt* propulser ■ **propeller** *n* hélice *f*

**proper** ['prɒpə(r)] *adj* (**a**) *(correct)* vrai; *(word)* correct; **the village p.** le village proprement dit (**b**) *(appropriate)* bon (*f* bonne); *(equipment)* adéquat; *(behaviour)* convenable (**c**) *Br (downright)* véritable ■ **properly** *adv (suitably)* convenablement; *(correctly)* correctement

**property** ['prɒpətɪ] **1** *(pl* **-ies***) n* (**a**) *(land, house)* propriété *f*; *(possessions)* biens *mpl* (**b**) *(quality)* propriété *f* **2** *adj (market)* immobilier, -ère; **p. developer** promoteur *m* immobilier

**prophecy** ['prɒfɪsɪ] *(pl* **-ies***) n* prophétie *f*

**prophet** ['prɒfɪt] *n* prophète *m*

**proportion** [prə'pɔ:ʃən] *n (ratio, part)* proportion *f*; **proportions** *(size)* proportions *fpl*; **in p.** proportionné (**to** avec); **out of p.** disproportionné (**to** par rapport à) ■ **proportional, proportionate** *adj* proportionnel, -elle (**to** à)

**proposal** [prə'pəʊzəl] *n* proposition *f*; *(plan)* projet *m*; *(for marriage)* demande *f* en mariage ■ **proposition** [prɒpə'zɪʃən] *n* proposition *f*

**propose** [prə'pəʊz] **1** *vt* proposer; **to p. to do sth, to p. doing sth** *(suggest)* proposer de faire qch; *(intend)* se proposer de faire qch **2** *vi* **to p. to sb** demander qn en mariage

**proprietor** [prə'praɪətə(r)] *n* propriétaire *mf*

**pros** [prəʊz] *npl* **the p. and cons** le pour et le contre

**prose** [prəʊz] *n* prose *f*; *Br (translation)* thème *m*

**prosecute** ['prɒsɪkju:t] *vt (in law court)* poursuivre (en justice) ■ **prosecution** *n (in law court)* poursuites *fpl* judiciaires; **the p.** *(lawyers)* ≃ le ministère public

**prospect¹** ['prɒspekt] *n (expectation, thought)* perspective *f*; *(chance, likelihood)* perspectives *fpl*; **(future) prospects** perspectives *fpl* d'avenir ■ **prospective** [prə'spektɪv] *adj (potential)* potentiel, -elle; *(future)* futur

**prospect²** [prə'spekt] *vi* **to p. for gold** chercher de l'or

**prospectus** [prə'spektəs] *n (publicity leaflet)* prospectus *m*; *Br (for university)* guide *m* (de l'étudiant)

**prosper** ['prɒspə(r)] *vi* prospérer ■ **prosperity** [-'sperətɪ] *n* prospérité *f* ■ **prosperous** *adj* prospère

**prostitute** ['prɒstɪtju:t] *n (woman)* prostituée *f*; **male p.** prostitué *m* ■ **prostitution** *n* prostitution *f*

**prostrate** ['prɒstreɪt] *adj (lying flat)* sur le ventre

**protagonist** [prəʊ'tægənɪst] *n* protagoniste *mf*

**protect** [prə'tekt] *vt* protéger (**from** *or* **against** de) ■ **protection** *n* protection *f* ■ **protective** *adj (clothes, screen)* de protection; *(person, attitude)* protecteur, -trice (**to** *or* **towards** envers)

**protein** ['prəʊti:n] *n* protéine *f*

**protest** [prə'test] **1** ['prəʊtest] *n* protestation *f* (**against** contre); **in p.** en signe de protestation (**at** contre) **2** *vt* protester contre; *(one's innocence)* protester de; **to p. that...** protester en disant que... **3** *vi* protester (**against** contre) ▪ **protester** *n* contestataire *mf*

**Protestant** ['prɒtɪstənt] *adj & n* protestant, -e *(mf)*

**protracted** [prə'træktɪd] *adj* prolongé

**protrude** [prə'tru:d] *vi* dépasser (**from** de); *(of tooth)* avancer ▪ **protruding** *adj (chin, veins, eyes)* saillant

**proud** [praʊd] (**-er, -est**) *adj (person)* fier (*f* fière) (**of** de) ▪ **proudly** *adv* fièrement

**prove** [pru:v] **1** *vt* prouver (**that** que); **to p. sb wrong** prouver que qn a tort **2** *vi* **to p. (to be) difficult** s'avérer difficile ▪ **proven** *adj (method)* éprouvé

**proverb** ['prɒvɜ:b] *n* proverbe *m*

**provide** [prə'vaɪd] **1** *vt (supply)* fournir; *(service)* offrir (**to** à); **to p. sb with sth** fournir qch à qn **2** *vi* **to p. for sb** *(sb's needs)* pourvoir aux besoins de qn; *(sb's future)* assurer l'avenir de qn; **to p. for sth** *(make allowance for)* prévoir qch ▪ **provided, providing** *conj* **p. (that)...** pourvu que... *(+ subjunctive)*

**province** ['prɒvɪns] *n* province *f*; **in the provinces** en province ▪ **provincial** [prə'vɪnʃəl] *adj & n* provincial, -e *(mf)*

**provision** [prə'vɪʒən] *n (clause)* disposition *f*; **provisions** *(supplies)* provisions *fpl*

**provisional** [prə'vɪʒənəl] *adj* provisoire

**provocation** [prɒvə'keɪʃən] *n* provocation *f*

**provocative** [prə'vɒkətɪv] *adj* provocateur, -trice

**provoke** [prə'vəʊk] *vt* provoquer; **to p. sb into doing sth** pousser qn à faire qch

**prowl** [praʊl] **1** *n* **to be on the p.** rôder **2** *vi* **to p. (around)** rôder

**proxy** ['prɒksɪ] (*pl* **-ies**) *n* **by p.** par procuration

**prudent** ['pru:dənt] *adj* prudent

**prudish** ['pru:dɪʃ] *adj* pudibond

**prune**[1] [pru:n] *n (dried plum)* pruneau *m*

**prune**[2] [pru:n] *vt (tree, bush)* tailler

**pry** [praɪ] **1** (*pt & pp* **pried**) *vt Am* **to p. open** forcer (avec un levier) **2** *vi* être indiscret, -ète; **to p. into sth** *(meddle)* mettre son nez dans qch; *(sb's reasons)* chercher à découvrir qch

**PS** [pi:'es] (*abbr* **postscript**) *n* PS *m*

**psalm** [sɑ:m] *n* psaume *m*

**pseudonym** ['sju:dənɪm] *n* pseudonyme *m*

**psychiatry** [saɪ'kaɪətrɪ] *n* psychiatrie *f* ▪ **psychiatric** [-kɪ'ætrɪk] *adj* psychiatrique ▪ **psychiatrist** *n* psychiatre *mf*

**psychic** ['saɪkɪk] *adj (paranormal)* paranormal

**psycho-** ['saɪkəʊ] *pref* psycho- ▪ **psychoanalyst** *n* psychanalyste *mf*

**psychology** [saɪ'kɒlədʒɪ] *n* psychologie *f* ▪ **psychological** [-kə'lɒdʒɪkəl] *adj* psychologique ▪ **psychologist** *n* psychologue *mf*

**psychopath** ['saɪkəʊpæθ] *n* psychopathe *mf*

**PTO** (*abbr* **please turn over**) TSVP

**pub** [pʌb] *n Br* pub *m*

**puberty** ['pju:bətɪ] *n* puberté *f*

**public** ['pʌblɪk] **1** *adj* public, -ique; *(library, swimming pool)* municipal; **p. holiday** jour *m* férié; **p. school** *Br* école *f* privée; *Am* école *f* publique; **p. transport** transports *mpl* en commun **2** *n* public *m*; **in p.** en public

**publication** [pʌblɪ'keɪʃən] *n* publication *f*

**publicity** [pʌ'blɪsətɪ] *n* publicité *f*

**publicize** ['pʌblɪsaɪz] *vt* faire connaître au public

**publicly** ['pʌblɪklɪ] *adv* publiquement; **p. owned** à capitaux publics

**publish** ['pʌblɪʃ] *vt* publier ▪ **publisher** *n (person)* éditeur, -trice *mf*; *(company)* maison *f* d'édition

**pudding** ['pʊdɪŋ] *n (dish)* pudding *m*; *Br (dessert)* dessert *m*

**puddle** ['pʌdəl] *n* flaque *f* (d'eau)

**puff** [pʌf] **1** *n (of smoke)* bouffée *f*; *(of wind, air)* souffle *m*; **p. pastry,** *Am* **p. paste** pâte *f* feuilletée **2** *vt* **to p. sth out** *(cheeks, chest)* gonfler qch **3** *vi (of person)* souffler; **to p. at a cigar** tirer sur un cigare

**puke** [pju:k] *vi Fam* dégueuler

**pull** [pʊl] **1** *n (attraction)* attraction *f*; **to give sth a p.** tirer qch **2** *vt (draw, tug)* tirer; *(tooth)* arracher; *(trigger)* appuyer sur; *(muscle)* se froisser; *Fig* **to p. sth apart** *or* **to bits** *or* **to pieces** démolir qch **3** *vi (tug)* tirer (**on** sur)

▸ **pull along** *vt sep (drag)* traîner (**to** jusqu'à)

▸ **pull away 1** *vt sep (move)* éloigner; *(snatch)* arracher (**from** à) **2** *vi (in vehicle)* démarrer

▸ **pull back 1** *vt sep* retirer; *(curtains)* ouvrir **2** *vi (withdraw)* se retirer

▸ **pull down** *vt sep (lower)* baisser; *(knock down)* faire tomber; *(demolish)* démolir

▸ **pull in 1** *vt sep (drag into room)* faire entrer (de force); *(rope)* ramener; *(stomach)* rentrer **2** *vi (arrive)* arriver; *(stop in vehicle)* s'arrêter

▸ **pull off** *vt sep (remove)* enlever; *Fig (plan, deal)* réaliser

▸ **pull on** *vt sep (boots, clothes)* mettre

▸ **pull out 1** *vt sep (tooth, hair)* arracher; *(cork, pin)* enlever (**from** de); *(from pocket, bag)* sortir (**from** de) **2** *vi (of car)* déboîter; *(of train)* partir; *(withdraw)* se retirer (**of** de)

▸ **pull over 1** *vt sep (drag)* traîner (**to** jusqu'à); *(knock down)* faire tomber **2** *vi (in vehicle)* s'arrêter

▸ **pull through** *vi (recover)* s'en tirer

▸ **pull together** *vt sep* **to p. oneself together** se ressaisir

▸ **pull up 1** *vt sep (socks, blinds)* remonter; *(haul up)* hisser; *(plant, tree)* arracher; *(stop)* arrêter **2** *vi (of car)* s'arrêter

**pullover** ['pʊləʊvə(r)] *n* pull-over *m*

**pulp** [pʌlp] *n (of fruit)* pulpe *f*

**pulse** [pʌls] *n Med* pouls *m*

**pump[1]** [pʌmp] **1** *n (machine)* pompe *f*; *Br* **petrol p.,** *Am* **gas p.** pompe *f* à essence **2** *vt* pomper; **to p. sth up** *(mattress)* gonfler qch

**pump[2]** [pʌmp] *n (flat shoe)* escarpin *m*; *(for sports)* tennis *f*

**pumpkin** ['pʌmpkɪn] *n* potiron *m*

**pun** [pʌn] *n* jeu *m* de mots

**punch[1]** [pʌntʃ] **1** *n (blow)* coup *m* de poing; **p. line** *(of joke, story)* chute *f* **2** *vt (person)* donner un coup de poing à; *(sb's nose)* donner un coup de poing sur ▪ **punch-up** *n Br Fam* bagarre *f*

**punch[2]** [pʌntʃ] **1** *n (for paper)* perforeuse *f*; *(for tickets)* poinçonneuse *f* **2** *vt (ticket)* poinçonner; *(with date)* composter; *(paper, card)* perforer; **to p. a hole in sth** faire un trou dans qch

**punch[3]** [pʌntʃ] *n (drink)* punch *m*

**punctual** ['pʌŋktʃʊəl] *adj* ponctuel, -elle ▪ **punctually** *adv* à l'heure

**punctuation** [pʌŋktjʊ'eɪʃən] *n* ponctuation *f*; **p. mark** signe *m* de ponctuation

**puncture** ['pʌŋktʃə(r)] **1** *n (in tyre)* crevaison *f*; **to have a p.** crever **2** *vt (tyre)* crever **3** *vi (of tyre)* crever

**pungent** ['pʌndʒənt] *adj* âcre

**punish** ['pʌnɪʃ] *vt* punir (**for** de); **to p. sb for doing sth** punir qn pour avoir fait qch

**punishment** ['pʌnɪʃmənt] *n* punition *f*; *(in law)* peine *f*

**punk** [pʌŋk] *n* punk *mf*; **p. (rock)** le punk

**punter** ['pʌntə(r)] *n Br (gambler)* parieur, -euse *mf*; *Fam (customer)* client, -e *m*

**puny** ['pju:nɪ] (**-ier, -iest**) *adj* chétif, -ive

**pupil[1]** ['pju:pəl] *n (student)* élève *mf*

**pupil[2]** ['pju:pəl] *n (of eye)* pupille *f*

**puppet** ['pʌpɪt] *n* marionnette *f*; **p. show** spectacle *m* de marionnettes

**puppy** ['pʌpɪ] (*pl* **-ies**) *n (dog)* chiot *m*

**purchase** ['pɜ:tʃɪs] **1** *n (action, thing bought)* achat *m* **2** *vt* acheter (**from** à) ▪ **purchaser** *n* acheteur, -euse *mf*

**pure** [pjʊə(r)] (**-er, -est**) *adj* pur

**purée** ['pjʊəreɪ] *n* purée *f*

**purely** ['pjʊəlɪ] *adv* purement

**purge** [pɜːdʒ] **1** *n* purge *f* **2** *vt* purger (**of** de)

**purify** ['pjʊərɪfaɪ] (*pt & pp* **-ied**) *vt* purifier

**puritanical** [pjʊərɪ'tænɪkəl] *adj* puritain

**purity** ['pjʊərətɪ] *n* pureté *f*

**purple** ['pɜːpəl] **1** *adj* violet, -ette **2** *n* violet *m*

**purpose** ['pɜːpəs] *n* (**a**) *(aim)* but *m*; **on p.** exprès; **for the purposes of** pour les besoins de (**b**) *(determination)* résolution *f*

**purposely** ['pɜːpəslɪ] *adv* exprès

**purr** [pɜː(r)] *vi* ronronner

**purse** [pɜːs] **1** *n (for coins)* porte-monnaie *m inv*; *Am (handbag)* sac *m* à main **2** *vt* **to p. one's lips** pincer les lèvres

**pursue** [pə'sjuː] *vt* poursuivre; *(fame, pleasure)* rechercher ■ **pursuit** *n (of person)* poursuite *f*; *(of pleasure, glory)* quête *f*; *(activity)* occupation *f*

**push** [pʊʃ] **1** *n (act of pushing, attack)* poussée *f*; **to give sb/sth a p.** pousser qn/qch; **at a p.** à la rigueur

**2** *vt* pousser (**to** *or* **as far as** jusqu'à); *(button)* appuyer sur; *(lever)* abaisser; *(product)* faire la promotion de; *Fam (drugs)* vendre; **to p. sth into/between** enfoncer qch dans/entre; *Fig* **to p. sb into doing sth** pousser qn à faire qch; **to p. sth off the table** faire tomber qch de la table (en le poussant)

**3** *vi* pousser; *(on button)* appuyer (**on** sur)

▸**push about, push around** *vt sep Fam* **to p. sb about** *or* **around** faire de qn ce que l'on veut

▸**push aside** *vt sep* écarter

▸**push down** *vt sep (button)* appuyer sur; *(lever)* abaisser

▸**push in** *vi Br (in queue)* resquiller

▸**push off** *vi Fam* ficher le camp

▸**push on** *vi (go on)* continuer; **to p. on with sth** continuer qch

▸**push over** *vt sep* faire tomber

▸**push up** *vt sep (lever, collar)* relever; *(sleeves)* remonter; *(increase)* augmenter ■ **push-button** *n* bouton *m*; *(of phone)* touche *f*; **p. phone** téléphone *m* à touches ■ **pushchair** *n Br* poussette *f* ■ **push-up** *n Am (exercise)* pompe *f*

**pushed** [pʊʃt] *adj* **to be p. for time** être très pressé

**pushy** ['pʊʃɪ] (**-ier, -iest**) *adj Fam* batailleur, -euse

**puss, pussy** ['pʊs, 'pʊsɪ] (*pl* **-ies**) *n Fam (cat)* minou *m*

**PUT** [pʊt] (*pt & pp* **put,** *pres p* **putting**) *vt* mettre; *(on flat surface)* poser; *(problem, argument)* présenter (**to** à); *(question)* poser (**to** à); *(say)* dire; *(estimate)* évaluer (**at** à); **to p. money on a horse** parier sur un cheval; **to p. a lot of work into sth** beaucoup travailler à qch; **to p. it bluntly** pour parler franc

▸**put across** *vt sep (message, idea)* faire comprendre (**to** à)

▸**put aside** *vt sep (money, object)* mettre de côté

▸**put away** *vt sep (tidy away)* ranger; **to p. sb away** *(criminal)* mettre qn en prison

▸**put back** *vt sep (replace, postpone)* remettre; *(telephone receiver)* raccrocher; *(clock)* retarder

▸**put by** *vt sep (money)* mettre de côté

▸**put down** *vt sep (on floor, table)* poser; *(a deposit)* verser; *(revolt)* réprimer; *(write down)* inscrire; *(attribute)* attribuer (**to** à); *(kill)* faire piquer; **to p. oneself down** se rabaisser

▸**put forward** *vt sep (clock, meeting, argument)* avancer; *(candidate)* proposer (**for** à)

▸**put in 1** *vt sep (into box)* mettre dedans; *(insert)* introduire; *(add)* ajouter; *(install)* installer; *(claim, application)* soumettre; *(time)* passer (**doing** à faire) **2** *vi* **to p. in for sth** *(new job, transfer)* faire une demande de qch

▸**put off** *vt sep (postpone)* remettre (à

plus tard); *(dismay)* déconcerter; **to p. off doing sth** retarder le moment de faire qch; **to p. sb off sth** dégoûter qn de qch

▸ **put on** *vt sep (clothes, shoe, record)* mettre; *(accent)* prendre; *(play, show)* monter; *(gas, radio)* allumer; *(clock)* avancer; **to p. on weight** prendre du poids; **she p. me on to you** elle m'a donné votre adresse; **p. me on to him!** *(on phone)* passez-le-moi!

▸ **put out** *vt sep (take outside)* sortir; *(arm, leg, hand)* tendre; *(gas, light)* éteindre; *(inconvenience)* déranger; *(upset)* vexer; *(report, statement)* publier; **to p. one's shoulder out** se démettre l'épaule

▸ **put through** *vt sep* **to p. sb through (to sb)** *(on phone)* passer qn (à qn)

▸ **put together** *vt sep (assemble)* assembler; *(meal, team)* composer; *(file, report)* préparer; *(collection)* rassembler

▸ **put up** *vt sep (lift)* lever; *(tent, fence)* monter; *(statue, ladder)* dresser; *(flag)* hisser; *(building)* construire; *(umbrella)* ouvrir; *(picture, poster)* mettre; *(price, numbers)* augmenter; *(resistance)* offrir; *(candidate)* présenter (**for** à); *(guest)* loger; **to p. sth up for sale** mettre qch en vente

▸ **put up with** *vt insep* supporter

---

**putting** ['pʌtɪŋ] *n (in golf)* putting *m*; **p. green** green *m*

**puzzle** ['pʌzəl] **1** *n (jigsaw)* puzzle *m*; *(game)* casse-tête *m inv*; *(mystery)* mystère *m* **2** *vt* laisser perplexe **3** *vi* **to p. over sth** essayer de comprendre qch ▪ **puzzled** *adj* perplexe

**PVC** [pi:vi:'si:] *n* PVC *m*

**pyjamas** [pə'dʒɑ:məz] *npl Br* pyjama *m*; **a pair of p.** un pyjama

**pylon** ['paɪlən] *n* pylône *m*

**pyramid** ['pɪrəmɪd] *n* pyramide *f*

**Pyrex®** ['paɪreks] *n* Pyrex® *m*; **P. dish** plat *m* en Pyrex®

# Qq

**Q, q** [kjuː] *n (letter)* Q, q *m inv*
**quack** [kwæk] *n (of duck)* coin-coin *m inv*
**quadruple** [kwɒ'druːpəl] *vti* quadrupler
**quaint** [kweɪnt] (**-er, -est**) *adj (picturesque)* pittoresque; *(old-fashioned)* vieillot, -otte; *(odd)* bizarre
**quake** [kweɪk] **1** *n Fam* tremblement *m* de terre **2** *vi* trembler (**with** de)
**Quaker** ['kweɪkə(r)] *n Rel* quaker, -eresse *mf*
**qualification** [kwɒlɪfɪ'keɪʃən] *n (diploma)* diplôme *m*; *(skill)* compétence *f*; *(modification)* précision *f*
**qualify** ['kwɒlɪfaɪ] (*pt & pp* **-ied**) **1** *vt* (**a**) *(make competent, in sport)* qualifier (**for sth** pour qch) (**b**) *(modify)* nuancer **2** *vi (of sportsperson)* se qualifier (**for** pour); **to q. as a doctor** obtenir son diplôme de médecin; **to q. for sth** *(be eligible)* avoir droit à qch ▪ **qualified** *adj (competent)* compétent; *(having diploma)* diplômé; *(support)* mitigé
**quality** ['kwɒlətɪ] (*pl* **-ies**) *n* qualité *f*
**quantity** ['kwɒntətɪ] (*pl* **-ies**) *n* quantité *f*
**quarantine** ['kwɒrəntiːn] *n* quarantaine *f*
**quarrel** ['kwɒrəl] **1** *n* dispute *f*, querelle *f* **2** (*Br* **-ll-**, *Am* **-l-**) *vi* se disputer (**with** avec); **to q. with sth** ne pas être d'accord avec qch
**quarry** ['kwɒrɪ] (*pl* **-ies**) *n (for stone)* carrière *f*
**quart** [kwɔːt] *n (liquid measurement)* *Br* = 1,14 l, *Am* = 0,95 l
**quarter¹** ['kwɔːtə(r)] *n* quart *m*; *(of fruit, moon)* quartier *m*; *(division of year)* trimestre *m*; *Am & Can (money)* pièce *f* de 25 cents; **q. (of a) pound** quart *m* de livre; *Br* **a q. past nine,** *Am* **a q. after nine** neuf heures et quart; **a q. to nine** neuf heures moins le quart
**quarter²** ['kwɔːtə(r)] *n (district)* quartier *m*; **(living) quarters** logements *mpl*; *(of soldier)* quartiers *mpl*
**quarterfinal** [kwɔːtə'faɪnəl] *n* quart *m* de finale
**quarterly** ['kwɔːtəlɪ] **1** *adj (magazine, payment)* trimestriel, -elle **2** *adv* tous les trimestres
**quartet(te)** [kwɔː'tet] *n (music, players)* quatuor *m*; **(jazz) q.** quartette *m*
**quartz** [kwɔːts] **1** *n* quartz *m* **2** *adj (watch)* à quartz
**quash** [kwɒʃ] *vt (rebellion)* réprimer; *(sentence)* annuler
**quasi-** ['kweɪzaɪ] *pref* quasi-
**quay** [kiː] *n* quai *m*
**queasy** ['kwiːzɪ] (**-ier, -iest**) *adj* **to feel** *or* **be q.** avoir mal au cœur
**Quebec** [kwɪ'bek] *n* le Québec
**queen** [kwiːn] *n* reine *f*
**queer** ['kwɪə(r)] (**-er, -est**) *adj (strange)* bizarre
**quench** [kwentʃ] *vt (thirst)* étancher
**query** ['kwɪərɪ] **1** (*pl* **-ies**) *n* question *f* **2** (*pt & pp* **-ied**) *vt* mettre en question
**quest** [kwest] *n* quête *f* (**for** de)
**question** ['kwestʃən] **1** *n* question *f*; **there's no q. of it, it's out of the q.** c'est hors de question; **the matter/person in q.** l'affaire/la personne en

question; **q. mark** point *m* d'interrogation **2** *vt* interroger (**about** sur); *(doubt)* mettre en question

**questionable** ['kwestʃənəbəl] *adj* discutable

**questionnaire** [kwestʃə'neə(r)] *n* questionnaire *m*

**queue** [kju:] *Br* **1** *n (of people)* queue *f*; *(of cars)* file *f*; **to form a q., to stand in a q.** faire la queue **2** *vi* **to q. (up)** faire la queue

**quiche** [ki:ʃ] *n* quiche *f*

**quick** [kwɪk] **1** (**-er, -est**) *adj (rapid)* rapide; *(clever)* vif (*f* vive); **be q.!** fais vite!; **to have a q. shower/meal** se doucher/manger en vitesse **2** (**-er, -est**) *adv Fam* vite

**quicken** ['kwɪkən] **1** *vt* accélérer **2** *vi* s'accélérer

**quickly** ['kwɪklɪ] *adv* vite

**quid** [kwɪd] *n inv Br Fam (pound)* livre *f*

**quiet** ['kwaɪət] **1** (**-er, -est**) *adj (silent, still, peaceful)* tranquille, calme; *(machine, vehicle)* silencieux, -euse; *(person, voice, music)* doux (*f* douce); **to be** *or* **keep q.** *(say nothing)* se taire; *(make no noise)* ne pas faire de bruit; **to keep q. about sth, to keep sth q.** ne rien dire au sujet de qch; **q.!** silence! **2** *n Fam* **on the q.** *(secretly)* en cachette

**quieten** ['kwaɪətən] *Br* **1** *vt* **to q. (down)** calmer **2** *vi* **to q. down** se calmer

**quietly** ['kwaɪətlɪ] *adv* tranquillement; *(gently, not loudly)* doucement; *(silently)* silencieusement; *(secretly)* en cachette; *(discreetly)* discrètement

**quilt** [kwɪlt] *n* édredon *m*; *Br* **(continental) q.** *(duvet)* couette *f*

**quip** [kwɪp] **1** *n* boutade *f* **2** *(pt & pp* **-pp-**) *vti* plaisanter

**quirk** [kwɜ:k] *n (of character)* particularité *f* ▪ **quirky** (**-ier, -iest**) *adj* bizarre

**quit** [kwɪt] *(pt & pp* **quit** *or* **quitted,** *pres p* **quitting**) **1** *vt (leave)* quitter; *Comptr* sortir de; **to q. doing sth** arrêter de faire qch **2** *vi (give up)* abandonner; *(resign)* démissionner; *Comptr* sortir

**quite** [kwaɪt] *adv (entirely)* tout à fait; *(really)* vraiment; *(fairly)* assez; **q. good** *(not bad)* pas mal du tout; **q. (so)!** exactement!; **q. a lot** pas mal (**of** de)

**quits** [kwɪts] *adj* quitte (**with** envers); **to call it q.** en rester là

**quiver** ['kwɪvə(r)] *vi (of voice)* trembler

**quiz** [kwɪz] **1** *(pl* **-zz-**) *n (on radio)* jeu *m* radiophonique; *(on TV)* jeu *m* télévisé; *(in magazine)* questionnaire *m* **2** *(pt & pp* **-zz-**) *vt* interroger

**quota** ['kwəʊtə] *n* quota *m*

**quotation** [kwəʊ'teɪʃən] *n (from author)* citation *f*; *(estimate)* devis *m*; **in q. marks** entre guillemets

**quote** [kwəʊt] **1** *n (from author)* citation *f*; *(estimate)* devis *m*; **in quotes** entre guillemets **2** *vt (author, passage)* citer; *(reference number)* rappeler; *(price)* indiquer **3** *vi* **to q. from** *(author, book)* citer

# Rr

**R, r** [ɑː(r)] *n (lettre)* R, r *m inv*
**rabbi** ['ræbaɪ] *n* rabbin *m*
**rabbit** ['ræbɪt] *n* lapin *m*
**rabies** ['reɪbiːz] *n* rage *f*
**raccoon** [rə'kuːn] *n* raton *m* laveur
**race**[1] [reɪs] **1** *n (contest)* course *f*
**2** *vt* **to r. (against** *or* **with) sb** faire une course avec qn
**3** *vi (run)* courir ■ **racecourse** *n* champ *m* de courses ■ **racehorse** *n* cheval *m* de course ■ **racetrack** *n Am (for horses)* champ *m* de courses; *Br (for cars, bicycles)* piste *f* ■ **racing** *n* courses *fpl*; **r. car** voiture *f* de course; **r. driver** coureur *m* automobile
**race**[2] [reɪs] *n (group)* race *f*; **r. relations** relations *fpl* interraciales ■ **racial** ['reɪʃəl] *adj* racial ■ **racism** *n* racisme *m* ■ **racist** *adj & n* raciste *(mf)*
**rack** [ræk] **1** *n (for bottles, letters, records)* casier *m*; *(for plates)* égouttoir *m*; **(luggage) r.** porte-bagages *m inv*; **(roof) r.** *(of car)* galerie *f* **2** *vt* **to r. one's brains** se creuser la cervelle
**racket**[1] ['rækɪt] *n (for tennis)* raquette *f*
**racket**[2] ['rækɪt] *n Fam* (**a**) *(din)* vacarme *m* (**b**) *(criminal activity)* racket *m*
**radar** ['reɪdɑː(r)] *n* radar *m*
**radiant** ['reɪdɪənt] *adj (person, face)* resplendissant (**with** de)
**radiate** ['reɪdɪeɪt] **1** *vt (heat, light)* dégager; *Fig (joy, health)* être rayonnant de **2** *vi* rayonner (**from** de) ■ **radiation** *n (radioactivity)* radiation *f*
**radiator** ['reɪdɪeɪtə(r)] *n (heater)* radiateur *m*
**radical** ['rædɪkəl] *adj & n* radical, -e *(mf)*
**radio** ['reɪdɪəʊ] **1** (*pl* **-os**) *n* radio *f*; **on the r.** à la radio; **r. cassette (player)** radiocassette *f* **2** (*pt & pp* **-oed**) *vt (message)* transmettre par radio (**to** à); **to r. sb** contacter qn par radio ■ **radio-controlled** *adj* radioguidé
**radioactivity** [reɪdɪəʊæk'tɪvətɪ] *n* radioactivité *f*
**radish** ['rædɪʃ] *n* radis *m*
**radius** ['reɪdɪəs] (*pl* **-dii**) *n* rayon *m*; **within a r. of 10 km** dans un rayon de 10 km
**RAF** [ɑːreɪ'ef] (*abbr* **Royal Air Force**) *n* = armée de l'air britannique
**raffle** ['ræfəl] *n* tombola *f*
**raft** [rɑːft] *n* radeau *m*
**rag** [ræg] *n* (**a**) *(piece of old clothing)* chiffon *m*; **in rags** *(clothes)* en loques; *(person)* en haillons (**b**) *Fam Pej (newspaper)* torchon *m*
**rage** [reɪdʒ] **1** *n (of person)* rage *f*; **to fly into a r.** entrer dans une rage folle; *Fam* **to be all the r.** *(of fashion)* faire fureur **2** *vi (be angry)* être furieux, -euse; *(of storm, battle)* faire rage ■ **raging** *adj (storm, fever, fire)* violent
**ragged** ['rægɪd] *adj (clothes)* en loques; *(person)* en haillons; *(edge)* irrégulier, -ère
**raid** [reɪd] **1** *n (military)* raid *m*; *(by police)* descente *f*; *(by thieves)* hold-up *m inv*; **air r.** raid *m* aérien **2** *vt* faire un raid/une descente/un hold-up dans
**rail** [reɪl] **1** *n* (**a**) *(for train)* rail *m*; **by r.** par le train (**b**) *(rod on balcony)* balustrade *f*; *(on stairs)* rampe *f*; *(curtain rod)* tringle *f* **2** *adj (ticket)* de chemin

de fer; *(strike)* des cheminots ▪ **railcard** *n* carte *f* d'abonnement de train
**railings** ['reɪlɪŋz] *npl* grille *f*
**railroad** ['reɪlrəʊd] *n Am (system)* chemin *m* de fer; *(track)* voie *f* ferrée
**railway** ['reɪlweɪ] *Br* **1** *n (system)* chemin *m* de fer; *(track)* voie *f* ferrée **2** *adj (ticket)* de chemin de fer; *(timetable)* des chemins de fer; *(network, company)* ferroviaire; **r. line** ligne *f* de chemin de fer; **r. station** gare *f*
**rain** [reɪn] **1** *n* pluie *f*; **in the r.** sous la pluie **2** *vi* pleuvoir; **it's raining** il pleut ▪ **rainbow** *n* arc-en-ciel *m* ▪ **raincoat** *n* imperméable *m* ▪ **rainfall** *n (amount)* précipitations *fpl* ▪ **rainforest** *n* forêt *f* tropicale humide ▪ **rainwater** *n* eau *f* de pluie ▪ **rainy** (**-ier, -iest**) *adj* pluvieux, -euse; *(day)* de pluie; **the r. season** la saison des pluies
**raise** [reɪz] **1** *vt (lift)* lever; *(child, family, voice)* élever; *(salary, price)* augmenter; *(temperature)* faire monter; *(question, protest)* soulever; *(taxes)* lever; **to r. money** réunir des fonds; **to r. the alarm** donner l'alarme **2** *n Am (pay rise)* augmentation *f* (de salaire)
**raisin** ['reɪzən] *n* raisin *m* sec
**rake** [reɪk] **1** *n* râteau *m* **2** *vt (soil)* ratisser; **to r. (up)** *(leaves)* ratisser
**rally** ['rælɪ] **1** (*pl* **-ies**) *n (political)* rassemblement *m*; *(car race)* rallye *m* **2** (*pt & pp* **-ied**) *vt (unite, win over)* rallier (**to** à) **3** *vi* se rallier (**to** à); *(recover)* reprendre ses forces; **to r. round sb** venir en aide à qn
**RAM** [ræm] (*abbr* **random access memory**) *n Comptr* mémoire *f* vive
**ram** [ræm] **1** *n (animal)* bélier *m* **2** (*pt & pp* **-mm-**) *vt (vehicle)* emboutir; *(ship)* aborder; **to r. sth into sth** enfoncer qch dans qch
**ramble** ['ræmbəl] **1** *n (hike)* randonnée *f* **2** *vi (hike)* faire une randonnée; **to r. on** *(talk)* divaguer ▪ **rambler** *n* randonneur, -euse *mf*
**rambling** ['ræmblɪŋ] *adj* (**a**) *(house)* plein de coins et de recoins; *(spread out)* vaste (**b**) *(speech)* décousu
**ramp** [ræmp] *n (for wheelchair)* rampe *f* d'accès; *(in garage)* pont *m* (de graissage); *(on road)* petit dos *m* d'âne
**rampant** ['ræmpənt] *adj* endémique
**ran** [ræn] *pt of* **run**
**ranch** [rɑːntʃ] *n* ranch *m*
**rancid** ['rænsɪd] *adj* rance
**random** ['rændəm] **1** *n* **at r.** au hasard **2** *adj (choice)* (fait) au hasard; *(sample)* prélevé au hasard
**rang** [ræŋ] *pt of* **ring**[2]
**range** [reɪndʒ] **1** *n* (**a**) *(of gun, voice)* portée *f*; *(of singer's voice)* registre *m*; *(of aircraft, ship)* rayon *m* d'action; *(of colours, prices, products)* gamme *f*; *(of sizes)* choix *m* (**b**) *(of mountains)* chaîne *f* (**c**) *(stove)* fourneau *m* (**d**) **(shooting) r.** champ *m* de tir **2** *vi (vary)* varier (**from** de; **to** à); *(extend)* s'étendre
**ranger** ['reɪndʒə(r)] *n* **(forest) r.** garde *m* forestier
**rank**[1] [ræŋk] **1** *n (position, class)* rang *m*; *(military grade)* grade *m*; *(row)* rangée *f*; *(for taxis)* station *f* **2** *vt* placer (**among** parmi) **3** *vi* compter (**among** parmi)
**rank**[2] [ræŋk] (**-er, -est**) *adj (smell)* fétide
**ransack** ['rænsæk] *vt (house)* mettre sens dessus dessous; *(shop, town)* piller
**ransom** ['rænsəm] **1** *n* rançon *f*; **to hold sb to r.** rançonner qn **2** *vt* rançonner
**rant** [rænt] *vi Fam* **to r. and rave** tempêter (**at** contre)
**rap** [ræp] **1** *n* (**a**) *(blow)* coup *m* sec (**b**) **r. (music)** rap *m* **2** *vi (hit)* frapper (**on** à)
**rape** [reɪp] **1** *n* viol *m* **2** *vt* violer ▪ **rapist** *n* violeur *m*
**rapid** ['ræpɪd] *adj* rapide ▪ **rapidly** *adv* rapidement
**rapids** ['ræpɪdz] *npl (of river)* rapides *mpl*
**rare** [reə(r)] *adj* (**a**) (**-er, -est**) *(uncommon)* rare (**b**) *(meat)* saignant

▪ **rarely** *adv* rarement ▪ **rarity** (*pl* **-ies**) *n (quality, object)* rareté *f*

**raring** ['reərɪŋ] *adj* **r. to do sth** impatient de faire qch

**rascal** ['rɑːskəl] *n* coquin, -e *mf*

**rash**[1] [ræʃ] *n (on skin) (red patches)* rougeurs *fpl*; *(spots)* (éruption *f* de) boutons *mpl*

**rash**[2] [ræʃ] (**-er, -est**) *adj (imprudent)* irréfléchi ▪ **rashly** *adv* sans réfléchir

**rasher** ['ræʃə(r)] *n Br* tranche *f (de bacon)*

**raspberry** ['rɑːzbərɪ] (*pl* **-ies**) *n (fruit)* framboise *f*

**rat** [ræt] *n* rat *m*; *Fig* **r. race** foire *f* d'empoigne

**rate** [reɪt] **1** *n (level, percentage)* taux *m*; *(speed)* rythme *m*; *(price)* tarif *m*; **interest r.** taux *m* d'intérêt; **at the r. of** au rythme de; *(amount)* à raison de; **at this r.** *(slow speed)* à ce train-là; **at any r.** en tout cas **2** *vt (regard)* considérer (**as** comme); *(deserve)* mériter; **to r. sb/sth highly** tenir qn/qch en haute estime

**rather** ['rɑːðə(r)] *adv (preferably, quite)* plutôt; **I'd r. stay** j'aimerais mieux rester (**than** que); **I r. liked it** j'ai bien aimé

**ratify** ['rætɪfaɪ] (*pt & pp* **-ied**) *vt* ratifier

**rating** ['reɪtɪŋ] *n (classification)* classement *m*

**ratio** ['reɪʃɪəʊ] (*pl* **-os**) *n* rapport *m*

**ration** ['ræʃən] **1** *n* ration *f*; **rations** *(food)* vivres *mpl* **2** *vt* rationner ▪ **rationing** *n* rationnement *m*

**rational** ['ræʃənəl] *adj (sensible)* raisonnable; *(sane)* rationnel, -elle ▪ **rationalize** *vt (organize)* rationaliser; *(explain)* justifier ▪ **rationally** *adv (behave)* raisonnablement

**rattle** ['rætəl] **1** *n (for baby)* hochet *m* **2** *vt (window)* faire vibrer; *(keys, chains)* faire cliqueter; *Fam* **to r. sth off** *(speech, list)* débiter qch **3** *vi (of window)* vibrer

**raucous** ['rɔːkəs] *adj (noisy, rowdy)* bruyant

**rave** [reɪv] **1** *n (party)* rave *f* **2** *vi (talk nonsense)* délirer; **to r. about sb/sth** *(enthuse)* ne pas tarir d'éloges sur qn/qch ▪ **raving** *adj* **to be r. mad** être complètement fou (*f* folle)

**raven** ['reɪvən] *n* corbeau *m*

**ravenous** ['rævənəs] *adj* **I'm r.** j'ai une faim de loup

**ravine** [rə'viːn] *n* ravin *m*

**ravioli** [rævɪ'əʊlɪ] *n* ravioli(s) *mpl*

**raw** [rɔː] (**-er, -est**) *adj (vegetable)* cru; *(data)* brut; **r. material** matière *f* première

**ray** [reɪ] *n (of light, sun)* rayon *m*; *Fig (of hope)* lueur *f*

**rayon** ['reɪɒn] *n* rayonne *f*

**razor** ['reɪzə(r)] *n* rasoir *m*; **r. blade** lame *f* de rasoir

**Rd** (*abbr* **road**) rue

**re** [riː] *prep Com* en référence à; **re your letter** suite à votre lettre

**reach** [riːtʃ] **1** *n* portée *f*; **within r. of** à portée de; *(near)* à proximité de; **within (easy) r.** *(object)* à portée de main; *(shops)* tout proche

**2** *vt (place, aim, distant object)* atteindre, arriver à; *(decision)* prendre; *(agreement)* aboutir à; *(contact)* joindre; **to r. a conclusion** arriver à une conclusion; **to r. out one's arm** tendre le bras

**3** *vi (extend)* s'étendre (**to** jusqu'à); **to r. (out) for sth** tendre le bras pour prendre qch

**react** [rɪ'ækt] *vi* réagir (**against** contre; **to** à) ▪ **reaction** *n* réaction *f*

**reactionary** [rɪ'ækʃənərɪ] (*pl* **-ies**) *adj & n* réactionnaire *(mf)*

**reactor** [rɪ'æktə(r)] *n* réacteur *m*

**read** [riːd] **1** (*pt & pp* **read** [red]) *vt* lire; *(meter)* relever; *(of instrument)* indiquer; *Br Univ (study)* étudier **2** *vi (of person)* lire (**about** sur); **to r. to sb** faire la lecture à qn **3** *n* **to be a good r.** être agréable à lire ▪ **readable** *adj (handwriting)* lisible; *(book)* facile à lire

▸ **read back** *vt sep* relire

▸ **read out** *vt sep* lire (à haute voix)

▸ **read over** *vt sep* relire

▸ **read through** *vt sep (skim)* parcourir

▸ **read up (on)** *vt insep (study)* étudier

**reader** ['ri:də(r)] *n* lecteur, -trice *mf*; *(book)* livre *m* de lecture

**readily** ['redɪlɪ] *adv (willingly)* volontiers; *(easily)* facilement

**reading** ['ri:dɪŋ] *n* lecture *f*; *(of meter)* relevé *m*; **r. glasses** lunettes *fpl* de lecture; **r. lamp** *(on desk)* lampe *f* de bureau; *(at bedside)* lampe *f* de chevet; **r. matter** de quoi lire

**readjust** [ri:ə'dʒʌst] **1** *vt (instrument)* régler **2** *vi (of person)* se réadapter (**to** à)

**ready** ['redɪ] **1** (**-ier, -iest**) *adj* prêt (**to do** à faire; **for sth** pour qch); **to get sb/sth r.** préparer qn/qch; **to get r.** se préparer (**for sth** pour qch; **to do** à faire); **r. cash, r. money** argent *m* liquide

**2** *n* **to be at the r.** être tout prêt (*f* toute prête) ▪ **ready-made** *adj (food)* tout prêt (*f* toute prête); **r. clothes** le prêt-à-porter ▪ **ready-to-wear** *adj* **r. clothes** le prêt-à-porter

**real** [rɪəl] **1** *adj* vrai; *(leather)* véritable; *(world, danger)* réel (*f* réelle); **in r. life** dans la réalité; *Am* **r. estate** immobilier *m* **2** *adv Fam* vraiment **3** *n Fam* **for r.** pour de vrai

**realistic** [rɪə'lɪstɪk] *adj* réaliste

**reality** [rɪ'ælətɪ] (*pl* **-ies**) *n* réalité *f*; **in r.** en réalité

**realization** [rɪəlaɪ'zeɪʃən] *n (awareness)* prise *f* de conscience

**realize** ['rɪəlaɪz] *vt* (**a**) *(become aware of)* se rendre compte de; **to r. that...** se rendre compte que... (**b**) *(carry out)* réaliser

**really** ['rɪəlɪ] *adv* vraiment

**ream** [ri:m] *n (of paper)* rame *f*

**reap** [ri:p] *vt (crop)* moissonner; *Fig (profits)* récolter

**reappear** [ri:ə'pɪə(r)] *vi* réapparaître

**rear**[1] [rɪə(r)] **1** *n (back part)* arrière *m*; **in** *or* **at the r.** à l'arrière (**of** de) **2** *adj (entrance, legs)* de derrière; *(lights, window)* arrière *inv*

**rear**[2] [rɪə(r)] **1** *vt (child, animals)* élever; *(one's head)* relever **2** *vi* **to r. (up)** *(of horse)* se cabrer

**rearrange** [ri:ə'reɪndʒ] *vt (hair, room)* réarranger; *(plans)* changer

**rearview** ['rɪəvju:] *n* **r. mirror** rétroviseur *m*

**reason** ['ri:zən] **1** *n (cause, sense)* raison *f*; **the r. for/why** la raison de/pour laquelle; **for no r.** sans raison; **it stands to r.** cela va de soi; **within r.** dans des limites raisonnables

**2** *vt* **to r. that...** estimer que...

**3** *vi* raisonner (**about** sur); **to r. with sb** raisonner qn ▪ **reasoning** *n* raisonnement *m*

**reasonable** ['ri:zənəbəl] *adj (fair)* raisonnable; *(quite good)* passable ▪ **reasonably** *adv (behave, act)* raisonnablement; *(quite)* plutôt

**reassure** [ri:ə'ʃʊə(r)] *vt* rassurer ▪ **reassuring** *adj* rassurant

**rebate** ['ri:beɪt] *n (discount)* rabais *m*; *(refund)* remboursement *m*

**rebel** **1** ['rebəl] *n* rebelle *mf* **2** ['rebəl] *adj (camp, chief, attack)* des rebelles **3** [rɪ'bel] (*pt & pp* **-ll-**) *vi* se rebeller (**against** contre) ▪ **rebellion** [rɪ'beljən] *n* rébellion *f*

**rebound** **1** ['ri:baʊnd] *n (of ball)* rebond *m* **2** [rɪ'baʊnd] *vi (of ball)* rebondir; *Fig (of lies, action)* se retourner (**on** contre)

**rebuild** [ri:'bɪld] (*pt & pp* **-built**) *vt* reconstruire

**rebuke** [rɪ'bju:k] **1** *n* réprimande *f* **2** *vt* réprimander

**recall** [rɪ'kɔ:l] **1** *n (calling back)* rappel *m* **2** *vt (remember)* se rappeler (**that** que; **doing** avoir fait); *(call back)* rappeler; **to r. sth to sb** rappeler qch à qn

**recap** ['ri:kæp] **1** *n* récapitulation *f* **2** (*pt & pp* **-pp-**) *vi* récapituler

**recapitulate** [ri:kə'pɪtjʊleɪt] *vti* récapituler

**recede** [rɪ'si:d] *vi (into the distance)* s'éloigner; *(of floods)* baisser ▪ **receding** *adj* **his hairline is r., he has a r. hairline** son front se dégarnit

**receipt** [rɪ'si:t] *n (for payment, object)* reçu *m* (**for** de); *(for letter, parcel)* récépissé *m*; **receipts** *(at box office)* recette *f*; **on r. of sth** dès réception de qch

**receive** [rɪ'si:v] *vt* recevoir; *(stolen goods)* receler

**receiver** [rɪ'si:və(r)] *n (of phone)* combiné *m*; *(radio)* récepteur *m*; **to pick up** *or* **lift the r.** *(of phone)* décrocher

**recent** ['ri:sənt] *adj* récent; *(development)* dernier, -ère; **in r. months** au cours des derniers mois ▪ **recently** *adv* récemment

**reception** [rɪ'sepʃən] *n (party, of radio)* réception *f*; *(welcome)* accueil *m*; **r. (desk)** réception *f* ▪ **receptionist** *n* réceptionniste *mf*

**receptive** [rɪ'septɪv] *adj* réceptif, -ive (**to** à)

**recess** [*Br* rɪ'ses, *Am* 'ri:ses] *n* (**a**) *(holiday)* vacances *fpl*; *Am (between classes)* récréation *f* (**b**) *(in wall)* renfoncement *m*; *(smaller)* recoin *m*

**recession** [rɪ'seʃən] *n Econ* récession *f*

**recharge** [ri:'tʃɑ:dʒ] *vt (battery, mobile phone)* recharger ▪ **rechargeable** *adj (battery)* rechargeable

**recipe** ['resɪpɪ] *n (for food) & Fig* recette *f* (**for sth** de qch)

**recipient** [rɪ'sɪpɪənt] *n (of gift, letter)* destinataire *mf*; *(of award)* lauréat, -e *mf*

**reciprocal** [rɪ'sɪprəkəl] *adj* réciproque ▪ **reciprocate 1** *vt* retourner **2** *vi* rendre la pareille

**recital** [rɪ'saɪtəl] *n (of music)* récital *m* (*pl* -als)

**recite** [rɪ'saɪt] *vt (poem)* réciter; *(list)* énumérer

**reckless** ['rekləs] *adj (rash)* imprudent

**reckon** ['rekən] **1** *vt (calculate)* calculer; *(consider)* considérer; *Fam (think)* penser (**that** que) **2** *vi* calculer, compter; **to r. with** *(take into account)* compter avec; *(deal with)* avoir affaire à; **to r. on sb/sth** *(rely on)* compter sur qn/qch ▪ **reckoning** *n (calculation)* calcul *m*

**reclaim** [rɪ'kleɪm] *vt (lost property, luggage)* récupérer; *(expenses)* se faire rembourser

**recline** [rɪ'klaɪn] *vi (be stretched out)* être allongé ▪ **reclining** *adj* **r. seat** siège *m* à dossier inclinable

**recluse** [rɪ'klu:s] *n* reclus, -e *mf*

**recognition** [rekəg'nɪʃən] *n* reconnaissance *f*; **to gain r.** être reconnu

**recognize** ['rekəgnaɪz] *vt* reconnaître ▪ **recognizable** *adj* reconnaissable

**recoil** [rɪ'kɔɪl] *vi (of person)* avoir un mouvement de recul

**recollect** [rekə'lekt] *vt* se souvenir de ▪ **recollection** *n* souvenir *m*

**recommend** [rekə'mend] *vt (praise, support, advise)* recommander (**to** à; **for** pour); **to r. sb to do sth** recommander à qn de faire qch ▪ **recommendation** *n* recommandation *f*

**recompense** ['rekəmpens] **1** *n* récompense *f* **2** *vt (reward)* récompenser

**reconcile** ['rekənsaɪl] *vt (person)* réconcilier (**with** *or* **to** avec); *(opinions, facts)* concilier; **to r. oneself to sth** se résigner à qch

**reconditioned** [ri:kən'dɪʃənd] *adj (engine, machine)* remis à neuf

**reconsider** [ri:kən'sɪdə(r)] **1** *vt* réexaminer **2** *vi* réfléchir

**reconstruct** [ri:kən'strʌkt] *vt (crime)* reconstituer

**record 1** ['rekɔ:d] *n* (**a**) *(disc)* disque *m*; **r. player** électrophone *m*

(**b**) *(best sporting performance)* record *m*

(**c**) *(report)* rapport *m*; *(background)* antécédents *mpl*; *(file)* dossier *m*; **to make** *or* **keep a r. of sth** garder une trace écrite de qch; **on r.** *(fact, event)* attesté; **(police) r.** casier *m* judiciaire; **(public) records** archives *fpl*

**2** ['rekɔ:d] *adj* record *inv*; **to be at a r. high/low** être à son taux le plus haut/bas

**3** [rɪ'kɔ:d] *vt (on tape, in register)* enregistrer; *(in diary)* noter

**4** [rɪˈkɔːd] *vi (on tape, of tape recorder)* enregistrer
**recorded** [rɪˈkɔːdɪd] *adj* enregistré; *(fact)* attesté; *(TV broadcast)* en différé; *Br* **to send sth (by) r. delivery** ≃ envoyer qch en recommandé avec accusé de réception
**recorder** [rɪˈkɔːdə(r)] *n (musical instrument)* flûte *f* à bec
**recording** [rɪˈkɔːdɪŋ] *n* enregistrement *m*
**recount** [rɪˈkaʊnt] *vt (relate)* raconter
**recoup** [rɪˈkuːp] *vt* récupérer
**recourse** [rɪˈkɔːs] *n* recours *m*; **to have r. to** avoir recours à
**recover** [rɪˈkʌvə(r)] **1** *vt (get back)* récupérer; *(one's appetite, balance)* retrouver **2** *vi (from illness, shock, surprise)* se remettre (**from** de); *(of economy, country)* se redresser; *(of sales)* reprendre ▪ **recovery** (*pl* **-ies**) *n* (**a**) *(from illness)* rétablissement *m*; *(of economy)* redressement *m* (**b**) *Br* **r. vehicle** dépanneuse *f*
**re-create** [riːkrɪˈeɪt] *vt* recréer
**recreation** [rekrɪˈeɪʃən] *n Sch (break)* récréation *f*
**recrimination** [rɪkrɪmɪˈneɪʃən] *n* récrimination *f*
**recruit** [rɪˈkruːt] **1** *n* recrue *f* **2** *vt* recruter
**rectangle** [ˈrektæŋgəl] *n* rectangle *m* ▪ **rectangular** *adj* rectangulaire
**rectify** [ˈrektɪfaɪ] (*pt & pp* **-ied**) *vt* rectifier
**rector** [ˈrektə(r)] *n (priest)* pasteur *m* anglican
**recuperate** [rɪˈkuːpəreɪt] *vi (from illness)* récupérer
**recur** [rɪˈkɜː(r)] (*pt & pp* **-rr-**) *vi (of event, problem)* se reproduire; *(of illness)* réapparaître; *(of theme)* revenir
**recycle** [riːˈsaɪkəl] *vt* recycler
**red** [red] **1** (**redder, reddest**) *adj* rouge; *(hair)* roux (*f* rousse); **to turn** *or* **go r.** rougir; **the R. Cross** la Croix-Rouge; **r. light** *(traffic light)* feu *m* rouge; *Fig* **r. tape** paperasserie *f* **2** *n (colour)* rouge *m*; **in the r.** *(in debt)* dans le rouge ▪ **red-handed** *adv* **to be caught r.** être pris la main dans le sac ▪ **redhead** *n* roux *m*, rousse *f* ▪ **red-hot** *adj* brûlant
**redcurrant** [redˈkʌrənt] *n* groseille *f*
**redecorate** [riːˈdekəreɪt] *vt (repaint)* refaire la peinture de
**redeem** [rɪˈdiːm] *vt (restore to favour, buy back, free)* racheter; *(gift token, coupon)* échanger; **his one redeeming feature is...** la seule chose qui le rachète, c'est...
**redirect** [riːdaɪˈrekt] *vt (mail)* faire suivre
**redo** [riːˈduː] (*pt* **-did**, *pp* **-done**) *vt* refaire
**reduce** [rɪˈdjuːs] *vt* réduire (**to** à; **by** de); *(temperature, price)* baisser; **at a reduced price** à prix réduit; **to be reduced to doing sth** en être réduit à faire qch ▪ **reduction** [-ˈdʌkʃən] *n (of temperature, price)* baisse *f*; *(discount)* réduction *f* (**in/on** de/sur)
**redundant** [rɪˈdʌndənt] *adj (not needed)* superflu; *Br* **to make sb r.** licencier qn ▪ **redundancy** (*pl* **-ies**) *n Br (of worker)* licenciement *m*; **r. pay** *or* **payment** *or* **money** prime *f* de licenciement
**reed** [riːd] *n (plant)* roseau *m*
**reef** [riːf] *n* récif *m*
**reek** [riːk] *vi* **to r. (of sth)** puer (qch)
**reel** [riːl] **1** *n (of thread, film)* bobine *f*; *(for fishing line)* moulinet *m* **2** *vt sep* **to r. off** *(names, statistics)* débiter
**re-elect** [riːɪˈlekt] *vt* réélire
**re-establish** [riːɪˈstæblɪʃ] *vt* rétablir
**ref** [ref] (*abbr* **referee**) *n Fam* arbitre *m*
**refectory** [rɪˈfektərɪ] (*pl* **-ies**) *n* réfectoire *m*
**refer** [rɪˈfɜː(r)] (*pt & pp* **-rr-**) **1** *vt* **to r. sth to sb** *(submit)* soumettre qch à qn; **to r. sb to a specialist** envoyer qn voir un spécialiste **2** *vt insep* **to r. to** *(allude to)* faire allusion à; *(mention)* parler de; *(apply to)* s'appliquer à; *(consult)* consulter
**referee** [refəˈriː] **1** *n (in sport)* arbitre *m*; **to give the names of two referees**

*(for job)* fournir deux références **2** *vti* arbitrer

**reference** ['refərəns] *n (source, consultation)* référence *f*; *(allusion)* allusion *f* (**to** à); *(mention)* mention *f* (**to** de); *(for employer)* lettre *f* de référence; **with** *or* **in r. to** concernant; **r. book** ouvrage *m* de référence

**referendum** [refə'rendəm] *n* référendum *m*

**refill 1** ['ri:fɪl] *n (for pen)* cartouche *f*; *(for lighter)* recharge *f*; **would you like a r.?** *(of drink)* je te ressers? **2** [ri:'fɪl] *vt (glass)* remplir à nouveau; *(lighter, pen)* recharger

**refine** [rɪ'faɪn] *vt (oil, sugar, manners)* raffiner; *(technique, machine)* perfectionner ▪ **refined** *adj (person, manners)* raffiné ▪ **refinement** *n (of person, manners)* raffinement *m*; **refinements** *(technical improvements)* améliorations *fpl*

**reflect** [rɪ'flekt] **1** *vt* (**a**) *(light, image)* refléter, réfléchir; *Fig (portray)* refléter; **to be reflected (in)** *(of light)* se refléter (dans) (**b**) **to r. that...** se dire que... **2** *vi* (**a**) **to r. on sb** *(of prestige, honour)* rejaillir sur qn; **to r. badly on sb** faire du tort à qn (**b**) *(think)* réfléchir (**on** à)

**reflection** [rɪ'flekʃən] *n* (**a**) *(image)* & *Fig* reflet *m* (**b**) *(thought, criticism)* réflexion (**on** sur); **on r.** tout bien réfléchi

**reflector** [rɪ'flektə(r)] *n (on bicycle, vehicle)* catadioptre *m*

**reflex** ['ri:fleks] *n* & *adj* réflexe (*m*); **r. action** réflexe *m*

**reflexive** [rɪ'fleksɪv] *adj (verb)* réfléchi

**reform** [rɪ'fɔ:m] **1** *n* réforme *f* **2** *vt* réformer; *(person, conduct)* corriger **3** *vi (of person)* se réformer

**refrain** [rɪ'freɪn] **1** *n (of song)* & *Fig* refrain *m* **2** *vi* s'abstenir (**from sth** de qch; **from doing** de faire)

**refresh** [rɪ'freʃ] *vt (of drink)* rafraîchir; *(of bath)* revigorer; *(of sleep, rest)* reposer; **to r. one's memory** se rafraîchir la mémoire ▪ **refreshing** *adj (drink)* rafraîchissant; *(bath)* revigorant; *(original)* nouveau (*f* nouvelle)

**refreshments** [rɪ'freʃmənts] *npl* rafraîchissements *mpl*

**refrigerate** [rɪ'frɪdʒəreɪt] *vt* réfrigérer ▪ **refrigerator** *n (domestic)* réfrigérateur *m*

**refuel** [ri:'fjʊəl] **1** (*Br* **-ll-**, *Am* **-l-**) *vt (aircraft)* ravitailler en carburant **2** *vi (of aircraft)* se ravitailler en carburant

**refuge** ['refju:dʒ] *n* refuge *m*; **to take r.** se réfugier (**in** dans)

**refugee** [refjʊ'dʒi:] *n* réfugié, -e *mf*

**refund 1** ['ri:fʌnd] *n* remboursement *m* **2** [rɪ'fʌnd] *vt* rembourser

**refurbish** [ri:'fɜ:bɪʃ] *vt* rénover

**refusal** [rɪ'fju:zəl] *n* refus *m*

**refuse**[1] [rɪ'fju:z] **1** *vt* refuser; **to r. to do sth** refuser de faire qch; **to r. sb sth** refuser qch à qn **2** *vi* refuser

**refuse**[2] ['refju:s] *n Br (rubbish)* ordures *fpl*; **r. collection** ramassage *m* des ordures

**refute** [rɪ'fju:t] *vt* réfuter

**regain** [rɪ'geɪn] *vt (lost ground, favour)* regagner; *(health, sight)* retrouver; **to r. consciousness** reprendre connaissance

**regal** ['ri:gəl] *adj* royal

**regard** [rɪ'gɑ:d] **1** *n (admiration)* respect *m*; *(consideration)* égard *m*; **to hold sb in high r.** tenir qn en haute estime; **with r. to** en ce qui concerne; **to give** *or* **send one's regards to sb** transmettre son meilleur souvenir à qn **2** *vt (admire, respect)* estimer; **to r. sb/sth as...** considérer qn/qch comme... ▪ **regarding** *prep* en ce qui concerne

**regardless** [rɪ'gɑ:dləs] **1** *adj* **r. of...** *(without considering)* sans tenir compte de... **2** *adv (all the same)* quand même

**regenerate** [rɪ'dʒenəreɪt] *vt* régénérer

**reggae** ['regeɪ] *n (music)* reggae *m*

**régime** [reɪ'ʒi:m] *n* régime *m*

**regiment** ['redʒɪmənt] *n* régiment *m*

**region** ['ri:dʒən] *n* région *f*; *Fig* **in the r.**

**of** *(about)* environ ▪ **regional** *adj* régional

**register** ['redʒɪstə(r)] **1** *n* registre *m*; *(in school)* cahier *m* d'appel; **electoral r.** liste *f* électorale; **to take the r.** *(of teacher)* faire l'appel
 **2** *vt (birth, death)* déclarer; *(record, note)* enregistrer; *(vehicle)* immatriculer; *(complaint)* déposer
 **3** *vi (enrol)* s'inscrire (**for** à); *(at hotel)* signer le registre; *(of voter)* s'inscrire sur les listes électorales ▪ **registered** *adj (member)* inscrit; *(letter, package)* recommandé; **to send sth by r. post** *or Am* **mail** envoyer qch en recommandé

**registration** [redʒɪ'streɪʃən] *n (enrolment)* inscription *f*; *Br* **r. (number)** *(of vehicle)* numéro *m* d'immatriculation; *Br* **r. document** *(of vehicle)* ≃ carte *f* grise

**registry** ['redʒɪstrɪ] *adj & n Br* **r. (office)** bureau *m* de l'état civil; **to get married in a r. office** se marier à la mairie

**regret** [rɪ'gret] **1** *n* regret *m* **2** *(pt & pp* **-tt-**) *vt* regretter (**to do** de faire; **that** que + *subjunctive*); **to r. doing sth** regretter d'avoir fait qch

**regrettable** [rɪ'gretəbəl] *adj* regrettable (**that** que + *subjunctive*)

**regroup** [ri:'gru:p] *vi* se regrouper

**regular** ['regjʊlə(r)] **1** *adj (steady, even, in grammar)* régulier, -ère; *(usual)* habituel, -elle; *(price)* normal; *(size)* moyen, -enne; *(listener, reader)* fidèle; *Am Fam* **a r. guy** un chic type **2** *n (in bar)* habitué, -e *mf* ▪ **regularly** *adv* régulièrement

**regulate** ['regjʊleɪt] *vt (adjust)* régler; *(control)* réglementer ▪ **regulations** *npl (rules)* règlement *m*

**rehabilitate** [ri:hə'bɪlɪteɪt] *vt* réhabiliter

**rehearse** [rɪ'hɜ:s] *vti* répéter ▪ **rehearsal** *n* répétition *f*

**reign** [reɪn] **1** *n* règne *m*; **in** *or* **during the r. of** sous le règne de **2** *vi* régner (**over** sur)

**reimburse** [ri:ɪm'bɜ:s] *vt* rembourser (**for** de)

**reindeer** ['reɪndɪə(r)] *n inv* renne *m*

**reinforce** [ri:ɪn'fɔ:s] *vt* renforcer (**with** de); **reinforced concrete** béton *m* armé ▪ **reinforcements** *npl (troops)* renforts *mpl*

**reinstate** [ri:ɪn'steɪt] *vt* réintégrer

**reiterate** [ri:'ɪtəreɪt] *vt* réitérer

**reject 1** ['ri:dʒekt] *n (object)* rebus *m* **2** [rɪ'dʒekt] *vt* rejeter; *(candidate, goods, offer)* refuser ▪ **rejection** [rɪ'dʒekʃən] *n* rejet *m*; *(of candidate, goods, offer)* refus *m*

**rejoice** [rɪ'dʒɔɪs] *vi* se réjouir (**over** *or* **at** de) ▪ **rejoicing** *n* réjouissance *f*

**rejoin** [rɪ'dʒɔɪn] *vt (join up with)* rejoindre

**rejuvenate** [rɪ'dʒu:vəneɪt] *vt* rajeunir

**relapse** ['ri:læps] *n* rechute *f*

**relate** [rɪ'leɪt] **1** *vt* (**a**) *(narrate)* raconter (**that** que); *(report)* rapporter (**that** que) (**b**) *(connect)* mettre en rapport (**to** avec)
 **2** *vi* **to r. to** *(apply to)* avoir rapport à; *(person)* avoir des affinités avec ▪ **related** *adj (linked)* lié (**to** à); *(languages, styles)* apparenté; **to be r. to sb** *(by family)* être parent de qn

**relation** [rɪ'leɪʃən] *n* (**a**) *(relative)* parent, -e *mf* (**b**) *(relationship)* rapport *m*; **international relations** relations *fpl* internationales

**relationship** [rɪ'leɪʃənʃɪp] *n (within family)* lien *m* de parenté; *(between people)* relation *f*; *(between countries)* relations *fpl*; *(connection)* rapport *m*

**relative** ['relətɪv] **1** *n* parent, -e *mf* **2** *adj (comparative)* relatif, -ive; *(respective)* respectif, -ive; **r. to** *(compared to)* relativement à ▪ **relatively** *adv* relativement

**relax** [rɪ'læks] **1** *vt (person, mind)* détendre; *(grip, pressure)* relâcher; *(law, control)* assouplir **2** *vi (of person)* se détendre; **r.!** *(calm down)* du calme! ▪ **relaxed** *adj (person, atmosphere)* détendu ▪ **relaxing** *adj* délassant

**relaxation** [riːlækˈseɪʃən] *n (of person)* détente *f*

**relay 1** [ˈriːleɪ] *n* **r. (race)** (course *f* de) relais *m* **2** [riːˈleɪ] *vt (information)* transmettre (**to** à)

**release** [rɪˈliːs] **1** *n (of prisoner)* libération *f*; *(of film)* sortie *f* (**of** de); *(film)* nouveau film *m*; *(record)* nouveau disque *m* **2** *vt (person)* libérer (**from** de); *(brake)* desserrer; *(film, record)* sortir; *(news)* communiquer; **to r. sb's hand** lâcher la main de qn

**relegate** [ˈrelɪgeɪt] *vt* reléguer (**to** à); *Br* **to be relegated** *(of team)* descendre en division inférieure

**relent** [rɪˈlent] *vi (of person)* céder

**relentless** [rɪˈlentləs] *adj* implacable

**relevant** [ˈreləvənt] *adj* (**a**) *(apt)* pertinent; **to be r. to sth** avoir rapport à qch; **that's not r.** ça n'a rien à voir (**b**) *(appropriate) (chapter)* correspondant; *(authorities)* compétent; *(qualifications)* requis (**c**) *(topical)* d'actualité ▪ **relevance** *n* pertinence *f* (**to** à); *(connection)* rapport *m* (**to** avec)

**reliable** [rɪˈlaɪəbəl] *adj (person, machine)* fiable; *(information)* sûr ▪ **reliability** *n (of person)* sérieux *m*; *(of machine)* fiabilité *f*

**relic** [ˈrelɪk] *n* relique *f*; *Fig* **relics** vestiges *mpl*

**relief** [rɪˈliːf] **1** *n (comfort)* soulagement *m*; *(help)* secours *m*; *(in art)* relief *m* **2** *adj (train, bus)* supplémentaire; *(work)* de secours; **r. map** carte *f* en relief; *Br* **r. road** route *f* de délestage

**relieve** [rɪˈliːv] *vt (alleviate)* soulager; *(boredom)* tromper; *(replace)* remplacer; *(free)* libérer; **to r. sb of sth** débarrasser qn de qch; *Hum* **to r. oneself** se soulager

**religion** [rɪˈlɪdʒən] *n* religion *f* ▪ **religious** *adj* religieux, -euse

**relinquish** [rɪˈlɪŋkwɪʃ] *vt (hope, habit, thought)* abandonner; *(share, claim)* renoncer à

**relish** [ˈrelɪʃ] **1** *n (pickle)* condiments *mpl*; *(pleasure)* goût *m* (**for** pour); **to do sth with r.** faire qch avec délectation **2** *vt* savourer

**reload** [riːˈləʊd] *vt (gun, camera)* recharger

**relocate** [*Br* riːləʊˈkeɪt, *Am* riːˈləʊkeɪt] *vi (of company)* être transféré; *(of person)* se déplacer

**reluctant** [rɪˈlʌktənt] *adj (greeting, promise)* accordé à contrecœur; **to be r. (to do sth)** être réticent (à faire qch) ▪ **reluctantly** *adv* à contrecœur

**rely** [rɪˈlaɪ] *(pt & pp* **-ied***) vi* **to r. (up)on** *(count on)* compter sur; *(be dependent on)* dépendre de

**remain** [rɪˈmeɪn] *vi (stay behind, continue to be)* rester; *(be left)* subsister ▪ **remaining** *adj* restant ▪ **remains** *npl* restes *mpl*

**remainder** [rɪˈmeɪndə(r)] *n* reste *m*; *(book)* invendu *m* soldé

**remark** [rɪˈmɑːk] **1** *n* remarque *f* **2** *vt* faire remarquer **3** *vi* **to r. on sth** *(comment)* faire un commentaire sur qch ▪ **remarkable** *adj* remarquable ▪ **remarkably** *adv* remarquablement

**remarry** [riːˈmærɪ] *(pt & pp* **-ied***) vi* se remarier

**remedy** [ˈremɪdɪ] **1** *(pl* **-ies***) n* remède *m* **2** *(pt & pp* **-ied***) vt* remédier à

**remember** [rɪˈmembə(r)] **1** *vt* se souvenir de, se rappeler; *(commemorate)* commémorer; **to r. that/doing** se rappeler que/d'avoir fait; **to r. to do sth** penser à faire qch; **to r. sb to sb** rappeler qn au bon souvenir de qn **2** *vi* se souvenir, se rappeler

**remind** [rɪˈmaɪnd] *vt* **to r. sb of sth** rappeler qch à qn; **to r. sb to do sth** rappeler à qn de faire qch ▪ **reminder** *n (letter, of event)* rappel *m*

**reminisce** [remɪˈnɪs] *vi* évoquer des souvenirs; **to r. about sth** évoquer qch ▪ **reminiscence** *n* souvenir *m*

**reminiscent** [remɪˈnɪsənt] *adj* **r. of** qui rappelle

**remittance** [rɪˈmɪtəns] *n (sum)* paiement *m*

**remorse** [rɪˈmɔːs] *n* remords *m*; **to feel r.** avoir du *ou* des remords

▪ **remorseless** *adj* impitoyable
**remote** [rɪ'məʊt] (**-er, -est**) *adj* (**a**) *(far-off)* éloigné (**from** de); **r. control** télécommande *f* (**b**) *(slight)* vague ▪ **remotely** *adv (slightly)* vaguement
**removable** [rɪ'mu:vəbəl] *adj (lining)* amovible
**removal** [rɪ'mu:vəl] *n* (**a**) *(of control, threat)* suppression *f*; *(of politician)* renvoi *m* (**b**) *Br* **r. van** camion *m* de déménagement
**remove** [rɪ'mu:v] *vt (clothes, stain, object)* enlever (**from sb** à qn; **from sth** de qch); *(obstacle, threat, word)* supprimer; *(fear, doubt)* dissiper; *(politician)* renvoyer
**remover** [rɪ'mu:və(r)] *n (for nail polish)* dissolvant *m*; *(for paint)* décapant *m*; *(for stains)* détachant *m*
**remunerate** [rɪ'mju:nəreɪt] *vt* rémunérer
**rename** [ri:'neɪm] *vt* rebaptiser; *Comptr (file)* renommer
**rendezvous** ['rɒndɪvu:, *pl* -vu:z] *n inv* rendez-vous *m inv*
**renew** [rɪ'nju:] *vt* renouveler; *(resume)* reprendre; *(library book)* renouveler le prêt de ▪ **renewed** *adj (efforts)* renouvelé; *(attempt)* nouveau (*f* nouvelle)
**renounce** [rɪ'naʊns] *vt (give up)* renoncer à; *(disown)* renier
**renovate** ['renəveɪt] *vt (house)* rénover; *(painting)* restaurer
**renowned** [rɪ'naʊnd] *adj* renommé (**for** pour)
**rent** [rent] **1** *n (for house, flat)* loyer *m* **2** *vt* louer; **to r. out** louer; **rented car** voiture *f* de location
**rental** ['rentəl] *n (of television, car)* location *f*; *(of telephone)* abonnement *m*
**reopen** [ri:'əʊpən] *vti* rouvrir
**reorganize** [ri:'ɔ:gənaɪz] *vt* réorganiser
**rep** [rep] *(abbr* **representative**) *n Fam* VRP *m*
**repair** [rɪ'peə(r)] **1** *n* réparation *f*; **under r.** en travaux **2** *vt* réparer
**repay** [ri:'peɪ] (*pt & pp* **-paid**) *vt (pay back)* rembourser; *(reward)* remercier (**for** de) ▪ **repayment** *n* remboursement *m*
**repeal** [rɪ'pi:l] *vt* abroger
**repeat** [rɪ'pi:t] **1** *n (of event)* répétition *f*; *(on TV, radio)* rediffusion *f*
**2** *vt* répéter (**that** que); *(promise, threat)* réitérer; *(class)* redoubler; *(TV programme)* rediffuser; **to r. oneself** se répéter
**3** *vi* répéter ▪ **repeated** *adj (attempts)* répété; *(efforts)* renouvelé ▪ **repeatedly** *adv* à maintes reprises
**repel** [rɪ'pel] (*pt & pp* **-ll-**) *vt* repousser ▪ **repellent 1** *adj (disgusting)* repoussant **2** *n* **insect r.** anti-moustiques *m inv*
**repent** [rɪ'pent] *vi* se repentir (**of** de) ▪ **repentant** *adj* repentant
**repercussions** [ri:pə'kʌʃənz] *npl* répercussions *fpl* (**on** sur)
**repertoire** ['repətwɑ:(r)] *n Theatre & Fig* répertoire *m* ▪ **repertory** [-tərɪ] (*pl* **-ies**) *n Theatre & Fig* répertoire *m*; **r. theatre** théâtre *m* de répertoire
**repetition** [repɪ'tɪʃən] *n* répétition *f* ▪ **repetitious, repetitive** [repə'tɪʃəs, rɪ'petɪtɪv] *adj* répétitif, -ive
**rephrase** [ri:'freɪz] *vt* reformuler
**replace** [rɪ'pleɪs] *vt (take the place of)* remplacer (**by** *or* **with** par); *(put back)* remettre (à sa place); **to r. the receiver** *(on phone)* raccrocher ▪ **replacement** *n (substitution)* remplacement *m* (**of** de); *(person)* remplaçant, -e *mf*; *(machine part)* pièce *f* de rechange
**replay 1** ['ri:pleɪ] *n (match)* nouvelle rencontre *f*; **(instant** *or* **action) r.** *(on TV)* = répétition d'une séquence précédente **2** [ri:'pleɪ] *vt (match)* rejouer
**replica** ['replɪkə] *n* réplique *f*
**reply** [rɪ'plaɪ] **1** (*pl* **-ies**) *n* réponse *f*; **in r.** en réponse (**to** à) **2** (*pt & pp* **-ied**) *vti* répondre (**to** à; **that** que)
**report** [rɪ'pɔ:t] **1** *n (analysis)* rapport *m*; *(account)* compte rendu *m*; *(in media)* reportage *m*; *Br* **(school) r.**, *Am* **r. card** bulletin *m* scolaire

**2** *vt (information)* rapporter; *(accident, theft)* signaler (**to** à); **to r. sb to the police** dénoncer qn à la police
**3** *vi (give account)* faire un rapport (**on** sur); *(of journalist)* faire un reportage (**on** sur); *(go)* se présenter (**to** à) ▪ **reported** *adj* **r. speech** *(in grammar)* discours *m* indirect; **it is r. that...** on dit que...; **to be r. missing** être porté disparu ▪ **reporter** *n* reporter *m*

**repossess** [riːpəˈzes] *vt* saisir

**represent** [reprɪˈzent] *vt* représenter ▪ **representation** *n* représentation *f*

**representative** [reprɪˈzentətɪv] **1** *adj* représentatif, -ive (**of** de) **2** *n* représentant, -e *mf*; *Am Pol* ≃ député *m*

**repress** [rɪˈpres] *vt* réprimer; *(memory, feeling)* refouler; **to be repressed** *(of person)* être un(e) refoulé(e) ▪ **repressive** *adj (régime)* répressif, -ive; *(measures)* de répression

**reprieve** [rɪˈpriːv] *n (cancellation of sentence)* commutation *f* de la peine capitale; *(temporary) & Fig* sursis *m*

**reprimand** [ˈreprɪmɑːnd] **1** *n* réprimande *f* **2** *vt* réprimander

**reprint 1** [ˈriːprɪnt] *n* réimpression *f* **2** [riːˈprɪnt] *vt* réimprimer

**reprisal** [rɪˈpraɪzəl] *n* représailles *fpl*; **as a r. for, in r. for** en représailles de

**reproach** [rɪˈprəʊtʃ] **1** *n (blame)* reproche *m* **2** *vt* faire des reproches à; **to r. sb with sth** reprocher qch à qn

**reproduce** [riːprəˈdjuːs] **1** *vt* reproduire **2** *vi* se reproduire ▪ **reproduction** [-ˈdʌkʃən] *n* reproduction *f*

**reptile** [ˈreptaɪl] *n* reptile *m*

**republic** [rɪˈpʌblɪk] *n* république *f* ▪ **republican** *adj & n* républicain, -e *(mf)*

**repugnant** [rɪˈpʌgnənt] *adj* répugnant

**repulsive** [rɪˈpʌlsɪv] *adj* repoussant

**reputable** [ˈrepjʊtəbəl] *adj* de bonne réputation ▪ **reputed** *adj* **she's r. to be wealthy** on la dit riche

**reputation** [repjʊˈteɪʃən] *n* réputation *f*

**request** [rɪˈkwest] **1** *n* demande *f* (**for** de); **on r.** sur demande; **at sb's r.** à la demande de qn; *Br* **r. stop** *(for bus)* arrêt *m* facultatif **2** *vt* demander; **to r. sb to do sth** prier qn de faire qch

**require** [rɪˈkwaɪə(r)] *vt (of task, problem, situation)* requérir; *(of person)* avoir besoin de; **to be required to do sth** être tenu de faire qch; **the required qualities** les qualités *fpl* requises ▪ **requirement** *n (need)* exigence *f*; *(condition)* condition *f* (requise)

**requisite** [ˈrekwɪzɪt] *adj* requis

**reschedule** [*Br* riːˈʃedjuːl, *Am* riːˈskedʒʊəl] *vt* changer la date/l'heure de

**rescue** [ˈreskjuː] **1** *n (action)* sauvetage *m* (**of** de); **to go/come to sb's r.** aller/venir au secours de qn **2** *adj (team, operation, attempt)* de sauvetage **3** *vt (save)* sauver; *(set free)* délivrer (**from** de)

**research** [rɪˈsɜːtʃ] **1** *n* recherches *fpl* (**on** *or* **into** sur) **2** *vi* faire des recherches (**on** *or* **into** sur) ▪ **researcher** *n* chercheur, -euse *mf*

**resemble** [rɪˈzembəl] *vt* ressembler à ▪ **resemblance** *n* ressemblance *f* (**to** avec)

**resent** [rɪˈzent] *vt* ne pas aimer ▪ **resentment** *n* ressentiment *m*

**reservation** [rezəˈveɪʃən] *n* (**a**) *(booking)* réservation *f*; **to make a r.** réserver (**b**) *(doubt)* réserve *f* (**c**) *(land for Indians, animals)* réserve *f*

**reserve** [rɪˈzɜːv] **1** *n* (**a**) *(reticence)* réserve *f* (**b**) *(stock, land)* réserve *f*; **r. (player)** *(in team)* remplaçant, -e *mf*; *Mil* **the reserves** les réservistes *mpl*; **in r.** en réserve; **r. tank** *(of vehicle, aircraft)* réservoir *m* de secours
**2** *vt (room, decision)* réserver; *(right)* se réserver ▪ **reserved** *adj (person, room)* réservé

**reservoir** [ˈrezəvwɑː(r)] *n (of water)* réservoir *m*

**reset** [riːˈset] *vt (counter)* remettre à zéro

**reshuffle** [riːˈʃʌfəl] *n* **(cabinet) r.** remaniement *m* (ministériel)

**reside** [rɪ'zaɪd] *vi* résider

**residence** ['rezɪdəns] *n (home)* résidence *f*; *(of students)* foyer *m*; *Br* **r. permit** permis *m* de séjour

**resident** ['rezɪdənt] **1** *n (of country, street)* habitant, -e *mf*; *(of hotel)* pensionnaire *mf*; *(foreigner)* résident, -e *mf* **2** *adj* **to be r. in London** résider à Londres

**residential** [rezɪ'denʃəl] *adj (neighbourhood)* résidentiel, -elle

**resign** [rɪ'zaɪn] **1** *vt (job)* démissionner de; **to r. oneself to sth/to doing sth** se résigner à qch/à faire qch **2** *vi* démissionner (**from** de) ▪ **resigned** *adj* résigné

**resignation** [rezɪg'neɪʃən] *n (from job)* démission *f*; *(attitude)* résignation *f*

**resilient** [rɪ'zɪlɪənt] *adj* élastique; *Fig (person)* résistant

**resist** [rɪ'zɪst] **1** *vt* résister à; **to r. doing sth** s'empêcher de faire qch **2** *vi* résister ▪ **resistance** *n* résistance *f* (**to** à) ▪ **resistant** *adj* résistant (**to** à)

**resit** [riː'sɪt] *(pt & pp* **-sat**, *pres p* **-sitting**) *vt Br (exam)* repasser

**resolute** ['rezəluːt] *adj* résolu ▪ **resolution** *n* résolution *f*

**resolve** [rɪ'zɒlv] **1** *n* résolution *f* **2** *vt (problem)* résoudre; **to r. to do sth** *(of person)* se résoudre à faire qch

**resort** [rɪ'zɔːt] **1** *n* (**a**) *(holiday place)* lieu *m* de villégiature; *Br* **seaside r.**, *Am* **beach r.** station *f* balnéaire (**b**) *(recourse)* **as a last r., in the last r.** en dernier ressort **2** *vi* **to r. to sth** avoir recours à qch; **to r. to doing sth** finir par faire qch

**resounding** [rɪ'zaʊndɪŋ] *adj (failure)* retentissant; *(success)* éclatant

**resource** [rɪ'sɔːs, rɪ'zɔːs] *n* ressource *f* ▪ **resourceful** *adj* ingénieux, -euse

**respect** [rɪ'spekt] **1** *n* respect *m* (**for** pour); *(aspect)* égard *m*; **in many respects** à bien des égards; **with r. to, in r. of** en ce qui concerne **2** *vt* respecter

**respectable** [rɪ'spektəbəl] *adj (decent, fairly large)* respectable; *(fairly good)* honorable

**respective** [rɪ'spektɪv] *adj* respectif, -ive ▪ **respectively** *adv* respectivement

**respond** [rɪ'spɒnd] *vi (answer)* répondre (**to** à); *(react)* réagir (**to** à); **to r. to treatment** bien réagir (au traitement) ▪ **response** *n (answer)* réponse *f*; *(reaction)* réaction *f*; **in r. to** en réponse à

**responsible** [rɪ'spɒnsəbəl] *adj* responsable (**for** de); *(job)* à responsabilités ▪ **responsibility** (*pl* **-ies**) *n* responsabilité *f* (**for** de) ▪ **responsibly** *adv* de façon responsable

**responsive** [rɪ'spɒnsɪv] *adj (reacting)* qui réagit bien; *(alert)* éveillé; **r. to** *(suggestion)* réceptif, -ive à

**rest**[1] [rest] **1** *n (relaxation)* repos *m*; *(support)* support *m*; **to have** *or* **take a r.** se reposer; **to set** *or* **put sb's mind at r.** tranquilliser qn; *Am* **r. room** toilettes *fpl*

**2** *vt (lean)* poser (**on** sur); *(horse)* laisser reposer

**3** *vi (relax)* se reposer; *(lean)* être posé (**on** sur); **to r. on** *(of argument, roof)* reposer sur; **a resting place** un lieu de repos

**rest**[2] [rest] **1** *n (remainder)* reste *m* (**of** de); **the r.** *(others)* les autres *mfpl* **2** *vi* **to r. with sb** *(of decision, responsibility)* incomber à qn

**restaurant** ['restərɒnt] *n* restaurant *m*; *Br* **r. car** *(on train)* wagon-restaurant *m*

**restful** ['restfəl] *adj* reposant

**restless** ['restləs] *adj* agité

**restore** [rɪ'stɔː(r)] *vt (give back)* rendre (**to** à); *(order, peace, rights)* rétablir; *(building, painting, monarchy)* restaurer

**restrain** [rɪ'streɪn] *vt (person, dog)* maîtriser; *(crowd, anger)* contenir; **to r. sb from doing sth** retenir qn pour qu'il ne fasse pas qch ▪ **restrained** *adj (manner)* réservé ▪ **restraint** *n (moderation)* mesure *f*; *(restriction)* restriction *f*

**restrict** [rɪ'strɪkt] *vt* restreindre; **to r. oneself to sth/doing sth** se limiter à qch/à faire qch ▪ **restricted** *adj* restreint ▪ **restriction** *n* restriction *f* (**on** à)

**result** [rɪ'zʌlt] **1** *n (outcome, success)* résultat *m*; **as a r.** en conséquence; **as a r. of** à la suite de **2** *vi* résulter (**from** de); **to r. in sth** aboutir à qch

**resume** [rɪ'zju:m] *vti* reprendre; **to r. doing sth** se remettre à faire qch ▪ **resumption** [-'zʌmpʃən] *n* reprise *f*

**résumé** ['rezjʊmeɪ] *n (summary)* résumé *m*; *Am (CV)* curriculum vitae *m inv*

**resurgence** [rɪ'sɜ:dʒəns] *n* réapparition *f*

**resurrect** [rezə'rekt] *vt Fig (fashion)* remettre au goût du jour ▪ **resurrection** *n Rel* résurrection *f*

**resuscitate** [rɪ'sʌsɪteɪt] *vt Med* ranimer

**retail** ['ri:teɪl] **1** *n* (vente *f* au) détail *m* **2** *adj (price)* de détail **3** *vi* se vendre (au détail) (**at** à) ▪ **retailer** *n* détaillant *m*

**retain** [rɪ'teɪn] *vt (keep)* conserver; *(hold in place)* retenir

**retaliate** [rɪ'tælɪeɪt] *vi* riposter ▪ **retaliation** *n* représailles *fpl*; **in r. for** en représailles à

**retch** [retʃ] *vi* avoir des haut-le-cœur

**rethink** [ri:'θɪŋk] (*pt & pp* **-thought**) *vt* repenser

**reticent** ['retɪsənt] *adj* peu communicatif, -ive

**retire** [rɪ'taɪə(r)] *vi* (**a**) *(from work)* prendre sa retraite (**b**) *(withdraw)* se retirer (**from** de; **to** à); *(go to bed)* aller se coucher ▪ **retired** *adj (no longer working)* retraité

**retirement** [rɪ'taɪəmənt] *n* retraite *f*; **r. age** l'âge *m* de la retraite

**retrace** [ri:'treɪs] *vt* **to r. one's steps** revenir sur ses pas

**retract** [rɪ'trækt] **1** *vt* (**a**) *(statement)* revenir sur (**b**) *(claws)* rentrer **2** *vi (of person)* se rétracter

**retrain** [ri:'treɪn] **1** *vt* recycler **2** *vi* se recycler ▪ **retraining** *n* recyclage *m*

**retreat** [rɪ'tri:t] **1** *n (withdrawal)* retraite *f*; *(place)* refuge *m* **2** *vi* se réfugier; *(of troops)* battre en retraite

**retribution** [retrɪ'bju:ʃən] *n* châtiment *m*

**retrieve** [rɪ'tri:v] *vt (recover)* récupérer

**retrospect** ['retrəspekt] *n* **in r.** rétrospectivement

**retrospective** [retrə'spektɪv] *adj* rétrospectif, -ive; *(law)* à effet rétroactif

**return** [rɪ'tɜ:n] **1** *n* retour *m*; *Fin (on investment)* rapport *m*; **returns** *(profits)* bénéfices *mpl*; *Br* **r. (ticket)** (billet *m*) aller et retour *m*; **many happy returns!** bon anniversaire!; **in r.** en échange (**for** de); **by r. of post** par retour du courrier

**2** *adj (trip, flight)* (de) retour; **r. match** match *m* retour

**3** *vt (give back)* rendre; *(put back)* remettre; *(bring back)* rapporter; *(send back)* renvoyer; **to r. sb's call** *(on phone)* rappeler qn

**4** *vi (come back)* revenir; *(go back)* retourner; *(go back home)* rentrer; **to r. to** *(subject)* revenir à

**reunion** [ri:'ju:njən] *n* réunion *f* ▪ **reunite** *vt* réconcilier; **to be reunited with sb** retrouver qn

**reuse** [ri:'ju:z] *vt* réutiliser

**reveal** [rɪ'vi:l] *vt (make known)* révéler (**that** que); *(make visible)* laisser voir ▪ **revealing** *adj (sign, comment)* révélateur, -trice

**revel** ['revəl] (*Br* **-ll-**, *Am* **-l-**) *vi* faire la fête; **to r. in sth** savourer qch

**revelation** [revə'leɪʃən] *n* révélation *f*

**revenge** [rɪ'vendʒ] **1** *n* vengeance *f*; **to have** *or* **get one's r. (on sb)** se venger (de qn); **in r.** pour se venger **2** *vt* venger

**revenue** ['revənju:] *n (income)* revenu *m*; *(from sales)* recettes *fpl*

**reverence** ['revərəns] *n* révérence *f*

**reversal** [rɪ'vɜ:səl] *n (of situation, roles)* renversement *m*; *(of policy, opinion)* revirement *m*; **r. (of fortune)** revers *m* (de fortune)

**reverse** [rɪˈvɜːs] **1** *adj (opposite)* contraire; *(image)* inverse; **in r. order** dans l'ordre inverse

**2** *n* contraire *m*; *(of coin)* revers *m*; *(of fabric)* envers *m*; *(of paper)* verso *m*; **in r. (gear)** *(when driving)* en marche arrière

**3** *vt (situation)* renverser; *(order, policy)* inverser; *(decision)* revenir sur; **to r. the car** faire marche arrière; *Br* **to r. the charges** *(when phoning)* téléphoner en PCV

**4** *vi Br (in car)* faire marche arrière; **to r. in/out** rentrer/sortir en marche arrière

**revert** [rɪˈvɜːt] *vi* **to r. to** revenir à

**review** [rɪˈvjuː] **1** *n* (**a**) *(of book, film)* critique *f*; **to be under r.** faire l'objet d'une révision (**b**) *(magazine)* revue *f* **2** *vt (book, film)* faire la critique de; *(troops)* passer en revue; *(situation)* faire le point sur; *(salary)* réviser ▪ **reviewer** *n* critique *m*

**revise** [rɪˈvaɪz] **1** *vt (opinion, notes, text)* réviser **2** *vi (for exam)* réviser (**for** pour) ▪ **revision** *n* révision *f*

**revival** [rɪˈvaɪvəl] *n (of custom, business, play)* reprise *f*; *(of fashion)* renouveau *m*

**revive** [rɪˈvaɪv] **1** *vt (person)* ranimer; *(custom, industry)* faire renaître; *(fashion)* relancer **2** *vi (of person)* reprendre connaissance; *(of industry)* connaître un renouveau; *(of interest)* renaître

**revolt** [rɪˈvəʊlt] **1** *n* révolte *f* **2** *vt (disgust)* révolter **3** *vi (rebel)* se révolter (**against** contre) ▪ **revolting** *adj* dégoûtant

**revolution** [revəˈluːʃən] *n* révolution *f* ▪ **revolutionary** (*pl* **-ies**) *adj & n* révolutionnaire *(mf)*

**revolve** [rɪˈvɒlv] *vi* tourner (**around** autour de) ▪ **revolving** *adj* **r. door(s)** porte *f* à tambour

**revolver** [rɪˈvɒlvə(r)] *n* revolver *m*

**revulsion** [rɪˈvʌlʃən] *n (disgust)* dégoût *m*

**reward** [rɪˈwɔːd] **1** *n* récompense *f* (**for** de) **2** *vt* récompenser (**for** de *ou* pour) ▪ **rewarding** *adj* intéressant

**rewind** [riːˈwaɪnd] (*pt & pp* **-wound**) *vt (tape, film)* rembobiner

**rewrite** [riːˈraɪt] (*pt* **-wrote,** *pp* **-written**) *vt* réécrire

**rhetoric** [ˈretərɪk] *n* rhétorique *f* ▪ **rhetorical** [rɪˈtɒrɪkəl] *adj* **r. question** question *f* de pure forme

**rheumatism** [ˈruːmətɪzəm] *n* rhumatisme *m*; **to have r.** avoir des rhumatismes

**rhinoceros** [raɪˈnɒsərəs] *n* rhinocéros *m*

**rhubarb** [ˈruːbɑːb] *n* rhubarbe *f*

**rhyme** [raɪm] **1** *n* rime *f*; *(poem)* vers *mpl* **2** *vi* rimer (**with** avec)

**rhythm** [ˈrɪðəm] *n* rythme *m* ▪ **rhythmic(al)** [ˈrɪðmɪk(əl)] *adj* rythmé

**rib** [rɪb] *n (bone)* côte *f*

**ribbon** [ˈrɪbən] *n* ruban *m*

**rice** [raɪs] *n* riz *m*; **r. pudding** riz *m* au lait

**rich** [rɪtʃ] **1** (**-er, -est**) *adj (person, food)* riche; **to be r. in sth** être riche en qch **2** *npl* **the r.** les riches *mpl* ▪ **riches** *npl* richesses *fpl*

**rid** [rɪd] (*pt & pp* **rid,** *pres p* **ridding**) *vt* débarrasser (**of** de); **to get r. of, to r. oneself of** se débarrasser de ▪ **riddance** [ˈrɪdəns] *n Fam* **good r.!** bon débarras!

**ridden** [ˈrɪdən] *pp of* **ride**

**riddle** [ˈrɪdəl] **1** *n (puzzle)* devinette *f*; *(mystery)* énigme *f* **2** *vt* cribler (**with** de); **riddled with mistakes** truffé de fautes

**ride** [raɪd] **1** *n (on horse)* promenade *f*; *(on bicycle, in car)* tour *m*; *(in taxi)* course *f*; **to go for a r.** aller faire un tour; **to give sb a r.** *(in car)* emmener qn en voiture; *Fam* **to take sb for a r.** mener qn en bateau

**2** (*pt* **rode,** *pp* **ridden**) *vt (horse, bicycle)* monter à; *(a particular horse)* monter; **to know how to r. a bicycle** savoir faire de la bicyclette

**3** *vi (on horse)* faire du cheval; *(on bicycle)* faire de la bicyclette; **to go**

**riding** *(on horse)* faire du cheval; **I ride to work** *(on bicycle)* je vais travailler à bicyclette

**rider** ['raɪdə(r)] *n (on horse)* cavalier, -ère *mf*; *(cyclist)* cycliste *mf*

**ridge** [rɪdʒ] *n (of mountain)* crête *f*

**ridicule** ['rɪdɪkjuːl] **1** *n* ridicule *m*; **to hold sb/sth up to r.** tourner qn/qch en ridicule **2** *vt* tourner en ridicule, ridiculiser

**ridiculous** [rɪ'dɪkjʊləs] *adj* ridicule

**riding** ['raɪdɪŋ] *n* **(horse) r.** équitation *f*

**rife** [raɪf] *adj (widespread)* répandu

**riffraff** ['rɪfræf] *n* racaille *f*

**rifle** ['raɪfəl] *n* fusil *m*

**rift** [rɪft] *n (in political party)* scission *f*; *(disagreement)* désaccord *m*

**rig** [rɪg] **1** *n* **(oil) r.** derrick *m*; *(at sea)* plate-forme *f* pétrolière **2** *(pt & pp* **-gg-***) vt Fam (result, election)* truquer; **to r. up** *(equipment)* installer

**right¹** [raɪt] **1** *adj* (**a**) *(correct)* bon (*f* bonne), exact; *(word)* juste; **to be r.** *(of person)* avoir raison (**to do** de faire); **it's the r. time** c'est l'heure exacte; **that's r.** c'est ça; **r.!** bon!
(**b**) *(appropriate)* bon (*f* bonne); **he's the r. man** c'est l'homme qu'il faut
(**c**) *(morally good)* bien *inv*; **to do the r. thing** faire ce qu'il faut
(**d**) *Fam (for emphasis)* véritable; **I felt a r. fool** je me suis vraiment senti stupide
(**e**) *Math* **r. angle** angle *m* droit
**2** *adv (straight)* (tout) droit; *(completely)* tout à fait; *(correctly)* correctement; **to put sth r.** *(rectify)* corriger qch; *(fix)* arranger qch; **to put sb r.** détromper qn; **r. round** tout autour (**sth** de qch); **r. behind** juste derrière; **r. here** ici même; **r. away, r. now** tout de suite
**3** *n* **to be in the r.** avoir raison; **r. and wrong** le bien et le mal
**4** *vt (error, wrong, boat, car)* redresser

**right²** [raɪt] **1** *adj (not left) (hand, side)* droit **2** *adv* à droite **3** *n* droite *f*; **on** *or* **to the r.** à droite (**of** de) ▪ **right-hand** *adj* de droite; **on the r. side** à droite (**of** de) ▪ **right-handed** *adj (person)* droitier, -ère ▪ **right-wing** *adj Pol* de droite

**right³** [raɪt] *n (entitlement)* droit *m* (**to do** de faire); **to have a r. to sth** avoir droit à qch; **to have (the) r. of way** *(on road)* avoir la priorité

**rightful** ['raɪtfəl] *adj* légitime

**rightly** ['raɪtlɪ] *adv (correctly)* bien; *(justifiably)* à juste titre

**rigid** ['rɪdʒɪd] *adj* rigide

**rigorous** ['rɪgərəs] *adj* rigoureux, -euse

**rim** [rɪm] *n (of cup)* bord *m*; *(of wheel)* jante *f*

**rind** [raɪnd] *n (of cheese)* croûte *f*; *(of bacon)* couenne *f*

**ring¹** [rɪŋ] *n (for finger, curtain)* anneau *m*; *(for finger, with stone)* bague *f*; *(on stove)* brûleur *m*; *(of people, chairs)* cercle *m*; *(of criminals)* bande *f*; *(at circus)* piste *f*; *(for boxing)* ring *m*; **to have rings under one's eyes** avoir les yeux cernés; *Br* **r. road** périphérique *m*

**ring²** [rɪŋ] **1** *n (sound)* **there's a r. at the door** on sonne à la porte; *Fam* **to give sb a r.** passer un coup de fil à qn
**2** *(pt* **rang,** *pp* **rung***) vt (bell)* sonner; *(alarm)* déclencher; **to r. sb** *(on phone)* téléphoner à qn; **to r. the doorbell** sonner à la porte; *Fam* **that rings a bell** ça me dit quelque chose
**3** *vi (of bell, phone, person)* sonner; *(of sound, words)* retentir; *(of ears)* bourdonner; *(make a phone call)* téléphoner ▪ **ringing** *adj Br* **r. tone** *(on phone)* sonnerie *f*

▸ **ring back 1** *vt sep* **to r. sb back** rappeler qn **2** *vi* rappeler

▸ **ring off** *vi (on phone)* raccrocher

▸ **ring out** *vi (of bell)* sonner; *(of voice, shout)* retentir

▸ **ring up 1** *vt sep* **to r. sb up** téléphoner à qn **2** *vi* téléphoner

**ringleader** ['rɪŋliːdə(r)] *n Pej (of rebellion, strike)* meneur, -euse *mf*

**rink** [rɪŋk] *n (for ice-skating)* patinoire *f*; *(for roller-skating)* piste *f*

**rinse** [rɪns] **1** *n* rinçage *m*; **to give sth a r.** rincer qch **2** *vt* rincer; **to r. one's hands** se rincer les mains; **to r. out** rincer

**riot** ['raɪət] **1** *n (uprising)* émeute *f*; **to run r.** se déchaîner **2** *vi (rise up)* faire une émeute; *(of prisoners)* se mutiner ▪ **rioter** *n* émeutier, -ère *mf*; *(vandal)* casseur *m* ▪ **rioting** *n* émeutes *fpl*

**rip** [rɪp] **1** *n* déchirure *f* **2** *(pt & pp* **-pp-***) vt* déchirer; **to r. sth off** arracher qch (**from** de); *Fam (steal)* faucher qch; *Fam* **to r. sb off** *(deceive)* rouler qn; **to r. sth up** déchirer qch **3** *vi (of fabric)* se déchirer ▪ **rip-off** *n Fam* arnaque *f*

**ripe** [raɪp] (**-er, -est**) *adj (fruit)* mûr; *(cheese)* fait ▪ **ripen** *vti* mûrir

**rise** [raɪz] **1** *n (in price, pressure)* hausse *f* (**in** de); *(slope in ground)* montée *f*; *(of leader, party)* ascension *f*; *Br* **(pay) r.** augmentation *f* (de salaire); **to give r. to sth** donner lieu à qch

**2** *(pt* **rose**, *pp* **risen** ['rɪzən]) *vi (of temperature, balloon, price)* monter; *(in society)* s'élever; *(of sun, theatre curtain)* se lever; *(of dough)* lever; *(get up from chair or bed)* se lever; **to r. (up)** *(rebel)* se soulever (**against** contre)

**rising** ['raɪzɪŋ] *adj (sun)* levant; *(number)* croissant; *(prices)* en hausse

**risk** [rɪsk] **1** *n* risque *m*; **at r.** *(person)* en danger; *(job)* menacé; **to run the r. of doing sth** courir le risque de faire qch **2** *vt (life, reputation)* risquer; **I can't r. going** je ne peux pas prendre le risque d'y aller ▪ **risky** (**-ier, -iest**) *adj* risqué

**rite** [raɪt] *n* rite *m*; *Rel* **the last rites** les derniers sacrements *mpl* ▪ **ritual** ['rɪtjʊəl] **1** *adj* rituel, -elle **2** *n* rituel *m*

**rival** ['raɪvəl] **1** *adj* rival **2** *n* rival, -e *mf* **3** (*Br* **-ll-**, *Am* **-l-**) *vt (equal)* égaler (**in** en) ▪ **rivalry** (*pl* **-ies**) *n* rivalité *f* (**between** entre)

**river** ['rɪvə(r)] **1** *n (small)* rivière *f*; *(flowing into sea)* fleuve *m* **2** *adj* **r. bank** rive *f* ▪ **riverside 1** *n* bord *m* de l'eau **2** *adj* au bord de l'eau

**riveting** ['rɪvɪtɪŋ] *adj Fig* fascinant

**Riviera** [rɪvɪ'eərə] *n* **the (French) R.** la Côte d'Azur

**road** [rəʊd] **1** *n* route *f*; *(small)* chemin *m*; *(in town)* rue *f*; *(roadway)* chaussée *f*; **the Paris r.** la route de Paris; **by r.** par la route; **to live across** *or* **over the r.** habiter en face

**2** *adj (map, safety)* routier, -ère; *(accident)* de la route; **r. sign** panneau *m* de signalisation; *Br* **r. works,** *Am* **r. work** travaux *mpl* de voirie ▪ **roadblock** *n* barrage *m* routier ▪ **roadside** *n* bord *m* de la route

**roam** [rəʊm] **1** *vt* parcourir; **to r. the streets** traîner dans les rues **2** *vi* errer

**roar** [rɔː(r)] **1** *n (of lion)* rugissement *m*; *(of person)* hurlement *m* **2** *vt* **to r. sth (out)** hurler qch **3** *vi (of lion, wind, engine)* rugir; *(of person, crowd)* hurler; **to r. with laughter** hurler de rire ▪ **roaring** *adj* **a r. fire** une belle flambée; **to do a r. trade** faire des affaires en or

**roast** [rəʊst] **1** *n (meat)* rôti *m* **2** *adj* rôti; **r. beef** rosbif *m* **3** *vt (meat, potatoes)* faire rôtir **4** *vi (of meat)* rôtir

**rob** [rɒb] *(pt & pp* **-bb-***) vt (person)* voler; *(shop, bank)* dévaliser; **to r. sb of sth** voler qch à qn; *Fig (deprive)* priver qn de qch ▪ **robber** *n* voleur, -euse *mf* ▪ **robbery** (*pl* **-ies**) *n* vol *m*; **it's daylight r.!** c'est du vol pur et simple!

**robe** [rəʊb] *n (of priest, judge)* robe *f*

**robin** ['rɒbɪn] *n (bird)* rouge-gorge *m*

**robot** ['rəʊbɒt] *n* robot *m*

**robust** [rəʊ'bʌst] *adj* robuste

**rock[1]** [rɒk] **1** *n (music)* rock *m* **2** *vt (boat)* balancer; *(building)* secouer **3** *vi (sway)* se balancer; *(of building, ground)* trembler ▪ **rocking** *adj* **r. chair** fauteuil *m* à bascule

**rock[2]** [rɒk] **1** *n (substance)* roche *f*; *(boulder, rock face)* rocher *m*; *Am (stone)* pierre *f*; *Br (sweet)* = sucrerie en forme de bâton parfumée à la menthe; **on the rocks** *(whisky)* avec des glaçons; *(marriage)* en pleine débâcle; **r. climbing** varappe *f*; **r. face** paroi *f* rocheuse

**rocket** ['rɒkɪt] **1** *n* fusée *f* **2** *vi (of prices, unemployment)* monter en flèche

**rocky** ['rɒkɪ] (**-ier, -iest**) *adj (road)* rocailleux, -euse; *Fig (relationship)* instable

**rod** [rɒd] *n (wooden)* baguette *f*; *(metal)* tige *f*; *(of curtain)* tringle *f*; *(for fishing)* canne *f* à pêche

**rode** [rəʊd] *pt of* **ride**

**rodent** ['rəʊdənt] *n* rongeur *m*

**rodeo** [*Br* 'rəʊdɪəʊ, *Am* rəʊ'deɪəʊ] (*pl* **-os**) *n Am* rodéo *m*

**rogue** [rəʊg] *n (dishonest)* crapule *f*; *(mischievous)* coquin, -e *mf*

**role** [rəʊl] *n* rôle *m*; **r. model** modèle *m*

**roll** [rəʊl] **1** *n (of paper)* rouleau *m*; *(of drum, thunder)* roulement *m*; *(bread)* petit pain *m*; *(list)* liste *f*; **r. of film** pellicule *f*; **to have a r. call** faire l'appel; **r. neck** col *m* roulé

**2** *vt (cigarette)* rouler; *(ball)* faire rouler

**3** *vi (of ball)* rouler; *(of camera)* tourner ▪ **rolling** *adj (hills)* ondulant; **r. pin** rouleau *m* à pâtisserie

▸ **roll down** *vt sep (car window)* baisser; *(sleeves)* redescendre

▸ **roll in** *vi Fam (flow in)* affluer; *(of person)* s'amener

▸ **roll on** *vi Fam* **r. on tonight!** vivement ce soir!

▸ **roll out** *vt sep (dough)* étaler

▸ **roll over** **1** *vt sep* retourner **2** *vi (many times)* se rouler; *(once)* se retourner

▸ **roll up** **1** *vt sep (map, cloth)* rouler; *(sleeve)* retrousser **2** *vi Fam (arrive)* s'amener

**roller** ['rəʊlə(r)] *n (for hair, painting)* rouleau *m*; **r. coaster** montagnes *fpl* russes; **r. skate** patin *m* à roulettes ▪ **roller-skate** *vi* faire du patin à roulettes

**rollerblades** ['rəʊləbleɪdz] *npl* patins *mpl* en ligne

**ROM** [rɒm] (*abbr* **read only memory**) *n Comptr* mémoire *f* morte

**Roman** ['rəʊmən] **1** *adj* romain **2** *n* Romain, -e *mf* **3** *adj & n* **R. Catholic** catholique *(mf)*

**romance** [rəʊ'mæns] *n (love)* amour *m*; *(affair)* aventure *f* amoureuse; *(story)* histoire *f* d'amour; *(charm)* poésie *f*

**Romania** [rəʊ'meɪnɪə] *n* la Roumanie ▪ **Romanian** **1** *adj* roumain **2** *n (person)* Roumain, -e *mf*; *(language)* roumain *m*

**romantic** [rəʊ'mæntɪk] **1** *adj (of love, tenderness)* romantique; *(fanciful, imaginary)* romanesque **2** *n* romantique *mf*

**romp** [rɒmp] *vi* s'ébattre

**rompers** ['rɒmpəz] *npl (for baby)* barboteuse *f*

**roof** [ru:f] *n (of building, vehicle)* toit *m*; *(of tunnel, cave)* plafond *m*; **r. rack** *(of car)* galerie *f* ▪ **rooftop** *n* toit *m*

**room** [ru:m, rʊm] *n* (**a**) *(in house)* pièce *f*; *(bedroom)* chambre *f*; *(large, public)* salle *f* (**b**) *(space)* place *f*; **to make r.** faire de la place (**for** pour) ▪ **roommate** *n* camarade *mf* de chambre ▪ **roomy** (**-ier, -iest**) *adj* spacieux, -euse

**roost** [ru:st] *vi* se percher

**rooster** ['ru:stə(r)] *n* coq *m*

**root** [ru:t] **1** *n (of plant, tooth, hair) & Math* racine *f*; *Fig (origin)* origine *f*; *(cause)* cause *f*; **to take r.** *(of plant, person)* prendre racine **2** *vt* **to r. sth out** supprimer qch

**rooted** ['ru:tɪd] *adj* **deeply r.** bien enraciné (**in** dans); **r. to the spot** *(immobile)* cloué sur place

**rope** [rəʊp] **1** *n* corde *f*; *(on ship)* cordage *m*; *Fam* **to know the ropes** connaître son affaire **2** *vt Fam* **to r. sb in** recruter qn

**rop(e)y** ['rəʊpɪ] (**-ier, -iest**) *adj Br Fam (thing)* minable; *(person)* patraque

**rosary** ['rəʊzərɪ] (*pl* **-ies**) *n Rel* chapelet *m*

**rose¹** [rəʊz] *n (flower)* rose *f*

**rose²** [rəʊz] *pt of* **rise**

**rosette** [rəʊ'zet] *n* rosette *f*

**roster** ['rɒstə(r)] *n* **(duty) r.** liste *f* de service

**rostrum** ['rɒstrəm] *n* tribune *f*; *(for prizewinner)* podium *m*

**rosy** ['rəʊzɪ] (**-ier, -iest**) *adj (pink)* rose; *Fig (future)* prometteur, -euse

**rot** [rɒt] **1** *n* pourriture *f*; *Br Fam (nonsense)* inepties *fpl* **2** (*pt & pp* **-tt-**) *vti* pourrir

**rota** ['rəʊtə] *n* roulement *m*

**rotary** ['rəʊtərɪ] **1** *adj* rotatif, -ive **2** (*pl* **-ies**) *n Am (for traffic)* rond-point *m*

**rotate** [rəʊ'teɪt] **1** *vt* faire tourner **2** *vi* tourner

**rotation** [rəʊ'teɪʃən] *n* **in r.** à tour de rôle

**rotten** ['rɒtən] *adj (fruit, egg, wood)* pourri; *Fam (bad)* nul (*f* nulle); *Fam (weather)* pourri; *Fam* **to feel r.** *(ill)* être mal fichu

**rough**[1] [rʌf] **1** (**-er, -est**) *adj (surface)* rugueux, -euse; *(ground)* accidenté; *(life)* rude; *(wine)* âpre; *(neighbourhood)* dur; *(sea)* agité; *(brutal)* brutal **2** *adv Br* **to sleep/live r.** coucher/vivre à la dure **3** *vt Fam* **to r. it** vivre à la dure

**rough**[2] [rʌf] **1** (**-er, -est**) *adj (approximate)* approximatif, -ive; **r. guess, r. estimate** approximation *f*; **r. copy, r. draft** brouillon *m*; **r. paper** papier *m* brouillon **2** *vt* **to r. sth out** *(plan)* ébaucher

**rough-and-ready** [rʌfən'redɪ] *adj (solution)* rudimentaire; *(accommodation)* sommaire

**roughen** ['rʌfən] *vt* rendre rugueux, -euse

**roughly**[1] ['rʌflɪ] *adv (brutally)* brutalement

**roughly**[2] ['rʌflɪ] *adv (approximately)* à peu près

**round** [raʊnd] **1** (**-er, -est**) *adj* rond; *Am* **r. trip** aller et retour *m*

**2** *adv* autour; **all r., right r.** tout autour; **all year r.** toute l'année; **the wrong way r.** à l'envers

**3** *prep* autour de; **r. here** par ici; **r. about** *(approximately)* environ

**4** *n Br (slice)* tranche *f*; *(in competition)* manche *f*; *(of golf)* partie *f*; *(in boxing)* round *m*; *(of talks)* série *f*; *(of drinks)* tournée *f*

**5** *vt* **to r. sth off** *(meal, speech)* terminer qch (**with** par); **to r. up** *(gather)* rassembler; *(price)* arrondir au chiffre supérieur

**roundabout** ['raʊndəbaʊt] **1** *adj (method, route)* indirect **2** *n Br (at funfair)* manège *m*; *(road junction)* rond-point *m*

**rounders** ['raʊndəz] *npl* = jeu similaire au base-ball

**rouse** [raʊz] *vt (awaken)* éveiller; **roused (to anger)** en colère

**rousing** ['raʊzɪŋ] *adj (speech)* vibrant

**route** [ru:t] *n* itinéraire *m*; *(of aircraft, ship)* route *f*; **bus r.** ligne *f* d'autobus

**routine** [ru:'ti:n] **1** *n (habit)* routine *f*; **the daily r.** le train-train quotidien **2** *adj (inquiry, work)* de routine; *Pej* routinier, -ère

**row**[1] [rəʊ] *n (line)* rangée *f*; **two days in a r.** deux jours d'affilée

**row**[2] [rəʊ] **1** *n Am* **r. boat** bateau *m* à rames **2** *vt (boat)* faire aller à la rame; *(person)* transporter en canot **3** *vi (in boat)* ramer

**row**[3] [raʊ] **1** *n (noise)* vacarme *m*; *(quarrel)* dispute *f* **2** *vi* se disputer (**with** avec)

**rowdy** ['raʊdɪ] (**-ier, -iest**) *adj* chahuteur, -euse

**rowing** ['rəʊɪŋ] *n (as sport)* aviron *m*; *Br* **r. boat** bateau *m* à rames

**royal** ['rɔɪəl] *adj* royal; **the R. Air Force** = l'armée de l'air britannique

**royalty** ['rɔɪəltɪ] **1** *n (rank, position)* royauté *f* **2** *npl* **royalties** *(from book)* droits *mpl* d'auteur

**rub** [rʌb] **1** *n (massage)* friction *f*; **to give sth a r.** frotter qch **2** (*pt & pp* **-bb-**) *vti* frotter

▸**rub down** *vt sep (person)* frictionner; *(wood, with sandpaper)* poncer

▸**rub in** *vt sep (cream)* faire pénétrer (en massant); *Fam* **to r. it in** retourner le couteau dans la plaie

▸**rub off** *vt sep (mark)* effacer
▸**rub out** *vt sep (mark, writing)* effacer

**rubber** ['rʌbə(r)] *n (substance)* caoutchouc *m*; *Br (eraser)* gomme *f*; *Am Fam (contraceptive)* capote *f*; **r. band** élastique *m*; **r. stamp** tampon *m*

**rubbish** ['rʌbɪʃ] *n Br (waste)* ordures *fpl*; *Fig (nonsense)* idioties *fpl*; *Fam* **that's r.** *(absurd)* c'est absurde; *(worthless)* ça ne vaut rien; **r. bin** poubelle *f*

**rubbishy** ['rʌbɪʃɪ] *adj (book, film)* nul (*f* nulle); *(goods)* de mauvaise qualité

**rubble** ['rʌbəl] *n* décombres *mpl*

**ruby** ['ru:bɪ] (*pl* **-ies**) *n (gem)* rubis *m*

**rucksack** ['rʌksæk] *n* sac *m* à dos

**rudder** ['rʌdə(r)] *n* gouvernail *m*

**ruddy** ['rʌdɪ] (**-ier, -iest**) *adj (complexion)* rose; *Br Fam (bloody)* fichu

**rude** [ru:d] (**-er, -est**) *adj (impolite)* impoli (**to** envers); *(indecent)* obscène

**rudiments** ['ru:dɪmənts] *npl* rudiments *mpl*

**ruffian** ['rʌfɪən] *n* voyou *m* (*pl* -ous)

**rug** [rʌg] *n* tapis *m*; *(over knees)* plaid *m*

**rugby** ['rʌgbɪ] *n* **r. (football)** rugby *m*

**rugged** ['rʌgɪd] *adj (terrain, coast)* accidenté; *(features)* rude

**ruin** ['ru:ɪn] **1** *n (destruction, rubble, building)* ruine *f*; **in ruins** *(building)* en ruine **2** *vt (health, country, person)* ruiner; *(clothes)* abîmer; *(effect, meal, party)* gâcher ▪ **ruined** *adj (person, country)* ruiné; *(building)* en ruine

**rule** [ru:l] **1** *n* (**a**) *(principle)* règle *f*; *(regulation)* règlement *m*; *(government)* autorité *f*; *Br* **against the rules** *or Am* **r.** contraire au règlement; **as a r.** en règle générale
(**b**) *(for measuring)* règle *f*
**2** *vt (country)* gouverner; *(decide) (of judge, referee)* décider (**that** que); **to r. sth out** *(exclude)* exclure qch
**3** *vi (of king)* régner (**over** sur); *(of judge)* statuer (**against** contre; **on** sur) ▪ **ruling 1** *adj Pol* **the r. party** le parti au pouvoir **2** *n (of judge, referee)* décision *f*

**ruler** ['ru:lə(r)] *n* (**a**) *(for measuring)* règle *f* (**b**) *(king, queen)* souverain, -e *mf*; *(political leader)* dirigeant, -e *mf*

**rum** [rʌm] *n* rhum *m*

**Rumania** [ru:'meɪnɪə] *see* **Romania**

**rumble** ['rʌmbəl] *vi (of train, thunder)* gronder; *(of stomach)* gargouiller

**rummage** ['rʌmɪdʒ] *vi* **to r. (about)** farfouiller; *Am* **r. sale** vente *f* de charité *(articles d'occasion uniquement)*

**rumour** ['ru:mə(r)] (*Am* **rumor**) *n* rumeur *f* ▪ **rumoured** (*Am* **rumored**) *adj* **it is r. that...** on dit que...

**rump** [rʌmp] *n (of horse)* croupe *f*; **r. steak** romsteck *m*

---

**RUN** [rʌn] **1** *n (series)* série *f*; *(running)* course *f*; *(outing)* tour *m*; *(for skiing)* piste *f*; *(in cricket, baseball)* point *m*; *(in stocking)* maille *f* filée; **to go for a r.** aller courir; **on the r.** *(prisoner)* en fuite; **in the long/short r.** à long/court terme
**2** (*pt* **ran**, *pp* **run**, *pres p* **running**) *vt (distance, race)* courir; *(machine)* faire fonctionner; *(business, country)* diriger; *(courses, events)* organiser; *Comptr (program)* exécuter; *(bath)* faire couler; **to r. one's hand over** passer la main sur; **to r. sb to the airport** conduire qn à l'aéroport
**3** *vi* courir; *(flee)* fuir; *(of river, nose, tap)* couler; *(of colour in washing)* déteindre; *(of ink)* baver; *(function) (of machine)* marcher; *(idle) (of engine)* tourner; **to r. down/in/out** descendre/entrer/sortir en courant; **to go running** faire du jogging; **to r. for president** être candidat à la présidence; **it runs in the family** c'est de famille

▸**run about** *vi* courir çà et là
▸**run across** *vt insep (meet)* tomber sur
▸**run along** *vi* **r. along!** filez!
▸**run around** *vi* = **run about**
▸**run away** *vi (flee)* s'enfuir (**from** de)
▸**run down** *vt sep (pedestrian)* renverser; *(knock over and kill)* écraser; *Fig (belittle)* dénigrer; *(restrict)* limiter peu à peu

▸ **run into** *vt insep (meet)* tomber sur; *(crash into) (of vehicle)* percuter
▸ **run off 1** *vt sep (print)* tirer **2** *vi (flee)* s'enfuir (**with** avec)
▸ **run out** *vi (of stocks)* s'épuiser; *(of lease)* expirer; *(of time)* manquer; **to r. out of time/money** manquer de temps/d'argent; **we've r. out of coffee** on n'a plus de café; **I ran out of petrol** *or Am* **gas** je suis tombé en panne d'essence
▸ **run over 1** *vt sep (kill)* écraser; *(knock down)* renverser **2** *vt insep (notes, text)* revoir **3** *vi (of liquid)* déborder
▸ **run round** *vt insep (surround)* entourer
▸ **run through** *vt insep (recap)* revoir
▸ **run up** *vt sep (debts, bill)* laisser s'accumuler

---

**runaway** ['rʌnəweɪ] **1** *n* fugitif, -ive *mf* **2** *adj (car, horse)* fou (*f* folle); *(inflation)* galopant
**run-down** [rʌn'daʊn] *adj (weak, tired)* fatigué; *(district)* délabré
**rung¹** [rʌŋ] *n (of ladder)* barreau *m*
**rung²** [rʌŋ] *pp of* **ring²**
**runner** ['rʌnə(r)] *n (athlete)* coureur *m*; *Br* **r. bean** haricot *m* d'Espagne
**runner-up** [rʌnər'ʌp] *n (in race)* second, -e *mf*
**running** ['rʌnɪŋ] **1** *n* course *f*; *(of business, country)* gestion *f*; **to be in/out of the r.** être/ne plus être dans la course **2** *adj* **six days r.** six jours de suite; **r. water** eau *f* courante; **r. costs** *(of factory)* frais *mpl* d'exploitation; *(of car)* dépenses *fpl* courantes
**runny** ['rʌnɪ] (**-ier, -iest**) *adj (cream, sauce)* liquide; *(nose)* qui coule
**run-up** ['rʌnʌp] *n* **in the r. to** *(elections, Christmas)* dans la période qui précède
**runway** ['rʌnweɪ] *n (for aircraft)* piste *f* (d'envol)
**rupture** ['rʌptʃə(r)] **1** *n (hernia)* hernie *f* **2** *vt* rompre
**rural** ['rʊərəl] *adj* rural
**ruse** [ru:z] *n* ruse *f*
**rush¹** [rʌʃ] **1** *n (demand)* ruée *f* (**for** vers; **on** sur); *(confusion)* bousculade *f*; **to be in a r.** être pressé (**to do** de faire); **r. hour** heures *fpl* de pointe
**2** *vt* **to r. sb** *(hurry)* bousculer qn; **to r. sb to hospital** *or Am* **the hospital** transporter qn d'urgence à l'hôpital; **to r. sth** *(job)* faire qch en vitesse; *(decision)* prendre qch à la hâte
**3** *vi (move fast, throw oneself)* se ruer (**at** sur; **towards** vers); *(hurry)* se dépêcher (**to do** de faire); *(of vehicle)* foncer; **to r. out** sortir précipitamment
**rush²** [rʌʃ] *n (plant)* jonc *m*
**rusk** [rʌsk] *n Br* biscotte *f*
**Russia** ['rʌʃə] *n* la Russie ▪ **Russian 1** *adj* russe **2** *n (person)* Russe *mf*; *(language)* russe *m*
**rust** [rʌst] **1** *n* rouille *f* **2** *vi* rouiller
**rustic** ['rʌstɪk] *adj* rustique
**rustle** ['rʌsəl] **1** *vt Fam* **to r. sth up** *(meal, snack)* improviser qch **2** *vi (of leaves)* bruire
**rustproof** ['rʌstpru:f] *adj* inoxydable
**rusty** ['rʌstɪ] (**-ier, -iest**) *adj* rouillé
**rut** [rʌt] *n* ornière *f*; *Fig* **to be in a r.** être encroûté
**ruthless** ['ru:θləs] *adj* impitoyable
**rye** [raɪ] *n* seigle *m*; **r. bread** pain *m* de seigle

# Ss

**S, s** [es] *n (letter)* S, s *m inv*
**sabotage** ['sæbətɑ:ʒ] **1** *n* sabotage *m* **2** *vt* saboter
**sachet** ['sæʃeɪ] *n* sachet *m*
**sack** [sæk] **1** *n (bag)* sac *m*; *Fam* **to get the s.** se faire virer **2** *vt Fam (dismiss)* virer
**sacred** ['seɪkrɪd] *adj* sacré
**sacrifice** ['sækrɪfaɪs] **1** *n* sacrifice *m* **2** *vt* sacrifier (**to** à)
**sad** [sæd] (**sadder, saddest**) *adj* triste ▪ **sadden** *vt* attrister ▪ **sadly** *adv (unhappily)* tristement; *(unfortunately)* malheureusement ▪ **sadness** *n* tristesse *f*
**saddle** ['sædəl] **1** *n* selle *f* **2** *vt (horse)* seller
**sadistic** [sə'dɪstɪk] *adj* sadique
**sae** [eseɪ'i:] (*abbr Br* **stamped addressed envelope**, *Am* **self-addressed envelope**) *n* enveloppe *f* timbrée
**safari** [sə'fɑ:rɪ] *n* safari *m*
**safe** [seɪf] **1** (**-er, -est**) *adj (person)* en sécurité; *(equipment, animal)* sans danger; *(place, investment, method)* sûr; **s. (and sound)** sain et sauf (*f* saine et sauve) **2** *n (for money)* coffre-fort *m* ▪ **safely** *adv (without risk)* en toute sécurité; *(drive)* prudemment; *(with certainty)* avec certitude
**safeguard** ['seɪfgɑ:d] **1** *n* garantie *f* (**against** contre) **2** *vt* sauvegarder
**safety** ['seɪftɪ] **1** *n* sécurité *f* **2** *adj (belt, device, margin)* de sécurité; *(pin, chain, valve)* de sûreté
**sag** [sæg] (*pt & pp* **-gg-**) *vi (of roof, bed)* s'affaisser
**saga** ['sɑ:gə] *n* saga *f*
**Sahara** [sə'hɑ:rə] *n* **the S. (desert)** le Sahara
**said** [sed] *pt & pp of* **say**
**sail** [seɪl] **1** *n (on boat)* voile *f*; **to set s.** prendre la mer **2** *vt (boat)* commander **3** *vi (of person, ship)* naviguer; *(leave)* prendre la mer ▪ **sailing** *n (sport)* voile *f*; **to go s.** faire de la voile; *Br* **s. boat** voilier *m* ▪ **sailboat** *n Am* voilier *m*
**sailor** ['seɪlə(r)] *n* marin *m*
**saint** [seɪnt] *n* saint *m*, sainte *f*
**sake** [seɪk] *n* **for my/your/his s.** pour moi/toi/lui; **for heaven's** *or* **God's s.!** pour l'amour de Dieu!; **(just) for the s. of eating** simplement pour manger
**salad** ['sæləd] *n* salade *f*; *Br* **s. cream** = sorte de mayonnaise; **s. dressing** = sauce pour salade
**salami** [sə'lɑ:mɪ] *n* salami *m*
**salary** ['sælərɪ] (*pl* **-ies**) *n* salaire *m*
**sale** [seɪl] *n (action, event)* vente *f*; *(at reduced price)* solde *m*; **on s.** en vente; **in the sales** en solde; **(up) for s.** à vendre; *Am* **sales check** *or* **slip** reçu *m* ▪ **salesclerk** *n Am* vendeur, -euse *mf* ▪ **salesman** (*pl* **-men**) *n (in shop)* vendeur *m*; *(for company)* représentant *m* ▪ **saleswoman** (*pl* **-women**) *n (in shop)* vendeuse *f*, *(for company)* représentante *f*
**salmon** ['sæmən] *n inv* saumon *m*
**salon** ['sælɒn] *n* **beauty s.** institut *m* de beauté; **hairdressing s.** salon *m* de coiffure
**saloon** [sə'lu:n] *n Am (bar)* bar *m*; *Br* **s. car** berline *f*

**salt** [sɔːlt] **1** *n* sel *m* **2** *vt* saler ▪ **salt-cellar** *n Br* salière *f* ▪ **salt-shaker** *n Am* salière *f* ▪ **saltwater** *adj (lake)* salé; *(fish)* de mer ▪ **salty** (**-ier, -iest**) *adj* salé

**salute** [sə'luːt] **1** *n* salut *m* **2** *vt (greet) & Mil* saluer **3** *vi* faire un salut

**salvage** ['sælvɪdʒ] *vt (ship)* sauver; *(waste material)* récupérer

**salvation** [sæl'veɪʃən] *n* salut *m*

**SAME** [seɪm] **1** *adj* même; **the (very) s. house as…** (exactement) la même maison que…

**2** *pron* **the s.** le même, la même, *pl* les mêmes; **I would have done the s.** j'aurais fait la même chose; **it's all the s. to me** ça m'est égal

**3** *adv* **to look the s.** *(of two things)* sembler pareils; **all the s.** *(nevertheless)* tout de même

**sample** ['sɑːmpəl] **1** *n* échantillon *m*; *(of blood)* prélèvement *m* **2** *vt (wine, cheese)* goûter

**sanction** ['sæŋkʃən] *n (penalty)* sanction *f*

**sanctuary** [*Br* 'sæŋktʃʊərɪ, *Am* -erɪ] (*pl* **-ies**) *n (for fugitive, refugee)* refuge *m*; *(for wildlife)* réserve *f*

**sand** [sænd] **1** *n* sable *m*; **s. castle** château *m* de sable **2** *vt* **to s. (down)** *(wood)* poncer

**sandal** ['sændəl] *n* sandale *f*

**sandwich** ['sænwɪdʒ] **1** *n* sandwich *m*; **cheese s.** sandwich *m* au fromage **2** *vt* **to be sandwiched between** *(of person, building)* être coincé entre

**sandy** ['sændɪ] (**-ier, -iest**) *adj* (**a**) *(beach)* de sable; *(ground)* sablonneux, -euse (**b**) *(hair)* blond roux *inv*

**sane** [seɪn] (**-er, -est**) *adj (person)* sain d'esprit

**sang** [sæŋ] *pt of* **sing**

**sanitary** [*Br* 'sænɪtərɪ, *Am* -erɪ] *adj (fittings)* sanitaire; *Br* **s. towel,** *Am* **s. napkin** serviette *f* hygiénique

**sanitation** [sænɪ'teɪʃən] *n* hygiène *f* publique; *(plumbing)* installations *fpl* sanitaires

**sanity** ['sænətɪ] *n* santé *f* mentale

**sank** [sæŋk] *pt of* **sink**[2]

**Santa Claus** ['sæntəklɔːz] *n* le Père Noël

**sap** [sæp] **1** *n (of tree, plant)* sève *f* **2** (*pt & pp* **-pp-**) *vt (weaken)* saper

**sapphire** ['sæfaɪə(r)] *n* saphir *m*

**sarcastic** [sɑː'kæstɪk] *adj* sarcastique

**sardine** [sɑː'diːn] *n* sardine *f*

**Sardinia** [sɑː'dɪnɪə] *n* la Sardaigne

**sat** [sæt] *pt & pp of* **sit**

**Satan** ['seɪtən] *n* Satan *m*

**satchel** ['sætʃəl] *n* cartable *m*

**satellite** ['sætəlaɪt] *n* satellite *m*; **s. dish** antenne *f* parabolique; **s. television** télévision *f* par satellite

**satin** ['sætɪn] *n* satin *m*

**satire** ['sætaɪə(r)] *n* satire *f* (**on** contre) ▪ **satirical** *adj* satirique

**satisfaction** [sætɪs'fækʃən] *n* satisfaction *f* ▪ **satisfactory** *adj* satisfaisant

**satisfy** ['sætɪsfaɪ] (*pt & pp* **-ied**) *vt* satisfaire; *(convince)* persuader (**that** que); *(condition)* remplir; **to be satisfied (with)** être satisfait (de) ▪ **satisfying** *adj* satisfaisant; *(meal, food)* substantiel, -elle

**satsuma** [sæt'suːmə] *n Br* mandarine *f*

**saturate** ['sætʃəreɪt] *vt* saturer (**with** de)

**Saturday** ['sætədeɪ] *n* samedi *m*

**sauce** [sɔːs] *n* sauce *f*; **mint s.** sauce à la menthe

**saucepan** ['sɔːspən] *n* casserole *f*

**saucer** ['sɔːsə(r)] *n* soucoupe *f*

**Saudi Arabia** [saʊdɪə'reɪbɪə] *n* l'Arabie *f* saoudite

**sauna** ['sɔːnə] *n* sauna *m*

**saunter** ['sɔːntə(r)] *vi* flâner

**sausage** ['sɒsɪdʒ] *n* saucisse *f*; *Br* **s. roll** feuilleté *m* à la viande

**savage** ['sævɪdʒ] **1** *adj (animal, person)* féroce; *(attack, criticism)* violent **2** *vt (physically)* attaquer

**save**[1] [seɪv] **1** *vt (rescue)* sauver (**from** de); *(keep)* garder; *(money)* économiser; *(time)* gagner; *Comptr* sauvegarder; **to s. sb's life** sauver la vie de qn; **to s. sb from doing sth** empêcher qn de faire qch **2** *vi* **to s. (up)** faire des économies (**for/on** pour/sur) **3** *n (by goalkeeper)* arrêt *m*

**save**[2] [seɪv] *prep Formal (except)* hormis

**saving** ['seɪvɪŋ] *n (of time, money)* économie *f*; **savings** *(money saved)* économies *fpl*; **savings account** compte *m* d'épargne

**saviour** ['seɪvjə(r)] (*Am* **savior**) *n* sauveur *m*

**savour** ['seɪvə(r)] (*Am* **savor**) *vt* savourer ▪ **savoury** (*Am* **savory**) *adj (not sweet)* salé

**saw**[1] [sɔː] **1** *n* scie *f* **2** (*pt* **sawed,** *pp* **sawn** *or* **sawed**) *vt* scier; **to s. sth off** scier qch ▪ **sawdust** *n* sciure *f*

**saw**[2] [sɔː] *pt of* **see**[1]

**sawn** [sɔːn] *pp of* **saw**[1]

**saxophone** ['sæksəfəʊn] *n* saxophone *m*

**say** [seɪ] **1** (*pt & pp* **said**) *vt* dire (**to** à; **that** que); *(of dial, watch)* indiquer; **to s. again** répéter; **that is to s.** c'est-à-dire

**2** *vi* dire; *Am Fam* **s.!** dis donc!; **that goes without saying** ça va sans dire

**3** *n* **to have one's s.** avoir son mot à dire; **to have no s.** ne pas avoir voix au chapitre (**in** concernant)

**saying** ['seɪɪŋ] *n* maxime *f*

**scab** [skæb] *n (of wound)* croûte *f*

**scaffolding** ['skæfəldɪŋ] *n* échafaudage *m*

**scald** [skɔːld] *vt* ébouillanter

**scale**[1] [skeɪl] **1** *n (of instrument, map)* échelle *f*; *(of salaries)* barème *m*; *Fig (of problem)* étendue *f*; **on a small/large s.** sur une petite/grande échelle **2** *vt* **to s. sth down** revoir qch à la baisse

**scale**[2] [skeɪl] *n (on fish)* écaille *f*; *(in kettle)* dépôt *m* calcaire

**scales** [skeɪlz] *npl (for weighing)* balance *f*; **(bathroom) s.** pèse-personne *m*

**scalp** [skælp] *n* cuir *m* chevelu

**scamper** ['skæmpə(r)] *vi* **to s. off** *or* **away** détaler

**scampi** ['skæmpɪ] *n* scampi *mpl*

**scan** [skæn] **1** *n* **to have a s.** passer une échographie **2** (*pt & pp* **-nn-**) *vt (look at briefly)* parcourir; *(scrutinize)* scruter; *Comptr* passer au scanner

**scandal** ['skændəl] *n (outrage)* scandale *m*; *(gossip)* ragots *mpl* ▪ **scandalous** *adj* scandaleux, -euse

**Scandinavia** [skændɪ'neɪvɪə] *n* la Scandinavie ▪ **Scandinavian 1** *adj* scandinave **2** *n* Scandinave *mf*

**scanner** ['skænə(r)] *n Med & Comptr* scanner *m*

**scant** [skænt] *adj* insuffisant ▪ **scanty** (**-ier, -iest**) *adj* insuffisant; *(bikini)* minuscule

**scapegoat** ['skeɪpgəʊt] *n* bouc *m* émissaire

**scar** [skɑː(r)] **1** *n* cicatrice *f* **2** (*pt & pp* **-rr-**) *vt* marquer d'une cicatrice; *Fig (of experience)* marquer

**scarce** [skeəs] (**-er, -est**) *adj* rare ▪ **scarcely** *adv* à peine; **s. anything** presque rien

**scare** [skeə(r)] **1** *n* **to give sb a s.** faire peur à qn **2** *vt* faire peur à; **to s. sb off** faire fuir qn ▪ **scared** *adj* effrayé; **to be s. of sb/sth** avoir peur de qn/qch

**scarf** [skɑːf] (*pl* **scarves**) *n (long)* écharpe *f*; *(square)* foulard *m*

**scarlet** ['skɑːlət] *adj* écarlate; **s. fever** scarlatine *f*

**scary** ['skeərɪ] (**-ier, -iest**) *adj Fam* effrayant

**scathing** ['skeɪðɪŋ] *adj (remark)* acerbe; **to be s. about sb/sth** faire des remarques acerbes sur qn/qch

**scatter** ['skætə(r)] **1** *vt (demonstrators)* disperser; *(corn, seed)* jeter à la volée; *(papers)* laisser traîner **2** *vi (of crowd)* se disperser

**scavenge** ['skævɪndʒ] *vi* **to s. for sth** fouiller pour trouver qch

**scenario** [sɪ'nɑːrɪəʊ] (*pl* **-os**) *n (of film)* scénario *m*

**scene** [siːn] *n (in book, film, play)* scène *f*; *(of event, crime, accident)* lieu *m*; *also Fig* **behind the scenes** dans les coulisses; **on the s.** sur les lieux; **to**

**make a s.** faire un scandale

**scenery** ['si:nərɪ] (*pl* **-ies**) *n (landscape)* paysage *m*; *(in play, film)* décors *mpl*

**scenic** ['si:nɪk] *adj* pittoresque; **s. route** route *f* touristique

**scent** [sent] *n (smell)* odeur *f*; *(perfume)* parfum *m*; *(in hunting)* fumet *m*

**sceptical** ['skeptɪkəl] (*Am* **skeptical**) *adj* sceptique

**schedule** [*Br* 'ʃedju:l, *Am* 'skedjʊl] **1** *n (plan)* programme *m*; *(for trains, buses)* horaire *m*; *(list)* liste *f*; **according to s.** comme prévu **2** *vt* prévoir; *(event)* fixer la date/l'heure de ▪ **scheduled** [*Br* 'ʃedju:ld, *Am* 'skedju:ld] *adj (planned)* prévu; *(service, flight, train)* régulier, -ère

**scheme** [ski:m] **1** *n (plan)* plan *m* (**to do** pour faire); *(plot)* complot *m*; *(arrangement)* arrangement *m* **2** *vi Pej* comploter ▪ **scheming** *Pej* **1** *adj* intrigant **2** *n* machinations *fpl*

**schizophrenic** [skɪtsəʊ'frenɪk] *adj & n* schizophrène *(mf)*

**scholar** ['skɒlə(r)] *n* érudit, -e *mf* ▪ **scholarly** *adj* érudit ▪ **scholarship** *n (learning)* érudition *f*; *(grant)* bourse *f* d'études

**school** [sku:l] **1** *n* école *f*; *(within university)* département *m*; *Am Fam (college)* université *f*; *Br* **secondary s.**, *Am* **high s.** établissement *m* d'enseignement secondaire
**2** *adj (year, book, equipment)* scolaire; **s. bag** cartable *m*; **s. fees** frais *mpl* de scolarité; *Am* **s. yard** cour *f* de récréation ▪ **schoolboy** *n* écolier *m* ▪ **schoolchildren** *npl* écoliers *mpl* ▪ **schoolfriend** *n* camarade *mf* de classe ▪ **schoolgirl** *n* écolière *f* ▪ **schoolteacher** *n (primary)* instituteur, -trice *mf*; *(secondary)* professeur *m*

**science** ['saɪəns] *n* science *f*; **to study s.** étudier les sciences; **s. fiction** science-fiction *f* ▪ **scientific** *adj* scientifique ▪ **scientist** *n* scientifique *mf*

**scissors** ['sɪzəz] *npl* ciseaux *mpl*

**scoff** [skɒf] **1** *vt* **to s. at sb/sth** se moquer de qn/qch **2** *vti Br Fam (eat)* bouffer

**scold** [skəʊld] *vt* gronder (**for doing** pour avoir fait)

**scone** [skəʊn, skɒn] *n Br* scone *m*

**scoop** [sku:p] **1** *n (for flour, sugar)* pelle *f*; *(for ice cream)* cuillère *f*; *(amount) (of ice cream)* boule *f* **2** *vt* **to s. sth out** *(hollow out)* évider qch; **to s. sth up** ramasser qch

**scooter** ['sku:tə(r)] *n (for child)* trottinette *f*; *(motorcycle)* scooter *m*

**scope** [skəʊp] *n (range)* étendue *f*; *(of action)* possibilité *f*

**scorch** [skɔ:tʃ] **1** *n* **s. (mark)** brûlure *f* **2** *vt* roussir ▪ **scorching** *adj (day)* torride; *(sun, sand)* brûlant

**score[1]** [skɔ:(r)] **1** *n (in sport)* score *m*; *(in music)* partition *f*; *(of film)* musique *f* **2** *vt (point, goal)* marquer; *(exam mark)* avoir; *(piece of music)* adapter (**for** pour) **3** *vi (score a goal)* marquer; *(count points)* marquer les points ▪ **scoreboard** *n* tableau *m* d'affichage ▪ **scorer** *n* marqueur *m*

**score[2]** [skɔ:(r)] *n* **a s.** *(twenty)* vingt; *Fam* **scores of** des tas de

**scorn** [skɔ:n] **1** *n* mépris *m* **2** *vt* mépriser ▪ **scornful** *adj* méprisant

**scorpion** ['skɔ:pɪən] *n* scorpion *m*

**Scot** [skɒt] *n* Écossais, -e *mf* ▪ **Scotland** *n* l'Écosse *f* ▪ **Scotsman** (*pl* **-men**) *n* Écossais *m* ▪ **Scotswoman** (*pl* **-women**) *n* Écossaise *f* ▪ **Scottish** *adj* écossais

**Scotch** [skɒtʃ] **1** *n (whisky)* scotch *m* **2** *adj Am* **S. tape®** Scotch® *m*

**scoundrel** ['skaʊndrəl] *n* crapule *f*

**scour** ['skaʊə(r)] *vt (pan)* récurer; *Fig (streets, house)* ratisser (**for** à la recherche de) ▪ **scourer** *n* tampon *m* à récurer

**scout** [skaʊt] *n* **(boy) s.** scout *m*, éclaireur *m*; *Am* **(girl) s.** éclaireuse *f*

**scowl** [skaʊl] *vi* lancer des regards noirs (**at** à)

**scram** [skræm] (*pt & pp* **-mm-**) *vi Fam* se tirer

**scramble** ['skræmbəl] **1** *vt* **scrambled eggs** œufs *mpl* brouillés **2** *vi* **to s. up a hill** gravir une colline en s'aidant des mains

**scrap** [skræp] **1** *n* (**a**) *(piece)* bout *m* (**of** de); *(of information)* bribe *f*; **scraps** *(food)* restes *mpl*; **s. paper** papier *m* brouillon

(**b**) **s. (metal)** ferraille *f*; **s. heap** tas *m* de ferraille; **s. dealer, s. merchant** ferrailleur *m*; **s. yard** casse *f*

**2** *(pt & pp* **-pp-***)* *vt (get rid of)* se débarrasser de; *(car)* envoyer à la casse; *Fig (plan, idea)* abandonner ▪ **scrapbook** *n* album *m (de coupures de presse etc)*

**scrape** [skreɪp] **1** *vt* gratter; *(skin)* érafler; **to s. a living** arriver tout juste à vivre **2** *vi* **to s. against sth** frotter contre qch

▸**scrape away, scrape off** *vt sep* racler

▸**scrape through** *vt insep & vi* **to s. through (an exam)** passer de justesse (à un examen)

▸**scrape together** *vt sep (money, people)* parvenir à rassembler

**scratch** [skrætʃ] **1** *n (mark, injury)* éraflure *f*; *(on glass, wood)* rayure *f*; *Fam* **to start from s.** repartir de zéro; **it isn't up to s.** ce n'est pas au niveau

**2** *vt (to relieve itching)* gratter; *(by accident)* érafler; *(glass)* rayer; *(with claw)* griffer; *(write, draw)* griffonner (**on** sur)

**3** *vi (of person)* se gratter; *(of pen, new clothes)* gratter ▪ **scratchcard** *n (lottery card)* carte *f* à gratter

**scrawl** [skrɔ:l] **1** *n* gribouillis *m* **2** *vt* gribouiller

**scream** [skri:m] **1** *n* hurlement *m* **2** *vt* hurler **3** *vi* hurler; **to s. at sb** crier après qn

**screech** [skri:tʃ] *vti* hurler

**screen** [skri:n] **1** *n (of TV set, computer, cinema)* écran *m*; *Comptr* **s. saver** économiseur *m* d'écran

**2** *vt (hide)* cacher (**from sb** à qn); *(protect)* protéger (**from** de); *(film)* projeter; *(visitors, calls)* filtrer; *(for disease)* faire subir un test de dépistage à ▪ **screening** *n (of film)* projection *f*; *(selection)* tri *m*; *(for disease)* dépistage *m* ▪ **screenplay** *n (of film)* scénario *m*

**screw** [skru:] **1** *n* vis *f* **2** *vt* visser (**to** à); **to s. sth down** *or* **on** visser qch; **to s. sth off** dévisser qch; **to s. sth up** *(paper)* chiffonner qch ▪ **screwdriver** *n* tournevis *m*

**scribble** ['skrɪbəl] **1** *n* griffonnage *m* **2** *vti* griffonner

**script** [skrɪpt] *n* (**a**) *(of film)* script *m*; *(of play)* texte *m*; *(in exam)* copie *f* (**b**) *(handwriting)* script *m*

**Scripture(s)** ['skrɪptʃə(z)] *n(pl) Rel* les saintes Écritures *fpl*

**scroll** [skrəʊl] **1** *n* rouleau *m*; *(manuscript)* manuscrit *m* **2** *vi Comptr* défiler; **to s. down/up** défiler vers le bas/haut

**scrounge** [skraʊndʒ] *vt Fam (meal)* se faire payer (**off** *or* **from sb** par qn); *(steal)* taper (**off** *or* **from sb** à qn); **to s. money off** *or* **from sb** taper qn ▪ **scrounger** *n Fam* parasite *m*

**scrub** [skrʌb] **1** *n* (**a**) **to give sth a s.** bien frotter qch; *Am* **s. brush** brosse *f* dure (**b**) *(land)* broussailles *fpl* **2** *(pt & pp* **-bb-***)* *vt (surface)* frotter; *(pan)* récurer; **to s. sth off** *(remove)* enlever qch (à la brosse *ou* en frottant)

**scrubbing** ['skrʌbɪŋ] *n* **s. brush** brosse *f* dure

**scruff** [skrʌf] *n* **by the s. of the neck** par la peau du cou

**scruffy** ['skrʌfɪ] (**-ier, -iest**) *adj (person)* peu soigné

**scrum** [skrʌm] *n (in rugby)* mêlée *f*

**scrupulous** ['skru:pjʊləs] *adj* scrupuleux, -euse

**scrutinize** ['skru:tɪnaɪz] *vt (document)* éplucher

**scuba** ['sku:bə] *n* **s. diving** la plongée sous-marine

**scuff** [skʌf] *vt* **to s. sth (up)** *(shoe)* érafler qch

**scuffle** ['skʌfəl] *n* bagarre *f*

**sculpt** [skʌlpt] *vti* sculpter ▪ **sculptor**

*n* sculpteur *m* ▪ **sculpture** *n (art, object)* sculpture *f*

**scum** [skʌm] *n* (**a**) *(froth)* écume *f* (**b**) *Fam Pej (people)* racaille *f*; *(person)* ordure *f*

**scurry** ['skʌrɪ] *vi (rush)* courir; **to s. off** se sauver

**sea** [siː] **1** *n* mer *f*; **(out) at s.** en mer; **by s.** par mer; **by** *or* **beside the s.** au bord de la mer

**2** *adj (level, breeze)* de la mer; *(water, fish, salt)* de mer; *(air)* marin; *(battle)* naval (*mpl* -als); *(route)* maritime; **s. bed, s. floor** fond *m* de la mer ▪ **seafood** *n* fruits *mpl* de mer ▪ **seafront** *n Br* front *m* de mer ▪ **seagull** *n* mouette *f* ▪ **seashell** *n* coquillage *m* ▪ **seaside** *n Br* bord *m* de la mer; **s. resort** station *f* balnéaire ▪ **seashore** *n* rivage *m* ▪ **seasick** *adj* **to be s.** avoir le mal de mer ▪ **seaweed** *n* algues *fpl*

**seal**[1] [siːl] *n (animal)* phoque *m*

**seal**[2] [siːl] **1** *n (stamp)* sceau *m*; *(device for sealing)* joint *m* d'étanchéité **2** *vt (document, container)* sceller; *(stick down)* cacheter; *(make airtight)* fermer hermétiquement; **to s. off an area** boucler un quartier

**seam** [siːm] *n (in cloth)* couture *f*

**search** [sɜːtʃ] **1** *n* recherches *fpl* (**for** de); *(of place)* fouille *f*; **in s. of** à la recherche de; *Comptr* **to do a s. for sth** rechercher qch; *Comptr* **s. engine** moteur *m* de recherche **2** *vt (person, place)* fouiller (**for** pour trouver) **3** *vi* chercher; **to s. for sth** chercher qch ▪ **searchlight** *n* projecteur *m*

**season**[1] ['siːzən] *n* saison *f*; *(of films)* cycle *m*; **in the peak s., in (the) high s.** en haute saison; **in the low** *or* **off s.** en basse saison; **s. ticket** abonnement *m*

**season**[2] ['siːzən] *vt (food)* assaisonner ▪ **seasoning** *n Culin* assaisonnement *m*

**seasonal** ['siːzənəl] *adj (work, change)* saisonnier, -ère

**seat** [siːt] **1** *n* siège *m*; *(of trousers)* fond *m*; **to take** *or* **have a s.** s'asseoir; **s. belt** ceinture *f* de sécurité **2** *vt (at table)* placer; *(on one's lap)* asseoir ▪ **seated** *adj (sitting)* assis ▪ **seating** *n (seats)* places *fpl* assises

**-seater** ['siːtə(r)] *suff* **two-s. (car)** voiture *f* à deux places

**secluded** [sɪ'kluːdɪd] *adj (remote)* isolé ▪ **seclusion** *n* solitude *f*

**second**[1] ['sekənd] **1** *adj* deuxième, second; **every s. week** une semaine sur deux; *Aut* **in s. (gear)** en seconde

**2** *adv (say)* deuxièmement; **to come s.** *(in competition)* se classer deuxième; **the s. biggest** le deuxième en ordre de grandeur

**3** *n (in series)* deuxième *mf*, second, -e *mf*; *(in month)* deux *m*; **Louis the S.** Louis Deux; **seconds** *(goods)* articles *mpl* défectueux

**4** *vt (motion, proposal)* appuyer ▪ **second-class** *adj (ticket on train)* de seconde (classe); *(mail)* non urgent; *(product)* de qualité inférieure ▪ **secondly** *adv* deuxièmement ▪ **second-rate** *adj* médiocre

**second**[2] ['sekənd] *n (part of minute)* seconde *f*; **s. hand** *(of clock, watch)* trotteuse *f*

**secondary** ['sekəndərɪ] *adj* secondaire; *Br* **s. school** établissement *m* secondaire

**second-hand** [sekənd'hænd] **1** *adj & adv (not new)* d'occasion **2** *adj (report, news)* de seconde main

**secrecy** ['siːkrəsɪ] *n (discretion, silence)* secret *m*

**secret** ['siːkrɪt] **1** *adj* secret, -ète **2** *n* secret *m*; **in s.** en secret ▪ **secretly** *adv* secrètement

**secretary** [*Br* 'sekrətərɪ, *Am* -erɪ] (*pl* **-ies**) *n* secrétaire *mf*; *Br* **Foreign S.,** *Am* **S. of State** ≃ ministre *m* des Affaires étrangères ▪ **secretarial** [-'teərɪəl] *adj (work)* administratif, -ive; *(job, course)* de secrétariat

**secretive** ['siːkrətɪv] *adj (person)* secret, -ète; **to be s. about sth** faire des cachotteries à propos de qch

**sect** [sekt] *n* secte *f*

**section** ['sekʃən] *n* partie *f*; *(of road)* tronçon *m*; *(of machine)* élément *m*; *(of organization)* département *m*; **the sports s.** *(of newspaper)* la page des sports
**sector** ['sektə(r)] *n* secteur *m*
**secular** ['sekjʊlə(r)] *adj (music, art)* profane
**secure** [sɪ'kjʊə(r)] **1** *adj (person)* en sécurité; *(investment, place)* sûr; *(door, window)* bien fermé **2** *vt (fasten)* attacher; *(window, door)* bien fermer; *(position, future)* assurer; *(support, promise)* procurer; **to s. sth (for oneself)** se procurer qch ▪ **securely** *adv (firmly)* solidement; *(safely)* en sûreté
**security** [sɪ'kjʊərətɪ] *(pl* **-ies***)* *n* sécurité *f*; *Fin (for loan, bail)* garantie *f*; **securities** *(stocks, bonds)* titres *mpl*
**sedan** [sɪ'dæn] *n Am (saloon)* berline *f*
**sedate** [sɪ'deɪt] **1** *adj* calme **2** *vt* mettre sous calmants
**sedative** ['sedətɪv] *n* calmant *m*
**seduce** [sɪ'dju:s] *vt* séduire ▪ **seductive** [-'dʌktɪv] *adj (person, offer)* séduisant

**SEE** [si:] *(pt* **saw**, *pp* **seen***)* *vti* voir; **we'll s.** on verra; **I can s. a hill** je vois une colline; **I saw him run(ning)** je l'ai vu courir; **to s. reason** entendre raison; **s. you (later)!** à tout à l'heure!; **to s. that...** *(make sure that)* faire en sorte que... *(+ subjunctive)*; *(check)* s'assurer que... *(+ indicative)*; **to s. sb to the door** accompagner qn jusqu'à la porte
▸ **see about** *vt insep (deal with)* s'occuper de; *(consider)* songer à
▸ **see off** *vt sep (say goodbye to)* dire au revoir à
▸ **see out** *vt sep* accompagner jusqu'à la porte
▸ **see through 1** *vt sep (task)* mener à bien **2** *vt insep* **to s. through sb** percer qn à jour
▸ **see to** *vt insep (deal with)* s'occuper de; *(mend)* réparer; **to s. to it that...** *(make sure that)* faire en sorte que... *(+ subjunctive)*; *(check)* s'assurer que... *(+ indicative)*

**seed** [si:d] *n* graine *f*; *(of fruit)* pépin *m*; *Fig (source)* germe *m*
**seedy** ['si:dɪ] (**-ier, -iest**) *adj* miteux, -euse
**seeing** ['si:ɪŋ] *conj* **s. (that)** vu que
**seek** [si:k] *(pt & pp* **sought***)* *vt* chercher (**to do** à faire); *(ask for)* demander (**from** à); **to s. sb out** dénicher qn
**seem** [si:m] *vi* sembler (**to do** faire); **it seems that...** *(impression)* il semble que... *(+ subjunctive)*; **it seems to me that...** il me semble que... *(+ indicative)*
**seemingly** ['si:mɪŋlɪ] *adv* apparemment
**seemly** ['si:mlɪ] *adj Formal* bienséant
**seen** [si:n] *pp of* **see**
**seep** [si:p] *vi* suinter; **to s. into sth** s'infiltrer dans qch
**seesaw** ['si:sɔ:] *n* balançoire *f* à bascule
**see-through** ['si:θru:] *adj* transparent
**segment** ['segmənt] *n* segment *m*; *(of orange)* quartier *m*
**segregate** ['segrɪgeɪt] *vt* séparer (**from** de) ▪ **segregation** *n* ségrégation *f*
**seize** [si:z] **1** *vt* saisir; *(power, land)* s'emparer de **2** *vi* **to s. (up)on** *(offer)* sauter sur; **to s. up** *(of engine)* se bloquer
**seizure** ['si:ʒə(r)] *n (of goods, property)* saisie *f*; *Med* crise *f*
**seldom** ['seldəm] *adv* rarement
**select** [sɪ'lekt] **1** *vt* sélectionner **2** *adj (exclusive)* sélect ▪ **selection** *n* sélection *f*
**selective** [sɪ'lektɪv] *adj* sélectif, -ive
**self** [self] *(pl* **selves** [selvz]*)* *n* **he's back to his old s.** il est redevenu comme avant ▪ **self-addressed** *n* **s. envelope** enveloppe *f* libellée à ses nom et adresse ▪ **self-assured** *adj* sûr de soi ▪ **self-catering** *adj Br (holiday)* en appartement meublé; *(accommodation)* meublé ▪ **self-centred** (*Am* **-centered**)

*adj* égocentrique ▪ **self-confidence** *n* confiance *f* en soi ▪ **self-confident** *adj* sûr de soi ▪ **self-conscious** *adj* gêné ▪ **self-contained** *adj (flat)* indépendant ▪ **self-control** *n* maîtrise *f* de soi ▪ **self-defence** (*Am* **-defense**) *n (in law)* légitime défense *f*; **in s.** en état de légitime défense ▪ **self-discipline** *n* autodiscipline *f* ▪ **self-employed** *adj* indépendant ▪ **self-esteem** *n* confiance *f* en soi ▪ **self-evident** *adj* évident ▪ **self-important** *adj* suffisant ▪ **self-indulgent** *adj* complaisant ▪ **self-interest** *n* intérêt *m* personnel ▪ **self-pity** *n* **to be full of s.** s'apitoyer sur son propre sort ▪ **self-portrait** *n* autoportrait *m* ▪ **self-raising** (*Am* **-rising**) *n* **s. flour** = farine contenant de la levure chimique ▪ **self-respect** *n* amour-propre *m* ▪ **self-righteous** *adj* suffisant ▪ **self-sacrifice** *n* abnégation *f* ▪ **self-satisfied** *adj* content de soi ▪ **self-service** *n & adj* libre-service *(m inv)* ▪ **self-sufficient** *adj* indépendant ▪ **self-taught** *adj* autodidacte

**selfish** ['selfɪʃ] *adj* égoïste; *(motive)* intéressé ▪ **selfishness** *n* égoïsme *m* ▪ **selfless** *adj* désintéressé

**sell** [sel] **1** (*pt & pp* **sold**) *vt* vendre; *Fig (idea)* faire accepter; **to s. sb sth, to s. sth to sb** vendre qch à qn; **she sold it to me for £20** elle me l'a vendu 20 livres **2** *vi (of product)* se vendre; *(of person)* vendre ▪ **sell-by** *adj* **s. date** date *f* limite de vente

▸**sell off** *vt sep* liquider

▸**sell out** *vt insep* **to have** *or* **be sold out of sth** n'avoir plus de qch; **to be sold out** *(of book, item)* être épuisé; *(of show, concert)* afficher complet

▸**sell up** *vi (sell home, business)* tout vendre

**seller** ['selə(r)] *n* vendeur, -euse *mf*

**Sellotape®** ['seləteɪp] *n Br* Scotch® *m*

**semblance** ['sembləns] *n* semblant *m*

**semen** ['si:mən] *n* sperme *m*

**semester** [sɪ'mestə(r)] *n* semestre *m*

**semi-** ['semɪ] *pref* semi-, demi- ▪ **semi-circle** *n* demi-cercle *m* ▪ **semi-colon** *n* point-virgule *m* ▪ **semi-detached** *adj Br* **s. house** maison *f* jumelée ▪ **semi-final** *n* demi-finale *f* ▪ **semi-skimmed** *adj (milk)* demi-écrémé

**seminar** ['semɪnɑ:(r)] *n* séminaire *m*

**semolina** [semə'li:nə] *n* semoule *f*

**senate** ['senɪt] *n* **the S.** le Sénat ▪ **senator** [-nətə(r)] *n* sénateur *m*

**send** [send] (*pt & pp* **sent**) *vt* envoyer (**to** à); **to s. sth to sb, to s. sb sth** envoyer qch à qn; **to s. sb home** renvoyer qn chez soi; *Fam* **to s. sb packing** envoyer promener qn ▪ **sender** *n* expéditeur, -trice *mf*

▸**send away 1** *vt sep (person)* renvoyer **2** *vi* **to s. away for sth** se faire envoyer qch

▸**send back** *vt sep* renvoyer

▸**send for** *vt insep* envoyer chercher; *(doctor)* faire venir; *(send away for)* se faire envoyer

▸**send in** *vt sep (form, invoice, troops)* envoyer; *(person)* faire entrer

▸**send off 1** *vt sep (letter)* envoyer (**to** à); *(player)* expulser **2** *vi* **to s. off for sth** se faire envoyer qch

▸**send on** *vt sep (letter)* faire suivre

▸**send out 1** *vt sep* envoyer **2** *vi* **to s. out for sth** envoyer chercher qch

▸**send up** *vt sep Br Fam (parody)* se moquer de

**senile** ['si:naɪl] *adj* sénile

**senior** ['si:nɪə(r)] **1** *adj (in age)* aîné; *(in position, rank)* supérieur; **to be sb's s., to be s. to sb** être l'aîné de qn; *(in rank, status)* être le supérieur de qn; **Brown s.** Brown père; **s. citizen** personne *f* âgée; *Am* **s. year** *(in school, college)* dernière année *f* **2** *n* aîné, -e *mf*; *Am (in last year of school or college)* étudiant, -e *mf* de dernière année; *(in sport)* senior *mf*

**sensation** [sen'seɪʃən] *n* sensation *f* ▪ **sensational** *adj* sensationnel, -elle

**sense** [sens] **1** *n (faculty, awareness, meaning)* sens *m*; **s. of smell** odorat *m*; **a s. of shame** un sentiment de honte; **s. of direction** sens de l'orientation; **to have a s. of humour** avoir le sens de l'humour; **to have the s. to do sth** avoir l'intelligence de faire qch; **to bring sb to his/her senses** ramener qn à la raison; **to make s.** être logique; **to make s. of sth** comprendre qch **2** *vt* sentir (**that** que)

**senseless** ['sensləs] *adj (pointless)* absurde

**sensibility** [sensɪ'bɪlətɪ] *n* sensibilité *f*

**sensible** ['sensəbəl] *adj (wise)* sensé; *(clothes, shoes)* pratique

**sensitive** ['sensɪtɪv] *adj (person)* sensible (**to** à); *(skin, question)* délicat; *(information)* confidentiel, -elle ▪ **sensitivity** *n* sensibilité *f*; *(touchiness)* susceptibilité *f*

**sensor** ['sənsə(r)] *n* détecteur *m*

**sensual** ['senʃʊəl] *adj* sensuel, -elle ▪ **sensuous** *adj* sensuel, -elle

**sent** [sent] *pt & pp of* **send**

**sentence** ['sentəns] **1** *n* (**a**) *(words)* phrase *f* (**b**) *(in prison)* peine *f* **2** *vt* *(criminal)* condamner; **to s. sb to three years (in prison)/to death** condamner qn à trois ans de prison/ à mort

**sentiment** ['sentɪmənt] *n* sentiment *m* ▪ **sentimental** [-'mentəl] *adj* sentimental

**separate 1** ['sepərət] *adj (distinct)* séparé; *(organization)* indépendant; *(occasion, entrance)* différent; *(room)* à part **2** ['sepəreɪt] *vt* séparer (**from** de) **3** ['sepəreɪt] *vi* se séparer (**from** de) ▪ **separately** ['sepərətlɪ] *adv* séparément ▪ **separation** *n* séparation *f*

**September** [sep'tembə(r)] *n* septembre *m*

**septic** ['septɪk] *adj (wound)* infecté; **to go** *or* **turn s.** s'infecter

**sequel** ['si:kwəl] *n (book, film)* suite *f*

**sequence** ['si:kwəns] *n (order)* ordre *m*; *(series)* succession *f*; *(in film) & Comptr, Mus & Cards* séquence *f*; **in s.** dans l'ordre

**sequin** ['si:kwɪn] *n* paillette *f*

**Serbia** ['sɜ:bɪə] *n* la Serbie

**serenade** [serə'neɪd] **1** *n* sérénade *f* **2** *vt* chanter la sérénade à

**serene** [sə'ri:n] *adj* serein

**sergeant** ['sɑ:dʒənt] *n Mil* sergent *m*; *(in police)* brigadier *m*

**serial** ['sɪərɪəl] *n (story, film)* feuilleton *m*; **s. killer** tueur *m* en série; **s. number** numéro *m* de série ▪ **serialize** *vt (in newspaper)* publier en feuilleton; *(on television or radio)* adapter en feuilleton

**series** ['sɪəri:z] *n inv* série *f*

**serious** ['sɪərɪəs] *adj (person)* sérieux, -euse; *(illness, mistake, tone)* grave; *(damage)* important; **to be s. about doing sth** envisager sérieusement de faire qch ▪ **seriously** *adv* sérieusement; *(ill, damaged)* gravement; **to take sb/sth s.** prendre qn/ qch au sérieux

**sermon** ['sɜ:mən] *n* sermon *m*

**servant** ['sɜ:vənt] *n* domestique *mf*

**serve** [sɜ:v] **1** *n (in tennis)* service *m*

**2** *vt (country, cause, meal, customer)* servir; *(prison sentence)* purger; *(apprenticeship)* faire; *Fam* **(it) serves you right!** ça t'apprendra!

**3** *vi* servir (**as** de); **to s. on** *(committee, jury)* être membre de ▪ **server** *n (in tennis)* serveur, -euse *mf*; *Comptr* serveur *m*

**service** ['sɜ:vɪs] **1** *n (with army, firm, in restaurant, in tennis) & Rel* service *m*; *(of machine)* entretien *m*; *(of car)* révision *f*; **to be at sb's s.** être au service de qn; **the (armed) services** les forces *fpl* armées; **s. charge** service *m*; *Br* **s. area** *(on motorway)* aire *f* de service; *Comptr* **s. provider** fournisseur *m* d'accès Internet; **s. station** station-service *f*

**2** *vt (machine)* entretenir; *(car)* réviser

**serviceman** ['sɜ:vɪsmən] (*pl* **-men**) *n* militaire *m*

**serviette** [sɜ:vɪ'et] *n Br* serviette *f* de table

**servile** ['sɜ:vaɪl] *adj* servile

**serving** ['sɜːvɪŋ] *n (of food)* portion *f*; **s. dish** plat *m*

**session** ['seʃən] *n (meeting, period)* séance *f*; *(university term)* trimestre *m*; *(university year)* année *f* universitaire

**set** [set] **1** *n (of keys, tools)* jeu *m*; *(of stamps, numbers)* série *f*; *(of people)* groupe *m*; *(of facts, laws) & Math* ensemble *m*; *(of books)* collection *f*; *(of dishes)* service *m*; *(kit)* trousse *f*; *(in theatre)* décor *m*; *(for film)* plateau *m*; *(in tennis)* set *m*; **chess s.** jeu *m* d'échecs; **tea s.** service *m* à thé; **television s.,TV s.** téléviseur *m*

**2** *adj (time, price)* fixe; *(lunch)* à prix fixe; *(school book)* au programme; *(ideas, purpose)* déterminé; **to be s. on doing sth** être résolu à faire qch; **to be dead s. against sth** être formellement opposé à qch; **to be all s.** être prêt (**to do** pour faire); **s. menu** menu *m*; **s. phrase** expression *f* figée

**3** (*pt & pp* **set,** *pres p* **setting**) *vt (put)* mettre, poser; *(date, limit, task)* fixer; *(homework)* donner (**for sb** à qn); *(jewel)* sertir; *(watch)* régler; *(alarm clock)* mettre (**for** pour); *(bone fracture)* réduire; *(trap)* tendre (**for** à); **to s. a record** établir un record; **to s. a precedent** créer un précédent; **to s. sb free** libérer qn

**4** *vi (of sun)* se coucher; *(of jelly)* prendre; *(of bone)* se ressouder

▸ **set about** *vt insep (begin)* se mettre à; **to s. about doing sth** se mettre à faire qch

▸ **set back** *vt sep (in time)* retarder; *Fam (cost)* coûter à

▸ **set down** *vt sep (object)* poser

▸ **set off 1** *vt sep (bomb)* faire exploser; *(mechanism)* déclencher; *Fig (beauty)* rehausser; **to s. sb off (crying)** faire pleurer qn **2** *vi (leave)* partir

▸ **set out 1** *vt sep (display, explain)* exposer; *(arrange)* disposer **2** *vi (leave)* partir; **to s. out to do sth** avoir l'intention de faire qch

▸ **set up 1** *vt sep (tent, statue)* dresser; *(roadblock)* mettre en place; *(company)* créer; *(meeting)* organiser; *(inquiry)* ouvrir **2** *vi* **to s. up in business** s'installer (**as** comme)

**setback** ['setbæk] *n* revers *m*

**settee** [se'tiː] *n* canapé *m*

**setting** ['setɪŋ] *n (surroundings)* cadre *m*; *(of sun)* coucher *m*; *(on machine)* réglage *m*

**settle** ['setəl] **1** *vt (put in place)* installer; *(decide, arrange, pay)* régler; *(date)* fixer; *(nerves)* calmer; *(land)* coloniser; **that settles it!** c'est décidé! **2** *vi (of person, family)* s'installer; *(of dust)* se déposer; *(of bird)* se poser ▪ **settled** *adj (weather, period)* stable; *(life)* rangé

▸ **settle down** *vi (in chair, house)* s'installer; *(become quieter)* s'assagir; *(of situation)* se calmer; **to s. down with sb** mener une vie stable avec qn; **to s. down to work** se mettre au travail

▸ **settle for** *vt insep* se contenter de

▸ **settle in** *vi (in new home)* s'installer

▸ **settle up** *vi (pay)* régler; **to s. up with sb** régler qn

**settlement** ['setəlmənt] *n (agreement)* accord *m*; *(payment)* règlement *m*; *(colony)* colonie *f*

**settler** ['setlə(r)] *n* colon *m*

**setup** ['setʌp] *n Fam (arrangement)* système *m*

**seven** ['sevən] *adj & n* sept *(m)* ▪ **seventh** *adj & n* septième *(mf)*

**seventeen** [sevən'tiːn] *adj & n* dix-sept *(m)* ▪ **seventeenth** *adj & n* dix-septième *(mf)*

**seventy** ['sevəntɪ] *adj & n* soixante-dix *(m)*; **s.-one** soixante et onze ▪ **seventieth** *adj & n* soixante-dixième *(mf)*

**sever** ['sevə(r)] *vt* couper; *Fig (relations)* rompre

**several** ['sevərəl] *adj & pron* plusieurs (**of** d'entre)

**severe** [sə'vɪə(r)] *adj (person, punishment, tone)* sévère; *(winter)* rigoureux, -euse; *(illness, injury)* grave; *(blow, pain)* violent; *(cold, frost)* intense

■ **severely** *adv (criticize, punish)* sévèrement; *(damaged, wounded)* gravement

**sew** [səʊ] (*pt* **sewed,** *pp* **sewn** *or* **sewed**) *vt* coudre; **to s. a button on a shirt** coudre un bouton à une chemise; **to s. sth up** recoudre qch ■ **sewing** *n* couture *f*; **s. machine** machine *f* à coudre

**sewage** ['suːɪdʒ] *n* eaux *fpl* d'égout ■ **sewer** *n* égout *m*

**sewn** [səʊn] *pp of* **sew**

**sex** [seks] **1** *n* sexe *m*; **to have s. with sb** coucher avec qn **2** *adj (education, life, act)* sexuel, -elle ■ **sexist** *adj & n* sexiste *(mf)*

**sexual** ['sekʃʊəl] *adj* sexuel, -elle ■ **sexuality** [seksjʊ'ælətɪ] *n* sexualité *f* ■ **sexy** ['seksɪ] (**-ier, -iest**) *adj Fam* sexy *inv*

**sh** [ʃ] *exclam* chut!

**shabby** ['ʃæbɪ] (**-ier, -iest**) *adj* miteux, -euse; *(behaviour, treatment)* mesquin

**shack** [ʃæk] *n* cabane *f*

**shade** [ʃeɪd] **1** *n* ombre *f*; *(of colour, meaning, opinion)* nuance *f*; *(for lamp)* abat-jour *m inv*; **in the s.** à l'ombre; **a s. faster/taller** un rien plus vite/plus grand **2** *vt (of tree)* ombrager ■ **shady** (**-ier, -iest**) *adj (place)* ombragé; *Fig (person, business)* louche

**shadow** ['ʃædəʊ] **1** *n* ombre *f* **2** *adj Br Pol* **s. cabinet** cabinet *m* fantôme **3** *vt* **to s. sb** *(follow)* filer qn

**shaft** [ʃɑːft] *n* (**a**) *(of tool)* manche *m*; **s. of light** rayon *m* de lumière (**b**) *(of mine)* puits *m*; *(of lift)* cage *f*

**shaggy** ['ʃægɪ] (**-ier, -iest**) *adj (hairy)* hirsute

**shake** [ʃeɪk] **1** *n* secousse *f*; **to give sth a s.** secouer qch

**2** (*pt* **shook,** *pp* **shaken**) *vt (move up and down)* secouer; *(bottle, fist)* agiter; *(building)* faire trembler; *Fig (belief, resolution)* ébranler; **to s. one's head** faire non de la tête; **to s. hands with sb** serrer la main à qn; **to s. off** *(dust)* secouer; *Fig (illness, pursuer)* se débarrasser de; **to s. up** *(reorganize)* réorganiser de fond en comble

**3** *vi (of person, windows, voice)* trembler (**with** de)

**shaken** ['ʃeɪkən] *pp of* **shake**

**shaky** ['ʃeɪkɪ] (**-ier, -iest**) *adj (voice)* tremblant; *(table, chair)* branlant; *(handwriting)* tremblé; *(health)* précaire

**SHALL** [ʃæl, *unstressed* ʃəl]

On trouve généralement **I/you/he/** etc **shall** sous leurs formes contractées **I'll/you'll/he'll/**etc. La forme négative correspondante est **shan't**, que l'on écrira **shall not** dans des contextes formels.

*v aux* (**a**) *(expressing future tense)* **I s. come, I'll come** je viendrai; **we s. not come, we shan't come** nous ne viendrons pas

(**b**) *(making suggestion)* **s. I leave?** veux-tu que je parte?; **let's go in, s. we?** entrons, tu veux bien?

(**c**) *Formal (expressing order)* **he s. do it if I order it** il le fera si je l'ordonne

**shallow** ['ʃæləʊ] (**-er, -est**) *adj (water, river)* peu profond; *Fig & Pej (argument, person)* superficiel, -elle

**sham** [ʃæm] **1** *n (pretence)* comédie *f* **2** *adj (false)* faux (*f* fausse); *(illness, emotion)* feint **3** (*pt & pp* **-mm-**) *vt* feindre **4** *vi* faire semblant

**shambles** ['ʃæmbəlz] *n* pagaille *f*

**shame** [ʃeɪm] **1** *n (guilt, disgrace)* honte *f*; **it's a s.** c'est dommage (**to do** de faire); **it's a s. (that)...** c'est dommage que... *(+ subjunctive)*; **what a s.!** quel dommage! **2** *vt (make ashamed)* faire honte à

**shameful** ['ʃeɪmfəl] *adj* honteux, -euse

**shameless** ['ʃeɪmləs] *adj* impudique

**shampoo** [ʃæm'puː] **1** *n* shampooing *m* **2** *vt (carpet)* shampouiner

**shandy** ['ʃændɪ] *n Br* panaché *m*

**shan't** [ʃɑːnt] = **shall not**

**shape** [ʃeɪp] **1** *n* forme *f*; **what s. is it?** quelle forme cela a-t-il?; **to take s.** *(of plan)* prendre forme; **to be in good/**

**bad s.** *(of person)* être en bonne/mauvaise forme; *(of business)* marcher bien/mal; **to keep in s.** garder la forme

2 *vt (clay)* modeler; *(wood)* façonner (**into** en); *Fig (events, future)* influencer

3 *vi* **to s. up** *(of person)* progresser; *(of teams, plans)* prendre forme ▪ **-shaped** *suff* **pear-s.** en forme de poire ▪ **shapeless** *adj* informe ▪ **shapely** (**-ier, -iest**) *adj* bien fait

**share** [ʃeə(r)] **1** *n* part *f* (**of** *or* **in** de); *Fin (in company)* action *f*; **to do one's (fair) s.** mettre la main à la pâte **2** *vt* partager; *(characteristic)* avoir en commun; **to s. sth out** partager qch **3** *vi* partager; **to s. in sth** avoir sa part de qch ▪ **shareholder** *n Fin* actionnaire *mf*

**shark** [ʃɑːk] *n (fish, crook)* requin *m*

**sharp** [ʃɑːp] **1** (**-er, -est**) *adj (knife)* bien aiguisé; *(pencil)* bien taillé; *(point)* aigu (*f* aiguë); *(claws)* acéré; *(rise, fall)* brusque; *(focus)* net (*f* nette); *(contrast)* marqué; *(eyesight)* perçant; *(taste)* acide; *(intelligent)* vif (*f* vive)

2 *adv* **five o'clock s.** cinq heures pile; **to turn s. right/left** tourner tout de suite à droite/à gauche

3 *n Mus* dièse *m*

**sharpen** [ˈʃɑːpən] *vt (knife)* aiguiser; *(pencil)* tailler

**sharply** [ˈʃɑːplɪ] *adv (rise, fall)* brusquement; *(contrast)* nettement

**shatter** [ˈʃætə(r)] **1** *vt (glass)* faire voler en éclats; *(health, hopes)* briser **2** *vi (of glass)* voler en éclats ▪ **shattered** *adj Fam (exhausted)* crevé ▪ **shattering** *adj (news, experience)* bouleversant

**shave** [ʃeɪv] **1** *n* **to have a s.** se raser **2** *vt (person, head)* raser **3** *vi* se raser ▪ **shaver** *n* rasoir *m* électrique ▪ **shaving** *n (strip of wood)* copeau *m*; **s. cream, s. foam** mousse *f* à raser

**shawl** [ʃɔːl] *n* châle *m*

**she** [ʃiː] **1** *pron* elle; **she's a happy woman** c'est une femme heureuse **2** *n Fam* **it's a s.** *(of baby)* c'est une fille

**sheaf** [ʃiːf] (*pl* **sheaves** [ʃiːvz]) *n (of corn)* gerbe *f*; *(of paper)* liasse *f*

**shear** [ʃɪə(r)] **1** *vt* tondre **2** *npl* **shears** cisaille *f*

**sheath** [ʃiːθ] (*pl* **-s** [ʃiːðz]) *n (for sword)* fourreau *m*; *(contraceptive)* préservatif *m*

**she'd** [ʃiːd] = **she had, she would**

**shed¹** [ʃed] *n (in garden)* abri *m*

**shed²** [ʃed] (*pt & pp* **shed**, *pres p* **shedding**) *vt (leaves)* perdre; *(tears, blood)* verser; *Fig* **to s. light on sth** éclairer qch

**sheep** [ʃiːp] *n inv* mouton *m* ▪ **sheepdog** *n* chien *m* de berger ▪ **sheepskin** *n* peau *f* de mouton

**sheepish** [ˈʃiːpɪʃ] *adj* penaud

**sheer** [ʃɪə(r)] *adj (pure)* pur; *(stockings)* très fin; *(cliff)* à pic; **by s. chance** tout à fait par hasard

**sheet** [ʃiːt] *n (on bed)* drap *m*; *(of paper)* feuille *f*; *(of glass, ice)* plaque *f*

**shelf** [ʃelf] (*pl* **shelves** [ʃelvz]) *n* étagère *f*; *(in shop)* rayon *m*

**shell** [ʃel] **1** *n* (**a**) *(of egg, snail, nut)* coquille *f*; *(of tortoise, lobster)* carapace *f*; *(on beach)* coquillage *m*; *(of peas)* cosse *f* (**b**) *(explosive)* obus *m* **2** *vt* (**a**) *(peas)* écosser; *(nut)* décortiquer (**b**) *(town)* bombarder

**she'll** [ʃiːl] = **she will, she shall**

**shellfish** [ˈʃelfɪʃ] *npl* fruits *mpl* de mer

**shelter** [ˈʃeltə(r)] **1** *n (place, protection)* abri *m*; **to take s.** se mettre à l'abri (**from** de) **2** *vt* abriter (**from** de); *(criminal)* accueillir **3** *vi* s'abriter (**from** de) ▪ **sheltered** *adj (place)* abrité

**shelve** [ʃelv] *vt (postpone)* mettre au placard

**shelving** [ˈʃelvɪŋ] *n* rayonnages *mpl*

**shepherd** [ˈʃepəd] *n* berger *m*; *Br* **s.'s pie** ≃ hachis *m* Parmentier

**sherbet** [ˈʃɜːbət] *n Br (powder)* poudre *f* acidulée; *Am (sorbet)* sorbet *m*

**sheriff** [ˈʃerɪf] *n Am* shérif *m*

**sherry** [ˈʃerɪ] *n* sherry *m*, xérès *m*

**shield** [ʃiːld] **1** *n (of warrior)* bouclier *m* **2** *vt* protéger (**from** de)

**shift** [ʃɪft] **1** *n (change)* changement *m* (**of** *or* **in** de); *(period of work)* poste *m*; *(workers)* équipe *f*; **s. key** *(on computer, typewriter)* touche *f* des majuscules

**2** *vt (move)* déplacer; *(stain)* enlever; *Am* **to s. gear(s)** *(in vehicle)* changer de vitesse

**3** *vi (move)* bouger ■ **shiftwork** *n* travail *m* posté

**shifty** ['ʃɪftɪ] (**-ier, -iest**) *adj (person)* louche

**shimmer** ['ʃɪmə(r)] *vi (of silk)* chatoyer; *(of water)* miroiter

**shin** [ʃɪn] *n* tibia *m*; **s. pad** *(of hockey player)* jambière *f*

**shine** [ʃaɪn] **1** *n* brillant *m*; *(on metal)* éclat *m* **2** *(pt & pp* **shone***) vt (polish)* faire briller; *(light, torch)* braquer **3** *vi* briller

**shiny** ['ʃaɪnɪ] (**-ier, -iest**) *adj* brillant

**ship** [ʃɪp] **1** *n* navire *m* **2** *(pt & pp* **-pp-***) vt (send)* expédier; *(transport)* transporter ■ **shipment** *n* cargaison *f* ■ **shipping** *n (traffic)* navigation *f*; *(ships)* navires *mpl* ■ **shipwreck** *n* naufrage *m* ■ **shipwrecked** *adj* naufragé; **to be s.** faire naufrage ■ **shipyard** *n* chantier *m* naval

**shirk** [ʃɜːk] **1** *vt (duty)* se dérober à; *(work)* éviter de faire **2** *vi* tirer au flanc

**shirt** [ʃɜːt] *n* chemise *f*; *(of woman)* chemisier *m*; *(of sportsman)* maillot *m*

**shiver** ['ʃɪvə(r)] **1** *n* frisson *m* **2** *vi* frissonner (**with** de)

**shoal** [ʃəʊl] *n (of fish)* banc *m*

**shock** [ʃɒk] **1** *n (impact, emotional blow)* choc *m*; **(electric) s.** décharge *f* (électrique) **2** *adj (wave, tactics, troops)* de choc; *Aut* **s. absorber** amortisseur *m* **3** *vt (offend)* choquer; *(surprise)* stupéfier ■ **shocking** *adj (outrageous)* choquant; *(very bad)* atroce

**shoddy** ['ʃɒdɪ] (**-ier, -iest**) *adj (goods)* de mauvaise qualité

**shoe** [ʃuː] *n* chaussure *f*; *(for horse)* fer *m* à cheval; **s. polish** cirage *m*; **s. shop** magasin *m* de chaussures ■ **shoelace** *n* lacet *m*

**shone** [*Br* ʃɒn, *Am* ʃəʊn] *pt & pp of* **shine**

**shoo** [ʃuː] **1** *(pt & pp* **shooed***) vt* **to s. (away)** chasser **2** *exclam* ouste!

**shook** [ʃʊk] *pt of* **shake**[1]

**shoot** [ʃuːt] **1** *n (of plant)* pousse *f* **2** *(pt & pp* **shot***) vt (bullet)* tirer; *(arrow)* lancer; *(film, scene)* tourner; **to s. sb** *(kill)* tuer qn par balle; *(wound)* blesser qn par balle; *(execute)* fusiller qn **3** *vi (with gun)* tirer (**at** sur); *(of footballer)* shooter ■ **shooting** *n (shots)* coups *mpl* de feu; *(incident)* fusillade *f*; *(of film, scene)* tournage *m*

▸ **shoot down** *vt sep (plane)* abattre

▸ **shoot off** *vi (leave quickly)* filer

▸ **shoot up** *vi (of price)* monter en flèche; *(of plant, child)* pousser vite; *(of rocket)* s'élever

**shop** [ʃɒp] **1** *n* magasin *m*; *(small)* boutique *f*; *(workshop)* atelier *m*; **at the baker's s.** à la boulangerie, chez le boulanger; *Br* **s. assistant** vendeur, -euse *mf*; **s. window** vitrine *f*

**2** *(pt & pp* **-pp-***) vi* faire ses courses (**at** chez); **to s. around** comparer les prix ■ **shopkeeper** *n* commerçant, -e *mf* ■ **shoplifter** *n* voleur, -euse *mf* à l'étalage ■ **shopper** *n (customer)* client, -e *mf* ■ **shopping 1** *n (goods)* achats *mpl*; **to go s.** faire des courses; **to do one's s.** faire ses courses **2** *adj (street, district)* commerçant; **s. bag** sac *m* à provisions; **s. centre** centre *m* commercial; **s. list** liste *f* des commissions

**shore** [ʃɔː(r)] *n (of sea)* rivage *m*; *(of lake)* bord *m*; **on s.** à terre

**short** [ʃɔːt] **1** (**-er, -est**) *adj* court; *(person, distance)* petit; *(impatient, curt)* brusque; **to be s. of sth** être à court de qch; **money/time is s.** l'argent/le temps manque; **a s. time** *or* **while ago** il y a peu de temps; **Tony is s. for Anthony** Tony est le diminutif d'Anthony; **in s.** bref; **s. cut** raccourci *m*; **s. story** nouvelle *f*

**2** *adv* **to cut s.** *(hair)* couper court; *(visit)* abréger; *(person)* couper la parole à; **to stop s. of doing sth** se retenir tout juste de faire qch; **to be running s. of sth** n'avoir presque plus de qch ▪ **shortbread** *n* sablé *m* ▪ **short-circuit 1** *n* court-circuit *m* **2** *vt* court-circuiter **3** *vi* se mettre en court-circuit ▪ **shortcoming** *n* défaut *m* ▪ **shorthand** *n* sténo *f*; **s. typist** sténodactylo *m* ▪ **short-lived** *adj* de courte durée ▪ **short-sighted** *adj* myope; *Fig (in one's judgements)* imprévoyant ▪ **short-sleeved** *adj* à manches courtes ▪ **short-staffed** *adj* à court de personnel ▪ **short-term** *adj* à court terme

**shortage** [ˈʃɔːtɪdʒ] *n* pénurie *f*

**shorten** [ˈʃɔːtən] *vt* raccourcir

**shortly** [ˈʃɔːtlɪ] *adv (soon)* bientôt; **s. before/after** peu avant/après

**shorts** [ʃɔːts] *npl* **(pair of) s.** short *m*; **boxer s.** caleçon *m*

**shot** [ʃɒt] **1** *pt & pp of* **shoot 2** *n (from gun)* coup *m*; *(with camera)* prise *f* de vue; *(in football)* coup *m* de pied; *Fam (injection)* piqûre *f*; **to fire a s.** tirer; **to be a good s.** *(of person)* être bon tireur; **to have a s. at sth/doing sth** essayer qch/de faire qch ▪ **shotgun** *n* fusil *m* de chasse

**SHOULD** [ʃʊd, *unstressed* ʃəd]

> La forme négative **should not** s'écrit **shouldn't** en forme contractée.

*v aux* (**a**) *(expressing obligation)* **you s. do it** vous devriez le faire; **I s. have stayed** j'aurais dû rester

(**b**) *(expressing possibility)* **the weather s. improve** le temps devrait s'améliorer; **she s. have arrived by now** elle devrait être arrivée à l'heure qu'il est

(**c**) *(expressing preferences)* **I s. like to stay** j'aimerais bien rester; **I s. like to** j'aimerais bien; **I s. hope so** j'espère bien

(**d**) *(in subordinate clauses)* **it's strange (that) she s. say no** il est étrange qu'elle dise non; **he insisted that she s. meet her parents** il a insisté pour qu'elle rencontre ses parents

(**e**) *(in conditional clauses)* **if he s. come, s. he come** s'il vient

(**f**) *(in rhetorical questions)* **why s. you suspect me?** pourquoi me soupçonnez-vous?; **who s. I meet but Martin!** et qui a-t-il fallu que je rencontre? Martin!

---

**shoulder** [ˈʃəʊldə(r)] **1** *n* épaule *f*; **s. bag** sac *m* besace; **s. pad** épaulette *f*; **s. strap** *(of garment)* bretelle *f* **2** *vt (responsibility)* endosser

**shout** [ʃaʊt] **1** *n* cri *m*; **to give sb a s.** appeler qn **2** *vt* **to s. sth (out)** crier qch **3** *vi* **to s. (out)** crier; **to s. to sb to do sth** crier à qn de faire qch; **to s. at sb** crier après qn ▪ **shouting** *n (shouts)* cris *mpl*

**shove** [ʃʌv] **1** *n* poussée *f*; **to give sb/sth a s.** pousser qn/qch **2** *vt* pousser; *Fam* **to s. sth into sth** fourrer qch dans qch **3** *vi* pousser; *Fam* **to s. over** *(move over)* se pousser

**shovel** [ˈʃʌvəl] **1** *n* pelle *f* **2** (*Br* **-ll-**, *Am* **-l-**) *vt* pelleter; **to s. leaves up** ramasser des feuilles à la pelle

**show** [ʃəʊ] **1** *n (concert, play)* spectacle *m*; *(on TV)* émission *f*; *(exhibition)* exposition *f*; *(of force, friendship)* démonstration *f*; *(pretence)* semblant *m* (**of** de); **to be on s.** être exposé; **to put sth on s.** exposer qch; **s. business** le monde du spectacle; **s. jumping** jumping *m*

**2** (*pt* **showed**, *pp* **shown**) *vt* montrer (**to** à; **that** que); *(in exhibition)* exposer; *(film)* passer; *(indicate)* indiquer; **to s. sb sth, to s. sth to sb** montrer qch à qn; **to s. sb to the door** reconduire qn à la porte

**3** *vi (be visible)* se voir; *(of film)* passer ▪ **showdown** *n* confrontation *f* ▪ **show-off** *n Pej* crâneur, -euse *mf* ▪ **showroom** *n* magasin *m* d'exposition

▸ **show around** *vt sep* **to s. sb around the town/the house** faire visiter la ville/la maison à qn

▸**show in** *vt sep (visitor)* faire entrer
▸**show off 1** *vt sep Pej (display)* étaler; *(highlight)* faire valoir **2** *vi Pej* crâner
▸**show out** *vt sep (visitor)* reconduire
▸**show round** *vt sep* = **show around**
▸**show up 1** *vt sep (embarrass)* faire honte à; *(reveal)* faire ressortir **2** *vi (stand out)* ressortir (**against** contre); *Fam (of person)* se présenter
**shower** ['ʃaʊə(r)] **1** *n (bathing, device)* douche *f*; *(of rain)* averse *f*; **to have** *or* **take a s.** prendre une douche; **s. gel** gel *m* de douche **2** *vt* **to s. sb with** *(gifts, abuse)* couvrir qn de ▪ **showery** *adj* pluvieux, -euse
**shown** [ʃəʊn] *pp of* **show**
**showy** ['ʃəʊɪ] (**-ier, -iest**) *adj* voyant
**shrank** [ʃræŋk] *pt of* **shrink**
**shred** [ʃred] **1** *n* lambeau *m*; **to tear sth to shreds** mettre qch en lambeaux; *Fig* **not a s. of truth** pas une once de vérité **2** (*pt & pp* **-dd-**) *vt* mettre en lambeaux; *(documents)* déchiqueter; *(food)* couper grossièrement
**shrewd** [ʃruːd] (**-er, -est**) *adj (person, plan)* astucieux, -euse
**shriek** [ʃriːk] **1** *n* cri *m* strident **2** *vi* pousser un cri strident; **to s. with pain/laughter** hurler de douleur/de rire
**shrill** [ʃrɪl] (**-er, -est**) *adj* aigu (*f* aiguë)
**shrimp** [ʃrɪmp] *n* crevette *f*
**shrine** [ʃraɪn] *n (place of worship)* lieu *m* saint; *(tomb)* tombeau *m*
**shrink** [ʃrɪŋk] **1** (*pt* **shrank** *or Am* **shrunk,** *pp* **shrunk** *or* **shrunken**) *vt (of clothes)* faire rétrécir **2** *vi* rétrécir
**shrivel** ['ʃrɪvəl] (*Br* **-ll-**, *Am* **-l-**) **1** *vt* **to s. (up)** dessécher **2** *vi* **to s. (up)** se dessécher
**shroud** [ʃraʊd] **1** *n* linceul *m* **2** *vt* **to be shrouded in sth** être enveloppé de qch
**Shrove** [ʃrəʊv] *adj* **S. Tuesday** mardi *m* gras
**shrub** [ʃrʌb] *n* arbuste *m*
**shrug** [ʃrʌg] **1** *n* haussement *m* d'épaules **2** (*pt & pp* **-gg-**) *vt* **to s. one's shoulders** hausser les épaules; **to s. sth off** dédaigner qch
**shrunk(en)** ['ʃrʌŋk(ən)] *pp of* **shrink**
**shudder** ['ʃʌdə(r)] *vi (of person)* frémir (**with** de); *(of machine)* vibrer
**shuffle** ['ʃʌfəl] **1** *vt (cards)* battre **2** *vti* **to s. (one's feet)** traîner les pieds
**shun** [ʃʌn] (*pt & pp* **-nn-**) *vt* fuir, éviter
**shush** [ʃʊʃ] *exclam* chut!
**shut** [ʃʌt] **1** (*pt & pp* **shut,** *pres p* **shutting**) *vt* fermer **2** *vi (of door)* se fermer; *(of shop, museum)* fermer
▸**shut away** *vt sep (lock away)* enfermer
▸**shut down 1** *vt sep* fermer (définitivement) **2** *vi* fermer (définitivement)
▸**shut in** *vt sep (lock in)* enfermer
▸**shut off** *vt sep (gas, electricity)* couper; *(engine)* arrêter; *(road)* fermer; *(isolate)* isoler
▸**shut out** *vt sep (keep outside)* empêcher d'entrer; *(exclude)* exclure (**of** *or* **from** de); **to s. sb out** enfermer qn dehors
▸**shut up 1** *vt sep (close)* fermer; *(confine)* enfermer; *Fam (silence)* faire taire **2** *vi Fam (be quiet)* se taire
**shutter** ['ʃʌtə(r)] *n (on window)* volet *m*; *(of shop)* store *m*; *(of camera)* obturateur *m*
**shuttle** ['ʃʌtəl] **1** *n (bus, train, plane)* navette *f*; **s. service** navette *f* **2** *vi* faire la navette
**shy** [ʃaɪ] **1** (**-er, -est**) *adj* timide **2** *vi* **to s. away from doing sth** éviter de faire qch
**sibling** ['sɪblɪŋ] *n (brother)* frère *m*; *(sister)* sœur *f*
**Sicily** ['sɪsɪlɪ] *n* la Sicile
**sick** [sɪk] **1** (**-er, -est**) *adj (ill)* malade; **to be s.** *(be ill)* être malade; *(vomit)* vomir; **to feel s.** avoir mal au cœur; **to be off s., to be on s. leave** être en congé de maladie; **to be s. of sb/sth** en avoir assez de qn/qch; *Fig* **he makes me s.** il m'écœure **2** *n Br Fam (vomit)* vomi *m* **3** *npl* **the s.** *(sick people)* les malades *mpl*
**sicken** ['sɪkən] **1** *vt* écœurer **2** *vi Br* **to**

**be sickening for something** couver quelque chose ■ **sickening** *adj* écœurant

**sickly** ['sɪklɪ] (**-ier, -iest**) *adj* maladif, -ive; *(pale, faint)* pâle; *(taste)* écœurant

**sickness** ['sɪknɪs] *n (illness)* maladie *f*

**side** [saɪd] **1** *n* côté *m*; *(of hill, animal)* flanc *m*; *(of road, river)* bord *m*; *(of question, character)* aspect *m*; *(team)* équipe *f*; **at** *or* **by the s. of** *(nearby)* à côté de; **at** *or* **by my s.** à côté de moi, à mes côtés; **s. by s.** l'un à côté de l'autre; **to move to one s.** s'écarter; **on this s.** de ce côté; **to take sides with sb** se ranger du côté de qn; **she's on our s.** elle est de notre côté
**2** *adj (lateral)* latéral; *(view, glance)* de côté; *(street)* transversal; *(effect, issue)* secondaire
**3** *vi* **to s. with sb** se ranger du côté de qn ■ **sideboard** *n* buffet *m* ■ **sideburns** *npl (hair)* pattes *fpl* ■ **-sided** *suff* **ten-sided** à dix côtés ■ **sidelight** *n Br (on vehicle)* feu *m* de position ■ **sideline** *n (activity)* activité *f* secondaire; *(around playing field)* ligne *f* de touche ■ **sidestep** (*pt & pp* **-pp-**) *vt* éviter ■ **sidetrack** *vt* distraire; **to get sidetracked** s'écarter du sujet ■ **sidewalk** *n Am* trottoir *m* ■ **sideways** *adv (look, walk)* de côté

**siege** [siːdʒ] *n (by soldiers, police)* siège *m*; **under s.** assiégé

**siesta** [sɪ'estə] *n* sieste *f*; **to take** *or* **have a s.** faire la sieste

**sieve** [sɪv] *n* tamis *m*; *(for liquids)* passoire *f*

**sift** [sɪft] **1** *vt (flour)* tamiser **2** *vi* **to s. through** *(papers)* examiner (à la loupe)

**sigh** [saɪ] **1** *n* soupir *m* **2** *vti* soupirer

**sight** [saɪt] **1** *n (faculty)* vue *f*; *(thing seen)* spectacle *m*; *(on gun)* viseur *m*; **to lose s. of sb/sth** perdre qn/qch de vue; **to catch s. of sb/sth** apercevoir qn/qch; **at first s.** à première vue; **by s.** de vue; **in s.** *(target, end, date)* en vue; **out of s.** *(hidden)* caché; *(no longer visible)* disparu; **he hates the s. of me** il ne peut pas me voir; **the (tourist) sights** les attractions *fpl* touristiques; **to set one's sights on** *(job)* viser **2** *vt (land)* apercevoir

**sightseer** ['saɪtsiːə(r)] *n* touriste *mf* ■ **sightseeing** *n* **to go s., to do some s.** faire du tourisme

**sign** [saɪn] **1** *n* signe *m*; *(notice)* panneau *m*; *(over shop, pub)* enseigne *f*; **no s. of** aucune trace de **2** *vt (put signature to)* signer; **to s. on** *or* **up** *(worker, soldier)* engager **3** *vi* signer; **to s. for** *(letter)* signer le reçu de; *Br* **to s. on** *(on the dole)* s'inscrire au chômage; **to s. on** *or* **up** *(of soldier, worker)* s'engager; *(for course)* s'inscrire

**signal** ['sɪgnəl] **1** *n* signal *m*; *Rail Br* **s. box,** *Am* **s. tower** poste *m* d'aiguillage
**2** (*Br* **-ll-**, *Am* **-l-**) *vt (be a sign of)* indiquer; *(make gesture to)* faire signe à
**3** *vi (make gesture)* faire signe (**to** à); *(of driver)* mettre son clignotant; **to s. (to) sb to do sth** faire signe à qn de faire qch

**signature** ['sɪgnətʃə(r)] *n* signature *f*; **s. tune** indicatif *m*

**significance** [sɪg'nɪfɪkəns] *n (meaning)* signification *f*; *(importance)* importance *f*

**significant** [sɪg'nɪfɪkənt] *adj (important, large)* important; *(meaningful)* significatif, -ive ■ **significantly** *adv (appreciably)* sensiblement

**signify** ['sɪgnɪfaɪ] (*pt & pp* **-ied**) *vt (mean, make known)* signifier (**that** que)

**signpost** ['saɪnpəʊst] **1** *n* poteau *m* indicateur **2** *vt* signaliser

**silence** ['saɪləns] **1** *n* silence *m*; **in s.** en silence **2** *vt* faire taire

**silent** ['saɪlənt] *adj* silencieux, -euse; *(film, anger)* muet (*f* muette); **to keep** *or* **be s.** garder le silence (**about** sur) ■ **silently** *adv* silencieusement

**silhouette** [sɪluː'et] *n* silhouette *f*

**silicon** ['sɪlɪkən] *n* silicium *m*; **s. chip** puce *f* électronique

**silk** [sɪlk] *n* soie *f* ■ **silky** (**-ier, -iest**) *adj* soyeux, -euse

**sill** [sɪl] *n (of window)* rebord *m*

**silly** ['sɪlɪ] (**-ier, -iest**) *adj* bête, idiot; **to do something s.** faire une bêtise; **to look s.** avoir l'air ridicule

**silver** ['sɪlvə(r)] **1** *n* argent *m*; *(plates)* argenterie *f* **2** *adj (spoon)* en argent, d'argent; *(colour)* argenté; **s. jubilee** vingt-cinquième anniversaire *m*; *Br* **s. paper** papier *m* d'argent ▪ **silver-plated** *adj* plaqué argent

**similar** ['sɪmɪlə(r)] *adj* semblable (**to** à) ▪ **similarity** [-'lærətɪ] (*pl* **-ies**) *n* ressemblance *f* (**between** entre; **to** avec) ▪ **similarly** *adv* de la même façon; *(likewise)* de même

**simile** ['sɪmɪlɪ] *n* comparaison *f*

**simmer** ['sɪmə(r)] **1** *vt (vegetables)* mijoter **2** *vi (of vegetables)* mijoter; *(of water)* frémir; *Fig (of revolt, hatred)* couver

**simple** ['sɪmpəl] (**-er, -est**) *adj (easy)* simple ▪ **simple-minded** *adj* simple d'esprit ▪ **simplicity** *n* simplicité *f*

**simplify** ['sɪmplɪfaɪ] (*pt & pp* **-ied**) *vt* simplifier

**simply** ['sɪmplɪ] *adv (plainly, merely)* simplement; *(absolutely)* absolument

**simulate** ['sɪmjʊleɪt] *vt* simuler

**simultaneous** [*Br* sɪməl'teɪnɪəs, *Am* saɪməl'teɪnɪəs] *adj* simultané ▪ **simultaneously** [*Br* sɪməl'teɪnɪəslɪ, *Am* saɪməl'teɪnɪəslɪ] *adv* simultanément

**sin** [sɪn] **1** *n* péché *m* **2** (*pt & pp* **-nn-**) *vi* pécher

**since** [sɪns] **1** *prep (in time)* depuis; **s. then** depuis **2** *conj (in time)* depuis que; *(because)* puisque; **it's a year s. I saw him** ça fait un an que je ne l'ai pas vu **3** *adv* **(ever) s.** depuis

**sincere** [sɪn'sɪə(r)] *adj* sincère ▪ **sincerely** *adv* sincèrement; *Br* **yours s.,** *Am* **s.** *(in letter)* veuillez agréer, Madame/Monsieur, mes salutations distinguées ▪ **sincerity** [-'serətɪ] *n* sincérité *f*

**sinful** ['sɪnfəl] *adj (act)* coupable; *(waste)* scandaleux, -euse

**sing** [sɪŋ] (*pt* **sang,** *pp* **sung**) *vti* chanter ▪ **singer** *n* chanteur, -euse *mf* ▪ **singing 1** *n (of bird, musical technique)* chant *m* **2** *adj* **s. lesson/teacher** leçon *f*/professeur *m* de chant

**singe** [sɪndʒ] *vt (cloth)* roussir; *(hair)* brûler

**single** ['sɪŋgəl] **1** *adj (only one)* seul; *(room, bed)* pour une personne; *(unmarried)* célibataire; **not a s. book** pas un seul livre; **every s. day** tous les jours sans exception; *Br* **s. ticket** aller *m* simple; **s. parent** père *m*/mère *f* célibataire

**2** *n Br (ticket)* aller *m* simple; *(record)* single *m*; **singles** *(in tennis)* simples *mpl*

**3** *vt* **to s. sb out** sélectionner qn ▪ **single-handedly** *adv* tout seul (*f* toute seule) ▪ **single-minded** *adj (person)* résolu; *(determination)* farouche ▪ **single-sex** *adj Br* **s. school** école *f* non mixte

**singly** ['sɪŋglɪ] *adv (one by one)* un à un

**singular** ['sɪŋgjʊlə(r)] **1** *adj (in grammar)* singulier, -ère; *(remarkable)* remarquable **2** *n* singulier *m*; **in the s.** au singulier

**sinister** ['sɪnɪstə(r)] *adj* sinistre

**sink**[1] [sɪŋk] *n (in kitchen)* évier *m*; *(in bathroom)* lavabo *m*

**sink**[2] [sɪŋk] (*pt* **sank,** *pp* **sunk**) **1** *vt (ship)* couler **2** *vi (of ship, person)* couler; *(of water level, sun, price)* baisser; *(collapse)* s'affaisser; **my heart sank** j'ai eu un pincement de cœur; **to s. (down) into** *(mud)* s'enfoncer dans; *(armchair)* s'affaler dans; *Fam* **it hasn't sunk in yet** je n'ai/il n'a/*etc* pas encore digéré la nouvelle

**sinner** ['sɪnə(r)] *n* pécheur(eresse) *mf*

**sinus** ['saɪnəs] *n Anat* sinus *m*

**sip** [sɪp] **1** *n* petite gorgée *f* **2** (*pt & pp* **-pp-**) *vt* siroter

**siphon** ['saɪfən] **1** *n* siphon *m* **2** *vt* **to s. sth off** *(liquid)* siphonner qch; *(money)* détourner qch

**sir** [sɜː(r)] *n* monsieur *m*; **S. Walter Raleigh** *(title)* sir Walter Raleigh

**siren** ['saɪərən] *n* sirène *f*

**sister** ['sɪstə(r)] *n* sœur *f*; *(nurse)* infirmière-chef *f* ▪ **sister-in-law** (*pl* **sisters-in-law**) *n* belle-sœur *f*

**sit** [sɪt] (*pt & pp* **sat**, *pres p* **sitting**) **1** *vt (child on chair)* asseoir; *Br (exam)* se présenter à **2** *vi (of person)* s'asseoir; *(for artist)* poser (**for** pour); *(of assembly)* siéger; **to be sitting** *(of person, cat)* être assis; **she was sitting reading, she sat reading** elle était assise à lire

▸ **sit around** *vi* rester assis à ne rien faire

▸ **sit back** *vi (in chair)* se caler; *(rest)* se détendre; *(do nothing)* ne rien faire

▸ **sit down 1** *vt* **to s. sb down** asseoir qn **2** *vi* s'asseoir; **to be sitting down** être assis

▸ **sit for** *vt insep Br (exam)* se présenter à

▸ **sit in on** *vt insep (lecture)* assister à

▸ **sit on** *vt insep (jury)* être membre de

▸ **sit out** *vt sep (dance)* ne pas prendre part à

▸ **sit through** *vt insep (film)* rester jusqu'au bout de

▸ **sit up** *vi* **to s. up (straight)** s'asseoir (bien droit); **to s. up waiting for sb** veiller jusqu'au retour de qn

**sitcom** ['sɪtkɒm] *n* sitcom *m*

**site** [saɪt] *n (position)* emplacement *m*; *(archaeological, on Internet)* site *m*; **(building) s.** chantier *m* (de construction)

**sitting** ['sɪtɪŋ] *n* séance *f*; *(in restaurant)* service *m*; **s. room** salon *m*

**situate** ['sɪtʃʊeɪt] *vt* situer; **to be situated** être situé ▪ **situation** *n* situation *f*

**six** [sɪks] *adj & n* six *(m)* ▪ **sixth** *adj & n* sixième *(mf)*; **a s.** *(fraction)* un sixième; *Br Sch* **(lower) s. form** ≃ classe *f* de première; *Br Sch* **(upper) s. form** ≃ classe *f* terminale

**sixteen** [sɪk'stiːn] *adj & n* seize *(m)* ▪ **sixteenth** *adj & n* seizième *(mf)*

**sixty** ['sɪkstɪ] *adj & n* soixante *(m)* ▪ **sixtieth** *adj & n* soixantième *(mf)*

**size** [saɪz] **1** *n (of person, animal, clothes)* taille *f*; *(of shoes, gloves)* pointure *f*; *(of shirt)* encolure *f*; *(measurements)* dimensions *fpl*; *(of packet)* grosseur *f*; *(of town, damage, problem)* étendue *f*; *(of sum)* montant *m*; **hip/chest s.** tour *m* de hanches/de poitrine **2** *vt* **to s. up** *(person)* jauger; *(situation)* évaluer ▪ **sizeable** *adj* non négligeable

**sizzle** ['sɪzəl] *vi* grésiller

**skate** [skeɪt] **1** *n (on foot)* patin *m* **2** *vi (on ice-skates)* faire du patin à glace; *(on roller-skates)* faire du roller ▪ **skateboard** *n* planche *f* à roulettes ▪ **skater** *n* patineur, -euse *mf* ▪ **skating** *n* patinage *m*; **to go s.** faire du patinage

**skeleton** ['skelɪtən] *n* squelette *m*; **s. staff** personnel *m* minimum

**skeptical** ['skeptɪkəl] *adj Am* sceptique

**sketch** [sketʃ] **1** *n (drawing)* croquis *m*; *(comic play)* sketch *m* **2** *vt* **to s. (out)** *(idea, view)* exposer brièvement **3** *vi* faire un/des croquis ▪ **sketchy** (**-ier, -iest**) *adj* vague

**skewer** ['skjuːə(r)] *n (for meat)* broche *f*; *(for kebab)* brochette *f*

**ski** [skiː] **1** (*pl* **skis**) *n* ski *m*; **s. boot** chaussure *f* de ski; **s. lift** remonte-pente *m*; **s. mask** cagoule *f*, passe-montagne *m*; **s. pants** fuseau *m*; **s. resort** station *f* de ski; **s. run** *or* **slope** piste *f* de ski

**2** (*pt* **skied** [skiːd], *pres p* **skiing**) *vi* skier, faire du ski ▪ **skier** *n* skieur, -euse *mf* ▪ **skiing 1** *n (sport)* ski *m* **2** *adj (clothes)* de ski

**skid** [skɪd] **1** *n* dérapage *m* **2** (*pt & pp* **-dd-**) *vi* déraper; **to s. into sth** déraper et heurter qch

**skill** [skɪl] *n (ability)* qualités *fpl*; *(technique)* compétence *f* ▪ **skilful** (*Am* **skillful**) *adj* habile (**at doing** à faire; **at sth** en qch) ▪ **skilled** *adj* habile (**at doing** à faire; **at sth** en qch); *(worker)* qualifié; *(work)* de spécialiste

**skim** [skɪm] (*pt & pp* **-mm-**) **1** *vt (milk)* écrémer; *(soup)* écumer; **to s. (over) sth** *(surface)* effleurer qch; **skimmed**

**milk** lait *m* écrémé **2** *vt insep* **to s. through** *(book)* parcourir

**skimp** [skɪmp] *vi (on food, fabric)* lésiner (**on** sur) ▪ **skimpy** (**-ier, -iest**) *adj (clothes)* étriqué; *(meal)* maigre

**skin** [skɪn] **1** *n* peau *f*; **s. diving** plongée *f* sous-marine **2** (*pt & pp* **-nn-**) *vt (fruit)* peler; *(animal)* écorcher ▪ **skin-tight** *adj* moulant

**skinflint** ['skɪnflɪnt] *n* avare *mf*

**skinhead** ['skɪnhed] *n Br* skinhead *mf*

**skinny** ['skɪnɪ] (**-ier, -iest**) *adj* maigre

**skint** [skɪnt] *adj Br Fam (penniless)* fauché

**skip¹** [skɪp] **1** (*pt & pp* **-pp-**) *vt (miss, omit)* sauter; **to s. classes** sécher les cours **2** *vi (hop about)* sautiller; *Br (with rope)* sauter à la corde; *Br* **skipping rope** corde *f* à sauter

**skip²** [skɪp] *n Br (for rubbish)* benne *f*

**skipper** ['skɪpə(r)] *n (of ship, team)* capitaine *m*

**skirt** [skɜːt] *n* jupe *f*

**skittle** ['skɪtəl] *n Br* quille *f*; **to play skittles** jouer aux quilles

**skulk** [skʌlk] *vi* rôder

**skull** [skʌl] *n* crâne *m*

**skunk** [skʌŋk] *n (animal)* moufette *f*

**sky** [skaɪ] *n* ciel *m* ▪ **skydiving** *n* parachutisme *m* en chute libre ▪ **skylight** *n* lucarne *f* ▪ **skyline** *n (horizon)* horizon *m* ▪ **skyscraper** *n* gratte-ciel *m inv*

**slack** [slæk] **1** (**-er, -est**) *adj (not tight)* mou (*f* molle); *(careless)* négligent; **to be s.** *(of rope)* avoir du mou; **business is s.** les affaires vont mal **2** *vi* **to s. off** *(in effort)* se relâcher

**slacken** ['slækən] **1** *vt* **to s. (off)** *(rope)* relâcher; *(pace, effort)* ralentir **2** *vi* **to s. (off)** *(in effort)* se relâcher; *(of production, demand, speed, enthusiasm)* diminuer

**slam** [slæm] **1** (*pt & pp* **-mm-**) *vt (door, lid)* claquer; *(hit)* frapper violemment; **to s. sth (down)** *(put down)* poser qch violemment; **to s. on the brakes** écraser la pédale de frein **2** *vi (of door)* claquer

**slander** ['slɑːndə(r)] **1** *n* calomnie *f* **2** *vt* calomnier

**slang** [slæŋ] **1** *n* argot *m* **2** *adj (word)* d'argot, argotique

**slant** [slɑːnt] **1** *n* pente *f*; *Fig (point of view)* perspective *f*; *Fig (bias)* parti *m* pris **2** *vi (of roof, handwriting)* être incliné ▪ **slanted, slanting** *adj* penché; *(roof)* en pente

**slap** [slæp] **1** *n (with hand)* claque *f*; **a s. in the face** une gifle **2** (*pt & pp* **-pp-**) *vt (person)* donner une claque à; **to s. sb's face** gifler qn; **to s. sb's bottom** donner une fessée à qn

**slapdash** ['slæpdæʃ] *adj (person)* négligent; *(work)* fait à la va-vite

**slapstick** ['slæpstɪk] *adj & n* **s. (comedy)** grosse farce *f*

**slash** [slæʃ] **1** *n* entaille *f* **2** *vt (cut)* taillader; *(reduce)* réduire considérablement

**slat** [slæt] *n* latte *f*

**slate** [sleɪt] *n* ardoise *f*

**slaughter** ['slɔːtə(r)] **1** *n (of people)* massacre *m*; *(of animal)* abattage *m* **2** *vt (people)* massacrer; *(animal)* abattre; *Fam (defeat)* massacrer

**slave** [sleɪv] **1** *n* esclave *mf* **2** *vi* **to s. (away)** trimer ▪ **slavery** *n* esclavage *m*

**sleazy** ['sliːzɪ] (**-ier, -iest**) *adj Fam* sordide

**sledge** [sledʒ] (*Am* **sled** [sled]) *n Br* luge *f*

**sledgehammer** ['sledʒhæmə(r)] *n* masse *f*

**sleek** [sliːk] (**-er, -est**) *adj (smooth)* lisse et brillant; *Pej (manner)* mielleux, -euse

**sleep** [sliːp] **1** *n* sommeil *m*; **to have a s., to get some s.** dormir; **to go to s.** *(of person)* s'endormir; **to put an animal to s.** *(kill)* faire piquer un animal

**2** (*pt & pp* **slept**) *vi* dormir; *Euph* **to s. with sb** coucher avec qn

**3** *vt* **this flat sleeps six** on peut dormir à six dans cet appartement ▪ **sleeping** *adj (asleep)* endormi; **s. bag** sac *m* de couchage; **s. car**

wagon-lit *m*; **s. pill** somnifère *m*

**sleeper** ['sli:pə(r)] *n* (**a**) **to be a light/sound s.** avoir le sommeil léger/lourd (**b**) *Br Rail (on track)* traverse *f*; *(bed in train)* couchette *f*; *(train)* train-couchettes *m* ■ **sleepless** *adj (night)* d'insomnie

**sleepy** ['sli:pɪ] (**-ier, -iest**) *adj (town, voice)* endormi; **to be s.** *(of person)* avoir sommeil

**sleet** [sli:t] **1** *n* neige *f* fondue **2** *vi* **it's sleeting** il tombe de la neige fondue

**sleeve** [sli:v] *n (of shirt, jacket)* manche *f*; *(of record)* pochette *f*; **long-/short-sleeved** à manches longues/courtes

**sleigh** [sleɪ] *n* traîneau *m*

**slender** ['slendə(r)] *adj (person)* svelte; *(neck, hand, waist)* fin; *Fig (small, feeble)* faible

**slept** [slept] *pt & pp of* **sleep**

**slice** [slaɪs] **1** *n* tranche *f*; *Fig (portion)* part *f* **2** *vt* **to s. sth (up)** couper qch en tranches; **to s. sth off** couper qch

**slick** [slɪk] **1** (**-er, -est**) *adj (campaign)* bien mené; *(reply, person)* habile **2** *n (on beach)* marée *f* noire

**slide** [slaɪd] **1** *n (in playground)* toboggan *m*; *(for hair)* barrette *f*; *Phot* diapositive *f*; *(in prices, popularity)* baisse *f* **2** (*pt & pp* **slid** [slɪd]) *vt* glisser (**into** dans); *(table, chair)* faire glisser **3** *vi* glisser ■ **sliding** *adj (door, panel)* coulissant

**slight** [slaɪt] **1** (**-er, -est**) *adj (small, unimportant)* léger, -ère; *(chance)* faible; **the slightest thing** la moindre chose; **not in the slightest** pas le moins du monde **2** *n* affront *m* (**on** à) **3** *vt (offend)* offenser; *(ignore)* bouder

**slightly** ['slaɪtlɪ] *adv* légèrement

**slim** [slɪm] **1** (**slimmer, slimmest**) *adj* mince **2** (*pt & pp* **-mm-**) *vi Br* suivre un régime

**slime** [slaɪm] *n* vase *f*; *(of snail)* bave *f* ■ **slimy** (**-ier, -iest**) *adj (muddy)* boueux (*f* boueuse); *Fig (sticky, smarmy)* visqueux, -euse

**sling** [slɪŋ] **1** *n (weapon)* fronde *f*; *(for injured arm)* écharpe *f*; **in a s.** en écharpe **2** (*pt & pp* **slung**) *vt (throw)* lancer

**slip** [slɪp] **1** *n (mistake)* erreur *f*; *(garment)* combinaison *f*; *(fall)* chute *f*; **a s. of paper** un bout de papier; *(printed)* un bordereau; **a s. of the tongue** un lapsus; *Br* **s. road** bretelle *f* **2** (*pt & pp* **-pp-**) *vt (slide)* glisser (**to** à; **into** dans); **it slipped my mind** ça m'est sorti de l'esprit **3** *vi* glisser; *Fam (of popularity, ratings)* baisser; **to let sth s.** *(chance, secret)* laisser échapper qch

▸ **slip away** *vi (escape)* s'éclipser

▸ **slip into** *vt insep (room)* se glisser dans; *(bathrobe)* passer

▸ **slip off** *vt sep (coat)* enlever

▸ **slip on** *vt sep (coat)* mettre

▸ **slip out** *vi (leave)* sortir furtivement; *(for a moment)* sortir (un instant); *(of secret)* s'éventer

▸ **slip up** *vi Fam* se planter

**slipper** ['slɪpə(r)] *n* pantoufle *f*

**slippery** ['slɪpərɪ] *adj* glissant

**slit** [slɪt] **1** *n* fente *f* **2** (*pt & pp* **slit,** *pres p* **slitting**) *vt (cut)* couper; **to s. open** *(sack)* éventrer

**slither** ['slɪðə(r)] *vi* glisser; *(of snake)* se couler

**slob** [slɒb] *n Fam (lazy person)* gros fainéant *m*; *(dirty person)* porc *m*

**slobber** ['slɒbə(r)] *vi (of dog, baby)* baver

**slog** [slɒg] *Br Fam* **1** *n* **a (hard) s.** *(effort)* un gros effort **2** (*pt & pp* **-gg-**) *vi* **to s. (away)** trimer

**slogan** ['sləʊgən] *n* slogan *m*

**slop** [slɒp] **1** (*pt & pp* **-pp-**) *vt* renverser **2** *vi* **to s. (over)** se renverser

**slope** [sləʊp] **1** *n* pente *f*; *(of mountain)* versant *m*; *(for skiing)* piste *f* **2** *vi (of ground, roof)* être en pente ■ **sloping** *adj (roof)* en pente

**sloppy** ['slɒpɪ] (**-ier, -iest**) *adj (work, appearance)* négligé; *(person)* négligent; *(sentimental)* sentimental

**slot** [slɒt] **1** *n (slit)* fente *f*; *(in schedule,*

*list)* créneau *m*; **s. machine** *(for vending)* distributeur *m* automatique; *(for gambling)* machine *f* à sous **2** (*pt & pp* **-tt-**) *vt (insert)* insérer (**into** dans) **3** *vi* s'insérer (**into** dans)

**slouch** [slaʊtʃ] *vi* ne pas se tenir droit; *(in chair)* être avachi

**slovenly** ['slʌvənlɪ] *adj* négligé

**slow** [sləʊ] **1** (**-er, -est**) *adj* lent; **in s. motion** au ralenti; **to be s.** *(of clock, watch)* retarder; **business is s.** les affaires tournent au ralenti **2** *adv* lentement **3** *vt* **to s. sth down** *or* **up** ralentir qch; *(delay)* retarder qch **4** *vi* **to s. down** *or* **up** ralentir ▪ **slowcoach** *n Br Fam* lambin, -e *mf* ▪ **slowly** *adv* lentement; *(bit by bit)* peu à peu

**sludge** [slʌdʒ] *n* gadoue *f*

**slug** [slʌg] **1** *n* (**a**) *(mollusc)* limace *f* (**b**) *Am Fam (bullet)* pruneau *m* **2** (*pt & pp* **-gg-**) *vt Am Fam (hit)* frapper

**sluggish** ['slʌgɪʃ] *adj (person)* amorphe; **business is s.** les affaires ne marchent pas très bien

**slum** [slʌm] *n (house)* taudis *m*; **the slums** les quartiers *mpl* délabrés

**slump** [slʌmp] **1** *n* baisse *f* soudaine (**in** de); *(in prices)* effondrement *m*; *(economic depression)* crise *f* **2** *vi (of person, prices)* s'effondrer

**slung** [slʌŋ] *pt & pp of* **sling**

**slur** [slɜː(r)] **1** *n (insult)* insulte *f* **2** (*pt & pp* **-rr-**) *vt* mal articuler ▪ **slurred** *adj (speech)* indistinct

**slush** [slʌʃ] *n (snow)* neige *f* fondue

**slut** [slʌt] *n Pej (promiscuous woman)* salope *f*; *(untidy woman)* souillon *f*

**sly** [slaɪ] **1** (**-er, -est**) *adj (deceitful)* sournois; *(cunning, crafty)* rusé **2** *n* **on the s.** en douce

**smack** [smæk] **1** *n (blow)* claque *f*; *(on bottom)* fessée *f* **2** *vt (person)* donner une claque à; **to s. sb's face** gifler qn; **to s. sb('s bottom)** donner une fessée à qn **3** *vi* **to s. of** *(be suggestive of)* avoir des relents de

**small** [smɔːl] **1** (**-er, -est**) *adj* petit; **s. change** petite monnaie *f*; **s. talk** banalités *fpl* **2** *adv (cut, chop)* menu; *(write)* petit **3** *n* **the s. of the back** la chute des reins ▪ **small-minded** *adj* à l'esprit étroit ▪ **small-scale** *adj (model)* réduit; *(research)* à petite échelle

**smallpox** ['smɔːlpɒks] *n* variole *f*

**smarmy** ['smɑːmɪ] (**-ier, -iest**) *adj Fam Pej* obséquieux, -euse

**smart**[1] [smɑːt] (**-er, -est**) *adj (in appearance)* élégant; *(clever)* intelligent; *(astute)* astucieux, -euse; *(quick)* rapide; **s. card** carte *f* à puce

**smart**[2] [smɑːt] *vi (sting)* brûler

**smarten** ['smɑːtən] **1** *vt* **to s. sth up** égayer qch **2** *vti* **to s. (oneself) up** se faire beau (*f* belle)

**smartly** ['smɑːtlɪ] *adv (dressed)* avec élégance

**smash** [smæʃ] **1** *n (accident)* collision *f*; *(in tennis)* smash *m* **2** *vt (break)* briser; *(shatter)* fracasser; *(record)* pulvériser **3** *vi* **to s. into sth** *(of vehicle)* entrer dans qch; **to s. into pieces** éclater en mille morceaux ▪ **smash-up** *n* collision *f*

▸**smash down, smash in** *vt sep (door)* enfoncer

▸**smash up** *vt sep (vehicle)* esquinter

**smashing** ['smæʃɪŋ] *adj Br Fam (wonderful)* génial

**smattering** ['smætərɪŋ] *n* **a s. of French** quelques notions *fpl* de français

**smear** [smɪə(r)] **1** *n (mark)* trace *f* **2** *vt (coat)* enduire (**with** de); *(stain)* tacher (**with** de); *(smudge)* faire une trace sur; **to s. sb** calomnier qn

**smell** [smel] **1** *n* odeur *f*; **(sense of) s.** odorat *m* **2** (*pt & pp* **smelled** *or* **smelt**) *vt* sentir; *(of animal)* flairer **3** *vi (stink)* sentir mauvais; *(have a smell)* sentir; **to s. of smoke** sentir la fumée ▪ **smelly** (**-ier, -iest**) *adj* **to be s.** sentir mauvais

**smelt** [smelt] *pt & pp of* **smell**

**smile** [smaɪl] **1** *n* sourire *m* **2** *vi* sourire (**at sb** à qn; **at sth** de qch)

**smirk** [smɜːk] *n (smug)* sourire *m* suffisant; *(scornful)* sourire *m* goguenard

**smog** [smɒg] *n* smog *m*

**smoke** [sməʊk] **1** *n* fumée *f*; **to have a s.** fumer; **s. detector** *or* **alarm** détecteur *m* de fumée **2** *vt (cigarette)* fumer; **smoked salmon** saumon *m* fumé **3** *vi* fumer; **'no smoking'** 'défense de fumer'; **smoking compartment** *(on train)* compartiment *m* fumeurs ▪ **smoker** *n* fumeur, -euse *mf* ▪ **smoky** (**-ier, -iest**) *adj (room, air)* enfumé

**smooth** [smu:ð] **1** (**-er, -est**) *adj (surface, skin)* lisse; *(cream, sauce)* onctueux, -euse; *(sea, flight)* calme; *Pej (person, manners)* doucereux, -euse; **the s. running of** *(machine, service, business)* la bonne marche de **2** *vt* **to s. sth down** *(hair, sheet, paper)* lisser qch; **to s. sth out** *(paper, sheet, dress)* lisser qch; *(crease)* faire disparaître qch ▪ **smoothly** *adv (without problems)* sans problèmes

**smother** ['smʌðə(r)] *vt (stifle)* étouffer; **to s. sth in sth** recouvrir qch de qch

**smoulder** ['sməʊldə(r)] (*Am* **smolder**) *vi (of fire, passion)* couver

**smudge** [smʌdʒ] **1** *n* tache *f* **2** *vt (paper)* faire des taches sur; *(ink)* étaler

**smug** [smʌg] (**smugger, smuggest**) *adj (person)* content de soi

**smuggle** ['smʌgəl] *vt* passer en fraude; **smuggled goods** contrebande *f* ▪ **smuggler** *n* contrebandier, -ère *mf*; *(of drugs)* trafiquant, -e *mf* ▪ **smuggling** *n* contrebande *f*

**smut** [smʌt] *n inv (obscenity)* cochonneries *fpl* ▪ **smutty** (**-ier, -iest**) *adj (joke)* cochon, -onne

**snack** [snæk] *n (meal)* casse-croûte *m inv*; **s. bar** snack-bar *m*

**snag** [snæg] *n (hitch)* problème *m*

**snail** [sneɪl] *n* escargot *m*

**snake** [sneɪk] *n* serpent *m*

**snap** [snæp] **1** *n Fam (photo)* photo *f*; **s. fastener** pression *f*; **cold s.** coup *m* de froid **2** *adj (judgement, decision)* hâtif, -ive **3** (*pt & pp* **-pp-**) *vt (break)* casser net; *(fingers)* faire claquer; **to s. up a bargain** sauter sur une occasion **4** *vi* se casser net; *Fig (of person)* parler sèchement (**at** à); **to s. off** se casser net; *Fam* **s. out of it!** secoue-toi!

**snare** [sneə(r)] *n* piège *m*

**snarl** [snɑ:l] *vi* grogner (en montrant les dents)

**snatch** [snætʃ] *vt (grab)* saisir; *(steal)* arracher; **to s. sth from sb** arracher qch à qn

**sneak** [sni:k] **1** *n Br Fam (telltale)* mouchard, -e *mf* **2** (*pt & pp* **sneaked** *or Am* **snuck**) *vi Br Fam (tell tales)* rapporter; **to s. in/out** entrer/sortir furtivement; **to s. off** s'esquiver

**sneaker** ['sni:kə(r)] *n Am (shoe)* chaussure *f* de sport

**sneer** [snɪə(r)] *vi* ricaner; **to s. at sb/sth** se moquer de qn/qch

**sneeze** [sni:z] *vi* éternuer

**snicker** ['snɪkə(r)] *vi Am* = **snigger**

**snide** [snaɪd] *adj* méprisant

**sniff** [snɪf] **1** *vt* renifler; **to s. glue** sniffer de la colle **2** *vi* renifler

**sniffle** ['snɪfəl] **1** *n Fam* **to have the sniffles** avoir un petit rhume **2** *vi* renifler

**snigger** ['snɪgə(r)] *vi* ricaner

**snip** [snɪp] **1** *n (cut)* petite entaille *f*; *Br Fam (bargain)* bonne affaire *f* **2** (*pt & pp* **-pp-**) *vt* **to s. sth (off)** couper qch

**snivel** ['snɪvəl] (*Br* **-ll-**, *Am* **-l-**) *vi* pleurnicher

**snob** [snɒb] *n* snob *mf* ▪ **snobbish** *adj* snob *inv*

**snooker** ['snu:kə(r)] *n (game)* = billard qui se joue avec vingt-deux billes

**snoop** [snu:p] *vi* fouiner; **to s. on sb** espionner qn

**snooze** [snu:z] **1** *n* petit somme *m*; **to have a s.** faire un petit somme **2** *vi* faire un petit somme

**snore** [snɔ:(r)] *vi* ronfler ▪ **snoring** *n* ronflements *mpl*

**snorkel** ['snɔ:kəl] **1** *n* tuba *m* **2** (*Br* **-ll-**, *Am* **-l-**) *vi* nager sous l'eau avec un tuba

**snort** [snɔ:t] *vi (of person)* grogner; *(of horse)* s'ébrouer

**snot** [snɒt] *n Fam* morve *f*

**snout** [snaʊt] *n* museau *m*

**snow** [snəʊ] **1** *n* neige *f* **2** *vi* **it's snowing** il neige **3** *vt* **to be snowed in** être bloqué par la neige; *Fig* **to be snowed under with work** être submergé de travail ▪ **snowball 1** *n* boule *f* de neige **2** *vi (increase)* faire boule de neige ▪ **snowdrop** *n (flower)* perce-neige *m ou f inv* ▪ **snowflake** *n* flocon *m* de neige ▪ **snowman** (*pl* **-men**) *n* bonhomme *m* de neige ▪ **snowplough** (*Am* **snowplow**) *n* chasse-neige *m inv* ▪ **snowshoe** *n* raquette *f* ▪ **snowstorm** *n* tempête *f* de neige

**snub** [snʌb] **1** *n* rebuffade *f* **2** (*pt & pp* **-bb-**) *vt (offer)* rejeter; **to s. sb** snober qn **3** *adj* **s. nose** nez *m* retroussé

**snuck** [snʌk] *Am pt & pp of* **sneak**

**snuff** [snʌf] **1** *n* tabac *m* à priser **2** *vt* **to s. (out)** *(candle)* moucher

**snug** [snʌg] (**snugger, snuggest**) *adj (house)* douillet, -ette; *(garment)* bien ajusté

**snuggle** ['snʌgəl] *vi* **to s. up to sb** se blottir contre qn

**so** [səʊ] **1** *adv (to such a degree)* si, tellement (**that** que); *(thus)* ainsi, comme ça; **to work/drink so much that...** travailler/boire tellement que...; **so much courage** tellement de courage (**that** que); **so many books** tant de livres (**that** que); **and so on** et ainsi de suite; **I think so** je crois que oui; **is that so?** c'est vrai?; **so am I** moi aussi; **I told you so** je vous l'avais bien dit; *Fam* **so long!** au revoir!

**2** *conj (therefore)* donc; *(in that case)* alors; **so what?** et alors?; **so that...** pour que... *(+ subjunctive)*; **so as to do sth** pour faire qch ▪ **So-and-so** *n* **Mr S.** Monsieur Untel ▪ **so-called** *adj* soi-disant *inv* ▪ **so-so** *adj & adv Fam* comme ci comme ça

**soak** [səʊk] **1** *vt (drench)* tremper; *(washing, food)* faire tremper; **to be soaked (through** *or* **to the skin)** être trempé (jusqu'aux os); **to s. sth up** absorber qch **2** *vi (of washing)* tremper ▪ **soaking** *adj & adv* **s. (wet)** trempé

**soap** [səʊp] *n* savon *m*; **s. opera** feuilleton *m* populaire; **s. powder** lessive *f* ▪ **soapsuds** *npl* mousse *f* de savon

**soar** [sɔː(r)] *vi (of bird)* s'élever; *(of price)* monter en flèche

**sob** [sɒb] **1** *n* sanglot *m* **2** (*pt & pp* **-bb-**) *vi* sangloter

**sober** ['səʊbə(r)] **1** *adj (sensible)* sobre; **he's s.** *(not drunk)* il n'est pas ivre **2** *vti* **to s. up** dessoûler

**soccer** ['sɒkə(r)] *n* football *m*

**sociable** ['səʊʃəbəl] *adj (person)* sociable; *(evening)* amical

**social** ['səʊʃəl] *adj* social; **to have a good s. life** sortir beaucoup; **S. Security** ≃ la Sécurité sociale; **s. security** *(aid)* aide *f* sociale; *Am (retirement pension)* pension *f* de retraite; **the s. services** les services *mpl* sociaux; **s. worker** assistant, -e *mf* social(e)

**socialist** ['səʊʃəlɪst] *adj & n* socialiste *(mf)*

**socialize** ['səʊʃəlaɪz] *vi* fréquenter des gens; **to s. with sb** fréquenter qn

**socially** ['səʊʃəlɪ] *adv* socialement; *(meet)* en société

**society** [sə'saɪətɪ] (*pl* **-ies**) *n (community, club, companionship)* société *f*; *(school/university club)* club *m*; **(high) s.** haute société *f*

**sociology** [səʊsɪ'ɒlədʒɪ] *n* sociologie *f*

**sock** [sɒk] *n* chaussette *f*

**socket** ['sɒkɪt] *n Br (of electric plug)* prise *f* de courant; *Br (of lamp)* douille *f*

**soda** ['səʊdə] *n Am* **s. (pop)** boisson *f* gazeuse; **s. (water)** eau *f* de Seltz

**sofa** ['səʊfə] *n* canapé *m*; **s. bed** canapé-lit *m*

**soft** [sɒft] (**-er, -est**) *adj (gentle, not stiff)* doux (*f* douce); *(butter, ground, paste, snow)* mou (*f* molle); *(wood, heart, colour)* tendre; *(indulgent)* indulgent; **s. drink** boisson *f* non alcoolisée; **s. drugs** drogues *fpl* douces; **s. toy** peluche *f* ▪ **soft-boiled** *adj (egg)* à la coque

**soften** ['sɒfən] **1** *vt (object)* ramollir;

*(colour, light, voice, skin)* adoucir **2** *vi* ramollir ▪ **softener** *n* adoucissant *m*
**softly** ['sɒftlɪ] *adv* doucement
**software** ['sɒftweə(r)] *n inv Comptr* logiciel *m*; **s. package** progiciel *m*
**soggy** ['sɒgɪ] (**-ier, -iest**) *adj* trempé
**soil** [sɔɪl] **1** *n (earth)* terre *f* **2** *vt (dirty)* salir
**solar** ['səʊlə(r)] *adj* solaire
**sold** [səʊld] *pt & pp of* **sell**
**soldier** ['səʊldʒə(r)] *n* soldat *m*
**sole[1]** [səʊl] **1** *n (of shoe)* semelle *f*; *(of foot)* plante *f* **2** *vt (shoe)* ressemeler
**sole[2]** [səʊl] *adj (only)* unique; *(rights, representative, responsibility)* exclusif, -ive ▪ **solely** *adv* uniquement
**solemn** ['sɒləm] *adj* solennel, -elle
**solicit** [sə'lɪsɪt] **1** *vt (seek)* solliciter **2** *vi (of prostitute)* racoler
**solicitor** [sə'lɪsɪtə(r)] *n Br (for wills)* notaire *m*
**solid** ['sɒlɪd] **1** *adj (not liquid)* solide; *(not hollow)* plein; *(gold, silver)* massif, -ive **2** *adv* **frozen s.** complètement gelé; **ten days s.** dix jours d'affilée **3** *n* solide *m*; **solids** *(food)* aliments *mpl* solides ▪ **solidly** *adv (built)* solidement; *(work)* sans interruption
**solidarity** [sɒlɪ'dærətɪ] *n* solidarité *f* (**with** avec)
**solitary** ['sɒlɪtərɪ] *adj (lonely, alone)* solitaire; *(only)* seul ▪ **solitude** *n* solitude *f*
**solo** ['səʊləʊ] **1** (*pl* **-os**) *n Mus* solo *m* **2** *adj (guitar, violin)* solo *inv* **3** *adv (play, sing)* en solo; *(fly)* en solitaire ▪ **soloist** *n Mus* soliste *mf*
**soluble** ['sɒljʊbəl] *adj (substance, problem)* soluble
**solution** [sə'lu:ʃən] *n* (**a**) *(to problem)* solution *f* (**to** de) (**b**) *(liquid)* solution *f*
**solve** [sɒlv] *vt (problem)* résoudre
**solvent** ['sɒlvənt] **1** *adj (financially)* solvable **2** *n Chem* solvant *m*
**sombre** ['sɒmbə(r)] (*Am* **somber**) *adj* sombre

**SOME** [sʌm] **1** *adj* (**a**) *(a quantity of)* du, de la, des; **s. wine** du vin; **s. water** de l'eau; **s. dogs** des chiens; **s. pretty flowers** de jolies fleurs
(**b**) *(unspecified)* un, une; **s. man (or other)** un homme (quelconque); **for s. reason or other** pour une raison ou pour une autre; **I have been waiting s. time** ça fait un moment que j'attends
(**c**) *(a few)* quelques; *(in contrast to others)* certains; **s. days ago** il y a quelques jours; **s. people think that...** certains pensent que...
**2** *pron* (**a**) *(a certain quantity)* en; **I want s.** j'en veux; **s. of my wine** un peu de mon vin; **s. of the time** une partie du temps
(**b**) *(as opposed to others)* certain(e)s; **some say...** certains disent...; **s. of the guests** certains invités
**3** *adv (about)* environ; **s. ten years** environ dix ans ▪ **somebody** *pron* quelqu'un; **s. small** quelqu'un de petit ▪ **someday** *adv* un jour ▪ **somehow** *adv (in some way)* d'une manière ou d'une autre; *(for some reason)* on ne sait pourquoi ▪ **someone** *pron* quelqu'un; **s. small** quelqu'un de petit ▪ **someplace** *adv Am* quelque part ▪ **something 1** *pron* quelque chose; **s. awful** quelque chose d'affreux **2** *adv* **she plays s. like...** elle joue un peu comme... ▪ **sometime** *adv* un jour; **s. in May** au mois de mai ▪ **sometimes** *adv* quelquefois, parfois ▪ **somewhat** *adv* quelque peu, assez ▪ **somewhere** *adv* quelque part; **s. about fifteen** *(approximately)* environ quinze

**somersault** ['sʌməsɔ:lt] *n (on ground)* roulade *f*; *(in air)* saut *m* périlleux
**son** [sʌn] *n* fils *m* ▪ **son-in-law** (*pl* **sons-in-law**) *n* gendre *m*
**sonata** [sə'nɑ:tə] *n* sonate *f*
**song** [sɒŋ] *n* chanson *f*; *(of bird)* chant *m*
**soon** [su:n] (**-er, -est**) *adv (in a short time)* bientôt; *(quickly)* vite; *(early)* tôt; **s. after** peu après; **as s. as...** aussitôt que...; **no sooner had he spoken than...** à peine avait-il parlé que...;

**I'd sooner leave** je préférerais partir; **sooner or later** tôt ou tard

**soot** [sʊt] *n* suie *f*

**soothe** [su:ð] *vt* calmer

**sophisticated** [sə'fɪstɪkeɪtɪd] *adj (person, taste)* raffiné; *(machine, method)* sophistiqué

**sophomore** ['sɒfəmɔ:(r)] *n Am* étudiant, -e *mf* de deuxième année

**sopping** ['sɒpɪŋ] *adj & adv* **s. (wet)** trempé

**soppy** ['sɒpɪ] (**-ier, -iest**) *adj Br Fam (sentimental)* sentimental

**soprano** [sə'prɑ:nəʊ] (*pl* **-os**) *n (singer)* soprano *mf*

**sordid** ['sɔ:dɪd] *adj* sordide

**sore** [sɔ:(r)] **1** (**-er, -est**) *adj (painful)* douloureux, -euse; *Am (angry)* fâché (**at** contre); **to have a s. throat** avoir mal à la gorge **2** *n (wound)* plaie *f*

**sorrow** ['sɒrəʊ] *n* chagrin *m*

**sorry** ['sɒrɪ] (**-ier, -iest**) *adj (sight, state)* triste; **to be s. (about sth)** *(regret)* être désolé (de qch); **to feel** *or* **be s. for sb** plaindre qn; **I'm s. she can't come** je regrette qu'elle ne puisse pas venir; **s.!** pardon!; **to say s.** demander pardon (**to** à)

**sort**[1] [sɔ:t] *n* sorte *f*; **a s. of** une sorte de; **all sorts of** toutes sortes de; **what s. of drink is it?** qu'est-ce que c'est comme boisson?; **s. of sad** *(somewhat)* plutôt triste

**sort**[2] [sɔ:t] **1** *vt (papers)* trier; **to s. out** *(classify, select)* trier; *(separate)* séparer (**from** de); *(organize)* ranger; *(problem)* régler **2** *vi* **to s. through letters/magazines** trier des lettres/magazines

**sought** [sɔ:t] *pt & pp of* **seek**

**soul** [səʊl] *n* âme *f*

**sound**[1] [saʊnd] **1** *n* son *m*; *(noise)* bruit *m*; **s. effects** bruitage *m* **2** *vt (bell, alarm)* sonner; *(bugle)* sonner de; **to s. one's horn** *(in vehicle)* klaxonner **3** *vi (seem)* sembler; **to s. like** sembler être; *(resemble)* ressembler à; **it sounds like** *or* **as if...** il semble que... *(+ subjunctive or indicative)*

**sound**[2] [saʊnd] **1** (**-er, -est**) *adj (healthy)* sain; *(in good condition)* en bon état; *(basis)* solide; *(argument)* valable; *(advice)* bon (*f* bonne); *(investment)* sûr

**2** *adv* **s. asleep** profondément endormi ▪ **soundly** *adv (asleep, sleep)* profondément

**sound**[3] [saʊnd] *vt (test, measure)* sonder; **to s. sb out** sonder qn (**about** sur)

**soundproof** ['saʊndpru:f] **1** *adj* insonorisé **2** *vt* insonoriser

**soundtrack** ['saʊndtræk] *n (of film)* bande *f* sonore

**soup** [su:p] *n* soupe *f*; **s. dish** *or* **plate** assiette *f* creuse

**sour** ['saʊə(r)] (**-er, -est**) *adj* aigre; *(milk)* tourné; **to turn s.** *(of milk)* tourner; *(of friendship)* se détériorer

**source** [sɔ:s] *n (origin)* source *f*

**south** [saʊθ] **1** *n* sud *m*; **(to the) s. of** au sud de

**2** *adj (coast)* sud *inv*; *(wind)* du sud; **S. America/Africa** l'Amérique *f*/l'Afrique *f* du Sud; **S. American** *adj* sud-américain; *n* Sud-Américain, -e *mf*; **S. African** *adj* sudafricain; *n* Sud-Africain, -e *mf*

**3** *adv* au sud; *(travel)* vers le sud ▪ **southbound** *adj (traffic)* en direction du sud; *Br (carriageway)* sud *inv* ▪ **south-east** *n & adj* sud-est *(m)* ▪ **southerly** *adj (direction)* du sud ▪ **southern** ['sʌðən] *adj (town)* du sud; *(coast)* sud *inv*; **S. Italy** le sud de l'Italie ▪ **southerner** ['sʌðənə(r)] *n* habitant, -e *mf* du sud ▪ **southward(s)** *adj & adv* vers le sud ▪ **south-west** *n & adj* sud-ouest *(m)*

**souvenir** [su:və'nɪə(r)] *n* souvenir *m*

**sovereign** ['sɒvrɪn] *n (monarch)* souverain, -e *mf* ▪ **sovereignty** [-rəntɪ] *n* souveraineté *f*

**sow**[1] [saʊ] *n (pig)* truie *f*

**sow**[2] [səʊ] (*pt* **sowed,** *pp* **sowed** *or* **sown** [səʊn]) *vt (seeds, doubt)* semer; *(land)* ensemencer (**with** de)

**soya** ['sɔɪə] *n Br* soja *m*; **s. bean** graine

*f* de soja ▪ **soybean** *n Am* graine *f* de soja

**spa** [spɑː] *n (town)* station *f* thermale

**space** [speɪs] **1** *n (gap, emptiness, atmosphere)* espace *m*; *(for parking)* place *f*; **to take up s.** prendre de la place; **blank s.** espace *m*, blanc *m*; **s. bar** *(on keyboard)* barre *f* d'espacement **2** *adj (voyage, capsule)* spatial **3** *vt* **to s. out** espacer ▪ **spaceship** *n* vaisseau *m* spatial ▪ **spacing** *n Typ* **in double/single s.** à double/simple interligne

**spacious** ['speɪʃəs] *adj* spacieux, -euse

**spade** [speɪd] *n* (**a**) *(for garden)* bêche *f* (**b**) *Cards* **spade(s)** pique *m*

**spaghetti** [spə'getɪ] *n* spaghettis *mpl*

**Spain** [speɪn] *n* l'Espagne *f*

**span** [spæn] *(pt & pp* **-nn-***) vt (of bridge)* enjamber; *Fig (in time)* couvrir

**Spaniard** ['spænjəd] *n* Espagnol, -e *mf* ▪ **Spanish 1** *adj* espagnol **2** *n (language)* espagnol *m*

**spank** [spæŋk] *vt* donner une tape sur les fesses à ▪ **spanking** *n* fessée *f*

**spanner** ['spænə(r)] *n Br (tool)* clef *f*

**spare** [speə(r)] **1** *adj (extra, surplus)* de ou en trop; *(reserve)* de rechange; *(wheel)* de secours; *(available)* disponible; **s. room** chambre *f* d'ami; **s. time** loisirs *mpl*

**2** *n* **s. (part)** *(for vehicle, machine)* pièce *f* détachée

**3** *vt (do without)* se passer de; *(efforts, sb's feelings)* ménager; **to s. sb sth** *(grief, details)* épargner qch à qn; **I can't s. the time** je n'ai pas le temps; **with five minutes to s.** avec cinq minutes d'avance

**sparingly** ['speərɪŋlɪ] *adv* en petite quantité

**spark** [spɑːk] **1** *n* étincelle *f*; *Aut* **s. plug** bougie *f* **2** *vt* **to s. off** *(cause)* provoquer

**sparkle** ['spɑːkəl] *vi* briller; *(of diamond, star)* scintiller ▪ **sparkling** *adj (wine, water)* pétillant

**sparrow** ['spærəʊ] *n* moineau *m*

**sparse** [spɑːs] *adj* clairsemé ▪ **sparsely** *adv (populated)* peu; **s. furnished** à peine meublé

**spasm** ['spæzəm] *n (of muscle)* spasme *m*

**spat** [spæt] *pt & pp of* **spit**

**spate** [speɪt] *n* **a s. of sth** *(of letters, calls)* une avalanche de qch; *(of crimes)* une vague de qch

**spatter** ['spætə(r)] *vt (clothes, person)* éclabousser (**with** de)

**speak** [spiːk] **1** *(pt* **spoke**, *pp* **spoken***) vt (language)* parler; *(say)* dire; **to s.one's mind** dire ce que l'on pense

**2** *vi* parler (**about** *or* **of** de); *(formally, in assembly)* prendre la parole; **so to s.** pour ainsi dire; **that speaks for itself** c'est évident; **Jayne speaking!** *(on the telephone)* Jayne à l'appareil!; **to s. out** *or* **up** *(boldly)* parler (franchement); **to s. up** *(more loudly)* parler plus fort

**speaker** ['spiːkə(r)] *n (at meeting)* intervenant, -e *mf*; *(at conference)* conférencier, -ère *mf*; *(loudspeaker)* enceinte *f*; **to be a Spanish s.** parler espagnol

**spear** [spɪə(r)] *n* lance *f*

**spearmint** ['spɪəmɪnt] *adj (sweet)* à la menthe; *(chewing gum)* mentholé

**spec** [spek] *n Br Fam* **on s.** à tout hasard

**special** ['speʃəl] **1** *adj* spécial; *(care, attention)* particulier, -ère; *Br* **by s. delivery** en exprès; **s. effects** effets *mpl* spéciaux **2** *n* **today's s.** *(in restaurant)* le plat du jour

**specialist** ['speʃəlɪst] **1** *n* spécialiste *mf* (**in** de) **2** *adj (dictionary, knowledge)* spécialisé; *(equipment)* de spécialiste ▪ **speciality** [-ʃɪ'ælɪtɪ] *(pl* **-ies***) n Br* spécialité *f*

**specialize** ['speʃəlaɪz] *vi* se spécialiser (**in** dans)

**specially** ['speʃəlɪ] *adv (specifically)* spécialement; *(particularly)* particulièrement

**specialty** ['speʃəltɪ] *(pl* **-ies***) n Am* spécialité *f*

**species** ['spiːʃiːz] *n inv* espèce *f*

**specific** [spəˈsɪfɪk] *adj* précis ▪ **specifically** *adv (explicitly)* expressément; *(exactly)* précisément; *(specially)* spécialement

**specify** [ˈspesɪfaɪ] (*pt & pp* **-ied**) *vt (state exactly)* préciser; *(stipulate)* stipuler ▪ **specification** [-fɪˈkeɪʃən] *n* spécification *f*

**specimen** [ˈspesɪmɪn] *n (individual example)* spécimen *m*; *(of urine, blood)* échantillon *m*

**speck** [spek] *n (stain)* petite tache *f*; *(of dust)* grain *m*; *(dot)* point *m*

**speckled** [ˈspekəld] *adj* tacheté

**specs** [speks] *npl Fam* lunettes *fpl*

**spectacle** [ˈspektəkəl] *n (sight)* spectacle *m* ▪ **spectacles** *npl (glasses)* lunettes *fpl*

**spectacular** [spekˈtækjʊlə(r)] *adj* spectaculaire

**spectator** [spekˈteɪtə(r)] *n* spectateur, -trice *mf*

**spectre** [ˈspektə(r)] *n* spectre *m* (**of** de)

**spectrum** [ˈspektrəm] (*pl* **-tra** [-trə]) *n* spectre *m*; *Fig (range)* gamme *f*

**speculate** [ˈspekjʊleɪt] **1** *vt* **to s. that...** *(guess)* conjecturer que... **2** *vi Fin* spéculer; **to s. about** *(make guesses)* faire des suppositions sur ▪ **speculation** *n* suppositions *fpl*; *Fin* spéculation *f*

**sped** [sped] *pt & pp of* **speed**

**speech** [spiːtʃ] *n (talk, lecture)* discours *m* (**on** *or* **about** sur); *(faculty)* parole *f*; *(diction)* élocution *f*; **to make a s.** faire un discours ▪ **speechless** *adj* muet (*f* muette) (**with** de)

**speed** [spiːd] **1** *n (rapidity, gear)* vitesse *f*; **at top** *or* **full s.** à toute vitesse; **s. limit** *(on road)* limitation *f* de vitesse

**2** (*pt & pp* **sped**) *vt* **to s. sth up** accélérer qch

**3** *vi* (**a**) **to s. up** *(of person)* aller plus vite; **to s. past sth** passer à toute vitesse devant qch

(**b**) (*pt & pp* **speeded**) *(exceed speed limit)* faire un excès de vitesse ▪ **speedboat** *n* vedette *f* ▪ **speeding** *n (in vehicle)* excès *m* de vitesse ▪ **speedometer** *n Br (in vehicle)* compteur *m* de vitesse

**speedy** [ˈspiːdɪ] (**-ier, -iest**) *adj* rapide

**spell¹** [spel] *n (magic words)* formule *f* magique; **to cast a s. on sb** jeter un sort à qn ▪ **spellbound** *adj* fasciné

**spell²** [spel] *n (period)* période *f*; **cold s.** vague *f* de froid

**spell³** [spel] (*pt & pp* **spelled** *or* **spelt** [spelt]) *vt (write)* écrire; *(say aloud)* épeler; *(of letters)* former; *Fig (mean)* signifier; **how do you s. it?** comment ça s'écrit?; **to s. sth out** *(word)* épeler qch; *Fig (explain)* expliquer clairement qch ▪ **spell-checker** *n Comptr* correcteur *m* d'orthographe ▪ **spelling** *n* orthographe *f*; **s. mistake** faute *f* d'orthographe

**spend** [spend] (*pt & pp* **spent**) *vt (money)* dépenser (**on** pour/en); *(time)* passer (**on sth** sur qch; **doing** à faire); *(energy)* consacrer (**on sth** à qch; **doing** à faire) ▪ **spending** *n* dépenses *fpl*; **s. money** argent *m* de poche ▪ **spendthrift** *n* **to be a s.** être dépensier, -ère

**spent** [spent] *pt & pp of* **spend**

**sperm** [spɜːm] *n* sperme *m*

**spew** [spjuː] *vt* vomir

**sphere** [sfɪə(r)] *n (of influence, action), Math & Pol* sphère *f* ▪ **spherical** [ˈsferɪkəl] *adj* sphérique

**spice** [spaɪs] **1** *n* épice *f*; *Fig (interest)* piquant *m* **2** *vt (food)* épicer; **to s. sth (up)** *(add interest to)* ajouter du piquant à qch ▪ **spicy** (**-ier, -iest**) *adj* épicé

**spider** [ˈspaɪdə(r)] *n* araignée *f*

**spike** [spaɪk] *n (of metal)* pointe *f* ▪ **spiky** (**-ier, -iest**) *adj (hair)* tout hérissé

**spill** [spɪl] (*pt & pp* **spilled** *or* **spilt** [spɪlt]) **1** *vt (liquid)* renverser **2** *vi* se répandre

▸ **spill out** *vt sep (empty)* vider

▸ **spill over** *vi (of liquid)* déborder

**spin** [spɪn] **1** *n (motion)* tournoiement *m*; *(on ball)* effet *m*; *Fam* **to go for a s.** *(in car)* aller faire un tour

2 (*pt & pp* **spun,** *pres p* **spinning**) *vt (wool, cotton)* filer; *(wheel, top)* faire tourner; *(spin-dry)* essorer; **to s. sth out** *(speech)* faire durer qch
3 *vi* tourner; **to s. round** *(of dancer, wheel, top, planet)* tourner; **my head's spinning** j'ai la tête qui tourne
**spinach** ['spɪnɪdʒ] *n* épinards *mpl*
**spin-dry** ['spɪndraɪ] *vt* essorer ▪ **spin-dryer** *n* essoreuse *f*
**spine** [spaɪn] *n (backbone)* colonne *f* vertébrale; *(of book)* dos *m*
**spinster** ['spɪnstə(r)] *n* vieille fille *f*
**spiral** ['spaɪərəl] **1** *n* spirale *f* **2** *adj* en spirale; *(staircase)* en colimaçon **3** (*Br* **-ll-,** *Am* **-l-**) *vi (of prices)* s'envoler
**spire** ['spaɪə(r)] *n (of church)* flèche *f*
**spirit** ['spɪrɪt] **1** *n (soul, ghost, mood)* esprit *m*; *Fig (determination)* courage *m*; **spirits** *(drink)* spiritueux *mpl*; **in good spirits** de bonne humeur **2** *adj (lamp)* à alcool; **s. level** niveau *m* (à bulle) ▪ **spirited** *adj (campaign, attack)* vigoureux, -euse; *(person, remark)* énergique
**spiritual** ['spɪrɪtʃʊəl] *adj* spirituel, -elle
**spit¹** [spɪt] **1** *n (on ground)* crachat *m*; *(in mouth)* salive *f* **2** (*pt & pp* **spat** *or* **spit,** *pres p* **spitting**) *vt* cracher; **to s. sth out** cracher qch; **to be the spitting image of sb** être le portrait (tout craché) de qn **3** *vi* cracher
**spit²** [spɪt] *n (for meat)* broche *f*
**spite** [spaɪt] **1** *n (dislike)* dépit *m*; **in s. of sb/sth** malgré qn/qch; **in s. of the fact that…** bien que… *(+ subjunctive)* **2** *vt* vexer ▪ **spiteful** *adj* vexant
**splash** [splæʃ] **1** *n (of liquid)* éclaboussure *f*; *Fig (of colour)* tache *f* **2** *vt (spatter)* éclabousser (**with** de) **3** *vi (of mud)* faire des éclaboussures; *(of waves)* clapoter; **to s. (about)** *(in river, mud)* patauger; *(in bath)* barboter; *Fam* **to s. out** *(spend money)* claquer des ronds
**splendid** ['splendɪd] *adj* splendide ▪ **splendour** (*Am* **splendor**) *n* splendeur *f*
**splint** [splɪnt] *n* attelle *f*
**splinter** ['splɪntə(r)] *n (of wood, glass)* éclat *m*; *(in finger)* écharde *f*
**split** [splɪt] **1** *n* fente *f*; *(tear)* déchirure *f*; *(in political party)* scission *f* **2** *adj* **in a s. second** en une fraction de seconde **3** (*pt & pp* **split,** *pres p* **splitting**) *vt (break apart)* fendre; *(tear)* déchirer; **to s. (up)** *(group)* diviser; *(money, work)* partager (**between** entre) **4** *vi* se fendre; *(tear)* se déchirer; **to s. (up)** *(of group)* se diviser (**into** en); **to s. up** *(because of disagreement) (of couple, friends)* se séparer; *(of crowd)* se disperser; **to s. up with sb** rompre avec qn
**spoil** [spɔɪl] (*pt & pp* **spoilt** *or* **spoiled**) *vt (ruin)* gâcher; *(indulge)* gâter ▪ **spoilsport** *n* rabat-joie *mf inv*
**spoilt** [spɔɪlt] *pt & pp of* **spoil**
**spoke¹** [spəʊk] *n (of wheel)* rayon *m*
**spoke²** [spəʊk] *pt of* **speak** ▪ **spoken 1** *pp of* **speak 2** *adj (language)* parlé ▪ **spokesman** (*pl* **-men**), ▪ **spokesperson, spokeswoman** (*pl* **-women**) *n* porte-parole *mf inv* (**for** *or* **of** de)
**sponge** [spʌndʒ] **1** *n* éponge *f*; *Br* **s. bag** trousse *f* de toilette; **s. cake** génoise *f* **2** *vt* **to s. sth down/off** laver/enlever qch avec une éponge **3** *vi Fam* **to s. off** *or* **on sb** vivre aux crochets de qn ▪ **sponger** *n Fam* parasite *m*
**sponsor** ['spɒnsə(r)] **1** *n* sponsor *m* **2** *vt* sponsoriser ▪ **sponsorship** *n* sponsoring *m*
**spontaneous** [spɒn'teɪnɪəs] *adj* spontané
**spooky** ['spu:kɪ] (**-ier, -iest**) *adj Fam* qui donne le frisson
**spoon** [spu:n] *n* cuillère *f* ▪ **spoonful** *n* cuillerée *f*
**sporadic** [spə'rædɪk] *adj* sporadique
**sport¹** [spɔ:t] *n* sport *m*; **to play** *Br* **s.** *or Am* **sports** faire du sport; **sports club** club *m* de sport; **sports car/ground** voiture *f*/terrain *m* de sport ▪ **sporting** *adj (attitude, person)* sportif, -ive ▪ **sportsman** (*pl* **-men**) *n* sportif *m*

■ **sportswoman** (*pl* **-women**) *n* sportive *f* ■ **sporty** (**-ier, -iest**) *adj* sportif, -ive

**sport²** [spɔ:t] *vt (wear)* arborer

**spot¹** [spɒt] *n (stain, mark)* tache *f*; *(dot)* point *m*; *(polka dot)* pois *m*; *(drop)* goutte *f*; *(pimple)* bouton *m*; *(place)* endroit *m*; **on the s.** sur place; *(at once)* sur le coup; **to be in a tight s.** *(difficulty)* être dans le pétrin

**spot²** [spɒt] (*pt & pp* **-tt-**) *vt (notice)* apercevoir

**spotless** ['spɒtləs] *adj (clean)* impeccable

**spotlight** ['spɒtlaɪt] *n* projecteur *m*; *(for photography)* spot *m*

**spotty** ['spɒtɪ] (**-ier, -iest**) *adj (face, person)* boutonneux, -euse

**spouse** [spaʊs, spaʊz] *n* époux *m*, épouse *f*

**spout** [spaʊt] **1** *n (of teapot, jug)* bec *m* **2** *vt Pej (say)* débiter

**sprain** [spreɪn] **1** *n* entorse *f* **2** *vt* **to s. one's ankle/wrist** se fouler la cheville/le poignet

**sprang** [spræŋ] *pt of* **spring¹**

**spray** [spreɪ] **1** *n (can, device)* vaporisateur *m*; *(water drops)* gouttelettes *fpl*; *(from sea)* embruns *mpl* **2** *vt (liquid, surface)* vaporiser; *(plant, crops)* pulvériser; *(car)* peindre à la bombe

**spread** [spred] **1** *n (of idea, religion, language)* diffusion *f*; *(of disease)* propagation *f*; *Fam (meal)* festin *m*; **cheese s.** fromage *m* à tartiner

**2** (*pt & pp* **spread**) *vt (stretch, open out)* étendre; *(legs, fingers)* écarter; *(paint, payment, visits, cards)* étaler; *(sand, fear)* répandre; *(news, illness)* propager; **to s. out** *(map, payments, visits)* étaler; *(fingers)* écarter

**3** *vi (of fog)* s'étendre; *(of fire, epidemic)* se propager; *(of news, fear)* se répandre; **to s. out** *(of people)* se disperser ■ **spreadsheet** *n Comptr* tableur *m*

**spree** [spri:] *n* **to go on a spending s.** faire des folies dans les magasins

**sprightly** ['spraɪtlɪ] (**-ier, -iest**) *adj* alerte

**spring¹** [sprɪŋ] **1** *n (device)* ressort *m*; *(leap)* bond *m* **2** (*pt* **sprang**, *pp* **sprung**) *vt (surprise)* faire (**on** à) **3** *vi (leap)* bondir; **to s. to mind** venir à l'esprit; **to s. from** *(stem from)* provenir de; **to s. up** *(appear)* surgir ■ **springboard** *n* tremplin *m*

**spring²** [sprɪŋ] *n (season)* printemps *m*; **in (the) s.** au printemps; *Br* **s. onion** petit oignon *m* ■ **spring-cleaning** *n* nettoyage *m* de printemps ■ **springtime** *n* printemps *m*

**spring³** [sprɪŋ] *n (of water)* source *f*; **s. water** eau *f* de source

**sprinkle** ['sprɪŋkəl] *vt (sand)* répandre (**on** *or* **over** sur); **to s. sth with water, to s. water on sth** arroser qch; **to s. sth with sth** *(sugar, salt, flour)* saupoudrer qch de qch

**sprint** [sprɪnt] *vi (run)* sprinter

**sprout** [spraʊt] **1** *n* **(Brussels) s.** chou *m* de Bruxelles **2** *vt (leaves)* pousser **3** *vi (of seed, bulb)* pousser

**spruce** [spru:s] **1** (**-er, -est**) *adj (neat)* impeccable **2** *vt* **to s. oneself up** se faire beau (*f* belle)

**sprung** [sprʌŋ] *pp of* **spring¹**

**spud** [spʌd] *n Fam (potato)* patate *f*

**spun** [spʌn] *pt & pp of* **spin**

**spur** [spɜ:(r)] **1** *n (of horse rider)* éperon *m*; *Fig (stimulus)* aiguillon *m*; **to do sth on the s. of the moment** faire qch sur un coup de tête **2** (*pt & pp* **-rr-**) *vt* **to s. sb on** *(urge on)* aiguillonner qn

**spurn** [spɜ:n] *vt* rejeter

**spurt** [spɜ:t] **1** *n (of energy)* regain *m*; **to put on a s.** foncer **2** *vi* **to s. (out)** *(of liquid)* gicler

**spy** [spaɪ] **1** (*pl* **-ies**) *n* espion, -onne *mf* **2** *adj (story, film)* d'espionnage **3** (*pt & pp* **-ied**) *vt (notice)* repérer **4** *vi* espionner; **to s. on sb** espionner qn ■ **spying** *n* espionnage *m*

**squabble** ['skwɒbəl] **1** *n* querelle *f* **2** *vi* se quereller (**over** à propos de)

**squad** [skwɒd] *n (of workmen, footballers)* équipe *f*; *(of soldiers)* section *f*; *(of police)* brigade *f*

**squalid** ['skwɒlɪd] *adj* sordide

▪ **squalor** *n (poverty)* misère *f*

**squander** ['skwɒndə(r)] *vt (money, resources)* gaspiller; *(time)* perdre

**square** ['skweə(r)] **1** *n* carré *m*; *(on chessboard, map)* case *f*; *(in town)* place *f* **2** *adj* carré; *Math* **s. root** racine *f* carrée **3** *vt (settle)* régler; *Math (number)* élever au carré **4** *vi (tally)* cadrer (**with** avec)

**squash** [skwɒʃ] **1** *n (game)* squash *m*; *(vegetable)* courge *f*; *Br* **lemon/orange s.** ≃ sirop *m* de citron/d'orange **2** *vt* écraser

**squat** [skwɒt] **1** *adj (person, object, building)* trapu **2** *(pt & pp* **-tt-**) *vi* squatter; **to s. (down)** s'accroupir; **to be squatting (down)** être accroupi

**squawk** [skwɔ:k] *vi* pousser un cri rauque

**squeak** [skwi:k] *vi (of person)* pousser un cri aigu; *(of door)* grincer

**squeal** [skwi:l] *vi* pousser un cri perçant

**squeamish** ['skwi:mɪʃ] *adj* de nature délicate

**squeeze** [skwi:z] **1** *n* **to give sth a s.** presser qch; **to give sb's hand/arm a s.** serrer la main/le bras à qn

**2** *vt (press)* presser; **to s. sb's hand** serrer la main à qn; **to s. sth into sth** faire rentrer qch dans qch; **to s. the juice (out)** faire sortir le jus (**of** de)

**3** *vi* **to s. through/into sth** *(force oneself)* se glisser par/dans qch; **to s. in** trouver de la place; **to s. up** se serrer (**against** contre)

**squelch** [skweltʃ] *vi* patauger

**squid** [skwɪd] *n inv* calmar *m*

**squint** [skwɪnt] **1** *n* **to have a s.** loucher **2** *vi* loucher; *(in the sunlight)* plisser les yeux

**squirm** [skwɜ:m] *vi (wriggle)* se tortiller

**squirrel** [*Br* 'skwɪrəl, *Am* 'skwɜ:rəl] *n* écureuil *m*

**squirt** [skwɜ:t] **1** *vt (liquid)* faire gicler **2** *vi (of liquid)* gicler

**St** (**a**) *(abbr* **Street**) rue (**b**) *(abbr* **Saint**) St, Ste

**stab** [stæb] **1** *n* **s. (wound)** coup *m* de couteau **2** *(pt & pp* **-bb-**) *vt (with knife)* poignarder

**stability** [stə'bɪlətɪ] *n* stabilité *f*

**stabilize** ['steɪbəlaɪz] **1** *vt* stabiliser **2** *vi* se stabiliser

**stable[1]** ['steɪbəl] (**-er, -est**) *adj* stable

**stable[2]** ['steɪbəl] *n* écurie *f*

**stack** [stæk] **1** *n (heap)* tas *m*; *Fam* **stacks of** *(lots of)* des tas de **2** *vt* **to s. (up)** entasser

**stadium** ['steɪdɪəm] *n* stade *m*

**staff** [stɑ:f] *n* personnel *m*; *(of school, university)* professeurs *mpl*; *Br* **s. room** *(in school)* salle *f* des professeurs

**stag** [stæg] *n* cerf *m*; **s. night** *or* **party** enterrement *m* de la vie de garçon

**stage[1]** [steɪdʒ] **1** *n (platform)* scène *f*; **on s.** sur scène **2** *vt (play)* monter; *Fig* organiser

**stage[2]** [steɪdʒ] *n (phase)* stade *m*

**stagger** ['stægə(r)] **1** *vt (holidays)* échelonner; *(astound)* stupéfier **2** *vi (reel)* chanceler ▪ **staggering** *adj* stupéfiant

**stagnant** ['stægnənt] *adj* stagnant ▪ **stagnate** *vi* stagner

**staid** [steɪd] *adj* collet monté *inv*

**stain** [steɪn] **1** *n (mark)* tache *f* **2** *vt (mark)* tacher (**with** de); *(dye)* teinter ▪ **stained-glass** *adj* **s. window** vitrail *m (pl* -aux) ▪ **stainless** *n* **s. steel** acier *m* inoxydable, Inox® *m*

**stair** [steə(r)] *n* **a s.** *(step)* une marche; **the stairs** *(staircase)* l'escalier *m* ▪ **staircase, stairway** *n* escalier *m*

**stake** [steɪk] **1** *n* (**a**) *(post)* pieu *m*; *(for plant)* tuteur *m* (**b**) *(in betting)* enjeu *m*; **to have a s. in sth** *(share)* avoir des intérêts dans qch; **at s.** en jeu **2** *vt (bet)* jouer (**on** sur)

**stale** [steɪl] (**-er, -est**) *adj (bread)* rassis; *(air)* vicié; *(joke)* éculé

**stalemate** ['steɪlmeɪt] *n (in chess)* pat *m*; *Fig* impasse *f*

**stalk** [stɔ:k] **1** *n (of plant)* tige *f*; *(of fruit)* queue *f* **2** *vt (animal, criminal)* traquer; *(celebrity)* harceler **3** *vi* **to s. out** *(walk* *angrily)* sortir d'un air furieux mais digne

**stall** [stɔːl] **1** *n (in market)* étal *m*; *Br (for newspapers, flowers)* kiosque *m*; *(in stable)* stalle *f*; *Br* **the stalls** *(in cinema, theatre)* l'orchestre *m* **2** *vt (engine, car)* caler **3** *vi (of car)* caler; **to s. (for time)** chercher à gagner du temps

**stamina** ['stæmɪnə] *n* résistance *f* physique

**stammer** ['stæmə(r)] **1** *n* **to have a s.** être bègue **2** *vi* bégayer

**stamp** [stæmp] **1** *n (for letter)* timbre *m*; *(mark)* cachet *m*; *(device)* tampon *m*; **s. collector** philatéliste *mf* **2** *vt (document)* tamponner; *(letter)* timbrer; *(metal)* estamper; **to s. one's foot** taper du pied; *Br* **stamped addressed envelope,** *Am* **stamped self-addressed envelope** enveloppe *f* timbrée libellée à ses noms et adresse **3** *vi* **to s. on sth** écraser qch

**stampede** [stæm'piːd] **1** *n* débandade *f* **2** *vi* se ruer

**stance** [stɑːns] *n* position *f*

**STAND** [stænd] **1** *n (opinion)* position *f*; *(support)* support *m*; *(stall)* étal *m*; *(at exhibition)* stand *m*; *(at sports ground)* tribune *f*; **to take a s.** prendre position

**2** (*pt & pp* **stood**) *vt (pain, journey)* supporter; *(put straight)* mettre debout; **to s. a chance** avoir des chances; **I can't s. him** je ne peux pas le supporter

**3** *vi (be upright)* se tenir debout; *(get up)* se mettre debout; *(remain)* rester debout; *(of building)* se trouver; *(of object)* être

▸**stand about, stand around** *vi (in street)* traîner

▸**stand aside** *vi* s'écarter

▸**stand back** *vi* reculer

▸**stand by 1** *vt insep (opinion)* s'en tenir à; *(person)* soutenir **2** *vi (do nothing)* rester sans rien faire; *(be ready)* être prêt

▸**stand down** *vi (withdraw)* se retirer

▸**stand for** *vt insep (mean)* signifier; *(represent)* représenter; *Br (be candidate for)* être candidat à; *(tolerate)* supporter

▸**stand in for** *vt insep (replace)* remplacer

▸**stand out** *vi (be visible)* ressortir (**against** sur)

▸**stand over** *vt insep (watch closely)* surveiller

▸**stand up 1** *vt sep* mettre debout; *Fam* **to s. sb up** poser un lapin à qn **2** *vi (get up)* se lever

▸**stand up for** *vt insep (defend)* défendre

▸**stand up to** *vt insep (resist)* résister à; *(defend oneself against)* tenir tête à

**standard** ['stændəd] **1** *n (norm)* norme *f*; *(level)* niveau *m*; **standards** *(principles)* principes *mpl* moraux; **s. of living, living standards** niveau *m* de vie **2** *adj (average)* ordinaire; *(model, size)* standard *inv* ▪ **standardize** *vt* standardiser

**stand-by** ['stændbaɪ] **1** (*pl* **-bys**) *n* **on s.** *(troops, emergency services)* prêt à intervenir **2** *adj (plane ticket)* en stand-by

**stand-in** ['stændɪn] *n* remplaçant, -e *mf* (**for** de); *(actor)* doublure *f* (**for** de)

**standing** ['stændɪŋ] **1** *adj (upright)* debout; *(permanent)* permanent; *Br* **s. order** virement *m* automatique **2** *n (reputation)* réputation *f*; *(social, professional)* rang *m*; **of long s.** de longue date

**stand-offish** [stænd'ɒfɪʃ] *adj* distant

**standpoint** ['stændpɔɪnt] *n* point *m* de vue

**standstill** ['stændstɪl] *n* **to bring sth to a s.** immobiliser qch; **to come to a s.** s'immobiliser; **at a s.** immobile; *(negotiations, industry)* paralysé

**stank** [stæŋk] *pt of* **stink**

**stanza** ['stænzə] *n* strophe *f*

**staple**[1] ['steɪpəl] *adj (basic)* de base; **s. food** *or* **diet** nourriture *f* de base

**staple**[2] ['steɪpəl] **1** *n (for paper)* agrafe *f* **2** *vt* agrafer ▪ **stapler** *n (for paper)* agrafeuse *f*

**star** [stɑː(r)] **1** *n* étoile *f*; *(famous person)* star *f*; *Br* **four-s. (petrol)** du super **2** *(pt & pp* **-rr-**) *vt (of film)* avoir pour vedette **3** *vi (of actor, actress)* être la vedette (**in** de)

**starboard** [ˈstɑːbəd] *n Naut* tribord *m*

**starch** [stɑːtʃ] *n* amidon *m*

**stare** [steə(r)] **1** *n* regard *m* fixe **2** *vi* **to s. at sb/sth** fixer qn/qch (du regard)

**stark** [stɑːk] **1** (**-er, -est**) *adj (place)* désolé; *(fact, reality)* brutal; **to be in s. contrast to** contraster nettement avec **2** *adv* **s. naked** complètement nu

**start**[1] [stɑːt] **1** *n* début *m*; *(of race)* départ *m*; **for a s.** pour commencer; **from the s.** dès le début; **to make a s.** commencer

**2** *vt* commencer; *(packet, conversation)* entamer; *(fashion, campaign, offensive)* lancer; *(engine, vehicle)* mettre en marche; *(business, family)* fonder; **to s. doing** *or* **to do sth** commencer à faire qch

**3** *vi* commencer (**with sth** par qch; **by doing** par faire); *(of vehicle)* démarrer; *(leave)* partir (**for** pour); *(in job)* débuter; **to s. with** *(firstly)* pour commencer; **starting from now/10 euros** à partir de maintenant/10 euros ▪ **starting** *adj (point, line, salary)* de départ; **s. post** *(in race)* ligne *f* de départ

▸**start off** *vi (leave)* partir (**for** pour); *(in job)* débuter

▸**start out** *vi (begin)* débuter; *(on journey)* se mettre en route

▸**start up** **1** *vt sep (engine, vehicle)* mettre en marche; *(business)* fonder **2** *vi (of engine, vehicle)* démarrer

**start**[2] [stɑːt] **1** *n (movement)* sursaut *m*; **to give sb a s.** faire sursauter qn **2** *vi* sursauter

**starter** [ˈstɑːtə(r)] *n (in vehicle)* démarreur *m*; *(in meal)* entrée *f*; *(runner)* partant, -e *mf*; *Fam* **for starters** *(firstly)* pour commencer

**startle** [ˈstɑːtəl] *vt* faire sursauter

**starvation** [stɑːˈveɪʃən] **1** *n* faim *f* **2** *adj (wage, ration)* de misère

**starve** [stɑːv] **1** *vt (make suffer)* faire souffrir de la faim; *Fig (deprive)* priver (**of** de) **2** *vi (suffer)* souffrir de la faim; **to s. to death** mourir de faim; *Fam* **I'm starving!** je meurs de faim!

**state**[1] [steɪt] **1** *n* (**a**) *(condition)* état *m*; *(situation)* situation *f*; **not in a (fit) s. to..., in no (fit) s. to...** hors d'état de... (**b**) **S.** *(nation)* État *m*; *Fam* **the States** les États-Unis *mpl* **2** *adj (secret)* d'État; *Br (school, education)* public, -ique; **s. visit** voyage *m* officiel ▪ **state-owned** *adj* étatisé

**state**[2] [steɪt] *vt* déclarer (**that** que); *(opinion)* formuler; *(problem)* exposer

**statement** [ˈsteɪtmənt] *n* déclaration *f*; *(in court)* déposition *f*; **(bank) s.** relevé *m* de compte

**statesman** [ˈsteɪtsmən] (*pl* **-men**) *n* homme *m* d'État

**static** [ˈstætɪk] *adj* statique

**station** [ˈsteɪʃən] **1** *n (for trains)* gare *f*; *(underground)* station *f*; *(social)* rang *m*; **bus s.** gare *f* routière; **radio s.** station *f* de radio; *Am* **s. wagon** break *m* **2** *vt (position)* placer; **to be stationed at/in** *(of troops)* être en garnison à/en

**stationary** [ˈsteɪʃənərɪ] *adj (vehicle)* à l'arrêt

**stationer** [ˈsteɪʃənə(r)] *n* papetier, -ère *mf*; **s.'s (shop)** papeterie *f* ▪ **stationery** *n (articles)* articles *mpl* de bureau; *(paper)* papier *m*

**statistic** [stəˈtɪstɪk] *n (fact)* statistique *f*; **statistics** *(science)* la statistique

**statue** [ˈstætʃuː] *n* statue *f*

**stature** [ˈstætʃə(r)] *n (importance)* envergure *f*

**status** [ˈsteɪtəs] *n (position)* situation *f*; *(legal, official)* statut *m*; *(prestige)* prestige *m*; **s. symbol** marque *f* de prestige

**staunch** [stɔːntʃ] (**-er, -est**) *adj (resolute)* convaincu; *(supporter)* ardent

**stave** [steɪv] *vt* **to s. sth off** *(disaster, danger)* conjurer qch; **to s. off hunger** tromper la faim

**stay** [steɪ] **1** *n (visit)* séjour *m* **2** *vi (remain)* rester; *(reside)* loger; *(visit)* séjourner; **to s. put** ne pas bouger

▸ **stay away** *vi* ne pas s'approcher (**from** de); **to s. away from school** ne pas aller à l'école

▸ **stay behind** *vi* rester en arrière

▸ **stay in** *vi (at home)* rester à la maison; *(of nail, screw, tooth)* tenir

▸ **stay out** *vi (outside)* rester dehors; *(not come home)* ne pas rentrer; **to s. out of sth** *(not interfere in)* ne pas se mêler de qch; *(avoid)* éviter qch

▸ **stay up** *vi (at night)* ne pas se coucher; *(of fence)* tenir; **to s. up late** se coucher tard

**stead** [sted] *n* **to stand sb in good s.** être bien utile à qn; **in sb's s.** à la place de qn

**steadfast** ['stedfɑːst] *adj* dévoué; *(opponent)* constant

**steady** ['stedɪ] **1** (**-ier, -iest**) *adj (firm, stable)* stable; *(hand, voice)* assuré; *(progress, speed, demand)* constant; **to be s. on one's feet** être solide sur ses jambes **2** *vt* faire tenir; **to s. one's nerves** se calmer; **to s. oneself** retrouver son équilibre ▪ **steadily** *adv (gradually)* progressivement; *(regularly)* régulièrement; *(continuously)* sans arrêt; *(walk)* d'un pas assuré

**steak** [steɪk] *n (beef)* steak *m*

**steal[1]** [stiːl] (*pt* **stole,** *pp* **stolen**) *vti* voler (**from sb** à qn)

**steal[2]** [stiːl] (*pt* **stole,** *pp* **stolen**) *vi* **to s. in/out** entrer/sortir furtivement

**stealthy** ['stelθɪ] (**-ier, -iest**) *adj* furtif, -ive

**steam** [stiːm] **1** *n* vapeur *f*; *(on glass)* buée *f*; *Fam* **to let off s.** se défouler; **s. engine/iron** locomotive *f*/fer *m* à vapeur **2** *vt (food)* cuire à la vapeur; **to get steamed up** *(of glass)* se couvrir de buée **3** *vi* **to s. up** *(of glass)* s'embuer ▪ **steamer** *n* bateau *m* à vapeur; *(for food)* panier *m* pour cuisson à la vapeur

**steel** [stiːl] **1** *n* acier *m* **2** *vt* **to s. oneself** s'armer de courage

**steep** [stiːp] **1** (**-er, -est**) *adj (stairs, slope)* raide; *(hill, path)* escarpé; *Fig (price)* excessif, -ive **2** *vt (soak)* tremper (**in** dans) ▪ **steeply** *adv (rise)* en pente raide; *Fig (of prices)* excessivement

**steeple** ['stiːpəl] *n* clocher *m*

**steer** [stɪə(r)] **1** *vt* diriger **2** *vi (of person)* conduire; *(of ship)* se diriger (**for** vers); **to s. clear of sb/sth** éviter qn/qch ▪ **steering** *n (in vehicle)* direction *f*; **s. wheel** volant *m*

**stem** [stem] **1** *n (of plant)* tige *f*; *(of glass)* pied *m* **2** (*pt & pp* **-mm-**) *vt (stop)* arrêter **3** *vi* **to s. from sth** provenir de qch

**stench** [stentʃ] *n* puanteur *f*

**step** [step] **1** *n (movement, sound)* pas *m*; *(of stairs)* marche *f*; *(on train, bus)* marchepied *m*; *(doorstep)* pas de la porte; *Fig (action)* mesure *f*; **(flight of) steps** *(indoors)* escalier *m*; *(outdoors)* perron *m*; *Br* **(pair of) steps** *(ladder)* escabeau *m*; **s. by s.** pas à pas **2** (*pt & pp* **-pp-**) *vi (walk)* marcher (**on** sur) ▪ **stepdaughter** *n* belle-fille *f* ▪ **stepfather** *n* beau-père *m* ▪ **stepladder** *n* escabeau *m* ▪ **stepmother** *n* belle-mère *f* ▪ **stepson** *n* beau-fils *m*

▸ **step aside** *vi* s'écarter

▸ **step back** *vi* reculer

▸ **step down** *vi* descendre (**from** de); *Fig (withdraw)* se retirer

▸ **step forward** *vi* faire un pas en avant

▸ **step in** *vi (intervene)* intervenir

▸ **step off** *vt insep (chair)* descendre de

▸ **step over** *vt insep (obstacle)* enjamber

▸ **step up** *vt sep (increase)* augmenter; *(speed up)* accélérer

**stereo** ['sterɪəʊ] **1** (*pl* **-os**) *n (hi-fi, record player)* chaîne *f* stéréo; **in s.** en stéréo **2** *adj (record)* stéréo *inv*; *(broadcast)* en stéréo

**stereotype** ['sterɪətaɪp] *n* stéréotype *m*

**sterile** [*Br* 'steraɪl, *Am* 'sterəl] *adj* stérile

**sterilize** ['sterəlaɪz] *vt* stériliser

**sterling** ['stɜ:lɪŋ] *n Br (currency)* livre *f* sterling

**stern¹** [stɜ:n] (**-er, -est**) *adj* sévère

**stern²** [stɜ:n] *n (of ship)* arrière *m*

**steroid** ['stɪərɔɪd] *n* stéroïde *m*

**stethoscope** ['steθəskəʊp] *n* stéthoscope *m*

**stew** [stju:] **1** *n* ragoût *m* **2** *vt (meat)* faire cuire en ragoût; *(fruit)* faire de la compote de; **stewed fruit** compote *f* **3** *vi* cuire

**steward** ['stju:əd] *n (on plane, ship)* steward *m* ▪ **stewardess** *n (on plane)* hôtesse *f*

**stick¹** [stɪk] *n (piece of wood, chalk, dynamite)* bâton *m*; *(for walking)* canne *f*

**stick²** [stɪk] **1** (*pt & pp* **stuck**) *vt (glue)* coller; *Fam (put)* fourrer; *Fam (tolerate)* supporter; **to s. sth into sth** fourrer qch dans qch **2** *vi* coller (**to** à); *(of food in pan)* attacher (**to** dans); *(of drawer)* se coincer

▸ **stick by** *vt insep* rester fidèle à

▸ **stick down** *vt sep (envelope, stamp)* coller

▸ **stick on** *vt sep (stamp, label)* coller

▸ **stick out 1** *vt sep (tongue)* tirer; *Fam (head or arm from window)* sortir **2** *vi (of shirt)* dépasser; *(of tooth)* avancer

▸ **stick up** *vt sep (notice)* coller; *Fam (hand)* lever

▸ **stick up for** *vt insep* défendre

**sticker** ['stɪkə(r)] *n* autocollant *m*

**sticky** ['stɪkɪ] (**-ier, -iest**) *adj* collant; *(label)* adhésif, -ive

**stiff** [stɪf] (**-er, -est**) *adj* raide; *(joint)* ankylosé; *(brush, paste)* dur; *Fig (person)* guindé; **to have a s. neck** avoir un torticolis; *Fam* **to be bored s.** s'ennuyer à mourir; *Fam* **frozen s.** complètement gelé

**stiffen** ['stɪfən] **1** *vt* raidir **2** *vi* se raidir

**stifle** ['staɪfəl] **1** *vt (feeling, person)* étouffer **2** *vi* **it's stifling** on étouffe

**stigma** ['stɪgmə] *n (moral stain)* flétrissure *f*

**stiletto** [stɪ'letəʊ] *adj Br* **s. heels** talons *mpl* aiguille

**still¹** [stɪl] *adv* encore, toujours; *(even)* encore; *(nevertheless)* tout de même; **better s., s. better** encore mieux

**still²** [stɪl] (**-er, -est**) *adj (not moving)* immobile; *(calm)* calme; *Br (drink)* non gazeux, -euse; **to stand s.** rester immobile; **s. life** nature *f* morte

**stilted** ['stɪltɪd] *adj (speech, person)* guindé

**stimulate** ['stɪmjʊleɪt] *vt* stimuler ▪ **stimulant** *n* stimulant *m* ▪ **stimulus** (*pl* **-li** [-laɪ]) *n (encouragement)* stimulant *m*; *(physiological)* stimulus *m inv*

**sting** [stɪŋ] **1** *n* piqûre *f* **2** (*pt & pp* **stung**) *vt (of insect, ointment, wind)* piquer **3** *vi* piquer

**stingy** ['stɪndʒɪ] (**-ier, -iest**) *adj* avare

**stink** [stɪŋk] **1** *n* puanteur *f* **2** (*pt & pp* **stank** *or* **stunk,** *pp* **stunk**) *vi* puer; *Fam (of book, film)* être infect **3** *vt* **to s. out** *(room)* empester

**stint** [stɪnt] **1** *n (period)* période *f* de travail; *(share)* part *f* de travail **2** *vi* **to s. on sth** lésiner sur qch

**stipulate** ['stɪpjʊleɪt] *vt* stipuler (**that** que) ▪ **stipulation** *n* stipulation *f*

**stir** [stɜ:(r)] **1** *n* **to give sth a s.** remuer qch; *Fig* **to cause a s.** faire du bruit **2** (*pt & pp* **-rr-**) *vt (coffee, leaves)* remuer; *Fig (excite)* exciter; *(incite)* inciter (**sb to do** qn à faire); **to s. up trouble** semer la zizanie; **to s. things up** envenimer les choses **3** *vi (move)* remuer, bouger ▪ **stirring** *adj (speech)* émouvant

**stirrup** ['stɪrəp] *n* étrier *m*

**stitch** [stɪtʃ] **1** *n* point *m*; *(in knitting)* maille *f*; *(in wound)* point *m* de suture; *(sharp pain)* point *m* de côté; *Fam* **to be in stitches** être plié (de rire) **2** *vt* **to s. (up)** *(sew up)* coudre; *Med* recoudre

**stock** [stɒk] **1** *n (supply)* provisions *fpl*; *Com* stock *m*; *Fin* valeurs *fpl*; *(soup)* bouillon *m*; *Fin* **stocks and shares** valeurs *fpl* mobilières; **in s.** *(goods)* en stock; **out of s.** *(goods)* épuisé; *Fig* **to take s.** faire le point (**of** de); **the S. Exchange** *or* **Market** la Bourse

**2** *vt (sell)* vendre; *(keep in store)* stocker; **to s. (up)** *(shop)* approvisionner; *(fridge, cupboard)* remplir

**3** *vi* **to s. up** s'approvisionner (**with** en) ▪ **stockbroker** *n* agent *m* de change ▪ **stockpile** *vt* faire des réserves de ▪ **stocktaking** *n Br Com* inventaire *m*

**stocky** ['stɒkɪ] (**-ier, -iest**) *adj* trapu

**stodgy** ['stɒdʒɪ] (**-ier, -iest**) *adj Fam (food)* bourratif, -ive; *Fig (book)* indigeste

**stole**[1] [stəʊl] *n (shawl)* étole *f*

**stole**[2] [stəʊl] *pt of* **steal**[1,2]

**stolen** ['stəʊlən] *pp of* **steal**[1,2]

**stomach** ['stʌmək] **1** *n* ventre *m*; *(organ)* estomac *m* **2** *vt (put up with)* supporter ▪ **stomachache** *n* mal *m* de ventre; **to have (a) s.** avoir mal au ventre

**stone** [stəʊn] *n* pierre *f*; *(pebble)* caillou *m*; *(in fruit)* noyau *m*; *Br (unit of weight)* = 6,348 kg ▪ **stone-cold** *adj* glacé ▪ **stone-deaf** *adj* sourd comme un pot

**stoned** [stəʊnd] *adj Fam (on drugs)* défoncé (**on** à)

**stony** ['stəʊnɪ] (**-ier, -iest**) *adj (path)* caillouteux, -euse; *Br Fam* **s. broke** *(penniless)* fauché

**stood** [stʊd] *pt & pp of* **stand**

**stool** [stu:l] *n* tabouret *m*

**stoop** [stu:p] *vi* se baisser; *Fig* **to s. to doing sth** s'abaisser à faire qch

**stop** [stɒp] **1** *n (place, halt)* arrêt *m*; *(for plane, ship)* escale *f*; **to put a s. to sth** mettre fin à qch; **to come to a s.** s'arrêter; **s. sign** *(on road)* stop

**2** (*pt & pp* **-pp-**) *vt* arrêter; *(end)* mettre fin à; *(cheque)* faire opposition à; **to s. sb/sth from doing sth** empêcher qn/qch de faire qch

**3** *vi* s'arrêter; *(of pain, bleeding)* cesser; *(stay)* rester; **to s. snowing** cesser de neiger ▪ **stopgap** *n* bouche-trou *m* ▪ **stopoff** *n* halte *f*; *(in plane journey)* escale *f* ▪ **stopover** *n* arrêt *m*; *(in plane journey)* escale *f* ▪ **stopwatch** *n* chronomètre *m*

▸ **stop by** *vi (visit)* passer (**sb's** chez qn)

▸ **stop off, stop over** *vi (on journey)* s'arrêter

▸ **stop up** *vt sep (sink, pipe, leak)* boucher

**stoppage** ['stɒpɪdʒ] *n (strike)* débrayage *m*; *Br (in pay)* retenue *f*; **s. time** *(in sport)* arrêts *mpl* de jeu

**stopper** ['stɒpə(r)] *n* bouchon *m*

**store** [stɔ:(r)] **1** *n (supply)* provision *f*; *Fig (of knowledge)* fonds *m*; *(warehouse)* entrepôt *m*; *(shop) Br* grand magasin *m*, *Am* magasin *m*; **to have sth in s. for sb** réserver qch à qn

**2** *vt (in warehouse)* stocker; *(furniture)* entreposer; *(food)* ranger; *Comptr (in memory)* mettre en mémoire ▪ **storage** *n* emmagasinage *m*; **s. space** espace *m* de rangement; *Comptr* **s. capacity** capacité *f* de mémoire

▸ **store away** *vt sep (put away, file away)* ranger; *(furniture)* entreposer

▸ **store up** *vt sep* accumuler

**storekeeper** ['stɔ:ki:pə(r)] *n Am (shopkeeper)* commerçant, -e *mf*

**storeroom** ['stɔ:ru:m] *n (in house)* débarras *m*; *(in office, shop)* réserve *f*

**storey** ['stɔ:rɪ] (*pl* **-eys**) *n Br (of building)* étage *m*

**stork** [stɔ:k] *n* cigogne *f*

**storm** [stɔ:m] **1** *n (bad weather)* tempête *f*; *(thunderstorm)* orage *m* **2** *vt (of soldiers, police)* prendre d'assaut **3** *vi* **to s. out** *(angrily)* sortir comme une furie ▪ **stormy** (**-ier, -iest**) *adj (weather, meeting)* orageux, -euse

**story**[1] ['stɔ:rɪ] (*pl* **-ies**) *n* histoire *f*; *(newspaper article)* article *m*

**story**[2] ['stɔ:rɪ] (*pl* **-ies**) *n Am (of building)* étage *m*

**stout** [staʊt] **1** (**-er, -est**) *adj (person)* corpulent; *(shoes)* solide **2** *n Br (beer)* bière *f* brune

**stove** [stəʊv] *n (for cooking)* cuisinière *f*; *(for heating)* poêle *m*

**stow** [stəʊ] **1** *vt (cargo)* arrimer; **to s. sth away** *(put away)* ranger qch **2** *vi*

**to s. away** *(on ship)* voyager clandestinement ▪ **stowaway** *n (on ship)* passager, -ère *mf* clandestin(e)

**straddle** ['strædəl] *vt (chair, fence)* se mettre à califourchon sur; *(step over, span)* enjamber

**straggle** ['strægəl] *vi (lag behind)* être à la traîne ▪ **straggler** *n* retardataire *mf*

**straight** [streɪt] **1** (**-er, -est**) *adj* droit; *(hair)* raide; *(honest)* honnête; *(answer)* clair; *(consecutive)* consécutif, -ive; *(conventional)* conformiste; *Fam (heterosexual)* hétéro

**2** *adv (in straight line)* droit; *(directly)* directement; *(immediately)* tout de suite; **s. away** *(at once)* tout de suite; *Br* **s. ahead** *or* **on** *(walk)* tout droit; **to look s. ahead** regarder droit devant soi

**straightaway** [streɪtə'weɪ] *adv* tout de suite

**straighten** ['streɪtən] *vt* **to s. (out)** *(wire)* redresser; **to s. (up)** *(tie, hair, room)* arranger

**straightforward** [streɪt'fɔːwəd] *adj (easy, clear)* simple; *(frank)* franc (*f* franche)

**strain** [streɪn] **1** *n* tension *f*; *(mental stress)* stress *m*

**2** *vt* (**a**) *(rope, wire)* tendre excessivement; *(muscle)* se froisser; *(ankle, wrist)* se fouler; *(eyes)* fatiguer; *(voice)* forcer; *Fig (patience, friendship)* mettre à l'épreuve; **to s. oneself** *(hurt oneself)* se faire mal; *(tire oneself)* se fatiguer (**b**) *(soup)* passer; *(vegetables)* égoutter

**3** *vi* faire un effort (**to do** pour faire)

**strained** [streɪnd] *adj (muscle)* froissé; *(ankle, wrist)* foulé; *(relations)* tendu

**strainer** ['streɪnə(r)] *n* passoire *f*

**strait** [streɪt] *n Geog* **strait(s)** détroit *m*; **in financial straits** dans l'embarras

**strand** [strænd] *n (of wool)* brin *m*; *(of hair)* mèche *f*; *Fig (of story)* fil *m*

**stranded** ['strændɪd] *adj (person, vehicle)* en rade

**strange** [streɪndʒ] (**-er, -est**) *adj (odd)* bizarre; *(unknown)* inconnu ▪ **strangely** *adv* étrangement; **s. (enough), she...** chose étrange, elle...

**stranger** ['streɪndʒə(r)] *n (unknown)* inconnu, -e *mf*; *(outsider)* étranger, -ère *mf*

**strangle** ['stræŋgəl] *vt* étrangler

**strap** [stræp] **1** *n* sangle *f*; *(on dress)* bretelle *f*; *(on watch)* bracelet *m*; *(on sandal)* lanière *f* **2** (*pt & pp* **-pp-**) *vt* **to s. (down** *or* **in)** attacher *(avec une sangle)*; **to s. sb in** attacher qn avec une ceinture de sécurité

**strapping** ['stræpɪŋ] *adj* robuste

**strategy** ['strætədʒɪ] (*pl* **-ies**) *n* stratégie *f* ▪ **strategic** [strə'tiːdʒɪk] *adj* stratégique

**straw** [strɔː] *n (from wheat, for drinking)* paille *f*

**strawberry** ['strɔːbərɪ] **1** (*pl* **-ies**) *n* fraise *f* **2** *adj (flavour, ice cream)* à la fraise; *(jam)* de fraises; *(tart)* aux fraises

**stray** [streɪ] **1** *adj (animal, bullet)* perdu; **a few s. cars** quelques rares voitures **2** *n (dog)* chien *m* errant; *(cat)* chat *m* égaré **3** *vi* s'égarer; **to s. from** *(subject, path)* s'écarter de

**streak** [striːk] *n (of paint, dirt)* traînée *f*; *(of light)* rai *m*; *(in hair)* mèche *f* ▪ **streaked** *adj (marked)* strié; *(stained)* taché (**with** de)

**stream** [striːm] **1** *n (brook)* ruisseau *m*; *(of light, blood)* jet *m*; *(of people)* flot *m* **2** *vi* ruisseler (**with** de); **to s. in** *(of sunlight, people)* entrer à flots

**streamer** ['striːmə(r)] *n (banner)* banderole *f*

**streamline** ['striːmlaɪn] *vt (work, method)* rationaliser ▪ **streamlined** *adj (shape)* aérodynamique; *(industry, production)* rationalisé

**street** [striːt] *n* rue *f*; **s. lamp, s. light** lampadaire *m*; **s. map** plan *m* des rues ▪ **streetcar** *n Am (tram)* tramway *m*

**strength** [streŋθ] *n* force *f*; *(of wood, fabric)* solidité *f* ▪ **strengthen** *vt (building, position)* renforcer; *(body, limb)* fortifier

**strenuous** ['strenjʊəs] *adj (effort)* vigoureux, -euse; *(work)* fatigant

**stress** [stres] **1** *n (physical)* tension *f*; *(mental)* stress *m*; *(emphasis, in grammar)* accent *m*; **under s.** *(person)* stressé, sous pression; *(relationship)* tendu **2** *vt* insister sur; *(word)* accentuer; **to s. that...** souligner que... ▪ **stressful** *adj* stressant

**stretch** [stretʃ] **1** *n (area)* étendue *f*; *(period of time)* période *f*; *(of road)* tronçon *m*
**2** *vt (rope, neck)* tendre; *(shoe, rubber)* étirer; *Fig (income, supplies)* faire durer; **to s. (out)** *(arm, leg)* tendre; *Fig* **to s. one's legs** se dégourdir les jambes; *Fig* **to s. sb** pousser qn à son maximum
**3** *vi (of person, elastic)* s'étirer; *(of influence)* s'étendre; **to s. (out)** *(of rope, plain)* s'étendre

**stretcher** ['stretʃə(r)] *n* brancard *m*

**strew** [stru:] (*pt* **strewed,** *pp* **strewed** *or* **strewn** [stru:n]) *vt (scatter)* éparpiller; **strewn with** *(covered)* jonché de

**stricken** ['strɪkən] *adj (town, region)* sinistré

**strict** [strɪkt] (**-er, -est**) *adj (severe, absolute)* strict ▪ **strictly** *adv* strictement; **s. forbidden** formellement interdit

**stride** [straɪd] **1** *n* pas *m*; *Fig* **to make great strides** faire de grands progrès **2** (*pt* **strode**) *vi* **to s. across** *or* **over** *(fields)* traverser à grandes enjambées; **to s. along/out** avancer/sortir à grands pas

**strike** [straɪk] **1** *n (of workers)* grève *f*; *Mil* raid *m*; **to go on s.** se mettre en grève **2** (*pt & pp* **struck**) *vt (hit, impress)* frapper; *(collide with)* heurter; *(gold, oil)* trouver; *(match)* craquer; **it strikes me that...** il me semble que... *(+ indicative)* **3** *vi (of workers)* faire grève; *(attack)* attaquer

▸ **strike at** *vt insep (attack)* attaquer

▸ **strike back** *vi (retaliate)* riposter

▸ **strike down** *vt sep (of illness)* terrasser

▸ **strike off** *vt sep (from list)* rayer (**from** de); **to be struck off** *(of doctor)* être radié

▸ **strike out** *vi* **to s. out at sb** essayer de frapper qn

▸ **strike up** *vt sep* **to s. up a friendship** se lier amitié (**with sb** avec qn)

**striker** ['straɪkə(r)] *n (worker)* gréviste *mf*; *(footballer)* buteur *m*

**striking** ['straɪkɪŋ] *adj (impressive)* frappant

**string** [strɪŋ] **1** *n* ficelle *f*; *(of apron)* cordon *m*; *(of violin, racket)* corde *f*; *(of questions)* série *f*; *Fig* **to pull strings** faire jouer ses relations **2** *adj (instrument, quartet)* à cordes **3** (*pt & pp* **strung**) *vt (beads)* enfiler ▪ **stringed** *adj (instrument)* à cordes

**stringent** ['strɪndʒənt] *adj* rigoureux, -euse

**strip** [strɪp] **1** *n (piece)* bande *f*; *(of metal)* lame *f*; *(of sports team)* tenue *f*; **s. cartoon** bande *f* dessinée **2** (*pt & pp* **-pp-**) *vt (undress)* déshabiller; *(deprive)* dépouiller (**of** de); **to s. off** *(remove)* enlever **3** *vi* **to s. (off)** *(get undressed)* se déshabiller ▪ **stripper** *n (woman)* strip-teaseuse *f*; **(paint) s.** *(substance)* décapant *m* ▪ **striptease** *n* strip-tease *m*

**stripe** [straɪp] *n* rayure *f*; *(indicating rank)* galon *m* ▪ **striped** *adj* rayé (**with** de)

**strive** [straɪv] (*pt* **strove,** *pp* **striven** ['strɪvən]) *vi* s'efforcer (**to do** de faire; **for** d'obtenir)

**strode** [strəʊd] *pt of* **stride**

**stroke** [strəʊk] **1** *n (movement)* coup *m*; *(of pen)* trait *m*; *(of brush)* touche *f*; *(caress)* caresse *f*; *Med (illness)* attaque *f*; **at a s.** d'un coup; **s. of luck** coup *m* de chance **2** *vt (caress)* caresser

**stroll** [strəʊl] **1** *n* promenade *f* **2** *vi* se promener; **to s. in** entrer sans se presser

**stroller** ['strəʊlə(r)] *n Am (for baby)* poussette *f*

**strong** [strɒŋ] **1** (**-er, -est**) *adj* fort;

*(shoes, chair, nerves)* solide; *(interest)* vif (*f* vive); *(measures)* énergique; *(supporter)* ardent **2** *adv* **to be going s.** aller toujours bien ▪ **strong-box** *n* coffre-fort *m* ▪ **stronghold** *n* bastion *m* ▪ **strongly** *adv (protest, defend)* énergiquement; *(advise, remind, desire)* fortement

**strove** [strəʊv] *pt of* **strive**

**struck** [strʌk] *pt & pp of* **strike**

**structure** ['strʌktʃə(r)] *n* structure *f*; *(building)* édifice *m* ▪ **structural** *adj* structural; *(building defect)* de construction

**struggle** ['strʌgəl] **1** *n (fight)* lutte *f* (**to do** pour faire); **to have a s. doing** *or* **to do sth** avoir du mal à faire qch **2** *vi (fight)* lutter (**with** avec); **to be struggling** *(financially)* avoir du mal; **to s. to do sth** s'efforcer de faire qch

**strung** [strʌŋ] *pt & pp of* **string**

**strut**[1] [strʌt] (*pt & pp* **-tt-**) *vi* **to s. (about** *or* **around)** se pavaner

**strut**[2] [strʌt] *n (for frame)* étai *m*

**stub** [stʌb] **1** *n (of pencil, cigarette)* bout *m*; *(of cheque)* talon *m* **2** (*pt & pp* **-bb-**) *vt* **to s. one's toe** se cogner l'orteil (**on** *or* **against** contre); **to s. out** *(cigarette)* écraser

**stubble** ['stʌbəl] *n (on face)* barbe *f* de plusieurs jours

**stubborn** ['stʌbən] *adj (person)* têtu

**stuck** [stʌk] **1** *pt & pp of* **stick**[2] **2** *adj (caught, jammed)* coincé; **s. in bed/indoors** cloué au lit/chez soi; **to get s.** être coincé; **to be s. with sb/sth** se farcir qn/qch

**stuck-up** [stʌ'kʌp] *adj Fam* snob

**stud**[1] [stʌd] *n (on football boot)* crampon *m*; *(earring)* clou *m* d'oreille ▪ **studded** *adj* **s. with** *(covered)* constellé de

**stud**[2] [stʌd] *n (farm)* haras *m*; *(stallion)* étalon *m*

**student** ['stju:dənt] **1** *n (at university)* étudiant, -e *mf*; *(at school)* élève *mf*; **music s.** étudiant, -e *mf* en musique **2** *adj (life, protest)* étudiant; *(restaurant, residence, grant)* universitaire

**studio** ['stju:dɪəʊ] (*pl* **-os**) *n* studio *m*; *(of artist)* atelier *m*; *Br* **s. flat**, *Am* **s. apartment** studio *m*

**studious** ['stju:dɪəs] *adj (person)* studieux, -euse

**study** ['stʌdɪ] **1** (*pl* **-ies**) *n* étude *f*; *(office)* bureau *m* **2** (*pp & pp* **-ied**) *vt (learn, observe)* étudier **3** *vi* étudier; **to s. to be a doctor** faire des études de médecine; **to s. for an exam** préparer un examen

**stuff** [stʌf] **1** *n (possessions)* affaires *fpl*; *Fam* **some s.** *(substance)* un truc; *(things)* des trucs; *Fam* **this s.'s good, it's good s.** c'est bien

**2** *vt (pocket)* remplir (**with** de); *(cushion)* rembourrer (**with** avec); *(animal)* empailler; *(chicken, tomatoes)* farcir; **to s. sth into sth** fourrer qch dans qch ▪ **stuffing** *n (padding)* bourre *f*; *(for chicken, tomatoes)* farce *f*

**stuffy** ['stʌfɪ] (**-ier, -iest**) *adj (room)* qui sent le renfermé; *(person)* vieux jeu *inv*

**stumble** ['stʌmbəl] *vi* trébucher; **to s. across** *or* **on** *(find)* tomber sur

**stump** [stʌmp] *n (of tree)* souche *f*; *(of limb)* moignon *m*; *(in cricket)* piquet *m*

**stun** [stʌn] (*pt & pp* **-nn-**) *vt (make unconscious)* assommer; *Fig (amaze)* stupéfier ▪ **stunned** *adj (amazed)* stupéfait (**by** par) ▪ **stunning** *adj Fam (excellent)* excellent; *Fam (beautiful)* superbe

**stung** [stʌŋ] *pt & pp of* **sting**

**stunk** [stʌŋk] *pt & pp of* **stink**

**stunt**[1] [stʌnt] *n (in film)* cascade *f*; *(for publicity)* coup *m* de pub; **s. man** cascadeur *m*

**stunt**[2] [stʌnt] *vt (growth)* retarder ▪ **stunted** *adj (person)* rabougri

**stupid** ['stju:pɪd] *adj* stupide; **to do/say a s. thing** faire/dire une stupidité ▪ **stupidity** *n* stupidité *f* ▪ **stupidly** *adv* bêtement

**sturdy** ['stɜ:dɪ] (**-ier, -iest**) *adj (person, shoe)* robuste

**stutter** ['stʌtə(r)] **1** *n* **to have a s.** être bègue **2** *vi* bégayer

**sty¹** [staɪ] *n (for pigs)* porcherie *f*
**sty², stye** [staɪ] *n (on eye)* orgelet *m*
**style** [staɪl] **1** *n* style *m*; *(sophistication)* classe *f* **2** *vt (design)* créer; **to s. sb's hair** coiffer qn
**stylish** ['staɪlɪʃ] *adj* chic *inv*
**stylist** ['staɪlɪst] *n* **(hair) s.** coiffeur, -euse *mf*
**sub-** [sʌb] *pref* sous-, sub-
**subconscious** [sʌb'kɒnʃəs] *adj & n* subconscient *(m)* ▪ **subconsciously** *adv* inconsciemment
**subcontract** [sʌbkən'trækt] *vt* sous-traiter
**subdivide** [sʌbdɪ'vaɪd] *vt* subdiviser (**into** en)
**subdue** [səb'djuː] *vt (country, people)* soumettre; *(feelings)* maîtriser ▪ **subdued** *adj (light)* tamisé; *(voice, tone)* bas (*f* basse); *(person)* inhabituellement calme
**subject¹** ['sʌbdʒɪkt] *n* (**a**) *(matter, in grammar)* sujet *m*; *(at school, university)* matière *f*; **s. matter** *(topic)* sujet *m*; *(content)* contenu *m* (**b**) *(of monarch)* sujet, -ette *mf*
**subject² 1** ['sʌbdʒekt] *adj* **to be s. to depression/jealousy** avoir tendance à la dépression/à la jalousie; **it's s. to my agreement** c'est sous réserve de mon accord **2** [səb'dʒekt] *vt* soumettre (**to** à)
**subjective** [səb'dʒektɪv] *adj* subjectif, -ive ▪ **subjectively** *adv* subjectivement
**subjunctive** [səb'dʒʌŋktɪv] *n* subjonctif *m*
**sublet** [sʌb'let] *(pt & pp* **-let,** *pres p* **-letting)** *vt* sous-louer
**sublime** [sə'blaɪm] *adj* sublime; *(utter)* suprême
**submarine** ['sʌbməriːn] *n* sous-marin *m*
**submerge** [səb'mɜːdʒ] *vt (flood, overwhelm)* submerger; *(immerse)* immerger (**in** dans)
**submit** [səb'mɪt] **1** *(pt & pp* **-tt-)** *vt* soumettre (**to** à) **2** *vi* se soumettre (**to** à) ▪ **submissive** *adj (person)* soumis; *(attitude)* de soumission
**subordinate** [sə'bɔːdɪnət] **1** *adj* subalterne; **s. to** subordonné à **2** *n* subordonné, -e *mf*
**subscribe** [səb'skraɪb] *vi (pay money)* cotiser (**to** à); **to s. to a newspaper** s'abonner à un journal ▪ **subscriber** *n (to newspaper, telephone)* abonné, -e *mf* ▪ **subscription** [sʌb'skrɪpʃən] *n (to newspaper)* abonnement *m*; *(to club)* cotisation *f*
**subsequent** ['sʌbsɪkwənt] *adj* ultérieur (**to** à); **our s. problems** les problèmes que nous avons eus par la suite ▪ **subsequently** *adv* par la suite
**subside** [səb'saɪd] *vi (of ground, building)* s'affaisser; *(of wind, flood, fever)* baisser ▪ **subsidence** *n (of ground)* affaissement *m*
**subsidiary** [*Br* səb'sɪdɪərɪ, *Am* -dɪerɪ] **1** *adj* subsidiaire **2** (*pl* **-ies**) *n (company)* filiale *f*
**subsidize** ['sʌbsɪdaɪz] *vt* subventionner ▪ **subsidy** (*pl* **-ies**) *n* subvention *f*
**substance** ['sʌbstəns] *n* substance *f*; *(solidity, worth)* fondement *m*
**substantial** [səb'stænʃəl] *adj* important; *(meal)* substantiel, -elle ▪ **substantially** *adv* considérablement
**substitute** ['sʌbstɪtjuːt] **1** *n (thing)* produit *m* de remplacement; *(person)* remplaçant, -e *mf* (**for** de) **2** *vt* **to s. sb/sth for** substituer qn/qch à **3** *vi* **to s. for sb** remplacer qn ▪ **substitution** *n* substitution *f*
**subtitle** ['sʌbtaɪtəl] **1** *n (of film)* sous-titre *m* **2** *vt (film)* sous-titrer
**subtle** ['sʌtəl] (**-er, -est**) *adj* subtil
**subtotal** [sʌb'təʊtəl] *n* sous-total *m*
**subtract** [səb'trækt] *vt* soustraire (**from** de) ▪ **subtraction** *n* soustraction *f*
**suburb** ['sʌbɜːb] *n* banlieue *f*; **the suburbs** la banlieue ▪ **suburban** [sə'bɜːbən] *adj (train, house)* de banlieue ▪ **suburbia** [sə'bɜːbɪə] *n* la banlieue; **in s.** en banlieue
**subversive** [səb'vɜːsɪv] *adj* subversif, -ive
**subway** ['sʌbweɪ] *n Br (under road)*

passage *m* souterrain; *Am (railroad)* métro *m*

**succeed** [sək'si:d] **1** *vt* **to s. sb** succéder à qn **2** *vi* réussir (**in doing** à faire; **in sth** dans qch); **to s. to the throne** monter sur le trône ▪ **succeeding** *adj (in past)* suivant; *(in future)* futur; *(consecutive)* consécutif, -ive

**success** [sək'ses] *n* succès *m*, réussite *f*; **he was a s.** il a eu du succès; **it was a s.** c'était réussi

**successful** [sək'sesfəl] *adj (effort, venture)* couronné de succès; *(outcome)* heureux, -euse; *(company, businessman)* prospère; *(candidate in exam)* admis, reçu; *(candidate in election)* élu; *(writer, film)* à succès; **to be s.** réussir; **to be s. in doing sth** réussir à faire qch ▪ **successfully** *adv* avec succès

**succession** [sək'seʃən] *n* succession *f*; **ten days in s.** dix jours consécutifs ▪ **successive** *adj* successif, -ive; **ten s. days** dix jours consécutifs ▪ **successor** *n* successeur *m* (**to** de)

**succinct** [sək'sɪŋkt] *adj* succinct

**succumb** [sə'kʌm] *vi* succomber (**to** à)

**such** [sʌtʃ] **1** *adj (of this or that kind)* tel (*f* telle); **s. a car** une telle voiture; **s. happiness/noise** tant de bonheur/bruit; **there's no s. thing** ça n'existe pas; **s. as** comme, tel que
**2** *adv (so very)* si; *(in comparisons)* aussi; **s. long trips** de si longs voyages
**3** *pron* **happiness as s.** le bonheur en tant que tel ▪ **suchlike** *pron & adj* **...and s.** ...et autres

**suck** [sʌk] **1** *vt* sucer; *(of baby)* téter; **to s. (up)** *(with straw, pump)* aspirer; **to s. up** *or* **in** *(absorb)* absorber **2** *vi (of baby)* téter

**suckle** ['sʌkəl] **1** *vt (of woman)* allaiter **2** *vi (of baby)* téter

**suction** ['sʌkʃən] *n* succion *f*

**sudden** ['sʌdən] *adj* soudain; **all of a s.** tout à coup ▪ **suddenly** *adv* tout à coup, soudain; *(die)* subitement

**suds** [sʌdz] *npl* mousse *f* de savon

**sue** [su:] **1** *vt* poursuivre (en justice) **2** *vi* engager des poursuites judiciaires

**suede** [sweɪd] *n* daim *m*

**suffer** ['sʌfə(r)] **1** *vt (loss, damage, defeat)* subir; *(pain)* ressentir; *(tolerate)* supporter **2** *vi* souffrir (**from** de); **your work will s.** ton travail s'en ressentira ▪ **sufferer** *n (from misfortune)* victime *f*; **AIDS s.** malade *mf* du SIDA ▪ **suffering** *n* souffrance *f*

**suffice** [sə'faɪs] *vi* suffire

**sufficient** [sə'fɪʃənt] *adj* suffisant; **s. money** *(enough)* suffisamment d'argent; **to be s.** suffire ▪ **sufficiently** *adv* suffisamment

**suffix** ['sʌfɪks] *n* suffixe *m*

**suffocate** ['sʌfəkeɪt] **1** *vt* étouffer **2** *vi* suffoquer

**sugar** ['ʃʊgə(r)] **1** *n* sucre *m*; **s. bowl** sucrier *m*; **s. lump** morceau *m* de sucre **2** *vt (tea)* sucrer

**suggest** [sə'dʒest] *vt (propose)* suggérer; *(imply)* indiquer ▪ **suggestion** *n* suggestion *f* ▪ **suggestive** *adj* suggestif, -ive; **to be s. of** évoquer

**suicide** ['su:ɪsaɪd] *n* suicide *m*; **to commit s.** se suicider

**suit**[1] [su:t] *n* (**a**) *(man's)* costume *m*; *(woman's)* tailleur *m*; **flying/diving/ski s.** combinaison *f* de vol/plongée/ski (**b**) *(in card games)* couleur *f*; *Fig* **to follow s.** faire de même (**c**) *(lawsuit)* procès *m*

**suit**[2] [su:t] *vt (please, be acceptable to)* convenir à; *(of dress, colour)* aller (bien) à; *(adapt)* adapter (**to** à); **suited to** *(job, activity)* fait pour; *(appropriate to)* qui convient à; **to be well suited** *(of couple)* être bien assorti

**suitable** ['su:təbəl] *adj* convenable (**for** à); *(candidate, date)* adéquat; *(example)* approprié; **this film is not s. for children** ce film n'est pas pour les enfants

**suitcase** ['su:tkeɪs] *n* valise *f*

**suite** [swi:t] *n (rooms)* suite *f*

**sulk** [sʌlk] *vi* bouder

**sullen** ['sʌlən] *adj* maussade

**sultana** [sʌl'tɑ:nə] *n (raisin)* raisin *m* de Smyrne

**sum** [sʌm] **1** *n (amount of money)* somme *f*; *(mathematical problem)* problème *m*; **s. total** somme *f* totale **2** *(pt & pp* **-mm-**) *vt* **to s. up** *(summarize)* résumer; *(assess)* évaluer **3** *vi* **to s. up** résumer

**summarize** ['sʌməraɪz] *vt* résumer ▪ **summary** *(pl* **-ies**) *n* résumé *m*

**summer** ['sʌmə(r)] **1** *n* été *m*; **in (the) s.** en été **2** *adj* d'été; *Am* **s. camp** colonie *f* de vacances; *Br* **s. holidays,** *Am* **s. vacation** grandes vacances *fpl* ▪ **summertime** *n* été *m*; **in (the) s.** en été

**summit** ['sʌmɪt] *n* sommet *m*

**summon** ['sʌmən] *vt (call)* appeler; *(meeting, person)* convoquer (**to** à); **to s. up one's courage/strength** rassembler son courage/ses forces

**summons** ['sʌmənz] **1** *n (in law)* assignation *f* à comparaître **2** *vt* assigner à comparaître

**sumptuous** ['sʌmptʃʊəs] *adj* somptueux, -euse

**sun** [sʌn] **1** *n* soleil *m*; **in the s.** au soleil; **the s. is shining** il fait soleil **2** *(pt & pp* **-nn-**) *vt* **to s. oneself** prendre le soleil ▪ **sunbathe** *vi* prendre un bain de soleil ▪ **sunbed** *n* lit *m* à ultraviolets ▪ **sunblock** *n (cream)* écran *m* total ▪ **sunburn** *n* coup *m* de soleil ▪ **sunburnt** *adj* brûlé par le soleil ▪ **sundial** *n* cadran *m* solaire ▪ **sunflower** *n* tournesol *m* ▪ **sunglasses** *npl* lunettes *fpl* de soleil ▪ **sunhat** *n* chapeau *m* de soleil ▪ **sunlamp** *n* lampe *f* à bronzer ▪ **sunlight** *n* lumière *f* du soleil ▪ **sunrise** *n* lever *m* du soleil ▪ **sunroof** *n (in car)* toit *m* ouvrant ▪ **sunset** *n* coucher *m* du soleil ▪ **sunshade** *n (on table)* parasol *m*; *(portable)* ombrelle *f* ▪ **sunshine** *n* soleil *m* ▪ **sunstroke** *n* insolation *f* ▪ **suntan** *n* bronzage *m*; **s. lotion/oil** crème *f*/huile *f* solaire ▪ **suntanned** *adj* bronzé

**Sunday** ['sʌndeɪ] *n* dimanche *m*; **S. school** ≃ catéchisme *m*

**sundry** ['sʌndrɪ] **1** *adj* divers **2** *n* **all and s.** tout le monde

**sung** [sʌŋ] *pp of* **sing**

**sunk** [sʌŋk] *pp of* **sink²** ▪ **sunken** *adj (rock, treasure)* submergé

**sunny** ['sʌnɪ] (**-ier, -iest**) *adj (day)* ensoleillé; **it's s.** il fait soleil; **s. periods** *or* **intervals** éclaircies *fpl*

**super** ['su:pə(r)] *adj Fam* super *inv*

**super-** ['su:pə(r)] *pref* super-

**superb** [su:'pɜ:b] *adj* superbe

**superficial** [su:pə'fɪʃəl] *adj* superficiel, -elle

**superfluous** [su:'pɜ:flʊəs] *adj* superflu

**superglue** ['su:pəglu:] *n* colle *f* extra-forte

**superior** [su:'pɪərɪə(r)] **1** *adj* supérieur (**to** à) **2** *n (person)* supérieur, -eure *mf* ▪ **superiority** [-rɪ'ɒrətɪ] *n* supériorité *f*

**superlative** [su:'pɜ:lətɪv] **1** *adj* sans pareil **2** *adj & n Gram* superlatif *(m)*

**supermarket** ['su:pəmɑ:kɪt] *n* supermarché *m*

**supernatural** [su:pə'nætʃərəl] *adj & n* surnaturel, -elle *(m)*

**superpower** ['su:pəpaʊə(r)] *n Pol* superpuissance *f*

**supersede** [su:pə'si:d] *vt* supplanter

**supersonic** [su:pə'sɒnɪk] *adj* supersonique

**superstition** [su:pə'stɪʃən] *n* superstition *f* ▪ **superstitious** *adj* superstitieux, -euse

**superstore** ['su:pəstɔ:r] *n* hypermarché *m*

**supervise** ['su:pəvaɪz] *vt (person, work)* surveiller; *(research)* superviser ▪ **supervisor** *n* surveillant, -e *mf*; *(in office)* chef *m* de service; *(in store)* chef *m* de rayon

**supper** ['sʌpə(r)] *n (meal)* dîner *m*; *(snack)* = casse-croûte pris avant d'aller se coucher

**supple** ['sʌpəl] *adj* souple

**supplement 1** ['sʌplɪmənt] *n* supplément *m* (**to** à) **2** ['sʌplɪment] *vt* compléter; **to s. one's income** arrondir ses fins de mois ▪ **supplementary** [-'mentərɪ] *adj* supplémentaire

**supplier** [sə'plaɪə(r)] *n Com* fournisseur *m*

**supply** [sə'plaɪ] **1** (*pl* **-ies**) *n (stock)* provision *f*; **s. and demand** l'offre *f* et la demande; *Br* **s. teacher** suppléant, -e *mf* **2** (*pt & pp* **-ied**) *vt (provide)* fournir; *(with gas, electricity, water)* alimenter (**with** en); *(equip)* équiper (**with** de); **to s. sb with sth, to s. sth to sb** fournir qch à qn

**support** [sə'pɔːt] **1** *n (backing, person supporting)* soutien *m*; *(thing supporting)* support *m*; **in s. of** *(person)* en faveur de; *(evidence, theory)* à l'appui de **2** *vt (bear weight of)* supporter; *(help, encourage)* soutenir; *(theory, idea)* appuyer; *(family, wife, husband)* subvenir aux besoins de

**supporter** [sə'pɔːtə(r)] *n* partisan *m*; *(of football team)* supporter *m*

**supportive** [sə'pɔːtɪv] *adj* **to be s. of sb** être d'un grand soutien à qn

**suppose** [sə'pəʊz] *vti* supposer (**that** que); **I'm supposed to be working** je suis censé travailler; **he's supposed to be rich** on le dit riche; **I s. (so)** je pense; **s.** *or* **supposing (that) you're right** supposons que tu aies raison

**suppress** [sə'pres] *vt (revolt, feelings, smile)* réprimer; *(fact, evidence)* faire disparaître

**supreme** [suː'priːm] *adj* suprême

**surcharge** ['sɜːtʃɑːdʒ] *n (extra charge)* supplément *m*

**sure** [ʃʊə(r)] (**-er, -est**) *adj* sûr (**of** de; **that** que); **she's s. to accept** c'est sûr qu'elle acceptera; **to make s. of sth** s'assurer de qch; **for s.** à coup sûr; *Fam* **s.!, s. thing!** bien sûr! ▪ **surely** *adv (certainly)* sûrement; **s. he didn't refuse?** il n'a quand même pas refusé?

**surf** [sɜːf] **1** *n (waves)* ressac *m* **2** *vt Comptr* **to s. the Net** naviguer sur l'Internet ▪ **surfboard** *n* planche *f* de surf ▪ **surfing** *n (sport)* surf *m*; **to go s.** faire du surf

**surface** ['sɜːfɪs] **1** *n* surface *f*; **s. area** superficie *f*; **on the s.** *(of water)* à la surface; *Fig (to all appearances)* en apparence **2** *vi (of swimmer)* remonter à la surface; *Fam (of person, thing)* réapparaître

**surge** ['sɜːdʒ] **1** *n (of enthusiasm)* vague *f*; *(of anger, pride)* bouffée *f* **2** *vi (of crowd)* déferler; *(of prices)* monter (soudainement); **to s. forward** *(of person)* se lancer en avant

**surgeon** ['sɜːdʒən] *n* chirurgien *m* ▪ **surgery** ['sɜːdʒərɪ] *n Br (doctor's office)* cabinet *m*; *(period, sitting)* consultation *f*; *(science)* chirurgie *f*; **to have heart s.** se faire opérer du cœur ▪ **surgical** *adj* chirurgical

**surly** ['sɜːlɪ] (**-ier, -iest**) *adj* revêche

**surmount** [sə'maʊnt] *vt* surmonter

**surname** ['sɜːneɪm] *n* nom *m* de famille

**surpass** [sə'pɑːs] *vt* surpasser (**in** en)

**surplus** ['sɜːpləs] **1** *n* surplus *m* **2** *adj (goods)* en surplus

**surprise** [sə'praɪz] **1** *n* surprise *f*; **to give sb a s.** faire une surprise à qn; **s. visit/result** visite *f*/résultat *m* inattendu(e)

**2** *vt* étonner, surprendre ▪ **surprised** *adj* surpris (**that** que + *subjunctive*; **at sth** de qch; **at seeing** de voir) ▪ **surprising** *adj* surprenant

**surrender** [sə'rendə(r)] **1** *n (of soldiers)* reddition *f* **2** *vt (town)* livrer; *(right, claim)* renoncer à **3** *vi (give oneself up)* se rendre (**to** à)

**surrogate** ['sʌrəgət] *n* substitut *m*; **s. mother** mère *f* porteuse

**surround** [sə'raʊnd] *vt* entourer (**with** de); *(of army, police)* cerner; **surrounded by** entouré de ▪ **surrounding** *adj* environnant ▪ **surroundings** *npl (of town)* environs *mpl*; *(setting)* cadre *m*

**surveillance** [sɜː'veɪləns] *n* surveillance *f*

**survey 1** ['sɜːveɪ] *n (investigation)* enquête *f*; *(of opinion)* sondage *m*; *(of house)* inspection *f*

**2** [sə'veɪ] *vt (look at)* regarder; *(review)* passer en revue; *(house)* inspecter; *(land)* faire un relevé de

■ **surveyor** *n (of land)* géomètre *m*; *(of house)* expert *m*

**survive** [sə'vaɪv] **1** *vt* survivre à **2** *vi* survivre ■ **survival** *n (act)* survie *f*; *(relic)* vestige *m* ■ **survivor** *n* survivant, -e *mf*

**susceptible** [sə'septəbəl] *adj (sensitive)* sensible (**to** à)

**suspect 1** ['sʌspekt] *n & adj* suspect, -ecte *(mf)* **2** [sə'spekt] *vt* soupçonner (**sb of sth** qn de qch; **sb of doing** qn d'avoir fait); *(have intuition of)* se douter de

**suspend** [sə'spend] *vt* (**a**) *(hang)* suspendre (**from** à) (**b**) *(service, employee, player)* suspendre; *(pupil)* renvoyer temporairement

**suspense** [sə'spens] *n (uncertainty)* incertitude *f*; *(in film, book)* suspense *m*; **to keep sb in s.** tenir qn en haleine

**suspicion** [sə'spɪʃən] *n* soupçon *m*; **to be under s.** être soupçonné

**suspicious** [sə'spɪʃəs] *adj (person)* soupçonneux, -euse; *(behaviour)* suspect; **to be s. of** *or* **about sth** se méfier de qch

**sustain** [sə'steɪn] *vt (effort, theory)* soutenir; *(weight)* supporter; *(life)* maintenir; *(damage, loss, attack)* subir; **to s. an injury** être blessé

**swagger** ['swægə(r)] *vi (walk)* se pavaner

**swallow**[1] ['swɒləʊ] **1** *vt* avaler; **to s. sth down** avaler qch **2** *vi* avaler

**swallow**[2] ['swɒləʊ] *n (bird)* hirondelle *f*

**swam** [swæm] *pt of* **swim**

**swamp** [swɒmp] **1** *n* marais *m* **2** *vt (flood, overwhelm)* submerger (**with** de)

**swan** [swɒn] *n* cygne *m*

**swap** [swɒp] **1** *n* échange *m* **2** *(pt & pp* **-pp-***) vt* échanger (**for** contre); **to s. seats** *or* **places** changer de place **3** *vi* échanger

**swarm** [swɔːm] **1** *n (of bees, people)* essaim *m* **2** *vi (of streets, insects, people)* fourmiller (**with** de)

**swat** [swɒt] *(pt & pp* **-tt-***) vt* écraser

**sway** [sweɪ] **1** *vt* balancer; *Fig (person, public opinion)* influencer **2** *vi* se balancer

**swear** [sweə(r)] **1** *(pt* **swore,** *pp* **sworn***) vt (promise)* jurer (**to do** de faire; **that** que); **to s. an oath** prêter serment **2** *vi (take an oath)* jurer (**to sth** de qch); **to s. at sb** injurier qn ■ **swearword** *n* juron *m*

**sweat** [swet] **1** *n* sueur *f* **2** *vi* suer ■ **sweatshirt** *n* sweat-shirt *m*

**sweater** ['swetə(r)] *n* pull *m*

**sweaty** ['swetɪ] (**-ier, -iest**) *adj (shirt)* plein de sueur; *(hand)* moite; *(person)* en sueur

**Swede** [swiːd] *n* Suédois, -e *mf* ■ **Sweden** *n* la Suède ■ **Swedish 1** *adj* suédois **2** *n (language)* suédois *m*

**sweep** [swiːp] **1** *(pt & pp* **swept***) vt (with broom)* balayer; *(chimney)* ramoner **2** *vi* balayer

▸ **sweep aside** *vt sep (opposition, criticism)* écarter

▸ **sweep away** *vt sep (leaves)* balayer; *(carry off)* emporter

▸ **sweep out** *vt sep (room)* balayer

▸ **sweep through** *vt insep (of fear)* saisir; *(of disease)* ravager

▸ **sweep up** *vt sep & vi* balayer

**sweeping** ['swiːpɪŋ] *adj (gesture)* large; *(change)* radical; *(statement)* trop général

**sweet** [swiːt] **1** (**-er, -est**) *adj* doux (*f* douce); *(tea, coffee, cake)* sucré; *(pretty, kind)* adorable; **to have a s. tooth** aimer les sucreries
**2** *n Br (piece of confectionery)* bonbon *m*; *Br (dessert)* dessert *m*; *Br* **s. shop** confiserie *f* ■ **sweetcorn** *n Br* maïs *m*

**sweeten** ['swiːtən] *vt (food)* sucrer; *Fig (person)* amadouer

**sweetheart** ['swiːthɑːt] *n* petit, -e ami, -e *mf*

**swell**[1] [swel] **1** *(pt* **swelled,** *pp* **swollen** *or* **swelled***) vt (river, numbers)* grossir **2** *vi (of hand, leg)* enfler; *(of wood)* gonfler; *(of river, numbers)* grossir; **to s. up** *(of body part)* enfler ■ **swelling** *n (on body)* enflure *f*

**swell²** [swel] *adj Am Fam (excellent)* super *inv*
**swelter** ['sweltə(r)] *vi* étouffer ■ **sweltering** *adj* étouffant; **it's s.** on étouffe
**swept** [swept] *pt & pp of* **sweep**
**swerve** [swɜːv] *vi (of vehicle)* faire une embardée; *(of player)* faire un écart
**swift** [swɪft] **1** (**-er, -est**) *adj* rapide **2** *n (bird)* martinet *m* ■ **swiftly** *adv* rapidement
**swill** [swɪl] *vt Fam (drink)* écluser; **to s. (out** *or* **down)** rincer à grande eau
**swim** [swɪm] **1** *n* **to go for a s.** aller nager
**2** (*pt* **swam,** *pp* **swum,** *pres p* **swimming**) *vt (river)* traverser à la nage; *(length, crawl)* nager
**3** *vi* nager; *(as sport)* faire de la natation; **to go swimming** aller nager; **to s. away** s'éloigner à la nage ■ **swimmer** *n* nageur, -euse *mf* ■ **swimming** *n* natation *f*; **s. cap** bonnet *m* de bain; *Br* **s. costume** maillot *m* de bain; *Br* **s. pool** piscine *f*; **s. trunks** slip *m* de bain
**swindle** ['swɪndəl] **1** *n* escroquerie *f* **2** *vt* escroquer ■ **swindler** *n* escroc *m*
**swine** [swaɪn] *n inv Pej (person)* salaud *m*
**swing** [swɪŋ] **1** *n (in playground)* balançoire *f*; *(movement)* balancement *m*; *(in opinion)* revirement *m*; *(of golfer)* swing *m*
**2** (*pt & pp* **swung**) *vt (arms, legs)* balancer; *(axe)* brandir
**3** *vi (sway)* se balancer; *(turn)* virer; **to s. round** *(turn suddenly)* se retourner
**swipe** [swaɪp] *vt (card)* passer dans un lecteur de cartes; *Fam* **to s. sth** *(steal)* faucher qch (**from sb** à qn)
**swirl** [swɜːl] *vi* tourbillonner
**Swiss** [swɪs] **1** *adj* suisse; *Br* **S. roll** roulé *m* **2** *n inv* Suisse *m*, Suissesse *f*; **the S.** les Suisses *mpl*
**switch** [swɪtʃ] **1** *n (electrical)* interrupteur *m*; *(change)* changement *m* (**in** de); *(reversal)* revirement *m* (**in** de) **2** *vt (money, employee)* transférer (**to** à); *(support, affection)* reporter (**to** sur); *(exchange)* échanger (**for** contre) **3** *vi* **to s. to** *(change to)* passer à ■ **switchboard** *n Tel* standard *m*; **s. operator** standardiste *mf*
▸ **switch off 1** *vt sep (lamp, gas, radio)* éteindre; *(engine)* arrêter; *(electricity)* couper **2** *vi (of appliance)* s'éteindre
▸ **switch on 1** *vt sep (lamp, gas, radio)* allumer; *(engine)* mettre en marche **2** *vi (of appliance)* s'allumer
▸ **switch over** *vi (change TV channels)* changer de chaîne; **to s. over to** *(change to)* passer à
**Switzerland** ['swɪtsələnd] *n* la Suisse
**swivel** ['swɪvəl] **1** (*Br* **-ll-**, *Am* **-l-**) *vi* **to s. (round)** *(of chair)* pivoter **2** *adj* **s. chair** chaise *f* pivotante
**swollen** ['swəʊlən] **1** *pp of* **swell¹ 2** *adj (leg)* enflé; *(stomach)* gonflé
**swoop** [swuːp] *vi* faire une descente (**on** dans); **to s. (down) on** *(of bird)* fondre sur
**swop** [swɒp] *n & vti* = **swap**
**sword** [sɔːd] *n* épée *f*
**swore** [swɔː(r)] *pt of* **swear**
**sworn** [swɔːn] *pp of* **swear**
**swot** [swɒt] *Br Fam Pej* **1** *n* bûcheur, -euse *mf* **2** (*pt & pp* **-tt-**) *vti* **to s. (up)** bûcher; **to s. up on sth** bûcher qch
**swum** [swʌm] *pp of* **swim**
**swung** [swʌŋ] *pt & pp of* **swing**
**sycamore** ['sɪkəmɔː(r)] *n (maple)* sycomore *m*; *Am (plane tree)* platane *m*
**syllable** ['sɪləbəl] *n* syllabe *f*
**syllabus** ['sɪləbəs] *n* programme *m*
**symbol** ['sɪmbəl] *n* symbole *m* ■ **symbolic** [-'bɒlɪk] *adj* symbolique ■ **symbolize** *vt* symboliser
**symmetrical** [sɪ'metrɪkəl] *adj* symétrique
**sympathetic** [sɪmpə'θetɪk] *adj (showing pity)* compatissant; *(understanding)* compréhensif, -ive; **s. to sb/sth** *(favourable)* bien disposé à l'égard de qn/qch
**sympathize** ['sɪmpəθaɪz] *vi* **I s. with you** *(pity)* je suis désolé (pour vous); *(understanding)* je vous comprends

**sympathy** ['sɪmpəθɪ] *n (pity)* compassion *f*; *(understanding)* compréhension *f*; **to have s. for sb** éprouver de la compassion pour qn

**symphony** ['sɪmfənɪ] **1** (*pl* **-ies**) *n* symphonie *f* **2** *adj (orchestra, concert)* symphonique

**symptom** ['sɪmptəm] *n Med & Fig* symptôme *m*

**synagogue** ['sɪnəgɒg] *n* synagogue *f*

**synchronize** ['sɪŋkrənaɪz] *vt* synchroniser

**syndicate** ['sɪndɪkət] *n* syndicat *m*

**syndrome** ['sɪndrəʊm] *n Med & Fig* syndrome *m*

**synonym** ['sɪnənɪm] *n* synonyme *m*

■ **synonymous** [-'nɒnɪməs] *adj* synonyme (**with** de)

**synopsis** [sɪ'nɒpsɪs] (*pl* **-opses** [-ɒpsi:z]) *n* résumé *m*; *(of film)* synopsis *m*

**synthetic** [sɪn'θetɪk] *adj* synthétique

**syphon** ['saɪfən] *n & vt* = **siphon**

**syringe** [sə'rɪndʒ] *n* seringue *f*

**syrup** ['sɪrəp] *n* sirop *m*; *Br* **(golden) s.** mélasse *f* raffinée

**system** ['sɪstəm] *n (structure) & Comptr* système *m*; *(human body)* organisme *m*; *(method)* méthode *f*; **the digestive s.** l'appareil *m* digestif; *Comptr* **systems analyst** analyste *m* programmeur

**systematic** [sɪstə'mætɪk] *adj* systématique

# Tt

**T, t** [ti:] *n (letter)* T, t *m inv*
**ta** [tɑ:] *exclam Br Fam* merci!
**tab** [tæb] *n* (**a**) *(label)* étiquette *f* (**b**) *Am Fam (bill)* addition *f* (**c**) *(on computer, typewriter)* tabulateur *m*; **t. key** touche *f* de tabulation
**table[1]** ['teɪbəl] *n* (**a**) *(furniture)* table *f*; *Br* **to set** *or* **lay/clear the t.** mettre/débarrasser la table; **(sitting) at the t.** à table; **t. tennis** tennis *m* de table; **t. wine** vin *m* de table (**b**) *(list)* table *f*; **t. of contents** table *f* des matières ▪ **tablecloth** *n* nappe *f* ▪ **tablespoon** *n* ≃ cuillère *f* à soupe ▪ **tablespoonful** *n* ≃ cuillerée *f* à soupe
**table[2]** ['teɪbəl] *vt Br (motion)* présenter; *Am (postpone)* ajourner
**tablet** ['tæblɪt] *n (pill)* comprimé *m*
**tabloid** ['tæblɔɪd] *n (newspaper)* tabloïd *m*
**taboo** [tə'bu:] (*pl* **-oos**) *adj & n* tabou *(m)*
**tack** [tæk] **1** *n (nail)* clou *m*; *Am (thumbtack)* punaise *f* **2** *vt* **to t. (down)** clouer
**tackle** ['tækəl] **1** *n (gear)* matériel *m*; *(in rugby)* placage *m*; *(in football)* tacle *m* **2** *vt (task, problem)* s'attaquer à; *(subject)* aborder; *(rugby player)* plaquer; *(football player)* tacler
**tacky** ['tækɪ] (**-ier, -iest**) *adj (sticky)* collant; *Fam (shoddy)* minable, moche
**tact** [tækt] *n* tact *m* ▪ **tactful** *adj (remark)* diplomatique; **to be t.** *(of person)* avoir du tact ▪ **tactless** *adj (person, remark)* qui manque de tact
**tactic** ['tæktɪk] *n* **a t.** une tactique; **tactics** la tactique ▪ **tactical** *adj* tactique
**tag** [tæg] **1** *n (label)* étiquette *f* **2** *vi* **to t. along with sb** venir avec qn
**tail** [teɪl] **1** *n (of animal)* queue *f*; **tails, t. coat** queue-de-pie *f*; **the t. end** la fin (**of** de) **2** *vt Fam (follow)* filer **3** *vi* **to t. off** *(lessen)* diminuer ▪ **tailback** *n Br (of traffic)* bouchon *m* ▪ **taillight** *n Am (of vehicle)* feu *m* arrière *inv*
**tailor** ['teɪlə(r)] **1** *n (person)* tailleur *m* **2** *vt (garment)* faire; *Fig (adjust)* adapter (**to** à)
**tainted** ['teɪntɪd] *adj (air)* pollué; *(food)* gâté; *Fig (reputation, system)* souillé

---

**TAKE** [teɪk] (*pt* **took**, *pp* **taken**) *vt* prendre; *(bring)* amener (**to** à); *(by car)* conduire (**to** à); *(escort)* accompagner (**to** à); *(lead away)* emmener (**to** à); *(exam)* passer; *(credit card)* accepter; *(contain)* avoir une capacité de; *(tolerate)* supporter; *Math (subtract)* soustraire (**from** de); **to t. sth to sb** apporter qch à qn; **to t. sth with one** emporter qch; **it takes an army/courage** il faut une armée/du courage (**to do** pour faire); **I took an hour to do it** j'ai mis une heure à le faire; **I t. it that...** je présume que... ▪ **takeaway** *Br* **1** *adj (meal)* à emporter **2** *n (shop)* restaurant *m* qui fait des plats à emporter; *(meal)* plat *m* à emporter ▪ **takeoff** *n (of plane)* décollage *m* ▪ **take-out** *adj & n Am* = **takeaway** ▪ **takeover** *n (of company)* rachat *m*
▸ **take after** *vt insep* **to t. after sb** ressembler à qn
▸ **take along** *vt sep (object)* emporter; *(person)* emmener

▸ **take apart** *vt sep (machine)* démonter

▸ **take away** *vt sep (thing)* emporter; *(person)* emmener; *(remove)* enlever (**from** à); *Math (subtract)* soustraire (**from** de)

▸ **take back** *vt sep* reprendre; *(return)* rapporter; *(statement)* retirer; *(accompany)* ramener (**to** à)

▸ **take down** *vt sep (object)* descendre; *(notes)* prendre

▸ **take in** *vt sep (chair, car)* rentrer; *(skirt)* reprendre; *(include)* inclure; *(understand)* saisir; *Fam (deceive)* rouler

▸ **take off 1** *vt sep (remove)* enlever; *(lead away)* emmener; *(mimic)* imiter; *Math (deduct)* déduire (**from** de) **2** *vi (of aircraft)* décoller

▸ **take on** *vt sep (work, staff, passenger, shape)* prendre

▸ **take out** *vt sep (from pocket)* sortir; *(tooth)* arracher; *(insurance policy, patent)* prendre; *Fam* **to t. it out on sb** passer sa colère sur qn

▸ **take over 1** *vt sep (become responsible for)* reprendre; *(buy out)* racheter; *(overrun)* envahir; **to t. over sb's job** remplacer qn **2** *vi (relieve)* prendre la relève (**from** de); *(succeed)* prendre la succession (**from** de)

▸ **take round** *vt sep (bring)* apporter (**to** à); *(distribute)* distribuer; *(visitor)* faire visiter

▸ **take to** *vt insep* **to t. to doing sth** se mettre à faire qch; **I didn't t. to him/it** il/ça ne m'a pas plu

▸ **take up 1** *vt sep (carry up)* monter; *(continue)* reprendre; *(space, time)* prendre; *(offer)* accepter; *(hobby)* se mettre à **2** *vi* **to t. up with sb** se lier avec qn

---

**taken** ['teɪkən] *adj (seat)* pris; *(impressed)* impressionné (**with** *or* **by** par); **to be t. ill** tomber malade

**takings** ['teɪkɪŋz] *n (money)* recette *f*

**talc** [tælk], **talcum powder** ['tælkəmpaʊdə(r)] *n* talc *m*

**tale** [teɪl] *n (story)* histoire *f*; *(lie)* salades *fpl*; **to tell tales** rapporter (**on sb** sur qn)

**talent** ['tælənt] *n* talent *m* ▪ **talented** *adj* talentueux, -euse

**talk** [tɔ:k] **1** *n (conversation)* conversation *f* (**about** à propos de); *(lecture)* exposé *m* (**on** sur); **talks** *(negotiations)* pourparlers *mpl*; **to have a t. with sb** parler avec qn

**2** *vt (nonsense)* dire; **to t. politics** parler politique; **to t. sb into doing/out of doing sth** persuader qn de faire/de ne pas faire qch; **to t. sth over** discuter (de) qch

**3** *vi* parler (**to/about** à/de); *(gossip)* jaser

**talkative** ['tɔ:kətɪv] *adj* bavard

**tall** [tɔ:l] (**-er, -est**) *adj (person)* grand; *(tree, house)* haut; *Fig* **a t. story** une histoire invraisemblable

**tally** ['tælɪ] (*pt & pp* **-ied**) *vi* correspondre (**with** à)

**tambourine** [tæmbə'ri:n] *n* tambourin *m*

**tame** [teɪm] **1** (**-er, -est**) *adj (animal)* apprivoisé; *Fig (book, play)* fade **2** *vt (animal)* apprivoiser

**tamper** ['tæmpə(r)] *vt insep* **to t. with** *(lock, car)* essayer de forcer; *(machine)* toucher à; *(documents)* trafiquer

**tampon** ['tæmpɒn] *n* tampon *m* (hygiénique)

**tan** [tæn] **1** *n (suntan)* bronzage *m* **2** *adj (colour)* marron clair *inv* **3** (*pt & pp* **-nn-**) *vt (skin)* hâler; *(leather)* tanner **4** *vi (of person, skin)* bronzer

**tangerine** [tændʒə'ri:n] *n* mandarine *f*

**tangible** ['tændʒəbəl] *adj* tangible

**tangle** ['tæŋgəl] *n* **to get into a t.** *(of rope)* s'enchevêtrer; *(of hair)* s'emmêler; *Fig (of person)* s'embrouiller ▪ **tangled** *adj* enchevêtré; *(hair)* emmêlé

**tango** ['tæŋgəʊ] (*pl* **-os**) *n* tango *m*

**tangy** ['tæŋɪ] (**-ier, -iest**) *adj* acidulé

**tank** [tæŋk] *n (container)* réservoir *m*; *(military vehicle)* tank *m*; **(fish) t.** aquarium *m*

**tanker** ['tæŋkə(r)] *n (lorry)* camion-citerne *m*; **(oil) t.** *(ship)* pétrolier *m*

**Tannoy**® ['tænɔɪ] *n Br* **over the T.** au haut-parleur

**tantalizing** ['tæntəlaɪzɪŋ] *adj* alléchant

**tantrum** ['tæntrəm] *n* caprice *m*

**tap¹** [tæp] **1** *n Br (for water)* robinet *m*; **t. water** eau *f* du robinet **2** *(pt & pp* **-pp-***) vt (resources)* puiser dans; *(phone)* placer sur écoute

**tap²** [tæp] **1** *n (blow)* petit coup *m*; **t. dancing** claquettes *fpl* **2** *(pt & pp* **-pp-***) vt (hit)* tapoter

**tape** [teɪp] **1** *n* (**a**) *(ribbon)* ruban *m*; **(sticky** *or* **adhesive) t.** ruban *m* adhésif; **t. measure** mètre *m* (à) ruban (**b**) *(for recording)* bande *f*; *(cassette)* cassette *f*; **t. deck** platine *f* cassette; **t. recorder** magnétophone *m*
**2** *vt* (**a**) *(stick)* scotcher (**b**) *(record)* enregistrer

**taper** ['teɪpə(r)] **1** *n (candle)* bougie *f* filée **2** *vi* s'effiler; *Fig* **to t. off** diminuer

**tapestry** ['tæpəstrɪ] *n* tapisserie *f*

**tar** [tɑ:(r)] *n* goudron *m*

**target** ['tɑ:gɪt] **1** *n* cible *f*; *(objective)* objectif *m* **2** *vt (campaign, product)* destiner (**at** à); *(age group)* viser

**tariff** ['tærɪf] *n (tax)* tarif *m* douanier; *Br (price list)* tarif *m*

**tarmac** ['tɑ:mæk] *n Br (on road)* macadam *m*; *(runway)* piste *f*

**tarnish** ['tɑ:nɪʃ] *vt* ternir

**tart** [tɑ:t] **1** (**-er, -est**) *adj (sour)* aigre **2** *n (pie) (large)* tarte *f*; *(small)* tartelette *f*

**tartan** ['tɑ:tən] **1** *n* tartan *m* **2** *adj (skirt, tie)* écossais

**task** [tɑ:sk] *n* tâche *f*

**tassel** ['tæsəl] *n* gland *m*

**taste** [teɪst] **1** *n* goût *m*; **in good/bad t.** de bon/mauvais goût; **to have a t. of sth** goûter à qch **2** *vt (detect flavour of)* sentir; *(sample)* goûter; *Fig (experience)* goûter à **3** *vi* **to t. of** *or* **like sth** avoir un goût de qch; **to t. good** être bon (*f* bonne)

**tasteful** ['teɪstfəl] *adj* de bon goût ▪ **tasteless** *adj (food)* insipide; *Fig (joke)* de mauvais goût ▪ **tasty** (**-ier, -iest**) *adj* savoureux, -euse

**tatters** ['tætəz] *npl* **in t.** *(clothes)* en lambeaux

**tattoo** [tæ'tu:] **1** *(pl* **-oos***) n (design)* tatouage *m* **2** *(pt & pp* **-ooed***) vt* tatouer

**tatty** ['tætɪ] (**-ier, -iest**) *adj Br Fam* minable

**taught** [tɔ:t] *pt & pp of* **teach**

**taunt** [tɔ:nt] **1** *n* raillerie *f* **2** *vt* railler

**taut** [tɔ:t] *adj* tendu

**tax¹** [tæks] **1** *n (on goods)* taxe *f*, impôt *m*; *(on income)* impôts *mpl*; *Br* **road t.** ≃ vignette *f* automobile
**2** *adj* fiscal; **t. collector** percepteur *m*; *Br* **(road) t. disc** ≃ vignette *f* automobile
**3** *vt (person)* imposer; *(goods)* taxer ▪ **taxable** *adj* imposable ▪ **taxation** *n (taxes)* impôts *mpl*; *(act)* imposition *f* ▪ **tax-free** *adj* exempt d'impôts ▪ **taxpayer** *n* contribuable *mf*

**tax²** [tæks] *vt (put under strain)* mettre à l'épreuve

**taxi** ['tæksɪ] *n* taxi *m*; *Br* **t. rank,** *Am* **t. stand** station *f* de taxis

**tea** [ti:] *n (plant, drink)* thé *m*; *Br (snack)* goûter *m*; *Br* **high t.** dîner *m (pris tôt dans la soirée)*; *Br* **t. break** ≃ pause-café *f*; **t. leaves** feuilles *fpl* de thé; **t. set** service *m* à thé; *Br* **t. towel** torchon *m* ▪ **teabag** *n* sachet *m* de thé ▪ **teacup** *n* tasse *f* à thé ▪ **teapot** *n* théière *f* ▪ **tearoom** *n* salon *m* de thé ▪ **teaspoon** *n* petite cuillère *f* ▪ **teaspoonful** *n* cuillerée *f* à café ▪ **teatime** *n* l'heure *f* du thé

**teach** [ti:tʃ] **1** *(pt & pp* **taught***) vt* apprendre (**sb sth** qch à qn; **that** que); *(in school, at university)* enseigner (**sb sth** qch à qn); **to t. sb (how) to do sth** apprendre à qn à faire qch **2** *vi* enseigner ▪ **teaching 1** *n* enseignement *m* **2** *adj (staff)* enseignant; *(method, material)* pédagogique

**teacher** ['ti:tʃə(r)] *n* professeur *m*; *(in primary school)* instituteur, -trice *mf*

**team** [ti:m] **1** *n* équipe *f*; *(of horses,*

*oxen)* attelage *m*; **t. mate** coéquipier, -ère *mf* **2** *vi* **to t. up** faire équipe (**with sb** avec qn) ▪ **teamwork** *n* travail *m* d'équipe

**tear¹** [teə(r)] **1** *n* déchirure *f* **2** (*pt* **tore,** *pp* **torn**) *vt (rip)* déchirer; *(snatch)* arracher (**from** à); **to t. off** *or* **out** arracher; **to t. up** déchirer **3** *vi* **to t. along/past** aller/passer à toute vitesse

**tear²** [tɪə(r)] *n* larme *f*; **in tears** en larmes

**tease** [ti:z] **1** *n (person)* taquin, -e *mf* **2** *vt* taquiner

**technical** ['teknɪkəl] *adj* technique

**technician** ['teknɪʃən] *n* technicien, -enne *mf*

**technique** [tek'ni:k] *n* technique *f*

**technology** [tek'nɒlədʒɪ] (*pl* **-ies**) *n* technologie *f* ▪ **technological** [-nə'lɒdʒɪkəl] *adj* technologique

**tedious** ['ti:dɪəs] *adj* fastidieux, -euse

**teem** [ti:m] *vi (swarm)* grouiller (**with** de); **to t. (with rain)** pleuvoir à torrents

**teenage** ['ti:neɪdʒ] *adj (boy, girl, behaviour)* adolescent; *(fashion, magazine)* pour adolescents ▪ **teenager** *n* adolescent, -e *mf* ▪ **teens** *npl* **to be in one's t.** être adolescent

**tee-shirt** ['ti:ʃɜ:t] *n* tee-shirt *m*

**teeth** [ti:θ] *pl of* **tooth**

**teethe** [ti:ð] *vi* faire ses dents

**teetotaller** [ti:'təʊtələ(r)] (*Am* **teetotaler**) *n* = personne qui ne boit jamais d'alcool

**telecommunications** [telɪkəmju:nɪ'keɪʃənz] *npl* télécommunications *fpl*

**telegram** ['telɪgræm] *n* télégramme *m*

**telegraph** ['telɪgrɑ:f] *adj* **t. pole/wire** poteau *m*/fil *m* télégraphique

**telephone** ['telɪfəʊn] **1** *n* téléphone *m*; **to be on the t.** *(speaking)* être au téléphone

**2** *adj (call, line, message)* téléphonique; *Br* **t. booth, t. box** cabine *f* téléphonique; **t. directory** annuaire *m* du téléphone; **t. number** numéro *m* de téléphone

**3** *vt (message)* téléphoner (**to** à); **to t. sb** téléphoner à qn

**4** *vi* téléphoner ▪ **telephonist** *n Br* téléphoniste *mf*

**telescope** ['telɪskəʊp] *n* télescope *m*

**teletext** ['telɪtekst] *n* télétexte *m*

**televise** ['telɪvaɪz] *vt* téléviser

**television** [telɪ'vɪʒən] **1** *n* télévision *f*; **on (the) t.** à la télévision **2** *adj (programme, screen)* de télévision; *(interview, report)* télévisé

**telex** ['teleks] **1** *n (service, message)* télex *m* **2** *vt (message)* télexer

**tell** [tel] **1** (*pt & pp* **told**) *vt* dire (**sb sth** qch à qn; **that** que); *(story)* raconter; *(distinguish)* distinguer (**from** de); **to t. sb to do sth** dire à qn de faire qch; **to t. the difference** voir la différence (**between** entre); **I could t. she was lying** je savais qu'elle mentait; *Fam* **to t. sb off** disputer qn

**2** *vi* dire; *(have an effect)* se faire sentir; **to t. of** *or* **about sb/sth** parler de qn/qch; **you can never t.** on ne sait jamais; *Fam* **to t. on sb** dénoncer qn

**telltale** ['telteɪl] **1** *adj* révélateur, -trice **2** *n* rapporteur, -euse *mf*

**telly** ['telɪ] *n Br Fam* télé *f*; **on the t.** à la télé

**temp** [temp] *Br Fam* **1** *n* intérimaire *mf* **2** *vi* faire de l'intérim

**temper** ['tempə(r)] **1** *n (mood, nature)* humeur *f*; *(bad mood)* mauvaise humeur *f*; **in a bad t.** de mauvaise humeur; **to lose one's t.** se mettre en colère **2** *vt (moderate)* tempérer

**temperament** ['tempərəmənt] *n* tempérament *m* ▪ **temperamental** [-'mentəl] *adj (person, machine)* capricieux, -euse

**temperate** ['tempərət] *adj (climate)* tempéré

**temperature** ['tempərətʃə(r)] *n* température *f*

**template** ['templət, -pleɪt] *n* gabarit *m*; *Comptr* modèle *m*

**temple¹** ['tempəl] *n (religious building)* temple *m*

**temple²** ['tempəl] *n Anat* tempe *f*

**tempo** ['tempəʊ] (*pl* **-os**) *n (of life, work)* rythme *m*; *Mus* tempo *m*

**temporary** [*Br* 'tempərərɪ, *Am* -erɪ] *adj* temporaire; *(secretary)* intérimaire ▪ **temporarily** [*Br* tempə'reərəlɪ, *Am* tempə'reərəlɪ] *adv* temporairement

**tempt** [tempt] *vt* tenter; **tempted to do sth** tenté de faire qch ▪ **temptation** *n* tentation *f* ▪ **tempting** *adj* tentant

**ten** [ten] *adj & n* dix *(m)*

**tenable** ['tenəbəl] *adj (argument, position)* défendable

**tenacious** [tə'neɪʃəs] *adj* tenace

**tenant** ['tenənt] *n* locataire *mf* ▪ **tenancy** *n (lease)* location *f*; *(period)* occupation *f*

**tend[1]** [tend] *vi* **to t. to do sth** avoir tendance à faire qch; **to t. towards** incliner vers ▪ **tendency** (*pl* **-ies**) *n* tendance *f* (**to do** à faire)

**tend[2]** [tend] *vt (look after)* s'occuper de

**tender[1]** ['tendə(r)] *adj (soft, delicate, loving)* tendre; *(painful)* sensible

**tender[2]** ['tendə(r)] **1** *n* **to be legal t.** *(of money)* avoir cours **2** *vt (offer)* offrir

**tenement** ['tenəmənt] *n* immeuble *m*

**tenner** ['tenə(r)] *n Br Fam* billet *m* de 10 livres

**tennis** ['tenɪs] *n* tennis *m*; **t. court** court *m* de tennis

**tenor** ['tenə(r)] *n Mus* ténor *m*

**tenpin** ['tenpɪn] *adj Br* **t. bowling** bowling *m*

**tense[1]** [tens] **1** (**-er, -est**) *adj (person, muscle, situation)* tendu **2** *vt* tendre; *(muscle)* contracter **3** *vi* **to t. (up)** *(of person, face)* se crisper ▪ **tension** *n* tension *f*

**tense[2]** [tens] *n (in grammar)* temps *m*

**tent** [tent] *n* tente *f*; *Br* **t. peg** piquet *m* de tente; *Br* **t. pole,** *Am* **t. stake** mât *m* de tente

**tentative** ['tentətɪv] *adj (not definite)* provisoire; *(hesitant)* timide

**tenth** [tenθ] *adj & n* dixième *(mf)*; **a t.** *(fraction)* un dixième

**tenuous** ['tenjʊəs] *adj (link)* ténu

**tepid** ['tepɪd] *adj (liquid) & Fig* tiède

**term** [tɜːm] **1** *n (word)* terme *m*; *(period)* période *f*; *Br (of school or university year)* trimestre *m*; *Am (semester)* semestre *m*; **terms** *(conditions)* conditions *fpl*; *(of contract)* termes *mpl*; **to be on good/bad terms** être en bons/mauvais termes (**with sb** avec qn); **in terms of** *(speaking of)* sur le plan de; **to come to terms with sth** se résigner à qch; **in the long/short/medium t.** à long/court/moyen terme **2** *vt* appeler

**terminal** ['tɜːmɪnəl] **1** *n (electronic) & Comptr* terminal *m*; *(of battery)* borne *f*; **(air) t.** aérogare *f* **2** *adj (patient, illness)* en phase terminale

**terminate** ['tɜːmɪneɪt] **1** *vt* mettre fin à; *(contract)* résilier; *(pregnancy)* interrompre **2** *vi* se terminer

**terminus** ['tɜːmɪnəs] *n* terminus *m*

**terrace** ['terɪs] *n (next to house, on hill)* terrasse *f*; *Br (houses)* = rangée de maisons attenantes; *Br* **the terraces** *(at football ground)* les gradins *mpl* ▪ **terraced** *n Br* **t. house** = maison située dans une rangée d'habitations attenantes

**terrain** [tə'reɪn] *n Mil & Geol* terrain *m*

**terrestrial** [tə'restrɪəl] *adj* terrestre

**terrible** ['terəbəl] *adj* terrible ▪ **terribly** *adv Fam (extremely)* terriblement; *(badly)* affreusement mal

**terrier** ['terɪə(r)] *n (dog)* terrier *m*

**terrific** [tə'rɪfɪk] *adj Fam (excellent)* super *inv* ▪ **terrifically** *adv Fam (extremely)* terriblement; *(extremely well)* terriblement bien

**terrify** ['terɪfaɪ] (*pt & pp* **-ied**) *vt* terrifier; **to be terrified of sb/sth** avoir une peur bleue de qn/qch ▪ **terrifying** *adj* terrifiant

**territory** ['terɪtərɪ] (*pl* **-ies**) *n* territoire *m*

**terror** ['terə(r)] *n* terreur *f* ▪ **terrorism** *n* terrorisme *m* ▪ **terrorist** *n & adj* terroriste *(mf)* ▪ **terrorize** *vt* terroriser

**test** [test] **1** *n (trial)* essai *m*; *(of product)* test *m*; *Sch & Univ* interrogation *f*; *(by doctor)* examen *m*; *(of blood)* analyse *f*

**2** *adj* **t. drive** essai *m* sur route; **t. tube** éprouvette *f*; **t. tube baby** bébé-éprouvette *m*

**3** *vt (try)* essayer; *(product, machine)* tester; *(pupil)* interroger; *(of doctor)* examiner; *(blood)* analyser; *Fig (try out)* mettre à l'épreuve; **to t. sb for AIDS** faire subir à qn un test de dépistage du SIDA

**4** *vi* **to t. positive** *(for drugs)* être positif, -ive

**testament** ['testəmənt] *n (will)* testament *m*; *(tribute)* preuve *f*; *Rel* **the Old/New T.** l'Ancien/le Nouveau Testament

**testicle** ['testɪkəl] *n Anat* testicule *m*

**testify** ['testɪfaɪ] (*pt & pp* **-ied**) **1** *vt* **to t. that...** témoigner que... **2** *vi (in law)* témoigner (**against** contre); **to t. to sth** *(be proof of)* témoigner de qch ▪ **testimony** ['testɪmənɪ] (*pl* **-ies**) *n* témoignage *m*

**tetanus** ['tetənəs] *n Med* tétanos *m*

**tether** ['teðə(r)] *n* **at the end of one's t.** à bout

**text** [tekst] *n* texte *m*; **t. message** message *m* texte, mini-message *m* ▪ **textbook** *n* manuel *m*

**textile** ['tekstaɪl] *adj & n* textile *(m)*

**texture** ['tekstʃə(r)] *n (of fabric, cake)* texture *f*; *(of paper, wood)* grain *m*

**Thames** [temz] *n* **the (River) T.** la Tamise

**than** [ðən, *stressed* ðæn] *conj* que; **happier t. me** plus heureux que moi; **he has more/less t. you** il en a plus/moins que toi; **more t. six** plus de six

**thank** [θæŋk] *vt* remercier (**for sth** de qch; **for doing** d'avoir fait); **t. you** merci; **no, t. you** (non) merci; **t. God!, t. heavens!, t. goodness!** Dieu merci! ▪ **thanks** *npl* remerciements *mpl*; **(many) t.!** merci (beaucoup)!; **t. to** *(because of)* grâce à

**thankful** ['θæŋkfəl] *adj* reconnaissant (**for** de); **to be t. that...** être heureux, -euse que... *(+ subjunctive)* ▪ **thankless** *adj* ingrat

**Thanksgiving** [θæŋks'gɪvɪŋ] *n Am* **T. (Day)** = quatrième jeudi de novembre, commémorant la première action de grâce des colons anglais

**THAT** [ðət, *stressed* ðæt] **1** *conj (souvent omise)* que; **she said t. she would come** elle a dit qu'elle viendrait

**2** *relative pron*

On peut omettre le pronom relatif **that** sauf s'il est en position sujet.

*(subject)* qui; *(object)* que; *(with preposition)* lequel, laquelle, *pl* lesquel(-le)s; **the boy t. left** le garçon qui est parti; **the book t. I read** le livre que j'ai lu; **the house t. she told me about** la maison dont elle m'a parlé; **the day/morning t. she arrived** le jour/matin où elle est arrivée

**3** (*pl* **those**) *demonstrative adj* ce, cet *(before vowel or mute h)*, cette; *(opposed to 'this')* ce...-là (*f* cette...-là); **t. woman** cette femme(-là); **t. day** ce jour-là; **t. one** celui-là *m*, celle-là *f*

**4** (*pl* **those**) *demonstrative pron* cela, *Fam* ça; **give me t.** donne-moi ça; **t.'s right** c'est exact; **who's t.?** qui est-ce?; **t.'s the house** voilà la maison; **what do you mean by t.?** qu'entends-tu par là?; **t. is (to say)...** c'est-à-dire...

**5** *adv Fam (so)* si; **not t. good** pas si bon que ça; **it cost t. much** ça a coûté tant que ça

**thatched** [θætʃt] *adj (roof)* de chaume; **t. cottage** chaumière *f*

**thaw** [θɔː] **1** *n* dégel *m* **2** *vt (snow, ice)* faire fondre; **to t. (out)** *(food)* se décongeler **3** *vi* dégeler; *(of snow, ice)* fondre; *(of food)* décongeler

**the** [ðə, *before vowel* ðɪ, *stressed* ðiː] *definite article* le, l', la, *pl* les; **of t., from t.** du, de l', de la, *pl* des; **to t., at t.** au, à l', à la, *pl* aux; **Elizabeth t. Second** Élisabeth Deux

**theatre** ['θɪətə(r)] (*Am* **theater**) *n (place, art)* théâtre *m*; *Br* **(operating) t.** *(in hospital)* salle *f* d'opération ▪ **theatrical** [θɪ'ætrɪkəl] *adj also Fig* théâtral

**theft** [θeft] *n* vol *m*
**their** [ðeə(r)] *possessive adj* leur, *pl* leurs ▪ **theirs** *possessive pron* le leur, la leur, *pl* les leurs; **this book is t.** ce livre est à eux *ou* est le leur; **a friend of t.** un ami à eux
**them** [ðəm, *stressed* ðem] *pron* les; *(after prep, 'than', 'it is')* eux *mpl*, elles *fpl*; **(to) t.** *(indirect)* leur; **I see t.** je les vois; **I gave it (to) t.** je le leur ai donné; **ten of t.** dix d'entre eux/elles; **all of t. came** tous sont venus, toutes sont venues; **I like all of t.** je les aime tous/toutes
**theme** [θi:m] *n* thème *m*; **t. tune** *(of TV, radio programme)* indicatif *m*; **t. park** parc *m* à thème
**themselves** [ðəm'selvz, *stressed* ðem'selvz] *pron* eux-mêmes *mpl*, elles-mêmes *fpl*; *(reflexive)* se, s'; *(after prep)* eux *mpl*, elles *fpl*; **they cut t.** ils/elles se sont coupé(e)s
**then** [ðen] **1** *adv (at that time)* à cette époque-là, alors; *(just a moment ago)* à ce moment-là; *(next)* ensuite, puis; *(therefore)* donc, alors; **from t. on** dès lors; **before t.** avant cela; **until t.** jusque-là, jusqu'alors **2** *adj* **the t. mayor** le maire d'alors
**theory** ['θɪərɪ] (*pl* **-ies**) *n* théorie *f*; **in t.** en théorie ▪ **theoretical** *adj* théorique
**therapy** ['θerəpɪ] (*pl* **-ies**) *n* thérapeutique *f* ▪ **therapeutic** [-'pju:tɪk] *adj* thérapeutique
**there** [ðeə(r)] *adv* là; **(down/over) t.** là-bas; **on t.** là-dessus; **she'll be t.** elle y sera; **t. is, t. are** il y a; *(pointing)* voilà; **t. he is** le voilà; **that man t.** cet homme-là; **t. (you are)!** *(take this)* tenez! ▪ **thereabouts** *adv* dans les environs; *(in amount)* à peu près ▪ **thereby** *adv Formal* ainsi ▪ **therefore** *adv* donc
**thermometer** [θə'mɒmɪtə(r)] *n* thermomètre *m*
**Thermos**® ['θɜ:məs] (*pl* **-moses** [-məsəz]) *n* **T. (flask)** Thermos® *f*
**thermostat** ['θɜ:məstæt] *n* thermostat *m*
**these** [ði:z] (*sing* **this**) **1** *demonstrative adj* ces; *(opposed to 'those')* ces…-ci; **t. men** ces hommes(-ci); **t. ones** ceux-ci *mpl*, celles-ci *fpl* **2** *demonstrative pron* ceux-ci *mpl*, celles-ci *fpl*; **t. are my friends** ce sont mes amis
**thesis** ['θi:sɪs] (*pl* **theses** ['θi:si:z]) *n* thèse *f*
**they** [ðeɪ] *pron* (**a**) *(subject)* ils *mpl*, elles *fpl*; *(stressed)* eux *mpl*, elles *fpl*; **t. are doctors** ce sont des médecins (**b**) *(people in general)* on ▪ **they'd** = **they had, they would** ▪ **they'll** = **they will**
**thick** [θɪk] **1** (**-er, -est**) *adj* épais (*f* épaisse); *Fam (stupid)* lourd **2** *adv (spread)* en couche épaisse ▪ **thickly** *adv (spread)* en couche épaisse
**thicken** ['θɪkən] **1** *vt* épaissir **2** *vi (of fog)* s'épaissir; *(of cream, sauce)* épaissir ▪ **thickness** *n* épaisseur *f*
**thick-skinned** [θɪk'skɪnd] *adj (person)* peu susceptible
**thief** [θi:f] (*pl* **thieves**) *n* voleur, -euse *mf* ▪ **thieving 1** *adj* voleur, -euse **2** *n* vol *m*
**thigh** [θaɪ] *n* cuisse *f*
**thimble** ['θɪmbəl] *n* dé *m* à coudre
**thin** [θɪn] **1** (**thinner, thinnest**) *adj (person, slice, paper)* mince; *(soup)* peu épais (*f* peu épaisse); *(crowd, hair)* clairsemé
**2** *adv (spread)* en couche mince; *(cut)* en tranches minces
**3** (*pt & pp* **-nn-**) *vt* **to t. (down)** *(paint)* diluer
**4** *vi* **to t. out** *(of crowd, mist)* s'éclaircir ▪ **thinly** *adv (spread)* en couche mince; *(cut)* en tranches minces
**thing** [θɪŋ] *n* chose *f*; **things** *(belongings, clothes)* affaires *fpl*; **poor little t.!** pauvre petit!; **how are things?**, *Fam* **how's things?** comment ça va?; **for one t.... and for another t....** d'abord… et ensuite…
**think** [θɪŋk] **1** (*pt & pp* **thought**) *vt* penser (**that** que); **I t. so** je pense *ou* crois que oui; **what do you t. of him?** que penses-tu de lui?; **to t. out** *(plan,*

*method)* élaborer; *(reply)* réfléchir sérieusement à; **to t. sth over** réfléchir à qch; **to t. sth up** *(invent)* inventer qch

**2** *vi* penser (**about/of** à); **to t. (carefully)** réfléchir (**about/of** à); **to t. of doing sth** penser à faire qch; **to t. highly of sb** penser beaucoup de bien de qn

**3** *n Fam* **to have a t.** réfléchir (**about** à)

**third** [θɜːd] **1** *adj* troisième; **the T. World** le tiers-monde **2** *n* troisième *mf*; **a t.** *(fraction)* un tiers **3** *adv* **to come t.** *(in race)* se classer troisième ▪ **thirdly** *adv* troisièmement

**third-party** [θɜːd'pɑːtɪ] *adj* **t. insurance** assurance *f* au tiers

**third-rate** [θɜːd'reɪt] *adj* très inférieur

**thirst** [θɜːst] *n* soif *f* (**for** de) ▪ **thirsty (-ier, -iest)** *adj* **to be** *or* **feel t.** avoir soif; **to make sb t.** donner soif à qn

**thirteen** [θɜː'tiːn] *adj & n* treize *(m)* ▪ **thirteenth** *adj & n* treizième *(mf)*

**thirty** ['θɜːtɪ] *adj & n* trente *(m)* ▪ **thirtieth** *adj & n* trentième *(mf)*

**this** [ðɪs] **1** *(pl* **these**) *demonstrative adj* ce, cet *(before vowel or mute h)*, cette; *(opposed to 'that')* ce...-ci; **t. man** cet homme(-ci); **t. one** celui-ci *m*, celle-ci *f*

**2** *(pl* **these**) *demonstrative pron (subject)* ce, ceci; *(object)* ceci; **I prefer t.** je préfère celui-ci; **who's t.?** qui est-ce?; **t. is Paul** c'est Paul; *(pointing)* voici Paul

**3** *adv (so)* **t. high** *(pointing)* haut comme ceci; **t. far** *(until now)* jusqu'ici

**thistle** ['θɪsəl] *n* chardon *m*

**thorn** [θɔːn] *n* épine *f*

**thorough** ['θʌrə] *adj (search, cleaning, preparation)* minutieux, -euse; *(knowledge, examination)* approfondi ▪ **thoroughly** *adv (completely)* tout à fait; *(carefully)* avec minutie; *(know, clean, wash)* à fond

**thoroughfare** ['θʌrəfeə(r)] *n Br* **'no t.'** 'passage interdit'

**those** [ðəʊz] **1** *(sing* **that**) *demonstrative adj* ces; *(opposed to 'these')* ces...-là; **t. men** ces hommes(-là); **t. ones** ceux-là *mpl*, celles-là *fpl*

**2** *(sing* **that**) *demonstrative pron* ceux-là *mpl*, celles-là *fpl*; **t. are my friends** ce sont mes amis

**though** [ðəʊ] **1** *conj* bien que *(+ subjunctive)*; **(even) t.** même si; **as t.** comme si; **strange t. it may seem** si étrange que cela puisse paraître **2** *adv (however)* pourtant

**thought** [θɔːt] **1** *pt & pp of* **think 2** *n* pensée *f*; **(careful) t.** réflexion *f*; **to have second thoughts** changer d'avis; *Br* **on second thoughts,** *Am* **on second t.** à la réflexion

**thoughtful** ['θɔːtfəl] *adj (considerate, kind)* attentionné; *(pensive)* pensif, -ive

**thoughtless** ['θɔːtləs] *adj* irréfléchi

**thousand** ['θaʊzənd] *adj & n* mille *(m) inv*; **a t. pages** mille pages; **two t. pages** deux mille pages; **thousands of** des milliers de

**thrash** [θræʃ] **1** *vt* **to t. sb** donner une correction à qn; *(defeat)* écraser qn **2** *vi* **to t. around** *or* **about** *(struggle)* se débattre ▪ **thrashing** *n (beating)* correction *f*

**thread** [θred] **1** *n (yarn) & Fig* fil *m*; *(of screw)* filetage *m* **2** *vt (needle, beads)* enfiler

**threat** [θret] *n* menace *f* ▪ **threaten 1** *vt* menacer (**to do** de faire; **with sth** de qch) **2** *vi* menacer ▪ **threatening** *adj* menaçant

**three** [θriː] *adj & n* trois *(m)* ▪ **three-dimensional** *adj* à trois dimensions ▪ **threefold 1** *adj* triple **2** *adv* **to increase t.** tripler ▪ **three-piece** *adj Br* **t. suite** canapé *m* et deux fauteuils assortis ▪ **three-quarters 1** *n* **t. (of)** les trois quarts *mpl* (de) **2** *adv* **it's t. full** c'est aux trois quarts plein

**threshold** ['θreʃhəʊld] *n* seuil *m*

**threw** [θruː] *pt of* **throw**

**thrifty** ['θrɪftɪ] (**-ier, -iest**) *adj* économe

**thrill** [θrɪl] **1** *n* frisson *m*; **to get a t. out of doing sth** prendre plaisir à faire qch **2** *vt (delight)* réjouir; *(excite)* faire frissonner ▪ **thrilled** *adj* ravi (**with sth** de qch; **to do** de faire) ▪ **thriller** *n* thriller *m* ▪ **thrilling** *adj* passionnant

**thrive** [θraɪv] *vi (of business, person, plant)* prospérer; **to t. on sth** avoir besoin de qch pour s'épanouir ▪ **thriving** *adj (business)* prospère

**throat** [θrəʊt] *n* gorge *f*

**throb** [θrɒb] (*pt & pp* **-bb-**) *vi (of heart)* palpiter; **my head is throbbing** j'ai une douleur lancinante dans la tête

**throes** [θrəʊz] *npl* **in the t. of** au milieu de; *(illness, crisis)* en proie à; **in the t. of doing sth** en train de faire qch

**throne** [θrəʊn] *n* trône *m*

**throttle** ['θrɒtəl] **1** *n (accelerator)* manette *f* des gaz **2** *vt (strangle)* étrangler

**through** [θru:] **1** *prep (place)* à travers; *(by means of)* par; *(because of)* à cause de; **t. the window/door** par la fenêtre/porte; **t. ignorance** par ignorance; *Am* **Tuesday t. Saturday** de mardi à samedi

**2** *adv* à travers; **to go t.** *(of bullet, nail)* traverser; **to let sb t.** laisser passer qn; **to be t. with sb/sth** *(finished)* en avoir fini avec qn/qch; **t. to** *or* **till** jusqu'à; **I'll put you t. (to him)** *(on telephone)* je vous le passe

**3** *adj (train, ticket)* direct; *Br* **'no t. road'** *(no exit)* 'voie sans issue'

**throughout** [θru:'aʊt] **1** *prep* **t. the neighbourhood** dans tout le quartier; **t. the day** pendant toute la journée **2** *adv (everywhere)* partout; *(all the time)* tout le temps

**throw** [θrəʊ] **1** *n (in sport)* lancer *m*; *(of dice)* coup *m* **2** (*pt* **threw,** *pp* **thrown**) *vt* jeter (**to/at** à); *(javelin, discus)* lancer; *(image, shadow)* projeter; *(of horse)* désarçonner; *(party)* donner; *Fam (baffle)* déconcerter

▸ **throw away** *vt sep (discard)* jeter; *Fig (life, chance)* gâcher

▸ **throw back** *vt sep (ball)* renvoyer (**to** à); *(one's head)* rejeter en arrière

▸ **throw in** *vt sep Fam (include as extra)* donner en prime

▸ **throw out** *vt sep (unwanted object)* jeter; *(suggestion)* repousser; *(expel)* mettre à la porte

▸ **throw up** *vi Fam (vomit)* vomir

**thrown** [θrəʊn] *pp of* **throw**

**thrush** [θrʌʃ] *n (bird)* grive *f*

**thrust** [θrʌst] **1** *n (movement)* mouvement *m* en avant; *(of argument)* idée *f* principale **2** (*pt & pp* **thrust**) *vt* **to t. sth into sth** enfoncer qch dans qch; **to t. sb/sth aside** écarter qn/qch

**thud** [θʌd] *n* bruit *m* sourd

**thug** [θʌg] *n* voyou *m* (*pl* -ous)

**thumb** [θʌm] **1** *n* pouce *m* **2** *vt Fam* **to t. a lift** *or* **a ride** faire du stop **3** *vi* **to t. through a book** feuilleter un livre

**thump** [θʌmp] **1** *n (blow)* coup *m*; *(noise)* bruit *m* sourd **2** *vt (hit)* frapper; **to t. one's head** se cogner la tête (**on** contre) **3** *vi* frapper, cogner (**on** sur); *(of heart)* battre la chamade

**thunder** ['θʌndə(r)] **1** *n* tonnerre *m* **2** *vi* tonner; **to t. past** *(of train, truck)* passer dans un bruit de tonnerre ▪ **thunderstorm** *n* orage *m*

**Thursday** ['θɜ:zdeɪ] *n* jeudi *m*

**thus** [ðʌs] *adv* ainsi

**thyme** [taɪm] *n* thym *m*

**tic** [tɪk] *n* tic *m*

**tick** [tɪk] **1** *n (of clock)* tic-tac *m inv*; *(mark)* ≃ croix *f*; *Fam (moment)* instant *m* **2** *vt* **to t. sth (off)** *(on list)* cocher qch **3** *vi* faire tic-tac; *Br* **to t. over** *(of engine, factory)* tourner au ralenti ▪ **ticking** *n (of clock)* tic-tac *m inv*

**tickle** ['tɪkəl] *vt* chatouiller; *Fig (amuse)* amuser ▪ **ticklish** *adj (person)* chatouilleux, -euse

**ticket** ['tɪkɪt] *n* billet *m*; *(for bus, metro)* ticket *m*; *Fam (for parking, speeding)* contravention *f*; **(price) t.** étiquette *f*; **t. collector** contrôleur, -euse *mf*; **t. office** guichet *m*

**tidbit** ['tɪdbɪt] *n Am (food)* bon morceau *m*

**tide** [taɪd] **1** *n* marée *f* **2** *vt* **to t. sb over** dépanner qn

**tidy** ['taɪdɪ] **1** (**-ier, -iest**) *adj (place, toys)* bien rangé; *(clothes, hair)* soigné; *(person) (methodical)* ordonné; *(in appearance)* soigné **2** *vt* **to t. sth (up** *or* **away)** ranger qch; **to t. sth out** mettre de l'ordre dans qch; **to t. oneself up** s'arranger **3** *vi* **to t. up** ranger ▪ **tidily** *adv (put away)* soigneusement, avec soin

**tie** [taɪ] **1** *n (garment)* cravate *f*; *(link)* lien *m*; *(draw)* égalité *f*; *(drawn match)* match *m* nul **2** *vt (fasten)* attacher (**to** à); *(knot)* faire (**in** à); *(shoe)* lacer **3** *vi (draw)* être à égalité; *(at end of match)* faire match nul; *(in race)* être ex aequo

▸ **tie down** *vt sep* attacher

▸ **tie in** *vi (of facts)* concorder

▸ **tie up** *vt sep (animal)* attacher; *(parcel)* ficeler; *(money)* immobiliser; *Fig* **to be tied up** *(busy)* être occupé

**tier** [tɪə(r)] *n (of seats)* gradin *m*; *(of cake)* étage *m*

**tiger** ['taɪgə(r)] *n* tigre *m*

**tight** [taɪt] **1** (**-er, -est**) *adj (clothes, knot, race, bend)* serré; *(control)* strict; *Fam (mean)* radin **2** *adv (hold, shut)* bien; *(squeeze)* fort; **to sit t.** ne pas bouger ▪ **tight-fitting** *adj (garment)* ajusté ▪ **tightly** *adv (hold)* bien; *(squeeze)* fort ▪ **tightrope** *n* corde *f* raide

**tighten** ['taɪtən] *vt* **to t. (up)** *(bolt)* serrer; *(rope)* tendre; *Fig (security)* renforcer

**tights** [taɪts] *npl Br (garment)* collant *m*

**tile** [taɪl] **1** *n (on roof)* tuile *f*; *(on wall, floor)* carreau *m* **2** *vt (wall, floor)* carreler ▪ **tiled** *adj (roof)* de tuiles; *(wall, floor)* carrelé

**till**[1] [tɪl] *prep & conj* = **until**

**till**[2] [tɪl] *n Br (for money)* caisse *f* enregistreuse

**tilt** [tɪlt] **1** *n* inclinaison *f* **2** *vti* pencher

**timber** ['tɪmbə(r)] *n Br (wood)* bois *m* (de construction)

**time** [taɪm] **1** *n* temps *m*; *(period, moment)* moment *m*; *(age)* époque *f*; *(on clock)* heure *f*; *(occasion)* fois *f*; *Mus* mesure *f*; **in t., with t.** avec le temps; **it's t. to do sth** il est temps de faire qch; **some of the t.** *(not always)* une partie du temps; **most of the t.** la plupart du temps; **all (of) the t.** tout le temps; **in a year's t.** dans un an; **a long t.** longtemps; **a short t.** peu de temps; **to have a good** *or* **a nice t.** s'amuser (bien); **to have t. off** avoir du temps libre; **in no t. (at all)** en un rien de temps; **(just) in t.** *(arrive)* à temps (**for sth** pour qch; **to do** pour faire); **from t. to t.** de temps en temps; **what t. is it?** quelle heure est-il?; **the right** *or* **exact t.** l'heure *f* exacte; **on t.** à l'heure; **at the same t.** en même temps (**as** que); *(simultaneously)* à la fois; **for the t. being** pour le moment; **at the** *or* **that t.** à ce moment-là; **at times** parfois; **(the) next t. you come** la prochaine fois que tu viendras; **(the) last t.** la dernière fois; **one at a t.** un à un; **ten times ten** dix fois dix; **t. difference** décalage *m* horaire; **t. limit** délai *m*; **t. zone** fuseau *m* horaire

**2** *vt (sportsman, worker)* chronométrer; *(activity, programme)* minuter; *(choose the time of)* choisir le moment de; *(plan)* prévoir ▪ **time-consuming** *adj* qui prend du temps

**timely** ['taɪmlɪ] *adj* à propos

**timer** ['taɪmə(r)] *n (device)* minuteur *m*; *(sand-filled)* sablier *m*; *(built into appliance)* programmateur *m*; *(plugged into socket)* prise *f* programmable

**timetable** ['taɪmteɪbəl] *n* horaire *m*; *(in school)* emploi *m* du temps

**timid** ['tɪmɪd] *adj* timide

**timing** ['taɪmɪŋ] *n (of election)* moment *m* choisi; *(of musician)* sens *m* du rythme

**tin** [tɪn] *n (metal)* étain *m*; *Br (can)*

boîte *f*; **cake t.** moule *m* à gâteaux; **t. opener** ouvre-boîtes *m inv* ▪ **tinfoil** *n* papier *m* aluminium

**tinge** [tɪndʒ] *n* pointe *f* ▪ **tinged** *adj* **t. with sth** teinté de qch

**tingle** ['tɪŋgəl] *vi* picoter

**tinker** ['tɪŋkə(r)] *vi* **to t. (about** *or* **around) with sth** bricoler qch

**tinkle** ['tɪŋkəl] *vi* tinter

**tinned** [tɪnd] *adj Br* **t. pears/salmon** poires *fpl*/saumon *m* en boîte; **t. food** conserves *fpl*

**tinsel** ['tɪnsəl] *n* guirlandes *fpl* de Noël

**tint** [tɪnt] *n* teinte *f*; *(for hair)* rinçage *m* ▪ **tinted** *adj (paper, glass)* teinté

**tiny** ['taɪnɪ] (**-ier, -iest**) *adj* minuscule

**tip¹** [tɪp] *n (end)* bout *m*; *(pointed)* pointe *f*

**tip²** [tɪp] **1** *n Br (rubbish dump)* décharge *f* **2** (*pt & pp* **-pp-**) *vt (pour)* déverser; **to t. sth up** *or* **over** renverser qch; **to t. sth out** *(liquid, load)* déverser qch (**into** dans) **3** *vi* **to t. (up** *or* **over)** *(tilt)* se renverser; *(overturn)* basculer

**tip³** [tɪp] **1** *n (money)* pourboire *m*; *(advice)* conseil *m*; *(information)* tuyau *m* **2** (*pt & pp* **-pp-**) *vt (waiter)* donner un pourboire à; **to t. off** *(police)* prévenir

**tipsy** ['tɪpsɪ] (**-ier, -iest**) *adj (drunk)* éméché, gai

**tiptoe** ['tɪptəʊ] **1** *n* **on t.** sur la pointe des pieds **2** *vi* marcher sur la pointe des pieds; **to t. into/out of a room** entrer dans une pièce/sortir d'une pièce sur la pointe des pieds

**tire¹** ['taɪə(r)] **1** *vt* fatiguer; **to t. sb out** épuiser qn **2** *vi* se fatiguer ▪ **tired** *adj* fatigué; **to be t. of sth/doing sth** en avoir assez de qch/de faire qch ▪ **tiredness** *n* fatigue *f* ▪ **tireless** *adj* infatigable ▪ **tiresome** *adj* ennuyeux, -euse ▪ **tiring** *adj* fatigant

**tire²** ['taɪə(r)] *n Am* pneu *m* (*pl* pneus)

**tissue** ['tɪʃuː] *n (handkerchief)* mouchoir *m* en papier; *Biol* tissu *m*; **t. paper** papier *m* de soie

**titbit** ['tɪtbɪt] *n Br (food)* bon morceau *m*

**titillate** ['tɪtɪleɪt] *vt* exciter

**title** ['taɪtəl] **1** *n (name, claim, in sport)* titre *m*; **t. role** *(in film, play)* rôle-titre *m* **2** *vt* intituler

**titter** ['tɪtə(r)] *vi* rire bêtement

---

**TO** [tə, *stressed* tuː] **1** *prep* (**a**) *(towards)* à; *(until)* jusqu'à; **give it to him/her** donne-le-lui; **to go to town** aller en ville; **to go to France/Portugal** aller en France/au Portugal; **to go to the butcher's** aller chez le boucher; **the road to London** la route de Londres; **the train to Paris** le train pour Paris; **kind/cruel to sb** gentil/cruel envers qn; **to my surprise** à ma grande surprise; **it's ten (minutes) to one** il est une heure moins dix; **ten to one** *(proportion)* dix contre un; **one person to a room** une personne par chambre

(**b**) *(with infinitive)* **to say/jump** dire/sauter; **(in order) to do sth** pour faire qch; **she tried to** elle a essayé

(**c**) *(with adjective)* **I'd be happy to do it** je serais heureux de le faire; **it's easy to do** c'est facile à faire

**2** *adv* **to push the door to** fermer la porte; **to go** *or* **walk to and fro** aller et venir

---

**toad** [təʊd] *n* crapaud *m*

**toadstool** ['təʊdstuːl] *n* champignon *m* vénéneux

**toast¹** [təʊst] **1** *n (bread)* pain *m* grillé **2** *vt (bread)* faire griller ▪ **toaster** *n* grille-pain *m inv*

**toast²** [təʊst] **1** *n (drink)* toast *m* **2** *vt (person)* porter un toast à; *(success, event)* arroser

**tobacco** [tə'bækəʊ] (*pl* **-os**) *n* tabac *m*; *Am* **t. store** (bureau *m* de) tabac ▪ **tobacconist** [-kənɪst] *n* buraliste *mf*; *Br* **t.'s (shop)** (bureau *m* de) tabac *m*

**toboggan** [tə'bɒgən] *n* luge *f*

**today** [tə'deɪ] *adv* aujourd'hui

**toddler** ['tɒdlə(r)] *n* enfant *mf* (en bas âge)

**toe** [təʊ] **1** *n* orteil *m* **2** *vt* **to t. the line** bien se tenir

**toffee** ['tɒfɪ] *n Br* caramel *m* (dur); **t. apple** pomme *f* d'amour

**together** [tə'geðə(r)] *adv* ensemble; *(at the same time)* en même temps

**toil** [tɔɪl] **1** *n* labeur *m* **2** *vi* travailler dur

**toilet** ['tɔɪlɪt] *n Br (room)* toilettes *fpl*; *(bowl, seat)* cuvette *f* des toilettes; *Br* **to go to the t.** aller aux toilettes; **t. paper** papier *m* hygiénique; **t. roll** rouleau *m* de papier hygiénique; *(paper)* papier *m* hygiénique ■ **toiletries** *npl* articles *mpl* de toilette

**token** ['təʊkən] **1** *n (for vending machine)* jeton *m*; *(symbol)* signe *m*; *Br* **book t.** chèque-livre *m* **2** *adj* symbolique

**told** [təʊld] **1** *pt & pp of* **tell** **2** *adv* **all t.** *(taken together)* en tout

**tolerable** ['tɒlərəbəl] *adj (bearable)* tolérable; *(fairly good)* acceptable

**tolerant** ['tɒlərənt] *adj* tolérant (**of** à l'égard de) ■ **tolerance** *n* tolérance *f*

**tolerate** ['tɒləreɪt] *vt* tolérer

**toll** [təʊl] **1** *n* (**a**) *(fee)* péage *m*; **t. road/bridge** route *f*/pont *m* à péage (**b**) **the death t.** le nombre de morts; *Fig* **to take its t.** faire des dégâts **2** *vi (of bell)* sonner ■ **toll-free** *Am* **1** *adj* **t. number** ≃ numéro *m* vert **2** *adv (call)* gratuitement

**tomato** [*Br* tə'mɑːtəʊ, *Am* tə'meɪtəʊ] (*pl* **-oes**) *n* tomate *f*; **t. sauce** sauce *f* tomate

**tomb** [tuːm] *n* tombeau *m* ■ **tombstone** *n* pierre *f* tombale

**tomorrow** [tə'mɒrəʊ] *adv & n* demain *(m)*; **t. morning/evening** demain matin/soir; **the day after t.** après-demain

**ton** [tʌn] *n* tonne *f*; *Fam* **tons of** *(lots of)* des tonnes de

**tone** [təʊn] **1** *n* ton *m*; *(of telephone, radio)* tonalité *f*; *(of answering machine)* signal *m* sonore; *Br* **the engaged t.** *(on telephone)* la sonnerie 'occupé' **2** *vt* **to t. sth down** atténuer qch; **to t. up** *(muscles, skin)* tonifier

**tongs** [tɒŋz] *npl* pinces *fpl*; **sugar t.** pince *f* à sucre; **curling t.** fer *m* à friser

**tongue** [tʌŋ] *n (in mouth, language)* langue *f*

**tonic** ['tɒnɪk] *n (medicine)* fortifiant *m*; **t. (water)** Schweppes® *m*; **gin and t.** gin-tonic *m*

**tonight** [tə'naɪt] *adv & n (this evening)* ce soir *(m)*; *(during the night)* cette nuit *(f)*

**tonne** [tʌn] *n (metric)* tonne *f*

**tonsil** ['tɒnsəl] *n* amygdale *f* ■ **tonsillitis** [-'laɪtɪs] *n* **to have t.** avoir une angine

**too** [tuː] *adv* (**a**) *(excessively)* trop; **t. tired to play** trop fatigué pour jouer; **t. much, t. many** trop; **t. much salt** trop de sel; **t. many people** trop de gens; **one t. many** un de trop (**b**) *(also)* aussi; *(moreover)* en plus

**took** [tʊk] *pt of* **take**

**tool** [tuːl] *n* outil *m*; **t. bag, t. kit** trousse *f* à outils

**tooth** [tuːθ] (*pl* **teeth**) *n* dent *f*; **t. decay** carie *f* dentaire ■ **toothache** *n* mal *m* de dents; **to have t.** avoir mal aux dents ■ **toothbrush** *n* brosse *f* à dents ■ **toothpaste** *n* dentifrice *m*

**top**[1] [tɒp] **1** *n (of mountain, tower, tree)* sommet *m*; *(of wall, ladder, page)* haut *m*; *(of table, box, surface)* dessus *m*; *(of list)* tête *f*; *(of bottle, tube)* bouchon *m*; *(crown cap)* capsule *f*; *(of pen)* capuchon *m*; *(garment)* haut *m*; **(at the) t. of the class** le premier/la première de la classe; **on t.** dessus; *(in bus)* en haut; **on t. of** sur; *Fig (in addition to)* en plus de; **from t. to bottom** de fond en comble; *Fam* **over the t.** *(excessive)* exagéré

**2** *adj (drawer, shelf)* du haut; *(step, layer)* dernier, -ère; *(upper)* supérieur; *(in rank, exam)* premier, -ère; *(chief)* principal; *(best)* meilleur; **on the t. floor** au dernier étage; **at t. speed** à toute vitesse; **t. hat** haut-de-forme *m* ■ **top-secret** *adj* top secret *inv* ■ **topsy-turvy** *adj & adv* sens dessus dessous [sɑ̃dsydsu]

**top²** [tɒp] (*pt & pp* **-pp-**) *vt (exceed)* dépasser; *Br* **to t. up** *(glass)* remplir (de nouveau); **topped with cream** nappé de crème ▪ **topping** *n (of pizza)* garniture *f*

**top³** [tɒp] *n* **(spinning) t.** toupie *f*

**topic** ['tɒpɪk] *n* sujet *m* ▪ **topical** *adj* d'actualité

**topple** ['tɒpəl] *vi* **to t. (over)** tomber

**torch** [tɔːtʃ] *n Br (electric)* lampe *f* de poche; *(flame)* torche *f*

**tore** [tɔː(r)] *pt of* **tear¹**

**torment 1** ['tɔːment] *n* supplice *m* **2** [tɔː'ment] *vt* tourmenter

**torn** [tɔːn] *pp of* **tear¹**

**tornado** [tɔː'neɪdəʊ] (*pl* **-oes**) *n* tornade *f*

**torpedo** [tɔː'piːdəʊ] **1** (*pl* **-oes**) *n* torpille *f* **2** *vt* torpiller

**torrent** ['tɒrənt] *n* torrent *m* ▪ **torrential** [tɒ'renʃəl] *adj* **t. rain** pluie *f* torrentielle

**tortoise** ['tɔːtəs] *n* tortue *f*

**tortuous** ['tɔːtʃʊəs] *adj* tortueux, -euse

**torture** ['tɔːtʃə(r)] **1** *n* torture *f*; *Fig* **it's (sheer) t.!** quel supplice! **2** *vt* torturer

**Tory** ['tɔːrɪ] *Pol* **1** *n* tory *m* **2** *adj* tory *inv*

**toss** [tɒs] **1** *vt (throw)* lancer (**to** à); *(pancake)* faire sauter; **to t. sb (about)** *(of boat, vehicle)* ballotter qn; **to t. a coin** jouer à pile ou face **2** *vi* **to t. (about), to t. and turn** *(in bed)* se tourner et se retourner; **let's t. up, let's t. (up) for it** jouons-le à pile ou face

**tot** [tɒt] **1** *n* **(tiny) t.** tout-petit *m* **2** (*pt & pp* **-tt-**) *vt Fam* **to t. up** *(total)* additionner

**total** ['təʊtəl] **1** *adj* total; **the t. sales** le total des ventes **2** *n* total *m*; **in t.** au total **3** (*Br* **-ll-**, *Am* **-l-**) *vt (of sum)* s'élever à; **to t. (up)** *(find the total of)* totaliser; **that totals $9** ça fait 9 dollars en tout ▪ **totally** *adv* totalement

**totter** ['tɒtə(r)] *vi* chanceler

**touch** [tʌtʃ] **1** *n (contact)* contact *m*; *(sense)* toucher *m*; *(of painter)* touche *f*; **a t. of** *(small amount)* une pointe de; **to have a t. of flu** être un peu grippé; **to be/get in t. with sb** être/se mettre en contact avec qn

**2** *vt* toucher; *(interfere with, eat)* toucher à

**3** *vi (of lines, hands, ends)* se toucher; **don't t.!** ne touche pas! ▪ **touchdown** *n (of aircraft)* atterrissage *m*; *(in American football)* but *m* ▪ **touched** *adj (emotionally)* touché (**by** de) ▪ **touching** *adj (moving)* touchant ▪ **touchline** *n* ligne *f* de touche

▸ **touch down** *vi (of plane)* atterrir

▸ **touch on** *vt insep* aborder

▸ **touch up** *vt sep (photo)* retoucher

**touchy** ['tʌtʃɪ] (**-ier, -iest**) *adj (sensitive)* susceptible (**about** à propos de)

**tough** [tʌf] (**-er, -est**) *adj (strict, hard)* dur; *(sturdy)* solide ▪ **toughen** *vt (body, person)* endurcir

**toupee** ['tuːpeɪ] *n* postiche *m*

**tour** [tʊə(r)] **1** *n (journey)* voyage *m*; *(visit)* visite *f*; *(by artiste, team)* tournée *f*; *(on bicycle, on foot)* randonnée *f*; **to go on t.** *(of artiste, team)* être en tournée; **(package) t.** voyage *m* organisé; **t. guide** guide *mf*; **t. operator** voyagiste *m* **2** *vt* visiter; *(of artiste, team)* être en tournée en/dans

**tourism** ['tʊərɪzəm] *n* tourisme *m* ▪ **tourist 1** *n* touriste *mf* **2** *adj (region)* touristique; **t. office** syndicat *m* d'initiative

**tournament** ['tʊənəmənt] *n (in sport) & Hist* tournoi *m*

**tout** [taʊt] **1** *n* racoleur, -euse *mf* **2** *vi* **to t. for trade** racoler des clients

**tow** [təʊ] *vt* remorquer; **to t. a car away** *(of police)* mettre une voiture à la fourrière

**toward(s)** [tə'wɔːd(z)] *prep* vers; *(of feelings)* envers; **cruel t. sb** cruel envers qn

**towel** ['taʊəl] *n* serviette *f* (de toilette); **(kitchen) t.** *(paper)* essuie-tout *m inv*

**tower** ['taʊə(r)] **1** *n* tour *f*; *Br* **t. block** tour **2** *vi* **to t. over sb/sth** dominer qn/qch

**town** [taʊn] *n* ville *f*; **to go into t.** aller en ville; **t. centre** centre-ville *m*; *Br* **t.**

**council** conseil *m* municipal; *Br* **t. hall** mairie *f*; *Br* **t. planning** urbanisme *m*

**toxic** ['tɒksɪk] *adj* toxique

**toy** [tɔɪ] **1** *n* jouet *m*; **t. shop** magasin *m* de jouets **2** *adj (gun)* d'enfant; *(car, train)* miniature **3** *vi* **to t. with an idea** caresser une idée

**trace** [treɪs] **1** *n* trace *f*; **without t.** sans laisser de traces **2** *vt (diagram, picture)* tracer; *(person)* retrouver la trace de; **to t. sth back to...** faire remonter qch à... ▪ **tracing** *n (drawing)* calque *m*; **t. paper** papier-calque *m*

**track** [træk] **1** *n (mark)* trace *f*; *(trail)* piste *f*; *(path)* chemin *m*, piste *f*; *(for trains)* voie *f*; *(of record, CD, tape)* morceau *m*; *Am (racetrack)* champ *m* de courses; **to keep t. of sth** surveiller qch; **to lose t. of** *(friend)* perdre de vue; **to be on the right t.** être sur la bonne voie; **t. event** *(in athletics)* épreuve *f* sur piste; *Fig* **t. record** passé *m*

**2** *vt* **to t. (down)** *(find)* retrouver ▪ **tracksuit** *n* survêtement *m*

**tractor** ['træktə(r)] *n* tracteur *m*

**trade** [treɪd] **1** *n* commerce *m*; *(job)* métier *m*; *(exchange)* échange *m*

**2** *adj (fair, balance, route)* commercial; *(price)* de (demi-)gros; *(secret)* de fabrication; *(barrier)* douanier, -ère; *Br* **t. union** syndicat *m*

**3** *vt (exchange)* échanger (**for** contre); **to t. sth in** *(old article)* faire reprendre qch

**4** *vi* faire du commerce (**with** avec); **to t. in** *(sugar)* faire le commerce de ▪ **trademark** *n* marque *f* de fabrique ▪ **trader** *n Br (shopkeeper)* commerçant, -e *mf*; *(on Stock Exchange)* opérateur, -trice *mf*; *Br* **street t.** vendeur, -euse *mf* de rue ▪ **tradesman** *(pl* **-men**) *n Br* commerçant *m*

**trading** ['treɪdɪŋ] **1** *n* commerce *m* **2** *adj (port, debts, activity)* commercial

**tradition** [trə'dɪʃən] *n* tradition *f* ▪ **traditional** *adj* traditionnel, -elle

**traffic** ['træfɪk] **1** *n* (**a**) *(on road)* circulation *f*; *(air, sea, rail)* trafic *m*; *Am* **t. circle** rond-point *m*; **t. island** refuge *m* (pour piétons); **t. jam** embouteillage *m*; **t. lights** feux *mpl* (de signalisation); **t. warden** contractuel, -elle *mf* (**b**) *Pej (trade)* trafic *m* (**in** de) **2** *(pt & pp* **-ck-**) *vi* trafiquer (**in** de) ▪ **trafficker** *n Pej* trafiquant, -e *mf*

**tragedy** ['trædʒədɪ] *(pl* **-ies**) *n* tragédie *f* ▪ **tragic** *adj* tragique

**trail** [treɪl] **1** *n (of smoke, blood, powder)* traînée *f*; *(path)* piste *f*, sentier *m*

**2** *vt (drag)* traîner; *(follow)* suivre

**3** *vi (drag)* traîner; *(of plant)* ramper; *(move slowly)* se traîner; **to be trailing (behind)** *(in sporting contest)* être mené ▪ **trailer** *n* (**a**) *(for car)* remorque *f*; *Am (caravan)* caravane *f*; *Am (camper)* camping-car *m* (**b**) *(advertisement for film)* bande-annonce *f*

**train** [treɪn] **1** *n* (**a**) *(engine, transport)* train *m*; *(underground)* rame *f*; **t. set** *(toy)* petit train *m* (**b**) *(procession)* file *f*; *(of events)* suite *f*; *(of dress)* traîne *f*; **my t. of thought** le fil de ma pensée

**2** *vt (person)* former (**to do** à faire); *(sportsman)* entraîner; *(animal)* dresser (**to do** à faire); **to t. oneself to do sth** s'entraîner à faire qch; **to t. sth on sb/sth** *(aim)* braquer qch sur qn/qch

**3** *vi (of sportsman)* s'entraîner; **to t. as a nurse** faire une formation d'infirmière ▪ **trained** *adj (skilled)* qualifié; *(nurse, engineer)* diplômé ▪ **training** *n* formation *f*; *(in sport)* entraînement *m*; *(of animal)* dressage *m*; **to be in t.** *(of sportsman)* s'entraîner

**trainee** [treɪ'ni:] *n & adj* stagiaire *(mf)*

**trainer** ['treɪnə(r)] *n (of athlete, racehorse)* entraîneur *m*; *(of animals)* dresseur *m*; *Br* **trainers** *(shoes)* chaussures *fpl* de sport

**traipse** [treɪps] *vi Fam* **to t. around** *(tiredly)* traîner les pieds; *(wander)* se balader

**trait** [treɪt] *n* trait *m* (de caractère)

**traitor** ['treɪtə(r)] *n* traître *m*, traîtresse *f*

**tram** [træm] *n* tram(way) *m*

**tramp** [træmp] **1** *n Br (vagrant)* clochard, -e *mf* **2** *vi* marcher d'un pas lourd

**trample** ['træmpəl] *vti* **to t. sth (underfoot), to t. on sth** piétiner qch

**trampoline** [træmpə'li:n] *n* trampoline *m*

**trance** [trɑ:ns] *n* **to be in a t.** être en transe

**tranquillizer** ['træŋkwɪlaɪzə(r)] (*Am* **tranquilizer**) *n* tranquillisant *m*

**transaction** [træn'zækʃən] *n* opération *f*, transaction *f*

**transatlantic** [trænzət'læntɪk] *adj* transatlantique

**transcend** [træn'send] *vt* transcender

**transfer 1** ['trænsfɜ:(r)] *n* transfert *m* (**to** à); *(of political power)* passation *f*; *Br (picture, design)* décalcomanie *f*; **credit t.** virement *m* bancaire

**2** [træns'fɜ:(r)] (*pt & pp* **-rr-**) *vt* transférer (**to** à); *(political power)* faire passer (**to** à)

**3** [træns'fɜ:(r)] *vi* être transféré (**to** à)

**transform** [træns'fɔ:m] *vt* transformer (**into** en) ▪ **transformation** [-fə'meɪʃən] *n* transformation *f* ▪ **transformer** *n El* transformateur *m*

**transfusion** [træns'fju:ʒən] *n* **(blood) t.** transfusion *f* (sanguine)

**transit** ['trænzɪt] *n* **in t.** en transit

**transition** [træn'zɪʃən] *n* transition *f*

**transitional** [træn'zɪʃənəl] *adj* de transition

**transitive** ['trænsɪtɪv] *adj (verb)* transitif

**translate** [trænz'leɪt] *vt* traduire (**from** de; **into** en) ▪ **translation** *n* traduction *f* ▪ **translator** *n* traducteur, -trice *mf*

**transmit** [trænz'mɪt] **1** (*pt & pp* **-tt-**) *vt* transmettre **2** *vti (broadcast)* émettre ▪ **transmission** *n* transmission *f*; *(broadcast)* émission *f* ▪ **transmitter** *n (for radio, TV)* émetteur *m*

**transparent** [træn'spærənt] *adj* transparent

**transpire** [træn'spaɪə(r)] *vi Fam (happen)* arriver; **it transpired that...** il s'est avéré que...

**transplant 1** ['trænsplɑ:nt] *n (surgical)* greffe *f*, transplantation *f* **2** [træns'plɑ:nt] *vt* transplanter

**transport 1** ['trænspɔ:t] *n* transport *m* (**of** de); *Br* **t. café** routier *m (restaurant)* **2** [træn'spɔ:t] *vt* transporter

**transpose** [træn'spəʊz] *vt* transposer

**transvestite** [trænz'vestaɪt] *n* travesti *m*

**trap** [træp] **1** *n* piège *m* **2** (*pt & pp* **-pp-**) *vt* prendre au piège; **to t. one's finger** se coincer le doigt (**in** dans) ▪ **trapdoor** *n* trappe *f*

**trappings** ['træpɪŋz] *npl* signes *mpl* extérieurs

**trash** [træʃ] *n (nonsense)* bêtises *fpl*; *(junk)* bric-à-brac *m inv*; *Am (waste)* ordures *fpl*; *(riffraff)* racaille *f*; *Am* **t. can** poubelle *f* ▪ **trashy** (**-ier, -iest**) *adj Fam* à la noix

**trauma** ['trɔ:mə] *n* traumatisme *m* ▪ **traumatic** [-'mætɪk] *adj* traumatisant ▪ **traumatize** *vt* traumatiser

**travel** ['trævəl] **1** *n* voyage *m*; **t. agent** agent *m* de voyages; **t. insurance** assurance *f* voyage; **t. sickness** *(in car)* mal *m* de la route; *(in aircraft)* mal *m* de l'air

**2** (*Br* **-ll-**, *Am* **-l-**) *vt (country, distance, road)* parcourir

**3** *vi (of person)* voyager; *(of vehicle, light, sound)* se déplacer ▪ **travelling** (*Am* **traveling**) **1** *n* voyages *mpl* **2** *adj (bag, clothes)* de voyage; *(expenses)* de déplacement; *(musician, circus)* ambulant

**traveller** ['trævələ(r)] (*Am* **traveler**) *n* voyageur, -euse *mf*; **t.'s cheque** chèque *m* de voyage

**travesty** ['trævəstɪ] (*pl* **-ies**) *n* parodie *f*; **a t. of justice** un simulacre de justice

**tray** [treɪ] *n* plateau *m*; *(in office)* corbeille *f*; **baking t.** plaque *f* de four

**treacherous** ['tretʃərəs] *adj (road, conditions)* très dangereux, -euse; *(person, action)* traître ▪ **treachery** (*pl* **-ies**) *n* traîtrise *f*

**treacle** ['tri:kəl] *n Br* mélasse *f*

**tread** [tred] **1** *n (footstep)* pas *m*; *(step of stairs)* marche *f*; *(of tyre)* chape *f* **2** (*pt* **trod,** *pp* **trodden**) *vt* **to t. sth into a carpet** étaler qch sur un tapis (avec ses chaussures) **3** *vi (walk)* marcher (**on** sur)

**treason** ['tri:zən] *n* trahison *f*

**treasure** ['treʒə(r)] **1** *n* trésor *m*; **t. hunt** chasse *f* au trésor **2** *vt (value)* tenir beaucoup à ■ **treasurer** *n* trésorier, -ère *mf*

**treat** [tri:t] **1** *n (pleasure)* plaisir *m*; *(gift)* cadeau *m*; **it's my t.** c'est moi qui régale **2** *vt (person, illness, product)* traiter; **to t. sb to sth** offrir qch à qn

**treatment** ['tri:tmənt] *n* traitement *m*

**treaty** ['tri:tɪ] (*pl* **-ies**) *n (international)* traité *m*

**treble** ['trebəl] **1** *adj* triple **2** *n* le triple; **it's t. the price** c'est le triple du prix **3** *vti* tripler

**tree** [tri:] *n* arbre *m*; **t. trunk** tronc *m* d'arbre

**trek** [trek] **1** *n (long walk)* randonnée *f* **2** (*pt & pp* **-kk-**) *vi* faire de la randonnée

**tremble** ['trembəl] *vi* trembler (**with** de)

**tremendous** [trə'mendəs] *adj (huge)* énorme; *(dreadful)* terrible; *(wonderful)* formidable

**trench** [trentʃ] *n* tranchée *f*

**trend** [trend] *n* tendance *f* (**towards** à); *(fashion)* mode *f* ■ **trendy** (**-ier, -iest**) *adj Br Fam* branché

**trespass** ['trespəs] *vi* = s'introduire illégalement dans une propriété privée; **'no trespassing'** 'entrée interdite'

**trial** ['traɪəl] **1** *n (in law)* procès *m*; *(test)* essai *m*; *(ordeal)* épreuve *f*; **to go** *or* **be on t., to stand t.** passer en jugement; **by t. and error** par tâtonnements **2** *adj (period, flight, offer)* d'essai

**triangle** ['traɪæŋgəl] *n* triangle *m* ■ **triangular** [-'æŋgjʊlə(r)] *adj* triangulaire

**tribe** [traɪb] *n* tribu *f*

**tribunal** [traɪ'bju:nəl] *n* tribunal *m*

**tribute** ['trɪbju:t] *n* hommage *m*; **to pay t. to** rendre hommage à

**trick** [trɪk] **1** *n (joke, deception, of conjurer)* tour *m*; *(clever method)* astuce *f*; *(in card game)* pli *m*; **to play a t. on sb** jouer un tour à qn **2** *vt (deceive)* duper; **to t. sb into doing sth** amener qn à faire qch par la ruse ■ **trickery** *n* ruse *f*

**trickle** ['trɪkəl] **1** *n (of liquid)* filet *m* **2** *vi (of liquid)* couler goutte à goutte; *Fig* **to t. in** *(of letters, people)* arriver en petit nombre

**tricky** ['trɪkɪ] (**-ier, -iest**) *adj (problem)* délicat

**tricycle** ['traɪsɪkəl] *n* tricycle *m*

**trifle** ['traɪfəl] **1** *n (insignificant thing)* bagatelle *f*; *Br (dessert)* = dessert où alternent génoise, fruits en gelée et crème anglaise **2** *adv* **a t. wide** un tantinet trop large **3** *vi* **to t. with** plaisanter avec ■ **trifling** *adj* insignifiant

**trigger** ['trɪgə(r)] **1** *n (of gun)* détente *f* **2** *vt* **to t. sth (off)** déclencher qch

**trilogy** ['trɪlədʒɪ] (*pl* **-ies**) *n* trilogie *f*

**trim** [trɪm] **1** (**trimmer, trimmest**) *adj (neat)* soigné; *(slim)* svelte **2** *n* **to give sb's hair a t.** faire une coupe d'entretien à qn **3** (*pt & pp* **-mm-**) *vt* couper (un peu); **to t. sth with sth** orner qch de qch ■ **trimmings** *npl (on clothes)* garniture *f*; *(of meal)* accompagnements *mpl* traditionnels

**trinket** ['trɪŋkɪt] *n* babiole *f*

**trio** ['tri:əʊ] (*pl* **-os**) *n* trio *m*

**trip** [trɪp] **1** *n (journey)* voyage *m*; *(outing)* excursion *f* **2** (*pt & pp* **-pp-**) *vt* **to t. sb up** faire trébucher qn **3** *vi* **to t. (over** *or* **up)** trébucher; **to t. over sth** trébucher sur qch

**triple** ['trɪpəl] **1** *adj* triple **2** *vti* tripler ■ **triplets** *npl (children)* triplés, -es *mfpl*

**triplicate** ['trɪplɪkət] *n* **in t.** en trois exemplaires

**tripod** ['traɪpɒd] *n* trépied *m*

**triumph** ['traɪəmf] **1** *n* triomphe *m* (**over** sur) **2** *vi* triompher (**over** de) ■ **triumphant** [traɪ'ʌmfənt] *adj* triomphant; *(success, welcome, return)* triomphal

**trivial** ['trɪvɪəl] *adj (unimportant)* insignifiant; *(trite)* banal *(mpl* -als)

**trod** [trɒd] *pt of* **tread**

**trodden** ['trɒdən] *pp of* **tread**

**trolley** ['trɒlɪ] *(pl* **-eys***) n Br* chariot *m*; *Br* **(tea) t.** table *f* roulante; *Am* **t. (car)** tramway *m*

**trombone** [trɒm'bəʊn] *n* trombone *m*

**troop** [tru:p] **1** *n* bande *f*; *(of soldiers)* troupe *f*; **the troops** *(soldiers)* les troupes *fpl* **2** *vi* **to t. in/out** entrer/sortir en groupe

**trophy** ['trəʊfɪ] *(pl* **-ies***) n* trophée *m*

**tropics** ['trɒpɪks] *n* **in the tropics** sous les tropiques ▪ **tropical** *adj* tropical

**trot** [trɒt] **1** *n* trot *m*; *Fam* **on the t.** *(consecutively)* de suite **2** *(pt & pp* **-tt-***) vt Fam* **to t. sth out** débiter qch **3** *vi (of horse)* trotter

**trouble** ['trʌbəl] **1** *n (difficulty)* ennui *m*; *(inconvenience)* problème *m*; *(social unrest, illness)* trouble *m*; **to be in t.** avoir des ennuis; **to get into t.** s'attirer des ennuis; **to have t. doing sth** avoir du mal à faire qch; **to go to the t. of doing sth** se donner la peine de faire qch; **it's no t.** pas de problème
**2** *vt (inconvenience)* déranger; *(worry)* inquiéter

**troublemaker** ['trʌbəlmeɪkə(r)] *n (in school)* élément *m* perturbateur; *(political)* fauteur *m* de troubles

**troublesome** ['trʌbəlsəm] *adj* pénible

**trough** [trɒf] *n (for drinking)* abreuvoir *m*; *(for feeding)* auge *f*

**troupe** [tru:p] *n (of actors)* troupe *f*

**trousers** ['traʊzəz] *npl Br* pantalon *m*; **a pair of t., some t.** un pantalon; **short t.** culottes *fpl* courtes

**trout** [traʊt] *n inv* truite *f*

**trowel** ['traʊəl] *n (for cement or plaster)* truelle *f*; *(for plants)* déplantoir *m*

**truant** ['tru:ənt] *n* **to play t.** faire l'école buissonnière

**truce** [tru:s] *n Mil* trêve *f*

**truck** [trʌk] *n (lorry)* camion *m*; **t. driver** camionneur *m*; *Am* **t. stop** *(restaurant)* routier *m* ▪ **trucker** *n Am* camionneur *m*

**trudge** [trʌdʒ] *vi* marcher péniblement

**true** [tru:] (**-er, -est**) *adj* vrai; *(genuine)* véritable; *(accurate)* exact; *(faithful)* fidèle (**to** à) ▪ **truly** *adv* vraiment; **well and t.** bel et bien

**trump** [trʌmp] *n* atout *m*

**trumpet** ['trʌmpɪt] *n* trompette *f*

**truncheon** ['trʌntʃən] *n Br* matraque *f*

**trundle** ['trʌndəl] *vti* **to t. along** rouler bruyamment

**trunk** [trʌŋk] *n (of tree, body)* tronc *m*; *(of elephant)* trompe *f*; *(case)* malle *f*; *Am (of vehicle)* coffre *m*; **trunks** *(for swimming)* slip *m* de bain

**trust** [trʌst] **1** *n (faith)* confiance *f* (**in** en) **2** *vt (believe in)* faire confiance à; **to t. sb with sth, to t. sth to sb** confier qch à qn; **I t. that...** j'espère que... **3** *vi* **to t. in sb** faire confiance à qn ▪ **trusted** *adj (method)* éprouvé

**trustworthy** ['trʌstwɜ:ðɪ] *adj* digne de confiance

**truth** [tru:θ] *(pl* **-s** [tru:ðz]) *n* vérité *f*; **there's some t. in...** il y a du vrai dans... ▪ **truthful** *adj (story)* véridique; *(person)* sincère

**try** [traɪ] **1** *(pl* **-ies***) n (attempt, in rugby)* essai *m*; **to have a t. at doing sth** essayer de faire qch; **it's worth a t.** ça vaut la peine d'essayer
**2** *(pt & pp* **-ied***) vt (attempt, sample)* essayer; *(food, drink)* goûter à; *(in law court)* juger (**for** pour); **to t. doing** *or* **to do sth** essayer de faire qch
**3** *vi* essayer ▪ **trying** *adj* difficile

▸ **try on** *vt sep (clothes, shoes)* essayer

▸ **try out** *vt sep (car, method, recipe)* essayer; *(person)* mettre à l'essai

**T-shirt** ['ti:ʃɜ:t] *n* tee-shirt *m*

**tub** [tʌb] *n (basin)* baquet *m*; *(bath)* baignoire *f*; *Br (for ice cream)* pot *m*; *Br (for flower, bush)* bac *m*

**tuba** ['tju:bə] *n Mus* tuba *m*

**tube** [tju:b] *n* tube *m*; *(of tyre)* chambre *f* à air; *Br Fam* **the t.** *(underground railway)* le métro

**tuberculosis** [tju:bɜ:kjʊ'ləʊsɪs] *n Med* tuberculose *f*

**tuck** [tʌk] **1** *vt (put)* mettre; **to t. sth away** *(put)* ranger qch; *(hide)* cacher qch; **to t. in** *(shirt, blanket)* rentrer; *(child)* border **2** *vi Br Fam* **to t. in** *(start eating)* attaquer

**Tuesday** ['tju:zdeɪ] *n* mardi *m*

**tuft** [tʌft] *n* touffe *f*

**tug** [tʌg] **1** *n* **to give sth a t.** tirer sur qch **2** *(pt & pp* **-gg-***) vt (pull)* tirer sur **3** *vi* tirer (**at** *or* **on** sur)

**tuition** [tju:'ɪʃən] *n (lessons)* cours *mpl*; *(fee)* frais *mpl* de scolarité

**tulip** ['tju:lɪp] *n* tulipe *f*

**tumble** ['tʌmbəl] **1** *n (fall)* chute *f*; *Br* **t. dryer** *or* **drier** sèche-linge *m inv* **2** *vi (of person)* faire une chute; *Fig (of prices)* chuter

**tumbler** ['tʌmblə(r)] *n (glass)* verre *m* droit

**tummy** ['tʌmɪ] *n Fam* ventre *m*

**tumour** ['tju:mə(r)] (*Am* **tumor**) *n* tumeur *f*

**tuna** ['tju:nə] *n* **t. (fish)** thon *m*

**tune** [tju:n] **1** *n (melody)* air *m*; **in t.** *(instrument)* accordé; **out of t.** *(instrument)* désaccordé; **to be** *or* **sing in t./out of t.** chanter juste/faux; *Fig* **to be in t. with sb/sth** être en harmonie avec qn/qch

**2** *vt* **to t. (up)** *(instrument)* accorder; *(engine)* régler

**3** *vi* **to t. in** brancher son poste (**to** sur)

**tuner** ['tju:nə(r)] *n (on TV, radio)* tuner *m*

**tunic** ['tju:nɪk] *n* tunique *f*

**Tunisia** [tju:'nɪzɪə] *n* la Tunisie

**tunnel** ['tʌnəl] **1** *n* tunnel *m* **2** (*Br* **-ll-**, *Am* **-l-**) *vi* creuser un tunnel (**into** dans)

**turban** ['tɜ:bən] *n* turban *m*

**turbulence** ['tɜ:bjʊləns] *n* turbulence *f*

**turf** [tɜ:f] *n (grass)* gazon *m*

**Turkey** ['tɜ:kɪ] *n* la Turquie ▪ **Turk** *n* Turc *m*, Turque *f* ▪ **Turkish 1** *adj* turc (*f* turque); **T. delight** des loukoums *mpl* **2** *n (language)* turc *m*

**turkey** ['tɜ:kɪ] (*pl* **-eys**) *n (bird)* dinde *f*

**turmoil** ['tɜ:mɔɪl] *n* **to be in t.** *(of person)* être dans tous ses états; *(of country)* être en ébullition

**turn** [tɜ:n] **1** *n (of wheel, in game, queue)* tour *m*; *(in road)* tournant *m*; *(of events)* tournure *f*; *Br Fam (fit)* crise *f*; **to take turns** se relayer; **in t.** à tour de rôle; **it's your t. (to play)** c'est à toi (de jouer); **the t. of the century** le tournant du siècle; **t. of phrase** tournure de phrase

**2** *vt* tourner; *(mechanically)* faire tourner; *(mattress, pancake)* retourner; **to t. sb/sth into sb/sth** changer qn/qch en qn/qch; **to t. sth red/black** rougir/noircir qch; **to t. sth on sb** *(aim)* braquer qch sur qn; **she has turned twenty** elle a vingt ans passés

**3** *vi (of wheel, driver)* tourner; *(of person)* se retourner; **to t. red/black** rougir/noircir; **to t. nasty** *(of person)* devenir méchant; *(of situation)* mal tourner; **to t. to sb** se tourner vers qn; **to t. into sb/sth** devenir qn/qch; **to t. against sb** se retourner contre qn ▪ **turn-off** *n (on road)* sortie *f* ▪ **turnout** *n (people)* assistance *f*; *(at polls)* participation *f* ▪ **turnover** *n Com (sales)* chiffre *m* d'affaires; *(of stock)* rotation *f*; *(of staff)* renouvellement *m* ▪ **turnup** *n Br (on trousers)* revers *m*

▸**turn around** *vi (of person)* se retourner

▸**turn away 1** *vt sep (eyes)* détourner (**from** de); *(person)* refuser **2** *vi* se détourner

▸**turn back 1** *vt sep (sheets)* rabattre; *(clock)* retarder **2** *vi (return)* faire demi-tour

▸**turn down** *vt sep (gas, radio)* baisser; *(fold down)* rabattre; *(refuse)* rejeter

▸**turn in 1** *vt sep (person)* livrer à la police **2** *vi Fam (go to bed)* aller au pieu

▸**turn off 1** *vt sep (light, radio)* éteindre; *(tap)* fermer; *(machine)* arrêter; *Fam* **to t. sb off** dégoûter qn **2** *vi* *(leave road)* sortir

▸**turn on 1** *vt sep (light, radio)* allumer; *(tap)* ouvrir; *(machine)* mettre en marche; *Fam* **to t. sb on** *(sexually)* exciter qn **2** *vi* **to t. on sb** *(attack)* attaquer qn

▸**turn out 1** *vt sep (light)* éteindre; *(pocket, box)* vider; *(produce)* produire **2** *vi (appear, attend)* se déplacer; **it turns out that...** il s'avère que...; **she turned out to be...** elle s'est révélée être...

▸**turn over 1** *vt sep (page)* tourner **2** *vi (of person)* se retourner; *(of car)* faire un tonneau

▸**turn round 1** *vt sep (head)* tourner; *(object)* retourner; *(situation)* renverser **2** *vi (of person)* se retourner; *(in vehicle)* faire demi-tour

▸**turn up 1** *vt sep (radio, heat)* mettre plus fort; *(collar)* remonter **2** *vi (arrive)* arriver; *(be found)* être retrouvé

**turning** ['tɜ:nɪŋ] *n Br (street)* petite rue *f*; *(bend in road)* tournant *m*; *Fig* **t. point** tournant *m*

**turnip** ['tɜ:nɪp] *n* navet *m*

**turnpike** ['tɜ:npaɪk] *n Am* autoroute *f* à péage

**turnstile** ['tɜ:nstaɪl] *n* tourniquet *m*

**turntable** ['tɜ:nteɪbəl] *n* platine *f*

**turquoise** ['tɜ:kwɔɪz] *adj* turquoise *inv*

**turret** ['tʌrɪt] *n* tourelle *f*

**turtle** ['tɜ:təl] *n Br* tortue *f* de mer; *Am* tortue *f*

**tusk** [tʌsk] *n* défense *f (dent)*

**tussle** ['tʌsəl] *n* bagarre *f*

**tutor** ['tju:tə(r)] **1** *n* professeur *m* particulier; *(in British university)* directeur, -trice *mf* d'études **2** *vt* donner des cours particuliers à ▪ **tutorial** [-'tɔ:rɪəl] *n Univ* ≃ travaux *mpl* dirigés

**tuxedo** [tʌk'si:dəʊ] *(pl* **-os***)* *n Am* smoking *m*

**TV** [ti:'vi:] *n* télé *f*; **on TV** à la télé

**tweed** [twi:d] *n* tweed *m*; **t. jacket** veste *f* en tweed

**tweezers** ['twi:zəz] *npl* pince *f* à épiler

**twelve** [twelv] *adj & n* douze *(m)* ▪ **twelfth** *adj & n* douzième *(mf)*

**twenty** ['twentɪ] *adj & n* vingt *(m)* ▪ **twentieth** *adj & n* vingtième *(mf)*

**twice** [twaɪs] *adv* deux fois; **t. as heavy (as)** deux fois plus lourd (que); **t. a month, t. monthly** deux fois par mois

**twiddle** ['twɪdəl] *vti* **to t. (with) sth** tripoter qch; **to t. one's thumbs** se tourner les pouces

**twig¹** [twɪg] *n (of branch)* brindille *f*

**twig²** [twɪg] *(pt & pp* **-gg-***) vti Br Fam* piger

**twilight** ['twaɪlaɪt] *n* crépuscule *m*

**twin** [twɪn] **1** *n* jumeau *m*, jumelle *f*; **t. brother** frère *m* jumeau; **t. sister** sœur *f* jumelle; **t. beds** lits *mpl* jumeaux; **t. town** ville *f* jumelée **2** *(pt & pp* **-nn-***) vt (town)* jumeler

**twine** [twaɪn] **1** *n (string)* ficelle *f* **2** *vi (twist)* s'enrouler (**round** autour de)

**twinge** [twɪndʒ] *n* **a t. (of pain)** un élancement; **a t. of remorse** un peu de remords

**twinkle** ['twɪŋkəl] *vi (of star)* scintiller; *(of eye)* pétiller

**twirl** [twɜ:l] **1** *vt* faire tournoyer; *(moustache)* tortiller **2** *vi* tournoyer

**twist** [twɪst] **1** *n (action)* tour *m*; *(bend)* tortillement *m*; *Fig (in story)* tour *m* inattendu

**2** *vt (wire, arm)* tordre; *(roll)* enrouler (**round** autour de); **to t. one's ankle** se tordre la cheville; *Fig* **to t. sb's arm** forcer la main à qn; **to t. sth off** *(lid)* dévisser qch

**3** *vi (wind)* s'entortiller (**round sth** autour de qch); *(of road, river)* serpenter ▪ **twisted** *adj (person, mind, logic)* tordu

**twit** [twɪt] *n Br Fam* andouille *f*

**twitch** [twɪtʃ] **1** *n (nervous)* tic *m* **2** *vi (of person)* avoir un tic; *(of muscle)* se contracter nerveusement

**twitter** ['twɪtə(r)] *vi (of bird)* pépier

**two** [tu:] *adj & n* deux *(m)* ▪ **two-dimensional** *adj* à deux dimensions ▪ **two-faced** *adj Fig* hypocrite ▪ **two-piece** *adj (suit, swimsuit)* deux-pièces ▪ **two-seater** *n (car)* voiture *f* à deux places

**twofold** ['tu:fəʊld] **1** *adj* double **2** *adv* **to increase t.** doubler

**twosome** ['tu:səm] *n* couple *m*

**tycoon** [taɪ'ku:n] *n* magnat *m*

**type**[1] [taɪp] *n* (**a**) *(sort)* genre *m*, type *m* (**b**) *(print)* caractères *mpl*; **in large t.** en gros caractères

**type**[2] [taɪp] **1** *vti (write)* taper (à la machine) **2** *vt* **to t. sth in** *(on computer)* entrer qch au clavier; **to t. sth out** *(letter)* taper qch ▪ **typewriter** *n* machine *f* à écrire ▪ **typewritten** *adj* dactylographié ▪ **typing** *n* dactylographie *f*; **t. error** faute *f* de frappe ▪ **typist** *n* dactylo *mf*

**typhoid** ['taɪfɔɪd] *n Med* typhoïde *f*

**typhoon** [taɪ'fu:n] *n* typhon *m*

**typical** ['tɪpɪkəl] *adj* typique (**of** de)

**tyrant** ['taɪrənt] *n* tyran *m*

**tyre** ['taɪə(r)] *n Br* pneu *m* (*pl* pneus)

# Uu

**U, u** [juː] *n (letter)* U, u *m inv*
**ugh** [ʌχ] *exclam* berk!
**ugly** [ˈʌglɪ] (**-ier, -iest**) *adj* laid
**UK** [juːˈkeɪ] (*abbr* **United Kingdom**) *n* **the UK** le Royaume-Uni
**ulcer** [ˈʌlsə(r)] *n* ulcère *m*
**ulterior** [ʌlˈtɪərɪə(r)] *adj* **u. motive** arrière-pensée *f*
**ultimate** [ˈʌltɪmət] *adj (last)* final; *(supreme, best)* absolu ▪ **ultimately** *adv (finally)* finalement; *(basically)* en fin de compte
**ultimatum** [ʌltɪˈmeɪtəm] *n* ultimatum *m*
**ultra-** [ˈʌltrə] *pref* ultra-
**ultraviolet** [ʌltrəˈvaɪələt] *adj* ultraviolet, -ette
**umbrella** [ʌmˈbrelə] *n* parapluie *m*
**umpire** [ˈʌmpaɪə(r)] *n* arbitre *m*
**umpteen** [ʌmpˈtiːn] *adj Fam* **u. times** je ne sais combien de fois ▪ **umpteenth** *adj Fam* énième
**UN** [juːˈen] (*abbr* **United Nations**) *n* **the UN** les Nations *fpl* unies
**unable** [ʌnˈeɪbəl] *adj* **to be u. to do sth** être incapable de faire qch
**unabridged** [ʌnəˈbrɪdʒd] *adj* intégral
**unacceptable** [ʌnəkˈseptəbəl] *adj* inacceptable
**unaccompanied** [ʌnəˈkʌmpənɪd] *adj (person)* non accompagné; *(singing)* sans accompagnement
**unaccustomed** [ʌnəˈkʌstəmd] *adj* inaccoutumé; **to be u. to sth/to doing sth** ne pas être habitué à qch/à faire qch
**unaided** [ʌnˈeɪdɪd] *adv* sans aide
**unanimous** [juːˈnænɪməs] *adj* unanime ▪ **unanimously** *adv* à l'unanimité
**unappetizing** [ʌnˈæpɪtaɪzɪŋ] *adj* peu appétissant
**unarmed** [ʌnˈɑːmd] *adj* non armé
**unashamedly** [ʌnəˈʃeɪmədlɪ] *adv* sans aucune honte
**unassuming** [ʌnəˈsjuːmɪŋ] *adj* sans prétention
**unattached** [ʌnəˈtætʃt] *adj (without partner)* sans attaches
**unattainable** [ʌnəˈteɪnəbəl] *adj* inaccessible
**unattended** [ʌnəˈtendɪd] *adj* **to leave sb/sth u.** laisser qn/qch sans surveillance
**unattractive** [ʌnəˈtræktɪv] *adj* peu attrayant
**unauthorized** [ʌnˈɔːθəraɪzd] *adj* non autorisé
**unavailable** [ʌnəˈveɪləbəl] *adj* **to be u.** ne pas être disponible
**unavoidable** [ʌnəˈvɔɪdəbəl] *adj* inévitable
**unaware** [ʌnəˈweə(r)] *adj* **to be u. of sth** ignorer qch; **to be u. that...** ignorer que... ▪ **unawares** *adv* **to catch sb u.** prendre qn au dépourvu
**unbalanced** [ʌnˈbælənst] *adj (mind, person)* instable
**unbearable** [ʌnˈbeərəbəl] *adj* insupportable
**unbeatable** [ʌnˈbiːtəbəl] *adj* imbattable
**unbeaten** [ʌnˈbiːtən] *adj (player)* invaincu; *(record)* jamais battu
**unbelievable** [ʌnbɪˈliːvəbəl] *adj* incroyable

**unbias(s)ed** [ʌn'baɪəst] *adj* impartial

**unblock** [ʌn'blɒk] *vt (sink, pipe)* déboucher

**unbolt** [ʌn'bəʊlt] *vt (door)* déverrouiller

**unborn** [ʌn'bɔːn] *adj* **u. child** enfant *mf* à naître

**unbreakable** [ʌn'breɪkəbəl] *adj* incassable ▪ **unbroken** *adj (intact)* intact; *(continuous)* continu; *(record)* jamais battu

**unbutton** [ʌn'bʌtən] *vt* déboutonner

**uncalled-for** [ʌn'kɔːldfɔː(r)] *adj* déplacé

**uncanny** [ʌn'kænɪ] (**-ier, -iest**) *adj* étrange

**uncertain** [ʌn'sɜːtən] *adj* incertain; **to be u. about sth** ne pas être certain de qch; **it's u. whether** *or* **that...** il n'est pas certain que... *(+ subjunctive)* ▪ **uncertainty** (*pl* **-ies**) *n* incertitude *f*

**unchanged** [ʌn'tʃeɪndʒd] *adj* inchangé ▪ **unchanging** *adj* immuable

**unclaimed** [ʌn'kleɪmd] *adj (luggage)* non réclamé

**uncle** ['ʌŋkəl] *n* oncle *m*

**unclear** [ʌn'klɪə(r)] *adj* vague; *(result)* incertain; **it's u. whether...** on ne sait pas très bien si...

**uncomfortable** [ʌn'kʌmftəbəl] *adj* inconfortable; *(heat, experience)* désagréable; **to feel u.** *(physically)* ne pas être à l'aise; *(ill at ease)* être mal à l'aise

**uncommon** [ʌn'kɒmən] *adj* peu commun

**uncompromising** [ʌn'kɒmprəmaɪzɪŋ] *adj* intransigeant

**unconditional** [ʌnkən'dɪʃənəl] *adj* sans condition

**unconfirmed** [ʌnkən'fɜːmd] *adj* non confirmé

**unconnected** [ʌnkə'nektɪd] *adj* sans lien

**unconscious** [ʌn'kɒnʃəs] **1** *adj (person)* sans connaissance; *(desire)* inconscient; **to be u. of sth** ne pas avoir conscience de qch **2** *n* **the u.** l'inconscient *m* ▪ **unconsciously** *adv* inconsciemment

**uncontrollable** [ʌnkən'trəʊləbəl] *adj* incontrôlable

**unconventional** [ʌnkən'venʃənəl] *adj* non conformiste

**unconvinced** [ʌnkən'vɪnst] *adj* **to be** *or* **remain u.** ne pas être convaincu (**of** de) ▪ **unconvincing** *adj* peu convaincant

**uncooked** [ʌn'kʊkt] *adj* cru

**uncooperative** [ʌnkəʊ'ɒpərətɪv] *adj* peu coopératif, -ive

**uncouth** [ʌn'kuːθ] *adj* fruste

**uncover** [ʌn'kʌvə(r)] *vt* découvrir

**undaunted** [ʌn'dɔːntɪd] *adj* nullement impressionné

**undecided** [ʌndɪ'saɪdɪd] *adj (person)* indécis (**about** sur); **I'm u. whether to do it or not** je n'ai pas décidé si je le ferai ou non

**undeniable** [ʌndɪ'naɪəbəl] *adj* indéniable

**under** ['ʌndə(r)] **1** *prep* sous; *(less than)* moins de; **children u. nine** les enfants de moins de neuf ans; **u. it** dessous; **u. (the command of) sb** sous les ordres de qn; **u. the circumstances** dans ces circonstances; **to be u. discussion/repair** être en discussion/réparation; **to be u. way** *(in progress)* être en cours; *(on the way)* être en route; **to get u. way** *(of campaign)* démarrer

**2** *adv* au-dessous

**undercharge** [ʌndə'tʃɑːdʒ] *vt* **I undercharged him (for it)** je ne (le) lui ai pas fait payer assez

**underclothes** ['ʌndəkləʊðz] *npl* sous-vêtements *mpl*

**undercooked** [ʌndə'kʊkt] *adj* pas assez cuit

**undercover** ['ʌndəkʌvə(r)] *adj* secret, -ète

**undercut** [ʌndə'kʌt] (*pt & pp* **-cut,** *pres p* **-cutting**) *vt* vendre moins cher que

**underdeveloped** [ʌndədɪ'veləpt] *adj (country, region)* sous-développé

**underdog** ['ʌndədɒg] *n (politically, socially)* opprimé, -e *mf*; *(likely loser)* outsider *m*
**underdone** [ʌndə'dʌn] *adj (food)* pas assez cuit; *(steak)* saignant
**underestimate** [ʌndər'estɪmeɪt] *vt* sous-estimer
**underfoot** [ʌndə'fʊt] *adv* sous les pieds
**undergo** [ʌndə'gəʊ] (*pt* **-went,** *pp* **-gone**) *vt* subir; **to u. surgery** être opéré
**undergraduate** [ʌndə'grædʒʊət] *n* étudiant, -e *mf* de licence
**underground 1** ['ʌndəgraʊnd] *adj (subterranean)* souterrain **2** ['ʌndəgraʊnd] *n Br (railway)* métro *m* **3** [ʌndə'graʊnd] *adv* sous terre; *Fig* **to go u.** *(of fugitive)* passer dans la clandestinité
**undergrowth** ['ʌndəgrəʊθ] *n* broussailles *fpl*
**underhand** [ʌndə'hænd] *adj* sournois
**underline** [ʌndə'laɪn] *vt* souligner
**underlying** [ʌndə'laɪɪŋ] *adj* sous-jacent
**undermine** [ʌndə'maɪn] *vt (weaken)* saper
**underneath** [ʌndə'ni:θ] **1** *prep* sous **2** *adv* (en) dessous; **the book u.** le livre d'en dessous **3** *n* **the u. (of)** le dessous (de)
**underpaid** [ʌndə'peɪd] *adj* sous-payé
**underpants** ['ʌndəpænts] *npl (male underwear)* slip *m*
**underpass** ['ʌndəpɑ:s] *n (for pedestrians)* passage *m* souterrain; *(for vehicles)* passage *m* inférieur
**underprivileged** [ʌndə'prɪvɪlɪdʒd] *adj* défavorisé
**underrate** [ʌndə'reɪt] *vt* sous-estimer
**underside** ['ʌndəsaɪd] *n* **the u. (of)** le dessous (de)
**understaffed** [ʌndə'stɑ:ft] *adj* **to be u.** manquer de personnel
**understand** [ʌndə'stænd] (*pt & pp* **-stood**) *vti* comprendre; **I u. that...** je crois comprendre que... ▪ **understanding 1** *n (act, faculty)* compréhension *f*; *(agreement)* accord *m*, entente *f*; *(sympathy)* entente *f*; **on the u. that...** à condition que... *(+ subjunctive)* **2** *adj (person)* compréhensif, -ive ▪ **understood** *adj (agreed)* entendu; *(implied)* sous-entendu
**understandable** [ʌndə'stændəbəl] *adj* compréhensible
**understatement** ['ʌndəsteɪtmənt] *n* euphémisme *m*
**undertake** [ʌndə'teɪk] (*pt* **-took,** *pp* **-taken**) *vt (task)* entreprendre; **to u. to do sth** entreprendre de faire qch
**undertaker** ['ʌndəteɪkə(r)] *n* entrepreneur *m* de pompes funèbres
**undertaking** [ʌndə'teɪkɪŋ] *n (task)* entreprise *f*; *(promise)* promesse *f*
**undertone** ['ʌndətəʊn] *n* **in an u.** à mi-voix
**underwater** [ʌndə'wɔ:tə(r)] *adv* sous l'eau
**underwear** ['ʌndəweə(r)] *n* sous-vêtements *mpl*
**undesirable** [ʌndɪ'zaɪərəbəl] *adj & n* indésirable *(mf)*
**undignified** [ʌn'dɪgnɪfaɪd] *adj* indigne
**undisciplined** [ʌn'dɪsɪplɪnd] *adj* indiscipliné
**undiscovered** [ʌndɪ'skʌvəd] *adj* **to remain u.** *(of crime, body)* ne pas être découvert
**undisputed** [ʌndɪ'spju:tɪd] *adj* incontesté
**undistinguished** [ʌndɪ'stɪŋgwɪʃt] *adj* médiocre
**undo** [ʌn'du:] (*pt* **-did,** *pp* **-done**) *vt* défaire; *(bound person)* détacher; *(parcel)* ouvrir; *(mistake, damage)* réparer; *Comptr (command)* annuler ▪ **undoing** *n* ruine *f* ▪ **undone** *adj* **to come u.** *(of knot)* se défaire; **to leave sth u.** *(work)* ne pas faire qch
**undoubtedly** [ʌn'daʊtɪdlɪ] *adv* indubitablement
**undress** [ʌn'dres] **1** *vt* déshabiller; **to get undressed** se déshabiller **2** *vi* se déshabiller
**undrinkable** [ʌn'drɪnkəbəl] *adj* imbuvable

**undue** [ʌn'dju:] *adj* excessif, -ive ▪ **unduly** *adv* excessivement
**unearth** [ʌn'ɜ:θ] *vt (from ground)* déterrer; *Fig (discover)* mettre à jour
**unearthly** [ʌn'ɜ:θlɪ] *adj Fam* **at an u. hour** à une heure impossible
**uneasy** [ʌn'i:zɪ] *adj (person)* mal à l'aise; *(silence)* gêné
**uneconomic(al)** [ʌni:kə'nɒmɪk(əl)] *adj* peu économique
**uneducated** [ʌn'edjʊkeɪtɪd] *adj (person)* sans éducation
**unemployed** [ʌnɪm'plɔɪd] **1** *adj* au chômage **2** *npl* **the u.** les chômeurs *mpl* ▪ **unemployment** *n* chômage *m*; *Br* **u. benefit** allocation *f* chômage
**unenthusiastic** [ʌnɪnθju:zɪ'æstɪk] *adj* peu enthousiaste
**unenviable** [ʌn'envɪəbəl] *adj* peu enviable
**unequal** [ʌn'i:kwəl] *adj* inégal
**unequivocal** [ʌnɪ'kwɪvəkəl] *adj* sans équivoque
**uneven** [ʌn'i:vən] *adj* inégal
**uneventful** [ʌnɪ'ventfəl] *adj* sans histoires
**unexpected** [ʌnɪk'spektɪd] *adj* inattendu ▪ **unexpectedly** *adv (arrive)* à l'improviste; *(fail, succeed)* contre toute attente
**unexplained** [ʌnɪk'spleɪnd] *adj* inexpliqué
**unfailing** [ʌn'feɪlɪŋ] *adj (optimism, courage)* à toute épreuve
**unfair** [ʌn'feə(r)] *adj* injuste (**to sb** envers qn); *(competition)* déloyal ▪ **unfairly** *adv* injustement
**unfaithful** [ʌn'feɪθfəl] *adj* infidèle (**to** à)
**unfamiliar** [ʌnfə'mɪlɪə(r)] *adj* inconnu; **to be u. with sth** ne pas connaître qch
**unfashionable** [ʌn'fæʃənəbəl] *adj* démodé
**unfasten** [ʌn'fɑ:sən] *vt* défaire
**unfavourable** [ʌn'feɪvərəbəl] (*Am* **unfavorable**) *adj* défavorable
**unfinished** [ʌn'fɪnɪʃt] *adj* inachevé
**unfit** [ʌn'fɪt] *adj (unsuitable)* inapte; *(in bad shape)* pas en forme; **to be u. to do sth** être incapable de faire qch
**unflattering** [ʌn'flætərɪŋ] *adj* peu flatteur, -euse
**unfold** [ʌn'fəʊld] **1** *vt* déplier; *(wings)* déployer **2** *vi (of story)* se dérouler
**unforeseeable** [ʌnfɔ:'si:əbəl] *adj* imprévisible ▪ **unforeseen** *adj* imprévu
**unforgettable** [ʌnfə'getəbəl] *adj* inoubliable
**unforgivable** [ʌnfə'gɪvəbəl] *adj* impardonnable
**unfortunate** [ʌn'fɔ:tʃənət] *adj* malchanceux, -euse; *(event)* fâcheux, -euse; **you were u.** tu n'as pas eu de chance ▪ **unfortunately** *adv* malheureusement
**unfounded** [ʌn'faʊndɪd] *adj (rumour)* sans fondement
**unfriendly** [ʌn'frendlɪ] *adj* peu aimable (**to** avec)
**unfulfilled** [ʌnfʊl'fɪld] *adj (plan, dream)* non réalisé
**unfurnished** [ʌn'fɜ:nɪʃt] *adj* non meublé
**ungainly** [ʌn'geɪnlɪ] *adj (clumsy)* gauche
**ungrateful** [ʌn'greɪtfəl] *adj* ingrat
**unhappy** [ʌn'hæpɪ] (**-ier, -iest**) *adj (sad, unfortunate)* malheureux, -euse; *(not pleased)* mécontent; **to be u. about doing sth** ne pas vouloir faire qch
**unharmed** [ʌn'hɑ:md] *adj* indemne
**unhealthy** [ʌn'helθɪ] (**-ier, -iest**) *adj (person)* maladif, -ive; *(climate, place, job)* malsain
**unheard-of** [ʌn'hɜ:dɒv] *adj (unprecedented)* inouï
**unhelpful** [ʌn'helpfəl] *adj (person)* peu serviable; *(advice)* peu utile
**unhurt** [ʌn'hɜ:t] *adj* indemne
**unhygienic** [ʌnhaɪ'dʒi:nɪk] *adj* contraire à l'hygiène
**uniform** ['ju:nɪfɔ:m] **1** *n* uniforme *m* **2** *adj (regular)* uniforme; *(temperature)* constant
**unify** ['ju:nɪfaɪ] (*pt & pp* **-ied**) *vt* unifier

**unilateral** [juːnɪˈlætərəl] *adj* unilatéral

**unimaginable** [ʌnɪˈmædʒɪnəbəl] *adj* inimaginable ▪ **unimaginative** *adj (person, plan)* qui manque d'imagination

**unimportant** [ʌnɪmˈpɔːtənt] *adj* sans importance

**uninhabitable** [ʌnɪnˈhæbɪtəbəl] *adj* inhabitable ▪ **uninhabited** *adj* inhabité

**uninhibited** [ʌnɪnˈhɪbɪtɪd] *adj (person)* sans complexes

**uninjured** [ʌnˈɪndʒəd] *adj* indemne

**uninspiring** [ʌnɪnˈspaɪərɪŋ] *adj (subject)* pas très inspirant

**unintelligible** [ʌnɪnˈtelɪdʒəbəl] *adj* inintelligible

**unintentional** [ʌnɪnˈtenʃənəl] *adj* involontaire

**uninterested** [ʌnˈɪntrɪstɪd] *adj* indifférent (**in** à) ▪ **uninteresting** *adj* inintéressant

**uninterrupted** [ʌnɪntəˈrʌptɪd] *adj* ininterrompu

**uninvited** [ʌnɪnˈvaɪtɪd] *adv (arrive)* sans invitation ▪ **uninviting** *adj* peu attrayant

**union** [ˈjuːnɪən] **1** *n* union *f*; *(trade union)* syndicat *m* **2** *adj* syndical; **the U. Jack** = le drapeau britannique

**unique** [juːˈniːk] *adj* unique

**unisex** [ˈjuːnɪseks] *adj (clothes)* unisexe

**unison** [ˈjuːnɪsən] *n* **in u.** à l'unisson (**with** de)

**unit** [ˈjuːnɪt] *n* unité *f*; *(of furniture)* élément *m*; *(system)* bloc *m*; *(group, team)* groupe *m*; **psychiatric/heart u.** *(of hospital)* service *m* de psychiatrie/cardiologie

**unite** [juːˈnaɪt] **1** *vt* unir; *(country, party)* unifier; **the United Kingdom** le Royaume-Uni; **the United Nations** les Nations *fpl* unies; **the United States (of America)** les États-Unis *mpl* (d'Amérique) **2** *vi* s'unir

**unity** [ˈjuːnətɪ] *n (cohesion)* unité *f*; *Fig (harmony)* harmonie *f*

**universal** [juːnɪˈvɜːsəl] *adj* universel, -elle

**universe** [ˈjuːnɪvɜːs] *n* univers *m*

**university** [juːnɪˈvɜːsətɪ] **1** (*pl* **-ies**) *n* université *f*; **to go to u.** aller à l'université; *Br* **at u.** à l'université **2** *adj (teaching, town, restaurant)* universitaire; *(student, teacher)* d'université

**unjust** [ʌnˈdʒʌst] *adj* injuste

**unjustified** [ʌnˈdʒʌstɪfaɪd] *adj* injustifié

**unkind** [ʌnˈkaɪnd] *adj* pas gentil (*f* pas gentille) (**to sb** avec qn)

**unknowingly** [ʌnˈnəʊɪŋlɪ] *adv* inconsciemment

**unknown** [ʌnˈnəʊn] **1** *adj* inconnu **2** *n (person)* inconnu, -e *mf*; *Math & Fig* **u. (quantity)** inconnue *f*

**unlawful** [ʌnˈlɔːfəl] *adj* illégal

**unleaded** [ʌnˈledɪd] *adj* sans plomb

**unleash** [ʌnˈliːʃ] *vt (emotion)* susciter

**unless** [ʌnˈles] *conj* à moins que *(+ subjunctive)*; **u. she comes** à moins qu'elle ne vienne; **u. you work harder, you'll fail** à moins de travailler plus dur, vous échouerez

**unlike** [ʌnˈlaɪk] *prep* **to be u. sb/sth** ne pas être comme qn/qch; **u. her brother, she...** à la différence de son frère, elle...; **it's very u. him to...** ça ne lui ressemble pas du tout de...

**unlikely** [ʌnˈlaɪklɪ] *adj* improbable; *(unbelievable)* invraisemblable; **she's u. to win** il est peu probable qu'elle gagne

**unlimited** [ʌnˈlɪmɪtɪd] *adj* illimité

**unlisted** [ʌnˈlɪstɪd] *adj Am (phone number)* sur liste rouge

**unload** [ʌnˈləʊd] *vti* décharger

**unlock** [ʌnˈlɒk] *vt* ouvrir

**unlucky** [ʌnˈlʌkɪ] (**-ier, -iest**) *adj (person)* malchanceux, -euse; *(number, colour)* qui porte malheur ▪ **unluckily** *adv* malheureusement

**unmade** [ʌnˈmeɪd] *adj (bed)* défait

**unmanageable** [ʌnˈmænɪdʒəbəl] *adj (child)* difficile; *(hair)* difficile à coiffer

**unmarried** [ʌnˈmærɪd] *adj* non marié

**unmistakable** [ʌnmɪˈsteɪkəbəl] *adj*

*(obvious)* indubitable; *(face, voice)* caractéristique
**unmoved** [ʌn'mu:vd] *adj* **to be u. by sth** rester insensible à qch
**unnatural** [ʌn'nætʃərəl] *adj (abnormal)* anormal; *(affected)* affecté
**unnecessary** [ʌn'nesəsərɪ] *adj* inutile; *(superfluous)* superflu
**unnerve** [ʌn'nɜ:v] *vt* troubler
**unnoticed** [ʌn'nəʊtɪst] *adv* **to go u.** passer inaperçu
**unobtainable** [ʌnəb'teɪnəbəl] *adj* impossible à obtenir
**unoccupied** [ʌn'ɒkjʊpaɪd] *adj (house)* inoccupé; *(seat)* libre
**unofficial** [ʌnə'fɪʃəl] *adj* officieux, -euse; *(visit)* privé; *(strike)* sauvage
**unorthodox** [ʌn'ɔ:θədɒks] *adj* peu orthodoxe
**unpack** [ʌn'pæk] **1** *vt (suitcase)* défaire; *(contents)* déballer **2** *vi* défaire sa valise
**unpaid** [ʌn'peɪd] *adj (bill, sum)* impayé; *(work, worker)* bénévole; *(leave)* non payé
**unparalleled** [ʌn'pærəleld] *adj* sans égal
**unplanned** [ʌn'plænd] *adj* imprévu
**unpleasant** [ʌn'plezənt] *adj* désagréable (**to sb** avec qn)
**unplug** [ʌn'plʌg] (*pt & pp* **-gg-**) *vt (appliance)* débrancher
**unpopular** [ʌn'pɒpjʊlə(r)] *adj* impopulaire; **to be u. with sb** ne pas plaire à qn
**unprecedented** [ʌn'presɪdentɪd] *adj* sans précédent
**unpredictable** [ʌnprɪ'dɪktəbəl] *adj* imprévisible; *(weather)* indécis
**unprepared** [ʌnprɪ'peəd] *adj* **to be u. for sth** *(not expect)* ne pas s'attendre à qch
**unprofessional** [ʌnprə'feʃənəl] *adj (person, behaviour)* pas très professionnel, -elle
**unprovoked** [ʌnprə'vəʊkt] *adj* gratuit
**unpublished** [ʌn'pʌblɪʃt] *adj (text, writer)* inédit
**unqualified** [ʌn'kwɒlɪfaɪd] *adj (teacher)* non diplômé; *(support)* sans réserve; *(success)* parfait; **to be u. to do sth** ne pas être qualifié pour faire qch
**unquestionable** [ʌn'kwestʃənəbəl] *adj* incontestable
**unravel** [ʌn'rævəl] (*Br* **-ll-**, *Am* **-l-**) *vt (threads)* démêler; *Fig (mystery)* éclaircir
**unreal** [ʌn'rɪəl] *adj* irréel, -elle
**unrealistic** [ʌnrɪə'lɪstɪk] *adj* irréaliste
**unreasonable** [ʌn'ri:zənəbəl] *adj (person, attitude)* déraisonnable
**unrecognizable** [ʌn'rekəgnaɪzəbəl] *adj* méconnaissable
**unrelated** [ʌnrɪ'leɪtɪd] *adj (facts)* sans rapport (**to** avec); **we're u.** il n'y a aucun lien de parenté entre nous
**unrelenting** [ʌnrɪ'lentɪŋ] *adj* incessant; *(person)* tenace
**unreliable** [ʌnrɪ'laɪəbəl] *adj* peu fiable
**unremarkable** [ʌnrɪ'mɑ:kəbəl] *adj* quelconque
**unrepentant** [ʌnrɪ'pentənt] *adj* impénitent
**unreservedly** [ʌnrɪ'zɜ:vɪdlɪ] *adv* sans réserve
**unrest** [ʌn'rest] *n* agitation *f*, troubles *mpl*
**unrestricted** [ʌnrɪ'strɪktɪd] *adj* illimité
**unrewarding** [ʌnrɪ'wɔ:dɪŋ] *adj* ingrat; *(financially)* peu rémunérateur, -trice
**unrivalled** [ʌn'raɪvəld] (*Am* **unrivaled**) *adj* hors pair *inv*
**unroll** [ʌn'rəʊl] **1** *vt* dérouler **2** *vi* se dérouler
**unruly** [ʌn'ru:lɪ] (**-ier, -iest**) *adj* indiscipliné
**unsafe** [ʌn'seɪf] *adj (place, machine)* dangereux, -euse
**unsaid** [ʌn'sed] *adj* **to leave sth u.** passer qch sous silence
**unsatisfactory** [ʌnsætɪs'fæktərɪ] *adj* peu satisfaisant ▪ **unsatisfied** *adj* insatisfait; **u. with sb/sth** peu satisfait de qn/qch

**unscheduled** [*Br* ʌn'ʃedu:ld, *Am* ʌn'skedjʊld] *adj* imprévu

**unscrew** [ʌn'skru:] *vt* dévisser

**unscrupulous** [ʌn'skru:pjʊləs] *adj (person)* peu scrupuleux, -euse

**unseemly** [ʌn'si:mlɪ] *adj* inconvenant

**unseen** [ʌn'si:n] *adv* **to do sth u.** faire qch sans qu'on vous voie

**unselfish** [ʌn'selfɪʃ] *adj (person, motive)* désintéressé

**unsettle** [ʌn'setəl] *vt (person)* troubler ▪ **unsettled** *adj (weather, situation)* instable

**unshak(e)able** [ʌn'ʃeɪkəbəl] *adj* inébranlable

**unshaven** [ʌn'ʃeɪvən] *adj* pas rasé

**unsightly** [ʌn'saɪtlɪ] *adj* laid

**unskilled** [ʌn'skɪld] *adj* non qualifié

**unsociable** [ʌn'səʊʃəbəl] *adj* peu sociable

**unsolved** [ʌn'sɒlvd] *adj (mystery)* inexpliqué; *(crime)* dont l'auteur n'est pas connu

**unsophisticated** [ʌnsə'fɪstɪkeɪtɪd] *adj* simple

**unsound** [ʌn'saʊnd] *adj (construction)* peu solide; *(method)* peu sûr; *(decision)* peu judicieux, -euse

**unspeakable** [ʌn'spi:kəbəl] *adj* indescriptible

**unspecified** [ʌn'spesɪfaɪd] *adj* non spécifié

**unsporting** [ʌn'spɔ:tɪŋ] *adj* qui n'est pas fair-play

**unstable** [ʌn'steɪbəl] *adj* instable

**unsteady** [ʌn'stedɪ] *adj (hand, voice, step)* mal assuré; *(table, ladder)* bancal (*mpl* -als) ▪ **unsteadily** *adv (walk)* d'un pas mal assuré

**unstuck** [ʌn'stʌk] *adj* **to come u.** *(of stamp)* se décoller; *Br Fam (of person, plan)* se casser la figure

**unsuccessful** [ʌnsək'sesfəl] *adj (attempt)* infructueux, -euse; *(outcome, candidate)* malheureux, -euse; *(application)* non retenu; **to be u.** ne pas réussir (**in doing** à faire); *(of book, film, artist)* ne pas avoir de succès ▪ **unsuccessfully** *adv* en vain, sans succès

**unsuitable** [ʌn'su:təbəl] *adj* qui ne convient pas (**for** à); *(manners, clothes)* peu convenable; **to be u. for sth** ne pas convenir à qch ▪ **unsuited** *adj* **to be u. to sth** ne pas être fait pour qch; **they're u. (to each other)** ils ne sont pas compatibles

**unsupervised** [ʌn'su:pəvaɪzd] *adv (play)* sans surveillance

**unsure** [ʌn'ʃʊə(r)] *adj* incertain (**of** *or* **about** de)

**unsympathetic** [ʌnsɪmpə'θetɪk] *adj* peu compatissant (**to** à); **u. to a cause/request** insensible à une cause/requête

**untangle** [ʌn'tæŋgəl] *vt (rope, hair)* démêler

**unthinkable** [ʌn'θɪŋkəbəl] *adj* impensable, inconcevable

**untidy** [ʌn'taɪdɪ] (**-ier, -iest**) *adj (clothes, hair)* peu soigné; *(room)* en désordre; *(person)* désordonné

**untie** [ʌn'taɪ] *vt (person, hands)* détacher; *(knot, parcel)* défaire

**until** [ʌn'tɪl] **1** *prep* jusqu'à; **u. now** jusqu'à présent; **u. then** jusque-là; **not u. tomorrow** pas avant demain; **I didn't see her u. Monday** c'est seulement lundi que je l'ai vue

**2** *conj* jusqu'à ce que *(+ subjunctive)*; **u. she comes** jusqu'à ce qu'elle vienne; **do nothing u. I come** ne fais rien avant que j'arrive

**untimely** [ʌn'taɪmlɪ] *adj (remark, question)* inopportun; *(death)* prématuré

**untold** [ʌn'təʊld] *adj (wealth, quantity)* incalculable

**untoward** [ʌntə'wɔ:d] *adj* fâcheux, -euse

**untrue** [ʌn'tru:] *adj* faux (*f* fausse) ▪ **untruthful** *adj (person)* menteur, -euse; *(statement)* mensonger, -ère

**unusable** [ʌn'ju:zəbəl] *adj* inutilisable

**unused**[1] [ʌn'ju:zd] *adj (new)* neuf (*f* neuve); *(not in use)* inutilisé

**unused**[2] [ʌn'juːst] *adj* **u. to sth/to doing sth** peu habitué à qch/à faire qch
**unusual** [ʌn'juːʒʊəl] *adj (not common)* inhabituel, -elle; *(strange)* étrange ▪ **unusually** *adv* exceptionnellement
**unveil** [ʌn'veɪl] *vt* dévoiler
**unwanted** [ʌn'wɒntɪd] *adj* non désiré
**unwarranted** [ʌn'wɒrəntɪd] *adj* injustifié
**unwelcome** [ʌn'welkəm] *adj (news)* fâcheux, -euse; *(gift, visit)* inopportun; *(person)* importun
**unwell** [ʌn'wel] *adj* souffrant
**unwieldy** [ʌn'wiːldɪ] *adj (package)* encombrant; *(system)* lourd
**unwilling** [ʌn'wɪlɪŋ] *adj* **to be u. to do sth** être réticent à faire qch ▪ **unwillingly** *adv* à contrecœur
**unwind** [ʌn'waɪnd] *(pt & pp* **-wound***)* **1** *vt (thread)* dérouler **2** *vi* se dérouler; *Fam (relax)* décompresser
**unwise** [ʌn'waɪz] *adj* imprudent
**unwittingly** [ʌn'wɪtɪŋlɪ] *adv* involontairement
**unworthy** [ʌn'wɜːðɪ] *adj* indigne (**of** de)
**unwrap** [ʌn'ræp] *(pt & pp* **-pp-***)* *vt* déballer
**unwritten** [ʌn'rɪtən] *adj (agreement)* verbal
**unzip** [ʌn'zɪp] *(pt & pp* **-pp-***)* *vt* ouvrir (la fermeture Éclair® de)

**UP** [ʌp] **1** *adv* en haut; **to come/go up** monter; **to walk up and down** marcher de long en large; **up there** là-haut; **up above** au-dessus; **further** *or* **higher up** plus haut; **up to** *(as far as)* jusqu'à; **to be up to doing sth** *(capable of)* être de taille à faire qch; **to feel up to doing sth** *(well enough)* être assez bien pour faire qch; **it's up to you to do it** c'est à toi de le faire; **it's up to you** *(you decide)* c'est à toi de décider; **where are you up to?** *(in book)* où en es-tu?; *Fam* **what are you up to?** que fais-tu?; *Fam* **to be well up in** *(versed in)* s'y connaître en
**2** *prep* **up a hill** en haut d'une colline; **up a tree** dans un arbre; **up a ladder** sur une échelle; **to live up the street** habiter plus loin dans la rue
**3** *adj (out of bed)* levé; **we were up all night** nous sommes restés debout toute la nuit; **the two weeks were up** les deux semaines étaient terminées; *Fam* **what's up?** qu'est-ce qu'il y a?
**4** *npl* **ups and downs** des hauts et des bas *mpl*
**5** *(pt & pp* **-pp-***)* *vt Fam (price, offer)* augmenter ▪ **up-and-coming** *adj* qui monte ▪ **upbeat** *adj Fam* optimiste ▪ **upbringing** *n* éducation *f* ▪ **update** *vt* mettre à jour ▪ **upgrade** *vt (job)* revaloriser; *(person)* promouvoir; *Comptr (hardware)* augmenter la puissance de ▪ **uphill 1** [ʌp'hɪl] *adv* **to go u.** monter **2** ['ʌphɪl] *adj Fig (struggle, task)* pénible ▪ **uphold** *(pt & pp* **-held***)* *vt (decision)* maintenir ▪ **upkeep** *n* entretien *m* ▪ **up-market** *adj Br (car, product)* haut de gamme *inv*; *(area, place)* chic *inv* ▪ **upright 1** *adv (straight)* droit **2** *adj (vertical, honest)* droit ▪ **uprising** *n* insurrection *f* ▪ **uproot** *vt (plant, person)* déraciner ▪ **upside** *adv* **u. down** à l'envers; **to turn sth u. down** retourner qch; *Fig* mettre qch sens dessus dessous ▪ **upstairs 1** [ʌp'steəz] *adv* en haut; **to go u.** monter **2** ['ʌpsteəz] *adj (people, room)* du dessus ▪ **upstream** *adv* en amont ▪ **uptight** *adj Fam (tense)* crispé; *(inhibited)* coincé ▪ **up-to-date** *adj* moderne; *(information)* à jour; *(well-informed)* au courant (**on** de) ▪ **upturn** *n (improvement)* amélioration *f* (**in** de) ▪ **upward** *adj (movement)* ascendant; *(path)* qui monte; *(trend)* à la hausse ▪ **upwards** *adv* vers le haut; **from 5 euros u.** à partir de 5 euros; **u. of fifty** cinquante et plus

**upheaval** [ʌp'hiːvəl] *n* bouleversement *m*
**upholstery** [ʌp'həʊlstərɪ] *n (padding)* rembourrage *m*; *(covering)* revêtement *m*; *(in car)* sièges *mpl*
**upon** [ə'pɒn] *prep* sur

**upper** ['ʌpə(r)] **1** *adj* supérieur; **u. class** aristocratie *f*; **to have/get the u. hand** avoir/prendre le dessus **2** *n (of shoe)* empeigne *f* ▪ **upper-class** *adj* aristocratique ▪ **uppermost** *adj* le plus haut (*f* la plus haute)

**uproar** ['ʌprɔ:(r)] *n* tumulte *m*

**upset 1** [ʌp'set] (*pt & pp* **-set,** *pres p* **-setting**) *vt (knock over, spill)* renverser; *(person, plans, schedule)* bouleverser

**2** [ʌp'set] *adj (unhappy)* bouleversé (**about** par); **to have an u. stomach** avoir l'estomac dérangé

**3** ['ʌpset] *n (disturbance)* bouleversement *m*; *(surprise)* défaite *f*; **to have a stomach u.** avoir l'estomac dérangé ▪ **upsetting** *adj* bouleversant

**upshot** ['ʌpʃɒt] *n* résultat *m*

**urban** ['ɜ:bən] *adj* urbain

**urge** [ɜ:dʒ] **1** *n* forte envie *f*; **to have an u. to do sth** avoir très envie de faire qch **2** *vt* **to u. sb to do sth** presser qn de faire qch

**urgency** ['ɜ:dʒənsɪ] *n* urgence *f*; **it's a matter of u.** il y a urgence

**urgent** ['ɜ:dʒənt] *adj* urgent ▪ **urgently** *adv* d'urgence

**urine** ['jʊərɪn] *n* urine *f* ▪ **urinate** *vi* uriner

**urn** [ɜ:n] *n* urne *f*; *(for coffee or tea)* fontaine *f*

**US** [ju:'es] (*abbr* **United States**) *n* **the US** les USA *mpl*

**us** [əs, *stressed* ʌs] *pron* nous; **(to) us** *(indirect)* nous; **she saw us** elle nous a vus; **he gave it (to) us** il nous l'a donné

**USA** [ju:es'eɪ] (*abbr* **United States of America**) *n* **the U.** les USA *mpl*

**usage** ['ju:sɪdʒ] *n* usage *m*

**use 1** [ju:s] *n (utilization)* emploi *m*, usage *m*; *(ability, permission to use)* emploi *m* ; **to have the u. of sth** avoir l'usage de qch; **to make (good) u. of sth** faire (bon) usage de qch; **to be of u. to sb** être utile à qn; **in u.** en usage; **not in u., out of u.** hors d'usage; **it's no u. crying** ça ne sert à rien de pleurer; **what's the u. of worrying?** à quoi bon s'inquiéter?

**2** [ju:z] *vt (utilize)* utiliser, se servir de; *(force, diplomacy)* avoir recours à; *(electricity)* consommer; **it's used to do** *or* **for doing sth** ça sert à faire qch; **it's used as...** ça sert de...; **to u. sth up** *(food, fuel)* finir; *(money)* dépenser ▪ **use-by** ['ju:zbaɪ] *adj* **u. date** date *f* limite de consommation

**used 1** *adj* (**a**) [ju:zd] *(second-hand)* d'occasion; *(stamp)* oblitéré (**b**) [ju:st] **to be u. to sth/to doing sth** être habitué à qch/à faire qch; **to get u. to sb/sth** s'habituer à qn/qch

**2** [ju:st] *v aux* **I u. to sing** avant, je chantais; **she u. to jog every Sunday** elle faisait du jogging tous les dimanches

**useful** ['ju:sfəl] *adj* utile (**to** à); **to come in u.** être utile; **to make oneself u.** se rendre utile ▪ **useless** *adj* inutile; *(person)* nul (*f* nulle) (**at** en)

**user** ['ju:zə(r)] *n (of train, telephone)* usager *m*; *(of road, machine)* utilisateur, -trice *mf* ▪ **user-friendly** *adj* convivial

**usher** ['ʌʃə(r)] **1** *n (in church, theatre)* ouvreur *m* **2** *vt* **to u. sb in** faire entrer qn ▪ **usherette** *n* ouvreuse *f*

**usual** ['ju:ʒʊəl] **1** *adj* habituel, -elle; **as u.** comme d'habitude **2** *n Fam* **the u.** *(food, excuse)* la même chose que d'habitude ▪ **usually** *adv* d'habitude

**usurp** [ju:'zɜ:p] *vt* usurper

**utensil** [ju:'tensəl] *n* ustensile *m*

**utility** [ju:'tɪlətɪ] *n* **(public) u.** service *m* public

**utilize** ['ju:tɪlaɪz] *vt* utiliser

**utmost** ['ʌtməʊst] **1** *adj* **the u. ease** *(greatest)* la plus grande facilité; **it is of the u. importance that...** il est de la plus haute importance que... *(+ subjunctive)*

**2** *n* **to do one's u.** faire de son mieux (**to do** pour faire)

**utter**[1] ['ʌtə(r)] *adj* total; *(folly, lie)* pur; **it's u. nonsense** c'est complètement absurde ▪ **utterly** *adv* complètement

**utter**[2] ['ʌtə(r)] *vt (cry, sigh)* pousser; *(word)* prononcer; *(threat)* proférer

**U-turn** ['ju:tɜ:n] *n (in vehicle)* demi-tour *m*; *Fig (change of policy)* virage *m* à 180°

# Vv

**V, v** [viː] *n (letter)* V, v *m inv*

**vacant** [ˈveɪkənt] *adj (room, seat)* libre; *(post)* vacant ▪ **vacancy** (*pl* **-ies**) *n (post)* poste *m* vacant; *(room)* chambre *f* libre

**vacate** [*Br* vəˈkeɪt, *Am* ˈveɪkeɪt] *vt* quitter

**vacation** [veɪˈkeɪʃən] *n Am* vacances *fpl*; **to take a v.** prendre des vacances

**vaccinate** [ˈvæksɪneɪt] *vt* vacciner ▪ **vaccination** *n* vaccination *f* ▪ **vaccine** [-ˈsiːn] *n* vaccin *m*

**vacuum** [ˈvækjʊəm] **1** *n* vide *m*; **v. cleaner** aspirateur *m*; *Br* **v. flask** Thermos® *f* **2** *vt (room)* passer l'aspirateur dans; *(carpet)* passer l'aspirateur sur

**vagabond** [ˈvægəbɒnd] *n* vagabond, -e *mf*

**vagina** [vəˈdʒaɪnə] *n Anat* vagin *m*

**vague** [veɪg] (**-er, -est**) *adj* vague; *(outline)* flou; **he was v. (about it)** il est resté vague ▪ **vaguely** *adv* vaguement

**vain** [veɪn] (**-er, -est**) *adj* (**a**) *(attempt, hope)* vain; **in v.** en vain; **her efforts were in v.** ses efforts ont été inutiles (**b**) *(conceited)* vaniteux, -euse

**valentine** [ˈvæləntaɪn] *n (card)* carte *f* de la Saint-Valentin; **(Saint) V.'s Day** la Saint-Valentin

**valid** [ˈvælɪd] *adj* valable ▪ **validate** *vt* valider

**valley** [ˈvælɪ] (*pl* **-eys**) *n* vallée *f*

**valuable** [ˈvæljʊəbəl] **1** *adj (object)* de valeur; *Fig (help, time)* précieux, -euse **2** *npl* **valuables** objets *mpl* de valeur

**value** [ˈvæljuː] **1** *n* valeur *f*; **to be of v.** avoir de la valeur; **to be good v. (for money)** être d'un bon rapport qualité-prix **2** *vt (appreciate)* apprécier; *(assess)* évaluer ▪ **valuation** [-jʊˈeɪʃən] *n (by expert)* expertise *f*

**valve** [vælv] *n (of machine, car)* soupape *f*; *(of pipe, tube)* valve *f*

**van** [væn] *n (vehicle)* camionnette *f*, fourgonnette *f*

**vandal** [ˈvændəl] *n* vandale *mf* ▪ **vandalism** *n* vandalisme *m* ▪ **vandalize** *vt* saccager

**vanilla** [vəˈnɪlə] **1** *n* vanille *f* **2** *adj (ice cream)* à la vanille

**vanish** [ˈvænɪʃ] *vi* disparaître

**vanity** [ˈvænətɪ] *n* vanité *f*

**vapour** [ˈveɪpə(r)] (*Am* **vapor**) *n* vapeur *f*

**variable** [ˈveərɪəbəl] *adj & n* variable *(f)*

**variant** [ˈveərɪənt] *n* variante *f*

**variation** [veərɪˈeɪʃən] *n* variation *f*

**varicose** [ˈværɪkəʊs] *adj* **v. veins** varices *fpl*

**varied** [ˈveəriːd] *adj* varié

**variety** [vəˈraɪətɪ] *n* (**a**) *(diversity)* variété *f*; **a v. of** toutes sortes de (**b**) **v. show** spectacle *m* de variétés

**various** [ˈveərɪəs] *adj* divers

**varnish** [ˈvɑːnɪʃ] **1** *n* vernis *m* **2** *vt* vernir

**vary** [ˈveərɪ] (*pt & pp* **-ied**) *vti* varier (**in/with** en/selon) ▪ **varying** *adj* variable

**vase** [*Br* vɑːz, *Am* veɪs] *n* vase *m*

**vast** [vɑːst] *adj* immense

**VAT** [viːeɪˈtiː, væt] (*abbr* **value added tax**) *n Br* TVA *f*

**vat** [væt] *n* cuve *f*
**Vatican** ['vætɪkən] *n* **the V.** le Vatican
**vault**[1] [vɔ:lt] *n (roof)* voûte *f*; *(tomb)* caveau *m*; *(cellar)* cave *f*; *(in bank)* salle *f* des coffres
**vault**[2] [vɔ:lt] *vti (jump)* sauter
**VCR** [vi:si:'ɑ:(r)] (*abbr* **video cassette recorder**) *n* magnétoscope *m*
**VDU** [vi:di:'ju:] (*abbr* **visual display unit**) *n Comptr* moniteur *m*
**veal** [vi:l] *n* veau *m*
**veer** [vɪə(r)] *vi (of car)* virer; **to v. off the road** quitter la route
**vegan** ['vi:gən] *n* végétalien, -enne *mf*
**vegetable** ['vedʒtəbəl] *n* légume *m* ▪ **vegetarian** [vedʒɪ'teərɪən] *adj & n* végétarien, -enne *(mf)* ▪ **vegetation** [vedʒɪ'teɪʃən] *n* végétation *f*
**vehicle** ['vi:ɪkəl] *n* véhicule *m*
**veil** [veɪl] *n (covering) & Fig* voile *m* ▪ **veiled** *adj* voilé
**vein** [veɪn] *n (in body)* veine *f*
**Velcro**® ['velkrəʊ] *n* Velcro® *m*
**velvet** ['velvɪt] **1** *n* velours *m* **2** *adj* de velours
**vending** ['vendɪŋ] *n* **v. machine** distributeur *m* automatique
**vendor** ['vendə(r)] *n* vendeur, -euse *mf*
**veneer** [və'nɪə(r)] *n (wood)* placage *m*; *Fig (appearance)* vernis *m*
**vengeance** ['vendʒəns] *n* vengeance *f*; **to take v. on sb** se venger de qn; *Fig* **with a v.** de plus belle
**venison** ['venɪsən] *n* venaison *f*
**venom** ['venəm] *n (poison) & Fig* venin *m*
**vent** [vent] *n* conduit *m*
**ventilate** ['ventɪleɪt] *vt* ventiler, aérer ▪ **ventilation** *n* ventilation *f*, aération *f*
**ventriloquist** [ven'trɪləkwɪst] *n* ventriloque *mf*
**venture** ['ventʃə(r)] **1** *n* entreprise *f* (hasardeuse) **2** *vt* risquer; **to v. to do sth** se risquer à faire qch **3** *vi* s'aventurer (**into** dans)
**venue** ['venju:] *n (for meeting, concert)* salle *f*; *(for football match)* stade *m*
**veranda(h)** [və'rændə] *n* véranda *f*
**verb** [vɜ:b] *n* verbe *m* ▪ **verbal** *adj* verbal
**verdict** ['vɜ:dɪkt] *n* verdict *m*
**verge** [vɜ:dʒ] **1** *n Br (of road)* bord *m*; **on the v. of ruin/tears** au bord de la ruine/des larmes; **to be on the v. of doing sth** être sur le point de faire qch **2** *vi* **to v. on** friser; *(of colour)* tirer sur
**verify** ['verɪfaɪ] (*pt & pp* **-ied**) *vt* vérifier
**vermin** ['vɜ:mɪn] *n (animals)* animaux *mpl* nuisibles; *(insects, people)* vermine *f*
**versatile** [*Br* 'vɜ:sətaɪl, *Am* 'vɜ:rsətəl] *adj* polyvalent
**verse** [vɜ:s] *n (poetry)* vers *mpl*; *(stanza)* strophe *f*; *(of Bible)* verset *m*
**versed** [vɜ:st] *adj* **(well) v. in sth** versé dans qch
**version** [*Br* 'vɜ:ʃən, *Am* 'vɜ:ʒən] *n* version *f*
**versus** ['vɜ:səs] *prep (in sport, law)* contre; *(compared to)* comparé à
**vertical** ['vɜ:tɪkəl] *adj* vertical
**very** ['verɪ] **1** *adv* très; **v. much** beaucoup; **the v. first** le tout premier (*f* la toute première); **the v. next day** le lendemain même; **at the v. least/most** tout au moins/plus; **at the v. latest** au plus tard
**2** *adj (emphatic use)* **this v. house** cette maison même; **at the v. end** tout à la fin
**vessel** ['vesəl] *n (ship)* vaisseau *m*; *(container)* récipient *m*
**vest** [vest] *n* maillot *m* de corps; *Am (waistcoat)* gilet *m*
**vested** ['vestɪd] *adj* **to have a v. interest in sth** avoir un intérêt personnel dans qch
**vestige** ['vestɪdʒ] *n* vestige *m*
**vet**[1] [vet] *n* vétérinaire *mf*
**vet**[2] [vet] (*pt & pp* **-tt-**) *vt Br* faire une enquête sur
**veteran** ['vetərən] *n Mil* ancien combattant *m*; *Fig* vétéran *m*
**veto** ['vi:təʊ] **1** (*pl* **-oes**) *n* veto *m inv* **2** (*pt & pp* **-oed**) *vt* mettre son veto à

**via** ['vaɪə, 'vɪə] *prep* via, par
**viable** ['vaɪəbəl] *adj* viable
**viaduct** ['vaɪədʌkt] *n* viaduc *m*
**vibrant** ['vaɪbrənt] *adj (colour)* vif (*f* vive)
**vibrate** [vaɪ'breɪt] *vi* vibrer ▪ **vibration** *n* vibration *f*
**vicar** ['vɪkə(r)] *n (in Church of England)* pasteur *m* ▪ **vicarage** [-rɪdʒ] *n* presbytère *m*
**vice** [vaɪs] *n (depravity, fault)* vice *m*; *Br (tool)* étau *m*
**vice-** [vaɪs] *pref* vice-
**vice versa** [vaɪs(ɪ)'vɜːsə] *adv* vice versa
**vicinity** [və'sɪnətɪ] *n* environs *mpl*; **in the v. of** aux environs de
**vicious** ['vɪʃəs] *adj (malicious)* méchant; *(violent)* brutal; **v. circle** cercle *m* vicieux
**victim** ['vɪktɪm] *n* victime *f*; **to be the v. of** être victime de
**victimize** ['vɪktɪmaɪz] *vt* persécuter
**Victorian** [vɪk'tɔːrɪən] **1** *adj* victorien, -enne **2** *n* Victorien, -enne *mf*
**victory** ['vɪktərɪ] (*pl* **-ies**) *n* victoire *f* ▪ **victorious** [-'tɔːrɪəs] *adj* victorieux, -euse
**video** ['vɪdɪəʊ] **1** (*pl* **-os**) *n (medium)* vidéo *f*; *(cassette)* cassette *f* vidéo; *(recorder)* magnétoscope *m*; **on v.** sur cassette vidéo
**2** *adj (camera, cassette, game)* vidéo *inv*; **v. recorder** magnétoscope *m*
**3** (*pt & pp* **-oed**) *vt (on camcorder)* filmer en vidéo; *(on video recorder)* enregistrer (sur magnétoscope) ▪ **videotape** *n* bande *f* vidéo
**vie** [vaɪ] (*pres p* **vying**) *vi* **to v. with sb (for sth/to do sth)** rivaliser avec qn (pour qch/pour faire qch)
**Vietnam** [*Br* vjet'næm, *Am* -'nɑːm] *n* le Viêt Nam
**view** [vjuː] **1** *n* vue *f*; *(opinion)* opinion *f*; **in my v.** *(opinion)* à mon avis; **in v. of** *(considering)* étant donné; **on v.** *(exhibit)* exposé; **with a v. to doing sth** dans l'intention de faire qch
**2** *vt (regard)* considérer; *(look at)* voir; *(house)* visiter ▪ **viewer** *n* (**a**) *TV* téléspectateur, -trice *mf* (**b**) *(for slides)* visionneuse *f* ▪ **viewfinder** *n (in camera)* viseur *m* ▪ **viewpoint** *n* point *m* de vue
**vigilant** ['vɪdʒɪlənt] *adj* vigilant
**vigorous** ['vɪgərəs] *adj* vigoureux, -euse
**vile** [vaɪl] (**-er, -est**) *adj (unpleasant)* abominable; *(food, drink)* infect
**villa** ['vɪlə] *n* villa *f*
**village** ['vɪlɪdʒ] *n* village *m* ▪ **villager** *n* villageois, -e *mf*
**villain** ['vɪlən] *n (scoundrel)* scélérat *m*; *(in story, play)* méchant *m*
**vindicate** ['vɪndɪkeɪt] *vt* justifier
**vindictive** [vɪn'dɪktɪv] *adj* vindicatif, -ive
**vine** [vaɪn] *n* vigne *f* ▪ **vineyard** ['vɪnjəd] *n* vigne *f*
**vinegar** ['vɪnɪgə(r)] *n* vinaigre *m*
**vintage** ['vɪntɪdʒ] **1** *n (year)* année *f*; *(wine)* cru *m* **2** *adj (wine)* de cru; *(car)* de collection *(datant généralement des années 1920)*
**vinyl** ['vaɪnəl] *n* vinyle *m*
**viola** [vɪ'əʊlə] *n Mus* alto *m*
**violate** ['vaɪəleɪt] *vt (agreement)* violer
**violence** ['vaɪələns] *n* violence *f* ▪ **violent** *adj* violent ▪ **violently** *adv* violemment
**violet** ['vaɪələt] **1** *adj (colour)* violet, -ette **2** *n (colour)* violet *m*; *(plant)* violette *f*
**violin** [vaɪə'lɪn] *n* violon *m* ▪ **violinist** *n* violoniste *mf*
**VIP** [viːaɪ'piː] (*abbr* **very important person**) *n* VIP *mf*
**viper** ['vaɪpə(r)] *n* vipère *f*
**virgin** ['vɜːdʒɪn] *n* vierge *f*
**virile** [*Br* 'vɪraɪl, *Am* 'vɪrəl] *adj* viril
**virtual** ['vɜːtʃʊəl] *adj* quasi; *Comptr* virtuel, -elle ▪ **virtually** *adv (almost)* quasiment
**virtue** ['vɜːtʃuː] *n (goodness, chastity)* vertu *f*; *(advantage)* mérite *m* ▪ **virtuous** [-tjʊəs] *adj* vertueux, -euse
**virus** ['vaɪərəs] *n Med & Comptr* virus *m*

**Visa®** ['vi:zə] *n* **V. (card)** carte *f* Visa®
**visa** ['vi:zə] *n* visa *m*
**visible** ['vɪzəbəl] *adj* visible ▪ **visibility** *n* visibilité *f*
**vision** ['vɪʒən] *n (eyesight)* vue *f*; *(foresight)* clairvoyance *f*; *(apparition)* vision *f*
**visit** ['vɪzɪt] **1** *n* visite *f*; **to pay sb a v.** rendre visite à qn
**2** *vt (place)* visiter; *(person)* rendre visite à
**3** *vi* **to be visiting** être de passage; *Br* **v. hours/card** heures *fpl*/carte *f* de visite ▪ **visitor** *n* visiteur, -euse *mf*; *(guest)* invité, -e *mf*
**visor** ['vaɪzə(r)] *n* visière *f*
**visual** ['vɪʒʊəl] *adj* visuel, -elle; **v. aid** support *m* visuel; **v. arts** arts *mpl* plastiques ▪ **visualize** *vt (imagine)* visualiser; *(foresee)* envisager
**vital** ['vaɪtəl] *adj* vital; **it's v. that...** il est vital que... *(+ subjunctive)*
**vitality** [vaɪ'tæləti] *n* vitalité *f*
**vitamin** [*Br* 'vɪtəmɪn, *Am* 'vaɪtəmɪn] *n* vitamine *f*
**vivacious** [vɪ'veɪʃəs] *adj* enjoué
**vivid** ['vɪvɪd] *adj* vif (*f* vive); *(description)* vivant; *(memory)* clair
**V-neck** ['vi:nek] *adj* à col en V
**vocabulary** [*Br* və'kæbjʊlərɪ, *Am* -erɪ] *n* vocabulaire *m*
**vocal** ['vəʊkəl] *adj (cords, music)* vocal; *(noisy, critical)* qui se fait entendre
**vocation** [vəʊ'keɪʃən] *n* vocation *f* ▪ **vocational** *adj* professionnel, -elle
**vociferous** [və'sɪfərəs] *adj* bruyant
**vodka** ['vɒdkə] *n* vodka *f*
**vogue** [vəʊg] *n* vogue *f*; **in v.** en vogue
**voice** [vɔɪs] **1** *n* voix *f*; **at the top of one's v.** à tue-tête **2** *vt (opinion, feelings)* exprimer
**void** [vɔɪd] **1** *n* vide *m* **2** *adj (deed, contract)* nul (*f* nulle)
**volatile** [*Br* 'vɒlətaɪl, *Am* 'vɒlətəl] *adj (person)* inconstant; *(situation)* explosif, -ive
**volcano** [vɒl'keɪnəʊ] (*pl* **-oes**) *n* volcan *m*
**volley** ['vɒlɪ] *n (in tennis)* volée ▪ **volleyball** *n* volley(-ball) *m*
**volt** [vəʊlt] *n* volt *m* ▪ **voltage** [-tɪdʒ] *n* voltage *m*
**volume** ['vɒlju:m] *n (book, capacity, loudness)* volume *m*
**voluntary** [*Br* 'vɒləntərɪ, *Am* -erɪ] *adj* volontaire; *(unpaid)* bénévole ▪ **voluntarily** *adv* volontairement; *(on an unpaid basis)* bénévolement
**volunteer** [vɒlən'tɪə(r)] **1** *n* volontaire *mf*; *(for charity)* bénévole *mf* **2** *vt (information)* donner spontanément **3** *vi* se porter volontaire (**for sth** pour qch; **to do** pour faire)
**vomit** ['vɒmɪt] **1** *n* vomi *m* **2** *vti* vomir
**vote** [vəʊt] **1** *n (choice)* vote *m*; *(election)* scrutin *m*; *(paper)* voix *f*; **to take a v. on sth** voter sur qch; **to have the v.** avoir le droit de vote **2** *vt (funds, bill)* voter **3** *vi* voter; **to v. Labour** voter travailliste ▪ **voter** *n (elector)* électeur, -trice *mf* ▪ **voting** *n (polling)* scrutin *m*
**vouch** [vaʊtʃ] *vi* **to v. for sb/sth** répondre de qn/qch
**voucher** ['vaʊtʃə(r)] *n* coupon *m*, bon *m*; **(gift-)v.** chèque-cadeau *m*
**vow** [vaʊ] **1** *n* vœu *m* **2** *vt* jurer (**to** à); **to v. to do sth** jurer de faire qch
**vowel** ['vaʊəl] *n* voyelle *f*
**voyage** ['vɔɪɪdʒ] *n* voyage *m*
**vulgar** ['vʌlgə(r)] *adj* vulgaire
**vulnerable** ['vʌlnərəbəl] *adj* vulnérable
**vulture** ['vʌltʃə(r)] *n* vautour *m*

# Ww

**W, w** ['dʌbəljuː] *n (letter)* W, w *m inv*
**wacky** ['wækɪ] (**-ier, -iest**) *adj Fam* farfelu
**wad** [wɒd] *n (of papers, banknotes)* liasse *f*; *(of cotton wool)* morceau *m*
**waddle** ['wɒdəl] *vi Fig (of duck, person)* se dandiner
**wade** [weɪd] *vi* **to w. through** *(mud, water)* patauger dans; *Fig (book)* venir péniblement à bout de
**wafer** ['weɪfə(r)] *n (biscuit)* gaufrette *f*; *Rel* hostie *f*
**waffle¹** ['wɒfəl] *n (cake)* gaufre *f*
**waffle²** ['wɒfəl] *Br Fam* **1** *n* remplissage *m* **2** *vi* faire du remplissage
**waft** [wɒft] *vi (of smell, sound)* parvenir
**wag** [wæg] *(pt & pp* **-gg-**) *vt* remuer, agiter; **to w. one's finger at sb** menacer qn du doigt
**wage** [weɪdʒ] **1** *n* **wage(s)** salaire *m*, paie *f*; **w. earner** salarié, -e; *mf*; *Br* **w. packet** *(money)* paie **2** *vt* **to w. war** faire la guerre (**on** à)
**wager** ['weɪdʒə(r)] **1** *n* pari *m* **2** *vt* parier (**that** que)
**waggle** ['wægəl] *vti* remuer
**wag(g)on** ['wægən] *n Br (of train)* wagon *m* (découvert); *(horse-drawn)* charrette *f*
**wail** [weɪl] *vi (of person)* gémir; *(of siren)* hurler
**waist** [weɪst] *n* taille *f* ▪ **waistcoat** *n Br* gilet *m* ▪ **waistline** *n* taille *f*
**wait** [weɪt] **1** *n* attente *f*; **to lie in w. for sb** guetter qn

**2** *vt* **to w. one's turn** attendre son tour

**3** *vi* (**a**) attendre; **to w. for sb/sth** attendre qn/qch; **to keep sb waiting** faire attendre qn; **w. till** *or* **until I've gone, w. for me to go** attends que je sois parti; **I can't w. to see her** j'ai vraiment hâte de la voir (**b**) **to w. on sb** servir qn ▪ **waiting 1** *n* attente *f*; *Br* **'no w.'** 'arrêt interdit' **2** *adj* **w. list/room** liste *f*/salle *f* d'attente

▸ **wait about, wait around** *vi* attendre
▸ **wait behind** *vi* rester
▸ **wait up** *vi* veiller; **to w. up for sb** attendre le retour de qn pour aller se coucher

**waiter** ['weɪtə(r)] *n* serveur *m* ▪ **waitress** *n* serveuse *f*
**wake¹** [weɪk] *(pt* **woke**, *pp* **woken**) **1** *vt* **to w. sb (up)** réveiller qn **2** *vi* **to w. (up)** se réveiller; **to w. up to sth** prendre conscience de qch
**wake²** [weɪk] *n (of ship)* sillage *m*; *Fig* **in the w. of sth** à la suite de qch
**Wales** [weɪlz] *n* le pays de Galles
**walk** [wɔːk] **1** *n (short)* promenade *f*; *(long)* marche *f*; *(gait)* démarche *f*; *(path)* avenue *f*; **to go for a w., to take a w.** aller se promener; **to take the dog for a w.** promener le chien; **five minutes' w. (away)** à cinq minutes à pied

**2** *vt* **to w. the dog** promener le chien; **to w. sb home** raccompagner qn; **I walked 3 miles** ≃ j'ai fait presque 5 km à pied

**3** *vi* marcher; *(as opposed to cycling, driving)* aller à pied; *(for exercise, pleasure)* se promener; **to w. home** rentrer à pied ▪ **walker** *n* marcheur, -euse *mf*; *(for pleasure)* promeneur, -euse *mf* ▪ **walking** *n* marche *f* (à pied); **w. stick** canne *f* ▪ **walkway** *n* passage *m* couvert; **moving w.** trottoir *m* roulant

▸ **walk away** *vi* s'en aller (**from** de)

▸ **walk in** *vi* entrer

▸ **walk off** *vi* s'en aller; **to w. off with sth** *(steal)* partir avec qch

▸ **walk out** *vi (leave)* sortir; *Br (of workers)* se mettre en grève; **to w. out on sb** quitter qn

▸ **walk over** *vi* **to w. over to** *(go up to)* s'approcher de

**Walkman®** ['wɔːkmən] (*pl* **-mans**) *n* baladeur *m*, Walkman® *m*

**wall** [wɔːl] **1** *n* mur *m*; *(of cabin, tunnel, stomach)* paroi *f* **2** *adj (map, hanging)* mural ▪ **wallpaper 1** *n* papier *m* peint **2** *vt* tapisser ▪ **wall-to-wall** *adj* **w. carpet(ing)** moquette *f*

**wallet** ['wɒlɪt] *n* portefeuille *m*

**wallow** ['wɒləʊ] *vi* se vautrer

**walnut** ['wɔːlnʌt] *n (nut)* noix *f*; *(tree, wood)* noyer *m*

**walrus** ['wɔːlrəs] (*pl* **-ruses** [-rəsəz]) *n* morse *m*

**waltz** [*Br* wɔːls, *Am* wɒlts] **1** *n* valse *f* **2** *vi* valser

**wand** [wɒnd] *n* **(magic) w.** baguette *f* magique

**wander** ['wɒndə(r)] **1** *vt* **to w. the streets** errer dans les rues **2** *vi (of thoughts)* vagabonder; *(of person)* errer, vagabonder; **to w. from** *(path, subject)* s'écarter de

▸ **wander about, wander around** *vi (roam)* errer, vagabonder; *(stroll)* flâner

▸ **wander off** *vi (go away)* s'éloigner

**wangle** ['wæŋgəl] *vt Br Fam (obtain)* se débrouiller pour avoir

**want** [wɒnt] **1** *n (lack)* manque *m* (**of** de); **for w. of** par manque de; **for w. of money/time** faute d'argent/de temps

**2** *vt* vouloir (**to do** faire); **I w. him to go** je veux qu'il parte; **the lawn wants cutting** la pelouse a besoin d'être tondue; **you're wanted on the phone** on vous demande au téléphone ▪ **wanted** *adj (criminal)* recherché par la police

**wanton** ['wɒntən] *adj (gratuitous)* gratuit

**war** [wɔː(r)] **1** *n* guerre *f*; **at w.** en guerre (**with** avec); **to declare w.** déclarer la guerre (**on** à) **2** *adj (wound, crime)* de guerre; **w. memorial** monument *m* aux morts

**ward¹** [wɔːd] *n (in hospital)* salle *f*

**ward²** [wɔːd] *vt* **to w. off** *(blow)* éviter; *(danger)* chasser

**warden** ['wɔːdən] *n (of institution, hostel)* directeur, -trice *mf*

**warder** ['wɔːdə(r)] *n Br* gardien *m* (de prison)

**wardrobe** ['wɔːdrəʊb] *n (cupboard)* penderie *f*; *(clothes)* garde-robe *f*

**warehouse** ['weəhaʊs] (*pl* **-ses** [-zɪz]) *n* entrepôt *m*

**wares** [weəz] *npl* marchandises *fpl*

**warfare** ['wɔːfeə(r)] *n* guerre *f*

**warm** [wɔːm] **1** (**-er, -est**) *adj* chaud; *Fig (welcome)* chaleureux, -euse; **to be** *or* **feel w.** avoir chaud; **to get w.** *(of person, room)* se réchauffer; **it's w.** *(of weather)* il fait chaud

**2** *vt* **to w. (up)** *(person, food)* réchauffer

**3** *vi* **to w. up** *(of person, room)* se réchauffer; *(of athlete)* s'échauffer ▪ **warmly** *adv (dress)* chaudement; *Fig (welcome, thank)* chaleureusement ▪ **warmth** *n* chaleur *f*

**warn** [wɔːn] *vt* avertir, prévenir (**that** que); **to w. sb against** *or* **of sth** mettre qn en garde contre qch ▪ **warning** *n (caution)* avertissement *m*; *(advance notice)* avis *m*; **without w.** sans prévenir; **w. light** *(on appliance)* voyant *m* lumineux; *Br* **(hazard) w. lights** feux *mpl* de détresse

**warp** [wɔːp] **1** *vt (wood)* gauchir; *Fig (judgement, person)* pervertir **2** *vi (of door)* gauchir

**warrant** ['wɒrənt] *n (in law)* mandat *m* ▪ **warranty** (*pl* **-ies**) *n Com* garantie *f*

**warren** ['wɒrən] *n* **(rabbit) w.** garenne *f*

**warrior** ['wɒrɪə(r)] *n* guerrier, -ère *mf*

**wart** [wɔːt] *n* verrue *f*

**wartime** ['wɔːtaɪm] *n* **in w.** en temps de guerre

**wary** ['weərɪ] (**-ier, -iest**) *adj* prudent; **to be w. of sb/sth** se méfier de qn/qch; **to be w. of doing sth** hésiter beaucoup à faire qch

**was** [wəz, *stressed* wɒz] *pt of* **be**

**wash** [wɒʃ] **1** *n* **to have a w.** se laver; **to give sth a w.** laver qch

**2** *vt* laver; **to w. one's hands** se laver les mains (**of sth** de qch)

**3** *vi (have a wash)* se laver ▪ **washbasin** *n Br* lavabo *m* ▪ **washcloth** *n Am* gant *m* de toilette ▪ **washing-up** *n Br* vaisselle *f*; **to do the w.** faire la vaisselle; **w. liquid** liquide *m* vaisselle ▪ **washroom** *n Am* toilettes *fpl*

▸ **wash down** *vt sep (car, deck)* laver à grande eau; *(food)* arroser (**with** de)

▸ **wash off 1** *vt sep* enlever **2** *vi* partir

▸ **wash out 1** *vt sep (bowl, cup)* rincer; *(stain)* faire partir (en lavant) **2** *vi (of stain)* partir (au lavage)

▸ **wash up 1** *vt sep Br (dishes, forks)* laver **2** *vi Br (do the dishes)* faire la vaisselle; *Am (have a wash)* se débarbouiller

**washable** ['wɒʃəbəl] *adj* lavable

**washer** ['wɒʃə(r)] *n (ring)* joint *m*

**washing** ['wɒʃɪŋ] *n (action)* lavage *m*; *(clothes)* linge *m*; **to do the w.** faire la lessive; **w. machine** machine *f* à laver; *Br* **w. powder** lessive *f*

**wasp** [wɒsp] *n* guêpe *f*

**waste** [weɪst] **1** *n* gaspillage *m*; *(of time)* perte *f*; *(rubbish)* déchets *mpl*; **w. material** *or* **products** déchets *mpl*; *Br* **w. ground** *(in town)* terrain *m* vague; **w. land** *(uncultivated)* terres *fpl* incultes; *(in town)* terrain *m* vague; **w. pipe** tuyau *m* d'évacuation

**2** *vt (money, food)* gaspiller; *(time)* perdre; *(opportunity)* gâcher; **to w. no time doing sth** ne pas perdre de temps pour faire qch

**3** *vi* **to w. away** dépérir ▪ **wasted** *adj (effort)* inutile

**wastebin** ['weɪstbɪn] *n (in kitchen)* poubelle *f*

**wasteful** ['weɪstfəl] *adj (person)* gaspilleur, -euse; *(process)* peu économique

**watch** [wɒtʃ] **1** *n* (**a**) *(timepiece)* montre *f* (**b**) **to keep a close w. on sb/sth** surveiller qn/qch de près

**2** *vt* regarder; *(observe)* observer; *(suspect, baby, luggage)* surveiller; *(be careful of)* faire attention à; **w. it!** attention!

**3** *vi* regarder; **to w. out for sb/sth** guetter qn/qch; **to w. out** *(take care)* faire attention (**for** à); **w. out!** attention!; **to w. over** surveiller ▪ **watchdog** *n* chien *m* de garde ▪ **watchstrap** *n* bracelet *m* de montre

**watchful** ['wɒtʃfəl] *adj* vigilant

**water** ['wɔːtə(r)] **1** *n* eau *f*; **under w.** *(road, field)* inondé; *(swim)* sous l'eau; **w. heater** chauffe-eau *m inv*; **w. pistol** pistolet *m* à eau; **w. polo** water-polo *m*; **w. skiing** ski *m* nautique; **w. wings** brassards *mpl* de natation

**2** *vt (plant)* arroser; **to w. sth down** *(wine)* diluer qch; *(text)* édulcorer qch

**3** *vi (of eyes)* larmoyer; **it makes my mouth w.** ça me met l'eau à la bouche ▪ **watercolour** (*Am* **-color**) *n* aquarelle *f* ▪ **watercress** *n* cresson *m* (de fontaine) ▪ **waterfall** *n* cascade *f* ▪ **watering** *n* **w. can** arrosoir *m* ▪ **watermark** *n* filigrane *m* ▪ **watermelon** *n* pastèque *f* ▪ **waterproof** *adj* imperméable; *(watch)* étanche ▪ **watertight** *adj (container)* étanche

**watery** ['wɔːtərɪ] *adj (soup)* trop liquide; *(coffee, tea)* insipide; *(colour)* délavé

**watt** [wɒt] *n* watt *m*

**wave** [weɪv] **1** *n (of water, crime)* vague *f*; *(in hair)* ondulation *f*; *Phys* onde *f* **2** *vt (arm, flag)* agiter; *(stick)* brandir **3** *vi (of person)* faire signe (de la main); **to w. to sb** *(signal)* faire signe de la main à qn; *(greet)* saluer qn de la main

■ **waveband** *n* bande *f* de fréquences ■ **wavelength** *n* longueur *f* d'onde; *Fig* **on the same w.** sur la même longueur d'onde

**waver** ['weɪvə(r)] *vi (of person, flame)* vaciller

**wavy** ['weɪvɪ] (**-ier, -iest**) *adj (line)* qui ondule; *(hair)* ondulé

**wax** [wæks] **1** *n* cire *f*; *(for ski)* fart *m* **2** *adj (candle, doll)* de cire; *Am* **w. paper** *(for wrapping)* papier *m* paraffiné **3** *vt* cirer; *(ski)* farter; *(car)* lustrer

**WAY** [weɪ] **1** *n* (**a**) *(path, road)* chemin *m* (**to** de); *(direction)* sens *m*, direction *f*; **the w. in** l'entrée *f*; **the w. out** la sortie; **the w. to the station** le chemin pour aller à la gare; **to ask sb the w.** demander son chemin à qn; **to show sb the w.** montrer le chemin à qn; **to lose one's w.** se perdre; **I'm on my w.** *(coming)* j'arrive; *(going)* je pars; **to make w. for sb** faire de la place à qn; **out of the w.** *(isolated)* isolé; **to get out of the w.** s'écarter; **to go all the w.** aller jusqu'au bout; **to give w.** céder; *Br (in vehicle)* céder le passage (**to** à); **it's a long w. away** *or* **off** c'est très loin; **it's the wrong w. up** c'est dans le mauvais sens; **this w.** par ici; **that w.** par là; **which w.?** par où?
(**b**) *(manner)* manière *f*; **in this w.** de cette manière; **by w. of** *(via)* par; *Fig (as)* comme; *Fig* **by the w.** à propos; *Fam* **no w.!** *(certainly not)* pas question!; **w. of life** mode *m* de vie
**2** *adv Fam* **w. behind** très en arrière; **w. ahead** très en avance (**of** sur)

**wayward** ['weɪwəd] *adj* difficile

**WC** [dʌbəlju:'si:] *n* W.-C. *mpl*

**we** [wi:] *pron* nous; *(indefinite)* on; **we teachers** nous autres professeurs; **we all make mistakes** tout le monde peut se tromper

**weak** [wi:k] (**-er, -est**) *adj* faible; *(tea, coffee)* léger, -ère; **to have a w. heart** avoir le cœur fragile ■ **weakling** *n (in body)* mauviette *f*; *(in character)* faible *mf* ■ **weakness** *n* faiblesse *f*; *(fault)* point *m* faible; **to have a w. for sb/sth** avoir un faible pour qn/qch

**weaken** ['wi:kən] **1** *vt* affaiblir **2** *vi* s'affaiblir

**wealth** [welθ] *n* richesse *f*; *Fig* **a w. of sth** une abondance de qch ■ **wealthy 1** (**-ier, -iest**) *adj* riche **2** *npl* **the w.** les riches *mpl*

**weapon** ['wepən] *n* arme *f*

**wear** [weə(r)] **1** *n* (**a**) **men's w.** vêtements *mpl* pour hommes; **evening w.** tenue *f* de soirée (**b**) *(use)* **w. and tear** usure *f* naturelle **2** (*pt* **wore,** *pp* **worn**) *vt (garment, glasses)* porter; **to w. black** porter du noir **3** *vi* **to w. thin** *(of clothing)* s'user; **to w. well** *(of clothing)* bien vieillir

▸ **wear down 1** *vt sep* user; **to w. sb down** avoir qn à l'usure **2** *vi* s'user

▸ **wear off** *vi (of colour, pain)* disparaître

▸ **wear out 1** *vt sep (clothes)* user; **to w. sb out** épuiser qn **2** *vi (of clothes)* s'user; *Fig (of patience)* s'épuiser

**weary** ['wɪərɪ] **1** (**-ier, -iest**) *adj* las (*f* lasse) (**of doing** de faire) **2** *vi* se lasser (**of** de)

**weather** ['weðə(r)] **1** *n* temps *m*; **what's the w. like?** quel temps fait-il?; **in hot w.** par temps chaud; **under the w.** *(ill)* patraque **2** *adj* **w. forecast** prévisions *fpl* météorologiques; **w. report** (bulletin *m*) météo *f* **3** *vt (storm)* essuyer; *Fig (crisis)* surmonter ■ **weatherman** (*pl* **-men**) *n (on TV, radio)* présentateur *m* météo

**weave** [wi:v] **1** (*pt* **wove,** *pp* **woven**) *vt (cloth, plot)* tisser; *(basket, garland)* tresser **2** *vi* tisser; *Fig* **to w. in and out of** *(crowd, cars)* se faufiler entre

**web** [web] *n (of spider)* toile *f*; *Fig (of lies)* tissu *m*; *Comptr* **the W.** le Web; **w. page** page *f* Web; **w. site** site *m* Web

**wed** [wed] (*pt & pp* **-dd-**) **1** *vt (marry)* épouser **2** *vi* se marier

**we'd** [wi:d] = **we had, we would**

**wedding** ['wedɪŋ] **1** *n* mariage *m*; **golden/silver w.** noces *fpl* d'or/d'argent **2** *adj (anniversary, present, cake)* de mariage; *(dress)* de mariée; **his/her w. day** le jour de son mariage; *Br* **w. ring,** *Am* **w. band** alliance *f*

**wedge** [wedʒ] **1** *n (of wheel, table)* cale *f* **2** *vt (wheel, table)* caler; *(push)* enfoncer (**into** dans); **to w. a door open** maintenir une porte ouverte avec une cale; **wedged (in) between** coincé entre

**Wednesday** ['wenzdeɪ] *n* mercredi *m*

**wee¹** [wi:] *adj Scot Fam (tiny)* tout petit (*f* toute petite)

**wee²** [wi:] *vi Br Fam* faire pipi

**weed** [wi:d] **1** *n (plant)* mauvaise herbe *f* **2** *vti* désherber; *Fig* **to w. sth out** éliminer qch (**from** de) ▪ **weed-killer** *n* désherbant *m* ▪ **weedy** (**-ier, -iest**) *adj Fam (person)* malingre

**week** [wi:k] *n* semaine *f*; **tomorrow w., a w. tomorrow** demain en huit ▪ **weekday** *n* jour *m* de semaine

**weekend** [wi:k'end] *n* week-end *m*; **at** *or* **on** *or* **over the w.** ce week-end; *(every weekend)* le week-end

**weekly** ['wi:klɪ] **1** *adj* hebdomadaire **2** *adv* toutes les semaines **3** *n (magazine)* hebdomadaire *m*

**weep** [wi:p] *(pt & pp* **wept**) *vi* pleurer

**weigh** [weɪ] **1** *vt* peser; **to w. sb/sth down** *(with load)* surcharger qn/qch (**with** de); **to w. up** *(chances)* peser **2** *vi* peser; **it's weighing on my mind** ça me tracasse ▪ **weighing-machine** *n* balance *f*

**weight** [weɪt] **1** *n* poids *m*; **to put on w.** grossir; **to lose w.** maigrir; *Fig* **to carry w.** *(of argument)* avoir du poids **2** *vt* **to w. sth (down)** *(hold down)* faire tenir qch avec un poids ▪ **weightlifter** *n* haltérophile *mf* ▪ **weightlifting** *n* haltérophilie *f*

**weighty** ['weɪtɪ] (**-ier, -iest**) *adj (serious, important)* grave

**weir** [wɪə(r)] *n* barrage *m*

**weird** [wɪəd] (**-er, -est**) *adj* bizarre

**welcome** ['welkəm] **1** *adj (person, news, change)* bienvenu; **to make sb w.** faire un bon accueil à qn; **w.!** bienvenue!; **you're w.!** *(after 'thank you')* il n'y a pas de quoi!; **you're w. to use my bike** mon vélo est à ta disposition

**2** *n* accueil *m*; **to give sb a warm w.** faire un accueil chaleureux à qn

**3** *vt (person)* souhaiter la bienvenue à; *(news, change)* accueillir favorablement ▪ **welcoming** *adj* accueillant; *(speech, words)* de bienvenue

**welfare** ['welfeə(r)] *n (wellbeing)* bien-être *m*; *Am Fam* **to be on w.** recevoir l'aide sociale; *Br* **the W. State** l'État *m* providence

**we'll** [wi:l] = **we will, we shall**

**well¹** [wel] *n (for water, oil)* puits *m*

**well²** [wel] **1** (**better, best**) *adj* bien; **to be w.** aller bien; **to get w.** se remettre; **it's just as w....** heureusement que...

**2** *adv* bien; **you'd do w. to refuse** tu ferais bien de refuser; **she might (just) as w. have stayed at home** elle aurait mieux fait de rester chez elle; **as w.** *(also)* aussi; **as w. as** aussi bien que; **as w. as two cats, he has...** en plus de deux chats, il a...

**3** *exclam* eh bien!; **w., w.!** *(surprise)* tiens, tiens!; **huge, w. quite big** énorme, enfin, assez grand ▪ **well-behaved** *adj* sage ▪ **well-being** *n* bien-être *m* ▪ **well-built** *adj (person, car)* solide ▪ **well-dressed** *adj* bien habillé ▪ **well-informed** *adj* bien informé ▪ **well-known** *adj* (bien) connu ▪ **well-meaning** *adj* bien intentionné ▪ **well-off** *adj* riche ▪ **well-paid** *adj* bien payé ▪ **well-read** *adj* instruit ▪ **well-timed** *adj* opportun ▪ **well-to-do** *adj* aisé ▪ **wellwisher** *n* sympathisant, -e *mf* ▪ **well-worn** *adj (clothes, carpet)* très usé

**wellington** ['welɪŋtən] (*Fam* **welly** [welɪ], *pl* **-ies**) *n Br* **w. (boot)** botte *f* de caoutchouc

**Welsh** [welʃ] **1** *adj* gallois **2** *n (language)* gallois *m*; **the W.** *(people)* les Gallois *mpl* ▪ **Welshman** (*pl* **-men**) *n* Gallois *m* ▪ **Welshwoman** (*pl* **-women**) *n* Galloise *f*

**went** [went] *pt of* **go**

**wept** [wept] *pt & pp of* **weep**
**were** [wə(r), *stressed* wɜ:(r)] *pt of* **be**
**we're** [wɪə(r)] = **we are**
**west** [west] **1** *n* ouest *m*; **(to the) w. of** à l'ouest de; *Pol* **the W.** l'Occident *m*
**2** *adj (coast)* ouest *inv*; *(wind)* d'ouest; **W. Africa** l'Afrique *f* occidentale; **W. Indian** *adj* antillais; *n* Antillais, -e *mf*; **the W. Indies** les Antilles *fpl*
**3** *adv* à l'ouest; *(travel)* vers l'ouest ▪ **westbound** *adj (traffic)* en direction de l'ouest; *Br (carriageway)* ouest *inv* ▪ **westerly** *adj (direction)* de l'ouest ▪ **western 1** *adj (coast)* ouest *inv*; *Pol (culture)* occidental; **W. Europe** l'Europe *f* de l'Ouest **2** *n (film)* western *m* ▪ **westerner** *n Pol* occidental, -e *mf* ▪ **westward** *adj & adv* vers l'ouest ▪ **westwards** *adv* vers l'ouest
**wet** [wet] **1** (**wetter, wettest**) *adj* mouillé; *(weather)* pluvieux, -euse; *(day)* de pluie; **to get w.** se mouiller; **to be w. through** être trempé; **it's w.** *(raining)* il pleut; **'w. paint'** 'peinture fraîche'; **w. suit** combinaison *f* de plongée **2** *n* **the w.** *(rain)* la pluie; *(damp)* l'humidité *f* **3** (*pt & pp* **-tt-**) *vt* mouiller
**we've** [wi:v] = **we have**
**whack** [wæk] *vt Fam* donner un grand coup à
**whale** [weɪl] *n* baleine *f*

**WHAT** [wɒt] **1** *adj* quel, quelle, *pl* quel(le)s; **w. book?** quel livre?; **w. a fool!** quel idiot!; **w. little she has** le peu qu'elle a
**2** *pron* (**a**) *(in questions) (subject)* qu'est-ce qui; *(object)* (qu'est-ce) que; *(after prep)* quoi; **w.'s happening?** qu'est-ce qui se passe?; **w. does he do?** qu'est-ce qu'il fait?, que fait-il?; **w. is it?** qu'est-ce que c'est?; **w.'s that book?** c'est quoi, ce livre?; **w.!** *(surprise)* quoi!, comment!; **w.'s it called?** comment ça s'appelle?; **w. for?** pourquoi?; **w. about going out for lunch?** si on allait déjeuner?
(**b**) *(in relative construction) (subject)* ce qui; *(object)* ce que; **I know w. will happen/w. she'll do** je sais ce qui arrivera/ce qu'elle fera; **w. I need...** ce dont j'ai besoin...

**whatever** [wɒt'evə(r)] **1** *adj* **w. (the) mistake** quelle que soit l'erreur; **of w. size** de n'importe quelle taille; **no chance w.** pas la moindre chance; **nothing w.** rien du tout **2** *pron (no matter what)* quoi que *(+ subjunctive)*; **w. you do** quoi que tu fasses; **do w. you want** fais tout ce que tu veux
**whatsit** ['wɒtsɪt] *n Fam* machin *m*
**whatsoever** [wɒtsəʊ'evə(r)] *adj* **for no reason w.** sans aucune raison; **none w.** aucun
**wheat** [wi:t] *n* blé *m*
**wheedle** ['wi:dəl] *vt* **to w. sb** enjôler qn (**into doing** pour qu'il/elle fasse); **to w. sth out of sb** obtenir qch de qn par la flatterie
**wheel** [wi:l] **1** *n* roue *f*; **to be at the w.** être au volant **2** *vt (push)* pousser ▪ **wheelbarrow** *n* brouette *f* ▪ **wheelchair** *n* fauteuil *m* roulant ▪ **wheelclamp** *n* sabot *m* de Denver
**wheeze** [wi:z] *vi* respirer bruyamment ▪ **wheezy** (**-ier, -iest**) *adj* poussif, -ive
**when** [wen] **1** *adv* quand **2** *conj (with time)* quand, lorsque; **w. I finish, w. I've finished** quand j'aurai fini; **the day/moment w.** le jour/moment où
**whenever** [wen'evə(r)] *conj (at whatever time)* quand; *(each time that)* chaque fois que
**where** [weə(r)] **1** *adv* où; **w. are you from?** d'où êtes-vous?
**2** *conj* où; **I found it w. she'd left it** je l'ai trouvé là où elle l'avait laissé; **the place/house w. I live** l'endroit/la maison où j'habite; ▪ **whereabouts 1** *adv* où **2** ['weərəbaʊts] *n* **his w.** l'endroit *m* où il est ▪ **whereas** *conj* alors que ▪ **whereby** *adv Formal* par quoi
**wherever** [weər'evə(r)] *conj* **w. you go** *(everywhere)* partout où tu iras, où que tu ailles; **I'll go w. you like** j'irai (là) où vous voudrez

**whet** [wet] *(pt & pp* **-tt-**) *vt (appetite, desire)* aiguiser

**whether** ['weðə(r)] *conj* si; **I don't know w. to leave** je ne sais pas si je dois partir; **w. she does it or not** qu'elle le fasse ou non; **it's doubtful w....** il est douteux que... *(+ subjunctive)*

---

**WHICH** [wɪtʃ] **1** *adj (in questions)* quel, quelle, *pl* quel(le)s; **w. book?** quel livre?; **w. one?** lequel/laquelle?; **in w. case** auquel cas

**2** *relative pron (subject)* qui; *(object)* que; *(after prep)* lequel, laquelle, *pl* lesquel(le)s; *(referring to a whole clause) (subject)* ce qui; *(object)* ce que; **the house, w. is old...** la maison, qui est vieille...; **the book w. I like...** le livre que j'aime...; **the table w. I put it on...** la table sur laquelle je l'ai mis...; **the film of w. she was speaking** le film dont *ou* duquel elle parlait; **she's ill, w. is sad** elle est malade, ce qui est triste; **he lies, w. I don't like** il ment, ce que je n'aime pas; **after w.** *(whereupon)* après quoi

**3** *interrogative pron (in questions)* lequel, laquelle, *pl* lesquel(le)s; **w. of us?** lequel/laquelle d'entre nous?; **w. are the best of the books?** quels sont les meilleurs de ces livres?

**4** *pron* **w. (one)** *(the one that) (subject)* celui qui, celle qui, *pl* ceux qui, celles qui; *(object)* celui que, celle que, *pl* ceux que, celles que; **I know w. (ones) you want** je sais ceux/celles que vous désirez

---

**whichever** [wɪtʃ'evə(r)] **1** *adj (no matter which)* **take w. books interest you** prenez les livres qui vous intéressent; **take w. one you like** prends celui/celle que tu veux **2** *pron (no matter which)* quel que soit celui qui (*f* quelle que soit celle qui); **w. you choose...** quel que soit celui que tu choisiras...; **take w. you want** prends celui/celle que tu veux

**while** [waɪl] **1** *conj (when)* pendant que; *(although)* bien que *(+ subjunctive)*; *(as long as)* tant que; *(whereas)* tandis que; **w. eating** en mangeant **2** *n* **a w.** un moment; **all the w.** tout le temps **3** *vt* **to w. away the time** passer le temps (**doing sth** à faire qch) ■ **whilst** *conj Br* = **while**

**whim** [wɪm] *n* caprice *m*; **on a w.** sur un coup de tête

**whimper** ['wɪmpə(r)] *vi* gémir

**whine** [waɪn] *vi* gémir

**whip** [wɪp] **1** *n* fouet *m* **2** *(pt & pp* **-pp-**) *vt* fouetter; **whipped cream** crème *f* fouettée

▸ **whip off** *vt sep Fam (clothes)* enlever rapidement

▸ **whip out** *vt sep Fam* sortir brusquement (**from** de)

▸ **whip up** *vt sep (interest)* susciter; *Fam (meal)* préparer rapidement

**whirl** [wɜːl] **1** *vt* **to w. sb/sth (round)** faire tourbillonner qn/qch **2** *vi* **to w. (round)** tourbillonner ■ **whirlpool** *n* tourbillon *m* ■ **whirlwind** *n* tourbillon *m*

**whirr** [wɜː(r)] *vi* ronfler

**whisk** [wɪsk] **1** *n (for eggs)* fouet *m* **2** *vt* battre; **to w. away** *or* **off** *(object)* enlever rapidement; *(person)* emmener rapidement

**whiskers** ['wɪskəz] *npl (of cat)* moustaches *fpl*; *(of man)* favoris *mpl*

**whisky** ['wɪskɪ] *(Am* **whiskey**) *n* whisky *m*

**whisper** ['wɪspə(r)] **1** *n* chuchotement *m* **2** *vti* chuchoter; **to w. sth to sb** chuchoter qch à l'oreille de qn

**whistle** ['wɪsəl] **1** *n* sifflement *m*; *(object)* sifflet *m* **2** *vti* siffler

**white** [waɪt] **1** (**-er, -est**) *adj* blanc (*f* blanche); **to go** *or* **turn w.** blanchir; *Br* **w. coffee** café *m* au lait; **w. lie** pieux mensonge *m*; **w. man** Blanc *m*; **w. woman** Blanche *f* **2** *n (colour, of egg, eye)* blanc *m* ■ **whitewash 1** *n (paint)* badigeon *m* à la chaux **2** *vt (paint)* badigeonner à la chaux; *Fig (person)* blanchir

**Whitsun** ['wɪtsən] *n Br* la Pentecôte

**whizz** [wɪz] **1** *vi (rush)* aller à toute vitesse; **to w. past** *or* **by** passer à toute vitesse **2** *adj Fam* **w. kid** petit prodige *m*

**who** [huː] *pron* qui; **w. did it?** qui (est-ce qui) a fait ça?; **the woman w. came** la femme qui est venue; **w. were you talking to?** à qui est-ce que tu parlais?

**whodun(n)it** [huː'dʌnɪt] *n Fam* polar *m*

**whoever** [huː'evə(r)] *pron (no matter who) (subject)* qui que ce soit qui; *(object)* qui que ce soit que; **w. has seen this** *(anyone who)* quiconque a vu cela; **w. you are** qui que vous soyez; **this man, w. he is** cet homme, quel qu'il soit

**whole** [həʊl] **1** *adj* entier, -ère; **the w. time** tout le temps; **the w. apple** toute la pomme, la pomme tout entière; **the w. world** le monde entier

**2** *n* totalité *f*; **the w. of the village** le village tout entier, tout le village; **on the w., as a w.** dans l'ensemble ▪ **wholefood** *n* aliment *m* complet ▪ **whole-hearted** *adj* sans réserve ▪ **wholemeal** (*Am* **wholewheat**) *adj (bread)* complet, -ète ▪ **wholesome** *adj (food, climate)* sain

**wholesale** ['həʊlseɪl] **1** *adj (price)* de gros; **w. business** *or* **trade** commerce *m* de gros **2** *adv (buy, sell)* au prix de gros

**wholly** ['həʊlɪ] *adv* entièrement

**whom** [huːm] *pron Formal (object)* que; *(in questions and after prep)* qui; **w. did she see?** qui a-t-elle vu?; **the man w. you know** l'homme que tu connais; **the man of w. we were speaking** l'homme dont nous parlions

**whooping** ['huːpɪŋ] *adj* **w. cough** coqueluche *f*

**whoops** [wʊps] *exclam* houp-là!

**whopping** ['wɒpɪŋ] *adj Fam (big)* énorme

**whore** [hɔː(r)] *n Fam* putain *f*

**whose** [huːz] *possessive pron & adj* à qui, de qui; **w. book is this?, w. is this book?** à qui est ce livre?; **w. daughter are you?** de qui es-tu la fille?; **the woman w. book I have** la femme dont j'ai le livre; **the man w. mother I spoke to** l'homme à la mère de qui j'ai parlé

**why** [waɪ] **1** *adv* pourquoi; **w. not?** pourquoi pas? **2** *conj* **the reason w. they...** la raison pour laquelle ils... **3** *exclam (surprise)* tiens!

**wick** [wɪk] *n (of candle, lighter, oil lamp)* mèche *f*

**wicked** ['wɪkɪd] *adj (evil)* méchant

**wicker** ['wɪkə(r)] *n* osier *m*

**wicket** ['wɪkɪt] *n (cricket stumps)* guichet *m*

**wide** [waɪd] **1** (**-er, -est**) *adj* large; *(choice, variety, knowledge)* grand; **to be 3 metres w.** avoir 3 mètres de large **2** *adv (fall, shoot)* loin du but; **w. open** *(eyes, mouth, door)* grand ouvert; **w. awake** complètement réveillé ▪ **widely** *adv (travel)* beaucoup; *(spread)* largement; **it's w. thought that...** on pense généralement que... ▪ **widen 1** *vt* élargir **2** *vi* s'élargir

**widespread** ['waɪdspred] *adj* répandu

**widow** ['wɪdəʊ] *n* veuve *f* ▪ **widower** *n* veuf *m*

**width** [wɪdθ] *n* largeur *f*

**wield** [wiːld] *vt (brandish)* brandir; *Fig* **to w. power** exercer le pouvoir

**wife** [waɪf] (*pl* **wives**) *n* femme *f*, épouse *f*

**wig** [wɪg] *n* perruque *f*

**wiggle** ['wɪgəl] **1** *vt* remuer **2** *vi (of worm)* se tortiller; *(of tail)* remuer

**wild** [waɪld] **1** (**-er, -est**) *adj (animal, flower, region)* sauvage; *(idea)* fou (*f* folle); **w. with joy/anger** fou de joie/colère; **to be w.** *(of person)* mener une vie agitée; *Fam* **I'm not w. about it** ça ne m'emballe pas; **the W. West** le Far West

**2** *adv* **to grow w.** *(of plant)* pousser à l'état sauvage; **to run w.** *(of animals)* courir en liberté; *(of crowd)* se déchaîner

**3** *n* **in the w.** à l'état sauvage; **in the wilds** en pleine brousse ▪ **wildlife** *n* nature *f*

**wilderness** ['wɪldənəs] *n* région *f* sauvage

**wildly** ['waɪldlɪ] *adv (cheer)* frénétiquement; *(guess)* au hasard

**wilful** ['wɪlfəl] (*Am* **willful**) *adj (intentional, obstinate)* volontaire

**WILL¹** [wɪl]

On trouve généralement **I/you/he/** etc **will** sous leurs formes contractées **I'll/you'll/he'll/**etc. La forme négative correspondante est **won't**, que l'on écrira **will not** dans des contextes formels.

*v aux (expressing future tense)* **he w. come, he'll come** il viendra; **you w. not come, you won't come** tu ne viendras pas; **w. you have some tea?** veux-tu du thé?; **w. you be quiet!** veux-tu te taire!; **it won't open** ça ne s'ouvre pas

**will²** [wɪl] *n (resolve, determination)* volonté *f*; *(legal document)* testament *m*; **free w.** libre arbitre *m*; **against one's w.** à contrecœur; **at w.** à volonté; *(cry)* à la demande

**willing** ['wɪlɪŋ] *adj (helper, worker)* plein de bonne volonté; **to be w. to do sth** bien vouloir faire qch ▪ **willingly** *adv (with pleasure)* volontiers; *(voluntarily)* de son plein gré ▪ **willingness** *n* bonne volonté *f*; **her w. to do sth** *(enthusiasm)* son empressement à faire qch

**willpower** ['wɪlpaʊə(r)] *n* volonté *f*

**wilt** [wɪlt] *vi (of plant)* dépérir

**wily** ['waɪlɪ] (**-ier, -iest**) *adj* rusé

**wimp** [wɪmp] *n Fam (weakling)* mauviette *f*

**win** [wɪn] **1** *n (victory)* victoire *f* **2** (*pt & pp* **won,** *pres p* **winning**) *vt (money, race, prize)* gagner; *(victory)* remporter; *(fame)* acquérir; *(friends)* se faire; *Br* **to w. sb over** *or* **round** gagner qn (**to** à) **3** *vi* gagner ▪ **winning 1** *adj (number, horse)* gagnant; *(team)* victorieux, -euse; *(goal)* décisif, -ive **2** *npl* **winnings** gains *mpl*

**wince** [wɪns] *vi* faire une grimace

**winch** [wɪntʃ] **1** *n* treuil *m* **2** *vt* **to w. (up)** hisser

**wind¹** [wɪnd] **1** *n* vent *m*; *(breath)* souffle *m*; **to have w.** *(in stomach)* avoir des gaz; **to get w. of sth** avoir vent de qch; *Mus* **w. instrument** instrument *m* à vent

**2** *vt* **to w. sb** *(of blow)* couper le souffle à qn ▪ **windcheater** (*Am* **windbreaker**) *n* coupe-vent *m inv* ▪ **windfall** *n (unexpected money)* aubaine *f* ▪ **windmill** *n* moulin *m* à vent ▪ **windscreen** (*Am* **windshield**) *n (of vehicle)* pare-brise *m inv*; **w. wiper** essuie-glace *m* ▪ **windsurfer** *n (person)* véliplanchiste *mf* ▪ **windsurfing** *n* **to go w.** faire de la planche à voile ▪ **windy** (**-ier, -iest**) *adj* **it's w.** *(of weather)* il y a du vent; **w. day** jour *m* de grand vent

**wind²** [waɪnd] **1** (*pt & pp* **wound**) *vt (roll)* enrouler (**round** autour de); *(clock)* remonter; **to w. a cassette back** rembobiner une cassette **2** *vi (of river, road)* serpenter ▪ **winding** *adj (road)* sinueux, -euse; *(staircase)* en colimaçon

▸ **wind down 1** *vt sep (car window)* baisser **2** *vi Fam (relax)* se détendre

▸ **wind up 1** *vt sep (clock)* remonter; *(meeting, speech)* terminer; *Br Fam* **to w. sb up** faire marcher qn **2** *vi (end up)* finir (**doing sth** par faire qch); **to w. up with sb/sth** se retrouver avec qn/qch

**window** ['wɪndəʊ] *n* fenêtre *f*; *(pane)* vitre *f*; *(of shop)* vitrine *f*; *(counter)* guichet *m*; *Br* **French w.** porte-fenêtre *f*; **w. box** jardinière *f*; *Br* **w. cleaner,** *Am* **w. washer** laveur, -euse *mf* de vitres; *Br* **w. ledge** rebord *m* de fenêtre ▪ **windowpane** *n* vitre *f*, carreau *m* ▪ **window-shopping** *n* **to go w.** faire du lèche-vitrines ▪ **windowsill** *n* rebord *m* de fenêtre

**wine** [waɪn] *n* vin *m*; **w. bar/bottle** bar *m*/bouteille *f* à vin; **w. cellar** cave *f* à vin; **w. list** carte *f* des vins; **w. tasting** dégustation *f*; **w. waiter** sommelier *m* ▪ **wineglass** *n* verre *m* à vin

**wing** [wɪŋ] *n* aile *f*; **the wings** *(in theatre)* les coulisses *fpl*

**wink** [wɪŋk] *vi* faire un clin d'œil (**at** à)

**winner** ['wɪnə(r)] *n* gagnant, -e *mf*

**winter** ['wɪntə(r)] **1** *n* hiver *m*; **in (the) w.** en hiver **2** *adj* d'hiver ▪ **wintertime** *n* hiver *m* ▪ **wintry** *adj* hivernal; **w. day** jour *m* d'hiver

**wipe** [waɪp] **1** *n* **to give sth a w.** essuyer qch **2** *vt* essuyer; **to w. one's feet/hands** s'essuyer les pieds/les mains; **to w. sth away** *or* **off** *or* **up** *(liquid)* essuyer qch; **to w. sth out** *(clean)* essuyer qch; *(destroy)* anéantir qch ▪ **wiper** *n* essuie-glace *m*

**wire** ['waɪə(r)] **1** *n* fil *m*; **w. mesh** *or* **netting** toile *f* métallique **2** *vt* **to w. (up)** *(house)* faire l'installation électrique de; **to w. sth (up) to sth** *(connect electrically)* relier qch à qch ▪ **wiring** *n (system)* installation *f* électrique

**wisdom** ['wɪzdəm] *n* sagesse *f*

**wise** [waɪz] (**-er, -est**) *adj (in knowledge)* sage; *(advisable)* prudent; **to be none the wiser** ne pas être plus avancé ▪ **wisely** *adv* sagement

**-wise** [waɪz] *suff (with regard to)* **money-w.** question argent

**wish** [wɪʃ] **1** *n (specific)* souhait *m*, vœu *m*; *(general)* désir *m*; **to do sth against sb's wishes** faire qch contre le souhait de qn; **best wishes, all good wishes** *(in letter)* amitiés *fpl*; **send him my best wishes** fais-lui mes amitiés

**2** *vt* souhaiter (**to do** faire); **I w. (that) you could help me** je voudrais que vous m'aidiez; **I w. she could come** j'aurais bien aimé qu'elle vienne; **I w. you (a) happy birthday/(good) luck** je vous souhaite bon anniversaire/bonne chance; **I w. I could** si seulement je pouvais

**3** *vi* **to w. for sth** souhaiter qch; **as you w.** comme vous voudrez ▪ **wishful** *adj* **it's w. thinking (on your part)** tu prends tes désirs pour des réalités

**wisp** [wɪsp] *n (of smoke)* traînée *f*; *(of hair)* mèche *f*

**wistful** ['wɪstfəl] *adj* nostalgique

**wit** [wɪt] *n (humour)* esprit *m*; *(person)* homme *m*/femme *f* d'esprit; **wits** *(intelligence)* intelligence *f*; **to be at one's wits'** *or* **w.'s end** ne plus savoir que faire

**witch** [wɪtʃ] *n* sorcière *f*

---

**WITH** [wɪð] *prep* (**a**) *(expressing accompaniment)* avec; **come w. me** viens avec moi; **w. no hat/gloves** sans chapeau/gants; **I'll be right w. you** je suis à vous dans une seconde; *Fam* **I'm w. you** *(I understand)* je te suis; *Fam* **to be w. it** *(up-to-date)* être dans le vent

(**b**) *(at the house, flat of)* chez; **she's staying w. me** elle loge chez moi

(**c**) *(expressing cause)* de; **to tremble w. fear** trembler de peur; **to be ill w. measles** être malade de la rougeole

(**d**) *(expressing instrument, means)* **to write w. a pen** écrire avec un stylo; **to fill w. sth** remplir de qch; **satisfied w. sb/sth** satisfait de qn/qch; **w. my own eyes** de mes propres yeux

(**e**) *(in description)* à; **a woman w. blue eyes** une femme aux yeux bleus

(**f**) *(despite)* malgré; **w. all his faults** malgré tous ses défauts

---

**withdraw** [wɪð'drɔː] **1** (*pt* **-drew,** *pp* **-drawn**) *vt* retirer (**from** de) **2** *vi* se retirer (**from** de) ▪ **withdrawal** *n* retrait *m* ▪ **withdrawn** *adj (person)* renfermé

**withhold** [wɪð'həʊld] (*pt & pp* **-held**) *vt (permission, help)* refuser (**from** à); *(decision)* différer; *(money)* retenir (**from** de); *(information)* cacher (**from** à)

**within** [wɪð'ɪn] **1** *prep (inside)* à l'intérieur de; **w. 10 km (of)** *(less than)* à moins de 10 km (de); *(inside an area of)* dans un rayon de 10 km (de); **w. a month** *(return)* avant un mois; *(finish)*

en moins d'un mois; **w. sight** en vue **2** *adv* à l'intérieur
**without** [wɪð'aʊt] **1** *prep* sans; **w. a tie** sans cravate; **w. doing sth** sans faire qch; **to do w. sb/sth** se passer de qn/qch **2** *adv* **to do w.** se priver
**withstand** [wɪð'stænd] (*pt & pp* **-stood**) *vt* résister à
**witness** ['wɪtnɪs] **1** *n (person)* témoin *m* **2** *vt (accident)* être témoin de; *(document)* signer (pour attester l'authenticité de)
**witty** ['wɪtɪ] (**-ier, -iest**) *adj* spirituel, -elle
**wives** [waɪvz] *pl of* **wife**
**wizard** ['wɪzəd] *n* magicien *m*; *Fig (genius)* as *m*
**wobble** ['wɒbəl] *vi (of chair)* branler; *(of jelly, leg)* trembler; *(of wheel)* tourner de façon irrégulière; *(of person)* chanceler ▪ **wobbly** *adj (table, chair)* branlant
**woe** [wəʊ] *n* malheur *m*
**wok** [wɒk] *n* poêle *f* chinoise
**woke** [wəʊk] *pt of* **wake**[1]
**woken** ['wəʊkən] *pp of* **wake**[1]
**wolf** [wʊlf] **1** (*pl* **wolves**) *n* loup *m* **2** *vt* **to w. (down)** *(food)* engloutir
**woman** ['wʊmən] (*pl* **women**) *n* femme *f*; **women's** *(clothes, attitudes, magazine)* féminin; **women's rights** droits *mpl* des femmes
**womb** [wu:m] *n Anat* utérus *m*
**women** ['wɪmɪn] *pl of* **woman**
**won** [wʌn] *pt & pp of* **win**
**wonder** ['wʌndə(r)] **1** *n (marvel)* merveille *f*; *(feeling)* émerveillement *m*; **it's no w.** ce n'est pas étonnant (**that** que + *subjunctive*); **it's a w. she wasn't killed** c'est un miracle qu'elle n'ait pas été tuée
**2** *vt (ask oneself)* se demander (**if** si; **why** pourquoi)
**3** *vi (ask oneself questions)* s'interroger (**about** au sujet de *ou* sur); **I was just wondering** je réfléchissais
**wonderful** ['wʌndəfəl] *adj* merveilleux, -euse
**wonky** ['wɒŋkɪ] (**-ier, -iest**) *adj Br Fam (table)* déglingué; *(hat, picture)* de travers
**won't** [wəʊnt] = **will not**
**woo** [wu:] (*pt & pp* **wooed**) *vt (voters)* chercher à plaire à
**wood** [wʊd] *n (material, forest)* bois *m* ▪ **wooded** *adj* boisé ▪ **wooden** *adj* en bois; *Fig (manner, dancer, actor)* raide ▪ **woodland** *n* région *f* boisée ▪ **woodwind** *n* **the w.** *(musical instruments)* les bois *mpl* ▪ **woodwork** *n (school subject)* menuiserie *f* ▪ **woodworm** *n* **it has w.** c'est vermoulu
**wool** [wʊl] *n* laine *f* ▪ **woollen** (*Am* **woolen**) **1** *adj (dress)* en laine **2** *npl* **woollens** (*Am* **woolens**) *(garments)* lainages *mpl* ▪ **woolly** (**-ier, -iest**) **1** *adj* en laine; *Fig (unclear)* nébuleux, -euse **2** *n Br Fam (garment)* lainage *m*
**word** [wɜ:d] **1** *n* mot *m*; *(promise)* parole *f*; **words** *(of song)* paroles *fpl*; **to have a w. with sb** parler à qn; **to keep one's w.** tenir sa promesse; **in other words** autrement dit; **w. for w.** *(report)* mot pour mot; *(translate)* mot à mot; **w. processing** traitement *m* de texte; **w. processor** machine *f* à traitement de texte
**2** *vt (express)* formuler ▪ **wording** *n* termes *mpl* ▪ **wordy** (**-ier, -iest**) *adj* prolixe
**wore** [wɔ:(r)] *pt of* **wear**
**work** [wɜ:k] **1** *n* travail *m*; *(literary, artistic)* œuvre *f*; **works** *(construction)* travaux *mpl*; **to be at w.** travailler; **it's hard w. (doing that)** ça demande beaucoup de travail (de faire ça); **to be out of w.** être sans travail; **a day off w.** un jour de congé; **w. permit** permis *m* de travail; **w. station** poste *m* de travail; **w. of art** œuvre *f* d'art
**2** *vt (person)* faire travailler; *(machine)* faire marcher; *(metal, wood)* travailler
**3** *vi (of person)* travailler; *(of machine)* marcher, fonctionner; *(of drug)* agir; **to w. loose** *(of knot, screw)* se desserrer; **to w. towards** *(result, agreement, aim)* travailler à ▪ **workaholic** [-ə'hɒlɪk] *n*

*Fam* bourreau *m* de travail ▪ **workforce** *n* main-d'œuvre *f* ▪ **workload** *n* charge *f* de travail ▪ **workman** (*pl* **-men**) *n* ouvrier *m* ▪ **workmanship** *n* travail *m* ▪ **workmate** *n Br* camarade *mf* de travail ▪ **workout** *n (sports training)* séance *f* d'entraînement ▪ **workshop** *n (place, study course)* atelier *m*

▸ **work at** *vt insep (improve)* travailler

▸ **work off** *vt sep (debt)* payer en travaillant; *(excess fat)* se débarrasser de (par l'exercice)

▸ **work on** *vt insep (book, problem)* travailler à; *(French)* travailler

▸ **work out 1** *vt sep (calculate)* calculer; *(problem)* résoudre; *(plan)* préparer; *(understand)* comprendre **2** *vi (succeed)* marcher; *(do exercises)* s'entraîner; **it works out at 50 euros** ça fait 50 euros

▸ **work up 1** *vt sep* **to w. up enthusiasm** s'enthousiasmer (**for** pour); **I worked up an appetite** ça m'a ouvert l'appétit; **to get worked up** s'énerver **2** *vi* **to w. up to sth** se préparer à qch

**worker** ['wɜːkə(r)] *n* travailleur, -euse *mf*; *(manual)* ouvrier, -ère *mf*; **(office) w.** employé, -e *mf* (de bureau)

**working** ['wɜːkɪŋ] **1** *adj (day, clothes)* de travail; **in w. order** en état de marche; **w. class** classe *f* ouvrière; **w. conditions** conditions *fpl* de travail **2** *npl* **the workings of** *(clock)* le mécanisme de ▪ **working-class** *adj* ouvrier, -ère

**world** [wɜːld] **1** *n* monde *m*; **all over the w.** dans le monde entier **2** *adj (war, production)* mondial; *(champion, record)* du monde; **the W. Cup** *(in football)* la Coupe du Monde ▪ **worldly** *adj (person)* qui a l'expérience du monde ▪ **worldwide 1** *adj* mondial **2** *adv* dans le monde entier

**worm** [wɜːm] **1** *n* ver *m* **2** *vt* **to w. one's way into** s'insinuer dans; **to w. sth out of sb** soutirer qch à qn

**worn** [wɔːn] **1** *pp of* **wear 2** *adj (clothes, tyre)* usé ▪ **worn-out** *adj (object)* complètement usé; *(person)* épuisé

**worry** ['wʌrɪ] **1** (*pl* **-ies**) *n* souci *m*; **it's a w.** ça me cause du souci

**2** (*pt & pp* **-ied**) *vt* inquiéter

**3** *vi* s'inquiéter (**about sth** de qch; **about sb** pour qn) ▪ **worried** *adj* inquiet, -ète (**about** au sujet de) ▪ **worrying** *adj* inquiétant

**worse** [wɜːs] **1** *adj* pire (**than** que); **to get w.** se détériorer; **he's getting w.** *(in health)* il va de plus en plus mal; *(in behaviour)* il se conduit de plus en plus mal

**2** *adv* plus mal (**than** que); **I could do w.** j'aurais pu tomber plus mal; **she's w. off (than before)** sa situation est pire (qu'avant); *(financially)* elle est encore plus pauvre (qu'avant)

**3** *n* **there's w. to come** le pire reste à venir; **a change for the w.** une détérioration

**worsen** ['wɜːsən] **1** *vt* aggraver **2** *vi* empirer

**worship** ['wɜːʃɪp] **1** *n* culte *m* **2** (*pt & pp* **-pp-**) *vt (person, god)* adorer; *Pej (money)* avoir le culte de

**worst** [wɜːst] **1** *adj* pire; **the w. book I've ever read** le plus mauvais livre que j'aie jamais lu **2** *adv* **(the) w.** le plus mal **3** *n* **the w. (one)** *(object, person)* le/la pire, le/la plus mauvais(e); **the w. (thing) is that...** le pire, c'est que...; **at (the) w.** au pire

**worth** [wɜːθ] **1** *adj* **to be w. sth** valoir qch; **how much** *or* **what is it w.?** ça vaut combien?; **the film's (well) w. seeing** le film vaut la peine d'être vu **2** *n* valeur *f*; **to buy 50 pence w. of chocolates** acheter pour 50 pence de chocolats; **to get one's money's w.** en avoir pour son argent ▪ **worthless** *adj* qui ne vaut rien

**worthwhile** ['wɜːθ'waɪl] *adj (book, film)* qui vaut la peine d'être lu/vu; *(activity)* qui vaut la peine; *(plan, contribution)* valable; *(cause)* louable; *(satisfying)* qui donne des satisfactions

**worthy** ['wɜːðɪ] (**-ier, -iest**) *adj (person)* digne; *(cause, act)* louable; **to be w. of sb/sth** être digne de qn/qch

**WOULD** [wʊd, *unstressed* wəd]

On trouve généralement **I/you/he** etc **would** sous leurs formes contractées **I'd/you'd/he'd** etc. La forme négative correspondante est **wouldn't**, que l'on écrira **would not** dans des contextes formels.

*v aux* (**a**) *(expressing conditional tense)* **I w. stay if I could** je resterais si je le pouvais; **he w. have done it** il l'aurait fait; **I said she'd come** j'ai dit qu'elle viendrait

(**b**) *(willingness, ability)* **w. you help me, please?** veux-tu bien m'aider?; **she wouldn't help me** elle n'a pas voulu m'aider; **w. you like some tea?** prendrez-vous du thé?; **the car wouldn't start** la voiture ne démarrait pas

(**c**) *(expressing past habit)* **I w. see her every day** je la voyais chaque jour

**wound[1]** [wuːnd] **1** *n* blessure *f* **2** *vt (hurt)* blesser; **the wounded** les blessés *mpl*

**wound[2]** [waʊnd] *pt & pp of* **wind[2]**

**wove** [wəʊv] *pt of* **weave**

**woven** ['wəʊvən] *pp of* **weave**

**wow** [waʊ] *exclam Fam* oh là là!

**wrap** [ræp] **1** *n Am* **plastic w.** film *m* plastique

**2** *(pt & pp* **-pp-***) vt* **to w. (up)** envelopper; *(parcel)* emballer; *Fig* **wrapped up in** *(engrossed)* absorbé par

**3** *vti* **to w. (oneself) up** *(dress warmly)* s'emmitoufler ▪ **wrapper** *n (of sweet)* papier *m* ▪ **wrapping** *n (action, material)* emballage *m*; **w. paper** papier *m* d'emballage

**wreath** [riːθ] *(pl* **-s** [riːðz]) *n* couronne *f*

**wreck** [rek] **1** *n (ship)* épave *f*; *(train)* train *m* accidenté; *(person)* épave *f* (humaine); **to be a nervous w.** être à bout de nerfs **2** *vt (break, destroy)* détruire; *Fig (spoil)* gâcher; *(career, hopes)* briser ▪ **wreckage** [-ɪdʒ] *n (of plane, train)* débris *mpl*

**wrench** [rentʃ] **1** *n Am (tool)* clef *f* (à écrous) **2** *vt* **to w. sth from sb** arracher qch à qn

**wrestle** ['resəl] *vi* lutter (**with sb** avec qn); *Fig* **to w. with a problem** se débattre avec un problème ▪ **wrestler** *n* lutteur, -euse *mf*; *(in all-in wrestling)* catcheur, -euse *mf* ▪ **wrestling** *n* lutte *f*; **(all-in) w.** *(with relaxed rules)* catch *m*

**wretch** [retʃ] *n (unfortunate person)* malheureux, -euse *mf*; *(rascal)* misérable *mf* ▪ **wretched** [-ɪd] *adj (poor, pitiful)* misérable; *(dreadful)* affreux, -euse; *Fam (annoying)* maudit

**wriggle** ['rɪgəl] **1** *vt (toes, fingers)* tortiller **2** *vi* **to w. (about)** se tortiller; *(of fish)* frétiller; **to w. out of sth** couper à qch

**wring** [rɪŋ] *(pt & pp* **wrung**) *vt* **to w. (out)** *(clothes)* essorer; **to w. one's hands** se tordre les mains

**wrinkle** ['rɪŋkəl] **1** *n (on skin)* ride *f*; *(in cloth, paper)* pli *m* **2** *vi (of skin)* se rider; *(of cloth)* faire des plis ▪ **wrinkled** *adj (skin)* ridé; *(cloth)* froissé

**wrist** [rɪst] *n* poignet *m* ▪ **wristwatch** *n* montre-bracelet *f*

**write** [raɪt] *(pt* **wrote,** *pp* **written**) *vti* écrire; **to w. to sb** écrire à qn ▪ **write-off** *n Br* **to be a (complete) w.** *(of vehicle)* être bon pour la casse

▸ **write away for** *vt insep (details)* écrire pour demander

▸ **write back** *vi* répondre

▸ **write down** *vt sep* noter

▸ **write in 1** *vt sep (insert)* inscrire **2** *vi (send letter)* écrire

▸ **write off** *vt sep (debt)* annuler

▸ **write out** *vt sep (list, recipe)* noter; *(cheque)* faire

▸ **write up** *vt sep (notes)* rédiger

**writer** ['raɪtə(r)] *n* auteur *m* (**of** de); *(literary)* écrivain *m*

**writing** ['raɪtɪŋ] *n (handwriting, action, profession)* écriture *f*; **to put sth (down) in w.** mettre qch par écrit; **w. pad** bloc-notes *m*; **w. paper** papier *m* à lettres

**written** ['rɪtən] *pp of* **write**

**wrong** [rɒŋ] **1** *adj (sum, idea)* faux (*f* fausse); *(direction, time)* mauvais; *(unfair)* injuste; **to be w.** *(of person)* avoir tort (**to do** de faire); **it's the w. road** ce n'est pas la bonne route; **the clock's w.** la pendule n'est pas à l'heure; **to get the w. number** *(on phone)* se tromper de numéro; **something's w. with the phone** le téléphone ne marche pas bien; **something's w. with her leg** elle a quelque chose à la jambe; **what's w. with you?** qu'est-ce que tu as?; **the w. way round** *or* **up** à l'envers

**2** *adv* mal; **to go w.** *(of plan)* mal tourner; *(of vehicle, machine)* tomber en panne; *(of person)* se tromper

**3** *n (injustice)* injustice *f*; **to be in the w.** être dans son tort; **right and w.** le bien et le mal

**4** *vt* faire du tort à ▪ **wrongful** *adj* **w. arrest** arrestation *f* arbitraire ▪ **wrongly** *adv (inform, translate)* mal; *(accuse, condemn, claim)* à tort

**wrote** [rəʊt] *pt of* **write**

**wrung** [rʌŋ] *pt & pp of* **wring**

**wry** [raɪ] (**wryer, wryest**) *adj* ironique

**X, x** [eks] *n (letter)* X, x *m inv*

**xenophobia** [*Br* zenə'fəʊbɪə, *Am* zi:nəʊ-] *n* xénophobie *f*

**Xerox®** ['zɪərɒks] **1** *n (copy)* photocopie *f* **2** *vt* photocopier

**Xmas** ['krɪsməs] *n Fam* Noël *m*

**X-ray** ['eksreɪ] **1** *n (picture)* radio *f*; **to have an X.** passer une radio **2** *vt* radiographier

**xylophone** ['zaɪləfəʊn] *n* xylophone *m*

# Yy

**Y, y** [waɪ] *n (letter)* Y, y *m inv*
**yacht** [jɒt] *n (sailing boat)* voilier *m*; *(large private boat)* yacht *m* ■ **yachting** *n* voile *f*
**yap** [jæp] *(pt & pp* **-pp-***) vi (of dog)* japper
**yard[1]** [jɑːd] *n (of house, farm, school, prison)* cour *f*; *(for working)* chantier *m*; *(for storage)* dépôt *m* de marchandises; *Am (garden)* jardin *m*
**yard[2]** [jɑːd] *n (measure)* yard *m (= 91,44 cm)*
**yarn** [jɑːn] *n (thread)* fil *m*; *Fam (tale)* histoire *f* à dormir debout
**yawn** [jɔːn] *vi* bâiller
**year** [jɪə(r)] *n* an *m*, année *f*; *(of wine)* année *f*; **school/tax y.** année *f* scolaire/fiscale; **in the y. 2004** en (l'an) 2004; **he's ten years old** il a dix ans; **New Y.** Nouvel An *m*; **New Y.'s Day** le jour de l'An; **New Y.'s Eve** la Saint-Sylvestre ■ **yearly 1** *adj* annuel, -elle **2** *adv* annuellement; **twice y.** deux fois par an
**yearn** [jɜːn] *vi* **to y. for sb** languir après qn; **to y. for sth** désirer ardemment qch; **to y. to do sth** brûler de faire qch
**yeast** [jiːst] *n* levure *f*
**yell** [jel] *vti* **to y. (out)** hurler; **to y. at sb** *(scold)* crier après qn
**yellow** ['jeləʊ] **1** *adj (in colour)* jaune; **y. card** *(in football)* carton *m* jaune **2** *n* jaune *m*
**yes** [jes] **1** *adv* oui; *(after negative question)* si **2** *n* oui *m inv*
**yesterday** ['jestədeɪ] **1** *adv* hier **2** *n* hier *m*; **y. morning/evening** hier matin/soir; **the day before y.** avant-hier
**yet** [jet] **1** *adv* (**a**) *(still)* encore; *(already)* déjà; **she hasn't arrived (as) y.** elle n'est pas encore arrivée; **the best y.** le meilleur jusqu'ici; **y. another mistake** encore une erreur; **not (just) y.** pas pour l'instant (**b**) *(in questions)* **has he come y.?** est-il arrivé? **2** *conj (nevertheless)* pourtant
**yew** [juː] *n (tree, wood)* if *m*
**yield** [jiːld] **1** *n (of field, shares)* rendement *m* **2** *vt (result)* donner; *(interest)* rapporter; *(territory, right)* céder; **to y. a profit** rapporter **3** *vi (surrender)* se rendre; *Am* **'y.'** *(road sign)* 'cédez le passage'
**yob** [jɒb], **yobbo** ['jɒbəʊ] *(pl* **yob(bo)s***) n Br Fam* loubard *m*
**yoga** ['jəʊgə] *n* yoga *m*
**yog(h)urt** [*Br* 'jɒgət, *Am* 'jəʊgərt] *n* yaourt *m*
**yolk** [jəʊk] *n* jaune *m* (d'œuf)
**you** [juː] *pron* (**a**) *(subject) (pl, polite form sing)* vous; *(familiar form sing)* tu; *(object)* vous, te, t', *pl* vous; *(after prep, 'than', 'it is')* vous, toi, *pl* vous; **(to) y.** *(indirect)* vous, te, t', *pl* vous; **I gave it (to) y.** je vous/te l'ai donné; **y. teachers** vous autres professeurs; **y. idiot!** espèce d'imbécile!
(**b**) *(indefinite)* on; *(object)* vous, te, t', *pl* vous; **y. never know** on ne sait jamais ■ **you'd** = **you had, you would** ■ **you'll** = **you will**
**young** [jʌŋ] **1** (**-er, -est**) *adj* jeune; **she's two years younger than me** elle a deux ans de moins que moi; **my**

**young(er) brother** mon (frère) cadet; **my youngest sister** la cadette de mes sœurs; **y. people** les jeunes *mpl*
**2** *n (of animals)* petits *mpl*; **the y.** *(people)* les jeunes *mpl*; **she's my youngest** *(daughter)* c'est ma petite dernière ▪ **youngster** *n* jeune *mf*

**your** [jɔ:(r)] *possessive adj (polite form sing, polite and familiar form pl)* votre, *pl* vos; *(familiar form sing)* ton, ta, *pl* tes; *(one's)* son, sa, *pl* ses

**yours** [jɔ:z] *possessive pron* le vôtre, la vôtre, *pl* les vôtres; *(familiar form sing)* le tien, la tienne, *pl* les tien(ne)s; **this book is y.** ce livre est à vous *ou* est le vôtre/ce livre est à toi *ou* est le tien; **a friend of y.** un ami à vous/toi

**yourself** [jɔ:'self] *pron (polite form)* vous-même; *(familiar form)* toi-même; *(reflexive)* vous, te, t'; *(after prep)* vous, toi; **you wash y.** vous vous lavez/tu te laves ▪ **yourselves** *pron pl* vous-mêmes; *(reflexive and after prep)* vous; **did you cut y.?** est-ce que vous vous êtes coupés?

**youth** [ju:θ] *(pl* **-s** [ju:ðz]) *n (age)* jeunesse *f*; *(young man)* jeune *m*; **y. club** centre *m* de loisirs pour les jeunes; **y. hostel** auberge *f* de jeunesse ▪ **youthful** *adj (person)* jeune

**you've** [ju:v] = **you have**

**yo-yo** ['jəʊjəʊ] *(pl* **yo-yos**) *n* Yo-Yo® *m inv*

**yuppie** ['yʌpɪ] *n* yuppie *mf*

# Zz

**Z, z** [*Br* zed, *Am* zi:] *n (letter)* Z, z *m inv*
**zany** ['zeɪnɪ] (**-ier, -iest**) *adj* loufoque
**zap** [zæp] (*pt & pp* **-pp-**) *vt Fam Comptr* effacer
**zeal** [zi:l] *n* zèle *m* ▪ **zealous** ['zeləs] *adj* zélé
**zebra** ['zi:brə, *Br* 'zebrə] *n* zèbre *m*; *Br* **z. crossing** passage *m* pour piétons
**zero** ['zɪərəʊ] (*pl* **-os**) *n* zéro *m*
**zest** [zest] *n (enthusiasm)* enthousiasme *m*; *(of lemon, orange)* zeste *m*
**zigzag** ['zɪgzæg] **1** *n* zigzag *m* **2** *adj & adv* en zigzag **3** (*pt & pp* **-gg-**) *vi* zigzaguer
**zinc** [zɪŋk] *n* zinc *m*
**zip** [zɪp] **1** *n Br* **z. (fastener)** fermeture *f* Éclair® **2** *adj Am* **z. code** code *m* postal **3** (*pt & pp* **-pp-**) *vt* **to z. sth (up)** remonter la fermeture Éclair® de qch **4** *vi* **to z. past** *(of car)* passer en trombe ▪ **zipper** *n Am* fermeture *f* Éclair®
**zit** [zɪt] *n Fam (pimple)* bouton *m*
**zodiac** ['zəʊdɪæk] *n* zodiaque *m*
**zone** [zəʊn] *n* zone *f*
**zoo** [zu:] (*pl* **zoos**) *n* zoo *m*
**zoom** [zu:m] **1** *n* **z. lens** zoom *m* **2** *vi* **to z. in** *(of camera)* faire un zoom avant (**on** sur); *Fam* **to z. past** passer comme une flèche
**zucchini** [zu:'ki:nɪ] (*pl* **-ni** *or* **-nis**) *n Am* courgette *f*

# French Verb Conjugations

## Regular Verbs

| | **-ER verbs** | **-IR verbs** | **-RE verbs** |
|---|---|---|---|
| *Infinitive* | *donn/er* | *fin/ir* | *vend/re* |
| 1 Present | je donne | je finis | je vends |
| | tu donnes | tu finis | tu vends |
| | il donne | il finit | il vend |
| | nous donnons | nous finissons | nous vendons |
| | vous donnez | vous finissez | vous vendez |
| | ils donnent | ils finissent | ils vendent |
| 2 Imperfect | je donnais | je finissais | je vendais |
| | tu donnais | tu finissais | tu vendais |
| | il donnait | il finissait | il vendait |
| | nous donnions | nous finissions | nous vendions |
| | vous donniez | vous finissiez | vous vendiez |
| | ils donnaient | ils finissaient | ils vendaient |
| 3 Past historic | je donnai | je finis | je vendis |
| | tu donnas | tu finis | tu vendis |
| | il donna | il finit | il vendit |
| | nous donnâmes | nous finîmes | nous vendîmes |
| | vous donnâtes | vous finîtes | vous vendîtes |
| | ils donnèrent | ils finirent | ils vendirent |
| 4 Future | je donnerai | je finirai | je vendrai |
| | tu donneras | tu finiras | tu vendras |
| | il donnera | il finira | il vendra |
| | nous donnerons | nous finirons | nous vendrons |
| | vous donnerez | vous finirez | vous vendrez |
| | ils donneront | ils finiront | ils vendront |
| 5 Subjunctive | je donne | je finisse | je vende |
| | tu donnes | tu finisses | tu vendes |
| | il donne | il finisse | il vende |
| | nous donnions | nous finissions | nous vendions |
| | vous donniez | vous finissiez | vous vendiez |
| | ils donnent | ils finissent | ils vendent |
| 6 Imperative | donne | finis | vends |
| | donnons | finissons | vendons |
| | donnez | finissez | vendez |
| 7 Present participle | donnant | finissant | vendant |
| 8 Past participle | donné | fini | vendu |

*Note* The conditional is formed by adding the following endings to the infinitive: **-ais**, **-ais**, **-ait**, **-ions**, **-iez**, **-aient**. The final **e** is dropped in infinitives ending **-re**.

# Irregular French Verbs

Listed below are those verbs considered to be the most useful. Forms and tenses not given are fully derivable, such as the third person singular of the **present tense** which is normally formed by substituting 't' for the final 's' of the first person singular, eg 'crois' becomes 'croit', 'dis' becomes 'dit'. Note that the endings of the **past historic** fall into three categories, the 'a' and 'i' categories shown at donner, and at finir and vendre, and the 'u' category which has the following endings: -us, -ut, -ûmes, -ûtes, -urent. Most of the verbs listed below form their past historic with 'u'.

The **imperfect** may usually be formed by adding -ais, -ait, -ions, -iez, -aient to the stem of the first person plural of the present tense, eg 'je buvais' etc may be derived from 'nous buvons' (stem 'buv-' and ending '-ons'); similarly, the **present participle** may generally be formed by substituting -ant for -ons (eg buvant). The **future** may usually be formed by adding -ai, -as, -a, -ons, -ez, -ont to the infinitive or to an infinitive without final 'e' where the ending is -re (eg conduire). The **imperative** usually has the same forms as the second persons singular and plural and first person plural of the present tense.

| | | | |
|---|---|---|---|
| 1 = Present | 2 = Imperfect | 3 = Past historic | 4 = Future |
| 5 = Subjunctive | 6 = Imperative | 7 = Present participle | 8 = Past participle |
| n = nous | v = vous | *verbs conjugated with **être** only | |

**abattre** *like* **battre**

**absoudre** 1 j'absous, n absolvons 2 j'absolvais<br>3 j'absolus *(rarely used)* 5 j'absolve 7 absolvant<br>8 absous, absoute

**s'abstenir** *like* **tenir**

**abstraire** 1 j'abstrais, n abstrayons 2 j'abstrayais 3 *none* 5 j'abstraie<br>7 abstrayant 8 abstrait

**accourir** *like* **courir**

**accroître** *like* **croître** *except* 8 accru

**accueillir** *like* **cueillir**

**acquérir** 1 j'acquiers, n acquérons 2 j'acquérais 3 j'acquis<br>4 j'acquerrai 5 j'acquière 7 acquérant 8 acquis

**adjoindre** *like* **joindre**

**admettre** *like* **mettre**

**advenir** *like* **venir** *(third person only)*

***aller** 1 je vais, tu vas, il va, n allons, v allez, ils vont 4 j'irai<br>5 j'aille, n allions, ils aillent 6 va, allons, allez (*but note* vas-y)

**apercevoir** *like* **recevoir**

**apparaître** *like* **connaître**

**appartenir** *like* **tenir**

**apprendre** *like* **prendre**
**asseoir** 1 j'assieds, il assied, n asseyons, ils asseyent 2 j'asseyais 3 j'assis 4 j'assiérai 5 j'asseye 7 asseyant 8 assis
**astreindre** *like* **atteindre**
**atteindre** 1 j'atteins, n atteignons, ils atteignent 2 j'atteignais 3 j'atteignis 4 j'atteindrai 5 j'atteigne 7 atteignant 8 atteint
**avoir** 1 j'ai, tu as, il a, n avons, v avez, ils ont 2 j'avais 3 j'eus 4 j'aurai 5 j'aie, il ait, n ayons, ils aient 6 aie, ayons, ayez 7 ayant 8 eu
**battre** 1 je bats, il bat, n battons 5 je batte
**boire** 1 je bois, n buvons, ils boivent 2 je buvais 3 je bus 5 je boive, n buvions 7 buvant 8 bu
**bouillir** 1 je bous, n bouillons, ils bouillent 2 je bouillais 3 je bouillis 5 je bouille 7 bouillant
**braire** (*defective*) 1 il brait, ils braient 4 il braira, ils brairont
**circonscrire** *like* **écrire**
**circonvenir** *like* **tenir**
**clore** *like* **éclore**
**combattre** *like* **battre**
**commettre** *like* **mettre**
**comparaître** *like* **connaître**
**complaire** *like* **plaire**
**comprendre** *like* **prendre**
**compromettre** *like* **mettre**
**concevoir** *like* **recevoir**
**conclure** 1 je conclus, n concluons, ils concluent 5 je conclue
**concourir** *like* **courir**
**conduire** 1 je conduis, n conduisons 3 je conduisis 5 je conduise 8 conduit
**confire** *like* **suffire**
**connaître** 1 je connais, il connaît, n connaissons 3 je connus 5 je connaisse 7 connaissant 8 connu
**conquérir** *like* **acquérir**
**consentir** *like* **mentir**
**construire** *like* **conduire**
**contenir** *like* **tenir**
**contraindre** *like* **craindre**
**contredire** *like* **dire** *except* 1 v contredisez
**convaincre** *like* **vaincre**
**convenir** *like* **tenir**
**corrompre** *like* **rompre**
**coudre** 1 je couds, il coud, n cousons, ils cousent 3 je cousis 5 je couse 7 cousant 8 cousu
**courir** 1 je cours, n courons 3 je courus 4 je courrai 5 je coure 8 couru
**couvrir** 1 je couvre, n couvrons 2 je couvrais 5 je couvre 8 couvert
**craindre** 1 je crains, n craignons, ils craignent 2 je craignais

| | | |
|---|---|---|
| | 3 je craignis 4 je craindrai 5 je craigne 7 craignant 8 craint | |
| **croire** | 1 je crois, n croyons, ils croient 2 je croyais 3 je crus 5 je croie, n croyions 7 croyant 8 cru | |
| **croître** | 1 je crois, il croît, n croissons 2 je croissais 3 je crûs 5 je croisse 7 croissant 8 crû, crue | |
| **cueillir** | 1 je cueille, n cueillons 2 je cueillais 4 je cueillerai 5 je cueille 7 cueillant | |
| **cuire** | 1 je cuis, n cuisons 2 je cuisais 3 je cuisis 5 je cuise 7 cuisant 8 cuit | |
| **débattre** | *like* | **battre** |
| **décevoir** | *like* | **recevoir** |
| **déchoir** | (*defective*) 1 je déchois 2 *none* 3 je déchus 4 je déchoirai 6 *none* 7 *none* 8 déchu | |
| **découdre** | *like* | **coudre** |
| **découvrir** | *like* | **couvrir** |
| **décrire** | *like* | **écrire** |
| **décroître** | *like* | **croître** *except* 8 décru |
| **se dédire** | *like* | **dire** |
| **déduire** | *like* | **conduire** |
| **défaillir** | 1 je défaille, n défaillons 2 je défaillais 3 je défaillis 5 je défaille 7 défaillant 8 défailli | |
| **défaire** | *like* | **faire** |
| **démentir** | *like* | **mentir** |
| **démettre** | *like* | **mettre** |
| **se départir** | *like* | **mentir** |
| **dépeindre** | *like* | **atteindre** |
| **déplaire** | *like* | **plaire** |
| **déteindre** | *like* | **atteindre** |
| **détenir** | *like* | **tenir** |
| **détruire** | *like* | **conduire** |
| ***devenir** | *like* | **tenir** |
| **se dévêtir** | *like* | **vêtir** |
| **devoir** | 1 je dois, n devons, ils doivent 2 je devais 3 je dus 4 je devrai 5 je doive, n devions 6 *not used* 7 devant 8 dû, due, *pl* dus, dues | |
| **dire** | 1 je dis, n disons, v dites 2 je disais 3 je dis 5 je dise 7 disant 8 dit | |
| **disconvenir** | *like* | **tenir** |
| **disjoindre** | *like* | **joindre** |
| **disparaître** | *like* | **connaître** |
| **dissoudre** | *like* | **absoudre** |
| **distraire** | *like* | **abstraire** |
| **dormir** | *like* | **mentir** |
| **échoir** | (*defective*) 1 il échoit 2 *none* 3 il échut, ils échurent 4 il échoira 6 *none* 7 échéant 8 échu | |
| **éclore** | 1 il éclôt, ils éclosent 8 éclos | |

| | | |
|---|---|---|
| **éconduire** | *like* | **conduire** |
| **écrire** | 1 j'écris, n écrivons 2 j'écrivais 3 j'écrivis 5 j'écrive 7 écrivant 8 écrit | |
| **élire** | *like* | **lire** |
| **émettre** | *like* | **mettre** |
| **émouvoir** | *like* | **mouvoir** *except* 8 ému |
| **enclore** | *like* | **éclore** |
| **encourir** | *like* | **courir** |
| **endormir** | *like* | **mentir** |
| **enduire** | *like* | **conduire** |
| **enfreindre** | *like* | **atteindre** |
| ***s'enfuir** | *like* | **fuir** |
| **enjoindre** | *like* | **joindre** |
| **s'enquérir** | *like* | **acquérir** |
| **s'ensuivre** | *like* | **suivre** (*third person only*) |
| **entreprendre** | *like* | **prendre** |
| **entretenir** | *like* | **tenir** |
| **entrevoir** | *like* | **voir** |
| **entrouvrir** | *like* | **couvrir** |
| **envoyer** | 4 j'enverrai | |
| ***s'éprendre** | *like* | **prendre** |
| **équivaloir** | *like* | **valoir** |
| **éteindre** | *like* | **atteindre** |
| **être** | 1 je suis, tu es, il est, n sommes, v êtes, ils sont 2 j'étais 3 je fus 4 je serai 5 je sois, n soyons, ils soient 6 sois, soyons, soyez 7 étant 8 été | |
| **étreindre** | *like* | **atteindre** |
| **exclure** | *like* | **conclure** |
| **extraire** | *like* | **abstraire** |
| **faillir** | (*defective*) 3 je faillis 4 je faillirai 8 failli | |
| **faire** | 1 je fais, n faisons, v faites, ils font 2 je faisais 3 je fis 4 je ferai 5 je fasse 7 faisant 8 fait | |
| **falloir** | (*impersonal*) 1 il faut 2 il fallait 3 il fallut 4 il faudra 5 il faille 6 *none* 7 *none* 8 fallu | |
| **feindre** | *like* | **atteindre** |
| **foutre** | 1 je fous, n foutons 2 je foutais 3 *none* 5 je foute 7 foutant 8 foutu | |
| **frire** | (*defective*) 1 je fris, tu fris, il frit 4 je frirai 6 fris 8 frit (*for other persons and tenses use* faire frire) | |
| **fuir** | 1 je fuis, n fuyons, ils fuient 2 je fuyais 3 je fuis 5 je fuie 7 fuyant 8 fui | |
| **geindre** | *like* | **atteindre** |
| **haïr** | 1 je hais, il hait, n haïssons | |
| **inclure** | *like* | **conclure** |
| **induire** | *like* | **conduire** |
| **inscrire** | *like* | **écrire** |
| **instruire** | *like* | **conduire** |

| | | |
|---|---|---|
| **interdire** | *like* | **dire** *except* 1 v interdisez |
| **interrompre** | *like* | **rompre** |
| **intervenir** | *like* | **tenir** |
| **introduire** | *like* | **conduire** |
| **joindre** | 1 je joins, n joignons, ils joignent 2 je joignais 3 je joignis 4 je joindrai 5 je joigne 7 joignant 8 joint | |
| **lire** | 1 je lis, n lisons 2 je lisais 3 je lus 5 je lise 7 lisant 8 lu | |
| **luire** | *like* | **nuire** |
| **maintenir** | *like* | **tenir** |
| **maudire** | 1 je maudis, n maudissons 2 je maudissais 3 je maudis 4 je maudirai 5 je maudisse 7 maudissant 8 maudit | |
| **méconnaître** | *like* | **connaître** |
| **médire** | *like* | **dire** *except* 1 v médisez |
| **mentir** | 1 je mens, n mentons 2 je mentais 5 je mente 7 mentant | |
| **mettre** | 1 je mets, n mettons 2 je mettais 3 je mis 5 je mette 7 mettant 8 mis | |
| **moudre** | 1 je mouds, il moud, n moulons 2 je moulais 3 je moulus 5 je moule 7 moulant 8 moulu | |
| ***mourir** | 1 je meurs, n mourons, ils meurent 2 je mourais 3 je mourus 4 je mourrai 5 je meure, n mourions 7 mourant 8 mort | |
| **mouvoir** | 1 je meus, n mouvons, ils meuvent 2 je mouvais 3 je mus 4 je mouvrai 5 je meuve, n mouvions 8 mû, mue, *pl* mus, mues | |
| ***naître** | 1 je nais, il naît, n naissons 2 je naissais 3 je naquis 4 je naîtrai 5 je naisse 7 naissant 8 né | |
| **nuire** | 1 je nuis, n nuisons 2 je nuisais 3 je nuisis 5 je nuise 7 nuisant 8 nui | |
| **obtenir** | *like* | **tenir** |
| **offrir** | *like* | **couvrir** |
| **omettre** | *like* | **mettre** |
| **ouvrir** | *like* | **couvrir** |
| **paître** | (*defective*) 1 il paît 2 ils paissait 3 *none* 4 il paîtra 5 il paisse 7 paissant 8 *none* | |
| **paraître** | *like* | **connaître** |
| **parcourir** | *like* | **courir** |
| **parfaire** | *like* | **faire** (*present tense, infinitive and past participle only*) |
| ***partir** | *like* | **mentir** |
| ***parvenir** | *like* | **tenir** |
| **peindre** | *like* | **atteindre** |
| **percevoir** | *like* | **recevoir** |
| **permettre** | *like* | **mettre** |
| **plaindre** | *like* | **craindre** |
| **plaire** | 1 je plais, il plaît, n plaisons 2 je plaisais 3 je plus 5 je plaise 7 plaisant 8 plu | |
| **pleuvoir** | (*impersonal*) 1 il pleut 2 il pleuvait 3 il plut 4 il pleuvra 5 il pleuve 6 *none* 7 pleuvant 8 plu | |

| | | |
|---|---|---|
| **poindre** | (*defective*) 1 il point 4 il poindra 8 point | |
| **poursuivre** | *like* | **suivre** |
| **pourvoir** | *like* | **voir** *except* 3 je pourvus *and* 4 je pourvoirai |
| **pouvoir** | 1 je peux *or* je puis, tu peux, il peut, n pouvons, ils peuvent 2 je pouvais 3 je pus 4 je pourrai 5 je puisse 6 *not used* 7 pouvant 8 pu | |
| **prédire** | *like* | **dire** *except* v prédisez |
| **prendre** | 1 je prends, il prend, n prenons, ils prennent 2 je prenais 3 je pris 5 je prenne 7 prenant 8 pris | |
| **prescrire** | *like* | **écrire** |
| **pressentir** | *like* | **mentir** |
| **prévaloir** | *like* | **valoir** *except* 5 je prévale |
| **prévenir** | *like* | **tenir** |
| **prévoir** | *like* | **voir** *except* 4 je prévoirai |
| **produire** | *like* | **conduire** |
| **promettre** | *like* | **mettre** |
| **promouvoir** | *like* | **mouvoir** *except* 8 promu |
| **proscrire** | *like* | **écrire** |
| ***provenir** | *like* | **tenir** |
| **rabattre** | *like* | **battre** |
| **rasseoir** | *like* | **asseoir** |
| **réapparaître** | *like* | **connaître** |
| **recevoir** | 1 je reçois, n recevons, ils reçoivent 2 je recevais 3 je reçus 4 je recevrai 5 je reçoive, n recevions, ils reçoivent 7 recevant 8 reçu | |
| **reconduire** | *like* | **conduire** |
| **reconnaître** | *like* | **connaître** |
| **reconquérir** | *like* | **acquérir** |
| **reconstruire** | *like* | **conduire** |
| **recoudre** | *like* | **coudre** |
| **recourir** | *like* | **courir** |
| **recouvrir** | *like* | **couvrir** |
| **récrire** | *like* | **écrire** |
| **recueillir** | *like* | **cueillir** |
| **redevenir** | *like* | **tenir** |
| **redire** | *like* | **dire** |
| **réduire** | *like* | **conduire** |
| **réécrire** | *like* | **écrire** |
| **réélire** | *like* | **lire** |
| **refaire** | *like* | **faire** |
| **rejoindre** | *like* | **joindre** |
| **relire** | *like* | **lire** |
| **reluire** | *like* | **nuire** |
| **remettre** | *like* | **mettre** |
| ***renaître** | *like* | **naître** |
| **rendormir** | *like* | **mentir** |

| | | |
|---|---|---|
| **renvoyer** | *like* | **envoyer** |
| **se repaître** | *like* | **paître** |
| **reparaître** | *like* | **connaître** |
| ***repartir** | *like* | **mentir** |
| **repeindre** | *like* | **atteindre** |
| **repentir** | *like* | **mentir** |
| **reprendre** | *like* | **prendre** |
| **reproduire** | *like* | **conduire** |
| **résoudre** | 1 je résous, n résolvons 2 je résolvais 3 je résolus 5 je résolve 7 résolvant 8 résolu | |
| **ressentir** | *like* | **mentir** |
| **resservir** | *like* | **mentir** |
| **ressortir** | *like* | **mentir** |
| **restreindre** | *like* | **atteindre** |
| **retenir** | *like* | **tenir** |
| **retransmettre** | *like* | **mettre** |
| ***revenir** | *like* | **tenir** |
| **revêtir** | *like* | **vêtir** |
| **revivre** | *like* | **vivre** |
| **revoir** | *like* | **voir** |
| **rire** | 1 je ris, n rions 2 je riais 3 je ris 5 je rie, n riions 7 riant 8 ri | |
| **rompre** | *regular except* 1 il rompt | |
| **rouvrir** | *like* | **couvrir** |
| **satisfaire** | *like* | **faire** |
| **savoir** | 1 je sais, n savons, il savent 2 je savais 3 je sus 4 je saurai 5 je sache 6 sache, sachons, sachez 7 sachant 8 su | |
| **séduire** | *like* | **conduire** |
| **sentir** | *like* | **mentir** |
| **servir** | *like* | **mentir** |
| **sortir** | *like* | **mentir** |
| **souffrir** | *like* | **couvrir** |
| **soumettre** | *like* | **mettre** |
| **sourire** | *like* | **rire** |
| **souscrire** | *like* | **écrire** |
| **soustraire** | *like* | **abstraire** |
| **soutenir** | *like* | **tenir** |
| ***se souvenir** | *like* | **tenir** |
| **subvenir** | *like* | **tenir** |
| **suffire** | 1 je suffis, n suffisons 2 je suffisais 3 je suffis 5 je suffise 7 suffisant 8 suffi | |
| **suivre** | 1 je suis, n suivons 2 je suivais 3 je suivis 5 je suive 7 suivant 8 suivi | |
| **surprendre** | *like* | **prendre** |
| ***survenir** | *like* | **tenir** |
| **survivre** | *like* | **vivre** |
| **taire** | 1 je tais, n taisons 2 je taisais 3 je tus 5 je taise 7 taisant 8 tu | |

**teindre** *like* **atteindre**

**tenir** 1 je tiens, ne tenons, ils tiennent 2 je tenais 3 je tins, tu tins, il tint, n tînmes, v tîntes, ils tinrent 4 je tiendrai 5 je tienne 7 tenant 8 tenu

**traduire** *like* **conduire**

**traire** *like* **abstraire**

**transcrire** *like* **écrire**

**transmettre** *like* **mettre**

**transparaître** *like* **connaître**

**tressaillir** *like* **défaillir**

**vaincre** 1 je vaincs, il vainc, n vainquons 2 je vainquais 3 je vainquis 5 je vainque 7 vainquant 8 vaincu

**valoir** 1 je vaux, il vaut, n valons 2 je valais 3 je valus 4 je vaudrai 5 je vaille 6 *not used* 7 valant 8 valu

***venir** *like* **tenir**

**vêtir** 1 je vêts, n vêtons 2 je vêtais 5 je vête 7 vêtant 8 vêtu

**vivre** 1 je vis, n vivons 2 je vivais 3 je vécus 5 je vive 7 vivant 8 vécu

**voir** 1 je vois, n voyons 2 je voyais 3 je vis 4 je verrai 5 je voie, n voyions 7 voyant 8 vu

**vouloir** 1 je veux, il veut, n voulons, ils veulent 2 je voulais 3 je voulus 4 je voudrai 5 je veuille 6 veuille, veuillons, veuillez 7 voulant 8 voulu

# Verbes anglais irréguliers

| Infinitif | Prétérit | Participe passé |
|---|---|---|
| arise | arose | arisen |
| awake | awoke | awoken |
| awaken | awoke, awakened | awakened, awoken |
| be | were/was | been |
| bear | bore | borne |
| beat | beat | beaten |
| become | became | become |
| begin | began | begun |
| bend | bent | bent |
| beseech | besought, beseeched | besought, beseeched |
| bet | bet, betted | bet, betted |
| bid | bade, bid | bidden, bid |
| bind | bound | bound |
| bite | bit | bitten |
| bleed | bled | bled |
| blow | blew | blown |
| break | broke | broken |
| breed | bred | bred |
| bring | brought | brought |
| build | built | built |
| burn | burnt, burned | burnt, burned |
| burst | burst | burst |
| bust | bust, busted | bust, busted |
| buy | bought | bought |
| cast | cast | cast |
| catch | caught | caught |
| chide | chided, chid | chided, chidden |
| choose | chose | chosen |
| cleave | cleaved, cleft, clove | cleaved, cleft, cloven |
| cling | clung | clung |
| clothe | clad, clothed | clad, clothed |
| come | came | come |
| cost | cost | cost |
| creep | crept | crept |
| crow | crowed, crew | crowed |
| cut | cut | cut |
| deal | dealt | dealt |
| dig | dug | dug |
| dive | dived, *Am* dove | dived |
| do | did | done |
| draw | drew | drawn |
| dream | dreamt, dreamed | dreamt, dreamed |
| drink | drank | drunk |
| drive | drove | driven |
| dwell | dwelt | dwelt |
| eat | ate | eaten |

| Infinitif | Prétérit | Participe passé |
|---|---|---|
| fall | fell | fallen |
| feed | fed | fed |
| feel | felt | felt |
| fight | fought | fought |
| find | found | found |
| flee | fled | fled |
| fling | flung | flung |
| fly | flew | flown |
| forget | forgot | forgotten |
| forgive | forgave | forgiven |
| forsake | forsook | forsaken |
| freeze | froze | frozen |
| get | got | got, *Am* gotten |
| gild | gilded, gilt | gilded, gilt |
| gird | girded, girt | girded, girt |
| give | gave | given |
| go | went | gone |
| grind | ground | ground |
| grow | grew | grown |
| hang | hung/hanged | hung/hanged |
| have | had | had |
| hear | heard | heard |
| hew | hewed | hewn, hewed |
| hide | hid | hidden |
| hit | hit | hit |
| hold | held | held |
| hurt | hurt | hurt |
| keep | kept | kept |
| kneel | knelt | knelt |
| knit | knitted, knit | knitted, knit |
| know | knew | known |
| lay | laid | laid |
| lead | led | led |
| lean | leant, leaned | leant, leaned |
| leap | leapt, leaped | leapt, leaped |
| learn | learnt, learned | learnt, learned |
| leave | left | left |
| lend | lent | lent |
| let | let | let |
| lie | lay | lain |
| light | lit | lit |
| lose | lost | lost |
| make | made | made |
| mean | meant | meant |
| meet | met | met |
| mow | mowed | mown |
| pay | paid | paid |
| plead | pleaded, *Am* pled | pleaded, *Am* pled |
| prove | proved | proved, proven |
| put | put | put |
| quit | quit | quit |
| read | read | read |

| **Infinitif** | **Prétérit** | **Participe passé** |
|---|---|---|
| rend | rent | rent |
| rid | rid | rid |
| ride | rode | ridden |
| ring | rang | rung |
| rise | rose | risen |
| run | ran | run |
| saw | sawed | sawn, sawed |
| say | said | said |
| see | saw | seen |
| seek | sought | sought |
| sell | sold | sold |
| send | sent | sent |
| set | set | set |
| sew | sewed | sewn |
| shake | shook | shaken |
| shear | sheared | shorn, sheared |
| shed | shed | shed |
| shine | shone | shone |
| shoe | shod | shod |
| shoot | shot | shot |
| show | showed | shown |
| shrink | shrank | shrunk |
| shut | shut | shut |
| sing | sang | sung |
| sink | sank | sunk |
| sit | sat | sat |
| slay | slew | slain |
| sleep | slept | slept |
| slide | slid | slid |
| sling | slung | slung |
| slink | slunk | slunk |
| slit | slit | slit |
| smell | smelled, smelt | smelled, smelt |
| smite | smote | smitten |
| sow | sowed | sown, sowed |
| speak | spoke | spoken |
| speed | sped, speeded | sped, speeded |
| spell | spelt, spelled | spelt, spelled |
| spend | spent | spent |
| spill | spilt, spilled | spilt, spilled |
| spin | span | spun |
| spit | spat, *Am* spit | spat, *Am* spit |
| split | split | split |
| spoil | spoilt, spoiled | spoilt, spoiled |
| spread | spread | spread |
| spring | sprang | sprung |
| stand | stood | stood |
| stave in | staved in, stove in | staved in, stove in |
| steal | stole | stolen |
| stick | stuck | stuck |
| sting | stung | stung |
| stink | stank, stunk | stunk |

| **Infinitif** | **Prétérit** | **Participe passé** |
|---|---|---|
| strew | strewed | strewed, strewn |
| stride | strode | stridden |
| strike | struck | struck |
| string | strung | strung |
| strive | strove | striven |
| swear | swore | sworn |
| sweep | swept | swept |
| swell | swelled | swollen, swelled |
| swim | swam | swum |
| swing | swung | swung |
| take | took | taken |
| teach | taught | taught |
| tear | tore | torn |
| tell | told | told |
| think | thought | thought |
| thrive | thrived, throve | thrived |
| throw | threw | thrown |
| thrust | thrust | thrust |
| tread | trod | trodden |
| wake | woke | woken |
| wear | wore | worn |
| weave | wove, weaved | woven, weaved |
| weep | wept | wept |
| wet | wet, wetted | wet, wetted |
| win | won | won |
| wind | wound | wound |
| wring | wrung | wrung |
| write | wrote | written |

# Verbes modaux anglais

## Formes

Les modaux sont : **can**, **could**, **may**, **might**, **will**, **would**, **shall**, **should**, **must**, **need**, **ought to**. Ils ont toujours la même forme et sont suivis d'un infinitif sans **to** (sauf la construction **ought to**).

Les formes contractées sont très courantes :

affirmatives : **'ll** (**will**), **'d** (**would**)
négatives : **can't**, **couldn't**, **won't** (**will not**), **wouldn't**, **shan't** (**shall not**), **shouldn't**, **mustn't**, **needn't**.

Les formes de remplacement **be able to**, **be allowed to** et **have to** se conjuguent normalement.

## Différents degrés de certitude

### * Certitude

| | |
|---|---|
| you must be joking! | vous voulez rire ! |
| we must have met before | on a dû déjà se rencontrer |
| you can't miss it, it's just opposite the station | vous ne pouvez pas le rater, c'est juste en face de la gare |

### * Probabilité et possibilité

| | |
|---|---|
| you may change your mind when you see it! | tu changera peut-être d'avis quand tu le verras ! |
| I might join you later | je vous rejoindrai peut-être plus tard |
| they might have forgotten altogether | ils ont peut-être carrément oublié |
| they should have arrived by now | ils devraient être arrivés maintenant |

### * Fait généralement ou parfois vrai

| | |
|---|---|
| the roads can get dangerous in the winter | les routes peuvent être dangereuses en hiver |

### * Certitude liée à certaines conditions

| | |
|---|---|
| if I had the time, I would take Chinese lessons | si j'avais le temps, je prendrais des cours de chinois |

## Obligation ou nécessité

| | |
|---|---|
| I must/have to/'ve got to be in London by Monday | je dois être à Londres pour lundi |
| do I have to stay? | dois-je rester ? |

## Interdiction

| | |
|---|---|
| children must not run near the swimming pool | les enfants ne doivent pas courir au bord de la piscine |
| drinks may not be taken into the cinema | les boissons sont interdites dans la salle de cinéma |
| I'm afraid you can't smoke in here | j'ai bien peur que vous ne puissiez pas fumer ici |
| dogs are not allowed in the shop | les chiens ne sont pas autorisés dans le magasin |

## Absence d'obligation ou de nécessité

| | |
|---|---|
| you needn't worry so much | ce n'est pas la peine de te faire autant de souci |
| you don't have to come if you don't want to | tu n'es pas obligé de venir si tu n'en as pas envie |

## Permission

**Could** est plus poli, et **may** plus formel.

| | |
|---|---|
| can I borrow your pen, please? | est-ce que je peux emprunter ton stylo ? |
| candidates may/are allowed to leave after one hour | les candidats sont autorisés à partir au bout d'une heure |

## Suggestion

### * Conseil

| | |
|---|---|
| you really ought to/should see a doctor | tu devrais aller voir un docteur |
| shall I open the window? | voulez-vous que j'ouvre la fenêtre ? |

### * Invitation

**Should** est moins insistant et **ought to** plus formel.

| | |
|---|---|
| you must come and see me some time | viens me voir un jour |

Notez ici l'emploi de **must** : il s'agit bien d'une invitation et non d'un ordre.

| | |
|---|---|
| I'll give you a lift if you want | je peux te déposer si tu veux |
| can I get you a drink? | je t'offre quelque chose à boire ? |

*** Proposition**

| | |
|---|---|
| would you like anything to drink? | est-ce que tu voudrais quelque chose à boire ? |
| will you pass me the salt, please? | veux-tu me passer le sel, s'il te plaît ? |
| shall we go to the cinema instead? | et si on allait au cinéma à la place ? |

**Capacité**

| | |
|---|---|
| he can be very irritating | il peut être vraiment agaçant quelquefois |
| you could have warned me! | tu aurais pu me prévenir ! |
| it's great being able to send files by e-mail | c'est génial de pouvoir envoyer des fichiers par e-mail |

# Numbers/Les Nombres

| Cardinal numbers | | Les nombres cardinaux |
|---:|:---:|:---|
| nought, zero | 0 | zéro |
| one | 1 | un |
| two | 2 | deux |
| three | 3 | trois |
| four | 4 | quatre |
| five | 5 | cinq |
| six | 6 | six |
| seven | 7 | sept |
| eight | 8 | huit |
| nine | 9 | neuf |
| ten | 10 | dix |
| eleven | 11 | onze |
| twelve | 12 | douze |
| thirteen | 13 | treize |
| fourteen | 14 | quatorze |
| fifteen | 15 | quinze |
| sixteen | 16 | seize |
| seventeen | 17 | dix-sept |
| eighteen | 18 | dix-huit |
| nineteen | 19 | dix-neuf |
| twenty | 20 | vingt |
| twenty-one | 21 | vingt et un |
| twenty-two | 22 | vingt-deux |
| thirty | 30 | trente |
| forty | 40 | quarante |
| fifty | 50 | cinquante |
| sixty | 60 | soixante |
| seventy | 70 | soixante-dix |
| eighty | 80 | quatre-vingts |
| eighty-one | 81 | quatre-vingt-un |
| ninety | 90 | quatre-vingt-dix |
| ninety-one | 91 | quatre-vingt-onze |
| a *or* one hundred | 100 | cent |
| a hundred and one | 101 | cent un |
| a hundred and two | 102 | cent deux |
| a hundred and fifty | 150 | cent cinquante |
| two hundred | 200 | deux cents |
| two hundred and one | 201 | deux cent un |

| | | |
|---|---|---|
| two hundred and two | 202 | deux cent deux |
| a *or* one thousand | 1,000 (1 000 ) | mille |
| a thousand and one | 1,001 (1 001) | mille un |
| a thousand and two | 1,002) (1 002) | mille deux |
| two thousand | 2,000 (2 000) | deux mille |
| a *or* one million | 1,000,000 (1 000 000) | un million |

## Ordinal numbers — Les nombres ordinaux

| | | | |
|---|---|---|---|
| first | 1st | 1er | premier |
| second | 2nd | 2e | deuxième |
| third | 3rd | 3e | troisième |
| fourth | 4th | 4e | quatrième |
| fifth | 5th | 5e | cinquième |
| sixth | 6th | 6e | sixième |
| seventh | 7th | 7e | septième |
| eighth | 8th | 8e | huitième |
| ninth | 9th | 9e | neuvième |
| tenth | 10th | 10e | dixième |
| eleventh | 11th | 11e | onzième |
| twelfth | 12th | 12e | douzième |
| thirteenth | 13th | 13e | treizième |
| fourteenth | 14th | 14e | quatorzième |
| fifteenth | 15th | 15e | quinzième |
| twentieth | 20th | 20e | vingtième |
| twenty-first | 21st | 21e | vingt et unième |
| twenty-second | 22nd | 22e | vingt deuxième |
| thirtieth | 30th | 30e | trentième |

| Examples of usage | Exemples d'emplois |
|---|---|
| three (times) out of ten | trois (fois) sur dix |
| ten at a time, in *or* by tens, ten by ten | dix par dix, dix à dix |
| the ten of us/you, we ten/you ten | nous/vous dix |
| all ten of them *or* us *or* you | tous les dix, toutes les dix |
| there are ten of us/them | nous sommes/elles sont dix |
| (between) the ten of them | à eux dix, à elles dix |
| ten of them were living together/came | ils vivaient/sont venus à dix |
| page ten | page dix |
| Charles the Tenth | Charles Dix |
| to live at number ten | habiter au (numéro) dix |
| to be the tenth to arrive/to leave | arriver/partir le dixième |
| to come tenth, to be tenth (*in a race*) | arriver dixième, être dixième |
| it's the tenth (today) | nous sommes le dix (aujourd'hui) |

| | |
|---|---|
| the tenth of May, May the tenth, *Am* May tenth | le dix mai |
| to arrive/be paid on the tenth | arriver/être payé le dix |
| to arrive/be paid on the tenth of May *or* on May the tenth *or Am* on May tenth | arriver/être payé le dix mai |
| by the tenth, before the tenth | avant le dix, pour le dix |
| it's ten (o'clock) | il est dix heures |
| it's half past ten | il est dix heures et demie |
| ten past ten, *Am* ten after ten | dix heures dix |
| ten to ten | dix heures moins dix |
| by ten (o'clock), before ten (o'clock) | pour dix heures, avant dix heures |
| to be ten (years old) | avoir dix ans |
| a child of ten, a ten-year-old (child) | un enfant de dix ans |

# Days and Months/
# Les Jours et les mois

| | |
|---|---|
| Monday | lundi |
| Tuesday | mardi |
| Wednesday | mercredi |
| Thursday | jeudi |
| Friday | vendredi |
| Saturday | samedi |
| Sunday | dimanche |
| January | janvier |
| February | février |
| March | mars |
| April | avril |
| May | mai |
| June | juin |
| July | juillet |
| August | août |
| September | septembre |
| October | octobre |
| November | novembre |
| December | décembre |

| **Examples of usage** | **Exemples d'emplois** |
|---|---|
| he arrives on Monday | il arrive lundi |
| (on) Mondays | le lundi |
| see you on Monday! | à lundi |
| by Monday, before Monday | avant lundi, pour lundi |
| Monday morning/evening | lundi matin/soir |
| a week/two weeks on Monday, *Am* a week/two weeks from Monday | lundi en huit/en quinze |
| it's Monday (today) | nous sommes (aujourd'hui) lundi |
| Monday the tenth of May, Monday May the tenth, *Am* Monday May tenth | le lundi dix mai |
| tomorrow is Tuesday | demain c'est mardi |
| in May | en mai, au mois de mai |
| every May, each May | tous les ans en mai, chaque année en mai |
| by May, before May | avant mai, pour mai |

# Time/L'Heure

| | |
|---|---|
| what time is it?, what's the time? | quelle heure est-il? |

| **Hours** | **Les heures** |
|---|---|
| it's one o'clock | il est une heure |
| it's 12 (noon) | il est midi |
| it's 12 (midnight) | il est minuit |
| at five o'clock | à cinq heures |
| at about ten o'clock | à dix heures environ |
| (at) around midday/midnight | vers midi/minuit |
| at exactly nine o'clock | à neuf heures précises, à neuf heures pile |

| **Half-hours** | **Les demi-heures** |
|---|---|
| it's half past nine, it's nine thirty, it's half nine (familier) | il est neuf heures et demie |

| **Quarter-hours** | **Les quarts d'heure** |
|---|---|
| it's a quarter to six | il est six heures moins le quart |
| it's a quarter past (*Br*)/after (*Am*) six | il est six heures et quart |

| **Minutes** | **Les minutes** |
|---|---|
| it's ten past seven, it's 7:10 | il est sept heures dix |
| it's ten to seven, it's 6:50 | il est sept heures moins dix |
| it's four minutes past two | il est deux heures quatre |

| **a.m. and p.m.** | **a.m. et p.m.** |
|---|---|
| a.m. | du matin |
| p.m. | de l'après-midi/du soir |
| it's 7 a.m., it's seven (o'clock) in the morning | il est sept heures du matin |
| it's 7 p.m., it's seven (o'clock) in the evening | il est sept heures du soir |

**L'heure sur 24 heures**

Les expressions du type quinze heures, etc (à la place de trois heures, etc) ne s'emploient pas dans l'anglais de tous les jours. On les rencontre cependant parfois dans les horaires et surtout dans le langage militaire (souvent suivies du mot **hours**) :

| | |
|---|---|
| o five hundred hours | 5 heures du matin |
| fifteen hundred hours | quinze heures |

**The 24-hour clock**

In French the use of the 24-hour clock is not restricted to military contexts and timetables. It is therefore not uncommon to hear French people use **seize heures**, rather than **quatre heures**, to refer to four p.m.

# Conversation guide

## Meeting people

**Hello, how are you?**
*Bonjour, comment ça va ?*

**Fine thanks, and you?**
*Ça va bien, merci, et vous/toi ?*

**What's your name?**
*Comment tu t'appelles ? / Comment vous vous appelez ?*

**My name's...**
*Je m'appelle...*

**Nice to meet you!**
*Enchanté(e) !*

**This is my wife/my brother.**
*Voici ma femme/mon frère.*

**How old are you?**
*Quel âge as-tu? / Quel âge avez-vous ?*

**I'm 15/21/40.**
*J'ai quinze ans/vingt-et-un ans/quarante ans.*

**Where are you from ?**
*D'où viens-tu ? / D'où venez-vous ?*

**I'm from Edinburgh.**
*Je viens d'Édimbourg.*

**We're English.**
*Nous sommes anglais(es).*

**We live in the north of England**
*Nous habitons au nord de l'Angleterre..*

**What do you do?**
*Qu'est-ce que tu fais / Qu'est-ce que vous faites dans la vie ?*

**I'm a student.**
*Je suis étudiant(e).*

**I'm a teacher.**
*Je suis professeur.*

**I work in a bank.**
*Je travaille dans une banque.*

**I like football/going to the cinema.**
*J'aime bien le foot/aller au cinéma.*

**I don't like beer/cycling.**
*Je n'aime pas la bière/faire du vélo.*

**Can I have your address?**
*Je peux avoir ton/votre adresse ?*

**You must come and visit us one day!**
*Vous devez venir nous voir un jour !*

**Here's my e-mail address.**
*Voici mon adresse e-mail.*

**See you soon/later.**
*À bientôt/plus tard.*

## Understanding

**Pardon?**
*Pardon ?*

**Could you repeat that, please?**
*Vous pouvez répéter ?*

**I don't understand.**
*Je ne comprends pas.*

**Do you speak English?**
*Parlez-vous anglais ?*

**I don't speak much French.**
*Je parle à peine français.*

**I can understand a little.**
*Je comprends un peu.*

**What does that mean?**
*Qu'est-ce que ça veut dire ?*

**How do you say ... in French?**
*Comment dit-on ... en français ?*

**I'm learning French.**
*J'apprends le français.*

**Could you write it down for me?**
*Pourriez-vous me l'écrire ?*

## Your stay

**We're on holiday.**
*Nous sommes en vacances.*

**I'm here on business.**
*Je suis ici pour mon travail.*

**I'm just here for the weekend.**
*Je ne suis ici que pour le weekend.*

**We're here for a week.**
*Nous sommes ici pour une semaine.*

**We have a house here.**
*Nous avons une maison ici.*

**I really like it here.**
*Je me plais beaucoup ici.*

**Have a good holiday!**
*Bonnes vacances !*

**Have fun!**
*Amuse-toi /Amusez-vous bien !*

## Asking for directions

**Excuse me, can you tell me where the bus station is, please?**
*Excusez-moi, pourriez-vous me dire où se trouve la gare routière ?*

**How do I get to the beach?**
*Comment je fais pour aller à la plage ?*

**Which way is it to the market?**
*Le marché, c'est par où ?*

**I'm looking for...**
*Je cherche...*

**Is there a bakery round here?**
*Y a-t-il une boulangerie par ici ?*

**Could you show me on the map?**
*Pourriez-vous me montrer sur la carte ?*

**Is it far to the next town?**
*C'est loin jusqu'à la prochaine ville ?*

***You may hear...***

**Continuez tout droit.**
Go straight on.

**Tournez à gauche/à droite.**
Turn left/right.

**Continuez jusqu'à...**
Carry on as far as...

**Prenez la prochaine sortie.**
Take the next exit.

## Requests, thanks, opinions

**Could I have a glass of water, please?**
*Est-ce que je pourrais avoir un verre d'eau ?*

**Would you be able to give me a lift?**
*Est-ce que vous pourriez m'emmener en voiture ?*

**Do you mind if I open the window?**
*Ça vous dérange si j'ouvre la fenêtre ?*

**Can you show me?**
*Vous pouvez me montrer ?*

**Is it ok if I smoke?**
*Je peux fumer ?*

**Thank you (very much)!**
*Merci (beaucoup) !*

**You're welcome!**
*De rien !*

**Merci, c'est très gentil.**
*Thanks, that's very kind of you.*

**Thanks a lot for your help.**
*Merci beaucoup pour votre aide.*

**I enjoyed it.**
*Je l'ai bien aimé.*

**I didn't enjoy it.**
*Ça ne m'a pas plu.*

**It's beautiful!**
*C'est très joli(e) !*

**It was boring.**
*C'était ennuyeux.*

**I agree/disagree.**
*Je suis d'accord/Je ne suis pas d'accord.*

**You're right.**
*Vous avez raison.*

**I think it's delicious!**
*Je le trouve délicieux !*

**It's not bad.**
*Ce n'est pas mal.*

**Really? That's interesting!**
*Ah bon ? C'est intéressant !*

**I think so/don't think so.**
*Je crois que oui/non.*

**I don't mind.**
*Ça m'est égal.*

**I don't know.**
*Je ne sais pas.*

## Travelling

**I'd like a ticket to Lille, please.**
*Je voudrais un billet pour Lille, s'il vous plaît.*

**A single/return ticket.**
*Un aller simple/aller-retour.*

**When's the next train to Paris?**
*À quelle heure est le prochain train pour Paris ?*

**Which platform does it go from?**
*Il part de quel quai ?*

**Do I have to change?**
*Est-ce qu'il y a une correspondance ?*

**Is this seat free?**
*Est-ce que cette place est libre ?*

**Sorry, there's someone sitting there.**
*Désolé(e), il y a déjà quelqu'un.*

**Where's the Easyjet check-in ?**
*Où est l'enregistrement pour Easyjet ?*

**I'd like an aisle/window seat.**
*Je voudrais une place côté couloir/côté hublot.*

**What time do we board?**
*À quelle heure embarque-t-on ?*

**I've missed my connection.**
*J'ai raté ma correspondance.*

**My luggage hasn't arrived.**
*Mes bagages ne sont pas arrivés.*

**Do you have a timetable/a map of the underground?**
*Avez-vous un dépliant avec les horaires/un plan du métro ?*

**Does this bus go to the station ?**
*Est-ce que ce bus va à la gare ?*

**Is this the stop for the market?**
*Est-ce que c'est l'arrêt pour le marché ?*

**Which line do I take?**
*Je prends quelle ligne ?*

**What time's the last bus/train?**
*À quelle heure part le dernier bus/train ?*

**I'd like to hire a car for a week.**
*Je voudrais louer une voiture pour une semaine.*

**Is there a petrol station near here ?**
*Ya-t-il une station-service près d'ici ?*

**We've run out of petrol.**
*On est en panne d'essence.*

**I've broken down.**
*Je suis tombé en panne.*

**We've got a puncture.**
*Nous avons crevé.*

**Is there a taxi rank near here?**
*Y a-t-il une station de taxis près d'ici ?*

**I'd like to go to the airport.**
*Je voudrais aller à l'aéroport.*

**How much will it be?**
*Ça va coûter combien ?*

**You can drop me off here, thanks.**
*Vous pouvez me déposer ici, merci.*

***You may hear...***

**Combien de bagages avez-vous ?**
How many bags do you have ?

**Votre passeport, s'il vous plaît.**
Can I see your passport, please ?

**Voici votre carte d'embarquement.**
Here's your boarding card.

**Embarquement immédiat à la porte numéro...**
Immediate boarding at gate...

**Vous avez une correspondance à Lyon.**
You have to change in Lyon.

**Le train à destination de...**
The train to...

**Prenez le bus numéro...**
Take bus number...

**Descendez au troisième arrêt.**
Get off at the third stop.

## Accommodation

**Have you got a room available for tonight?**
*Avez-vous une chambre de libre pour ce soir ?*
**I'd like to book a double/single room for three nights.**
*Je voudrais réserver une chambre double/individuelle pour trois nuits.*

**I'd like an ensuite room.**
*Je voudrais une chambre avec salle de bains.*

**I have a reservation in the name of...**
*J'a fait une réservation au nom de...*

**Do you have family rooms ?**
*Avez-vous des chambres familiales ?*

**Don't you have anything cheaper?**
*Vous n'avec rien de moins cher ?*

**Is breakfast included?**
*Est-ce que le petit déjeuner est compris ?*

**What time is breakfast?**
*À quelle heure est le petit déjeuner ?*

**What time do we have to check out?**
*À quelle heure doit-on libérer la chambre ?*

**There's a problem with the shower/the air conditioning.**
*Il y a un problème avec la douchella climatisation.*

**It's broken.**
*C'est cassé.*

**It doesn't work.**
*Ça ne marche pas.*

**Can we pay, please?**
*Nous venons régler.*

**Can I leave my bags here?**
*Je peux laisser mes bagages ici ?*

**We'd like to rent a cottage in the country.**
*Nous voudrons louer une gîte rurale.*

**Are sheets and towels provided?**
*Les draps et serviettes sont-ils fournis ?*

**Is there a pool?**
*Est-ce qu'il y a une piscine ?*

**Is there a campsite nearby?**
*Est-ce qu'il y a un camping par ici ?*

**Can we pitch our tent here?**
*Pouvons-nous monter notre tente ici ?*

***You may hear...***

**C'ést à quel nom?**
What's the name?

**Désolé, on est complet.**
Sorry, we're fully booked.

**La chambre sera disponible à 14 heures.**
The room will be ready at 2pm.

**La chambre doit être libérée à midi.**
Check-out is at midday.

**Le petit déjeuner est servi de sept heures à dix heures.**
Breakfast is from 7 to 10.

## Eating and drinking

**Can you recommend a good restaurant?**
*Pouvez-vous me recommander un bon restaurant ?*

**I'd like to book a table for two for tomorrow night.**
*Je voudrais réserver une table pour deux personnes pour demain soir.*

**Do you have a table for four ?**
*Avez-vous une table pour quatre ?*

**I've booked a table, the name's...**
*J'ai réservé une table au nom de...*

**We're ready to order now.**
*Nous avons choisi.*

**I'll have the salmon.**
*Je vais prendre le saumon.*

**I'm vegetarian.**
*Je suis végétarien(enne).*

**I'm allergic to shellfish.**
*Je suis allergique aux fruits de mer.*

**What's "bouillabaisse"?**
*C'est quoi, la bouillabaisse ?*

**What are today's specials?**
*Quels sont les plats du jour ?*

**A bottle of red/white wine.**
*Une bouteille de vin rouge/blanc.*

**Two beers and a Coke®, please.**
*Deux bières et un Coca®, s'il vous plaît.*

**Could we have some more bread/water?**
*Est-ce qu'on pourrait avoir encore du pain/de l'eau ?*

**What desserts do you have?**
*Qu'est-ce que vous avez comme desserts ?*

**That was delicious.**
*C'était délicieux.*

**Excuse me!**
*S'il vous plaît !*

**Could we have the bill, please?**
*L'addition, s'il vous plaît.*

**Excuse me, where are the toilets?**
*Où sont les toilettes, s'il vous plaît ?*

***You may hear...***

**Vous avez réservé ?**
Have you booked?

**À quel nom ?**
What's the name?

**À quelle heure ?**
For what time?

**Désolé, on est complet.**
Sorry, we're full.

**Vous avez choisi ?**
Are you ready to order?

**Cette table-ci vous convient ?**
Is this table here all right for you?

**Pour combien de personnes ?**
For how many people?

**Qu'est-ce que vous voulez boire ?**
What would you like to drink?

**Bon appétit !**
Enjoy your meal!

**Vous voulez un dessert ?**
Would you like a dessert?

**Ça a été ?**
Was everything ok?

## Shopping

**Do you sell stamps/milk?**
*Est-ce que vous vendez des timbres/du lait ?*

**I'd like some of that cheese.**
*Je voudrais un peu de ce fromage-là.*

**How much is it?**
*Ça coûte combien ?*

**Four apples, please.**
*Quatre pommes, s'il vous plaît.*

**A bit more/less.**
*Un peu plus/moins.*

**That's all, thanks.**
*Ce sera tout, merci.*

**Can I try it on?**
*Est-ce que je peux essayer ?*

**No thanks, I'm just looking.**
*Non merci, je regarde seulement.*

**I need a size 12.**
*Je fais du 40.*

**I'm a size 5.** *(in shoes)*
*Je chausse du 38.*

**Do you have it in a bigger/smaller size?**
*Est-ce que vous l'avez dans une plus grande/plus petite taille ?*

**That's fine, I'll take it.**
*C'est bon, je le/la prends.*

**No, I don't like it.**
*No, je ne l'aime pas.*

**Do you take credit cards?**
*Est-ce qu'on peut payer par carte ?*

**Can I have a plastic bag?**
*Je peux avoir un sac plastique ?*

***You may hear...***

**Je peux vous aider ?**
Can I help you?

**Et avec ceci ?**
Will there be anything else?

**Vous n'avez pas plus petit ?**
Don't you have anything smaller?

**C'est pour offrir ?**
Is it for a present?

## Health

**Where can I find a doctor?**
*Où est-ce que je peux trouver un médecin ?*

**I need an ambulance!**
*J'ai besoin d'une ambulance !*

**I'd like to make an appointment.**
*Je voudrais prendre rendez-vous.*

**I have an appointment with Dr...**
*J'ai rendez-vous avec le Docteur...*

**As soon as possible.**
*Le plus tôt possible.*

**I don't feel well.**
*Je ne me sens pas bien.*

**I've got a headache/stomachache.**
*J'ai mal à la tête/au ventre.*

**I've got a sore throat/back.**
*J'ai mal à la gorge/au dos.*

**I feel sick.**
*J'ai envie de vomir.*

**I've got a temperature.**
*J'ai de la fièvre.*

**It hurts.**
*Ça fait mal.*

**I have asthma/diabetes.**
*J'ai de l'asthme/du diabète.*

**I'm four months pregnant.**
*Je suis enceinte de quatre mois.*

**It's been three days.**
*Ça fait trois jours.*

**I'm allergic to penicillin.**
*Je suis allergique à la pénicilline.*

**It's got worse.**
*Ça s'est aggravé.*

**Where's the nearest pharmacy?**
*Où est la pharmacie la plus proche ?*

**I need some plasters/aspirin.**
*J'ai besoin de pansements/d'aspirine.*

**Do you have anything for a cold/diarrhoea ?**
*Pouvez-vous me donner quelque chose contre le rhume/la diarrée ?*

***You may hear...***

**Prenez place dans la salle d'attente.**
Take a seat in the waiting room.

**Où est-ce que ça fait mal ?**
Where does it hurt?

**Respirez bien fort.**
Take a deep breath.

**Allongez-vous.**
Lie down.

**Ça devrait passer dans quelques jours.**
It should clear up in a few days.

**Je vais vous faire une ordonnance.**
I'll write you a prescription.

**Revenez me voir dans une semaine.**
Come back and see me in a week.

**Prenez-le trois fois par jour avant les repas.**
Take it three times a day before meals.

## Emergencies

**Help!**
*Au secours !*

**Fire!**
*Au feu !*

**Stop, thief!**
*Au voleur !*

**There's been an accident.**
*Il y a eu un accident.*

**It's an emergency!**
*C'est urgent !*

**Where's the nearest police station/hospital?**
*Où est le commissariat/l'hôpital le plus proche ?*

**Can you help me?**
*Est-ce que vous pouvez m'aider ?*

**My bag/passport's been stolen.**
*On m'a volé mon sac/mon passeport.*

**I've lost my car keys.**
*J'ai perdu mes clés de voiture.*

**My son/daughter is missing.**
*Mon fils/Ma fille a disparu.*

**There's someone following me.**
*Il y a quelqu'un qui me suit.*

**I want to report a theft.**
*Je voudrais faire une déclaration de vol.*

**What do I have to do?**
*Qu'est-ce que je dois faire ?*

**I need a document from the police for my insurance company.**
*J'ai besoin d'un certificat de police pour ma compagnie d'assurances.*

***You may hear...***

**Qu'est-ce qui s'est passé ?**
What happened?

**Quand cela est-il passé ?**
When did it happen?

**Pouvez-vous le/la décrire ?**
Can you describe him/her ?

**Qu'est-ce qu'il vous manque ?**
What's missing?

**Vous devez remplir ce formulaire.**
You need to fill in this form.

# Guide de conversation

## Rencontres

**Bonjour, comment ça va ?**
*Hello, how are you?*

**Ça va bien, merci, et vous / toi ?**
*Fine thanks, and you?*

**Comment tu t'appelles/vous vous appelez ?**
*What's your name?*

**Je m'appelle...**
*My name's...*

**Enchanté(e) !**
*Nice to meet you!*

**Voici mon mari/ma sœur.**
*This is my husband/my sister.*

**Quel âge as-tu/avez-vous ?**
*How old are you?*

**J'ai 15/21/40 ans.**
*I'm fifteen/twenty-one/forty.*

**D'où viens-tu/venez-vous ?**
*Where are you from ?*

**Je viens de Bordeaux.**
*I'm from Bordeaux.*

**Nous sommes français(es).**
*We're French.*

**Nous habitons dans le sud de la France.**
*We live in the south of France.*

**Qu'est-ce que tu fais/vous faites dans la vie ?**
*What do you do?*

**Je suis étudiant(e).**
*I'm a student.*

**Je suis professeur.**
*I'm a teacher.*

**Je travaille dans une banque.**
*I work in a bank.*

**J'aime bien le foot/aller au cinéma.**
*I like football/going to the cinema.*

**Je n'aime pas la bière/faire du vélo.**
*I don't like beer/cycling.*

**Je peux avoir ton/votre adresse ?**
*Can I have your address?*

**Vous devez venir nous voir un jour !**
*You must come and visit us one day!*

**Voici mon adresse e-mail.**
*Here's my e-mail address.*

**À bientôt/plus tard.**
*See you soon/later.*

## Comprendre

**Pardon ?**
*Pardon?*

**Je ne comprends pas.**
*I don't understand.*

**Je parle à peine anglais.**
*I don't speak much English.*

**Qu'est-ce que ça veut dire ?**
*What does that mean?*

**J'apprends l'anglais.**
*I'm learning English.*

**Vous pouvez répéter ?**
*Could you repeat that, please?*

**Parlez-vous français ?**
*Do you speak French?*

**Je comprends un peu.**
*I can understand a little.*

**Comment dit-on ... en anglais ?**
*How do you say ... in English?*

**Pourriez-vous me l'écrire ?**
*Could you write it down for me?*

## Votre séjour

**Nous sommes en vacances.**
*We're on holiday.*

**Je suis ici pour mon travail.**
*I'm here on business.*

**Je ne suis ici que pour le weekend.**
*I'm only here for the weekend.*

**Nous sommes ici pour une semaine.**
*We're here for a week.*

**Nous avons des amis/de la famille ici.**
*We have friends/family here.*

**Je me plais beaucoup ici.**
*I really like it here.*

**Bonnes vacances !**
*Have a good holiday!*

**Amuse-toi / Amusez-vous bien !**
*Have fun!*

## Demander son chemin

**Excusez-moi, pourriez-vous me dire où se trouve la gare routière ?**
*Excuse me, can you tell me where the bus station is, please?*

**Comment je fais pour aller au zoo ?**
*How do I get to the zoo?*

**Le marché, c'est par où ?**
*Which way is it to the market?*

**Je cherche...**
*I'm looking for...*

**Y a-t-il une papeterie par ici ?**
*Is there a newsagent's round here?*

**Pourriez-vous me montrer sur la carte ?**
*Could you show me on the map?*

**C'est loin jusqu'à la prochaine ville ?**
*Is it far to the next town?*

***Vous entendrez peut-être...***

**Go straight on.**
Continuez tout droit.

**Turn left/right.**
Tournez à gauche/à droite.

**Carry on as far as...**
Continuez jusqu'à...

**Take the next exit.**
Prenez la prochaine sortie.

## Demandes, remerciements, opinions

**Est-ce que pourrais avoir de l'eau?**
*Could I have some water, please?*

**Est-ce que vous pourriez m'emmener en voiture ?**
*Would you be able to give me a lift?*

**Vous pouvez me montrer ?**
*Can you show me?*

**Je peux fumer ?**
*Is it ok if I smoke?*

**Ça vous dérange si j'ouvre la fenêtre ?**
*Do you mind if I open the window?*

**Merci (beaucoup) !**
*Thank you (very much)!*

**De rien !**
*You're welcome!*

**Merci, c'est très gentil.**
*Thanks, that's very kind of you.*

**Merci beaucoup pour votre aide.**
*Thanks a lot for your help.*

**Je l'ai bien aimé.**
*I enjoyed it.*

**Ça ne m'a pas plu.**
*I didn't enjoy it.*

**C'est très joli(e) !**
*It's beautiful!*

**C'était ennuyeux.**
*It was boring.*

**Je suis/ne suis pas d'accord.**
*I agree/disagree.*

**Vous avez raison.**
*You're right.*

**Je le trouve délicieux !**
*I think it's delicious!*

**Ce n'est pas mal.**
*It's not bad.*

**Ah bon ? C'est intéressant !**
*Really? That's interesting!*

**Je crois que oui/non.**
*I think so/don't think so.*

**Ça m'est égal.**
*I don't mind.*

**Je ne sais pas.**
*I don't know.*

## Voyages

**Un billet pour York, s'il vous plaît.**
*I'd like a ticket to York, please.*

**Un aller simple/aller-retour.**
*A single/return ticket.*

**À quelle heure est le prochain train pour Birmingham ?**
*When's the next train to Birmingham?*

**Il part de quel quai ?**
*Which platform does it go from?*

**Est-ce qu'il y a une correspondance ?**
*Do I have to change?*

**Est-ce que cette place est libre ?**
*Is this seat free?*

**Désolé(e), il y a déjà quelqu'un.**
*Sorry, there's someone sitting there.*

**Où est l'enregistrement pour Easyjet ?**
*Where's the Easyjet check-in ?*

**À quelle heure embarque-t-on ?**
*What time do we board?*

**Je voudrais une place côté couloir/côté hublot.**
*I'd like an aisle/window seat please.*

**J'ai raté ma correspondance.**
*I've missed my connection.*

**Mes bagages ne sont pas arrivés.**
*My luggage hasn't arrived.*

**Avez-vous un dépliant avec les horaires/un plan du métro ?**
*Do you have a timetable/a map of the underground?*

**Est-ce que ce bus va à la gare ?**
*Does this bus go to the station?*

**Je prends quelle ligne ?**
*Which line do I take?*

**Est-ce que c'est l'arrêt pour le musée ?**
*Is this the stop for the museum?*

**À quelle heure part le dernier bus/train ?**
*What time is the last bus/train?*
**Je voudrais louer une voiture pour une semaine.**
*I'd like to hire a car for a week.*

**Y a-t-il une station-service près d'ici ?**
*Is there a petrol station near here ?*

**On est en panne d'essence.**
*We've run out of petrol.*

**Je suis tombé en panne.**
*I've broken down.*

**Nous avons crevé.**
*We've got a puncture.*

**Y a-t-il une station de taxis près d'ici ?**
*Is there a taxi rank near here?*

**Je voudrais aller à l'aéroport.**
*I'd like to go to the airport.*

**Ça va coûter combien ?**
*How much will it be?*

**Vous pouvez me déposer ici, merci.**
*You can drop me off here, thanks.*

***Vous entendrez peut-être...***

**How many bags do you have ?**
Combien de bagages avez-vous ?

**Can I see your passport, please ?**
Votre passeport, s'il vous plaît.

**Here's your boarding card.**
Voici votre carte d'embarquement.

**Immediate boarding at gate...**
Embarquement immédiat à la porte numéro...

**You have to change at Peterborough.**
Vous avez une correspondance à Peterborough.

**The train to...**
Le train à destination de...

**Take bus number...**
Prenez le bus numéro...

**Get off at the third stop.**
Descendez au troisième arrêt.

## Logement

**Avez-vous une chambre de libre pour ce soir ?**
*Have you got a room available for tonight?*

**Je voudrais réserver une chambre double/individuelle pour trois nuits.**
*I'd like to book a double/single room for three nights.*

**Je voudrais une chambre avec salle de bains.**
*I'd like an ensuite room.*

**J'a fait une réservation au nom de...**
*I have a reservation in the name of...*

**Avez-vous des chambres familiales ?**
*Do you have family rooms ?*

**Vous n'avez rien de moins cher ?**
*Don't you have anything cheaper?*

**Est-ce que le petit déjeuner est compris ?**
*Is breakfast included?*

**À quelle heure est le petit déjeuner ?**
*What time is breakfast?*

**À quelle heure doit-on libérer la chambre ?**
*What time do we have to check out?*

**Je peux laisser mes bagages ici ?**
*Can I leave my bags here?*

**Il y a un problème avec la douche/la climatisation.**
*There's a problem with the shower/the air conditioning.*

**C'est cassé.**
*It's broken.*

**Ça ne marche pas.**
*It doesn't work.*

**Je viens régler.**
*I'd like to pay, please.*

**Il n'y a pas de papier toilette.**
*There's no toilet paper.*

**Nous voudrons louer une gîte rurale.**
*We'd like to rent a cottage in the country.*

**Les draps et serviettes sont-ils fournis ?**
*Are sheets and towels provided?*

**Est-ce qu'on a besoin d'une voiture ?**
*Do you need a car?*

**Est-ce qu'il y a un camping par ici ?**
*Is there a campsite nearby?*

**Pouvons-nous monter notre tente ici?**
*Can we pitch our tent here?*

*Vous entendrez peut-être...*

**What's the name?**
C'ést à quel nom ?

**I'm afraid we're fully booked.**
Désolé, on est complet.

**The room will be ready at 2 o'clock.**
La chambre sera disponible à 14 heures.

**Check-out is at midday.**
La chambre doit être libérée à midi.

**Breakfast is from seven to ten.**
Le petit déjeuner est servi de 7h à 10h.

## Manger et boire

**Pouvez-vous me recommander un bon restaurant ?**
*Can you recommend a good restaurant?*

**Je voudrais réserver une table pour deux personnes pour demain soir.**
*I'd like to book a table for two for tomorrow night.*

**Avez-vous une table pour quatre ?**
*Do you have a table for four ?*

**J'ai réservé une table au nom de...**
*I've booked a table, the name's...*

**Nous avons choisi.**
*We're ready to order now.*

**Je vais prendre le saumon.**
*I'll have the salmon.*

**Je suis végétarien(enne).**
*I'm vegetarian.*

**Je suis allergique aux produits laitiers.**
*I'm allergic to dairy products.*

**C'est quoi, le « black pudding » ?**
*What's black pudding?*

**Quels sont les plats du jour ?**
*What are today's specials?*

**A bottle of red/white wine.**
*Une bouteille de vin rouge/ blanc.*

**Two beers and a Coke®, please.**
*Deux bières et un Coca®, s'il vous plaît.*

**Est-ce qu'on pourrait avoir encore du pain/de l'eau ?**
*Could we have some more bread/water?*

**Vous avez quoi comme desserts ?**
*What desserts do you have?*

**C'était délicieux.**
*That was delicious.*

**S'il vous plaît !**
*Excuse me!*

**L'addition, s'il vous plaît.**
*Could we have the bill, please?*

**Où sont les toilettes, s'il vous plaît ?**
*Excuse me, where are the toilets?*

***Vous entendrez peut-être...***

**Do you have a reservation?**
Vous avez réservé ?

**What's the name?**
À quel nom?

**For what time?**
À quelle heure ?

**For how many people?**
Pour combien de personnes ?

**Sorry, we're full.**
Désolé, on est complet.

**Are you ready to order?**
Vous avez choisi ?

**Is this table here all right for you?**
Cette table-ci vous convient ?

**What would you like to drink?**
Qu'est-ce que vous voulez boire ?

**Enjoy your meal!**
Bon appétit !

**Would you like a dessert?**
Vous voulez un dessert ?

**Was everything ok?**
Ça a été ?

## Achats

**Est-ce que vous vendez des timbres/du lait ?**
*Do you sell stamps/milk?*

**Je voudrais un peu de ce fromage-là.**
*I'd like a bit of that cheese.*

**Ça coûte combien ?**
*How much is it?*

**Four apples, please.**
*Quatre pommes, s'il vous plaît.*

**Un peu plus/moins.**
*A bit more/less.*

**Ce sera tout, merci.**
*That's all, thanks.*

**Est-ce que je peux essayer ?**
*Can I try it on?*
**Non merci, je regarde seulement.**
*No thanks, I'm just looking.*

**Je fais du 40. (vêtements)**
*I'm a size 12.*

**Je chausse du 38.**
*I take a size 5.*

**Est-ce que vous l'avez dans une plus grande/plus petite taille?**
*Do you have it in a bigger/smaller size?*

**C'est bon, je le/la prends.**
*That's fine, I'll take it.*

**No, je ne l'aime pas.**
*No, I don't like it.*

**Est-ce qu'on peut payer par carte ?**
*Do you take credit cards?*

**Je peux avoir un sac plastique ?**
*Can I have a (plastic) bag?*

***Vous entendrez peut-être...***

**Can I help you?**
Je peux vous aider ?

**Will there be anything else?**
Et avec ceci ?

**Don't you have anything smaller?**
Vous n'avez pas plus petit ?

**Would you like a bag?**
Voulez-vous un sac en plastique ?

## Santé

**J'ai besoin de voir un médecin.**
*I need to see a doctor.*

**J'ai besoin d'une ambulance !**
*I need an ambulance!*

**Je voudrais prendre rendez-vous.**
*I'd like to make an appointment.*

**J'ai rendez-vous avec le Docteur...**
*I have an appointment with Dr...*

**Le plus tôt possible.**
*As soon as possible.*

**Je ne me sens pas bien.**
*I don't feel well.*

**J'ai mal au ventre/à la tête.**
*I've got stomachache/a headache.*

**J'ai mal à la gorge/au dos.**
*I've got a sore throat/back.*

**J'ai envie de vomir.**
*I feel sick.*

**J'ai de la fièvre.**
*I've got a temperature.*

**Ça fait mal.**
*It hurts.*

**J'ai de l'asthme/du diabète.**
*I have asthma/diabetes.*

**Je suis enceinte de quatre mois.**
*I'm four months pregnant.*

**Je suis allergique à la pénicilline.**
*I'm allergic to penicillin.*

**Ça fait trois jours.**
*It's been three days.*

**Ça s'est aggravé.**
*It's got worse.*

**Où est la pharmacie la plus proche ?**
*Where's the nearest pharmacy?*

**J'ai besoin de pansements/d'aspirine.**
*I need some plasters/aspirin.*

**Pouvez-vous me donner quelque chose contre le rhume/la diarrée ?**
*Do you have anything for a cold/diarrhoea ?*

***Vous entendrez peut-être...***

**Take a seat in the waiting room.**
Prenez place dans la salle d'attente.

**Where does it hurt ?**
Où est-ce que ça fait mal ?

**Take a deep breath.**
Respirez bien fort.

**Lie down.**
Allongez-vous.

**It should clear up in a few days.**
Ça devrait passer dans quelques jours.

**I'll write you a prescription.**
Je vais vous faire une ordonnance.

**Come back and see me in a week.**
Revenez me voir dans une semaine.

**Take it three times a day before meals.**
Prenez-le trois fois par jour avant les repas.

## Urgences

**Au secours !**
*Help!*

**Au feu !**
*Fire!*

**Au voleur !**
*Stop, thief!*

**Il y a eu un accident.**
*There's been an accident.*

**C'est urgent !**
*It's an emergency!*

**Où est le commissariat/l'hôpital le plus proche ?**
*Where's the nearest police station/hospital?*

**Est-ce que vous pouvez m'aider ?**
*Can you help me?*

**On m'a volé mon sac/mon passeport.**
*My bag/passport's been stolen.*

**J'ai perdu mes clés de voiture.**
*I've lost my car keys.*

**Mon fils/Ma fille a disparu.**
*My son/daughter is missing.*

**Il y a quelqu'un qui me suit.**
*There's someone following me.*

**Qu'est-ce que je dois faire ?**
*What do I have to do?*

**Je voudrais faire une déclaration de vol.**
*I want to report a theft.*

**J'ai besoin d'un certificat de police pour ma compagnie d'assurances.**
*I need a document from the police for my insurance company.*

***Vous entendrez peut-être...***

**What happened?**
Qu'est-ce qui s'est passé ?

**When did it happen?**
Quand cela est-il passé ?

**What's missing?**
Qu'est-ce qu'il vous manque ?

**Can you describe him/her?**
Pouvez-vous le/la décrire ?

**You need to fill in this form.**
Vous devez remplir ce formulaire.

# Conversion tables

•

# Tables de conversion

Note that when writing numbers in French, commas are used instead of decimal points. For example, **2.5** would be written **2,5** in French and pronounced *deux virgule cinq*.

***

Notez que les chiffres en anglais s'écrivent avec un point là ou en français on utilise une virgule. Par exemple, **2,5** s'écrira **2.5** en anglais et se prononcera *two point five*.

## Measurements *Mesures*

**Length** *Longueur*

1 cm ≈ 0.4 inches    1 inch (*pouce*) ≈ 2,5 cm

30 cm ≈ 1 foot (*pied*)

Lengths in France are always given in metres and centimetres.

***

Les Britanniques et les Américains se mesurent normalement en **feet** et en **inches**. On dira donc « he's 6 foot four » (6 pieds et 4 pouces, ou 1m90).

## **Distance** *Distance*

On French road signs, distances are always shown in kilometres.

***

Sur les panneaux de route britanniques et américains, les distances sont toujours données en miles.

1 m ≈ 1 yard

1 km ≈ 0.6 miles 1 mile ≈ 1,6 km

To convert kilometers into miles, divide by 8 and then multiply by 5.

*Pour convertir des kilomètres en miles, divisez par 8 puis multipliez par 5.*

| **km** | 1 | 2 | 5 | 10 | 20 | 50 | 100 |
|---|---|---|---|---|---|---|---|
| **miles** | 0.6 | 1.25 | 3.1 | 6.25 | 12.5 | 31.25 | 62.5 |

To convert miles into kilometers, divide by 5 and then multiply by 8.

*Pour convertir des miles en kilomètres, divisez par 5 puis multipliez par 8.*

| **miles** | 1 | 2 | 5 | 10 | 20 | 50 | 100 |
|---|---|---|---|---|---|---|---|
| **km** | 1.6 | 3.2 | 8 | 16 | 32 | 80 | 160 |

## **Weight** *Poids*

Weights in France are always in kilos (or grams for small amounts).

***

Les fruits et légumes se vendent par livres (**pounds**). Pour parler du poids d'une personne, les britanniques utilisent le plus souvent les **stones** (14 livres = 1 stone). On dira donc « I weigh nine stone ten » (neuf stones et dix livres, ou 61kg). Aux États-Unis, on emploie les pounds pour les personnes.

25 g ≈ 1 oz (ounce/*once*)
1 kg ≈ 2 lb (pound/*livre*) 1lb ≈ 0.5 kg
6 kg ≈ 1 stone

To convert kilos into pounds, divide by 5 and then multiply by 11.
*Pour convertir des kilos en livres, divisez par 5 puis multipliez par 11.*

| **kilos** | 1 | 2 | 10 | 20 | 60 | 80 |
|---|---|---|---|---|---|---|
| **pounds** | 2.2 | 4.4 | 2.2 | 44 | 132 | 176 |
| **kilos** | 10 | 20 | 50 | 60 | 75 | 90 |
| **stone** | 1.6 | 3.2 | 8 | 9.4 | 11.8 | 14 |

To convert pounds into kilos, divide by 11 and then multiply by 5.
*Pour convertir des livres en kilos, divisez par 11 puis multipliez par 5.*

| **pounds** | 1 | 2 | 10 | 20 | 60 | 80 |
|---|---|---|---|---|---|---|
| **kilos** | 0.45 | 0.9 | 4.5 | 9 | 27 | 36 |

| **stone** | 1 | 2 | 8 | 10 | 12 | 14 |
|---|---|---|---|---|---|---|
| **kilos** | 6.35 | 12.7 | 50.8 | 63.5 | 76 | 89 |

## Liquids *Liquides*

1 litre ≈ 2 pints  1 pint ≈ 0.5 litres
1 gallon (*Br*) ≈ 4.54 litres, (*Am*) ≈ 3.78 litres

## Temperatures *Températures*

To convert Celsius into Fahrenheit, divide by 5, multiply by 9 and then add 32.
*Pour convertir des degrés Celsius en degrés Fahrenheit, divisez par 5, multipliez par 9 puis ajoutez 32.*

To convert Fahrenheit into Celsius, subtract 32, multiply by 5 and then divide by 9.
*Pour convertir des degrés Fahrenheit en degrés Celsius, soustrayez 32, multipliez par 5 puis divisez par 9.*

| °C | 0 | 10 | 20 | 30 | 37 | 40 | 100 |
|---|---|---|---|---|---|---|---|
| °F | 32 | 50 | 68 | 104 | 98.6 | 80 | 212 |

## Clothes sizes *Tailles de vêtements*

Clothes in France may also be labelled with the English-language abbreviations XS, S, M, L and XL, or with the numbers 1 to 4 (increasing in size).

***

Vous connaissez sans doute déjà les abréviations XS (extra small), S (small), M (medium), L (large) et XL (extra large).

**Women's clothes** *Vêtements pour femmes*

| UK | 6 | 8 | 10 | 12 | 14 | 16 |
|---|---|---|---|---|---|---|
| US | 4 | 6 | 8 | 10 | 12 | 14 |
| Europe | 38 | 36 | 38 | 40 | 42 | 44 |

**Bras** *Soutiens-gorge*

| UK/US | 32 | 34 | 36 | 38 | 40 |
|---|---|---|---|---|---|
| France | 85 | 90 | 95 | 100 | 105 |
| Europe | 70 | 75 | 80 | 85 | 90 |

Cup sizes are the same.
*La taille de bonnet est identique.*

**Men's clothes** *Vêtements pour hommes*

| UK/US | 30 | 32 | 34 | 36 | 38 | 40 |
|---|---|---|---|---|---|---|
| Europe | 40 | 42 | 44 | 46 | 48 | 50 |

**Men's shirts** *Chemises pour hommes*

| UK/US | 14 | 15 | 16 | 17 | 18 |
|---|---|---|---|---|---|
| Europe | 36 | 38 | 41 | 43 | 48 |

**Women's shoes** *Chaussures de femmes*

| UK | 4 | 5 | 6 | 7 | 8 |
|---|---|---|---|---|---|
| US | 6 | 7 | 8 | 9 | 10 |
| Europe | 37 | 38 | 39 | 40 | 41 |

**Men's shoes** *Chaussures d'hommes*

| UK | 7 | 8 | 9 | 10 | 11 |
|---|---|---|---|---|---|
| US | 8 | 9 | 10 | 11 | 12 |
| Europe | 40 | 41 | 42 | 43 | 44 |

## **Currency** *Monnaie*

£1 (pound) = 100 pence
$1 (dollar) = 100 cents
€1 (euro) = 100 cents

As exchange rates vary, we have left blanks in the following tables for you to fill in with the most up-to-date figures.

***

Comme les taux de change varient, nous avons laissé des blancs dans ces tableaux que vous pouvez remplir avec les chiffres les plus récentes.

| £ | 1 | 5 | 10 | 25 | 50 | 100 |
|---|---|---|---|---|---|---|
| $ | 1 | 5 | 10 | 25 | 50 | 100 |
| € | | | | | | |

| € | 1 | 5 | 10 | 25 | 50 | 100 |
|---|---|---|---|---|---|---|
| £ | | | | | | |
| $ | | | | | | |

# FRANÇAIS-ANGLAIS

# Aa

**A, a** [ɑ] *nm inv* A, a; **A1** *(autoroute) Br* ≃ M1, *Am* ≃ I1

**a** [a] *voir* **avoir**

**À** [a]

**à + le = au** [o], **à + les = aux** [o]

*prép* (**a**) *(indique la direction)* to; **aller à Paris** to go to Paris; **partir au Venezuela** to leave for Venezuela; **de Paris à Lyon** from Paris to Lyons

(**b**) *(indique la position)* at; **être au bureau/à la ferme/à Paris** to be at *or* in the office/on *or* at the farm/in Paris; **à la maison** at home

(**c**) *(dans l'expression du temps)* **à 8 heures** at 8 o'clock; **du lundi au vendredi** from Monday to Friday, *Am* Monday through Friday; **au vingt-et-unième siècle** in the twenty-first century; **à mon arrivée** on (my) arrival; **à lundi!** see you (on) Monday!

(**d**) *(dans les descriptions)* **l'homme à la barbe** the man with the beard; **verre à vin** wine glass

(**e**) *(introduit le complément d'objet indirect)* **donner qch à qn** to give sth to sb, to give sb sth; **penser à qn/qch** to think about *or* of sb/sth

(**f**) *(devant infinitif)* **apprendre à lire** to learn to read; **avoir du travail à faire** to have work to do; **maison à vendre** house for sale; **prêt à partir** ready to leave

(**g**) *(indique l'appartenance)* **un ami à moi** a friend of mine; **c'est à lui** it's his; **c'est à vous de...** *(il vous incombe de)* it's up to you to...; *(c'est votre tour)* it's your turn to...

(**h**) *(indique le moyen, la manière)* **à bicyclette** by bicycle; **à pied** on foot; **à la main** by hand; **au crayon** in pencil; **deux à deux** two by two

(**i**) *(prix)* **pain à 1 euro** loaf for 1 euro

(**j**) *(poids)* **vendre au kilo** to sell by the kilo

(**k**) *(vitesse)* **100 km à l'heure** 100 km an *or* per hour

(**l**) *(pour appeler)* **au voleur!** (stop) thief!; **au feu!** (there's a) fire!

---

**abaisser** [abese] **1** *vt (levier, pont-levis)* to lower; *(store)* to pull down **2 s'abaisser** *vpr* (**a**) *(barrière)* to lower (**b**) *(être en pente)* to slope down

**abandon** [abɑ̃dɔ̃] *nm (d'enfant, de projet)* abandonment; *(de lieu)* neglect; *(de sportif)* withdrawal; *Ordinat* abort ▪ **abandonner 1** *vt (personne, animal, lieu)* to desert, to abandon; *(pouvoir, combat)* to give up; *(projet)* to abandon; **a. ses études** to drop out (of school) **2** *vi (renoncer)* to give up; *(sportif)* to withdraw

**abasourdi, -e** [abazurdi] *adj* stunned

**abat-jour** [abaʒur] *nm inv* lampshade

**abats** [aba] *nmpl* offal; *(de volaille)* giblets

**abattement** [abatmɑ̃] *nm (mental)* dejection; *(physique)* exhaustion; **a. fiscal** tax allowance

**abattoir** [abatwar] *nm* slaughterhouse

**abattre*** [abatr] **1** *vt (arbre)* to cut down; *(personne)* to kill; *(animal de boucherie)* to slaughter; *(animal blessé ou malade)* to destroy; *(avion)* to shoot down; *Fig (déprimer)* to demoralize **2**

**s'abattre** *vpr (tomber)* to crash down (**sur** on); *(pluie)* to pour down (**sur** on)
**abattu, -e** [abaty] *adj (mentalement)* dejected; *(physiquement)* exhausted
**abbaye** [abei] *nf* abbey
**abcès** [apsɛ] *nm* abscess
**abdomen** [abdɔmɛn] *nm* abdomen ▪ **abdominal, -e, -aux, -ales** *adj* abdominal
**abeille** [abɛj] *nf* bee
**aberrant, -e** [aberɑ̃, -ɑ̃t] *adj* absurd
**abîme** [abim] *nm* abyss
**abîmer** [abime] **1** *vt* to spoil, to damage **2 s'abîmer** *vpr (object)* to get spoilt; *(fruit)* to go bad
**abject, -e** [abʒɛkt] *adj* despicable
**abolir** [abɔlir] *vt* to abolish ▪ **abolition** *nf* abolition
**abominable** [abɔminabl] *adj* appalling
**abondant, -e** [abɔ̃dɑ̃, -ɑ̃t] *adj* plentiful, abundant ▪ **abondance** *nf* abundance (**de** of) ▪ **abonder** *vi* to be plentiful
**abonné, -e** [abɔne] *nmf (d'un journal, du téléphone)* subscriber; *(du gaz)* consumer ▪ **abonnement** *nm (de journal)* subscription; *(de téléphone)* line rental ▪ **s'abonner** *vpr (à un journal)* to subscribe (**à** to)
**abord** [abɔr] *nm* (**a**) *(accès)* **d'un a. facile** easy to approach; **abords** *(d'un bâtiment)* surroundings; *(d'une ville)* outskirts (**b**) *(expressions)* **au premier a., de prime a.** at first sight; **d'a., tout d'a.** *(pour commencer)* at first, to begin with; *(premièrement)* first (and foremost)
**abordable** [abɔrdabl] *adj (prix, marchandises)* affordable
**aborder** [abɔrde] **1** *vt (personne, lieu, virage)* to approach; *(problème)* to tackle **2** *vi* to land
**aborigène** [abɔriʒɛn] *nm (d'un pays)* native; **les Aborigènes d'Australie** the (Australian) Aborigines
**aboutir** [abutir] *vi (réussir)* to be successful; **a. à qch** *(avoir pour résultat)* to result in sth ▪ **aboutissement** *nm* *(succès)* success; *(résultat)* outcome
**aboyer** [abwaje] *vi* to bark
**abréger** [abreʒe] *vt (texte)* to shorten; *(visite)* to cut short; *(mot)* to abbreviate ▪ **abrégé** *nm (d'un texte)* summary; *(livre)* abstract; **en a.** *(mot)* in abbreviated form
**abréviation** [abrevjɑsjɔ̃] *nf* abbreviation
**abri** [abri] *nm* shelter; **mettre qn/qch à l'a.** to shelter sb/sth; **se mettre à l'a.** to take shelter; **être à l'a. de qch** to be sheltered from sth; **sans a.** homeless ▪ **abriter 1** *vt (protéger)* to shelter (**de** from); *(loger)* to house **2 s'abriter** *vpr* to (take) shelter (**de** from)
**abricot** [abriko] *nm* apricot
**abroger** [abrɔʒe] *vt* to repeal
**abrupt, -e** [abrypt] *adj (pente)* steep
**abrutir** [abrytir] *vt (hébéter)* to daze ▪ **abrutissant, -e** *adj* mind-numbing
**absence** [apsɑ̃s] *nf (d'une personne)* absence; *(manque)* lack ▪ **absent, -e 1** *adj (personne)* absent (**de** from); *(chose)* missing **2** *nmf* absentee ▪ **s'absenter** *vpr* to go away
**absolu, -e** [apsɔly] *adj* absolute ▪ **absolument** *adv* absolutely
**absorber** [apsɔrbe] *vt (liquid)* to absorb; *(nourriture)* to eat; *(boisson)* to drink; *(médicament)* to take ▪ **absorbant, -e** *adj (papier)* absorbent; *(travail)* absorbing ▪ **absorption** *nf (de liquide)* absorption; *(de nourriture)* eating; *(de boisson)* drinking; *(de médicament)* taking
**abstenir*** [apstənir] **s'abstenir** *vpr (ne pas voter)* to abstain; **s'a. de qch/de faire qch** to refrain from sth/from doing sth ▪ **abstention** *nf Pol* abstention
**abstrait, -e** [apstrɛ, -ɛt] *adj* abstract ▪ **abstraction** *nf* abstraction
**absurde** [apsyrd] *adj* absurd ▪ **absurdité** *nf* absurdity; **dire des absurdités** to talk nonsense
**abus** [aby] *nm (excès)* overindulgence (**de** in); *(pratique)* abuse (**de** of); **a. de pouvoir** abuse of power; **a. d'alcool**

alcohol abuse; **a. de confiance** breach of trust ■ **abuser 1** *vi* to go too far; **a. de** *(situation, personne)* to take unfair advantage of; *(autorité)* to abuse; *(nourriture)* to overindulge in **2 s'abuser** *vpr* **si je ne m'abuse** if I am not mistaken

**abusif, -ive** [abyzif, -iv] *adj* excessive; *(mère)* possessive

**académie** [akademi] *nf* academy; *(administration scolaire)* ≃ local education authority; **l'A. française** = learned society responsible for promoting the French language and imposing standards

**acajou** [akaʒu] *nm* mahogany

**accabler** [akɑble] *vt* to overwhelm (**de** with); **accablé de dettes** (over)-burdened with debt ■ **accablant, -e** *adj (chaleur)* oppressive; *(témoignage)* damning

**accalmie** [akalmi] *nf* lull

**accaparer** [akapare] *vt (personne)* to monopolize

**accéder** [aksede] *vi* **a. à** *(lieu)* to reach; *(rang)* to gain; *(requête)* to comply with; *Ordinat (programme)* to access; **a. au trône** to accede to the throne

**accélérer** [akselere] **1** *vt (allure, pas)* to quicken **2** *vi (en voiture)* to accelerate **3 s'accélérer** *vpr* to speed up ■ **accélérateur** *nm (de voiture, d'ordinateur)* accelerator ■ **accélération** *nf* acceleration

**accent** [aksɑ̃] *nm (prononciation)* accent; *(sur une syllabe)* stress; *Fig* **mettre l'a. sur qch** to stress sth; **a. aigu/circonflexe/grave** acute/circumflex/grave (accent) ■ **accentuation** *nf (sur lettre)* accentuation; *(de phénomène)* intensification ■ **accentuer 1** *vt (syllabe)* to stress; *(lettre)* to put an accent on; *Fig (renforcer)* to emphasize **2 s'accentuer** *vpr* to become more pronounced

**accepter** [aksepte] *vt* to accept; **a. de faire qch** to agree to do sth ■ **acceptable** *adj (recevable)* acceptable ■ **acceptation** *nf* acceptance

**acception** [aksɛpsjɔ̃] *nf (de mot)* meaning

**accès** [aksɛ] *nm* (**a**) *(approche) & Ordinat* access (**à** to); **avoir a. à qch** to have access to sth; **'a. interdit'** 'no entry'; **'a. aux quais'** to the trains (**b**) *(de folie, de colère)* fit; *(de fièvre)* bout ■ **accessible** *adj (lieu, livre)* accessible

**accession** [aksɛsjɔ̃] *nf* accession (**à** to); **a. à la propriété** home ownership

**accessoire** [akseswar] *adj* minor ■ **accessoires** *nmpl (de théâtre)* props; *(de mode, de voiture)* accessories; **a. de toilette** toilet accessories

**accident** [aksidɑ̃] *nm* accident; **a. de chemin de fer** train crash; **a. de la route** road accident; **a. du travail** industrial accident; **a. de parcours** hitch; **par a.** by accident, by chance ■ **accidenté, -e 1** *adj (terrain)* uneven; *(voiture)* damaged **2** *nmf* accident victim ■ **accidentel, -elle** *adj* accidental

**acclamer** [aklame] *vt* to cheer ■ **acclamations** *nfpl* cheers

**acclimater** [aklimate] **1** *vt Br* to acclimatize, *Am* to acclimate (**à** to) **2 s'acclimater** *vpr* to become *Br* acclimatized *or Am* acclimated (**à** to) ■ **acclimatation** *nf Br* acclimatization, *Am* acclimation (**à** to)

**accolade** [akɔlad] *nf (embrassade)* embrace; *(signe)* curly bracket

**accommoder** [akɔmɔde] **1** *vt (nourriture)* to prepare; *(restes)* to use up **2** *vi (œil)* to focus **3 s'accommoder** *vpr* **s'a. de qch** to put up with sth ■ **accommodant, -e** *adj* accommodating

**accompagner** [akɔ̃paɲe] *vt (personne)* to accompany; **a. qn à la gare** *(en voiture)* to take sb to the station ■ **accompagnateur, -trice** *nmf (musical)* accompanist; *(de touristes)* guide; *(d'enfants)* group leader ■ **accompagnement** *nm (de musique)* accompaniment

**accomplir** [akɔ̃plir] *vt (tache)* to carry out; *(formalités)* to go through ■ **accompli, -e** *adj (parfait)* accomplished

**accord** [akɔr] *nm (traité, entente) &*

*Gram* agreement; *(autorisation)* consent; *(musical)* chord; **être d'a.** to agree (**avec** with); **d'a.!** all right! ▪ **accorder 1** *vt (instrument)* to tune; **a. qch à qn** *(faveur)* to grant sb sth; *(prêt)* to authorize sth to sb **2 s'accorder** *vpr (se mettre d'accord)* to agree (**avec/sur** with/on); *Gram (mots)* to agree (**avec** with); **s'a. qch** to allow oneself sth

**accordéon** [akɔrdeɔ̃] *nm* accordion

**accoster** [akɔste] **1** *vt (personne)* to approach **2** *vi Naut* to dock

**accotement** [akɔtmɑ̃] *nm (de route)* verge; *(de voie ferrée)* shoulder

**accoucher** [akuʃe] *vi* to give birth (**de** to) ▪ **accouchement** *nm* delivery

**accouder** [akude] **s'accouder** *vpr* **s'a. à** *ou* **sur qch** to lean one's elbows on sth ▪ **accoudoir** *nm* armrest

**accoupler** [akuple] **s'accoupler** *vpr (animaux)* to mate

**accourir*** [akurir] *vi* to run up

**accoutrement** [akutrəmɑ̃] *nm Péj* rig-out

**accoutumer** [akutyme] **1** *vt* **a. qn à qch** to get sb accustomed to sth **2 s'accoutumer** *vpr* to get accustomed (**à** to) ▪ **accoutumance** *nf (adaptation)* familiarization (**à** with); *Méd (dépendance)* addiction ▪ **accoutumé, -e** *adj* usual; **comme à l'accoutumée** as usual

**accroc** [akro] *nm (déchirure)* tear; *(difficulté)* hitch; **sans a.** without a hitch

**accrocher** [akrɔʃe] **1** *vt (déchirer)* to catch; *(fixer)* to hook (**à** onto); *(suspendre)* to hang up (**à** on)

**2** *vi (achopper)* to hit a stumbling block; *(se remarquer)* to grab one's attention

**3 s'accrocher** *vpr (se fixer)* to fasten; *Fam (persévérer)* to stick at it; **s'a. à qn/qch** *(s'agripper)* to cling to sb/sth ▪ **accrochage** *nm (de véhicules)* minor accident ▪ **accrocheur, -euse** *adj (personne)* tenacious; *(titre, slogan)* catchy

**accroître*** [akrwatr] **1** *vt* to increase **2 s'accroître** *vpr* to increase ▪ **accroissement** *nm* increase (**de** in)

**accroupir** [akrupir] **s'accroupir** *vpr* to squat (down)

**accueil** [akœj] *nm (bureau)* reception; *(manière)* welcome; **faire un bon a. à qn** to give sb a warm welcome ▪ **accueillant, -e** *adj* welcoming ▪ **accueillir*** *vt (personne, proposition)* to greet; *(sujet: hôtel)* to accommodate

**acculer** [akyle] *vt* **a. qn à qch** to drive sb to sth

**accumuler** [akymyle] *vt*, **s'accumuler** *vpr* to accumulate ▪ **accumulation** *nf* accumulation

**accuser** [akyze] *vt (dénoncer)* to accuse; *(accentuer)* to bring out; *(baisse)* to show; **a. qn de qch/de faire qch** to accuse sb of sth/of doing sth ▪ **accusateur, -trice 1** *adj (regard)* accusing **2** *nmf* accuser ▪ **accusation** *nf* accusation ▪ **accusé, -e** *nmf* **l'a.** the accused; *(au tribunal)* the defendant

**achalandé, -e** [aʃalɑ̃de] *adj* **bien a.** *(magasin)* well-stocked

**acharner** [aʃarne] **s'acharner** *vpr* **s'a. sur** *ou* **contre qn** *(persécuter)* to persecute sb; **s'a. à faire qch** to try very hard to do sth ▪ **acharné, -e** *adj (effort, travail)* relentless; *(combat)* fierce ▪ **acharnement** *nm* relentlessness; *(dans un combat)* fury

**achat** [aʃa] *nm* purchase; **faire l'a. de qch** to buy sth; **achats** *(paquets)* shopping

**acheter** [aʃəte] **1** *vt* to buy; **a. qch à qn** *(faire une transaction)* to buy sth from sb; *(faire un cadeau)* to buy sth for sb **2** *vi* to buy **3 s'acheter** *vpr* **je vais m'acheter une glace** I'm going to buy (myself) an ice cream ▪ **acheteur, -euse** *nmf* buyer; *(dans un magasin)* shopper

**achever** [aʃəve] **1** *vt* (**a**) *(finir)* to end; *(travail)* to complete; **a. de faire qch** to finish doing sth (**b**) *(tuer) (animal malade)* to put out of its misery; **a. qn** to finish sb off **2 s'achever** *vpr* to end ▪ **achèvement** *nm* completion

**acide** [asid] **1** *adj* acid(ic); *(au goût)* sour **2** *nm* acid ▪ **acidité** *nf* acidity; *(au goût)* sourness

**acier** [asje] *nm* steel; **a. inoxydable** stainless steel ▪ **aciérie** *nf* steelworks

**acné** [akne] *nf* acne

**acompte** [akɔ̃t] *nm* down payment; **verser un a.** to make a down payment

**à-coup** [aku] (*pl* **à-coups**) *nm* jolt; **sans à-coups** smoothly; **par à-coups** *(avancer)* in fits and starts

**acoustique** [akustik] *nf (qualité)* acoustics *(pluriel)*

**acquérir*** [akerir] *vt (acheter)* to purchase; *(obtenir)* to acquire; **a. de la valeur** to increase in value; **tenir qch pour acquis** to take sth for granted ▪ **acquéreur** *nm* purchaser ▪ **acquis** *nm (expérience)* experience; **les a. sociaux** social benefits ▪ **acquisition** *nf (action)* acquisition; *(bien acheté)* purchase

**acquitter** [akite] **1** *vt (accusé)* to acquit; *(dette)* to pay **2 s'acquitter** *vpr* **s'a. d'un devoir** to fulfil a duty ▪ **acquittement** *nm (d'un accusé)* acquittal; *(d'une dette)* payment

**âcre** [ɑkr] *adj (goût)* bitter; *(odeur)* acrid

**acrobate** [akrɔbat] *nmf* acrobat ▪ **acrobatie** *nf* acrobatics *(sing)*; **acrobaties aériennes** aerobatics *(sing)*

**acrylique** [akrilik] *nm* acrylic

**acte** [akt] *nm (action) & Théât* act; **faire a. de candidature** to apply; **prendre a. de qch** to take note of sth; **a. terroriste** terrorist act; **a. unique européen** Single European Act; **a. de naissance** birth certificate

**acteur** [aktœr] *nm* actor

**actif, -ive** [aktif, -iv] **1** *adj* active **2** *nm Gram* active; *Com (d'une entreprise)* assets

**action** [aksjɔ̃] *nf (acte)* action; *(en Bourse)* share; **bonne a.** good deed; **passer à l'a.** to take action ▪ **actionnaire** *nmf* shareholder ▪ **actionner** *vt (mettre en marche)* to start up

**activer** [aktive] **1** *vt (accélérer)* to speed up; *Ordinat (option)* to select **2 s'activer** *vpr (être actif)* to be busy

**activité** [aktivite] *nf* activity; **en a.** *(personne)* working; *(volcan)* active

**actrice** [aktris] *nf* actress

**actualisation** [aktɥalizasjɔ̃] *nf (de texte)* updating

**actualité** [aktɥalite] *nf (d'un problème)* topicality; **l'a.** current affairs; **les actualités** *(à la radio, à la télévision)* the news; **d'a.** topical

**actuel, -elle** [aktɥɛl] *adj (présent)* present; *(d'actualité)* topical ▪ **actuellement** *adv* at present

**acupuncture** [akypɔ̃ktyr] *nf* acupuncture ▪ **acupuncteur, -trice** *nmf* acupuncturist

**adapter** [adapte] **1** *vt* to adapt (**à** to) **2 s'adapter** *vpr (s'acclimater)* to adapt (**à** to); **s'a. à qn/qch** to get used to sb/sth ▪ **adaptateur** *nm* adapter ▪ **adaptation** *nf* adaptation; **faculté d'a.** adaptability

**additif** [aditif] *nm (substance)* additive

**addition** [adisjɔ̃] *nf* addition (**à** to); *(de restaurant) Br* bill, *Am* check ▪ **additionner** *vt* to add (up) (**à** to)

**adepte** [adept] *nmf* follower

**adéquat, -e** [adekwa, -at] *adj* appropriate; *(quantité)* adequate

**adhérer** [adere] *vi* **a. à qch** *(coller)* to stick to sth; *(s'inscrire)* to join sth ▪ **adhérent, -e** *nmf* member

**adhésif, -ive** [adezif, -iv] *adj* adhesive ▪ **adhésion** *nf (inscription)* joining (**à** of)

**adieu, -x** [adjø] **1** *exclam* farewell **2** *nm* farewell; **faire ses adieux** to say one's goodbyes

**adjacent, -e** [adʒasɑ̃, -ɑ̃t] *adj* adjacent (**à** to)

**adjectif** [adʒɛktif] *nm* adjective

**adjoint, -e** [adʒwɛ̃, -ɛ̃t] *nmf* assistant; **a. au maire** deputy mayor

**adjuger** [adʒyʒe] **1** *vt* **a. qch à qn** *(prix, contrat)* to award sth to sb; *(aux enchères)* to knock sth down to sb **2 s'adjuger** *vpr* **s'a. qch** to appropriate sth

**admettre*** [admɛtr] *vt (accueillir,*

*reconnaître)* to admit; *(autoriser)* to allow; **être admis à un examen** to pass an exam

**administrer** [administre] *vt (gérer)* to administer ▪ **administrateur, -trice** *nmf (de société)* director ▪ **administration** *nf* administration; **l'A.** *(service public)* ≃ the Civil Service; *(fonctionnaires)* civil servants

**admirer** [admire] *vt* to admire ▪ **admirable** *adj* admirable ▪ **admirateur, -trice** *nmf* admirer ▪ **admiratif, -ive** *adj* admiring ▪ **admiration** *nf* admiration; **être en a. devant qn/qch** to be filled with admiration for sb/sth

**admissible** [admisibl] *adj (tolérable)* acceptable, admissible; *Scol & Univ* **candidats admissibles** = candidates who have qualified for the oral examination ▪ **admission** *nf* admission (**à/dans** to)

**adolescent, -e** [adɔlesɑ̃, -ɑ̃t] *nmf* adolescent, teenager ▪ **adolescence** *nf* adolescence

**adonner** [adɔne] **s'adonner** *vpr* **s'a. à qch** to devote oneself to sth; **s'a. à la boisson** to be an alcoholic

**adopter** [adɔpte] *vt* to adopt ▪ **adoptif, -ive** *adj (enfant, patrie)* adopted; *(parents)* adoptive ▪ **adoption** *nf* adoption

**adorer** [adɔre] **1** *vt (dieu)* to worship; *(chose, personne)* to adore; **a. faire qch** to adore doing sth **2 s'adorer** *vpr* **ils s'adorent** they adore each other ▪ **adorable** *adj* adorable

**adosser** [adose] **s'adosser** *vpr* **s'a. à qch** to lean (back) against sth

**adoucir** [adusir] **1** *vt (traits, peau)* to soften; *(caractère)* to take the edge off **2 s'adoucir** *vpr (temps)* to turn milder; *(voix)* to soften; *(caractère)* to mellow

**adresse** [adrɛs] *nf* (**a**) *(domicile)* address; **a. électronique** e-mail address (**b**) *(habileté)* skill ▪ **adresser 1** *vt (lettre, remarque)* to address (**à** to); **a. qch à qn** *(lettre)* to send sb sth; **a. la parole à qn** to speak to sb **2 s'adresser** *vpr* **s'a. à qn** *(parler)* to speak to sb; *(aller trouver)* to go and see sb; *(être destiné à)* to be aimed at sb

**Adriatique** [adriatik] *nf* **l'A.** the Adriatic

**adroit, -e** [adrwa, -at] *adj (habile)* skilful

**adulte** [adylt] **1** *adj (personne, animal)* adult **2** *nmf* adult

**adultère** [adyltɛr] *nm* adultery

**advenir*** [advənir] *(aux* **être***) v impersonnel* to happen; **a. de qn** *(devenir)* to become of sb

**adverbe** [advɛrb] *nm* adverb

**adversaire** [advɛrsɛr] *nmf* opponent ▪ **adverse** *adj* opposing

**aérer** [aere] **1** *vt (pièce, lit)* to air **2 s'aérer** *vpr* to get some fresh air ▪ **aération** *nf* ventilation

**aérien, -enne** [aerjɛ̃, -ɛn] *adj (transport, attaque, défense)* air; *(photo)* aerial; *(câble)* overhead

**aérobic** [aerɔbik] *nm* aerobics *(sing)* ▪ **aérodynamique** *adj* aerodynamic ▪ **aérogare** *nf* air terminal ▪ **aéroglisseur** *nm* hovercraft ▪ **aérogramme** *nm* airmail letter ▪ **aéroport** *nm* airport ▪ **aérosol** *nm* aerosol

**affable** [afabl] *adj* affable

**affaiblir** [afeblir] *vt*, **s'affaiblir** *vpr* to weaken ▪ **affaiblissement** *nm* weakening

**affaire** [afɛr] *nf (question)* matter, affair; *(marché)* deal; *(firme)* business; *(scandale)* affair; *(procès)* case; **affaires** *(commerce)* business *(sing)*; *(effets personnels)* belongings; **les Affaires étrangères** *Br* ≃ the Foreign Office, *Am* ≃ the State Department; **avoir a. à qn/qch** to have to deal with sb/sth; **faire une bonne a.** to get a bargain; **c'est mon a.** that's my business; **ça fera l'a.** that will do nicely; **a. de cœur** love affair

**affairer** [afere] **s'affairer** *vpr* to busy oneself ▪ **affairé, -e** *adj* busy

**affaisser** [afese] **s'affaisser** *vpr (personne, bâtiment)* to collapse; *(sol)* to subside

**affaler** [afale] **s'affaler** *vpr* to collapse; **affalé dans un fauteuil** slumped in an armchair

**affamé, -e** [afame] *adj* starving

**affecter** [afɛkte] *vt* (**a**) *(employé)* to appoint (**à** to); *(soldat)* to post (**à** to); *(fonds)* to assign (**à** to) (**b**) *(feindre, émouvoir)* to affect ▪ **affectation** *nf (d'employé)* appointment (**à** to); *(de soldat)* posting (**à** to); *(de fonds)* assignment (**à** to); *Péj (pose)* affectation ▪ **affecté, -e** *adj Péj (manières, personne)* affected

**affection** [afɛksjɔ̃] *nf (attachement)* affection; *(maladie)* ailment; **avoir de l'a. pour qn** to be fond of sb ▪ **affectionner** *vt* to be fond of ▪ **affectueux, -euse** *adj* affectionate

**affiche** [afiʃ] *nf* notice; *(publicitaire)* poster; **être à l'a.** *(spectacle)* to be on ▪ **afficher** *vt (avis)* to put up; *(prix, horaire, résultat) & Ordinat (message)* to display; *Péj (sentiment)* to show; **a. complet** *(sujet: spectacle)* to be sold out ▪ **affichage** *nm* bill-posting; *Ordinat* display

**affiliation** [afiljɑsjɔ̃] *nf* affiliation ▪ **affilié, -e** *adj* affiliated

**affiner** [afine] **1** *vt (métal, goût)* to refine **2 s'affiner** *vpr (goût)* to become more refined; *(visage)* to get thinner

**affinité** [afinite] *nf* affinity

**affirmatif, -ive** [afirmatif, -iv] *adj (réponse) & Gram* affirmative

**affirmer** [afirme] **1** *vt (manifester)* to assert; *(soutenir)* to maintain **2 s'affirmer** *vpr (personne)* to assert oneself; *(tendance)* to be confirmed ▪ **affirmation** *nf* assertion

**affliger** [afliʒe] *vt (peiner)* to distress; *(atteindre)* to afflict (**de** with)

**affluence** [aflyɑ̃s] *nf (de personnes)* crowd; *(de marchandises)* abundance

**affluer** [aflye] *vi (sang)* to rush (**à** to); *(gens)* to flock (**vers** to)

**afflux** [afly] *nm (de sang)* rush; *(de visiteurs)* flood; *(de capitaux)* influx

**affoler** [afɔle] **1** *vt* to throw into a panic **2 s'affoler** *vpr* to panic ▪ **affolant, -e** *adj* terrifying ▪ **affolement** *nm* panic

**affranchir** [afrɑ̃ʃir] *vt (timbrer)* to put a stamp on; *(émanciper)* to free ▪ **affranchissement** *nm (tarif)* postage

**affreux, -euse** [afrø, -øz] *adj (laid)* hideous; *(atroce)* dreadful

**affront** [afrɔ̃] *nm* insult; **faire un a. à qn** to insult sb

**affronter** [afrɔ̃te] **1** *vt* to confront; *(mauvais temps)* to brave **2 s'affronter** *vpr (ennemis, équipes)* to clash ▪ **affrontement** *nm* confrontation

**affût** [afy] *nm Fig* **à l'a. de** on the lookout for

**affûter** [afyte] *vt* to sharpen

**Afghanistan** [afganistɑ̃] *nm* **l'A.** Afghanistan ▪ **afghan, -e 1** *adj* Afghan **2** *nmf* **A., Afghane** Afghan

**afin** [afɛ̃] **1** *prép* **a. de faire qch** in order to do sth **2** *conj* **a. que...** *(+ subjunctive)* so that...

**Afrique** [afrik] *nf* **l'A.** Africa ▪ **africain, -e 1** *adj* African **2** *nmf* **A., Africaine** African

**agacer** [agase] *vt (personne)* to irritate ▪ **agaçant, -e** *adj* irritating

**âge** [ɑʒ] *nm* age; **quel â. as-tu?** how old are you?; **d'un certain â.** middle-aged ▪ **âgé, -e** *adj* old; **être â. de six ans** to be six years old; **un enfant â. de six ans** a six-year-old child

**agence** [aʒɑ̃s] *nf* agency; *(de banque)* branch; **a. de voyage** travel agent's; **a. immobilière** *Br* estate agent's, *Am* real estate office

**agencer** [aʒɑ̃se] *vt* to arrange; **bien agencé** *(maison)* well laid-out

**agenda** [aʒɛ̃da] *nm Br* diary, *Am* datebook

**agenouiller** [aʒənuje] **s'agenouiller** *vpr* to kneel (down); **être agenouillé** to be kneeling (down)

**agent** [aʒɑ̃] *nm (employé, espion)* agent; **a. de police** police officer; **a. de change** stockbroker; **a. immobilier** *Br* estate agent, *Am* real estate agent; **a. secret** secret agent

**agglomération** [aglɔmerɑsjɔ̃] *nf (ville)* built-up area, town; **l'a. parisienne** Paris and its suburbs

**aggraver** [agrave] **1** *vt (situation, maladie)* to make worse; *(difficultés)* to increase **2 s'aggraver** *vpr (situation, maladie)* to get worse; *(état de santé)* to deteriorate; *(difficultés)* to increase ▪ **aggravation** *nf (de maladie)* aggravation; *(de conflit)* worsening

**agile** [aʒil] *adj* agile, nimble ▪ **agilité** *nf* agility, nimbleness

**agir** [aʒir] **1** *vi* to act **2 s'agir** *v impersonnel* **de quoi s'agit-il?** what is it about?; **il s'agit de se dépêcher** we have to hurry

**agitateur, -trice** [aʒitatœr, -tris] *nmf* agitator

**agitation** [aʒitɑsjɔ̃] *nf (fébrilité)* restlessness; *(troubles)* unrest

**agiter** [aʒite] **1** *vt (remuer)* to stir; *(secouer)* to shake; *(brandir)* to wave; *(troubler)* to agitate **2 s'agiter** *vpr (enfant)* to fidget ▪ **agité, -e** *adj (mer)* rough; *(personne)* restless; *(enfant)* fidgety; *(period)* unsettled

**agneau, -x** [aɲo] *nm* lamb

**agonie** [agɔni] *nf* death throes; **être à l'a.** to be at death's door ▪ **agoniser** *vi* to be dying

**agrafe** [agraf] *nf (pour vêtement)* hook; *(pour papiers)* staple ▪ **agrafer** *vt (vêtement)* to fasten; *(papiers)* to staple ▪ **agrafeuse** *nf* stapler

**agrandir** [agrɑ̃dir] **1** *vt (rendre plus grand)* to enlarge; *(grossir)* to magnify **2 s'agrandir** *vpr (entreprise)* to expand; *(ville)* to grow ▪ **agrandissement** *nm (d'entreprise)* expansion; *(de ville)* growth; *(de maison)* extension; *(de photo)* enlargement

**agréable** [agreabl] *adj* pleasant

**agréer** [agree] *vt (fournisseur)* to approve; **veuillez a. l'expression de mes salutations distinguées** *(dans une lettre) (à quelqu'un dont on ne connaît pas le nom) Br* yours faithfully, *Am* sincerely; *(à quelqu'un dont on connaît le nom) Br* yours sincerely, *Am* sincerely ▪ **agréé, -e** *adj (fournisseur, centre)* approved

**agrémenter** [agremɑ̃te] *vt* to adorn (**de** with)

**agrès** [agrɛ] *nmpl (de voilier)* tackle; *Gym Br* apparatus, *Am* equipment

**agresser** [agrese] *vt* to attack; **se faire a.** to be attacked; *(pour son argent)* to be mugged ▪ **agresseur** *nm* attacker; *(dans un conflit)* aggressor ▪ **agression** *nf* attack; *(pour de l'argent)* mugging; *(d'un État)* aggression; **être victime d'une a.** to be attacked; *(pour son argent)* to be mugged

**agressif, -ive** [agresif, -iv] *adj* aggressive ▪ **agressivité** *nf* aggressiveness

**agricole** [agrikɔl] *adj* agricultural; *(ouvrier, machine)* farm; **travaux agricoles** farm work

**agriculteur, -trice** [agrikyltœr, -tris] *nmf* farmer ▪ **agriculture** *nf* farming, agriculture

**agripper** [agripe] **s'agripper** *vpr* **s'a. à qn/qch** to cling on to sb/sth

**agrume** [agrym] *nm* citrus fruit

**aguerri, -e** [ageri] *adj* seasoned, hardened

**aguets** [age] **aux aguets** *adv* on the lookout

**aguichant, -e** [agiʃɑ̃, -ɑ̃t] *adj* seductive

**ahurir** [ayrir] *vt (étonner)* to astound

**ai** [ɛ] *voir* **avoir**

**aide** [ɛd] **1** *nf* help, assistance; **à l'a. de qch** with the aid of sth; **appeler à l'a.** to call for help; **a. humanitaire** aid **2** *nmf (personne)* assistant; **a. de camp** aide-de-camp ▪ **aide-mémoire** *nm inv* notes ▪ **aide-soignante** (*pl* **aides-soignantes**) *nf Br* nursing auxiliary, *Am* nurse's aid

**aider** [ede] **1** *vt* to help; **a. qn à faire qch** to help sb to do sth **2 s'aider** *vpr* **s'a. de qch** to use sth

**aïe** [aj] *exclam* ouch!

**aie(s), aient** [ɛ] *voir* **avoir**

**aigle** [ɛgl] *nm* eagle

**aigre** [ɛgr] *adj (acide)* sour; *(parole)* cutting; **d'un ton a.** sharply ▪ **aigreur**

*nf (de goût)* sourness; *(de ton)* sharpness; **aigreurs d'estomac** heartburn

**aigri, -e** [ɛgri] *adj (personne)* embittered

**aigu, -ë** [egy] *adj (douleur, crise, accent)* acute; *(son)* high-pitched

**aiguille** [egɥij] *nf (à coudre)* needle; *(de montre)* hand; *(de balance)* pointer; **a. (rocheuse)** peak; **a. de pin** pine needle

**aiguiller** [egɥije] *vt (train) Br* to shunt, *Am* to switch; *Fig (personne)* to steer (**vers** towards) ▪ **aiguillage** *nm (appareil) Br* points, *Am* switches ▪ **aiguilleur** *nm (de trains)* signalman; **a. du ciel** air-traffic controller

**aiguiser** [egize] *vt (outil)* to sharpen; *Fig (appétit)* to whet

**ail** [aj] *nm* garlic

**aile** [ɛl] *nf* wing; *(de moulin)* sail; *(de voiture) Br* wing, *Am* fender ▪ **ailé, -e** *adj* winged ▪ **aileron** *nm (de requin)* fin; *(d'avion)* aileron ▪ **ailier** *nm (au football)* winger; *(au rugby)* wing

**aille(s), aillent** [aj] *voir* **aller**[1]

**ailleurs** [ajœr] *adv* somewhere else, elsewhere; **d'a.** *(du reste)* besides, anyway; **par a.** *(en outre)* moreover; *(par d'autres côtés)* in other respects

**aimable** [ɛmabl] *adj (gentil)* kind

**aimant**[1] [ɛmɑ̃] *nm* magnet ▪ **aimanter** *vt* to magnetize

**aimant**[2]**, -e** [emɑ̃, -ɑ̃t] *adj* loving

**aimer** [eme] **1** *vt* to love; **a. bien qn/qch** to like sb/sth; **a. faire qch** to like doing sth; **j'aimerais qu'il vienne** I would like him to come; **a. mieux qch** to prefer sth **2 s'aimer** *vpr* **ils s'aiment** they're in love

**aine** [ɛn] *nf* groin

**aîné, -e** [ene] **1** *adj (de deux enfants)* elder; *(de plus de deux)* eldest **2** *nmf (de deux enfants)* elder; *(de plus de deux)* eldest

**ainsi** [ɛ̃si] *adv (de cette façon)* in this way; *(alors)* so; **a. que...** as well as...; **et a. de suite** and so on; **pour a. dire** so to speak; **a. soit-il!** amen!

**air** [ɛr] *nm* (**a**) *(gaz)* air; **prendre l'a.** to get some fresh air; **au grand a.** in the fresh air; **en plein a.** outside; **en l'a.** *(jeter)* (up) in the air; *(paroles, menaces)* empty; **regarder en l'a.** to look up (**b**) *(expression)* look, appearance; **avoir l'a. content** to look happy; **avoir l'a. de s'ennuyer** to look bored; **a. de famille** family likeness (**c**) *(mélodie)* tune

**aire** [ɛr] *nf (surface) & Math* area; *(d'oiseau)* eyrie; **a. de jeux** (children's) play area; **a. de lancement** launch pad; **a. de repos** *(sur autoroute)* rest area; **a. de stationnement** lay-by

**aisance** [ɛzɑ̃s] *nf (facilité)* ease; *(prospérité)* affluence

**aise** [ɛz] *nf* **à l'a.** *(dans un vêtement)* comfortable; *(dans une situation)* at ease; *(fortuné)* comfortably off; **mal à l'a.** uncomfortable, ill at ease ▪ **aisé, -e** [ɛze] *adj (fortuné)* comfortably off; *(facile)* easy ▪ **aisément** *adv* easily

**aisselle** [ɛsɛl] *nf* armpit

**ait** [ɛ] *voir* **avoir**

**ajourner** [aʒurne] *vt* to postpone; *(après le début de la séance)* to adjourn

**ajout** [aʒu] *nm* addition (**à** to) ▪ **ajouter 1** *vti* to add (**à** to) **2 s'ajouter** *vpr* **s'a. à qch** to add to sth

**ajuster** [aʒyste] *vt (appareil, outil)* to adjust; *(vêtement)* to alter

**alarme** [alarm] *nf* alarm; **donner l'a.** to raise the alarm; **a. antivol/d'incendie** burglar/fire alarm ▪ **alarmer 1** *vt* to alarm **2 s'alarmer** *vpr* **s'a. de qch** to become alarmed at sth

**Albanie** *nf* **l'A.** Albania ▪ **albanais, -e 1** *adj* Albanian **2** *nmf* **A., Albanaise** Albanian

**album** [albɔm] *nm* album; **a. de photos** photo album

**alcool** [alkɔl] *nm Chim* alcohol; *(spiritueux)* spirits; **a. à 90°** *Br* surgical spirit, *Am* rubbing alcohol; **a. à brûler** *Br* methylated spirits, *Am* wood alcohol ▪ **alcoolique** *adj & nmf* alcoholic ▪ **alcoolisée** *adj f* **boisson a.** alcoholic drink; **boisson non a.** soft drink ▪ **alcoolisme** *nm* alcoholism ▪ **Alcootest®**

*nm (test)* breath test; *(appareil)* Breathalyzer®

**alcôve** [alkov] *nf* alcove

**aléas** [alea] *nmpl* hazards ▪ **aléatoire** *adj (résultat)* uncertain; *(nombre) & Ordinat* random

**alentour** [alɑ̃tur] *adv* round about; **les villages a.** the surrounding villages ▪ **alentours** *nmpl* surroundings; **aux a. de la ville** in the vicinity of the town

**alerte** [alɛrt] **1** *adj (leste)* sprightly; *(éveillé)* alert **2** *nf* alarm; **en état d'a.** on the alert; **donner l'a.** to give the alarm; **a. à la bombe** bomb scare; **fausse a.** false alarm ▪ **alerter** *vt* to alert (**de** to)

**alezan, -e** [alzɑ̃, -an] *adj & nmf (cheval)* chestnut

**algèbre** [alʒɛbr] *nf* algebra

**Algérie** [alʒeri] *nf* **l'A.** Algeria ▪ **algérien, -enne 1** *adj* Algerian **2** *nmf* **A., Algérienne** Algerian

**algues** [alg] *nfpl* seaweed

**alias** [aljɑs] *adv* alias

**alibi** [alibi] *nm* alibi

**aliéner** [aljene] **1** *vt* to alienate **2 s'aliéner** *vpr* **s'a. qn** to alienate sb

**aligner** [aliɲe] **1** *vt* to line up; *(politique)* to align (**sur** with) **2 s'aligner** *vpr (personnes)* to line up; *(pays)* to align oneself (**sur** with) ▪ **alignement** *nm* alignment

**aliment** [alimɑ̃] *nm* food ▪ **alimentaire** *adj (ration, industrie)* food; **produits alimentaires** foods ▪ **alimentation** *nf (action)* feeding; *(en eau, en électricité)* supply(ing); *(régime)* diet; *(nourriture)* food; **magasin d'a.** grocer's, grocery store ▪ **alimenter** *vt (nourrir)* to feed; *(fournir)* to supply (**en** with); *(débat, feu)* to fuel

**alité, -e** [alite] *adj* bedridden

**allaiter** [alete] *vt (femme)* to breastfeed

**allécher** [aleʃe] *vt* to tempt

**allée** [ale] *nf (de parc)* path; *(de ville)* avenue; *(de cinéma, de supermarché)* aisle; *(devant une maison)* driveway; **allées et venues** comings and goings

**allégation** [alegɑsjɔ̃] *nf* allegation

**alléger** [aleʒe] *vt (impôt)* to reduce; *(fardeau)* to lighten ▪ **allégé, -e** *adj (fromage)* low-fat

**allégorie** [alegɔri] *nf* allegory

**allègre** [alɛgr] *adj* lively, cheerful

**allégresse** [alegrɛs] *nf* joy

**Allemagne** [almaɲ] *nf* **l'A.** Germany ▪ **allemand, -ande 1** *adj* German **2** *nmf* **A., Allemande** German **3** *nm (langue)* German

---

**ALLER[1*]** [ale] **1** *(aux* **être***) vi* to go; **a. à Paris** to go to Paris; **a. à la pêche** to go fishing; **a. faire qch** to go and do sth; **a. à qn** *(convenir à)* to suit sb; **a. avec** *(vêtement)* to go with; **a. bien/mieux** *(personne)* to be well/better; **comment vas-tu?, (comment) ça va?** how are you?; **ça va!** all right!, fine!; **allez-y** go ahead

**2** *v aux (futur proche)* **a. faire qch** to be going to do sth; **il va venir** he'll come; **il va partir** he's about to leave

**3 s'en aller** [sɑ̃nale] *vpr (personne)* to go away; *(tache)* to come out

---

**aller[2]** [ale] *nm* outward journey; **a. (simple)** *Br* single (ticket), *Am* one-way (ticket); **a. (et) retour** *Br* return (ticket), *Am* round-trip (ticket)

**allergie** [alɛrʒi] *nf* allergy ▪ **allergique** *adj* allergic (**à** to)

**alliage** [aljaʒ] *nm* alloy

**alliance** [aljɑ̃s] *nf (anneau)* wedding ring; *(mariage)* marriage; *(de pays)* alliance

**allier** [alje] **1** *vt (associer)* to combine (**à** with); *(pays)* to ally (**à** with); *(famille)* to unite by marriage **2 s'allier** *vpr (couleurs)* to combine; *(pays)* to become allied (**à** with); **s'a. à contre qn/qch** to unite against sb/sth ▪ **allié, -e** *nmf* ally

**allô** [alo] *exclam* hello!

**allocation** [alɔkɑsjɔ̃] *nf (somme)* allowance; **a. (de) chômage** unemployment benefit; **a. (de) logement** housing benefit; **allocations familiales** child benefit

**allocution** [alɔkysjɔ̃] *nf* address

**allonger** [alɔ̃ʒe] **1** *vt (bras)* to stretch out; *(sauce)* to thin; **a. le pas** to quicken one's pace **2** *vi (jours)* to get longer **3 s'allonger** *vpr (jours)* to get longer; *(personne)* to lie down ▪ **allongé, -e** *adj (étiré)* elongated; **être a.** *(personne)* to be lying down

**allouer** [alwe] *vt* **a. qch à qn** *(ration)* to allocate sb sth; *(indemnité)* to grant sb sth

**allumer** [alyme] **1** *vt (feu, pipe)* to light; *(électricité, radio)* to switch on; *(incendie)* to start **2 s'allumer** *vpr (lumière, lampe)* to come on ▪ **allumage** *nm (de feu)* lighting; *(de moteur)* ignition

**allumette** [alymɛt] *nf* match

**allure** [alyr] *nf (vitesse)* speed; *(démarche)* gait, walk; *(maintien)* bearing; **à toute a.** at top speed; **avoir de l'a.** to look stylish

**allusion** [alyzjɔ̃] *nf (référence)* allusion (**à** to); *(voilée)* hint; **faire a. à qch** to allude to sth; *(en termes voilés)* to hint at sth

**aloi** [alwa] *nm* **de bon a.** *(plaisanterie)* in good taste

**alors** [alɔr] *adv (donc)* so; *(à ce moment-là)* then; *(dans ce cas)* in that case; **a. que...** *(lorsque)* when...; *(tandis que)* whereas...; **et a.?** so what?

**alouette** [alwɛt] *nf* lark

**alourdir** [alurdir] **1** *vt (chose)* to make heavier **2 s'alourdir** *vpr* to get heavy

**alpage** [alpaʒ] *nm* mountain pasture ▪ **Alpes** *nfpl* **les A.** the Alps ▪ **alpestre, alpin, -e** [alpɛ̃, -in] *adj* alpine

**alphabet** [alfabɛ] *nm* alphabet ▪ **alphabétique** *adj* alphabetical

**alphanumérique** [alfanymerik] *adj* alphanumeric

**alpinisme** [alpinism] *nm* mountaineering; **faire de l'a.** to go mountaineering ▪ **alpiniste** *nmf* mountaineer

**altérer** [altere] **1** *vt* (**a**) *(viande, vin)* to spoil (**b**) *(changer)* to affect **2 s'altérer** *vpr (relations)* to deteriorate

**alternatif, -ive** [altɛrnatif, -iv] *adj (successif)* alternating; *(de remplacement)* alternative ▪ **alternative** *nf* alternative ▪ **alternativement** *adv* alternately

**alterner** [altɛrne] **1** *vt (crops)* to rotate **2** *vi (se succéder)* to alternate (**avec** with); *(personnes)* to take turns (**avec** with) ▪ **alternance** *nf* alternation; **en a.** alternately

**Altesse** [altɛs] *nf* **son A. royale** His/Her Royal Highness

**altier, -ère** [altje, -ɛr] *adj* haughty

**altitude** [altityd] *nf* altitude; **prendre de l'a.** to climb

**aluminium** [alyminjɔm] *nm Br* aluminium, *Am* aluminum; **papier (d')a.** tinfoil

**amabilité** [amabilite] *nf* kindness

**amaigrir** [amɛgrir] *vt* to make thin *or* thinner ▪ **amaigri, -e** *adj* gaunt

**amande** [amɑ̃d] *nf* almond

**amant** [amɑ̃] *nm* lover

**amarre** [amar] *nf* (mooring) rope; **amarres** moorings

**amas** [amɑ] *nm* heap, pile ▪ **amasser** **1** *vt* to amass **2 s'amasser** *vpr (preuves, foule)* to build up; *(neige)* to pile up

**amateur** [amatœr] **1** *nm (non professionnel)* amateur; **a. de tennis** tennis enthusiast; **faire de la photo en a.** to be an amateur photographer **2** *adj* **une équipe a.** an amateur team

**amazone** [amazɔn] *nf* horsewoman; **monter en a.** to ride sidesaddle

**ambages** [ɑ̃baʒ] **sans ambages** *adv* without beating about the bush

**ambassade** [ɑ̃basad] *nf* embassy ▪ **ambassadeur, -drice** *nmf* ambassador

**ambiance** [ɑ̃bjɑ̃s] *nf* atmosphere ▪ **ambiant, -e** *adj* surrounding; **température a.** room temperature

**ambidextre** [ɑ̃bidɛkstr] *adj* ambidextrous

**ambigu, -ë** [ɑ̃bigy] *adj* ambiguous ▪ **ambiguïté** *nf* ambiguity

**ambitieux, -euse** [ɑ̃bisjø, -øz] *adj* ambitious ▪ **ambition** *nf* ambition ▪ **ambitionner** *vt* to aspire to

**ambre** [ɑ̃br] *nm (résine)* amber
**ambulance** [ɑ̃bylɑ̃s] *nf* ambulance
**ambulant, -e** [ɑ̃bylɑ̃, -ɑ̃t] *adj* travelling, itinerant; **marchand a.** (street) hawker
**âme** [ɑm] *nf* soul; **rendre l'â.** to give up the ghost; **â. sœur** soul mate
**améliorer** [ameljɔre] *vt*, **s'améliorer** *vpr* to improve ▪ **amélioration** *nf* improvement
**amen** [amɛn] *adv* amen
**aménager** *vt (changer)* to adjust, *(maison)* to convert (**en** into) ▪ **aménagement** *nm (changement)* adjustment; *(de pièce)* conversion (**en** into); **a. du temps de travail** flexibility of working hours
**amende** [amɑ̃d] *nf* fine; **infliger une a. à qn** to impose a fine on sb
**amender** [amɑ̃de] *vt (texte de loi)* to amend
**amener** [amne] **1** *vt (apporter)* to bring; *(causer)* to bring about; *(tirer à soi)* to pull in; **a. qn à faire qch** *(sujet: personne)* to get sb to do sth; **ce qui nous amène à parler de…** which brings us to the issue of… **2 s'amener** *vpr Fam* to turn up
**amenuiser** [amənɥize] **s'amenuiser** *vpr* to dwindle; *(écart)* to get smaller
**amer, -ère** [amɛr] *adj* bitter
**Amérique** [amerik] *nf* **l'A.** America; **l'A. du Nord/du Sud** North/South America; **l'A. latine** Latin America ▪ **américain, -e 1** *adj* American **2** *nmf* **A., Américaine** American
**amertume** [amɛrtym] *nf* bitterness
**ameublement** [amœbləmɑ̃] *nm (meubles)* furniture
**ami, -e** [ami] **1** *nmf* friend; **petit a.** boyfriend; **petite amie** girlfriend **2** *adj* friendly; **être a. avec qn** to be friends with sb
**amiable** [amjabl] **à l'amiable 1** *adj* amicable **2** *adv* amicably
**amical, -e, -aux, -ales** [amikal, -o] *adj* friendly ▪ **amicale** *nf* association
**amincir** [amɛ̃sir] *vt* to make thin *or* thinner; **cette robe t'amincit** that dress makes you look thinner
**amiral, -aux** [amiral, -o] *nm* admiral
**amitié** [amitje] *nf* friendship; **mes amitiés à votre mère** give my best wishes to your mother
**amnésie** [amnezi] *nf* amnesia
**amnistie** [amnisti] *nf* amnesty
**amoindrir** [amwɛ̃drir] *vt*, **s'amoindrir** *vpr* to diminish
**amonceler** [amɔ̃sle] *vt*, **s'amonceler** *vpr* to pile up ▪ **amoncellement** *nm* heap, pile
**amont** [amɔ̃] **en amont** *adv* upstream (**de** from)
**amoral, -e, -aux, -ales** [amɔral, -o] *adj* amoral
**amorce** [amɔrs] *nf (début)* start; *(de pêcheur)* bait; *(détonateur)* detonator; *(de pistolet d'enfant)* cap ▪ **amorcer 1** *vt (commencer)* to start; *(hameçon)* to bait; *(bombe)* to arm; *Ordinat* to boot up **2 s'amorcer** *vpr* to start
**amortir** [amɔrtir] *vt (coup)* to absorb; *(bruit)* to deaden; *(chute)* to break; *(achat)* to recoup the costs of; *Fin (dette)* to pay off ▪ **amortissement** *nm (d'un emprunt)* redemption ▪ **amortisseur** *nm (de véhicule)* shock absorber
**amour** [amur] *nm (sentiment, liaison)* love; **faire l'a. avec qn** to make love with *or* to sb; **pour l'a. du ciel!** for heaven's sake!; **mon a.** my darling, my love ▪ **amour-propre** *nm* self-respect ▪ **amoureux, -euse 1** *adj* **être a. de qn** in love with sb; **tomber a. de qn** to fall in love with sb **2** *nm* boyfriend; **un couple d'a.** a pair of lovers
**amovible** [amɔvibl] *adj* removable, detachable
**amphétamine** [ɑ̃fetamin] *nf* amphetamine
**amphithéâtre** [ɑ̃fiteɑtr] *nm (romain)* amphitheatre; *(à l'université)* lecture hall
**ample** [ɑ̃pl] *adj (vêtement)* full; *(geste)* sweeping; **de plus amples renseignements** more detailed information ▪ **amplement** *adv* amply, fully; **c'est a. suffisant** it is more than enough

■ **ampleur** *nf (de vêtement)* fullness; *(importance)* scale, extent; **prendre de l'a.** to grow in size

**amplifier** [ɑ̃plifje] **1** *vt (son)* to amplify; *(phénomène)* to intensify **2 s'amplifier** *vpr (son)* to increase; *(phénomène)* to intensify ■ **amplificateur** *nm* amplifier ■ **amplification** *nf (de son)* amplification; *(de phénomène)* intensification

**amplitude** [ɑ̃plityd] *nf (de désastre)* magnitude; *(variation)* range

**ampoule** [ɑ̃pul] *nf (électrique)* (light) bulb; *(sur la peau)* blister; *(de médicament)* phial

**amputer** [ɑ̃pyte] *vt (membre)* to amputate; **a. qn de la jambe** to amputate sb's leg ■ **amputation** *nf (de membre)* amputation

**amuser** [amyze] **1** *vt* to amuse **2 s'amuser** *vpr* to amuse oneself; **s'a. avec qn/qch** to play with sb/sth; **s'a. à faire qch** to amuse oneself doing sth; **bien s'a.** to have a good time ■ **amusant, -e** *adj* amusing ■ **amusement** *nm* amusement

**amygdales** [amidal] *nfpl* tonsils

**an** [ɑ̃] *nm* year; **il a dix ans** he's ten (years old); **par a.** per year; **en l'an 2005** in the year 2005; **bon a., mal a.** on average over the years

**anachronisme** [anakrɔnism] *nm* anachronism

**anagramme** [anagram] *nf* anagram

**analogie** [analɔʒi] *nf* analogy

**analogue** [analɔg] *adj* similar (**à** to)

**analphabète** [analfabɛt] *adj & nmf* illiterate

**analyse** [analiz] *nf* analysis; **a. de sang/d'urine** blood/urine test ■ **analyser** *vt* to analyse

**ananas** [anana(s)] *nm* pineapple

**anarchie** [anarʃi] *nf* anarchy ■ **anarchiste 1** *adj* anarchistic **2** *nmf* anarchist

**anatomie** [anatɔmi] *nf* anatomy ■ **anatomique** *adj* anatomical

**ancestral, -e, -aux, -ales** [ɑ̃sɛstral, -o] *adj* ancestral

**ancêtre** [ɑ̃sɛtr] *nm* ancestor

**anchois** [ɑ̃ʃwa] *nm* anchovy

**ancien, -enne** [ɑ̃sjɛ̃, -ɛn] **1** *adj (vieux)* old; *(meuble)* antique; *(qui n'est plus)* former, old; **dans l'a. temps** in the old days; **a. combattant** *Br* ex-serviceman, *Am* veteran **2** *nmf (par l'âge)* elder ■ **anciennement** *adv* formerly ■ **ancienneté** *nf (âge)* age; *(expérience)* seniority

**ancre** [ɑ̃kr] *nf* anchor ■ **ancrer** *vt (navire)* to anchor

**Andorre** [ɑ̃dɔr] *nf* Andorra

**andouille** [ɑ̃duj] *nf* (**a**) *(charcuterie)* = sausage made from pigs' intestines (**b**) *Fam (idiot)* twit

**âne** [ɑn] *nm (animal)* donkey

**anéantir** [aneɑ̃tir] *vt (ville)* to destroy; *(armée)* to crush; *(espoirs)* to shatter ■ **anéanti, -e** *adj (épuisé)* exhausted; *(accablé)* overwhelmed ■ **anéantissement** *nm (de ville)* destruction

**anecdote** [anɛkdɔt] *nf* anecdote ■ **anecdotique** *adj* anecdotal

**anémie** [anemi] *nf* an(a)emia ■ **anémique** *adj* an(a)emic

**anémone** [anemɔn] *nf* anemone

**ânerie** [ɑnri] *nf (parole)* stupid remark; *(action)* stupid act

**anesthésie** [anɛstezi] *nf* an(a)esthesia; **être sous a.** to be under ana(e)sthetic; **a. générale/locale** general/local an(a)esthetic ■ **anesthésier** *vt* to an(a)esthetize ■ **anesthésiste** *nmf Br* an(a)esthetist, *Am* anesthesiologist

**ange** [ɑ̃ʒ] *nm* angel; **être aux anges** to be in seventh heaven; **a. gardien** guardian angel ■ **angélique 1** *adj* angelic **2** *nf Culin* angelica

**angine** [ɑ̃ʒin] *nf* sore throat; **a. de poitrine** angina (pectoris)

**anglais, -e** [ɑ̃glɛ, -ɛz] **1** *adj* English **2** *nmf* **A., Anglaise** Englishman, Englishwoman; **les A.** the English **3** *nm (langue)* English **4** *nf Fam* **filer à l'anglaise** to slip away

**angle** [ɑ̃gl] *nm (point de vue) & Math* angle; *(coin de rue)* corner; **la maison**

**qui fait l'a.** the house on the corner; *Aut* **a. mort** blind spot

**Angleterre** [ɑ̃glətɛr] *nf* **l'A.** England

**anglican, -e** [ɑ̃glikɑ̃, -an] *adj & nmf* Anglican

**anglo-normand, -e** [ɑ̃glonɔrmɑ̃, -ɑ̃d] *adj* **les îles anglo-normandes** the Channel Islands

**anglophone** [ɑ̃glofɔn] **1** *adj* English-speaking **2** *nmf* English speaker

**anglo-saxon, -onne** [ɑ̃glosaksɔ̃, -ɔn] (*mpl* **anglo-saxons,** *fpl* **anglo-saxonnes**) *adj & nmf* Anglo-Saxon

**angoisse** [ɑ̃gwas] *nf* anguish; **une crise d'a.** an anxiety attack ▪ **angoissant, -e** *adj (nouvelle)* distressing; *(attente)* agonizing; *(livre)* frightening ▪ **angoissé, -e** *adj (personne)* anxious; *(cri, regard)* anguished ▪ **angoisser 1** *vt* **a. qn** to make sb anxious **2 s'angoisser** *vpr* to get anxious

**angora** [ɑ̃gɔra] *nm (laine)* angora; **pull en a.** angora sweater

**anguille** [ɑ̃gij] *nf* eel

**anguleux, -euse** [ɑ̃gylø, -øz] *adj (visage)* angular

**anicroche** [anikrɔʃ] *nf* hitch, snag

**animal, -aux** [animal, -o] **1** *nm* animal; **a. domestique** pet **2** *adj (règne, graisse)* animal

**animateur, -trice** [animatœr, -tris] *nmf (de télévision, de radio)* presenter; *(de club)* leader

**animer** [anime] **1** *vt (débat)* to lead; *(jeu télévisé)* to present; *(inspirer)* to prompt **2 s'animer** *vpr (rue)* to come to life; *(visage)* to light up; *(conversation)* to get more lively ▪ **animation** *nf (vie)* life; *(divertissement)* event; *Cin* animation; **mettre de l'a. dans une soirée** to liven up a party ▪ **animé, -e** *adj (personne, conversation)* lively; *(rue, quartier)* busy

**animosité** [animozite] *nf* animosity

**anis** [ani(s)] *nm* aniseed

**ankylosé, -e** [ɑ̃kiloze] *adj* stiff

**annales** [anal] *nfpl* annals

**anneau, -x** [ano] *nm (bague)* ring; *(de chaîne)* link; *Gym* **les anneaux** the rings

**année** [ane] *nf* year; **les années 90** the nineties

**annexe** [anɛks] **1** *nf (bâtiment)* annexe; *(de lettre)* enclosure; *(de livre)* appendix; **document en a.** enclosed document **2** *adj (pièces)* enclosed; *(revenus)* supplementary; **bâtiment a.** annex(e) ▪ **annexer** *vt (pays)* to annex; *(document)* to append

**annihiler** [aniile] *vt (ville, armée)* to annihilate

**anniversaire** [anivɛrsɛr] **1** *nm (d'événement)* anniversary; *(de naissance)* birthday **2** *adj* **date a.** anniversary

**annonce** [anɔ̃s] *nf (déclaration)* announcement; *(publicitaire)* advertisement; *(indice)* sign; **passer une a. dans un journal** to put an ad(vertisement) in a newspaper; **petites annonces** classified advertisements, *Br* small ads ▪ **annoncer 1** *vt (déclarer)* to announce; *(dans la presse) (soldes, exposition)* to advertise; *(indiquer)* to herald; **a. qn** *(visiteur)* to show sb in **2 s'annoncer** *vpr* **ça s'annonce bien/mal** things aren't looking too bad/good ▪ **annonceur** *nm (publicitaire)* advertiser

**annuaire** [anɥɛr] *nm (d'organisme)* yearbook; *(liste d'adresses)* directory; **a. téléphonique** telephone directory; **a. électronique** = telephone directory available on Minitel®

**annuel, -elle** [anɥɛl] *adj* annual, yearly

**annuité** [anɥite] *nf (d'emprunt)* annual repayment

**annulaire** [anylɛr] *nm* ring finger

**annuler** [anyle] **1** *vt (commande, rendez-vous)* to cancel; *(dette)* to write off; *(mariage)* to annul; *(jugement)* to quash **2 s'annuler** *vpr* to cancel each other out ▪ **annulation** *nf (de commande, de rendez-vous)* cancellation; *(de dette)* writing off; *(de mariage)* annulment; *(de jugement)* quashing; *Ordinat* deletion

**anodin, -e** [anɔdɛ̃, -in] *adj (remarque)* harmless; *(personne)* insignificant

**anomalie** [anɔmali] *nf (bizarrerie)* anomaly

**anonymat** [anɔnima] *nm* anonymity; **garder l'a.** to remain anonymous ▪ **anonyme** *adj & nmf* anonymous

**anorak** [anɔrak] *nm* anorak

**anorexie** [anɔrɛksi] *nf Méd* anorexia ▪ **anorexique** *adj & nmf Méd* anorexic

**anormal, -e, -aux, -ales** [anɔrmal, -o] *adj (non conforme)* abnormal; *(mentalement)* educationally subnormal; *(injuste)* unfair

**anse** [ɑ̃s] *nf (de tasse, de panier)* handle

**antagonisme** [ɑ̃tagɔnism] *nm* antagonism

**antan** [ɑ̃tɑ̃] **d'antan** *adj Littéraire* of yesteryear

**antarctique** [ɑ̃tarktik] *nm* **l'A.** the Antarctic, Antarctica

**antécédent** [ɑ̃tesedɑ̃] *nm Gram* antecedent; **antécédents** *(de personne)* past record; **antécédents médicaux** medical history

**antenne** [ɑ̃tɛn] *nf (de radio, de satellite)* aerial, antenna; *(d'insecte)* antenna, feeler; *(société)* branch; **être à l'a.** to be on the air; **a. parabolique** satellite dish

**antérieur, -e** [ɑ̃terjœr] *adj (période)* former; *(année)* previous; *(date)* earlier; *(placé devant)* front; **a. à qch** prior to sth

**anthologie** [ɑ̃tɔlɔʒi] *nf* anthology

**anthropologie** [ɑ̃trɔpɔlɔʒi] *nf* anthropology

**antiaérien, -enne** [ɑ̃tiaerjɛ̃, -ɛn] *adj* **abri a.** air-raid shelter

**antiatomique** [ɑ̃tiatɔmik] *adj* **abri a.** fallout shelter

**antibiotique** [ɑ̃tibjɔtik] *nm* antibiotic

**antibrouillard** [ɑ̃tibrujar] *adj & nm* **(phare) a.** fog lamp

**antichambre** [ɑ̃tiʃɑ̃br] *nf* antechamber

**antichoc** [ɑ̃tiʃɔk] *adj inv* shock-proof

**anticipation** [ɑ̃tisipasjɔ̃] *nf* anticipation; **d'a.** *(roman, film)* futuristic ▪ **anticipé, -e** *adj (retraite, retour)* early; *(paiement)* advance

**anticommuniste** [ɑ̃tikɔmynist] *adj* anti-communist

**anticonformiste** [ɑ̃tikɔ̃fɔrmist] *adj & nmf* nonconformist

**anticonstitutionnel, -elle** [ɑ̃tikɔ̃stitysjɔnɛl] *adj* unconstitutional

**anticorps** [ɑ̃tikɔr] *nm* antibody

**anticyclone** [ɑ̃tisiklon] *nm* anticyclone

**antidépresseur** [ɑ̃tidepresœr] *nm* antidepressant

**antidérapant, -e** [ɑ̃tiderapɑ̃, -ɑ̃t] *adj (surface, pneu)* non-skid; *(semelle)* non-slip

**antidopage** [ɑ̃tidɔpaʒ] *adj* **contrôle a.** drug detection test

**antidote** [ɑ̃tidɔt] *nm* antidote

**antigel** [ɑ̃tiʒɛl] *nm* antifreeze

**antihistaminique** [ɑ̃tiistaminik] *adj Méd* antihistamine

**anti-inflamatoire** [ɑ̃tiɛ̃flamatwar] *adj Méd* anti-inflammatory

**Antilles** [ɑ̃tij] *nfpl* **les A.** the West Indies ▪ **antillais, -e 1** *adj* West Indian **2** *nmf* **A., Antillaise** West Indian

**antilope** [ɑ̃tilɔp] *nf* antelope

**antimite** [ɑ̃timit] *nm* **de l'a.** mothballs

**antinucléaire** [ɑ̃tinykleɛr] *adj* antinuclear

**antipathique** [ɑ̃tipatik] *adj* unpleasant; **elle m'est a.** I find her unpleasant

**antipodes** [ɑ̃tipɔd] *nmpl* antipodes; **être aux a. de** to be on the other side of the world from; *Fig* to be the exact opposite of

**antique** [ɑ̃tik] *adj (de l'Antiquité)* ancient ▪ **antiquaire** *nmf* antique dealer ▪ **antiquité** *nf (objet ancien)* antique; **l'a. grecque/romaine** ancient Greece/Rome; **antiquités** *(de musée)* antiquities

**antirabique** [ɑ̃tirabik] *adj Méd* antirabies

**antireflet** [ɑ̃tirəflɛ] *adj inv* nonreflecting

**antiseptique** [ɑ̃tisɛptik] *adj & nm* antiseptic

**antisocial, -e, -aux, -ales** [ɑ̃tisɔsjal, -o] *adj* antisocial

**antitabac** [ɑ̃titaba] *adj inv* **lutte a.** anti-smoking campaign
**antiterroriste** [ɑ̃titerɔrist] *adj* antiterrorist
**antithèse** [ɑ̃titɛz] *nf* antithesis
**antivol** [ɑ̃tivɔl] *nm* anti-theft device
**Anvers** [ɑ̃ver(s)] *nm ou f* Antwerp
**anxiété** [ɑ̃ksjete] *nf* anxiety ▪ **anxieux, -euse** *adj* anxious
**août** [u(t)] *nm* August
**apaiser** [apeze] **1** *vt (personne)* to calm (down); *(douleur)* to soothe; *(craintes)* to allay **2 s'apaiser** *vpr (personne, colère)* to calm down; *(tempête, douleur)* to subside ▪ **apaisant, -e** *adj* soothing
**apanage** [apanaʒ] *nm* prerogative
**aparté** [aparte] *nm Théât* aside; *(dans une réunion)* private exchange; **en a.** in private
**apathique** [apatik] *adj* apathetic
**apercevoir*** [apɛrsəvwar] **1** *vt* to see; *(brièvement)* to catch a glimpse of **2 s'apercevoir** *vpr* **s'a. de qch** to realize sth; **s'a. que…** to realize that… ▪ **aperçu** *nm (idea)* general idea
**apéritif** [aperitif] *nm* aperitif; **prendre un a.** to have a drink before lunch/ dinner
**à-peu-près** [apøprɛ] *nm inv* vague approximation
**apeuré, -e** [apœre] *adj* frightened, scared
**aphone** [afɔn] *adj* voiceless; **je suis complètement a.** I've lost my voice
**aphrodisiaque** [afrɔdizjak] *nm* aphrodisiac
**aphte** [aft] *nm* mouth ulcer
**aphteuse** [aftøz] *adj f* **fièvre a.** foot-and-mouth disease
**apiculture** [apikyltyr] *nf* beekeeping ▪ **apiculteur, -trice** *nmf* beekeeper
**apitoyer** [apitwaje] **1** *vt* **a. qn** to move sb to pity **2 s'apitoyer** *vpr* **s'a. sur qn** to feel sorry for sb; **s'a sur son sort** to feel sorry for oneself
**aplanir** [aplanir] *vt (terrain)* to level; *(difficulté)* to iron out
**aplatir** [aplatir] **1** *vt* to flatten **2 s'aplatir** *vpr (être plat)* to be flat; *(devenir plat)* to go flat; **s'a. contre qch** to flatten oneself against sth ▪ **aplati, -e** *adj* flat
**aplomb** [aplɔ̃] *nm (assurance)* self-confidence; *Péj* cheek; **mettre qch d'a.** to stand sth up straight
**apocalypse** [apɔkalips] *nf* apocalypse; **d'a.** *(vision)* apocalyptic
**apogée** [apɔʒe] *nm (d'orbite)* apogee; *Fig* **être à l'a. de sa carrière** to be at the height of one's career
**apostrophe** [apɔstrɔf] *nf (signe)* apostrophe ▪ **apostropher** *vt (pour attirer l'attention)* to shout at
**apothéose** [apɔteoz] *nf (consécration)* crowning glory
**apparaître*** [aparɛtr] *(aux* **être***) vi (se montrer, sembler)* to appear; **il m'apparaît comme le seul capable d'y parvenir** he seems to me to be the only person capable of doing it
**appareil** [aparɛj] *nm (instrument, machine)* apparatus; *(téléphone)* telephone; *(avion)* aircraft; **qui est à l'a.?** *(au téléphone)* who's speaking?; **a. (dentaire)** *(correctif)* brace; **a. photo** camera; **appareils ménagers** household appliances
**apparence** [aparɑ̃s] *nf* appearance; **en a.** outwardly; **sauver les apparences** to keep up appearances ▪ **apparemment** *adv* apparently ▪ **apparent, -e** *adj* apparent
**apparenter** [aparɑ̃te] **s'apparenter** *vpr (ressembler)* to be akin (**à** to)
**apparition** [aparisjɔ̃] *nf (manifestation)* appearance; *(fantôme)* apparition; **faire son a.** *(personne)* to make one's appearance
**appartement** [apartəmɑ̃] *nm Br* flat, *Am* apartment
**appartenance** [apartənɑ̃s] *nf (de groupe)* belonging (**à** to); *(de parti)* membership (**à** of)
**appartenir*** [apartənir] **1** *vi* to belong (**à** to) **2** *v impersonnel* **il vous appartient de prendre la décision** it's up to you to decide
**appât** [apɑ] *nm (amorce)* bait; *Fig*

*(attrait)* lure ▪ **appâter** *vt (hameçon)* to bait; *(animal)* to lure; *Fig (personne)* to entice

**appauvrir** [apovrir] **1** *vt* to impoverish **2 s'appauvrir** *vpr* to become impoverished ▪ **appauvrissement** *nm* impoverishment

**appel** [apɛl] *nm (cri, attrait)* call; *(invitation) & Jur* appeal; *Mil (recrutement)* call-up; *(pour sauter)* take-off; **faire l'a.** *(à l'école)* to take the register; *Mil* to have a roll call; **faire a. à qn** to appeal to sb; *(plombier, médecin)* to send for sb; **a. au secours** call for help; **a. gratuit** *Br* freefone call, *Am* toll-free call; **a. téléphonique** telephone call ▪ **appeler 1** *vt (personne, nom)* to call; *(en criant)* to call out to; *Mil (recruter)* to call up; *(nécessiter)* to call for; **a. qn à l'aide** to call to sb for help; **a. qn au téléphone** to call sb **2 s'appeler** *vpr* to be called; **comment vous appelez-vous?** what's your name?; **je m'appelle David** my name is David ▪ **appellation** *nf (nom)* term; **a. contrôlée** *(de vin)* guaranteed vintage ▪ **appelé** *nm Mil* conscript

**appendice** [apɛ̃dis] *nm (du corps, de livre)* appendix; *(d'animal)* appendage ▪ **appendicite** *nf* appendicitis

**appesantir** [apəzɑ̃tir] **s'appesantir** *vpr* to become heavier; **s'a. sur** *(sujet)* to dwell upon

**appétit** [apeti] *nm* appetite (**de** for); **couper l'a. à qn** to spoil sb's appetite; **manger de bon a.** to tuck in; **bon a.!** enjoy your meal! ▪ **appétissant, -e** *adj* appetizing

**applaudir** [aplodir] *vti* to applaud ▪ **applaudissements** *nmpl* applause

**applicable** [aplikabl] *adj* applicable (**à** to) ▪ **application** *nf (action, soin)* application; *(de loi)* enforcement; **entrer en a.** to come into force

**applique** [aplik] *nf* wall light

**appliquer** [aplike] **1** *vt* to apply (**à/sur** to); *(loi, décision)* to enforce **2 s'appliquer** *vpr (se concentrer)* to apply oneself (**à** to); **s'a. à faire qch** to take pains to do sth; **cette décision s'applique à...** *(concerne)* this decision applies to... ▪ **appliqué, -e** *adj (personne)* hard-working; *(écriture)* careful; *(sciences)* applied

**appoint** [apwɛ̃] *nm* (**a**) **faire l'a.** to give the exact money (**b**) **d'a.** extra

**apport** [apɔr] *nm* contribution (**à** to)

**apporter** [apɔrte] *vt* to bring (**à** to); *(preuve)* to provide; *(modification)* to bring about

**apposer** [apoze] *vt (sceau, signature)* to affix (**à** to); *(affiche)* to put up

**apprécier** [apresje] *vt (aimer, percevoir)* to appreciate; *(évaluer)* to estimate ▪ **appréciable** *adj* appreciable ▪ **appréciation** *nf (opinion de professeur)* comment (**sur** on); *(évaluation)* valuation; *(augmentation de valeur)* appreciation

**appréhender** [apreɑ̃de] *vt (craindre)* to dread (**de faire qch** doing sth); *(arrêter)* to arrest; *(comprendre)* to grasp ▪ **appréhension** *nf (crainte)* apprehension (**de** about)

**apprendre*** [aprɑ̃dr] *vti (étudier)* to learn; *(nouvelle)* to hear; *(mariage, mort)* to hear of; **a. à faire qch** to learn to do sth; **a. qch à qn** *(enseigner)* to teach sb sth; *(informer)* to tell sb sth; **a. à qn à faire qch** to teach sb to do sth; **a. que...** to learn that...; *(être informé)* to hear that...

**apprenti, -e** [aprɑ̃ti] *nmf* apprentice ▪ **apprentissage** *nm (professionnel)* training; *(chez un artisan)* apprenticeship; *(d'une langue)* learning (**de** of); **faire l'a. de qch** to learn about sth

**apprivoiser** [aprivwaze] **1** *vt* to tame **2 s'apprivoiser** *vpr* to become tame

**approbation** [aprɔbasjɔ̃] *nf* approval ▪ **approbateur, -trice** *adj* approving

**approche** [aprɔʃ] *nf* approach; **approches** *(de ville)* outskirts

**approcher** [aprɔʃe] **1** *vt (objet)* to bring up; *(personne)* to approach, to get close to; **a. qch de qn** to bring sth near to sb **2** *vi* to approach, to get closer; **a. de qn/qch** to approach sb/sth

**3 s'approcher** *vpr* to approach, to get closer; **s'a. de qn/qch** to approach sb/sth; **il s'est approché de moi** he came up to me

**approfondir** [aprɔfɔ̃dir] *vt (question, idée)* to go thoroughly into ▪ **approfondi, -e** *adj (étude, examen)* thorough

**approprié, -e** [aprɔprije] *adj* appropriate (**à** for)

**approprier** [aprɔprije] **s'approprier** *vpr* **s'a. qch** to appropriate sth

**approuver** [apruve] *vt (facture, contrat)* to approve; *(décision)* to approve of

**approvisionner** [aprɔvizjɔne] **1** *vt (ville, armée)* to supply (**en** with); *(magasin)* to stock (**en** with); *(compte bancaire)* to pay money into

**2 s'approvisionner** *vpr* to get supplies (**en** of) ▪ **approvisionnement** *nm (d'une ville, d'une armée)* supplying (**en** with); *(d'un magasin)* stocking (**en** with)

**approximatif, -ive** [aprɔksimatif, -iv] *adj* approximate ▪ **approximation** *nf* approximation

**appui** [apɥi] *nm* support; **prendre a. sur qch** to lean on sth; **à l'a. de qch** in support of sth; **a. de fenêtre** window sill ▪ **appui-tête** (*pl* **appuis-tête**) *nm* headrest

**appuyer** [apɥije] **1** *vt (poser)* to lean, to rest; *Fig (proposition)* to second; **a. qch sur qch** *(poser)* to rest sth on sth; *(presser)* to press sth on sth **2** *vi (presser)* to press; **a. sur un bouton** to press a button **3 s'appuyer** *vpr* **s'a. sur qch** to lean on sth, to rest on sth; *Fig (être basé sur)* to be based on sth

**âpre** [ɑpr] *adj* sour; *Fig (lutte)* fierce

**après** [aprɛ] **1** *prép (dans le temps)* after; *(dans l'espace)* beyond; **a. tout** after all; **a. avoir mangé** after eating; **a. qu'il t'a vu** after he saw you; **d'a.** *(selon)* according to

**2** *adv* after(wards); **l'année d'a.** the following year; **et a.?** *(et ensuite)* and then what?; *(et alors)* so what? ▪ **après-demain** *adv* the day after tomorrow ▪ **après-guerre** *nm* post-war period; **d'a.** post-war ▪ **après-midi** *nm ou f inv* afternoon; **trois heures de l'a.** three o'clock in the afternoon ▪ **après-rasage** (*pl* **après-rasages**) *nm* aftershave ▪ **après-shampooing** *nm inv* conditioner ▪ **après-ski** (*pl* **après-skis**) *nm* snowboot ▪ **après-vente** *adj inv Com* **service a.** after-sales service

**âpreté** [ɑprəte] *nf* sourness; *Fig (lutte)* fierceness

**à-propos** [aprɔpo] *nm* aptness; **avoir l'esprit d'a.** to have presence of mind

**apte** [apt] *adj* **a. à qch/à faire qch** fit to sth/for doing sth ▪ **aptitude** *nf* aptitude (**à** *ou* **pour** for); **avoir des aptitudes pour qch** to have an aptitude for sth

**aquarelle** [akwarɛl] *nf* watercolour

**aquarium** [akwarjɔm] *nm* aquarium

**aquatique** [akwatik] *adj* aquatic

**arabe 1** *adj (peuple, litterature)* Arab; *(langue)* Arabic **2** *nmf* **A.** Arab **3** *nm (langue)* Arabic ▪ **Arabie** *nf* **l'A.** Arabia; **l'A. Saoudite** Saudi Arabia

**arable** [arabl] *adj* arable

**arachide** [araʃid] *nf* peanut

**araignée** [areɲe] *nf* spider

**arbitraire** [arbitrɛr] *adj* arbitrary

**arbitre** [arbitr] *nm (de football)* referee; *(de tennis)* umpire ▪ **arbitrage** *nm (de football)* refereeing; *(de tennis)* umpiring

**arborer** [arbɔre] *vt (insigne)* to sport

**arbre** [arbr] *nm (végétal)* tree; *Tech* shaft; **a. fruitier** fruit tree; **a. de transmission** transmission shaft ▪ **arbuste** *nm* shrub

**arc** [ark] *nm (arme)* bow; *(voûte)* arch; *(de cercle)* arc ▪ **arcade** *nf* archway; **arcades** *(de place)* arcade

**arc-boutant** [arkbutɑ̃] (*pl* **arcs-boutants**) *nm* flying buttress

**arc-en-ciel** [arkɑ̃sjɛl] (*pl* **arcs-en-ciel**) *nm* rainbow

**archaïque** [arkaik] *adj* archaic

**arche** [arʃ] *nf (voûte)* arch; **l'a. de Noé** Noah's ark

**archéologie** [arkeɔlɔʒi] *nf* archaeology ▪ **archéologique** *adj* archaeological ▪ **archéologue** *nmf* archaeologist

**archet** [arʃɛ] *nm (de violon)* bow

**architecte** [arʃitɛkt] *nm* architect ▪ **architecture** *nf* architecture

**archives** [arʃiv] *nfpl* archives, records

**arctique** [arktik] **1** *adj* arctic **2** *nm* **l'A.** the Arctic

**ardent, -e** [ardɑ̃, -ɑ̃t] *adj (désir)* burning; *(soleil)* scorching ▪ **ardeur** *nf (passion)* fervour, ardour; *(du soleil)* intense heat

**ardoise** [ardwaz] *nf* slate

**ardu, -e** [ardy] *adj* arduous

**arène** [arɛn] *nf (pour taureaux)* bullring; *(romaine)* arena; **arènes** bullring; *(romaines)* amphitheatre

**arête** [arɛt] *nf (de poisson)* bone; *(de cube)* edge; *(de montagne)* ridge

**argent** [arʒɑ̃] **1** *nm (métal)* silver; *(monnaie)* money; **a. liquide** cash; **a. de poche** pocket money **2** *adj (couleur)* silver ▪ **argenté, -e** *adj (plaqué)* silver-plated; *(couleur)* silvery ▪ **argenterie** *nf* silverware

**Argentine** [arʒɑ̃tin] *nf* **l'A.** Argentina ▪ **argentin, -e 1** *adj* Argentinian **2** *nmf* **A., Argentine** Argentinian

**argile** [arʒil] *nf* clay

**argot** [argo] *nm* slang ▪ **argotique** *adj (terme)* slang

**argument** [argymɑ̃] *nm* argument

**argumenter** [argymɑ̃te] *vi* to argue

**aride** [arid] *adj (terre)* arid, barren; *(sujet)* dry

**aristocrate** [aristɔkrat] *nmf* aristocrat ▪ **aristocratie** [-asi] *nf* aristocracy ▪ **aristocratique** *adj* aristocratic

**arithmétique** [aritmetik] *nf* arithmetic

**armature** [armatyr] *nf (charpente)* framework; *(de lunettes, de tente)* frame

**arme** [arm] *nf* weapon; **prendre les armes** to take up arms; *Fig* **à armes égales** on equal terms; **a. à feu** firearm; **a. blanche** knife ▪ **armes** *nfpl (blason)* (coat of) arms

**armée** [arme] *nf* army; **être à l'a.** to be doing one's military service; **a. de l'air** air force; **a. de terre** army; **a. active/de métier** regular/professional army

**armer** [arme] **1** *vt (personne)* to arm (**de** with); *(fusil)* to cock; *(appareil photo)* to set **2 s'armer** *vpr* to arm oneself (**de** with); **s'a. de patience** to summon up one's patience ▪ **armements** *nmpl (armes)* armaments

**armistice** [armistis] *nm* armistice

**armoire** [armwar] *nf (penderie) Br* wardrobe, *Am* closet; **a. à pharmacie** medicine cabinet

**armure** [armyr] *nf* armour

**aromate** [arɔmat] *nm (herbe)* herb; *(épice)* spice

**aromathérapie** [arɔmaterapi] *nf* aromatherapy

**aromatique** [arɔmatik] *adj* aromatic

**arôme** [arom] *nm (goût)* flavour; *(odeur)* aroma

**arpenter** [arpɑ̃te] *vt (parcourir)* to pace up and down

**arqué, -e** [arke] *adj (jambes)* bandy

**arraché** [araʃe] *nm* **gagner à l'a.** to snatch victory

**arrache-pied** [araʃpje] **d'arrache-pied** *adv* relentlessly

**arracher** [araʃe] *vt (plante)* to uproot; *(clou, dent, mauvaise herbe)* to pull out; *(page)* to tear out; **a. qch à qn** *(objet)* to snatch sth from sb; *(promesse)* to force sth out of sb; **se faire a. une dent** to have a tooth out

**arrangement** [arɑ̃ʒmɑ̃] *nm (disposition) & Mus* arrangement; *(accord)* agreement

**arranger** [arɑ̃ʒe] **1** *vt (fleurs)* to arrange; *(col)* to straighten; *(réparer)* to repair; **ça m'arrange** that suits me (fine) **2 s'arranger** *vpr (se mettre d'accord)* to come to an agreement; *(finir bien)* to turn out fine; *(s'organiser)* to manage

**arrestation** [arɛstɑsjɔ̃] *nf* arrest

**arrêt** [arɛ] *nm (halte, endroit)* stop; *(action)* stopping; *Jur* judgement; **temps d'a.** pause; **à l'a.** stationary; **sans a.**

continuously; **a. du cœur** cardiac arrest; *Sport* **a. de jeu** stoppage; **a. de mort** death sentence; **a. de travail** *(congé)* sick leave
**arrêté**[1] [arete] *nm (décret)* order, decree
**arrêté**[2]**, -e** [arete] *adj (idées)* fixed
**arrêter** [arete] **1** *vt (personne, animal, véhicule)* to stop; *(criminel)* to arrest; *(moteur)* to turn off; *(date)* to fix; *(études)* to give up **2** *vi* to stop; **a. de faire qch** to stop doing sth **3 s'arrêter** *vpr* to stop; **s'a. de faire qch** to stop doing sth
**arriéré, -e** [arjere] **1** *adj (pays, idées, enfant)* backward **2** *nm (dette)* arrears
**arrière** [arjɛr] **1** *nm (de maison)* back, rear; *(de bâteau)* stern; *(au football)* full back; **à l'a.** in/at the back
**2** *adj inv (siège)* back, rear; **feu a.** rear light
**3** *adv* **en a.** *(marcher, tomber)* backwards; *(rester)* behind; *(regarder)* back, behind; **en a. de qn/qch** behind sb/sth ▪ **arrière-goût** (*pl* **arrière-goûts**) *nm* aftertaste ▪ **arrière-pays** *nm inv* hinterland ▪ **arrière-pensée** (*pl* **arrière-pensées**) *nf* ulterior motive ▪ **arrière-plan** *nm* background; **à l'a.** in the background ▪ **arrière-saison** (*pl* **arrière-saisons**) *nf Br* late autumn, *Am* late fall
**arriver** [arive] **1** *(aux* **être***) vi (venir)* to arrive; **a. à** *(lieu)* to reach; *(résultat)* to achieve; **a. à faire qch** to manage to do sth
**2** *v impersonnel (survenir)* to happen; **a. à qn** to happen to sb; **qu'est-ce qu'il t'arrive?** what's wrong with you? ▪ **arrivage** *nm* consignment ▪ **arrivée** *nf* arrival; *(ligne, poteau)* winning post ▪ **arriviste** *nmf Péj* social climber
**arrogant, -e** [arɔgɑ̃, -ɑ̃t] *adj* arrogant ▪ **arrogance** *nf* arrogance
**arroger** [arɔʒe] **s'arroger** *vpr (droit)* to claim
**arrondir** [arɔ̃dir] *vt (chiffre, angle)* to round off; **a. qch** to make sth round; **a. à l'euro supérieur/inférieur** to round up/down to the nearest euro; *Fam* **a. ses fins de mois** to supplement one's income ▪ **arrondi, -e** *adj* round
**arrondissement** [arɔ̃dismɑ̃] *nm* = administrative subdivision of Paris, Lyons and Marseilles
**arroser** [aroze] *vt (plante)* to water; *(pelouse)* to sprinkle; *Fam (succès)* to drink to ▪ **arrosage** *nm (de plante)* watering; *(de pelouse)* sprinkling ▪ **arrosoir** *nm* watering can
**arsenal, -aux** [arsənal, -o] *nm Mil* arsenal
**arsenic** [arsənik] *nm* arsenic
**art** [ar] *nm* art; **critique d'a.** art critic; **arts martiaux** martial arts; **arts ménagers** home economics; **arts plastiques** fine arts
**artère** [artɛr] *nf (veine)* artery; *(rue)* main road
**artichaut** [artiʃo] *nm* artichoke; **fond d'a.** artichoke heart
**article** [artikl] *nm (de presse, de contrat) & Gram* article; *Com* item; **articles de toilette** toiletries; **articles de voyage** travel goods
**articuler** [artikyle] **1** *vt (mot)* to articulate **2 s'articuler** *vpr (membre)* to articulate; **s'a. autour de qch** *(théorie)* to centre on ▪ **articulation** *nf (de membre)* joint; *(prononciation)* articulation
**artifice** [artifis] *nm* trick
**artificiel, -elle** [artifisjɛl] *adj* artificial
**artillerie** [artijri] *nf* artillery ▪ **artilleur** *nm* artilleryman
**artisan** [artizɑ̃] *nm* craftsman, artisan ▪ **artisanal, -e, -aux, -ales** *adj* **objet a.** object made by craftsmen; **bombe artisanale** homemade bomb ▪ **artisanat** *nm* craft industry
**artiste** [artist] *nmf* artist; *(acteur, musicien)* performer, artiste ▪ **artistique** *adj* artistic
**as** [ɑs] *nm (carte, champion)* ace
**ascendant** [asɑ̃dɑ̃] **1** *adj* ascending; *(mouvement)* upward **2** *nm (influence)* influence; **ascendants** ancestors ▪ **ascendance** *nf (ancêtres)* ancestry

**ascenseur** [asɑ̃sœr] *nm Br* lift, *Am* elevator

**ascension** [asɑ̃sjɔ̃] *nf (escalade)* ascent; *Rel* **l'A.** Ascension Day

**Asie** [azi] *nf* **l'A.** Asia ▪ **asiatique 1** *adj* Asian **2** *nmf* **A.** Asian

**asile** [azil] *nm (abri)* refuge, shelter; *(pour vieillards)* home; *Péj* **a. (d'aliénés)** (lunatic) asylum; **a. politique** (political) asylum

**aspect** [aspɛ] *nm (air)* appearance; *(perspective)* aspect

**asperger** [aspɛrʒe] **1** *vt (par jeu ou accident)* to splash (**de** with); **se faire a.** to get splashed **2 s'asperger** *vpr* **s'a. de parfum** to splash oneself with perfume

**asperges** [aspɛrʒ] *nfpl* asparagus

**asphalte** [asfalt] *nm* asphalt

**asphyxie** [asfiksi] *nf* asphyxiation ▪ **asphyxier** *vt*, **s'asphyxier** *vpr* to suffocate

**aspirateur** [aspiratœr] *nm* vacuum cleaner, *Br* Hoover®; **passer l'a. dans la maison** to vacuum the house

**aspirer** [aspire] **1** *vt (liquide)* to suck up; *(air)* to breathe in, to inhale **2** *vi* **a. à qch** *(bonheur, gloire)* to aspire to sth ▪ **aspiration** *nf (inhalation)* inhalation; *(ambition)* aspiration (**à** for)

**aspirine** [aspirin] *nf* aspirin

**assaillir** [asajir] *vt* to attack ▪ **assaillant** *nm* attacker, assailant

**assainir** [asenir] *vt (purifier)* to clean up; *(marché, économie)* to stabilize

**assaisonner** [asezɔne] *vt* to season ▪ **assaisonnement** *nm* seasoning

**assassin** [asasɛ̃] *nm* murderer; *(de politicien)* assassin ▪ **assassinat** *nm* murder; *(de politicien)* assassination ▪ **assassiner** *vt* to murder; *(politicien)* to assassinate

**assaut** [aso] *nm* attack, assault; *Mil* charge

**assécher** [aseʃe] **1** *vt* to drain **2 s'assécher** *vpr* to dry up

**assemblée** [asɑ̃ble] *nf (personnes réunies)* gathering; *(réunion)* meeting; **a. générale** *(de compagnie)* annual general meeting; **l'A. nationale** *Br* ≃ the House of Commons, *Am* ≃ the House of Representatives

**assembler** [asɑ̃ble] **1** *vt* to put together, to assemble **2 s'assembler** *vpr* to gather ▪ **assemblage** *nm (montage)* assembly; *(réunion d'objets)* collection

**asséner** [asene] *vt* **a. un coup à qn** to deliver a blow to sb

**asseoir*** [aswar] **1** *vt (personne)* to seat (**sur** on); *Fig (autorité)* to establish **2** *vi* **faire a. qn** to ask sb to sit down **3 s'asseoir** *vpr* to sit (down)

**assermenté, -e** [asɛrmɑ̃te] *adj* sworn; *(témoin)* under oath

**asservir** [asɛrvir] *vt* to enslave

**assez** [ase] *adv* (**a**) *(suffisament)* enough; **a. de pain/de gens** enough bread/people; **j'en ai a. (de)** I've had enough (of); **a. grand/intelligent (pour faire qch)** big/clever enough (to do sth) (**b**) *(plutôt)* quite, rather

**assidu, -e** [asidy] *adj (toujours présent)* regular; *(appliqué)* diligent; **a. auprès de qn** attentive to sb ▪ **assiduité** *nf (d'élève)* regularity

**assiéger** [asjeʒe] *vt (ville, magasin)* to besiege

**assiette** [asjɛt] *nf (récipient)* plate; *Culin* **a. anglaise** *Br* (assorted) cold meats, *Am* cold cuts

**assigner** [asiɲe] *vt (attribuer)* to assign (**à** to); *(en justice)* to summon ▪ **assignation** *nf Jur* summons

**assimiler** [asimile] *vt (aliments, savoir, immigrés)* to assimilate

**assis, -e¹** [asi, -iz] (*pp de* **asseoir**) *adj* sitting (down), seated; **rester a.** to remain seated; **place assise** seat

**assise²** [asiz] *nf (base)* foundation; **assises** *(d'un parti)* congress; *Jur* **les assises** the assizes

**assistance** [asistɑ̃s] *nf* (**a**) *(public)* audience (**b**) *(aide)* assistance

**assister** [asiste] **1** *vt (aider)* to assist **2** *vi* **a. à** *(réunion, cours)* to attend; *(accident)* to witness ▪ **assistant, -e** *nmf* assistant; **assistante sociale** social worker; **assistante maternelle** *Br* child minder, *Am* baby-sitter ▪ **assisté, -e** *adj* **a. par ordinateur** computer-aided

**association** [asɔsjasjɔ̃] *nf* association; *Com* partnership; **a. de parents d'élèves** parent-teacher association; **a. sportive** sports club

**associer** [asɔsje] **1** *vt* to associate (**à** with); **a. qn à** *(travaux)* to involve sb in **2 s'associer** *vpr* to join forces (**à** *ou* **avec** with); *Com* **s'a. avec qn** to enter into partnership with sb ▪ **associé, -e** *nmf* partner, associate

**assoiffé, -e** [aswafe] *adj* thirsty (**de** for)

**assombrir** [asɔ̃brir] **1** *vt (obscurcir)* to darken; *(attrister)* to cast a shadow over **2 s'assombrir** *vpr (ciel, visage)* to cloud over; *(personne)* to become gloomy

**assommer** [asɔme] *vt* **a. qn** to knock sb unconscious; *Fig (ennuyer)* to bore sb to death ▪ **assommant, -e** *adj* very boring

**Assomption** [asɔ̃psjɔ̃] *nf Rel* **l'A.** the Assumption

**assortir** [asɔrtir] *vt (harmoniser)* to match ▪ **assorti, -e** *adj (objet semblable)* matching; *(bonbons)* assorted; **a. de** accompanied by ▪ **assortiment** *nm* assortment

**assoupir** [asupir] **s'assoupir** *vpr* to doze off

**assouplir** [asuplir] **1** *vt (cuir, muscles)* to make supple; *(corps)* to limber up; *Fig (réglementation)* to relax **2 s'assouplir** *vpr (personne, cuir)* to get supple ▪ **assouplissement** *nm* **exercices d'a.** warm-up exercises

**assourdissant, -e** [asurdisɑ̃, -ɑ̃t] *adj* deafening

**assouvir** [asuvir] *vt* to satisfy

**assujettir** [asyʒetir] *vt (soumettre)* to subject (**à** to); *(peuple)* to subjugate; *(objet)* to fix (**à** to)

**assumer** [asyme] **1** *vt (tâche, rôle)* to assume, to take on; *(risque)* to take **2 s'assumer** *vpr* to come to terms with oneself

**assurance** [asyrɑ̃s] *nf (confiance)* (self-)assurance; *(promesse)* assurance; *(contrat)* insurance; **prendre une a.** to take out insurance; **a. au tiers/tous risques** third-party/comprehensive insurance; **a. maladie/vie** health/life insurance

**assurer** [asyre] **1** *vt (garantir) Br* to ensure, *Am* to insure; *(par contrat)* to insure; **a. qn de qch, a. qch à qn** to assure sb of sth; **un service régulier est assuré** there is a regular service **2 s'assurer** *vpr (par contrat)* to insure oneself; **s'a. de qch/que...** to make sure of sth/that... ▪ **assuré, -e 1** *adj (succès)* guaranteed; *(air, personne)* confident **2** *nmf* policyholder ▪ **assurément** *adv* certainly

**asthme** [asm] *nm* asthma ▪ **asthmatique** *adj & nmf* asthmatic

**asticot** [astiko] *nm Br* maggot, *Am* worm

**astiquer** [astike] *vt* to polish

**astre** [astr] *nm* star

**astreindre*** [astrɛ̃dr] **1** *vt* **a. qn à faire qch** to compel sb to do sth **2 s'astreindre** *vpr* **s'a. à faire qch** to force oneself to do sth ▪ **astreignant, -e** *adj* exacting ▪ **astreinte** *nf* constraint

**astrologie** [astrɔlɔʒi] *nf* astrology

**astrologue** [astrɔlɔg] *nm* astrologer

**astronaute** [astrɔnot] *nmf* astronaut ▪ **astronautique** *nf* space travel

**astronomie** [astrɔnɔmi] *nf* astronomy ▪ **astronome** *nm* astronomer

**astuce** [astys] *nf (truc)* trick; *(plaisanterie)* witticism ▪ **astucieux, -euse** *adj* clever

**atelier** [atəlje] *nm (d'ouvrier)* workshop; *(de peintre)* studio; *(personnel)* workshop staff; **a. de montage** assembly shop; **a. de réparation** repair shop

**athée** [ate] **1** *adj* atheistic **2** *nmf* atheist

**Athènes** [atɛn] *nm ou f* Athens

**athlète** [atlɛt] *nmf* athlete ▪ **athlétique** *adj* athletic ▪ **athlétisme** *nm* athletics *(sing)*

**atlantique** [atlɑ̃tik] **1** *adj* Atlantic **2** *nm* **l'A.** the Atlantic

**atlas** [atlɑs] *nm* atlas

**atmosphère** [atmɔsfɛr] *nf* atmosphere ▪ **atmosphérique** *adj* atmospheric

**atome** [atom] *nm* atom ▪ **atomique** *adj* atomic

**atomiser** [atɔmize] *vt (liquide)* to spray; *(région)* to destroy with nuclear weapons ▪ **atomiseur** *nm* spray

**atout** [atu] *nm* trump; *Fig (avantage)* asset

**âtre** [ɑtr] *nm (foyer)* hearth

**atroce** [atrɔs] *adj* atrocious; *(douleur)* excruciating ▪ **atrocité** *nf (cruauté)* atrociousness; **les atrocités de la guerre** the atrocities committed in wartime

**attabler** [atable] **s'attabler** *vpr* to sit down at a/the table

**attache** [ataʃ] *nf (lien)* fastener

**attaché, -e** [ataʃe] **1** *adj (fixé)* fastened; *(chien)* chained up; **être a. à qn** to be attached to sb **2** *nmf* attaché; **a. de presse** press officer

**attaché-case** [ataʃekɛz] (*pl* **attachés-cases**) *nm* attaché case

**attacher** [ataʃe] **1** *vt* **a. qch à qch** to fasten sth to sth; *(avec de la ficelle)* to tie sth to sth; *(avec une chaîne)* to chain sth to sth; **a. de l'importance à qch** to attach great importance to sth

**2** *vi (en cuisant)* to stick (to the pan)

**3 s'attacher** *vpr (se fixer)* to be fastened; **s'a. à qn** to get attached to sb ▪ **attachant, -e** *adj* engaging ▪ **attachement** *nm (affection)* attachment (**à** to)

**attaque** [atak] *nf* attack; **a. aérienne** air raid ▪ **attaquer 1** *vt (physiquement, verbalement)* to attack **2** *vi* to attack **3 s'attaquer** *vpr* **s'a. à** *(adversaire)* to attack; *(problème)* to tackle ▪ **attaquant, -e** *nmf* attacker

**attarder** [atarde] **s'attarder** *vpr* to linger ▪ **attardé, -e** *adj (enfant)* mentally retarded

**atteindre*** [atɛ̃dr] *vt (parvenir à)* to reach; *(cible)* to hit; **être atteint d'une maladie** to be suffering from a disease

**atteinte** [atɛ̃t] *nf* attack (**à** on); **porter a. à** to undermine; **hors d'a.** *(objet, personne)* out of reach

**atteler** [atle] **1** *vt (bêtes)* to harness **2 s'atteler** *vpr* **s'a. à une tâche** to apply oneself to a task

**attenant, -e** [atnɑ̃, -ɑ̃t] *adj* **a. (à)** adjoining

**attendre** [atɑ̃dr] **1** *vt (personne, train)* to wait for; **a. son tour** to wait one's turn; **elle attend un bébé** she's expecting a baby; **a. que qn fasse qch** to wait for sb to do sth; **a. qch de qn** to expect sth from sb

**2** *vi* to wait; **faire a. qn** to keep sb waiting; **en attendant** meanwhile; **en attendant que...** *(+ subjunctive)* until...

**3 s'attendre** *vpr* **s'a. à qch** to expect sth; **s'a. à ce que qn fasse qch** to expect sb to do sth ▪ **attendu, -e 1** *adj (prévu)* expected **2** *prép Formel* considering

**attendrir** [atɑ̃drir] **1** *vt (émouvoir)* to move **2 s'attendrir** *vpr* to be moved (**sur** by) ▪ **attendri, -e** *adj* compassionate ▪ **attendrissant, -e** *adj* moving

**attentat** [atɑ̃ta] *nm* attack; **a. à la bombe** bombing; **a. à la pudeur** indecent assault

**attente** [atɑ̃t] *nf (fait d'attendre)* waiting; *(période)* wait; **en a.** *(au téléphone)* on hold; **contre toute a.** against all expectations

**attentif, -ive** [atɑ̃tif, -iv] *adj* attentive; **a. à qch** to pay attention to sth

**attention** [atɑ̃sjɔ̃] *nf (soin, amabilité)* attention; **faire a. à qch** to pay attention to sth; **faire a. (à ce) que...** *(+ subjunctive)* to be careful that...; **a.!** watch out!; **a. à la voiture!** watch out for the car!; **à l'a. de qn** *(sur lettre)* for the attention of sb ▪ **attentionné, -e** *adj* considerate

**atténuer** [atenɥe] **1** *vt (effet, douleur)* to reduce **2 s'atténuer** *vpr (douleur)* to ease

**atterrir** [aterir] *vi* to land; **a. en catastrophe** to make an emergency landing ▪ **atterrissage** *nm* landing; **a. forcé** forced landing

**attester** [atɛste] *vt* to testify to; **a. que...** to testify that... ▪ **attestation** *nf (document)* certificate

**attirail** [atiraj] *nm* equipment; *Fam Péj* gear

**attirance** [atirɑ̃s] *nf* attraction (**pour** for)

**attirer** [atire] **1** *vt (sujet: aimant, personne)* to attract; *(sujet: matière, pays)* to appeal to; **a. l'attention de qn** to catch sb's attention; **a. qn dans un piège** to lure sb into a trap **2 s'attirer** *vpr (mutuellement)* to be attracted to each other; **s'a. des ennuis** to get oneself into trouble ▪ **attirant, -e** *adj* attractive

**attitré, -e** [atitre] *adj (représentant)* appointed

**attitude** [atityd] *nf (conduite, position)* attitude

**attraction** [atraksjɔ̃] *nf (force, centre d'intérêt)* attraction

**attrait** [atrɛ] *nm* attraction

**attraper** [atrape] *vt (ballon, maladie, voleur)* to catch; **a. froid** to catch cold

**attrayant, -e** [atrɛjɑ̃, -ɑ̃t] *adj* attractive

**attribuer** [atribɥe] *vt (allouer)* to assign (**à** to); *(prix, bourse)* to award (**à** to); *(œuvre)* to attribute (**à** to); **a. de l'importance à qch** to attach importance to sth ▪ **attribution** *nf (allocation)* assigning (**à** to); *(de prix)* awarding (**à** to); *(d'une œuvre)* attribution (**à** to); **attributions** *(fonctions)* duties

**attribut** [atriby] *nm (caractéristique)* attribute

**attrister** [atriste] *vt* to sadden

**attrouper** [atrupe] **s'attrouper** *vpr* to gather ▪ **attroupement** *nm* crowd

**au** [o] *voir* **à**

**aube** [ob] *nf* dawn; **dès l'a.** at the crack of dawn

**auberge** [obɛrʒ] *nf* inn; **a. de jeunesse** youth hostel

**aubergine** [obɛrʒin] *nf Br* aubergine, *Am* eggplant

**aucun, -e** [okœ̃, -yn] **1** *adj* no, not any; **il n'a a. talent** he has no talent; **a. professeur n'est venu** no teacher came **2** *pron* none; **il n'en a a.** he has none (at all); **a. d'entre nous** none of us; **a. des deux** neither of the two

**audace** [odas] *nf (courage)* daring, boldness; *(impudence)* audacity ▪ **audacieux, -euse** *adj (courageux)* daring, bold

**au-dehors** [odəɔr] *adv* outside

**au-delà** [odəla] **1** *adv* beyond; **100 euros mais pas a.** 100 euros but no more **2** *prép* **a. de** beyond **3** *nm* **l'a.** the next world

**au-dessous** [odəsu] **1** *adv (à l'étage inférieur)* downstairs; *(moins, dessous)* below, under **2** *prép* **a. de** *(dans l'espace)* below, under, beneath; *(âge, prix)* under; *(température)* below

**au-dessus** [odəsy] **1** *adv* above; *(à l'étage supérieur)* upstairs **2** *prép* **a. de** above; *(âge, température, prix)* over; *(posé sur)* on top of

**au-devant** [odəvɑ̃] *prép* **aller a. de** *(personne)* to go to meet; *(danger)* to court; *(désirs de qn)* to anticipate

**audible** [odibl] *adj* audible

**audience** [odjɑ̃s] *nf (entretien)* audience; *(de tribunal)* hearing; *Jur* **l'a. est suspendue** the case is adjourned

**audiovisuel, -elle** [odjɔvizɥɛl] **1** *adj (méthodes)* audiovisual; *(de radio, de télévision)* radio and television **2** *nm* **l'a.** radio and television

**auditeur, -trice** [oditœr, -tris] *nmf (de radio)* listener ▪ **audition** *nf (ouïe)* hearing; *(d'acteurs)* audition; **passer une a.** to have an audition ▪ **auditionner** *vti* to audition ▪ **auditoire** *nm* audience ▪ **auditorium** *nm* concert hall

**augmenter** [ɔgmɑ̃te] **1** *vt* to increase (**de** by); **a. qn** to give sb a *Br* rise *or Am* raise **2** *vi* to increase (**de** by); *(prix,* *population)* to rise ■ **augmentation** *nf* increase (**de** in, of); **a. de salaire** *Br* (pay) rise, *Am* raise; **être en a.** to be on the increase

**augure** [ɔgyr] *nm (présage)* omen; **être de bon/mauvais a.** to be a good/bad omen

**aujourd'hui** [oʒurdɥi] *adv* today; *(de nos jours)* nowadays, today; **a. en quinze** two weeks from today

**auparavant** [oparavɑ̃] *adv (avant)* before(-hand); *(d'abord)* first

**auprès** [oprɛ] **auprès de** *prép (près de)* by, next to; **se renseigner a. de qn** to ask sb

**auquel** [okɛl] *voir* **lequel**

**aura, aurait** [ora, ore] *voir* **avoir**

**auréole** [ɔreɔl] *nf (de saint)* halo; *(tache)* ring

**auriculaire** [ɔrikylɛr] *nm* little finger

**aurore** [ɔrɔr] *nf* dawn, daybreak; **à l'a.** at dawn

**auspices** [ospis] *nmpl* **sous les a. de** under the auspices of

**aussi** [osi] **1** *adv* (**a**) *(comparaison)* as; **a. lourd que...** as heavy as... (**b**) *(également)* too, as well; **moi a.** so do/can/am/*etc* I; **a. bien que...** as well as... (**c**) *(tellement)* so; **un repas a. délicieux** such a delicious meal (**d**) *(quelque)* **a. bizarre que cela paraisse** however odd this may seem

**2** *conj (donc)* therefore

**aussitôt** [osito] *adv* immediately, straight away; **a. que...** as soon as...; **a. dit, a. fait** no sooner said than done

**austère** [ɔstɛr] *adj (vie, style)* austere; *(vêtement)* severe ■ **austérité** *nf (de vie, de style)* austerity; *(de vêtement)* severity; **mesure d'a.** austerity measures

**austral, -e, -als, -ales** [ostral] *adj* southern

**Australie** [ostrali] *nf* **l'A.** Australia ■ **australien, -enne 1** *adj* Australian **2** *nmf* **A., Australienne** Australian

---

**AUTANT** [otɑ̃] *adv* (**a**) **a. de... que** *(quantité)* as much... as; *(nombre)* as many... as; **il a a. d'argent/de pommes que vous** he has as much money/as many apples as you

(**b**) **a. de** *(tant de)* so much; *(nombre)* so many; **je n'ai jamais vu a. d'argent/de pommes** I've never seen so much money/so many apples; **pourquoi manges-tu a.?** why are you eating so much?

(**c**) **a. que** *(quantité)* as much as; *(nombre)* as many as; **il lit a. que vous/que possible** he reads as much as you/as possible; **il n'a jamais souffert a.** he's never suffered as *or* so much

(**d**) *(expressions)* **d'a. (plus) que...** all the more (so) since...; **en faire a.** to do the same; **j'aimerais a. aller au musée** I'd just as soon go to the museum

---

**autel** [otɛl] *nm* altar

**auteur** [otœr] *nm (de livre)* author, writer; *(de chanson)* composer

**authenticité** [otɑ̃tisite] *nf* authenticity ■ **authentique** *adj* genuine, authentic

**autiste** [otist] *adj* autistic

**autobiographie** [otobjɔgrafi] *nf* autobiography ■ **autobiographique** *adj* autobiographical

**autobus** [otobys] *nm* bus

**autocar** [otokar] *nm* bus, *Br* coach

**autocollant, -e** [otokɔlɑ̃, -ɑ̃t] **1** *adj* self-adhesive; *(enveloppe, timbre)* self-seal **2** *nm* sticker

**autodéfense** [otodefɑ̃s] *nf* self-defence

**autodidacte** [otodidakt] *nmf* self-taught person

**auto-école** [otoekɔl] (*pl* **auto-écoles**) *nf* driving school, *Br* school of motoring

**autographe** [otograf] *nm* autograph

**automation** [ɔtɔmasjɔ̃] *nf* automation ■ **automatiser** *vt* to automate

**automatique** [ɔtɔmatik] *adj* automatic ■ **automatiquement** *adv* automatically

**automatisation** [ɔtɔmatizasjɔ̃] *nf* = **automation**

**automne** [otɔn] *nm* autumn, *Am* fall

**automobile** [otɔmɔbil] *nf* car, *Br* motorcar, *Am* automobile; **l'a.** *(industrie)* the car industry ▪ **automobiliste** *nmf* motorist

**autonettoyant, -e** [otonetwajɑ̃, -ɑ̃t] *adj* **four a.** self-cleaning oven

**autonome** [otonɔm] *adj (région)* autonomous, self-governing; *(personne)* self-sufficient ▪ **autonomie** *nf (de région)* autonomy; *(de personne)* self-sufficiency

**autopsie** [ɔtɔpsi] *nf* autopsy, post-mortem

**autoradio** [otoradjo] *nm* car radio

**autoriser** [otorize] *vt* **a. qn à faire qch** to authorize *or* permit sb to do sth ▪ **autorisation** *nf (permission)* permission, authorization; *(document)* authorization; **demander à qn l'a. de faire qch** to ask sb permission to do sth; **donner à qn l'a. de faire qch** to give sb permission to do sth ▪ **autorisé, -e** *adj (qualifié)* authoritative; *(permis)* permitted, allowed

**autorité** [otorite] *nf (fermeté, domination)* authority; **faire qch d'a.** to do sth on one's own authority

**autoroute** [otorut] *nf Br* motorway, *Am* highway, *Am* freeway; **a. à péage** *Br* toll motorway, *Am* turnpike (road); *Ordinat* **a. de l'information** information superhighway ▪ **autoritaire** *adj* authoritarian

**auto-stop** [otostɔp] *nm* hitchhiking; **faire de l'a.** to hitchhike ▪ **auto-stoppeur, -euse** *nmf* hitchhiker

**autour** [otur] **1** *adv* around; **tout a.** all around **2** *prép* **a. de** around, round; *(environ)* around, round about

**AUTRE** [otr] *adj & pron* other; **un a. livre** another book; **un a.** another (one); **d'autres** others; **d'autres livres** other books; **quelqu'un d'a.** somebody else; **personne/rien d'a.** no one/nothing else; **a. chose/part** something/somewhere else; **qui/quoi d'a.?** who/what else?; **l'un ou l'a.** either (of them); **ni l'un ni l'a.** neither (of them)

**autrefois** [otrəfwa] *adv* in the past, once

**autrement** [otrəmɑ̃] *adv (différemment)* differently; *(sinon)* otherwise; *(plus)* far more (**que** than)

**Autriche** [otriʃ] *nf* **l'A.** Austria ▪ **autrichien, -enne 1** *adj* Austrian **2** *nmf* **A., Autrichienne** Austrian

**autruche** [otryʃ] *nf* ostrich

**autrui** [otrɥi] *pron* others, other people

**auvent** [ovɑ̃] *nm (toit)* porch roof; *(de tente, de magasin)* awning, canopy

**aux** [o] *voir* **à**

**auxiliaire** [ɔksiljɛr] **1** *adj (machine, troupes)* auxiliary **2** *nm (verbe)* auxiliary **3** *nmf (aide)* assistant; *(d'hôpital)* auxiliary; *(dans l'administration)* temporary worker

**auxquels, -elles** [okɛl] *voir* **lequel**

**av.** (*abrév* **avenue**) Ave

**avait** [avɛ] *voir* **avoir**

**aval** [aval] *nm* downstream section; **en a. (de)** downstream (from)

**avalanche** [avalɑ̃ʃ] *nf* avalanche

**avaler** [avale] *vti* to swallow

**avance** [avɑ̃s] *nf (progression, acompte)* advance; *(avantage)* lead; **faire une a. à qn** *(donner de l'argent)* to give sb an advance; **avoir de l'a. sur qn** to be ahead of sb; **à l'a., d'a., par a.** in advance; **en a.** early; **avoir une heure d'a.** to be an hour early

**avancé, -e** [avɑ̃se] *adj* advanced; **à un âge/stade a.** at an advanced age/stage

**avancée** [avɑ̃se] *nf (saillie)* projection; *(progression, découverte)* advance

**avancement** [avɑ̃smɑ̃] *nm (de personne)* promotion; *(de travail)* progress

**avancer** [avɑ̃se] **1** *vt (dans le temps)* to bring forward; *(dans l'espace)* to move forward; *(pion, thèse)* to advance; *(montre)* to put forward; **a. de l'argent à qn** to lend sb money

**2** *vi (aller de l'avant)* to move forward; *(armée)* to advance; *(faire des progrès)* to progress; *(faire saillie)* to jut out (**sur** over); **a. (de cinq minutes)** *(montre)* to be (five minutes) fast

**3 s'avancer** *vpr* to move forward; **s'a. vers qch** to head towards sth

**AVANT** [avɑ̃] **1** *prép* before; **a. de faire qch** before doing sth; **je vous verrai a. de partir/que vous (ne) partiez** I'll see you before I/you leave; **a. tout** above all

**2** *adv (auparavant)* before; *(d'abord)* beforehand; **a. j'avais les cheveux longs** I used to have long hair; **en a.** *(mouvement)* forward; *(en tête)* ahead; **en a. de** in front of; **la nuit d'a.** the night before

**3** *nm (de navire, de voiture)* front; *(joueur de football)* forward; **à l'a.** in (the) front; **aller de l'a.** to get on with it

**4** *adj inv (pneu, roue)* front ▪ **avant-bras** *nm inv* forearm ▪ **avant-centre** (*pl* **avants-centres**) *nm (au football)* centre-forward ▪ **avant-dernier, -ère** (*mpl* **avant-derniers,** *fpl* **avant-dernières**) *adj & nmf* second last ▪ **avant-hier** *adv* the day before yesterday ▪ **avant-première** (*pl* **avant-premières**) *nf* preview ▪ **avant-propos** *nm inv* foreword

---

**avantage** [avɑ̃taʒ] *nm* advantage; **être/tourner à l'a. de qn** to be/turn to sb's advantage; **avantages sociaux** social security benefits ▪ **avantager** *vt* **a. qn** *(favoriser)* to give sb an advantage over; *(faire valoir)* to show sb off to advantage ▪ **avantageux, -euse** *adj (offre)* attractive; *(prix)* reasonable

**avare** [avar] **1** *adj* miserly **2** *nmf* miser ▪ **avarice** *nf* miserliness, avarice

**avaries** [avari] *nf* damage; **subir une a.** to be damaged ▪ **avarié, -e** *adj (aliment)* rotten

**avec** [avɛk] *prép* with; **méchant/aimable a. qn** nasty/kind to sb; **a. enthousiasme** with enthusiasm, enthusiastically; *Fam* **et a. ça?** *(dans un magasin)* anything else?

**avenant, -e** [avnɑ̃, -ɑ̃t] **1** *adj (personne, manières)* pleasing **2** *nm* **à l'a. (de)** in keeping (with)

**avènement** [avɛnmɑ̃] *nm (d'une ère)* advent; *(d'un roi)* accession

**avenir** [avnir] *nm* future; **à l'a.** *(désormais)* in future; **d'a.** *(métier)* with good prospects

**aventure** [avɑ̃tyr] *nf* adventure; *(en amour)* affair; **dire la bonne a. à qn** to tell sb's fortune ▪ **aventurer** *vpr* **s'aventurer** to venture (**dans** into) ▪ **aventurier, -ère** *nmf* adventurer

**avenue** [avny] *nf* avenue

**avérer** [avere] **s'avérer** *vpr (se révéler)* to prove to be; **il s'avère que...** it turns out that... ▪ **avéré, -e** *adj (fait)* established

**averse** [avɛrs] *nf* shower

**aversion** [avɛrsjɔ̃] *nf* aversion (**pour** to)

**avertir** [avertir] *vt* **a. qn de qch** *(informer)* to inform sb of sth; *(danger)* to warn sb of sth ▪ **avertissement** *nm* warning; *(de livre)* foreword ▪ **avertisseur** *nm (klaxon®)* horn

**aveu, -x** [avø] *nm* confession

**aveugle** [avœgl] **1** *adj* blind; **devenir a.** to go blind; **avoir une confiance a. en qn** to trust sb implicitly **2** *nmf* blind man, *f* blind woman; **les aveugles** the blind ▪ **aveuglement** *nm (moral, mental)* blindness ▪ **aveuglément** *adv* blindly ▪ **aveugler** *vt (éblouir) & Fig* to blind; **aveuglé par la colère** blind with rage

**aveuglette** [avœglɛt] **à l'aveuglette** *adv* blindly; **chercher qch à l'a.** to grope for sth

**aviateur, -trice** [avjatœr, -tris] *nmf* aviator ▪ **aviation** *nf (secteur)* aviation; *(armée de l'air)* air force; **l'a.** *(activité)* flying

**avide** [avid] *adj (cupide)* greedy; *(passionné)* eager (**de** for) ▪ **avidité** *nf (voracité, cupidité)* greed; *(passion)* eagerness

**avilir** [avilir] *vt* to degrade

**avion** [avjɔ̃] *nm* plane, *Br* aeroplane, *Am* airplane; **par a.** *(sur lettre)* airmail;

**en a., par a.** *(voyager)* by plane, by air; **a. à réaction** jet; **a. de tourisme** private plane

**aviron** [avirɔ̃] *nm* oar; **l'a.** *(sport)* rowing; **faire de l'a.** to row

**avis** [avi] *nm* opinion; *(communiqué)* notice; *(conseil)* advice; **à mon a.** in my opinion, to my mind; **être de l'a. de qn** to be of the same opinion as sb; **changer d'a.** to change one's mind; **sauf a. contraire** unless I/you/*etc* hear to the contrary

**aviser** [avize] **1** *vt* **a. qn de qch/que...** to inform sb of sth/that... **2 s'aviser** *vpr* **s'a. de qch** to become aware of sth; **s'a. que...** to notice that... ▪ **avisé, -e** *adj* wise (**de faire** to do); **bien/mal a.** well-/ill-advised

**avocat[1], -e** [avɔka, -at] *nmf Jur* lawyer; *Fig* advocate

**avocat[2]** [avɔka] *nm (fruit)* avocado

**avoine** [avwan] *nf* oats

**AVOIR*** [avwar] **1** *v aux* to have; **je l'ai vu** I have *or* I've seen him

**2** *vt (posséder)* to have; *(obtenir)* to get; *(porter)* to wear; *Fam (tromper)* to take for a ride; **qu'est-ce que tu as?** what's the matter with you?; **j'ai à faire** I have things to do; **il n'a qu'à essayer** he only has to try; **a. faim/chaud** to be *or* feel hungry/hot; **a. cinq ans** to be five (years old); **a. du diabète** to be diabetic

**3** *v impersonnel* **il y a** there is, *pl* there are; **il y a six ans** six years ago; **il n'y a pas de quoi!** *(en réponse à 'merci')* don't mention it!; **qu'est-ce qu'il y a?** what's the matter?

**4** *nm* assets, property; *(d'un compte)* credit

---

**avoisiner** [avwazine] *vt (dans l'espace)* to border on; *(en valeur)* to be close to ▪ **avoisinant, -e** *adj* neighbouring, nearby

**avorter** [avɔrte] *vi (subir une IVG)* to have an abortion; *Fig (projet)* to fall through; **se faire a.** to have an abortion ▪ **avortement** *nm* abortion

**avouer** [avwe] **1** *vt (crime)* to confess to; **il faut a. que...** it must be admitted that... **2 s'avouer** *vpr* **s'a. vaincu** to acknowledge defeat

**avril** [avril] *nm* April

**axe** [aks] *nm (géométrique)* axis; *(essieu)* axle; **les grands axes** *(routes)* the main roads ▪ **axer** *vt* to centre (**sur** on)

**ayant** [ɛjɑ̃], **ayez** [ɛje], **ayons** [ɛjɔ̃] *voir* **avoir**

**azote** [azɔt] *nm* nitrogen

# Bb

**B, b** [be] *nm inv* B, b
**babiller** [babije] *vi (enfant)* to babble
**babines** [babin] *nfpl (lèvres)* chops
**bâbord** [babɔr] *nm* port (side); **à b.** to port
**baby-foot** [babifut] *nm inv* table football
**baby-sitting** [babisitiŋ] *nm* baby-sitting ▪ **baby-sitter** *(pl* **baby-sitters**) *nmf* baby-sitter
**bac**[1] [bak] *nm (bateau)* ferry(boat); *(cuve)* tank; **b. à glace** ice tray
**bac**[2] [bak] *(abrév* **baccalauréat**) *nm Fam* = secondary school examination qualifying for entry to university, *Br* ≃ A-levels, *Am* ≃ high school diploma
**baccalauréat** [bakalɔrea] *nm* = secondary school examination qualifying for entry to university, *Br* ≃ A-levels, *Am* ≃ high school diploma
**bâche** [baʃ] *nf (de toile)* tarpaulin; *(de plastique)* plastic sheet ▪ **bâcher** *vt* to cover *(with a tarpaulin or plastic sheet)*
**bachelier, -ère** [baʃəlje, -ɛr] *nmf* = student who has passed the "baccalauréat
**bâcler** [bakle] *vt Fam* to botch (up)
**bactérie** [bakteri] *nf* bacterium
**badaud, -aude** [bado, -od] *nmf (promeneur)* stroller; *(curieux)* onlooker
**badge** [badʒ] *nm Br* badge, *Am* button
**badigeonner** [badiʒɔne] *vt (surface)* to daub (**de** with); *(mur)* to whitewash; *Culin* to brush (**de** with); *(plaie)* to paint (**de** with)
**badinage** [badinaʒ] *nm* banter
**badine** [badin] *nf* switch
**badiner** [badine] *vi* to jest
**baffle** [bafl] *nm* speaker
**bafouer** [bafwe] *vt (person)* to jeer at; *(autorité)* to flout
**bafouiller** [bafuje] *vti* to stammer
**bagages** [bagaʒ] *nmpl (valises)* luggage, baggage; **faire ses b.** to pack (one's bags)
**bagarre** [bagar] *nf* fight, brawl ▪ **se bagarrer** to fight ▪ **bagarreur, -euse** *adj (personne, caractère)* aggressive
**bague** [bag] *nf (anneau)* ring; *(de cigare)* band ▪ **baguer** *vt (oiseau, arbre)* to ring
**baguette** [bagɛt] *nf (canne)* stick; *(de chef d'orchestre)* baton; *(pain)* baguette; **baguettes** *(de tambour)* drumsticks; *(pour manger)* chopsticks
**bahut** [bay] *nm (buffet)* sideboard
**baie**[1] [bɛ] *nf Géog* bay
**baie**[2] [bɛ] *nf (fruit)* berry
**baie**[3] [bɛ] *nf* **b. vitrée** picture window
**baignade** [bɛɲad] *nf (activité)* swimming, *Br* bathing; **'b. interdite'** 'no swimming'
**baigner** [beɲe] **1** *vt (pied, blessure)* to bathe; *(enfant) Br* to bath, *Am* to bathe; *(sujet: mer)* to wash **2** *vi (tremper)* to soak (**dans** in) **3 se baigner** *vpr (nager)* to have a swim ▪ **baigneur, -euse 1** *nmf* swimmer **2** *nm (poupée)* baby doll ▪ **baignoire** *nf* bath (tub)
**bail** [baj] *(pl* **baux** [bo]) *nm* lease; *Fam* **ça fait un b. que je ne l'ai pas vu** I haven't seen him for ages ▪ **bailleur** *nm* **b. de fonds** financial backer

**bâiller** [bɑje] *vi* to yawn; *(col)* to gape; *(porte)* to be ajar

**bâillon** [bɑjɔ̃] *nm* gag; **mettre un b. à qn** to gag sb ▪ **bâillonner** *vt (victime, presse)* to gag

**bain** [bɛ̃] *nm* bath; **prendre un b.** to have *or* take a bath; **prendre un b. de soleil** to sunbathe; **petit/grand b.** *(de piscine)* small/large pool

**baiser** [beze] *nm* kiss

**baisse** [bes] *nf* fall, drop (**de** in); **en b.** *(température)* falling; *(popularité)* declining

**baisser** [bese] **1** *vt (rideau, vitre, prix)* to lower; *(radio, chauffage)* to turn down; **b. la tête** to lower one's head; **b. les yeux** to look down **2** *vi (prix, niveau, température)* to fall; *(vue, mémoire)* to fail; *(popularité, qualité)* to decline **3 se baisser** *vpr* to bend down; *(pour éviter quelque chose)* to duck

**baissier** [besje] *adj m Fin* **marché b.** bear market

**bal** [bal] *(pl* **bals***) nm (élégant)* ball; *(populaire)* dance; **b. costumé, b. masqué** fancy dress ball; **b. populaire** = dance, usually outdoors, open to the public

**balade** [balad] *nf Fam (à pied)* walk; *(en voiture)* drive; **faire une b.** *(à pied)* to go for a walk; *(en voiture)* to go for a drive ▪ **balader** *Fam* **1** *vi* **envoyer qn b.** to send sb packing **2 se balader** *vpr (à pied)* to go for a walk; *(en voiture)* to go for a drive ▪ **baladeur** *nm* personal stereo

**balafre** [balafr] *nf (cicatrice)* scar; *(coupure)* gash ▪ **balafrer** *vt* to gash

**balai** [balɛ] *nm* broom; **donner un coup de b.** to give the floor a sweep

**balance** [balɑ̃s] *nf* (**a**) *(instrument)* (pair of) scales (**b**) **la B.** *(signe)* Libra

**balancer** [balɑ̃se] **1** *vt (bras, jambe)* to swing **2 se balancer** *vpr (arbre, bateau)* to sway; *(sur une balançoire)* to swing ▪ **balancement** *nm* swaying

**balancier** [balɑ̃sje] *nm (d'horloge)* pendulum

**balançoire** [balɑ̃swar] *nf (suspendue)* swing; *(bascule)* see-saw

**balayer** [baleje] *vt (pièce)* to sweep; *(feuilles, saletés)* to sweep up ▪ **balayage** *nm (nettoyage)* sweeping; *(coiffure)* highlighting

**balayeur, -euse** [balɛjœr, -øz] *nmf (personne)* road-sweeper

**balbutier** [balbysje] *vti* to stammer ▪ **balbutiement** *nm* **balbutiement(s)** stammering

**balcon** [balkɔ̃] *nm* balcony; *(de théâtre)* circle, *Am* mezzanine; **premier/deuxième b.** dress/upper circle

**Baléares** [balear] *nfpl* **les B.** the Balearic Islands

**baleine** [balɛn] *nf (animal)* whale; *(de corset)* whalebone; *(de parapluie)* rib

**balèze** [balɛz] *adj Fam (grand et fort)* hefty; *(intelligent)* brainy

**balise** [baliz] *nf Naut* beacon; *Aviat* light; *(de piste de ski)* marker; *Ordinat* tag ▪ **balisage** *nm (signaux) Naut* beacons; *Aviat* lights ▪ **baliser** *vt (chenal)* to beacon; *(aéroport)* to equip with lights; *(route)* to mark out with beacons; *(piste de ski)* to mark out; *Ordinat* to tag

**balivernes** [balivɛrn] *nfpl* twaddle

**Balkans** [balkɑ̃] *nmpl* **les B.** the Balkans

**ballant, -e** [balɑ̃, -ɑ̃t] *adj (bras, jambes)* dangling

**ballast** [balast] *nm (de route, de voie ferrée)* ballast

**balle** [bal] *nf (pour jouer)* ball; *(d'arme)* bullet; **b. de tennis** tennis ball; **b. perdue** stray bullet

**ballet** [balɛ] *nm* ballet ▪ **ballerine** *nf (danseuse)* ballerina; *(chaussure)* pumps

**ballon** [balɔ̃] *nm (balle, dirigeable)* balloon; *(verre)* round wine glass; **jouer au b.** to play with a ball; **b. de football** *Br* football, *Am* soccer ball

**ballonné** [balɔne] *adj m (ventre, personne)* bloated

**ballottage** [balɔtaʒ] *nm Pol* **il y a b.** there will be a second ballot

**ballotter** [balɔte] *vt (bateau)* to toss about; *(passagers)* to shake about

**balluchon** [balyʃɔ̃] *nm* bundle; **faire son b.** to pack one's bags

**balnéaire** [balneɛr] *adj* **station b.** *Br* seaside resort, *Am* beach resort

**balourd, -e** [balur, -urd] *adj* oafish

**balte** [balt] *adj* **les États baltes** the Baltic states

**Baltique** [baltik] *nf* **la (mer) B.** the Baltic (Sea)

**baluchon** [balyʃɔ̃] *nm* = **balluchon**

**balustrade** [balystrad] *nf (de pont)* railing; *(de balcon)* balustrade

**bambou** [bɑ̃bu] *nm* bamboo

**ban** [bɑ̃] *nm (applaudissements)* round of applause; **bans** *(de mariage)* banns

**banal, -e, -als, -ales** [banal] *adj (objet, gens)* ordinary; *(idée)* trite, banal; **pas b.** unusual ■ **banalité** *nf (d'objet, de gens)* ordinariness; *(d'idée)* triteness

**banaliser** [banalize] *vt (rendre commun)* to trivialize

**banane** [banan] *nf (fruit)* banana; *(coiffure)* quiff ■ **bananier** *nm (arbre)* banana tree

**banc** [bɑ̃] *nm (siège)* bench; *(établi)* (work-)bench; *(de poissons)* shoal; **b. des accusés** dock; **b. d'essai** *Ind* test bed; *Fig* testing ground; **b. de sable** sandbank

**bancaire** [bɑ̃kɛr] *adj (opération)* banking; *(chèque, compte)* bank

**bancal, -e, -als, -ales** [bɑ̃kal] *adj (meuble)* wobbly; *Fig (raisonnement)* unsound

**bandage** [bɑ̃daʒ] *nm (pansement)* bandage

**bande** [bɑ̃d] *nf* (**a**) *(de tissu, de papier, de terre)* strip; *(pansement)* bandage; *(pellicule)* film; **b. magnétique** tape; *Aut* **b. d'arrêt d'urgence** *Br* hard shoulder, *Am* shoulder; **b. dessinée** comic strip; **b. sonore** soundtrack

(**b**) *(de personnes)* band, group; *(de voleurs)* gang; *(de loups)* pack; **faire b. à part** *(agir seul)* to do one's own thing ■ **bande-annonce** (*pl* **bandes-annonces**) *nf* trailer (**de** for) ■ **bande-son** (*pl* **bandes-son**) *nf* soundtrack

**bandeau, -x** [bɑ̃do] *nm (pour cheveux)* headband; *(sur les yeux)* blindfold

**bander** [bɑ̃de] *vt (blessure, main)* to bandage; *(arc)* to bend; **b. les yeux à qn** to blindfold sb

**banderole** [bɑ̃drɔl] *nf (de manifestants)* banner; *(publicitaire)* streamer

**bandit** [bɑ̃di] *nm (escroc)* crook

**bandoulière** [bɑ̃duljɛr] *nf (de sac)* shoulder strap; **en b.** slung across the shoulder

**banlieue** [bɑ̃ljø] *nf* suburbs; **la b. parisienne** the suburbs of Paris; **de b.** *(maison, magasin)* suburban; **train de b.** commuter train ■ **banlieusard, -e** *nmf (habitant)* suburbanite; *(voyageur)* commuter

**bannière** [banjɛr] *nf* banner; **la b. étoilée** the Star-spangled Banner

**bannir** [banir] *vt (personne, idée)* to banish (**de** from)

**banque** [bɑ̃k] *nf (établissement)* bank; **la b.** *(activité)* banking; **employé de b.** bank clerk; *Ordinat* **b. de données** data bank

**banqueroute** [bɑ̃krut] *nf* bankruptcy; **faire b.** to go bankrupt

**banquet** [bɑ̃kɛ] *nm* banquet

**banquette** [bɑ̃kɛt] *nf (siège)* (bench) seat

**banquier, -ère** [bɑ̃kje, -ɛr] *nmf* banker

**banquise** [bɑ̃kiz] *nf* ice floe

**baptême** [batɛm] *nm* christening, baptism ■ **baptiser** *vt* to christen, to baptize

**baquet** [bakɛ] *nm (cuve)* tub

**bar**[1] [bar] *nm (café, comptoir)* bar

**bar**[2] [bar] *nm (poisson)* bass

**baraque** [barak] *nf (cabane)* hut, shack; *(de foire)* stall ■ **baraquement** *nm* shacks; *Mil* camp

**baratin** [baratɛ̃] *nm Fam (verbiage)* waffle; *(de séducteur)* sweet talk; *(de vendeur)* sales talk ■ **baratiner** *vt Fam* to chatter; *(sujet: séducteur) Br* to chat up, *Am* to hit on

**barbare** [barbar] **1** *adj (cruel, sauvage)* barbaric **2** *nmf* barbarian ▪ **barbarie** *nf (cruauté)* barbarity

**barbe** [barb] *nf* beard; **b. à papa** *Br* candyfloss, *Am* cotton candy

**barbecue** [barbəkju] *nm* barbecue

**barbelés** [barbəle] *nmpl* barbed wire

**barber** [barbe] *Fam* **1** *vt* **b. qn** to bore sb stiff **2 se barber** *vpr* to be bored stiff

**barbiche** [barbiʃ] *nf* goatee

**barbiturique** [barbityrik] *nm* barbiturate

**barboter** [barbɔte] *vi* to splash about ▪ **barboteuse** *nf* rompers

**barbouiller** [barbuje] *vt (salir)* to smear (**de** with)

**barbu, -e** [barby] **1** *adj* bearded **2** *nm* bearded man

**barder[1]** [barde] *vt Culin* to bard; *Fig* **bardé de décorations** covered with decorations

**barder[2]** [barde] *v impersonnel Fam* **ça va b.!** there's going to be trouble!

**barème** [barɛm] *nm (de notes, de salaires, de prix)* scale; *(pour calculer)* ready reckoner

**baril** [baril] *nm (de pétrole, de vin)* barrel; *(de lessive)* drum

**bariolé, -e** [barjɔle] *adj* multicoloured

**barjo(t)** [barʒo] *adj inv Fam (fou)* nutty

**barman** [barman] (*pl* **-men** [-men] *ou* **-mans**) *nm Br* barman, *Am* bartender

**baromètre** [barɔmɛtr] *nm* barometer

**baron** [barɔ̃] *nm* baron; *Fig* **b. de la finance** financial tycoon ▪ **baronne** *nf* baroness

**baroque** [barɔk] **1** *adj (édifice, style, musique)* baroque **2** *nm Archit & Mus* **le b.** the baroque

**baroudeur** [barudœr] *nm Fam (combattant)* fighter; *(voyageur)* keen traveller

**barque** [bark] *nf* (small) boat ▪ **barquette** *nf (de fruit)* punnet; *(de plat cuisiné)* container

**barrage** [baraʒ] *nm (sur l'eau)* dam; **b. de police** police roadblock; **b. routier** roadblock

**barre** [bar] *nf (de fer, de bois)* bar; *(de danse)* barre; *(trait)* line, stroke; *Naut (volant)* helm; **b. chocolatée** chocolate bar; *Mus* **b. de mesure** bar (line); *Jur* **b. des témoins** *Br* witness box, *Am* witness stand; **b. d'appui** *(de fenêtre)* rail; **b. d'espacement** *(de clavier)* space bar; *Ordinat* **b. d'outils** tool bar; *Ordinat* **b. de sélection** menu bar

**barreau, -x** [baro] *nm (de fenêtre, de cage)* bar; *(d'échelle)* rung; *Jur* **le b.** the bar; **être derrière les barreaux** *(en prison)* to be behind bars

**barrer** [bare] **1** *vt (voie)* to block off; *(porte)* to bar; *(chèque)* to cross; *(mot)* to cross out; *Naut (bateau)* to steer; **b. le passage** *ou* **la route à qn** to bar sb's way; **'route barrée'** 'road closed' **2 se barrer** *vpr Fam* to beat it

**barrette** [barɛt] *nf (pour cheveux) Br* (hair)slide, *Am* barrette

**barricade** [barikad] *nf* barricade ▪ **barricader 1** *vt (rue, porte)* to barricade **2 se barricader** *vpr* to barricade oneself (**dans** in)

**barrière** [barjɛr] *nf (obstacle)* barrier; *(de passage à niveau)* gate; *(clôture)* fence

**barrique** [barik] *nf* (large) barrel

**barrir** [barir] *vi (éléphant)* to trumpet

**baryton** [baritɔ̃] *nm Mus* baritone

**BAS[1], BASSE[1]** [bɑ, bɑs] **1** *adj (dans l'espace, en quantité, en intensité) & Mus* low; *(origine)* lowly; *Péj (acte)* mean, low; **à b. prix** cheaply; **enfant en b. âge** young child; **avoir la vue basse** to be short-sighted

**2** *adv (dans l'espace)* low (down); *(dans une hiérarchie)* low; *(parler)* quietly; **plus b.** further *or* lower down; **voir plus b.** *(sur document)* see below; **en b.** at the bottom; **en b. de** at the bottom of; **à b. les dictateurs!** down with dictators!

**3** *nm (partie inférieure)* bottom; **l'étagère du b.** the bottom shelf; **au b. de** at the bottom of; **de b. en haut** upwards

**bas²** [bɑ] *nm (chaussette)* stocking; *Fig* **b. de laine** *(économies)* nest egg

**basané, -e** [bazane] *adj (bronzé)* tanned

**bas-côté** [bɑkote] *(pl* **bas-côtés**) *nm (de route)* verge; *(d'église)* (side)aisle

**bascule** [baskyl] *nf (balançoire)* seesaw; *(balance)* weighing machine; **fauteuil à b.** rocking chair ▪ **basculer 1** *vt (chargement)* to tip over; *(benne)* to tip up **2** *vi (tomber)* to topple over; **faire b.** *(personne)* to knock over; *(chargement)* to tip over

**base** [bɑz] *nf (partie inférieure) & Chim, Math & Mil* base; *(de parti politique)* rank and file; *(principe)* basis; **avoir de bonnes bases en anglais** to have a good grounding in English; **de b.** basic; **salaire de b.** basic pay; *Ordinat* **b. de données** database ▪ **baser 1** *vt* to base (**sur** on) **2 se baser** *vpr* **se b. sur qch** to base oneself on sth

**bas-fond** [bɑfɔ̃] *(pl* **bas-fonds**) *nm (de mer, de rivière)* shallow; *Péj* **les bas-fonds** *(de ville)* the rough areas

**basic** [bazik] *nm Ordinat* BASIC

**basilic** [bazilik] *nm (plante, aromate)* basil

**basilique** [bazilik] *nf* basilica

**basket-ball** [basketbol] *nm* basketball

**baskets** [basket] *nmpl ou nfpl (chaussures)* baseball boots

**basque¹** [bask] **1** *adj* Basque **2** *nmf* **B.** Basque

**basque²** [bask] *nfpl (de veste)* tail; *Fig* **être toujours pendu aux basques de qn** to be always at sb's heels

**basse²** [bɑs] **1** *voir* **bas¹ 2** *nf Mus (contrebasse)* (double) bass; *(guitare)* bass (guitar)

**basse-cour** [bɑskur] *(pl* **basses-cours**) *nf Br* farmyard, *Am* barnyard

**bassesse** [basɛs] *nf (d'action)* lowness; *(action)* low act

**bassin** [basɛ̃] *nm* (**a**) *(pièce d'eau)* ornamental lake; *(de fontaine)* basin; *(récipient)* bowl, basin; **petit b.** *(de piscine)* children's pool; **grand b.** *(de piscine)* large pool (**b**) *(du corps)* pelvis (**c**) *(région)* basin; **le b. parisien** the Paris Basin ▪ **bassine** *nf* bowl

**basson** [bɑsɔ̃] *nm (instrument)* bassoon; *(musicien)* bassoonist

**bastion** [bastjɔ̃] *nm aussi Fig* bastion

**bas-ventre** [bɑvɑ̃tr] *nm* lower abdomen

**bat** [ba] *voir* **battre**

**bataille** [bataj] *nf (lutte)* battle; *(jeu de cartes)* ≃ beggar-my-neighbour ▪ **batailleur, -euse** *adj* aggressive

**bataillon** [batajɔ̃] *nm Mil* batallion

**bâtard, -e** [bɑtar, -ard] **1** *adj (enfant)* illegitimate; *(solution)* hybrid **2** *nmf (enfant)* illegitimate child; *Péj* bastard; *(chien)* mongrel; *(pain)* = small, thick baguette

**bateau, -x** [bato] **1** *nm (embarcation)* boat; *(grand)* ship; **faire du b.** to go boating; **b. à moteur** motorboat; **b. à voiles** *Br* sailing boat, *Am* sailboat; **b. de plaisance** pleasure boat **2** *adj inv Fam (sujet)* hackneyed; **col b.** boat neck ▪ **bateau-mouche** *(pl* **bateaux-mouches**) *nm* river boat *(on the Seine)*

**bâtiment** [bɑtimɑ̃] *nm (édifice)* building; *(navire)* vessel; **le b., l'industrie du b.** the building trade

**bâtir** [bɑtir] *vt (construire)* to build; *Couture* to tack; **terrain à b.** building plot ▪ **bâti, -e 1** *adj* **bien b.** *(personne)* well-built **2** *nm (charpente)* frame; *Couture* tacking ▪ **bâtisse** *nf Péj* ugly building

**bâton** [bɑtɔ̃] *nm (canne)* stick; *(de maréchal)* baton; *(d'agent de police) Br* truncheon, *Am* nightstick; *(trait)* vertical line; **donner des coups de b. à qn** to beat sb (with a stick); **b. de rouge** lipstick; **bâtons de ski** ski sticks ▪ **bâtonnet** *nm* stick

**battant¹** [batɑ̃] *nm* (**a**) *(de porte, de volet)* leaf; **porte à deux battants** double door (**b**) *(personne)* fighter

**battant², -e** [batɑ̃, -ɑ̃t] *adj* **pluie b.** driving rain; **porte b.** *Br* swing door, *Am* swinging door

**battement** [batmɑ̃] *nm* (**a**) *(de tambour)* beat(ing); *(de porte)* banging;

*(de paupières)* blink(ing); *(d'ailes)* flapping (**b**) *(délai)* gap

**batterie** [batri] *nf (d'orchestre)* drums; *(ensemble) & Mil, Él* battery; *(de questions)* series; **être à la b.** *(sujet: musicien)* to be on drums; **élevage en b.** battery farming; **b. de cuisine** kitchen utensils

**batteur** [batœr] *nm (musicien)* drummer; *(de cuisine)* mixer

**battre*** [batr] **1** *vt (frapper, vaincre)* to beat; *(œufs)* to whisk; *(beurre)* to churn; *(record)* to break; *(cartes)* to shuffle; *Mus* **b. la mesure** to beat time

**2** *vi (cœur)* to beat; *(porte, volet)* to bang; **b. des mains** to clap one's hands; **b. des ailes** to flap its wings

**3 se battre** *vpr* to fight (**avec** with); **se b. au couteau** to fight with a knife

**battu, -e**[1] [baty] *adj (femme, enfant)* battered

**battue**[2] [baty] *nf (à la chasse)* beat; *(recherche)* search

**baume** [bom] *nm aussi Fig* balm

**baux** [bo] *voir* **bail**

**bavard, -e** [bavar, -ard] **1** *adj (qui parle beaucoup)* chatty **2** *nmf (qui parle beaucoup)* chatterbox ▪ **bavardage** *nm (action)* chatting; *(commérage)* gossiping; **bavardages** *(paroles)* chats ▪ **bavarder** *vi (parler)* to chat; *(commérer)* to gossip

**bave** [bav] *nf (de personne)* dribble; *(de chien)* slaver; *(de chien enragé)* froth ▪ **baver** *vi (personne)* to dribble; *(chien)* to slaver; *(chien enragé)* to foam at the mouth; *(stylo)* to leak; *Fam* **en b.** to have a hard time of it

**bavette** [bavɛt] *nf (de bébé)* bib; *(de bœuf)* skirt (of beef)

**baveux, -euse** [bavø, -øz] *adj (omelette)* runny

**bavoir** [bavwar] *nm* bib

**bavure** [bavyr] *nf (tache)* smudge; *(erreur)* slip-up

**bayer** [baje] *vi* **b. aux corneilles** to stare into space

**bazar** [bazar] *nm (marché)* bazaar; *(magasin)* general store; *Fam (désordre)* shambles *(sing)*; *Fam (affaires)* gear; *Fam* **mettre du b. dans qch** to make a shambles of sth

**BCG** [beseʒe] *nm Méd* BCG

**BD** [bede] *(abrév* **bande dessinée***) nf* comic strip

**bd** *abrév* **boulevard**

**béant, -e** [beɑ̃, -ɑ̃t] *adj (gouffre)* yawning

**béat, -e** [bea, -at] *adj Hum (heureux)* blissful; *Péj (niais)* inane; **être b. d'admiration** to be open-mouthed in admiration ▪ **béatement** *adv (sourire)* inanely

**beau, belle** [bo, bel] *(pl* **beaux, belles***)*

**bel** is used before masculine singular nouns beginning with a vowel or h mute.

**1** *adj* (**a**) *(femme, enfant, fleur, histoire)* beautiful; *(homme)* handsome, good-looking; *(spectacle, discours)* fine; *(maison, voyage, temps)* lovely; **une belle somme** a tidy sum; **se faire b.** to smarten oneself up; **c'est trop b. pour être vrai** it's too good to be true; **c'est le plus b. jour de ma vie!** it's the best day of my life!

(**b**) *(expressions)* **au b. milieu de** right in the middle of; **bel et bien** *(complètement)* well and truly

**2** *adv* **il fait b.** the weather's nice; **j'ai b. crier…** it's no use (my) shouting…

**3** *nm* **le b.** *(la beauté)* beauty

**4** *nf* **belle** *(jeu, partie)* decider ▪ **beau-fils** *(pl* **beaux-fils***) nm (gendre)* son-in-law; *(après remariage)* stepson ▪ **beau-frère** *(pl* **beaux-frères***) nm* brother-in-law ▪ **beau-père** *(pl* **beaux-pères***) nm (père du conjoint)* father-in-law; *(après remariage)* stepfather ▪ **beaux-arts** *nmpl* fine arts; **école des b., les B.** art school ▪ **beaux-parents** *nmpl* parents-in-law

**beaucoup** [boku] *adv (intensément, en grande quantité)* a lot; **aimer b. qch** to like sth very much; **s'intéresser b. à qch** to be very interested in sth; **b.**

**d'entre nous** many of us; **b. de** *(quantité)* a lot of; *(nombre)* many, a lot of; **pas b. d'argent** not much money; **pas b. de gens** not many people; **j'en ai b.** *(quantité)* I have a lot; *(nombre)* I have lots; **b. plus/moins (que)** much more/less (than), a lot more/less (than); *(nombre)* many *or* a lot more/ a lot fewer (than)

**beauté** [bote] *nf (qualité, femme)* beauty

**bébé** [bebe] *nm* baby ▪ **bébé-éprouvette** (*pl* **bébés-éprouvette**) *nm* test-tube baby

**bec** [bɛk] *nm (d'oiseau)* beak, bill; *(de pot)* lip; *(de flûte)* mouthpiece; *Fam (bouche)* mouth; *Fam* **clouer le b. à qn** to shut sb up; **b. verseur** spout ▪ **bec-de-lièvre** (*pl* **becs-de-lièvre**) *nm* harelip

**bêche** [bɛʃ] *nf* spade ▪ **bêcher** *vt* to dig

**bedonnant, -e** [bədɔnɑ̃, -ɑ̃t] *adj* pot-bellied, paunchy

**bée** [be] *adj f* **j'en suis resté bouche b.** I was speechless

**beffroi** [befrwa] *nm* belfry

**bégayer** [begeje] *vi* to stutter, to stammer

**bègue** [bɛg] **1** *adj* **être b.** to stutter, to stammer **2** *nmf* stutterer, stammerer

**beige** [bɛʒ] *adj & nm* beige

**beignet** [beɲe] *nm* fritter; *(au sucre, à la confiture)* doughnut

**Beijing** [beidʒiŋ] *nm ou f* Beijing

**bel** [bel] *voir* **beau**

**bêler** [bɛle] *vi* to bleat

**belette** [bəlɛt] *nf* weasel

**Belgique** [bɛlʒik] *nf* **la B.** Belgium ▪ **belge 1** *adj* Belgian **2** *nmf* **B.** Belgian

**bélier** [belje] *nm (animal, machine)* ram; **le B.** *(signe)* Aries

**belle** [bɛl] *voir* **beau** ▪ **belle-famille** (*pl* **belles-familles**) *nf* in-laws ▪ **belle-fille** (*pl* **belles-filles**) *nf (épouse du fils)* daughter-in-law; *(après remariage)* stepdaughter ▪ **belle-mère** (*pl* **belles-mères**) *nf (mère du conjoint)* mother-in-law; *(après remariage)* stepmother ▪ **belle-sœur** (*pl* **belles-sœurs**) *nf* sister-in-law

**belvédère** [belvedɛr] *nm (construction)* gazebo; *(sur site naturel)* viewpoint

**bémol** [bemɔl] *nm Mus* flat

**bénédiction** [benediksjɔ̃] *nf Rel & Fig* blessing

**bénéfice** [benefis] *nm (financier)* profit; *(avantage)* benefit; **accorder le b. du doute à qn** to give sb the benefit of the doubt

**bénéficiaire** [benefisjɛr] **1** *nmf (de chèque)* payee; *Jur* beneficiary **2** *adj (entreprise)* profit-making; *(compte)* in credit

**bénéficier** [benefisje] *vi* **b. de qch** *(profiter de)* to benefit from sth; *(avoir)* to have sth

**bénéfique** [benefik] *adj* beneficial (**à** to)

**Bénélux** [benelyks] *nm* **le B.** the Benelux

**bénévolat** [benevɔla] *nm* voluntary work

**bénévole** [benevɔl] **1** *adj (travail, infirmière)* voluntary **2** *nmf* volunteer, voluntary worker

**bénin, -igne** [benɛ̃, -iɲ] *adj (accident, opération)* minor; *(tumeur)* benign

**bénir** [benir] *vt* to bless; **que Dieu te bénisse!** God bless you! ▪ **bénit, -e** *adj* **eau bénite** holy water

**benne** [bɛn] *nf (de camion)* tipping body; *(de téléphérique)* cable car; **b. à ordures** bin lorry

**BEP** [beəpe] (*abrév* **brevet d'études professionnelles**) *nm Scol* = vocational diploma taken at 18

**BEPC** [beəpese] (*abrév* **brevet d'études du premier cycle**) *nm Scol* = former school leaving certificate taken at 15

**béquille** [bekij] *nf (canne)* crutch; *(de moto)* stand

**berceau, -x** [bɛrso] *nm (de bébé)* cradle; *Fig (de civilisation)* birthplace

**bercer** [bɛrse] **1** *vt (bébé)* to rock **2 se bercer** *vpr* **se b. d'illusions** to delude oneself ▪ **berceuse** *nf* lullaby

**béret** [berɛ] *nm* beret
**berge** [bɛrʒ] *nf (rive)* bank
**berger** [bɛrʒe] *nm* shepherd; **b. allemand** German shepherd, *Br* Alsatian ▪ **bergère** *nf* shepherdess
**berline** [bɛrlin] *nf (voiture) Br* (four-door) saloon, *Am* sedan
**berlingot** [bɛrlɛ̃go] *nm (bonbon) Br* boiled sweet, *Am* hard candy; *(de lait)* carton
**bermuda** [bɛrmyda] *nm* Bermuda shorts
**Bermudes** [bɛrmyd] *nfpl* **les B.** Bermuda
**berner** [bɛrne] *vt* to fool
**besogne** [bəzɔɲ] *nf* job, task; *Fig* **aller vite en b.** to jump the gun
**besoin** [bəzwɛ̃] *nm* need; **avoir b. de qn/qch** to need sb/sth; **avoir b. de faire qch** to need to do sth; **au b., si b. est** if necessary, if need be
**bestial, -e, -aux, -ales** [bestjal, -o] *adj* bestial ▪ **bestiaux** *nmpl* livestock
**bestiole** [bɛstjɔl] *nf (insecte) Br* creepy-crawly, *Am* creepy-crawler
**bétail** [betaj] *nm* livestock
**bête**[1] [bɛt] *adj* stupid, silly
**bête**[2] [bɛt] *nf* animal; *(insecte)* bug; **b. féroce** wild animal; **b. noire** *Br* pet hate, *Am* pet peeve ▪ **bêtement** *adv* stupidly; **tout b.** quite simply ▪ **bêtise** *nf (manque d'intelligence)* stupidity; *(action, parole)* stupid thing; **faire une b.** to do something stupid; **dire des bêtises** to talk nonsense
**béton** [betɔ̃] *nm (matériau)* concrete; **mur en b.** concrete wall
**bette** [bɛt] *nf* Swiss chard
**betterave** [betrav] *nf (plante) Br* beetroot, *Am* beet; **b. sucrière** sugar beet
**beur** [bœr] *nmf* = North African born in France of immigrant parents
**beurre** [bœr] *nm* butter ▪ **beurrer** *vt* to butter
**bévue** [bevy] *nf* slip-up
**biais** [bjɛ] *nm (de mur)* slant; *(moyen)* way; *(aspect)* angle; **regarder qn de b.** to look sideways at sb; **par le b. de** through
**biaiser** [bjeze] *vi (ruser)* to dodge the issue
**bibelot** [biblo] *nm* small ornament
**biberon** [bibrɔ̃] *nm* (feeding) bottle; **nourrir un bébé au b.** to bottle-feed a baby
**bible** [bibl] *nf* bible; **la B.** the Bible ▪ **biblique** *adj* biblical
**bibliographie** [biblijɔgrafi] *nf* bibliography
**bibliothèque** [biblijɔtɛk] *nf (bâtiment, salle)* library; *(meuble)* bookcase; **b. municipale** public library ▪ **bibliothécaire** *nmf* librarian
**Bic®** [bik] *nm* ballpoint, *Br* biro®
**bicarbonate** [bikarbɔnat] *nm Chim* bicarbonate; **b. de soude** bicarbonate of soda
**biceps** [biseps] *nm* biceps
**biche** [biʃ] *nf (animal)* doe, hind
**bicolore** [bikɔlɔr] *adj* two-coloured
**bicyclette** [bisiklɛt] *nf* bicycle; **faire de la b.** to go cycling
**bidet** [bidɛ] *nm (cuvette)* bidet
**bidon** [bidɔ̃] **1** *nm (d'essence, d'huile)* can; *(de lait)* churn; **b. d'essence** petrol can, jerry can **2** *adj inv Fam (simulé)* phoney, fake
**bidonville** [bidɔ̃vil] *nf* shantytown
**bidule** [bidyl] *nm Fam (chose)* whatsit; **B.** *(personne)* what's-his-name, *f* what's-her-name

**BIEN** [bjɛ̃] **1** *adv* (**a**) *(convenablement)* well; **il joue b.** he plays well; **je vais b.** I'm fine *or* well; **écoutez-moi b.!** listen carefully
(**b**) *(moralement)* right; **b. se conduire** to behave (well); **vous avez b. fait** you did the right thing; **tu ferais b. de te méfier** you would be wise to behave
(**c**) *(très)* very
(**d**) *(beaucoup)* a lot, a great deal; **b. plus/moins** much more/less; **b. des gens** a lot of people; **b. des fois** many times; **tu as b. de la chance** you're really lucky!; **merci b.!** thanks very much!
(**e**) *(en intensif)* **regarder qn b. en**

**face** to look sb right in the face; **je sais b.** I'm well aware of it; **je vous l'avais b. dit** I told you so!; **nous verrons b.!** we'll see!; **c'est b. fait pour lui** it serves him right; **c'est b. ce que je pensais** that's what I thought

(**f**) *(locutions)* **b. que...** *(+ subjunctive)* although, though; **b. entendu, b. sûr** of course; **b. sûr que non!** of course, not!; **b. sûr que je viendrai!** of course, I'll come!

**2** *adj inv (satisfaisant)* good; *(à l'aise)* comfortable; *(en forme)* well; *(moral)* decent; *(beau)* attractive; **être b. avec qn** *(en bons termes)* to be on good terms with sb; **on est b. ici** it's nice here; **ce n'est pas b. de mentir** it's not nice to lie; **elle est b. sur cette photo** she looks good on this photo

**3** *exclam* fine!, right!; **eh b.!** well!

**4** *nm Phil & Rel* good; *(chose, capital)* possession; *Jur* asset; **le b. et le mal** good and evil; *Jur* **biens** property; **faire le b.** to do good; **ça te fera du b.** it will do you good; **dire du b. de qn** to speak well of sb; **c'est pour ton b.** it's for your own good; **biens de consommation** consumer goods; **biens immobiliers** real estate *or* property ▪ **bien-aimé, -e** (*mpl* **bien-aimés,** *fpl* **bien-aimées**) *adj & nmf* beloved ▪ **bien-être** *nm* well-being

---

**bienfaisance** [bjɛ̃fəzɑ̃s] *nf* **œuvre de b.** charity

**bienfaisant, -e** [bjɛ̃fəzɑ̃, -ɑ̃t] *adj (remède)* beneficial; *(personne)* charitable

**bienfait** [bjɛ̃fɛ] *nm (acte)* kindness; *(avantage)* benefit

**bienfaiteur, -trice** [bjɛ̃fɛtœr, -tris] *nmf* benefactor, *f* benefactress

**bien-fondé** [bjɛ̃fɔ̃de] *nm* validity

**bienheureux, -euse** [bjɛ̃nœrø, -øz] *adj* blissful; *Rel* blessed

**bienséance** [bjɛ̃seɑ̃s] *nf* propriety

**bientôt** [bjɛ̃to] *adv* soon; **à b.!** see you soon!

**bienveillant, -e** [bjɛ̃vɛjɑ̃, -ɑ̃t] *adj* kind ▪ **bienveillance** *nf* kindness

**bienvenu, -e[1]** [bjɛ̃vny] **1** *adj (repos, explication)* welcome **2** *nmf* **soyez le b.!** welcome!

**bienvenue[2]** [bjɛ̃vny] *nf* welcome; **souhaiter la b. à qn** to welcome sb

**bière[1]** [bjɛr] *nf (boisson)* beer; **b. blonde** lager; **b. brune** *Br* brown ale, *Am* dark beer; **b. pression** *Br* draught beer, *Am* draft beer

**bière[2]** [bjɛr] *nf (cercueil)* coffin

**biffer** [bife] *vt* to cross out

**bifteck** [biftɛk] *nm* steak; **b. haché** *Br* mince, *Am* mincemeat

**bifurquer** [bifyrke] *vi (route, chemin)* to fork; *(automobiliste)* to turn off ▪ **bifurcation** *nf* fork

**bigamie** [bigami] *nf* bigamy

**bigarré, -e** [bigare] *adj (étoffe)* multicoloured; *(foule)* motley

**bigorneau, -x** [bigɔrno] *nm* winkle

**bigoudi** [bigudi] *nm* (hair) curler *or* roller

**bijou, -x** [biʒu] *nm* jewel; *Fig* gem ▪ **bijouterie** *nf (boutique) Br* jeweller's shop, *Am* jewelry shop; *(commerce, fabrication)* jeweller's trade ▪ **bijoutier, -ère** *nmf Br* jeweller, *Am* jeweler

**bilan** [bilɑ̃] *nm (de situation)* assessment; *(résultats)* results; *(d'un accident)* toll; *Com* **déposer son b.** to file for bankruptcy; *Fin* **b. (comptable)** balance sheet

**bilatéral, -e, -aux, -ales** [bilateral, -o] *adj* bilateral

**bile** [bil] *nf* bile

**bilingue** [bilɛ̃g] *adj* bilingual

**billard** [bijar] *nm (jeu)* billiards; *(table)* billiard table; **b. américain** pool; **b. électrique** pinball

**bille** [bij] *nf (de verre)* marble; *(de billard)* billiard ball

**billet** [bijɛ] *nm* ticket; **b. (de banque)** *Br* (bank)note, *Am* bill; **b. d'avion/de train** plane/train ticket; **b. de première/seconde** first-class/second-class ticket; **b. simple** single ticket, *Am* one-way ticket; **b. aller retour** return ticket, *Am* round trip ticket

**billetterie** [bijɛtri] *nf (lieu)* ticket

office; **b. automatique** *(de billet de transport)* ticket machine
**billion** [biljɔ̃] *nm* trillion
**bimensuel, -elle** [bimɑ̃sɥɛl] *adj* bimonthly, *Br* fortnightly
**bimoteur** [bimɔtœr] *adj* twin-engined
**binaire** [binɛr] *adj Math* binary
**biner** [bine] *vt* to hoe
**binocle** [binɔkl] *nm* pince-nez
**biochimie** [bjɔʃimi] *nf* biochemistry
**biodégradable** [bjɔdegradabl] *adj* biodegradable
**biodiversité** [bjodivɛrsite] *nf* biodiversity
**biographie** [bjɔgrafi] *nf* biography ▪ **biographique** *adj* biographical
**bio-industrie** [bjoɛ̃dystri] *(pl* **bio-industries**) *nf* biotechnology industry
**biologie** [bjɔlɔʒi] *nf* biology ▪ **biologique** *adj* biological; *(sans engrais chimiques)* organic ▪ **biologiste** *nmf* biologist
**biotechnologie** [bjotɛknoloʒi] *nf* biotechnology
**bip** [bip] *nm (son)* beep; *(appareil)* beeper
**bipède** [bipɛd] *nm* biped
**Birmanie** [birmani] *nf* **la B.** Burma ▪ **birman, -e 1** *adj* Burmese **2** *nmf* **B., Birmane** Burmese
**bis¹** [bis] *adv (au théâtre)* encore; *(en musique)* repeat; **4 bis** *(adresse)* ≃ 4A
**bis², bise¹** [bi, biz] *adj Br* greyish-brown, *Am* grayish-brown
**biscornu, -e** [biskɔrny] *adj (objet)* oddly shaped; *Fam (idée)* cranky
**biscotte** [biskɔt] *nf* rusk
**biscuit** [biskɥi] *nm Br* biscuit, *Am* cookie
**bise²** [biz] *nf (vent)* north wind
**bise³** [biz] *nf Fam (baiser)* kiss; **faire la b. à qn** to kiss sb on both cheeks
**bisexuel, -elle** [bisɛksɥɛl] *adj* bisexual
**bison** [bizɔ̃] *nm* bison
**bisou** [bizu] *nm Fam* kiss
**bissextile** [bisɛkstil] *adj f* **année b.** leap year
**bistro(t)** [bistro] *nm Fam* bar
**bitume** [bitym] *nm (revêtement)* asphalt
**bizarre** [bizar] *adj* odd
**blafard, -e** [blafar, -ard] *adj* pallid
**blague** [blag] *nf (plaisanterie)* joke; **faire une b. à qn** to play a joke on sb
**blaguer** [blage] *vi Fam* to joke ▪ **blagueur, -euse** *nmf Fam* joker
**blaireau, -x** [blɛro] *nm (animal)* badger; *(brosse)* shaving brush
**blâme** [blɑm] *nm (reproche)* blame; *(sanction)* reprimand ▪ **blâmer** *vt (désapprouver)* to blame; *(sanctionner)* to reprimand
**blanc, blanche** [blɑ̃, blɑ̃ʃ] **1** *adj* white; *(peau)* pale; *(page)* blank
**2** *nm (couleur)* white; *(espace)* blank; *(vin)* white wine; **(article de) b.** *(linge)* linen; **en b.** *(chèque)* blank; **tirer à b.** to fire blanks; **b. d'œuf** egg white; **b. de poulet** chicken breast
**3** *nf (note de musique) Br* minim, *Am* half-note
**4** *nmf* **B.** *(personne)* White man, *f* White woman; **les B.** the Whites ▪ **blanchâtre** *adj* whitish ▪ **blancheur** *nf* whiteness
**blanchiment** [blɑ̃ʃimɑ̃] *nm (d'argent)* laundering
**blanchir** [blɑ̃ʃir] **1** *vt* to whiten; *(mur)* to whitewash; *(linge)* to launder; *Culin* to blanch; *Fig (argent)* to launder; **b. qn** *(disculper)* to clear sb **2** *vi* to turn white ▪ **blanchisserie** *nf (lieu)* laundry ▪ **blanchisseur, -euse** *nmf* laundryman, *f* laundrywoman
**blanquette** [blɑ̃kɛt] *nf* **b. de veau** = blanquette of veal; **b. de Limoux** = sparkling white wine from Limoux
**blasé, -e** [blɑze] *adj* blasé
**blason** [blazɔ̃] *nm* coat of arms
**blasphème** [blasfɛm] *nm* blasphemy ▪ **blasphémer** *vi* to blaspheme
**blatte** [blat] *nf* cockroach
**blazer** [blazœr] *nm* blazer
**bld** *(abrév* **boulevard**) Blvd
**blé** [ble] *nm* wheat, *Br* corn
**blême** [blɛm] *adj* sickly pale; **b. de colère** livid ▪ **blêmir** *vi* to turn pale

**blesser** [blese] **1** *vt (dans un accident)* to injure, to hurt; *(par arme)* to wound; *(offenser)* to hurt

**2 se blesser** *vpr (par accident)* to hurt *or* injure oneself; *(avec une arme)* to wound oneself; **se b. au bras** to hurt one's arm ▪ **blessant, -e** *adj* hurtful ▪ **blessé, -e** *nmf (victime d'accident)* injured person; *(victime d'aggression)* wounded person; **les blessés** the injured/wounded ▪ **blessure** *nf (dans un accident)* injury; *(par arme)* wound

**blette** [blɛt] *nf* = **bette**

**bleu, -e** [blø] *(mpl* **-s**) **1** *adj* blue; *(steak)* very rare **2** *n (couleur)* blue; *(ecchymose)* bruise; *(fromage)* blue cheese; *Fam (novice)* novice; **b. de travail** *Br* overalls, *Am* overall; **b. ciel** sky blue; **b. marine** navy blue; **b. roi** royal blue

**bleuet** [bløɛ] *nm (plante)* cornflower

**blinder** [blɛ̃de] *vt (véhicule)* to armour-plate ▪ **blindé, -e 1** *adj Mil* armoured, armour-plated; *(voiture)* bulletproof **2** *nm Mil* armoured vehicle

**bloc** [blɔk] *nm (de pierre, de bois)* block; *(de papier)* pad; *(de maison) & Pol* bloc; **en b.** *(démissionner)* all together; **à b.** *(visser, serrer)* as tightly as possible; **b. opératoire** operating theatre ▪ **bloc-notes** *(pl* **blocs-notes**) *nm* notepad

**blocage** [blɔkaʒ] *nm (de mécanisme)* jamming; *(de freins, de roues)* locking

**blocus** [blɔkys] *nm* blockade; **lever le b.** to raise the blockade

**blond, -e** [blɔ̃, -ɔ̃d] **1** *adj (cheveux, personne)* blond; *(sable)* golden **2** *nm (homme)* fair-haired *or* blond man; *(couleur)* blond; **b. cendré** ash blond; **b. vénitien** strawberry blond **3** *nf (femme)* fair-haired woman, blonde ▪ **blondeur** *nf* fairness, blondness

**bloquer** [blɔke] **1** *vt (route, ballon, compte)* to block; *(porte, mécanisme)* to jam; *(roue)* to lock; *(salaires, prix, crédits)* to freeze; *(grouper)* to group together; **b. le passage à qn** to block sb's way; **bloqué par la neige** snowbound

**2 se bloquer** *vpr (machine)* to get stuck

**blottir** [blɔtir] **se blottir** *vpr* to snuggle up; **se b. contre qn** to snuggle up to sb

**blouse** [bluz] *nf (tablier)* overall; *(corsage)* blouse; **b. blanche** *(de médecin, de biologiste)* white coat ▪ **blouson** *nm* short jacket; **b. en cuir** leather jacket; **b. d'aviateur** bomber jacket

**bluff** [blœf] *nm* bluff ▪ **bluffer** *vi (aux cartes) & Fam* to bluff

**boa** [bɔa] *nm (serpent, tour de cou)* boa

**bobard** [bɔbar] *nm Fam* tall story

**bobine** [bɔbin] *nf (de ruban, de fil)* reel; *(de machine à coudre)* bobbin; *(de film, de papier)* roll; *(de machine à écrire)* spool; *Él* coil

**bocal, -aux** [bɔkal, -o] *nm* jar; *(aquarium)* bowl

**bœuf** [bœf] *(pl* **bœufs** [bø]) *nm (animal)* bullock; *(de trait)* ox *(pl* oxen); *(viande)* beef

**bogue** [bɔg] *nm Ordinat* bug

**bohème** [bɔɛm] *adj & nmf* bohemian ▪ **bohémien, -enne** *adj & nmf* gypsy

**boire*** [bwar] **1** *vt (sujet: personne)* to drink; *(sujet: plante)* to soak up

**2** *vi (sujet: personne)* to drink; *(sujet: plante)* to soak in; *Fam* **b. un coup** to have a drink

**3 se boire** *vpr* to be drunk

**4** *nm* **le b. et le manger** food and drink

**bois** [bwa] *nm (matériau, forêt)* wood; *(de raquette)* frame; **en** *ou* **de b.** wooden; **les b.** *(d'un cerf)* the antlers; *(d'un orchestre)* woodwind instruments; **b. de chauffage** firewood; **b. de construction** timber ▪ **boisé, -e** *adj* wooded ▪ **boiseries** *nfpl Br* panelling, *Am* paneling

**boisson** [bwasɔ̃] *nf* drink

**boit** [bwa] *voir* **boire**

**boîte** [bwat] *nf* (**a**) *(récipient)* box; **b. d'allumettes** *(pleine)* box of matches; *(vide)* matchbox; **des haricots en b.** canned *or Br* tinned beans; **b. à bijoux** jewel box; **b. à gants** glove compartment; **b. à** *ou* **aux lettres** *Br* postbox, *Am* mailbox; **b. de conserve** can, *Br* tin; *Aut* **b. de vitesses** gearbox; **b. postale** Post Office Box; **b. vocale** voice mail (**b**) *Fam (entreprise)* firm; **b. de nuit** nightclub ■ **boîtier** *nm (de montre)* case

**boiter** [bwate] *vi* to limp ■ **boiteux, -euse** *adj (personne)* lame; *Fig (raisonnement)* shaky

**boive** [bwav] *subjonctif de* **boire**

**bol** [bɔl] *nm (récipient, contenu)* bowl

**bolide** [bɔlid] *nm (voiture)* racing car

**Bolivie** [bɔlivi] *nf* **la B.** Bolivia ■ **bolivien, -enne 1** *adj* Bolivian **2** *nmf* **B., Bolivienne** Bolivian

**bombardement** [bɔ̃bardəmɑ̃] *nm (avec des bombes)* bombing; *(avec des obus)* shelling

**bombarder** [bɔ̃barde] *vt (avec des bombes)* to bomb; *(avec des obus)* to shell; **b. qn de questions** to bombard sb with questions ■ **bombardier** *nm (avion)* bomber

**bombe** [bɔ̃b] *nf* (**a**) *(explosif)* bomb; *Fig* **faire l'effet d'une b.** to be a bombshell (**b**) *(atomiseur)* spray (can) (**c**) *(chapeau)* riding hat

**bomber** [bɔ̃be] **1** *vt* **b. le torse** to throw out one's chest **2** *vi (mur)* to bulge; *(planche)* to warp

**BON[1], BONNE[1]** [bɔ̃, bɔn] **1** *adj* (**a**) *(satisfaisant)* good; **c'est b.** *(d'accord)* that's fine

(**b**) *(agréable)* nice, good; **passer une bonne soirée** to spend a pleasant evening; **b. anniversaire!** happy birthday!; **bonne année!** Happy New Year!

(**c**) *(charitable)* kind, good (**avec qn** to sb)

(**d**) *(correct)* right

(**e**) *(apte)* fit; **b. à manger** fit to eat; **elle n'est bonne à rien** she's useless

(**f**) *(prudent)* wise, good; **juger b. de partir** to think it wise to leave

(**g**) *(compétent)* good; **b. en français** good at French

(**h**) *(profitable) (investissement, conseil, idée)* good; **c'est b. à savoir** it's worth knowing

(**i**) *(valable)* valid

(**j**) *(en intensif)* **un b. rhume** a bad cold; **dix bonnes minutes** a good ten minutes; **j'ai mis un b. moment à comprendre** it took me a while to understand

(**k**) *(locutions)* **à quoi b.?** what's the point?; **quand b. vous semble** whenever you like; **pour de b.** *(partir, revenir)* for good; **tenir b.** *(personne)* to hold out; **elle est bien bonne!** that's a good one!

**2** *nm* **avoir du b.** to have some good points; **un b. à rien** a good-for-nothing; **les bons et les méchants** the goodies and the baddies

**3** *adv* **sentir b.** to smell good; **il fait b.** it's nice and warm

**4** *exclam* **b.! on y va?** right, shall we go?; **ah b., je ne le savais pas** really? I didn't know; **ah b.?** is that so?

**bon[2]** [bɔ̃] *nm (papier)* coupon, *Br* voucher; *Fin (titre)* bond; **b. d'achat** gift voucher; **b. de réduction** money-off coupon

**bonbon** [bɔ̃bɔ̃] *nm Br* sweet, *Am* candy

**bonbonne** [bɔ̃bɔn] *nf (bouteille)* demijohn; *(de gaz)* cylinder

**bond** [bɔ̃] *nm* leap, jump; *(de balle)* bounce; **faire un b.** to leap up; **se lever d'un b.** *(du lit)* to jump out of bed; *(d'une chaise)* to leap up; **faire faux b. à qn** to leave sb in the lurch

**bonde** [bɔ̃d] *nf (bouchon)* plug; *(trou)* plughole

**bondé, -e** [bɔ̃de] *adj* packed, crammed

**bondir** [bɔ̃dir] *vi* to leap, to jump; **b. sur qn/qch** to pounce on sb/sth

**bonheur** [bɔnœr] *nm (bien-être)* happiness; *(chance)* good fortune; **porter b. à qn** to bring sb luck; **par b.** luckily

**bonhomie** [bɔnɔmi] *nf* good-naturedness

**bonhomme** [bɔnɔm] (*pl* **bonshommes** [bɔ̃zɔm]) *nm* fellow, guy; **b. de neige** snowman

**bonjour** [bɔ̃ʒur] *nm & exclam (le matin)* hello, good morning; *(l'après-midi)* hello, good afternoon

**bonne**[1] [bɔn] *voir* **bon**[1]

**bonne**[2] [bɔn] *nf (domestique)* maid; **b. d'enfants** nanny

**bonnement** [bɔnmɑ̃] *adv* **tout b.** simply

**bonnet** [bɔnɛ] *nm (coiffure)* hat; *(de soutien-gorge)* cup; *Fam* **gros b.** bigshot; **b. de bain** bathing cap ▪ **bonneterie** *nf (bas)* hosiery

**bonniche** [bɔniʃ] *nf* = **boniche**

**bonsoir** [bɔ̃swar] *nm & exclam (en rencontrant quelqu'un)* hello, good evening; *(en partant)* goodbye; *(au coucher)* goodnight

**bonté** [bɔ̃te] *nf* kindness, goodness

**bonus** [bɔnys] *nm (de salaire)* bonus; *(d'assurance)* no-claims bonus

**bord** [bɔr] *nm (limite)* edge; *(de chapeau)* brim; *(de verre)* rim; **le b. du trottoir** *Br* the kerb, *Am* the curb; **au b. de la route** at the side of the road; **au b. de la rivière** beside the river; **au b. de la mer** at the seaside; **au b. des larmes** on the verge of tears; **à b. d'un bateau/d'un avion** on board a boat/a plane; **monter à b.** to go on board; **par-dessus b.** overboard

**bordeaux** [bɔrdo] **1** *nm (vin)* Bordeaux (wine); *(rouge)* claret **2** *adj inv* burgundy

**bordée** [bɔrde] *nf Naut (salve)* broadside; *Fig (d'injures)* torrent

**border** [bɔrde] *vt (lit)* to tuck in; *(sujet: arbres)* to line

**bordereau, -x** [bɔrdəro] *nm Fin & Com* note

**bordure** [bɔrdyr] *nf (bord)* edge; *(de vêtement)* border; **en b. de route** by the roadside

**borgne** [bɔrɲ] *adj (personne)* one-eyed

**borne** [bɔrn] *nf (limite)* boundary marker; *(pierre)* boundary stone; *Él* terminal; *Fam (kilomètre)* kilometer; *Fig* **sans bornes** boundless; *Fig* **dépasser les bornes** to go too far

**borné, -e** [bɔrne] *adj (personne)* narrow-minded; *(esprit)* narrow

**borner** [bɔrne] **1** *vt (terrrain)* to mark out **2 se borner** *vpr* **se b. à qch/à faire qch** *(personne)* to restrict oneself to sth/to doing sth; **se b. à qch** *(chose)* to be limited to sth

**Bosnie** [bɔzni] *nf* **la B.** Bosnia

**bosquet** [bɔskɛ] *nm* grove

**bosse** [bɔs] *nf (de bossu, de chameau)* hump; *(enflure)* bump, lump; *(de terrain)* bump

**bosseler** [bɔsle] *vt (déformer)* to dent

**bosser** [bɔse] *vi Fam* to work

**bosseur, -euse** [bɔsœr, -øz] *nmf Fam* hard-worker

**bossu, -e** [bɔsy] **1** *adj (personne)* hunchbacked **2** *nmf* hunchback

**botanique** [bɔtanik] **1** *adj* botanical **2** *nf* botany

**botte** [bɔt] *nf (chaussure)* boot; *(de fleurs, de radis)* bunch; **bottes en caoutchouc** rubber boots ▪ **botter** *vt* **botté de cuir** wearing leather boots; *Fam* **b. le derrière à qn** to boot sb up the backside ▪ **bottillon** *nm*, **bottine** *nf* ankle boot

**Bottin**® [bɔtɛ̃] *nm* phone book

**bouc** [buk] *nm (animal)* billy goat; *(barbe)* goatee; **b. émissaire** scapegoat

**boucan** [bukɑ̃] *nm Fam* din, row; **faire du b.** to kick up a row

**bouche** [buʃ] *nf* mouth; **de b. à oreille** by word of mouth; **b. d'égout** manhole; **b. d'incendie** *Br* fire hydrant, *Am* fireplug ▪ **bouchée** *nf* mouthful ▪ **bouche-à-bouche** *nm* mouth-to-mouth resuscitation

**boucher**[1] [buʃe] **1** *vt (fente, trou)* to fill in; *(conduite, fenêtre)* to block up; *(vue, rue, artère)* to block; *(bouteille)* to cork **2 se boucher** *vpr (conduite)* to get blocked up; **se b. le nez** to hold one's nose ▪ **bouché, -e** *adj (conduite)* blocked; *Fam (personne)* dense; **j'ai le nez b.** my nose is stuffed up ▪ **bouche-trou** (*pl* **bouche-trous**) *nm Fam* stopgap

**boucher²,** **-ère** [buʃe, -ɛr] *nmf* butcher ▪ **boucherie** *nf* butcher's (shop); *Fig (carnage)* butchery

**bouchon** [buʃɔ̃] *nm* (**a**) *(à vis)* cap, top; *(de tonneau)* stopper; *(de liège)* cork; *(de canne à pêche)* float (**b**) *(embouteillage)* traffic jam ▪ **bouchonner** *vt Fam* **ça bouchonne** *(sur la route)* there's congestion

**boucle** [bukl] *nf (de ceinture)* buckle; *(de cheveu)* curl; *(méandre)* loop; **b. d'oreille** earring

**boucler** [bukle] **1** *vt (ceinture, valise)* to buckle; *(quartier)* to seal off; **b. ses valises** *(se préparer à partir)* to pack one's bags **2** *vi (cheveux)* to be curly ▪ **bouclé, -e** *adj (cheveux)* curly

**bouclier** [buklije] *nm* shield

**bouddhiste** [budist] *adj & nmf* Buddhist

**bouder** [bude] **1** *vi* to sulk **2** *vt (personne)* to refuse to talk to; **b. une élection** to refuse to vote ▪ **boudeur, -euse** *adj* sulky

**boudin** [budɛ̃] *nm* **b. noir** *Br* black pudding, *Am* blood sausage; **b. blanc** white pudding

**boue** [bu] *nf* mud ▪ **boueux, -euse** *adj* muddy

**bouée** [bwe] *nf Naut* buoy; **b. de sauvetage** lifebelt; **b. (gonflable)** *(d'enfant)* (inflatable) rubber ring

**bouffe** [buf] *nf Fam (nourriture)* grub

**bouffée** [bufe] *nf (de fumée)* puff; *(de parfum)* whiff; *Fig (de colère)* outburst; *Méd* **b. de chaleur** *Br* hot flush, *Am* hot flash

**bouffer¹** [bufe] *vti Fam (manger)* to eat

**bouffer²** [bufe] *vi (manche, jupe)* to puff out ▪ **bouffi, -e** *adj (yeux, visage)* puffy

**bouffon, -onne** [bufɔ̃, -ɔn] **1** *adj* farcical **2** *nm* buffoon ▪ **bouffonneries** *nfpl (actes)* antics

**bougeoir** [buʒwar] *nm* candlestick

**bougeotte** [buʒɔt] *nf Fam* **avoir la b.** to be fidgety

**bouger** [buʒe] **1** *vti* to move; **rester sans b.** to keep still **2 se bouger** *vpr Fam (se déplacer)* to move; *(s'activer)* to get a move on

**bougie** [buʒi] *nf (en cire)* candle; *(de moteur)* spark plug

**bougonner** [bugɔne] *vi Fam* to grumble

**bouillabaisse** [bujabɛs] *nf* bouillabaisse, = Provençal fish soup

**bouilli, -e¹** [buji] *adj* boiled

**bouillie²** [buji] *nf (pour bébé)* baby food; *(à base de céréales)* baby cereal

**bouillir*** [bujir] *vi* to boil; **faire b. qch** to boil sth; **b. de colère** to be seething (with anger) ▪ **bouillant, -e** *adj (qui bout)* boiling; *(très chaud)* boiling hot

**bouilloire** [bujwar] *nf* kettle

**bouillon** [bujɔ̃] *nm (aliment)* stock; *(bulles)* bubbles ▪ **bouillonner** *vi* to bubble

**bouillotte** [bujɔt] *nf* hot-water bottle

**boulanger, -ère** [bulɑ̃ʒe, -ɛr] *nmf* baker ▪ **boulangerie** *nf* baker's (shop)

**boule** [bul] *nf (sphère)* ball; **boules** *(jeu)* bowls; **b. de neige** snowball; *Fig* **faire b. de neige** to snowball; **boules Quiès®** earplugs

**bouledogue** [buldɔg] *nm* bulldog

**boulet** [bulɛ] *nm (de forçat)* ball and chain; **b. de canon** cannonball

**boulette** [bulɛt] *nf (de papier)* ball; *(de viande)* meatball

**boulevard** [bulvar] *nm* boulevard

**bouleverser** [bulvɛrse] *vt (émouvoir)* to move deeply; *(perturber)* to distress; *(projets, habitudes)* to disrupt; *(vie)* to turn upside down ▪ **bouleversant, -e** *adj (émouvant)* deeply moving, *(perturbant)* distressing

**boulimie** [bulimi] *nf Méd* bulimia ▪ **boulimique** *adj* **être b.** to have bulimia

**boulon** [bulɔ̃] *nm* bolt

**boulot¹** [bulo] *nm Fam (emploi)* job; *(travail)* work

**boulot², -otte** [bulo, -ɔt] *adj Fam* tubby

**bouquet** [bukɛ] *nm (fleurs)* bunch of flowers; *(d'arbres)* clump; *(de vin)* bouquet; *Fig* **c'est le b.!** that takes the *Br* biscuit *or Am* cake!

**bouquin** [bukɛ̃] *nm Fam* book ■ **bouquiner** *vti Fam* to read ■ **bouquiniste** *nmf* second-hand bookseller

**bourbier** [burbje] *nm (lieu, situation)* quagmire

**bourde** [burd] *nf Fam (gaffe)* blunder; **faire une b.** to put one's foot in it

**bourdon** [burdɔ̃] *nm (insecte)* bumblebee ■ **bourdonnement** *nm (d'insecte)* buzz(ing) ■ **bourdonner** *vi (insecte, oreilles)* to buzz

**bourg** [bur] *nm* market town ■ **bourgade** *nf* village

**bourgeois, -e** [burʒwa, -waz] **1** *adj* middle-class **2** *nmf* middle-class person ■ **bourgeoisie** *nf* middle class

**bourgeon** [burʒɔ̃] *nm* bud ■ **bourgeonner** *vi* to bud

**bourgogne** [burgɔɲ] *nm (vin)* Burgundy

**bourrage** [buraʒ] *nm Fam* **b. de crâne** brainwashing

**bourrasque** [burask] *nf* squall, gust of wind

**bourratif, -ive** [buratif, -iv] *adj Fam* stodgy

**bourre** [bur] *nf (pour rembourrer)* stuffing

**bourreau, -x** [buro] *nm* executioner; **b. de travail** workaholic

**bourrelet** [burlɛ] *nm (contre les courants d'air)* weather strip; **b. de graisse** spare *Br* tyre *or Am* tire

**bourrer** [bure] **1** *vt (coussin)* to stuff (**de** with); *(sac)* to cram (**de** with); *(pipe)* to fill; **b. qn de qch** *(gaver)* to fill sb up with sth **2 se bourrer** *vpr* **se b. de qch** *(se gaver)* to stuff oneself up with ■ **bourré, -e** *adj* (**a**) *(plein)* **b. à craquer** full to bursting (**b**) *Fam (ivre)* plastered

**bourrique** [burik] *nf* she-ass; *Fam* **faire tourner qn en b.** to drive sb crazy

**bourru, -e** [bury] *adj* surly

**bourse** [burs] *nf (sac)* purse; *Scol & Univ* **b. (d'étude)** grant; **la B.** the Stock Exchange ■ **boursier, -ère 1** *adj* **opération boursière** Stock Exchange transaction **2** *nmf (élève, étudiant)* grant holder

**boursouflé, -e** [bursufle] *adj (visage, yeux)* puffy

**bous** [bu] *voir* **bouillir**

**bousculer** [buskyle] **1** *vt (pousser)* to jostle; *(presser)* to rush; *Fig (habitudes)* to disrupt **2 se bousculer** *(foule)* to push and shove ■ **bousculade** *nf (agitation)* pushing and shoving

**bousiller** [buzije] *vt Fam* to wreck

**boussole** [busɔl] *nf* compass

**bout**[1] [bu] *voir* **bouillir**

**bout**[2] [bu] *nm (extrémité)* end; *(de langue, de doigt)* tip; *(morceau)* bit; **faire un b. de chemin** to go part of the way; **d'un b. à l'autre** from one end to the other; **au b. de la rue** at the end of the street; **au b. d'un moment** after a while; *Fam* **au b. du fil** *(au téléphone)* on the other end; **jusqu'au b.** *(lire, rester)* (right) to the end; **à b. de forces** exhausted; **à b. de souffle** out of breath; **pousser qn à b.** to push sb too far

**boutade** [butad] *nf (plaisanterie)* quip

**boute-en-train** [butɑ̃trɛ̃] *nm inv (personne)* live wire

**bouteille** [butɛj] *nf* bottle; *(de gaz)* cylinder

**boutique** [butik] *nf Br* shop, *Am* store; *(de couturier)* boutique; **fermer b.** to shut up shop ■ **boutiquier, -ère** *nmf Br* shopkeeper, *Am* storekeeper

**bouton** [butɔ̃] *nm (bourgeon)* bud; *(au visage)* spot; *(de vêtement)* button; *(de porte, de télévision)* knob; **b. de manchette** cufflink ■ **bouton-d'or** (*pl* **boutons-d'or**) *nm* buttercup ■ **boutonner** *vt*, **se boutonner** *vpr (vêtement)* to button (up) ■ **boutonnière** *nf* buttonhole

**bouture** [butyr] *nf* cutting

**bovins** [bɔvɛ̃] *nmpl* cattle

**bowling** [boliŋ] *nm (jeu) Br* tenpin bowling, *Am* tenpins; *(lieu)* bowling alley

**box** [bɔks] (*pl* **boxes**) *nm (d'écurie)* stall;

*(de dortoir)* cubicle; *(garage)* lock-up garage; *Jur* **b. des accusés** dock

**boxe** [bɔks] *nf* boxing ▪ **boxer** *vi* to box ▪ **boxeur** *nm* boxer

**boyau, -x** [bwajo] *nm (intestin)* gut; *(corde)* catgut; *(de vélo)* tubular *Br* tyre or *Am* tire; *(de mine)* narrow gallery

**boycotter** [bɔjkɔte] *vt* to boycott ▪ **boycottage** *nm* boycott

**BP** [bepe] *(abrév* **boîte postale**) *nf* PO Box

**bracelet** [braslɛ] *nm (bijou)* bracelet; *(rigide)* bangle; *(de montre) Br* strap, *Am* band ▪ **bracelet-montre** (*pl* **bracelets-montres**) *nm* wristwatch

**braconner** [brakɔne] *vi* to poach ▪ **braconnier** *nm* poacher

**brader** [brade] *vt* to sell off cheaply ▪ **braderie** *nf* clearance sale

**braguette** [bragɛt] *nf (de pantalon)* fly, *Br* flies

**braille** [brɑj] *nm* Braille; **en b.** in Braille

**brailler** [brɑje] *vti* to yell

**braire*** [brɛr] *vi (âne)* to bray

**braises** [brɛz] *nfpl* embers ▪ **braiser** *vt Culin* to braise

**brancard** [brɑ̃kar] *nm (civière)* stretcher; *(de charrette)* shaft

**branche** [brɑ̃ʃ] *nf (d'arbre, de science)* branch; *(de lunettes)* side piece ▪ **branchages** *nmpl (des arbres)* branches; *(coupés)* cut branches

**brancher** [brɑ̃ʃe] **1** *vt (à une prise)* to plug in; *(à un réseau)* to connect **2 se brancher** *vpr* **se b. sur** *(station de radio)* to tune in to ▪ **branchement** *nm (fils)* connection

**brandir** [brɑ̃dir] *vt* to brandish

**branle** [brɑ̃l] *nm* **mettre qch en b.** *(mécanisme, procédure)* to set sth in motion ▪ **branlant, -e** *adj (chaise, escalier)* rickety ▪ **branler** *vi (chaise, escalier)* to be rickety

**braquer** [brake] **1** *vt (diriger)* to point (**sur** at); *(regard)* to fix (**sur** on); *Fam (banque)* to hold up; **b. qn contre qn/qch** to turn sb against sb/sth **2** *vi Aut* to turn the steering wheel

**braquet** [brakɛ] *nm* gear ratio

**bras** [bra] *nm* arm; **b. dessus b. dessous** arm in arm; **les b. croisés** with one's arms folded; *Fig* **b. droit** *(assistant)* right-hand man

**brasier** [brɑzje] *nm* blaze, inferno

**brassard** [brasar] *nm* armband

**brasse** [bras] *nf (nage)* breaststroke; *(mouvement)* stroke; **b. papillon** butterfly stroke

**brassée** [brase] *nf* armful

**brasser** [brase] *vt (mélanger)* to mix; *(bière)* to brew ▪ **brassage** *nm (mélange)* mixing; *(de la bière)* brewing

**brasserie** [brasri] *nf (usine)* brewery; *(café)* brasserie

**brassière** [brasjɛr] *nf (de bébé) Br* vest, *Am* undershirt

**bravade** [bravad] *nf* bravado

**brave** [brav] **1** *adj (courageux)* brave; *(bon)* good **2** *nm (héros)* brave man

**braver** [brave] *vt (personne)* to defy; *(danger)* to brave

**bravo** [bravo] *exclam* bravo!

**bravoure** [bravur] *nf* bravery

**break** [brek] *nm (voiture) Br* estate car, *Am* station wagon

**brebis** [brəbi] *nf* ewe; *Fig* **b. galeuse** black sheep

**brèche** [brɛʃ] *nf* gap; *(dans la coque d'un bateau)* hole

**bréchet** [breʃɛ] *nm* breastbone

**bredouille** [brəduj] *adj* empty-handed

**bredouiller** [brəduje] *vti* to mumble

**bref, brève** [bref, brɛv] **1** *adj* brief, short **2** *adv* in short; **enfin b....** in a word...

**Brésil** [brezil] *nm* **le B.** Brazil ▪ **brésilien, -enne 1** *adj* Brazilian **2** *nmf* **B., Brésilienne** Brazilian

**Bretagne** [brətaɲ] *nf* **la B.** Brittany ▪ **breton, -onne 1** *adj* Breton **2** *nmf* **B., Bretonne** Breton

**bretelle** [brətɛl] *nf* strap; **bretelles** *(de pantalon) Br* braces, *Am* suspenders; **b. (d'accès)** *(route)* access road

**breuvage** [brœvaʒ] *nm* potion

**brève** [brɛv] *voir* **bref**

**brevet** [brəvɛ] *nm (certificat)* certificate; *(diplôme)* diploma; *Scol* **b. des collèges** = exam taken at 14; **b. de technicien supérieur** = advanced vocational training certificate; **b. (d'invention)** patent ▪ **breveter** *vt* to patent

**bric-à-brac** [brikabrak] *nm inv (vieux objets)* odds and ends

**bricole** [brikɔl] *nf (objet, futilité)* trifle

**bricoler** [brikɔle] **1** *vt (construire)* to put together; *(réparer)* to fix **2** *vi* to do-it-yourself ▪ **bricolage** *nm (travail)* DIY, do-it-yourself; **faire du b.** to do some DIY ▪ **bricoleur, -euse 1** *adj* **être b.** to be good with one's hands **2** *nmf* handyman, *f* handywoman

**bride** [brid] *nf (de cheval)* bridle ▪ **brider** *vt (cheval)* to bridle; *(personne, désir)* to curb; **avoir les yeux bridés** to have slanting eyes

**bridge** [bridʒ] *nm (jeu, prothèse)* bridge

**brièvement** [briɛvmɑ̃] *adv* briefly ▪ **brièveté** *nf* brevity

**brigade** [brigad] *nf (de gendarmerie)* squad; *Mil* brigade ▪ **brigadier** *nm (de police)* police sergeant; *Mil* corporal

**brigand** [brigɑ̃] *nm (bandit)* brigand

**briguer** [brige] *vt (honneur, poste)* to sollicit

**brillant, -e** [brijɑ̃, -ɑ̃t] **1** *adj (luisant)* shining; *(couleur)* bright; *(cheveux, cuir)* shiny; *Fig (remarquable)* brilliant **2** *nm (éclat)* shine; *(diamant)* diamond; **b. à lèvres** lip gloss ▪ **brillamment** [-amɑ̃] *adv* brilliantly

**briller** [brije] *vi* to shine; **faire b. qch** to polish sth

**brimer** [brime] *vt* to bully ▪ **brimades** *nfpl (vexations)* bullying

**brin** [brɛ̃] *nm (d'herbe)* blade; *(de muguet)* spray; *(de fil)* strand; *Fig* **un b. de qch** a bit of sth; **faire un b. de toilette** to have a quick wash

**brindille** [brɛ̃dij] *nf* twig

**bringue**[1] [brɛ̃g] *nf Fam* **faire la b.** to go on a binge

**bringue**[2] [brɛ̃g] *nf Fam* **grande b.** *(fille)* beanpole

**brio** [brijo] *nm* brilliance

**brioche** [brijɔʃ] *nf* brioche ▪ **brioché** *adj* **pain b.** = milk bread

**brique** [brik] *nf (de construction)* brick; **mur de briques** brick wall

**briquer** [brike] *vt (nettoyer)* to scrub down

**briquet** [brikɛ] *nm* (cigarette) lighter

**bris** [bri] *nm (de verre)* breaking; **b. de glaces** broken windows

**brise** [briz] *nf* breeze

**briser** [brize] **1** *vt* to break; *(opposition, résistance)* to crush; *(espoir, carrière)* to wreck; *(fatiguer)* to exhaust **2 se briser** *vpr* to break ▪ **brise-glace** *nm inv (navire)* ice breaker ▪ **brise-lames** *nm inv* breakwater

**britannique** [britanik] **1** *adj* British **2** *nmf* **B.** Briton; **les Britanniques** the British

**broc** [bro] *nm* pitcher, jug

**brocante** [brɔkɑ̃t] *nf (commerce)* second-hand trade ▪ **brocanteur** *nm* secondhand dealer

**broche** [brɔʃ] *nf (pour rôtir)* spit; *(bijou)* brooch; *(pour fracture)* pin; **faire cuire qch à la b.** to spit-roast sth ▪ **brochette** *nf (tige)* skewer; *(plat)* kebab

**broché, -e** [brɔʃe] *adj* **livre b.** paperback

**brochet** [brɔʃɛ] *nm* pike

**brochure** [brɔʃyr] *nf* brochure, pamphlet

**brocolis** [brɔkɔli] *nmpl* broccoli

**broder** [brɔde] *vt* to embroider (**de** with) ▪ **broderie** *nf (activité)* embroidery

**broncher** [brɔ̃ʃe] *vi* **il n'a pas bronché** he didn't bat an eyelid

**bronches** [brɔ̃ʃ] *nfpl* bronchial tubes ▪ **bronchite** *nf* bronchitis; **avoir une b.** to have bronchitis

**bronze** [brɔ̃z] *nm* bronze

**bronzer** [brɔ̃ze] *vi* to tan ▪ **bronzage** *nm* (sun)tan

**brosse** [brɔs] *nf* brush; **donner un**

**coup de b. à qch** to give sth a brush; **cheveux en b.** crew cut; **b. à dents** toothbrush ▪ **brosser 1** *vt (tapis, cheveux)* to brush; **b. un tableau de qch** to give an outline of sth **2 se brosser** *vpr* **se b. les dents/les cheveux** to brush one's teeth/one's hair

**brouette** [bruɛt] *nf* wheelbarrow

**brouhaha** [bruaa] *nm* hubbub

**brouillard** [brujar] *nm* fog; **il y a du b.** it's foggy

**brouiller** [bruje] **1** *vt (idées)* to muddle up; *(vue)* to blur; *(émission)* to jam **2 se brouiller** *vpr (vue)* to get blurred; *(se disputer)* to fall out (**avec** with) ▪ **brouillé, -e** *adj (teint)* blotchy; **être b. avec qn** to have fallen out with sb

**brouillon, -onne** [brujɔ̃, -ɔn] **1** *adj (mal organisé)* disorganized; *(mal présenté)* untidy **2** *nm* rough draft; **(papier) b.** *Br* scrap paper, *Am* scratch paper

**broussailles** [brusɑj] *nfpl* scrub

**brousse** [brus] *nf* **la b.** the bush

**brouter** [brute] *vti* to graze

**broyer** [brwaje] *vt* to grind; *(doigt, bras)* to crush

**bru** [bry] *nf* daughter-in-law

**brugnon** [bryɲɔ̃] *nm* nectarine

**bruine** [brɥin] *nf* drizzle ▪ **bruiner** *v impersonnel* to drizzle; **il bruine** it's drizzling

**bruissement** [brɥismɑ̃] *nm (de feuilles)* rustle, rustling

**bruit** [brɥi] *nm* noise, sound; *(nouvelle)* rumour; **faire du b.** to make a noise ▪ **bruitage** *nm Cin* sound effects

**brûlant, -e** [brylɑ̃, -ɑ̃t] *adj (objet, soupe)* burning hot; *(soleil)* scorching; *Fig (sujet)* burning

**brûlé, -e** [bryle] *nm* **odeur de b.** burnt smell; **sentir le b.** to smell burnt

**brûle-pourpoint** [brylpurpwɛ̃] **à brûle-pourpoint** *adv* point-blank

**brûler** [bryle] **1** *vt (sujet: flamme, acide)* to burn; *(feu rouge)* to go through **2** *vi* to burn **3 se brûler** *vpr* to burn oneself; **se b. la langue** to burn one's tongue

**brûlure** [brylyr] *nf* burn

**brume** [brym] *nf* mist, haze ▪ **brumeux, -euse** *adj* misty, hazy

**brun, -e** [brœ̃, bryn] **1** *adj (cheveux)* dark, brown; *(personne)* dark-haired; **être b. de peau** to be dark-skinned
**2** *nm (couleur)* brown
**3** *nmf* dark-haired man, *f* dark-haired woman ▪ **brunette** *nf* brunette ▪ **brunir** *vi (personne, peau)* to tan; *(cheveux)* to darken

**brushing®** [brœʃiŋ] *nm* blow-dry; **faire un b. à qn** to blow-dry sb's hair

**brusque** [brysk] *adj* abrupt ▪ **brusquement** [-əmɑ̃] *adv* abruptly ▪ **brusquer** *vt (décision)* to rush ▪ **brusquerie** *nf* abruptness

**brut, -e** [bryt] *adj (pétrole)* crude; *(diamant)* rough; *(poids, salaire)* gross; *(champagne)* extra-dry; **à l'état b.** in its raw state

**brutal, -e, -aux, -ales** [brytal, -o] *adj (personnes, manières, paroles)* brutal; *(franchise, réponse)* crude, blunt; *(changement)* abrupt; **être b. avec qn** to be rough with sb ▪ **brutalement** *adv (violemment)* brutally; *(avec brusquerie)* bluntly; *(soudainement)* abruptly ▪ **brutaliser** *vt* to ill-treat ▪ **brutalité** *nf (violence, acte)* brutality; *(soudaineté)* abruptness ▪ **brute** *nf* brute

**Bruxelles** [brysɛl] *nm ou f* Brussels

**bruyant, -e** [brɥijɑ̃, -ɑ̃t] *adj* noisy ▪ **bruyamment** [-amɑ̃] *adv* noisily

**bruyère** [bryjɛr] *nf (plante)* heather; *(terrain)* heath

**BTS** [beteɛs] (*abrév* **brevet de technicien supérieur**) *nm* = advanced vocational training certificate

**bu, -e** [by] *pp de* **boire**

**buanderie** [bɥɑ̃dri] *nf (lieu)* laundry

**bûche** [byʃ] *nf* log; **b. de Noël** Yule log ▪ **bûcher** *nm (à bois)* woodshed; *(de supplice)* stake

**bûcheron** [byʃrɔ] *nm* woodcutter

**bûcheur, -euse** [byʃœr, -øz] *nmf Br* swot, *Am* grind

**budget** [bydʒɛ] *nm* budget ▪ **budgétaire** *adj* budgetary; *(année)* financial

**buée** [bɥe] *nf (sur vitre)* condensation; *(sur miroir)* mist

**buffet** [byfɛ] *nm (meuble bas)* sideboard; *(meuble haut)* dresser; *(repas)* buffet

**buffle** [byfl] *nm* buffalo

**buisson** [bɥisɔ̃] *nm* bush

**buissonnière** [bɥisɔnjɛr] *adj f* **faire l'école b.** *Br* to play truant, *Am* to play hookey

**bulbe** [bylb] *nm* bulb

**Bulgarie** [bylgari] *nf* **la B.** Bulgaria ▪ **bulgare 1** *adj* Bulgarian **2** *nmf* **B.** Bulgarian

**bulldozer** [byldozœr] *nm* bulldozer

**bulle** [byl] *nf (d'air, de savon)* bubble; *(de bande dessinée)* balloon; **faire des bulles** to blow bubbles

**bulletin** [byltɛ̃] *nm (communiqué, revue)* bulletin; **b. d'informations** news bulletin; **b. de paie** *ou* **de salaire** *Br* pay slip, *Am* pay stub; **b. de santé** medical bulletin; **b. de vote** ballot paper; **b. météo** weather report; **b. scolaire** *Br* school report, *Am* report card

**bureau, -x** [byro] *nm (table)* desk; *(lieu)* office; *(comité)* committee; **b. de change** bureau de change; **b. de poste** post office; **b. de tabac** *Br* tobacconist's (shop), *Am* tobacco store

**bureaucratie** [byrokrasi] *nf* bureaucracy ▪ **bureaucratique** *adj* bureaucratic

**Bureautique®** [byrotik] *nf* office automation

**burette** [byrɛt] *nf (pour huile)* oilcan; *(de chimiste)* burette

**burin** [byrɛ̃] *nm (de graveur)* burin; *(pour découper)* (cold) chisel

**buriné, -e** [byrine] *adj (visage)* seamed

**burlesque** [byrlɛsk] *adj (idée)* ludicrous; *(genre)* burlesque

**bus**[1] [bys] *nm* bus

**bus**[2] [by] *pt de* **boire**

**buste** [byst] *nm (torse)* chest; *(sculpture)* bust ▪ **bustier** *nm (corsage)* bustier

**but**[1] [by(t)] *nm (objectif)* aim, goal; *(intention)* purpose; *Sport* goal

**but**[2] [by] *pt de* **boire**

**butane** [bytan] *nm* butane

**buter** [byte] **1** *vt* **b. qn** to put sb's back up **2** *vi* **b. contre qch** *(cogner)* to bump into sth; *(trébucher)* to stumble over sth; *Fig (difficulté)* to come up against sth **3 se buter** *vpr (s'entêter)* to dig one's heels in ▪ **buté, -e** *adj* obstinate

**butin** [bytɛ̃] *nm (de voleur)* loot; *(de pillards)* spoils; *(d'armée)* booty

**butoir** [bytwar] *nm (pour train)* buffer; *(de porte)* stopper, *Br* stop

**buvard** [byvar] *nm* blotting paper

**buvette** [byvɛt] *nf* refreshment bar

**buveur, -euse** [byvœr, -øz] *nmf* drinker; **un grand b.** a heavy drinker

**buviez** [byvje] *voir* **boire**

# Cc

**C, c** [se] *nm inv* C, c
**c'** [s] *voir* **ce²**

**ÇA** [sa] *(abrév* **cela***) pron démonstratif (pour désigner)* that; *(plus près)* this; *(sujet indéfini)* it, that; **où/quand ça?** where?/when?; **ça dépend** it depends; **ça va?** how are things?; **ça va!** fine!, OK!; **c'est ça** that's right

**çà** [sa] **çà et là** *adv* here and there
**cabane** [kaban] *nf (baraque)* hut; *(en rondin)* cabin; *(de jardin)* shed; **c. à outils** tool shed
**cabaret** [kabarɛ] *nm* cabaret
**cabillaud** [kabijo] *nm* (fresh) cod
**cabine** [kabin] *nf (de bateau)* cabin; **c. d'essayage** fitting room; **c. de pilotage** cockpit; **c. téléphonique** phone box
**cabinet** [kabinɛ] *nm (de médecin) Br* surgery, *Am* office; *(d'avocat)* firm; *(de ministre)* departmental staff; **c. de toilette** (small) bathroom; *Fam* **les cabinets** *Br* the loo, *Am* the john
**câble** [kɑbl] *nm* cable; *TV* **le c.** cable ▪ **câbler** *vt TV (ville, quartier)* to install cable television in
**cabrer** [kabre] **se cabrer** *vpr (cheval)* to rear (up)
**cabriole** [kabriɔl] *nf (saut)* caper; **faire des cabrioles** to caper about
**cabriolet** [kabriɔlɛ] *nm (auto)* convertible
**cacah(o)uète** [kakawɛt] *nf* peanut
**cacao** [kakao] *nm (poudre)* cocoa
**cache** [kaʃ] *nf* hiding place ▪ **cache-cache** *nm inv* **jouer à c.** to play hide and seek ▪ **cache-nez** *nm inv* scarf
**cachemire** [kaʃmir] *nm (laine)* cashmere
**cacher** [kaʃe] **1** *vt* to hide (**à** from) **2 se cacher** *vpr* to hide
**cachet** [kaʃɛ] *nm (sceau)* seal; *(de fabrication)* stamp; *(comprimé)* tablet; *(d'acteur)* fee; *(originalité)* character; **c. de la poste** postmark ▪ **cacheter** *vt* to seal
**cachette** [kaʃɛt] *nf* hiding place; **en c.** in secret
**cachot** [kaʃo] *nm* dungeon
**cachotteries** [kaʃɔtri] *nfpl* **faire des cachotteries** to be secretive
**cactus** [kaktys] *nm* cactus
**cadavre** [kadɑvr] *nm* corpse ▪ **cadavérique** *adj (teint)* deathly pale
**caddie®** [kadi] *nm Br* trolley, *Am* cart
**cadeau, -x** [kado] *nm* present, gift; **faire un c. à qn** to give sb a present
**cadenas** [kadnɑ] *nm* padlock
**cadence** [kadɑ̃s] *nf (taux, vitesse)* rate; *(de chanson)* rhythm
**cadet, -ette** [kade, -ɛt] **1** *adj (de deux)* younger; *(de plus de deux)* youngest **2** *nmf (de deux)* younger (one); *(de plus de deux)* youngest (one); *Sport* junior
**cadran** [kadrɑ̃] *nm (de téléphone)* dial; *(de montre)* face; **c. solaire** sundial
**cadre** [kɑdr] *nm* (**a**) *(de photo, de vélo)* frame; *(décor)* setting; **dans le c. de** within the framework of (**b**) *(d'entreprise)* executive; **les cadres** the management; *Mil* the officers
**cadrer** [kɑdre] **1** *vt (photo)* to centre **2** *vi (correspondre)* to tally (**avec** with)
**caduc, caduque** [kadyk] *adj (feuille)* deciduous

**cafard** [kafar] *nm (insecte)* cockroach

**café** [kafe] *nm (produit, boisson)* coffee; *(bar)* café; **c. au lait, c. crème** *Br* white coffee, *Am* coffee with milk; **c. noir** black coffee; **c. soluble** *ou* **instantané** instant coffee ▪ **caféine** *nf* caffeine ▪ **cafétéria** *nf* cafeteria ▪ **cafetier** *nm* café owner ▪ **cafetière** *nf (récipient)* coffeepot; *(électrique)* coffee machine

**cage** [kaʒ] *nf (d'oiseau, de zoo)* cage; *(d'ascenseur)* shaft; *Sport* goal; **c. d'escalier** stairwell

**cageot** [kaʒo] *nm* crate

**cagneux** [kaɲø] *adj* **avoir les genous c.** to have knock-knees

**cagnotte** [kaɲɔt] *nf (caisse commune)* kitty; *(de jeux)* pool

**cagoule** [kagul] *nf (de bandit)* hood; *(d'enfant) Br* balaclava, *Am* ski mask

**cahier** [kaje] *nm* notebook; *(d'écolier)* exercise book; **c. de brouillon** *Br* rough book, *Am* ≃ scratch pad; *Scol* **c. d'appel** register

**cahin-caha** [kaɛ̃kaa] *adv Fam* **aller c.** *(se déplacer)* to struggle along

**caille** [kɑj] *nf (oiseau)* quail

**cailler** [kɑje] *vi (lait)* to curdle ▪ **caillot** *nm (de sang)* clot

**caillou, -x** [kaju] *nm* stone; *(sur la plage)* pebble

**Caire** [kɛr] *nm* **le C.** Cairo

**caisse** [kɛs] *nf* (**a**) *(boîte)* case; *(d'outils)* box; *(cageot)* crate (**b**) *(de magasin)* cash desk; *(de supermarché)* checkout; **c. d'épargne** savings bank; **c. enregistreuse** cash register

**caissier, -ère** [kesje, -ɛr] *nmf* cashier; *(de supermarché)* checkout operator

**cajoler** [kaʒɔle] *vt* to cuddle

**cajou** [kaʒu] *nm* **noix de c.** cashew nut

**calamité** [kalamite] *nf (fléau)* calamity; *(malheur)* great misfortune

**calcaire** [kalkɛr] **1** *adj (eau)* hard; *(terrain)* chalky **2** *nm Géol* limestone; *(dépôt)* fur

**calciné, -e** [kalsine] *adj* burnt to a cinder

**calcium** [kalsjɔm] *nm* calcium

**calcul** [kalkyl] *nm* (**a**) *(opérations, estimation)* calculation; *Scol* **le c.** arithmetic; **faire un c.** to make a calculation (**b**) *Méd* stone; **c. rénal** kidney stone

**calculatrice** [kalkylatris] *nf* **c. (de poche)** (pocket) calculator

**calculer** [kalkyle] *vt (prix, superficie)* to calculate; *(chances, conséquences)* to weigh (up)

**calculette** [kalkylɛt] *nf* (pocket) calculator

**cale** [kal] *nf* (**a**) *(de meuble, de porte)* wedge (**b**) *(de navire)* hold

**caleçon** [kalsɔ̃] *nm* boxer shorts

**calembour** [kalɑ̃bur] *nm* pun, play on words

**calendrier** [kalɑ̃drije] *nm (mois et jours)* calendar; *(programme)* timetable

**calepin** [kalpɛ̃] *nm* notebook

**caler** [kale] **1** *vt (meuble, porte)* to wedge; *(chargement)* to secure **2** *vi (moteur)* to stall **3 se caler** *vpr (dans un fauteuil)* to settle oneself comfortably

**calfeutrer** [kalføtre] *vt (brèches)* to block up

**calibre** [kalibr] *nm (diamètre)* calibre; *(d'œuf, de fruit)* grade; *(outil)* gauge

**Californie** [kalifɔrni] *nf* **la C.** California

**califourchon** [kalifurʃɔ̃] **à califourchon** *adv* astride; **se mettre à c. sur qch** to sit astride sth

**câlin, -e** [kɑlɛ̃, -in] **1** *adj* affectionate **2** *nm* cuddle; **faire un c. à qn** to give sb a cuddle

**calmant** [kalmɑ̃] *nm (pour les nerfs)* sedative

**calmar** [kalmar] *nm* squid

**calme** [kalm] **1** *adj (flegmatique)* calm, cool; *(tranquille)* quiet; *(mer)* calm **2** *nm* calm(ness); **garder/perdre son c.** to keep/lose one's calm; **du c.!** *(taisez-vous)* keep quiet!; *(pas de panique)* keep calm!

**calmer** [kalme] **1** *vt (douleur)* to soothe; *(inquiétude)* to calm; *(faim)* to appease; **c. qn** to calm sb down **2 se calmer** *vpr (personne)* to calm down; *(vent)* to die down; *(mer)* to become calm; *(douleur)* to subside

**calomnie** [kalɔmni] *nf (en paroles)* slander; *(par écrit)* libel ▪ **calomnier** *vt (en paroles)* to slander; *(par écrit)* to libel ▪ **calomnieux, -euse** *adj (paroles)* slanderous; *(écrits)* libellous

**calorie** [kalɔri] *nf* calorie

**calotte** [kalɔt] *nf (chapeau rond)* skullcap

**calque** [kalk] *nm (copie)* tracing; **(papier-)c.** tracing paper

**calvaire** [kalvɛr] *nm Rel* calvary; *Fig* ordeal

**calvitie** [kalvisi] *nf* baldness

**camarade** [kamarad] *nmf* friend; **c. de classe** classmate; **c. d'école** school friend; **c. de jeu** playmate ▪ **camaraderie** *nf* camaraderie

**Cambodge** [kɑ̃bɔdʒ] *nm* **le C.** Cambodia

**cambouis** [kɑ̃bwi] *nm* dirty oil

**cambrer** [kɑ̃bre] **1** *vt* to arch **2 se cambrer** *vpr* to arch one's back ▪ **cambrure** *nf (du pied, du dos)* arch

**cambrioler** [kɑ̃brijɔle] *vt Br* to burgle, *Am* to burglarize ▪ **cambriolage** *nm* burglary ▪ **cambrioleur, -euse** *nmf* burglar

**camée** [kame] *nm* cameo

**caméléon** [kameleɔ̃] *nm* chameleon

**camelot** [kamlo] *nm* street peddler *or Br* hawker, *Am* huckster ▪ **camelote** *nf (pacotille)* junk; *(marchandise)* stuff

**camembert** [kamɑ̃bɛr] *nm (fromage)* Camembert (cheese)

**caméra** [kamera] *nf* camera ▪ **cameraman** (*pl* **-mans** *ou* **-men**) *nm* cameraman

**Caméscope®** [kameskɔp] *nm* camcorder

**camion** [kamjɔ̃] *nm Br* lorry, *Am* truck; **c. de déménagement** *Br* removal van, *Am* moving van ▪ **camion-citerne** (*pl* **camions-citernes**) *nm Br* tanker, *Am* tank truck ▪ **camionnette** *nf* van ▪ **camionneur** *nm (conducteur) Br* lorry driver, *Am* truck driver; *(entrepreneur) Br* haulier, *Am* trucker

**camomille** [kamɔmij] *nf (plante)* camomile; *(tisane)* camomile tea

**camoufler** [kamufle] *vt Mil* to camouflage ▪ **camouflage** *nm Mil* camouflage

**camp** [kɑ̃] *nm (campement)* camp; *(de parti, de jeu)* side; **c. de concentration** concentration camp; **c. de prisonniers** prison camp

**campagne** [kɑ̃paɲ] *nf* (**a**) *(par opposition à la ville)* country; *(paysage)* countryside; **à la c.** in the country; **en pleine c.** deep in the countryside (**b**) *Mil, Com & Pol* campaign; **c. de presse/publicité** press/publicity campaign ▪ **campagnard, -e** *adj* country

**camper** [kɑ̃pe] **1** *vi* to camp **2** *vt (chapeau)* to plant **3 se camper** *vpr* to plant oneself (**devant** in front of) ▪ **campeur, -euse** *nmf* camper

**camping** [kɑ̃piŋ] *nm (activité)* camping; *(terrain)* camp(ing) site; **faire du c.** to go camping; **c. sauvage** unauthorized camping ▪ **camping-car** (*pl* **camping-cars**) *nm* camper

**campus** [kɑ̃pys] *nm* campus

**Canada** [kanada] *nm* **le C.** Canada ▪ **canadien, -enne 1** *adj* Canadian **2** *nmf* **C., Canadienne** Canadian

**canal, -aux** [kanal, -o] *nm (cours d'eau)* canal; *(conduite)* conduit; *Fig* channel

**canaliser** [kanalize] *vt (rivière, fleuve)* to canalize; *Fig (foule, énergie)* to channel ▪ **canalisation** *nf (conduite)* pipe

**canapé** [kanape] *nm* (**a**) *(siège)* sofa, couch (**b**) *(pour l'apéritif)* canapé ▪ **canapé-lit** (*pl* **canapés-lits**) *nm* sofa bed

**canard** [kanar] *nm* duck; *(mâle)* drake; *Fam (journal)* rag

**canari** [kanari] *nm* canary

**cancaner** [kɑ̃kane] *vi* to gossip

**cancans** [kɑ̃kɑ̃] *nmpl* gossip

**cancer** [kɑ̃sɛr] *nm (maladie)* cancer; **c.**

**de l'estomac** stomach cancer; **avoir un c.** to have cancer; **le C.** *(signe)* Cancer ▪ **cancéreux, -euse 1** *adj* cancerous **2** *nmf* cancer patient ▪ **cancérigène** *adj* carcinogenic

**candeur** [kɑ̃dœr] *nf* guilelessness

**candidat, -e** [kɑ̃dida, -at] *nmf (d'examen, d'élection)* candidate (**à** for); *(de poste)* applicant (**à** for); **être c. aux élections** to stand for election ▪ **candidature** *nf (à un poste)* application (**à** for); *(aux élections)* candidature (**à** for); **poser sa c.** to apply (**à** for); **c. spontanée** unsolicited application

**candide** [kɑ̃did] *adj* guileless

**cane** [kan] *nf* (female) duck ▪ **caneton** *nm* duckling

**canette** [kanɛt] *nf (boîte)* can

**canevas** [kanva] *nm (toile)* canvas

**caniche** [kaniʃ] *nm* poodle

**canicule** [kanikyl] *nf* heatwave

**canif** [kanif] *nm* penknife

**canine** [kanin] **1** *adj f (espèce, race)* canine **2** *nf (dent)* canine (tooth)

**caniveau, -x** [kanivo] *nm* gutter

**canne** [kan] *nf (tige)* cane; *(pour marcher)* (walking) stick; **c. à pêche** fishing rod; **c. à sucre** sugar cane

**cannelle** [kanɛl] *nf* cinnamon

**cannette** [kanɛt] *nf* = **canette**

**cannibale** [kanibal] *nmf* cannibal

**canoë-kayak** [kanɔekajak] *nm* canoeing

**canon**[1] [kanɔ̃] *nm* gun; *(ancien, à boulets)* cannon; *(de fusil)* barrel

**canon**[2] [kanɔ̃] *nm Rel & Fig (règle)* canon

**canot** [kano] *nm* boat; **c. de sauvetage** lifeboat; **c. pneumatique** rubber dinghy

**cantatrice** [kɑ̃tatris] *nf* opera singer

**cantine** [kɑ̃tin] *nf* (**a**) *(réfectoire)* canteen; *(d'école)* dining hall (**b**) *(coffre)* trunk

**canton** [kɑ̃tɔ̃] *nm (en France)* canton *(division of a department)*; *(en Suisse)* canton *(semi-autonomous region)*

**cantonade** [kɑ̃tɔnad] **à la cantonade** *adv* to everyone present

**cantonner** [kɑ̃tɔne] **1** *vt (troupes)* to quarter; **c. qn dans/à** to confine sb to **2 se cantonner** *vpr* **se c. dans/à** to confine oneself to ▪ **cantonnement** *nm (lieu)* quarters

**canular** [kanylar] *nm Fam* hoax

**CAO** [seao] *(abrév* **conception assistée par ordinateur**) *nf Ordinat* CAD

**caoutchouc** [kautʃu] *nm* rubber; *(élastique)* rubber band

**CAP** [seape] *(abrév* **certificat d'aptitude professionnelle**) *nm Scol* = vocational training certificate

**cap** [kap] *nm Géog* cape, headland; *Naut (direction)* course

**capable** [kapabl] *adj* capable, able; **c. de qch** capable of sth; **c. de faire qch** able to do sth, capable of doing sth ▪ **capacité** *nf* capacity; *(aptitude)* ability

**CAPES** [kapɛs] *(abrév* **certificat d'aptitude professionnelle à l'enseignement secondaire**) *nm* = postgraduate teaching certificate

**capillaire** [kapilɛr] *adj* **huile/lotion c.** hair oil/lotion

**capitaine** [kapitɛn] *nm* captain

**capital, -e, -aux, -ales** [kapital, -o] **1** *adj (essentiel)* major **2** *adj f* **lettre capitale** capital letter **3** *nm Fin* capital ▪ **capitale** *nf (lettre, ville)* capital

**capitalisme** [kapitalism] *nm* capitalism ▪ **capitaliste** *adj & nmf* capitalist

**capiteux, -euse** [kapitø, -øz] *adj (parfum)* heady

**capitonné, -e** [kapitɔne] *adj* padded

**capituler** [kapityle] *vi* to surrender ▪ **capitulation** *nf* surrender

**caporal, -aux** [kapɔral, -o] *nm Mil* corporal

**capot** [kapo] *nm Aut Br* bonnet, *Am* hood

**capote** [kapɔt] *nf Aut (de décapotable)* top, *Br* hood

**capoter** [kapɔte] *vi (véhicule)* to overturn

**câpre** [kɑpr] *nf* caper

**caprice** [kapris] *nm* whim; **faire un c.** to throw a tantrum ▪ **capricieux,**

**-euse** *adj (personne)* capricious
**Capricorne** [kaprikɔrn] *nm* **le C.** *(signe)* Capricorn
**capsule** [kapsyl] *nf (spatiale, de médicament)* capsule; *(de bouteille)* cap
**capter** [kapte] *vt (signal, radio)* to pick up; *(attention)* to capture
**captif, -ive** [kaptif, -iv] *adj & nmf* captive ▪ **captivité** *nf* captivity; **en c.** in captivity
**captiver** [kaptive] *vt* to captivate ▪ **captivant, -e** *adj* captivating
**capture** [kaptyr] *nf* capture ▪ **capturer** *vt* to capture
**capuche** [kapyʃ] *nf* hood ▪ **capuchon** *nm (de manteau)* hood; *(de stylo, de tube)* cap, top
**caqueter** [kakte] *vi (poule)* to cackle
**car**[1] [kar] *conj* because, for
**car**[2] [kar] *nm* bus, *Br* coach; **c. de police** police van
**carabine** [karabin] *nf* rifle; **c. à air comprimé** air gun
**caractère**[1] [karaktɛr] *nm (lettre)* character; **en caractères gras** in bold characters; **caractères d'imprimerie** block letters
**caractère**[2] [karaktɛr] *nm (tempérament, nature)* character, nature; **avoir bon c.** to be good-natured; **avoir mauvais c.** to be bad-tempered
**caractériser** [karakterize] **1** *vt* to characterize **2 se caractériser** *vpr* **se c. par** to be characterized by
**caractéristique** [karakteristik] *adj & nf* characteristic
**carafe** [karaf] *nf (pour l'eau, le vin)* carafe
**carambolage** [karɑ̃bɔlaʒ] *nm* pile-up
**caramel** [karamɛl] *nm* caramel ▪ **caraméliser** *vti* to caramelize
**carapace** [karapas] *nf (de tortue) & Fig* shell
**carat** [kara] *nm* carat; **or à 18 carats** 18-carat gold
**caravane** [karavan] *nf (pour camper) Br* caravan, *Am* trailer; *(dans le désert)* caravan ▪ **caravaning** *nm* caravanning; **faire du c.** to go caravanning
**carbone** [karbɔn] *nm* carbon; **(papier) c.** carbon (paper) ▪ **carbonique** *adj* **gaz c.** carbon dioxide; **neige c.** dry ice
**carbonisé, -e** [karbɔnize] *adj (nourriture)* burnt to a cinder
**carburant** [karbyrɑ̃] *nm* fuel ▪ **carburateur** *nm Aut Br* carburettor, *Am* carburetor
**carcasse** [karkas] *nf (os)* carcass; *(d'immeuble)* shell
**carcéral, -e, -aux, -ales** [karseral, -o] *adj* prison
**cardiaque** [kardjak] **1** *adj (arrêt, massage)* cardiac; **être c.** to have a heart condition **2** *nmf* heart patient
**cardigan** [kardigɑ̃] *nm* cardigan
**cardinal, -e, -aux, -ales** [kardinal, -o] **1** *adj (nombre, point, vertu)* cardinal **2** *nm Rel* cardinal
**cardiologie** [kardjɔlɔʒi] *nf* cardiology
**carême** [karɛm] *nm Rel* **le c.** Lent; **faire c.** to fast
**carence** [karɑ̃s] *nf (manque)* deficiency
**caresse** [karɛs] *nf* caress; **faire des caresses à qn** to caress sb
**caresser** [karese] *vt (personne)* to caress; *(animal)* to stroke; *Fig (espoir)* to cherish
**cargaison** [kargɛzɔ̃] *nf* cargo
**caricature** [karikatyr] *nf* caricature
**carie** [kari] *nf* **c. (dentaire)** tooth decay; **avoir une c.** to have a cavity
**carillon** [karijɔ̃] *nm (sonnerie)* chimes; *(horloge)* chiming clock; *(de porte)* door chime
**caritatif, -ive** [karitatif, -iv] *adj* charitable
**carlingue** [karlɛ̃g] *nf (d'avion)* cabin
**carnage** [karnaʒ] *nm* carnage
**carnassier, -ère** [karnasje, -ɛr] **1** *adj* flesh-eating **2** *nm* carnivore
**carnaval, -als** [karnaval] *nm* carnival
**carnet** [karnɛ] *nm* notebook; *(de tickets)* = book of tickets; **c. d'adresses** address book; **c. de chèques** cheque book; **c. de notes** *Br* school report, *Am* report card

**carnivore** [karnivɔr] **1** *adj* carnivorous **2** *nm* carnivore

**carotte** [karɔt] *nf* carrot

**carpette** [karpɛt] *nf* rug

**carré, -e** [kare] **1** *adj* square; *(épaules)* square, broad; **mètre c.** square metre **2** *nm* square; **avoir une coupe au c.** to have (one's hair in) a bob; *Culin* **c. d'agneau** rack of lamb

**carreau, -x** [karo] *nm (motif)* square; *(sur tissu)* check; *(de céramique)* tile; *(vitre)* (window) pane; *Cartes (couleur)* diamonds; **tissu à carreaux** check(ed) material

**carrefour** [karfur] *nm* crossroads *(sing)*

**carrelage** [karlaʒ] *nm (sol)* tiled floor; *(carreaux)* tiles

**carrelet** [karlɛ] *nm Br* plaice, *Am* flounder

**carrément** [karemɑ̃] *adv Fam (franchement)* straight out; *(très)* really

**carrière** [karjɛr] *nf* (**a**) *(lieu)* quarry (**b**) *(métier)* career; **faire c. dans** to make a career in

**carrosse** [karɔs] *nm Hist* (horse-drawn) carriage ▪ **carrosserie** *nf (de véhicule)* bodywork

**carrure** [karyr] *nf (de personne)* build; *(de vêtement)* width across the shoulders

**cartable** [kartabl] *nm* school bag

**carte** [kart] *nf* (**a**) *(carton, document officiel, informatisé) & Ordinat* card; *(géographique)* map; *(marine, météo)* chart; *Fig* **avoir c. blanche** to have a free hand; **c. (à jouer)** (playing) card; **jouer aux cartes** to play cards; **c. à puce** smart card; **c. de crédit** credit card; **c. d'identité** identity card; **c. de séjour** residence permit; **c. de téléphone** phonecard; **c. de visite** *Br* visiting card, *Am* calling card; *(professionnelle)* business card; **c. de vœux** greetings card; **c. postale** postcard; **c. routière** road map
(**b**) *(de restaurant)* menu; **manger à la c.** to eat à la carte; **c. des vins** wine list

**cartel** [kartɛl] *nm Écon* cartel

**cartomancien, -enne** [kartɔmɑ̃sjɛ̃, -ɛn] *nmf* fortune-teller *(who uses cards)*

**carton** [kartɔ̃] *nm (matière)* cardboard; *(boîte)* cardboard box; **c. à dessin** portfolio; **c. jaune/rouge** *(au football)* yellow/red card ▪ **cartonné** *adj* **livre c.** hardback

**cartouche** [kartuʃ] *nf* cartridge; *(de cigarettes)* carton

**cas** [kɑ] *nm* case; **en tout c.** in any case; **en c. de besoin** if need be; **en c. d'accident** in the event of an accident; **en c. d'urgence** in an emergency; **au c. où elle tomberait** if she should fall

**casanier, -ère** [kazanje, -ɛr] *adj* stay-at-home

**cascade** [kaskad] *nf* (**a**) *(d'eau)* waterfall; **en c.** in succession (**b**) *(de cinéma)* stunt ▪ **cascadeur, -euse** *nmf* stunt man, *f* stunt woman

**case** [kɑz] *nf* (**a**) *(de tiroir)* compartment; *(d'échiquier)* square; *(de formulaire)* box (**b**) *(hutte)* hut

**caser** [kaze] *Fam* **1** *vt (placer)* to fit in **2** **se caser** *vpr (se marier)* to get married and settle down

**caserne** [kazɛrn] *nf* barracks; **c. de pompiers** fire station

**casier** [kɑzje] *nm* compartment; *(pour courrier)* pigeonhole; *(pour vêtements)* locker; **c. à bouteilles** bottle rack; *Jur* **c. judiciaire** criminal *or* police record

**casino** [kazino] *nm* casino

**casque** [kask] *nm* helmet; **c. (à écouteurs)** headphones

**casquette** [kaskɛt] *nf* cap

**cassation** [kɑsɑsjɔ̃] *nf Jur* annulment

**casse** [kɑs] *nf (objets cassés)* breakages; **aller à la c.** to go for scrap

**casser** [kɑse] **1** *vt* (**a**) *(briser)* to break; *(noix)* to crack; *(voix)* to strain; *Fam* **c. les pieds à qn** to get on sb's nerves
(**b**) *Jur (verdict)* to quash; *(mariage)* to annul
**2** *vi* to break
**3** **se casser** *vpr* to break; **se c. la jambe** to break one's leg; *Fam* **se c. la figure** *(tomber)* to fall flat on one's face

■ **cassant, -e** *adj (fragile)* brittle; *(brusque)* curt, abrupt ■ **casse-cou** *nmf inv (personne)* daredevil ■ **casse-croûte** *nm inv Fam* snack ■ **casse-noisettes, casse-noix** [kasnwa] *nm inv* nutcrackers ■ **casse-pieds** *nmf inv Fam (personne)* pain (in the neck) ■ **casse-tête** *nm inv (problème)* headache; *(jeu)* puzzle ■ **casseur** *nm (manifestant)* rioter

**casserole** [kasrɔl] *nf* (sauce)pan

**cassette** [kasɛt] *nf (magnétique)* cassette, tape; **enregistrer qch sur c.** to tape sth; **c. video** video cassette

**cassis** [kasis] *nm (fruit)* blackcurrant; *(boisson)* blackcurrant liqueur

**cassoulet** [kasule] *nm* cassoulet, = stew of beans, pork and goose

**cassure** [kɑsyr] *nf* break

**castagnettes** [kastaɲɛt] *nfpl* castanets

**caste** [kast] *nf* caste

**castor** [kastɔr] *nm* beaver

**castrer** [kastre] *vt* to castrate; *(chat, chien)* to neuter

**catalogue** [katalɔg] *nm Br* catalogue, *Am* catalog ■ **cataloguer** *vt Br* to catalogue, *Am* to catalog; *Fig & Péj* to label

**catalyseur** [katalizœr] *nm Chim & Fig* catalyst

**catalytique** [katalitik] *adj Aut* **pot c.** catalytic converter

**catapulte** [katapylt] *nf* catapult

**catastrophe** [katastrɔf] *nf* disaster, catastrophe ■ **catastrophique** *adj* disastrous, catastrophic

**catch** [katʃ] *nm* wrestling ■ **catcheur, -euse** *nmf* wrestler

**catéchisme** [kateʃism] *nm Rel* catechism

**catégorie** [kategɔri] *nf* category; *(d'hôtel)* grade

**catégorique** [kategɔrik] *adj* categorical; **c'est lui, je suis c.** I'm positive it's him

**cathédrale** [katedral] *nf* cathedral

**catholicisme** [katɔlisism] *nm* Catholicism ■ **catholique** *adj & nmf* (Roman) Catholic

**catimini** [katimini] **en catimini** *adv* on the sly

**cauchemar** [koʃmar] *nm aussi Fig* nightmare; **faire un c.** to have a nightmare

**cause** [koz] *nf (origine)* cause; *(procès, parti)* case; **à c. de qn/qch** because of sb/sth

**causer**[1] [koze] *vt (provoquer)* to cause

**causer**[2] [koze] *vi (bavarder)* to chat (**de** about); *(cancaner)* to talk ■ **causerie** *nf* talk

**caustique** [kostik] *adj (substance, esprit)* caustic

**caution** [kosjɔ̃] *nf (d'appartement)* deposit; *Jur* bail; *(personne)* guarantor; *Fig (appui)* backing; *Jur* **sous c.** on bail ■ **cautionner** *vt Fig (approuver)* to back

**cavalier, -ère** [kavalje, -ɛr] **1** *nmf (à cheval)* rider; *Échecs* knight; *(de bal)* partner, escort; *Fig* **faire c. seul** to go it alone **2** *adj (manière, personne)* cavalier

**cave** [kav] *nf* cellar ■ **caveau, -x** *nm (sépulture)* burial vault

**caverne** [kavɛrn] *nf* cave, cavern; **homme des cavernes** caveman

**caviar** [kavjar] *nm* caviar

**cavité** [kavite] *nf* hollow, cavity

**CCP** [sesepe] (*abrév* **compte chèque postal**) *nm Br* ≃ PO Giro account, *Am* ≃ Post Office checking account

**CD** [sede] (*abrév* **disque compact**) *nm* CD

**CD-Rom** [sederɔm] *nm inv Ordinat* CD-Rom

**CE** [seə] **1** (*abrév* **cours élémentaire**) *nm Scol* **CE1** = second year of primary school; **CE2** = third year of primary school **2** (*abrév* **Communauté européenne**) *nf* EC

**CE[1], CETTE, CES** [sə, sɛt, se]

**cet** is used before a masculine singular adjective beginning with a vowel or mute h.

*adj démonstratif* this, that, *pl* these, those; **cet homme** this/that man; **cet**

**homme-ci** this man; **cet homme-là** that man

**CE²** [sə]

**ce** becomes **c'** before a vowel.

*pron démonstratif* (**a**) *(pour désigner, pour qualifier)* it, that; **c'est facile** it's easy; **c'est exact** that's right; **c'est mon père** that's my father; *(au téléphone)* it's my father; **ce sont eux qui...** they are the people who...; **qui est-ce?** *(en général)* who is it?; *(en désignant)* who is that?; **ce faisant** in so doing; **sur ce** thereupon

(**b**) *(après une proposition)* **ce que..., ce qui...** what...; **je sais ce qui est bon/ce que tu veux** I know what is good/what you want; **ce que c'est beau!** it's so beautiful!

**ceci** [səsi] *pron démonstratif* this; **c. étant dit** having said this

**cécité** [sesite] *nf* blindness

**céder** [sede] **1** *vt (donner)* to give up (**à** to); *(par testament)* to leave (**à** to); **'cédez le passage'** *Br* 'give way', *Am* 'yield'; **'à céder'** 'for sale' **2** *vi (personne)* to give in (**à/devant** to); *(branche, chaise)* to give way

**cédérom** [sederɔm] *nm Ordinat* CD-ROM

**cèdre** [sɛdr] *nm (arbre, bois)* cedar

**CEI** [seøi] *(abrév* **Communauté d'États Indépendants**) *nf* CIS

**ceinture** [sɛ̃tyr] *nf (accessoire)* belt; *(taille)* waist; **c. de sécurité** *(de véhicule)* seatbelt

**cela** [s(ə)la] *pron démonstratif (pour désigner)* that; *(sujet indéfini)* it, that; **c. m'attriste que...** it saddens me that...; **quand/comment c.?** when?/how?

**célèbre** [selɛbr] *adj* famous ▪ **célébrité** *nf* fame; *(personne)* celebrity

**célébrer** [selebre] *vt* to celebrate ▪ **célébration** *nf* celebration (**de** of)

**céleri** [sɛlri] *nm* celery

**céleste** [selɛst] *adj* celestial, heavenly

**célibat** [seliba] *nm (de prêtre)* celibacy ▪ **célibataire 1** *adj (non marié)* single, unmarried **2** *nmf* bachelor, *f* single woman

**celle** *voir* **celui**

**cellier** [selje] *nm* storeroom

**Cellophane®** [selɔfan] *nf* cellophane®; **sous c.** cellophane®-wrapped

**cellule** [selyl] *nf (de prison) & Biol* cell ▪ **cellulaire** *adj Biol* cell; **téléphone c.** cellular phone

**celte** [sɛlt] *adj* Celtic

**celui, celle, ceux, celles** [səlɥi, sɛl, sø, sɛl] *pron démonstratif* the one, *pl* those, the ones; **c. de Jean** Jean's (one); **ceux de Jean** Jean's (ones), those of Jean; **c. qui appartient à Jean** the one that belongs to Jean; **c.-ci** this one; *(le dernier)* the latter; **c.-là** that one; *(le premier)* the former

**cendre** [sɑ̃dr] *nf* ash

**cendrier** [sɑ̃drije] *nm* ashtray

**censé, -e** [sɑ̃se] *adj* **être c. faire qch** to be supposed to do sth

**censeur** [sɑ̃sœr] *nm (de films, de journaux)* censor; *(de lycée) Br* deputy head, *Am* assistant principal ▪ **censure** *nf (activité)* censorship; *(comité)* board of censors ▪ **censurer** *vt (film)* to censor

**cent** [sɑ̃] *adj & nm* a hundred; **c. pages** a *or* one hundred pages; **deux cents pages** two hundred pages; **cinq pour c.** five per cent ▪ **centaine** *nf* **une c. (de)** about a hundred; **des centaines de** hundreds of ▪ **centenaire 1** *adj* hundred-year-old; **être c.** to be a hundred **2** *nmf* centenarian **3** *nm (anniversaire)* centenary ▪ **centième** *adj & nmf* hundredth

**centigrade** [sɑ̃tigrad] *adj* centigrade

**centimètre** [sɑ̃timɛtr] *nm* centimetre; *(ruban)* tape measure

**central, -e, -aux, -ales** [sɑ̃tral, -o] **1** *adj* central **2** *nm* **c. téléphonique** telephone exchange ▪ **centrale** *nf* **c. électrique** *Br* power station, *Am* power plant; **c. nucléaire** nuclear *Br* power station *or Am* power plant ▪ **centraliser** *vt* to centralize

**centre** [sɑ̃tr] *nm* centre; **c. aéré** outdoor activity centre; **c. commercial** shopping centre; **c. hospitalo-universitaire** ≃ teaching hospital ▪ **centre-ville** (*pl* **centres-villes**) *nm* town centre; *(de grande ville) Br* city centre, *Am* downtown ▪ **centrer** *vt* to centre

**centuple** [sɑ̃typl] *nm* **x est le c. de y** x is a hundred times y; **au c.** a hundredfold

**cependant** [səpɑ̃dɑ̃] *conj* however, yet

**céramique** [seramik] *nf (matière)* ceramic; *(art)* ceramics *(sing)*; **de** *ou* **en c.** ceramic

**cercle** [sɛrkl] *nm (forme, groupe)* circle; **le c. polaire arctique** the Arctic Circle; **c. vicieux** vicious circle

**cercueil** [sɛrkœj] *nm* coffin

**céréale** [sereal] *nf* cereal

**cérébral, -e, -aux, -ales** [serebral, -o] *adj* cerebral

**cérémonie** [seremɔni] *nf* ceremony

**cerf** [sɛr] *nm* stag ▪ **cerf-volant** (*pl* **cerfs-volants**) *nm (jeu)* kite

**cerise** [səriz] *nf* cherry ▪ **cerisier** *nm* cherry tree

**cerne** [sɛrn] *nm* ring ▪ **cerner** *vt* to surround; *(problème)* to define; **avoir les yeux cernés** to have rings under one's eyes

**certain, -e** [sɛrtɛ̃, -ɛn] **1** *adj (sûr)* certain; **il est c. que tu réussiras** you're certain to succeed; **je suis c. de réussir** I'm certain I'll be successful *or* of being successful; **être c. de qch** to be certain of sth

**2** *adj indéfini (avant nom)* certain; **un c. temps** a while

**3** *pron indéfini* **certains pensent que…** some people think that…; **certains d'entre nous** some of us ▪ **certainement** *adv* most probably

**certificat** [sɛrtifika] *nm* certificate

**certifier** [sɛrtifje] *vt* to certify; **je te certifie que…** I assure you that…

**certitude** [sɛrtityd] *nf* certainty; **avoir la c. que…** to be certain that…

**cerveau, -x** [sɛrvo] *nm (organe)* brain; *(intelligence)* mind, brain(s); *Fam (de projet)* mastermind

**cervelle** [sɛrvɛl] *nf (substance)* brain; *(plat)* brains

**CES** [seəes] (*abrév* **collège d'enseignement secondaire**) *nm Anciennement* = secondary school for pupils aged 12 to 15

**ces** *voir* **ce**[1]

**César** [sezar] *nm Cin* = French cinema award

**césarienne** [sezarjɛn] *nf Méd* Caesarean (section)

**cesse** [sɛs] *nf* **sans c.** constantly

**cesser** [sese] *vti* to stop; **faire c. qch** to put a stop to sth; **c. de faire qch** to stop doing sth ▪ **cessez-le-feu** *nm inv* cease-fire

**c'est-à-dire** [setadir] *conj* that is (to say)

**cet, cette** *voir* **ce**[1]

**ceux** *voir* **celui**

**chacun, -e** [ʃakœ̃, -yn] *pron indéfini* each (one), every one; *(tout le monde)* everyone; **(à) c. son tour!** wait your turn!

**chagrin** [ʃagrɛ̃] *nm* grief, sorrow; **avoir du c.** to be upset ▪ **chagriner** *vt (peiner)* to grieve; *(contrarier)* to bother

**chahut** [ʃay] *nm Fam* racket ▪ **chahuter** *Fam* **1** *vi* to make a racket **2** *vt (professeur)* to bait

**chaîne** [ʃɛn] *nf (attache, décoration, série)* chain; *(de montagnes)* chain, range; **réaction en c.** chain reaction; **travailler à la c.** to work on the assembly line; *Aut* **chaînes** (snow) chains; **c. de montage** assembly line; **c. de télévision** television channel; **c. (hi-fi)** hi-fi (system) ▪ **chaînette** *nf* (small) chain ▪ **chaînon** *nm* link

**chair** [ʃɛr] *nf* flesh; **(couleur) c.** flesh-coloured; **en c. et en os** in the flesh; **avoir la c. de poule** to have *Br* goose pimples *or Am* goose bumps

**chaire** [ʃɛr] *nf (d'université)* chair; *(d'église)* pulpit

**chaise** [ʃɛz] *nf* chair; **c. longue** deckchair; **c. roulante** wheelchair

**châle** [ʃɑl] *nm* shawl
**chalet** [ʃalɛ] *nm* chalet
**chaleur** [ʃalœr] *nf* heat; *(de personne, de couleur, de voix)* warmth; **coup de c.** heatstroke ▪ **chaleureux, -euse** *adj* warm
**challenge** [ʃalɑ̃ʒ] *nm Sport* tournament; *(défi)* challenge
**chaloupe** [ʃalup] *nf* launch
**chalumeau, -x** [ʃalymo] *nm* blowtorch, *Br* blowlamp
**chalutier** [ʃalytje] *nm* trawler
**chamailler** [ʃamɑje] **se chamailler** *vpr* to squabble
**chambre** [ʃɑ̃br] *nf* bedroom; *(de tribunal)* division; **c. (d'hôtel)** (hotel) room; **c. à coucher** *(pièce)* bedroom; *(mobilier)* bedroom suite; **c. d'ami** spare room; **c. d'hôte** ≃ guest house; **C. de commerce** Chamber of Commerce; *Pol* **C. des députés** = lower chamber of Parliament ▪ **chambrer** *vt (vin)* to bring to room temperature
**chameau, -x** [ʃamo] *nm* camel
**champ** [ʃɑ̃] *nm (étendue) & Él, Ordinat* field; *Fig (portée)* scope; *Fig* **laisser le c. libre à qn** to leave the field free for sb; **c. de bataille** battlefield; **c. de courses** *Br* racecourse, *Am* racetrack
**champagne** [ʃɑ̃paɲ] *nm* champagne
**champêtre** [ʃɑ̃pɛtr] *adj* rustic
**champignon** [ʃɑ̃piɲɔ̃] *nm (végétal)* mushroom; *Méd* fungus; **c. de Paris** button mushroom; **c. vénéneux** toadstool, poisonous mushroom
**champion, -onne** [ʃɑ̃pjɔ̃, -ɔn] **1** *nmf* champion **2** *adj* **l'équipe championne du monde** the world champions ▪ **championnat** *nm* championship
**chance** [ʃɑ̃s] *nf (sort favorable)* luck; *(possibilité)* chance; **avoir de la c.** to be lucky; **ne pas avoir de c.** to be unlucky; **par c.** luckily ▪ **chanceux, -euse** *adj* lucky
**chanceler** [ʃɑ̃sle] *vi* to stagger
**chancelier** [ʃɑ̃səlje] *nm Pol* chancellor
**chandail** [ʃɑ̃daj] *nm* sweater
**Chandeleur** [ʃɑ̃dlœr] *nf* **la C.** Candlemas
**chandelier** [ʃɑ̃dəlje] *nm (à une branche)* candlestick; *(à plusieurs branches)* candelabra
**chandelle** [ʃɑ̃dɛl] *nf* candle
**change** [ʃɑ̃ʒ] *nm Fin* exchange
**changer** [ʃɑ̃ʒe] **1** *vt (modifier, remplacer, convertir)* to change; **c. qch de place** to move sth
**2** *vi* to change; **c. de voiture/d'adresse** to change one's car/address; **c. de vitesse/de couleur** to change gear/colour
**3 se changer** *vpr* to change (one's clothes); **se c. en qch** to change into sth ▪ **changeant, -e** *adj (temps)* unsettled ▪ **changement** *nm* change; *Aut* **c. de vitesse** *(levier) Br* gear lever, *Am* gear shift
**chanson** [ʃɑ̃sɔ̃] *nf* song ▪ **chant** *nm (art)* singing; *(chanson)* song; **c. de Noël** Christmas carol
**chanter** [ʃɑ̃te] **1** *vt (chanson)* to sing; *(exploits)* to sing of **2** *vi (personne, oiseau)* to sing; *(coq)* to crow; **faire c. qn** to blackmail sb ▪ **chantage** *nm* blackmail ▪ **chanteur, -euse** *nmf* singer
**chantier** [ʃɑ̃tje] *nm* (building) site; *(sur route)* roadworks; **mettre qch en c.** to get sth under way; **c. naval** shipyard
**chantilly** [ʃɑ̃tiji] *nf* whipped cream
**chantonner** [ʃɑ̃tɔne] *vti* to hum
**chaos** [kao] *nm* chaos ▪ **chaotique** *adj* chaotic
**chapeau, -x** [ʃapo] *nm* hat; **c. de paille** straw hat; **c. melon** bowler hat
**chapelle** [ʃapɛl] *nf* chapel; **c. ardente** chapel of rest
**chapelure** [ʃaplyr] *nf* breadcrumbs
**chapiteau, -x** [ʃapito] *nm (de cirque)* big top; *(pour expositions)* tent, *Br* marquee
**chapitre** [ʃapitr] *nm* chapter
**chaque** [ʃak] *adj* each, every
**char** [ʃar] *nm (romain)* chariot; *(de carnaval)* float; *Mil* **c. (d'assaut)** tank

**charabia** [ʃarabja] *nm Fam* gibberish
**charbon** [ʃarbɔ̃] *nm* coal; **c. de bois** charcoal
**charcuterie** [ʃarkytri] *nf (magasin)* pork butcher's shop; *(aliments)* cooked (pork) meats ▪ **charcutier, -ère** *nmf* pork butcher
**chardon** [ʃardɔ̃] *nm (plante)* thistle
**charge** [ʃarʒ] *nf (poids)* load; *(responsabilité)* responsibility; *(d'une arme) & Él, Mil* charge; *(fonction)* office; **être en c. de qch** to be in charge of sth; **prendre qn/qch en c.** to take charge of sb/sth; **être à la c. de qn** *(personne)* to be dependent on sb; *(frais)* to be payable by sb; **charges sociales** *Br* national insurance contributions, *Am* Social Security contributions
**charger** [ʃarʒe] **1** *vt (véhicule, marchandises, arme) & Ordinat* to load; *(batterie) & Mil* to charge; **c. qn de qch** to entrust sb with; **c. qn de faire qch** to give sb the responsibility of doing sth
**2** *vi Ordinat* to load up; *Mil* to charge
**3 se charger** *vpr (s'encombrer)* to weigh oneself down; **se c. de qn/qch** to take care of sb/sth; **se c. de faire qch** to undertake to do sth ▪ **chargé, -e 1** *adj (véhicule)* loaded (**de** with); *(arme)* loaded; *(journée, programme)* busy; **être c. de faire qch** to be responsible for doing sth **2** *nmf Univ* **c. de cours** = part-time lecturer ▪ **chargement** *nm (action)* loading; *(marchandises)* load; *(de bateau)* cargo
**chariot** [ʃarjo] *nm (de supermarché) Br* trolley, *Am* cart; *(de ferme)* waggon; *(de machine à écrire)* carriage; **c. à bagages** luggage trolley
**charisme** [karism] *nm* charisma
**charitable** [ʃaritabl] *adj* charitable (**envers** towards)
**charité** [ʃarite] *nf (vertu)* charity; **faire la c.** to give to charity
**charme** [ʃarm] *nm (attrait)* charm; *(magie)* spell
**charmer** [ʃarme] *vt* to charm ▪ **charmant, -e** *adj* charming ▪ **charmeur, -euse 1** *adj (sourire, air)* charming **2** *nmf* charmer
**charnel, -elle** [ʃarnɛl] *adj* carnal
**charnier** [ʃarnje] *nm* mass grave
**charnière** [ʃarnjɛr] *nf* hinge
**charnu, -e** [ʃarny] *adj* fleshy
**charpente** [ʃarpɑ̃t] *nf* framework; *(de personne)* build ▪ **charpentier** *nm* carpenter
**charpie** [ʃarpi] *nf* **mettre qch en c.** to tear sth to shreds
**charrette** [ʃarɛt] *nf* cart
**charrier** [ʃarje] *vt (transporter)* to cart; *(rivière)* to carry along
**charrue** [ʃary] *nf Br* plough, *Am* plow
**charter** [ʃartɛr] *nm (vol)* charter (flight); *(avion)* charter plane
**chasse¹** [ʃas] *nf (activité)* hunting; *(événement)* hunt; *(poursuite)* chase; **aller à la c.** to go hunting; **c. à courre** hunting; **c. au trésor** treasure hunt; **c. gardée** private hunting ground
**chasse²** [ʃas] *nf* **c. d'eau** flush; **tirer la c.** to flush the toilet
**chassé-croisé** [ʃasekrwaze] (*pl* **chassés-croisés**) *nm (de personnes)* comings and goings
**chasser** [ʃase] **1** *vt (animal)* to hunt; *(faisan, perdrix)* to shoot; **c. qn** *(expulser)* to chase sb away; *(employé)* to dismiss sb **2** *vi* to hunt ▪ **chasse-neige** *nm inv Br* snowplough, *Am* snowplow ▪ **chasseur, -euse 1** *nmf* hunter; **c. de têtes** headhunter **2** *nm (d'hôtel) Br* pageboy, *Am* bellboy; *(avion)* fighter
**châssis** [ʃɑsi] *nm* frame; *(d'automobile)* chassis
**chat** [ʃa] *nm* cat; **c. sauvage** wildcat
**châtaigne** [ʃɑtɛɲ] *nf* chestnut ▪ **châtaignier** *nm* chestnut tree ▪ **châtain** *adj (cheveux)* (chestnut) brown; *(personne)* brown-haired
**château, -x** [ʃɑto] *nm (forteresse)* castle; *(manoir)* mansion
**châtiment** [ʃɑtimɑ̃] *nm* punishment; **c. corporel** corporal punishment
**chaton** [ʃatɔ̃] *nm* (**a**) *(chat)* kitten (**b**) *(de bague)* bezel (**c**) *(d'arbre)* catkin
**chatouiller** [ʃatuje] *vt* to tickle

▪ **chatouilleux, -euse** *adj* ticklish

**chatoyer** [ʃatwaje] *vi* to shimmer; *(pierre)* to sparkle

**châtrer** [ʃɑtre] *vt* to castrate

**chatte** [ʃat] *nf* (female) cat

**chaud, -e** [ʃo, ʃod] **1** *adj* (**a**) *(modérément)* warm; *(intensément)* hot (**b**) *Fig (couleur)* warm; *(voix)* sultry **2** *nm* **avoir c.** to be hot; **il fait c.** it's hot ▪ **chaudement** *adv (s'habiller, féliciter)* warmly

**chaudière** [ʃodjɛr] *nf* boiler

**chauffage** [ʃofaʒ] *nm* heating; *(de voiture)* heater

**chauffard** [ʃofar] *nm* reckless driver

**chauffer** [ʃofe] **1** *vt* to heat (up); *(moteur)* to warm up
**2** *vi* to heat (up); *(s'échauffer) (moteur)* to overheat; **faire c. qch** to heat sth up
**3 se chauffer** *vpr* to warm oneself ▪ **chauffant, -e** *adj* **couverture chauffante** electric blanket; **plaque chauffante** hot plate ▪ **chauffé, -e** *adj (piscine)* heated ▪ **chauffe-eau** *nm inv* water heater; **c. électrique** immersion heater ▪ **chauffe-plat** (*pl* **chauffe-plats**) *nm* hotplate ▪ **chaufferie** *nf* boiler room

**chauffeur** [ʃofœr] *nm (de véhicule)* driver; *(employé)* chauffeur; **c. de taxi** taxi driver

**chaume** [ʃom] *nm (pour toits)* thatch; **toit de c.** thatched roof ▪ **chaumière** *nf (à toit de chaume)* thatched cottage; *(maison pauvre)* cottage

**chaussée** [ʃose] *nf* road(way)

**chausser** [ʃose] **1** *vt (chaussures, lunettes, skis)* to put on; **c. qn** to put shoes on sb; **c. du 40** to take a size 40 shoe **2 se chausser** *vpr* to put one's shoes on

**chaussette** [ʃosɛt] *nf* sock

**chausson** [ʃosɔ̃] *nm (pantoufle)* slipper; *(de danse)* ballet shoe; *(de bébé)* bootee; *Culin* **c. aux pommes** apple turnover

**chaussure** [ʃosyr] *nf* shoe; **chaussures de ski** ski boots

**chauve** [ʃov] **1** *adj* bald **2** *nm* bald (-headed) man

**chauve-souris** [ʃovsuri] (*pl* **chauves-souris**) *nf* bat

**chauvin, -e** [ʃovɛ̃, -in] **1** *adj* chauvinistic **2** *nmf* chauvinist

**chaux** [ʃo] *nf* lime; **blanchir qch à la c.** to whitewash sth

**chavirer** [ʃavire] *vti (bateau)* to capsize

**chef** [ʃɛf] *nm* (**a**) *(de parti, de bande)* leader; *(de tribu)* chief; **rédacteur en c.** editor in chief; **le c. du gouvernement** the head of government; **c. d'entreprise** company head; **c. d'État** head of state; **c. d'orchestre** conductor (**b**) *(cuisinier)* chef

**chef-d'œuvre** [ʃedœvr] (*pl* **chefs-d'œuvre**) *nm* masterpiece

**chef-lieu** [ʃɛfljø] (*pl* **chefs-lieux**) *nm* = administrative centre of a 'département'

**chemin** [ʃəmɛ̃] *nm (route étroite)* path, track; *(itinéraire)* way (**de** to); **à mi-c.** half-way; **en c., c. faisant** on the way; **c. de grande randonnée** hiking trail; **c. de terre** track ▪ **chemin de fer** (*pl* **chemins de fer**) *nm Br* railway, *Am* railroad

**cheminée** [ʃəmine] *nf (âtre)* fireplace; *(encadrement)* mantelpiece; *(sur le toit)* chimney

**cheminot** [ʃəmino] *nm Br* railwayman, *Am* railroader

**chemise** [ʃəmiz] *nf (vêtement)* shirt; *(classeur)* folder; **c. de nuit** *(de femme)* nightdress ▪ **chemisier** *nm (corsage)* blouse

**chenal, -aux** [ʃənal, -o] *nm* channel

**chêne** [ʃɛn] *nm (arbre, bois)* oak

**chenil** [ʃəni(l)] *nm Br* kennels, *Am* kennel

**chenille** [ʃənij] *nf (insecte)* caterpillar; *(de char)* caterpillar track

**chèque** [ʃɛk] *nm Br* cheque, *Am* check; **faire un c. à qn** to write sb a cheque; **payer qch par c.** to pay sth by cheque; **c. de voyage** *Br* traveller's cheque, *Am* traveler's check ▪ **chèque-repas** (*pl* **chèques-repas**), **chèque-restaurant** (*pl* **chèques-restaurants**) *nm Br* luncheon voucher,

*Am* meal ticket ▪ **chéquier** *nm Br* cheque book, *Am* checkbook

**cher, chère** [ʃɛr] **1** *adj* (**a**) *(aimé)* dear (**à** to); **C. Monsieur** *(dans une lettre)* Dear Mr X; *(officiel)* Dear Sir (**b**) *(coûteux)* expensive, dear **2** *adv* **coûter c.** to be expensive **3** *nmf* **mon c., ma chère** my dear ▪ **chèrement** *adv (à un prix élevé)* dearly

**chercher** [ʃɛrʃe] **1** *vt* to look for; *(dans ses souvenirs)* to try to think of; *(dans un dictionnaire)* to look up; **aller c. qn/qch** to (go and) fetch sb/sth; **c. à faire qch** to try to do sth **2 se chercher** *vpr (chercher son identité)* to try to find oneself ▪ **chercheur, -euse** *nmf (scientifique)* researcher; **c. d'or** gold digger

**chérir** [ʃerir] *vt* to cherish ▪ **chéri, -e** *adj* dear

**cherté** [ʃɛrte] *nf* high cost

**chétif, -ive** [ʃetif, -iv] *adj (personne)* puny

**cheval, -aux** [ʃəval, -o] *nm* horse; **à c.** on horseback; **faire du c.** *Br* to go horse riding, *Am* to go horseback riding; **c. de course** racehorse; *Aut* **c. (-vapeur)** horsepower

**chevalet** [ʃəvalɛ] *nm (de peintre)* easel

**chevalier** [ʃəvalje] *nm* knight

**chevalière** [ʃəvaljɛr] *nf* signet ring

**chevaline** [ʃəvalin] *adj f* **boucherie c.** horse butcher's (shop)

**chevaucher** [ʃəvoʃe] **1** *vt* to straddle **2** *vi* **se chevaucher** *vpr* to overlap

**chevelu, -e** [ʃəvly] *adj* long-haired ▪ **chevelure** *nf* (head of) hair

**chevet** [ʃəvɛ] *nm* bedhead; **rester au c. de qn** to stay at sb's bedside

**cheveu, -x** [ʃəvø] *nm* **un c.** a hair; **cheveux** hair; **avoir les cheveux noirs** to have black hair

**cheville** [ʃəvij] *nf (partie du corps)* ankle

**chèvre** [ʃɛvr] **1** *nf* goat **2** *nm* goat's cheese

**chevreau, -x** [ʃəvro] *nm* kid

**chèvrefeuille** [ʃɛvrəfœj] *nm* honeysuckle

**chevreuil** [ʃəvrœj] *nm* roe deer; *(viande)* venison

**chevronné, -e** [ʃəvrɔne] *adj* experienced

**chez** [ʃe] *prép* **c. qn** at sb's house; **il n'est pas c. lui** he isn't at home; **elle est rentrée c. elle** she's gone home; **c. Mme Dupont** *(adresse)* c/o Mme Dupont ▪ **chez-soi** *nm inv* **son petit c.** one's own little home

**chic** [ʃik] **1** *adj inv* smart, stylish; *Fam (gentil)* decent **2** *nm (élégance)* style; **avoir le c. pour faire qch** to have the knack of doing sth

**chicaner** [ʃikane] *vi* **c. sur qch** to quibble over sth

**chicorée** [ʃikɔre] *nf (en poudre)* chicory

**chien, chienne** [ʃjɛ̃, ʃjɛn] *nmf* dog, *f* bitch; *Fam* **quel temps de c.!** what foul weather!; **c. d'aveugle** guide dog; **c. de berger** sheepdog; **c. de garde** guard dog; **c. policier** police dog

**chiendent** [ʃjɛ̃dɑ̃] *nm (plante)* couch grass

**chiffon** [ʃifɔ̃] *nm* rag; **passer un coup de c. sur qch** to give sth a dust; **c. (de poussière)** *Br* duster, *Am* dustcloth

**chiffonner** [ʃifɔne] *vt* to crumple; *Fig (ennuyer)* to bother

**chiffre** [ʃifr] *nm (nombre)* figure, number; *(total)* total; **chiffres romains/arabes** Roman/Arabic numerals; **c. d'affaires** turnover ▪ **chiffrer 1** *vt (montant)* to work out; *(réparations)* to assess **2 se chiffrer** *vpr* **se c. à** to amount to

**chignon** [ʃiɲɔ̃] *nm* bun, chignon

**Chili** [ʃili] *nm* **le C.** Chile ▪ **chilien, -enne 1** *adj* Chilean **2** *nmf* **C., Chilienne** Chilean

**chimie** [ʃimi] *nf* chemistry ▪ **chimique** *adj* chemical ▪ **chimiste** *nmf* (research) chemist

**chimiothérapie** [ʃimjɔterapi] *nf Méd* chemotherapy

**chimpanzé** [ʃɛ̃pɑ̃ze] *nm* chimpanzee

**Chine** [ʃin] *nf* **la C.** China ▪ **chinois, -e 1** *adj* Chinese **2** *nmf* **C., Chinoise**

Chinese; **les C.** the Chinese **3** *nm (langue)* Chinese

**chiot** [ʃjo] *nm* puppy, pup

**chipoter** [ʃipɔte] *vi (contester)* to quibble (**sur** about)

**chips** [ʃips] *nf Br* (potato) crisp, *Am* (potato) chip

**chiromancien, -enne** [kirɔmɑ̃sjɛ̃, -ɛn] *nmf* palmist

**chirurgie** [ʃiryrʒi] *nf* surgery; **c. esthétique** plastic surgery ▪ **chirurgical, -e, -aux, -ales** *adj* surgical ▪ **chirurgien, -enne** *nmf* surgeon ▪ **chirurgien-dentiste** (*pl* **chirurgiens-dentistes**) *nm* dental surgeon

**chlem** [ʃlɛm] *nm Sport* **le grand c.** the grand slam

**chlore** [klɔr] *nm* chlorine

**choc** [ʃɔk] **1** *nm (coup)* impact; *(forte émotion)* shock; *Fig (conflit)* clash; **faire un c. à qn** to give sb a shock; **c. pétrolier** oil crisis **2** *adj* **image-c.** shocking image; **'prix-chocs'** 'drastic reductions'

**chocolat** [ʃɔkɔla] **1** *nm* chocolate; **gâteau au c.** chocolate cake; **c. à croquer** *Br* plain chocolate, *Am* bittersweet chocolate; **c. au lait** milk chocolate **2** *adj inv* chocolate(-coloured) ▪ **chocolaté, -e** *adj* chocolate

**chœur** [kœr] *nm (chanteurs, nef)* choir; *(d'opéra)* chorus; **en c.** *(chanter)* in chorus; *(répéter)* (all) together

**choisir** [ʃwazir] *vt* to choose, to pick; **c. de faire qch** to choose to do sth ▪ **choisi, -e** *adj (œuvres)* selected; *(langage)* careful

**choix** [ʃwa] *nm* choice; *(assortiment)* selection; **avoir le c.** to have a choice

**cholestérol** [kɔlɛsterɔl] *nm Méd* cholesterol

**chômer** [ʃome] *vi* **vous n'avez pas chômé!** you've not been idle!; **jour chômé** (public) holiday ▪ **chômage** *nm* unemployment; **être au c.** to be unemployed ▪ **chômeur, -euse** *nmf* unemployed person; **les chômeurs** the unemployed

**choquer** [ʃɔke] *vt (scandaliser)* to shock ▪ **choquant, -e** *adj* shocking

**choral, -e, -aux** *ou* **-als, -ales** [kɔral] *adj* choral ▪ **chorale** *nf (club)* choral society; *(chanteurs)* choir ▪ **choriste** *nmf* chorister

**chorégraphe** [kɔregraf] *nmf* choreographer

**chose** [ʃoz] *nf* thing; **avant toute c.** first of all

**chou, -x** [ʃu] *nm* cabbage; **choux de Bruxelles** Brussels sprouts; **c. à la crème** cream puff ▪ **chou-fleur** (*pl* **choux-fleurs**) *nm* cauliflower

**choucroute** [ʃukrut] *nf* sauerkraut

**chouette** [ʃwɛt] **1** *nf (oiseau)* owl **2** *adj Fam (chic)* great **3** *exclam* great!

**choyer** [ʃwaje] *vt* to pamper

**chrétien, -enne** [kretjɛ̃, -ɛn] *adj & nmf* Christian ▪ **Christ** [krist] *nm* **le C.** Christ ▪ **christianisme** *nm* Christianity

**chrome** [krom] *nm* chromium; **chromes** *(de voitures)* chrome

**chronique[1]** [krɔnik] *adj (malade, chômage)* chronic

**chronique[2]** [krɔnik] *nf (de journal)* column; *(annales)* chronicle

**chronologie** [krɔnɔlɔʒi] *nf* chronology ▪ **chronologique** *adj* chronological

**chronomètre** [krɔnɔmɛtr] *nm* chronometer; *(pour le sport)* stopwatch ▪ **chronométrer** *vt* to time

**chrysanthème** [krizɑ̃tɛm] *nm* chrysanthemum

**chuchoter** [ʃyʃɔte] *vti* to whisper ▪ **chuchotement** *nm* whisper

**chuinter** [ʃwɛ̃te] *vi (siffler)* to hiss

**chut** [ʃyt] *exclam* sh!, shush!

**chute** [ʃyt] *nf* fall; *(d'histoire drôle)* punchline; *(de tissu)* scrap; **c. de neige** snowfall; **c. libre** free fall ▪ **chuter** *vi (diminuer)* to fall, to drop; *Fam (tomber)* to fall

**Chypre** [ʃipr] *nm ou f* Cyprus ▪ **chypriote 1** *adj* Cypriot **2** *nmf* **C.** Cypriot

**ci** [si] *pron démonstratif* **comme ci comme ça** so so

**-ci** [si] *adv* (**a**) **par-ci, par-là** here and

there (**b**) *voir* **ce**[1], **celui** ▪ **ci-après** *adv* below ▪ **ci-contre** *adv* opposite ▪ **ci-dessous** *adv* below ▪ **ci-dessus** *adv* above ▪ **ci-gît** *adv* here lies... *(on gravestones)* ▪ **ci-joint, -e** (*mpl* **ci-joints,** *fpl* **ci-jointes**) **1** *adj* **le document c.** the enclosed document **2** *adv* **vous trouverez c. copie de...** please find enclosed a copy of...

**cible** [sibl] *nf* target

**ciboulette** [sibulet] *nf* chives

**cicatrice** [sikatris] *nf* scar

**cicatriser** [sikatrize] *vti*, **se cicatriser** *vpr* to heal ▪ **cicatrisation** *nf* healing

**cidre** [sidr] *nm* cider

**Cie** (*abrév* **compagnie**) Co

**ciel** [sjɛl] *nm* (**a**) (*pl* **ciels**) sky; **à c. ouvert** open-air (**b**) (*pl* **cieux** [sjø]) *(paradis)* heaven

**cierge** [sjɛrʒ] *nm Rel* candle

**cigale** [sigal] *nf* cicada

**cigare** [sigar] *nm* cigar ▪ **cigarette** *nf* cigarette

**cigogne** [sigɔɲ] *nf* stork

**cil** [sil] *nm* eyelash

**cime** [sim] *nf (d'arbre)* top; *(de montagne)* peak

**ciment** [simɑ̃] *nm* cement

**cimetière** [simtjɛr] *nm* cemetery; *(d'église)* graveyard

**cinéaste** [sineast] *nm* film maker ▪ **ciné-club** (*pl* **ciné-clubs**) *nm* film club ▪ **cinéphile** *nmf Br* film *or Am* movie enthusiast

**cinéma** [sinema] *nm (art, industrie) Br* cinema, *Am* movies; *(salle) Br* cinema, *Am* movie theater; **faire du c.** to be a film actor/actress; **aller au c.** to go to the *Br* cinema *or Am* movies ▪ **cinématographique** *adj* film; **industrie c.** film industry

**cinglé, -e** [sɛ̃gle] *adj Fam* crazy

**cingler** [sɛ̃gle] *vt* to lash ▪ **cinglant, -e** *adj (pluie)* lashing; *(remarque)* cutting

**cinq** [sɛ̃k] **1** *adj inv* five **2** *nm inv* five ▪ **cinquième** *adj & nmf* fifth; **un c.** a fifth

**cinquante** [sɛ̃kɑ̃t] *adj & nm inv* fifty ▪ **cinquantaine** *nf* **une c. (de)** about fifty; **avoir la c.** to be about fifty ▪ **cinquantenaire** *nm (anniversaire)* fiftieth anniversary ▪ **cinquantième** *adj & nmf* fiftieth

**cintre** [sɛ̃tr] *nm* coathanger

**cirage** [siraʒ] *nm* (shoe) polish

**circonscription** [sirkɔ̃skripsjɔ̃] *nf* division, district; **c. (électorale)** *Br* constituency, *Am* district

**circonscrire*** [sirkɔ̃skrir] *vt (encercler)* to encircle; *(incendie)* to contain

**circonspect, -e** [sirkɔ̃spɛ, -ɛkt] *adj* cautious, circumspect

**circonstance** [sirkɔ̃stɑ̃s] *nf* circumstance; **en pareilles circonstances** under such circumstances

**circuit** [sirkɥi] *nm Él & Sport* circuit; *(chemin)* way; **c. automobile** racing circuit; **c. touristique** (organized) tour

**circulaire** [sirkylɛr] **1** *adj* circular **2** *nf (lettre)* circular

**circulation** [sirkylɑsjɔ̃] *nf (du sang, de l'information, de billets)* circulation; *(d'autos)* traffic; **c. routière/aérienne** road/air traffic ▪ **circuler** *vi (sang, air, information)* to circulate; *(voyageur)* to travel; *(train, bus)* to run

**cire** [sir] *nf* wax; *(pour meubles)* polish ▪ **ciré** *nm (vêtement)* oilskin(s) ▪ **cirer** *vt* to polish ▪ **cireux, -euse** *adj* waxy

**cirque** [sirk] *nm (spectacle)* circus

**cisailles** [sizɑj] *nfpl* (garden) shears ▪ **ciseau, -x** *nm (de menuisier)* chisel; **(une paire de) ciseaux** (a pair of) scissors

**ciseler** [sizle] *vt* to chisel; *(or, argent)* to chase

**citadelle** [sitadɛl] *nf* citadel ▪ **citadin, -e 1** *adj* city **2** *nmf* city dweller

**cité** [site] *nf (ville)* city; *(immeubles) Br* housing estate, *Am* housing development; **c. universitaire** *Br* (students') halls of residence, *Am* university dormitory complex

**citer** [site] *vt (auteur, texte)* to quote; *(énumérer)* to name ▪ **citation** *nf* quotation

**citerne** [sitɛrn] *nf* tank

**citoyen, -enne** [sitwajɛ̃, -ɛn] *nmf* citizen ▪ **citoyenneté** *nf* citizenship

**citron** [sitrɔ̃] *nm* lemon; **c. pressé** = freshly squeezed lemon juice served with water and sugar; **c. vert** lime ▪ **citronnade** *nf Br* lemon squash, *Am* lemonade

**citrouille** [sitruj] *nf* pumpkin

**civet** [sivɛ] *nm* stew

**civière** [sivjɛr] *nf* stretcher

**civil, -e** [sivil] **1** *adj (guerre, mariage, droits)* civil; *(non militaire)* civilian; *(courtois)* civil; **année civile** calendar year **2** *nm* civilian; **dans le c.** in civilian life; **en c.** *(policier)* in plain clothes ▪ **civilité** *nf* civility

**civilisation** [sivilizasjɔ̃] *nf* civilization ▪ **civilisé, -e** *adj* civilized

**civique** [sivik] *adj* civic; *Scol* **instruction c.** civics

**clair, -e** [klɛr] **1** *adj (net, limpide, évident)* clear; *(éclairé, pâle)* light; **bleu/vert c.** light blue/green **2** *adv (voir)* clearly; **il fait c.** it's light **3** *nm* **en c.** in plain language; **c. de lune** moonlight

**clairière** [klerjɛr] *nf* clearing

**clairon** [klɛrɔ̃] *nm* bugle; *(soldat)* bugler

**clairsemé, -e** [klɛrsəme] *adj (auditoire, population)* sparse

**clairvoyant, -e** [klɛrvwajɑ̃, -ɑ̃t] *adj* perceptive

**clameur** [klamœr] *nf* clamour

**clan** [klɑ̃] *nm (tribu)* clan; *Péj (groupe)* clique

**clandestin, -e** [klɑ̃dɛstɛ̃, -in] *adj (rencontre)* clandestine; *(mouvement)* underground; *(travailleur)* illegal

**clapier** [klapje] *nm* (rabbit) hutch

**clapoter** [klapɔte] *vi (vagues)* to lap

**claque** [klak] *nf Fam* slap

**claquer** [klake] **1** *vt (porte)* to slam **2** *vi (porte)* to slam; *(drapeau)* to flap; *(talons)* to click; *(coup de feu)* to ring out; **elle claque des dents** her teeth are chattering **3 se claquer** *vpr* **se c. un muscle** to pull a muscle ▪ **claquement** *nm (de porte)* slam(ming)

**claquettes** [klakɛt] *nfpl* tap dancing; **faire des c.** to do tap dancing

**clarifier** [klarifje] *vt* to clarify ▪ **clarification** *nf* clarification

**clarinette** [klarinɛt] *nf* clarinet

**clarté** [klarte] *nf (lumière)* light; *(transparence)* clearness; *Fig (d'explications)* clarity; **avec c.** clearly

**classe** [klɑs] *nf (catégorie, leçon, élèves)* class; **en c. de sixième** *Br* in the first year, *Am* in fifth grade; **aller en c.** to go to school; **avoir de la c.** *(personne)* to have class; **(salle de) c.** classroom; **de première c.** *(billet, compartiment)* first-class; **c. ouvrière/moyenne** working/middle class; **c. sociale** social class

**classer** [klɑse] **1** *vt (objets)* to classify; *(papiers)* to file; **c. une affaire** to consider a matter closed **2 se classer** *vpr* **se c. parmi les meilleurs** to rank among the best; *Sport* **se c. troisième** to be placed third ▪ **classé, -e** *adj (monument)* listed; *(au tennis)* seeded ▪ **classement** *nm* classification; *(de papiers)* filing; *(rang)* place; *Sport* table ▪ **classeur** *nm (meuble)* filing cabinet; *(portefeuille)* ring binder

**classifier** [klasifje] *vt* to classify ▪ **classification** *nf* classification

**classique** [klasik] **1** *adj (période)* classical; *(typique, conventionnel)* classic **2** *nm (œuvre)* classic; *(auteur)* classical author

**claustrophobe** [klostrɔfɔb] *adj* claustrophobic

**clavecin** [klavsɛ̃] *nm* harpsichord

**clavicule** [klavikyl] *nf* collarbone

**clavier** [klavje] *nm* keyboard

**clé, clef** [kle] **1** *nf (de porte)* key; *(outil) Br* spanner, *Am* wrench; **fermer qch à c.** to lock sth; **c. de contact** ignition key; *Mus* **c. de sol** treble clef; *Fig* **c. de voûte** cornerstone **2** *adj* key; **poste c.** key post

**clément, -e** [klemɑ̃, -ɑ̃t] *adj (juge)* clement; *(temps)* mild ▪ **clémence** *nf (de juge)* clemency; *(de temps)* mildness

**clémentine** [klemɑ̃tin] *nf* clementine
**clerc** [klɛr] *nm Rel* cleric; **c. de notaire** ≃ solicitor's clerk ▪ **clergé** *nm* clergy ▪ **clérical, -e, -aux, -ales** *adj* clerical
**cliché** [kliʃe] *nm (photo)* photo; *(negative)* negative; *(idée)* cliché
**client, -e** [klijɑ̃, -ɑ̃t] *nmf (de magasin)* customer; *(d'avocat)* client; *(d'hôtel)* guest; *(de taxi)* fare ▪ **clientèle** *nf (de magasin)* customers; *(d'avocat)* practice
**cligner** [kliɲe] *vi* **c. des yeux** to blink; **c. de l'œil** to wink
**clignoter** [kliŋɔte] *vi (lumière, voyant)* to flash ▪ **clignotant** *nm (de voiture) Br* indicator, *Am* flasher; **mettre son c.** to indicate
**climat** [klima] *nm (de région) & Fig* climate ▪ **climatique** *adj* climatic
**climatisation** [klimatizɑsjɔ̃] *nf* air-conditioning ▪ **climatisé, -e** *adj* air-conditioned
**clin d'œil** [klɛ̃dœj] (*pl* **clins d'œil**) *nm* wink; **faire un c. à qn** to wink at sb; **en un c.** in a flash
**clinique** [klinik] *nf (hôpital)* clinic
**clinquant, -e** [klɛ̃kɑ̃, -ɑ̃t] *adj* flashy
**clip** [klip] *nm (vidéo)* (music) video
**cliquer** [klike] *vi Ordinat* to click
**cliqueter** [klikte] *vi (monnaie, clefs)* to jingle ▪ **cliquetis** *nm (de monnaie, de clefs)* jingling
**clivage** [klivaʒ] *nm (de société)* divide; *(de parti)* split
**clochard, -e** [klɔʃar, -ard] *nmf* tramp
**cloche** [klɔʃ] *nf (d'église)* bell; **c. à fromage** covered cheese dish ▪ **clocher 1** *nm (d'église)* bell tower, steeple **2** *vi Fam* **il y a quelque chose qui cloche** there's something wrong somewhere
**cloche-pied** [klɔʃpje] **à cloche-pied** *adv* **sauter à c.** to hop
**cloison** [klwazɔ̃] *nf (entre pièces)* partition
**cloître** [klwɑtr] *nm (de monastère)* cloister; *(pour moines)* monastery; *(pour religieuses)* convent
**clone** [klon] *nm Biol* clone
**clopin-clopant** [klɔpɛ̃klɔpɑ̃] *adv* **aller c.** to hobble along
**cloque** [klɔk] *nf (au pied)* blister
**clore*** [klɔr] *vt (réunion)* to conclude; *(débat)* to close; *Ordinat* **c. une session** to log off
**clos, -e** [klo, kloz] **1** *adj (porte, volets)* closed; **l'incident est c.** the matter is closed; **espace c.** enclosed space **2** *nm* enclosure
**clôture** [klotyr] *nf (barrière)* fence; *(de réunion)* conclusion; *(de débat)* closing; *(de Bourse)* close ▪ **clôturer** *vt (terrain)* to enclose
**clou** [klu] *nm (pointe)* nail; *(de spectacle)* main attraction; **les clous** *(passage) Br* the pedestrian crossing, *Am* the crosswalk; **c. de girofle** clove ▪ **clouer** *vt (au mur)* to nail up; *(ensemble)* to nail together; **cloué au lit** confined to (one's) bed
**clown** [klun] *nm* clown; **faire le c.** to clown around
**club** [klœb] *nm* club
**cm** (*abrév* **centimètre**) cm
**coalition** [kɔalisjɔ̃] *nf* coalition
**cobaye** [kɔbaj] *nm (animal) & Fig* guinea pig
**cocaïne** [kɔkain] *nf* cocaine
**coccinelle** [kɔksinɛl] *nf (insecte) Br* ladybird, *Am* ladybug; *(voiture)* Beetle
**cocher¹** [kɔʃe] *vt Br* to tick, *Am* to check
**cocher²** [kɔʃe] *nm* coachman
**cochon, -onne** [kɔʃɔ̃, -ɔn] **1** *nm (animal)* pig; *(viande)* pork; **c. d'Inde** guinea pig **2** *nmf (personne sale)* pig **3** *adj (histoire, film)* dirty ▪ **cochonnerie** *nf (chose sans valeur)* trash, *Br* rubbish; *(obscénité)* smutty remark; **manger des cochonneries** to eat junk food
**cocktail** [kɔktɛl] *nm (boisson)* cocktail; *(réunion)* cocktail party; **c. de fruits** fruit cocktail
**coco** [kɔko] *nm* **noix de c.** coconut
**cocu, -e** [kɔky] **1** *adj* **il est c.** his wife's cheating on him **2** *nm* cuckold
**code** [kɔd] *nm (symboles, lois) & Ordinat* code; **passer le c.** *(du permis de*

*conduire)* = to sit the written part of one's driving test; **codes** *Br* dipped headlights, *Am* low beams; **le C. de la route** *Br* the Highway Code, *Am* the traffic regulations; *Jur* **c. civil/pénal** civil/penal code; **c. confidentiel** security code; *(de carte bancaire)* PIN; **c. postal** *Br* postcode, *Am* zip code ▪ **code-barres** (*pl* **codes-barres**) *nm* bar code ▪ **coder** *vt* to code

**coéquipier, -ère** [kɔekipje, -ɛr] *nmf* team-mate

**cœur** [kœr] *nm* heart; *Cartes (couleur)* hearts; **avoir mal au c.** to feel sick; **par c.** (off) by heart; **de bon c.** *(volontiers)* willingly; *(rire)* heartily

**coexister** [kɔegziste] *vi* to coexist

**coffre** [kɔr] *nm (meuble)* chest; *(pour objets de valeur)* safe; *(de voiture) Br* boot, *Am* trunk; **c. à bagages** *(d'avion)* baggage compartment; **c. à jouets** toy box ▪ **coffre-fort** (*pl* **coffres-forts**) *nm* safe ▪ **coffret** *nm (petit coffre)* box; **c. à bijoux** *Br* jewellery *or Am* jewelry box

**cogner** [kɔɲe] **1** *vt (heurter)* to knock **2** *vi (buter)* to bang (**sur/contre** on) **3 se cogner** *vpr* to bang oneself; **se c. la tête contre qch** to bang one's head on sth; **se c. à qch** to bang into sth

**cohabiter** [kɔabite] *vi* to live together; **c. avec qn** to live with sb

**cohérent, -e** [kɔerɑ̃, -ɑ̃t] *adj (discours)* coherent; *(attitude)* consistent ▪ **cohérence** *nf (de discours)* coherence; *(d'attitude)* consistency ▪ **cohésion** *nf* cohesion

**cohue** [kɔy] *nf* crowd

**coiffe** [kwaf] *nf* headdress

**coiffer** [kwafe] **1** *vt Fig (surmonter)* to cap; *(service)* to head; **c. qn de qch** to put sth on sb's head; **elle est bien coiffée** her hair is lovely **2 se coiffer** *vpr* to do one's hair; **se c. de qch** to put sth on

**coiffeur, -euse**[1] [kwafœr, -øz] *nmf* hairdresser ▪ **coiffeuse**[2] *nf (meuble)* dressing table ▪ **coiffure** *nf (chapeau)* headgear; *(coupe de cheveux)* hairstyle

**coin** [kwɛ̃] *nm (angle)* corner; *(endroit)* spot; *(cale)* wedge; **faire le c.** to be on the corner; **dans le c.** in the area; *Fam* **le petit c.** *(toilettes)* the smallest room in the house

**coincer** [kwɛ̃se] **1** *vt (mécanisme, tiroir)* to jam; *(caler)* to wedge **2** *vi (mécanisme, tiroir)* to jam **3 se coincer** *vpr (mécanisme)* to jam; **se c. le doigt dans la porte** to catch one's finger in the door ▪ **coincé, -e** *adj (mécanisme, tiroir)* stuck, jammed

**coïncider** [kɔɛ̃side] *vi* to coincide (**avec** with) ▪ **coïncidence** *nf* coincidence

**col** [kɔl] *nm (de chemise)* collar; *Géog* col; **c. en V** V-neck; **c. roulé** *Br* polo neck, *Am* turtleneck

**colère** [kɔlɛr] *nf* anger; **être en c. (contre qn)** to be angry (with sb); **se mettre en c.** to get angry (**contre** with) ▪ **coléreux, -euse** *adj (personne)* quick-tempered

**colimaçon** [kɔlimasɔ̃] **en colimaçon** *adv* **escalier en c.** spiral staircase

**colin** [kɔlɛ̃] *nm (merlu)* hake; *(lieu noir)* coley

**colique** [kɔlik] *nf Br* diarrhoea, *Am* diarrhea

**colis** [kɔli] *nm* parcel

**collaborer** [kɔlabɔre] *vi* collaborate (**avec** with); **c. à qch** *(projet)* to take part in sth ▪ **collaborateur, -trice** *nmf (aide)* assistant ▪ **collaboration** *nf (aide)* collaboration

**collage** [kɔlaʒ] *nm (œuvre, jeu)* collage

**collant, -e** [kɔlɑ̃, -ɑ̃t] **1** *adj (papier)* sticky; *(vêtement)* skin-tight **2** *nm Br* tights, *Am* pantihose

**colle** [kɔl] *nf (transparente)* glue; *(blanche)* paste; *Fam (question)* poser; *Fam (retenue)* detention

**collecte** [kɔlɛkt] *nf* collection ▪ **collecter** *vt* to collect

**collectif, -ive** [kɔlɛktif, -iv] *adj* collective ▪ **collectivité** *nf (groupe)* community

**collection** [kɔlɛksjɔ̃] *nf (ensemble)* collection; **faire la c. de qch** to collect

sth ▪ **collectionner** *vt* to collect ▪ **collectionneur, -euse** *nmf* collector
**collège** [kɔlɛʒ] *nm (école)* school ▪ **collégien** *nm* schoolboy ▪ **collégienne** *nf* schoolgirl
**collègue** [kɔlɛg] *nmf* colleague
**coller** [kɔle] **1** *vt (timbre)* to stick; *(à la colle transparente)* to glue; *(à la colle blanche)* to paste; *(enveloppe)* to stick (down); *(deux objets)* to stick together; *(affiche)* to stick up; *Fam* **c. un élève** *(en punition)* to keep a pupil in; *Fam* **être collé** *(à un examen)* to fail **2 se coller** *vpr* **se c. contre un mur** to flatten oneself against a wall
**collier** [kɔlje] *nm (bijou)* necklace; *(de chien)* collar
**colline** [kɔlin] *nf* hill
**collision** [kɔlizjɔ̃] *nf (de véhicules)* collision; **entrer en c. avec qch** to collide with sth
**colloque** [kɔlɔk] *nm (conférence)* seminar
**colmater** [kɔlmate] *vt* to fill in
**colombe** [kɔlɔ̃b] *nf* dove
**Colombie** [kɔlɔ̃bi] *nf* **la C.** Columbia ▪ **colombien, -enne 1** *adj* Columbian **2** *nmf* **C., Colombienne** Columbian
**colon** [kɔlɔ̃] *nm (pionnier)* settler, colonist
**colonel** [kɔlɔnɛl] *nm (d'infanterie)* colonel
**colonial, -e, -aux, -ales** [kɔlɔnjal, -jo] *adj* colonial
**colonie** [kɔlɔni] *nf* colony; **c. de vacances** *Br* (children's) holiday camp, *Am* summer camp
**coloniser** [kɔlɔnize] *vt* to colonize
**colonne** [kɔlɔn] *nf* column; *Anat* **c. vertébrale** spine
**colorer** [kɔlɔre] *vt* to colour; **c. qch en vert** to colour sth green ▪ **colorant, -e** *nm (pour teindre)* colorant; *(alimentaire)* colouring ▪ **colorier** *vt (dessin)* to colour (in) ▪ **coloris** *nm (nuance)* shade
**colosse** [kɔlɔs] *nm* giant ▪ **colossal, -e, -aux, -ales** *adj* colossal
**colporter** [kɔlpɔrte] *vt (marchandises)* to hawk; *(rumeur)* to spread
**colza** [kɔlza] *nm* rape
**coma** [kɔma] *nm* coma; **être dans le c.** to be in a coma
**combat** [kɔ̃ba] *nm (bataille) & Fig* fight; **c. de boxe** boxing match ▪ **combatif, -ive** *adj* combative
**combattre*** [kɔ̃batr] **1** *vt (personne, incendie)* to fight (against); *(maladie)* to fight **2** *vi* to fight ▪ **combattant, -e 1** *adj (troupes)* fighting **2** *nmf* combattant; **anciens combattants** veterans
**combien** [kɔ̃bjɛ̃] **1** *adv* (**a**) *(en quantité)* how much; *(en nombre)* how many; **c. d'argent** how much money; **c. de temps** how long; **c. de gens** how many people; **c. y a-t-il d'ici à...?** how far is it to...? (**b**) *(comme)* how; **tu verras c. il est bête** you'll see how silly he is **2** *nm inv Fam* **le c. sommes-nous?** what's the date?
**combinaison** [kɔ̃binɛzɔ̃] *nf (assemblage)* combination; *(vêtement de travail) Br* boiler suit, *Am* coveralls; **c. de ski** ski suit
**combiner** [kɔbine] **1** *vt (unir)* to combine **2 se combiner** *vpr* to combine ▪ **combiné** *nm (de téléphone)* receiver
**comble** [kɔ̃bl] **1** *adj (salle, bus)* packed; *Théât* **faire salle c.** to have a full house **2** *nm* **le c. du bonheur** the height of happiness; **c'est un** *ou* **le c.!** that's the last straw!
**combler** [kɔ̃ble] *vt (trou)* to fill in; *(lacune)* to fill; *(désir)* to satisfy
**combustible** [kɔ̃bystibl] **1** *adj* combustible **2** *nm* fuel ▪ **combustion** *nf* combustion
**comédie** [kɔmedi] *nf* comedy; **jouer la c.** to act; **c. musicale** musical ▪ **comédien** *nm* actor ▪ **comédienne** *nf* actress
**comestible** [kɔmɛstibl] *adj* edible
**comète** [kɔmɛt] *nf* comet
**comique** [kɔmik] **1** *adj (amusant)* funny, comical; *(acteur, rôle)* comedy **2** *nm (genre)* comedy; *(acteur)* comic actor
**comité** [kɔmite] *nm* committee; **c.**

**d'entreprise** works council

**commandant** [kɔmɑ̃dɑ̃] *nm (de navire)* captain; *(grade) (dans l'infanterie)* major; *(dans l'aviation)* squadron leader; *Aviat* **c. de bord** captain

**commande** [kɔmɑ̃d] *nf* (**a**) *(achat)* order; **sur c.** to order; **passer une c.** to place an order (**b**) *Tech (action, manette)* control; *Ordinat* command; **c. à distance** remote control; **à c. vocale** voice-activated

**commandement** [kɔmɑ̃dmɑ̃] *nm (ordre, autorité)* command; *Rel* Commandment

**commander** [kɔmɑ̃de] **1** *vt (diriger, exiger)* to command; *(marchandises)* to order (**à** from) **2** *vi* **c. à qn de faire qch** to command sb to do sth

**commando** [kɔmɑ̃do] *nm* commando

---

**COMME** [kɔm] **1** *adv* (**a**) *(devant nom, pronom)* like; **c. moi/elle** like me/her; **c. cela** like that; **qu'as-tu c. diplômes?** what do you have in the way of certificates?; **les femmes c. les hommes** men and women alike; **P c. pomme** p as in 'pomme'

(**b**) *(devant proposition)* as; **il écrit c. il parle** he writes as he speaks; **c. si** as if; **c. pour faire qch** as if to do sth

**2** *adv (exclamatif)* **regarde c. il pleut!** look how it's raining!; **c. c'est petit!** isn't it small!

**3** *conj (cause)* as, since; **c. tu es mon ami...** as *or* since you're my friend...; **c. elle entrait** (just) as she was coming in

---

**commémorer** [kɔmemɔre] *vt* to commemorate ▪ **commémoration** *nf* commemoration

**commencer** [kɔmɑ̃se] *vti* to begin, to start (**à faire** to do, doing; **par qch** with sth; **par faire** by doing); **pour c.** to begin with ▪ **commencement** *nm* beginning, start; **au c.** at the beginning *or* start

**comment** [kɔmɑ̃] *adv* how; **c. le sais-tu?** how do you know?; **c. t'appelles-tu?** what's your name?; **c. est-il?** what is he like?; **c. va-t-il?** how is he?; **c. faire?** what's to be done?; **c.?** *(pour faire répéter)* pardon?

**commentaire** [kɔmɑ̃tɛr] *nm (remarque)* comment; *(de radio, de télévision)* commentary ▪ **commentateur, -trice** *nmf* commentator ▪ **commenter** *vt* to comment (up)on

**commérages** [kɔmeraʒ] *nmpl* gossip

**commerçant, -e** [kɔmɛrsɑ̃, -ɑ̃t] **1** *nmf* trader; *(de magasin)* shopkeeper **2** *adj* **rue commerçante** shopping street

**commerce** [kɔmɛrs] *nm (activité, secteur)* trade; *(affaires, magasin)* business; **c. de proximité** *Br* local shop, *Am* local store ▪ **commercial, -e, -aux, -ales** *adj* commercial ▪ **commercialisation** *nf* marketing ▪ **commercialiser** *vt* to market

**commère** [kɔmɛr] *nf* gossip

**commettre*** [kɔmɛtr] *vt (meurtre)* to commit; *(erreur)* to make

**commis** [kɔmi] *nm (de magasin)* shop assistant; *(de bureau)* clerk

**commissaire** [kɔmisɛr] *nm (de course)* steward; **c. (de police)** *Br* ≃ police superintendent, *Am* ≃ police captain ▪ **commissariat** *nm* **c. (de police)** (central) police station

**commission** [kɔmisjɔ̃] *nf (course)* errand; *(message)* message; *(comité)* commission, committee; *Com (pourcentage)* commission (**sur** on); **faire les commissions** to go shopping

**commode** [kɔmɔd] **1** *adj (pratique)* handy; **pas c.** *(pas aimable)* awkward; *(difficile)* tricky **2** *nf Br* chest of drawers, *Am* dresser ▪ **commodité** *nf* convenience

**commun, -e** [kɔmœ̃, -yn] **1** *adj (non exclusif, répandu, vulgaire)* common; *(cuisine)* shared; *(démarche)* joint; **peu c.** uncommon; **ami c.** mutual friend; **en c.** in common; **mettre qch en c.** to share sth **2** *nm* **hors du c.** out of the ordinary

**communauté** [kɔmynote] *nf (collectivité)* community; **la C. (économique) européenne** the (European) Economic

Community; **la C. d'États indépendants** the Commonwealth of Independent States ■ **communautaire** *adj (de la CE)* Community; **vie c.** community life

**commune** [kɔmyn] *nf (municipalité)* commune ■ **communal, -e, -aux, -ales** *adj Br* ≃ council, *Am* ≃ district; **école communale** ≃ local *Br* primary *or Am* grade school

**communicatif, -ive** [kɔmynikatif, -iv] *adj (personne)* communicative; *(rire)* infectious

**communication** [kɔmynikɑsjɔ̃] *nf* communication; **c. téléphonique** telephone call; **je vous passe la c.** I'll put you through; **la c. est mauvaise** the line is bad

**communion** [kɔmynjɔ̃] *nf* communion; *Rel* (Holy) Communion

**communiquer** [kɔmynike] **1** *vt* to communicate (**à** to); *(maladie)* to pass on (**à** to) **2** *vi (personne, pièces)* to communicate (**avec** with) **3 se communiquer** *vpr* to spread (**à** to) ■ **communiqué** *nm (avis)* communiqué; **c. de presse** press release

**communisme** [kɔmynism] *nm* communism ■ **communiste** *adj & nmf* communist

**commutateur** [kɔmytatœr] *nm (bouton)* switch

**compact, -e** [kɔ̃pakt] **1** *adj (foule, amas)* dense; *(appareil)* compact **2** *nm (CD)* compact disc

**compagne** [kɔ̃paɲ] *nf (camarade)* companion; *(concubine)* partner

**compagnie** [kɔ̃paɲi] *nf (présence, société, soldats)* company; **tenir c. à qn** to keep sb company

**compagnon** [kɔ̃paɲɔ̃] *nm* companion; *(concubin)* partner; **c. de jeu** playmate; **c. de route** travelling companion

**comparaître*** [kɔ̃parɛtr] *vi (devant tribunal)* to appear (in court) (**devant** before)

**comparer** [kɔ̃pare] *vt* to compare (**à** to, with) ■ **comparable** *adj* comparable (**à** to, with) ■ **comparaison** *nf* comparison (**avec** with); **en c. de...** in comparison with...

**compartiment** [kɔ̃partimɑ̃] *nm* compartment; **c. à bagages** *(de car)* luggage compartment; **c. fumeurs** smoking compartment

**compas** [kɔ̃pa] *nm Math Br* (pair of) compasses, *Am* compass; *Naut* compass

**compassion** [kɔ̃pɑsjɔ̃] *nf* compassion

**compatible** [kɔ̃patibl] *adj* compatible (**avec** with) ■ **compatibilité** *nf* compatibility

**compatir** [kɔ̃patir] *vi* to sympathize ■ **compatissant, -e** *adj* compassionate, sympathetic

**compatriote** [kɔ̃patrijɔt] *nmf* compatriot

**compenser** [kɔ̃pɑ̃se] **1** *vt (perte, défaut)* to make up for, to compensate for **2** *vi* to compensate ■ **compensation** *nf (de perte)* compensation; **en c.** in compensation (**de** for)

**compétent, -e** [kɔ̃petɑ̃, -ɑ̃t] *adj* competent ■ **compétence** *nf* competence; **compétences** *(connaissances)* skills, abilities

**compétition** [kɔ̃petisjɔ̃] *nf (rivalité)* competition; *(épreuve sportive)* event; **être en c. avec qn** to compete with sb; **sport de c.** competitive sport ■ **compétitif, -ive** *adj* competitive

**compiler** [kɔ̃pile] *vt* to compile

**complaire*** [kɔ̃plɛr] **se complaire** *vpr* **se c. dans qch/à faire qch** to delight in sth/in doing sth

**complaisant, -e** [kɔ̃plɛzɑ̃, -ɑ̃t] *adj (bienveillant)* kind, obliging; *(satisfait)* complacent ■ **complaisance** *nf (bienveillance)* kindness; *(vanité)* complacency

**complément** [kɔ̃plemɑ̃] *nm (reste)* rest; *Gram* complement; **un c. d'information** additional information; **c. d'objet direct/indirect** direct/indirect object ■ **complémentaire** *adj* complementary; *(détails)* additional

**complet, -ète** [kɔ̃plɛ, -ɛt] **1** *adj (entier,*

*absolu)* complete; *(train, hôtel, théâtre)* full; *(pain)* wholemeal **2** *nm (costume)* suit

**compléter** [kɔ̃plete] **1** *vt (collection, formation)* to complete; *(formulaire)* to fill in; *(somme)* to make up **2 se compléter** *vpr* to complement each other

**complexe** [kɔ̃plɛks] **1** *adj* complex **2** *nm (sentiment, construction)* complex; **avoir des complexes** to have a hang-up ▪ **complexé, -e** *adj Fam* hung up (**par** about) ▪ **complexité** *nf* complexity

**complication** [kɔ̃plikɑsjɔ̃] *nf (ennui) & Méd* complication; *(complexité)* complexity

**complice** [kɔ̃plis] **1** *nm* accomplice **2** *adj (regard)* knowing; *(silence)* conniving; **être c. de qch** to be a party to sth ▪ **complicité** *nf* complicity

**compliment** [kɔ̃plimɑ̃] *nm* compliment; **faire des compliments à qn** to pay sb compliments ▪ **complimenter** *vt* to compliment (**sur** on)

**compliquer** [kɔ̃plike] **1** *vt* to complicate **2 se compliquer** *vpr (situation)* to get complicated; **se c. la vie** to make life complicated for oneself ▪ **compliqué, -e** *adj* complicated

**complot** [kɔ̃plo] *nm* conspiracy (**contre** against)

**comporter** [kɔ̃pɔrte] **1** *vt (contenir)* to contain; *(être constitué de)* to consist of **2 se comporter** *vpr (personne)* to behave ▪ **comportement** [-əmɑ̃] *nm* behaviour

**composer** [kɔ̃poze] **1** *vt (faire partie de)* to make up; *(musique, poème)* to compose; *(numéro de téléphone)* to dial; *Typ* to set; **être composé de qch** to be made up *or* composed of sth

**2** *vi (étudiant)* to take a test

**3 se composer** *vpr* **se c. de qch** to be made up *or* composed of sth ▪ **composant** *nm* component ▪ **composante** *nf* component

**compositeur, -trice** [kɔ̃pozitœr, -tris] *nmf (musicien)* composer; *(typographe)* typesetter

**composition** [kɔ̃pozisjɔ̃] *nf (de musique, de poème)* composing; *Typ* typesetting; *(éléments)* composition; *(d'aliment)* ingredients; *(examen)* test

**composter** [kɔ̃pɔste] *vt (billet)* to cancel

**compote** [kɔ̃pɔt] *nf Br* stewed fruit, *Am* sauce; **c. de pommes** *Br* stewed apples, *Am* applesauce

**compréhensible** [kɔ̃preɑ̃sibl] *adj (justifié)* understandable; *(clair)* comprehensible ▪ **compréhensif, -ive** *adj* understanding ▪ **compréhension** *nf* understanding

**comprendre*** [kɔ̃prɑ̃dr] **1** *vt (par l'esprit, par les sentiments)* to understand; *(être composé de)* to consist of; *(comporter)* to include; **mal c. qch** to misunderstand sth; **je n'y comprends rien** I can't make head or tail of it **2 se comprendre** *vpr* **ça se comprend** that's understandable

**compresse** [kɔ̃prɛs] *nf* compress

**comprimé** [kɔ̃prime] *nm (médicament)* tablet

**comprimer** [kɔ̃prime] *vt (gaz, artère)* to compress

**compris, -e** [kɔ̃pri, -is] **1** *pp voir* **comprendre 2** *adj (inclus)* included (**dans** in); **y c.** including

**compromettre*** [kɔ̃prɔmɛtr] *vt (personne)* to compromise; *(sécurité)* to jeopardize ▪ **compromis** *nm* compromise

**comptabiliser** [kɔ̃tabilize] *vt (compter)* to count

**comptabilité** [kɔ̃tabilite] *nf (comptes)* accounts; *(science)* book-keeping, accounting; *(service)* accounts department ▪ **comptable** *nmf* accountant

**comptant** [kɔ̃tɑ̃] **1** *adv* **payer c.** to pay (in) cash **2** *nm* **acheter au c.** to buy for cash

**COMPTE** [kɔ̃t] *nm* (**a**) *(de banque, de commerçant)* account; *(calcul)* calculation; **avoir un c. en banque** to have a bank account; **faire ses comptes** to do one's accounts; **c. chèque** *Br*

current account, *Am* checking account; **c. à rebours** countdown (**b**) *(expressions)* **en fin de c.** all things considered; **tenir c. de qch** to take sth into account; **c. tenu de qch** considering sth; **se rendre c. de qch** to realize sth; **rendre c. de qch** *(exposer)* to report on sth; *(justifier)* to account for sth; **travailler à son c.** to be self-employed; *Fig* **être loin du c.** to be wide of the mark ■ **compte-gouttes** *nm inv* dropper; *Fig* **au c.** in dribs and drabs

**compter** [kɔ̃te] **1** *vt (calculer)* to count; *(prévoir)* to allow; *(include)* to include; **c. faire qch** *(espérer)* to expect to do sth; *(avoir l'intention de)* to intend to do sth; **c. qch à qn** *(facturer)* to charge sb for sth; **sans c....** *(sans parler de)* not to mention...
**2** *vi (calculer, être important)* to count; **c. sur qn/qch** to count *or* rely on sb/sth; **à c. de demain** as from tomorrow
**3 se compter** *vpr* **ses membres se comptent par milliers** it has thousands of members ■ **compteur** *nm* meter; **c. de gaz** gas meter; *Aut* **c. kilométrique** *Br* milometer, *Am* odometer; *Aut* **c. de vitesse** speedometer

**compte rendu** [kɔ̃trɑ̃dy] (*pl* **comptes rendus**) *nm* report; *(de livre, de film)* review

**comptoir** [kɔ̃twar] *nm (de magasin)* counter; *(de café)* bar

**comte** [kɔ̃t] *nm (noble)* count; *(en Grande-Bretagne)* earl ■ **comtesse** *nf* countess

**concéder** [kɔ̃sede] *vt (victoire, but)* to concede; **c. qch à qn** to grant sb sth

**concentrer** [kɔ̃sɑ̃tre] **1** *vt* to concentrate; *(attention)* to focus **2 se concentrer** *vpr (réfléchir)* to concentrate ■ **concentration** *nf* concentration ■ **concentré, -e 1** *adj (lait)* condensed; *(attentif)* concentrating (hard) **2** *nm* **c. de tomates** tomato purée

**concept** [kɔ̃sɛpt] *nm* concept ■ **conception** *nf (d'idée)* conception; *(création)* design; **c. assistée par ordinateur** computer-aided design

**concerner** [kɔ̃sɛrne] *vt* to concern; **en ce qui me concerne** as far as I'm concerned ■ **concernant** *prép* concerning

**concert** [kɔ̃sɛr] *nm (de musique)* concert

**concerter** [kɔ̃sɛrte] **se concerter** *vpr* to consult together ■ **concertation** *nf* consultation

**concession** [kɔ̃sesjɔ̃] *nf (compromis)* concession (**à** to); *(terrain)* plot ■ **concessionnaire** *nmf* dealer

**concevoir*** [kɔ̃səvwar] **1** *vt (enfant, plan, idée)* to conceive; *(produit)* to design; *(comprendre)* to understand **2 se concevoir** *vpr* **ça se conçoit** that's understandable ■ **concevable** *adj* conceivable

**concierge** [kɔ̃sjɛrʒ] *nmf* caretaker, *Am* janitor

**concilier** [kɔ̃silje] *vt (choses)* to reconcile

**concis, -e** [kɔ̃si, -is] *adj* concise

**conclure*** [kɔ̃klyr] *vt (terminer)* to conclude; *(accord)* to finalize; *(marché)* to clinch ■ **concluant, -e** *adj* conclusive ■ **conclusion** *nf* conclusion; **tirer une c. de qch** to draw a conclusion from sth

**concombre** [kɔ̃kɔ̃br] *nm* cucumber

**concorder** [kɔ̃kɔrde] *vi (preuves, dates, témoignages)* to tally (**avec** with)

**concourir*** [kɔ̃kurir] *vi Sport* to compete (**pour** for); *(converger)* to converge; **c. à qch/faire qch** to contribute to sth/to do sth

**concours** [kɔ̃kur] *nm (examen)* competitive examination; *(jeu)* competition; *(aide)* assistance; **c. de beauté** beauty contest

**concret, -ète** [kɔ̃kre, -ɛt] *adj* concrete ■ **concrétiser 1** *vt (rêve)* to realize; *(projet)* to carry out **2 se concretiser** *vpr* to materialize

**conçu, -e** [kɔ̃sy] **1** *pp de* **concevoir 2** *adj* **c. pour faire qch** designed to do sth

**concubine** [kɔ̃kybin] *nf Jur* cohabitant ▪ **concubinage** *nm* cohabitation; **vivre en c.** to cohabit

**concurrent, -e** [kɔ̃kyrɑ̃, -ɑ̃t] *nmf* competitor ▪ **concurrence** *nf* competition; **faire c. à** to compete with; **jusqu'à c. de 100 euros** up to the amount of 100 euros ▪ **concurrencer** *vt* to compete with

**condamnation** [kɔ̃danɑsjɔ̃] *nf Jur (jugement)* conviction (**pour** for); *(peine)* sentence (**à** to); *(critique)* condemnation; **c. à mort** death sentence

**condamner** [kɔ̃dane] *vt (blâmer)* to condemn; *Jur* to sentence (**à** to); *(porte)* to block up; **c. qn à une amende** to fine sb; **c. qn à qch** *(forcer à)* to force sb into sth ▪ **condamné, -e 1** *adj (malade)* terminally ill **2** *nmf (prisonnier)* convicted person

**condensation** [kɔ̃dɑ̃sasjɔ̃] *nf* condensation

**condescendant, -e** [kɔ̃desɑ̃dɑ̃, -ɑ̃t] *adj* condescending

**condition** [kɔ̃disjɔ̃] *nf (état, stipulation, sort)* condition; *(classe sociale)* station; **conditions** *(circonstances)* conditions; *(de contrat)* terms; **à c. de faire qch, à c. que l'on fasse qch** providing *or* provided (that) one does sth ▪ **conditionnel, -elle 1** *adj* conditional **2** *nm Gram* conditional

**conditionner** [kɔ̃disjɔne] *vt (être la condition de)* to govern; *(emballer)* to package; *(personne)* to condition ▪ **conditionnement** *nm (emballage)* packaging; *(de personne)* conditioning

**condoléances** [kɔ̃dɔleɑ̃s] *nfpl* condolences

**conducteur, -trice** [kɔ̃dyktœr, -tris] **1** *nmf (de véhicule, de train)* driver **2** *adj Él* **fil c.** lead (wire)

**conduire*** [kɔ̃dɥir] **1** *vt (troupeau)* to lead; *(voiture)* to drive; *(moto)* to ride; *(électricité)* to conduct; **c. qn à** *(accompagner)* to take sb to **2** *vi (en voiture)* to drive; **c. à** *(lieu)* to lead to **3 se conduire** *vpr* to behave

**conduit** [kɔ̃dɥi] *nm (tuyau)* pipe

**conduite** [kɔ̃dɥit] *nf (de véhicule)* driving (**de** of); *(d'entreprise)* management; *(tuyau)* pipe; *(comportement)* conduct, behaviour; **c. à gauche/droite** *(volant)* left-hand/right-hand drive; **c. de gaz** gas main

**cône** [kon] *nm* cone

**confection** [kɔ̃fɛksjɔ̃] *nf (réalisation)* making (**de** of); *(industrie)* clothing industry; **vêtements de c.** ready-to-wear clothes ▪ **confectionner** *vt* to make

**confédération** [kɔ̃federɑsjɔ̃] *nf* confederation

**conférence** [kɔ̃ferɑ̃s] *nf (réunion)* conference; *(exposé)* lecture; **c. de presse** press conference

**conférer** [kɔ̃fere] *vt (titre)* to confer (**à** on)

**confesser** [kɔ̃fese] *Rel* **1** *vt* to confess **2 se confesser** *vpr* to confess (**à** to) ▪ **confession** *nf* confession

**confettis** [kɔ̃feti] *nmpl* confetti

**confiance** [kɔ̃fjɑ̃s] *nf* confidence; **faire c. à qn, avoir c. en qn** to trust sb; **de c.** *(mission)* of trust; *(personne)* trustworthy; **c. en soi** self-confidence; **avoir c. en soi** to be self-confident ▪ **confiant, -e** *adj (qui fait confiance)* trusting; *(optimiste)* confident; *(qui a confiance en soi)* self-confident

**confidence** [kɔ̃fidɑ̃s] *nf* confidence; **faire une c. à qn** to confide in sb ▪ **confident, -e** *nmf* confidant, *f* confidante ▪ **confidentiel, -elle** *adj* confidential

**confier** [kɔ̃fje] **1** *vt* **c. qch à qn** *(laisser)* to entrust sb with sth; *(dire)* to confide sth to sb **2 se confier** *vpr* **se c. à qn** to confide in sb

**configuration** [kɔ̃figyrɑsjɔ̃] *nf (disposition)* layout; *Ordinat* configuration

**confiner** [kɔ̃fine] **1** *vt* to confine **2** *vi* **c. à** to border on **3 se confiner** *vpr* **se c. chez soi** to shut oneself up indoors

**confins** [kɔ̃fɛ̃] *nmpl* confines; **aux c. de** on the edge of

**confirmation** [kɔ̃firmasjɔ̃] *nf* confirmation

**confirmer** [kɔ̃firme] **1** *vt* to confirm (**que** that) **2 se confirmer** *vpr (nouvelle)* to be confirmed; *(tendance)* to continue

**confiserie** [kɔ̃fizri] *nf (magasin) Br* sweetshop, *Am* candy store; **confiseries** *(bonbons) Br* sweets, *Am* candy ▪ **confiseur** *nm* confectioner

**confisquer** [kɔ̃fiske] *vt* to confiscate (**à qn** from sb)

**confit, -e** [kɔ̃fi] **1** *adj (fruits)* candied **2** *nm* **c. d'oie** potted goose

**confiture** [kɔ̃fityr] *nf* jam; **c. de fraises** strawberry jam

**conflit** [kɔ̃fli] *nm* conflict; **conflits sociaux** industrial disputes ▪ **conflictuel, -elle** *adj (intérêts)* conflicting

**confondre** [kɔ̃fɔ̃dr] **1** *vt (choses, personnes)* to mix up, to confuse; *(consterner)* to astound; *(démasquer)* to confound; **c. qn/qch avec qn/qch** to mistake sb/sth for sb/sth
**2 se confondre** *vpr (couleurs, intérêts)* to merge; **se c. en excuses** to apologize profusely

**conforme** [kɔ̃fɔrm] *adj* **c. à** in accordance with; *(modèle)* true to ▪ **conformément** *adv* **c. à** in accordance with

**conformer** [kɔ̃fɔrme] **1** *vt* to model **2 se conformer** *vpr* to conform (**à** to)

**conformiste** [kɔ̃fɔrmist] *adj & nmf* conformist

**conformité** [kɔ̃fɔrmite] *nf* conformity (**à** with)

**confort** [kɔ̃fɔr] *nm* comfort ▪ **confortable** *adj* comfortable

**confrère** [kɔ̃frɛr] *nm (de profession)* colleague

**confronter** [kɔ̃frɔ̃te] *vt (personnes)* to confront; *(expériences, résultats)* to compare; **confronté à** *(difficulté)* confronted with ▪ **confrontation** *nf (face-à-face)* confrontation; *(comparaison)* comparison

**confus, -e** [kɔ̃fy, -yz] *adj (esprit, situation, explication)* confused; *(gêné)* embarrassed ▪ **confusion** *nf (désordre, méprise)* confusion; *(gêne)* embarrassment

**congé** [kɔ̃ʒe] *nm (vacances) Br* holiday, *Am* vacation; *(arrêt de travail)* leave; *(avis de renvoi)* notice; **donner son c. à qn** *(employé, locataire)* to give notice to sb; **c. de maladie** sick leave; **c. de maternité** maternity leave; **c. de paternité** paternity leave; **congés payés** *Br* paid holidays, *Am* paid vacation

**congédier** [kɔ̃ʒedje] *vt* to dismiss

**congeler** [kɔ̃ʒle] *vt* to freeze ▪ **congélateur** *nm* freezer

**congère** [kɔ̃ʒɛr] *nf* snowdrift

**Congo** [kɔ̃go] *nm* **le C.** Congo ▪ **congolais, -e 1** *adj* Congolese **2** *nmf* **C., Congolaise** Congolese

**congratuler** [kɔ̃gratyle] *vt* to congratulate (**sur** on)

**congrès** [kɔ̃grɛ] *nm* conference; **le C.** *(aux États-Unis)* the Congress

**conique** [kɔnik] *adj* conical

**conjoint, -e** [kɔ̃ʒwɛ̃, -wɛ̃t] **1** *adj* joint **2** *nm* spouse; **conjoints** husband and wife

**conjonction** [kɔ̃ʒɔ̃ksjɔ̃] *nf (union)* union; *Gram* conjunction

**conjonctivite** [kɔ̃ʒɔ̃ktivit] *nf Méd* conjunctivitis

**conjoncture** [kɔ̃ʒɔ̃ktyr] *nf* circumstances

**conjugal, -e, -aux, -ales** [kɔ̃ʒygal, -o] *adj (bonheur)* marital; *(vie)* married; *(devoir)* conjugal

**conjuguer** [kɔ̃ʒyge] **1** *vt (verbe)* to conjugate; *(efforts)* to combine **2 se conjuguer** *vpr (verbe)* to be conjugated ▪ **conjugaison** *nf Gram* conjugation

**conjurer** [kɔ̃ʒyre] *vt (danger)* to avert; *(mauvais sort)* to ward off; **c. qn de faire qch** to beg sb to do sth ▪ **conjuré, -e** *nmf* conspirator

**connaissance** [kɔnɛsɑ̃s] *nf (savoir)* knowledge; *(personne)* acquaintance; **à ma c.** to my knowledge; **avoir c. de qch** to be aware of sth; **faire c. avec qn** to get to know sb; **perdre/**

reprendre c. to lose/regain consciousness; **sans c.** unconscious ■ **connaisseur** *nm* connoisseur

**connaître*** [kɔnɛtr] **1** *vt (personne, endroit, faits)* to know; *(rencontrer)* to meet; *(famine, guerre)* to experience; **faire c. qch** to make sth known; **faire c. qn** *(présenter)* to introduce sb; *(rendre célèbre)* to make sb known
**2 se connaître** *vpr* **nous nous connaissons déjà** we've met before; **s'y c. en qch** to know all about sth

**connecter** [kɔnɛkte] *vt (appareil électrique)* to connect; *Ordinat* **connecté** on line ■ **connexion** *nf* connection

**connu, -e** [kɔny] **1** *pp de* **connaître 2** *adj (célèbre)* well-known

**conquérir*** [kɔ̃kerir] *vt (pays, sommet)* to conquer; *(marché)* to capture ■ **conquérant, -e** *nmf* conqueror ■ **conquête** *nf* conquest

**consacrer** [kɔ̃sakre] **1** *vt (temps)* to devote (**à** to); *(église)* to consecrate; *(entériner)* to establish **2 se consacrer** *vpr* **se c. à** to devote oneself to

**consciemment** [kɔ̃sjamɑ̃] *adv* consciously

**conscience** [kɔ̃sjɑ̃s] *nf* (**a**) *(esprit)* consciousness; **avoir/prendre c. de qch** to be/become aware of sth; **perdre c.** to lose consciousness (**b**) *(morale)* conscience; **avoir bonne/mauvaise c.** to have a clear/guilty conscience ■ **consciencieux, -euse** *adj* conscientious

**conscient, -e** [kɔ̃sjɑ̃, -ɑ̃t] *adj (lucide)* conscious; **c. de qch** aware *or* conscious of sth

**conscrit** [kɔ̃skri] *nm* conscript

**consécutif, -ive** [kɔ̃sekytif, -iv] *adj* consecutive; **c. à** following upon

**conseil** [kɔ̃sɛj] *nm* (**a**) **un c.** *(recommandation)* a piece of advice; **des conseils** advice (**b**) *(assemblée)* council, committee; **c. d'administration** board of directors; *Scol* **c. de classe** = staff meeting with participation of class representatives; *Pol* **c. des ministres** cabinet meeting

**conseiller¹** [kɔ̃seje] *vt (guider)* to advise; **c. qch à qn** to recommend sth to sb; **c. à qn de faire qch** to advise sb to do sth

**conseiller², -ère** [kɔ̃seje, -ɛr] *nmf (expert)* consultant, adviser; **c. d'orientation** careers adviser

**consentir*** [kɔ̃sɑ̃tir] **1** *vi* **c. à qch/à faire qch** to consent to sth/to do sth **2** *vt (prêt)* to grant (**à** to) ■ **consentement** *nm* consent

**conséquence** [kɔ̃sekɑ̃s] *nf* consequence; **en c.** accordingly; **sans c.** *(sans importance)* of no importance

**conservateur, -trice** [kɔ̃servatœr, -tris] **1** *adj & nmf Pol* Conservative **2** *nmf (de musée)* curator; *(de bibliothèque)* librarian **3** *nm (alimentaire)* preservative

**conservatoire** [kɔ̃sɛrvatwar] *nm* school, academy

**conserve** [kɔ̃sɛrv] *nf* **conserves** canned *or Br* tinned food; **en c.** canned, *Br* tinned

**conserver** [kɔ̃sɛrve] **1** *vt* to keep; *(fruits, tradition)* to preserve **2 se conserver** *vpr (aliment)* to keep

**considérable** [kɔ̃siderabl] *adj* considerable

**considérer** [kɔ̃sidere] *vt* to consider (**que** that); **tout bien considéré** all things considered ■ **considération** *nf (respect)* regard, esteem; **prendre qch en c.** to take sth into consideration

**consigne** [kɔ̃siɲ] *nf (instructions)* orders; *(de bouteille)* deposit; **c. (à bagages)** *Br* left-luggage office, *Am* checkroom; **c. automatique** lockers ■ **consigner** *vt (bouteille)* to charge a deposit on; *(bagages) Br* to deposit in the left-luggage office, *Am* to check; *(écrire)* to record; *(punir) (soldat)* to confine to barracks

**consistant, -e** [kɔ̃sistɑ̃, -ɑ̃t] *adj (sauce, bouillie)* thick; *(repas)* substantial ■ **consistance** *nf* consistency

**consister** [kɔ̃siste] *vi* **c. en qch** to consist of sth; **c. à faire qch** to consist in doing sth

**consœur** [kɔ̃sœr] *nf* female colleague

**console** [kɔ̃sɔl] *nf (d'ordinateur, de jeux)* console

**consoler** [kɔ̃sɔle] **1** *vt* to comfort, to console **2 se consoler** *vpr* **se c. de qch** to get over sth ▪ **consolation** *nf* comfort, consolation

**consolider** [kɔ̃sɔlide] *vt (mur, position)* to strengthen ▪ **consolidation** *nf* strengthening

**consommateur, -trice** [kɔ̃sɔmatœr, -tris] *nmf* consumer; *(au café)* customer ▪ **consommation** *nf (de nourriture, d'électricité)* consumption; *(de voiture)* fuel consumption; *(boisson)* drink

**consommer** [kɔ̃sɔme] **1** *vt (aliment, carburant)* to consume; *(mariage)* to consumate **2** *vi (au café)* to drink

**consonne** [kɔ̃sɔn] *nf* consonant

**consortium** [kɔ̃sɔrsjɔm] *nm (entreprises)* consortium

**conspirer** [kɔ̃spire] *vi (comploter)* to conspire (**contre** against); **c. à faire qch** *(concourir)* to conspire to do sth ▪ **conspirateur, -trice** *nmf* conspirator ▪ **conspiration** *nf* conspiracy

**constant, -e** [kɔ̃stɑ̃, -ɑ̃t] **1** *adj* constant **2** *nf* **constante** *Math* constant ▪ **constamment** [-amɑ̃] *adv* constantly ▪ **constance** *nf* constancy

**constat** [kɔ̃sta] *nm* (official) report

**constater** [kɔ̃state] *vt (observer)* to note (**que** that); *Jur (enregistrer)* to record; *(décès)* to certify ▪ **constatation** *nf (remarque)* observation

**constellation** [kɔ̃stɛlɑsjɔ̃] *nf* constellation

**consterner** [kɔ̃stɛrne] *vt* to dismay

**constipation** [kɔ̃stipɑsjɔ̃] *nf* constipation

**constituer** [kɔ̃stitɥe] **1** *vt (composer)* to make up; *(équivaloir à)* to constitute; *(former)* to form; **constitué de** made up of **2 se constituer** *vpr* **se c. prisonnier** to give oneself up

**constitution** [kɔ̃stitysjɔ̃] *nf (santé, lois)* constitution; *(de gouvernement)* formation ▪ **constitutionnel, -elle** *adj* constitutional

**constructeur** [kɔ̃stryktœr] *nm (bâtisseur)* builder; *(fabricant)* maker (**de** of); **c. automobile** car manufacturer ▪ **constructif, -ive** *adj* constructive ▪ **construction** *nf (de pont, de route, de maison)* building, construction (**de** of); *(édifice)* building; **en c.** under construction

**construire*** [kɔ̃strɥir] *vt (maison, route)* to build

**consul** [kɔ̃syl] *nm* consul ▪ **consulat** *nm* consulate

**consulter** [kɔ̃sylte] **1** *vt* to consult **2** *vi (médecin)* to see patients, *Br* to take surgery **3 se consulter** *vpr (discuter)* to confer ▪ **consultation** *nf* consultation

**consumer** [kɔ̃syme] *vt (brûler)* to consume

**contact** [kɔ̃takt] *nm* contact; **être en c. avec qn** to be in contact with sb; **prendre c.** to get in touch (**avec** with); *Aut* **mettre/couper le c.** to switch on/off ▪ **contacter** *vt* to contact

**contagieux, -euse** [kɔ̃taʒjø, -øz] *adj (maladie, personne)* contagious

**contaminer** [kɔ̃tamine] *vt* to contaminate ▪ **contamination** *nf* contamination

**conte** [kɔ̃t] *nm* tale; **c. de fées** fairy tale

**contempler** [kɔ̃tɑ̃ple] *vt* to gaze at, to contemplate

**contemporain, -e** [kɔ̃tɑ̃pɔrɛ̃, -ɛn] *adj & nmf* contemporary

**contenance** [kɔ̃tnɑ̃s] *nf* (**a**) *(de récipient)* capacity (**b**) *(allure)* bearing

**contenir*** [kɔ̃tnir] *vt (renfermer)* to contain; *(contrôler)* to hold back, to contain ▪ **conteneur** *nm* container

**content, -e** [kɔ̃tɑ̃, -ɑ̃t] **1** *adj* pleased, happy (**de** with; **de faire** to do); **être c. de soi** to be pleased with oneself **2** *nm* **avoir son c.** to have had one's fill (**de** of)

**contenter** [kɔ̃tɑ̃te] **1** *vt (satisfaire)* to satisfy; *(faire plaisir à)* to please **2 se contenter** *vpr* **se c. de qch** to content oneself with sth ▪ **contentement** *nm* contentment, satisfaction

**contentieux** [kɔ̃tɑ̃sjø] *nm (querelles)* dispute; *Jur* litigation; *(service)* legal department

**contenu** [kɔ̃tny] *nm (de paquet, de bouteille)* contents; *(de lettre, de film)* content

**conter** [kɔ̃te] *vt* to tell (**à** to) ▪ **conteur, -euse** *nmf* storyteller

**contestable** [kɔ̃testabl] *adj* debatable

**contestation** [kɔ̃tɛstasjɔ̃] *nf* protest

**conteste** [kɔ̃tɛst] **sans conteste** *adv* indisputably

**contester** [kɔ̃teste] **1** *vt* to dispute **2** *vi* **faire qch sans c.** to do sth without protest ▪ **contesté, -e** *adj (théorie, dirigeant)* controversial

**contexte** [kɔ̃tɛkst] *nm* context

**contigu, -ë** [kɔ̃tigy] *adj (maisons)* adjoining; **c. à qch** adjoining sth

**continent** [kɔ̃tinɑ̃] *nm* continent; *(opposé à une île)* mainland ▪ **continental, -e, -aux, -ales** *adj (climat, plateau)* continental

**contingent** [kɔ̃tɛ̃ʒɑ̃] *nm Mil* contingent; *(quota)* quota

**continu, -e** [kɔ̃tiny] *adj* continuous ▪ **continuel, -elle** *adj (ininterrompu)* continuous; *(qui se répète)* continual ▪ **continuellement** *adv (de façon ininterrompue)* continuously; *(de façon répétitive)* continually

**continuer** [kɔ̃tinɥe] **1** *vt (études, efforts, politique)* to continue, to carry on with; **c. à** *ou* **de faire qch** to continue *or* carry on doing sth **2** *vi* to continue, to go on ▪ **continuation** *nf* continuation

**continuité** [kɔ̃tinɥite] *nf* continuity

**contour** [kɔ̃tur] *nm* outline

**contourner** [kɔ̃turne] *vt* to go round; *Fig (difficulté, loi)* to get round

**contraceptif, -ive** [kɔ̃trasɛptif, -iv] *adj & nm* contraceptive

**contracter** [kɔ̃trakte] **1** *vt (muscle, habitude, dette)* to contract **2 se contracter** *vpr (muscle)* to contract; *(personne)* to tense up ▪ **contraction** *nf* contraction

**contractuel, -elle** [kɔ̃traktɥɛl] **1** *adj (politique)* contractual **2** *nmf Br* ≃ traffic warden, *Am* ≃ traffic policeman, *f* traffic policewoman

**contradiction** [kɔ̃tradiksjɔ̃] *nf* contradiction; **être en c. avec qch** to contradict sth ▪ **contradictoire** *adj* contradictory

**contraindre*** [kɔ̃trɛ̃dr] **1** *vt* to compel, to force (**à faire** to do) **2 se contraindre** *vpr* to compel *or* force oneself (**à faire** to do) ▪ **contraignant, -e** *adj* restricting ▪ **contrainte** *nf (obligation, limitation)* constraint; **sous la c.** under duress

**contraire** [kɔ̃trɛr] **1** *adj (opposé)* conflicting; **c. à qch** contrary to sth; **en sens c.** in the opposite direction **2** *nm* opposite; **(bien) au c.** on the contrary ▪ **contrairement** *adv* **c. à** contrary to; **c. à qn** unlike sb

**contrarier** [kɔ̃trarje] *vt (projet, action)* to thwart; *(personne)* to annoy ▪ **contrariant, -e** *adj (situation)* annoying; *(personne)* contrary ▪ **contrariété** *nf* annoyance

**contraste** [kɔ̃trast] *nm* contrast ▪ **contraster** *vi* to contrast (**avec** with)

**contrat** [kɔ̃tra] *nm* contract

**contravention** [kɔ̃travɑ̃sjɔ̃] *nf (amende)* fine; *(pour stationnement interdit)* (parking) ticket

**contre** [kɔ̃tr] **1** *prép* against; *(en échange de)* (in exchange) for; **échanger qch c. qch** to exchange sth for sth; **fâché c. qn** angry with sb; **six voix c. deux** six votes to two; **Nîmes c. Arras** *(match)* Nîmes versus *or* against Arras; **sirop c. la toux** cough mixture; *Fam* **par c.** on the other hand **2** *nm (au volley, au basket)* block ▪ **contre-attaque** *nf* counter-attack ▪ **contre-attaquer** *vt* to counterattack

**contrebalancer** [kɔ̃trəbalɑ̃se] *vt* to counterbalance; *Fig (compenser)* to offset

**contrebande** [kɔ̃trəbɑ̃d] *nf (activité)* smuggling; *(marchandises)* contraband; **tabac de c.** smuggled tobacco;

**faire de la c.** to smuggle goods ▪ **contrebandier, -ère** *nmf* smuggler
**contrebas** [kɔ̃trəbɑ] **en contrebas** *adv & prép* (down) below; **en c. de** below
**contrebasse** [kɔ̃trəbɑs] *nf (instrument)* double-bass
**contrecarrer** [kɔ̃trəkare] *vt* to thwart
**contrecœur** [kɔ̃trəkœr] **à contrecœur** *adv* reluctantly
**contrecoup** [kɔ̃trəku] *nm* repercussions
**contre-courant** [kɔ̃trəkurɑ̃] **à contre-courant** *adv (nager)* against the current
**contredire*** [kɔ̃trədir] **1** *vt* to contradict **2 se contredire** *vpr (soi-même)* to contradict oneself; *(l'un l'autre)* to contradict each other
**contrée** [kɔ̃tre] *nf Littéraire (region)* region; *(pays)* land
**contre-espionnage** [kɔ̃trɛspjɔnaʒ] *nm* counter-espionage
**contrefaçon** [kɔ̃trəfasɔ̃] *nf (pratique)* counterfeiting; *(produit)* fake ▪ **contrefaire*** *vt (écriture)* to disguise; *(argent)* to counterfeit; *(signature)* to forge
**contre-jour** [kɔ̃trəʒur] **à contre-jour** *adv* against the light
**contremaître** [kɔ̃trəmɛtr] *nm* foreman
**contre-offensive** [kɔ̃trɔfɑ̃siv] (*pl* **contre-offensives**) *nf* counter-offensive
**contrepartie** [kɔ̃trəparti] *nf* compensation; **en c.** in return (**de** for)
**contre-pied** [kɔ̃trəpje] *nm Sport* **prendre son adversaire à c.** to wrongfoot one's opponent
**contreplaqué** [kɔ̃trəplake] *nm* plywood
**contrepoids** [kɔ̃trəpwa] *nm* counterbalance
**contrepoison** [kɔ̃trəpwazɔ̃] *nm* antidote
**contrer** [kɔ̃tre] *vt (personne, attaque)* to counter
**contresens** [kɔ̃trəsɑ̃s] *nm* misinterpretation; *(en traduisant)* mistranslation; **prendre une rue à c.** to go down/up a street the wrong way
**contresigner** [kɔ̃trəsiɲe] *vt* to countersign
**contretemps** [kɔ̃trətɑ̃] *nm* hitch, mishap
**contrevenir*** [kɔ̃trəvnir] *vi* **c. à** to contravene
**contribuable** [kɔ̃tribɥabl] *nmf* taxpayer
**contribuer** [kɔ̃tribɥe] *vi* to contribute (**à** to); **c. à faire qch** to help (to) do sth
**contribution** [kɔ̃tribysjɔ̃] *nf* contribution (**à** to); *(impôt)* tax; **contributions** *(administration)* tax office
**contrôle** [kɔ̃trol] *nm (vérification)* checking (**de** of); *(surveillance)* monitoring; *(maîtrise)* control; *Scol* test; **avoir le c. de qch** to have control of sth; **le c. des naissances** birth control; **c. de soi** self-control; **c. fiscal** tax inspection
**contrôler** [kɔ̃trole] **1** *vt (vérifier)* to check; *(surveiller)* to monitor; *(maîtriser)* to control **2 se contrôler** *vpr* to control oneself ▪ **contrôleur, -euse** *nmf (de train, de bus) Br* (ticket) inspector, *Am* conductor; **c. aérien** air-traffic controller
**controverse** [kɔ̃trɔvɛrs] *nf* controversy ▪ **controversé, -e** *adj* controversial
**contumace** [kɔ̃tymas] **par contumace** *adv Jur* in absentia
**contusion** [kɔ̃tyzjɔ̃] *nf* bruise
**convaincre*** [kɔ̃vɛ̃kr] *vt* to convince (**de** of); **c. qn de faire qch** to persuade sb to do sth ▪ **convaincant, -e** *adj* convincing ▪ **convaincu, -e** *adj* convinced (**de** of; **que** that); *(partisan)* committed
**convalescent, -e** [kɔ̃valɛsɑ̃, -ɑ̃t] *adj & nmf* convalescent ▪ **convalescence** *nf* convalescence
**convenable** [kɔ̃vnabl] *adj (approprié)* suitable; *(acceptable, décent)* decent
**convenance** [kɔ̃vnɑ̃s] *nf* **faire qch à sa c.** to do sth at one's own convenience
**convenir*** [kɔ̃vnir] **1** *vi* **c. à** *(être fait pour)* to be suitable for; *(plaire à, aller*

*à)* to suit; **c. de qch** *(lieu, prix)* to agree upon sth; **c. de faire qch** to agree to do sth; **c. que...** to admit that...
**2** *v impersonnel* **il convient de...** it is advisable to...; *(selon les usages)* it is proper to...; **il fut convenu que...** *(décidé)* it was agreed that... ▪ **convenu, -e** *adj (décidé)* agreed

**convention** [kɔ̃vɑ̃sjɔ̃] *nf (accord)* agreement; *(règle)* convention; **c. collective** collective agreement

**conventionné, -e** [kɔ̃vɑ̃sjɔne] *adj (médecin, clinique)* attached to the health system, *Br* ≃ NHS; **médecin non c.** private doctor

**conventionnel, -elle** [kɔ̃vɑ̃sjɔnɛl] *adj* conventional

**convergence** [kɔ̃vɛrʒɑ̃s] *nf* convergence ▪ **converger** *vi* to converge (**vers** on)

**conversation** [kɔ̃vɛrsasjɔ̃] *nf* conversation

**conversion** [kɔ̃vɛrsjɔ̃] *nf (changement)* conversion (**en** into); *(à une doctrine)* conversion (**à** to) ▪ **convertible 1** *adj* convertible (**en** into) **2** *nm* sofa bed ▪ **convertir 1** *vt (changer)* to convert (**en** into); *(à une doctrine)* to convert (**à** to) **2 se convertir** *vpr (à une doctrine)* to be converted (**à** to)

**conviction** [kɔ̃viksjɔ̃] *nf (certitude, croyance)* conviction; **avoir la c. que...** to be convinced that...

**convier** [kɔ̃vje] *vt Formel* to invite (**à** to; **à faire** to do)

**convive** [kɔ̃viv] *nmf* guest

**convivial, -e, -aux, -ales** [kɔ̃vivjal, -jo] *adj* convivial; *Ordinat* user-friendly

**convoi** [kɔ̃vwa] *nm (véhicules, personnes)* convoy; *(train)* train; **c. funèbre** funeral procession

**convoiter** [kɔ̃vwate] *vt (poste, richesses)* to covet

**convoquer** [kɔ̃vɔke] *vt (employé, postulant)* to call in; **c. qn à un examen** to notify sb of an examination ▪ **convocation** *nf (lettre)* notice to attend; **c. à un examen** notification of an examination

**convoyer** [kɔ̃vwaje] *vt (troupes)* to convoy; *(fonds)* to transport under armed guard

**convulsion** [kɔ̃vylsjɔ̃] *nf* convulsion

**coopérer** [kɔɔpere] *vi* to cooperate (**à** in, **avec** with) ▪ **coopératif, -ive** *adj & nf* cooperative ▪ **coopération** *nf* cooperation (**entre** between); *Pol* overseas development

**coordonner** [kɔɔrdɔne] *vt* to coordinate (**à** *ou* **avec** with) ▪ **coordination** *nf* coordination ▪ **coordonnées** *nfpl (adresse, téléphone)* address and phone number

**copain** [kɔpɛ̃] *nm Fam (camarade)* pal; *(petit ami)* boyfriend

**copeau, -x** [kɔpo] *nm (de bois)* shaving

**copie** [kɔpi] *nf (manuscrit, double)* copy; *Scol (devoir, examen)* paper

**copier** [kɔpje] *vt (texte, musique, document) & Scol (à un examen)* to copy (**sur** from) ▪ **copieur, -euse 1** *nmf (élève)* copier **2** *nm (machine)* photocopier

**copieux, -euse** [kɔpjø, -øz] *adj (repas)* copious; *(portion)* generous

**copine** [kɔpin] *nf Fam (camarade)* pal; *(petite amie)* girlfriend

**copropriété** [kɔprɔprijete] *nf* joint ownership

**coq** [kɔk] *nm* cock, *Am* rooster

**coque** [kɔk] *nf (de noix)* shell; *(de navire)* hull; *(fruit de mer)* cockle

**coquelet** [kɔklɛ] *nm* cockerel

**coquelicot** [kɔkliko] *nm* poppy

**coqueluche** [kɔklyʃ] *nf (maladie)* whooping cough

**coquet, -ette** [kɔkɛ, -ɛt] *adj (intérieur)* charming; *Fam (somme)* tidy

**coquetier** [kɔktje] *nm* egg-cup

**coquille** [kɔkij] *nf* shell; *(faute d'imprimerie)* misprint; *Culin* **c. Saint-Jacques** scallop ▪ **coquillage** *nm (mollusque)* shellfish *inv*; *(coquille)* shell

**coquin, -e** [kɔkɛ̃, -in] **1** *adj (sourire, air)* mischievous; *(sous-vêtements)* naughty **2** *nmf* rascal

**cor** [kɔr] *nm (instrument)* horn; *(durillon)* corn

**corail, -aux** [kɔraj, -o] *nm* coral

**Coran** [kɔrɑ̃] *nm* **le C.** the Koran

**corbeau, -x** [kɔrbo] *nm (oiseau)* crow

**corbeille** [kɔrbɛj] *nf* (**a**) *(panier)* basket; **c. à pain** breadbasket; **c. à papier** wastepaper basket (**b**) *(à la Bourse)* trading floor (**c**) *Théât* dress circle

**corbillard** [kɔrbijar] *nm* hearse

**corde** [kɔrd] *nf (lien)* rope; *(de raquette, de violon)* string; **c. à linge** washing *or* clothes line; **c. à sauter** *Br* skipping rope, *Am* jump-rope; **cordes vocales** vocal cords ▪ **cordée** *nf* roped party ▪ **corder** *vt (raquette)* to string

**cordial, -e, -aux, -ales** [kɔrdjal, -o] **1** *adj (accueil, personne)* cordial **2** *nm (remontant)* tonic

**cordon** [kɔrdɔ̃] *nm (de tablier, de sac)* string; *(de rideau)* cord; *(de policiers)* cordon; *Anat* **c. ombilical** umbilical cord ▪ **cordon-bleu** (*pl* **cordons-bleus**) *nm Fam* gourmet cook

**cordonnier** [kɔrdɔnje] *nm* shoe repairer ▪ **cordonnerie** *nf (boutique)* shoe repairer's shop

**Corée** [kɔre] *nf* **la C.** Korea ▪ **coréen, -enne 1** *adj* Korean **2** *nmf* **C., Coréenne** Korean

**coriace** [kɔrjas] *adj (viande, personne)* tough

**corne** [kɔrn] *nf (d'animal, matière, instrument)* horn; *(au pied, à la main)* hard skin; **c. de brume** foghorn

**corneille** [kɔrnɛj] *nf* crow

**cornemuse** [kɔrnəmyz] *nf* bagpipes

**corner**[1] [kɔrne] *vt (page)* to turn down the corner of; *(abîmer)* to make dog-eared

**corner**[2] [kɔrner] *nm (au football)* corner; **tirer un c.** to take a corner

**cornet** [kɔrnɛ] *nm (glace)* cone, *Br* cornet

**corniche** [kɔrniʃ] *nf (de rocher)* ledge; *(route)* coast road; *(en haut d'un mur)* cornice

**cornichon** [kɔrniʃɔ̃] *nm* gherkin

**cornu, -e** [kɔrny] *adj (diable, animal)* horned

**corporation** [kɔrpɔrɑsjɔ̃] *nf* corporate body

**corporel, -elle** [kɔrpɔrɛl] *adj (besoin)* bodily; *(hygiène)* personal

**corps** [kɔr] *nm (organisme, cadavre) & Chim* body; *(partie principale)* main part; **c. et âme** body and soul; **c. d'armée/diplomatique** army/diplomatic corps; **c. enseignant** teaching profession; **c. gras** fat

**corpulent, -e** [kɔrpylɑ̃, -ɑ̃t] *adj* stout, corpulent

**correct, -e** [kɔrɛkt] *adj (exact, courtois)* correct; *Fam (acceptable)* reasonable ▪ **correctement** *adv (sans faire de fautes, décemment)* correctly; *Fam (de façon acceptable)* reasonably

**correcteur, -trice** [kɔrɛktœr, -tris] **1** *adj* **verres correcteurs** corrective lenses **2** *nmf (d'examen)* examiner; *(en typographie)* proofreader **3** *nm Ordinat* **c. d'orthographe** spellchecker

**correction** [kɔrɛksjɔ̃] *nf (rectification)* correction; *(punition)* beating; *(décence, courtoisie)* correctness; *Scol (de devoirs, d'examens)* marking

**correctionnel, -elle** [kɔrɛksjɔnɛl] **1** *adj* **tribunal c.** criminal court **2** *nf* **correctionnelle** criminal court; **passer en c.** to go before a criminal court

**correspondance** [kɔrɛspɔ̃dɑ̃s] *nf (relation, lettres)* correspondence; *(de train, d'autocar) Br* connection, *Am* transfer

**correspondre** [kɔrɛspɔ̃dr] *vi* **c. à qch** to correspond to sth; **c. avec qn** *(par lettres)* to correspond with sb ▪ **correspondant, -e 1** *adj* corresponding (**à** to) **2** *nmf (reporter)* correspondent; *(par lettres)* pen friend, pen pal; *(au téléphone)* caller; **c. de guerre** war correspondent

**corrida** [kɔrida] *nf* bullfight

**corridor** [kɔridɔr] *nm* corridor

**corriger** [kɔriʒe] **1** *vt (texte, erreur, myopie, injustice)* to correct; *(exercice, devoir)* to mark; **c. qn** to give sb a beating; **c. qn de qch** to cure sb of sth **2 se corriger** *vpr* to mend one's ways; **se c. de qch** to cure oneself of sth ▪ **corrigé** *nm (d'exercice)* correct answers (**de** to)

**corrompre*** [kɔrɔ̃pr] *vt (personne, goût)* to corrupt; *(soudoyer)* to bribe ▪ **corrompu, -e** *adj* corrupt ▪ **corruption** *nf* corruption

**corrosion** [kɔrozjɔ̃] *nf* corrosion ▪ **corrosif, -ive** *adj* corrosive

**corsage** [kɔrsaʒ] *nm* blouse

**Corse** [kɔrs] *nf* **la C.** Corsica ▪ **corse 1** *adj* Corsican **2** *nmf* **C.** Corsican

**corser** [kɔrse] **1** *vt (plat)* to spice up; *Fig (récit)* to liven up **2 se corser** *vpr* **ça se corse** things are getting complicated ▪ **corsé, -e** *adj (café)* full-flavoured; *Fig (histoire)* spicy

**corset** [kɔrsɛ] *nm* corset

**cortège** [kɔrtɛʒ] *nm (défilé)* procession

**corvée** [kɔrve] *nf* chore; *Mil* fatigue duty

**cosmétique** [kɔsmetik] *adj & nm* cosmetic

**cosmique** [kɔsmik] *adj* cosmic ▪ **cosmonaute** *nmf* cosmonaut

**cosmopolite** [kɔsmɔpɔlit] *adj* cosmopolitan

**cossu, -e** [kɔsy] *adj (personne)* well-to-do; *(maison, intérieur)* opulent

**costaud** [kɔsto] *adj* sturdy

**costume** [kɔstym] *nm (habit)* costume; *(complet)* suit

**cotation** [kɔtasjɔ̃] *nf* **c. (en Bourse)** quotation (on the Stock Exchange)

**cote** [kɔt] *nf (marque de classement)* classification mark; *(valeur)* quotation; *(liste)* share index; *(de cheval)* odds; *(altitude)* altitude

**coté, -e** [kɔte] *adj* **bien c.** highly rated; **c. en Bourse** quoted on the Stock Market

**côte** [kot] *nf* (**a**) *(os)* rib; **à côtes** *(étoffe)* ribbed; **c. à c.** side by side; **c. d'agneau/de porc** lamb/pork chop; **c. de bœuf** rib of beef (**b**) *(de montagne)* slope (**c**) *(littoral)* coast; **la C. d'Azur** the French Riviera

**côté** [kote] *nm* side; **de l'autre c.** on the other side (**de** of); *(partir)* the other way; **de ce c.** *(passer)* this way; **du c. de** *(près de)* near; **à c.** close by, nearby; *(pièce)* in the other room; *(maison)* next door; **la maison d'à c.** the house next door; **à c. de qn/qch** next to sb/sth; *(en comparaison de)* compared to sb/sth; **passer à c.** *(balle)* to fall wide (**de** of); **mettre qch de c.** to put sth aside

**coteau, -x** [kɔto] *nm* hill; *(versant)* hillside

**côtelé, -e** [kotle] *adj* **velours c.** corduroy

**côtelette** [kotlɛt] *nf (d'agneau, de porc)* chop

**coter** [kɔte] *vt (prix, action)* to quote

**côtier, -ère** [kotje, -ɛr] *adj* coastal; *(pêche)* inshore

**cotiser** [kɔtize] **1** *vi (à un cadeau, pour la retraite)* to contribute (**à** to; **pour** towards) **2 se cotiser** *vpr Br* to club together, *Am* to club in ▪ **cotisation** *nf (de club)* dues, subscription; *(de retraite, de chômage)* contribution

**coton** [kɔtɔ̃] *nm* cotton; **c. hydrophile** *Br* cotton wool, *Am* absorbent cotton

**côtoyer** [kotwaje] *vt (personnes)* to mix with

**cou** [ku] *nm* neck

**couchage** [kuʃaʒ] *nm* **sac de c.** sleeping bag

**couchant** [kuʃɑ̃, -ɑ̃t] **1** *adj m* **soleil c.** setting sun **2** *nm* **le c.** *(ouest)* the west

**couche** [kuʃ] *nf* (**a**) *(épaisseur)* layer; *(de peinture)* coat; **la c. d'ozone** the ozone layer (**b**) *(linge de bébé) Br* nappy, *Am* diaper ▪ **couche-culotte** (*pl* **couches-culottes**) *nf Br* disposable nappy, *Am* disposable diaper

**coucher** [kuʃe] **1** *nm (moment)* bedtime; **l'heure du c.** bedtime; **au c.** at bedtime; **c. de soleil** sunset

**2** *vt (allonger)* to lay down; **c. qn** to put sb to bed

**3** *vi* to sleep (**avec** with)

**4 se coucher** *vpr (personne)* to go to

bed; *(s'allonger)* to lie down; *(soleil)* to set, to go down; **aller se c.** to go to bed ▪ **couché, -e** *adj* **être c.** to be in bed; *(étendu)* to be lying (down)

**couchette** [kuʃɛt] *nf (de train)* couchette; *(de bateau)* bunk

**coude** [kud] *nm* elbow; *(tournant)* bend; **donner un coup de c. à qn** to nudge sb

**cou-de-pied** [kudpje] *(pl* **cous-de-pied***) nm* instep

**coudre*** [kudr] *vti* to sew

**couette**[1] [kwɛt] *nf (édredon)* duvet

**couette**[2] [kwɛt] *nf Fam (coiffure)* bunch

**couffin** [kufɛ̃] *nm (de bébé) Br* Moses basket, *Am* bassinet

**coulée** [kule] *nf* **c. de lave** lava flow

**couler** [kule] **1** *vt* (**a**) *(métal, statue)* to cast; *(liquide, ciment)* to pour (**b**) *(navire)* to sink **2** *vi* (**a**) *(eau, rivière)* to flow; *(nez, sueur)* to run; *(robinet)* to leak (**b**) *(bateau, nageur)* to sink

**couleur** [kulœr] *nf (teinte) Br* colour, *Am* color; *(colorant)* paint; *(pour cheveux)* dye; *Cartes* suit; **de quelle c. est…?** what colour is…?; **télévision c.** *ou* **en couleurs** colour television (set)

**couleuvre** [kulœvr] *nf* grass snake

**coulisse** [kulis] *nf (de porte)* runner; **porte à c.** sliding door; *Théât* **les coulisses** the wings ▪ **coulissant, -e** *adj* sliding

**couloir** [kulwar] *nm (de maison, de train)* corridor; *(en natation, en athlétisme)* lane; **c. de bus** bus lane

**COUP** [ku] *nm* (**a**) *(choc)* blow; *(essai)* attempt, go; **donner un c. à qn** to hit sb; **se donner un c. contre qch** to knock against sth; **donner un c. de couteau à qn** to knife sb; **c. de pied** kick; **donner un c. de pied à qn** to kick sb; **c. de poing** punch; **donner un c. de poing à qn** to punch sb; **c. de tête** header

(**b**) *(action soudaine, événement soudain)* **c. de vent** gust of wind; **donner un c. de frein** to brake; **prendre un c. de soleil** to get sunburned; *Fig* **ça a été le c. de foudre** it was love at first sight; **c. d'État** coup; **c. de théâtre** coup de théâtre

(**c**) *(bruit)* **c. de feu** shot; **c. de fusil** shot; **c. de sifflet** whistle; **c. de tonnerre** clap of thunder; **l'horloge sonna deux coups** the clock struck two

(**d**) *(expressions)* **après c.** after the event; **sur le c.** *(alors)* at the time; **tué sur le c.** killed outright; **tout à c., tout d'un c.** suddenly; **d'un seul c.** *(avaler)* in one go; *(soudain)* all of a sudden; **du premier c.** at the first attempt; **sous le c. de la colère** in a fit of anger; **tenir le c.** to hold out; **tomber sous le c. de la loi** to be an offence; **c. d'envoi** *(au football, au rugby)* kickoff; **c. de maître** masterstroke; **c. droit** *(au tennis)* forehand; **c. franc** *(au football)* free kick; **c. monté** put-up job

**coupable** [kupabl] **1** *adj* guilty (**de** of); *(négligence)* culpable; **se sentir c.** to feel guilty **2** *nmf* culprit

**coupant, -e** [kupɑ̃, -ɑ̃t] *adj* sharp

**coupe**[1] [kup] *nf (trophée)* cup; *(récipient)* bowl; **la C. du monde** the World Cup; **c. à champagne** champagne glass

**coupe**[2] [kup] *nf (de vêtement)* cut; *(plan)* section; **c. de cheveux** haircut ▪ **coupe-papier** *nm inv* paper knife ▪ **coupe-vent** *nm inv (blouson) Br* windcheater, *Am* Windbreaker ®

**couper** [kupe] **1** *vt (trancher, supprimer)* to cut; *(arbre)* to cut down; **c. la parole à qn** to interrupt sb; **nous avons été coupés** *(au téléphone)* we were cut off

**2** *vi (être tranchant)* to be sharp; *(aux cartes)* to cut; *(prendre un raccourci)* to take a short cut; **ne coupez pas!** *(au téléphone)* hold the line!

**3 se couper** *vpr (routes)* to intersect; **se c. au doigt** to cut one's finger; **se c. les cheveux** to cut one's hair ▪ **coupé** *nm (voiture)* coupé

**couperet** [kuprɛ] *nm (de boucher)* cleaver; *(de guillotine)* blade

**couple** [kupl] *nm* couple
**couplet** [kuplɛ] *nm* verse
**coupole** [kupɔl] *nf* dome
**coupon** [kupɔ̃] *nm (tissu)* remnant; **c. de réduction** money-off coupon; **c.-réponse** reply coupon
**coupure** [kupyr] *nf (blessure)* cut; **5 000 euros en petites coupures** 5,000 euros in small notes; **c. d'électricité** *ou* **de courant** blackout, *Br* power cut; **c. de presse** newspaper cutting
**cour** [kur] *nf* (**a**) *(de maison, de ferme)* yard; **c. de récréation** *Br* playground, *Am* schoolyard (**b**) *(de roi, tribunal)* court; **c. d'appel** court of appeal (**c**) **faire la c. à qn** to court sb
**courage** [kuraʒ] *nm* courage; **bon c.!** good luck! ▪ **courageux, -euse** *adj (brave)* courageous; *(énergique)* spirited
**couramment** [kuramɑ̃] *adv (parler)* fluently; *(généralement)* commonly
**courant, -e** [kurɑ̃, -ɑ̃t] **1** *adj (common)* common; *(en cours)* current **2** *nm (de rivière)* current; **être au c. de qch** to know about sth; **mettre qn au c. de qch** to tell sb about sth; **c. d'air** *Br* draught, *Am* draft; **c. électrique** electric current
**courbature** [kurbatyr] *nf* ache; **avoir des courbatures** to be aching (all over)
**courbe** [kurb] **1** *adj* curved **2** *nf* curve; **c. de niveau** contour line ▪ **courber 1** *vt* to bend **2 se courber** *vpr (personne)* to bend down; **se c. en deux** to bend double
**courgette** [kurʒɛt] *nf Br* courgette, *Am* zucchini
**courir*** [kurir] **1** *vi* to run; *(à une course automobile)* to race; **c. après qn/qch** to run after sb/sth; **descendre une colline en courant** to run down a hill; **le bruit court que...** rumour has it that...
**2** *vt* **c. un risque** to run a risk; **c. le 100 mètres** to run the 100 metres ▪ **coureur, -euse** *nmf (sportif)* runner; *(cycliste)* cyclist; **c. automobile** racing driver; **c. de jupons** womanizer
**couronne** [kurɔn] *nf (de roi, de reine)* crown; *(pour enterrement)* wreath; *(de dent)* crown ▪ **couronnement** *nm (de roi)* coronation; *Fig (réussite)* crowning achievement ▪ **couronner** *vt (roi)* to crown; *(auteur, ouvrage)* to award a prize to; **et pour c. le tout...** and to crown it all...
**courrier** [kurje] *nm (lettres)* mail, *Br* post; **par retour du c.** *Br* by return of post, *Am* by return mail; *Journ* **c. du cœur** problem page; **c. électronique** electronic mail, e-mail
**courroie** [kurwa] *nf (attache)* strap
**cours** [kur] *nm* (**a**) *(de rivière, d'astre)* course; *(de monnaie)* currency; *Fin (d'action)* price; **suivre son c.** to run its course; **avoir c.** *(monnaie)* to be legal tender; *(pratique)* to be current; **en c.** *(travail)* in progress; *(année)* current; *(affaires)* outstanding; **au c. de qch** in the course of sth; **c. d'eau** river, stream
(**b**) *(leçon)* class; *(série de leçons)* course; *(conférence)* lecture; *(établissement)* school; **suivre un c.** to take a course; **c. particulier** private lesson
(**c**) *(allée)* avenue
**course**[1] [kurs] *nf (action de courir)* running; *Sport (épreuve)* race; *(discipline)* racing; *(trajet en taxi)* journey; *(de projectile, de planète)* course; **les courses de chevaux** the races; **faire la c. avec qn** to race sb; **c. automobile** motor race; **c. cycliste** cycle race
**course**[2] [kurs] *nf (commission)* errand; **courses** *(achats)* shopping; **faire une c.** to get something from the shops; **faire les courses** to do the shopping
**coursier, -ère** [kursje, -ɛr] *nmf* messenger
**court, -e** [kur, kurt] **1** *adj* short **2** *adv* short; **à c. d'argent** short of money **3** *nm* **c. (de tennis)** tennis court ▪ **court-circuit** (*pl* **courts-circuits**) *nm* short-circuit
**courtier, -ère** [kurtje, -ɛr] *nmf* broker
**courtisan** [kurtizɑ̃] *nm Hist* courtier

■ **courtiser** *vt (femme)* to court

**courtois, -e** [kurtwa, -az] *adj* courteous ■ **courtoisie** *nf* courtesy

**couru, -e** [kury] *adj (spectacle, lieu)* popular

**cousin, -e** [kuzɛ̃, -in] **1** *nmf* cousin; **c. germain** first cousin **2** *nm (insecte)* mosquito

**coussin** [kusɛ̃] *nm* cushion

**cousu, -e** [kuzy] *adj* sewn; **c. main** hand-sewn

**coût** [ku] *nm* cost; **le c. de la vie** the cost of living ■ **coûter** *vti* to cost; **ça coûte combien?** how much is it?, how much does it cost?

**couteau, -x** [kuto] *nm* knife; **c. à pain** breadknife; **c.-scie** serrated knife

**coûteux, -euse** [kutø, -øz] *adj* costly, expensive

**coutume** [kutym] *nf (habitude, tradition)* custom; **avoir c. de faire qch** to be accustomed to doing sth; **comme de c.** as usual

**couture** [kutyr] *nf (activité)* sewing, needlework; *(raccord)* seam; **faire de la c.** to sew ■ **couturier** *nm* fashion designer ■ **couturière** *nf* dressmaker

**couvent** [kuvɑ̃] *nm (de religieuses)* convent; *(de moines)* monastery; *(pensionnat)* convent school

**couver** [kuve] **1** *vt (œufs)* to sit on; *(maladie)* to be coming down with **2** *vi (poule)* to brood; *(feu) Br* to smoulder, *Am* to smolder ■ **couveuse** *nf (pour nouveaux-nés)* incubator

**couvercle** [kuvɛrkl] *nm* lid; *(vissé)* cap

**couvert**[1] [kuvɛr] *nm* (**a**) **mettre le c.** to set *or Br* lay the table; **table de cinq couverts** table set *or Br* laid for five; **couverts** *(ustensiles)* cutlery (**b**) **sous le c. de** *(sous l'apparence de)* under cover of; **se mettre à c.** to take cover

**couvert**[2]**, -e** [kuvɛr, -ɛrt] **1** *pp de* **couvrir 2** *adj* covered (**de** with *or* in); *(ciel)* overcast; **être bien c.** *(habillé chaudement)* to be warmly dressed

**couverture** [kuvɛrtyr] *nf (de lit)* blanket; *(de livre, de magazine)* cover; *(de bâtiment)* roofing; *Journ* coverage; **c. chauffante** electric blanket; **c. sociale** social security cover

**couvrir*** [kuvrir] **1** *vt* to cover (**de** with); *(bruit)* to drown **2 se couvrir** *vpr (s'habiller)* to wrap up; *(se coiffer)* to cover one's head; *(ciel)* to cloud over ■ **couvre-feu** (*pl* **couvre-feux**) *nm* curfew ■ **couvre-lit** (*pl* **couvre-lits**) *nm* bedspread

**cow-boy** [kɔbɔj] (*pl* **cow-boys**) *nm* cowboy

**crabe** [krab] *nm* crab

**crachat** [kraʃa] *nm* gob of spit; **crachats** spit

**cracher** [kraʃe] **1** *vt* to spit out **2** *vi (personne)* to spit; *(stylo)* to splutter; *(radio)* to crackle

**crachin** [kraʃɛ̃] *nm* (fine) drizzle

**craie** [krɛ] *nf (matière)* chalk; *(bâton)* stick of chalk

**craindre*** [krɛ̃dr] *vt (redouter)* to be afraid of, to fear; *(chaleur, froid)* to be sensitive to; **c. de faire qch** to be afraid of doing sth; **je crains qu'elle ne soit partie** I'm afraid she's left; **ne craignez rien** *(n'ayez pas peur)* don't be afraid; *(ne vous inquiétez pas)* don't worry

**crainte** [krɛ̃t] *nf* fear; **de c. de faire qch** for fear of doing sth

**craintif, -ive** [krɛ̃tif, -iv] *adj* timid

**crampe** [krɑ̃p] *nf* cramp

**crampon** [krɑ̃pɔ̃] *nm (de chaussure)* stud; *(pour l'alpinisme)* crampon

**cramponner** [krɑ̃pɔne] **se cramponner** *vpr* to hold on; **se c. à qn/qch** to hold on to sb/sth

**cran** [krɑ̃] *nm* (**a**) *(entaille)* notch; *(de ceinture)* hole; **c. d'arrêt** *ou* **de sûreté** safety catch (**b**) *(de cheveux)* wave (**c**) *Fam (courage)* guts; **avoir du c.** to have guts (**d**) *Fam* **être à c.** *(excédé)* to be wound up

**crâne** [kran] *nm* skull

**crapaud** [krapo] *nm* toad

**crapule** [krapyl] *nf* villain, scoundrel

**craquer** [krake] **1** *vt (allumette)* to strike **2** *vi (branche)* to crack; *(escalier)* to creak; *(se casser)* to snap; *(se déchirer)* to rip ▪ **craquements** *nmpl (de branches)* cracking; *(d'escalier)* creaking

**crasse** [kras] *nf* filth ▪ **crasseux, -euse** *adj* filthy

**cratère** [kratɛr] *nm* crater

**cravate** [kravat] *nf* tie

**crawlé** [krole] *adj m* **dos c.** backstroke

**crayon** [krɛjɔ̃] *nm (en bois)* pencil; *(en cire)* crayon

**créancier, -ère** [kreɑ̃sje, -ɛr] *nmf* debtor

**créateur, -trice** [kreatœr, -tris] **1** *adj* creative **2** *nmf* creator ▪ **création** *nf* creation; **1000 créations d'emplois** 1,000 new jobs

**créature** [kreatyr] *nf (être vivant)* creature

**crèche** [krɛʃ] *nf (de Noël)* manger, *Br* crib; *(garderie)* (day) nursery, *Br* crèche

**crédible** [kredibl] *adj* credible

**crédit** [kredi] *nm (prêt, influence)* credit; **crédits** *(somme d'argent)* funds; **à c.** on credit ▪ **créditer** *vt (compte)* to credit (**de** with); *Fig* **c. qn de qch** to give sb credit for sth ▪ **créditeur, -trice** *adj* **solde c.** credit balance; **être c.** to be in credit

**crédule** [kredyl] *adj* credulous ▪ **crédulité** *nf* credulity

**créer** [kree] *vt* to create

**crémaillère** [kremajɛr] *nf* **pendre la c.** to have a housewarming (party)

**crématorium** [krematɔrjɔm] *nm Br* crematorium, *Am* crematory

**crème** [krɛm] **1** *nf (de lait, dessert, cosmétique)* cream; **c. Chantilly** whipped cream; **c. glacée** ice cream; **c. à raser** shaving cream **2** *adj inv* cream (-coloured) **3** *nm Fam* coffee with milk, *Br* white coffee ▪ **crémerie** *nf (magasin)* dairy ▪ **crémeux, -euse** *adj* creamy

**créneau, -x** [kreno] *nm Com* niche; *TV & Radio* slot

**créole** [kreɔl] **1** *adj* creole **2** *nmf* Creole **3** *nm (langue)* Creole

**crêpe** [krɛp] **1** *nf* pancake, crêpe **2** *nm (tissu)* crepe ▪ **crêperie** *nf* pancake restaurant

**crépiter** [krepite] *vi (feu)* to crackle ▪ **crépitement** *nm (du feu)* crackling

**crépu, -e** [krepy] *adj* frizzy

**crépuscule** [krepyskyl] *nm* twilight

**cresson** [kresɔ̃] *nm* watercress

**Crète** [krɛt] *nf* **la C.** Crete

**crête** [krɛt] *nf (de montagne, d'oiseau, de vague)* crest

**creuser** [krøze] **1** *vt (trou, puits)* to dig; *(évider)* to hollow (out); *Fig (idée)* to look into **2** *vi* to dig **3 se creuser** *vpr (joues)* to become hollow; *Fam* **se c. la tête** *ou* **la cervelle** to rack one's brains

**creux, -euse** [krø, -øz] **1** *adj (tube, joues, arbre, paroles)* hollow; *(sans activité)* slack; **assiette creuse** soup plate **2** *nm* hollow; *(moment)* slack period

**crevaison** [krəvɛzɔ̃] *nf (de pneu)* flat, *Br* puncture

**crevasse** [krəvas] *nf (trou)* crack; *(de glacier)* crevasse

**crever** [krəve] **1** *vt (ballon, bulle)* to burst; *Fam (épuiser)* to wear out **2** *vi (bulle, ballon, pneu)* to burst ▪ **crevé, -e** *adj (ballon, pneu)* burst; *Fam (épuisé)* worn out

**crevette** [krəvɛt] *nf (grise)* shrimp; *(rose)* prawn

**cri** [kri] *nm (de personne)* cry, shout; *(perçant)* scream; *(d'animal)* cry ▪ **criard, -e** *adj (son)* shrill; *(couleur)* loud

**crier** [krije] **1** *vt (injure, ordre)* to shout (**à** to) **2** *vi (personne)* to shout, to cry out; *(fort)* to scream; *(parler très fort)* to shout; **c. au secours** to shout for help

**crime** [krim] *nm* crime; *(assassinat)* murder ▪ **criminalité** *nf* crime ▪ **criminel, -elle 1** *adj* criminal **2** *nmf* criminal; *(assassin)* murderer

**crinière** [krinjɛr] *nf* mane

**crique** [krik] *nf* creek

**crise** [kriz] *nf* crisis; *(de maladie)* attack; **c. de nerfs** fit of hysteria

**crisper** [krispe] **1** *vt (poing)* to clench; *(muscle)* to tense **2 se crisper** *vpr (visage)* to tense; *(personne)* to get tense ■ **crispé, -e** *adj (personne)* tense

**crisser** [krise] *vi (pneu, roue)* to squeal; *(neige)* to crunch

**cristal, -aux** [kristal, -o] *nm* crystal; *Tech* **cristaux liquides** liquid crystal ■ **cristallin, -e** *adj (eau, son)* crystal-clear

**critère** [kritɛr] *nm* criterion

**critique** [kritik] **1** *adj (situation, phase)* critical **2** *nf (reproche)* criticism; *(de film, de livre)* review; **faire la c. de** *(film)* to review **3** *nm* critic ■ **critiquer** *vt* to criticize

**croasser** [krɔase] *vi* to caw

**Croatie** [krɔasi] *nf* **la C.** Croatia

**croc** [kro] *nm (crochet)* hook; *(dent)* fang

**croche** [krɔʃ] *nf Mus Br* quaver, *Am* eighth (note)

**croche-pied** [krɔʃpje] *nm* trip; **faire un c. à qn** to trip sb up

**crochet** [krɔʃɛ] *nm (pour accrocher, en boxe)* hook; *(aiguille)* crochet hook; *(parenthèse)* square bracket; **faire du c.** to crochet; **faire un c.** *(détour)* to make a detour; *(route)* to make a sudden turn ■ **crocheter** *vt (serrure)* to pick

**crochu, -e** [krɔʃy] *adj (nez)* hooked; *(doigts)* claw-like

**crocodile** [krɔkɔdil] *nm* crocodile

**croire*** [krwar] **1** *vt* to believe; *(penser)* to think (**que** that); **j'ai cru la voir** I thought I saw her; **je crois que oui** I think *or* believe so

**2** *vi* to believe (**à** *ou* **en** in)

**3 se croire** *vpr* **il se croit malin** he thinks he's smart

**croisé**[1] [krwaze] *nm Hist* crusader ■ **croisade** *nf Hist* crusade

**croiser** [krwaze] **1** *vt (passer)* to pass; *(ligne)* to cross; *(espèce)* to cross-breed; **c. les jambes** to cross one's legs; **c. les bras** to fold one's arms; *Fig* **c. les doigts** to keep one's fingers crossed

**2** *vi (navire)* to cruise

**3 se croiser** *vpr (voitures)* to pass each other; *(lignes, routes)* to cross, to intersect; *(lettres)* to cross; *(regards)* to meet ■ **croisé**[2], **-e** *adj (bras)* folded; *(veston)* double-breasted ■ **croisement** *nm (de routes)* crossroads *(sing)*, intersection; *(d'animaux)* crossing

**croisière** [krwazjɛr] *nf* cruise

**croître*** [krwatr] *vi (plante)* to grow; *(augmenter)* to grow, to increase (**de** by); *(lune)* to wax ■ **croissance** *nf* growth ■ **croissant, -e 1** *adj (nombre)* growing **2** *nm* crescent; *(pâtisserie)* croissant

**croix** [krwa] *nf* cross; **la C.-Rouge** the Red Cross

**croquer** [krɔke] **1** *vt (manger)* to crunch **2** *vi (fruit)* to be crunchy; **c. dans qch** to bite into sth ■ **croquant, -e** *adj* crunchy ■ **croque-monsieur** *nm inv* = toasted cheese and ham sandwich

**croquis** [krɔki] *nm* sketch

**crosse** [krɔs] *nf (de fusil)* butt; *(de hockey)* stick; *(d'évêque)* crook

**crotte** [krɔt] *nf (de mouton, de lapin)* droppings; **c. de chien** dog dirt ■ **crottin** *nm* dung

**crouler** [krule] *vi (édifice)* to crumble; **c. sous le travail** to be snowed under with work ■ **croulant, -e** *adj (mur)* crumbling

**croupe** [krup] *nf* rump

**croupier** [krupje] *nm* croupier

**croupir** [krupir] *vi (eau)* to stagnate

**croustiller** [krustije] *vi* to be crunchy; *(pain)* to be crusty ■ **croustillant, -e** *adj* crunchy; *(pain)* crusty; *Fig (histoire)* spicy

**croûte** [krut] *nf (de pain)* crust; *(de fromage)* rind; *(de plaie)* scab; *Fam* **casser la c.** to have a snack ■ **croûton** *nm (de pain)* end; **croûtons** *(pour la soupe)* croûtons

**croyable** [krwajabl] *adj* credible, believable ■ **croyance** *nf* belief (**en** in) ■ **croyant, -e 1** *adj* **être c.** to be a believer **2** *nmf* believer

**CRS** [seɛrɛs] (*abrév* **compagnie républicaine de sécurité**) *nm* = French riot policeman
**cru[1], -e[1]** [kry] *pp de* **croire**
**cru[2], -e[2]** [kry] **1** *adj (aliment)* raw; *(lait)* unpasteurized; *(lumière)* garish; *(propos)* crude; **monter à c.** to ride bareback **2** *nm (vignoble)* vineyard; **un grand c.** *(vin)* a vintage wine; **vin du c.** local wine
**cruauté** [kryote] *nf* cruelty (**envers** to)
**cruche** [kryʃ] *nf* pitcher, jug
**crucial, -e, -aux, -ales** [krysjal, -o] *adj* crucial
**crucifier** [krysifje] *vt* to crucify ▪ **crucifix** *nm* crucifix ▪ **crucifixion** *nf* crucifixion
**crudités** [krydite] *nfpl (légumes)* assorted raw vegetables
**crue** [kry] *nf (montée)* swelling; *(inondation)* flood; **en c.** *(rivière, fleuve)* in spate
**cruel, -elle** [kryɛl] *adj* cruel (**envers** *ou* **avec** to) ▪ **cruellement** *adv* cruelly
**crûment** [krymɑ̃] *adv (sans détour)* bluntly; *(grossièrement)* crudely
**crustacés** [krystase] *nmpl Culin* shellfish *inv*
**crypte** [kript] *nf* crypt
**crypté, -e** [kripte] *adj (message) & TV* coded
**Cuba** [kyba] *n* Cuba ▪ **cubain, -e 1** *adj* Cuban **2** *nmf* **C., Cubaine** Cuban
**cube** [kyb] **1** *nm* cube; *(de jeu)* building block **2** *adj* **mètre c.** cubic metre ▪ **cubique** *adj* cubic
**cueillir*** [kœjir] *vt* to pick, to gather
**cuiller, cuillère** [kɥijɛr] *nf* spoon; *(mesure)* spoonful; **c. à café, petite c.** teaspoon; **c. à soupe** tablespoon ▪ **cuillerée** *nf* spoonful; **c. à café** teaspoonful; **c. à soupe** tablespoonful
**cuir** [kɥir] *nm* leather; *(d'éléphant)* hide; **pantalon en c.** leather trousers; **c. chevelu** scalp
**cuirassé** [kɥirase] *nm Naut* battleship
**cuire*** [kɥir] **1** *vt (aliment, plat)* to cook; **c. qch à l'eau** to boil sth; **c. qch au four** to bake sth; *(viande)* to roast sth **2** *vi (aliment)* to cook; **faire c. qch** to cook sth
**cuisant, -e** [kɥizɑ̃, -ɑ̃t] *adj (douleur)* burning; *(affront)* stinging
**cuisine** [kɥizin] *nf (pièce)* kitchen; *(art)* cookery, cooking; **faire la c.** to do the cooking ▪ **cuisiner** *vti* to cook
**cuisinier, -ère[1]** [kɥizinje, -ɛr] *nmf* cook
**cuisinière[2]** [kɥizinjɛr] *nf (appareil)* stove, *Br* cooker
**cuisse** [kɥis] *nf* thigh; **c. de poulet** chicken leg; **cuisses de grenouilles** frogs' legs
**cuisson** [kɥisɔ̃] *nm (d'aliments)* cooking; *(de pain)* baking
**cuit, -e** [kɥi, kɥit] **1** *pp de* **cuire 2** *adj* cooked; **bien c.** well done
**cuivre** [kɥivr] *nm (rouge)* copper; *(jaune)* brass; *Mus* **les cuivres** the brass ▪ **cuivré, -e** *adj* copper-coloured
**culbuter** [kylbyte] *vi (personne)* to take a tumble
**cul-de-sac** [kydsak] (*pl* **culs-de-sac**) *nm* dead end, *Br* cul-de-sac
**culinaire** [kylinɛr] *adj* culinary
**culminer** [kylmine] *vi (tension, crise)* to peak; **la montagne culmine à 3 000 mètres** the mountain is 3,000 metres at its highest point ▪ **culminant** *adj* **point c.** *(de montagne)* highest point
**culot** [kylo] *nm (d'ampoule, de lampe)* base; *Fam (audace)* nerve, *Br* cheek
**culotte** [kylɔt] *nf (de femme)* knickers, *Am* panties; *(d'enfant)* pants; **culottes courtes** *Br* short trousers, *Am* short pants
**culpabiliser** [kylpabilize] **1** *vt* **c. qn** to make sb feel guilty **2 se culpabiliser** *vpr* to feel guilty ▪ **culpabilité** *nf* guilt
**culte** [kylt] **1** *nm (de dieu)* worship; *(religion)* religion **2** *adj* **film c.** cult film
**cultiver** [kyltive] **1** *vt (terre, amitié)* to cultivate; *(plantes)* to grow **2 se cultiver** *vpr* to improve one's mind ▪ **cultivateur, -trice** *nmf* farmer ▪ **cultivé, -e**

*adj (terre)* cultivated; *(esprit, personne)* cultured, cultivated

**culture** [kyltyr] *nf* (**a**) *(action)* farming, cultivation; *(de plantes)* growing; **cultures** *(terres)* fields under cultivation; *(plantes)* crops (**b**) *(éducation, civilisation) & Biol* culture; **c. générale** general knowledge; **c. physique** physical training ▪ **culturel, -elle** *adj* cultural

**culturisme** [kyltyrism] *nm* bodybuilding

**cumulatif, -ive** *adj* cumulative ▪ **cumuler** *vt* **c. deux fonctions** to hold two offices **cupide** [kypid] *adj* avaricious

**cure** [kyr] *nf (traitement)* (course of) treatment

**curé** [kyre] *nm* parish priest

**curer** [kyre] **1** *vt* to clean out **2 se curer** *vpr* **se c. les dents** to clean one's teeth ▪ **cure-dents** *nm inv* toothpick

**curieux, -euse** [kyrjø, -øz] **1** *adj (bizarre)* curious; *(indiscret)* inquisitive, curious (**de** about) **2** *nmf* inquisitive person; *(badaud)* onlooker ▪ **curiosité** *nf* curiosity; *(chose)* curio

**curriculum vitae** [kyrikylɔmvite] *nm inv Br* curriculum vitae, *Am* résumé

**curseur** [kyrsœr] *nm Ordinat* cursor

**cutané, -e** [kytane] *adj* **maladie cutanée** skin condition

**cuti** [kyti] *nf* skin test

**cuve** [kyv] *nf* tank; *(de fermentation)* vat ▪ **cuvée** *nf (récolte)* vintage ▪ **cuvette** *nf (récipient) & Géog* basin; *(des cabinets)* bowl

**CV** [seve] *(abrév* **curriculum vitae**) *nm Br* CV, *Am* résumé

**cyanure** [sjanyr] *nm* cyanide

**cybercafé** [sibɛrkafe] *nm* cybercafé

**cycle** [sikl] *nm* (**a**) *(série, movement)* cycle (**b**) **premier/second c.** *Scol* = lower/upper classes in secondary school; *Univ* = first/last two years of a degree course (**c**) *(bicyclette)* cycle ▪ **cyclable** *adj* **piste c.** cycle path

**cyclisme** [siklism] *nm* cycling ▪ **cycliste 1** *nmf* cyclist **2** *adj* **course c.** cycle race

**cyclomoteur** [siklɔmɔtœr] *nm* moped

**cyclone** [siklon] *nm* cyclone

**cygne** [siɲ] *nm* swan

**cylindre** [silɛ̃dr] *nm* cylinder; *(rouleau)* roller ▪ **cylindrée** *nf* (cubic) capacity ▪ **cylindrique** *adj* cylindrical

**cymbale** [sɛ̃bal] *nf* cymbal

**cynique** [sinik] **1** *adj* cynical **2** *nmf* cynic

**cyprès** [siprɛ] *nm* cypress

**cypriote** [siprijɔt] **1** *adj* Cypriot **2** *nmf* **C.** Cypriot

# Dd

**D, d** [de] **1** *nm inv* D, d **2** (*abrév* **route départementale**) = designation of a secondary road

**dactylo** [daktilo] *nf (personne)* typist; *(action)* typing

**daigner** [deɲe] *vt* **d. faire qch** to deign to do sth

**daim** [dɛ̃] *nm (animal)* fallow deer; *(mâle)* buck; *(cuir)* suede

**dalle** [dal] *nf (de pierre)* paving stone; *(de marbre)* slab

**daltonien, -enne** [daltɔnjɛ̃, -ɛn] *adj* colour-blind

**dame** [dam] *nf (femme)* lady; *Cartes* queen; *(au jeu de dames)* king; **dames** *(jeu) Br* draughts, *Am* checkers

**damner** [dane] *vt* to damn

**Danemark** [danmark] *nm* **le D.** Denmark ▪ **danois, -e 1** *adj* Danish **2** *nmf* **D., Danoise** Dane **3** *nm (langue)* Danish

**danger** [dɑ̃ʒe] *nm* danger; **en d.** in danger ▪ **dangereux, -euse** *adj* dangerous (**pour** to)

---

**DANS** [dɑ̃] *prép* (**a**) in; *(changement de lieu)* into; *(à l'intérieur de)* inside

(**b**) *(provenance)* from, out of; **boire d. un verre** to drink out of a glass

(**c**) *(exprime la temporalité)* in; **d. deux jours** in two days' time

(**d**) *(exprime une approximation)* **d. les dix euros** about ten euros

---

**danse** [dɑ̃s] *nf* dance; **la d.** *(art)* dancing; **d. classique** ballet ▪ **danser** *vti* to dance ▪ **danseur, -euse** *nmf* dancer

**dard** [dar] *nm (d'insecte)* sting

**date** [dat] *nf* date; **d. de naissance** date of birth; **d. limite** deadline; **d. limite de vente** sell-by date ▪ **dater 1** *vt (lettre)* to date **2** *vi* **à d. du 15** as from the 15th

**datte** [dat] *nf* date

**daube** [dob] *nf* **bœuf en d.** braised beef stew

**dauphin** [dofɛ̃] *nm (animal)* dolphin

**davantage** [davɑ̃taʒ] *adv* more; **d. de temps/d'argent** more time/money

---

**DE¹** [də]

**de** becomes **d'** before vowel and h mute; de + le = **du**, de + les = **des**.

*prép* (**a**) *(complément de nom)* of; **le livre de Paul** Paul's book; **un livre de Flaubert** a book by Flaubert; **le train de Londres** the London train; **une augmentation de salaire** an increase in salary

(**b**) *(complément d'adjectif)* **digne de qn** worthy of sb; **content de qn/qch** pleased with sb/sth; **heureux de partir** happy to leave

(**c**) *(complément de verbe)* **parler de qn/qch** to speak of sb/sth; **se souvenir de qn/qch** to remember sb/sth; **décider de faire qch** to decide to do sth; **empêcher qn de faire qch** to stop sb from doing sth

(**d**) *(indique la provenance)* from; **venir de...** to come from...; **sortir de qch** to come out of sth; **le train de Londres** the train from London

(**e**) *(introduit l'agent)* **accompagné de qn** accompanied by sb; **entouré de qch** surrounded by *or* with sth (**f**) *(introduit le moyen)* **armé de qch** armed with sth

(**g**) *(introduit la manière)* **d'une voix douce** in a gentle voice

(**h**) *(introduit la cause)* **puni de son impatience** punished for his/her impatience; **mourir de faim** to die of hunger

(**i**) *(introduit le temps)* **travailler de nuit** to work by night; **six heures du matin** six o'clock in the morning

(**j**) *(mesure)* **avoir six mètres de haut, être haut de six mètres** to be six metres high; **homme de trente ans** thirty-year-old man; **gagner cent francs de l'heure** to earn a hundred francs an hour

---

**DE²** [də] *article partitif* some; **elle boit du vin** she drinks (some) wine; **il ne boit pas de vin** he doesn't drink (any) wine; **est-ce que vous buvez du vin?** do you drink (any) wine?

---

**DE³** [də] *article indéfini* **de, des** some; **des fleurs** (some) flowers; **de jolies fleurs** (some) pretty flowers; **d'agréables soirées** (some) pleasant evenings

---

**dé** [de] *nm (à jouer)* dice; *(à coudre)* thimble

**déballer** [debale] *vt* to unpack

**débarbouiller** [debarbuje] **se débarbouiller** *vpr* to wash one's face

**débardeur** [debardœr] *nm (vêtement)* vest

**débarquer** [debarke] **1** *vt (passagers)* to land; *(marchandises)* to unload **2** *vi (passagers)* to disembark ▪ **débarquement** *nm (de passagers, de troupes)* landing; *(de marchandises)* unloading

**débarras** [debara] *nm* storeroom ▪ **débarrasser 1** *vt (chambre, table)* to clear (**de** of); **d. qn de qch** to relieve sb of sth **2 se débarrasser** *vpr* **se d. de qn/qch** to get rid of sb/sth

**débat** [deba] *nm* debate

**débattre*** [debatr] **1** *vt* to discuss, to debate; **d. de qch** to discuss sth **2 se débattre** *vpr* to struggle

**débaucher** [deboʃe] *vt* **d. qn** *(licencier)* to lay sb off; *(inciter à la débauche)* to corrupt sb

**débit** [debi] *nm Fin* debit; *(de fleuve)* flow; *(de personne)* delivery; **d. de tabac** *Br* tobacconist's (shop), *Am* tobacco store

**débiter** [debite] *vt (découper)* to cut up (**en** into); *(compte)* to debit; *Péj (dire)* to spout ▪ **débiteur** *adj m* **solde d.** debit balance; **mon compte est d.** my account is in debit

**débloquer** [deblɔke] *vt (mécanisme)* to unjam; *(compte, prix)* to unfreeze

**déboiser** [debwaze] *vt (terrain)* to clear of trees

**déboîter** [debwate] **1** *vt (tuyau)* to disconnect **2** *vi (véhicule)* to pull out **3 se déboîter** *vpr* **se d. l'épaule** to dislocate one's shoulder

**déborder** [debɔrde] **1** *vi (fleuve, liquide)* to overflow; *(en bouillant)* to boil over **2** *vt (dépasser)* to stick out from; **débordé de travail** snowed under with work

**débouché** [debuʃe] *nm (carrière)* opening; *(de produit)* outlet

**déboucher** [debuʃe] **1** *vt (bouteille)* to uncork; *(bouchon vissé)* to uncap; *(lavabo, tuyau)* to unblock **2** *vi (surgir)* to emerge (**de** from); **d. sur** *(rue)* to lead out onto/into

**debout** [dəbu] *adv (personne)* standing; *(objet)* upright; **se mettre d.** to stand up; **rester d.** to stand; **être d.** *(hors du lit)* to be up

**déboutonner** [debutɔne] **1** *vt* to unbutton **2 se déboutonner** *vpr (personne)* to undo one's coat/jacket/*etc*

**débraillé, -e** [debraje] *adj* slovenly

**débrancher** [debrɑ̃ʃe] *vt* to unplug

**débrayer** [debreje] *vi* (**a**) *Aut* to release the clutch (**b**) *(se mettre en grève)* to stop work ▪ **débrayage** (**a**) *Aut* declutching (**b**) *(grève)* stoppage

**débris** [debri] *nmpl (de voiture, d'avion)* debris

**débrouiller** [debruje] **1** *vt (fil, mystère)* to unravel **2 se débrouiller** *vpr Fam* to manage; **se d. pour faire qch** to manage to do sth ▪ **débrouillard, -e** *adj Fam* resourceful

**début** [deby] *nm* beginning, start; **au d. (de)** at the beginning (of); **dès le d.** (right) from the start *or* beginning

**débuter** [debyte] *vi* to start, to begin (**par** with); *(dans une carrière)* to start out ▪ **débutant, -e** *nmf* beginner

**deçà** [dəsa] **en deçà 1** *adv* (on) this side **2** *prép* **en d. de** (on) this side of

**décadent, -e** [dekadɑ̃, -ɑ̃t] *adj* decadent

**décaféiné, -e** [dekafeine] *adj* decaffeinated

**décaler** [dekale] **1** *vt (dans le temps)* to change the time of; *(dans l'espace)* to shift, to move **2 se décaler** *vpr* to move, to shift ▪ **décalage** *nm (écart)* gap (**entre** between); **d. horaire** time difference; **souffrir du d. horaire** to have jet lag

**décalquer** [dekalke] *vt* to trace

**décaper** [dekape] *vt (avec un produit)* to strip; *(au papier de verre)* to sand (down); *(four)* to clean

**décapiter** [dekapite] *vt (personne)* to decapitate

**décapotable** [dekapɔtabl] *adj & nf* convertible

**décapsuleur** [dekapsylœr] *nm* bottle opener

**décédé, -e** [desede] *adj* deceased

**déceler** [desle] *vt (trouver)* to detect

**décembre** [desɑ̃br] *nm* December

**décence** [desɑ̃s] *nf (de comportement)* propriety; *(d'habillement)* decency

**décennie** [deseni] *nf* decade

**décent, -e** [desɑ̃, -ɑ̃t] *adj (comportement)* proper; *(vêtements)* decent

**décentralisation** [desɑ̃tralizɑsjɔ̃] *nf* decentralization

**déception** [desɛpsjɔ̃] *nf* disappointment

**décerner** [desɛrne] *vt (prix)* to award (**à** to)

**décès** [desɛ] *nm* death

**décevant, -e** [desvɑ̃, -ɑ̃t] *adj* disappointing

**décevoir*** [desəvwar] *vt* to disappoint

**déchaîner** [deʃene] **1** *vt (colère, violence)* to unleash **2 se déchaîner** *vpr (tempête)* to rage; *(personne)* to fly into a rage (**contre** with)

**décharge** [deʃarʒ] *nf* **d. (électrique)** (electric) shock; **d. (publique)** *Br* (rubbish) dump, *Am* (garbage) dump

**décharger** [deʃarʒe] **1** *vt (camion, navire, cargaison)* to unload; **d. qn de qch** *(tâche, responsabilité)* to relieve sb of **2 se décharger** *vpr (batterie)* to go flat

**déchausser** [deʃose] **1** *vt* **d. qn** to take sb's shoes off **2 se déchausser** *vpr (personne)* to take one's shoes off

**déchéance** [deʃeɑ̃s] *nf (déclin)* decline

**déchets** [deʃɛ] *nmpl* scraps; **d. radioactifs** radioactive waste

**déchiffrer** [deʃifre] *vt (message, écriture)* to decipher

**déchiqueté, -e** [deʃikte] *adj (tissu)* torn to shreds

**déchirer** [deʃire] **1** *vt (accidentellement)* to tear; *(volontairement)* to tear up **2 se déchirer** *vpr (tissu, papier)* to tear

**déchirure** [deʃiryr] *nf* tear

**déchoir*** [deʃwar] *vi (personne)* to demean oneself

**déchu, -e** [deʃy] *adj* **être d. de qch** to be stripped of sth

**décidé, -e** [deside] *adj (personne, air)* determined; *(fixé)* settled; **être d. à faire qch** to be determined to do sth

**décidément** [desidemɑ̃] *adv* really

**décider** [deside] **1** *vt* **d. quand/que...** to decide when/that... **2** *vi* **d. de qch** to decide on sth; **d. de faire qch** to decide to do sth **3 se décider** *vpr* **se d. (à faire qch)** to make up one's mind (to do sth)

**décimal, -e, -aux, -ales** [desimal, -o] *adj* decimal

**décimer** [desime] *vt* to decimate

**décimètre** [desimɛtr] *nm* decimetre

**décisif, -ive** [desizif, -iv] *adj (bataille)* decisive; *(moment)* critical ▪ **décision**

*nf* decision (**de faire** to do); **prendre une d.** to make a decision

**déclaration** [deklarɑsjɔ̃] *nf (annonce)* statement; *(de naissance, de décès)* registration; *(à la police)* report; **d. d'impôts** income tax return

**déclarer** [deklare] **1** *vt (annoncer)* to declare (**que** that); *(naissance, décès)* to register; **d. qn coupable** to find sb guilty (**de** of); **d. la guerre** to declare war (**à** on); **rien à d.** *(en douane)* nothing to declare **2 se déclarer** *vpr (incendie, maladie)* to break out

**déclencher** [deklɑ̃ʃe] **1** *vt (appareil)* to start; *(mécanisme)* to activate; *(sonnerie)* to set off; *(révolte)* to trigger off; *(attaque)* to launch **2 se déclencher** *vpr (alarme, sonnerie)* to go off; *(incendie)* to start

**déclic** [deklik] *nm (bruit)* click

**déclin** [deklɛ̃] *nm* decline; **être en d.** to be in decline

**décliner** [dekline] **1** *vi (forces)* to decline; *(jour)* to draw to a close **2** *vt (refuser)* to decline

**décocher** [dekɔʃe] *vt (flèche)* to shoot

**décoder** [dekɔde] *vt* to decode ▪ **décodeur** *nm TV* decoder

**décoiffer** [dekwafe] **1** *vt* **d. qn** to mess up sb's hair **2 se décoiffer** *vpr (se dépeigner)* to mess up one's hair; *(ôter son chapeau)* to remove one's hat

**décoincer** [dekwɛ̃se] *vt*, **se décoincer** *vpr (tiroir, mécanisme)* to loosen

**décollage** [dekɔlaʒ] *nm (d'avion)* takeoff

**décoller** [dekɔle] **1** *vt (enlever)* to peel off **2** *vi (avion)* to take off **3 se décoller** *vpr* to peel off

**décolleté, -e** [dekɔlte] **1** *adj (robe)* low-cut **2** *nm (de robe)* low neckline

**décolorer** [dekɔlɔre] **1** *vt (cheveux)* to bleach **2 se décolorer** *vpr (tissu)* to fade; **se d. les cheveux** to bleach one's hair

**décombres** [dekɔ̃br] *nmpl* ruins, debris

**décommander** [dekɔmɑ̃de] **1** *vt (marchandises, invitation)* to cancel; *(invité)* to put off **2 se décommander** *vpr* to cancel

**décomposer** [dekɔ̃poze] **1** *vt Chim* to decompose **2 se décomposer** *vpr (pourrir)* to decompose ▪ **décomposition** *nf* decomposition

**décompression** [dekɔ̃prɛsjɔ̃] *nf* decompression

**décompte** [dekɔ̃t] *nm (soustraction)* deduction; *(détail)* breakdown ▪ **décompter** *vt* to deduct (**de** from)

**déconcentrer** [dekɔ̃sɑ̃tre] **se déconcentrer** *vpr* to lose concentration

**déconcerter** [dekɔ̃sɛrte] *vt* to disconcert

**décongeler** [dekɔ̃ʒle] *vt* to thaw, to defrost

**décongestionner** [dekɔ̃ʒɛstjɔne] *vt (rue, poumons)* to relieve congestion in

**déconnecter** [dekɔnɛkte] *vt (appareil, fil)* to disconnect

**déconseiller** [dekɔ̃seje] *vt* **d. qch à qn** to advise sb against sth; **d. à qn de faire qch** to advise sb against doing sth

**déconsidérer** [dekɔ̃sidere] *vt* to discredit

**décontaminer** [dekɔ̃tamine] *vt* to decontaminate

**décontracter** [dekɔ̃trakte] **1** *vt (muscle)* to relax **2 se décontracter** *vpr* to relax ▪ **décontracté, -e** *adj (ambiance, personne)* relaxed; *(vêtement)* casual

**décor** [dekɔr] *nm (de maison)* decor; *(paysage)* surroundings; *Théât* **décors** scenery, set

**décorer** [dekɔre] *vt (maison, soldat)* to decorate (**de** with) ▪ **décorateur, -trice** *nmf* (interior) decorator; *Théât* stage designer ▪ **décoratif, -ive** *adj* decorative ▪ **décoration** *nf (action, ornement, médaille)* decoration

**décortiquer** [dekɔrtike] *vt (riz, orge)* to hull; *(crevette, noisette)* to shell

**découdre*** [dekudr] **1** *vt (ourlet, vêtement)* to unstitch; *(bouton)* to take off **2 se découdre** *vpr (ourlet, vêtement)* to come unstitched; *(bouton)* to come off

**découler** [dekule] *vi* **d. de qch** to follow from sth

**découper** [dekupe] *vt (viande)* to carve; *(gâteau, papier)* to cut up ▪ **découpé, -e** *adj (irrégulier)* jagged

**décourager** [dekuraʒe] **1** *vt (dissuader)* to discourage (**de faire** from doing); *(démoraliser)* to dishearten, to discourage **2 se décourager** *vpr* to get discouraged *or* disheartened ▪ **découragement** *nm* discouragement

**décousu, -e** [dekuzy] *adj (ourlet, vêtement)* unstitched; *Fig (propos)* disjointed

**découvert, -e** [dekuvɛr, -ɛrt] **1** *adj (terrain)* open; *(tête, épaule)* bare **2** *nm (de compte)* overdraft

**découverte** [dekuvɛrt] *nf* discovery; **faire une d.** to make a discovery

**découvrir*** [dekuvrir] **1** *vt (trouver, apprendre à connaître)* to discover; *(secret)* to uncover; **faire d. qch à qn** to introduce sb to sth **2 se découvrir** *vpr (ciel)* to clear

**décrire*** [dekrir] *vt (représenter)* to describe

**décrocher** [dekrɔʃe] **1** *vt (détacher)* to unhook; *(tableau, rideau)* to take down; **d. (le téléphone)** *(pour répondre)* to pick up the phone; *(pour ne pas être dérangé)* to take the phone off the hook **2 se décrocher** *vpr (tableau, rideau)* to come unhooked

**décroître*** [dekrwatr] *vi (forces, nombre)* to decrease; *(jours)* to get shorter

**décrypter** [dekripte] *vt* to decipher

**déçu, -e** [desy] **1** *pp de* **décevoir 2** *adj* disappointed

**décupler** [dekyple] *vti* to increase tenfold

**dédaigner** [dedeɲe] *vt (offre, richesses)* to scorn; *(conseil)* to disregard ▪ **dédaigneux, -euse** *adj* scornful, disdainful (**de** of)

**dédain** [dedɛ̃] *nm* scorn, disdain (**pour/de** for)

**dedans** [dədɑ̃] *adv* inside; **de d.** from (the) inside; **en d.** on the inside; **tomber d.** *(trou)* to fall in (it)

**dédicace** [dedikas] *nf* dedication ▪ **dédicacer** *vt (signer)* to sign (**à** for)

**dédier** [dedje] *vt* to dedicate (**à** to)

**dédommager** [dedɔmaʒe] *vt* to compensate (**de** for) ▪ **dédommagement** *nm* compensation

**dédouaner** [dedwane] *vt (marchandises)* to clear through customs

**déduire*** [dedɥir] *vt (retirer)* to deduct (**de** from); *(conclure)* to deduce (**de** from) ▪ **déductible** *adj* deductible ▪ **déduction** *nf (raisonnement, décompte)* deduction

**déesse** [deɛs] *nf* goddess

**défaillir*** [defajir] *vi (s'évanouir)* to faint; *(faiblir)* to fail ▪ **défaillance** *nf (évanouissement)* fainting fit; *(faiblesse)* weakness; *(panne)* failure; **avoir une d.** *(s'évanouir)* to faint; *(faiblir)* to feel weak

**défaire*** [defɛr] **1** *vt (nœud)* to undo; *(valises)* to unpack **2 se défaire** *vpr (nœud)* to come undone

**défait, -e**[1] [defɛ, -ɛt] *adj (lit)* unmade; *(visage)* haggard

**défaite**[2] [defɛt] *nf* defeat

**défaut** [defo] *nm (de personne)* fault, shortcoming; *(de machine)* defect; *(de diamant, de raisonnement)* flaw; **à d. de qch** for lack of sth; **ou, à d.…** or, failing that…; **d. de fabrication** manufacturing fault; **d. de prononciation** speech impediment

**défavorable** [defavɔrabl] *adj* unfavourable (**à** to) ▪ **défavorisé, -e** *adj (milieu)* underprivileged ▪ **défavoriser** *vt* to put at a disadvantage

**défection** [defɛksjɔ̃] *nf (de soldat, d'espion)* defection; **faire d.** *(soldat, espion)* to defect

**défectueux, -euse** [defɛktɥø, -øz] *adj* faulty, defective

**défendre** [defɑ̃dr] **1** *vt (protéger, soutenir)* to defend (**contre** against); **d. à qn de faire qch** to forbid sb to do sth; **d. qch à qn** to forbid sb sth **2 se défendre** *vpr* to defend oneself

**défense¹** [defɑ̃s] *nf (protection) Br* defence, *Am* defense; **sans d.** *Br* defenceless, *Am* defenseless; **'d. de fumer'** 'no smoking'
**défense²** [defɑ̃s] *nf (d'éléphant)* tusk
**défenseur** [defɑ̃sœr] *nm* defender
**défensif, -ive** [defɑ̃sif, -iv] **1** *adj* defensive **2** *nf* **sur la défensive** on the defensive
**déferler** [defɛrle] *vi (vagues)* to break
**défi** [defi] *nm* challenge (**à** to); **lancer un d. à qn** to challenge sb; **mettre qn au d. de faire qch** to defy sb to do sth
**défiance** [defjɑ̃s] *nf* mistrust
**déficience** [defisjɑ̃s] *nf* deficiency
**déficit** [defisit] *nm* deficit; **être en d.** to be in deficit; **d. commercial** trade deficit ▪ **déficitaire** *adj (budget)* in deficit; *(entreprise)* loss-making; *(compte)* in debit
**défier** [defje] *vt (provoquer)* to challenge; *(danger, mort)* to defy; **d. qn de faire qch** to defy sb to do sth
**défiguré, -e** [defigyre] *adj (personne)* disfigured
**défilé** [defile] *nm (cortège)* procession; *(de manifestants)* march; *Mil* parade; *Géog* pass; **d. de mode** fashion show
**définir** [definir] *vt* to define ▪ **défini, -e** *adj* definite ▪ **définition** *nf* definition; *(de mots croisés)* clue
**définitif, -ive** [definitif, -iv] **1** *adj (version)* final; *(fermeture)* permanent **2** *nf* **en définitive** in the final analysis ▪ **définitivement** *adv (partir, exclure)* for good
**déflagration** [deflagrɑsjɔ̃] *nf* explosion
**défoncer** [defɔ̃se] *vt (porte, mur)* to smash in; *(trottoir)* to break up ▪ **défoncé, -e** *adj (route)* bumpy
**déformation** [defɔrmɑsjɔ̃] *nf (de membre)* deformation; *(de fait)* distortion
**déformer** [defɔrme] **1** *vt (membre)* to deform; *(vêtement, chaussures)* to put out of shape; *(image)* to distort; *(propos)* to twist **2 se déformer** *vpr* to lose its shape ▪ **déformé, -e** *adj (objet)* misshapen; *(corps)* deformed
**défricher** [defriʃe] *vt (terrain)* to clear
**défriser** [defrize] *vt (cheveux)* to straighten
**défroisser** [defrwase] *vt* to smooth out
**défunt, -e** [defœ̃, -œ̃t] **1** *adj (mort)* departed; **mon d. mari** my late husband **2** *nmf* **le d., la défunte** the deceased
**dégager** [degaʒe] **1** *vt (passage, voie)* to clear (**de** of); *(odeur, chaleur)* to emit; **d. qn de** *(décombres)* to free sb from **2 se dégager** *vpr (odeur)* to be given off; *(ciel)* to clear; **se d. de qch** *(personne)* to free oneself from sth ▪ **dégagé, -e** *adj (ciel)* clear; *(ton)* casual; *(vue)* open ▪ **dégagement** *nm (action)* clearing; *(de chaleur)* emission
**dégainer** [degene] *vti* to draw
**dégarnir** [degarnir] **se dégarnir** *vpr (personne)* to go bald
**dégâts** [degɑ] *nmpl* damage
**dégel** [deʒɛl] *nm* thaw ▪ **dégeler 1** *vt* to thaw; *(surgelé)* to defrost; *(crédits)* to unfreeze **2** *vi* to thaw; **faire d. qch** *(surgelé)* to defrost sth **3** *v impersonnel* **il dégèle** it's thawing **4 se dégeler** *vpr Fig (atmosphère)* to become less chilly
**dégénérer** [deʒenere] *vi* to degenerate (**en** into)
**dégonfler** [degɔ̃fle] **1** *vt (pneu)* to let the air out of **2 se dégonfler** *vpr (pneu)* to go flat ▪ **dégonflé, -e** *adj (pneu)* flat
**dégouliner** [deguline] *vi* to trickle
**dégourdir** [degurdir] **se dégourdir** *vpr* **se d. les jambes** to stretch one's legs ▪ **dégourdi, -e** *adj (malin)* smart
**dégoût** [degu] *nm* disgust
**dégoûter** [degute] *vt (moralement)* to disgust; *(physiquement)* to turn sb's stomach; **d. qn de qch** to put sb off sth ▪ **dégoutant, -e** *adj* disgusting ▪ **dégouté, -e** *adj* disgusted; **être d. de qch** to be sick of sth
**dégradation** [degradɑsjɔ̃] *nf (de matériel)* damage (**de** to)
**dégrader** [degrade] **1** *vt (matériel)* to

damage **2 se dégrader** *vpr (situation)* to deteriorate ▪ **dégradant, -e** *adj* degrading

**dégrafer** [degrafe] **1** *vt (vêtement)* to undo **2 se dégrader** *vpr (vêtement)* to come undone

**degré** [dəgre] *nm (d'angle, de température)* degree; *(d'alcool)* proof; *(d'échelle)* rung; **au plus haut d.** in the extreme

**dégrèvement** [degrɛvmɑ̃] *nm* **d. fiscal** tax relief

**dégrossir** [degrɔsir] *vt (travail)* to rough out

**déguiser** [degize] **1** *vt (pour tromper)* to disguise; **d. qn en qch** *(costumer)* to dress sb up as sth **2 se déguiser** *vpr (pour s'amuser)* to dress oneself up (**en** as) ▪ **déguisement** *nm* disguise; *(de bal costumé)* fancy dress

**déguster** [degyste] *vt (savourer)* to savour ▪ **dégustation** *nf* tasting

**dehors** [dəɔr] **1** *adv* outside; *(pas chez soi)* out; *(en plein air)* out of doors; **en d. de la ville** out of town; *Fig* **en d. de** *(excepté)* apart from **2** *nm (extérieur)* outside; **au d.** on the outside; *(se pencher)* out

**déjà** [deʒa] *adv* already; **est-il d. parti?** has he left yet *or* already?; **elle l'a d. vu** she's seen it before, she's already seen it

**déjeuner** [deʒœne] **1** *nm* lunch; **petit d.** breakfast **2** *vi (à midi)* to have lunch; *(le matin)* to have breakfast

**déjouer** [deʒwe] *vt (intrigue)* to foil

**délabré, -e** [delabre] *adj (bâtiment)* dilapidated

**délacer** [delase] **1** *vt (chaussure)* to untie **2 se délacer** *vpr (chaussure)* to come untied

**délai** [delɛ] *nm (laps de temps)* time allowed; *(sursis)* extension; **dans les plus brefs délais** as soon as possible; **dernier d.** final date

**délaisser** [delese] *vt (négliger)* to neglect

**délasser** [delɑse] *vt*, **se délasser** *vpr* to relax

**délavé, -e** [delave] *adj (tissu, jean)* faded; *(couleur, ciel)* watery

**délayer** [deleje] *vt (poudre)* to add water to; *(liquide)* to water down

**délecter** [delɛkte] **se délecter** *vpr* **se d. de qch** to take delight in sth

**déléguer** [delege] *vt* to delegate (**à** to) ▪ **délégation** *nf* delegation ▪ **délégué, -e** *nmf* delegate; *Scol* **d. de classe** = pupil elected to represent his or her class at class meetings

**délibération** [deliberɑsjɔ̃] *nf* deliberation

**délibéré, -e** [delibere] *adj (intentionnel)* deliberate

**délicat, -e** [delika, -at] *adj (santé, travail)* delicate; *(question)* tricky, delicate; *(peau)* sensitive; *(geste)* tactful ▪ **délicatesse** *nf (tact)* tact

**délice** [delis] *nm* delight ▪ **délicieux, -euse** *adj (mets)* delicious; *(parfum)* delightful

**délier** [delje] *vt* to untie

**délimiter** [delimite] *vt (terrain)* to mark off; *(sujet)* to define

**délinquant, -e** [delɛ̃kɑ̃, -ɑ̃t] *nmf* delinquent ▪ **délinquance** *nf* delinquency

**délire** [delir] *nm Méd* delirium; *(exaltation)* frenzy

**délit** [deli] *nm Br* offence, *Am* offense

**délivrer** [delivre] *vt* (**a**) *(captif)* to rescue; **d. qn de qch** to rid sb of sth (**b**) *(marchandises)* to deliver; *(passeport)* to issue (**à** to) ▪ **délivrance** *nf (soulagement)* relief; *(de passeport)* issue

**déloger** [delɔʒe] *vt (envahisseur)* to drive out (**de** from)

**déloyal, -e, -aux, -ales** [delwajal, -o] *adj (personne)* disloyal; *(concurrence)* unfair

**deltaplane** [deltaplan] *nm* hang-glider; **faire du d.** to go hang-gliding

**déluge** [delyʒ] *nm (de pluie)* downpour; *(de paroles)* flood; *(d'insultes)* torrent

**demain** [dəmɛ̃] *adv* tomorrow; **d. soir** tomorrow evening; **à d.!** see you tomorrow!

**demande** [dəmɑ̃d] *nf (requête)* request (**de** for); *Écon* demand; **faire une d. de qch** *(prêt, permis)* to apply for sth; **demandes d'emploi** *(dans le journal)* jobs wanted, *Br* situations wanted

**demander** [dəmɑ̃de] **1** *vt (conseil)* to ask for; *(prix, raison)* to ask; *(nécessiter)* to require; **d. son chemin/l'heure** to ask the way/the time; **d. qch à qn** to ask sb for sth; **d. à qn de faire qch** to ask sb to do sth; **d. qn en mariage** to propose (marriage) to sb

**2 se demander** *vpr* to wonder, to ask oneself (**pourquoi** why; **si** if) ▪ **demandeur, -euse** *nmf* **d. d'emploi** job seeker

**démanger** [demɑ̃ʒe] *vti* to itch ▪ **démangeaisons** *nfpl* **avoir des d.** to be itching

**démanteler** [demɑ̃tle] *vt* to break up

**démaquiller** [demakije] **se démaquiller** *vpr* to remove one's make-up ▪ **démaquillant** *nm* cleanser

**démarcation** [demarkɑsjɔ̃] *nf* demarcation

**démarche** [demarʃ] *nf (allure)* walk, gait; *(requête)* step; **faire les démarches nécessaires pour…** to take the necessary steps to…

**démarcheur, -euse** [demarʃœr, -øz] *nmf (vendeur)* door-to-door salesman, *f* saleswoman

**démarquer** [demarke] *vt (marchandises)* to mark down

**démarrer** [demare] *vi (moteur)* to start; *(voiture)* to move off; *Fig (entreprise)* to get off the ground ▪ **démarrage** *nm (de moteur)* starting; **au d.** when moving off; **d. en côte** hill start ▪ **démarreur** *nm Aut* starter

**démasquer** [demaske] *vt* to unmask

**démêler** [demele] *vt* to untangle

**déménager** [demenaʒe] **1** *vi* to move **2** *vt (meubles)* to move ▪ **déménagement** *nm* move ▪ **déménageur** *nm Br* removal man, *Am* (furniture) mover

**démener** [demne] **se démener** *vpr (s'agiter)* to thrash about

**dément, -e** [demɑ̃, -ɑ̃t] *adj* insane ▪ **démentiel, -elle** *adj* insane

**démentir** [demɑ̃tir] *vt (nouvelle, fait)* to deny ▪ **démenti** *nm* denial

**démesuré, -e** [deməzyre] *adj* excessive

**démettre*** [demɛtr] **1** *vt* **d. qn de ses fonctions** to remove sb from his/her post **2 se démettre** *vpr* **se d. l'épaule** to dislocate one's shoulder

**demeurant** [dəmœrɑ̃] **au demeurant** *adv (malgré tout)* for all that

**demeure** [dəmœr] *nf (belle maison)* mansion

**demeurer** [dəmœre] *vi* (**a**) *(aux* **être**) *(rester)* to remain (**b**) *(aux* **avoir**) *Formel (habiter)* to reside

**demi, -e** [dəmi] **1** *adj* half; **une heure et demie** *(90 minutes)* an hour and a half; *(à l'horloge)* half past one, one-thirty

**2** *adv* **(à) d. plein** half-full; **à d. nu** half-naked

**3** *nmf (moitié)* half

**4** *nm (au football)* midfielder; **un d.** *(bière)* a beer, *Br* a half(-pint); **d. de mêlée** *(au rugby)* scrum half

**5** *nf* **à la demie** *(à l'horloge)* at half-past ▪ **demi-cercle** (*pl* **demi-cercles**) *nm* semicircle ▪ **demi-douzaine** (*pl* **demi-douzaines**) *nf* **une d. (de)** half a dozen ▪ **demi-écrémé** *adj* semi-skimmed ▪ **demi-finale** (*pl* **demi-finales**) *nf Sport* semi-final ▪ **demi-frère** (*pl* **demi-frères**) *nm* half brother ▪ **demi-heure** (*pl* **demi-heures**) *nf* **une d.** half an hour ▪ **demi-journée** (*pl* **demi-journées**) *nf* half-day ▪ **demi-pension** *nf Br* half-board, *Am* breakfast and one meal ▪ **demi-pensionnaire** (*pl* **demi-pensionnaires**) *nmf Br* = pupil who has school dinners ▪ **demi-sœur** (*pl* **demi-sœurs**) *nf* half sister ▪ **demi-tarif** (*pl* **demi-tarifs**) *nm* half-price ▪ **demi-tour** (*pl* **demi-tours**) *nm Br* about turn, *Am* about face; *(en voiture)* U-turn; **faire d.** *(à pied)* to turn back; *(en voiture)* to do a U-turn

**démission** [demisjɔ̃] *nf* resignation; **donner sa d.** to hand in one's resignation ▪ **démissionner** *vi* to resign

**démocrate** [demɔkrat] **1** *adj* democratic **2** *nmf* democrat ▪ **démocratie** [-asi] *nf* democracy ▪ **démocratique** *adj* democratic

**démodé, -e** [demɔde] *adj* old-fashioned

**démographie** [demɔgrafi] *nf* demography

**demoiselle** [dəmwazɛl] *nf (jeune fille)* young lady; **d. d'honneur** bridesmaid

**démolir** [demɔlir] *vt (bâtiment)* to pull down, to demolish ▪ **démolition** *nf* demolition

**démon** [demɔ̃] *nm* demon; **le d.** the Devil

**démonstratif, -ive** [demɔ̃stratif, -iv] *adj* demonstrative

**démonstration** [demɔ̃strɑsjɔ̃] *nf* demonstration

**démonter** [demɔ̃te] **1** *vt (mécanisme, tente)* to dismantle **2 se démonter** *vpr (mécanisme)* to come apart

**démontrer** [demɔ̃tre] *vt* to demonstrate

**démoraliser** [demɔralize] **1** *vt* to demoralize **2 se démoraliser** *vpr* to become demoralized

**démordre** [demɔrdr] *vi* **ne pas d. de qch** to stick to sth

**démouler** [demule] *vt (gâteau)* to turn out

**démuni, -e** [demyni] *adj* penniless

**démunir** [demynir] **se démunir** *vpr* **se d. de qch** to part with sth

**démystifier** [demistifje] *vt* to demystify

**dénier** [denje] *vt (responsabilité)* to deny; **d. qch à qn** to deny sb sth

**dénigrer** [denigre] *vt* to denigrate

**dénivellation** [denivelɑsjɔ̃] *nf* difference in level; **dénivellations** *(relief)* bumps

**dénombrer** [denɔ̃bre] *vt* to count

**dénommer** [denɔme] *vt* to name

**dénoncer** [denɔ̃se] **1** *vt (injustice, abus, malfaiteur)* to denounce (**à** to); *(élève)* to tell on (**à** to) **2 se dénoncer** *vpr (malfaiteur)* to give oneself up (**à** to); *(élève)* to own up (**à** to)

**dénoter** [denɔte] *vt* to denote

**dénouement** [denumɑ̃] *nm (de livre)* ending; *(de pièce de théâtre)* dénouement; *(d'affaire)* outcome

**dénouer** [denwe] **1** *vt (nœud, corde)* to undo, to untie; *(cheveux)* to let down, to undo; *Fig (intrigue)* to unravel **2 se dénouer** *vpr (nœud)* to come undone; *(cheveux)* to come down

**denrée** [dɑ̃re] *nf* foodstuff; **denrées alimentaires** foodstuffs; **denrées périssables** perishable goods

**dense** [dɑ̃s] *adj* dense ▪ **densité** *nf* density

**dent** [dɑ̃] *nf* tooth (*pl* teeth); *(de roue)* cog; *(de fourchette)* prong; **d. de lait/sagesse** milk/wisdom tooth; **faire ses dents** *(enfant)* to be teething; **en dents de scie** serrated; *Fig (résultats)* uneven ▪ **dentaire** *adj* dental

**dentelé, -e** [dɑ̃tle] *adj (côte, feuille)* jagged

**dentelle** [dɑ̃tɛl] *nf* lace

**dentier** [dɑ̃tje] *nm* (set of) false teeth, dentures

**dentifrice** [dɑ̃tifris] *nm* toothpaste

**dentiste** [dɑ̃tist] *nmf* dentist

**dénuder** [denyde] *vt* to (lay) bare ▪ **dénudé, -e** *adj* bare

**dénué, -e** [denɥe] *adj* **d. d'intérêt** devoid of interest

**dénuement** [denymɑ̃] *nm* destitution; **dans le d.** poverty-stricken, destitute

**déodorant** [deɔdɔrɑ̃] *nm* deodorant

**dépanner** [depane] *vt (machine)* to repair ▪ **dépannage** *nm* (emergency) repairs; **voiture/service de d.** breakdown vehicle/service ▪ **dépanneur** *nm (de télévision)* repairman; *(de voiture)* breakdown mechanic ▪ **dépanneuse** *nf (voiture) Br* breakdown lorry, *Am* wrecker

**dépareillé, -e** [depareje] *adj (chaussure)* odd

**départ** [depar] *nm* departure; *(de*

*course)* start; **les grands départs** = the mass exodus of people from major cities at the beginning of the holiday period; **point/ligne de d.** starting point/post; **au d.** at the outset, at the start; **au d. de Paris** *(excursion)* leaving from Paris

**départager** [departaʒe] *vt* to decide between

**département** [departəmɑ̃] *nm* department *(division of local government)* ▪ **départemental, -e, -aux, -ales** *adj* departmental; **route départementale** secondary road, *Br* ≃ B road

**départir*** [departir] **se départir** *vpr* **il ne s'est jamais départi de son calme** his calm never deserted him

**dépasser** [depɑse] **1** *vt (véhicule) Br* to overtake, *Am* to pass; *(endroit)* to go past; *(vitesse)* to exceed; **d. qn** *(en hauteur)* to be taller than sb **2** *vi (clou)* to stick out ▪ **dépassé, -e** *adj (démodé)* outdated; *(incapable)* unable to cope

**dépayser** [depeize] *vt Br* to disorientate, *Am* to disorient

**dépêche** [depɛʃ] *nf* dispatch ▪ **dépêcher 1** *vt* to dispatch **2 se dépêcher** *vpr* to hurry (up); **se d. de faire qch** to hurry to do sth

**dépendant, -e** [depɑ̃dɑ̃, -ɑ̃t] dependent (**de** on) ▪ **dépendance** *nf* dependence; **sous la d. de qn** under sb's domination ▪ **dépendances** *nfpl (bâtiments)* outbuildings

**dépendre** [depɑ̃dr] *vi* to depend (**de** on *or* upon); **d. de** *(appartenir à)* to belong to; *(être soumis à)* to be dependent on

**dépens** [depɑ̃] *nmpl* **apprendre qch à ses d.** to learn sth to one's cost

**dépense** [depɑ̃s] *nf (frais)* expense, expenditure; **faire des dépenses** to spend money ▪ **dépenser 1** *vt (argent)* to spend; *(forces)* to exert **2 se dépenser** *vpr* to burn up energy

**dépensier, -ère** [depɑ̃sje, -ɛr] *adj* extravagant

**dépérir** [deperir] *vi (personne)* to waste away; *(plante)* to wither

**dépeupler** [depœple] **1** *vt* to depopulate **2 se dépeupler** *vpr* to become depopulated

**dépilatoire** [depilatwar] *nm* hair-remover

**dépister** [depiste] *vt (maladie)* to detect ▪ **dépistage** *nm (de maladie)* screening

**dépit** [depi] *nm* spite; **en d. de qn/qch** in spite of sb/sth

**dépité, -e** [depite] *adj* annoyed

**déplacement** [deplasmɑ̃] *nm (voyage)* trip; **être en d.** *(homme d'affaires)* to be on a business trip; **frais de d.** *Br* travelling *or Am* traveling expenses

**déplacer** [deplase] **1** *vt (objet)* to move **2 se déplacer** *vpr (aiguille de montre)* to move; *(personne, animal)* to move (about); *(marcher)* to walk (around); *(voyager)* to travel ▪ **deplacé, -e** *adj (mal à propos)* out of place; **personne déplacée** *(réfugié)* displaced person

**déplaire*** [deplɛr] **1** *vi* **d. à qn** to displease sb; **ça me déplaît** I don't like it **2 se déplaîre** *vpr* **il se déplaît à Paris** he doesn't like it in Paris ▪ **déplaisant, -e** *adj* unpleasant

**déplier** [deplije] *vt* to open out, to unfold ▪ **dépliant** *nm (prospectus)* leaflet

**déplorer** [deplɔre] *vt (regretter)* to deplore; **d. que...** *(+ subjunctive)* to deplore the fact that...; **d. la mort de qn** to mourn sb's death

**déployer** [deplwaje] *vt (ailes)* to spread; *(journal, carte)* to unfold; *(troupes)* to deploy ▪ **déploiement** *nm (démonstration)* display; *(d'une armée)* deployment

**dépoli, -e** [depɔli] *adj* **verre d.** frosted glass

**déporter** [depɔrte] *vt* **d. qn** to send sb to a concentration camp

**déposer** [depoze] **1** *vt (poser)* to put down; *(gerbe)* to lay; *(projet de loi)* to introduce; *(souverain)* to depose; **d. qn** *(en voiture)* to drop sb off; **d. de l'argent sur un compte** to deposit money in an account; **d. une plainte contre qn** to lodge a complaint against sb **2**

*vi Jur* to testify; *(liquide)* to leave a deposit **3 se déposer** *vpr* to settle

**dépositaire** [depɔzitɛr] *nmf (vendeur)* agent

**déposséder** [depɔsede] *vt* to deprive, to dispossess (**de** of)

**dépôt** [depo] *nm (de vin)* deposit, sediment; *(entrepôt)* depot; *(prison)* jail; **faire un d.** *(d'argent)* to make a deposit; **d. de munitions** munitions depot

**dépouille** [depuj] *nf (d'animal)* hide, skin; **d. mortelle** *(de personne)* mortal remains

**dépouiller** [depuje] **1** *vt (animal)* to skin; *(analyser)* to go through; **d. qn de qch** to deprive sb of sth; **d. un scrutin** to count the votes **2 se dépouiller** *vpr* **se d. de qch** to rid oneself of sth ▪ **dépouillé, -e** *adj (style)* austere ▪ **dépouillement** *nm (de documents)* analysis; *(privation)* deprivation; *(sobriété)* austerity; **d. du scrutin** counting of the votes

**dépourvu, -e** [depurvy] *adj* **d. de qch** devoid of sth; **prendre qn au d.** to catch sb off guard

**dépoussiérer** [depusjere] *vt* to dust

**dépraver** [deprave] *vt* to deprave

**déprécier** [depresje] **se déprécier** *vpr (valeurs, marchandises)* to depreciate

**dépression** [depresjɔ̃] *nf (creux, maladie)* depression; **d. économique** slump; **d. nerveuse** nervous breakdown; **faire de la d.** to be suffering from depression ▪ **dépressif, -ive** *adj* depressive

**déprimer** [deprime] *vt* to depress ▪ **déprimé, -e** *adj* depressed

**DEPUIS** [dəpɥi] **1** *prép* since; **d. lundi/2001** since Monday/2001; **j'habite ici d. un mois** I've been living here for a month; **d. quand êtes-vous là?, d. combien de temps êtes-vous là?** how long have you been here?; **d. peu/longtemps** for a short/long time

**2** *adv* since (then), ever since

**3** *conj* **d. que** since

**député** [depyte] *nm Pol* deputy, *Br* ≃ MP, *Am* ≃ representative; **d. du Parlement européen** Member of the European Parliament

**déraciner** [derasine] *vt (arbre, personne)* to uproot

**dérailler** [deraje] *vi (train)* to leave the rails; **faire d. un train** to derail a train

**déranger** [derɑ̃ʒe] **1** *vt (affaires)* to disturb; **je viendrai si ça ne te dérange pas** I'll come if that's all right with you; **ça vous dérange si je fume?** do you mind if I smoke?

**2 se déranger** *vpr* to put oneself to a lot of trouble (**pour faire** to do); *(se déplacer)* to move; **ne te dérange pas!** don't bother! ▪ **dérangement** *nm (gêne)* trouble; **en d.** *(téléphone)* out of order

**déraper** [derape] *vi (véhicule)* to skid; *(personne)* to slip

**dérégler** [deregle] **1** *vt (mécanisme)* to cause to malfunction **2 se dérégler** *vpr (mécanisme)* to go wrong

**dérider** [deride] *vt*, **se dérider** *vpr* to cheer up

**dérision** [derizjɔ̃] *nf* derision; **tourner qch en d.** to deride sth ▪ **dérisoire** *adj (somme)* derisory

**dérive** [deriv] *nf Naut* drift; **à la d.** adrift

**dériver** [derive] **1** *vt (cours d'eau)* to divert **2** *vi Naut* to drift

**dermatologue** [dermatɔlɔg] *nmf* dermatologist

**dernier, -ère** [dernje, -ɛr] **1** *adj (ultime)* last; *(marquant la fin)* final; *(nouvelles, mode)* latest; *(étage)* top; *(degré)* highest; **le d. rang** the back *or* last row; **ces derniers mois** these past few months; **les dix dernières minutes** the last ten minutes; **en d.** last

**2** *nmf* last; **ce d.** *(de deux)* the latter; *(de plusieurs)* the last-mentioned

**dérober** [derɔbe] **1** *vt (voler)* to steal (**à** from); *(cacher)* to hide (**à** from) **2 se dérober** *vpr (s'esquiver)* to slip away; *(éviter de répondre)* to dodge the issue

**dérogation** [derɔgasjɔ̃] *nf* exemption (**à** from)

**déroger** [derɔʒe] *vi* **d. à une règle** to depart from a rule

**dérouler** [derule] **1** *vt (tapis)* to unroll; *(fil)* to unwind **2 se dérouler** *vpr (tapis)* to unroll; *(fil)* to unwind

**déroute** [derut] *nf (d'armée)* rout

**dérouter** [derute] *vt (avion, navire)* to divert, to reroute; *(poursuivant)* to throw off the scent; *Fig (étonner)* to throw

**derrière** [derjɛr] **1** *prép & adv* behind; **d. moi** behind me; **assis d.** *(dans une voiture)* sitting in the back; **par d.** *(attaquer)* from behind, from the rear **2** *nm (de maison)* back, rear; *(fesses)* behind; **roue de d.** back *or* rear wheel

**des** [dɛ] *voir* **de, un**

**dès** [dɛ] *prép* from; **d. le début** (right) from the start; **d. maintenant** from now on; **d. le VIe siècle** as early as *or* as far back as the sixth century; **d. lors** *(dans le temps)* from then on; *(en conséquence)* consequently; **d. leur arrivée** as soon as they arrive/arrived; **d. qu'elle viendra** as soon as she comes

**désabusé, -e** [dezabyze] *adj* disillusioned

**désaccord** [dezakɔr] *nm* disagreement; **être en d. avec qn** to disagree with sb

**désaffecté, -e** [dezafɛkte] *adj* disused

**désaffection** [dezafɛksjɔ̃] *nf* disaffection (**à l'égard de** with)

**désagréable** [dezagreabl] *adj* unpleasant

**désagrément** [dezagremɑ̃] *nm (gêne)* trouble; *(souci, aspect négatif)* problem

**désaltérer** [dezaltere] **1** *vt* **d. qn** to quench sb's thirst **2 se désaltérer** *vpr* to quench one's thirst

**désamorcer** [dezamɔrse] *vt (bombe, conflit)* to defuse

**désapprouver** [dezapruve] **1** *vt* to disapprove of **2** *vi* to disapprove ▪ **désapprobateur, -trice** *adj* disapproving ▪ **désapprobation** *nf* disapproval

**désarmer** [dezarme] **1** *vt (soldat, nation)* to disarm; *Fig* **d. qn** *(franchise, attitude)* to disarm sb **2** *vi (pays)* to disarm ▪ **désarmement** *nm (de nation)* disarmament

**désarroi** [dezarwa] *nm* confusion

**désastre** [dezastr] *nm* disaster ▪ **désastreux, -euse** *adj* disastrous

**désavantage** [dezavɑ̃taʒ] *nm* disadvantage ▪ **désavantager** *vt* to put at a disadvantage

**désavouer** [dezavwe] *vt (renier)* to disown

**désaxé, -e** [dezakse] *nmf* unbalanced person

**desceller** [desele] **1** *vt (pierre)* to loosen **2 se desceller** *vpr* to come loose

**descendant, -e** [desɑ̃dɑ̃, -ɑ̃t] *nmf* descendant ▪ **descendance** *nf (enfants)* descendants; *(origine)* descent

**descendre** [desɑ̃dr] **1** *(aux* **être***) vi* to come/go down (**de** from); *(d'un train)* to get off (**de** from); *(d'un arbre)* to climb down (**de** from); *(marée)* to go out; **d. à l'hôtel** to put up at a hotel; **d. de** *(être issu de)* to be descended from
**2** *(aux* **avoir***) vt (escalier)* to come/go down; *(objet)* to bring/take down

**descente** [desɑ̃t] *nf (d'avion)* descent; *(en parachute)* drop; *(pente)* slope; *(de police)* raid (**dans** upon); **d. de lit** bedside rug

**descriptif, -ive** [deskriptif, -iv] *adj* descriptive ▪ **description** *nf* description

**désemparé, -e** [dezɑ̃pare] *adj (personne)* at a loss

**désemplir** [dezɑ̃plir] *vi* **ce magasin ne désemplit pas** this shop is always crowded

**désenchanté, -e** [dezɑ̃ʃɑ̃te] *adj* disillusioned ▪ **désenchantement** *nm* disenchantment

**déséquilibre** [dezekilibr] *nm* imbalance; **en d.** unsteady ▪ **déséquilibré, -e 1** *adj* unbalanced **2** *nmf* unbalanced person ▪ **déséquilibrer** *vt* to throw off balance

**désert, -e** [dezɛr, -ɛrt] **1** *adj (lieu)* deserted; *(région)* uninhabited; **île déserte** desert island **2** *nm* desert ▪ **désertique** *adj* **région d.** desert region

**déserter** [dezɛrte] *vti* to desert ▪ **désertion** *nf* desertion

**désespérer** [dezɛspere] **1** *vt* to drive to despair **2** *vi* to despair (**de** of) **3 se désespérer** *vpr* to despair ▪ **désespérant, -e** *adj (situation, personne)* hopeless ▪ **désespéré, -e** *adj (personne)* in despair; *(cas, situation, efforts)* desperate ▪ **désespérément** *adv* desperately

**désespoir** [dezɛspwar] *nm* despair; **en d. de cause** in desperation

**déshabiller** [dezabije] *vt*, **se déshabiller** *vpr* to undress

**désherber** [dezɛrbe] *vti* to weed

**déshériter** [dezerite] *vt* to disinherit

**déshonneur** [dezɔnœr] *nm* dishonour

**déshonorer** [dezɔnɔre] *vt* to disgrace ▪ **déshonorant, -e** *adj* dishonourable

**déshydrater** [dezidrate] **1** *vt* to dehydrate **2 se déshydrater** *vpr* to become dehydrated

**désigner** [deziɲe] *vt (montrer)* to point to; *(choisir)* to choose; *(nommer)* to appoint; **d. qn par son nom** to refer to sb by name ▪ **désignation** *nf* designation

**désillusion** [dezilyzjɔ̃] *nf* disillusion ▪ **désillusionner** *vt* to disillusion

**désinfecter** [dezɛ̃fɛkte] *vt* to disinfect ▪ **désinfectant** *nm* disinfectant

**désinformation** [dezɛ̃fɔrmɑsjɔ̃] *nf* disinformation

**désintégrer** [dezɛ̃tegre] **se désintégrer** *vpr* to disintegrate

**désintéresser** [dezɛ̃terese] **se désintéresser** *vpr* **se d. de qch** to lose interest in sth ▪ **désintéressé, -e** *adj (altruiste)* disinterested ▪ **désintérêt** *nm* lack of interest

**désintoxiquer** [dezɛ̃tɔksike] *vt (alcoolique, drogué)* to treat for alcoholism/drug abuse

**désinvolte** [dezɛ̃vɔlt] *adj (dégagé)* casual; *(insolent)* offhand ▪ **désinvolture** *nf* casualness; *(insolence)* offhandedness

**désir** [dezir] *nm* desire ▪ **désirable** *adj* desirable ▪ **désirer** *vt* to wish; *(convoiter)* to desire

**désireux, -euse** [desirø, -øz] *adj* **d. de faire qch** anxious to do sth

**désistement** [dezistəmɑ̃] *nm* withdrawal

**désister** [deziste] **se désister** *vpr* to withdraw

**désobéir** [dezɔbeir] *vi* to disobey; **d. à qn** to disobey sb ▪ **désobéissant, -e** *adj* disobedient

**désobligeant, -e** [dezɔbliʒɑ̃, -ɑ̃t] *adj* disagreeable

**désodorisant** [dezɔdɔrizɑ̃] *nm* air freshener

**désœuvré, -e** [dezœvre] *adj* idle

**désoler** [dezɔle] **1** *vt* to upset **2 se désoler** *vpr* to be upset (**de** at) ▪ **désolant, -e** *adj* upsetting ▪ **désolé, -e** *adj (région)* desolate; *(affligé)* upset; **être d. que...** *(+ subjunctive)* to be sorry that...; **je suis d. de vous déranger** I'm sorry to disturb you

**désolidariser** [desɔlidarize] **se désolidariser** *vpr* to dissociate oneself (**de** from)

**désordonné, -e** [dezɔrdɔne] *adj (personne, chambre)* untidy

**désordre** [dezɔrdr] *nm (manque d'ordre)* mess; *(manque d'organisation)* disorder; **en d.** untidy, messy; **de graves désordres** *(émeutes)* serious disturbances

**désorganiser** [dezɔrganize] *vt* to disorganize ▪ **désorganisation** *nf* disorganization ▪ **désorganisé, -e** *adj* disorganized

**désorienter** [dezɔrjɑ̃te] *vt* **d. qn** to bewilder sb

**désormais** [dezɔrmɛ] *adv* from now on, in future

**despote** [despɔt] *nm* despot

**desquels, desquelles** [dekɛl] *voir* **lequel**

**dessaisir** [desezir] **se dessaisir** *vpr* **se**

**d. de qch** to relinquish sth

**dessaler** [desale] *vt (poisson)* to remove the salt from *(by soaking)*

**dessécher** [deseʃe] **1** *vt (peau)* to dry up; *(végétation)* to wither **2 se dessécher** *vpr (peau)* to dry up; *(végétation)* to wither

**dessein** [desɛ̃] *nm* intention; **à d.** intentionally

**desserrer** [desere] **1** *vt (ceinture)* to loosen; *(poing)* to unclench; *(frein)* to release **2 se desserrer** *vpr (ceinture)* to come loose

**dessert** [desɛr] *nm* dessert, *Br* pudding

**desserte** [desɛrt] *nf* **assurer la d. de** *(village)* to provide a service to

**desservir** [desɛrvir] *vt (table)* to clear (away); **d. qn** to do sb a disservice; **le car dessert ce village** the bus stops at this village; **ce quartier est bien desservi** this district is well served by public transport

**dessin** [desɛ̃] *nm* drawing; *(rapide)* sketch; *(motif)* design, pattern; *(contour)* outline; **d. animé** cartoon; **d. humoristique** *(de journal)* cartoon

**dessinateur, -trice** [desinatœr, -tris] *nmf* drawer; **d. industriel** *Br* draughtsman, *Am* draftsman

**dessiner** [desine] **1** *vt* to draw; *(rapidement)* to sketch; *(meuble, robe)* to design; *(indiquer)* to outline; **d. (bien) la taille** *(vêtement)* to show off the figure **2 se dessiner** *vpr (colline)* to stand out; *(projet)* to take shape

**dessous** [dəsu] **1** *adv* underneath; **en d.** underneath; **en d. de** below **2** *nm* underside; **des d.** *(sous-vêtements)* underwear ■ **dessous-de-plat** *nm inv* table mat ■ **dessous-de-table** *nm inv* bribe, *Br* backhander

**dessus** [dəsy] **1** *adv (marcher, écrire)* on it/them; *(monter)* on top (of it/them), on it/them; *(passer)* over it/them; **de d. la table** off *or* from the table **2** *nm* top; *(de chaussure)* upper; **avoir le d.** to have the upper hand; **reprendre le d.** *(se remettre)* to get over it

**déstabiliser** [destabilize] *vt* to destabilize

**destin** [dɛstɛ̃] *nm* fate, destiny ■ **destinée** *nf* destiny

**destinataire** [dɛstinatɛr] *nmf* addressee

**destination** [dɛstinasjɔ̃] *nf (lieu)* destination; **trains à d. de...** trains to...; **arriver à d.** to reach one's destination

**destiner** [dɛstine] **1** *vt* **d. qch à qn** to intend sth for sb; **d. qn à** *(carrière, fonction)* to intend *or* destine sb for **2 se destiner** *vpr* **se d. à** *(carrière)* to intend to take up

**destituer** [dɛstitɥe] *vt (fonctionnaire)* to remove from office

**destructeur, -trice** [dɛstryktœr, -tris] *adj* destructive

**destruction** [dɛstryksjɔ̃] *nf* destruction

**désuet, -ète** [desɥe, -ɛt] *adj* obsolete ■ **désuétude** *nf* **tomber en d.** *(expression)* to become obsolete

**désunir** [dezynir] *vt (famille, personnes)* to divide

**détachant** [detaʃɑ̃] *nm* stain remover

**détachement** [detaʃmɑ̃] *nm* (**a**) *(indifférence)* detachment (**b**) *(de fonctionnaire)* secondment; *(de troupes)* detachment

**détacher¹** [detaʃe] **1** *vt (ceinture, vêtement)* to undo; *(mains)* to untie; *(ôter)* to take off; *(mots)* to pronounce clearly; **d. qn** *(libérer)* to untie sb; *(affecter)* to transfer sb (on assignment) (**à** to)
**2 se détacher** *vpr (chien, prisonnier)* to break loose; *(se dénouer)* to come undone; **se d.** *(fragment)* to come off (**de qch** sth); **se d. de qn** to break away from sb; **se d. sur qch** *(ressortir)* to stand out against sth ■ **détaché, -e** *adj (air, ton)* detached

**détacher²** [detaʃe] *vt (linge)* to remove the stains from

**détail** [detaj] *nm* detail; **en d.** in detail; **entrer dans les détails** to go into detail; **prix de d.** retail price

**détaillant** [detajɑ̃] *nm* retailer

**détailler** [detaje] *vt (énumérer)* to detail ▪ **détaillé, -e** *adj (récit, description)* detailed; *(facture)* itemized

**détaxer** [detakse] *vt* to exempt from tax; **produit détaxé** duty-free article

**détecter** [detɛkte] *vt* to detect ▪ **détecteur** *nm (appareil)* detector

**détective** [detɛktiv] *nm* **d. (privé)** (private) detective

**déteindre*** [detɛ̃dr] *vi (couleur, tissu)* to run

**détendre** [detɑ̃dr] **1** *vt (corde)* to slacken; *(arc)* to unbend; **d. qn** to relax sb **2 se détendre** *vpr (corde)* to slacken; *(arc)* to unbend; *(atmosphère)* to become less tense; *(personne)* to relax ▪ **détendu, -e** *adj (visage, atmosphère)* relaxed; *(ressort, câble)* slack

**détenir*** [detənir] *vt (record, pouvoir, titre, prisonnier)* to hold; *(secret, objet volé)* to be in possession of ▪ **détenteur, -trice** *nmf (de record)* holder ▪ **détention** *nf (d'armes)* possession; *(captivité)* detention; **d. provisoire** detention pending trial, remand ▪ **détenu, -e** *nmf* prisoner

**détente** [detɑ̃t] *nf* (**a**) *(repos)* relaxation; *(entre deux pays)* détente (**b**) *(saut)* spring (**c**) *(gâchette)* trigger

**détergent** [detɛrʒɑ̃] *nm* detergent

**détériorer** [deterjɔre] **1** *vt* to damage **2 se détériorer** *vpr* to deteriorate ▪ **détérioration** *nf* damage (**de** to); *(de situation)* deterioration (**de** in)

**détermination** [detɛrminɑsjɔ̃] *nf (fermeté)* determination

**déterminer** [detɛrmine] *vt (préciser)* to determine; *(causer)* to bring about ▪ **déterminant, -e** *adj* decisive ▪ **déterminé, -e** *adj (précis)* specific; *(résolu)* determined

**déterrer** [detere] *vt* to dig up

**détester** [detɛste] *vt* to hate, to detest; **d. faire qch** to hate doing *or* to do sth ▪ **détestable** *adj* foul

**détonation** [detɔnɑsjɔ̃] *nf* explosion; *(d'arme)* bang

**détonner** [detɔne] *vi (contraster)* to clash

**détour** [detur] *nm (crochet)* detour; *(de route)* bend, curve

**détourner** [deturne] **1** *vt (dévier)* to divert; *(avion)* to hijack; *(conversation, sens)* to change; *(fonds)* to embezzle; *(coup)* to ward off; **d. la tête** to turn one's head away; **d. les yeux** to look away; **d. qn de** *(son devoir)* to take sb away from; *(sa route)* to lead sb away from

**2 se détourner** *vpr* to turn away ▪ **détourné, -e** *adj (chemin, moyen)* roundabout, indirect ▪ **détournement** [-əmɑ̃] *nm (de cours d'eau)* diversion; **d. d'avion** hijack(ing); **d. de fonds** embezzlement

**détracteur, -trice** [detraktœr, -tris] *nmf* detractor

**détraquer** [detrake] **1** *vt (mécanisme)* to put out of order **2 se détraquer** *vpr (machine)* to go wrong

**détresse** [detrɛs] *nf* distress; **en d.** *(navire)* in distress

**détriment** [detrimɑ̃] **au détriment de** *prép* to the detriment of

**détritus** [detritys] *nmpl Br* rubbish, *Am* garbage

**détroit** [detrwa] *nm* strait

**détromper** [detrɔ̃pe] **1** *vt* **d. qn** to put sb right **2 se détromper** *vpr* **détrompez-vous!** don't you believe it!

**détrôner** [detrone] *vt (souverain)* to dethrone; *(supplanter)* to supersede

**détruire*** [detrɥir] *vt (ravager)* to destroy; *(tuer)* to kill

**dette** [dɛt] *nf* debt; **avoir des dettes** to be in debt; **faire des dettes** to run into debt

**DEUG** [døg] *(abrév* **diplôme d'études universitaires générales**) *nm* = degree gained after two years' study at university

**deuil** [dœj] *nm (affliction, vêtements)* mourning; *(décès)* bereavement; **être en d.** to be in mourning

**deux** [dø] *adj inv & nm inv* two; **d. fois** twice; **mes d. sœurs** both my sisters, my two sisters; **tous (les) d.** both ▪ **deux-pièces** *nm inv (maillot de bain)* bikini; *(appartement)* two-roomed *Br* flat *or Am* apartment ▪ **deux-roues** *nm inv* two-wheeled vehicle

**deuxième** [døzjɛm] *adj & nmf* second

**dévaler** [devale] *vt (escalier)* to hurtle down

**dévaliser** [devalize] *vt (personne, banque)* to rob

**dévaloriser** [devalɔrize] **1** *vt (monnaie, diplôme)* to devalue **2 se dévaloriser** *vpr (monnaie)* to depreciate ▪ **dévalorisation** *nf (de diplôme)* loss of value

**dévaluer** [devalɥe] *vt (monnaie)* to devalue ▪ **dévaluation** *nf Fin* devaluation

**devancer** [dəvɑ̃se] *vt (concurrent)* to be ahead of; *(arriver avant)* to arrive before

**devant** [dəvɑ̃] **1** *prép & adv* in front (of); **passer d. une église** to go past a church; **marcher d. qn** to walk in front of sb; **assis d.** *(dans une voiture)* sitting in the front

**2** *nm* front; **roue/porte de d.** front wheel/door; **prendre les devants** *(action)* to take the initiative

**devanture** [dəvɑ̃tyr] *nf (vitrine)* window; *(façade)* front

**dévaster** [devaste] *vt* to devastate ▪ **dévastation** *nf* devastation

**développer** [devlɔpe] *vt*, **se développer** *vpr* to develop ▪ **développement** *nm* development; *(de photo)* developing; **en plein d.** *(entreprise, pays)* growing fast

**devenir*** [dəvnir] (*aux* **être**) *vi* to become; **d. médecin** to become a doctor; **d. vieux** to get *or* grow old; **d. tout rouge** to go all red; **qu'est-elle devenue?** what has become of her?

**dévergondé, -e** [devergɔ̃de] *adj* shameless

**déverser** [deverse] **1** *vt (liquide)* to pour out; *(ordures)* to dump **2 se déverser** *vpr (liquide, rivière)* to empty (**dans** into)

**dévêtir** [devetir] *vt*, **se dévêtir** *vpr* to undress

**dévier** [devje] **1** *vt (circulation)* to divert; *(coup, rayons)* to deflect **2** *vi (balle)* to deflect; *(véhicule)* to veer; **d. de sa route** to veer off course ▪ **déviation** *nf (itinéraire) Br* diversion, *Am* detour

**devin** [dəvɛ̃] *nm* soothsayer

**deviner** [dəvine] *vt* to guess (**que** that) ▪ **devinette** *nf* riddle

**devis** [dəvi] *nm* estimate

**dévisager** [devizaʒe] *vt* **d. qn** to stare at sb

**devise** [dəviz] *nf (légende)* motto; *(monnaie)* currency; **devises étrangères** foreign currency

**dévisser** [devise] **1** *vt* to unscrew **2 se dévisser** *vpr (bouchon)* to unscrew; *(par accident)* to come unscrewed

**dévoiler** [devwale] **1** *vt (statue)* to unveil; *Fig (secret)* to disclose **2 se dévoiler** *vpr (mystère)* to come to light

**DEVOIR*[1]** [dəvwar] *v aux* (**a**) *(indique la nécessité)* **je dois refuser** I must refuse, I have (got) to refuse; **j'ai dû refuser** I had to refuse

(**b**) *(indique une forte probabilité)* **il doit être tard** it must be late; **elle a dû oublier** she must have forgotten; **cela devait arriver** it had to happen

(**c**) *(indique l'obligation)* **tu dois apprendre tes leçons** you must learn your lessons; **vous devriez rester** you should stay, you ought to stay; **il aurait dû venir** he should have come, he ought to have come

(**d**) *(indique l'intention)* **elle doit venir** she's supposed to be coming, she's due to come; **le train devait arriver à midi** the train was due (to arrive) at noon; **je devais le voir** I was (due) to see him

**devoir*[2]** [dəvwar] **1** *vt* to owe; **d. qch à qn** to owe sb sth, to owe sth to sb

**2 se devoir** *vpr* **comme il se doit** as is proper

**3** *nm (obligation)* duty; **présenter ses devoirs à qn** to pay one's respects to sb; *Scol* **devoirs** homework; **faire ses**

**devoirs** to do one's homework
**dévorer** [devɔre] *vt (manger)* to devour
**dévotion** [devosjɔ̃] *nf (adoration)* devotion
**dévouer** [devwe] **se dévouer** *vpr (se sacrifier)* to volunteer; *(se consacrer)* to devote oneself (**à** to) ▪ **dévoué, -e** *adj (ami, femme)* devoted (**à** to) ▪ **dévouement** [-umɑ̃] *nm* devotion; *(de héros)* devotion to duty
**dextérité** [dɛksterite] *nf* dexterity, skill
**diabète** [djabɛt] *nm Méd* diabetes ▪ **diabétique** *adj & nmf* diabetic
**diable** [djɑbl] *nm* devil; **le d.** the Devil ▪ **diabolique** *adj* diabolical
**diadème** [djadɛm] *nm* tiara
**diagnostic** [djagnɔstik] *nm* diagnosis ▪ **diagnostiquer** *vt* to diagnose
**diagonal, -e, -aux, -ales** [djagɔnal, -o] *adj* diagonal ▪ **diagonale** *nf* diagonal (line); **en d.** diagonally
**dialecte** [djalɛkt] *nm* dialect
**dialogue** [djalɔg] *nm Br* dialogue, *Am* dialog; *(conversation)* conversation ▪ **dialoguer** *vi* to communicate; *Ordinat* to interact
**diamant** [djamɑ̃] *nm* diamond
**diamètre** [djamɛtr] *nm* diameter
**diapason** [djapazɔ̃] *nm Mus (appareil)* tuning fork
**diapositive** [djapozitiv] *nf* slide
**diarrhée** [djare] *nf* diarrhoea
**dictateur** [diktatœr] *nm* dictator ▪ **dictatorial, -e, -aux, -ales** *adj* dictatorial ▪ **dictature** *nf* dictatorship
**dicter** [dikte] *vt* to dictate (**à** to) ▪ **dictée** *nf* dictation
**diction** [diksjɔ̃] *nf* diction
**dictionnaire** [diksjɔnɛr] *nm* dictionary
**dièse** [djɛz] *adj & nm Mus* sharp
**diesel** [djezɛl] *adj & nm* **(moteur) d.** diesel (engine)
**diète** [djɛt] *nf (partielle)* diet; *(totale)* fast; **être à la d.** to be on a diet/to be fasting
**diététicien, -enne** [djetetisjɛ̃, -ɛn] *nmf* dietician ▪ **diététique 1** *nf* dietetics *(sing)* **2** *adj* **aliment** *ou* **produit d.** health food; **magasin d.** health-food shop
**dieu, -x** [djø] *nm* god; **D.** God; **le bon D.** God
**diffamation** [difamɑsjɔ̃] *nf (en paroles)* slander; *(par écrit)* libel ▪ **diffamatoire** *adj (paroles)* slanderous; *(écrit)* libellous
**différé** [difere] *nm* **en d.** *(émission)* prerecorded
**différence** [diferɑ̃s] *nf* difference (**de** in); **à la d. de qn/qch** unlike sb/sth; **faire la d. entre** to make a distinction between
**différencier** [diferɑ̃sje] **1** *vt* to differentiate (**de** from) **2 se différencier** *vpr* to differ (**de** from)
**différend** [diferɑ̃] *nm* difference of opinion
**différent, -e** [diferɑ̃, -ɑ̃t] *adj* different; **différents** *(divers)* different, various; **d. de** different from ▪ **différemment** [-amɑ̃] *adv* differently (**de** from)
**différer** [difere] **1** *vt (remettre)* to postpone; *(paiement)* to defer **2** *vi* to differ (**de** from)
**difficile** [difisil] *adj* difficult; *(exigeant)* fussy; **c'est d. à faire** it's hard *or* difficult to do ▪ **difficilement** *adv* with difficulty
**difficulté** [difikylte] *nf* difficulty (**à faire** in doing); **en d.** in a difficult situation; **avoir de la d. à faire qch** to have difficulty (in) doing sth
**difforme** [difɔrm] *adj* deformed, misshapen ▪ **difformité** *nf* deformity
**diffus, -e** [dify, -yz] *adj (lumière)* diffuse; *(impression)* vague
**diffuser** [difyze] *vt (émission)* to broadcast; *(nouvelle)* to spread; *(lumière, chaleur)* to diffuse ▪ **diffusion** *nf (d'émission)* broadcasting; *(de lumière, de chaleur)* diffusion
**digérer** [diʒere] **1** *vt* to digest **2** *vi* to digest
**digestif, -ive** [diʒɛstif, -iv] **1** *adj (tube,*

*sucs)* digestive **2** *nmf* after-dinner liqueur

**digestion** [diʒɛstjɔ̃] *nf* digestion

**Digicode®** [diʒikɔd] *nm* door code *(for entrance to building)*

**digne** [diɲ] *adj (air, attitude)* dignified; **d. de qn/qch** worthy of sb/sth; **d. d'admiration** worthy of *or* deserving of admiration ▪ **dignement** [-əmɑ̃] *adv* with dignity

**dignitaire** [diɲitɛr] *nm* dignitary

**dignité** [diɲite] *nf* dignity

**digue** [dig] *nf* dike, dyke; *(en bord de mer)* sea wall

**dilapider** [dilapide] *vt* to squander

**dilater** [dilate] *vt*, **se dilater** *vpr (pupille)* to dilate

**dilemme** [dilɛm] *nm* dilemma

**diluer** [dilɥe] *vt (liquide, substance)* to dilute (**dans** in)

**dimanche** [dimɑ̃ʃ] *nm* Sunday

**dimension** [dimɑ̃sjɔ̃] *nf (mesure, aspect)* dimension; *(taille)* size; **à deux dimensions** two-dimensional; **prendre les dimensions de qch** to measure sth up

**diminuer** [diminɥe] **1** *vt (réduire)* to reduce, to decrease; *(affaiblir)* to affect **2** *vi (réserves, nombre)* to decrease, to diminish; *(jours)* to get shorter; *(prix, profits)* to decrease, to drop ▪ **diminution** *nf* reduction, decrease (**de** in)

**diminutif** [diminytif] *nm (nom)* diminutive

**dinde** [dɛ̃d] *nf (volaille, viande)* turkey ▪ **dindon** *nm* turkey (cock)

**dîner** [dine] **1** *nm (repas du soir)* dinner; *(repas de midi)* lunch; *(soirée)* dinner party **2** *vi* to have dinner; *Belg & Can* to (have) lunch

**dinosaure** [dinozɔr] *nm* dinosaur

**diplomate** [diplɔmat] **1** *adj* diplomatic **2** *nmf* diplomat ▪ **diplomatie** [-asi] *nf (tact)* diplomacy; *(carrière)* diplomatic service ▪ **diplomatique** *adj* diplomatic

**diplôme** [diplom] *nm* diploma; *(d'université)* degree ▪ **diplômé, -e** **1** *adj* qualified; *Univ* **être d. (de)** to be a graduate (of) **2** *nmf* holder of a diploma; *Univ* graduate

---

**DIRE*** [dir] **1** *nm* **au d. de** according to; **selon ses dires** according to him/her

**2** *vt (mot)* to say; *(vérité, secret)* to tell; **d. des bêtises** to talk nonsense; **d. qch à qn** to tell sb sth, to say sth to sb; **d. à qn que...** to tell sb that..., to say to sb that...; **d. à qn de faire qch** to tell sb to do sth; **d. du mal/du bien de qn** to speak ill/well of sb; **on dirait un château** it looks like a castle; **on dirait du cabillaud** it tastes like cod; **autrement dit** in other words; **à vrai d.** to tell the truth

**3 se dire** *vpr* **il se dit malade** he says he's ill; **comment ça se dit en anglais?** how do you say that in English?

---

**direct, -e** [dirɛkt] **1** *adj* direct **2** *nm Radio & TV* live broadcasting; **en d. (de)** live (from) ▪ **directement** [-əmɑ̃] *adv (sans intermédiaire)* directly; *(sans détour)* straight

**directeur, -trice** [dirɛktœr, -tris] **1** *nmf* director; *(de magasin, de service)* manager; *(de journal)* editor; *(d'école) Br* headmaster, *f* headmistress, *Am* principal **2** *adj (principe)* guiding; *(idées)* main; *(équipe)* management

**direction** [dirɛksjɔ̃] *nf* (**a**) *(sens)* direction; **train en d. de Lille** train to Lille (**b**) *(de société, de club)* running, management; *(de parti)* leadership; *Aut* steering; **sous la d. de** under the supervision of; *(orchestre)* conducted by; **un poste de d.** a management post; **d. du personnel** personnel department

**dirigeant, -e** [diriʒɑ̃, -ɑ̃t] **1** *adj (classe)* ruling **2** *nm (de pays)* leader; *(d'entreprise, de club)* manager

**diriger** [diriʒe] **1** *vt (entreprise, club)* to run, to manage; *(pays, parti)* to lead; *(orchestre)* to conduct; *(travaux)* to supervise; *(acteur)* to direct; *(orienter)* to turn (**vers** to); *(arme, lumière)* to

point (**sur** at); *(véhicule)* to steer **2 se diriger** *vpr* **se d. vers** *(lieu, objet)* to head for; *(personne)* to go up to; *(dans une carrière)* to go into
**dis, disant** [di, dizɑ̃] *voir* **dire**
**discerner** [disɛrne] *vt (voir)* to make out; *(différencier)* to distinguish (**de** from) ▪ **discernement** [-əmɑ̃] *nm* discernment
**disciple** [disipl] *nm* disciple
**discipline** [disiplin] *nf (règle, matière)* discipline
**discipliner** [disipline] **1** *vt (enfant)* to control **2 se discipliner** *vpr* to discipline oneself ▪ **discipliné, -e** *adj* well-disciplined
**discontinu, -e** [diskɔ̃tiny] *adj (ligne)* broken; *(bruit)* intermittent ▪ **discontinuer** *vi* **sans d.** without stopping
**discorde** [diskɔrd] *nf* discord
**discothèque** [diskɔtɛk] *nf (organisme)* record library; *(club)* disco
**discours** [diskur] *nm* speech; *(écrit littéraire)* discourse; **faire un d.** to make a speech
**discréditer** [diskredite] **1** *vt* to discredit **2 se discréditer** *vpr (personne)* to discredit oneself
**discret, -ète** [diskre, -ɛt] *adj (personne, manière)* discreet; *(vêtement)* simple ▪ **discrètement** *adv (avec retenue)* discreetly; *(sobrement)* simply
**discrétion** [diskresjɔ̃] *nf* discretion; **laisser qch à la d. de qn** to leave sth to sb's discretion
**discrimination** [diskriminɑsjɔ̃] *nf* discrimination
**disculper** [diskylpe] *vt* to exonerate (**de** from)
**discussion** [diskysjɔ̃] *nf* discussion; **avoir une d.** to have a discussion (**sur** about)
**discutable** [diskytabl] *adj* questionable
**discuter** [diskyte] **1** *vt* to discuss; *(contester)* to question **2** *vi* to discuss; *(protester)* to argue; **d. de qch avec qn** to discuss sth with sb **3 se discuter** *vpr* **ça se discute** that's debatable

**dise, disent** [diz] *voir* **dire**
**disgrace** [disgras] *nf* **tomber en d.** to fall into disfavour ▪ **disgracier** *vt* to disgrace ▪ **disgracieux, -euse** *adj* ungainly
**disjoint, -e** [disʒwɛ̃, -ɛ̃t] *adj* separated
**disjoncter** [disʒɔ̃kte] *vi (circuit électrique)* to fuse ▪ **disjoncteur** *nm* circuit breaker
**dislocation** [dislɔkɑsjɔ̃] *nf (de membre)* dislocation
**disloquer** [dislɔke] **1** *vt (membre)* to dislocate **2 se disloquer** *vpr* **se d. le bras** to dislocate one's arm
**disons** [dizɔ̃] *voir* **dire**
**disparaître*** [disparɛtr] *vi* to disappear; *(être porté manquant)* to go missing; *(mourir)* to die; *(coutume)* to die out; **faire d. qch** to get rid of sth ▪ **disparition** *nf* disappearance; *(mort)* death ▪ **disparu, -e 1** *adj (personne)* missing; **être porté d.** to be reported missing **2** *nmf (absent)* missing person; *(mort)* departed
**disparité** [disparite] *nf* disparity (**entre** *ou* **de** between)
**dispensaire** [dispɑ̃sɛr] *nm* community health centre
**dispense** [dispɑ̃s] *nf (d'obligation)* exemption ▪ **dispenser 1** *vt (soins, bienfaits)* to dispense; **d. qn de qch** to exempt sb from sth; **d. qn de faire qch** to exempt sb from doing sth **2** *vpr* **se d. de qch** to get out of sth; **se d. de faire qch** to get out of doing sth
**disperser** [dispɛrse] **1** *vt (papiers, foule)* to scatter; *(brouillard)* to disperse; *(collection)* to break up **2 se disperser** *vpr (foule)* to scatter, to disperse ▪ **dispersion** *nf (d'armée, de manifestants, de brouillard)* dispersal
**disponible** [dispɔnibl] *adj (article, place, personne)* available ▪ **disponibilité** *nf* availability; **disponibilités** *(fonds)* available funds
**dispos** [dispo] *adj m* **frais et d.** hale and hearty
**disposé, -e** [dispoze] *adj* **bien/mal d.**

in a good/bad mood; **d. à faire qch** disposed to do sth

**disposer** [dispoze] **1** *vt (objets)* to arrange; **d. qn à (faire) qch** to dispose sb to (do) sth **2** *vi* **d. de qch** to have sth at one's disposal **3 se disposer** *vpr* **se d. à faire qch** to prepare to do sth

**dispositif** [dispozitif] *nm (mécanisme)* device

**disposition** [dispozisjɔ̃] *nf* arrangement; *(tendance)* tendency (**à** to); *(de maison, de page)* layout; **être** *ou* **rester** *ou* **se tenir à la d. de qn** to be *or* remain at sb's disposal; **dispositions** *(aptitudes)* ability, aptitude (**pour** for)

**disproportionné, -e** [disprɔpɔrsjɔne] *adj* disproportionate

**dispute** [dispyt] *nf* quarrel ■ **disputer** **1** *vt (match)* to play; *(rallye)* to compete in; *(combat de boxe)* to fight; *(droit)* to contest; **d. qch à qn** *(prix, première place)* to fight with sb for *or* over sth **2 se disputer** *vpr* to quarrel (**avec** with); *(match)* to take place; **se d. qch** to fight over sth

**disqualifier** [diskalifje] *vt (équipe, athlète)* to disqualify ■ **disqualification** *nf* disqualification

**disque** [disk] *nm (de musique)* record; *(cercle) Br* disc, *Am* disk; *Ordinat* disk; *Sport* discus; **d. compact** compact *Br* disc *or Am* disk; **d. dur** hard disk ■ **disquaire** *nmf* record dealer ■ **disquette** *nf Ordinat* floppy (disk), diskette

**disséminer** [disemine] *vt (graines, mines)* to scatter

**disséquer** [diseke] *vt* to dissect

**dissertation** [disɛrtɑsjɔ̃] *nf* essay

**dissident, -e** [disidɑ̃, -ɑ̃t] *nmf* dissident

**dissimuler** [disimyle] **1** *vt (cacher)* to conceal (**à** from) **2 se dissimuler** *vpr* to be hidden ■ **dissimulation** *nf* concealment; *(duplicité)* deceit

**dissiper** [disipe] **1** *vt (nuages)* to disperse; *(brouillard)* to clear; *(malentendu)* to clear up; *(craintes)* to dispel; **d. qn** to lead sb astray **2 se dissiper** *vpr* *(nuage)* to disperse; *(brume)* to clear; *(craintes)* to vanish; *(élève)* to misbehave ■ **dissipé, -e** *adj (élève)* unruly

**dissocier** [disɔsje] *vt* to dissociate (**de** from)

**dissolu, -e** [disɔly] *adj (vie)* dissolute

**dissolution** [disɔlysjɔ̃] *nf* dissolution

**dissolvant** [disɔlvɑ̃] *nm* solvent; *(pour vernis à ongles)* nail polish remover

**dissoudre*** [disudr] *vt*, **se dissoudre** *vpr* to dissolve

**dissuader** [disɥade] *vt* to dissuade (**de qch** from sth; **de faire** from doing) ■ **dissuasif, -ive** *adj* deterrent; **avoir un effet d.** to be a deterrent ■ **dissuasion** *nf* dissuasion; *Mil* **force de d.** deterrent

**distance** [distɑ̃s] *nf* distance; **à deux mètres de d.** two metres apart; **à d.** at *or* from a distance; **garder ses distances** to keep one's distance (**vis-à-vis de** from); **commandé à d.** remote-controlled

**distancer** [distɑ̃se] *vt* to outstrip; **se laisser d.** to fall behind

**distant, -e** [distɑ̃, -ɑ̃t] *adj* distant; *(personne)* aloof, distant; **d. de dix kilomètres** *(éloigné)* ten kilometres away; *(à intervalles)* ten kilometres apart

**distendre** [distɑ̃dr] *vt*, **se distendre** *vpr* to stretch

**distiller** [distile] *vt* to distil ■ **distillerie** *nf (lieu)* distillery

**distinct, -e** [distɛ̃, -ɛ̃kt] *adj (différent)* distinct, separate (**de** from); *(net)* clear, distinct ■ **distinctif, -ive** *adj* distinctive ■ **distinction** *nf (différence, raffinement)* distinction

**distinguer** [distɛ̃ge] **1** *vt (différencier)* to distinguish; *(voir)* to make out; *(choisir)* to single out; **d. le bien du mal** to tell good from evil **2 se distinguer** *vpr (s'illustrer)* to distinguish oneself; **se d. de qn/qch (par)** to be distinguishable from sb/sth (by) ■ **distingué, -e** *adj (bien élevé, éminent)* distinguished

**distorsion** [distɔrsjɔ̃] *nf* distortion

**distraction** [distraksjɔ̃] *nf (étourderie)* absent-mindedness ■ **distraire*** **1** *vt (divertir)* to entertain; **d. qn** to distract sb (**de** from) **2 se distraire** *vpr* to amuse oneself ■ **distrait, -e** *adj* absent-minded ■ **distrayant, -e** *adj* entertaining

**distribuer** [distribɥe] *vt (donner) & Com* to distribute; *(courrier)* to deliver; *(cartes)* to deal; *(tâches)* to allocate; *(eau)* to supply

**distributeur** [distribytœr] *nm Com* distributor; **d. automatique** vending machine; **d. de billets** *(de train)* ticket machine; *(de billets de banque)* cash machine

**distribution** [distribysjɔ̃] *nf* distribution; *(du courrier)* delivery; *(de l'eau)* supply; *(acteurs de cinéma)* cast; **d. des prix** prizegiving

**district** [distrikt] *nm* district

**dit[1], dite** [di, dit] **1** *pp de* **dire** **2** *adj (convenu)* agreed; *(surnommé)* called

**dit[2], dites** [di, dit] *voir* **dire**

**divaguer** [divage] *vi (dérailler)* to rave

**divan** [divɑ̃] *nm* divan, couch

**divergent, -e** [diverʒɑ̃, -ɑ̃t] *adj (lignes)* divergent; *(opinions)* differing ■ **divergence** *nf (de lignes)* divergence; *(d'opinions)* difference ■ **diverger** *vi* to diverge (**de** from)

**divers, -e** [diver, -ers] *adj (varié)* varied; **divers(es)** *(plusieurs)* various

**diversifier** [diversifje] *vt*, **se diversifier** *vpr* to diversify

**diversion** [diversjɔ̃] *nf* diversion; **faire d.** to create a diversion

**diversité** [diversite] *nf* diversity

**divertir** [divertir] **1** *vt* to entertain **2 se divertir** *vpr* to enjoy oneself ■ **divertissement** *nm* entertainment, amusement

**divin, -e** [divɛ̃, -in] *adj* divine ■ **divinité** *nf* divinity

**diviser** [divize] *vt*, **se diviser** *vpr* to divide (**en** into) ■ **division** *nf* division

**divorce** [divɔrs] *nm* divorce ■ **divorcer** *vi* to get divorced; **d. d'avec qn** to divorce sb ■ **divorcé, -e** **1** *adj* divorced (**d'avec** from) **2** *nmf* divorcee

**divulguer** [divylge] *vt* to divulge

**dix** [dis] ([di] *before consonant*, [diz] *before vowel*) *adj & nm* ten ■ **dix-huit** *adj & nm* eighteen ■ **dixième** *adj & nmf* tenth; **un d.** a tenth ■ **dix-neuf** *adj & nm* nineteen ■ **dix-sept** *adj & nm* seventeen

**dizaine** [dizen] *nf* **une d. (de)** about ten

**do** [do] *nm inv (note)* C

**docile** [dɔsil] *adj* docile

**docteur** [dɔktœr] *nm (en médecine, d'université)* doctor (**ès/en** of) ■ **doctorat** *nm* doctorate, ≃ PhD (**ès/en** in)

**doctrine** [dɔktrin] *nf* doctrine

**document** [dɔkymɑ̃] *nm* document ■ **documentaire** *adj & nm* documentary ■ **documentaliste** *nmf* archivist; *(à l'école)* (school) librarian

**documentation** [dɔkymɑ̃tɑsjɔ̃] *nf (documents)* documentation, *(brochures)* literature ■ **se documenter** *vpr* to gather information *or* material (**sur** on)

**dodu, -e** [dɔdy] *adj* chubby, plump

**doigt** [dwa] *nm* finger; **d. de pied** toe; **petit d.** little finger, *Am & Scot* pinkie; **un d. de vin** a drop of wine; **montrer qn du d.** to point at sb

**doigté** [dwate] *nm Mus* fingering; *(savoir-faire)* tact

**dois, doit** [dwa] *voir* **devoir[1,2]**

**doléances** [dɔleɑ̃s] *nfpl (plaintes)* grievances

**dollar** [dɔlar] *nm* dollar

**domaine** [dɔmen] *nm (terres)* estate, domain; *(matière)* field, domain; **être du d. public** to be in the public domain

**dôme** [dom] *nm* dome

**domestique** [dɔmestik] **1** *adj (vie, marché, produit)* domestic; **travaux domestiques** housework **2** *nmf* servant ■ **domestiquer** *vt* to domesticate

**domicile** [dɔmisil] *nm* home; *(demeure légale)* abode; **sans d. fixe** of no fixed abode; *Jur* **d. conjugal** marital home

**dominateur, -trice** [dɔminatœr, -tris] *adj* domineering ▪ **domination** *nf* domination

**dominer** [dɔmine] **1** *vt* to dominate; *(situation, sentiment)* to master; *(être supérieur à)* to surpass **2** *vi (être le plus fort)* to be dominant; *(être le plus important)* to predominate **3 se dominer** *vpr* to control oneself ▪ **dominant, -e** *adj* dominant

**dommage** [dɔmaʒ] *nm (tort)* harm; **dommages** *(dégâts)* damage; **quel d.!** what a pity, what a shame!; **c'est (bien) d. qu'elle ne soit pas venue** it's a (great) pity *or* shame she didn't come; **dommages-intérêts** damages

**dompter** [dɔ̃te] *vt (animal)* to tame

**DOM-TOM** [dɔmtɔm] *(abrév* **départements et territoires d'outre-mer**) *nmpl* = French overseas departments and territories

**don** [dɔ̃] *nm (cadeau, aptitude)* gift; *(à un musée, à une œuvre)* donation; **faire d. de qch** to give sth; **d. du sang** blood donation

**donateur, -trice** [dɔnatœr, -tris] *nmf* donor ▪ **donation** *nf* donation

**donc** [dɔ̃(k)] *conj* so, then; *(par conséquent)* so, therefore; **asseyez-vous d.!** *(intensif)* do sit down!

**donjon** [dɔ̃ʒɔ̃] *nm* keep

**données** [dɔne] *nfpl Ordinat* data

---

**DONNER** [dɔne] **1** *vt* to give; *(récolte, résultat)* to produce; *(cartes)* to deal; *(pièce, film)* to put on; **pourriez-vous me d. l'heure?** could you tell me the time?; **d. un coup à qn** to hit sb; **d. à manger à qn** *(animal, enfant)* to feed sb; **elle m'a donné de ses nouvelles** she told me how she was doing; **ça donne soif/faim** it makes you thirsty/hungry; **étant donné...** considering..., in view of...; **étant donné que...** seeing (that), considering (that)...; **à un moment donné** at some stage

**2** *vi* **d. sur** *(fenêtre)* to overlook, to look out onto; *(porte)* to open onto

**3 se donner** *vpr (se consacrer)* to devote oneself (**à** to); **se d. du mal** to go to a lot of trouble (**pour faire** to do)

---

**donneur, -euse** [dɔnœr, -øz] *nmf (de sang, d'organe)* donor

**dont** [dɔ̃] (= **de qui, duquel, de quoi**) *pron relatif (exprime la partie d'un tout) (personne)* of whom; *(chose)* of which; *(exprime l'appartenance) (personne)* whose, of whom; *(chose)* of which, whose; **une mère d. le fils est malade** a mother whose son is ill; **la fille d. il est fier** the daughter he is proud of *or* of whom he is proud; **les outils d. j'ai besoin** the tools I need; **la façon d. elle joue** the way (in which) she plays; **cinq enfants d. deux filles** five children two of whom are daughters, five children including two daughters; **voici ce d. il s'agit** here's what it's about

**doper** [dɔpe] **1** *vt* to dope **2 se doper** *vpr* to take drugs ▪ **dopage** *nm (action)* doping; *(de sportif)* drug-taking

**dorénavant** [dɔrenavɑ̃] *adv* from now on

**dorer** [dɔre] **1** *vt (objet)* to gild **2** *vi (à la cuisson)* to brown **3 se dorer** *vpr* **se d. au soleil** to sunbathe ▪ **doré, -e** *adj (objet)* gilt, gold; *(couleur)* golden

**dormir*** [dɔrmir] *vi* to sleep; *(être endormi)* to be asleep; *Fig (argent)* to lie idle

**dortoir** [dɔrtwar] *nm* dormitory

**dos** [do] *nm (de personne, d'animal)* back; *(de livre)* spine; **'voir au d.'** *(verso)* 'see over'

**dose** [doz] *nf* dose; *(dans un mélange)* proportion ▪ **doser** *vt (médicament, ingrédients)* to measure out

**dossard** [dosar] *nm (de sportif)* number *(worn by player or competitor)*

**dossier** [dosje] *nm (de siège)* back; *(documents)* file

**dot** [dɔt] *nf* dowry

**doter** [dɔte] *vt (équiper)* to equip (**de** with); **doté d'une grande intelligence** endowed with great intelligence

**douane** [dwan] *nf* customs; **passer la d.** to go through customs ▪ **douanier, -ère** *nmf* customs officer

**doublage** [dublaʒ] *nm (de film)* dubbing

**double** [dubl] **1** *adj* double; *(rôle, avantage)* twofold, double; **en d. exemplaire** in duplicate **2** *adv* double **3** *nm (de personne)* double; *(copie)* copy, duplicate; **le d. (de)** *(quantité)* twice as much (as); **je l'ai en d.** I have two of them

**doubler** [duble] **1** *vt (augmenter)* to double; *(vêtement)* to line; *(film)* to dub; *(acteur)* to dub the voice of; *(classe à l'école)* to repeat **2** *vi (augmenter)* to double **3** *vti (en voiture) Br* to overtake, *Am* to pass **4 se doubler** *vpr* **se d. de** to be coupled with

**doublure** [dublyr] *nf (étoffe)* lining; *(au théâtre)* understudy; *(au cinéma)* stand-in

**douce** [dus] *voir* **doux** ■ **doucement** *adv (délicatement)* gently; *(bas)* softly; *(lentement)* slowly; *(sans bruit)* quietly ■ **douceur** *nf (de miel)* sweetness; *(de peau)* softness; *(de temps)* mildness; *(de personne)* gentleness

**douche** [duʃ] *nf* shower; **prendre une d.** to have *or* take a shower ■ **doucher se doucher** *vpr* to have *or* take a shower

**doué, -e** [dwe] *adj* gifted, talented (**en** at); **être d. pour qch** to have a gift for sth

**douille** [duj] *nf (d'ampoule)* socket; *(de cartouche)* case

**douillet, -ette** [dujɛ, -ɛt] *adj (lit) Br* cosy, *Am* cozy

**douleur** [dulœr] *nf (mal)* pain; *(chagrin)* sorrow, grief ■ **douloureux, -euse** *adj* painful

**doute** [dut] *nm* doubt; **sans d.** no doubt, probably; **sans aucun d.** without (any) doubt; **mettre qch en d.** to cast doubt on sth

**douter** [dute] **1** *vi* to doubt; **d. de qn/qch** to doubt sb/sth **2** *vt* **je doute qu'il soit assez fort** I doubt whether he's strong enough **3 se douter** *vpr* **se d. de quelque chose** to suspect something

**douteux, -euse** [dutø, -øz] *adj (peu certain)* doubtful; *(louche, médiocre)* dubious

**Douvres** [duvr] *nm ou f* Dover

**doux, douce** [du, dus] *adj (miel, son)* sweet; *(peau, lumière)* soft; *(temps, climat)* mild; *(personne, pente)* gentle

**douze** [duz] *adj & nm* twelve ■ **douzaine** *nf (douze)* dozen; *(environ)* about twelve; **une d. d'œufs** a dozen eggs

**dragée** [draʒe] *nf* sugared almond

**dragon** [dragɔ̃] *nm (animal, personne acariâtre)* dragon

**drainer** [drene] *vt* to drain

**drame** [dram] *nm (genre littéraire)* drama; *(catastrophe)* tragedy ■ **dramatique 1** *adj* dramatic; **auteur d.** playwright, dramatist **2** *nf* drama

**drap** [dra] *nm (de lit)* sheet; *(tissu)* cloth; **d.-housse** fitted sheet; **d. de bain** bath towel

**drapeau, -x** [drapo] *nm* flag

**dresser** [drese] **1** *vt (échelle, statue)* to put up, to erect; *(liste)* to draw up; *(piège)* to set, to lay; *(animal)* to train; **d. les oreilles** to prick up one's ears **2 se dresser** *vpr (personne)* to stand up; *(statue, montagne)* to rise up ■ **dressage** *nm* training ■ **dresseur, -euse** *nmf* trainer

**drogue** [drɔg] *nf (stupéfiant) & Péj (médicament)* drug; **d. dure/douce** hard/soft drug ■ **drogué, -e** *nmf* drug addict ■ **droguer 1** *vt (victime)* to drug; *(malade)* to dose up **2 se droguer** *vpr* to take drugs

**droguerie** [drɔgri] *nf* hardware *Br* shop *or Am* store ■ **droguiste** *nmf* hardware dealer

**droit[1]** [drwa] *nm (privilège)* right; *(d'inscription)* fee(s); **le d.** *(science juridique)* law; **avoir d. à qch** to be entitled to sth; **avoir le d. de faire qch** to be entitled to do sth, to have the right to do sth; **droits de douane** (customs) duty; **droits de l'homme** human rights

**droit[2], droite[1]** [drwa, drwat] **1** *adj*

*(route, ligne)* straight; *(angle)* right; *Fig (honnête)* upright **2** *adv* straight; **tout d.** straight *or* right ahead; **aller d. au but** to go straight to the point

**droit**[3]**, droite**[2] [drwa, drwat] *adj (côté, bras)* right

**droite**[3] [drwat] *nf (ligne)* straight line

**droite**[4] [drwat] *nf* **la d.** *(côté)* the right (side); *Pol* the right (wing); **à d.** *(tourner)* (to the) right; *(rouler, se tenir)* on the right, on the right(-hand) side; **de d.** *(fenêtre)* right-hand; *(candidat)* right-wing; **à d. de** on *or* to the right of

**droitier, -ère** [drwatje, -ɛr] **1** *adj* right-handed **2** *nmf* right-handed person

**droiture** [drwatyr] *nf* rectitude

**drôle** [drol] *adj* funny ▪ **drôlement** *adv* funnily; *Fam (extrêmement)* terribly, dreadfully

**dru, drue** [dry] **1** *adj (herbe)* thick, dense **2** *adv* **tomber d.** *(pluie)* to pour down heavily; **pousser d.** to grow thickly

**du** [dy] *voir* **de**[1,2]

**dû, due** [dy] **1** *adj* **d. à qch** due to sth; **en bonne et due forme** in due form **2** *nm* due

**duc** [dyk] *nm* duke ▪ **duchesse** *nf* duchess

**duel** [dɥɛl] *nm* duel

**dûment** [dymɑ̃] *adv* duly

**dune** [dyn] *nf* (sand) dune

**duo** [dɥo] *nm Mus* duet

**dupe** [dyp] **1** *adj* **être d. de** to be taken in by; **il n'est pas d.** he's well aware of it **2** *nf* dupe ▪ **duper** *vt* to fool, to dupe

**duplex** [dyplɛks] *nm Br* maisonette, *Am* duplex

**duplicata** [dyplikata] *nm inv* duplicate

**duquel** [dykɛl] *voir* **lequel**

**dur, dure** [dyr] **1** *adj (substance)* hard; *(difficile)* hard, tough; *(viande)* tough; *(hiver, ton)* harsh; *(personne)* hard, harsh; **d. d'oreille** hard of hearing **2** *adv (travailler)* hard ▪ **durement** *adv* harshly ▪ **dureté** *nf (de substance)* hardness; *(d'hiver, de ton)* harshness; *(de viande)* toughness

**durable** [dyrabl] *adj* lasting

**durant** [dyrɑ̃] *prép* during; **d. l'hiver** during the winter; **des heures d.** for hours and hours

**durcir** [dyrsir] *vti*, **se durcir** *vpr* to harden

**durée** [dyre] *nf (de film, d'événement)* length; *(période)* duration; **de longue d.** *(bonheur)* lasting; **de courte d.** *(attente)* short; *(bonheur)* short-lived

**durer** [dyre] *vi* to last

**duvet** [dyvɛ] *nm (d'oiseau)* down; *(sac)* sleeping bag

**dynamique** [dinamik] *adj* dynamic

**dynamite** [dinamit] *nf* dynamite

**dynamo** [dinamo] *nf* dynamo

**dynastie** [dinasti] *nf* dynasty

**dyslexique** [dislɛksik] *adj* dyslexic

# Ee

**E, e** [ə] *nm inv* E, e

**EAO** [əao] (*abrév* **enseignement assisté par ordinateur**) *nm inv* CAL

**eau, -x** [o] *nf* water; **sports d'e. vive** whitewater sports; **e. de toilette** eau de toilette; **e. du robinet** tap water; **e. douce** fresh water ■ **eau-de-vie** (*pl* **eaux-de-vie**) *nf* brandy

**ébahir** [ebair] *vt* to astound

**ébattre** [ebatr] **s'ébattre** *vpr* to frolic

**ébaucher** [eboʃe] *vt (tableau, roman)* to rough out

**ébéniste** [ebenist] *nm* cabinetmaker

**éblouir** [ebluir] *vt* to dazzle

**éboueur** [ebwœr] *nm Br* dustman, *Am* garbage collector

**ébouillanter** [ebujɑ̃te] **1** *vt* to scald **2 s'ébouillanter** *vpr* to scald oneself

**ébouler** [ebule] **s'ébouler** *vpr (falaise)* to collapse; *(tunnel)* to cave in ■ **éboulement** *nm (écroulement)* collapse; *(de mine)* cave-in

**ébouriffé, -e** [eburife] *adj* dishevelled

**ébranler** [ebrɑ̃le] **1** *vt (mur, confiance, personne)* to shake **2 s'ébranler** *vpr (train, cortège)* to move off

**ébrécher** [ebreʃe] *vt (assiette)* to chip; *(lame)* to nick

**ébriété** [ebrijete] *nf* **en état d'é.** under the influence of drink

**ébrouer** [ebrue] **s'ébrouer** *vpr (chien)* to shake itself; *(cheval)* to snort

**ébruiter** [ebrɥite] *vt (nouvelle)* to spread

**EBS** [øbeɛs] (*abrév* **encéphalite bovine spongiforme**) *nf* BSE

**ébullition** [ebylisjɔ̃] *nf* boiling; **être en é.** *(eau)* to be boiling; **porter qch à é.** to bring sth to the boil

**écaille** [ekɑj] *nf (de poisson)* scale ■ **écailler 1** *vt (poisson)* to scale **2 s'écailler** *vpr (peinture)* to peel (off)

**écarquiller** [ekarkije] *vt* **é. les yeux** to open one's eyes wide

**écart** [ekar] *nm (intervalle)* gap, distance; *(différence)* difference (**de** in; **entre** between); **faire le grand é.** to do the splits; **à l'é.** out of the way; **à l'é. de qch** away from sth

**écartelé, -e** [ekartəle] *adj* **é. entre** *(tiraillé)* torn between

**écartement** [ekartəmɑ̃] *nm (espace)* gap, distance (**de** between)

**écarter** [ekarte] **1** *vt (objets, personnes)* to move apart; *(jambes, doigts)* to spread; *(rideaux)* to draw (back); *(idée)* to brush aside; *(proposition)* to turn down; **é. qch de qch** to move sth away from sth

**2 s'écarter** *vpr* (**a**) *(se séparer) (personnes)* to move apart (**de** from); *(foule)* to part

(**b**) *(piéton)* to move away (**de** from); **s'é. du sujet** to wander from the subject ■ **écarté, -e** *adj* **les jambes écartées** with his/her legs (wide) apart

**ecclésiastique** [eklezjastik] *nm* clergyman

**écervelé, -e** [esɛrvəle] **1** *adj* scatterbrained **2** *nmf* scatterbrain

**échafaudage** [eʃafodaʒ] *nm* scaffolding; **des échafaudages** scaffolding

**échalote** [eʃalɔt] *nf* shallot

**échancré, -e** [eʃɑ̃kre] *adj* low-cut ■ **échancrure** *nf* low neckline

**échange** [eʃɑ̃ʒ] *nm* exchange; **en é.** in exchange (**de** for) ■ **échanger** *vt* to exchange (**contre** for)

**échangeur** [eʃɑ̃ʒœr] *nm* interchange

**échantillon** [eʃɑ̃tijɔ̃] *nm* sample

**échapper** [eʃape] **1** *vi* **é. à qn** to escape from sb; **son nom m'échappe** his/her name escapes me; **ça lui a échappé des mains** it slipped out of his/her hands

**2** *vt* **il l'a échappé belle** he had a narrow escape

**3 s'échapper** *vpr (personne, gaz, eau)* to escape (**de** from) ■ **échappée** *nf (de cyclistes)* breakaway

**écharde** [eʃard] *nf* splinter

**écharpe** [eʃarp] *nf* scarf; *(de maire)* sash; **avoir le bras en é.** to have one's arm in a sling

**échasse** [eʃas] *nf (bâton)* stilt

**échauffer** [eʃofe] **1** *vt (moteur)* to overheat **2 s'échauffer** *vpr (sportif)* to warm up

**échauffourée** [eʃofure] *nf* clash, brawl, skirmish

**échéance** [eʃeɑ̃s] *nf (de facture, de dette)* date of payment; **à brève/longue é.** *(projet, emprunt)* short-/long-term

**échéant** [eʃeɑ̃] **le cas échéant** *adv* if need be

**échec** [eʃɛk] *nm* failure; **faire é. à qch** to hold sth in check; **les échecs** *(jeu)* chess; **é.!** check!; **é. et mat!** checkmate!

**échelle** [eʃɛl] *nf* (**a**) *(marches)* ladder (**b**) *(de carte)* scale; **à l'é. nationale** on a national scale

**échelon** [eʃlɔ̃] *nm (d'échelle)* rung; *(d'employé)* grade; *(d'organisation)* echelon; **à l'é. régional** on a regional level

**échelonner** [eʃlɔne] **1** *vt (paiements)* to spread **2 s'échelonner** *vpr* to be spread out

**échevelé, -e** [eʃəvle] *adj (ébouriffé)* dishevelled

**échiquier** [eʃikje] *nm (plateau)* chessboard

**écho** [eko] *nm (de son)* echo; **échos** *(de presse)* gossip column

**échographie** [ekografi] *nf* (ultrasound) scan; **passer une é.** to have a scan

**échoir*** [eʃwar] *vi* **é. à qn** to fall to sb

**échouer** [eʃwe] **1** *vi* to fail; **é. à** *(examen)* to fail **2** *vi,* **s'échouer** *vpr (navire)* to run aground

**éclabousser** [eklabuse] *vt* to splash, to spatter (**avec** with) ■ **éclaboussure** *nf* splash

**éclair** [eklɛr] **1** *nm* (**a**) *(lumière)* flash; *(d'orage)* flash of lightning (**b**) *(gâteau)* éclair **2** *adj inv* **visite é.** lightning visit

**éclairage** [eklɛraʒ] *nm* lighting

**éclaircie** [eklɛrsi] *nf* sunny spell

**éclaircir** [eklɛrsir] **1** *vt (couleur)* to lighten; *(mystère)* to clear up **2 s'éclaircir** *vpr (ciel)* to clear; *(mystère)* to be cleared up; **s'é. la voix** to clear one's throat ■ **éclaircissement** *nm (explication)* explanation

**éclairer** [eklere] **1** *vt (pièce)* to light (up); **é. qn** *(avec une lampe)* to give sb some light; *(informer)* to enlighten sb (**sur** about)

**2** *vi (lampe)* to give light; **é. bien/mal** to give good/poor light

**3 s'éclairer** *vpr (visage)* to light up; **s'é. à la bougie** to use candlelight; **s'é. à l'électricité** to have electric lighting ■ **éclairé, -e** *adj (averti)* enlightened; **bien/mal é.** *(illuminé)* well-/badly lit

**éclaireur, -euse** [eklɛrœr, -øz] **1** *nmf* (boy) scout, (girl) guide **2** *nm (soldat)* scout

**éclat** [ekla] *nm* (**a**) *(de lumière)* brightness; *(de phare)* glare; *(de diamant)* flash (**b**) *(de verre)* splinter; **é. de rire** burst of laughter

**éclatant, -e** [eklatɑ̃, -ɑ̃t] *adj (lumière, succès)* brilliant; **être é. de santé** to be glowing with health

**éclater** [eklate] *vi (pneu)* to burst; *(bombe)* to go off, to explode; *(verre)* to shatter; *(guerre)* to break out; *(orage, scandale)* to break; *(parti)* to break up; **é. de rire** to burst out laughing; **é. en sanglots** to burst into tears ▪ **éclatement** *nm (de pneu)* bursting; *(de bombe)* explosion; *(de parti)* break-up

**éclectique** [eklɛktik] *adj* eclectic

**éclipse** [eklips] *nf* eclipse ▪ **éclipser** *vt* to eclipse

**éclore*** [eklɔr] *vi (œuf)* to hatch; *(fleur)* to open (out), to blossom

**écluse** [eklyz] *nf (de canal)* lock

**écœurer** [ekœre] *vt* **é. qn** *(aliment)* to make sb feel sick; *(moralement)* to sicken sb ▪ **écœurant, -e** *adj* disgusting, sickening ▪ **écœurement** *nm (nausée)* nausea; *(indignation)* disgust

**école** [ekɔl] *nf* school; **à l'é.** at school; **faire é.** to gain a following; **les grandes écoles** = university-level colleges specializing in professional training; **é. de dessin** art school; **é. privée** private school, *Br* public school; **é. publique** *Br* state school, *Am* public school ▪ **écolier, -ère** *nmf* schoolboy, *f* schoolgirl

**écologie** [ekɔlɔʒi] *nf* ecology ▪ **écologique** *adj* ecological ▪ **écologiste** *adj & nmf* environmentalist

**économe** [ekɔnɔm] *adj* thrifty, economical

**économie** [ekɔnɔmi] *nf (activité, vertu)* economy; **économies** *(argent)* savings; **faire des économies** to save (up) ▪ **économique** *adj* (**a**) *(relatif à l'économie)* economic; **science é.** economics *(sing)* (**b**) *(avantageux)* economical

**économiser** [ekɔnɔmize] **1** *vt (forces, argent, énergie)* to save **2** *vi* to economize (**sur** on)

**écoper** [ekɔpe] *vi Fam* **é. de qch** *(punition, amende)* to get sth

**écorce** [ekɔrs] *nf (d'arbre)* bark; *(de fruit)* peel; **l'é. terrestre** the earth's crust

**écorcher** [ekɔrʃe] **1** *vt (érafler)* to graze; *Fig (mot)* to mispronounce **2 s'écorcher** *vpr* to graze oneself; **s'é. le genou** to graze one's knee

**Écosse** [ekɔs] *nf* **l'É.** Scotland ▪ **écossais, -e 1** *adj* Scottish; *(tissu)* tartan **2** *nmf* **É., Écossaise** Scot

**écouler** [ekule] **1** *vt (se débarrasser de)* to dispose of **2 s'écouler** *vpr (eau)* to flow out, to run out; *(temps)* to pass ▪ **écoulé, -e** *adj (passé)* past ▪ **écoulement** *nm (de liquide)* flow; *(de marchandises)* sale

**écourter** [ekurte] *vt (séjour)* to cut short; *(texte, tige)* to shorten

**écoute** [ekut] *nf* listening; **être à l'é.** to be listening in (**de** to); **écoutes téléphoniques** phone tapping

**écouter** [ekute] **1** *vt* to listen to; **faire é. qch à qn** *(disque)* to play sb sth **2 s'écouter** *vpr* **si je m'écoutais** if I did what I wanted ▪ **écouteur** *nm (de téléphone)* earpiece; **écouteurs** *(casque)* headphones

**écran** [ekrɑ̃] *nm* screen; **à l'é.** on screen; **le petit é.** television; **é. publicitaire** commercial break; **é. total** sun block

**écraser** [ekraze] **1** *vt (broyer, vaincre)* to crush; *(fruit, insecte)* to squash; *(cigarette)* to put out; *(piéton)* to run over; **se faire é. par une voiture** to get run over by a car **2 s'écraser** *vpr (avion)* to crash (**contre** into) ▪ **écrasant, -e** *adj (victoire, chaleur)* overwhelming

**écrémer** [ekreme] *vt (lait)* to skim

**écrevisse** [ekrəvis] *nf* crayfish *inv*

**écrier** [ekrije] **s'écrier** *vpr* to exclaim, to cry out (**que** that)

**écrin** [ekrɛ̃] *nm* (jewel) case

**écrire*** [ekrir] **1** *vt* to write; *(noter)* to write down **2** *vi* to write **3 s'écrire** *vpr (mot)* to be spelt; **comment ça s'écrit?** how do you spell it? ▪ **écrit** *nm (document)* written document; *(examen)* written examination; **par é.** in writing

**écriteau, -x** [ekrito] *nm* notice, sign

**écriture** [ekrityr] *nf (système)* writing; *(calligraphie)* (hand)writing; *Com* **écritures** accounts; **les Écritures** *(la Bible)* the Scriptures

**écrivain** [ekrivɛ̃] *nm* writer

**écrou** [ekru] *nm (de boulon)* nut

**écrouer** [ekrue] *vt* to imprison

**écrouler** [ekrule] **s'écrouler** *vpr (édifice, personne)* to collapse ▪ **écroulement** *nm* collapse

**écru, -e** [ekry] *adj (beige)* écru; *(naturel)* unbleached

**ÉCU** [eky] *(abrév* **European Currency Unit)** *nm Anciennement* ECU

**écueil** [ekœj] *nm (rocher)* reef; *Fig (obstacle)* pitfall

**écuelle** [ekɥɛl] *nf* bowl

**écume** [ekym] *nf (de mer)* foam ▪ **écumer 1** *vt (piller)* to plunder **2** *vi* to foam (**de rage** with anger)

**écureuil** [ekyrœj] *nm* squirrel

**écurie** [ekyri] *nf* stable

**écusson** [ekysɔ̃] *nm (en étoffe)* badge

**écuyer, -ère** [ekɥije, -ɛr] *nmf (cavalier)* rider

**édifice** [edifis] *nm* edifice ▪ **édifier** *vt (bâtiment)* to erect; *(théorie)* to construct

**Édimbourg** [edɛ̃bur] *nm ou f* Edinburgh

**éditer** [edite] *vt (publier)* to publish; *Ordinat* to edit ▪ **éditeur, -trice** *nmf (dans l'édition)* publisher ▪ **édition** *nf (livre, journal)* edition; *(métier, diffusion)* publishing

**éditorial, -aux** [editɔrjal, -o] *nm (article)* editorial, *Br* leader ▪ **éditorialiste** *nmf* editorial *or Br* leader writer

**éducateur, -trice** [edykatœr, -tris] *nmf* educator

**éducatif, -ive** [edykatif, -iv] *adj* educational

**éducation** [edykɑsjɔ̃] *nf (enseignement)* education; *(des parents)* upbringing; **avoir de l'é.** to have good manners; **l'É. nationale** ≃ the Department of Education; **é. physique** physical education *or* training ▪ **éduquer** *vt (à l'école)* to educate; *(à la maison)* to bring up

**EEE** [əəə] *(abrév* **Espace économique européen)** *nm* EEA

**effacé, -e** [efase] *adj (modeste)* self-effacing

**effacer** [efase] **1** *vt (avec une gomme)* to rub out, to erase; *(avec un chiffon)* to wipe away; *Fig (souvenir)* to blot out, to erase **2 s'effacer** *vpr (souvenir)* to fade; *(se placer en retrait)* to step aside

**effarant, -e** [efarɑ̃, -ɑ̃t] *adj* astounding

**effaroucher** [efaruʃe] **1** *vt* to scare away **2 s'effaroucher** *vpr* to take fright

**effectif, -ive** [efɛktif, -iv] **1** *adj (réel)* effective **2** *nm (de classe)* size; *(employés)* staff ▪ **effectivement** *adv (en effet)* actually

**effectuer** [efɛktɥe] *vt (expérience, geste difficile)* to carry out, to perform; *(paiement, trajet)* to make

**efféminé, -e** [efemine] *adj* effeminate

**effervescent, -e** [efɛrvesɑ̃, -ɑ̃t] *adj (médicament)* effervescent

**effet** [efɛ] *nm (résultat)* effect; *(impression)* impression (**sur** on); **en e.** indeed, in fact; **e. de serre** greenhouse effect; **e. secondaire** side effect; *Cin* **effets spéciaux** special effects

**efficace** [efikas] *adj (mesure)* effective; *(personne)* efficient ▪ **efficacité** *nf (de mesure)* effectiveness; *(de personne)* efficiency

**effilocher** [efilɔʃe] **s'effilocher** *vpr* to fray

**effleurer** [eflœre] *vt (frôler)* to touch lightly; **e. qn** *(pensée)* to cross sb's mind

**effondrer** [efɔ̃dre] **s'effondrer** *vpr (tomber, chuter)* to collapse; *(plan)* to fall through; *Fig (perdre ses forces)* to go to pieces; **s'e. en larmes** to break down and cry ▪ **effondrement** *nm (chute)* collapse; *(sentiment)* dejection

**efforcer** [efɔrse] **s'efforcer** *vpr* **s'e. de faire qch** to try hard to do sth

**effort** [efɔr] *nm* effort; **faire des efforts** to make an effort

**effraction** [efraksjɔ̃] *nf* **entrer par e.** to break in; **vol avec e.** housebreaking

**effrayer** [efreje] **1** *vt* to frighten, to scare **2 s'effrayer** *vpr* to be frightened *or* scared ▪ **effrayant, -e** *adj* frightening, scary

**effriter** [efrite] **s'effriter** *vpr* to crumble

**effronté, -e** [efrɔ̃te] *adj (personne)* impudent

**effroyable** [efrwajabl] *adj* dreadful

**effusion** [efyzjɔ̃] *nf* **e. de sang** bloodshed

**égal, -e, -aux, -ales** [egal, -o] **1** *adj* equal (**à** to); *(régulier)* even; **ça m'est é.** it's all the same to me **2** *nmf (personne)* equal ▪ **également** *adv (au même degré)* equally; *(aussi)* also, as well ▪ **égaler** *vt* to equal, to match (**en** in); **3 plus 4 égale(nt) 7** 3 plus 4 equals 7

**égaliser** [egalize] *vi Sport* to equalize

**égalité** [egalite] *nf* equality; *(régularité)* evenness; *(au tennis)* deuce; *Sport* **à é.** even, equal (in points) ▪ **égalitaire** *adj* egalitarian

**égard** [egar] *nm* **à l'é. de** *(envers)* towards; **à cet é.** in this respect; **par é. pour qn** out of consideration for sb

**égarer** [egare] **1** *vt (objet)* to mislay; *(personne)* to mislead **2 s'égarer** *vpr (personne, lettre)* to get lost; *(objet)* to go astray

**égayer** [egeje] **1** *vt (pièce)* to brighten up; **é. qn** to cheer sb up **2 s'égayer** *vpr (s'animer)* to cheer up

**église** [egliz] *nf* church

**égoïste** [egɔist] **1** *adj* selfish **2** *nmf* selfish person

**égorger** [egɔrʒe] *vt* to cut *or* slit the throat of

**égout** [egu] *nm* sewer

**égoutter** [egute] **1** *vt* to drain **2** *vi*, **s'égoutter** *vpr* to drain ▪ **égouttoir** *nm (panier)* drainer

**égratigner** [egratiɲe] **1** *vt* to scratch **2 s'égratigner** *vpr* to scratch oneself ▪ **égratignure** *nf* scratch

**Égypte** [eʒipt] *nf* **l'É.** Egypt ▪ **égyptien, -enne 1** *adj* Egyptian **2** *nmf* **É., Égyptienne** Egyptian

**éjecter** [eʒɛkte] *vt* to eject

**élaborer** [elabɔre] *vt (plan, idée)* to develop ▪ **élaboration** *nf (de plan, d'idée)* development

**élan** [elɑ̃] *nm (vitesse)* momentum; *(course)* run-up; **prendre son é.** to take a run-up

**élancé, -e** [elɑ̃se] *adj (personne)* slender

**élancer** [elɑ̃se] **1** *vi (abcès)* to give shooting pains **2 s'élancer** *vpr (bondir)* to rush forward; *Sport* to take a run-up ▪ **élancement** *nm (douleur)* shooting pain

**élargir** [elarʒir] **1** *vt (chemin)* to widen; *(vêtement)* to let out **2 s'élargir** *vpr (sentier)* to widen out; *(vêtement)* to stretch

**élastique** [elastik] **1** *adj (tissu)* elastic **2** *nm (lien)* rubber band, *Br* elastic band; *(pour la couture)* elastic

**élection** [elɛksjɔ̃] *nf* election; **é. partielle** by-election ▪ **électeur, -trice** *nmf* voter, elector ▪ **électoral, -e, -aux, -ales** *adj* **campagne électorale** election campaign; **liste électorale** electoral roll ▪ **électorat** *nm (électeurs)* electorate, voters

**électricien, -enne** [elɛktrisjɛ̃, -ɛn] *nmf* electrician ▪ **électricité** *nf* electricity ▪ **électrifier** *vt (voie ferrée)* to electrify ▪ **électrique** *adj (pendule, décharge) & Fig* electric; *(courant, fil)* electric(al)

**électrocuter** [elɛktrɔkyte] *vt* to electrocute

**électroménager** [elɛktrɔmenaʒe] **1** *adj m* **appareil é.** household electrical appliance **2** *nm* household appliances

**électronique** [elɛktrɔnik] **1** *adj* electronic **2** *nf* electronics *(sing)*

**élégant, -e** [elegɑ̃, -ɑ̃t] *adj (bien habillé)* smart, elegant ▪ **élégance** *nf* elegance

**élément** [elemɑ̃] *nm (composante, personne) & Chim* element; *(de meuble)* unit

**élémentaire** [elemɑ̃tɛr] *adj* basic

**éléphant** [elefɑ̃] *nm* elephant

**élevage** [elvaʒ] *nm (production)* breeding (**de** of); *(ferme)* farm

**élevé, -e** [elve] *adj (haut)* high; *(noble)* noble; **bien/mal é.** well-/bad-mannered

**élève** [elɛv] *nmf (à l'école)* pupil

**élever** [elve] **1** *vt (objection)* to raise; *(enfant)* to bring up; *(animal)* to breed **2 s'élever** *vpr (montagne)* to rise; *(monument)* to stand; **s'é. à** *(prix)* to amount to; **s'é. contre** to rise up against

**éleveur, -euse** [elvœr, -øz] *nmf* breeder

**éliminer** [elimine] *vt* to eliminate ▪ **éliminatoire** *adj* **épreuve é.** *Sport* qualifying round, heat; *Scol* qualifying exam; *Scol* **note é.** disqualifying mark ▪ **éliminatoires** *nfpl Sport* qualifying rounds

**élire*** [elir] *vt* to elect (**à** to)

**élite** [elit] *nf* elite (**de** of)

**elle** [ɛl] *pron personnel* (**a**) *(sujet)* she; *(chose, animal)* it; **elles** they (**b**) *(complément)* her; *(chose, animal)* it; **elles** them ▪ **elle-même** *pron (personne)* herself; *(chose, animal)* itself; **elles-mêmes** themselves

**éloge** [elɔʒ] *nm (compliment)* praise ▪ **élogieux, -euse** *adj* laudatory

**éloigné, -e** [elwaɲe] *adj (lieu)* far away, remote; **é. de** *(village, maison)* far (away) from; *(très différent)* far removed from

**éloignement** [elwaɲəmɑ̃] *nm (distance)* remoteness, distance; *(absence)* separation (**de** from)

**éloigner** [elwaɲe] **1** *vt (chose, personne)* to move away (**de** from); *(malade)* to keep away; **é. qn de qch** *(sujet, but)* to take sb away from sth **2 s'éloigner** *vpr (partir)* to move away (**de** from); *(dans le passé)* to become (more) remote; **s'é. de qch** *(sujet, but)* to wander from sth

**éloquent, -e** [elɔkɑ̃, -ɑ̃t] *adj* eloquent

**élu, -e** [ely] **1** *pp de* **élire 2** *nmf Pol* elected member *or* representative

**élucider** [elyside] *vt* to elucidate

**Élysée** [elize] *nm* **(le palais de) l'É.** the Élysée palace *(French President's residence)*

**e-mail** [imɛl] *nm* e-mail; **envoyer un e.** to send an e-mail (**à** to)

**émail, -aux** [emaj, -o] *nm* enamel

**émanations** [emanɑsjɔ̃] *nfpl* **des é.** *(odeurs)* smells; *(vapeurs)* fumes

**émanciper** [emɑ̃sipe] **1** *vt (femmes)* to emancipate **2 s'émanciper** *vpr* to become emancipated

**émaner** [emane] *vt* **é. de qch** to emanate from sth

**emballer** [ɑ̃bale] **1** *vt (dans une boîte)* to pack; *(dans du papier)* to wrap (up) **2 s'emballer** *vpr (cheval)* to bolt; *(moteur)* to race ▪ **emballage** *nm (action)* packing; *(dans du papier)* wrapping; *(boîte)* packaging; **papier d'e.** wrapping paper

**embarcadère** [ɑ̃barkadɛr] *nm* landing stage

**embarcation** [ɑ̃barkɑsjɔ̃] *nf* (small) boat

**embarquer** [ɑ̃barke] **1** *vt (passagers)* to take on board; *(marchandises)* to load **2** *vi*, **s'embarquer** *vpr* to (go on) board ▪ **embarquement** *nm (de passagers)* boarding

**embarras** [ɑ̃bara] *nm (gêne)* embarrassment; **dans l'e.** in an awkward situation; *(financièrement)* in financial difficulties

**embarrasser** [ɑ̃barase] **1** *vt (encombrer)* to clutter up; *(mettre mal à l'aise)* to embarrass **2 s'embarrasser** *vpr* **s'e. de qch** to burden oneself with sth ▪ **embarrassant, -e** *adj (paquet)* cumbersome; *(question)* embarrassing

**embauche** [ɑ̃boʃ] *nf (action)* hiring; *(travail)* work ▪ **embaucher** *vt (ouvrier)* to hire, to take on

**embaumer** [ɑ̃bome] **1** *vt (parfumer)* to give a sweet smell to **2** *vi* to smell sweet

**embellir** [ɑ̃bɛlir] **1** *vt (pièce, personne)* to make more attractive **2** *vi (personne)* to grow more attractive

**embêter** [ɑ̃bete] *Fam* **1** *vt (agacer)* to annoy; *(ennuyer)* to bore **2 s'embêter** *vpr (s'ennuyer)* to get bored ▪ **embêtant, -e** *adj Fam* annoying

**emblée** [ɑ̃ble] **d'emblée** *adv* right away

**emblème** [ɑ̃blɛm] *nm* emblem

**emboîter** [ɑ̃bwate] **1** *vt* to fit together **2 s'emboîter** *vpr* to fit together

**embouchure** [ɑ̃buʃyr] *nf (de fleuve)* mouth

**embourber** [ɑ̃burbe] **s'embourber** *vpr (véhicule)* to get bogged down

**embouteillage** [ɑ̃butɛjaʒ] *nm* traffic jam

**emboutir** [ɑ̃butir] *vt (voiture)* to crash into

**embranchement** [ɑ̃brɑ̃ʃmɑ̃] *nm (de voie)* junction

**embraser** [ɑ̃braze] **1** *vt* to set ablaze **2 s'embraser** *vpr (prendre feu)* to flare up

**embrasser** [ɑ̃brase] **1** *vt* **e. qn** *(donner un baiser à)* to kiss sb; *(serrer contre soi)* to embrace *or* hug sb **2 s'embrasser** *vpr* to kiss (each other)

**embrasure** [ɑ̃brazyr] *nf (de fenêtre, de porte)* aperture; **dans l'e. de la porte** in the doorway

**embrayer** [ɑ̃breje] *vi Aut* to engage the clutch ▪ **embrayage** *nm (mécanisme, pédale)* clutch

**embrouiller** [ɑ̃bruje] **1** *vt (fils)* to tangle (up); **e. qn** to confuse sb, to get sb muddled **2 s'embrouiller** *vpr* to get confused *or* muddled (**dans** in *or* with)

**embroussaillé, -e** [ɑ̃brusaje] *adj (barbe, chemin)* bushy

**embûches** [ɑ̃byʃ] *nfpl (difficultés)* traps, pitfalls

**embuer** [ɑ̃bɥe] *vt (vitre)* to mist up

**embusquer** [ɑ̃byske] **s'embusquer** *vpr* to lie in ambush ▪ **embuscade** *nf* ambush

**émeraude** [emrod] *nf & adj inv* emerald

**émerger** [emɛrʒe] *vi* to emerge (**de** from)

**émerveiller** [emɛrveje] **1** *vt* to amaze, to fill with wonder **2 s'émerveiller** *vpr* to marvel, to be filled with wonder (**de** at)

**émettre*** [emɛtr] *vt (lumière, son)* to give out, to emit; *(message radio)* to broadcast; *(monnaie)* to issue; *(vœu)* to express; *(chèque)* to draw; *(emprunt)* to float ▪ **émetteur** *nm Radio* transmitter

**émeute** [emøt] *nf* riot

**émietter** [emjete] *vt*, **s'émietter** *vpr (pain)* to crumble

**émigrer** [emigre] *vi (personne)* to emigrate ▪ **émigrant, -e** *nmf* emigrant ▪ **émigration** *nf* emigration ▪ **émigré, -e 1** *adj* **travailleur é.** migrant worker **2** *nmf* exile, émigré

**éminent, -e** [eminɑ̃, -ɑ̃t] *adj* eminent ▪ **éminence** *nf (colline)* hill; **son É.** *(cardinal)* his Eminence

**émissaire** [emisɛr] *nm* emissary

**émission** [emisjɔ̃] *nf (de radio)* programme; *(diffusion)* transmission; *(de lumière, de son)* emission (**de** of)

**emmanchure** [ɑ̃mɑ̃ʃyr] *nf* armhole

**emmêler** [ɑ̃mele] **1** *vt (fil, cheveux)* to tangle (up) **2 s'emmêler** *vpr* to get tangled

**emménager** [ɑ̃menaʒe] *vi* to move in; **e. dans** to move into

**emmener** [ɑ̃mne] *vt* to take (**à** to); *(prisonnier)* to take away; **e. qn faire une promenade** to take sb for a walk; **e. qn en voiture** to give sb a *Br* lift *or Am* ride

**emmitoufler** [ɑ̃mitufle] **s'emmitoufler** *vpr* to wrap (oneself) up (**dans** in)

**émotion** [emosjɔ̃] *nf (sentiment)* emotion ▪ **émotif, -ive** *adj* emotional

**émoussé, -e** [emuse] *adj (pointe)* blunt

**émouvoir*** [emuvwar] **1** *vt (affecter)* to move, to touch **2 s'émouvoir** *vpr* to be moved *or* touched ▪ **émouvant, -e** *adj* moving, touching

**empailler** [ɑ̃paje] *vt (animal)* to stuff

**empaqueter** [ɑ̃pakte] *vt* to pack

**emparer** [ɑ̃pare] **s'emparer** *vpr* **s'e. de** *(lieu, personne, objet)* to seize; *(sujet: émotion)* to take hold of

**empêcher** [ɑ̃peʃe] *vt* to prevent, to stop; **e. qn de faire qch** to prevent *or* stop sb from doing sth ▪ **empêchement** [-ɛʃmɑ̃] *nm* hitch; **il a/j'ai eu un e.** something came up

**empereur** [ɑ̃prœr] *nm* emperor
**empester** [ɑ̃pɛste] **1** *vt (tabac)* to stink of; *(pièce)* to stink out **2** *vi* to stink
**empêtrer** [ɑ̃petre] **s'empêtrer** *vpr* to get entangled (**dans** in)
**empiéter** [ɑ̃pjete] *vi* **e. sur** to encroach (up)on
**empiler** [ɑ̃pile] **1** *vt* to pile up (**sur** on) **2 s'empiler** *vpr* to pile up (**sur** on); **s'e. dans** *(passagers)* to cram into
**empire** [ɑ̃pir] *nm (territoires)* empire; *(autorité)* hold, influence
**empirer** [ɑ̃pire] *vi* to worsen, to get worse
**emplacement** [ɑ̃plasmɑ̃] *nm (de construction)* site, location; *(de stationnement)* place
**emplettes** [ɑ̃plɛt] *nfpl* **faire des e.** to do some shopping
**emplir** [ɑ̃plir] *vt*, **s'emplir** *vpr* to fill (**de** with)
**emploi** [ɑ̃plwa] *nm* (**a**) *(usage)* use; **e. du temps** timetable (**b**) *(travail)* job; **sans e.** unemployed
**employer** [ɑ̃plwaje] **1** *vt (utiliser)* to use; *(personne)* to employ **2 s'employer** *vpr (expression)* to be used ■ **employé, -e** *nmf* employee; **e. de banque** bank clerk; **e. de bureau** office worker ■ **employeur, -euse** *nmf* employer
**empocher** [ɑ̃pɔʃe] *vt* to pocket
**empoigner** [ɑ̃pwaɲe] *vt (saisir)* to grab
**empoisonner** [ɑ̃pwazɔne] **1** *vt (personne, aliment)* to poison **2 s'empoisonner** *vpr (par accident)* to be poisoned; *(volontairement)* to poison oneself ■ **empoisonnement** *nm* poisoning
**emporter** [ɑ̃pɔrte] **1** *vt (prendre)* to take (**avec soi** with one); *(transporter)* to take away; *(entraîner)* to carry along *or* away; *(par le vent)* to blow off *or* away; *(par les vagues)* to sweep away; **pizza à e.** takeaway pizza; **l'e. sur qn** to get the upper hand over sb **2 s'emporter** *vpr* to lose one's temper (**contre** with)
**empreinte** [ɑ̃prɛ̃t] *nf* mark; **e. digitale** fingerprint
**empresser** [ɑ̃prese] **s'empresser** *vpr* **s'e. de faire qch** to hasten to do sth
**emprise** [ɑ̃priz] *nf* hold (**sur** over)
**emprisonner** [ɑ̃prizɔne] *vt* to imprison ■ **emprisonnement** *nm* imprisonment
**emprunt** [ɑ̃prœ̃] *nm (argent)* loan; **faire un e.** *(auprès d'une banque)* to take out a loan ■ **emprunter** *vt (argent, objet)* to borrow (**à qn** from sb); *(route)* to take
**ému, -e** [emy] **1** *pp de* **émouvoir 2** *adj (attendri)* moved; *(attristé)* upset; *(apeuré)* nervous; **une voix émue** a voice charged with emotion

---

**EN[1]** [ɑ̃] *prép* (**a**) *(indique le lieu)* in; *(indique la direction)* to
(**b**) *(indique le temps)* in
(**c**) *(indique le moyen)* by; *(indique l'état)* in; **en avion** by plane; **en fleur** in flower; **en congé** on leave
(**d**) *(indique la matière)* in; **en bois** made of wood, wooden; **chemise en Nylon®** nylon shirt; **c'est en or** it's (made of) gold
(**e**) *(domaine)* **étudiant en anglais** English student; **docteur en médecine** doctor of medicine
(**f**) *(comme)* **en cadeau** as a present; **en ami** as a friend
(**g**) *(+ participe présent)* **en souriant** smiling, with a smile; **en chantant** while singing; **en apprenant que...** on hearing that...; **sortir en courant** to run out
(**h**) *(transformation)* into; **traduire en français** to translate into French

---

**EN[2]** [ɑ̃] *pron* (**a**) *(indique la provenance)* from there; **j'en viens** I've just come from there
(**b**) *(remplace les compléments introduits par 'de')* **en parler** to talk about it; **il en est content** he's pleased with it/him/them; **il s'en souviendra** he'll remember it
(**c**) *(partitif)* some; **j'en ai** I have

some; **en veux-tu?** do you want some? **donne-m'en** give some to me

**ENA** [ena] *(abrév* **École nationale d'administration**) *nf* = university-level college preparing students for senior positions in law and economics

**encadrer** [ɑ̃kadre] *vt (tableau)* to frame; *(mot)* to circle; *(personnel)* to manage; *(prisonnier)* to flank ▪ **encadrement** *nm (de porte, de photo)* frame

**encaisser** [ɑ̃kese] *vt (argent)* to collect; *(chèque)* to cash

**encart** [ɑ̃kar] *nm* **e. publicitaire** insert

**encastré, -e** [ɑ̃kastre] *adj (cuisinière, lave-linge)* built-in

**enceinte**[1] [ɑ̃sɛ̃t] *adj f (femme)* pregnant

**enceinte**[2] [ɑ̃sɛ̃t] *nf (muraille)* (surrounding) wall; *(espace)* enclosure; **dans l'e. de** within, inside; **e. (acoustique)** speaker

**encercler** [ɑ̃sɛrkle] *vt (lieu, ennemi)* to surround, to encircle; *(mot)* to circle

**enchaîner** [ɑ̃ʃene] **1** *vt (animal, prisonnier)* to chain up; *(idées)* to link (up)
**2** *vi (continuer à parler)* to continue
**3 s'enchaîner** *vpr (idées)* to be linked (up) ▪ **enchaînement** [-ɛnmɑ̃] *nm (succession)* chain, series; *(liaison)* link (ing) (**de** between *or* of)

**enchanter** [ɑ̃ʃɑ̃te] *vt (ravir)* to delight, to enchant; *(ensorceler)* to bewitch ▪ **enchanté, -e** *adj (ravi)* delighted (**de** with; **que** + *subjunctive* that); *(magique)* enchanted; **e. de faire votre connaissance!** pleased to meet you! ▪ **enchantement** *nm (ravissement)* delight; *(sortilège)* magic spell

**enchère** [ɑ̃ʃɛr] *nf (offre)* bid; **vente aux enchères** auction; **mettre qch aux enchères** to put sth up for auction, to auction sth

**enchérir** [ɑ̃ʃerir] *vi* to make a higher bid; **e. sur qn** to outbid sb

**enchevêtrer** [ɑ̃ʃvetre] **s'enchevêtrer** *vpr* to get entangled (**dans** in)

**enclencher** [ɑ̃klɑ̃ʃe] *vt* to engage

**enclin, -e** [ɑ̃klɛ̃, -in] *adj* **e. à** inclined to

**enclos** [ɑ̃klo] *nm (terrain, clôture)* enclosure

**encoche** [ɑ̃kɔʃ] *nf* notch (**à** in)

**encolure** [ɑ̃kɔlyr] *nf (de cheval, de vêtement)* neck; *(tour du cou)* collar (size)

**encombre** [ɑ̃kɔ̃br] **sans encombre** *adv* without a hitch

**encombrer** [ɑ̃kɔ̃bre] **1** *vt (pièce, couloir)* to clutter up (**de** with); *(rue, passage)* to block; **e. qn** to hamper sb
**2 s'encombrer** *vpr* **s'e. de qch** to load oneself down with sth ▪ **encombrant, -e** *adj (paquet)* bulky, cumbersome ▪ **encombré, -e** *adj (lignes téléphoniques, route)* jammed ▪ **encombrement** [-əmɑ̃] *nm (d'objets)* clutter; *(embouteillage)* traffic jam; *(volume)* bulk(iness)

**encontre** [ɑ̃kɔ̃trə] **à l'encontre de** *prép* against

**ENCORE** [ɑ̃kɔr] *adv* (**a**) *(toujours)* still
(**b**) *(avec négation)* **pas e.** not yet; **je ne suis pas e. prêt** I'm not ready yet
(**c**) *(de nouveau)* again
(**d**) *(de plus, en plus)* **e. un café** another coffee; **e. une fois** (once) again, once more; **e. un** another (one), one more; **e. du pain** (some) more bread; **quoi e.?** what else?
(**e**) *(avec comparatif)* even, still; **e. mieux** even better, better still
(**f**) *(aussi)* **mais e.** but also
(**g**) **et e.** *(à peine)* if that, only just
(**h**) **e. que...** *(+ subjunctive)* although...

**encourager** [ɑ̃kuraʒe] *vt* to encourage (**à faire** to do) ▪ **encourageant, -e** *adj* encouraging ▪ **encouragement** *nm* encouragement

**encrasser** [ɑ̃krase] **1** *vt* to clog up (with dirt) **2 s'encrasser** *vpr* to get clogged up

**encre** [ɑ̃kr] *nf* ink

**encyclopédie** [ɑ̃siklɔpedi] *nf* encyclopedia

**endetter** [ɑ̃dete] **s'endetter** *vpr* to get

into debt ▪ **endettement** *nm* debts

**endimanché, -e** [ɑ̃dimɑ̃ʃe] *adj* in one's Sunday best

**endive** [ɑ̃div] *nf* chicory *inv*, endive

**endoctriner** [ɑ̃dɔktrine] *vt* to indoctrinate

**endolori, -e** [ɑ̃dɔlɔri] *adj* painful

**endommager** [ɑ̃dɔmaʒe] *vt* to damage

**endormir*** [ɑ̃dɔrmir] **1** *vt (enfant)* to put to sleep; *(ennuyer)* to send to sleep **2 s'endormir** *vpr* to fall asleep, to go to sleep ▪ **endormi, -e** *adj* asleep, sleeping

**endosser** [ɑ̃dose] *vt (vêtement)* to put on; *(chèque)* to endorse

**endroit** [ɑ̃drwa] *nm* (**a**) *(lieu)* place, spot; **par endroits** in places (**b**) *(de tissu)* right side; **à l'e.** *(vêtement)* the right way round

**enduire*** [ɑ̃dɥir] *vt* to smear, to coat (**de** with) ▪ **enduit** *nm* coating; *(de mur)* plaster

**endurant, -e** [ɑ̃dyrɑ̃, -ɑ̃t] *adj* hardy, tough ▪ **endurance** *nf* stamina; **course d'e.** endurance race

**endurcir** [ɑ̃dyrsir] **1** *vt* **e. qn à** *(douleur)* to harden sb to **2 s'endurcir** *vpr (moralement)* to become hard; *(physiquement)* to toughen up

**endurer** [ɑ̃dyre] *vt* to endure, to bear

**énergie** [enɛrʒi] *nf* energy ▪ **énergétique** *adj* **aliment é.** energy food; **ressources énergétiques** energy resources ▪ **énergique** *adj (personne)* energetic; *(mesure, ton)* forceful

**énerver** [enɛrve] **1** *vt* **é. qn** *(irriter)* to get on sb's nerves; *(rendre nerveux)* to make sb nervous **2 s'énerver** *vpr* to get worked up ▪ **énervé, -e** *adj (agacé)* irritated; *(excité)* on edge, agitated

**enfance** [ɑ̃fɑ̃s] *nf* childhood ▪ **enfantillages** *nmpl* childish behaviour ▪ **enfantin, -e** *adj (voix, joie)* childlike; *(langage)* children's; *(simple)* easy

**enfant** [ɑ̃fɑ̃] *nmf* child (*pl* children); **attendre un e.** to be expecting a baby; **e. unique** only child

**enfer** [ɑ̃fɛr] *nm* hell

**enfermer** [ɑ̃fɛrme] **1** *vt (personne, chose)* to shut up; **e. qn/qch à clef** to lock sb/sth up **2 s'enfermer** *vpr* **s'e. dans** *(chambre)* to shut oneself (up) in; **s'e. à clef** to lock oneself in

**enfiler** [ɑ̃file] *vt (aiguille)* to thread; *(perles)* to string; *Fam (vêtement)* to slip on

**enfin** [ɑ̃fɛ̃] *adv (à la fin)* finally, at last; *(en dernier lieu)* lastly; *(en somme)* in a word; *(de résignation)* well; *Fam* **e. bref…** *(en somme)* in a word…; **(mais) e.!** for heaven's sake!

**enflammer** [ɑ̃flame] **1** *vt* to set fire to; *(allumette)* to light **2 s'enflammer** *vpr* to catch fire

**enfler** [ɑ̃fle] *vi (membre)* to swell (up) ▪ **enflure** *nf* swelling

**enfoncer** [ɑ̃fɔ̃se] **1** *vt (clou)* to bang in; *(porte)* to smash in; **e. dans qch** *(couteau, mains)* to plunge into sth **2 s'enfoncer** *vpr (s'enliser)* to sink (**dans** into); *(couteau)* to go in; **s'e. dans** *(pénétrer)* to disappear into

**enfouir** [ɑ̃fwir] *vt* to bury

**enfourner** [ɑ̃furne] *vt* to put in the oven

**enfreindre*** [ɑ̃frɛ̃dr] *vt* to infringe

**enfuir*** [ɑ̃fɥir] **s'enfuir** *vpr* to run away (**de** from)

**engager** [ɑ̃gaʒe] **1** *vt (discussion, combat)* to start; *(bijou)* to pawn; *(clef)* to insert (**dans** into); **e. qn** *(embaucher)* to hire sb

**2 s'engager** *vpr (dans l'armée)* to enlist; *(prendre position)* to commit oneself; *(partie)* to start; **s'e. à faire qch** to undertake to do sth; **s'e. dans** *(voie)* to enter; *(affaire)* to get involved in ▪ **engagé, -e** *adj (écrivain)* committed ▪ **engageant, -e** *adj* engaging ▪ **engagement** *nm (promesse)* commitment; *(de soldats)* enlistment; *(au football)* kick-off; **prendre l'e. de faire qch** to undertake to do sth

**engelure** [ɑ̃ʒlyr] *nf* chilblain

**engendrer** [ɑ̃ʒɑ̃dre] *vt (causer)* to generate, to engender; *(procréer)* to father

**engin** [ɑ̃ʒɛ̃] *nm (machine)* machine; *(outil)* device; **e. explosif** explosive device; **e. spatial** spacecraft

**englober** [ɑ̃glɔbe] *vt* to include

**engloutir** [ɑ̃glutir] *vt (nourriture)* to wolf down; *(bateau, village)* to submerge

**engorger** [ɑ̃gɔrʒe] *vt* to block up, to clog

**engouement** [ɑ̃gumɑ̃] *nm* craze (**pour** for)

**engouffrer** [ɑ̃gufre] **s'engouffrer** *vpr* **s'e. dans** to rush into

**engourdir** [ɑ̃gurdir] **s'engourdir** *vpr (membre)* to go numb

**engrais** [ɑ̃grɛ] *nm* fertilizer

**engraisser** [ɑ̃grese] *vt (animal, personne)* to fatten up

**engrenage** [ɑ̃grənaʒ] *nm Tech* gears; *Fig* chain; *Fig* **pris dans l'e.** caught in a trap

**énigme** [enigm] *nf (devinette)* riddle; *(mystère)* enigma ▪ **énigmatique** *adj* enigmatic

**enjamber** [ɑ̃ʒɑ̃be] *vt* to step over; *(sujet: pont) (rivière)* to span ▪ **enjambée** *nf* stride

**enjeu, -x** [ɑ̃ʒø] *nm (mise)* stake; *Fig (de pari, de guerre)* stakes

**enjoliver** [ɑ̃ʒɔlive] *vt* to embellish

**enjoué, -e** [ɑ̃ʒwe] *adj* playful

**enlacer** [ɑ̃lɑse] *vt (mêler)* to entwine; *(embrasser)* to clasp

**enlaidir** [ɑ̃ledir] **1** *vt* to make ugly **2** *vi* to grow ugly

**enlevé, -e** [ɑ̃lve] *adj (style, danse)* lively

**enlever** [ɑ̃l(ə)ve] **1** *vt* to remove; *(meubles)* to take away, to remove; *(vêtement, couvercle)* to take off, to remove; *(tapis)* to take up; *(rideau)* to take down; *(enfant)* to kidnap, to abduct; *(ordures)* to collect **2 s'enlever** *vpr (tache)* to come out; *(vernis)* to come off ▪ **enlèvement** [-ɛvmɑ̃] *nm (d'enfant)* kidnapping, abduction; *(d'objet)* removal

**enliser** [ɑ̃lize] **s'enliser** *vpr (véhicule) & Fig* to get bogged down (**dans** in)

**enneigé, -e** [ɑ̃neʒe] *adj* snow-covered

**ennemi, -e** [enmi] **1** *nmf* enemy **2** *adj (personne)* hostile (**de** to)

**ennui** [ɑ̃nɥi] *nm (lassitude)* boredom; *(souci)* problem; **avoir des ennuis** *(soucis)* to be worried; *(problèmes)* to have problems

**ennuyer** [ɑ̃nɥije] **1** *vt (agacer)* to annoy; *(préoccuper)* to bother; *(lasser)* to bore **2 s'ennuyer** *vpr* to get bored ▪ **ennuyé, -e** *adj (air)* bored ▪ **ennuyeux, -euse** *adj (contrariant)* annoying; *(lassant)* boring

**énoncer** [enɔ̃se] *vt* to state

**énorme** [enɔrm] *adj* enormous, huge ▪ **énormément** *adv (travailler, pleurer)* an awful lot; **je le regrette é.** I'm awfully sorry about it; **il n'a pas é. d'argent** he hasn't got a huge amount of money ▪ **énormité** *nf (de demande, de crime, de somme)* enormity; *(faute)* glaring mistake

**enquête** [ɑ̃kɛt] *nf (de policiers, de journalistes)* investigation; *(judiciaire, administrative)* inquiry; *(sondage)* survey ▪ **enquêter** *vi (policier, journaliste)* to investigate; **e. sur qch** to investigate sth

**enraciner** [ɑ̃rasine] **s'enraciner** *vpr* to take root; **enraciné dans** *(personne, souvenir)* rooted in

**enrager** [ɑ̃raʒe] *vi* to be furious (**de faire** about doing); **faire e. qn** to get on sb's nerves ▪ **enragé, -e** *adj (chien)* rabid

**enrayer** [ɑ̃reje] **1** *vt (maladie)* to check **2 s'enrayer** *vpr (fusil)* to jam

**enregistrer** [ɑ̃r(ə)ʒistre] *vt (par écrit, sur bande)* to record; *(afficher)* to register; **faire e. ses bagages** *(à l'aéroport)* to check in, to check one's baggage in ▪ **enregistrement** [-əmɑ̃] *nm (sur bande)* recording; **l'e. des bagages** *(à l'aéroport)* (baggage) check-in; **se présenter à l'e.** to check in

**enrhumer** [ɑ̃ryme] **s'enrhumer** *vpr* to catch a cold; **être enrhumé** to have a cold

**enrichir** [ɑ̃riʃir] **1** *vt* to enrich (**de** with) **2 s'enrichir** *vpr (personne)* to get rich

**enrober** [ɑ̃rɔbe] *vt* to coat (**de** in)

**enrouer** [ɑ̃rwe] **s'enrouer** *vpr* to get hoarse

**enrouler** [ɑ̃rule] **1** *vt (fil)* to wind **2 s'enrouler** *vpr* **s'e. dans qch** *(couvertures)* to wrap oneself up in sth; **s'e. sur** *ou* **autour de qch** to wind round sth

**ensabler** [ɑ̃sable] **s'ensabler** *vpr (port)* to silt up

**ensanglanté, -e** [ɑ̃sɑ̃glɑ̃te] *adj* bloodstained

**enseignant, -e** [ɑ̃sɛɲɑ̃, -ɑ̃t] **1** *nmf* teacher **2** *adj* **corps e.** teaching profession

**enseigne** [ɑ̃sɛɲ] **1** *nf (de magasin)* sign; **e. lumineuse** neon sign **2** *nm* **e. de vaisseau** *Br* lieutenant, *Am* ensign

**enseigner** [ɑ̃seɲe] **1** *vt* to teach; **e. qch à qn** to teach sb sth **2** *vi* to teach ▪ **enseignement** [-ɛɲmɑ̃] *nm* education; *(action, métier)* teaching; **e. par correspondance** distance learning; **e. privé** private education; **e. public** *Br* state *or Am* public education

**ensemble** [ɑ̃sɑ̃bl] **1** *adv* together; **aller (bien) e.** *(couleurs)* to go (well) together; *(personnes)* to be well-matched **2** *nm (d'objets)* group, set; *Math* set; *(vêtement)* outfit; *(harmonie)* unity; **l'e. du personnel** *(totalité)* the whole (of the) staff; **l'e. des enseignants** all (of) the teachers; **dans l'e.** on the whole

**ensevelir** [ɑ̃səvlir] *vt* to bury

**ensoleillé, -e** [ɑ̃sɔleje] *adj (endroit, journée)* sunny

**ensommeillé, -e** [ɑ̃sɔmeje] *adj* sleepy

**ensorceler** [ɑ̃sɔrsəle] *vt (envoûter, séduire)* to bewitch

**ensuite** [ɑ̃sɥit] *adv (puis)* next, then; *(plus tard)* afterwards

**ensuivre*** [ɑ̃sɥivr] **s'ensuivre** *v impersonnel* **il s'ensuit que...** it follows that...

**entailler** [ɑ̃taje] *vt (fendre)* to notch; *(blesser)* to gash, to slash

**entamer** [ɑ̃tame] *vt (pain)* to cut into; *(bouteille, boîte)* to open; *(négociations)* to enter into

**entartrer** [ɑ̃tartre] *vt*, **s'entartrer** *vpr (chaudière) Br* to fur up, *Am* to scale

**entasser** [ɑ̃tɑse] *vt*, **s'entasser** *vpr (objets)* to pile up, to heap up

**entendre** [ɑ̃tɑ̃dr] **1** *vt* to hear; *(comprendre)* to understand; **e. parler de qn/qch** to hear of sb/sth; **e. dire que...** to hear (it said) that... **2 s'entendre** *vpr (être entendu)* to be heard; *(être compris)* to be understood; **s'e.** *(être d'accord)* to agree (**sur** on); **(bien) s'e. avec qn** to get along *or Br* on with sb

**entendu, -e** [ɑ̃tɑ̃dy] *adj (convenu)* agreed; *(sourire, air)* knowing; **e.!** all right!; **bien e.** of course

**entente** [ɑ̃tɑ̃t] *nf (accord)* agreement, understanding; **(bonne) e.** *(amitié)* harmony

**entériner** [ɑ̃terine] *vt* to ratify

**enterrer** [ɑ̃tere] *vt (défunt)* to bury; *Fig (projet)* to scrap ▪ **enterrement** [-ɛrmɑ̃] *nm (ensevelissement)* burial; *(funérailles)* funeral

**en-tête** [ɑ̃tɛt] (*pl* **en-têtes**) *nm (de papier)* heading; **papier à e.** headed paper, letterhead

**entêter** [ɑ̃tete] **s'entêter** *vpr* to persist (**à faire** in doing) ▪ **entêté, -e** *adj* stubborn

**enthousiasme** [ɑ̃tuzjasm] *nm* enthusiasm ▪ **enthousiaste** *adj* enthusiastic

**enticher** [ɑ̃tiʃe] **s'enticher** *vpr* **s'e. de qn/qch** to become infatuated with sb/sth

**entier, -ère** [ɑ̃tje, -ɛr] **1** *adj (total)* whole, entire; *(intact)* intact; *(absolu)* absolute, complete; *(caractère)* uncompromising; **le pays tout e.** the whole *or* entire country **2** *nm* **en e.** in its entirety, completely

**entonner** [ɑ̃tɔne] *vt (air)* to start singing

**entonnoir** [ɑ̃tɔnwar] *nm* funnel

**entorse** [ɑ̃tɔrs] *nf Méd* sprain; **se faire une e. à la cheville** to sprain one's ankle

**entortiller** [ɑ̃tɔrtije] **1** *vt* to wrap (**dans** in) **2 s'entortiller** *vpr (lierre)* to coil (**autour de** round)

**entourage** [ɑ̃turaʒ] *nm (proches)* circle of family and friends

**entourer** [ɑ̃ture] **1** *vt* to surround (**de** with); *(envelopper)* to wrap (**de** in); **entouré de** surrounded by **2 s'entourer** *vpr* **s'e. de** to surround oneself with

**entracte** [ɑ̃trakt] *nm Br* interval, *Am* intermission

**entraide** [ɑ̃trɛd] *nf* mutual aid ■ **s'entraider** *vpr* to help each other

**entraînant, -e** [ɑ̃trɛnɑ̃, -ɑ̃t] *adj (musique)* lively

**entraîner** [ɑ̃trene] **1** *vt* (**a**) *(charrier)* to carry away; *(causer)* to bring about; *(dépenses)* to entail; **e. qn** *(emmener)* to lead sb away; *(de force)* to drag sb away; *(attirer)* to lure sb; **se laisser e.** to allow oneself to be led astray
(**b**) *(athlète, cheval)* to train (**à** for)
**2 s'entraîner** *vpr* to train oneself (**à faire qch** to do sth); *Sport* to train ■ **entraînement** [-ɛnmɑ̃] *nm Sport* training; *(élan)* impulse ■ **entraîneur** [-ɛnœr] *nm (d'athlète)* coach; *(de cheval)* trainer

**entraver** [ɑ̃trave] *vt* to hinder, to hamper

**entre** [ɑ̃tr] *prép* between; *(parmi)* among(st); **l'un d'e. vous** one of you; **se dévorer e. eux** *(réciprocité)* to devour each other

**entrebâiller** [ɑ̃trəbɑje] *vt (porte)* to open slightly

**entrecôte** [ɑ̃trəkot] *nf* rib steak

**entrecouper** [ɑ̃trəkupe] *vt (entremêler)* to punctuate (**de** with)

**entrée** [ɑ̃tre] *nf (action)* entry, entrance; *(porte)* entrance; *(vestibule)* entrance hall, entry; *(accès)* admission, entry (**de** to); *Ordinat* input; *(plat)* starter; **faire son e.** to make one's entrance; **'e. interdite'** 'no entry', 'no admittance'; **'e. libre'** 'admission free'; **e. de service** service *or Br* tradesmen's entrance; **e. des artistes** stage door

**entrelacer** [ɑ̃trəlase] *vt*, **s'entrelacer** *vpr* to intertwine

**entremêler** [ɑ̃trəmele] *vt*, **s'entremêler** *vpr* to intermingle

**entremets** [ɑ̃trəmɛ] *nm (plat)* dessert, *Br* sweet

**entreposer** [ɑ̃trəpoze] *vt* to store ■ **entrepôt** *nm* warehouse

**entreprendre*** [ɑ̃trəprɑ̃dr] *vt (travail, voyage)* to undertake; **e. de faire qch** to undertake to do sth ■ **entreprenant, -e** [-ənɑ̃, -ɑ̃t] *adj (dynamique)* enterprising; *(galant)* forward

**entrepreneur** [ɑ̃trəprənœr] *nm (en bâtiment)* contractor; *(chef d'entreprise)* entrepreneur

**entreprise** [ɑ̃trəpriz] *nf (firme)* company, firm

**entrer** [ɑ̃tre] **1** *vi (aux* **être**) *(aller)* to go in, to enter; *(venir)* to come in, to enter; **e. dans** to go into; *(pièce)* to come/go into, to enter; **e. à l'université** to start university; **e. dans les détails** to go into detail; **entrez!** come in!
**2** *vt (aux* **avoir**) *Ordinat* **e. des données** to enter data (**dans** into)

**entresol** [ɑ̃trəsɔl] *nm* mezzanine floor

**entre-temps** [ɑ̃trətɑ̃] *adv* meanwhile

**entretenir*** [ɑ̃trətnir] **1** *vt (voiture, maison, famille)* to maintain; *(relations)* to keep; **e. qn de qch** to talk to sb about sth **2 s'entretenir** *vpr* **s'e. de qch** to talk about sth (**avec** with) ■ **entretenu, -e** *adj* **bien/mal e.** *(maison)* well-kept/badly kept

**entretien** [ɑ̃trətjɛ̃] *nm (de route, de maison)* maintenance, upkeep; *(dialogue)* conversation; *(entrevue)* interview

**entrevoir*** [ɑ̃trəvwar] *vt (rapidement)* to catch a glimpse of; *(pressentir)* to foresee

**entrevue** [ɑ̃trəvy] *nf* interview

**entrouvrir*** [ɑ̃truvrir] *vt*, **s'entrouvrir** *vpr* to half-open ■ **entrouvert, -e** *adj (porte, fenêtre)* half-open

**énumérer** [enymere] *vt* to list ▪ **énumération** *nf* listing
**envahir** [ɑ̃vair] *vt (pays)* to invade; *(marché)* to flood; **e. qn** *(doute, peur)* to overcome sb ▪ **envahissant, -e** *adj (personne)* intrusive ▪ **envahisseur** *nm* invader
**enveloppant, -e** [ɑ̃vlɔpɑ̃, -ɑ̃t] *adj (séduisant)* captivating
**enveloppe** [ɑ̃vlɔp] *nf (pour lettre)* envelope
**envelopper** [ɑ̃vlɔpe] **1** *vt* to wrap (up) (**dans** in) **2 s'envelopper** *vpr* to wrap oneself (up) (**dans** in)
**envenimer** [ɑ̃vnime] **s'envenimer** *vpr (plaie)* to turn septic; *Fig* to become acrimonious
**envergure** [ɑ̃vɛrgyr] *nf (d'avion, d'oiseau)* wingspan; *(de personne)* calibre; *(ampleur)* scope
**envers** [ɑ̃vɛr] **1** *prép Br* towards, *Am* toward(s), to **2** *nm (de tissu)* wrong side; **à l'e.** *(chaussette)* inside out; *(pantalon)* back to front; *(la tête en bas)* upside down
**envie** [ɑ̃vi] *nf (jalousie)* envy; *(désir)* desire; **avoir e. de qch** to want sth; **avoir e. de faire qch** to feel like doing sth ▪ **envier** *vt* to envy (**qch à qn** sb sth) ▪ **envieux, -euse** *adj* envious
**environ** [ɑ̃virɔ̃] *adv (à peu près)* about ▪ **environs** *nmpl* outskirts, surroundings; **aux e. de qch** around sth, in the vicinity of sth
**environnant, -e** [ɑ̃virɔnɑ̃, -ɑ̃t] *adj* surrounding
**environnement** [ɑ̃virɔnmɑ̃] *nm* environment
**envisager** [ɑ̃vizaʒe] *vt (considérer)* to consider; *(projeter) Br* to envisage, *Am* to envision; **e. de faire qch** to consider doing sth
**envoi** [ɑ̃vwa] *nm (action)* sending; *(paquet)* package; *(marchandises)* consignment
**envoler** [ɑ̃vɔle] **s'envoler** *vpr (oiseau)* to fly away; *(avion)* to take off; *(chapeau, papier)* to blow away; *Fig (espoir)* to vanish
**envoûter** [ɑ̃vute] *vt* to bewitch
**envoyer*** [ɑ̃vwaje] *vt* to send; *(lancer)* to throw; **e. chercher qn** to send for sb ▪ **envoyé, -e** *nmf* envoy; **e. spécial** *(reporter)* special correspondent ▪ **envoyeur** *nm* sender; **retour à l'e.** 'return to sender'
**épais, -aisse** [epɛ, -ɛs] *adj* thick ▪ **épaisseur** *nf* thickness; **avoir 1 mètre d'é.** to be 1 metre thick ▪ **épaissir** [epesir] **1** *vt* to thicken **2** *vi*, **s'épaissir** *vpr* to thicken; *(grossir)* to fill out; **le mystère s'épaissit** the mystery is deepening
**épanouir** [epanwir] **s'épanouir** *vpr (fleur)* to bloom; *Fig (personne)* to blossom; *(visage)* to beam ▪ **épanoui, -e** *adj (fleur, personne)* in full bloom; *(visage)* beaming ▪ **épanouissement** *nm (de fleur)* full bloom; *(de personne)* blossoming
**épargne** [eparɲ] *nf (action, vertu)* saving; *(sommes)* savings ▪ **épargnant, -e** *nmf* saver ▪ **épargner** *vt (argent, provisions)* to save; *(ennemi)* to spare; **e. qch à qn** *(ennuis, chagrin)* to spare sb sth
**éparpiller** [eparpije] *vt*, **s'éparpiller** *vpr* to scatter; *(efforts)* to dissipate
**épaule** [epol] *nf* shoulder ▪ **épauler 1** *vt (fusil)* to raise (to one's shoulder); **é. qn** *(aider)* to back sb up **2** *vi* to take aim ▪ **épaulette** *nf (de veste)* shoulder pad
**épave** [epav] *nf (bateau, personne)* wreck
**épée** [epe] *nf* sword
**épeler** [eple] *vt* to spell
**éperon** [eprɔ̃] *nm (de cavalier, de coq)* spur
**épi** [epi] *nm (de blé)* ear; *(de cheveux)* tuft of hair
**épice** [epis] *nf* spice ▪ **épicé, -e** *adj (plat, récit)* spicy ▪ **épicer** *vt* to spice
**épicier, -ère** [episje, -ɛr] *nmf* grocer ▪ **épicerie** *nf (magasin) Br* grocer's (shop), *Am* grocery (store); **é. fine** delicatessen
**épidémie** [epidemi] *nf* epidemic

**épier** [epje] *vt (observer)* to watch closely; *(occasion)* to watch out for; **é. qn** to spy on sb

**épiler** [epile] **s'épiler** *vpr* to remove unwanted hair; **s'é. les jambes à la cire** to wax one's legs

**épilogue** [epilɔg] *nm* epilogue

**épinards** [epinar] *nmpl* spinach

**épine** [epin] *nf (de plante)* thorn; *(d'animal)* spine, prickle ■ **épineux, -euse** *adj (tige, question)* thorny; *(poisson)* spiny

**épingle** [epɛ̃gl] *nf* pin; **é. à nourrice** safety pin; **é. à linge** *Br* clothes peg, *Am* clothes pin ■ **épingler** *vt* to pin

**Épiphanie** [epifani] *nf* **l'É.** Epiphany

**épique** [epik] *adj* epic

**épiscopal, -e, -aux, -ales** [episkɔpal, -o] *adj* episcopal

**épisode** [epizɔd] *nm* episode ■ **épisodique** *adj (intermittent)* occasional

**épitaphe** [epitaf] *nf* epitaph

**éplucher** [eplyʃe] *vt (carotte, pomme)* to peel ■ **épluchure** *nf* peeling

**éponge** [epɔ̃ʒ] *nf* sponge; *Fig* **jeter l'é.** to throw in the towel ■ **éponger 1** *vt (liquide)* to mop up; *(dette)* to absorb **2 s'éponger** *vpr* **s'é. le front** to mop one's brow

**époque** [epɔk] *nf (date)* time, period; *(historique)* age; **meubles d'é.** period furniture; **à l'é.** at the *or* that time

**épouse** [epuz] *nf* wife

**épouser** [epuze] *vt* to marry

**épousseter** [epuste] *vt* to dust

**épouvantable** [epuvɑ̃tabl] *adj* appalling

**épouvantail** [epuvɑ̃taj] *nm (de jardin)* scarecrow

**épouvante** [epuvɑ̃t] *nf* terror ■ **épouvanter** *vt* to terrify

**époux** [epu] *nm* husband; **les é.** the husband and wife

**éprendre*** [eprɑ̃dr] **s'éprendre** *vpr* **s'é. de qn** to fall in love with sb

**épreuve** [eprœv] *nf (essai, examen)* test; *(sportive)* event; *(malheur)* ordeal, trial; *(photo)* print; **mettre qn à l'é.** to put sb to the test; **à toute é.** *(patience)* unfailing; *(nerfs)* rock-solid; **à l'é. du feu** fireproof

**éprouver** [epruve] *vt (méthode, personne)* to test; *(sentiment)* to feel; *(difficultés)* to meet with ■ **éprouvant, -e** *adj (pénible)* trying

**éprouvette** [epruvɛt] *nf* test tube

**EPS** [əpeɛs] *(abrév* **éducation physique et sportive**) *nf* PE

**épuiser** [epɥize] **1** *vt (personne, provisions, sujet)* to exhaust **2 s'épuiser** *vpr (réserves, patience)* to run out; **s'é. à faire qch** to exhaust oneself doing sth ■ **épuisant, -e** *adj* exhausting ■ **épuisé, -e** *adj* exhausted; *(marchandise)* sold out; *(édition)* out of print

**épuisette** [epɥizɛt] *nf* landing net

**épurer** [epyre] *vt (eau, gaz)* to purify; *(minerai)* to refine ■ **épuration** *nf* purification; *(de minerai)* refining

**équateur** [ekwatœr] *nm* equator; **sous l'é.** at the equator

**équation** [ekwɑsjɔ̃] *nf Math* equation

**équerre** [ekɛr] *nf* **é. (à dessin)** *Br* set square, *Am* triangle

**équestre** [ekɛstr] *adj (statue, sports)* equestrian

**équilibre** [ekilibr] *nm* balance; **garder/perdre l'é.** to keep/lose one's balance

**équilibrer** [ekilibre] *vt (charge, composition, budget)* to balance

**équinoxe** [ekinɔks] *nm* equinox

**équipage** [ekipaʒ] *nm (de navire, d'avion)* crew

**équipe** [ekip] *nf* team; *(d'ouvriers)* gang; **faire é. avec qn** to team up with sb; **é. de nuit** night shift; **é. de secours** rescue team ■ **équipier, -ère** *nmf* team member

**équiper** [ekipe] **1** *vt* to equip (**de** with) **2 s'équiper** *vpr* to equip oneself (**de** with) ■ **équipement** *nm* equipment

**équitable** [ekitabl] *adj* fair, equitable

**équitation** [ekitɑsjɔ̃] *nf Br* (horse) riding, *Am* (horseback) riding; **faire de l'é.** to go riding

**équivalent, -e** [ekivalɑ̃, -ɑ̃t] *adj & nm*

equivalent ■ **équivalence** *nf* equivalence ■ **équivaloir*** *vi* **é. à qch** to be equivalent to sth

**équivoque** [ekivɔk] **1** *adj (ambigu)* equivocal; *(douteux)* dubious **2** *nf* ambiguity

**érable** [erabl] *nm (arbre, bois)* maple

**érafler** [erafle] *vt* to graze, to scratch ■ **éraflure** *nf* graze, scratch

**ère** [ɛr] *nf* era; **avant notre è.** BC; **en l'an 800 de notre è.** in the year 800 AD

**éreinter** [erɛ̃te] **1** *vt (fatiguer)* to exhaust **2 s'éreinter** *vpr* **s'é. à faire qch** to wear oneself out doing sth

**ériger** [eriʒe] **1** *vt* to erect **2 s'ériger** *vpr* **s'é. en qch** to set oneself up as sth

**érosion** [erozjɔ̃] *nf* erosion ■ **éroder** *vt* to erode

**errer** [ɛre] *vi* to wander ■ **errant** *adj m* **chien/chat e.** stray dog/cat

**erreur** [ɛrœr] *nf (faute)* mistake, error; **par e.** by mistake; **e. judiciaire** miscarriage of justice

**érudit, -e** [erydi, -it] **1** *adj* scholarly, erudite **2** *nmf* scholar ■ **érudition** *nf* scholarship, erudition

**éruption** [erypsjɔ̃] *nf (de volcan)* eruption; *(de boutons)* rash

**es** [ɛ] *voir* **être**

**ès** [ɛs] *prép* of; **licencié ès lettres** ≃ BA; **docteur ès lettres** ≃ PhD

**escabeau, -x** [ɛskabo] *nm (marchepied)* stepladder, *Br* (pair of) steps; *(tabouret)* stool

**escadrille** [ɛskadrij] *nf Aviat (unité)* flight

**escadron** [ɛskadrɔ̃] *nm* squadron

**escalade** [ɛskalad] *nf* climbing; *(de prix, de violence)* escalation ■ **escalader** *vt* to climb, to scale

**escale** [ɛskal] *nf Aviat* stopover; *Naut (lieu)* port of call; **faire e. à** *(avion)* to stop (over) at; *(navire)* to put in at; **vol sans e.** non-stop flight

**escalier** [ɛskalje] *nm (marches)* stairs; *(cage)* staircase; **l'é., les escaliers** the stairs; **e. mécanique** *ou* **roulant** escalator; **e. de secours** fire escape

**escalope** [ɛskalɔp] *nf* escalope

**escamoter** [ɛskamɔte] *vt (faire disparaître)* to make vanish; *(esquiver)* to dodge

**escapade** [ɛskapad] *nf* jaunt

**escargot** [ɛskargo] *nm* snail

**escarpé, -e** [ɛskarpe] *adj* steep ■ **escarpement** [-əmɑ̃] *nm (côte)* steep slope

**escarpin** [ɛskarpɛ̃] *nm (soulier)* pump, *Br* court shoe

**esclave** [ɛsklav] *nmf* slave ■ **esclavage** *nm* slavery

**escompte** [ɛskɔ̃t] *nm* discount; **taux d'e.** bank discount rate ■ **escompter** *vt (espérer)* to anticipate (**faire** doing), to expect (**faire** to do)

**escorte** [ɛskɔrt] *nf* escort ■ **escorter** *vt* to escort

**escrime** [ɛskrim] *nf* fencing; **faire de l'e.** to fence ■ **escrimeur, -euse** *nmf* fencer

**escrimer** [ɛskrime] **s'escrimer** *vpr* **s'e. à faire qch** to struggle to do sth

**escroc** [ɛskro] *nm* crook, swindler ■ **escroquer** *vt* **e. qn** to swindle sb; **e. qch à qn** to swindle sb out of sth ■ **escroquerie** *nf (action)* swindling; *(résultat)* swindle

**espace** [ɛspas] *nm* space; **e. aérien** air space; **e. vert** garden, park

**espacer** [ɛspase] **1** *vt* to space out; **espacés d'un mètre** one metre apart **2 s'espacer** *vpr (maisons, visites)* to become less frequent

**espadrille** [ɛspadrij] *nf* = rope-soled sandal

**Espagne** [ɛspaɲ] *nf* **l'E.** Spain ■ **espagnol, -e 1** *adj* Spanish **2** *nmf* **E., Espagnole** Spaniard **3** *nm (langue)* Spanish

**espèce** [ɛspɛs] *nf (race)* species; *(genre)* kind, sort ■ **espèces** *nfpl (argent)* cash; **en e.** in cash

**espérance** [ɛsperɑ̃s] *nf* hope; **e. de vie** life expectancy

**espérer** [ɛspere] **1** *vt* to hope for; **e. que...** to hope that...; **e. faire qch** to hope to do sth **2** *vi* to hope; **j'espère (bien)!** I hope so!

**espiègle** [ɛspjɛgl] *adj* mischievous
**espion, -onne** [ɛspjɔ̃, -ɔn] *nmf* spy ▪ **espionnage** *nm* spying, espionage ▪ **espionner 1** *vt* to spy on **2** *vi* to spy
**espoir** [ɛspwar] *nm* hope; **avoir l'e. de faire qch** to have hopes of doing sth
**esprit** [ɛspri] *nm (attitude, fantôme)* spirit; *(intellect)* mind; *(humour)* wit; **venir à l'e. de qn** to cross sb's mind; **avoir de l'e.** to be witty; **avoir l'e. large/étroit** to be broad-/narrow-minded
**esquimau, -aude, -aux, -audes** [ɛskimo, -od] **1** *adj* Eskimo, *Am* Inuit **2** *nmf* **E., Esquimaude** Eskimo, *Am* Inuit **3** *nm* **Esquimau®** *(glace) Br* ≃ choc-ice *(on a stick)*, *Am* ≃ ice-cream bar
**esquisse** [ɛskis] *nf (croquis, plan)* sketch ▪ **esquisser** *vt* to sketch; **e. un geste** to make a (slight) gesture
**esquiver** [ɛskive] **1** *vt (coup, problème)* to dodge **2 s'esquiver** *vpr* to slip away
**essai** [esɛ] *nm (test)* test, trial; *(tentative, au rugby)* try; *(ouvrage)* essay; **à l'e.** *(objet)* on a trial basis
**essaim** [esɛ̃] *nm* swarm
**essayer** [eseje] *vt* to try (**de faire** to do); *(vêtement)* to try on; *(méthode)* to try out ▪ **essayage** [-ɛjaʒ] *nm (de vêtement)* fitting
**essence** [esɑ̃s] *nf (carburant) Br* petrol, *Am* gas; *(extrait) & Phil* essence; **e. sans plomb** unleaded; **e. ordinaire** *Br* two-star petrol, *Am* regular gas
**essentiel, -elle** [esɑ̃sjɛl] **1** *adj* essential (**à/pour** for) **2** *nm* **l'e.** *(le plus important)* the main thing; *(le minimum)* the essentials
**essor** [esɔr] *nm (d'oiseau)* flight; *(de pays, d'entreprise)* rapid growth; **en plein e.** booming; **prendre son e.** to take off
**essorer** [esɔre] *vt (dans une essoreuse)* to spin-dry; *(dans une machine à laver)* to spin
**essouffler** [esufle] **1** *vt* to make out of breath **2 s'essouffler** *vpr* to get out of breath
**essuyer** [esɥije] **1** *vt (objet, surface)* to wipe; *(liquide)* to wipe up; *(larmes)* to wipe away; *(défaite)* to suffer; *(refus)* to meet with; **e. la vaisselle** to dry the dishes **2 s'essuyer** *vpr* to wipe oneself; **s'e. les yeux** to wipe one's eyes ▪ **essuie-glace** (*pl* **essuie-glaces**) *nm Br* windscreen wiper, *Am* windshield wiper
**est**[1] [ɛ] *voir* **être**
**est**[2] [ɛst] **1** *nm* east; **à l'e.** in the east; *(direction)* (to the) east (**de** of); **d'e.** *(vent)* east(erly); **de l'e.** eastern **2** *adj inv (côte)* east(ern)
**estampe** [ɛstɑ̃p] *nf* print
**estampille** [ɛstɑ̃pij] *nf (de produit)* mark; *(de document)* stamp
**esthéticienne** [ɛstetisjɛn] *nf* beautician
**estime** [ɛstim] *nf* esteem, regard
**estimer** [ɛstime] **1** *vt (tableau)* to value (**à** at); *(prix, distance, poids)* to estimate; *(dommages, besoins)* to assess; *(juger)* to consider (**que** that); **e. qn** to esteem sb
**2 s'estimer** *vpr* **s'e. heureux** to consider oneself happy ▪ **estimable** *adj* respectable ▪ **estimation** *nf (de mobilier)* valuation; *(de prix, de distance, de poids)* estimation; *(de dommages, de besoins)* assessment
**estival, -e, -aux, -ales** [ɛstival, -o] *adj* **température estivale** summer temperature ▪ **estivant, -e** *nmf Br* holidaymaker, *Am* vacationer
**estomac** [ɛstɔma] *nm* stomach
**estomper** [ɛstɔ̃pe] **1** *vt (rendre flou)* to blur **2 s'estomper** *vpr* to become blurred
**estrade** [ɛstrad] *nf* platform
**estragon** [ɛstragɔ̃] *nm* tarragon
**esturgeon** [ɛstyrʒɔ̃] *nm* sturgeon
**et** [e] *conj* and; **vingt et un** twenty-one; **et moi?** what about me?
**établi** [etabli] *nm* workbench
**établir** [etablir] **1** *vt (paix, relations, principe)* to establish; *(liste)* to draw up; *(record)* to set; *(démontrer)* to establish, to prove **2 s'établir** *vpr (pour habiter)* to settle; *(pour exercer un*

*métier)* to set up in business ▪ **établissement** *nm (de paix, de relations, de principe)* establishment; *(entreprise)* business, firm; **é. scolaire** school

**étage** [etaʒ] *nm (d'immeuble)* floor, *Br* storey, *Am* story; *(de fusée)* stage; **à l'é.** upstairs; **au premier é.** on the *Br* first *or Am* second floor; **maison à deux étages** *Br* two-storeyed *or Am* two-storied house

**étagère** [etaʒɛr] *nf* shelf; *(meuble)* shelving unit

**étain** [etɛ̃] *nm (métal)* tin; *(de gobelet)* pewter

**étais, était** [etɛ] *voir* **être**

**étal** [etal] *(pl* **étals***) nm (au marché)* stall

**étalage** [etalaʒ] *nm* display; *(vitrine)* display window

**étaler** [etale] **1** *vt (disposer)* to lay out; *(en vitrine)* to display; *(beurre)* to spread; *(vacances, paiements)* to stagger **2 s'étaler** *vpr* **s'é. sur** *(congés, paiements)* to be spread over ▪ **étalement** *nm (de vacances, de paiements)* staggering

**étanche** [etɑ̃ʃ] *adj* watertight; *(montre)* waterproof

**étancher** [etɑ̃ʃe] *vt (sang)* to stop the flow of; *(soif)* to quench

**étang** [etɑ̃] *nm* pond

**étant** [etɑ̃] *p prés de* **être**

**étape** [etap] *nf (de voyage)* stage; *(lieu)* stop(over); **faire é. à** to stop off *or* over at; **par étapes** in stages

**état** [eta] *nm* (**a**) *(condition, manière d'être)* state; **à l'é. neuf** as new; **en bon é.** in good condition; **é. d'esprit** state *or* frame of mind; **é. des lieux** inventory of fixtures; **é. civil** register office (**b**) *(autorité centrale)* **É.** *(nation)* State

**état-major** [etamaʒɔr] *(pl* **états-majors***) nm Mil* (general) staff; *(de parti)* senior staff

**États-Unis** [etazyni] *nmpl* **les É.** the United States; **les É. d'Amérique** the United States of America

**étau, -x** [eto] *nm (instrument) Br* vice, *Am* vise

**été**[1] [ete] *nm* summer

**été**[2] [ete] *pp de* **être**

**éteindre*** [etɛ̃dr] **1** *vt (feu, cigarette)* to put out, to extinguish; *(lampe)* to switch off; *(gaz)* to turn off **2** *vi* to switch off **3 s'éteindre** *vpr (feu)* to go out; *(personne)* to pass away ▪ **éteint, -e** *adj (feu, bougie)* out; *(lampe, lumière)* off; *(volcan)* extinct

**étendre** [etɑ̃dr] **1** *vt (linge)* to hang out; *(agrandir)* to extend; **é. le bras** to stretch out one's arm; **é. qn** to stretch sb out **2 s'étendre** *vpr (personne)* to lie down; *(plaine)* to stretch; *(feu)* to spread; **s'é. sur qch** *(sujet)* to dwell on sth

**étendu, -e**[1] [etɑ̃dy] *adj (forêt, vocabulaire)* extensive; *(personne)* lying

**étendue**[2] [etɑ̃dy] *nf (importance)* extent; *(surface)* area

**éternel, -elle** [etɛrnɛl] *adj* eternal ▪ **s'éterniser** *vpr (débat)* to drag on endlessly; *Fam (visiteur)* to stay for ever ▪ **éternité** *nf* eternity

**éternuer** [etɛrnɥe] *vi* to sneeze

**êtes** [ɛt] *voir* **être**

**Éthiopie** [etjɔpi] *nf* **l'É.** Ethiopia ▪ **éthiopien, -enne 1** *adj* Ethiopian **2** *nmf* **É., Éthiopienne** Ethiopian

**ethnie** [ɛtni] *nf* ethnic group ▪ **ethnique** *adj* ethnic

**étinceler** [etɛ̃sle] *vi* to sparkle ▪ **étincelle** *nf* spark

**étiqueter** [etikte] *vt* to label ▪ **étiquette** *nf (marque)* label; *(protocole)* (diplomatic *or* court) etiquette

**étirer** [etire] **1** *vt* to stretch **2 s'étirer** *vpr* to stretch (oneself)

**étoffe** [etɔf] *nf* material, fabric

**étoffer** [etɔfe] **1** *vt* to fill out; *(texte)* to make more meaty **2 s'étoffer** *vpr (personne)* to fill out

**étoile** [etwal] *nf* star; **à la belle é.** in the open; **é. de mer** starfish; **é. filante** shooting star

**étonner** [etɔne] **1** *vt* to surprise **2 s'étonner** *vpr* to be surprised (**de qch** at sth; **que** + *subjunctive* that) ▪ **étonnant, -e** *adj (ahurissant)* surprising;

*(remarquable)* amazing ▪ **étonnement** *nm* surprise

**étouffant, -e** [etufɑ̃, -ɑ̃t] *adj (air)* stifling

**étouffer** [etufe] **1** *vt (tuer)* to suffocate; *Fig (révolte)* to stifle; *Fig (scandale)* to hush up **2** *vi* to suffocate **3 s'étouffer** *vpr (en mangeant)* to choke (**avec** on); *(mourir)* to suffocate

**étourdi, -e** [eturdi] **1** *adj* scatterbrained **2** *nmf* scatterbrain ▪ **étourderie** *nf* absent-mindedness; **une é.** a thoughtless blunder

**étourdissant, -e** [eturdisɑ̃, -ɑ̃t] *adj (bruit)* deafening; *(beauté)* stunning

**étourdissement** [eturdismɑ̃] *nm (malaise)* dizzy spell

**étrange** [etrɑ̃ʒ] *adj* strange, odd ▪ **étranger, -ère 1** *adj (d'un autre pays)* foreign; *(non familier)* strange (**à** to) **2** *nmf (d'un autre pays)* foreigner; *(inconnu)* stranger; **à l'é.** abroad

**étrangler** [etrɑ̃gle] **1** *vt* **é. qn** *(tuer)* to strangle sb **2 s'étrangler** *vpr (de colère, en mangeant)* to choke ▪ **étranglé, -e** *adj (voix)* choking

**ÊTRE*** [ɛtr] **1** *vi* to be; **il est professeur** he's a teacher; **est-ce qu'elle vient?** is she coming?; **il vient, n'est-ce pas?** he's coming, isn't he?; **est-ce qu'il aime le thé?** does he like tea?; **nous sommes dix** there are ten of us; **nous sommes le dix** today is the tenth; **il a été à Paris** *(il y est allé)* he has been to Paris; **elle est de Paris** she's from Paris; **il est cinq heures** it's five (o'clock); **c'est à lire pour demain** this has to be read for tomorrow; **c'est à lui** it's his

**2** *v aux (avec 'venir', 'partir' etc)* to have/to be; **elle est arrivée** she has arrived; **elle est née en 1999** she was born in 1999

**3** *nm (personne)* being; **les êtres chers** the loved ones; **ê. humain** human being; **ê. vivant** living being

**étreindre*** [etrɛ̃dr] *vt* to grip; *(avec amour)* to embrace

**étrennes** [etrɛn] *nfpl* New Year gift; *(gratification)* ≃ Christmas tip *or Br* box

**étrier** [etrije] *nm* stirrup

**étroit, -e** [etrwa, -at] *adj* narrow; *(vêtement)* tight; *(lien, collaboration)* close; **être à l'é.** to be cramped

**étude** [etyd] *nf (action, ouvrage)* study; *(de notaire)* office; *Scol (pièce)* study room; *(période)* study period; **à l'é.** *(projet)* under consideration; **faire des études de français** to study French; **faire une é. de marché** to do market research

**étudiant, -e** [etydjɑ̃, -ɑ̃t] **1** *nmf* student **2** *adj (vie)* student

**étudier** [etydje] *vti* to study

**étui** [etɥi] *nm (à lunettes, à cigarettes)* case; *(de revolver)* holster

**eu, eue** [y] *pp de* **avoir**

**eurent** [yr] *voir* **avoir**

**euro** [əro] *nm (monnaie)* Euro

**euro-** [øro] *préf* Euro-

**eurodéputé** [ørodepyte] *nm* Euro MP

**Europe** [ørɔp] *nf* **l'E.** Europe; **l'E. verte** European Union agriculture ▪ **européen, -enne 1** *adj* European **2** *nmf* **E., Européenne** European

**eut** [y] *voir* **avoir**

**euthanasie** [øtanazi] *nf* euthanasia

**eux** [ø] *pron personnel (sujet)* they; *(complément)* them; *(réfléchi, emphase)* themselves ▪ **eux-mêmes** *pron* themselves

**évacuer** [evakɥe] *vt (bâtiment)* to evacuate; *(liquide)* to drain off ▪ **évacuation** *nf* evacuation

**évader** [evade] **s'évader** *vpr* to escape (**de** from) ▪ **évadé, -e** *nmf* escaped prisoner

**évaluer** [evalɥe] *vt (fortune)* to estimate; *(bien)* to value ▪ **évaluation** *nf* estimation; *(de bien)* valuation

**évangile** [evɑ̃ʒil] *nm* gospel; **l'É.** the Gospel

**évanouir** [evanwir] **s'évanouir** *vpr (personne)* to faint; *Fig (espoir, crainte)* to vanish ▪ **évanoui, -e** *adj* unconscious ▪ **évanouissement** *nm (syncope)* fainting fit

**évaporer** [evapɔre] **s'évaporer** *vpr* to evaporate; *Fig (disparaître)* to vanish into thin air

**évasé, -e** [evaze] *adj (jupe)* flared

**évasif, -ive** [evazif, -iv] *adj* evasive

**évasion** [evazjɔ̃] *nf* escape (**de** from); *(de la réalité)* escapism; **é. fiscale** tax evasion

**éveil** [evɛj] *nm* awakening; **être en é.** to be alert

**éveiller** [eveje] **1** *vt (susciter)* to arouse **2 s'éveiller** *vpr* to awaken (**à** to) ▪ **éveillé, -e** *adj* awake; *(vif)* alert

**événement** [evɛnmɑ̃] *nm* event

**éventail** [evɑ̃taj] *nm (instrument)* fan; *(choix)* range

**éventuel, -elle** [evɑ̃tɥɛl] *adj* possible ▪ **éventualité** *nf* possibility ▪ **éventuellement** *adv* possibly

**évêque** [evɛk] *nm* bishop

**évertuer** [evɛrtɥe] **s'évertuer** *vpr* **s'é. à faire qch** to endeavour to do sth

**éviction** [eviksjɔ̃] *nf (de concurrent, de président)* ousting; *(de locataire)* eviction

**évident, -e** [evidɑ̃, -ɑ̃t] *adj* obvious (**que** that) ▪ **évidemment** [-amɑ̃] *adv* obviously ▪ **évidence** *nf* obviousness; **une é.** an obvious fact; **en é.** in a prominent position

**évier** [evje] *nm* (kitchen) sink

**évincer** [evɛ̃se] *vt (concurrent)* to oust (**de** from)

**éviter** [evite] *vt* to avoid (**de faire** doing); **é. qch à qn** to spare *or* save sb sth

**évoluer** [evɔlɥe] *vi (changer)* to develop; *(société, situation)* to evolve; *(se déplacer)* to move around ▪ **évolué, -e** *adj (pays)* advanced; *(personne)* enlightened ▪ **évolution** *nf (changement)* development; *Biol* evolution

**évoquer** [evɔke] *vt* to evoke

**exact, -e** [ɛgzakt] *adj (quantité, poids, nombre)* exact, precise; *(rapport, description)* exact, accurate; *(mot)* right, correct; *(ponctuel)* punctual ▪ **exactement** [-əmɑ̃] *adv* exactly ▪ **exactitude** *nf (précision, fidélité)* exactness; *(justesse)* correctness; *(ponctualité)* punctuality

**ex æquo** [ɛgzeko] **1** *adj inv Sport* **être classés e.** to tie, to be equally placed **2** *adv Sport* **être troisième e.** to tie for third place

**exagérer** [ɛgzaʒere] **1** *vt* to exaggerate **2** *vi (parler)* to exaggerate; *(agir)* to go too far ▪ **exagération** *nf* exaggeration ▪ **exagéré, -e** *adj* excessive

**exalter** [ɛgzalte] *vt (passionner)* to stir ▪ **exaltant, -e** *adj* stirring ▪ **exalté, -e** *adj (sentiment)* impassioned

**examen** [ɛgzamɛ̃] *nm* examination; **e. blanc** mock exam; **e. de la vue** eye test ▪ **examinateur, -trice** *nmf* examiner ▪ **examiner** *vt (considérer, regarder)* to examine

**exaspérer** [ɛgzaspere] *vt (personne)* to exasperate

**exaucer** [ɛgzose] *vt (désir)* to grant

**excavation** [ɛkskavɑsjɔ̃] *nf (trou, action)* excavation

**excéder** [ɛksede] *vt (dépasser)* to exceed; **é. qn** *(énerver)* to exasperate sb ▪ **excédent** *nm* surplus, excess ▪ **excédentaire** *adj* **poids e.** excess weight

**excellent, -e** [ɛkselɑ̃, -ɑ̃t] *adj* excellent ▪ **excellence** *nf* excellence ▪ **exceller** *vi* to excel (**en** at)

**excentrique** [ɛksɑ̃trik] *adj & nmf* eccentric

**excepté[1]** [ɛksɛpte] *prép* except

**excepté[2], -e** *adj* except (for)

**exception** [ɛksɛpsjɔ̃] *nf* exception; **à l'e. de** except (for), with the exception of ▪ **exceptionnel, -elle** *adj* exceptional

**excès** [ɛksɛ] *nm* excess; **e. de vitesse** speeding ▪ **excessif, -ive** *adj* excessive

**exciter** [ɛksite] **1** *vt (faire naître)* to arouse; **e. qn** *(énerver)* to excite sb **2 s'exciter** *vpr (devenir nerveux)* to get excited ▪ **excitant, -e** *nm* stimulant ▪ **excitation** *nf (agitation)* excitement ▪ **excité, -e** *adj* excited

**exclamer** [ɛksklame] **s'exclamer** *vpr* to

exclaim ▪ **exclamation** *nf* exclamation

**exclure*** [ɛksklyr] *vt (écarter)* to exclude (**de** from); *(chasser)* to expel (**de** from) ▪ **exclu, -e** *adj (solution)* out of the question; *(avec une date)* exclusive

**exclusif, -ive** [ɛksklyzif, -iv] *adj (droit, modèle)* exclusive ▪ **exclusivité** *nf Com* exclusive rights; *(dans la presse)* scoop; **en e.** *(film)* having an exclusive showing (**à** at)

**exclusion** [ɛksklyzjɔ̃] *nf* exclusion; **à l'e. de** with the exception of

**excursion** [ɛkskyrsjɔ̃] *nf* trip, excursion; *(de plusieurs jours)* tour; **faire une e.** to go on a trip/tour

**excuse** [ɛkskyz] *nf (prétexte)* excuse; **excuses** *(regrets)* apology; **faire des excuses** to apologize (**à** to) ▪ **excuser 1** *vt (justifier, pardonner)* to excuse (**qn d'avoir fait/qn de faire** sb for doing) **2 s'excuser** *vpr* to apologize (**de** for; **auprès de** to); **excusez-moi!, je m'excuse!** excuse me!

**exécrer** [ɛgzekre] *vt* to loathe ▪ **exécrable** *adj* atrocious

**exécuter** [ɛgzekyte] **1** *vt (tâche)* to carry out; *(jouer)* to perform; **e. qn** to execute sb **2 s'exécuter** *vpr* to comply ▪ **exécutant, -e** *nmf (ouvrier, employé)* subordinate ▪ **exécution** *nf (de tâche)* carrying out; *(de musique)* performance; *(de condamné)* execution

**exécutif** [ɛgzekytif] **1** *adj m* **pouvoir e.** executive power **2** *nm* **l'e.** the executive

**exemplaire** [ɛgzɑ̃plɛr] **1** *adj* exemplary **2** *nm (livre)* copy

**exemple** [ɛgzɑ̃pl] *nm* example; **par e.** for example, for instance; **donner l'e.** to set an example (**à** to)

**exempt, -e** [ɛgzɑ̃, -ɑ̃t] *adj* **e. de** *(dispensé de)* exempt from; *(sans)* free from ▪ **exempter** [ɛgzɑ̃te] *vt* to exempt (**de** from) ▪ **exemption** *nf* exemption

**exercer** [ɛgzɛrse] **1** *vt (voix, droits)* to exercise; *(autorité, influence)* to exert (**sur** on); *(profession)* to practise; **e. qn à qch** to train sb in sth **2** *vi (médecin)* to practise **3 s'exercer** *vpr (s'entraîner)* to train; **s'e. à qch** to practise sth; **s'e. à faire qch** to practise doing sth

**exercice** [ɛgzɛrsis] *nm (physique) & Scol* exercise; *Mil* drill; **en e.** *(fonctionnaire)* in office; *(médecin)* in practice; **prendre de l'e.** to exercise

**exhiber** [ɛgzibe] *vt (documents, passeport)* to produce; *Péj (savoir, richesses)* to show off, to flaunt

**exiger** [ɛgziʒe] *vt (exiger)* to demand (**de** from); *(nécessiter)* to require ▪ **exigeant, -e** *adj* demanding, exacting ▪ **exigence** *nf (caractère)* exacting nature; *(condition)* demand

**exigu, -ë** [ɛgzigy] *adj* cramped, tiny

**exil** [ɛgzil] *nm* exile ▪ **exilé, -e** *nmf (personne)* exile ▪ **exiler 1** *vt* to exile **2 s'exiler** *vpr* to go into exile

**existence** [ɛgzistɑ̃s] *nf (fait d'exister)* existence; *(vie)* life; **moyen d'e.** means of existence ▪ **existant, -e** *adj* existing ▪ **exister 1** *vi* to exist **2** *v impersonnel* **il existe...** there is/are...

**exode** [ɛgzɔd] *nm* exodus

**exonérer** [ɛgzɔnere] *vt* to exempt (**de** from) ▪ **exonération** *nf* exemption

**exorbitant, -e** [ɛgzɔrbitɑ̃, -ɑ̃t] *adj* exorbitant

**exotique** [ɛgzɔtik] *adj* exotic

**expansif, -ive** [ɛkspɑ̃sif, -iv] *adj* expansive

**expansion** [ɛkspɑ̃sjɔ̃] *nf (de commerce, de pays, de gaz)* expansion; **en (pleine) e.** (fast *or* rapidly) expanding

**expatrier** [ɛkspatrije] **s'expatrier** *vpr* to leave one's country

**expédier** [ɛkspedje] *vt (envoyer)* to send, to dispatch; *(affaires, client)* to deal promptly with ▪ **expéditeur, -trice** *nmf* sender ▪ **expéditif, -ive** *adj* hasty ▪ **expédition** *nf (envoi)* dispatch; *(voyage)* expedition

**expérience** [ɛksperjɑ̃s] *nf (connaissance)* experience; *(scientifique)* experiment; **faire l'e. de qch** to experience sth; **avoir de l'e.** to have experience ▪ **expérimental, -e, -aux, -ales** *adj* experimental

**expérimenter** [ɛksperimɑ̃te] *vt (remède, vaccin)* to try out (**sur** on) ▪ **expérimenté, -e** *adj* experienced

**expert, -e** [ɛkspɛr, -ɛrt] **1** *adj* expert, skilled (**en** in) **2** *nm* expert (**en** on *or* in); *(d'assurances)* valuer ▪ **expert-comptable** (*pl* **experts-comptables**) *nm Br* ≃ chartered accountant, *Am* ≃ certified public accountant

**expertise** [ɛkspɛrtiz] *nf (évaluation)* valuation; *(rapport)* expert's report; *(compétence)* expertise

**expier** [ɛkspje] *vt (péchés)* to expiate, to atone for

**expirer** [ɛkspire] **1** *vti* to breathe out **2** *vi (mourir)* to pass away; *(finir, cesser)* to expire ▪ **expiration** *nf (respiration)* breathing out; *(échéance) Br* expiry, *Am* expiration

**explication** [ɛksplikɑsjɔ̃] *nf* explanation; *(mise au point)* discussion

**explicite** [ɛksplisit] *adj* explicit

**expliquer** [ɛksplike] **1** *vt* to explain (**à** to; **que** that) **2 s'expliquer** *vpr* to explain oneself; *(discuter)* to talk things over (**avec** with); **s'e. qch** *(comprendre)* to understand sth ▪ **explicatif, -ive** *adj* explanatory

**exploit** [ɛksplwa] *nm* feat

**exploiter** [ɛksplwate] *vt (champs)* to farm; *(ferme)* to run; *(mine)* to work; *Fig & Péj (personne, situation)* to exploit ▪ **exploitant, -e** *nmf* **e. agricole** farmer ▪ **exploitation** *nf (de champs)* farming; *(de ferme)* running; *(de mine)* working; *Péj* exploitation; **e. agricole** farm

**explorer** [ɛksplɔre] *vt* to explore ▪ **explorateur, -trice** *nmf* explorer

**exploser** [ɛksploze] *vi (gaz, bombe)* to explode; **faire e. qch** to explode sth ▪ **explosif, -ive** *adj & nm* explosive ▪ **explosion** *nf* explosion; *(de colère)* outburst

**exporter** [ɛkspɔrte] *vt* to export (**vers** to; **de** from) ▪ **exportateur, -trice 1** *nmf* exporter **2** *adj* exporting ▪ **exportation** *nf (produit)* export; *(action)* export(ation)

**exposer** [ɛkspoze] **1** *vt (tableau)* to exhibit; *(marchandises)* to display; *(théorie)* to set out; *Phot (film)* to expose **2 s'exposer** *vpr* **s'e. au danger** to put oneself in danger; **s'e. à la critique** to lay oneself open to criticism ▪ **exposé, -e 1** *adj* **e. au sud** facing south **2** *nm (compte rendu)* account (**de** of); *(présentation)* talk; *Scol* paper

**exposition** [ɛkspozisjɔ̃] *nf (d'objets d'art)* exhibition; *(de marchandises)* display; *Phot* exposure (**à** to); *(de maison)* aspect

**exprès[1]** [ɛksprɛ] *adv* on purpose, intentionally; *(spécialement)* specially

**exprès[2], -esse** [ɛksprɛs] *adj (ordre, condition)* express ▪ **expressément** *adv* expressly

**exprès[3]** [ɛksprɛs] *adj inv* **lettre e.** special delivery letter

**express** [ɛksprɛs] *adj & nm inv (train)* express; *(café)* espresso

**expressif, -ive** [ɛkspresif, -iv] *adj* expressive ▪ **expression** *nf (phrase, mine)* expression ▪ **exprimer 1** *vt* to express **2 s'exprimer** *vpr* to express oneself

**expulser** [ɛkspylse] *vt* to expel (**de** from); *(joueur)* to send off ▪ **expulsion** *nf* expulsion; *(de joueur)* sending off

**exquis, -e** [ɛkski, -iz] *adj (nourriture)* exquisite

**extase** [ɛkstɑz] *nf* ecstasy ▪ **s'extasier** *vpr* to be in raptures (**sur** over *or* about)

**extensible** [ɛkstɑ̃sibl] *adj (métal)* tensile; *(tissu)* stretch ▪ **extension** *nf (de muscle)* stretching; *(de durée, de contrat)* extension

**exténué, -e** [ɛkstenɥe] *adj* exhausted

**extérieur, -e** [ɛksterjœr] **1** *adj (monde)* outside; *(surface)* outer, external; *(signe)* outward, external; *(politique)* foreign **2** *nm* outside, exterior; **à l'e. (de)** outside; **à l'e.** *(match)* away ▪ **extérieurement** *adv (dehors)* externally;

*(en apparence)* outwardly ▪ **extérioriser** *vt* to express

**exterminer** [ɛkstɛrmine] *vt* to exterminate

**externat** [ɛkstɛrna] *nm (école)* day school

**externe** [ɛkstɛrn] **1** *adj* external **2** *nmf (élève)* day pupil; *Méd* = non-resident hospital medical student, *Am* extern

**extincteur** [ɛkstɛ̃ktœr] *nm* fire extinguisher ▪ **extinction** *nf (de feu)* extinguishing; *(de race)* extinction; **e. de voix** loss of voice

**extorquer** [ɛkstɔrke] *vt* to extort (**à** from) ▪ **extorsion** *nf* extortion; **e. de fonds** extortion

**extradition** [ɛkstradisjɔ̃] *nf* extradition ▪ **extrader** *vt* to extradite

**extraire*** [ɛkstrɛr] *vt* to extract (**de** from); *(charbon)* to mine ▪ **extrait** *nm* extract; **e. de naissance** birth certificate

**extralucide** [ɛkstralysid] *adj & nmf* clairvoyant

**extraordinaire** [ɛkstraɔrdinɛr] *adj* extraordinary

**extraterrestre** [ɛkstraterɛstr] *adj & nmf* extraterrestrial

**extravagant, -e** [ɛkstravagɑ̃, -ɑ̃t] *adj (idée, comportement)* extravagant

**extraverti, -e** [ɛkstravɛrti] *nmf* extrovert

**extrême** [ɛkstrɛm] **1** *adj* extreme; *Pol* **l'e. droite/gauche** the far *or* extreme right/left **2** *nm* extreme ▪ **Extrême-Orient** *nm* **l'E.** the Far East ▪ **extrémiste** *adj & nmf* extremist ▪ **extrémité** *nf (bout)* extremity, end; **extrémités** *(pieds et mains)* extremities

**exulter** [ɛgzylte] *vi* to exult, to rejoice

# Ff

**F, f** [ɛf] *nm inv* F, f
**fa** [fɑ] *nm (note)* F
**fabricant, -e** [fabrikɑ̃, -ɑ̃t] *nmf* manufacturer ▪ **fabrication** *nf* manufacture
**fabrique** [fabrik] *nf* factory
**fabriquer** [fabrike] *vt (objet)* to make; *(en usine)* to manufacture
**fabuleux, -euse** [fabylø, -øz] *adj (légendaire, incroyable)* fabulous
**façade** [fasad] *nf* façade
**face** [fas] *nf (visage)* face; *(de cube, de montagne)* side; *(de pièce de monnaie)* head; **en f.** opposite; **en f. de** opposite, facing; *(en présence de)* in front of; **f. à** *(vis-à-vis)* facing; **f. à f.** face to face; **faire f. à qch** to face up to sth; **sauver/perdre la f.** to save/lose face
**facette** [fasɛt] *nf (de diamant, de problème)* facet
**fâcher** [fɑʃe] **se fâcher** *vpr* to get angry (**contre** with); **se f. avec qn** to fall out with sb ▪ **fâché, -e** *adj (air)* angry; *(personnes)* on bad terms; **f. contre qn** angry with sb
**facile** [fasil] *adj* easy; **f. à vivre** easy to get along with ▪ **facilité** *nf (simplicité)* easiness; *(aisance)* ease ▪ **faciliter** *vt* to make easier, to facilitate
**façon** [fasɔ̃] *nf (manière)* way; **la f. dont elle parle** the way (in which) she talks; **de quelle f.?** how?; **de toute f.** anyway, anyhow; **de f. à** so as to; **de f. générale** generally speaking; **d'une f. ou d'une autre** one way or another; **à ma f.** my way, (in) my own way
**façonner** [fasɔne] *vt (former)* to shape; *(fabriquer)* to make
**facteur** [faktœr] *nm* (**a**) *(employé) Br* postman, *Am* mailman (**b**) *(élément)* factor
**facture** [faktyr] *nf Com* bill, invoice ▪ **facturer** *vt* to bill, to invoice
**facultatif, -ive** [fakyltatif, -iv] *adj (travail)* optional; *Scol* **matière facultative** optional subject
**faculté** [fakylte] *nf* (**a**) *(aptitude)* faculty (**b**) *(d'université)* faculty; **à la f.** *Br* at university, *Am* at school
**fade** [fad] *adj* insipid
**faible** [fɛbl] **1** *adj* weak, feeble; *(voix)* faint; *(chances)* slight; *(revenus)* small **2** *nm* weakling; **f. d'esprit** feeble-minded person ▪ **faiblesse** *nf (physique, morale)* weakness
**faiblir** [fɛblir] *vi (forces)* to weaken; *(courage, vue)* to fail; *(vent)* to drop
**faïence** [fajɑ̃s] *nf (matière)* earthenware; **faïences** *(objets)* earthenware
**faille¹** [faj] *nf Géol* fault; *Fig* flaw
**faille²** [faj] *voir* **falloir**
**faillir*** [fajir] *vi* **il a failli tomber** he almost *or* nearly fell
**faillite** [fajit] *nf Com* bankruptcy; **faire f.** to go bankrupt
**faim** [fɛ̃] *nf* hunger; **avoir f.** to be hungry
**fainéant, -e** [feneɑ̃, -ɑ̃t] **1** *adj* idle **2** *nmf* idler

**FAIRE*** [fɛr] **1** *vt (faute, gâteau, voyage, repas)* to make; *(devoir, ménage)* to do; *(rêve, chute)* to have; *(sourire)* to give; *(promenade, sieste)* to have, to take; *(guerre)* to wage, to make; **ça fait 10 mètres de large** it's 10 metres wide; **ça fait 10 euros** it's *or* that's 10 euros; **2 et 2 font 4** 2 and 2 are 4; **que f.?** what's to be done? **f. du tennis/du piano** to play tennis/the piano; **f. du droit** to study law; **f. du bien à qn** to do sb good; **f. du mal à qn** to hurt *or* harm sb; **ça ne fait rien** that doesn't matter; **comment as-tu fait pour...?** how did you manage to...?; **'oui', fit-elle** 'yes', she said

**2** *vi (agir)* to do; *(paraître)* to look; **f. comme chez soi** to make oneself at home; **elle ferait bien de partir** she'd do well to leave

**3** *v impersonnel* **il fait beau/froid** it's fine/cold; **il fait du vent** it's windy; **quel temps fait-il?** what's the weather like?; **ça fait deux ans que je ne l'ai pas vu** I haven't seen him for two years, it's (been) two years since I saw him

**4** *v aux (+ infinitive)* **f. construire une maison** to have a house built (**à qn** for sb; **par qn** by sb); **f. souffrir qn** to make sb suffer

**5 se faire** *vpr (fabrication)* to be made; *(activité)* to be done; **se f. couper les cheveux** to have one's hair cut; **se f. renverser** to get knocked down; **se f. des amis** to make friends; **il se fait tard** it's getting late; **comment se fait-il que...?** how is it that...?; **ça se fait beaucoup** people do that a lot; **se f. à qch** to get used to sth; **ne t'en fais pas!** don't worry! ▪ **faire-part** *nm inv* announcement

---

**fais, fait** [fɛ] *voir* **faire**

**faisable** [fəzabl] *adj* feasible

**faisan** [fəzɑ̃] *nm* pheasant

**faisceau, -x** [fɛso] *nm (rayons)* beam

**fait, -e** [fɛ, fɛt] **1** *pp de* **faire 2** *adj (fromage)* ripe; *(ongles)* polished; **tout f.** ready made **3** *nm (événement)* event; *(donnée, réalité)* fact; **du f. de** on account of; **au f.** *(à propos)* by the way; **en f.** in fact; **prendre qn sur le f.** to catch sb red-handed *or* in the act; *Journ* **faits divers** ≃ news in brief

**faîte** [fɛt] *nm (haut)* top; *Fig (apogée)* height

**faites** [fɛt] *voir* **faire**

**falaise** [falɛz] *nf* cliff

---

**FALLOIR*** [falwar] **1** *v impersonnel* **il faut qn/qch** I/you/we/*etc* need sb/sth; **il te faut un stylo** you need a pen; **il faut partir** I/you/we/*etc* have to go; **il faut que je parte** I have to go; **il faudrait qu'elle reste** she ought to stay; **il faut un jour** it takes a day (**pour faire** to do); **comme il faut** *(adjectif)* proper; *(adverbe)* properly; **s'il le faut** if need be

**2 s'en falloir** *vpr* **il s'en est fallu de peu qu'il ne pleure** he almost cried; **tant s'en faut** far from it

---

**famé** [fame] **mal famé, -e** *adj* disreputable

**fameux, -euse** [famø, -øz] *adj (célèbre)* famous

**familial, -e, -aux, -ales** [familjal, -o] *adj (atmosphère, ennuis)* family; *(entreprise)* family-run

**familier, -ère** [familje, -ɛr] *adj (connu)* familiar (**à** to); *(désinvolte)* informal (**avec** with); *(locution)* colloquial ▪ **familiariser 1** *vt* to familiarize (**avec** with) **2 se familiariser** *vpr* to familiarize oneself (**avec** with)

**famille** [famij] *nf* family

**famine** [famin] *nf* famine

**fanatique** [fanatik] **1** *adj* fanatical **2** *nmf* fanatic

**faner** [fane] **se faner** *vpr (fleur, beauté)* to fade ▪ **fané, -e** *adj* faded

**fanfare** [fɑ̃far] *nf (orchestre)* brass band

**fantaisie** [fɑ̃tezi] *nf (imagination)* imagination; **bijoux f.** costume jewellery

**fantastique** [fɑ̃tastik] *adj (imaginaire, excellent)* fantastic

**fantôme** [fɑ̃tom] **1** *nm* ghost, phantom **2** *adj* **ville/train f.** ghost town/train

**faon** [fɑ̃] *nm* fawn

**farce**[1] [fars] *nf (tour)* practical joke, prank; **faire une f. à qn** to play a practical joke *or* a prank on sb ▪ **farceur, -euse** *nmf (blagueur)* practical joker

**farce**[2] [fars] *nf Culin* stuffing ▪ **farcir** *vt (poulet)* to stuff

**fardeau, -x** [fardo] *nm* burden, load

**farder** [farde] **1** *vt (maquiller)* to make up **2 se farder** *vpr (se maquiller)* to put on one's make-up; **se f. les yeux** to put eyeshadow on

**farine** [farin] *nf (de blé)* flour

**farouche** [faruʃ] *adj (personne)* shy; *(animal)* timid; *(haine)* fierce

**fart** [far] *nm* wax

**fascicule** [fasikyl] *nm (de publication)* instalment; *(brochure)* brochure

**fasciner** [fasine] *vt* to fascinate ▪ **fascination** *nf* fascination

**fascisme** [faʃism] *nm* fascism ▪ **fasciste** *adj & nmf* fascist

**fasse(s), fassent** [fas] *voir* **faire**

**faste** [fast] **1** *nm* splendour **2** *adj* **jour f.** lucky day

**fastidieux, -euse** [fastidjø, -øz] *adj* tedious

**fatal, -e, -als, -ales** [fatal] *adj (mortel)* fatal; *(inévitable)* inevitable; *(moment)* fateful ▪ **fataliste** *adj* fatalistic ▪ **fatalité** *nf (destin)* fate ▪ **fatidique** *adj (jour, date)* fateful

**fatigant, -e** [fatigɑ̃, -ɑ̃t] *adj (épuisant)* tiring; *(ennuyeux)* tiresome

**fatigue** [fatig] *nf* tiredness

**fatiguer** [fatige] **1** *vt (épuiser)* to tire; *(yeux)* to strain; *(ennuyer)* to bore **2** *vi (personne)* to get tired; *(moteur)* to labour **3 se fatiguer** *vpr (s'épuiser, se lasser)* to get tired (**de** of); **se f. à faire qch** to tire oneself out doing sth; **se f. les yeux** to strain one's eyes ▪ **fatigué, -e** *adj* tired (**de** of)

**faucher** [foʃe] *vt (herbe)* to mow; *(blé)* to reap

**faucon** [fokɔ̃] *nm* hawk, falcon

**faudra, faudrait** [fodra, fodrɛ] *voir* **falloir**

**faufiler** [fofile] **se faufiler** *vpr* to work one's way (**dans** through *or* into; **entre** between)

**faune** [fon] *nf* wildlife, fauna

**faussaire** [fosɛr] *nm* forger

**fausse** [fos] *voir* **faux**[1]

**fausser** [fose] *vt (réalité)* to distort

**fausseté** [foste] *nf (hypocrisie)* duplicity

**faut** [fo] *voir* **falloir**

**faute** [fot] *nf (erreur)* mistake; *(responsabilité) & (au tennis)* fault; *(au football)* foul; **c'est de ta f.** it's your fault; **f. de mieux** for want of anything better; **faire une f.** to make a mistake

**fauteuil** [fotœj] *nm* armchair; *(de président)* chair; **f. roulant** wheelchair

**fautif, -ive** [fotif, -iv] *adj (personne)* at fault; *(erroné)* faulty

**fauve** [fov] *nm* big cat

**faux, fausse** [fo, fos] **1** *adj (pas vrai)* false, untrue; *(inexact)* wrong; *(inauthentique)* false; *(monnaie)* forged; *(tableau)* fake; **faire une fausse couche** to have a miscarriage; **f. départ** false start

**2** *adv (chanter)* out of tune

**3** *nm (tableau)* fake; *(document)* forgery ▪ **faux-filet** (*pl* **faux-filets**) *nm* sirloin ▪ **faux-monnayeur** (*pl* **faux-monnayeurs**) *nm* counterfeiter

**faveur** [favœr] *nf* favour; **en f. de** *(au profit de)* in aid of; **être en f. de qch** to be in favour of sth ▪ **favorable** *adj* favourable (**à** to) ▪ **favori, -e** *adj & nmf* favourite ▪ **favoriser** *vt* to favour

**fax** [faks] *nm (appareil, message)* fax ▪ **faxer** *vt (message)* to fax

**fécond, -e** [fekɔ̃, -ɔ̃d] *adj (femme, idée)* fertile ▪ **fécondité** *nf* fertility

**fédéral, -e, -aux, -ales** [federal, -o] *adj* federal ▪ **fédération** *nf* federation

**fée** [fe] *nf* fairy ▪ **féerique** *adj (personnage, monde)* fairy; *(vision)* enchanting

**feindre*** [fɛ̃dr] *vt* to feign; **f. de faire qch** to pretend to do sth ▪ **feint, -e** *adj* feigned ▪ **feinte** *nf (ruse)* ruse

**fêler** [fele] *vt*, **se fêler** *vpr* to crack

**féliciter** [felisite] *vt* to congratulate (**de** *ou* **sur** on) ▪ **félicitations** *nfpl* congratulations (**pour** on)

**félin** [felɛ̃] *nm* feline

**fêlure** [felyr] *nf* crack

**femelle** [fəmɛl] *adj & nf* female

**féminin, -e** [feminɛ̃, -in] *adj (prénom, hormone)* female; *(trait, intuition, pronom)* feminine; *(mode)* women's ▪ **féministe** *adj & nmf* feminist ▪ **féminité** *nf* femininity

**femme** [fam] *nf* woman (*pl* women); *(épouse)* wife; **f. de ménage** cleaning lady, maid; **f. au foyer** housewife

**fendiller** [fɑ̃dije] **se fendiller** *vpr* to crack

**fendre** [fɑ̃dr] **1** *vt (bois, lèvre)* to split; *Fig (cœur)* to break **2 se fendre** *vpr (se fissurer)* to crack

**fenêtre** [fənɛtr] *nf* window

**fenouil** [fənuj] *nm* fennel

**fente** [fɑ̃t] *nf (de tirelire, de palissade)* slit; *(de rocher)* split, crack

**féodal, -e, -aux, -ales** [feɔdal, -o] *adj* feudal

**fer** [fɛr] *nm* iron; *(partie métallique)* metal (part); **barre de** *ou* **en f.** iron bar; **f. à cheval** horseshoe; **f. forgé** wrought iron; **f. à repasser** iron

**fera, ferait** *etc* [fəra, fərɛ] *voir* **faire**

**férié** [ferje] *adj m* **jour f.** (public) holiday

**ferme¹** [fɛrm] *nf* farm; *(maison)* farm(-house)

**ferme²** [fɛrm] **1** *adj (fruit, beurre, décision)* firm; *(autoritaire)* firm (**avec** with) **2** *adv (travailler)* hard; **s'ennuyer f.** to be bored stiff

**fermenter** [fɛrmɑ̃te] *vi* to ferment

**fermer** [fɛrme] **1** *vt* to close, to shut; *(gaz, radio)* to turn *or* switch off; *(passage)* to block; **f. qch à clef** to lock sth; **f. un magasin** *(définitivement)* to close *or* shut (down) a shop **2** *vi*, **se fermer** *vpr* to close, to shut ▪ **fermé, -e** *adj (porte, magasin)* closed, shut; *(route, circuit)* closed; *(gaz)* off

**fermeté** [fɛrməte] *nf* firmness

**fermeture** [fɛrmətyr] *nf* closing, closure; *(heure)* closing time; *(mécanisme)* catch; **f. annuelle** annual closing; **f. Éclair®** *Br* zip (fastener), *Am* zipper

**fermier, -ère** [fɛrmje, -ɛr] *nmf* farmer

**fermoir** [fɛrmwar] *nm* clasp

**féroce** [ferɔs] *adj* ferocious ▪ **férocité** *nf* ferocity

**feront** [fərɔ̃] *voir* **faire**

**ferraille** [fɛrɑj] *nf* scrap iron; **mettre qch à la f.** to scrap sth

**ferronnerie** [fɛrɔnri] *nf* ironwork

**ferroviaire** [ferɔvjɛr] *adj* **compagnie f.** *Br* railway company, *Am* railroad company

**ferry** [fɛri] (*pl* **ferrys** *ou* **ferries**) *nm* ferry

**fertile** [fɛrtil] *adj (terre, imagination)* fertile ▪ **fertiliser** *vt* to fertilize ▪ **fertilité** *nf* fertility

**ferveur** [fɛrvœr] *nf* fervour

**fesse** [fɛs] *nf* buttock; **fesses** *Br* bottom, *Am* butt ▪ **fessée** *nf* spanking

**festin** [fɛstɛ̃] *nm* feast

**festival, -als** [fɛstival] *nm* festival

**festivités** [fɛstivite] *nfpl* festivities

**fête** [fɛt] *nf (civile)* holiday; *(religieuse)* festival, feast; *(entre amis)* party; **jour de f.** (public) holiday; **les fêtes (de Noël et du nouvel an)** the Christmas holidays; **faire la f.** to have a good time; **c'est sa f.** it's his/her saint's day; **la f. des Mères** Mother's Day; **la f. du Travail** Labour Day ▪ **fêter** *vt (événement)* to celebrate

**feu, -x** [fø] *nm* fire; *(de réchaud)* burner; *Aut, Naut & Aviat (lumière)* light; **en f.** on fire, ablaze; **faire du f.** to light *or* make a fire; **mettre le f. à qch** to set fire to sth; **prendre f.** to catch fire; **donner du f. à qn** to give sb a light; **avez-vous du f.?** have you got a light?; **faire cuire qch à f. doux** to cook sth on a low heat; **au f.!** (there's a) fire!; *Aut* **f. rouge** *(lumière)* red light; *(objet)* traffic lights

**feuille** [fœj] *nf* leaf; *(de papier)* sheet; *(de journal)* newssheet; **f. de maladie** = form given by doctor to patient for claiming reimbursement from the Social Security; **f. de paie** *Br* pay slip, *Am* pay stub ▪ **feuillage** *nm* leaves, foliage

**feuilleté** [fœjte] *nm* **f. au fromage** cheese pastry

**feuilleter** [fœjte] *vt (livre)* to flip through

**feuilleton** [fœjtɔ̃] *nm (roman, film)* serial; **f. télévisé** television serial

**feutre** [føtr] *nm* felt; **(crayon) f.** felt-tip(ped) pen

**fève** [fɛv] *nf* (broad) bean

**février** [fevrije] *nm* February

**fiable** [fjabl] *adj* reliable

**fiancer** [fjɑ̃se] **se fiancer** *vpr* to become engaged (**avec** to) ▪ **fiabilité** *nf* reliability ▪ **fiançailles** *nfpl* engagement ▪ **fiancé** *nm* fiancé; **fiancés** engaged couple ▪ **fiancée** *nf* fiancée

**fibre** [fibr] *nf* fibre; **f. de verre** fibreglass; **fibres optiques** optical fibres

**ficelle** [fisɛl] *nf (de corde)* string; *(pain)* = long thin loaf ▪ **ficeler** *vt* to tie up

**fiche** [fiʃ] *nf* (**a**) *(carte)* index card; *(papier)* form; **f. de paie** *Br* pay slip, *Am* pay stub (**b**) *Él (broche)* pin; *(prise)* plug ▪ **fichier** *nm* card index, file; *Ordinat* file

**ficher** [fiʃe] *vt (enfoncer)* to drive in; *(mettre sur fiche)* to put on file

**fictif, -ive** [fiktif, -iv] *adj* fictitious ▪ **fiction** *nf* fiction

**fidèle** [fidɛl] **1** *adj* faithful (**à** to) **2** *nmf* faithful supporter; **les fidèles** *(croyants)* the faithful; *(à l'église)* the congregation ▪ **fidélité** *nf* fidelity, faithfulness

**fier**[1] [fje] **se fier** *vpr* **se f. à qn/qch** to trust sb/sth

**fier**[2]**, fière** [fjɛr] *adj* proud (**de** of) ▪ **fierté** *nf* pride

**fièvre** [fjɛvr] *nf (maladie)* fever; **avoir de la f.** to have a temperature *or* a fever ▪ **fiévreux, -euse** *adj* feverish

**figer** [fiʒe] **1** *vt (liquide)* to congeal **2** **se figer** *vpr (liquide)* to congeal; *Fig (sourire, personne)* to freeze

**figue** [fig] *nf* fig

**figurant, -e** [figyrɑ̃, -ɑ̃t] *nmf (de film)* extra

**figure** [figyr] *nf (visage)* face; *(personnage)* figure

**figurer** [figyre] **1** *vt* to represent **2** *vi* to appear **3** **se figurer** *vpr* to imagine; **figure-toi que...?** would you believe that...?

**fil** [fil] *nm* (**a**) *(de coton, de pensée)* thread; *(lin)* linen; **f. dentaire** dental floss (**b**) *(métallique)* wire; **f. de fer** wire (**c**) *(expressions)* **au f. de l'eau** with the current; **au bout du f.** *(au téléphone)* on the line

**file** [fil] *nf* line; *Aut (couloir)* lane; **f. d'attente** *Br* queue, *Am* line; **être en double f.** to be double-parked

**filer** [file] **1** *vt (coton)* to spin; **f. qn** to shadow sb **2** *vi (partir)* to rush off; *(aller vite)* to speed along; *(collant)* to run, *Br* to ladder

**filet** [filɛ] *nm* (**a**) *(en maille)* net; **f. à provisions** string bag (**b**) *(d'eau)* trickle (**c**) *(de poisson, de viande)* fillet

**filial, -e, -aux, -ales** [filjal, -o] *adj* filial ▪ **filiale** *nf* subsidiary (company)

**filière** [filjɛr] *nf (voie obligée)* channels; *(domaine d'études)* field of study; *(organisation clandestine)* network; **suivre la f. normale** to go through the official channels

**fille** [fij] *nf (enfant)* girl; *(descendante)* daughter; **petite f.** (little *or* young) girl; **jeune f.** girl, young lady ▪ **fillette** *nf* little girl

**film** [film] *nm (œuvre)* film, movie; *(pour photo)* film; **f. muet** silent film; **f. policier** thriller ▪ **filmer** *vt (personne, scène)* to film

**fils** [fis] *nm* son

**filtre** [filtr] *nm* filter; **bout f.** filter tip ▪ **filtrer 1** *vt (liquide, lumière)* to filter; *(personne, nouvelles)* to screen **2** *vi (liquide)* to filter (through); *(nouvelle)* to leak out

**fin**[1] [fɛ̃] *nf* (**a**) *(conclusion)* end; **mettre f. à qch** to put an end to sth; **prendre f.** to come to an end; **à la f.** in the end; **f. mai** at the end of May (**b**) *(but)* end, aim

**fin**[2]**, fine** [fɛ̃, fin] **1** *adj (pointe, tissu)* fine; *(couche)* thin; *(visage, mets)* delicate; *(oreille)* sharp; *(intelligent)* subtle **2** *adv (couper, moudre)* finely

**final, -e, -aux** *ou* **-als, -ales** [final, -o] *adj* final ▪ **finale** *nf Sport* final ▪ **finaliste** *nmf Sport* finalist

**finance** [finɑ̃s] *nf* finance ▪ **financement** *nm* financing ▪ **financer** *vt* to finance

**financier, -ère** [finɑ̃sje, -ɛr] **1** *adj* financial **2** *nm* financier

**finesse** [finɛs] *nf (de pointe)* fineness; *(de taille)* thinness; *(de visage)* delicacy; *(intelligence)* subtlety

**finir** [finir] **1** *vt* to finish; *(discours, vie)* to end, to finish **2** *vi* to finish, to end; **f. de faire qch** to finish doing sth; **f. par faire qch** to end up doing sth; **f. par qch** to finish (up) *or* end (up) with sth ▪ **fini, -e** *adj (produit)* finished; *(univers) & Math* finite

**Finlande** [fɛ̃lɑ̃d] *nf* **la F.** Finland ▪ **finlandais, -e 1** *adj* Finnish **2** *nmf* **F., Finlandaise** Finn

**firme** [firm] *nf* firm

**fisc** [fisk] *nm Br* ≃ Inland Revenue, *Am* ≃ Internal Revenue ▪ **fiscal, -e, -aux, -ales** *adj* **charges fiscales** taxes; **fraude fiscale** tax fraud *or* evasion ▪ **fiscalité** *nf* tax system

**fissure** [fisyr] *nf* crack ▪ **se fissurer** *vpr* to crack

**fixation** [fiksɑsjɔ̃] *nf (action)* fixing; *(dispositif)* fastening, binding; *(idée fixe)* fixation; **faire une f. sur qn/qch** to be fixated on sb/sth

**fixe** [fiks] *adj* fixed ▪ **fixement** [-əmɑ̃] *adv* **regarder qn/qch f.** to stare at sb/sth

**fixer** [fikse] **1** *vt (attacher)* to fix (**à** to); *(date, règle)* to decide, to fix; **f. qn/qch du regard** to stare at sb/sth; **être fixé** *(décidé)* to be decided **2 se fixer** *vpr (regard)* to become fixed; *(s'établir)* to settle

**flacon** [flakɔ̃] *nm* small bottle

**flageolet** [flaʒɔlɛ] *nm (haricot)* flageolet bean

**flagrant, -e** [flagrɑ̃, -ɑ̃t] *adj (injustice)* flagrant, blatant; **pris en f. délit** caught in the act *or* red-handed

**flair** [flɛr] *nm (de chien)* (sense of) smell, scent; *(de personne)* intuition, flair ▪ **flairer** *vt* to smell, to sniff at

**flamand, -e** [flamɑ̃, -ɑ̃d] **1** *adj* Flemish **2** *nmf* **F., Flamande** Fleming **3** *nm (langue)* Flemish

**flamant** [flamɑ̃] *nm* **f. rose** flamingo

**flambant** [flɑ̃bɑ̃] *adv* **f. neuf** brand new

**flambeau, -x** [flɑ̃bo] *nm* torch

**flamber** [flɑ̃be] *vi* to blaze

**flamboyer** [flɑ̃bwaje] *vi* to blaze

**flamme** [flam] *nf* flame; **en flammes** on fire

**flan** [flɑ̃] *nm* baked custard

**flanc** [flɑ̃] *nm* side; *(d'armée, d'animal)* flank

**Flandre** [flɑ̃dr] *nf* **la F., les Flandres** Flanders

**flâner** [flɑne] *vi* to stroll

**flanquer** [flɑ̃ke] *vt* to flank (**de** with)

**flaque** [flak] *nf (d'eau)* puddle

**flash** [flaʃ] (*pl* **flashes**) *nm Phot* flashlight; *Radio & TV* **f. d'informations** (news)flash

**flatter** [flate] *vt* to flatter ▪ **flatterie** *nf* flattery ▪ **flatteur, -euse** *adj* flattering

**fléau, -x** [fleo] *nm (catastrophe)* scourge

**flèche** [flɛʃ] *nf (projectile)* arrow; *(d'église)* spire; **monter en f.** *(prix)* to shoot up ▪ **fléchette** *nf* dart; **fléchettes** *(jeu)* darts

**fléchir** [fleʃir] **1** *vt (ployer)* to bend **2** *vi (ployer)* to bend; *(faiblir)* to give way; *(baisser)* to fall

**flétrir** [fletrir] *vt*, **se flétrir** *vpr* to wither

**fleur** [flœr] *nf* flower; *(d'arbre, d'arbuste)* blossom; **en fleur(s)** in flower, in bloom; *(arbre)* in blossom

**fleurir** [flœrir] **1** *vt (table)* to decorate with flowers; *(tombe)* to lay flowers on **2** *vi (plante)* to flower, to bloom; *(arbre)* to blossom; *Fig (prospérer)* to flourish ▪ **fleuri, -e** *adj (fleur, jardin)* in bloom; *(tissu)* floral

**fleuriste** [flœrist] *nmf* florist

**fleuve** [flœv] *nm* river

**flexible** [flɛksibl] *adj* flexible ▪ **flexibilité** *nf* flexibility

**flocon** [flɔkɔ̃] *nm* flake; **f. de neige** snowflake

**floraison** [flɔrɛzɔ̃] *nf* flowering; **en pleine f.** in full bloom ▪ **floral, -e, -aux, -ales** *adj* floral

**flore** [flɔr] *nf* flora

**florissant, -e** [flɔrisɑ̃, -ɑ̃t] *adj* flourishing

**flot** [flo] *nm (de larmes)* flood, stream; **les flots** *(la mer)* the waves; **à f.** *(bateau)* afloat; *Fig* **couler à flots** *(argent, vin)* to flow freely

**flotte** [flɔt] *nf (de bateaux, d'avions)* fleet

**flotter** [flɔte] *vi (bateau)* to float; *(drapeau)* to fly ▪ **flotteur** *nm* float

**flou, -e** [flu] *adj (image)* fuzzy, blurred; *(idée)* vague

**fluet, -ette** [flye, -ɛt] *adj* thin, slender

**fluide** [flɥid] *adj & nm (liquide)* fluid

**fluorescent, -e** [flyɔresɑ̃, -ɑ̃t] *adj* fluorescent

**flûte** [flyt] *nf (instrument)* flute; *(verre)* champagne glass ▪ **flûtiste** *nmf Br* flautist, *Am* flutist

**flux** [fly] *nm (abondance)* flow; **f. et reflux** ebb and flow

**foi** [fwa] *nf* faith; **être de bonne/mauvaise f.** to be sincere/insincere

**foie** [fwa] *nm* liver; **f. gras** foie gras; **crise de f.** bout of indigestion

**foin** [fwɛ̃] *nm* hay

**foire** [fwar] *nf* fair

**fois** [fwa] *nf* time; **une f.** once; **deux f.** twice; **trois f.** three times; **deux f. trois** two times three; **chaque f. que...** whenever..., each time (that)...; **une f. qu'il sera arrivé** once he has arrived; **à la f.** at the same time, at once; **il était une fois...** once upon a time there was...

**foisonner** [fwazɔne] *vi* to abound (**de** *ou* **en** in)

**fol** [fɔl] *voir* **fou**

**folie** [fɔli] *nf* madness; **aimer qn à la f.** to be madly in love with sb

**folklore** [fɔlklɔr] *nm* folklore ▪ **folklorique** *adj (costume)* traditional; *(musique, danse)* folk

**folle** [fɔl] *voir* **fou**

**foncé, -e** [fɔ̃se] *adj* dark

**foncer** [fɔ̃se] **1** *vi (aller vite)* to tear *or* charge along; **f. sur qn/qch** to swoop on sb/sth **2** *vti (couleur)* to darken

**foncier, -ère** [fɔ̃sje, -ɛr] *adj (taxe)* land

**fonction** [fɔ̃ksjɔ̃] *nf* function; *(emploi)* office; **en f. de** according to; **faire f. de** *(personne)* to act as; *(objet)* to serve *or* act as; **prendre ses fonctions** to take up one's duties; **la f. publique** the civil service ▪ **fonctionnaire** *nmf* civil servant; **haut f.** high-ranking civil servant ▪ **fonctionnel, -elle** *adj* functional

**fonctionner** [fɔ̃ksjɔne] *vi (machine)* to work, to function; **faire f. qch** to operate sth ▪ **fonctionnement** *nm (de machine)* working; **en état de f.** in working order

**fond** [fɔ̃] *nm (de boîte, de jardin, de vallée)* bottom; *(de salle, d'armoire)* back; *(arrière-plan)* background; **au f. de** *(boîte, jardin)* at the bottom of; *(salle)* at the back of; *Fig* **au f., dans le f.** basically; **à f.** *(connaître)* thoroughly; **de f. en comble** from top to bottom; **course de f.** long-distance race; **ski de f.** cross-country skiing; **bruits de f.** background noise; **f. sonore** background music

**fondamental, -e, -aux, -ales** [fɔ̃damɑ̃tal, -o] *adj* fundamental, basic

**fonder** [fɔ̃de] **1** *vt (ville)* to found; *(commerce)* to set up; *(famille)* to start; **f. qch sur qch** to base sth on sth **2 se fonder** *vpr* **se f. sur qch** *(sujet: théorie)* to be based on sth ▪ **fondateur, -trice** *nmf* founder ▪ **fondation** *nf (création, œuvre)* foundation (**de** of); **fondations** *(de bâtiment)* foundations ▪ **fondement** *nm* foundation

**fondre** [fɔ̃dr] **1** *vt (métal)* to melt down; *(neige)* to melt; **faites f. le chocolat** melt the chocolate **2** *vi (se liquéfier)* to melt; **f. en larmes** to burst into tears; **f. sur qch** to swoop on sth **3 se fondre** *vpr* **se f. dans qch** *(disparaître)* to merge into sth ▪ **fondant, -e** *adj (aliment)* which melts in the mouth

**fonds** [fɔ̃] **1** *nm (organisme)* fund; *(de bibliothèque)* collection; **f. de commerce** business; **F. monétaire international** International Monetary Fund **2** *nmpl (argent)* funds; **être en f.** to be in funds

**font** [fɔ̃] *voir* **faire**

**fontaine** [fɔ̃tɛn] *nf (construction)* fountain; *(source)* spring

**fonte** [fɔ̃t] *nf* (**a**) *(de neige)* melting; *(d'acier)* smelting (**b**) *(alliage)* cast iron; **en f.** *(poêle)* cast-iron (**c**) *Typ* font

**football** [futbol] *nm Br* football, *Am* soccer ▪ **footballeur, -euse** *nmf Br* footballer, *Am* soccer player

**forage** [fɔraʒ] *nm* drilling, boring

**forain** [fɔrɛ̃] *nm* fairground stallholder

**force** [fɔrs] *nf (violence) & Phys* force; *(vigueur)* strength; **de toutes ses forces** with all one's strength; **de f.** by force, forcibly; **à f. de faire qch** through doing sth; **les forces armées** the armed forces ▪ **forcément** *adv* inevitably; **pas f.** not necessarily

**forcer** [fɔrse] **1** *vt (obliger)* to force; *(porte)* to force open; *(voix)* to strain; **f. qn à faire qch** to force sb to do sth **2** *vi (appuyer, tirer)* to force it; *(se surmener)* to overdo it **3 se forcer** *vpr* to force oneself (**à faire** to do)

**forer** [fɔre] *vt* to drill, to bore

**forêt** [fɔrɛ] *nf* forest

**forfait** [fɔrfɛ] *nm* (**a**) *(prix)* all-in price; *(de ski)* pass; **f. week-end** weekend package (**b**) *(crime)* heinous crime ▪ **forfaitaire** *adj (indemnités)* basic; **prix f.** all-in price

**forge** [fɔrʒ] *nf* forge ▪ **forger** *vt (métal, liens)* to forge; *Fig (caractère)* to form ▪ **forgeron** [-ərɔ̃] *nm* (black)smith

**formaliser** [fɔrmalize] **se formaliser** *vpr* to take offence (**de** at)

**formalité** [fɔrmalite] *nf* formality

**format** [fɔrma] *nm* format

**formater** [fɔrmate] *vt Ordinat* to format

**formation** [fɔrmɑsjɔ̃] *nf (de roche, de mot)* formation; *(éducation)* education; **f. permanente** continuing education; **f. professionnelle** vocational training ▪ **formateur, -trice 1** *adj* formative **2** *nmf* trainer

**forme** [fɔrm] *nf (contour)* shape, form; *(manière, bonne santé)* form; **en f. de qch** in the shape of sth; **en f. de poire** pear-shaped; **sous f. de qch** in the form of sth; **en (pleine) f.** *(en bonne santé)* on (top) form

**formel, -elle** [fɔrmɛl] *adj (structure)* formal; *(personne, preuve)* positive; *(interdiction)* strict

**former** [fɔrme] **1** *vt (groupe, caractère)* to form; *(apprenti)* to train **2 se former** *vpr (apparaître)* to form; *(association, liens)* to be formed; *(apprendre son métier)* to train oneself

**formidable** [fɔrmidabl] *adj (fantastique)* great; *(gigantesque)* tremendous

**formulaire** [fɔrmylɛr] *nm* form

**formule** [fɔrmyl] *nf Math* formula; *(phrase)* expression; *(solution)* method; **nouvelle f.** *(menu)* new-style; **f. magique** magic formula ▪ **formulation** *nf* formulation ▪ **formuler** *vt* to formulate

**fort[1], -e** [fɔr, fɔrt] **1** *adj (vigoureux)* strong; *(gros, important)* large; *(pluie, mer, chute de neige)* heavy; *(voix)* loud; *(fièvre)* high; *(pente)* steep; **être f. en qch** *(doué)* to be good at sth

**2** *adv (frapper, pleuvoir)* hard; *(parler)* loud(ly); *(serrer)* tight; **sentir f.** to have a strong smell; **respirer f.** to breathe heavily

**3** *nm (spécialité)* strong point

**fort[2]** [fɔr] *nm Hist & Mil* fort ▪ **forteresse** *nf* fortress

**fortifié, -e** [fɔrtifje] *adj (ville, camp)* fortified ▪ **fortification** *nf* fortification

**fortifier** [fɔrtifje] *vt (mur, ville)* to fortify; *(corps)* to strengthen ▪ **fortifiant** *nm* tonic

**fortune** [fɔrtyn] *nf (richesse, hasard)*

fortune; **faire f.** to make one's fortune

**fosse** [fos] *nf (trou)* pit; **f. d'orchestre** orchestra pit

**fossé** [fose] *nm* ditch; *(de château)* moat; *Fig (désaccord)* gulf

**fossette** [fosɛt] *nf* dimple

**fossoyeur** [foswajœr] *nm* gravedigger

**fou, folle** [fu, fɔl]

**fol** is used before masculine singular nouns beginning with a vowel or h mute.

**1** *adj (personne, projet)* mad, insane; *(succès, temps)* tremendous; *(envie)* wild, mad; *(espoir)* foolish; **f. de qch** *(musique, personne)* mad about sth; **f. de joie** beside oneself with joy

**2** *nmf* madman, *f* madwoman

**3** *nm (bouffon)* jester; *Échecs* bishop

**foudre** [fudr] *nf* **la f.** lightning ▪ **foudroyant,-e** *adj (succès, vitesse)* staggering ▪ **foudroyer** *vt* to strike; **f. qn du regard** to give sb a withering look

**fouet** [fwɛ] *nm* whip; *Culin* whisk; **coup de f.** lash (with a whip); **de plein f.** head-on ▪ **fouetter** *vt* to whip; *(sujet: pluie)* to lash (against); **crème fouettée** whipped cream

**fougère** [fuʒɛr] *nf* fern

**fougue** [fug] *nf* fire, spirit ▪ **fougueux, -euse** *adj* fiery, ardent

**fouille** [fuj] **1** *nf (de personne, de bagages)* search **2** *nfpl* **fouilles archéologiques** excavations, dig ▪ **fouiller 1** *vt (personne, maison)* to search **2** *vi* **f. dans qch** *(tiroir)* to search through sth **3** *vti (creuser)* to dig

**fouillis** [fuji] *nm* jumble

**foulard** [fular] *nm* (head)scarf

**foule** [ful] *nf* crowd; **une f. de** *(objets)* a mass of

**foulée** [fule] *nf (de coureur, de cheval)* stride

**fouler** [fule] **1** *vt (sol)* to tread; **f. qch aux pieds** to trample sth underfoot **2 se fouler** *vpr* **se f. la cheville** to sprain one's ankle ▪ **foulure** *nf* sprain

**four** [fur] *nm (de cuisine)* oven; *(de potier)* kiln; **petit f.** *(gâteau)* (small) fancy cake

**fourche** [furʃ] *nf (outil, embranchement)* fork; **faire une f.** to fork ▪ **fourcher** *vi (arbre)* to fork ▪ **fourchette** *nf (pour manger)* fork; *(de salaires)* bracket ▪ **fourchu, -e** *adj* forked

**fourgon** [furgɔ̃] *nm (camion)* van; **f. cellulaire** *Br* prison van, *Am* patrol wagon

**fourmi** [furmi] *nf (insecte)* ant; **avoir des fourmis dans les jambes** to have pins and needles in one's legs ▪ **fourmiller** *vi* to teem, to swarm (**de** with)

**fourneau, -x** [furno] *nm (de cuisine)* stove

**fournir** [furnir] *vt (approvisionner)* to supply (**en** with); *(alibi, preuve, document)* to provide; *(effort)* to make; **f. qch à qn** to provide sb with sth; **pièces à f.** required documents ▪ **fourni, -e** *adj (barbe)* bushy; **bien f.** *(boutique)* well-stocked ▪ **fournisseur** *nm (commerçant)* supplier; *Ordinat* **f. d'accès** access provider ▪ **fournitures** *nfpl* **f. de bureau** office supplies; **f. scolaires** school stationery

**fourrage** [furaʒ] *nm* fodder

**fourré, -e** [fure] **1** *adj (vêtement)* furlined; *(gâteau)* jam-/cream-filled **2** *nm Bot* thicket

**fourreau, -x** [furo] *nm (gaine)* sheath

**fourrer** [fure] **1** *vt (vêtement)* to furline; *(gâteau)* to fill **2 se fourrer** *vpr Fam* to put oneself (**dans** in); **où est-il allé se f.?** where's he got to? ▪ **fourretout** *nm inv (sac) Br* holdall, *Am* carryall

**fourrière** [furjɛr] *nf (lieu)* pound; **mettre à la f.** *(voiture)* to impound; *(chien)* to put in the pound

**fourrure** [furyr] *nf* fur

**foyer** [fwaje] *nm (maison)* home; *(d'étudiants)* residence; *(de travailleurs)* hostel; *(de théâtre)* foyer; *(de lunettes)* focus; *(de chaleur, d'infection)* source; *(d'incendie)* seat; *(âtre)* hearth; *(famille)* family

**fracas** [fraka] *nm* crash ▪ **fracassant, -e** *adj (nouvelle, révélation)* shattering

■ **fracasser** *vt*, **se fracasser** *vpr* to smash

**fraction** [fraksjɔ̃] *nf* fraction; *(partie)* part ■ **fractionner** *vt*, **se fractionner** *vpr* to split (up)

**fracture** [fraktyr] *nf* fracture ■ **fracturer 1** *vt (porte)* to break open; *(os)* to fracture **2 se fracturer** *vpr* **se f. la jambe** to fracture one's leg

**fragile** [fraʒil] *adj (objet, matériau)* fragile; *(santé, équilibre)* delicate; *(personne) (physiquement)* frail; *(mentalement)* sensitive ■ **fragilité** *nf (d'objet, de matériau)* fragility; *(de personne) (physique)* frailty; *(mentale)* sensitivity

**fragment** [fragmɑ̃] *nm* fragment

**fraîcheur** [frɛʃœr] *nf (d'aliments)* freshness; *(de température)* coolness

**frais[1], fraîche** [frɛ, frɛʃ] **1** *adj (aliment, fleurs)* fresh; *(vent, air)* cool, fresh; *(nouvelles)* recent; *(peinture)* wet

**2** *adv* **servir f.** *(vin)* to serve chilled

**3** *nm* **mettre qch au f.** to put sth in a cool place; *(au réfrigérateur)* to refrigerate sth; **il fait f.** it's cool ■ **fraîchir** *vi (temps)* to freshen

**frais[2]** [frɛ] *nmpl* expenses; **à mes f.** at my (own) expense; **faire des f.** to go to great expense; **f. de scolarité** school fees

**fraise** [frɛz] *nf (fruit)* strawberry; *(de dentiste)* drill ■ **fraisier** *nm (plante)* strawberry plant; *(gâteau)* strawberry cream cake

**framboise** [frɑ̃bwaz] *nf* raspberry ■ **framboisier** *nm* raspberry bush

**franc[1], franche** [frɑ̃, frɑ̃ʃ] *adj* (**a**) *(sincère)* frank; *(visage)* open (**b**) *(net) (couleur)* pure (**c**) *(zone, ville, port)* free ■ **franchement** *adv (sincèrement)* frankly; *(vraiment)* really; *(sans ambiguïté)* clearly

**franc[2]** [frɑ̃] *nm Anciennement (monnaie)* franc

**France** *nf* **la F.** France ■ **français, -e 1** *adj* French **2** *nmf* **F.** Frenchman; **Française** Frenchwoman; **les F.** the French **3** *nm (langue)* French

**franchir** [frɑ̃ʃir] *vt (obstacle)* to get over; *(fossé)* to jump over; *(frontière, ligne d'arrivée)* to cross; *(porte)* to go through; *(distance)* to cover

**franchise** [frɑ̃ʃiz] *nf (sincérité)* frankness; *(exonération)* exemption; *Com* franchise; **f. postale** ≃ postage paid

**franc-maçon** [frɑ̃masɔ̃] *(pl* **francs-maçons)** *nm* freemason

**francophone** [frɑ̃kɔfɔn] **1** *adj* French-speaking **2** *nmf* French speaker

**franc-parler** [frɑ̃parle] *nm* **avoir son f.** to speak one's mind

**frange** [frɑ̃ʒ] *nf (de cheveux) Br* fringe, *Am* bangs; *(de vêtement)* fringe

**frappe** [frap] *nf (sur machine à écrire)* typing; *(sur ordinateur)* keying; **faute de f.** typing error

**frapper** [frape] **1** *vt (battre)* to strike, to hit; *(monnaie)* to mint; **f. qn** *(impressionner)* to strike sb; *(impôt, mesure)* to hit sb **2** *vi (donner un coup)* to strike, to hit; **f. du pied** to stamp (one's foot); **f. du poing sur la table** to bang (on) the table; **f. à une porte** to knock on a door; **'entrez sans f.'** 'go straight in' ■ **frappant, -e** *adj* striking ■ **frappé, -e** *adj (boisson)* chilled

**fraternel, -elle** [fraternɛl] *adj* fraternal, brotherly ■ **fraternité** *nf* fraternity, brotherhood

**fraude** [frod] *nf* fraud; **passer qch en f.** to smuggle sth in; **f. fiscale** tax evasion ■ **frauder 1** *vt* **f. le fisc** to evade tax **2** *vi* to cheat (**sur** on) ■ **fraudeur, -euse** *nmf* defrauder ■ **frauduleux, -euse** *adj* fraudulent

**frayer** [frɛje] **se frayer** *vpr* **se f. un chemin** to clear a way (**à travers/dans** through)

**frayeur** [frɛjœr] *nf* fright

**fredonner** [frədɔne] *vti* to hum

**frein** [frɛ̃] *nm* brake; **donner un coup de f.** to put on the brakes; **f. à main** handbrake ■ **freiner 1** *vt (véhicule)* to slow down; *(chute)* to break; *Fig (inflation)* to curb **2** *vi* to brake

**frelaté, -e** [frəlate] *adj (vin) & Fig* adulterated

**frêle** [frɛl] *adj* frail
**frémir** [fremir] *vi (personne)* to tremble (**de** with); *(feuilles)* to rustle; *(eau chaude)* to simmer ▪ **frémissement** *nm (de peur)* shudder; *(de plaisir)* thrill; *(de colère)* quiver; *(de feuilles)* rustle; *(d'eau chaude)* simmering
**frénétique** [frenetik] *adj* frenzied
**fréquent, -e** [frekɑ̃, -ɑ̃t] *adj* frequent ▪ **fréquence** *nf* frequency
**fréquenter** [frekɑ̃te] **1** *vt (lieu)* to frequent; **f. qn** to see sb regularly **2 se fréquenter** *vpr (se voir régulièrement)* to see each other socially ▪ **fréquentation** *nf (de lieu)* frequenting; **fréquentations** *(relations)* company ▪ **fréquenté, -e** *adj* **mal f.** disreputable, of ill repute; **bien f.** reputable, of good repute
**frère** [frɛr] *nm* brother
**friable** [frijabl] *adj* crumbly
**friand, -e** [frijɑ̃, -ɑ̃d] **1** *adj* **f. de qch** fond of sth **2** *nm (salé)* = small savoury pastry ▪ **friandise** *nf Br* titbit, *Am* tidbit
**friction** [friksjɔ̃] *nf (massage)* rubdown; *(de cuir chevelu)* scalp massage; *(désaccord)* friction ▪ **frictionner** *vt (partie du corps)* to rub; *(personne)* to rub down
**Frigidaire**® [friʒidɛr] *nm* fridge
**frileux, -euse** [frilø, -øz] *adj* **être f.** to feel the cold
**friper** [fripe] **1** *vt* to crumple **2 se friper** *vpr* to get crumpled ▪ **fripé, -e** *adj* crumpled
**frire*** [frir] **1** *vt* to fry **2** *vi* to fry; **faire f. qch** to fry sth
**friser** [frize] **1** *vt (cheveux)* to curl; *(effleurer)* to skim; **f. la catastrophe** to come within an inch of disaster **2** *vi (cheveux)* to curl; *(personne)* to have curly hair ▪ **frisé, -e** *adj (cheveux)* curly; *(personne)* curly-haired
**frisson** [frisɔ̃] *nm (de froid, de peur)* shiver; *(de plaisir)* thrill ▪ **frissonner** *vi (de froid, de peur)* to shiver
**frit, -e** [fri, -it] **1** *pp de* **frire 2** *adj* fried ▪ **frites** *nfpl Br* chips, *Am* French fries ▪ **friture** *nf (mode de cuisson)* frying; *(aliment)* fried food
**frivole** [frivɔl] *adj* frivolous
**froid, -e** [frwa, frwad] **1** *adj* cold **2** *nm* cold; **avoir f.** to be/catch cold; **il fait f.** it's cold
**froisser** [frwase] **1** *vt (tissu)* to crumple, to crease **2 se froisser** *vpr (tissu)* to crease, to crumple; **se f. un muscle** to strain a muscle
**frôler** [frole] *vt (effleurer)* to brush against, to touch lightly; *Fig (catastrophe)* to come close to
**fromage** [frɔmaʒ] *nm* cheese; **f. de chèvre** goat's cheese; **f. blanc** soft cheese; **f. frais** fromage frais ▪ **fromager, -ère** *nmf (fabricant)* cheesemaker; *(commerçant)* cheese seller ▪ **fromagerie** *nf (magasin)* cheese shop
**froment** [frɔmɑ̃] *nm* wheat
**froncer** [frɔ̃se] *vt (tissu)* to gather; **f. les sourcils** to frown
**front** [frɔ̃] *nm (du visage)* forehead; *(avant), Mil & Pol* front; **de f.** *(heurter)* head-on; *(côte à côte)* abreast; *(à la fois)* (all) at once; **faire f. à qn/qch** to face up to sb/sth; **f. de mer** sea front ▪ **frontal, -e, -aux, -ales** *adj (collision)* head-on
**frontière** [frɔ̃tjɛr] **1** *nf (de pays)* border **2** *adj inv* **ville f.** border town ▪ **frontalier, -ère** *adj* **ville frontalière** border *or* frontier town
**frotter** [frɔte] **1** *vt* to rub; *(plancher)* to scrub; *(allumette)* to strike **2** *vi* to rub (**contre** against) **3 se frotter** *vpr* to rub oneself; **se f. le dos** to scrub one's back
**fructifier** [fryktifje] *vi (arbre, capital)* to bear fruit ▪ **fructueux, -euse** *adj* fruitful
**frugal, -e, -aux, -ales** [frygal, -o] *adj* frugal
**fruit** [frɥi] *nm* fruit; **des fruits** fruit; **un f.** a piece of fruit; **fruits de mer** seafood; **fruits secs** dried fruit ▪ **fruité, -e** *adj* fruity ▪ **fruitier** *adj m* **arbre f.** fruit tree

**frustrer** [frystre] *vt* **f. qn** to frustrate sb; **f. qn de qch** to deprive sb of sth ▪ **frustration** *nf* frustration ▪ **frustré, -e** *adj* frustrated

**fuel** [fjul] *nm* fuel oil

**fugitif, -ive** [fyʒitif, -iv] **1** *adj (passager)* fleeting **2** *nmf* runaway, fugitive

**fugue** [fyg] *nf* **faire une f.** *(enfant)* to run away ▪ **fuguer** *vi Fam* to run away

**fuir*** [fɥir] **1** *vt (pays)* to flee; *(personne)* to run away from; *(guerre)* to escape **2** *vi (s'échapper)* to run away (**devant** from); *(gaz, robinet, stylo)* to leak ▪ **fuite** *nf (évasion)* flight (**devant** from); *(de gaz)* leak; **en f.** on the run; **prendre la f.** to take flight

**fulgurant, -e** [fylgyrɑ̃, -ɑ̃t] *adj (progrès)* spectacular; *(douleur)* shooting

**fumer** [fyme] **1** *vt (cigarette, poisson)* to smoke; **f. la pipe** to smoke a pipe **2** *vi (fumeur, moteur)* to smoke; *(liquide brûlant)* to steam ▪ **fumé, -e** *adj (poisson, verre)* smoked ▪ **fumée** *nf* smoke; *(vapeur)* steam ▪ **fumeur, -euse** *nmf* smoker

**fumeux, -euse** [fymø, -øz] *adj Fig (idée)* hazy

**fumier** [fymje] *nm (engrais)* manure, dung

**funambule** [fynɑ̃byl] *nmf* tightrope walker

**funèbre** [fynɛbr] *adj (lugubre)* gloomy; **marche f.** funeral march ▪ **funérailles** *nfpl* funeral ▪ **funéraire** *adj* funeral

**funiculaire** [fynikylɛr] *nm* funicular

**fur** [fyr] **au fur et à mesure** *adv* as one goes along, progressively; **au f. et à mesure que...** as...

**furent** [fyr] *voir* **être**

**furie** [fyri] *nf (colère)* fury ▪ **furieux, -euse** *adj (en colère)* furious (**contre** with)

**fuseau, -x** [fyzo] *nm (pantalon)* ski pants; *(bobine)* spindle; **f. horaire** time zone

**fusée** [fyze] *nf* rocket

**fuselage** [fyzlaʒ] *nm (d'avion)* fuselage

**fusible** [fyzibl] *nm* fuse

**fusil** [fyzi] *nm* rifle, gun; *(de chasse)* shotgun ▪ **fusillade** *nf (tirs)* gunfire ▪ **fusiller** *vt (exécuter)* to shoot

**fusion** [fyzjɔ̃] *nf* (**a**) *(de métal)* melting; *Phys* fusion; **métal en f.** molten metal (**b**) *(de sociétés)* merger ▪ **fusionner** *vti (sociétés)* to merge

**fut** [fy] *voir* **être**

**futile** [fytil] *adj (personne)* frivolous; *(prétexte)* trivial

**futur, -ure** [fytyr] **1** *adj* future; **future mère** mother-to-be **2** *nmf* **mon f./ma future** my intended **3** *nm (avenir)* future

**fuyant** [fɥijɑ̃] *p prés de* **fuir** ▪ **fuyant, -e** *adj (front)* receding; *(personne)* evasive ▪ **fuyard, -e** *nmf* runaway

# Gg

**G, g** [ʒe] *nm inv* G, g
**gabarit** [gabari] *nm (dimension)* size
**gâcher** [gɑʃe] *vt (gâter)* to spoil; *(gaspiller)* to waste ■ **gâchis** *nm* waste
**gâchette** [gɑʃɛt] *nf* trigger
**gadget** [gadʒɛt] *nm* gadget
**gadoue** [gadu] *nf* mud
**gag** [gag] *nm* gag
**gage** [gaʒ] *nm (garantie)* guarantee; *(au jeu)* forfeit; *(preuve)* token
**gagnant, -e** [gaɲɑ̃, -ɑ̃t] **1** *adj (billet, cheval)* winning **2** *nmf* winner
**gagner** [gaɲe] **1** *vt (par le travail)* to earn; *(par le jeu)* to win; *(obtenir)* to gain; *(atteindre)* to reach; *(sujet: feu, épidémie)* to spread to; **g. sa vie** to earn one's living; **g. du temps** *(aller plus vite)* to save time; *(temporiser)* to gain time; **g. du terrain** to gain ground; **g. de la place** to save space **2** *vi (être vainqueur)* to win ■ **gagne-pain** *nm inv* livelihood
**gai, -e** [gɛ] *adj* cheerful ■ **gaieté** *nf* cheerfulness
**gaillard** [gajar] *nm (homme)* fellow; **un grand g.** a strapping man
**gain** [gɛ̃] *nm (profit)* gain, profit; *(succès)* winning; **gains** *(à la Bourse)* profits; *(au jeu)* winnings
**gaine** [gɛn] *nf (étui)* sheath
**gala** [gala] *nm* gala
**galant, -e** [galɑ̃, -ɑ̃t] *adj (homme)* gallant; *(rendez-vous)* romantic ■ **galanterie** *nf* gallantry
**galaxie** [galaksi] *nf* galaxy
**galerie** [galri] *nf (passage, salle)* gallery; *(de taupe)* tunnel; **g. d'art** art gallery; **g. marchande** (shopping) mall
**galet** [galɛ] *nm* pebble; **plage de galets** shingle beach
**galette** [galɛt] *nf (gâteau)* butter biscuit; *(crêpe)* buckwheat pancake; **g. des Rois** = Twelfth Night cake
**Galles** [gal] *nm* **pays de G.** Wales ■ **gallois, -e 1** *adj* Welsh **2** *nmf* **G.** Welshman; **Galloise** Welshwoman **3** *nm (langue)* Welsh
**galon** [galɔ̃] *nm (ruban)* braid; *(de soldat)* stripe
**galop** [galo] *nm* gallop; **aller au g.** to gallop ■ **galoper** *vi (cheval)* to gallop
**gambader** [gɑ̃bade] *vi* to leap *or* frisk about
**Gambie** [gɑ̃bi] *nf* **la G.** The Gambia
**gamelle** [gamɛl] *nf (de chien)* bowl; *(d'ouvrier)* billy(can); *(de soldat)* mess tin
**gamin, -e** [gamɛ̃, -in] *nmf (enfant)* kid
**gamme** [gam] *nf Mus* scale; *(éventail)* range; **téléviseur haut/bas de g.** top-of-the-range/bottom-of-the-range television
**gang** [gɑ̃g] *nm* gang
**gant** [gɑ̃] *nm* glove; **g. de toilette** ≃ facecloth
**garage** [garaʒ] *nm (de voitures)* garage ■ **garagiste** *nmf (mécanicien)* garage mechanic; *(propriétaire)* garage owner
**garant, -e** [garɑ̃, -ɑ̃t] *nmf Jur (personne)* guarantor; **se porter g. de qn** to stand guarantor for sb; **se porter g. de qch** to vouch for sth
**garantie** [garɑ̃ti] *nf* guarantee; *Fig (précaution)* safeguard; **sous g.** under

guarantee ▪ **garantir** *vt* to guarantee; *(emprunt)* to secure; **g. à qn que...** to guarantee sb that...

**garçon** [garsɔ̃] *nm* boy; *(jeune homme)* young man; *(serveur)* waiter; **g. de café** waiter; **g. d'honneur** best man; **g. manqué** tomboy

**garde** [gard] **1** *nm (gardien)* guard; *(soldat)* guardsman; **g. du corps** bodyguard

**2** *nf* (**a**) *(d'enfants, de bagages)* care, custody (**de** of); **avoir la g. de** to be in charge of; **prendre g.** to pay attention (**à qch** to sth); **être de g.** to be on duty; *(soldat)* to be on guard duty; **médecin de g.** duty doctor

(**b**) *(escorte, soldats)* guard

**3** *nm* **g. de nuit** *(de malade)* night nurse ▪ **garde-à-vous** *nm inv Mil* (position of) attention; **se mettre au g.** to stand to attention ▪ **garde-chasse** (*pl* **gardes-chasses**) *nm* gamekeeper ▪ **garde-côte** (*pl* **garde-côtes**) *nm (bateau)* coastguard vessel ▪ **garde-manger** *nm inv (armoire)* food safe; *(pièce)* pantry, *Br* larder ▪ **garde-robe** (*pl* **garde-robes**) *nf* wardrobe

**garder** [garde] **1** *vt (conserver)* to keep; *(vêtement)* to keep on; *(habitude)* to keep up; *(surveiller)* to look after; *(défendre)* to protect **2 se garder** *vpr (aliment)* to keep; **se g. de qch** to beware of sth; **se g. de faire qch** to take care not to do sth

**garderie** [gardəri] *nf Br* (day) nursery, *Am* daycare center

**gardien, -enne** [gardjɛ̃, -ɛn] *nmf (d'immeuble, d'hôtel)* caretaker, *Am* janitor; *(de prison)* (prison) guard, *Br* warder; *(de zoo)* keeper; *(de musée) Br* attendant, *Am* guard; **g. de but** *(au football)* goalkeeper; **gardienne d'enfants** child minder, baby-sitter; **g. de nuit** night watchman; **g. de la paix** policeman

**gare** [gar] *nf (pour trains)* station; **g. routière** bus *or Br* coach station

**garer** [gare] **1** *vt (voiture)* to park **2 se garer** *vpr (automobiliste)* to park

**gargariser** [gargarize] **se gargariser** *vpr* to gargle

**gargouiller** [garguje] *vi (fontaine, eau)* to gurgle; *(ventre)* to rumble

**garnir** [garnir] *vt (décorer)* to trim (**de** with); *(équiper)* to fit out (**de** with); *(couvrir)* to cover; *(remplir)* to fill ▪ **garniture** *nf Culin* garnish

**garnison** [garnizɔ̃] *nf* garrison

**gaspiller** [gaspije] *vt* to waste ▪ **gaspillage** *nm* waste

**gastronomie** [gastrɔnɔmi] *nf* gastronomy

**gâté, -e** [gɑte] *adj (dent, fruit)* bad; **enfant g.** spoilt child

**gâteau, -x** [gɑto] *nm* cake; **g. sec** *Br* biscuit, *Am* cookie

**gâter** [gɑte] **1** *vt* to spoil **2 se gâter** *vpr (aliment, dent)* to go bad; *(temps)* to take a turn for the worst

**gâteux, -euse** [gɑtø, -øz] *adj* senile

**gauche**[1] [goʃ] **1** *adj (côté, main)* left

**2** *nf* **la g.** *(côté)* the left (side); *Pol* the left (wing); **à g.** *(tourner)* (to the) left; *(marcher)* on the left, on the left(-hand) side; **de g.** *(fenêtre, colonne)* left-hand; *(parti, politique)* left-wing; **à g. de** on *or* to the left of ▪ **gaucher, -ère 1** *adj* left-handed **2** *nmf* left-hander ▪ **gauchiste** *adj & nmf Pol* (extreme) leftist

**gauche**[2] [goʃ] *adj (maladroit)* awkward

**gaufre** [gofr] *nf* waffle ▪ **gaufrette** *nf* wafer (biscuit)

**gaver** [gave] **1** *vt (animal)* to force-feed; *Fig (personne)* to stuff (**de** with) **2 se gaver** *vpr* to stuff oneself (**de** with)

**gaz** [gɑz] *nm inv* gas; **masque à g.** gas mask; **g. carbonique** carbon dioxide; **g. d'échappement** exhaust fumes ▪ **gazeux, -euse** *adj (état)* gaseous; *(boisson)* fizzy, carbonated; *(eau)* sparkling

**gazole** [gɑzɔl] *nm* diesel oil

**gazon** [gɑzɔ̃] *nm (herbe)* grass; *(surface)* lawn

**gazouiller** [gazuje] *vi (oiseau)* to

chirp; *(bébé, ruisseau)* to babble
**géant, -e** [ʒeɑ̃, -ɑ̃t] *adj & nmf* giant
**geindre*** [ʒɛ̃dr] *vi (gémir)* to moan
**gel** [ʒɛl] *nm* (**a**) *(temps, glace)* frost (**b**) *(pour cheveux)* gel ▪ **gelé, -e** *adj* frozen; *Méd* frostbitten ▪ **gelée** *nf* (**a**) frost; **g. blanche** ground frost (**b**) *(de fruits, de viande)* jelly ▪ **geler 1** *vt* to freeze **2** *vi* to freeze; **on gèle ici** it's freezing here **3** *v impersonnel* **il gèle** it's freezing
**Gémeaux** [ʒemo] *nmpl* **les G.** *(signe)* Gemini
**gémir** [ʒemir] *vi* to groan, to moan ▪ **gémissement** *nm* groan, moan
**gênant, -e** [ʒɛnɑ̃, -ɑ̃t] *adj (objet)* cumbersome; *(présence, situation)* awkward; *(bruit, personne)* annoying
**gencive** [ʒɑ̃siv] *nf* gum
**gendarme** [ʒɑ̃darm] *nm* gendarme, policeman ▪ **gendarmerie** *nf (corps)* police force; *(local)* police headquarters
**gendre** [ʒɑ̃dr] *nm* son-in-law
**gène** [ʒɛn] *nm Biol* gene
**gêne** [ʒɛn] *nf (trouble physique)* discomfort; *(confusion)* embarrassment; *(dérangement)* inconvenience
**gêné, -e** [ʒene] *adj (intimidé)* embarrassed; *(silence, sourire)* awkward
**généalogie** [ʒenealɔʒi] *nf* genealogy ▪ **généalogique** *adj* genealogical; **arbre g.** family tree
**gêner** [ʒene] **1** *vt (déranger, irriter)* to bother; *(troubler)* to embarrass; *(mouvement)* to hamper; *(circulation)* to hold up; **ça ne me gêne pas** I don't mind (**si** if) **2 se gêner** *vpr (se déranger)* to put oneself out
**général, -e, -aux, -ales** [ʒeneral, -o] **1** *adj* general; **en g.** in general **2** *nm Mil* general ▪ **généralité** *nf* generality
**généralisation** [ʒeneralizɑsjɔ̃] *nf* generalization ▪ **généraliser 1** *vti* to generalize **2 se généraliser** *vpr* to become widespread ▪ **généraliste** *nmf (médecin)* general practitioner, GP
**générateur** [ʒeneratœr] *nm Él* generator
**génération** [ʒenerɑsjɔ̃] *nf* generation
**génératrice** [ʒeneratris] *nf Él* generator
**générer** [ʒenere] *vt* to generate
**généreux, -euse** [ʒenerø, -øz] *adj* generous (**de** with)
**générique** [ʒenerik] **1** *nm (de film)* credits **2** *adj* **produit g.** generic product
**générosité** [ʒenerozite] *nf* generosity
**génétique** [ʒenetik] **1** *nf* genetics *(sing)* **2** *adj* genetic; **manipulation g.** genetic engineering ▪ **génétiquement** *adv* **g. modifié** genetically modified
**Genève** [ʒənɛv] *nm ou f* Geneva
**génial, -e, -aux, -ales** [ʒenjal, -jo] *adj (personne, invention)* brilliant
**génie** [ʒeni] *nm* (**a**) *(aptitude, personne)* genius; **avoir le g. pour faire qch** to have a genius for doing sth (**b**) **g. civil** civil engineering; **g. génétique** genetic engineering (**c**) *(esprit)* genie, spirit
**genou, -x** [ʒ(ə)nu] *nm* knee; **être à genoux** to be kneeling (down); **se mettre à genoux** to kneel (down)
**genre** [ʒɑ̃r] *nm (espèce)* kind, sort; *(attitude)* manner; *Beaux-Arts* genre; *Gram* gender; **le g. humain** mankind
**gens** [ʒɑ̃] *nmpl* people
**gentil, -ille** [ʒɑ̃ti, -ij] *adj (aimable)* nice (**avec** to); *(sage)* good ▪ **gentillesse** *nf* kindness; **avoir la g. de faire qch** to be kind enough to do sth ▪ **gentiment** *adv (aimablement)* kindly; *(sagement)* nicely
**géographie** [ʒeɔgrafi] *nf* geography ▪ **géographique** *adj* geographical
**geôlier, -ère** [ʒolje, -jɛr] *nmf* jailer
**géologie** [ʒeɔlɔʒi] *nf* geology ▪ **géologique** *adj* geological
**géomètre** [ʒeɔmɛtr] *nm* surveyor
**géométrie** [ʒeɔmetri] *nf* geometry ▪ **géométrique** *adj* geometric(al)
**gérant, -e** [ʒerɑ̃, -ɑ̃t] *nmf* manager, *f* manageress
**gerbe** [ʒɛrb] *nf (de blé)* sheaf; *(de fleurs)* bunch; *(d'eau)* spray

**gercer** [ʒɛrse] *vi*, **se gercer** *vpr (peau, lèvres)* to chap ▪ **gerçure** *nf* chap, crack

**gérer** [ʒere] *vt* to manage

**germe** [ʒɛrm] *nm (microbe)* germ; *(de plante)* shoot ▪ **germer** *vi (graine)* to start to grow; *(pomme de terre)* to sprout

**geste** [ʒɛst] *nm* gesture; **faire un g.** *(bouger, agir)* to make a gesture; **ne pas faire un g.** *(ne pas bouger)* not to make a move

**gestion** [ʒɛstjɔ̃] *nf (action)* management ▪ **gestionnaire** *nmf* administrator

**Ghana** [gana] *nm* **le G.** Ghana

**gibier** [ʒibje] *nm* game

**giboulée** [ʒibule] *nf* sudden shower; **giboulées de mars** ≃ April showers

**gicler** [ʒikle] *vi (liquide)* to spurt out; *(boue)* to splash up

**gifle** [ʒifl] *nf* slap in the face ▪ **gifler** *vt* **g. qn** to slap sb in the face

**gigantesque** [ʒigɑ̃tɛsk] *adj* gigantic

**gigot** [ʒigo] *nm* leg of mutton/lamb

**gilet** [ʒilɛ] *nm (cardigan)* cardigan; *(de costume) Br* waistcoat, *Am* vest; **g. pare-balles** bulletproof vest; **g. de sauvetage** life jacket

**gingembre** [ʒɛ̃ʒɑ̃br] *nm* ginger

**girafe** [ʒiraf] *nf* giraffe

**giratoire** [ʒiratwar] *adj Aut* **sens g.** *Br* roundabout, *Am* traffic circle

**girofle** [ʒirɔfl] *nm* **clou de g.** clove

**gisement** [ʒizmɑ̃] *nm (de minerai)* deposit; **g. de pétrole** oilfield

**gitan, -e** [ʒitɑ̃, -an] *nmf* gipsy

**gîte** [ʒit] *nm (abri)* resting place; **g. rural** gîte, = self-catering holiday cottage or apartment

**givre** [ʒivr] *nm* frost ▪ **givré, -e** *adj* frost-covered

**glace** [glas] *nf* (**a**) *(eau gelée)* ice; *(crème glacée)* ice cream (**b**) *(vitre)* window; *(miroir)* mirror

**glacer** [glase] *vt (durcir)* to freeze; *(gâteau)* to ice ▪ **glaçage** *nm (de gâteau)* icing ▪ **glacé, -e** *adj (eau, pièce)* ice-cold, icy; *(vent)* freezing, icy; *(thé, café)* iced; *(papier)* glazed

**glacial, -e, -aux, -ales** [glasjal, -o] *adj* icy

**glacier** [glasje] *nm* (**a**) *Géol* glacier (**b**) *(vendeur)* ice-cream seller

**glacière** [glasjɛr] *nf (boîte)* icebox

**glaçon** [glasɔ̃] *nm Culin* ice cube; *Géol* block of ice; *(sur toit)* icicle

**glande** [glɑ̃d] *nf* gland

**glaner** [glane] *vt (blé, renseignement)* to glean

**glisse** [glis] *nf* **sports de g.** = sports involving sliding and gliding motion, eg skiing, surfing etc

**glisser** [glise] **1** *vt (introduire)* to slip (**dans** into); *(murmurer)* to whisper **2** *vi (involontairement)* to slip; *(volontairement) (sur glace)* to slide; *(sur l'eau)* to glide; **ça glisse** it's slippery **3 se glisser** *vpr* **se g. dans/sous qch** to slip into/under sth ▪ **glissade** *nf (involontaire)* slip; *(volontaire)* slide ▪ **glissant, -e** *adj* slippery ▪ **glissement** *nm* **g. de terrain** landslide

**glissière** [glisjɛr] *nf Tech* runner, slide; **porte à g.** sliding door

**global, -e, -aux, -ales** [glɔbal, -o] *adj* total, global ▪ **globalement** *adv* overall

**globe** [glɔb] *nm* globe; **g. terrestre** *(mappemonde)* globe

**globuleux, -euse** [glɔbylø, -øz] *adj* **yeux g.** protruding eyes

**gloire** [glwar] *nf (renom)* glory; *(personne célèbre)* celebrity ▪ **glorieux, -euse** *adj* glorious ▪ **glorifier 1** *vt* to glorify **2 se glorifier** *vpr* **se g. de qch** to glory in sth

**glousser** [gluse] *vi (poule)* to cluck; *(personne)* to chuckle

**glouton, -onne** [glutɔ̃, -ɔn] **1** *adj* greedy, gluttonous **2** *nmf* glutton

**gluant, -e** [glyɑ̃, -ɑ̃t] *adj* sticky

**goal** [gol] *nm (au football)* goalkeeper

**gobelet** [gɔblɛ] *nm* tumbler; *(de plastique, de papier)* cup

**goéland** [gɔelɑ̃] *nm* (sea)gull

**golf** [gɔlf] *nm* golf; *(terrain)* golf course ▪ **golfeur, -euse** *nmf* golfer

**golfe** [gɔlf] *nm* gulf, bay
**gomme** [gɔm] *nf (pour effacer)* eraser, *Br* rubber ▪ **gommer** *vt (effacer)* to rub out, to erase
**gond** [gɔ̃] *nm (de porte)* hinge
**gondoler** [gɔ̃dɔle] **1** *vi (planche)* to warp; *(papier)* to crinkle **2 se gondoler** *vpr (planche)* to warp; *(papier)* to crinkle
**gonflable** [gɔ̃flabl] *adj* inflatable
**gonfler** [gɔ̃fle] **1** *vt* to swell; *(pneu)* to inflate **2** *vi* to swell ▪ **gonflé, -e** *adj* swollen ▪ **gonflement** *nm* swelling
**gorge** [gɔrʒ] *nf* throat; *Géog* gorge; **avoir la g. serrée** to have a lump in one's throat
**gorgé, -e** [gɔrʒe] *adj* **g. de qch** *(saturé)* gorged with sth
**gorgée** [gɔrʒe] *nf* mouthful; **petite g.** sip
**gorger** [gɔrʒe] **1** *vt (remplir)* to stuff (**de** with) **2 se gorger** *vpr* **se g. de qch** to gorge oneself with sth
**gorille** [gɔrij] *nm (animal)* gorilla
**gothique** [gɔtik] *adj & nm* Gothic
**goudron** [gudrɔ̃] *nm* tar
**gouffre** [gufr] *nm* abyss
**goulot** [gulo] *nm (de bouteille)* neck; **boire au g.** to drink from the bottle
**goulu, -e** [guly] *adj* greedy
**goupille** [gupij] *nf (de grenade)* pin
**gourde** [gurd] *nf (à eau)* water bottle, flask
**gourmand, -e** [gurmɑ̃, -ɑ̃d] **1** *adj* fond of eating; **g. de qch** fond of sth **2** *nmf* hearty eater ▪ **gourmandise** *nf* fondness for food; **gourmandises** *(mets)* delicacies
**gourmet** [gurmɛ] *nm* gourmet; **fin g.** gourmet
**gousse** [gus] *nf* **g. d'ail** clove of garlic
**goût** [gu] *nm* taste; **de bon g.** in good taste; **par g.** by choice; **avoir du g.** *(personne)* to have (good) taste; **avoir un g. de noisette** to taste of hazelnut
**goûter** [gute] **1** *vt (aliment)* to taste; *(apprécier)* to enjoy; **g. à qch** to taste (a little of) sth **2** *vi* to have an afternoon snack, *Br* to have tea **3** *nm* afternoon snack, *Br* tea
**goutte** [gut] *nf (de liquide)* drop; **couler g. à g.** to drip ▪ **goutte-à-goutte** *nm inv Méd* drip ▪ **gouttelette** *nf* droplet ▪ **goutter** *vi* to drip
**gouttière** [gutjɛr] *nf (le long du toit)* gutter; *(le long du mur)* drainpipe
**gouvernail** [guvɛrnaj] *nm (pale)* rudder; *(barre)* helm
**gouvernante** [guvɛrnɑ̃t] *nf* governess
**gouvernants** [guvɛrnɑ̃] *nmpl* rulers
**gouvernement** [guvɛrnəmɑ̃] *nm* government ▪ **gouvernemental, -e, -aux, -ales** *adj* **politique gouvernementale** government policy
**gouverner** [guvɛrne] *vti Pol & Fig* to govern, to rule ▪ **gouverneur** *nm* governor
**grâce** [grɑs] **1** *nf (charme) & Rel* grace; *(acquittement)* pardon; **de bonne/mauvaise g.** with good/bad grace; **délai de g.** period of grace **2** *prép* **g. à** thanks to
**gracier** [grasje] *vt (condamné)* to pardon
**gracieux, -euse** [grasjø, -øz] *adj (élégant)* graceful; *(aimable)* gracious; *(gratuit)* gratuitous; **à titre g.** free (of charge) ▪ **gracieusement** *adv (avec élégance)* gracefully; *(aimablement)* graciously; *(gratuitement)* free (of charge)
**grade** [grad] *nm (militaire)* rank; **monter en g.** to be promoted ▪ **gradé** *nm Mil* non-commissioned officer
**gradins** [gradɛ̃] *nmpl (d'amphithéâtre)* rows of seats; *(de stade) Br* terraces, *Am* bleachers
**graduel, -elle** [gradɥɛl] *adj* gradual
**graduer** [gradɥe] *vt (règle)* to graduate; *(augmenter)* to increase gradually
**graffiti** [grafiti] *nmpl* graffiti
**grain** [grɛ̃] *nm* (**a**) *(de blé) & Fig* grain; *(de café)* bean; *(de poussière)* speck; **g. de beauté** mole; *(sur le visage)* beauty spot; **g. de raisin** grape (**b**) *(averse)* shower
**graine** [grɛn] *nf* seed
**graisse** [grɛs] *nf* fat; *(lubrifiant)* grease

▪ **graisser** *vt* to grease ▪ **graisseux, -euse** *adj (vêtement)* greasy, oily; *(tissu)* fatty

**grammaire** [gramɛr] *nf* grammar ▪ **grammatical, -e, -aux, -ales** *adj* grammatical

**gramme** [gram] *nm* gram(me)

**GRAND, -E** [grɑ̃, grɑ̃d] **1** *adj* big, large; *(en hauteur)* tall; *(chaleur, découverte, âge, mérite, ami)* great; *(bruit)* loud; *(différence)* big, great; *(adulte)* grown-up, big; *(illustre)* great; **g. frère** *(plus âgé)* big brother; **le g. air** the open air; **il est g. temps que je parte** it's high time that I left; **il n'y avait pas g. monde** there were not many people

**2** *adv* **g. ouvert** *(yeux, fenêtre)* wide open; **ouvrir g.** to open wide; **en g.** on a grand *or* large scale

**3** *nmf (enfant)* senior; *(adulte)* grown-up ▪ **grandement** *adv (beaucoup)* greatly; *(généreusement)* grandly ▪ **grand-mère** (*pl* **grands-mères**) *nf* grandmother ▪ **grand-père** (*pl* **grands-pères**) *nm* grandfather ▪ **grands-parents** *nmpl* grandparents

**grand-chose** [grɑ̃ʃoz] *pron* **pas g.** not much

**Grande-Bretagne** [grɑ̃dbrətaɲ] *nf* **la G.** Great Britain

**grandeur** [grɑ̃dœr] *nf (importance, gloire)* greatness; *(dimension)* size; *(majesté, splendeur)* grandeur; **g. nature** life-size

**grandiose** [grɑ̃djoz] *adj* imposing

**grandir** [grɑ̃dir] **1** *vi (en taille)* to grow; *(en âge)* to grow up; **g. de 2 cm** to grow 2 cm **2** *vt* **g. qn** *(faire paraître plus grand)* to make sb look taller

**grange** [grɑ̃ʒ] *nf* barn

**granit(e)** [granit] *nm* granite

**graphique** [grafik] **1** *adj (signe, art)* graphic **2** *nm* graph; *Ordinat* graphic

**grappe** [grap] *nf (de fruits)* cluster; **g. de raisin** bunch of grapes

**gras, grasse** [grɑ, grɑs] **1** *adj (personne, ventre)* fat; *(aliment)* fatty; *(graisseux)* greasy, oily; *(toux)* loose; **faire la grasse matinée** to have a lie-in **2** *nm (de viande)* fat ▪ **grassement** *adv* **g. payé** handsomely paid ▪ **grassouillet, -ette** *adj* plump

**gratifier** [gratifje] *vt* **g. qn de qch** to present sb with sth ▪ **gratification** *nf (prime)* bonus

**gratin** [gratɛ̃] *nm (plat)* = baked dish with a cheese topping; **chou-fleur au g.** cauliflower cheese

**gratis** [gratis] *adv* free (of charge)

**gratitude** [gratityd] *nf* gratitude

**gratte-ciel** [gratsjɛl] *nm inv* skyscraper

**gratter** [grate] **1** *vt (avec un outil)* to scrape; *(avec les ongles, les griffes)* to scratch; *(effacer)* to scratch out; *Fam* **ça me gratte** it's itchy **2** *vi (tissu)* to be scratchy **3 se gratter** *vpr* to scratch oneself

**gratuit, -e** [gratɥi, -it] *adj (billet, entrée)* free; *(acte)* gratuitous ▪ **gratuité** *nf* **la g. de l'enseignement** free education ▪ **gratuitement** *adv (sans payer)* free (of charge); *(sans motif)* gratuitously

**gravats** [gravɑ] *nmpl* rubble, debris

**grave** [grav] *adj (maladie, faute)* serious; *(visage)* grave; *(voix)* deep, low; **ce n'est pas g.!** it's not important! ▪ **gravement** *adv (malade)* seriously; *(dignement)* gravely

**graver** [grave] *vt (sur métal)* to engrave; *(sur bois)* to carve; *(disque)* to cut ▪ **graveur** *nm* engraver

**gravier** [gravje] *nm* gravel ▪ **gravillon** *nm* piece of gravel; **gravillons** gravel, *Br* (loose) chippings

**gravir** [gravir] *vt* to climb

**gravité** [gravite] *nf (de situation)* seriousness; *(solennité)* & *Phys* gravity; *Phys* **centre de g.** centre of gravity

**graviter** [gravite] *vi* to revolve (**autour** around)

**gravure** [gravyr] *nf (image)* print; *(action, art)* engraving; **g. sur bois** *(action)* woodcarving; *(objet)* woodcut

**gré** [gre] *nm* **de son plein g.** of one's

own free will; **de bon g.** willingly; **contre le g. de qn** against sb's will; **bon g. mal g.** whether we/you/*etc* like it or not; **de g. ou de force** one way or another

**Grèce** [grɛs] *nf* **la G.** Greece ▪ **grec, grecque 1** *adj* Greek **2** *nmf* **G., Grecque** Greek **3** *nm (langue)* Greek

**greffe** [grɛf] **1** *nf (de peau, d'arbre)* graft; *(d'organe)* transplant **2** *nm Jur* record office ▪ **greffer** *vt (peau) & Bot* to graft (**à** on to); *(organe)* to transplant ▪ **greffier** *nm Jur* clerk (of the court)

**grêle**[1] [grɛl] *nf* hail ▪ **grêler** *v impersonnel* to hail; **il grêle** it's hailing ▪ **grêlon** *nm* hailstone

**grêle**[2] [grɛl] *adj (jambes)* skinny; *(voix)* shrill

**grelot** [grəlo] *nm* (small) bell

**grelotter** [grəlɔte] *vi* to shiver (**de** with)

**grenade** [grənad] *nf (fruit)* pomegranate; *(projectile)* grenade

**grenier** [grənje] *nm (de maison)* attic; *(pour le fourrage)* granary

**grenouille** [grənuj] *nf* frog

**grès** [grɛ] *nm (roche)* sandstone; *(poterie)* stoneware

**grésiller** [grezije] *vi (huile)* to sizzle

**grève**[1] [grɛv] *nf (arrêt du travail)* strike; **faire g.** to be on strike; **g. de la faim** hunger strike; **g. du zèle** *Br* work-to-rule, *Am* rule-book slowdown ▪ **gréviste** *nmf* striker

**grève**[2] [grɛv] *nf (de mer)* shore; *(de rivière)* bank

**gribouiller** [gribuje] *vti* to scribble

**grief** [grijɛf] *nm (plainte)* grievance; **faire g. de qch à qn** to hold sth against sb

**grièvement** [grijɛvmɑ̃] *adv* seriously, badly

**griffe** [grif] *nf (ongle)* claw; *(de couturier)* (designer) label; *Fig (style)* stamp ▪ **griffer** *vt* to scratch

**griffonner** [grifɔne] *vt* to scribble, to scrawl

**grignoter** [griɲɔte] *vti* to nibble

**gril** [gril] *nm (ustensile) Br* grill, *Am* broiler ▪ **grillade** *nf (viande) Br* grilled meat, *Am* broiled meat ▪ **grille-pain** *nm inv* toaster ▪ **griller 1** *vt (viande) Br* to grill, *Am* to broil; *(pain)* to toast; *(ampoule électrique)* to blow; *Fam* **g. un feu rouge** to jump the lights; **2** *vi (viande)* to grill; *(pain)* to toast

**grille** [grij] *nf (clôture)* railings; *(porte)* gate; *(de foyer)* grate; *Fig (de salaires)* scale ▪ **grillage** *nm* wire mesh *or* netting

**grillon** [grijɔ̃] *nm* cricket

**grimace** [grimas] *nf (pour faire rire)* (funny) face; *(de douleur)* grimace; **faire la g.** to pull a face ▪ **grimacer** *vi* to make a face; *(de douleur)* to wince (**de** with)

**grimer** [grime] **se grimer** *vpr* to put one's make-up on

**grimper** [grɛ̃pe] **1** *vi* to climb (**à qch** up sth) **2** *vt (escalier)* to climb

**grincer** [grɛ̃se] *vi* to creak; **g. des dents** to grind one's teeth ▪ **grincement** *nm* creaking

**grincheux, -euse** [grɛ̃ʃø, -øz] *adj* grumpy

**grippe** [grip] *nf (maladie)* flu, influenza; **prendre qn en g.** to take a strong dislike to sb ▪ **grippé, -e** *adj* **être g.** to have (the) flu

**gripper** [gripe] **se gripper** *vpr (moteur)* to seize up

**gris, -e** [gri, griz] **1** *adj Br* grey, *Am* gray; *(temps)* dull, grey; *(ivre)* tipsy **2** *nm Br* grey, *Am* gray ▪ **grisaille** *nf (caractère morne)* dreariness

**grisonner** [grizɔne] *vi (cheveux, personne)* to go *Br* grey *or Am* gray

**grivois, -e** [grivwa, -waz] *adj* bawdy

**Groenland** [grɔɛnlɑ̃d] *nm* **le G.** Greenland

**grog** [grɔg] *nm* hot toddy

**grogner** [grɔɲe] *vi (personne)* to grumble (**contre** at); *(cochon)* to grunt ▪ **grognement** *nm (de personne)* growl; *(de cochon)* grunt ▪ **grognon, -onne** *adj* grumpy

**grommeler** [grɔm(ə)le] *vti* to mutter

**gronder** [grɔ̃de] **1** *vt (réprimander)* to scold, to tell off **2** *vi (chien)* to growl; *(tonnerre)* to rumble

**GROS, GROSSE** [gro, gros] **1** *adj (corpulent, important)* big; *(gras)* fat; *(épais)* thick; *(effort, progrès)* great; *(somme, fortune)* large; *(rhume, mer)* heavy; *(faute)* serious, gross; *(traits, laine)* coarse; **g. mot** swearword

**2** *adv* **risquer g.** to take a big risk; **écrire g.** to write big; **en g.** *(globalement)* roughly; *(écrire)* in big letters; *(vendre)* in bulk, wholesale

**3** *nmf (personne)* fat man, *f* fat woman

**4** *nm* **le g. de** the bulk of; **prix de g.** wholesale prices

---

**groseille** [grozɛj] *nf* redcurrant

**grossesse** [grosɛs] *nf* pregnancy

**grosseur** [grosœr] *nf (volume)* size; *(tumeur)* lump

**grossier, -ère** [grosje, -ɛr] *adj (tissu, traits)* rough, coarse; *(personne, manières)* rude, coarse; *(erreur)* gross; *(ruse, instrument)* crude ▪ **grossièrement** *adv (calculer)* roughly; *(répondre)* coarsely, rudely; *(se tromper)* grossly ▪ **grossièreté** *nf (incorrection, vulgarité)* coarseness; *(mot)* rude word

**grossir** [grosir] **1** *vt (sujet: verre, loupe)* to magnify **2** *vi (personne)* to put on weight; *(fleuve)* to swell; *(bosse, foule)* to get bigger ▪ **grossissement** *nm (augmentation de taille)* increase in size; *(de microscope)* magnification

**grossiste** [grosist] *nmf Com* wholesaler

**grosso modo** [grosomɔdo] *adv (en gros)* roughly

**grotesque** [grɔtɛsk] *adj* ludicrous

**grotte** [grɔt] *nf* cave

**grouiller** [gruje] *vi (se presser)* to swarm around; **g. de qch** to swarm with sth

**groupe** [grup] *nm* group; **g. sanguin** blood group ▪ **groupement** *nm (action)* grouping; *(groupe)* group ▪ **grouper 1** *vt* to group (together) **2** **se grouper** *vpr (en association)* to form a group

**grue** [gry] *nf (machine, oiseau)* crane

**grumeau, -x** [grymo] *nm (dans une sauce)* lump

**Guadeloupe** [gwadlup] *nf* **la G.** Guadeloupe

**Guatemala** [gwatemala] *nm* **le G.** Guatemala

**gué** [ge] *nm* ford

**guenon** [gənɔ̃] *nf* female monkey

**guépard** [gepar] *nm* cheetah

**guêpe** [gɛp] *nf* wasp

**guère** [gɛr] *adv* **(ne...) g.** *(pas beaucoup)* not much; *(pas longtemps)* hardly, scarcely; **il n'a g. d'amis** he hasn't got many friends

**guéri, -e** [geri] *adj* cured

**guérilla** [gerija] *nf* guerrilla warfare

**guérir** [gerir] **1** *vt (personne, maladie)* to cure (**de** of); *(blessure)* to heal **2** *vi (personne)* to get better, to recover; *(blessure)* to heal; *(rhume)* to get better **3** **se guérir** *vpr* to get better ▪ **guérison** *nf (rétablissement)* recovery ▪ **guérisseur, -euse** *nmf* faith healer

**Guernesey** [gɛrnzɛ] *nf* Guernsey

**guerre** [gɛr] *nf* war; *(technique)* warfare; **en g.** at war (**avec** with); **faire la g.** to wage *or* make war (**à** on *or* against); *(soldat)* to fight; **crime de g.** war crime; **g. d'usure** war of attrition ▪ **guerrier, -ère 1** *adj* **danse guerrière** war dance; **chant g.** battle song; **2** *nmf* warrior

**guet** [gɛ] *nm* **faire le g.** to be on the lookout ▪ **guetter** *vt (occasion)* to watch out for; *(gibier)* to lie in wait for

**guet-apens** [gɛtapɑ̃] (*pl* **guets-apens**) *nm* ambush

**gueule** [gœl] *nf (d'animal, de canon)* mouth

**gui** [gi] *nm* mistletoe

**guichet** [giʃɛ] *nm (de gare, de banque)* window; **g. automatique** *(de banque)* cash dispenser ▪ **guichetier, -ère** *nmf (de banque) Br* counter clerk, *Am* teller; *(de gare)* ticket clerk

**guide** [gid] *nm (personne, livre)* guide;

**g. touristique** tourist guide ■ **guider** *vt* to guide

**guidon** [gidɔ̃] *nm* handlebars

**guignol** [giɲɔl] *nm (spectacle)* ≃ Punch and Judy show

**guillemets** [gijmɛ] *nmpl Typ* inverted commas, quotation marks; **entre g.** in inverted commas, in quotation marks

**guillotine** [gijɔtin] *nf* guillotine ■ **guillotiner** *vt* to guillotine

**guimauve** [gimov] *nf (confiserie)* marshmallow

**guindé, -e** [gɛ̃de] *adj (peu naturel)* stiff; *(style)* stilted

**Guinée** [gine] *nf* **la G.** Guinea

**guirlande** [girlɑ̃d] *nf* garland; **g. de Noël** piece of tinsel

**guise** [giz] *nf* **n'en faire qu'à sa g.** to do just as one pleases; **en g. de** by way of

**guitare** [gitar] *nf* guitar ■ **guitariste** *nmf* guitarist

**Guyane** [gɥijan] *nf* **la G.** Guiana

**gymnase** [ʒimnɑz] *nm* gymnasium ■ **gymnaste** *nmf* gymnast ■ **gymnastique** *nf* gymnastics *(sing)*

**gynécologue** [ʒinekɔlɔg] *nmf Br* gynaecologist, *Am* gynecologist

# Hh

**H, h** [aʃ] *nm inv* H, h

**habile** [abil] *adj* skilful, *Am* skillful (**à qch** at sth); **h. de ses mains** good with one's hands ▪ **habileté** *nf* skill

**habilité, -e** [abilite] *adj* (legally) authorized (**à faire** to do)

**habillé, -e** [abije] *adj* dressed (**de** in; **en** as); *(costume, robe)* smart

**habiller** [abije] **1** *vt (vêtir)* to dress (**de** in); *(fournir en vêtements)* to clothe **2 s'habiller** *vpr* to dress, to get dressed; *(avec élégance)* to dress up ▪ **habillement** *nm (vêtements)* clothes

**habit** [abi] *nm (tenue de soirée)* evening dress, tails; **habits** *(vêtements)* clothes

**habitable** [abitabl] *adj* (in)habitable; *(maison)* fit to live in

**habitat** [abita] *nm (d'animal, de plante)* habitat; *(conditions)* housing conditions

**habitation** [abitɑsjɔ̃] *nf (lieu)* dwelling; *(fait de résider)* living

**habiter** [abite] **1** *vt (maison, région)* to live in **2** *vi* to live (**à/en** in) ▪ **habitant, -e** *nmf (de pays)* inhabitant ▪ **habité, -e** *adj (région)* inhabited; *(maison)* occupied

**habitude** [abityd] *nf* habit; **avoir l'h. de qch** to be used to sth; **avoir l'h. de faire qch** to be used to doing sth; **prendre l'h. de faire qch** to get into the habit of doing sth; **d'h.** usually; **comme d'h.** as usual

**habituel, -elle** [abitɥɛl] *adj* usual, customary

**habituer** [abitɥe] **1** *vt* **h. qn à qch** to accustom sb to sth; **être habitué à qch/à faire qch** to be used to sth/to doing sth **2 s'habituer** *vpr* **s'h. à qn/qch** to get used to sb/sth ▪ **habitué, -e** *nmf* regular

**hache** ['aʃ] *nf* axe, *Am* ax

**hacher** ['aʃe] *vt (au couteau)* to chop up; *(avec un appareil) Br* to mince, *Am* to grind ▪ **haché, -e** *adj (viande) Br* minced, *Am* ground ▪ **hachis** *nm* **h. Parmentier** ≃ cottage pie

**hachurer** ['aʃyre] *vt* to hatch

**haie** ['ɛ] *nf (clôture)* hedge; *(en équitation)* fence; **400 mètres haies** *(épreuve d'athlétisme)* 400-metre hurdles; **h. d'honneur** guard of honour

**haine** ['ɛn] *nf* hatred, hate ▪ **haineux, -euse** *adj* full of hatred

**haïr*** ['air] *vt* to hate ▪ **haïssable** *adj* hateful

**hâle** ['ɑl] *nm* suntan ▪ **hâlé, -e** *adj* suntanned

**haleine** [alɛn] *nf* breath; **reprendre h.** to get one's breath back

**haleter** ['alte] *vi* to pant, to gasp ▪ **haletant, -e** *adj* panting, gasping

**hall** ['ol] *nm (de maison)* entrance hall; *(d'hôtel)* lobby; **h. de gare** station concourse

**halle** ['al] *nf* (covered) market; **les halles** the central food market

**hallucination** [alysinɑsjɔ̃] *nf* hallucination ▪ **hallucinant, -e** *adj* extraordinary

**halogène** [alɔʒɛn] *nm (lampe)* halogen lamp

**halte** ['alt] *nf (arrêt)* stop; *Mil* halt; *(lieu)* stopping place; *Mil* halting place; **faire h.** to stop

**haltère** [altɛr] *nm* dumbbell ▪ **haltérophile** *nmf* weightlifter ▪ **haltérophilie** *nf* weightlifting

**hamac** ['amak] *nm* hammock

**hamburger** ['ɑ̃bœrgœr] *nm* (ham-)burger

**hameau, -x** ['amo] *nm* hamlet

**hameçon** [amsɔ̃] *nm* (fish-)hook

**hamster** ['amstɛr] *nm* hamster

**hanche** ['ɑ̃ʃ] *nf* hip

**handball** ['ɑ̃dbal] *nm Sport* handball

**handicap** ['ɑ̃dikap] *nm (physique, mental)* disability; *Fig* handicap ▪ **handicapé, -e 1** *adj* disabled **2** *nmf* disabled person; **h. physique/mental** physically/mentally handicapped person

**hangar** ['ɑ̃gar] *nm (entrepôt)* shed

**hanter** ['ɑ̃te] *vt (sujet: fantôme, souvenir)* to haunt ▪ **hantise** *nf* **avoir la h. de qch** to really dread sth

**harasser** ['arase] *vt* to exhaust

**harceler** ['arsəle] *vt (importuner)* to harass; *(insister auprès de)* to pester ▪ **harcèlement** *nm* harassment

**hardi, -e** ['ardi] *adj* bold

**hargneux, -euse** ['arɲø, -øz] *adj* bad-tempered

**haricot** ['ariko] *nm* bean; *Culin* **h. de mouton** mutton stew; **h. rouge** kidney bean; **h. vert** green bean, *Br* French bean

**harmonica** [armɔnika] *nm* harmonica, mouthorgan

**harmonie** [armɔni] *nf* harmony ▪ **harmonieux, -euse** *adj* harmonious ▪ **harmoniser** *vt*, **s'harmoniser** *vpr* to harmonize

**harnais** ['arnɛ] *nm (de cheval, de bébé)* harness

**harpe** ['arp] *nf* harp

**harpon** ['arpɔ̃] *nm* harpoon

**hasard** ['azar] *nm* **le h.** chance; **un h.** a coincidence; **par h.** by chance; **au h.** *(choisir, répondre)* at random; *(marcher)* aimlessly; **à tout h.** *(par précaution)* just in case; *(pour voir)* on the off chance ▪ **hasarder 1** *vt (remarque)* to venture **2 se hasarder** *vpr* **se h. dans** to venture into; **se h. à faire qch** to risk doing sth ▪ **hasardeux, -euse** *adj* risky, hazardous

**hâte** ['ɑt] *nf* haste; **à la h.** hastily; **en (toute) h.** hurriedly; **avoir h. de faire qch** to be eager to do sth ▪ **hâter 1** *vt (pas, départ)* to hasten **2 se hâter** *vpr* to hurry (**de faire** to do) ▪ **hâtif, -ive** *adj (trop rapide)* hasty

**hausse** ['os] *nf* rise (**de** in); **en h.** rising ▪ **hausser 1** *vt (prix, voix)* to raise; *(épaules)* to shrug **2 se hausser** *vpr* **se h. sur la pointe des pieds** to stand on tiptoe

---

**HAUT, -E** ['o, 'ot] **1** *adj* high; *(en taille)* tall; **h. de 5 mètres** 5 metres high *or* tall; **à haute voix, à voix haute** aloud; **en haute mer** out at sea; **la mer est haute** it's high tide; **la haute couture** designer fashion; **un instrument de haute précision** a precision instrument; **un renseignement de la plus haute importance** news of the utmost importance; **haute trahison** high treason

**2** *adv (dans l'espace) & Mus* high; *(dans une hiérarchie)* highly; *(parler)* loud, loudly; **tout h.** *(lire, penser)* out loud; **h. placé** *(personne)* in a high position; **plus h.** *(dans un texte)* above

**3** *nm (partie haute)* top; **en h. de** at the top of; **en h.** *(loger)* upstairs; *(regarder)* up; *(mettre)* on (the) top; **d'en h.** *(de la partie haute, du ciel)* from high up, from up above; **avoir 5 mètres de h.** to be 5 metres high *or* tall; *Fig* **des hauts et des bas** ups and downs ▪ **haut-parleur** (*pl* **haut-parleurs**) *nm* loudspeaker

---

**hautain, -e** ['otɛ̃, -ɛn] *adj* haughty

**hautbois** ['obwa] *nm* oboe

**haut-de-forme** ['odfɔrm] (*pl* **hauts-de-forme**) *nm* top hat

**hautement** ['otmɑ̃] *adv (très)* highly ▪ **hauteur** *nf* height; *(colline)* hill; *Péj (orgueil)* haughtiness; **à la h. de** *(objet)* level with; *(rue)* opposite; **arriver**

**à la h. de qch** *(mesurer)* to reach (the level of) sth; **il n'est pas à la h.** he isn't up to it

**Haye** ['ɛ] *nf* **La H.** The Hague

**hebdomadaire** [ɛbdɔmadɛr] *adj & nm* weekly

**héberger** [ebɛrʒe] *vt* to put up

**hébreu, -x** [ebrø] **1** *adj m* Hebrew **2** *nm (langue)* Hebrew

**hectare** [ɛktar] *nm* hectare *(= 2.47 acres)*

**hélas** ['elɑs] *exclam* unfortunately

**héler** ['ele] *vt (taxi)* to hail

**hélice** [elis] *nf (d'avion, de navire)* propeller

**hélicoptère** [elikɔptɛr] *nm* helicopter

**helvétique** [ɛlvetik] *adj* Swiss

**hémisphère** [emisfɛr] *nm* hemisphere

**hémophilie** [emɔfili] *nf Méd* haemophilia

**hémorragie** [emɔraʒi] *nf Méd* haemorrhage; *Fig (de capitaux)* drain; **faire une h.** to haemorrhage; **h. cérébrale** stroke

**hémorroïdes** [emɔrɔid] *nfpl* piles, haemorrhoids

**hennir** ['enir] *vi (cheval)* to neigh

**herbe** [ɛrb] *nf* grass; **mauvaise h.** weed; *Culin* **fines herbes** herbs

**herbivore** [ɛrbivɔr] *adj* herbivorous

**hérédité** [eredite] *nf* heredity ▪ **héréditaire** *adj* hereditary

**hérésie** [erezi] *nf* heresy ▪ **hérétique** **1** *adj* heretical **2** *nmf* heretic

**hérisser** ['erise] **1** *vt (poils)* to bristle up; *Fig* **h. qn** *(irriter)* to get sb's back up **2 se hérisser** *vpr (animal, personne)* to bristle; *(poils, cheveux)* to stand on end ▪ **hérissé, -e** *adj (cheveux)* bristly; **h. de** bristling with

**hérisson** ['erisɔ̃] *nm* hedgehog

**hériter** [erite] **1** *vt* to inherit (**qch de qn** sth from sb) **2** *vi* **h. de qch** to inherit sth ▪ **héritage** *nm (biens)* inheritance; *Fig (culturel)* heritage; **faire un h.** to come into an inheritance ▪ **héritier** *nm* heir (**de** to) ▪ **héritière** *nf* heiress (**de** to)

**hermétique** [ɛrmetik] *adj* hermetically sealed; *Fig (obscur)* impenetrable

**héros** ['ero] *nm* hero ▪ **héroïne** *nf (femme)* heroine; *(drogue)* heroin ▪ **héroïque** *adj* heroic ▪ **héroïsme** *nm* heroism

**hésiter** [ezite] *vi* to hesitate (**sur** over *or* about; **entre** between; **à faire** to do) ▪ **hésitant, -e** *adj* hesitant ▪ **hésitation** *nf* hesitation; **avec h.** hesitatingly

**hétérogène** [eterɔʒɛn] *adj* mixed

**hêtre** ['ɛtr] *nm (arbre, bois)* beech

---

**HEURE** [œr] *nf (mesure)* hour; *(moment)* time; **quelle h. est-il?** what time is it?; **il est six heures** it's six (o'clock); **six heures moins cinq** five to six; **six heures cinq** *Br* five past six, *Am* five after six; **à l'h.** *(arriver)* on time; *(être payé)* by the hour; **100 km à l'h.** 100 km an hour; **de bonne h.** early; **nouvelle de dernière h.** latest *or* last-minute news; **tout à l'h.** *(futur)* in a few moments, later; *(passé)* a moment ago; **à tout à l'h.!** *(au revoir)* see you soon!; **à toute h.** *(continuellement)* at all hours; **24 heures sur 24** 24 hours a day; **d'h. en h.** hourly, hour by hour; **faire des heures supplémentaires** to work *or* do overtime; **heures d'affluence, heures de pointe** *(circulation)* rush hour; *(dans les magasins)* peak period; **heures creuses** off-peak *or* slack periods; **h. d'été** *Br* summer time, *Am* daylight-saving time

---

**heureux, -euse** [œrø, -øz] **1** *adj* happy (**de** with); *(chanceux)* lucky, fortunate; *(issue)* successful **2** *adv (vivre, mourir)* happily ▪ **heureusement** *adv (par chance)* fortunately, luckily (**pour** for); *(avec succès)* successfully

**heurter** ['œrte] **1** *vt (cogner)* to hit (**contre** against); *(entrer en collision avec)* to collide with; **h. qn** *(choquer)* to offend sb **2 se heurter** *vpr* to collide (**à** *ou* **contre** against); *Fig* **se h. à qch** to meet with sth

**hexagone** [ɛgzagɔn] *nm* hexagon; *Fig* **l'H.** France

**hiberner** [ibɛrne] *vi* to hibernate
**hibou, -x** ['ibu] *nm* owl
**hier** [ijɛr] *adv* yesterday; **h. soir** yesterday evening
**hiérarchie** ['jerarʃi] *nf* hierarchy
**hi-fi** ['ifi] *adj inv & nf inv* hi-fi
**hilare** [ilar] *adj* grinning ▪ **hilarant, -e** *adj* hilarious ▪ **hilarité** *nf* hilarity, mirth
**hindou, -e** [ɛ̃du] *adj & nmf* Hindu
**hippie** ['ipi] *nmf* hippie, hippy
**hippique** [ipik] *adj* **concours h.** horse show
**hippodrome** [ipɔdrom] *nm Br* racecourse, *Am* racetrack
**hippopotame** [ipɔpɔtam] *nm* hippopotamus
**hirondelle** [irɔ̃dɛl] *nf* swallow
**hisser** ['ise] **1** *vt* to hoist up **2 se hisser** *vpr* to heave oneself up
**histoire** [istwar] *nf (science, événements)* history; *(récit)* story
**historien, -enne** [istɔrjɛ̃, -ɛn] *nmf* historian
**historique** [istɔrik] **1** *adj (concernant l'histoire)* historical; *(important)* historic **2** *nm* historical account
**hiver** [ivɛr] *nm* winter ▪ **hivernal, -e, -aux, -ales** *adj* winter; *(temps)* wintry
**HLM** ['aʃɛlɛm] *(abrév* **habitation à loyer modéré**) *nm ou f Br* ≃ council flats, *Am* ≃ low-rent apartment building
**hocher** ['ɔʃe] *vt* **h. la tête** *(pour dire oui)* to nod; *(pour dire non)* to shake one's head
**hockey** ['ɔkɛ] *nm* hockey; **h. sur glace** ice hockey; **h. sur gazon** *Br* hockey, *Am* field hockey
**hold-up** ['ɔldœp] *nm inv* hold-up
**Hollande** ['ɔlɑ̃d] *nf* **la H.** Holland ▪ **hollandais, -e 1** *adj* Dutch **2** *nmf* **H.** Dutchman; **Hollandaise** Dutchwoman; **les H.** the Dutch **3** *nm (langue)* Dutch
**homard** ['ɔmar] *nm* lobster
**homéopathie** [ɔmeɔpati] *nf* homoeopathy
**homicide** [ɔmisid] *nm* homicide; **h. involontaire** *ou* **par imprudence** manslaughter; **h. volontaire** murder
**hommage** [ɔmaʒ] *nm* homage (**à** to); **rendre h. à qn** to pay homage to sb; **faire qch en h. à qn** to do sth as a tribute to sb *or* in homage to sb
**homme** [ɔm] *nm* man (*pl* men); **l'h.** *(genre humain)* man(kind); **des vêtements d'h.** men's clothes; **h. d'affaires** businessman; **h. politique** politician ▪ **homme-grenouille** (*pl* **hommes-grenouilles**) *nm* frogman
**homogène** [ɔmɔʒɛn] *adj* homogeneous
**homologue** [ɔmɔlɔg] *nmf* counterpart, opposite number
**homologuer** [ɔmɔlɔge] *vt (décision, accord, record)* to ratify
**homonyme** [ɔmɔnim] *nm (mot)* homonym
**homosexuel, -elle** [ɔmɔsɛksɥɛl] *adj & nmf* homosexual
**Hongrie** ['ɔ̃gri] *nf* **la H.** Hungary ▪ **hongrois, -e 1** *adj* Hungarian **2** *nmf* **H., Hongroise** Hungarian **3** *nm (langue)* Hungarian
**honnête** [ɔnɛt] *adj (intègre)* honest; *(vie, gens)* decent; *(prix)* fair ▪ **honnêtement** *adv (avec intégrité)* honestly; *(raisonnablement)* decently ▪ **honnêteté** *nf (intégrité)* honesty
**honneur** [ɔnœr] *nm* honour; **en l'h. de qn** in honour of sb; **invité d'h.** guest of honour
**honorable** [ɔnɔrabl] *adj* honourable; *Fig (résultat, salaire)* respectable
**honoraires** [ɔnɔrɛr] *nmpl* fees
**honorer** [ɔnɔre] *vt* to honour (**de** with); **h. qn** *(conduite)* to be a credit to sb ▪ **honorifique** *adj* honorary
**honte** ['ɔ̃t] *nf* shame; **avoir h.** to be *or* feel ashamed (**de qch/de faire qch** of sth/to do *or* of doing sth); **faire h. à qn** to put sb to shame ▪ **honteux, -euse** *adj (personne)* ashamed (**de** of); *(conduite, acte)* shameful
**hôpital, -aux** [ɔpital, -o] *nm* hospital; **à l'h.** *Br* in hospital, *Am* in the hospital

**hoquet** ['ɔkɛ] *nm* hiccup; **avoir le h.** to have the hiccups

**horaire** [ɔrɛr] **1** *adj (salaire)* hourly; *(vitesse)* per hour **2** *nm* timetable, schedule; **horaires de travail** working hours

**horizon** [ɔrizɔ̃] *nm* horizon; *(vue, paysage)* view; **à l'h.** on the horizon ▪ **horizontal, -e, -aux, -ales** *adj* horizontal

**horloge** [ɔrlɔʒ] *nf* clock

**hormone** [ɔrmɔn] *nf* hormone

**horoscope** [ɔrɔskɔp] *nm* horoscope

**horreur** [ɔrœr] *nf* horror; **avoir h. de qch** to hate *or* loathe sth; **quelle h.!** how horrible!

**horrible** [ɔribl] *adj (effrayant)* horrible; *(laid)* hideous ▪ **horriblement** [-əmɑ̃] *adv (défiguré)* horribly; *(cher, froid)* terribly

**horrifié, -e** [ɔrifje] *adj* horrified

**hors** ['ɔr] *prép* **h. de** *(maison, boîte)* outside; *Fig (danger, haleine)* out of; *(au football)* **être h. jeu** to be offside ▪ **hors-bord** *nm inv* speedboat ▪ **hors-d'œuvre** *nm inv (plat)* hors-d'œuvre, starter ▪ **hors-jeu** *nm inv (au football)* offside ▪ **hors-la-loi** *nm inv* outlaw ▪ **hors-piste** *nm inv Ski* off-piste skiing ▪ **hors service** *adj inv (appareil)* out of order ▪ **hors taxe** *adj inv (magasin, objet)* duty-free

**horticulteur, -trice** [ɔrtikyltœr, -tris] *nmf* horticulturist ▪ **horticulture** *nf* horticulture

**hospice** [ɔspis] *nm (asile)* home

**hospitalier, -ère** [ɔspitalje, -ɛr] *adj (accueillant)* hospitable; **centre h.** hospital (complex); **personnel h.** hospital staff ▪ **hospitaliser** *vt* to hospitalize ▪ **hospitalité** *nf* hospitality

**hostile** [ɔstil] *adj* hostile (**à** to *or* towards) ▪ **hostilité** *nf* hostility (**envers** to *or* towards)

**hôte** [ot] **1** *nm (qui reçoit)* host **2** *nmf (invité)* guest ▪ **hôtesse** *nf* hostess; **h. de l'air** air hostess

**hôtel** [otɛl] *nm* hotel; **h. particulier** mansion, town house; **h. de ville** *Br* town hall, *Am* city hall ▪ **hôtelier, -ère 1** *nmf* hotel-keeper, hotelier **2** *adj* **industrie hôtelière** hotel industry ▪ **hôtellerie** *nf (auberge)* inn; *(métier)* hotel trade

**hotte** ['ɔt] *nf (panier)* basket *(carried on back)*; *(de cheminée)* hood; **h. aspirante** extractor hood

**houille** ['uj] *nf* coal; **h. blanche** hydroelectric power ▪ **houiller, -ère** *adj* **bassin h.** coalfield

**houleux, -euse** ['ulø, -øz] *adj (mer)* rough; *Fig (réunion)* stormy

**housse** ['us] *nf* (protective) cover

**houx** ['u] *nm* holly

**hublot** ['yblo] *nm (de navire, d'avion)* porthole

**huer** ['ɥe] *vt* to boo ▪ **huées** *nfpl* boos

**huile** [ɥil] *nf* oil; **h. d'arachide/d'olive** groundnut/olive oil; **h. essentielle** essential oil; **h. solaire** suntan oil ▪ **huiler** *vt* to oil ▪ **huileux, -euse** *adj* oily

**huis** [ɥi] *nm* **à h. clos** behind closed doors; *Jur* in camera

**huissier** [ɥisje] *nm (portier)* usher; *Jur* bailiff

**huit** ['ɥit, 'ɥi *before consonant*] *adj & nm inv* eight; **h. jours** a week ▪ **huitième** *adj, nm & nmf* eighth; **un h.** an eighth; *Sport* **h. de finale** last sixteen

**huître** [ɥitr] *nf* oyster

**humain, -e** [ymɛ̃, -ɛn] **1** *adj (relatif à l'homme)* human; *(compatissant)* humane **2** *nmpl* **les humains** humans ▪ **humainement** *adv (relatif à l'homme)* humanly; *(avec bonté)* humanely ▪ **humanitaire** *adj* humanitarian ▪ **humanité** *nf (genre humain, sentiment)* humanity

**humble** [œ̃bl] *adj* humble

**humecter** [ymɛkte] *vt* to moisten

**humer** ['yme] *vt (respirer)* to breathe in; *(sentir)* to smell

**humeur** [ymœr] *nf (disposition)* mood; **être de bonne/mauvaise h.** to be in a good/bad mood

**humide** [ymid] *adj (linge)* damp, wet; *(climat, temps)* humid ▪ **humidifier** *vt* to humidify ▪ **humidité** *nf (de maison)* dampness; *(de climat)* humidity

**humilier** [ymilje] *vt* to humiliate ▪ **humiliant, -e** *adj* humiliating ▪ **humiliation** *nf* humiliation ▪ **humilité** *nf* humility

**humour** [ymur] *nm* humour; **avoir le sens de l'h.** to have a sense of humour ▪ **humoriste** *nmf* humorist ▪ **humoristique** *adj (récit, ton)* humorous

**hurler** ['yrle] **1** *vt (slogans, injures)* to yell **2** *vi (loup, vent)* to howl; *(personne)* to scream ▪ **hurlement** [-əmɑ̃] *nm (de loup, de vent)* howl; *(de personne)* scream

**hutte** ['yt] *nf* hut

**hybride** [ibrid] *adj & nm* hybrid

**hydrater** [idrate] *vt (peau)* to moisturize

**hydraulique** [idrolik] *adj* hydraulic

**hydravion** [idravjɔ̃] *nm* seaplane

**hydrocarbure** [idrokarbyr] *nm* hydrocarbon

**hydrophile** [idrɔfil] *adj* **coton h.** *Br* cotton wool, *Am* (absorbent) cotton

**hyène** [jɛn] *nf* hyena

**hygiène** [iʒjɛn] *nf* hygiene ▪ **hygiénique** *adj* hygienic; *(serviette, conditions)* sanitary

**hymne** [imn] *nm* hymn; **h. national** national anthem

**hypermarché** [ipɛrmarʃe] *nm* hypermarket

**hypermétrope** [ipɛrmetrɔp] *adj* long-sighted

**hypnose** [ipnoz] *nf* hypnosis ▪ **hypnotiser** *vt* to hypnotize

**hypocrisie** [ipɔkrizi] *nf* hypocrisy ▪ **hypocrite 1** *adj* hypocritical **2** *nmf* hypocrite

**hypodermique** [ipɔdɛrmik] *adj* hypodermic

**hypothèque** [ipɔtɛk] *nf* mortgage

**hypothèse** [ipɔtɛz] *nf* hypothesis; **dans l'h. où...** supposing (that)...

# Ii

**I, i** [i] *nm inv* I, i
**iceberg** [isbɛrg, ajsbɛrg] *nm* iceberg
**ici** [isi] *adv* here; **par i.** *(passer)* this way; *(habiter)* around here; **jusqu'i.** *(temps)* up to now; *(lieu)* as far as this *or* here; **d'i. à mardi** by Tuesday; **d'i. peu** before long
**icône** [ikon] *nf Rel & Ordinat* icon
**idéal, -e, -aux** *ou* **-als, -ales** [ideal, -o] **1** *adj* ideal **2** *n* ideal; **l'i. serait de/que...** the ideal *or* best solution would be to/if... ■ **idéaliser** *vt* to idealize ■ **idéaliste 1** *adj* idealistic **2** *nmf* idealist
**idée** [ide] *nf* idea (**de** of; **que** that); **i. fixe** obsession
**identifier** [idɑ̃tifje] *vt*, **s'identifier** *vpr* to identify (**à** with) ■ **identification** *nf* identification
**identique** [idɑ̃tik] *adj* identical (**à** to)
**identité** [idɑ̃tite] *nf* identity
**idéologie** [ideɔlɔʒi] *nf* ideology
**idiot, -e** [idjo, -ɔt] **1** *adj* silly, idiotic **2** *nmf* idiot
**idole** [idɔl] *nf* idol
**idyllique** [idilik] *adj* idyllic
**igloo** [iglu] *nm* igloo
**ignare** [iɲar] **1** *adj* ignorant **2** *nmf* ignoramus
**ignoble** [iɲɔbl] *adj* vile
**ignorant, -e** [iɲɔrɑ̃, -ɑ̃t] *adj* ignorant (**de** of) ■ **ignorance** *nf* ignorance
**ignorer** [iɲɔre] *vt* not to know; **j'ignore si...** I don't know if...; **je n'ignore pas les difficultés** I am not unaware of the difficulties; **i. qn** *(mépriser)* to ignore sb ■ **ignoré, -e** *adj (inconnu)* unknown

**il** [il] *pron personnel (personne)* he; *(chose, animal, impersonnel)* it; **il est** he/it is; **il pleut** it's raining; **il est vrai que...** it's true that...; **il y a...** there is/are...; **il y a six ans** six years ago; **il y a une heure qu'il travaille** he has been working for an hour; **qu'est-ce qu'il y a?** what's the matter?, what's wrong?; **il n'y a pas de quoi!** don't mention it!
**île** [il] *nf* island; **les îles Anglo-Normandes** the Channel Islands; **les îles Britanniques** the British Isles
**illégal, -e, -aux, -ales** [il(l)egal, -o] *adj* illegal
**illégitime** [il(l)eʒitim] *adj (enfant, revendication)* illegitimate; *(demande)* unwarranted
**illettré, -e** [il(l)etre] *adj & nmf* illiterate
**illicite** [il(l)isit] *adj* unlawful, illicit
**illimité, -e** [il(l)imite] *adj* unlimited
**illisible** [il(l)izibl] *adj (écriture)* illegible; *(livre) & Ordinat* unreadable
**illogique** [il(l)ɔʒik] *adj* illogical
**illuminer** [il(l)ymine] **1** *vt* to light up, to illuminate **2 s'illuminer** *vpr (visage, ciel)* to light up ■ **illumination** *nf (action, lumière)* illumination ■ **illuminé, -e** *adj (monument)* floodlit
**illusion** [il(l)yzjɔ̃] *nf* illusion (**sur** about); **se faire des illusions** to delude oneself (**sur** about); **i. d'optique** optical illusion ■ **illusionniste** *nmf* conjurer ■ **illusoire** *adj* illusory
**illustre** [il(l)ystr] *adj* illustrious
**illustrer** [il(l)ystre] **1** *vt (livre, récit)* to illustrate (**de** with) **2 s'illustrer** *vpr* to distinguish oneself (**par** by) ■ **illustration** *nf* illustration ■ **illustré, -e** *adj*

*(livre, magazine)* illustrated

**îlot** [ilo] *nm (île)* small island; *(maisons)* block

**ils** [il] *pron personnel mpl* they; **i. sont ici** they are here

**image** [imaʒ] *nf* picture; *(ressemblance, symbole)* image; *(dans une glace)* reflection; *Ordinat* **i. de synthèse** computer-generated image ▪ **imagé, -e** *adj (style)* colourful, full of imagery

**imaginable** [imaʒinabl] *adj* imaginable ▪ **imaginaire** *adj* imaginary ▪ **imaginatif, -ive** *adj* imaginative

**imagination** [imaʒinɑsjɔ̃] *nf* imagination

**imaginer** [imaʒine] **1** *vt (se figurer)* to imagine; *(inventer)* to devise **2 s'imaginer** *vpr (se figurer)* to imagine (**que** that); *(se voir)* to picture oneself

**imbattable** [ɛ̃batabl] *adj* unbeatable

**imbécile** [ɛ̃besil] **1** *adj* idiotic **2** *nmf* idiot, imbecile ▪ **imbécillité** *nf (état)* imbecility; **une i.** *(action, parole)* an idiotic thing

**imberbe** [ɛ̃bɛrb] *adj* beardless

**imbiber** [ɛ̃bibe] *vt* to soak (**de** with *or* in)

**imbriquer** [ɛ̃brike] **s'imbriquer** *vpr (s'emboîter)* to overlap

**imbu, -e** [ɛ̃by] *adj* **i. de soi-même** full of oneself

**imbuvable** [ɛ̃byvabl] *adj* undrinkable

**imiter** [imite] *vt* to imitate; *(signature)* to forge; **i. qn** *(pour rire)* to mimic sb; *(faire comme)* to do the same as sb; *(imitateur professionnel)* to impersonate sb ▪ **imitateur, -trice** *nmf* imitator; *(professionnel)* impersonator ▪ **imitation** *nf* imitation

**immaculé, -e** [imakyle] *adj (sans tache, sans péché)* immaculate

**immangeable** [ɛ̃mɑ̃ʒabl] *adj* inedible

**immanquable** [ɛ̃mɑ̃kabl] *adj* inevitable

**immatriculer** [imatrikyle] *vt* to register; **se faire i.** to register ▪ **immatriculation** *nf* registration

**immédiat, -e** [imedja, -jat] **1** *adj* immediate **2** *nm* **dans l'i.** for the time being ▪ **immédiatement** *adv* immediately

**immense** [imɑ̃s] *adj* immense ▪ **immensément** *adv* immensely ▪ **immensité** *nf* immensity

**immerger** [imɛrʒe] *vt* to immerse ▪ **immersion** *nf* immersion (**dans** in)

**immeuble** [imœbl] *nm* building; *(appartements) Br* block of flats, *Am* apartment block

**immigrant, -e** [imigrɑ̃, -ɑ̃t] *nmf* immigrant ▪ **immigration** *nf* immigration ▪ **immigré, -e** *adj & nmf* immigrant; **travailleur i.** immigrant worker

**imminent, -e** [iminɑ̃, -ɑ̃t] *adj* imminent

**immiscer** [imise] **s'immiscer** *vpr* to interfere (**dans** in)

**immobile** [imɔbil] *adj* still, motionless

**immobilier, -ère** [imɔbilje, -ɛr] **1** *adj* **marché i.** property market **2** *nm* **l'i.** *Br* property, *Am* real estate

**immobiliser** [imɔbilize] **1** *vt (blessé)* to immobilize; *(train)* to bring to a stop; *(voiture) (avec un sabot)* to clamp **2 s'immobiliser** *vpr* to come to a stop

**immonde** [i(m)mɔ̃d] *adj (sale)* foul; *(ignoble, laid)* vile

**immoral, -e, -aux, -ales** [i(m)mɔral, -o] *adj* immoral ▪ **immoralité** *nf* immorality

**immortel, -elle** [i(m)mɔrtɛl] *adj* immortal ▪ **immortaliser** *vt* to immortalize ▪ **immortalité** *nf* immortality

**immuable** [i(m)mɥabl] *adj* immutable, unchanging

**immuniser** [i(m)mynize] *vt* to immunize (**contre** against) ▪ **immunitaire** *adj Méd (déficience, système)* immune ▪ **immunité** *nf* immunity

**impact** [ɛ̃pakt] *nm* impact (**sur** on)

**impair, -e** [ɛ̃pɛr] **1** *adj (nombre)* odd, uneven **2** *nm (maladresse)* blunder

**imparable** [ɛ̃parabl] *adj (coup)* unavoidable

**impardonnable** [ɛ̃pardɔnabl] *adj* unforgivable

**imparfait, -e** [ɛ̃parfɛ, -ɛt] *adj* *(connaissance)* imperfect

**impartial, -e, -aux, -ales** [ɛ̃parsjal, -o] *adj* impartial, unbiased ▪ **impartialité** *nf* impartiality

**impartir** [ɛ̃partir] *vt* **dans le temps qui nous est imparti** within the allotted time

**impasse** [ɛ̃pas] *nf (rue)* dead end; *Fig (situation)* impasse; **être dans une i.** to be deadlocked

**impassible** [ɛ̃pasibl] *adj* impassive

**impatient, -e** [ɛ̃pasjɑ̃, -ɑ̃t] *adj* impatient; **i. de faire qch** impatient to do sth ▪ **impatience** *nf* impatience ▪ **impatienter 1** *vt* to annoy **2 s'impatienter** *vpr* to get impatient

**impayé, -e** [ɛ̃peje] *adj* unpaid

**impeccable** [ɛ̃pekabl] *adj* impeccable

**impénétrable** [ɛ̃penetrabl] *adj (forêt, mystère)* impenetrable

**impensable** [ɛ̃pɑ̃sabl] *adj* unthinkable

**impératif, -ive** [ɛ̃peratif, -iv] *adj (consigne, besoin)* imperative; *(ton)* imperious

**impératrice** [ɛ̃peratris] *nf* empress

**imperceptible** [ɛ̃pɛrsɛptibl] *adj* imperceptible (**à** to)

**imperfection** [ɛ̃pɛrfɛksjɔ̃] *nf* imperfection

**impérial, -e, -aux, -ales** [ɛ̃perjal, -o] *adj* imperial ▪ **impérialisme** *nm* imperialism

**impérieux, -euse** [ɛ̃perjø, -øz] *adj (autoritaire)* imperious; *(besoin)* pressing

**impérissable** [ɛ̃perisabl] *adj (souvenir)* enduring

**imperméable** [ɛ̃pɛrmeabl] **1** *adj* impervious (**à** to); *(tissu, manteau)* waterproof **2** *nm* raincoat

**impersonnel, -elle** [ɛ̃pɛrsɔnɛl] *adj* impersonal

**impertinent, -e** [ɛ̃pɛrtinɑ̃, -ɑ̃t] *adj* impertinent (**envers** to) ▪ **impertinence** *nf* impertinence

**imperturbable** [ɛ̃pɛrtyrbabl] *adj (personne)* imperturbable

**impitoyable** [ɛ̃pitwajabl] *adj* merciless

**implacable** [ɛ̃plakabl] *adj (personne, vengeance)* implacable; *(avancée)* relentless

**implanter** [ɛ̃plɑ̃te] **1** *vt (installer)* to establish; *(chirurgicalement)* to implant **2 s'implanter** *vpr* to become established ▪ **implantation** *nf* establishment

**implicite** [ɛ̃plisit] *adj* implicit

**impliquer** [ɛ̃plike] *vt (entraîner)* to imply; **i. que...** to imply that...; **i. qn** to implicate sb (**dans** in) ▪ **implication** *nf (conséquence)* implication; *(participation)* involvement

**implorer** [ɛ̃plɔre] *vt* to implore (**qn de faire** sb to do)

**impoli, -e** [ɛ̃pɔli] *adj* rude, impolite

**impolitesse** [ɛ̃pɔlitɛs] *nf* impoliteness, rudeness

**impopulaire** [ɛ̃pɔpylɛr] *adj* unpopular

**import** [ɛ̃pɔr] *nm* import

**important, -e** [ɛ̃pɔrtɑ̃, -ɑ̃t] **1** *adj (personnage, événement)* important; *(quantité, somme, ville)* large; *(dégâts, retard)* considerable **2** *nm* **l'i., c'est de...** the important thing is to... ▪ **importance** *nf* importance; *(taille)* size; *(de dégâts)* extent; **ça n'a pas d'i.** it doesn't matter

**importer[1]** [ɛ̃pɔrte] **1** *vi* to matter (**à** to) **2** *v impersonnel* **il importe de faire qch** it's important to do sth; **il importe que vous y soyez** it is important that you're there; **peu importe, n'importe** it doesn't matter; **n'importe qui/quoi/où/quand/comment** anyone/anything/anywhere/any time/anyhow

**importer[2]** [ɛ̃pɔrte] *vt (marchandises)* to import (**de** from) ▪ **importateur, -trice 1** *adj* importing **2** *nmf* importer ▪ **importation** *nf (objet)* import; *(action)* importing, importation

**importun, -e** [ɛ̃pɔrtœ̃, -yn] **1** *adj*

*(personne, question)* importunate **2** *nmf* nuisance

**imposer** [ɛ̃poze] **1** *vt (condition)* to impose; *(taxer)* to tax; **i. qch à qn** to impose sth on sb **2** *vi* **en i. à qn** to impress sb **3 s'imposer** *vpr (faire reconnaître sa valeur)* to assert oneself; *(gagner)* to win; *(être nécessaire)* to be essential; *Péj (chez quelqu'un)* to impose; **s'i. de faire qch** to make it a rule to do sth ▪ **imposant, -e** *adj* imposing

**impossible** [ɛ̃pɔsibl] **1** *adj* impossible (**à faire** to do); **il est i. que...** *(+ subjunctive)* it is impossible that... **2** *nm* **tenter l'i.** to attempt the impossible ▪ **impossibilité** *nf* impossibility

**imposteur** [ɛ̃pɔstœr] *nm* impostor ▪ **imposture** *nf* deception

**impôt** [ɛ̃po] *nm* tax; **(service des) impôts** tax authorities; **impôts locaux** local taxes; **i. sur le revenu** income tax

**impraticable** [ɛ̃pratikabl] *adj (chemin)* impassable; *(projet)* impracticable

**imprécis, -e** [ɛ̃presi, -iz] *adj* imprecise ▪ **imprécision** *nf* imprecision

**imprégner** [ɛ̃preɲe] **1** *vt* to impregnate (**de** with); *Fig* **être imprégné de qch** to be full of sth **2 s'imprégner** *vpr* to become impregnated (**de** with)

**imprenable** [ɛ̃prənabl] *adj (forteresse)* impregnable; *(vue)* unobstructed

**impression** [ɛ̃presjɔ̃] *nf* (**a**) *(sensation)* impression; **avoir l'i. que...** to have the impression that...; **faire bonne i. à qn** to make a good impression on sb (**b**) *(de livre)* printing

**impressionner** [ɛ̃presjɔne] *vt (bouleverser)* to upset; *(frapper)* to impress ▪ **impressionnable** *adj* easily upset ▪ **impressionnant, -e** *adj* impressive

**imprévisible** [ɛ̃previzibl] *adj (temps, réaction, personne)* unpredictable; *(événement)* unforeseeable ▪ **imprévu, -e 1** *adj* unexpected, unforeseen **2** *nm* **en cas d'i.** in case of anything unexpected

**imprimer** [ɛ̃prime] *vt (livre, tissu)* to print; *Ordinat* to print (out) ▪ **imprimante** *nf* printer ▪ **imprimé** *nm (formulaire)* printed form ▪ **imprimerie** *nf (technique)* printing; *(lieu) Br* printing works, *Am* print shop ▪ **imprimeur** *nm* printer

**improbable** [ɛ̃prɔbabl] *adj* improbable, unlikely

**impropre** [ɛ̃prɔpr] *adj* inappropriate; **i. à qch** unfit for sth; **i. à la consommation** unfit for human consumption

**improviser** [ɛ̃prɔvize] *vt & vi* to improvise ▪ **improvisation** *nf* improvisation

**improviste** [ɛ̃prɔvist] **à l'improviste** *adv* unexpectedly

**imprudent, -e** [ɛ̃prydɑ̃, -ɑ̃t] *adj (personne, action)* rash; **il est i. de...** it is unwise to... ▪ **imprudemment** [-amɑ̃] *adv* rashly ▪ **imprudence** *nf* rashness

**impudique** [ɛ̃pydik] *adj* shameless

**impuissant, -e** [ɛ̃pɥisɑ̃, -ɑ̃t] *adj* powerless; *Méd* impotent

**impulsif, -ive** [ɛ̃pylsif, -iv] *adj* impulsive ▪ **impulsion** *nf* impulse

**impunément** [ɛ̃pynemɑ̃] *adv* with impunity ▪ **impuni, -e** *adj* unpunished

**impur, -e** [ɛ̃pyr] *adj* impure ▪ **impureté** *nf* impurity

**imputer** [ɛ̃pyte] *vt* to attribute (**à** to); *(frais)* to charge (**à** to)

**inabordable** [inabɔrdabl] *adj (prix)* prohibitive; *(lieu)* inaccessible; *(personne)* unapproachable

**inacceptable** [inaksɛptabl] *adj* unacceptable

**inaccessible** [inaksesibl] *adj (lieu)* inaccessible; *(personne)* unapproachable

**inachevé, -e** [inaʃve] *adj* unfinished

**inactif, -ive** [inaktif, -iv] *adj (personne)* inactive; *(remède)* ineffective ▪ **inaction** *nf* inaction ▪ **inactivité** *nf* inactivity

**inadapté, -e** [inadapte] **1** *adj (socialement)* maladjusted; *(physiquement, mentalement)* handicapped; *(matériel)* unsuitable (**à** for) **2** *nmf (socialement)* maladjusted person

**inadmissible** [inadmisibl] *adj* inadmissible
**inadvertance** [inadvɛrtɑ̃s] **par inadvertance** *adv* inadvertently
**inamical, -e, -aux, -ales** [inamikal, -o] *adj* unfriendly
**inanimé, -e** [inanime] *adj (mort)* lifeless; *(évanoui)* unconscious; *(matière)* inanimate
**inaperçu, -e** [inapɛrsy] *adj* **passer i.** to go unnoticed
**inappréciable** [inapresjabl] *adj* invaluable
**inapte** [inapt] *adj (intellectuellement)* unsuited (**à** for); *(médicalement)* unfit (**à** for) ▪ **inaptitude** *nf (intellectuelle)* inaptitude; *(médicale)* unfitness (**à** for)
**inattendu, -e** [inatɑ̃dy] *adj* unexpected
**inattention** [inatɑ̃sjɔ̃] *nf* lack of attention
**inaudible** [inodibl] *adj* inaudible
**inaugurer** [inogyre] *vt (édifice)* to inaugurate ▪ **inaugural, -e, -aux, -ales** *adj* inaugural
**inavouable** [inavwabl] *adj* shameful
**incalculable** [ɛ̃kalkylabl] *adj* incalculable
**incapable** [ɛ̃kapabl] *adj* incapable; **i. de faire qch** incapable of doing sth ▪ **incapacité** *nf (impossibilité)* inability (**de faire** to do); *(invalidité)* disability; **être dans l'i. de faire qch** to be unable to do sth
**incarcérer** [ɛ̃karsere] *vt* to incarcerate ▪ **incarcération** *nf* incarceration
**incarnation** [ɛ̃karnɑsjɔ̃] *nf* incarnation
**incarné, -e** [ɛ̃karne] *adj (ongle)* ingrown
**incarner** [ɛ̃karne] *vt* to embody
**incassable** [ɛ̃kɑsabl] *adj* unbreakable
**incendie** [ɛ̃sɑ̃di] *nm* fire; **i. criminel** arson; **i. de forêt** forest fire ▪ **incendiaire 1** *adj (bombe)* incendiary **2** *nmf* arsonist ▪ **incendier** *vt* to set on fire
**incertain, -e** [ɛ̃sɛrtɛ̃, -ɛn] *adj (résultat)* uncertain; *(temps)* unsettled; *(personne)* indecisive ▪ **incertitude** *nf* uncertainty
**incessamment** [ɛ̃sesamɑ̃] *adv* very soon
**incessant, -e** [ɛ̃sesɑ̃, -ɑ̃t] *adj* incessant
**inchangé, -e** [ɛ̃ʃɑ̃ʒe] *adj* unchanged
**incidence** [ɛ̃sidɑ̃s] *nf (influence)* impact (**sur** on); *Méd* incidence
**incident** [ɛ̃sidɑ̃] *nm* incident; *(accroc)* hitch; **i. de parcours** minor setback
**incinérer** [ɛ̃sinere] *vt (ordures)* to incinerate; *(cadavre)* to cremate ▪ **incinération** *nf (d'ordures)* incineration; *(de cadavre)* cremation
**inciser** [ɛ̃size] *vt (peau)* to make an incision in; *(abcès)* to lance ▪ **incision** *nf (entaille)* incision
**incisif, -ive**[1] [ɛ̃sizif, -iv] *adj* incisive
**incisive**[2] [ɛ̃siziv] *nf (dent)* incisor (tooth)
**inciter** [ɛ̃site] *vt* to encourage (**à faire** to do) ▪ **incitation** *nf* incitement (**à** to)
**incliner** [ɛ̃kline] **1** *vt (pencher)* to tilt; **i. la tête** *(approuver)* to nod; *(saluer)* to bow one's head **2 s'incliner** *vpr (se pencher)* to lean forward; *(pour saluer)* to bow; *Fig (se soumettre)* to give in (**devant** to) ▪ **inclinaison** *nf* incline, slope ▪ **inclination** *nf (tendance)* inclination
**inclure*** [ɛ̃klyr] *vt* to include; *(dans un courrier)* to enclose (**dans** with) ▪ **inclus, -e** *adj* **du 4 au 10 i.** from the 4th to the 10th inclusive; **jusqu'à lundi i.** *Br* up to and including Monday, *Am* through Monday ▪ **inclusion** *nf* inclusion
**incognito** [ɛ̃kɔɲito] *adv* incognito
**incohérent, -e** [ɛ̃kɔerɑ̃, -ɑ̃t] *adj (propos)* incoherent; *(histoire)* inconsistent ▪ **incohérence** *nf (de propos)* incoherence; *(d'histoire)* inconsistency
**incolore** [ɛ̃kɔlɔr] *adj* colourless; *(vernis, verre)* clear
**incomber** [ɛ̃kɔ̃be] *vi* **i. à qn** *(devoir)* to fall to sb; **il lui incombe de faire qch** it falls to him/her to do sth
**incommoder** [ɛ̃kɔmɔde] *vt* to bother

**incomparable** [ɛ̃kɔ̃parabl] *adj* matchless

**incompatible** [ɛ̃kɔ̃patibl] *adj* incompatible (**avec** with)

**incompétent, -e** [ɛ̃kɔ̃petɑ̃, -ɑ̃t] *adj* incompetent ▪ **incompétence** *nf* incompetence

**incomplet, -ète** [ɛ̃kɔ̃plɛ, -ɛt] *adj* incomplete

**incompréhensible** [ɛ̃kɔ̃preɑ̃sibl] *adj* incomprehensible ▪ **incompréhension** *nf* incomprehension

**incompris, -e** [ɛ̃kɔ̃pri, -iz] **1** *adj* misunderstood **2** *nmf* **être un i.** to be misunderstood

**inconcevable** [ɛ̃kɔ̃səvabl] *adj* inconceivable

**inconciliable** [ɛ̃kɔ̃siljabl] *adj (théorie)* irreconcilable; *(activité)* incompatible

**inconditionnel, -elle** [ɛ̃kɔ̃disjɔnɛl] *adj* unconditional; *(supporter)* staunch

**inconfortable** [ɛ̃kɔ̃fɔrtabl] *adj* uncomfortable

**inconnu, -e** [ɛ̃kɔny] **1** *adj* unknown (**de** to) **2** *nmf (étranger)* stranger; *(auteur)* unknown **3** *nm* **l'i.** the unknown **4** *nf Math* **inconnue** unknown (quantity)

**inconscient, -e** [ɛ̃kɔ̃sjɑ̃, -ɑ̃t] **1** *adj (sans connaissance)* unconscious; *(imprudent)* reckless; **i. de qch** unaware of sth **2** *nm* **l'i.** the unconscious ▪ **inconsciemment** [-amɑ̃] *adv (dans l'inconscient)* subconsciously ▪ **inconscience** *nf (perte de connaissance)* unconsciousness; *(irréflexion)* recklessness

**inconséquence** [ɛ̃kɔ̃sekɑ̃s] *nf (manque de prudence)* recklessness; *(manque de cohérence)* inconsistency

**inconsidéré, -e** [ɛ̃kɔ̃sidere] *adj* thoughtless

**inconsistant, -e** [ɛ̃kɔ̃sistɑ̃, -ɑ̃t] *adj (personne)* weak; *(film, roman)* flimsy; *(sauce, crème)* thin

**inconsolable** [ɛ̃kɔ̃sɔlabl] *adj* inconsolable

**inconstant, -e** [ɛ̃kɔ̃stɑ̃, -ɑ̃t] *adj* fickle

**incontestable** [ɛ̃kɔ̃tɛstabl] *adj* indisputable ▪ **incontesté, -e** *adj* undisputed

**incontournable** [ɛ̃kɔ̃turnabl] *adj Fig (film)* unmissable; *(auteur)* who cannot be ignored

**incontrôlé, -e** [ɛ̃kɔ̃trole] *adj* unchecked ▪ **incontrôlable** *adj (invérifiable)* unverifiable; *(indomptable)* uncontrollable

**inconvenant, -e** [ɛ̃kɔ̃vnɑ̃, -ɑ̃t] *adj* improper

**inconvénient** [ɛ̃kɔ̃venjɑ̃] *nm (désavantage)* drawback; **l'i., c'est que...** the annoying thing is that...

**incorporer** [ɛ̃kɔrpɔre] *vt (insérer)* to insert (**à** in); *(troupes)* to draft; **i. qch à qch** to blend sth into sth ▪ **incorporation** *nf (mélange)* blending (**de qch dans qch** of sth into sth); *Mil* conscription

**incorrect, -e** [ɛ̃kɔrɛkt] *adj (inexact)* incorrect; *(grossier)* impolite; *(inconvenant)* improper ▪ **incorrection** *nf (impolitesse)* impoliteness; *(propos)* impolite remark; *(faute de grammaire)* mistake

**incorrigible** [ɛ̃kɔriʒibl] *adj* incorrigible

**incorruptible** [ɛ̃kɔryptibl] *adj* incorruptible

**incrédule** [ɛ̃kredyl] *adj* incredulous ▪ **incrédulité** *nf* incredulity

**incriminer** [ɛ̃krimine] *vt (personne)* to accuse

**incroyable** [ɛ̃krwajabl] *adj* incredible

**incrusté, -e** [ɛ̃kryste] *adj* **i. de** *(orné)* inlaid with

**incubation** [ɛ̃kybɑsjɔ̃] *nf* incubation

**inculper** [ɛ̃kylpe] *vt (accuser)* to charge (**de** with) ▪ **inculpation** *nf* charge, indictment ▪ **inculpé, -e** *nmf* **l'i.** the accused

**inculquer** [ɛ̃kylke] *vt* to instil (**à qn** in sb)

**inculte** [ɛ̃kylt] *adj (terre, personne)* uncultivated

**incurable** [ɛ̃kyrabl] *adj* incurable

**incursion** [ɛ̃kyrsjɔ̃] *nf (invasion)* incursion; *Fig (entrée soudaine)* intrusion

**Inde** [ɛ̃d] *nf* **l'I.** India

**indécent, -e** [ɛ̃desɑ̃, -ɑ̃t] *adj* indecent ▪ **indécence** *nf* indecency

**indéchiffrable** [ɛ̃deʃifrabl] *adj (illisible)* undecipherable

**indécis, -e** [ɛ̃desi, -iz] *adj (personne) (de caractère)* indecisive; *(ponctuellement)* undecided ▪ **indécision** *nf (de caractère)* indecisiveness; *(ponctuelle)* indecision

**indéfendable** [ɛ̃defɑ̃dabl] *adj* indefensible

**indéfini, -e** [ɛ̃defini] *adj (illimité)* indefinite; *(imprécis)* undefined ▪ **indéfiniment** *adv* indefinitely ▪ **indéfinissable** *adj* indefinable

**indélébile** [ɛ̃delebil] *adj* indelible

**indélicat, -e** [ɛ̃delika, -at] *adj (grossier)* insensitive; *(malhonnête)* unscrupulous

**indemne** [ɛ̃dɛmn] *adj* unhurt, unscathed

**indemniser** [ɛ̃dɛmnize] *vt* to compensate (**de** for) ▪ **indemnisation** *nf* compensation ▪ **indemnité** *nf (dédommagement)* compensation; *(allocation)* allowance; **i. de licenciement** redundancy payment

**indéniable** [ɛ̃denjabl] *adj* undeniable

**indépendant, -e** [ɛ̃depɑ̃dɑ̃, -ɑ̃t] *adj* independent (**de** of); *(chambre)* self-contained; *(travailleur)* self-employed ▪ **indépendamment** [-amɑ̃] *adv* independently; **i. de** apart from ▪ **indépendance** *nf* independence

**indescriptible** [ɛ̃dɛskriptibl] *adj* indescribable

**indésirable** [ɛ̃dezirabl] *adj & nmf* undesirable

**indestructible** [ɛ̃dɛstryktibl] *adj* indestructible

**indéterminé, -e** [ɛ̃detɛrmine] *adj (date, heure)* unspecified; *(raison)* unknown

**index** [ɛ̃dɛks] *nm (doigt)* forefinger, index finger; *(liste) & Ordinat* index

**indicateur, -trice** [ɛ̃dikatœr, -tris] **1** *nm Tech* indicator, gauge; *Écon* indicator; *(espion)* informer **2** *adj* **panneau i.** road sign

**indicatif, -ive** [ɛ̃dikatif, -iv] **1** *adj* indicative (**de** of) **2** *nm Radio* theme tune; **i. téléphonique** *Br* dialling code, *Am* area code

**indication** [ɛ̃dikɑsjɔ̃] *nf* indication (**de** of); *(renseignement)* (piece of) information; *(directive)* instruction; **indications...** *(de médicament)* suitable for...

**indice** [ɛ̃dis] *nm (signe)* sign; *(d'enquête)* clue

**indien, -enne** [ɛ̃djɛ̃, -ɛn] **1** *adj* Indian **2** *nmf* **I., Indienne** Indian

**indifférent, -e** [ɛ̃diferɑ̃, -ɑ̃t] *adj* indifferent (**à** to) ▪ **indifférence** *nf* indifference (**à** to)

**indigène** [ɛ̃diʒɛn] *adj & nmf* native

**indigent, -e** [ɛ̃diʒɑ̃, -ɑ̃t] *adj* destitute ▪ **indigence** *nf* destitution

**indigeste** [ɛ̃diʒɛst] *adj* indigestible ▪ **indigestion** *nf* **avoir une i.** to have a stomach upset

**indignation** [ɛ̃diɲɑsjɔ̃] *nf* indignation

**indigne** [ɛ̃diɲ] *adj (personne)* unworthy; *(conduite)* shameful; **i. de qn/qch** unworthy of sb/sth ▪ **indignité** *nf (de personne)* unworthiness; *(de conduite)* shamefulness; *(action)* shameful act

**indigner** [ɛ̃diɲe] **1** *vt* **i. qn** to make sb indignant **2 s'indigner** *vpr* to be indignant (**de** at) ▪ **indigné, -e** *adj* indignant

**indiquer** [ɛ̃dike] *vt (sujet: personne)* to point out; *(sujet: panneau)* to show, to indicate; *(sujet: compteur)* to read; *(donner) (date, adresse)* to give; **i. le chemin à qn** to tell sb the way ▪ **indiqué, -e** *adj (conseillé)* advisable; **à l'heure indiquée** at the appointed time

**indirect, -e** [ɛ̃dirɛkt] *adj* indirect

**indiscipline** [ɛ̃disiplin] *nf* indiscipline ▪ **indiscipliné, -e** *adj* unruly

**indiscret, -ète** [ɛ̃diskrɛ, -ɛt] *adj Péj (curieux)* inquisitive; *(qui parle trop)* indiscreet ▪ **indiscrétion** *nf* indiscretion

**indiscutable** [ɛ̃diskytabl] *adj* indisputable

**indispensable** [ɛ̃dispɑ̃sabl] *adj* essential, indispensable (**à qch** for sth); **i. à qn** indispensable to sb

**indisponible** [ɛ̃dispɔnibl] *adj* unavailable

**indisposer** [ɛ̃dispoze] *vt (contrarier)* to annoy; **i. qn** *(odeur, climat)* to make sb feel ill ▪ **indisposé, -e** *adj (malade)* indisposed, unwell ▪ **indisposition** *nf* indisposition

**indistinct, -e** [ɛ̃distɛ̃(kt), -ɛ̃kt] *adj* indistinct ▪ **indistinctement** [-ɛ̃ktəmɑ̃] *adv (voir, parler)* indistinctly; *(également)* equally

**individu** [ɛ̃dividy] *nm* individual; *Péj* individual, character

**individualiste** [ɛ̃dividɥalist] **1** *adj* individualistic **2** *nmf* individualist

**individualité** [ɛ̃dividɥalite] *nf* individuality

**individuel, -elle** [ɛ̃dividɥɛl] *adj* individual; *(maison)* detached

**indivisible** [ɛ̃divizibl] *adj* indivisible

**Indochine** [ɛ̃dɔʃin] *nf* **l'I.** Indo-China

**indolent, -e** [ɛ̃dɔlɑ̃, -ɑ̃t] *adj* lazy

**indolore** [ɛ̃dɔlɔr] *adj* painless

**indomptable** [ɛ̃dɔ̃(p)tabl] *adj (animal)* untamable

**Indonésie** [ɛ̃dɔnezi] *nf* **l'I.** Indonesia

**indue** [ɛ̃dy] *adj f* **rentrer à des heures indues** to come home at all hours of the night

**induire*** [ɛ̃dɥir] *vt* **i. qn en erreur** to lead sb astray

**indulgent, -e** [ɛ̃dylʒɑ̃, -ɑ̃t] *adj* indulgent ▪ **indulgence** *nf* indulgence

**industrie** [ɛ̃dystri] *nf* industry ▪ **industrialisé, -e** *adj* industrialized ▪ **industriel, -elle 1** *adj* industrial **2** *nm* industrialist

**inébranlable** [inebrɑ̃labl] *adj Fig (certitude, personne)* unshakeable

**inédit, -e** [inedi, -it] *adj (texte)* unpublished

**inefficace** [inefikas] *adj (mesure)* ineffective; *(personne)* inefficient ▪ **inefficacité** *nf (de mesure)* ineffectiveness; *(de personne)* inefficiency

**inégal, -e, -aux, -ales** [inegal, -o] *adj (parts, lutte)* unequal; *(sol, humeur)* uneven; *Fig (travail)* inconsistent ▪ **inégalable** *adj* incomparable ▪ **inégalé, -e** *adj* unequalled ▪ **inégalité** *nf (injustice)* inequality; *(physique)* disparity (**de** in); *(de sol)* unevenness

**inéluctable** [inelyktabl] *adj* inescapable

**inepte** [inɛpt] *adj (remarque, histoire)* inane; *(personne)* inept ▪ **ineptie** [inɛpsi] *nf (de comportement, de film)* inanity; *(remarque)* stupid remark

**inépuisable** [inepɥizabl] *adj* inexhaustible

**inespéré, -e** [inɛspere] *adj* unhoped-for

**inestimable** [inɛstimabl] *adj (objet d'art)* priceless

**inévitable** [inevitabl] *adj* inevitable, unavoidable

**inexact, -e** [inɛgzakt] *adj (erroné)* inaccurate; *(calcul)* wrong ▪ **inexactitude** *nf (caractère erroné, erreur)* inaccuracy; *(manque de ponctualité)* unpunctuality

**inexcusable** [inɛkskyzabl] *adj* inexcusable

**inexistant, -e** [inɛgzistɑ̃, -ɑ̃t] *adj* non-existent

**inexpérience** [inɛksperjɑ̃s] *nf* inexperience ▪ **inexpérimenté, -e** *adj* inexperienced

**inexplicable** [inɛksplikabl] *adj* inexplicable ▪ **inexpliqué, -e** *adj* unexplained

**inexploré, -e** [inɛksplɔre] *adj* unexplored

**inexprimable** [inɛksprimabl] *adj* inexpressible

**inextricable** [inɛkstrikabl] *adj* inextricable

**infaillible** [ɛ̃fajibl] *adj* infallible

**infaisable** [ɛ̃fəzabl] *adj (travail)* impossible

**infâme** [ɛ̃fɑm] *adj (personne)* despicable; *(acte)* unspeakable; *(taudis)* squalid; *(aliment)* revolting
**infantile** [ɛ̃fɑ̃til] *adj (maladie)* childhood; *Péj (comportement, personne)* infantile
**infarctus** [ɛ̃farktys] *nm Méd* heart attack
**infatigable** [ɛ̃fatigabl] *adj* tireless
**infect, -e** [ɛ̃fɛkt] *adj* foul
**infecter** [ɛ̃fɛkte] **1** *vt (atmosphère)* to contaminate; *Méd* to infect **2 s'infecter** *vpr* to become infected ▪ **infection** *nf Méd* infection; *(odeur)* stench
**inférieur, -e** [ɛ̃ferjœr] **1** *adj (étagère, niveau)* bottom; *(étage, lèvre, membre)* lower; *(qualité, marchandises)* inferior; **i. à la moyenne** below average; **à l'étage i.** on the floor below **2** *nmf* inferior ▪ **infériorité** *nf* inferiority
**infernal, -e, -aux, -ales** [ɛ̃fɛrnal, -o] *adj (de l'enfer) & Fig (chaleur, bruit)* infernal
**infidèle** [ɛ̃fidɛl] *adj* unfaithful (**à** to) ▪ **infidélité** *nf* unfaithfulness, infidelity
**infiltrer** [ɛ̃filtre] **1** *vt (party)* to infiltrate **2 s'infiltrer** *vpr (liquide)* to seep (**dans** into); *(lumière)* to filter in; *Fig* **s'i. dans** *(groupe, esprit)* to infiltrate ▪ **infiltration** *nf (de liquide, d'espions)* infiltration
**infime** [ɛ̃fim] *adj* tiny
**infini, -e** [ɛ̃fini] **1** *adj* infinite **2** *nm Math & Phot* infinity; *Phil* infinite; **à l'i.** *(discuter)* ad infinitum; *Math* to infinity ▪ **infiniment** *adv* infinitely; **je regrette i.** I'm very sorry ▪ **infinité** *nf* **une i. de** an infinite number of
**infirme** [ɛ̃firm] **1** *adj* disabled **2** *nmf* disabled person ▪ **infirmité** *nf* disability
**infirmer** [ɛ̃firme] *vt* to invalidate
**infirmerie** [ɛ̃firməri] *nf (d'école, de bateau)* sick room; *(de caserne, de prison)* infirmary ▪ **infirmier** *nm* male nurse ▪ **infirmière** *nf* nurse
**inflammable** [ɛ̃flamabl] *adj* (in)flammable
**inflammation** [ɛ̃flamɑsjɔ̃] *nf Méd* inflammation
**inflation** [ɛ̃flɑsjɔ̃] *nf Écon* inflation
**infléchir** [ɛ̃fleʃir] *vt (courber)* to bend; *(politique)* to change the direction of ▪ **inflexion** *nf (de courbe, de voix)* inflection
**inflexible** [ɛ̃flɛksibl] *adj* inflexible
**infliger** [ɛ̃fliʒe] *vt* to inflict (**à** on); *(amende)* to impose (**à** on)
**influence** [ɛ̃flyɑ̃s] *nf* influence ▪ **influençable** *adj* easily influenced ▪ **influencer** *vt* to influence ▪ **influent, -e** *adj* influential ▪ **influer** *vi* **i. sur qch** to influence sth
**informaticien, -enne** [ɛ̃fɔrmatisjɛ̃, -ɛn] *nmf* computer scientist
**information** [ɛ̃fɔrmɑsjɔ̃] *nf* information; *(nouvelle)* piece of news; *Ordinat* data, information; *Radio & TV* **les informations** the news *(sing)*
**informatique** [ɛ̃fɔrmatik] **1** *nf (science)* computer science; *(technique)* data processing **2** *adj* **programme i.** computer program ▪ **informatisation** *nf* computerization ▪ **informatiser** *vt* to computerize
**informe** [ɛ̃fɔrm] *adj* shapeless
**informer** [ɛ̃fɔrme] **1** *vt* to inform (**de** of *or* about; **que** that) **2 s'informer** *vpr (se renseigner)* to inquire (**de** about; **si** if *or* whether)
**inforoute** [ɛ̃fɔrut] *nf* information superhighway
**infortune** [ɛ̃fɔrtyn] *nf* misfortune ▪ **infortuné, -e** *adj* unfortunate
**infraction** [ɛ̃fraksjɔ̃] *nf (à un règlement)* infringement; *(délit) Br* offence, *Am* offense
**infranchissable** [ɛ̃frɑ̃ʃisabl] *adj (mur, fleuve)* impassable; *Fig (difficulté)* insurmountable
**infrarouge** [ɛ̃fraruʒ] *adj* infrared
**infrastructure** [ɛ̃frastryktyr] *nf (de bâtiment)* substructure; *(équipements)* infrastructure
**infructueux, -euse** [ɛ̃fryktɥø, -øz] *adj* fruitless
**infuser** [ɛ̃fyze] *vi (thé)* to brew; *(tisane)*

to infuse ▪ **infusion** *nf (tisane)* herb tea

**ingénier** [ɛ̃ʒenje] **s'ingénier** *vpr* to strive (**à faire** to do)

**ingénieur** [ɛ̃ʒenjœr] *nm* engineer ▪ **ingénierie** [-iri] *nf* engineering

**ingénieux, -euse** [ɛ̃ʒenjø, -øz] *adj* ingenious ▪ **ingéniosité** *nf* ingenuity

**ingénu, -e** [ɛ̃ʒeny] *adj* ingenuous

**ingérer** [ɛ̃ʒere] **s'ingérer** *vpr* to interfere (**dans** in) ▪ **ingérence** *nf* interference (**dans** in)

**ingrat, -e** [ɛ̃gra, -at] *adj (personne)* ungrateful (**envers** to); *(tâche)* thankless; *(sol)* barren; *(visage)* unattractive; **l'âge i.** the awkward age ▪ **ingratitude** *nf* ingratitude

**ingrédient** [ɛ̃gredjɑ̃] *nm* ingredient

**inhabitable** [inabitabl] *adj* uninhabitable ▪ **inhabité, -e** *adj* uninhabited

**inhabituel, -elle** [inabitɥɛl] *adj* unusual

**inhérent, -e** [inerɑ̃, -ɑ̃t] *adj* inherent (**à** in)

**inhibé, -e** [inibe] *adj* inhibited ▪ **inhibition** *nf* inhibition

**inhospitalier, -ère** [inɔspitalje, -ɛr] *adj* inhospitable

**inhumain, -e** [inymɛ̃, -ɛn] *adj (cruel, terrible)* inhuman

**inhumer** [inyme] *vt* to bury

**inimaginable** [inimaʒinabl] *adj* unimaginable

**inimitable** [inimitabl] *adj* inimitable

**inimitié** [inimitje] *nf* enmity

**ininflammable** [inɛ̃flamabl] *adj* non-flammable

**inintelligible** [inɛ̃teliʒibl] *adj* unintelligible

**ininterrompu, -e** [inɛ̃terɔ̃py] *adj* continuous

**initial, -e, -aux, -ales** [inisjal, -o] *adj* initial ▪ **initiale** *nf* initial

**initialiser** [inisjalize] *vt Ordinat (disque)* to initialize; *(ordinateur)* to boot

**initiation** [inisjɑsjɔ̃] *nf* initiation

**initiative** [inisjativ] *nf* initiative; **de ma propre i.** on my own initiative

**initier** [inisje] **1** *vt (former)* to introduce (**à** to); *(rituellement)* to initiate (**à** into) **2 s'initier** *vpr* **s'i. à qch** to start learning sth

**injecter** [ɛ̃ʒɛkte] *vt* to inject (**dans** into) ▪ **injection** *nf* injection

**injure** [ɛ̃ʒyr] *nf* insult ▪ **injurier** *vt* to insult, to abuse ▪ **injurieux, -euse** *adj* abusive, insulting (**pour** to)

**injuste** [ɛ̃ʒyst] *adj (contraire à la justice)* unjust; *(non équitable)* unfair ▪ **injustice** *nf* injustice

**injustifiable** [ɛ̃ʒystifjabl] *adj* unjustifiable ▪ **injustifié, -e** *adj* unjustified

**inlassable** [ɛ̃lɑsabl] *adj* untiring

**inné, -e** [ine] *adj* innate, inborn

**innocent, -e** [inɔsɑ̃, -ɑ̃t] **1** *adj* innocent (**de** of) **2** *nmf (non coupable)* innocent person; *(idiot)* simpleton ▪ **innocence** *nf* innocence ▪ **innocenter** *vt* **i. qn** to clear sb (**de** of)

**innombrable** [inɔ̃brabl] *adj* countless, innumerable; *(foule)* huge

**innommable** [inɔmabl] *adj (conduite, actes)* unspeakable; *(nourriture, odeur)* vile

**innover** [inɔve] *vi* to innovate ▪ **innovateur, -trice 1** *adj* innovative **2** *nmf* innovator ▪ **innovation** *nf* innovation

**inoccupé, -e** [inɔkype] *adj* unoccupied

**inoculer** [inɔkyle] *vt* **i. qch à qn** to inoculate sb with sth; **i. qn contre qch** to inoculate sb against sth

**inodore** [inɔdɔr] *adj* odourless

**inoffensif, -ive** [inɔfɑ̃sif, -iv] *adj* harmless

**inonder** [inɔ̃de] *vt (lieu)* to flood; *Fig (marché)* to flood, to inundate (**de** with); **inondé de soleil** bathed in sunlight ▪ **inondation** *nf* flood; *(action)* flooding

**inopérable** [inɔperabl] *adj* inoperable

**inopiné, -e** [inɔpine] *adj* unexpected

**inopportun, -e** [inɔpɔrtœ̃, -yn] *adj* inopportune

**inoubliable** [inublijabl] *adj* unforgettable

**inouï, -e** [inwi] *adj* incredible

**Inox®** [inɔks] *nm* stainless steel; **couteau en I.** stainless-steel knife ▪ **inoxydable** *adj (couteau)* stainless-steel

**inqualifiable** [ɛ̃kalifjabl] *adj* unspeakable

**inquiet, -ète** [ɛ̃kjɛ, -ɛt] *adj* worried, anxious (**de** about)

**inquiéter** [ɛ̃kjete] **1** *vt (préoccuper)* to worry **2 s'inquiéter** *vpr* to worry (**de** about); **s'i. pour qn** to worry about sb ▪ **inquiétant, -e** *adj* worrying

**inquiétude** [ɛ̃kjetyd] *nf* anxiety, worry

**insaisissable** [ɛ̃sezisabl] *adj* elusive

**insalubre** [ɛ̃salybr] *adj (climat, habitation)* insalubrious

**insatiable** [ɛ̃sasjabl] *adj* insatiable

**insatisfait, -e** [ɛ̃satisfɛ, -ɛt] *adj (personne)* dissatisfied

**inscription** [ɛ̃skripsjɔ̃] *nf (action)* entering; *(immatriculation)* registration; *(sur écriteau, mur, tombe)* inscription

**inscrire*** [ɛ̃skrir] **1** *vt (renseignements, date)* to write down; *(dans un journal, sur un registre)* to enter; *(graver)* to inscribe; **i. qn à un club** to *Br* enrol *or Am* enroll sb in a club

**2 s'inscrire** *vpr* to put one's name down; *(à une activité) Br* to enrol, *Am* to enroll (**à** at); *(à l'université)* to register (**à** at); **s'i. à un club** to join a club

**insecte** [ɛ̃sɛkt] *nm* insect

**insécurité** [ɛ̃sekyrite] *nf* insecurity

**insensé, -e** [ɛ̃sɑ̃se] *adj (projet, idée)* crazy; *(espoir)* wild

**insensible** [ɛ̃sɑ̃sibl] *adj (indifférent)* insensitive (**à** to); *(imperceptible)* imperceptible

**inséparable** [ɛ̃separabl] *adj* inseparable (**de** from)

**insérer** [ɛ̃sere] *vt* to insert (**dans** in) ▪ **insertion** [ɛ̃sɛrsjɔ̃] *nf* insertion

**insidieux, -euse** [ɛ̃sidjø, -øz] *adj* insidious

**insigne** [ɛ̃siɲ] *nm* badge

**insignifiant, -e** [ɛ̃siɲifjɑ̃, -jɑ̃t] *adj* insignificant

**insinuer** [ɛ̃sinɥe] **1** *vt Péj* to insinuate (**que** that) **2 s'insinuer** *vpr (froid)* to creep (**dans** into); *(personne)* to worm one's way (**dans** into)

**insipide** [ɛ̃sipid] *adj* insipid

**insister** [ɛ̃siste] *vi* to insist (**pour faire** on doing); **i. sur qch** to stress sth; **i. pour que...** *(+ subjunctive)* to insist that... ▪ **insistance** *nf* insistence

**insolation** [ɛ̃sɔlɑsjɔ̃] *nf Méd* sunstroke

**insolent, -e** [ɛ̃sɔlɑ̃, -ɑ̃t] *adj (impoli)* insolent; *(luxe)* unashamed ▪ **insolence** *nf* insolence

**insolite** [ɛ̃sɔlit] *adj* unusual, strange

**insoluble** [ɛ̃sɔlybl] *adj* insoluble

**insomnie** [ɛ̃sɔmni] *nf* insomnia ▪ **insomniaque** *nmf* insomniac

**insondable** [ɛ̃sɔ̃dabl] *adj* unfathomable

**insonoriser** [ɛ̃sɔnɔrize] *vt* to soundproof

**insouciant, -e** [ɛ̃susjɑ̃, -ɑ̃t] *adj* carefree ▪ **insouciance** *nf* carefree attitude

**insoumis, -e** [ɛ̃sumi, -iz] *adj (personne)* rebellious; *Mil* absentee

**insoupçonnable** [ɛ̃supsɔnabl] *adj* beyond suspicion

**insoutenable** [ɛ̃sutnabl] *adj (spectacle, odeur)* unbearable; *(théorie)* untenable

**inspecter** [ɛ̃spɛkte] *vt* to inspect ▪ **inspecteur, -trice** *nmf* inspector ▪ **inspection** *nf* inspection

**inspirer** [ɛ̃spire] **1** *vt* to inspire; **i. qch à qn** to inspire sb with sth **2** *vi* to breathe in **3 s'inspirer** *vpr* **s'i. de qn/qch** to take one's inspiration from sb/sth ▪ **inspiration** *nf (idée)* inspiration; *(respiration)* breathing in ▪ **inspiré, -e** *adj* inspired

**instable** [ɛ̃stabl] *adj* unstable; *(temps)* changeable ▪ **instabilité** *nf* instability; *(de temps)* changeability

**installer** [ɛ̃stale] **1** *vt (appareil, meuble)* to install, to put in; *(étagère)* to put up; *(cuisine)* to fit out; **i. qn** *(dans une fonction, dans un logement)* to install sb (**dans** in)

**2 s'installer** *vpr (s'asseoir)* to settle

down; *(dans un bureau)* to install oneself; *(médecin)* to set oneself up; **s'i. à la campagne** to settle in the country ▪ **installation** *nf (de machine)* installation; *(de cuisine)* fitting out; *(emménagement)* move; **installations** *(appareils)* fittings; *(bâtiments)* facilities

**instant** [ɛ̃stɑ̃] *nm* moment, instant; **à l'i.** a moment ago; **à l'i. où...** just as...; **pour l'i.** for the moment ▪ **instantané, -e 1** *adj* instantaneous; **café i.** instant coffee **2** *nm (photo)* snapshot

**instar** [ɛ̃star] *nm* **à l'i. de qn** after the fashion of sb

**instaurer** [ɛ̃stɔre] *vt* to establish

**instigateur, -trice** [ɛ̃stigatœr, -tris] *nmf* instigator

**instinct** [ɛ̃stɛ̃] *nm* instinct; **d'i.** by instinct ▪ **instinctif, -ive** *adj* instinctive

**instituer** [ɛ̃stitɥe] *vt* to establish

**institut** [ɛ̃stity] *nm* institute; **i. de beauté** beauty salon

**instituteur, -trice** [ɛ̃stitytœr, -tris] *nmf Br* primary *or Am* elementary school teacher

**institution** [ɛ̃stitysjɔ̃] *nf (création)* establishment; *(coutume)* institution; *(école)* private school ▪ **institutionnel, -elle** *adj* institutional

**instructif, -ive** [ɛ̃stryktif, -iv] *adj* instructive

**instruction** [ɛ̃stryksjɔ̃] *nf (éducation)* education; *Mil* training; *Jur* preliminary investigation; **instructions** *(ordres)* instructions; **i. civique** civics *(sing)* ▪ **instructeur** *nm* instructor

**instruire*** [ɛ̃strɥir] **1** *vt* to teach, to educate; *Mil* to train; *Jur* to investigate; **i. qn de qch** to inform sb of sth **2 s'instruire** *vpr* to educate oneself ▪ **instruit, -e** *adj* educated

**instrument** [ɛ̃strymɑ̃] *nm* instrument; **i. à vent** wind instrument ▪ **instrumental, -e, -aux, -ales** *adj Mus* instrumental

**insu** [ɛ̃sy] **à l'insu de** *prép* without the knowledge of; **à mon/son i.** *(sans m'en/s'en apercevoir)* without my/his/her being aware of it

**insuffisant, -e** [ɛ̃syfizɑ̃, -ɑ̃t] *adj (en quantité)* insufficient; *(en qualité)* inadequate ▪ **insuffisance** *nf (manque)* insufficiency; *(de moyens)* inadequacy

**insulaire** [ɛ̃sylɛr] **1** *adj* insular **2** *nmf* islander

**insulte** [ɛ̃sylt] *nf* insult (**à** to) ▪ **insulter** *vt* to insult

**insupportable** [ɛ̃sypɔrtabl] *adj* unbearable

**insurger** [ɛ̃syrʒe] **s'insurger** *vpr* to rise up (**contre** against)

**insurmontable** [ɛ̃syrmɔ̃tabl] *adj* insurmountable

**insurrection** [ɛ̃syrɛksjɔ̃] *nf* insurrection, uprising

**intact, -e** [ɛ̃takt] *adj* intact

**intarissable** [ɛ̃tarisabl] *adj* inexhaustible

**intégral, -e, -aux, -ales** [ɛ̃tegral, -o] *adj (paiement)* full; *(édition)* unabridged; **version intégrale** *(de film)* uncut version ▪ **intégralement** *adv* in full, fully ▪ **intégralité** *nf* whole (**de** of)

**intègre** [ɛ̃tɛgr] *adj* upright, honest ▪ **intégrité** *nf* integrity

**intégrer** [ɛ̃tegre] **1** *vt* to integrate (**dans** in); *(école)* to get into **2 s'intégrer** *vpr* to become integrated ▪ **intégrante** *adj f* **faire partie i. de qch** to be an integral part of sth ▪ **intégration** *nf (au sein d'un groupe)* integration

**intégrisme** [ɛ̃tegrism] *nm* fundamentalism

**intellectuel, -elle** [ɛ̃telɛktɥɛl] *adj & nmf* intellectual

**intelligent, -e** [ɛ̃teliʒɑ̃, -ɑ̃t] *adj* intelligent, clever ▪ **intelligence** *nf (faculté)* intelligence; **avoir l'i. de faire qch** to have the intelligence to do sth; *Ordinat* **i. artificielle** artificial intelligence

**intelligible** [ɛ̃teliʒibl] *adj* intelligible

**intempéries** [ɛ̃tɑ̃peri] *nfpl* **les i.** the bad weather

**intempestif, -ive** [ɛ̃tɑ̃pɛstif, -iv] *adj* untimely

**intenable** [ɛ̃tnabl] *adj (position)* untenable

**intendant, -e** [ɛ̃tɑ̃dɑ̃, -ɑ̃t] *nmf Scol* bursar

**intense** [ɛ̃tɑ̃s] *adj* intense; *(circulation)* heavy ▪ **intensif, -ive** *adj* intensive ▪ **intensité** *nf* intensity

**intensifier** [ɛ̃tɑ̃sifje] *vt*, **s'intensifier** *vpr* to intensify

**intenter** [ɛ̃tɑ̃te] *vt Jur* **i. un procès à qn** to institute proceedings against sb

**intention** [ɛ̃tɑ̃sjɔ̃] *nf* intention; *Jur* intent; **avoir l'i. de faire qch** to intend to do sth ▪ **intentionné, -e** *adj* **bien i.** well-intentioned; **mal i.** ill-intentioned ▪ **intentionnel, -elle** *adj* intentional

**interactif, -ive** [ɛ̃tɛraktif, -iv] *adj Ordinat* interactive

**interaction** [ɛ̃tɛraksjɔ̃] *nf* interaction

**intercaler** [ɛ̃tɛrkale] *vt* to insert

**intercéder** [ɛ̃tɛrsede] *vt* to intercede (**auprès de** with; **en faveur de** on behalf of)

**intercepter** [ɛ̃tɛrsɛpte] *vt* to intercept

**interchangeable** [ɛ̃tɛrʃɑ̃ʒabl] *adj* interchangeable

**interdire*** [ɛ̃tɛrdir] *vt* to forbid (**qch à qn** sb sth); *(film, meeting)* to ban; **i. à qn de faire qch** *(personne)* to forbid sb to do sth ▪ **interdiction** *nf* ban (**de** on); **'i. de fumer'** 'no smoking' ▪ **interdit, -e** *adj* (**a**) *(défendu)* forbidden; **'stationnement i.'** 'no parking' (**b**) *(étonné)* disconcerted

**intéresser** [ɛ̃terese] **1** *vt (captiver)* to interest; *(concerner)* to concern **2 s'intéresser** *vpr* **s'i. à qn/qch** to be interested in sb/sth ▪ **intéressant, -e 1** *adj (captivant)* interesting; *(prix)* attractive
**2** *nmf Péj* **faire l'i.** to show off ▪ **intéressé, -e 1** *adj (avide)* self-interested; *(motif)* selfish; *(concerné)* concerned **2** *nmf* **l'i.** the person concerned

**intérêt** [ɛ̃terɛ] *nm* interest; *Fin* **intérêts** interest; **tu as i. à le faire** you'd do well to do it; **sans i.** *(personne, film)* uninteresting

**intérieur, -eure** [ɛ̃terjœr] **1** *adj (escalier, paroi)* interior; *(cour, vie)* inner; *(poche)* inside; *(partie)* internal; *(vol)* internal, domestic; *(mer)* inland **2** *nm (de boîte, de maison)* inside (**de** of); *(de pays)* interior; *(maison)* home; **à l'i. (de)** inside; **d'i.** *(vêtement, jeux)* indoor

**intérim** [ɛ̃terim] *nm (travail temporaire)* temporary work; **président par i.** acting president ▪ **intérimaire 1** *adj (fonction, employé)* temporary **2** *nmf (travailleur)* temporary worker; *(secrétaire)* temp

**interlocuteur, -trice** [ɛ̃tɛrlɔkytœr, -tris] *nmf (de conversation)* speaker; *(de négociation)* discussion partner; **mon i.** the person I am/was speaking to

**intermède** [ɛ̃tɛrmɛd] *nm* interlude

**intermédiaire** [ɛ̃tɛrmedjɛr] **1** *adj* intermediate **2** *nmf* intermediary; *Com* middleman; **par l'i. de** through; **sans i.** directly

**interminable** [ɛ̃tɛrminabl] *adj* interminable

**intermittent, -e** [ɛ̃tɛrmitɑ̃, -ɑ̃t] *adj* intermittent ▪ **intermittence** *nf* **par i.** intermittently

**internat** [ɛ̃tɛrna] *nm (école)* boarding school; *(concours de médecine)* = entrance examination for *Br* a housemanship *or Am* an internship ▪ **interne 1** *adj (douleur)* internal; *(oreille)* inner **2** *nmf (élève)* boarder; **i. des hôpitaux** *Br* house doctor, *Am* intern

**international, -e, -aux, -ales** [ɛ̃tɛrnasjɔnal, -o] **1** *adj* international **2** *nm (footballeur)* international

**interner** [ɛ̃tɛrne] *vt (prisonnier)* to intern; *(aliéné)* to commit ▪ **internement** [-əmɑ̃] *nm (emprisonnement)* internment; *(d'aliéné)* confinement

**Internet** [ɛ̃tɛrnɛt] *nm* Internet; **sur (l')I.** on the Internet ▪ **internaute** *nmf* Internet surfer

**interpeller** [ɛ̃tɛrpəle] *vt (appeler)* to

call out to; *(dans une réunion)* to question; **i. qn** *(police)* to take sb in for questioning ■ **interpellation** *nf* sharp address; *(dans une réunion)* question

**interposer** [ɛ̃tɛrpoze] **s'interposer** *vpr (intervenir)* to intervene (**dans** in)

**interprète** [ɛ̃tɛrprɛt] *nmf (traducteur)* interpreter; *(chanteur)* singer; *(musicien, acteur)* performer ■ **interprétariat** *nm* interpreting ■ **interprétation** *nf (de texte, de rôle, de rêve)* interpretation; *(traduction)* interpreting ■ **interpréter** *vt (texte, rôle, musique, rêve)* to interpret; *(chanter)* to sing

**interroger** [ɛ̃tɛrɔʒe] *vt* to question; *(élève)* to test; *Ordinat (banque de données)* to query ■ **interrogateur, -trice** *adj (air)* questioning ■ **interrogation** *nf (question)* question; *(de prisonnier)* questioning; *Scol* **i. écrite/orale** written/oral test ■ **interrogatoire** *nm* interrogation

**interrompre*** [ɛ̃tɛrɔ̃pr] **1** *vt* to interrupt **2 s'interrompre** *vpr* to break off ■ **interrupteur** *nm* switch ■ **interruption** *nf* interruption; *(de négociations)* breaking off; **sans i.** continuously; **i. volontaire de grossesse** termination

**intersection** [ɛ̃tɛrsɛksjɔ̃] *nf* intersection

**intervalle** [ɛ̃tɛrval] *nm (dans l'espace)* gap, space; *(dans le temps)* interval; **dans l'i.** *(entretemps)* in the meantime; **par intervalles** (every) now and then, at intervals

**intervenir*** [ɛ̃tɛrvənir] *vi (agir, prendre la parole)* to intervene; *(survenir)* to occur; **être intervenu** *(accord)* to be reached ■ **intervention** *nf* intervention; *(discours)* speech; **i. chirurgicale** operation

**intervertir** [ɛ̃tɛrvɛrtir] *vt* to invert

**interview** [ɛ̃tɛrvju] *nm ou f* interview ■ **interviewer** [-vjuve] *vt* to interview

**intestin** [ɛ̃tɛstɛ̃] *nm* intestine

**intime** [ɛ̃tim] **1** *adj* intimate; *(ami)* close; *(cérémonie)* quiet **2** *nmf* close friend ■ **intimement** [-əmɑ̃] *adv* intimately; **i. liés** *(problèmes)* closely linked ■ **intimité** *nf (familiarité)* intimacy; *(vie privée)* privacy; **dans l'i.** in private

**intimider** [ɛ̃timide] *vt* to intimidate

**intituler** [ɛ̃tityle] **1** *vt* to give a title to **2 s'intituler** *vpr* to be entitled

**intolérable** [ɛ̃tɔlerabl] *adj* intolerable ■ **intolérance** *nf* intolerance ■ **intolérant, -e** *adj* intolerant

**intoxiquer** [ɛ̃tɔksike] **1** *vt (empoisonner)* to poison **2 s'intoxiquer** *vpr* to poison oneself ■ **intoxication** *nf (empoisonnement)* poisoning; **i. alimentaire** food poisoning

**intraitable** [ɛ̃trɛtabl] *adj* uncompromising

**intransigeant, -e** [ɛ̃trɑ̃ziʒɑ̃, -ɑ̃t] *adj* intransigent

**intrépide** [ɛ̃trepid] *adj* fearless, intrepid

**intrigue** [ɛ̃trig] *nf* intrigue; *(de film, roman)* plot ■ **intriguer 1** *vt* **i. qn** to intrigue sb **2** *vi* to scheme

**introduire*** [ɛ̃trɔdɥir] **1** *vt (insérer)* to insert (**dans** into); *(marchandises)* to bring in; *(réforme, mode)* to introduce; *(visiteur)* to show in **2 s'introduire** *vpr* **s'i. dans une maison** to get into a house ■ **introduction** *nf (texte, action)* introduction

**introuvable** [ɛ̃truvabl] *adj (produit)* unobtainable; *(personne)* nowhere to be found

**introverti, -e** [ɛ̃trɔvɛrti] *nmf* introvert

**intrus, -e** [ɛ̃try, -yz] *nmf* intruder ■ **intrusion** *nf* intrusion (**dans** into)

**intuition** [ɛ̃tɥisjɔ̃] *nf* intuition ■ **intuitif, -ive** *adj* intuitive

**inuit** [inɥit] **1** *adj inv* Inuit **2** *nmf inv* **I.** Inuit

**inusable** [inyzabl] *adj* hard-wearing

**inusité, -e** [inyzite] *adj (mot, forme)* uncommon

**inutile** [inytil] *adj (qui ne sert à rien)* useless; *(précaution, bagage)* unnecessary; **c'est i. de crier** it's pointless shouting ■ **inutilement** *adv* needlessly ■ **inutilité** *nf* uselessness

**inutilisable** [inytilizabl] *adj* unusable ■ **inutilisé, -e** *adj* unused

**invaincu, -e** [ɛ̃vɛ̃ky] *adj Sport* unbeaten

**invalide** [ɛ̃valid] **1** *adj* disabled **2** *nmf* disabled person

**invalider** [ɛ̃valide] *vt* to invalidate

**invariable** [ɛ̃varjabl] *adj* invariable

**invasion** [ɛ̃vɑzjɔ̃] *nf* invasion

**invendable** [ɛ̃vɑ̃dabl] *adj* unsellable ▪ **invendu, -e 1** *adj* unsold **2** *nmpl* **invendus** unsold articles; *(journaux)* unsold copies

**inventaire** [ɛ̃vɑ̃tɛr] *nm Com (liste)* inventory; **faire l'i.** to do the stocktaking (**de** of)

**inventer** [ɛ̃vɑ̃te] *vt (créer)* to invent; *(concept)* to think up; *(histoire, excuse)* to make up ▪ **inventeur, -trice** *nmf* inventor ▪ **inventif, -ive** *adj* inventive ▪ **invention** *nf* invention

**inverse** [ɛ̃vɛrs] **1** *adj (sens)* opposite; *(ordre)* reverse; *Math* inverse **2** *nm* **l'i.** the reverse, the opposite ▪ **inversement** [-əmɑ̃] *adv* conversely ▪ **inverser** *vt (ordre)* to reverse ▪ **inversion** *nf* inversion

**investigation** [ɛ̃vɛstigɑsjɔ̃] *nf* investigation

**investir** [ɛ̃vɛstir] **1** *vt (capitaux)* to invest (**dans** in); *(édifice, ville)* to besiege **2** *vi* to invest (**dans** in) ▪ **investissement** *nm Fin* investment

**invincible** [ɛ̃vɛ̃sibl] *adj* invincible

**invisible** [ɛ̃vizibl] *adj* invisible

**inviter** [ɛ̃vite] *vt* to invite; **i. qn à faire qch** *(prier)* to request sb to do sth; *(inciter)* to urge sb to do sth; **i. qn à dîner** to invite sb to dinner ▪ **invitation** *nf* invitation ▪ **invité, -e** *nmf* guest

**involontaire** [ɛ̃vɔlɔ̃tɛr] *adj (geste)* involuntary; *(témoin)* unwilling

**invoquer** [ɛ̃vɔke] *vt (argument)* to put forward; *(loi, texte)* to refer to; *(divinité)* to invoke ▪ **invocation** *nf* invocation (**à** to)

**invraisemblable** [ɛ̃vrɛsɑ̃blabl] *adj (extraordinaire)* incredible; *(alibi)* implausible ▪ **invraisemblance** *nf (improbabilité)* unlikelihood; *(d'alibi)* implausibility

**invulnérable** [ɛ̃vylnerabl] *adj* invulnerable

**ira, irait** *etc* [ira, irɛ] *voir* **aller[1]**

**Irak** [irak] *nm* **l'I.** Iraq ▪ **irakien, -enne 1** *adj* Iraqi **2** *nmf* **I., Irakienne** Iraqi

**Iran** [irɑ̃] *nm* **l'I.** Iran ▪ **iranien, -enne 1** *adj* Iranian **2** *nmf* **I., Iranienne** Iranian

**iris** [iris] *nm (plante) & Anat* iris

**Irlande** [irlɑ̃d] *nf* **l'I.** Ireland; **l'I. du Nord** Northern Ireland ▪ **irlandais, -e 1** *adj* Irish **2** *nmf* **I.** Irishman; **Irlandaise** Irishwoman; **les I.** the Irish **3** *nm (langue)* Irish

**ironie** [irɔni] *nf* irony ▪ **ironique** *adj* ironic(al)

**iront** [irɔ̃] *voir* **aller[1]**

**irrationnel, -elle** [irasjɔnɛl] *adj* irrational

**irréalisable** [irealizabl] *adj (projet)* impracticable

**irréaliste** [irealist] *adj* unrealistic

**irrécusable** [irekyzabl] *adj (preuve)* indisputable; *Jur (témoignage)* unimpeachable

**irréductible** [iredyktibl] **1** *adj (ennemi)* implacable **2** *nm* diehard

**irréel, -elle** [ireɛl] *adj* unreal

**irréfléchi, -e** [irefleʃi] *adj* rash

**irréfutable** [irefytabl] *adj* irrefutable

**irrégulier, -ère** [iregylje, -ɛr] *adj (rythme, verbe, procédure)* irregular; *(sol)* uneven; *(résultats)* inconsistent ▪ **irrégularité** *nf* irregularity; *(de sol)* unevenness

**irrémédiable** [iremedjabl] *adj* irreparable

**irremplaçable** [irɑ̃plasabl] *adj* irreplaceable

**irréparable** [ireparabl] *adj (véhicule)* beyond repair; *(tort, perte)* irreparable

**irrépressible** [irepresibl] *adj* irrepressible

**irréprochable** [ireprɔʃabl] *adj* irreproachable

**irrésistible** [irezistibl] *adj (personne, charme)* irresistible

**irrésolu, -e** [irezɔly] *adj (personne)* indecisive; *(problème)* unresolved

**irrespirable** [irɛspirabl] *adj (air)* unbreathable; *Fig (atmosphère)* unbearable

**irresponsable** [irɛspɔ̃sabl] *adj (personne)* irresponsible

**irréversible** [ireversibl] *adj* irreversible

**irrévocable** [irevɔkabl] *adj* irrevocable

**irrigation** [irigasjɔ̃] *nf* irrigation

**irriter** [irite] **1** *vt* to irritate **2 s'irriter** *vpr (s'énerver)* to get irritated (**de** with; **contre** at); *(s'enflammer)* to become irritated ▪ **irritable** *adj* irritable ▪ **irritation** *nf (colère) & Méd* irritation

**irruption** [irypsjɔ̃] *nf* **faire i. dans** to burst into

**Islam** [islam] *nm* **l'I.** Islam ▪ **islamique** *adj* Islamic

**Islande** [islɑ̃d] *nf* **l'I.** Iceland ▪ **islandais, -e 1** *adj* Icelandic **2** *nmf* **I., Islandaise** Icelander

**isolant, -e** [izɔlɑ̃, -ɑ̃t] **1** *adj* insulating **2** *nm* insulating material

**isoler** [izɔle] **1** *vt* to isolate (**de** from); *(du froid) & Él* to insulate **2 s'isoler** *vpr* to isolate oneself ▪ **isolation** *nf* insulation ▪ **isolé, -e** *adj (personne, endroit, maison)* isolated; *(du froid)* insulated; **i. de** cut off *or* isolated from ▪ **isolement** *nm (de personne)* isolation; ▪ **isolément** *adv (agir)* in isolation; *(interroger des gens)* individually

**isoloir** [izɔlwar] *nm Br* polling *or Am* voting booth

**Israël** [israel] *nm* Israel ▪ **israélien, -enne 1** *adj* Israeli **2** *nmf* **I., Israélienne** Israeli ▪ **israélite 1** *adj* Jewish **2** *nmf* Jew

**issu, -e** [isy] *adj* **être i. de** to come from

**issue** [isy] *nf (sortie)* exit; *Fig (solution)* way out; *(résultat)* outcome; **à l'i. de** at the end of; **i. de secours** emergency exit

**isthme** [ism] *nm* isthmus

**Italie** [itali] *nf* **l'I.** Italy ▪ **italien, -enne 1** *adj* Italian **2** *nmf* **I., Italienne** Italian **3** *nm (langue)* Italian

**italique** [italik] **1** *adj (lettre)* italic **2** *nm* italics; **en i.** in italics

**itinéraire** [itinerɛr] *nm* route, itinerary

**IUT** [iyte] (*abrév* **institut universitaire de technologie**) *nm* = vocational higher education college

**IVG** [iveʒe] (*abrév* **interruption volontaire de grossesse**) *nf* abortion, termination

**ivoire** [ivwar] *nm* ivory; **statuette en i.** *ou* **d'i.** ivory statuette

**ivre** [ivr] *adj* drunk (**de** with); *Fig* **i. de joie** wild with joy ▪ **ivresse** *nf* drunkenness; **en état d'i.** under the influence of drink ▪ **ivrogne** *nmf* drunk(ard)

# Jj

**J, j** [ʒi] *nm inv* J, j; **le jour J.** D-day
**j'** [ʒ] *voir* **je**
**jadis** [ʒadis] *adv Littéraire* in times past
**jaillir** [ʒajir] *vi (liquide)* to gush out; *(étincelles)* to shoot out
**jalonner** [ʒalɔne] *vt (marquer)* to mark out; *(border)* to line
**jaloux, -ouse** [ʒalu, -uz] *adj* jealous (**de** of) ■ **jalousie** *nf (sentiment)* jealousy
**Jamaïque** [ʒamaik] *nf* **la J.** Jamaica
**jamais** [ʒamɛ] *adv* (**a**) *(négatif)* never; **elle ne sort j.** she never goes out; **sans j. sortir** without ever going out
(**b**) *(positif)* ever; **à tout j.** for ever; **si j.** if ever; **le film le plus drôle que j'aie j. vu** the funniest film I have ever seen
**jambe** [ʒɑ̃b] *nf* leg
**jambon** [ʒɑ̃bɔ̃] *nm* ham
**janvier** [ʒɑ̃vje] *nm* January
**Japon** [ʒapɔ̃] *nm* **le J.** Japan ■ **japonais, -e 1** *adj* Japanese **2** *nmf* **J., Japonaise** Japanese *inv*; **les J.** the Japanese **3** *nm (langue)* Japanese
**jardin** [ʒardɛ̃] *nm* garden; **j. d'enfants** kindergarten; **j. public** gardens ■ **jardinage** *nm* gardening ■ **jardinier** *nm* gardener
**jargon** [ʒargɔ̃] *nm* jargon
**jasmin** [ʒasmɛ̃] *nm* jasmine; **thé au j.** jasmine tea
**jaune** [ʒon] **1** *adj* yellow **2** *nm (couleur)* yellow; **j. d'œuf** (egg) yolk
**Javel** [ʒavɛl] **eau de Javel** *nf* bleach
**javelot** [ʒavlo] *nm* javelin
**jazz** [dʒaz] *nm* jazz
**je** [ʒə]

> j' is used before a word beginning with a vowel or h mute.

*pron personnel* I; **je suis ici** I'm here
**jean** [dʒin] *nm* (pair of) jeans; **veste en j.** denim jacket
**Jersey** [ʒɛrzɛ] *nf* Jersey
**jet** [ʒɛ] *nm (de pierre)* throwing; *(de vapeur, de liquide)* jet; **j. d'eau** fountain
**jetable** [ʒətabl] *adj* disposable
**jetée** [ʒəte] *nf* pier, jetty
**jeter** [ʒəte] **1** *vt* to throw (**à** to; **dans** into); *(à la poubelle)* to throw away; *(sort)* to cast; **j. un coup d'œil à qn/qch** to have a quick look at sb/sth
**2 se jeter** *vpr (personne)* to throw oneself; **se j. sur qn** to throw oneself at sb; *Fig* to pounce on sb; **se j. sur qch** *(occasion)* to jump at sth; **se j. contre** *(véhicule)* to crash into; **se j. dans** *(fleuve)* to flow into
**jeton** [ʒətɔ̃] *nm (pièce)* token; *(au jeu)* chip
**jeu, -x** [ʒø] *nm* (**a**) *(amusement)* play; *(activité, au tennis)* game; *(d'acteur)* acting; **le j.** *(au casino)* gambling; **en j.** *(en cause)* at stake; *(forces)* at work; **j.-concours** competition; **j. électronique** computer game; **j. de hasard** game of chance; **j. de mots** play on words, pun; **jeux de société** board games; **j. télévisé** television game show; *(avec questions)* television quiz show; **j. vidéo** video game
(**b**) *(série complète)* set; *(de cartes)* deck, *Br* pack; *(cartes en main)* hand; **j. d'échecs** *(boîte, pièces)* chess set
(**c**) *Tech (de ressort, de verrou)* play

**jeudi** [ʒødi] *nm* Thursday
**jeun** [ʒœ̃] **à jeun 1** *adv* on an empty stomach **2** *adj* **être à j.** to have eaten no food
**jeune** [ʒœn] **1** *adj* young; *(apparence)* youthful; **jeunes gens** young people **2** *nmf* young person; **les jeunes** young people ▪ **jeunesse** *nf* youth; *(apparence)* youthfulness; **la j.** *(les jeunes)* the young
**jeûner** [ʒøne] *vi* to fast
**joaillier, -ère** [ʒɔaje, -ɛr] *nmf Br* jeweller, *Am* jeweler ▪ **joaillerie** *nf (bijoux) Br* jewellery, *Am* jewelry; *(magasin) Br* jewellery shop, *Am* jewelry store
**jockey** [ʒɔkɛ] *nm* jockey
**jogging** [dʒɔgiŋ] *nm Sport* jogging; *(survêtement)* jogging suit
**joie** [ʒwa] *nf* joy, delight; **avec j.** with pleasure, gladly
**joindre*** [ʒwɛ̃dr] **1** *vt (réunir)* to join; *(ajouter)* to add (**à** to); *(dans une enveloppe)* to enclose (**à** with); **j. qn** *(contacter)* to get in touch with sb
**2 se joindre** *vpr* **se j. à qn** to join sb ▪ **joint, -e 1** *adj* **à pieds joints** with feet together; **pièces jointes** *(de lettre)* enclosures **2** *nm Tech (articulation)* joint; *(d'étanchéité)* seal; *(de robinet)* washer; **j. de culasse** gasket
**joker** [ʒɔkɛr] *nm Cartes* joker
**joli, -e** [ʒɔli] *adj* pretty
**jonché** [ʒɔ̃ʃe] *adj* **j. de** strewn with
**jonction** [ʒɔ̃ksjɔ̃] *nf* junction
**jongler** [ʒɔ̃gle] *vi* to juggle (**avec** with)
**jonquille** [ʒɔ̃kij] *nf* daffodil
**Jordanie** [ʒɔrdani] *nf* **la J.** Jordan
**joue** [ʒu] *nf (du visage)* cheek
**jouer** [ʒwe] **1** *vt (musique, carte, rôle)* to play; *(pièce de théâtre)* to perform; *(film)* to show; *(parier)* to stake (**sur** on); *(cheval)* to bet on
**2** *vi* to play; *(acteur)* to act; *(au tiercé)* to gamble; *(être important)* to count; **j. au tennis/aux cartes** to play tennis/cards; **j. du piano/du violon** to play the piano/violin; **à toi de j.!** it's your turn (to play)!
**3 se jouer** *vpr (film, pièce)* to be on
**jouet** [ʒwɛ] *nm* toy
**joueur, -euse** [ʒwœr, -øz] *nmf* player; *(au tiercé)* gambler
**jouir** [ʒwir] *vi* **j. de qch** to enjoy sth
**jour** [ʒur] *nm (journée, date)* day; *(clarté)* daylight; *(éclairage)* light; **il fait j.** it's (day)light; **de j. en j.** day by day; **du j. au lendemain** overnight; **en plein j., au grand j.** in broad daylight; **de nos jours** nowadays, these days; *Fig* **sous un j. nouveau** in a different light; **mettre qch à j.** to bring sth up to date; **quel j. sommes-nous?** what day is it?; **il y a dix ans j. pour j.** ten years ago to the day; **le j. de l'an** New Year's Day
**journal, -aux** [ʒurnal, -o] *nm* (news)-paper; *(spécialisé)* journal; *(intime)* diary; **j. télévisé** (TV) news *(sing)* ▪ **journalisme** *nm* journalism ▪ **journaliste** *nmf* journalist
**journalier, -ère** [ʒurnalje, -ɛr] *adj* daily
**journée** [ʒurne] *nf* day; **pendant la j.** during the day(time); **toute la j.** all day (long)
**jovial, -e, -aux, -ales** [ʒɔvjal, -o] *adj* jovial, jolly
**joyau, -x** [ʒwajo] *nm* jewel
**joyeux, -euse** [ʒwajø, -øz] *adj* joyful; **j. anniversaire!** happy birthday!; **j. Noël!** merry *or Br* happy Christmas!
**jubiler** [ʒybile] *vi* to be jubilant
**jucher** [ʒyʃe] *vt*, **se jucher** *vpr* to perch (**sur** on)
**judicieux, -euse** [ʒydisjø, -øz] *adj* judicious
**judo** [ʒydo] *nm* judo
**juge** [ʒyʒ] *nm* judge; **j. de touche** *(au football)* linesman, assistant referee
**jugé** [ʒyʒe] **au jugé** *adv (calculer)* roughly
**jugement** [ʒyʒmɑ̃] *nm (opinion, discernement)* judgement; *(verdict)* sentence; **porter un j. sur qch** to pass judgement on sth; *Jur* **passer en j.** to stand trial
**juger** [ʒyʒe] **1** *vt (personne, question)*

to judge; *(au tribunal)* to try; *(estimer)* to consider (**que** that) **2** *vi* **j. de** to judge; **jugez de ma surprise!** imagine my surprise!

**juif, juive** [ʒɥif, ʒɥiv] **1** *adj* Jewish **2** *nmf* **J.** Jew

**juillet** [ʒɥijɛ] *nm* July

**juin** [ʒɥɛ̃] *nm* June

**jumeau, -elle, -x, -elles** [ʒymo, -ɛl] **1** *adj* **frère j.** twin brother; **sœur jumelle** twin sister; **lits jumeaux** twin beds **2** *nmf* twin ▪ **jumeler** *vt (villes)* to twin ▪ **jumelles** *nfpl (pour regarder)* binoculars

**jument** [ʒymɑ̃] *nf* mare

**jungle** [ʒœ̃gl] *nf* jungle

**junior** [ʒynjɔr] *nm & adj inv Sport* junior

**jupe** [ʒyp] *nf* skirt

**jurer** [ʒyre] **1** *vt (promettre)* to swear (**que** that; **de faire** to do) **2** *vi (dire un gros mot)* to swear (**contre** at); *(contraster)* to clash (**avec** with); **j. de qch** to swear to sth ▪ **juré, -e 1** *adj* **ennemi j.** sworn enemy **2** *nm Jur* juror

**juriste** [ʒyrist] *nmf* legal expert

**juron** [ʒyrɔ̃] *nm* swearword

**jury** [ʒyri] *nm Jur* jury; *(d'examen)* board of examiners

**jus** [ʒy] *nm (de fruits)* juice; *(de viande)* gravy; **j. d'orange** orange juice

**jusque** [ʒysk] **1** *prép* **jusqu'à** *(espace)* as far as, (right) up to; *(temps)* until, (up) till, to; *(même)* even; **jusqu'en mai** until May; **jusqu'où?** how far?; **jusqu'ici** as far as this; *(temps)* up till now; **j. chez moi** as far as my place **2** *conj* **jusqu'à ce qu'il vienne** until he comes

**juste** [ʒyst] **1** *adj (équitable)* fair, just; *(exact)* right, correct; *(étroit)* tight; *(raisonnement)* sound; **un peu j.** *(quantité, qualité)* barely enough **2** *adv (deviner, compter)* correctly, right; *(chanter)* in tune; *(précisément, à peine)* just; **à trois heures j.** on the stroke of three; **un peu j.** *(mesurer, compter)* a bit on the short side ▪ **justement** [-əmɑ̃] *adv (précisément)* exactly; *(avec justesse, avec justice)* justly; **j. j'allais t'appeler** I was just going to ring you

**justesse** [ʒystɛs] *nf (exactitude)* accuracy; **de j.** *(éviter, gagner)* just

**justice** [ʒystis] *nf (équité)* justice; **la j.** *(autorité)* the law; **rendre j. à qn** to do justice to sb

**justifier** [ʒystifje] **1** *vt* to justify **2 se justifier** *vpr* to justify oneself (**de** of) ▪ **justification** *nf (explication)* justification; *(preuve)* proof

**juteux, -euse** [ʒytø, -øz] *adj* juicy

# Kk

**K, k** [kɑ] *nm inv* K, k
**kangourou** [kɑ̃guru] *nm* kangaroo
**karaté** [karate] *nm* karate
**karting** [kartiŋ] *nm* karting
**kasher** [kaʃɛr] *adj inv Rel* kosher
**kayak** [kajak] *nm (bateau de sport)* canoe
**Kenya** [kenja] *nm* **le K.** Kenya
**kermesse** [kɛrmɛs] *nf* charity fair *or Br* fête; *(en Belgique)* village fair
**kérosène** [kerozɛn] *nm* kerosene
**kidnapper** [kidnape] *vt* to kidnap ▪ **kidnappeur, -euse** *nmf* kidnapper
**kilo** [kilo] *nm* kilo ▪ **kilogramme** *nm* kilogram(me)
**kilomètre** [kilɔmɛtr] *nm* kilometre ▪ **kilométrage** *nm Aut* ≃ mileage ▪ **kilométrique** *adj* **borne k.** ≃ milestone
**kilo-octet** [kilɔɔktɛ] (*pl* **kilo-octets**) *nm Ordinat* kilobyte
**kilowatt** [kilɔwat] *nm* kilowatt
**kinésithérapeute** [kineziterapøt] *nmf* physiotherapist
**kiosque** [kjɔsk] *nm (à fleurs)* kiosk, *Br* stall; **k. à journaux** news-stand
**kit** [kit] *nm* (self-assembly) kit; **en k.** in kit form
**kiwi** [kiwi] *nm (oiseau, fruit)* kiwi
**Klaxon**® [klaksɔn] *nm* horn ▪ **klaxonner** *vi* to sound one's horn
**km** (*abrév* **kilomètre**) km
**km/h** (*abrév* **kilomètre-heure**) kph, ≃ mph
**Koweït** [kɔwɛjt] *nm* **le K.** Kuwait ▪ **koweïtien, -enne 1** *adj* Kuwaiti **2** *nmf* **K., Koweïtienne** Kuwaiti

# Ll

**L, l** [ɛl] *nm inv* L, l
**l', la**[1] [l, la] *voir* **le**
**la**[2] [la] *nm inv (note)* A
**là** [la] **1** *adv (là-bas)* there; *(ici)* here; **c'est là que…** *(lieu)* that's where…; **à 5 mètres de là** 5 metres away **2** *exclam* **oh là là!** oh dear! **3** *voir* **ce**[1], **celui**
**là-bas** [labɑ] *adv* over there
**laboratoire** [labɔratwar] *nm* laboratory
**labourer** [labure] *vt (terre) Br* to plough, *Am* to plow
**lac** [lak] *nm* lake
**lacet** [lasɛ] *nm (de chaussure)* lace; **faire ses lacets** to tie one's laces
**lâche** [lɑʃ] **1** *adj (nœud)* loose, slack; *Péj (personne, acte)* cowardly **2** *nmf* coward ▪ **lâcheté** *nf* cowardice; **une l.** *(action)* a cowardly act
**lâcher** [lɑʃe] **1** *vt (ne plus tenir)* to let go of; *(bombe)* to drop; *(poursuivant)* to shake off; *(dans une course)* to leave behind; **l. prise** to let go **2** *vi (corde)* to break
**là-dedans** [ladədɑ̃] *adv (lieu)* in there, inside
**là-dessous** [ladəsu] *adv* underneath
**là-dessus** [ladəsy] *adv* on there; *(monter)* on top
**là-haut** [lao] *adv* up there; *(à l'étage)* upstairs
**laid, -e** [lɛ, lɛd] *adj (physiquement)* ugly ▪ **laideur** *nf* ugliness
**laine** [lɛn] *nf* wool; **de l., en l.** *Br* woollen, *Am* woolen ▪ **lainage** *nm (vêtement)* jumper
**laisse** [lɛs] *nf* lead, leash
**laisser** [lese] **1** *vt* to leave; **l. qn partir** *(permettre)* to let sb go; **l. qch à qn** *(confier, donner)* to leave sth with sb **2 se laisser** *vpr* **se l. aller** to let oneself go; **se l. faire** to be pushed around
**lait** [lɛ] *nm* milk; **l. entier/demi-écrémé/écrémé** whole/semi-skimmed/skimmed milk ▪ **laitier** *adj m* **produit l.** dairy product
**laitue** [lety] *nf* lettuce
**lame** [lam] *nf (de couteau, de rasoir)* blade; *(vague)* wave
**lamelle** [lamɛl] *nf* thin strip
**lamenter** [lamɑ̃te] **se lamenter** *vpr* to moan ▪ **lamentable** *adj (mauvais)* terrible, deplorable; *(voix, cri)* mournful; *(personne)* pathetic
**lampadaire** [lɑ̃padɛr] *nm Br* standard lamp, *Am* floor lamp; *(de rue)* street lamp
**lampe** [lɑ̃p] *nf* lamp; **l. de poche** *Br* torch, *Am* flashlight
**lance** [lɑ̃s] *nf* spear
**lancer** [lɑ̃se] **1** *vt (jeter)* to throw (**à** to); *(fusée, produit)* to launch; *(appel)* to issue
**2 se lancer** *vpr (se précipiter)* to rush; **se l. dans** *(aventure)* to launch into
**3** *nm Sport* **l. du javelot** throwing the javelin; **l. franc** *(au basket)* free throw ▪ **lancement** *nm (de fusée, de produit)* launch(ing)
**landau, -s** [lɑ̃do] *nm Br* pram, *Am* baby carriage
**langage** [lɑ̃gaʒ] *nm* language; *Ordinat* **l. machine/naturel** computer/natural language
**langer** [lɑ̃ʒe] *vt (bébé)* to change

**langouste** [lãgust] *nf* crayfish ▪ **langoustine** *nf* langoustine

**langue** [lãg] *nf Anat* tongue; *Ling* language; **de l. anglaise/française** English-/French-speaking; **l. maternelle** mother tongue; **langues vivantes** modern languages ▪ **languette** *nf (patte)* tongue

**lanière** [lanjɛr] *nf* strap; *(d'étoffe)* strip

**lapin** [lapɛ̃] *nm* rabbit

**laque** [lak] *nf (pour cheveux)* hair spray

**laquelle** [lakɛl] *voir* **lequel**

**lard** [lar] *nm (viande)* bacon ▪ **lardon** *nm Culin* strip of bacon

**large** [larʒ] **1** *adj (route, porte, chaussure)* wide; *(considérable)* **l. de 6 mètres** 6 metres wide

**2** *nm* **avoir 6 mètres de l.** to be 6 metres wide; **au l. de Cherbourg** off Cherbourg ▪ **largement** [-əmɑ̃] *adv (répandu, critiqué)* widely; *(payer, servir)* generously; *(dépasser)* by a long way; **avoir l. le temps** to have plenty of time ▪ **largeur** *nf (dimension)* width, breadth; **en l., dans la l.** widthwise

**larguer** [large] *vt (bombe)* to drop; *Naut* **l. les amarres** to cast off

**larme** [larm] *nf* tear; **en larmes** in tears; **rire aux larmes** to laugh till one cries

**las, lasse** [lɑ, lɑs] *adj* weary (**de** of) ▪ **lassant, -e** *adj* tiresome ▪ **lasser 1** *vt* to tire **2 se lasser** *vpr* **se l. de qch/de faire qch** to get tired of sth/of doing sth

**laser** [lazɛr] *nm* laser

**latéral, -e, -aux, -ales** [lateral, -o] *adj* side

**latin, -e** [latɛ̃, -in] **1** *adj* Latin **2** *nmf* **L., Latine** Latin **3** *nm (langue)* Latin

**lavabo** [lavabo] *nm* washbasin; **lavabos** *(toilettes) Br* toilet(s), *Am* washroom

**lavande** [lavɑ̃d] *nf* lavender

**lave** [lav] *nf* lava

**laver** [lave] **1** *vt* to wash; **l. qch à l'eau froide** to wash sth in cold water **2 se laver** *vpr* to wash (oneself), *Am* to wash up; **se l. les mains** to wash one's hands ▪ **lavable** *adj* washable ▪ **lavage** *nm* washing ▪ **lave-auto** *(pl* **lave-autos**) *nm Can* carwash ▪ **lave-linge** *nm inv* washing machine ▪ **laverie** *nf (automatique) Br* launderette, *Am* Laundromat® ▪ **laveur** *nm* **l. de vitres** window *Br* cleaner *or Am* washer ▪ **lave-vaisselle** *nm inv* dishwasher

**LE, LA, LES** [lə, la, le]

**l'** is used instead of **le** or **la** before a word beginning with a vowel or h mute.

**1** *article défini* (**a**) *(pour définir le nom)* the; **le garçon** the boy; **la fille** the girl; **les petits** the little ones

(**b**) *(avec les notions)* **la vie** life; **la France** France; **les Français** the French; **les hommes** men; **aimer le café** to like coffee

(**c**) *(avec les parties du corps)* **il ouvrit la bouche** he opened his mouth; **se blesser au pied** to hurt one's foot; **avoir les cheveux blonds** to have blond hair

(**d**) *(distributif)* **10 euros le kilo** 10 euros a kilo

(**e**) *(dans les compléments de temps)* **elle vient le lundi** she comes on Mondays; **l'an prochain** next year

**2** *pron (homme)* him; *(femme)* her; *(chose, animal)* it; **les** them; **je la vois** I see her/it; **je le vois** I see him/it; **je les vois** I see them

**lécher** [leʃe] *vt* to lick

**leçon** [ləsɔ̃] *nf* lesson

**lecteur, -trice** [lɛktœr, -tris] *nmf* reader; *Univ* foreign language assistant; **l. de cassettes/de CD** cassette/CD player; *Ordinat* **l. de disques** *ou* **de disquettes** disk drive ▪ **lecture** *nf* reading

**légal, -e, -aux, -ales** [legal, -o] *adj* legal ▪ **légaliser** *vt* to legalize ▪ **légalité** *nf* legality (**de** of)

**légende** [leʒɑ̃d] *nf (histoire)* legend; *(de carte)* key; *(de photo)* caption

**léger, -ère** [leʒe, -ɛr] **1** *adj* light; *(blessure, odeur)* slight; *(café, thé)* weak; *(bière, tabac)* mild; *(frivole)* frivolous; *(irréfléchi)* thoughtless

**2** *adv* **manger l.** to have a light meal

**3** *nf* **prendre qch à la légère** to make light of sth ▪ **légèrement** *adv (inconsidérément)* lightly; *(un peu)* slightly ▪ **légèreté** *nf (poids)* lightness; *(de blessure)* slightness; *(d'attitude)* thoughtlessness

**légion** [leʒjɔ̃] *nf Mil* legion ▪ **légionnaire** *nm (de la Légion étrangère)* legionnaire

**législatif, -ive** [leʒislatif, -iv] *adj* legislative; *(élections)* parliamentary

**légitime** [leʒitim] *adj (action, enfant)* legitimate; *(héritier)* rightful; *(colère)* justified; **être en état de l. défense** to be acting in *Br* self-defence *or Am* self-defense

**léguer** [lege] *vt* to bequeath (**à** to)

**légume** [legym] *nm* vegetable

**lendemain** [lɑ̃dmɛ̃] *nm* **le l.** the next day; **le l. de** the day after; **le l. matin** the next morning

**lent, -e** [lɑ̃, lɑ̃t] *adj* slow

**lentille** [lɑ̃tij] *nf (plante, graine)* lentil; *(verre)* lens; **lentilles de contact** contact lenses

**lequel, laquelle** [ləkɛl, lakɛl] (*mpl* **lesquels,** *fpl* **lesquelles** [lekɛl])

> **lequel** and **lesquel(le)s** contract with **à** to form **auquel** and **auxquel(le)s**, and with **de** to form **duquel** and **desquel(le)s**.

**1** *pron relatif (chose, animal)* which; *(personne)* who; *(indirect)* whom; **dans l.** in which; **parmi lesquels** *(choses, animaux)* among which; *(personnes)* among whom

**2** *pron interrogatif* which (one); **l. préférez-vous?** which (one) do you prefer?

**les** [le] *voir* **le**

**lessive** [lɛsiv] *nf (produit)* washing powder; *(liquide)* liquid detergent; *(linge)* washing; **faire la l.** to do the washing

**lettre** [lɛtr] *nf (missive, caractère)* letter; **les lettres** *(discipline)* arts, humanities

**leur** [lœr] **1** *adj possessif* their; **l. chat** their cat; **leurs voitures** their cars **2** *pron possessif* **le l., la l., les leurs** theirs **3** *pron personnel (indirect)* to them; **donne-l. ta carte** give them your card

**lever** [ləve] **1** *vt (objet)* to lift, to raise; *(blocus, immunité)* to lift; *(séance)* to close; *(impôts)* to levy

**2** *vi (pâte)* to rise

**3 se lever** *vpr* to get up; *(soleil)* to rise; *(jour)* to break; *(brouillard)* to clear, to lift

**4** *nm* **le l. du soleil** sunrise; *Théât* **l. de rideau** curtain up ▪ **levé, -e** *adj* **être l.** *(debout)* to be up ▪ **levée** *nf (d'interdiction)* lifting; *(du courrier)* collection

**levier** [ləvje] *nm* lever; *Aut* **l. de vitesse** *Br* gear lever, *Am* gearshift

**lèvre** [lɛvr] *nf* lip

**lévrier** [levrije] *nm* greyhound

**levure** [ləvyr] *nf* yeast

**lézard** [lezar] *nm* lizard ▪ **lézarder se lézarder** *vpr* to crack

**liaison** [ljɛzɔ̃] *nf (rapport)* connection; *(entre mots) & Mil* liaison; **l. aérienne/ferroviaire** air/rail link; **l. amoureuse** love affair

**Liban** [libɑ̃] *nm* **le L.** (the) Lebanon ▪ **libanais, -e 1** *adj* Lebanese **2** *nmf* **L., Libanaise** Lebanese

**libeller** [libele] *vt (chèque)* to make out

**libéral, -e, -aux, -ales** [liberal, -o] *adj & nmf* liberal

**libérer** [libere] **1** *vt (prisonnier)* to free, to release; *(pays)* to liberate (**de** from); *(chambre)* to vacate **2 se libérer** *vpr* to free oneself (**de** from); **je n'ai pas pu me l.** I couldn't get away ▪ **libération** *nf (de prisonnier)* release; *(de pays)* liberation

**liberté** [libɛrte] *nf* freedom, liberty; **mettre qn en l.** to set sb free

**libraire** [librɛr] *nmf* bookseller ▪ **librairie** *nf (magasin)* bookshop

**libre** [libr] *adj (personne, siège)* free (**de qch** from sth; **de faire** to do);

*(voie)* clear; **radio l.** independent radio ▪ **libre-échange** *nm Écon* free trade ▪ **libre-service** *(pl* **libres-services***) nm (système, magasin)* self-service

**Libye** [libi] *nf* **la L.** Libya ▪ **libyen, -enne 1** *adj* Libyan **2** *nmf* **L., Libyenne** Libyan

**licence** [lisɑ̃s] *nf Sport* permit; *Com Br* licence, *Am* license; *Univ* (bachelor's) degree; **l. ès lettres/sciences** arts/ science degree

**licencier** [lisɑ̃sje] *vt (employé)* to lay off, *Br* to make redundant ▪ **licenciement** *nm* lay-off, *Br* redundancy

**lien** [ljɛ̃] *nm (rapport)* link, connection; *(attache)* bond; **l. de parenté** family relationship; *Ordinat* **l. hypertexte** hypertext link

**lier** [lje] **1** *vt (attacher)* to tie up; *(contrat)* to be binding on; *(personnes)* to bind together; *(paragraphes)* to connect, to link; **l. qn** *(unir, engager)* to bind sb; **être très lié avec qn** to be great friends with sb **2 se lier** *vpr* **se l. d'amitié** to become friends

**lierre** [ljɛr] *nm* ivy

**lieu[1], -x** [ljø] *nm* place; **les lieux** *(locaux)* the premises; **être sur les lieux** to be on the spot; **avoir l.** to take place; **au l. de qch** instead of sth; **au l. de faire qch** instead of doing sth; **en dernier l.** lastly; **l. de naissance** place of birth; **l. public** public place

**lieu[2], -s** [ljø] *nm (poisson)* **l. noir** coalfish

**lieutenant** [ljøtnɑ̃] *nm* lieutenant

**lièvre** [ljɛvr] *nm* hare

**ligne** [liɲ] *nf (trait)* line; *(silhouette)* figure; *(rangée)* row, line; **les grandes lignes** *(de train)* the main lines; *Fig (idées principales)* the broad outline; **aller à la l.** to begin a new paragraph; *Fig* **sur toute la l.** completely; **l. d'autobus** bus service; *(parcours)* bus route; **l. de chemin de fer** *Br* railway *or Am* railroad line; *Sport* **l. de touche** touchline

**ligoter** [ligɔte] *vt* to tie up (**à** to)

**liguer** [lige] **se liguer** *vpr (États)* to form a league (**contre** against); *(personnes)* to gang up (**contre** against)

**lilas** [lilɑ] *nm & adj inv* lilac

**limace** [limas] *nf* slug

**limande** [limɑ̃d] *nf* dab

**lime** [lim] *nf (outil)* file; **l. à ongles** nail file

**limitation** [limitɑsjɔ̃] *nf* limitation; **l. de vitesse** speed limit

**limite** [limit] **1** *nf* limit (**à** to); *(de propriété)* boundary; **sans l.** unlimited, limitless; **dans la l. des stocks disponibles** while stocks last **2** *adj (vitesse, âge)* maximum

**limiter** [limite] **1** *vt (restreindre)* to limit, to restrict (**à** to); *(territoire)* to bound **2 se limiter** *vpr* **se l. à qch/à faire qch** to limit *or* restrict oneself to sth/to doing sth

**limoger** [limɔʒe] *vt* to dismiss

**limonade** [limɔnad] *nf (boisson)* lemonade

**limpide** [lɛ̃pid] *adj (eau, explication)* clear, crystal-clear

**lin** [lɛ̃] *nm (tissu)* linen

**linge** [lɛ̃ʒ] *nm (vêtements)* linen; *(à laver)* washing; **l. de corps** underwear ▪ **lingerie** *nf (de femmes)* underwear

**lingot** [lɛ̃go] *nm* **l. d'or** gold bar

**lion** [ljɔ̃] *nm* lion; **le L.** *(signe)* Leo

**liqueur** [likœr] *nf* liqueur

**liquide** [likid] **1** *adj* liquid **2** *nm* liquid; *(argent)* cash; **payer en l.** to pay cash

**liquider** [likide] *vt (stock)* to clear ▪ **liquidation** *nf (de stock)* clearing; *Com* **l. totale** stock clearance

**lire[1]*** [lir] **1** *vt* to read; **l. qch à qn** to read sth to sb **2** *vi* to read

**lire[2]** [lir] *nf (monnaie)* lira

**lis, lisant, lise(nt)** *etc* [li, lizɑ̃, liz] *voir* **lire[1]**

**lisible** [lizibl] *adj (écriture)* legible

**lisière** [lizjɛr] *nf* edge

**lisse** [lis] *adj* smooth

**liste** [list] *nf* list; **l. d'attente** waiting list; **l. électorale** electoral roll

**lit[1]** [li] *nm* bed; **se mettre au l.** to go to bed; **faire son l.** to make one's bed; **l. de camp** *Br* camp bed, *Am* cot; **l. d'enfant**

*Br* cot, *Am* crib; **lits superposés** bunk beds

**lit²** [li] *voir* **lire¹**

**litière** [litjɛr] *nf (d'animal)* litter

**litige** [litiʒ] *nm (conflit)* dispute

**litre** [litr] *nm Br* litre, *Am* liter

**littéraire** [literɛr] *adj* literary ▪ **littérature** *nf* literature

**littoral, -e, -aux, -ales** [litɔral, -o] **1** *adj* coastal **2** *nm* coast(line)

**livraison** [livrɛzɔ̃] *nf* delivery

**livre** [livr] **1** *nm* book; *Naut* **l. de bord** logbook; **l. de poche** paperback (book) **2** *nf (monnaie, poids)* pound

**livrer** [livre] **1** *vt (marchandises)* to deliver (**à** to); **l. qn à la police** to hand sb over to the police **2 se livrer** *vpr (se rendre)* to give oneself up (**à** to) ▪ **livreur, -euse** *nmf* delivery man, *f* delivery woman

**livret** [livrɛ] *nm (livre)* booklet; **l. d'épargne** bankbook, *Br* passbook; **l. scolaire** school report book

**local, -e, -aux, -ales** [lɔkal, -o] **1** *adj* local **2** *nm (pièce)* room; **locaux** *(bâtiment)* premises

**localité** [lɔkalite] *nf* locality

**locataire** [lɔkatɛr] *nmf* tenant; *(chez le propriétaire)* lodger, *Am* roomer

**location** [lɔkɑsjɔ̃] *nf (de maison) (par le locataire)* renting; *(par le propriétaire)* renting out, *Br* letting; *(de voiture)* renting, *Br* hiring; *(logement)* rented *Br* accommodation *or Am* accommodations; *(loyer)* rent; *(pour spectacle)* booking; **bureau de l.** booking office; **en l.** on hire; **voiture de l.** rented *or Br* hired car

**locomotion** [lɔkɔmosjɔ̃] *nf* **moyen de l.** means of transport

**locomotive** [lɔkɔmotiv] *nf (de train)* engine

**loge** [lɔʒ] *nf (de concierge)* lodge; *(d'acteur)* dressing-room; *Théât (de spectateur)* box

**loger** [lɔʒe] **1** *vt (recevoir, mettre)* to accommodate; *(héberger)* to put up; **être logé et nourri** to have board and lodging

**2** *vi (temporairement)* to stay; *(en permanence)* to live

**3 se loger** *vpr* **trouver à se l.** to find somewhere to live; *(temporairement)* to find somewhere to stay ▪ **logement** *nm (habitation)* lodging, *Br* accommodation, *Am* accommodations; **le l.** housing

**logiciel** [lɔʒisjɛl] *nm Ordinat* software *inv*

**logique** [lɔʒik] **1** *adj* logical **2** *nf* logic

**loi** [lwa] *nf* law; **faire la l.** to lay down the law (**à** to)

**loin** [lwɛ̃] *adv* far (away *or* off) (**de** from); **Nice est l. de Paris** Nice is a long way away from Paris; **plus l.** further, farther; **au l.** in the distance, far away; **de l.** from a distance ▪ **lointain, -e** *adj* distant, far-off; *(rapport)* remote

**loisirs** [lwazir] *nmpl (temps libre)* spare time, leisure (time); *(distractions)* leisure *or* spare-time activities

**Londres** [lɔ̃dr] *nm ou f* London ▪ **londonien, -enne 1** *adj* London, of London **2** *nmf* **L., Londonienne** Londoner

**long, longue** [lɔ̃, lɔ̃g] **1** *adj* long; **l. de 2 mètres** 2 metres long

**2** *nm* **avoir 2 mètres de l.** to be 2 metres long; **le l. de qch** along sth; **de l. en large** *(marcher)* up and down

**3** *adv* **en savoir l. sur qch** to know a lot about sth ▪ **long-courrier** (*pl* **long-courriers**) *nm (avion)* long-haul aircraft

**longer** [lɔ̃ʒe] *vt (sujet: personne, voiture)* to go along; *(mur, côte)* to hug; *(sujet: sentier, canal)* to run alongside

**longtemps** [lɔ̃tɑ̃] *adv* (for) a long time; **trop l.** too long; **aussi l. que** as long as

**longue** [lɔ̃g] *voir* **long** ▪ **longuement** *adv (expliquer)* at length; *(réfléchir)* for a long time ▪ **longueur** *nf* length; *Radio* **l. d'onde** wavelength ▪ **longue-vue** (*pl* **longues-vues**) *nf* telescope

**lopin** [lɔpɛ̃] *nm* **l. de terre** plot *or* patch of land

**loquet** [lɔkɛ] *nm* latch

**lorgner** [lɔrɲe] *vt (regarder)* to eye; *(convoiter)* to have one's eye on

**lors** [lɔr] *adv* **l. de** at the time of; **dès l.** from then on; **dès l. que** *(puisque)* since

**lorsque** [lɔrsk(ə)] *conj* when

**losange** [lɔzɑ̃ʒ] *nm (forme)* diamond

**lot** [lo] *nm (de marchandises)* batch; *(de loterie)* prize; **gros l.** jackpot

**loterie** [lɔtri] *nf* lottery

**lotion** [losjɔ̃] *nf* lotion

**lotissement** [lɔtismɑ̃] *nm (terrain)* building plot; *(habitations)* housing *Br* estate *or Am* development

**loto** [lɔto] *nm (jeu)* lotto; *(jeu national)* national lottery

**louange** [lwɑ̃ʒ] *nf* praise

**louche**[1] [luʃ] *nf (cuillère)* ladle

**louche**[2] [luʃ] *adj (suspect)* dodgy

**loucher** [luʃe] *vi* to squint

**louer**[1] [lwe] *vt (prendre en location) (maison, appartement)* to rent; *(voiture)* to rent, *Br* to hire; *(donner en location) (logement)* to rent out, *Br* to let; *(voiture)* to rent out, *Br* to hire out; *(réserver)* to book; **maison/chambre à l.** house/room to rent *or Br* to let

**louer**[2] [lwe] **1** *vt (exalter)* to praise (**de** for) **2 se louer** *vpr* **se l. de qch** to be highly satisfied with sth

**loup** [lu] *nm* wolf

**loupe** [lup] *nf* magnifying glass

**lourd, -e** [lur, lurd] **1** *adj* heavy (**de** with); *(temps)* close **2** *adv* **peser l.** *(personne, objet)* to be heavy ▪ **lourdement** [-əmɑ̃] *adv* heavily ▪ **lourdeur** *nf* heaviness; **avoir des lourdeurs d'estomac** to feel bloated

**loyal, -e, -aux, -ales** [lwajal, -o] *adj (honnête)* fair (**envers** to); *(dévoué)* loyal (**envers** to) ▪ **loyauté** *nf (honnêteté)* fairness; *(dévouement)* loyalty (**envers** to)

**loyer** [lwaje] *nm* rent

**lu** [ly] *pp de* **lire**[1]

**lubrifier** [lybrifje] *vt* to lubricate

**lucarne** [lykarn] *nf (fenêtre)* dormer window; *(de toit)* skylight

**lucide** [lysid] *adj* lucid ▪ **lucidité** *nf* lucidity

**lucratif, -ive** [lykratif, -iv] *adj* lucrative

**lueur** [lɥœr] *nf (lumière) & Fig* glimmer

**luge** [lyʒ] *nf Br* sledge, *Am* sled, toboggan

---

**LUI** [lɥi] *pron personnel* (**a**) *(objet indirect)* (to) him; *(femme)* (to) her; *(chose, animal)* (to) it; **je le l. ai montré** I showed it to him/her

(**b**) *(complément direct)* him; **elle n'aime que l.** she only loves him

(**c**) *(après une préposition)* him; **pour/avec l.** for/with him; **elle pense à l.** she thinks of him; **ce livre est à l.** this book is his

(**d**) *(dans les comparaisons)* **elle est plus grande que l.** she's taller than he is *or* than him

(**e**) *(sujet)* **l., il ne viendra pas** *(emphatique)* HE won't come; **c'est l. qui me l'a dit** he is the one who told me ▪ **lui-même** *pron* himself; *(chose, animal)* itself

---

**luire*** [lɥir] *vi* to shine ▪ **luisant, -e** *adj (métal)* shiny

**lumière** [lymjɛr] *nf* light; **à la l. de** by the light of

**lumineux, -euse** [lyminø, -øz] *adj (idée, ciel)* bright, brilliant; *(cadran)* luminous

**lunaire** [lynɛr] *adj* lunar

**lundi** [lœ̃di] *nm* Monday

**lune** [lyn] *nf* moon; **l. de miel** honeymoon

**lunette** [lynɛt] *nf (astronomique)* telescope; **lunettes** *(de vue)* glasses, spectacles; *(de protection, de plongée)* goggles; **l. arrière** *(de voiture)* rear window; **lunettes de soleil** sunglasses

**lustre** [lystr] *nm (lampe)* chandelier; *(éclat)* lustre

**lutte** [lyt] *nf* fight, struggle; *Sport* wrestling ▪ **lutter** *vi* to fight, to struggle; *Sport* to wrestle

**luxation** [lyksɑsjɔ̃] *nf Méd* dislocation

**luxe** [lyks] *nm* luxury; **modèle de l.** de luxe model ▪ **luxueux, -euse** *adj* luxurious

**Luxembourg** [lyksɑ̃bur] *nm* **le L.** Luxembourg

**lycée** [lise] *nm Br* ≃ secondary school, *Am* ≃ high school; **l. technique** *ou* **professionnel** vocational *or* technical school ▪ **lycéen, -enne** *nmf* pupil *(at a lycée)*

# Mm

**M[1], m[1]** [ɛm] *nm inv* M, m

**m'** [m] *voir* **me**

**M[2]** (*abrév* **Monsieur**) Mr

**m[2]** (*abrév* **mètre(s)**) m

**ma** [ma] *voir* **mon**

**macérer** [masere] *vti* to steep

**mâcher** [mɑʃe] *vt* to chew

**machine** [maʃin] *nf (appareil)* machine; **m. à calculer** calculator; **m. à coudre** sewing machine; **m. à écrire** typewriter; **m. à laver** washing machine; **m. à laver la vaisselle** dishwasher; **m. à** *ou* **de traitement de texte** word processor ▪ **machiniste** *nm (conducteur)* driver

**mâchoire** [mɑʃwar] *nf* jaw

**mâchonner** [mɑʃɔne] *vt* to chew

**maçon** [masɔ̃] *nm (de briques)* bricklayer; *(de pierres)* mason ▪ **maçonnerie** *nf (travaux)* building work; *(ouvrage de briques)* brickwork; *(de pierres)* masonry, stonework

**Madagascar** [madagaskar] *nf* Madagascar

**madame** [madam] (*pl* **mesdames**) *nf (en apostrophe)* madam; **bonjour mesdames** good morning(, ladies); **M. Legras** Mrs Legras; **M.** *(dans une lettre)* Dear Madam

**madeleine** *nf* (small) sponge cake

**mademoiselle** [madmwazɛl] (*pl* **mesdemoiselles**) *nf (avant nom)* Miss; **M. Legras** Miss Legras; **M.** *(dans une lettre)* Dear Madam

**magasin** [magazɛ̃] *nm Br* shop, *Am* store; *(entrepôt)* warehouse; *(d'arme) & Phot* magazine; **grand m.** department store; **en m.** in stock

**magazine** [magazin] *nm (revue)* magazine

**magie** [maʒi] *nf* magic ▪ **magicien, -enne** *nmf* magician ▪ **magique** *adj (surnaturel)* magic; *(enchanteur)* magical

**magistrat** [maʒistra] *nm* magistrate

**magnanime** [maɲanim] *adj* magnanimous

**magnat** [magna] *nm* tycoon, magnate

**magnésium** [maɲezjɔm] *nm* magnesium

**magnétique** [maɲetik] *adj* magnetic

**magnétophone** [maɲetɔfɔn] *nm* tape recorder; **m. à cassettes** cassette recorder

**magnétoscope** [maɲetɔskɔp] *nm Br* video (recorder), *Am* VCR

**magnifique** [maɲifik] *adj* magnificent

**mai** [mɛ] *nm* May

**maigre** [mɛgr] *adj (personne, corps)* thin; *(viande)* lean; *(fromage)* low-fat; *(salaire)* meagre ▪ **maigrir** *vi* to get thinner

**maillot** [majo] *nm (de sportif)* jersey, shirt; **m. de bain** *(de femme)* swimsuit; *(d'homme)* (swimming) trunks; **m. jaune** *(du Tour de France)* yellow jersey

**main** [mɛ̃] **1** *nf* hand; **à la m.** *(faire, écrire)* by hand; **tenir qch à la m.** to hold sth in one's hand; **en mains propres** in person; **donner la m. à qn** to hold sb's hand; **haut les mains!** hands up! **2** *adj* **fait m.** hand-made ▪ **main-d'œuvre** (*pl* **mains-d'œuvre**) *nf* labour

**maintenant** [mɛ̃tənɑ̃] *adv* now; *(de nos jours)* nowadays; **m. que...** now that...; **dès m.** from now on

**maintenir*** [mɛ̃tənir] **1** *vt (conserver)* to keep, to maintain; *(retenir)* to hold in position; *(affirmer)* to maintain (**que** that) **2 se maintenir** *vpr (durer)* to remain ▪ **maintien** *nm (action)* maintenance (**de** of); *(allure)* bearing

**maire** [mɛr] *nm* mayor ▪ **mairie** *nf Br* town hall, *Am* city hall; *(administration) Br* town council, *Am* city hall

**mais** [mɛ] *conj* but; **m. oui, m. si** of course; **m. non** definitely not

**maïs** [mais] *nm Br* maize, *Am* corn

**maison** [mɛzɔ̃] **1** *nf (bâtiment, famille)* house; *(foyer)* home; *(entreprise)* company; **à la m.** at home; **rentrer à la m.** to go/come (back) home; **m. de la culture** arts centre; **m. d'édition** publishing house; **m. de retraite** old people's home; **m. de santé** nursing home **2** *adj inv (artisanal)* home-made

**maître** [mɛtr] *nm* master; **être m. de la situation** to be in control of the situation; **m. d'hôtel** *(de restaurant)* head waiter; **m. de maison** host; **m. chanteur** blackmailer; **m. nageur (sauveteur)** swimming instructor (and lifeguard)

**maîtresse** [mɛtrɛs] **1** *nf* mistress; **être m. de la situation** to be in control of the situation; **m. d'école** teacher; **m. de maison** hostess **2** *adj f (idée, poutre)* main; *(carte)* master

**maîtrise** [mɛtriz] *nf (contrôle, connaissance)* mastery (**de** of); *(diplôme)* ≃ master's degree (**de** in); **m. de soi** self-control ▪ **maîtriser 1** *vt (incendie, passion)* to control; *(peur)* to overcome; *(sujet)* to master; *(véhicule)* to have under control; **m. qn** to overpower sb **2 se maîtriser** *vpr* to control oneself

**majesté** [maʒɛste] *nf* majesty; **Votre M.** *(titre)* Your Majesty

**majeur, -e** [maʒœr] **1** *adj (important)* & *Mus* major; *Jur* **être m.** to be of age; **la majeure partie de** most of **2** *nm (doigt)* middle finger

**majorer** [maʒɔre] *vt* to increase

**majorette** [maʒɔrɛt] *nf* (drum) majorette

**majoritaire** [maʒɔritɛr] *adj* majority; **être m.** to be in the majority

**majorité** [maʒɔrite] *nf* majority (**de** of); *(gouvernement)* government, party in office; **en m.** *(pour la plupart)* in the main

**Majorque** [maʒɔrk] *nf* Majorca

**majuscule** [maʒyskyl] **1** *adj* capital **2** *nf* capital letter

---

**MAL, MAUX** [mal, mo] **1** *nm (douleur)* pain; *(préjudice)* harm; *(maladie)* illness; *(malheur)* misfortune; *Phil* **le m.** evil; **avoir m. à la tête/à la gorge** to have a headache/sore throat; **ça me fait m., j'ai m.** it hurts (me); **avoir le m. de mer** to be seasick; **faire du m. à qn** to harm sb; **avoir du m. à faire qch** to have trouble doing sth; **avoir le m. du pays** to be homesick; **m. de gorge** sore throat; **m. de tête** headache

**2** *adv (avec médiocrité)* badly; *(incorrectement)* wrongly; **aller m.** *(personne)* to be ill; **m. comprendre** to misunderstand; **se trouver m.** to faint; *Fam* **pas m.** *(beaucoup)* quite a lot (**de** of)

---

**malade** [malad] **1** *adj* ill, sick; *(arbre, dent)* diseased; **être m. du cœur** to have a bad heart **2** *nmf* sick person; *(de médecin)* patient; **les malades** the sick ▪ **maladie** *nf* illness, disease

**maladroit, -e** [maladrwa, -at] *adj (malhabile)* clumsy, awkward; *(indélicat)* tactless ▪ **maladresse** *nf (manque d'habileté)* clumsiness, awkwardness; *(indélicatesse)* tactlessness; *(bévue)* blunder

**malaise** [malɛz] *nm (angoisse)* uneasiness, malaise; *(indisposition)* feeling of sickness; *(étourdissement)* dizzy spell; **avoir un m.** to feel faint

**Malaisie** [malɛzi] *nf* **la M.** Malaysia

**malchance** [malʃɑ̃s] *nf* bad luck; **jouer de m.** to have no luck at all ▪ **malchanceux, -euse** *adj* unlucky

**mâle** [mal] **1** *adj (du sexe masculin)* male; *(viril)* manly **2** *nm* male

**malédiction** [malediksjɔ̃] *nf* curse
**maléfique** [malefik] *adj* evil
**malencontreux, -euse** [malɑ̃kɔ̃trø, -øz] *adj* unfortunate
**malentendant, -e** [malɑ̃tɑ̃dɑ̃, -ɑ̃t] *nmf* person who is hard of hearing
**malentendu** [malɑ̃tɑ̃dy] *nm* misunderstanding
**malfaçon** [malfasɔ̃] *nf* defect
**malfaisant, -e** [malfəzɑ̃, -ɑ̃t] *adj* harmful
**malfaiteur** [malfɛtœr] *nm* criminal
**malgré** [malgre] *prép* in spite of; **m. tout** for all that, after all
**malhabile** [malabil] *adj* clumsy
**malheur** [malœr] *nm (drame)* misfortune; *(malchance)* bad luck; **par m.** unfortunately; **porter m. à qn** to bring sb bad luck ■ **malheureusement** *adv* unfortunately ■ **malheureux, -euse 1** *adj (triste)* unhappy, miserable; *(malchanceux)* unlucky **2** *nmf (infortuné)* poor wretch; *(indigent)* needy person
**malhonnête** [malɔnɛt] *adj* dishonest ■ **malhonnêteté** *nf* dishonesty
**malice** [malis] *nf* mischievousness ■ **malicieux, -euse** *adj* mischievous
**malin, -igne** [malɛ̃, -iɲ] *adj (astucieux)* clever, smart; *Méd (tumeur)* malignant
**malintentionné, -e** [malɛ̃tɑ̃sjɔne] *adj* ill-intentioned (**à l'égard de** towards)
**malle** [mal] *nf (coffre)* trunk; *(de véhicule) Br* boot, *Am* trunk
**mallette** [malɛt] *nf* briefcase
**malmener** [malməne] *vt* to manhandle, to treat badly
**malnutrition** [malnytrisjɔ̃] *nf* malnutrition
**malpoli, -e** [malpɔli] *adj Fam* rude
**malsain, -e** [malsɛ̃, -ɛn] *adj* unhealthy
**Malte** [malt] *nf* Malta ■ **maltais, -e 1** *adj* Maltese **2** *nmf* **M., Maltaise** Maltese
**maltraiter** [maltrɛte] *vt* to ill-treat
**malveillant, -e** [malvɛjɑ̃, -ɑ̃t] *adj* malevolent
**maman** [mamɑ̃] *nf Br* mum, *Am* mom
**mamie** [mami] *nf* grandma, granny
**mammifère** [mamifɛr] *nm* mammal
**Manche** [mɑ̃ʃ] *nf* **la M.** the Channel
**manche**[1] [mɑ̃ʃ] *nf (de vêtement)* sleeve; *Sport & Cartes* round ■ **manchette** *nf (de chemise)* cuff; *(de journal)* headline
**manche**[2] [mɑ̃ʃ] *nm (d'outil)* handle; **m. à balai** broomstick; *(d'avion, d'ordinateur)* joystick
**manchot, -e** [mɑ̃ʃo, -ɔt] **1** *adj* one-armed **2** *nmf* one-armed person
**mandarine** [mɑ̃darin] *nf (fruit)* mandarin (orange)
**mandat** [mɑ̃da] *nm (de député)* mandate; *(de président)* term of office; **m. postal** *Br* postal order, *Am* money order
**manège** [manɛʒ] *nm (de foire)* merry-go-round, *Br* roundabout; *Équitation* riding school
**manette** [manɛt] *nf* lever
**manger** [mɑ̃ʒe] **1** *vt* to eat; *(corroder)* to eat into **2** *vi* to eat; **donner à m. à qn** to give sb sth to eat **3** *nm (nourriture)* food ■ **mangeable** *adj (médiocre)* eatable
**mangue** [mɑ̃g] *nf* mango
**maniaque** [manjak] *adj* fussy
**manie** [mani] *nf (habitude)* odd habit; *(idée fixe)* mania (**de** for)
**manier** [manje] *vt* to handle ■ **maniable** *adj (outil)* handy; *(véhicule)* easy to handle
**manière** [manjɛr] *nf* way, manner; **la m. dont elle parle** the way (in which) she talks; **manières** *(politesse)* manners; **de toute m.** anyway, anyhow; **de cette m.** (in) this way; **à la m. de** in the style of; **d'une m. générale** generally speaking ■ **maniéré, -e** *adj* affected
**manifeste** [manifɛst] **1** *adj* manifest, obvious **2** *nm Pol* manifesto
**manifester** [manifɛste] **1** *vt (exprimer)* to show **2** *vi (protester)* to demonstrate **3 se manifester** *vpr (maladie)* to show *or* manifest itself; *(personne)* to make oneself known ■ **manifestant,**

**-e** *nmf* demonstrator ▪ **manifestation** *nf (défilé)* demonstration; *(réunion, fête)* event

**manipuler** [manipyle] *vt (appareils, produits)* to handle ▪ **manipulation** *nf (d'appareils, de produits)* handling; **manipulations génétiques** genetic engineering

**manivelle** [manivɛl] *nf* crank

**mannequin** [mankɛ̃] *nm (personne)* model; *(statue)* dummy

**manœuvre** [manœvr] **1** *nm (ouvrier)* unskilled worker **2** *nf (opération) & Mil Br* manoeuvre, *Am* maneuver ▪ **manœuvrer 1** *vt (véhicule, personne) Br* to manoeuvre, *Am* to maneuver; *(machine)* to operate **2** *vi Br* to manoeuvre, *Am* to maneuver

**manoir** [manwar] *nm* manor house

**manque** [mɑ̃k] *nm (insuffisance)* lack (**de** of); *(lacune)* gap; **par m. de qch** through lack of sth; **être en m.** *(drogué)* to have withdrawal symptoms

**manquer** [mɑ̃ke] **1** *vt (cible, train, chance)* to miss; *(échouer)* to fail

**2** *vi (faire défaut)* to be lacking; *(être absent)* to be missing; *(échouer)* to fail; **m. de** *(pain, argent)* to be short of; *(attention, cohérence)* to lack; **tu me manques** I miss you; **ne m. de rien** to have all one needs

**3** *v impersonnel* **il manque/il nous manque dix tasses** there are/we are ten cups short; **il manque quelques pages** there are a few pages missing ▪ **manquant, -e** *adj* missing ▪ **manqué, -e** *adj (occasion)* missed; *(tentative)* unsuccessful

**mansarde** [mɑ̃sard] *nf* attic

**manteau, -x** [mɑ̃to] *nm* coat

**manucure** [manykyr] *nmf (personne)* manicurist

**manuel, -elle** [manɥɛl] **1** *adj (travail)* manual **2** *nm (livre)* handbook, manual; **m. scolaire** textbook

**manufacture** [manyfaktyr] *nf* factory ▪ **manufacturé, -e** *adj (produit)* manufactured

**manuscrit** [manyskri] *nm* manuscript; *(tapé à la machine)* typescript

**maquereau, -x** [makro] *nm (poisson)* mackerel

**maquiller** [makije] **1** *vt (personne, visage)* to make up **2** **se maquiller** *vpr* to put one's make-up on ▪ **maquillage** *nm (fard)* make-up

**maraîcher, -ère** [mareʃe, -ɛr] **1** *nmf Br* market gardener, *Am* truck farmer **2** *adj* **culture maraîchère** *Br* market gardening, *Am* truck farming

**marais** [marɛ] *nm* marsh

**marathon** [maratɔ̃] *nm* marathon

**marbre** [marbr] *nm* marble ▪ **marbré, -e** *adj (surface)* marbled; **gâteau m.** marble cake

**marc** [mar] *nm* **m. de café** coffee grounds

**marchand, -e** [marʃɑ̃, -ɑ̃d] **1** *nmf Br* shopkeeper, *Am* storekeeper; *(de vins)* merchant; *(de voitures, de meubles)* dealer; **m. de journaux** *(dans la rue)* newsvendor; *(dans un magasin) Br* newsagent, *Am* newsdealer **2** *adj* **valeur marchande** market value

**marchander** [marʃɑ̃de] **1** *vt (objet, prix)* to haggle over **2** *vi* to haggle

**marchandises** [marʃɑ̃diz] *nfpl* goods, merchandise

**marche** [marʃ] *nf* (**a**) *(d'escalier)* step, stair (**b**) *(action)* walking; *(promenade)* walk; *Mus* march; **un train en m.** a moving train; **la bonne m. de** *(opération)* the smooth running of; **mettre qch en m.** to start sth (up); **faire m. arrière** *(en voiture) Br* to reverse, *Am* to back up; *Fig* to backtrack; **fermer la m.** to bring up the rear; **m. à suivre** procedure

**marché** [marʃe] **1** *nm (lieu) & Écon* market; *(contrat)* deal; **faire son** *ou* **le m.** to go shopping; **vendre qch au m. noir** to sell sth on the black market; **le m. du travail** the labour market; **le M. commun** the Common Market; **le M. unique européen** the Single European Market; **m. des changes** foreign exchange market

**2** *adj inv* **être bon m.** to be cheap;

**c'est meilleur m.** it's cheaper

**marcher** [marʃe] *vi (personne)* to walk; *(machine)* to run; *(plans)* to work; **faire m. qch** to operate sth ▪ **marcheur, -euse** *nmf* walker

**mardi** [mardi] *nm* Tuesday; **M. gras** Shrove Tuesday

**mare** [mar] *nf (étang)* pond

**marécage** [marekaʒ] *nm* marsh

**maréchal, -aux** [mareʃal, -o] *nm* **m. de France** field marshal ▪ **maréchal-ferrant** (*pl* **maréchaux-ferrants**) *nm* blacksmith

**marée** [mare] *nf* tide; *(poissons)* fresh seafood; **m. haute/basse** high/low tide; **m. noire** oil slick

**margarine** [margarin] *nf* margarine

**marge** [marʒ] *nf (de page)* margin; **en m. de** *(en dehors de)* on the fringes of; **avoir de la m.** to have some leeway; **m. de manœuvre** room for *Br* manoeuvre *or Am* maneuver ▪ **marginal, -e, -aux, -ales 1** *adj (secondaire)* marginal; *(personne)* on the fringes of society **2** *nmf* dropout

**marguerite** [margərit] *nf (fleur)* daisy

**mari** [mari] *nm* husband

**mariage** [marjaʒ] *nm (union)* marriage; *(cérémonie)* wedding; *Fig (de couleurs)* blend

**marier** [marje] **1** *vt (couleurs)* to blend; **m. qn** *(sujet: prêtre, maire)* to marry sb; *(sujet: père)* to marry sb off **2 se marier** *vpr* to get married; **se m. avec qn** to get married to sb, to marry sb ▪ **marié, -e 1** *adj* married **2** *nm* (bride)-groom; **les mariés** the bride and groom ▪ **mariée** *nf* bride

**marin, -e** [marɛ̃, -in] **1** *adj (flore)* marine; *(mille)* nautical; **air m.** sea air **2** *nm* sailor, seaman; **m. pêcheur** (deep-sea) fisherman ▪ **marine 1** *nf* **m. de guerre** navy; **m. marchande** merchant navy **2** *adj & nm inv* **bleu m.** *(couleur)* navy (blue)

**mariner** [marine] *vti Culin* to marinate

**marionnette** [marjɔnɛt] *nf* puppet; *(à fils)* marionette

**maritalement** [maritalmɑ̃] *adv* **vivre m.** to cohabit

**maritime** [maritim] *adj (droit, climat)* maritime; **port m.** seaport; **gare m.** harbour station; *Can* **les Provinces maritimes** the Maritime Provinces

**marmelade** [marməlad] *nf Br* stewed fruit, *Am* fruit compote

**marmite** [marmit] *nf* (cooking) pot

**Maroc** [marɔk] *nm* **le M.** Morocco ▪ **marocain, -e 1** *adj* Moroccan **2** *nmf* **M., Marocaine** Moroccan

**maroquinerie** [marɔkinri] *nf (magasin)* leather goods shop

**marque** [mark] *nf (trace, signe)* mark; *(de confiance)* sign; *(de produit)* brand; *(de voiture)* make; *Sport (points)* score; **de m.** *(hôte, visiteur)* distinguished; *(produit)* of quality; **m. déposée** (registered) trademark

**marquer** [marke] **1** *vt (par une marque)* to mark; *(écrire)* to note down; *(indiquer)* to show; *Sport (point, but)* to score; **m. les points** to keep (the) score **2** *vi (laisser une trace)* to leave a mark; *(date, événement)* to stand out; *Sport* to score ▪ **marquant, -e** *adj (remarquable)* outstanding; *(épisode)* significant ▪ **marqué, -e** *adj (différence, accent)* marked; *(visage)* lined ▪ **marqueur** *nm (stylo)* marker

**marquis** [marki] *nm* marquis ▪ **marquise** *nf* (**a**) *(personne)* marchioness (**b**) *(auvent)* canopy

**marraine** [marɛn] *nf* godmother

**marre** [mar] *adv Fam* **en avoir m.** to be fed up (**de** with)

**marron** [marɔ̃] **1** *nm (fruit)* chestnut; *(couleur)* (chestnut) brown **2** *adj inv (couleur)* (chestnut) brown ▪ **marronnier** *nm* (horse) chestnut tree

**mars** [mars] *nm* March

**marteau, -x** [marto] *nm* hammer; **m. piqueur** pneumatic drill ▪ **marteler** *vt* to hammer

**martial, -e, -aux, -ales** [marsjal, -o] *adj* martial; **cour martiale** court martial

**Martinique** [martinik] *nf* **la M.** Martinique ▪ **martiniquais, -e 1** *adj* Martinican **2** *nmf* **M., Martiniquaise**

Martinican

**martyriser** [martirize] *vt* to torture; *(enfant)* to batter

**masculin, -e** [maskylɛ̃, -in] **1** *adj (sexe, mode)* male; *(caractère, femme, nom)* masculine **2** *nm (en grammaire)* masculine

**masochiste** [mazɔʃist] **1** *adj* masochistic **2** *nmf* masochist

**masque** [mask] *nm* mask; **m. à gaz** gas mask ▪ **masquer** *vt (dissimuler)* to mask (**à** from); *(cacher à la vue)* to block off

**massacre** [masakr] *nm (tuerie)* massacre ▪ **massacrer** *vt* to massacre

**massage** [masaʒ] *nm* massage

**masse** [mas] *nf* (**a**) *(volume)* mass; *(gros morceau, majorité)* bulk (**de** of); **de m.** *(culture, communication)* mass; **en m.** en masse (**b**) *Él Br* earth, *Am* ground

**masser** [mase] **1** *vt (rassembler)* to assemble; *(pétrir)* to massage **2 se masser** *vpr (foule)* to form ▪ **masseur** *nm* masseur ▪ **masseuse** *nf* masseuse

**massif, -ive** [masif, -iv] **1** *adj* massive; *(or, chêne)* solid **2** *nm (d'arbres, de fleurs)* clump; *Géog* massif

**mastic** [mastik] *nm (pour vitres)* putty; *(pour bois)* filler ▪ **mastiquer** *vt (mâcher)* to chew

**mat[1], mate** [mat] *adj (papier, couleur)* matt

**mat[2]** [mat] *adj m inv & nm Échecs* (check-)mate; **faire m.** to (check)mate

**mât** [mɑ] *nm (de navire)* mast; *(poteau)* pole

**match** [matʃ] *nm Sport Br* match, *Am* game; **m. nul** draw; **faire m. nul** to draw; **m. aller** first leg; **m. retour** return leg

**matelas** [matla] *nm* mattress; **m. pneumatique** air bed

**matelot** [matlo] *nm* sailor

**mater** [mate] *vt (dominer)* to bring to heel

**matérialiser** [materjalize] *vt*, **se matérialiser** *vpr* to materialize

**matérialiste** [materjalist] **1** *adj* materialistic **2** *nmf* materialist

**matériau, -x** [materjo] *nm* material; **matériaux** *(de construction)* building material(s)

**matériel, -elle** [materjɛl] **1** *adj (confort, dégâts, besoins)* material; *(problème)* practical **2** *nm (de camping)* equipment; *Ordinat* **m. informatique** computer hardware ▪ **matériellement** *adv* materially; **m. impossible** physically impossible

**maternel, -elle** [maternɛl] **1** *adj (amour, femme)* maternal; *(langue)* native **2** *adj & nf* **(école) maternelle** *Br* nursery school, *Am* kindergarten ▪ **maternité** *nf (hôpital)* maternity hospital

**mathématiques** [matematik] *nfpl* mathematics *(sing)* ▪ **maths** *nfpl Fam Br* maths, *Am* math

**matière** [matjɛr] *nf (à l'école)* subject; *(de livre)* subject matter; *(substance)* material; *Phys* **la m.** matter; **en m. de qch** as regards sth; **m. première** raw material; **matières grasses** fat

**Matignon** [matiɲɔ̃] *nm* **(l'hôtel) M.** = the French Prime Minister's offices

**matin** [matɛ̃] *nm* morning; **le m.** *(chaque matin)* in the morning(s); **le mardi matin** every Tuesday morning; **tous les matins** every morning; **le 8 au m.** on the morning of the 8th; **à sept heures du m.** at seven in the morning; **au petit m.** very early (in the morning) ▪ **matinal, -e, -aux, -ales** *adj (heure)* early; **être m.** to be an early riser

**matinée** [matine] *nf* morning; *Théât & Cin* matinée; **dans la m.** in the course of the morning

**matraque** [matrak] *nf* bludgeon; *(de policier) Br* truncheon, *Am* nightstick ▪ **matraquage** *nm* **m. publicitaire** hype

**matrimonial, -e, -aux, -ales** [matrimɔnjal, -o] *adj* matrimonial

**maturité** [matyrite] *nf* maturity; **arriver à m.** *(fromage, vin)* to mature; *(fruit)* to ripen

**maudire*** [modir] *vt* to curse ▪ **mau-**

**dit, -e** *adj (damné)* cursed
**Maurice** [moris] *nf* **l'île M.** Mauritius
**maussade** [mosad] *adj (personne)* sullen; *(temps)* gloomy
**mauvais, -e** [move, -ɛz] **1** *adj* bad; *(santé, vue)* poor; *(méchant)* nasty; *(mal choisi)* wrong; *(mer)* rough; **plus m. que...** worse than...; **le plus m.** the worst; **être m. en anglais** to be bad at English; **être en mauvaise santé** to be in bad *or* ill *or* poor health
**2** *adv* **il fait m.** the weather's bad; **ça sent m.** it smells bad
**3** *nm* **le bon et le m.** the good and the bad
**mauve** [mov] *adj & nm (couleur)* mauve
**maux** [mo] *pl de* **mal**
**maximum** [maksimɔm] (*pl* **maxima** [-a] *ou* **maximums**) **1** *nm* maximum; **faire le m.** to do one's very best; **au m.** at the most **2** *adj* maximum
**mayonnaise** [majɔnɛz] *nf* mayonnaise
**mazout** [mazut] *nm* (fuel) oil
**me** [mə]

**m'** is used before a vowel or mute h.

*pron personnel* (**a**) *(complément direct)* me; **il me voit** he sees me (**b**) *(complément indirect)* (to) me; **elle me parle** she speaks to me; **tu me l'as dit** you told me (**c**) *(réfléchi)* myself; **je me lave** I wash myself (**d**) *(avec les pronominaux)* **je me suis trompé** I made a mistake
**mécanicien** [mekanisjɛ̃] *nm* mechanic; *(de train) Br* train driver, *Am* engineer
**mécanique** [mekanik] **1** *adj* mechanical **2** *nf (science)* mechanics *(sing)*; *(mécanisme)* mechanism ▪ **mécanisme** *nm* mechanism
**mécène** [mesɛn] *nm* patron (of the arts)
**méchant, -e** [meʃɑ̃, -ɑ̃t] *adj (personne, remarque)* nasty; *(enfant)* naughty; *(chien)* vicious; **'attention! chien m.'** 'beware of the dog' ▪ **méchanceté** *nf* nastiness; **une m.** *(parole)* a nasty remark; *(acte)* a nasty action
**mèche** [mɛʃ] *nf* (**a**) *(de cheveux)* lock (**b**) *(de bougie)* wick; *(de pétard)* fuse; *(de perceuse)* bit
**méconnaître*** [mekɔnɛtr] *vt (fait)* to fail to take into account; *(talent)* to fail to recognize ▪ **méconnaissable** *adj* unrecognizable ▪ **méconnu, -e** *adj* unrecognized
**mécontent, -e** [mekɔ̃tɑ̃, -ɑ̃t] *adj (insatisfait)* displeased (**de** with); *(contrarié)* annoyed ▪ **mécontenter** *vt (ne pas satisfaire)* to displease; *(contrarier)* to annoy
**Mecque** [mɛk] *nf* **La M.** Mecca
**médaille** [medaj] *nf (décoration, bijou) & Sport* medal; *(portant le nom)* pendant *(with name engraved on it)*; *(de chien)* name tag; *Sport* **être m. d'or/d'argent** to be a gold/silver medallist ▪ **médaillé, -e** *nmf* medal holder ▪ **médaillon** *nm (bijou)* locket; *(de viande)* medallion
**médecin** [medsɛ̃] *nm* doctor, physician; **m. généraliste** general practitioner; **m. traitant** consulting physician ▪ **médecine** *nf* medicine; **médecines douces** alternative medicine; **étudiant en m.** medical student ▪ **médical, -e, -aux, -ales** *adj* medical ▪ **médicament** *nm* medicine ▪ **médicinal, -e, -aux, -ales** *adj* medicinal
**média** [medja] *nm* medium; **les médias** the media ▪ **médiatique** *adj* **campagne m.** media campaign ▪ **médiatiser** *vt* to give media coverage to
**médiateur, -trice** [medjatœr, -tris] *nmf* mediator
**médiéval, -e, -aux, -ales** [medjeval, -o] *adj* medieval
**médiocre** [medjɔkr] *adj* mediocre ▪ **médiocrité** *nf* mediocrity
**médire*** [medir] *vi* **m. de qn** to speak ill of sb ▪ **médisance** *nf (action)* gossiping; **médisances** *(propos)* gossip
**méditer** [medite] **1** *vt (réfléchir à)* to contemplate **2** *vi* to meditate (**sur** on) ▪ **méditation** *nf* meditation

**Méditerranée** [mediterane] *nf* **la M.** the Mediterranean ▪ **méditerranéen, -enne** *adj* Mediterranean

**médium** [medjɔm] *nmf (voyant)* medium

**méduse** [medyz] *nf* jellyfish

**méfiance** [mefjɑ̃s] *nf* distrust, mistrust

**méfier** [mefje] **se méfier** *vpr* to be careful; **se m. de qn** not to trust sb; **se m. de qch** to watch out for sth; **méfie-toi!** watch out!, beware! ▪ **méfiant, -e** *adj* suspicious, distrustful

**mégaoctet** [megaɔktɛ] *nm Ordinat* megabyte

**mégarde** [megard] **par mégarde** *adv* inadvertently

**mégot** [mego] *nm* cigarette butt *or* end

**meilleur, -e** [mejœr] **1** *adj* better (**que** than); **le m. résultat/moment** the best result/moment **2** *nmf* **le m., la meilleure** the best (one) **3** *adv* **il fait m.** it's warmer

**mél** [mel] *nm (courrier)* e-mail

**mélancolie** [melɑ̃kɔli] *nf* melancholy ▪ **mélancolique** *adj* melancholy

**mélange** [melɑ̃ʒ] *nm (résultat)* mixture; *(opération)* mixing ▪ **mélanger 1** *vt (mêler)* to mix; *(brouiller)* to mix up **2 se mélanger** *vpr (s'incorporer)* to mix; *(idées)* to get mixed up

**mêler** [mele] **1** *vt* to mix (**à** with); *(odeurs, thèmes)* to combine; **m. qn à qch** *(affaire, conversation)* to involve sb in sth

**2 se mêler** *vpr* to combine (**à** with); **se m. à qch** *(foule)* to mingle with sth; *(conversation)* to join in sth; **se m. de qch** to get involved in sth; **mêle-toi de tes affaires!** mind your own business! ▪ **mêlé, -e** *adj* mixed (**de** with) ▪ **mêlée** *nf (au rugby)* scrum(mage)

**mélodie** [melɔdi] *nf* melody

**mélodramatique** [melɔdramatik] *adj* melodramatic

**melon** [məlɔ̃] *nm (fruit)* melon; **(chapeau) m.** *Br* bowler (hat), *Am* derby

**membre** [mɑ̃br] *nm (bras, jambe)* limb; *(de groupe)* member

**MÊME** [mɛm] **1** *adj (identique)* same; **en m. temps** at the same time (**que** as); **le m. jour** the same day; **le jour m.** *(exact)* the very day; **lui-m./vous-m.** himself/yourself

**2** *pron* **le/la m.** the same (one); **j'ai les mêmes** I have the same (ones); **cela revient au m.** it amounts to the same thing

**3** *adv (y compris, aussi)* even; **m. si...** even if...; **ici m.** in this very place; **tout de m.,** *Fam* **quand m.** all the same; **de m.** likewise; **de m. que...** just as...; **être à m. de faire qch** to be in a position to do sth

**mémoire** [memwar] **1** *nf* memory; **de m.** *(citer)* from memory; **à la m. de** in memory of; *Ordinat* **m. morte/vive** read-only/random access memory **2** *nm (rapport)* report; *Univ* dissertation; **Mémoires** *(chronique)* memoirs ▪ **mémorable** *adj* memorable

**mémorial, -aux** [memɔrjal, -o] *nm (monument)* memorial

**menaçant, -e** [mənasɑ̃, -ɑ̃t] *adj* threatening

**menace** [mənas] *nf* threat ▪ **menacer** *vt* to threaten (**de faire** to do)

**ménage** [menaʒ] *nm (entretien)* housekeeping; *(couple)* couple, household; **faire le m.** to do the housework

**ménager[1], -ère** [menaʒe, -ɛr] **1** *adj (équipement)* household **2** *nf* **ménagère** *(femme)* housewife

**ménager[2]** [menaʒe] **1** *vt (argent)* to use sparingly; *(forces)* to save; *(sortie)* to provide; **m. qn** to treat sb carefully; **ne pas m. sa peine** to put in a lot of effort **2 se ménager** *vpr (prendre soin de soi)* to look after oneself; *(se réserver)* to set aside

**ménagerie** [menaʒri] *nf* menagerie

**mendier** [mɑ̃dje] **1** *vt* to beg for **2** *vi* to beg ▪ **mendiant, -e** *nmf* beggar

**mener** [məne] **1** *vt (personne)* to take (**à** to); *(course, vie)* to lead; *(enquête)* to carry out; *Fig* **m. qch à bien** to carry sth through **2** *vi Sport* to lead; **m. à un lieu** to lead to a place ▪ **meneur, -euse** *nmf (de révolte)* ringleader

**méningite** [menɛ̃ʒit] *nf* meningitis

**menottes** [mənɔt] *nfpl* handcuffs

**mensonge** [mɑ̃sɔ̃ʒ] *nm (propos)* lie; *(action)* lying ▪ **mensonger, -ère** *adj (propos)* untrue; *(publicité)* misleading

**mensuel, -elle** [mɑ̃sɥɛl] **1** *adj* monthly **2** *nm (revue)* monthly ▪ **mensualité** *nf* monthly payment

**mensurations** [mɑ̃syrɑsjɔ̃] *nfpl* measurements

**mental, -e, -aux, -ales** [mɑ̃tal, -o] *adj* mental ▪ **mentalité** *nf* mentality

**menthe** [mɑ̃t] *nf* mint

**mention** [mɑ̃sjɔ̃] *nf (fait de citer)* mention; *(à un examen)* ≃ distinction; *Scol* **m. passable/assez bien/bien/très bien** ≃ C/B/A; **faire m. de qch** to mention sth; **'rayez les mentions inutiles'** 'delete as appropriate' ▪ **mentionner** *vt* to mention

**mentir*** [mɑ̃tir] *vi* to lie (**à** to) ▪ **menteur, -euse 1** *adj* lying **2** *nmf* liar

**menton** [mɑ̃tɔ̃] *nm* chin

**menu[1]** [məny] *nm (de restaurant)* set menu; *Ordinat* menu; **par le m.** in detail

**menu[2], -e** [məny] **1** *adj (petit)* tiny; *(mince)* slim **2** *adv (hacher)* small, finely

**menuisier** [mənɥizje] *nm* carpenter, joiner ▪ **menuiserie** *nf (atelier)* joiner's workshop; *(boiseries)* woodwork

**mépris** [mepri] *nm* contempt (**pour** for), scorn (**pour** for); **au m. de qch** without regard to sth ▪ **méprisable** *adj* despicable ▪ **méprisant, -e** *adj* contemptuous, scornful ▪ **mépriser** *vt* to despise

**méprise** [mepriz] *nf* mistake

**mer** [mɛr] *nf* sea; *(marée)* tide; **en (haute) m.** at sea; **par m.** by sea; **aller à la m.** to go to the seaside; **prendre la m.** to set sail

**mercatique** [mɛrkatik] *nf* marketing

**mercenaire** [mɛrsənɛr] *nm* mercenary

**mercerie** [mɛrsəri] *nf (magasin) Br* haberdasher's, *Am* notions store

**merci** [mɛrsi] **1** *exclam* thank you, thanks (**de** *ou* **pour** for); **non m.** no thank you; **m. bien** thanks very much **2** *nf* **à la m. de qn/qch** at the mercy of sb/sth; **sans m.** merciless

**mercredi** [mɛrkrədi] *nm* Wednesday

**mercure** [mɛrkyr] *nm* mercury

**mère** [mɛr] *nf* mother; *Com* **maison m.** parent company; **m. porteuse** surrogate mother

**méridional, -e, -aux, -ales** [meridjɔnal, -o] **1** *adj* southern **2** *nmf* southerner

**mérite** [merit] *nm* merit; *(honneur)* credit; **avoir du m. à faire qch** to deserve credit for doing sth ▪ **mériter** *vt (être digne de)* to deserve; *(demander)* to be worth; **m. réflexion** to be worth thinking about; **ce livre mérite d'être lu** this book is worth reading

**merle** [mɛrl] *nm* blackbird

**merlu** [mɛrly] *nm* hake

**merveille** [mɛrvɛj] *nf* wonder, marvel; **à m.** wonderfully (well)

**merveilleux, -euse** [mɛrvejø, -øz] *adj* wonderful, *Br* marvellous, *Am* marvelous

**mes** [me] *voir* **mon**

**mésaventure** [mezavɑ̃tyr] *nf* misadventure

**mesdames** [medam] *pl de* **madame**

**mesdemoiselles** [medmwazɛl] *pl de* **mademoiselle**

**mésestimer** [mezɛstime] *vt* to underestimate

**mesquin, -e** [meskɛ̃, -in] *adj* mean, petty ▪ **mesquinerie** *nf* meanness, pettiness; **une m.** an act of meanness

**mess** [mes] *nm inv Mil (salle)* mess

**message** [mesaʒ] *nm* message; **m. publicitaire** advertisement ▪ **messager, -ère** *nmf* messenger ▪ **messagerie** *nf* courier company; **m. électronique** electronic mail service; **m. vocale** voice mail

**messe** [mɛs] *nf (office, musique)* mass;

**aller à la m.** to go to mass
**messeigneurs** [mesɛɲœr] *pl de* **monseigneur**
**messieurs** [mesjø] *pl de* **monsieur**
**mesure** [məzyr] *nf (dimension)* measurement; *(moyen)* measure; *(retenue)* moderation; *Mus (temps)* time; *Mus (division)* bar; **sur m.** *(vêtement)* made to measure; **être en m. de faire qch** to be in a position to do sth; **prendre des mesures** to take measures; **à m. que...** as...; **dans la m. où...** in so far as...; **dans la m. du possible** as far as possible
**mesurer** [məzyre] **1** *vt (dimension, taille)* to measure; *(déterminer)* to assess **2** *vi* **m. 1 mètre 83** *(personne)* ≃ to be 6 feet tall; *(objet)* ≃ to measure 6 feet **3 se mesurer** *vpr Fig* **se m. à** *ou* **avec qn** to pit oneself against sb
**met** [mɛ] *voir* **mettre**
**métal, -aux** [metal, -o] *nm* metal ▪ **métallique** *adj (éclat, reflet)* metallic ▪ **métallisé, -e** *adj* **bleu m.** metallic blue
**métallurgie** [metalyrʒi] *nf (industrie)* steel industry; *(science)* metallurgy ▪ **métallurgiste** *nm* metalworker
**métamorphoser** [metamɔrfoze] *vt*, **se métamorphoser** *vpr* to transform (**en** into)
**météo** [meteo] *nf Fam (bulletin)* weather forecast
**météorologie** [meteɔrɔlɔʒi] *nf (science)* meteorology; *(service)* weather bureau ▪ **météorologique** *adj* meteorological; **bulletin m.** weather report
**méthode** [metɔd] *nf (manière, soin)* method; *(livre)* course ▪ **méthodique** *adj* methodical
**méticuleux, -euse** [metikylø, -øz] *adj* meticulous
**métier** [metje] *nm (manuel, commercial)* trade; *(intellectuel)* profession; *(savoir-faire)* experience; **homme de m.** specialist; **tailleur de son m.** tailor by trade; **être du m.** to be in the business; **m. à tisser** loom
**métrage** [metraʒ] *nm (action)* measuring; *(tissu)* length; **long m.** feature film; **court m.** short film
**mètre** [mɛtr] *nm (mesure) Br* metre, *Am* meter; **m. carré/cube** square/cubic metre ▪ **métrique** *adj (système)* metric
**métro** [metro] *nm Br* underground, *Am* subway
**métropole** [metrɔpɔl] *nf (ville)* metropolis; *(pays)* mother country ▪ **métropolitain, -e** *adj* metropolitan
**mets** [mɛ] *nm (aliment)* dish
**metteur** [metœr] *nm* **m. en scène** director

**METTRE*** [mɛtr] **1** *vt* to put; *(vêtement, lunettes)* to put on; *(chauffage, radio)* to switch on; *(réveil)* to set (**à** for); **j'ai mis une heure** it took me an hour; **m. qn en colère** to make sb angry; **m. qn à l'aise** to put sb at ease; **m. qch plus fort** to turn sth up; **m. de la musique** to put some music on; **mettons que...** *(+ subjunctive)* let's suppose that...
**2 se mettre** *vpr (se placer)* to put oneself; *(debout)* to stand; *(assis)* to sit; *(objet)* to go; **se m. en pyjama** to get into one's pyjamas; **se m. à table** to sit (down) at the table; **se m. à l'aise** to make oneself comfortable; **se m. au salon** to go into the dining room; **se m. au travail** to start work; **se m. à faire qch** to start doing sth; **le temps s'est mis au beau** the weather has turned fine

**meuble** [mœbl] *nm* piece of furniture; **meubles** furniture ▪ **meublé** *nm* furnished *Br* flat *or Am* apartment ▪ **meubler** *vt* to furnish
**meule** [møl] *nf (d'herbe)* stack; *(de moulin)* millstone; **m. de foin** haystack
**meunier, -ère** [mønje, -ɛr] *nmf* miller
**meurt** [mœr] *voir* **mourir**
**meurtre** [mœrtr] *nm* murder ▪ **meurtrier, -ère 1** *nmf* murderer **2** *adj* murderous; *(épidémie)* deadly
**meurtrir** [mœrtrir] *vt* to bruise

**meute** [møt] *nf* pack
**Mexique** [mɛksik] *nm* **le M.** Mexico ▪ **mexicain, -e 1** *adj* Mexican **2** *nmf* **M., Mexicaine** Mexican
**mi** [mi] *nm inv (note)* E
**mi-** [mi] *préf* **la mi-mars** mid March; **à mi-distance** midway; **cheveux mi-longs** shoulder-length hair
**miauler** [mjole] *vi (chat)* to miaow
**mi-chemin** [miʃmɛ̃] **à mi-chemin** *adv* halfway
**mi-clos, -e** [miklo, -oz] (*mpl* **mi-clos,** *fpl* **mi-closes**) *adj* half-closed
**micro** [mikro] *nm (microphone)* mike ▪ **microphone** *nm* microphone
**microbe** [mikrɔb] *nm* germ, microbe
**microfilm** [mikrɔfilm] *nm* microfilm
**micro-informatique** [mikroɛ̃fɔrmatik] *nf* microcomputing
**micro-ondes** [mikrɔɔ̃d] *nm inv* microwave; **four à m.** microwave oven
**micro-ordinateur** [mikroɔrdinatœr] (*pl* **micro-ordinateurs**) *nm* microcomputer
**microprocesseur** [mikroprɔsɛsœr] *nm Ordinat* microprocessor
**microscope** [mikrɔskɔp] *nm* microscope ▪ **microscopique** *adj* microscopic
**midi** [midi] *nm* (**a**) *(heure)* twelve o'clock, midday; *(heure du déjeuner)* lunchtime; **entre m. et deux heures** at lunchtime (**b**) *(sud)* south; **le M.** the South of France
**mie** [mi] *nf (de pain)* soft part
**miel** [mjɛl] *nm* honey
**mien, mienne** [mjɛ̃, mjɛn] **1** *pron possessif* **le m., la mienne** mine, *Br* my one; **les miens, les miennes** mine, *Br* my ones; **les deux miens** my two **2** *nmpl* **les miens** *(ma famille)* my family
**miette** [mjɛt] *nf (de pain)* crumb
**mieux** [mjø] **1** *adv* better (**que** than); **aller m.** to be (feeling) better; **de m. en m.** better and better; **le/la/les m.** *(de plusieurs)* the best; *(de deux)* the better; **le m. serait de…** the best thing would be to…; **le plus tôt sera le m.** the sooner the better **2** *adj inv* better; *(plus beau)* better-looking; **si tu n'as rien de m. à faire** if you've got nothing better to do **3** *nm (amélioration)* improvement; **faire de son m.** to do one's best; **faites au m.** do the best you can
**mignon, -onne** [miɲɔ̃, -ɔn] *adj (charmant)* cute
**migraine** [migrɛn] *nf* headache; *Méd* migraine
**migration** [migrɑsjɔ̃] *nf* migration
**mijoter** [miʒɔte] **1** *vt (avec soin)* to cook (lovingly); *(lentement)* to simmer **2** *vi* to simmer
**mil** [mil] *adj inv* **l'an deux m.** the year two thousand
**milieu, -x** [miljø] *nm (centre)* middle; *(cadre, groupe social)* environment; *(entre extrêmes)* middle course; *Phys* medium; **milieux littéraires** literary circles; **au m. de** in the middle of; **le juste m.** the happy medium; **le m.** *(la pègre)* the underworld
**militaire** [militɛr] **1** *adj* military **2** *nm* serviceman; *(de l'armée de terre)* soldier
**militer** [milite] *vi (personne)* to campaign (**pour** for; **contre** against)
**mille** [mil] **1** *adj inv & nm inv* thousand; **m. hommes** a *or* one thousand men; **deux m.** two thousand; **je vous le donne en m.!** you'll never guess! **2** *nm (de cible)* bull's eye; **m. (marin)** nautical mile ▪ **mille-feuille** (*pl* **mille-feuilles**) *nm Br* ≃ vanilla slice, *Am* ≃ napoleon ▪ **millième** *adj, nm & nmf* thousandth; **un m.** a thousandth ▪ **millier** *nm* thousand; **un m. (de)** a thousand or so; **par milliers** in their thousands
**millénaire** [milenɛr] *nm* millennium
**milliard** [miljar] *nm* billion ▪ **milliardaire** *adj & nmf* billionaire
**millimètre** [milimɛtr] *nm* millimetre
**million** [miljɔ̃] *nm* million; **un m. de francs** a million francs; **deux millions** two million; **par millions** in millions ▪ **millionnaire** *nmf* millionaire

**mime** [mim] **1** *nm (art)* mime **2** *nmf (artiste)* mime ▪ **mimer** *vti (exprimer)* to mime

**minable** [minabl] *adj (lieu, personne)* shabby

**mince** [mɛ̃s] *adj* thin; *(élancé)* slim; *(insuffisant)* slight ▪ **minceur** *nf* thinness; *(sveltesse)* slimness ▪ **mincir** *vi* to get slimmer

**mine** [min] *nf* (**a**) *(physionomie)* look; **avoir bonne/mauvaise m.** to look well/ill (**b**) *(gisement) & Fig* mine; **m. de charbon** coalmine (**c**) *(de crayon)* lead (**d**) *(engin explosif)* mine

**miner** [mine] *vt (terrain)* to mine; *Fig (saper)* to undermine; **m. qn** *(chagrin, maladie)* to wear sb down

**minerai** [minrɛ] *nm* ore

**minéral, -e, -aux, -ales** [mineral, -o] *adj & nm* mineral

**minéralogique** [mineralɔʒik] *adj* **plaque m.** *(de véhicule) Br* number *or Am* license plate

**mineur, -e** [minœr] **1** *nm (ouvrier)* miner; **m. de fond** underground worker **2** *adj (secondaire) & Mus* minor; *(de moins de 18 ans)* underage **3** *nmf Jur* minor ▪ **minière** *adj f* **industrie minière** mining industry

**miniature** [minjatyr] **1** *nf* miniature **2** *adj* **train m.** miniature train

**minigolf** [minigɔlf] *nm* crazy golf

**minijupe** [miniʒyp] *nf* miniskirt

**minimum** [minimɔm] (*pl* **minima** [-a] *ou* **minimums**) **1** *nm* minimum; **le m. de** *(force)* the minimum (amount of); **faire le m.** to do the bare minimum; **en un m. de temps** in as short a time as possible; **au m.** at the very least; **le m. vital** a minimum to live on; **les minima sociaux** = basic income support **2** *adj* minimum

**ministère** [ministɛr] *nm (département)* ministry; *(gouvernement)* government, cabinet; **m. des Affaires étrangères** *Br* ≃ Foreign Office, *Am* ≃ State Department; **m. de l'Intérieur** *Br* ≃ Home Office, *Am* ≃ Department of the Interior ▪ **ministériel, -elle** *adj* ministerial

**ministre** [ministr] *nm Pol & Rel* secretary, *Br* minister; **m. des Affaires étrangères** *Br* ≃ Foreign Secretary, *Am* ≃ Secretary of State; **m. de l'Intérieur** *Br* ≃ Home Secretary, *Am* ≃ Secretary of the Interior

**Minitel**® [minitɛl] *nm* = consumer information network accessible via home computer terminal

**minorité** [minɔrite] *nf* minority ▪ **minoritaire** *adj* **être m.** to be in the minority

**minuit** [minɥi] *nm* midnight, twelve o'clock

**minuscule** [minyskyl] **1** *adj (petit)* tiny, minute **2** *adj & nf* **(lettre) m.** small letter

**minute** [minyt] *nf* minute; **à la m.** *(tout de suite)* this (very) minute; **d'une m. à l'autre** any minute (now) ▪ **minuterie** *nf (d'éclairage)* time switch

**minutie** [minysi] *nf* meticulousness ▪ **minutieux, -euse** *adj* meticulous

**mirabelle** [mirabɛl] *nf* mirabelle plum

**miracle** [mirɑkl] *nm* miracle; **par m.** miraculously ▪ **miraculeux, -euse** *adj* miraculous

**mirage** [miraʒ] *nm* mirage

**mire** [mir] *nf* **point de m.** *(cible) & Fig* target

**miroir** [mirwar] *nm* mirror

**mis, mise**[1] [mi, miz] **1** *pp de* **mettre 2** *adj* **bien m.** *(vêtu)* well-dressed

**mise**[2] [miz] *nf* (**a**) *(placement)* putting; **m. au point** *(de rapport)* finalization; *Phot* focusing; *(de moteur)* tuning; *(de technique)* perfecting; *Fig (clarification)* clarification; **m. en garde** warning; **m. en scène** *Théât* production; *Cin* direction (**b**) *(argent)* stake (**c**) **être de m.** to be acceptable

**miser** [mize] *vt (argent)* to stake (**sur** on); **m. sur qn/qch** *(parier)* to bet on sb/sth; *(compter sur)* to count on sb/sth

**misère** [mizɛr] *nf* extreme poverty; **être dans la m.** to be poverty-stricken ▪ **misérable 1** *(pitoyable)* miserable; *(pauvre)* destitute; *(existence)* wretched; *(logement, quartier)* seedy, slummy **2** *nmf (indigent)* poor wretch; *(scélérat)* scoundrel

**missile** [misil] *nm* missile

**mission** [misjɔ̃] *nf (tâche, organisation)* mission; *(d'employé)* task; **partir en m.** *(cadre)* to go away on business; *(diplomate)* to go off on a mission ▪ **missionnaire** *nmf & adj* missionary

**mistral** [mistral] *nm* **le m.** the mistral

**mite** [mit] *nf* moth

**mi-temps** [mitɑ̃] **1** *nf inv Sport (pause)* half-time; *(période)* half **2** *nm inv* part-time job; **travailler à m.** to work part-time

**mitigé, -e** [mitiʒe] *adj (accueil)* lukewarm

**mitoyen, -enne** [mitwajɛ̃, -ɛn] *adj* common, shared

**mitraillette** [mitrajɛt] *nf* submachine gun

**mitrailleur** [mitajœr] *adj m* **fusil m.** machine gun

**mitrailleuse** [mitrajøz] *nf* machine gun

**mi-voix** [mivwa] **à mi-voix** *adv* in a low voice

**mixer**[1] [mikse] *vt (à la main)* to mix; *(au mixer)* to blend

**mixer**[2], **mixeur** [miksœr] *nm (pour mélanger)* (food) mixer; *(pour rendre liquide)* liquidizer

**mixte** [mikst] *adj* mixed; *(école)* co-educational, *Br* mixed

**mixture** [mikstyr] *nf* mixture

**MJC** [ɛmʒise] *(abrév* **maison des jeunes et de la culture**) *nf* = youth club and arts centre

**Mlle** *(abrév* **Mademoiselle**) Miss

**MM** *(abrév* **Messieurs**) Messrs

**mm** *(abrév* **millimètre(s)**) mm

**Mme** *(abrév* **Madame**) Mrs

**mobile** [mɔbil] **1** *adj (pièce, cible)* moving; *(panneau)* movable; *(personne)* mobile; *(feuillets)* loose **2** *nm (décoration)* mobile; *(motif)* motive (**de** for)

**mobilier** [mɔbilje] *nm* furniture

**mobiliser** [mɔbilize] *vt*, **se mobiliser** *vpr* to mobilize

**Mobylette**® [mɔbilɛt] *nf* moped

**mode**[1] [mɔd] *nf (tendance)* fashion; *(industrie)* fashion industry; **à la m.** fashionable; **à la m. de** in the manner of

**mode**[2] [mɔd] *nm (manière)* mode; **m. d'emploi** instructions; **m. de transport** mode of transport; **m. de vie** way of life

**modèle** [mɔdɛl] **1** *nm (schéma, exemple, personne)* model; *(au tricot)* pattern; **grand/petit m.** *(de vêtement)* large/small size; **m. déposé** registered design **2** *adj* **élève m.** model pupil ▪ **modeler 1** *vt* to model (**sur** on) **2 se modeler** *vpr* **se m. sur qn** to model oneself on sb

**modem** [mɔdɛm] *nm Ordinat* modem

**modérer** [mɔdere] **1** *vt (passions, désirs)* to moderate, to restrain; *(vitesse)* to reduce **2 se modérer** *vpr* to calm down ▪ **modération** *nf (retenue)* moderation; *(réduction)* reduction; **avec m.** in moderation ▪ **modéré, -e** *adj* moderate

**moderne** [mɔdɛrn] *adj* modern ▪ **moderniser** *vt*, **se moderniser** *vpr* to modernize ▪ **modernité** *nf* modernity

**modeste** [mɔdɛst] *adj* modest ▪ **modestie** *nf* modesty

**modifier** [mɔdifje] **1** *vt* to alter, to modify **2 se modifier** *vpr* to alter ▪ **modification** *nf* alteration, modification; **apporter une m. à qch** to make an alteration to sth

**modulation** [mɔdylasjɔ̃] *nf (de son, d'amplitude)* modulation; *Radio* **m. de fréquence** frequency modulation

**moelle** [mwal] *nf (d'os)* marrow; **m. épinière** spinal cord; **m. osseuse** bone marrow

**moelleux, -euse** [mwalø, -øz] *adj (lit, tissu)* soft

**mœurs** [mœr(s)] *nfpl (morale)* morals; *(habitudes)* customs; **entrer dans les m.** to become part of everyday life

**moi** [mwa] **1** *pron personnel* (**a**) *(après une préposition)* me; **pour/avec m.** for/with me; *Fam* **un ami à m.** a friend of mine

(**b**) *(complément direct)* me; **laissez-m.** leave me

(**c**) *(complément indirect)* (to) me; **montrez-le-m.** show it to me, show me it

(**d**) *(sujet)* I; **c'est m. qui vous le dis!** I'm telling you!; **il est plus grand que m.** he's taller than I am *or* than me

**2** *nm inv* self, ego ▪ **moi-même** *pron* myself

**moindre** [mwɛ̃dr] *adj (comparatif)* lesser; *(prix)* lower; *(quantité)* smaller; **le/la m.** *(superlatif)* the least; **la m. erreur** the slightest mistake; **dans les moindres détails** in the smallest detail; **c'est la m. des choses** it's the least I/we/*etc* can do

**moineau, -x** [mwano] *nm* sparrow

**MOINS** [mwɛ̃] **1** ([mwɛ̃z] *before vowel*) *adv (comparatif)* less (**que** than); **m. de** *(temps, travail)* less (**que** than); *(gens, livres)* fewer (**que** than); **le/la/les m.** *(superlatif)* the least; **le m. grand, la m. grande, les m. grand(e)s** the smallest; **au m., du m.** at least; **qch de m., qch en m.** *(qui manque)* sth missing; **dix ans de m.** ten years less; **en m.** *(personne, objet)* less; *(personnes, objets)* fewer; **les m. de vingt ans** those under twenty, the under-twenties; **à m. que...** *(+ subjunctive)* unless...

**2** *prép Math* minus; **deux heures m. cinq** five to two; **il fait m. 10 (degrés)** it's minus 10 (degrees)

**mois** [mwa] *nm* month; **au m. de juin** in (the month of) June

**moisir** [mwazir] *vi* to go *Br* mouldy *or Am* moldy ▪ **moisi, -e 1** *adj Br* mouldy, *Am* moldy **2** *nm Br* mould, *Am* mold; *(sur un mur)* mildew; **sentir le m.** to smell musty ▪ **moisissure** *nf Br* mould, *Am* mold

**moisson** [mwasɔ̃] *nf* harvest; **faire la m.** to harvest ▪ **moissonner** *vt (céréales)* to harvest; *(champ)* to reap ▪ **moissonneuse-batteuse** (*pl* **moissonneuses-batteuses**) *nf* combine harvester

**moite** [mwat] *adj* sticky

**moitié** [mwatje] *nf* half; **la m. de la pomme** half (of) the apple; **à m.** *(remplir)* halfway; **à m. plein/vide** half-full/-empty; **à m. prix** (at) half-price

**moka** [mɔka] *nm (café)* mocha; *(gâteau)* coffee cake

**mol** [mɔl] *voir* **mou**

**molaire** [mɔlɛr] *nf* molar

**molécule** [mɔlekyl] *nf* molecule

**molester** [mɔlɛste] *vt* to manhandle

**molle** [mɔl] *voir* **mou**

**mollet**[1] [mɔlɛ] *nm (de jambe)* calf

**mollet**[2] [mɔlɛ] *adj* **œuf m.** soft-boiled egg

**mollusque** [mɔlysk] *nm* mollusc

**moment** [mɔmɑ̃] *nm (instant, durée)* moment; **un petit m.** a little while; **en ce m.** at the moment; **pour le m.** for the moment, for the time being; **sur le m.** at the time; **à ce m.-là** *(à ce moment précis)* at that (very) moment, at that time; *(dans ce cas)* then; **à un m. donné** at one point; **le m. venu** *(dans le future)* when the time comes; **d'un m. à l'autre** any moment; **dans ces moments-là** at times like that; **par moments** at times; **au m. de partir** when just about to leave; **au m. où...** just as...; **jusqu'au m. où...** until...; **du m. que...** *(puisque)* seeing that... ▪ **momentané, -e** *adj (temporaire)* momentary; *(bref)* brief ▪ **momentanément** *adv (temporairement)* temporarily; *(brièvement)* briefly

**mon, ma, mes** [mɔ̃, ma, me]

**ma** becomes **mon** [mɔ̃n] before a vowel or mute h.

*adj possessif* my; **m. père** my father; **ma mère** my mother; **m. ami(e)** my friend; **mes parents** my parents

**Monaco** [mɔnako] *nm* Monaco

**monarque** [mɔnark] *nm* monarch ▪ **monarchie** *nf* monarchy

**monastère** [mɔnastɛr] *nm* monastery

**mondain, -e** [mɔ̃dɛ̃, -ɛn] *adj* **réunion mondaine** society gathering ▪ **mondanités** *nfpl (événements)* social life;

*(conversations)* social chitchat

**monde** [mɔ̃d] *nm* world; *(gens)* people; **dans le m. entier** worldwide, all over the world; **tout le m.** everybody; **il y a du m.** there are a lot of people; **venir au m.** to come into the world ■ **mondial, -e, -aux, -ales** *adj (crise, renommée)* worldwide; **guerre mondiale** world war ■ **mondialisation** *nf* globalization

**monégasque** [mɔnegask] **1** *adj* Monegasque **2** *nmf* **M.** Monegasque

**monétaire** [mɔnetɛr] *adj* monetary

**mongolien, -enne** [mɔ̃gɔljɛ̃, -ɛn] **1** *adj* **être m.** to have Down's syndrome **2** *nmf* person with Down's syndrome

**moniteur, -trice** [mɔnitœr, -tris] **1** *nmf* instructor; *(de colonie) Br* assistant, *Am* camp counselor **2** *nm Ordinat (écran)* monitor

**monnaie** [mɔnɛ] *nf (argent)* money; *(de)* currency; *(pièces)* change; **petite m.** small change; **faire de la m.** to get change; **avoir la m. de 100 euros** to have change for 100 euros; **m. électronique** plastic money; **m. unique** single currency

**monoparentale** [mɔnoparɑ̃tal] *adj f* **famille m.** one-parent family

**monoplace** [mɔnɔplas] *adj & nmf* single-seater

**monopole** [mɔnɔpɔl] *nm* monopoly; **avoir le m. de qch** to have a monopoly on sth ■ **monopoliser** *vt* to monopolize

**monoski** [mɔnoski] *nm* mono-ski; **faire du m.** to mono-ski

**monotone** [mɔnɔtɔn] *adj* monotonous ■ **monotonie** *nf* monotony

**monseigneur** [mɔ̃seɲœr] *(pl* **messeigneurs**) *nm (évêque)* His/Your Lordship; *(prince)* His/Your Highness

**monsieur** [məsjø] *(pl* **messieurs**) *nm (homme quelconque)* gentleman; **M. Legras** Mr Legras; **bonsoir, messieurs-dames!** good evening!; **M.** *(dans une lettre)* Dear Sir

**monstre** [mɔ̃str] *nm* monster; **m. sacré** giant ■ **monstrueux, -euse** *adj (mal formé, scandaleux)* monstrous; *(énorme)* huge

**mont** [mɔ̃] *nm* mount

**montage** [mɔ̃taʒ] *nm Tech* assembling; *Cin* editing; *(image truquée)* montage

**montagne** [mɔ̃taɲ] *nf* mountain; **la m.** *(zone)* the mountains; **à la m.** in the mountains; **en haute m.** high in the mountains; **montagnes russes** *(attraction foraine)* rollercoaster ■ **montagnard, -e** *nmf* mountain dweller ■ **montagneux, -euse** *adj* mountainous

**montant, -e 1** *adj (marée)* rising; *(col)* stand-up **2** *nm (somme)* amount; *(de barrière)* post; **montants compensatoires** subsidies

**monte-charge** [mɔ̃tʃarʒ] *(pl* **monte-charges**) *nm* service *Br* lift *or Am* elevator

**montée** [mɔ̃te] *nf (ascension)* climb, ascent; *(chemin)* slope; *(des prix, du fascisme)* rise; **la m. des eaux** the rise in the water level

**monter** [mɔ̃te] **1** *(aux* **avoir**) *vt (côte)* to climb (up); *(objet)* to bring/take up; *(cheval)* to ride; *(son)* to turn up; *(tente)* to put up; *(machine)* to assemble; *(pièce de théâtre)* to stage; **m. l'escalier** to go/come upstairs *or* up the stairs

**2** *(aux* **être**) *vi (personne)* to go/come up; *(prix)* to rise; *(marée)* to come in; *(avion)* to climb; **faire m. qn** to show sb up; **m. dans un véhicule** to get in(to) a vehicle; **m. sur qch** to climb onto sth; **m. sur** *ou* **à une échelle** to climb up a ladder; **m. en courant** to run up; *Sport* **m. à cheval** to ride (a horse)

**3 se monter** *vpr* **se m. à** *(s'élever à)* to amount to

**monteur, -euse** [mɔ̃tœr, -øz] *nmf Cin* editor

**montre** [mɔ̃tr] *nf (instrument)* (wrist-) watch; *Sport & Fig* **course contre la m.** race against the clock

**Montréal** [mɔ̃real] *nm ou f* Montreal

**montrer** [mɔ̃tre] **1** *vt* to show (**à** to); **m. qn/qch du doigt** to point at sb/sth; **m.**

**le chemin à qn** to show sb the way **2 se montrer** *vpr* to show oneself; **se m. courageux** to be courageous

**monture** [mɔ̃tyr] *nf (de lunettes)* frame; *(de bijou)* setting

**monument** [mɔnymɑ̃] *nm* monument; **m. historique** ancient monument; **m. aux morts** war memorial ▪ **monumental, -e, -aux, -ales** *adj (imposant, énorme)* monumental

**moquer** [mɔke] **se moquer** *vpr* **se m. de qn** to make fun of sb; **se m. de qch** *(rire de)* to make fun of sth; *(ne pas se soucier)* not to care about sth ▪ **moquerie** *nf* mockery ▪ **moqueur, -euse** *adj* mocking

**moquette** [mɔkɛt] *nf Br* fitted carpet, *Am* wall-to-wall carpeting

**moral, -e, -aux, -ales** [mɔral, -o] **1** *adj* moral **2** *nm* **avoir le m.** to be in good spirits ▪ **morale** *nf (d'histoire)* moral; *(principes)* morals; *(règles)* morality; **faire la m. à qn** to lecture sb ▪ **moralité** *nf (mœurs)* morality; *(de récit)* moral

**morceau, -x** [mɔrso] *nm* piece, bit; *(de sucre)* lump; *(de viande)* cut; **tomber en morceaux** to fall to pieces ▪ **morceler** *vt (terrain)* to divide up

**mordiller** [mɔrdije] *vt* to nibble

**mordre** [mɔrdr] **1** *vti* to bite; **m. qn au bras** to bite sb's arm; **2 se mordre** *vpr Fig* **se m. les doigts d'avoir fait qch** to kick oneself for doing sth

**mordu, -e** [mɔrdy] *pp de* **mordre**

**morgue** [mɔrg] *nf (d'hôpital)* mortuary; *(pour corps non identifiés)* morgue

**moribond, -e** [mɔribɔ̃, -ɔ̃d] **1** *adj* dying **2** *nmf* dying person

**morne** [mɔrn] *adj (temps)* dismal; *(silence)* gloomy; *(personne)* glum

**morose** [mɔroz] *adj* morose

**mors** [mɔr] *nm (de harnais)* bit

**morse** [mɔrs] *nm (code)* Morse (code)

**morsure** [mɔrsyr] *nf* bite

**mort**[1] [mɔr] *nf* death; **se donner la m.** to take one's own life; **un silence de m.** a deathly silence ▪ **mortalité** *nf* death rate, mortality ▪ **mortel, -elle 1** *adj (hommes, ennemi, danger)* mortal; *(accident)* fatal **2** *nmf* mortal ▪ **mortellement** *adv (blessé)* fatally

**mort**[2]**, morte** [mɔr, mɔrt] **1** *adj (personne, plante, ville)* dead; **m. de fatigue** dead tired; **m. de froid** numb with cold; **m. de peur** frightened to death; **m. ou vif** dead or alive **2** *nmf* dead man, *f* dead woman; **les morts** the dead; **de nombreux morts** *(victimes)* many deaths; **le jour** *ou* **la fête des Morts** All Souls' Day ▪ **morte-saison** (*pl* **mortes-saisons**) *nf* off-season ▪ **mort-né, -e** (*mpl* **mort-nés,** *fpl* **mort-nées**) *adj (enfant)* stillborn

**morue** [mɔry] *nf* cod

**mosaïque** [mɔzaik] *nf* mosaic

**Moscou** [mɔsku] *nm ou f* Moscow

**mot** [mo] *nm* word; **envoyer un m. à qn** to drop sb a line; **m. à m.** word for word; **avoir le dernier m.** to have the last word; **mots croisés** crossword (puzzle); **m. de passe** password

**motel** [mɔtɛl] *nm* motel

**moteur**[1] [mɔtœr] *nm (de véhicule)* engine; *(électrique)* motor

**moteur**[2]**, -trice** [mɔtœr, -tris] **1** *adj (nerf, muscle)* motor; **voiture à quatre roues motrices** four-wheel drive (car) **2** *nf* **motrice** *(de train)* engine

**motif** [mɔtif] *nm (raison)* reason (**de** for); *(dessin)* pattern

**motiver** [mɔtive] *vt (inciter, causer)* to motivate; *(justifier)* to justify ▪ **motivation** *nf* motivation ▪ **motivé, -e** *adj* motivated

**moto** [mɔto] *nf* motorbike ▪ **motocycliste** *nmf* motorcyclist

**motte** [mɔt] *nf (de terre)* lump, clod; *(de beurre)* block

**mou, molle** [mu, mɔl]

> **mol** is used before masculine singular nouns beginning with a vowel or h mute.

*adj* soft; *(sans énergie)* feeble ▪ **mollesse** *nf (de matelas)* softness; *(de personne)* lethargy

**mouche** [muʃ] *nf (insecte)* fly; **faire m.** to hit the bull's-eye ▪ **moucheron** *nm* midge

**moucher** [muʃe] **1** *vt* **m. qn** to wipe sb 's nose **2 se moucher** *vpr* to blow one's nose

**moucheté, -e** [muʃte] *adj* speckled

**mouchoir** [muʃwar] *nm* handkerchief; **m. en papier** tissue

**moudre*** [mudr] *vt* to grind

**mouette** [mwɛt] *nf* (sea)gull

**moufle** [mufl] *nf* mitten, mitt

**mouiller** [muje] **1** *vt* to wet **2** *vi Naut* to anchor **3 se mouiller** *vpr* to get wet ▪ **mouillé, -e** *adj* wet (**de** with)

**moule[1]** [mul] *nm Br* mould, *Am* mold; **m. à gâteaux** cake tin ▪ **moulage** *nm (objet)* cast ▪ **moulant, -e** *adj (vêtement)* tight-fitting ▪ **mouler** *vt Br* to mould, *Am* to mold; *(statue)* to cast

**moule[2]** [mul] *nf (mollusque)* mussel

**moulin** [mulɛ̃] *nm* mill; **m. à café** coffee grinder; **m. à vent** windmill

**moulinet** [mulinɛ] *nm (de canne à pêche)* reel

**moulu, -e** [muly] **1** *pp de* **moudre 2** *adj (café)* ground

**mourir*** [murir] *(aux* **être**) *vi* to die (**de** of *or* from); **m. de froid** to die of exposure; *Fig* **m. de fatigue** to be dead tired; *Fig* **m. de peur** to be frightened to death; *Fig* **je meurs de faim!** I'm starving! ▪ **mourant, -e 1** *adj* dying; *(voix)* faint **2** *nmf* dying person

**mousse** [mus] **1** *nf (plante)* moss; *(écume)* foam; *(de bière)* head; *(de savon)* lather; **m. à raser** shaving foam; *Culin* **m. au chocolat** chocolate mousse **2** *nm (marin)* ship's boy ▪ **mousser** *vi (bière)* to froth; *(savon)* to lather ▪ **mousseux, -euse 1** *adj (vin)* sparkling **2** *nm* sparkling wine

**moustache** [mustaʃ] *nf (d'homme) Br* moustache, *Am* mustache; *(de chat)* whiskers ▪ **moustachu, -e** *adj* with a *Br* moustache *or Am* mustache

**moustique** [mustik] *nm* mosquito ▪ **moustiquaire** *nf* mosquito net; *(en métal)* screen

**moutarde** [mutard] *nf* mustard

**mouton** [mutɔ̃] *nm* sheep *inv*; *(viande)* mutton; **moutons** *(écume) Br* white horses, *Am* whitecaps; *(poussière)* fluff; **peau de m.** sheepskin

**mouvement** [muvmɑ̃] *nm (geste, groupe, déplacement)* movement; *(élan)* impulse; *(de gymnastique)* exercise; **en m.** in motion; **m. de colère** fit of anger; **mouvements sociaux** workers' protest movements ▪ **mouvementé, -e** *adj (vie, voyage)* eventful

**mouvoir*** [muvwar] *vi*, **se mouvoir** *vpr* to move; **mû par** *(mécanisme)* driven by

**MOYEN[1], -ENNE** [mwajɛ̃, -ɛn] **1** *adj* average; *(format, entreprise)* medium(-sized)

**2** *nf* **moyenne** average; **en moyenne** on average; **la moyenne d'âge** the average age; **avoir la moyenne** *(à un examen) Br* to get a pass mark, *Am* to get a pass; *(à un devoir)* to get 50 percent, *Br* to get half marks; **le M. Âge** the Middle Ages

**moyen[2]** [mwajɛ̃] *nm (procédé, façon)* means, way (**de faire** of doing *or* to do); **moyens** *(capacités mentales)* ability; *(argent, ressources)* means; **je n'ai pas les moyens** *(argent)* I can't afford it; **au m. de qch** by means of sth

**Mozambique** [mɔzɑ̃bik] *nm* **le M.** Mozambique

**MST** [ɛmɛste] *(abrév* **maladie sexuellement transmissible**) *nf* STD

**muer** [mɥe] **1** *vi (animal) Br* to moult, *Am* to molt; *(voix)* to break **2 se muer** *vpr* **se m. en qch** to change into sth

**muet, muette** [mɥe, mɥɛt] **1** *adj (infirme)* dumb; *(de surprise)* speechless; *(film)* silent **2** *nmf* mute

**muguet** [mygɛ] *nm* lily of the valley

**mule** [myl] *nf (pantoufle, animal)* mule ▪ **mulet** *nm (équidé)* mule; *(poisson)* mullet

**multicolore** [myltikɔlɔr] *adj Br* multicoloured, *Am* multicolored

**multinationale** [myltinasjɔnal] *nf* multinational

**multiple** [myltipl] *adj (nombreux)* numerous; *(varié)* multiple ▪ **multiplication** *nf (calcul)* multiplication; *(augmentation)* increase ▪ **multiplier 1** *vt* to multiply **2 se multiplier** *vpr* to increase; *(se reproduire)* to multiply

**multitude** [myltityd] *nf* multitude

**municipal, -e, -aux, -ales** [mynisipal, -o] *adj* municipal ▪ **municipalité** *nf (maires et conseillers)* local council; *(commune)* municipality

**munir** [mynir] **1** *vt* **m. de qch** *(personne)* to provide with sth **2 se munir** *vpr* **se m. de qch** to take sth

**munitions** [mynisjɔ̃] *nfpl* ammunition

**mur** [myr] *nm* wall; *Fig* **au pied du m.** with one's back to the wall; **m. du son** sound barrier ▪ **muraille** *nf* (high) wall ▪ **mural, -e, -aux, -ales** *adj* **carte murale** wall map; **peinture murale** mural (painting) ▪ **murer** *vt (porte)* to wall up

**mûr, mûre**[1] [myr] *adj (fruit)* ripe; *(personne)* mature; **d'âge m.** middle-aged ▪ **mûrir** *vti (fruit)* to ripen; *(personne)* to mature

**mûre**[2] [myr] *nf (baie)* blackberry

**muret** [myrɛ] *nm* low wall

**murmure** [myrmyr] *nm* murmur ▪ **murmurer** *vti* to murmur

**muscle** [myskl] *nm* muscle ▪ **musclé, -e** *adj (bras)* muscular ▪ **musculaire** *adj (force, douleur)* muscular ▪ **musculature** *nf* muscles

**museau, -x** [myzo] *nm (de chien, de chat)* muzzle ▪ **museler** *vt (animal, presse)* to muzzle

**musée** [myze] *nm* museum; **m. de peinture** art gallery ▪ **muséum** *nm* natural history museum

**music-hall** [myzikol] *(pl* **music-halls***) nm (genre, salle)* music hall

**musique** [myzik] *nf* music ▪ **musical, -e, -aux, -ales** *adj* musical ▪ **musicien, -enne 1** *nmf* musician **2** *adj* musical

**musulman, -e** [myzylmɑ̃, -an] *adj & nmf* Muslim, Moslem

**muter** [myte] *vt* to transfer ▪ **mutant, -e** *adj & nmf* mutant ▪ **mutation** *nf (d'employé)* transfer; *Biol* mutation

**mutiler** [mytile] *vt* to mutilate, to maim; **être mutilé** to be disabled

**mutin** [mytɛ̃] *nm (rebelle)* mutineer ▪ **mutinerie** *nf* mutiny

**mutisme** [mytism] *nm* silence

**mutuel, -elle** [mytɥɛl] **1** *adj (réciproque)* mutual **2** *nf* **mutuelle** mutual insurance company ▪ **mutuellement** *adv* each other

**myope** [mjɔp] *adj* shortsighted

**myrtille** [mirtij] *nf (baie)* bilberry

**mystère** [mistɛr] *nm* mystery ▪ **mystérieux, -euse** *adj* mysterious

**mystique** [mistik] **1** *adj* mystical **2** *nmf (personne)* mystic

**mythe** [mit] *nm* myth ▪ **mythique** *adj* mythical ▪ **mythologie** *nf* mythology ▪ **mythologique** *adj* mythological

# Nn

**N¹, n** [ɛn] *nm inv* N, n
**N²** *(abrév* **route nationale)** M
**n'** [n] *voir* **ne**
**nacelle** [nasɛl] *nf (de ballon)* basket
**nacre** [nakr] *nf* mother-of-pearl ▪ **nacré, -e** *adj* pearly
**nage** [naʒ] *nf* (swimming) stroke; **traverser une rivière à la n.** to swim across a river; **n. libre** freestyle
**nageoire** [naʒwar] *nf (de poisson)* fin; *(de dauphin)* flipper
**nager** [naʒe] *vti* to swim ▪ **nageur, -euse** *nmf* swimmer
**naïf, naïve** [naif, naiv] *adj* naïve
**nain, naine** [nɛ̃, nɛn] *adj & nmf* dwarf
**naissance** [nɛsɑ̃s] *nf (de personne, d'animal)* birth; **donner n. à** *(enfant)* to give birth to; **de n.** from birth
**naître*** [nɛtr] *vi* to be born; *(sentiment, difficulté)* to arise (**de** from); *(idée)* to originate
**naïveté** [naivte] *nf* naïvety
**nantir** [nɑ̃tir] *vt* **n. qn de qch** to provide sb with sth ▪ **nanti, -e 1** *adj* well-to-do **2** *nmpl Péj* **les nantis** the well-to-do
**nappe** [nap] *nf (de table)* tablecloth; **n. de brouillard** fog patch; **n. d'eau** expanse of water; **n. de pétrole** layer of oil; *(de marée noire)* oil slick
**napper** [nape] *vt* to coat (**de** with)
**narguer** [narge] *vt* to taunt
**narine** [narin] *nf* nostril
**narquois, -e** [narkwa, -az] *adj* sneering
**nasal, -e, -aux, -ales** [nazal, -o] *adj* nasal
**nasillard, -e** [nazijar, -ard] *adj (voix)* nasal
**natal, -e, -als, -ales** [natal] *adj* native
**natalité** [natalite] *nf* birth rate
**natation** [natɑsjɔ̃] *nf* swimming
**natif, -ive** [natif, -iv] *adj & nmf* native; **être n. de** to be a native of
**nation** [nasjɔ̃] *nf* nation; **les Nations unies** the United Nations ▪ **national, -e, -aux, -ales** *adj* national ▪ **nationale** *nf (route) Br* ≃ A road, *Am* ≃ highway ▪ **nationaliser** *vt* to nationalize ▪ **nationaliste 1** *adj* nationalistic **2** *nmf* nationalist ▪ **nationalité** *nf* nationality
**natte** [nat] *nf (de cheveux) Br* plait, *Am* braid
**naturaliser** [natyralize] *vt* to naturalize ▪ **naturalisation** *nf* naturalization
**nature** [natyr] **1** *nf (univers, caractère)* nature; *(campagne)* country; **contre n.** unnatural; **en pleine n.** in the middle of the country; **payer en n.** to pay in kind; **n. morte** still life **2** *adj inv (omelette, yaourt)* plain; *(thé)* without milk
**naturel, -elle** [natyrɛl] **1** *adj* natural; **mort naturelle** death from natural causes **2** *nm (caractère)* nature; *(simplicité)* naturalness ▪ **naturellement** *adv* naturally
**naufrage** [nofraʒ] *nm* (ship)wreck; **faire n.** *(bateau)* to be wrecked; *(marin)* to be shipwrecked
**nausée** [noze] *nf* nausea, sickness; **avoir la n.** to feel sick
**nautique** [notik] *adj* nautical
**naval, -e, -als, -ales** [naval] *adj* naval
**navet** [navɛ] *nm (légume)* turnip

**navette** [navɛt] *nf (véhicule)* shuttle; **faire la n.** *(véhicule, personne)* to shuttle back and forth (**entre** between); **n. spatiale** space shuttle

**navigable** [navigabl] *adj (fleuve)* navigable

**navigant, -e** [navigɑ̃, -ɑ̃t] *adj Aviat* **personnel n.** flight crew

**navigateur** [navigatœr] *nm (marin)* navigator ▪ **navigation** *nf* navigation

**naviguer** [navige] *vi (bateau)* to sail; **n. sur Internet** to surf the Net

**navire** [navir] *nm* ship

**navrer** [navre] *vt* to appal ▪ **navrant, -e** *adj* appalling ▪ **navré, -e** *adj (air)* distressed; **je suis n.** I'm terribly sorry

**ne** [nə]

> **n'** before vowel or mute h; used to form negative verb with **pas, jamais, personne, rien** etc.

*adv* **ne... pas** not; **il ne boit pas** he does not *or* doesn't drink; **elle n'ose (pas)** she doesn't dare; **ne... que** only; **je crains qu'il ne parte** I'm afraid he'll leave

**né, -e** [ne] **1** *pp de* **naître** born; **il est né en 2001** he was born in 2001; **née Dupont** née Dupont **2** *adj* born; **c'est un poète-né** he's a born poet

**néanmoins** [neɑ̃mwɛ̃] *adv* nevertheless

**néant** [neɑ̃] *nm* nothingness; *(sur formulaire)* ≃ none

**nécessaire** [nesesɛr] **1** *adj* necessary **2** *nm* **le n.** the necessities; **faire le n.** to do what's necessary; **n. de toilette** toilet bag

**nécessité** [nesesite] *nf* necessity ▪ **nécessiter** *vt* to require, to necessitate

**nectarine** [nektarin] *nf* nectarine

**néerlandais, -e** [neɛrlɑ̃dɛ, -ɛz] **1** *adj* Dutch **2** *nmf* **N.** Dutchman; **Néerlandaise** Dutchwoman **3** *nm (langue)* Dutch

**nef** [nɛf] *nf (d'église)* nave

**néfaste** [nefast] *adj* harmful (**à** to)

**négatif, -ive** [negatif, -iv] **1** *adj* negative **2** *nm (de photo)* negative

**négligeable** [negliʒabl] *adj* negligible; **non n.** *(quantité)* significant

**négligent, -e** [negliʒɑ̃, -ɑ̃t] *adj* careless, negligent ▪ **négligence** *nf (défaut)* carelessness, negligence

**négliger** [negliʒe] **1** *vt (personne, travail, conseil)* to neglect; **n. de faire qch** to neglect to do sth **2 se négliger** *vpr* to neglect oneself ▪ **négligé, -e** *adj (tenue)* untidy; *(travail)* careless

**négocier** [negɔsje] *vti* to negotiate ▪ **négociable** *adj* negotiable ▪ **négociant, -e** *nmf* merchant, dealer ▪ **négociateur, -trice** *nmf* negotiator ▪ **négociation** *nf* negotiation

**neige** [nɛʒ] *nf* snow; **aller à la n.** to go skiing; **n. fondue** sleet ▪ **neiger** *v impersonnel* to snow; **il neige** it's snowing

**néon** [neɔ̃] *nm (gaz)* neon; *(enseigne)* neon sign; **éclairage au n.** neon lighting

**néo-zélandais, -e** [neɔzelɑ̃dɛ, -ɛz] *(mpl* **néo-zélandais,** *fpl* **néo-zélandaises)** **1** *adj* New Zealand **2** *nmf* **N., Néo-Zélandaise** New Zealander

**nerf** [nɛr] *nm* nerve ▪ **nerveux, -euse** *adj* nervous ▪ **nervosité** *nf* nervousness

**n'est-ce pas** [nɛspɑ] *adv* isn't he?/don't you?/won't they?/*etc*; **tu viendras, n.?** you'll come, won't you?; **il fait beau, n.?** the weather's nice, isn't it?

**Net** [nɛt] *nm* **le N.** the Net

**net, nette** [nɛt] **1** *adj (propre)* clean; *(image, refus)* clear; *(écriture)* neat; *(prix, salaire)* net; **n. d'impôt** net of tax **2** *adv (casser, couper)* clean; *(tuer)* outright; *(refuser)* flatly; **s'arrêter n.** to stop dead ▪ **nettement** *adv (avec précision)* clearly; *(incontestablement)* definitely; **il va n. mieux** he's much better ▪ **netteté** *nf (propreté, précision)* cleanness; *(de travail)* neatness

**nettoyer** [netwaje] **1** *vt* to clean **2 se nettoyer** *vpr* **se n. les oreilles** to clean one's ears ▪ **nettoyage** *nm* cleaning; **n. à sec** dry-cleaning

**neuf**[1], **neuve** [nœf, nœv] **1** *adj* new; **quoi de n.?** what's new? **2** *nm* **remettre qch à n.** to make sth as good as new

**neuf**[2] [nœf, nœv *before* **heures, ans**] *adj & nm* nine ▪ **neuvième** *adj & nmf* ninth

**neutre** [nøtr] **1** *adj (pays, personne)* neutral **2** *nm Él* neutral ▪ **neutraliser** *vt* to neutralize ▪ **neutralité** *nf* neutrality

**neveu, -x** [nəvø] *nm* nephew

**nez** [ne] *nm* nose; **n. à n.** face to face (**avec** with); **rire au n. de qn** to laugh in sb's face; **parler du n.** to speak through one's nose

**ni** [ni] *conj* **ni... ni...** neither... nor...; **ni Pierre ni Paul ne sont venus** neither Pierre nor Paul came; **il n'a ni faim ni soif** he's neither hungry nor thirsty; **sans manger ni boire** without eating or drinking; **ni l'un(e) ni l'autre** neither (of them)

**Nicaragua** [nikaragwa] *nm* **le N.** Nicaragua

**niche** [niʃ] *nf (de chien) Br* kennel, *Am* doghouse; *(cavité)* niche, recess

**nicher** [niʃe] **1** *vi (oiseau)* to nest **2 se nicher** *vpr (oiseau)* to nest ▪ **nichée** *nf (chiens)* litter; *(oiseaux)* brood

**nickel** [nikɛl] *nm (métal)* nickel

**nicotine** [nikɔtin] *nf* nicotine

**nid** [ni] *nm* nest

**nièce** [njɛs] *nf* niece

**nier** [nje] **1** *vt* to deny (**que** that) **2** *vi (accusé)* to deny the charge

**Niger** [niʒɛr] *nm* **le N.** *(pays)* Niger

**Nigéria** [niʒerja] *nm* **le N.** Nigeria

**Nil** [nil] *nm* **le N.** the Nile

**n'importe** [nɛ̃pɔrt] *voir* **importer**[1]

**nippon, -one** *ou* **-onne** [nipɔ̃, -ɔn] *adj* Japanese

**niveau, -x** [nivo] *nm (hauteur, étage, degré)* level; *Scol* standard; **au n. de la mer** at sea level; **n. de vie** standard of living ▪ **niveler** *vt (surface)* to level

**noble** [nɔbl] **1** *adj* noble **2** *nmf* nobleman, *f* noblewoman ▪ **noblesse** *nf (caractère, classe)* nobility

**noce** [nɔs] *nf* wedding; **noces d'or** golden wedding

**nocif, -ive** [nɔsif, -iv] *adj* harmful ▪ **nocivité** *nf* harmfulness

**nocturne** [nɔktyrn] **1** *adj (animal)* nocturnal **2** *nf (de magasin)* late-night opening; *Sport* **(match en) n.** evening match

**Noël** [nɔɛl] *nm* Christmas; **arbre de N.** Christmas tree; **le père N.** Father Christmas, Santa Claus

**nœud** [nø] *nm* (**a**) *(entrecroisement)* knot; *(ruban)* bow; **n. papillon** bow tie (**b**) *Naut (vitesse)* knot

**noir, -e** [nwar] **1** *adj* black; *(sombre)* dark; *(idées)* gloomy; *(misère)* dire; **il fait n.** it's dark; **film n.** film noir **2** *nm (couleur)* black; *(obscurité)* dark; **N.** *(homme)* Black (man); **3** *nf* **noire** *(note) Br* crotchet, *Am* quarter note; **Noire** *(femme)* Black (woman) ▪ **noircir 1** *vt* to blacken **2** *vi* to turn black

**noisette** [nwazet] *nf* hazelnut

**noix** [nwa] *nf (du noyer)* walnut; **n. de coco** coconut

**nom** [nɔ̃] *nm* name; *Gram* noun; **au n. de qn** on sb's behalf; **n. de famille** surname; **n. de jeune fille** maiden name

**nomade** [nɔmad] **1** *adj* nomadic **2** *nmf* nomad

**nombre** [nɔ̃br] *nm* number; **être au** *ou* **du n. de** to be among; **ils sont au n. de dix** there are ten of them; **le plus grand n. de** the majority of; **bon n. de** a good many; *Math* **n. premier** prime number

**nombreux, -euse** [nɔ̃brø, -øz] *adj (amis, livres)* numerous, many; *(famille, collection)* large; **peu n.** few; **venir n.** to come in large numbers

**nombril** [nɔ̃bri] *nm* navel

**nominal, -e, -aux, -ales** [nɔminal, -o] *adj* nominal

**nomination** [nɔminɑsjɔ̃] *nf (à un poste)* appointment; *(pour récompense)* nomination

**nommer** [nɔme] **1** *vt (appeler)* to name; **n. qn** *(désigner)* to appoint sb (**à un poste** to a post); **n. qn président**

to appoint sb chairman **2 se nommer** *vpr (s'appeler)* to be called

**non** [nɔ̃] *adv* no; **tu viens ou n.?** are you coming or not?; **n. seulement** not only; **n. (pas) que...** *(+ subjunctive)* not that...; **n. loin** not far; **je crois que n.** I don't think so; **(ni) moi n. plus** neither do/am/can/*etc* I

**nonante** [nɔnɑ̃t] *adj & nm (en Belgique, en Suisse)* ninety

**nonchalant, -e** [nɔ̃ʃalɑ̃, -ɑ̃t] *adj* nonchalant

**non-fumeur, -euse** [nɔ̃fymœr, -øz] **1** *adj* non-smoking **2** *nmf* non-smoker

**non-retour** [nɔ̃rətur] *nm* **point de n.** point of no return

**non-violence** [nɔ̃vjɔlɑ̃s] *nf* non-violence

**non-voyants** [nɔ̃vwajɑ̃] *nmpl* **les n.** the unsighted

**nord** [nɔr] **1** *nm* north; **au n.** in the north; *(direction)* (to the) north (**de** of); **du n.** *(vent, direction)* northerly; *(ville)* northern; *(gens)* from/in the north; **l'Afrique du N.** North Africa; **l'Europe du N.** Northern Europe; **le grand N.** the Frozen North
**2** *adj inv (côte)* north; *(régions)* northern ▪ **nord-africain, -e** (*mpl* **nord-africains,** *fpl* **nord-africaines**) **1** *adj* North African **2** *nmf* **N., Nord-Africaine** North African ▪ **nord-américain, -e** (*mpl* **nord-américains,** *fpl* **nord-américaines**) **1** *adj* North American **2** *nmf* **N., Nord-Américaine** North American ▪ **nord-est** *nm & adj inv* northeast ▪ **nord-ouest** *nm & adj inv* northwest

**nordique** [nɔrdik] **1** *adj* Scandinavian **2** *nmf* **N.** Scandinavian; *Can* Northern Canadian

**normal, -e, -aux, -ales** [nɔrmal, -o] *adj* normal ▪ **normale** *nf* norm; **au-dessus/au-dessous de la n.** above/below average; *Fam* **N. Sup** = university-level college preparing students for senior posts in teaching ▪ **normalement** *adv* normally ▪ **normaliser** *vt (uniformiser)* to standardize; *(relations)* to normalize

**normand, -e** [nɔrmɑ̃, -ɑ̃d] **1** *adj* Norman **2** *nmf* **N., Normande** Norman ▪ **Normandie** *nf* **la N.** Normandy

**norme** [nɔrm] *nf* norm; **normes de sécurité** safety standards

**Norvège** [nɔrvɛʒ] *nf* **la N.** Norway ▪ **norvégien, -enne 1** *adj* Norwegian **2** *nmf* **N., Norvégienne** Norwegian **3** *nm (langue)* Norwegian

**nos** [no] *voir* **notre**

**nostalgie** [nɔstalʒi] *nf* nostalgia ▪ **nostalgique** *adj* nostalgic

**notable** [nɔtabl] *adj & nm* notable

**notaire** [nɔtɛr] *nm* lawyer, *Br* notary (public)

**notamment** [nɔtamɑ̃] *adv* notably

**note** [nɔt] *nf (annotation, communication) & Mus* note; *Scol Br* mark, *Am* grade; *(facture) Br* bill, *Am* check; **prendre n. de qch** to make a note of sth; **prendre des notes** to take notes; **n. de frais** expenses

**noter** [nɔte] *vt (remarquer)* to note; *(écrire)* to note down; *(devoir) Br* to mark, *Am* to grade

**notice** [nɔtis] *nf (mode d'emploi)* instructions; *(de médicament)* directions

**notifier** [nɔtifje] *vt* **n. qch à qn** to notify sb of sth

**notion** [nosjɔ̃] *nf* notion; **notions** *(éléments)* rudiments; **avoir des notions de qch** to know the basics of sth

**notoriété** [nɔtɔrjete] *nf (renom)* fame; **il est de n. publique que...** it's common knowledge that...

**notre, nos** [nɔtr, no] *adj possessif* our

**nôtre** [notr] **1** *pron possessif* **le/la n., les nôtres** ours **2** *nmpl* **les nôtres** *(parents)* our family

**nouer** [nwe] **1** *vt (lacets)* to tie; *(cravate)* to knot; *Fig (relation)* to establish **2 se nouer** *vpr (intrigue)* to take shape

**nougat** [nuga] *nm* nougat

**nouilles** [nuj] *nfpl* noodles

**nourrice** [nuris] *nf (assistante maternelle)* (children's) nurse, *Br* childminder; *(qui allaite)* wet nurse

**nourrir** [nurir] **1** *vt (alimenter)* to feed; *Fig (espoir)* to cherish **2 se nourrir** *vpr* to eat; **se n. de qch** to feed on sth
**nourrisson** [nurisɔ̃] *nm* infant
**nourriture** [nurityr] *nf* food
**nous** [nu] *pron personnel* (**a**) *(sujet)* we; **n. sommes ici** we are here
(**b**) *(complément direct)* us; **il n. connaît** he knows us
(**c**) *(complément indirect)* (to) us; **il n. l'a donné** he gave it to us, he gave us it
(**d**) *(réfléchi)* ourselves; **n. n. lavons** we wash ourselves; **n. n. habillons** we get dressed
(**e**) *(réciproque)* each other; **n. n. détestons** we hate each other ▪ **nous-mêmes** *pron* ourselves
**nouveau, -elle**[1], **-x, -elles** [nuvo, -ɛl]

**nouvel** is used before masculine singular nouns beginning with a vowel or mute h.

**1** *adj* new; *(mode)* latest; **on craint de nouvelles inondations** *(d'autres)* further flooding is feared
**2** *nmf (à l'école)* new boy, *f* new girl
**3** *nm* **du n.** something new
**4** *adv* **de n., à n.** again ▪ **nouveau-né, -e** (*mpl* **nouveau-nés,** *fpl* **nouveau-nées**) **1** *adj* newborn **2** *nmf* newborn baby
**nouveauté** [nuvote] *nf* novelty; **nouveautés** *(livres)* new books; *(disques)* new releases
**nouvelle**[2] [nuvɛl] *nf* (**a**) **une n.** *(annonce)* a piece of news; **la n. de sa mort** the news of his/her death; **les nouvelles** the news *(sing)*; **avoir des nouvelles de qn** *(directement)* to have heard from sb (**b**) *(récit)* short story
**Nouvelle-Calédonie** [nuvɛlkaledɔni] *nf* **la N.** New Caledonia
**Nouvelle-Zélande** [nuvɛlzelɑ̃d] *nf* **la N.** New Zealand
**novateur, -trice** [nɔvatœr, -tris] *adj* innovative
**novembre** [nɔvɑ̃br] *nm* November
**noyade** [nwajad] *nf* drowning
**noyau, -x** [nwajo] *nm (de fruit)* stone, *Am* pit; *(d'atome, de cellule)* nucleus; *(groupe)* group; **n. dur** *(de groupe)* hard core
**noyauter** [nwajote] *vt* to infiltrate
**noyé, -e** [nwaje] *nmf* drowned person
**noyer**[1] [nwaje] **1** *vt (personne)* to drown; *(terres)* to flood **2 se noyer** *vpr* to drown; **se n. dans les détails** to get bogged down in details
**noyer**[2] [nwaje] *nm (arbre)* walnut tree
**nu, -e** [ny] **1** *adj (personne, vérité)* naked; *(mains, chambre)* bare; **tout nu** (stark) naked, (in the) nude; **tête nue, nu-tête** bare-headed; **aller pieds nus** to go barefoot **2** *nm* nude; **mettre qch à nu** to expose sth
**nuage** [nɥaʒ] *nm* cloud; *Fig* **être dans les nuages** to have one's head in the clouds ▪ **nuageux, -euse** *adj (ciel)* cloudy
**nuance** [nɥɑ̃s] *nf (de couleur)* shade; *(de sens)* nuance; *(de regret)* tinge ▪ **nuancé, -e** *adj (jugement)* qualified ▪ **nuancer** *vt (pensée)* to qualify
**nucléaire** [nykleɛr] **1** *adj* nuclear **2** *nm* nuclear energy
**nudiste** [nydist] *nmf* nudist ▪ **nudité** *nf (de personne)* nudity, nakedness
**nuée** [nɥe] *nf* **une n. de** *(foule)* a horde of; *(groupe compact)* a cloud of
**nuire*** [nɥir] *vi* **n. à qn/qch** to harm sb/sth ▪ **nuisible** *adj* harmful (**à** to)
**nuit** [nɥi] *nf* night; *(obscurité)* dark(-ness); **la n.** *(se promener)* at night; **cette n.** *(hier)* last night; *(aujourd'hui)* tonight; **avant la n.** before nightfall; **il fait n.** it's dark; **il fait n. noire** it's pitch-black; **bonne n.!** good night! ▪ **nuitée** *nf* overnight stay
**nul, nulle** [nyl] **1** *adj (médiocre)* hopeless, useless; *(risque)* non-existent, nil; *Jur (non valable)* null (and void); **être n. en qch** to be hopeless at sth
**2** *adj indéfini Littéraire (aucun)* no; **sans n. doute** without any doubt
**3** *pron indéfini m Littéraire (aucun)* no one ▪ **nulle part** *adv* nowhere; **n. ailleurs** nowhere else
**numérique** [nymerik] *adj* numerical;

*(montre, clavier, données)* digital

**numéro** [nymero] *nm (chiffre)* number; *(de journal)* issue, number; *(au cirque)* act; *Tél* **n. vert** *Br* ≃ Freefone® number, *Am* ≃ toll-free number; **n. de téléphone** telephone number ▪ **numéroter** *vt (pages, sièges)* to number

**nuptial, -ale, -aux, -ales** [nypsjal, -jo] *adj (chambre)* bridal; **cérémonie nuptiale** wedding ceremony

**nuque** [nyk] *nf* back of the neck

**nutrition** [nytrisjɔ̃] *nf* nutrition

**Nylon®** [nilɔ̃] *nm (fibre)* nylon; **chemise en N.** nylon shirt

# Oo

**O, o** [o] *nm inv* O, o

**obéir** [ɔbeir] *vi* to obey; **o. à qn/qch** to obey sb/sth ▪ **obéissance** *nf* obedience (**à** to) ▪ **obéissant, -e** *adj* obedient

**obèse** [ɔbɛz] *adj* obese ▪ **obésité** [ɔbesite] *nf* obesity

**objecter** [ɔbʒɛkte] *vt* **o. que...** to object that... ▪ **objecteur** *nm* **o. de conscience** conscientious objector ▪ **objection** *nf* objection; **si vous n'y voyez pas d'o.** if you have no objections

**objectif, -ive** [ɔbʒɛktif, -iv] **1** *adj* objective **2** *nm (but)* objective; *(d'appareil photo)* lens ▪ **objectivité** *nf* objectivity

**objet** [ɔbʒɛ] *nm (chose, sujet, but)* object; **faire l'o. de** *(étude, critiques)* to be the subject of; *(soins, surveillance)* to be given; **o. d'art** objet d'art; **objets trouvés** *(bureau) Br* lost property, *Am* lost and found

**obligation** [ɔbligasjɔ̃] *nf (contrainte)* obligation; *Fin* bond; **se trouver dans l'o. de faire qch** to be obliged to do sth; **sans o. d'achat** no purchase necessary ▪ **obligatoire** *adj* compulsory, obligatory

**obliger** [ɔbliʒe] **1** *vt (contraindre)* to force (**à faire** to do); **être obligé de faire qch** to be obliged to do sth **2 s'obliger** *vpr* **s'o. à faire qch** to force oneself to do sth ▪ **obligé, -e** *adj (obligatoire)* necessary

**oblique** [ɔblik] *adj* oblique

**oblitéré, -e** [ɔblitere] *adj (timbre)* used

**obscène** [ɔpsɛn] *adj* obscene ▪ **obscénité** *nf* obscenity

**obscur, -e** [ɔpskyr] *adj (sombre)* dark; *(confus, inconnu)* obscure ▪ **obscurcir 1** *vt (rendre sombre)* to darken; *(rendre confus)* to obscure **2 s'obscurcir** *vpr (ciel)* to darken ▪ **obscurité** *nf (noirceur)* darkness; **dans l'o.** in the dark

**obséder** [ɔpsede] *vt* to obsess ▪ **obsédant, -e** *adj* haunting; *(pensée)* obsessive

**obsèques** [ɔpsɛk] *nfpl* funeral

**observateur, -trice** [ɔpsɛrvatœr, -tris] **1** *adj* observant **2** *nmf* observer

**observation** [ɔpsɛrvasjɔ̃] *nf (étude, remarque)* observation; *(reproche)* remark; *(respect)* observance

**observatoire** [ɔpsɛrvatwar] *nm* observatory

**observer** [ɔpsɛrve] *vt (regarder, respecter)* to observe; *(remarquer)* to notice; **faire o. qch à qn** to point sth out to sb

**obsession** [ɔpsesjɔ̃] *nf* obsession ▪ **obsessionnel, -elle** *adj* obsessional

**obstacle** [ɔpstakl] *nm* obstacle; **faire o. à qch** to stand in the way of sth

**obstétricien, -enne** [ɔpstetrisjɛ̃, -ɛn] *nmf* obstetrician

**obstiner** [ɔpstine] **s'obstiner** *vpr* to persist (**à faire** in doing) ▪ **obstination** *nf* stubbornness, obstinacy ▪ **obstiné, -e** *adj* stubborn, obstinate

**obstruction** [ɔpstryksjɔ̃] *nf* obstruction ▪ **obstruer** *vt* to obstruct

**obtempérer** [ɔptɑ̃pere] *vi* **o. à qch** to comply with sth

**obtenir*** [ɔptənir] *vt* to get, to obtain ▪ **obtention** *nf* obtaining

**obus** [ɔby] *nm (projectile)* shell

**occasion** [ɔkazjɔ̃] *nf* (**a**) *(chance)* chance, opportunity (**de faire** to do); *(moment)* occasion; **à l'o.** when the occasion arises; **à l'o. de qch** on the occasion of sth; **pour les grandes occasions** for special occasions (**b**) *(affaire)* bargain; *(objet non neuf)* second-hand item; **d'o.** second-hand

**occasionner** [ɔkazjɔne] *vt* to cause; **o. qch à qn** to cause sb sth

**occident** [ɔksidɑ̃] *nm* **l'O.** the West ▪ **occidental, -e, -aux, -ales 1** *adj Géog & Pol* western **2** *nmpl Pol* **les Occidentaux** Westerners

**occulte** [ɔkylt] *adj* occult

**occupant, -e** [ɔkypɑ̃, -ɑ̃t] **1** *adj (armée)* occupying **2** *nmf (habitant)* occupant **3** *nm Mil* **l'o.** the occupying forces

**occupation** [ɔkypasyɔ̃] *nf (activité, travail) & Mil* occupation

**occupé, -e** [ɔkype] *adj* busy (**à faire** doing); *(place, maison)* occupied; *(ligne téléphonique) Br* engaged, *Am* busy

**occuper** [ɔkype] **1** *vt (bâtiment, pays)* to occupy; *(place)* to take up, to occupy; *(poste)* to hold; **o. qn** *(jeu, travail)* to keep sb busy *or* occupied

**2 s'occuper** *vpr* to keep oneself busy (**à faire** doing); **s'o. de** *(affaire, problème)* to deal with; **s'o. de qn** *(malade)* to take care of sb; *(client)* to see to sb

**océan** [ɔseɑ̃] *nm* ocean; **l'o. Atlantique/Pacifique** the Atlantic/Pacific Ocean

**octante** [ɔktɑ̃t] *adj & nm inv (en Belgique, en Suisse)* eighty

**octet** [ɔktɛ] *nm Ordinat* byte; **milliard d'octets** gigabyte

**octobre** [ɔktɔbr] *nm* October

**octogonal, -e, -aux, -ales** [ɔktɔgɔnal, -o] *adj* octagonal

**oculaire** [ɔkylɛr] *adj* **témoin o.** eyewitness ▪ **oculiste** *nmf* eye specialist

**odeur** [ɔdœr] *nf* smell; *(de fleur)* scent ▪ **odorat** *nm* sense of smell

**odieux, -euse** [ɔdjø, -øz] *adj* odious

**œil** [œj] (*pl* **yeux** [jø]) *nm* eye; **avoir les yeux verts** to have green eyes; **avoir de grands yeux** to have big eyes; **lever/baisser les yeux** to look up/down; **coup d'o.** *(regard)* look, glance; **jeter un coup d'o. sur qch** to have a look at sth; **à vue d'o.** visibly; **regarder qn dans les yeux** to look sb in the eye; *Fig* **o. au beurre noir** black eye

**œillères** [œjɛr] *nfpl (de cheval) Br* blinkers, *Am* blinders

**œillet** [œjɛ] *nm (fleur)* carnation

**œuf** [œf] (*pl* **œufs** [ø]) *nm* egg; **œufs** *(de poissons)* (hard) roe; **o. à la coque** boiled egg; **o. sur le plat** fried egg; **o. dur** hard-boiled egg; **œufs brouillés** scrambled eggs; **o. de Pâques** Easter egg

**œuvre** [œvr] *nf (travail, livre)* work; **o. d'art** work of art; **o. de charité** *(organisation)* charity

**offense** [ɔfɑ̃s] *nf* insult ▪ **offensant, -e** *adj* offensive ▪ **offenser 1** *vt* to offend **2 s'offenser** *vpr* **s'o. de qch** to take *Br* offence *or Am* offense at sth

**offensif, -ive** [ɔfɑ̃sif, -iv] **1** *adj* offensive **2** *nf* **offensive** offensive; **passer à l'o.** to go on the offensive

**offert, -e** [ɔfɛr, -ɛrt] *pp de* **offrir**

**office** [ɔfis] *nm* (**a**) *Rel* service (**b**) *(pièce)* pantry (**c**) *(établissement)* office, bureau; **o. du tourisme** tourist information centre (**d**) *(charge)* office; **d'o.** without having any say; **faire o. de qch** to serve as sth

**officiel, -elle** [ɔfisjɛl] *adj & nm* official

**officier** [ɔfisje] *nm (dans l'armée)* officer

**officieux, -euse** [ɔfisjø, -øz] *adj* unofficial

**offre** [ɔfr] *nf* offer; *(aux enchères)* bid; *Écon* **l'o. et la demande** supply and demand; *Fin* **o. publique d'achat** takeover bid; **offres d'emploi** *(de journal)* job vacancies, *Br* situations vacant ▪ **offrande** *nf* offering

**offrir*** [ɔfrir] **1** *vt (donner)* to give;

*(proposer)* to offer; **o. qch à qn** *(donner)* to give sb sth, to give sth to sb; *(proposer)* to offer sb sth, to offer sth to sb; **o. de faire qch** to offer to do sth **2 s'offrir** *vpr (cadeau)* to treat oneself to; *(se proposer)* to offer oneself (**comme** as) ▪ **offrant** *nm* **au plus o.** to the highest bidder

**OGM** [ɔʒeɛm] (*abrév* **organisme génétiquement modifié**) *nm* GMO

**oie** [wa] *nf* goose (*pl* geese)

**oignon** [ɔɲɔ̃] *nm (légume)* onion

**oiseau, -x** [wazo] *nm* bird; **o. de proie** bird of prey

**oisif, -ive** [wazif, -iv] *adj* idle ▪ **oisiveté** *nf* idleness

**oléoduc** [ɔleɔdyk] *nm* pipeline

**olive** [ɔliv] **1** *nf* olive **2** *adj inv* **vert o.** olive (green) ▪ **olivier** *nm (arbre)* olive tree

**olympique** [ɔlɛ̃pik] *adj* Olympic; **les jeux Olympiques** the Olympic games

**ombilical, -e, -aux, -ales** [ɔ̃bilikal, -o] *adj* umbilical

**ombrage** [ɔ̃braʒ] *nm (ombre)* shade

**ombre** [ɔ̃br] *nf (forme)* shadow; *(zone sombre)* shade; **30° à l'o.** 30° in the shade; **sans l'o. d'un doute** without the shadow of a doubt; **pas l'o. d'un reproche/remords** not a trace of blame/remorse

**ombrelle** [ɔ̃brɛl] *nf* sunshade, parasol

**omelette** [ɔmlɛt] *nf* omelette; **o. norvégienne** baked Alaska

**omettre*** [ɔmɛtr] *vt* to omit (**de faire** to do) ▪ **omission** *nf* omission

**omnibus** [ɔmnibys] *adj & nm* **(train) o.** slow train *(stopping at all stations)*

**omnipotent, -e** [ɔmnipɔtɑ̃, -ɑ̃t] *adj* omnipotent

**omniprésent, -e** [ɔmniprezɑ̃, ɑ̃t] *adj* omnipresent

**omnisports** [ɔmnispɔr] *adj inv* **centre o.** sports centre

**omnivore** [ɔmnivɔr] *adj* omnivorous

**on** [ɔ̃] (*sometimes* **l'on** [lɔ̃]) *pron indéfini (les gens)* they, people; *(nous)* we, one; *(vous)* you, one; **on m'a dit que...** I was told that...; **on me l'a donné** somebody gave it to me

**oncle** [ɔ̃kl] *nm* uncle

**onctueux, -euse** [ɔ̃ktɥø, -øz] *adj* smooth

**onde** [ɔ̃d] *nf (à la radio) & Phys* wave; **grandes ondes** long wave; **ondes courtes/moyennes** short/medium wave; **o. de choc** shock wave

**ondée** [ɔ̃de] *nf* sudden downpour

**on-dit** [ɔ̃di] *nm inv* rumour, hearsay

**ondoyer** [ɔ̃dwaje] *vi* to undulate

**ondulé, -e** [ɔ̃dyle] *adj* wavy

**onduler** [ɔ̃dyle] *vi* to undulate; *(cheveux)* to be wavy

**onéreux, -euse** [ɔnerø, -øz] *adj* costly

**ONG** [oɛnʒe] (*abrév* **organisation non gouvernementale**) *nf* NGO

**ongle** [ɔ̃gl] *nm* (finger)nail

**ont** [ɔ̃] *voir* **avoir**

**ONU** [ɔny] (*abrév* **Organisation des Nations unies**) *nf* UN

**onze** [ɔ̃z] *adj & nm* eleven ▪ **onzième** *adj & nmf* eleventh

**OPA** [ɔpeɑ] (*abrév* **offre publique d'achat**) *nf Fin* takeover bid

**opaque** [ɔpak] *adj* opaque

**opéra** [ɔpera] *nm (musique)* opera; *(édifice)* opera house

**opérateur, -trice** [ɔperatœr, -tris] *nmf (personne)* operator; *Cin* cameraman

**opération** [ɔperɑsjɔ̃] *nf (action) & Méd, Mil & Math* operation ▪ **opérationnel, -elle** *adj* operational

**opérer** [ɔpere] **1** *vt (exécuter)* to carry out; *(choix)* to make; *(patient)* to operate on (**de** for); **se faire o.** to have an operation **2** *vi (agir)* to work; *(procéder)* to proceed; *(chirurgien)* to operate

**ophtalmologue** [ɔftalmɔlɔg] *nmf* ophthalmologist

**opiniâtre** [ɔpinjɑtr] *adj* stubborn

**opinion** [ɔpinjɔ̃] *nf* opinion (**sur** about *or* on); **mon o. est faite** my mind is made up; **o. publique** public opinion

**opportun, -e** [ɔpɔrtœ̃, -yn] *adj* opportune, timely ▪ **opportunité** *nf* timeliness

**opposant, -e** [ɔpɔzɑ̃, -ɑ̃t] *nmf* opponent (**à** of)

**opposé, -e** [ɔpoze] **1** *adj (direction)* opposite; *(intérêts)* conflicting; *(armées, équipe)* opposing; **être o. à qch** to be opposed to sth **2** *nm* **l'o.** the opposite (**de** of); **à l'o.** *(côté)* on the opposite side (**de** to); **à l'o. de** *(contrairement à)* contrary to

**opposer** [ɔpoze] **1** *vt (résistance, argument)* to put up (**à** against); **o. qn à qn** to set sb against sb; **match qui oppose...** match between... **2 s'opposer** *vpr (équipes)* to confront each other; **s'o. à qch** to be opposed to sth; **je m'y oppose** I'm opposed to it

**opposition** [ɔpozisjɔ̃] *nf* opposition (**à** to); **faire o. à** to oppose; *(chèque)* to stop; **par o. à** as opposed to

**oppresser** [ɔprese] *vt (gêner)* to oppress ▪ **oppressant, -e** *adj* oppressive ▪ **oppresseur** *nm* oppressor ▪ **oppression** *nf* oppression ▪ **opprimer** *vt (peuple, nation)* to oppress ▪ **opprimés** *nmpl* **les o.** the oppressed

**opter** [ɔpte] *vi* **o. pour qch** to opt for sth

**opticien, -enne** [ɔptisjɛ̃, -ɛn] *nmf* optician

**optimal, -e, -aux, -ales** [ɔptimal, -o] *adj* optimal

**optimiser** [ɔptimize] *vt* to optimize

**optimisme** [ɔptimism] *nm* optimism ▪ **optimiste 1** *adj* optimistic **2** *nmf* optimist

**option** [ɔpsjɔ̃] *nf (choix)* option; *(chose)* optional extra; *Scol Br* optional subject, *Am* elective (subject)

**optique** [ɔptik] **1** *adj (nerf)* optic; *(verre, fibres)* optical **2** *nf* optics *(sing)*; **d'o.** *(instrument, appareil)* optical

**opulent, -e** [ɔpylɑ̃, -ɑ̃t] *adj* opulent ▪ **opulence** *nf* opulence

**or**[1] [ɔr] *nm* gold; **montre en or** gold watch; **règle/âge d'or** golden rule/age; **cœur d'or** heart of gold; **mine d'or** gold mine; **affaire en or** bargain; **or noir** *(pétrole)* black gold

**or**[2] [ɔr] *conj (cependant)* now, well

**orage** [ɔraʒ] *nm* (thunder)storm ▪ **orageux, -euse** *adj* stormy

**oral, -e, -aux, -ales** [ɔral, -o] **1** *adj* oral **2** *nm Scol & Univ* oral

**orange** [ɔrɑ̃ʒ] **1** *nf* orange; **o. pressée** (fresh) orange juice **2** *adj & nm inv (couleur)* orange ▪ **oranger** *nm* orange tree

**orateur** [ɔratœr] *nm* speaker, orator

**orbite** [ɔrbit] *nf (d'astre)* orbit; *(d'œil)* socket; **mettre qch sur o.** *(fusée)* to put sth into orbit

**orchestre** [ɔrkɛstr] *nm (classique)* orchestra; *(de jazz)* band; *Théât (places) Br* stalls, *Am* orchestra ▪ **orchestrer** *vt (organiser) & Mus* to orchestrate

**ordinaire** [ɔrdinɛr] *adj (habituel, normal)* ordinary, *Am* regular; *(médiocre)* ordinary, average; **d'o., à l'o.** usually; **comme d'o., comme à l'o.** as usual

**ordinateur** [ɔrdinatœr] *nm* computer; **o. individuel** personal computer; **o. portable** laptop

**ordonnance** [ɔrdɔnɑ̃s] *nf (de médecin)* prescription; *(disposition)* arrangement

**ordonner** [ɔrdɔne] *vt* (**a**) *(commander)* to order (**que** + *subjunctive* that); **o. à qn de faire qch** to order sb to do sth (**b**) *(ranger)* to organize (**c**) *(prêtre)* to ordain; **il a été ordonné prêtre** he has been ordained (as) a priest ▪ **ordonné, -e** *adj (personne, maison)* tidy

**ordre** [ɔrdr] *nm (organisation, discipline, catégorie, commandement)* order; *(absence de désordre)* tidiness; **en o.** *(chambre)* tidy; **mettre de l'o. dans qch** to tidy sth up; **rentrer dans l'o.** to return to normal; **jusqu'à nouvel o.** until further notice; **de l'o. de** *(environ)* of the order of; **du même o.** of the same order; **de premier o.** first-rate; **par o. d'âge** in order of age; **assurer le maintien de l'o.** to maintain order; *Rel* **entrer dans les ordres** to take holy orders; **o. du jour** agenda; **l'o. public** law and order

**ordures** [ɔrdyr] *nfpl (déchets) Br* rubbish, *Am* garbage; **mettre qch aux o.** to throw sth out (in the *Br* rubbish *or Am* garbage)

**oreille** [ɔrɛj] *nf* ear; **faire la sourde o.** to turn a deaf ear

**oreiller** [ɔrɛje] *nm* pillow

**oreillons** [ɔrɛjɔ̃] *nmpl (maladie)* mumps

**ores et déjà** [ɔrzedeʒa] **d'ores et déjà** *adv* already

**orfèvrerie** [ɔrfɛvrəri] *nf (magasin)* goldsmith's/silversmith's shop; *(objets)* gold/silver plate

**organe** [ɔrgan] *nm Anat & Fig* organ; ▪ **organisme** *nm (corps)* body; *Biol* organism; *(bureaux)* organization

**organisateur, -trice** [ɔrganizatœr, -tris] *nmf* organizer

**organisation** [ɔrganizɑsjɔ̃] *nf (arrangement, association)* organization

**organiser** [ɔrganize] **1** *vt* to organize **2 s'organiser** *vpr* to get organized ▪ **organisé, -e** *adj* organized

**orge** [ɔrʒ] *nf* barley

**orgue** [ɔrg] **1** *nm* organ **2** *nfpl* **orgues** organ

**orgueil** [ɔrgœj] *nm* pride ▪ **orgueilleux, -euse** *adj* proud

**orient** [ɔrjɑ̃] *nm* **l'O.** the Orient, the East; **en O.** in the East ▪ **oriental, -e, -aux, -ales 1** *adj (côte, région)* eastern; *(langue)* oriental **2** *nmf* **O., Orientale** Oriental

**orientation** [ɔrjɑ̃tɑsjɔ̃] *nf (de position)* orientation; *(d'antenne)* positioning; *(de maison)* aspect; **avoir le sens de l'o.** to have a good sense of direction; **o. professionnelle** careers guidance

**orienter** [ɔrjɑ̃te] **1** *vt (bâtiment)* to orientate; *(canon, télescope)* to point (**vers** at); **o. ses recherches sur** to direct one's research on
**2 s'orienter** *vpr* to get one's bearings; **s'o. vers** *(carrière)* to specialize in ▪ **orienté, -e** *adj (peu objectif)* slanted; **o. à l'ouest** *(appartement)* facing west

**orifice** [ɔrifis] *nm* opening

**originaire** [ɔriʒinɛr] *adj* **être o. de** *(natif)* to be a native of

**original, -e, -aux, -ales** [ɔriʒinal, -o] **1** *adj (idée, artiste, version)* original **2** *nm (texte, tableau)* original **3** *nmf (personne)* eccentric ▪ **originalité** *nf* originality

**origine** [ɔriʒin] *nf* origin; **à l'o.** originally; **être à l'o. de qch** to be at the origin of sth; **d'o.** *(pneu)* original; **être d'o. française** to be of French origin ▪ **originel, -elle** *adj* original

**ornement** [ɔrnəmɑ̃] *nm* ornament ▪ **ornemental, -e, -aux, -ales** *adj* ornamental

**orner** [ɔrne] *vt* to decorate (**de** with)

**orphelin, -e** [ɔrfəlɛ̃, -in] *nmf* orphan ▪ **orphelinat** *nm* orphanage

**orteil** [ɔrtɛj] *nm* toe

**orthodoxe** [ɔrtɔdɔks] *adj* orthodox

**orthographe** [ɔrtɔgraf] *nf* spelling ▪ **orthographier** *vt* to spell; **mal o. qch** to misspell sth

**ortie** [ɔrti] *nf* nettle

**os** [ɔs, *pl* o *ou* ɔs] *nm* bone

**oscar** [ɔskar] *nm (récompense)* Oscar

**osciller** [ɔsile] *vi Tech* to oscillate; *(pendule)* to swing; *(aiguille, flamme)* to flicker; *Fig (varier)* to fluctuate (**entre** between)

**oser** [oze] *vt* to dare; **o. faire qch** to dare (to) do sth ▪ **osé, -e** *adj* daring

**osier** [ozje] *nm* wicker; **panier d'o.** wicker basket

**ossements** [ɔsmɑ̃] *nmpl* bones

**osseux, -euse** [ɔsø, -øz] *adj (maigre)* bony

**otage** [ɔtaʒ] *nm* hostage; **prendre qn en o.** to take sb hostage

**OTAN** [ɔtɑ̃] *(abrév* **Organisation du traité de l'Atlantique Nord**) *nf* NATO

**ôter** [ote] *vt* to take away, to remove (**à qn** from sb); *(vêtement)* to take off; *(déduire)* to take (away)

**otite** [ɔtit] *nf* ear infection

**ou** [u] *conj* or; **ou elle ou moi** either her or me

**où** [u] *adv & pron relatif* where; **le jour**

**où...** the day when...; **la table où...** the table on which...; **l'état où...** the condition in which...; **par où?** which way?; **d'où?** where from?; **le pays d'où je viens** the country from which I come

**ouate** [wat] *nf (pour pansement) Br* cotton wool, *Am* absorbent cotton

**oubli** [ubli] *nm (trou de mémoire)* oversight; *(lacune)* omission; **tomber dans l'o.** to fall into oblivion

**oublier** [ublije] *vt* to forget (**de faire** to do); *(omettre)* to leave out

**oubliettes** [ublijɛt] *nfpl (de château)* dungeons

**ouest** [wɛst] **1** *nm* west; **à l'o.** in the west; *(direction)* (to the) west (**de** of); **d'o.** *(vent)* west(erly); **de l'o.** western **2** *adj inv (côte)* west; *(région)* western

**Ouganda** [ugɑ̃da] *nm* **l'O.** Uganda

**oui** [wi] **1** *adv* yes; **ah, ça o.!** oh yes (indeed!); **je crois que o.** I think so **2** *nm inv* **pour un o. pour un non** for the slightest thing

**ouï-dire** [widir] *nm* hearsay; **par o.** by hearsay

**ouïe** [wi] *nf* hearing

**ouïes** [wi] *nfpl (de poisson)* gills

**ouragan** [uragɑ̃] *nm* hurricane

**ourlet** [urlɛ] *nm* hem

**ours** [urs] *nm* bear; **o. blanc** polar bear; **o. en peluche** teddy bear ▪ **ourse** *nf* she-bear; **la Grande O.** the Great Bear

**oursin** [ursɛ̃] *nm* sea urchin

**outil** [uti] *nm* tool ▪ **outillage** *nm* tools; *(d'usine)* equipment ▪ **outiller** *vt* to equip

**outrage** [utraʒ] *nm* insult (**à** to)

**outrance** [utrɑ̃s] *nf (excès)* excess; **à o.** to excess ▪ **outrancier, -ère** *adj* excessive

**outre** [utr] **1** *prép* besides; **o. mesure** unduly **2** *adv* **en o.** besides; **passer o.** to take no notice (**à** of) ▪ **outre-Manche** *adv* across the Channel ▪ **outre-mer** *adv* overseas; **d'o.** *(marché)* overseas; **territoires d'o.** overseas territories

**outré, -e** [utre] *adj (révolté)* outraged; *(excessif)* exaggerated

**outrepasser** [utrəpɑse] *vt* to go beyond, to exceed

**ouvert, -e** [uvɛr, -ɛrt] **1** *pp de* **ouvrir 2** *adj* open; *(robinet, gaz)* on ▪ **ouverture** *nf* opening; *(trou)* hole

**ouvrable** [uvrabl] *adj* **jour o.** working or *Am* work day

**ouvrage** [uvraʒ] *nm (travail, livre, objet)* work; *(couture)* (needle)work; **un o.** *(travail)* a piece of work

**ouvreuse** [uvrøz] *nf* usherette

**ouvrier, -ère** [uvrije, -ɛr] **1** *nmf* worker; **o. qualifié/spécialisé** skilled/semi-skilled worker; **o. agricole** farm worker **2** *adj (quartier)* working-class

**ouvrir*** [uvrir] **1** *vt* to open; *(gaz, radio)* to turn on; *(hostilités)* to begin; *(appétit)* to whet **2** *vi* to open **3 s'ouvrir** *vpr (porte, boîte, fleur)* to open ▪ **ouvre-boîtes** *nm inv Br* tin opener, *Am* can opener ▪ **ouvre-bouteilles** *nm inv* bottle opener

**ovale** [ɔval] *adj & nm* oval

**ovation** [ɔvɑsjɔ̃] *nf* (standing) ovation

**ovni** [ɔvni] *(abrév* **objet volant non identifié**) *nm* UFO

**oxyder** [ɔkside] *vt*, **s'oxyder** *vpr* to oxidize

**oxygène** [ɔksiʒɛn] *nm* oxygen; **masque/tente à o.** oxygen mask/tent ▪ **oxygéné, -e** *adj* **eau oxygénée** (hydrogen) peroxide; **cheveux blonds oxygénés** peroxide blonde hair, bleached hair

**ozone** [ozon] *nm Chim* ozone

# Pp

**P, p** [pe] *nm inv* P, p

**pacifique** [pasifik] **1** *adj (manifestation)* peaceful; *(personne, peuple)* peace-loving; *(côte)* Pacific **2** *nm* **le P.** the Pacific

**pacifiste** [pasifist] *adj & nmf* pacifist

**pacte** [pakt] *nm* pact

**pagaie** [page] *nf* paddle

**pagaïe, pagaille** [pagaj] *nf Fam (désordre)* mess; **semer la p.** to cause chaos

**pagayer** [pageje] *vi* to paddle

**page** [paʒ] *nf (de livre)* page; *Ordinat* **p. d'accueil** home page; **les Pages Jaunes®** *(de l'annuaire)* the Yellow Pages®; *Radio* **p. de publicité** commercial break

**paie** [pɛ] *nf* pay, wages

**paiement** [pemɑ̃] *nm* payment

**païen, -enne** [pajɛ̃, -ɛn] *adj & nmf* pagan, heathen

**paillasson** [pajasɔ̃] *nm* (door)mat

**paille** [pɑj] *nf* straw; *(pour boire)* (drinking) straw

**paillette** [pajɛt] *nf (d'habit)* sequin; **paillettes** *(de savon, lessive)* flakes; *(d'or)* gold dust

**pain** [pɛ̃] *nm* bread; **un p.** a loaf (of bread); **petit p.** roll; **p. au chocolat** = chocolate-filled pastry; **p. complet** wholemeal bread; **p. d'épices** ≃ gingerbread; **p. grillé** toast; **p. de mie** sandwich loaf

**pair, -e** [pɛr] **1** *adj (numéro)* even **2** *nm (personne)* peer; **hors p.** unrivalled; **aller de p.** to go hand in hand (**avec** with); **au p.** *(étudiante)* au pair; **travailler au p.** to work as an au pair

**paire** [pɛr] *nf* pair (**de** of)

**paisible** [pezibl] *adj (vie, endroit)* peaceful; *(caractère, personne)* quiet

**paître*** [pɛtr] *vi* to graze

**paix** [pɛ] *nf* peace; **en p.** *(vivre, laisser)* in peace (**avec** with)

**Pakistan** [pakistɑ̃] *nm* **le P.** Pakistan ▪ **pakistanais, -e 1** *adj* Pakistani **2** *nmf* **P., Pakistanaise** Pakistani

**palace** [palas] *nm* luxury hotel

**palais** [palɛ] *nm (château)* palace; *Anat* palate; **P. de justice** law courts; **p. des sports** sports centre

**pâle** [pɑl] *adj* pale

**Palestine** [palɛstin] *nf* **la P.** Palestine ▪ **palestinien, -enne 1** *adj* Palestinian **2** *nmf* **P., Palestinienne** Palestinian

**palette** [palɛt] *nf (de peintre)* palette; *(pour marchandises)* pallet

**pâleur** [pɑlœr] *nf (de lumière)* paleness; *(de personne)* pallor

**palier** [palje] *nm (niveau)* level; *(d'escalier)* landing; *(phase)* plateau; **par paliers** in stages

**pâlir** [pɑlir] *vi* to turn pale (**de** with)

**palissade** [palisad] *nf* fence

**pallier** [palje] **1** *vt (difficultés)* to alleviate **2** *vi* **p. à qch** to compensate for sth

**palmarès** [palmarɛs] *nm* prize list; *(de chansons)* charts

**palme** [palm] *nf (de palmier)* palm (branch); *(de nageur)* flipper

**palmier** [palmje] *nm* palm (tree)

**palourde** [palurd] *nf* clam

**palper** [palpe] *vt* to feel ▪ **palpable** *adj* palpable

**palpiter** [palpite] *vi (cœur)* to flutter; *(plus fort)* to throb

**pamplemousse** [pɑ̃pləmus] *nm* grapefruit

**panaché, -e** [panaʃe] **1** *adj* multicoloured; **p. de blanc** streaked with white **2** *nm* shandy

**Panama** [panama] *nm* **le P.** Panama

**pancarte** [pɑ̃kart] *nf* sign, notice; *(de manifestant)* placard

**pané, -e** [pane] *adj (poisson)* breaded

**panier** [panje] *nm (ustensile, contenu)* basket; **p. à linge** *Br* linen basket, *Am* (clothes) hamper

**panique** [panik] **1** *nf* panic; **pris de p.** panic-stricken **2** *adj* **peur p.** panic

**panne** [pan] *nf* breakdown; **tomber en p.** to break down; **être en p.** to have broken down; **tomber en p. sèche** to run out of *Br* petrol *or Am* gas; **p. d'électricité** blackout, *Br* power cut

**panneau, -x** [pano] *nm (écriteau)* sign, notice, board; *(de porte)* panel; **p. d'affichage** *Br* notice board, *Am* bulletin board; **p. de signalisation** road sign ▪ **panonceau, -x** *nm (enseigne)* sign

**panoplie** [panɔpli] *nf (jouet)* outfit; *(gamme)* set

**panorama** [panɔrama] *nm* panorama ▪ **panoramique** *adj* panoramic; *Cin* **écran p.** wide screen

**panser** [pɑ̃se] *vt (main)* to bandage; *(plaie)* to dress; **p. qn** to dress sb's wounds ▪ **pansement** *nm* dressing; **faire un p. à qn** to put a dressing on sb; **p. adhésif** *Br* sticking plaster, *Am* Band-aid®

**pantalon** [pɑ̃talɔ̃] *nm Br* trousers, *Am* pants; **deux pantalons** two pairs of *Br* trousers *or Am* pants

**panthère** [pɑ̃tɛr] *nf* panther

**pantoufle** [pɑ̃tufl] *nf* slipper

**paon** [pɑ̃] *nm* peacock

**papa** [papa] *nm* dad(dy)

**pape** [pap] *nm* pope

**papeterie** [papɛtri] *nf (magasin)* stationer's shop; *(articles)* stationery; *(fabrique)* paper mill

**papi** [papi] *nm* = **papy**

**papier** [papje] *nm (matière)* paper; **un p.** *(feuille)* a piece of paper; *(formulaire)* a form; *(de journal)* an article; **p. hygiénique** toilet paper; **papiers d'identité** identity papers; **p. à lettres** writing paper; **p. peint** wallpaper

**papillon** [papijɔ̃] *nm (insecte)* butterfly; **p. de nuit** moth

**papy** [papi] *nm* grand(d)ad

**Pâque** [pɑk] *nf Rel* **la P. juive, P.** Passover

**paquebot** [pakbo] *nm* liner

**pâquerette** [pɑkrɛt] *nf* daisy

**Pâques** [pɑk] *nm sing & nfpl* Easter

**paquet** [pakɛ] *nm (sac)* packet; *(de sucre)* bag; *(de cigarettes)* packet, *Am* pack; *Br (postal)* parcel, package

---

**PAR** [par] *prép* (**a**) *(indique l'agent, la manière, le moyen)* by; **frappé p. qn** hit by sb; **p. mer** by sea; **p. le train** by train; **p. la force** by *or* through force; **commencer p. qch** *(récit)* to begin with sth; **p. erreur** by mistake; **p. chance** by a stroke of luck

(**b**) *(à travers)* through; **p. la porte** through the door; **jeter/regarder p. la fenêtre** to throw/look out (of) the window; **p. ici/là** *(aller)* this/that way; *(habiter)* around here/there; **p. les rues** through the streets

(**c**) *(à cause de)* out of, from; **p. pitié** out of pity

(**d**) *(pendant)* **p. ce froid** in this cold; **p. le passé** in the past

(**e**) *(distributif)* **dix fois p. an/mois** ten times a *or* per year/month; **50 euros p. personne** 50 euros per person; **deux p. deux** two by two; **p. deux fois** twice

(**f**) *(avec 'trop')* **p. trop aimable** far too kind

---

**parachute** [paraʃyt] *nm* parachute; **p. ascensionnel** parascending ▪ **parachutisme** *nm* parachute jumping ▪ **parachutiste** *nmf* parachutist; *(soldat)* paratrooper

**parade** [parad] *nf (défilé)* parade; *(étalage)* show

**paradis** [paradi] *nm* heaven

**paradoxe** [paradɔks] *nm* paradox
**parafer** [parafe] *vt* = **parapher**
**paraffine** [parafin] *nf* paraffin (wax)
**parages** [paraʒ] *nmpl Naut* waters; **dans les p. de** in the vicinity of
**paragraphe** [paragraf] *nm* paragraph
**Paraguay** [paragwe] *nm* **le P.** Paraguay
**paraître*** [parɛtr] **1** *vi (sembler)* to seem, to appear; *(apparaître)* to appear; *(livre)* to come out, to be published **2** *v impersonnel* **il paraît qu'il va partir** it appears *or* seems (that) he's leaving; **à ce qu'il paraît** apparently
**parallèle** [paralɛl] **1** *adj* parallel (**à** with *or* to); *(police, marché)* unofficial **2** *nf* parallel (line) **3** *nm (comparaison) & Géog* parallel; **mettre qch en p. avec qch** to draw a parallel between sth and sth ▪ **parallèlement** *adv* **p. à** parallel to; *(simultanément)* at the same time as
**paralyser** [paralize] *vt Br* to paralyse, *Am* to paralyze ▪ **paralysie** *nf* paralysis ▪ **paralytique** *adj & nmf* paralytic
**paramédical, -e, -aux, -ales** [paramedikal, -o] *adj* paramedical
**paramilitaire** [paramilitɛr] *adj* paramilitary
**parapente** [parapɑ̃t] *nm (activité)* paragliding; **faire du p.** to go paragliding
**parapet** [parapɛ] *nm* parapet
**parapher** [parafe] *vt* to initial
**parapluie** [paraplɥi] *nm* umbrella
**parasite** [parazit] **1** *nm (organisme, personne)* parasite; **parasites** *(à la radio)* interference **2** *adj* parasitic
**parasol** [parasɔl] *nm* sunshade, parasol; *(de plage)* beach umbrella
**paratonnerre** [paratɔnɛr] *nm* lightning *Br* conductor *or Am* rod
**paravent** [paravɑ̃] *nm* screen
**parc** [park] *nm (jardin)* park; *(de château)* grounds; *(de bébé)* playpen; **p. d'attractions** amusement park; **p. de stationnement** *Br* car park, *Am* parking lot; **p. naturel** nature reserve
**parcelle** [parsɛl] *nf* small piece; *(terrain)* plot
**parce que** [parsəkə] *conj* because
**parchemin** [parʃəmɛ̃] *nm* parchment
**par-ci, par-là** [parsiparla] *adv* here, there and everywhere
**parcmètre** [parkmɛtr] *nm* (parking) meter
**parcourir*** [parkurir] *vt (lieu)* to walk round; *(pays)* to travel through; *(mer)* to sail; *(distance)* to cover; *(texte)* to glance through; **p. qch des yeux** *ou* **du regard** to glance at sth; **il reste 2 km à p.** there are 2 km to go ▪ **parcours** *nm (itinéraire)* route; **p. de golf** *(terrain)* golf course
**par-delà** [pardəla] *prép & adv* beyond
**par-derrière** [parderjɛr] **1** *prép* behind **2** *adv (attaquer)* from behind; *(se boutonner)* at the back; **passer p.** to go in the back door
**par-dessous** [pardəsu] *prép & adv* underneath
**pardessus** [pardəsy] *nm* overcoat
**par-dessus** [pardəsy] **1** *prép* over; **p. tout** above all **2** *adv* over
**par-devant** [pardəvɑ̃] *adv (attaquer)* from the front; *(se boutonner)* at the front
**pardon** [pardɔ̃] *nm* forgiveness; **p.!** *(excusez-moi)* sorry!; **p.?** *(pour demander)* excuse me?, *Am* pardon me?; **demander p.** to apologize (**à** to) ▪ **pardonner** *vt* to forgive; **p. qch à qn** to forgive sb for sth; **elle m'a pardonné d'avoir oublié** she forgave me for forgetting
**pare-balles** [parbal] *adj inv* **gilet p.** bulletproof *Br* jacket *or Am* vest
**pare-brise** [parbriz] *nm inv Br* windscreen, *Am* windshield
**pare-chocs** [parʃɔk] *nm inv* bumper
**pareil, -eille** [parɛj] **1** *adj* (**a**) *(identique)* the same; **p. à** the same as (**b**) *(tel)* such; **en p. cas** in such cases
**2** *adv Fam* the same
**3** *nmf (personne)* equal; **sans p.** unparalleled, unique
**4** *nf* **rendre la pareille à qn** *(se venger)* to get one's own back on sb ▪ **pareillement** *adv (de la même manière)* in

the same way; *(aussi)* likewise

**parent, -e** [parɑ̃, -ɑ̃t] **1** *nmf (oncle, tante, cousin)* relative, relation **2** *nmpl* **parents** *(père et mère)* parents **3** *adj* related (**de** to) ▪ **parental, -e, -aux, -ales** *adj* parental ▪ **parenté** *nf* relationship; **avoir un lien de p.** to be related

**parenthèse** [parɑ̃tɛz] *nf (signe)* bracket, parenthesis; **entre parenthèses** in brackets

**parer[1]** [pare] **1** *vt (coup)* to parry **2** *vi* **p. à toute éventualité** to prepare for any contingency

**parer[2]** [pare] *vt (orner)* to adorn (**de** with)

**paresseux, -euse** [parɛsø, -øz] **1** *adj* lazy **2** *nmf* lazy person

**parfaire*** [parfɛr] *vt* to finish off ▪ **parfait, -e** *adj* perfect ▪ **parfaitement** *adv (sans fautes, complètement)* perfectly; *(certainement)* certainly

**parfois** [parfwa] *adv* sometimes

**parfum** [parfœ̃] *nm (essence)* perfume; *(senteur)* fragrance; *(de glace)* flavour ▪ **parfumer 1** *vt (embaumer)* to scent; *(glace)* to flavour (**à** with) **2 se parfumer** *vpr* to put perfume on ▪ **parfumerie** *nf (magasin)* perfumery

**pari** [pari] *nm* bet; **faire un p.** to make a bet; **p. mutuel** *Br* ≃ tote, *Am* ≃ parimutuel ▪ **parier** *vti* to bet (**sur** on; **que** that); **il y a fort à p. que...** the odds are that...

**Paris** [pari] *nm ou f* Paris ▪ **parisien, -enne 1** *adj* Parisian **2** *nmf* **P., Parisienne** Parisian

**parking** [parkiŋ] *nm Br* car park, *Am* parking lot; **'p. payant'** *Br* ≃ 'pay-and-display car park'

**parlement** [parləmɑ̃] *nm* **le P.** Parliament ▪ **parlementaire 1** *adj* parliamentary **2** *nmf* member of parliament

**parlementer** [parləmɑ̃te] *vi* to negotiate (**avec** with)

**parler** [parle] **1** *vi* to talk, to speak (**de** about *or* of; **à** to); **sans p. de...** not to mention...

**2** *vt (langue)* to speak; **p. affaires** to talk business

**3 se parler** *vpr (langue)* to be spoken; *(l'un l'autre)* to talk to each other

**4** *nm* speech; *(régional)* dialect

**parloir** [parlwar] *nm* visiting room

**parmi** [parmi] *prép* among(st)

**paroi** [parwa] *nf* wall; *(de rocher)* (rock) face

**paroisse** [parwas] *nf* parish

**parole** [parɔl] *nf (mot, promesse)* word; *(faculté, langage)* speech; **paroles** *(de chanson)* words, lyrics; **adresser la p. à qn** to speak to sb; **prendre la p.** to speak; **tenir p.** to keep one's word

**parquet** [parkɛ] *nm (sol)* wooden floor

**parrain** [parɛ̃] *nm Rel* godfather; *(de sportif, de club)* sponsor ▪ **parrainer** *vt (sportif, membre)* to sponsor

**pars** [par] *voir* **partir**

**parsemer** [parsəme] *vt* to scatter (**de** with)

**part[1]** [par] *voir* **partir**

**part[2]** [par] *nf (portion)* share, part; *(de gâteau)* slice; **prendre p. à** *(activité)* to take part in; **faire p. de qch à qn** to inform sb of sth; **de toutes parts** on all sides; **de p. et d'autre** on both sides; **d'une p.... d'autre p....** on the one hand... on the other hand...; **d'autre p.** *(d'ailleurs)* moreover; **de la p. de qn** from sb; **c'est de la p. de qui?** *(au téléphone)* who's calling?; **pour ma p.** as for me; **à p.** *(mettre)* aside; *(excepté)* apart from; *(personne)* different; **prendre qn à p.** to take sb aside

**partage** [partaʒ] *nm (action)* dividing up; *(de gâteau, de responsabilités)* sharing out; **faire le p. de qch** to divide sth up

**partager** [partaʒe] **1** *vt (avoir en commun)* to share (**avec** with); *(répartir)* to divide (up); **p. qch en deux** to divide sth in two; **p. l'avis de qn** to share sb's opinion

**2 se partager** *vpr (bénéfices)* to share (between themselves); **se p. entre** to divide one's time between ▪ **partagé, -e** *adj (amour)* mutual; **les avis sont partagés** opinions are divided

**partance** [partɑ̃s] **en partance** *adv*

*(train)* about to depart; **en p. pour...** for...

**partenaire** [partənɛr] *nmf* partner ▪ **partenariat** *nm* partnership

**parterre** [partɛr] *nm (de fleurs)* flower bed; *Théât Br* stalls, *Am* orchestra; *Fam (sol)* floor

**parti** [parti] *nm (camp)* side; **tirer p. de qch** to make good use of sth; **p. (politique)** (political) party

**partial, -e, -aux, -ales** [parsjal, -o] *adj* biased ▪ **partialité** *nf* bias

**participer** [partisipe] *vi* **p. à** *(jeu)* to take part in, to participate in; *(bénéfices, joie)* to share (in); *(financièrement)* to contribute to ▪ **participant, -e** *nmf* participant ▪ **participation** *nf* participation; *(d'élection)* turnout; **p. aux frais** contribution towards costs

**particularité** [partikylarite] *nf* peculiarity

**particule** [partikyl] *nf* particle

**particulier, -ère** [partikylje, -ɛr] **1** *adj (propre)* characteristic (**à** of); *(remarquable)* unusual; *(soin, intérêt)* particular; *(maison, voiture, leçon)* private; *Péj (bizarre)* peculiar; **en p.** *(surtout)* in particular; *(à part)* in private; **cas p.** special case **2** *nm* private individual; **vente de p. à p.** private sale ▪ **particulièrement** *adv* particularly; **tout p.** especially

**partie** [parti] *nf (morceau)* part; *(jeu)* game; *(domaine)* field; **en p.** partly, in part; **en grande p.** mainly; **faire p. de** to be a part of; *(club)* to belong to; *(comité)* to be on ▪ **partiel, -elle** *adj* partial

**partir*** [partir] *(aux* **être**) *vi (s'en aller)* to go, to leave; *(se mettre en route)* to set off; *(s'éloigner)* to go away; *(coup de feu)* to go off; *(tache)* to come out; *(peinture)* to come off; **p. en voiture** to go by car, to drive; **p. en courant** to run off; **p. de** *(lieu)* to leave from; *(commencer par)* to start (off) with; **à p. de** *(date, prix)* from

**partisan** [partizɑ̃] **1** *nm* supporter; *(combattant)* partisan **2** *adj (esprit)* partisan; **être p. de qch/de faire qch** to be in favour of sth/of doing sth

**partition** [partisjɔ̃] *nf Mus* score

**partout** [partu] *adv* everywhere; **p. où je vais** everywhere *or* wherever I go; **un peu p.** all over the place

**paru, -e** [pary] *pp de* **paraître** ▪ **parution** *nf* publication

**parure** [paryr] *nf (ensemble)* set

**parvenir*** [parvənir] *(aux* **être**) *vi* **p. à** *(lieu)* to reach; *(objectif)* to achieve; **p. à faire qch** to manage to do sth

---

**PAS[1]** [pɑ] *adv (de négation)* **(ne...) p.** not; **je ne sais p.** I do not *or* don't know; **je n'ai p. compris** I didn't understand; **je voudrais ne p. sortir** I would like not to go out; **p. de pain** no bread; **p. du tout** not at all; **elle chantera – p. moi!** she'll sing – no I won't!

---

**pas[2]** [pɑ] *nm* (**a**) *(enjambée)* step; *(allure)* pace; *(bruit)* footstep; *(trace)* footprint; **p. à p.** step by step; **à p. de loup** stealthily; **à deux p. (de)** close by; **aller au p.** to go at a walking pace; **rouler au p.** *(véhicule)* to crawl along; **faire un faux p.** *(en marchant)* to trip; **revenir sur ses p.** to retrace one's steps; **marcher à grands p.** to stride along (**b**) *(de vis)* pitch (**c**) **le p. de Calais** the Straits of Dover

**passable** [pɑsabl] *adj* passable, fair

**passage** [pɑsaʒ] *nm (chemin, extrait)* passage; *(ruelle)* alley(way); *(traversée)* crossing; **être de p. dans une ville** to be passing through a town; **p. clouté** *ou* **pour piétons** *Br* (pedestrian) crossing, *Am* crosswalk; **p. souterrain** *Br* subway, *Am* underpass; **p. à niveau** *Br* level crossing, *Am* grade crossing; **'p. interdit'** 'no through traffic'; **'cédez le p.'** *(au carrefour) Br* 'give way', *Am* 'yield'

**passager, -ère** [pasaʒe, -ɛr] **1** *adj* momentary **2** *nmf* passenger; **p. clandestin** stowaway

**passant, -e** [pɑsɑ̃, -ɑ̃t] **1** *adj (rue)* busy **2** *nmf* passer-by **3** *nm (de ceinture)* loop

**passe** [pɑs] *nf (au football)* pass; *Fig* **une mauvaise p.** a bad patch

**passé, -e** [pɑse] **1** *adj (temps)* past; *(couleur)* faded; **la semaine passée** last week; **il est dix heures passées** it's after *or Br* gone ten o'clock; **p. de mode** out of fashion **2** *nm (temps, vie passée)* past; **par le p.** in the past **3** *prép* after; **p. huit heures** after eight o'clock

**passe-montagne** [pɑsmɔ̃taɲ] *(pl* **passe-montagnes***) nm Br* balaclava, *Am* ski mask

**passe-partout** [pɑspartu] *nm inv* master key

**passeport** [pɑspɔr] *nm* passport

**PASSER** [pɑse] **1** *(aux* **avoir***) vt (pont, frontière)* to go over; *(porte, douane)* to go through; *(ballon)* to pass; *(vêtement)* to slip on; *(film)* to show; *(disque)* to play; *(vacances)* to spend; *(examen)* to take; *(commande)* to place; *(visite médicale)* to have; *(omettre)* to leave out; **p. qch à qn** *(prêter)* to pass sth to sb; *Aut* **p. la seconde** to change into second; **p. son temps à faire qch** to spend one's time doing sth

**2** *(aux* **être***) vi (se déplacer)* to go past; *(disparaître)* to go; *(facteur)* to come; *(temps)* to pass (by), to go by; *(film, programme)* to be on; *(douleur)* to pass; *(courant)* to flow; **laisser p. qn** to let sb through; **p. de qch à qch** to go from sth to sth; **p. devant qn/qch** to go past sb/sth; **p. par Paris** to pass through Paris; **p. chez le boulanger** to go round to the baker's; **p. à la radio** to be on the radio; **p. pour** *(riche)* to be taken for; **faire p. qn pour** to pass sb off as; **faire p. qch sous/dans qch** to slide/push sth under/into sth; **p. sur** *(détail)* to pass over

**3 se passer** *vpr (se produire)* to happen; **se p. de qn/qch** to do without sb/sth; **ça s'est bien passé** it went off well

**passerelle** [pɑsrɛl] *nf (pont)* footbridge; **p. d'embarquement** *(de navire)* gangway; *(d'avion)* steps

**passe-temps** [pɑstɑ̃] *nm inv* pastime

**passeur, -euse** [pɑsœr, -øz] *nmf (batelier)* ferryman, *f* ferrywoman; *(contrebandier)* smuggler

**passif, -ive** [pasif, -iv] *adj* passive

**passion** [pɑsjɔ̃] *nf* passion; **avoir la p. des voitures** to have a passion for cars

**passionner** [pɑsjɔne] **1** *vt* to fascinate **2 se passionner** *vpr* **se p. pour qch** to have a passion for sth ▪ **passionnant, -e** *adj* fascinating ▪ **passionné, -e** *adj* passionate; **p. de qch** passionately fond of sth

**passivité** [pasivite] *nf* passiveness, passivity

**passoire** [pɑswar] *nf (pour liquides)* sieve; *(à thé)* strainer; *(à légumes)* colander

**pastel** [pastɛl] *adj inv & nm* pastel

**pastèque** [pastɛk] *nf* watermelon

**pasteurisé, -e** [pastœrize] *adj* pasteurized

**pastille** [pastij] *nf* pastille; *(médicament)* lozenge

**patauger** [patoʒe] *vi (s'embourber)* to squelch; *(barboter)* to splash about

**pâte** [pɑt] *nf (pour tarte)* pastry; *(pour pain)* dough; *(pour gâteau)* mixture; **p. d'amandes** marzipan; **p. feuilletée** puff pastry; **pâtes (alimentaires)** pasta

**pâté** [pɑte] *nm (charcuterie)* pâté; *(tache d'encre)* blot; **p. en croûte** ≃ meat pie; **p. de maisons** block of houses

**pâtée** [pɑte] *nf (pour chien)* dog food; *(pour chat)* cat food

**paternel, -elle** [paternɛl] *adj* paternal ▪ **paternité** *nf (état)* paternity, fatherhood; *(de livre)* authorship

**pathétique** [patetik] *adj* moving

**pathologique** [patɔlɔʒik] *adj* pathological

**patience** [pasjɑ̃s] *nf* patience; **avoir de la p.** to be patient; **perdre p.** to lose patience

**patient, -e** [pasjɑ̃, -ɑ̃t] **1** *adj* patient **2** *nmf (malade)* patient ▪ **patienter** *vi* to wait

**patin** [patɛ̃] *nm (de patineur)* skate; **p. à glace** ice skate; **p. à roulettes** roller skate

**patiner** [patine] *vi Sport* to skate; *(véhicule)* to skid ▪ **patinage** *nm Sport* skating; **p. artistique** figure skating ▪ **patineur, -euse** *nmf* skater ▪ **patinoire** *nf* skating rink, ice rink

**pâtir** [pɑtir] *vi* **p. de** to suffer because of

**pâtisserie** [pɑtisri] *nf (gâteau)* pastry, cake; *(magasin)* cake shop; *(art)* pastry-making ▪ **pâtissier, -ère 1** *nmf* pastry cook; *(commerçant)* confectioner **2** *adj* **crème pâtissière** confectioner's custard

**patrie** [patri] *nf* homeland

**patrimoine** [patrimwan] *nm* heritage; *(biens)* property

**patriote** [patrijɔt] **1** *adj* patriotic **2** *nmf* patriot ▪ **patriotique** *adj* patriotic ▪ **patriotisme** *nm* patriotism

**patron, -onne** [patrɔ̃, -ɔn] **1** *nmf (chef)* boss; *(propriétaire)* owner (**de** of); *(gérant)* manager, *f* manageress; *(de bar)* landlord, *f* landlady **2** *nm Couture* pattern

**patronat** [patrɔna] *nm* employers ▪ **patronal, -e, -aux, -ales** *adj* employers'

**patrouille** [patruj] *nf* patrol ▪ **patrouiller** *vi* to patrol

**patte** [pat] *nf* (**a**) *(membre)* leg; *(de chat, de chien)* paw (**b**) *(languette)* tab; *(de poche)* flap ▪ **pattes** *nfpl (favoris)* sideburns

**pâturage** [patyraʒ] *nm* pasture

**paume** [pom] *nf* palm

**paupière** [popjɛr] *nf* eyelid

**paupiette** [popjɛt] *nf* **p. de veau** veal olive

**pause** [poz] *nf (arrêt)* break; *(en parlant)* pause

**pauvre** [povr] **1** *adj (personne, sol, excuse)* poor; *(meubles)* shabby; **p. en** *(calories)* low in; *(ressources)* low on **2** *nmf* poor man, *f* poor woman; **les pauvres** the poor ▪ **pauvreté** [-əte] *nf* poverty

**pavaner** [pavane] **se pavaner** *vpr* to strut about

**paver** [pave] *vt* to pave ▪ **pavé** *nm* paving stone

**pavillon** [pavijɔ̃] *nm* (**a**) *(maison)* detached house; *(d'hôpital)* wing; *(d'exposition)* pavilion (**b**) *(drapeau)* flag

**payable** [pejabl] *adj* payable

**paye** [pɛj] *nf* pay, wages ▪ **payement** *nm* = **paiement**

**payer** [peje] **1** *vt (personne, somme)* to pay; *(service, objet)* to pay for; *(récompenser)* to repay; **se faire p.** to get paid **2** *vi* to pay ▪ **payant, -e** [pejɑ̃, -ɑ̃t] *adj (hôte, spectateur)* paying

**pays** [pei] *nm* country; *(région)* region; **du p.** *(vin, gens)* local

**paysage** [peizaʒ] *nm* landscape, scenery

**paysan, -anne** [peizɑ̃, -an] **1** *nmf* farmer **2** *adj* **coutume paysanne** rural *or* country custom; **le monde p.** the farming community

**Pays-Bas** [peibɑ] *nmpl* **les P.** the Netherlands

**P-DG** [pedeʒe] *(abrév* **président-directeur général***) nm Br* (chairman and) managing director, *Am* chief executive officer

**péage** [peaʒ] *nm (droit)* toll; *(lieu)* tollbooth; **pont à p.** toll bridge; *TV* **chaîne à p.** pay channel

**peau, -x** [po] *nf* skin; *(de fruit)* peel, skin; *(cuir)* hide ▪ **Peau-Rouge** (*pl* **Peaux-Rouges**) *nmf* Red Indian

**péché** [peʃe] *nm* sin ▪ **pécher** *vi* to sin

**pêche**[1] [pɛʃ] *nf (activité)* fishing; *(poissons)* catch; **p. à la ligne** angling; **aller à la p.** to go fishing ▪ **pêcher** [peʃe] **1** *vt (attraper)* to catch; *(chercher à prendre)* to fish for **2** *vi* to fish ▪ **pêcheur** *nm* fisherman; *(à la ligne)* angler

**pêche**[2] [pɛʃ] *nf (fruit)* peach ▪ **pêcher** [peʃe] *nm (arbre)* peach tree

**pectoraux** [pektoro] *nmpl* chest muscles

**pédagogie** [pedagɔʒi] *nf (discipline)* pedagogy ▪ **pédagogique** *adj* educational ▪ **pédagogue** *nmf* teacher

**pédale** [pedal] *nf (de voiture, de piano)* pedal; **p. de frein** brake pedal

**Pédalo®** [pedalo] *nm* pedal boat, pedalo

**pédestre** [pedɛstr] *adj* **randonnée p.** hike

**pédiatre** [pedjatr] *nmf* paediatrician

**pédicure** [pedikyr] *nmf Br* chiropodist, *Am* podiatrist

**pègre** [pɛgr] *nf* **la p.** the underworld

**peigne** [pɛɲ] *nm* comb; **se donner un coup de p.** to give one's hair a comb ■ **peigner 1** *vt (cheveux)* to comb; **p. qn** to comb sb's hair **2 se peigner** *vpr* to comb one's hair

**peignoir** [pɛɲwar] *nm Br* dressing gown, *Am* bathrobe; **p. de bain** bathrobe

**peindre*** [pɛ̃dr] **1** *vt* to paint **2** *vi* to paint

**peine** [pɛn] *nf* (**a**) *(châtiment)* punishment; **p. de mort** death penalty; **p. de prison** prison sentence; **'défense d'entrer sous p. d'amende'** 'trespassers will be prosecuted'
(**b**) *(chagrin)* sorrow; **avoir de la p.** to be upset; **faire de la p. à qn** to upset sb
(**c**) *(effort)* trouble; *(difficulté)* difficulty; **se donner de la p.** *ou* **beaucoup de p.** to go to a lot of trouble (**pour faire** to do); **avec p.** with difficulty; **ça vaut la p. d'attendre** it's worth waiting; **ce n'est pas** *ou* **ça ne vaut pas la p.** it's not worth it
(**d**) **à p.** hardly, scarcely; **à p. arrivée, elle...** no sooner had she arrived than she... ■ **peiner 1** *vt* to upset **2** *vi* to labour

**peintre** [pɛ̃tr] *nm (artiste)* painter; **p. en bâtiment** painter and decorator ■ **peinture** *nf (tableau, activité)* painting; *(matière)* paint; **p. à l'huile** oil painting; **'p. fraîche'** 'wet paint'

**Pékin** [pekɛ̃] *nm ou f* Peking, Beijing

**pelage** [pəlaʒ] *nm* coat, fur

**pelé, -e** [pəle] *adj* bare

**peler** [pəle] **1** *vt* to peel **2** *vi (personne, peau)* to peel

**pelle** [pɛl] *nf* shovel; *(d'enfant)* spade; **p. à tarte** cake server

**pellicule** [pelikyl] *nf (pour photos)* film; *(couche)* thin layer; **pellicules** *(de cheveux)* dandruff

**pelote** [plɔt] *nf (de laine)* ball; *(à épingles)* pincushion; *Sport* **p. basque** pelota

**peloton** [p(ə)lɔtɔ̃] *nm (de ficelle)* ball; *(de cyclistes)* pack; *Mil* platoon; **p. d'exécution** firing squad

**pelotonner** [pəlɔtɔne] **se pelotonner** *vpr* to curl up (into a ball)

**pelouse** [pəluz] *nf* lawn

**peluche** [pəlyʃ] *nf (tissu)* plush; **(jouet en) p.** soft toy; **peluches** *(de pull)* fluff, lint

**pelure** [pəlyr] *nf (de légumes)* peelings; *(de fruits)* peel

**pénal, -e, -aux, -ales** [penal, -o] *adj* penal ■ **pénaliser** *vt* to penalize ■ **pénalité** *nf* penalty

**penalty** [penalti] *nm Sport* penalty

**penchant** [pɑ̃ʃɑ̃] *nm (préférence)* penchant (**pour** for); *(tendance)* propensity (**pour** for)

**penché, -e** [pɑ̃ʃe] *adj* leaning

**pencher** [pɑ̃ʃe] **1** *vt (objet)* to tilt; *(tête)* to lean **2** *vi (arbre)* to lean over **3 se pencher** *vpr* to lean over; **se p. par la fenêtre** to lean out of the window; **se p. sur qch** *(problème)* to examine sth

**pendaison** [pɑ̃dɛzɔ̃] *nf* hanging

**pendant¹** [pɑ̃dɑ̃] *prép (au cours de)* during; **p. deux mois** for two months; **p. tout le trajet** for the whole journey; **p. que...** while...

**pendant², -e 1** *adj* hanging; *(langue)* hanging out **2** *nm* **le p. de** the companion piece to

**pendentif** [pɑ̃dɑ̃tif] *nm (collier)* pendant

**penderie** [pɑ̃dri] *nf Br* wardrobe, *Am* closet

**pendre** [pɑ̃dr] **1** *vti* to hang (**à** from); **p. qn** to hang sb **2 se pendre** *vpr (se suicider)* to hang oneself; *(se suspendre)* to hang (**à** from) ■ **pendu, -e** *adj (objet)* hanging (**à** from)

**pendule** [pɑ̃dyl] **1** *nf* clock **2** *nm (balancier)* pendulum

**pénétrer** [penetre] **1** *vi* **p. dans** to enter; *(profondément)* to penetrate (into) **2** *vt (sujet: pluie)* to penetrate **3 se pénétrer** *vpr* **se p. d'une idée** to become convinced of an idea ▪ **pénétration** *nf* penetration

**pénible** [penibl] *adj (difficile)* difficult; *(douloureux)* painful, distressing; *(ennuyeux)* tiresome ▪ **péniblement** [-əmɑ̃] *adv* with difficulty

**péniche** [peniʃ] *nf* barge

**pénicilline** [penisilin] *nf* penicillin

**péninsule** [penɛ̃syl] *nf* peninsula

**pénitencier** [penitɑ̃sje] *nm* prison, *Am* penitentiary

**pensée** [pɑ̃se] *nf (idée)* thought; **à la p. de faire qch** at the thought of doing sth

**penser** [pɑ̃se] **1** *vi (réfléchir)* to think (**à** of *or* about); **p. à qn/qch** to think of *or* about sb/sth; **p. à faire qch** *(ne pas oublier)* to remember to do sth; **penses-tu!** what an idea!

**2** *vt (estimer)* to think (**que** that); *(concevoir)* to think out; **je pensais rester** I was thinking of staying; **que pensez-vous de...?** what do you think of *or* about...?; **p. du bien de qn/qch** to think highly of sb/sth ▪ **pensif, -ive** *adj* thoughtful, pensive

**pension** [pɑ̃sjɔ̃] *nf* (**a**) *(école)* boarding school; **mettre un enfant en p.** to send a child to boarding school (**b**) *(hôtel)* **p. de famille** boarding house; **p. complète** *Br* full board, *Am* American plan (**c**) *(allocation)* pension; **p. alimentaire** maintenance, alimony ▪ **pensionnaire** *nmf (élève, résident)* boarder ▪ **pensionnat** *nm* boarding school

**pente** [pɑ̃t] *nf* slope; **être en p.** to be sloping

**Pentecôte** [pɑ̃tkot] *nf Rel Br* Whitsun, *Am* Pentecost

**pénurie** [penyri] *nf* shortage (**de** of)

**pépé** [pepe] *nm* grandpa

**pépin** [pepɛ̃] *nm (de fruit) Br* pip, *Am* seed, pit

**pépinière** [pepinjɛr] *nf (pour plantes)* nursery

**pépite** [pepit] *nf (d'or)* nugget; **p. de chocolat** chocolate chip

**perçant, -e** [pɛrsɑ̃, -ɑ̃t] *adj (cri, froid)* piercing; *(vue)* sharp

**percée** [pɛrse] *nf (ouverture)* opening; *Mil, Sport & Tech* breakthrough

**perceptible** [pɛrsɛptibl] *adj* perceptible (**à** to)

**perception** [pɛrsɛpsjɔ̃] *nf* (**a**) *(bureau)* tax office; *(d'impôt)* collection (**b**) *(sensation)* perception

**percer** [pɛrse] **1** *vt (trouer)* to pierce; *(avec une perceuse)* to drill; *(trou, ouverture)* to make; *(abcès)* to lance; *(mystère)* to solve; **p. une dent** *(bébé)* to cut a tooth; **p. qch à jour** to see through sth **2** *vi (soleil)* to break through; *(abcès)* to burst; *(acteur)* to make a name for oneself ▪ **perceuse** *nf* drill

**percevoir*** [pɛrsəvwar] *vt* (**a**) *(sensation)* to perceive; *(son)* to hear (**b**) *(impôt)* to collect

**perche** [pɛrʃ] *nf (bâton)* pole

**percher** [pɛrʃe] **1** *vi (oiseau)* to perch **2 se percher** *vpr (oiseau, personne)* to perch

**percuter** [pɛrkyte] **1** *vt (véhicule)* to crash into **2** *vi* **p. contre** to crash into **3 se percuter** *vpr* to crash into each other

**perdant, -e** [pɛrdɑ̃, -ɑ̃t] **1** *adj* losing **2** *nmf* loser

**perdre** [pɛrdr] **1** *vt* to lose; *(habitude)* to get out of; **p. qn/qch de vue** to lose sight of sb/sth **2** *vi* to lose **3 se perdre** *vpr (s'égarer)* to get lost; *(disparaître)* to die out; **se p. dans les détails** to get lost in details ▪ **perdu, -e** *adj (égaré)* lost; *(gaspillé)* wasted; *(malade)* finished; *(lieu)* out-of-the-way

**père** [pɛr] *nm* father; **de p. en fils** from father to son; *Rel* **mon p.** father; **p. de famille** father

**péremption** [perɑ̃psjɔ̃] *nf* **date de p.** use-by date

**perfection** [pɛrfɛksjɔ̃] *nf* perfection; **à la p.** to perfection

**perfectionner** [pɛrfɛksjɔne] **1** *vt* to improve, to perfect **2 se perfectionner** *vpr* **se p. en anglais** to improve one's English ▪ **perfectionné, -e** *adj* advanced ▪ **perfectionnement** *nm* improvement (**de** in; **par rapport à** on); **cours de p.** proficiency course

**perfectionniste** [pɛrfɛksjɔnist] *nmf* perfectionist

**perforer** [pɛrfɔre] *vt (pneu, intestin)* to perforate; *(billet)* to punch; **carte perforée** punch card

**performance** [pɛrfɔrmɑ̃s] *nf* performance ▪ **performant, -e** *adj* highly efficient

**perfusion** [pɛrfyzjɔ̃] *nf* drip; **être sous p.** to be on a drip

**péril** [peril] *nm* danger, peril; **à tes risques et périls** at your own risk; **mettre qch en p.** to endanger sth ▪ **périlleux, -euse** *adj* dangerous, perilous

**périmé, -e** [perime] *adj (billet)* expired; *(nourriture)* past its sell-by date

**période** [perjɔd] *nf* period ▪ **périodique 1** *adj* periodic **2** *nm (revue)* periodical

**périphérie** [periferi] *nf (limite)* periphery; *(banlieue)* outskirts

**périphérique** [periferik] **1** *adj* peripheral; **radio p.** = radio station broadcasting from outside France **2** *nm & adj* **(boulevard) p.** *Br* ring road, *Am* beltway

**périr** [perir] *vi* to perish ▪ **périssable** *adj (denrée)* perishable

**perle** [pɛrl] *nf (bijou)* pearl; *(de bois, de verre)* bead

**permanent, -e** [pɛrmanɑ̃, -ɑ̃t] **1** *adj* permanent; *Cin (spectacle)* continuous; *(comité)* standing **2** *nf* **permanente** perm ▪ **permanence** *nf* permanence; *(salle d'étude)* study room; *(service, bureau)* duty office; **être de p.** to be on duty; **en p.** permanently

**perméable** [pɛrmeabl] *adj* permeable (**à** to)

**permettre*** [pɛrmɛtr] **1** *vt* to allow, to permit; **p. à qn de faire qch** to allow sb to do sth; **vous permettez?** may I? **2 se permettre** *vpr* **se p. de faire qch** to take the liberty of doing sth; **je ne peux pas me le p.** I can't afford it

**permis, -e** [pɛrmi, -iz] **1** *adj* allowed, permitted **2** *nm Br* licence, *Am* license, permit; **p. de conduire** *Br* driving licence, *Am* driver's license; **passer son p. de conduire** to take one's driving test

**permission** [pɛrmisjɔ̃] *nf* permission; *Mil* leave; *Mil* **en p.** on leave; **demander la p.** to ask permission (**de faire** to do)

**permuter** [pɛrmyte] **1** *vt (lettres, chiffres)* to transpose **2** *vi* to exchange posts

**Pérou** [peru] *nm* **le P.** Peru

**perpendiculaire** [pɛrpɑ̃dikylɛr] *adj & nf* perpendicular (**à** to)

**perpétrer** [pɛrpetre] *vt* to perpetrate

**perpétuel, -elle** [pɛrpetɥɛl] *adj* perpetual; *(membre)* permanent ▪ **perpétuer** *vt* to perpetuate ▪ **perpétuité** *adv* **à p.** in perpetuity; **condamnation à p.** life sentence

**perplexe** [pɛrplɛks] *adj* perplexed, puzzled

**perquisition** [pɛrkizisjɔ̃] *nf* search ▪ **perquisitionner** *vi* to make a search

**perron** [perɔ̃] *nm* steps *(leading to a building)*

**perroquet** [perɔkɛ] *nm* parrot

**perruche** [peryʃ] *nf Br* budgerigar, *Am* parakeet

**perruque** [peryk] *nf* wig

**persan, -e** [pɛrsɑ̃, -an] **1** *adj* Persian **2** *nm (langue)* Persian

**persécuter** [pɛrsekyte] *vt* to persecute ▪ **persécution** *nf* persecution

**persévérer** [pɛrsevere] *vi* to persevere (**dans** in) ▪ **persévérance** *nf* perseverance ▪ **persévérant, -e** *adj* persevering

**persil** [pɛrsi] *nm* parsley

**Persique** [pɛrsik] *adj* **le golfe P.** the Persian Gulf

**persister** [pɛrsiste] *vi* to persist (**à**

**faire** in doing; **dans qch** in sth) ▪ **persistance** *nf* persistence

**personnage** [pɛrsɔnaʒ] *nm (de fiction, individu)* character; *(personnalité)* important person; **p. célèbre** celebrity; **p. officiel** VIP

**personnaliser** [pɛrsɔnalize] *vt* to personalize; *(voiture)* to customize

**personnalité** [pɛrsɔnalite] *nf (caractère, personnage)* personality; **avoir de la p.** to have lots of personality

**personne** [pɛrsɔn] **1** *nf* person; **deux personnes** two people; **p. âgée** elderly person; **en p.** in person **2** *pron indéfini (de négation)* **(ne...) p.** nobody, no one; **je ne vois p.** I don't see anybody *or* anyone; **p. ne saura** nobody *or* no one will know

**personnel, -elle** [pɛrsɔnɛl] **1** *adj* personal; *(joueur, jeu)* individualistic **2** *nm (de firme, d'école)* staff; *(d'usine)* workforce; **manquer de p.** to be understaffed; **p. au sol** ground personnel

**personnifier** [pɛrsɔnifje] *vt* to personify ▪ **personnification** *nf* personification

**perspective** [pɛrspɛktiv] *nf (de dessin)* perspective; *(idée)* prospect (**de** of); *Fig (point de vue)* viewpoint; **perspectives d'avenir** future prospects

**perspicace** [pɛrspikas] *adj* shrewd ▪ **perspicacité** *nf* shrewdness

**persuader** [pɛrsɥade] *vt* **p. qn (de qch)** to persuade sb (of sth); **p. qn de faire qch** to persuade sb to do sth; **être persuadé de qch/que...** to be convinced of sth/that... ▪ **persuasif, -ive** *adj* persuasive ▪ **persuasion** *nf* persuasion

**perte** [pɛrt] *nf* loss; *(destruction)* ruin; **une p. de temps** a waste of time; **à p. de vue** as far as the eye can see; **vendre qch à p.** to sell sth at a loss

**pertinent, -e** [pɛrtinɑ̃, -ɑ̃t] *adj* relevant, pertinent ▪ **pertinemment** [-amɑ̃] *adv* **savoir qch p.** to know sth for a fact ▪ **pertinence** *nf* relevance, pertinence

**perturber** [pɛrtyrbe] *vt (trafic, cérémonie)* to disrupt; *(personne)* to disturb ▪ **perturbateur, -trice 1** *adj* disruptive **2** *nmf* troublemaker ▪ **perturbation** *nf* disruption

**péruvien, -enne** [peryvjɛ̃, -jɛn] **1** *adj* Peruvian **2** *nmf* **P., Péruvienne** Peruvian

**pervers, -e** [pɛrvɛr, -ɛrs] **1** *adj* perverse **2** *nmf* pervert ▪ **perversion** *nf* perversion ▪ **perversité** *nf* perversity ▪ **pervertir** *vt* to pervert

**pesant, -e** [pəzɑ̃, -ɑ̃t] **1** *adj* heavy, weighty **2** *nm* **valoir son p. d'or** to be worth one's weight in gold ▪ **pesanteur** *nf* heaviness; *Phys* gravity

**pesée** [pəze] *nf* weighing; *(pression)* force

**peser** [pəze] **1** *vt* to weigh **2** *vi* to weigh; **p. 2 kilos** to weigh 2 kilos; **p. lourd** to be heavy; *Fig (argument)* to carry weight; **p. sur** *(appuyer)* to press on; *(influer)* to bear upon; **p. sur qn** *(menace)* to hang over sb ▪ **pèse-personne** (*pl* **pèse-personnes**) *nm* (bathroom) scales

**pessimisme** [pesimism] *nm* pessimism ▪ **pessimiste 1** *adj* pessimistic **2** *nmf* pessimist

**pester** [peste] *vi* **p. contre qn/qch** to curse sb/sth

**pétale** [petal] *nm* petal

**pétanque** [petɑ̃k] *nf (jeu)* ≃ bowls

**pétard** [petar] *nm (feu d'artifice)* firecracker, *Br* banger

**pétiller** [petije] *vi (yeux, vin)* to sparkle ▪ **pétillant, -e** *adj (gazeux)* sparkling

**petit, -e** [pəti, -it] **1** *adj* small, little; *(taille, distance)* short; *(bruit, coup)* slight; *(somme)* small; *(accident)* minor; *(mesquin)* petty; **tout p.** tiny; **mon p. frère** my little brother

**2** *nmf* (little) boy, *f* (little) girl; *(personne)* small person; *Scol* junior; **petits** *(d'animal)* young; *(de chien)* pups; *(de chat)* kittens

**3** *adv* **écrire p.** to write small; **p. à p.** little by little ▪ **petite-fille** (*pl* **petites-filles**) *nf* granddaughter ▪ **petit-fils** (*pl*

**petits-fils**) *nm* grandson ▪ **petits-enfants** *nmpl* grandchildren

**pétition** [petisjɔ̃] *nf* petition

**pétrifier** [petrifje] *vt* to petrify

**pétrir** [petrir] *vt* to knead

**pétrole** [petrɔl] *nm* oil, petroleum ▪ **pétrolier, -ère 1** *adj* **industrie pétrolière** oil industry **2** *nm* oil tanker ▪ **pétrolifère** *adj* **gisement p.** oilfield

---

**PEU** [pø] **1** *adv (avec un verbe)* not much; *(avec un adjectif, un adverbe)* not very; *(un petit nombre)* few; **elle mange p.** she doesn't eat much; **p. intéressant/souvent** not very interesting/often; **p. ont compris** few understood; **p. de sel/de temps** not much salt/time, little salt/time; **p. de gens/de livres** few people/books; **p. à p.** little by little, gradually; **à p. près** more or less; **p. après/avant** shortly after/before; **sous p.** shortly; **pour p. que...** *(+ subjunctive)* if by chance...
**2** *nm* **un p.** a little, a bit; **un p. grand** a bit big; **un p. de fromage** a little cheese, a bit of cheese; **un (tout) petit p.** a (tiny) little bit; **le p. de fromage que j'ai** the little cheese I have; **reste encore un p.** stay a little longer

---

**peuplade** [pœplad] *nf* tribe

**peuple** [pœpl] *nm (nation, citoyens)* people; **les gens du p.** ordinary people

**peupler** [pœple] *vt (habiter)* to inhabit ▪ **peuplé, -e** *adj (région)* inhabited (**de** by); **très/peu p.** highly/sparsely populated

**peuplier** [pøplije] *nm (arbre, bois)* poplar

**peur** [pœr] *nf* fear; **avoir p.** to be afraid *or* frightened (**de qn/qch** of sb/sth; **de faire qch** to do sth *or* of doing sth); **faire p. à qn** to frighten *or* scare sb; **de p. qu'il ne parte** for fear that he would leave; **de p. de faire qch** for fear of doing sth ▪ **peureux, -euse** *adj* easily fearful

**peut** [pø] *voir* **pouvoir 1**

**peut-être** [pøtɛtr] *adv* perhaps, maybe; **p. qu'il viendra, p. viendra-t-il** perhaps *or* maybe he'll come; **p. que oui** perhaps; **p. que non** perhaps not

**peuvent, peux** [pœv, pø] *voir* **pouvoir 1**

**phare** [far] **1** *nm (pour bateaux)* lighthouse; *(de véhicule)* headlight; **faire un appel de phares** to flash one's lights **2** *adj* **épreuve-p.** star event

**pharmacie** [farmasi] *nf (magasin) Br* chemist, *Am* drugstore; *(armoire)* medicine cabinet ▪ **pharmaceutique** *adj* pharmaceutical ▪ **pharmacien, -enne** *nmf Br* chemist, pharmacist, *Am* druggist

**phase** [fɑz] *nf* phase

**phénomène** [fenɔmɛn] *nm* phenomenon

**philharmonique** [filarmɔnik] *adj* philharmonic

**Philippines** [filipin] *nfpl* **les P.** the Philippines

**philosophe** [filɔzɔf] **1** *nmf* philosopher **2** *adj* philosophical ▪ **philosopher** *vi* to philosophize (**sur** about) ▪ **philosophie** *nf* philosophy ▪ **philosophique** *adj* philosophical

**photo** [fɔto] **1** *nf (cliché)* photo; *(art)* photography; **prendre une p. de qn/qch, prendre qn/qch en p.** to take a photo of sb/sth; **p. d'identité** ID photo **2** *adj inv* **appareil p.** camera ▪ **photogénique** *adj* photogenic ▪ **photographe** *nmf* photographer ▪ **photographie** *nf (art)* photography; *(cliché)* photograph ▪ **photographier** *vt* to photograph; **se faire p.** to have one's photo taken ▪ **photographique** *adj* photographic

**photocopie** [fɔtɔkɔpi] *nf* photocopy ▪ **photocopier** *vt* to photocopy ▪ **photocopieur** *nm*, **photocopieuse** [fotokɔpjøz] *nf* photocopier

**Photomaton**® [fɔtɔmatɔ̃] *nm* photo booth

**phrase** [frɑz] *nf* sentence

**physicien, -enne** [fizisjɛ̃, -ɛn] *nmf* physicist

**physique** [fizik] **1** *adj* physical **2** *nm (de personne)* physique **3** *nf (science)* physics *(sing)*

**pianiste** [pjanist] *nmf* pianist

**piano** [pjano] *nm* piano; **p. droit/à queue** upright/grand piano ▪ **pianoter** *vi* **p. sur qch** *(table)* to drum one's fingers on sth

**pic** [pik] *nm (cime)* peak; *(outil)* pick(-axe); *(oiseau)* woodpecker; **couler à p.** to sink like a stone; **tomber à p.** *(falaise)* to go straight down; **p. à glace** ice pick

**pichet** [piʃɛ] *nm Br* jug, *Am* pitcher

**picorer** [pikɔre] *vt* to peck

**picoter** [pikɔte] *vt* **j'ai la gorge qui (me) picote** I've got a tickle in my throat

**pièce** [pjɛs] *nf (de maison)* room; *(morceau, objet)* piece; *(de pantalon)* patch; *(de dossier)* document; **p. (de monnaie)** coin; **p. (de théâtre)** play; **5 euros (la) p.** 5 euros each; **mettre qch en pièces** to tear sth to pieces; **p. d'identité** proof of identity; **pièces détachées** *ou* **de rechange** spare parts

**pied** [pje] *nm (de personne)* foot (*pl* feet); *(de lit, d'arbre, de colline)* foot; *(de meuble)* leg; *(de verre, de lampe)* base; **à p.** on foot; **aller à p.** to walk, to go on foot; **au p. de** at the foot *or* bottom of; **sur un p. d'égalité** on an equal footing; **avoir p.** to be within one's depth; **mettre qch sur p.** to set sth up

**piédestal, -aux** [pjedɛstal, -o] *nm* pedestal

**piège** [pjɛʒ] *nm (pour animal) & Fig* trap ▪ **piéger** *vt (animal)* to trap; *(voiture)* to booby-trap; **voiture/lettre piégée** car/letter bomb

**pierre** [pjɛr] *nf* stone; *(de bijou)* gem, stone; **p. précieuse** precious stone, gem ▪ **pierreries** *nfpl* gems, precious stones ▪ **pierreux, -euse** *adj* stony

**piétiner** [pjetine] **1** *vt* **p. qch** *(en trépignant)* to stamp on sth; *(en marchant)* to trample on sth **2** *vi (ne pas avancer)* to stand around; **p. d'impatience** to stamp one's feet impatiently

**piéton** [pjetɔ̃] *nm* pedestrian ▪ **piétonne, piétonnière** [pjetɔnjɛr] *adj f* **rue p.** pedestrian(ized) street; **zone p.** pedestrian precinct

**pigeon** [piʒɔ̃] *nm* pigeon

**pile** [pil] **1** *nf* (**a**) **p. (électrique)** battery; **radio à piles** battery radio (**b**) *(tas)* pile; **en p.** in a pile (**c**) *(de pièce)* **p. ou face?** heads or tails?; **jouer à p. ou face** to toss for it **2** *adv Fam* **s'arrêter p.** to stop dead; *Fam* **à deux heures p.** at two on the dot

**piler** [pile] *vt (broyer)* to crush; *(amandes)* to grind

**pilier** [pilje] *nm* pillar

**piller** [pije] *vt* to loot, to pillage ▪ **pillage** *nm* looting, pillaging

**pilon** [pilɔ̃] *nm (de poulet)* drumstick

**pilonner** [pilɔne] *vt (bombarder)* to bombard

**pilote** [pilɔt] **1** *nm (d'avion, de bateau)* pilot; *(de voiture)* driver; **p. automatique** automatic pilot; **p. de chasse** fighter pilot; **p. d'essai** test pilot; **p. de ligne** airline pilot **2** *adj* **usine(-)p.** pilot factory ▪ **pilotage** *nm* piloting ▪ **piloter** *vt (avion)* to fly, to pilot; *(bateau)* to pilot; *(voiture)* to drive

**pilule** [pilyl] *nf* pill; **prendre la p.** to be on the pill

**piment** [pimɑ̃] *nm* chilli ▪ **pimenté, -e** *adj (épicé)* spicy

**pin** [pɛ̃] *nm (arbre, bois)* pine; **pomme de p.** pine cone; *(de sapin)* fir cone

**pince** [pɛ̃s] *nf (outil)* pliers; *(sur vêtement)* dart; *(de crustacé)* pincer; **p. à épiler** tweezers; **p. à linge** (clothes) *Br* peg *or Am* pin

**pincé, -e** [pɛ̃se] *adj (air)* stiff; *(sourire)* tight-lipped

**pinceau, -x** [pɛ̃so] *nm* (paint)brush

**pincer** [pɛ̃se] **1** *vt* to pinch **2 se pincer** *vpr* **se p. le doigt** to get one's finger caught (**dans** in); **se p. le nez** to hold one's nose ▪ **pincée** *nf* pinch (**de** of)

**ping-pong** [piŋpɔ̃g] *nm* table tennis, Ping-Pong®

**pintade** [pɛ̃tad] *nf* guinea fowl

**pioche** [pjɔʃ] *nf (outil)* pick(axe); *Cartes* stock, pile ▪ **piocher** *vt (creuser)* to dig *(with a pick)*; **p. une carte** to draw a card

**pion** [pjɔ̃] *nm (au jeu de dames)* piece; *Échecs & Fig* pawn

**pionnier** [pjɔnje] *nm* pioneer

**pipe** [pip] *nf (de fumeur)* pipe

**pipeau, -x** [pipo] *nm (flûte)* pipe

**piquant, -e** [pikɑ̃, -ɑ̃t] **1** *adj (au goût)* spicy, hot; *(plante, barbe)* prickly; *(détail)* spicy **2** *nm (de plante)* prickle, thorn; *(d'animal)* spine

**pique** [pik] **1** *nm Cartes (couleur)* spades **2** *nf (allusion)* cutting remark; *(arme)* pike

**pique-nique** [piknik] (*pl* **pique-niques**) *nm* picnic ▪ **pique-niquer** *vi* to picnic

**piquer** [pike] **1** *vt (percer)* to prick; *(langue, yeux)* to sting; *(sujet: moustique)* to bite; **p. qch dans** *(enfoncer)* to stick sth into; **la fumée me pique les yeux** the smoke is making my eyes sting **2** *vi (moutarde)* to be hot **3** **se piquer** *vpr* to prick oneself; **se p. au doigt** to prick one's finger

**piquet** [pikɛ] *nm (pieu)* stake, post; *(de tente)* peg; **p. de grève** picket

**piqûre** [pikyr] *nf (d'abeille)* sting; *(de moustique)* bite; *(d'épingle)* prick; *(de tissu)* stitching; *(de rouille)* spot; *Méd* injection; **faire une p. à qn** to give sb an injection

**pirate** [pirat] **1** *nm (des mers)* pirate; **p. de l'air** hijacker; **p. informatique** hacker **2** *adj* **radio p.** pirate radio; **édition/CD p.** pirated edition/CD ▪ **pirater** *vt (enregistrement)* to pirate; *Ordinat* to hack

**pire** [pir] **1** *adj* worse (**que** than); **c'est de p. en p.** it's getting worse and worse **2** *nmf* **le/la p.** the worst (one); **le p. de tout** the worst thing of all; **au p.** at (the very) worst; **s'attendre au p.** to expect the (very) worst

**pirogue** [pirɔg] *nf* canoe, dugout

**pis**[1] [pi] *nm (de vache)* udder

**pis**[2] [pi] *adv* **aller de mal en p.** to go from bad to worse

**piscine** [pisin] *nf* swimming pool

**pistache** [pistaʃ] *nf* pistachio

**piste** [pist] *nf (traces)* track, trail; *(indices)* lead; *(de magnétophone) & Sport* track; *(de cirque)* ring; *(de ski)* run, piste; *(pour chevaux) Br* racecourse, *Am* racetrack; *Sport* **tour de p.** lap; **p. d'atterrissage** runway; **p. cyclable** *Br* cycle path, *Am* bicycle path; **p. de danse** dance floor

**pistolet** [pistɔlɛ] *nm* gun, pistol; *(de peintre)* spray gun; **p. à eau** water pistol

**pitié** [pitje] *nf* pity; **avoir de la p. pour qn** to pity sb; **il me fait p.** I feel sorry for him; **être sans p.** to be ruthless ▪ **pitoyable** *adj* pitiful ▪ **piteux, -euse** *adj* pitiful; **en p. état** in a sorry state

**piton** [pitɔ̃] *nm (d'alpiniste)* piton; **p. (rocheux)** (rocky) peak

**pittoresque** [pitɔrɛsk] *adj* picturesque

**pivoter** [pivɔte] *vi* to pivot, to swivel; **faire p. qch** to swivel sth round

**pizza** [pidza] *nf* pizza ▪ **pizzeria** *nf* pizzeria

**placard** [plakar] *nm (armoire) Br* cupboard, *Am* closet; **p. publicitaire** large display advertisement

**place** [plas] *nf (endroit, rang) & Sport* place; *(lieu public)* square; *(espace)* room; *(siège)* seat; *(emploi)* job, post; **à la p.** instead (**de** of); **à votre p.** in your place; **se mettre à la p. de qn** to put oneself in sb's position; **sur p.** on the spot; **en p.** *(objet)* in place; **mettre qch en p.** to put sth in place; **changer de p.** to change places; **faire de la p.** to make room (**à** for); **faire p. à qn/qch** to give way to sb/sth; **prendre p.** to take a seat; **p. de parking** parking space; **p. de train/bus** train/bus fare; **p. assise** seat

**placer** [plase] **1** *vt (mettre)* to put, to place; *(faire asseoir)* to seat; *(trouver un emploi à)* to place; *(argent)* to invest (**dans** in) **2** **se placer** *vpr (debout)* to stand; *(s'asseoir)* to sit ▪ **placé, -e** *adj (objet) & Sport* placed; **bien/mal p.**

**pour faire qch** well/badly placed to do sth ▪ **placement** *nm (d'argent)* investment

**plafond** [plafɔ̃] *nm* ceiling ▪ **plafonner** *vi (prix)* to peak; *(salaires)* to have reached a ceiling (**à** of) ▪ **plafonnier** *nm* ceiling light

**plage** [plaʒ] *nf (grève)* beach; *(surface)* area; *(de disque)* track; **p. de sable** sandy beach; **p. horaire** time slot

**plaider** [plede] *vti Jur (défendre)* to plead; **p. coupable** to plead guilty ▪ **plaidoyer** *nm Jur* speech for the *Br* defence *or Am* defense

**plaie** [plɛ] *nf (blessure)* wound

**plaindre*** [plɛ̃dr] **1** *vt* to feel sorry for, to pity **2 se plaindre** *vpr (protester)* to complain (**de** about; **que** that); **se p. de** *(douleur)* to complain of ▪ **plainte** *nf* complaint; *(gémissement)* moan; **porter p. contre qn** to lodge a complaint against sb

**plaine** [plɛn] *nf* plain

**plaintif, -ive** [plɛ̃tif, -iv] *adj* plaintive

**plaire*** [plɛr] **1** *vi* **elle me plaît** I like her; **ça me plaît** I like it **2** *v impersonnel* **il me plaît de le faire** I like doing it; **s'il vous/te plaît** please; **comme il vous plaira** as you like it **3 se plaire** *vpr (l'un l'autre)* to like each other; **se p. à Paris** to like it in Paris

**plaisance** [plɛzɑ̃s] *nf* **navigation de p.** yachting

**plaisant, -e** [plɛzɑ̃, -ɑ̃t] **1** *adj (drôle)* amusing; *(agréable)* pleasing **2** *nm* **mauvais p.** joker ▪ **plaisanter** *vi* to joke (**sur** about) ▪ **plaisanterie** *nf* joke; **par p.** for a joke ▪ **plaisantin** *nm* joker

**plaisir** [plɛzir] *nm* pleasure; **faire p. à qn** to please sb; **pour le p.** for the fun of it; **au p. (de vous revoir)** see you again sometime; **faites-moi le p. de...** would you be good enough to...

**plan** [plɑ̃] *nm (projet, dessin, organisation)* plan; *(de ville)* map; *Math* plane; **au premier p.** in the foreground; *Phot* **au second p.** in the background; **sur le p. politique, au p. politique** from the political viewpoint; **sur le même p.** on the same level; **de premier p.** of importance, major; *Phot & Cin* **gros p.** close-up; **p. d'eau** stretch of water; *Fin* **p. d'épargne** savings plan

**planche** [plɑ̃ʃ] *nf (en bois)* plank; *(plus large)* board; *(illustration)* plate; **faire la p.** to float on one's back; **p. à dessin** drawing board; **p. à roulettes** skateboard; **p. à voile** sailboard; **faire de la p. à voile** to go windsurfing

**plancher** [plɑ̃ʃe] *nm* floor

**planer** [plane] *vi (oiseau, planeur)* to glide

**planète** [planɛt] *nf* planet

**planeur** [planœr] *nm (avion)* glider

**planifier** [planifje] *vt* to plan

**plant** [plɑ̃] *nm (de plante)* seedling

**plantation** [plɑ̃tɑsjɔ̃] *nf (action)* planting; *(exploitation agricole)* plantation

**plante** [plɑ̃t] *nf Bot* plant; **jardin des plantes** botanical gardens; **p. du pied** sole (of the foot)

**planter** [plɑ̃te] *vt (fleur, arbre)* to plant; *(clou, couteau)* to drive in; *(tente)* to put up; *(mettre)* to put (**sur** on; **contre** against)

**plaque** [plak] *nf* plate; *(de verre, de métal)* sheet, plate; *(de verglas)* sheet; *(de marbre)* slab; *(de chocolat)* bar; *(commémorative)* plaque; *(sur la peau)* blotch; **p. chauffante** hotplate; *Aut* **p. minéralogique, p. d'immatriculation** *Br* number *or Am* license plate

**plaquer** [plake] **1** *vt (métal, bijou)* to plate; *(bois)* to veneer; *(cheveux)* to plaster down; *(au rugby)* to tackle; *(aplatir)* to flatten (**contre** against) **2 se plaquer** *vpr* **se p. contre** to flatten oneself against ▪ **plaqué, -e 1** *adj (bijou)* plated; **p. or** gold-plated **2** *nm* **p. or** gold plate

**plasma** [plasma] *nm Biol* plasma

**plastic** [plastik] *nm* plastic explosive ▪ **plastiquer** *vt* to bomb

**plastifier** [plastifje] *vt* to laminate

**plastique** [plastik] *adj & nm* plastic

**plat, -e** [pla, plat] **1** *adj* flat; *(mer)* calm,

smooth; *(ennuyeux)* flat, dull; **à p. ventre** flat on one's face; **à p.** *(pneu, batterie)* flat; **poser qch à p.** to lay sth (down) flat

**2** *nm* (**a**) *(de la main)* flat (**b**) *(récipient, nourriture)* dish; *(partie du repas)* course; **p. de résistance** main course ▪ **plate-bande** (*pl* **plates-bandes**) *nf* flower bed ▪ **plate-forme** (*pl* **plates-formes**) *nf* platform; **p. pétrolière** oil rig

**plateau, -x** [plato] *nm* tray; *(de balance)* pan; *TV & Cin* set; *Géog* plateau; **p. à fromages** cheeseboard

**platine**[1] [platin] **1** *nm (métal)* platinum **2** *adj inv* platinum; **blond p.** platinum blond

**platine**[2] [platin] *nf (d'électrophone, de magnétophone)* deck; **p. laser** CD player

**platitude** [platityd] *nf (propos)* platitude

**plâtre** [plɑtr] *nm (matière)* plaster; **un p.** *(de jambe cassée)* a plaster cast; **les plâtres** *(de maison)* the plasterwork ▪ **plâtrer** *vt (mur)* to plaster; *(membre)* to put in plaster

**plausible** [plozibl] *adj* plausible

**play-back** [plɛbak] *nm inv* **chanter en p.** to mime

**plein, -e** [plɛ̃, plɛn] **1** *adj (rempli, complet)* full; *(solide)* solid; **p. de** full of; **p. à craquer** full to bursting; **en pleine mer** out at sea, on the open sea; **en pleine figure** right in the face; **en pleine nuit** in the middle of the night; **en p. jour** in broad daylight; **en p. hiver** in the depths of winter; **en p. soleil** in the full heat of the sun; **être en p. travail** to be hard at work; **à la pleine lune** at full moon; **travailler à p. temps** to work full-time; **p. sud** due south; **p. tarif** full price; *(de transport)* full fare

**2** *adv* **de l'argent p. les poches** pockets full of money; **du chocolat p. la figure** chocolate all over one's face

**3** *nm Aut* **faire le p. (d'essence)** to fill up (the tank)

**pleurer** [plœre] **1** *vi* to cry, to weep (**sur** over) **2** *vt (personne)* to mourn (for) ▪ **pleurs** *mpl* **en p.** in tears

**pleuvoir*** [pløvwar] **1** *v impersonnel* to rain; **il pleut** it's raining; *Fig* **il pleut des cordes** it's raining cats and dogs **2** *vi (coups)* to rain down (**sur** on)

**Plexiglas**® [plɛksiglɑs] *nm Br* Perspex®, *Am* Plexiglas®

**pli** [pli] *nm* (**a**) *(de papier, de rideau, de la peau)* fold; *(de jupe, de robe)* pleat; *(de pantalon, de bouche)* crease; **(faux) p.** crease; **mise en plis** set *(hairstyle)* (**b**) *(enveloppe)* envelope; *(lettre)* letter (**c**) *Cartes* trick

**plier** [plije] **1** *vt (draps, vêtements)* to fold; *(parapluie)* to fold up; *(courber)* to bend; **p. bagages** to pack one's bags (and leave) **2** *vi (branche)* to bend **3 se plier** *vpr (lit, chaise)* to fold up; **se p. à** to submit to ▪ **pliable** *adj* foldable ▪ **pliage** *nm (manière)* fold; *(action)* folding ▪ **pliant, -e 1** *adj (chaise)* folding **2** *nm* folding stool

**plisser** [plise] *vt (lèvres)* to pucker; *(front)* to wrinkle; *(yeux)* to screw up ▪ **plissé, -e** *adj (jupe)* pleated

**plomb** [plɔ̃] *nm (métal)* lead; *(fusible) Br* fuse, *Am* fuze; *(pour rideau)* lead weight; **plombs** *(de chasse)* lead shot; *Fig* **de p.** *(sommeil)* heavy; *(soleil)* blazing

**plomber** [plɔ̃be] *vt (dent)* to fill; *(mettre des plombs à)* to weigh with lead ▪ **plombage** *nm (de dent)* filling

**plombier** [plɔ̃bje] *nm* plumber ▪ **plomberie** *nf (métier, installations)* plumbing

**plonger** [plɔ̃ʒe] **1** *vi (personne)* to dive (**dans** into); *(oiseau, avion)* to dive (**sur** onto) **2** *vt (enfoncer)* to plunge (**dans** into) **3 se plonger** *vpr* **se p. dans** *(lecture)* to immerse oneself in; **plongé dans l'obscurité** plunged in darkness ▪ **plongée** *nf* diving; *(de sous-marin)* dive; **p. sous-marine** skin *or* scuba diving ▪ **plongeoir** *nm* diving board ▪ **plongeon** *nm* dive; **faire un p.** to dive ▪ **plongeur, -euse** *nmf (nageur)* diver

**plu** [ply] *pp de* **plaire, pleuvoir**

**pluie** [plɥi] *nf* rain; **sous la p.** in the rain; **p. fine** drizzle

**plume** [plym] *nf (d'oiseau)* feather; *(de stylo)* nib ▪ **plumer** *vt (volaille)* to pluck

**plupart** [plypar] **la plupart** *nf* most; **la p. du temps** most of the time; **la p. d'entre eux** most of them; **pour la p.** mostly

**PLUS[1]** [ply] ([plyz] *before vowel*, [plys] *in end position*) *adv* (**a**) *(comparatif)* more (**que** than); **p. d'un kilo/de dix** more than a kilo/ten; **p. de thé** more tea; **p. beau/rapidement** more beautiful/quickly (**que** than); **p. tard** later; **p. petit** smaller; **de p. en p.** more and more; **de p. en p. vite** quicker and quicker; **p. ou moins** more or less; **en p.** in addition (**de** to); **au p.** at most; **de p.** more (**que** than); *(en outre)* moreover; **les enfants de p. de dix ans** children over ten; **j'ai dix ans de p. qu'elle** I'm ten years older than she is; **il est p. de cinq heures** it's after five (o'clock); **p. il crie, p. il s'enroue** the more he shouts, the more hoarse he gets

(**b**) *(superlatif)* **le p.** (the) most; **le p. beau** the most beautiful (**de** in); *(de deux)* the more beautiful; **le p. grand** the biggest (**de** in); *(de deux)* the bigger; **j'ai le p. de livres** I have (the) most books; **j'en ai le p.** I have the most

**PLUS[2]** [ply] *adv (négation)* **(ne...) p.** no more; **il n'a p. de pain** he has no more bread, he doesn't have any more bread; **il n'y a p. rien** there's nothing left; **elle ne le fait p.** she no longer does it, she doesn't do it any more *or* any longer; **je ne la reverrai p.** I won't see her again; **je ne voyagerai p. jamais** I'll never travel again

**plus[3]** [plys] **1** *conj* plus; **deux p. deux font quatre** two plus two are four; **il fait p. 2 (degrés)** it's 2 degrees above freezing **2** *nm* **le signe p.** the plus sign

**plusieurs** [plyzjœr] *adj & pron* several

**plutôt** [plyto] *adv* rather (**que** than)

**pluvieux, -euse** [plyvjø, -jøz] *adj* rainy, wet

**pneu** [pnø] (*pl* **pneus**) *nm (de roue) Br* tyre, *Am* tire ▪ **pneumatique** *adj (gonflable)* inflatable

**poche** [pɔʃ] *nf (de vêtement)* pocket; *(de kangourou)* pouch ▪ **pochette** *nf (sac)* bag; *(d'allumettes)* book; *(de disque)* sleeve; *(sac à main)* (clutch) bag; *(mouchoir)* pocket handkerchief

**pocher** [pɔʃe] *vt (œufs)* to poach

**poêle** [pwal] **1** *nm (chauffage)* stove **2** *nf* **p. (à frire)** frying pan

**poème** [pɔɛm] *nm* poem ▪ **poésie** *nf (art)* poetry; *(poème)* poem ▪ **poète** *nm* poet

**poids** [pwa] *nm* weight; *Sport* shot; **au p.** by weight; **prendre/perdre du p.** to gain/lose weight; **p. lourd** *(camion) Br* lorry, *Am* truck; *(en boxe)* heavyweight; **p. plume** *(en boxe)* featherweight

**poignant, -e** [pwaɲɑ̃, -ɑ̃t] *adj* poignant

**poignard** [pwaɲar] *nm* dagger; **coup de p.** stab ▪ **poignarder** *vt* to stab

**poignée** [pwaɲe] *nf (quantité)* handful (**de** of); *(de porte, de casserole)* handle; *(d'épée)* hilt; **p. de main** handshake

**poignet** [pwaɲɛ] *nm* wrist; *(de chemise)* cuff

**poil** [pwal] *nm* hair; *(pelage)* coat; **poils** *(de brosse)* bristles; *(de tapis)* pile; **p. à gratter** itching powder ▪ **poilu, -e** *adj* hairy

**poinçonner** [pwɛ̃sɔne] *vt (billet)* to punch; *(bijou)* to hallmark

**poing** [pwɛ̃] *nm* fist

**POINT** [pwɛ̃] *nm (lieu, score, question)* point; *(sur i, à l'horizon)* dot; *(tache)* spot; *(de notation)* mark; *(de couture)* stitch; **être sur le p. de faire qch** to be about to do sth; **à p.** *(steak)* medium; **déprimé au p. que...** depressed to such an extent that...; **mettre au p.** *(appareil photo)* to focus; *(moteur)* to tune; *(technique)* to perfect; **être au p.** to be up to scratch; **au p. où j'en suis...** at the stage I've reached...; **au plus haut p.** extremely; **p. de côté** stitch; **p. de départ** starting point; **p. de vue** *(opinion)* point of view, viewpoint; *(endroit)* viewing point; **p. faible/fort** weak/strong point

**pointe** [pwɛ̃t] *nf (extrémité)* tip, point; *(clou)* nail; *Géog* headland; *Fig (maximum)* peak; **une p. d'humour** a touch of humour; **sur la p. des pieds** on tiptoe; **en p.** pointed; **de p.** *(technologie, industrie)* state-of-the-art; **vitesse de p.** top speed; *Fig* **à la p. de** *(progrès)* in *or* at the forefront of; **faire des pointes** *(danseuse)* to dance on points; **p. de vitesse** burst of speed

**pointer** [pwɛ̃te] **1** *vt (cocher) Br* to tick off, *Am* to check (off); *(braquer)* to point (**sur/vers** at) **2** *vi (employé) (à l'arrivée)* to clock in; *(à la sortie)* to clock out

**pointillé** [pwɛ̃tije] *nm* dotted line

**pointu, -e** [pwɛ̃ty] *adj (en pointe)* pointed; *(voix)* shrill; *Fig (spécialisé)* specialized

**pointure** [pwɛ̃tyr] *nf* size

**poire** [pwar] *nf (fruit)* pear ▪ **poirier** *nm* pear tree

**poireau, -x** [pwaro] *nm* leek

**pois** [pwa] *nm (légume)* pea; *(dessin)* (polka) dot; **à p.** *(vêtement)* polka-dot; **petits p.** *Br* (garden) peas, *Am* peas; **p. de senteur** sweet pea; **p. chiche** chickpea

**poison** [pwazɔ̃] *nm* poison

**poisson** [pwasɔ̃] *nm* fish; **les Poissons** *(signe)* Pisces; **p. d'avril** April fool; **p. rouge** goldfish ▪ **poissonnerie** *nf* fish shop ▪ **poissonnier, -ère** *nmf* fishmonger

**poitrine** [pwatrin] *nf* chest; *(seins)* bust; *Culin (de veau)* breast

**poivre** [pwavr] *nm* pepper ▪ **poivrer** *vt* to pepper ▪ **poivrière** *nf* pepper pot

**poivron** [pwavrɔ̃] *nm* pepper

**pôle** [pol] *nm Géog* pole; **p. Nord/Sud** North/South Pole ▪ **polaire** *adj* polar

**polémique** [pɔlemik] **1** *adj* polemical **2** *nf* heated debate

**poli, -e** [pɔli] *adj (courtois)* polite (**avec** to *or* with); *(lisse)* polished

**police** [pɔlis] *nf* police; *Typ & Ordinat* **p. de caractères** font; **p. secours** emergency services ▪ **policier, -ère 1** *adj* **enquête policière** police inquiry; **roman p.** detective novel **2** *nm* policeman, detective

**polir** [pɔlir] *vt* to polish

**politesse** [pɔlitɛs] *nf* politeness

**politique** [pɔlitik] **1** *adj* political **2** *nf (activité, science)* politics *(sing)*; *(mesure)* policy; **faire de la p.** to be in politics **3** *nmf* politician ▪ **politicien, -enne** *nmf Péj* politician

**pollen** [pɔlɛn] *nm* pollen

**polluer** [pɔlɥe] *vt* to pollute ▪ **polluant** *nm* pollutant ▪ **pollueur, -euse 1** *adj* polluting **2** *nmf* polluter ▪ **pollution** *nf* pollution

**Pologne** [pɔlɔɲ] *nf* **la P.** Poland ▪ **polonais, -e 1** *adj* Polish **2** *nmf* **P., Polonaise** Pole **3** *nm (langue)* Polish

**polycopier** [pɔlikɔpje] *vt* to duplicate

**polyester** [pɔliɛstɛr] *nm* polyester

**polygame** [pɔligam] *adj* polygamous

**Polynésie** [pɔlinezi] *nf* **la P.** Polynesia

**polyvalent, -e** [pɔlivalɑ̃, -ɑ̃t] **1** *adj (salle)* multi-purpose; *(personne)* versatile **2** *adj & nf* **(école) polyvalente** *Br* = secondary school, *Am* = high school

**pommade** [pɔmad] *nf* ointment

**pomme** [pɔm] *nf* (**a**) *(fruit)* apple; *Anat* **p. d'Adam** Adam's apple; **p. de terre** potato; **pommes chips** *Br* (potato) crisps, *Am* (potato) chips; **pommes frites** *Br* chips, *Am* (French) fries; **pommes vapeur** steamed potatoes (**b**) *(d'arrosoir)* rose ▪ **pommier** *nm* apple tree

**pompe**[1] [pɔ̃p] **1** *nf (machine)* pump; **p. à essence** *Br* petrol *or Am* gas station; **p. à vélo** bicycle pump **2** *nfpl* **pompes funèbres** undertaker's; **entrepreneur des pompes funèbres** *Br* undertaker, *Am* mortician

**pompe**[2] [pɔ̃p] *nf* **en grande p.** with great ceremony

**pomper** [pɔ̃pe] **1** *vt (eau, air)* to pump; *(faire monter)* to pump up; *(évacuer)* to pump out **2** *vi* to pump

**pompeux, -euse** [pɔ̃pø, -øz] *adj* pompous

**pompier** [pɔ̃pje] *nm* fireman; **voiture des pompiers** fire engine

**pompiste** [pɔ̃pist] *nmf Br* petrol *or Am* gas station attendant

**ponce** [pɔ̃s] *nf* **pierre p.** pumice stone

**ponctuel, -elle** [pɔ̃ktɥɛl] *adj (à l'heure)* punctual; *(unique) Br* one-off, *Am* one-of-a-kind ▪ **ponctualité** *nf* punctuality

**ponctuer** [pɔ̃ktɥe] *vt* to punctuate (**de** with)

**pondre** [pɔ̃dr] *vt (œuf)* to lay

**poney** [pɔne] *nm* pony

**pont** [pɔ̃] *nm* bridge; *(de bateau)* deck; *Fig* **faire le p.** to make a long weekend of it ▪ **pont-levis** (*pl* **ponts-levis**) *nm* drawbridge

**populaire** [pɔpylɛr] *adj (personne, gouvernement)* popular; *(quartier, milieu)* working-class; *(expression)* vernacular ▪ **populariser** *vt* to popularize ▪ **popularité** *nf* popularity (**auprès de** with)

**population** [pɔpylɑsjɔ̃] *nf* population

**porc** [pɔr] *nm (animal)* pig; *(viande)* pork

**porcelaine** [pɔrsəlɛn] *nf* china, porcelain

**porche** [pɔrʃ] *nm* porch

**pornographie** [pɔrnɔgrafi] *nf* pornography

**port** [pɔr] *nm* (**a**) *(pour bateaux)* port, harbour; *Ordinat* port (**b**) *(d'armes)* carrying; *(de barbe)* wearing; *(prix)* carriage, postage; *(attitude)* bearing

**portable** [pɔrtabl] **1** *adj (ordinateur)* portable; *(téléphone)* mobile **2** *nm (ordinateur)* laptop; *(téléphone)* mobile

**portail** [pɔrtaj] *nm (de jardin)* gate; *(de cathédrale)* portal

**portant, -e** [pɔrtɑ̃, -ɑ̃t] *adj* **bien p.** in good health

**portatif, -ive** [pɔrtatif, -iv] *adj* portable

**porte** [pɔrt] *nf* door, *(de jardin, de ville, de slalom)* gate; **mettre qn à la p.** *(jeter dehors)* to throw sb out; *(renvoyer)* to fire sb; **p. d'embarquement** *(d'aéroport)* (departure) gate; **p. d'entrée** front door

**portée** [pɔrte] *nf* (**a**) *(de fusil)* range; *Fig* scope; **à la p. de qn** within reach of sb; **à p. de la main** within reach; **hors de p.** out of reach (**b**) *(animaux)* litter (**c**) *(impact)* significance (**d**) *Mus* stave

**portefeuille** [pɔrtəfœj] *nm Br* wallet, *Am* billfold; *(de ministre, d'actions)* portfolio

**portemanteau, -x** [pɔrtmɑ̃to] *nm (sur pied)* coat stand; *(crochet)* coat rack

**porter** [pɔrte] **1** *vt* to carry; *(vêtement, lunettes)* to wear; *(moustache, barbe)* to have; *(trace, responsabilité, fruits)* to bear; *(regard)* to cast; *(inscrire)* to enter; **p. qch à qn** to take/bring sth to sb; **p. bonheur/malheur** to bring good/bad luck; **p. son attention sur qch** to turn one's attention to sth; **tout (me) porte à croire que...** everything leads me to believe that...; **se faire p. malade** to report sick

**2** *vi (voix)* to carry; *(coup)* to strike home; **p. sur** *(concerner)* to be about

**3 se porter** *vpr (vêtement)* to be worn; **se p. bien** to be well; **comment te portes-tu?** how are you?; **se p. candidat** *Br* to stand *or Am* to run as a candidate ▪ **porté, -e** *adj* **p. à croire** inclined to believe; **p. sur qch** fond of sth ▪ **porte-bonheur** *nm inv* (lucky) charm ▪ **porte-clefs** *nm inv* key ring ▪ **porte-monnaie** *nm inv* purse ▪ **porte-parole** *nmf inv* spokesperson (**de** for) ▪ **porte-voix** *nm inv* megaphone

**porteur, -euse** [pɔrtœr, -øz] **1** *nm (de bagages)* porter **2** *nmf (malade)* carrier; *(de nouvelles, de chèque)* bearer

**portier** [pɔrtje] *nm* doorkeeper, porter ■ **portière** *nf (de véhicule, de train)* door ■ **portillon** *nm* gate

**portion** [pɔrsjɔ̃] *nf* portion

**Porto Rico** [pɔrtoriko] *nm ou f* Puerto Rico

**portrait** [pɔrtrɛ] *nm (peinture, dessin, photo)* portrait; *(description)* description; **faire le p. de qn** to do sb's portrait ■ **portrait-robot** *(pl* **portraits-robots***) nm* identikit picture, Photofit®

**Portugal** [pɔrtygal] *nm* **le P.** Portugal ■ **portugais, -e 1** *adj* Portuguese **2** *nmf* **P., Portugaise** Portuguese *inv*; **les P.** the Portuguese **3** *nm (langue)* Portuguese

**pose** [poz] *nf* (**a**) *(de rideau, de papier peint)* putting up; *(de moquette)* laying (**b**) *(pour photo, portrait)* pose; *Phot* exposure; **prendre la p.** to pose

**posé, -e** [poze] *adj (calme)* composed, staid

**poser** [poze] **1** *vt* to put down; *(papier peint, rideaux)* to put up; *(mine, moquette, fondations)* to lay; *(bombe)* to plant; *(conditions, principe)* to lay down; **p. qch sur qch** to put sth on sth; **p. une question à qn** to ask sb a question; **p. sa candidature** *(à une élection)* to put oneself forward as a candidate; *(à un emploi)* to apply (**à** for)

**2** *vi (modèle)* to pose (**pour** for)

**3 se poser** *vpr (oiseau, avion)* to land; *(problème, question)* to arise; **se p. sur** *(sujet: regard)* to rest on; **se p. des questions** to ask oneself questions

**positif, -ive** [pozitif, -iv] *adj* positive

**position** [pozisjɔ̃] *nf* position; *Fig* **prendre p.** to take a stand (**contre** against)

**posséder** [pɔsede] *vt (biens, talent)* to possess; *(sujet)* to have a thorough knowledge of; *(langue)* to have mastered ■ **possession** *nf* possession; **en p. de qch** in possession of sth; **prendre p. de qch** to take possession of sth

**possibilité** [pɔsibilite] *nf* possibility; **avoir la p. de faire qch** to have the chance *or* opportunity of doing sth

**possible** [pɔsibl] **1** *adj* possible (**à faire** to do); **il (nous) est p. de le faire** it is possible (for us) to do it; **il est p. que...** *(+ subjunctive)* it is possible that...; **si p.** if possible; **le plus tôt p.** as soon as possible; **autant que p.** as far as possible; **le plus p.** as much/as many as possible; **le moins de détails p.** as few details as possible **2** *nm* **faire (tout) son p.** to do one's utmost (**pour faire** to do)

**postal, -e, -aux, -ales** [pɔstal, -o] *adj* postal; *(train)* mail

**poste**[1] [pɔst] *nf (service)* mail, *Br* post; *(bureau)* post office; **la P.** the postal services; **par la p.** by mail, *Br* by post; **p. aérienne** airmail; **p. restante** *Br* poste restante, *Am* general delivery

**poste**[2] [pɔst] *nm* (**a**) *(lieu, emploi)* post; **être à son p.** to be at one's post; **p. d'essence** *Br* petrol *or Am* gas station; **p. d'incendie** fire point; **p. de police** police station; **p. de secours** first-aid post (**b**) **p. (de radio/télévision)** radio/television set (**c**) *(de standard)* extension

**poster**[1] [pɔste] *vt (lettre)* to mail, *Br* to post

**poster**[2] [pɔste] **1** *vt (sentinelle, troupes)* to post, to station **2 se poster** *vpr* to take up a position

**poster**[3] [pɔstɛr] *nm* poster

**postérieur, -e** [pɔsterjœr] *adj (dans le temps)* later; *(de derrière)* back; **p. à** after

**postérité** [pɔsterite] *nf* posterity

**postier, -ère** [pɔstje, -ɛr] *nmf* postal worker

**postillonner** [pɔstijɔne] *vi* to splutter

**postuler** [pɔstyle] **1** *vt Math* to postulate **2** *vi* **p. à un emploi** to apply for a job ■ **postulant, -e** *nmf* applicant (**à** for)

**posture** [pɔstyr] *nf* posture

**pot** [po] *nm* pot; *(en verre)* jar; *(de bébé)* potty; **p. d'échappement** *Br* exhaust pipe, *Am* tail pipe

**potable** [pɔtabl] *adj* drinkable; **eau p.** drinking water

**potage** [pɔtaʒ] *nm* soup

**potager, -ère** [pɔtaʒe, -ɛr] **1** *adj* **jardin p.** vegetable garden; **plante potagère** vegetable **2** *nm* vegetable garden

**pot-au-feu** [pɔtofø] *nm inv* = boiled beef with vegetables

**pot-de-vin** [podvɛ̃] (*pl* **pots-de-vin**) *nm* bribe

**poteau, -x** [pɔto] *nm* post; **p. électrique** electricity pylon; **p. indicateur** signpost; **p. télégraphique** telegraph pole

**potelé, -e** [pɔtle] *adj* plump, chubby

**potence** [pɔtɑ̃s] *nf (gibet)* gallows *(sing)*

**potentiel, -elle** [pɔtɑ̃sjɛl] *adj & nm* potential

**poterie** [pɔtri] *nf (art, objets)* pottery; *(objet)* piece of pottery ▪ **potier, -ère** *nmf* potter

**potion** [posjɔ̃] *nf* potion

**potiron** [pɔtirɔ̃] *nm* pumpkin

**pot-pourri** [popuri] (*pl* **pots-pourris**) *nm (chansons)* medley

**pou, -x** [pu] *nm* louse (*pl* lice)

**poubelle** [pubɛl] *nf Br* dustbin, *Am* garbage can; **mettre qch à la p.** to throw sth out

**pouce** [pus] *nm (doigt)* thumb

**poudre** [pudr] *nf (poussière, explosif)* powder; **en p.** *(lait)* powdered; *(chocolat)* drinking; **p. à récurer** scouring powder ▪ **poudrer 1** *vt* to powder **2 se poudrer** *vpr* to powder one's face ▪ **poudreux, -euse 1** *adj* powdery **2** *nf* **poudreuse** *(neige)* powder snow

**poulain** [pulɛ̃] *nm* foal

**poule**[1] [pul] *nf (animal)* hen; *Culin* fowl

**poule**[2] [pul] *nf (groupe)* group

**poulet** [pulɛ] *nm (animal)* chicken

**poulie** [puli] *nf* pulley

**pouls** [pu] *nm Méd* pulse; **prendre le p. de qn** to take sb's pulse

**poumon** [pumɔ̃] *nm* lung; **à pleins poumons** *(respirer)* deeply

**poupée** [pupe] *nf* doll

**POUR** [pur] **1** *prép* for; **p. toi/moi** for you/me; **faites-le p. lui** do it for him, do it for his sake; **partir p. Paris/l'Italie** to leave for Paris/Italy; **elle part p. cinq ans** she's leaving for five years; **elle est p.** she's all for it, she's in favour of it; **p. faire qch** (in order) to do sth; **p. que tu le voies** so (that) you may see it; **p. quoi faire?** what for?; **assez grand p. faire qch** big enough to do sth; **p. affaires** on business; **p. cela** for that reason; **p. ma part** as for me; **jour p. jour/heure p. heure** to the day/hour; **dix p. cent** ten percent

**2** *nm* **le p. et le contre** the pros and cons

**pourboire** [purbwar] *nm* tip

**pourcentage** [pursɑ̃taʒ] *nm* percentage

**pourchasser** [purʃase] *vt* to pursue

**pourparlers** [purparle] *nmpl* negotiations, talks

**pourquoi** [purkwa] **1** *adv & conj* why; **p. pas?** why not? **2** *nm inv* reason (**de** for); **le p. et le comment** the whys and wherefores

**pourra, pourrait** [pura, purɛ] *voir* **pouvoir 1**

**pourrir** [purir] *vti* to rot ▪ **pourri, -e** *adj (fruit, temps)* rotten ▪ **pourriture** *nf* rot

**poursuite** [pursɥit] **1** *nf (chasse)* pursuit; *(continuation)* continuation; **se lancer à la p. de qn** to set off in pursuit of sb **2** *nfpl Jur* **poursuites (judiciaires)** legal proceedings (**contre** against); **engager des poursuites contre qn** to start proceedings against sb

**poursuivre*** [pursɥivr] **1** *vt (chercher à atteindre)* to pursue; *(sujet: idée, crainte)* to haunt; *(sujet: malchance)* to dog; *(harceler)* to pester; *(continuer)* to continue, to go on with; *Jur* **p. qn (en justice)** to bring proceedings against sb; *(au criminel)* to prosecute sb **2 se poursuivre** *vpr* to continue, to go on

**pourtant** [purtɑ̃] *adv* yet, nevertheless; **et p.** and yet

**pourtour** [purtur] *nm* perimeter

**pourvoir*** [purvwar] **1** *vt* to provide (**de** with); **être pourvu de** to be provided with **2** *vi* **p. à** *(besoins)* to provide for **3 se pourvoir** *vpr Jur* **se p. en cassation** to take one's case to the Court of Appeal ▪ **pourvoyeur, -euse** *nmf* supplier

**pourvu** [purvy] **pourvu que** *conj* (**a**) *(condition)* provided (that) (**b**) *(souhait)* **p. qu'elle soit là!** I just hope (that) she's there!

**pousse** [pus] *nf (croissance)* growth; *(bourgeon)* shoot, sprout

**poussée** [puse] *nf (pression)* pressure; *(coup)* push; *(d'ennemi)* thrust, push; *(de fièvre)* outbreak

**pousser** [puse] **1** *vt (presser)* to push; *(moteur)* to drive hard; **p. qn à qch** to drive sb to sth; **p. qn à faire qch** *(sujet: faim)* to drive sb to do sth; *(sujet: personne)* to urge sb to do sth; **p. un cri** to shout; **p. un soupir** to sigh

**2** *vi (presser)* to push; *(croître)* to grow; **faire p. qch** *(plante)* to grow sth; **se laisser p. les cheveux** to let one's hair grow

**3 se pousser** *vpr (pour faire de la place)* to move over ▪ **poussé, -e** *adj (études)* thorough

**poussette** [puset] *nf Br* pushchair, *Am* stroller

**poussière** [pusjɛr] *nf* dust; **une p.** a speck of dust ▪ **poussiéreux, -euse** *adj* dusty

**poussin** [pusɛ̃] *nm (animal)* chick

**poutre** [putr] *nf (en bois)* beam; *(en acier)* girder

**POUVOIR*** [puvwar] **1** *v aux (être capable de)* can, to be able to; *(avoir la permission)* can, may, to be allowed; **tu peux entrer** you may *or* can come in

**2** *v impersonnel* **il peut neiger** it may snow; **il se peut qu'elle parte** she might leave

**3** *nm (puissance, attributions)* power; **au p.** *(parti)* in power; **p. d'achat** purchasing power; **les pouvoirs publics** the authorities

**poux** [pu] *pl de* **pou**

**prairie** [preri] *nf* meadow

**praline** [pralin] *nf* praline

**pratique** [pratik] **1** *adj (méthode, personne)* practical; *(outil)* handy **2** *nf (application, procédé, coutume)* practice; *(expérience)* practical experience; **la p. de la natation/du golf** swimming/golfing; **mettre qch en p.** to put sth into practice; **dans la p.** *(en réalité)* in practice ▪ **pratiquement** *adv (presque)* practically; *(en réalité)* in practice

**pratiquer** [pratike] **1** *vt (religion) Br* to practise, *Am* to practice; *(activité)* to take part in; *(langue)* to use; *(sport)* to play; **p. la natation** to go swimming **2** *vi (médecin, avocat) Br* to practise, *Am* to practice ▪ **pratiquant, -e 1** *adj* practising **2** *nmf* practising Christian/Jew/Muslim/*etc*

**pré** [pre] *nm* meadow

**préalable** [prealabl] **1** *adj* prior, previous; **p. à** prior to **2** *nm* precondition, prerequisite; **au p.** beforehand

**préavis** [preavi] *nm* (advance) notice (**de** of); **p. de grève** strike notice; **p. de licenciement** notice of dismissal

**précaire** [prekɛr] *adj* precarious; *(santé)* delicate ▪ **précarité** *nf* precariousness; **p. de l'emploi** lack of job security

**précaution** [prekosjɔ̃] *nf (mesure)* precaution; *(prudence)* caution; **par p.** as a precaution; **pour plus de p.** to be on the safe side; **prendre des précautions** to take precautions

**précédent, -e** [presedɑ̃, -ɑ̃t] **1** *adj* previous **2** *nmf* previous one **3** *nm* precedent; **sans p.** unprecedented ▪ **précéder** *vti* to precede

**prêcher** [preʃe] *vti* to preach

**précieux, -euse** [presjø, -øz] *adj* precious

**précipice** [presipis] *nm* chasm, abyss; *(de ravin)* precipice

**précipiter** [presipite] **1** *vt (hâter)* to hasten; *(jeter)* to hurl down **2 se précipiter** *vpr (se jeter)* to rush (**vers/sur**

towards/at); *(se hâter)* to rush; **les événements se sont précipités** things started happening quickly ▪ **précipitamment** [-amɑ̃] *adv* hastily ▪ **précipitation** *nf* haste; **précipitations** *(pluie)* precipitation ▪ **précipité, -e** *adj* hasty

**précis, -e** [presi, -iz] **1** *adj* precise, exact; *(mécanisme)* accurate, precise; **à deux heures précises** at two o'clock sharp *or* precisely **2** *nm (résumé)* summary; *(manuel)* handbook ▪ **précision** *nf* precision; *(de mécanisme, d'information)* accuracy; *(détail)* detail; **donner des précisions sur qch** to give precise details about sth; **demander des précisions sur qch** to ask for further information about sth

**préciser** [presize] **1** *vt* to specify (**que** that) **2 se préciser** *vpr* to become clear(er)

**précoce** [prekɔs] *adj (fruit, été)* early; *(enfant)* precocious

**préconiser** [prekɔnize] *vt* to advocate (**que** that)

**précurseur** [prekyrsœr] **1** *nm* forerunner, precursor **2** *adj* **signe p.** forewarning

**prédécesseur** [predesesœr] *nm* predecessor

**prédestiné, -e** [predestine] *adj* predestined (**à faire** to do)

**prédilection** [predilɛksjɔ̃] *nf* predilection; **de p.** favourite

**prédire*** [predir] *vt* to predict (**que** that) ▪ **prédiction** *nf* prediction

**prédisposer** [predispoze] *vt* to predispose (**à qch** to sth; **à faire** to do) ▪ **prédisposition** *nf* predisposition (**à** to)

**préfabriqué, -e** [prefabrike] *adj* prefabricated

**préface** [prefas] *nf* preface (**de** to)

**préfecture** [prefɛktyr] *nf* prefecture; **la P. de police** police headquarters

**préférable** [preferabl] *adj* preferable (**à** to)

**préférence** [preferɑ̃s] *nf* preference (**pour** for); **de p.** preferably; **de p. à** in preference to ▪ **préférentiel, -elle** *adj* preferential

**préférer** [prefere] *vt* to prefer (**à** to); **p. faire qch** to prefer to do sth; **je préférerais rester** I would rather stay, I would prefer to stay ▪ **préféré, -e** *adj & nmf* favourite

**préfet** [prefɛ] *nm* prefect *(chief administrator in a 'département')*; **p. de police** = chief commissioner of police

**préhistorique** [preistɔrik] *adj* prehistoric

**préjudice** [preʒydis] *nm (à une cause)* prejudice; *(à une personne)* harm; **porter p. à qn** to do sb harm

**préjugé** [preʒyʒe] *nm* prejudice; **avoir des préjugés** to be prejudiced (**contre** against)

**prélasser** [prelɑse] **se prélasser** *vpr* to lounge

**prélever** [prel(ə)ve] *vt (échantillon)* to take (**sur** from); *(somme)* to deduct (**sur** from) ▪ **prélèvement** *nm (d'échantillon)* taking; *(de somme)* deduction; **p. automatique** *Br* direct debit, *Am* automatic deduction; **prélèvements obligatoires** = tax and social security contributions

**préliminaire** [preliminɛr] **1** *adj* preliminary **2** *nmpl* **préliminaires** preliminaries

**prélude** [prelyd] *nm* prelude (**à** to)

**prématuré, -e** [prematyre] **1** *adj* premature **2** *nmf* premature baby

**préméditer** [premedite] *vt* to premeditate ▪ **préméditation** *nf* premeditation; **meurtre avec p.** premeditated murder

**premier, -ère** [prəmje, -ɛr] **1** *adj* first; *(enfance)* early; *(page de journal)* front; *(qualité)* prime; *(état)* original; *(danseuse, rôle)* leading; *(marche)* bottom; **le p. rang** the front row; **les trois premiers mois** the first three months; **à la première occasion** at the earliest opportunity; **en p.** firstly; **P. ministre** Prime Minister

**2** *nm (étage) Br* first *or Am* second floor; **le p. juin** June the first; **le p. de l'an** New Year's Day

**3** *nmf* first (one); **arriver le p.** *ou* **en p.** to arrive first

**4** *nf* **première** *(wagon, billet)* first class; *(vitesse)* first (gear); *(événement historique)* first; *(de chaussure)* insole; *Théât* opening night; *Cin* première; *Scol Br* ≃ lower sixth, *Am* ≃ eleventh grade

**prémonition** [premɔnisjɔ̃] *nf* premonition

**prénatal, -e, -als, -ales** [prenatal] *adj Br* antenatal, *Am* prenatal

**PRENDRE*** [prɑ̃dr] **1** *vt* to take (**à qn** from sb); *(attraper)* to catch; *(repas, boisson, douche)* to have; *(nouvelles)* to get; *(air)* to put on; *(bonne)* to take on; **p. qch dans un tiroir** to take sth out of a drawer; **p. qn pour** to take sb for; **p. feu** to catch fire; **p. du temps/une heure** to take time/an hour; **p. de la place** to take up room; **p. du poids/de la vitesse** to put on weight/gather speed; **p. l'eau** *(bateau, chaussure)* to be leaking

**2** *vi (feu)* to catch; *(ciment, gelée)* to set; *(greffe, vaccin, plante)* to take; *(mode)* to catch on; **p. sur soi** to restrain oneself

**3 se prendre** *vpr (médicament)* to be taken; *(s'accrocher)* to get caught; **se p. les pieds dans qch** to get one's feet caught in sth; **s'y p. bien avec qn** to know how to handle sb; **s'en p. à qn** to take it out on sb

**prénom** [prenɔ̃] *nm* first name ▪ **prénommer** *vt* to name; **il se prénomme Daniel** his first name is Daniel

**préoccuper** [preɔkype] **1** *vt (inquiéter)* to worry **2 se préoccuper** *vpr* **se p. de qn/qch** to concern oneself with sb/sth ▪ **préoccupant, -e** *adj* worrying ▪ **préoccupation** *nf* preoccupation, concern ▪ **préoccupé, -e** *adj* worried (**par** about)

**préparatifs** [preparatif] *nmpl* preparations (**de** for) ▪ **préparation** *nf* preparation ▪ **préparatoire** *adj* preparatory

**préparer** [prepare] **1** *vt* to prepare (**qch pour** sth for); *(examen)* to study for; **p. qch à qn** to prepare sth for sb; **plats tout préparés** ready-cooked meals

**2 se préparer** *vpr (être imminent)* to be in the offing; *(s'apprêter)* to prepare oneself (**à** *ou* **pour qch** for sth); **se p. à faire qch** to prepare to do sth; **se p. qch** *(boisson)* to make oneself sth

**préposé, -e** [prepoze] *nmf* employee; *(facteur)* postman, *f* postwoman

**préretraite** [prerətrɛt] *nf* early retirement

**près** [prɛ] *adv* **p. de qn/qch** near sb/sth, close to sb/sth; **p. de deux ans** nearly two years; **p. de partir** about to leave; **tout p.** nearby (**de qn/qch** sb/sth), close by (**de qn/qch** sb/sth); **de p.** *(suivre, examiner)* closely; **à peu de chose p.** more or less; **à cela p.** except for that; **voici le chiffre à un euro p.** here is the figure, give or take a euro; **calculer au euro p.** to calculate to the nearest euro

**présage** [prezaʒ] *nm* omen, sign ▪ **présager** *vt* **ça ne présage rien de bon** it doesn't bode well

**presbyte** [prɛsbit] *adj* long-sighted

**presbytère** [prɛsbitɛr] *nm* presbytery

**prescrire*** [preskrir] *vt (médicament)* to prescribe ▪ **prescription** *nf (ordonnance)* prescription

**présence** [prezɑ̃s] *nf* presence; *(à l'école)* attendance (**à** at); **en p. de** in the presence of; **faire acte de p.** to put in an appearance; **p. d'esprit** presence of mind

**présent, -e** [prezɑ̃, -ɑ̃t] **1** *adj (non absent, actuel)* present **2** *nm (temps)* present; **à p.** at present, now; **dès à p.** as from now

**présenter** [prezɑ̃te] **1** *vt (montrer)* to show, to present; *(facture)* to submit; *(arguments)* to present; **p. qn à qn** to introduce sb to sb

**2 se présenter** *vpr (dire son nom)* to introduce oneself (**à** to); *(chez qn)* to show up; *(occasion)* to arise; **se p. à**

*(examen)* to take, *Br* to sit for; *(élections)* to run in; *(emploi)* to apply for; *(autorités)* to report to; **ça se présente bien** it looks promising ■ **présentable** *adj* presentable ■ **présentateur, -trice** *nmf* presenter ■ **présentation** *nf* presentation; *(de personnes)* introduction; **faire les présentations** to make the introductions; **p. de mode** fashion show

**préserver** [prezɛrve] *vt* to protect, to preserve (**de** from) ■ **préservation** *nf* protection, preservation

**présidence** [prezidɑ̃s] *nf (de nation)* presidency; *(de firme)* chairmanship ■ **président, -e** *nmf (de nation)* president; *(de firme)* chairman, *f* chairwoman; **p.-directeur général** *Br* (chairman and) managing director, *Am* chief executive officer; **p. du jury** *(d'examen)* chief examiner; *(de tribunal)* foreman of the jury ■ **présidentiel, -elle** *adj* presidential

**présider** [prezide] *vt (réunion)* to chair; *(conseil)* to preside over

**presque** [prɛsk] *adv* almost, nearly; **p. jamais/rien** hardly ever/anything

**presqu'île** [prɛskil] *nf* peninsula

**pressant, -e** [prɛsɑ̃, -ɑ̃t] *adj* urgent, pressing

**presse** [prɛs] *nf Tech* press; *Typ* (printing) press; **la p.** *(journaux)* the press

**pressé, -e** [prese] *adj (personne)* in a hurry; *(air)* hurried

**pressentir*** [presɑ̃tir] *vt (deviner)* to sense (**que** that) ■ **pressentiment** *nm* presentiment; *(de malheur)* foreboding

**pressing** [presiŋ] *nm* dry cleaner's

**pression** [prɛsjɔ̃] *nf Tech* pressure; *(bouton)* snap (fastener); **faire p. sur qn** to put pressure on sb, to pressurize sb

**pressuriser** [presyrize] *vt (avion)* to pressurize

**prestataire** [prɛstatɛr] *nmf Ordinat* **p. d'accès** access provider

**prestation** [prɛstɑsjɔ̃] *nf* (**a**) *(allocation)* benefit; **prestations** *(services)* services; **prestations sociales** *Br* social security benefits, *Am* welfare payments (**b**) *(de comédien)* performance

**prestidigitateur, -trice** [prɛstidiʒitatœr, -tris] *nmf* conjurer ■ **prestidigitation** *nf* **tour de p.** conjuring trick

**prestige** [prɛstiʒ] *nm* prestige ■ **prestigieux, -euse** *adj* prestigious

**présumer** [prezyme] *vt* to presume (**que** that); **p. de qch** to overestimate sth

**prêt[1], -e** [prɛ, prɛt] *adj (préparé)* ready (**à faire** to do; **à qch** for sth); **être fin p.** to be all set ■ **prêt-à-porter** *nm* ready-to-wear clothes

**prêt[2]** [prɛ] *nm (somme)* loan

**prétendre** [pretɑ̃dr] **1** *vt (déclarer)* to claim (**que** that); *(vouloir)* to intend (**faire** to do); **à ce qu'il prétend** according to him **2** *vi* **p. à** *(titre)* to lay claim to **3 se prétendre** *vpr* to claim to be ■ **prétendu, -e** *adj (progrès)* so-called; *(coupable)* alleged

**prétentieux, -euse** [pretɑ̃sjø, -øz] *adj* pretentious ■ **prétention** *nf (vanité)* pretension; *(revendication, ambition)* claim; **sans p.** *(film, robe)* unpretentious

**prêter** [prete] **1** *vt (argent, objet)* to lend (**à** to); *(aide)* to give (**à** to); *(propos, intention)* to attribute (**à** to); **p. attention** to pay attention (**à** to); **p. serment** to take an oath; **p. main-forte à qn** to lend sb a hand **2** *vi* **p. à confusion** to give rise to confusion **3 se prêter** *vpr* **se p. à** *(consentir)* to agree to; *(convenir)* to lend itself to

**prétexte** [pretɛkst] *nm* excuse, pretext; **sous p. de/que** on the pretext of/that; **sous aucun p.** under no circumstances ■ **prétexter** *vt* to plead (**que** that)

**prêtre** [prɛtr] *nm* priest

**preuve** [prœv] *nf* piece of evidence; **preuves** evidence; **faire p. de qch** to prove sth; **faire p. de courage** to show courage; **faire ses preuves** *(personne)* to prove oneself; *(méthode)* to be tried and tested

**prévaloir*** [prevalwar] *vi* to prevail (**sur** over)

**prévenant, -e** [prevnɑ̃, -ɑ̃t] *adj* considerate

**prévenir*** [prevnir] *vt* (**a**) *(mettre en garde)* to warn; *(aviser)* to inform (**de** of *or* about) (**b**) *(maladie)* to prevent; *(accident)* to avert ▪ **préventif, -ive** *adj* preventive ▪ **prévention** *nf* prevention; **p. routière** road safety

**prévisible** [previzibl] *adj* foreseeable

**prévision** [previzjɔ̃] *nf* forecast; **en p. de** in expectation of; **prévisions météorologiques** weather forecast

**prévoir*** [prevwar] *vt (météo)* to forecast; *(difficultés, retard, réaction)* to expect; *(organiser)* to plan; **la réunion est prévue pour demain** the meeting is scheduled for tomorrow; **comme prévu** as planned; **plus tôt que prévu** earlier than expected; **prévu pour** *(véhicule, appareil)* designed for

**prévoyant, -e** [prevwajɑ̃, -ɑ̃t] *adj* far-sighted ▪ **prévoyance** *nf* foresight

**prier** [prije] **1** *vi Rel* to pray **2** *vt (Dieu)* to pray to; *(supplier)* to beg; **p. qn de faire qch** to ask sb to do sth; **je vous en prie** *(faites-le)* please; *(en réponse à 'merci')* don't mention it

**prière** [prijɛr] *nf Rel* prayer; *(demande)* request

**primaire** [primɛr] **1** *adj* primary; **école p.** *Br* primary school, *Am* elementary school **2** *nm Scol Br* primary *or Am* elementary education; **entrer en p.** to be at *Br* primary *or Am* elementary school

**prime** [prim] **1** *nf (sur salaire)* bonus; *(d'État)* subsidy; **en p.** *(cadeau)* as a free gift; **p. (d'assurance)** (insurance) premium; **p. de fin d'année** ≃ Christmas bonus; **p. de licenciement** severance allowance; **p. de transport** transport allowance **2** *adj* **de p. abord** at the very first glance

**primé, -e** [prime] *adj (film, animal)* prizewinning

**primer** [prime] *vi* to come first; **p. sur qch** to take precedence over sth

**primitif, -ive** [primitif, -iv] *adj (société, art)* primitive; *(état, sens)* original

**primordial, -e, -aux, -ales** [primɔrdjal, -jo] *adj* vital (**de faire** to do)

**prince** [prɛ̃s] *nm* prince ▪ **princesse** *nf* princess ▪ **princier, -ère** *adj* princely ▪ **principauté** *nf* principality

**principal, -e, -aux, -ales** [prɛ̃sipal, -o] **1** *adj* main, principal; *(rôle)* leading **2** *nm (de collège)* principal, *Br* headmaster, *f* headmistress; **le p.** *(l'essentiel)* the main thing

**principe** [prɛ̃sip] *nm* principle; **en p.** theoretically, in principle; **par p.** on principle

**printemps** [prɛ̃tɑ̃] *nm* spring; **au p.** in the spring

**priorité** [priɔrite] *nf* priority (**sur** over); *Aut* right of way; *Aut* **avoir la p.** to have (the) right of way; *Aut* **p. à droite** right of way to traffic coming from the right; **'cédez la p.'** *Br* 'give way', *Am* 'yield'; **en p.** as a matter of priority ▪ **prioritaire** *adj* **secteur p.** priority sector; **être p.** to have priority; *Aut* to have (the) right of way

**pris, -e**[1] [pri, priz] **1** *pp de* **prendre 2** *adj (place)* taken; **avoir le nez p.** to have a blocked nose; **être p.** *(occupé)* to be busy; *(candidat)* to be accepted; **p. de** *(peur)* seized with; **p. de panique** panic-stricken

**prise**[2] [priz] *nf (action)* taking; *(objet saisi)* catch; *(manière d'empoigner)* grip; *(de judo)* hold; *(de tabac)* pinch; **lâcher p.** to lose one's grip; **p. de sang** blood test; *Él* **p. (de courant)** *(mâle)* plug; *(femelle)* socket; *Él* **p. multiple** adaptor; **p. d'otages** hostage-taking

**prison** [prizɔ̃] *nf* prison, jail; *(peine)* imprisonment; **mettre qn en p.** to put sb in prison, to jail sb ▪ **prisonnier, -ère** *nmf* prisoner; **faire qn p.** to take sb prisoner; **p. de guerre** prisoner of war

**privation** [privasjɔ̃] *nf* deprivation (**de** of); **privations** *(manque)* hardship

**privatiser** [privatize] *vt* to privatize

■ **privatisation** *nf* privatization
**privé, -e** [prive] **1** *adj* private **2** *nm* **le p.** the private sector; *Scol* the private education system; **en p.** in private; **dans le p.** privately; *(travailler)* in the private sector
**priver** [prive] **1** *vt* to deprive (**de** of) **2 se priver** *vpr* **se p. de** to do without, to deprive oneself of
**privilège** [privilɛʒ] *nm* privilege ■ **privilégié, -e** *adj* privileged
**prix** [pri] *nm (coût)* price; *(récompense)* prize; **à tout p.** at all costs; **hors de p.** exorbitant; **attacher du p. à qch** to attach importance to sth
**probable** [prɔbabl] *adj* likely, probable; **peu p.** unlikely ■ **probabilité** *nf* probability, likelihood; **selon toute p.** in all probability
**probant, -e** [prɔbɑ̃, -ɑ̃t] *adj* conclusive
**probité** [prɔbite] *nf* integrity
**problème** [prɔblɛm] *nm* problem ■ **problématique** *adj* problematic
**procédé** [prɔsede] *nm (technique)* process; *(méthode)* method
**procéder** [prɔsede] *vi (agir)* to proceed; **p. à** *(enquête, arrestation)* to carry out; **p. par élimination** to follow a process of elimination ■ **procédure** *nf (méthode)* procedure; *(règles juridiques)* procedure; *(procès)* proceedings
**procès** [prɔsɛ] *nm (criminel)* trial; *(civil)* lawsuit; **faire un p. à qn** to take sb to court
**procession** [prɔsesjɔ̃] *nf* procession
**processus** [prɔsesys] *nm* process
**procès-verbal** [prɔsɛvɛrbal] (*pl* **procès-verbaux** [-o]) *nm (amende)* fine
**prochain, -e** [prɔʃɛ̃, -ɛn] *adj* next; *(mort, arrivée)* impending ■ **prochainement** *adv* shortly, soon
**proche** [prɔʃ] *adj (dans l'espace)* near, close; *(dans le temps)* near, imminent; *(parent, ami)* close; **p. de** near (to), close to; **de p. en p.** step by step; **le P.-Orient** the Middle East ■ **proches** *nmpl* close relations
**proclamer** [prɔklame] *vt* to proclaim (**que** that) ■ **proclamation** *nf* proclamation
**procréer** [prɔkree] *vi* to procreate ■ **procréation** *nf* procreation; **p. médicalement assistée** assisted conception
**procuration** [prɔkyrɑsjɔ̃] *nf* power of attorney; **par p.** by proxy
**procurer** [prɔkyre] **1** *vt* **p. qch à qn** *(sujet: personne)* to get sth for sb; *(sujet: chose)* to bring sb sth **2 se procurer** *vpr* **se p. qch** to obtain sth
**prodige** [prɔdiʒ] *nm (miracle)* wonder; *(personne)* prodigy; **tenir du p.** to be extraordinary ■ **prodigieux, -euse** *adj* prodigious
**prodiguer** [prɔdige] *vt* **p. qch à qn** to lavish sth on sb; **p. des conseils à qn** to pour out advice to sb
**production** [prɔdyksjɔ̃] *nf* production; *(produit)* product; *(d'usine)* output ■ **producteur, -trice 1** *nmf* producer **2** *adj* producing; **pays p. de pétrole** oil-producing country ■ **productif, -ive** *adj* productive ■ **productivité** *nf* productivity
**produire*** [prɔdɥir] **1** *vt (marchandise, émission, gaz)* to produce; *(effet, résultat)* to produce, to bring about **2 se produire** *vpr (événement)* to happen, to occur; *(acteur)* to perform ■ **produit** *nm (article)* product; *(de vente, de collecte)* proceeds; **p. de beauté** cosmetic; **p. chimique** chemical; **produits ménagers** cleaning products
**profane** [prɔfan] **1** *adj* secular **2** *nmf* lay person
**profaner** [prɔfane] *vt* to desecrate
**proférer** [prɔfere] *vt* to utter
**professer** [prɔfese] *vt* to profess (**que** that)
**professeur** [prɔfɛsœr] *nm* teacher; *(à l'université)* professor; **p. principal** *Br* class *or* form teacher, *Am* homeroom teacher
**profession** [prɔfɛsjɔ̃] *nf* occupation, profession; *(manuelle)* trade; **sans p.** not gainfully employed; **p. libérale**

profession ▪ **professionnel, -elle 1** *adj* professional; *(enseignement)* vocational **2** *nmf* professional

**profil** [prɔfil] *nm* profile; **de p.** (viewed) from the side ▪ **se profiler** *vpr* to be outlined (**sur** against)

**profit** [prɔfi] *nm* profit; **tirer p. de qch** to benefit from sth; **mettre qch à p.** to put sth to good use ▪ **profitable** *adj* profitable (**à** to) ▪ **profiter** *vi* **p. de** to take advantage of; **p. de la vie** to make the most of life; **p. à qn** to benefit sb, to be of benefit to sb

**profond, -e** [prɔfɔ̃, -ɔ̃d] **1** *adj* deep; *(joie, erreur)* profound; *(cause)* underlying; **p. de 2 mètres** 2 metres deep **2** *adv* deep ▪ **profondément** *adv* deeply; *(dormir)* soundly; *(triste, ému)* profoundly; *(creuser)* deep ▪ **profondeur** *nf* depth; **faire 6 mètres de p.** to be 6 metres deep; **à 6 mètres de p.** at a depth of 6 metres

**profusion** [prɔfyzjɔ̃] *nf* profusion; **à p.** in profusion

**programmable** [prɔgramabl] *adj* programmable ▪ **programmation** *nf Radio & TV* programme planning; *Ordinat* programming

**programmateur** [prɔgramatœr] *nm Tech* automatic control (device)

**programme** [prɔgram] *nm Br* programme, *Am* program; *(de parti politique)* manifesto; *Scol* curriculum; *(d'un cours)* syllabus; *Ordinat* program ▪ **programmer** *vt Ordinat* to program; *Radio, TV & Cin* to schedule ▪ **programmeur, -euse** *nmf* (computer) programmer

**progrès** [prɔgrɛ] *nm & nmpl* progress; **faire des p.** to make (good) progress ▪ **progresser** *vi* to progress ▪ **progressif, -ive** *adj* progressive ▪ **progression** *nf* progression ▪ **progressiste** *adj & nmf* progressive ▪ **progressivement** *adv* progressively

**prohiber** [prɔibe] *vt* to prohibit, to forbid ▪ **prohibitif, -ive** *adj* prohibitive ▪ **prohibition** *nf* prohibition

**proie** [prwa] *nf* prey; **être la p. des flammes** to be consumed by fire

**projecteur** [prɔʒɛktœr] *nm (de monument, de stade)* floodlight; *(de prison, d'armée)* searchlight; *Théât* spotlight; *Cin* projector

**projectile** [prɔʒɛktil] *nm* missile

**projection** [prɔʒeksjɔ̃] *nf (d'objet, de film)* projection; *(séance)* screening

**projet** [prɔʒɛ] *nm (intention)* plan; *(étude)* project; **faire des projets d'avenir** to make plans for the future; **p. de loi** bill

**projeter** [prɔʒte] *vt (lancer)* to project; *(liquide, boue)* to splash; *(lumière)* to flash; *(film)* to show; *(ombre)* to cast; *(prévoir)* to plan; **p. de faire qch** to plan to do sth

**proliférer** [prɔlifere] *vi* to proliferate ▪ **prolifération** *nf* proliferation

**prolonger** [prɔlɔ̃ʒe] **1** *vt (vie, débat, séjour)* to prolong; *(mur, route)* to extend **2 se prolonger** *vpr (séjour)* to be prolonged; *(réunion)* to go on; *(rue)* to continue ▪ **prolongation** *nf (de séjour)* extension; **prolongations** *(au football)* extra time ▪ **prolongement** *nm (de rue)* continuation; *(de mur)* extension; **prolongements** *(d'affaires)* repercussions

**promenade** [prɔmənad] *nf (à pied)* walk; *(courte)* stroll; *(avenue)* promenade; **faire une p.** to go for a walk; **faire une p. à cheval** to go for a ride

**promener** [prɔməne] **1** *vt (personne, chien)* to take for a walk; *(visiteur)* to show around; **p. qch sur qch** *(main, regard)* to run sth over sth **2 se promener** *vpr (à pied)* to go for a walk ▪ **promeneur, -euse** *nmf* stroller, walker

**promesse** [prɔmɛs] *nf* promise; **tenir sa p.** to keep one's promise

**promettre*** [prɔmɛtr] **1** *vt* to promise (**qch à qn** sb sth; **que** that); **p. de faire qch** to promise to do sth; **c'est promis** it's a promise **2** *vi Fig* to be promising **3 se promettre** *vpr* **se p. qch** *(à soi-même)* to promise oneself sth; *(l'un l'autre)* to promise each other sth

■ **prometteur, -euse** *adj* promising
**promoteur** [prɔmɔtœr] *nm* **p. (immobilier)** property developer
**promotion** [prɔmosjɔ̃] *nf* (**a**) *(avancement) & Com* promotion; **en p.** *(produit)* on (special) offer; **p. sociale** upward mobility (**b**) *(d'une école) Br* year, *Am* class ■ **promouvoir*** *vt (personne, produit)* to promote; **être promu** *(employé)* to be promoted (**à** to)
**prompt, -e** [prɔ̃, prɔ̃t] *adj* prompt; **p. à faire qch** quick to do sth
**promulguer** [prɔmylge] *vt* to promulgate
**prononcer** [prɔnɔ̃se] **1** *vt (articuler)* to pronounce; *(dire)* to utter; *(discours)* to deliver; *(jugement)* to pronounce **2 se prononcer** *vpr (mot)* to be pronounced; *(personne)* to give one's opinion (**sur** about *or* on); **se p. pour/contre qch** to come out in favour of/against sth ■ **prononcé, -e** *adj* pronounced, marked ■ **prononciation** *nf* pronunciation
**pronostic** [prɔnɔstik] *nm* forecast; *Méd* prognosis ■ **pronostiquer** *vt* to forecast
**propagande** [prɔpagɑ̃d] *nf* propaganda
**propager** [prɔpaʒe] *vt*, **se propager** *vpr* to spread ■ **propagation** *nf* spreading
**prophète** [prɔfɛt] *nm* prophet ■ **prophétie** [-fesi] *nf* prophecy ■ **prophétique** *adj* prophetic
**propice** [prɔpis] *adj* favourable (**à** to); **le moment p.** the right moment
**proportion** [prɔpɔrsjɔ̃] *nf* proportion; **en p. de** in proportion to; **hors de p.** out of proportion (**avec** to) ■ **proportionné, -e** *adj* proportionate (**à** to); **bien p.** well-proportioned ■ **proportionnel, -elle 1** *adj* proportional (**à** to) **2** *nf* **proportionnelle** *(scrutin)* proportional representation
**propos** [prɔpo] *nm (sujet)* subject; *(intention)* purpose; **des p.** *(paroles)* talk, words; **à p. de qn/qch** about sb/sth; **à p.** *(arriver)* at the right time; **à p.** by the way
**proposer** [prɔpoze] **1** *vt (suggérer)* to suggest, to propose (**qch à qn** sth to sb; **que** + *subjunctive* that); *(offrir)* to offer (**qch à qn** sb sth; **de faire** to do); **je te propose de rester** I suggest (that) you stay **2 se proposer** *vpr* to offer one's services; **se p. pour faire qch** to offer to do sth; **se p. de faire qch** to propose to do sth ■ **proposition** *nf* suggestion, proposal; *(offre)* offer; **faire une p. à qn** to make a suggestion to sb
**propre**[1] [prɔpr] **1** *adj* clean; *(soigné)* neat; **p. comme un sou neuf** spick and span **2** *nm* **mettre qch au p.** to make a fair copy of sth ■ **proprement** [-əmɑ̃] *adv (avec propreté)* cleanly; *(avec soin)* neatly ■ **propreté** [-əte] *nf* cleanliness; *(soin)* neatness
**propre**[2] [prɔpr] **1** *adj (à soi)* own; **mon p. argent** my own money; **être p. à qn/qch** *(particulier)* to be characteristic of sb/sth; **au sens p.** literally **2** *nm* **le p. de** *(qualité)* the distinctive quality of; **au p.** *(au sens propre)* literally ■ **proprement** [-əmɑ̃] *adv (strictement)* strictly; **à p. parler** strictly speaking; **le village p. dit** the village proper
**propriétaire** [prɔprijetɛr] *nmf* owner; *(de location)* landlord, *f* landlady; **p. foncier** landowner
**propriété** [prɔprijete] *nf (fait de posséder)* ownership; *(chose possédée)* property; *(caractéristique)* property; **p. privée** private property
**propulser** [prɔpylse] *vt* to propel
**proscrire*** [prɔskrir] *vt* to proscribe, to ban
**prospecter** [prɔspɛkte] *vt (sol)* to prospect; *(clients)* to canvass
**prospectus** [prɔspɛktys] *nm* leaflet
**prospère** [prɔspɛr] *adj* prosperous; *(santé)* glowing ■ **prospérer** *vi* to prosper ■ **prospérité** *nf* prosperity
**prosterner** [prɔstɛrne] **se prosterner** *vpr* to prostrate oneself (**devant** before)
**prostituée** [prɔstitɥe] *nf* prostitute ■ **prostitution** *nf* prostitution

**protecteur, -trice** [prɔtɛktœr, -tris] **1** *nmf* protector; *(mécène)* patron **2** *adj (geste, crème)* protective ▪ **protection** *nf* protection; **de p.** *(écran)* protective; **assurer la p. de qn** to ensure sb's safety ▪ **protectionnisme** *nm Écon* protectionism

**protéger** [prɔteʒe] **1** *vt* to protect (**de** from; **contre** against) **2 se protéger** *vpr* to protect oneself ▪ **protégé** *nm* protégé ▪ **protégée** *nf* protégée

**protestant, -e** [prɔtɛstɑ̃, -ɑ̃t] *adj & nmf* Protestant

**protester** [prɔtɛste] *vi* to protest (**contre** against); **p. de son innocence** to protest one's innocence ▪ **protestataire** *nmf* protester ▪ **protestation** *nf* protest (**contre** against); **en signe de p.** as a protest

**prothèse** [prɔtɛz] *nf* prosthesis; **p. auditive** hearing aid; **p. dentaire** false teeth

**protocole** [prɔtɔkɔl] *nm* protocol

**prototype** [prɔtɔtip] *nm* prototype

**prouesse** [pruɛs] *nf* feat

**prouver** [pruve] *vt* to prove (**que** that)

**Provence** [prɔvɑ̃s] *nf* **la P.** Provence ▪ **provençal, -e, -aux, -ales 1** *adj* Provençal **2** *nmf* **P., Provençale** Provençal

**provenir*** [prɔvənir] *vi* **p. de** to come from ▪ **provenance** *nf* origin; **en p. de** from

**proverbe** [prɔvɛrb] *nm* proverb

**providence** [prɔvidɑ̃s] *nf* providence ▪ **providentiel, -elle** *adj* providential

**province** [prɔvɛ̃s] *nf* province; **la p.** the provinces; **en p.** in the provinces; **de p.** *(ville)* provincial ▪ **provincial, -e, -aux, -ales** *adj & nmf* provincial

**proviseur** [prɔvizœr] *nm Br* headmaster, *f* headmistress, *Am* principal

**provision** [prɔvizjɔ̃] *nf* (**a**) *(réserve)* supply, stock; **provisions** *(nourriture)* shopping; **sac à provisions** shopping bag; **faire des provisions de qch** to stock up on sth (**b**) *(somme)* credit; *(acompte)* deposit

**provisoire** [prɔvizwar] *adj* temporary; **à titre p.** temporarily

**provoquer** [prɔvɔke] *vt (incendie, mort)* to cause; *(réaction)* to provoke; *(colère, désir)* to arouse ▪ **provocant, -e** *adj* provocative ▪ **provocateur** *nm* troublemaker ▪ **provocation** *nf* provocation

**proximité** [prɔksimite] *nf* closeness, proximity; **à p.** close by; **à p. de** close to; **de p.** local

**prude** [pryd] **1** *adj* prudish **2** *nf* prude

**prudent, -e** [prydɑ̃, -ɑ̃t] *adj (personne)* cautious, careful; *(décision)* sensible ▪ **prudence** *nf* caution, care; **par p.** as a precaution

**prune** [pryn] *nf (fruit)* plum ▪ **prunier** *nm* plum tree

**pruneau, -x** [pryno] *nm* prune

**pseudonyme** [psødɔnim] *nm* pseudonym

**psychanalyse** [psikanaliz] *nf* psychoanalysis ▪ **psychanalyste** *nmf* psychoanalyst

**psychiatre** [psikjatr] *nmf* psychiatrist ▪ **psychiatrie** *nf* psychiatry ▪ **psychiatrique** *adj* psychiatric

**psychique** [psiʃik] *adj* psychic

**psychologie** [psikɔlɔʒi] *nf* psychology ▪ **psychologique** *adj* psychological ▪ **psychologue** *nmf* psychologist

**psychose** [psikoz] *nf* psychosis

**pu** [py] *pp de* **pouvoir 1**

**puant, -e** [pɥɑ̃, pɥɑ̃t] *adj* stinking ▪ **puanteur** *nf* stink, stench

**public, -ique** [pyblik] **1** *adj* public; **dette publique** national debt **2** *nm (de spectacle)* audience; **le grand p.** the general public; **film grand p.** film suitable for the general public; **en p.** in public; *(émission)* before a live audience

**publication** [pyblikasjɔ̃] *nf (action, livre)* publication ▪ **publier** *vt* to publish

**publicité** [pyblisite] *nf (secteur)* advertising; *(annonce)* advertisement, advert; *Radio & TV* commercial; **agence de p.** advertising agency; **faire de la**

**p. pour qch** to advertise sth ▪ **publicitaire 1** *adj* **film p.** promotional film **2** *nmf* advertising executive

**puce** [pys] *nf (insecte)* flea; *Ordinat* (micro-)chip; **le marché aux puces, les puces** the flea market

**pudeur** [pydœr] *nf* modesty; **par p.** out of a sense of decency ▪ **pudibond, -e** *adj* prudish ▪ **pudique** *adj* modest

**puer** [pɥe] **1** *vt* to stink of **2** *vi* to stink

**puériculture** [pɥerikyltyr] *nf* child care ▪ **puéricultrice** *nf* nursery nurse

**puéril, -e** [pɥeril] *adj* puerile ▪ **puérilité** *nf* puerility

**puis** [pɥi] *adv* then; **et p.** *(ensuite)* and then; *(en plus)* and besides

**puiser** [pɥize] **1** *vt* to draw (**à/dans** from) **2** *vi* **p. dans qch** to dip into sth

**puisque** [pɥisk(ə)] *conj* since, as

**puissant, -e** [pɥisɑ̃, -ɑ̃t] *adj* powerful ▪ **puissance** *nf (force, nation) & Math* power; **en p.** *(meurtrier)* potential; *Math* **dix p. quatre** ten to the power of four

**puisse(s), puissent** [pɥis] *voir* **pouvoir 1**

**puits** [pɥi] *nm* well; *(de mine)* shaft; **p. de pétrole** oil well

**pull-over** [pylɔver] (*pl* **pull-overs**), **pull** [pyl] *nm* sweater, *Br* jumper

**pulluler** [pylyle] *vi (abonder)* to swarm

**pulmonaire** [pylmɔnɛr] *adj* pulmonary

**pulpe** [pylp] *nf (de fruits)* pulp

**pulvériser** [pylverize] *vt (vaporiser)* to spray; *(broyer)* to pulverize ▪ **pulvérisateur** *nm* spray

**punaise** [pynɛz] *nf (insecte)* bug; *(clou) Br* drawing pin, *Am* thumbtack

**punir** [pynir] *vt* to punish; **p. qn de qch** *(bêtise, crime)* to punish sb for sth ▪ **punition** *nf* punishment

**pupille** [pypij] **1** *nf (de l'œil)* pupil **2** *nmf (enfant)* ward

**pupitre** [pypitr] *nm (d'écolier)* desk; *(d'orateur)* lectern

**pur, -e** [pyr] *adj* pure; *(alcool)* neat, straight ▪ **pureté** *nf* purity

**purée** [pyre] *nf* purée; **p. (de pommes de terre)** mashed potatoes, *Br* mash

**purge** [pyrʒ] *nf (à des fins médicales, politiques)* purge

**purger** [pyrʒe] *vt (patient)* to purge; *(radiateur)* to bleed; *(peine de prison)* to serve

**purifier** [pyrifje] *vt* to purify ▪ **purification** *nf* purification; **p. ethnique** ethnic cleansing

**puriste** [pyrist] *nmf* purist

**puritain, -e** [pyritɛ̃, -ɛn] *adj & nmf* puritan

**pur-sang** [pyrsɑ̃] *nm inv* thoroughbred

**pus**[1] [py] *nm (liquide)* pus, matter

**pus**[2]**, put** [py] *voir* **pouvoir 1**

**putréfier** [pytrefje] *vt*, **se putréfier** *vpr* to putrefy

**puzzle** [pœzl] *nm* (jigsaw) puzzle

**pyjama** [piʒama] *nm Br* pyjamas, *Am* pajamas; **un p.** a pair of *Br* pyjamas *or Am* pajamas

**pyramide** [piramid] *nf* pyramid

**Pyrénées** [pirene] *nfpl* **les P.** the Pyrenees

**Pyrex**® [pireks] *nm* Pyrex®; **plat en P.** Pyrex® dish

**pyromane** [pirɔman] *nmf* arsonist

# Qq

**Q, q** [ky] *nm inv* Q, q
**qu'** [k] *voir* **que**
**quadrillage** [kadrijaʒ] *nm (de carte)* grid
**quadriller** [kadrije] *vt (quartier, ville)* to put under tight surveillance; *(papier)* to mark into squares ▪ **quadrillé, -e** *adj (papier)* squared
**quadrupède** [k(w)adrypɛd] *adj & nm* quadruped
**quadruple** [k(w)adrypl] **1** *adj* fourfold **2** *nm* **le q. (de)** *(quantité)* four times as much (as); *(nombre)* four times as many (as) ▪ **quadrupler** *vti* to quadruple ▪ **quadruplés, -es** *nmfpl* quadruplets
**quai** [kɛ] *nm (de port)* quay; *(de fleuve)* embankment; *(de gare, de métro)* platform
**qualification** [kalifikɑsjɔ̃] *nf (action, d'équipe, de sportif)* qualification; *(désignation)* description
**qualifier** [kalifje] **1** *vt (équipe)* to qualify (**pour qch** for sth; **pour faire** to do); *(décrire)* to describe (**de** as) **2 se qualifier** *vpr (équipe)* to qualify (**pour** for) ▪ **qualifié, -e** *adj (équipe)* that has qualified; **q. pour faire qch** qualified to do sth
**qualité** [kalite] *nf (de personne, de produit)* quality; *(occupation)* occupation; **produit de q.** quality product; **de bonne q.** of good quality; **en q. de** in his/her/*etc* capacity as
**quand** [kɑ̃] *conj & adv* when; **q. je viendrai** when I come
**quant** [kɑ̃] **quant à** *prép* as for
**quantité** [kɑ̃tite] *nf* quantity; **une q., des quantités** *(beaucoup)* a lot (**de** of)
**quarante** [karɑ̃t] *adj & nm inv* forty; **un q.-cinq tours** *(disque)* a single ▪ **quarantaine** *nf* (**a**) **une q. (de)** *(nombre)* (about) forty; **avoir la q.** *(âge)* to be about forty (**b**) *Méd* quarantine; **mettre qn en q.** to quarantine sb ▪ **quarantième** *adj & nmf* fortieth
**quart** [kar] *nm* (**a**) *(fraction)* quarter; **q. de litre** quarter litre, quarter of a litre; **q. d'heure** quarter of an hour; **une heure et q.** an hour and a quarter; **il est une heure et q.** it's a quarter *Br* past *or Am* after one; **une heure moins le q.** quarter to one; *Sport* **quarts de finale** quarter finals (**b**) *Naut* **être de q.** to be on watch ▪ **quart-monde** *nm* **le q.** the least-developed countries
**quartier** [kartje] *nm* (**a**) *(de ville)* district; **de q.** local; **q. général** headquarters (**b**) *(de lune)* quarter; *(de pomme)* piece; *(d'orange)* segment (**c**) *(expression)* **avoir q. libre** to be free
**quartz** [kwarts] *nm* quartz; **montre à q.** quartz watch
**quasi** [kazi] *adv* almost
**quasiment** [kazimɑ̃] *adv* almost
**quatorze** [katɔrz] *adj & nm inv* fourteen ▪ **quatorzième** *adj & nmf* fourteenth
**quatre** [katr] *adj & nm inv* four ▪ **quatrième** *adj & nmf* fourth
**quatre-vingt** [katrəvɛ̃] *adj & nm* eighty; **quatre-vingts ans** eighty years; **q.-un** eighty-one; **page q.** page eighty ▪ **quatre-vingt-dix** *adj & nm inv* ninety

**QUE** [kə]

**que** becomes **qu'** before a vowel or mute h.

**1** *conj* (**a**) *(complétif)* that; **je pense qu'elle restera** I think (that) she'll stay; **qu'elle vienne ou non** whether she comes or not; **qu'il s'en aille!** let him leave!; **ça fait un an q. je suis là** I've been here for a year

(**b**) *(de comparaison)* than; *(avec 'aussi', 'même', 'tel', 'autant')* as; **plus/moins âgé q. lui** older/younger than him; **aussi sage/fatigué q. toi** as wise/tired as you; **le même q. Pauline** the same as Pauline

(**c**) **(ne...) que** only; **tu n'as qu'un stylo** you only have one pen

**2** *adv* **(ce) qu'il est bête!** *(comme)* he's really stupid!

**3** *pron relatif (chose)* that, which; *(personne)* that, whom; *(temps)* when; **le livre q. j'ai** the book (that *or* which) I have; **l'ami q. j'ai** the friend (that *or* whom) I have

**4** *pron interrogatif* what; **q. fait-il?, qu'est-ce qu'il fait?** what is he doing?; **q. préférez-vous?** which do you prefer?

**Québec** [kebɛk] *nm* **le Q.** Quebec

**quel, quelle** [kɛl] **1** *adj interrogatif (chose)* what, which; *(personne)* which; **q. livre préférez-vous?** which *or* what book do you prefer?; **q. est cet homme?** who is that man?; **je sais q. est ton but** I know what your aim is; **je ne sais à q. employé m'adresser** I don't know which clerk to ask

**2** *pron interrogatif* which (one); **q. est le meilleur?** which (one) is the best?

**3** *adj exclamatif* **q. idiot!** what a fool!

**4** *adj relatif* **q. qu'il soit** *(chose)* whatever it may be; *(personne)* whoever it *or* he may be

**quelconque** [kɛlkɔ̃k] **1** *adj indéfini* any; **donne-moi un livre q.** give me any book **2** *adj (insignifiant)* ordinary

**quelque** [kɛlk] **1** *adj indéfini* some; **quelques** some, a few; **les quelques amies qu'elle a** the few friends she has **2** *adv (environ)* about, some; **q. peu** somewhat; *Fam* **100 euros et q.** 100 euros and a bit

**quelque chose** [kɛlkəʃoz] *pron indéfini* something; **q. d'autre** something else; **q. de grand** something big; **q. de plus pratique/de moins lourd** something more practical/less heavy

**quelquefois** [kɛlkəfwa] *adv* sometimes

**quelque part** [kɛlkəpar] *adv* somewhere; *(dans les questions)* anywhere

**quelques-uns, -unes** [kɛlkəzœ̃, -yn] *pron* some

**quelqu'un** [kɛlkœ̃] *pron indéfini* someone, somebody; *(dans les questions)* anyone, anybody; **q. d'intelligent** someone clever

**querelle** [kərɛl] *nf* quarrel; **chercher q. à qn** to try to pick a fight with sb ▪ **se quereller** *vpr* to quarrel

**question** [kɛstjɔ̃] *nf (interrogation)* question; *(affaire)* matter, question; **il n'en est pas q.** it's out of the question; **en q.** in question ▪ **questionnaire** *nm* questionnaire ▪ **questionner** *vt* to question (**sur** about)

**quête** [kɛt] *nf* (**a**) *(collecte)* collection; **faire la q.** to collect money (**b**) *(recherche)* quest (**de** for); **en q. de** in quest *or* search of ▪ **quêter** [kete] **1** *vt* to seek **2** *vi* to collect money

**queue** [kø] *nf* (**a**) *(d'animal)* tail; *(de fleur, de fruit)* stalk; *(de train)* rear; **à la q. leu leu** in single file; **q. de cheval** *(coiffure)* ponytail (**b**) *(file) Br* queue, *Am* line; **faire la q.** *Br* to queue up, *Am* to stand in line

**QUI** [ki] **1** *pron interrogatif (personne)* who; *(en complément)* whom; **q. (est-ce qui) est là?** who's there?; **q. désirez-vous voir?, q. est-ce que vous désirez voir?** who(m) do you want to see?; **à q. est ce livre?** whose book is this?; **je demande q. a téléphoné** I'm asking who phoned

**2** *pron relatif* (**a**) *(sujet) (personne)*

who, that; *(chose)* which, that; **l'homme q. est là** the man who's here *or* that's here; **la maison q. se trouve en face** the house which is *or* that's opposite

(**b**) *(sans antécédent)* **q. que vous soyez** whoever you are

(**c**) *(après une préposition)* **la femme de q. je parle** the woman I'm talking about

---

**quiconque** [kikɔ̃k] *pron (sujet)* whoever; *(complément)* anyone

**quille** [kij] *nf (de navire)* keel; *(de jeu)* (bowling) pin, *Br* skittle; **jouer aux quilles** to bowl, *Br* to play skittles

**quincaillerie** [kɛ̃kajri] *nf (magasin)* hardware shop; *(objets)* hardware

**quinquennal, -e, -aux, -ales** [kɛ̃kenal, -o] *adj* **plan q.** five-year plan ▪ **quinquennat** *nm Pol* five-year term (of office)

**quintuple** [kɛ̃typl] **1** *adj* **q. de** fivefold **2** *nm* **le q. (de)** *(quantité)* five times as much (as); *(nombre)* five times as many (as) ▪ **quintupler** *vti* to increase fivefold

**quinze** [kɛ̃z] *adj & nm inv* fifteen; **q. jours** two weeks, *Br* a fortnight ▪ **quinzaine** *nf* **une q. (de)** (about) fifteen; **une q. (de jours)** two weeks, *Br* a fortnight ▪ **quinzième** *adj & nmf* fifteenth

**quittance** [kitɑ̃s] *nf (reçu)* receipt

**quitte** [kit] *adj* quits (**envers** with); **q. à faire qch** even if it means doing sth; **en être q. pour qch** to get off with sth

**quitter** [kite] **1** *vt (personne, lieu, poste)* to leave; **ne pas q. qn des yeux** to keep one's eyes on sb **2** *vi* **ne quittez pas!** *(au téléphone)* hold the line! **3 se quitter** *vpr* to part; **ils ne se quittent plus** they are inseparable

---

**QUOI** [kwa] *pron* what; *(après une préposition)* which; **à q. penses-tu?** what are you thinking about?; **après q.** after which; **de q. manger** something to eat; *(assez)* enough to eat; **de q. écrire** something to write with; **q. que je dise** whatever I say; **q. qu'il en soit** be that as it may; **il n'y a pas de q.!** *(en réponse à 'merci')* don't mention it!; **q.?** what?

---

**quoique** [kwak] *conj* (al)though; **quoiqu'il soit pauvre** (al)though he's poor

**quota** [kwɔta] *nm* quota

**quotidien, -enne** [kɔtidjɛ̃, -ɛn] **1** *adj* daily **2** *nm* daily (paper)

# Rr

**R, r** [er] *nm inv* R, r
**rabâcher** [rabɑʃe] **1** *vt* to repeat endlessly **2** *vi* to say the same thing over and over again
**rabais** [rabɛ] *nm* reduction, discount ▪ **rabaisser 1** *vt (dénigrer)* to belittle **2 se rabaisser** *vpr* to belittle oneself
**rabattre*** [rabatr] **1** *vt (col)* to turn down; *(couvercle)* to close **2 se rabattre** *vpr (se refermer)* to close; *(véhicule)* to pull back in; *Fig* **se r. sur qch** to fall back on sth
**rabbin** [rabɛ̃] *nm* rabbi
**rabougri, -e** [rabugri] *adj (personne, plante)* stunted
**raccommoder** [rakɔmɔde] *vt (linge)* to mend; *(chaussette)* to darn
**raccompagner** [rakɔ̃paɲe] *vt* to take back
**raccord** [rakɔr] *nm (dispositif)* connection; *(de papier peint)* join; *(de peinture)* touch-up ▪ **raccordement** [-əmɑ̃] *nm (action, lien)* connection ▪ **raccorder** *vt*, **se raccorder** *vpr* to link up (**à** to)
**raccourcir** [rakursir] **1** *vt* to shorten **2** *vi* to get shorter ▪ **raccourci** *nm* short cut; **en r.** in brief
**raccrocher** [rakrɔʃe] **1** *vt (objet tombé)* to hang back up; *(téléphone)* to put down **2** *vi (au téléphone)* to hang up **3 se raccrocher** *vpr* **se r. à qch** to catch hold of sth; *Fig* to cling to sth
**race** [ras] *nf (ethnie)* race; *(animale)* breed; **chien de r.** pedigree dog ▪ **racial, -e, -aux, -ales** *adj* racial ▪ **racisme** *nm* racism ▪ **raciste** *adj & nmf* racist
**rachat** [raʃa] *nm (de voiture, d'appartement)* repurchase; *(de firme)* buy-out ▪ **racheter 1** *vt (acheter davantage)* to buy some more; *(remplacer)* to buy another; *(firme)* to buy out; *(faute)* to make up for **2 se racheter** *vpr* to make amends, to redeem oneself
**racine** [rasin] *nf (de plante, de personne) & Math* root
**racler** [rɑkle] **1** *vt* to scrape; *(peinture, boue)* to scrape off **2 se racler** *vpr* **se r. la gorge** to clear one's throat ▪ **raclette** *nf (outil)* scraper; *(plat)* raclette *(Swiss dish consisting of potatoes and melted cheese)*
**raconter** [rakɔ̃te] *vt (histoire, mensonge)* to tell; *(événement)* to tell about; **r. qch à qn** *(histoire)* to tell sb sth; *(événement)* to tell sb about sth; **r. à qn que...** to tell sb that... ▪ **racontars** *nmpl* gossip
**radar** [radar] *nm* radar; **contrôle r.** radar speed check
**rade** [rad] *nf* harbour
**radeau, -x** [rado] *nm* raft
**radiateur** [radjatœr] *nm* radiator; **r. électrique** electric heater
**radiation** [radjɑsjɔ̃] *nf Phys* radiation; *(suppression)* removal (**de** from) ▪ **radier** *vt* to strike off (**de** from)
**radical, -e, -aux, -ales** [radikal, -o] *adj* radical
**radieux, -euse** [radjø, -øz] *adj (personne, visage, soleil)* radiant; *(temps)* glorious
**radio** [radjo] **1** *nf* (**a**) *(poste)* radio; *(station)* radio station; **à la r.** on the radio (**b**) *Méd* X-ray; **passer une r.** to

have an X-ray **2** *nm (opérateur)* radio operator ▪ **radio-réveil** (*pl* **radios-réveils**) *nm* radio alarm, clock radio

**radioactif, -ive** [radjoaktif, -iv] *adj* radioactive ▪ **radioactivité** *nf* radioactivity

**radiodiffuser** [radjodifyse] *vt* to broadcast ▪ **radiodiffusion** *nf* broadcasting

**radiographie** [radjografi] *nf (photo)* X-ray; *(technique)* radiography ▪ **radiographier** *vt* to X-ray ▪ **radiologie** *nf Méd* radiology ▪ **radiologue** *nmf (technicien)* radiographer; *(médecin)* radiologist

**radiophonique** [radjofɔnik] *adj* **émission r.** radio broadcast

**radis** [radi] *nm* radish

**radoucir** [radusir] **se radoucir** *vpr (personne)* to calm down; *(temps)* to become milder

**rafale** [rafal] *nf (vent)* gust; *(de mitrailleuse)* burst

**raffermir** [rafɛrmir] **1** *vt (autorité)* to strengthen; *(muscles)* to tone up **2 se raffermir** *vpr (muscle)* to become stronger

**raffiné, -e** [rafine] *adj* refined ▪ **raffinement** *nm* refinement

**raffiner** [rafine] *vt* to refine ▪ **raffinage** *nm* refining

**raffinerie** [rafinri] *nf* refinery

**rafle** [rɑfl] *nf* raid

**rafraîchir** [rafrɛʃir] **1** *vt (rendre frais)* to chill; *(pièce)* to air; *(raviver)* to freshen up **2** *vi* to cool down **3 se rafraîchir** *vpr (temps)* to get cooler; *(se laver)* to freshen up ▪ **rafraîchissant, -e** *adj* refreshing ▪ **rafraîchissement** *nm (boisson)* cold drink

**rage** [raʒ] *nf (colère)* rage; *(maladie)* rabies; **faire r.** *(incendie, tempête)* to rage

**ragoût** [ragu] *nm Culin* stew

**raid** [rɛd] *nm* raid

**raide** [rɛd] **1** *adj (rigide, guindé)* stiff; *(côte)* steep; *(cheveux)* straight **2** *adv (grimper)* steeply; **tomber r.** to fall to the ground ▪ **raideur** *nf (rigidité)* stiffness; *(de côte)* steepness ▪ **raidir 1** *vt (bras, jambe)* to brace; *(corde)* to tauten **2 se raidir** *vpr (membres)* to stiffen; *(corde)* to tauten; *(personne)* to tense up

**raie** [rɛ] *nf (motif)* stripe; *(de cheveux)* *Br* parting, *Am* part

**rail** [rɑj] *nm* rail; **le r.** *(chemins de fer)* rail; **r. de sécurité** crash barrier

**raisin** [rɛzɛ̃] *nm* **raisin(s)** grapes; **r. sec** raisin

**raison** [rɛzɔ̃] *nf* (**a**) *(faculté, motif)* reason; **la r. de mon absence** the reason for my absence; **la r. pour laquelle...** the reason (why)...; **en r. de** *(cause)* on account of; **à r. de** *(proportion)* at the rate of; **à plus forte r.** all the more so

(**b**) **avoir r.** to be right (**de faire** to do *or* in doing); **donner r. à qn** to agree with sb

**raisonnable** [rɛzɔnabl] *adj* reasonable

**raisonner** [rɛzɔne] *vi (penser)* to reason ▪ **raisonnement** *nm (faculté, activité)* reasoning; *(argumentation)* argument

**rajeunir** [raʒœnir] **1** *vt (moderniser)* to modernize; **r. qn** *(faire paraître plus jeune)* to make sb look younger; *(donner moins que son âge à)* to underestimate how old sb is **2** *vi* to look younger ▪ **rajeunissement** *nm (après traitement)* rejuvenation; *(de population)* decrease in age

**rajouter** [raʒute] *vt* to add (**à** to)

**rajuster** [raʒyste] *vt (vêtements, lunettes)* to straighten, to adjust

**ralentir** [ralɑ̃tir] *vti* to slow down ▪ **ralenti** *nm Cin & TV* slow motion; **au r.** in slow motion; *(travailler)* at a slower pace; **tourner au r.** *(moteur, usine)* *Br* to tick over, *Am* to turn over ▪ **ralentissement** *nm* slowing down; *(embouteillage)* hold-up

**rallier** [ralje] **1** *vt (réunir)* to rally; *(regagner)* to return to; **r. qn à qch** *(convertir)* to win sb over to sth **2 se rallier** *vpr* **se r. à** *(avis)* to come round to; *(cause)* to rally to

**rallonge** [ralɔ̃ʒ] *nf (de table)* extension; *(fil électrique)* extension (lead) ▪ **rallonger** *vti* to lengthen

**rallumer** [ralyme] **1** *vt (feu, pipe)* to light again; *(lampe)* to switch on again **2 se rallumer** *vpr (lumière)* to come back on; *(incendie)* to flare up again

**ramasser** [ramɑse] **1** *vt (prendre, réunir)* to pick up; *(ordures, copies)* to collect; *(fruits, coquillages)* to gather **2 se ramasser** *vpr (se pelotonner)* to curl up; *(se relever)* to pick oneself up ▪ **ramassage** *nm (d'ordures)* collection; **r. scolaire** school bus service

**rame** [ram] *nf (aviron)* oar; *(de métro)* train ▪ **ramer** *vi* to row ▪ **rameur, -euse** *nmf* rower

**ramener** [ramne] *vt (amener)* to bring back; *(raccompagner)* to take back; *(ordre, calme)* to restore; **r. qch à qch** to reduce sth to sth; **r. qn à la vie** to bring sb back to life

**ramollir** [ramɔlir] *vt*, **se ramollir** *vpr* to soften

**ramoner** [ramɔne] *vt (cheminée)* to sweep

**rampe** [rɑ̃p] *nf (d'escalier)* banister; *(pente)* slope; **r. d'accès** *(de pont)* access ramp

**ramper** [rɑ̃pe] *vi* to crawl

**rancœur** [rɑ̃kœr] *nf* rancour, resentment

**rançon** [rɑ̃sɔ̃] *nf* ransom ▪ **rançonner** *vt* to hold to ransom

**rancune** [rɑ̃kyn] *nf* spite; **garder r. à qn** to bear sb a grudge ▪ **rancunier, -ère** *adj* spiteful

**randonnée** [rɑ̃dɔne] *nf (à pied)* hike; *(en vélo)* ride

**rang** [rɑ̃] *nm (rangée)* row; *(classement, grade)* rank; **par r. de taille** in order of size; **de haut r.** high-ranking; **se mettre en r.** to line up (**par trois** in threes) ▪ **rangée** *nf* row

**ranger** [rɑ̃ʒe] **1** *vt (papiers, vaisselle)* to put away; *(chambre)* to tidy (up); *(classer)* to rank (**parmi** among) **2 se ranger** *vpr (se disposer)* to line up; *(s'écarter)* to stand aside ▪ **rangé, -e** *adj (chambre)* tidy; *(personne)* steady ▪ **rangement** *nm* putting away; *(de chambre)* tidying (up); **rangements** *(placards)* storage space

**ranimer** [ranime] *vt (personne) (après évanouissement)* to bring round; *(après arrêt cardiaque)* to resuscitate; *(feu)* to rekindle; *(souvenir)* to reawaken; *(débat)* to revive

**rapace** [rapas] **1** *nm (oiseau)* bird of prey **2** *adj (personne)* grasping

**rapatrier** [rapatrije] *vt* to repatriate

**râpé, -e** [rɑpe] *adj (fromage, carottes)* grated ▪ **râper** *vt (fromage)* to grate; *(bois)* to rasp

**rapetisser** [raptise] **1** *vt (rendre plus petit)* to make smaller; *(faire paraître plus petit)* to make look smaller **2** *vi (vêtement, personne)* to shrink

**rapide** [rapid] **1** *adj* fast; *(progrès)* rapid; *(esprit, lecture)* quick **2** *nm (train)* express (train); *(de fleuve)* rapid ▪ **rapidité** *nf* speed

**rappel** [rapɛl] *nm (de diplomate)* recall; *(d'événement, de promesse)* reminder; *(au théâtre)* curtain call; *(vaccin)* booster; **descendre en r.** *(en alpinisme)* to abseil down

**rappeler** [raple] **1** *vt (pour faire revenir, au téléphone)* to call back; *(souvenir, diplomate)* to recall; **r. qch à qn** to remind sb of sth **2** *vi (au téléphone)* to call back **3 se rappeler** *vpr* **se r. qn/qch** to remember sb/sth; **se r. que...** to remember that...

**rapport** [rapɔr] *nm* (**a**) *(lien)* connection, link; **par r. à** compared with; **rapports** *(entre personnes)* relations; **rapports (sexuels)** (sexual) intercourse (**b**) *(profit)* return, yield (**c**) *(compte rendu)* report

**rapporter** [rapɔrte] **1** *vt (rendre)* to bring back; *(remporter)* to take back; *(raconter)* to report; *(profit)* to yield; **r. de l'argent** to be profitable; *(moralement)* to bring sb sth; **on rapporte que...** it is reported that... **2** *vi (chien)* to retrieve

**3 se rapporter** *vpr* **se r. à qch** to relate to sth; **s'en r. à qn/qch** to rely on sb/sth

**rapprocher** [raprɔʃe] **1** *vt (objet)* to move closer (**de** to); *(réconcilier)* to bring together; *(comparer)* to compare (**de** to *or* with)
**2 se rapprocher** *vpr* to get closer (**de** to); *(se réconcilier)* to be reconciled; *(ressembler)* to be similar (**de** to) ▪ **rapproché, -e** *adj* close; *(yeux)* close-set ▪ **rapprochement** *nm (réconciliation)* reconciliation; *(rapport)* connection

**rapt** [rapt] *nm* abduction

**raquette** [rakɛt] *nf (de tennis)* racket; *(de ping-pong)* bat; *(de neige)* snowshoe

**rare** [rar] *adj* rare; *(argent, main-d'œuvre)* scarce; *(barbe, végétation)* sparse; **c'est r. qu'il pleuve ici** it rarely rains here ▪ **rarement** *adv* rarely, seldom ▪ **rareté** *nf (objet rare)* rarity; *(de main-d'œuvre)* scarcity; *(de phénomène)* rareness

**ras, -e** [rɑ, rɑz] **1** *adj (cheveux)* close-cropped; *(herbe, barbe)* short; *(mesure)* full; **à r. bord** to the brim; **pull (au) r. du cou** crew-neck sweater **2** *nm* **au r. de, à r. de** level with; **voler au r. du sol** to fly close to the ground **3** *adv (coupé)* short

**raser** [rɑse] **1** *vt (menton, personne)* to shave; *(barbe, moustache)* to shave off; *(démolir)* to raze to the ground; *(frôler)* to skim **2 se raser** *vpr* to shave ▪ **rasé, -e** *adj* **être bien r.** to be clean-shaven

**rasoir** [rɑzwar] *nm* razor; *(électrique)* shaver

**rassasier** [rasazje] *vt (faim, curiosité)* to satisfy

**rassembler** [rasɑ̃ble] **1** *vt (gens, objets)* to gather (together) **2 se rassembler** *vpr* to gather, to assemble ▪ **rassemblement** [-əmɑ̃] *nm (action, groupe)* gathering

**rasseoir*** [raswar] **se rasseoir** *vpr* to sit down again

**rassis, -e** [rasi, -iz] *adj (pain)* stale

**rassurer** [rasyre] **1** *vt* to reassure **2 se rassurer** *vpr* **rassure-toi** don't worry ▪ **rassurant, -e** *adj* reassuring

**rat** [ra] *nm* rat

**ratatiner** [ratatine] **se ratatiner** *vpr* to shrivel up

**ratatouille** [ratatuj] *nf Culin* **r. (niçoise)** ratatouille

**râteau, -x** [rɑto] *nm* rake

**râtelier** [rɑtəlje] *nm (pour outils, pour armes)* rack

**rater** [rate] *vt (bus, cible, occasion)* to miss; *(travail, gâteau)* to ruin; *(examen)* to fail; *(vie)* to waste ▪ **raté, -e** *nmf* loser

**ratifier** [ratifje] *vt* to ratify

**ration** [rɑsjɔ̃] *nf* ration ▪ **rationnement** *nm* rationing

**rationaliser** [rasjɔnalize] *vt* to rationalize

**rationnel, -elle** [rasjɔnɛl] *adj* rational

**ratisser** [ratise] *vt (allée)* to rake; *(feuilles)* to rake up

**rattacher** [rataʃe] **1** *vt (lacets)* to tie up again; *(région)* to unite (**à** with) **2 se rattacher** *vpr* **se r. à** to be linked to

**rattraper** [ratrape] **1** *vt* to catch; *(prisonnier)* to recapture; **r. qn** *(rejoindre)* to catch up with sb; **r. le temps perdu** to make up for lost time **2 se rattraper** *vpr (se retenir)* to catch oneself in time; *(après une faute)* to make up for it; **se r. à qch** to catch hold of sth ▪ **rattrapage** *nm Scol* **cours de r.** remedial class

**raturer** [ratyre] *vt* to cross out, to delete

**rauque** [rok] *adj (voix)* hoarse

**ravages** [ravaʒ] *nmpl* devastation; *(du temps, de maladie)* ravages; **faire des r.** to wreak havoc; *(femme)* to break hearts ▪ **ravager** *vt* to devastate

**ravaler** [ravale] *vt (façade)* to clean

**ravi, -e** [ravi] *adj* delighted (**de** with; **de faire** to do; **que** that)

**ravin** [ravɛ̃] *nm* ravine

**ravir** [ravir] *vt (emporter)* to snatch (**à**

from); *(plaire à)* to delight; **chanter à r.** to sing delightfully ■ **ravissement** *nm (extase)* ecstasy ■ **ravisseur, -euse** *nmf* kidnapper

**raviser** [ravize] **se raviser** *vpr* to change one's mind

**ravitailler** [ravitaje] **1** *vt (personnes)* to supply; *(avion)* to refuel **2 se ravitailler** *vpr* to get in supplies ■ **ravitaillement** *nm (action)* supplying; *(d'avion)* refuelling; *(denrées)* supplies

**raviver** [ravive] *vt (feu, sentiment)* to rekindle; *(douleur)* to revive; *(couleur)* to brighten up

**rayer** [rɛje] *vt (érafler)* to scratch; *(mot)* to cross out ■ **rayé, -e** *adj (verre, disque)* scratched; *(tissu, pantalon)* striped ■ **rayure** *nf (éraflure)* scratch; *(motif)* stripe; **à rayures** striped

**rayon** [rɛjɔ̃] *nm* (**a**) *(de lumière)* ray; *(de cercle)* radius; *(de roue)* spoke; **dans un r. de** within a radius of; **r. X** X-ray; **r. de soleil** sunbeam (**b**) *(d'étagère)* shelf; *(de magasin)* department; *(de ruche)* honeycomb ■ **rayonnage** *nm* shelving, shelves

**rayonner** [rɛjɔne] *vi (avenue, douleur)* to radiate; *(dans une région)* to travel around *(from a central base)*; *(soleil)* to beam; *Fig* **r. de joie** to beam with joy ■ **rayonnant, -e** *adj (soleil)* radiant; *Fig (visage)* beaming (**de** with) ■ **rayonnement** *nm (du soleil)* radiance; *(influence)* influence

**raz de marée** [rɑdmare] *nm inv* tidal wave; **r. électoral** landslide

**ré** [re] *nm inv (note)* D

**réacteur** [reaktœr] *nm (d'avion)* jet engine; *(nucléaire)* reactor

**réaction** [reaksjɔ̃] *nf* reaction; **moteur à r.** jet engine

**réagir** [reaʒir] *vi* to react (**contre** against; **à** to); *Fig (se secouer)* to shake oneself out of it

**réaliser** [realize] **1** *vt (projet)* to realize; *(rêve, ambition) Br* to fulfil, *Am* to fulfill; *(bénéfices)* to make; *(film)* to direct; *(comprendre)* to realize (**que** that) **2 se réaliser** *vpr (vœu)* to come true; *(personne) Br* to fulfil *or Am* fulfill oneself ■ **réalisable** *adj (plan)* workable; *(rêve)* attainable ■ **réalisateur, -trice** *nmf (de film)* director ■ **réalisation** *nf (de projet)* realization; *(de rêve)* fulfilment; *(de film)* direction

**réalité** [realite] *nf* reality; **en r.** in reality

**réanimation** [reanimɑsjɔ̃] *nf* resuscitation; **(service de) r.** intensive care unit ■ **réanimer** *vt* to resuscitate

**rebattu, -e** [rəbaty] *adj (sujet)* hackneyed

**rebelle** [rəbɛl] **1** *adj (personne)* rebellious; *(mèche)* unruly **2** *nmf* rebel ■ **se rebeller** *vpr* to rebel (**contre** against) ■ **rébellion** *nf* rebellion

**rebondir** [rəbɔ̃dir] *vi* to bounce; *(par ricochet)* to rebound

**rebondissement** [rəbɔ̃dismɑ̃] *nm* new development (**de** in)

**rebord** [rəbɔr] *nm* edge; *(de plat)* rim; *(de vêtement)* hem; **r. de fenêtre** windowsill

**reboucher** [rəbuʃe] *vt (flacon)* to put the top back on; *(trou)* to fill in again

**rebours** [rəbur] **à rebours** *adv* the wrong way

**rébus** [rebys] *nm* rebus

**rebut** [rəby] *nm* **mettre qch au r.** to throw sth out

**rebuter** [rəbyte] *vt (décourager)* to put off

**récapituler** [rekapityle] *vti* to recapitulate

**recel** [rəsɛl] *nm* receiving stolen goods ■ **receler, recéler** *vt (mystère, secret)* to conceal; *(objet volé)* to receive; *(criminel)* to harbour

**recenser** [rəsɑ̃se] *vt (population)* to take a census of ■ **recensement** *nm (de population)* census

**récent, -e** [resɑ̃, -ɑ̃t] *adj* recent

**récepteur** [resɛptœr] *nm (téléphone)* receiver ■ **réceptif, -ive** *adj* receptive (**à** to) ■ **réception** *nf (accueil, soirée) & Radio* reception; *(de lettre)* receipt; *(d'hôtel)* reception (desk); **dès r. de**

on receipt of; **avec accusé de r.** with acknowledgement of receipt ▪ **réceptionniste** *nmf* receptionist

**récession** [resesjɔ̃] *nf Écon* recession

**recette** [rəsɛt] *nf Culin & Fig* recipe (**de** for); *(argent, bénéfice)* takings; **recettes** *(gains)* takings

**recevoir*** [rəsəvwar] **1** *vt (amis, lettre, proposition, coup de téléphone)* to receive; *(gifle, coup)* to get; *(client)* to see; *(candidat)* to admit; *(station de radio)* to pick up; **r. la visite de qn** to have a visit from sb; **être reçu à un examen** to pass an exam; **être reçu premier** to come first

**2** *vi (faire une fête)* to have guests ▪ **receveur, -euse** *nmf (de bus)* (bus) conductor; **r. des Postes** postmaster, *f* postmistress

**rechange** [rəʃɑ̃ʒ] **de rechange** *adj (pièce)* spare

**recharge** [rəʃarʒ] *nf (de stylo)* refill ▪ **rechargeable** *adj (briquet)* refillable; *(pile)* rechargeable ▪ **recharger** *vt (fusil, appareil photo, camion)* to reload; *(briquet, stylo)* to refill; *(pile)* to recharge

**réchaud** [reʃo] *nm* (portable) stove

**réchauffer** [reʃofe] **1** *vt (personne, aliment)* to warm up **2 se réchauffer** *vpr (personne)* to get warm ▪ **réchauffement** *nm (de température)* rise (**de** in); **le r. de la planète** global warming

**rêche** [rɛʃ] *adj* rough

**recherche** [rəʃɛrʃ] *nf* (**a**) *(quête)* search (**de** for); **à la r. de** in search of (**b**) *(scientifique)* research (**sur** into); **faire de la r.** to do research (**c**) **recherches** *(de police)* search, hunt; **faire des recherches** to make inquiries (**d**) *(raffinement)* elegance

**rechercher** [rəʃɛrʃe] *vt (personne, objet)* to search for; *(emploi)* to look for; *(honneurs)* to seek ▪ **recherché, -e** *adj* (**a**) *(très demandé)* in demand; *(rare)* sought-after; **r. pour meurtre** wanted for murder (**b**) *(élégant)* elegant

**rechute** [rəʃyt] *nf* relapse ▪ **rechuter** *vi* to have a relapse

**récidive** [residiv] *nf (de malfaiteur)* repeat *Br* offence *or Am* offense; *(de maladie)* recurrence (**de** of) ▪ **récidiver** *vi (malfaiteur)* to reoffend ▪ **récidiviste** *nmf (malfaiteur)* repeat offender

**récif** [resif] *nm* reef

**récipient** [resipjɑ̃] *nm* container

**réciproque** [resiprɔk] *adj (sentiments)* mutual; *(concessions)* reciprocal

**récit** [resi] *nm (histoire)* story; *(compte rendu)* account; **faire le r. de qch** to give an account of sth

**récital, -als** [resital] *nm* recital

**réciter** [resite] *vt* to recite

**réclame** [reklam] *nf (publicité)* advertising; *(annonce)* advertisement; **en r.** on special offer

**réclamer** [reklame] **1** *vt (demander)* to ask for; *(exiger)* to demand; *(nécessiter)* to require **2** *vi* to complain ▪ **réclamation** *nf* complaint; **(bureau des) réclamations** complaints department

**réclusion** [reklyzjɔ̃] *nf* **r. (criminelle) à perpétuité** life imprisonment

**recoin** [rəkwɛ̃] *nm (de lieu)* nook

**recoller** [rəkɔle] *vt (objet cassé)* to stick back together

**récolte** [rekɔlt] *nf (action)* harvesting; *(produits)* harvest; **faire la r.** to harvest the crops ▪ **récolter** *vt* to harvest

**recommandable** [rəkɔmɑ̃dabl] *adj* **peu r.** disreputable

**recommandation** [rəkɔmɑ̃dɑsjɔ̃] *nf (appui, conseil)* recommendation

**recommander** [rəkɔmɑ̃de] *vt (appuyer)* to recommend (**à** to; **pour** for); **r. à qn de faire qch** to advise sb to do sth ▪ **recommandé, -e 1** *adj (lettre)* registered **2** *nm* **en r.** registered

**recommencer** [rəkɔmɑ̃se] *vti* to start *or* begin again ▪ **recommencement** *nm* renewal (**de** of)

**récompense** [rekɔ̃pɑ̃s] *nf* reward (**pour** *ou* **de** for); *(prix)* award ▪ **récompenser** *vt* to reward (**de** *ou* **pour** for)

**réconcilier** [rekɔ̃silje] **1** *vt* to reconcile (**avec** with) **2 se réconcilier** *vpr* to become reconciled, *Br* to make it up (**avec** with) ▪ **réconciliation** *nf* reconciliation

**reconduire*** [rəkɔ̃dɥir] *vt (contrat)* to renew; **r. qn (à la porte)** to show sb out ▪ **reconduction** *nf (de contrat)* renewal

**réconfort** [rekɔ̃fɔr] *nm* comfort ▪ **réconfortant, -e** *adj* comforting ▪ **réconforter** *vt* to comfort

**reconnaissable** [rəkɔnɛsabl] *adj* recognizable (**à qch** by sth)

**reconnaissant, -e** [rəkɔnɛsɑ̃, -ɑ̃t] *adj* grateful (**à qn de qch** to sb for sth) ▪ **reconnaissance** *nf (gratitude)* gratitude (**pour** for); *(de droit, de gouvernement)* recognition; *Mil* reconnaissance; **r. de dette** IOU

**reconnaître*** [rəkɔnɛtr] **1** *vt (identifier, admettre)* to recognize (**à qch** by sth); *(enfant, erreur)* to acknowledge; *Mil (terrain)* to reconnoitre; **être reconnu coupable** to be found guilty
**2 se reconnaître** *vpr (soi-même)* to recognize oneself; *(l'un l'autre)* to recognize each other ▪ **reconnu, -e** *adj* recognized

**reconquérir*** [rəkɔ̃kerir] *vt (territoire)* to reconquer

**reconsidérer** [rəkɔ̃sidere] *vt* to reconsider

**reconstituer** [rəkɔ̃stitɥe] *vt (armée, parti)* to reconstitute; *(crime)* to reconstruct ▪ **reconstitution** *nf (de crime)* reconstruction; **r. historique** historical reconstruction

**reconstruire*** [rəkɔ̃strɥir] *vt* to rebuild ▪ **reconstruction** *nf* rebuilding

**reconvertir** [rəkɔ̃vɛrtir] **1** *vt (entreprise)* to convert; *(personne)* to retrain **2 se reconvertir** *vpr (personne)* to retrain ▪ **reconversion** *nf (d'usine)* conversion; *(de personne)* retraining

**recopier** [rəkɔpje] *vt (mettre au propre)* to copy out; *(faire un double de)* to recopy

**record** [rəkɔr] *nm & adj inv* record

**recoucher** [rəkuʃe] **se recoucher** *vpr* to go back to bed

**recoudre*** [rəkudr] *vt (bouton)* to sew back on; *(vêtement, plaie)* to stitch up

**recouper** [rəkupe] **1** *vt (couper de nouveau)* to recut; *(confirmer)* to confirm **2 se recouper** *vpr (témoignages)* to tally ▪ **recoupement** *nm* crosscheck; **par r.** by crosschecking

**recourber** [rəkurbe] *vt*, **se recourber** *vpr* to bend ▪ **recourbé, -e** *adj (bec)* curved

**recours** [rəkur] *nm* recourse; **avoir r. à** *(chose)* to resort to; *(personne)* to turn to; **en dernier r.** as a last resort ▪ **recourir*** *vi* **r. à** *(moyen, violence)* to resort to; *(personne)* to turn to

**recouvrer** [rəkuvre] *vt (santé, bien)* to recover; *(vue)* to regain

**recouvrir*** [rəkuvrir] *vt (revêtir, inclure)* to cover (**de** with); *(couvrir de nouveau)* to re-cover

**récréation** [rekreɑsjɔ̃] *nf Scol Br* break, *Am* recess; *(pour les plus jeunes)* playtime

**recroqueviller** [rəkrɔkvije] **se recroqueviller** *vpr (personne)* to huddle up

**recrue** [rəkry] *nf* recruit ▪ **recrutement** *nm* recruitment ▪ **recruter** *vt* to recruit

**rectangle** [rɛktɑ̃gl] *nm* rectangle ▪ **rectangulaire** *adj* rectangular

**rectifier** [rɛktifje] *vt (calcul, erreur)* to correct; *(compte)* to adjust ▪ **rectification** *nf (de calcul, d'erreur)* correction

**recto** [rɛkto] *nm* front; **r. verso** on both sides

**rectorat** [rɛktɔra] *nm Br* ≃ local education authority, *Am* ≃ board of education

**reçu, -e** [rəsy] **1** *pp de* **recevoir 2** *adj (idée)* received; *(candidat)* successful **3** *nm (récépissé)* receipt

**recueil** [rəkœj] *nm (de poèmes, de chansons)* collection (**de** of)

**recueillir*** [rəkœjir] **1** *vt (argent, renseignements)* to collect; *(personne, animal)* to take in **2 se recueillir** *vpr* to meditate; *(devant un monument)* to stand in silence ▪ **recueillement** *nm* meditation

**recul** [rəkyl] *nm (d'armée, de négociateur, de maladie)* retreat; *(de canon)* recoil; *(déclin)* decline; **avoir un mouvement de r.** to recoil

**reculer** [rəkyle] **1** *vi (personne)* to move back; *(automobiliste)* to reverse, *Am* to back up; *(armée)* to retreat; *(épidémie)* to lose ground; *(renoncer)* to back down, to retreat; *(diminuer)* to decline; **faire r. la foule** to move the crowd back

**2** *vt (meuble)* to move back; *(paiement, décision)* to postpone ■ **reculé, -e** *adj (endroit)* remote

**reculons** [rəkylɔ̃] **à reculons** *adv* backwards

**récupérer** [rekypere] **1** *vt (objet prêté)* to get back, to recover; *(bagages)* to retrieve; *(forces)* to recover; *(recycler)* to salvage; *Péj (détourner à son profit)* to exploit **2** *vi (reprendre des forces)* to recover ■ **récupération** *nf (d'objet)* recovery; *(de déchets)* salvage

**recycler** [rəsikle] **1** *vt (matériaux)* to recycle **2 se recycler** *vpr (personne)* to retrain ■ **recyclage** *nm (de matériaux)* recycling; *(de personne)* retraining

**rédacteur, -trice** [redaktœr, -tris] *nmf* writer; *(de journal)* editor ■ **rédaction** *nf (action)* writing; *(de contrat)* drawing up; *(journalistes)* editorial staff; *(bureaux)* editorial offices

**redemander** [rədəmɑ̃de] *vt* to ask for more; **il faut que je le lui redemande** *(que je pose la question à nouveau)* I'll have to ask him/her again

**redémarrer** [rədemare] *vi (voiture)* to start again

**redescendre** [rədesɑ̃dr] **1** *(aux* **avoir***) vt (objet)* to bring/take back down **2** *(aux* **être***) vi* to come/go back down

**redevance** [rədəvɑ̃s] *nf (de télévision)* licence fee

**redevenir*** [rədəvənir] *(aux* **être***) vi* to become again

**rediffusion** [rədifyzjɔ̃] *nf (de film)* repeat

**rédiger** [rediʒe] *vt* to write; *(contrat)* to draw up

**redire*** [rədir] **1** *vt* to repeat **2** *vi* **avoir** *ou* **trouver à r. à qch** to find fault with sth

**redoublant, -e** [rədublɑ̃, -ɑ̃t] *nmf* pupil repeating a year *or Am* a grade

**redoubler** [rəduble] **1** *vt* to increase; *Scol* **r. une classe** to repeat a year *or Am* a grade **2** *vi Scol* to repeat a year *or Am* a grade ■ **redoublement** *nm* increase (**de** in)

**redouter** [rədute] *vt* to dread (**de faire** doing) ■ **redoutable** *adj (adversaire, arme)* formidable; *(maladie)* dreadful

**redresser** [rədrese] **1** *vt (objet tordu)* to straighten (out); *(économie, situation)* to put right; **r. la tête** to hold up one's head **2 se redresser** *vpr (personne)* to straighten up; *(pays, économie)* to recover ■ **redressement** [-ɛsmɑ̃] *nm* **r. fiscal** tax adjustment

**réduction** [redyksjɔ̃] *nf* reduction (**de** in); *(rabais)* discount

**réduire*** [redɥir] **1** *vt* to reduce (**à** to; **de** by); **r. qch en cendres** to reduce sth to ashes; **r. qn à qch** *(misère, désespoir)* to reduce sb to sth **2** *vi (sauce)* to reduce **3 se réduire** *vpr* **se r. à** *(se ramener à)* to come down to ■ **réduit, -e** **1** *adj (prix, vitesse)* reduced **2** *nm (pièce)* small room

**réécrire*** [reekrir] *vt* to rewrite

**rééduquer** [reedyke] *vt (personne)* to rehabilitate ■ **rééducation** *nf (de personne)* rehabilitation; **faire de la r.** to have physiotherapy

**réel, -elle** [reɛl] *adj* real

**réélire*** [reelir] *vt* to re-elect

**réévaluer** [reevalɥe] *vt (monnaie)* to revalue; *(salaires)* to reassess

**réexpédier** [reɛkspedje] *vt (faire suivre)* to forward; *(à l'envoyeur)* to return

**refaire*** [rəfɛr] *vt (exercice, travail)* to do again, to redo; *(chambre)* to do up; *(erreur, voyage)* to make again; **r. sa vie** to make a new life for oneself; **r. du riz** to make some more rice

**réfectoire** [refɛktwar] *nm* dining hall, refectory

**référence** [referɑ̃s] *nf* reference; **faire r. à qch** to refer to sth
**référer** [refere] **se référer** *vpr* **se r. à** to refer to
**refermer** [rəfɛrme] *vt*, **se refermer** *vpr* to close *or* shut again
**réfléchir** [refleʃir] **1** *vt (image, lumière)* to reflect; **r. que...** to realize that... **2** *vi* to think (**à** *ou* **sur** about) **3 se réfléchir** *vpr* to be reflected ▪ **réfléchi, -e** *adj (personne)* thoughtful; *(action, décision)* carefully thought-out; **tout bien r.** all things considered
**reflet** [rəflɛ] *nm (image) & Fig* reflection; *(lumière)* glint; **reflets** *(de cheveux)* highlights ▪ **refléter 1** *vt* to reflect **2 se refléter** *vpr* to be reflected
**réflexe** [reflɛks] *nm & adj* reflex
**réflexion** [reflɛksjɔ̃] *nf (d'image, de lumière)* reflection; *(pensée)* thought, reflection; *(remarque)* remark; **faire une r. à qn** to make a remark to sb; **r. faite, à la r.** on second *Br* thoughts *or Am* thought
**reflux** [rəfly] *nm (de marée)* ebb; *(de foule)* backward surge
**réforme** [refɔrm] *nf* reform ▪ **réformer** *vt (loi)* to reform; *(soldat)* to discharge as unfit
**refouler** [rəfule] *vt (personnes)* to force *or* drive back; *(étrangers)* to turn away; *(sentiment)* to repress; *(larmes)* to hold back
**refrain** [rəfrɛ̃] *nm (de chanson)* chorus, refrain
**réfrigérateur** [refriʒeratœr] *nm* refrigerator
**refroidir** [rəfrwadir] **1** *vt* to cool (down) **2** *vi (devenir froid)* to get cold; *(devenir moins chaud)* to cool down **3 se refroidir** *vpr (temps)* to get colder ▪ **refroidissement** *nm (de température)* drop in temperature; *(de l'eau)* cooling
**refuge** [rəfyʒ] *nm* refuge; *(de montagne)* (mountain) hut
**réfugier** [refuʒje] **se réfugier** *vpr* to take refuge ▪ **réfugié, -e** *nmf* refugee
**refus** [rəfy] *nm* refusal ▪ **refuser 1** *vt* to refuse (**qch à qn** sb sth; **de faire** to do); *(offre, invitation)* to turn down; *(proposition)* to reject; *(candidat)* to fail; *(client)* to turn away **2 se refuser** *vpr (plaisir)* to deny oneself; **se r. à faire qch** to refuse to do sth
**regagner** [rəgaɲe] *vt (récupérer)* to regain, to get back; *(revenir à)* to get back to
**régaler** [regale] **se régaler** *vpr* **je me régale** *(en mangeant)* I'm really enjoying it
**regard** [rəgar] *nm (coup d'œil, expression)* look; **jeter un r. sur** to glance at
**regarder** [rəgarde] **1** *vt* to look at; *(émission, film)* to watch; *(considérer)* to consider, to regard (**comme** as); *(concerner)* to concern; **r. qn fixement** to stare at sb
**2** *vi (observer)* to look; **r. par la fenêtre** *(du dedans)* to look out of the window
**3 se regarder** *vpr (soi-même)* to look at oneself; *(l'un l'autre)* to look at each other
**régénérer** [reʒenere] *vt* to regenerate
**régie** [reʒi] *nf (entreprise)* state-owned company; *TV (organisation)* production management; *(lieu)* control room
**régime** [reʒim] *nm (politique)* (form of) government; *(de bananes)* bunch; **r. (alimentaire)** diet; **suivre un r.** to be on a diet
**régiment** [reʒimɑ̃] *nm (de soldats)* regiment
**région** [reʒjɔ̃] *nf* region, area ▪ **régional, -e, -aux, -ales** *adj* regional
**registre** [rəʒistr] *nm* register
**réglable** [reglabl] *adj* adjustable ▪ **réglage** *nm (de siège, de machine)* adjustment; *(de moteur, de télévision)* tuning
**règle** [rɛgl] *nf* (**a**) *(principe)* rule; **en r.** *(papiers d'identité)* in order; **en r. générale** as a (general) rule (**b**) *(instrument)* ruler
**règlement** [rɛgləmɑ̃] *nm* (**a**) *(règles)* regulations (**b**) *(de conflit)* settling; *(paiement)* payment; *Fig* **r. de**

**comptes** settling of scores ▪ **réglementaire** *adj* in accordance with the regulations; *Mil* **tenue r.** regulation uniform ▪ **réglementation** *nf (règles)* regulations ▪ **réglementer** *vt* to regulate

**régler** [regle] **1** *vt (problème, conflit)* to settle; *(mécanisme)* to adjust; *(moteur, télévision)* to tune; *(payer)* to pay; **r. qn** to settle up with sb **2** *vi* to pay **3 se régler** *vpr* **se r. sur qn** to model oneself on sb

**réglisse** [reglis] *nf Br* liquorice, *Am* licorice

**règne** [rɛɲ] *nm (de souverain)* reign; *(animal, minéral, végétal)* kingdom ▪ **régner** *vi (roi, silence)* to reign (**sur** over); *(prédominer)* to prevail; **faire r. l'ordre** to maintain law and order

**regorger** [rəgɔrʒe] *vi* **r. de** to be overflowing with

**regret** [rəgrɛ] *nm* regret; **à r.** with regret; **avoir le r.** *ou* **être au r. de faire qch** to be sorry to do sth ▪ **regrettable** *adj* regrettable ▪ **regretter** [rəgrɛte] *vt* to regret; **r. qn** to miss sb; **je regrette, je le regrette** I'm sorry; **r. que...** *(+ subjunctive)* to be sorry that...

**regrouper** [rəgrupe] *vt*, **se regrouper** *vpr* to gather together

**régulariser** [regylarize] *vt (situation)* to regularize

**régulier, -ère** [regylje, -ɛr] *adj (intervalles, visage)* regular; *(constant)* steady; *(légal)* legal ▪ **régularité** *nf (exactitude)* regularity; *(constance)* steadiness

**réhabituer** [reabitɥe] **se réhabituer** *vpr* **se r. à qch/à faire qch** to get used to sth/to doing sth again

**rein** [rɛ̃] *nm* kidney; **les reins** *(dos)* the lower back

**reine** [rɛn] *nf* queen; **la r. Élisabeth** Queen Elizabeth

**réinsertion** [reɛ̃sɛrsjɔ̃] *nf* reintegration; **r. sociale** rehabilitation

**réintégrer** [reɛ̃tegre] *vt (fonctionnaire)* to reinstate; *(lieu)* to return to

**rejaillir** [rəʒajir] *vi* to spurt out

**rejet** [rəʒɛ] *nm (refus) & Méd* rejection ▪ **rejeter** *vt (relancer)* to throw back; *(offre, candidature, greffe, personne)* to reject; *(blâme)* to shift (**on** to)

**rejoindre*** [rəʒwɛ̃dr] **1** *vt (personne)* to meet; *(rue, rivière)* to join; *(lieu)* to reach; *(concorder avec)* to coincide with **2 se rejoindre** *vpr (personnes)* to meet up; *(rues, rivières)* to join up

**réjouir** [reʒwir] **1** *vt* to delight **2 se réjouir** *vpr* to be delighted (**de** at; **de faire** to do) ▪ **réjoui, -e** *adj* joyful ▪ **réjouissance** *nf* rejoicing; **réjouissances** festivities

**relâche** [rəlɑʃ] *nf* **faire r.** *Théât & Cin* to be closed; *Naut* to put in (**dans un port** at a port); **sans r.** without a break

**relâcher** [rəlɑʃe] **1** *vt (corde, étreinte)* to loosen; *(discipline)* to relax; *(prisonnier)* to release **2** *vi Naut* to put into port **3 se relâcher** *vpr (corde)* to slacken; *(discipline)* to become lax; *(employé)* to slack off

**relais** [rəlɛ] *nm (dispositif émetteur)* relay; *Sport* **(course de) r.** relay (race); **passer le r. à qn** to hand over to sb; **prendre le r.** to take over (**de** from); **r. routier** *Br* transport café, *Am* truck stop (café)

**relancer** [rəlɑ̃se] *vt (lancer à nouveau)* to throw again; *(rendre)* to throw back; *(production)* to boost; *(moteur)* to restart

**relatif, -ive** [rəlatif, -iv] *adj* relative (**à** to)

**relation** [rəlɑsjɔ̃] *nf (rapport)* relationship; *(ami)* acquaintance; **être en r. avec qn** to be in touch with sb; **avoir des relations** *(amis)* to have contacts; **r. (amoureuse)** (love) affair; **relations extérieures** foreign affairs; **relations internationales** international relations

**relayer** [rəleje] **1** *vt (personne)* to take over from; *(émission)* to relay **2 se relayer** *vpr* to take turns (**pour faire** doing); *Sport* to take over from one another

**relevé** [rəlve] *nm* list; *(de compteur)* reading; **r. de compte** bank statement; *Scol* **r. de notes** list of *Br* marks *orAm* grades

**relève** [rəlɛv] *nf* relief; **prendre la r.** to take over (**de** from)

**relèvement** [rəlɛvmɑ̃] *nm (d'économie, de pays)* recovery; *(de salaires)* raising

**relever** [rəlve] **1** *vt (ramasser)* to pick up; *(personne)* to help back up; *(pays)* to revive; *(copies)* to collect; *(faute)* to pick out; *(empreinte)* to find; *(défi)* to accept; *(sauce)* to spice up; *(copier)* to note down; *(compteur)* to read; *(relayer)* to relieve; *(augmenter)* to raise; **r. la tête** to look up; **r. qn de ses fonctions** to relieve sb of his/her duties

**2** *vi* **r. de** *(dépendre de)* to come under; *(maladie)* to be recovering from

**3 se relever** *vpr (après une chute)* to get up

**relief** [rəljɛf] *nm (de paysage)* relief; **en r.** in relief; *Fig* **mettre qch en r.** to highlight sth

**relier** [rəlje] *vt* to connect, to link (**à** to); *(idées, faits)* to link together; *(livre)* to bind

**religion** [rəliʒjɔ̃] *nf* religion ▪ **religieuse** *nf (femme)* nun; *(gâteau)* cream puff ▪ **religieux, -euse 1** *adj* religious; **mariage r.** church wedding **2** *nm (moine)* monk

**relire*** [rəlir] *vt* to reread

**reliure** [rəljyr] *nf (couverture)* binding; *(art)* bookbinding

**reluire*** [rəlɥir] *vi* to shine, to gleam; **faire r. qch** to polish sth up

**remanier** [rəmanje] *vt (texte)* to revise; *(ministère)* to reshuffle ▪ **remaniement** *nm (de texte)* revision; **r. ministériel** cabinet reshuffle

**remarier** [rəmarje] **se remarier** *vpr* to remarry ▪ **remariage** *nm* remarriage

**remarquable** [rəmarkabl] *adj* remarkable (**par** for)

**remarque** [rəmark] *nf* remark; **faire une r.** to make a remark

**remarquer** [rəmarke] *vt (apercevoir)* to notice (**que** that); *(dire)* to remark (**que** that); **faire r. qch** to point sth out (**à** to); **se faire r.** to attract attention

**rembobiner** [rɑ̃bɔbine] *vt*, **se rembobiner** *vpr* to rewind

**rembourser** [rɑ̃burse] *vt (personne)* to pay back; *(billet, frais)* to refund ▪ **remboursement** [-əmɑ̃] *nm* repayment; *(de billet)* refund

**remède** [rəmɛd] *nm* cure, remedy (**contre** for) ▪ **remédier** *vi* **r. à qch** to remedy sth

**remémorer** [rəmemɔre] **se remémorer** *vpr* to remember

**remercier** [rəmɛrsje] *vt (dire merci à)* to thank (**de** *ou* **pour qch** for sth); **je vous remercie d'être venu** thank you for coming ▪ **remerciements** *nmpl* thanks

**remettre*** [rəmɛtr] **1** *vt (replacer)* to put back; *(vêtement)* to put back on; *(disque)* to put on again; *(différer)* to postpone (**à** until); *(ajouter)* to add (**dans** to); **r. qch à qn** *(lettre)* to deliver sth to sb; *(rapport)* to submit sth to sb; *(démission)* to hand sth in to sb; **r. qn en liberté** to set sb free; **r. qch en question** to call sth into question; **r. qch en état** to repair sth; **r. qch à jour** to bring sth up to date

**2 se remettre** *vpr* **se r. à qch** to start sth again; **se r. à faire qch** to start to do sth again; **se r. de qch** to recover from sth

**remise** [rəmiz] *nf* (**a**) *(de lettre)* delivery; **r. à neuf** *(de machine)* reconditioning; **r. en question** questioning; **r. en état** *(de maison)* restoration (**b**) *(rabais)* discount (**c**) *Jur* **r. de peine** reduction of sentence (**d**) *(local)* shed

**remontée** [rəmɔ̃te] *nf* **r. mécanique** ski lift

**remonter** [rəmɔ̃te] **1** *(aux* **être***) vi* to come/go back up; *(niveau, prix)* to rise again, to go back up; *(dans le temps)* to go back (**à** to); **r. dans** *(voiture)* to get back in(to); *(bus, train)* to get back on(to); **r. à dix ans** to go back ten years

**2** *(aux* **avoir**) *vt (escalier, pente)* to come/go back up; *(porter)* to bring/take back up; *(montre)* to wind up; *(relever)* to raise; *(objet démonté)* to put back together, to reassemble; **r. le moral à qn** to cheer sb up ▪ **remonte-pente** (*pl* **remonte-pentes**) *nm* ski lift

**remords** [rəmɔr] *nm* remorse; **avoir des r.** to feel remorse

**remorque** [rəmɔrk] *nf (de voiture)* trailer ▪ **remorquer** *vt (voiture, bateau)* to tow ▪ **remorqueur** *nm* tug(-boat)

**rempart** [rɑ̃par] *nm* rampart; **remparts** walls

**remplacer** [rɑ̃plase] *vt* to replace (**par** with); *(professionnellement)* to stand in for ▪ **remplaçant, -e** *nmf (personne)* replacement; *(enseignant)* substitute teacher, *Br* supply teacher; *(joueur)* substitute ▪ **remplacement** *nm* replacement; **en r. de** in place of

**remplir** [rɑ̃plir] **1** *vt* to fill (up) (**de** with); *(formulaire)* to fill out, *Br* to fill in; *(promesse)* to fulfil **2 se remplir** *vpr* to fill (up) (**de** with)

**remporter** [rɑ̃pɔrte] *vt (objet)* to take back; *(prix, victoire)* to win

**remuer** [rəmɥe] **1** *vt (bouger)* to move; *(terre)* to turn over **2** *vi* to move; *(gigoter)* to fidget

**rémunérer** [remynere] *vt (personne)* to pay; *(travail)* to pay for ▪ **rémunération** *nf* payment (**de** for)

**renaître*** [rənɛtr] *vi (personne)* to be born again; *(espoir, industrie)* to revive ▪ **renaissance** *nf* rebirth; *(des arts)* renaissance

**renard** [rənar] *nm* fox

**renchérir** [rɑ̃ʃerir] *vi (dire plus)* to go one better (**sur** than)

**rencontre** [rɑ̃kɔ̃tr] *nf (de personnes)* meeting; *(match) Br* match, *Am* game; **aller à la r. de qn** to go to meet sb ▪ **rencontrer 1** *vt (personne)* to meet; *(difficulté)* to come up against, to encounter; *(trouver)* to come across

**2 se rencontrer** *vpr* to meet

**rendement** [rɑ̃dmɑ̃] *nm (de champ)* yield; *(d'investissement)* return, yield; *(de personne, de machine)* output

**rendez-vous** [rɑ̃devu] *nm inv (rencontre)* appointment; *(amoureux)* date; *(lieu)* meeting place; **donner r. à qn** to arrange to meet sb; **prendre r. avec qn** to make an appointment with sb; **recevoir sur r.** *(médecin)* to see patients by appointment

**rendormir*** [rɑ̃dɔrmir] **se rendormir** *vpr* to go back to sleep

**rendre** [rɑ̃dr] **1** *vt (restituer)* to give back, to return (**à** to); *(jugement)* to deliver; *(armes)* to surrender; *(invitation)* to return; *(santé)* to restore; *(exprimer)* to render; *(vomir)* to bring up; **r. célèbre** to make famous; **r. la monnaie à qn** to give sb his/her change; **r. l'âme** to pass away; **r. les armes** to surrender

**2** *vi (vomir)* to vomit

**3 se rendre** *vpr (criminel)* to give oneself up (**à** to); *(soldats)* to surrender (**à** to); *(aller)* to go (**à** to); **se r. à l'évidence** *(être lucide)* to face facts; **se r. malade** to make oneself ill

**renfermer** [rɑ̃fɛrme] *vt* to contain ▪ **renfermé, -e 1** *adj (personne)* withdrawn **2** *nm* **sentir le r.** to smell musty

**renforcer** [rɑ̃fɔrse] *vt* to strengthen, to reinforce

**renfort** [rɑ̃fɔr] *nm* **des renforts** *(troupes)* reinforcements; *Fig* **à grand r. de** with (the help of) a great deal of

**renfrogner** [rɑ̃frɔɲe] **se renfrogner** *vpr* to scowl

**renier** [rənje] *vt (ami, pays)* to disown; *(foi)* to deny

**renifler** [rənifle] *vti* to sniff ▪ **reniflement** [-əmɑ̃] *nm (bruit)* sniff

**renne** [rɛn] *nm* reindeer

**renom** [rənɔ̃] *nm* renown; **de r.** *(ouvrage, artiste)* famous, renowned ▪ **renommé, -e** *adj* famous, renowned (**pour** for) ▪ **renommée** *nf* fame, renown

**renoncer** [rənɔ̃se] *vi* **r. à qch** to give

sth up, to abandon sth; **r. à faire qch** to give up doing sth

**renouer** [rənwe] **1** *vt (lacet)* to tie again **2** *vi* **r. avec qch** *(tradition)* to revive sth; **r. avec qn** to take up with sb again

**renouveau, -x** [rənuvo] *nm* revival

**renouveler** [rənuvəle] **1** *vt* to renew; *(expérience)* to repeat **2 se renouveler** *vpr (incident)* to happen again, to recur; *(cellules, sang)* to be renewed ▪ **renouvelable** *adj* renewable ▪ **renouvellement** [-ɛlmɑ̃] *nm* renewal

**rénover** [renɔve] *vt (édifice, meuble)* to renovate ▪ **rénovation** *nf (d'édifice, de meuble)* renovation

**renseigner** [rɑ̃seɲe] **1** *vt* to give some information to (**sur** about) **2 se renseigner** *vpr* to make inquiries (**sur** about) ▪ **renseignement** [-əmɑ̃] *nm* piece of information; **renseignements** information; **les renseignements (téléphoniques)** *Br* directory inquiries, *Am* information; **demander des renseignements** to make inquiries

**rentable** [rɑ̃tabl] *adj* profitable ▪ **rentabilité** *nf* profitability

**rente** [rɑ̃t] *nf* (private) income; *(pension)* pension

**rentrée** [rɑ̃tre] *nf* **r. des classes** start of the new school year

**rentrer** [rɑ̃tre] **1** *(aux* **être***) vi (entrer)* to go/come in; *(entrer de nouveau)* to go/come back in; *(chez soi)* to go/come (back) home; **r. en France** to return to France; **en rentrant de l'école** on my/his/her/*etc* way home from school; **r. dans qch** *(pénétrer)* to get into sth; *(sujet: voiture)* to crash into sth; **r. dans une catégorie** to fall into a category

**2** *(aux* **avoir***) vt (linge, troupeau)* to bring/take in; *(chemise)* to tuck in; *(griffes)* to retract

**renverse** [rɑ̃vɛrs] **à la renverse** *adv (tomber)* backwards

**renverser** [rɑ̃vɛrse] **1** *vt (faire tomber)* to knock over; *(liquide)* to spill; *(piéton)* to run over; *(tendance, situation)* to reverse; *(gouvernement)* to overthrow **2 se renverser** *vpr (récipient)* to fall over; *(véhicule)* to overturn

**renvoi** [rɑ̃vwa] *nm (de marchandise, de lettre)* return; *(d'employé)* dismissal; *(d'élève)* expulsion; *(rot)* belch, burp ▪ **renvoyer*** *vt (lettre, cadeau)* to send back, to return; *(employé)* to dismiss; *(élève)* to expel; *(balle)* to throw back; *(lumière, image)* to reflect

**réorganiser** [reɔrganize] *vt* to reorganize ▪ **réorganisation** *nf* reorganization

**repaître*** [rəpɛtr] **se repaître** *vpr Fig* **se r. de qch** to revel in sth

**répandre** [repɑ̃dr] **1** *vt (liquide)* to spill; *(odeur)* to give off; *(chargement)* to shed; *(bienfaits)* to lavish **2 se répandre** *vpr (nouvelle, peur)* to spread; *(liquide)* to spill; **se r. dans** *(fumée, odeur)* to spread through ▪ **répandu, -e** *adj (opinion, usage)* widespread

**reparaître*** [rəparɛtr] *vi* to reappear

**réparer** [repare] *vt (objet, machine)* to repair, to mend; *(faute)* to make amends for; **faire r. qch** to get sth repaired ▪ **réparable** *adj (machine)* repairable ▪ **réparateur, -trice 1** *nmf* repairer **2** *adj (sommeil)* refreshing ▪ **réparation** *nf (action)* repairing; *(résultat)* repair; *(dédommagement)* reparation; **en r.** under repair

**repartir*** [rəpartir] *(aux* **être***) vi (continuer)* to set off again; *(s'en retourner)* to go back; *(machine)* to start again

**répartir** [repartir] *vt (poids, charge)* to distribute; *(tâches, vivres)* to share (out); *(classer)* to divide (up); *(étaler dans le temps)* to spread (out) (**sur** over) ▪ **répartition** *nf (de poids)* distribution; *(de tâches)* sharing; *(classement)* division

**repas** [rəpɑ] *nm* meal

**repasser** [rəpɑse] **1** *vi* to come/go back; **r. chez qn** to drop in on sb again **2** *vt (montagne, frontière)* to go across again; *(examen)* to take again, *Br* to resit; *(film)* to show again; *(disque,* *cassette)* to play again; *(linge)* to iron ▪ **repassage** *nm* ironing

**repêcher** [rəpeʃe] *vt (objet)* to fish out

**repeindre*** [rəpɛ̃dr] *vt* to repaint

**répercuter** [reperkyte] **1** *vt (son)* to reflect; *(augmentation)* to pass **2 se répercuter** *vpr (son, lumière)* to be reflected; *Fig* **se r. sur** to have repercussions on

**repère** [rəper] *nm* mark; **point de r.** *(espace, temps)* reference point ▪ **repérer 1** *vt (endroit)* to locate **2 se repérer** *vpr* to get one's bearings

**répertoire** [repertwar] *nm (liste)* index; *(carnet)* (indexed) notebook; *Théât* repertoire

**répéter** [repete] **1** *vt* to repeat; *(pièce de théâtre, rôle)* to rehearse; **r. à qn que...** to tell sb again that...

**2** *vi (redire)* to repeat; *(acteur)* to rehearse

**3 se répéter** *vpr (radoter)* to repeat oneself; *(événement)* to happen again ▪ **répétition** *nf (redite)* repetition; *Théât* rehearsal; **r. générale** dress rehearsal

**répit** [repi] *nm* rest, respite; **sans r.** ceaselessly

**replacer** [rəplase] *vt* to replace, to put back

**replanter** [rəplɑ̃te] *vt* to replant

**repli** [rəpli] *nm (de vêtement, de terrain)* fold; *(d'armée)* withdrawal; *(de monnaie)* fall

**replier** [rəplije] **1** *vt (objet)* to fold up; *(couteau)* to fold away; *(ailes)* to fold; *(jambes)* to tuck up **2 se replier** *vpr (objet)* to fold up; *(armée)* to withdraw

**réplique** [replik] *nf (réponse)* retort; *(d'acteur)* lines; *(copie)* replica; **sans r.** *(argument)* unanswerable ▪ **répliquer 1** *vt* **r. que...** to reply that... **2** *vi* to reply; *(avec impertinence)* to answer back

**répondre** [repɔ̃dr] **1** *vi* to answer, to reply; *(avec impertinence)* to answer back; *(réagir)* to respond (**à** to); **r. à qn** to answer sb, to reply to sb; *(avec impertinence)* to answer sb back; **r. à** *(lettre, question, objection)* to answer, to reply to; *(besoin)* to meet; **r. au téléphone** to answer the phone; **r. de qn/qch** to answer for sb/sth

**2** *vt (remarque)* to answer *or* reply with; **r. que...** to answer *or* reply that... ▪ **répondeur** *nm* **r. (téléphonique)** answering machine

**réponse** [repɔ̃s] *nf* answer, reply; *(réaction)* response (**à** to)

**reportage** [rəpɔrtaʒ] *nm (article, émission)* report; *(métier)* reporting

**reporter**[1] [rəpɔrte] **1** *vt (objet)* to take back; *(réunion)* to put off, to postpone (**à** until); *(transcrire)* to transfer (**sur** to) **2 se reporter** *vpr* **se r. à** *(texte)* to refer to

**reporter**[2] [rəpɔrtɛr] *nm* reporter

**repos** [rəpo] *nm (détente)* rest; *(tranquillité)* peace

**reposer** [rəpoze] **1** *vt (objet)* to put back down; *(problème, question)* to raise again; *(délasser)* to rest, to relax; **r. sa tête sur** *(appuyer)* to lean one's head on

**2** *vi (être enterré)* to lie; **r. sur** *(bâtiment)* to be built on; *(théorie)* to be based on; **laisser r.** *(liquide)* to allow to settle

**3 se reposer** *vpr* to rest; **se r. sur qn** to rely on sb ▪ **reposant, -e** *adj* restful, relaxing ▪ **reposé, -e** *adj* rested

**repousser** [rəpuse] **1** *vt (en arrière)* to push back; *(sur le côté)* to push away; *(attaque, ennemi)* to beat off; *(offre)* to reject; *(dégoûter)* to repel **2** *vi (cheveux, feuilles)* to grow again

**reprendre*** [rəprɑ̃dr] **1** *vt (objet)* to take back; *(évadé, ville)* to recapture; *(activité)* to take up again; *(vêtement)* to alter; *(corriger)* to correct; **r. de la viande** to take some more meat

**2** *vi (recommencer)* to start again; *(affaires)* to pick up; *(continuer de parler)* to go on, to continue

**3 se reprendre** *vpr (se ressaisir)* to get a grip on oneself; *(se corriger)* to correct oneself; **s'y r. à deux fois** to have another go (at it)

**représenter** [rəprezɑ̃te] **1** *vt* to represent; *(pièce de théâtre)* to perform **2 se représenter** *vpr (s'imaginer)* to imagine ▪ **représentant, -e** *nmf* representative ▪ **représentatif, -ive** *adj* representative (**de** of) ▪ **représentation** *nf* representation; *Théât* performance

**répression** [represjɔ̃] *nf (d'émeute)* suppression; *(mesures de contrôle)* repression ▪ **répressif, -ive** *adj* repressive ▪ **réprimer** *vt (sentiment, révolte)* to suppress

**réprimander** [reprimɑ̃de] *vt* to reprimand

**reprise** [rəpriz] *nf (recommencement)* resumption; *(de l'économie)* recovery; *(de locataire)* = money for fixtures and fittings *(paid by outgoing tenant)*; *(de marchandise)* taking back; *(pour nouvel achat)* part exchange, trade-in; **faire une r. à qch** to darn sth; **à plusieurs reprises** on several occasions ▪ **repriser** *vt (chaussette)* to darn

**réprobateur, -trice** [reprɔbatœr, -tris] *adj* disapproving

**reproche** [rəprɔʃ] *nm* reproach; **sans r.** beyond reproach ▪ **reprocher** *vt* **r. qch à qn** to blame *or* reproach sb for sth

**reproduire*** [rəprɔdɥir] **1** *vt (modèle, son)* to reproduce **2 se reproduire** *vpr (animaux)* to reproduce; *(incident)* to happen again ▪ **reproduction** *nf (d'animaux, de son)* reproduction; *(copie)* copy

**reptile** [rɛptil] *nm* reptile

**repu, -e** [rəpy] *adj (rassasié)* satiated

**république** [repyblik] *nf* republic ▪ **républicain, -e** *adj & nmf* republican

**répugnant, -e** [repyɲɑ̃, -ɑ̃t] *adj* repulsive ▪ **répugner** *vi* **r. à qn** to be repugnant to sb; **r. à faire qch** to be loath to do sth

**réputation** [repytasjɔ̃] *nf* reputation; **avoir la r. d'être franc** to have a reputation for being frank *or* for frankness ▪ **réputé, -e** *adj (célèbre)* renowned (**pour** for)

**requête** [rəkɛt] *nf* request

**requin** [rəkɛ̃] *nm (animal)* shark

**réquisitionner** [rekizisjɔne] *vt* to requisition, to commandeer

**rescapé, -e** [rɛskape] **1** *adj* surviving **2** *nmf* survivor

**réseau, -x** [rezo] *nm* network

**réservation** [rezɛrvasjɔ̃] *nf* reservation, booking

**réserve** [rezɛrv] *nf (provision, discrétion)* reserve; *(entrepôt)* storeroom; *(de bibliothèque)* stacks; *(de chasse, de pêche)* preserve; *(restriction)* reservation; *Mil* **la r.** the reserve; **en r.** in reserve; **sans r.** *(admiration)* unqualified; **sous r. de** subject to; **sous toutes réserves** without guarantee; **r. naturelle** nature reserve

**réserver** [rezɛrve] **1** *vt* to reserve; *(garder)* to save, to keep (**à** for); *(marchandises)* to put aside (**à** for); *(sort, surprise)* to hold in store (**à** for) **2 se réserver** *vpr* **se r. pour qch** to save oneself for sth ▪ **réservé, -e** *adj (personne, place, chambre)* reserved

**réservoir** [rezɛrvwar] *nm (lac)* reservoir; *(cuve)* tank; **r. d'essence** *Br* petrol *or Am* gas tank

**résidence** [rezidɑ̃s] *nf* residence; **r. secondaire** second home; **r. universitaire** *Br* hall of residence, *Am* dormitory ▪ **résident, -e** *nmf* resident ▪ **résidentiel, -elle** *adj (quartier)* residential ▪ **résider** *vi* to reside; **r. dans** *(consister en)* to lie in

**résidu** [rezidy] *nm* residue

**résigner** [reziɲe] **se résigner** *vpr* to resign oneself (**à qch** to sth; **à faire** to doing) ▪ **résignation** *nf* resignation

**résistance** [rezistɑ̃s] *nf* resistance (**à** to); *Hist* **la R.** the Resistance

**résister** [reziste] *vi* **r. à** *(attaque, agresseur, tentation)* to resist; *(chaleur, fatigue, souffrance)* to withstand; *(mauvais traitement)* to stand up to ▪ **résistant, -e 1** *adj* tough; **r. à la chaleur** heat-resistant **2** *nmf Hist* Resistance fighter

**résolu, -e** [rezɔly] **1** *pp de* **résoudre 2**

*adj* determined, resolute; **r. à faire qch** determined to do sth ▪ **résolution** *nf (décision)* resolution; *(fermeté)* determination

**résonance** [rezɔnɑ̃s] *nf* resonance

**résonner** [rezɔne] *vi (cri)* to resound; *(salle, voix)* to echo (**de** with)

**résoudre*** [rezudr] **1** *vt (problème)* to solve; *(difficulté)* to resolve; **r. de faire qch** to resolve to do sth **2 se résoudre** *vpr* **se r. à faire qch** to resolve to do sth

**respect** [rɛspɛ] *nm* respect (**pour/de** for) ▪ **respectable** *adj (honorable, important)* respectable ▪ **respecter** *vt* to respect; **r. la loi** to abide by the law; **faire r. la loi** to enforce the law ▪ **respectueux, -euse** *adj* respectful (**envers** to; **de** of)

**respirer** [rɛspire] **1** *vi* to breathe **2** *vt* to breathe (in) ▪ **respiration** *nf* breathing; *(haleine)* breath

**responsable** [rɛspɔ̃sabl] **1** *adj* responsible (**de qch** for sth; **devant qn** to sb) **2** *nmf (chef)* person in charge; *(d'organisation)* official; *(coupable)* person responsible (**de** for) ▪ **responsabilité** *nf* responsibility; *(légale)* liability

**ressaisir** [rəsezir] **se ressaisir** *vpr* to pull oneself together

**ressemblance** [rəsɑ̃blɑ̃s] *nf* likeness, resemblance (**avec** to) ▪ **ressembler 1** *vi* **r. à** to look like, to resemble **2 se ressembler** *vpr* to look alike

**ressentir*** [rəsɑ̃tir] *vt* to feel

**resserrer** [rəsere] **1** *vt (nœud, boulon)* to tighten; *Fig (liens)* to strengthen **2 se resserrer** *vpr (nœud)* to tighten

**resservir*** [rəsɛrvir] **1** *vi (outil)* to come in useful (again) **2 se resservir** *vpr* **se r. de** *(plat)* to have another helping of

**ressort** [rəsɔr] *nm (objet)* spring; **du r. de** within the competence of; **en dernier r.** *(décider)* as a last resort

**ressortir*** [rəsɔrtir] **1** *(aux* **être**) *vi (personne)* to go/come back out; *(film)* to be shown again; *(se voir)* to stand out; **faire r. qch** to bring sth out; **il ressort de...** *(résulte)* it emerges from... **2** *(aux* **avoir**) *vi (vêtement)* to get out again

**ressortissant, -e** [rəsɔrtisɑ̃, -ɑ̃t] *nmf* national

**ressource** [rəsurs] **1** *nfpl* **ressources** *(moyens, argent)* resources; **être sans ressources** to be without means **2** *nf (possibilité)* possibility (**de faire** of doing); **avoir de la r.** to be resourceful; **en dernière r.** as a last resort

**ressusciter** [resysite] *vi* to rise from the dead

**restant, -e** [rɛstɑ̃, -ɑ̃t] **1** *adj* remaining **2** *nm* **le r.** the rest, the remainder; **un r. de viande** some leftover meat

**restaurant** [rɛstɔrɑ̃] *nm* restaurant

**restaurateur, -trice** [rɛstɔratœr, -tris] *nmf (hôtelier, hôtelière)* restaurant owner; *(de tableaux)* restorer

**restaurer** [rɛstɔre] **1** *vt (réparer, rétablir)* to restore **2 se restaurer** *vpr* to have something to eat ▪ **restauration** *nf (hôtellerie)* catering; *(de tableau)* restoration

**reste** [rɛst] *nm* rest, remainder (**de** of); **restes** remains (**de** of); *(de repas)* leftovers; **au r., du r.** moreover, besides

**rester** [rɛste] *(aux* **être**) *vi* to stay, to remain; *(calme, jeune)* to keep, to stay, to remain; *(subsister)* to be left, to remain; **il reste du pain** there's some bread left (over); **il me reste une pomme** I have one apple left; **l'argent qui lui reste** the money he/she has left; **il me reste deux choses à faire** I still have two things to do

**restituer** [rɛstitɥe] *vt (rendre)* to return (**à** to); *(argent)* to repay ▪ **restitution** *nf (d'objet)* return

**restriction** [rɛstriksjɔ̃] *nf* restriction; **sans r.** *(approuver)* unreservedly

**résultat** [rezylta] *nm* result; **avoir qch pour r.** to result in sth ▪ **résulter 1** *vi* **r. de** to result from **2** *v impersonnel* **il en résulte que...** the result of this is that...

**résumer** [rezyme] **1** *vt (abréger)* to summarize; *(récapituler)* to sum up **2**

**se résumer** *vpr (orateur)* to sum up; **se r. à qch** *(se réduire à)* to boil down to sth ▪ **résumé** *nm* summary; **en r.** in short

**rétablir** [retablir] **1** *vt (communications, ordre)* to restore; *(vérité)* to re-establish; *(employé)* to reinstate **2 se rétablir** *vpr (malade)* to recover ▪ **rétablissement** *nm (d'ordre, de dynastie)* restoration; *(de vérité)* re-establishment; *(de malade)* recovery

**retard** [rətar] *nm (de personne)* lateness; *(sur horaire)* delay; **en r.** late; **en r. sur qn/qch** behind sb/sth; **rattraper** *ou* **combler son r.** to catch up; **avoir du r.** to be late; *(sur un programme)* to be behind (schedule); *(montre)* to be slow; **avoir une heure de r.** to be an hour late; **prendre du r.** *(personne)* to fall behind

**retarder** [rətarde] **1** *vt (faire arriver en retard)* to delay; *(date, montre, départ)* to put back; **r. qn** *(dans une activité)* to put sb behind **2** *vi (montre)* to be slow; **r. de cinq minutes** to be five minutes slow

**retenir*** [rətənir] **1** *vt (personne)* to keep; *(eau, chaleur)* to retain; *(cotisation)* to deduct (**sur** from); *(suggestion)* to adopt; *(larmes, foule)* to hold back; *Math (chiffre)* to carry; *(se souvenir de)* to remember; *(réserver)* to reserve; **r. qn prisonnier** to keep sb prisoner; **r. l'attention de qn** to catch sb's attention; **r. qn de faire qch** to stop sb (from) doing sth

**2 se retenir** *vpr (se contenir)* to restrain oneself; **se r. de faire qch** to stop oneself (from) doing sth; **se r. à qn/qch** to cling to sb/sth

**retenue** [rətəny] *nf (modération)* restraint; *(de salaire)* deduction; *Scol (punition)* detention

**retirer** [rətire] **1** *vt* to withdraw; *(faire sortir)* to take out; *(ôter)* to take off; *(éloigner)* to take away; *(aller chercher)* to pick up; **r. qch à qn** *(permis)* to take sth away from sb; **r. qch de qch** *(gagner)* to derive sth from sth **2 se retirer** *vpr* to withdraw (**de** from); *(mer)* to ebb

**retomber** [rətɔ̃be] *vi* to fall again; *(après un saut)* to land; *(intérêt)* to slacken; **r. dans** *(l'oubli)* to sink back into

**retouche** [rətuʃ] *nf (de vêtement)* alteration ▪ **retoucher** *vt (vêtement, texte)* to alter; *(photo, tableau)* to touch up

**retour** [rətur] *nm* return; *(trajet)* return journey; **être de r.** to be back (**de** from); **à mon r.** when I get/got back (**de** from); **r. à l'envoyeur** return to sender; **match r.** return *Br* match *or Am* game

**retourner** [rəturne] **1** *(aux* **avoir***) vt (matelas, steak)* to turn over; *(terre)* to turn; *(vêtement, sac)* to turn inside out; *(compliment)* to return; **r. qch contre qn** *(argument)* to turn sth against sb; *(arme)* to turn sth on sb

**2** *(aux* **être***) vi* to go back, to return

**3 se retourner** *vpr (pour regarder)* to turn round; *(sur le dos)* to turn over; *(dans son lit)* to toss and turn; *(voiture)* to overturn; *Fig* **se r. contre** to turn against

**retrait** [rətrɛ] *nm* withdrawal; *(de bagages, de billets)* collection; *(des eaux)* receding; **en r.** *(maison)* set back; **rester en r.** to stay in the background

**retraite** [rətrɛt] *nf (d'employé)* retirement; *(pension)* (retirement) pension; *(refuge)* retreat, refuge; *(d'armée)* retreat; **prendre sa r.** to retire; **être à la r.** to be retired; **r. anticipée** early retirement ▪ **retraité, -e 1** *adj* retired **2** *nmf* senior citizen, *Br* (old age) pensioner

**retraitement** [rətrɛtmɑ̃] *nm*

**retrancher** [rətrɑ̃ʃe] **1** *vt (passage, nom)* to remove (**de** from); *(argent, quantité)* to deduct (**de** from) **2 se retrancher** *vpr (soldats)* to dig in; *Fig* **se r. dans/derrière qch** to hide in/behind sth

**retransmettre*** [rətrɑ̃smɛtr] *vt* to broadcast ▪ **retransmission** *nf* broadcast

**rétrécir** [retresir] **1** *vt (vêtement)* to take in **2** *vi (au lavage)* to shrink **3 se rétrécir** *vpr (rue)* to narrow

**rétroactif, -ive** [retrɔaktif, -iv] *adj* retroactive

**rétrograder** [retrograde] **1** *vt (fonctionnaire, officier)* to demote **2** *vi (automobiliste)* to change down

**rétrospectif, -ive** [retrɔspɛktif, -iv] **1** *adj* retrospective **2** *nf* **rétrospective** retrospective

**retrouver** [rətruve] **1** *vt (objet)* to find again; *(personne)* to meet again; *(forces, santé)* to regain; *(se rappeler)* to recall; *(découvrir)* to rediscover **2 se retrouver** *vpr (être)* to find oneself; *(trouver son chemin)* to find one's way (**dans** round); *(se rencontrer)* to meet; **se r. à la rue** to find oneself homeless

**rétroviseur** [retrɔvizœr] *nm* rear-view mirror

**Réunion** [reynjɔ̃] *nf* **la R.** Réunion

**réunion** [reynjɔ̃] *nf (séance)* meeting; *(d'objets)* collection, gathering; *(jonction)* joining; **être en r.** to be in a meeting; **r. de famille** family gathering

**réunir** [reynir] **1** *vt (objets)* to put together; *(documents)* to gather together; *(fonds)* to raise; *(amis, famille)* to get together; *(après une rupture)* to reunite; *(avantages, qualités)* to combine; **r. qch à qch** to join sth to sth **2 se réunir** *vpr (personnes)* to meet; **se r. autour de qn/qch** to gather round sb/sth

**réussir** [reysir] **1** *vt (bien faire)* to make a success of; *(examen)* to pass **2** *vi* to succeed, to be successful (**à faire** in doing); **r. à un examen** to pass an exam ▪ **réussi, -e** *adj* successful ▪ **réussite** *nf* success; *Cartes* **faire des réussites** to play patience

**revaloriser** [rəvalɔrize] *vt (monnaie)* to revalue; *(salaires, profession)* to upgrade

**revanche** [rəvɑ̃ʃ] *nf* revenge; *(de match)* return game; **prendre sa r.** to get one's revenge (**sur** on); **en r.** on the other hand

**rêve** [rɛv] *nm* dream; **faire un r.** to have a dream

**réveil** [revɛj] *nm (de personnes)* waking; *(pendule)* alarm (clock); **à son r.** on waking

**réveiller** [reveje] **1** *vt (personne)* to wake (up); *Fig (douleur)* to revive; *Fig (sentiment, souvenir)* to revive **2 se réveiller** *vpr (personne)* to wake (up); *(nature)* to reawaken; *Fig (douleur)* to come back ▪ **réveillé, -e** *adj* awake ▪ **réveille-matin** *nm inv* alarm clock

**réveillon** [revɛjɔ̃] *nm (repas)* midnight supper; *(soirée)* midnight party *(on Christmas Eve or New Year's Eve)* ▪ **réveillonner** *vi* to see in Christmas/the New Year

**révéler** [revele] **1** *vt* to reveal (**que** that) **2 se révéler** *vpr (personne)* to reveal oneself; *(talent)* to be revealed; **se r. facile** to turn out to be easy ▪ **révélateur, -trice** *adj* revealing; **r. de qch** indicative of sth ▪ **révélation** *nf (action, découverte)* revelation; *(personne)* discovery; **faire des révélations** to disclose important information

**revendiquer** [rəvɑ̃dike] *vt* to claim; *(attentat)* to claim responsibility for ▪ **revendication** *nf* claim

**revendre** [rəvɑ̃dr] *vt* to resell

**revenir*** [rəvənir] (*aux* **être**) *vi (personne)* to come back, to return; *(date)* to come round again; **le dîner nous est revenu à 50 euros** the dinner cost us 50 euros; **r. cher** to work out expensive; **r. à** *(activité, sujet)* to go back to, to return to; *(se résumer à)* to boil down to; **r. à qn** *(forces, mémoire)* to come back to sb; *(honneur)* to fall to sb; **r. de** *(surprise)* to get over; **r. sur** *(décision, promesse)* to go back on; *(passé, question)* to go back over; **r. sur ses pas** to retrace one's steps

**revenu** [rəvəny] *nm* income (**de** from); *(d'un État)* revenue (**de** from)

**rêver** [reve] **1** *vt* to dream (**que** that) **2** *vi* to dream (**de** of; **de faire** of doing)

**réverbère** [revɛrbɛr] *nm* street lamp

**révérence** [reverɑ̃s] *nf (respect)* reverence; *(salut)* curtsey
**rêverie** [rɛvri] *nf* daydream
**revers** [rəvɛr] *nm (de veste)* lapel; *(de pantalon) Br* turn-up, *Am* cuff; *(d'étoffe)* wrong side; *(de pièce)* reverse; *(coup du sort)* setback; *(au tennis)* backhand; **d'un r. de la main** with the back of one's hand; *Fig* **le r. de la médaille** the other side of the coin
**reverser** [rəvɛrse] *vt (café, vin)* to pour more; *Fig (argent)* to transfer (**sur un compte** into an account)
**réversible** [revɛrsibl] *adj* reversible
**revêtir*** [rəvɛtir] *vt* to cover (**de** with); *(habit)* to don; *(caractère, forme)* to assume; **r. qn** *(habiller)* to dress sb (**de** in) ▪ **revêtement** *nm (surface)* covering; *(de route)* surface
**rêveur, -euse** [rɛvœr, -øz] **1** *adj* dreamy **2** *nmf* dreamer
**revient** [rəvjɛ̃] *nm* **prix de r.** *Br* cost price, *Am* wholesale price
**revirement** [rəvirmɑ̃] *nm (changement) Br* about-turn, *Am* about-face; *(de situation, d'opinion, de politique)* reversal
**réviser** [revize] *vt (leçon)* to revise; *(machine, voiture)* to service; *(jugement, règlement)* to review ▪ **révision** *nf (de leçon)* revision; *(de machine)* service; *(de jugement)* review
**revivre*** [rəvivr] **1** *vt (incident)* to relive **2** *vi* to live again; **faire r. qch** to revive sth
**revoici** [rəvwasi] *prép* **me r.** here I am again
**revoilà** [rəvwala] *prép* **la r.** there she is again
**revoir*** [rəvwar] *vt* to see (again); *(texte, leçon)* to revise; **au r.** goodbye
**révolte** [revɔlt] *nf* revolt ▪ **révolter 1** *vt* to appal **2 se révolter** *vpr* to rebel, to revolt (**contre** against)
**révolu, -e** [revɔly] *adj (époque)* past; **avoir trente ans révolus** to be over thirty
**révolution** [revɔlysjɔ̃] *nf (changement, rotation)* revolution ▪ **révolutionner** *vt (transformer)* to revolutionize
**revolver** [revɔlvɛr] *nm* revolver
**revue** [rəvy] *nf (magazine)* magazine; *(spécialisée)* journal; *(spectacle)* revue; *Mil* review; **passer qch en r.** to review sth
**rez-de-chaussée** [redəʃose] *nm inv Br* ground floor, *Am* first floor
**Rhin** [rɛ̃] *nm* **le R.** the Rhine
**rhinocéros** [rinɔserɔs] *nm* rhinoceros
**Rhône** [ron] *nm* **le R.** the Rhône
**rhumatisme** [rymatism] *nm* rheumatism; **avoir des rhumatismes** to have rheumatism
**rhume** [rym] *nm* cold; **r. des foins** hay fever
**ri** [ri] *pp de* **rire**
**ricaner** [rikane] *vi (sarcastiquement) Br* to snigger, *Am* to snicker; *(bêtement)* to giggle
**riche** [riʃ] **1** *adj (personne, pays, aliment)* rich; **r. en** *(vitamines, minérai)* rich in **2** *nmf* rich person; **les riches** the rich ▪ **richesse** *nf (de personne, de pays)* wealth; *(d'étoffe, de sol)* richness; **richesses** *(trésor)* riches; *(ressources)* wealth
**ricocher** [rikɔʃe] *vi* to rebound, to ricochet ▪ **ricochet** *nm* rebound, ricochet; *Fig* **par r.** indirectly
**ride** [rid] *nf (de visage)* wrinkle ▪ **ridé, -e** *adj* wrinkled ▪ **rider 1** *vt (visage, peau)* to wrinkle; *(eau)* to ripple **2 se rider** *vpr (visage, peau)* to wrinkle
**rideau, -x** [rido] *nm* curtain; *(métallique)* shutter; *Fig (écran)* screen (**de** of)
**ridicule** [ridikyl] **1** *adj* ridiculous, ludicrous **2** *nm (moquerie)* ridicule; *(absurdité)* ridiculousness; **tourner qn/qch en r.** to ridicule sb/sth ▪ **ridiculiser 1** *vt* to ridicule **2 se ridiculiser** *vpr* to make a fool of oneself

**RIEN** [rjɛ̃] **1** *pron* nothing; **il ne sait r.** he knows nothing, he doesn't know anything; **r. du tout** nothing at all; **r. d'autre/de bon** nothing else/good; **r. de tel** nothing like it; **de r.!** *(je vous en* *prie)* don't mention it!; **ça ne fait r.** it doesn't matter; **pour r. au monde** never in a thousand years; **comme si de r. n'était** as if nothing had happened

**2** *nm* (mere) nothing, trifle; **un r. de** a little; **en un r. de temps** in no time

**rieur, -euse** [rijœr, -øz] *adj* cheerful
**rigide** [riʒid] *adj* rigid; *(carton)* stiff; *(éducation)* strict
**rigole** [rigɔl] *nf (conduit)* channel; *(filet d'eau)* rivulet
**rigueur** [rigœr] *nf (d'analyse)* rigour; *(de climat)* harshness; *(de personne)* strictness; **être de r.** to be the rule; **à la r.** if need be ▪ **rigoureux, -euse** *adj (analyse)* rigorous; *(climat, punition)* harsh; *(personne, morale, neutralité)* strict
**rillettes** [rijɛt] *nfpl* potted minced pork
**rimer** [rime] *vi* to rhyme (**avec** with)
**rincer** [rɛ̃se] *vt* to rinse; *(verre)* to rinse (out)
**ring** [riŋ] *nm* (boxing) ring
**riposte** [ripɔst] *nf (réponse)* retort; *(attaque)* counterattack ▪ **riposter 1** *vt* **r. que...** to retort that... **2** *vi* to counterattack; **r. à** *(attaque)* to counter; *(insulte)* to reply to
**rire*** [rir] **1** *nm* laugh; **rires** laughter; **le fou r.** the giggles **2** *vi* to laugh (**de** at); *(s'amuser)* to have a good time; *(plaisanter)* to joke; **r. aux éclats** to roar with laughter; **faire qch pour r.** to do sth for a joke *or* laugh
**risible** [rizibl] *adj* laughable
**risque** [risk] *nm* risk; **au r. de faire qch** at the risk of doing sth; **à vos risques et périls** at your own risk; **assurance tous risques** comprehensive insurance
**risquer** [riske] **1** *vt* to risk; *(question)* to venture; **r. de faire qch** to stand a good chance of doing sth **2 se risquer** *vpr* **se r. à faire qch** to dare to do sth ▪ **risqué, -e** *adj (dangereux)* risky; *(osé)* risqué
**rivage** [rivaʒ] *nm* shore
**rival, -e, -aux, -ales** [rival, -o] *adj & nmf* rival ▪ **rivaliser** *vi* to compete (**avec** with; **de** in) ▪ **rivalité** *nf* rivalry
**rive** [riv] *nf (de fleuve)* bank; *(de lac)* shore
**riverain, -e** [rivərɛ̃, -ɛn] **1** *adj (de rivière)* riverside; *(de lac)* lakeside **2** *nmf (près d'une rivière)* riverside resident; *(près d'un lac)* lakeside resident; *(de rue)* resident
**rivière** [rivjɛr] *nf* river
**riz** [ri] *nm* rice; **r. blanc/complet** white/brown rice; **r. au lait** rice pudding ▪ **rizière** *nf* paddy (field), ricefield
**RMI** [ɛrɛmi] (*abrév* **revenu minimum d'insertion**) *nm Br* ≃ income support, *Am* ≃ welfare
**RN** (*abrév* **route nationale**) *nf Br* main road, A-road, *Am* (state) highway
**robe** [rɔb] *nf (de femme)* dress; *(d'ecclésiastique, de juge)* robe; *(pelage)* coat; **r. du soir** evening dress; **r. de chambre** *Br* dressing gown, *Am* bathrobe; **pomme de terre en r. des champs** jacket potato, baked potato
**robinet** [rɔbinɛ] *nm Br* tap, *Am* faucet
**robot** [rɔbo] *nm* robot; **r. ménager** food processor
**robuste** [rɔbyst] *adj* robust
**roc** [rɔk] *nm* rock
**rocaille** [rɔkɑj] *nf (terrain)* rocky ground; *(de jardin)* rockery ▪ **rocailleux, -euse** *adj* rocky, stony; *(voix)* harsh
**roche** [rɔʃ] *nf* rock ▪ **rocher** *nm (bloc, substance)* rock ▪ **rocheux, -euse** *adj* rocky
**rock** [rɔk] **1** *nm (musique)* rock **2** *adj inv* **chanteur/opéra r.** rock singer/opera ▪ **rockeur, -euse** *nmf (musicien)* rock musician
**roder** [rɔde] *vt (moteur, voiture) Br* to run in, *Am* to break in
**rôder** [rode] *vi* to be on the prowl ▪ **rôdeur, -euse** *nmf* prowler
**rognon** [rɔɲɔ̃] *nm* kidney
**roi** [rwa] *nm* king; **fête des Rois** Twelfth Night

**rôle** [rol] *nm* role, part; *(de père)* job; **à tour de r.** in turn

**romain, -e** [rɔmɛ̃, -ɛn] **1** *adj* Roman **2** *nmf* **R., Romaine** Roman **3** *nf* **romaine** *(laitue) Br* cos (lettuce), *Am* romaine

**roman** [rɔmɑ̃] *nm* novel; *Fig (histoire)* story ▪ **romancier, -ère** *nmf* novelist

**romanesque** [rɔmanɛsk] *adj* romantic; *(incroyable)* fantastic

**romantique** [rɔmɑ̃tik] *adj* romantic

**romarin** [rɔmarɛ̃] *nm* rosemary

**rompre*** [rɔ̃pr] **1** *vt* to break; *(pourparlers, relations)* to break off **2** *vi (casser)* to break; *(digue)* to burst; *(fiancés)* to break it off **3 se rompre** *vpr (corde)* to break; *(digue)* to burst

**ronces** [rɔ̃s] *nfpl (branches)* brambles

**rond, -e**[1] [rɔ̃, -ɔ̃d] **1** *adj* round; *(gras)* plump; **chiffre r.** whole number **2** *adv* **10 euros tout r.** 10 euros exactly **3** *nm (cercle)* circle; **en r.** *(s'asseoir)* in a circle ▪ **rondement** *adv* briskly ▪ **rond-point** (*pl* **ronds-points**) *nm Br* roundabout, *Am* traffic circle

**ronde**[2] [rɔ̃d] *nf (de soldat)* round; *(de policier)* beat; *(danse)* round (dance); *Mus Br* semibreve, *Am* whole note; **faire sa r.** *(gardien)* to do one's rounds

**rondelle** [rɔ̃dɛl] *nf (tranche)* slice

**ronfler** [rɔ̃fle] *vi (personne)* to snore

**ronger** [rɔ̃ʒe] **1** *vt* to gnaw (at); *(ver, mer, rouille)* to eat into; **r. qn** *(maladie, chagrin)* to consume sb **2 se ronger** *vpr* **se r. les ongles** to bite one's nails ▪ **rongeur** *nm* rodent

**ronronner** [rɔ̃rɔne] *vi* to purr

**roquette** [rɔkɛt] *nf Mil* rocket

**rosace** [rozas] *nf* rosette; *(d'église)* rose window

**rosbif** [rɔzbif] *nm* **du r.** *(rôti)* roast beef; *(à rôtir)* roasting beef; **un r.** a joint of roast/roasting beef

**rose** [roz] **1** *adj (couleur)* pink; *(situation, teint)* rosy **2** *nm (couleur)* pink **3** *nf (fleur)* rose ▪ **rosé, -e 1** *adj* pinkish **2** *adj & nm (vin)* rosé

**roseau, -x** [rozo] *nm* reed

**rosée** [roze] *nf* dew

**rossignol** [rɔsiɲɔl] *nm (oiseau)* nightingale

**rôti** [roti] *nm* **du r.** roasting meat; *(cuit)* roast meat; **un r.** a joint; **r. de bœuf** (joint of) roast beef

**rotin** [rɔtɛ̃] *nm* rattan

**rôtir** [rotir] *vti* to roast; **faire r. qch** to roast sth

**roue** [ru] *nf* wheel; **r. dentée** cogwheel; **être en r. libre** to freewheel; **les deux roues** two-wheeled vehicles

**rouge** [ruʒ] **1** *adj* red; *(fer)* red-hot **2** *nm (couleur)* red; **le feu est au r.** the (traffic) lights are at red; **r. à lèvres** lipstick

**rougeur** [ruʒœr] *nf* redness; *(due à la honte)* blush; *(due à l'émotion)* flush; **rougeurs** *(irritation)* rash, red blotches

**rougir** [ruʒir] **1** *vt (visage)* to redden **2** *vi (de honte)* to blush (**de** with); *(d'émotion)* to flush (**de** with)

**rouille** [ruj] **1** *nf* rust **2** *adj inv (couleur)* rust(-coloured) ▪ **rouillé, -e** *adj* rusty ▪ **rouiller 1** *vi* to rust **2 se rouiller** *vpr* to rust

**rouleau, -x** [rulo] *nm (outil, vague)* roller; *(de papier, de pellicule)* roll; **r. à pâtisserie** rolling pin; **r. compresseur** steamroller

**roulement** [rulmɑ̃] *nm (bruit)* rumbling, rumble; *(de tambour, de tonnerre)* roll; *(ordre)* rotation; **par r.** in rotation; *Tech* **r. à billes** ball bearing

**rouler** [rule] **1** *vt* to roll; *(crêpe, ficelle, manches)* to roll up **2** *vi (balle)* to roll; *(train, voiture)* to go, to travel **3 se rouler** *vpr* to roll; **se r. dans** *(couverture)* to roll oneself (up) in ▪ **roulant, -e** *adj (escalier)* moving

**roulette** [rulɛt] *nf (de meuble)* castor; *(de dentiste)* drill; *(jeu)* roulette

**roulotte** [rulɔt] *nf (de gitan)* caravan

**Roumanie** [rumani] *nf* **la R.** Romania ▪ **roumain, -e 1** *adj* Romanian **2** *nmf* **R., Roumaine** Romanian **3** *nm (langue)* Romanian

**rousse** [rus] *voir* **roux**

**rousseur** [rusœr] *nf* **tache de r.** freckle ▪ **roussi** *nm* **ça sent le r.** there's a smell of burning ■ **roussir 1** *vt (brûler)* to scorch, to singe **2** *vi (feuilles)* to turn brown

**route** [rut] *nf* road (**de** to); *(itinéraire)* way, route; *Fig (chemin)* path; **grand-r., grande r.** main road; **code de la r.** *Br* Highway Code, *Am* traffic regulations; **en r.** on the way, en route; **par la r.** by road; *Fig* **faire fausse r.** to be on the wrong track; **mettre qch en r.** *(voiture)* to start sth (up); **se mettre en r.** to set out (**pour** for); **une heure de r.** *(en voiture)* an hour's drive; **faire r. vers Paris** to head for Paris; **r. départementale** secondary road, *Br* B road; **r. nationale** *Br* main road, A-road, *Am* (state) highway

**routier, -ère** [rutje, -ɛr] **1** *adj* **carte/ sécurité routière** road map/safety; **réseau r.** road network **2** *nm (camionneur)* (long-distance) *Br* lorry *or Am* truck driver; *(restaurant) Br* transport café, *Am* truck stop

**routine** [rutin] *nf* routine; **contrôle de r.** routine check ■ **routinier, -ère** *adj* **travail r.** routine work; **être r.** *(personne)* to be set in one's ways

**rouvrir*** [ruvrir] *vti*, **se rouvrir** *vpr* to reopen

**roux, rousse** [ru, rus] **1** *adj (cheveux)* red, ginger; *(personne)* red-haired **2** *nmf* redhead

**royal, -e, -aux, -ales** [rwajal, -jo] *adj (famille, palais)* royal; *(cadeau, festin)* fit for a king; *(salaire)* princely

**royaume** [rwajom] *nm* kingdom ■ **Royaume-Uni** *nm* **le R.** the United Kingdom

**royauté** [rwajote] *nf (monarchie)* monarchy

**ruban** [rybɑ̃] *nm* ribbon; *(de chapeau)* band; **r. adhésif** sticky *or* adhesive tape

**rubis** [rybi] *nm (pierre)* ruby; *(de montre)* jewel

**rubrique** [rybrik] *nf (article de journal)* column; *(catégorie, titre)* heading

**ruche** [ryʃ] *nf* beehive

**rude** [ryd] *adj (pénible)* tough; *(hiver, voix)* harsh; *(rêche)* rough

**rue** [ry] *nf* street; **être à la r.** *(sans domicile)* to be on the streets ■ **ruelle** *nf* alley(way)

**ruer** [rɥe] **1** *vi (cheval)* to kick (out) **2** **se ruer** *vpr (foncer)* to rush (**sur** at) ■ **ruée** *nf* rush; **la r. vers l'or** the gold rush

**rugby** [rygbi] *nm* rugby ■ **rugbyman** [rygbiman] *(pl* **-men** [-mɛn]*)* *nm* rugby player

**rugir** [ryʒir] *vi* to roar ■ **rugissement** *nm* roar

**rugueux, -euse** [rygø, -øz] *adj* rough

**ruine** [rɥin] *nf (décombres, destruction, faillite)* ruin; **en r.** *(bâtiment)* in ruins; **tomber en r.** *(bâtiment)* to become a ruin ■ **ruiner 1** *vt (personne, santé, pays)* to ruin **2** **se ruiner** *vpr (perdre tout son argent)* to ruin oneself; *(dépenser beaucoup d'argent)* to spend a fortune ■ **ruineux, -euse** *adj (goûts, projet)* ruinously expensive; *(dépense)* ruinous; **ce n'est pas r.** it won't ruin me/you/*etc*

**ruisseau, -x** [rɥiso] *nm* stream; *(caniveau)* gutter ■ **ruisseler** *vi* to stream (**de** with)

**rumeur** [rymœr] *nf (murmure)* murmur; *(nouvelle)* rumour

**ruminer** [rymine] **1** *vt (herbe)* to chew **2** *vi (vache)* to chew the cud

**rupture** [ryptyr] *nf* breaking; *(de fiançailles, de relations)* breaking off; *(de pourparlers)* breakdown (**de** in); *(dispute)* break-up; **être en r. de stock** to be out of stock

**rural, -e, -aux, -ales** [ryral, -o] *adj (population)* rural; **vie rurale** country life

**ruse** [ryz] *nf (subterfuge)* trick; **la r.** *(habileté)* cunning; *(fourberie)* trickery ■ **rusé, -e** *adj* cunning, crafty

**Russie** [rysi] *nf* **la R.** Russia ■ **russe 1** *adj* Russian **2** *nmf* **R.** Russian **3** *nm (langue)* Russian

**rythme** [ritm] *nm* rhythm; *(de travail)* rate; *(allure)* pace ■ **rythmé, -e** *adj* rhythmic(al)

# Ss

**S, s** [ɛs] *nm inv* S, s
**s'** [s] *voir* **se, si**
**sa** [sa] *voir* **son**[3]
**sable** [sabl] *nm* sand; **sables mouvants** quicksands
**sablé** [sable] *nm* shortbread *Br* biscuit *or Am* cookie ▪ **sablée** *adj f* **pâte sablée** shortcrust pastry
**sablier** [sablije] *nm* hourglass; *Culin* egg timer
**saborder** [sabɔrde] *vt (navire)* to scuttle
**sabot** [sabo] *nm (de cheval)* hoof; *(chaussure)* clog; **s. de Denver** wheel clamp
**saboter** [sabɔte] *vt (machine, projet)* to sabotage ▪ **sabotage** *nm* sabotage ▪ **saboteur, -euse** *nmf* saboteur
**sabre** [sɑbr] *nm* sabre
**sac** [sak] *nm* bag; *(grand, en toile)* sack; **s. à main** handbag; **s. à dos** rucksack; **s. de voyage** travelling bag
**saccade** [sakad] *nf* jerk, jolt; **par saccades** in fits and starts ▪ **saccadé, -e** *adj* jerky
**saccager** [sakaʒe] *vt (détruire)* to wreak havoc in
**sachant, sache(s), sachent** [saʃɑ̃, saʃ] *voir* **savoir**
**sachet** [saʃɛ] *nm* (small) bag; **s. de thé** teabag
**sacre** [sakr] *nm (de roi)* coronation ▪ **sacrer** *vt (roi)* to crown
**sacré, -e** [sakre] *adj (saint)* sacred ▪ **sacrement** *nm Rel* sacrament
**sacrifice** [sakrifis] *nm* sacrifice ▪ **sacrifier 1** *vt* to sacrifice (**à** to) **2** *vi* **s. à la mode** to be a slave to fashion **3 se sacrifier** *vpr* to sacrifice oneself (**pour** for)
**sacrilège** [sakrilɛʒ] **1** *adj* sacrilegious **2** *nm* sacrilege
**sadique** [sadik] **1** *adj* sadistic **2** *nmf* sadist
**safari** [safari] *nm* safari; **faire un s.** to go on safari
**safran** [safrɑ̃] *nm* saffron
**sage** [saʒ] **1** *adj (avisé)* wise; *(tranquille)* good **2** *nm* wise man ▪ **sage-femme** (*pl* **sages-femmes**) *nf* midwife ▪ **sagesse** *nf (philosophie)* wisdom; *(calme)* good behaviour
**Sagittaire** [saʒitɛr] *nm* **le S.** *(signe)* Sagittarius
**saigner** [seɲe] *vi* to bleed; **s. du nez** to have a nosebleed ▪ **saignant, -e** *adj (viande)* rare
**saillant, -e** [sajɑ̃, -ɑ̃t] *adj* projecting ▪ **saillie** *nf (partie avant)* projection
**sain, -e** [sɛ̃, sɛn] *adj* healthy; *(nourriture)* wholesome, healthy; **s. et sauf** safe and sound
**saint, -e** [sɛ̃, sɛ̃t] **1** *adj (lieu)* holy; *(personne)* saintly; **s. Jean** Saint John; **la Sainte Vierge** the Blessed Virgin **2** *nmf* saint ▪ **Saint-Esprit** *nm* **le S.** the Holy Spirit ▪ **Saint-Sylvestre** *nf* **la S.** New Year's Eve
**sainteté** [sɛ̃tәte] *nf (de lieu)* holiness; *(de personne)* saintliness
**sais** [sɛ] *voir* **savoir**
**saisie** [sezi] *nf (de biens)* seizure; *Ordinat* **s. de données** data capture, keyboarding
**saisir** [sezir] **1** *vt* to take hold of; *(brusquement)* to grab; *(occasion)* to seize,

to grasp; *(comprendre)* to grasp; *Jur* to seize; *(viande)* to seal **2 se saisir** *vpr* **se s. de qn/qch** to take hold of sb/sth; *(brusquement)* to grab sb/sth ■ **saisissant, -e** *adj (film)* gripping; *(contraste, ressemblance)* striking

**saison** [sɛzɔ̃] *nf* season; **en/hors s.** in/out of season; **en haute/basse s.** in the high/low season; **la s. des pluies** the rainy season ■ **saisonnier, -ère** *adj* seasonal

**sait** [sɛ] *voir* **savoir**

**salade** [salad] *nf (laitue)* lettuce; **s. verte** green salad; **s. de fruits** fruit salad; **s. niçoise** salade niçoise

**salaire** [salɛr] *nm (mensuel)* salary

**salarié, -e** [salarje] **1** *adj (payé mensuellement)* salaried **2** *nmf (payé mensuellement)* salaried employee; **salariés** *(de société)* employees

**sale** [sal] *adj* dirty; *(dégoûtant)* filthy ■ **salement** *adv (se conduire, manger)* disgustingly ■ **saleté** *nf (manque de soin)* dirtiness; *(crasse)* dirt; **saletés** *(détritus) Br* rubbish, *Am* garbage; **faire des saletés** to make a mess

**saler** [sale] *vt* to salt ■ **salé, -e** *adj (goût, plat)* salty; *(aliment)* salted

**salir** [salir] **1** *vt* to (make) dirty **2 se salir** *vpr* to get dirty ■ **salissant, -e** *adj (travail)* dirty, messy; *(étoffe)* that shows the dirt

**salle** [sal] *nf* room; *(très grande, publique)* hall; *(de cinéma) Br* cinema, *Am* movie theater; *(d'hôpital)* ward; **s. à manger** dining room; **s. de bain(s)** bathroom; **s. de classe** classroom; **s. de concert** concert hall; **s. de jeux** *(pour enfants)* games room; *(de casino)* gaming room; **s. de spectacle** auditorium; **s. d'embarquement** *(d'aéroport)* departure lounge; **s. d'opération** *(d'hôpital)* operating *Br* theatre or *Am* room

**salon** [salɔ̃] *nm* living room, *Br* lounge; *(exposition)* show; **s. de coiffure** hairdressing salon; **s. de thé** tea room

**salopette** [salɔpɛt] *nf Br* dungarees, *Am* overalls

**salubre** [salybr] *adj* healthy ■ **salubrité** *nf* healthiness; **s. publique** public health

**saluer** [salɥe] *vt* to greet; *(en partant)* to take one's leave of; *(de la main)* to wave to; *(de la tête)* to nod to; *Mil* to salute

**salut** [saly] **1** *nm* greeting; *(de la main)* wave; *(de la tête)* nod; *Mil* salute; *(sauvegarde)* rescue; *Rel* salvation **2** *exclam Fam* hi!; *(au revoir)* bye!

**salutaire** [salytɛr] *adj* salutary

**samedi** [samdi] *nm* Saturday

**SAMU** [samy] (*abrév* **service d'aide médicale d'urgence**) *nm* emergency medical service

**sanctifier** [sɑ̃ktifje] *vt* to sanctify

**sanction** [sɑ̃ksjɔ̃] *nf (approbation, peine)* sanction ■ **sanctionner** *vt (approuver)* to sanction; *(punir)* to punish

**sanctuaire** [sɑ̃ktɥɛr] *nm* sanctuary

**sandale** [sɑ̃dal] *nf* sandal

**sandwich** [sɑ̃dwitʃ] *nm* sandwich

**sang** [sɑ̃] *nm* blood ■ **sang-froid** *nm* self-control; **garder son s.** to keep calm; **tuer qn de s.** to kill sb in cold blood ■ **sanglant, -e** *adj* bloody

**sangle** [sɑ̃gl] *nf* strap

**sanglier** [sɑ̃glije] *nm* wild boar

**sanglot** [sɑ̃glo] *nm* sob ■ **sangloter** *vi* to sob

**sanguin, -e** [sɑ̃gɛ̃, -in] *adj (tempérament)* full-blooded; **vaisseau s.** blood vessel

**sanguinaire** [sɑ̃ginɛr] *adj* bloodthirsty

**sanitaire** [sanitɛr] *adj (conditions)* sanitary; *(personnel)* medical; **règlement s.** health regulations

**sans** [sɑ̃] ([sɑ̃z] *before vowel and mute h*) *prép* without; **s. faire qch** without doing sth; **s. qu'il le sache** without him *or* his knowing; **s. cela, s. quoi** otherwise; **s. importance/travail** unimportant/unemployed; **s. argent/manches** penniless/sleeveless ■ **sans-abri** *nmf inv* homeless person; **les s.** the homeless ■ **sans-faute** *nm inv Fig* **faire un s.** not to put a foot wrong

■ **sans-gêne 1** *adj inv* ill-mannered **2** *nm inv* lack of manners ■ **sans-papiers** *nmf inv* illegal immigrant

**santé** [sɑ̃te] *nf* health; **en bonne/mauvaise s.** in good/bad health; **(à votre) s.!** *(en trinquant)* cheers!

**saoul** [su] *adj & nm* = **soûl**

**saper** [sape] *vt* to undermine; **s. le moral à qn** to sap sb's morale

**sapeur-pompier** [sapœrpɔ̃pje] (*pl* **sapeurs-pompiers**) *nm* fireman, firefighter

**saphir** [safir] *nm* sapphire

**sapin** [sapɛ̃] *nm (arbre, bois)* fir; **s. de Noël** Christmas tree

**Sardaigne** [sardɛɲ] *nf* **la S.** Sardinia ■ **sarde 1** *adj* Sardinian **2** *nmf* **S.** Sardinian

**sardine** [sardin] *nf* sardine

**sarrasin** [sarazɛ̃] *nm (plante)* buckwheat

**Satan** [satɑ̃] *nm* Satan

**satellite** [satelit] *nm* satellite; **télévision par s.** satellite television

**satiété** [sasjete] *nf* **boire/manger à s.** to eat/drink one's fill

**satin** [satɛ̃] *nm* satin

**satire** [satir] *nf* satire (**contre** on) ■ **satirique** *adj* satirical

**satisfaction** [satisfaksjɔ̃] *nf* satisfaction; **donner s. à qn** to give sb (complete) satisfaction ■ **satisfaire* 1** *vt* to satisfy **2** *vi* **s. à qch** *(conditions)* to satisfy sth; *(obligation)* to fulfil sth, *Am* to fulfill sth ■ **satisfaisant, -e** *adj (acceptable)* satisfactory ■ **satisfait, -e** *adj* satisfied (**de** with)

**saturer** [satyre] *vt* to saturate (**de** with) ■ **saturation** *nf* saturation; **arriver à s.** to reach saturation point

**sauce** [sos] *nf* sauce

**saucisse** [sosis] *nf* sausage; **s. de Francfort** frankfurter ■ **saucisson** *nm* (cold) sausage

**sauf**[1] [sof] *prép* except; **s. erreur** if I'm not mistaken

**sauf**[2]**, sauve** [sof, sov] *adj* **avoir la vie sauve** to be unharmed

**saumon** [somɔ̃] **1** *nm* salmon **2** *adj inv (couleur)* salmon (pink)

**sauna** [sona] *nm* sauna

**saupoudrer** [sopudre] *vt* to sprinkle (**de** with)

**saur** [sɔr] *adj m* **hareng s.** smoked herring

**saura, saurait** [sora, sorɛ] *voir* **savoir**

**saut** [so] *nm* jump, leap; **faire un s.** to jump, to leap; **s. à la corde** *Br* skipping, *Am* jumping rope; **s. à l'élastique** bungee jumping; **s. en hauteur** high jump; **s. en longueur** long jump; **s. en parachute** parachute jump; *(activité)* parachute jumping

**sauter** [sote] **1** *vt (franchir)* to jump (over); *(mot, repas, classe, ligne)* to skip **2** *vi (personne, animal)* to jump, to leap; *(bombe)* to go off, to explode; *(fusible)* to blow; **faire s. qch** *(pont, mine)* to blow sth up; *(serrure)* to force sth; **s. à la corde** *Br* to skip, *Am* to jump rope; **s. en parachute** to do a parachute jump

**sauterelle** [sotrɛl] *nf* grasshopper

**sautes** [sot] *nfpl (d'humeur, de température)* sudden changes (**de** in)

**sauvage** [sovaʒ] *adj (animal, plante)* wild; *(tribu, homme)* primitive; *(cruel)* savage; *(farouche)* unsociable; *(illégal)* unauthorized ■ **sauvagerie** *nf (insociabilité)* unsociability; *(cruauté)* savagery

**sauve** [sov] *adj voir* **sauf**[2]

**sauvegarde** [sovgard] *nf* safeguard (**contre** against); *Ordinat* backup ■ **sauvegarder** *vt* to safeguard; *Ordinat* to save

**sauver** [sove] **1** *vt (personne)* to save, to rescue (**de** from); *(matériel)* to salvage **2 se sauver** *vpr (s'enfuir)* to run away; *(s'échapper)* to escape ■ **sauvetage** *nm (de personne)* rescue ■ **sauveteur** *nm* rescuer

**sauvette** [sovɛt] **à la sauvette** *adv (pour ne pas être vu)* on the sly; **vendre qch à la s.** to peddle sth illegally on the streets

**sauveur** [sovœr] *nm* saviour

**savant, -e** [savɑ̃, -ɑ̃t] **1** *adj (érudit)*

learned; *(habile)* clever **2** *nm (scientifique)* scientist

**saveur** [savœr] *nf (goût)* flavour

**Savoie** [savwa] *nf* **la S.** Savoy

**SAVOIR*** [savwar] **1** *vt* to know; *(nouvelle)* to have heard; **s. lire/nager** to know how to read/swim; **faire s. à qn que...** to inform sb that...; **à s.** *(c'est-à-dire)* that is, namely; **pas que je sache** not that I know of; **je n'en sais rien** I have no idea, I don't know; **en s. long sur qn/qch** to know a lot about sb/sth

**2** *nm (culture)* learning, knowledge ▪ **savoir-faire** *nm inv* know-how

**savon** [savɔ̃] *nm* soap ▪ **savonnette** *nf* bar of soap ▪ **savonneux, -euse** *adj* soapy

**savourer** [savure] *vt* to savour ▪ **savoureux, -euse** *adj* tasty

**savoyard, -e** [savwajar, -ard] **1** *adj* Savoyard **2** *nmf* **S., Savoyarde** Savoyard

**saxophone** [saksɔfɔn] *nm* saxophone

**scalpel** [skalpɛl] *nm* scalpel

**scandale** [skɑ̃dal] *nm* scandal ▪ **scandaleux, -euse** *adj* scandalous ▪ **scandaliser 1** *vt* to scandalize, to shock **2 se scandaliser** *vpr* to be shocked *or* scandalized (**de** by)

**Scandinavie** [skɑ̃dinavi] *nf* **la S.** Scandinavia ▪ **scandinave 1** *adj* Scandinavian **2** *nmf* **S.** Scandinavian

**scanner 1** [skanɛr] *nm* scanner **2** [skane] *vt* to scan

**scaphandrier** [skafɑ̃drije] *nm* diver

**sceau, -x** [so] *nm* seal ▪ **sceller** *vt (document)* to seal

**scénario** [senarjo] *nm* script, screenplay ▪ **scénariste** *nmf* scriptwriter

**scène** [sɛn] *nf* (**a**) *(de théâtre)* scene; *(plateau)* stage; *(action)* action; **mettre qch en s.** *(pièce)* to stage sth; *(film)* to direct sth; *Fig* **sur la s. internationale** on the international scene (**b**) *(dispute)* scene; **faire une s.** to make a scene; **s. de ménage** domestic quarrel

**sceptique** [sɛptik] **1** *adj Br* sceptical, *Am* skeptical **2** *nmf Br* sceptic, *Am* skeptic

**schéma** [ʃema] *nm* diagram ▪ **schématique** *adj* schematic

**schizophrène** [skizɔfrɛn] *adj & nmf* schizophrenic

**scie** [si] *nf (outil)* saw ▪ **scier** *vt* to saw

**sciemment** [sjamɑ̃] *adv* knowingly

**science** [sjɑ̃s] *nf* science; *(savoir)* knowledge; **sciences humaines** social sciences; **sciences naturelles** biology ▪ **science-fiction** *nf* science fiction ▪ **scientifique 1** *adj* scientific **2** *nmf* scientist

**scinder** [sɛ̃de] **se scinder** *vpr* to split up (**en** into)

**scintiller** [sɛ̃tije] *vi* to sparkle; *(étoile)* to twinkle ▪ **scintillement** *nm* sparkling; *(d'étoile)* twinkling

**scission** [sisjɔ̃] *nf (de parti)* split (**de** in); **s. de l'atome** splitting of the atom

**sclérose** [skleroz] *nf Méd* sclerosis; *Fig* ossification; **s. en plaques** multiple sclerosis

**scolaire** [skɔlɛr] *adj* **année s.** school year; **enfant d'âge s.** child of school age ▪ **scolariser** *vt (enfant)* to send to school ▪ **scolarité** *nf* schooling; **pendant ma s.** during my school years

**scooter** [skuter] *nm* (motor) scooter; **s. des mers** jet ski

**score** [skɔr] *nm* score

**scorpion** [skɔrpjɔ̃] *nm* scorpion; **le S.** *(signe)* Scorpio

**Scotch®** [skɔtʃ] *(ruban adhésif) Br* sellotape®, *Am* scotch tape® ▪ **scotcher** *vt Br* to sellotape, *Am* to tape

**scout, -e** [skut] *adj & nm* scout

**script** [skript] *nm (écriture)* printing; *Cin* script

**scrupule** [skrypyl] *nm* scruple; **sans scrupules** *(être)* unscrupulous; *(agir)* unscrupulously ▪ **scrupuleux, -euse** *adj* scrupulous

**scruter** [skryte] *vt* to scrutinize

**scrutin** [skrytɛ̃] *nm (vote)* ballot; *(élection)* poll; *(système)* voting system; **premier tour de s.** first ballot *or* round; **s. majoritaire** first-past-the-post voting system

**sculpter** [skylte] *vt (statue, pierre)* to sculpt; *(bois)* to carve; **s. qch dans qch** to sculpt/carve sth out of sth ▪ **sculpteur** *nm* sculptor ▪ **sculpture** *nf (art, œuvre)* sculpture

**SDF** [ɛsdeɛf] *(abrév* **sans domicile fixe**) *nm* person of no fixed abode

**SE** [sə]

**se** becomes **s'** before vowel or mute h.

*pron personnel* (**a**) *(complément direct)* himself; *(féminin)* herself; *(non humain)* itself; *(indéfini)* oneself, *pl* themselves; **il se lave** he washes himself; **ils** *ou* **elles se lavent** they wash themselves

(**b**) *(indirect)* to himself/herself/itself/oneself; **il se lave les mains** he washes his hands; **elle se lave les mains** she washes her hands

(**c**) *(réciproque)* each other; *(indirect)* to each other; **ils s'aiment** they love each other; **ils** *ou* **elles se parlent** they speak to each other

(**d**) *(passif)* **ça se fait** that is done; **ça se vend bien** it sells well

**séance** [seɑ̃s] *nf (de cinéma)* showing, performance; *(d'assemblée, de travail)* session

**seau, -x** [so] *nm* bucket

**sec, sèche** [sɛk, sɛʃ] **1** *adj* dry; *(fruits, légumes)* dried; *(ton)* curt; **frapper un coup s.** to knock sharply **2** *adv (boire) Br* neat, *Am* straight; *(frapper, pleuvoir)* hard **3** *nm* **à s.** dry; **au s.** in a dry place

**sécession** [sesesjɔ̃] *nf* secession; **faire s.** to secede

**sèche** [sɛʃ] *voir* **sec**

**sécher** [seʃe] **1** *vti* to dry **2 se sécher** *vpr* to dry oneself ▪ **séchage** *nm* drying ▪ **sèche-cheveux** *nm inv* hair dryer ▪ **sèche-linge** *nm inv Br* tumble dryer, *Am* (clothes) dryer

**sécheresse** [seʃrɛs] *nf (d'air, de sol, de peau)* dryness; *(de ton)* curtness; *(manque de pluie)* drought

**séchoir** [seʃwar] *nm (appareil)* dryer; **s. à linge** clothes horse

**second, -e**[1] [səgɔ̃, -ɔ̃d] **1** *adj & nmf* second

**2** *nm (adjoint)* second in command; *(étage) Br* second floor, *Am* third floor

**3** *nf* **seconde** *Rail* second class; *Scol Br* ≃ fifth form, *Am* ≃ tenth grade; *Aut (vitesse)* second (gear) ▪ **secondaire** *adj* secondary; **école s.** *Br* secondary school, *Am* high school

**seconde**[2] [səgɔ̃d] *nf (instant)* second

**seconder** [sgɔ̃de] *vt* to assist

**secouer** [səkwe] *vt* to shake; *(poussière)* to shake off; **s. qch de qch** *(enlever)* to shake sth out of sth; **s. la tête** *(réponse affirmative)* to nod (one's head); *(réponse négative)* to shake one's head

**secourir** [səkurir] *vt* to assist, to help ▪ **secourable** *adj* helpful ▪ **secourisme** *nm* first aid ▪ **secouriste** *nmf* first-aid worker

**secours** [səkur] *nm* help; *(financier, matériel)* aid; *Mil* **les s.** *(renforts)* relief; **au s.!** help!; **porter s. à qn** to give sb help; **roue de s.** spare wheel

**secousse** [səkus] *nf* jolt, jerk; *(de tremblement de terre)* tremor

**secret, -ète** [səkrɛ, -ɛt] **1** *adj* secret; *(cachottier)* secretive **2** *nm* secret; **en s.** in secret, secretly

**secrétaire** [səkretɛr] *nmf* secretary; **s. d'État** Secretary of State ▪ **secrétariat** *nm (bureau)* secretary's office; *(d'organisation internationale)* secretariat; *(métier)* secretarial work

**sectaire** [sɛktɛr] *adj & nmf Péj* sectarian

**secte** [sɛkt] *nf* sect

**secteur** [sɛktœr] *nm (zone)* area; *Écon* sector; *Él* mains

**section** [sɛksjɔ̃] *nf* section; *(de ligne d'autobus)* stage; *Mil* platoon ▪ **sectionner** *vt (couper)* to sever

**séculaire** [sekylɛr] *adj (tradition)* age-old

**sécurité** [sekyrite] *nf (absence de danger)* safety; *(tranquillité)* security; **S.**

**sociale** *Br* Social Security, *Am* Welfare; **en s.** *(hors de danger)* safe
**séduire*** [sedɥir] *vt* to charm; *(plaire à)* to appeal to; *(abuser de)* to seduce ■ **séduisant, -e** *adj* attractive ■ **séducteur, -trice** *nmf* seducer, *f* seductress ■ **séduction** *nf* attraction
**ségrégation** [segregɑsjɔ̃] *nf* segregation
**seigle** [sɛgl] *nm* rye; **pain de s.** rye bread
**seigneur** [sɛɲœr] *nm Hist (noble, maître)* lord; *Rel* **le S.** the Lord
**sein** [sɛ̃] *nm* breast; **donner le s. à** *(enfant)* to breastfeed; **au s. de** within
**Seine** [sɛn] *nf* **la S.** the Seine
**séisme** [seism] *nm* earthquake
**seize** [sɛz] *adj & nm inv* sixteen ■ **seizième** *adj & nmf* sixteenth
**séjour** [seʒur] *nm* stay; **s. linguistique** language-learning trip; **(salle de) s.** living room ■ **séjourner** *vi* to stay
**sel** [sɛl] *nm* salt; *Fig (piquant)* spice; **s. de mer** sea salt; **sels de bain** bath salts
**sélectif, -ive** [selɛktif, -iv] *adj* selective ■ **sélection** *nf* selection ■ **sélectionner** *vt* to select ■ **sélectionneur** *nm* selector
**self** [sɛlf] *nm* self-service restaurant
**selle** [sɛl] *nf (de cheval, de vélo)* saddle
**selon** [səlɔ̃] *prép* according to; **s. que...** depending on whether...
**semaine** [səmɛn] *nf* week; **en s.** in the week
**semblable** [sɑ̃blabl] *adj* similar (**à** to); **de semblables propos** such remarks
**semblant** [sɑ̃blɑ̃] *nm* **faire s.** to pretend (**de faire** to do)
**sembler** [sɑ̃ble] **1** *vi* to seem (**à** to); **il (me) semble vieux** he seems *or* looks old (to me); **s. faire qch** to seem to do sth **2** *v impersonnel* **il semble que...** it seems that...; **il me semble que...** it seems to me that...
**semelle** [səmɛl] *nf (de chaussure)* sole; *(intérieure)* insole
**semer** [səme] *vt (graines)* to sow; *Fig (poursuivant)* to shake off; *Fig* **semé de** strewn with ■ **semence** *nf* seed
**semestre** [səmɛstr] *nm* half-year; *Univ* semester
**séminaire** [seminɛr] *nm Univ* seminar; *Rel* seminary
**semi-remorque** [səmirəmɔrk] (*pl* **semi-remorques**) *nm (camion) Br* articulated lorry, *Am* semi(trailer), trailer truck
**semoule** [səmul] *nf* semolina
**sénat** [sena] *nm* senate ■ **sénateur** *nm* senator
**sénile** [senil] *adj* senile

---

**SENS** [sɑ̃s] *nm* (**a**) *(faculté, raison, instinct)* sense; **avoir le s. de l'humour** to have a sense of humour; **avoir du bon s.** to be sensible; **bon sens** common sense
(**b**) *(signification)* meaning, sense; **ça n'a pas de s.** that doesn't make sense
(**c**) *(direction)* direction; *Aut* **s. giratoire** *Br* roundabout, *Am* traffic circle, *Am* rotary; **s. interdit** *ou* **unique** *(rue)* one-way street; **'s. interdit'** 'no entry'; **à s. unique** *(rue)* one-way; **dans le s. des aiguilles d'une montre** clockwise; **dans le s. inverse des aiguilles d'une montre** *Br* anticlockwise, *Am* counterclockwise

---

**sensation** [sɑ̃sɑsjɔ̃] *nf* feeling, sensation; **faire s.** to create a sensation
**sensé, -e** [sɑ̃se] *adj* sensible
**sensible** [sɑ̃sibl] *adj* sensitive (**à** to); *(douloureux)* tender, sore; *(perceptible)* perceptible; *(progrès)* noticeable ■ **sensibiliser** *vt* **s. qn à qch** *(problème)* to make sb aware of sth ■ **sensibilité** *nf* sensitivity
**sensuel, -elle** [sɑ̃sɥɛl] *adj* sensual ■ **sensualité** *nf* sensuality
**sentence** [sɑ̃tɑ̃s] *nf Jur (jugement)* sentence
**sentier** [sɑ̃tje] *nm* path
**sentiment** [sɑ̃timɑ̃] *nm* feeling; **avoir le s. que...** to have a feeling that... ■ **sentimental, -e, -aux, -ales** *adj* sentimental; **vie sentimentale** love life
**sentinelle** [sɑ̃tinɛl] *nf* sentry

**sentir*** [sɑ̃tir] **1** *vt (douleur)* to feel; *(odeur)* to smell; **s. le moisi** to smell musty; **s. le poisson** to smell of fish **2** *vi* to smell; **s. bon/mauvais** to smell good/bad **3 se sentir** *vpr* **se s. humilié** to feel humiliated

**séparation** [separɑsjɔ̃] *nf* separation; *(départ)* parting

**séparer** [separe] **1** *vt* to separate (**de** from) **2 se séparer** *vpr (couple)* to separate; *(cortège)* to disperse, to break up; **se s. de qn/qch** *(donner, jeter)* to part with sb/sth ▪ **séparé, -e** *adj (distinct)* separate; *(époux)* separated (**de** from)

**sept** [sɛt] *adj & nm inv* seven

**septante** [sɛptɑ̃t] *adj (en Belgique, en Suisse)* seventy

**septembre** [sɛptɑ̃br] *nm* September

**septième** [sɛtjɛm] *adj & nmf* seventh; **un s.** a seventh

**sépulture** [sepyltyr] *nf* burial; *(lieu)* burial place

**séquelles** [sekɛl] *nfpl (de maladie)* after-effects

**séquence** [sekɑ̃s] *nf* sequence

**séquestrer** [sekɛstre] *vt* **s. qn** to keep sb locked up

**sera, serait** [səra, sərɛ] *voir* **être**

**Serbie** [sɛrbi] *nf* **la S.** Serbia ▪ **serbe 1** *adj* Serbian **2** *nmf* **S.** Serbian

**serein, -e** [sərɛ̃, -ɛn] *adj* serene

**sérénade** [serenad] *nf* serenade

**sérénité** [serenite] *nf* serenity

**sergent** [sɛrʒɑ̃] *nm Mil* sergeant

**série** [seri] *nf* series; *(ensemble)* set; **de s.** *(article, voiture)* standard; **fin de s.** discontinued line; **fabrication en s.** mass production; **numéro hors s.** special issue

**sérieux, -euse** [serjø, -jøz] **1** *adj (personne, doute)* serious; *(de bonne foi)* genuine, serious; *(fiable)* reliable; **de sérieuses chances de...** a good chance of... **2** *nm (application)* seriousness; *(fiabilité)* reliability; **prendre qn/qch au s.** to take sb/sth seriously

**seringue** [sərɛ̃g] *nf* syringe

**serment** [sɛrmɑ̃] *nm (affirmation solennelle)* oath; *(promesse)* pledge; **prêter s.** to take an oath; **faire le s. de faire qch** to swear to do sth; *Jur* **sous s.** on *or* under oath

**sermon** [sɛrmɔ̃] *nm (de prêtre)* sermon ▪ **sermonner** *vt (faire la morale à)* to lecture

**séropositif, -ive** [seropozitif, -iv] *adj Méd* HIV positive ▪ **séronégatif, -ive** *adj Méd* HIV negative

**serpent** [sɛrpɑ̃] *nm* snake

**serpenter** [sɛrpɑ̃te] *vi (sentier)* to meander

**serre** [sɛr] *nf* greenhouse

**serrer** [sere] **1** *vt (tenir)* to grip; *(nœud, vis)* to tighten; *(poing)* to clench; **s. la main à qn** to shake hands with sb; **s. qn** *(sujet: vêtement)* to be too tight for sb
**2** *vi* **s. à droite** to keep (to the) right
**3 se serrer** *vpr (se rapprocher)* to squeeze up; **se s. contre** to squeeze up against ▪ **serré, -e** *adj (nœud, vêtement)* tight; *(gens)* packed (together); *(lutte)* close ▪ **serre-tête** *nm inv* headband

**serrure** [seryr] *nf* lock

**serveur, -euse** [sɛrvœr, -øz] **1** *nmf* waiter, *f* waitress; *(de bar)* barman, *f* barmaid **2** *nm Ordinat* server

**serviable** [sɛrvjabl] *adj* helpful, obliging

**service** [sɛrvis] *nm* service; *(travail)* duty; *(pourboire)* service (charge); *(d'entreprise)* department; *(au tennis)* serve, service; **un s.** *(aide)* a favour; **rendre s.** to be of service (**à qn** to sb); **être de s.** to be on duty; **faire son s. (militaire)** to do one's military service; **s. à café** coffee set; **s. (non) compris** service (not) included; **s. après-vente** aftersales service

**serviette** [sɛrvjɛt] *nf (pour s'essuyer)* towel; *(sac)* briefcase; **s. de bain/de toilette** bath/hand towel; **s. de table** napkin, *Br* serviette ▪ **serviette-éponge** (*pl* **serviettes-éponges**) *nf* terry towel

**servir*** [sɛrvir] **1** *vt* to serve (**qch à qn** sb with sth, sth to sb); *(convive)* to wait on
**2** *vi* to serve; **s. à qch/à faire qch** to be used for sth/to do *or* for doing sth; **ça ne sert à rien** it's useless, it's no good *or* use (**de faire** doing); **s. de qch** to be used for sth, to serve as sth
**3 se servir** *vpr (à table)* to help oneself (**de** to); **se s. de qch** *(utiliser)* to use sth

**serviteur** [sɛrvitœr] *nm* servant

**ses** [se] *voir* **son²**

**session** [sesjɔ̃] *nf* session

**set** [sɛt] *nm (au tennis)* set; **s. de table** place mat

**seuil** [sœj] *nm (entrée)* doorway; *Fig (limite)* threshold; *Fig* **au s. de** on the threshold of

**seul, -e** [sœl] **1** *adj (sans compagnie)* alone; *(unique)* only; **tout s.** by oneself, on one's own, all alone; **se sentir s.** to feel lonely *or* alone; **la seule femme** the only woman; **un s. chat** only one cat; **une seule fois** only once; **pas un s. livre** not a single book; **seuls les garçons...** only the boys...
**2** *adv* **(tout) s.** *(rentrer, vivre)* by oneself, alone, on one's own; *(parler)* to oneself
**3** *nmf* **le s., la seule** the only one; **un s., une seule** only one, one only; **pas un s.** not (a single) one

**seulement** [sœlmɑ̃] *adv* only; **non s.... mais encore...** not only... but (also)...

**sève** [sɛv] *nf (de plante)* sap

**sévère** [sevɛr] *adj* severe; *(parents, professeur)* strict ▪ **sévérité** *nf* severity; *(de parents)* strictness

**sévices** [sevis] *nmpl* ill-treatment; **s. à enfant** child abuse

**sexe** [sɛks] *nm (catégorie, sexualité)* sex; *(organes)* genitals ▪ **sexiste** *adj & nmf* sexist ▪ **sexualité** *nf* sexuality ▪ **sexuel, -elle** *adj* sexual

**shampooing** [ʃɑ̃pwɛ̃] *nm* shampoo; **s. colorant** rinse; **faire un s. à qn** to shampoo sb's hair

**shooter** [ʃute] *vti (au football)* to shoot

**short** [ʃɔrt] *nm* (pair of) shorts

**SI¹** [si]

**si** becomes **s'** [s] before **il, ils**.

**1** *conj* if; **si je pouvais** if I could; **s'il vient** if he comes; **si j'étais roi** if I were *or* was king; **je me demande si...** I wonder whether *or* if...; **si on restait?** *(suggestion)* what if we stayed?; **si oui** if so; **si non** if not; **si seulement** if only
**2** *adv* (**a**) *(tellement)* so; **pas si riche que tu crois** not as rich as you think; **un si bon dîner** such a good dinner; **si bien que...** so much so that...
(**b**) *(après négative)* yes; **tu ne viens pas? – si!** you're not coming? – yes (I am)!

**si²** [si] *nm inv (note)* B

**siamois, -e** [sjamwa, -waz] *adj* Siamese; **frères s., sœurs siamoises** Siamese twins

**Sicile** [sisil] *nf* **la S.** Sicily

**SIDA** [sida] (*abrév* **syndrome immunodéficitaire acquis**) *nm* AIDS; **virus du S.** AIDS virus

**sidérurgie** [sidɛryrʒi] *nf* iron and steel industry

**siècle** [sjɛkl] *nm* century

**siège** [sjɛʒ] *nm* (**a**) *(meuble, centre) & Pol* seat; *(d'autorité, de parti)* headquarters; **s. social** head office (**b**) *Mil* siege; **faire le s. de** to lay siege to

**siéger** [sjeʒe] *vi (assemblée)* to sit

**sien, sienne** [sjɛ̃, sjɛn] **1** *pron possessif* **le s., la sienne, les sien(ne)s** *(d'homme)* his; *(de femme)* hers; *(de chose)* its; **les deux siens** his/her two **2** *nmpl* **les siens** *(sa famille)* one's family **3** *nfpl* **faire des siennes** to be up to one's tricks again

**sieste** [sjɛst] *nf* siesta; **faire la s.** to have a nap

**siffler** [sifle] **1** *vi* to whistle; *(avec un sifflet)* to blow one's whistle; *(gaz, serpent)* to hiss
**2** *vt (chanson)* to whistle; *(chien)* to whistle at; *Sport (faute, fin de match)* to blow one's whistle for; *(acteur,*

*pièce)* to boo; **se faire s.** *(acteur)* to be booed ▪ **sifflement** [-əmɑ̃] *nm* whistling; *(de serpent, de gaz)* hissing

**sifflet** [siflɛ] *nm (instrument)* whistle; **sifflets** *(de spectateurs)* booing ▪ **siffloter** *vti* to whistle

**sigle** [sigl] *nm (initiales)* abbreviation; *(acronyme)* acronym

**signal, -aux** [siɲal, -o] *nm* signal; **s. d'alarme** alarm signal; **s. lumineux** warning light; **s. sonore** warning sound

**signalement** [siɲalmɑ̃] *nm* description, particulars

**signaler** [siɲale] **1** *vt (faire remarquer)* to point out (**à qn** to sb; **que** that); *(par panneau)* to signpost; *(dire à la police)* to report (**à** to) **2 se signaler** *vpr* **se s. par qch** to distinguish oneself by sth

**signalisation** [siɲalizɑsjɔ̃] *nf (sur les routes)* signposting; **s. routière** *(signaux)* road signs

**signature** [siɲatyr] *nf* signature; *(action)* signing

**signe** [siɲ] *nm (indice)* sign, indication; **en s. de protestation** as a sign of protest; **faire s. à qn** *(geste)* to motion (to) sb (**de faire** to do); *(contacter)* to get in touch with sb; **faire s. que oui** to nod (one's head); **faire s. que non** to shake one's head; **s. particulier** distinguishing mark; **s. astrologique** astrological sign

**signer** [siɲe] **1** *vt* to sign **2 se signer** *vpr* to cross oneself

**signification** [siɲifikɑsjɔ̃] *nf* meaning ▪ **significatif, -ive** *adj* significant, meaningful

**signifier** [siɲifje] *vt* to mean (**que** that)

**silence** [silɑ̃s] *nm* silence; *Mus* rest; **en s.** in silence; **garder le s.** to keep quiet *or* silent (**sur** about) ▪ **silencieux, -euse 1** *adj* silent **2** *nm (de voiture) Br* silencer, *Am* muffler; *(d'arme)* silencer

**silhouette** [silwɛt] *nf* outline; *(en noir)* silhouette; *(du corps)* figure

**sillonner** [sijɔne] *vt (parcourir)* to criss-cross

**similaire** [similɛr] *adj* similar ▪ **similitude** *nf* similarity

**simple** [sɛ̃pl] *adj (facile, crédule, sans prétention)* simple; *(fait d'un élément)* single; *(employé, particulier)* ordinary ▪ **simplicité** *nf* simplicity

**simplifier** [sɛ̃plifje] *vt* to simplify ▪ **simplification** *nf* simplification

**simpliste** [sɛ̃plist] *adj* simplistic

**simuler** [simyle] *vt (reproduire)* to simulate; *(feindre)* to feign

**simultané, -e** [simyltane] *adj* simultaneous

**sincère** [sɛ̃sɛr] *adj* sincere ▪ **sincérité** *nf* sincerity; **en toute s.** quite sincerely

**Singapour** [sɛ̃gapur] *nm* Singapore

**singe** [sɛ̃ʒ] *nm* monkey; **grand s.** ape

**singulariser** [sɛ̃gylarize] **se singulariser** *vpr* to draw attention to oneself

**singulier, -ère** [sɛ̃gylje, -ɛr] *adj (peu ordinaire)* peculiar, odd ▪ **singularité** *nf* peculiarity

**sinistre** [sinistr] **1** *adj (effrayant)* sinister; *(triste)* grim **2** *nm* disaster; *(incendie)* fire; *Jur (dommage)* damage ▪ **sinistré, -e 1** *adj (population, région)* disaster-stricken **2** *nmf* disaster victim

**sinon** [sinɔ̃] *conj (autrement)* otherwise, or else; *(sauf)* except (**que** that); *(si ce n'est)* if not

**sinueux, -euse** [sinɥø, -øz] *adj* winding

**sinusite** [sinyzit] *nf* sinusitis; **avoir une s.** to have sinusitis

**siphon** [sifɔ̃] *nm* siphon; *(d'évier)* trap, *Br* U-bend

**sirène** [sirɛn] *nf (d'usine)* siren; *(femme)* mermaid

**sirop** [siro] *nm* syrup; *(à diluer)* (fruit) cordial; **s. contre la toux** cough mixture

**sismique** [sismik] *adj* seismic; **secousse s.** earth tremor

**site** [sit] *nm (endroit)* site; *(pittoresque)* beauty spot; **s. touristique** place of interest; **s. classé** conservation area; *Ordinat* **s. Web** website

**sitôt** [sito] *adv* **s. que...** as soon as...; **s. levée, elle partit** as soon as she was up, she left; **pas de s.** not for some time

**situation** [sitɥasjɔ̃] *nf* situation, position; *(emploi)* position; **s. de famille** marital status ▪ **situé, -e** *adj (maison)* situated (**à** in) ▪ **situer 1** *vt (placer)* to situate; *(trouver)* to locate; *(dans le temps)* to set **2 se situer** *vpr (se trouver)* to be situated

**six** [sis] ([si] *before consonant,* [siz] *before vowel) adj & nm inv* six ▪ **sixième** [sizjɛm] **1** *adj & nmf* sixth; **un s.** a sixth **2** *nf Scol Br* ≃ first form, *Am* ≃ sixth grade

**sketch** [skɛtʃ] *(pl* **sketches**) *nm* sketch

**ski** [ski] *nm (objet)* ski; *(sport)* skiing; **faire du s.** to ski; **s. alpin** downhill skiing; **s. de fond** cross-country skiing; **s. nautique** water skiing ▪ **skiable** *adj (piste)* skiable, fit for skiing ▪ **skier** *vi* to ski ▪ **skieur, -euse** *nmf* skier

**slalom** [slalɔm] *nm Sport* slalom

**slave** [slav] **1** *adj* Slav; *(langue)* Slavonic **2** *nmf* **S.** Slav

**slip** [slip] *nm (d'homme)* briefs, underpants; *(de femme)* panties, *Br* knickers

**slogan** [slɔgɑ̃] *nm* slogan

**Slovaquie** [slɔvaki] *nf* **la S.** Slovakia

**Slovénie** [slɔveni] *nf* **la S.** Slovenia

**SMIC** [smik] *(abrév* **salaire minimum interprofessionnel de croissance**) *nm* guaranteed minimum wage

**smoking** [smɔkiŋ] *nm (veston, costume)* dinner jacket, *Am* tuxedo

**SNCF** [ɛsɛnseef] *(abrév* **Société nationale des chemins de fer français**) *nf* = French national railway company

**snob** [snɔb] **1** *adj* snobbish **2** *nmf* snob ▪ **snobisme** *nm* snobbery

**sobre** [sɔbr] *adj* sober ▪ **sobriété** *nf* sobriety

**sociable** [sɔsjabl] *adj* sociable ▪ **sociabilité** *nf* sociability

**social, -e, -aux, -ales** [sɔsjal, -o] *adj* social ▪ **socialisme** *nm* socialism ▪ **socialiste** *adj & nmf* socialist

**société** [sɔsjete] *nf (communauté)* society; *(compagnie)* company; **s. anonyme** *Br* (public) limited company, *Am* corporation ▪ **sociétaire** *nmf (membre)* member

**sociologie** [sɔsjɔlɔʒi] *nf* sociology ▪ **sociologique** *adj* sociological ▪ **sociologue** *nmf* sociologist

**sœur** [sœr] *nf* sister; *(religieuse)* sister, nun

**sofa** [sɔfa] *nm* sofa, settee

**soi** [swa] *pron personnel* oneself; **chacun pour s.** every man for himself; **chez s.** at home; **cela va de soi** it's self-evident (**que** that) ▪ **soi-même** *pron* oneself

**soi-disant** [swadizɑ̃] **1** *adj inv* so-called **2** *adv* supposedly

**soie** [swa] *nf (tissu)* silk

**soient** [swa] *voir* **être**

**soif** [swaf] *nf* thirst (**de** for); **avoir s.** to be thirsty

**soigner** [swaɲe] **1** *vt* to look after, to take care of; *(sujet: médecin) (malade, maladie)* to treat; *(présentation, travail)* to take care over; **se faire s.** to have (medical) treatment
**2 se soigner** *vpr* to take care of oneself, to look after oneself ▪ **soigné, -e** *adj (personne, vêtement)* neat, tidy; *(travail)* careful

**soigneux, -euse** [swaɲø, -øz] *adj (attentif)* careful (**de** with); *(propre)* neat, tidy

**soin** [swɛ̃] *nm (attention)* care; *Méd* **soins** treatment, care; **avoir** *ou* **prendre s. de qch/de faire qch** to take care of sth/to do sth; **avec s.** carefully, with care

**soir** [swar] *nm* evening; **le s.** *(chaque soir)* in the evening(s); **à neuf heures du s.** at nine in the evening; **repas du s.** evening meal

**soirée** [sware] *nf* evening; *(réunion)* party

**sois, soit**[1] [swa] *voir* **être**

**soit**[2] **1** [swa] *conj (à savoir)* that is (to say); **s.... s....** either... or... **2** [swat] *adv (oui)* very well

**soixante** [swasɑ̃t] *adj & nm inv* sixty

▪ **soixantaine** *nf* **une s. (de)** *(nombre)* (about) sixty; **avoir la s.** *(âge)* to be about sixty
**soixante-dix** [swasɑ̃tdis] *adj & nm inv* seventy ▪ **soixante-dixième** *adj & nmf* seventieth
**soixantième** [swasɑ̃tjɛm] *adj & nmf* sixtieth
**soja** [sɔʒa] *nm (plante)* soya; **germes** *ou* **pousses de s.** beansprouts
**sol**[1] [sɔl] *nm* ground; *(plancher)* floor; *(territoire, terrain)* soil
**sol**[2] [sɔl] *nm inv (note)* G
**solaire** [sɔlɛr] *adj* solar; **huile s.** sun(-tan) oil
**soldat** [sɔlda] *nm* soldier
**solde** [sɔld] **1** *nm (de compte, à payer)* balance; **en s.** *(acheter)* in the sales, *Am* on sale; **soldes** *(marchandises)* sale goods; *(vente)* (clearance)sale(s) **2** *nf (de soldat)* pay
**solder** [sɔlde] **1** *vt (articles)* to clear, to sell off; *(compte)* to pay the balance of **2 se solder** *vpr* **se s. par un échec** to end in failure ▪ **soldé, -e** *adj (article)* reduced
**sole** [sɔl] *nf (poisson)* sole
**soleil** [sɔlɛj] *nm* sun; *(chaleur, lumière)* sunshine; **au s.** in the sun; **il fait s.** it's sunny
**solennel, -elle** [sɔlanɛl] *adj* solemn
**solidaire** [sɔlidɛr] *adj* **être s.** *(ouvriers)* to show solidarity (**de** with) ▪ **solidarité** *nf (entre personnes)* solidarity
**solide** [sɔlid] **1** *adj (objet, état)* solid; *(amitié)* strong; *(nerfs)* sound; *(personne)* sturdy **2** *nm (corps)* solid ▪ **solidité** *nf (d'objet)* solidity
**soliste** [sɔlist] *nmf Mus* soloist
**solitaire** [sɔlitɛr] **1** *adj (par choix)* solitary; *(involontairement)* lonely **2** *nmf* loner; **en s.** on one's own ▪ **solitude** *nf* solitude; **aimer la s.** to like being alone
**solliciter** [sɔlisite] *vt (audience)* to request; *(emploi)* to apply for; **s. qn** *(faire appel à)* to appeal to sb (**de faire** to do) ▪ **sollicitation** *nf* request
**sollicitude** [sɔlisityd] *nf* solicitude, concern
**soluble** [sɔlybl] *adj (substance, problème)* soluble
**solution** [sɔlysjɔ̃] *nf (de problème)* solution (**de** to); *(mélange chimique)* solution
**sombre** [sɔ̃br] *adj* dark; *(triste)* sombre, gloomy; **il fait s.** it's dark
**sombrer** [sɔ̃bre] *vi (bateau)* to sink; *Fig* **s. dans** *(folie, sommeil)* to sink into
**sommaire** [sɔmɛr] **1** *adj* summary; *(repas)* basic **2** *nm (table des matières)* contents
**somme** [sɔm] **1** *nf* sum; **faire la s. de** to add up; **en s., s. toute** in short **2** *nm (sommeil)* nap; **faire un s.** to have a nap
**sommeil** [sɔmɛj] *nm* sleep; **avoir s.** to feel sleepy; **être en plein s.** to be fast asleep ▪ **sommeiller** *vi* to doze
**sommelier** [sɔməlje] *nm* wine waiter
**sommer** [sɔme] *vt* **s. qn de faire qch** to summon sb to do sth
**sommes** [sɔm] *voir* **être**
**sommet** [sɔmɛ] *nm* top; *(de montagne)* summit, top
**sommier** [sɔmje] *nm (de lit)* base
**sommité** [sɔmite] *nf* leading light (**de** in)
**somnambule** [sɔmnɑ̃byl] *nmf* sleepwalker; **être s.** to sleepwalk
**somnifère** [sɔmnifɛr] *nm* sleeping pill
**somnoler** [sɔmnɔle] *vi* to doze
**somptueux, -euse** [sɔ̃ptɥø, -øz] *adj* sumptuous
**son**[1] [sɔ̃] *nm (bruit)* sound
**son**[2] [sɔ̃] *nm (de grains)* bran
**son**[3], **sa, ses** [sɔ̃, sa, se]

sa becomes **son** [sɔ̃n] before a vowel or mute h.

*adj possessif (d'homme)* his; *(de femme)* her; *(de chose)* its; *(indéfini)* one's; **s. père/sa mère** his/her/one's father/mother; **s. ami(e)** his/her/one's friend
**sondage** [sɔ̃daʒ] *nm (de terrain)* drilling; **s. (d'opinion)** opinion poll
**sonder** [sɔ̃de] *vt (rivière)* to sound; *(terrain)* to drill; *Fig (personne, l'opinion)* to sound out

**songe** [sɔ̃ʒ] *nm* dream
**songer** [sɔ̃ʒe] **1** *vi* **s. à qch/à faire qch** to think of sth/of doing sth **2** *vt* **s. que...** to think that... ▪ **songeur, -euse** *adj* thoughtful, pensive
**sonner** [sɔne] **1** *vi* to ring; *(cor, cloches)* to sound; **on a sonné (à la porte)** there's someone at the door **2** *vt (cloche)* to ring; *(domestique)* to ring for; *(cor)* to sound; *(l'heure)* to strike
**sonnerie** [sɔnri] *nf (son)* ring(ing); *(de cor)* sound; *(appareil)* bell; *(de téléphone) Br* ringing tone, *Am* ring
**sonnette** [sɔnɛt] *nf* bell; **coup de s.** ring; **s. d'alarme** alarm (bell)
**sonore** [sɔnɔr] *adj (rire)* loud; *(voix)* resonant; **effet s.** sound effect ▪ **sonorité** *nf (de salle)* acoustics; *(de violon)* tone
**sont** [sɔ̃] *voir* **être**
**sophistiqué, -e** [sɔfistike] *adj* sophisticated
**soporifique** [sɔpɔrifik] *adj (médicament, discours)* soporific
**sorbet** [sɔrbɛ] *nm* sorbet
**sorcellerie** [sɔrsɛlri] *nf* witchcraft, sorcery ▪ **sorcier** *nm* sorcerer ▪ **sorcière** *nf* witch
**sordide** [sɔrdid] *adj (acte, affaire)* sordid; *(maison)* squalid
**sort** [sɔr] *nm (destin)* fate; *(condition)* lot; *(maléfice)* spell
**sortant, -e** [sɔrtɑ̃, -ɑ̃t] *adj (numéro)* winning; *(député)* outgoing
**sorte** [sɔrt] *nf* sort, kind (**de** of); **toutes sortes de** all sorts *or* kinds of; **en quelque s.** in a way, as it were; **de (telle) s. que tu apprennes** so that *or* in such a way that you may learn; **faire en s. que...** *(+ subjunctive)* to see to it that...
**sortie** [sɔrti] *nf (porte)* exit, way out; *(action de sortir)* leaving, exit, departure; *(promenade)* walk; *(de film, de disque)* release; *(de livre)* appearance; **être de s.** to be out; **s. de bain** bathrobe; **s. de secours** emergency exit
**sortir*** [sɔrtir] **1** *(aux* **être***) vi* to go out, to leave; *(pour s'amuser)* to go out; *(film)* to come out; *(numéro gagnant)* to come up; **s. de** *(endroit)* to leave; *(université)* to be a graduate of; *(famille, milieu)* to come from; *(rails)* to come off; **s. de l'ordinaire** to be out of the ordinary
**2** *(aux* **avoir***) vt* to take out (**de** of); *(film, livre)* to bring out
**3 se sortir** *vpr* **s'en s.** *(malade)* to pull through
**SOS** [ɛsoɛs] *nm* SOS; **lancer un SOS** to send (out) an SOS
**sosie** [sozi] *nm* double
**sottise** [sɔtiz] *nf* foolishness; *(action, parole)* foolish thing
**souche** [suʃ] *nf (d'arbre)* stump; *(de carnet)* stub, counterfoil; *(de virus)* strain
**souci** [susi] *nm (inquiétude)* worry, concern; *(préoccupation)* concern (**de** for); **se faire du s.** to worry, to be worried ▪ **se soucier** *vpr* **se s. de** to be worried *or* concerned about ▪ **soucieux, -euse** *adj* worried, concerned (**de qch** about sth)
**soucoupe** [sukup] *nf* saucer
**soudain, -e** [sudɛ̃, -ɛn] **1** *adj* sudden **2** *adv* suddenly ▪ **soudaineté** *nf* suddenness
**Soudan** [sudɑ̃] *nm* **le S.** Sudan
**souder** [sude] **1** *vt (par alliage)* to solder; *(par soudure autogène)* to weld; **lampe à s.** blowlamp **2 se souder** *vpr (os)* to knit (together) ▪ **soudure** *nf (par alliage)* soldering; *(autogène)* welding
**souffle** [sufl] *nm (d'air, de vent)* breath, puff; *(respiration)* breathing; *(de bombe)* blast; **reprendre son s.** to get one's breath back ▪ **souffler 1** *vi* to blow; *(haleter)* to puff; **laisser s. qn** *(se reposer)* to give sb time to catch his/her breath **2** *vt (bougie)* to blow out; *(fumée, verre)* to blow; *(faire exploser)* to blast; *(chuchoter)* to whisper
**souffrance** [sufrɑ̃s] *nf* suffering; **en s.** *(colis)* unclaimed
**souffrir*** [sufrir] *vi* to suffer; **s. de** to suffer from; **faire s. qn** *(physiquement)*

to hurt sb; *(moralement)* to make sb suffer ■ **souffrant, -e** *adj* unwell

**souhait** [swɛ] *nm* wish; **à vos souhaits!** *(après un éternuement)* bless you! ■ **souhaitable** *adj* desirable ■ **souhaiter** *vt (bonheur)* to wish for; **s. qch à qn** to wish sb sth; **s. faire qch** to hope to do sth; **s. que...** *(+ subjunctive)* to hope that...

**soûl, -e** [su, sul] **1** *adj* drunk **2** *nm* **tout son s.** *(boire)* to one's heart's content ■ **se soûler** *vpr* to get drunk

**soulager** [sulaʒe] *vt* to relieve (**de** of) ■ **soulagement** *nm* relief

**soulever** [sulәve] **1** *vt* to lift (up); *(question)* to raise **2 se soulever** *vpr (personne)* to lift oneself (up); *(se révolter)* to rise up ■ **soulèvement** [-ɛvmɑ̃] *nm (révolte)* uprising

**soulier** [sulje] *nm* shoe

**souligner** [suliɲe] *vt (d'un trait)* to underline; *(faire remarquer)* to emphasize

**soumettre*** [sumɛtr] **1** *vt (pays, rebelles)* to subdue; *(rapport, demande)* to submit (**à** to); **s. qn à** *(assujettir)* to subject sb to
**2 se soumettre** *vpr* to submit (**à** to) ■ **soumis, -e** *adj (docile)* submissive; **s. à** subject to ■ **soumission** *nf (à une autorité)* submission; *(docilité)* submissiveness

**soupçon** [supsɔ̃] *nm* suspicion; **au-dessus de tout s.** above suspicion ■ **soupçonner** *vt* to suspect (**de** of; **d'avoir fait** of doing) ■ **soupçonneux, -euse** *adj* suspicious

**soupe** [sup] *nf* soup; **s. populaire** soup kitchen ■ **soupière** *nf* (soup) tureen

**souper** [supe] **1** *nm* supper **2** *vi* to have supper

**soupir** [supir] *nm* sigh ■ **soupirer** *vi* to sigh

**souple** [supl] *adj (corps, personne)* supple; *(branche)* flexible ■ **souplesse** *nf (de corps)* suppleness; *(de branche)* flexibility

**source** [surs] *nf* (**a**) *(point d'eau)* spring; **prendre sa s.** *(rivière)* to rise (**à** at) (**b**) *(origine)* source

**sourcil** [sursi] *nm* eyebrow ■ **sourciller** *vi Fig* **ne pas s.** not to bat an eyelid

**sourd, -e** [sur, surd] **1** *adj (personne)* deaf (**à** to); *(douleur)* dull; **bruit s.** thump **2** *nmf* deaf person ■ **sourd-muet, sourde-muette** (*mpl* **sourds-muets,** *fpl* **sourdes-muettes**) **1** *adj* deaf-and-dumb **2** *nmf* deaf mute

**sourire*** [surir] **1** *nm* smile; **faire un s. à qn** to give sb a smile **2** *vi* to smile (**à** at)

**souris** [suri] *nf (animal) & Ordinat* mouse (*pl* mice)

**sournois, -e** [surnwa, -waz] *adj* sly, underhand

**sous** [su] *prép (position)* under, underneath, beneath; *(rang)* under; **s. la pluie** in the rain; **nager s. l'eau** to swim underwater; **s. le nom de** under the name of; **s. Charles X** under Charles X; **s. peu** *(bientôt)* shortly

**sous-bois** [subwa] *nm* undergrowth

**sous-chef** [suʃɛf] (*pl* **sous-chefs**) *nmf* second-in-command

**souscrire*** [suskrir] *vi* **s. à** *(payer, approuver)* to subscribe to ■ **souscription** *nf* subscription

**sous-développé, -e** [sudevlɔpe] (*mpl* **sous-développés,** *fpl* **sous-développées**) *adj (pays)* underdeveloped

**sous-directeur, -trice** [sudirɛktœr, -tris] (*pl* **sous-directeurs**) *nmf* assistant manager

**sous-entendre** [suzɑ̃tɑ̃dr] *vt* to imply

**sous-entendu** [suzɑ̃tɑ̃dy] (*pl* **sous-entendus**) *nm* insinuation

**sous-estimer** [suzɛstime] *vt* to underestimate

**sous-jacent, -e** [suʒasɑ̃, -ɑ̃t] (*mpl* **sous-jacents,** *fpl* **sous-jacentes**) *adj* underlying

**sous-louer** [sulwe] *vt (sujet: locataire)* to sublet

**sous-marin, -e** [sumarɛ̃, -in] (*mpl* **sous-marins,** *fpl* **sous-marines**) **1** *adj* underwater **2** *nm* submarine

**sous-préfet** [suprefɛ] (*pl* **sous-préfets**) *nm* subprefect ■ **sous-préfecture** *nf* subprefecture

**soussigné, -e** [susiɲe] *adj & nmf* undersigned; **je s.** I the undersigned
**sous-sol** [susɔl] (*pl* **sous-sols**) *nm (d'immeuble)* basement; *Géol* subsoil
**sous-titre** [sutitr] (*pl* **sous-titres**) *nm* subtitle
**soustraire*** [sustrɛr] **1** *vt* to remove; *Math* to take away, to subtract (**de** from); **s. qn à** *(danger)* to shield *or* protect sb from **2 se soustraire** *vpr* **se s. à** to escape from; *(devoir, obligation)* to avoid ▪ **soustraction** *nf Math* subtraction
**soustraitant** [sutretɑ̃] *nm* subcontractor
**sous-vêtement** [suvɛtmɑ̃] *nm* undergarment; **sous-vêtements** underwear
**soutenir*** [sutənir] *vt* to support, to hold up; *(candidat)* to back; *(thèse)* to defend; *(regard)* to hold; **s. que...** to maintain that... ▪ **soutenu, -e** *adj (attention, effort)* sustained
**souterrain, -e** [suterɛ̃, -ɛn] **1** *adj* underground **2** *nm* underground passage
**soutien** [sutjɛ̃] *nm* support; *(personne)* supporter ▪ **soutien-gorge** (*pl* **soutiens-gorge**) *nm* bra
**soutirer** [sutire] *vt* **s. qch à qn** to extract sth from sb
**souvenir**[1] [suvnir] *nm* memory, recollection; *(objet)* memento; *(cadeau)* keepsake; *(pour touristes)* souvenir; **en s. de** in memory of
**souvenir**[2]* [suvnir] **se souvenir** *vpr* **se s. de qn/qch** to remember sb/sth; **se s. que...** to remember that...
**souvent** [suvɑ̃] *adv* often; **peu s.** seldom; **le plus s.** usually, more often than not
**souverain, -e** [suvərɛ̃, -ɛn] *nmf* sovereign ▪ **souveraineté** *nf* sovereignty
**soviétique** [sɔvjetik] *Anciennement* **1** *adj* Soviet; **l'Union s.** the Soviet Union **2** *nmf* Soviet citizen
**soyeux, -euse** [swajø, -øz] silky
**soyons, soyez** [swajɔ̃, swaje] *voir* **être**
**spacieux, -euse** [spasjø, -øz] *adj* spacious, roomy
**spaghettis** [spageti] *nmpl* spaghetti
**sparadrap** [sparadra] *nm (pour pansement) Br* sticking plaster, *Am* adhesive tape
**spatial, -e, -aux, -ales** [spasjal, -o] *adj* **station spatiale** space station; **engin s.** spaceship, spacecraft
**spécial, -e, -aux, -ales** [spesjal, -o] *adj* special; *(bizarre)* peculiar ▪ **spécialement** *adv (exprès)* specially; *(en particulier)* especially, particularly
**spécialiser** [spesjalize] **se spécialiser** *vpr* to specialize (**dans** in) ▪ **spécialisation** *nf* specialization ▪ **spécialiste** *nmf* specialist ▪ **spécialité** *nf Br* speciality, *Am* specialty
**spécifier** [spesifje] *vt* to specify (**que** that)
**spécifique** [spesifik] *adj* specific
**spécimen** [spesimɛn] *nm* specimen; *(livre)* specimen copy
**spectacle** [spɛktakl] *nm* (**a**) *(vue)* sight, spectacle (**b**) *(représentation)* show; **le s.** *(industrie)* show business ▪ **spectateur, -trice** *nmf* spectator; *(au théâtre, au cinéma)* member of the audience; **spectateurs** *(au théâtre, au cinéma)* audience
**spectaculaire** [spɛktakylɛr] *adj* spectacular
**spéculer** [spekyle] *vi* to speculate ▪ **spéculateur, -trice** *nmf* speculator ▪ **spéculation** *nf* speculation
**spéléologie** [speleɔlɔʒi] *nf (activité) Br* potholing, caving, *Am* spelunking
**sphère** [sfɛr] *nf (boule, domaine)* sphere
**spirituel, -elle** [spiritɥɛl] *adj (amusant)* witty; *(pouvoir, vie)* spiritual
**spiritueux** [spiritɥø] *nmpl (boissons)* spirits
**splendide** [splɑ̃did] *adj* splendid ▪ **splendeur** *nf* splendour
**spontané, -e** [spɔ̃tane] *adj* spontaneous ▪ **spontanéité** *nf* spontaneity
**sport** [spɔr] *nm* sport; **faire du s.** to play *Br* sport *or Am* sports; **voiture/**

**terrain de s.** sports car/ground; **sports de combat** combat sports; **sports d'équipe** team sports; **sports d'hiver** winter sports; **aller aux sports d'hiver** to go skiing; **sports mécaniques** motor sports *(on land, in the air, on water)* ▪ **sportif, -ive 1** *adj (personne)* fond of *Br* sport *or Am* sports; *(esprit)* sporting; *(association, journal, résultats)* sports, sporting; *(allure)* athletic **2** *nmf* sportsman, *f* sportswoman

**spot** [spɔt] *nm (lampe)* spotlight; **s. publicitaire** commercial

**square** [skwar] *nm* public garden

**squash** [skwaʃ] *nm (jeu)* squash

**squatter 1** [skwate] *vi* to squat **2** [skwatœr] *nm* squatter ▪ **squatteur, -euse** *nmf* squatter

**squelette** [skəlɛt] *nm* skeleton

**stable** [stabl] *adj* stable ▪ **stabiliser** *vt*, **se stabiliser** *vpr* to stabilize ▪ **stabilité** *nf* stability

**stade** [stad] *nm Sport* stadium; *(phase)* stage

**stage** [staʒ] *nm (période)* training period; *(cours)* (training) course; **faire un s.** to undergo training; **être en s.** to be on a training course ▪ **stagiaire** *adj & nmf* trainee

**stagner** [stagne] *vi* to stagnate

**stand** [stɑ̃d] *nm (d'exposition)* stand, stall; **s. de tir** *(de foire)* shooting range

**standard** [stɑ̃dar] **1** *nm (téléphonique)* switchboard **2** *adj inv (modèle)* standard ▪ **standardiste** *nmf* (switchboard) operator

**standing** [stɑ̃diŋ] *nm* standing, status; **immeuble de (grand) s.** *Br* luxury block of flats, *Am* luxury apartment building

**station** [stɑsjɔ̃] *nf (de métro, d'observation, de radio)* station; *(de ski)* resort; *(d'autobus)* stop; **s. de taxis** *Br* taxi rank, *Am* taxi stand ▪ **station-service** (*pl* **stations-service**) *nf* service station, *Br* petrol *or Am* gas station

**stationnaire** [stasjɔnɛr] *adj* stationary

**stationner** [stasjɔne] *vi (être garé)* to be parked ▪ **stationnement** *nm* parking

**statistique** [statistik] **1** *adj* statistical **2** *nf (donnée)* statistic; **la s.** *(science)* statistics *(sing)*

**statue** [staty] *nf* statue

**statut** [staty] *nm (position)* status; **statuts** *(règles)* statutes

**steak** [stɛk] *nm* steak

**sténographie** [stenɔgrafi] *nf* shorthand, stenography

**stéréo** [stereo] *nf* stereo; **en s.** in stereo ▪ **stéréophonique** *adj* stereophonic

**stéréotype** [stereɔtip] *nm* stereotype ▪ **stéréotypé, -e** *adj* stereotyped

**stérile** [steril] *adj* sterile; *(terre)* barren ▪ **stérilisation** *nf* sterilization ▪ **stériliser** *vt* to sterilize ▪ **stérilité** *nf* sterility; *(de terre)* barrenness

**stéthoscope** [stetɔskɔp] *nm* stethoscope

**steward** [stiwart] *nm (d'avion, de bateau)* steward

**stigmatiser** [stigmatize] *vt (dénoncer)* to stigmatize

**stimuler** [stimyle] *vt* to stimulate ▪ **stimulation** *nf* stimulation

**stimulus** [stimylys] (*pl* **stimuli** [-li]) *nm (physiologique)* stimulus

**stipuler** [stipyle] *vt* to stipulate (**que** that)

**stock** [stɔk] *nm* stock (**de** of); **en s.** in stock ▪ **stockage** *nm* stocking ▪ **stocker** *vt (provisions)* to stock

**stop** [stɔp] **1** *exclam* stop **2** *nm Aut (panneau)* stop sign; *(feu arrière)* brake light, *Br* stoplight ▪ **stopper** *vti* to stop

**stratagème** [strataʒɛm] *nm* stratagem, ploy

**stratège** [stratɛʒ] *nm* strategist ▪ **stratégie** *nf* strategy ▪ **stratégique** *adj* strategic

**stress** [strɛs] *nm inv* stress ▪ **stressant, -e** *adj* stressful ▪ **stressé, -e** *adj* under stress

**strict, -e** [strikt] *adj (principes, professeur)* strict; *(tenue)* plain; **le s.**

**minimum** the bare minimum ▪ **strictement** [-əmɑ̃] *adv* strictly; *(vêtu)* plainly

**strident, -e** [stridɑ̃, -ɑ̃t] *adj* shrill, strident

**structure** [stryktyr] *nf* structure ▪ **structural, -e, -aux, -ales** *adj* structural ▪ **structurer** *vt* to structure

**studieux, -euse** [stydjø, -øz] *adj* studious; *(vacances)* devoted to study

**studio** [stydjo] *nm (de cinéma, de télévision, de peintre)* studio; *(logement) Br* studio flat, *Am* studio apartment

**stupéfait, -e** [stypefɛ, -ɛt] *adj* amazed, astounded (**de** at *or* by) ▪ **stupéfaction** *nf* amazement

**stupéfier** [stypefje] *vt* to amaze, to astound ▪ **stupéfiant, -e 1** *adj* amazing, astounding **2** *nm* drug, narcotic

**stupeur** [stypœr] *nf (étonnement)* amazement; *(inertie)* stupor

**stupide** [stypid] *adj* stupid ▪ **stupidité** *nf* stupidity; *(action, parole)* stupid thing

**style** [stil] *nm* style; **meubles de s.** period furniture ▪ **stylé, -e** *adj* well-trained ▪ **styliste** *nmf (de mode)* designer ▪ **stylistique** *adj* stylistic

**stylo** [stilo] *nm* pen; **s. à bille** ballpoint (pen), *Br* biro®; **s. à encre, s.-plume** fountain pen

**su, -e** [sy] *pp de* **savoir**

**subdiviser** [sybdivize] *vt* to subdivide (**en** into) ▪ **subdivision** *nf* subdivision

**subir** [sybir] *vt* to undergo; *(conséquences, défaite, perte, tortures)* to suffer; *(influence)* to be under; **faire s. qch à qn** to subject sb to sth

**subit, -e** [sybi, -it] *adj* sudden

**subjectif, -ive** [sybʒɛktif, -iv] *adj* subjective ▪ **subjectivité** *nf* subjectivity

**subjuguer** [sybʒyge] *vt* to subjugate, to subdue; *(envoûter)* to captivate

**sublime** [syblim] *adj & nm* sublime

**submerger** [sybmɛrʒe] *vt* to submerge; *Fig (envahir)* to overwhelm; *Fig* **submergé de travail** snowed under with work

**submersible** [sybmɛrsibl] *nm* submarine

**subside** [sypsid] *nm* grant, subsidy

**subsistance** [sybzistɑ̃s] *nf* subsistence

**subsister** [sybziste] **1** *vi (chose)* to remain; *(personne)* to subsist **2** *v impersonnel* to remain; **il subsiste un doute** there remains some doubt

**substance** [sypstɑ̃s] *nf* substance; *Fig* **en s.** in essence ▪ **substantiel, -elle** *adj* substantial

**substituer** [sypstitɥe] **1** *vt* to substitute (**à** for) **2 se substituer** *vpr* **se s. à qn** to take the place of sb, to substitute for sb ▪ **substitution** *nf* substitution; **produit de s.** substitute (product)

**substitut** [sypstity] *nm (produit)* substitute (**de** for); *(magistrat)* deputy public prosecutor

**subtil, -e** [syptil] *adj* subtle ▪ **subtilité** *nf* subtlety

**subvenir*** [sybvənir] *vi* **s. à** *(besoins, frais)* to meet

**subvention** [sybvɑ̃sjɔ̃] *nf* subsidy ▪ **subventionner** *vt* to subsidize

**subversif, -ive** [sybvɛrsif, -iv] *adj* subversive ▪ **subversion** *nf* subversion

**suc** [syk] *nm (gastrique, de fruit)* juice; *(de plante)* sap

**succéder** [syksede] **1** *vi* **s. à qn** to succeed sb; **s. à qch** to follow sth, to come after sth **2 se succéder** *vpr (choses, personnes)* to follow one another

**succès** [syksɛ] *nm* success; **s. de librairie** *(livre)* best-seller; **avoir du s.** to be successful; **à s.** *(auteur, film)* successful

**successeur** [syksesœr] *nm* successor ▪ **successif, -ive** *adj* successive ▪ **succession** *nf* succession (**de** of; **à** to); *(série)* sequence (**de** of); *(patrimoine)* inheritance, estate; **prendre la s. de qn** to succeed sb

**succinct, -e** [syksɛ̃, -ɛ̃t] *adj* succinct, brief

**succomber** [sykɔ̃be] *vi (mourir)* to die; **s. à** *(céder à)* to succumb to

**succulent, -e** [sykylɑ̃, -ɑ̃t] *adj* succulent

**succursale** [sykyrsal] *nf (de magasin)* branch; **magasin à succursales multiples** chain store

**sucer** [syse] *vt* to suck ▪ **sucette** *nf* lollipop; *(tétine) Br* dummy, *Am* pacifier

**sucre** [sykr] *nm* sugar; *(morceau)* sugar lump; **s. en poudre, s. semoule** *Br* castor *or* caster sugar, *Am* finely ground sugar; **s. d'orge** barley sugar

**sucrer** [sykre] *vt* to sugar, to sweeten ▪ **sucré, -e** *adj* sweet, sugary; *(artificiellement)* sweetened; *Fig (doucereux)* sugary, syrupy

**sucrerie** [sykrəri] *nf (usine)* sugar refinery; **sucreries** *(bonbons) Br* sweets, *Am* candy

**sucrier** [sykrije] *nm (récipient)* sugar bowl

**sud** [syd] **1** *nm* south; **au s.** in the south; *(direction)* (to the) south (**de** of); **du s.** *(vent, direction)* southerly; *(ville)* southern; *(gens)* from *or* in the south; **l'Afrique du S.** South Africa
**2** *adj inv (côte)* south(ern) ▪ **sud-africain, -e** (*mpl* **sud-africains,** *fpl* **sud-africaines**) **1** *adj* South African **2** *nmf* **S., S.-Africaine** South African ▪ **sud-américain, -e** (*mpl* **sud-américains,** *fpl* **sud-américaines**) **1** *adj* South American **2** *nmf* **S., S.-Américaine** South American ▪ **sud-est** *nm & adj inv* south-east ▪ **sud-ouest** *nm & adj inv* south-west

**Suède** [sɥɛd] *nf* **la S.** Sweden ▪ **suédois, -e 1** *adj* Swedish **2** *nmf* **S., Suédoise** Swede **3** *nm (langue)* Swedish

**suer** [sɥe] *vi (personne, mur)* to sweat ▪ **sueur** *nf* sweat; **(tout) en s.** sweating

**suffire*** [syfir] **1** *vi* to be enough (**à** for); **ça suffit!** that's enough! **2** *v impersonnel* **il suffit de faire qch** one only has to do sth; **il suffit d'une goutte/d'une heure pour faire qch** a drop/an hour is enough to do sth **3 se suffire** *vpr* **se s. à soi-même** to be self-sufficient

**suffisance** [syfizɑ̃s] *nf (vanité)* conceit

**suffisant, -e** [syfizɑ̃, -ɑ̃t] *adj (satisfaisant)* sufficient, adequate; *(vaniteux)* conceited ▪ **suffisamment** [-amɑ̃] *adv* sufficiently; **s. de** enough, sufficient

**suffoquer** [syfɔke] *vti* to choke, to suffocate

**suffrage** [syfraʒ] *nm Pol (voix)* vote; **s. universel** universal suffrage

**suggérer** [sygʒere] *vt (proposer)* to suggest (**à** to; **de faire** doing; **que** + *subjunctive* that) ▪ **suggestif, -ive** *adj* suggestive ▪ **suggestion** *nf* suggestion

**suicide** [sɥisid] *nm* suicide ▪ **se suicider** *vpr* to commit suicide

**suie** [sɥi] *nf* soot

**suinter** [sɥɛ̃te] *vi* to ooze ▪ **suintement** *nm* oozing

**suis** [sɥi] *voir* **être, suivre**

**Suisse** [sɥis] *nf* **la S.** Switzerland; **S. allemande/romande** German-speaking/French-speaking Switzerland ▪ **suisse 1** *adj* Swiss **2** *nmf* **S.** Swiss; **les Suisses** the Swiss ▪ **Suissesse** *nf* Swiss *inv*

**suite** [sɥit] *nf (reste)* rest; *(continuation)* continuation; *(de film, de roman)* sequel; *(série)* series, sequence; *(appartement, escorte)* suite; *(cohérence)* order; **suites** *(séquelles)* effects; *(résultats)* consequences; **faire s. (à)** to follow; **donner s. à** *(demande)* to follow up; **par la s.** afterwards; **par s. de** as a result of; **à la s.** one after another; **à la s. de** *(derrière)* behind; *(événement, maladie)* as a result of; **de s.** *(deux jours)* in a row

**suivant, -e** [sɥivɑ̃, -ɑ̃t] **1** *adj* next, following; *(ci-après)* following **2** *nmf* next (one); **au s.!** next!, next person! ▪ **suivant** *prép (selon)* according to

**suivi, -e** [sɥivi] *adj (régulier)* regular, steady; *(cohérent)* coherent; **peu/très s.** *(cours)* poorly/well attended

**suivre*** [sɥivr] **1** *vt* to follow; *(accompagner)* to go with, to accompany; *(cours)* to attend, to go to; **s.**

**qn/qch des yeux** *ou* **du regard** to watch sb/sth; **s. l'exemple de qn** to follow sb's example; **s. l'actualité** to follow events *or* the news **2** *vi* to follow; **faire s.** *(courrier, lettre)* to forward; **'à s.'** 'to be continued' **3 se suivre** *vpr* to follow each other

**sujet**[1]**, -ette** [syʒɛ, -ɛt] **1** *adj* **s. à** *(maladie)* subject to; **s. à caution** *(information, nouvelle)* unconfirmed **2** *nmf (personne)* subject

**sujet**[2] [syʒɛ] *nm* (**a**) *(question)* subject; *(d'examen)* question; **au s. de** about; **à quel s.?** about what? (**b**) *(raison)* cause; **sujet(s) de dispute** grounds for dispute (**c**) *(individu)* subject; **un brillant s.** a brilliant student

**super** [sypɛr] *nm (supercarburant) Br* four-star (petrol), *Am* premium *ou* high-test gas

**superbe** [sypɛrb] *adj* superb

**supercherie** [sypɛrʃəri] *nf* deception

**supérette** [syperɛt] *nf* convenience store

**superficie** [sypɛrfisi] *nf* surface; *(dimensions)* area ▪ **superficiel, -elle** *adj* superficial

**superflu, -e** [sypɛrfly] *adj* superfluous

**supérieur, -e** [sypɛrjœr] **1** *adj (étages, partie)* upper; *(qualité, air, ton)* superior; **à l'étage s.** on the floor above; **s. à** *(meilleur que)* superior to, better than; *(plus grand que)* above, greater than; **s. à la moyenne** above average; **études supérieures** higher *ou* university studies **2** *nmf* superior ▪ **supériorité** *nf* superiority

**supermarché** [sypɛrmarʃe] *nm* supermarket

**superposer** [sypɛrpoze] *vt (objets)* to put on top of each other; *(images)* to superimpose

**superproduction** [sypɛrprɔdyksjɔ̃] *nf (film)* blockbuster

**superpuissance** [sypɛrpɥisɑ̃s] *nf Pol* superpower

**supersonique** [sypɛrsɔnik] *adj* supersonic

**superstar** [sypɛrstar] *nf* superstar

**superstitieux, -euse** [sypɛrstisjø, -øz] *adj* superstitious ▪ **superstition** *nf* superstition

**superviser** [sypɛrvize] *vt* to supervise

**supplanter** [syplɑ̃te] *vt* to take the place of

**suppléer** [syplee] *vi* **s. à** *(compenser)* to make up for ▪ **suppléant, -e** *adj & nmf (personne)* substitute, replacement; **(professeur) s.** substitute *or Br* supply teacher

**supplément** [syplemɑ̃] *nm (argent)* extra charge, supplement; *(de revue, de livre)* supplement; **en s.** extra; **un s. de** *(information, de travail)* extra, additional ▪ **supplémentaire** *adj* extra, additional

**supplice** [syplis] *nm* torture ▪ **supplier** *vt* **s. qn de faire qch** to beg *or* implore sb to do sth; **je vous en supplie!** I beg *or* implore you!

**support** [sypɔr] *nm* support; *(d'instrument)* stand

**supporter**[1] [sypɔrte] *vt (malheur, conséquences)* to bear, to endure; *(chaleur)* to withstand; **je ne peux pas la s.** I can't bear her ▪ **supportable** *adj* bearable; *(excusable, passable)* tolerable

**supporter**[2] [sypɔrtɛr] *nm (de football)* supporter

**supposer** [sypoze] *vt* to suppose, to assume (**que** that); *(impliquer)* to imply (**que** that); **à s.** *ou* **en supposant que...** *(+ subjunctive)* supposing (that)... ▪ **supposition** *nf* assumption, supposition

**supprimer** [syprime] **1** *vt* to get rid of, to remove; *(mot, passage)* to cut out, to delete; *(train)* to cancel; *(tuer)* to do away with; **s. des emplois** to axe jobs; **s. qch à qn** to take sth away from sb

**2 se supprimer** *vpr (se suicider)* to do away with oneself ▪ **suppression** *nf* removal; *(de mot)* deletion; *(de train)* cancellation; *(d'emplois)* axing

**suprématie** [sypremasi] *nf* supremacy

**suprême** [syprɛm] *adj* supreme
**sur** [syr] *prép* on, upon; *(par-dessus)* over; *(au sujet de)* on, about; **six s. dix** six out of ten; **un jour s. deux** every other day; **six mètres s. dix** six metres by ten; **s. votre gauche** to *or* on your left; **mettre/monter s. qch** to put/ climb on (to) sth
**sûr, -e** [syr] *adj* sure, certain (**de** of; **que** that); *(digne de confiance)* reliable; *(lieu)* safe; *(goût)* discerning; *(main)* steady; **s. de soi** self-assured; **bien s.!** of course!
**surcharge** [syrʃarʒ] *nf* (**a**) *(poids)* excess weight; **s. de travail** extra work; **en s.** *(passagers)* extra (**b**) *(correction)* alteration; *(à payer)* surcharge ▪ **surcharger** *vt (voiture, personne)* to overload (**de** with)
**surchauffer** [syrʃofe] *vt* to overheat
**surcroît** [syrkrwa] *nm* increase (**de** in); **de s., par s.** in addition
**surdité** [syrdite] *nf* deafness
**surdose** [syrdoz] *nf (de drogue)* overdose
**surélever** [syrelve] *vt* to raise
**surestimer** [syrɛstime] *vt* to overestimate; *(tableau)* to overvalue
**sûreté** [syrte] *nf* safety; *(de l'État)* security; *(garantie)* surety; *(de geste)* sureness; **être en s.** to be safe; **mettre qn/qch en s.** to put sb/sth in a safe place; **pour plus de s.** to be on the safe side
**surexcité, -e** [syrɛksite] *adj* overexcited
**surf** [sœrf] *nm Sport* surfing; **faire du s.** to surf, to go surfing ▪ **surfer** *vi* **s. sur le Net** to surf the Net
**surface** [syrfas] *nf* surface; *(étendue)* (surface) area; **faire s.** *(sous-marin)* to surface; **(magasin à) grande s.** hypermarket; **de s.** *(politesse)* superficial
**surfait, -e** [syrfɛ, -ɛt] *adj* overrated
**surgelé, -e** [syrʒəle] *adj* frozen ▪ **surgelés** *nmpl* frozen foods
**surgir** [syrʒir] *vi* to appear suddenly (**de** from)
**surhomme** [syrɔm] *nm* superman ▪ **surhumain, -e** *adj* superhuman
**sur-le-champ** [syrləʃɑ̃] *adv* immediately
**surlendemain** [syrlɑ̃dəmɛ̃] *nm* **le s.** two days later; **le s. de** two days after
**surligner** [syrliɲe] *vt* to highlight ▪ **surligneur** *nm* highlighter (pen)
**surmener** [syrməne] *vt*, **se surmener** *vpr* to overwork ▪ **surmenage** *nm* overwork
**surmonter** [syrmɔ̃te] *vt (être placé sur)* to surmount; *Fig (obstacle, peur)* to overcome
**surnaturel, -elle** [syrnatyrɛl] *adj & nm* supernatural
**surnom** [syrnɔ̃] *nm* nickname
**surpasser** [syrpɑse] **1** *vt* to surpass (**en** in) **2 se surpasser** *vpr* to surpass oneself
**surpeuplé, -e** [syrpœple] *adj* overpopulated
**surplomb** [syrplɔ̃] *nm* **en s.** overhanging ▪ **surplomber** *vti* to overhang
**surplus** [syrply] *nm* surplus
**surprendre*** [syrprɑ̃dr] *vt (étonner)* to surprise; *(prendre sur le fait)* to catch ▪ **surprenant, -e** *adj* surprising ▪ **surpris, -e** *adj* surprised (**de** at; **que** + *subjunctive* that); **je suis s. de te voir** I'm surprised to see you ▪ **surprise** *nf* surprise; **prendre qn par s.** to catch sb unawares
**surréaliste** [syrrealist] *adj (poète, peintre)* surrealist
**sursaut** [syrso] *nm* (sudden) start *ou* jump; **se réveiller en s.** to wake up with a start ▪ **sursauter** *vi* to jump, start
**sursis** [syrsi] *nm (à l'armée)* deferment; *Fig (répit)* reprieve; **un an (de prison) avec s.** a one-year suspended sentence
**surtout** [syrtu] *adv* especially; *(avant tout)* above all; **s. pas** certainly not
**surveiller** [syrveje] *vt (garder)* to watch, to keep an eye on; *(contrôler)* to supervise; *(épier)* to watch ▪ **surveillance** *nf* watch (**sur** over); *(de travaux, d'ouvriers)* supervision; *(de*

*police)* surveillance ▪ **surveillant, -e** *nmf (de lycée)* supervisor (in charge of discipline); *(de prison)* (prison) guard, *Br* warder
**survenir*** [syrvənir] *vi* to occur; *(personne)* to turn up
**survêtement** [syrvɛtmɑ̃] *nm* tracksuit
**survie** [syrvi] *nf* survival ▪ **survivre*** *vi* to survive (**à qch** sth); **s. à qn** to outlive sb ▪ **survivant, -e** *nmf* survivor
**survoler** [syrvɔle] *vt* to fly over; *Fig (question)* to skim over
**susceptible** [sysɛptibl] *adj (ombrageux)* touchy, sensitive; **s. de** *(interprétations)* open to; **s. de faire qch** likely *ou* liable to do sth; *(capable)* able to do sth ▪ **susceptibilité** *nf* touchiness, sensitivity
**susciter** [sysite] *vt (sentiment)* to arouse; *(ennuis, obstacles)* to create
**suspect, -e** [syspɛ, -ɛkt] **1** *adj* suspicious, suspect; **s. de qch** suspected of sth **2** *nmf* suspect ▪ **suspecter** *vt (personne)* to suspect (**de qch** of sth; **de faire** of doing)
**suspendre** [syspɑ̃dr] **1** *vt (accrocher)* to hang (up) (**à** on); *(destituer, interrompre)* to suspend **2 se suspendre** *vpr* **se s. à** to hang from ▪ **suspendu, -e** *adj* **s. à** hanging from; **pont s.** suspension bridge
**suspens** [syspɑ̃] **en suspens** *adv (affaire, travail)* in abeyance; *(en l'air)* suspended
**suspense** [syspɛns] *nm* suspense
**suspension** [syspɑ̃sjɔ̃] *nf (d'hostilités, d'employé, de véhicule)* suspension
**suspicion** [syspisjɔ̃] *nf* suspicion
**suture** [sytyr] *nf Méd* **point de s.** stitch
**SVP** [ɛsvepe] *(abrév* **s'il vous plaît**) please

**symbole** [sɛ̃bɔl] *nm* symbol ▪ **symbolique** *adj* symbolic; *(salaire, cotisation, loyer)* nominal; **geste s.** symbolic *ou* token gesture ▪ **symboliser** *vt* to symbolize
**sympathie** [sɛ̃pati] *nf (affinité)* liking; *(condoléances)* sympathy; **avoir de la s. pour qn** to be fond of sb ▪ **sympathique** *adj* nice; *(accueil)* friendly ▪ **sympathiser** *vi* to get along well, *Br* to get on well (**avec** with)
**symphonie** [sɛ̃fɔni] *nf* symphony
**symptôme** [sɛ̃ptom] *nm Méd & Fig* symptom
**synagogue** [sinagɔg] *nf* synagogue
**synchroniser** [sɛ̃krɔnize] *vt* to synchronize
**syndicat** [sɛ̃dika] *nm (d'ouvriers)* (*Br* trade *or Am* labor) union; *(de patrons)* association; **s. d'initiative** tourist (information) office ▪ **syndicaliste** *nmf Br* trade *or Am* labor unionist
**syndiquer** [sɛ̃dike] **1** *vt* to unionize **2 se syndiquer** *vpr (adhérer)* to join a (*Br* trade *or Am* labor) union ▪ **syndiqué, -e** *nmf* (*Br* trade *or Am* labor) union member
**syndrome** [sɛ̃drom] *nm Méd & Fig* syndrome; **s. immunodéficitaire acquis** acquired immune deficiency syndrome
**synthèse** [sɛ̃tɛz] *nf* synthesis ▪ **synthétique** *adj* synthetic
**synthétiseur** [sɛ̃tetizœr] *nm* synthesizer
**Syrie** [siri] *nf* **la S.** Syria ▪ **syrien, -enne 1** *adj* Syrian **2** *nmf* **S., Syrienne** Syrian
**système** [sistɛm] *nm (structure, réseau) & Anat* system; *Ordinat* **s. d'exploitation** operating system ▪ **systématique** *adj* systematic ▪ **systématiquement** *adv* systematically

# Tt

**T, t** [te] *nm inv* T, t
**t'** [t] *voir* **te**
**ta** [ta] *voir* **ton**[1]
**tabac** [taba] *nm* tobacco; *(magasin) Br* tobacconist's (shop), *Am* tobacco store
**table** [tabl] *nf* (**a**) *(meuble)* table; *(d'école)* desk; **mettre/débarrasser la t.** to set *or Br* lay/clear the table; **être à t.** to be sitting at the table; **à t.!** food's ready!; **t. à repasser** ironing board; **t. de nuit/d'opération** bedside/operating table (**b**) *(liste)* table; **t. des matières** table of contents
**tableau, -x** [tablo] *nm* (**a**) *(peinture)* picture, painting; *(image, description)* picture; **t. de maître** *(peinture)* old master (**b**) *(panneau)* board; *(liste)* list; *(graphique)* chart; **t. (noir)** (black)board; **t. d'affichage** *Br* notice board, *Am* bulletin board
**tabler** [table] *vi* **t. sur qch** to count *or* rely on sth
**tablette** [tablɛt] *nf (de chocolat)* bar, slab; *(de lavabo)* shelf; *(de cheminée)* mantelpiece
**tablier** [tablije] *nm (vêtement)* apron; *(d'écolier)* smock
**tabouret** [taburɛ] *nm* stool
**tache** [taʃ] *nf* mark; *(salissure)* stain ▪ **tacher** *vt*, **se tacher** *vpr (tissu)* to stain
**tâche** [tɑʃ] *nf* task, job; **tâches ménagères** housework
**tâcher** [tɑʃe] *vi* **t. de faire qch** to try *or* endeavour to do sth
**tacheté, -e** [taʃte] *adj* speckled (**de** with)
**tact** [takt] *nm* tact; **avoir du t.** to be tactful
**tactique** [taktik] **1** *adj* tactical **2** *nf* tactics *(sing)*; **une t.** a tactic
**Tahiti** [taiti] *nm* Tahiti ▪ **tahitien, -enne** [taisjɛ̃, -ɛn] **1** *adj* Tahitian **2** *nmf* **T., Tahitienne** Tahitian
**taillader** [tajade] *vt* to gash
**taille**[1] [tɑj] *nf* (**a**) *(hauteur)* height; *(dimension, mesure)* size; **de haute t.** *(personne)* tall; **de petite t.** short; **de t. moyenne** medium-sized (**b**) *(ceinture)* waist; **tour de t.** waist measurement
**taille**[2] [tɑj] *nf* cutting; *(de haie)* trimming; *(d'arbre)* pruning ▪ **tailler** *vt* to cut; *(haie, barbe)* to trim; *(arbre)* to prune; *(crayon)* to sharpen
**taille-crayon** [tɑjkrɛjɔ̃] *nm inv* pencil sharpener
**tailleur** [tɑjœr] *nm (personne)* tailor; *(costume)* suit
**taire*** [tɛr] **1** *vt* to say nothing about **2** *vi* **faire t. qn** to silence sb **3 se taire** *vpr (ne rien dire)* to keep quiet (**sur qch** about sth); *(cesser de parler)* to stop talking, to fall silent; **tais-toi!** be quiet!
**Taiwan** [tajwan] *nm ou f* Taiwan
**talc** [talk] *nm* talcum powder
**talent** [talɑ̃] *nm* talent; **avoir du t.** to be talented ▪ **talentueux, -euse** *adj* talented
**talkie-walkie** [talkiwalki] (*pl* **talkies-walkies**) *nm* walkie-talkie
**talon** [talɔ̃] *nm* (**a**) *(de chaussure)* heel; **(chaussures à) talons hauts** high heels, high-heeled shoes; **talons**

**aiguilles** stiletto heels (**b**) *(de chèque)* stub, counterfoil

**tambour** [tɑ̃bur] *nm (de machine, instrument de musique)* drum ▪ **tambourin** *nm* tambourine

**Tamise** [tamiz] *nf* **la T.** the Thames

**tamiser** [tamize] *vt (farine)* to sift; *(lumière)* to filter

**tampon** [tɑ̃pɔ̃] *nm* (**a**) *(marque, instrument)* stamp; **t. encreur** ink pad (**b**) *(bouchon)* plug, stopper; *(de coton)* wad, pad; *(pour pansement)* swab; **t. hygiénique** tampon (**c**) *(de train) & Fig* buffer; **état t.** buffer state

**tamponner** [tɑ̃pɔne] **1** *vt (lettre, document)* to stamp; *(visage)* to dab; *(plaie)* to swab; *(train, voiture)* to crash into **2** **se tamponner** *vpr* to crash into each other ▪ **tamponneuses** *adj fpl* **autos t.** Dodgems®

**tandem** [tɑ̃dɛm] *nm (bicyclette)* tandem; *Fig (duo)* duo

**tandis** [tɑ̃di] **tandis que** *conj (simultanéité)* while; *(contraste)* whereas, while

**tanière** [tanjɛr] *nf* den, lair

**tank** [tɑ̃k] *nm* tank

**tanker** [tɑ̃kɛr] *nm (navire)* tanker

**tanner** [tane] *vt (cuir)* to tan ▪ **tanné, -e** *adj (visage)* weather-beaten

**TANT** [tɑ̃] *adv (travailler)* so much (**que** that); **t. de** *(pain, temps)* so much (**que** that); *(gens, choses)* so many (**que** that); **t. de fois** so often, so many times; **t. que** *(autant que)* as much as; *(aussi fort que)* as hard as; *(aussi longtemps que)* as long as; **en t. que** *(considéré comme)* as; **t. mieux!** so much the better!; **t. pis!** too bad!, pity!; **t. mieux pour toi!** good for you!; **t. soit peu** (even) remotely *or* slightly; **un t. soit peu** somewhat; **t. s'en faut** far from it

**tante** [tɑ̃t] *nf* aunt

**tantinet** [tɑ̃tinɛ] *nm & adv* **un t.** a tiny bit (**de** of)

**tantôt** [tɑ̃to] *adv* (**a**) **t....t....** sometimes... sometimes... (**b**) *(cet après-midi)* this afternoon

**taon** [tɑ̃] *nm* horsefly, gadfly

**tapage** [tapaʒ] *nm* din, uproar ▪ **tapageur, -euse** *adj (bruyant)* rowdy; *(criard)* flashy

**tape** [tap] *nf* slap

**taper** [tape] **1** *vt (frapper)* to hit; *(marteler)* to bang; **t. qch à la machine** to type sth **2** *vi (soleil)* to beat down; **t. du pied** to stamp one's foot; **t. à la machine** to type; **t. sur qch** to bang on sth ▪ **tapant, -e** *adj* **à huit heures tapantes** at eight sharp

**tapis** [tapi] *nm* carpet; **envoyer qn au t.** *(abattre)* to floor sb; **mettre qch sur le t.** *(sujet)* to bring sth up for discussion; **t. de bain** bath mat; **t. roulant** *(pour marchandises)* conveyor belt; *(pour personnes)* moving walkway

**tapisser** [tapise] *vt (mur)* to (wall)paper ▪ **tapisserie** *nf (papier peint)* wallpaper; *(broderie)* tapestry

**tapoter** [tapɔte] **1** *vt* to tap; *(joue)* to pat **2** *vi* **t. sur** to tap (on)

**taquin, -e** [takɛ̃, -in] *adj* teasing ▪ **taquiner** *vt* to tease ▪ **taquineries** *nfpl* teasing

**tard** [tar] *adv* late; **plus t.** later (on); **au plus t.** at the latest; **sur le t.** late in life

**tarder** [tarde] **1** *vi (lettre, saison)* to be a long time coming; **sans t.** without delay; **t. à faire qch** to take one's time doing sth; **elle ne va pas t.** she won't be long **2** *v impersonnel* **il me tarde de le faire** I long to do it

**tardif, -ive** [tardif, -iv] *adj* late; *(regrets)* belated ▪ **tardivement** *adv* late

**tare** [tar] *nf (poids)* tare; *Fig (défaut)* defect

**targuer** [targe] **se targuer** *vpr* **se t. de faire qch** to pride oneself on doing sth

**tarif** [tarif] *nm (prix)* rate; *(de train)* fare; *(tableau)* price list, *Br* tariff; **plein t.** full price; *(de train, bus)* full fare ▪ **tarification** *nf* pricing

**tartare** [tartar] *adj* **sauce t.** tartar sauce

**tarte** [tart] *nf* (open) pie, tart ▪ **tartelette** [-əlɛt] *nf* (small) tart

**tartine** [tartin] *nf* slice of bread; **t. de**

**confiture** slice of bread and jam ▪ **tartiner** *vt (beurre)* to spread; **fromage à t.** cheese spread

**tas** [tɑ] *nm* pile, heap

**tasse** [tɑs] *nf* cup; **t. à café** coffee cup; **t. à thé** teacup

**tasser** [tɑse] **1** *vt* to pack (**dans** into) **2** **se tasser** *vpr (se serrer)* to squeeze up; *(sol)* to sink, to collapse; *(se voûter)* to become bowed

**tâter** [tɑte] *vt* to feel

**tâtonner** [tɑtɔne] *vi* to grope about ▪ **tâtons** *adv* **avancer à t.** to feel one's way (along); **chercher qch à t.** to grope for sth

**tatouer** [tatwe] *vt (corps, dessin)* to tattoo; **se faire t.** to get a tattoo ▪ **tatouage** *nm (dessin)* tattoo; *(action)* tattooing

**taudis** [todi] *nm* slum

**taupe** [top] *nf (animal, espion)* mole

**taureau, -x** [tɔro] *nm* bull; **le T.** *(signe)* Taurus ▪ **tauromachie** *nf* bull-fighting

**taux** [to] *nm* rate; **t. de cholestérol** cholesterol level; **t. d'intérêt** interest rate; **t. de natalité** birth rate

**taxe** [taks] *nf (impôt)* tax; **t. à la valeur ajoutée** value-added tax ▪ **taxation** *nf* taxation

**taxer** [takse] *vt (produit, personne, firme)* to tax; **t. qn de qch** to accuse sb of sth ▪ **taxé, -e** *adj (produit)* taxed

**taxi** [taksi] *nm* taxi

**Tchécoslovaquie** [tʃekɔslɔvaki] *nf Anciennement* **la T.** Czechoslovakia ▪ **tchèque 1** *adj* Czech; **la République t.** the Czech Republic **2** *nmf* **T.** Czech **3** *nm (langue)* Czech

**te** [tə]

**t'** is used before a word beginning with a vowel or h mute.

*pron personnel* (**a**) *(complément direct)* you; **je te vois** I see you (**b**) *(indirect)* (to) you; **il te parle** he speaks to you; **elle te l'a dit** she told you (**c**) *(réfléchi)* yourself; **tu te laves** you wash yourself

**technicien, -enne** [tɛknisjɛ̃, -ɛn] *nmf* technician ▪ **technique 1** *adj* technical **2** *nf* technique ▪ **technologie** *nf* technology ▪ **technologique** *adj* technological

**teckel** [tekɛl] *nm* dachshund

**tee-shirt** [tiʃœrt] *nm* tee-shirt

**teindre*** [tɛ̃dr] **1** *vt* to dye; **t. qch en rouge** to dye sth red **2** **se teindre** *vpr* **se t. (les cheveux)** to dye one's hair

**teint** [tɛ̃] *nm (de visage)* complexion; **bon** *ou* **grand t.** *(tissu)* colourfast

**teinte** [tɛ̃t] *nf* shade, tint ▪ **teinter** *vt* to tint; *(bois)* to stain

**teinture** [tɛ̃tyr] *nf* dyeing; *(produit)* dye ▪ **teinturerie** [-rri] *nf (boutique)* (dry) cleaner's

---

**TEL, TELLE** [tɛl] *adj* such; **un t. livre/homme** such a book/man; **de tels mots** such words; **t. que** such as, like; **t. que je l'ai laissé** just as I left it; **laissez-le t. quel** leave it just as it is; **en tant que t., comme t.** as such; **t. ou t.** such and such; **rien de t. que...** (there's) nothing like...; **t. père t. fils** like father like son

---

**télé** [tele] *nf Fam* TV, *Br* telly; **à la t.** on TV, *Br* on the telly

**Télécarte®** [telekart] *nf* phone card

**télécommande** [telekɔmɑ̃d] *nf* remote control ▪ **télécommandé, -e** *adj* remote-controlled

**télécommunications** [telekɔmynikɑsjɔ̃] *nfpl* telecommunications

**télécopie** [telekɔpi] *nf* fax ▪ **télécopieur** *nm* fax (machine)

**téléfilm** [telefilm] *nm* TV movie

**télégramme** [telegram] *nm* telegram

**télégraphe** [telegraf] *nm* telegraph ▪ **télégraphique** *adj* **poteau/fil t.** telegraph pole/wire

**téléguider** [telegide] *vt* to operate by remote control

**télépathie** [telepati] *nf* telepathy

**téléphérique** [teleferik] *nm* cable car

**téléphone** [telefɔn] *nm* (tele)phone; **coup de t.** (phone) call; **passer un coup de t. à qn** to give sb a ring *or* a call; **au t.** on the (tele)phone; **avoir le t.** to be on the (tele)phone; **t. portable** mobile phone; **t. sans fil** cordless phone ■ **téléphoner 1** *vt (nouvelle)* to (tele)phone (**à** to) **2** *vi* to (tele)phone; **t. à qn** to (tele)phone sb, to call sb (up) ■ **téléphonique** *adj* **appel t.** telephone call

**télescope** [telɛskɔp] *nm* telescope ■ **télescopique** *adj* telescopic

**télescoper** [telɛskɔpe] **1** *vt (voiture, train)* to smash into **2 se télescoper** *vpr (voiture, train)* to concertina

**télésiège** [telesjɛʒ] *nm* chair lift

**téléski** [telɛski] *nm* ski tow

**téléspectateur, -trice** [telespɛktatœr, -tris] *nmf* (television) viewer

**télétravail** [teletravaj] *nm* teleworking

**téléviser** [televize] *vt* to televise ■ **téléviseur** *nm* television (set) ■ **télévision** *nf* television; **à la t.** on (the) television; **regarder la t.** to watch (the) television; **programme de t.** television programme

**télex** [telɛks] *nm (service, message)* telex

**telle** [tɛl] *voir* **tel** ■ **tellement** *adv (si)* so; *(tant)* so much; **t. grand que...** so big that...; **crier t. que...** to shout so much that...; **t. de travail** so much work; **t. de soucis** so many worries; **tu aimes ça? – pas t.!** *(pas beaucoup)* do you like it? – not much *or* a lot!; **personne ne peut le supporter, t. il est bavard** nobody can stand him, he's so talkative

**tellurique** [telyrik] *adj* **secousse t.** earth tremor

**téméraire** [temerɛr] *adj* reckless ■ **témérité** *nf* recklessness

**témoigner** [temwaɲe] **1** *vt (gratitude)* to show (**à qn** (to) sb); **t. que...** *(attester)* to testify that... **2** *vi Jur* to give evidence, to testify (**contre** against); **t. de qch** *(personne, attitude)* to testify to sth ■ **témoignage** *nm Jur* evidence, testimony; *(récit)* account; **faux t.** *(délit)* perjury; **en t. de qch** as a token of sth

**témoin** [temwɛ̃] **1** *nm* (**a**) *Jur* witness; **être t. de qch** to witness sth (**b**) *(de relais)* baton **2** *adj* **appartement t.** *Br* show flat, *Am* model apartment

**tempérament** [tɑ̃peramɑ̃] *nm (caractère)* temperament; **acheter qch à t.** to buy sth on *Br* hire purchase *or Am* on the installment plan

**température** [tɑ̃peratyr] *nf* temperature; **avoir de la t.** to have a temperature

**tempérer** [tɑ̃pere] *vt (ardeurs)* to moderate ■ **tempéré, -e** *adj (climat, zone)* temperate

**tempête** [tɑ̃pɛt] *nf* storm

**tempêter** [tɑ̃pete] *vi (crier)* to storm, to rage (**contre** against)

**temple** [tɑ̃pl] *nm (romain, grec)* temple; *(protestant)* church

**temporaire** [tɑ̃pɔrɛr] *adj* temporary

**temporel, -elle** [tɑ̃pɔrɛl] *adj* temporal; *(terrestre)* wordly

---

**TEMPS[1]** [tɑ̃] *nm (durée, période, moment)* time; *(étape)* stage; **en t. de guerre** in wartime, in time of war; **avoir le t.** to have (the) time (**de faire** to do); **il est t.** it is time (**de faire** to do); **il était t.!** it was about time (too)!; **il est (grand) t. que vous partiez** it's (high) time you left; **ces derniers t.** lately; **de t. en t.** [dətɑ̃zɑ̃tɑ̃], **de t. à autre** [dətɑ̃zaotr] from time to time, now and again; **en t. utile** [ɑ̃tɑ̃zytil] in due course; **en t. voulu** in due course; **en même t.** at the same time (**que** as); **à t.** *(arriver)* in time; **à plein t.** *(travailler)* full-time; **à t. partiel** *(travailler)* part-time; **dans le t.** *(autrefois)* in the old days; **avec le t.** *(à la longue)* in time; **tout le t.** all the time; **de mon t.** in my time; **t. d'arrêt** pause, break; **t. libre** free time

---

**temps[2]** [tɑ̃] *nm (climat)* weather; **il fait beau/mauvais t.** the weather's fine/bad; **quel t. fait-il?** what's the weather like?

**tenace** [tənas] *adj* stubborn, tenacious ■ **ténacité** *nf* stubbornness, tenacity

**tenailles** [tənɑj] *nfpl (outil)* pincers

**tenant, -e** [tənɑ̃, -ɑ̃t] **1** *nmf* **le t. du**

**titre** *(champion)* the title holder **2** *nm (partisan)* supporter (**de** of)

**tendance** [tɑ̃dɑ̃s] *nf (penchant)* tendency; *(évolution)* trend (**à** towards); **avoir t. à faire qch** to tend to do sth, to have a tendency to do sth

**tendre**[1] [tɑ̃dr] **1** *vt* to stretch; *(main)* to hold out (**à qn** to sb); *(bras, jambe)* to stretch out; *(cou)* to strain, to crane; *(muscle)* to tense; *(arc)* to bend; *(piège)* to set, to lay; *(filet)* to spread; **t. qch à qn** to hold out sth to sb; *Fig* **t. l'oreille** to prick up one's ears

**2** *vi* **t. à qch/à faire qch** to tend towards sth/to do sth

**3 se tendre** *vpr (rapports)* to become strained ▪ **tendu, -e** *adj (corde)* tight, taut; *(personne, situation, muscle)* tense; *(rapports)* strained

**tendre**[2] [tɑ̃dr] *adj (personne)* affectionate (**avec** to); *(parole, regard)* tender, loving; *(viande)* tender; *(bois, couleur)* soft; **depuis ma plus t. enfance** since I was a young child ▪ **tendresse** *nf (affection)* affection, tenderness

**teneur** [tənœr] *nf (de lettre)* content; **t. en alcool** alcohol content (**de** of)

**TENIR*** [tənir] **1** *vt (à la main)* to hold; *(promesse, comptes, hôtel)* to keep; *(rôle)* to play

**2** *vi (nœud)* to hold; *(neige, coiffure)* to last, to hold; *(résister)* to hold out; **t. à qn/qch** to be attached to sb/sth; **t. à faire qch** to be anxious to do sth; **t. dans qch** *(être contenu)* to fit into sth; **t. de qn** to take after sb; **tenez!** *(prenez)* here (you are)!; **tiens!** *(surprise)* well!, hey!

**3** *v impersonnel* **il ne tient qu'à vous de le faire** it's up to you to do it

**4 se tenir** *vpr (avoir lieu)* to be held; *(rester)* to remain; **se t. debout** to stand (up); **se t. droit** to stand up/sit up straight; **se t. par la main** to hold hands; **se t. bien** to behave oneself; **se t. à qch** to hold on to sth

**tennis** [tenis] **1** *nm* tennis; *(terrain)* (tennis) court; **t. de table** table tennis **2** *nmpl Br (chaussures)* tennis shoes

**tension** [tɑ̃sjɔ̃] *nf* tension; **t. artérielle** blood pressure; **avoir de la t.** to have high blood pressure

**tente** [tɑ̃t] *nf* tent

**tenter**[1] [tɑ̃te] *vt (essayer)* to try; **t. de faire qch** to try *or* attempt to do sth ▪ **tentative** *nf* attempt

**tenter**[2] [tɑ̃te] *vt (faire envie à)* to tempt; **tenté de faire qch** tempted to do sth ▪ **tentant, -e** *adj* tempting ▪ **tentation** *nf* temptation

**tenture** [tɑ̃tyr] *nf* (wall) hanging; *(de porte)* drape, curtain

**tenu, -e** [təny] **1** *pp de* **tenir 2** *adj* **t. de faire qch** obliged to do sth; **bien/mal t.** *(maison)* well/badly kept

**ténu, -e** [teny] *adj (fil)* fine; *(différence)* tenuous; *(voix)* thin

**tenue** [təny] *nf* (**a**) *(vêtements)* clothes, outfit; **t. de soirée** evening dress (**b**) *(conduite)* (good) behaviour; *(maintien)* posture (**c**) *(de maison, d'hôtel)* running; *(de comptes)* keeping (**d**) **t. de route** *(de véhicule)* road-holding

**ter** [tɛr] *adj* **4 t.** ≃ 4B

**terme** [tɛrm] *nm* (**a**) *(mot)* term (**b**) *(date limite)* time (limit); *(fin)* end; **mettre un t. à qch** to put an end to sth; **à court/long t.** *(conséquences, projet)* short-/long-term (**c**) **moyen t.** *(solution)* middle course (**d**) **en bons/mauvais termes** on good/bad terms (**avec qn** with sb) (**e**) *(loyer)* rent; *(jour)* rent day; *(période)* rental period

**terminal, -e, -aux, -ales** [tɛrminal, -o] **1** *adj* final; *(phase de maladie)* terminal **2** *adj & nf Scol* **(classe) terminale** *Br* ≃ sixth form, *Am* ≃ twelfth grade **3** *nm (d'ordinateur, pétrolier)* terminal

**terminer** [tɛrmine] **1** *vt* to end; *(achever)* to finish, to complete **2 se terminer** *vpr* to end (**par** with; **en** in) ▪ **terminaison** *nf (de mot)* ending

**terminologie** [tɛrminɔlɔʒi] *nf* terminology

**terminus** [tɛrminys] *nm* terminus
**terne** [tɛrn] *adj (couleur, journée)* dull, drab; *(personne)* dull ▪ **ternir 1** *vt (métal, réputation)* to tarnish; *(meuble, miroir)* to dull **2 se ternir** *vpr (métal)* to tarnish
**terrain** [terɛ̃] *nm (sol) & Fig* ground; *(étendue)* land; *(à bâtir)* plot, site; *(pour opérations militaires) & Géol* terrain; **un t.** a piece of land; **gagner/perdre du t.** *(armée) & Fig* to give/gain/lose ground; **t. de camping** campsite; **t. de football/rugby** football/rugby pitch; **t. de golf** golf course; **t. de jeu(x)** *(pour enfants)* playground; *(stade) Br* playing field, *Am* athletic field; **t. de sport** *Br* sports ground, *Am* athletic field
**terrasse** [teras] *nf (balcon, plateforme)* terrace; *(toit)* terrace (roof); *(de café) Br* pavement *or Am* sidewalk area; **à la t.** outside
**terrassement** [terasmɑ̃] *nm (travail)* excavation
**terrasser** [terase] *vt (adversaire)* to floor; *Fig (accabler)* to overcome
**terre** [tɛr] *nf (matière, monde)* earth; *(sol)* ground; *(opposé à mer, étendue)* land; **terres** *(domaine)* land, estate; *Él Br* earth, *Am* ground; **la t.** *(le monde)* the earth; **la T.** *(planète)* Earth; **à** *ou* **par t.** *(tomber)* to the ground; *(poser)* on the ground; **par t.** *(assis, couché)* on the ground; **sous t.** underground; **t. cuite** (baked) clay, earthenware; **t. battue** *(de court de tennis)* clay ▪ **terre-à-terre** *adj inv* down-to-earth ▪ **terre-plein** (*pl* **terres-pleins**) *nm* (earth) platform; *(de route) Br* central reservation, *Am* median strip
**terrer** [tere] **se terrer** *vpr (fugitif, animal)* to go to earth
**terrestre** [terɛstr] *adj (vie, joies)* earthly; **transport t.** land transportation
**terreur** [tɛrœr] *nf* terror ▪ **terrible** *adj* awful, terrible
**terrien, -enne** [terjɛ̃, -ɛn] **1** *adj* landowning; **propriétaire t.** landowner **2** *nmf (habitant de la terre)* earthling
**terrier** [terje] *nm (de lapin)* burrow; *(chien)* terrier
**terrifier** [terifje] *vt* to terrify ▪ **terrifiant, -e** *adj* terrifying
**terrine** [terin] *nf (récipient)* terrine; *(pâté)* pâté
**territoire** [teritwar] *nm* territory ▪ **territorial, -e, -aux, -ales** *adj* territorial
**terroir** [terwar] *nm (sol)* soil; *(région)* region
**terroriser** [terɔrize] *vt* to terrorize ▪ **terrorisme** *nm* terrorism ▪ **terroriste** *adj & nmf* terrorist
**tertiaire** [tersjɛr] *adj* tertiary
**tes** [te] *voir* **ton**[1]
**test** [tɛst] *nm* test ▪ **tester** *vt (élève, produit)* to test
**testament** [tɛstamɑ̃] *nm (document)* will; *Rel* **Ancien/Nouveau T.** Old/New Testament
**testicule** [tɛstikyl] *nm Anat* testicle
**tête** [tɛt] *nf* head; *(visage)* face; *(cerveau)* brain; *(de lit, de clou, de cortège)* head; *(de page, de liste)* top, head; *(au football)* header; **à la t. de** *(entreprise, parti)* at the head of; *(classe)* at the top of; **de la t. aux pieds** from head *or* top to toe; **t. nue** bare-headed; **en t.** *(d'une course)* in the lead; *Fig* **perdre la t.** to lose one's head ▪ **tête-à-tête** *nm inv* tête-à-tête; **en t.** in private
**téter** [tete] *vt (lait, biberon)* to suck; **donner à t. à qn** to feed sb ▪ **tétée** *nf (de bébé)* feed ▪ **tétine** *nf (de biberon) Br* teat, *Am* nipple; *(sucette) Br* dummy, *Am* pacifier
**têtu, -e** [tety] *adj* stubborn, obstinate
**texte** [tɛkst] *nm* text; *(de théâtre)* lines ▪ **textuellement** *adv* word for word
**textile** [tɛkstil] *adj & nm* textile
**texture** [tɛkstyr] *nf* texture
**TGV** [teʒeve] (*abrév* **train à grande vitesse**) *nm* high-speed train
**Thaïlande** [tailɑ̃d] *nf* **la T.** Thailand ▪ **thaïlandais, -e 1** *adj* Thai **2** *nmf* **T., Thaïlandaise** Thai
**thé** [te] *nm (boisson, réunion)* tea ▪ **théière** *nf* teapot

**théâtre** [teɑtr] *nm (art, lieu)* theatre; *(œuvres)* drama; **faire du t.** to act ▪ **théâtral, -e, -aux, -ales** *adj* theatrical

**thème** [tɛm] *nm* theme

**théologie** [teɔlɔʒi] *nf* theology

**théorie** [teɔri] *nf* theory; **en t.** in theory

**théorique** [teɔrik] *adj* theoretical

**thérapeutique** [terapøtik] **1** *adj* therapeutic **2** *nf (traitement)* therapy ▪ **thérapie** *nf* therapy

**thermal, -e, -aux, -ales** [tɛrmal, -o] *adj* **station thermale** spa

**thermique** [tɛrmik] *adj (énergie, unité)* thermal

**thermomètre** [tɛrmɔmɛtr] *nm* thermometer

**Thermos®** [tɛrmɔs] *nm ou f* Thermos® (*Br* flask *or Am* bottle)

**thermostat** [tɛrmɔsta] *nm* thermostat

**thèse** [tɛz] *nf (proposition, ouvrage)* thesis

**thon** [tɔ̃] *nm* tuna (fish)

**thym** [tɛ̃] *nm (plante, aromate)* thyme

**Tibet** [tibɛ] *nm* **le T.** Tibet

**tic** [tik] *nm (contraction)* twitch, tic; *Fig (manie)* mannerism

**ticket** [tikɛ] *nm* ticket

**tiède** [tjɛd] *adj* lukewarm, tepid; *(vent, climat)* mild ▪ **tiédir** *vti (refroidir)* to cool down; *(réchauffer)* to warm up

**tien, tienne** [tjɛ̃, tjɛn] **1** *pron possessif* **le t., la tienne, les tien(ne)s** yours; **les deux tiens** your two **2** *nmpl* **les tiens** *(ta famille)* your family

**tiens, tient** [tjɛ̃] *voir* **tenir**

**tiercé** [tjɛrse] *nm (pari)* place betting *(on the horses)*; **jouer/gagner au t.** to bet/win on the horses

**tiers, tierce** [tjɛr, tjɛrs] **1** *adj* third **2** *nm (fraction)* third; *(personne)* third party ▪ **Tiers-Monde** *nm* **le T.** the Third World

**tige** [tiʒ] *nf (de plante)* stem, stalk; *(barre)* rod

**tigre** [tigr] *nm* tiger ▪ **tigresse** *nf* tigress

**tilleul** [tijœl] *nm (arbre)* lime tree; *(infusion)* lime blossom tea

**timbre** [tɛ̃br] *nm* (**a**) *(vignette)* stamp; *(pour traitement médicale)* patch (**b**) *(sonnette)* bell (**c**) *(d'instrument, de voix)* tone (quality) ▪ **timbrer** *vt (lettre)* to put a stamp on; *(document)* to stamp

**timide** [timid] *adj (gêné)* shy; *(protestations)* timid ▪ **timidité** *nf* shyness

**tinter** [tɛ̃te] *vi (cloche)* to tinkle; *(clefs, monnaie)* to jingle; *(verres)* to chink

**tique** [tik] *nf* tick

**tir** [tir] *nm (sport)* shooting; *(action)* firing, shooting; *(au football)* shot; **t. (forain)** shooting *or* rifle range; **t. à l'arc** archery

**tirade** [tirad] *nf (au théâtre) & Fig Br* monologue, *Am* monolog

**tirage** [tiraʒ] *nm* (**a**) *(de journal)* circulation; *(de livre)* print run; *Typ & Phot (impression)* printing (**b**) *(de loterie)* draw; **t. au sort** drawing lots

**tirailler** [tirɑje] **1** *vt* to pull at; *Fig* **tiraillé entre** *(possibilités)* torn between **2** *vi* **j'ai la peau qui tiraille** my skin feels tight

**tire** [tir] *nf* **vol à la t.** pickpocketing

**tirelire** [tirlir] *nf Br* moneybox, *Am* coin bank

**tirer** [tire] **1** *vt* to pull; *(langue)* to stick out; *(trait, rideaux, conclusion)* to draw; *(balle)* to fire; *(gibier)* to shoot; *(journal, épreuves de livre, photo)* to print; **t. qch de qch** to pull sth out of sth; *(nom, origine)* to derive sth from sth; *(produit)* to extract sth from sth; **t. qn de qch** *(danger, lit)* to get sb out of sth

**2** *vi* to pull (**sur** on/at); *(faire feu)* to shoot, to fire (**sur** at); *(cheminée)* to draw; **t. au sort** to draw lots; **t. à sa fin** to draw to a close

**3 se tirer** *vpr* **se t. de qch** *(travail, problème)* to cope with sth; *(danger, situation)* to get out of sth ▪ **tiré, -e** *adj (traits, visage)* drawn ▪ **tire-bouchon** (*pl* **tire-bouchons**) *nm* corkscrew

**tireur** [tirœr] *nm* gunman; **t. d'élite** marksman

**tiroir** [tirwar] *nm (de commode)* drawer

**tisane** [tizan] *nf* herbal tea

**tisser** [tise] *vt* to weave ▪ **tissage** *nm* *(action)* weaving

**tissu** [tisy] *nm* material, cloth; *Biol* tissue

**titre** [titr] *nm (nom, qualité)* title; *Fin* security; *(diplôme)* qualification; **(gros) t.** *(de journal)* headline; **à t. d'exemple** as an example; **à t. exceptionnel** exceptionally; **à t. indicatif** for general information; **à juste t.** rightly; **t. de transport** ticket

**titrer** [titre] *vt (film)* to title; *(journal)* to run as a headline ▪ **titré, -e** *adj (personne)* titled

**tituber** [titybe] *vi* to stagger

**titulaire** [titylɛr] **1** *adj (enseignant)* tenured; **être t. de** *(permis)* to be the holder of; *(poste)* to hold **2** *nmf (de permis, de poste)* holder (**de** of) ▪ **titulariser** *vt (fonctionnaire)* to give tenure to

**toast** [tost] *nm (pain grillé)* piece *or* slice of toast; *(allocution)* toast; **porter un t. à** to drink (a toast) to

**toboggan** [tɔbɔgɑ̃] *nm (d'enfant)* slide; *Can (traîneau)* toboggan; *(voie de circulation) Br* flyover, *Am* overpass

**toc** [tɔk] *nm* **du t.** *(camelote)* trash; **bijou en t.** imitation jewel

**toi** [twa] *pron personnel* (**a**) *(après une préposition)* you; **avec t.** with you (**b**) *(sujet)* you; **t., tu peux** you may; **c'est t. qui...** it's you who... (**c**) *(réfléchi)* **assieds-t.** sit (yourself) down; **dépêche-t.** hurry up ▪ **toi-même** *pron* yourself

**toile** [twal] *nf* (**a**) *(étoffe)* cloth; *(à voile, sac)* canvas; **une t.** a piece of cloth *or* canvas; *Théât & Fig* **t. de fond** backdrop; **t. cirée** oil cloth (**b**) *(tableau)* painting, canvas (**c**) **t. d'araignée** (spider's) web, cobweb

**toilette** [twalɛt] *nf (action)* wash(ing); *(vêtements)* clothes, outfit; **faire sa t.** to wash (and dress); **les toilettes** *(W-C) Br* the toilet(s), *Am* the men's/ladies' room

**toit** [twa] *nm* roof ▪ **toiture** *nf* roof(ing)

**tôle** [tol] *nf* sheet metal; **t. ondulée** corrugated iron

**tolérer** [tɔlere] *vt (permettre)* to tolerate ▪ **tolérable** *adj* tolerable ▪ **tolérance** *nf* tolerance ▪ **tolérant, -e** *adj* tolerant (**à l'égard de** of)

**tomate** [tɔmat] *nf* tomato

**tombe** [tɔ̃b] *nf* grave; *(avec monument)* tomb ▪ **tombale** *adj f* **pierre t.** gravestone, tombstone ▪ **tombeau, -x** *nm* tomb

**tomber** [tɔ̃be] (*aux* **être**) *vi* to fall; *(température)* to drop, to fall; *(vent)* to drop (off); **t. malade** to fall ill; **t. par terre** to fall (down); **faire t.** *(personne)* to knock over; *(gouvernement, prix)* to bring down; **laisser t.** *(objet)* to drop; *Fig* **laisser t. qn** to let sb down; **t. un lundi** to fall on a Monday; **t. sur qch** *(trouver)* to come across sth ▪ **tombée** *nf* **la t. de la nuit** nightfall

**tome** [tɔm] *nm (livre)* volume

**ton[1], ta, tes** [tɔ̃, ta, te]

> **ta** becomes **ton** [tɔ̃n] before a vowel or mute h.

*adj possessif* your; **t. père** your father; **ta mère** your mother; **t. ami(e)** your friend

**ton[2]** [tɔ̃] *nm (de voix)* tone; *(de couleur)* shade, tone; *Mus (gamme)* key; *(hauteur de son)* pitch ▪ **tonalité** *nf (timbre, impression)* tone; *(de téléphone) Br* dialling tone, *Am* dial tone

**tondre** [tɔ̃dr] *vt (mouton)* to shear; *(gazon)* to mow ▪ **tondeuse** *nf* shears; *(à cheveux)* clippers; **t. (à gazon)** (lawn)mower

**tonifier** [tɔnifje] *vt (muscles, peau)* to tone up; *(personne)* to invigorate

**tonique** [tɔnik] **1** *adj (froid, effet)* tonic, invigorating **2** *nm (médicament)* tonic; *(cosmétique)* tonic lotion

**tonnage** [tɔnaʒ] *nm (de navire)* tonnage

**tonne** [tɔn] *nf (poids)* metric ton, tonne

**tonneau, -x** [tɔno] *nm* (**a**) *(récipient)* barrel, cask (**b**) *(acrobatie)* roll; **faire un t.** to roll over

**tonner** [tɔne] **1** *vi (canons)* to thunder; *Fig (crier)* to thunder, to rage (**contre**

against) **2** *v impersonnel* **il tonne** it's thundering ▪ **tonnerre** *nm* thunder

**tonus** [tɔnys] *nm (énergie)* energy, vitality

**top** [tɔp] *nm (signal sonore)* beep

**topographie** [tɔpɔgrafi] *nf* topography

**toque** [tɔk] *nf (de fourrure)* fur hat; *(de jockey)* cap; *(de cuisinier)* hat

**torche** [tɔrʃ] *nf (flamme)* torch; **t. électrique** *Br* torch, *Am* flashlight

**torchon** [tɔrʃɔ̃] *nm (à vaisselle)* dish towel, *Br* tea towel

**tordre** [tɔrdr] **1** *vt* to twist; *(linge, cou)* to wring; *(barre)* to bend **2 se tordre** *vpr* to twist; *(barre)* to bend; **se t. de douleur** to be doubled up with pain; **se t. (de rire)** to split one's sides (laughing); **se t. la cheville** to twist *or* sprain one's ankle ▪ **tordu, -e** *adj* twisted; *(esprit)* warped

**tornade** [tɔrnad] *nf* tornado

**torpille** [tɔrpij] *nf* torpedo ▪ **torpiller** *vt (navire, projet)* to torpedo

**torrent** [tɔrɑ̃] *nm* torrent; *Fig* **un t. de larmes** a flood of tears; **il pleut à torrents** it's pouring (down) ▪ **torrentiel, -elle** *adj (pluie)* torrential

**torride** [tɔrid] *adj (chaleur)* torrid

**torse** [tɔrs] *nm Anat* chest; **t. nu** stripped to the waist

**tort** [tɔr] *nm (dommage)* wrong; *(défaut)* fault; **avoir t.** to be wrong (**de faire** to do, in doing); **être dans son t.** *ou* **en t.** to be in the wrong; **faire du t. à qn** to harm sb; **à t.** wrongly; **à t. ou à raison** rightly or wrongly

**torticolis** [tɔrtikɔli] *nm* **avoir le t.** to have a stiff neck

**tortiller** [tɔrtije] **1** *vt* to twist; *(moustache)* to twirl **2 se tortiller** *vpr (ver, personne)* to wriggle

**tortionnaire** [tɔrsjɔnɛr] *nm* torturer

**tortue** [tɔrty] *nf Br* tortoise, *Am* turtle; *(de mer)* turtle

**torture** [tɔrtyr] *nf* torture ▪ **torturer** *vt* to torture

**tôt** [to] *adv* early; **au plus t.** at the earliest; **le plus t. possible** as soon as possible; **t. ou tard** sooner or later; **je n'étais pas plus t. sorti que...** no sooner had I gone out than...

**total, -e, -aux, -ales** [tɔtal, -o] *adj & nm* total; **au t.** all in all, in total; *(somme toute)* all in all ▪ **totaliser** *vt* to total ▪ **totalité** *nf* entirety; **la t. de** all of; **en t.** *(détruit)* entirely; *(payé)* fully

**totalitaire** [tɔtalitɛr] *adj (État, régime)* totalitarian

**touche** [tuʃ] *nf (de clavier)* key; *(de téléphone)* (push-)button; *(au football & au rugby)* throw-in; **téléphone à touches** push-button phone; **une t. de** *(un peu de)* a touch *or* hint of

**toucher** [tuʃe] **1** *nm (sens)* touch; **au t.** to the touch **2** *vt* to touch; *(paie)* to draw; *(chèque)* to cash; *(émouvoir)* to touch, to move; *(concerner)* to affect **3** *vi* **t. à** to touch; *(sujet)* to touch on; *(but, fin)* to approach **4 se toucher** *vpr (lignes, mains)* to touch ▪ **touchant, -e** *adj (émouvant)* moving, touching

**touffe** [tuf] *nf (de cheveux, d'herbe)* tuft ▪ **touffu, -e** *adj (barbe, haie)* thick, bushy

**toujours** [tuʒur] *adv (exprime la continuité, la répétition)* always; *(encore)* still; **pour t.** for ever

**tour**[1] [tur] *nf (bâtiment) & Ordinat* tower; *(immeuble)* tower block, high-rise; *Échecs* castle, rook

**tour**[2] [tur] *nm* (**a**) *(mouvement, ordre, tournure)* turn; *(de magie)* trick; *(excursion)* trip, outing; *(à pied)* stroll, walk; *(en voiture)* drive; **t. (de piste)** *(de course)* lap; **de dix mètres de t.** ten metres round; **faire le t. de** to go round; **faire le t. du monde** to go round the world; **faire un t.** *(à pied)* to go for a stroll *or* walk; *(en voiture)* to go for a drive; **à t. de rôle** in turn; **t. à t.** in turn, by turns (**b**) *Tech* lathe; *(de potier)* wheel

**tourbillon** [turbijɔ̃] *nm (de vent)* whirlwind; *(d'eau)* whirlpool; *(de sable)* swirl ▪ **tourbillonner** *vi* to whirl

**tourisme** [turism] *nm* tourism; **faire du t.** to do some touring ■ **touriste** *nmf* tourist ■ **touristique** *adj* **guide/menu t.** tourist guide/menu; **route t., circuit t.** scenic route

**tourmenter** [turmɑ̃te] **1** *vt* to torment **2 se tourmenter** *vpr* to worry

**tournage** [turnaʒ] *nm (de film)* shooting, filming

**tournant** [turnɑ̃] *nm (de route)* bend; *Fig (moment)* turning point (**de** in)

**tourne-disque** [turnədisk] (*pl* **tourne-disques**) *nm* record player

**tournée** [turne] *nf (de facteur, de boissons)* round; *(spectacle)* tour; **faire sa t.** to do one's rounds; **faire la t. de** *(magasins, musées)* to go to, *Br* to go round

**tourner** [turne] **1** *vt* to turn; *(film)* to shoot, to make; *(difficulté)* to get round; **t. qn/qch en ridicule** to ridicule sb/sth

**2** *vi* to turn; *(tête, toupie)* to spin; *(Terre)* to revolve, to turn; *(moteur, usine)* to run; *(lait)* to go off; **t. autour de** *(objet)* to go round; *(maison, personne)* to hang around; *(question)* to centre on; **t. bien/mal** *(évoluer)* to turn out well/badly; **t. au froid** *(temps)* to turn cold

**3 se tourner** *vpr* to turn (**vers** to, towards)

**tournesol** [turnəsɔl] *nm* sunflower

**tournevis** [turnəvis] *nm* screwdriver

**tourniquet** [turnikɛ] *nm (barrière)* turnstile; *(pour arroser)* sprinkler

**tournoi** [turnwa] *nm (de tennis) & Hist* tournament

**tournoyer** [turnwaje] *vi* to swirl (round)

**tournure** [turnyr] *nf (expression)* turn of phrase; **t. d'esprit** way of thinking; **t. des événements** turn of events

**Toussaint** [tusɛ̃] *nf* **la T.** All Saints' Day

**tousser** [tuse] *vi* to cough

**TOUT, TOUTE, TOUS, TOUTES** [tu, tut, tu, tut] **1** *adj* all; **tous les livres** all the books; **t. l'argent/le temps/le village** all the money/time/village; **toute la nuit** all night, the whole (of the) night; **tous (les) deux** both; **tous (les) trois** all three

**2** *adj indéfini (chaque)* every, each; *(n'importe quel)* any; **tous les ans/jours** every *or* each year/day; **tous les deux mois** every two months, every second month; **tous les cinq mètres** every five metres; **t. homme** [tutɔm] every *ou* any man

**3** *pron pl* **tous** [tus] all; **ils sont tous là, tous sont là** they're all there

**4** *pron m sing* **tout** everything; **dépenser t.** to spend everything, to spend it all; **t. ce qui est là** everything that's here; **t. ce que je sais** everything that *or* all that I know; **en t.** *(au total)* in all

**5** *adv (tout à fait)* quite; *(très)* very; **t. simplement** quite simply; **t. petit** very small; **t. neuf** brand new; **t. seul** all alone; **t. droit** straight ahead; **t. autour** all around, right round; **t. au début** right at the beginning; **le t. premier** the very first; **t. au plus/moins** at the very most/least; **t. en chantant** while singing; **t. rusé qu'il est** *ou* **soit** however sly he may be; **t. à coup** suddenly, all of a sudden; **t. à fait** completely, quite; **t. de suite** at once

**6** *nm* **le t.** everything, the lot; **un t.** a whole; **le t. est que…** *(l'important)* the main thing is that…; **pas du t.** not at all; **rien du t.** nothing at all; **du t. au t.** *(changer)* entirely, completely

---

**toutefois** [tutfwa] *adv* nevertheless, however ■ **tout-puissant, toute-puissante** (*mpl* **tout-puissants,** *fpl* **toutes-puissantes**) *adj* all-powerful ■ **tout-terrain 1** (*pl* **tout-terrains**) *adj* **véhicule t.** off-road *or* all terrain vehicle; **vélo t.** mountain bike **2** *nm* **faire du t.** to do off-road racing

**toux** [tu] *nf* cough

**toxicomane** [tɔksikɔman] *nmf* drug addict ■ **toxicomanie** *nf* drug addiction

**toxique** [tɔksik] *adj* poisonous, toxic

**trac** [trak] *nm* **le t.** *(peur)* the jitters; *(de candidat)* exam nerves; *(d'acteur)* stage fright; **avoir le t.** to be nervous

**trace** [tras] *nf (quantité, tache, vestige)* trace; *(marque)* mark; *(de fugitif)* trail; **traces** *(de bête, de pneus)* tracks; **traces de pas** footprints; **disparaître sans laisser de traces** to disappear without trace

**tracer** [trase] *vt (dessiner)* to draw; *(écrire)* to trace; **t. une route** to mark out a route; *(frayer)* to open up a route ▪ **tracé** *nm (plan)* layout; *(ligne)* line

**tract** [trakt] *nm* leaflet

**tractations** [traktɑsjɔ̃] *nfpl* dealings

**tracter** [trakte] *vt* to tow

**tracteur** [traktœr] *nm* tractor

**tradition** [tradisjɔ̃] *nf* tradition ▪ **traditionnel, -elle** *adj* traditional

**traduire*** [tradɥir] *vt* to translate (**de** from; **en** into) ▪ **traducteur, -trice** *nmf* translator ▪ **traduction** *nf* translation

**trafic** [trafik] *nm (automobile, ferroviaire)* traffic; *(de marchandises)* traffic, trade ▪ **trafiquant, -e** *nmf* trafficker, dealer

**tragédie** [traʒedi] *nf (pièce de théâtre, événement)* tragedy ▪ **tragique** *adj* tragic; **prendre qch au t.** *(remarque)* to take sth too much to heart

**trahir** [trair] **1** *vt* to betray; *(secret)* to give away, to betray; *(sujet: forces)* to fail **2 se trahir** *vpr* to give oneself away ▪ **trahison** *nf* betrayal; *(crime)* treason

**train** [trɛ̃] *nm* (**a**) *(de voyageurs, de marchandises)* train; **t. à grande vitesse** high-speed train; **t. corail** express train; **t. couchettes** sleeper (**b**) **en t.** *(en forme)* on form; **être en t. de faire qch** to be (busy) doing sth (**c**) *(allure)* pace; **t. de vie** life style (**d**) *(de pneus)* set; *(de péniches, de véhicules)* string (**e**) **t. d'atterrissage** *(d'avion)* undercarriage

**traînard, -e** [trɛnar, -ard] *nmf Br* slowcoach, *Am* slowpoke

**traîne** [trɛn] *nf (de robe)* train

**traîneau, -x** [trɛno] *nm* sleigh, *Br* sledge, *Am* sled

**traînée** [trɛne] *nf (de peinture, dans le ciel)* streak

**traîner** [trɛne] **1** *vt* to drag; *(wagon)* to pull

**2** *vi (jouets, papiers)* to lie around; *(s'attarder)* to lag behind, to dawdle; *(errer)* to hang around; *(subsister)* to linger on; **t. par terre** *(robe)* to trail (on the ground); **t. en longueur** to drag on

**3 se traîner** *vpr (avancer)* to drag oneself (along); *(par terre)* to crawl; *(durer)* to drag on ▪ **traînant, -e** *adj (voix)* drawling

**traire*** [trɛr] *vt (vache)* to milk

**trait** [trɛ] *nm* line; *(en dessinant)* stroke; *(caractéristique)* feature, trait; **traits** *(du visage)* features; **d'un t.** *(boire)* in one gulp, in one go; **avoir t. à qch** to relate to sth

**traite** [trɛt] *nf (de vache)* milking; *(lettre de change)* bill, draft; **d'une (seule) t.** *(sans interruption)* in one go; **t. des Noirs** slave trade

**traité** [trete] *nm (accord)* treaty; *(ouvrage)* treatise (**sur** on); **t. de paix** peace treaty

**traiter** [trete] **1** *vt (se comporter envers, soigner)* to treat; *(problème, sujet)* to deal with; *(marché)* to negotiate; *(matériau, produit)* to treat, to process; **t. qn de tous le noms** to call sb all the names under the sun

**2** *vi* to negotiate, to deal (**avec** with); **t. de** *(sujet)* to deal with ▪ **traitement** [trɛtmɑ̃] *nm (de personne, de maladie)* treatment; *(de matériau)* processing; *(gains)* salary; **t. de données/de texte** data/word processing; **machine à t. de texte** word processor

**traiteur** [trɛtœr] *nm (fournisseur)* caterer; **chez le t.** at the delicatessen

**traître** [trɛtr] **1** *nm* traitor; **en t.** treacherously **2** *adj (dangereux)* treacherous; **être t. à une cause** to be a traitor to a cause ▪ **traîtrise** *nf* treachery

**trajectoire** [traʒɛktwar] *nf* path, trajectory

**trajet** [traʒɛ] *nm* journey; *(distance)* distance; *(itinéraire)* route

**tramer** [trame] **se tramer** *vpr* **il se trame**

**quelque chose** something's afoot

**trampoline** [trɑ̃pɔlin] *nm* trampoline

**tramway** [tramwɛ] *nm Br* tram, *Am* streetcar

**tranche** [trɑ̃ʃ] *nf (morceau)* slice; *(bord)* edge; *(partie)* portion; *(de salaire, d'impôts)* bracket; **t. d'âge** age bracket

**tranchée** [trɑ̃ʃe] *nf* trench

**trancher** [trɑ̃ʃe] **1** *vt* to cut; *(difficulté, question)* to settle **2** *vi (décider)* to decide; *(contraster)* to contrast (**sur** with) ▪ **tranchant, -e 1** *adj (couteau)* sharp; *(ton)* curt **2** *nm* (cutting) edge; *Fig* **à double t.** double-edged ▪ **tranché, -e** *adj (couleurs)* distinct; *(opinion)* clear-cut

**tranquille** [trɑ̃kil] *adj* quiet; *(mer)* calm, still; *(esprit)* easy; **avoir la conscience t.** to have a clear conscience; **soyez t.** don't worry; **laisser qn/qch t.** to leave sb/sth alone

**tranquilliser** [trɑ̃kilize] *vt* to reassure ▪ **tranquillisant** *nm* tranquillizer

**tranquillité** [trɑ̃kilite] *nf* (peace and) quiet; *(d'esprit)* peace of mind

**transaction** [trɑ̃zaksjɔ̃] *nf (opération)* transaction; *Jur* compromise

**transatlantique** [trɑ̃zatlɑ̃tik] **1** *adj* transatlantic **2** *nm (paquebot)* transatlantic liner; *(chaise)* deckchair ▪ **transat** *nm (chaise)* deckchair

**transcrire*** [trɑ̃skrir] *vt* to transcribe ▪ **transcription** *nf* transcription; *(document)* transcript

**transe** [trɑ̃s] *nf* **en t.** *(mystique)* in a trance; *(excité)* very excited; **entrer en t.** to go into a trance

**transférer** [trɑ̃sfere] *vt* to transfer (**à** to) ▪ **transfert** *nm* transfer

**transformer** [trɑ̃sfɔrme] **1** *vt* to transform; *(maison, au rugby)* to convert; *(matière première)* to process; **t. qch en qch** to turn sth into sth **2 se transformer** *vpr* to change, to be transformed (**en** into) ▪ **transformateur** *nm Él* transformer ▪ **transformation** *nf* change, transformation; *(de maison)* alteration

**transfuge** [trɑ̃sfyʒ] *nmf* defector

**transfusion** [trɑ̃sfyzjɔ̃] *nf* **t. (sanguine)** (blood) transfusion

**transgresser** [trɑ̃sgrese] *vt (ordres)* to disobey; *(loi)* to infringe

**transi, -e** [trɑ̃zi] *adj (personne)* numb with cold

**transiger** [trɑ̃ziʒe] *vi* to compromise

**transistor** [trɑ̃zistɔr] *nm* transistor

**transit** [trɑ̃zit] *nm* transit; **en t.** in transit

**transition** [trɑ̃zisjɔ̃] *nf* transition ▪ **transitoire** *adj (qui passe)* transient; *(provisoire)* transitional

**transmettre*** [trɑ̃smɛtr] **1** *vt (message, héritage)* to pass on (**à** to); *Radio & TV (informations)* to transmit; *(émission)* to broadcast **2 se transmettre** *vpr (maladie, tradition)* to be passed on ▪ **transmetteur** *nm (appareil)* transmitter ▪ **transmission** *nf* transmission

**transparaître*** [trɑ̃sparɛtr] *vi* to show (through)

**transparent, -e** [trɑ̃sparɑ̃, -ɑ̃t] *adj* clear, transparent ▪ **transparence** *nf* transparency; **voir qch par t.** to see sth showing through

**transpercer** [trɑ̃spɛrse] *vt* to pierce

**transpirer** [trɑ̃spire] *vi (suer)* to sweat, to perspire ▪ **transpiration** *nf* perspiration

**transplanter** [trɑ̃splɑ̃te] *vt (organe, plante)* to transplant

**transport** [trɑ̃spɔr] *nm (action)* transport, transportation (**de** of); **transports** *(moyens)* transport; **transports en commun** public transport; **moyen de t.** means of transport

**transporter** [trɑ̃spɔrte] *vt (passagers, troupes, marchandises)* to transport, to carry ▪ **transporteur** *nm* **t. (routier)** *Br* haulier, *Am* trucker

**transposer** [trɑ̃spoze] *vt* to transpose ▪ **transposition** *nf* transposition

**trapèze** [trapɛz] *nm (de cirque)* trapeze

**trappe** [trap] *nf (de plancher)* trap door

**trappeur** [trapœr] *nm* trapper

**trapu, -e** [trapy] *adj (personne)* stocky, thickset

**traquer** [trake] *vt* to hunt (down)

**traumatiser** [tromatize] *vt* to traumatize ▪ **traumatisant, -e** *adj* traumatic ▪ **traumatisme** *nm (choc)* trauma

**travail, -aux** [travaj, -o] *nm (activité, lieu)* work; *(à effectuer)* job, task; *(emploi)* job; *(façonnage)* working (**de** of); *(ouvrage, étude)* work, publication; *Écon & Méd* labour; **travaux** work; *(dans la rue) Br* roadworks, *Am* roadwork; *(aménagement)* alterations; *Scol & Univ* **travaux pratiques** practical work; *Scol & Univ* **travaux dirigés** tutorial; *Scol* **travaux manuels** handicrafts; **travaux ménagers** housework

**travailler** [travaje] **1** *vi (personne)* to work (**à qch** on sth); *(bois)* to warp **2** *vt (discipline, rôle, style)* to work on; *(façonner)* to work ▪ **travailleur, -euse 1** *adj* hard-working **2** *nmf* worker

**travailliste** [travajist] *Pol* **1** *adj* Labour **2** *nmf* member of the Labour party

**travers** [travɛr] **1** *prép & adv* **à t.** through; **en t. (de)** across **2** *adv* **de t.** *(chapeau, nez)* crooked; **j'ai avalé de t.** it went down the wrong way

**traverser** [travɛrse] *vt* to cross; *(foule, période, mur)* to go through ▪ **traversée** *nf (voyage)* crossing

**travesti** [travɛsti] *nm (acteur)* female impersonator; *(homosexuel)* transvestite

**travestir** [travɛstir] *vt* to disguise

**trébucher** [trebyʃe] *vi* to stumble (**sur** over); **faire t. qn** to trip sb (up)

**trèfle** [trɛfl] *nm (plante)* clover; *Cartes (couleur)* clubs

**treillis** [trɛji] *nm* (**a**) *(treillage)* lattice(-work); *(en métal)* wire mesh (**b**) *(tenue militaire)* combat uniform

**treize** [trɛz] *adj & nm inv* thirteen ▪ **treizième** *adj & nmf* thirteenth

**tréma** [trema] *nm* di(a)eresis

**trembler** [trɑ̃ble] *vi* to shake, to tremble; *(de froid, peur)* to tremble (**de** with); *(flamme, lumière)* to flicker; *(voix)* to tremble, to quaver; *(avoir peur)* to be afraid (**que** + *subjunctive* that); **t. pour qn** to fear for sb ▪ **tremblement** [-əmɑ̃] *nm (action, frisson)* shaking, trembling; **t. de terre** earthquake ▪ **trembloter** *vi* to quiver

**tremper** [trɑ̃pe] **1** *vt* to soak, to drench; *(plonger)* to dip (**dans** in); *(acier)* to temper **2** *vi* to soak; **faire t. qch** to soak sth; *Péj* **t. dans** *(participer)* to be mixed up in

**tremplin** [trɑ̃plɛ̃] *nm* springboard

**trente** [trɑ̃t] *adj & nm inv* thirty; **un t.-trois tours** *(disque)* an LP; **se mettre sur son t. et un** to get all dressed up ▪ **trentaine** *nf* **une t. (de)** *(nombre)* (about) thirty; **avoir la t.** *(âge)* to be about thirty ▪ **trentième** *adj & nmf* thirtieth

**très** [trɛ] ([trɛz] *before vowel or mute h*) *adv* very; **t. aimé/critiqué** *(with past participle)* much *or* greatly liked/criticized

**trésor** [trezɔr] *nm* treasure; **le T. (public)** *(service)* public revenue (department); *(finances)* public funds; **des trésors de patience** boundless patience ▪ **trésorerie** [-rri] *nf (bureaux d'un club)* accounts department; *(gestion)* accounting; *(capitaux)* funds ▪ **trésorier, -ère** *nmf* treasurer

**tressaillir*** [tresajir] *vi (frémir)* to shake, to quiver; *(de joie, de peur)* to tremble (**de** with); *(sursauter)* to jump, to start

**tresse** [trɛs] *nf (cordon)* braid; *(cheveux) Br* plait, *Am* braid ▪ **tresser** [trese] *vt* to braid; *Br (cheveux)* to plait, *Am* to braid

**trêve** [trɛv] *nf (de combat)* truce

**tri** [tri] *nm* sorting (out); **faire le t. de** to sort (out); **(centre de) t.** *(des postes)* sorting office ▪ **triage** *nm* sorting (out)

**triangle** [trijɑ̃gl] *nm* triangle ▪ **triangulaire** *adj* triangular

**tribord** [tribɔr] *nm (de bateau, d'avion)* starboard

**tribu** [triby] *nf* tribe ▪ **tribal, -e, -aux, -ales** *adj* tribal

**tribunal, -aux** [tribynal, -o] *nm Jur* court; *(militaire)* tribunal

**tribune** [tribyn] *nf (de salle publique)* gallery; *(de stade)* (grand)stand; *(d'orateur)* rostrum

**tribut** [triby] *nm* tribute (**à** to)

**tricher** [triʃe] *vi* to cheat ▪ **tricherie** *nf* cheating, trickery ▪ **tricheur, -euse** *nmf* cheat, *Am* cheater

**tricolore** [trikɔlɔr] *adj (cocarde)* red, white and blue; **le drapeau/l'équipe t.** the French flag/team

**tricot** [triko] *nm (activité, ouvrage)* knitting; *(chandail)* sweater, *Br* jumper; *(ouvrage)* piece of knitting; **en t.** knitted; **t. de corps** *Br* vest, *Am* undershirt ▪ **tricoter** *vti* to knit

**trier** [trije] *vt (lettres)* to sort; *(vêtements)* to sort through

**trilingue** [trilɛ̃g] *adj* trilingual

**trimestre** [trimɛstr] *nm* quarter; *Scol* term; *Scol* **premier/second/troisième t.** *Br* autumn *or Am* fall/winter/summer term ▪ **trimestriel, -elle** *adj (revue)* quarterly; **bulletin t.** end-of-term *Br* report *or Am* report card

**Trinité** [trinite] *nf* **la T.** *(fête)* Trinity; *(dogme)* the Trinity

**trinquer** [trɛ̃ke] *vi* to chink glasses; **t. à la santé de qn** to drink to sb's health

**trio** [trijo] *nm (groupe) & Mus* trio

**triomphe** [trijɔ̃f] *nm* triumph (**sur** over) ▪ **triomphal, -e, -aux, -ales** *adj* triumphal ▪ **triomphant, -e** *adj* triumphant ▪ **triompher** *vi* to triumph (**de** over); *(jubiler)* to be jubilant

**triple** [tripl] **1** *adj* treble, triple; *Sport* **t. saut** triple jump **2** *nm* **le t.** three times as much (**de** as) ▪ **tripler** *vti* to treble, to triple ▪ **triplés, -es** *nmfpl* triplets

**triste** [trist] *adj* sad; *(sinistre)* dreary; *(lamentable)* unfortunate ▪ **tristesse** *nf* sadness; *(du temps)* dreariness

**trivial, -e, -aux, -ales** [trivjal, -o] *adj* coarse, vulgar

**troc** [trɔk] *nm* exchange; *(système économique)* barter

**trois** [trwɑ] *adj & nm inv* three; **les t. quarts (de)** three-quarters (of) ▪ **troisième 1** *adj & nmf* third; **le t. âge** *(vieillesse)* the retirement years; **personne du t. âge** senior citizen **2** *nf Scol* **la t.** *Br* ≃ fourth year, *Am* ≃ eighth grade; *Aut (vitesse)* third gear ▪ **troisièmement** *adv* thirdly

**trombe** [trɔ̃b] *nf* **trombe(s) d'eau** *(pluie)* rainstorm, downpour

**trombone** [trɔ̃bɔn] *nm (instrument)* trombone; *(agrafe)* paper clip

**trompe** [trɔ̃p] *nf (d'éléphant)* trunk; *(d'insecte)* proboscis; *(instrument de musique)* horn

**tromper** [trɔ̃pe] **1** *vt (abuser)* to fool (**sur** about); *(être infidèle à)* to be unfaithful to; *(échapper à)* to elude

**2 se tromper** *vpr* to be mistaken; **se t. de route** to take the wrong road; **se t. de jour** to get the day wrong ▪ **tromperie** [-pri] *nf* deceit, deception ▪ **trompeur, -euse** *adj (apparences)* deceptive, misleading; *(personne)* deceitful

**trompette** [trɔ̃pɛt] *nf* trumpet ▪ **trompettiste** *nmf* trumpet player

**tronc** [trɔ̃] *nm (d'arbre) & Anat* trunk; *(boîte)* collection box

**tronçon** [trɔ̃sɔ̃] *nm* section ▪ **tronçonner** *vt* to cut into sections

**trône** [tron] *nm* throne ▪ **trôner** *vi Fig (vase, personne)* to occupy the place of honour

**trop** [tro] *adv (avec adjectif, adverbe)* too; *(avec verbe)* too much; **t. dur/loin** too hard/far; **t. fatigué pour jouer** too tired to play; **lire t.** to read too much; **t. de sel** too much salt; **t. de gens** too many people; **du fromage en t.** too much cheese; **un verre en t.** one glass too many; **t. souvent** too often; **t. peu** not enough ▪ **trop-plein** (*pl* **trop-pleins**) *nm (excédent)* overflow; *(dispositif)* overflow pipe

**trophée** [trɔfe] *nm* trophy

**tropique** [trɔpik] *nm* tropic; **sous les tropiques** in the tropics ▪ **tropical, -e, -aux, -ales** *adj* tropical

**troquer** [trɔke] *vt* to exchange (**contre** for)

**trot** [tro] *nm* trot; **aller au t.** to trot ▪ **trotter** *vi (cheval)* to trot

**trottoir** [trɔtwar] *nm Br* pavement, *Am* sidewalk

**trou** [tru] *nm* hole; *(d'aiguille)* eye; *Fig* **t. de mémoire** memory lapse

**trouble** [trubl] **1** *adj (liquide)* cloudy; *(image)* blurred; *(affaire)* shady **2** *adv* **voir t.** to see things blurred **3** *nm (désarroi)* distress; *(désordre)* confusion; **troubles** *(de santé)* trouble; *(révolte)* disturbances, troubles

**troubler** [truble] **1** *vt* to disturb; *(vue)* to blur; *(liquide)* to make cloudy; *(esprit)* to unsettle; *(projet)* to upset; *(inquiéter)* to trouble **2 se troubler** *vpr (liquide)* to become cloudy; *(personne)* to become flustered ▪ **troublant, -e** *adj (détail)* disturbing, disquieting

**trouer** [true] *vt* to make a hole/holes in

**troupe** [trup] *nf (de soldats)* troop; *(de théâtre)* company, troupe

**troupeau, -x** [trupo] *nm (de vaches)* herd; *(de moutons)* flock

**trousse** [trus] *nf (étui)* case, kit; *(d'écolier)* pencil case; **t. à pharmacie** first-aid kit; **t. de toilette** toilet bag

**trousseau, -x** [truso] *nm (de mariée)* trousseau; **t. de clefs** bunch of keys

**trouvaille** [truvaj] *nf* (lucky) find

**trouver** [truve] **1** *vt* to find; **aller t. qn** to go and see sb; **je trouve que...** I think that...; **comment la trouvez-vous?** what do you think of her?

**2 se trouver** *vpr* to be; *(être situé)* to be situated; **se t. dans une situation difficile** to find oneself in a difficult situation; **se t. mal** *(s'évanouir)* to faint; **se t. petit** to consider oneself small

**3** *v impersonnel* **il se trouve que...** it happens that...

**trucage** [trykaʒ] *nm* = **truquage**

**truffe** [tryf] *nf (champignon, confiserie)* truffle; *(de chien)* nose

**truffer** [tryfe] *vt (remplir)* to stuff (**de** with)

**truite** [trɥit] *nf* trout

**truquer** [tryke] *vt (photo)* to fake; *(élections, match)* to rig ▪ **truquage** *nm (de cinéma)* (special) effect; *(action)* faking; *(d'élections)* rigging ▪ **truqué, -e** *adj (élections, match)* rigged; **photo truquée** fake photo

**trust** [trœst] *nm Com (cartel)* trust

**tsar** [dzar] *nm* tsar, czar

**tsigane** [tsigan] **1** *adj* gipsy **2** *nmf* **T.** gipsy

**tu**[1] [ty] *pron personnel* you *(familiar form of address)*

**tu**[2] [ty] *pp de* **taire**

**tuba** [tyba] *nm (instrument de musique)* tuba; *(de plongée)* snorkel

**tube** [tyb] *nm* tube; **t. à essai** test tube

**tuer** [tɥe] **1** *vt* to kill **2 se tuer** *vpr* to kill oneself; *(dans un accident)* to be killed ▪ **tuerie** *nf* slaughter ▪ **tueur, -euse** *nmf* killer

**tulipe** [tylip] *nf* tulip

**tumeur** [tymœr] *nf* tumour

**tunique** [tynik] *nf* tunic

**Tunisie** [tynizi] *nf* **la T.** Tunisia ▪ **tunisien, -enne 1** *adj* Tunisian **2** *nmf* **T., Tunisienne** Tunisian

**tunnel** [tynɛl] *nm* tunnel; **le t. sous la Manche** the Channel Tunnel

**turban** [tyrbɑ̃] *nm* turban

**turbulent, -e** [tyrbylɑ̃, -ɑ̃t] *adj (enfant)* boisterous

**Turquie** [tyrki] *nf* **la T.** Turkey ▪ **turc, turque 1** *adj* Turkish **2** *nmf* **T., Turque** Turk **3** *nm (langue)* Turkish

**turquoise** [tyrkwaz] *adj inv* turquoise

**tuteur, -trice** [tytœr, -tris] **1** *nmf (de mineur)* guardian **2** *nm (bâton)* stake, prop

**tutoyer** [tytwaje] *vt* **t. qn** to address sb using the familiar "tu" form ▪ **tutoiement** *nm* = use of the familiar "tu" instead of the more formal "vous"

**tutu** [tyty] *nm* tutu

**tuyau, -x** [tɥijo] *nm* pipe; **t. d'arrosage** hose(pipe); **t. d'échappement** *(de véhicule)* exhaust (pipe)

**TVA** [tevea] (*abrév* **taxe à la valeur ajoutée**) *nf* VAT

**type** [tip] **1** *nm (genre)* type; *Fig* **le t. même de** the very model of **2** *adj inv* typical; **lettre t.** standard letter ▪ **typique** *adj* typical (**de** of)

**typographie** [typɔgrafi] *nf* typography, printing

**tyran** [tirɑ̃] *nm* tyrant ▪ **tyrannie** *nf* tyranny ▪ **tyranniser** *vt* to tyrannize

**tzigane** [tzigan] *adj & nmf* = **tsigane**

# Uu

**U, u** [y] *nm inv* U, u

**UE** [yø] (*abrév* **Union européenne**) *nf* EU

**Ukraine** [ykrɛn] *nf* **l'U.** the Ukraine

**ulcère** [ylsɛr] *nm* ulcer

**ULM** [yɛlɛm] (*abrév* **ultraléger motorisé**) *nm inv Aviat* microlight

**ultérieur, -e** [ylterjœr] *adj* later, subsequent (**à** to) ▪ **ultérieurement** *adv* later (on), subsequently

**ultimatum** [yltimatɔm] *nm* ultimatum; **lancer un u. à qn** to give sb *or* issue sb with an ultimatum

**ultime** [yltim] *adj* last; *(préparatifs)* final

**ultramoderne** [yltramodɛrn] *adj* high-tech

**ultrason** [yltrasɔ̃] *nm* ultrasound

**ultraviolet, -ette** [yltravjɔlɛ, -ɛt] *adj & nm* ultraviolet

---

**UN, UNE** [œ̃, yn] **1** *article indéfini* a; *(devant voyelle)* an; **une page** a page; **un ange** [œ̃nɑ̃ʒ] an angel

**2** *adj* one; **la page un** page one; **un kilo** one kilo; **un par un** one by one

**3** *pron & nmf* one; **l'un** one; **les uns** some; **le numéro un** number one; **j'en ai un** I have one; **l'un d'eux, l'une d'elles** one of them; *Journ* **la une** the front page, page one

---

**unanime** [ynanim] *adj* unanimous ▪ **unanimité** *nf* unanimity; **à l'u.** unanimously

**uni, -e** [yni] *adj (famille, couple)* close; *(couleur, étoffe)* plain

**unième** [ynjɛm] *adj* first; **trente et u.** thirty-first; **cent u.** hundred and first

**unifier** [ynifje] *vt* to unify ▪ **unification** *nf* unification

**uniforme** [ynifɔrm] **1** *adj (expression)* uniform; *(sol)* even; *(mouvement)* regular **2** *nm* uniform ▪ **uniformément** *adv* uniformly ▪ **uniformiser** *vt* to standardize ▪ **uniformité** *nf (de couleurs)* uniformity; *(monotonie)* monotony

**unilatéral, -e, -aux, -ales** [ynilateral, -o] *adj (décision)* unilateral; *(contrat)* one-sided; *(stationnement)* on one side of the road/street only

**union** [ynjɔ̃] *nf (de partis, de consommateurs)* union, association; *(entente)* unity; *(mariage)* marriage; **l'U. européenne** the European Union; **u. monétaire** monetary union; **u. libre** cohabitation

**unique** [ynik] *adj* (**a**) *(fille, fils)* only; *(espoir, souci)* only, sole; *(prix, parti, salaire, marché)* single (**b**) *(exceptionnel)* unique; **u. en son genre** completely unique ▪ **uniquement** *adv* only, just

**unir** [ynir] **1** *vt (personnes, territoires)* to unite; *(marier)* to join in marriage; *(efforts, qualités)* to combine (**à** with) **2 s'unir** *vpr (s'associer)* to unite; *(se marier)* to be joined in marriage; **s'u. à qn** to join forces with sb

**unitaire** [ynitɛr] *adj (prix)* per unit

**unité** [ynite] *nf (de mesure, élément, régiment)* unit; *(cohésion)* unity; **u. de longueur** unit of measurement

**univers** [ynivɛr] *nm* universe; *Fig* world ▪ **universel, -elle** *adj* universal

**université** [ynivɛrsite] *nf* university; **à**

**l'u.** *Br* at university, *Am* in college ▪ **universitaire 1** *adj* **ville/restaurant u.** university town/refectory **2** *nmf* academic

**uranium** [yranjɔm] *nm* uranium

**urbain, -e** [yrbɛ̃, -ɛn] *adj* urban ▪ **urbaniser** *vt* to urbanize ▪ **urbanisme** *nm Br* town planning, *Am* city planning

**urgent, -e** [yrʒɑ̃, -ɑ̃t] *adj* urgent ▪ **urgence** *nf (de décision, de tâche)* urgency; *(cas d'hôpital)* emergency; **d'u.** urgently; *Pol* **état d'u.** state of emergency; **(service des) urgences** *(d'hôpital) Br* casualty (department), *Am* emergency room

**urne** [yrn] *nf (vase)* urn; *(pour voter)* ballot box; **aller aux urnes** to go to the polls

**Uruguay** [yrygwe] *nm* **l'U.** Uruguay

**usage** [yzaʒ] *nm (utilisation)* use; *(coutume)* custom; *(de mot)* usage; **faire u. de qch** to make use of sth; **d'u.** *(habituel)* customary; **à l'u. de** for (the use of); **hors d'u.** out of order ▪ **usagé, -e** *adj (vêtement)* worn; *(billet)* used ▪ **usager** *nm* user

**user** [yze] **1** *vt (vêtement)* to wear out; *(personne)* to wear down; *(consommer)* to use (up) **2** *vi* **u. de qch** to use sth **3 s'user** *vpr (tissu, machine)* to wear out; *(talons, personne)* to wear down ▪ **usé, -e** *adj (tissu)* worn out; *(sujet)* stale; *(personne)* worn out; **eaux usées** dirty *or* waste water

**usine** [yzin] *nf* factory; **u. à gaz** gasworks; **u. métallurgique** ironworks

**ustensile** [ystɑ̃sil] *nm* implement, tool; **u. de cuisine** kitchen utensil

**usuel, -elle** [yzɥɛl] *adj* everyday

**usure** [yzyr] *nf (de pneu)* wear

**usurper** [yzyrpe] *vt* to usurp

**utile** [ytil] *adj* useful (**à** to)

**utiliser** [ytilize] *vt* to use ▪ **utilisateur, -trice** *nmf* user ▪ **utilisation** *nf* use ▪ **utilité** *nf* usefulness; **d'une grande u.** very useful

**utilitaire** [ytilitɛr] *adj* utilitarian

**utopie** [ytɔpi] *nf (idéal)* utopia; *(projet, idée)* utopian plan/idea ▪ **utopique** *adj* utopian

**UV** [yve] *(abrév* **ultraviolet***) nm inv* UV

# Vv

**V, v** [ve] *nm inv* V, v

**va** [va] *voir* **aller**[1]

**vacances** [vakɑ̃s] *nfpl Br* holiday(s), *Am* vacation; **partir en v.** to go on *Br* holiday *or Am* vacation; **les grandes v.** the summer *Br* holidays *or Am* vacation ▪ **vacancier, -ère** *nf Br* holidaymaker, *Am* vacationer

**vacant, -e** [vakɑ̃, -ɑ̃t] *adj* vacant

**vacarme** [vakarm] *nm* din, uproar

**vaccin** [vaksɛ̃] *nm* vaccine; **faire un v. à qn** to vaccinate sb ▪ **vaccination** *nf* vaccination ▪ **vacciner** *vt* to vaccinate; **se faire v.** to get vaccinated (**contre** against)

**vache** [vaʃ] *nf* cow; **maladie de la v. folle** mad cow disease

**vaciller** [vasije] *vi* to sway; *(flamme, lumière)* to flicker

**vagabond, -e** [vagabɔ̃, -ɔ̃d] *nmf (clochard)* vagrant, tramp ▪ **vagabonder** *vi* to roam, to wander

**vague**[1] [vag] *adj* vague; *(regard)* vacant; *(souvenir)* dim, vague

**vague**[2] [vag] *nf (de mer) & Fig* wave; **v. de chaleur** heat wave; **v. de froid** cold spell *or* snap

**vaille, vailles** *voir* **valoir**

**vain, -e** [vɛ̃, vɛn] *adj (sans résultat)* futile; *(vaniteux)* vain; **en v.** in vain ▪ **vainement** *adv* in vain

**vaincre*** [vɛ̃kr] *vt (adversaire)* to defeat; *Fig (maladie, difficulté)* to overcome ▪ **vaincu, -e** *nmf* defeated man/woman; *(de match)* loser ▪ **vainqueur** *nm* victor; *(de match)* winner

**vais** [ve] *voir* **aller**[1]

**vaisseau, -x** [vɛso] *nm Anat* vessel; *(bateau)* ship, vessel; **v. spatial** spaceship

**vaisselle** [vɛsɛl] *nf* crockery; **faire la v.** to do the washing up, to do the dishes

**valable** [valabl] *adj (billet, motif)* valid

**valet** [valɛ] *nm Cartes* jack; **v. de chambre** valet

**valeur** [valœr] *nf (prix, qualité)* value; *(mérite)* worth; **avoir de la v.** to be valuable; **mettre qch en v.** *(faire ressortir)* to highlight sth; **objets de v.** valuables

**valide** [valid] *adj (personne)* fit, able-bodied; *(billet)* valid ▪ **valider** *vt* to validate; *(titre de transport)* to stamp ▪ **validité** *nf* validity

**valise** [valiz] *nf* suitcase; **faire ses valises** to pack (one's bags)

**vallée** [vale] *nf* valley

**valoir*** [valwar] **1** *vi (avoir pour valeur)* to be worth; *(s'appliquer)* to apply (**pour** to); **v. mille euros/cher** to be worth a thousand euros/a lot; **il vaut mieux rester** it's better to stay; **il vaut mieux que j'attende** I'd better wait; **faire v. qch** *(faire ressortir)* to highlight sth; *(droit)* to assert sth **2** *vt* **v. qch à qn** *(ennuis)* to bring sb sth **3 se valoir** *vpr (objets, personnes)* to be as good as each other

**valse** [vals] *nf* waltz

**valve** [valv] *nf* valve

**vampire** [vɑ̃pir] *nm* vampire

**vandale** [vɑ̃dal] *nmf* vandal ▪ **vandalisme** *nm* vandalism

**vanille** [vanij] *nf* vanilla

**vanité** [vanite] *nf (orgueil)* vanity

▪ **vaniteux, -euse** *adj* vain, conceited
**vanter** [vɑ̃te] **1** *vt* to praise **2 se vanter** *vpr* to boast, to brag (**de** about, of)
**vapeur** [vapœr] *nf* **v. (d'eau)** steam; **cuire qch à la v.** to steam sth
**vaporiser** [vapɔrize] *vt* to spray ▪ **vaporisateur** *nm (appareil)* spray
**vaquer** [vake] *vi* **v. à qch** to attend to sth; **v. à ses occupations** to go about one's business
**varappe** [varap] *nf* rock-climbing
**variable** [varjabl] **1** *adj* variable; *(humeur, temps)* changeable **2** *nf* variabie ▪ **variation** *nf* variation
**varicelle** [varisɛl] *nf* chickenpox
**varier** [varje] *vti* to vary (**de** from) ▪ **varié, -e** *adj (diversifié)* varied
**variété** [varjete] *nf* variety
**variole** [varjɔl] *nf* smallpox
**vas** [va] *voir* **aller**[1]
**vase**[1] [vaz] *nm (récipient)* vase
**vase**[2] [vaz] *nf (boue)* mud, silt
**vaste** [vast] *adj* vast, huge
**Vatican** [vatikɑ̃] *nm* **le V.** the Vatican
**vaut** [vo] *voir* **valoir**
**veau, -x** [vo] *nm (animal)* calf; *(viande)* veal
**vécu, -e** [veky] **1** *pp de* **vivre 2** *adj (histoire)* real-life **3** *nm* real-life experience
**vedette** [vədɛt] *nf* (**a**) *(acteur)* star; **être en v.** *(dans un spectacle)* to top the bill (**b**) *(bateau)* launch
**végétal, -e, -aux, -ales** [veʒetal, -o] **1** *adj* **huile végétale** vegetable oil **2** *nm* plant ▪ **végétalien, -enne** *nmf* vegan ▪ **végétarien, -enne** *adj & nmf* vegetarian ▪ **végétation** *nf* vegetation
**véhément, -e** [veemɑ̃, -ɑ̃t] *adj* vehement ▪ **véhémence** *nf* vehemence
**véhicule** [veikyl] *nm* vehicle; **v. tout-terrain** off-road *or* all-terrain vehicle
**veille** [vɛj] *nf* (**a**) *(jour précédent)* **la v.** the day before (**de qch** sth); **la v. de Noël** Christmas Eve; **à la v. de qch** *(événement)* on the eve of sth (**b**) *(état)* wakefulness
**veillée** [veje] *nf (soirée)* evening
**veiller** [veje] **1** *vi* to stay up *or* awake; **v. à qch** to see to sth; **v. à ce que...** *(+ subjunctive)* to make sure that...; **v. sur qn** to watch over sb **2** *vt (malade)* to sit up with
**veine** [vɛn] *nf Anat, Bot & Géol* vein
**véliplanchiste** [veliplɑ̃ʃist] *nmf* windsurfer
**vélo** [velo] *nm* bike, bicycle; *(activité)* cycling; **faire du v.** to cycle, to go cycling; **v. tout-terrain** mountain bike ▪ **vélomoteur** *nm* moped
**velours** [vəlur] *nm* velvet; **v. côtelé** corduroy ▪ **velouté, -e 1** *adj* velvety **2** *nm* **v. d'asperges** cream of asparagus soup
**velu, -e** [vəly] *adj* hairy
**venaison** [vənɛzɔ̃] *nf* venison
**vendange** [vɑ̃dɑ̃ʒ] *nf (récolte)* grape harvest; *(raisin récolté)* grapes (harvested); **vendanges** *(période)* grape-harvesting time; **faire les vendanges** to harvest *or* pick the grapes ▪ **vendanger** *vi* to pick the grapes ▪ **vendangeur, -euse** *nmf* grape picker
**vendre** [vɑ̃dr] **1** *vt* to sell; **v. qch à qn** to sell sb sth, to sell sth to sb; **v. qch 10 euros** to sell sth for 10 euros; **'à v.'** 'for sale' **2 se vendre** *vpr* to be sold; **ça se vend bien** it sells well ▪ **vendeur, -euse** *nmf (de magasin) Br* sales *or* shop assistant, *Am* sales clerk; *(non professionnel)* seller
**vendredi** [vɑ̃drədi] *nm* Friday; **V. saint** Good Friday
**vénéneux, -euse** [venenø, -øz] *adj* poisonous
**vénérable** [venerabl] *adj* venerable
**venger** [vɑ̃ʒe] **1** *vt* to avenge **2 se venger** *vpr* to get one's revenge (**de qn** on sb; **de qch** for sth) ▪ **vengeance** *nf* revenge, vengeance
**venin** [vənɛ̃] *nm* poison, venom ▪ **venimeux, -euse** *adj* poisonous, venomous

**VENIR*** [vənir] **1** *(aux* **être***) vi* to come (**de** from); **v. faire qch** to come to do sth; **viens me voir** come and see me; **je viens/venais d'arriver** I've/I'd just arrived; **les jours qui viennent**

the coming days; **faire v. qn** to send for sb

**2** *v impersonnel* **s'il venait à pleuvoir** if it happened to rain

**vent** [vɑ̃] *nm* wind; **il y a** *ou* **il fait du v.** it's windy

**vente** [vɑ̃t] *nf* sale; **en v.** *(en magasin)* on sale; **mettre qch en v.** to put sth up for sale; **v. aux enchères** auction (sale); **v. par correspondance** mail order

**ventilateur** [vɑ̃tilatœr] *nm (électrique)* fan ▪ **ventilation** *nf* ventilation ▪ **ventiler** *vt* to ventilate

**ventre** [vɑ̃tr] *nm* stomach, belly; **à plat v.** flat on one's face; **avoir du v.** to have a paunch; **avoir mal au v.** to have a sore stomach

**ventriloque** [vɑ̃trilɔk] *nmf* ventriloquist

**venu, -e** [vəny] **1** *pp de* **venir 2** *adj* **bien v.** *(à propos)* timely; **mal v.** untimely **3** *nmf* **nouveau v., nouvelle venue** newcomer; **le premier v.** anyone **4** *nf* **venue** *(de personne, de printemps)* coming

**ver** [vɛr] *nm* worm; *(larve)* grub; *(de fruits, de fromage)* maggot; **v. de terre** (earth)worm; **v. à soie** silkworm

**véranda** [verɑ̃da] *nf* veranda(h); *(en verre)* conservatory

**verbe** [vɛrb] *nm* verb

**verdict** [vɛrdikt] *nm* verdict

**verdir** [vɛrdir] *vti* to turn green ▪ **verdure** *nf (végétation)* greenery

**verger** [vɛrʒe] *nm* orchard

**verglas** [vɛrgla] *nm Br* (black) ice, *Am* glaze ▪ **verglacé, -e** *adj (route)* icy

**véridique** [veridik] *adj* truthful

**vérifier** [verifje] **1** *vt* to check, to verify; *(comptes)* to audit **2 se vérifier** *vpr* to prove correct ▪ **vérifiable** *adj* verifiable ▪ **vérification** *nf* checking, verification; *(de comptes)* audit(ing)

**véritable** [veritabl] *adj (histoire, ami)* true, real; *(cuir, or, nom)* real, genuine; *(en intensif)* real

**vérité** [verite] *nf (de déclaration)* truth; *(sincérité)* sincerity; **en v.** in fact; **dire la v.** to tell the truth

**verni, -e** [vɛrni] *adj (meuble, parquet)* varnished

**vernir** [vɛrnir] *vt (bois)* to varnish; *(céramique)* to glaze ▪ **vernis** *nm* varnish; *(pour céramique)* glaze; **v. à ongles** nail polish *or Br* varnish ▪ **vernissage** *nm (d'exposition)* opening

**verra, verrait** [vera, verɛ] *voir* **voir**

**verre** [vɛr] *nm (substance, récipient)* glass; **prendre un v.** to have a drink; **v. de bière** glass of beer; **v. à bière/à vin** beer/wine glass; **v. de contact** contact lens ▪ **verrière** *nf (toit)* glass roof

**verrou** [vɛru] *nm* bolt; **fermer qch au v.** to bolt sth; **sous les verrous** behind bars

**verrouiller** [vɛruje] *vt (porte)* to bolt; *(quartier)* to seal off

**verrue** [vɛry] *nf* wart; **v. plantaire** verruca

**vers[1]** [vɛr] *prép (direction)* toward(s); *(approximation)* around, about

**vers[2]** [vɛr] *nm (de poème)* line; **des vers** *(poésie)* verse

**versant** [vɛrsɑ̃] *nm* slope, side

**verse** [vɛrs] **à verse** *adv* **la pluie tombait à v.** the rain was coming down in torrents

**Verseau** [vɛrso] *nm (signe)* Aquarius

**verser** [vɛrse] *vt* to pour (out); *(larmes, sang)* to shed; *(argent)* to pay (**sur un compte** into an account) ▪ **versement** *nm* payment

**version** [vɛrsjɔ̃] *nf (de film, d'incident)* version; *Cin* **en v. originale** in the original language; **en v. française** dubbed *(into French)*

**verso** [vɛrso] *nm* back (of the page); **'voir au v.'** 'see overleaf'

**vert, verte** [vɛr, vɛrt] **1** *adj* green; *(pas mûr)* unripe; **aller en classe verte** to go on a school trip to the countryside **2** *nm* green; *Pol* **les Verts** the Greens

**vertical, -e, -aux, -ales** [vertikal, -o] *adj & nf* vertical; **à la verticale** vertically

**vertige** [vɛrtiʒ] *nm (étourdissement)*

(feeling of) dizziness *or* giddiness; *(peur du vide)* vertigo; **vertiges** dizzy spells; **avoir le v.** to be *or* feel dizzy *or* giddy ▪ **vertigineux, -euse** *adj (hauteur)* giddy, dizzy

**vertu** [vɛrty] *nf* virtue; **en v. de** in accordance with ▪ **vertueux, -euse** *adj* virtuous

**verveine** [vɛrvɛn] *nf (plante)* verbena; *(tisane)* verbena tea

**vessie** [vesi] *nf* bladder

**veste** [vɛst] *nf* jacket, coat

**vestiaire** [vɛstjɛr] *nm (de théâtre)* cloakroom; *(de piscine, de stade)* changing room, *Am* locker room

**vestibule** [vɛstibyl] *nm* (entrance) hall

**vestiges** [vɛstiʒ] *nmpl (ruines)* remains; *(traces)* relics

**veston** [vɛstɔ̃] *nm* (suit) jacket

**vêtement** [vɛtmɑ̃] *nm* garment, article of clothing; **vêtements** clothes; **vêtements de sport** sportswear

**vétéran** [veterɑ̃] *nm* veteran

**vétérinaire** [veterinɛr] **1** *adj* veterinary **2** *nmf* vet, *Br* veterinary surgeon, *Am* veterinarian

**vêtir*** [vetir] *vt*, **se vêtir** *vpr* to dress

**veto** [veto] *nm inv* veto; **opposer son v. à qch** to veto sth

**vêtu, -e** [vety] *adj* dressed (**de** in)

**vétuste** [vetyst] *adj* dilapidated

**veuf, veuve** [vœf, vœv] **1** *adj* widowed **2** *nm* widower **3** *nf* widow

**veuille(s), veuillent** [vœj] *voir* **vouloir**

**veut, veux** [vø] *voir* **vouloir**

**vexer** [vɛkse] **1** *vt* to upset, to hurt **2 se vexer** *vpr* to get upset (**de** at)

**VF** [veɛf] *(abrév* **version française***) nf* **film en VF** film dubbed into French

**viable** [vjabl] *adj (entreprise, enfant)* viable

**viaduc** [vjadyk] *nm* viaduct

**viande** [vjɑ̃d] *nf* meat

**vibrer** [vibre] *vi* to vibrate; *(être ému)* to be stirred (**de** with); **faire v. qn** to stir sb ▪ **vibrant, -e** *adj (hommage)* stirring ▪ **vibration** *nf* vibration

**vice** [vis] *nm (perversité)* vice; *(défectuosité)* defect

**vice versa** [vis(e)versa] *adv* vice versa

**vicié, -e** [visje] *adj (air, atmosphère)* polluted

**vicieux, -euse** [visjø, -øz] *adj (pervers)* depraved; *(perfide)* underhand

**victime** [viktim] *nf* victim; *(d'accident)* casualty; **être v. de** *(accident, attentat)* to be the victim of

**victoire** [viktwar] *nf* victory; *(en sport)* win ▪ **victorieux, -euse** *adj* victorious; *(équipe)* winning

**vidange** [vidɑ̃ʒ] *nf* emptying, draining; *(de véhicule)* oil change ▪ **vidanger** *vt* to empty, to drain

**vide** [vid] **1** *adj* empty **2** *nm (espace)* empty space; *(d'emploi du temps)* gap; *Phys* vacuum; **regarder dans le v.** to stare into space; **emballé sous v.** vacuum-packed; **à v.** empty

**vidéo** [video] *adj inv & nf* video ▪ **vidéocassette** *nf* video (cassette) ▪ **vidéoclip** *nm* video

**vider** [vide] *vt*, **se vider** *vpr* to empty ▪ **vide-ordures** *nm inv Br* rubbish *or Am* garbage chute ▪ **videur** *nm (de boîte de nuit)* bouncer

**vie** [vi] *nf* life; *(durée)* lifetime; **en v.** living; **à v., pour la v.** for life

**vieil, vieille** [vjɛj] *voir* **vieux**

**vieillard** [vjɛjar] *nm* old man; **les vieillards** old people ▪ **vieillerie** *nf (objet)* old thing ▪ **vieillesse** *nf* old age

**vieillir** [vjejir] **1** *vi* to grow old; *(changer)* to age; *(théorie, mot)* to become old-fashioned **2** *vt* **v. qn** *(vêtement)* to make sb look old(er) ▪ **vieilli, -e** *adj (démodé)* old-fashioned ▪ **vieillissant, -e** *adj* ageing ▪ **vieillissement** *nm* ageing

**vieillot, -otte** [vjɛjo, -ɔt] *adj* old-fashioned

**Vienne** [vjɛn] *nm ou f* Vienna

**viens, vient** [vjɛ̃] *voir* **venir**

**vierge** [vjɛrʒ] **1** *adj (femme, neige)* virgin; *(feuille de papier, film)* blank; **être v.** *(femme, homme)* to be a virgin **2** *nf* virgin; **la V.** *(signe)* Virgo

**Viêt-nam** [vjɛtnam] *nm* **le V.** Vietnam ■ **vietnamien, -enne 1** *adj* Vietnamese **2** *nmf* **V., Vietnamienne** Vietnamese

**vieux, vieille, vieux, vieilles** [vjø, vjɛj]

**vieil** is used before masculine singular nouns beginning with a vowel or mute h.

**1** *adj* old; **être v. jeu** *(adj inv)* to be old-fashioned; **se faire v.** to get old **2** *nm* old man; **les vieux** old people **3** *nf* **vieille** old woman

**vif, vive** [vif, viv] **1** *adj (personne)* lively; *(imagination)* vivid; *(intelligence, vent, douleur)* sharp; *(intérêt, satisfaction)* great; *(couleur, lumière)* bright; *(froid)* biting; *(pas, mouvement)* quick; **brûler qn v.** to burn sb alive **2** *nm* **entrer dans le v. du sujet** to get to the heart of the matter; **à v.** *(plaie)* open

**vigilant, -e** [viʒilɑ̃, -ɑ̃t] *adj* vigilant ■ **vigilance** *nf* vigilance

**vigile** [viʒil] *nm* watchman

**vigne** [viɲ] *nf (plante)* vine; *(plantation)* vineyard ■ **vigneron, -onne** [-ərɔ̃, -ɔn] *nmf* wine grower ■ **vignoble** *nm* vineyard; *(région)* vineyards

**vignette** [viɲɛt] *nf (de véhicule)* road tax sticker, *Br* ≃ road tax disc; *(de médicament)* label *(for reimbursement by Social Security)*

**vigueur** [vigœr] *nf* vigour; **entrer en v.** *(loi)* to come into force ■ **vigoureux, -euse** *adj (personne)* vigorous

**vilain, -e** [vilɛ̃, -ɛn] *adj (laid)* ugly; *(peu sage)* naughty

**villa** [vila] *nf* villa

**village** [vilaʒ] *nm* village ■ **villageois, -e** *nmf* villager

**ville** [vil] *nf* town; *(grande)* city; **aller/être en v.** to go (in)to/be in town; **v. d'eaux** spa (town)

**vin** [vɛ̃] *nm* wine ■ **vinicole** *adj (région)* wine-growing

**vinaigre** [vinɛgr] *nm* vinegar ■ **vinaigrette** *nf (sauce)* vinaigrette, *Br* French dressing, *Am* Italian dressing

**vingt** [vɛ̃] ([vɛ̃t] *before vowel or mute h and in numbers 22–29*) *adj & nm inv* twenty; **v. et un** twenty-one ■ **vingtaine** *nf* **une v. (de)** *(nombre)* about twenty ■ **vingtième** *adj & nmf* twentieth

**viol** [vjɔl] *nm* rape; *(de lieu)* violation ■ **violation** *nf* violation ■ **violer** *vt (femme)* to rape ■ **violeur** *nm* rapist

**violent, -e** [vjɔlɑ̃, -ɑ̃t] *adj* violent; *(effort)* strenuous ■ **violence** *nf* violence; **acte de v.** act of violence

**violet, -ette** [vjɔlɛ, -ɛt] **1** *adj & nm (couleur)* purple **2** *nf* **violette** *(fleur)* violet

**violon** [vjɔlɔ̃] *nm* violin ■ **violoncelle** *nm* cello ■ **violoncelliste** *nmf* cellist ■ **violoniste** *nmf* violinist

**vipère** [vipɛr] *nf* adder, viper

**virage** [viraʒ] *nm (de route)* bend

**virer** [vire] **1** *vi* to turn; **v. au bleu** to turn blue **2** *vt Fin (somme)* to transfer (**à** to) ■ **virement** *nm Fin* transfer

**virgule** [virgyl] *nf (ponctuation)* comma; *Math* (decimal) point; **2 v. 5** 2 point 5

**viril, -e** [viril] *adj* virile; *(force)* male ■ **virilité** *nf* virility

**virtuel, -elle** [virtɥɛl] *adj* potential; *(image)* virtual; **réalité virtuelle** virtual reality

**virtuose** [virtɥoz] *nmf* virtuoso

**virulent, -e** [virylɑ̃, -ɑ̃t] *adj* virulent

**virus** [virys] *nm Méd & Ordinat* virus

**vis**[1] [vi] *voir* **vivre, voir**

**vis**[2] [vis] *nf* screw

**visa** [viza] *nm (de passeport)* visa

**visage** [vizaʒ] *nm* face

**vis-à-vis** [vizavi] **1** *prép* **v. de** *(en face de)* opposite; *(envers)* towards **2** *nm inv (personne)* person opposite

**viser** [vize] **1** *vt (cible)* to aim at; *(concerner)* to be aimed at **2** *vi* to aim (**à** at); **v. à faire qch** to aim to do sth

**visible** [vizibl] *adj* visible ■ **visibilité** *nf* visibility

**visière** [vizjɛr] *nf (de casquette)* peak; *(en plastique)* eyeshade; *(de casque)* visor

**vision** [vizjɔ̃] *nf (conception, image)* vision; *(sens)* sight ▪ **visionnaire** *adj & nmf* visionary ▪ **visionner** *vt (film)* to view

**visite** [vizit] *nf* visit; *(personne)* visitor; *(examen)* inspection; **rendre v. à qn** to visit sb; **avoir de la v.** to have a visitor/visitors; **v. médicale** medical examination; **v. guidée** guided tour ▪ **visiter** *vt (lieu touristique, patient)* to visit ▪ **visiteur, -euse** *nmf* visitor

**vison** [vizɔ̃] *nm* mink

**visqueux, -euse** [viskø, -øz] *adj* viscous; *(surface)* sticky

**visser** [vise] *vt* to screw on

**visuel, -elle** [vizɥɛl] *adj* visual ▪ **visualiser** *vt* to visualize

**vit** [vi] *voir* **vivre, voir**

**vital, -e, -aux, -ales** [vital, -o] *adj* vital ▪ **vitalité** *nf* vitality

**vitamine** [vitamin] *nf* vitamin

**vite** [vit] *adv (rapidement)* quickly, fast; *(sous peu)* soon; **v.!** quick(ly)!

**vitesse** [vitɛs] *nf* speed; *(de moteur)* gear; **à toute v.** at top full speed

**viticole** [vitikɔl] *adj (région)* wine-growing ▪ **viticulteur** *nm* wine grower ▪ **viticulture** *nf* wine growing

**vitre** [vitr] *nf* (window)pane; *(de véhicule, de train)* window ▪ **vitrage** *nm (vitres)* windows ▪ **vitrail, -aux** *nm* stained-glass window ▪ **vitré, -e** *adj* **porte vitrée** glass door ▪ **vitrier** *nm* glazier

**vitrine** [vitrin] *nf (de magasin)* (shop) window; *(meuble)* display cabinet

**vivace** [vivas] *adj (plante)* perennial ▪ **vivacité** *nf* liveliness; *(d'imagination)* vividness; *(d'intelligence)* sharpness; *(de couleur)* brightness; *(emportement)* petulance; **v. d'esprit** quick-wittedness

**vivant, -e** [vivɑ̃, -ɑ̃t] **1** *adj (en vie)* alive, living; *(récit, rue, enfant)* lively; *(être, matière)* living **2** *nm* **de son v.** in one's lifetime; **les vivants** the living

**vive[1]** [viv] *voir* **vif**

**vive[2]** [viv] *exclam* **v. le roi!** long live the king!

**vivement** [vivmɑ̃] *adv* quickly; *(ré[illegible] quer)* sharply; *(regretter)* deeply

**vivier** [vivje] *nm* fish pond

**vivifier** [vivifje] *vt* to invigorate

**vivisection** [vivisɛksjɔ̃] *nf* vivisecti[illegible]

**vivre*** [vivr] **1** *vi* to live; **elle vit enco[illegible]** she's still alive *or* living; **faire v. qn** *([illegible] mille)* to support sb; **v. vieux** to live [illegible] be old; **v. de** *(fruits)* to live on; *(trava[illegible])* to live by **2** *vt (vie)* to live; *(aventu[illegible] époque)* to live through; *(éprouver)* [illegible] experience ▪ **vivres** *nmpl* food, su[illegible]plies

**VO** [veo] *(abrév* **version originale***)* [illegible] **film en VO** film in the original lan[illegible]guage

**vocal, -e, -aux, -ales** [vɔkal, -o] *a[illegible]* vocal

**vocation** [vɔkɑsjɔ̃] *nf* vocation, cal[illegible]ing

**vociférer** [vɔsifere] *vti* to shout an[illegible]grily

**vœu, -x** [vø] *nm (souhait)* wish; *(pro[illegible] messe)* vow; **faire un v.** to make [illegible] wish; **tous mes vœux!** best wishes!

**vogue** [vɔg] *nf* fashion, vogue; **en v.** in vogue

**voici** [vwasi] *prép* here is/are; **me v.** here I am; **v. dix ans** ten years ago; **v. dix ans que...** it's ten years since...

**voie** [vwa] *nf (route)* road; *(rails)* track, line; *(partie de route)* lane; *(chemin)* way; *(de gare)* platform; *(de communication)* line; *(moyen)* means, way; **pays en v. de développement** developing country; **v. sans issue** dead end

**voilà** [vwala] *prép* there is/are; **les v.** there they are; **le v. parti** he has left now; **v. dix ans** ten years ago; **v. dix ans que...** it's ten years since...

**voile[1]** [vwal] *nm (étoffe, coiffure)* veil ▪ **voilé, -e** *adj (femme, allusion)* veiled; *(photo, lumière)* hazy ▪ **voiler** [vwale] **1** *vt (visage, vérité)* to veil **2 se voiler** *vpr (personne)* to wear a veil; *(ciel)* to cloud over

**voile[2]** [vwal] *nf (de bateau)* sail; *(sport)* sailing; **faire de la v.** to sail ▪ **voilier** *nm* sailing boat; *(de plaisance)* yacht

**oiler** [vwale] *vt*, **se voiler** *vpr (roue)* to buckle

**VOIR*** [vwar] **1** *vt* to see; **faire v. qch** to show sth; **v. qn faire qch** to see sb do/doing sth

**2** *vi* to see; **fais v.** let me see, show me; **ça n'a rien à v. avec ça** that's got nothing to do with that

**3 se voir** *vpr (soi-même)* to see oneself; *(se fréquenter)* to see each other; *(objet, attitude)* to be seen; *(reprise, tache)* to show

**voisin, -e** [vwazɛ̃, -in] **1** *adj (pays, village) Br* neighbouring, *Am* neighboring; *(maison, pièce)* next (**de** to); *(état)* similar (**de** to) **2** *nmf Br* neighbour, *Am* neighbor ▪ **voisinage** *nm (quartier, voisins) Br* neighbourhood, *Am* neighborhood; *(proximité)* closeness, proximity ▪ **voisiner** *vi* **v. avec** to be side by side with

**voiture** [vwatyr] *nf* car; *(de train)* carriage, *Br* coach, *Am* car; **en v.!** *(dans le train)* all aboard!; **v. de course** racing/private car

**voix** [vwa] *nf* voice; *(d'électeur)* vote; **à v. basse** in a whisper; **à haute v.** aloud

**vol** [vɔl] *nm* (**a**) *(d'avion, d'oiseau)* flight; *(groupe d'oiseaux)* flock, flight; **attraper qch au v.** to catch sth in the air (**b**) *(délit)* theft; **v. à main armée** armed robbery

**volaille** [vɔlɑj] *nf* **la v.** poultry; **une v.** a fowl

**volatiliser** [vɔlatilize] **se volatiliser** *vpr* to vanish into thin air

**volcan** [vɔlkɑ̃] *nm* volcano ▪ **volcanique** *adj* volcanic

**voler[1]** [vɔle] *vi (oiseau, avion)* to fly ▪ **volant** *nm (de véhicule)* (steering) wheel; *(de badminton)* shuttlecock; *(de jupe)* flounce ▪ **volée** *nf (de flèches)* flight; *(de coups)* thrashing

**voler[2]** [vɔle] **1** *vt (prendre)* to steal (**à** from); **v. qn** to rob sb **2** *vi (prendre)* to steal

**volet** [vɔlɛ] *nm (de fenêtre)* shutter; *(de programme)* section, part

**voleur, -euse** [vɔlœr, -øz] *nmf* thief; **au v.!** stop thief!

**volière** [vɔljɛr] *nf* aviary

**volley-ball** [vɔlebol] *nm* volleyball ▪ **volleyeur, -euse** *nmf* volleyball player

**volontaire** [vɔlɔ̃tɛr] **1** *adj (geste, omission)* deliberate; *(travail)* voluntary; *(opiniâtre) Br* wilful, *Am* willful **2** *nmf* volunteer ▪ **volontairement** *adv (spontanément)* voluntarily; *(exprès)* deliberately

**volontariat** [volɔ̃tarja] *nm* voluntary work

**volonté** [vɔlɔ̃te] *nf (faculté, intention)* will; *(détermination)* willpower; *(souhait)* wish; **bonne v.** willingness; **mauvaise v.** unwillingness; **à v.** *(quantité)* as much as desired

**volontiers** [vɔlɔ̃tje] *adv* gladly, willingly; **v.!** *(oui)* I'd love to!

**volte-face** [vɔltəfas] *nf inv* **faire v.** to turn round; *Fig* to do a U-turn

**voltiger** [vɔltiʒe] *vi (feuilles)* to flutter

**volume** [vɔlym] *nm (de boîte, de son, livre)* volume ▪ **volumineux, -euse** *adj* bulky, voluminous

**volupté** [vɔlypte] *nf* sensual pleasure ▪ **voluptueux, -euse** *adj* voluptuous

**vomir** [vɔmir] **1** *vt* to bring up, to vomit **2** *vi* to vomit, *Br* to be sick ▪ **vomissements** *nmpl* **avoir des v.** to vomit

**vont** [vɔ̃] *voir* **aller[1]**

**vorace** [vɔras] *adj* voracious

**vos** [vo] *voir* **votre**

**vote** [vɔt] *nm (action)* vote, voting; *(suffrage)* vote; *(de loi)* passing; *Br* **bureau de v.** polling station, *Am* polling place ▪ **votant, -e** *nmf* voter ▪ **voter 1** *vt (loi)* to pass; *(crédits)* to vote **2** *vi* to vote

**votre, vos** [vɔtr, vo] *adj possessif* your ▪ **vôtre 1** *pron possessif* **le** *ou* **la v., les vôtres** yours; **à la v.!** cheers! **2** *nmpl* **les vôtres** *(votre famille)* your family

**voudra, voudrait** [vudra, vudrɛ] *voir* **vouloir**

**vouer** [vwe] **1** *vt (promettre)* to vow (**à** to); *(consacrer)* to dedicate (**à** to) **2 se**

**vouer** *vpr* **se v. à** to dedicate oneself to

**VOULOIR*** [vulwar] *vt* to want (**faire** to do); **je veux qu'il parte** I want him to go; **v. dire** to mean (**que** that); **je voudrais un pain** I'd like a loaf of bread; **je voudrais rester** I'd like to stay; **je veux bien attendre** I don't mind waiting; **voulez-vous me suivre** will you follow me; **si tu veux** if you like *or* wish; **en v. à qn d'avoir fait qch** to be angry with sb for doing sth; **v. du bien à qn** to wish sb well; **sans le v.** unintentionally

**voulu, -e** [vuly] *adj (requis)* required; *(délibéré)* deliberate, intentional

**vous** [vu] *pron personnel* (**a**) *(sujet, complément direct)* you; **v. êtes ici** you are here; **il v. connaît** he knows you

(**b**) *(complément indirect)* (to) you; **il v. l'a donné** he gave it to you, he gave you it

(**c**) *(réfléchi)* yourself, *pl* yourselves; **v. v. lavez** you wash yourself/yourselves

(**d**) *(réciproque)* each other; **v. v. aimez** you love each other ▪ **vous-même** *pron* yourself ▪ **vous-mêmes** *pron pl* yourselves

**voûte** [vut] *nf (arch)* vault ▪ **voûté, -e** *adj (personne)* bent, stooped

**vouvoyer** [vuvwaje] *vt* **v. qn** to address sb as "vous" ▪ **vouvoiement** *nm* = use of the formal "vous" instead of the more familiar "tu"

**voyage** [vwajaʒ] *nm* trip, journey; *(par mer)* voyage; **aimer les voyages** to like *Br* travelling *or Am* traveling; **faire un v., partir en v.** to go on a trip; **être en v.** to be (away) *Br* travelling *or Am* traveling; **bon v.!** have a pleasant trip!; **v. de noces** honeymoon; **v. organisé** (package) tour ▪ **voyager** *vi* to travel ▪ **voyageur, -euse** *nmf Br* travell *Am* traveler; *(passager)* passenger; **de commerce** *Br* travelling *or Am* tr veling salesman, *Br* commercial tr veller ▪ **voyagiste** *nm* tour operator

**voyant, -e**[1] [vwajɑ̃, -ɑ̃t] **1** *adj (couleu* gaudy, loud **2** *nm (signal)* (warnin light; *(d'appareil électrique)* pilot ligh

**voyant, -e**[2] [vwajɑ̃, -ɑ̃t] *nmf* clairvo ant

**voyou** [vwaju] *nm* hooligan

**vrac** [vrak] **en vrac** *adv (en désordre)* a muddle; *(au poids)* loose

**vrai** [vrɛ] *adj* true; *(réel)* real; *(authen tique)* genuine ▪ **vraiment** *adv* really

**vraisemblable** [vrɛsɑ̃blabl] *adj (pro bable)* likely, probable; *(crédible* credible ▪ **vraisemblablement** *ad* probably ▪ **vraisemblance** *nf* likeli hood; *(crédibilité)* credibility

**vrombir** [vrɔ̃bir] *vi* to hum ▪ **vrombis sement** *nm* hum(ming)

**VTT** [vetete] *(abrév* **vélo tout terrain**) *nm inv* mountain bike

**vu, -e**[1] [vy] **1** *pp de* **voir 2** *adj* **bien vu** well thought of; **mal vu** frowned upon **3** *prép* in view of; **vu que...** seeing that...

**vue**[2] [vy] *nf (sens)* (eye)sight; *(panorama, photo)* view; **en v.** *(proche)* in sight; *(en évidence)* on view; *Fig (personne)* in the public eye; **avoir qn/qch en v.** to have sb/sth in mind; **à v.** *(tirer)* on sight; *(payable)* at sight; **à première v.** at first sight; **à v. d'œil** *(grandir)* visibly; **de v.** *(connaître)* by sight; **v. d'ensemble** overall view

**vulgaire** [vylgɛr] *adj (grossier)* vulgar; *(ordinaire)* common ▪ **vulgariser** *vt* to popularize ▪ **vulgarité** *nf* vulgarity

**vulnérable** [vylnerabl] *adj* vulnerable ▪ **vulnérabilité** *nf* vulnerability

# Ww

**W, w** [dubləve] *nm inv* W, w

**wagon** [vagɔ̃] *nm (de voyageurs)* carriage, *Br* coach, *Am* car; *(de marchandises) Br* wagon, *Am* freight car ▪ **wagon-lit** (*pl* **wagons-lits**) *nm* sleeping car, sleeper ▪ **wagon-restaurant** (*pl* **wagons-restaurants**) *nm* dining *or* restaurant car

**Walkman®** [wɔkman] *nm* Walkman®, personal stereo

**wallon, -onne** [walɔ̃, -ɔn] **1** *adj* Walloon **2** *nmf* **W., Wallonne** Walloon

**watt** [wat] *nm Él* watt

**w-c** [(dublə)vese] *nmpl Br* toilet, *Am* bathroom

**week-end** [wikɛnd] (*pl* **week-ends**) *nm* weekend; **partir en w.** to go away for the weekend

**whisky** [wiski] (*pl* **-ies** *ou* **-ys**) *nm Br* whisky, *Am* whiskey

**wysiwyg** [wiziwig] *adj & nm Ordinat* WYSIWYG

**X, x** [iks] *nm inv* (*lettre, personne ou nombre inconnus*) X, x; **x fois** umpteen times

**xénophobe** [gsenɔfɔb] *adj* xenophobic ▪ **xénophobie** *nf* xenophobia

**xylophone** [gsilɔfɔn] *nm* xylophone

# Yy

**Y, y**[1] [igrɛk] *nm inv* Y, y

**y**[2] [i] **1** *adv* there; *(dedans)* in it/them; *(dessus)* on it/them; **elle y vivra** she'll live there; **j'y entrai** I entered (it); **allons-y** let's go **2** *pron* **j'y pense** I'm thinking about it; **je m'y attendais** I was expecting it; **ça y est!** that's it!

**yacht** [jɔt] *nm* yacht

**yaourt** [jaurt] *nm* yoghurt

**Yémen** [jemɛn] *nm* **le Y.** Yemen

**yen** [jɛn] *nm* yen

**yeux** [jø] *voir* **œil**

**yoga** [jɔga] *nm* yoga; **faire du y.** to do yoga

**yog(h)ourt** [jɔgurt] *nm* = **yaourt**

**Yo-Yo**® [jojo] *nm inv* yo-yo

# Zz

**Z, z** [zɛd] *nm inv* Z, z
**Zaïre** [zair] *nm* **le Z.** Zaïre
**zèbre** [zɛbr] *nm* zebra
**zèle** [zɛl] *nm* zeal; **faire du z.** to overdo it ▪ **zélé, -e** *adj* zealous
**zéro** [zero] *nm* *(chiffre)* zero, *Br* nought; *(de numéro de téléphone)* *Br* 0 [əʊ], *Am* zero; *(température)* zero; *Fig* *(personne)* nonentity; **deux buts à z.** *(au football)* *Br* two nil, *Am* two zero
**zeste** [zɛst] *nm* **un z. de citron** a piece of lemon peel
**zigzag** [zigzag] *nm* zigzag; **en z.** *(route)* zigzag(ging) ▪ **zigzaguer** *vi* to zigzag
**Zimbabwe** [zimbabwe] *nm* **le Z.** Zimbabwe
**zinc** [zɛ̃g] *nm* *(métal)* zinc
**zipper** [zipe] *vt Ordinat* to zip
**zodiaque** [zɔdjak] *nm* zodiac; **sign du z.** sign of the zodiac
**zone** [zon] *nf* zone; **de seconde z.** second-rate; **z. industrielle** industrial *Br* estate *or Am* park; **z. fumeurs/non-fumeurs** smoking/no-smoking area
**zoo** [zo(o)] *nm* zoo ▪ **zoologie** *nf* zoology ▪ **zoologique** *adj* zoological; **parc z.** zoo
**zoom** [zum] *nm* *(objectif)* zoom lens

Imprimé en Italie par

LA TIPOGRAFICA VARESE
Società per Azioni
Varese
Dépôt legal : Mai 2010
304477-04/11016902 - Janvier 2011

BASEBALL'S BELTERS

# JACKSON★SCHMIDT PARKER★BRETT

BASEBALL'S BELTERS

# JACKSON★SCHMIDT PARKER★BRETT

BILL GUTMAN

tempo books
GROSSET & DUNLAP
A Filmways Company
Publishers • New York

BASEBALL BELTERS: JACKSON, SCHMIDT, PARKER, BRETT


ISBN: 0-448-17325-5
A Tempo Books Original
Tempo Books is registered in the U.S. Patent Office
Printed in the United States of America
Published simultaneously in Canada

Cover photos by FOCUS ON SPORTS

**Acknowledgments**

The author would like to thank the following for providing background information helpful in the preparation of this book. The public relations departments of the New York Yankees, Kansas City Royals, and Pittsburgh Pirates. Also, Chris Wheeler and Larry Shenk of the Philadelphia Phillies, and Joan Frey, secretary to George Brett. And special thanks to George Brett's mother, Mrs. Ethel Johnson, and Mike Schmidt's father, Jack Schmidt, for taking the time to speak openly and freely about their famous sons.

## CONTENTS

# REGGIE JACKSON

Of all the major professional sports, baseball undoubtedly relies on statistics more than any of the others. The records go back a long way, to the turn of the century and earlier. Today, stats are often used to compare one player with another, even if the two performed some twenty or thirty years apart.

Whether you enjoy reading stats, using them to back you in an argument, or to settle a bet, anyone can have fun with baseball stats. Although stats can be used as a measuring stick to compare the capabilities of various players, in many instances, they tell just a portion of the whole story. For example, take the case of Reggie Jackson, the star slugger of the New York Yankees.

Looking at the stats for the decade of the 1970s, you find that Reggie has hit 292 home runs during that ten-year span, more than any other player in the major leagues with the exception of Pittsburgh Pirate star Willie Stargell, who had 296. You also find that Reggie drove home 922 runs during that period, best in the American League, right behind Johnny Bench, Tony Perez, and Lee May, all of whom toiled in the National League. A very impressive record.

Wait, there's more. In the whole, long history of baseball, Reggie Jackson is one of just four players to have 400 homers and 200 stolen bases in a career. The other three are Hank Aaron, Willie Mays, and Frank Robinson. Pretty fast company! Since coming to the big leagues for good in 1968, Reggie has been in on five World Series wins: three with Oakland, and two with the Yankees.

So just using the stats, you can conclude that Reginald Martinez Jackson is a great ballplayer, a future Hall of Famer, and one of the top sluggers in the game today. All that is true. So much for the statistics. For there is a great deal more to the Reggie Jackson story, things that fans reading the stats some thirty years from now may never know, unless they see fit to look beyond the numbers and the totals.

Reggie Jackson is a handsome, intelligent, articulate man with worldly tastes. He is a compassionate man who won't forget his roots or those who are less fortunate than he. He is also an astute businessman who should continue to prosper long after his playing career ends. He is a man who has strong opinions and the courage to express them, and he is a man with a tremendous ego and an equal amount of pride.

In other words, Reggie Jackson is an extremely complex human being, one who has had a career wrought with controversy. Admittedly, he has been the center of the storm on many occasions, both in Oakland and in New York. There is no real middle ground with Reggie. People either like him or dislike him, and that goes for his managers, teammates, and the fans.

There is little doubt about the baseball side of Reggie. As his former teammate and close friend, Dave Duncan, once said, "Reggie is so strong that he should be able to hit thirty home runs a year just by accident."

It hasn't always been that simple. Reggie's career has seen a series of ups and downs that could have destroyed a less resolute man. When he hit forty-seven homers his second full season in 1969 with the Oakland Athletics, and after challenging the Ruth-Maris home run marks for much of the year, a great deal was expected of him. But the pressures on a young player were great, and salary disputes with A's owner Charles O. Finley didn't help. Within a year or two there was some talk about

Reggie going back to the minors.

In 1971 Reggie pinch-hit at the annual All-Star Game in Detroit, and he hit a shot off pitcher Dock Ellis that left the entire baseball world in awe of his raw power. The ball cleared the stands in rightcenter and would have gone completely out of the park had it not hit a generator box on the top of a light tower, some five hundred feet from home plate. It was such a mammoth shot that the crowd at Tiger Stadium was shocked to silence.

A year later Reggie injured his leg in the playoffs. He was on crutches as Oakland went to the World Series for the first time since the franchise moved there. But there were championships the next two years, then more salary disputes, and finally a trade to Baltimore.

Reggie was there for a year before opting for free agency and a huge, long-term pact with the N.Y. Yankees. He thought he'd finally found peace and security at last, but he didn't count on running into a pair of volatile personalities in Yankee owner George Steinbrenner and Manager Billy Martin. Hence more ups and downs, such as his near fistfight with Martin in the Yankee dugout during a game on national television, and his three homers on three pitches to clinch the 1977 World Series for the Bronx Bombers.

So, wherever Reggie has gone, the excitement hasn't been too far behind. Now, that he is an elder statesman in the final phase of his career, hopefully the controversies that have marked his years in baseball are behind him. To see how they came about it is necessary to go back to the beginning.

Reggie was born in Wyncote, Pennsylvania, a suburb of Philadelphia, on May 18, 1946. His father, Martinez C. Jackson, was of Spanish ancestry on his mother's side. When Reggie was still an infant, the family moved to Cheltenham, another suburb of Philly and a rather high-class neighborhood. Mr. Jackson had a dry-cleaning delivery route there and that's where Reggie grew up.

When Reggie was four his parents were divorced and

the family broke up. Three of Reggie's brothers and sisters went to live with their mother, Clara, while Reggie, an older brother and sister, stayed with their father. Fortunately, the family was not in a tough neighborhood where a kid on his own much of the time could get into trouble.

"There were very few blacks in the neighborhood," Reggie recalls, "but I guess there had to be someone to do the work. I never felt much prejudice. Since I was the only black, I guess there was more or less no need for it. And since that time, I've always been a well-known athlete, so that's helped keep me away from it. But I did know what it was like to be poor, especially since we were in such a rich place. Everyone around there had more than we did."

Since his father had to work very hard, Reggie learned to do things for himself at an early age, and he also learned that things wouldn't be given to him. He had to earn them.

"If I wanted a quarter to go to the movies or something, my father would always make me earn it. Sometimes I'd work on his delivery truck, but then it was too late for the movies anyway. He was strict with me, but I respected him for it. He made me see the value of money."

It wasn't long before Reggie was playing ball. Bob Tremble, later the athletic director at Cheltenham High, knew Reggie from the time he was in the third grade and coached him during those early days.

"Reggie Jackson was always a terrific kid," Tremble recalls. "He never caused any trouble and always had a lot of friends. Of course, he was a good ballplayer. You could see the speed and good hands right from the first. When he was in the fifth grade I tried making him a switch hitter, but after practicing awhile, he went back to the left side.

"Even then, in the fifth and sixth grades, he was willing to help others. He would always play catch with the younger kids or throw passes to them and show them the various skills he had learned from me. I've got nothing but good things to say about Reggie Jackson."

By the time Reggie began his sophomore year at Cheltenham High in 1961 he was already an exceptional all-around athlete, participating in baseball, football, and track. His baseball coach there, Chuck Mehelich remembers the skills Reggie brought to the team as a sophomore.

"He started in the outfield for me right away," Mehelich said. "He had great speed and a great arm, and he hit well. His arm was so strong that he pitched some relief for us, too. I remember one practice game when he struck out seventeen batters in twelve innings. I think he could have made the grade as a pitcher if he wanted to."

By the next year he was a bonafide star and the only black player on both the baseball and football teams. He had many friends and met with no prejudice. Academically, he stayed in the upper third of his class and was a very good student. Plus his athletic exploits were being noticed more and more. As a halfback on the unbeaten Cheltenham football team in 1962, he averaged about eight yards a carry and scored a slew of touchdowns. He was tough and showed the ability to play with and return from minor injuries.

The baseball team that spring had a 13-3 mark and won their league title. Reggie hit well over .300 and although there were no fences and the outfielders could play a mile deep, he hit about six long, rolling home runs. Before the year was out, there were some veteran baseball scouts nosing around the Cheltenham practice sessions.

At the end of his junior year Reggie was hit by a pitch during batting practice and he went down like a shot.

"I thought at first that it caught him in the temple," said Chuck Mehelich. "He wasn't wearing a helmet and I saw blood spurting from his mouth. I carried him to my car and rushed him to the hospital. The doctors found that his jaw was broken in three places.

"They wired it and sent him home. Well, I think the wire lasted about three days. He was right back in school and made speedy recovery. The amazing part is, that as soon as he began playing baseball again, he dug right in there. He wasn't gun-shy in the least."

This was the stuff pros were made of, and he showed it all over again as a senior. The scouts continued coming to the games and Reggie knew that the time for a decision was close at hand. Offers to turn pro weren't tempting, and the big money signings hadn't come in yet. But Reggie did have some forty-eight scholarship offers to play college football. Since he wasn't completely sold on a baseball career, he and his father agreed that by attending college, he might raise his market value in both sports.

Some of the schools that wanted him for football were Notre Dame, Penn State, Syracuse, and Michigan State. Quite an impressive list. But they didn't want him doubling in baseball. That's when Arizona State came along to say he could play both sports.

"That's what Reggie really wanted," said Chuck Mehelich. "He had a football scholarship with an eye to baseball. Arizona State played about 50 or 60 games a year, so he could really have a complete season. That's where he decided to go."

So in the autumn of 1964, Reggie packed his bags and left Philadelphia for the wide open spaces of Tempe, Arizona. He joined the freshman football team and was a starting halfback until a knee injury sidelined him for a few games. When he returned, they put him on defense. Before his injury, he carried 21 times for 161 yards and a 7.7 average. Now, that's running. Defensively, he was a hard-nosed tackler and good ballhawk.

He couldn't play baseball as a freshman, but he worked out with the varsity twice a week and there met baseball coach Bobby Winkles for the first time.

"I knew he was a great prospect right away," said Winkles. "You could see he had tremendous power, though off-speed pitches gave him trouble. We had Sal

Bando, Rick Monday and Duffy Dyer on the varsity then, but I had a hunch a couple of them might sign and leave after the season, so I really looked forward to getting Reggie full time next year."

Winkles was right. Both Bando and Monday signed with the Kansas City A's after the season and left school. Reggie returned in the fall, as a starting safety for the Sun Devil gridders, and then took over Monday's old spot in centerfield for the baseball team. Once the season started, it became obvious that Reggie was a college superstar. He was the power man in the Sun Devil attack, and his blazing speed on the basepaths and in the outfield began to impress the scouts once again.

By the time the 1966 season ended, Reggie had firmly established himself as one of the top major league prospects in the country. In fifty-two games, he had come to bat 202 times, banging out sixty-six hits for a .327 average. He also had nine doubles, six triples, and a school record of fifteen home runs, as well as 65 RBI's. His only negative statistic was sixty-two strikeouts, but that's to be expected from a young powerhitter.

"Reggie was admired and respected by all his teammates," Winkles recalls. "He was always ready to help his teammates, and he often lectured at junior high and high schools, telling kids to work hard and stick with it.

"He was also an intense competitor who sometimes got down on himself, but if you sat down and talked things out with him, man to man, that usually snapped him out of it."

At the end of the season Reggie learned he had been drafted by the A's, the team that had signed Bando and Monday. The ballclub offered him a bonus of $60,000 to sign, and when he hesitated, they raised the ante. When it reached $95,000, he said yes. Reggie was already a tough negotiator, and now he was a pro.

"I wasn't happy to lose a ballplayer and fine young man like Reggie," said Bobby Winkles. "But it was the best move for him and I advised him to sign."

Reggie left school in June of 1966 and was assigned to Lewiston, Idaho, a Class A team in the Rookie League. Twelve games later he was moved to Modesto, a Class A team in the California League. In fifty-six games there, he hit .299 with 21 homers among his 66 hits, driving in 60 runs. He was still a free swinger, striking out seventy-one times, but the A's loved his potential.

He was at Birmingham in the Southern League for the main part of the 1967 season, where he batted .293 with 17 homers and 58 RBIs. He also had the amazing total of seventeen triples, a further tribute to his speed and baserunning ability. Toward the end of the season he was brought up to Kansas City for his first shot at the Big Leagues. And just as he arrived in K.C., he learned he had been named Southern League Player of the Year.

So Reggie was in the majors at 21, and to be truthful about it, he was rather wild and undisciplined. He played in 35 games, batting a miniscule .178 and striking out 46 times in 118 times at bat. He had just one homer, six RBI's, and only one stolen base. Yet his potential must have shined through, because a club spokesman went so far as to say, "Yes, we expect Reggie to be the regular rightfielder next season."

Before the 1968 season began, it was learned that owner Charles O. Finley had received permission to move the team from Kansas City to Oakland, California. The team had finished last in 1967 with a 66-99 record, yet had some fine young players, including Sal Bando and Rick Monday, Reggie's old pals from Arizona State. And sure enough like the club spokesman said, Reggie had a good spring and was the A's starting rightfielder on opening day.

Reggie was the model of inconsistency in 1968. His raw talent produced some tremendous homers, some great catches, and some exciting baserunning, but there were also days of bad mistakes, including temper tantrums. So the fans cheered him one day and booed him the next.

"Reggie's just a kid trying to find himself," said Manager Bob Kennedy, attempting to explain the situation. "Just have patience with him. When he realizes just how good he can be, watch out. He's really gonna be something."

Though inconsistent, the A's stuck with him, and when the 1968 season ended he had a .250 batting average in 154 games, with 29 homers and 74 RBI's, good numbers for a raw rookie. But on the other hand, he struck out 171 times, coming within four whiffs of the then major league record. He made eighteen outfield errors, but had fourteen assists. So the talent was there.

Reggie came under a lot of criticism for his spotty playing and his ever-changing temperament. One day he seemed not to care, the next he'd explode. But, as usual, Reggie knew himself pretty well and talked about it.

"Let me tell you something, I care," he said. "But sometimes I tend to hold things back until I finally explode. I haven't made friends easily up here and I've found it difficult to confide in people. There are so many people telling me what to do that I just don't know who to listen to. I've just got to get a better grip on myself and I think it will happen as I get older."

Oakland improved its record to 82-80 in 1968, surprising everyone, and before the 1969 season, Reggie asked for a raise of $23,000. Finley offered him $18,000 and that's when Reggie's first holdout began.

Both parties made some mild threats (Reggie claiming he didn't need baseball and could do other things), but it wasn't long before he finally came to terms and settled for about $22,000. And as soon as the season began, it was apparant that he was earning his increase and much more. He began tearing the American League apart with his bat, and by June 1, he had sixteen homers and a slugging percentage of .713. He was *hitting a ton*, as they say, and the whole baseball world was taking notice.

By All-Star game time, Reggie had clubbed a fantastic 39 homers and was running some twenty-five or so games ahead of Babe Ruth's famous 60-home-run pace. There was already speculation that he'd finish with between 65-70 homers, and Reggie was loving every minute of his new-found success.

"No problem with a temper this year," he said. "But I must admit that it's a lot easier to live at the top than down at the bottom."

It was the first year of divisional play, and the surprising A's were challenging the Minnesota Twins for the American League West crown. So after starting in the All-Star Game, Reggie went back to the business of trying to help his team to a title. But shortly after the midseason All-Star break, the bubble burst. It had to.

American League pitchers were getting tired of craning their necks to watch Reggie's long home runs sail over distant fences. Before long, they were throwing him curveballs and nibbling around the corners, not worrying whether he walked or not. There wouldn't be any more three-homer, ten-RBI days, like he had against Boston during the first half of the year.

In fact, after belting thirty-nine homers through July, Reggie hit just eight more the rest of the way. It wasn't only the pitchers. He had lost the magic to a good, old-fashioned slump.

"I knew what the pitchers were doing," Reggie said. "But I'm a home run hitter and I have to swing big. I know I'll begin to hit more homers off curveballs, then I'll see the fastballs again. Most sluggers don't reach their peaks until they're about 30 anyway, so that gives me another six years or so to learn."

The A's finished the '69 season with an 88-74 mark, second to the Twins in the division, and no one could criticize the contribution made by Reggie Jackson. He ended up third in the league with 47 homers, scored 123 in runs and 24 intentional walks, had 36 doubles, three triples, 118 big runs batted in, and a solid batting average of .275. Plus he had cut his strikeouts down to 142. It was truly quite a year.

He even enjoyed his off-season as there were now demands for him at dinners, speaking engagements, and for personal appearances. He was also interested in real estate and land development in Tempe, Arizona, where he formerly went to college. So, at last, things really seemed to be coming together.

The start of another season brought negotiations once again with Charley Finley and problems arose. Reggie wanted $60,000 and Finley offered $40,000. So it soon became a heated battle and Reggie was a holdout for a second straight year. The bickering continued and it lingered, two, then four, then six weeks. Reggie was losing valuable training time and Finley kept telling him he wanted too much too soon.

"Maybe I'm asking too much," Reggie admitted, "but not when I see what some other guys are getting for lesser accomplishments. Unfortunately, I have no choice over what team has the rights to me and I can't move on. But if the A's can't afford to pay me, why don't they trade me to a team that can?" And Charlie Finley certainly wasn't about to trade a player like Reggie Jackson. The situation has certainly changed since today players can act as free agents and can make their own career decisions. Finally, as the holdout was into a seventh week, Reggie signed. The terms were a $47,000 base pay and a season-long rent on a $400-a-month apartment in Oakland.

"Sure, I felt like I'd given in," Reggie said. "But there was certainly an obligation on my part. I owed it to the guys to report and I wanted to play baseball. I just didn't have much time to get in shape."

And it showed. When the season opened, Reggie was seven weeks behind the other players. His timing was off and he didn't make much of an impression at the plate. He just wasn't producing and before long he was benched. Word had it that Finley ordered new manager John McNamara to take that step. Then Finley added:

"I can't really say Reggie's been helping the club. If he doesn't start hitting at least righthanders, he might have to go down to the minors to get it back."

It was a real low point for Reggie, maybe the lowest ever to that time. He was being used solely as a pinch runner and late-inning replacement, and he was growing bitter.

"I don't think I did anything wrong, except try to get the best possible contract for myself," he said. "I think I deserve another chance. Even the players are kidding me about being the game's only $50,000 pinch-runner. Maybe everyone expects too much from me. I'm just 24. Who do they think I should be, Henry Aaron?"

So Reggie remained on the bench. There were rumors of an impending trade, but Finley said no way. The young slugger now dreamed of playing elsewhere, and sometimes he dreamed about not playing at all.

"I don't want to give all this up," he told a reporter, "but the few years I've been in baseball are slowly breaking my spirit. A lot of the joy has gone out of the game for me. I should be on the threshold of my best years, but instead I find myself thinking of leaving the game."

Even then, Reggie's emotions were often up and down, and when he didn't feel wanted or appreciated, they were always down. Soon he began keeping quiet, waiting for a chance to get back in the line-up. His attitude had changed again.

"It's funny," he said, "the more the game's taken away from me, the more I want it."

Finally, in mid-June, he regained his starting job full-time, still working to break his slump, something he had to fight all year. The A's finished 1970 with an 89-73 mark, closer to the Twins, but still second best. And Reggie finished his poorest season with a .237 batting average, getting just 101 hits in 426 times up. The power department had fallen to 23 homers and 66 RBI's, about half of his production of a year earlier. He had to be optimistic now. The only way he could go was up.

That winter he played ball in Puerto Rico, for a team managed by Frank Robinson, one of the superstars of baseball. Robinson's guidance and encouragement bolstered Reggie tremendously, and when he returned to the A's for 1971, he was anxious to play ball and make up for lost time.

The A's had a new manager again, Dick Williams, who was a tough, no-nonsense field boss, and a new star pitcher, Vida Blue, a hard-throwing lefthander who had seen some action in 1970. Blue began blowing the ball past American League hitters with awesome frequency, having the kind of start Reggie had in 1969. His emergence took a lot of pressure off Jackson, since the media now came after Vida and not Reggie, allowing him to relax more, and slowly assume leadership of the hitters once again.

By All-Star time, Blue had a 17-3 record and was the talk of baseball. Reggie had a solid .272 average, with 17 homers and 40 RBI's. So he was quietly getting the job done. But his mammoth All-Star homer at Tiger Stadium caused him to make the headlines once again.

Blue tailed off the second half, somewhat as Reggie had done in '69, but still finished at 24-8 and helped the A's to their first American League West crown with a 101-60 mark. What Reggie found in '71 was consistency. He finished at .277 with 32 home runs and 80 runs batted in, his second half just about equal with the first. And he also impressed his new manager.

"I found Reggie Jackson to be a hustling fool," said Williams. "I was also impressed by his leadership ability. He never gives up and the other guys respect and follow him. The fans still expect too much from him, but he didn't get down at all during the season. In addition, he's maturing as a hitter, learning to go with the pitch, protect the plate with two strikes, and handling the off-speed stuff. He wants to learn everything he can about the entire game."

The A's met the Baltimore Orioles in the playoffs that year and found themselves outclassed by a strong veteran team. They were beaten three straight, despite a pair of homers and a .333 average by Reggie. Still, the A's had good reason to look forward to 1972. They were building a fine, all-around team, with a balance of pitching and hitting.

The 1971 season was an important one for Reggie. He

quietly re-established himself as a player of the first rank. And, as one Oakland newsman put it:

"Reggie didn't have the real big numbers, but he did the little things that characterize an outstanding ballplayer. Vida Blue got most of the attention, but Reggie did as much to help the team. He's the man they look up to now."

Dick Williams told people that Reggie was never too busy to help young players, even rookies who didn't have much chance to make the team.

"Maybe it was some of the experiences he had before I got here," said Williams, "but he has more humility than any superstar I ever met. He knows he's not the only one of the team. Yet he loves playing the game and he wants to be the best at what he does. The result of that is he makes all those around him go harder."

The more reporters talked to Reggie, the more they began to see his sensitivity, and the complex nature of his character. He was certainly more than a one-dimensional ballplayer. For instance, someone asked him about having a white roommate, pitcher Chuck Dobson.

"Prejudice has eaten me alive," Reggie said. "Because of my background and my prominence as an athlete, I haven't really been exposed to it. But what has been directed to me and what I have seen has moved me to tears."

And when talking about himself and his actions, Reggie said: "There have been some things I've said and done that I wish I could take back. I'm basically a thin-skinned person and afraid of being hurt. And I was always a loner. Now I think I pop off sometimes to keep people from getting too close to me. I've often hurt the feelings of people who mean quite a lot to me."

It's not often that a top player, or any person for that matter, is as painfully honest about himself, especially in the public forum. But Reggie was, and in 1972 he saw Vida Blue going through the same thing he did in 1970. Coming off a super year, Vida and owner Finley could not agree on a contract and Blue held out.

Fortunately, the A's picked up Ken Holtzman to join Catfish Hunter in the rotation, and despite the fact that Blue never did find himself and finished at 6-10, the team won another divisional crown with a 93-62 record. Reggie missed a number of games to injury and wound up batting .265 in 135 games, with 25 homers and 75 RBIs. But manager Williams still thought very highly of his young star.

"As far as I'm concerned," he said, "Reggie Jackson had a superstar year. He lost playing time to illness and injury and no one steps right back into that good groove. But he was a complete player this year. When we had problems in centerfield (the team had traded Rick Monday), Reggie volunteered to go out there and he did an outstanding job."

The A's were quickly becoming a unique team. At a time when facial hair was still frowned upon in baseball, many members of the team began growing mustaches. Finally, they all did, including manager Williams, and they gave their sport a rather new look. That, and Finley's green-and-gold uniforms certainly put the club in the limelight.

So did their ability on the field. They had to meet Detroit in the playoffs that year, and won the first two games, 3-2, and 5-0, before losing the third, 3-0. The Tigers then won the fourth in 10 innings, so there was one game left to determine the American League pennant. Blue Moon Odom started game five for the A's against Woody Fryman of the Tigers.

In the second inning, Reggie walked, stole second, went to third on a fly to right, and surprised everyone at Tiger Stadium by stealing home. It was daring, exciting baseball and it gave the A's a crucial lead. The Oakland dugout erupted in cheers, then stopped suddenly. Reggie was on the ground and not getting up. He was holding the back of his left leg.

He was helped off the field, and without him, the A's went on to win, 2-1, giving the club its first American

League championship. In a strange bit of irony, that wouldn't come full cycle for a number of years yet, Reggie made his way on crutches to the Detroit dressing room to congratulate the losers and their manager, Billy Martin.

"You're one heck of a guy," Martin is reported to have said. "Believe me, I don't like playing against you. You really showed me a lot of class. I like guys like you."

When Reggie went to the hospital he learned the bad news. He had a badly torn hamstring muscle and would definitely miss the World Series.

"I changed my slide just before I hit Freehan (the Detroit catcher)," Reggie said. "It felt like someone reached inside my leg and just pulled everything apart. When I got to the clubhouse, I just started to cry. It's a rotten feeling to work your butt off all year and then have this happen. But I've got to accept it. I'm hurt and I can't help the team in the Series."

Because Reggie felt so badly about not playing in the Series, Manager Williams and the rest of the A's asked him to sit on the bench, in civilian clothes, the first time an injured player has done that. He was introduced with the rest of the team and before the final game took the line-up card to the plate. It was the least they could do to show him how they felt.

In the Series, the A's were underdogs to the Cincinnati Reds. But the A's pulled together, and in a hard-fought series, won it in seven games. Oakland fans who had come to Cincy for the finale went wild, and national TV cameras caught Charley Finley hugging and kissing his wife atop the A's dugout, and he was soon joined by Dick Williams and his wife.

But those with sharp eyes caught another small drama being played out at home plate. The injured Reggie Jackson had come out on his crutches and was talking to the Reds' outstanding catcher, Johnny Bench, at home plate. The two young superstars were good friends, and they spoke quietly, arms around each other's shoulders.

The wounded gladiator and the losing gladiator, consoling each other and maybe planning an off-season get-together.

In a way, it was a very touching scene. The two young men, each about twenty-five years of age, one expected to be jubilant in victory, the other despondent in defeat. Yet they spoke quietly, almost detached from the bedlam around them. Both are fierce competitors, both have the drive and desire to go all out and play their hardest, every day. But both also have acquired the maturity to put their sport in perspective. Human communication was more important to them than uncontrolled emotion.

Reggie was relaxed in the off-season, though he still regretted having missed the Series and wanted to be back there in '73. He also said he wanted to be the A's first $100,000 player, but with Charley Finley, that might not be so easy. The big thing for him was producing. Though he was considered by many to be a superstar, he still wanted to bring his numbers back to the level of 1969.

Though Reggie's moods and emotions sometimes seemed to change from day to day, one local writer who had known the slugger since the beginning, said this about him before the 1973 season started:

"Reggie has become very much more cooperative with newsmen, even those he doesn't particularly like. He's very intelligent and doesn't shy away from talk outside of the baseball world. In fact, one of his favorite expressions is that he likes to have his mind 'stretched.' I find him affable and eager to please, a much more settled person than he was five years ago.

"But in a sense he's worked to subdue his temperament, alter his public personality to please Mr. Finley. I think it has cost him some of his spark. There's often an unnatural calm about, a suppression of feelings which some people define as maturity."

It was an interesting analysis. First of all, it showed that Reggie was much more than an ordinary, run-of-the-mill jock. And secondly, it hinted at the inevitable . . . that the rocky marriage between Reggie and Charles O. Finley probably couldn't go on forever.

The team got off to a terrible start in '73. By the first week in June, the A's were just 23-21 and tied for fourth place in the division, and just some four games from the top. It was a horserace. Williams began shuffling his players, giving leftfielder Joe Rudi a "rest," then giving Reggie a rest, and invariably, the "rested" player began griping. As Reggie said:

"Rest! Why should I need a rest. I'm 27, not 37, and I'm not tired. I'm hitting .285 and driving in runs. How can he (Williams) say I need a rest?"

No one was happy with the way the team was performing. Reggie, of course, wasn't out of the line-up for long, and when he returned he began hitting very well. By the first of July even though the club was just 37-32, none of the other teams could pull away and the A's were right in there. Shortly after, the A's began winning and by mid-August it was obvious that Reggie was finally having the year everyone hoped for. Oakland was battling Kansas City for the top spot in the division and Reggie was battling K.C.'s John Mayberry for the home run and RBI lead in the American League.

The team was getting outstanding pitching from its big three of Blue, Hunter, and Holtzman, all headed for 20-win seasons, and in the last week of August they moved into first place for good. At the same time, Reggie belted his 30th homer and eased past the 100-RBI mark. He seemed to be en route to a really big year. Then in mid-September, lady luck turned her face away once again. Reggie pulled the same hamstring that had shelved him the year before. It wasn't as severe an injury, but Manager Williams didn't want to lose his star for the playoffs. So he kept Reggie on the bench most of the remaining weeks.

A short time later, the A's wrapped up their third straight divisional title. And when the season ended, Reggie had turned in his best season since 1969. Despite missing time at the end, Reggie had 158 hits in 539 trips for a .293 average. He scored 99 runs, had 28 doubles, two triples, 32 homers and 117 runs batted in. Third baseman Bando, catcher Gene Tenace, and designated hitter Deron Johnson all had fine power years as well.

In the playoffs, the A's beat the Orioles in five tough games, Hunter pitching a 3-0 shutout in the finale. Reggie's bat was strangely silent in the five games. He had just three singles in 21 at bats for an anemic .143 average. Hopefully, he would fare better when the A's met the underdog New York Mets, who had surprised the Reds in the playoffs on the strength of their great pitching.

With centerfielder Bill North out, Reggie opened the series in North's position as Ken Holtzman faced Jon Matlack of the Mets. It was a close game all the way, the A's leading 2-1 in the fourth when Reggie made a spectacular catch in deep center, backhanding the ball and saving a run. Holtzman hung on and the A's took the opener.

The Mets got even in game two, winning a loose contest, 10-7, in 12 innings. There was more controversy when the A's journeyman infielder Mike Andrews made two straight errors, in effect, costing the A's the game. When it was over, Charlie Finley decided to punish Andrews by railroading him off the team with a fake shoulder injury. The infielder was placed on the disabled list and the rest of the team rebelled.

They traveled to New York and showed up at their first practice with Andrews' number 17 taped to all their uniforms, and threatened to boycott the series. Manager Williams backed his players and the battle lines were drawn. The press had a field day as the battling A's were at it again.

"I'm a man divided," Reggie told reporters. "Half of me is concentrating on the Andrews business, the other half on the ballgame. But we'll be ready. Nothing that happens on this team surprises anyone."

Finally, it was Finley who backed down. He made a

personal call to Andrews and asked him to rejoin the team. Then the A's went out and won game three in 11 innings, 3-2. Reggie had a bad day, as Mets ace Tom Seaver fanned him three times.

"He was beating me all night," said the honest Jackson. "I thought I'd see more fastballs, but he threw me a lot of curves, good curves. He's a super pitcher."

In the fourth game, the Mets' Rusty Staub drove in five runs and Matlack pitched the New Yorkers to a 6-1 victory. The Series was tied once more. Then the Mets forged ahead on a three-hit shutout by Jerry Koosman and Tug McGraw, winning 2-0, as Reggie went hitless again. Now it was back to Oakland and the A's had their backs against the wall.

It was Hunter and Seaver in game six and this time Reggie finally asserted himself. He doubled home Rudi in the first and Bando in the third. His third hit came in the eighth and he wound up scoring the insurance run in a 3-1 victory. It was now down to a seventh game, Ken Holtzman facing Jon Matlack for a third time.

In the Mets' second, Reggie made another great catch, a shoestring grab of a Jerry Grote liner. Then in the A's third, shortstop Bert Campaneris slammed a two-run homer to give Oakland the lead. Rudi followed with a single and up came Reggie. He timed a Matlack fastball and hit a long, majestic drive deep into the right centerfield seats for another round-tripper. The A's suddenly had established a 4-0 lead. But Reggie wasn't through yet. He made another great catch after shifting over to right, then watched as his team closed out another championship with a 5-2 victory. Here's how one columnist described Reggie's enjoyment of the victory:

"For the rest of the afternoon Reggie Jackson basked in the glory that was his in his own fashion. He slipped two baseballs to his fans. He doffed his cap and cheered them as they cheered him. When they streamed on the field prematurely, he tackled a kid who lifted his cap and ran down a girl who picked up his glove. When they engulfed him as the game ended, he lingered among them as though he was one of them until a burly friend escorted him off."

After missing the '72 Series, this was his finest hour, and it was compounded for him when he was chosen the Series Most Valuable Player. At that time it was also revealed that he had played the Series under a death threat which police felt was very serious. That made for more pressure.

Yet Reggie wasn't through yet. A few weeks later he learned that he had unanimously been chosen as the Most Valuable Player in the American League for 1973. He summed up his feelings about the Series and the whole season in his usual candid manner.

"One reason I was glad I could lead in the Series was that I need approval," he said. "If we lost and I was hitless I'd still be able to do the same things. But because we won and I did well, more people are going to admire and love me, and I'll admit that makes me glad."

Reggie had batted .310 in the Series with nine hits, a homer, and six RBIs. Then came the league MVP prize.

"This is the icing on the cake," he said, smiling, "a culmination of things that make it my most exciting moment. I've been on a team that won the world's championship two years in a row, then was named the most valuable in the series, and now this. It's a hard act to follow.

"But there are still other things. I haven't hit .300 yet, haven't hit fifty homers in a season and haven't swiped forty bases. So there is a lot to be done and until I do them I feel I'll be shortchanging myself, the fans, the owners, the team, and everyone else. In other words, I want to be the best."

So Reggie was coming off an MVP season, and despite the problems with owner Finley and the usual grumblings among his teammates, he came away from 1973 on a very high note. By continuing to pursue even higher goals, he gave every indication that his problems were behind him and he was about to attain the kind of consistency that would mark him as a true superstar.

But, of course, there couldn't be peace in Oakland for long. The 1974 season was marked by the revolt of Catfish Hunter. The star righthander claimed that Finley was not honoring all the terms of his contract and he finally decided to sue the owner, claiming breach of contract and asking to be declared a free agent. The pending lawsuit dragged on, yet during the season, the redoubtable Hunter continued to be about the best pitcher in the American League.

There were the other usual grumblings, mainly by various players claiming to be underpaid, and though the team didn't overpower the opposition as it had the past two seasons, they were still the best of the Western Division. Reggie was en route to another good, but not great season. By All-Star Game time, he was the top vote getter in the entire league and the starting rightfielder once again.

Despite their bickering, the A's nevertheless beat back any challengers and won the divisional crown for the fourth year in a row, though they did it with just 88 victories on the season. Hunter led the pitchers with a 25-12 record and would win the Cy Young Award, despite his suit against Finley. Lefthander Holtzman won 19.

As for Reggie, he wound up with a .286 average in 148 games, collecting 146 hits, 29 homers and 93 RBIs. So his production was down from the MVP season of 1973, and because he had set his goals so high, Reggie was disappointed with it. In addition, there was increasing dissatisfaction with conditions on the club and a number of the star players were talking about leaving Oakland. People began wondering just how long Finley could hold his championship club together.

In the playoffs that year, the A's met the Baltimore Orioles and showed once again that they were the best when the chips are down. They disposed of the Orioles in four games, Reggie hitting a dismal .167 in the championship series. But now the club was headed for the World Series once again, and this time they would be bidding to become the first team to take three straight Series since the New York Yankees won five straight from 1949 to 1953.

But it wouldn't be easy. This time the A's would be meeting the Los Angeles Dodgers, a team that really put it together in '74, winning 104 games during the regular season and then whipping the hard-hitting Pittsburgh Pirates, three games to one in the playoffs.

Veteran manager Walt Alston would be fielding a well-balanced and potent ballclub. He had a twenty-game winner in Andy Messersmith and a nineteen-gamer in Don Sutton. They were backed by relief ace Mike Marshall, who set an incredible major league record by appearing in 106 games during the regular season, and who would win the Cy Young Award for his efforts, the first reliever to achieve that distinction.

The hitters were led by Steve Garvey, who hit .312 with 111 RBIs for the year. He was backed by power-hitting Jimmy Wynn, Bill Buckner, Ron Cey, Davey Lopes, and Bill Russell. Despite the fact that the A's had taken two straight world titles, the Dodgers were favorites to win it all in '74. After all, the A's were staying right in character. Right before game one, there was a big clubhouse brawl between pitchers Rollie Fingers and Blue Moon Odom. But then again, when the A's fight, they usually also win.

Game one was in Los Angeles, and Ken Holtzman faced Andy Messersmith. Reggie had not come into the Series in top shape. He was hampered by another hamstring pull, but insisted on playing. In the first inning of the first game, he picked out a Messersmith fastball and stroked a home run to the opposite field, giving the A's a one-run lead and setting the tempo for what was to follow.

Oakland got a second run in the fifth when shortstop Campaneris squeezed Holtzman home on a perfect bunt. A Dodger run in the bottom of the inning closed the gap to 2-1, but the A's made it 3-1 in the eighth, the run coming home on a throwing error by third baseman

Cey. A Wynn homer in the ninth made it 3-2, and when the Dodgers got another runner on base, Catfish Hunter was summoned from the bullpen in a surprise move. The Cat fanned Joe Ferguson to end the game and the A's had a 1-0 lead.

Game two was just the reverse, Don Sutton pitching the Dodgers to a 3-2 victory to tie the Series. The teams traveled up the "freeway" to Oakland, for game three, Catfish facing the Dodgers' Al Downing. Once again it was a close game. Several defensive lapses by the Dodgers allowed the A's to take another 3-2 victory, giving them a one-game advantage once more.

It was Holtzman and Messersmith again in game four. The Oakland lefty helped his own cause with a homer, but the Dodgers came back to take a 2-1 lead. In the sixth the A's pushed across four big runs and Holtzman held on to record a 5-2 victory, giving his club a commanding 3-1 lead in the Series. The big difference between the teams at this point was that the A's were performing brilliantly in the field, while the Dodgers were shaky. Oakland second baseman Dick Green was especially outstanding, making several incredible plays to snuff out Dodger rallies.

Game five saw Vida Blue take the mound for the first time against the Dodgers Don Sutton. The A's wanted to win it in front of their home fans. A sacrifice fly by Sal Bando gave Oakland a 1-0 lead in the first inning, and a Ray Fosse homer extended it to 2-0 in the second. But the Dodgers refused to quit and a single by Steve Garvey drove in the tying run in the sixth. Joe Rudi came right back, hitting a solo shot off Mike Marshall in the A's seventh. Relief ace Rollie Fingers then shut the Dodgers down in the eighth and ninth, making the A's world champions for the third straight year.

Reggie did not have a real good Series. His homer in the first inning of the first game was to be his only RBI, and he wound up with just four hits in fourteen at bats for a .286 average. He did walk five times, showing the respect the Dodger pitchers had for his always potentially potent bat. And with the team winning for a third time in three years, Reggie was satisfied.

Though the A's were now being proclaimed as one of the great teams of the past quarter-century, there were signs that the club just could not stay together much longer. Most of the top stars were unhappy with the salaries they were getting from owner Finley. And despite three straight world titles, the club's attendance record was quite low. In fact, it was a standing joke around Oakland that the reason the team won was simple. The players all had a rallying point, a common bond, and that was their intense dislike of Charles O. Finley. As Reggie was to say a short time later:

"I find it hard to believe some of the things we had to put up with under Finley. But I'll say this; he's the most strong-willed person I've ever known. Even if he loses all of us, he'll probably still land on his feet."

It didn't take long for the dissatisfied players to leave. To everyone's surprise, Catfish Hunter won his lawsuit against Finley and was declared a free agent. Before the 1975 season started, the Cat signed a huge, multi-year deal with the New York Yankees, making him an instant millionaire and causing all his ex-teammates to drool with envy. Now the rest of them saw that life without Finley could be quite lucrative, and many of them would soon follow the same route as Hunter.

Even without the Cat, the A's were still good enough to top the rest of the west in '75, though the Kansas City Royals made a strong run at them. Reggie had a strange year. While taking pot-shots at the owner all season long, he nevertheless stayed healthy and played 157 games, the most of his career. And while hitting with tremendous power, his batting average fell. In the end he hit just .253, but tied for the A.L. lead in homers with 36 and drove home 104 runs, as the A's took their fifth consecutive Western Division crown.

But too much had happened for the club to rally for another big effort. In the playoffs, they were routed by the Boston Red Sox in three straight games, despite a five for twelve effort by Reggie, including a homer and three RBIs and a .417 average. The dominance of the A's was over.

That winter, there was a historic decision that would change the entire face of baseball and eventually push Reggie Jackson into the limelight of the entire sports world. Dodger pitcher Andy Messersmith took baseball to court, claiming a player should be allowed to become a free agent under certain circumstances and not be bound to a team for life unless that team decides to move him. Messersmith won, and the baseball powers set about changing the system, allowing veteran players to become free agents after playing out the options on their current contracts.

The free agent draft would begin before the 1977 season, enabling a number of teams to choose the self-proclaimed free agents, who would then be allowed to negotiate with each team and sign the best offer. It would prove to be a veritable gold mine in the coming years, not only for the top stars, but for the average ballplayer as well.

This had to be on Reggie Jackson's mind as he reported to spring training for the 1976 season. After all, for years he had dreamed about getting away from Finley. Suddenly that dream was possible. He could play out his option and become a free agent for the 1977 season. But for whatever faults Charley Finley had as an owner, he was certainly no fool. He could see the handwriting on the wall and he wasn't about to lose star players through the new ruling without getting something in return. So on April 2, just before the start of the season, he made a shocking move. He traded Reggie Jackson and Ken Holtzman to the Baltimore Orioles for Don Baylor, Mike Torrez, and Paul Mitchell.

Reggie was totally stunned by the sudden deal, especially with it coming practically on the eve of a new season. By this time, his salary at Oakland had risen to about the $140,000 bracket, but in view of the prospect of free agency, that wasn't much. He was really confused, and his first reaction was not to report to the Orioles, a fine team led by the fiery manager Earl Weaver. He asked the Orioles for a rather large, multi-year contract, but when they refused, he became a holdout.

So the Orioles opened the season without Reggie, as he pondered his baseball future. His holdout didn't endear him to the Baltimore fans, who were initially pleased to know that the powerful slugger was headed to their town. What they didn't realize was how complex an individual Reggie had become. He was considering many more factors than just coming to the ballpark every day. When faced with changing his address, he just couldn't see leaving the West Coast, where he felt comfortable among friends and business associates, and a place conducive to his lifestyle.

Finally, Reggie made his decision. He would report to the Orioles and play for them in 1976. But he would remain under his old contract with the A's, putting him in his option year and making him eligible for free agency in 1977. Of course, the Orioles sweetened the pot by raising his salary for the one year without affecting his option. And, on May 2, 1976, Reggie Jackson played his first major league baseball game in a uniform other than that of the Oakland A's.

Reggie admitted that he had taken a gamble. The late start could mean a poor season, and a poor season would greatly diminish his value on the free agent market. When he did, indeed, get off to a poor start, it was not greeted with much enthusiasm by the fans, or some of his new teammates. This made it quite a very uncomfortable situation for him.

"I had an uneasy feeling every time I walked into the clubhouse," he admitted. "I felt like a stranger, that I was playing on the road for the whole season. My teammates were saying things about me that I didn't like and the fans were really booing me. I remember hitting a grand slam one day and I was booed the very next time at bat. Early on I was pressing at the plate and there's no way you can get into a groove when you're doing that."

By the All-Star break, Reggie was hitting just .242 and showing only flashes of his awesome power. Needless to say, it was the first year he had failed to be included on the All-Star Team since 1970. A fire in his condominium in Oakland, just before the All-Star break, caused a considerable amount of damage. Most of his wardrobe was destroyed and some treasured World Series mementos from his days with the A's were lost. As Reggie himself admitted:

"The fire really kicked h--- out of me mentally for about three weeks."

All these factors—the fans, teammates, the fire, the slow start—would have made it easy for Reggie to quit, to go through the motions and write the season off as a lost cause. And there was the added pressure of impending free agency.

"Suppose I never came out of it," Reggie said. "Suppose August rolled around and I was hitting down around .200. Then the holdout and everything else might cost me a cool million."

But it wasn't only the money. Reggie has another quality, one that all the great ones seem to possess in abundance—an excess of pride. Reggie Jackson simply knew he was more than a .240 hitter. Shortly after the All-Star break he began to come to life. In the next month he practically carried the club into contention, as the O's began challenging the New York Yankees and Boston Red Sox for the top spot in the American League East.

From the break through the month of August, Reggie hit over .300, belted 13 home runs, and drove home 39 runs. He was finally showing the fans of Baltimore and his Oriole teammates what the real Reggie Jackson could do. His spurt gave him 22 homers and 78 RBIs for the year, putting him back among the league leaders in those all-important categories. He was also putting people in the stands. One analyst noted that Oriole attendance was up some 67,000 over the previous season, while crowds in Oakland had diminished by some

300,000 from a year earlier.

And now that Reggie had turned his season around, more and more talk centered around his upcoming free agency. It was almost a foregone conclusion that he would not be remaining in Baltimore, for a number of reasons. One of them was touched on by Oriole catcher Dave Duncan, a good friend and former teammate of Reggie's at Oakland.

"Baltimore is a very conservative town," Duncan said. "Anytime you're traded there's an adjustment to be made, but for Reggie, Baltimore was a particularly tough adjustment because it just isn't the type of town Reggie is used to."

Reggie himself agreed that where he played was as important to him as the size of his contract.

"Suppose that one team offers me, say, $1.7 million and another team $2 million," he said, "but the team that made the higher offer is in Georgia and the lower offer came from a team in my own backyard, say, San Francisco. Well, in that case I'd probably want to play in my backyard. Let's face it, a couple of hundred thousand dollars isn't gonna make much difference when you're talking about those kinds of figures. What it amounts to is that I'll soon be an overpaid athlete. I'll probably get a million more than I should, but I didn't make the rules. I'm just taking advantage of them."

As usual, Reggie was being totally candid in discussing his situation. He might be a controversial figure to some, but he'll always say what's on his mind. And he continued to give his opinions about his upcoming entry into the free agent market.

"I also want to go to a place with a liberal attitude," he said. "I don't like sectarian living, where certain people live among themselves—Jews here, Poles there, blacks over there. I'm not interested in playing in a town that has that. I'm not crazy about playing in the South, and the Midwest would be impractical because all my business interests are either on the West Coast or in the East."

What Reggie was doing, in effect, was telling certain teams not to bother drafting him, because he wouldn't even consider their offers. He seemed to know just what he wanted, and he narrowed it down even further when he said:

"I'm not sure I'd fit in with teams like the Mets or the Dodgers that emphasize organization over individual personality. Who knows, they may not even want a guy like me. But I can see myself with a team like the Phillies, because with all their stars—the Schmidts and Luzinskis—there wouldn't be so much pressure on me. I'd also like to be on a contender and a team that draws well. Even with three World Series wins in Oakland, we never really drew that well.

"I also like getting involved in a community, doing youth work. I've taken so much out of this game that it often weighs on my mind. Therefore, I'd like to give something back to the town in which I'm playing. I would like nothing better than to settle down and really be part of things."

That kind of straight talk probably angered some fans, who wondered where a ballplayer comes off saying where he will and will not play. But free agency had created a whole new way of looking at things. For the first time in the long history of the game, a player *did* have a say in where he would play, and as Reggie admitted, he didn't makes the rules, but he was willing to take advantage of them. And since he would be the first big name everyday player on the free agent market, he was creating a lot of stir.

The second half of the 1976 season was vintage Reggie. He had re-emerged as one of the top sluggers in the league, and although it became obvious that the Orioles wouldn't catch the Yankees and Red Sox, who were battling for the top spot, Reggie's surge made his team more competitive.

"If we had Reggie going full steam all season," said Manager Weaver, "there's no question in my mind that we'd be five games closer to the top."

In the final weeks of the season, the Orioles surged past the fading Red Sox into second place, but the rejuvenated New York Yankees had it all but wrapped up. The Bronx Bombers, baseball's dominant team from the 1920s into the 1960s, took their first title since 1964, finishing with a 97-62 record. The O's finished second at 88-74, some 10½ games off the pace.

As for Reggie, he wound up playing in 134 games and batting .277, with 27 home runs and 91 RBIs. Projected over a full season, without the holdout and the resultant slow start, it had to be considered an outstanding year, ranking with his best. So he was in an excellent position for the upcoming free agent draft.

Though a number of teams picked Reggie, it seemed to many that the handwriting was already on the wall. Reggie had once remarked half jokingly, that if he ever played in New York they would name a candy bar after him. At the time, Reggie never thought there was even a remote chance of him playing in the Big Apple nor that the candy bar idea would become a reality. But times had changed.

The New York Yankees had been baseball's glamour team since the 1920s, when sluggers Babe Ruth and Lou Gehrig spearheaded a wrecking crew known as "Murderers' Row." When Ruth left, Gehrig continued and was joined by Joe DiMaggio, as well as a group of slightly lesser stars in the '30s and 40s. Then in the 1950's along came Mickey Mangle, and later Roger Maris, as the team continued to win pennant after pennant and World Series after World Series. They took four straight from 1936 to '39, and five straight from 1949 to 1953. They won another five straight pennants from 1960 to '64, giving them 29 pennants and 20 World Series wins from 1921 through 1964.

But then, suddenly, the team collapsed, and for the first time since the days of the Babe, replacements for aging stars were not waiting in the wings. The team plummeted to sixth in 1965 and tenth the following year. Then began the long struggle to return the club to respectability. In 1973, a group of businessmen, headed by Cleveland shipping magnate George Steinbrenner, purchased the Yankees from CBS. Steinbrenner's first comment was, "We plan absent ownership. I'll stick to shipbuilding." But his promise was not kept. Steinbrenner soon became obsessed with returning the Yankees to their former lofty status, and he quickly became one of the most active owners in the league.

With the farm system weakened, Steinbrenner looked elsewhere for players, and soon began opening his wallet and making trades, acquiring veteran ballplayers and beginning with Catfish Hunter in 1975, obtaining free agents. And, looking for the right formula to get his club back in the hunt, he also began changing managers. Veteran Yankee skipper Ralph Houk was still in harness when Steinbrenner took over the club. But the team was going nowhere, and Houk resigned after the 1973 season. Steinbrenner then signed Dick Williams, who had just managed Reggie and the Oakland A's to a second world's championship. But Finley wouldn't let Williams out of his contract, and Steinbrenner turned to Bill Virdon, who had recently managed the Pittsburgh Pirates.

Virdon stayed at the helm until August of 1975, when he was fired, to be replaced by Billy Martin, a fiery competitor who was the Yankee second baseman in the early 1950s. Martin had managed at Detroit, Minnesota, and Texas, always getting the maximum out of his players, but also running into trouble with the front office and winding up on the block. Now he was coming back to New York, the only managerial job he says he ever really wanted.

The question was whether the combative, strong-willed Martin could survive with the equally strong-willed Steinbrenner. But it looked good when Billy the Kid brought the team home with an 83-77 record in '75, and then piloted them to their first pennant in twelve years the following season. The Yanks lost the World Series to the powerful Cincinnati Reds that year in four straight, but the team was headed in the right direction.

That's when Steinbrenner decided to pursue Reggie Jackson.

Even without Reggie, the Yanks had a fine incumbent ballclub. The 1976 pennant club featured pitchers Catfish Hunter, Ed Figueroa, Dock Ellis, and Sparky Lyle. Catcher Thurman Munson was the team leader and an acknowledged superstar. Infielders Chris Chambliss, Graig Nettles, and Willie Randolph were all outstanding, while centerfielder Mickey Rivers was a real catalyst for the offense and had ample support from Lou Piniella and Roy White.

Even a lineup like that wasn't enough for owner Steinbrenner. He decided to go after the free agents. He signed lefthanded fastballer Don Gullett, who had won the first game of the '76 Series against the Yanks for the Cincinnati Reds. Gullett was a youngster of vast potential, but also had a series of past injuries. The Yanks were hoping.

Next, Steinbrenner wanted Reggie Jackson. Word had it that Manager Martin didn't want Reggie, his feeling being that Jackson wasn't his kind of ballplayer. But the owner had the last word and just weeks after the Series ended, Reggie signed a huge, five-year pact with the Yanks, estimated to be worth some $2.9 million, which at that time made him the highest paid player in the game.

Naturally, there was a big press conference with all the trappings of a Hollywood extravaganza. Reggie was delighted to be in New York and with the Yankees. He knew he was on the spot and would have to produce. But having experienced performing under pressure all his life, he wasn't worried now. Yet he had no idea what a pressure-cooker playing for the Yanks would be. Before the season was over, Reggie's character and his ability to persevere would be tested as never before. Some of the problems would be of his own making.

Reggie hit New York with a great deal of hoopla. It wasn't long after his signing that a candy manufacturer, remembering his statement earlier about a candy being named after him if he ever played in New York, made a deal in which his name was used, and the "Reggie Bar" was born. It was a great gimmick for both Reggie and the manufacturer, and things seemed to be going his way. The press and media wanted him, his refreshing personality, intelligence, and candor making him a much sought after interview. This same personality combined with his good looks also began getting him offers of endorsements and commercials. So it soon seemed that the marriage between Reggie and the Yanks was going to work out.

But the problems began again as soon as he hit training camp. Many of the established Yankees resented him, probably due somewhat to his huge contract, and all the excitement he was causing. Many treated him rather coolly and Reggie had a big job ahead of him, mainly to prove that he was the kind of player the media made him out to be. Many waited to see how Reggie and catcher Thurman Munson would get along. Munson was the Yankee leader and a tremendous competitor. He also had the reputation of being surly and not always the friendliest of sorts. It was very important for clubhouse harmony, that a homogeneous relationship be established between the two.

There was a definite coolness between the two players during spring training, but, as the season neared, they seemed to be getting on a lot better. The Yanks had made some other acquisitions by then, picking up shortstop Bucky Dent from the White Sox, veteran outfielder Paul Blair, and shortly after the season opened, pitcher Mike Torrez. Things hopefully began to fall into place.

As it turns out, there were already problems between owner Steinbrenner and Manager Martin involving some of the late player moves, which apparently Steinbrenner was making without Martin's blessing. Early in the regular season, some claimed that Martin was using Reggie to get back at Steinbrenner.

It began because Steinbrenner felt Reggie should bat fourth, the traditional clean-up spot. Martin responded by moving Reggie around in the batting order, everywhere but fourth, and the result was that Reggie wasn't hitting. The team was off to a slow start and Reggie was beginning to struggle in the field.

In mid-April, Reggie's elbow began bothering him. The team was in Milwaukee and Reggie told reporters he could play, at least as the designated hitter. But Martin took the opportunity to bench him, and the consensus of some was that he did it to show Steinbrenner who was running the team on the field. Reggie found himself in the middle of a seemingly difficult situation.

"I don't know why I'm not playing," Reggie told the press, after the official Yankee line was that his elbow was bad. "I could play." When asked if he was upset, Reggie replied, "No comment. I'm going along with the program."

The Martin-Steinbrenner confrontation definitely caused a split among the players. As one Yankee said, preferring to remain anonymous, "The Man (Steinbrenner) better stay off his (Martin's) back. One thing Billy has going for him is that he has more players on his side than the owner has."

Reggie may not have been one of those players. After all, it was Steinbrenner who gave him the big contract and brought him to New York. So the manager-owner conflict did not help his situation. Shortly afterward, there arose another crisis. In a story published early in the season and written during spring training with *Sport* magazine, Reggie apparently had said he thought Thurman Munson was jealous of him. He also made a statement that would haunt him all year.

"I'm the straw that stirs the drink," the magazine article quoted him as saying. "It all comes back to me. Maybe I should say me and Munson, but really he doesn't enter into it. . . Munson thinks he can be the straw that stirs the drink, but he can only stir it bad."

Naturally, when the magazine hit the stands, it didn't go over too well with Munson. The team's two best hitters and leaders were feuding. Reggie was later to say it was a definite mistake and the worst thing that happened to him all year. What made him say such a thing is still a mystery. Perhaps it has to do with the fragile egos that drive so many superstar athletes. But it really put the ice into the Yankee clubhouse. Backup catcher Fran Healy, who was to become Reggie's closest friend on the club, remembers Munson parading around the clubhouse, the magazine in his hand, exclaiming:

"Can you believe this? Can you believe this?"

The situation continued to worsen. How could the team expect to win games if its two best players weren't even talking? To make matters worse, Reggie's hitting was affected and the team trailed Boston and Baltimore in the standings. Now the impatient fans began to show their displeasure causing Reggie to sulk.

The next crisis came on June 18, which could have been the end of everything, since all the animosities from early in the year were still simmering beneath the surface. The Yankees were playing the Red Sox in a nationally televised game, a big one at that, as they trailed Boston by a game and a half in the standings.

Midway through the game a Red Sox batter hit a bloop to shallow rightfield. Reggie came in slowly and the ball dropped in front of him for a hit. An angry Martin came to the top step of the dugout and motioned Reggie in. For a minute Reggie didn't know what to do. The inning wasn't over, but Martin kept motioning him to come off the field. Finally, he trotted slowly to the dugout, where Martin informed him he was removing him from the game for not hustling after the pop fly. Paul Blair had already gone to right to replace him.

Reggie sat down, then said something to the manager, who had gone to the far end of the dug-out. The two began shouting. Suddenly Martin lost his famous temper and charged at Reggie, while TV cameras beamed the entire incident across the nation. Only the intervention of coach Ellie Howard prevented Martin from attacking Reggie. Even with Howard holding him, Martin continued to struggle to get at Reggie. It was an embarrassing and humiliating scene, witnessed by a huge TV audience, and people couldn't help wondering if Reggie, Martin, and the Yankees could recover from it.

Of course, the story was splashed all over the papers the next day. Reggie denied not hustling, but declined to say too much more. Martin claimed it was an act of defiance, and two days later George Steinbrenner said, "The team looks out of control." General Manager Gabe Paul said that Martin's job was still secure. The Yanks were making the old Battling A's look like angels. The strain of the entire season was really beginning to affect Reggie. He withdrew even more, rarely talking and just seeing a few close friends.

"I didn't know how to talk to him," said pitcher Ron Guidry. "He just didn't seem to fit in with the rest of the guys. He was him and we were us."

By July it grew worse. Reggie recalls just how bad it had become.

"It was pure horror," he says. "I lost my confidence and I was afraid. I didn't know how to manipulate or move around anymore, how to adjust to what was happening. My mother and father couldn't go to the games, couldn't deal with it, either. Old friends were asking me, 'What's happened to you? Who's this monster that's been created?' If it wasn't for Fran Healy I'd have lost my mind. The Bible, Fran, and my agent, Gary Walker, probably saved me. It seemed I was the center of the storm every day, every moment. But I couldn't quit, couldn't give up. There was a coldness in the clubhouse, on the field, and in the stands. It was just awful."

To make matters worse, a 14-year-old boy lodged criminal harassment charges against Reggie, claiming he had roughed him up outside the Stadium. Reggie was found not guilty, but the added burden didn't help matters Gary Walker recalls really worrying about Reggie's health during this trying period.

"There was a stiffness about him, an enormous tenseness I'd never seen before," Walker said. "Reggie had a rigid expression on his face and he walked with a rigid gait. For awhile I thought he was on the verge of a mental breakdown."

So the exciting prospect of free agency, the huge contract, all the hoopla of coming to New York, all of that had turned into a gigantic nightmare for Reggie. And by July, no one seemed to know just how it would be resolved.

But at the end of July, Steinbrenner struck again. He issued seven rules that he expected Martin to follow if he was wanted to continue as Yankee manager. They become known as the Seven Commandments. The whole thing was beginning to look like some kind of sordid circus act.

"I don't know what's important anymore," Thurman Munson was quoted as saying. "But I know I don't like being laughed at. And when a grown man managing a ballclub has to have seven rules thrown at him, people are going to laugh at that team."

No one liked what was going on by this time. Everyone just wished it would end so the team could play ball and win or lose the division on the field. By August 10, the Yanks had a 61-49 record, but still trailed the Red Sox by five games. Finally, some of the players took the bull by the horn. Led by the outspoken Lou Piniella, they went to Martin and asked him to stop juggling the line-up, to put Reggie in the clean-up spot and let him stay there. At this point they had nothing to lose.

Martin listened, then agreed. He also decided to make the hard-hitting Piniella an everyday player instead of platooning him, as he had done for most of the season. So the die was cast. Reggie had waited more than half a season to bat clean-up. Again, his great pride and to an extent his ego, made him feel this was his rightful place in the line-up. Perhaps he placed too much importance on where he hit, but to Reggie, batting fourth seemed to represent respect, and a feeling of being needed, two things which were always very important to him.

Many people figured that 1977 would be a lost year

for Reggie, that no matter where he hit it was too late to shake off the various problems and confrontations that had occurred. But those people may have forgotten Reggie's great natural talent, and the ability, like that of many superstars, to reach down deep within himself for that little something extra.

Shortly after being installed in the clean-up spot, Reggie began to hit, and hit with a vengeance. It was as if he was trying to make up for the entire season in two short months. Once again he was hitting those majestic home runs, the kind that are gone from the second they leave the bat. And as is his style, Reggie was again watching them sail out before starting his home run trot.

Other Yankees also began responding. Piniella, Munson, Rivers, and Chambliss were also coming alive, while Graig Nettles was headed for his best RBI season. The club was also getting good pitching now from Gullett, Figueroa, Torrez, and young Ron Guidry, a real surprise, as well as outstanding relief work from Dick Tidrow and especially Sparky Lyle. As the club began winning, much of the tension and animosity began to melt away. Now there was a pennant race to contend with and it looked as if everyone was finally going to relax and play baseball.

Play they did. Led by Reggie, the Yanks caught fire down the stretch, winning 39 of their final 52 games, finishing at 100-62, and nipping both Boston and Baltimore at the wire. They were American League East champs once again.

For Reggie, it had to be a miracle finish. His great surge in the final two months gave him a more than respectable finish. Playing in 146 games, he batted a solid .286, clubbing out 32 home runs and driving home a team-leading 110 runs. He also had 39 doubles, two triples, and scored 93 runs.

"I always hit, was always able to produce," he said, when it was over. "I was in a position where, if I failed, the fans and the press would have buried me. And here they don't just let you escape with minor scratches and bruises. They put real scars on you. Come to the Big Apple and have a bite. I had to either learn to digest, or choke."

Reggie had certainly tasted the bad part of playing in New York under the Steinbrenner-Martin dictatorship, and now he was finally tasting the good, though the best was still yet to come.

He had plenty of help in the Yanks divisional win. Piniella batted .333, Rivers .326, and Munson .308 with 100 RBIs. Chambliss hit .287 with 90 RBIs, while Nettles stroked 37 homers and drove in 107. Roy White, Willie Randolph, Bucky Dent and the bench also contributed. Pitching wise, the team also did well. Reliever Lyle was 13-5 with a 2.16 ERA and a slew of saves. Young Guidry surprised at 16-7, Figueroa was 16-11, Gullett 14-4, Torrez 17-13, and Tidrow 11-4. Now the club was ready to do battle with the Kansas City Royals for the American League crown.

Kansas City was a young team, an expansion club from the 1960s, created in Kansas City when the A's moved from there to Oakland. They had some fine young ballplayers and had just taken their first divisional crown. The Yanks were solid favorites to win, but KC wouldn't be an easy opponent.

In game one, the Yanks started Don Gullett against the Royals' Paul Splittorff, a noted Yankee killer. Gullett didn't have it, a stiff shoulder forcing him from the mound after Kansas City scored four runs in two innings. The Royals got two more off Dick Tidrow in the top of the third, and from there coasted to a 7-2 win behind Splittorff, who had his usual mastery over the Yanks, and over Reggie, who was 0-4 in the opener.

The Yanks got even in game two. Ron Guidry, their best pitcher in the second-half of the year, threw a three-hitter at the Royals, the Yanks winning it, 6-2. Munson with three hits, Cliff Johnson with a homer and two hits, and Willie Randolph with a pair of safeties paced the attack. Reggie got a single and stolen base in four trips, but he still wasn't stinging the ball that well.

After splitting the first two in New York, the teams moved to Kansas City for game three, Mike Torrez pitching against KC's twenty-game winner, Dennis Leonard. Torrez didn't have it, and the Royals chipped away for single runs in the second, third, and fifth, en route to an easy, 6-2 victory, as Leonard hurled a two-hitter. A frustrated Reggie went 0-3, and the Yanks were one game away from elimination.

But the Bombers wouldn't die. Sparky Lyle was the hero of game four, coming on in the fourth inning to retire the always dangerous George Brett with two men on. From there, Lyle breezed home, pitching 5 1/3 innings of two-hit relief as the Yanks won, 6-4. So there would be a fifth and final game for the American League pennant, and the pitchers would be Ron Guidry, going with two days rest, against Paul Splittorff, the winner of game one.

Then right before the game there was another bombshell. Manager Martin made out the starting line-up and Reggie wasn't in it. Paul Blair was starting in right. The biggest game of the year for the Yanks and Reggie Jackson was benched!

Martin claimed he made the bold move because Reggie had a history of not hitting Splittorff, and Blair was undeniably the superior defensive outfielder, Reggie tried to keep a low profile. "I've never been a good pinch-hitter," he said, "but I guess I'll have to change that tonight." And owner Steinbrenner calmly said, "Billy's the manager. If we win, he gets the credit. If we lose, he has to accept the blame."

For most of the game it looked as if he'd get the blame. Starter Guidry just didn't have it on two days rest. The Royals got a pair of tallies in the first. A single by Munson made it 2-1 in the top of the third. But in the bottom of the third, the Royals got another and bumped Guidry, Mike Torrez taking over. Fortunately, Torrez had it and checked the Royals right there.

But the Yanks could do little with Splittorff, who was once again proving a Yankee killer. Then when Willie

Randolph led off the eighth with a single, Manager Whitey Herzog replaced Splittorff with righthander Doug Bird, who promptly fanned Thurman Munson for the first out. The Royals were just five outs away from a pennant. But Lou Piniella came up and singled to center, with Randolph stopping at third. Then out came Reggie to bat for DH Cliff Johnson. The pressure was really on.

Bird worked the count to 1-2. Then Reggie hit a looper to center which dropped in front of Amos Otis. Randolph raced home with the second run. But after another pitching change to left-hander Steve Mingori, Nettles flied out and Chambliss grounded to second to end the inning.

It was still 3-2 in the ninth as Blair led off against Dennis Leonard, the KC ace. The veteran rightfielder blooped a single to center and then Roy White walked. Lefty Larry Gura came in to pitch and Mickey Rivers singled to right, driving in the tying run. Then Randolph hit a sacrifice fly to give the Yanks a 4-3 lead. When Piniella bounced to third, Brett threw the ball into the stands, letting the fifth run come home. Sparky Lyle set the Royals down in the bottom of the ninth, and the Yanks had won the pennant in dramatic fashion. They went wild in celebration.

The incredible victory helped soften Reggie's anger at being benched. "It must have been a tough decision for Billy to make," he said. "The easiest thing would have been to play me, and if I went 0-for-4 and we lost, he wouldn't get any heat. But he really showed some guts. He did it because he wanted to win. Still, I have to admit that not playing gave me an empty feeling."

Reggie's good friend, Fran Healy, added this. "Reggie took the benching like a man. He's a complex person, but he has a great deal of class and he showed it in his response."

In truth, Reggie didn't help much. He was just two for sixteen for a .125 average and one RBI. The Yanks would have to get a lot more production from his big bat in the World Series. For their opponent would be the Los Angeles Dodgers, their old rivals from when the team was in Brooklyn. Whenever these two teams met it was total war. As Dodger star Steve Garvey said:

"These are the two classic teams of the past. There is so much nostalgia about these clubs . . . I think this is the World Series the people wanted."

Reggie, of course, had played against the Dodgers in 1974 when he was with the A's. Many of those same players remained and it was another fine Dodger team, this time under Manager Tom Lasorda. The hitters were led by Garvey, Ron Cey, Dusty Baker, Davey Lopes, Reggie Smith, and Bill Russell, while on the mound the club had solid starters in Tommy John, Don Sutton, Burt Hooton, Doug Rau, and Rick Rhoden. Since the National League had no designated hitter rule, it was used in alternate Series, and in this Series the pitchers would have to hit. This could possibly help the Dodgers.

In game one, Martin tabbed Don Gullett to go up against Don Sutton. Gullett had been experiencing shoulder problems, but Martin had little choice. His best late-season pitchers, Guidry and Torrez, needed more rest.

The Series opened at Yankee Stadium and the Dodgers promptly touched up Gullett for a pair in the first. Singles by Munson, Reggie, and Chris Chambliss got one back in the Yankee half of the inning. After his terrible playoff series against the Royals, it was important for Reggie to get off to a good start. So the hit in the opening inning made him feel good.

Both pitchers settled down until the sixth, when Willie Randolph lined a homer to left for a 2-2 tie. The Yankees took the lead in the eighth when the busy Randolph walked and Munson drove him home with a clutch, hit-and-run double. Then in the top of the ninth, Manager Martin removed Reggie in favor of Paul Blair for defensive strength. This didn't make Reggie happy.

"I just do my job," he said. "I do what the manager wants. I just play here—sometimes. If they don't want me to play I won't play."

For awhile it looked as if the move might backfire when the Dodgers scored a run to tie the game, and now Reggie's bat was on the bench. But in the last of the 12th inning, Randolph doubled off Rick Rhoden, Munson was intentionally walked, and Blair, batting in Reggie's clean-up spot, singled to left to win the game. The Yanks had gone one game up.

The Dodgers went to Burt Hooton in game two, and Martin, with a tired staff, surprised everyone by choosing veteran Catfish Hunter, who had had a mediocre 9-9 record on the season, and to some, appeared finished. When he took a three-homer drubbing in 2 1/3 innings, giving the Dodgers a 5-0 lead, Martin's gamble had backfired. The Dodgers went on to a 6-1 victory which tied the Series at a game apiece. Reggie took the collar in four trips and must have been wondering if it was the playoffs all over again.

In the pivotal third game, held in Los Angeles, the Yanks sent Mike Torrez to the mound against twenty-game winner Tommy John. The New Yorkers showed little respect for John's record. In the first, Rivers doubled to right, Munson doubled him home, Reggie singled Munson home, went to second on an error, and scored on a base hit by Piniella. The Yanks had a quick, 3-0, lead.

The Dodgers showed their guts by bouncing back in the third, getting three runs on a home run by Dusty Baker. But the Yanks weren't about to let it get away. They got single tallies in the fourth and fifth, as Torrez settled down and pitched outstanding ball the rest of the way for a complete game victory and a 2-1 Yank lead in the Series.

Reggie had one hit, but to him it was a big one. "I was really glad to get that hit in the first inning," he said. "I know there's pressure and I just have to try and deal with it the best I can."

There was still another conflict with Martin when

Reggie apparently second-guessed him about using Hunter in game two. Yankee turmoil seemed to go on, no matter what the circumstance.

"It's between me and the manager," Reggie said. "Everything's fine now. I've had enough. I just want to play baseball."

Then in game four, things turned around for Reggie. Ron Guidry pitched for the Yanks against lefty Doug Rau of the Dodgers. Leading off the second inning, Reggie slammed a double, igniting a three-run rally that finished Rau and brought in Rick Rhoden. By the sixth, the Dodgers had fought back to make it a 3-2 game, but up came Reggie and promptly slammed a long home run, his first of the Series, giving the Yanks and Guidry an insurance run. The thin, hard-throwing lefthander made it stand up, finishing with a four-hitter and a 4-2 victory. The Yanks now had a commanding 3-1 lead in the World Series.

With a chance to wrap it up in L.A., the Yanks sent Don Gullett back to the mound to face Don Sutton. But the Dodgers weren't ready to quit. They got a run in the first, then rocked Gullett with four in the fourth and three more in the fifth. Ken Clay and Dick Tidrow followed, but they were also hit hard, as the Dodgers won going away, 10-4. In the eighth, Munson and Reggie slammed back-to-back homers off Sutton, and Reggie added a single. His bat was definitely coming to life. The clubs now headed back to New York where the Yanks hoped to take it in six.

But they didn't return unscathed. There was still more controversy. A national magazine article appeared claiming that Reggie said he wouldn't play for the Yankees in 1978 if Billy Martin were still the manager. The team didn't need this now, especially since there were rumors that George Steinbrenner was the source of the story.

"It's an out-and-out lie," Reggie said, strongly. "It's a shame for anybody to report stuff like this . . . I never talked to anyone from the magazine. People must think I'm stupid if they'd think I'd talk about that. I can't wait till next year to play for the man (Martin). I'm excited about it."

So once again the Yanks were sniping at each other, from owner to manager to players. It was incredible that they could continue playing competitive ball, let alone have a lead in the Series. But it seemed that Reggie and Billy were trying. After game four, Reggie remarked that Martin deserved "the Nobel Peace Prize" for managing the Yanks, and the manager answered by saying that Jackson should get "The Good Guy Award." But it was truly like a continuing soap opera.

The sixth game pitchers were Mike Torrez for the Yanks and Burt Hooton for the Dodgers. Hooton had the extra day rest, but the strong-armed Torrez had come through in the playoffs with a tired arm. And the Yanks wanted to end it right here and now. A seventh game was just too risky.

In the first inning it looked as if Torrez might not have it. An error, a passed ball, a walk, and a triple by Steve Garvey gave the Dodgers a fast, two-run lead. But in the Yankee second, Reggie drew a walk, then Chris Chambliss slammed a 400-foot home run into the right centerfield bleachers to tie the game at two-all.

Reggie Smith took one downtown off Torrez in the third, giving L.A. a 3-2 advantage. But in the Yankee fourth, Munson opened with a single and Reggie came up. He promptly lined Hooton's first pitch into the rightfield grandstand, a two-run shot, giving the lead back to the Yanks at 4-3. It was Reggie's third homer of the Series and third in his last seven at bats.

The Yanks got another run in the inning off reliever Elias Sosa to make it 5-3, and the tension started to build. The players and the fans sensed world championship, and they could just taste it.

In the fifth, Reggie was up again, facing Sosa. Once again he went after the first pitch, and once again the ball sailed into the rightfield stands, this time into the upper deck. It was another two-run shot and it increased the Yankee lead to 7-3. Reggie circled the bases slowly, savoring every moment as the packed house went wild.

The score remained 7-3 when Reggie came to bat again in the eighth inning. Knuckleballer Charley Hough was on the mound for the Dodgers. He threw the flutterball and Reggie swung again, hitting a high deep, majestic drive to almost dead center. It sailed into the bleachers some 440 feet from home plate, his third homer on just three pitches from three different hurlers. The crowd went completely berserk, screaming REGGIE ... REGGIE ... REGGIE, and a grateful Jackson came back out of the dugout to tip his cap to the cheering throng.

His third homer in a game had tied a Series record, and his five shots set a new mark. An inning later Torrez finished off the Dodgers and the Yanks were World Champs for the first time since 1962. And the Most Valuable Player in the Series was obviously Reggie Jackson, who finished with nine hits in 20 trips for a .450 average, five homers and eight RBIs.

It was a glorious finish to a nightmarish season. Reggie had turned it all around with his big bat. After the game, he was the center of attention, the reporters and newsmedia gathered around, as they would for days to come.

"Ernest Hemingway, one of the greatest writers in the world, couldn't have written a better ending for me," Reggie said. "I just didn't dream of three home runs. Whenever we're in a big game I always think of winning it with a home run, or hitting a right field double for big runs, or making a great catch. But not three home runs."

Then Reggie added some serious thoughts that he wanted everyone to hear. "Early in the year I told myself, 'I'm going to dedicate all the good things I do to Jackie Robinson.' When the free agent thing came along I thought of the man who made it all possible for blacks. In fact, I have this little Jackie Robinson button and I wore it during the entire Series."

Reggie continued, switching to another theme. "I'd like to be accepted as a great person, more than a ballplayer. I'd like my accomplishments to be treated humanistically, what they mean to people, to mankind, to black people . . . What happened to me this year has strengthened my character and changed my personality."

A few days later the Yanks announced that Billy Martin would be back, and they gave him a $50,000 bonus. Now that they were champs, the Yanks seemed to be mending fences.

"I think it's well deserved," Reggie said of Martin's bonus and vote of confidence. "I don't say I'm sympathetic to Billy, but I know what he's gone through. He's been through even more than me. The season has aged him. Now he can start being 49 instead of 99."

So the Yanks departed with apparent good will all around after an up-and-down season that couldn't have ended on a higher note. It was hoped that 1978 would be without all the internal problems and that the club could concentrate on simply playing baseball.

For Reggie, it must have been one of the best off-seasons of his life. He was in the limelight constantly, his exploits from the Series were still marveled at and shown repeatedly all over the place. Plus he was beginning to realize all the fringe benefits of playing in New York. His good looks, pleasing personality, and easy manner made him a natural for TV appearances, commercials, and other endorsements. He was now not only a sports superstar, but a genuine media personality as well.

Then spring training rolled around and the Yanks were ready to go again. They had caught another plum in the free agent market, fireballing relief star Rich "Goose" Gossage, who signed a huge contract and would join Sparky Lyle, who had taken the 1977 Cy Young Award as the best pitcher in the league, in the Yankee bullpen. But Lyle quickly questioned whether there would be room enough for both of them, and the first conflict of the year emerged.

Aside from that, the Yankees seemed to put past differences aside. And it was a relaxed Reggie Jackson who began working out in preparation for his eleventh full season in the big leagues.

"I'll be 32 this year," Reggie said, "so I have to work harder all winter and spring to be ready. I don't want to fall back this year, I want to win again. That's why I'm here. I'm a professional athlete and I only enjoy my work when I win.

"But there's a lot less pressure this year. Last year I had to prove to people and to myself that I was worth the money. Other things are better now, too. There is a lot more kidding going on between Thurman, Graig and myself. We're not talking about what happened last year, we have just made an adjustment and have taken it from there. So I'm happy with everything. The World Series certainly helped. Now people respect my performance and they respect me as a man. I'm comfortable and I'm proud of myself."

The team got off the mark slowly, and early in the year minor injuries began striking, at first on the pitching staff. Mike Torrez had left the team via the free agent route and had subsequently signed with arch rival Boston. So his durable right arm was missing. Gullett, Hunter, Figueroa and newcomer Andy Messersmith were all ailing early. In fact, Messersmith and Gullett were soon down for the count and in the early months the pitching staff was dotted with names like Jim Beattie, Bob Kammeyer, Larry McCall, and Dave Rajsich.

On May 18, the surprising Detroit Tigers were in first place with a 21-9 mark, followed by the Red Sox at 23-12, and the Yanks at 19-13. On May 24, the Bosox took over the lead and settled in for a long run at the top, with the Milwaukee Brewers, the Orioles, the Yanks, and the fading Tigers in pursuit.

Reggie was also having his problems. A slow start at the plate, plus bigger difficulties in the outfield were making the storybook finish of '77 slowly fade over the horizon. When the Red Sox got hot in late May and into June, the Yanks began falling further behind, even though Reggie was picking up his pace, hitting homers and driving in runs once again.

But the injuries also kept mounting. Centerfielder Mickey Rivers, shortstop Dent and second baseman Randolph all made trips to the disabled list during this time, and catcher Munson was beginning to show the wear and tear of all the years behind the plate. There was talk of finding another part-time position for him, and Martin began spotting him in rightfield, with Reggie serving as the DH.

In late June and early July, the club lost a pair of series to the Red Sox, one pitcher, Dennis Eckersley, beating them three times in twelve days. By All-Star break time on July 9, the Red Sox had a 57-26 record, best in the majors. They had a nine-game lead over surprising Milwaukee, and led the 46-38 Yanks by 11½ games.

That wasn't the only problem. Once again the Yanks were having internal trouble. There were rumors that Manager Martin was drinking too much and his health wasn't good. Reggie had fallen into a bad slump, perhaps brought on by his shuffling between the outfield and designated hitter spot. He was hitting under .200 for the month, and Martin had even benched him on a number of occasions. It was said that he had been informed that his future with the Yanks was probably as a DH, and he promptly said he had better things to do with his life than play in that spot for three years.

That wasn't the only problem. George Steinbrenner could never take losing and he began sniping again at Martin and his players, several of whom were complaining over lack of playing time. That and the injuries were really taking a toll. The Red Sox lead seemed insurmountable. Reggie himself remarked to the press that "even Affirmed (the Triple Crown winning racehorse) couldn't catch them."

On July 17, the Yanks were playing the Royals at the

Stadium. The game was tied at 5-5 with the Yanks batting in the tenth inning. Munson was on first with none out, Reggie at bat. Martin put the bunt on, but Reggie took the pitch from Al Hrabosky for a ball. Then the manager changed his mind, and relayed the hit sign to third base coach Dick Howser, who flashed the sign to Reggie. Yet when Hrabosky delivered, Reggie bunted the ball foul.

This time Howser came halfway down the line and spoke with Reggie directly. He told him again to hit away. But the next pitch came and Reggie bunted foul again. Another pitch, another bunt, and this was caught in foul territory by catcher Darrell Porter. That's when everything erupted.

Reggie walked back to the bench, waiting for Martin to explode. This time the manager controlled himself. He sent coach Gene Michael over to Reggie to tell him he was out of the game.

"It was the maddest I've ever been in my life," said Martin. "No player ever challenged me like that before. I know what I would have done in private."

The Yanks lost the game in the 11th, and Martin immediately went to Yankee President Al Rosen to relate the incident. Shortly afterward, the team announced that Reggie had been suspended for five days. It was widely thought that he had openly defied his manager. That, he denied.

"I hadn't been playing regularly and I wasn't swinging the bat very well," he said. "Under the circumstances, I thought bunting was the best thing I could do. Even after I was told to hit away by Howser, I didn't realize just what the consequences would be. But I didn't consider what I did an act of defiance and I don't feel I did anything wrong."

So once again the delicate balance of pride and ego had been shattered. Reggie was prepared for anything.

"I can't win, no matter what I do. I come off as a big, greedy moneymaker . . . Martin doesn't want me around here anymore, so he should be happy. I'm not going to fight this. I'm just going back to California to get away from this mess."

It was a no-win situation. Whatever motivated Reggie is hard to say. Martin, too, was under tremendous pressure from Steinbrenner to win again, and on the day Reggie was suspended, July 18, the Yanks fell fourteen-games behind the Red Sox. It seemed as if there was no way they could ever catch them.

"Injury after injury have broken us down," Martin said.

Steinbrenner thought otherwise, and kept the pressure on. Oddly enough, the Yanks won four straight while Reggie was gone, cutting into the Red Sox lead and enabling them to slip past Baltimore into third place. Then, with the suspension ending, Reggie flew to Chicago to rejoin the team. He would be in uniform again the next day, Sunday.

In the clubhouse, Reggie again refused to admit to reporters that his bunt was intended as an act of defiance. This again angered the tense Martin, who said about Reggie, "If he doesn't shut his mouth he won't play, and I don't care what George says. He can replace me right now if he doesn't like it."

This outburst came at the airport as the team was preparing to leave town. Forty-five minutes later, the reporters resumed their questions and Martin made his now infamous statement about Reggie and Steinbrenner, saying that "one's a born liar and the other's convicted." The "convicted" part referred to a guilty plea Steinbrenner made in 1974 after being accused of violating the election campaign-funding law.

That was the final straw. Martin had gone too far. The next day, July 24, Billy the Kid resigned as manager and a day later former White Sox skipper and Hall of Fame pitcher Bob Lemon was named to replace him. But would this move finally bring peace to the Yankees at last.

It seemed so, because Lemon was the complete opposite of Martin. Calm, controlled, a man of few words, he pressed the managerial buttons, but preferred to allow his players to perform without interference. Lemon's first game at the helm was on July 26, and the line-up had Thurman Munson in right field and Reggie as the designated hitter. That was Steinbrenner's idea, and it continued only until they saw that Munson could not be relied upon to make the plays in right. But this didn't help Reggie's ego, either.

The next Yankee shocker came on July 29, at the club's celebrated Old Timers Day. In a move that took everyone by surprise, Billy Martin was brought out and announced as the Yankee manager beginning in 1980, when Lemon would become general manager. The fans went wild. They loved vulnerable Billy, and their reaction to his resignation must have prompted Steinbrenner to announce his pending return, with a year and a half off to get his health and emotions back together. Some guessed it was just a political move, so much could happen before 1980 and Martin would never return.

But whatever, it was done. Now the Yanks began playing ball, and for the first time all year, the Red Sox actually began faltering. While it was the Yanks who had the early season injuries, the Sox players were suddenly dropping like flies, as the Yanks were getting well. By July 30, the Sox lead was down to 7½ over Milwaukee, with the Yanks right behind.

There were many positive things happening for the Yanks in spite of everything. For one thing, lefty Ron Guidry had emerged as the best pitcher in baseball in 1978. Guidry had won his first thirteen games to single-handedly keep the Yanks in the race. And by July 30, when the Yanks began moving, his record was 15-1. He was virtually unhittable. He was getting help from Ed Figueroa, who also began pitching extremely well, and the veteran Catfish Hunter, whose mysterious shoulder ailment had suddenly disappeared. Goose Gossage was proving an awesome late-inning reliever, and he moved past Sparky Lyle as the Bombers' bullpen ace.

And they were getting the hitting, too. Reggie was beginning to come alive again, and he was getting support from Munson, Chambliss, Nettles, Piniella, and others. All through August the Yanks chipped away at the Red Sox lead. They slipped past Milwaukee into second place and now had a genuine chance to catch the Sox. In fact, in the last week of August, the Sox lost second baseman Jerry Remy and rightfielder Dwight Evans to injury. They were really hurting.

On September 8, the Yanks came into Boston for a four-game series, and the lead was down to just four games. Since July 17, the Bombers had compiled a 35-14 mark, while the Sox were 25-24. So the Yanks had sliced ten full games off the once insurmountable Boston lead. A sweep at Fenway Park would tie it up.

Though a sweep seemed impossible, the Yanks went to work in the best tradition of the Bronx Bombers. They won the first game by a 15-3 count, getting twenty hits; took the second, 13-2, with eighteen safeties; won the third, 7-0, behind Guidry, who was now 21-2; then took the fourth, 7-4, for a sweep. In four games they had scored forty-two runs on sixty-seven hits, while the Sox had just nine runs and twenty-one hits and committed twelve errors.

Reggie was back in right and contributing mightily. His three-run homer in the second game helped put the icing on the cake, and he swung the bat well through the entire series. Now the Sox looked dead.

"I can't believe this is happening," said Yankee scout Clyde King, who had watched the Red Sox all year. "I could understand if an expansion team fell apart like this, but Boston had the best record in baseball. It can't go on."

The next weekend at the Stadium Guidry shut the Sox out again on two hits, and Hunter won the next day, as Reggie tied the game at 2-2 with a homer in the fifth and the Yanks won on a sacrifice fly by Munson in the ninth. The Red Sox salvaged the final game of the set, but they still trailed by 2½ games with only thirteen remaining.

It was a one-game lead with six left. The Red Sox

finally pulled themselves together and won all their games. The Yanks won their first five, then lost the last one to Cleveland. So the teams finished the season in a dead heat at 99-63. There would be a one-game playoff at Fenway for the A.L. East crown.

Guidry was on the mound for the Yanks with three days rest facing ex-Yankee Mike Torrez, the World Series pitching star of a year before. With so little rest, Guidry didn't have his real good stuff and the Sox took a 1-0 lead on a Carl Yastrzemski homer in the second. It stayed that way until the sixth when Jim Rice singled home the second Red Sox run. It looked as if the Yanks were in trouble as Torrez was setting them down. Going into the seventh he was working on a two-hit shutout.

Then with one out Chris Chambliss singled to left, followed by a Roy White base hit to center. Jim Spencer flied out and shortstop Bucky Dent came up. He surprised everyone by belting a three-run homer over the short left field wall to give the Yanks a 3-2 lead. A walk to Rivers finished Torrez, then Munson whacked a double off reliever Bob Stanley to make it 4-2.

In the eighth Reggie came up and poled a tremendous home run into the centerfield seats to give the Yanks insurance at 5-2. They needed it, for the Sox rallied to make it 5-4 in the eighth against Gossage. They got two on in the ninth, but Gossage got the dangerous Yastrzemski to foul out to Nettles and the Yankees had done it!

It was an incredible comeback, especially in light of all the turmoil of the past season, Reggie's suspension, Martin's resignation, the various players who carped about playing time and asked to be traded. But in the final accounting, talent had won out.

Reggie had fallen off slightly from his performance of '77. Playing in 139 games, he batted .274 with 27 homers and 97 RBIs. But Nettles had 93 RBIs, Chambliss 90, Munson 71, Piniella 69, so it was a balanced effort.

Guidry, of course, was the mainstay of the pitching staff with an incredible year, a 25-3 record, 248 strikeouts, a league leading 1.74 ERA, nine shutouts, and a Cy Young Award. He had help from Figueroa at 20-9, Hunter at 12-6, and Gossage with a barrelful of saves. Now the team had to meet Kansas City once again in the playoffs.

Manager Lemon gambled in the opener, using rookie Jim Beattie on the mound to rest his veterans. It worked. Beattie and young Ken Clay pitched well and Reggie supplied the power with a three-run homer as the Yanks won easily, 7-1.

Game two was no contest. The Royals teed off on Ed Figueroa and relievers, winning easily, 10-4. Then came the third back at Yankee Stadium, and this one was a dogfight, the lead changing hands a number of times. When the Royals took a 5-4 lead in the top of the eighth it spelled trouble. But in the bottom of the inning Munson belted a huge two-run homer to Death Valley in leftcenter and won the game, 6-5. The Yanks held a 2-1 lead with ace Ron Guidry ready for Game four.

Solo homers by Nettles and White gave the Yanks a 2-1 victory, closing out the playoffs in four. The Yanks were A.L. champs for a third straight year. Reggie had been a big factor once again. He was six for 13 for a .462 average, with a pair of homers and six RBIs. In the big third game, the one Munson broke up with his titanic shot, Reggie also had a homer, single, and three RBIs. It was ironic that Reggie and Munson were the heroes, but since their so-called feud of a year earlier, the two had become somewhat closer.

"We have a good relationship now," Reggie said. "There's respect on both sides. You can't play with a man like that and not like him. I like Thurman and I respect him."

So it was World Series time again, and it would be a repeat of 1977, the Yankees and the Dodgers. Once again there would be excitement, and Reggie Jackson would probably be in the middle of it.

Game one, played in Dodger Stadium, was a rout. The Dodgers scored three times off Ed Figueroa in the second, three times off Ken Clay in the fourth, and three times off Paul Linblad in the seventh en route to an easy, 11-5, victory behind Tommy John. But Reggie showed he was ready again. Used as a designated hitter, he blasted a homer and two other hits in a losing effort. Mr. October a nickname given him, was back!

Catfish Hunter started against Burt Hooton in the second game. The Yanks were hurting, having already lost second baseman Willie Randolph for the Series with a leg injury, Mickey Rivers and Chris Chambliss soon joined also with injuries. The Yanks took the lead when Reggie doubled home a pair of runs in the third, but L.A. came back with one in the fourth and a three-run homer by Ron Cey to make it 4-2 in the sixth. Reggie drove home the third Yankee run on an infield out in the seventh and it stayed that way into the ninth.

And then the drama came. The Yanks had two on and two out, Reggie coming up, facing Dodger rookie Bob Welch, a kid with a blazing fastball and a lot of heart. Could Reggie, who had driven in all the Yankee runs, do it again? Welch fired for a strike. The next pitch was high and tight. Ball one. Three more fastballs and three fouls. It was one-and-two. The confrontation continued, with 57,000 fans and millions more at home, living and dying with each pitch.

Welch's sixth straight fastball was high and tight, the count was even at 2-2. In came the next one, and Reggie fouled it off. The eighth pitch came in, off the plate, ball three. The count was full. Reggie stepped out and stared at Welch. Then he dug in again.

The young righthander kicked and fired. Reggie swung . . . and MISSED! He had fanned, and the Dodger crowd went berserk, the L.A. players mobbing young Welch. A disgruntled Reggie flung the bat and stormed into the dugout. The Dodgers had won, 4-3, and took a commanding 2-0 lead in the Series.

"I was trying to get a piece of the ball," Reggie said, "but he just made good pitches and that's why he got me out."

Steve Garvey, the Dodgers star first baseman, added a postscript. "That's the kind of a situation I'd like to be in. It's what the game is all about. But don't forget, Reggie's won those a lot of times, and he will again."

Now the Yanks had a long road back. But at least they were returning to Yankee Stadium and they had their ace, Ron Guidry, ready to take the mound. Hopefully, the long season and playoff hadn't taken too much out of his left arm. Don Sutton was on the mound for the Dodgers.

The Yanks broke early, with single runs in the first and second, but the Dodgers got one back in the third. After that, Guidry held them, even though he didn't have his best stuff, and the Yanks broke it open with three in the seventh to win, 5-1.

Game four had Ed Figueroa facing Tommy John again. It was scoreless until the top of the fifth, when Reggie Smith put the Dodgers on top with a three-run homer. Then in the New York sixth, Roy White singled, Munson walked, and Reggie drove in the first Yankee run with a single. Piniella was next and hit a low liner to short. It popped out of shortstop Bill Russell's glove. He picked it up, touched second for a force, then fired toward first. But the ball never got there. It hit Reggie on the hip and scooted away, allowing Munson to score the second Yankee run.

A big argument followed. The Dodgers said Reggie moved into the ball, in which case the runner would be out. But the ump said he was hit accidentally, so the ball remained in play and the run counted. After the game, Reggie would explain it all with a little smile.

"I'm a slow runner and a slow thinker," he said, tongue in cheek. "That's why I'm a DH. I didn't move too quickly. I just froze."

But to many, it seemed as if he did lean into the ball, and it turned out to be a smart play . . . or a lucky play, whichever way you look at it. The Yanks tied it on a Munson double in the eighth, and they won it in the tenth when Lou Piniella drove home Roy White with a clutch single. Goose Gossage got the win and the game two hero, Bob Welch, took the loss.

Now the Series was tied and the next day the Yanks untied it, losing an 18-hit barrage and winning, 12-2, behind surprise starter Jim Beattie. Now they headed back to L.A., hoping to wrap it up in six once again.

Veteran Catfish Hunter got the call for the Yanks and the Dodgers pinned their hopes on Don Sutton. When Davey Lopes homered off the Cat in the first it looked like trouble. But Hunter got out of an ensuing jam. The Yanks then got three in the second, with Randolph's sub, Brian Doyle, driving in one, and Bucky Dent (who was to be Series MVP) driving in the other two. L.A. clawed back for one in the third, but marvelous fielding by the Yanks shut them down.

After that, Hunter settled down and in the Yankee sixth Doyle singled home Piniella, and Dent drove home Doyle, making it 5-2. In the eighth, the Yanks got their final two, and a fitting final pair of runs. Reggie hit a mammoth, two-run homer off Bob Welch, the pitcher who fanned him in the second game confrontation, and Goose Gossage came on to nail down the victory for the Yanks and Catfish, 7-2. The New Yorkers were champs once more.

"This team has a certain mental toughness," Reggie said, afterward. "The players all have a certain desire in life. Otherwise, we never would have made it."

The Yanks certainly looked like a complete team. Doyle was brilliant subbing for Randolph. Nettles put on another amazing fielding exhibition at third. Veterans like Roy White and Catfish Hunter contributed mightily, and Reggie Jackson was again Mr. October, getting nine for 23, for a .391 average, with a pair of homers and a team leading eight RBIs. It was the fifth championship team he had played on in his career.

Now it would seem the Yanks were finally settled. Steinbrenner still wanted to upgrade the team and he acquired free agent pitcher Tommy John from the Dodgers. Sparky Lyle was also gone, traded to Texas after losing stopper job to Gossage. But with Lemon's low-key managing style and two world championships under the belt, it seemed the controversy would be over.

It didn't work out that way though. The team got off to a horrendous start. John was pitching well, but Ron Guidry wasn't, not up to the form of '78. Then, early in the year, a clubhouse scuffle erupted between Gossage and big Cliff Johnson. As a result, the Goose tore ligaments in his right thumb and needed surgery. He'd be out a good part of the year. Without the big man, the bullpen fell apart and Guidry volunteered for duty there. In addition, Catfish Hunter appeared finished and Ed Figueroa went down with elbow problems that eventually needed surgery.

With the team still struggling in mid-June, George Steinbrenner struck again. He dismissed Lemon and brought Billy Martin back, a year earlier than planned, saying, "If anyone can turn things around, it's Billy."

By this time the Yanks were far behind the high-flying Baltimore Orioles and it just didn't seem possible that there were any miracles left. Reggie was having a good, but not great season, and was himself sidelined by minor injuries on a number of occasions. Then, on August 2, the final and most devastating blow was struck.

The team had an off day to return to the Stadium from Chicago. Thurman Munson chose to make a stop at his home in Canton, Ohio. He decided to go to the airport in Akron, Ohio, to practice take-offs and landings in his Cessna Citation, a twin engine jet which he piloted. During one of the landings the plane went out of control and crashed. Munson was killed instantly. The news of the Yankee captain's death shocked the baseball world and especially the Yanks. There were tributes to him everywhere, and the team won an emotional game the next night. But there was no way Munson's talents could be replaced.

Reggie, too, was deeply saddened. The old animosity between him and the catcher had all but disappeared. He wept openly at the funeral and at a tribute at the

Stadium, and he cited the enormous mutual respect the two had for one another.

"I was just glad we eventually got along so well," he said.

On the playing field the team never fully recovered. They finished the year with an 89-71 record, in fourth place and 13½ games behind division winning Baltimore. Playing in 131 games, Reggie had a .297 batting average, the best mark of his career. He belted 29 homers and drove home 89 runs. So in spite of everything, he had a very good year.

Now the Yanks would have time to lick their emotional and physical moves, and perhaps make some more big player changes. But controversy was never far behind. Just a short time after the season ended, Manager Martin got in another of his famous fights, this one with a marshmallow salesman in a Minnesota hotel. While the other man supposedly started it, Steinbrenner had had enough. On October 28, he dismissed Martin once again. A short time later it was announced that Dick Howser, a former coach, would be the new manager, and another former coach, Gene Michael, would be taking over as general manager. As for Martin, he wasn't out of work for long. He surfaced as manager of Reggie's old team, the Oakland A's.

There were indeed many player moves in the off-season. A big trade with Toronto brought catcher Rick Cerone and pitcher Tom Underwood to the team, sending first baseman Chris Chambliss packing. Free agent Rudy May rejoined the club after being away several years, pitching for Baltimore and Montreal. Another free agent, Bob Watson, was signed. He was a fine hitter at Houston for ten years and spent half a season with the Red Sox. He was a first baseman, designated hitter.

Another big trade with Seattle saw centerfielder Rupport Jones join the Yanks, as Mickey Rivers departed. Outfielder Oscar Gamble had also rejoined the team, and a year earlier former Yankee Bobby Murcer had come back. But the key men were Cerone, who had the giant task of filling Munson's shoes; Jones, who was counted on for dependable play in center; Watson, to give the Yanks the big righty bat they missed; and pitchers May and Underwood, to solidify a staff that had Guidry, John, and Gossage, and many question marks after that.

Well, it turned into a very strange kind of season. The team got off fast and took the early lead in the division, widening the gap into May and June. But the injuries started again. Gamble broke a toe. Ruppert Jones went down to abdominal surgery. Reggie strained a muscle in his right thigh and had to miss thirteen games. He then became the DH. Young players such as Bobby Brown, Joe Lefebvre, and Dennis Werth were seeing action, but the team held up, having the best record in baseball.

There were also some problems with veteran players who were carping about lack of playing time. Howser believed in platoon baseball, and wouldn't hesitate to pinch hit for a proven stick like Lou Piniella if a right-handed pitcher was in the game. Some of the players began privately criticizing this practice. Though the team was still winning, it all remained pretty much low key.

But for one man, it was a dream season. For the first time since coming to New York, Reggie Jackson was at peace, free from the controversy that had surrounded him his three previous seasons. Except for the injury, he was having an outstanding year, up among the homer and RBI leaders, and threatening to hit .300 for the first time in his career. He was now cheered by the fans and had assumed the role of a leader on the ballclub. Quite a change from the stormy days of '77 and '78.

"I look forward to getting to the ballpark now," he said. "It's fun getting there early, talking baseball, fooling around. I'm just enjoying baseball more this year. I like it here now. I'm finally comfortable."

And he was playing well. Batting coach Charley Lau said the best of Reggie was still ahead.

"Reggie is getting better and better with age," Lau

said. "Each at bat is a pleasure to behold. You can see the preparation, the discipline, the concentration at bat after at bat. When everything is in place, in the proper sequence, he's awesome. In a season of 450 at bats, maybe 1,200 swings, you can only count on maybe twenty perfect swings a year. When he does it, I get goose pimples."

Now, Reggie was more outgoing with teammates, helping younger players, giving advice, leading.

"Reggie honestly believes that he's the man who had to do it for us to win," said Willie Randolph, "and that keeps him going. He believes he's the leader, and that's the way he carries himself. He leads by example—by going out and coming through."

Tommy John, who had pitched against Reggie early in his career, noticed a big difference.

"He was a dead pull hitter when I pitched against him years ago at Oakland," John said. "Now he'll go the other way for his base hit. And he's more patient. That's the mark of a mature ballplayer, a confident ballplayer."

Always busy with off-field work, making many commercials and doing charity work that doesn't always get publicized, Reggie was not a big socializer, often preferring a quiet meal after a game in a restaurant with a few friends. At age 34, he takes good care of himself and doesn't burn the candle at both ends. But being out in New York can cause problems.

In early June, Reggie became embroiled in an argument over a parking space and a scuffle ensued. Before it was over, one of the men involved pulled a gun and fired three wild shots. Fortunately, no one was hurt.

On August 11, Reggie came out of a restaurant on 76th street and a young man approached him carrying a gun. He demanded, "Gimme everything you got." As Reggie said, "It was the biggest gun I ever saw. I flinched. He was pointing it at my head. I really thought he was going to shoot me."

The young man reached into Reggie's silver and blue

Rolls Royce to get the keys and Reggie pushed the car door against him. The man lost his balance, then recovered and started running. Reggie and several other men gave chase, but couldn't catch him.

It was a sobering incident, coming just hours after Reggie reached another milestone, belting the 400th home run of his great career. He was beginning to get up there with the best of them.

The Orioles made a run at the Yanks in August, when the team fell off a bit. During one series, owner Steinbrenner criticized the team and even included Reggie, but he failed to note how carefully the Oriole hurlers had pitched around Reggie. He was seeing fewer good pitches to hit.

Though in September it looked as if the Yanks would hold on to win it, some people saw chinks in the armor. Centerfielder Ruppert Jones returned from surgery, but soon after went down again after colliding with a wall. He was through for the year, and his replacement, Bobby Brown, was prone to mistakes. Third baseman Nettles had contracted hepatitis earlier in the year and that position was unsettled, with journeymen Aurelio Rodriquez and Eric Soderholm sharing the spot. The pitching staff couldn't seem to get it together at once. The team leaders were Reggie and catcher Cerone, who was having a brilliant season in spite of the pressure of replacing Munson.

In the end, the Yanks won 103 games, their best effort since 1963, and took their fourth A.L. East title in five years. And Reggie had an absolutely outstanding season. It was beginning to look as if Charley Lau was right. He was getting better with age.

Reggie had 154 hits in 514 at bats to reach one of his goals, a .300 season. He hit that right on the nose. And in the power department he had one of his finest seasons, blasting 41 big homers to tie Ben Oglivie of Milwaukee for the league lead. It was his second best home run season in the majors, his best since 1969. And he drove home 111 runs, third best mark of his career. Had he not lost time to injury, and had he not been pitched around when some other players were hurt, he would have had an even greater year.

He had some good support among his mates. For example, Bob Watson hit .307 with 68 RBIs. Willie Randolph had a .294 average and a great on-base percentage. Rick Cerone hit .277 and drove in 85 runs in his first year as a Yankee. Veteran Bobby Murcer, in a part-time role, had 13 homers and 57 RBIs, plus a slew of game-winning hits, second only to Reggie in that department.

The pitchers were led by Tommy John with 22 wins, Guidry with 17, Rudy May with 15 and a league leading ERA, and Tom Underwood with 13. Plus there was still Gossage, coming out of the bullpen. They were certainly a solid Yankee team.

Yet in the playoffs they again went up against the Kansas City Royals, and this time the Yanks came up short. Kansas City simply outplayed them in every phase of the game, getting the key hits, the big play, the clutch pitching. They beat the New Yorkers three straight times and advanced to the World Series.

To some, the Yanks' luck simply ran out. To others, it showed that K.C. had the better ballclub and that the Yanks were an aging team with many holes to be filled. One man who fumed was owner Steinbrenner, who hates to lose as much as anyone. He vowed to make changes once again, and by November 1980 he made a big one, announcing that rookie manager Dick Howser was stepping down and GM Gene Michael would take over as field manager. To most observers, Howser was out and out fired, though the Yanks tried to soft soap the whole thing.

Some of the players commented on the dismissal, with pro and con opinions, but for once, Reggie Jackson stayed clear of controversy.

"I enjoyed playing for Dick," he said, simply. "He was easy to work for and we respected each other. But I anticipate no problems with Gene. He's cut from the same mold and we already know each other well."

So perhaps Reggie was settling into the role of elder statesman. He wants to play for a few more years at least, and will be looking for one more big contract with the Yanks, hopefully before the 1981 season begins. Then the Yanks signed free agent outfielder Dave Winfield, giving him a long-term contract that made him the highest paid player in the game. But the new Reggie seemed unconcerned. He is more aware of himself and his role than ever before.

"I earn the money I make because I've hit 375 home runs and I've played on a certain number of winners and I've put a certain number of people in the ballpark," Reggie said, early in 1980. "I make the money I make because of my production."

No truer statement could have been made. Despite all the controversies surrounding Reggie Jackson's career, first in Oakland, then in New York, he had always produced, especially when the chips were down and the game was on the line. One has to wonder just how many of the five championship teams Reggie has played on would have gotten there and gone all the way without him?

No matter what else you might have to say about Reggie Jackson, the man is a winner. Make no mistake about that.

## MIKE SCHMIDT

When a player comes into the big leagues and in his first full season hits eighteen homers and drives home fifty-two runs in just 367 at bats, it would seem that he had a pretty bright future going for him. But when that same set of stats reveals 136 strikeouts and a .196 batting average, then one begins to wonder.

Obviously, several things can happen to the player. He can learn to correct the flaws that caused the strikeouts and the low batting average, and slowly become a bona fide power hitter with a load of homers and RBIs. But, in some cases, it doesn't happen. The player just can't seem to improve and it is the pitchers who do the catching up. Then, the low batting average might get even lower, and the homers and RBIs diminish.

And in a few cases, the player levels off to become a mediocre or fringe player, who was better than the .196 average, but not really a bona fide power man.

So when Mike Schmidt of the Philadelphia Phillies compiled those stats as a rookie in 1973, the jury was out on what exactly would happen to him in the ensuing years. He seemed to be a player of great promise. A muscular, 6'-2", 200-pounder who had all the natural physical tools—strength, coordination, speed and quickness—to be a star, but in the strange world of baseball, you can never be sure.

"I was tight as a drum as a rookie," recalls Mike. "All I did all year was try to kill the ball."

Some players never break early habits, and Mike Schmidt knew he had a great deal of work to do. Yet some eight years later, the same Mike Schmidt is standing atop the mountain. He had just completed the 1980 season and there isn't a player in the world who could ask for more. In the regular campaign he led the National League in home runs with 48 and in RBIs with 121. He was the big hero as his team won the divisional title, and he helped them into the World Series.

When they won the Series in six games, it marked the first time in the history of the franchise that the Phillies were world champions . . . and Mike Schmidt was named the Most Valuable Player in the Fall Classic. Then, a short time later, he was named the Most Valuable Player in the National League in just the second unanimous vote in league history.

Sweet success, obviously. But not easy success. For the Mike Schmidt story is beset with frustration and disappointment. It is also the story of the growth and maturation of a sensitive athlete and it involves many more elements than balls and strikes, hits and errors. It's the story of a team and a city, and how fans treat their athletic heroes. Mike Schmidt, since 1974, has hit more home runs than any other player in the game during that same time span, but it took until 1980 for him to be fully recognized as the superstar he has become.

Michael Jack Schmidt was born on September 27, 1949, in Dayton, Ohio. He was the first child born to Jack and Lois Schmidt, who later also had a daughter, Sally. So Mike never had any older brothers to follow around and learn sports from, but that didn't really stop him. His family operated a swim club and restaurant in Dayton, and little Mike was in the water at about six months and swimming by the time he was two.

Shortly afterwards, he began playing ball. "He must have been about three when his Grandmother Schmidt used to play with him in the backyard," said his father, Jack Schmidt. "She would play catch with him and before long we got him a little baseball uniform to wear.

He used to wear it everywhere, even when he was just watching TV."

Jack Schmidt also played catch with his son and says he knew immediately that he was going to be a good athlete. Before long, Mike was heading across the street to Ridge Crest Park to play ball with other boys from the neighborhood. As with most youngsters, they played whatever was in season—baseball, football, or basketball, and Mike became good at them all.

When he was about six years old, the old story of boys-will-be-boys almost got him in big trouble.

"Mike decided to climb this tree," recalls Mr. Schmidt. "And when he got part way up he grabbed at this wire that was there. Well, it was a high-tension wire and it knocked Mike right out of the tree. The fall didn't really hurt him much, but he had severe burns on the hands and legs from the electric shock. But I guess we were all lucky. It could have been much worse."

When Mike was eight, his father signed him up for Little League, his first time with an organized team. He was the third baseman that year, and as he got older, he shifted to short and did a lot of pitching. Already one of the best players in the league, there was little doubt that he was going to be a fine athlete.

He continued to spend a lot of his time playing ball, but he was also interested in music and always did well with his studies in school. He was at the Loos School in Dayton from first to eighth grade, then moved on to Fairview High School. While he was in high school, he began to follow the exploits of a young player with the nearby Cincinnati Reds. Pete Rose was an early idol and Mike probably never dreamed the two would be teammates some day.

At Fairview, Mike played baseball and football for Coach Dave Palsgrove and basketball for Donald Barger. But there would be a problem at Fairview—injuries.

During his sophomore year he made the football team. Early in the season he dropped back to receive a punt. Taking the ball upfield he was tackled near the sidelines. He came up gimping on a knee. By midnight he was in the hospital having his first knee operation. Fortunately, the surgery was successful and his father recalls that despite the operation Mike was already playing some basketball by late that winter.

In his junior year he was back out for football where he was being worked in at quarterback. Injured once again in practice, Mike had surgery performed on his other knee.

"The doctor said that Mike had worked so hard to rehabilitate the first knee he injured that he might have weakened the other one," Jack Schmidt recalls. "And I think his knees did hamper him all through high school, though he kept going and returned to action as soon as he could. But it had to affect his baseball somewhat."

Yet, Mike was still becoming a fine player. He played mostly third base in high school and was already a powerful hitter. In fact, he even experimented with switch-hitting while in high school.

"That was my suggestion," said Jack Schmidt. "I thought if Mike could adopt himself to switch-hitting he'd have a better chance to go further. He had good power from the left side, but never the consistency that he has as a right-handed batter."

Mike had no scouts come see him while in high school, perhaps because of the knee injuries, or perhaps because they just can't get everywhere. He didn't have any college offers, either, since there isn't as much money passed out for baseball as there is for football. He was planning on college anyway and finally decided to attend Ohio University. It was close to home and had a fine baseball program and an outstanding coach in Bob Wren. So in the fall of 1967, Mike enrolled at Ohio University in nearby Athens, Ohio.

"I think Mike already had the desire to play pro ball then," said Mr. Schmidt. "He and I both felt he had the natural ability. It was just a matter of him developing and then getting somebody to notice him."

He played on the freshman team that spring, continuing to play mostly third base, and in August, Philadelphia Phillies scout Ed French filed his first report on Mike. It read:

"Big, strong boy. Good hands and wrists. Strong arms. Hustles; good competitor. Challenges the pitchers. Has good power from both sides. Good bat control. Will follow."

So the Phils had their eyes on him and he hadn't reached nineteen-years-old yet. The report mentioned Mike's power from both sides, so he was obviously still trying some switch-hitting. This ended the next year when he made the varsity and Coach Wren suggested Mike work solely as a righthanded batter. Mike was moved to short as he made the starting lineup, and put together a big year, hitting over .300 and leading the team in homers. He also fielded well, showing a strong arm and good hands. Sure enough, the Phils sent another scout, Tony Lucadello, to look at him. Again, the report was good.

"Swings a good bat with power," said Lucadello. "Can develop into a good power hitter. Third base is his spot."

So while he still played short, the scouts figured if he turned pro they'd have to move him over to the hot corner. As his career at Ohio U. continued, it's quite interesting to follow the continuing scouting reports that were geared to deliver him to the big leagues.

As a junior, he became an all-American, a big step toward going further in the game, and this time a pair of Philadelphia scouts visited the Athens campus to take another long look at Mike. The first was Ed French, who had seen him two years earlier as a freshman.

"Big boned, strong, hard-nosed kid," wrote French. "Real good power. Has poise and confidence. Good reflexes. Not quite quick enough for shortstop. Should be at third or first."

French's report indicated Mike's growing maturity at Ohio U., by mentioning his poise and confidence. It also showed the prevalent opinion that he couldn't make it as a big league shortstop. And, in truth, there aren't too many shortstops with Mike's size and muscular build. Those kinds of players are just not quick enough, as the report said, to play short.

A month later, in May of 1970, another scout, Bill Schlesinger, also filed a report on Mike. It looked as if the Phillies really wanted him.

Schlesinger's report said: "Very aggressive. Ball jumps off his bat. Good power. Good actions, just average arm, 4.2 down the line. Good desire."

The only strange part of that report was the declaration of an average arm. Perhaps Mike was hurting then, because he has one of the finest arms among all third basemen playing today.

At any rate, Mike completed his senior year in fine style, and shortly after learned he was the Phils' second choice in the 1971 draft. He knew by that time that he wanted to give pro ball a crack and signed with scout Tony Lucadello for a modest bonus. But unlike many athletes, who just want to get that pro contract and not worry about anything else, Mike continued his academic work and graduated with his class in 1971, earning a bachelor's degree in business administration.

Now it was time to play ball. Mike's first stop was Reading, Pennsylvania, in the low minors, where he would finish out the 1971 season. It's a big jump for a player going from college to the minors the very same year. The atmosphere is different and the player suddenly has different people coaching him. In many cases he has to learn new positions defensively. In Mike's case he was being tried at both second and third, and he had to concentrate on learning the characteristics of each spot.

As a consequence, his hitting suffered. In 74 games at Reading, he hit just .211, getting fifty hits in 237 at bats. He had just seven doubles, one triple, but showed promise of power with eight homers and 31 RBIs. He also struck out 66 times, something that would open him to criticism for many years to come.

But in spite of his low batting average, the Phillies apparently liked what they saw. They promoted Mike to Eugene (Oregon) of the Pacific Coast League for the 1972 season. Playing mostly second base there, he began to blossom. He hit very well, though he was still striking out too much. But he began to show the awesome kind of power he would later display in the majors. The ball did, indeed, seem to jump off his bat, and the homers and RBIs often came in bunches when he'd get hot.

He became the PCL's All-Star second baseman that year, not so much for his fielding, but because of his big bat. In 131 games he had 127 hits in 436 at bats for a solid, .291 average. He had 23 doubles, six triples, banged out 26 homers and drove home 91 runs. He seemed to have a good eye, walking 87 times, but his free swinging produced 145 strikeouts, a very high number for that amount of at bats.

Still, at the tail end of the 1972 season, the Phillies brought him up for his first taste of major league action. He played in just thirteen games and had seven hits in 34 at bats for a .206 average. But he did get a feel for the big time and also hit his first major league home run, which made him feel awfully good. He also felt he had a good chance to stick with the club in 1973.

To some, sticking with the Philadelphia Phillies was no bargain. The club had deteriorated into one of the poorest in the league. In addition, there had not really been a whole lot of past successes in the long history of the franchise to give the faithful fans of the Phillies much joy to look back upon. In fact, the team had never won a World Series, and had reached the fall classic only twice, in 1915 and 1950.

Then in 1964 the team seemed to have a lock on the National League pennant for most of the season. But in the final two weeks came an unexpected, but complete collapse. The club just couldn't buy a victory and the St. Louis Cardinals sneaked in under the wire to take the flag. That foldup was still being talked about when Mike arrived on the scene late in 1972.

Despite everything, the fans of Philadelphia kept coming out. The A's, of course, eventually moved to Oakland, where they were in the process of becoming the best team in baseball. The Phils were also playing in a brand-new, modern stadium then, Veterans Stadium, but more than anything else the fans wanted a winner.

And it didn't look as if they were about to get one in the near future. In 1971, the team had finished dead last in the National League's Eastern Division with a 67-95 mark. When Mike arrived, the club was in the process of finishing last again, and would do so with a dismal, 65-97 record. It was even more discouraging when one looks at the stats and discovers that one pitcher, Steve Carlton, had compiled a 27-10 record with such a terrible team. Carlton was simply overpowering and dominating. If you took away his record, the rest of the club was 38-87. It seemed, indeed, like a hopeless situation.

Yet when Mike reported for spring training in 1973, there were signs that the Phils were starting to pick up some good young players. Besides Mike, there were a couple of promising infielders in Larry Bowa, a shortstop; second baseman Denny Doyle; and Bob Boone looked as if he might be the catcher of the future. In the outfield, Greg Luzinski was showing promise of being an outstanding power hitter; Willie Montanez, Bill Robinson, and Oscar Gamble all showed signs of being able to do the job. Carlton, hopefully, would have some help from veteran Jim Lonborg, young Ken Brett, and Barry Lersch. But there was still that long climb uphill.

So, Mike was installed at third base at the outset of the 1973 season, and he stayed there on a more or less regular basis for most of the season. He was benched from time to time when his performance was not quite up to par. There was also a great deal of pressure on Mike almost from the beginning. First of all, most of the early publicity releases regarding him always described him as a player of "unlimited potential." This wasn't always easy for him, because he felt from the beginning that he had something to live up to.

When a player in Mike's position joins a weak team like the Phils, there are no proven veterans to carry the load and stabilize the rookies, taking the pressure off them. If Mike had joined a winning club, he could have been worked in and not expected to produce right away. There would have been no feeling of having to carry a certain load.

Though the team was improved in some areas, the Phils were still losing and floundering in last place in their division. Young Greg Luzinski was beginning to look like a genuine slugger, and perhaps Mike felt he had to try to keep up with the man who would become known as "The Bull." So, as he had always done since he was a kid, he tried to kill the ball. And when he did connect for one of his long homers, everyone would get excited. But then he'd start trying too hard and strike out again.

Mike's batting average was hovering around the .200 mark most of the year and he was striking out about one of three times at bat. Manager Danny Ozark believed strongly in Mike and his ability, and he tried to help the youngster all he could. But in doing so, he became a bit overbearing and Mike often found it hard to take.

"I know Danny was trying hard to help me," Mike says. "But I often found myself wishing that he would just leave me alone. It was like I was in the Little League and he was my father. He was continually on me."

And occasionally the manager would do something which he felt was for the good of the ballclub, but it also served to rob Mike of some of his confidence. For instance, one time the Phils had a man on third with one out, and Ozark had the runner break for home on a grounder right at the third baseman. It was a strategy foreign to all the basics of the game, and when Ozark was asked why he played it that way, he said:

"Because Schmidt was the next hitter and he strikes out a lot!"

No wonder Mike would tend to brood and get down on himself.

"It was just a sore-thumb year for me," Mike said,

later. "I was scrutinized for everything, even the way I walked. I remember one time there was a conference at the mound and I stayed at third, my arms folded, my glove under one of them. There was a picture of me that way in the paper the next day and the caption read: 'Does he really care?' I remember being criticized for that. But it's part of my nature. I know what's going to be said, so why should I walk to the mound every time? But I guess there has to be some static around a losing team and in 1973 a lot of it was around me."

Danny Ozark also remembers '73, and admits that he took on Mike as a personal project.

"I bragged about Mike all the time and maybe helped bring on some of his problems," said Ozark. "I guess I was a little stubborn with him. I'd say things like, 'If I had your ability, I know what I'd do . . . ' I was kind of trying to cram things into him and I talked to him almost every other day. I guess I liked him so much that I tried to school him too rapidly. It was like trying to cram four years of school into five months. In some ways, the more I pushed, the more he resisted. I remember him once telling me that I was trying to be a father to him and he preferred it if I just treated him like a player."

So the Phils continued to flounder for most of the season. When it ended, they were in a familiar position—last place. But the record had improved a bit to 71-91, and some of the young players got a valuable learning experience. Greg Luzinski was especially productive. The 225-pound outfielder seemed ready to blossom into one of the young sluggers of the National League. In just his second full season, he batted .285, with 29 homers and 97 RBIs. He was really a welcomed surprise.

As for Mike, well, there was still the old phrase, "unlimited potential." Surely, he had shown flashes. He finished the year with 72 hits in 367 at bats for a .196 average. You've got to be Superman in the field to stay in the league with that kind of hitting. But he partly atoned with 18 homers and 52 RBIs, while playing in 132 games. Again, on the negative side, were his 136 strikeouts. That's a lot of Ks. So when he looks back at that season, it's not with fond memories.

"It was a plain and simple bad time for me," he says. "The team was scraping the bottom of the barrel professionally, and to tell the truth, I knew nothing about myself as a ballplayer then. I didn't know the pitchers, how they planned to pitch me, and I couldn't hit a breaking ball anyway. I wasn't married then, so I was spending a lot of time in the streets doing things that weren't exactly conducive to playing well the next day."

Yet GM Paul Owens wasn't about to quit on Mike, and with Luzinski's development, he began to see the future, as stated by Philly Public Relations Director, Larry Shenk.

"We knew then that someday Mike and Greg would be big stars," Shenk said. "They would be the kingpins that we would fill in around. They were both young and would be our nucleus for many years."

But the problem was that one-half of the nucleus was coming off a .196 season and that just wouldn't do. In fact, his average was the lowest among the regulars in both leagues. That, in itself, had to be embarrassing to a guy with Mike's pride.

He was planning to play winter ball in Puerto Rico, hoping to regain his lost confidence and work on learning how to hit the breaking ball, a feat that some young players of potential have never been able to master. But before he left, he met someone who would also have a stabilizing influence on his life. He had just finished a round of golf with Steve Carlton and Barry Lersch and the three of them went to a local restaurant for a beer and a bite to eat. At the restaurant was a part-time singer named Donna Wightman. She and Mike hit it off immediately, and they were married before the start of the 1974 season.

But there was still winter ball. Without the pressure of the Bigs, Mike tried to put it all together. And suddenly, without warning, he found something.

"I found a swing that made things happen," he recalls. "One day I was at the plate, completely relaxed, and took an easy cut and that sucker went off my bat a mile. It was the first time I could remember hitting a ball that far without muscling it. After that, I began to find myself. And I was still stubborn then. I wanted to prove to everyone that I didn't need coaching just to walk out of the dugout."

They were still trying to coach him down there, but Mike was convinced that his batting style was something he would have to work out for himself.

"They tried to level my swing by making me lay the bat flat on my shoulder the way Nate Colbert (a former National League slugger) used to do," Mike recalls. "They thought I could hit .300 if I did that. But we shook that theory real fast. You know, you can hit one hundred line drives in batting practice and feel real good about it. It seems like a confidence builder, but it really doesn't change the fundamentals. In a game the adrenalin starts flowing and that ball isn't sitting on a tee. The pitcher is doing things with it that take you out of a grooved swing. It doesn't take long for you to revert to what's natural for you."

So Mike came to spring training with renewed optimism. After all, he had fallen in love and been married, and he had found a swing. What more could a ballplayer want? Try a winning team. Mike wanted that, too, and so did the rest of the Philly organization. There was a positive move when the team acquired second baseman Dave Cash, a sure-handed fielder, though with somewhat limited range, but an outstanding hitter who was usually up around the 200-hit mark and on base a great deal. On the negative side, Greg Luzinski tore ligaments in his knee and would miss nearly half the season. When that happened, there was immediately increased pressure on Mike, since he was now being looked to as the main power man.

In spring training, Manager Ozark and the coaches were still fooling with Mike's batting style, and he still resisted, preferring to do it his way.

"I was pretty stubborn in spring training that year," he recalls. "At first I tried it their way a few times, but I always felt uncomfortable. Finally, I decided I had to take a stand. I told them they could send me back to Triple A if they wanted, but I had to hit my own way. What it came down to was they said fine, do it your way. But if you hit .196 again you will be back down in Triple A."

That was the way Mike wanted it. He would sink or swim on his own. Despite the problems he had as a rookie, he basically had a great deal of confidence in himself and his ability to hit major league pitching.

"I felt I always had the ability," he says. "It was just a matter of putting the ability and the confidence together. When I did that, everything started falling into place. I was able to relax more when I batted, had a clear head, and allowed my natural instincts to take over. What it amounted to was that I stopped thinking so much and I started hitting. I learned that all I had to do was meet the ball."

He started meeting the ball more right from the start. In fact, the change in Mike was startling. He still struck out quite frequently, and always would, as most power hitters seem to do. But instead of hitting .200, he was hitting close to .300. In the early going, it was obvious that he had become a really dangerous hitter, a force. Whereas he had batted eighth most of 1973, he was now operating out of the third slot, and it seemed that whenever he came up he had Bowa and/or Cash on base with an opportunity to drive them home.

The Philadelphia fans couldn't believe it. Their perennial last place team was suddenly flirting with the .500 mark and actually playing good, sound, exciting baseball. They began coming out to Veterans Stadium in droves, sensing that perhaps something big was going to happen at the Vet very soon.

There must have been a great deal of breath holding around the Phils in '74, as if people were waiting for the bubble to burst. But it wasn't bursting. In fact, the Phils were remaining within striking distance of the division lead. And in the forefront of the surge was Mike Schmidt, whose consistent slugging had him near the top of the league in both homers and RBIs. My, how opinions about him had changed.

"I'm Mike's biggest fan," crowed Manager Ozark. "And I'm finished giving him advice. Right now I probably believe in him more than he believes in himself."

But Mike did believe in himself. No more doubting that he could cut the mustard as a big leaguer. He also appreciated his natural talents, which people were now accepting and not trying to change.

"What I have is a gift," he said. "I'd be foolish to treat it as anything else. The smart thing for me now is to try to perfect it. It's something that God gave to me and I always had. Sometimes it's downright scary. Like I can just pick up a golf club and swing it the way you're supposed to. I've never fired a gun, but I know, with my hand-eye coordination, I could be an expert marksman."

This wasn't a conceited braggart talking. It was an exceptional athlete who had always taken to physical endeavors easily. In fact, over the years, several Phillies have remarked that Mike is the best natural athlete on the team.

On June 10, the Phils were in Houston, playing the Astros in the "eighth wonder of the world," that great enclosed stadium: the Houston Astrodome. Mike was up, standing squared away on the right side of the plate. He got a pitch to his liking, stepped into it and swung. He could tell immediately that it was one of those rare moments when everything was just right, the perfect coordination of hand and eye, of mind and body. The bat hit the ball on the fat part of the bat, at just the right second.

The ball took off toward dead center. It was a majestic drive, high and going deep. Centerfielder Cesar Cedeno, one of the best in the game, knew immediately.

He didn't even move. This ball was gone . . . and it was going to go a long way out.

But it never made it. The ball was already some 300 feet from home plate and about 117 feet high when it slammed into a public address speaker that was suspended from the roof. The ball came straight down, and there was Mike, standing on first base . . . with a single! It was the first time a ball had hit anything that high on the dome. Those who saw it figured Mike's smash might have traveled some 600 feet unimpeded. Naturally, the blast was reported in all the papers, and more people than ever began to learn of the awesome power in the bat wielded by Mike Schmidt.

"I think that people will start to realize that I'm around now," Mike said, with a wink.

The Phils continued to battle the rest of the division and the .500 mark. No longer were they league patsies, and it was a good feeling. The pitching was still not deep, and there were some holes on the bench, but the starting club had become a strong one. Luzinski was about ready to return to the line-up and young Bob Boone was looking more like a major league catcher, though still sharing the position with Mike Ryan.

But it was the infield that was the team's strong point. Mike was also a much improved third baseman, who was quick to both his right and left, and charged slow-hit balls very well. He also had a powerful, but accurate throwing arm. And he had plenty of company in an infield that was considered one of the best in baseball.

Larry Bowa was quickly becoming one of the best shortstops in the league. He had great range and a sure pair of hands. Cash, though limited somewhat in range, made all the plays well, and could turn the double-play. Montanez had moved from the outfield to first, and fielded his position as well as anyone, in addition to heading for a .300 season at the plate. And as is usually the case, winning breeds camaraderie.

Mike and Dave Cash had become especially close, and would often kid each other, Cash often telling Mike that he could be the game's next white superstar. Mike, in turn, would play along with Cash, a black man, and the two would often have the rest of the clubhouse breaking up.

Mike was becoming more and more his own man. He was also becoming a fast favorite with the fans of Philadelphia. It was almost All-Star time and the fans were collecting their ballots in order to vote. The ballots listed the players by position, at least all the players the commissioner's office felt would merit votes. Because of the dismal year Mike had in '73, he wasn't even listed on the ballot.

To the Philly fans, this was a personal affront, and they embarked on an intense write-in campaign to get Mike on the team. Ballot stuffing is not uncommon at All-Star time, a practice that has led for an annual call to change the system. Anyway, it was reported that an engineer at a Philadelphia radio station personally wrote Mike's name on some 30,000 All-Star ballots. The team also got behind the fans and hired a helicopter to airlift 100,000 votes to All-Star headquarters just before the voting deadline. Mike wound up with the most write-in votes in All-Star history to that time, and finished second in the balloting to Ron Cey of the Dodgers. This prompted Mets' Manager Yogi Berra, who would be handling the All-Star squad, to name Mike to the team.

"The guy is having a fantastic year," Yogi said, "and besides, I don't want to get shot the next time I'm in Philadelphia."

(Mike got into the game and walked in both his plate appearances.)

Then it was back to business. By the time the team had played 106 games they had a record of 54-52, and incredibly, were second in a close divisional race, just a game behind the 55-51 Cardinals. Mike was still around the .300 mark and becoming increasingly optimistic about the possibilities for the future.

"Before the season started I was hoping to hit .250, with about 20 to 25 home runs and maybe 80 RBIs, play a decent third base and help the club a little," he said. "All of a sudden I find I can hit .300 and that a load of homers and RBIs come with an average like that. Now I think I can hit more than .300, maybe .340 or .350. And I never thought all this would happen so fast."

The motto around the Vet was "Yes, we can!" and there was talk about Mike winning the Most Valuable Player prize, especially if the Phils could go all the way to the division title. Manager Ozark had joined everyone else in hopping on the Schmidt bandwagon.

"I don't want to black-cat the kid," said the manager, "but if Mike continues to progress the way he has, he'll be the highest-paid player in this game some day. The front office won't be able to find enough money to pay him."

Even with the return of Luzinski, whose injury prevented him from completely regaining his form of a year earlier, the Phils didn't have quite enough firepower and pitching to go all the way. They continued to play around .500 ball and stayed fairly close, but it wasn't quite enough. When it ended, they had an 80-82 record, good for third place behind the Pirates and Cards. Yet they had ended their string of last-place finishes and had played better than anyone dreamed. Plus, they had unveiled a new star. Mike Schmidt had put together a great season.

Despite tailing off slightly in September, he still finished with a .282 batting average while playing in all 162 games. He had 160 hits in 568 at bats. He scored 108 runs, had 28 doubles and seven triples. In the power department you couldn't ask for much more. Mike led the major leagues in home runs with 36 and was second in the National League with 116 big RBIs. He also showed his good eye by walking 106 times. He still had 138 strikeouts, two more than the year before, but he also came to the plate some 200 times more. All in all, it was a fantastic year.

"Last year I was single," Mike said, in explaining one of the differences since '73. "There were times when I'd be out till all hours of the morning. But things have changed now that I have a wife to go home to. I'm not concerned with anything now except baseball and loving my wife."

Now, perhaps Mike faced an even greater task than he had a year earlier. At that time he was making it big after a dismal rookie year. But how many players, stars and superstars, have said that getting there isn't as difficult as staying there. Mike would be striving for consistency, and he was hoping for a .300 season. If he could hit .300, he knew everything else would fall into place.

The team also had high hopes for '75. After their surprising finish of a year earlier, and playing in a well-balanced division, they felt they would be strong contenders for the title. They hadn't rested on their laurels, either. Before the season they made two important moves. The first brought centerfielder Garry Maddox to the team. Maddox was a good hitter, but perhaps more important, considered by many the best defensive centerfielder in the game. The second move brought relief ace Tug McGraw over from the Mets, where he had had several outstanding seasons.

Sure enough, the Phils were an improved team once again in '75, and it wasn't long before it became obvious that they would be challenging the Pirates for the top spot in the East. Luzinski was back to full strength and hitting a ton. McGraw had joined righty Gene Garber to give the club a one-two punch out of the bullpen. Carlton still wasn't as dominating as he had been in '72, but remained the ace of the staff, and he was beginning to get help. Even shortstop Bowa was shattering his reputation of good field-not hit, and heading for a .300 year.

Mike, too, was hitting the long ball again, but he wasn't doing it consistently. In fact, his average was down, and he was again striking out too much . . . way too much. His hitting hadn't collapsed completely, but his average was hovering in the mid .200's, around the

.250 mark, and he couldn't seem to get it much higher. He seemed to have reverted somewhat to lunging at pitches and trying to kill the ball instead of just meeting it.

Nevertheless, the team hung in there, and Mike was contributing, just not quite to the extent he would have liked. Fortunately, Luzinski was having a super year, heading for a .300 season and leading the league in RBIs. He was also battling Mike and the Mets' Dave Kingman for the home run crown. Mike finally got hot in August and belted twelve circuits during the month to move himself right back up there.

Once again the Phils found themselves chasing the Pirates. They fall short once again but finished second with their best reçord in years, an 86-76 slate. They also had some fine individual performances. Luzinski was consistent all year, hitting .300, with 34 homers and a major league best of 120 runs batted in. He would finish second to Joe Morgan of Cincinnati in the MVP balloting.

That wasn't all. Shortstop Bowa had his best year, hitting .305, Maddox hit a solid .272, and several other players produced. The pitching was still a bit thin, especially with Carlton having a mediocre 15-14 mark, but the team was obviously still improving.

As for Mike, well, it was a strange year. He once again led the majors in home runs with 38, but he had only hit .249 in 158 games, and that was the lowest average by a National League home run king in some twenty-three years. He still managed a respectable 95 RBIs, but the thing that really hurt was a major league leading 180 strikeouts, almost a record. In fact, someone figured out that Mike was striking out at a higher rate than former Yankee great Mickey Mantle, who holds the career mark for whiffs.

Mike talked about his old nemesis—the strikeout.

"One hundred and eighty strikeouts is a ridiculous number. No one with my kind of hand-eye coordination should strike out that much. That's what makes it so hard to take. I do so many things well that I can't understand why hitting a baseball is so difficult. I've got to find what it takes to make me do what I know I have to do.

"I figure that eighty fewer strikeouts would have given me twenty more hits this past year and probably some four more homers. And I can't count how many times I might have advanced a runner with an out or gotten on because of an error. A strikeout is just nowhere."

Although Mike obviously felt that hitting a baseball should be easier he should be reminded that many people feel it is the singularly most difficult skill to master in all of sports. And while his batting average and number of strikeouts distressed him, Mike should have been happy that he was becoming a fine all-around player. He was second in the Gold Glove balloting for the top fielding third sacker in the league, and he had also become a fine baserunner, swiping 23 sacks in 1974 and 29 in 1975. So he was contributing in other ways, not just with his bat.

Still, he vowed to improve upon things in 1976. He and his teammates figured they were now ready to go all the way to the top. Everyone was pleased with the year to year improvement. But there comes a time when that improvement has to lead to a title, and in 1976, the Phils felt they were ready to cross that line.

And they were right. No longer did the Phillies resemble a three-ring circus. They were a solid, well-balanced, and increasingly deep ballclub. It wasn't long before they jumped on top of the pack with every indication that they would stay right there. As for Mike, he was off to a good start. The strikeouts were down, the average was up, and he was driving in a lot of runs.

On April 17, the Phils were in Wrigley Field (a small ballpark with no lights), to meet the home-standing Cubs. All games are played during the day at Wrigley, and the hitters love it. On this day, Mike Schmidt loved it more than anyone else. In four trips to the plate, Mike belted four consecutive home runs, tying a major league record. He was in the midst of a hot streak which would see him belt seven in four games.

Yet a short time later, Mike was striking out again at a rate that Manager Ozark felt was too high. He promptly dropped his slugger from third to sixth in the batting order, saying, "He'll stay there until he cuts down on his strikeouts."

Like many sluggers, Mike would experience hot and cold streaks. When he was hot, the homers, RBIs, and other hits would come in bunches. And when he lost the groove, he begins overswinging, striking out too much, and hitting a lot of harmless pops. For that reason, Mike still got down on himself and admired contact hitters who didn't worry about homers. For instance, when he was hitting his four homers in Chicago and receiving all kinds of accolades for his feat, he still took time to compare himself with Cub third baseman Bill Madlock, the National League batting champion.

"I'm sure Bill has no idea of the frustrations I experience," Mike said. "He goes up there and gets his base hits almost every day. Guys like him don't have to think. They just react."

There were obviously many National League hurlers who feared him when he stepped into the batter's box. For one thing, he was always capable of turning a game around or winning it with one sweep of the bat. And for another, a man with Mike's strength and power could take a pitcher's head off if he hit the ball just right. So obviously, with his drive to improve and excel, Mike was selling himself short. The strikeouts still depressed him, as did his failure to maintain a .300 batting average over the course of a season. But he also had to realize that batting .300 wasn't necessarily his role. As GM Paul Owens said:

"If Mike drives in 100 runs, I don't care what he hits."

Mike was an all-star again in '76, after missing that distinction the year before. And after the midsummer classic, he helped the Phillies complete their drive to the division title, their first win of any kind since 1950. And they did it in fine style, finishing with a 101-61 record, one of the best in baseball.

For Mike it was another outstanding year. Once again he led the major leagues in homers, blasting 38, the same as the year before, and marking the third consecutive year he had that honor. He did it with a .262 batting average, disappointing to him, perhaps, but not that bad. He also scored 112 times, had 31 doubles, four triples and drove home 107 runs. He also managed 100 walks. On the negative side were 149 strikeouts, making him the league leader in that category for the third straight year, but at least it was down from his 180 of the season before.

He had plenty of help. Garry Maddox put together a sensational .330 season with 68 RBIs, Luzinski batted .304 with 21 homers and 95 RBIs; outfielder Jay Johnstone hit .318 in 129 games, and catcher Bob Boone was maturing with a .271 average. Pitching-wise, Carlton reverted to form with a 20-7 season; Jim Lonborg was 18-10 and young Larry Christenson 13-8. Garber was 9-3 and McGraw 7-6 out of the pen. And there was a lot of help from the guys on the bench.

But before everyone celebrated too much, the Phils had to return to action in the playoffs, and that wouldn't be easy. They would have to meet the defending World Champion Cincinnati Reds in a best of five series to determine which club went to the World Series. And the Big Red Machine was a powerhouse, sporting the likes of Pete Rose, Johnny Bench, Tony Perez, George Foster, Joe Morgan, Dave Concepcion, and Ken Griffey. The Reds were considered the best team in baseball and were heavy favorites.

The first two games were scheduled for the Vet, so there was hope. But in the opener the Phils played like amateurs, making one mistake after another, especially in the field, as the Reds won, 6-3. The next day Philly took a 2-0 lead on a Luzinski homer, but Cincy stormed back to take a 4-2 lead in the sixth and went on to win it 6-2. Then a disheartened Philadelphia team traveled to Cincinnati where they promptly lost and were eliminated.

So a glorious season ended suddenly with a real downer, a sweep by the Reds in three quick days. And after winning their first title of any kind in more than a quarter of a century, their season was over. The team's only consolation was that they were a solid ballclub and had an excellent chance of being right back in the same position the next year.

Mike was as distraught as the rest of his teammates, though he had a good playoff with four hits in 13 trips for a .308 average with two doubles and two RBIs. He only struck out once. But none of that mattered. Everyone now looked to 1977.

Even with an outstanding season behind them, the Philly brass didn't want to stand pat. The team lost second baseman Dave Cash to Montreal via the free agent route and brought in veteran Ted Sizemore to replace him. They also picked up hard-hitting Richie Hebner to be the new first baseman and shortly after the season started got speedy outfielder Bake McBride from St. Louis. So with a few new players, they were ready for another run at the rest of the National League.

Before the 1977 season started, Mike made some big news. He and the Phils had come to terms on a new, long-term contract. The big slugger signed a six-year pact, calling for more than $3 million, all of which made him the highest-paid player on the team and at the time one of the three or four best paid players in the game. There was little doubt that he had reached superstar status. It also showed the Phils were not going to take any chances losing him to the new free agent set-up which was beginning in earnest.

But there was a negative aspect for Mike getting such a huge contract. Many fans and even some members of the press expected Mike to carry the team, especially when other players began to go sour, and to some extent, Mike began believing this, too.

"There have been plenty of times when I've tried to hit a three-run homer with no one on base," he said, added in a self-mocking tone, "and that's pretty hard to do."

What Mike was referring to was his old habit of trying too hard, trying to kill the ball, just as he had as a kid. He constantly had to monitor himself, keep himself from falling into the trap. He began to believe in something he called the KISS theory, and if that sounds strange, it's not. KISS stands for "Keep it simple, stupid," something that Mike was always reminding himself about. He still tended to put a great deal of pressure on himself. As his friend and teammate, Larry Bowa, said:

"You can't play this game if you're trying too hard. If you're squeezing the sawdust out of the bat, you're not going to get hits."

Mike controlled himself pretty well in 1977. Perhaps one reason was that many of his teammates were producing fine seasons and the club was again running away with the National League East. For the second straight year, the Phils won the division title with a 101-61 record.

It also had to be a very satisfying season for Mike. In spite of the new pact and the ensuing pressure, he still produced a solid .274 season. Although he didn't win the home run title (Cincy's George Foster had 52), he showed his consistency by banging out 38 for the third straight year. He also drove home 101 runs, scored 114 times, walked 104 times, and cut his strikeouts down to a career low of 122. So he had no complaints.

And as mentioned before, he had the support. Luzinski had his greatest season, with a .309 average, 39 homers, and 130 big RBIs. Behind him were McBride with a .315 average, Maddox at .292 with 74 RBIs, Richie Hebner with 18 homers, and solid .281 and .280 seasons by the keystone combination of Sizemore and Bowa. Pitching-wise it was Carlton at 23-10 with another Cy Young Award season, Christenson at 19-6, Lonborg 11-4, and the great bullpen of Garber and McGraw. The Phillies were good.

Now it was on to the playoffs once again, only this time their opponents would not be Cincinnati. The Reds had been dethroned by the rejuvenated Los Angeles Dodgers, a powerful and speedy team, which in 1977 had four players—Steve Garvey, Reggie Smith, Dusty Baker, and Ron Cey—who blasted 30 or more homers. They also had a 20-game winner in Tommy John and a sound club defensively. But after the debacle of 1976, the Phils figured it was their year.

It was a battle of 20-gamers in game one, Carlton vs. John, with the series opening at Dodger Stadium in Los Angeles. The Phils wasted no time, as Luzinski blasted a two-run homer in the very first inning. They made it 4-0 with a pair in the fourth and 5-0 as they got one in the fifth. Meanwhile, Carlton was sailing along without a problem.

Then in the fifth the Dodgers got one back, and in the last of the seventh they loaded the bases with Ron Cey up. Cey caught a fastball and drove it deep into the leftfield stands, a grand slam home run that tied the game, as the Dodger fans went wild. Were the Phils coming apart already? Fortunately, the Philadelphia bullpen came to the rescue, as Garber, and then McGraw did the job. The Phils pushed across a pair of runs in the ninth and had drawn first blood, 7-5. Mike had one hit in five trips, but knocked in one of the key runs.

So the Phils were up by a game, a luxury they didn't have a year earlier. Now if they could manage another pair of victories, they'd be headed for the World Series. In game two they started Jim Lonborg against the Dodgers' Don Sutton. It was scoreless until the third, when both clubs got single tallies, but then in the bottom of the fourth, the Dodgers broke it as Dusty Baker belted another grand slam homer. Single runs in the sixth and seventh gave L.A. a 7-1 victory, as Sutton pitched a strong game and held Mike hitless in four trips.

Now it was back to Philly for the pivotal third game, and the Phils were hoping that some 60,000 cheering fans at the Vet would give them an added advantage. The Dodgers started Burt Hooton and the Phils countered with Larry Christenson. It would be a game remembered for a long time at the Vet and throughout the City of Brotherly Love.

In the top of the second, Garvey singled and Dusty Baker doubled to leftcenter. Garvey was trying to score and the relay home seemed to get there in time, but the umpire called him safe and the Dodgers had the lead. With two out, catcher Steve Yeager singled Baker home and the Dodgers had a 2-0 lead.

But the Phils battled right back. In their half of the inning Luzinski led off with a single. A force play followed and Maddox whiffed for the second out. But Bob Boone singled and Ted Sizemore walked to load the bases. Pitcher Christenson, a good hitter, was up next. Hooton worked the count to 1-2, then threw two pitches he felt hit the strike zone. But the umpire called each a ball, and a rattled Hooton then walked Christenson to force in a run. Still rattled, Hooton then argued two more called before walking McBride to get the tying run home.

Hooton tried, but just couldn't settle down. He then walked Bowa to force in the third run, and Rick Rhoden had to come in to put out the fire. The Dodgers then tied it in the fourth, knocking out Christenson. The game remained scoreless until the Philly eighth.

Richie Hebner opened the inning with a double to right. Then a base hit by Maddox brought Hebner home with the go-ahead run. Ron Cey then made a throwing error on Boone, allowing Maddox to come around with a second run, making it 5-3. Now the Phils were just three outs away from taking a 2-1 lead in the series and they had their bullpen ace, Gene Garber, on the mound as the Dodgers came up in the ninth.

Garber got the first two batters easily. One more out to go and the Phils would be *thisclose* to making the World Series. The hitter was veteran Vic Davalillo, who caught everyone sleeping by bunting for a basehit. Another pinch hitter, 39-year-old Manny Mota, promptly sent a drive to deep left. Luzinski trapped the ball as it came off the wall, and when his throw got past Sizemore at second, Davalillo scored and Mota went all the way to third. It was now a 5-4 game.

Davey Lopes was next and he hit a shot right at Mike. It bounced off his glove, but Bowa grabbed it and threw to first. It was one of those plays that could have gone either way, but the umpire called Lopes safe and Mota came in with the tying run. Now the Phils were in trouble. They couldn't let this game slip away. A defeat here might be something they couldn't get over.

Garber looked in at the next hitter, Bill Russell, then suddenly whirled and tried to pick Lopes off first. He threw the ball past Hebner and the speedy Lopes streaked into second. When Russell slammed a solid single, Lopes came home with the go-ahead run. The Dodgers had scored three times after two were out in the ninth and had taken a 6-5 lead. The stunned Phillies went down meekly in the last of the ninth and had lost the game. Now they trailed by 2-1 in the best of five series.

No one could believe what had happened. As reliever Tug McGraw said, "It was like watching Shock Theatre at 2am and being eight years old again. I wasn't believing what I was seeing. I was not believing anything."

The Phils really had their backs to the wall. They still argued that safe call to Lopes but could do nothing about that now. The team was suddenly under tremendous pressure, and so was Mike, who was just 1-for-13 in the series. If ever he felt he was letting the team down it had to be then. But he looked at it philosophically before the start of the fourth game.

"It's very simple," he said. "We have to win tonight.

If we're a championship team, we will win. I still can't believe what happened yesterday. I was wondering if this was a dream and if this was happening to me or not. We really have our backs to the wall now and we have to show what we're made of."

Nearly 65,000 fans crammed into the Vet to witness Steve Carlton hook up with Tommy John for a second time. The Phils had the man they wanted on the mound. It was do or die for them and they knew it. The game was played in a damp, steady rain, the kind of game that would have been called off quickly in the regular season, but because of tight post-season scheduling, the game went on.

In the top of the second the Dodgers broke the ice. Ron Cey walked and after Garvey flied out, Dusty Baker belted a two-run homer, and a strange silence fell over the huge stadium, as the rain continued to fall. Finally, in the bottom of the fourth, the Phils got to John for the first time. Luzinski singled, Hebner doubled, and Garry Maddox got the run in with a ground out. So it was 2-1, with the Dodgers coming up in the fifth.

Once again they put runners on and Carlton couldn't stem the tide. Before the inning ended they had two more runs across and a 4-1 lead. For the second straight year the Phils felt it all slipping away. And the rain continued, making playing conditions even worse as the game went on. As Mike noted, after catching a pop in the ill-fated fifth.

"It was raining so hard I almost couldn't see the ball as it came down to me. I was lucky to catch it."

What the Phils and Mike couldn't do was hit. Tommy John, with his sinker working to perfection, shut the Phillies down the rest of the way and the Dodgers had themselves a 4-1 win and a ticket to the World Series.

What a bitter pill for the Phils to swallow. It was hard for all of them, but perhaps hardest of all for Mike because of the way he performed, or more accurately, didn't perform. In four games he had gotten just a single hit, and that was in the opener. He finished with a 1-for-16 log for an .063 average. With his new contract and his own desire to lead, it had to be a mammoth disappointment to him. The big man is expected to produce in the clutch. That's something all the great ones have done.

Now there was nothing to do but follow the old axiom, *wait till next year.* Those long suffering Philadelphia fans were also waiting, yet they remained loyal, with well over two million coming out to the Vet each year. But how long could they wait for the Phils to win the big one?

Whereas in '76 and '77, the team broke from the gate quickly and led virtually all the way, in 1978 they started slowly. Things were just not going right. Perhaps the club was demoralized from their two straight playoff losses. At any rate, they weren't playing well. In fact, they were under .500 for awhile and had to struggle just to get even. Fortunately, none of the other teams in the division could break away, and the Phils hung close.

Finally, on June 23, the team went into first place, but they were still not playing well. The pitching had suddenly become thin and the club was forced to trade reliever Garber to Atlanta to get former Phillies pitcher, Dick Ruthven, so he could join the starting rotation. Second baseman Sizemore broke a hand and would miss a lot of action. And there was still another Phil who was not producing. His name was Mike Schmidt.

For the first time in his career, Mike was having injury problems. He had a strained knee and a pulled hamstring, and the injuries lingered. He hung in the lineup, but wasn't hitting with his usual power. His average dropped down around the .250 mark, but this time he wasn't compensating with his usual power pace.

That made it extremely difficult for him, especially with the kind of pressure he always put on himself. As usual, it resulted in his trying too hard at the plate.

"My perennial nemesis is my lack of ability to stay within myself," was the way Mike put it, "to play the game relaxed and use the pressure as a positive force."

That was important. Pressure usually drives the superstar to excel even more, but with Mike, it always seemed to hold him back. And, of course, problems usually lead to more problems. When Mike stopped hitting well, the fans of Philadelphia began letting him know it by booing him, something that made him press even more.

"The first time it happened I couldn't believe it," he said. "I wondered how in the world they could boo me. I was trying; it wasn't a lack of effort that was causing my problems. I just had to realize that they were booing the guy who plays third for the Phillies. I couldn't let myself take it personally. You can't block out a hostile crowd, but you can find ways to deal with its reaction to you. When I don't deserve negative crowd reaction it disappoints me. When I do deserve it, fine.

"People pay their money to come to games and they have certain expectations. If I don't live up to them, well, they can do what they want. You've got to remember that we have a lot of people here who live and die by the team."

The Phils remained in the lead, but they couldn't pull away as they had in the past. As the season began winding down, the Pittsburgh Pirates began chasing them in earnest and the club had to make sure it didn't do the "el foldo" routine. Mike still hadn't regained his old touch at the plate, but though the injuries still bothered him, he still hung in there. He still excelled in the field, and he was now recognized as one of the best in the business at his position. He was well on his way to winning a third straight Golden Glove award.

General Manager Paul Owens said that Mike's fielding probably saved the team fifteen to eighteen runs a year. "He's one of the finest third basemen in the game, especially going to his left," Owens claimed. And shortstop Larry Bowa concurred, saying, "Mike makes my job easier because he goes to his left so well that I can cheat a little more to my left. To tell the truth, I'm getting a little spoiled having him out there."

By the final weekend of the season, the Phils led the Pirates by four games, but would be meeting their cross-state rivals in a wrap-up four-game series. If the Bucs could sweep, they would force the Phils to a playoff. When the Pirates took the first two, many fans thought about the 1964 collapse and the playoff results of the past two seasons. But the team pulled itself together and won the third game, 10-8, clinching the division crown for a third straight year.

It hadn't been a good year all around. Many of the Phils fell short of previous production levels. Mike, too, wanted to forget the season.

The team was in the playoffs again, nevertheless, and would be meeting the Dodgers in a rematch of 1977. Manager Ozark was so brash as to predict the club would win in three straight, and Mike came out and said the Phils were "ready for an offensive explosion."

The explosion came, all right, in the first game. Only it was the Dodgers who exploded, routing the Phils by a 9-5 count and immediately bringing back the haunting memories of the last two playoffs. The next day Tommy John took to the mound for the Dodgers and had his famous sinker working to the tune of 21 ground outs. When it ended the Phils had been shut out by a 4-0 score and were already on the ropes.

"I was just in the players' lounge," said Tug McGraw, after the game. "A bunch of the guys there were asking what happens to us in these playoffs. We couldn't come up with an answer. In fact, the question is still on the table."

To make matters worse, the club had lost the first two in front of their loyal fans at the Vet. Now they were on their way to Los Angeles. With Steve Carlton pitching, they managed to come alive for a 9-4 victory. In game four, young Randy Lerch faced veteran Doug Rau of the Dodgers.

The first inning was typical of the Phils' playoff futility. They loaded the bases with none out . . . and didn't score! The Dodgers then took a 1-0 lead in the second, but in the third Luzinski slammed a two-run homer to give his team a 2-1 lead. Cey homered in the fourth to tie the game and Steve Garvey slammed one in the sixth to give the Dodgers a 3-2 lead. But Bake McBride got it even again with a pinch-hit homer in the seventh.

It stayed that way into the 10th inning, and everyone was on the edge of their seats. The Phillies were hanging on by a thread and the Dodgers didn't want to go into a fifth game. With Tug McGraw pitching, both Reggie Smith and Garvey, dangerous hitters, made out. Then Ron Cey walked, but when Dusty Baker lofted a fly to short center, it seemed the inning would be over.

But the Dodgers' won it when the usually sure-handed Garry Maddox made a pair of errors. With runners on first and second, Bill Russell slammed a hit up the middle. Cey scored and the game and playoffs were over. One of the best centerfielders in the game had let it get away.

But Maddox wasn't the only one at fault. No one played well. Mike had another terrible playoff game, with just three hits in fifteen trips for a .200 average. And he hadn't hit a single homer in three championship series.

"We haven't won a playoff game at home in three years," lamented PR man Larry Shenk. "The fans and media have come down pretty hard on us. The worst thing about it is we haven't really been competitive in the playoffs. If we had lost three straight to the Dodgers we might have had a lot of fan trouble next year. But we did win the one game, and there's always next year."

But how long could it go on? Sometimes a team can become snake pit, psychologically defeated, and it won't change unless there are wholesale changes. The Philly brass didn't want to do that, but they did decide to make one dramatic move.

They signed a free agent, a 38-year-old one at that, but a very special kind of player. He was Pete Rose, the long-time star of the Cincinnati Reds, a fiery competitor and a proven winner. To get this incredible player, the Phils agreed to pay him some $800,000 a year for four years. Despite his age Pete was still in great shape and had all his skills in tact. But they didn't only want him for his 200 hits and .300 batting average. They wanted him for his fiery leadership, the kind of qualities some felt were missing on the present Phillies' club. In fact, one national magazine, previewing the 1979 season, said this about the Phils, quoting a source said to be close to the team:

"With Dick Butkus in football and Jerry Sloan in basketball, Rose is the greatest competitor of all-time in sports. There's something about him under pressure—he doesn't think he can fail."

The source went on to say the team hoped this quality of Pete's would rub off on two players in particular, Mike Schmidt and Greg Luzinski. The source was then quoted as saying.

"They (Schmidt and Luzinski) heard they needed a leader so much that, out of spite, they got too cool, trying to prove they didn't. When they finally needed some emotion, they couldn't muster it up, especially Mike. Greg was fooled a lot but went on ferocious power streaks; Mike did nothing all year. He beats himself; he swung at bad pitches, overthought, brooded. He's like Garry Maddox and Bake McBride. They should all be in their salad years but none of them really *likes* to play, there's no joy in it. It's a job, and they don't like pressure and high visibility. Now that Rose has the spotlight, maybe they'll relax and have some fun."

Like most opinions, only part of what was said rang true. For instance, there was no mention made of Mike's injuries. And wasn't he entitled to an off year? He had been remarkably consistent for the four previous seasons. Any player who worried about carrying the team, who wanted to hit .300, who felt he had to produce, had to care about playing the game. When a team loses the way the Phils had for three straight years, the players might well try to cover up their disappointment and embarrassment by acting as if they don't really care. But with almost all professional athletes, winning is the ultimate achievement. So why should it be any different with Mike and the rest of the Phillies?

But while all this speculation was going on, Mike was working hard to come back in '79. Since he had never experienced the debilitating effects of a nagging injury before, he began working extra hard in the off-season, using all the facilities available to the team, including various types of Nautilus machines. When he came to camp that year, catcher Bob Boone saw the difference immediately.

"I can see a lot of change in Mike," he said. "He put a lot of hard work and commitment into training. When you work like that, you have a tremendous desire coming into a season."

Mike and his wife also had their first child in December, and that event also seemed to make him a more settled man. However, early in spring training the team tried an experiment. They had him playing some second base. He didn't like it much, especially when he began hurting his arm when attempting the double play pivot and throw. Fortunately, a trade with the Cubs brought the slick-fielding Manny Trillo to the Phils and Mike was returned to third.

When the season started, he began playing very well, hitting with his old authority, and taking charge on the field. Rose was playing first for the Phils, and doing exactly what was expected of him, but the team still wasn't winning. The other players and the pitching staff were having their problems. Larry Christenson, for one, had broken a collarbone in the off-season and would be out of action for a good part of the season.

There were other injuries. At one time or another, Bowa, Trillo, Luzinski and Boone were all on the shelf. The only two players really doing a big job were the incredible Rose and Mike Schmidt. Yet the team still trailed Montreal, Pittsburgh, the Cubs and Cardinals.

The three-time division winners found themselves in fifth place.

By the end of June, while the team was still struggling, Mike had already passed his 1978 total of 21 homers and was close to 50 RBIs. And Larry Bowa admitted that the addition of Rose might have helped Mike.

"Mike is playing more relaxed this year," said Bowa. "A lot of the pressure at being the highest paid Phillie has now been channeled toward Pete Rose."

It wasn't all gravy for Mike. By mid-August he had slammed his 39th homer, a career high, but was beset by a painful groin injury that wouldn't heal as long as he stayed in the line-up. But he stayed. He was also in another battle with Dave Kingman for the home run leadership. In fact, Mike had hit 36 homers by the end of July, and that tied a league record. As usual, people said he would be a totally devastating hitter if he could always have this kind of consistency.

"I get a kick out of people telling me that my home runs come in bunches," Mike said. "Hey, all home run hitters hit them in bunches. If they didn't, wouldn't it make sense that some guy would figure out how to hit 162 of them, one in every game. Seriously, though, I can't deny that I'm streaky. I can hit about .400 during one month. But since my lifetime batting average is about .255, there have obviously been some valleys along the way."

Mike definitely seemed to have a more relaxed attitude at last, judging by the way he was answering these types of questions, questions that used to bother him in past seasons. For instance, another popular one was whether he'd rather hit homers or .300. Certainly, he'd like to do both, but he no longer went on long discourses about it.

"I don't swing for homers," he said. "I swing the same way all the time. When I make good contact, it can turn into a homer as easily as a single. The home run just takes longer to watch."

But in spite of his success, 1979 wasn't a fun season,

because by August it was becoming increasingly obvious that the Phils weren't going to make it four straight. And Mike's groin injury was beginning to affect his performance. As he said to one reporter toward the end of the so-called dog days:

"I'm having trouble getting into a very good mood right now. It's about 100 degrees and we're playing doubleheaders and struggling. This is the grinding time for ballplayers. It makes it tough to get ready to play, and tough to always act the way people expect."

There was another major event taking place late in the season. The team fired long-time manager Danny Ozark, and replaced him with Dallas Green, a former Phils pitcher who was working within the organization. The feeling was that Ozark was too easy with the players, and that they needed someone to shake them up. Green would do the job. He wasn't out to win a popularity contest and he proved that in 1980.

The long season finally ended for the Phils. They had fallen back to an 84-78 record, finishing an embarrassing fourth in the division, some fourteen games behind the Pirates. It was even more embarrassing when the Bucs did what the Phils had been unable to do the previous three years, winning the playoffs and going on to take the World Series.

A quick look at the stats showed the kind of year it was. Bowa hit just .241, Luzinski was at .252 with just 18 homers and 81 RBIs, Trillo was at .260. Carlton led the pitchers at 18-11, but there wasn't much else behind him. Pete Rose had done all that was asked of him. He batted .331 with 208 hits, but he couldn't pull the rest with him.

Mike also had an outstanding year. The groin injury slowed him in September and he finished with a .253 average, playing in 160 games despite the injury. Powerwise, he was awesome, with a career high 45 homers, three less than Kingman, and 114 RBIs. He also led the league with 120 walks and had his strikeouts down to a respectable 115. Though the team fared poorly, Mike had to be satisfied with many aspects of his performance.

Now came the business of regrouping for 1980. Dallas Green showed quickly that he was the boss, and although the players didn't agree with all his methods, he wouldn't bend. There would be manager-player conflicts all year, some of them culminating in harsh words, often aired in the press. But maybe this is what the team needed.

For one thing, Green wanted more contributions from his bench. He acquired veterans such as Greg Gross and Del Unser, who wouldn't rattle in tough situations. He also had productive youngsters such as Keith Moreland, Lonnie Smith, Bob Walk, and Dickie Noles. The new manager had certain expectations and felt his players should live up to them.

The team did not get off well. For the first couple of months it seemed like a rerun of '79. None of the contending teams seemed to be able to pull away. The Phils, Pirates, and Expos each took turns at getting hot, then cooling off. The club was again playing with various injuries, the biggest being a knee injury to Luzinski that shelved him for several months. Fortunately, rookie Lonnie Smith played very well in his place, hitting well over .300 and giving the club another stolen base threat.

There were still problems with the pitching staff. Carlton was brilliant again, the best in the league, and Dick Ruthven was doing a good job. Rookie Bob Walk picked up some of the slack in the early going, and Marty Bystrom, another rookie, did it near the end. The bullpen suffered somewhat as Tug McGraw had to go on the disabled list for some time.

Aside from Carlton, one other Phillie was having an outstanding year. Mike was finally putting it all together. He was leading the league in homers and RBIs, but also hitting well, up around .290 for much of the year. And while the team couldn't get a solid streak going, there was a strong feeling that the club had to do it in 1980. They were no longer a young team, but a veteran club, with many of the starters now past their thirtieth birthdays. Carlton was 35 and still the workhorse of the staff. Rose was nearing 40 and playing everyday. McGraw was 36 and Mike was approaching his 31st birthday. It was the outspoken McGraw who voiced a sentiment felt by many.

"Time is beginning to pass us by, and we don't want to have to look back on these years as wasted," he said.

In April, the team had a 6-9 mark; in May, they were 17-9, to go over the .500 mark; in June they were just 14-14; and in July they were 15-14. That wouldn't be good enough, as both Pittsburgh and Montreal were hanging in there with them. They knew they couldn't win it unless they played better ball.

But when they dropped a doubleheader to Pittsburgh on August 10, making their season record 55-52, and dropping them six games off the pace, things began looking bleak. After the game, Manager Green exploded, chewing out many of the players, a number of whom resented him for it. But as the manager said:

"We have a penchant for ripping guys in the papers. But we do this for exercise. It flushes our minds."

The battle continued. Once again the Pirates and Expos faltered and the Phils gained ground. By September 1, they were in striking distance of the top, but General Manager Paul Owens didn't like what he saw and called a team meeting. He, too, pointed a finger at several veterans, claiming they weren't really interested in winning.

"You've been wanting to win this thing for yourself and for every other reason the last five months," he shouted. "Well, I want you to win this thing now for Ruly Carpenter (the team owner) and for me, the guys who put this team together."

That seemed to shake everyone. They won that day in San Francisco and moved into first place, at least temporarily. But they were playing well again. By the middle of the month it looked as if the defending champion Pirates were out of the race. Only the young Montreal Expos stood in the way. They had battled the

Pirates to the wire the year before, and seemed intent on going all the way this time around. The two clubs began their stretch runs.

The last week in September there was a key series between the clubs in Philadelphia. In the first game, Bake McBride, who was having a fine season, homered in the ninth to give the Phils a 2-1 victory. That put them up by 1 ½ games, and two in the loss column. If they could win the next two, they'd be in good shape.

But that didn't happen. Montreal beat Carlton, 4-3, then bombed the Phils, 8-3, in the third game to retake the lead by one-half game. Was this the foldup? Many of the fans might have thought so. Four key players were in batting slumps. At the conclusion of the Montreal set, Rose was 3-for-31, Luzinski 2-for-21, Mike 2-for-16, and Bob Boone 0-for-20. If this kept up there was no way they could win it.

In spite of his mild slump, Mike already had 44 homers, 114 RBIs, and a .281 average. But none of that would mean anything if the team didn't pull out of their slump and win the race. The Phils were scheduled to meet the Expos in another three-game series to end the season, but they had to hang tight for another week. The night after losing the lead to the Expos they bounced back to score three runs in a 15th inning game to edge the Chicago Cubs, 6-5. This time they didn't fold.

"This came at a time we really needed it," said Manager Green. "We really had our backs to the wall and if we lost it, we would have been in trouble. We already knew that Montreal won when we were going into the 15th."

Finally it came down to the final three games. The two teams were deadlocked with identical 89-70 records. Both starting pitchers, Dick Ruthven of the Phils, and Scott Sanderson of the Expos, would be gunning for their seventeenth wins. So it was an even matchup.

Mike came into the game feeling real good. In spite of his mild slump of a week earlier, he had an outstanding September, slugging thirteen homers during the month.

And he had hit a homer in each of the last two games before Montreal. If he could just keep it up a little longer.

The Phils wasted no time. In the first inning Rose led off with a single and McBride doubled him to third. Mike was next to bat. Going with the pitch, he hit a fly to right. Rose tagged and scored, giving Philly a 1-0 lead before Sanderson shut the door. It stayed that way until the sixth inning. Mike was up to bat again.

Sanderson worked carefully, but Mike waited for his pitch. He got what he wanted and with his smooth swing sent the ball high over the leftfield fence for his 47th home run of the year, and a 2-0 lead. It proved to be the game-winner, as the Expos got one back in the bottom half of the inning. But veteran reliever Sparky Lyle, who had been recently acquired from Texas, shut the door and pitched the seventh. McGraw pitched brilliantly in the eighth and ninth and the Phils had won it, putting them a game up with two left.

After the game, Mike held court with the reporters. "When you win a game like this," he explained, "the first thing you do is say there's a lot of baseball still to be played; there's still all that pressure everyone says is supposed to come with a crucial series. And for us, this is a new experience. We've never really been in a pennant race before. When we won the other years, we never had games we had to win. If we lost then, we'd just drop from seven ahead to six ahead. This year, we've been in must win situations all along."

So it was back to the well the next day. Larry Christenson, who had missed much of the year with injuries, was on the mound for the Phils against Montreal ace Steve Rogers. It was raining in Montreal and the start of the game was held up for more than three hours. Finally the two teams took to the field at almost 5:30pm.

Both teams mounted threats in the first two innings, but neither scored. Then in the third McBride singled and Mike bounced a double off the centerfield wall. It looked like another RBI, but McBride was thrown out on a perfect relay to quell the opportunity. Then in the bottom of the inning, Montreal outfielder Jerry White belted a two-run homer to give the Expos the early lead.

The Phils cut it in half in the fourth as Pete Rose drove home the tally. Philly then loaded the bases with none out, but Rogers caught Mike looking at a third strike and got Luzinski to line into a double play. Finally, in the seventh, the Phils broke through. Rose, McBride, and Mike all singled to load the bases with one out. Luzinski then drilled a basehit to give Philly a 3-2 lead before a double play ended the inning.

It was becoming a see-saw game. The Expos got the runs back in the bottom of the inning, Rodney Scott doubling home the go-ahead tally, giving Montreal a 4-3 advantage. The Phils had just six outs left.

It was down to three and finally one. With two out and a man on second in the ninth, Bob Boone lined a clutch single to tie the game once again. Now it would go into extra innings. McGraw was pitching again for the Phils and Stan Bahnsen for Montreal as the game went into the 11th, still tied at 4-4.

Then Pete Rose did what he does so well. He got on base to start things off. After McBride went out, Mike stepped in again. Bahnsen pitched carefully, and Mike didn't offer at the first two, both balls. Then the Montreal righthander tried a fastball and Mike was ready. He hit a drive to deep left, way back . . . and gone! When Tug McGraw retired the Expos in the bottom of the inning, the Phils were National League East champs once more.

His teammates mobbed Mike after the game. He had really come through. Someone pointed out that his home run, the 48th of the year for him, had set a new record for third baseman, breaking the old mark of 47 held by Eddie Matthews of the Braves. It was also the 283rd of his career. When he heard that, Mike said:

"It might be the 283rd, but to me it will always be number one!"

The Phils lost the final game, but it didn't matter.

They were champs with a 91-71 record and Mike Schmidt had produced the greatest year of his career. He led the majors with 48 homers; led the National League in runs batted in with 121; in slugging average with .624; and in total bases with 342. He had seventeen game winning hits, scored 104 runs, cut his strikeouts to 119, and perhaps best of all, batted .286, the best mark of his career.

And from September 1, to the end, when the Phils ran up a 23-10 mark to take the title, Mike batted .304 with 27 runs batted in. He had finally learned to cope with the pressure and like other great stars, had played better because of it.

"Winning this year means more to me than ever before," he said. "There were times during the season when people gave up on us. Yet we came back and won it. We made believers of a lot of people. We had to have intensity throughout the year and overcome a lot of problems. And we did it!"

Once the joy of winning the division quieted down, the Phils realized they had to get another monkey off their backs, the inability to win the playoffs. They'd be meeting a new team this time, the Houston Astros, who had beaten the Dodgers in a one-game playoff. The Astros were a scrappy bunch, so there was no time to rest on any laurels.

There had to be tremendous pressure on the Phils as they got ready for the first game at Veterans Stadium. They had never won a playoff game at home and couldn't really afford to lose the opener. They had Steve Carlton, coming off a 24-9 season, ready to go against Houston's Ken Forsch.

A playoff record 65,277 fans squeezed into the huge stadium as both pitchers matched goose eggs for two innings. In the third the Astros pushed across a run when Gary Woods singled home Jose Cruz from second. Carlton didn't seem sharp and the Phils wondered if Houston was going to really nail him.

But being a great pitcher, "Lefty," as he is called,

worked out of several jams. Finally, in the bottom of the sixth, Pete Rose singled. After McBride and Mike were retired, Luzinski came up. The Bull had a dismal .228, nineteen-homer season, but this time he connected with a Forsch fastball and drove it into the leftfield seats for a two-run homer and a 2-1 Philadelphia lead.

In the seventh Garry Maddox reached third and came home when pinch-hitter Greg Gross singled to left. Tug McGraw came on to hold Houston in the final two, and the Phils finally had a playoff win at home. It was a great feeling. Mike, however, was hitless in three trips and must have wondered if his playoff blues were starting all over again.

Game two had Dick Ruthven on the mound against Houston fireballer Nolan Ryan. This game was a seesaw job from the start. Houston got one run in the third and the Phils got two in the fourth. The Astros tied it in the seventh, and took a 3-2 lead off McGraw in the eighth. But the Phils came right back to tie in their half of the eighth. They were leaving runners on base in droves, three in the seventh, two in the eighth, three more in the ninth, and two in the tenth.

The game went into extra innings. Philly had a chance to win it in the ninth when Lonnie Smith singled with Bake McBride on second. But McBride hesitated when he wasn't sure if the ball would drop and he stopped at third. Then Manny Trillo struck out and Maddox fouled out to end the inning.

Finally, in the tenth, Houston broke it open against Ron Reed with four runs. The Phils battled back to score one, but with two on and Mike at the plate with the tying run, he flied to deep right to end the game, a 7-4 Houston win.

Mike had two hits in six trips, but had fanned with the bases loaded in the seventh and then ended the game. So, again, he wasn't happy and now the series was tied and heading back to the Astrodome in Houston. But Mike said that his teammates were still confident.

"We've played well in Houston the last two years," he

said. "And nobody on this team is demoralized because nobody expected it to be easy. If we're as good a team as we think, we shouldn't be worrying. If we can't win two of three in the Astrodome, knowing what's at stake, then we don't deserve to be in the World Series. It's as simple as that."

Larry Christenson started against knuckleballer Joe Niekro in the third game and both pitchers had great stuff. Neither team could break through and at the end of nine innings it was still a scoreless tie. Once again the team battled into extra innings. Tug McGraw was again on the mound for the Phils, beginning his third inning of work in the last of the 11th. The first batter to face him was veteran Joe Morgan.

Morgan whacked a long fly to deep right. McBride went to the wall and leaped, just missing the catch, and Morgan with a leg injury limped into third with a triple. Rafael Landestoy ran for Morgan, as McGraw intentionally passed Jose Cruz and Art Howe to load the bases and set up a force or double play. Pinch-hitter Danny Walling crossed them up by hitting a fly to leftfield. Landestoy tagged and came home with the only run of the game. Houston had won it and now led, 2-1, putting the Phils in the hole again, as Mike had another quiet day with one hit in five trips.

With their backs against the wall, the Phils sent Steve Carlton to the mound in game four to square off against Houston righty Vern Ruhle. It was a scoreless game for the first three innings. But in the Philly fourth came a memorable play.

McBride led off with a single and went to second on a basehit by Manny Trillo. Garry Maddox was up next. He hit a soft, low liner back to the mound. Ruhle bent down and grabbed the ball at his shoetops, turned and threw to first. No one knew at first base whether Ruhle had caught the ball in the air or on a bounce. But both umps at first and third said he got it in the air, and the throw to first doubled off Trillo.

In the meantime, McBride had run to third, and so

first baseman Art Howe ran the ball to second and touched the bag, seeming to complete a triple play. A twenty-minute argument ensued, and it was ruled that McBride could stay on third because the home plate umpire hadn't made the call on the catch, confusing the runner on second. Despite some luck on their side, the Phils didn't score.

In the fourth and fifth innings, Houston broke through for single runs. But in the eighth the Phils came back with singles by Greg Gross and Lonnie Smith. Rose singled for the first run. Mike then got a key hit to deep second, scoring Smith with the tying run. When Trillo lined out to right, Rose tagged at third and scored the go-ahead run. The Phils led, 3-2.

But the game still wasn't in the bag for either team. Houston tied it in the last on the ninth, scoring off reliever Warren Brusstar, and for the third straight game, the teams went into extra innings. Only this time it didn't last as long as the previous ones. Rose singled with one down, and Mike lined out to left. Luzinski came up to pinch hit and drilled a double down the left field line, scoring Rose. A hit by Trillo produced the second run and Tug McGraw was called to the mound to hold the Astros. The Phils had won the game, 5-3, and tied the playoffs at two games apiece.

"It has been written and said that the Phillies have no character," said Manager Green. "You would believe this team had no character only if you turned off your TV sets early. It was one of those frustrating games where we struggled early. And after they tied us in the ninth we could have quit, but we didn't."

Now it was down to a single game. The Phils gambled and started rookie Marty Bystrom, who was 5-0 after coming up late in the year. The Astros countered with veteran Nolan Ryan. It was a wild game, as most of them had been and it went into extra innings.

It started calmly enough, the Astros getting one in the first, Philly bouncing back for two in the second, the Astros tying it in the sixth. In the seventh, Houston scored three times, giving them a 5-2 lead. It looked as if the pennant was wrapped up. Ryan was still on the mound and he was an awfully tough customer with a late-inning lead. The Phils were down to their last six outs.

Bowa led off the eighth with a single. Boone singled and Gross loaded the bases with a surprise bunt. Rose worked for a walk to force one run home and knocked out Ryan. Ace reliever Joe Sambito was called in. Keith Moreland hit into a force, Boone scoring to make it 5-4. Then Ken Forsch came in to face Mike.

Once again he was up in a big spot, but on three pitches, Forsch struck him out, the last one on a called strike. He walked slowly back to the dugout, having let the team down in a most crucial situation. Had the club lost, it would have been a devastating blow to Mike.

Fortunately, they weren't through. Del Unser pinch-hit an RBI single and Manny Trillo tripled to left, scoring two more and making it a big, five-run inning. The Phils had taken a 7-5 lead. Now it looked as if the Astros were finished. No such luck, for Houston stormed back to tie it in the eighth on singles by Landestoy and Cruz.

Neither team scored in the ninth, Dick Ruthven pitching against Frank LaCorte. Then in the tenth Mike led off. He struck out again, making him 0-for-5 on the night. Del Unser followed with a double, and after a fly out by Trillo, Garry Maddox doubled home Unser with the go-ahead run. Ruthven held the Astros in the last of the tenth and the Phils were National League champs. Finally!

It was a joyous occasion, and Mike joined his teammates in celebration. But he couldn't have been happy. He was just 5-for-24 in the five games, for a .208 average and one RBI. And he had left many runners stranded. But the club was in the World Series, and that's what really counted. Later, he would say that the playoff failure was again his old problem.

"I was trying too hard. I was carrying too much on my shoulders."

If that was the case, it would be hard to see how he could shake it as the Phils met the Kansas City Royals, a team that had also broken a jinx by beating the New York Yankees in the playoffs after three straight failures. They were led by the marvelous George Brett, who had hit .390 during the regular season, and a supporting cast of fine players. And the Royals, just like the Phillies, wanted to break their jinx.

The World Series opened in Philadelphia, as the fans of the city were really ecstatic. Their team was finally in the big one and they wanted it badly, almost as badly as the players. Because of the tough Houston series, rookie Bob Walk was the Phils' starter against twenty-game winner Dennis Leonard of the Royals.

It was a wild game for the opener. K.C. broke on top when Amos Otis hit a two-run homer in the second inning, and they increased the lead to 4-0 on a two-run shot by Willie Aikens in the third. But after the Houston series, the Phils seemed to be making comebacks a habit. They went to work on Leonard in the bottom of the third.

Bowa singled with one out, stole second, and scored on a double by Boone. Then Lonnie Smith singled to left and Boone scored when Brett mishandled a rundown on Smith between first and second. Now Rose was up. He was promptly hit by a pitch which he didn't really try to avoid. It hit him on the leg and he glared menacingly at Leonard before trotting to first.

Mike was next. Leonard didn't want to take chances and he walked him. McBride then stepped in and belted a long homer to right, giving the Phils a five-run inning and a 5-4 lead. A double by Boone in the fourth and a sacrifice fly by Maddox in the fifth increased the lead to 7-4. Aikens hit another two-run homer in the eighth, but Tug McGraw came to the rescue once again, getting the final six outs and giving the Phils their first victory, 7-6. Mike had a hit in two trips, and scored two runs. He seemed relaxed and swinging better.

Steve Carlton took to the mound in the second game

against K.C. lefty Larry Gura. Both pitchers matched goose eggs for four. Then Philly pushed across a pair in the fifth. K.C. got one back in the sixth, then got to Carlton for three in the seventh and a 4-3 lead. Could the Phils come back again?

In the eighth, Boone opened with a walk. Del Unser then doubled him home to make it 4-3. Rose advanced Unser with a ground out and then McBride got the tying run home with a single over second. Mike was next. He was facing righty submariner Dan Quisenberry, a tough man for righties to hit. But Mike waited for his pitch and then lined a double off the wall in leftcenter, scoring McBride with the go-ahead run. Keith Moreland then singled home Mike with an insurance run and Ron Reed held the Royals in the ninth. Philly won, 6-4, to make a two-game lead, as Mike had a pair of hits and a RBI. He was coming alive.

"No player ever played well when he tried too hard," Mike said, after the game. "The guys who always play well under pressure are the guys who block out the pressure, and I guarantee you there was pressure out there tonight. But I was relaxed."

He then recalled striking out with the bases loaded in the Houston series.

"My whole year flashed in front of me when that happened. It struck me as ironic, the year I had and then failing like that. I was completely humbled."

But it was Larry Bowa who expressed sentiments felt by many. "Mike wasn't happy that he didn't contribute during the playoffs," Bowa said. "But if it wasn't for him we wouldn't have been there and maybe a hit like this tonight will carry him on."

Now the teams were headed back to Kansas City for game three. There was some concern about Royals' star George Brett, who had a bad case of hemorrhoids, and had minor surgery before the third game, but he was ready. And so were the Royals. With their backs against the wall they survived. Each team pecked away for single runs in three different innings. It was tied a 3-3 at the end of nine. Then in the 10th, Kansas City finally got to Tug McGraw, Willie Aikens driving home the winning run, and bringing the Philly lead back to 2-1. Mike, however, showed he was coming, by leading off the fifth with his first post-season homer ever. It felt good, but in game three, it wasn't enough.

Then, in the fourth game, Willie Aikens took over, hitting another pair of homers. The Royals got rid of Larry Christenson with four in the first and went on to take it behind Dennis Leonard, 5-3, evening the Series at two games each. Mike had another RBI, but now his club was in a dogfight and he'd have to bear down even harder.

The pivotal fifth game had rookie Marty Bystrom facing Larry Gura. Both pitchers were solid through three innings, then in the fourth, the Phils broke on top. They did it when Mike blasted a long, two-run homer off Gura, Bob Boone scoring ahead of him. Now he seemed to be getting in a real groove which was bad news for the Royals.

The men from Kansas City wouldn't give up. They got a run in the fifth and two more in the sixth to retake the lead at 3-2. It was still that way going into the ninth, relief ace Dan Quisenberry on the mound for the Royals and Mike leading off.

This time he hit a ball in the hole which Brett knocked down but couldn't pick up to throw. It was a base-hit. Del Unser came up next as a pinch hitter and promptly doubled to right, scoring Mike with the tying run. Unser was sacrificed to third and scored on a hit by Manny Trillo. The Phils had scored twice to take a 4-3 lead. It was unreal. They were becoming a heart-stopping, late-inning team.

Tug McGraw was on the mound again. In spite of all his post-season appearances, the screwballing lefthander shut the door again, and the Phils had taken a 3-2 lead in the Series. Mike was 2-for-4 with a pair of RBIs, and was slowly emerging as the hitting star of the Series. Now it was back to Philadelphia, and the Phils would like nothing better than to wrap it up in front of their long-suffering home fans.

They had their ace, Lefty Carlton on the mound against young Rich Gale, so it looked as if they were in the driver's seat. Nearly 66,000 fans were on hand, screaming and yelling from the opening pitch. They really began hooting in the Philly third. A walk to Boone and an error on Lonnie Smith by Frank White put two men on with none out. Rose then bunted for a hit which loaded the bases. They could break it open right here. And who was up, none other than Mike Schmidt.

Again Mike was facing a difficult righthander, but instead of overswinging, he went with the pitch, lining a double into rightcenter as two runs scored, giving the Phils the lead. Reliever Rene Martin got out of the inning, but Philly had momentum and Mike Schmidt had given it to them.

With Carlton on the mound they were sailing. They got another in the fifth, and one more in the sixth for a 4-0 lead. When K.C. got a run off Carlton in the eighth, McGraw came in and did his thing for the last time. He shut the door and the Phils were *World Champions!*

The whole city went wild, celebrating the team's first World Series win ever. And shortly after the game ended, it was announced that Mike Schmidt had been chosen the Most Valuable Player in the Series. He had collected eight hits in 21 at bats for a .381 average, in addition to hitting two homers and driving home seven key runs.

"I'm in a coma," said Mike. "It hasn't really sunk in yet. Maybe it will in about two weeks. What I would like to do is chop the award up in twenty-five pieces and pass it around. This could have gone to six or seven guys on our team. I wasn't outstanding, really, but I did something in every game."

Of his double in the final game, Mike said, "It was a fastball in on me and I decided to just try to get my bat on it. I guess that's the biggest hit I ever got in my life."

So Mike had finally come through when it mattered

most, and at long last he might have finally relaxed, eliminated the tremendous pressure that had dogged him for so long. The post-season accolades kept coming. Early in November he was named National League Player of the Year by the Associated Press, and shortly after that was named the Most Valuable Player in the National League by an unanimous vote.

"This year we found a way to win at an important time in the season," he said. "That's more important than great statistics. It's what every team wants to find—a way to win."

Mike was grateful for the MVP prize and all the other things that had come his way. He made sure to thank his parents for all they had done for him, and referred again to his wife and two children as the greatest joys in his life. He finally seemed to be a completely happy and fulfilled man.

But he also knows that in sports, memories are short. The Phils will soon be at spring training and everyone will want them to do it one more time. If they don't, the talk will begin again. Only this time Mike Schmidt will be able to handle it. In a way, his story tells a lot about the world of sports. He's an extremely gifted athlete, an intelligent thinking athlete, to whom things always came easily. But when he became a pro, he still had to deal with the intangibles, the pressures, the expectations, the criticisms, the booing, the injuries.

Like most superstars, Mike Schmidt didn't have an easy time of it. But also like most of them, he learned to cope and then conquer, and that was the hardest lesson of all.

# DAVE PARKER

They are a loud, raucous, almost irreverent bunch. Their locker room has been legendary around the major leagues for several years now for the merciless needing that goes on, usually at a decible level that would cause the average person to seek out a pair of ear plugs. Disco music is continually blaring from a radio or casette recorder, with the team anthem being a number called "We Are Family."

The "family" is the Pittsburgh Pirates, and in 1979 they were the champions of the baseball world, a close-knit, racially mixed team that showed the entire sporting world what a team should truly be like, especially in this day and age of the what's-in-it-for-me athlete.

After all, the Pirates do have a superstar who could be considered above the rest of the team. His name is David Gene Parker, who, prior to the 1979 season, became the highest-paid player in all of baseball at that time.

Dave Parker is a 6'-5", 230-pound giant of a man, a man whose chest is three inches bigger and reach ten inches longer than Muhammad Ali's. But he is more than just a giant. He is a multitalented ballplayer, a classic combination of power and speed, and a man almost universally acclaimed by his peers as the best all-around player in the game today. He can do it all—hit for average, hit with power, drive in runs, steal bases, and throw with anyone. He is a two-time batting champion, a Most Valuable Player, an All-Star Game MVP, and a man who sets his goals extremely high.

"I'm always applying myself," he says, "and I haven't peaked yet. I'm the lead talent in baseball today. I'm going to get 3,000 hits. I'm going to win the Triple Crown. I'm probably going to bat .400 one day. It may sound unreal, but I think in terms of dreams that are dreamed to be lived."

At first glance a statement like this appears to be coming from a cocky, self-promoting athlete, the kind who constantly brags about his abilities and invariably finds someone else to blame for his shortcomings. Not so with Dave Parker. Dave is a man who believes in setting the ultimate goals—what many would consider dreams—and he honestly believes he can achieve them. But the thing that sets him apart from other dreamers is that he never stops working to reach his stars.

Listen to what one of his teammates, pitcher Jim Rooker, has to say: "Dave is worth every penny he gets. What makes him so rare is that he's a superstar who's not a jerk. Most are. Three years ago he was a lousy outfielder. But he's worked, and now he's made himself a great one."

Dave's manager, Chuck Tanner, echoes Rooker's thoughts. "Sure, Dave Parker has talent," says Tanner, "but he's worked as hard as any man I've ever seen play this game to develop his abilities. He's getting better every day, and he hasn't even hit his prime yet. That's why five years from now, we'll look back on his MVP season of '78 and say, 'That was just an ordinary Parker year.' "

In a way, Dave Parker was born to be a Pirate. The Pittsburgh team has had a tradition of strong hitting going back to the days of Honus Wagner. Just take a look at the all-time Pittsburgh batting leaders and you find names such as Wagner, Paul Waner, Pie Traynor, Max Carey, Ralph Kiner, Roberto Clemente, and Willie Stargell.

Stargell, of course, is still active, and along with Dave, one of the leaders of the present-day Pirates. Willie is also a big man and a long-ball hitter, and the two men have different styles of leading that complement each other beautifully.

"Willie is the silent leader and I'm the loud leader," says Dave.

The Pirate clubhouse of the last few years was well known among the ballplayers, but not to the fans, especially those outside of Pittsburgh. It took the 1979 season to bring everything out in the open. That's when the Pirates won a grueling divisional race with the Montreal Expos, went on to defeat the Cincinnati Reds in the playoffs to win the National League pennant, and finally beat the Baltimore Orioles in the World Series, after being down three games to one.

But before getting to the details of the dramatic season that really brought Dave Parker and his teammates into the limelight, let's look at the long road that brought Dave to the Pirates and superstardom.

Jackson, Mississippi, was where Dave was born on June 9, 1951. When he was still a youngster his family moved to the South Cummingsville ghetto of Cincinnati, and that's where he grew up.

"I always played ball," Dave recalls. "When I was just a little kid we lived about two streets from Crosley Field, where the Reds played then. I already loved the team. Frank Robinson and Vada Pinson were my idols, and I remember standing there, dumbfounded, one time when they were getting out of a car by the ballpark. Frank gave me a glove, and that really tripped me out. I was about nine then, and I told my mother I was going to be a ballplayer when I grew up and would buy her a house."

Dave and his friends always wanted to be as close to Crosley Field as they could. They played ball on the streets outside the stadium, and that made certain aspects of the game very difficult.

"I learned to slide on concrete," says Dave. "We just

played in blue jeans, and it took some technique to keep yourself in one piece. But after a while I very seldom skinned myself."

Unfortunately, playing ball wasn't the only thing that occupied Dave's time. Living in a ghetto area, he learned fast that it was necessary to be tough. And always being a big kid, he could be tough very well. Besides being a gifted athlete, he was a gifted street fighter, a hard case, as someone described him then, and a guy that you didn't mess with too often.

Dave remembers the way he was then. He doesn't brag about it, but accepts it as a fact of life. "I was a bully who got respect by treating everyone the way I wanted to be treated. I was sort of a neighborhood equalizer and the leader of a club called the Mod Spot."

There was never any big trouble with the law, just some minor things like broken windows, the kind of trouble any kid can get into, though in a ghetto area, bigger and badder things are usually lurking right around the corner. Fortunately, Dave managed to avoid this kind of thing, though he was once held overnight at a juvenile detention center.

During this growing period Dave was often at odds with his father. Dick Parker was also a large man, a shipping clerk who had a strong sense of right and wrong and how he thought his son should behave. Dave remembers this very clearly and is thankful that the hard feelings didn't last.

"It's a competitive thing to live in a ghetto," he said. "You're always thinking about getting out somehow. My dad struggled for the things he had, and he and I had some misunderstandings. In fact, I moved in with some relatives for a while, but there was always a lot of love between us, and there still is."

Dave was playing a lot of ball by then. That's one reason he came home. His sister, Dorothy, told him that his mother missed him and that he had a career to get on with. It made sense, and Dave moved back home.

At Courter Tech High School Dave was a big star in

both baseball and football until his junior year. That season he rushed for 1,365 yards as a power back, but tore ligaments in his knee. It finished his football career, and he decided to concentrate on baseball.

Baseball, of course, had always been his primary love. He continued to follow the Reds and was even a vendor for a while at Crosley Field. "I never sold any hot dogs," he recalls, "I just watched Frank Robinson and Vada Pinson, and fantasized about being like them."

Dave was not yet 19 years old when the 1970 free agent draft rolled around. He was a big kid with a world of raw talent, but he had no idea just where he'd go in the draft. He knew he had been scouted in high school and in the Connie Mack World Series, but there were no certainties. He just held his breath and hoped.

In the early rounds nothing happened. Dave continued to wait. Finally, on the fourteenth round, he was chosen by the Pirates. Players taken that low are usually just shots in the dark. The stars, the prospects, the so-called "can't miss" boys go early. On the later rounds there are retreads and players who can be signed cheap. But every once in a while you get a sleeper, so it's worth the risk.

Dave figured that many teams were hesitant to choose him because of the knee injury he had suffered in football. And because he came out of the Cincinnati ghetto, there were stories that he was a hoodlum and a militant. However, Pittsburgh's executive vice-president Pete Peterson and scout Howie Haak say there was more to it than that.

They claim that at the time Dave didn't look like much of a prospect. He had difficulty hitting the ball in the air and indeed did have a reputation as a tough player to coach and work with. So the reputation as a militant might have had some validity. Howie Haak said later, "The Reds had been watching him all along, and they laughed at us when we took him."

But none of that really mattered. The important thing for Dave was that he would be getting an opportunity to play professional baseball, and he knew he would not get any more out of it than he was willing to put in. So he signed with the Pirates for a mere $6,500. It would be interesting to compile a list of lesser players and men who never made it, who signed for more money than Dave. The figure sounds almost embarrassing, especially by today's standards, but as a fourteenth-round draft choice, Dave wasn't in a position to bargain. He signed and went to Bradenton, Florida, to play in the rookie league for the remainder of the 1970 season.

The purpose of the rookie league is to learn, and Dave began going about his business very diligently. He worked with the coaches there on both his offense and defense and the other fine points of the game. Before long, he was batting over .300 and beginning to look like a bargain at any price. Then tragedy struck. His sister, Dorothy, died during childbirth, and it caused a real trauma in Dave's life.

"I was closer to Dorothy than anyone," he says. "I began having bad dreams after she died, and they kept me from concentrating on baseball."

Dave had his average up to .318 when his sister died. He was in a good groove and getting better. But when the dreams worsened, he suddenly up and left the club. It could have been a real problem had not his mother intervened. She was the one who talked him into returning, and Dave himself knew it would have been what Dorothy wanted.

So he returned to Bradenton and finished out the year in fine style. In 61 games he batted .314, getting 75 hits in 239 at bats, including eight doubles, three triples, six homers, and 41 RBIs. He also stole six bases, showing he could really move for a man his size. For his efforts he was named the league's Most Valuable Player. The Dave Parker era had begun.

The next year he was assigned to Waterbury in AA ball. That spring he worked out with the Pirate veterans and remembers meeting one of his longtime idols, Roberto Clemente.

"I remember working out with Roberto in the outfield. He would say things to me like, 'Wooo, I used to be able to throw like that.' I found that to be a very reassuring and relaxing thing for me.

But at Waterbury Dave found himself in a bit too deep. He hit just .228 in 30 games, striking out 27 times and not hitting a single homer. The Pirates felt they had brought him along too fast and dropped him to Monroe, in Class A ball. There he was in his element, and he burned up the league with a .358 average in 71 games, hitting 11 homers and driving in 48 runs. And there was more encouragement from the home front. That year Willie Stargell, the Pirates' 30-year-old superslugger, belted 48 home runs during the regular season, but he still found time to talk about the big kid down on the farm.

"I read several times where people would tell Willie he was going great," recalls Dave, "and he would say there was a guy in the minor leagues named Parker who was going to rewrite the record books."

Things like that gave Dave a tremendous boost in confidence. He also had good reason for wanting to make the parent club. The Pirates were world champions in 1971, defeating the Baltimore Orioles in a memorable World Series in which Roberto Clemente was the star and MVP. The club had also won its division the year before and were destined to win the N.L. East again in '72. So they had one of the best teams in baseball.

But they still didn't feel Dave was ready. They assigned him to Salem in the Class A Carolina League for the 1972 season. For the volatile Parker, that presented a problem. Dave had a great spring, hitting nearly .400 in the Pirates' training camp. He reasoned that was good enough to stay with the parent club, or, at the very least, earn him a promotion to the team's Triple A team at Charleston. So when he heard that he was headed for Salem, he lost his temper.

"I threw my bat when they told me," he recalls. "One of the team officials told me to pick up the bat, yelling that I had been around for just two years and thought I knew everything. Iwas walking to get the bat and he told me to run. So I snapped again.

"I said to him, 'You talk to me like a man. I'm a man first. There are other things I could be doing with my life.' At that point he got mad and looked like he was going to grab me. So I said to him, 'Go ahead, grab me. Give me a reason to punch you.' That ended it for then, and I guess we both cooled down. Shortly after, I reported to Salem."

Dave was in full control of himself again. By his performance he showed that he not only didn't have a bad attitude, but that he had a great one, for he continued to concentrate, work, and learn, in a situation where he could have easily brooded. In a nutshell, he proceeded to tear up the Carolina League.

Playing 135 games for Salem in 1972, he led the league with a .310 average, 523 at bats, 91 runs scored, 162 hits, and 30 doubles. He also had 22 homers, a league-leading 101 runs batted in, and he startled everyone by also leading the loop with 38 stolen bases. For his efforts he was named Carolina League Player of the Year as well as being named to the Class A All-Star team.

The next year he once again went about his business of making the Pirates. He had another good spring, but was again sent down, this time to Charleston in Triple A, the place he wanted to be the year before. That didn't mean he was happy now. The only place Dave wanted to be was the bigs. But once again he attended to business, batting .317 in 84 games. He was confident now, knew he could handle himself anywhere, and felt he was ready for the majors..

He kept following the parent club. The Pirates were having an off year in '73, following three straight divisional titles and one World Series victory. One reason for this was a tragedy, the death of longtime superstar Roberto Clemente in a plane crash on December 31, 1972. Clemente was on a mercy mission to help the victims of an earthquake in Nicaragua when he was lost. At age 38 he was still an outstanding hitter and the team's spiritual leader, who had finally earned the respect of his peers and the fans after a long and highly successful career.

Without Roberto the Pirates floundered and were in fourth place shortly after midseason. Dave saw all this and decided it was time for him to be promoted.

"I'd hit .300 everywhere I'd been in the organization," he said. "The Pirates were in fourth place and going nowhere the second half of the season. I figured they had nothing to lose by bringing me up. I'd already given them three and a half years and felt I had earned a shot. So when they refused, I jumped the Charleston team."

The Pirates must have realized that they had a determined kid and a talented one. For once they relented and brought him up. Dave was in the major leagues at last. Now he laughs about the entire incident.

"Sure, it was a power play on my part," he says, "but I was convinced I was ready and doing the right thing."

Dave got into 54 games the remainder of the '73 season, and he did well. He batted a respectable .288 with 40 hits in 139 trips. He didn't do much in the power department, with just nine doubles, a triple, four homers, and 14 RBIs. But he survived his first test. He was in the majors and held his own, as the team limped home third with an 80-82 mark.

When Dave came to spring training in 1974, he felt secure for the first time in his baseball career. He had a job. Now he would be with the Pirates for a full season with a chance to win the right field job, previously held with such distinction by Roberto Clemente.

He was joining a close-knit group of men who played hard and had fun at the same time, and it didn't take him long to become part of the whole scene.

"When I first joined the team Dock Ellis was the verbalizer," Dave recalls, "I sat back and watched him. He took a lot of heat from the media, but he told the truth. Soon he and I began to exchange rips in the clubhouse, and the other guys began looking forward to it.

"Now, I'm the verbalizer. About 95 percent of the needling in the clubhouse is done by me, because I can challenge anybody and get away with it."

That was still a couple of years away, though. In 1974 Dave was still learning about the clubhouse and about his game. He became a starter early in the season, already exhibiting that big, aggressive batting stroke that earned him the nickname Cobra.

"My approach is this," he says. "I see something I like and I attack it. So I might be hacking at anything that goes by, high, low, or in between."

In the outfield he was still having problems. He covered a huge amount of ground for a big man and had an arm that left everyone in awe. But he often battled fly balls as if they were an archenemy, and this bothered him. So he applied the old fashioned work ethic again and took as much extra fielding practice as he could.

Playing right field also put some added pressure on Dave, because he was the first genuine candidate to try to fill the shoes of the great Clemente, and he knew there would be comparisons. That made him dig in all the harder.

Then, just when it looked like he was on his way to a successful season, disaster struck. Dave sustained a severe hamstring injury that was to become a series of hamstring problems. All told, it kept him out of the lineup for some ten weeks, about two and a half months of the season.

It was a bitter pill for him to swallow, since things had been going so well. At the advice of Dock Ellis, he had begun keeping a book on all the pitchers he faced, and you couldn't write that book when you weren't in the lineup. But Dave just had to grin and bear it. With the Pirates driving for another Eastern Division title, he wanted to be ready come playoff and, hopefully, World Series time.

Sure enough, the Bucs came back from their poor 1973 season to recapture the N.L. East with an 88-74 mark. It wasn't the greatest record in baseball, but as usual the division was tough with several teams in contention all the way. Now they'd be meeting the explosive Los Angeles Dodgers in the playoffs.

Dave was ready, having gotten back in the lineup late in the season. His injuries limited him to just 73 games, however, yet he still managed to bat a respectable .282. One ingredient that was missing was his power. He had just ten doubles, four homers, and 29 runs batted in. He also struck out 53 times in just 220 at bats. But he still had all that potential, and considering the injuries, it wasn't a bad year.

In the playoffs that year, the Pirates went up against the Dodgers, a well-balanced club that could beat you several ways. The pitching was led by Andy Messersmith, Don Sutton, and reliever Mike Marshall, while hitters Jim Wynn, Steve Garvey, Ron Cey, Bill Buckner, and Davey Lopes could produce runs.

Of course, the Pirates also had plenty of hitting, led by Stargell, Al Oliver, Manny Sanguillen, Richie Zisk, Rennie Stennett, Richie Hebner, and Dave. Their starting pitching was spotty, but the bullpen, with Giusti, was solid. It was expected to be a close, hard-fought series.

Unfortunately for the Pirates, it didn't turn out that way. Sutton twirled an easy, 3-0 shutout for the Dodgers in game one, and Messersmith stopped the Bucs with help from Marshall in the second, 5-2. Pittsburgh bounced back to take the third game, but the Dodgers and Sutton wrapped it up in the fourth, humiliating the Pirates, 12-1, to move on to the World Series. For the Bucs the season was over, and they could only look to 1975.

Dave was looking at '75 as well. The hamstring injuries had put a damper on the preceding season, and he wanted to stay healthy and find out just what he could do over a full year. The rest of the Pirates wanted to know as well. They felt it was time for the big guy to start contributing.

It was quickly obvious that Dave was a much improved player in 1975. He was the starting rightfielder, playing every day and producing. On May 9 he had a tremendous day against the Dodgers, getting three hits, including a long homer and a double, and driving home six runs. He was definitely a force to be reckoned with.

The Pirates were driving toward another Eastern Division title, and Dave was in the forefront of the thrust. In a year he had gone from a part-time injured player to a star up among the league leaders in hitting, homers, and RBIs. When the season ended, the Pirates were on top with a 92-69 record.

As for Dave, he finished the year by playing in 148 games and getting 172 hits in 558 trips for a .308 average, eleventh best in the league. He had 25 homers and 101 runs batted in, good for fifth best in each category, and his slugging percentage of .541 was the best in the entire loop.

This time in the playoffs the Pirates would be going up against old rivals, the Cincinnati Reds, winners in the West, and another power-laden ballclub, much like the Bucs. Dave was especially anxious for the playoffs. Against the Dodgers in '74, he had played in three games and had just one hit in eight tries. Against the Reds, he wanted to do much better.

But once again the Pirates' pitching failed and their bats were strangely silent. Cincinnati buried them in three straight by scores of 8-3, 6-1, and 5-3. The Bucs also got absolutely no help from their young rightfielder. Dave was atrocious, taking the collar in ten at bats.

In 1976 the Pirates were up against a new force in the National League East, the Philadelphia Phillies. The Phils had been quietly building a fine team and were set to challenge the Pirates for divisional supremacy.

The Phillies, as expected, got off to a fast start in 1976 with the Pirates chasing them. This was to be the pattern for the next three years. Dave was once again playing well, his terrible performance in the past playoff series forgotten. His play in the outfield had improved tremendously, and very few players in the league dared run on his rifle arm.

He had also improved his baserunning. He was one of the fastest men in the league for his size and was learning the art of basestealing. On the basepaths he was a holy terror, and league catchers were beginning to be very wary of the big man when he headed for home plate. Several catchers had to leave the game after trying to block the plate against Dave, and a 1976 brush with Parker left Philadelphia's John Oates with a broken collarbone.

"I thought I could hit Dave low," Oates said, "then tag him as he went over me. Needless to say, it didn't work. Dave never gave me a chance to apply my strategy. He simply went through me and left me lying there."

Parker was also becoming more verbal by now, often shouting of his own virtues and at the same time belittling those of his teammates. But there was a method in his loudness.

"I do it to get up for the game," he explains. "I'll get in the clubhouse before a game and really start airing it out, saying things like, 'I'm wall to wall and tree-top tall. Two things for sure, the sun's gonna shine and I'm going three for four.' "

If that kind of talk sounds like another great athlete, Muhammad Ali, it should, for Dave uses some of the same kind of psychology as the former heavyweight champ.

"Ali often says the reason he talks a lot is that he puts himself on the line and then has to go out and back it up," Dave says. "I push myself in that same regard. It makes me really want to go out there and back up my mouth.

"As for the other guys, I'm cracking on everyone. I tell them, nobody better get around the sword when it's swinging. If you first meet me in the clubhouse you're going to think I'm a very loud, insulting guy, and with my size, probably even a bully. I'll start yelling things at a guy, like telling him he can't hit or can't throw, but it helps the club. The guy begins thinking about it and trying to improve. They all know they can't be thin-skinned and be a Pirate at the same time."

But even Dave's prodding and his big bat couldn't help the Pirates in 1976. The Phillies had a big year, going 101-61 to win the division handily. The Bucs checked in at 92-70 to finish second, nine games out, as attendance barely topped a million. But those who did come to Three Rivers Stadium saw a budding superstar in Dave Parker.

Though injuries again limited him, this time to 138 games, Dave nevertheless hit a career-high .313. His power was off slightly, to 13 homers and 90 RBIs, but he swiped 19 bases and was much improved in all other facets of the game. At age 25 he seemed ready to explode, and 1977 seemed like the year in which to do it.

The team was changing then. Richie Zisk, Manny Sanguillen, and Richie Hebner were gone, as young players such as catcher Ed Ott, centerfielder Omar Moreno, and infielder Phil Garner moved into the lineup. Ott and Moreno came up through the organization, while Garner came over in a trade with Oakland. The pitching, as always, seemed questionable, but the bullpen was strong with Kent Tekulve and veteran Grant Jackson. The team also had a new manager, Chuck Tanner, who had previous experience managing at Chicago and Oakland in the American League.

Of course, the big problem was still the Phillies. Though the Philadelphians lost in the playoffs to the Reds in '76, they still had a powerful club and would be tough to catch. Sure enough, the same pattern emerged, the Phils breaking on top and the Pirates, after a slow start, trying to catch them.

This time Dave was healthy and stayed that way all year. He was hitting very well, up near the top of the league most of the year and showing the kind of all-around ability that marks one of the best players in the game. He was always a threat to steal a base, and he was throwing out runners from the outfield with increasing regularity. In fact, from a less than average fielder several years earlier, he had become one of the best in the National League. On two separate occasions during the year, he put together 22-game hitting streaks, longest in the league in '77.

In July he was the National League's starting rightfielder in the All-Star Game, getting a hit and scoring a run in a National League win. When he belted a homer, triple, and double in a September 11 victory over Montreal, he became the first Pirate since Clemente in 1967 to get 20 homers and 200 hits in the same season. He was also driving toward the league batting crown, which also hadn't been won by a Pirate since Clemente ten years earlier.

There was only one problem. The Bucs still couldn't catch the Phillies. They were playing good ball, but the Phils were en route to another 100-win season. Pittsburgh finished with a 96-66 record, but still they were five games out.

That was the only thing that put a damper on Dave Parker's season. Playing in 159 games, Dave won the National League batting title with a .338 average, leading the league with 215 hits in 637 at bats. He also had the most doubles with 44, hit 21 homers, and drove home 88 runs. In addition, he had 26 outfield assists and won a Gold Glove for his outstanding work in the field.

In one way, Dave had come into his own at just the right time. His present contract was running out, and he would be up for a new pact in 1979. There was already talk about his going the free agent route since so many teams were passing out the megabucks to even lesser talents. And many other clubs drooled at the thought of having Dave Parker added to their rosters, no matter what the cost. Dave himself made no bones about leaving Pittsburgh, and his agent, Tom Reich, began negotiations early, negotiations that would continue right through the 1978 season and into the winter of '79.

Fortunately, none of these activities affected Dave's

play or his interactions with his teammates. He continued to play outstanding baseball, and the Pirate clubhouse was still the loudest in the league.

But the team as a whole fell into a familiar pattern in 1978. They got off to a horrendous start in still another attempt to catch the Phillies, favorites to take a third straight. Even Dave was off to a rather slow start, batting below .300 in the early going. By the end of May the team had a 20-25 record and was in fifth place in the division, a step away from the bottom, but strangely enough, just 4½ games from the top. The Phils also started slowly in '78, and no one seemed to want to break on top and take command.

The Pirates were still struggling in late June when they came to New York for a series with the Mets. In one of the games Dave wound up on third and tagged on a short fly to left. After the catch he broke for home, determined to make it no matter who was in his path.

This time it was John Stearns, a rugged catcher who used to be a defensive back at Colorado. Willie Stargell, who was on deck, remembers seeing the play develop.

"The look in Dave's eyes was eerie," says Stargell. "I saw this kind of wildness, and then it was like an A-bomb went off."

Dave's explanation was quite simple. "John had the ball and he had a satisfied look on his face. So my running back instincts came back. I tried to put my face in his face."

The ensuing collision was of the bone-crunching variety, one of the hardest home-plate smashups in years. Stearns was shaken badly and had to leave the game. And for the first time in his career, Dave had gotten the worst of it. His left cheekbone had been shattered and blood was coming out of his left eye. His teammates had visions of him being lost for the season, perhaps even his career ending. He was led from the field right into the nearest operating room.

Within days of the operation Dave was back in the clubhouse, though his head was swollen and he really looked as if he had been through the mill. It was anticipated that he would be out a month, maybe six weeks. He had been voted a starting berth on the All-Star team once again, but missed the game due to the injury. However, he was shortly back in the lineup, having missed only 11 games.

It was an almost miraculous recovery. Of course, he had to be careful. He played with a special batting helmet, fitted with a football-type faceguard to protect him from baseballs and whatever else he might encounter. It was certain that Dave would not change his style of play. In fact, to protect himself during batting and pregame practice, he wore a hockey goalie's mask.

At the halfway mark the Bucs were still struggling. They were at 40-41, 7½ games behind the Phillies. The hitting had been adequate, but the pitching spotty, a usual situation for the club. But the good news was that Dave was back with his usual zest and swinging the bat very well.

"I gave this team my cheek," he kidded in the clubhouse. "Before this happened I was pretty. But I'm crazy about these guys. For Willie [Stargell] and me to both hit 30 home runs and drive in 100 runs this year, I'd give up a batting title for that."

But enthusiasm wasn't enough to fire up the club. On August 12 the club hit rock bottom, having just come through a stretch where they lost 17 of 21 games. They had fallen ten games below .500 at 51-61 and were 11½ games behind the front-running Phils. It looked as if the Pirates could close the book on 1978.

Then, when it appeared too late, they suddenly started winning. And the victories came in bunches. The pitching, led by John Candelaria, Bert Blyleven, rookie Don Robinson, and reliever Kent Tekulve, was suddenly solid. The good hitting was always there, and it now had the benefit of Dave Parker on a real tear.

Dave was walloping the hide off the ball, hitting homers, doubles, singles, and driving in runs. His average was over .300 again and climbing fast. The club won 12 of 13 games to climb over .500 at 63-62 and move within 3½ games of the top. Now there was a pennant race, and the Bucs were in the thick of it.

The Phils responded to the challenge and also began winning. After their first surge, the Bucs dropped a pair, then won three more as August ended. They were 4½ out, and during the month Dave batted .381 to lead the charge. He was also thinking about another batting title, saying things like, "When the leaves turn brown, I'll have the N.L. batting crown!"

At the outset of September the Bucs won eight more in a row, extending their winning streak to 11, and 23 of 26. They were now a game off the pace. A five-game slide dropped them to five out, but then they surged again, winning eight of nine and pulling to within a game and a half of the top.

Dave was hitting even better in September, topping .400 for the month and projecting himself into the thick of the batting race, and he was doing it all with the birdcage helmet to protect the still-healing cheekbone.

With 11 games left, plus a makeup if necessary to the outcome, the Bucs prepared for their final thrust. They stalled at first, splitting a pair with the Cubs and then dropping two to the Montreal Expos. But they rallied again, taking three straight from Chicago behind Candelaria, Robinson, and Jerry Reuss. Now there were four games left with the Phillies. The Bucs were 3½ out. If they swept and then won a makeup game, they could take it.

When the Bucs won the first two, 5-4 and 2-1, it began to look as if a miracle was in the offing. In the third game of the series the Pirates took a 4-3 lead in the sixth inning only to have the Phils get three back to make it 6-4, then four more in the eighth for a 10-4 lead. It appeared to be over.

But the Pirates weren't quitters. They rallied for four runs in the ninth inning before reliever Ron Reed shut the door for a 10-8 Philly win. So the Phils took their third straight Eastern title. Pittsburgh won the final game to finish at 88-73, just 1½ games off the pace.

As for Dave Parker, he had done everything humanly possible to help his team win. In September he batted a .415 to raise his season's average to .334, good for a second straight National League batting championship. He played in 148 games, missing some because of the broken cheek, but still managed to finish third in the league in home runs with 30 and second in RBIs with 117. He led the league with 340 total bases and had a career high of 20 stolen bases. He also had 13 more assists, half his total from the year before because very few runners would dare challenge his arm. And he won a second Gold Glove for his play in the outfield.

Shortly after the season ended, Dave learned he was a landslide choice for the league's Most Valuable Player award, receiving 21 of 24 first-place votes in the election. Now he had truly arrived as perhaps the best all-around player in baseball.

As soon as the season ended, Dave's agent, Tom Reich, began negotiating in earnest with the Buc brass for a new, long-term contract for his superstar client. During the winter, agreement was reached, and the pact was a whopper. Depending on the source, Dave's new contract was estimated to be between $6 and $7.5 million over five years. The difference in the estimates stems from a complicated bonus system within the pact, but it was obvious that Dave would become at least a million-dollar-a-year man and the highest paid player in baseball. And everyone was happy.

"We wanted to make sure Dave was financially secure for life, but not set in concrete," said agent Reich. "When this contract is over, Dave will only be 32."

"I might have made more money in another city," said a jubilant Dave, "but I want to know where my roots are. Plus the Pirates are my kind of team. The Dodgers, for instance, couldn't take me in the clubhouse. The Yankees, with their situation of internal bickering, they couldn't take me either.

"I wanted to make sure I received the highest salary in

baseball. But I know I can live up to it. The public needs to see a player who's gotten security and then still goes out and applies himself. It's what I feel for the game that makes me give 110 percent every time I go out there, not the money. With my attitude and potential, I think I can possibly be the greatest ever to have played. I like to think of myself as one of the greats now, not that I have the longevity yet. But I always set goals and push myself, and if I stay healthy, I feel I can do whatever I say I can do. I know I'm always going to push my God-given ability. In other words, I'm pursuing the ultimate."

Of course, Dave was besieged by the press and media after signing his mammoth contract. He knew the pressure would be on him to produce, but he was never a man to shy away from the pressure of a challenge. He also remembered the years of struggle to reach his lofty position.

"People ask me about the money I'm making, but I've paid my dues," he said. "You don't get to all this without sacrifice, without playing ball 11 months a year for $500 in the minors and winter leagues. I may be a millionaire now, but there was a time when I couldn't pay my electric bill. One week all I had to live on was one package of instant mashed potatoes and five cans of pinto beans."

With his contract finally settled, Dave and his teammates could look to 1979. They were determined to end the three-year reign of the Phillies and re-establish themselves as the top team in the N.L. East. It was a strong Pirate team that came to spring training that year, a balance of veteran and younger players, with the usual strong hitting and hopefully improved pitching. The club also stressed togetherness from the beginning, hoping not only to win their division, but win back the fans of Pittsburgh. Attendance had dipped under a million in '78, and the Steel City was being referred to as a football town and nothing else.

"Most teams in transition go down," manager Tanner said. "We've turned over 15 of our 25 players in three years and never missed a beat as a contender. We play like h . . . in the second half because we play basically with 12 men in the lineup and they last longer."

That was true. Behind the plate Tanner alternated youngsters Ed Ott and Steve Nicosia, with veteran Manny Sanguillen returning to the team to back them up. Stargell was the first baseman, but when he needed a rest or had an injury, John Milner, who came over from the Mets in '78, and Bill Robinson, filled in. Those two also alternated in left field. Omar Moreno, the base-stealing king, was the centerfielder, with Dave holding down the fort in right. Young Mike Easler was also available for outfield duty and pinch-hitting.

A pair of trades made after the start of the season would really solidify the infield. The first was the acquisition of shortstop Tim Foli from the Mets on April 19, and the second was the acquisition of third baseman and two-time National League batting champ Bill Madlock from the Giants on June 28. Scrappy Phil Garner was the second baseman, with veteran Rennie Stennett and young Dale Berra backing up.

There were some question marks among the starting pitchers, expected to be John Candelaria, Don Robinson, Bert Blyleven, Jim Bibby, and Bruce Kison. But the bullpen of Kent Tekulve, Grant Jackson, and Enrique Romo was among the best. The Pirates were strong, no doubt about it.

And they had the Pittsburgh spirit more than ever. Early in the year the team adopted the disco tune, "We Are Family," as their official anthem, and the feeling of togetherness grew. Through it all, two men emerged more strongly than ever as the team leaders: Dave Parker and Willie Stargell.

The two had distinctly different styles. Stargell was the wise philosopher, the man they called "Pops," who had the utmost respect of everyone in baseball. Dave, on the other hand, was the holler guy, the noisemaker, the one who gave the hop in the tail whenever and wherever it was needed. Plus the two had tremendous mutual respect, as evidenced by Stargell's statements at Dave's signing. Dave also had great reverence for Stargell and actually considered Willie the team leader.

"I'll probably be a Pirate until the day I die," Dave said. "One day I may succeed Willie as the leader. But right now he's a legend. He doesn't say much, but he leads by what he does. He plays hurt and he's an exceptional individual. And he's been a major influence on me. Among other things he taught me how to play the outfield and how to go to right field as a hitter."

Dave's foil in much of the clubhouse banter was Phil Garner, the little infielder the players call "Scrap Iron." He and Dave usually have something going, and it winds up helping the team. For instance, when Dave showed up late for spring training, Garner went berserk, screaming at him, "We've all been here busting out tails for two days and where were you?"

"If I hit like you do, I'd have been here since Christmas!" Dave hollered in return. And that's some of the milder stuff.

"Our needling has a purpose," Garner says. "It's the way Dave gets up for a game and it gets everyone else up. If you feel down, sorry for yourself, Dave gets the spark going in you. He's found that picking on someone, mostly me, makes guys rally around and laugh. Suddenly they're ready. It's a kind of group therapy. Dave has a sixth sense when someone needs a kick in the butt, and he knows how to smooth it over if he goes too far."

In return Dave says, "Phil has great mental toughness. I know he'll just shrug at most of what I say. He knows his strong points, so I pick on his weak ones and it helps him to think about them."

If all this sounds relatively mild, listen to how one writer described the atmosphere in the Pittsburgh clubhouse early in 1979:

"Pittsburgh traditionally has the loudest, trashiest-mouthed, loosest, most uproarious dressing room in baseball. Balls of tape fly through the air, people are forever doing unflattering imitations of each other, lifting each other up bodily, defaming each other's ethnic heritages, and threatening each other's lives."

Perhaps it was Garner who summed it up the best. "Brotherly love is so much bull," he said. "You get 25 guys together, some from Puerto Rico and some from the ghetto and some from rich white neighborhoods and some from poor white neighborhoods, and a lot of them are bitter about the way they grew up. Are you going to tell me they will all love each other? But this team gets it out into the open and brings everybody into it."

Now the trick was to bring everyone into the pennant race. Much of the focus was on Dave and his big contract as spring training ended. And because of all the media attention, a very sick, sordid tale began to emerge. It seems that ten days before the Pirates broke camp in Florida, Dave's home in suburban Pittsburgh was broken into and burglarized. Then it was learned that since his signing he had been receiving a great deal of hate mail, including a number of death threats and many racial slurs. It's happened before in sports, but it still left Dave both puzzled and angry.

"I knew things would be different because of the contract," he said. "I expected to be under a magnifying glass, but I never expected this kind of thing. I don't know what will happen now, but I know that I've got to sleep in my home without fear, and I've got to know that when I go home my house will be there. The only way I can fight back is by playing as hard as I can. Maybe then people will appreciate who I am and what I've accomplished."

So this was the atmosphere that Dave and his teammates found surrounding the beginning of the 1979 season. And they got off to a terrible start. After 20 games the team had an 8-12 record and was dead last in the division. There were the usual problems with the pitchers, and the hitters weren't doing their job, either. Dave was among those struggling, batting in the mid .200s and appearing to feel the pressure of his contract.

But there was still a quiet confidence about the club. Tim Foli recalls the situation when he first came to the Bucs in the April 19 deal with the Mets.

"We lost 11 of 15 games shortly after I got here," he said. "But I was the only guy worried. Everybody else kept saying, 'Don't worry about us. We'll be there.' "

By mid-June the club finally got over .500, at 29-28, and were in fourth place, but just 4½ games out in a tight race. The Phils were having problems, and it was the surprising Montreal Expos who led the pack, with the Phils, Pirates, Cubs, and Cardinals all in the hunt.

No team seemed to want to take charge. Manager Tanner was still using his platoon system in several areas, and the team got a big boost when Madlock came over from the Giants at the end of June. Dave's average had crept up into the .290s, but he still wasn't having the kind of season he wanted.

Pitching remained the big problem. Don Robinson, the rookie sensation of '78, was having arm problems. John Candelaria had his annual bad back. Bert Blyleven was pitching well but not winning the close ones, and ace reliever Tekulve was in a mild slump during the first half. As Tanner said, "Before midseason we had eight starting pitchers and didn't even have a rotation."

On July 8 the team was at 40-38, in fourth place, and 7½ games behind Montreal. It looked like the same old Pirates, and the fans were once again staying away. Then the club won six of its next seven before the All-Star break, giving them a 46-39 mark and leaving them four games out of first place. It looked like a second-half race again.

Though Dave was hitting just .297, he was nevertheless the starting rightfielder in the fiftieth midseason classic, as the National League went after its eighth straight victory over its American League counterparts. Steve Carlton of the Phillies and Nolan Ryan of the Angels were the starting pitchers in a game that usually sees a parade of hurlers before it ends.

Since the game was being played at Seattle, an American League city, the National batted first, and Ryan promptly fanned Los Angeles's Davey Lopes and then Parker, who was batting second. But then Steve Garvey of the Dodgers walked, and Mike Schmidt of the Phils tripled him home. A double by George Foster of Cincinnati brought home the second run before Ryan got out of the inning.

But the Americans came right back against Carlton on a walk to George Brett, a double by Don Baylor, and a two-run homer by Boston's Fred Lynn. So after just one inning, the American League held a 3-2 lead.

In the second, the Nationals loaded the bases with one out and Dave came up again. He picked out a Ryan fastball and swung, getting just under it and lofting a fly to right. Larry Bowa of the Phils tagged and scored after the catch. So Dave had driven in the tying run. The Nationals took a 4-3 lead in the third, but the A.L. came right back in their half of the inning, getting two and taking a 5-4 lead. The game looked as if it was going to be a high-scoring donnybrook.

But then there were a pair of quiet innings before the National tied it up with a run in the sixth. No sooner had that happened than the American scored to make it 6-5 at the end of six. The Nationals didn't score in the top of the seventh. But in the bottom of the inning Boston's great slugger, Jim Rice, lined one to the opposite field, down the right-field line. As Dave chased the ball down in the corner, Rice rounded second and went for third. Dave uncorked a throw that seemed to have rockets on it. The ball never got more than a few feet off the ground and beat Rice to the bag by a split second. The huge crowd was stunned to silence. Many had never seen a throw like that in their lives.

"I told Dave after he made the throw that he had all the instinctive moves of a great outfielder," said National League manager Tom Lasorda. "When he turned and threw the ball to third without even looking, it came like it was shot out of a cannon. He's just a tremendous player."

But Dave wasn't through yet. The Nationals tied the game at 6-6 in the top of the eighth when the Mets' Lee Mazzilli pinch-hit a home run. But in the bottom of the inning, the Americans threatened to take the lead once again. Brian Downing of the Angels was on second and took off on a basehit to right. When he rounded third he seemed to cinch a score. But Dave fielded the ball and launched another rocket toward home. Once again the throw arrived before the runner, and Montreal's Gary Carter applied the tag that killed the rally. This time the partisan American League crowd couldn't control themselves. They cheered Dave and his great arm.

The National won the game in the ninth when Texas's Jim Kern walked the bases loaded and the Yanks' Ron Guidry walked home the winning run. Dave had been the second of the walks, receiving an intentional pass after Kern balked Joe Morgan to second. With the 7-6 victory in the bag, Dave learned he had been voted the game's Most Valuable Player, mainly because of his two great throws, and again his peers couldn't say enough about him.

"You definitely have to admire Dave," said Gary Carter, "that he makes all that money, that he has all that security, and he still goes out and busts his butt. He works and hustles and has all that personal pride which makes him want to do well."

As for Dave, he, too, talked about pride taking precedence over money. "I never even thought about making X number of dollars while I was out there. Pride takes over. It's a pleasure and an honor to be here. Anybody who's not here is missing something."

With yet another prize under his belt, Dave then rejoined the rest of his teammates for the run for the divisional crown. It was no surprise that the Pirates had started slowly and were now coming on. The surprise was the Phillies. Despite the signing of free agent superstar Pete Rose during the off-season, the Phils could not get it going. Injuries and slumps had taken a toll on the team, and they were barely playing .500 ball. It was the young Montreal Expos who had jumped to the fore and refused to fold. As the season wore on, it began to look as if the Expos would be the team the Bucs had to catch.

By September it was obviously a two-team race, Montreal and Pittsburgh. The Pirates were getting their usual fine hitting. Stargell was having another great year, though not in the lineup every day. And there were major offensive contributions from Garner, Foli, Madlock, Moreno, Milner, Robinson, and Ott.

Then there was Dave. Though he kept telling people that he'd win a third straight batting crown, it was obvious he was struggling. A knee injury slowed him somewhat in the second half. He never complained and never left the lineup, but as Stargell and others testified, he was often playing on a knee that looked more like a grapefruit. His average stayed right around .300, and he was leading the team in RBIs as well as hitting his share of home runs, but he wasn't quite having the super season of a year earlier, and with his contract, there was naturally some criticism. But unlike some so-called superstars, Dave is and always has been a team player first, and his primary concern was seeing his team win.

So the dogfight continued. On September 17 the Bucs were shut out by Pete Falcone of the Mets. They had just won 15 of 19 to take over first place by a half game. But the loss to the Mets put them back in second by percentage points.

"The Mets may be a last-place team," said Dave, who had a double in four trips, "but they've got a lot of talent and I'll never degrade them."

Dave knew that every game was a big one, and that any team in the league could play the role of spoilers. The next night he singled home the first run and Stargell homered for the second as the Pirates, behind Don Robinson, stopped the Expos in a head-to-head duel to take back the league lead.

A week later the two teams were at it again at Three Rivers Stadium. The fans of Pittsburgh were finally responding to their team, as more than 47,000 of them came out for the doubleheader. By now the familiar sound of "We Are Family" would blare over the loudspeakers, and everyone in the big ballpark would join in. The Steel City finally had baseball fever.

The Pirates won the first game, 5-2, and had a 6-2 lead in the second. Had they won, they would have been 1½ games up. But the young Expos refused to fold. They rallied to win the second, 7-6, and reclaim a half-game lead. It was shaping up as one of the best divisional races in years.

On the next two days the Pirates used a tried and true method of playing. They took out the lumber and went to work. In the first game Stargell blasted two home runs to lead the way to a 10-4 Buc win. The team was now 95-62, with a half-game lead and five left to play.

"I love September," Stargell said afterward, "especially when we're in it."

They were in it, all right. The next night they blasted the Expos again, this time by a 10-1 score, with Garner and Foli driving in three runs each and Bruce Kison doing the pitching. Everyone was contributing.

But the next afternoon there was a letdown and a 9—5 loss to the Cards, cutting the lead to one. It was going down to the wire. And when the Bucs lost a 7-6 heartbreaker to the Cubs on September 29, the lead was again a game. Pittsburgh had one left, while the Expos had three, two of them makeup games. So if the Bucs won on the final day and Montreal lost, it would be over and the Expos wouldn't even bother to play the makeups.

With Bruce Kison starting and Kent Tekulve finishing, the Pirates did their share. They whipped the Cubs, 5-3, as Stargell belted a three-run homer and Bill Robinson singled in the two runs that made the difference. At the same time, Steve Carlton of Philadelphia was shutting out Montreal, 2-0. The Bucs had done it. They were divisional champions once more!

As a team the Bucs were 98-64, and everyone had a hand in their fine season. Dave finished with a rush to get his final average up to .310, with 193 hits, 109 runs scored, 25 homers, and a team leading 95 RBIs. It would be hard to complain about a season like that, but Dave still felt he should have done better.

Dave himself admitted to the pressures. "There were a lot of things that sidetracked me from baseball this year, including the contract and the media coverage it got. Then there was a lot of hate mail, a death threat in Philly, and things like that. Willie was a great inspiration to me. He helped me keep my head up. I know I should be hitting .330, and I'm as disappointed as anyone else about [only hitting .310]. I know I've got to have great mental toughness to achieve my goals."

In 1979 Dave had plenty of help from his teammates. Here are some of the batting average, homer and RBI figures the other Pirates compiled: Stargell (.281, 32, 81), Madlock (.299, 14, 85), Garner (.294, 11, 59), Foli (.287, 1, 65), Moreno (.282, 8, 69), Milner (.276, 16, 60), Robinson (.264, 24, 74). This club could hit.

In the playoffs the Bucs would be meeting the Cincinnati Reds, old rivals. The Reds had won the West after a season-long battle with the Houston Astros. The game one pitchers were John Candelaria for the Bucs and veteran Tom Seaver for the Reds.

The game was scoreless for two, then the Bucs broke through for a pair, Garner and Foli getting the RBIs. The Reds came back to tie it in the fourth on the two-run homer by slugger George Foster. Then it settled into a pitcher's duel. Candelaria lasted seven innings and Seaver eight. Then the relievers took over, and it was still a 2-2 game going into the eleventh.

Foli started it off with a single. Dave then singled, putting runners on first and second, Stargell up. Willie picked out Tom Hume's first pitch and sent it high and deep over the right-field wall for a three-run homer. The Bucs had a 5-2 lead. But with two out in the last of the eleventh, Cincy loaded the bases. Ray Knight was up against Don Robinson, and the young righty struck Knight out. The Pirates had drawn first blood.

Game two saw the Bucs pitch veteran Jim Bibby, with

rookie Frank Pastore on the mound for Cincy. This time the Reds got a run in the second to take the lead. But the Bucs evened things in the third and took a 2-1 lead in the fourth. Both starting pitchers were sharp, and it was still a 2-1 game going into the last of the ninth, but back-to-back doubles by Heity Cruz and Dave Collins tied it. In came Don Robinson to put out the fire again, but it was extra innings for the second game in a row.

Moreno led off the Pirate tenth with a basehit. Foli then sacrificed him to second, bringing Dave up to face righty Doug Bair. Dave went with the pitch and drove a basehit to left, bringing home Moreno with what proved to be the winning run. The Pirates now had a two-game lead.

"I'm not thinking sweep or anything like that," Dave said after the game. "I was just trying to win this one and wanted to hit the ball where it was pitched. To tell the truth, I don't understand how they're pitching me in this series. Instead of giving me breaking stuff inside like they usually do, they're giving me fastballs away, so I'm just going with the pitch."

The third game was no contest as ageless Willie Stargell was the star again. "Pops" had a homer, double, and three RBIs as the Bucs behind Bert Blyleven's complete game made it look easy, 7-1. Dave was one for three with an RBI, giving him four hits in 12 trips for a .333 average as the Bucs clinched the National League pennant. So the wild Bucs celebrated, and when it all died down they began to think about the upcoming World Series. That wouldn't be as easy. They'd be meeting the Baltimore Orioles, a team many considered the best in baseball in 1979.

The Orioles, under manager Earl Weaver, had made a shambles of the American League East, possibly the toughest division in baseball, and they had beaten the California Angels in four games to take the pennant. Possessed of a deep and talented pitching staff, the Birds were baseball's winningest team. They also had timely hitting and a good defense. They would surely be formidable foes.

In game one the Pirates sent Bruce Kison, who was 13—7 on the year and always a great September pitcher, against the Orioles' 23-game-winning Mike Flanagan. What happened in the opening inning could have been enough to take the starch out of any team. The game was played at a cold, wet Memorial Stadium in Baltimore with the temperature hovering around the 40-degree mark.

After the Pirates went out in the first, Al Bumbry led off for the Birds with a single to left. Shortstop Mark Belanger walked, and then big Ken Singleton hit a comebacker to the mound that looked like a double-play ball. But it bounced out of Kison's glove, and when he picked it up he only had time to get Singleton at first.

A walk to Eddie Murray loaded the bases, and John Lowenstein hit a grounder to second which again looked like a potential twin killing. But second baseman Garner threw the ball over Foli's head into left field. Two runs scored and the Birds had the lead. A wild pitch brought Murray home with the third run, and then Doug DeCinces belted a long two-run homer to left. The Bucs had hardly had time to breathe before they trailed, 5-0. Kison left the game after the next batter singled, but after that the Pirate relievers held the Birds in check.

That's when the Pirates showed they wouldn't quit. They began to peck away at the Baltimore lead. A pair of singles and two grounders got a run home in the fourth. Then in the sixth Dave singled to center, and Bill Robinson singled to right. After Stargell fanned and Madlock popped out, catcher Steve Nicosia chopped one to DeCinces's left, and the third baseman booted it for an error. Garner then singled two runs home, making it 5-3, before Flanagan shut the door.

In the eighth Stargell belted a long homer to make it a 5-4 game. Then came the ninth. Foli grounded out, but Dave singled for his fourth hit of the game. He then tried to steal second, but Flanagan saw it coming and threw to first, catching him off base. Dave continued to second anyway and slid hard into shortstop Belanger, who dropped the ball. He went to third on Robinson's groundout and was the tying run with Stargell up, two out.

But Flanagan bore down and fanned Willie with a fastball. The Orioles had won the opener, but had to hang on to do it. Now the Bucs would send 12-game-winner Bert Blyleven to the mound against longtime Orioles star, Jim Palmer, who won ten games in '79 while missing much of the year with a bad arm.

This time the Bucs drew first blood. In the second, singles by Stargell, Milner, and Madlock brought home one run, and a sacrifice fly by Ed Ott made it 2-0. The Orioles bounced back with a run in their half of the inning and another in the sixth. It was still a 2-2 game going into the ninth. Relief ace Don Stanhouse was now on the mound for the Birds. He retired the first two Bucs, but then Ott got a bad-hop basehit and Garner walked. Veteran Manny Sanguillen came up to pinch-hit and promptly rapped a single to score Ott with what proved to be the winning run. The Series was tied.

Both clubs moved on to Pittsburgh for game three, and it turned into no contest. The Bucs jumped on lefty Scott McGregor for a run in the first on a sacrifice fly by Dave, which drove in Moreno. In the second they got two more when Garner doubled home Stargell and Nicosia.

Then the Birds took over. They got a pair in the third and knocked out starter John Candelaria in the fourth when they scored five more runs to take the lead at 7-3. The game ended with an 8-4 Oriole win and a 2-1 lead in the Series. That made the fourth game pivotal.

Dennis Martinez was the Oriole starter, and big Jim Bibby got the call for the Bucs. And once again it was the Pirates who went to work first, knocking out Martinez with a four-run second inning. Baltimore came back with three in the third, but when the Pirates got single runs in the fifth and sixth to take a 6-3 lead, it looked as if they were on the brink of evening the Series.

Don Robinson was pitching when the Orioles came to bat in the eighth. Kiko Garcia started things with a single. A single by Singleton and forceout at second followed. Then a walk loaded the bases, and relief ace Kent Tekulve came in.

The thin sidearmer just didn't have it. Pinch-hitting John Lowenstein doubled home two runs, making it 6-5. Another walk loaded the bases once more, and a second pinch-hitter, Terry Crowley, followed with another double, giving the Birds the lead at 7-6. Another single and a forceout got two more in, making it a six-run inning and giving Baltimore a 9-6 lead. That's the way it ended.

Now it looked bleak for the Bucs. They were down three games to one, and only a handful of teams have ever overcome that kind of deficit. In addition, they had stopped producing in the clutch. They had 17 hits to Baltimore's 12, yet scored just six runs, leaving ten men on base. Dave had two hits, including a double, and an RBI, while Stargell had three hits, including two homers. But it wasn't enough. Now every game would be sudden death.

Before game five the team suffered another blow. Manager Tanner learned that his ailing mother had just died. So he was under intense pressure when he sent his team out onto the field, veteran Jim Rooker pitching against Mike Flanagan of the Orioles.

The game stayed scoreless until the fifth, when the Birds broke through for a run, putting even more pressure on the Bucs. But in the bottom of the sixth the Bucs went ahead, 2-1, as Bill Madlock drove home the go-ahead run. In the seventh they made it 4-1, Dave doubling home the fourth tally. Three more in the eighth made the final 7-1, as the Pirates pulled a step closer at 3-2. Rooker pitched five strong innings, and Blyleven finished up to ice it.

"We needed to win convincingly," Dave said after getting two more hits. "We needed to overpower them.

We got kicked in the rear the other day, so we needed to play up to our potential, and we did."

Manager Tanner talked about Dave when asked about the death of his mother.

"I especially thought of her when Dave was up in the seventh," the manager said. "I remember how he had phoned her for her seventieth birthday last May and how she was so happy then. He was her favorite ballplayer, and she told everybody how she had talked to Superman. So when he came up in the seventh I said to myself, 'Hit one for Grandma,' and he lined that double to put us ahead, 4-1."

Now it was back to Baltimore for game six. It wouldn't be easy winning a pair of games in the Birds' backyard, but that's all the Bucs were thinking about. Candelaria was the starter against veteran Jim Palmer. Both pitchers were magnificent for six innings, neither team able to get on the scoreboard. It was anybody's game.

Then in the seventh Moreno singled to right with one out. Foli bounced one over the mound which Palmer tipped, just enough to throw the infielders off. Foli beat it out. Dave was up next, and he slammed a hot one toward second. Rich Dauer got set to field the ball when it suddenly took a crazy hop and went past him, Moreno scoring the first run. Stargell followed with a sacrifice fly, and the Bucs had a 2—0 lead. The Bucs got two more in the eighth, and Kent Tekulve came on to shut the Orioles down in the final three innings. Pittsburgh had won it, tying the Series at three games each.

Everyone agreed that Dave's bad-hop hit had been the key. No hop and it might have been an inning-ending double play.

"When I hit the ball I thought it was right at him and was afraid it would be a double play," said Dave. "My only thought was to get to first base ahead of the ball."

Manager Tanner was excited after game six, and he sensed a similar feeling in his team.

"I've never seen them up like this since I came here

three years ago," he said. "When they got beat in the late innings in game four, it was Dave Parker who wouldn't let them hang back and sulk in the dugout. He came along and told them, 'What are you guys sitting on the bench for? Don't you know this is a seven-game World Series?' Now, it is."

So Dave was continuing to fire up his teammates. Game seven would have Jim Bibby of the Pirates going against Scott McGregor, who had beaten the Bucs in game four. Both teams began cautiously. The pitchers were throwing well and neither team scored in the first two innings. Then in the Oriole third Rich Dauer caught hold of a Bibby fastball and sent it into the left-field seats as the large Baltimore crowd roared its approval.

It stayed that way until the Pittsburgh sixth. With one out, Bill Robinson singled off the glove of shortstop Garcia. That brought up Stargell. The old man of the Pirates went after McGregor's first pitch and sent a long drive to deep right. It cleared the glove of a leaping Ken Singleton for a home run. The Pirates led, 2-1.

The Orioles threatened in a tense eighth inning. They had the bases loaded with two out and slugger Eddie Murray up. Tekulve was on the mound, and Murray hit a drive to deep right. Dave seemed to have it lined up, but he lost his footing. Oriole fans had visions on three runs scoring, but somehow Dave recovered and made a backhand catch while reaching high over his head. It saved the game.

In the ninth Garner doubled, and Moreno singled him home, making it 3-1. A walk put two men on with Dave up. Reliever Tippy Martinez came on and hit Robinson with a pitch, forcing in the fourth run. Stargell ended it by grounding into a double play.

But the Bucs had a 4-1 lead, and Tekulve then went out and retired the Orioles in the last of the ninth, making the Pirates world champions!

The Bucs had become just the fourth team in baseball history to win the Series after trailing three games to one. Led by the man they call Pops, the family team had stuck together and persevered.

Stargell had 12 hits in 30 at bats, including a record seven extra-base hits, and was named Most Valuable Player. He would later be named co-winner of the league's MVP prize with the Cardinals' Keith Hernandez.

Other Bucs had also excelled. Garner had 12 hits and five RBIs. Moreno had 11 hits, and Foli picked up ten. And Dave Parker had a fine World Series as well. Dave had ten hits in 29 trips for a .345 average, including three doubles and four RBIs. He hadn't disappointed anyone, and his spiritual leadership was in evidence as usual, as witnessed by Tanner's statement about how Dave fired up the team after game four.

Afterward, someone asked Dave if it was hard playing in the cold, wet conditions that prevailed for much of the Series.

"Under normal circumstances, it would have been awful," he said. "But in the World Series it could be 25 below and you wouldn't care. You work so hard to get there that you'd play it in any weather."

Dave had worked hard for everything, and now he was a very happy member of a world championship team. Though he still had his personal goals and wanted to improve upon his performance in 1980, he finished the season a very happy and fulfilled man. He didn't know at the time that the next season would be perhaps the most trying and frustrating of his life.

He and his teammates came to spring training full of optimism. The "Family" was in tact and they all expected to take a real shot at repeating as champions. The team was relaxed and confident. The club hadn't made any major trades, but since they were a balanced team with a strong bench, major changes weren't dictated.

Soon the team came north and opened the season, expecting once more to be in a dogfight with the Phillies and Expos for the N.L. East crown.

In the early going the teams jockeyed for position, with the Cardinals making it a four-team race. It was much like 1979, with one team getting hot, another slumping. Meanwhile the fans waited for the Pirates to take charge, many thinking it would be even easier than last year.

But it wasn't long before the team began having problems. For one thing, a number of regulars just weren't hitting as well as they had in '79. Willie Stargell began finding age and injuries limiting his playing time, and the leader of the "Family" was often on the shelf. Pitchers Bert Blyleven, John Candelaria, and Don Robinson, all key hurlers, were having problems winning. And in the bullpen, Kent Tekulve, while still effective, was not nearly as awesome as he had been the year before.

It was also becoming a difficult year for Dave. His left knee began bothering him almost from the beginning, limiting his mobility and his speed. The fans were booing him again, and worse than that, several ominous incidents had occurred. He began getting hate mail regularly, vilifying him for his huge contract and often containing racial slurs. One day he found the tires slashed on both his Mercedes. It was hard for him to understand.

"People in Pittsburgh know Dave's the best player in the game," Manager Tanner said. "It's a shame these kinds of things have to happen. People don't realize that Dave plays a lot of times when he can hardly walk into the clubhouse. But anytime he can go out there he makes our team better. He's the man who makes the wheels go around for the Pirates."

But Dave was not producing the super year people expected once he got that pact, which was now almost starting to haunt him. Before long, some fans in the right field stands at Three Rivers Stadium began throwing objects at him. The situation was growing worse. Once someone tossed a sock filled with nuts and bolts that weighed five pounds in his direction. Things were getting dangerous, and he often had to wear his batting helmet out on the field. And for the first time, the man who just a year earlier said he'd probably be a Pirate for life, talked of playing elsewhere.

"People don't really identify baseball as a job," Dave said. "Baseball is a heck of a job. It's mind-consuming. It strips you of your personal life. That's a major sacrifice, no matter how much money you make. People forget about us being human beings, too. I'll deal with the fans response because I have an obligation I can't get out of immediately. But I'll still be a young man in 1983 (when his contract will be up). If it hasn't improved dramatically, I'll do something, go elsewhere."

Some felt the fans of Pittsburgh, traditionally a blue collar town, resented Dave's flamboyant style and personality, the fact that he always wore a number of gold chains around his neck and a diamond stud in his left ear. And it didn't help when it was learned that Dave was going through a messy "divorce" from his common law wife. The story was all over the front pages of the local papers, and the booing continued.

"Any guy who's boisterous and black is gonna have it tough," said teammate Bill Robinson, also a black man, but one who adhered to a quiet lifestyle. "Name me any city where this isn't the case."

That undoubtedly had something to do with it. Plus the fact that the team continued to struggle didn't help, either. It reached a peak in late July. The Pirates were at Three Rivers, hosting the Los Angeles Dodgers. Dave was in right field. At the time he was hitting .284 with 12 homers and 52 RBI's, good numbers, but not Parker-type numbers.

In the eighth inning of the first game of a twin bill, Dave felt something whiz by his ear in right. He looked around and saw a transistor radio battery on the ground near him. With that, he walked off the field and said he wouldn't play in the second game. Afterward, he held a press conference where he publically asked to be traded.

"It is in the best interests of both parties—the City of Pittsburgh and myself—to complete my career without bodily harm. This has been going on too long now. Last year I was hit in the back of the head with a gas valve from a pellet gun. A couple of years ago someone tossed a bat. Then it was the sock full of nuts and bolts, now the battery.

"Maybe it's the money. But everybody else in baseball respects me. It hasn't happened all year except in Pittsburgh and I find that hard to digest because that's where I live.

"Hey, I love the city and I'd love to stay here. But the fact is I've got to go out there everyday and put my career on the line. I'll do everything I can to help the Pirates win, but I've reached the point of no return."

It was surely a critical situation. Manager Tanner felt Dave had become the target of a sick person. Luckily, cooler heads prevailed for the moment. Dave agreed to return to the lineup and remain in Pittsburgh for the time, hoping the situation would improve.

Unfortunately, it was his knee that didn't improve. It got worse and became increasingly obvious that he'd need surgery after the season. It was the same knee he hurt in high school playing football. Now the knee was swelling, had calcium deposits, strained ligaments, and arthritis. Yet he continued to play as often as he could.

"I can't afford to sit," was the way Dave put it, because Stargell was missing a good deal of the second half of the season. And manager Tanner said:

"When the players see him go out there with the knee he has, there's no way they can't run out a ball and give their best."

But in 1980, it wasn't enough. The problems continued. At one point Blyleven left the team because he felt he was being yanked out of games too soon. Bill Madlock was suspended for shoving an umpire. There were more injuries, and the bullpen continued to be less than it had been.

With nineteen games left, the club was third to the Expos and Phillies, but still had a chance. Dave was over .300 for the first time all year and was trying to spur his team on.

"I'm a strong finisher," he said. "And I'm right back where I belong. I even have an outside shot at the batting title."

With sixteen games left the club still trailed the Expos and Phils by five games. Dave was up to .306, with 16 homers and 74 RBI's, and batting over .400 in September. He was still the hollar guy in the clubhouse and everyone expected the team to make its title drive. But it never happened. Instead, the team went into a final tailspin, Dave included, and they finished the year with just an 83-79 mark, some nine games behind the division-winning Phillies.

It was a tremendous disappointment for everyone. Dave had even slumped the final weeks and wound up at .295, with 18 homers and 79 RBI's. It was the first time he finished below .300 since 1974.

But he wasn't the only one. Omar Moreno fell from .282 to .249. Tim Foli went from .291 to .265; Madlock from .298 to .277; and Phil Garner from .293 to .259. Stargell, in his brief appearances, batted just .262. Plus the power was down from all these players.

Of the pitchers, only Jim Bibby had an outstanding year at 19-6. Candelaria was 11-14, Blyleven 8-13, Robinson 7-10, and Tekulve 8-12. There was just no way the team could have won it with the dropoff in individual performances.

After the season, Dave had his knee surgery and it was pronounced a success. For the time being, he has stopped his talk of leaving. He just wants to rehabilitate the knee and come back strong.

The next season could see a partial breakup of the "Family." The team could decide to deal for new players, and no one knows yet whether Pops Stargell will be back. He'll probably wait to see how his aging body feels in the spring.

As for Dave, the 1981 season may well be the most challenging of his entire sports life. He has an awful lot to prove, to himself and to his many fans. Let us not forget that there are still many pro-Parker people out there. Unfortunately, the ones who behave badly get the publicity.

But Dave has never been one to duck a challenge. In addition, he's a man who has always set higher and higher goals for himself. After the 1979 season he said he hadn't reached his peak yet, and despite the frustrating and painful season of 1980, he still believes that. He has always been a man given to hard work, no matter what the circumstances and no matter how much money he is being paid. So there's no reason to think he'll change. If anyone can bounce back from adversity, Dave Parker can, because that is the very essence of the man.

# GEORGE BRETT

Shortly after the completion of the 1941 baseball season, the Japanese Air Force attacked Pearl Harbor and the United States was plunged into the ravages of World War II. Though major league baseball continued throughout the duration of the war, many of the top players were in the service and the quality of play was undeniably less than the best. As far as baseball was concerned, these were the war years, and in many ways, highly forgettable.

But that 1941 season was different. In the last full year before Uncle Sam claimed many of baseball's best, there were two achievements of monumental proportions. The first occurred during a two-month period when New York Yankee centerfielder Joe DiMaggio hit safely in 56 consecutive games, an incredible record that many experts feel will never be broken.

The second was an uncertainty until the very last day of the season. That's when Boston Red Sox outfielder Ted Williams rapped out six hits in a doubleheader to finish the year with a batting average of .406, becoming the first major leaguer in eleven years to reach that coveted mark.

In the thirty-nine seasons that have since passed, several players have made runs at DiMaggio's hitting streak and all have come up short. By the same token, several players have flirted with the magical .400 mark and they, too, have failed. Just as some baseball people feel that DiMaggio's streak will stand forever, there are those who say that the present-day game, with its hectic travel schedule and the profusion of night games, will make it extremely difficult for a player ever to hit .400 again.

What does this have to do with 1980? In 1980 there was a player who not only made a modest run at DiMaggio's record, but he also sat poised on the brink of becoming baseball's first .400 hitter since Ted Williams. And in approaching these two great achievements, he put together one of the most remarkable seasons in recent memory.

His name is George Brett, the third baseman of the American League champion team the Kansas City Royals, and as of 1980, he has become known as the best all-around hitter in baseball. He is also the man who kept the baseball fans of America on the edge of their seats over the final two months of the season, providing added drama to an already exciting year of diamond action, as baseball continued to reclaim its position as the national pastime.

Of course, it's no secret that George Brett fell short in his quest for a .400 average, but he didn't miss by much. In fact, he came closer than any player in the previous thirty-eight seasons. He finished the year batting a torrid .390, with 175 hits in 449 at bats. Because of several debilitating injuries, he played in just 117 games, yet upon returning from his injuries, he hit as if he'd never been away.

That wasn't all that made George Brett's 1980 season a totally incredible one. At one point in the year he put together a thirty-game hitting streak, which made people think of the DiMaggio achievement all over again. And when it all ended, George became the first player in thirty years to drive in more runs than games played. He had 118 RBIs in 117 games. It's no wonder that in 1980, George Brett was voted the Most Valuable Player in the American League.

Just who is this man who seems to have burst into

superstardom overnight? Actually, he has been one of the game's finest hitters for the past several years, having won his first batting title in 1976. But because he played in Kansas City and has kept a relatively low profile, he lacked the recognition given to many lesser talents. That isn't the case any longer.

George Howard Brett was born in Glendale, West Virginia, on May 15, 1953. He was the fourth son born to Jack and Ethel Brett, who were both accountants. When George was born his oldest brother John was six, then came Ken at four, and Bob who was two. So the boys were close in age and would remain very close as they grew up.

"I don't know if you could call us a close-knit family," Jack Brett once said. "But we all pulled for each other and all the kids wanted to be winners when they played ball."

Of course, there was no way of predicting the future for any of the boys, but George's mother recalls finding a photograph of him taken when he was about a year and a half old.

"George was standing there in a diaper," she says, "and he was already holding one of his brother's baseball gloves. The glove was almost as big as he was, but he wouldn't put it down when we took the picture."

When George was about two, there was a big change in his life. His father got a new job and the family moved from West Virginia to El Segundo, California, which is theoretically a suburb of Los Angeles, but not really like the big city at all. On one side of town is the giant Los Angeles Airport and on the other side the ocean. So El Segundo is effectively cut off from the rest of L.A. and often gives one the feeling of a sleepy little town on the Pacific.

"In a way we're almost like a small Midwestern town," said George's brother, Bob. "The way we're isolated makes it rather unusual for this area. There's just one high school here, one weekly newspaper."

Fortunately, there were plenty of parks and playing

fields, and a lot of kids who loved sports. It wasn't long before the Brett boys joined them. They all started early, playing football, baseball, and basketball, though baseball probably had the edge with all of them. One by one, as they were old enough, they began playing Little League, and worked their way up from there.

George, being the youngest, would tag along after his brothers, doing all he could to emulate their ways.

"When the older boys were in Little League, George and his friends would go out on the field before and after the games and run around the bases," said his mother, now Mrs. Ethel Johnson. "They would slide into each base and try to do everything the older boys did. Naturally, they'd come home all dirty and beat up."

Pretty soon George was old enough for Little League, and as soon as he began playing he had something to live up to. His brothers were all well known in El Segundo, and brother Ken was emerging as a real standout athlete, the best in the town. In fact, he spearheaded his Babe Ruth League team to a national title and received even more notoriety in the area.

"I was always being compared to one of my brothers," said George. "So when my brothers began playing, it was almost mandatory that I follow. My father always backed all of us all the way. We always had the best gloves, though mine were hand-me-downs from Bobby and John.

"We were middle class I guess, but my father never made us get jobs in the summer. He told us that it was time to enjoy ourselves. I don't ever recall getting an allowance, but if I needed something, I got it. For instance, there was no stereo or television in my room, but if I wanted three dollars to go to the movies, I'd get it."

When Ken reached El Segundo High he began to really make headlines. As George says, "He was the best thing ever to come out of my hometown. He was better than anyone in everything in high school — baseball, football, you name it."

Even Jack Brett was excited about Ken's success at

that time. "In my mind," he said, "Ken was going to be Mickey Mantle's replacement. Mantle was getting ready to retire and I thought Ken would replace him. If you had to say which of my kids was the best athlete, I think you would have to say Ken."

But at the time Ken was rewriting the El Segundo High record books, George and his friends discovered another love—the beach.

"We went to the beach all we could then," he recalls. "In the summer we'd go from ten in the morning until four in the afternoon. Then I'd come home, help clean up the house a bit, eat dinner, then play ball the rest of the night. Every day it was the same thing. It was really living."

At the beach there was volleyball and body surfing. So the beach and ballplaying occupied almost all of George's time.

"George was never a scholar," says his mother. "He always did what was asked of him at school, but no more. And he never had an interest in music, didn't play an instrument. But I can't complain about it. All my boys played sports and it always kept them out of trouble. There was no drinking, no drugs, no trouble with the law. My biggest problem with them was patching up the bumps and bruises, the broken fingers, things like that."

Jack Brett has this to add about the sports programs in El Segundo. "I really can't take credit for my sons' successes," he says. "El Segundo was a fantastic town for kids and sports. They always had great coaching at all levels. We encouraged them and their coaches taught them, and they did the rest."

After brother Ken rewrote the El Segundo record books, he signed a professional contract to join the Boston Red Sox organization, and in 1966 began his pro career as a lefthanded pitcher at Oneonta. He was still a fine hitter, but felt his future was as a pitcher. As George recalls, "He could really blow the ball past the hitters then."

A year later, Ken was at Winston-Salem, then moved up to Pittsfield, where he was outstanding, with a 10-7 record and 1.80 earned run average. He was so impressive that late in the year the Red Sox brought him up as a nineteen-year-old rookie. It was a year in which the Bosox would win the American League pennant and face the St. Louis Cardinals in the World Series, and young Ken Brett was a member of the team, eligible to play in the fall classic.

"The whole family went up to St. Louis when the Red Sox came in there. Ken got into two games as a relief pitcher and the whole thing was very inspirational to George," his mother recalls. "He even told me that someday he was going to play in a World Series."

Ken's early success seemed to spur George on. Once home again, he began playing with more determination. He still went to the beach, but baseball seemed to be getting a strong hold on him. And when he recalls those days, he realizes the effect that Ken's career had on him.

"I was only about twelve when Ken left home to play baseball, so I really didn't know him as a man then. When he played in the Series I realized all over again just how good he was. That's when I really started looking up to him. In fact, I idolized him.

"I also thought he had it made then. He'd come home, driving a GTO and pulling out a roll of bills, and I'd say, 'Look, he's got it made.' That's when I decided if there was anything I wanted to be, it was a ballplayer."

So George continued to play, and finally he followed Ken into El Segundo High School to play under John Stevenson. He was a reserved, self-effacing youngster then, who, according to his mother, didn't have a superego. "George was always kind of lackadaisical," she said. "He had a take-it-as-it-comes attitude."

But once he reached El Segundo High he found himself being compared with Ken all over again, and he began to feel there was a great deal that he had to live up to. For a time, in fact, his mother worried that Ken's success might begin to work in reverse and turn him against sports. Fortunately, George's easygoing attitude kept him from succumbing to this kind of pressure, and he began playing baseball, football, and basketball at El Segundo with a good deal of his own success.

Though Ken was the big record-setter, George nevertheless had a fine athletic career as a high schooler. Ethel Johnson recalls that her son rarely talked about himself, but she once talked to Coach Stevenson who told her what a fine ballplayer George had become, a record-setter in his own right.

As a footballer, one of his teammates was Jim O'Bradovich, now a receiver with the Tampa Bay Buccaneers, and on the baseball team he played alongside Scott McGregor, the outstanding lefthanded pitcher for the Baltimore Orioles.

George still wasn't a top student. He did the required work and got passing grades, but he just wasn't geared in that direction. According to his mother, there was never any thought of college and no serious scholarship offers coming to him. But in his senior year the baseball scouts began coming around, many of them simply because he was Ken Brett's brother and Ken had been such an outstanding player.

By then, George had become a fine player in his own right. He was a shortstop with good hands, good range, and with a powerful, but erratic arm. He batted from the left side of the plate, and his smooth swing produced line drives all over the lot. In addition, he was still filling out, getting bigger and stronger, and was undoubtedly a fine prospect.

George's mother remembers that the family felt it couldn't happen again, that a second Brett couldn't become a pro. It was 1971 then and Ken was with the Red Sox, but he was struggling. He had had some arm trouble and was just 8-9 in 1970 and having even more problems during the current season. It was beginning to look as if he was not going to repeat his schoolboy exploits in the big leagues.

Despite Ken's struggles and his own laid-back attitude, George felt he would be signed, but he felt his chances of making it to the majors were minimal. Yet after his final season at El Segundo High, he learned he had been drafted by the Kansas City Royals and soon after signed for a modest bonus. He then reported to Billings, Montana, to finish the 1971 season in the low minors.

Being drafted by Kansas City could not have excited George at the time. After all, El Segundo was next to Los Angeles, where the glamourous Dodgers played to huge crowds. Up the coast was the Oakland A's, building an American League dynasty in the early '70s, and back East there were teams like the Yankees, Red Sox, while in between dwelled the Cincinnati Reds and Pittsburgh Pirates, the kinds of clubs most youngsters would want to join.

The Royals, on the other hand, were an expansion team, which began play only in 1969, replacing the A's, who had moved from Kansas City to Oakland prior to that year. Like all expansion teams, the Royals experienced some very bleak seasons at the beginning, trying to put together a blend of veteran and young players, win a few games, and build for the future. At the same time, the club was trying to create an identity of its own and attract a following in K.C., where the A's had played in futility for so long.

"When George was in the minors he called us constantly," his mother remembers. "Things didn't always go well, but he had confidence in himself. And whenever we could manage it, we went to see him play."

At Billings, George was almost immediately converted from a shortstop to a third baseman. He didn't have quite enough speed to play short, but he had the quickness and the strong arm needed to play the hot corner. In 68 games at Billings in 1971, the eighteen-year-old Brett batted .291, with 75 hits in 258 at bats, five homers and 44 RBIs.

"I was strictly a pull hitter then, in fact, during my

whole tenure in the minors," George recalls. "I went for the long ball. But why not? The power alleys in my high school days were just 320 feet from home plate."

The next year, 1972, George was back in California, playing at San Jose, and he had a pretty good year, hitting .274 in 117 games, with 10 homers and 68 RBIs. He was also improving at third, most of his errors coming on throws. It was beginning to look as if he might have a future in the game after all. He had grown into a solid six-footer, weighing about 200 pounds, and as one writer described him, "the weight distributed like a running back's — broad shoulders, low center of gravity, thick, strong legs."

George's idols in those days were Brooks Robinson, the incredible third baseman of the Baltimore Orioles, and Carl Yastrzemski, the slugging outfielder of the Boston Red Sox.

"I started trying to hit like Yaz in high school", George says, "you know, bat held high, wanting to pull everything. I kept hitting that way right through the minors and even when I first joined the Royals. It took me quite a while to realize I didn't have the strength, the quickness, or the experience to hit like that."

Yet he was hitting well enough at Omaha in 1973 to get the parent club to take notice. Omaha was a Triple-A club, a step away from the majors, and George showed he could handle the pitching. But there was a problem with his teammates that he almost couldn't handle. It almost prompted George to jump the club.

The team was playing in Indianapolis and George went down swinging at a bad pitch. He really got mad and halfway back to the bench he removed his batting helmet and fired it into the dugout.

"I guess it was another bad throw on my part," recalls George. "It took a bad hop and hit one of the players who'd been in Triple-A for years and years and years. Needless to say, he was mad."

That night, George was playing cards in a hotel room with some of his teammates. He went down to the bar to get some beer. A few veteran players were down there and one said, "Hey, George, if the beer isn't cold enough, don't throw it at us." Now George got mad. He recalls what happened next.

"I was at the cash register and right next to it were all these saucers and coffee cups. Suddenly I just started grabbing the saucers and throwing them at the table where the guys were sitting. Then I left. The next day when I went to the ballpark, nobody would play catch with me during warmups, nobody. I didn't know it at the time but about three guys were arrested and I was the one who had been throwing the stuff."

When his teammates gave him the cold shoulder, George stomped off the field. He went into the locker-room, took his uniform off, dressed, and left. He was all ready to catch a plane for El Segundo when Omaha manager Harry Malmberg and general manager Bill Gorman found out about it. They intercepted the still angry Brett and after some fast talking, persuaded him to rejoin the club. Fortunately, all was forgiven and everyone went back to the business of playing baseball. It was an uncharacteristic show of temper for the usually placid Brett, but he was just twenty years old and not used to these kinds of situations.

Yet in 117 games for Omaha that year he batted .284 with eight homers and 64 RBIs. He was already showing his fine batting eye by striking out just 45 times in 405 at bats. The Royals were so pleased with his progress that they brought him up to the parent club at the tail end of the season. At age twenty, George Brett was in the major leagues!

"I couldn't believe I was there," he recalls. "Yet I still didn't think I'd be anything but a utility player and a bullpen catcher. I wasn't hitting well and I wasn't fielding well, but I sat out there in the bullpen, shooting the breeze with the other guys. I was just a kid, getting $15,000 a year to have fun, and I loved it. I didn't really care about anything else."

George got into thirteen games before the year ended, collecting just five hits in forty trips for a .125 average. But it was a pleasant taste, and he hoped he'd be around again in '74, even if it was in a full-time utility role once again.

But the Royals weren't fooling around. The team had progressed very quickly for an expansion club, actually battling the Oakland A's for the division lead well into August before fading in September. The club seemed to have a future and the brass wanted solid ballplayers, youngsters who would develop and help them continue to improve.

When the 1974 season opened, George found himself at Omaha again, but some two weeks into the season he got the call and reported back to the Royals. A short time later he was installed at third base. The job was his as long as he could hold onto it. He could hardly believe it. Barely twenty-one years old, he had become an everyday player, a regular with a team that seemed to be on the brink of being a real contender.

For awhile it didn't look as if George would hold onto the job. Still trying to "hit like Yaz," he was struggling. Trying to pull every pitch, he was often overswinging, hitting harmless grounders and pop flies. His average hovered around the .200 mark for the first several months of the year and he began wondering if he'd soon reclaim his old seat in the bullpen. If that happened, could thoughts of El Segundo be far behind?

Fortunately, there was someone to rescue George just when he really began floundering. He was the Royals' batting coach, Charley Lau, who had himself been a journeyman ballplayer with around a .250 lifetime batting mark. But Lau had some definite theories on hitting, and he was beginning to really help some of the younger K.C. players.

"After the first two months or so of the season," recalls George, "I was hitting around the .200 mark. Charley had been leaving me alone till then. I guess he wanted me to realize my way wasn't working. Finally, he told me that when my average got down to .199, he'd step in."

Lau took George aside and told him he had been watching him carefully in the early part of the year. "You've got some tools," he said, "but to use them better you've got to change a few things and it isn't going to be easy."

It didn't take much to convince George that he should listen. For one thing, there was his own average, which was ready to send him back to the bench. In addition, he saw other evidence around him. One case in point was Hal McRae, an outfielder-designated hitter who had come over from Cincinnati as a part-time player. McRae hit .278 at Cincy in 1972, but batted fewer than 100 times. His first year with the Royals he played more, but hit just .234. Then he began working with Lau and in 1974 was playing regularly and on his way to a .300 season.

The first thing Lau did was to change George's stance. He had him stand further off the plate and put more weight on his rear leg. He also had him lower the bat. Instead of holding it high over his head, George dropped it so it was almost parallel to the ground. His new stance was not unlike that of Rod Carew, then with the Minnesota Twins, who was another lefthanded batter and considered by many the best all-round hitter in baseball.

Once he had changed George's stance, Lau began discussing his theories of hitting with his new pupil. He wanted him to go with the ball, not try to pull everything. He stressed patience at the plate, a tension-free swing, and hitting through the ball. Many of Lau's charges will let go of the bat with their top hand as they follow through, assuring that they swing through the ball in correct fashion.

George joined the rest of Lau's pupils and began working very hard. The group would be out there at three o'clock if the game was at night, taking batting practice and going over the mechanics of hitting time and again. George soon began feeling more comfortable at the plate. He was using the entire field, spraying more line drives, and he still felt he could pull the ball if he wanted to.

"All of a sudden, I started to hit," he said. "It felt good. And before every at bat I would talk to Charley about what to expect from the pitcher, whether I can pull him, go with the pitch or take him to the opposite field. You might say I pre-program myself in the on-deck circle."

As the second half of the season began, George was a different hitter, and there was no longer a question of sending him back to the bench. His average was on the rise. Lau had hoped to bring him up to .250 by the end of the year, but he was rising so quickly it now looked as if he could do better. He was also working very hard on his fielding, again trying to harness his natural talents. Throwing proved to be his troublepoint. Some scatterarms can never straighten out. Steve Garvey, the outstanding star of the Dodgers, had to move from third to first because his throwing was so inconsistent. But George kept working, hoping to find the consistency he knew he needed.

The Royals as a team were disappointing in '74. The club had surprised everyone with an 88-74 mark in '73, an exceptional record for a club playing in just its fifth season. But this time around they were struggling to reach .500. This sometimes happens when a team is growing and maturing. There were some other fine ballplayers on the club, like slugging first baseman John Mayberry, centerfielder Amos Otis, shortstop Fred Patek, second baseman Cookie Rojas, and pitchers Paul Splittorff and Steve Busby.

George continued his fine hitting in the second half of the year and was quickly becoming an integral part of the team. He was settling in and very happy. What made it even better was that brother Ken seemed to have found himself in the National League. Traded to the

Phillies in 1973 Ken had his best year with a 13-9 mark, and was on his way to an identical record with the Pittsburgh Pirates in '74. So both brothers were doing well.

There was another big change in George's style in 1974, and again it had to do with his new teammate, Hal McRae. Up to that point, George had been, admittedly, a lackadaisical type of ballplayer. McRae, on the other hand, was and is one of the most aggressive players in the major leagues. Infielders hate to see him bearing down on them when they're trying to complete a double-play or in a similar situation. He knows only one way to play the game and it soon began rubbing off on George, who recalls his impressions.

"I watched Hal hustling all over the place, breaking up double plays, stretching singles into doubles, and doubles into triples, and I finally said, 'Hey, I can do that, too.' I'd never been that kind of ballplayer before, not in high school or in the minor leagues, and I hadn't been thus far with the Royals. But when I saw how effective Hal was with his style, I began copying it. Now I don't think I can play any other way but all out.

"Baseball just isn't fun if you don't go out there and be, how can I say it, berserk. I enjoy the game so much because I'm putting everything into it. It's a great feeling when you're standing out there on second or third knowing you've just stretched a hit with hustle. I probably have just a little better than average speed, but I try to get every ounce from it that I can."

So 1974 turned into quite a season for George, if not for all the Royals. The club dropped back to fifth in the division with a 77-85 mark, but George had come through his rookie year with flying colors. Playing in 133 games, he batted a solid .282, collecting 129 hits in 457 at bats. He had 21 doubles, five triples, two homers, and 47 RBIs. In addition, he walked just 21 times and fanned on only 38 occasions. So he went up there swinging and usually made contact.

Though he didn't show a great deal of power working with Lau, it was generally considered a matter of first things first. Once he learned how to hit, then his natural power would begin to show through. Lau's other prize pupil, Hal McRae, also showed the results of the new program. His average went from .234 to .310, making him a very important part of the K.C. offensive machine.

The Royals hoped to bounce back in '75 and challenge the A's for supremacy in the American League West. Oakland had taken the division four straight times and had completed a string of three consecutive World Series triumphs in 1974. So the Royals would be chasing the best team in baseball once again in '75.

Still working with Charley Lau and concentrating on improving his overall game, George got off the mark quickly in 1975. There was no question that he was now the Royals third baseman of the future, as well as the present, and he was in the line-up every day. The team was also playing well, showing signs of maturity, and moving over the .500 mark and up near the top of the division.

On May 1, George went hitless for the second straight game. He would not go two games without a hit the rest of the year, and would carry that trait well into 1976. He continued to follow Charley Lau's instructions, and was banging out base hits to every field. Pitchers were finding it tougher and tougher to outsmart him at the plate, and he was still exceedingly difficult to strike out. He was still having some problems throwing from third, but continued working hard to improve.

The team really put it together in 1975. Playing steady ball all year long they really gave the A's a scare, though Oakland managed to pull away at the end. Yet the Royals finished with an impressive, 91-71 record, good for second in the A.L. West, some seven games behind the division-winning A's, who took their fifth straight.

Several members of the Kansas City team had outstanding years. McRae was over .300 again, and big John Mayberry was an important run producer. Amos Otis continued to play about the best centerfield in the league and hit very well. Splittorff and Steve Busby were outstanding on the mound, and George Brett had emerged as one of the bright young stars in all of baseball.

Playing in 159 games, George batted a solid .308, leading the league in hits with 195 and at bats with 634. He also had 35 doubles, tied for the league lead with 13 triples, and upped his power production to 11 homers and 89 RBIs. He struck out just forty-nine times all year and showed he could run the bases when he had to with thirteen steals. What it amounted to was great all-around ability, the only drawback continuing to be his erratic throwing from third.

George was extremely pleased with his success. He hadn't expected it, especially so soon, and felt he owed much of it to Charley Lau.

"I just wish there was some way to repay people like Charley for what they've done for me," he said. "But in some ways I guess a coach just considers it part of his job."

The Royals had a definite goal as the 1976 season approached. They felt they were ready to dethrone the A's as Western Division champs. Oakland was beginning to lose some of its longtime stars, most of whom were constantly battling with owner Charles Finley, usually over money. Catfish Hunter and Reggie Jackson were already gone, and others were following suit. So there were signs that the A's were ready to be taken.

Plus the Royals had improved themselves by adding more players, more depth, and more balance. Youngsters like second baseman Frank White and outfielder Al Cowens were ready to make major contributions, as were pitchers Dennis Leonard and Al Fitzmorris. And the nucleus of Mayberry, Otis, Patek, Brett, and McRae were hopefully still getting better.

George picked up about where he left off, hitting very well and for an even better average. He was becoming one of the toughest outs in baseball, and as the season began wearing on, it was obvious that he was a strong candidate for the American League batting crown.

The team was playing at about the same pace of a year earlier, but as expected, the A's were sliding back, and the Royals jumped atop the division. And George was beginning to show everyone that when he went on a tear, no one could get him out.

In six straight games from May 8 through May 13, he had three or more hits. Surprisingly enough, no one knew whether that was a record or not. With all the statistics kept in baseball, there was no listing for consecutive three-hit games. At any rate, from May 4 through May 13, George had an incredible .605 batting average, putting his season mark up around .350, and he was battling teammate McRae for the league lead.

George was also showing some of the top American League hurlers that he could not be fooled at the plate. In a game against the Baltimore Orioles, he was facing the great Jim Palmer. It was the first inning and the Royals had Tom Poquette on third with one out. Palmer threw a fast ball for a strike. Then he thought about the book on George.

He figured that George liked to take inside pitches to left to cross up the opposition, so he jammed him with a hard slider on the wrists. But instead of trying to poke it the opposite way, George swung through the ball and pulled it to right for a base hit, driving home Poquette with the first run of the game.

Manager White Herzog couldn't say enough about his young star. "George Brett may be the best all-around player in the league right now," Herzog said. "And unless there is a bone sticking out of him, he's ready to play every day." And a proud Charley Lau added to that, "George Brett does not have a definite weakness as a hitter."

In the field, he continued to work on his fielding and seemed to be throwing better than a year earlier. Royals' coach Chuck Hiller said he had to tell George to cut short his practice sessions on more than one occasion because he felt George was working too hard and too long and might wear himself down. But diminutive shortstop Fred Patek said he was beginning to appreciate having George play alongside him because the youngster was learning the hitters and improving his range. He even went so far as to mention George in the same breath as his early idol, Brooks Robinson.

"I can see where a Mark Belanger (the Orioles shortstop) would appreciate a Brooks Robinson," said Patek. "When a third baseman can reach balls in the hole, it takes a lot of the strain off a shortstop's arm. George has been doing more and more of that this year."

His fine play resulted in his first All-Star Game appearance in 1976, and although he was hitless in two at bats, with a walk, it was nevertheless a big thrill. There was also another event that George knew he would face in 1976, and he looked forward to this with mixed emotions.

Brother Ken was back in the American League. He was 9-5 for the Pirates in '75, then was traded to the New York Yankees during the off-season. Ken was becoming more of a journeyman player and would move on to the White Sox before the year was out. But George had never faced his brother before in a real game.

"Ken used to kid us that he was still the best hitter in the family," George says. "In fact, when he was with the Phils in 1973, he set a record for a pitcher by hitting a home run in four consecutive starts. So when I faced him for the first time that spring, I was determined to hit it out or fall flat on my face."

Sure enough, George swung from the heels for one of the few times all year and sent a long drive over the right field fence. That's something they still talk about in the Brett family. But the homer aside, George was happy to have Ken in the A.L. They were closer than ever and whenever they played against each other they spent all the time they could with each other.

"Ken liked to have me call him 'The King.' " George remembers, "and he'd often call me in the middle of the night and say, 'This is the King speaking.' "

The two brothers often socialized together, double-dated, and had fun. As George said, "We look alike, so the same girls who like him should like me, too."

On the field, of course, George was all business. As the season wore down, it was obvious that the Royals were going to win the Western Division title for the first time. And George was in a dogfight with teammates Hal McRae and superhitter Rod Carew for the batting title. Each wanted to win it very badly.

It came down to the final game, with all three players having a chance to take it. George had two hits already against Minnesota, and on his final at bat he lofted a fly to left. Twins outfielder Steve Brye hesitated, misjudged the ball, and it dropped for George's third hit of the day. It gave him a final batting mark of .333 and the title, as McRae finished at .332 and Carew at .331. But it wasn't as simple as that.

The intensely proud and competitive McRae was bitterly disappointed at not having won, and when he thought about George's final hit, he began wondering out loud to his teammates and the media whether Brye might have misplayed the ball intentionally so that George would win the batting title. The reason he gave was racial, that Brye, a white man, wanted to see another white win the crown instead of McRae, a black.

McRae did not mean it as a reflection on George, who obviously was just trying for a hit. He may not have realized also, that George admired him greatly, and considered him something of a role model. His insinuation really crushed George.

"It took a lot of the fun out of winning the title," George said. "I respect Hal so much. But a week later we were kidding about the whole thing. He'd say to me, 'You know you won it because you're white.' And later, when I got the silver bat given to the batting champ, he said to me, 'OK, let's cut it in half.'

McRae later said he'd gotton over the whole thing, and emphasized, "It caused no damage to my relationship with George."

But the rest of the season had been great. The Royals were A.L. West champs with a 90-72 record, and George Brett had emerged as one of baseball's best. He once again played in 159 games, led the league with 215 hits and 645 at bats. He had 34 doubles, a league leading 14 triples, seven homers and 67 RBIs. He also scored 94 runs, stole a career high 21 bases, and struck out only 36 times in 645 at bats. And for a free swinger who didn't want the walk, either, that's an incredible statistic.

Now the Royals had one more hurdle to cross before going to the World Series. They'd have to meet the powerful New York Yankees in the best-of-five playoff series. The Yanks had also just completed a rebuilding process and hadn't won anything since 1964. But owner George Steinbrenner was determine to restore the Bronx Bombers to their former lofty position in the baseball world, and he was putting together a fine team, boasting the likes of Thurman Munson, Graig Nettles, Chris Chambliss, Willie Randolph, Mickey Rivers, Catfish Hunter, Ed Figueroa, Sparky Lyle, and Dock Ellis. They'd be tough to beat.

In the first game, George became the goat in the very first inning. It was his old nemesis, his arm, that betrayed him. He made a pair of throwing errors, allowing the Yanks to score a couple of unearned runs and take a 2-0 lead. From there, Catfish Hunter pitched them to a 4-1 victory, and George's three hits did not make up for the pair of miscues in the first.

Game two saw things turned around. This time it was the Yanks coming apart, making five errors and leaving 11 runners stranded on base. A determined George crashed a long triple in the sixth inning, driving home the go-ahead runs, and lefty Paul Splittorff protected the 7-3 victory with five and two-thirds innings of fine relief. The series was tied at a game apiece.

The two clubs split the next pair, with the Yanks winning, 5-3, then the Royals coming back to take a 7-4 verdict. George continued his fine hitting. Now it was down to one game, sudden death, and the Royals had their ace, Dennis Leonard, who was 17-10 in the regular season, going against Ed Figueroa.

Both teams scored a pair in the first. The Royals got another in the second, but the Yanks came back with two in the third and two more in the sixth to make it a 6-3 game. They were six outs from a pennant when the Royals came to bat in the eighth inning.

K.C. rallied, putting a pair of runners on base. Up stepped George, in perhaps the biggest pressure situation of his life. Sure enough, he came through with flying colors, belting a lone home run into the right-field stands at Yankee Stadium to tie the game. As he circled the bases, the huge ballpark was strangely quiet, the people wondering just who this young upstart was who was trying to keep the Yanks from their first pennant in twelve years.

On the bench, his teammates mobbed George, who had saved them from extinction with one swing of the bat. But they could score no more in the inning, or in the ninth, and when Chris Chambliss stepped up to lead off the last of the ninth against the Royals' Mark Littell, it was still anybody's game.

But not for long. Littell's first pitch was a fastball down the middle and Chambliss jumped on it. He sent a high, long drive to right centerfield. Cowens and Otis started to converge, then stopped as the ball sailed into the bleachers for a dramatic, pennant-clinching home run. The Yanks were American League champions!

It was a bitter loss for K.C., and for George, who had only a few short minutes to enjoy his heroics of the previous inning. But the team had come a long way, and so had its young third baseman. Getting national exposure for the first time, George showed the baseball world just what kind of a hitter he had become. In five games against the Yanks, he had eight hits in 18 at bats for a .444 average. Among them was a double, a triple, his big homer, and five RBIs. Despite the loss, he had emerged as the Royals' leader and prime offensive threat.

The Royals came to spring training in 1977 with essentially the same team. They did make one major deal that brought catcher Darrell Porter from Milwaukee. Porter was a strong lefthanded hitter, who would team with George and Mayberry from the portside. Otis, McRae, and Al Cowens were all strong righty hitters. The club was well balanced and seemed on the brink of becoming one of baseball's best. They had power, good speed, and were fine defensively. It didn't seem that anyone in their division could stop them. Even in the spring, their thoughts were to the Yankees, and getting revenge if the two teams met again in the playoffs.

Kansas City became a powerful team in 1977. They had definitely taken over from Oakland as the dominant team in the A.L. West. The balance Manager Herzog had sought was paying off. If there was a weakness it was with the pitching, especially the bullpen, but the K.C. hurlers were by no means a futile lot.

So the Royals were a steamroller. They hit a soft spot after the All-Star break, but came on to win going away, finishing with a 102-60 record. It was obvious that Kansas City could now compete with anyone in baseball. Just look at the 1977 stats.

Rightfielder Al Cowens emerged to have a great year, finishing at .312, with 23 homers and 112 RBIs. McRae was .298, 21, 91; Porter .272, 16, 60; Otis .253, 17, 79; Mayberry .232, 23, 82. There were also fine contributions from Patek, Frank White, and Tom Poquette. Of the pitchers, Dennis Leonard finished at 20-12, with 244 strikeouts. Paul Splittorff was 16-6, Jim Colborn a surprise at 18-14, and Marty Pattin 10-3. The club was good.

As for George, he had another fine year, though he blended in with the rest of the Royals. He also missed a number of games due to some minor injuries, but in 139 contests he hit .312 with a career high 22 home runs and 88 RBIs. He struck out just 24 times in 564 at bats. He was an All-Star again and during the second half of the year he and the rest of the league witnessed something that George would remember quite well in the future.

Rod Carew of the Minnesota Twins captured the attention of all baseball fans when he made a strong bid for a .400 batting average. On July 1, Carew was batting .411. In the past, Carew had batted .350, .364, and .359. He had flirted with .400 before, and everyone agreed he had the talent to do it. So when he made his move in 1977, everyone began watching, and stories of Ted Williams' drive to .406 in 1941 were told again and again.

The Twins were also chasing the Royals, but in August, both the Twins and Carew dropped off. By August 30, Carew was down to .377 and his bid all but by the boards. Still, he had a very strong finish, batting .441 over the final twenty-eight games to finish the year with a .388 mark. When it ended, he had missed batting .400 by the margin of just eight hits. Though he didn't make it, he showed everyone that a modern ballplayer was capable of reaching .400, something many people figured couldn't happen again. So in a sense, Carew blazed the trail for George's bid, which would come three years later.

It was an interesting season all around. And now that the Royals had won it again, they had their second wish. They'd have a chance to get even with the New York Yankees.

So it was time for the two clubs to go at it again. And this time the Kansas City players swore things would be different.

It sure looked that way in the game one. The Yanks started sore-shouldered Don Gullett against K.C.'s Paul Splittorff, who had a reputation as something of a Yankee killer. Splittorff was in complete control as the Royals won easily, 7-2. Homers by McRae, Cowens, and Mayberry highlighted the Kansas City attack.

Then in game two the outcome was reversed. The Yanks won, 6-2, as Ron Guidry bested Andy Hassler. But there was some controversy. In the Royals' sixth, Hal McRae was on first, Patek on second with George up. He hit a grounder to third. Graig Nettles fielded the ball and went to second. But just as Willie Randolph took the throw, McRae barreled into him with a hard block, knocking him down and allowing Patek to score what was at the time the tying run.

The Yankees began screaming, claiming it was a dirty play and a cheap shot. They then erupted for three runs in their half of the inning and went on to take it from there.

"I'm an aggressive player," McRae said after the game. "That's the only way I know how to play. We played that way in Cincinnati before I came here. I've done it for eight years and I've never been called anything but a clean player. And I'm not the only one who plays that way. George Brett plays that way, too."

George had made an error in the game and had gotten just one hit, so he wasn't happy when it was over. But when someone mentioned that McRae had said he played the same aggressive ball, he perked up and said, "Well, thank you."

So things were tied once more and it looked as if the two teams would again battle to the wire. The pivotal third game saw Dennis Leonard up against Mike Torrez of the Yanks. Buoyed by their return to Kansas City, the Royals pecked away for single runs in the second, third, and fifth, two in the sixth and one more in the seventh, as they took a 6-2 victory of their own, Leonard tossing a two-hitter. George had a pair of hits in this one and his hustle on the basepaths led to a run in the seventh. He seemed to be warming up.

K.C. was now in the driver's seat. The Royals just had to win one of the remaining two games to take the pennant. They sent ex-Yankee Larry Gura to the mound against Ed Figueroa. But the Yanks broke on top, getting a run in the first, two in the second, and one in the third. They had a quick 4-0 lead, but the Royals wouldn't quit.

K.C. got a pair in the third, and after the Yanks got another in the top of the fourth, the Royals got two more. George had a key triple to drive in one of the third-inning runs. He was up again in the fourth with runners at first and third, and two out. K.C. already had a pair in to cut the lead to 5-4, and Manager Martin called on relief ace Sparky Lyle.

He pitched George carefully, and finally got him on a fly to left, ending the rally. Lyle was superb the rest of the way, limiting the Royals to just two hits in the remaining five innings, and forcing a fifth and final game for the second straight year. With all the marbles on the line, the Royals called on Paul Splittorff to face the Yanks' Ron Guidry, who would be pitching with just two days rest.

Two days wasn't enough for the slim lefthander. In the Royals' first, McRae singled and George promptly tripled to center, driving in the first K.C. run. There was a play on him at third and he came up punching at Yankee third sacker Graig Nettles. Both benches emptied, but the combatants were quickly separated.

"He came in hard and I hit him with my leg, then he threw a punch," Nettles said.

George told it a bit differently. "He tried to push me off the bag. I was just defending myself."

The flare-up showed how badly each club wanted the game. Al Cowens followed with a bouncer to third and George raced home with the second run. The Yanks got one back in the third, but in the bottom of the inning Cowens singled McRae home, finishing Guidry and bringing in Mike Torrez. K.C. had a 3-1 lead with Yankee nemesis Paul Splittorff on the mound. It looked good.

It was still a 3-1 game as Splittorff pitched into the eighth inning. The Royals were six outs away from being champions. But when Willie Randolph opened the inning with a basehit, Manager Herzog went to reliever Doug Bird. Bird promptly struck out Munson, but Lou Piniella singled and Reggie Jackson came up to pinch hit. He slapped a single to center, scoring Randolph and making it 3-2. A great play by Frank White got the Royals out of the inning. They had a one-run lead and needed just three more outs.

In the ninth, Herzog brought in Dennis Leonard to try to close it out. But Paul Blair opened with a single and Roy White walked. Larry Gura came in to pitch to Mickey Rivers, and the large Kansas City crowd held its collective breath. Rivers faked a bunt, then singled to right, scoring Blair with the tying run. Was victory going to slip away from the Royals again?

Mark Littell came in to pitch to Willie Randolph, who lofted a sacrifice fly to right, scoring White and giving the Yanks a 4-3 lead. The Royals couldn't believe it was happening. Piniella then hit one to third. George picked it up and promptly threw it into the stands behind first. His old problem. Rivers came across with an insurance run before the Yanks were retired. But the Bombers had scored three times and took a 5-3 lead. Now it was the Royals who were down to their last three outs.

Once again it was Sparky Lyle, the Cy Young reliever, who came out of the pen and got the Royals easily, Patek ending the game by hitting into a double play. The Royals and their fans were stunned. They had let the Yankees get away, get off the hook that was two-thirds of the way in. It was perhaps the most demoralizing moment George and his teammates had ever experienced, a horrendous end to what had been a glorious season. And the fans wondered if their club could come back in '78.

George had a good series, though he wasn't as commanding at the plate as he had been a year earlier. He was six for 20 for a .300 mark, with a pair of triples and two RBIs. Now all he or anyone else could do was prepare to start all over again in 1978.

The club made a few changes. They sent big John Mayberry to Toronto and brought in a pair of highly touted rookies, Willie Wilson and Clint Hurdle. And they wanted more playing time for catcher-first baseman-outfielder John Wathan. George was raring to go again, also, hoping for a big year and another crack at the Yankees.

He didn't know it then, but he was about to embark on one of the most difficult years of his career. This time the problem would be a relatively new one for him — injuries. The culprits were a painfully bruised left shoulder and bone chips in the thumb of his right hand.

Because of the injuries he missed a number of games, and often played with pain. The thumb prevented him from getting a real good grip on the bat, though sometimes it was worse than others. Still, he hit better than most players in the league and the Royals still played well enough to take a third straight West title with a 92-70 slate.

With his injuries limiting him to just 128 games, George fell below the .300 mark for the first time since 1975, hitting .294. He also dropped off to nine homers and 62 RBIs. But he managed to lead the league with 45 doubles and stole a career high 23 bases. So he was still a force despite his various hurts.

"It wasn't an easy year for me," George said. "But playing hurt is part of the game and I won't use the injuries as an excuse. I'll say one thing, it will all feel a lot better if we can beat the Yankees this time."

That's right. The Royals would get a third crack at the Yanks, who had staged an amazing comeback amidst their usual turmoil, coming from 14 games back to catch the Red Sox and finally beating them in a one-game playoff.

When the Yanks started a rookie, Jim Beattie, in game one against ace Dennis Leonard, and came away with a 7-1 victory, the handwriting seemed to be on the wall once again. George had a double in four trips, but he and his teammates had to be wondering just what they had to do to beat the Yanks. This was becoming an awfully bad habit.

They broke it temporarily in the second game, pounding out 16 hits en route to a 10-4 victory, tying the series at a game apiece. It might have been the tonic they needed. George was really up for game three.

Paul Splittorff prepared to face Catfish Hunter. Facing the Cat in the first inning, he went after a 1-1 fastball and sent it into the right field seats for a home run and a 1-0 K.C. lead.

The Yanks tied it in the second as Reggie Jackson belted one, then George came up against Hunter again in the third. This time he really sent one downtown, a tremendous shot into the centerfield bleachers for his second homer. By the time he came up for a third time in the fifth inning, the Yanks had regained the lead at 3-2.

Hunter was still pitching and George was still hitting. A stunned Yankee Stadium crowd watched the graceful lefty hitter stroke his third straight homer, this one a line shot into the lower deck in right to tie the game. It was a record-setting performance. Off-season or not, George had just shown everyone that he was still one of the great hitters in the game, and an awesome hitter in the clutch.

Unfortunately, the Yanks wouldn't quit, either. They retook the lead in the sixth and George came up again in the seventh, this time facing ace reliever Goose Gossage. Again he hit the ball well, a long drive to rightcenter, only this time Paul Blair flagged it down right in front of the fence. But he had come close.

To the Royals credit, they wouldn't die. In the eighth they retook the lead with a pair of runs on a double by Otis and singles by Porter and Hurdle. But with Doug Bird pitching in the bottom of the inning, Thurman Munson hit a tremendous home run with a man on to give the Yanks a 6-5 lead. In the ninth, Gossage set the Royals down in order, but George hit another long fly that was caught near the wall. Still the Yanks had won and taken a 2-1 lead.

After the game the reporters gathered around George to ask him about his record-setting performance.

"I will remember this day for the rest of my life," he said, "but I'd be happier if I'd gone 0-for-4 with three errors and we'd won the game."

Even the Yanks were in awe of George's performance.

Manager Bob Lemon, who had taken over from Martin in midseason, said:

"We were lucky. The way he was swinging the bat he could have easily had five. Those last two didn't miss by much."

That was to be the Royals last hurrah. The next day the Yanks pitched Ron Guidry, who had an incredible 25-3 mark during the regular season, and he shut the door, beating Dennis Leonard, who also pitched well, 2-1, on solo homers by Nettles and White. The Yanks were A.L. champs for the third straight year, and each time they had done it at the expense of the Royals. After the final game, George talked to reporters. As usual, he was patient and cooperative. He had hit .389 in the playoffs, coming through in the clutch once again.

"This time it wasn't as bad as the last two years," he said. "This wasn't as climactic, maybe because it didn't go to a fifth game. And maybe we're just getting used to it. Maybe we've resigned ourselves to their superiority.

"After awhile, when you've been losing and losing and losing to the same team, they get a psychological edge on you. It seems as if the Yankees have it on us. They also have a lot of players who play their best under pressure. We have no complaints, no excuses. They are better than we are is all anyone will say. The only way we can beat these guys now is to win 10-1. That way, there's no chance to blow things. They seem to always win the close ones."

George had a problem of his own in the off-season. He needed surgery to remove the bone chips in his right thumb. Then he had to work hard to rehabilitate the hand and thumb. Because of the effects of the operation, he missed all of spring training and when the season started he had to wear a protective device on the thumb when he batted. In fact, he had to wear it for most of the season.

Because he missed so much time he started very slowly. So did the rest of the Royals. The problem with the hand was also causing him to make more bad throws from third, especially early in the year. He even used to kid about his fielding.

"If I can stay healthy long enough I have a chance to be the first player to get 3,000 hits and make 1,000 errors."

But teammate Paul Splittorff said this kind of talk was something of a cover.

"George is sensitive about his fielding," the pitcher said. "It's the only thing he's ever been criticized for and I think he does take it personally. Everybody looks for a weakness in people, and George doesn't have many. His fielding is actually pretty good, but it just doesn't measure up to his hitting. And when you think about it, what could? He's just an amazing clutch hitter. Ask the Palmers and the Guidrys. They'll say he's the toughest they've ever faced in the clutch situations. That's high praise. But George seems to have a higher gear he slips into, and he just takes over."

By the middle of May he still hadn't slipped into any kind of gear. He was hitting around .240 and that just wasn't George Brett. Yet it wasn't long after that when he began finding the groove. Suddenly, the hits were coming in bunches once again. He began doing it all with the bat.

There was something else that was different in 1979. Charley Lau was no longer with the Royals. He had gone to, of all teams, the Yankees. But in a way, it might have been a good thing at this point in his career for George to be on his own.

"I'm kind of reacting differently with Charley gone," George admitted. "When Charley was here I'd be up in a certain situation and he'd tell me to try to hit the ball between second and third and up the middle. If the pitcher threw me three fastballs on the inside corner, I'd still be trying to hit up the middle like he suggested. Now, I find myself trying to hit the ball where it's pitched. I can go up and try to pull for a home run if the time is right."

He was showing more power in '79, and by midseason

he was beginning to hang up the numbers once again. Unfortunately, other members of the team weren't, and it was the California Angels who looked as if they might finally win a divisional title, unless the Royals went on a real tear. By late August K.C. was within striking distance, but still having trouble putting together a real streak. George, however, had overcome the thumb injury and was in the midst of what could easily become his greatest season.

Though he was now getting more recognition in the media and off the field, he was still a fun-loving, easygoing guy. There was none of the superstar syndrome about him. One of his best friends was Royals utilityman Jamie Quirk, who marvelled at the way George never changed.

"I've known George since we played in the instructional league together," Quirk said. "He's my closest friend on the team now and he's the same guy who was making $500 a month when I first met him. He knows he's a public figure now and he can't be too outrageous, but he still enjoys going out. I'm just a run-of-the-mill player and he's a superstar, but he has never let that come between us. Wherever we go, he's recognized, but he always makes sure that I'm introduced to everyone. That's makes a guy feel good. In fact, he's always been one of the guys around here, not the sort of superstar who'll walk in five minutes before the game."

No, indeed. George continued to work hard and refused to rest on his laurels. He wanted to keep improving as a hitter and always worked to stabilize his throwing in the field. He hit a ton the second half of the '79 season, trying his hardest to put the Royals over the top. But it was just one of those years when the team couldn't put it together. They tried, but finished at 85-77, three games behind the division-winning Angels. Ironically, the same thing happened to the Yanks, and they lost the East crown to the Orioles.

But George had never been better. Playing in 154 games he batted a solid .329, leading the league with 212 hits in 645 at bats. He scored 119 runs, had 42 doubles, led the league with an amazing 20 triples, and had career highs of 23 homers and 107 RBIs. And he still had the eye, striking out just 36 times. You couldn't ask for much more offense from a single player. He was happy with his season and still proud of the pace at which he played the game.

"This is the third time I've led the league in triples," he said. "And if I were to guess, I'd say that seven or eight of my triples this past year were really just doubles. But I stretched them."

There were some changes with the Royals during the off-season. Longtime manager Whitney Herzog was gone and would be replaced by Jim Frey, who was a coach in the Oriole organization for some ten years. The club also traded with the Angels for slugging first baseman Willie Mays Aikens, hoping to add some more lefthanded power. In addition, U.L. Washington would be taking over at shortstop for the aging Fred Patek, who went to California in the Aikens deal. Plus speedy leftfielder Willie Wilson seemed on the verge of becoming a real force, a catalyst type player and possible superstar. Young pitchers Rich Gale and Rene Martin were expected to help the pitching staff, and the club was looking to submariner Dan Quisenberry to give the team a stopper out of the bullpen.

But these moves, while important, didn't excite George as much as another one did. In the off-season, the Royals had acquired the contract of George's brother, Ken. He had become a real journeyman pitcher. The Royals would be his 10th big league team and his lifetime record was a mediocre 82-84. Yet the prospect of having his brother as a teammate really turned George on. He looked forward to 1980, not fully realizing it was going to be the greatest year of his life in more ways than one.

At the outset, there were troubles for everyone. It started in spring training. First, catcher Darrell Porter, who had a .291, 20 homer, 112 RBI season in '79, left the team, citing personal problems as the reason. Soon after he disclosed that he had become addicted to alcohol and drugs and was undergoing treatment at a rehabilitation center in Arizona. He would not rejoin the team until late April. But it was a courageous admission for any player, especially one who was considered to be a star.

Next centerfielder Amos Otis incurred a freak injury when he was hit by a ball thrown by, of all things, an automatic pitching machine. He ruptured a tendon in the little finger of his right hand and couldn't play until late May.

George started slowly again. The players had struck part of spring training, so he wasn't really in a groove. He was still hitting in the mid .200s on April 25, when he slid into second in a game against Baltimore. The result was a severely bruised heel, and that slowed him up, put him in and out of the line-up for almost three weeks. He didn't return full time until May 16. And by then Hal McRae was out. He had torn a calf muscle on May 12. And on May 13, pitcher Paul Splittorff collapsed with back spasms. He would be out two weeks.

So the team was struggling because of the injuries and slow starts. For awhile in the early going they trailed the rejuvenated Oakland A's, now piloted by former Yank skipper Billy Martin. Hopefully, the walking wounded would all return and players like Willie Aikens, who was coming back from off-season knee surgery, would start hitting.

By May 21, George's average was just .247, but he wasn't worried. "I was hitting about .240 this time last year, too, then I caught fire and they never put me out."

There was little doubt that George had his confidence as a hitter. And he was right. He suddenly began hitting, and his average rose quickly and sharply. Like Rod Carew and a few other top hitters in the game, when George Brett gets hot there's really no one who can stop him. And this tear was the real thing.

In the three weeks following his May 21 low of .247 he hit safely in 16 of 18 games, driving in 24 runs, and gathering five doubles, a triple, and six homers among his hits. His average during that time was a cool .440! The streak had brought his season's average up to .337, and it was beginning to look as if he was headed for another outstanding season. His bat also helped bring the Royals alive, and the team moved out to a short lead over Oakland.

Then on June 10, it all came to a halt. The Royals were playing Cleveland and George was on first. He decided to steal and broke for second. George recalls what happened next.

"I saw their shortshop coming across the base and I was distracted. It caused me to slide late, and I hit the bag and bounced back. Then I heard a big pop!"

The big pop was no joke. It was the sound of a ligament tearing in George's right ankle. He had to be helped from the field. Word was that he would be out of action at least a month. The Royals tried to take his loss philosophically.

"George gets hurt a lot because he's so aggressive," said General Manager Joe Burke. "But then again, he wouldn't be as good as he is if he weren't so aggressive, so what can you do?"

"I wish he had one less stolen base," said Manager Frey.

George worked hard to rehabilitate the ankle. Without him, the Royals continued to struggle, barely playing .500 ball and still not able to pull away from the rest of the division. The injuries kept George out some thirty-five games, and without him the Royals managed just a 19-16 log, not really championship baseball, and they were still back with the rest of the pack in the A.L. West. Now the target date for George's return was July 10, the first game after the All-Star break. In about half a season, he had missed thirty-nine games. He'd have to be in there the rest of the way if he wanted to have enough plate appearances to qualify for the batting title.

There was something else to worry about. When a player misses that much time, he often loses his timing and the first month or so of his return is like spring training all over again. What if George reverted to being a .247 hitter again. The Royals needed his spark badly.

George returned as scheduled on July 10, in a game against Detroit. He promptly banged out a pair of hits. The next day he had three more. Then after a one-hit game, he came back with three, two, two, and four. In his first seven games back he had 17 hits in 28 at bats for a scorching .607 clip, raising hit batting average to .374. It was an amazing return, and everyone seemed to be waiting for the bubble to burst. In addition, the club was winning and beginning to open some daylight with the rest of the division.

Then on July 17, he was hitless in four trips against the Red Sox, but the next game he again banged out four hits in five tries to go up to .377. That game saw him embark on a hitting streak, which soon began attracting a great deal of attention. George Brett was hot and the whole baseball world knew it.

The streak reached ten games on July 27, though his average had actually dropped four points to .373. But when it reached 15 games on August 2, his average was up to .388. While all this was happening, the Royals had finally broken away from the pack and were obviously headed for their fourth division title in five years. Their archrivals, the Yanks, were also well ahead in the East, and it looked like a fourth October showdown between the two clubs.

Because of the lack of a tight divisional race, more and more attention began centering on the exploits of George Brett, who was fast becoming a national media celebrity. His hot hitting continued without letup. By August 12, the hitting streak had reached 25 games and out came all the stories about DiMaggio's great streak in 1941, and some of the others, including Pete Rose's 44-game run at it just a few years earlier. And it was beginning to bother George that he was getting so much publicity to the detriment of his teammates.

"When the streak got to 20 or 25 games," he said,

"there would be 25 reporters around my locker even if I'd only gotten one hit. So I'd look at them and say, 'What's everybody talking to me for. Willie Aikens just drove in four runs, you know.' I just didn't think it was fair."

But he kept hitting. And when he got four hits in four trips on August 17 against Toronto, the streak reached 29 and his batting average went over the magic mark. He was now batting .401. The next day against Texas he had three more hits. His hitting streak had reached 30 and his batting average was up to .404. The excitement was really starting.

"I've seen players get hot and go on hitting streaks," said Manager Frey. "But I've never seen anyone go out and hit like George has hit since the All-Star break. He's been doing it night after night, week after week."

Royals' coach Gordy MacKenzie added, "I've been in baseball a long time and everytime George comes up I think he's going to get a hit. I've never felt that way about anybody before."

American League pitchers were also trying to figure a way to slow down this hitting machine from Kansas City. Facing his old high school teammate, Scott McGregor, who was trying to protect a one-run lead, George stepped in with a man on first. Five times he swung and fouled pitches off. Finally he got the one he wanted, slamming a triple down the line in right and driving home the tying run.

"I gave him some of my best stuff," McGregor said, "but George kept hanging in there until he got the pitch he wanted."

The next night in Texas the streak ended. Lefthander Jon Matlack turned the trick, stopping George in three at bats and ending the skein at thirty games. When he went out for the final time, the fans in Texas gave him a standing ovation, attesting to his popularity all over the league. But the competitive Brett was not happy it was over and he was determined not to be let down.

"I kept telling myself I was hot all through the

streak," he said. "My thing the whole time was not to put any pressure on myself. Now I've got to avoid a dry spell. I've got to be patient and avoid swinging at first pitches, or change-ups, or chase bad balls. I would be putting added pressure on myself if I tried to do things differently just to try to hit .400. Right now I'm not going to count on doing it. I'm just going to enjoy myself running around those bases."

George was right. There would be no letdown. The night after the streak ended he simply went out and got three hits in three trips, bringing his average up to a season high of .406. With the streak over, the excitement about a .400 season was really building.

For those who don't already know, a .400 average is one of the rarest and most difficult of baseball achievements. Only eight different players have reached that mark on 13 occasions since 1900, and most of those occurred before 1925. The names of this elite group reads like a Who's Who of baseball greats: Nap Lajoie, Joe Jackson, Ty Cobb, George Sisler, Rogers Hornsby, Harry Heilmann, Bill Terry, Ted Williams.

Cobb and Hornsby reached the incredible level three times each, while Sisler did it twice. The others made it one time only. Eleven of those occasions occurred before 1925, then Terry did it in 1930 and Williams in 1941. No one since. There have been a few challenges, Carew's being the last in 1977. But of all those, many felt that George Brett had the best chance.

There was no doubt that he was battling. He fell to .399 with an 0-3 day against Cleveland on August 23. He had one hit the next day and two the next, bringing him back to .398. Then in a game against Milwaukee on August 26, he exploded for five straight hits, shooting his average back to .407. It was now a quest in earnest.

"There's still a long way to go," George told the persistent reporters, who gathered around him with increasing frequency. "I'd certainly like to do it. It would be a once-in-a-lifetime thing. I'm just going to try to stay up there as long as I can and hope I'm still there at the end of the season. The big thing is I don't want to fold completely and go down to .320 or something."

Everything had to be right for an assault on .400, including a little luck. Another element was the personality of the players. The hitters of the past didn't have the same kind of media blitz to put up with, but they had pressures. One writer put it this way.

"Like all .400 hitters of the past, Brett has an air of determination, combined with tremendous pride and confidence. Without it, everyday pressure of the baseball world would certainly take a toll. Williams carried it to the point of arrogance, as did Bill Terry. In fact, all eight .400 hitters of the century had it."

There was another kind of give and take. Playing on the fast artificial surface at Royals Stadium gave George an advantage. But then again, the huge, modern gloves the fielders wore took it away. In the old days, the fielders wore small gloves of poor quality. So there was a strange kind of balance struck.

Ted Williams recalled his 1941 success and discussed the advantage he had over Brett. "I didn't have to worry about a media blitz like he does and I also didn't realize the importance of hitting .400. It had happened only eleven years earlier, [Bill Terry 1930] and then five years before that [in 1925]. George has thirty-nine years [of baseball history] to look back on, so it's got to be a bigger deal for him then it was for me at the time.

"I think he's also find that September will be very tough for him. It's the hardest time for hitters anyway, with the weather getting a little colder and the sunlight getting lower, creating shadows that didn't exist in the summer. It also seems to me that many of the pitchers get a little stronger in cool weather."

It wasn't going to be a piece of cake, that's for sure. But the Royals sweetened the pot a bit. During his assault on .400 they reportedly signed him to a new contract, a five-year pact calling for $1 million per year, and they also added $250,000 a year to each of the remaining two years of his current contract.

The club also called Ken Brett up from Omaha, where he had spent most of the year. Having big brother around to run interference and keep an eye on George was also a good thing for him. The brothers were very close and Ken provided George with another source of confidence.

Reporters, of course, asked him any and all kinds of questions, and when one asked George to map out his plans for the next five years, he answered quickly.

"Hit .400 and win the World Series. Ditto on that for five years. As for off the field, I'd like to get married, have a couple of children, move to a ranch, have some horses, my hunting dogs, my jeep, my station wagon for the wife. I want to have hard work to do, but no particular times to do it."

George also said it hasn't been easy for him to get to the position he now occupied.

"It didn't happen overnight. I know it was tough. There were a lot of things I'd have liked to have done in '74, '75, '76, '77 besides going to the ballpark every day at 3:30 to take batting practice. There were a lot of things I could have done, and probably would have preferred to do. But I knew if I was going to become successful in baseball, *I* had to do it, *I* had to work at it."

The Brett watch was on in earnest now. Every day the newspapers, television reporters, and other media people honed in on every at bat, instantly figuring his average and counting his plate appearances to see how close he'd be to qualify for the official batting title. When he went 1-for-4 against Cleveland on September 5, his average dipped below .400 to .399. The next day he was 0-for-3 and down to .396. At this stage of the season if it slips away, it's awfully hard to get back. For instance, even though Rod Carew batted .441 over his final twenty-eight games in 1977, his average only rose eleven points to .388.

But dropping to .396 wasn't the only negative thing that happened at Cleveland. George hurt his right hand during his third at bat. Suddenly, he was on the shelf again. It was really incredible. Never had a player had such a fantastic year, but had it so interrupted by injury. This one was a sprain, bad enough to keep him from swinging the bat. And once again there was a question of whether George would have enough at bats to qualify.

And during all this, there were still great demands on George's spare time. Local people wanted him for promotions. National companies begged him for endorsements. In a presidential election year, *George Brett For President* bumper stickers appeared all over Kansas City. Yet he weathered the storm, saying only, "The closer the season comes to the end, the more pressure's going to be around and that's when I'm going to need more time for myself, to do the things I want to do. I don't want to find myself coming to the ballpark angry."

Others connected with the game couldn't believe how well George was conducting himself through the fuss and hoopla. Former teammate Buck Martinez, who had roomed with George at Omaha in the minor leagues, said:

"George really hasn't changed much. It's great to see a guy who attains that kind of success and still maintain the same personality. He just hasn't changed."

Umpire Ken Kaiser expressed the sentiments of most non-playing baseball people.

"George is just a super person," Kaiser said. "He's good for baseball, a gentleman on and off the field. The way he treats young umpires is just amazing. I hope he hits 9,000."

The big problem was the hand. The injury responded slowly and George missed eight games. He still needed 55 plate appearances to qualify for the batting title. Now there was the remote possibility that he would bat .400, but not have it recognized because of too few plate appearances. On September 16, the doctors said that George had developed tendonitis in the hand and should sit out until he was free of pain.

But he was back a few days later. He was still hitting well, but not in bunches like before. The average dipped slowly, finally going below .390. It looked as if another bid for .400 was by the boards. But George kept stroking. On October 1, he had a 3-for-3 day against the Mariners. With four games remaining he was batting .391. He had qualified for the batting title, so that wasn't a problem. But he would need nine hits in his final 12 at bats or better to make .400.

He didn't quite do it, but what an incredible season he had, finishing with 175 hits in 449 at bats for a .390 average. Just five more hits and he would have made history. He also had career highs of 24 home runs and 118 RBIs. Since he played in just 117 games, he became the first player in thirty years to get a ribby per game. His batting eye was as good as ever. He struck out just 22 times all year. The .390 average also raised his lifetime batting mark to .319, one of the best among active players.

He got plenty of help from his teammates as the Royals won the division with a 97-65 record. Willie Wilson had a .326 average, 230 hits, and 79 stolen bases. Willie Mays Aikens had 20 homers and 98 RBIs. McRae hit .297 with 14 homers and 83 RBI's. John Wathan hit .305 and Clint Hurdle checked in at .294. The club could hit. They also had a 20-game winner in Dennis Leonard, while Larry Gura was 18-10, and reliever Quisenberry blossomed to a 12-7 mark with 33 big saves.

All that was well and good. But now George and the entire team looked ahead. They would get another chance to beat the hated Yankees in the playoffs, though publically the players tried to downplay the revenge motive. And to those who felt the Yanks had the Royals' number, George answered this way.

"We beat them eight out of 12 during the regular season, but I don't hear anyone talk about that. Instead, everyone keeps bringing up 1976, '77, and '78. Let's forget past history. It doesn't even matter that we beat them eight of 12. But I'll say this. They should be a little tighter than we are because nobody expects us to win."

The Yanks started ace Ron Guidry in game one. He hadn't lost a game since August, and he'd be facing the Royals' Larry Gura, who hadn't won since August. So the Yanks were favorites. Both teams were scoreless in the first, but neither pitcher looked particularly sharp. Then in the second, the Yanks struck.

Catcher Rick Cerone, in his first playoff at bat ever, lined a home run into the left field stands. Lou Piniella was next, and he promptly homered, giving the Yanks a 2-0 lead and the Royals a feeling of here-we-go-again. But Guidry couldn't hold it. With two on and two out, Frank White blooped a double to left, tying the game.

Guidry was wild in the third. With two on and two out again, he intentionally walked John Wathan to get at Willie Aikens. Willie singled to left, driving in two more, and the Royals led, 4-2. When the Yanks came out for the fourth, Ron Davis had replaced Guidry.

The score remained 4-2 until the seventh. That's when George came up to face Davis. He already had a single to his credit, and this time he took Davis downtown, belting a long homer to leftcenter, making it 5-2. Kansas City got a pair of insurance runs in the eighth and Gura hung on to pitch a gritty, ten-hitter, as the Royals drew first blood, 7-2. Maybe this would finally be K.C.'s year.

Dennis Leonard got the call in the second game, facing lefty Rudy May of the Yanks, and this one was close all the way. May, in fact, pitched brilliantly, except for one inning, the third. In that inning, Darrel Porter singled, White singled, and Willie Wilson stepped up, batting righthanded against the southpaw May. Rudy jammed him, but Wilson inside-outed the swing and sent a drive between Bob Watson and the first base bag for a two-run double. U.L. Washington then doubled to score Wilson and K.C. had a 3-0 lead.

In the Yankee fourth, Graig Nettles came up with one out. It was Nettles first game since coming down with hepatitis in May, and he hit a shot to deep right. Wathan tried to make a leaping catch at the wall, but the ball bounced away and Nettles circled the bases as centerfielder Otis ran the ball down. It was an inside-the-park homer, as Nettles staggered across the plate.

Then with two out, Bobby Brown walked, and he scored when Randolph lined a double in front of Wathan in right. That made it 3-2 before Leonard got the side out. From there it was a pitching duel until the eighth. That's when the Yanks threatened again.

Randolph singled with one out. After Bobby Murcer fanned, Bob Watson came up. He lined one down the left field line and Randolph, a fast man, took off. Willie Wilson raced to the wall and played the carom perfectly. He threw to the cut-off man, shortstop Washington. But the throw was sailing high, and seeing that, third base coach Mike Ferraro waved Randolph home. As Willie rounded third, the throw did sail over Washington's head. But it came right to George, who was playing about 20 yards behind U.L. He grabbed the ball, whirled, and fired home. It was a perfect relay, and catcher Porter applied the tag a split second before Randolph's foot touched home. He was out!

The play saved the game. Dan Quisenberry came on to retire the Yanks in the ninth and the Royals had won it, 3-2, to take a commanding, 2-0, lead in the playoffs. So even though he was 0-for-4 at the plate, George had saved the game with his perfect relay throw. Now the teams returned to New York, where Paul Splittorff would be facing Tommy John in game three.

For the first four innings the game was scoreless, the tension mounting. Then the Royals drew first blood in the fifth when Frank White lined a homer into the left field seats. That might have awakened the Yanks, for in the sixth they came alive. After Watson lined out, Reggie Jackson doubled to left. Manager Frey quickly made a move, replacing Splittorff with relief ace Quisenberry. Oscar Gamble pinch hit and bounced one up the middle. White raced behind the bag and grabbed the ball. Having no play at first he threw toward third, hoping to get

Jackson rounding the bag. But the throw was wild and Reggie came home with the tying run, Gamble moving to second.

When Rick Cerone followed with a run scoring single to left, giving the Yanks a 2-1 lead, the Royals began worrying. They remembered their three previous losses. This was the game they wanted. Quisenberry then got out of the inning and the Royals came up in the seventh.

John got the first two outs and seemed to be sailing along. But Wilson then doubled to right and Manager Dick Howser called on his stopper, the awesome fireballer, Goose Gossage. U.L. Washington came up. He chopped a 3-2 pitch over Gossage's head and beat it out with determined hustle. The next batter was George Brett. But George was 0-for-7 since his homer in the first game. He was struggling at the plate for one of the few times all year.

It was the classic confrontation, the big fastballer coming off an awesome year, and the best hitter in baseball, coming off a near .400 season.

"I knew he was gonna try to throw it by me," George said. "But I feel I can hit a fastball as well as anyone. The harder they throw it, the better I like it."

Gossage stretched and threw as hard as he could. George stepped into the ball and whipped his bat around in that smooth, effortless motion. At the crack, some 57,000 heads turned and watched. It was a long, high drive to right . . . and it was GONE! George had belted a dramatic, three-run homer to give the Royals a 4-2 lead. His teammates mobbed him at home plate. It was as if they had just won the World Series.

But the Yanks still had three more at bats. Quisenberry had no problem in the seventh, but in the eighth the Yanks loaded the bases with none out. Was this the inevitable comeback? Rick Cerone was up, and he hit a line shot toward short. Washington grabbed it and fired to second, doubling up Jackson. The other runners held. Then Jim Spencer grounded out to end the inning.

In the ninth, Quisenberry was perfect, retiring the

Yanks in order. The Royals had done it. They had beaten the Yankees three straight. They were headed for the World Series at last.

It was wild in the Kansas City clubhouse after the game. Like everyone else, George couldn't hold back his joy.

"I went over .400 on August 17," he said, "and hitting .400 was one of my priorities. I wanted it, but not as bad as I wanted this. For us to beat the New York Yankees is the ultimate for our town. And when I say that, I don't mean just the mayor or the fans or the players. I mean the whole town of Kansas City. I'll cherish this as long as I live."

In the losers locker room, a disconsolate Goose Gossage put it simply. "If I'm gonna get beat, I guess I can't get beat by a better hitter. It was power against power. I feel I'm the best, and he's the best, and he beat me this time."

The Royals were flying. As Amos Otis said, "This is the ultimate high, and ain't nobody gonna take this away from us."

It was almost as if they had forgotten there was still a World Series to play. And for awhile they probably had. But soon they would have to get themselves up again. They'd be meeting the Philadelphia Phillies, who, like the Royals, had been snake bit until 1980. Just like K.C., Philly had lost in the playoffs in 1976, '77, and '78. They didn't make it in 1979, but now were back and had beaten Houston in the National League playoffs. The ancient franchise had never won a World Series and they wanted it very badly.

In the opener, the Royals sent Dennis Leonard to the mound and the Phils were forced to counter with a rookie, Bob Walk. K.C. took the early lead on two-run homers by Willie Aikens and Amos Otis, but the Phils erupted for five in the third to KO Leonard and take the lead. They added single tallies in the fourth and fifth and survived another two-run shot by Aikens to win the opener, 7-6. George had a double in four at bats.

Then, before the second game, the news came out that George was suffering from a painful case of hemorrhoids, which are the swelling of blood vessels in the rectum. It was so painful, the report said, he might miss the rest of the Series. But he gave it a try as Larry Gura faced Steve Carlton.

The game was scoreless until the Philly fifth, when Gura gave up two runs. But K.C. came back, getting one in the sixth and three in the seventh on Otis' two-run double and a sacrifice fly by Wathan. Yet the Phils wouldn't quit. Once again they rallied, getting four in the eighth off Quisenberry to win, 6-4, and take a two-game lead.

George had started, smacked a pair of singles and walked before coming out of the game when the pain became nearly unbearable. "It hurt a little at the start of the game but got worse every inning," he said. "I thought it best to come out."

With a day off for travel, George checked into the hospital for minor surgery, to have the inflamed areas lanced. Hopefully this would alleviate the pain enough for him to play. And he was in the starting line-up as young Rich Gale of the Royals faced veteran Dick Ruthven.

This was a tight one, each club pecking away for single runs three times, and it was a 3-3 deadlock at the end of nine. In the tenth, U.L. Washington singled and Willie Wilson walked. Tug McGraw was on the mound and on the next pitch Washington tried to steal third. He was nailed, Bob Boone to Schmidt. Then Frank White fanned for the second out.

George was up now and Wilson promptly stole second. Then the Phils walked Brett intentionally, bringing up lefthanded batting Aikens. But the move backfired when Aikens singled to bring home Wilson with the winning run. The Royals were back in it. George had played the entire game, going 2-for-4, including a homer that made it a 1-0 game in the first inning. He was now 5-for-10 in the Series.

K.C. tied it in the fourth game, getting all five runs in the first two innings, as Willie Aikens crashed two more homers and Leonard pitched them to a 5-3 victory. George was just 1-for-5 in this one, but had another RBI. Now came the pivotal fifth game.

Once again the Phillies struck late. The Royals had taken a 3-2 lead against rookie Marty Bystrom and had Larry Gura on the mound. Quisenberry replaced him in the seventh and was in there when the Phils came up for their final turn. Schmidt opened with a single and was promptly doubled home by Del Unser. Unser went to third on a sacrifice, and came on a single by Manny Trillo. Tug McGraw held the lead and the Phils had won, 4-3. George was 1-for-5 for a second day, with an RBI.

Next was a travel day back to Philadelphia. That's where the Phils won it, with Steve Carlton and McGraw combining to whip the Royals, 4-1, Mike Schmidt driving in a pair of runs. George had two more hits in the finale, but it was all over.

There were those who felt the Royals were so intent on beating the Yanks that they might have let down in the Series. Actually, they had hit well, with a team average of .290. Despite the painful hemorrhoid condition, George was nine of 24 for a .375 mark. Otis, Aikens, McRae, and Hurdle all hit very well. It was just that the pitchers couldn't get it done in the clutch.

But it was George who expressed the sentiments felt by many. "In Kansas City," he said, "winning the playoffs against the Yankees *was* the World Series. But I enjoyed playing in the Series. I think it was great. We have nothing to be ashamed of. I think we made the people of Kansas City happy and I'm sure we made the rest of the country happy, too. By the way, what are Reggie and the Yankees doing about now?"

So there was still that thing with the Yanks. But K.C. could be proud. It had been a good year, and the club is still a relatively young one. There's a good chance they will be back, that is, if they can get by the Yanks again.

As for George Brett, he had put together a simply marvelous year. In the minds of many, he has taken over from Rod Carew as the best all-around hitter in the game. And at age 27, there's a good chance he'll get better. He also impressed everyone with his stable and refreshing personality, and with his ability to handle the tremendous pressure put upon him.

In November he learned that he had been voted the American League's Most Valuable Player in spite of the fact that he played in just 117 games. But could there really have been another choice?

"It's a tremendous thrill," George said, upon being informed of his selection. Then he repeated a familiar theme. "But I still have to say it was a bigger thrill to beat the Yankees in the playoffs."

But that's George, always a team player first. He later named *The Sporting News* Player of the Year and made a member of the Major League All-Star Team for 1980.

George is happy and content in Kansas City, and right now the fans have a love affair going with him and the Royals. Some 10,000 people greeted the team when they returned from losing the World Series. You don't find that kind of support everywhere. It should serve to make George Brett work even harder. And it won't surprise anyone that come next summer, or the summer after, or the one after that, that all of baseball begins another Brett watch as this great hitter begins another assault on the magical .400 mark. He may make it yet.

# STATISTICS

## Reggie Jackson

| Year | Club | G | AB | R | H | 2B | 3B | HR | RBI | BA |
|---|---|---|---|---|---|---|---|---|---|---|
| 1966 | Lewiston | 12 | 48 | 14 | 3 | 2 | 2 | 11 | .292 | |
| 1966 | Modesto | 56 | 221 | 50 | 66 | 6 | 0 | 21 | 60 | .299 |
| 1967 | Birmingham | 114 | 413 | 84 | 121 | 26 | 17 | 17 | 58 | .293 |
| 1967 | Kansas City | 35 | 118 | 13 | 21 | 4 | 4 | 1 | 6 | .178 |
| 1968 | Oakland | 154 | 553 | 82 | 138 | 13 | 6 | 29 | 74 | .250 |
| 1969 | Oakland | 152 | 549 | 123 | 151 | 36 | 3 | 47 | 118 | .275 |
| 1970 | Oakland | 149 | 426 | 57 | 101 | 21 | 2 | 23 | 66 | .237 |
| 1971 | Oakland | 150 | 567 | 87 | 157 | 29 | 3 | 32 | 80 | .277 |
| 1972 | Oakland | 135 | 499 | 72 | 132 | 25 | 2 | 25 | 75 | .265 |
| 1973 | Oakland | 151 | 539 | 99 | 158 | 28 | 2 | 32 | 117 | .293 |
| 1974 | Oakland | 148 | 506 | 90 | 146 | 25 | 1 | 29 | 93 | .286 |
| 1975 | Oakland | 157 | 593 | 91 | 150 | 39 | 3 | 36 | 104 | .253 |
| 1976 | Baltimore | 134 | 498 | 84 | 138 | 27 | 2 | 27 | 91 | .277 |
| 1977 | New York | 146 | 525 | 93 | 150 | 39 | 2 | 32 | 110 | .286 |
| 1978 | New York | 139 | 511 | 82 | 140 | 13 | 5 | 27 | 97 | .274 |
| 1979 | New York | 131 | 465 | 8 | 138 | 24 | 2 | 29 | 89 | .297 |
| 1980 | New York | 143 | 514 | 94 | 154 | 22 | 4 | 41 | 111 | .300 |
| Major League Totals | | 1924 | 6863 | 1145 | 1874 | 345 | 41 | 410 | 1232 | .273 |

# STATISTICS

## Mike Schmidt

| Year | Club | G | AB | R | H | 2B | 3B | HR | RBI | BA |
|---|---|---|---|---|---|---|---|---|---|---|
| 1971 | Reading | 74 | 237 | 27 | 50 | 7 | 1 | 8 | 31 | .211 |
| 1972 | Eugene | 131 | 436 | 80 | 127 | 23 | 6 | 26 | 91 | .291 |
| 1972 | Phillies | 13 | 34 | 2 | 7 | 0 | 0 | 1 | 3 | .206 |
| 1973 | Phillies | 132 | 367 | 43 | 72 | 11 | 0 | 18 | 52 | .196 |
| 1974 | Phillies | 162 | 568 | 108 | 160 | 28 | 7 | 36 | 116 | .282 |
| 1975 | Phillies | 158 | 562 | 93 | 140 | 34 | 3 | 38 | 95 | .249 |
| 1976 | Phillies | 160 | 584 | 112 | 153 | 31 | 4 | 38 | 107 | .262 |
| 1977 | Phillies | 154 | 544 | 114 | 149 | 27 | 11 | 38 | 101 | .274 |
| 1978 | Phillies | 145 | 513 | 93 | 129 | 27 | 2 | 21 | 78 | .251 |
| 1979 | Phillies | 160 | 541 | 109 | 137 | 25 | 4 | 45 | 114 | .253 |
| 1980 | Phillies | 150 | 548 | 104 | 157 | 25 | 8 | 48 | 121 | .286 |
| Major League Totals | | 1234 | 4261 | 778 | 1104 | 208 | 19 | 283 | 787 | .259 |

# STATISTICS

## Dave Parker

| Year | Club | G | AB | R | H | 2B | 3B | HR | RBI | BA |
|---|---|---|---|---|---|---|---|---|---|---|
| 1970 | Bradenton | 61 | 239 | 34 | 75 | 8 | 3 | 6 | 41 | .314 |
| 1971 | Waterbury | 30 | 114 | 10 | 26 | 4 | 1 | 0 | 7 | .228 |
| 1971 | Monroe | 71 | 268 | 49 | 96 | 16 | 4 | 11 | 48 | .358 |
| 1972 | Salem | 135 | 523 | 91 | 162 | 30 | 6 | 22 | 101 | .310 |
| 1973 | Charleston | 84 | 309 | 44 | 98 | 20 | 7 | 9 | 57 | .317 |
| 1973 | Pittsburgh | 54 | 139 | 17 | 40 | 9 | 1 | 4 | 14 | .288 |
| 1974 | Pittsburgh | 73 | 220 | 27 | 62 | 10 | 3 | 4 | 29 | .282 |
| 1975 | Pittsburgh | 148 | 558 | 75 | 172 | 35 | 10 | 25 | 101 | .308 |
| 1976 | Pittsburgh | 138 | 537 | 82 | 168 | 28 | 10 | 13 | 90 | .313 |
| 1977 | Pittsburgh | 159 | 637 | 107 | 215 | 44 | 8 | 21 | 88 | .338 |
| 1978 | Pittsburgh | 148 | 581 | 102 | 194 | 32 | 12 | 30 | 117 | .334 |
| 1979 | Pittsburgh | 158 | 622 | 109 | 193 | 45 | 7 | 25 | 94 | .310 |
| 1980 | Pittsburgh | 139 | 518 | 71 | 153 | 31 | 1 | 17 | 79 | .295 |
| Major League Totals | | 1017 | 3812 | 590 | 1197 | 234 | 52 | 139 | 612 | .314 |

# STATISTICS

## George Brett

| Year | Club | G | AB | R | H | 2B | 3B | HR | RBI | BA |
|---|---|---|---|---|---|---|---|---|---|---|
| 1971 | Billings | 68 | 258 | 44 | 75 | 8 | 5 | 5 | 44 | .291 |
| 1972 | San Jose | 117 | 431 | 66 | 118 | 13 | 5 | 10 | 68 | .274 |
| 1973 | Omaha | 117 | 405 | 65 | 115 | 16 | 4 | 8 | 64 | .284 |
| 1973 | Kansas City | 13 | 40 | 2 | 5 | 2 | 0 | 0 | 0 | .125 |
| 1974 | Omaha | 16 | 64 | 9 | 17 | 2 | 0 | 2 | 14 | .266 |
| 1974 | Kansas City | 133 | 457 | 49 | 129 | 21 | 5 | 2 | 47 | .282 |
| 1975 | Kansas City | 159 | 634 | 84 | 195 | 35 | 13 | 11 | 89 | .308 |
| 1976 | Kansas City | 159 | 645 | 94 | 215 | 34 | 14 | 7 | 67 | .333 |
| 1977 | Kansas City | 139 | 564 | 105 | 176 | 32 | 13 | 22 | 88 | .312 |
| 1978 | Kansas City | 128 | 510 | 79 | 150 | 45 | 8 | 9 | 62 | .294 |
| 1979 | Kansas City | 154 | 645 | 119 | 212 | 42 | 20 | 23 | 107 | .329 |
| 1980 | Kansas City | 117 | 449 | 87 | 175 | 33 | 9 | 24 | 118 | .390 |
| Major League Totals | | 1002 | 3944 | 619 | 1257 | 244 | 82 | 98 | 578 | .319 |

TEMPO BOOKS

# SPORTS

## BIOGRAPHIES

Get all the facts on your favorite superstars—complete career records plus a look at the personal side of today's top names in sports.

| | | | | |
|---|---|---|---|---|
| ☐ 17170 | **THE AWESOME FOURSOME:** Harris, Bell, Pastorini, Fouts | Gutman | $1.95 |
| ☐ 17142 | **GIANTS OF SOCCER:** Cruyff, Beckenbauer, Rote, Chinaglia | Goldstein | $1.95 |
| ☐ 17201 | **CHAIRMEN OF THE BOARDS:** Erving, Bird, Malone, Johnson | Gutman | $1.95 |
| ☐ 17191 | **THURMAN MUNSON:** An Autobiography | Munson, Appel | $2.50 |
| ☐ 17061 | **WHERE HAVE THEY GONE:** Football Stars | Tully | $1.95 |
| ☐ 17103 | **WHERE HAVE THEY GONE:** Hockey Stars | Fischler | $1.95 |
| ☐ 17084 | **ERIC HEIDEN:** America's Olympic Golden Boy | Munshower | $2.50 |
| ☐ 17325 | **BASEBALL'S BELTERS:** Jackson, Schmidt, Parker, Brett | Gutman | $1.95 |

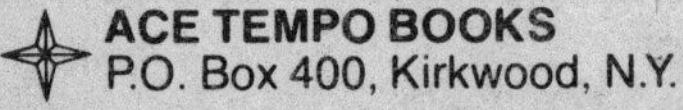

**ACE TEMPO BOOKS** T-01

P.O. Box 400, Kirkwood, N.Y. 13795

Please send me the titles checked above. I enclose ____________.
Include 75¢ for postage and handling if one book is ordered; 50¢ per book for two to five. If six or more are ordered, postage is free. California, Illinois, New York and Tennessee residents please add sales tax.

NAME________________________________________

ADDRESS_____________________________________

CITY____________________STATE______ZIP_________

# SHARK BAIT!

The shiny yellow raft stood out bright against the white surface of the water, attractive and inviting. It was going to be an easy kill.

"Jesus Christ! What was that?" Rick exclaimed. "Did we hit something?"

"Oh, no" Buck cried, pointing to the towering fin that had just surfaced fifteen feet from the boat. "Look how big that sonofabitch is. He must be twenty or thirty feet long."

Slowly the shark circled the raft. He was right; there *was* food inside.

Frantic, Buck leaned over and started hand-paddling furiously. Five feet from the splashing man, the enormous predator raised its head. Its hinged jaws jutted out in rows of curved saw-like teeth. Trying to avoid the inevitable, Buck leaned away from the onslaught. The jaws sliced through the raft as if it never existed, then clamped down on Buck's pelvis and abdomen turning the water crimson with blood.

Terrified, Rick started swimming away from the oncoming fish. But the shark caught him in the legs and pushed him through the water screaming and crying until he was seen no more.

The tiger shark had had his final catch of the day—but tomorrow was only a couple of hours away . . .

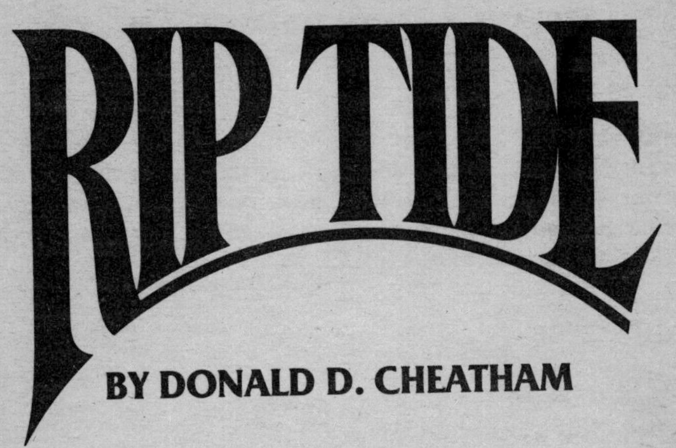


# RIP TIDE

BY DONALD D. CHEATHAM

ZEBRA BOOKS
KENSINGTON PUBLISHING CORP.

ZEBRA BOOKS

are published by

Kensington Publishing Corp.
475 Park Avenue South
New York, N.Y. 10016



First printing: September 1984

Printed in the United States of America

*For my wife, Lois, and my brother, Gene, who have always believed.*

# ACKNOWLEDGMENTS

The author wishes to extend his thanks to the management and staff of the Riverfront Holiday Inn, in St. Louis, Missouri, for their cooperation and assistance in writing this book.

The author also wishes to thank Dr. Perry Gilbert and the staff of the Mote Marine Science Center, Sarasota, Florida, who provided much of the research material needed to write *Riptide*.

RIP TIDE

"If the identity of every shark attacking man in the tropical Atlantic were known, the tiger shark might well be responsible for more of them than any other."

—Dr. John E. Randall, author of
"Dangerous Sharks of the Western Atlantic,"
Sharks and Survival

"At least some level of identification of the attacker was possible in 267 cases (out of approximately 1500 in the Shark Attack File). As popular belief would have it, the great white (*Carcharodon carcharias*) was cited most often, with 32 known attacks to its discredit. The ubiquitous tiger shark (*Galeocerdo cuvieri*) was close behind, having been identified as the attacker in 27 cases including some of the most dramatic accounts held in the SAF.

—Dr. H. David Baldridge, author of
"Shark Attack: A Program of Data Reduction and Analysis"

# 1. ALFA

The Red Tide had first appeared in the Gulf of Mexico on Tuesday, about ten miles offshore of Pinellas County, the heart of Florida's tourist-oriented Suncoast. It had turned the water reddish brown, killed the fish that swam through it, and created huge floating masses of fish bodies destined to defile the sugar-white sands of Surfside, Clearwater, and St. Petersburg Beaches. The Department of Natural Resources had not been expecting the outbreak so soon. The Red Tide was a common occurrence every year in the spring and fall when the water was a little cooler; but this fall the water temperature had remained much warmer than usual. They had thought they were going to get through the summer tourist season without incident. They were wrong.

On Thursday, a helicopter survey showed the Red Tide spreading and breaking out in new areas. Tampa Bay seemed to be having its own separate outbreak and prevailing currents were shoving the Tide southward. Scattered patches were found lying in pockets just north of Longboat Key. DNR spokesman Larry Smith decided to call a news conference.

"We are," Smith said, standing in front of the TV cameras crowded in his St. Petersburg office, "placing a ban on shellfishing in the following counties: Pinellas, Hillsborough, Manatee, and Sarasota." He pointed to an oversized map on an easel showing several large shaded circles lying just off the Suncoast and covering much of Tampa Bay. "These are the patches of Red Tide at the moment. We hoped the one off Pinellas County would dissipate, but we just didn't have any luck. It's grown and aerial reports now place it only five miles offshore. I hope it will not continue and that it will be short-lived. We'll just have to see.

"Maybe the storms the weather bureau is forecasting will put enough fresh water into the Gulf to force the organisms a little further from shore so they'll be less of a problem for us."

"Mr. Smith," a reporter questioned, "what causes the Red Tide and how dangerous is it?"

"The Red Tide is caused by a microscopic organism naturally present in saltwater called *ptychodiscus brevis*," the portly Smith replied. "For some reason that we don't yet understand, there is a sudden concentration or *bloom* of the organism which produces a poison that suffocates fish and turns the water a reddish color.

"It is not, as far as we know, unsafe to swim in—as long as you're not a fish—but it does cause some problems. Besides littering the beaches with dead fish—which aren't too nice to smell—it also releases a spore or something in the air that causes irritation of the nose, throat, eyes, and lungs. There are a few scientists who say this isn't true. Maybe they know more than I do, but I invite them to interview people on the beaches when we've had a bad outbreak.

"Let me add, though, if you eat shellfish that have been contaminated by Red Tide, you're in trouble! I'm talking about bi-valved mollusks such as coquinas and clams, not crabs, lobsters, or scallops. The symptoms of Red Tide illness, which generally affects the nervous system, include headache, nausea, diarrhea and general malaise. Sometimes there's a tingling sensation on the tongue. It's a lot like stomach flu."

"What about sharks, Mr. Smith."

"I hate to disappoint you, ladies and gentlemen, but sharks are not affected by the Red Tide. In fact, if anything, the dead fish attract more of them. I'd say they feel the Red Tide is a special banquet table God created just for them. A polluted area looks like a shark convention hall! I don't believe any of you would want to swim in a mass of smelly dead fish, but if you've had any thoughts along those lines, think again."

They all laughed, closed their notebooks, turned off the camera lights and prepared to leave.

Three and a half miles off Surfside Beach, eighteen inches of sinister fin broke the surface of the muddy red water and cut a swathe through the solid mile-wide mass of dead fish. The twenty-six foot tiger shark drifted through the water easily, taking in one basket-sized mouthful of fish after another. Suddenly, the small groups of sensory cells protruding in the delicate hair processes that made up his lateral line—the shark's ear—told him there was another shark feeding at the far end of the mass of dead fish.

The four-hundred-pound bull shark also sensed the much larger predator. Abruptly, he discontinued feeding and headed for the safer waters of Surfside Bay.

The huge tiger shark followed.

The bull shark knew he was in trouble, but thought he could outwit his pursuer. Never varying his speed, he swam swiftly and deliberately toward shore, toward the pass and the inside of Surfside Bay. His primitive brain knew that if he stayed calm and gave no sign of fear, there was a good chance he could make it into the shallow bay waters and find safety among the docks and pilings.

The bull was lucky. A half mile into the bay, along an exclusive residential district, he found a new dock built on a disorganized mass of old abandoned pilings. Twenty yards from shore the water was still only a few feet deep. The narrow access through the jumbled pilings made it impossible for the much larger fish to follow.

The tiger wasn't frustrated at all. He'd been eluded before and had learned to wait. Sooner or later the prey always panicked and made an ill-fated dash for survival. It was just a matter of time. He cruised up and down the channel in front of the docks waiting. Patiently waiting.

"I'm tired of playing housewife!" Gloria Johncourt shouted at her husband, Alex. Her lean spa-built body was shaking with anger. "And I'm tired of sitting around here trying to amuse myself while you're out playing basketball, football, volleyball, or any other kind of ball except the kind of ball I want. I thought I married a schoolteacher, not a professional athlete. I'm beginning to wonder why you want to spend all your time in the locker room with your boyfriends."

"That's enough, damn it!" Alex slammed the kitchen table with his fist. "Coaching the intramural teams is part of my job and you know that I like it, too. You thought it was fine until Ed Bilsters got transferred last month. Now, suddenly, you want me home all the time."

"Are you accusing me of something?"

"Let's just say I'm not dumb and that you'd better get the hell off my back!"

"Is that a threat?"

"Yes, by God, it is! If we can't straighten this marriage out, I think it's time to give up on it. I'm tired of the battle, Gloria. It's not worth it. Think about that for a while!"

Alex stalked out the front door across the front lawn, crossed Gulf Boulevard and stood in the empty public beach access lot. The island was less than three hundred yards wide in front of his home. He walked past the sea oats onto the beach.

The sun hung over the Gulf of Mexico like a deep-red heart bleeding into the sea. Above it, the clouds turned into cottony ribbons of vibrant color that stretched lazily across the horizon. Below, the aquamarine Gulf was slowly turning into deep blues that actually bordered more on purples. The evening colors blended and washed richly over Alex's face.

Tonight, the gentle thunder of the waves crashing on the beach and the soothing colors of the sky had no calming effect on Alex; tonight, the noise made him even more irritated. He kicked sand at the setting sun and returned across the highway to his sodded one-day-wonder Florida lawn, complete with mole crickets and sand fleas. Another fight. They kept increasing in number and intensity. Alex was at a loss as to what to do with Gloria. What would it take to make her happy? First, he'd changed job after job until he'd inherited his father's estate; then he'd moved to the Suncoast, bought her a bay-side house, a good-sized boat—and still she wanted more! Nothing was ever enough for her!

He shuffled moodily past his open front door and onto the wooden boat dock behind his house. He hesitated at the cabin cruiser they seldom used, then walked past it and settled himself heavily at the end of the pier. Alex sat there, tears in his eyes, a knot in his stomach, his bright blue-and-yellow striped sneakers dangling less than a foot above the high tide.

Suddenly the water boiled beside the dock and a yawning mouth full of glistening white curved razor-sharp teeth snagged Alex's legs just below the knees. He was whisked from the dock and pulled under the water in a fraction of a second. There hadn't been time for a scream; the splash was minimal. No one standing more than fifty feet away could have known what had happened. And no one did—but Alex.

The bay's absolutely calm surface uncannily masked the horror that was going on below. Alex was shoved through the water at a backbreaking speed of fifteen miles an hour. Desperately, he fought for his life. The pain and the pressure on his legs was almost unbearable.

"I can still get away! The shark hasn't bitten off my legs yet," he told himself. "Not yet. There's still a chance. I still might save them!" Straining against the crushing weight of the water rushing past him, Alex managed to jam his left hand down into the shark's mouth. He recoiled in terror, fighting the nausea that welled up in his stomach. Row after row of needle-sharp teeth had acted like a paper shredder, slicing the flesh on his palm and fingers to the bone. An explosion of white-hot pain hit his brain momentarily blinding him to any thought or action, but urgency forced him back to his senses. With his remaining hand he poked furiously at the shark's eye, or at the place where he thought it might be. It didn't faze the shark. He jabbed at the gill openings, hoping that would make the monster turn him loose. Again! Nothing happened. He couldn't see in the dark turbid water and realized he was getting weak from lack of oxygen. It seemed like hours since he'd been ripped from the docks. "I have to do something—do something quick," he thought faintly, "or I'm not going to make it!"

Suddenly, the momentum stopped. The jaws shifted their position on his legs only to clamp down more tightly. Alex felt his bones crunch. He was shaken violently from side to side like a rag doll. Luckily, he slipped from consciousness just before the giant tiger shark snapped off his legs and swallowed him with two more savage wrenching bites.

Three hundred yards from the dock a thin film of blood floated to the surface and dissipated. It evoked only the curiosity of other neighboring sharks and small fish that had collected to snap up the remnants of the larger fish's feeding. The sun slipped into the Gulf, the sky turned red, pink, and then black before allowing the stars to bloom. Alex's problems had all been solved.

## 2. BRAVO

"Detective Liza Sallings, I'd like you to meet your new partner, Detective Michael Stark," Captain Blanchert said. "Detective Sallings is Surfside's first detective and first female police officer. I think she was on vacation when you were here for your interview; wasn't she, Stark?"

"That's right, I didn't get to meet you," Stark said to the surprisingly pretty woman. "They said you were taking a well-earned vacation for a couple of weeks."

"I sure was! Welcome aboard, Stark. I can use the help, 'cause I don't get much around here." Sallings smiled broadly and stuck out her hand in a welcoming handshake.

"Hey, now come on," Captain Blanchert said jokingly. "We've been carrying you for two years now and you know it."

"Don't listen to him," Sallings said to Stark. "In a week you'll find out he wants twenty-six-hour days out of everyone who works here." She looked the new man over. After ten years of law enforcement, you got to where you could tell if you liked someone by just sizing him up; by observing the way he held himself, watching the way he looked at you, and using that cop sixth sense. In practice, it turned out to be accurate much more often than not. Then, too, Stark had a reputation for doggedly stalking, catching, and killing the St. Louis Sniper—the worst mass murderer in U.S. history.

Stark looked good, Sallings thought. He was maybe a fraction of an inch taller than her five-feet-nine-inch frame, but the difference was lost with her heels. He wasn't as muscular or as stocky as she had expected; nor as young, but he had his own imposing presence. His features were sharp; he was lean and hard looking. His big brown eyes were friendly, but they opened you up like an Xray. The sharp crease in his slacks, the expensive linen sport coat and the spit-shine on his shoes told Sallings that she had herself a no-nonsense partner and she was going to like the change. She was tired of cops who either looked like storm troopers or slobs who slept in their clothes. "I think you'll like it here, Detective. On the whole, I'd say we have a pretty nice town here—wouldn't you say so, Captain."

"I'd be lying if I said different. I'm sure not ready to leave."

"I'm sure I'll like it," Stark said, shaking hands with his new partner. He was surprised at the strength of her handshake; she was no cream-puff. When he had interviewed for the job earlier in the year, he had gone over her record fairly closely. He'd liked what he'd read and had heard nothing but good things about her from the city commissioners and the captain. Sallings had held down the detective post in Surfside singlehandedly for the last two years. She'd had to overcome a lot of hostility from the men on the force, but Captain Blanchert said she'd won everyone's respect and was probably the finest cop on the force. Stark also couldn't detect any resentment in the woman's ice-blue eyes that said she wished someone in the department had been promoted instead of bringing in an outsider to fill the job. She also didn't seem to mind sharing her detective status with him. He had hoped that would not be a problem and it looked as if it wasn't going to be; a few days would tell.

Stark hadn't really known what to expect. He'd worked with females before and it hadn't always been enjoyable. It seemed they were either dikeish and ball-busters or on the make and incompetent as hell. From the record, her photograph, and what people had told him, he'd decided that she didn't fit the mold. It was a big gamble for him in terms of his ego, accepting a detective position with a woman as senior partner. It looked like he'd gambled and won. "Just maybe," he thought, "this will be the place where I can settle down and grow old."

"You're from Missouri, aren't you Stark?" Sallings asked.

"I was once. I've been to quite a few places since then. But yes, I used to live in what was essentially a large resort community, a suburb of about fifty-thousand people just outside St. Louis called Cottonwood Hollow. It was nice. The town was built around one end of a lake that was three miles wide and five miles long. It had three championship golf courses, a race track and two country clubs. But it was nothing like this. Our beaches were made of grainy brown river sand. We didn't have palm trees and all the tropical plants that you have here. And in winter, of course, the only thing that was green was the envy of the people who couldn't afford to come down here."

"I'm due at a city commission meeting," Captain Blanchert interrupted, mopping his forehead and placing a hand on both detectives' shoulders. Fifty pounds of excess fat made him break out in sweat with the slightest increase in heat or exertion. He wanted to get across the street to the Mayor's office before the morning sun got any higher. "I'll let you two get down to work. In a few days, when you get settled in, we can all go out and have a drink or something."

"Fine, sir," Stark replied, shaking his hand. "Thanks for everything."

"Don't mention it. If you two do half the job here I think you can, it'll be me owing you the thanks. You'd better not disappoint me. I've put my ass on the line hiring two detectives for this burg and a male-female team to boot."

"We'll try," Stark and Sallings echoed as the captain left the station.

Stark turned to Sallings and rubbed his hands together in anticipation of work. "Well, Detective, how about filling me in on the action around here. I'm going to have to follow you around like a lost puppy until I find out where everything is and learn what is what."

"Don't worry, Stark. Believe me, it won't take long. Miami, this ain't!"

"If it were, I wouldn't be here," Stark replied with

a grin.

"You're not alone," Sallings concurred. "I was offered a job down there a few years ago. They pay well, but no way! A friend of mine works there and he says it's a living nightmare being a cop. You have blacks and Haitians, Cubans, Colombians, and a lot of others from South America down there. They're all poor and they're all desperate. They hate each other and they all hate you if you're a cop. You know, they'll kill six people without blinking an eye, just to rob them of pocket change!"

"Yeah, I've heard that, too."

"Let's hope it all stays down there! Talking about major crime," Sallings added sarcastically, "let's see what happened in our bustling metropolis last night."

The station house proper was one big room. A chest-high working counter sectioned off a large space into a second room. At the left end of the counter was a door marked JAIL. At the right of the counter was a door marked EMERGENCY EXIT ONLY—ALARM WILL SOUND. Behind the counter was a series of desks. File cabinets lined the back wall interrupted by three office doors.

Sallings pointed to the offices at the rear of the room. "I'm sure you've figured out that the office with CAPTAIN over it is not ours. The middle office is the radio room and the other office is ours. You get your own desk and two of the walls to hang your stuff on."

"Charming," Stark said. "Charming. It's just like the movies!"

"You've got it," Sallings laughed, "It's the big time! I think we're gonna get along fine."

"I don't see why not." Stark's near perfect teeth

flashed white in a big grin. "I'm glad you have a sense of humor."

"You've got to. That's half the entertainment in this burg. This isn't exactly the cultural center of the southeast. Well, maybe I shouldn't say that. They're trying. We're growing fast around here and it's taking a while to catch up. We'll get there in another hundred years or so."

"Don't complain. St. Louis used to be pretty much of a cow-town once, and you should see it now. Since the Arch, they've really expanded. There's one convention after another; there're new hotels all along the waterfront, including one with a revolving restaurant; there's a new shopping complex in the old Union Station—Hell, they've even got a McDonald's on a paddle-wheeled river boat just down from the Holiday Inn. You wouldn't believe what a few years can do to a place that's on the move."

"Let's just say I'm eagerly awaiting being moved."

Sallings led the new detective through the swinging doors and into the inner office. The three desks in the middle of the room were empty. "These are shared by the patrolmen. They need a place to dump things, write reports and all that stuff too."

Stark nodded.

She led him to a young officer who sat looking up expectantly from his desk in the middle office cubicle. "Detective Stark, I'd like you to meet our night radio operator, Officer Petit."

Petit, an awkward but amiable beanpole, jumped to attention beside his desk, catching the star-set telephone headphone on his chair arm and jerking it off the side of his head. "Damn! Excuse me, I'm sorry—I sure am glad to meet you, Detective!"

"Sit down, sit down," Stark replied, shaking the young man's eagerly offered hand.

"Well, Officer Petit," Sallings said, rolling her eyes playfully and looking at him seductively. "What exciting news do you have for us today?"

Petit blushed. "I've typed you a summary of everything and put it on your desk."

"Thanks, but let's hear it from you." Sallings winked at Stark and perched on the corner of Petit's desk. "It so much more fun that way."

"Okay" he replied, picking up a clipboard from his desk and looking nervously back and forth between his two superiors. "There's not a whole lot here. It was sort of quiet last night. There was a wreck on Oasis Street. The Grandall kid sideswiped a parked car, careened across the street, plowed through old man Davidson's hedge, and hit that big oak tree in his front yard. The kid wasn't hurt, but he totalled the car and old man Davidson is mad as hell.

"Then Mrs. Carver, on Gulfview, called in a complaint at twelve-thirty-nine about a loud party on the beach in front of her house. I let it stew for about thirty minutes and called her back before I sent anyone over. She said they'd packed up and left." Petit grinned sheepishly, "She thanked me for clearing them out. I told her it was no trouble at all.

"And Gloria Johncourt called and said she and her husband Alex had had a big row, that he'd walked out and had never come back. She's worried because he didn't take either his wallet or the car. She thinks he's been kidnapped or something."

"Kidnapped?" Sallings said incredulously. "Kidnapped! Who in the hell would want to kidnap him? He's a schoolteacher, for Christ's sake."

"That's what I thought. I started to call all the bars and motels, but I thought maybe we'd better stay out of a family squabble until we had to get into it."

Sallings swung off Petit's desk, absently giving him a fleeting glance up her skirt. He turned crimson when she caught his eyes riveted between her legs.

Sallings decided not to hassle him. "That was good thinking, Petit. Why don't you call her back when we're finished and see if he's wandered back home. What else? Any burglaries? Muggings? Bank robberies? Anything exciting?"

"No, I'm afraid that's about it." Petit wiped the perspiration from his forehead.

"Oh, come on, Petit!" Sallings replied. "Are you trying to make Stark look like he's not needed the first day he's here?"

"Well, you can work on that missing persons case."

"You've got to be kidding," she said, stalking off to her office. "I've got better stuff than that in my file from a month ago."

"Glad to meet you, Petit," Stark said, as he followed his sassy new partner into their office. "So this is it?" he asked, looking at the bare desk and two blank walls that were his.

"What'd you expect? A suite at the Fountainebleau?"

"Nope! Suits me fine," After seeing Petit get caught, Stark made a conscious effort to avoid looking at her 36D bustline as she stretched her arms up and over her head and ran her hands back through her sandy-blond hair. "If you don't mind, I need to start setting up shop. Afterward, maybe you and I can take a bird's-eye tour of the town."

"Sounds good to me. I'll try to get caught up on some reports and phone calls—unless you need some help with your stuff?"

"No, go ahead with your work. I'm as fussy as an old hen and I need to do most of it myself. Thanks, anyway."

The sun glistened on the Gulf of Mexico in all its morning splendor. At ten, the inshore water was as smooth as a giant cookie sheet. Patchy clouds drifted overhead, changing the water from mint to kelly to emerald green as they passed.

"You turkey!" Pete Blanchert, the police captain's son sputtered, coughing out a mouthful of briny seawater after someone had grabbed his ankles and upended him.

"Caught ya!" Billy Wheaton shouted, bursting from the water.

"Caught you, shit! Who the hell's playing tag?"

"Wheaton, you're a pain in the ass," James Dodd, the reverend's son said.

"So are you, Preacher Baby," Billy answered with a splash of saltwater in Dodd's eyes.

"You rat," Dodd laughed as he grabbed at the splashing hands. "Get him, Pete, and let's drown the little bugger!" Between the two of them they managed to hoist him shoulder high above the water, then plunged him deep underneath in a flurry of flailing legs, arms, and foaming water.

A quarter of a mile out in the Gulf, the giant tiger

shark turned towards the beach and the low-frequency vibrations in the water. The twenty-six foot faintly-striped body whipped snakelike through the water, building up speed and closing the distance to within a few hundred yards in less than a minute. At this distance, the sensory cells in his lateral line told him that there was definitely a lot of disturbance in the water that needed probing. He cruised alongside the boys, two hundred feet farther out and in deeper water. Their antics had carried them increasingly further from the shore into chest-deep water.

"You're going to get it," Billy laughed, coming up and trying to get away from the other two.

"Who's going to get it?" Dodd teased, as they shoved him back under again.

Billy decided to scare them. He drifted motionless, face-down in the water, doing a dead-man's float while the others stood unphased, quietly waiting for him to run out of air.

The shark hesitated when all the noise ceased. He drifted in closer and glided silently past the white blobs in the water, starting a lazy two-hundred-yard circle for his third and final pass. He had decided that the splashing objects were probably injured and edible—Alex Johncourt had been. In the final quarter of his circle, a subtle Gulf current a mile away brought the unmistakable smell of fish blood. A wounded fish. This was familiar food. With a sudden swirl of water, felt only as a slight bit of pressure by the clowning adolescents, the great shark abruptly changed direction and swept out to sea after his new prey.

"What was that?" Billy cried, splashing upright from his dead-man's position.

"What was what?" Pete replied.

"There was something down there—huge!"

"There was something down there. Huge!" the others mocked in feigned hysteria.

"You pansy-ass. What do think is there? Jaws or something?" Dodd asked scornfully.

"Yeah, Baby Billy!" Pete echoed. "You know, Baby Billy couldn't even get into Jennifer's pants last night because he spent all night looking over her shoulder for the boogeyman or the cops to look in his car. I heard he couldn't even get it up."

"I hear she gave up on him and did herself—she had to; she was stuck with our little nerd here," Dodd taunted.

"I really don't give a damn what you creeps say," Billy replied. "I'm getting out of here." He turned toward shore and started running out of the water—fighting it all the way. He hesitated halfway, winded, looked over his shoulder, and started running again.

"Will you look at that," Dodd said. "He's going to run up there and sit with the girls. God knows what kind of garbage he'll feed them."

"Who cares? He's afraid of everything—and the more he shows it, the better it makes us look. Understand?"

The eight-hundred-pound hammerhead shark was in trouble. He'd been hooked at Dunedin Reef, brought alongside a boat and gaffed several times before twisting the fishline, breaking it, and getting free. He was wobbling along miserably through the water trailing a stream of blood and pure panic behind him.

Blind instinct had sent him as far from the reef as he could go; but, already exhausted and confused, he was weakening and slowing down.

The warmer shallower water seemed to refresh him and he swept his strange T-shaped head back away from the shore line. He went to the bottom and tried to rub or shake loose the line that was twisted around his head and over his widely set nostils. Working agitatedly at the steel leader and hooks, he didn't see the deadly shadow hurtling toward him.

Sensing that something was wrong, the hammerhead arched his thirteen-foot body, turned upwards and tried to escape the unseen danger. He lost. The tiger shark hit him at full speed behind the left pectoral fin, almost ripping him in half with the power of the impact.

The massive shark glided, letting his momentum slowly subside with the added drag of the smaller shark in his mouth. He shook the hammerhead forcefully, ripping a crescent-shaped bite the size of a garbage can from its leathery hide. The wounded shark, its body connected only by à thin strip of flesh, dropped twisting, turning, and still snapping to the sandy bottom as the tiger shark hovered protectively above it swallowing the first mouthful. The huge mottled and scarred monster turned his nose downward and finished the smaller shark with a shattering series of violent hits and tearing bites.

James and Pete, tired of their horseplay, trudged through the water to the beach blanket to join their companions. They had not seen the shark the first time, nor had they seen him return. Less than thirty feet from their blanket, he was cruising inside a channel four feet deep formed by the shoreline and a close-to-surface sandbar. The tip of the triangular-shaped fin broke the water twice, but it was obscured by the waves that were starting to form because of the developing onshore breeze.

# 3. CHARLIE

Stark spent most of the morning arranging his office. He pushed the desk from one side of the room to the other. He hung his degrees on the back wall, his certifications, licenses and honors on another, and turned to Sallings for help. "Hey Sallings, are even half of these level? It seems the more I work at it, the worse they get."

"They look fine, really! You've done as good a job as I could have—at least they're up there."

The wall was as sparkling white as a new canvas from the paint job Sallings had given it a few days earlier. "It looks like they painted the wall for us," Stark said.

"*They* didn't do anything, brother. That wall got that way on my day off."

"Thanks," Stark replied. "I appreciate that. You didn't have to go to that much trouble—I would have helped after I moved in."

"I thought it was only fair that you had a decent, clean office for starters. And if you knew how hard

I've been pushing to get another detective on the staff—I damn near carpeted it for you, too. Anyway, you owe me a drink for painting it."

"You've got a deal."

After filling the desk with his personal stuff, Stark sat looking at a gold-framed photo of his ex-wife and two boys. He was trying to decide what to do with it. He could stick it away and ask Barbara to have a photo of just the boys taken. But, at the same time, he liked this one. He still cared a lot for Barbara even though he didn't want to live with her any longer. "Anyway," he thought, "that damn picture has been on my desk through a lot of hard times. I've lost myself in it, calmed myself with it, and used it as a security blanket more than once. I'll put it on the desk and be damned. People can just wonder about it and keep their lousy mouths shut."

"Stark, we've got a bit of a problem," Sallings said sticking her head in the door. "It's close to two o'clock and Gloria Johncourt just called again. Alex still hasn't come home and she's really worried. She says it wasn't that big a fight, the car is still in the garage, and she's sure something's happened to him."

"What do you think?"

"I don't know, really. I thought he'd show up by now. How about you and me checking around the major hotels and their cocktail lounges? Maybe we can find someone who ran into him last night. It'd be a way of introducing you to people and showing you around a little bit."

"Great! I'd like to get out, meet some people, and see what's what."

They started out at the Holiday Inn, a seventeen-story hotel in the very center of the beach area. The parking lot was filled with the cars of late summer visitors. Tourism had really been good this year and August was the wrap-up month of the summer season. In September the kids went back to school and things slowed down until the Christmas season.

"Hi, Detective!" the desk clerk greeted them as Stark and Sallings came in the door. "Is this our famous new detective?"

"He sure is!" Sallings replied. "Detective Stark, I'd like you to meet Rusty Hatten, the desk clerk here at the Holiday. If you ever need information, give him a call. He's helped me more than once."

"Glad to meet you, Detective," Hatten reached across the counter and shook Stark's hand. "If you weren't on duty, I'd offer you a drink. But I'll give you a raincheck on it if you want to come by after work sometime."

"We'll take you up on it," Stark replied with a wink.

"You'd better believe it," Sallings answered. "But it's help we need right now. I'm—*we're* trying to run someone down: Alex Johncourt. He and his wife had a fight last night; he walked out and hasn't returned. Know anything about it?"

"I haven't seen him in about a week. And then it was in the hardware store. Why don't you ask Hanibal Jones? He was the bartender on duty last night and he's out by the pool. There's not too many come in that he misses, no matter how busy we are."

A tanned and muscular Hanibal Jones was sitting at the end of the pool by the bar and Jacuzzi. "Hi, Detective!" he said, as he saw Sallings approach.

"Hi, Hanibal. How ya doin'?"

"Great. Are you here showing our new detective all the luscious bodies that populate this place?" He grinned at the girls around him. "You're welcome to join us or are you hard at work?"

"Unfortunately, the latter. Can you spare us a minute, Hanibal? I know how it hurts you to leave this harem even for a moment."

"Bring him back, Detective Sallings," one sultry blonde cooed, folding her arms over the bartender's shoulder and running her hands through his curly permed hair. "Hanibal's our ringmaster and he has to go back to work in just a few hours."

"Janice," Sallings said cupping her hand under the young woman's chin, "I'll return him in just a minute. I promise. And I'll even introduce you to our new bachelor detective!"

"Ooh!" she said, taking a step backwards. She took off her sunglasses and looked at Stark seductively. "Promise?"

"It's a promise."

Sallings explained to Jones about the schoolteacher's disappearance and asked if he had seen him the previous evening or knew where he might be. Jones shook his head. "I wish I could help you; I just can't. But that doesn't sound like Alex at all. Really. I don't believe he went too many places other than here and the Hilton. And I can tell you that, in the past two years, I've never seen him in either one without Gloria. He just wasn't that type of guy. I agree with Gloria. I'd bet more on something bad happening to him, like getting mugged or maybe taking a swim and getting swept off in the undertow or something. He wouldn't be out playing around with a chiquita somewhere—not Alex."

"Well, thanks and no thanks," Sallings replied.

"Yeah," Stark joined. "I don't like the alternatives."

"Neither do I," Hanibal said seriously. "I wish I could tell you something else. I'll ask around a little. Discreetly. Can I buy you a drink? Coke or something?"

"You're on," Stark answered quickly. He was getting hot standing in the sun. "Anyway, we told your harem we'd bring you back. And besides, I was promised an introduction, remember."

"You're gonna enjoy that," Hanibal promised. "Once those cats gets their claws into you, you're gonna be here the rest of the day. They're nice, though. Really."

"If you don't mind a loose usage of the word," Sallings added with a laugh.

"Well, who wants to spoil the fun?" Stark agreed.

Two hours later Stark and Sallings had checked the Hilton, a half dozen other likely lounges, and talked to Alex's closest friends. They drew one blank after another. "Well it looks like we've got a real live missing person," Stark said. "I hope he's alive, anyway."

"Me, too!"

"Surfside Three to Central," Stark spoke into the car radio.

"This is Central, Detective. Go ahead."

"Have you heard anything more on our missing person, Alex Johncourt?"

"No, sir; not a thing."

"What about his wife? Have you heard from her in

the last hour or so?"

"No, sir."

"How about giving her a call then getting back to us?"

"Ten-four, Detective. I'll get right on it."

A few minutes later the day radio dispatcher was back on the air with another negative report. The hair on the back of Stark's neck rose and a shiver ran down his spine. Ignoring the danger signals, he mused to himself, "This is just what the doctor ordered—retirement without retiring; a challenge, but not too much of one. Big deal of the day is a runaway schoolteacher!" Surfside was turning out to be everything he had hoped for. Early retirement with pay! Even though Surfside was a town filled mostly with midwesterners, its atmosphere was still definitely southern: it was laid back and relaxed, not rushing anything. "And after all the trouble in St. Louis, I deserve it," Stark thought. "No one should have to go through what I did."

He was right. Stark had been through hell. He had been the detective in charge when St. Louis was besieged by a mad sniper. The maniac had butchered people with an M-16, a Springfield Rifle, and a shotgun loaded with deer slugs for ten and a half months. He had slaughtered twelve people in one afternoon, driving down the street in a stolen car. He had struck erratically, occasionally killing at long range with a scope; and one time, opening up at point-blank range with a shotgun, he'd fired on a group of children waiting for their schoolbus. He had shot people on freeways and in shopping malls and before he was finished, he had killed one hundred and twenty-five.

There had been no consistency to the death sprees except the killer's need for publicity and his glee in telling Stark what he was going to do only minutes before he did it.

At one point, the chief of detectives had pulled Stark off the case—partly because there didn't seem to be a lot of progress being made, partly because the F.B.I. had entered the investigation when a postal worker was shot on the job, and partly because Stark had become too *involved*. The sniper reacted with rage to Stark's removal and shot five pregnant women in retaliation. He'd called Stark and said he would eliminate all the pregnant women in St. Louis if Stark wasn't put back on the job. An hour later every TV and radio station in St. Louis announced Stark's reassignment.

By using computers, eliminating possibilities, and tying off every loose end, Stark had finally gotten close to finding out who the man was. It all ended one night when he got a call at home. Today, many years later, it still seemed like yesterday:

"Stark?" the hauntingly familiar voice questioned dryly into the phone.

"You know it's me," Stark answered.

A dirty laugh. "Yeah, I know it's you. You ready to end this?"

"If you are."

"Don't play games with me; I'll turn the Mississippi red with blood."

"You're sick!"

"And you're scared! You know I can do it."

"I'm not scared of you—a coward who shoots kids and pregnant women then hides like an old woman.

When you get some balls, call me back!"

"You hang up on me Stark, you're gonna be sorry. I'm lookin at a long line of people waiting to get into a theatre—I'd love to waste 'em."

"You're really sick."

"You already said that Stark. Let's cut the crap. You know this is all between me and you. If you want to settle it, you keep your friggin' hand on the phone. I'll call you back when you can't trace me."

"There's no trace—" Stark stared emptily at the dial tone. Ten minutes later his phone rang again.

"Stark here."

"I know who it is. Just shut up and listen or go take a bath in the blood I'm about to spill. I'm calling from the Frontenac Shopping Center, so if you want to sic your cadet chihuahuas on me go ahead. I'll add them to your bill."

"I told you that I wasn't tracing."

"Bullshit!"

"Whatever you say, I'm still not tracing. Okay?"

"Doesn't matter, tonight it goes down. Ten o'clock. Go to the base of the steps on the north end of the Arch and look for a bottle of Muscatel with a note inside. Follow the directions. If you don't, or if you bring anyone with you—and you can screw department regulations—I'll fill St. Louis with more bodies tomorrow than the earthquake did in San Francisco." The sniper slammed the handset into the pastry shop's pay phone, glared at the waitress who'd partially overheard, and stormed out.

Stark stared into the dial tone emitting from the handset for a minute then started calling in favors. "Holiday Inn, Riverfront?"

"Yes, sir!"

"This is Detective Michael Stark. Let me speak to Dan."

There was a slight pause and the click of lines being switched. "Hi! Michael, what's up? What can I do for you?"

"I need a room for a half hour or so, twenty floors or higher and on the southeast corner, at about ten-thirty tonight. I also need a key to the service elevator. Dan, I don't want to lean on you, but I want anyone I bump into to forget that I'm there."

"You've got it. Just give me a second with the computer. What's up? Not the sniper?"

"You've got it. Just cover me."

"Don't worry, pal. That's what friends are for."

Stark's next call was to the Texas Antelope Gun Shack. "Greaser?" he asked as the gravel-voiced man answered the phone.

"Yeah, whatta you want?"

"This is Stark and I'm calling in some markers. I overlooked those three Uzi automatics that left your shop last week with no papers. It's time to pay."

"Come on Stark! I don't make enough dough on that shit to get shook down. You know that. Whatta you want, my Class Three license? What's that gonna get ya?"

"Nothing! Shut up and listen! In less than an hour I want you to deliver a Colt AR-15 modified or a fully automatic M-16 with plenty of clips of armor-piercing ammunition to the Riverfront Holiday Inn in my name. I also want a good pair of night glasses. Ten o'clock, get it?"

"Stark, I'm forty-five minutes from the shop!"

"Then speed! Break the law, as if you didn't know how. Get your ass off the phone and put the gear in a box that doesn't look like World War II. If you don't, tomorrow you can head for Anheuser-Busch and stand in line for a job application."

"You're gonna owe *me!*"

"If your lookin' to die, Greaser, think of it that way."

Less than an hour later Stark walked through the revolving doors of the Holiday, duffle bag in hand. "Hi, Dan. Whatta you got for me?"

Dan placed a large cardboard carton on the counter. "A guy just dropped this off and said to give it to you. He also said if it didn't fit, you'd know where to stick it. You know, you have some strange friends, Stark?"

"Yeah, that's what my wife tells me. Where've you got me?"

"In 2412. It's on the southeast corner of the building. It ought to give you a good view.

"Thank's, Dan."

"Here's the service elevator key."

In 2412, Stark turned off the lights then opened the drapes on the east and south windows. The city and riverfront unfolded beneath him; the Arch rose in the southeast. Michael trained his glasses on the riverfront, starting south of the McDonald's boat, traveling past the *Robert E. Lee* and up to the Arch. The sniper had kept his word. He was stupid, daring, or uncaring; but he was sitting on the bottom tier of steps dressed in camouflage fatigues with a rifle case across his lap acting as if he hadn't a care in the world. Stark respected his arrogance, feared his record just a little, and didn't call headquarters. He opened Greaser's box, found his M-16, ammo, and a surprise pack of camouflage fatigues and grease paint that he hadn't asked for. It made the game even.

Wearing a London Fog raincoat that hid his clothing and the M-16, Stark crossed I-95 and made his way into the Archway park. Once past the Interstate streetlights, Stark stashed his raincoat and M-16 case beneath a tree then circled the park's northern pond. He slipped off the grass, crossed the street to the cobblestoned riverfront. Screeching wildly, a hail of .556 M-16 ammunition whizzed past his ears and ricocheted off the centuries-old brick.

Stark rolled downhill with the natural contour of the riverfront, hugging his weapon close to protect it from the hard surface. The sniper's bullets danced behind him like an electrical light display, exploding a parked Firebird sports car Stark had taken momentary refuge behind. As he rolled closer to the river, the ricochetting projectiles exploded a helicopter sitting beside the docked riverboat, *Tom Sawyer*.

Stark realized the sniper had a nightscope and knew he had to get away from him. He rolled just a few feet into the freezing October river, holding his weapon just above the surface as he inched along trying to keep himself hidden between the line of cars parked above and the last sight of fire. It didn't work. The screech of bullets spent on brick and the sparks above his head told him the sniper was homing in. Stark took a deep breath and sank beneath the swift dark water of the Mississippi. He swam thirty yards out, surfaced briefly, then swam thirty more, letting the current carry him. He prayed that he wouldn't hit a whirlpool as he drifted past the *Robert E. Lee* and angled in behind McDonald's.

Time was short. This was downtown and Stark knew the precinct cars were on their way. He sloshed out of the river startling tourists who had come outside to see what was going on, grabbed the McDonald's retaining chain, and quickly made his way to the street above. He was met by another barrage of fire and again rolled halfway down the riverfront between the two riverboats.

The sniper saw him in his scope, fired a continous clip at Michael's fleeing form, then jammed in a second clip and emptied it as he saw Stark advancing past the *Robert E. Lee.*

On the lower level of the *Robert E. Lee*, steakhouse patrons who had tried to ignore the commotion unexpectedly ate a dinner of shattered window glass, china, and crystal. Others, fleeing to taxis and private cars, were cut down as they crossed the catwalk to the riverfront. Stark managed to disappear amid the screams and confusion.

The first two precinct cars rolled to a squealing stop on the riverfront, one of them less than a hundred feet from the sniper. A hand grenade arced through the darkness, was illuminated briefly by the burning helicopter and Firebird, then dropped between the two patrolmen. They heard it hit the ground, but the explosion was the sound that died in their ears.

The distraction had given Stark the time and space he needed. Quickly making his way to the street, he crawled beneath the cars until he saw a shadow squatting in the open end of a Ford van. He took an extra clip from his belt, threw it over several cars toward the river and spotted the night scope following it. Before the sniper had a chance to track its source, Stark fired a full clip into the van, blowing both van and sniper into an explosive mixture of gasoline, blistering copper-jacketed bullets, and ninety-eight-degree flesh.

The sniper turned out to be a Vietnam buddy. Stark had turned evidence against him in the Mai Lai Massacre investigations. He'd wanted his personal vengeance against Stark and the world. The fifteen-minute firefight up and down the waterfront killed twelve innocent bystanders, two policemen, and left twenty-nine others wounded.

The newspapers and national TV had a field day with Stark's ordeal. Some called him a hero; others claimed he was as mad as the man he'd killed. Within two days of the incident, his unauthorized actions and the death of the bystanders had earned him a month's suspension from the force.

There had been some positive aspects to the experience, though. For one, Stark had become nationally known; secondly, he had settled an old score: his guilt over Viet Nam and Mai Lai, the feeling that he had to make up for it somehow. It had also buried any feelings of inadequacy he'd had over not being able to catch the sniper—now those were all in the past!

On the other side of the scale, Stark had lost his wife in the process. Under the pressure of those difficult times, they had seen sides of each other that neither had particularly liked or felt they could live with. Barbara Stark had found that her husband didn't share her aspirations for greater and more glittering heights.

Barbara had urged him to exploit his fame, to revel in the money and become part of the old Veiled Prophet's society of St. Louis in which she'd been raised. Michael wasn't interested. He wasn't society before the sniper and he didn't want to be now. More than a few of Barbara's friends considered him the town barbarian. Barbara felt she could never understand him or his stubborn drive for independence, and she was tired of trying. Michael had found that, under pressure, he couldn't count on Barbara being there when he needed her, either physically or emotionally. So they had parted and he had made a futile attempt at a new life in the Southwest.

His childhood fantasy of becoming a modern-day cowboy had evaporated in New Mexico. After a year of sand, cactus, tumbleweed, a boiling hot sun in summer and a miserable winter, he realized he'd made a big mistake. Stark decided that he wanted to be comfortable for a change—to take life a little easier and to enjoy it for once. He started looking over the trade journals for a new place and a new job.

"And here I am," Stark thought, "smack in the middle of Florida's Suncoast, one of the prettiest places I've ever seen. It's paradise! I really like it. Admittedly," he continued musing to himself, "paradise is a bit tacky here and there, but that adds a bit of character. It's almost like an old movie."

Stark also enjoyed the southern attitude toward police. Sheriffs, detectives, and other police officers commanded respect in the South—as much as any other professional in the community. It was a far cry from St. Louis, where cops were *pigs* and just about anyone could shout at them, berate them and treat them a hell of a lot like personal servants. It seemed everyone felt that they, individually, paid a cop's salary and that he was two rungs down the social ladder. It was different here and he was going to like it! This was his kind of town and he wasn't going to let the anxiety of not being able to find Alex Johncourt spoil his first day.

"Okay, Detective Sallings," Stark said, coming from another hotel lounge. "I've had it. If it's all right with you, let's drop this for now and let someone else pick it up. I'd like to get back to the office, meet some more people, go over the manuals, and sort of settle in a little bit. And I don't know about you, but I'm starved to death. Where're all the good places to eat around here?"

"What do you want?" Sallings said. "A sandwich? A hot meal? Something more? You know, a formal twenty-or thirty-dollar meal with wine and everything? We've got it all."

"I'd like to know about all of them, really. But right now I'd settle for a good hamburger or some barbecue to take back to the office with me."

# 4. DELTA

By mid-afternoon a squall line of thunderstorms had rolled eastward across the Gulf of Mexico, blotting out the sky. Lightning slashed out in jagged blinding flashes. Gale force winds exceeding seventy miles an hour and gusting past hurricane strength in brief moments of intensity hurtled outward from the forward-edge of the thunderstorm. The Gulf reacted with passion. The gentle three-foot swells started tumbling over each other and piled up until they became twelve to fifteen feet tall. A one-foot width of fifteen-foot-high wave is over nine hundred pounds of water. And a hundred-foot-wide swell that high is ninety thousand pounds of the devil himself!

The evil black storm was less than five miles from the four men shark fishing too far from shore. From the boat, the squall line looked like a wall of boiling black fog hurtling toward them. The deadly black mass began at the top of the waves and its thunderheads reached forty thousand feet into the sky. It was moving fast. The center of it had turned into one of those small intense Gulf monsters that ship captains have nightmares about. They don't last long, but they don't need to! The bottom drops out of the barometer, the winds screech like banshees and seem to go in every direction at once. If you're caught in one and survive, you're a boater of incredible skill and even more incredible luck. A storm such as this on May 9, 1980, tossed the six-hundred-and-eight-foot, twenty-thousand-ton *Summit Venture* out of the Mullet Key Channel and into the Sunshine Skyway Bridge at the mouth of Tampa Bay, sending eight hundred and sixty-four feet of the bridge, a Greyhound Bus, other vehicles, and thirty-five people tumbling one hundred and fifty feet to their deaths.

Rick Reames, David Barker, Buck Taylor and Rod Bancoff were about to meet their first and last Gulf monster storm. The men had seen the storm coming from their twenty-four-foot Bayliner cabin cruiser, *Neptune's Delight*, but had thought it might pass them by. Rick, the captain, had bought the 2450 Ciera Command Bridge model in March. It had cost him twenty grand and it was much more boat than he was captain. Rick only had weekends free; he wasn't used to the boat yet and certainly not to rough-weather boating. Big waves—anything past the three-to four-feet range as far as Rick was concerned—scared the hell out of him, especially when he was on the command bridge. He felt better operating the boat from up there where he could see more easily, but his weight added to the pitch and roll of the boat in the high swells.

Rick decided not to chance it; to weigh anchor and head home in spite of his friends' protests. He turned on his engine blowers to exhaust the bilge of any gasoline vapors. The four minutes required seemed like hours as he watched the sky. The storm was approaching more rapidly than he had thought possible. Rick didn't know that much about weather, either.

He decided to jump the time ahead a minute and start the engine without waiting any longer. It coughed, sputtered, and died the first time he turned the key. The second time it cranked several times, sputtered, and died again. A knot of tension started balling up in his stomach. He knew the batteries were not in the best of shape. He had run them down to almost dead more than once and hadn't checked their water level for months. Cursing himself, remembering the appliances, he yelled at John over the rising wind, "Go down below and turn off the air-conditioner and refrigerator!"

He turned the key again and blanched as it cranked and ground itself down into a sickening clicking sound. Panicking, he turned the key again, holding it until there was virtually no sound at all. "The son of a bitch is dead," he whispered hoarsely to Buck, as his companion joined him on the command bridge to see if he could help. "Tell them to batten things down and let's get below. We're in for a hell of a storm. Look at that!

"Wait a minute," Rick shouted as Buck was about to disappear inside the boat. "I forgot about the auxiliary engine. Get me a life jacket and let's see if we can get it started."

The men scrambled to the stern of the boat. "Hold onto me while I get down on the swim-platform and try to start it." Rick strapped on the jacket and stepped onto the slippery eighteen-inch piece of fiberglass. The boat was starting to fight the waves and buck at its anchor line.

"This bastard is brand-new so it ought to start." He gave the fifteen-horsepower Mercury engine a strong pull on the starter rope and it coughed promisingly. A second pull and it roared as solidly as a chainsaw. A cheer went up from the men who'd come out on deck. "All right, you guys," Rick yelled with a wide smile on his face. "Get below and stay there. Buck, pull up the anchor and let's get the hell out of here."

Buck was slammed first into the starboard cabin windows. Then he found himself frantically holding onto the upper-helm handrail, trying to keep his balance on the almost nonexistent walkway that led to the bow. The waves were now nine feet high, dark, ugly and growing. The boat was bouncing as wildly as a cork in the water. When Buck tried to pull the twenty-pound Danforth anchor in, he found he had to hold onto the bow railing with one hand and pull the anchor up with the other. He couldn't do it. Frustrated, but knowing this was not a time for indecision, he fished out his pocketknife, cut the line, and let the anchor go.

From the stern, Rick felt the pounding against the anchor line cease and the boat pitch to one side. He knew the anchor was free and with a deathgrip on the railing, he lowered the engine into the greenish-black water with his free hand. He twisted the throttle to full speed trying to outrun the mountain of water he saw welling up behind him. The boat made it three-quarters of the way up the wave in front of him, was caught by a gust of wind, and toppled over the crest.

The canvas roof of the command bridge hung crazily to one side for a few seconds, then was ripped from its supports and blown into the sea. The ring buoy mounted on the cabin door soared off over Buck's head as he inched his way back around the cabin.

Rick was totally confused. He was trying to operate the outboard engine from the swim-platform and he could only see to the sides and in back of him. Everywhere he looked water towered high above his head. Feeling the boat being blown over the wave and starting to roll down the forward side, he kept the engine throttle wide open, hoping that somehow it might save them.

The sea was unforgiving. The wave crest caught the boat sideways, causing it to broach, capsizing it, plunging it beneath the surface, and rolling it over and over like an empty bottle. The force of the wave swept Rick from the swim-platform as easily as someone would pluck a piece of lint from a suit coat. The wave plunged him deep underwater despite the life jacket he had donned.

Likewise, Buck was washed from the stern deck in an instant. One minute he was gripping the railing; the next thing he knew, he was vomiting seawater and his arm was wrapped over something large, round and slick. He couldn't see it at first, but when he felt the twisted fibers of a rope in his hand, Buck knew a miracle had happened—the rubber raft that had been lashed to the top of the command bridge had somehow gotten under his arm! He didn't know how, but he was grateful. Coughing and choking, he hauled himself over its edge and sloshed into the bottom, never letting loose his grip on the rope that encircled the sides.

"Help me! Buck, help me!" a voice cried behind him. He looked back. A mere ten feet away Rick bobbed erratically in a bright international orange life vest flailing his arms at the water. Buck leaned over the side and tried to paddle the raft in his direction. For several minutes they fought the storm: Rick splashed wildly at the water and Buck paddled the raft with one hand in circles. They would get to within a few feet of each other and a wave crest would appear between them; they would slide down opposite sides and be separated again.

"I can't control the raft," Buck yelled at Rick, exhausted from his efforts. He realized the storm was starting to subside. "The waves aren't as bad. Do you think you could dump the life jacket and swim to the raft?"

"I'll try," Rick shouted. He managed to dunk himself several times before freeing himself from the straps but once out of the life vest, he found he could swim the short distance between them with relative ease.

"Did you see the others? The ship?" Rick asked, sprawled across the back of the bright yellow raft with a deathgrip on the rope on each side.

"No, I didn't see anything. One minute, I was on the side of the boat; the next, I was climbing onto the raft."

"Me, too." Rick said. "It was almost like someone slammed a door against me or hit me with a car. I had one hand on the railing and one on the engine; then, all of a sudden, I couldn't see anything but water and the boat was gone."

"Yeah, it seemed like I was rolling over and over

under the water for hours; then, out of nowhere, I was on the raft watching you bobbing around in the water.

"I guess they didn't make it—them or the boat. Would it sink just like that?"

"Yeah," Rick nodded his head dejectedly. "Just like that. But let's keep looking anyway."

After a few hours, the waves had subsided almost completely and the sky was crisp and sparkling. Visibility was excellent. And with it came good news: directly in front of them, two and a half miles away, streched the long white shoreline of Surfside Beach. In the center of the island the twenty-story condos and beachfront hotels stood out as familiar beacons. The men let out a whoop of joy and started slapping the water with their hands, paddling across the now smooth surface toward home.

Twenty-three feet below the surface of the Gulf, the predacious tiger shark circled the sunken boat. He had been drawn to the thudding sounds of the waves crashing against the boat and the boat bucking up and down against its anchor line. When it capsized with a roar—the fiberglass bursting and the braces straining and breaking—the shark had quickened its race toward the sounds. He instinctively sensed a catastrophe and, being at the top of the list of predators, catastrophe meant food for him. He circled the boat several times. David Barker, Rod Bancoff, and contents of the cabin had been tossed around like kernels of popcorn in a popper before the boat had sunk. The whiskey bottles on the cabin table had exploded when

Barker was thrown face-first into their midst and the overhead glass-rack had almost severed Rod's right hand when he grabbed it in his panic. Minute droplets of blood had seeped into the water around the boat.

The tiger shark's olfactory sacs picked up the scent. His instinct had been right! Agitated, the shark circled the boat faster. Butting and nudging the boat with his broad flat snout, he tried to make more of the exciting scents come forth. Not satisfied, he protruded his massive jaw and clamped down on the port side of the teak railing. He gave the boat a shake, rocking it, splintering the railing, swallowing the mouthful of wood, and swishing a bit more of the blood into the open water. It excited him even further. Frustrated by the lack of real food, he bit off another piece of teak and continued looking around the boat for something moving—for the source of the blood.

He heard an unfamiliar slapping noise coming from the surface a few hundred yards shoreward; but still he smelled blood and once more bit at the boat, angrily tearing chunks of fiberglass from the swim-platform. The slapping continued. Buck and Rick, one on each side of the rubber raft, were settling into a steady rhythm of paddling to shore with their hands. The shark hesitated again. A wounded fish? More disaster sounds? Food. It was moving—and not far away; the boat would wait.

The shark sped through the water toward the new sound. The shiny yellow raft stood out bright against the white surface of the water—it was attractive and inviting. He watched the hands dip-splash at the water in-almost perfect unison as the men slowly made their way toward shore. The shark knew this creature was not capable of moving swiftly through the water. It was going to be an easy kill. Although he was not familiar with rubber rafts, he could sense it was inanimate—just a barrier between him and his prey. Testing it, the shark gently nudged the raft from underwater and behind, bouncing it forward five feet in the process.

"Jesus Christ! What was that?" Rick exclaimed. "What happened? Did we hit something?"

"I don't know," Buck replied, untangling himself from Rick. They had both been thrown forward into the raft, on top of each other. "Either that or something hit us."

"You think we might have bumped into something floating just beneath the surface—maybe part of the boat?" Rick's face was starting to pale with panic. They were so close to home and neither wanted to say what they both were thinking.

"Oh God! Oh God! No!" Buck cried, pointing to the towering fin that had just surfaced fifteen feet from the boat. "Oh, Christ! Look how big that sonofabitch is! He must be twenty or thirty feet long. What kind of shark is it?"

"I don't know. I've never seen a shark that big. It's not a white, because his eye wasn't black. It's sure as hell not a hammerhead. It looks sort of like a tiger—it had a flat nose.

"It is a tiger shark! I saw some faint markings on its back."

"It can't be. They don't get that big, do they?"

"Tell him that! They're not supposed to—not very often, anyway. It looks like we just got lucky. For God's sake, don't move or make any more noise than you have to. They're mean sonofabitches."

The shark slowly circled the raft. He was right; there was food inside the big yellow thing and it was panicking. He could sense the fear through the rubber bottom. The men were whispering and shaking; he could see them above the edge of the raft watching, turning their heads, and following his circle. He glided within inches, his twenty-six-foot body dwarfing both raft and men. It would be easy, he decided. The raft was soft and squishy, like open flesh. He submerged, made a lazy half circle away from the raft, turned, and zeroed in on it, his fin breaking the surface once more a hundred yards from the men.

"You sonofabitch! Please God, not when we're so close to home," Rick cried, tears streaming down his face. "He's coming after us, Buck! Hold on tight!"

Buck leaned over the side and started paddling furiously in a vain attempt to outrun the shark. He had to make some effort to ward off the attack.

Five feet from the splashing man the enormous shark raised its head half way out of the water, its hinged jaws jutted out in massive rows of curved sawlike teeth as sharp as honed Solingen steel. They were aimed directly at Buck. Trying to avoid the inevitable, he leaned away from the onslaught. The jaws sliced through the raft as if it had never existed, clamped around Buck's pelvis and lower abdomen and continued on through the other side, cutting the raft in half.

Rick watched as his friend looked at him wild-eyed, speechless, one arm trapped in the massive jaws and the other flailing helplessly at the shark. Unable to scream, Buck could only look terrified as he was thrust under the water and the sea turned crimson with blood.

"Sweet Mother of God," Rick said out loud to himself. The water became calm again. Rick tightened his grip around the remaining section of the raft, thankful for its many compartments and hoping the shark had been satisfied with his friend. The water erupted ten feet away from him. The shark stuck his head above the surface with the top third of Buck's body in his mouth. The lower half had already been devoured. The shark looked at Rick, and shook the remaining piece of his friend, splattering Rick with blood and letting him hear Buck's skull crunch as he chewed, swallowed, and finished off his meal.

Rick vomited into the water, held onto the raft, and prayed. It was the wrong day for prayers. Twenty feet away the fin reappeared and started toward him. He let the raft go and started swimming frantically away from the oncoming fish. The shark caught him in his legs and pushed him screaming and crying across the surface for two hundred yards before pulling him under. Rick was his final catch of the day.

"This is Coast Guard Helicopter, Whiskey-Alpha-Bravo, One-Niner-One to Clearwater Coast Guard Station!"

"This is Clearwater Coast Guard—go ahead, One-Niner-One."

"We've located some flotsom two miles off Honeymoon Island; eighty-two degrees fifty-three minutes west, twenty-eight degrees and zero-four minutes North. I can make out an ice-cooler, a couple of vest-type PFD's, a ring buoy and other top-deck trappings from a small vessel. It looks like the Bayliner we're after—or what's left of it. I'd guess it capsized and went under."

"Have you located any survivors?"

"Negative. We haven't found anyone in spite of it being pretty flat out here. Can you get a vessel to our position? We'll remain here till she gets here, and we'll search further for them and for that missing sailboat."

"Detectives," Petit said, sticking his head inside their office door. "I just got a call from the Coast Guard. They said they've found some wreckage from Rick Reames's boat. It looks like it went down in that thunderstorm."

"Who all was in it?" Stark asked, leaning his elbows on his desk and rubbing his hands over his slightly hawkish nose.

"Didn't I tell you?"

"No. You told me the name of the boat and that was it. I don't read minds, old buddy."

"I forgot you wouldn't know who it was. I'm sorry, Detective Stark. Detective Sallings knows 'em." The young man self-consciously rubbed the stubble of a mustache he was trying to grow. "It was Rick Reames. Maybe I shouldn't say *was* yet; he's the brother-in-law of City Commissioner Barker. Reames, Barker, and two other guys were out there before the storm came up and they never came back in last night."

"Christ, I thought you people said this place was quiet!"

"It's supposed to be. I don't know what's going on.

Must be a full moon."

"This also isn't exactly East Podunk, either. We have almost thirty thousand people here in Surfside alone, you know." Sallings got up and sat on the corner of her desk. "They didn't find any survivors?"

"No, Ma'am."

"Bodies?"

"No, Ma'am I'd guess they're all inside, deep-sixed with the boat. You want me to call their wives?"

"No. Let's wait a while—No, that's not fair either. Send a car around to pick them up and take them to the Coast Guard station if they're not already there. Why don't you check with the captain and see if we can send that new officer we got last week, Officer Juanita—What's her name?"

"Hernandez."

"Yeah, Hernandez. See if the captain will have her pick them up. And ask her to keep us informed."

"Oh, Detective Stark," the radio man added, starting to leave. "One other thing—a reporter from the newspaper called and wanted to set up an interview with you to talk about the sniper thing, and how you like it here in Surfside, and all that stuff."

"I'd like it a hell of a lot better if everyone would forget St. Louis and that damned sniper and let me do the same."

"That's what I thought, but I didn't tell them that. Maybe I shouldn't have scheduled him to see you tomorrow morning. And besides, it wasn't a him, it was a her. You want me to call her back and tell her you're just too busy right now?"

"Probably not. I'm not going to like talking about it any better a week or a month from now. Maybe if we let them get the gore out of their system, they'll drop it once and for all. And it's a her? Jesus! Is the whole world turning female? I don't want to sound prejudiced, but—"

"You do sound prejudiced," Sallings replied with a grin, plopping back down into her chair. "And for your information, the whole world is not turning female—only the good part of it."

"I think I'll get out of here," Petit replied with a grin, "because she gets mean!"

"Is that right?" Stark folded his arms up over his head protectively. "If you start throwing things, you have to promise me a two-minute warning."

"Two-minute warning, my foot!" Sallings replied. "I don't throw things, I shoot. I may not be so hot with an M-16, but I can shoot the wings off a gnat with my revolver."

Stark held up his hands in surrender. "That's good enough for me!"

Half an hour later Petit stuck his head in their office again, "I hate to interrupt you two again but I just got another call from Coast Guard and they found the couple who were on that sailboat. Thought you'd want to know."

"Sure. Were they alive? Okay?"

"Yeah. No boat. They were bobbing along in their life jackets. The Coast Guard said they'd probably need hospitalization for exposure. I guess they were floating out there all night.

"And," Petit added with a grin, "they were nude. A lot of sailboaters go nude. It looks like they lost their clothes and a little dignity in the process."

"They're damned lucky that's all they lost," Sallings said sarcastically.

"They were tied together with ropes. Pretty smart. They didn't get separated that way."

"Was that before or after the storm hit," Stark asked.

"Cute. All you men think alike." She shook her head in mock disgust. "Petit, has anyone notified their families?"

"Someone did. They were at the Coast Guard Station, I think. The C.G. said something to that effect."

"Well, that's fine," Sallings said. "I'm ready to call it a day. How about you, Stark?"

"I agree. I'll stop by the captain's office and do all the polite things."

"You don't really think he's still here, do you?"

"Well, I—"

"Stark, you've got a lot to learn. This may not be Miami, but St. Louis it ain't either. That bastard was at the country club hours ago."

"Great! Then I'm gonna get out of here, too. Maybe I'll cruise around in the little bit of daylight that's left and get the flavor of Surfside. Petit, if you hear anything new about the commissioner—or have any troubles, let me know. I'll be in the car."

"Yeah. Call him, not me." Sallings added. "Either I'm not going to be in the car or the radio isn't going to be working. Understand?"

Petit nodded.

"Have you notified the mayor?"

"Yes, Ma'am! He asked me to keep him posted."

"Great! Maybe if we get out of here, we'll save something of this day after all! See ya later."

# 5. ECHO

Stark eased the new compact police car to the intersection at Gulf Boulevard. An almost solid line of cars parted to let the obviously unmarked police car through. Stark smiled and waved a "thank you" at the driver. "It's just as busy as Sallings said it would be," he thought. She had told Stark that you could pull onto Gulf Boulevard at anytime—even three or four in the morning—and count on seeing a car coming at you from one direction or the other.

He pulled off Gulf Boulevard to drive in and around the back streets of Surfside. He looked at the houses, at the cars parked in the driveways and on the gravel lawns, at the garages overflowing with boxes and boats, taking it all in. There seemed to be three fairly distinct districts on this incredibly narrow island. On the west side of Gulf Boulevard there were no side streets. It had a central business district of plush hotels and high-rise condominiums. On the southern end of the business district was a two-mile section of palatial homes. The streets were never more than a couple of hundred yards from the Gulf, allowing for plenty of beach and providing lawn space for the big homes—the ideal spot for a pool or tennis court. On the northern end of the business district was the two-mile park that the city kept as a nature refuge.

Newer homes were distinguished from older ones not only by obvious signs of wear and tear but also by their stilts. Insurance regulations demanded that new homes be built twelve-feet above sea level. Builders, therefore, had resorted to different styles of architecture to incorporate the stilts. There were massive homes on wooden pilings, some on concrete pilings, some with see-through parking areas underneath, and others with their parking areas enclosed. "The older homes," Stark thought, "still seem to have a little more charm and grace in spite of their age and impracticality during floods."

On the east side of Gulf Boulevard were streets whose length varied with the width of the island. The homes that lined the Intercoastal Waterway were nice—some as nice as the ones sitting directly on the Gulf. Sallings said they cost almost as much, too. They didn't have a Gulf view, but they did have direct water access. Some homeowners on the Intercoastal had rights extending as far as five hundred feet out into the water; they could build docks and keep their boats at home. And most of the homes along Surfside Bay had their boat docks filled. The docks were pegged with large sailboats and motor yachts, thirty, forty and even fifty feet long. Smaller boats dangled out over the water from davits that raised and lowered them into the bay.

Those who lived on the Gulf did not own the beachfront. The beach from the mean high-tide line to the water was public property. It was a constant source of irritation to the Surfside Police Department. There were calls about it almost every day of the year. New homeowners and renters would shout at them to do something: someone was walking on, sitting on, partying or fornicating on their private beach! The unlucky officer who took the call would have to patiently explain that the beaches belonged to *all* the people of the United States, that the "intruders" could *not* be evicted and advise them to please write their Congressman or woman.

The area between the Gulffront and Bayfront was much poorer than its two waterfront sisters. It had much smaller homes. Many were duplexes and converted motels that hadn't made it. Some had been built just for rental income. The majority were not nearly as nice or as well kept as the homes in other parts of Surfside, yet they still commanded high rents. Stark thought the City Commission could do a little better here.

The business district on Gulf Boulevard was lined with fine restaurants, shopping centers, convenience stores and tourist traps that the snowbirds couldn't seem to resist.

"Would you look at some of these places," Stark thought, driving back into the middle district. "They're so gaudy, they're almost pretty." He drove down one of the kaleidoscopic side streets, looking at the houses, walled yards and lawn ornaments. South Florida was a land of make-believe. It had its own Disneyesque charm. The houses were not real—not in the sense that most northerners thought of them. They were all

CBS homes, as the realty people called them—concrete block stucco—no basements; just a cement slab walled in with concrete blocks and pasted over with stucco. The stucco was painted every conceivable shade of turquoise, pink, red, green, yellow and blue. Gravel lawn after gravel lawn sported garish pink plaster flamingos or turquoise-and-black swordfish. One couldn't say that good taste was overabundant in the middle sector of the island; but in spite of its garishness, it held a certain charm.

Stark was fortunate. He was among that lucky few who lived on the water. He lived on the Gulf, very high above the Gulf—twenty-one stories up to be exact. Although the sniper and St. Louis had become a nightmare and a disaster for him, they had also been his salvation. Magazines and newspapers had paid him handsomely for interviews. For a time, he was a hero and a much-sought-after public speaker at five hundred dollars an evening. But after half a dozen speeches and receptions, it became pretty apparent that being a celebrity was not Stark's strong suit. He didn't like it and it showed. His big financial break came with television and the movies. Several national TV interviews paid him very well; and he became financially secure for a lifetime when, with his help, they wrote a book and made a movie about his experience in St. Louis.

But it hadn't worked. Money simply had not had the magic effect on Stark. It didn't change him. Somehow the money and fame had settled on the wrong shoulders: Stark was still Stark. He was still a small-town cop. Being a police detective in a town the size of Surfside was all he'd ever wanted to be. And that fact had driven his wife, Barbara, up the wall.

The money had made the divorce easier. He had to admit that. It had also enabled him to buy his large and luxurious condominium overlooking the Gulf and allowed him to have a maid come in to clean the place three times a week. He had tried to cook for a while shortly after Barbara and the boys had left, but found that he couldn't stand eating alone.

There were about the same number of shirts in the closet and shoes on the rack as he had always owned. That hadn't changed either. He had the money to buy whatever he wanted—he just didn't want a hell of a lot more than he had ever had. Barbara couldn't understand it and Stark didn't try.

"Central to Surfside One," Stark's radio announced with a stacatto of static.

"This is One. Go ahead, Central," he answered.

"Detective, I've got problems. Officer Hernandez just called from a pay phone. She was taking those women to the Coast Guard Station like you and Sallings asked and she stopped at a drug store so one of them could refill a nerve pill prescription—" Petit hesitated.

"What's the problem with that?" Stark queried into the silence.

"Well, while they were inside—Well, you see they were working on clearing this building next to the drugstore, and this guy was backing this bulldozer up, and he went too far or he didn't hit the brakes or something."

"Don't tell me," Stark said into the handset.

"Yes, sir. He went right off the lot, over Hernandez's car and into the side of a refrigerated grocery van!"

"Is anyone hurt?"

"Not yet. But I'm afraid there's going to be if someone doesn't get to Hernandez quick. I think she's going to shoot him. You wouldn't believe what she said over the phone."

"Yes, I would. I'll get over there. What's the ten-twenty?"

"It's on Blue Heron about four blocks this side of your condo. And Blue Heron is the second street off Gulf Boulevard."

"I know where Blue Heron is," Stark snapped. "I'm on Blue Heron now."

Stark's slightly irritable mood evaporated as quickly as a summer rain when he arrived at the scene. There was a crowd of nearly a hundred people ringing the flattened police car and the bulldozer that was sticking out of the side of the vegetable truck. When he saw what was happening, he doubled up with laughter. He knew he shouldn't—but he couldn't help it. The police cruiser looked very much like a stomped soft drink can and the grocery truck looked like an opened can of vegetables. There were tomatoes, watermelons, and heads of lettuce strewn all over the street and on top of the bulldozer. In the middle of this, Hernandez had a young shirtless dirt—streaked man in a construction hard-hat assuming a very slippery position against the side of the truck. Words were coming from her mouth faster than an M-16 could spit bullets. Her uniform was soiled with vegetable splatter and she was walking from one side of the young man to the other, writing on her pad and screaming at the top of her voice as she went.

"And what are *you* doing here?" she shouted at Stark as he came through the crowd, trying to wipe the last traces of laughter from his face.

"I'm Detective Stark," he replied, flipping open his wallet and displaying his shield.

"I know who you are! I met you when you applied."

"I heard there was a hell of a sale on vegetables down here, and I just decided to clean up, if you'll excuse the pun."

"That's not funny! And I can handle this by myself. You wouldn't be here if it was one of the men on the force."

"Heyyy Lady!" Stark said in a low menacing tone. "Let's don't lose it. They said an officer needed help and that's the only damned reason I'm here. What's between your legs has nothing to do with it!" Leaving her some dignity, Stark dropped the anger, took off his sunglasses, leaned down picked up an apple, polished it on the inside of his sport coat, winked at Hernandez, and took a bite. "Hungry?" he said, with a grin. "At least we get a new cruiser."

The worried look on her face broke. "I'm sorry, Detective! Really I'm sorry."

"You think you're sorry," Stark said. "What about old macho man here?"

"It is funny!" Officer Hernandez started to laugh. "It really is. I was pissed off with everyone else laughing, but it is funny."

"Good." Stark slapped her on the back and eyed the crowd. "You probably have more cool than I do—I'd probably have shot the sonofabitch."

"Well, this turkey has his own little plastic baggie of

pot and he's high as a kite." She gave the bulldozer driver's foot a subtle nudge in the slippery vegetables and he plopped face-first in the street with a splat.

"Book him!" Stark said with another wink. "I'll give you some help straightening up."

# 6. FOXTROT

Police Detective Michael Stark called it a day. He pulled the unmarked car in front of his condominium and got out.

"Hi, Detective!" the valet said, opening his door.

"Hi, Bob." Stark handed him two dollars as he got out of the car.

"You going out again later?"

"Yes, but I'll probably be taking my own car."

"I thought you were allowed to drive the city car so you'd have the radio and be able to keep in touch."

"You're right," Stark replied. "And that's why I'm taking my own car. I work enough all on my own. If I had the cruiser out, I'd have the radio on and be in the middle of everything. I'm too damned nosey for my own good. It's my own way of exercising self-control."

"Gotcha, Detective. I'll have your car ready for you."

To Bob Delacourte, having the car ready meant *having it ready*. He had worked as a waiter in the French Quarter in New Orleans when he was younger and he knew what service was. For the good tippers and the nice people he kept a bucket of soapy water, a hand vacuum and a note pad on hand. When they brought in their cars or told him they were going out later in the evening, he gave their cars a quick once over. He vacuumed the inside, wiped off any obvious dirt with the soapy cloth, rinsed it off quickly with a hose, and checked inside to make sure the car had plenty of gas and oil. The whole procedure took only ten or fifteen minutes; but it brought or bought, however one wished to term it, grateful patrons and generous tips.

Delacourte didn't do this for everyone. He couldn't have, even if he had wanted to. The condominium had eight units on each floor and was twenty-five stories high with twenty floors of living space. The bottom five were parking and storage. Fifty years old, it was all Bob could do to keep up with the traffic. Some people, like Stark, tipped rather well, some not quite so well, and some not at all. Since he worked solely on tips, like a good waiter, he rendered adequate and efficient service to the stingy and pampered the generous. He had secured the lucrative five P.M. to one A.M. shift, Saturday through Monday. And if his guess was right, he made as much money parking cars as did some of the people who owned them.

Upstairs, Stark fixed himself a drink, opened the patio doors in the living rooms, and stepped outside to the sound of crashing surf many stories below. The late summer tourists were doing the chicken walk down the beach—walking ten feet, bobbing down for a shell, rising up and looking around, walking another ten feet, and repeating the whole process again. The usual frisbee and volleyball groups were augmented today by twenty youths playing a serious game of touch football. Stark ignored them and turned his Celestron telescope toward the north end of the beach where the park was located. He was horny. The last mile of beachfront on Surfside's north end had no houses and was owned by the city. The city fathers had decided to leave the land untouched, not to build any kind of public facilities or picnic areas on it—no pathways except for those that the people and animals created.

The park was a haven for nude sunbathers. Over the years it had become common practice for anyone who wanted to sunbathe topless or nude to do so in this area. Residents knew that if they didn't want to be offended, they should walk on other stretches of beachfront. Conversely, the nude sunbathers didn't sunbathe within sight of the regular public beach or the street. Sallings had told Stark that there had been occasional complaints from startled tourists, but on the whole, they didn't have any trouble with it at all. Stark had teased her about sunbathing there.

"Are you kidding?" she had replied. "I go there only on official business. It's tough enough being a female detective in this burg without doing something like that. You might not get fired for it, but you'd have every male on the force trying to play grab-ass forever after!"

The town had laws against lewd and lascivious behavior but didn't consider nude sunbathing as such. The judges had confirmed it, and in fact, most had said if there was a ticket to be issued it should be for voyeurism. The complaints had noticeably decreased after those rulings, Sallings had said. Also, she had added, everyone knew it was good for business. Surfside's hotels boasted more foreign guests than any other city on the Suncoast. They had found that most foreign tourists were used to and wanted the option of sunning themselves in the nude—and would stay where it was available. Much to the hotel owners' surprise, they discovered there were a considerable number of American tourists who wanted the same thing and another sizable group who just wanted to look. As a consequence, when other places along the Suncoast were hurting for tourists, people were begging for places to stay in Surfside. The city fathers had levied a fairly hefty hotel surtax and it kept the city coffers full, while the tourists' spending kept the merchants flush. Although small in size, Surfside boasted some of the state's nicest hotels, finest restaurants, and most exclusive shops—and without question, it had the highest employment rate in the whole state of Florida. It didn't boast that it also had the state's highest prices.

The City Police kept a close eye on their golden money-making unofficial nude beach. Sallings had told Stark that they tried to keep sexual play to a minimum and homosexuality in check. But mainly they were just doing their duty—protecting the residents and tourists from harm. On most days at the north end of the beach, the police jeep was either in sight or soon would be. Anyone could go there, even children, without fear of being molested.

Stark thought it an excellent idea. Besides, with the Celestron he was able to bring the north end of the beach right onto his patio. That was a little secret he had discovered in the week before he had started duty. It was also one that he hadn't shared with his female partner. He just wasn't sure how to take her yet. She seemed all right: female, funny, not uptight about sex, not overly conscious about male/female roles; a woman of incredible beauty, wit, charm, and intelligence who seemed very honest, down to earth and unpretentious in spite of her wealthy family background. Stark said to himself, "The facts are, old buddy, she scares the hell out of you and you don't want to admit it."

Suddenly, in the early evening summer sun, a bronzed body filled his telescopic lens and made him suck in his breath. He adjusted the focus. Light blond hair, high cheekbones, and square shoulders looked directly at him just as plainly as if she were across the room. She could easily have been a movie star.

Stark was beside himself—his breathing deepened considerably. The woman was sitting on a beach towel looking him straight in the eye from a mile away. He moved the telescope downward revealing full, uplifted breasts crowned with hard dark nipples. He moved the telescope further down to a flat stomach lightly covered with downy sunbleached hair and sprinkled with dewdrops of perspiration. The telescope and Stark bottomed out to a mass of short blond pubic hair forming a perfect V between the woman's legs.

Stark lifted his eye from the sight and wiped his brow. Almost as if sensing her unknown voyeur, the woman slid a hand down over her pubis, trailed a finger down through her nether lips, brought it back up and played absent-mindedly with her uppermost pubic hair, idly turning it over and over, twisting it between her fingers. Disconcertingly, a wet male arm appeared around her shoulders. Stark turned the Celestron to the side to find a dripping companion and a second towel he hadn't noticed before. She kissed the intruder briefly and turned on her stomach to talk as he dried off and sat beside her. She was every bit as pretty from the backside as she was from the front, Stark decided. She stretched lazily, stood up on the towel, turned her back to the telescope, and reached down to pick up her shorts. Her boyfriend slid his hand up her leg and out of Stark's sight. She slapped playfully at him, wiggled into her shorts, and pulled a pale blue T-shirt over her head.

"Christ!" Stark said out loud. "It's been longer than I thought." He left the telescope and walked across the room to the wet bar, unbuttoning his khaki shirt as he went. He fixed himself a straight Jack Daniels Black with ice and picked up the telephone. "Sallings," he said into the phone. "Do you have a date tonight?"

"No, not really. Why?"

"Neither do I, goddamnit. So where are we going to dinner?" Even Stark was astounded by his boldness.

Stark liked the feel of Brannigan's Irish Pub. It had lots of brass, stained-glass, and antiques. The bar proper had a real brass footrail. One side was lined with old-time bar stools; the other was strictly a stand-up affair. Opposite the bar and half a level below was a row of video-game and backgammon tables.

Stark stirred his Bloody Mary, leaned one elbow on

the bar, and turned to Sallings. "Do they serve all their drinks in these quart jars?"

"Yeah!" She nodded. "It's sort of neat, but you have to watch it during happy hour."

"Why's that?"

"At happy hour these babies have over four ounces of booze and Brannigan's doesn't cheat you."

Stark let out a low whistle. "Thanks for warning me. Is this where we're going to eat?"

"No—although this is a decent place to eat, you use it mainly to pick up a date," Sallings replied. "And it's not *de rigueur* to eat in the same restaurant or bar where you make your kill."

"I see." A sardonic smile crossed his face. "Well, when in Rome,—"

"That's right," Sallings replied. "They've got it down to quite an art. See those phones on the tables?"

"Uh-huh."

"Well, each table on this side of the place has a number and each has a telephone. If you go by a table with a good looking hunk at it—or in your case, a pretty female—you note the number and when you get back to your table, you can give them a ring. That way they can turn around and take a look, no one has to get rebuffed in person. And if you don't want any phone calls, all you have to do is turn the phone off with the button at the side."

"Jesus," Stark laughed and shook his head, "times sure have changed."

"Come on," Sallings kidded him. You're not that out of touch!"

"The hell I'm not! What have you women and the younger generation done to this world, anyway?"

"Jesus, Stark!" Sallings laughed. "You sound like my Dad or a vacation Bible-school teacher."

"All right, damnit. I'll show you I'm not. Let's go sit at one of those butcher blocks."

They hailed the hostess and followed her in single file from the bar to one of the drinking-dining areas. "Bobbie will be with you in just a minute," she said. "Is this table okay?"

"It's fine," Stark replied with a self-conscious smile. "Just fine."

"Good. Here are the menus. The specialty drinks are in the front. Tonight is Margarita Night. They're two for a dollar all night long."

"Thanks," Sallings said.

"You're welcome." The hostess gave Stark a flirtatious bow as she left.

"It doesn't really cost a dime to call another table?" Stark pointed to the coin slot on the side of the phone. "You gotta be kidding me."

"Fat chance, brother. They make as much off these damned phones as they do the bar."

Stark nailed the phone on the first ring. "Should I?" he asked, looking at her out of the corner of his eye, a smile creasing his tanned hard face.

"Be my guest."

"Hi, Liza," a voice purred seductively in the phone. "Are you going to buy us a drink and introduce us to your sexy little playmate or do we have to come over and introduce ourselves?"

"I think you've got the playmate," Stark said, his face turning slightly pink as he caught Sallings watching him. He handed her the phone.

A pretty brunette jerked sharply around at a table

twenty feet away and looked at Stark's table. "Liza," she said. "I'm so embarrassed."

"Kara, darling," Sallings said into the phone, shaking her head. "That's what you get for talking to one person and watching another. Cats that don't look where they leap end up in the kitty litter."

"Tell him I'm sorry. I thought it was you."

"Kara—that femme-fatale at the back table by the window," Sallings said to Stark and the phone at the same time. "She says to tell you that she wants your bod so bad, she'd do anything for it, including buying you a drink."

"Liza!" the voice shouted from the phone.

A little embarrassed, but having fun and settling into the ambience of the place, Stark replied, "Should I ask for more or sell myself for a drink?"

"Sold!" Sallings said into the phone. "See, that's how easy it is to buy a male detective nowadays. They're easy. Come on over, gals."

After a few pats at their hair, a quick check of mascara, lipstick, and eye shadow, the two women smoothed out their dresses, folded up shop, and came over to Stark's and Sallings' table. Kara was the taller of the two women, but Olivia was the prettier of the two. Stark was definitely physically attracted to her. She was wearing a full-skirted southern-style dress with a wide-brimmed straw hat set jauntily on one side of her head. Chestnut hair cascaded from under the hat, was caught into a ponytail that hung over one shoulder and fell midway to her waist. Stark estimated she was about five-three and couldn't tip the scales at more than a hundred pounds. There were no visible scars or identifying marks, just dimples and a mischievous look in her eyes.

"Hi!" Kara said to Stark as he stood beside the table to greet them. Her dark eyes flashed excitement and fun. "I'm Kara and this is Ollie and we won't wait on this butch cop to introduce us."

"Butch!" Liza exclaimed indignantly. "If you go to bed with one of Kara's old boyfriends, she never forgives you."

"Old boyfriend! Try ex-husband! It doesn't matter; it was probably the most excitement he's had in the past ten years. Too bad it didn't get to his heart. It would have served you both right."

"Kara!"

"Well, if you feel it; say it! Hello, handsome."

"Hellooo, Kara. Hello, Ollie," Stark bowed slightly and pulled out a chair for each of them. "I'm Michael Stark."

"Look! My God, he even has manners," Ollie said, pointing to the offered chair.

"Yes," Liza replied. "It looks like there is a little good breeding left in the world. That's why he got my personal recommendation for the job."

"I'll bet," Kara replied. "What do you think, Ollie?"

"No, chance. He's got to have more than manners to get old Law and Order interested."

"That's below the belt!" Sallings said.

"That's what we were referring to," Ollie laughed.

Liza shook her head and feigned anger. "And to think I honestly call these female tigers my friends—friends like these, I ought to lock up. I must be losing my mind. Do you think I'm becoming a masochist or something? Maybe I'll call that radio-psychologist tomorrow and ask him what's wrong with me."

"Well, how about it?" Sallings asked, a pitcher of Margaritas and two hours later. "Do you ladies think we ought to buy this gentleman dinner? Think he's worth it?"

"Why not?" Kara answered. "You name the place, Liza, since you have first rights to him."

"Oh, no. That's not allowed on the job. No fraternization."

"That's right," Stark replied. "It's called look and and don't touch."

"Sure!" The other two women echoed.

"Let's go to the Laughing Gull," Kara said, "It's a revolving restaurant on top of the Hilton. I think he'll like it. They specialize in seafood and Spanish food. Have you been there yet, Michael?"

"Nope, but it sounds good. Is that all right with you, Liza?"

"Fine with me."

"Then we're off," he said, getting up to help them with their chairs.

Beneath the blackened waters of the Gulf of Mexico the tiger shark was searching for prey. During the afternoon, he had consumed several dozen horseshoe crabs and small conches, an assortment of beer cans and beach litter, a Labrador Retriever that had strayed too far from shore, and he was still hungry. Keeping more than five thousand pounds of body weight in constant motion meant the huge fish had to be constantly searching for food. Night was his natural feeding time and he knew the bigger fish were in close to shore. He turned in that direction.

On Clearwater's Big Pier 60, a young man high on alcohol and drugs took a midnight plunge into the Gulf waters. His friends begged him to stop—to swim in! He refused, shouting over and over, "I'm shark bait! I'm shark bait!"

Suddenly his shouting stopped. His friends couldn't see him in the dark water, but the tiger shark had. The huge fish was a little less hungry and there was another missing person on the Suncoast.

Michael Stark's left eye opened briefly before shutting down tightly to avoid the morning sunlight. It opened again and dully focused on the clock beside the bed. It was eight o'clock, two hours past his normal waking time. It was also Sunday morning and the sound of the surf hitting far below was like the gentle thud of a sledgehammer on the top of his skull. "Oh Jesus," he thought, "to be bitten by the wicked witch Margarita is to suffer miserably the next morning."

"Female!" he sensed, and reached out beside him without opening the other eye or turning his head. She was there. He raised up on his elbows and forced both eyes to focus. It was Ollie. Her long hair splashed down her body, split over one rose-nippled breast, closed again and disappeared beneath the tangled blue sheets of Stark's king-sized bed.

Stark wanted to make love again but the hammering on the top of his head wouldn't stop and his mouth tasted like a garbage can on a hot July afternoon. He got up, wobbled, cursed his age, stuck his arms out for balance, and made his way gingerly into the bathroom. After a shave, a toothbrush, two swallows of mouthwash, four aspirin, and a glass of tomato juice, he started to feel a little bit human again. In fact, the sea breeze and salt air were returning the warmth to his loins.

Ollie never heard Stark rumbling and bumbling through the house. She slept on as easily as if she had lived in his condo all her life. The morning heat filled the room through the open patio doors and Ollie had kicked the sheets down to where they covered only one leg from the knee to just above her ankle. She was sleeping three-quarters on her back, one breast peeking through her long chestnut hair, the other just barely exposed from under her body.

"Just perfect," Stark thought. "Ten years too young, but perfect. Wouldn't look like that if she were ten years older. Then she'd be like me—starting to show a little wear." He slid under the sheet and felt her nestle against him as she woke up.

"What are you up to?"

He rolled over on top of her. "That's the best pun of the day, if you're ready for this."

"Try me."

They made love for the third time since they'd met the night before. And it was even better.

Ollie stepped out of the shower and grabbed a towel. "I'm hungry. Can we go somewhere and get some breakfast or do you have to go to work?"

"Police detectives over thirty-five years of age don't have to work on Sundays," Stark said with a smile, dabbing the towel at a few shower drops left between her breasts. "Didn't you know that? It's in their contract— *No Sundays, Holidays, or dangerous assignments. . . . This man is just two steps from retirement.*"

"Michael!" She slapped at him with her towel. "I thought you were serious!"

"I was. I just wish it were true. No, Sallings and I only have to work every other Saturday or Sunday—barring any emergency, and this is our Sunday off.

"Where do you want to eat breakfast? I'm still learning to find my way around this place. Where's a good place to go?"

"Well, the Holiday has a fantastic champagne brunch."

"Sounds fine."

Four more Excedrins, another glass of tomato juice, and walking to the Holiday instead of driving, made it possible for Stark to look at the brunch table with feigned enthusiasm. Ollie was feeling great—damnably great. Stark was realizing what the years did to one's resiliency.

"Isn't it fantastic!" Ollie said excitedly, "Look at everything. There's always twice as many things that look good to me as I can eat. And of course," she added in a sexy whisper, "a night with you and a third round in the morning helps whet the appetite."

"I think you're right. Although, it helps if you don't hit the Margarita wagon quite so heavily the night before."

"Load up your plate. You'll feel better with something in your stomach."

"You're right." Stark loaded his plate with scrambled eggs, bacon, fried potatoes, and cantaloupe. He knew he'd feel better after he ate—he always did.

They took a table overlooking the beach and the surging waves.

Stark started having a case of the guilts. It bothered him that Ollie was so young and that he didn't want to get involved. Casual sex always unsettled him the next day. "I have a sort of confession to make. Last night I wanted to be an old pro or to seem like one, but I guess I'm a fake." The waiter interrupted his speech, pouring them each a glass of André Pink Champagne and leaving the bottle in a plastic ice-bucket.

Ollie looked down at her plate. "What do you mean? You don't owe me any explanations and certainly not any apologies—I'm not complaining at all, as long as you ask me out again."

"It's not an apology, really. It's just that I feel sort of dishonest and it bothers me. I'm not a big swinging single. Last night I wanted to act suave, sophisticated, and swashbuckling, but I'm really not. You see, my wife and I split up some time back, and to tell the truth, you're one of the few women I've been to bed with since then. I'm new at all of this. And to be honest, I guess I'm not too hot to get involved again."

Ollie looked at Stark warmly. She squeezed his hand across the table. "I knew that without your telling me. And if you eliminated all the people in Brannigan's who were faking being as sophisticated as they seem, Brannigan's would be out of business in a week! I just wanted someone honest to be with last night—and as far as committments go, I've been married and divorced, too. I'm not ready to go that route again, either."

"Thanks. I just didn't feel right. Maybe I'll learn."

"I hope not. That's why I went home with you instead of alone like I usually do."

# 7. GOLF

The telephone was ringing when Stark walked into his condo. "Hi, Detective Stark! I hope I didn't wake you up," Petit said cheerfully into the phone. "Detective Sallings said you'd probably be up long before now."

"At twelve-thirty in the afternoon; who are you kidding? Anyway, Petit, don't you ever go home?"

"I have to work every other Sunday, same as you; unless you want to put in a recommendation that I ought to get a better deal than that."

"Oh, you'd rather work every Sunday, then."

"Your ass, too!"

"What do you need, Petit?"

"They've located Reames's boat. They're going to send divers down and Detective Sallings is going out there to watch on her boat."

"Her boat?"

"Yeah, she has quite a boat and she wanted to know if you wanted to go with her. And if you do, I'm supposed to tell you that she'll be at the marina. Her boat is at that marina near your place—Cormorant Hole Marina."

"I know where it is."

"O.K., the name of her boat is *Sunday's Grouper.*"

*Sunday's Grouper* turned out to be quite a boat in Stark's opinion. It was a thirty-six-foot aft-cabin cruiser by Carver. It was plush, lean, and sleek. It also looked brand-new and raised a few questions in Stark's mind when he saw it.

"Permission to come aboard, Captain?" Stark saluted as he stood looking the craft over.

"Permission granted."

Stark let out a long appreciative whistle, "This is some boat!"

"Thanks."

"Jesus," he said, peeking around the rail. "It looks brand-new. Is it?"

"Almost, damnit. Now tell me what you really wanted to ask and didn't."

"I didn't ask a thing!" Stark knew he was caught.

"You were thinking it and don't deny it. Half the damn town thinks I'm running drugs or taking payoffs on the side."

"All right then, I'll bite," Stark poked his head inside the boat. "How many bales does she hold?"

"Damn you. Exactly none!" Sallings closed the cabin door. "But I'll have to admit, she is a little bit of an embarrassment. You see, last December my Dad visited me for Christmas. He owns the Orinco Pharmaceutical Company. Ever heard of it?"

"Just every time I walk into a drugstore."

"Well, I happen to be this black sheep daughter—you know, the one who wouldn't join the company or become a doctor, the one who wouldn't settle down after college and get married like a good little girl should. Instead I decided I wanted to be a cop. And as you can guess, that didn't thrill my Dad too much. But I'm still the one Dad has the most fun with; and in some ways, he respects me more for doing what I wanted than he does my brothers and sisters.

"To make a long story short, we went fishing one Sunday on a charter boat and Dad caught over two hundred pounds of grouper and red snapper. He had a ball! I think he had more fun that day last Christmas than I've seen him have in years. I really enjoyed it, too. And enjoyed being with him! I think that was the closest we'd been in years and I told him I wished I had a boat big enough to take him out on any time he wanted to come down and go fishing. Two days after he left town, a boat dealer in Clearwater called me and said my boat was ready and that they had delivered it to my slip. When I got down here—there sat *Sunday's Grouper* with a Christmas Card that said the slip was paid for for five years and that the boat went with it! Merry Christmas, from Dad! He'd see me next summer!"

"Wow! Tell your old man that if he wants to adopt another kid, you know someone who's willing and able! That's one hell of a Christmas present!"

Stark wasn't kidding. The inside of the boat was as nice as a lot of houses and had more room that some Stark had seen. It had bunks in the forward section. The middle was a galley complete with a microwave oven, refrigerator, and ice-maker; a few stairs up from the center section was the living-dining room—the inside or lower helm—with a built-in stereo system and wet bar. At the rear, of course, was the aft-cabin with an oversized double bed.

Stark had drooled over a boat almost identical to this one in a large on-the-water boat show in Jacksonville earlier that summer. He had felt the boat was probably large enough so that he really wouldn't be afraid to go out in the Gulf or ocean on it. Stark was just a little intimidated by those huge bodies of water. They were a hell of a lot bigger than the lakes in Missouri or the Mississippi River; and besides, the fish down here bit back. Once he'd had a bad experience with that. But the bottom line was that Stark was not willing to risk over a hundred thousand dollars on a boat he didn't know that much about. Stark wasn't even positive that he wouldn't get seasick on the open seas. He had decided against the boat, but still longed for the beauty and freedom it represented.

He took a couple of steps up the ladder to look at the upper helm. "I looked at a boat like this once—just looked, mind you. I've forgotten how fast the salesman said it'd go."

"They tell you around thirty-five knots, but I'd say it's closer to thirty. As far as that goes, there are not that many days you can get anywhere near that speed. Pounds the hell out of you if there's any chop to amount to anything."

"And your Dad has never been on it?" Stark asked incredulously.

"Nope. I guess he was on it when he bought it. But that's it. I kept hoping he'd come on down like he promised, but he says he's too busy. He keeps saying maybe next month or the next or the next."

Stark shook his head and looked about him with wonderment and a touch of envy. "How did you learn how to run it? I mean you don't just hop on one of these things and take off, do you?"

"Well, you can," Sallings replied. "That's one of Florida's dumbest laws."

"What do you mean?"

"Well, you have to take a written test, a vision test, and a driving test to take a hundred-dollar junker-car out on the road. But you can take two-hundred-thousand-dollars worth of boat, pile twenty people on it and take off for Hell and there are absolutely no requirements, except paying for the registration slips and having the right equipment on board. You can be ninety-years old, deaf, half-blind, and have never ever set foot on a boat in your life. Now, isn't that crazy?"

"Yeah, it is. I'll watch out for deaf, half-blind, ninety-year-old boat captains from now on. But, you still didn't tell me how you learned how to use it. Did you take a course or something?"

"I grew up in Milwaukee—Whitefish Bay. And Dad always owned a thirty- or forty-foot boat. When I was a teenager, I was running the hell out of them on Lake Michigan. But yes, I did take a Coast Guard course, anyway. It teaches you a lot of stuff and lowers the insurance rates."

"Good enough, Captain. What can I do to help get her underway?"

"If you'll cast off the bowlines, I'll cast off the stern. The bowlines are the ones on the front of the boat," Sallings grinned.

"Cute! Whether you know it or not, I had a sixteen-foot boat in St. Louis and I do know a little bit about these things. Well," he paused, looking around again, "maybe not much about boats quite this big, but I do know where the damned bow is."

"Then I dub you First Mate. Now, let's see how much we can bang it up against the pilings trying to get it out of here."

"Sounds good, Captain. Bang away."

Sallings pulled slickly out of the berth without ever coming close to the dock pilings. Stark was impressed.

It was one of those doldrum-days of summer when the afternoon brought no breeze at all. Old-time residents on the beach knew it was a time to dread. Normally the afternoon sea breeze kept the mosquito menace to a minimum, but on calm days it was open season on citizens. All the protected mangrove swamps on the bay side of Surfside and the mushy spoil islands between Surfside and the mainland were the Promised Land for Florida's famous and vicious mosquitoes. More than once they had driven jailbreakers out of swamps that sheriff's posses and alligators couldn't reach. They had sent hardened fishermen home empty-handed and campers high-tailing it for the nearest motel with locked windows and air-conditioning. Window screens were little protection against the indomitable creatures. As one old-timer had told Stark at a campground in Naples, "If'n they can't find a way in or around that screen, they'll just up and bite a hole right through it, sharpenin' their beak on the way through!"

The old-timer had been talking about the worst of

all Florida mosquitoes—the saltwater variety. During these windless summer days, instead of being blown down into the trees or across the bay to pester some poor mainlander, they rose out of the mangroves, out of the marshes, out of the tidal pools in great grey clouds and traveled wherever they wished. They descended on beach residents like the sons of Nippon on Pearl Harbor. They came in wave after wave, avoiding determined swats with aerobatic agility to relentlessly nail their prey. When they attacked, the fire department was deluged with calls, the Police department got calls—anyone who would answer a phone got a call. The next morning the county helicopter would spray the area, but the number of mosquitoes they were able to kill and the number surviving and hatching to take their place were at odds. It was a pyrrhic victory. Each day brought newly-hatched mosquitoes—each generation just a little more tolerant to insecticide than their predecessors.

Once Sallings had piloted *Sunday's Grouper* out of the marina's No Wake Zone where the wash from her engine would rock and damage moored boats, she opened the throttle. "What's down there?" Stark asked with raised eyebrows as the bow came out of the water and the *apparent* wind cut across the bridge.

"It has twin 454-Chevy gas engines. Thank God, Dad spared me the diesel and all the fumes." Sallings lowered the trim tabs and settled the craft back to a flatter plane.

Stark acted defeated and disgusted. "It must be nice, is all I can say; to be a police detective, look like a beauty queen, have a rich old man, and a boat like this. And I guess you have to beat the men off with a stick. And don't tell me—you have an eighteen-room mansion complete with servants, on the Gulf, too."

"Don't I wish!" Sallings laughed.

Sallings looked a lot better to Stark in her bikini than she did in street clothes. Stark was having trouble keeping his eyes from where they shouldn't be and maintaining his objectivity. Sallings seemed more at ease on the water than on land.

"I'm so rich," Liza said, "that I moved out of my apartment and onto the boat so I could get out of paying rent. I live on this thing."

"Really?"

"I sure do. Just because my Dad's rich, doesn't mean I am. I guess I will be some day, but that's a long way off. I wasn't sure that I'd like living on it at first, but now I don't think I could move back on land."

"I think I'll stick to land for a while. Maybe later on I can get you to teach me how to run one of these jobs."

"Sure, sit down and enjoy yourself. There are premixed Bloody-Marys, Margaritas, and Manhattans down in the refrigerator and beside the couch is a bar that has a brand new bottle of Jack Daniels Black."

"No, thanks!" Stark rubbed his stomach. "After last night, I think I'll pass for a day or two."

"Well, there're soft drinks in there, too. Just what did you two do last night, or maybe I shouldn't ask?"

"Let's just say I found out how old I am and leave it at that."

Sallings laughed.

Stark saw the blush on her face, "I'll tell her you told me all about her."

"Michael! You wouldn't!"

"Of course not," he teased, "as long as she tells me all the inside stuff about you."

"Oh, Jesus. You are a bastard. You know that? How would you like to try walking back to shore once we get to the salvage site?"

"I think I understand your meaning perfectly, Captain. Your name will never be mentioned."

"Smart man! You know, you're more of a tease than I am?"

"I wouldn't say that; but since you're the boss, I'll have to accept it."

The upper helm, the flying bridge, had three plush custom-leather chairs. Sallings was at the controls in the middle one. Stark settled into the chair on the right, popping the top on a can of Tab.

Sallings patted the back of his seat. "You know ninety-five percent of my passengers sit in that seat rather than the one on the left. I guess after years of sitting on the right-hand side of a person at the steering-wheel of a car, you only feel comfortable in that spot."

"That fits," Stark replied, not sure he wanted to be like ninety-five percent of the rest of the populace. "I would guess that's also a little more comfortable from your perspective."

"You've got it. I'm uneasy if someone gets in the left-hand chair. Crazy, isn't it?"

Michael nodded his head and became introspective as the backside of the island slid past. He had been watching Sallings out of the corner of his eye. Her brief bikini and tanned body were bothering him. He knew that he couldn't get involved and keep his job—that if there were a choice to be made between them, she had all the history and friends on her side. But he didn't understand why she was in a bikini. His paranoia said to watch out for some sort of trap, but he couldn't believe it. He'd told her he had no desire for her job—that he didn't want to be chief of detectives and he thought she believed him. "After all," he told himself, "she's the one that asked for me to be put on the force. Essentially she's the one who got me the job." Stark decided she was more comfortable on the boat. It was her home and probably that was how one went boating down here. He was determined that it wasn't going to become a stumbling block. The sexual thing had never been a problem for him before. He'd had several female partners, but none who looked like Sallings or whom he enjoyed being with as much as he did her.

Feeling the silence and realizing that Stark was physically attracted to her, Sallings sort of wished she had worn something a little less revealing but still, she liked the attention and admiration. To make up for it, she started a running commentary as they went. "You've got to be real careful back here and follow the channel markers closely. You know, the bay is about three miles wide at this point and it looks like it ought to be deep; but at low tide there's hardly a place that's over two feet deep."

"You're kidding. Where's the tide now?"

"We're pretty close to high tide, so I have a little leeway." Sallings cut the engine to avoid a couple of kids on a catamaran who were sailing across her path.

"Damn it! They ought to change the law on those damned things, too. Even when the tide's up there's still not that much water out here. You'll ground out in most places. But the law says you have to give up right of way to anything with a sail."

"I know." Stark watched the kids cut closely in front of the boat. "My son used to have one of them."

In a few minutes they rounded the end of the island, passed through the channel, and slid into the Gulf. "We can let her roll now," Sallings said. She pushed the throttles all the way forward, adjusted the trim again, and eased back the speed just a bit. The spear-headed white craft sliced effortlessly through the undulating green blanket of water. Behind them the twin engines plowed boiling white furrows into a long foamy V with Stark and Sallings at it's apex.

A big smile cut across Stark's face and he leaned back in the chair. "Now this is style! This is what real boating is all about."

"I like it, too," Sallings smiled. "Now, why don't you take the helm."

"Are you sure?"

"Sure, try it!" She got up from the middle seat and stood behind it.

Stark slid across, took the wheel, and felt the power and majesty of the craft below him. "My sixteen-foot bowrider wasn't quite like this," he said admiringly.

"I never dreamed I'd have a boat like this. You can't imagine how much I've enjoyed it."

"I'll bet. And I'll bet it doesn't impress the men or anything either, does it?"

"Now that's a low blow," her tan hid the tinge of a blush that rose to her face. "But it's true. I'll have to admit it. You can drop anchor a couple of hundred yards off the beach, turn on the stereo, break out the Bloody Marys, and before you can get one down, you'll have one of those tanned beachies bumping his inflatable mattress against the swim-platform asking to see the boat. It's great for your ego the first couple of times, but that's it! I know it's a clichè, but I like to be liked for me and not just for my body or my boat or because it's a huge conquest to bed down a lady cop. So in some ways it's not so great. I get hit on a lot and I'm never sure why."

"You ever hear of looking a gift horse in the mouth? You know, you could look like Godzilla and spend all your evenings with the boob-tube."

"Yeah."

"Then shut up and enjoy it! Here take the helm back before I sink this thing for you."

"Who's lucky and who's rich? Just wait, my friend. Maybe I have *boat* personality, but you're gonna get a taste of the old-fashioned *four-wheel* personality with your brand new Lincoln Town Car. You know, there's not that many people your age with your money, your condo, your car. And being a big he-man hero cop on top of it—are you ever gonna get hit on a lot."

"Break my heart! See if you hear me cry—"

"Son-of-a-bitch!" Sallings interrupted, a momentary look of alarm on her face. "Hold on, Michael!" She spun the wheel and turned the boat hard to port, as a huge, dark underwater mass slid by the side of the boat.

"What the hell was that," Stark asked, jumping up and holding onto the aluminum struts of the Bimini top. "Was it a log? It wasn't a fish, was it? Tell me it wasn't a fish."

"I don't know what it was. But I sure as hell almost collided with it. Let's take a look. If it was a log, at the speed we were going, it would have gone through us like a torpedo!"

She turned the yacht in a tight circle and cut the throttle as she neared her wake. The boat sat down in the water and slowed to a crawl almost immediately. Both of them stood up and searched the water as Sallings inched the craft forward.

"It was a fish, wasn't it?" Stark asked. "That wasn't a log. It was a fish. A goddamned shark! I've seen that shadow before!"

"What? Where?"

"A little girl was killed right in front of me in Galveston. I saw it happen."

"I'm sorry, Stark. I didn't know about that. Was she a friend?"

"No. She was just a pretty little kid who was bitten almost in two not even three feet away from me. I saw the shadow, saw him grab the kid, and I just stood there. There wasn't anything I could do, it was over so fast. I still feel like I should have done something, though."

"Christ! Did they get the shark or anything?"

"As far as I know that's the last they saw of either one of them—the body was never found. I guess the bastard ate her. But I haven't been too fond of sharks since then."

"So maybe it wasn't a log; but that doesn't mean it was a huge shark."

"Then what the hell do you think it was? A giant guppy? Come on, Liza, I tell you that shadow was a shark! I may be from St. Louis, damnit, but I'm not naive!"

"For Christ's sake, Stark! Okay. Let's not fight over it. Look, it could have been. but that's no big deal. We have a lot of sharks here. And some hammerheads and tigers get pretty big. But I didn't see any shark. Did you? Now, really. Did you see a fin above the water or anything? It was probably a pilot whale or maybe several dolphins close together. They'll fool you that way. Honest."

Surfside Police Detective Michael Stark sat back down in the chair decidedly more uncomfortable than he had been a few minutes earlier. He had that feeling again that he'd had in St. Louis after the very first sniper killing—something was not right in his world. He could feel the goose-bumps on his arms and the shivers running down his spine.

Sallings checked her chart and compass. "Well, they ought to be dead ahead, just about here." She jabbed a finger at a spot on the chart, trying to distract Stark and change his mood.

Stark remained silent, staring at the water in front of him and only barely nodding to Sallings's incessant commentary. He had a lot of private thoughts and he was not voicing them. A picture was forming, vaguely coming into focus in the back of his mind, and he didn't like how it was making him feel. So far, the picture was one big finned grey cloud of foreboding.

The Galveston incident had unnerved him a lot more than he had told Sallings. Initially, he had felt good about himself and what had happened in St. Louis; but after losing his job, being crucified by the press, and losing his wife and children, Stark had started feeling personally inadequate again. And when he had stood frozen in fear and just watched the small child be carried out to sea, he had started having some doubts about himself. He had even wondered if he had to do it again, if he would have the guts to face the sniper.

"There they are!" Sallings stood and pointed to the horizon. Stark raised the binoculars to his eyes. Through the exaggerated bouncing of the lenses he could make out the cluster of boats and the salvage derrick.

"*Mangrove Snapper*, this is *Sunday's Grouper*, Whiskey-Foxtrot-Romeo-Four-Nine-Three-Six.

"Go ahead, Detective," the radio rasped back at her.

"I'm about four miles away from your position. I have you in sight. What's happening, Jim?"

"Nothing much so far. I can see you, too. We're sitting over the wreck. It's only twenty-three feet down. A couple of divers went down on it, but they couldn't get inside. The cabin door is locked or jammed or something. They're hooking lines to it now so they can get it to the surface."

"O.K., we'll be there in a minute. *Sunday's Grouper*, Whiskey-Foxtrot-Romeo-Four-Nine-Three-Six, clearing Channel 16 and out."

Sallings eased her boat next to the *Mangrove Snapper*, a big beautiful motor yacht that looked like a ship compared to her boat. "That's a Hatteras sixty-five-foot motor yacht. Nice, isn't it?"

"I'll say," Stark replied. "Looks like a damned oceanliner! It's fantastic!"

"Yeah. The guy who owns it is Jim Rainford. He

sells them. He owns Surfside Yacht Sales and is one of the city commissioners. Hell of a nice guy, too. I'll introduce you in just a minute."

A big burly man wearing white, lambchop sideburns and a little blue Greek fishing cap tossed Stark a line. "Drop your fenders and tie up alongside, mate."

"He means the rubber things that keep the boats from scratching each other, Detective Michael."

"I know what he means," Stark said, trying to toss off his gloomy mood. He even managed to laugh and add a touch of disdain to his voice. "How the hell am I going to get you to come off that crap? Make you walk the plank or something?"

"Detective? Michael?" Lambchops asked. "Are you Detective Stark?"

"Last time I looked." Stark extended his hand over his head in a handshake as he clumsily lashed the two boats together.

"I'm Jim Rainford—Captain Jim, most people call me." The muscular man climbed down onto Liza's boat. "But I'll settle for just Jim. The captain part is mostly advertising. Glad to meet you. I've heard a lot about you."

"Have you?" Stark said guardedly, behind a smile. "Good or bad?"

"Good! Good! I'm on the City Commission, but I was down in the Bahamas when you interviewed and didn't get a chance to meet you. Everyone else thought you were just super and that we were lucky to get you. I've been meaning to stop in and introduce myself. I just haven't gotten caught up since I've been back. You know how that goes."

"You better believe I do."

"Well, it doesn't matter. It's more fun to meet you out here anyway—even if it's not the happiest of occasions. I'm glad you took the job."

"Now watch it," Sallings said. "You're going to swell his head like a balloon. You see, the only reason I brought him out here was so I could be captain of the boat and teach him that men are really unnecessary. In a few years, we women will clone people and make the male obsolete."

Stark just grinned and shook his head.

"I've been teaching him the finer points of boating, such as where the port and starboard sides are, that the anchor is not a large fish hook, and all sorts of good stuff like that. He's from St. Louis, you know. That's Huck Finn country—where you race matchbox sailboats on frog ponds."

Rainford looked at Stark and laughed, clasping his shoulder with a calloused hand. "And you took this job for these kinds of wisecracks—right?"

"That's all I've heard since I stepped on this damned thing." Stark finished winding the line around the rear cleat. "Unless you own the Queen Mary or were born and raised on the ocean or the glorious Great Lakes, this broad won't give you credit for knowing a boat from a bathtub and thinks you'd put a motor on either one."

"I believe it. I was boating when she was wearing diapers and she even hassles me."

Stark took a close look at Jim Rainford. He was a little awed by him, yet felt he was a little too friendly, certainly a little too familiar with Sallings. In addition to owning the Suncoast's largest yacht dealership, Rainford was reputed to be a millionaire; some said a millionaire several times over. Stark knew you didn't get that rich being the world's nicest guy. Still, Captain Blanchert had told Stark that Jim's money had not gone to his head. Rainford still had the same friends he'd always had, in spite of living much more expensively, having a Rolls, this boat, and a huge home. Captain Blanchert had added that Rainford was willing to work as a salesman, a parts manager, an ad-man—and even a janitor if he saw something dirty in his shop. He worked Saturdays, Sundays, and burnt a lot of midnight oil. He spent a lot of time on his boats. He knew what he sold. He believed in them or he didn't sell them.

Stark could identify with a lot of that in himself; but there was still something about Jim Rainford that made him wary. He liked the man, wanted to be his friend; but something was wrong, he had that uneasy feeling again. Something inside kept telling him to keep this man at a distance. It puzzled him, but Stark had learned in Vietnam that you lived a lot longer if you listened to those little voices inside you.

"If this gal hassles you too much," Rainford said to Stark, "tell her to go take a flying leap and give me a call. You can go out with me and I won't hassle you. I go out almost everyday and you're welcome anytime. Just give me a call."

"It's a deal, as long as I don't have to swab all that deck!"

"Don't worry," Jim said. "I have a fifteen-year-old boy and a fourteen-year-old daughter. You'd be stealing their jobs if you even thought about it."

"Tell them not to worry! It's all theirs."

"See here," Liza said, making herself comfortable

in one of the plush aft-deck chairs she'd bought for the Carver with her six month bonus. "Between the two of us, we're going to make a yachtsman out of him yet. He already knows what work to avoid—probably thinks scrubbing is woman's work. Nevertheless, in another year we'll have him trading that condo of his for one of those sixty-five-foot jobs like you have."

"You should have seen the shark we saw on the way out here," Stark said.

"Is that right?" Jim looked at Liza.

"I don't know," she said. "We saw something pretty big, but I couldn't tell what it was. Stark is sure it was a shark. Of course, if I'd had a night like his, I'd be seeing sharks, elephants, and giraffes, too."

"Jesus. Isn't anything private?" Stark laughed.

"What happened?" Jim asked.

"Oh, nothing much." Sallings propped her feet on the teak cockpit table. "Kara, Ollie and I took him out for dinner and a few drinks and now he has a case of traumatic post-margarita-itis."

"You have my sympathy," Rainford replied. "You've got more guts than I do, going out with that crew. I think I'd be seeing sharks in the water and in the trees, behind bushes—even in my own bathtub."

"Tell you what," Sallings said seriously. "The more I think about it, the more I think Stark may have been right. That shadow did look a hell of a lot like a shark. I've seen a few from this boat—and let me tell you, it wasn't a hell of a lot smaller than this boat either."

"Oh, come on!" Rainford interrupted. "Get serious. That's all Surfside needs is a hysterical female and a freshwater baby for it's detective force." He laughed and slapped Stark on the back, "You two sound like a couple of kids camping out and scaring each other with stories about the boogey-man. Come on now. Don't you guys go spreading any tall tales like that around town. Tourist business is bad enough as it is."

Rainford pointed to the salvage operation. "There's what we have to worry about right down there. It's not sharks, but dumb fools in little bitty boats who go offshore where they shouldn't and when they shouldn't—and I'll bet you a dime to a dollar they didn't have the radio on and never heard the storm warnings. Let me go get you both a drink while we wait for them to get that boat up."

"No! No," Sallings protested, "We have plenty on board. What do you want?"

Stark was pretty sure he didn't like Rainford at all; he just wondered why Sallings did.

## 8. HOTEL

The island of Surfside was teeming with beachgoers. Sunday afternoon was the busiest time of the week. The causeway was a solid ribbon of cars going westward from ten in the morning until three in the afternoon and then around four, like a changing tide, the ribbon reversed itself; the westward lanes thinned out and those eastward became solid steel, fiberglass, sweat, and screaming kids. Tempers, out in the sun too long and soaked with one beer to many, flared easily. Horns blared, drivers yelled curses and jabbed fuck-you fingers in their rear view mirrors. The crunching of fenders pierced the air with startling regularity. It happened every Sunday from February through September. The natives were ready for it to end.

On the beach itself, the frosted sand had turned into thousands of yards of towels, blankets, and oiled skin stretching endlessly; punctuated every so often by bright beach umbrellas and multi-colored covered cabanas. They were owned and rented out by a deeply-tanned blond beach-bum type with a beard of the same color. He ranged restlessly through the crowd with a notebook in one hand and a metal box in the other. Although he looked shiftless; inefficient, he was not. With an unerring accuracy he had developed through years of plying his trade, he remembered everyone who had rented a cabana or an umbrella during the course of the day and those who had not. He went from one to the other, and when he found one occupied by the wrong person—a cabana that the previous renters had left early and someone had tried to slide into without paying for—he went up to them with a jocular smile, pulled his hat from his head in a sweeping bow and said, "Good afternoon, folks! I'm Coconut. It looks as if you folks would like to rent an umbrella. They're nice, aren't they? It'll cost you two bucks an hour or you can have it all day for eight. The only thing is, you can't give it to someone else when you leave. Fair enough? I have to eat too, you know." It worked! Almost all of them forked over the money for at least one hour.

The Gulf was bathwater temperature; warm and toasty in the afternoon sun. The beach was a zoo! Frizbees fought the sea gulls for airspace and radios competed with seven-year-olds as attention-getters. The strollers strutted. The blanket-bound admired. And if you were in a lucky position, you might even be able to see the water or hear the waves.

Surfside's shoreline followed a familiar pattern. It was the same as most of the other barrier islands along Florida's west coast. It started out very shallow. You had to go a long way out into the Gulf to hit water that one would really call deep. Usually the water would go from nothing to waist deep or chest high within fifty to a hundred yards off shore; and then, an underwater island suddenly appeared. At mean low tide the underwater island would become exposed as a sandbar or be only an inch or two under water. People would be walking along a hundred-and-fifty yards from shore in water that was, at times, only ankle deep. From the shore, it gave the illusion they were walking on water. The kids loved to play in the trough of water three to four deet deep between the sandbar and shore.

This underwater contour was beautiful, fun, and dangerous! When the waves were high, pushed in by the winds and offshore storms, the water would pile up behind the sandbar. Sometimes the water behind the bar became a significant and dangerous few inches higher than the rest of the Gulf. When it did, it had to escape back out to sea. It would search for a weak spot in the underwater sandbar, a place of least resistance—particularly a pier or pilings that would break the incoming flow of waves and create an outflow that could be used to shoot the piled up water back out to sea. If there was no pier or piling, the trapped water would seek out a weak spot in the bar itself; a spot where the bar was scarred or a place there was a dent made by grass, shells or the natural sweep of the current—anything that made it a little more narrow than the rest of the bar.

Through this weak point the water would start, flowing in a steady stream out to sea. It would begin digging a tiny trench only a few inches wide and a few inches deep. As the waves continued to pile up and the pressure kept increasing, the outflow would become greater and greater and the trench would grow deeper and wider. And, depending on the size of the body of water trapped behind the bar and the amount and speed of the waves replenishing it, the current could become dangerously strong. *Undertow*, the uninformed called it; *rip-current* was the term used by scientists. Regardless, it was a giant mass of water reaching from the bottom of the trench to the surface that was racing back out to sea, expending itself anywhere from one hundred and fifty yards to a quarter of a mile offshore. Sometimes the rip-current was only a few yards wide; other times it was much wider. Sometimes the current was only strong enough to startle a wader; other times it swept the strongest swimmers out to sea.

The sandbars and accompanying troughs of water held another danger, too—sharks! The Shark Attack File is replete with accounts of sharks cruising or being trapped in the shallow channel between the shoreline and the offshore sandbars. Only a few miles south of Surfside, on Siesta Key at Sarasota, on July 23, 1958, young Douglas Lawton was savagely mauled by a tiger shark as he played in a four-foot trough of water like the one at Surfside. Today history was about to repeat itself.

Carol Swenson had been in Surfside for almost two weeks. She had come down with her sixteen-year-old twin brother, Sean, and their mother from La Crosse, Wisconsin, for a two-week vacation at the Surfside

Hilton. Everyday they played in the Gulf and worked at getting as much of a tan as was possible in order to impress everyone back home. Neither of the kids had tasted saltwater before and they were awed by the white beaches, the towering buildings, and the surrounding ring of glittering green water. "Come on, let's swim," Sean said to his sister, standing in the inch-deep water on the offshore sandbar and pointing out towards the Gulf.

"I'm afraid to go out any further," Carol said. "It gets deep and there may be sharks out there."

"Oh come on," Sean taunted. "Don't be such a sissy. They don't have sharks on public beaches for Christ's sake. If they did, they wouldn't have any tourists."

"I'm still afraid."

"Maybe this will help motivate you." He stepped behind her; with one hand at the neck knot and another at the back knot, he whipped away his sister's bikini top with one swift swipe, leaving her topless.

Two hundred yards away, at the end of the sandbar, a foot-long mullet and dozens of baitfish lept from the water as if it were boiling.

"Sean!" Carol shouted, folding an arm across her fully developed young breasts. "Give me my top back!" That magic phrase turned ever male head within earshot.

"Come after it." Sean dove into the fifty-yard channel between the sandbar and the shore and surfaced twenty feet away in chest-deep water dangling the red-and-white striped bikini top at his sister. "You can either try to take it away from me or go without it like they do at the end of the beach."

"Sean, you bastard!" Carol was a little mad, a little embarrassed, and at the same time, a little aroused by finding herself suddenly topless among all these strangers. In fact, she probably enjoyed the admiration a bit more than she was annoyed at the embarrassment. Throwing her modesty out to sea, she raised her arms above her head and dove into the water, giving the crowd a fleeting glimpse of her darkly-tanned breasts capped with white bikini-markings. She came out of the water ten feet in front of her brother, boldly jutting her breasts out and tossing her long blond hair back with a flip of her head. "All right, damn you. Give me back my top, right now!"

"And ruin all this fun?" Sean teased, waving the bikini top at the crowd of spectators.

Succumbing to the embarrassment of having several hundred people watch her argue topless, she hunched down in the water to cover her breasts and uttered a low guttural threat, "You little rat. If you don't give me my top back, I'm going to tell mother that I woke up and caught you playing with me while I was asleep."

"You weren't asleep," he whispered back. "You were just pre . . ." Sean lost his voice. The fin surfaced for just a second or two before it disappeared, stopping Sean's retort in mid-sentence. It had towered over a foot above the water but had disappeared so quickly that, for a second, Sean wondered if it weren't his imagination. But others had seen it too and for a moment all noise ceased except for two women who were facing the opposite direction talking about a restaurant they had gone to. Their inane chatter sounded shrill in the still air of silence.

Seeing the look of terror on her brother's face, Carol twisted sideways in the water to see what was behind her. She first heard someone scream "Shark!" just as the huge fish hit her with the impact of a mid-sized car, tearing through the water at ten miles per hour. He burst from the water, his bloody curved teeth clamped in Carol's left buttock and the back-half of her lower abdomen. Her striped bikini bottom dangled loosely from the side of the shark's mouth, leaving her now cruelly and completely naked in the struggle.

But being naked was Carol Swenson's last concern. She just wanted loose! To get rid of the crushing pressure and pain in her waist and hip. She pounded as hard as she could on the shark's blunt nose but her slim hands registered no effect. "Please, God! Help me, Sean! I don't want to die! Oh, it hurts! Please!"

Shaking his head violently, the tropical demon plunged underwater in a pink spray of blood, drowning the girl's pleas. A man standing close to Sean vomited into the water; a woman screamed, followed by dozens more; a man began to cry and hundreds of people stampeded to shore—and no one helped! Sean jumped in front of the shark as it turned and came back past him in the shallow water, only to be bumped completely out of the water by the impact. Landing across the shark's back he wrapped his leg around the great fin and grasped desperately at the gills for a handhold. For a moment he had Carol's hand in his, but he lost it as the fish went under. He dug deeply into the gills with his hands and it seemed to force the shark to the surface again. Carol was still crying.

"Ohhhh, Sean! God, stop him! Sean, don't let him get me."

The respite was momentary; her screams were smothered as the shark went back down, steadily making his way toward the end of the sandbar and into deeper water. Sean stuck his left hand down in the sharks mouth in a desperate attempt to pull his sister free. His ineffective, ingenuous action sealed his fate with excruciating pain as the cockscomb teeth sliced through his hand. The shark's abrasive skin and the hurtling speed ripped him off its back and from his sister's grasp.

On the Gulf side of the sandbar, Pete Blanchert and James Dodd had been watching the topless girl from Dodd's sixteen-foot boat when the attack began. Both boys acted swiftly. Dodd started the seventy-five-horse Mercury engine. Blanchert cut the anchor line with a fishing knife. James gunned the engine, speeding to the end of the sandbar. Almost flipping the boat, he made a tight U-turn to intercept the fish and girl. The shark turned sideways from the approaching boat; Dodd threw the throttle wide open and rammed the huge fish. They hit with such force that both boys were thrown to the floor of the boat. The shark stopped dead in the water with the bow of the boat resting on top of him. The mountainous scarred fin stood out like a giant scythe ready to slice into the boat. The tiger shark raised its head and the front of the boat came high out of the water, forcing the stern under and drowning out the engine when the water poured over the transom. The boat slid backwards off the shark's nose.

The monster turned and, from inches away, looked

at the boys. The protective nictitan slid down to cover the shark's eye; it was like looking into the blind eye of Hell. No one moved. Everyone was silent. Then almost defiantly, with the girl still in his mouth, the huge tiger shark jerked his head sideways, tearing at Carol's body, and started slowly past the boat, his back just inches below the water. The fin trailed a rippled bloody path in the lime green water—and another through Blanchert's and Dodd's memories forever.

Pete, a muscular body-builder, poised himself on the bow of the boat. Just as the shark passed, he leaned over the side and caught a handful of Carol's long blond hair in one hand and her arm in the other. Twisting quickly sideways, he flicked her body from the shark's mouth and whirled with it in a high-arching circle towards the boat. She was so light he could barely keep the momentum of the swing from carrying her body over the other side of the boat. He looked in his hands and saw why—only the top half was there.

James, the windshield, the boat cushions, and the engine were spattered with blood from the futile rescue attempt. It was too much for James. He hung over the transom never noticing how badly he was burning his hand on the engine as he retched into the sea.

Pete sank dull-eyed into the inch of water that had swamped the boat, clutching the lifeless naked half-woman to his stomach. He tried to speak but no words would come out. Absently, he pulled his beach towel from the seat and covered her breasts. He brushed the hair from her face, rocked back and forth, and cried.

The bottom half of Carol was still going steadily down the shark's gullet as he meandered out to sea.

"This is the United States Coast Guard Station, Clearwater, calling *Sunday's Grouper*. This is Clearwater-Coast-Guard-Station-calling *Sunday's Grouper!*"

"Now what do they want," Sallings complained, setting her drink on the table and getting out of her chair. "I guess I better go find out." Rather than climb to the upper helm, she decided to answer the call on the inside lower-helm radio, away from the noise of the salvage operation. She closed the custom-glass door behind her to keep in the air-conditioning. Stark and Rainford sat and waited. When Sallings switched on the inside radio, it cut off the one on the upper helm. The men were still able to faintly hear the conversation coming from the outside radio on Jim's boat.

"Clearwater Coast Guard, this is *Sunday's Grouper, WFR—Four-Nine-Three-Six.*"

"*Sunday's Grouper*, is this Captain Sallings?"

"Affirmative, this is Captain Sallings—over."

"Skipper, can you switch to Channel 22?"

"I'm switching now. WFR—Four-Nine-Three-Six, *Sunday's Grouper*, clearing Channel 16."

Jim's radio returned to its low-level staccato of silence as the conversation continued on the other channel.

Stark and Jim were watching the salvage efforts when a white-faced Sallings slid the door open. "Hey! You guys better get in here and hear this." Stark and

Rainford scrambled across the deck and down into the living room/control room of the aft-cabin cruiser. Sallings was back at the radio. "Clearwater Coast Guard. Clearwater Coast Guard. This is Captain Sallings, *Sunday's Grouper*. Would you repeat that message, please."

"Will do, Skipper. We just received an emergency call from your office, from Captain Blanchert, asking us to contact you and Detective Stark immediately. A large fish, reportedly a shark, has attacked one or more swimmers on Surfside beach. Captain Blanchert says he can't confirm how many casualties there are or if anyone has been killed at this time. He says the incident is causing a panic, and that a lot of people were hurt trying to leave the water, and more are being injured in car crashes in the parking lot and on the causeway. Your dispatcher says you wouldn't believe the mess they have out there. The police captain said to tell you he needs all the help he can get as fast as he can get it. Do you want us to send our chopper out after you? Please advise?"

Stark leaned back against the bulkhead speechless, a succession of looks: horror, disgust, and anger racing across his face. He slammed his first against the back of Liza's couch. His eyes flashed with the fury of a fire-bomb behind his dark sunglasses. He wanted to kill. "That bastard! That son-of-a-bitch!"

Liza pounded the inside helm. "Let's get him!"

The whole ordeal had lasted less than a few minutes and everyone on the beach who had seen it felt as if they were in suspended animation, unable to act.

Then suddenly, as if on cue, everyone had panicked and fled the water at once. Selfishness and self-preservation had prevailed—boyfriend had deserted girlfriend, husband had deserted wife, mother had deserted daughter. Each person's only thought was to escape the monster in the water.

The tiger shark's abrasive skin had scoured the flesh from Sean's arm and ribs to the bone. His left hand was almost completely severed and he was bleeding from another scrape the size of a basketball on his stomach. He was crying and covered with blood as he stumbled out of the water toward his dazed mother and the frantic crowd. He knew his sister was dead and he staggered with his arms outstretched in defeat. "Momma, Momma, I tried!"

"I know you did, Baby," she replied, reaching out to him, her contorted face not allowing any tears. "Sean you're hurt—Oh God, you're hurt bad!"

"Momma, I tried to stop him," he cried, not hearing her. "I tried. I had a hold of him—I had her in my hand—I just couldn't save her. I just want to die!"

"Don't say that, Sean. You did everything—everything you could. We've got to do something for you now."

"You don't understand, Momma. You didn't hear her begging me to help her."

"Mrs. Swenson realized her son was in shock and couldn't help himself. She folded her arms around him and screamed at the crowd, "Help me! Help me! Please someone, help my boy!"

A paramedic squeezed his way through the crowd and urged the people following him to back away as he started dressing the boy's wounds. Sean never saw him; the trauma and the loss of blood had been too much—he died with his head in his mother's lap.

Stark's knuckles turned white as his fingers dug into the velvet back of the couch. He pounded the top of it again. "I knew it! I knew it! I told you," he whipped off his sunglasses and shook them at Rainford. If we'd called in, this might not have happened!"

"That's right!" Sallings said, angrily slamming the microphone into its holder. "I didn't want to admit it, but I knew that shadow was a shark too. It's my fault."

"*Sunday's Grouper!* Skipper Sallings! Did you copy our transmission?" the Clearwater Coast Guard operator asked.

"This is Sallings. Yes I did. Give me a minute please."

"Stark, if we go all the way around to the marina, it's going to take us a while. But if we go straight into the beach, I can nose into shore and we'll be there in a few minutes—even before the helicopter could get here. We could drop anchor and see what we can do."

"Oh no!" Stark slid his sunglasses back over his nose. "I may be pissed at myself, but I'm not stupid. You've lost your damned mind if you think I'm wading through that fucking water between the boat and the beach. No way! Tell them to get that helicopter out here.

"Clearwater Coast Guard, this is *Sunday's Grouper*, let me give you our location and send that helicopter please."

"We have your location, Skipper. We'll have the helicopter there as soon as possible and we'll assist in any way we can. This is the United States Coast Guard at Clearwater clearing 22."

They went out onto the aft-deck. Stark and Sallings were angry; Rainford just seemed worried. "This is really unfortunate," Jim said. "But to tell you the truth, it's really not all that unusual, you know. And I'm sort of counting on you two to handle it with a little aplomb and delicacy."

"It's not *what?*" Stark asked incredulously.

"Well, I don't mean to make this sound like an everyday happening," Jim replied defensively. "But this is the damned Gulf you know, and it's full of stingrays, jellyfish, sea-snakes, and sharks. And if you load up the water with people the way we do, they're bound to run into each other; and sooner or later you're going to have an accident."

"An accident?" Stark extended his arms in a full circle above his head. "Being eaten alive by a shark with a mouth this big is an accident?"

"Yeah," Sallings added. "It sure as hell won't be such a blasé event if it's someone you know instead of a tourist, now will it? Come on Jim, there's a difference between being eaten alive and dying in a car wreck—that's an accident!"

"Now, you come on," Rainford said consolingly. "We don't even know that it was a shark for sure yet or how big it was—let alone that it ate somebody alive."

"The hell we don't," Stark lowered his voice. "We saw him on our way out here. Didn't we, Liza? She knows it—and you know it, too."

Sallings shook her head affirmatively. "He's right, I'd bet a year's pay on it."

"Jim, why don't you get back on your vessel. We'll start in and let the Coast Guard intercept us. That'll be a little faster, and the quicker one of us gets there and finds out what has happened, the better off we'll all be."

"Sure thing," Rainford replied. "You want me to tell the Coast Guard what you're doing so you don't have to bother calling them?"

"I'd appreciate that.

"Stark, think you can run this thing toward shore while I change out of this bikini?"

"Yeah, if you can get it started and away from the boats, I can handle it in the open water.

"Detective Stark," Jim said. "I'm really sorry this has happened. I mean it! This kind of thing doesn't happen down here often. It's a freak accident. When you get finished with this mess, let's get together for a drink or something."

"Sure," Stark said softly, not really answering. He stood blankly extending his hand for a handshake and seeing the St. Louis Arch in the night, hearing the nightmarish sounds of an M-16 splattering death across his Mississippi waterfront.

The pandemonium and confusion on the beach had to be the worst Stark had ever seen. Fear and panic had spread utter disaster for four solid miles across the causeway. The beach parking lot looked like a demolition derby racetrack. Stark had seen bad traffic jams in St. Louis, but this made them look like a child's crossword puzzle. Slowly, the city police, aided by sheriff's deputies and the highway patrol, started the traffic flowing again. The flashing red lights and uniforms brought a calm to the tempest and restored a semblance of order.

"Christ!" Stark thought, a foot on the bumper of a rammed car, "It'll be a two-week job just filling out the reports, filing them, and following up on the accidents here in this parking lot alone!" After most of the snarl had been untangled, he called Sallings on his shoulder radio and asked her to pick him up.

"I'll be there in just a minute, Stark. I'm in the middle of the causeway on the emergency road. Some idiot just ran over one of our auxiliary policemen who was directing traffic."

"Is he dead?"

"No, but he appears to have been bumped pretty bad. I don't know if he's broken anything. But I'm insisting he stay off his feet and waits here until an emergency vehicle can get him to a hospital."

"Okay, I'll catch a ride to the office with someone else. See you later."

# 9. INDIA

Stark was still in his office at eleven o'clock that evening. He was also still wearing a swimming suit under a pair of blue walking-shorts and a T-shirt that had a picture of palm trees, birds, and a sunset with the logo NASSAU, BAHAMAS under it. He looked haggard and decidedly older under the wash of the neon light. On his desk were twenty-seven eyewitness accounts of what had happened. He had read each one and called each individual personally to check the report. Afterward, he had diligently added his own notes in the margins.

"You look like hell," Sallings boomed cheerfully through the doorway.

"Thanks, sweetheart, I love you too. You ought to see me from the inside."

"Me, too. Really. How about a drink?"

"Where do they serve them in gallon buckets?"

Sallings suggested Brannigan's but Stark opted for somewhere closer to home since he didn't have his car with him. They settled on Captain David's Wharf, a restaurant and nightclub on the bay. It was built on a long two-level pier that extended into the bay and boasted fish nets, harpoons, parts of boats, lots of mounted fish, and a dozen sets of shark jaws on the walls. It was all polished wood and mirrors, with an outside dining area to finish it off. The sign at the entrance said the restaurant had a limited capacity of 650 people but still there was a line waiting to get in.

"Hey, I'd say I'm a little under-dressed for here, wouldn't you?" Stark looked down at his T-shirt and shorts. Sallings had been able to change into a blouse and slacks on the boat.

"No, no, she placated, fishing a business card from her purse. She handed it to the hostess and said something to her quietly. The girl left immediately. "This is a tourist town," Liza continued, "and you can dress anyway you please. Anyhow, these are nice people here. As long as you pay the bill, they're happy to have you."

The hostess returned and spoke to Liza in a voice loud enough for the others in line to hear, "The manager said he's been expecting you and would you please come to his table."

They followed her through several rooms to one on the far end. "That was really terrible on the beach today, wasn't it, detective?" she asked solicitously.

"It sure was," Sallings replied.

"You officers look beat. Is this table okay?"

"Sure. And thanks."

"Wait a minute," Stark interrupted, looking at a huge tiger-shark's jaw grinning at him from four feet above the table. "If you don't mind," he said, pointing a thumb at the jaws, "I'd just as soon sit at a table outside. I don't think I wantta sit under those. Not tonight."

"Neither do I," Sallings said, looking up at the glistening rows of curved white serrated teeth.

"Anyway," Stark said, running his hands lightly over the teeth, repelled yet fascinated, "these are wierd looking. They don't even look like teeth. The way they're curved, they look more like rows of daggers."

"That's because you're not a tiger shark," Sallings laughed. "Come on, let's go out on the deck."

They settled in padded captain's chairs and relaxed under the whirling blades of a large overhead fan that kept them cool and free from insects. "You know," Stark said, "I talked to every last person who gave an eyewitness report and you wouldn't believe the differences in what they saw!"

"Yes, I would."

"I mean it. There was even one woman who was positive that it was a giant turtle's head that got the girl! Now just what the hell do you do with that?"

Sallings laughed.

"What's more, I have three people who are sure there were at least two or three sharks out there, while all the others say just one. The size ranges from four feet to just under the size of a battleship and they're all willing to swear to it."

"What do you make of it, Michael? I never got to the beach. After the helicopter picked you up, the captain called me again and said the causeway was a mess and would I help out there. As soon as I got back to the marina, I went straight to the causeway and never got away from it. I haven't even read any of the reports on the attack, for that matter. All I've seen is twelve million traffic accident reports."

"Let me tell you, you're not going to enjoy reading about those kids. It's not too nice. I don't know. I'm trying to be level-headed about this and not let what happened in Galveston influence me." Stark paused. "But I'll be truthful—it's not working so well."

"I can believe that! How bad was it? I've heard bits and pieces, no pun intended, and it sounds pretty awful," Sallings grinned sheepishly.

"Sallings, you're sick!" Stark grinned back, unable to keep the smile from his face. "It was awful, damnit—as bad as your sick humor."

"Okay, then. Tell me about the shark. How big was he?"

"Jesus, now you're sounding like Ed McMahon.

"I'd guess if you took an average and discounted a little for fear and surprise, the shark was at least sixteen feet long—maybe longer, if that's possible. The guys who grabbed the girl's body said it passed by their sixteen-foot boat and they're positive it was at least as long as the boat. One of them, the guy who owns the boat, says he's certain he could see big portions of the shark at either end of the boat at the same time. That seems a little fantastic. I don't think the shark we saw was that big, was it?"

Liza hunched her shoulders in a question mark. "I don't know. I was just making sure we didn't hit it. I wasn't worried about how big it was."

"Well, they at least, had a measurable point of reference. Of course, they were scared out of their wits."

"Either way, that's a big one for these waters. From what I know, that pretty well narrows it down to being a hammerhead or a tiger shark, too. They're the only ones that get that big—well, a friend of mine tells me Makos do, but she says that we don't get very many of them—that they seldom come in that close to shore. And I guess great whites get that big, but I don't think one of them has ever been seen here on the west coast of Florida."

"Of course, all of the people I talked to are just sure it's a great white. I told them all the same thing—that great whites don't frequent the Gulf of Mexico, but they're still sure it's just like the shark they saw in the movies."

"Did anyone say anything about it having a funny head? Anything that might identify it as a hammerhead?"

"No. But really, all most of them saw was the girl. Their eyes were riveted on her. A few of them couldn't even remember seeing the shark at all. And those kids on the boat I was telling you about? One of them is still pretty much in a state of shock and sort of hazy with his statements. The boy who thought he saw the shark beyond both ends of the boat—that's all he remembers about the fish besides its teeth and her body in them."

"Maybe we'll find out more after the autopsy tomorrow. Who do we have who's not related to them who can identify the bodies?"

Stark thought for a minute and rubbed the creases in his forehead. "I think Hernandez said she'd located two people from the hotel staff who'd gotten to know the family. She said they were willing to make a tentative ID for us."

"The captain wants one of us to go to the autopsy

and talk to the medical examiner."

"Are you going to go?"

"Are you kidding? Not a chance. I'm pulling seniority, old buddy. You get the dirty work this time."

"Thanks, pal," Stark said sarcastically.

Stark pulled into the innocuous, undistinguished building that sat a good 3-iron golf shot from the city-block-sized sheriff's office. It was quiet except for the steady stream of traffic on Ulmerton Road. There were two cars in the dozen or so spaces alotted to the Medical Examiner's Building. It looked deserted. The Australian pines softened the blacktop with their long brown needles. It didn't look at all the house of horrors that it should have.

"Dr. Cook will be with you in just a few minutes, Detective Stark," the receptionist said, rising from her chair. "Would you mind waiting in the conference room?"

She led Stark to a long rectangular room adjoining the entrance foyer. It was at the end of a long dimly-lit hallway. And true to its name, the conference room held a long conference table encircled by chairs. "If you'll have a seat, Detective, it'll only be a few minutes."

Stark didn't feel like sitting. He wasn't exactly at ease in this place and, like any cop, he was curious and wanted to look around. The long side walls and one end wall of the rectangular room were lined with bookshelves half-filled with books. The other was not a wall at all but a picture window overlooking a highway clogged with tourist-season traffic. A small metal table held a Kodak slide projector propper up with past issues of the *Morbidity and Mortality Weekly Report.* The bookshelves held a scattered assortment of titles that Stark tried to scan quickly before Dr. Cook arrived. One section immediately caught his eye. It contained *Crimes of Passion* by DeSade, a number of other studies of the criminal mind, and copies of the *Florida Uniform Crime Report.* Beside them was a display case containing newspaper clippings about various incidents of food poisoning in the county and a display of different drugs, from antihistamines to heroin. There were photos of marijuana, a plant leaf, and a discolored home-rolled marijuana cigarette.

The bookshelves on the opposite wall were much less interesting. They were filled with forensic pathology journals, medical books, and other trade materials. But beside them, Stark found the section he'd been looking for—the shelves that held the staff's personal books and magazines. They told him more about the people who worked in this grim profession than all the others combined. There was an Algebra I textbook, a National Geographic, and a couple of women's magazines. Stark was just about to check out the address labels and see who matched what when the door opened.

"Detective Stark, I'm Dr. Jean Cook," a tired-looking woman in her late forties said. "I'm the County Medical Examiner. And from the look on your face, no one told you that M. E. was a woman, did they?"

Stark blushed.

"Well, don't feel bad. That's a little trick they play around here on every new policeman. They think it's cute to let them walk in and meet me cold. Am I that much of a shock? What's a nice lady like me doing in a job like this, right?"

"Guilty!" Stark threw his arms up in mock surrender.

"Don't be embarrassed, I've heard it before. Well, I'll tell you. Truthfully, when I first started, I didn't know if I was going to last. The job really bothered me. I would work here all day. I'd see what terrible things people did to each other; see how horrible, brutal, and sick they could be; I'd go home at night and I couldn't sleep. But, I've found that after a while you get used to it. In some ways I think it would be harder now for me to go back to being a practicing physician and deal with live people who are suffering and expect me to help them."

"Yes, ma'am. I think I can understand that."

"Well, that doesn't matter. You're here on the shark attack, right?"

Stark nodded his head as the receptionist knocked on the open door. "Dr. Cook, the other people for the beach accident are here. Shall I send them in or do you want me to hold them a minute?"

"Send them in—unless you had something private you wanted to say first, Detective."

"No, no. Send them on in."

A desk clerk and a tanned lifeguard from the hotel where the Swenson family had been staying stepped into the room. They all shook hands and Dr. Cook briefed them. "I'm sure you've heard by now that we only have a partial body on the girl. What's left is covered and only her face will be exposed; but it's still going to be quite a shock. She's been cleaned up, but a large portion of her cheek is missing—rubbed bare to the bone—and one eye is completely gone. The boy looks fine. All his wounds were below the neck. Legally, all I need you to do is to make a simple statement. If you recognize her, I need you to say to me 'that is Carol Swenson,' and the same for Sean Swenson, all right?

"Do you all think you'll be okay? It's pretty grim. Do you want me to ask an aide to come down with us in case you feel faint?"

All three said no and followed her down the hall. The remains of the bodies were on rolling ambulance beds parked beside a viewing window inside a refrigerated room. What was left of Carol's body was swathed in white sheets. Her long blond hair was covered by the sheets, too. The refrigeration and harsh lights turned her skin a faded blue-gray. "I know it's her," the lifeguard said. He put his hand over his mouth trying to choke down the nausea that was welling up in his throat. "It just doesn't look like her."

"Take your time," Dr. Cook reassured. "You have to be sure."

Both of the men took a deep breath, walked to the far end of the window and looked back at the body as full face as possible; both woodenly repeated the same message, "That's Carol Swenson." They looked at Sean, paused, and repeated the procedure. Shaken and as pale as the corpses they had identified, they asked if they could leave.

"Certainly, "Dr. Cook replied. "Are you going to be all right? You can sit or lie down on a couch for a few minutes if you wish. I'll call your boss."

"No ma'am. We'd just like to get out of here," the

lifeguard said. "No offense."

"Okay, no offense. Thank you both for coming down."

She turned to Stark after they left the building, "Do you want to watch the autopsy? We're going to start now."

"How about my telephoning you later? I'm really backed up with paperwork on this one."

"I understand. Certainly. It was nice meeting you, Detective."

"But I'd like to see the wounds, if that's okay?"

"They're not very pretty." She led him into the room.

"Try a tour of Nam."

Cook raised the sheets. "Christ Almighty!" Stark shook his head in disbelief. "That's worse than Nam. What the hell denuded the flesh like that?"

"The shark's skin and the force of the impact—it's like a giant sander."

"It's one I think I'll try to avoid. Thanks Doc. What time should I give you a call?"

"Suppose I call you?"

"Sounds great. Thanks again."

Stark's private line rang at his desk. He hesitated before answering, letting the phone ring twice more while his hand rested on top of it.

"Detective Stark?" Dr. Cook asked from the other end of the line.

"Yes, Ma'am."

"Hi! This is Jean Cook!"

"Oh. Hi, Doctor. What do you have for me?"

"Well, I wish I could be more helpful, but not much!"

"What do you mean?"

"Well, technically speaking, both kids died from loss of blood; but obviously, it was from a shark attack. That's all you'll find in the official report. But that poor girl went through hell according to the eyewitness reports you gave me. And if you had seen the body—how the abdomen was literally bitten in half—Jesus! She must have experienced one of the most terrifying deaths I can imagine. I think my swimming days are over!"

"That's two of us! Can you tell me anything else—like what kind of shark it was, how big, or anything like that?"

"I wish I could, Detective; but I'm a physician, a medical examiner, not a shark expert. I can give you the dimensions of the wound and that sort of thing, but telling you anything more is really out of my field."

"All right. Thanks, Doc. Let me buy you a drink sometime under better circumstances."

"I accept, but in the meantime, I have a suggestion for you. A very pretty and pleasant one. And if I didn't like you, I wouldn't even make it."

"What's that? And why do I feel like I'm being set up?"

"Now you're sounding like a cop again."

"Guilty again! You're getting good at this, maybe you're in the wrong field. What's your suggestion?"

"Dr. Carolyn Goodwin, from the Marine Lab in Naples is lecturing at the University of South Florida tonight. She just happens to be a very good friend of mine, and I happen to know that she's one of the world's leading shark experts!"

"You're kidding."

"No, I'm not. If you'd like, I'll give her a call and tell her you'll treat her to dinner if she'll let you pick her brain. And if she'll take a look at the bodies. Of course, you guys will have to foot her hotel bill if she agrees to stay over an extra day."

"You're talking my language!"

"I'll give her a call and see what I can arrange. I'm sure she's dying to get into the middle of this, anyway."

"I'll love you for life."

"I'll remember that!"

# 10. JULIETT

Dr. Carolyn Goodwin, like Dr. Cook, turned out to be a big surprise to Stark. She was not at all what he had pictured a shark expert would be. When he had pulled up to her hotel in Tampa, he had expected a husky, rather severe, athletic woman, capable of swimming and fighting with sharks—or bears if need be. He also thought she'd be hiding a dull and pedantic personality behind a pair of horn-rimmed glasses and under a pile of hair wound in a bun on the top of her head.

Stark's intuition was rusty. When he asked at the desk for Dr. Goodwin, the woman who rose from a couch to greet him was a tall slender beauty who turned every male head within sight. She had short auburn hair and aquamarine eyes that captivated him on contact. Instead of the mannish tweed suit Stark had expected, she wore a white silk dress cut high and straight across her collarbones in front and low enough in back to expose suntanned skin to the top of her hips—with no suit marks! Four strands of gold chain gave the dress and the woman just the right touch of class. Stark was in heaven.

"Have you been to Bern's before, Dr. Goodwin?" Stark asked.

"Yes, I have, Detective. A couple of times. Have you?"

"No, but it's where Dr. Cook and my partner told me to take you. It looks great!"

"Damn her! Excuse me, she's a fantastic medical examiner—She really is. But she's also an incurable matchmaker. I hope that's not what she's doing with us."

"Oh, no!" Stark exclaimed. "Don't get the wrong idea. We're not on the make—I mean Dr. Cook is not on the make, or I'm not. You know what I mean. Really! We're just desperate for help!"

"Okay, I know." Goodwin smiled. "And Jean takes in all the weary, the homeless, and the restless."

"Something like that. But I really do need your help. The captain is all over our rear ends about this. He wants it wound up in a hurry. We had two teenagers killed by a shark yesterday."

"I heard. It was on the radio, on TV, and in all the papers."

The waiter served their salad and onion soup, opened the bottle of Moet & Chandon White Star that Dr. Goodwin had ordered, and told them their steaks would be ready shortly.

"Can we dispense with the formalities?" Dr. Goodwin asked Stark.

"Sounds good to me. I've answered to Michael a lot longer than to Detective."

"Good! Across a dinner table, I respond to Carolyn

a lot better than Doctor!"

"It's a deal."

"Well, Michael, let me begin with sharks in general. If I get boring, say so. Promise?

"You come from the Midwest, don't you?

Stark nodded.

"Then you probably don't know a whole lot about saltwater animals."

"Let's just say they're not too prolific along the St. Louis waterfront."

"Okay, I get your point. Then let me explain some things to you about the Gulf of Mexico. To begin with, the Gulf of Mexico is saltier than the Atlantic; it's warmer and a whole lot of other things I'm sure you're not much interested in. We have a different shark population here than we do in the Atlantic. Sharks are a lot like people—there are many kinds of them and they behave differently. And some species behave differently when in different parts of the world. There are over two hundred different species of sharks known to man and we're sure there are some we've never studied or even classified. Are you sure you're ready for my lecture?"

"Shoot!"

"Let's start with their history—way far back. I'll make it brief, I promise. I'm sure you've heard it said that sharks have been around for three hundred million years or so.

Stark nodded again.

"Well, that's only true to a certain degree. Some so-called experts like to be quoted saying that this perfect eating machine, this perfect predator—the shark—hasn't changed in three or four-hundred-million years.

Like I said, horsefeathers! It sounds great in the newspapers the first time someone is bitten by a shark, but it just isn't so."

"How's that?"

"Well sharklike creatures have existed since the Devonian Period, which ended about two hundred seventy-five million years ago. In fact they started developing in the Silurian Period about four hundred million years ago. But sharks, as we know them, didn't appear until about seventy to one hundred million years ago! So it hasn't been nearly as long as some would like to suggest. And then the white shark, his ancestor (maybe I should say *her* ancestor since the female is the largest in the species) only appeared on the scene just before the Eocene Age, fifty million years ago. This prehistoric monster was called *Carcharodon megalodon* and he or she was a true monster! Have you ever seen the picture of the giant jaws in the American Museum of Natural History, in New York?'

"Is that the one with all the people inside?"

"That's it. It shows six full-grown men standing inside the reconstructed jaws! Those jaws are nine feet wide and the largest teeth average six inches high. Think of that, a tooth that size and only one of a nine-foot jawful; layer after layer of them, each tooth weighing almost a pound! This monster was estimated to reach a length in excess of forty-five feet.

"I don't want to press your paranoia buttons," Dr. Goodwin continued, "but I'm not too sure how damned extinct monsters such as these are."

"What?" Stark sat up with concern.

"I'll tell you more about that later. First, if you have any, let me set aside your fears about great whites. White sharks, this one's descendant, are very rare in Florida and even more so in the Gulf. If I remember one study of the Florida shark fishery correctly, there were only twenty-seven identified white sharks caught during a ten-year period and that was out of close to one hundred thousand large sharks recorded. What is that—something like less than one out of every ten thousand large sharks caught in Florida is a white shark?"

Stark nodded his head, not wanting to deal with the math.

"Well, let me give you the side of the story no one ever reads or hears about. The one I've never given in an interview or in a public lecture—and if you ever quote me, I'll publicly say you had too much champagne and have a fuzzy memory—but Jean asked me to level with you."

"Good, I need that. After I saw what that shark did to those two kids, I'm not sure I even want to get in a bathtub. Just level with me. Tell me what I'm dealing with. I've heard so much talk that, frankly, I don't know what to believe."

"I understand. I don't know how much of this will be gospel and how much will be educated speculation on my part; but I'll tell you, off the record, what I know and think."

"I'll be forever in your debt, and I'm not being melodramatic! I don't like stumbling around in the dark."

"Okay, a little more history first. The great white, as we know him, has been around for a long time. In fact, we have evidence that his ancestor, the forty-five foot monster, was around as recently as fifteen million years ago. And in terms of geological history, that's yesterday!

"Now here are some of the things that are kept pretty quiet; that we're not supposed to comment on. On the dramatic side are the jaws of the great white caught in Port Fairy, Australia. The British Museum says they come from a great white, over thirty-six feet long, caught somewhere before 1870. It's just not so. Dr. Perry Gilbert, one of our leading shark experts, measured the jaws against those of known size and determined the Port Fairy shark to be only a little over sixteen feet long. But still, don't kid yourself, a shark three times as long as you are tall is still a monster!

"Gilbert says the largest white that he could find on record is one reported by Luis Howell-Rivero, a respected Cuban ichthyologist. Rivero said it was twenty-one feet long and weighed close to seven thousand pounds. They used a length and girth measurement to come up with weight—but computer analysis later proved the shark couldn't have weighed quite that much and was probably somewhere between four and five thousand pounds. Scary isn't it?"

Stark wiped a line of perspiration from his forehead. "Yeah."

"I'm sorry. I guess it's upsetting if you don't know that much about them. Is there something else wrong?"

Stark told her about his incident with the shark in Galveston and how it had affected him.

"I can understand why this has shaken you up."

"I'm not sure how shook up I am, but I can guarantee you that I don't care to see a repeat performance," he replied.

"I don't blame you."

"Yeah, you don't whip out in the squad car, arrest and cuff a monster shark!"

Carolyn laughed. "Okay, now for some more of what I won't tell reporters. And you're going to forget I told it to you, right? I don't want to be accused of being inflammatory or whatever."

"Agreed!" Stark leaned on his elbows. "What's said here, you never said."

"You've probably heard that if there can be a twenty-one foot shark, then why not a twenty-five-foot one; if a twenty-five-footer, why not a thirty and so on."

"Yeah," Stark said. "But by that logic you can have sharks the size of oceanliners and men who are eighteen feet tall."

"That's right, except there is a lot more basis for a shark that size than for an eighteen-foot man."

"You're kidding!"

"I wish I were," she said, stopping as the waiter returned to their table. With practiced unobtrusiveness, he cleared the table, served the main course, and refilled the champagne glasses.

"Time and again white sharks have been brought up beside boats and determined to be twenty to thirty feet long," Goodwin continued. "One fellow brought one almost entirely out of the water and measured him against a measuring line on his boat. He was at least twenty-nine feet long! We've also found bite marks on whale carcasses to support sharks of that size. And for further evidence of the possibility of monster sharks, there's an account by one Australian authority who interviewed a group of fishermen—men intimate with the sea, with sharks, whales, and other creatures that inhabit it. These men had been at work in some fishing grounds in pretty deep water when a giant shark erupted from the water, and ate one three-and-a-half-foot spiny-lobster pot after another. All of them said they had never seen a monster such as this; and remember now, these were seamen, not landlubbers. They were scared to death! They described the monster shark as being somewhere between one hundred and three hundred feet long! Now grant you, they were scared, but these fellows know what a one-hundred-foot whale looks like—what a fifty-foot boat looks like. And even if they were exaggerating out of fear by fifty percent that still leaves a monster between fifty and one hundred and fifty feet!"

"Oh, Christ!" Stark laughed sarcastically, dropping his fork and feeling the wrinkles in his forehead deepening a quarter of an inch. "You're making my day, Goodwin. Remind me not to become a cop in Australia."

"So you want to know what this has to do with the price of potatoes in Idaho, right?" Carolyn continued. "Why am I telling you all this if there are no great whites in Florida?" she asked, attacking the last of her ten-ounce Delmonico as if it was her last meal.

"Good question, Doctor." Stark was still working his way through the first half of his steak.

"Carolyn, remember?"

"I'm sorry."

"First, in all probability the shark you had at Surfside was a tiger shark. I'll tell you for sure after I examine the corpse tomorrow. We have a lot of tiger sharks and hammerheads here on the Gulf Coast and they get big. They've been caught up in the eighteen-to twenty-foot range. Now, realize that is almost as large as the largest white caught! And a tiger shark, for all practical purposes, has the same personality as the great white—if not worse! They'll eat absolutely anything they come across. We've opened them up and found everything imaginable. They've contained coils of copper wire, driftwood, clothing, nuts and bolts, heads of crocodiles, lumps of coal, birds, sea snakes, conches, horseshoe crabs, octopus and squid, porpoise—and a hell of a lot of people."

"You're kidding?"

"I wish I were, but I'm not. The list of things they consume just goes on and on. They eat other sharks, including their own species. They are virtually moving garbage disposals.

"And let me tell you, the tiger shark is as mean and as vicious as any animal alive, and that includes great whites. You know, we don't know the identity, for sure, of most of the sharks that have attacked people. Most people don't recognize them, most of them are not even seen, and a whole lot of shark attacks are just never reported. But I'll tell you that if somehow you could go out and find out about every shark attack that had ever happened and what kind of shark was responsible; you'd find out that, by far and away, the tiger shark was the worst in the water. They are incredibly aggressive. Small ones won't even hesitate to attack a boat many times larger than they are and to keep it up repeatedly. So you can imagine what one in the twenty-foot range would be like?"

"We really have sharks that size here?" Stark asked.

"You better believe it! It's my opinion that one of

the reasons they don't have records of the larger sharks is that they're just simply unable to catch them. Go to any commercial marina and you'll hear about massive shark hooks straightened, long lines destroyed, etc. Face it, a monster that size you are not going to bring in."

"Yes, but people would see them," Stark countered.

"And they have!" she said, pounding the table with her fork in her hand. She looked around at the turned heads and lowered her voice. "Michael, we have report after report of sharks this size! We can't admit to them until we have them on a dock and can stretch a tape measure down their backs. Damn it! It's common knowledge in Tampa Bay that there's a hammerhead with distinctive markings that veteran Bay fishermen call Old Hitler. He's been measured at close to twenty feet time and time again. He's torn up one fishing rig after another, and he still comes and goes as he pleases. They've seen another one that size or larger up by Anclote Key at Tarpon Springs. And they've caught a lot of tiger sharks in that size range here—including the shark they showed on the docks in the original movie *Jaws*. It was caught off Sarasota!

"In 1982, a fishing guide and his wife—Gettig, I think their name was—were tarpon fishing off Anna Maria Island just south of you. They were in his twety-foot boat when he caught a one-hundred-fifty-pound tarpon that he battled for two hours; it towed them two miles out in the Gulf. He almost had him in, about fifty feet from the boat, when his line went slack. He climbed up in his sighting tower and saw a shark big enough to park his boat on. He said the one-hundred-fifty-pound tarpon looked like a minnow in the mouth of a bass. Gettig thought it was probably a tiger. It had an asymmetrical tail like a tiger—and of course, he knew it wasn't a hammerhead. Gettig said that was all he needed to see; it was easily larger than his boat, and he was afraid he might be the shark's next meal. He got out of there fast. So yes, we do have sharks that size."

Stark shook his head in amazement. "I'll have to admit, I'm getting some education tonight."

"Well, the question I pose to you," Goodwin said, polishing off the rest of her steak and vegetable," is this. If we know for sure, that white sharks can grow much larger than those we've been able to catch—then why can't the same be true for a similar shark of a different species? How do we know there isn't a tiger shark thirty, forty, or fifty feet long lurking somewhere out there just off our shores? You know, quite a few fisherman believe there is—or maybe I should make that plural and say there *are*. And I agree."

After a drink of champagne, Goodwin flashed her aquamarine eyes at Stark across the top of her glass, "Did you know there is no place in the world that has as many shark attacks as Florida and does as little about it? Even in Africa they have watch towers and they net the beaches—here we just feed them our missing swimmers and errant tourists."

"It's not that bad," Stark protested, feeling he should protect the police department a little.

"It's not that good," Dr. Goodwin replied. "I feel shark attacks are like rapes—they are some of the most under-reported statistics in this state. Unless you have twenty-seven notary publics willing to swear to someone being killed or bitten by a shark, they won't admit to it. In Florida it's called a boat-propellor accident, a brush with a sting-ray or a blue fish, a coral or barnacle injury or whatever.

"Who are we trying to kid? In this nice warm water people go swimming, supposedly drown, and somehow never float to the surface and wash into shore—they just disappear. Now who's kidding who? In 1981, there were at least sixteen reported attacks in the Florida area, including a fatal one right here at the mouth of Tampa Bay. And I'll bet three to five times that number never made it to the newspapers. In '83, they chomped their way up and down the coast and damned little publicity ever came of it. One woman from Key Haven received close to two-hundred stitches in a really savage attack. You know, the nude hotels and nude beaches in Key West got more coverage?"

Stark laughed.

"It's not funny."

"I'm sorry. I was being sarcastic. I don't find it funny, either."

Goodwin grimmaced, "It's not. As I said, a fifteen-foot tiger shark will atack a fifty-foot boat without thinking twice about it. Now what happens to the people in a sixteen-foot pleasure boat five miles offshore who run into Gettig's twenty-foot tiger or a shark half again that size? What happens to someone in a life raft that a shark that size decides to eat? Think about it? Who reports the shark attack? No one! The victims are just missing or presumed drowned."

"Why don't you go public with this and get something done? I'll work with you."

"First, I like my job and I want to keep it. This is Florida, remember? I'm not dumb. Secondly, it's not *that* bad. It seems that way to you—but from my side of the fence, terrible as it is, it's not that big a deal. When you consider the number of sharks out there, the size of them, the number of people we feed into the Gulf as appetizers, I find it incredible they eat as few people as they do. Frankly, I don't think they particularly care for human flesh or our beaches would be a different color than white.

"And you know, Michael, from my perspective, the public is pretty dumb in their attitude toward sharks—they're wild animals just like lions, tigers, or cheetahs. Now, if you took a park the size of a city block—which I guess would be about the size of the swimming area off one of our average beaches—if you took this hypothetical park and told people that there was a one-thousand-pound lion running wild in it and maybe a couple of dozen smaller lions and tigers; if you said, 'But don't worry about them. Just don't make too much unneccessary noise. Don't act frightened. Don't annoy them. Don't walk around with open wounds they can smell, and most likely they'll stay in the bushes and you'll never see them.' Now how many people do you think would go in that park?"

"Not many, I'd say."

"You're damned, right. But when they do the same thing in the Gulf or the Atlantic and someone gets bitten, then they're on every marine biologist's back, saying, 'What's wrong? Why can't you guys do something about this.' "

"Are there really that many sharks out there or are

you exaggerating?"

"I'm not exaggerating. There are literally dozens and dozens in the water around every beach. It's their home, not ours. Most of them are under the five-foot size; some are quite a bit bigger, but at five feet you're still looking at a mouth the size of a basketball, lined with teeth that are designed to slice you up like surgeon's scalpels.

"A USF biologist said that he was able to net twenty to thirty sharks every time he went out to catch them. And he was setting his net in four feet of water only a quarter of a mile from St. Petersburg's pier and Spa Beach on the bay. You better'd believe they're out there."

"Then why in the hell are we letting people swim out there?"

"Don't ask me. I guess it's because of what I said earlier—most sharks just don't like eating people. Personally, I think netting the beaches and keeping them offshore makes a hell of a lot more sense—except I'm not saying it!"

The waiter cleaned the table and asked if they would like dessert and an after-dinner drink. "I've been waiting for it all evening," she told the waiter. "What'll you have, Michael?"

"I'll have a cappucino."

"I think I'll have the banana cheese pie. You ought to try it; it's fantastic!"

"No, the cappucino is all I can handle right now. I have to fight the beltline battle as well as the sharks." The waiter smiled weakly and left.

"Well, Doctor Goodwin," Stark continued dryly, drawing himself upright in his chair. "Back to your question: 'What does this have to do with the price of potatoes in Idaho?' Just what the hell is going on in Surfside? I've just had two teenagers slaughtered on my beach in front of dozens of people and I have a schoolteacher and at least four other people who are unaccounted for! What's the bottom line?"

"That's easy," she smiled." You have a rogue—what we call a bank loafer. And I hate to tell you this," she swallowed a half-dollar-size bite of banana cheese pie, "but your troubles have just begun!"

# 11. KILO

The National Hurricane Center in Miami watched the storm develop slowly for several days. Dr. Logan, the center's director, had first noticed it as a large low pressure area fifteen degrees north and twenty-five degrees west, just south of the Cape Verde Islands. It was not a good sign. A low pressure area that large, in that position, at this time of year meant a probable hurricane.

Dr. Logan was pleased and displeased with his predictions of what would happen—pleased that the storm had developed as he had expected and displeased at what he believed was going to happen next. The massive windstorm had steadily gained strength since the first satellite photos had come in. At first it was just a disorganized cloud mass drifting away from the African mainland. As it drifted slowly across the warm water it picked up speed, strength, and a little organization, becoming a tropical depression. Finally it had drifted a little further south and west before whipping up winds of forty-five miles an hour and becoming the season's newest tropical storm, Eleuthera.

Ironically, Eleuthera was a name they had fought over. They had argued whether it should really be considered since the name might give the Bahamian Island of Eleuthera a bad name. The assistant director's daughter bore the same name and that settled the question—but not the storm.

Now, Eleuthera was sitting fat and low in the belly of the North Atlantic sucking up heat from the hot tropical waters. Plotters had her at twelve degrees north and forty-four degrees west; and Dr. Logan didn't like where she was at all. There was a Bermuda high sitting too far south. He was pretty sure that if Eleuthera kept developing (and he was sure she would) she was going to turn into a full fledged hurricane in a hurry. And, from her position, he was just as sure she wasn't going to curve off the East Coast of the States and dissipate in the North Atlantic; either she was going to ravage Central America or go right down the throat of the Gulf of Mexico. With a storm the size he saw developing, he was worrying a whole lot about the latter. Something told him this was not an ordinary storm—he had a feeling that this was going to be a great hurricane. Logan's stomach got a little tighter after he noted each new photo and position on the map.

Islanders in Grenada, Barbados, St. Vincent, St. Lucia and Martinique were not waiting. They looked at the clouds, sniffed the winds; they watched the birds and the waves. They brought out the plywood and started preparing for Hurricane Eleuthera. Years of living and dying at the hands of the West Indian wind god, Huraken, had given them a sixth sense Miami's computers would never learn.

# 12. LIMA

Stark pulled into the Tampa Hyatt at eight the next morning. He had the valet park his car across the street. He had planned to go inside, phone Dr. Goodwin's room, and have a cup of coffee while he waited the customary fifteen to twenty minutes it would take her to finish packing, get ready, and check out. As he walked through the sliding glass doors and turned into the lobby, he met his first surprise of the day.

Dressed in a crisp rust-colored business suit that matched her hair, Dr. Goodwin was sitting in the lobby holding a press conference. Beside her chair was a folding luggage bag and a flight bag; on the other side was a table with a cup of coffee and an open briefcase. Ringed in front of her were reporters from the *St. Petersburg Times*, the *Miami Herald*, the *Clearwater Sun* and *The Tampa Tribune*. Behind them, the *Action News* camera from Channel 10 was jockeying for position with the camera crew from Channel 44's *Eyewitness News*.

"Dr. Goodwin, I'm Mike Todd from Channel 10,

*Action News.*" He stepped from the side and in front of the reporters making sure the camera could get all of them in focus. "Unofficially, many regard you as the world's leading expert on sharks in the western hemisphere. Could we have a few words from you about what happened in Surfside? Can you tell us what kind of shark it was—if it was a great white and whether these attacks will continue?"

"Just which of your many questions do you want me to reply to first Mr. Todd?"

"How about all of them," he grinned.

"Let's start with the *world's leading shark expert of the western hemisphere*. If I'm anything, I'm just an authority on sharks of the tropical Atlantic, Caribbean, and the Gulf of Mexico."

"You're too modest."

"No, I'm not. Really. And as far as what kind of shark (if it was a shark—and that has not been conclusively proved yet), I won't be able to tell you that until I examine the bodies; and even then, I may not be able to make a positive identification. Will it happen again? Not likely; but anything is possible."

Arms shot in the air as the reporters shouted "Dr. Goodwin!" in unison.

"Yes, ma'am," Goodwin pointed to a woman on the end.

"Dr. Goodwin, Nancy Balaboa from the *Clearwater Sun*. These two kids from Surfside will be the eighth and ninth shark-attack victims here in Florida, and the fourth and fifth fatal ones—although the only attacks we have had here on our coast. Is something happening? Last year there were only two fatal attacks here in the whole year. Are they increasing or is it just better reporting?"

Goodwin wiped a thin line of perspiration from her forehead. Stark wondered whether it was from the questioning or the camera lights. He wondered how much further she should let this continue.

"Again, Ms. Balaboa, I can't say at this time, with certainty, that it was a shark attack. But granted, from the newspaper accounts and the police reports, it does appear to be. You are right, shark attacks are up slightly this year. We don't know why, but shark attacks seem to follow a cyclical pattern and judging by that, we've expected a few more incidents this year than we had last."

"Then you mean you were expecting this attack?" another reporter interrupted.

"No, sir, we were not expecting this particular attack. You're putting words in my mouth and you are also not waiting your turn!" A flush of anger colored her face. "Yes, Sir." She pointed to a tall handsome man who towered over the rest of the people in the room. He moved forward with his microphone.

"Dr. Goodwin, I'm Greg Sanderson from *Eyewitness News*. You just mentioned police reports as well as newspaper accounts. Is it true that the Surfside Police Department has asked you to aid in the investigation? Of course, all of us assume they have—that's why we're here. And is it true that Detective Michael Stark, the man who single-handedly stopped the St. Louis Sniper, has been placed in charge of the investigation and that you will be working with him?"

"Mr. Sanderson," she smiled, "why don't you ask Detective Stark? He's standing back there beside your camera crew."

Heads jerked around and the two camera teams stumbled over each other trying to focus on their new target. Stark's stomach felt as if someone had just yanked the bottom out of it. "Damn her!" he muttered as he took a deep breath to steady himself.

"Detective Stark!" Sanderson asked. "Would you join us up here for just a few questions please."

Breathing deeply to steady himself, Stark walked around the reporters and stood next to Goodwin and Sanderson. He fished a handkerchief from an inside vest pocket and wiped his forehead and palms before shaking hands with Sanderson. "It's been a few years since I've done any news interviews and especially unexpected ones. I didn't know you people were going to be here this morning."

"Frankly, we didn't either. But Dr. Goodwin was nice enough to allow us a few minutes of her time before she left this morning. How about it? Have you been placed in charge of the investigation? I understand that you were there or arrived shortly after the attack. What did you see and hear that you can tell us about?"

"First, let me tell you that I am not in charge of the investigation. My senior partner, Detective Liza Sallings, is the officer in charge. As far as what happened, I'm not at liberty to comment on that just yet. Detective Sallings will schedule a news conference later this week when the investigation is more complete. I'm just here to pick up Dr. Goodwin and I'm sorry, but I can't comment any further than that."

"Could we talk to you about the St. Louis Sniper and just how you happen to be here on the Suncoast?"

"Why don't you call me at my office and let's see if

we can arrange that another day?"

"Thank you, Detective Stark. I'll do that."

"Gentlemen and ladies," Goodwin said, rising from her chair. "We're running late. Let's talk again later in the week when we have a little more time and information."

Big Eddie Repucci felt great again this morning! After twenty hard years in the restaurant business he had decided he'd had it. One morning he woke up and told himself, "I have a wife who is always on my back. She's forty pounds overweight and not worth the trouble. I have a restaurant that not one of my three kids wants and I'm tired to working like a slave." So he went to the south side of Chicago, looked up a few old school friends, and that evening, had his restaurant burned to the ground. He paid off his torch, divorced his wife, left her the house, took the insurance money, and took off on a permanent vacation.

Big Eddie had just gotten to Surfside last night. It looked fantastic and people said the fishing was grand slam for this time of year. He had been worried earlier in the morning because there had been fairly heavy thunderstorms from about four-thirty on. But by seven the storms had lost their lightning and had settled down to gusty winds and a drizzling rain. "It might run the sunbathers inside," he thought, "but you're really a pansy of a fisherman if you're afraid of getting wet." He got his rod, reel and dip net from the trunk of the car, bought a bucket of live shrimp from the marina, and walked out on the stone jetty that extended a hundred yards into the Gulf at the edge of the

Holiday Inn's property.

Each time Big Eddie tried to cast into the wind he found his line blown back to within ten feet of the jetty. He considered fishing the other side so he could cast with the wind, but the lady at the baithouse had told him to fish the north side if he wanted to catch the big ones—so one way or another, he was determined to fish the north side. Eddie looked at the water and decided it probably wasn't over his head at this point, and that if he waded out a short way, he would be a little closer to deeper water and lower into the wind. He hung his tackle box and net over the back of the DANGEROUS CURRENTS sign and stepped down into the water. He was only knee deep when he slipped on the rocks and pitched face forward into the rip-current that was raging past the jetty like a locomotive. He rolled over in the water, came up face-first and screamed for help. Two other fisherman tried to snag him with their poles as he was whipped past them, but were unable to do so. They were veteran Florida fishermen and knew better than to jump in and try to save him. One ran for help while the other tried to keep Big Eddie in sight. But a quarter of a mile out, the high waves had quickly whisked Eddie from the second fisherman's sight and directly into the visual range of a fifteen-foot tiger shark.

Eddie knew he was in trouble. He was a long way from shore and, in these waves, he knew there was no chance of swimming in. He was just not that strong a swimmer. "But," he thought, "people saw me. If I can just stay afloat, they'll have the Coast Guard pick me up in a few minutes." He decided to make his treading water and floating easier. He reached down, pulled off his sneakers, and started removing his heavy wet clothes.

On the first pass, ten feet below Eddie, the tiger opened it's mouth and swallowed both sneakers as they drifted toward the bottom. Eddie felt a sharp tug and was yanked three feet under the water. On his second pass the tiger had bitten off Big Eddie's left leg midway up his thigh. Eddie surfaced spitting saltwater and wiping his eyes. He knew he was injured, but it didn't seem to hurt too badly, and he was afraid to touch his leg. The blood started spreading around him and he couldn't bear it any longer. He reached down to touch his knee with his hands and they came together in the open space. "Oh, my God, No!" he cried. He ran his hand down his thigh and felt it end twelve inches below his hip. He couldn't believe it and moved his hand around the stump, vomiting as he felt the raw flesh and splintered bone.

"Help! God, help quick!" he shouted. He started to yell again as the small tiger snapped off his frantically-kicking right foot just above the ankle, again popping him below the water like a hooked fish does a cork. Eddie came up screaming with all the strength he could muster. He knew he had to attract some attention in a hurry.

Below the surface, the wrong kind of attention arrived. The giant tiger shark glided by his much smaller relative and on toward the bleeding, frenzied Eddie. The cavernous mouth gaped open, closed momentarily on Eddie's waist, shifted to just below his chin, and snapped shut like a monstrous razored bear trap. Big Eddie's head, eyes still wide open in terror, dropped slowly to the bottom like a soggy basketball.

The crabs were already scurrying sideways toward their prize.

"Is this a car or an airplane," Goodwin asked Stark, running her fingers lightly across the row of buttons that spanned the Continental's dashboard. "What are all of these, for God's sake?"

"It's sort of an inboard computer. It can tell you all kinds of things. If you set a distance on it, of say five hundred miles, then you can get all kinds of information." He swelled a little with pride, seeing her admiration. "Look! If you hit this button it turns the digital speedometer from miles an hour to kilometers an hour. And if you hit this one—see?"

She nodded.

"It shows that our fuel economy in town has been seventeen-point-five miles to the gallon and look, now it's switching to a constant readout—we're getting twenty-two-point-five here on the highway."

"I'm impressed."

"It can also tell you how long you have been gone, what your average speed was, when you should arrive at the end of your five-hundred-mile journey and a lot of other stuff." Stark smiled self-consciously, realizing she was not nearly as interested as he was. "It's mainly another toy within what is already a very big toy."

"Let me tell you: toys like this, I like!" Goodwin settled back into the padded velvet seat and watched Tampa Bay slide by as they crossed the causeway.

"Why did you agree to that interview?" Stark looked at the split in her skirt that revealed half her thigh.

"Well, the Marine Lab depends fairly heavily on private donations to keep going. And anytime we, or I, can get it any publicity and call attention to our work, that's worth a lot. I get hassled a lot, but on the whole, the press has been pretty good to me. You don't realize it, but half my work is public relations. We have to do it to survive."

"Are you really that famous? They were talking about you like you were God's personal marine biologist or something."

"I'm not nearly as big a deal as they want me to be. I'm good, but not that good. No one is! One of the big things I have going for me is being female. Most people think shark experts should be male, but that never has been true. Nevertheless, they enjoy splashing my picture across the paper and quoting their local expert, as long as she says what they want to hear.

"What about you, Stark?" She looked at the lean hard middle-aged man seated comfortably behind the wheel. The sunglasses hid his eyes, but she had seen a real person there the night before. She had seen concern, passion, and fire in his penetrating eyes. She was not sure what kind of man she was dealing with. At times he seemed as open as a priest, but in an instant he could close the doors and become all cop: shutdown, emotionless, questioning—a person that no one could get close to. "Let's return to the question. Are you as famous as they say you are? The hero that they say you are? I remember the St. Louis Sniper. Are you really the one who tracked him down and shot him? Did you really do it single—handedly like they said?"

"Didn't anyone ever tell you it's the cops who are

supposed to ask the questions?"

"The same people who told me women weren't supposed to become shark experts. Now answer the question."

"Touché! Well, maybe I was a little famous for a while, but not anymore. And if killing someone you served with in Vietnam makes you a hero, then I guess I qualify. I never have been able to make people understand that it wasn't something I deserved a damned medal for. I just did a job that needed to be done and it wasn't a very pleasant one. A lot of people got hurt and I caught a lot of flak about it, but I got a psycho off the streets."

"Wasn't he a friend of yours?"

"No!" Stark's eyes flashed anger behind the glasses. "He was someone I served with. He was as nuts in Nam as he was here. I had heard that he was really on a rampage and, finally, personally witnessed him killing innocent civilians. I should have wasted him then and there rather than turn evidence in a court martial. It would have saved me and the city of St. Louis a lot of grief.

"But I'm not famous anymore," he continued. "I just work my butt off and hope that's enough to keep me on the force and out of retirement. I also like the work. You know, most people don't realize it, but a good part of every cop's day is spent being a plain, old good Samaritan—helping people out. I like people; I like helping them. And I don't like the filth and the trash that mucks up the place I live in. I enjoy taking it off the streets."

"I'm glad you do. Not to say you're wrong—from the cops I've met, you're the exception; not the rule.

Most of the cops I run into are just out to slap you with a ticket for speeding and don't seem to care about crime."

"Then you need to meet some new cops. The ones I know aren't out there risking their lives everyday because they enjoy writing traffic tickets."

Goodwin could hear the anger in his voice. "I'm sorry, Michael. I didn't mean anything bad about cops. Really."

"Forget it!" he replied sarcastically, but with some of the anger defused. "I'm sure some of your best friends are cops."

Carolyn laughed.

They pulled into the Medical Examiner's Building parking lot next to Salling's unmarked car.

"My senior partner, Liza Sallings, the one who's in charge of the investigation, is here. That's her car. And if you think I'm an exception to the standardized cop, wait until you meet her." Stark laughed, throwing off the rest of his anger. "She can kick-ass better than a marine drill sergeant. She has a mouth that can turn as dirty as a veteran sailor's, and she's more fun to work with than any two men. She's also one of the best cops I ever met—for a woman."

"Is that right?"

"You'd better believe it!" Stark opened the door, admitting Dr. Carolyn Goodwin into the waiting room-reception area. Liza was seated in a corner chair.

"Carolyn!" Liza exploded throwing her arms wide.

"Liza!" Goodwin exclaimed in return. The two women wrapped their arms around each other, hugged a couple of times, held each other at arm's length, then hugged again.

"You know each other?" echoed an astounded Stark and Dr. Cook, who had just entered the room.

"Try next door neighbors and close friends all the way through high school," Liza said. "I couldn't wait for you to get here. What has this oaf been doing with you all morning? Not trying to put the make on you, I hope. If he has, I'll shoot him where it'll solve the problem."

"What a snow job this dame has been doing on me. You should have heard the scenario she put me through on the way over here. You two are out of the same mold!" Stark shook his head. "Did you know all about this, Liza? Did you set this all up?"

"Now, would I do that to you?" Sallings laughed.

Eleuthera went quickly through her phases of life. In a matter of days she turned from a massive tropical storm into a fast-developing savage hurricane. Dr. Troy Logan and the Hurricane Center had her plotted at a latitude of twelve degrees north and a longitude of fifty-two-point-seven degrees west. This placed the storm approximately four hundred seventy-five miles west of Barbados.

It was time for action and more information. The National Hurricane Center at Miami sent two P-3 Orion aircraft and a C-30 to gather information. Late in the afternoon Assistant Director Robert Cowley announced their findings: It's not good. Eleuthera is a very dangerous hurricane. Our planes continue flying back and forth through her gathering information. They will probably make one hundred penetrations during the twenty-four- to thirty-six-hour period they are testing.

Right now they have reported the barometric pressures within the hurricane at nine hundred fifty-one millibars—twenty-eight-point-nine inches. Eleuthera has sustained winds of one hundred fifteen miles an hour and gale force winds extending one hundred fifty miles from her center.

We are issuing a hurricane watch for Barbados and the rest of the Windward Islands. The storm is traveling at slightly less than ten miles an hour and conditions for her to strengthen are favorable. I'd say Eleuthera is going to be one of the most intense storms to ever threaten the Lesser Antilles.

## 13. MIKE

It was steamy in South Florida. The temperature was ninety-seven degrees and it had been that way for a month. The humidity ranged from eighty to ninety percent, depending on the time of day. In the heat, the elderly were cashing in their lives the way a gambler does his baccarat chips. A lot of them just refused to accept their limitations and forged on as usual in the heat, ignoring warnings that combinations of high humidity and temperature raised body heat in a manner that mirrored the wind-chill factor in winter. The police department was busy. Phones were ringing almost contantly and the whole force was tied up investigating one death after another, ruling out homicide or suicide. Stark walked into the nearly deserted Police Department and found Sallings sitting at Petit's desk talking patiently on the phone. He mopped his forehead in protest against faltering air-conditioning as he waited for her to finish. "Where in hell is everyone? What are you doing at Petit's desk?"

"Glad you asked that." She stretched back, her off-white rayon blouse soaked with perspiration only reminded Stark how miserably hot it was in the station house.

"You look like you're about to die!"

"Try melting, frying, cooking, boiling! I've only been here two hours and I'm past medium on my way to being well-done. If they don't get this fixed in a hurry, it's going to be impossible to stay here."

"Why the hell don't they have windows you can open? I don't believe they'd build anything that didn't have windows that opened in this sub-tropical climate; you know, louvers, overhead fans—all that tropical stuff."

"You watch too many movies, Stark. This isn't the '30s. We have progress now; right up to the point of idiocy. Where the hell have you been, anyway?"

"I radioed Petit that I was checking out a lead on Alex Johncourt. The bartender at the Hilton said a friend of Alex's saw him in Sarasota, so I ran the guy down."

"And?"

"Well, it took me most of the morning and then it turned up blank. He said he saw a guy that looked like Alex, not that he saw Alex. You know how that goes. And then Petit had me running on three different heat-exhaustion dry runs, and checking out a B&E at the Surfside Gold & Coin Shop. I think it was an inside job. No alarms went off. The door had been pried, but it hadn't been forced open that way. Someone used a key.

"You never did tell me where Petit and everyone else is. I thought we were supposed to meet Cook and Goodwin here?"

Sallings sat up, pulled her sticky blouse away from her body and blew down it. "Even that feels good. Petit is up on the roof with the air-conditioning man. It was either him helping or waiting until tomorrow when the guy could get a helper. I guess they're as busy as we are. Everyone else is out on investigations—including Captain Blanchert. Do you believe that?

"Dr. Cook called and said she's busy, too, and that they just got the bodies of Bancoff and Barker in down there. I called Blanchert and he suggested that we all meet at the country club about seven to talk about what we've got and what we're going to do."

Stark looked at his watch and saw that it read six-fifteen. "That gives me plenty of time to go home, shower and change—maybe even have a little drink."

"As Johnny Carson would say, 'Wrong, buzzard breath!' You forget who's the senior officer here. You get the phone and I go home."

"Liza! You're not gonna pull rank on me."

"Watch me, love!" She shouted over she shoulder, hips swaying and her suit jacket draped over her arm as she crossed the room. "See you tonight."

Liza slid the glass door shut on the cabin of her boat and pulled the drapes. The front windows were already covered with white canvas that kept out the heat and protected the glass from the corrosive salt water. The air-conditioning felt good. The walk across the marina's asphalt parking lot had been a journey through a giant frying pan. The morning storms had added to the humidity and only made things worse.

She walked to the refrigerator, put a glass under the automatic ice-maker, filled it with ice, then half-filled it again with Stolichnaya. She draped her blouse over the galley sink and unbottoned her skirt as she walked back to the lounge. She let both skirt and half-slip slide into a crumpled mass on the floor, then peeled down her pantyhose and tossed them over the steering wheel of the inside helm. Turning, she looked at herself in the rope-framed mirror hanging over the couch. "Not bad," she thought, cupping her hands under her breasts. Her nipples hardened to her touch in the cool air. "I haven't lost it yet. My stomach's still hard and flat. My boobs haven't started to sag much yet, but it gets harder every year—especially to keep the weight off." She tossed a throw pillow into the corner of the couch and laid back to relax, taking a sizable drink of vodka and letting the first swallow burn slightly as it slid down her throat.

She was uneasy and didn't know why. "I ought to be up," she told herself. "I'll be seeing Carolyn. The captain is popping for dinner. I'm out of that damned hothouse downtown—and Stark's stuck there." She grinned widely to herself. "I enjoy kidding and sparring with him. He's one of the few men who can kid and leave it at that. Looks like I made a good choice in my recommendation for my assistant. Strange though," she continued musing to herself, "that he doesn't have any further ambitions—that he doesn't want to be chief of detectives, the captain's assistant or anything—just a detective." A rememberance hit her. "The first time I can work it in," she told herself, "I want to ask him about that Muscatel bottle that kept coming up at his disciplinary hearings in St. Louis."

Tossing down the rest of her drink she emptied the ice into the disposal, sat the glass down, changed her mind, fixed herself another and headed for her shower.

Stark walked through the ten-foot-high doors of the country club. It was much like a hotel. The carpet sank beneath his feet as he walked to a counter that had two twenty-year-old females corralled behind it. Across the room stood half a dozen muscular tuxedoed young men looking eager to escort guests somewhere within the vast confines of the club or to show intruders out the door.

"Hi there!" he smiled.

"Hi there, back," the blonder of the two girls replied, getting up from her desk. As she stepped to the counter, Stark admired her version of the tuxedo—a velvet skirt that swirled when she walked and a matching top cut into a V that reached the waistline both in front and back. The velvet bowed out in front, to reveal three quarters of her breast—but teasingly hiding the nipple that was only a fraction of an inch away.

"And how can I help you," she asked innocently.

"You're too young to ask that question and I'm too old to answer it." Stark flipped open his wallet, exposing his shield and I.D. "I'm Detective Michael Stark. I'm supposed to meet Police Captain Blanchert and some other guests here. I've never been here before and I haven't the slightest idea where I'm supposed to go."

"How about going with me?" A coy smile crossed her face, belying her years. "I'll take him, Ted," she said to the young man who had started toward Stark. "I think all of your party are here except you. What about that Dr. Carolyn Goodwin? How does someone that pretty become a doctor? Wow!"

"I don't know, but she is good looking, isn't she?"

"Good looking? She's gorgeous! She looks like a movie star. I wish I looked like that!"

Stark took another look at the half-exposed breast and the girl's svelte body. "She looks good. But someday you oughta look in a mirror—you're missing one of the prettiest women I've seen in this town. If I were ten years younger, I'd be calling you every night."

"Thank you. You're sweet." She gave his arm a squeeze as she ushered him into the private dining room. "Don't let age stop you. It doesn't me."

Stark was beginning to believe casual sex might have its merits after all.

"Well, look who's here," Sallings said, raising a glass in a toast. "And he's brought his daughter."

"Liza!" Goodwin said, placing a hand on her arm. "I happen to like him!"

"So do I, but for different reasons."

Carolyn blushed and the hostess looked like she'd been slapped. The girl disengaged her arm from Stark's. "I'm sorry. I should have had one of the guys bring you down."

"Are you kidding?" Stark replied. "You're probably the only good thing that's happened to me today—and most likely, for the rest of the evening. These people aren't friends. They're taskmasters. He slipped a folded ten-dollar bill and his business card into her hand. "Thanks and no thanks for finding me this group."

The young hostess left the room and Sallings immediately apologized. "Michael, I'm sorry! Really! I didn't mean that the way it sounded. I was just kidding. Really."

Stark grinned across the table at her. "Forget it! If you don't think I know enough to roll with a punch like that after working with you this long, then you oughta be cannin' me. I know you don't mean it. After all, I know I'm the only man in your life—right after Bill; Joe; Ted, the lifeguard; Hanibal; Josey—should I go on?"

"Would you believe," Blanchert interrupted, turning to Goodwin and Cook, "that this is what half my day revolves around? That I hear this from seven or eight o'clock in the morning until I go home at six?"

Stark and Sallings were noticeably quiet about the six. "He loves it," Sallings said. "With the exception of paid club staff, we're the only excitement he has."

"Okay, okay," Blanchert interrupted. "We're not here to discuss sex, or my sex life, or God knows, Sallings, not yours! We don't have that much time. Let's order, get something to eat, and discuss what Dr. Cook and Dr. Goodwin have to tell us. I'm really starved."

The waiter cleared the table and everyone ordered an after-dinner drink. "How about leaving us alone for a while," Blanchert asked. "If we need something, we'll give you a buzz."

"Yes, sir!" the waiter replied, sweeping a silver tray

full of dishes through the doorway and closing the door behind him.

"Okay," Blanchert said, turning to Dr. Cook and Dr. Goodwin. "Tell us everything we don't want to hear."

"What I have to say is not all that dramatic," Dr. Cook replied. "Most of it you know already. The two kids died from loss of blood, presumably from a shark attack. Bancoff and Barker are a different matter. They were pretty cut up, but both men died from drowning. Their wounds were filled with glass. I haven't had time to compare it yet, but I would guess it came from the glassware in the galley or the liquor bottles. From what I could tell from the wounds, and Dr. Goodwin confirmed my findings, they didn't come from a shark attack—they were purely accidental. My biggest problem right now is not shark attacks but the number of people who are dying in the heat and substandard housing in this county—the ones who'd rather die than pay the damned electric company!"

"I appreciate that," Blanchert replied. "It's driving us nuts, too. I was even out in the field today. But it's the shark attack that has all the media people on our backs. Right now, the whole goddamned world can only think of that shark attack and two people dying from it.

"Then let's hear from the expert," Dr. Cook said. "Although I'm not sure any of you are going to like what she's got to say. I sure didn't."

"Shoot!" Blanchert nodded to Goodwin.

She turned to Michael. "Remember the other night at Bern's, I said you had a bank loafer?"

Stark nodded.

"I still think that's true, but I'm afraid the problem is a lot worse than I thought."

"Oh no," Blanchert dropped his head forward as if he had been shot. "You're not telling me this bloody business is going to continue?"

"No, no, not really. It could, but I just don't know."

"What the hell kind of an answer is that?"

Goodwin's eyes flashed anger. "A truthful one, damn it! Do you want the truth or not?"

"Carolyn—Dr. Goodwin." Stark jumped in. "How about explaining to all of us what a bank loafter is and what kind of a problem we do or don't have here. The captain wasn't implying we're not grateful for your help."

"I know that. I'm just a little irritable tonight, that's all. Probably just tense. I've had a long trip and this is a hell of a way to finish it up.

"I guess I'm also a little uptight about telling you what I have to say—I don't think you're going to like it."

"Try us," Stark asked. Blanchert and Sallings nodded in in agreement.

Goodwin swirled the champagne in the glass that she had ordered. "Let's go back to the bank loafter. Let me tell you what he is."

They all nodded again.

"Well—"

"Excuse me," Blanchert interrupted. "If you don't mind, Dr. Goodwin, I think it would be a good idea if Stark and Sallings took notes. This isn't a specialty area of ours. The City Commission sort of dumped this thing on us."

"I don't mind," she said, brushing reddish hair from her eye, as Stark and Sallings dug for notepads and pens. "As you know, I limit my expertise specifically to sharks of the tropical Atlantic, the Caribbean, and the Gulf of Mexico. And as a whole, we divide the total population of each migratory species of sharks in this region into two categories. In ichthyological circles they are known as the principal and accessory populations. Let me explain to you what those are. The principal population is the main breeding population—the sort of core of the species, so to speak. They are the ones that maintain their numbers, follow all the regular patterns of migration, distribution, and habit. The accessory population is made up of sharks from the principal population who are lost, usually permanently. They become this way from disorientation in seasonal migrations or just from wandering out of their geographical range. As you might guess, their numbers fluctuate, but not a hell of a lot. Here in Florida, fishermen refer to them as bank loafers.

"As most shark fisherman can tell you, bank loafers are scattered everythere. They will also tell you that they catch more of them in closer to shore than any other shark—in other words, he or she is the shark who shouldn't even be in this area at this time. And they are usually very young or very old.

"As I said to Michael the other night, so what does this have to do with the price of potatoes in Idaho, right?"

"Don't stop now," Blanchert interjected.

"Well, I feel—I know that sharks from the accessory population are represented in shark attacks much more than those of the principal populations. Sharks of the accessory populations are the ones we find close to shore feeding on what we would classify as non-normal food. Their feeding habits are completely different and unpredictable and they're just as unpredictable in their behavior."

Dr. Carolyn Goodwin looked each person at the table squarely in the face, searching his or her eyes before continuing.

"The tiger shark is undoubtedly the worst shark in any of our waters—the whole species is considered a group of bank loafers. They conform to none of the patterns that we try to fit them into. Although they prefer to stay in deeper water, they're renowned as the most vicious, voracious, and prolific beach attackers. I'm a shark expert—I admire them, but they scare me to death. As I was telling Michael the other night, they will eat anything they come across in the water and they're not afraid of the Devil himself!"

"You're not telling us that this is what we have at Surfside?" Sallings asked.

"It sure is. And not just a tiger shark, but a monster. From the wounds on the bodies, I'd say you have something out there in the plus twenty-foot range, maybe bigger. And tooth fragments confirm it is *Galeocerdo cuvieri*—the tiger shark."

"Goddamn!" said Blanchert. "Just what the hell do we do?"

"Well, that's the only good news I have for you. From what I've been able to gather, those kids have been the only victims—"

"What about the other missing people?" Stark interjected.

"We always have missing people." Sallings replied. "This is a tourist town and a fishing town; one way or another, people constantly manage to make themselves missing."

Dr. Goodwin continued, "Judging that there have been no more attacks before or since, I would guess the shark has either returned to its principal population and has changed its feeding habits or possibly, its feeding grounds. So, with a little luck, your problems may be over. I told Michael the other night that they had just begun, but it looks like I was a little premature."

The door reverberated with the pounding of an insistent person. "See who it is," Blanchert said.

Stark reached the door an instant before Sallings to find Jim Rainford standing in the doorway, a piece of teak railing in his hand, with a curved tooth the size of a silver dollar imbedded in it.

"I don't believe it!" Blanchert said rising from the table. "I absolutely refuse to believe it!"

"I thought I'd better bring this thing to you, first off," Jim said. "My men brought it up after the reporters had left. Looks like a shark got the boat or at least Buck and Rick. It looks like you were right after all, Stark." He looked at Blanchert. "Whatta you think? Maybe we should close the beaches for a while?"

Sallings made a mental note that Rainford had said it looked like *Stark* was right, not the two of them.

They passed the teak railing and tooth to Goodwin. The silence in the room, was broken only by the loud hum of an air-conditioner that no one had noticed before. She looked quizzically at Rainford.

"I'm sorry, Dr. Goodwin," Blanchert said. "This is Jim Rainford. He's one of our city commissioners, probably one of our best businessmen, and certainly someone who's very concerned about Surfside."

After polite exchanges, Goodwin continued. "I know the spot you guys are in; but, you're asking me for professional opinions—on the record. Stuff that you're going to put in a report, right?"

Blanchert and Rainford both nodded. Sallings and Cook looked at the table; Stark took a drink of his Bloody Mary and looked out the window.

"That tooth in that railing doesn't mean anything. It could have come from the same tiger shark that attacked those kids or it could have come from a hundred others you have off your beach! And realistically, closing the beaches doesn't make any sense. If all the sharks out there wanted to eat people, you couldn't let someone get ankle deep in the Gulf. More than likely, the shark that attacked those kids has wandered on up or down the coast somewhere. He was really big! He requires a lot of food. And right now, you don't have the attacks to substantiate his appetite. I'd say he's probably left the area—anyway, how can you protect a beach from a shark by closing it? The people have already done that. There hasn't been anyone in the water since the attack. Like I said, I'd put my money on his being long gone—or let's hope he is!"

"She makes sense to me," Rainford said, raising from his chair. "I don't want to be rude, but I've had a long tough day and need some rest. I just wanted to get this over to you right away."

"Thanks, Jim," Blanchert replied. "I'm tired too. I think all of us are. Dr. Goodwin, thank you for your help and send us a bill."

"Agreed," she said, shaking hands around the table.

"Do you have a ride home?" Blanchert added.

"Yes. Thanks, Captain. I'm staying with Liza. We grew up together."

"You don't say!" Blanchert replied, a look of surprise on his face. "Why didn't I know that?"

"Because a good pinochle player always keeps a few trump cards close to his chest," Sallings replied.

Lisa and Carolyn stepped aboard *Sundays Grouper*. "Liza," Carolyn said turning around in the salon, "you don't know how much I think of you—and envy you—you and your fabulous boat! Do you realize how lucky you are?"

Liza started peeling off her clothes and tossing them over the couch. "I'm not all that sure I do. When you look at it from my side of the fence, I see you in that elegant condo on the beach in Naples, flying all over the United States and the world, for that matter, investigating this or that, or giving a talk on this or that—whatever; it don't look so bad."

Carolyn laughed. "When you put it that way, I guess it doesn't, but this looks so relaxing—so bohemian and free. I think I'd trade you."

"If we did, we'd probably both be unhappy."

"Can I take a shower? I feel like I haven't had one in a month."

"Sure, go ahead," Liza replied, picking up the newspaper. "I think I'd like to relax a little before I take mine. I'll have a drink and read the paper while you're in there."

"Fine, I'll fix a scotch on the rocks when I get out if you have any."

"How does Pinch sound."

"Liza, did you buy that just for me?"

"It wasn't for me!"

"I do love you," Carolyn hugged Liza. "You're the only sister I've ever had—I don't know what I'd do without you."

"Me, too." Liza answered. "Why do we see each other so seldom when we're only hours apart."

"I don't know! Let's make a deal that we end that now. I need you, really."

Carolyn went down into the aft-cabin to the shower and Liza punched in a Bertie Higgens tape, sank back on the couch, and began reading the newspaper. Subheadlines across the bottom half of the page, read: "*Martinique & Dominica To Feel Eleuthera's Fury.*" She read on:

> SAN JUAN, Puerto Rico (AP)—Eleuthera blazed by Barbados in the early morning hours and set her sights on the tropical paradise islands of Martinique and Dominica. At 6 A.M. this morning, the U.S. National Weather Service reported that Eleuthera was less than 50 miles from Martinique, but had slowed considerably and was just drifting towards the islands.
>
> The National Hurricane Center at Miami said that Eleuthera now has sustained winds of 140 miles per hour and conditions were still favorable for her to strengthen even further. Assistant Director Robert Cowley said Eleuthera is undoubtedly one of the worst storms to hit this region in

this century.

Barbados, already saturated with tourists, was lashed with gale-force winds and heavy rains. The Marriott's Sam Lord's Castle Resort was a refuge for many. The elegant resort, filled with fine Chippendale furniture, was piled high with suitcases, crowded with tourists in soggy clothes and had become a shelter for a pampered group of whimpering pets. Boards covered the windows and pool furniture was crammed in the hotel's hallways. There was extensive flooding and minor damage in Barbados, but the main body of the storm was passing to the north. Martinique was reporting heavy rain and increasing winds.

The National Hurricane Center in Miami has posted an additional warning for the French island of Guadeloupe. It has discontinued warnings for the southern islands of St. Lucia, St. Vincent and the Grenadines, as well as Barbados.

Concerned and curious, Liza crossed the room, turned on her marine radio and switched it to the weather channel. The radio crackled and screeched as she adjusted the squelch. "This is the National Oceanic and Atmospheric Administration in Ruskin, Florida. The voice of the National Weather Service! This is tropical weather advisory number nine. Great Hurricane Eleuthera is now approaching the northeast coast of Martinique and the southern coast of Dominica. Great Hurricane Eleuthera has sustained winds of one hundred sixty miles an hour and is traveling from the southeast to the northwest at ten miles an hour. Her position at ten P.M. this evening is fifteen degrees north latitude and sixty-two degrees west longitude." Liza switched the radio off as she heard the shower stop. There was something about Eleuthera that bothered her.

In Miami, Dr. Troy Logan felt the same way.

# 14. NOVEMBER

Carolyn Goodwin hugged Liza as she heard the Eastern Airlines flight attendant announce that the flight to Fort Meyers was boarding. "Well, it's off from here to a three day meeting at South Seas Plantation on Captiva Island, then back to the lab in Naples for a week, and then on to Miami."

"Don't you ever stop?"

"It's like I was telling Michael. The name of the game is funding and it comes in at the same rate we put out. If we slow down, it does, too. So it's sort of a constant hassle. It's getting to where we do as much fund raising as we do research." She reached down and picked up her briefcase and Liza handed her the folding bag from the seat beside her.

The cop in Liza sized up her friend. She was a little taller and lots thinner than she was. "She also has a lot of class," Liza thought. "Even though I come from a family that had as much, was as cultured, and I got my share of college—she still has class I don't have. And it only hurts when I think about it; so I won't."

Wearing boat pants and deck shoes, she walked beside the stylish woman. "Well, I have to get back too. I go in at noon, only work till six, thank God, and then I have a date!"

"Anyone I know?" Carolyn's face showed a flash of jealousy.

"If you mean Stark, the answer is no. Fraternization is not only bad business, but it's not allowed on our force. Are you interested in him?"

"I could be." She blushed at being caught so easily. "I have a good friend who likes him, too."

"Then I wouldn't—"

"Na, na, na." A mischievous twinkle sparkled in Salling's eye. "When it comes to men, everyone is on his own. If you like him, he's yours if you can get your cuffs on him."

"I might just try that."

"I'll put in a good word for you."

"Liza! Don't you dare!"

They hugged again and Goodwin waved good bye as she entered the boarding ramp to the plane.

South Seas Plantation sprawled over the northern tip of Captiva Island. One of the nicest luxury resorts on the Suncoast, its primary emphasis was tennis. No less a tennis star than Virginia Wade was it's touring pro. But economics and good sense had prompted the management to continue expanding facilities. The ever-present salt-white sand was there, but a beautiful nine-hole golf course, complete with carts, adjoined it.

At South Seas, one didn't just check into a hotel. It wasn't that plebeian, nor nearly that easy. Guests were confronted with a variety of places to stay and an even more confusing array of prices. There were Tennis Villas (privately owned condominiums rented out through the management) with several different arrangements, including a two-bedroom, two-bath upstairs-downstairs model with a loft, a kitchen, screened in porch, and a pool—the works); there were Golf Villas, Beach Villas, Marina Villas, Private Homes and even a Plantation House that resembled a hotel. None of them had restaurants or shops—these were all in a separate shopping area.

Chadwick's Restaurant, at the entrance to the resort, was also considered one of Florida's best. But to most palates, there was nothing wrong with either of the other two restaurants housed there. The most informal was Captain Al's Pub, which sat on the marina and offered both indoor and outdoor dining overlooking one of the best selections of private yachts to be found on the coast—fifty-,sixty-, seventy-, and eighty-footers abounded. Millions of dollars might be displayed in one boat alone.

Goodwin was savoring it. It was cocktail hour. Brief shorts covered the bottom half of her black bathing suit; the spandex top passed for a blouse. It was all that was needed here. People were sitting on the decks of their boats having cocktails, talking, and playing backgammon in bathing suits. Half the crowd at the outside tables were as casually clad. Those at the tables both envied and enjoyed looking at those on the boats; those on the boats luxuriated in the attention.

Carolyn's slim runner's legs were propped on the chair opposite her on the right hand side of the table. She held her arms outstretched in front of her and was happy to see that they had gotten a tinge of pink from the sun. She always lost a tan almost as fast as she could get one. While some people could tan in one day a week it took her, working at it, at least three days out of seven.

"May I join you?" A tall blond deeply-tanned muscular man in his mid-thirties stood with his hands on the chair to her left.

She had to crane her neck to the side to see him fully and hesitated before replying.

"Excuse me," he said again. "I don't mean to be offensive—or pushy. I have a boat out there and I've been on the damned thing fishing for a week—just me and another guy. I don't know anyone here. I was watching you. I thought maybe you were alone—I just wanted to talk to a female for a change. I'm sorry if I'm mistaken."

"No, no." Goodwin got up to shake hands. She was almost as tall as he was in her bare feet. "I was just sort of spacing out and you startled me, that's all." She offered a handshake. "My name's Carolyn—Carolyn Goodwin. What's yours?"

"I'm Rex Archer. The Rex stands for Reginald, but I don't often admit it. That's my boat over there. I call her *Sagittarius*. Bet you can't guess why?"

A light laugh broke Carolyn's speech. "Sit down, Mr. Sagittarius Rex Archer! Have a drink. I'm here for a meeting and none of my group has arrived yet—it doesn't look like they're going to, for a while at least."

"Business, huh?" He settled back in the chair as if it were home.

"Yep. But you have to admit, this isn't a bad place to do business."

His green eyes looked at her searchingly. "You come here often?"

"Once or twice a year, if I'm lucky. How about you?"

"Oh," he replied, not expecting the question. "I come here a lot—I don't mean to be pretentious or anything like that. I live in Fort Meyers, so it's just a matter of chugging across the bay."

Carolyn took another look at the *Sagittarius.* "I don't think I would call traveling in a forty-eight-foot Hatteras Long Range Cruiser exactly chugging. How did you get that thing in here by yourself? That must have taken some skill."

He was impressed with her knowledge. "The skill is called a lot of practice, help from the dock people, and hoping no one is watching too closely. Where did you learn so much about boats?"

"I grew up in Whitefish Bay, Wisconsin. They have a lot of big boats there." She looked at him closely. Being from Fort Meyers and owning a boat or whatever, only cut so much ice with Goodwin. She had traveled too much to become too friendly or to give out any more information than she already had. "Do you work in Fort Meyers, Mr. Archer, or just live there?"

"Neither, really. Please call me Rex." He saw the look of alarm on her face. "Let me explain. I just keep my boat in Fort Meyers behind a friend's home. I own the Chichen Itza beach resort on Sanibel."

"Then what are you doing here? I've heard that place is gorgeous. Isn't that the new one shaped like a Mexican pyramid?"

"Mayan, really. That's the one. But you have to realize that being there is work—being here is fun!"

Carolyn laughed. "Do you have a business card? We'll make a trade."

He motioned to the waiter as he pulled a brass card case from his pocket. "Hi, Mr. Archer. Welcome back," the waiter said. "I saw your boat when I came on duty a while ago. Can I get you both a drink?"

"Thanks, Bill. Yeah, get me the usual and whatever—My God," he said looking at the business card Carolyn had handed him. "Get Dr. Goodwin a refill on whatever she's drinking."

He sat up in the chair after the waiter had left. "You're Dr. Goodwin? *The* Dr. Goodwin who's always on television and in the newspapers?"

"Do I look that much worse in person?" she kidded.

"No, honest! You look different; you've always been in a suit and behind a bank of microphones and stuff."

"I get it," she teased, feeling more comfortable and safe with him. "You don't recognize me with my clothes off."

"Now you're going after me! I think you look great both ways. I just don't believe that I've run into you. In fact, I was just thinking about you the other day."

"I'll just bet you were," she continued teasing.

"No, I really was." He leaned back with the drink the waiter had brought. "My ex-brother in law—my wife was killed in a plane crash last year in the Bahamas—that's why I'm saying ex-brother in law. We'd been on a trip up along the coast and were passing about eight miles off of Pinellas County when we came through a fish kill that you wouldn't believe. I figured it must have been Red Tide. I knew they had some there, but this one section was at least three miles long and so wide that we couldn't see past it."

"That's what the conference is about. When was this exactly?"

"Yesterday morning. Let me tell you the rest of the story. Pretty far out in the fish kill I spotted this big shark fin. The damned thing looked like it was sticking twenty feet out of the water, it was so big." Carolyn didn't laugh at his obvious exaggeration "I really can't say how big it was, but my brother-in-law was looking through the binoculars and he said it looked like a submarine."

"You didn't get any closer?"

"Not a chance. You should have smelled that. We were both wheezing, coughing, and sneezing like mad. That stuff really bothers me."

"Could you tell what kind of shark it was."

"We weren't that close. But Bob thought it must have been a big tiger—they're the only ones we have around here that get that big, aren't they."

"Well, hammerheads—"

"Bob's a seasoned fisherman—he would have recognized a hammerhead's fin, as distinctive as it is. But that's right, they do get pretty big, too."

Goodwin's relaxed face turned tense. She had brought her feet out of the chair and one fist was clenched. "Mr. Archer, I don't want to be rude. If you're going to be here for the weekend, let's get together again. But I have some important work that won't wait."

Captain Blanchert woke at six-thirty to the incessant ringing of the telephone. "Do you want me to get it, dear?" his wife asked.

He lumbered around the bed, "No. You know it's not for you, damnit." He picked up the phone and cleared his voice. "Blanchert residence."

"Captain Blanchert, this is Dr. Goodwin. I apologize for waking you up so early, but I was afraid I'd miss you."

"No problem at all," he lied. "Just finished breakfast. What's the problem."

"It's the same one."

"I thought you said that was over with. We haven't had any more trouble."

"Maybe so, but I'm afraid you're going to. Remember, I said I thought the shark had moved on out of the area because people are not a shark's natural food to begin with, and that the beaches were practically empty, and there just wasn't enough food in close to shore this time of year to feed a fish that size?"

"And so?" He covered the phone and cleared his throat again.

"I think I'm going to have to change my story in light of some new evidence. I talked with a fellow here at Captiva Island who saw a large shark feeding in a massive Red Tide kill about eight miles off Pinellas County. I'm pretty sure it's the same shark. I've had my staff up most of the night and we've discovered that there are an unusual number of people missing and a few boats unaccounted for from Anclote to Sarasota.

"That also coincides with the Red Tide outbreaks we've been having. I think this shark may be old or diseased or something; he's hunting easy game. I think he's feeding on whatever he can get—sort of going back and forth between the beaches and the Tide kills."

"Oh, Christ!"

"Yes. Oh, Christ! I think you're going to have him hanging around the coast for some time—at least until the Tide breaks. If I were you, I'd quietly get together as many fishermen as I could and catch him before I had any more incidents. I'd also tell them not to play macho—not to try to bring him up to the boat or anything like that. If you can get him, you'd better kill him as quickly as you can."

"I'll talk to the commission about it. We have a meeting this morning at ten."

"One favor."

"Sure, you've got it."

"When you get him, give me a call immediately. I want to be there when they bring him in to dock."

"No problem. I'll ask the sheriff to send a chopper after you. Thanks for the bad news," he laughed.

"Sure." Goodwin didn't laugh back. She was afraid it might be worse than she'd said. And she felt a little responsible.

Five and a half hours earlier, at one o'clock that morning, two brothers, Gary and Rob, were drinking beer and shark fishing at the Fairway Anchorage about ten miles out from the Edgemont Key entrance to Tampa Bay. They were both a little tight and tired. Rob, the older brother, tossed another frozen gallon milk-carton of fish blood over the side and tethered it to a cleat with a long line. He chug a lugged another beer. "I'm going below to get some sleep. Wake me in a couple of hours will you? I just can't take the heat any longer. They're just not biting, anyway."

His brother reeled in his line and got another beer for himself. Gary wasn't quitting yet. He'd just gotten a new Penn 16.0 reel and one-thousand yards of one hundred-thirty-pound test line for his birthday; he wanted to catch a big one with it. He had downed the beer and was rummaging through the ice chest for another, listening to his brother snoring loudly below. He just barely heard the tether line on the chum bucket snap. "Damn!" he thought. "I've got a chance." He reached in the bait well, grabbed two halves of bonito, placed one on each hook, and flailed them over the side. He strapped on his body harness, ignored the fighting chair, and went to the railing to wait. "Is Rob gonna be surprised when he sees what I've caught!"

There was a slight tug on the rod and a steady pull on the reel. The ratchet sound of the spinning reel slowed and stopped. It cranked another turn or two, stopped again, and then started spinning rapidly. Gary set the lock then threw all the muscle and weight his one hundred-fifty-pound body could muster into setting the hook hard. The spinning kept going. He increased the drag to its maximum, stepped on a beer can, stumbled forward, caught his hand in the line, and was yanked off the back of the boat before he even knew he was caught. He was being pulled through the water and the line was cutting deeply into his wrist. Two hundred yards away the towing stopped; his brand-new five-hundred-dollar shark-fishing rig sank to the bottom and settled into the sand. Coughing sea water, scared, and hoarse, he shouted for help and started swimming toward the running lights of the boat.

Rob snored steadily through a dream of women, sharks, and tournament scales tipping with his victories.

Gary never saw the great tiger tearing up behind him. He could feel him. He knew he was there. Like most shark fishermen, Gary didn't like swimming in the Gulf—and falling overboard at night in a stream of chum was absolutely terrifying. Gary glanced behind him and saw the white wash of water around the fin as it closed on him. He fought the water furiously trying to get back to the boat, glancing anxiously over his shoulder as he went. There was nothing. He stopped, remaining motionless in the water, telling himself to be calm and not make any unnecessary commotion. "Rob!" Gary cried in a hoarse bellowing whisper. "Rob! Goddamnit! Help me!"

There was silence from the boat that bobbed seventy-five yards from him. "I'm gonna hafta swim it to the boat real easy," Gary told himself, taking a quick three hundred-sixty degree look around himself and finding only black wavecrests. "But first, I've gotta get this damned line unwrapped from my wrist and forearm."

The tiger, circling, ran into the one hundred-thirty-pound test line ten feet below Gary and rolled over in it several times, yanking the fisherman headfirst, arm outstretched beneath the water. Gary only felt a minimum of pain as the shark bit off the top of his body from his head to to just above the waist.

Four hours later Rob awoke, assumed his brother had fallen overboard and radioed the Coast Guard for assistance in finding him. Forty-six feet below, smaller sharks were finishing off Gary's remains.

In Dominica and Martinique many people had died last night, too. During the evening hours the center of Eleuthera had slowly blown its way through the southern half of the thirty-mile-wide Dominican Channel that separates the two islands. It had then veered a little to the north, managing to ravage both islands before bursting out into the Caribbean.

Stark woke up in Ollie's bed. He looked out the bedroom window of her condominium at the Gulf of Mexico. It was whitecapped and green in the early morning sun. Ollie sat up beside him and wrapped her arms around him. She really liked Stark; she knew she didn't love him, but she did enjoy him. "He's just not there, though," she thought. "You only get so close and then you hit a stone wall. There seems to be a limit to just how much he'll let anyone in. He knows all the right words. He's nice, polite, and all that; but he's someone I'm afraid to get too attached to—I'm afraid of being hurt. There's something about him that's not just right."

"How do you make enough money as a nurse to afford a place like this?"

"You idiot!" She shoved him off the edge of the bed and onto the floor with a thud.

"Damn! What are trying to do, kill me?"

"Just don't play prying cop, mister."

"I wasn't prying. I was just curious."

"My ex-husband was a plastic surgeon. This place, a sizable chunk of money, and other property, I got in the divorce."

"Other property? What property? Does he live here?"

Ollie's face turned red with anger. "Do you want to know if he was a hot lover too?" She jumped off the other side of the bed and jerked open a closet door. "Do you want to know how often we made it?"

"Hey," Stark stood up and rubbed his rear. "What's eating you?" He picked up his undershorts and pulled them on, suddenly aware of his nakedness. "All I did was ask a few innocent questions."

Ollie turned, naked, eyes flashing, hands on her hips. "Oh come on, Michael. Have I ever asked you about your ex-wife? Have I asked you how much money you make? Have I? Have I asked you where you got the money you have? If I had, you would have been furious! You would have told me it was none of my damned business."

"That's not true," he replied. He started across the room with arms outstretched.

"No, Michael. I don't want you to hug me. I don't want to be touched."

"Ollie! What do you want? Do you want to see my tax returns? You want to see my family photo album? What's the matter?"

"I don't know." The phone rang. "Hello. Yes, Liza, he's here." She handed the phone to Stark.

"Christ, that was abrupt," Liza spoke into the phone. "Did I interrupt something—"

"Just a fight!"

"I'm sorry."

"So am I. I guess that's what I get for getting involved with kids. What's the matter?"

"Blanchert called me before seven this morning. He said he wants both of us at the City Commission meeting at ten."

"We had a homicide yesterday! We need to be on that!"

"I told him that and he told me when I become captain, then I can decide where we work and to get our asses to that meeting and not to be late."

"It's his ballgame."

"Kid!" Ollie exploded from the other side of the room. "Kid! Well I can promise you this kid can do without a parent like you for a long time!" She slammed the bathroom door.

Stark was disgusted. This was not how he liked to start his days.

Liza turned on the TV in the aft-cabin. She wanted to watch the news while she dressed for work. She turned to Channel 44; the UHF Channel came in best on her boat. "After these messages we will have a special report on Great Hurricane Eleuthera." She stepped quickly into the shower stall, showered, skipped her hair, and came back out into the cabin to catch the News Special Report.

"Here in Puerto Rico the reports of the destruction in Martinique are sketchy, but from what we have heard it is massive.

"One amateur ham radio operator from Dominica reported that the island was hit by one hundred sixty-five mile-an-hour winds. He said most of the flimsy native shacks have been flattened and are without electricity. Many are thought to have died in floods and avalanches. The island suffered from huge tidal surges. Commercial and government communications have been knocked out and the nation's banana crop, its chief source of income, is flattened.

"Another ham from Martinique reported much the same conditions there. He said roofs and trees were sailing through the streets and there was heavy flooding. As soon as we can get you a visual report, we will.

"The National Hurricane Center in Miami said the storm had weakened to one hundred-fifty mile-an-hour winds after hitting the islands, but that it was still a Great Hurricane. Assistant Director Bob Cowley said that Eleuthera is expected to strengthen now that she is back over open water.

"Hurricane warnings have been issued for Puerto Rico and the island of Hispaniola, occupied by Haiti and the Dominican Republic. The storm has picked up a forward speed of ten miles an hour. The Hurricane Center says that if she does hit Hispaniola, the storm's intensity might be weakened considerably by the island's ten thousand-foot mountain chain—"

Liza switched off the set. Hurricanes bothered her, even when they were thousands of miles away. She lived on a boat and knew what would happen to her home if one ever hit Surfside.

# 15. OSCAR

The City Commission sat around a large walnut half-moon-shaped table. In front of each member was a microphone, but today the mikes were turned off since this was a private meeting. Sallings and Stark were seated in two comfortable chairs in front of the table. Rainford stood up and turned to the commission members. "I agree with the rest of you; the shark attacks have not been a problem again. And we want to keep it that way. All of you have lived here long enough to know that people's memories are short. In a week or two everyone will forget about it and it'll be back to business as usual. But we can't let it happen again. We have to do something about it. You guys don't realize how much money left this island on that one day. When they check out of the hotels, and don't eat in the restaurants, and don't shop in the shops, it hurts. It's bad enough that we have to contend with weather—we can't do anything about that. But this we can. Agreed?" They all nodded their heads.

Rainford pointed his finger at Stark and Sallings.

"We're counting on you to get this thing straightened out. We want it stopped in a hurry. Now you two are supposed to be crackerjacks, able to do just about anything. Let's see it! We want results. As acting Mayor until Mayor Feeney gets back from Europe, I'm telling you guys to bust ass on this one—you agree, Blanchert?" Captain Blanchert nodded his head silently. "And Detective Sallings, I know you're not particularly pleased with what we've asked you to do, but to use a line from *Gone With the Wind*, 'Frankly, my dear, I don't give a damn.' I do a lot of things I don't want to do, too. So let's get going, okay. Am I understood?" Stark and Sallings both nodded. Sallings' face was scorching red.

"That's all as far as the two of you are concerned, unless you want them to stay for something else, Captain Blanchert?"

"No," Blanchert shifted his portly body in his chair. "Although I'd like to say I don't have any qualms about them being able to get the job done. Both of these officers are every bit as good as I told you they would be."

"I agree," Rainford said. The rest of the commission echoed the same. "Maybe what I said didn't come out quite like I meant it. I think both of you are fine cops and I know this is not what you'd call regular police duty, but you're all we've got and you get the job. I agree with Captain Blanchert—I have complete faith in you."

"Do you believe that bunch of tight bastards?" Sallings said, walking out of the City Administration

Building. She slammed the car door shut and waited for Stark to close his before starting the engine. "Let's get something to eat and maybe something to drink before we start the afternoon." She hammered the steering wheel. "I just don't believe it. They want *me* to organize a group of fishermen to go out and catch that damned shark; keep it all on the QT; and get them to do it by just paying for their gasoline! Do you think those bastards would work just for gasoline?"

"Yeah." Stark noticed her driving speed increased in proportion to her anger. "But they did have a point. The person who gets that fish is going to have himself a record and a charter-boat business like you wouldn't believe."

"That's not the point! Those people are my friends. And Jim and Blanchert are taking advantage of me. They're asking me to lean on them to work for essentially nothing."

"Talking about friends," Stark interrupted. "I thought Rainford was supposed to be one. Is he always that way? It's almost schizophrenic the way he can change from being nice and shaking your hand to being domineering and shaking his finger at you."

"Jim's just had a bad year. He has a lot of money in business places along the beach and this winter really hurt him, as cold as it was. And now, these shark attacks right at the end of the summer tourist season, have him really—Hey, learn how to drive, stupid!" Liza hit the horn as an Illinois license plate switched lanes without signalling.

"Hey, don't get down on the tourists?" Stark said. "I've lived here just long enough to realize our livelihoods depend on them. They're our bread and butter.

Whatta you so pissed off about anyway, Liza, if it's any of my business?"

"You're right, it's none of your business. It's private. Let's just say my love life is not at its peak. I'm sorry. I'm dumping on you."

"No problem. What would make you happy?"

"A chili-dog with onions, ketchup, mustard, and relish," she said, pulling into the beach concession parking lot."

"I give up. You're hopeless. You're gonna have ulcers by Christmas. Want to flip for who pays?"

"Come on Stark, a man always buys lunch for the little lady."

"Not when the little lady is both a piranha and his boss—heads or tails?"

"Heads."

Stark peered at the quarter under his clasped hand. Some days a guy just can't win."

"That's the way it goes Stark. You wanna tell me what happened between you and Ollie or—hey, you know what I'd really like?"

"No, I don't want to tell you what happened between me and Ollie. I don't even want to think about what happened between me and Ollie, and I'm not too sure if I want to know what you'd really like."

"What I'd really like is to catch that shark!"

"So what's new? We all would."

"I mean me—us, personally, catch that bastard. Everything was sailing fine around here until he drifted into the scene. How about me and you taking him out?"

"Are you serious?"

"Dead serious! I know about shark fishing. Why

not? The captain says he wants this all cleared up—that'd clear it up."

"I know absolutely zero about shark fishing, Liza. And from what Carolyn told me, this baby is no fish to fool around with."

"Come on, Stark. I'm a woman. I'm a cop. Now who in the hell am I gonna get to go shark fishing with me? You're not afraid, are you? You know what a feather it would be in our caps if we brought that sucker in? Come on, you're the guy who got the St. Louis Sniper." She wolfed down the last of the chili-dog, much like Goodwin had her steak. "Do you mind if I ask you a question about that? Sort of personal—sort of professional?"

Stark's eyes hardened and grew as dark as the tint in his sunglasses. "You can ask."

"I was just sort of rerunning some mental tapes the other night. You know, going back over old material? Well, I was remembering what I had read in your files—about the discipline committee in St. Louis?"

Stark nodded and took another bite of his chili-dog, watching the waves fling themselves at the beach.

"There was one reference after another to a Muscatel bottle at the Arch. And something about a message; but it never became clear. A lot of it was struck out as inaudible."

Stark took a look at the people around them waiting for food. "Let's go sit on a bench." He led her away from the crowd before he began. "The sniper, his name was Raymond Furster, left a note in an empty bottle of Muscatel at the bottom of the Arch. I was supposed to pick it up. It said, 'wait for me at the doorway entrance of the *Robert E. Lee*. I want to give myself up and surrender to you alone, peacefully."

"Oh, no!"

"Oh, yes! I didn't pick up the note. I knew better, Liza. I had pretty well narrowed it down to who it had to be; and when I saw him from the hotel with my night glasses, I knew who it was! This guy spoke fluent Vietnamese. One of his tricks was to sucker gooks out from cover and then blow them away! There was no way I was going near that bottle. And I'll be honest; that night, I wasn't taking prisoners."

"I don't blame you."

"All the secrecy and hoopla was about the note. Everyone was worried that we were going to be sued no end because I didn't let Furster surrender or shoot me standing there on the *Lee*."

"I'd have done the same. I was just wondering what all the vague references were about."

"That's it. You serious about getting that shark?"

"Were you serious about the sniper?"

"When?"

"Let's see if we can get our desks cleaned off in the next couple of days and I'll have Petit cover for us. After all, it is police business, isn't it?"

"That's what the captain says."

Eleuthera's winds increased to one hundred-seventy-five miles an hour. Her spiral-banded clouds covered a huge section of the Caribbean. She edged up on the Haitian side of Hispaniola, her winds whipping at the mountainsides, her waters flooding the lowlands.

Again it was the poor who suffered. Along the coastal regions the tidal surge inundated and swept away the debris the natives lived in. Torrential rains caused floods and avalanches that wiped the mountainsides clean. In Petionville, wind-spewn splintered shacks and metal roofs cut people down like an invading army. In Port-au-Prince hundreds more died.

Then as if fearing La Citadelle—the legendary fortress King Henri Christophe had built three thousand feet in the mountains to defend Haiti—Eleuthera backed away from the island and went three hundred miles southwest into the Colombian Basin. The National Hurricane Center had her plotted at fifteen degrees north latitude and seventy-six degrees west longitude.

"What's the latest?" Assistant Director Cowley asked, coming into the Center's operations room.

A young female assistant came up and handed him the newest satellite photographs and reconnaissance data. "Eleuthera took a beating on Haiti's mountains. They knocked her winds back down to one hundred-fifty miles an hour. But then she reversed directions and for some crazy reason went down into the Colombian Basin, here." She jabbed at a map. "That was two hours ago. Now she's rebuilt her winds to one hundred-eighty miles an hour and is headed northwest towards Yucatan. That's why I called you. Dr. Logan says some decisions must be made."

Cowley wiped his eyes with one hand and ran the other over the imaginary hair that was no longer on his head. "Do you know what would happen if that storm tore straight across Cuba, through the Keys, and into Miami? Or up the west coast?"

With one hand behind her back, she pulled her T-shirt a little tighter by wadding it in her hand. She hoped Cowley would notice and admire the absent bra and the effects of the air-conditioning. He didn't. "Isn't your daughter named Eleuthera?" she asked in a seductive petulant tone. The tone was missed, but the question wasn't.

"Don't remind me. Where's Logan?"

Stark walked into his condo and saw that the digital message recorder on his PhoneMate three thousand read *three*. He pushed the playback button and turned up the volume. "Michael, I've been trying to reach you all afternoon," Ollie's voice thundered from the machine. Stark readjusted the volume. "My mother has to have emergency surgery in Kansas City. My father is scared to death and I'm flying out there immediately. I'm sorry about the fight. You're right, I was on edge and out of line. Please forgive me. I'll give you a call when I get back. I'll probably be gone for at least a week. Michael, I care a lot for you."

The second caller hung up. The third was Liza. "Guess who, sweetheart. Thought I'd call and make your day. Know that homicide you were working on? While you were eating dinner tonight—at someplace where you didn't tell anyone you were going—well, a witness ID'd the suspect and said he was in a bar three blocks away from the crime scene. Hernandez and I made the collar. A signed confession is on your desk. Good night!"

Stark looked at Sallings seated next to him in the cruiser. "She really looks good," he thought. "She's fun to be with; has a body that won't quit and near perfect teeth; always dresses nicely. What the hell am I doing ignoring it and not doing anything about it? Is departmental policy always that crucial and always that right?" He decided not to think about her anymore in her presence. Too many times he had thought about something too hard and someone had managed to pick up on his thinking. It reminded him of when he'd been a kid in school and the teacher had asked the one question he couldn't answer. He'd start thinking "Please not me! Please not me!" Invariably, the teacher would zero in on him like a sidewinder missle. Stark was too late.

"You're looking at my body, aren't you?" Sallings challenged, loving having caught him.

Stark decided to challenge back. "Yeah, I was. Not bad for a woman your age. Not a teeny-bopper body, but not bad!"

"Oh, you—Not bad for a woman my age! That's below the belt. Anyway, I think you're just horny because Ollie took off on you. Talk about teeny-boppers, you oughta be thankful that Ollie likes old men."

"Now who's fighting dirty? You're the one who introduced me to her. She's the first woman I've ever gone out with who was that much younger than I am. And personally I perfer women your age—and Goodwin's."

"Oh, Goodwin!" Liza's radar went into instant readiness. "Goodwin! I thought I saw a difference in the way you were acting when she was around. Goodwin! Now let's see—you're sleeping with Ollie, you've got your sights on Carolyn and, of course, you've got the perennial hots for me and anything in a bikini on the beach—just what kind of record are you aiming for anyway, Don Juan?"

"You are something else!" Stark threw a wadded Kleenex at her which she batted back at him. "Let's go to the Hilton for lunch. At least from the dining room there, I can look at the bodies in the pool and not get hassled."

"Here we go to the younger competition again. I thought you said you preferred bodies like mine and Carolyn's."

"I do. I'll admit it looks like Whitefish Bay turned out some pretty good models there for a while. But right now, this model sitting next to me is covered up in a business suit and the chiquitas at the pool are wearing next-to-nothing bikinis. No offense, I prefer bikinis to Polly Prude outfits."

Stark stopped Liza in the lobby of the Hilton as they were leaving. "I never did ask you how it went with the fishermen. Are they going to go after the shark?"

"It went perfectly." Liza had a tinge of disgust in her voice. "Captain Blanchert and our temporary mayor were right. They jumped at the news that the shark is still here. Every last one of them is dying to be the one to catch him. I told them they were under no obligations and I thought they oughta demand more than gas money; but they acted like I was doing them a personal favor. Between the fishermen and the Suncoast Sharkers, they've got about thirty boats all together. They're night fishing and keeping it quiet. Of course, that's when you catch sharks, anyway—at night."

"Then why are we going fishing during the day?"

"Because that's when we can get off. And because I don't have fishing rigs big enough to catch a fish that size. And that means I intend to see which one of us is the best shot, because we're gonna shoot him. Anyway, I don't own a charter boat—I don't want a rod-and-reel record, I just want to kill it stone-cold dead."

"Aye, aye, Captain; but I think we might be wasting our time. I think Carolyn may be wrong on this one. We sure haven't had any more trouble and no one has seen hide or hair of your shark. But I'll tell you what; just to keep the public safe, whatta you think about me taking an hour or so off to patrol the north end of the beach."

"You're an incurable voyeur! You know that? You just want to go down and look at the nudies!"

"Guilty. What can I say? But seriously, I need to sort some things out."

"Fine." She let him help her on with her suit jacket. "But how are you going to get back to the station?"

"I've got the portable radio. I'll catch a ride with someone or give you a call to pick me up."

"Who do you think I am, your personal chauffeur? Your private taxi?"

"Liza!" Stark folded his hands over his heart. "You know how much you mean to me!"

She slammed the car door and cracked the window. "One hour. If you're not back here in one hour, don't bother using that radio!"

Michael walked along the beach just above the water's edge where the sand was solid. Walking through the white powder was almost impossible. It was great for sunbathing because it was so soft and deep; but trying to walk in it was like trying to walk through mud.

The north end was pretty packed for a weekday. The initial scare of the shark attack had worn off and the water had close to a hundred people in it. Eight or nine times that many were sunning on chairs, blankets, beach towels, hotel towels, and rattan mats. Almost all were completely nude. Stark couldn't keep his head from going in all directions at once. This was his second time up here; the first time, the beach had been relatively empty. There was a difference in watching through the telescope and being here. He became fairly uneasy about being dressed in a shirt and tie with a sport coat slung over his shoulder. He felt like the pepper in the proverbial saltshaker. In order to make his presence seem official, he took his detective's badge from its case and pinned it to his belt.

At the very tip of the island the current in the three hundred-yard channel between Surfside and the next island was running fairly swiftly. Signs were posted advising swimmers that the currents were strong, that the channel was deep, and to avoid swimming in it. Most were obeying. Along the Gulf edge of the island the beach sloped gently down into the water, but here on the channel it dropped quickly and the water went to twenty feet almost immediately. It was low tide. The difference between high and low tide had left a ledge of shells and sand. Stark picked it as a place to sit, watch the water, and think. "I really have to straighten out my sex life," he thought. "I really am attracted to Carolyn. I want to go out with her so bad it hurts, but I don't want to give up Ollie. A couple of weeks ago I still thought it was strange to go to bed with someone I wasn't married to, and the other night I was slipping my business card to a girl young enough to be my daughter."

Stark drew circles in the sand that ended in an inward slash like a "G." He rubbed them out. "That's it. She's it," he thought. "She's the one I'd like; but I'm afraid. She seems on another plane, so professional and proper and all; and she's Liza's best friend. Wonder if I could edge Liza into helping me a little with her."

Stark jabbed at a balled-up mass of sea grass with a stick of driftwood that was at his side. He felt it slide into something and become stuck. He raised it up and all the sea grass came with it. Slightly curious about what he had found, assuming it was probably an exciting soda can at the most, Stark started somewhat absently pulling away the sea grass and watching a twenty-year-old Eurasian beauty saunter up the beach towards him. She had smooth tanned hips, a perfect triangle of coal-black pubic hair, a tiny waist with a flat stomach, full breasts with hard dark brown nipples, long straight black hair, the high cheekbones of a model, and a beautiful smile that turned to a look of horror and disgust as she neared Stark. She put her hand to her mouth and recoiled from him.

Stark was embarrassed and confused. First he looked down at himself and then at what he had in his hands. One was full of sea grass and the other held the driftwood stick—impaled through an eye-socket on it was a decomposed and partly denuded head. "Aaaaaahhh" Stark gagged, dropped the stick and shoved the head away from him, all at the same time. Seeing it tumble into the water, he grabbed at it way too late. It had already rolled to the bottom of the channel.

The girl screamed; Stark radioed headquarters; and a crowd formed. Three hours later the divers gave up searching for the head. The current was becoming stronger and visibility was becoming worse.

# 16. PAPA

Great Hurricane Eleuthera majestically took her time sliding across the stomach of the Caribbean. She snaked slowly out of the Colombian Basin on a northerly course. She threatened Jamaica with whirling winds and driving rain but proved to be fickle again and tacked westward toward Guatemala and Belize. Then she charged capriciously toward the north, picked up surface speed and roared across the tip of Yucatan before stalling in the southwest Gulf of Mexico.

Bob Cowley looked at the latest satellite photograph of the great storm just before Eleuthera struck Yucatan. "By God, she's pretty, isn't she!" He turned sideways so Director Troy Logan could see the photo, too. "Absolutely perfect. Deadly as a cobra, but perfect. Look at those bands. Have you ever seen an eye like that? I'm gonna have a copy of this framed for our house!"

Logan's admiration for the storm's beauty was lost in his concern for what this hot-headed, vicious lady was going to do. "Just where is she going," he thought, "and whom is she going to turn on next?" Eleuthera was proving to be one of the most unpredictable as well as one of the most devastating storms of the century. She had changed directions—almost reversing them—slowed down when she shouldn't have, and sped up when no one expected her to. Director Logan did not like Eleuthera at all. The only photograph he wanted to see of her was one of disorganized and dissipating winds.

"I'm going on out to start the news conference. Okay?"

Logan nodded and went back in to pour over his maps and data.

"Ladies and gentlemen of the press. As you all know, Great Hurricane Eleuthera has crossed the tip of Yucatan and has temporarily stalled in the Gulf of Mexico." Cowley loved being on TV and reading his name in the newspapers. He walked over to an easel and flipped back the top cover to show a picture of Eleuthera sitting northwest of Merida, the principal city of the Yucatan Peninsula. "As you can see by comparing these photographs," he flipped another page to a photo of the storm just before she hit Yucatan, "Eleuthera took a beating in Yucatan. So did Yucatan, for that matter." He smiled. Cowley was becoming as proud of Eleuthera as he was of his daughter. She had become famous.

"As I've told you before, Eleuthera is a Great Hurricane. She has winds exceeding one hundred-fifty miles an hour. And she is great in other respects, too. Not only has she visited some of the greatest damage we have ever known on the Caribbean; she has also demonstrated the ability to take a punch and recover like Muhammed Ali. She faltered in the mountains of Haiti and recovered. She bulldozed through Yucatan, came out bruised and battered, and now she's sitting out there getting a second wind—please excuse my pun—before plaguing us elsewhere. Eleuthera is truly a great storm—one that will go down in the history books and that we'll all remember."

Listening from the next room, Logan decided he needed to defuse his associate's zeal for both his subject and the cameras. That would have to wait, though. For now, Eleuthera was much more important.

Cowley pointed to another map that showed the coastal states bordering the Gulf of Mexico and the island of Cuba. "In accordance with our new policy of giving percentages of where a hurricane might strike, let me call your attention to the following numbers." He went around the coast calling out the percentages for each. "But let me remind you, that Great Eleuthera has been rather capricious. She is her own weather system. You know you have high and low pressure systems that affect storms, but Eleuthera is so massive, so strong that she is her own weather system and could well be stronger than any system opposing her. Predicting exactly what she is going to do—again, excuse the pun—is like throwing straws in the wind. You're really not sure where they're gonna fall."

Cowley flipped all the photos back over on the easel. "We have, however, notified all cities and civil defense personnel in coastal cities of the present situation. We will update that information as soon as we see where Great Eleuthera wishes to go."

"Mr. Cowley," a reporter's hand shot in the air.

"Yes."

"John Drake, *Miami Herald.* Where would you say, in spite of your percentages, the hurricane is likely to go?"

"Well, I hate to argue with percentages and computers, don't you? But personally, judging from history, I don't believe I'd want to live in the Galveston-Houston area or the New Orleans-Pass Christian area, would you?"

A day later, late in the evening, acting Mayor Jim Rainford returned Captain Blanchert's phone call. "Hi, Blanchert. What's up? I hate to call you at home, but I just never got a chance all day."

"We got a call from the National Hurricane Center in Miami. They say that Eleuthera has drifted up the west side of the Gulf and they're now giving us a forty-percent chance of being hit."

"A Forty per-cent chance of being hit? Where did they dig up that number anyway? Is God running some kind of crap game that he's cut them in on?"

"Well, they said it's all involved with temperatures and steering currents and stuff like that. They suggested starting a partial evacuation of all barrier islands such as Surfside."

"Come on, Blanchert!" Rainford bellowed into the phone. "That storm is all the way across the Gulf. You've lived here as long as I have and you know that damn Hurricane Center cries wolf half a dozen times a year. Logan is always around here saying how unsafe the islands are and how hard it's going to be to get people out. You also know as well as I do, that that storm is going to go off through the middle of Texas just like all the rest of them do. Now, we've had enough trouble around here without adding evacuation to our problems. Do you have any idea what that would do to the economy? Do you have the manpower to protect the abandoned property?"

"Not really." Blanchert never liked talking to Rainford, especially when he was upset.

"Then you'd better not call an evacuation until you can see that goddamned hurricane out your window coming straight at you."

Rainford dropped the phone in the cradle and wiped the perspiration from his face. He was angry. "Just how the hell does anyone down here accomplish anything without any guts?" he thought. "Guts! That's one four-letter word this city doesn't even know how to spell! These people don't even know what risk is. They ought to get into big business once."

Liza picked up her morning paper and returned to the galley for a cup of coffee. She opened the page and saw the headlines, KILLER ELEUTHERA STRIKES AGAIN! She took a drink of coffee and read on:

> MIAMI (AP)—Great Hurricane Eleuthera ravaged the jungle peninsula of Yucatan before going stationary in the Gulf of Mexico. Authorities estimate the great storm took an additional 500 to 1,000 lives in Yucatan alone. Many fear the toll will be much worse when dead and miss-

> ing are all accounted for. Totally, it looks like Eleuthera has already taken the lives of nearly 4,000 people since she started her deadly trek into the Lesser Antilles!
>
> Hardest hit at last report were the resort islands of Cancun, Isla Mujeres and Isla de Cozumel. In Cancun, the massive waves smashed into the coral rock behind the famous Camino Real and tossed over the top of the grand hotel. The Space Needle tower at the convention center has been destroyed and several condominiums have been washed into the sea. The new Hotel Blanco was washed completely away along with more than 200 guests and others who had taken shelter there.
>
> The city of Cancun, a ramshackle collection of village huts, modern store-fronts, and tented tourist shops fell as quickly to Eleuthera as the Mayans did to the Spanish. Not a window was left in the city and very few walls remained standing. The town looks much like the familiar Mayan ruins of a soon to be forgotten city.
>
> In Cozumel, the reports are much the same. One ham radio operator advises of complete destruction. Oddly enough, though, he says he came through Tulum earlier in the day and found the ancient ruins on the sea virtually unscathed by the storm. See KILLER STORM on inside page.

Liza decided to pass. She was more worried about a killer shark. Clearwater beach had reported two swimmers missing, and a sixteen-foot boat had disappeared at midnight; Madiera Beach had a missing hotel guest who was last seen swimming a hundred yards offshore; and to Liza's dismay, the biggest fish her shark-fishing fleet had been able to bring in was a twelve-foot hammerhead.

# 17. QUEBEC

Captain Blanchert put his suit coat on and stepped outside the station house to talk to the newspaper reporters. Actually, he wanted to have his photograph taken beside the Surfside Police Department logo on the outside of the building. He posed for one photograph with a bit of a smile and tried to a look a little more stern and businesslike in the second. The photographer said, "Thanks, Captain. I'm going to take off and leave you with the two villains."

"Okay, Bob," Blanchert replied. "Have a another tough day snapping pictures!"

He turned to the two reporters. "Let me tell you two what we know so far and then, if you have any questions, I'll try to answer them. First off, let me thank you for playing this down somewhat. I'll treat you right for taking care of us. Off the record, we don't have any more clues. It's going to be a tough case. It's like I told you last night: Detective Stark was poking around in some seaweed and a human head rolled out of there into the channel. It was badly decomposed and he didn't get a chance to look at it closely to determine if it was male or female.

"Without the head, it's impossible to conclude if it was a homicide, a boat accident, or whatever. As you know, we just had our first homicide for the year. This may be our second. And you also know, Surfside has had more than its share of bad publicity in recent weeks, including a rape night before last. So if you can keep playing it down as much as possible—until we know for sure—then I'll get you in here with first cracks at everything."

"Captain," the tallest of the two male reporters pressed. "Again, off the record, whatta you think? Homicide? That shark again? What?"

"I'd guess homicide. That's how we're treating it here. Although there is a sixteen-foot boat missing off of Clearwater that had a two hundred-horse engine on it. That's overloading a boat that size and a propeller that big sure could decapitate you. But we haven't found the rest of the body. When we do, I'll give you a call."

The second reporter put down his note pad. "Besides searching for the body, what else are you doing?"

"I'm beefing up the patrols up and down the beaches—I'd appreciate it if you didn't put that in. And we're searching for clues sort of surreptitiously. Again, I don't want to go up there, rope off half the beach and scare the hell out of the rest of the tourists when we aren't even sure there's been a crime."

"Yeah, I can understand that. We'll sort of play it along behind yesterday's story as police still investigating finding a body in the bay. That way it even leaves the beach out of it."

"Thanks, fellows." Blanchert wiped his brow in the heat. "Like I said, I'll do right by you." He shook their hands and went back into the station house.

"Stark! Sallings!" Blanchert bellowed across the room. "I want to see you in my office."

Sallings turned in her chair and looked at Stark. "Oh boy!" She drew a slashing finger across her throat. They hit the floor at once and went to Blanchert's office.

Blanchert took off his suit coat, loosened his tie, and rolled up the sleeves of his Dior shirt. He enjoyed dressing a little flamboyantly. "Shut the door and sit down.

They obeyed.

Blanchert leaned forward, elbows on his desk, and twisted a pencil in his hand. "Stark, let me say that I'm less than pleased with your handling of this one."

Sallings choked down a laugh at his choice of words.

"Just what were you doing up on the north end of the beach in the middle of the afternoon, anyway?"

"It was early afternoon, Sir. It was my lunch hour," Stark lied.

"I thought, according to the radio log, that the two of you checked out ten-seven for lunch at the Holiday Inn?"

"We did, but I had to catch someone right at noon so I left Sallings."

Sallings nodded corroborating the lie.

Blanchert shook his head. "It really doesn't matter, but what in blazes were you doing? They don't serve lunch up there. Just what the hell were you doing, detective; crotch watching or what?"

Liza choked down another throatful of laughter.

Blanchert drummed his fingers on the desk. "You expect me to believe you had that head in your hands and panicked like some old lady or little kid and dropped the damned thing in the channel? Jesus Christ, man! You're a police detective, not a tourist!"

Stark's face burned with heat; he was boiling. He didn't like being chewed out in front of Liza. Something inside him wanted to stuff Blanchert's fat face in the wastepaper basket and stomp on it. He sat on his anger. "I'm sorry, sir. It won't happen again."

"It damn well better not." He turned in his chair to Sallings. "And now you. You know your date the other night?"

Sallings looked back and forth from Blanchert to Stark with a quizzical look. "Which date? Which night?"

"The tall thin Latin fellow. The one who stayed all night on your boat. Ramon Lopez?"

Stark's anger abated; he became amused as Sallings began to squirm in her seat.

"Yeah, what about it?" she replied defensively. "Don't tell me you're snooping on my love life."

"Don't get smart!" Blanchert snapped the pencil. "Don't flatter yourself to think I'd be that interested in your love life! But I got a call from the Federal Narcotics people. They tell me your Latin lover is a big coke dealer. They're real interested in what he's doing with one of my detectives—especially one with a boat."

"Oh, damn!" She put her face in her hands and

shook her head. "I just met the guy, Captain. Kara and I were at Brannigan's and he just came up and introduced himself to us. Sally was the bartender on duty. She can back it up. The guy said he was from Tampa. He had Hillsborough County license plates. I had no idea he was dealing. I don't think I even told him I was a cop."

Blanchert shook his head and looked up at the ceiling. "No matter. The Feds are going to drop by your place tonight to get a statement. Be a little more careful in the future, okay. Just remember that your's is not the only career in this department?"

"Yes, sir."

Blanchert picked up a fresh pencil, tossed the broken one at the waste basket and missed. "Back to our homicide or whatever. Whether you two know it or not, I have Jim Rainford and the City Commission all over me. This town has received more bad publicity in the past month than it has in the past ten years. And that adds up to lost dollars—tax dollars and payroll dollars—budget dollars. And let me tell you they're not being too coy about it, either. I don't have to tell you that we live off the tourists. Agreed?

Stark and Sallings nodded their heads.

"Well, from the commission's standpoint, I—we don't look good. Can't say that I blame them. The way they see it we've had a shark tear up our beach, a pothead flatten a police car with a bulldozer, a rapist on our nude beach, a detective fumble a head into the channel, and we've got a homicide with the murderer sitting on his ass drinking beer within pissing range of the police investigating the crime. For some reason, they don't see that as a spectacular record. The shark's still not been caught, neither the head nor the body has been found, the rapist is still loose, and everyone who knows anything is just a bit edgy. They want it all tidied up so everyone can get back to business as usual. Do I make myself clear?"

They both nodded.

"Where do you want us to start, Captain?" Stark asked, realizing Blanchert was right.

Blanchert sat back in his chair and turned to Liza. "For beginners, Liza, I want you to get someone to call all the charter boats up and down the coast. The commission has authorized paying fifty boats one-hundred dollars a night to find that shark—if they find him. And only fifty dollars a night if no one turns him up."

"All right!" Liza slapped the arm of her chair. "They'll get him."

"And," Blanchert added. "let them know that anyone who talks this up might find himself having a real hard time getting a business license next year or passing his boat safety inspection.

"Secondly, I want you to to cover the north end of the beach with a fine tooth comb. See who's up there. There's a good chance that either one of those weird bastards are up there right now staking out a new victim."

"It's possible," Stark interjected, "that the guy who committed the rape is the same guy who did the number on the head. I read that rape report."

"Yeah, so did I," Sallings added. "I'd like to be alone in a cell with him for about five minutes."

"Well," Blanchert said. "You're starting to sound like cops again. Now, let's get to work. If there are any clues to who that rapist is anywhere on that beach—I want them. If that homicide happened up there, you'd better find out. This evening after everyone is gone, I have three boats that are going to scour the channel and bay area with drag lines. The commission doesn't want them out there in the middle of the day. All we need is for everyone to see us pull a headless body from the water or to wait until it gasses up and floats in somewhere.

"While you're up there—God help you—don't you dare cause any confusion or uproar. Don't let people know that you're looking for clues in a homicide or rape case—don't even mention them or that you're cops. Pretend you're looking for a wedding ring or a diamond earring or something, but comb that goddamned beach good. If there's anything up there, you better not miss it this time. Understand?"

"Aren't we going to be a little obvious in our clothes, walking around putting things in little plastic bags?" Sallings asked with just a tinge of sarcasm.

"Don't use little plastic bags," Blanchert replied with an equal amount of sarcasm. "Use a beach bag. Be creative! And take your clothes off so you look like tourists." He leaned back in his chair; a big grin crossed his face.

"Captain!" Liza stood up. "That's not in the line of duty!"

"Sit down, Detective Sallings." Blanchert sat back up in his chair. "I decide what's in the line of duty. You know as well as I do there are a lot of things you have to do out of the line duty, whether it's a one-on-one hunt for someone like Stark did in St. Louis or working a big narcotics hit. Let me tell you, if I had a dollar for every cop who's had to go to bed with someone in order to pull off a big bust, I'd be rich. There're lot's of things you have to do *out* of the line of duty that're *in* the line of duty. Walking around nude on a nude beach so you don't scare the hell out of people is not much to ask. Anyway, it's Stark's favorite hangout. Have him introduce you around. And take Hernandez with you.

"Captain," Liza interjected. "I'm one thing, but Hernandez is another. She just wouldn't do it. She'd quit. She'd sue us."

"No she won't." Blanchert replied. "I already talked to her. She thinks it sounds like fun. Now get out of here."

Stark drove Sallings to her boat to pick up her bathing suit, beach bag, and beach towel. "I almost quit," he said to Sallings as they got back into the car. He held his first finger and his thumb an inch apart. "I was just that far from telling Blanchert where to go."

Sallings was surprised. "Why? Not over being chewed out, for Christ's sake. Surely you've been chewed on before. It's not over the nudity, is it?"

"No. I have trouble being chewed out in front of someone. I feel like I've taken too much garbage. I think there's a little bit of the old me coming back, and the old me wasn't as nice a guy as I am now."

"Well," Sallings said, coming out of Stark's condo, after he'd donned his bathing suit and grabbed a beach towel. "If you want to get mean, fine. But don't get stupid. Believe it or not, there has to be some bad stuff going on in the City Commission. Blanchert likes you a lot—I know it. And he's the best captain this department has ever had. He'll back you up to the limit."

"I hope you're right." Stark replied, pulling the Lincoln into the traffic. "If you're not, I think we're in trouble. I've got a feelin that things are going to get real hot before this one's over."

"Glad you're thinking that way—cause you're right. Our ass is on the line and I want everyone doing anything and everything they can to get things back on an even keel. And if the Captain wants us nude, fine! I'll walk on my hands if I have to. We're gonna lean on everyone in this department to give us every ounce of help they can. Understand?"

Stark nodded. "I might quit, but I'll be damned if I'm gonna be fired from a job that I've just started. Where does Hernandez live?"

Hernandez, Sallings and Stark spread out their beach towels on the end of the beach. The sun was blistering. The waves were unusually high and frothy, churned up and sent across the Gulf by Hurricane Eleuthera. Right now, Surfside was living up to its name; surfers from all over Florida had come to ride the rising waves. The breeze was brisk and alleviated a lot of the midday sun's frying rays. Slickly oiled, tanned, and naked bodies were everywhere. Stark put a thumb in each side of his suit's waistband and hesitated. "I'm not sure I'm ready for this."

Hernandez had already dropped the top of her bikini on the towel and was wiggling out of the bottom. Stark tried not to stare, then relaxed; she was attractive. She picked up a bottle of suntan lotion. "This thing you have never done?" she asked in a soft Spanish accent. "You have not sunbathed in the nude?"

"No." Stark replied a little self-consciously as he watched her rub the oil over her breasts and through her pubic area. "I never have—at least not publicly like this."

She leaned down and rubbed the oil up and down her legs. "I grew up in Tampa and we used to go to Lake Como, the nudist camp there. But in the Gulf you could not go; it was against the law. And then Surfside changed the law, but I had become a policewoman and could not go. And now I get to go and be paid for it. It is fantastic, is it not?" She turned around, held her hair above her head with one hand and handed Liza the bottle of suntan oil. "Do my back for me, please."

Hernandez turned around to Stark and Sallings who were still clothed. "Come on, you two. This thing frightens everyone at first. You will see. In ten minutes you will not notice how nude you are."

"Why don't I believe that?" Stark said, looking around at all the nude bodies beside him. "Well, why not. There's got to be a time to try everything—I guess the time has come." He slipped the suit down to the towel and stepped out of it.

"Turn around." Hernandez said. "I will oil you." She started pouring the hot suntan oil over his shoulders and it felt good as she rubbed it in.

"You should not feel bad." Hernandez worked the oil down his back. "You are nice without your clothes. You do not have a big belly like most men your age."

"That's a nice way of putting it," Liza teased.

" 'For a man your age.' "

As Hernandez rubbed the oil around Stark's lower back he felt stirrings but was surprised at how easily the erection process was wiped out by the presence of so many people. "You do your front," Hernandez handed him the bottle.

Stark kicked his suit at Liza. "What's with you, Miss Prude? You're the only one out here who's still dressed." He sat down on his towel to finish putting on the lotion, stealing another look at Juanita. Her body was lean and solid. He could tell she worked out. "Come on Liza," he taunted. "Don't tell me you're the chicken."

"I'm just saving the best for last." She stood up on her beach towel. "This is what you've been waiting all your life for, Stark. Don't miss it." She reached behind her back for her bikini top strings. They fell to her side and she lifted the top over her head and tossed it at Stark.

"Not bad! Not bad!" he said with a smile of admiration. He wouldn't admit that she was right; that he had indeed thought about this minute more than once.

"Now don't have a heart attack on me, Michael. Just enjoy it." Liza reached down, pulled the strings at each hip, and let the bikini bottom drop.

Stark pursed his lips in a silent whistle. "So you're a blonde there, too." He looked unabashedly at the blonde triangle between her legs. "I'll say it again. They did turn out some decent women in Whitefish Bay."

"Okay, Stark. There's a difference between looking and leering. If you don't want a swift kick, you'd better cool it."

"I was just trying not to have a heart attack."

"Well, start by getting in gear. We've got a job to do."

"Lead on, boss lady."

Liza stood with Stark and Hernandez at the tip of the island. "Let's think a minute." She scanned the beach up and down, and from bay to Gulf.

"Well!" Stark startled her out of her thoughts. "What are you thinking? How do you want to go about this? We can't rope if off or anything."

"No, we can't. Since the head was your screw up, why don't you take the first twenty feet from the island's tip. That's where you found your prize. I'll take the next twenty feet, and Juanita will take the next. Let's work slowly from the Gulf to the bay and try not to be too obvious. Remember, we're looking for my wedding band. Don't ask anyone to move or anything like that, but if they do, go over and look where they've been—"

"Shark! Shark! Four of them!" came a shout from fifty yards down the beach. Liza, Michael, and Juanita started towards the commotion in the water at a dead run.

There were half a dozen people standing dripping at the water's edge and another two dozen still in the water. They were laughing. "Where's the shark?" Liza panted, catching up to Stark and Hernandez.

"No shark." Hernandez pointed toward the Gulf. "Dolphin. A whole school of them there, at the mouth of the channel."

"I thought I was going to have a heart attack," Liza

gasped.

"I did!" Stark wheezed, starting back toward the end of the island.

The dolphins had not been playing. They had just streaked through the channel at top speed. Not far behind them trailed twenty-six feet of certain death. The huge tiger shark had just eaten two slow pelicans and chased a large grouper halfway through Surfside Bay before losing him. There he had picked up the school of feeding dolphin and began chasing them. One, a small one, was in trouble and the tiger could sense it. It was moving erratically and couldn't keep up with the rest of the school—it had been injured.

At the bay side entrance to the channel, the baby dolphin's luck came to an abrupt end. Emitting a final burst of weak plaintive squeaks, it died when the huge tiger caught it at the surface. The great shark burst from the water with the small dolphin clamped between his teeth, then went to the bottom of the deep channel to finish his catch. Dolphin was the hardest prey to get, but his favorite food.

All eyes but those of a five-year-old boy were focused on the dolphins in the Gulf end of the channel. They hadn't seen the shark; he had. "Mommy! Mommy!" He yanked at his naked mother's hand. "A shark ate Flipper, Mommy! A shark ate Flipper!"

"No, he didn't." She smiled, reached down and picked him up, holding him on her hip and brushing the hair back from his eyes. "Look out there." She pointed to the end of the channel. "Flipper's out there."

"No, Mommy," the little boy insisted, pointing back towards the bay. "The shark ate him back there."

"Oh, Adrian," she laughed. "You just never stop, do you?"

Back at the tip of the island, Liza, Michael, and Juanita had begun their search for clues. Fifteen feet behind Liza at the water's edge, a little girl sat slapping the water with a yellow plastic sand-shovel and shrilly calling the dolphins to come back and play with her.

The dolphin had really whetted the tiger shark's appetite. He snapped at the water where traces of the mammal's blood remained. He heard the rhythmic slapping at the surface and streaked for it. Many times during the past month he had learned it was food.

Stark was walking along the beach with a button and a strip of clothing he had found, possible evidence in the rape or homicide cases. As he dropped them in Liza's beach bag, he saw the shadow bolting through the water. In a fraction of a second, he realized it wasn't aimed at him but at the small child. He screamed and grabbed the little girl just as the great fin first broke the surface. Stark swung the little girl high in the air as the shark broke completely out of the water and half-beached itself on the white sand. Snapping his teeth shut, he twisted from side to side, trying both to get at someone and get back in the water.

Screams started down the beach like an echo in a canyon. They began at the north end of the beach and traveled faintly down toward the hotels. Liza started giving CPR—cardiopulmonary resuscitation—to a man in his fifties who had a heart attack. Stark stood with clenched fists only five feet from the snapping jaws that still had bloody fragments of baby dolphin wedged between its teeth. The rest of the crowd hung back another twenty feet behind them cringing in fear of the snapping monster.

"Hernandez!" Liza shouted. Get our suits and get us some help here!"

"Don't get close to him." Stark cautioned Hernandez as she edged between him and the shark. "Look at that thing. You could drive a tractor into that mouth. Why in God's name don't we have a gun? Why! Juanita, get us rifles. Tell them we need M-16's with armor-piercing bullets—"

"Get a move on, Hernandez!" Liza shouted from twenty feet away.

Stark picked up a five-foot piece of driftwood and splintered it across the shark's head, narrowly missing getting his hand bitten off as the shark caught a bit of a wave and managed to move toward him before sliding back into the water. "You son-of-a-bitch!" He picked up a rock and bounced it off the shark's back. Angry and frustrated, he walked down the beach looking for another rock. The crowd followed fifteen yards back on the beach; the shark followed fifteen feet out in the water.

"Juanita?" Stark asked as she handed him his suit. "Is that bastard following me?"

"I think so, Michael. I think it is not good that you stay so close to the water."

"Get me that rifle."

Juanita took off at a miler's pace down the beach.

Liza, dressed, had handed over the CPR to a sunbathing nurse and joined Stark at the water's edge.

"The son-of-a-bitch is stalking you, Stark."

"Let's see if he is." He turned and walked to the tip of the island. The tiger followed. Stark walked around the tip to the bay. The tiger continued and here, where it was deeper, he came within three feet of the shore. He and Stark looked each other directly in the eye. Both glared hatred. Stark turned and walked back around to the Gulf. Again the tiger paced him, waiting.

Stark felt he was being dared and something in him rose to the challenge. He wanted to kill this fish more than he wanted anything else in his life at this moment. "I think I can tease and keep this bastard here. If I can, we'll kill this son-of-a-bitch right now!"

He put on his bathing suit and continued walking back and forth along the same section of beach, occasionally splashing the water a little. The crowd began throwing stones at the shark. "Stop it!" Stark shouted, waving his hands in the air. "Stop it! I'm a police officer. I'm trying to keep this damned thing here until we can get a rifle and kill it."

Almost as if he understood Stark's words, the water boiled and the massive tiger shark disappeared from sight. Two minutes later Hernandez and a Surfside Police Jeep arrived with two more officers, M-16's, and extra ammunition.

Stark grabbed an M-16; Liza grabbed another and wrapped a belted .357 Magnum around her waist. "Get out of the goddamned jeep," she shouted at the khaki-suited beach patrolman. She hopped behind the steering wheel and pointed the M-16 at the patrolman with her left hand. "You let me know if you see him again. You understand?"

The man turned pale with the gun barrel pointed in his face. "Yes, sir—Yes ma'am, Detective!"

She turned to Stark, "You ready to go fishing, Michael?"

"Can't wait!"

Sallings slid the police Jeep to a stop broadside behind her boat, blocking three cars, and left it. "Toss off the lines, Stark. I'll get us started."

Michael handed his rifle up to Sallings on the flybridge, dashed to the bow, and threw the front lines over her holding rope. He ran sideways to the stern as the engines roared to life. "Ready?" he shouted.

"Toss 'em!"

Stark threw the port line on the dock; the starboard line was yanked out of his hand and fell into the water as Liza blasted out of the slip. Ignoring No Wake regulations, she tore full speed out of the marina, her wake tossing boats around like a violent summer storm. On-board captains tumbled topside, shaking their fists and shouting curses.

Trim tabs down, they rocketed through the bay, into the pass, then slowed in the Gulf in the face of the high waves. Expertly, Sallings threaded the breakers. "I want to stay in close to shore. As rough as it is, we're not going to see anything deep anyway. I just think he's along the beach here and we've got a lot of it. He was defying us, Michael. He was daring us to get in *his* water."

"That's how I felt," Stark replied, one hand on the rail to steady himself, the other holding the M-16. "All I want is one clean shot. Just one clean shot!"

"That's two of us. I'd like to run this boat back and forth across his head about a half a dozen times."

"Looks like you got your wish." Stark pointed toward the northern tip of the beach a quarter of a mile away where he could barely make out beach patrolmen with arms outstretched. "It looks like they're shooting at something." He snapped back the M-16, loading a live round into the chamber.

"Michael, I hate to tell you this; but with seas this high, I can't get into that channel. Why the hell didn't they tell us what was going on?"

"Did you bring a radio?"

"No. Did you?"

Stark shook his head disgustedly. "They're in the jeep."

Liza got the Coast Guard on the marine radio and had them patch her through to Hernandez on the beach. "Juanita. What's going on?"

"Liza. He has gone inside the bay again. I have shot him twice. He doesn't even know it!"

"Stay away from him. Don't get close to the water. You saw how he came out of it. He could do it again." The sounds of gunfire popped and snapped over the radio.

"Liza! He come out! He come out!"

"I'm going up front," Stark said.

"Put on a life jacket, Michael. In these seas you could be tossed overboard pretty easily."

"What? And float around for that bastard's dessert? No way, lady. You put one on if you want to."

"Liza," Juanita's voice boomed on the radio; the patch had somehow gotten better.

"Yes, Hernandez."

"*Cuidado!* Be careful. He is headed straight for your boat."

"Thanks," Liza answered softly into the mike. "Stark! Stark, can you hear me?" she asked over the front of the bridge.

"Yeah!" he answered, waving his left hand in acknowledgment, yet never taking his eyes from the water.

"We should be right on top of him—or he should be right on top of us."

Stark waved his hand again.

Sallings loaded a copper-jacketed .556 into the M-16, checked the cylinder of her Magnum and laid it on the seat beside her.

"Liza, do you see anything?" Juanita's voice implored on the radio.

"Not a thing, Juanita. It's hard in these seas. It's like riding a roller coaster."

"I can see your boat bouncing. This is me. I'm right beside you on the shore about a hundred yards away. It is safe?"

"Yes, it's safe." Liza waved to her. "Just watch and watch out!"

Stark had inched out onto the pointed teak bow pulpit and now squatted, an arm over each railing, holding his rifle underneath and across his lap. "You see anything at all, Liza?"

"Nothing! I'm gonna watch the stern. Be careful out there."

"Don't worry."

Liza turned and looked south down the beach over the stern of the boat. The view was the same: rolling breakers, shadows, and people lined the beach about ten feet from the surf line.

"Liza! Liza" Juanita yelled into the radio. "He's here. He's right here! He's turning toward you."

Liza had the radio turned to full volume and Stark heard the call. He lept to his feet, caught his foot under the anchor-windlass and pitched sideways, throwing his M-16 into the Gulf as he tried to keep his balance. He teetered precariously for a second then tumbled after the gun. Survival instinct flowed with fear. Stark clawed at everything as he fell; his hand clamped the side of the bow pulpit railing like a vise, leaving him dangling just above the water and bouncing with the boat.

Liza had only glimpsed the fall. She turned and saw Stark bouncing up and down wildly above the waves, a tantalizing bait for the tiger shark that was heading straight for him. "Hold on, Michael," she shouted raising the rifle to her shoulder. "Don't let go!" A wave bounced the boat as she fired a burst of bullets at the oncoming shadow. They splashed the water ten feet from the shark. She fired again, emptying the clip and cutting her starboard railing in half as another wave bounced the boat and almost pitched her overboard.

Stark's hand didn't even feel tired; it was locked permanently around the railing. He heard Liza shout, but didn't hear what she said. He saw her aim the rifle and turned to see where she hit, knowing what was there. He saw the bullets splash before he saw the fin barely cut the surface and then rise above the waves like the conning tower of a submarine. "Liza!" Stark shouted, never taking his eyes from the fin. He heard the rifle fire a second and longer burst and sounds of the railing exploding further down the boat. "Oh God, Liza!" He looked at her, terror washing his face as the shark closed to within twenty feet of him. He pulled himself as high as he could with his one hand, and kept trying to get a hand-hold with the the other to keep from being knocked free of the boat.

Liza regained her footing and grabbed the .357 Magnum. She held onto the railing with her left and fired two shots into the shark before it slid beneath Stark. The shark sliced its devilish fin between Michael's legs before he submerged and swam off unconcerned into deeper water.

"Michael, are you okay?" Liza grabbed the front of his shorts and his belt and yanked him up to the gunwale of the boat. Stark managed to wrap a leg around the railing and wrap his other arm around Liza's shoulder. She rolled him over onto the deck where he lay doubled up massaging his aching shoulder.

"I think I wrenched it pretty badly, but at least I didn't go in. What about—?" He looked down at his groin. "How close was it?"

Liza grinned in spite of ths severity of the trauma. "You don't want to know, my friend. Let me tell you; you don't want to know!"

"Why didn't he get me? He could have?" Stark sat up, still rubbing his shoulder. "He could have nailed me easily if he'd wanted to. Do you think your shots stopped him?"

"Who knows? I doubt it. I'm not even sure I hit him. I think maybe he likes you, Stark. Maybe he thinks you're his playmate."

"Like hell he does? Are we going on after him?"

"Do you feel up to it?"

"Never felt better in my life." Stark grabbed the railing with the wrenched arm and fell back to a sitting position as the pain tore through his body.

Liza shook her head in disbelief and headed for the helm where the radio was blasting a message to *Sunday's Grouper* from the Clearwater Coast Guard. Captain Blanchert wanted them back in port immediately.

# 18. ROMEO

It was seven P.M. and Stark was glad to be home. He was hot, tired, sore, and disgusted with the day. He hung up his sport coat, dropped the rest of his clothes in a pile on the bathroom floor, stepped into his shower, and turned on the cold-water tap full blast. It was lukewarm but refreshing just the same. It lifted his spirits and he was even managing to whistle an off-key tune when the phone rang. "Hi!" Sallings said cheerfully before he could speak. "I've got good news and bad news—which one you want first?"

"The good news is that Blanchert's been eaten by the shark and they've made me captain. The bad news is you've been named mayor and you're still above me."

"Close, want to try again?"

"Liza, what I want is a drink. Are you going to spit it out or do you wantta hold the phone till I fix one?"

"Don't have time to wait. The bad news is that Jim Rainford is calling an informal commission meeting on his boat. He wants me, you, and Blanchert to attend."

Liza, I've had a bad day! Tonight I'm not sure I have the stomach for that bunch of mealy-mouthed self-interested self-important bureaucrats. Why don't you take them shark fishing and use them as bait."

Liza laughed. "Oh come on, Stark. It's not the end of the world. This won't be that bad. They're not out for blood—they're just scared and, believe it or not, concerned about you. They all want to see that you're okay. Come on and take some bows. And anyway, Jim always has the place decked out with food and drink. So come hungry and thirsty."

"I thought you said there was some good news."

"Blanchert got the Sheriff to send his helicopter down to pick up Carolyn. She's gonna be there, too."

A smile crossed Stark's face and he felt his pulse quicken. "Now, that is good news."

"You owe me one, old buddy. I was the one who suggested it."

"Anything you ask!"

"You're gonna be sorry you said that!" Liza laughed. "Be there at eight o'clock—sharp."

"What!"

Liza had hung up.

Stark didn't know what to expect when he reached the *Mangrove Snapper's* slip. He had rushed and was fifteen minutes early. Being late for appointments was not one of Stark's faults. The tide was high and the *Mangrove Snapper* sat majestically above the docks. Compared to the other yachts beside it, it looked like a cruise ship. The *Snapper* was easily the largest in Cormorant Hole Marina. A tall set of wooden stairs on rollers sat beside the bow of the boat and Stark could see a doorway beside them. He climbed the stairs, found a bell with a rope on it, rang twice, and waited before stepping aboard.

"Come aboard, Detective." Jim opened the door and held out a hand for a shake. "How you doin'? How's the arm?"

"It's a lot better, thanks. A hot shower helped."

"That was a close one—save the story for when everyone gets here. Come on inside and let's get a drink." They walked across the teak pilothouse and entered the salon. "You're the first one here."

"Liza said eight o'clock."

"Son, this is the South. Ain't nobody ever gonna get anywhere on time down here. If any of them gets here before eight-thirty, I owe you a drink. Anyway, whatcha drinkin?" He led him through the salon into the enclosed aft-deck and a full-sized wet bar.

"Jack Daniels and water if you have it." He looked around at the interior of the boat.

"Sure do."

Rainford emanated down-home friendship and an intimacy Stark didn't trust. It was too smooth, too much of a change of heart. Stark decided to play along and be wary. "Jesus," he said. "I've never seen a boat like this. This is fabulous. It's like a house!"

"Want the grand tour while we wait?"

"Sure!"

"Well this is aft-deck, of course, and in here is the salon or living room and dining room."

"I'm not kiddin'," Stark said. "It's fantastic! Huge."

"Thanks. I'm proud of it. It is big. Remember, this mother's sixty-five feet long and almost eighteen feet across the beam. That's a lot of boat. Come on down below." Through a hatchway in the corner of the room, a flight of stairs led below decks. "This is the master stateroom with a queen-size bed. Look in here. It has full-sized cedar-lined closets and a full-sized head with tub and shower."

"This is unbelievable." Stark said.

Jim led the way through a door and into a hallway. "Look at these." He opened doors on each side of the hallway and Stark could see huge sparkling-clean engines in rooms large enough to stand up in. "These are GM 6-71N Diesels and this baby carries twenty seven thousand gallons of fuel."

"I'll bet they like to see you at the gas tanks." Stark said, sticking his head inside the port engine room and then looking in its identical starboard twin.

"That they do." Jim chuckled and went on down the hall. "This is another guest stateroom here on the right; and another with a head and shower here on the left. That's your washer and dryer there, behind the louvered doors."

Stark poked his head into each stateroom. They were all elaborately and richly furnished.

"This is another head and shower here on the right; and up here," he said pointing to the bow, "is supposed to be another stateroom, but I had it customized into an office to hold books, files, my computers, and stuff."

"Nice."

"And these stairs go back up to the pilothouse. Did you see the galley when you came through? It was right behind the pilothouse. It's like any other kitchen; you know, microwave, dishwasher, range, side-by-side refrigerator, and all that stuff—even has a trash compacter."

"I'm impressed," Stark said following him back up the stairs. "It's like a floating hotel."

They heard voices in the salon and found Liza and Dr. Goodwin sitting on the velvet couch, drinks in hand. Jim walked over, shook hands, and gave them each a kiss on the cheek. "Dr. Goodwin, didn't we meet at that conference at Frenchman's Reef in St. Thomas last year?"

Carolyn beamed, pleased to be remembered. "Yes, sir. And Dr. Harvey said to tell you 'Hi,' and to thank you for your contribution to the Institute again this summer."

"I can't think of a better place to spend my money. I just gave Detective Stark a grand tour—want to see my pride and joy?"

A half hour later the rest of the guests had assembled and had downed a drink or two. "Let's get down to business," Jim said, setting his drink on the coffee table. "I asked you all to come over here so we could keep this private. We've got to do something about that damn shark. Dr. Goodwin, how can we get him? Can we poison him? Can you predict when he's going to hit again? We have to stop him somehow. We're getting national attention. This evening we were on the evening news of all three networks and that's not the kind of publicity Surfside needs."

"Yeah," Stark interjected. "Can we kill him by shooting him? If I'd had my pistol, could I have killed him today when he was beached?"

Dr. Goodwin started to answer when Rainford interrupted. "That's a good question." He looked at Stark and then at Liza. "Why didn't you shoot the hell out of him if he was following you up and down the beach."

"We didn't have our pieces," Liza answered.

"You didn't have your guns?" Jim was surprised. "Why not?"

Blanchert laughed. "They didn't have anyplace to carry them—they didn't have any clothes on."

"What?" Jim asked incredulously.

Blanchert laughed again. "You guys were all up in the air about that rape and the possible homicide. And you threatened to virtually dissolve the police force if we caused any more stir on the beach. Well, it had to be searched, so I sent them up there and told them to strip and act like tourists while they searched for evidence."

Stark and Sallings both turned red. "How do you get a job like that?" Rainford kidded. "Hell, I'm in the wrong profession." They all laughed. "But seriously," he turned back to Dr. Goodwin, "what about Stark's question? Can we shoot this shark and kill him?"

"Probably not with a handgun. Liza thinks she may have hit him but if she did, it didn't affect him much. If you had a high-powered rifle and if you hit the right spot, you might get lucky. I think it's your best bet. From the measurements Michael made on the beach, this shark is in the mid-twenty-foot range. There's not much chance that your fishermen are going to bring him in even if they hook him. Personally, I don't think I'd want to catch that one. Not unless I was on an ocean liner."

"Then what do we do?" Stark asked. "And what were all the dolphins doing there anyway? I thought they killed sharks."

Goodwin smiled. "That's one of the oldest myths around. Dolphins don't attack sharks. They don't kill them. In fact, the opposite is true. Sharks often kill and eat older, slower dolphins or very young ones. Both sharks and dolphin feed on fish. It's not at all unusual to have them feeding within sight of each other. We even have data on shark attacks with dolphins being sighted in the same area at the same time.

"But back to your original question. I'd suggest that you get as many civil defense people or police or whoever you can, arm them with rifles, get them on fairly large boats and go after this shark. This guy is a bank loafer, he's decided this is his feeding territory and he's not going to leave. I'd take the rap on the publicity, tell people that they're swimming at their own risk, and have those guys out there chumming day and night."

"Boy, I don't know." Rainford shook his head. "There're problems with that. I don't think we can afford that kind of publicity. If we have an armada of boats just offshore filled with armed men—the news media would have a ball with that one. Anyway, the damned civil defense people are so busy worrying about that goddamned hurricane all the way over on the other side of the Gulf that you can't get them to talk about anything but evacuating the island."

"Maybe that wouldn't be such a bad idea." Goodwin said. "It would clear the beaches."

"Yeah, and everyone in the country would think we did it solely because of the shark."

"Well, you can try something else, too."

"What's that?" Blanchert asked.

"Dynamite! Sharks are attracted to explosions in the water. They'll rush to the area to pick up the free lunch. You could set off charges, systematically, about a half a mile apart up and down the shore and bay, and hope your friend shows up. You're going to catch a lot of flack from the environmentalists, but it looks like you're going to catch flack with just about anything you do."

"I vote for taking your suggestion, but for doing it at night," Rainford said.

"If you insist." Goodwin replied. "But you're gonna have a much better chance of seeing him and getting a clean shot during the day."

"But there'd be less hulaballoo about it at night. We can at least try it for a day or—" The bell rang. "Come on in!" Rainford shouted.

Hernandez rounded the pilothouse and galley and walked into the salon holding a surfboard with a jagged seat-cushion-sized bite taken out of it. "This was just brought into the station by the girlfriend of the boy who owned it. She says he went surfing early this morning and didn't come back. She went to the beach and found this tossed up on the sand."

Rainford stood up and held the surfboard. "Gentlemen, when I'm wrong, I'm wrong. I say we start with Dr. Goodwin's plan first thing in the morning. Everyone agree?"

Carolyn, Liza, and Michael were standing at his car after the meeting. "How about a sandwich somewhere?" Stark asked. "Rainford didn't come up with any food besides potato chips and dip."

"Not me," Liza said. "I have a date and I'm already an hour late."

"A date?" Stark asked. "At this time of night? Who is it? The Latin Romeo or the Narcs?"

"Cute." She tossed her hair over her shoulder and started towards her boat slip. "Don't go anywhere with him, Carolyn. He's a lech!" she shouted down the docks.

"I'll tell you what," he said to Carolyn. "If you think you can stand another steak dinner with me, I'll treat you to one."

"You're on."

Stark opened the door to his condo and flipped on the lights. "I'm afraid I'm going to have to apologize for a little mess. My cleaning lady was here today, but I left in a rush for that meeting tonight and I didn't pick up after myself." He grabbed a bathtowel from a kitchen barstool, went to the bathroom, collected clothes from the floor, and tossed them in the clothes hamper.

"You don't have to apologize. We all live this way, I think."

"How about a B&B on the rocks. We can go outside and watch the surf in the lights. I've never seen it this high here."

Carolyn paused for a moment, then stood up from the couch. She put her hand behind her back and pulled at the zipper on her dress. "Michael, I'm not very good at these things." Her aquamarine eyes were sparkling wet and as deep as the Gulf. "I'm lousy at small talk, but I want very much to go to bed with you—if you want to. That's really why I'm here, isn't it? I'm not here to have a drink or to watch the surf, am I?"

Stark's face was answer enough. She pulled the zipper the rest of the way down as he crossed the room. The dress floated in a gentle circle around her feet as he folded her into his arms. Michael's hands caressed her face; his fingers ran through her rich dark red hair. "God, you're pretty." He gently kissed one eye, then the other, and then kissed her fully on the lips. "You don't know how many times I've thought of doing this since that first dinner with you." He ran his hands down her back, unhooked her bra, and pulled it away as she stepped back a few inches to give him room. Her breasts were small and firm—they cupped perfectly in his hands. He leaned down and kissed her right breast, hesitated, then kissed the other. Michael knelt in front of her and carefully slid her pantyhose down her legs. She kicked off her high-heeled shoes and lifted each foot so he could slide the hose from her feet. She did it again when he rolled her panties down her legs. Still kneeling, Michael wrapped his arms around her back and buttocks, hugging her to him. He leaned back and looked at her. She smiled. He hugged her again, kissed a circle around her navel, and nuzzled his face in her pubic hair. "I'm going to enjoy this."

Carolyn held his face in her hands. "Not yet, darling. Come up here." Stark wouldn't stop fondling her breasts; she had to slide her hands in between his to unbutton his shirt. She stopped when she couldn't get past his belt. Michael's hands rolling back and forth across her nipples were making it hard for her to do anything. There was a giddy feeling in her stomach and she could feel the wetness between her legs. "Michael stop," she squealed in pleasure. "Wait."

"Okay." He feigned a look of hurt.

"You can do that the rest of the night if you want—see if I stop you. But right now I want to make love." She tugged at his belt, unsnapped the pants, and pulled down the zipper. Tugging his pants down around his ankles, Carolyn reached for his underpants. She pulled them down and clasped her fingers around his turgid member. Michael moaned. "I love the feel of it," she said. "It feels wonderful."

"No more, Carolyn. No more. I'll come."

"Do you want to?"

He knelt in front of her. "Yes, but in here." He brought his hand up between her legs. She was soaked. He ran his fingers back and forth through her wetness. "I can't wait any longer." Michael pushed her gently backwards on to the carpet, then moved between her legs, his pants still wrapped around his ankles, making love as furiously as a teenager in the back seat of a car.

"I'm going to come. Michael, I'm going to come." Carolyn gasped. Perspiration covered her body and she shook her head wildly from side to side.

"So am I." A groan of passion came from deep in his throat. Exhausted, he dropped on her breast.

"I think I could do that the rest of my life." Carolyn trailed a finger up and down Stark's chest.

"Too often like that would be the end of me." He cupped her breast in his hand. "You're perfect to look at and even more perfect to make love to."

"It's always that way the first time, when you like someone or really want them bad. But you could be married to me for six months and I'd end up having to pry you from the TV to get you in bed."

"I wouldn't count on that." He thought to himself that he'd really like to find out the truth to that question.

From Tampico, Mexico to New Orleans they were boarding up windows, emptying grocery shelves, and preparing to ride out the fury of Eleuthera. The great storm had mated with the hot Gulf waters and was refreshed once more. Brownsville and Galveston had emptied most of their beach-front homes. The highways inland were clogged with traffic slowed by the incessant downpour. Eleuthera was sitting at 26.5 degrees north latitude; 94.2 degrees west longitude, and she was becoming impatient. She had whipped her sustained winds into a two hundred and five mile-an-hour circle of destruction that was already flooding lowlands and taking lives along a thousand miles of coastline.

Eleuthera's American debut was just beginning. She started picking up surface speed and rolling across the warm water toward land. In less than one hour the swirling mass of deadly winds had gone from drifting lazily across the water to a forward speed of more than fifteen miles an hour. In the next hour Eleuthera would double that—and her direction was due east.

## 19. SIERRA

The phone rang far away on a desk in the midst of Stark's dream. Hazily, slowly, he realized that the phone was for real and that the dream was not. Reluctantly, he untangled himself from Carolyn's arms and snatched at the loud plastic intruder. "Detective Stark," he answered, his voice cracking with lack of sleep.

"Detective Stark, I've . . ."

Stark cut him off. He was angry and worried that Carolyn would be awakened. "Petit. Do you have any idea what time it is? What do you want?" He spoke softly into a cupped hand.

"We're having an emergency. It looks like that damned hurricane might hit us."

"You're kidding," he whispered loudly.

"Well," Petit hedged. "The civil defense people say so, although Rainford and Blanchert say they're off their nuts. Nevertheless, Blanchert said to get you guys down here. We have to mobilize if they're right. Blanchert says to hit it!"

"I'll hit it, all right," Stark snarled into the phone. Although the evening had given him a slightly more positive feeling toward Blanchert and Rainford, he now found those feelings considerably diminished. "How soon do I have to be there?"

"Now, I guess. By the way, I have some good news for you!"

"You're kidding."

"You know that button and piece of cloth you found?"

"Yeah."

"They match the clothing of the rape victim. And, the lab in Tampa thinks the clothing has a print that can be raised. They've sent it on to the FBI."

"Fat chance that it's the rapist's."

"Don't be negative. It's time to go to work."

Stark hung up on him.

The rolling waves and rising tide were preceding the storm by hours. They were already lapping at the top of the sea wall in front of Stark's condominium. He didn't see them as he stumbled to his car with two hours sleep and the scent of Carolyn still in his nostrils. He just wanted to check in, check out, then slide back into bed next to her. He had told his sleep-drugged companion that he had an emergency and would be back in a couple of hours. Stark kissed her, took a lingering last look at her face and lovely body, then stumbled out into the elevator still not believing how happy he was.

The station house was filled with off-duty patrolmen and civil defense personnel. Blanchert was lean-ng against his doorway. He saw Stark enter and waved him to his office.

"Well, it's Sleeping Beauty in a ragamuffin outfit." Sallings laughed, pointing to Stark's inside-out T-shirt.

Blanchert smiled as he reversed it. "Stark, let me update you on what's happening. The National Hurricane Center called an hour ago and issued a hurricane warning for the area between Cape Romano and Apalachee Bay, with the most probable hit on Sarasota.

"The CD Director and I called there personally, and some guy named Cowley said, quote, 'this storm is really going to kick ass. You'd better batten down the hatches.' I don't know who this weirdo is, but he seemed delighted! Anyway, he said this was the worst storm in the Gulf since Camille and could be even worse."

"So what does it mean?" Stark asked. "We didn't have hurricanes in the midwest. Tornadoes, but not hurricanes."

"It means," said a man in military fatigues with a CD emblem on his chest, "that it's time to evacuate the islands and clear out of here. This storm is coming in on a high tide and if she hits when Logan predicts, you can expect over twenty-foot waves. You know how much higher that is than this building? You know where this place is gonna be in a few hours? You'd better haul ass to the Administration Building, Pronto!"

"Oh come on, Pete," Rainford said, having just entered the office. "Let's don't get panicky. If we'd listened to you, this would have been the millionth time in the past five years that we would have ordered an evacuation. Although I agree—I think you're right this time; but let's not get all bent out of shape. They're saying the storm is heading even further south now, with a landfall predicted at Punta Gorda."

"That still means, on a high tide, you're going to have high winds and flooding like you won't believe, and people in single-story houses are going to go under."

"What about your boat, Liza?" Stark asked.

"The guy next to me is going to watch after it. He said he'd loosen the lines when they needed to be. And if it takes any damage—well, that's why you carry insurance. This is Florida, you know. It's part of the life-style."

"No, I don't know."

"All right, Pete." Blanchert stood up, yawned, and stretched. "This is your big night. What do you want us to do?"

"Well, who are your best people?"

"Who do you think?" Blanchert asked disgustedly. "The ones I've called in here. Stark and Sallings—and Hernandez? Hey, Hernandez! Get in here!"

Pete was enjoying tonight as much as Assistant Director Cowley was. He adjusted his army cap and walked over to a map of Surfside on the wall. "Do you have a map pointer, Captain?"

"No, I don't have a 'map pointer, Captain'; where the hell do you think you are, Pete? New York City? We all know where Surfside is, for Christ's sake. Get on with it."

Unperturbed, Pete went back to the map, shook his head, turned, and looked out at the room full of people. "I suggest one of you take a team of CD workers and start evacuating the island from the south end and another start at the north. Your so-called *police presence* will give them added authority. Another man can take over the landside end of the causeway and the last can handle the island end of it."

"That's four people. We need another person." Stark noticed.

"I'm him." Pete answered. "I thought you and I, Stark, had better be the ones to evacuate the island. Men have more authority than women. Sallings and what's-her-name can do the causeway."

"Captain!" Sallings stood in front of Pete, hands on hips, eyes blazing defiance. "I don't—we don't have to take that kind of guff from this Mickey Mouse, mush-head."

"All right, all right." Blanchert put a hand on Sallings' shoulder and one on Pete's. "That wasn't called for from either one of you. Settle your personal differences another time. Now hit the streets!"

The seas had been rough and Liza's shark fishing fleet had called the hunt off until after the storm. The *Night Dragon*, a forty-two-foot shark-fishing charter boat was the last to slide through the north end of Surfside pass and into the calmer bay waters. "Am I glad to be back here," Chucky Ratzle, the captain, said.

"Me, too!" echoed his first mate. "I don't think I've ever gotten seasick; but tonight, I was starting to wonder."

Fat Chucky popped the top of a Miller Lite. "Flip on the lights. There may be some trash back here.

Anyway, this Loran ain't been acting right. I don't want to hit no marker poles."

First Mate Spinelli dropped his can of beer. "Damn, we've got him!"

"What?"

"We've got him. Look out there!" He pointed to the huge tiger shark swimming fifty yards in front of the boat. "Think you can get up beside him? I'll get the rifle."

"It's still too rough." Chucky tried to peer through the driving rain. "You won't get off any kind of shot. You'll just scare him away. Let's tag along behind him. We'll be in calmer waters in just a few minutes."

Spinelli came from below decks carrying an ancient 30-06 Springfield rifle. "I'm going up on the bow. Soon as it smooths out, I'm gonna give that bastard some of this. Get the gaffs ready. If we shoot him, we don't want to lose him." Spinelli held the rifle high above his head and shook it. "Do you want some of this, you sonofabitch? Get me up there, Chucky!"

The shark couldn't hear Spinelli, but he could hear the boat. He could feel the vibrations of the engines, the reverberations of the props. He didn't like it. He didn't like being followed and he didn't like being harassed. The shark remained near the surface, but increased his speed.

Spinelli shook his rifle in the air and waved Chucky to close in on the shark.

Chucky pushed the throttles slightly forward, adjusting the starboard engine to correct for the wind. At the same time, he tried to adjust the spotlights to keep them trained on the shark when he saw he was overrunning his prey.

"Whoopee!" Spinelli shouted as the bouncing bow came within fifty feet of the shark. He fired off a round that went through the caudal fin. "I got him! Goddamn! I got him. Get the gaff!"

The shark felt the sting of the bullet, but was more aggravated by the boat hassling him. It was invading his territory. The great tiger felt threatened as well as annoyed. He sank to the bottom of the channel and swam two hundred yards away.

"Damn it," Spinelli exploded. He crossed the foredeck of the Chris Craft 421 Commander Convertible and grabbed the base of the searchlight with one hand to steady his balance. Over the pounding of the rain he shouted up to Chucky on the fly-bridge, "Shut the engines down and let's see if he surfaces again. I think I got him pretty good."

It was not prey the primitive monster attacked; it was the enemy. And the *Night Dragon* was his unsuspecting victim—sitting still in the water, vulnerable and waiting. The tiger shark built up momentum as he closed in on the boat. The collision brought an explosion of broken shark's teeth and bursting fiberglass. He wrenched out a chunk of the boat and let it drop into the turbid bay waters. Still angry, the shark chewed out another piece. Water poured into the craft, quickly filling the engine compartment, drowning out the engines, and shorting the lights. The craft was steadily sinking.

Chucky saw Spinelli go overboard just as he himself was thrown against the plastic side-curtains of the fly-bridge and onto the floor. "I don't want to die he thought as he tried to regain his footing. He fell again as the shark shook the boat a second time. A sharp pain brought tears to his eyes and caused him to double up when he reached to lift himself from the floor. He grabbed his throbbing left arm and tried to lift it with his right. Again the pain arched through his shoulder, arm, and back. "Oh no," he said to himself. "I've broken my shoulder. He twisted sideways, grasped a seat, and pulled himself first to his knees, then to his feet with his right hand. Painfully, he climbed down the ladder to assess the damage and see if he could find Spina. "What the devil hit us?" he wondered. "I'll bet we took a hit by a piling or a palm tree. Lucky the boat's not going down any faster than it is. I would guess we're in water shallow enough that, if I can climb back up to the bridge or the sighting tower, I'll still be able to stay far enough above the water."

He took a life ring and leaned over the transom to see if he could spot his first-mate. "Spina!" he shouted as loud as he could. The boat was sinking and the water was nearing the top of the transom. Chucky knew it would start pouring over in just a few minutes. He tried again. "Spina!" He leaned against the transom. A flash of lightning lit the sky and in that instant he saw the angered tiger shark burst through the transom as he insanely attacked the boat again. Without thinking, Chucky jumped over the side and away from the shark. He still held the life ring in his good arm. Twisting and turning, he tried to spot the shark, couldn't, started swimming, and then stopped. "What the hell am I doing?" he thought. "I know better than to make a commotion in the water and advertise where I am. I'll just hang onto the ring and float into shore."

Chucky never knew the tiger passed less than two

feet below him on the first pass. He felt a brief, sharp pain in his stomach and groin and thought for an instant that something had hit him. He was right. On the second pass the tiger had opened and protruded his jaws, jutting out the rows of curved teeth that slashed viciously at his victim. The shark wasn't feeding; he was attacking. The pain intensified and Chucky reached to his middle with his broken arm. Painfully, he ran it from his chest to below his waist. Chucky was sick. The rows of serrated teeth had opened his abdomen like a surgeon's scalpel. His severed penis and testicles slid down his pant leg as he tried to hold his intestines inside his body. They were hot and oozing around his hands as he slipped from consciousness and sank beneath the water.

Spinelli had just gotten a glimpse of the shark before it attacked the boat. He swam as steadily as he could toward what he knew had to be shallower water. "I just hope I can reach a spoil island before the shark can reach me," he thought. "If I can, I'll beat that bastard yet." A flash of lightning revealed a line of Australian pines directly in front of him at about the same time he struck bottom with his hands. He was sure this was the luckiest night of his life as he waded out into the pine trees. He leaned against one, waiting for the sky to lighten. Spinelli was a little worried that the winds seemed to be increasing and the tide was quickly eating at his island. "I wonder if old Chucky made it on in," he mused. "I'd guess he'll have someone out here looking for me within half an hour."

Five hundred yards away, Chucky's butchered body slid slowly to the bottom of the bay. The angry shark swam out the channel and into the Gulf.

# 20. TANGO

Driving along Gulf Boulevard, Stark noticed the wind was really strong. It rocked his car and plastered it with raindrops. Through quick swipes of clear windshield he could see that most of the beachfront had shrunk to the encroaching tide. He went to the end of the street, turned at the bridge, switched on his flashing lights, and started down his section of the street broadcasting the evacuation order.

"*Attention! Attention! This is an evacuation order issued by the Surfside Police Department and the City Commission. You are ordered to leave your homes and condominiums immediately. Follow the evacuation signs and proceed to the nearest emergency shelter at once. Take only your personal belongings and no pets.*" Stark released the mike, moved the car to the middle of the block, and repeated the message.

Up and down the Suncoast, other cities were following suit. WSUN, the primary radio emergency broadcasting system in the bay area, released its squealing warning of an impending alert message. Other radio and TV stations started broadcasting the same message, telling people what routes to take. The emergency sirens wailed into the wind.

Within minutes the streets were filled with cars, and then the trouble began. People were panicked and confused. Few knew the evacuation routes or how to find them. Daily they passed the small blue signs, barely noticing them, and not caring to remember where they were. Now they turned in wrong directions, ran into dead ends, and created traffic jams. Few cars had more than one or two occupants and, with the tourists, there were thousands more cars than the roads could hold. On the wet pavements, one slid into another. The traffic arteries were as clogged as a by-pass patient's and threatened just as certain death if something wasn't done.

Inside the new Administration Building, built to highest hurricane standards, Blanchert and Pete's assistant were giving orders. "Sallings. Did you get that bridge-tender to lock down the causeway bridge?" Blanchert barked into the station's home-base radio.

"Yes, sir. It's locked down." Sallings voice cracked over the radio.

"What's wrong with his phone?"

"Some crazy bastard skidded off this end of the bridge, hit a telephone pole, and knocked it down. It's also blocking traffic at the landside exit. The GTE people are on their way and they're bringing a chainsaw."

"Watch the language on the air."

"Sure, Captain. If you could see the mess out here with people crying and fistfights breaking out—I need to be ten more people."

"I'll see what I can do."

There was a sudden break in the clouds and sunlight came through for a few minutes. "Maybe," Stark thought, "Just maybe we're gonna get a break. If this could clear up for a while, we'd get most of this mess straightened out." He peered between the condominiums out over the Gulf and saw nothing but blackness stretching from the horizon to far overhead. Then, just as quickly as it had bestowed the sunlight, the rolling mass eclipsed it again. "My God," Stark said, looking at his watch and the streetlights. "It's eight in the morning and dark as midnight!" He started driving down the sidewalk toward the next group of condominiums and houses to broadcast the useless evacuation order. "Surfside One to Central."

"This is Central, Stark." Blanchert answered. "What's happening out there?"

"Everything and nothing. These dodos are panicking. There's an accident at every intersection. People are getting mired down trying to drive across their own lawns. It's crazy!"

"I know, I know. Just do what you can."

Stark drove the sidwalk to one of Gulf Boulevard's major intersections and found an accident clogging a small canal-street bridge. Two cars had rammed and were wedged crossways blocking both lanes of the street. A bumper to bumper line started six inches away from them. A new Mercedes was first in line; a new Cadillac, second. Stark walked up to the man in the Mercedes, flashed his badge, motioned for him to roll his window down, and waved the man in the Cadillac to follow. The Mercedes was a young fellow who looked like a professional wrestler; the Cadillac was a graying, fortyish overweight businessman. "I want you," Stark said to the younger man, "to start pushing those cars. Don't ram them, but start pushing gently and increase speed until we can move them off the bridge and get traffic moving." "And I want you," he turned to the Cadillac owner, "to start pushing him if he needs help."

"Have you lost your mind, buddy? Do you know how much money this car costs? Call a damned wrecker out here!" the Mercedes owner exploded.

"My sentiments, exactly." The businessman echoed.

"Mister! There are no wreckers! Now do what I said."

"I'll stomp your goddamned ass, cop or not!" The Mercedes door swung wide.

Stark took three steps backwards, pulled his nickle-plated .357 Magnum from its holster, cocked the trigger, and pointed it straight at the younger man's face—quickly to the older man's head, and then back, dead-center, to the muscular young giant's forehead. "You get back in that damn car and you do exactly what I told you. I don't know what those cars cost and I don't care. But I'll guarantee you that they're going to cost you your life in less than sixty seconds because, if you don't get your ass moving, I'm gonna waste you and get two other people to drive them for me."

Cursing and shaking, they both jumped for their

cars and began pushing the wrecked vehicles from the bridge.

A young woman pounded on the window of Hernandez's car. "Officer! Officer!"

"Yes, ma'am."

"See that six-story condo over there?"

"Si. What is wrong?"

"What's wrong is that there's about eighty people in the top floor rec room. They've decided to have a hurricane party. And my sister is one of them. Can't you do something?"

Hernandez called Blanchert and told him the problem. "Just what the hell are you doing there?" Blanchert asked. "You were supposed to be at the island end of the causeway."

"I traded jobs with Petit."

"Hernandez! One of these days you're going to be working in Tampa instead of here! Go up and tell them the situation is serious. If they don't want to leave—leave them. Get your butt back to the causeway and send Petit back there. Tell him to start helping the senior citizens in the Bayway Condos get onto the municipal buses.

"Yes, sir. Ten-four."

Hernandez followed the scared young woman and knocked on the Sand Dunes' recreation room door. She could hear the sound of bongo drums and reggae music inside. The door swung wide and the smell of pot rolled out with the increased chant of the music. "Good afternoon, Officer!" A tall thin deeply-tanned man swept a straw hat from his bearded blond head and bowed cavalierly. "The name's Coconut! Would you like to join our stalwart band of hardy souls? We are celebrating the impending arrival of the good lady Eleuthera and the probable loss of my job and income."

"What you are all going to lose is your lives." Hernandez snapped. "You people are crazy, no? Do you not know how bad this storm she is? You are all going to die if you stay here."

"My sweet Spanish lady," Coconut said, leaning back yet still towering over, "I have lived here for twenty years and I've heard that about every thunderstorm and tornado that has ever hit the Suncoast. And the only ones that die are the oldies."

Hernandez pointed to the glass walls of the recreation room. "Look at those walls. They shake like the trees outside."

"They always do that," Coconut made a wave to the crowd that had gathered round. "What a bummer. Now take that uniform off and join the party! You were the one up on the nude beach the other day, weren't you?"

Hernandez eyes flashed and grew wide. "If you want to die, Mr. Coconut, that is good. I think you are going to do so. But this girl's sister, you are not going to take with you. Give her to me."

"What if I say no." Coconut placed his hat on his head and folded his arms in front of him as the bongo player and a lifeguard joined him.

"Then I will arrest you."

"All of us," Coconut laughed. "That's a pretty big job for you, isn't it, little lady?"

Hernandez unbuckled the strap over her service revolver and faced the crowd. She pointed her finger. "All of you! If I have to, I will shoot you; and you, Mr. Coconut, I shoot first. You have exactly one second! I have no time for your games."

"Hey, Coconut," a short burly man with long dirty black hair pushed out in front of the crowd and stood beside him. "Let's grab her and add a little Spanish spice to the party."

Instinctively, almost faster than an eyeblink, Hernandez whipped the .357 Magnum from its holster. The high pitched explosion smothered even Eleuthera's incessant howling. The blood, bone, and cartilige of the man's right knee splattered the crowd; the slug continued through his knee and smashed another's ankle.

It was not the right day to confront the Surfside Police Force. "Get the girl!" Coconut shouted as his friend twisted and turned like a worm on a hook in a fast-forming pool of blood on the floor. "Get Nan out here, fast!"

# 21. UNIFORM

Five hundred miles west of Surfside, ninety degrees north latitude and twenty-five degrees west longitude, Eleuthera slowed momentarily, fed on the hot Gulf waters, and built her sustained winds. The tightly compressed eye was the picture of horror itself. The barometric pressure had dropped to twenty-six-point-three-five millibars. Within the eye the winds went from dead calm to two hundred twenty-five miles an hour in less than the distance of a football field. The swirling column of death hurled waterspouts in all directions and the suncoast was splattered by a dozen tornados.

After three-quarters of an hour of hesitation, Great Hurricane Eleuthera whipped up her skirts and took aim at Surfside. She increased her forward speed to thirty-two miles an hour and started pushing a colossal blister of angry black water fifty miles wide and twenty-five feet high in front of her eye. The National Hurricane Center notified the Suncoast immediately.

* * *

"Captain Blanchert! Captain Blanchert!" Civil Defense Director Pete Southwell's assistant yelled.

"Will you shut up?" Blanchert glared at the man. He didn't like him much more than he did Pete. "Can't you see I'm on the radio?"

Blanchert finished his conversation with Hernandez. "I don't care what you have to do, but get that traffic moving across the bridge and causeway."

"All right now, what is it?" He turned to the short skinny mustached man.

He was shaking a paper in his hands. "It's all over with. Eleuthera has picked up speed and is heading straight for us. Her winds are over two-hundred miles an hour. She'll be here in less than five or six hours."

"How far away is she and how fast is she coming at us?"

"She's less than five-hundred miles away and going over thirty miles an hour."

Blanchert tapped at his calculator. "Five hundred divided by thirty comes to a little more than sixteen hours, not five or six!"

"Captain, that's the center! This lady is big. She's gargantuan. We're gonna start getting gale winds almost immediately. I suggest that we start rolling down the metal hurricane shutters on this building immediately. Is the causeway under water?"

"I don't know. Hernandez is on her way there now. Petit is there, but his handset's not working and I can't get a hold of Sallings over on the other side."

The electricity went off and Blanchert saw the city turn black. The emergency generator turned theirs back on. "What happened?"

"I guess the county gave Florida Power the order

to cut all power in the lines. When those twelve thousand-volt distribution lines start falling, if they're live, they'll cook people like hot dogs at a wienie roast."

Blanchert heard Hernandez on the Radio. "Captain the CD man here, he says the tide has risen five feet in the last forty-five minutes. The causeway, it is already under a couple of feet of water. Should I not turn them back?"

"No, not yet. Let as many get through as you can. When we turn them back, there's only going to be more confusion."

The door burst open and Pete, drenched under his yellow rubber slicker, staggered into the room. His assistant gave him the note from the National Hurricane Center. "Get them in, Blanchert." Pete said woodenly. "Get our people off the streets and back here, or to as safe a place as you can. We're not going to make it."

"What about all those people out there?"

"We made a mistake, that's all. We gave it our best shot and we lost."

"What the hell do you mean, 'we gave it our best shot and we lost?' " Blanchert slammed the chair he was leaning on into the desk.

"For years Director Logan has been saying that he wasn't sure if it was a good idea to try to evacuate if we didn't really have all the time we needed. That instead, it might be better to just seek shelter in the strongest, safest building you could find. We've got that type of situation here. We've got a freak storm that's going like hell; we've got the streets and highways jammed with people; and all the evacuation routes are going to go down in less than an hour—if they're not gone already. It's not just happening here, Blanchert; it's going on all over Tampa Bay. When this is over, it's going to make the Galveston hurricane with six thousand dead look like a firefight compared to a war. We just took a calculated risk and lost."

Blanchert's face was lobster-red and looked as if it would explode. "A calculated risk? You want to go back out there and tell those people that their lives are calculated risks?"

"Now, don't get mad at me." He held up his hands in surrender as Blanchert lowered his fist. Pete took out his pipe and stuck it in the corner of his mouth. "For two decades we've been telling you people not to build out here on these sand-spit islands and not to build in the lowlands. Still, everyone wants to live on the beach and not a soul has ever listened to us." He tamped in the tobacco, lit a match, and puffed furiously. "Ain't our fault, Blanchert—ain't our fault."

Stark was in the second-story parking garage of the Hurricane Watch Hotel when he heard the announcement on the squad car radio to all units. "This is Captain Blanchert. Surfside Civil Defense Director Pete Southwell and I have ordered all personnel off the streets. Return here to the Administration Building or seek shelter immediately. No more can be done. We don't want any heroes out there. We will need you even more after the storm than we do now. Let me repeat. All personnel, both Civil Defense and Police, return to the Administration Building or seek shelter immediately. Leave your vehicles only if you have to—we will need them, too."

"How do you expect me to get it back? It's a car, not a boat!" Stark shouted into the hand mike, then groaned as the wind whipped the door shut on his leg.

"Stark, is that you?" Blanchert asked.

"No! It's Captain Ahab!" he moaned into the mike, rubbing his badly bruised calf.

"Are you all right?" Blanchert could hear his pain.

Silence.

"Stark! Are you all right?"

Stark squeezed the tears out of his eyes. "I'm fine. No big deal. The goddamned wind slammed the car door shut on my leg and almost cut it off—that's all."

"Where are you? Can you get back to base? We need you here."

"I need to be there! I'm at the Hurricane Watch Hotel, trying to keep from being killed in this crazy storm."

"What? Come on in, you're less than a mile from us."

"Captain, when's the last time you looked outside?"

Blanchert wiped his forehead. He was getting to where he didn't like talking to Stark anymore than he did to Rainford. "The hurricane shutters are down. I can't see outside."

"I'm sorry, but my squad car doesn't have any hurricane shutters and I *can* see outside. The reason I'm here is because, if you don't know it, Gulf Boulevard is already under three feet of water. Your damned squad car was drowning out, so I pulled up under the Hurricane Watch Hotel before it gave out on me completely. It's an open parking area, but at least it's above the tide."

"Okay then, walk on in."

"Captain! Get serious. I told you I almost broke my leg. The ocean's in the streets! There's four-foot waves rolling right across everything. If you want me, come and get me. I'm not goin' anywhere. Come and get me in a boat. Or send Sallings in hers. Where's Sallings, anyway?"

"She was on landside, but I can't seem to get in touch with—"

That was all Stark heard. A gale-force gust of wind toppled the squad car and turned it upside down, smashing the antenna and killing the engine on the first roll. The second time it rolled over, it smashed hard against the side of the concrete downramp. Stark heard the sparks up front, smelled the gasoline, released his seatbelt, opened the door, and rolled down the ramp into the surging water just before the squad car exploded.

"Stark! Surfside One! Stark, answer me!" Blanchert shouted into the radio mike. There was no response. He felt a little queasy and wiped the sweat from his brow. A CD aide put a hand on his shoulder that he slapped away.

Stark turned over in the water. "My God," he thought; he was just able to touch bottom with his feet and keep his head above the waves. "This is close to five feet deep—Sallings! She's at landside. Goodwin! Goodwin! My God, Goodwin! She's still in my condo." He slammed into a palm tree behind the hotel, grabbed it, and held on. He looked at the vaguely familiar surroundings. "My condo is just five buildings down from this one. All I have to do is methodically get from one tree to the next, from one building to another. I wonder why they turned off all the lights?"

The orange-and-yellow raft floated straight toward him. Inching as high as he could on the palm and keeping his feet locked around it, Stark reached as far out in the water as he could to grasp it. He succeeded in twisting its string in his fingers and reeled it in. As he brought it up against himself, the yellow raft turned into a yellow slicker that revolved, exposing the face of a seventeen-year-old boy with staring eyes. Stark took a deep breath, but didn't shove his prize away. He pulled the slicker from the youth, unsnapped the life jacket it covered, and let the kid slide under the water. Using the life jacket as a float, he kicked and paddled his way from tree to tree between the wave crests.

Coughing seawater and exhausted, Stark stumbled into the elevator of his condo. Although the water was lapping in the lower lobby, the automatic generator was going in the upper one and had not affected the elevator yet. He punched the button for the twentieth floor and sagged against the wall. In a few seconds the elevator stopped and he staggered into his hall. As he did, the elevator's lights went out and he heard it wheeze as it settled on its cushion of oil all the way to the bottom. "Looks like a long walk down," he mused. Remembering why he was here, he rushed to his apartment.

"Carolyn!" he shouted into the darkened rooms. "Carolyn!" He fumbled through a kitchen closet, found a flashlight, and searched one room after another with no success. He pressed the talk-button on his shoulder radio to call Blanchert or Sallings and met more futility. It was as dead as the seventeen-year-old he had let wash into the bay.

Stark walked over to the shimmering patio doors; through the bolts of lightning he could see five-foot waves rolling across the top of his sea-wall. The condo next to him was faring no better; the cars parked on the streets and even on the second-story parking levels were doing much worse. The five-foot waves were riding a twelve-foot tide, sweeping automobiles from the island like cigarette butts from a gutter. Stark knew his Lincoln was somewhere down there. The thought made him sick, but his second thought made him sicker—as far as he knew, he was here alone. And he was trapped!

Five blocks due east of Stark's condominium, Reverend William Dodd tried to gather his family around him under the sheltering blanket of his religion. "James," he said to his son. "Come in here and let's all pray."

"Dad!" his son shouted above the ever-increasing wail of the wind. "This isn't the time for prayers. We need to do something. This stupid stilt house is already three feet deep in water and that storm's not even close yet. Either we have to get to a higher building or we've got to get out of here on the boat."

The elder Dodd had seen panic in the faces of El Salvadorian refugees and he knew the look. "James, James, don't fall victim to the Devil's impatience. Remember, not a sparrow falls from the sky without the nod of God's head."

"Well, I'm afraid the Old Man upstairs is shaking it like hell today," James spit back irreverently, "And I don't want to join his crew."

"Wait," Reverend Dodd said, turning his ear towards the front of the house. They had boarded all the windows, but they could hear a definite patter on them and on the door. "Is that hail? It couldn't be a group of people knocking, could it?"

"Where would they be coming from, Dad? A prayer meeting?"

The bullish broad-shouldered reverend walked to the door. "I'm going to find out. No one will be turned away from my door." He opened the door and the first wave hit him in the stomach like a boxer with a second wind in the twelfth round. He staggered for a second and was then cut down by the pebbles whipped from the roofs of Stark's condominium, the Hurricane Watch Hotel, and the Holiday Inn. They peppered his body like the FBI did Bonnie and Clyde. He spun around from the door, holes in his face, chest, and arms. He was dead before he hit the water.

James saw from the kitchen and cringed behind the refrigerator. As his father floated past, he could see the pebbles in a couple of the wounds and in a few deductive moments, he knew what had happened.

Gloria Johncourt was about to lose her spoiled, play-baby game of life. She had tried to leave the island, but she was too late. Three blocks from her house, her car had been rammed by a *Clearwater Sun* newspaper delivery truck. It wouldn't start, and even if it had, it would have taken an experienced wrecking crew to bend the bumper back far enough from the front axle to allow the right wheel to turn. Disgustedly, she had abandoned the car and sloshed through the deepening water back home. She thought of Ed Bilsters and of her missing husband, Alex. "No one's here, not one reliable person. When they need me, I always happen to be here; but when I need them, there's no one here!"

She grabbed a bottle of gin from the cabinet, dumped one ice cube in a Collins glass and filled it to the top, skipping the mix and the lime. "What am I going to do? The water was almost up to my hips. I guess the boat's still here."

She heard the front windows shatter as the wind machine gunned the pebbles from the highrise condominium and hotel roofs. "I've got to get out of here before the house goes," she shouted to the empty room. She drained the glass in one long swallow, ducked out the back door and headed for the cabin cruiser. Running across the porch to the corner stairs, she got halfway down to the water before the pebbles cut her down, turning her lean expensively-maintained body into a bloody pegboard of lifeless flesh.

## 22. VICTOR

In the howling wind and driving rain, Sallings could barely make out the school bus filled with elderly people from the Setting Sun condominium. It topped the bridge that sat a couple of hundred yards from the landside end of the causeway. The driver slowed almost to a crawl before again entering the water that covered the road. He had turned the lumbering yellow giant sideways a mile back, blocking the road before a trash disposal truck helped slide him back onto the pavement. The water had risen to just over the first step of the bus before he hit the bridge and he wondered how high it would be on this side.

"Come on! Come on!." Sallings shouted into the wind. "It's going to get deeper, not more shallow, and it's two miles back to the island." She pounded the hood of the squad car and waved, in spite of knowing the driver couldn't see her.

The bus edged into the water and the engine coughed. The sixty-year-old driver panicked and jammed the accelerator to the floor. The flat nose of the bus smashed into the water with a jolt that threw half of the senior citizens into the aisle. Eyeglasses, hearing aides, and false teeth popped onto the floor; brittle bones cracked and fractured; incontinent bladders and intestines let loose their contents. The bus filled with moans, screams, and the stench of a Porta-potty.

"Dumb! Dumb! Dumb!" Liza shouted at the driver. She reached for the radio as she saw traffic behind the bus grind to a halt. "Central, I have a problem."

There was no answer and Liza's problem got worse. The churning water had gotten deeper, the waves higher, and the wind stronger. The water was a third of the way up the side of the bus. A gust of wind broke the first wave midway up the side windows and scooted the bus to the edge of the road. The second wave rolled the bus slowly and gently over into the bay. Liza was horrified as she saw it bob slowly down the bay, steadily sinking out of sight in the heavy rain.

"Central! Central!" She shouted into the mike. "Can anyone hear me?"

"Liza," Hernandez's voice came popping over the radio. "A CD man told me Central's radio is out. Something hit the antenna and their generator works no longer. Can I be of help?"

"Close the causeway! Close the causeway! It's under water. A school bus full of people was just washed into the bay. Start turning them around and tell them to seek safety."

"Did you not hear the captain's announcement, Liza?"

"Juanita, I've been outside my car and I can't hear anything over this wind."

"He say to quit and come in. That it is no longer safe to be out and that they will need us more after the storm than before. You should come back at once."

"I can't. I can't get back across the causeway. I'll have to try to get to the county shelter. What are you still doing there."

"I was waiting for you."

"Hernandez, get out of there."

"But what about all these people?"

"You can't do anything about them and if you get yourself killed, then you're not helping anyone. Get out of there."

"Good luck, Liza."

A gust of wind slammed Liza's car three feet across the pavement and into a concrete streetlight. She dropped the mike. "Don't die on me now." She prayed, turning the ignition key. She dropped the gearshift to drive and skidded off toward the County Civil Defense Headquarters just as the light pole crashed inches behind her car. Liza drove up the hill through Surfside's sister city, Surfview, on the Pinellas Peninsula. She rounded the corner at Sabal and Cabbage doing forty miles an hour on the slick street when her headlights spotted the overturned trash dumpsters blocking her way. She slammed on the brakes, wrenched the steering wheel hard to the left, let it slide, and then stomped hard on the gas, executing a perfect whiskey-runner's turn. Rounding the corner again, she went ninety degrees in the opposite direction, through downtown, and down an alternate route.

Every window in the downtown section was shattered. It had been the custom in the past half-dozen years to build the exterior of almost every new building out of solid mirrored glass. Some were smoke-gray, some were amber-colored, and the rest were the shiny standard reflective mirror-finish. Today they were all the same—broken. So was every other window in the downtown section that was not boarded up.

Although downtown Surfview was fifteen feet above sea level and safe from the tides at present, the gale-force winds were already taking their toll. As in Surfside, the pebble rooftops were spraying the city like giant machine-guns. The decorative palm trees planted up and down the center boulevards of every major street yielded their dead and weak fronds to the lethal fusillade. Flower pots joined decorative awnings and even empty beer cans became deadly missiles on this dark Suncoast day.

On Surfside beach, another idiocy was occurring. Longtime Suncoast fishermen—used to storms but ignorant of hurricanes, since no severe ones had visited in almost a century—had tied themselves to palm trees and Australian Pines, donned life jackets and taken the opportunity to fish for bull drum, a giant Gulf fish particularly fond of feeding in surging, turbulent waters. But in the strong surges, their lifelines were misnomers. One after another, they snapped like kite twine. And today the floundering fishermen and feeding fish had company. The twenty-six-foot tiger shark was having an equally good time in the surf. In the turbulent water the drum, swept up in their own feeding frenzy, never saw the tiger until the final shadow shut their eyes.

Already, the pounding surf was filling with bodies. Those that had fled their drowned cars along the beachfront evacuation route, stumbled into potholes quickly dug by the tide or tried to reach the safety of the highrise beach-front condominiums, only to fall victim to deepening waters or deadly water-bound debris. Between the frenzied drum, the irrational fishermen, and the panicked evacuees, the tiger found himself at a veritable banquet of fools.

# 23. WHISKEY

The wind shook and rattled the windows of Stark's condominium with each strong gust. He knew he was trapped and had to save himself. "The first thing I have to do," he thought, "is to secure the windows." Besides the patio door, the corner unit had a living room window and another in each of the three bedrooms. When Stark had purchased the unit, the condo salesman had suggested placing roll-down metal hurricane shutters on all the windows. At this height, he had said, the wind during the summer storms was awfully hard on the windows; the shutters would help protect them. They also blocked out the sunlight for more efficient cooling. The hurricane shutters were guaranteed to withstand one hundred-fifty miles-an-hour winds.

The realtor had also recommended the installation of inside bolts with wing nuts that would hold half-inch plywood panels over the windows and a complete "Condo Hurricane Kit" that contained duct tape, tubes of caulking, a caulking gun, cans of Sterno camping fuel, hurricane-oil lamps, water purification tablets, other assorted odds and ends, and instructions for everything. Stark was green to Florida; he had bought the whole package, read the instructions, packed away the plywood and the big metal locker full of supplies, and had been kidded about being taken by everyone who found out about it. Today he wanted to give the realtor a tip!

He found the switch to the patio shutters with the flashlight and pressed the botton. They didn't budge. "Damn, what am I thinking about. There's no electricity!" He pulled the "Condo Hurricane Kit" from a deep corner of the hall closet, opened it, and rummaged through until he found the instructions and the manual shutter-crank. The bedroom and living room windows cranked down fairly easily. But in the force of the wind, Stark was afraid the hand-crank would break before he could get the patio shutter to the bottom.

Stark followed the rest of the instructions carefully. He caulked around all the windows, starred them with duct tape, placed the protective panels over the inside bolts, and fastened the plywood tight with the wing nuts, diligently spraying each one with WD-40 before doing so. He lit a hurricane lamp and sat on the floor, beaming and smug in the yellow glow from the flame. "It's time for a drink. I've been at this for a full hour. I'm beat and need to calm down and relax a little." He walked to the wet bar to fill his glass with ice and Jack Daniels Black. "Oh, Christ. I forgot to fill the sinks and bathtubs with water." A turn of the handle revealed it was too late. All that came out was a gurgling sound and a drop or two caught in the exterior part of the faucet. "Well, I have a case of JD whiskey, a couple dozen bottles of wine, a couple of bottles of Stoly, and the two bottles of Pinch I bought for Carolyn. I won't die of thirst—maybe cirrhosis of the liver—but it looks like I'll go out in style!"

Stark noticed that the large patio door was still making noises and vibrating. The largest of the windows, it was also the most vulnerable. "If I get the mattress off the king-size bed, place it against the window and then wedge it tight with the couch and the dining room table, that ought to do it." A half-hour later he had finished the job, braced the other windows with couch cushions and the remaining furniture. Tired and caring a whole lot less what happened, Michael fixed his third drink and settled on a barstool to await whatever would happen.

Great Hurricane Eleuthera thundered straight for Surfside and the beautiful Suncoast as if she wanted revenge—to make up for the century of having no major storms in this section of Florida. She sent her minions before her to wreak the first devastating waves of destruction on the coast. Tornados ripped through trailer courts on the mainland, opening the metal houses like cans of pork and beans and scattering their contents for miles. When the pressure dropped so suddenly, the mobile homes would bulge and explode with a tremendous roar. Many of the trailer dwellers were chopped up by the whirling trash-filled winds—others, cringing in worthless hiding places, were snatched up into the violent vortex, tossed through the air, and smashed against buildings and trees blocks away.

On the beachfront, Eleuthera was taking her toll. The smaller, weaker structures were the first to succumb. Only the highrises, strong two-story buildings and stilt-homes remained—and Eleuthera was chewing away at them. The waves ate at the traditional concrete slabs beneath the two-story homes and pounded incessantly on the oceanside walls of the buildings. Jim Rainford's huge home was no exception. First, a poorly secured window burst; water started quickly filling the house, seeping under the door and sloshing through the broken window with the attack of each new wave. Another window broke, splintering the plywood covering; and finally, the thick oak door gave way. The water surged back and forth inside, snatching up the contents and using them to batter down the inside walls as those on the ocean side continued to weaken.

Further beneath the surface, the sugar-white sand slid from the sides and out from under the concrete-slab foundation. The home's base became more unstable and insecure with each passing wavefront. Although the building was strong enough to withstand the pounding of the waves, it became undermined. As the sand disappeared from under the slab, the building's structural footing was broken, allowing it a minute or two to totter and sway in the wind before splitting and crumbling beneath the sea.

Stark's ego-extension, his car, had met the same fate as other vehicles in the lower parking areas. Waves, especially hurricane waves, have a tendency to bury all that they can't push or batter down in front of them. Stark's fawn-colored Lincoln Continental Town Car was no exception. It was just another obstruction in Great Eleuthera's upcoming passage. The wind first rolled the boxey car from the Gulf side of the parking lot to the bay side and halfway down the bay-side exit. It smashed the windows and mangled the antenna and outside rear-view mirrors. The distinctive grill ruptured itself on the bumpers of a half dozen cars. The rising tide then snatched the Lincoln from its downramp resting place and floated it toward the higher center of the still intact island. It sank quickly in the window-deep water, settling on the sandy bottom in the very spot where a construction trailer had stood earlier in the day. And, like a bather who lies in the surf during high waves, the Lincoln found itself being quickly buried. With each passing wave the return flow of the water dragged the sand from beneath it and the next tried to cover it up. Slowly and methodically, the car sank deeper and deeper until it disappeared.

Captain Blanchert wasn't worried. He had thought it was extravagant to spend the money to build the Administration Building to maximum hurricane standards. He had also objected to tearing down a beautiful old house across from the Police Station just so they could place the new city building on the highest part of the island. Now he was glad they had. For weeks, they had pounded giant concrete pillars reinforced with steel far beneath the surface of the island. The noise had driven Blanchert to take a week's vacation in order to escape it. For two years they had fought lawsuits with neighboring homes and business establishments who claimed the pounding had cracked their foundations and accused the city of negligence—of ordering twice as many pilings as were actually needed and causing even more damage. The city lost and had to float bonds to pay the lawsuits. Today those bonds were paying off handsomely. While other buildings were faltering—especially those whose owners had not used winnings to repair their cracked foundations—the City Administration Building was holding firm.

Pete walked into the room. "We got the generator fixed."

Blanchert shouted at him. It was getting increasingly hard to hear over the roar of the storm. "What'd you say?"

"I said, we got the generator fixed!"

"Jesus, Pete, I sort of figured you did when the lights came back on. How high is the water down there?"

"It's lapping at the steps a few feet from the second story door."

"Do you think we ought to sandbag it?"

"Nah. Won't do no good. Water's gonna get a lot higher before this is over with. Right now I'd bet that the waves are breaking over the top of any single-story structures that are left on the island—if there are any left. With that wind, I doubt it." Pete jabbed his pipe in the corner of his mouth and pulled his cylindrical lighter from his pocket.

"Don't light that thing. You know the air-conditioning is out. It's going to get stuffy as hell in here as it is without people smoking."

"You're right." He laid the pipe on the desk.

"Think the building will hold?" Blanchert was becoming a little less confident.

"No problem. Way this baby is built, it'd take a nuke to blow her off this island."

Blanchert mopped the sweat that was running down his neck. It was also getting warm in the building. "How many people we got in here?"

"We've got a couple of hundred refugees, all of my people, and all of yours except Stark and Sallings. What happened to them? I thought they were your prima donna material."

"They are. I don't know what happened to them."

Hernandez overheard the conversation. "Detective Liza, she could not get back to this side. She is taking refuge in the county facility."

"Then that leaves Mr. Stark out there in his Lincoln, doesn't it?" Pete said sarcastically.

Hernandez was pushed to her limit. She was tired, scared, and now furious. She took a step backwards and placed her hand on her revolver once more, and she was equally serious. "I don't think I like you, Mr. Pete!" she shouted, dark brown eyes flashing hatred. "And I don't think it will go good for you to be nasty about my friends dying."

Pete pulled Blanchert in front of him. "I'm sorry! I'm sorry. Really, I'm sorry. I didn't mean it that way. I'm as concerned for Detective Stark's life as anyone. I don't want to see anyone hurt."

Blanchert held up his hand for Hernandez to stop. "Okay, Juanita. I don't blame you, but this is not the place for that kind of stuff. How about seeing if you can help Dr. Goodwin on the next floor. She's got a woman up there who's about to have a baby. Screw Pete. There are others that need your help."

Hernandez wheeled and headed for the stairs, fire still in her eyes, her hand still on the butt of her pistol.

"That crazy cop would have killed me, Blanchert. Did you see that?"

Blanchert grabbed him by the lapels of his fatigue shirt and bent him backwards over the desk. "And I should have let her! You better come up with a quick change of attitude, Pete, or you're gonna turn up missing some day. And frankly, I don't think anyone would give a damn!"

Tempers were short everywhere. Full of bull drum and fishermen, the large tiger shark swam angrily across the beach parking lot. It was eight feet under water and full of trash. The shark snapped at garbage cans and slashed at unfamiliar underwater objects. He bit off the Blue Heron street sign and swam across the island into Surfside Bay. The bay was not much different. It was filled with flotsam and soggy materials drifting just below the surface.

Bob Delacourte was strapped securely in a Type I PFD, or life jacket. Bob had always been afraid of the water but loved fishing and loved going boating. To salve his fears, he had shelled out fifty dollars to buy the best life jacket he could find. His fishing buddies laughed when he wore it, and he took a lot of kidding; but he knew that if anything happened, it would keep him alive with his head above water, even if he were unconscious.

When Eleuthera's waves poked out his living room windows, he knew enough about hurricanes to know that his house was soon to follow. He strapped on his cumbersome PFD, stepped out of his house and was blown quickly from his porch into the swirling black waters that in seconds became Surfside Bay.

Bob topped the crest of one wave after another. It was like riding a liquid roller coaster. In spite of his terror of the storm, his fear of water, his horror of what was happening to his home and Surfside, Bob Delacourte found that he was enjoying himself. He liked the roller coaster ride and he was ecstatic over the performance of his PFD. He was certain he would be washed to shore and safety. At the top of a wave, a flash of lightning revealed the back and fin of the huge tiger shark.

"What the hell is he doing here?" Bob thought. Are there sharks in all this garbage, too? And why is that one here? Here by me, for God's sake."

Another bolt of lightning showed the shark repeatedly striking a large white object in the water. "I don't believe it." Delacourte thought. "That thing is attacking a sailboat that won't go under. And I hope there's no one on it. I hope he keeps after it and doesn't see me."

The next flash of lightning brought no sign of either the shark or the sailboat. Delacourte silently thanked the lord he didn't believe in and prayed he'd make it to the other side of the bay.

Captain Don Sanders talked to the group of sturdy volunteers in the second floor room of the bay-side Pilot House condominium. "Can ya'll hear me over the wind?" The candles and hurricane lamps flickered, but he could see the heads nodding yes. "Okay, sailors, let me lay it out to you straight and simple. I'm as guilty as anyone else at laying out a line of bull to make money. You all know that. Most of you have lived here in the Pilot House, while I've operated my dinner-cruise boat for the past ten years. Well, tonight the time for exaggeration is over. I spent many a year in the Caribbean before I landed here; I've seen storms come and go—but I've never seen one like this. She's worse than anything I've ever seen, and she ain't even mad yet.

"Let me tell you, folks," Captain Don looked at the two hundred-odd people crowded into the rec room: old people hanging on to each other, young mothers feeding babies bottles, singles standing nervously with their hands in their pockets. "Eleuthera is gonna savage this island. I own a place here just like the rest of you, but the time for kiddin is over—it ain't gonna be here tomorrer. This storm's gonna wipe this place as clean as a deacon's table, and that includes the Pilot House. Tomorrer there ain't gonna be nothin' here but sand."

A rumble of alarm and protest bubbled from the crowd.

"Hey!" Don pounded the rec room podium. "I ain't up here to argue whether I'm right or wrong. I know I'm right, and I don't care what you think. What I'm doin' is offerin you a chance to get out. Now do you want it or not?"

The overwhelming bellow of yeses answered his question. "That's what I wanted to hear. Let me set something straight, though. Most of you have taken a dinner cruise on my *Sand Egret*, so you know what she's like. She's a fine ship—a dinner-tug for fair weather in the bay. She's old, she's wooden, and she ain't no stormy-weather craft. But as far as I'm concerned, she's a hell of a lot better than this concrete coffin we're standin' in. Everybody who wants to go—stay in this room. Forget what's up in your condo. We don't have time to get it. This is it, folks." He pulled his white captain's hat down on his head at a rakish angle and looked at his Seiko Chronograph. "You have two minutes. Those of you who want to go with me, start linin' up toward the door. There's water and waves out there. I want you to lock hands, forearm to forearm, so we can wade onto the boat.

"Those of you who want to stay—God be with you; we'll meet somewhere else on another day."

The *Sand Egret* was licensed for one hundred-ten people. Tonight she carried one hundred forty-seven. Captain Don had already downed three more straight scotches than he should have. He knew it and worried about it as he churned the heated engines into reverse. His human cargo was soaked to the skin and shivering from the wind and the fright of their voyage. Getting to the boat through the chest-high water had been the difficult part. The *Sand Egret* was docked on the bay side of the docks so cutting loose and getting away from the docks was a joke. Captain Don felt as if he hadn't even tossed off the last stern line before the wind and engines had him halfway across the four-mile expanse of the bay.

He was wrong. He was only a quarter of a mile from Surfview when Eleuthera sent her minions on the

*Sand Egrets* trail. Her winds whipped the old wooden vessel sideways into the swells. Don's engines, built for bay-side puttering, fought a losing battle to tack into the seas.

A tornado flitted a thousand yards to her port side, illuminated in violent slashes of lightning. "By Morgan's grandma, will you look at that!" Captain Don edged his elbow into the side of the pretty young twenty-year-old from the second floor who'd come up to stand with him at the helm. "I be damned. 'Tis a waterspout in the midst of a hurricane!"

Captain Don's next line remained a thought. A brilliant flash of lightning streaked from the tornado, hit the *Sand Egret's* faultily grounded radar mast, and traveled through the ship's interior thru a loosely-laid piece of copper tubing left carelessly over the emergency gas tanks and the old metal aft-side plumbing.

The explosion lit the sky like a dozen lightning flashes. It rocked the bay bottom with the impact of a meteorite. Fire broke out almost instantaneously all over the ship. The sound of the disaster was heard for a mile around. The giant tiger raced to the scene, followed by a score of smaller tigers, blacktips, hammerheads, lemons, bulls, and bonnetheads.

Passengers were torn between burning and being eaten. The flames from the *Egret* illuminated the proliferation of fins around the burning vessel. The high waves added to the panic, making footing unstable. A young mother and baby pitched forward into the water to dissappear beneath a mass of fins. An elderly physician backed too close to a burning bulkhead, turned into a human torch, and went running wildly into the midst of those too panicked to move. When another explosion sent the *Egret* listing fatally to port, her passengers' fates were sealed. Another dozen jumped into the water to escape the flames. The sharks were in a frenzy. Arms, legs, heads, torsos, hands, and feet, drifted in all directions for the incensed sharks to feed on. The giant tiger took his choice, which included any smaller shark who happened to cross his path.

A twelve-foot hammerhead raked an elderly grandmother across her buttocks, sliced down her thigh, and opened her leg like a buzz saw. The giant tiger followed, snapping off the bleeding leg. A five-foot bull ripped a soccerball-sized bite out of her side.

Captain Don threw a life ring to a young couple swimming back toward the burning boat. The husband placed it over his wife and held the rope as Don tried to pull them in. The woman's body toppled over the top of the life ring, spewing blood in her husband's face—she had been bitten twice; the second bite had completely severed both her legs. She never screamed, but just sank silently beneath the water.

The sky was a strange mixture of fire and blackness, at times too bright to see; at others, too dark. A second explosion sent Captain Don flying into the midst of frenzy. The choppy water was thick with blood, bits of flesh, and tattered clothing. As soon as Don hit, the sharks were on him. A smaller blacktip snapped off the first three fingers of his hand. A marauding bull raked him across the head, tearing off his ear and scalping the back of his skull.

In only a few minutes all one hundred forty-seven residents of the Pilot House condominium had fallen victim to the fire, the sharks, or the sea.

# 24. XRAY

Eleuthera's banshee winds deafened Stark. Although he'd had several shots of Jack Daniels, he still couldn't stand the high ear-piercing sound. Rummaging through the bathroom medicine cabinet, he found a roll of cotton, tore off pieces, and stuffed them into his ears. "Why am I doing this?" he asked himself. "In the hall closet are ear protectors for my Magnum and M-16. If they don't screen out the whine, nothing will." Cotton still wadded in his ears, he found the headphone-like protectors, put them on, and went back into the living room.

"Big choice I have," He said out loud, unable to hear himself because of the cotton, the ear-protectors, and wind. "Just what do I do now? Have another drink? If I do and the condo goes down, I'll be half tight and not functioning like I should. I'll die for sure! Should I have a Tab, instead, and sober up even more? . . . If the condo goes down, I'm going to die, drunk or sober. At least it won't feel so bad this way!"

He filled his brandy glass with ice and lacking

water, filled the empty space with straight Jack Daniels.

Thirty minutes later, Eleuthera had systematically destroyed much of the Suncoast. Surfside, in the grip of a high tide raised and bloated by the hurricane winds, was already under fifteen feet of water. Only the largest buildings were still standing or visible.

At Cormorant Hole Marina, the floating docks (the only municipal floating docks on the coast) had fared well in the beginning. They had risen with the tide and the boats had risen with them. They rode the waves and tossed in the wind, but they withstood the initial tides.

Boats moored at fixed docks had long ago popped their lines: boats smashed pilings; pilings smashed boats; and loosened boats smashed into each other. Millions of dollars worth of boat loans turned into splintered teak and fiberglass in a matter of minutes. It would be months before insurance companies would be able to assess the true damage, and even longer before they assessed the actual worth of the boats that they had too quickly and greedily insured.

The next ten minutes brought chaos to Cormorant Hole Marina, too. Rainford's yacht, the *Mangrove Snapper*, was the end boat on the first dock. The deeper water here gave him more room to maneuver the huge ship into its berth. Eleuthera used that position to her advantage. She first broke Jim's lines, never designed for hurricane strength winds. Then, with waves rolling straight across the island and into the marina, Eleuthera used the huge sixty-five-foot, twelve thousand-pound craft to batter down the retaining pilings and pull the rest of the docks with her. The pilings leaned and broke; the other boats—many of which had already snapped their lines and were jousting with each other across a metal walkway—added their weight and wind resistance to that of the *Mangrove Snapper*. With an awesome wrenching roar the docks broke loose. Boats rolled in the water, gouged holes in each other, and slid beneath the surface. Others were caught in the wind, whipped from their berths and flung faster across the bay than their engines could have taken them.

Mako Don, Liza's slipmate, had seen what was coming. He knew the boats in dock were going to fare less well than those out—or at the least, they were all going to go down! He pulled a machete from the wall of his Gulfstar Sailmaster 39, went topside, and was rolled across the stern by the winds. He pulled himself across his craft until he could grasp the safety harness, strapped himself into it, and then let the wind slide him back across toward Liza's boat. Feeling a little sick at what he was doing, he inched to the bow of the Carver, cut the lines, returned to the stern, and cut those and the spring line. Feeling even sicker, he returned to his own craft and did the same.

Eleuthera had slowed for a moment before unleashing her first deathblow to the Suncoast. Her deadly winds and waves had skirted in front of her, leveling and inundating much in her path. But now she was ready to show the world her fury.

"Logan! Logan!" Assistant Hurricane Director Bob

Cowley shouted across the room at National Hurricane Center. "Look at this! Eleuthera's sustained winds are two hundred-thirty miles an hour! God knows what she's gusting to. The Orions won't even touch her. They say she's too strong to penetrate and that this close to land, it's way too dangerous. Have you ever seen a storm like this?"

"No, and I don't want to, Cowley. You and I have a lot of talking to do after we get finished with this mess. What have you heard from the Suncoast?"

Cowley knew he was in trouble. The stern look on the man with the stern square jaw spelled disaster for him as well as the Suncoast. He wondered how he could smooth things over. After all, Eleuthera wasn't his fault.

"We haven't heard anything, sir, for the past hour or so. You got the last reports. Pete Southwell at Surfside said to tell the world good-bye for him—but you know he's always been a little melodramatic."

"I'm afraid that today he just might not be that melodramatic." Logan rubbed his face and ran his hand up over his head. He was tired and worn. Eleuthera had given him almost no sleep in the past four days.

At Surfside, all of the major hotels and highrise condominiums were still standing in the face of the wind and towering waves. Only the very strongest buildings were left. The concrete and steel electric poles were twisted and crumbled. Wooden poles had turned into surface torpedoes. Anything remotely floatable or not riveted deeply in the earth had either been washed into the bay or buried beneath the sand. Surfside was devoid of automobiles, trash dumpsters, newspaper vendors, postal boxes, Australian Pines, palm trees or other shrubbery. Where great homes had faced the Gulf, a new beach waited beneath the waters. Where houses built on stilts had faced the initial fury of wind and water, there remained only pilings sticking up into the high tide like crazily-laid birthday candles. The line of cars that had jammed Gulf Boulevard and the causeway clogged it no more. They were deep below the dark bay waters, hiding occupants who had clawed at windows and car ceilings for their last breath of air.

The same scene was being repeated in town after town from Clearwater to Sarasota. Not only were the beach communities taking a beating from this female pugilist; the mainland was taking a pummeling as well. McDill Air Force Base had long before evacuated its top security fighter planes, including the fighter-bombers that were not supposed to be there. Tampa International Airport was not only closed—it was under water!

In downtown Surfview, the two hundred-mile-an-hour winds stripped the bark from those trees that had somehow managed to withstand the wind. Buildings collapsed under the pressure and the continual onslaught. Two miles from the bay, swimming pools were blown dry; garbage cans, pool chairs, and lawn mowers became as deadly as the sea. They were whipped from an owner's yard to be smashed through a neighbor's house like giant cannon balls, killing rooms full of people. Pets, tied or chained outside, were choked and decapitated.

The tornado-velocity winds skewered mobile-home parks like shish-kebabs. The tied-down metal houses were penetrated, gutted, and dispatched quickly. In half an hour, throughout the Suncoast, over ten thousand mobile-home residents surrendered their lives in a violent sacrifice to Eleuthera.

Bob Delacourte's feet touched bottom! He staggered and was blown up the shore on Surfview's bay coastline. Through the flashes of lightning, he could see the outline of buildings on the bluff. They blackened slowly as he recoiled from the blow of a palm frond on the back of his head. Delacourte staggered to his knees and pitched face-forward into the mud of the twenty-foot incline up the hill.

Eleuthera showed no mercy. Like a gladiator in the Coliseum, she pressed her advantage. With her increased winds she punished Delacourte, stripping the clothes from his body, and beating him with wind-driven debris. Ten minutes later, Delacourte's body was stripped not only of his life vest and clothing but also his top layers of flesh. He didn't bleed much—the wind blew the blood away, too. He didn't feel much, either—Bob Delacourte was dead.

At the Sand Dunes the party had grown wild—bacchanalian! The stereo system had been turned up to its limit to compete with the howling wind and vibrating windows. The Sand Dunes' owner, being more responsible than most, had installed many narrow panes of windows rather than large panoramic ones. Combined with reinforced metal strips and made of tempered glass, they were proudly withstanding Eleuthera's first intensive winds.

The unrealness of the night—the kerosene hurricane lamps, the screaming winds, the sound of the waves thudding against the bottom floors, the proliferation of coke and pot combined to cause all to lose their inhibitions in the recreation room. A young woman danced naked on the bar while her husband fondled their next door neighbor's breast. A mother of three lay spread-eagled on a pool table, glassy-eyed, staring at the ceiling, and humping furiously back at Coconut who knelt between her legs as two other men sucked on her breasts. Couples danced together; couples danced apart; singles danced by themselves. Others drank and drunkenly told stories no one wanted to hear.

The window by the door gave first. It had a slight imperfection in its curing and Eleuthera found it. The glass pane shattered like a car windshield, spraying the room with bullet-sized pieces of glass. The dancer on the bar turned from deep tan to blood-red as the glass cut her. Screams shrieked from all sides of the room. The twenty-one-year-old condo manager, Coconut's roommate, barely touched the big double doors on the other side of the room when they burst open and tore from their hinges, creating a voracious wind tunnel. The manager was speared by the chrome metal legs of a small stool and buried beneath more tables and chairs. The dancer on the bar was flung into the back bar, smashing the mirror, and shattering bottles in all directions. Stoned and unaware, the pool table mother continued humping vacant space for a minute after Coconut had been ripped from her body and slammed into the concrete wall. His head exploded like a dropped watermelon.

Deep in the Gulf, Eleuthera prepared her massive strike at the Suncoast. Directly in front of her, she pushed the huge wall of water called the tidal surge—the storm surge. The surge was not a tidal wave but a monstrous wall of water rising fifteen feet above the Gulf riding on a seventeen-foot tide. It was being pushed by two hundred twenty-five mile-an-hour winds and was traveling with a twenty-mile-an-hour storm, giving it a velocity of close to two hundred fifty miles an hour. The fat black swell in the Gulf was twenty-six miles wide and thirty-two feet high!

A sizable portion of the Suncoast's ninety thousand island residents were already dead. Another large segment of the population of the lower coastal areas in Tampa Bay lay beside them. Many more were doomed to follow.

The mountain of water first surged over the beaches. Condominiums, hotels, businesses, and homes that had withstood the initial onslaught of Eleuthera, succumbed to her knock-out blow. The weight of the water, pushed by the enormous winds, was too much. The tall buildings, like drunken giants, staggered, tottered, leaned into the wind, hesitated a second or two, then crumbled into the churning water one by one.

The Sand Dunes condominium shifted briefly sideways and slid under the water. Those who hadn't died when the windows exploded, got their chance when the tidal surge hit. The Hurricane Watch Hotel, the

Police Department, Brannigan's, and dozens of other buildings followed suit. Like dominoes in a roll, they toppled as the surge passed through.

# 25. YANKEE

Outside of Stark's condo, the winds screamed from the bowels of hell. Windows, not secured like his, shattered and shredded the wallpaper on the opposite walls of the apartments. Doors burst open and apartment contents funnelled into hallways and out opposite side units and hallway windows.

Michael Stark heard it vaguely in a fog. With cotton in his ears, ear-protectors covering them, and a belly full of Jack Daniels he really didn't give a damn at this particular moment. People were dying all over Surfside—more were dying in the greater Tampa Bay area—and Michael Stark was thinking how nice it was there were so many pretty, available women in the world. "I love it!" he thought, cradling the bottle of Jack Daniels like a baby. "I'm becoming a real hedonist!"

Michael's drunken dreams turned to cold steely reality as he felt the building shift significantly with the impact of the tidal surge. "What the 'ell was that? Ain't nothin' could bother this buildin' like that. I need another drink."

Stark rose from his seated position in front of the upturned couch, leaned against it to steady himself, then walked into the kitchen with a third-empty quart of Jack Daniels in his hand. He was surprised at how sober he was. He filled his glass, felt the building shift once more, and poured his drink down the sink. "Good God," he thought, "this whole building's gonna go. I wonder what happened to everyone else?" On second thought, he repoured the drink and sat down against the couch, hoping he was adding extra bracing to the glass door. In a few minutes, he nodded off to sleep without taking a drink. A few minutes later, he was jolted awake by the sound of total and absolute silence.

Stark felt the plywood on the inside of his windows—no vibrations. He touched the wood on the sliding glass door and got the same results. Two quick turns of the wing-nut bolts brought some common sense to his still liquor-clouded mind. "If this is the eye and not the end of the storm; if I open these, then I'm never gonna get them shut again. There are apartments all over this place that I can look outside from and not take any chances."

He stepped into the hallway and found it filled with rainwater, furniture, clothing, and bodies of people who had decided to ride out the storm. He stepped over the pretty blond corpse of a thirty-year-old divorcee who lived two units away from him. The wind had stripped off her clothing and the glass had cut her severely; but still Stark found himself oddly attracted to her. He passed. Stark was more interested in what was outside.

Her door had been blown off its hinges and down the hall toward the open window, leaving him an open invitation to go inside. The interior was a stripped, jumbled mess. Anything not fastened down had been tossed across the room or into the hallway. The heavier stuff was piled in masses; the floor was covered with glass. Stark walked to the patio, felt it give slightly and stepped quickly back inside. The storm's violent winds had given way to hot humid breezes. The killer waves had subsided to gentle summer swells. Sunlight bathed everything in an ethereal light. A look around him, below and to the horizon, proved the benign weather conditions to be disingenuous. Twenty stories below, toward Surfview, he could see the roofs of houses floating through deep water. To the north nothing but water showed where the nude beach had been. To the south, Cormorant Hole Marina looked the same. Most of the major hotels and high rises were still standing, although several were leaning at precarious angles.

Stark ran back to his apartment, grabbed his binoculars, and returned to the opened apartment. A closer inspection showed the gentle muddied waters to be full of bodies and debris. "Oh my God," he thought, "I've got to do something!" He dashed for the stairs and went down them two at a time, just barely holding the handrail. At the fourth floor he sidestepped a snarling raccoon; half a floor further down, he had to edge around two more. The stairwell had become increasingly dark as he left the top floor windows behind him. He heard the hissing before his foot hit the snake. He could feel it strike at his shoe—his foot was inches from its head. The whole stairwell was alive with rattles and hisses. It smelled like a goat. Swallowing a wave of nausea, Stark leaped three stairs upward, tore past the raccoons back to the twentieth floor, and slammed the door.

He stole another look at the blond body in the hallway and went back into her apartment to take another look outside. In the Gulf, the ominous sheer wall of black clouds edged closer to the coast. The survivors far below had little time to catch their breath or find a better handhold—the second page of hell was about to write their story.

Stark had read the hurricane preparedness pamphlets and knew what was coming. He rushed back into his condo, checked his windows, locked the doors, piled extra furniture against them, and waited. He had only minutes to go.

On the spoil island behind Surfside, First Mate Spinelli had lived a short, charmed life. The island was close enough to Surfside to bask in the diminished waves of Eleuthera—close enough that the waves had neither a chance to hit the spoil island directly nor to build up again as they did on the landside of the bay. When Eleuthera's eye passed over, shining her warm, soothing sun as treacherous and beguiling as a siren's song, Spinelli climbed half way down from the top of his Australian pine and whooped with joy. He had survived the boat; he had survived the shark; and now, he had survived Eleuthera. He felt the sky darkening, looked behind him and saw a wall of black clouds reaching from the Gulf to three stories above heaven. Bewildered and transfixed, he sat on his tree limb. The menacing clouds hung at his shoulder. They seemed to sit there forever; then suddenly, in less than thirty seconds, the humid breezes whirled into a vicious, windy whirlpool of death. Spinelli was ripped from his treetop sanctuary and tossed far into the bay. Coughing seawater from his lungs, he fought his way to the top of the giant waves. He managed to take in one deep lungful of air before one of the cresote pilings from Alex Johncourt's dock topped a wavecrest and smashed through his face. Spinelli's classic Mediterranean looks flattened on the end of the piling and his luck slid in a mass of blood and brains down through the weathered splits of the pole.

Eleuthera's winds exploded from tranquility to disaster in the breath of a minute. Stark had settled back to a sitting position, refilled his drink—and then wet his pants when he heard the roar and felt the condominium shake. The winds came from the opposite direction. There had been no warning, no gradual build up—just instant disaster. In Surfside and up and down the Suncoast, people had come outside their homes to see the damage. They had rolled up their hurricane shutters and peered through broken windows at devastated yards and neighborhoods. Taking advantage of their ignorance, Eleuthera's back wall had struck them standing in their yards, prying into their garages, gaping through unshuttered windows and wide-open doors. Another five thousand people died within the next five minutes.

Tampa and Old Tampa Bay had fared little better than the sandspit islands of the Suncoast. While there was little left of the barrier islands but sand from Anclote Key to Punta Gorda, the mainland was just as distorted. First, it had parried and lost with half a dozen tornados; then, it had fought a losing battle with the tides. The knockout came with the tidal surge which was compressed in the narrow confines of Tampa Bay, raising it to unbelievable heights of over forty feet. It popped homes from their foundations in Oldsmar and flattened the Tampa International and St. Petersburg/Clearwater airports into giant concrete parking lots void of buildings, cars, or planes.

The surge razed the exclusive districts of Hyde Park and Davis Island as it smashed its way through downtown Tampa; some old buildings stood regal and firm, but others sank with age and died in the sea. New buildings fought valiantly against the surge; those few which were well-constructed suffered heavily, but survived. Those thrown quickly together with safety standards hidden by cement mixed with saltwater became grist for Eleuthera's circular mill.

When the winds switched violently in the opposite direction—when they accelerated from near calm to over two hundred miles an hour—a second disaster began to unfold. The waters piled up high in Tampa Bay, in Surfside Bay, in St. Joseph's Sound and were held there by *seiche effect* —a phenomenon which occurs when the pressure inside a hurricane is so low that is actually sucks the water up to a much higher level than would be expected under normal hurricane conditions. When the eye passed, the pressure rose and the winds shifted behind the pent-up water, forcing it out from the bays and intercoastal intrapments. At first the waves washed over the islands with the same unbelievable speed at which they had arrived—driven by Eleuthera's savage winds. But as the islands began to surface, the water—like a herculean riptide—found there was too much wind and volume behind it; and there were not enough channels to exit through. Again, like the treacherous riptides of the Gulf coast, the pent-up waters sought out the weak spots in the islands—the places where the land was most narrow—and gutted them like groupers on a cleaning board. Surfside split in its narrowest section at Cormorant Hole Marina through a natural pass made by Stark's condominium and the tall Holiday Inn six blocks away. Both buildings had been built on sturdy deep-rooted pilings and had small concrete slab structures in between. Where the smaller buildings had been, a very wide and deep channel was opened. The winds kept blowing until the bays blew dry, exposing only small rivers criss-crossing their bellies. Then the storm moved inward, the winds diminished and the seas regained their ground.

At five that evening it was over. Eleuthera had claimed thirty thousand lives on the Suncoast and was upping her toll in Cocoa Beach and Melbourne. She had stalled over the Atlantic and was strengthening again. In Surfside, a bronze sky shone in the west. Stark tried to unfasten his windows and found he couldn't. He grabbed a fireman's axe from the end of the hallway and chopped his way through the plywood and tangled metal hurricane shutter. He couldn't believe what he saw. Stepping carefully out onto the patio, he looked up and down at what had been Surfside. "My God, it's not real!" he said out loud. "It doesn't even look like the same place."

Out in front of him was a channel almost a half a mile wide. On the island across the channel he finally recognized the Holiday Inn tilted slightly toward the sea like the leaning tower of Pisa. There were no streets. The houses were gone. There were no cars and no people. He grabbed his binoculars and started counting. There were only three highrises, including his own, left out of ten; there were only two big hotels left out of twenty. The trees were gone; the shrubbery was gone; the marina was gone; the Administration Building and the Coast Guard station were still there and the rest was sand—pure white sand—just what the environmentalists wanted, a pure, natural beach once again.

Stark knew he had to get out of the condo before he lost his mind. He couldn't stand it anymore. Between feeling trapped and being curious, he was at his limit. He started for the stairs, then remembered the snakes and the raccoons. "Oh no! Not that again. How do I get past them?" He thought for a second and decided to attack. He went into the bedroom, yanked several blankets out of the closet and wound them around a broom. He poured oil from the hurricane lamp over it, grabbed his service revolver, and headed for the stairs.

At the fourth floor he could hear the hissing. At the third his flashlight picked up the snakes. The raccoons had left when they heard him coming down the stairs.

Michael lit the blanket. It exploded with an amazing burst of flame, turning into a three-foot ball of fire that scorched his hand. He let it slide on the steps, kicking it and the slithering snakes down the next two floors. Repelled by them, Stark emptied his revolver into those that had not fled at the bottom of the stairs.

Outside, he found nothing but sand. He walked to the channel, sat, and waited. He knew he was in shock—he felt much as he had felt after a day of shelling in Nam.

# 26. ZULU

The following day, Stark, Liza, and Hernandez joined the rescue teams searching for bodies. They climbed into the police jeep. Stark took the driver's seat, Liza plopped next to him, and Juanita scrambled into the back. Stark turned to the two women before he started the engine. "Captain Blanchert has asked us to stay out here in the field. He says that the National Guard really doesn't have enough men to send us any—anyway, ain't hardly anyone here but us."

"You'd be surprised if you knew how many people are planning on coming back immediately," Liza said.

"You're kidding."

"No, I'm not. They're lined up on the mainland, waiting for the first opportunity to return."

Stark started down the nonexistent roads.

"She is right," Hernandez said. "I just came from the administration Building. The nasty fellow, Pete, he was telling someone on the radio that they should tell people that not one is coming over here until we have finished searching for the victims."

"Damn, it's hot in this jeep!" Liza looked around out both windows "It's like a desert over here."

Stark drove across the pontoon bridge that had been erected earlier that morning to link the two halves of Surfside. "What are all the poles with the flags?" Hernandez asked. "They are not plotting out land so soon?"

"No." Stark grimaced. "Those indicate something metal below—most probably a car. When we get to the end of the island, you'll see what they're doing. They have a line of guys walking along with big metal poles and they're boring them down into the sand. When they hit something, they put a stake out with a flag on it. They're supposed to airlift us a couple of tractors with backhole diggers and power winches later today."

"That's terrible," Liza said. "I don't think I particularly want to be around when they start pulling things up."

"Neither do I," Stark agreed. "What we're going to have to do today is going to be as bad. They haven't checked those other two highrises beside mine except for a quick run-through last night. They got the survivors out, but those that didn't make it are still in there."

"And I guess the snakes, they are there too?" Juanita asked.

Stark nodded and pulled up in front of where the Pelican Roost condominium's parking ramp used to be.

"How do we get in here?" Sallings asked. "That's two stories straight up and there's no stairs. I'm not Wonder Woman, you know."

Stark grinned. "Didn't think I'd ever hear you admit that! The CD people said they left a ladder out here somewhere. Let's find it."

Liza turned to Hernandez, "Juanita, get the shotguns and the fire-extinguishers. The CD people say they'll immobilize the snakes. Pete says all you have to do is hit them with the $CO_2$ then brush them out of the way. Personally, I don't trust what he says. I'm banking on a shotgun."

Stark laughed, placing the ladder against the building. "I'm with you. Ladies, and bosses first, sweetheart. Up the ladder you go."

"You chauvinist pig!"

"Oh, no," Stark protested. "Just the opposite. I'm showing you that I believe in equality. But to show you I'm still a gentleman, I'll hold the ladder steady for you."

"Thanks."

"This should be good," Hernandez laughed.

"Oh—my—God! Stark. Get up here! Bring another couple of extinguishers with you. Juanita bring the shotguns."

Stark heard the blasts from Liza's $CO_2$ cannister as he crawled through the window. On the floor was a shredded woman and baby covered with foam and the twisting bodies of short brownish-black snakes who tried to slither under them, away from the cold carbon dioxide. Liza gave them another blast. "Grim, isn't it?" she said.

"Yeah," he looked through the doorway into the hall. All the doors had been ripped from their hinges. "Have you looked in the other rooms?"

"More snakes. The husband's in the kitchen—or

what's left of him. Wind smashed the refrigerator against him. Popped both eyes out and severed his arm against the door jamb—it's in the hallway. God, it stinks in here."

"Let's see what else is here," Stark replied, taking the shotguns from Juanita as she stepped through the window. "I wonder if there's a chance the CD people overlooked someone last night. That maybe there's someone still alive? I doubt it, though. From the outside every window looked blown in. Come on."

Stark stepped into the hallway over a snake that was fighting to get out of his way. He took his broom and scooted two more to the opposite side of the hall. "I don't think we'd better waste that $CO_2$. These are mostly water snakes. If we run into a rattler or a cottonmouth, I want to have it."

"Don't worry brother," Liza replied. "If we run into one of those, they're gonna buy a bellyful of buckshot."

Past the third floor the snakes disappeared. On the ninth, they found another of the proverbial hurricane parties. In the hallway outside one room laid the battered bodies of two men and a woman. Inside the apartment were the grotesque remains of a mass murder—bodies were smashed, twisted, and turned into every concievable position. Flesh was mixed with furniture; arms and legs entwined in impossible positions. It took them a half and hour to determine just how many people had actually been in the room. The later and hotter it became, the worse the stench got.

"Okay, you guys. I'm not sure it's healthy to be here," Liza said. "There's bound to be all kinds of disease brewing in this heat. Let's move it. Hit each room quickly, make sure no one's alive, and let's get the hell out of here."

Later that evening, Liza sat at her temporary desk in the Administration Building, waiting for the return boat to the mainland. She was reading the accounts of the storm in Miami's newspaper. The front page was filled with half a dozen columns, photographs, and the promise of a special section inside. "Hey, Stark!" she said, pitching the newspaper across to him. "Read that column on the far right."

Michael picked up the paper and read:

"TAMPA BAY, Fla.(AP)—Great Hurricane Eleuthera has taken seventy five thousand lives on the Suncoast. Officials fear the toll might be much worse . . . extensive looting in Tampa . . . National Guardsman shoots man with bag of bejeweled fingers, earlobes, and gold teeth . . . fifty-cent bags of ice are selling at two dollars apiece and people are lined up for blocks to purchase them . . . Sterno and canned goods are virtually non-existent anywhere in Florida except on the black market . . . bodies are being stacked up in piles at Tampa International Airport to be flown to refrigeration elsewhere and identified later."

Stark put the paper down. "I don't think I care to read it or look at the glossies, thank you. I've had my fill."

"Yeah," Sallings took her feet off the desk, stood up, and stretched. "I'm ready to get out of here. You never did say where you're stayin—I'm staying with

Juanita. She said her house in Surfview was just barely damaged."

"I'm staying there, too—until they get power back over here and I can move back."

"Jesus, Juanita is as naive as the hospital planners."

Stark got up and stretched, too. "It's only temporary, Liza. And we all have separate bedrooms. Anyway, as soon as I can move back in, Ollie's going to fly back and stay with me until she can get another place . . . what'd you mean about the hospitals?"

"Well, evidently the same genius who sneaks around the country building civil defense shelters and schools on fault lines in California—the wise little man or men who invented plea bargaining to get criminals off—well, he managed to put Tampa General Hospital, Clearwater's Morton Plant Hospital, St. Petersburg's Bayfront Hospital and two others down there all just a few feet above sea level—they ain't there no more. I hear Ollie's ex-husband was in one of them too—that he's among the missing."

"Break my heart." Stark replied grimly.

In the weeks following Eleuthera, nature worked her indefatigable magic on the island. The sea oats, cactus, and water grass started staking their claims. The city started adding its touch with the planting of coconut palms, oleanders, and mangrove seedlings. The island was slowly taking shape again. They finally erected a temporary bridge to the mainland. That would allow real construction to begin. Florida Power rigged new lines across the bay and Surfview completed temporary water and sewage lines.

Stark had been able to return to his condo; Sallings had purchased another boat with her insurance money, and Goodwin had returned to Naples to help repair the damage Eleuthera had done to her Marine Lab.

In true cavalier fashion, Stark wrestled with his sexual desires for Ollie, Carolyn, Liza, and Juanita. "What the hell," he thought. "I almost bought it last month. I'm gonna do what I want. To hell with what's right and on with what's possible. I'll go out with and to bed with any of them that I can—and when I can. If one of them doesn't like that, then I'll deal with that problem when it arises." It was easy for him to say with Ollie staying in his condo and the other women preoccupied.

Whistling, Stark drove his jeep across the pontoon bridge from his condo to the other half of Surfside. He had another early morning meeting with Blanchert, Sallings, the City Commission and the new planners and developers they had hired from Miami. Stark rode the elevator to the third floor conference room of the Administration Building.

"Gentlemen—and ladies," Jim Rainford said, standing proudly beside a large easel at the end of the conference table. "I want to show you something today that will put Surfside back on the map. We have before us the chance to make it the model beach city in all of the United States—a tourist mecca for all the world!" He flipped over the first page on the large easel, revealing a sketch of an ultra-modern city, its business district exclusively on one half of the island, its residential district on the other. "We are, with Federal help, going to make Surfside what we have always dreamed it could be—and you are all going to be on the ground floor."

Stark stifled a yawn. Nights with Ollie were nights without sleep.

Three miles offshore and a mile north of Surfside, in the bright morning sunlight, eighteen inches of deadly fin broke the calm Gulf surface and trailed a V-shaped ripple of water behind it. The huge tiger shark sensed that he was in familiar waters. The bottom and islands had changed, but it still felt familiar. He steadily headed for what was once the popular and now deserted Surfside Beach.

Stark had kissed Ollie good-bye before he left. "I'll be back by noon. We'll go somewhere and get something to eat."

"What about eating in?"

"You're killing me."

She blew him a kiss as he left and proceeded cleaning the condo. An hour later she finished, put on her swimming suit, and went to the beach to do her daily aerobic swimming.

Two hundred yards further out in the Gulf, the giant tiger shark heard the rhythmic slapping of the water. He was right. He had found the easy food that was indigenous to this area.

There was another missing person in Surfside.

Critical acclaim for Celestine Sibley's

# STRAIGHT AS AN ARROW

"No words are wasted and no loose threads are left unsnipped."
—*Cleveland Plain Dealer*

"The variety of characters, well depicted locals and strong heroine are a pleasure to read about."
—*Booklist*

# and AH, SWEET MYSTERY

"[Kate Mulcay is an] appealing new sleuth. . . . 'Sweet' is the right word. . . Choice characterizations."
—*The New York Times*

"[Sibley's] spirit has always represented what was finest and most human in the South."
—Pat Conroy

"A charming, neatly crafted mystery. . . A beguiling mosaic as intrepid Kate fits them together."
—*Publishers Weekly*

"Sibley has a wonderful feel for the way Southerners talk, and her sadness for the passing of the rural South is so palpable you want to run right down there and punch out a few developers. . . . Sibley is a pro."
—*San Jose Mercury-News*

## ALSO BY CELESTINE SIBLEY

Straight as an Arrow
Ah, Sweet Mystery
The Malignant Heart
Christmas in Georgia
Dear Store
A Place Called Sweet Apple
Especially at Christmas
Mothers Are Always Special
Sweet Apple Gardening Book
Daby by Day
Small Blessings
Jincey
Children, My Children
Young'uns
The Magical Realm of Sallie Middleton (coauthor)
Turned Funny
Tokens of Myself
Peachtree Street U.S.A.
For All Seasons

# DIRE HAPPENINGS AT SCRATCH ANKLE

CELESTINE SIBLEY

HarperPaperbacks
*A Division of* HarperCollins*Publishers*

This is a work of fiction. The characters, incidents, and dialogues are products of the author's imagination and are not to be construed as real. Any resemblance to actual events or persons, living or dead, is entirely coincidental.

HarperPaperbacks *A Division of* HarperCollins*Publishers*
10 East 53rd Street, New York, N.Y. 10022



A hardcover edition of this book was published in 1993 by HarperCollins*Publishers*.

Cover illustration by Merrit Deckle

First HarperPaperbacks printing: October 1994

Printed in the United States of America

HarperPaperbacks and colophon are trademarks of HarperCollins*Publishers*

❖ 10 9 8 7 6 5 4 3 2 1

This book is dedicated to James A. Mackay, his daughter and law partner Kathy, and their friends Jim Youmans and Ken Pennington. They introduced me to the beauties and perils of northwest Georgia and the excitement of rappelling and caving. They are, however, in no way responsible for any errors I have made. I know that they will forgive me and I hope that all the other people who know and love Dade County will forgive me for the liberties I took with its geography, especially moving the courthouse from Trenton to Rising Fawn, and populating it with purely fictional characters.

# Dire Happenings at Scratch Ankle

KATE MULCAY HAD NOT covered Georgia politics in a long time and she didn't particularly want to. The calling had become pallid and self-righteous. There hadn't been a voting scandal of any scope since a south Georgia county had collected votes from a cemetery full of tombstones in a long-ago governor's race. There hadn't been a memorable sex shocker since a much-married governor had declined to divorce his wife and marry his pretty young mistress when she became pregnant but had smiled on her tenderly, called the state patrol, and asked them to send a trooper over to marry her.

Wicked. Shocking. Kate agreed, but it had sure made newspapering interesting and as she sat in the Georgia House of Representatives chamber that winter afternoon, she thought a little malefaction wouldn't be bad.

The old chamber was tired. It was getting on toward the end of the forty-day session and Kate wondered if the skipper of this old ark, Speaker Frank Pitts, had not long since dispatched a dove to the outside world and seen it come winging back with an olive twig in its beak, indicating mellow weather in life beyond the capitol.

Kate sighed and tilted back in the press section swivel chair and looked around. On the other side of the glass that segregated the press, the people's representatives appeared listless and bored. Some of them read the afternoon paper. Some of them were furtively cleaning out their desks against the time not many days off when the Speaker's gavel would fall and he would intone the final words of the session: "This House now stands adjourned sine die!" Then, according to custom, the members would fling a snowfall of papers into the air, let out a fusillade of Rebel yells, and, jostling and backslapping, work their way out of the capitol toward their respective homes in Georgia's far-flung 159 counties.

Kate was the only newspaper reporter she knew who had genuinely enjoyed covering the General Assembly. When other people were removed from that assignment, they heaved great sighs of relief and treated the pressroom corps to celebratory drinks. When Kate was ordered back to the office to write an editorial page column, she mourned at cleaning out her desk in the pressroom and turning it and her telephone over to a lanky kid newly graduated from the University of Georgia's journalism school.

Being in the capitol in lawmaking season was, to Kate, to be in the heart of the state and intensely alive. She found herself homesick for the place, the tall chamber with its long windows now heavily swathed with draperies but once open and looking out on the capitol lawn, with its blooming borders and old gray monuments and with pigeons preening dingy feathers and cooing along the window ledge. She delighted in the ancient rituals of lawmaking borrowed from the British Parliament. The daily bit of theater when the members recessed for the night and the Speaker left the podium and went to the floor and bowed to the left, bowed to the right, and ran from the chamber was one of those remnants of the past that unfailingly pleased Kate. She liked the fact that the Governor could only enter the House by invitation, like the British monarch and the House of Commons, and she enjoyed the clarion call of the doorkeeper from the center aisle, "Mistah Speakah! His excellency the

Governor of Georgia asks permission to enter the House of Representatives!" In a way it was playacting; in a way it was a nice nod to the past and Mother England with a sort of Magna Carta flavor. Most of all, Kate liked knowing the members, most of them leaders in cities and country towns from all parts of the state. In her day at the capitol the membership was exclusively male, except one session when there were a couple of women members battling to get their sex admitted to jury duty.

There had always been a sprinkling of elegant, old-fashioned orators whose speeches were rich in imagery and eloquence. There were also "wool-hat boys" with the flavor of the soil in their speech and the courthouse crowd back home dictating their every move. Kate enjoyed them all.

She remembered with affection the old retired postmaster from a little south Georgia county whose one and only appearance in the well of the House was to defeat a bill to erect a monument to the brutal Confederate commandant of the infamous prison camp at Andersonville.

The old gentleman, silver-haired and blue-serge-suited, had been shy but invincible. He told the still somewhat chauvinistic House that his grandfather had been a Confederate soldier assigned as a guard at Andersonville prison and had personally witnessed and been sickened by the atrocities committed by the commandant, Major Henry Wirz, against Union prisoners. His grandfather had never forgotten cruelties to helpless prisoners of war which, he contended, ranked alongside Hitler's brutalities.

He spoke in the quiet, courteous tone of a grandfather reasoning with recalcitrant grandchildren. Then he gathered steam:

"Honor that fiend with a monument?" he cried. "Oh, the shame, the disgrace to our state and the honorable men who fought for the Confederacy! I beg you gentlemen to show that you deplore such heinous atrocities. I beg you to reject this resolution!"

And then, lifting his faded old blue eyes to the House ceiling, he echoed that southern hero Patrick Henry: "A monument to Henry Wirz? Forbid it, Almighty God!"

He sat down, pink-faced and flustered, to a storm of applause. Kate heard later that he had gone home and had a fatal heart attack, but he had defeated the effort to honor a sadist, even one who happened to be wearing the gray.

Now back in the present-day House chamber listening to the reading clerk's singsong litany about some land dispute somewhere,

Kate wondered if there were any shy, brave old gentlemen down there at the little Victorian desks with their glowing maple spindles and lift-lid tops. The current membership looked generally young with smart blow-dry haircuts, conservatively tailored suits, and the sheen of higher education on their brows. More than that, they were considerably diluted with blacks and women.

Kate rejoiced in the high incidence of women and blacks entrusted with the people's business nowadays, but as a reporter she mourned their lack of color—and humor. They took themselves and their jobs seriously. They knew that the day when the electorate cherished clowns and cutups was long gone, and rightly so. But Kate couldn't help it; she missed the rogues and scoundrels, but most of all the funny ones.

There was the representative who was an undertaker "back home" and tried to camouflage his dolorous calling by wearing loud plaid suits with electric bow ties. He had a whole rainbow of loafers in colors to match every outfit.

"I'm just a dirt-road sport," he had remarked to Kate one time in wry self-assessment.

And there was the exuberant, bombastic old-timer who wasn't in his accustomed seat on opening day. His name was missing from the roll call. Wondering about him, Kate found him, listless and lonely, in the capitol coffee shop and asked him the reason for his absence.

"Oh, I didn't come back," he said morosely. "For reasons of health. The voters got sick of me."

It wasn't likely that any of the current crop of lawmakers talked like that, Kate thought. She heard them sometimes on television and they were always earnest and usually self-congratulatory.

She wondered how the reporters who succeeded her could abide them. Then she noticed that one of the few reporters remaining in the press box this late in the day, a fellow named Gary Boone from the afternoon paper, was sound asleep. And the gorgeous blonde who represented one of the television stations was catching up on her homework for whatever degree she was seeking at Georgia State. They all had so many degrees, Kate thought guiltily. She had been a college dropout. But they didn't seem to be savoring the Georgia General Assembly as she always had, before a new city editor, thinking he was promoting her, misguidedly transferred her to columnizing. Anyhow, the legislature seemed to have lost its pizzazz.

The reading clerk fell silent and the Speaker

said, "Chair recognizes the gentleman from the First."

A tall lean young fellow with dark eyes in the murky hollows of a bony face and a shock of black hair was approaching the well of the House. Kate idly checked her legislative directory. She didn't expect much of him or of any of the proceedings this dull day. She was only there filling in for Johnny Weaver, the regular capitol reporter, whose wife was having a baby. He had told her nothing much was coming up, but Shell Shellnut, the city editor, running her in as a substitute, said, "Any little thing, Kate. I doubt if there'll be a good murder for you, although God knows we'd welcome anything. News is nonexistent today."

"I can skip the murder, Shell," Kate said, putting on her jacket. But she knew Shell didn't believe her. She had helped her late husband, Homicide detective Benjamin Mulcay, investigate so many murders, her colleagues on the paper pretended to believe it was a major hobby with her.

Clearly there would be no murder in this somnolent lawmaking body today. Members seemed as drowsy as her neighbor in the press section. But the gentleman approaching the microphone in the well of the House did look tense and keyed up.

She found his name in the little directory:

Rep. R. Pickett. That was brief. Most members listed a couple of given names and often a nickname.

Her neighbor, Gary, was coming to life, already seasoned enough as a reporter to have that built-in automatic response to action on the floor.

"Who is this?" she asked.

He yawned. "Return Pickett. Indian warrior. They call him Turn."

"He does look like a Native American," Kate admitted.

"He's no more native than the rest of us," Gary said, yawning again. "He's a freshman and he's been on the warpath ever since he got here. The boys"—he nodded toward the floor—"are getting tired of it. But I think the female members consider him sexy and they think it's kind of a nice change when he's down there looking at them with those haunted bedroom eyes."

"What's his cause?" Kate asked.

"Oh, you know, the same old dead horse they've been beating for years. They must have been at it when you covered the capitol. Tennessee is stealing Georgia blind."

Kate looked startled and then she remembered. There had been a recurring rhubarb about some land in downtown Chattanooga that was part of a tract that belonged to

Georgia's state-owned railroad. It had become valuable—to Tennessee—commercial property. That was an ancient legal hassle that had been mediated half a century ago. But what now? Suddenly she started laughing. "Not the General again, is it?"

Gary shook his head. "You mean Walt Disney's *Great Locomotive Chase*? I don't think so. I wasn't here, but I believe Pickett said the courts gave that one back to Georgia. It's in a museum around the Kennesaw Mountain battlefield somewhere, I believe."

Kate nodded.

The little wood-burning locomotive had been stolen by a party of plainclothes Union spies while its Confederate crew breakfasted at a place called Big Shanty on the road to Chattanooga. The Confederates chased them on foot and by handcar and an unexpectedly appropriated engine or two, finally retrieving the little engine just short of the Tennessee line. The Union raiders fled but were subsequently caught and hanged. Many years after the war, Georgia leased the little train to the Louisville & Nashville railroad for show purposes and it toured the nation, returning to the South, where Tennessee laid claim to it with such enthusiasm and affection that it was on exhibition at Tennessee's newly renovated depot and medals of it were struck for souvenirs. Chattanooga's mayor had its likeness emblazoned on his official stationery and even the city's fire trucks wore pictures of the General.

Georgia went forth to battle once more, this time in the courts, and finally the little engine came home. There was bitterness in Tennessee. Some women wept and swore they would never cross the state line into Georgia again, even to shop.

It couldn't be at issue again, Kate thought, turning her attention to the young man at the microphone.

She could see why women in the capitol regarded the representative from the First as sexy. He had that lean, rangy Gary Cooper build with a bronzed face and those dark eyes that gleamed with a fanatical fire. A long bony hand chopped the turgid air of the chamber and his deep voice rumbled over a theme about rape.

"Rape, did he say?" asked Gary, come to life again.

"I think rape of the land," said Kate.

"Oh, that," said the young reporter, slouching back in his chair. "He talks about that a lot. His ancestors were in the Trail of Tears."

That sad old drama, a blot on the state's history which citizens had been shamed by and had grieved over for more than a century and a half, Kate mused. The Cherokee Indians had lost their homes and lands in north Georgia and had been driven to a government reservation in the West, a death march for thousands of them, now dramatized as the Trail of Tears.

But it was over and done with in 1838 or '39, so what was there to be said about it now? She listened attentively.

"And I say to you, ladies and gentlemen," the young zealot thundered, "my people were robbed of their homes—murdered, robbed, raped. And it is happening again! I submit to you that history is repeating itself! Georgia is being invaded. The state line is a joke, a farce. We have lost once more the lands of my people. Even before the infamous Trail of Tears my ancestors had cause to weep tears of blood. Their very graves are on alien soil."

Gary Boone stirred restively. "Here we go again. Dragging Canoe."

"Dragging what?" asked Kate.

"Oh, some old Indian chief," Gary said. "Turn's great-great-great-somebody. He's obsessed."

But the young man in the well didn't look obsessed now. He was silent for a moment and smiling slightly, an almost shy, crooked smile that showed a flash of very white teeth.

He was gathering steam for the finish.

"I'm asking this House," he said with sudden gravity, "to pass this resolution calling for realignment of our state's northern boundary, to send a committee from this General Assembly to see what injustice is being done to our citizens, and to report back that we may, ladies and gentlemen, *act!*"

He made as if to resume his seat, but then he turned to the microphone once more.

"You all know that beautiful mountainside, that Eden, that heaven on Earth that artists call Plum Nelly. It was a fun name meaning that it was 'plumb out of Tennessee and nelly out of Georgia.' That was back when a little woman named Fannie Mennen lived and painted there on beautiful Lookout Mountain. But, my fellow members, if we don't move fast, that wondrous spot called Plum Nelly will be plumb out of Georgia and plumb *in* that state to the north of us!"

"So what?" mumbled Gary, getting to his feet and preparing to leave for the pressroom just as a voice in back of the chamber cried, "Mister Speaker! I move that House Resolution 389-983 be recommitted to the State Institutions and Property Committee for further study!"

Representative Pickett paused on his way back to his seat and looked stunned as the House by voice vote promptly shelved his resolution. Not so Native American that he didn't register disappointment, Kate thought, getting to her feet. Impassivity must have been bred out of Dragging Canoe's great-great-great-descendant.

Back at the office Kate learned that there had been another protest march about replacing the Confederate battle flag as the state flag and the photo department had come up with some fine pictures of people in shabby Confederate uniforms marching and singing in a cold drizzle of sleet and rain. Shell wanted to play them big, so there was not much room for Representative Pickett's resolution and not much interest, either. Feuding with Tennessee and sometimes with North Carolina was old stuff that had had its day.

As Kate walked away from the city desk, Shell called after her: "Say, what is this Plum Nelly? Who's this Nelly broad?"

"Aw, Shell," Kate said with a laugh, "don't you know 'nelly' is the approved southern pronunciation of 'nearly'?"

"No, thank God, I came from Ohio," said the city editor, pushing Kate's story to one side.

But Kate, on her way to her log cabin home in the woods twenty-five miles north of Atlanta, could not get the young legislator with the fierce eyes off her mind. Was he nuts, or did he really have something besides the ancient Cherokee grievance to base his resolution on? It wasn't much of a story, after all these years of the bickering, which the newspaper faithfully covered. There were some legislators, busy with more urgent matters, who privately said Georgia was paranoid on the subject. Kate smiled to herself, remembering that the coastal ones fought to save the famed "Marshes of Glynn"; the city ones fought new soft drink taxes, which would be bound to alienate that reliable benefactor, the Coca-Cola Company; and the ones from the tobacco belt raged against additional cigarette taxes as if they would undermine pure drinking water and southern womanhood.

Each to his own, Kate thought, turning down the dirt road that led to her little cabin. The sight of her cabin, as always, caused Kate's heart to lift with affection and pride. The weathered old log walls looked welcoming in the light of the setting sun. They had survived a century and a half of summer suns and winter rain and sleet, and Kate always fancied that their shabby gray and lichened runnels and furrows held some of the color and life of the passing seasons. She and her late husband, Benjy, had found the cabin, long deserted and dilapidated, twenty years before his death.

Together they had shored it up and made it as snug and comfortable as its old shake roof and the gaping spaces between the logs permitted. It was small, but it accommodated their books and the country possessions of old cupboards and braided rugs they had loved and painstakingly acquired at auctions and old house sales through the years. Now Kate lived in it alone, and as she parked her car and walked toward the kitchen door, she thought of the young legislator named Return. Maybe he had such a feeling for home. She stopped to pat her almost-Dalmatian dog named Pepper, who rushed out to meet her, and paused as she pushed the kitchen door open to speak respectfully to her white cat named Sugar, who, against house rules, dozed on the old homemade hunt board where her mother's yellowed and veined ironstone tureen held a bunch of forsythia branches she was trying to force into early bloom.

One day, she thought, Sugar would knock that tureen off the table and break it.

"You do that," she threatened him, rubbing his ears, "and I'll give you to the subdividers."

It was a much smaller loss and invasion, she thought, than the one Representative Pickett's ancestors, the Cherokee Indians, had suffered when they were driven off their lands, but she thought she had an inkling of how they felt when developers had arrived in her woods and populated them with elegant million- and half-million-dollar houses.

She kicked off her shoes, got a beer out of the refrigerator, and made a resolution. *Tomorrow,* she decided, *I will talk to Mr. Pickett.* Crazy and illogical as his attempt was to take back lands belonging to the neighboring state of Tennessee, at least there was feeling there, perhaps akin to her own profound feeling for home. There had to be a story or maybe a column in it.

The next day was Friday and the legislature adjourned early. Kate caught Representative Pickett as he wandered, looking lost, up the splendid marble stairway to the capitol's fourth floor. "You going to look over the museum?" she asked him. He nodded gravely.

"There are things that belonged..." He paused and gulped, and a slight flush touched his high bronzed cheekbones.

"Oh, yes," said Kate. "I remember pottery and arrowheads." She grinned to show she was making a joke. "Are you going to ask that those be returned, too?"

The young legislator, surprisingly, smiled back and Kate once again admired the flash of white teeth in the dark face. "You think I'm bonkers, don't you?"

"I don't know," said Kate frankly. "I thought it might be a strong feeling for home and I understand that, loving my own primitive digs."

"I know you live in a log cabin," the legislator said, surprising her again. "I've read about it in your column. Maybe my people built it, you know. The Cherokees lived in houses instead of in tepees."

"No, you can't claim my house," Kate said firmly as they reached the stop of the stairs. "I know its history. White settlers came over the mountains from 'Ca'lina in kivered wagons' and cut the logs and hauled the rocks and built it themselves five or six years after . . . don't you call it The Removal?"

"Probably on Cherokee land," Pickett said dryly. "But don't worry, I won't contest your right to it. I would," he said with his crooked smile, "like to see it someday." And then to answer her question: "Yes, the government called it The Removal, but Trail of Tears is more accurate. You do know that it was one of the most barbarous, cold-blooded crimes in this country's history?"

Kate nodded. "I saw the pageant up in North Carolina one summer. But you can't undo what happened a hundred and fifty years ago, you know."

"Read the history books," the young man

said. "You'll see the greed and hatred that led to it and . . . " he paused in front of a painting of an Indian chief in a fine feathered bonnet, "you'll see the kind of cruelties I think you can never forget. Four thousand or more people died, many of them children. My great-great-great-grandmother carried her dead baby for two days before she let them bury it on alien land in Tennessee."

"Is that why you are resuming that old fight with Tennessee?" Kate asked.

The afternoon light slanting down from the capitol's gilded rotunda touched his shining black hair and dark face, which seemed to have an underlayer of crimson.

Redskins, they called them. Incongruous for such a well-tailored, well-barbered young man. Only his rugged half boots suggested that he might be an outdoorsman.

"Did you grow up on the reservation?"

"Born there," he said, "and named Return because they hoped I'd come back and avenge them."

"But Tennessee?" said Kate. "I thought most of the Cherokee Nation was in Georgia."

"I live here," he said, "in the Free State of Dade. I hope to bring family members back to Rising Fawn to live where our ancestors lived, hoping they will reclaim some of their land. If I marry, I hope I will have children who will feel a blood affinity for the land, especially that area now claimed by Tennessee but which is in reality Georgia's. Our ancestor, a chief, lies there—in alien soil, his grave unknown."

"Dragging Canoe?" Kate ventured.

He lifted his black crow's-wing eyebrows. "How did you know?"

Kate shrugged. "I guess we've had stories."

"He was a very brave man," said Pickett. "A great war chief. Different from another forefather, Attacullaculla. You've heard of him?" Kate shook her head. "He was a peace chief, who fought on the side of the white man, even going to England to meet the king as a child. He hoped for peace. He signed a treaty giving millions of acres to whites, but he warned them. Ah, he warned them!"

The dark head tilted upward; the dark eyes examined the rotunda. "He told them," he said softly, "'You have bought a fair and beautiful land, but you will find its settlement dark and bloody.'"

Standing there among the museum's cases of tattered flags and stained and worn uniforms from four wars, Kate shivered a little. It was as if one of the snakes from the wildlife case a few feet away had slithered toward her. So many wars, so many turbulent upheavals had come to the "fair and beautiful land," wars not just Cherokee in origin. The peace chief's words sounded like a curse—and she didn't believe in curses.

She tried for logic.

"Do you think it's reasonable to change the state line, at probably great expense, to satisfy the remembered wrongs of a handful of people?"

"I do," said the young man. "For more reasons than that. The first and foremost is that it's right."

"Well," conceded Kate, "you can't beat right. Or can you?"

"You can try," said Pickett somberly. And then he smiled. "Why don't you come up to the State of Dade and let me show you what I'm talking about? I could meet you in Rising Fawn early Saturday morning."

The name of the little town was so beautiful Kate was tempted. Or maybe she was tempted by the strange attraction of the dark young man named Return.

"I'll have to see," she said tentatively.

"In the meantime," he said, "it's getting late and the traffic is still heavy. Why don't you let me buy you a drink? Firewater."

Kate laughed. "For an Indian you are mighty knowledgeable about some of our better white customs here at the capitol. Newspaper reporters and some members of the General Assembly often do what we call 'waiting out traffic' at the end of the day by having a beer at some gracious hole in Underground Atlanta. I never heard them call it 'firewater,' however."

"I went to Georgia Tech," he said, "but I cling to a few archaic expressions."

Waiting out traffic took an hour and Kate found herself in the curiously partisan position of wanting to believe Representative Pickett. (Only now she was calling him Turn and he had stopped putting the "Miss" before Kate.) They parted by the big fountain outside Underground. He said he was leaving for Rising Fawn and Kate promised to meet him there early Saturday morning. It is a town so magically small, he had said, smiing proudly, that when she arrived inside the city limits he would most certainly know it. But to be sure, she could park on the main street and he would see her, if she had not already spotted his dusty red pickup truck, which would also be parked on the main street, probably in front of Miss Pearlie's Café.

Maybe he was bonkers, as he had suggested, Kate thought as she climbed the steps to Whitehall Street and threaded her way through fruit carts along the curb, past the Five Points MARTA station toward the newspaper office. Maybe there was no story there, as Shell indicated in the office, but it wouldn't hurt to see. She was looking forward to seeing Turn again, even if he was in the grip of an obsession, and after all, for all her travels over the state for the newspaper, she had somehow missed Rising Fawn. Such a pretty name, she mused, a town named for a Cherokee councilman, Turn had said, who was by Cherokee custom named for the first thing his parents saw after his birth. His father had looked out of their house at dawn and seen a beautiful baby deer struggling to stand on its slender legs at the edge of the clearing. Rising Fawn, beautiful name—and when the baby grew up he became a respected Cherokee representative in the Indians' dealings with the whites, Turn had said.

Back at the office, Shell, as Kate had anticipated, settled for a couple of small stories she had on General Assembly actions but rejected Representative Return Pickett's crusade.

"The customers get tired of the same old state line feud year after year," he said. "It stops being news."

Kate found she wasn't tired of it. She called Reference and was lucky enough to get Richard, a young fellow who didn't weary of history. Did he remember Georgia–Tennessee squabbles over anything besides football? she asked impudently.

"Sure do," said Richard. "What can I send you?"

"Anything you've got on boundary disputes."

Within a few minutes a pneumatic tube from Reference plummeted into a basket in the newsroom and Kate hurried over to see if it had her name on it. It did, and she took out a sheaf of copies of stories going back to the 1950s and stuffed them in her briefcase. She would read them when she got home.

On the way up the expressway toward her cabin in north Fulton County she found the name Rising Fawn running through her head. A poem? A song? When she reached the turnoff at Roswell she remembered it—a poem a long-ago southern poet had done in the style of Stephen Vincent Benét's ode to American names. His name was Daniel Whitehead Hicky and his poem had gone:

*O, Dewy Rose and Talking Rock.*
*O, rain-wet Rising Fawn.*

There was more saluting such Georgia names as Social Circle and Ty Ty and Ringgold. She couldn't remember how it went, but from her own knowledge of Georgia's geography she bet Georgia place names could outpicturesque the rest of the country's, except possibly Mr. Benét's line, "Bury my heart at Wounded Knee." She thought he might have liked Benevolence and Enigma and Between and Doerun and Flowery Branch and Dooling and Deepstep.

The Hicky poem had ended:

*May all the names I love best*
*Drift back in music over me*
*For one who loves each door, each lane*

. . . What else? It didn't matter. She was turning in her own lane, approaching her door. She would have a bath, find something to eat, and settle down to read the clippings in her briefcase in preparation for meeting Turn.

There was a light on in her kitchen and her heart sank. The Gandy sisters—Sheena, age twelve, and Kim Sue, eleven—must have preceded her. Pepper had not even come out to meet her. Some watchdog, she thought irritably. Probably on the sofa being cosseted by the girls.

It wasn't quite that bad. He was under the kitchen table on which the Gandys had spread a jigsaw puzzle which they appeared absorbed in, while their feet stirred around in Pepper's salt-and-pepper hide, alternately roughing it up and smoothing it, a most delectable treatment for a dog.

"Well, girls . . . " began Kate helplessly, "what are you doing here?"

"Um," said Sheena, fitting a piece of red rooftop in place, "we come to see you."

"We didn't even light the fire," said Kim Sue smugly. "We knowed the danger."

Kate had forbidden fire-lighting in her cabin when she wasn't at home. At least they had obeyed that rule. But still . . .

"Look, girls, I love you and I'm always glad to see you, but I think you'd better run along home tonight. I have some reading to do and I leave early in the morning for Lookout Mountain. I need a bath and a bite of something and then I have to get busy."

"Aw, shoot," said Kim Sue, her freckled face downcast as she carefully substituted the word "shoot" for the word she knew Kate disapproved.

"We told Mommer you'd just as soon have us as not," the older sister, Sheena, explained bleakly.

"Ah, you know I always love to have you," said Kate, putting an arm around each pair of skinny shoulders. "But tonight . . . well, Lookout Mountain is a sort of working trip and—"

"Lookout mounting?" Sheena repeated the destination like it was nirvana. "You going all the way up yonder? We ain't never been

"We had a cousin went onct," put in Kim Sue.

"Said it was mighty educational," interposed Sheena, knowing Kate's high regard for learning—at least for them.

"Well, yes, I suppose it is," said Kate tiredly. "But now you all scoot. I need a bath."

"Yes'm," they said dolefully, brushing their puzzle into its box and turning toward the door.

"Have a good one," Kim Sue offered politely.

"See you later, alligator," said Sheena.

Kate smiled but pointedly refrained from playing their after-a-while-crocodile game. They didn't need any encouragement, and as much as she loved them and valued their help in solving a neighbor's murder a year or so ago, there were times when she valued most being alone. Two grubby little country girls, the descendants of one of the last old farm families left in the settlement when the subdivisions came, they were fine in their way, but there were times when if Kate couldn't have Major Benjamin Mulcay, she wanted no one. After a marriage of twenty years, it was sometimes easier to adjust to nobody than to somebody.

She climbed the narrow steps to her bedroom and began divesting herself of her town-going work suit, piling everything on the bed and kicking her shoes under it as she headed for the bathroom and a shower. Once, over the sound of the water—which sometimes gushed and sometimes trickled, due to the idiosyncratic plumbing done by a man whose specialty was homicide detection—she heard a stirring on the stairs. She attributed it to Pepper and went on lathering herself.

When she came out, wrapped in the pride of her meager linen closet, a sheet-sized towel, she found her suit on a hanger, suspended from the closet door, and her shoes side by side on the little rack put there for the purpose.

"What on earth?" she muttered, and peered over the stair rail.

The Gandy sisters sat together on her sofa, a zipper bag, which they often brought for overnight visits, between them.

"Girls?" she said ineffectually. "You're back."

"Yes, ma'am," said Sheena. "Mommer's got to go hep midwife our aint. She's having her seventh young'un and the doctor won't come no more. She said it wasn't no telling how long it would take and we just as well go with you."

"Besides," said Kim Sue, "we ain't never seen Rock City. She says it's near 'bout as good as Disney World."

"Oh, but I'm not going to Rock City,"

protested Kate. "It's the other end of Lookout Mountain where I'm going."

"It don't matter," said Sheena soothingly, as if Kate were apologizing. "Same mounting. Couldn't be far."

She stood up. "We fixed you some supper. Come on and set down."

Kate was touched that they had made her a peanut butter and jelly sandwich, placed it neatly on one of her best plates, and lined up precisely beside it a bottle of beer. Was her pleasure in an occasional beer so noticeable the children thought she had to have it? She pushed it aside as she picked up the jelly-dripping sandwich before she realized she was still wearing nothing but a towel.

"Wait a minute, I'll light the fire," said Kim Sue, who was a junior-grade pyromaniac anyhow.

"And I'll git you a josie," said Sheena, using the country word for any covering garment. She headed for the stairs.

Kate chewed peanut butter, jelly, and slightly stale bread and looked at the girls helplessly. She couldn't send them home if their mother had gone off to midwife for their "aint" and she wasn't certain how Representative Return Pickett would feel about them horning in on his tour of onetime Cherokee lands.

It didn't matter, she decided after a while.

The weekend was her time off from the paper and if she chose to go sightseeing with the Gandy sisters, it was her own business.

She smiled over her sandwich at the two freckled faces. "Did you bring enough clothes for two days?" she asked.

The Gandy sisters, realizing that there had been a change in the climate, wriggled with delight. "Yes, ma'am!" they said together. "The jeans we've got on are clean and we brought dresses like you like for church."

It was both a concession to her archaic churchgoing habit, Kate realized, and assurance that they were ready for any exigency.

"Okay," she said, yawning. "Jackets because it's going to be cold and tough shoes for climbing rocky places. Got it?"

"I think they got their paths paved at Rock City," Kim Sue offered in a small hopeful voice.

"Hush up," ordered Sheena. "Miss Kate may not be a-going to Rock City."

"No," said Kate, now that she had been pampered with supper and a fire and a robe, deciding to mollify them. "We are going to a most interesting spot very few people in Georgia know. It is said to be the smallest and one of the most beautiful counties in the state. It used to be called the 'lost county' because there was no Georgia road leading to it. You had to go to Tennessee or Alabama to get there.

"There's a legend that when Georgia was slow to secede from the Union before the Civil War, the people of Dade County went ahead and voted themselves out of the United States. They didn't get back in for eighty-five years. They called this county the 'Free State of Dade.'"

She could tell her little guests weren't mesmerized by her history lesson. To give it a little glamour she added, "They had a party when they decided to return to the Union and it was on the radio all over the country!"

Her audience brightened, but not much.

"Not the teevee?" asked Sheena.

"Didn't have it then," said Kate. "That was a long time ago on the Fourth of July in 1945."

The girls were yawning. Kate shooed them up to bed. They would sleep on her bed and she would get a pillow and cover and bed down on the sofa. It would be easy to read there by the fire anyhow.

The girls fought spiritedly over taking turns in the bathroom. Although subdividers had paid a nice chunk of money for their grandfather's old cornfield, in a burst of reverse economy the Gandys had opted for two automobiles instead of one bathroom.

Once she had tucked her guests under the old quilts, some inherited from her mother, some given to her by their neighbor, Miss Willie Wilcox, she got a pillow and a comforter and settled on the sofa by the fire.

The story she had just told the girls about Dade's secession from the United States was widely believed and a favorite of hers, but she knew it was of dubious historical accuracy. Nevertheless, the people of the county liked it and, according to one of her clippings, citizens of the mountainous county "from Sitton's Gulch to Wildwood" came down from the hills to the county seat of Rising Fawn to vote for and celebrate "the return of Dade" to the Union.

*Lot of "returning" around here,* Kate said to herself as she shuffled her clippings. First the whole county and now one lone, very appealing young man. Kate wished that at her age she wasn't so susceptible to handsome young men. When she looked in the mirror, always accidentally, and saw her fast-graying hair, her sagging jawline, and the crow's feet around her eyes, she knew that they thought of her as a mother or grandmother figure and that wasn't at all the way she felt. It wasn't that she aspired to romance. Benjy had provided that. It was just that she didn't feel so far gone into age that she couldn't have a pleasant conversation, drink, or even an evening with a young man if he was interesting.

Return Pickett, now, what was he, about thirty or thirty-five? Younger? She couldn't tell, but their time in Underground was no-age. She even thought it would have been agreeable if he had held her hand a moment longer when they parted. Then she looked at her hands: rough and red from wood-getting and gardening, short nails, a callus on one forefinger, and freckles—or were they what the ads used to call "horrid age spots"? *Ha,* she jeered at herself. Nobody would ever hold one of those hands again!

She turned her attention back to the clippings. Georgia and Tennessee and possibly even North Carolina got into a land squabble as early as 1818 when a surveyor, according to legend, got drunk and drew the Thirty-fifth Parallel, making the state boundary too far south. Nothing was resolved then. One story in 1964 quoted the state attorney general as saying sixty square miles of land, including valuable deposits in the area of Copper Hill, rightfully belonged to Georgia. He was prepared to file suit in the U.S. Supreme Court to reclaim it, but the then governor decided litigation would be too costly and directed the attorney general to drop the matter.

Was that the land Return was pushing the legislature to retrieve?

The "return" commanding the most newspaper space and generating the most emotion was the return of the little Civil War locomotive and Kate was tired of that, even if the president of the United States, then governor of Georgia, Jimmy Carter, welcomed the General home in 1972.

She sighed and dropped the clippings to the floor and pulled up her comforter. Too bad Return didn't want something that would capture the public imagination like a little locomotive. What did he want? How many acres? Where? Most of all, why? Would the descendants of the Trail of Tears come trailing back?

Kate punched her pillow and drew up her feet, which were always cold when she slept on the sofa, and eventually slept.

Getting Sheena and Kim Sue up and dressed and on the road the next morning in the predawn darkness was not much trouble. They still harbored the delusion that they were going to Rock City.

"I remember when we had a birdhouse that said, 'See Rock City' on it," Kim Sue said dreamily.

"You do not," Sheena contradicted her.

"We never had no birdhouse in our family except some tacky old martin gourds."

"Well, I knowed somebody who had 'See Rock City' painted on the roof of their barn," Kim Sue persisted. "Was pretty, too. They got to go see it free for having it painted on their barn."

"My," said Kate absently, looking for the exit to Dade County. "That would be nice."

"How far is Rock City from where you got to go?" Sheena asked after a long silence.

"Honey, I don't know!" wailed Kate in exasperation. "I think it is a long way. Lookout Mountain is a very big mountain—about ninety miles long."

There was silence in the backseat for a mile or two and then Kate heard Kim Sue whisper, "I'm so hongry I a-perishing!"

Kate had anticipated that.

"Here," she said, throwing back two packages of Oreo cookies. "That'll do you till we get to Rising Fawn. The man I'm supposed to meet said they have good breakfasts there. How about hotcakes and sausage?"

The girls weren't thrilled, but they were quiet.

They passed through a little settlement with a funny sign Kate pointed out. "Look," she said, "'Exciting Naomi'! We are entering 'Exciting Naomi'! Look at it and tell me what you see. Is it really exciting?"

"If you ask me," Sheena said judiciously a moment later as they left Naomi, "they are trying to pull our leg."

Kate ransacked her mind for another diversion.

"When I was your age," she said, "we used to always sing on car trips. Let's sing. What do you like?"

"Miss Kate, you know you cain't sing," Kim Sue pointed out. It was so true Kate had to laugh. She loved to sing, but she knew this pair came from a long line of country music makers and had no patience with her tuneless croaking. They didn't even know the songs she liked—jolly camp tunes from her own childhood, Cole Porter and Irving Berlin songs to court by, church hymns. They probably were too young for Bing Crosby and Perry Como.

"Well, let me hear you all sing," she said. "It will cheer me up for a long working day." She was to recognize the fantasy in that later.

They were launched on something about a snow white dove when Kate hit the main street of Rising Fawn.

There was no dusty red pickup truck in sight. There were a few cars and trucks in front of Pearlie's Café, where Kate, mindful of the "perishing" girls, parked. It was early. She would take the girls in for breakfast where Turn would easily find them.

Pearlie was a plump lady wearing a blue sweat suit and eye shadow to match. She greeted Kate and the girls enthusiastically and found them a table by a window where they had a good view of the street.

"Have you seen Representative Turn Pickett this morning?" Kate asked as they were seated.

"No, I haven't," said Pearlie. "He must be a-lawing in Atlanta."

"I don't think so." Kate made her contradiction polite. "The legislature is in recess for the weekend. He said he would meet us here this morning."

A man with a group at a big table in the middle of the room spoke up.

"You must be that newspaper lady from Atlanta. Turn told me he was expecting you. The pretty little girls threw me off. Wasn't expecting them. But we're mighty glad to have them. Why don't you all come and sit with us over here? This is the community table. Turn always sits with us."

Sheena and Kim Sue were pleased to be asked and went over, flipping their stringy, sun-faded hair back with the air of models preening satin tresses.

Kate followed them.

"I'm Kate Mulcay," she said. "These are my neighbors, Sheena and Kim Sue Gandy. And you . . . ?"

"Pauling Merritt, called PawPaw," said the big man, standing and extending a surprisingly soft and well-manicured hand. "This little lady over here is Edie Putnam, and these rascals"—waving at two young men—"are Joe and Frank Priestley. Whit there"—pointing at a young man in a green jumpsuit—"used to be a forest ranger, so we call him—guess what—Smokey."

The little girls gasped.

"Did you ever see Smokey the Bear?" asked Kim Sue boldly.

The young man pushed a green hunting cap up on his head and smiled.

"Yes, ma'am," he said. "We are big buddies."

"Oooh!" breathed Kim Sue. "Could we see him?"

"Might," said the man, "but he's usually sleeping this time of year."

Everybody smiled benignly on the little girls and PawPaw pulled out chairs for them and for Kate and called to Pearlie, "More grub, hon. I bet these Atlanta folks is starving for a good breakfast."

Nice people, Kate thought happily, looking around the table. Edie appeared to be the youngest, a tanned piquant face and blond hair cropped short. The Priestleys—brothers, she supposed—had startlingly blue eyes, and such hair as she could see around the edges of the caps they didn't remove at table was fair. Their hands, which only briefly let up manipulating their forks as PawPaw made the introductions, were tanned and work-callused.

"This is a regular breakfast club?" she asked, and Edie explained.

"Most of the men around here come every morning. Some of us can only make it on Saturdays. I teach school. We're cavers and we're planning a big ridge walk today, hoping to check out a couple of unexplored caves. A lot of others will be along shortly."

"And Turn, is he a caver, too?"

"Was," said Smokey, "but he got hurt rescuing a girl who was rappelling out of control over on Pigeon Mountain and his leg hasn't healed too well."

"Limps," said Pearlie, putting plates of grits and eggs and country ham and biscuits before Kate and the girls.

"He'll be back with us sooner or later. He's especially interested in caves on the Tennessee side of the mountain," one of the Priestleys said.

"I just met him at the capitol the other day," ventured Kate, "but I didn't notice that he limps."

"Hides it pretty well," said Jim, one of the cavers, "until he gets real tired and it starts hurting bad."

Kate buttered a biscuit and let her eyes rest on Edie, wondering if she was Turn's girlfriend. Pretty, probably still in her twenties, and apparently the kind of steady sensible girl men liked.

"Are you the only female caver?" she asked.

"Gosh, no!" said Edie. "The wives of these fellows come with us when they can park their kids with grandparents, and there's always a crowd from Atlanta. We have a woman pediatrician and a woman police officer and one of our best is a beauty. Former Miss Dade County."

No end of possibilities for the handsome Turn, Kate thought, leaning over to cut Kim Sue's ham and push the fig preserves back from Sheena's plate. "When does Turn usually get here?"

"'Bout always early," said a Priestley, looking at the big watch on his wrist.

"Yeah, usually beats us all here," said Smokey. "Says he likes to get Pearlie's first making of coffee."

"Aw, you know how it is," said PawPaw. "Send a feller to Atlanta and he gits himself a set of new ways. I bet Turn is over yonder in his trailer sleeping in."

"Ringing for room service," joked Smokey.

They all laughed and PawPaw stood up and reached for the check.

"Oh, no," said Kate. "That's mine. You were good to let us join you, but I can't let you buy our breakfast."

"Company, ain't you?" said the big man. "We always try to feed up company. Next time, you or your boss down there at Atlanta newspapers can treat." He ruffled the girls' hair and they giggled.

"Let him have it," said Frank. "He's our tycoon. Or do you call that typhoon? Anyhow, he's the richest man in town."

Kate took another look at PawPaw's jeans and plaid shirt under what could have been a very expensive sport coat and his peaked cap with BUD emblazoned across the front. *They're kidding me,* she thought. *Big business doesn't dress like that.*

Edie's eyes were fixed on her with a glimmer of amusement in their amber depths. "Is," she murmured, and then added, "Would you like to look around town and view our views while you wait?"

"Yes, thank you," said Kate. "That would be wonderful."

Outside the restaurant the group stood a moment, looking at the great blue silhouette of Lookout Mountain rising above them. The valley was still swathed in mist, but the mist was, they all agreed, lifting as the eastern sky lightened and the sun stained the clouds with rose and gold, proof that it was rising over there somewhere.

Edie suggested that they go in her Blazer, a perky little half truck, half station wagon. The girls climbed in enthusiastically.

The business street was quiet. The half dozen stores had not opened, but a teenage kid was hoisting the flag in front of the brick post office and Edie stopped and lowered her window.

"Hi, Ira!" she called. "How's your granny?"

"Tolerable," said the boy. "She's coming in to open up, but she can't rest till this flag is flying. She'll put up the mail herself. Always does."

He got the flag to the top of the pole, secured the rope, and as they drove away Kate saw that he stood back and saluted it.

"He's one of my brightest students," Edie said. "Eagle Scout, too."

The girls had turned in the seat to watch him and they murmured together, "I pledge allegiance to the flag of the United States of America . . ."

Sometimes a strange and illogical affection for them welled up in her and brought a dampness to Kate's eyes. *Little brats,* she thought. *Wonderful little brats.*

The sun was now almost full out, making the mountains that encompassed the valley more blue than violet.

"We'll go by Turn's place first," Edie said. "He lives on old Scratch Ankle Road in a trailer in a very pretty spot." After a moment she added, "'Bout the prettiest spot on Scratch Ankle."

"What a fine name," mused Kate. "Indian in origin?"

"No," said Edie. "I've always heard miners gave it that name. It is a trail down to the old coal mine and it used to be all grown up with the most vicious briars you ever saw. Miners went to work and went home so mutilated by the thorns they were bloody. They named it."

The road climbed to a rocky shelf overlooking the valley and Edie slowed the car to let them see the view. Then she turned abruptly down a winding dirt road.

"Scratch Ankle?" Kate asked.

"Almost," Edie said. "Leads to it."

Pines and hemlocks and rhododendrons crowded close to the road and made a dark canopy over it. It crossed a narrow rocky trail and came out in a clearing. There, with its back to a wall of tremendous gleaming rocks, stood a neat trailer, freshly painted and with small Burford holly bushes anchoring it to the ground. An old whiskey barrel by the walk held a mass of cold-defying pansies. A red pickup truck stood in the yard.

"I guess he's here," Edie said, tapping her

horn. Nobody appeared. "Maybe he is still asleep or out walking in the woods. I'll go see."

She walked to the door and started to knock, but she found it ajar. Pushing it open and calling his name, she stepped inside. Kate heard her scream and within seconds she was back in the open door, white-faced and trembling. Kate scrambled out of the Blazer and ran to the trailer.

"Blood," stammered Edie, retching. "Blood everywhere. You look."

Kate brushed past her and into the small foyer. There was an immaculate kitchen on one side. Across from it the door opened into a small living room. Kate started in and then stopped, aghast. She closed her eyes for a second to shut out the appalling sight. A sofa covered in gray tweed was drenched with blood. There was blood on the floor and blood on a crushed lampshade on the floor and on the lamp base that stood on a table at the end of the sofa. A small Navajo rug in front of the sofa was streaked with crimson.

A pile of papers on the floor at one end of the sofa seemed to be still wet with blood. Kate took a step forward, involuntarily reaching for them. And then she backed off. As the wife of a homicide detective she should know better than that. As a reporter she had an overwhelming desire to examine them.

"The sheriff . . ." she faltered. "We should call the sheriff. The phone . . ."

"In the kitchen," said Edie. "And there's one in the bedroom, too."

Kate heard the voices of the little girls approaching the trailer.

"Oh, God," she moaned, "make them go back." Then she called to them, "Sheena, Kim Sue, get back in the car! I'll be there in a minute! Go sit in the car!"

Then to Edie, "We must not touch anything in here. Is there a neighbor anywhere close?"

"Not close," said Edie despairingly. "And if I move the car, won't that mess up any tracks in the yard?"

"You're right," said Kate. "Let's use the kitchen phone." Turning from the bloody room to stand in the doorway where the cold wind from the mountain swept in, she said, "You call. You know the sheriff."

She heard Edie dial and she watched the girls dragging their feet toward the Blazer, where they leaned against the hood looking sulky.

"Why cain't we see, too?" Kim Sue complained.

"'Cause it's prob'ly another murder," muttered Sheena.

In the kitchen Edie chokily asked for the

sheriff. Kate turned to listen, waiting because she was afraid the young schoolteacher in her shock and—was it grief?—might topple over.

"He's coming," Edie said, turning from the phone and leaning against the door facing.

*No!* Kate started to say. There might be fingerprints there. Instead she said, "Let's go wait in the car."

She put an arm around Edie and led her across the yard to the Blazer. Kim Sue and Sheena were not in it.

"Oh, my lord!" she cried. "They'll fall off the mountain! Sheena! Kim Sue! Where are you? Come back this minute!"

There was a rustle in the bushes next to the road and the girls came out, holding aloft a bitter weed.

"Look what we found by the road," Sheena said. "It's got blood on it!"

It was dried and brownish but probably blood, Kate decided, and took the uprooted weed from them.

"Where did you find this?"

"C'mon," said Sheena. "We'll show you."

"No," Kate said decisively. "We'll wait for the sheriff. You all get back in the car. We mustn't touch another thing to disturb this place!"

"Scene of the crime," said Sheena knowingly.

Kate threw her a shut-up look. Edie had her back to them, looking out the car window at the trailer. Kate knew she must be crying. In any case she didn't need to hear any comments from little girls about the hideous thing that must have happened to her neighbor, friend . . . lover?

For the first time Kate thought of the handsome young man with the white teeth and the crooked smile who had persuaded her to come to these mountains as the person whose blood washed over that room.

Had he been murdered? If not, whose blood was that? Why his absence from the trailer he called home?

The sheriff's office and jail were in a new building back of the pretty little courthouse in Rising Fawn—miles away over tortuous mountain roads—but it did not take Sheriff Jeff Atkins and his single deputy, who followed him, blue lights whirling, long to get there. They pulled up at the edge of the clearing but did not drive into the yard, careful not to obliterate any important tire marks. The sheriff was a young man, new in his job and very polite. He took off his baseball cap and bowed courteously to the women and children as he approached the Blazer.

"You called, Miss Edie?"

Edie wiped her eyes and blew her nose and nodded toward the trailer. "I think somebody has killed Turn. You look . . . blood everywhere."

"The body . . . ?" began the sheriff.

Kate shook her head. They hadn't looked. There were probably two bedrooms and a bathroom and even closets they could have searched, but they hadn't.

"We didn't go beyond the living room, Sheriff," she said. "Except Edie did use the phone in the kitchen to call you. From the amount of blood it didn't seem likely anybody could have been alive in there, but maybe we should have looked."

"You did right, lady," the young sheriff said, putting on his cap and turning to the trailer. He went in. His deputy waited at the doorsteps. When he emerged, he looked as pale and shaken as Edie and, Kate presumed, she herself had looked. She had seen murder scenes in her time, but nothing to compare with this.

Deputy Byron King, belatedly introduced by Edie, who had grown up with him, looked over Turn's red truck and then accepted the bloody weed, which Kate had left on the hood of the Blazer. He asked the little girls to show him where they found it. Sheena and Kim Sue jumped out with alacrity and led them all, Kate and Edie following, to a spot where a footpath diverged into the woods.

A few yards into the path they found the gravelly soil scuffed up and blood on the ground and on bushes along the path.

"Good God!" said Deputy King. "He must have got away and run this far!"

Edie was sobbing now. "Losing all that blood . . . his leg hurting! Oh, I can't stand it!"

The sheriff took off his cap again and waited a moment for Edie to regain control of herself. Then he asked her very gently to move her car back to the big road while he and his assistant stretched yellow tape around the house and yard.

"Now," he said, looking uncertain but, with almost a boyish resolve, putting his cap back on, "I'll call Atlanta for forensic help and see if I can get together a search party to look for Representative Pickett . . . or his body."

"The cavers, Jeff," Edie said. "A lot of them are coming to Dade County today for a big ridge walk. If we hurry, we might catch them before they start out. Some may still be at Pearlie's."

"Right," said the sheriff. "They know these mountains better than anybody else and if he is alive, they can get to him and help him. I'll call on them."

Kate couldn't imagine how much time had elapsed since they themselves had left Pearlie's. It felt like a long day already, but the sun wasn't high and her watch showed a few minutes to ten. Too early for her to find anybody in the office on Saturday, but she felt the old pressure, present in all such emergencies, to reach the city desk. She'd better try Shell at home, and somebody should call the Speaker of the House and maybe even the Governor. They had practically made fun of the young representative, but he was one of their own and they would certainly do something. Kate wasn't sure what.

Deputy King was assigned to stay at the scene, keeping a patrol car for mobility and its radio for communication. It would also serve, as he shiveringly found out, to give him shelter against the biting north wind.

Edie agreed to round up all the cavers she could find and get them to the sheriff's office. Now that she had work to do she seemed calmer, and only her little red nose and her swollen eyes showed that she had been crying.

The Gandys were mercifully quiet.

As soon as they reached the city limits, Kate began looking for a telephone. "I think I'm probably going to need a motel," she said to Edie. "Can you suggest one?"

"Oh, good!" breathed Kim Sue. "Miss Kate, git one with a swimming pool!"

"Dumb-dumb," jibed Sheena. "You feel that cold?"

"I don't know," said Edie doubtfully. "There's some kind of big festival or convention or something in Chattanooga and all the cavers are coming here. I think the people have overflowed to all the motels in the area, even as far as our town. But we'll find something."

"I'm not particular," said Kate. "Anything with a phone."

"And television," Kim Sue tried again.

Edie smiled. "I'll take you to your car and I guess we'd better go to Pearlie's. Smokey and Jim and some of the others might still be there."

There was still a gathering at the community table and Pearlie had acquired a couple of schoolgirls to help in the kitchen. Edie, followed by Kate, stood a moment at the edge of the crowd, seemingly unable to break the news.

Pearlie was the first to notice.

"What's the matter, sugarfoot? You look like somebody's stole your candy."

Suddenly Edie crumpled against Pearlie's ample bosom.

"He's dead, Pearlie! Turn is dead!"

Conversation at the big table ceased. A half dozen men got to their feet and surrounded Edie. The story came tumbling out. One by one the men picked up their jackets and headed for pickup trucks and vans parked at the door.

"Have some coffee, you all," Pearlie offered.

Edie shook her head. "I'm going with the others. Will you tell Kate where to find a phone and a motel?"

"Damn right," said Pearlie. "She can use my phone and I'll check out Mountain View and Big Rock. There might be something nicer close to Chattanooga, but the way the people have been coming in here I expect all the beds are full."

"I'll start with the phone," Kate said, "and I'll take you up on the coffee."

Shell was down at Bobby Jones Golf Course playing, his wife speculated, or maybe just hanging around.

"I had chores for him to do today," Dora Lee reported petulantly. "This is his way of getting out of them."

"This is Kate Mulcay," Kate began.

"Oh, hi, Kate, what's up? What big story you got for the big city editor this morning?"

"I think it's murder. Will you try to get hold of Shell? A legislator named Turn Pickett, and his trailer here near Rising Fawn is covered with blood. A big search party of cavers is heading out and I think I should go with them. But I'm going to need help—

another reporter and, of course, a photographer, maybe two. After all, it is a legislator."

"I'll have him paged and if that doesn't get him I'll run down there and look for him," Dora Lee said promptly, now in her role as the well-trained city editor's wife.

"I'll call back as soon as I find a place to stay," Kate said. "Meanwhile, if Shell tries to reach me, tell him to try the office of Sheriff Jeff Atkins in Rising Fawn."

Pearlie, with a portable phone tucked under her dangling blue plastic earring, had made her calls while she turned bacon and flipped hotcakes. They had yielded nothing. The only thing she could suggest was an old-fashioned tourist cabin over near the Tennessee River.

"It ain't the Henry Grady Hotel," Pearlie said, "but it's a roof and a bed."

Kate wanted to tell her that she was glad it wasn't the Henry Grady. That famous old state-owned hostelry, center of the state's political life for generations, had been demolished a decade ago to make room for a gleaming mirrored tower called the Plaza.

"Whatever you find will be all right," she assured Pearlie. "I hope it has a telephone."

"Aw, probably not in the room," said Pearlie. "It ain't that up-to-date. But Addie Armentrout runs it and I know she has a phone in the office. You can use that."

That was discouraging, but Kate thought it would have to do until she could do better. If she had known what she was running into she would have brought a portable computer, but a phone anywhere would serve. She had dictated from phones in all kinds of places, the worst probably from a roadside pay station with a broken-down door and chicken trucks thundering by in a smelly procession. It had been impossible to hear herself, much less anything the rewrite man back at the office had to say.

"Would you give me directions and ask Mrs. Armentrout to hold a cabin for me?" Kate asked. "I need to get to the sheriff's office now, but I'll get to her place later."

Kate walked into the sheriff's office to find eight or ten cavers in their boots and hard hats standing around the sheriff's desk.

"Call came for you, Kate," said Edie. "I think it was your boss. Said call him back."

For once Shell seemed excited over what her colleagues called "one of Kate's murders."

"The Speaker has appointed a special committee of House members to come up there and help with the search, if necessary," Shell said. "He's going to ask the Governor to dispatch the Georgia Bureau of Investigation and it could be he'll alert the civil defense.

Now I need a quick story for the Sunday paper. All that you know about this Pickett fellow, circumstances of the killing . . . you know."

"Until the body is found," Kate said carefully, aware that all the cavers were listening, "we can only assume that it was a killing. I know very little about Representative Pickett now, but I'll get on it and call you back. First deadline for Sunday?"

"You got it," Shell said. He was leaving for the office to mobilize the photographic staff and find a reporter to help out at that end. "Did you get a room? Got a telephone number?"

Kate turned to the caver group. "Anybody know Miss Armentrout's telephone number?"

"Oh, good Lord, is that where you're staying?" asked Edie.

Kate turned back to the phone and told Shell, "I'll get back to you with that number," and hung up.

"Honey, you'd do better if the sheriff here put you in jail," said Smokey.

"I haven't seen the place," Kate admitted. "But Miss Pearlie said it was the only thing left. I haven't any time to look. I have to call the office back with something on Mr. Pickett. What can you all tell me?"

One of them looked up the number of the tourist court, which was called "Home in the

Pines"—formerly, one young man said with a leer, the "No Tell Inn."

"I don't care about its sordid past," Kate said. "I just need a place for the night. Now about Mr. Pickett."

They were willing to cooperate, but they really didn't know much. They thought he was about thirty years old. He had come to Georgia from the Indian reservation in Oklahoma or somewhere out there. Nobody was sure where. He attended Georgia Tech and after graduation came to find a place in the mountains. He immediately claimed Rising Fawn for his home, bought a trailer from a coal mining family that was moving, and established residency.

"Work?" said Kate, scribbling in a notebook.

"He was an engineer," said Edie. "Worked some with the highway department and left there to work with the Forest Service. I think he liked that best of all."

"A good caver," put in somebody else. "Jim taught him to rappel a while back and he spent a lot of weekends doing that. Hurt himself saving a young girl who didn't know what she was doing and got out of control on Pigeon Mountain. Liked to be by himself a lot and surprised us all by getting enough votes to be elected to the legislature. He ran on the platform of getting Georgia land back from Tennessee."

The man laughed. "We're all for that."

"Family?" asked Kate.

They all looked at Edie.

"He spoke of family," she said, flushing a little. "I think he meant tribal family. He said his parents are dead. I don't know any names or addresses."

"I was gon' ask you, Edie," said the sheriff, coming to his door. "Do you know his next of kin?"

Edie shook her head miserably.

"We got to notify somebody," the sheriff said.

"Have you asked at the post office?" asked Kate. "He must have received and sent mail. And the Forest Service? Doesn't the state require a lot of vital statistics when they hire somebody?"

"Good idea, ma'am," said the sheriff. "This is my first case like this and I appreciate all the help I can get."

"Share and share alike," said Kate, smiling at him. "I've got to dictate a story pretty soon and facts like that will be important."

The cavers were still there and directionless when Jim arrived. A wave of relief seemed to pass over the group, washing over the young sheriff. He thrust out a hand, although he had probably seen and spoken to Jim already that day.

"Man, I'm glad to see you!" he said unabashedly. "I didn't know where to tell them to start. I know you know how to look for a person, dead or alive."

"We can try," said Jim gravely. "I'm sorry it's Turn."

"Well, I leave it to you all. Just be careful of anything that might be evidence. You know, tracks, people, or vehicles. We'll make the Blue Hole the . . . what's the term for it?"

"Meeting place," said Jim, grinning.

"Yeah, meeting place," said the sheriff, relieved that it was something so simple and untechnical.

The cavers filed out and climbed into two four-wheel-drive trucks at the curb. Edie collected a hard hat, a flashlight, a coil of rope, and some other gear from her car and climbed in with them. The sheriff, busy on the phone to the post office, motioned Kate and the Gandy girls into his office.

"You can have this phone in a minute, Mrs. Mulcay," the sheriff said. "As soon as I get an affirmative from the state crime lab and the GBI, I'll be out in the field with the search party. Take my chair and if you need a typewriter . . . " He waved to one on a stand by the window.

His eyes fell on Sheena and Kim Sue.

"Young ladies, you want a Coke? Here, be my guest!" He pulled some coins out of his pocket and pointed to the drink stand in the outer office.

Kate had almost forgotten the girls and now she damned their irresponsible mother for parking them on her without so much as a by-your-leave. They had relatives by the dozen. Young Mrs. Gandy didn't seem to realize that when Kate had to work, she didn't need two little girls along. But then—Kate's better nature surfaced—she hadn't known she was going to have to work and the girls, thinking of Rock City, might have overpersuaded their mother.

The sheriff hung up the phone and reached for his jacket. "They're sending a helicopter from Atlanta," he said. He patted his belt, which held a beeper in addition to such other gear as a pistol and a flashlight. "My girl is off today, but I've called her to come in special and she'll call me if need be. Name's Lorena."

He got to the door and turned back. "Mrs. Harbin at the post office said the only mail Turn ever got was from around here. If he heard from anybody out West she didn't know it. Forest Service had the shortest kind of bio. They needed rangers and he had been to Tech and was a minority besides."

"Oh, yes," said Kate. "Cherokee. That

would give him some kind of priority, I suppose. And Tech is bound to have something on his application and at least whatever they put in the yearbook."

She dialed Shell.

"Get somebody to check Georgia Tech and the Department of Transportation. He also worked for the Forest Service and they must have something in their personnel files. The clerk's office in the House of Representatives will at least have a short bio. If you can't find anybody in on Saturday, try the clerk at home. Wait, I have his number." She fumbled in her bag and brought out an address book and read the clerk's number to Shell, who wrote it down and hung up.

The sheriff got as far as the outside door, where he met a tall, doleful-looking woman with blue-black hair piled in an intricate arrangement on top of her head and deep shadows under her eyes. She was divesting herself of a handsome fur coat.

"Mrs. Mulcay, this is Lorena," the sheriff called over his shoulder. "She runs the office. Lorena, help Mrs. Mulcay any way you can. She's from the *Atlanta Searchlight.*"

Kate stood up from the sheriff's desk chair and extended a hand.

"I'm Kate. Glad to meet you."

Lorena nodded, noncommittal. She put her

coat in a cleaner's bag, which hung from a rack on the office wall.

"These your children?" she asked, looking disapprovingly at Sheena and Kim Sue, who occupied the one big rocker in the room, sucking away on Coke cans.

"Neighbors," said Kate. "Sheena and Kim Sue Gandy. We were just coming up here for a look at the mountains—nice weekend trip—when all this happened and I had to get to work."

"Was going to see Rock City," said Kim Sue dolefully.

"Well, it ain't all that great," said Lorena. "Say you can see seven states from up there, but I never have. You can put your foot, your own foot, on three states here in Dade County."

"Oooh!" gasped the girls together. "Miss Kate, can we—"

Kate shook her head. "Not now." She returned to her notes. In a few minutes she was ready to dictate a story to a hastily conscripted rewrite man.

"Here's the place for his background," she directed after she had dictated a few paragraphs. "Shell has somebody checking that. And then develop that part about his effort to get the legislature to study the Georgia-Tennessee line and act to reclaim a chunk of mountain, which he said was stolen from his Cherokee ancestors. His grandfather was the famous Cherokee war chief named Dragging Canoe."

"Are you kidding?" The rewrite man laughed. "Nobody ever had a name like that, Cherokee or not."

"Wanta bet?" said Kate. "You ever hear of Going Snake or Hanging Maw?"

"My God, it gets worse," muttered the rewrite man.

"Or better," said Kate. "Depends on how you feel about Native Americans. I like them to have colorful names. Oh, be sure to add a line that Representative Pickett's resolution was recommitted to the House State Institutions and Property Committee for further study. The chairman of that committee is Representative Tolbert Keys of Waycross. Tell Shell. Somebody ought to call him for comment."

Before the rewrite man checked his computer for spelling and released Kate, Shell came on the line.

"We've called that statesman in south Georgia. Half the committee is on the way to Rising Fawn in a state helicopter."

*Poor old Turn,* thought Kate, turning from the phone when the call was ended. *Not much attention in life. But now that they think he's dead they're going all-out.*

She collected hers and the little girls' jackets from the rack where Lorena's fur coat hung encased in plastic.

"Pretty coat," she said to make conversation with the melancholy woman who sat at a desk in the corner, her elbows on a typewriter she hadn't uncovered yet.

Kate didn't really like furs herself, but she recognized that, as furs went, this one was excellent. How did this plain gaunt woman clerk in an office in the smallest county in the state afford such opulence?

"I hate it," said Lorena surprisingly. "It's what men give you when they leave you."

"Oh," said Kate weakly. She supposed she had been left a time or two in her life before that endurer, Benjy, had stayed the course. But nobody ever gave her a fur coat. "You ought to write a song about it," she told Lorena. It might not make Broadway, but it seemed a natural for Nashville.

Back in the car she realized she had not asked directions for the motel or the cavers' meeting place, the Blue Hole. They shouldn't be hard to find.

First for the "Home in the Pines" to cinch a room for the night. The road climbed and instead of the altitude bringing them closer to the sun, the great brassy globe they had seen from the valley disappeared and rain was falling.

"Look for a lot of pine trees, girls," she said. "And a sign that says 'Home in the Pines.' That will be our home for the night."

"Will there be a swimming pool?" Kim Sue asked.

Kate threw her a derisive look and Sheena gave her the brutal truth. "Neither that or teevee, either, I bet."

"Aw, shi . . . OOT!" said Kim Sue, correcting herself.

Kate sighed. "Look," she said, "this is not going to be one of those fun days. We're going to see if we can help the sheriff and all those other people find a poor man who may be lost in the mountains, badly hurt. I'd hate to think that you were the kind of girls who worried about things for your own pleasure when you could be helping somebody else."

Even as she talked, she knew that Turn Pickett's body would be what they found and she didn't want the children to see that. She couldn't get their mother to come and take them off her hands because even if the BMW ran—and it had been practically totaled twice when their father, as the family put it, "took on a little too much"—young Mrs. Gandy was doing bedside service for her baby-having sister.

*I'll think of something,* Kate promised herself even as a battered sign with air rifle holes pockmarking it in rust appeared. The marksman must have been trying to hit the "I" in PINES, Kate thought. That would have only been sporting.

She turned in on an unpaved, pine-needle-carpeted driveway to a vibrantly blue hut with a sagging sign which said OFFICE. She knocked on the door and a strident voice called out, "Hell-o, babee!" Startled, Kate stepped back involuntarily as the girls yelled, "Here she comes, Miss Kate! Here the lady comes!"

Kate wasn't sure "lady" was the term she would have applied to the enormously fat woman in a flowered shift, a World War II Army jacket, and rubber waders used for trout fishing. But she had to appreciate her cordiality.

"Why, Kate Mulcay!" cried Addie Armentrout. "I'm as tickled as a jaybird in whistling time to meet you! I read your colyum just about every time I git my hands on the Atlanta paper. You all charging so high," she said in a confidential whisper, "I mostly have to wait for one of my guests to leave one behind."

"Ah, that's nice of you," said Kate. "I appreciate your going to that trouble. Did Pearlie at the restaurant call about my little girls and me?"

"Good God, yes!" cried the lady, just as the voice in the office shrieked "Hell-o, babee!"

again. She smiled proudly in that direction. "My mynah bird." And then she went on in her businesslike tone, "She didn't mention no young'uns. Does your'n wet the bed?"

"Not in years," said Kate, smiling.

"Well, I reckon I can let you have a roll-away—five dollars extry. How's that?"

"Maybe I should see the cabin first," said Kate doubtfully, her eyes on the row of sagging little shacks, one painted silver and the others in pastel rose, blue, and yellow, with one a deep pulsing purple.

Sheena and Kim Sue were already out of the car walking toward them. Children of the Holiday Inn age, what were they likely to say of this remnant of Model-T Fords and dirt roads? Surprisingly, they were ecstatic.

"Looka yonder, Miss Kate, they're doll-houses!" caroled Sheena.

The mynah bird shrilled "Hell-o-o, babee!" and the girls were stopped in their tracks, big-eyed and excited. They rushed back to the office and peered through the window.

"Oooh!" they squealed together. "You're the purtiest thing!"

Mrs. Armentrout looked very proud. "I got a baby bear, too," she whispered. "Don't tell nobody. Them governmints would take it—or me one. Say it's agin the law, but feller who rented from me were a hunter and he killed its ma. So tenderhearted he brought me the cub. I keep it back yonder in the woods so nobody will see it and report me. But you girls . . . if you're quiet-like and gentle, I reckon you could play with it some."

The excitement and appeal on the freckled faces was too much, Kate thought. "We gon' stay, ain't we?" asked Sheena. Mindful of the fact that there were no other accommodations within miles, Kate relented.

"Sure," she said. Whatever the condition of the cabin short of downright filth and squalor, she supposed it was theirs for one night, at least.

"The silver one, the silver one!" chanted Sheena, pulling herself away from the window and the mynah bird.

"No, purple, purple!" shouted Kim Sue.

"No, not purple," Kate said decisively. She didn't want to explain that she hated purple in all things except lilacs and violets and iris and wisteria. She just didn't feel lucky or secure enough to face sleeping enveloped in purple.

"Silver, then," said Sheena triumphantly.

"It is the closest to the office and the telephone Pearlie said you'd want to use," said Mrs. Armentrout, justifying the choice. "They're all nice," she added modestly. "I kinda like silver myself. I was thinking about maybe painting them all silver and renaming my place the Silver Comet."

"Nice," said Kate feebly, thinking the cabin she approached looked like the radiator grill on a 1938 Buick.

The interior was surprisingly fresh and clean. The one window was open to the cold outside air and the rain. Mrs. Armentrout pulled it down.

"Had a drunk last week," she explained. "Takes a time to air out the stink."

But the double bed under a chenille spread with a flamboyant peacock worked in a dozen bright colors looked clean. The little dresser was topped by a plastic scarf with ruffles on it. There was a bathroom, shower instead of tub, and except for the inevitable rust stains, it appeared to have been well scrubbed. Linoleum covered the floor and a small potbellied stove, anchored in a box of sand, occupied one wall.

"Wood outside," said Mrs. Armentrout. "I reckon you know how to build a fire if you need it."

"If you'll let us have a rollaway bed," Kate said, "we can manage fine here. Now can we see the baby bear?"

"I'm gon' take you there right soon," said the proprietor. "But first, wouldn't you like to sample one of my fried peach pies? I made 'em this morning because my grand-young'uns usually come stay with me on

Saturday. You all will like them. Boy and a girl. He's the oldest, named Kevin, fourteen years old. She's Debbie, about your age," looking at Sheena. "Prettiest yeller curly hair."

Kate could see interest in the fourteen-year-old boy sparking between age twelve and eleven. "Hurry and see the bear, girls," she said, "and ask Mrs. Armentrout to let you take the fried pies with you. I've got to hurry to the Blue Hole and see what the search party is doing."

"They could stay here with me," Mrs. Armentrout offered. "My grandkids would be tickled to death to have company and there's lots to see. We even got a little cave in the back where they can make a playhouse."

"Oh, may I see that?" asked Kate. "If I'm going to leave them with you . . . "

The cave was a shallow scoop at the base of the mountain, the kind country people in the days before electric freezers stored their winter fruits and vegetables in. It had a heavy door and a clean white sand floor with no dark corners. It seemed safe enough, but Kate hesitated. This comfortable, hospitable woman was, after all, a stranger.

"Oh, please, Miss Kate, let us stay," begged Sheena. "Please!"

"Please!" echoed Kim Sue.

The alternative, Kate thought, was taking them into the wilds of Scratch Ankle where a body might be found—no suitable Saturday outing for little girls.

"Well, I guess it will be all right," she said slowly. "And it's very nice of Mrs. Armentrout to invite you."

"You can pay me now," said Mrs. Armentrout briskly. "Advance is when it's due—twenty-five dollars for the cabin and five for the rollaway bed. I throw in the baby-sitting."

That was a false note in the great wash of hospitality, Kate thought as she handed over $30. But the woman was right. She would be baby-sitting.

"I'll get back as soon as I can. And I may bring some more people with me, photographers from the paper and maybe some legislators, if they haven't managed reservations in Chattanooga or with friends."

"Anything, anybody," said Mrs. Armentrout. "I've got four more vacancies."

Kate got directions to the Blue Hole and drove out, with the little girls waving happily and heading for the wooded area back of the cluster of cabins, where presumably the offspring of Smokey the Bear awaited them.

The Blue Hole was the prettiest little stream Kate thought she had ever seen, sapphire water which seemed to be flowing from a rock on the side of the mountain. Kate couldn't see its source—no waterfall, no cascading stream, simply bright blue water cupped in a little rocky pool and flowing jauntily into a grassy field, where the state helicopter and four legislators had already landed.

Kate walked toward them. She recognized a couple of them, one an old-timer who once had run for lieutenant governor—unsuccessfully—and a bumptious young fellow from one of the twenty counties in the metropolitan Atlanta area. They waved and seemed on the verge of greeting her gaily until they apparently remembered the gravity of their mission, the disappearance and possible death of one of their number, a young man who had now taken on the aura of sterling character and incalculable value to their state.

The two she knew greeted Kate with more cordiality than she thought their acquaintance warranted—Representative Cecil Hawkins from the tobacco belt in south Georgia and Representative Motley Banks from urban Gwinnett County. They introduced Representative Harry Hinson, who came from neighboring Walker County just across the line from Dade, and Representative Trent Goodman, who had the good fortune to be from the peach- and cotton-growing area where the celebrated U.S. Senator Walter George had lived. Georgia politicians enjoyed invoking the name of the late senator because he had made history during the Roosevelt administration by opposing the president's effort to expand the U.S. Supreme Court and then dealing a smashing defeat to the man the president chose to take Senator George's place in the Senate. Even people who liked Mr. Roosevelt rejoiced in the old senator's defiance and his triumph.

Goodman was a handsome, white-haired man with a heavy, well-fleshed body and a voice that rang out independent of microphones when he chose to speak in the House. His speech had an excessively fulsome flavor even in ordinary conversation.

Now he grabbed both of Kate's hands and looked deeply into her eyes, intoning sonorously, "Mrs. Mulcay, you know what a grievous thing this is! You understand our travail! We are here to do everything in the Georgia General Assembly's power to find that young man and to vindicate the heinous crime that has been done to him!"

Kate wanted to say *I'm not ready to quote you yet, Representative,* but the young fellow from the county next door was getting in his licks: "You better believe we gon' vindicate! Turn was fighting for our Georgia land and I, for one, am gon' see that he did not . . . "—he started to say *die in vain,* Kate thought, but he quickly changed course—"didn't fight in vain. I'm on the State Institutions and Property Committee and I glory in the responsibility we carry to be vigilant about the state's property."

He pointed toward the mountain, but Kate had a feeling that he wasn't sure of his directions. It was very confusing, this end of the ninety-mile-long Lookout Mountain and its neighbor, Sand Mountain. She was far from figuring out north and south, and as for the famed Rock City the girls yearned to see and the more famous Chickamauga battlefield, which she would like to see, she would have to get a map to find them.

The other two members of the delegation were busy hauling overnight bags and briefcases out of the helicopter and did not commit themselves.

"We couldn't make a hotel reservation," Representative Banks said. "But that's all right, we're rugged fellows, aren't we, boys? I brought along some camping equipment. A tent and a stove and some sleeping bags. You know a good camp spot?"

Kate had seen charred remnants of an old campfire across the little creek flowing from the Blue Hole. She pointed it out.

"This is supposed to be the meeting place of the cavers who are doing the searching," she said. "I'm expecting one of our photographers to meet me here. There is a kind of primitive motel about five miles from here. I got a room and the proprietor said she had four vacancies available when I left. But this may be handier for the search."

The portly Representative Goodman looked at the falling rain, laced with sleet. Clearly not an outdoorsman, he said, "Where did you say that motel is?"

"I can go home," said Representative Hinson, who was a Chickamauga real estate salesman. "I live only about twenty miles from here. I've asked them"—he nodded toward his colleagues—"but they want to stay on the ground."

Kate rested her eyes on the magical Blue Hole and the towering rocks above it. The little creek flowing from it was glazed with ice around the edges, but when they got the tent up and a fire built, it might beat the multicolored cabins by a mile. The luxury-loving girls might even be charmed by it, although Kate, an old camper herself, couldn't be sure about that.

At that moment she saw a red-clad figure swinging by a rope halfway down the mountainside. She went closer and the figure landed.

It was Edie.

A sharp intake of breath, and Kate went closer. "You could have fallen!"

"Sure," said the schoolteacher, grinning. "You can do that, all right. But I had good instruction. Jim. And I've done it lots of times. I came down to start some hot coffee and food arrangements for the rest of them. They still haven't found any trace of Turn."

She divested herself of rappelling gear. "Where are the girls?"

"Oh, I abandoned those brats," said Kate flippantly. And then seriously, "I left them with that nice Mrs. Armentrout. She was gon' give them fried pies and let them play with her bear cub and grandson and -daughter."

Edie dropped a rope and took a deep breath.

"Kate," she said urgently, "Addie Armentrout does not have any grandchildren. And that bear cub she had grew up and returned to the wild ten or fifteen years ago! Kate, we'd better—"

But Kate was running for her car.

As KATE REACHED HER CAR, Representative Hinson saw her from across the creek and came running, teetering precariously on the footlog that crossed the creek. "What's the trouble? Can I help?"

"No . . . yes! I don't know," cried Kate. "Two little girls I brought with me. . . I left them with a woman. . . . She may be crazy. I've got to go!"

"I'll go with you," Hinson cried, jumping in the passenger seat.

Edie was wresting open the back door even as the car moved toward the highway.

"Where is this place?" asked Hinson.

"Oh, I hope I can remember. . . . " muttered Kate through clenched teeth.

"I know," said Edie. "Scratch Ankle Road. I don't know why Pearlie sent you there. The woman is crazy."

"The place was clean," babbled Kate, "and fried pies . . . "

"Yes," said Edie. "It may be all right. She hasn't hurt anybody that I ever heard of and the motel brings her a living. But she is crazy. It's best that we go and see."

Kate was holding back tears. A sob caught in her throat and she said chokily, "I shouldn't . . . I shouldn't have left them."

"It's probably all right," said Edie. "She's a strange old thing, but I don't know that there's any harm in her. That about the grandchildren and the cub . . . that worries me a little. And her family has always lived on Scratch Ankle Road."

"What does that mean?" asked Hinson.

"Coal miners," said Edie. "Going back to the days when the owners leased convict labor and made them work in chains and shackles. You can see signs on the rocks where they dragged their chains."

"Oh, dear God!" cried Kate. "Generations of anger and hostility and grudges."

"Maybe not," said Edie. "I'm not sure that her granddaddy was one of those they starved and beat."

"Oh, dear God!" cried Kate again, and tromped down on the accelerator.

The little tourist court seemed peaceful—too peaceful. The door to the office was locked and so were the multicolored cabins. Kate ran from one to the other, trying the doors. Edie, standing on tiptoe to peer in the office window, saw no movement and heard no sound but the mynah bird's jubilant "Hell-o, babee!" when it realized it had an audience.

Kate ran toward the woods, calling the girls' names.

Edie and Hinson searched the driveway for footprints, but the rain had begun to fall harder and there was scant chance of any recognizable tracks in the gravelly soil.

Kate turned to Edie and Hinson, rigid with fear. "The sheriff . . . " she said, "I want to call the sheriff."

"Yes," said Edie, "the sheriff." And she picked up a rock and sent it through a pane of glass in the office door.

"Good shot," approbated Kate, poking her hand though the jagged glass and fumbling for the door lock.

"I don't know. Should you have done that?" protested Representative Hinson weakly.

"Damned right she should have," said Kate, searching for the door lock. Her hand refused to find it, but by stretching she could barely reach an old-fashioned black telephone.

She pulled it through the broken window and dialed 911. An answer was a long time coming. Perhaps everybody was out on the mountain search for Return Pickett. After a long spate of futile ringing, Lorena answered in a dull and listless voice. She said she would try to get the sheriff on the radio or on his beeper.

"Please hurry," begged Kate. "There's no sign of my girls or of that Mrs. Armentrout and I'm worried."

"Addie Armentrout?" asked Lorena. "Good God a'mighty! I'll git somebody there right away—or come myself."

Lorena's reaction was alarming. What did she know about Addie Armentrout? As for coming herself, Kate had little hope that Lorena in her consolation fur coat would be of much help, but she welcomed anybody. The way the wind had risen and the rain was whipping across the valley, she almost wished for the fur coat herself.

The three of them huddled under the only big pine tree in the yard. It was meager protection, but they couldn't bring themselves to leave the front of the office for the shelter of the car. Maybe the phone would ring or maybe Addie and the girls would emerge from the Scratch Ankle undergrowth.

The sheriff arrived faster than Kate had hoped.

"I was at Turn's trailer with the guys from the state crime lab," he explained. "What's this about Addie Armentrout killing some young'uns?"

Kate turned pale and grabbed hold of Edie and Hinson to keep from falling. "Killed?" she stammered.

The young sheriff's face went blank. "I thought Lorena said . . . Well, what is the problem?"

"Sheriff, the woman and the little girls have simply disappeared," put in Representative Hinson. "Kate is worried because apparently the woman told her some tall tales and she is afraid that the woman might be . . . well, deranged."

"Well, yeah, she *is* that," said the sheriff. "Nuts. Whole family was. But I don't know if she would harm anybody."

"Kidnap," said Kate weakly. "Would she try to kidnap them?"

Edie closed her eyes and opened them in shock and disbelief, as if, Kate thought, she believed it had happened.

"You think she would?" Kate said.

"No, no, I don't know," said Edie. "But you know women who are crazy about kids and never had any . . . I just thought the way Addie was making up those fictitious grandchildren."

The sheriff interrupted the grim imagining. "Let me call for some help and start looking," he said. "Edie, Harry, you want to stay or come with me?"

"Okay to leave you?" Edie asked, and Kate nodded. Whatever they could do to find the children was what was important. She dared not leave.

Representative Hinson said he would hitch a ride with the sheriff back to the Blue Hole and enlist the help of the other legislators. They were probably only waiting there for some direction from the cavers, and the sheriff might put them to work.

The three of them got in the sheriff's car, but then Edie jumped out and ran toward Kate, pulling off her down vest.

"Here, I've got another jacket in my car. This will keep you a little warmer."

Kate slipped the vest on under her own jacket, grateful for its warmth, and sat down on the single step to the little office. Oh, those children would be cold, wherever they were. She remembered reading that Anne Lindbergh, distraught over the disappearance of her little baby, worried a lot that he had been taken with nothing on but his sleepers and he might be cold. It was a small consideration. If only they were safe, she wouldn't worry that they might be a little sick. You could treat colds and croup, but suppose they never came back . . . suppose they were dead?

She thought she ought to call their mother, but perhaps it was pointless to get her upset and frightened so soon. She looked at her watch. It had been only a couple of hours since the girls had waved her a cheery goodbye and gone toward the woods to see the baby bear.

That bear . . . She stood up. Edie said it had been years since Addie's bear was a cub. It had grown up and now eluded hunters in the dense woods along the mountaintop. But suppose the girls went looking and got lost back there? Suppose there really was a cub and its mother attacked them?

She took the path around the cluster of cabins to the woods beyond. She passed the cave and noticed that its big timbered door was closed. She went on by means of awkward handholds and slipping feet, clutching at big rocks and using her knees when her feet skidded out from under her. Vicious briars tore at her clothes and the rain made the great sandstone rocks slippery. Her hands and her knees, striving for purchase, were skinned and bloody.

A slender cedar tree grew out of a cleft in the rock and Kate grabbed for its trunk to hoist herself up.

It was then she heard voices—young girl voices!

"Sheena! Kim Sue!" she shouted. "Where are you?"

There was no answer, and then there was a faint "Here, Miss Kate, in a hole in the ground!"

"Oh, thank God!" Kate breathed. "Are you all right? Can you get out?"

"We all right," faltered Kim Sue, "but we cain't find no way out of this hole. Rocks keep a-falling and penning us up."

Their voices seemed to come from a big rock right in front of Kate. There was, in truth, no opening.

"Be still. Be very still," said Kate. "If you wiggle around, you might dislodge a big rock, and that would make it harder for us to get you out." But displaying more optimism than she felt, she added, "We're going to get you out—and soon!"

"There was this rock we stepped on," said Sheena. "We was just climbing looking for a way out—and it fell!" Her voice broke and Kate thought, *Not Sheena crying; she never cries! Poor babies, poor scared meddlesome young'uns!*

"You stay put," she said, "and I'll run and find somebody who knows about caves and can get you out without any trouble."

"Miss Kate, don't leave us," pleaded Kim Sue, and Kate thought she might cry. "Oh, honey, I'll be right back with someone who can get you out," she said. "Don't worry."

She didn't notice the brambles or the rocks on the way down. She simply sat down and slid halfway, and when sliding was impossible she found a tree branch and swung over a big crevass she hadn't noticed on the way up.

There was a car in the yard when Kate got there. In it were Lorena and the big man called PawPaw, and emerging from the motel office was . . . Addie Armentrout!

The sheriff arrived as Kate, ready to throttle her, reached Addie's side.

"Do you know what you did to my little girls?" she shouted. "They're trapped in a cave!"

"What's that?" said the sheriff. "You've found the children?"

Kate pointed wordlessly to the cave. The sheriff strode to the barred door in the side of the hill, with Kate at his heels and PawPaw close behind them. Lorena stayed behind with Addie, who was humming as she unwrapped birdseed for her mynah bird.

With the bar lifted and the big door open, the cave was fairly light, and the sheriff, training his flashlight upward, saw that two rocks had been dislodged—the first one apparently by the girls themselves, who moved it to investigate the possibility of an exit. It had fallen back in place, jarring loose a second one, which effectively trapped them.

The sheriff turned helplessly to PawPaw. "I'm no caver, but I'm willing to go up there and try to pull those rocks out."

"I know how to do it," said PawPaw, but, looking down at his substantial girth, he added, "I don't believe I can fit in that shaft."

"I can," said Kate. "I'll go up there. Just tell me what to do."

The men were peering at the jagged chunk of sandstone that the girls had dislodged.

"The danger," said PawPaw, "is that you might set off an avalanche when you start pulling at that first rock. We don't know if it's loose. Let me go find Jim and Smokey."

"Hey, girls," called Kate, "can you hear us? We'll be getting you out soon."

"Yes'm," said one of them meekly.

*Oh, Lord,* thought Kate, *now they are getting meek. They must really be scared.* And the early winter twilight was falling. *Suppose we can't get them out before dark?*

"Sheriff," she said in a panic, "it's getting dark!"

"Don't worry, honey," he said, unexpectedly putting his arm around her shoulders. "We got floodlights on the way. Also, Jim and Smokey have been notified and they'll be here any minute. They are our best cavers, always know what to do in a tight situation."

Kate took up a post inside the shallow cave

where the children thought they were going to have a playhouse. Seated on the ground, she looked upward at the impenetrable ceiling and talked to them. The answers were mumbled and barely distinct, but she talked anyway, wanting to ask questions but making herself shout reassurances instead.

The rescue truck from the fire department whirled up and presently the hillside was illuminated like a stage. Somebody built a fire between the office and the mouth of the cave, and Mrs. Armentrout, followed by Lorena, moved close to warm herself.

"What are these people doing in my yard?" she demanded. "Might be ruining my business."

Kate dared not speak to her, but the sheriff did. "Lorena says she found you shopping at Wal-Mart when she went out on her break. Why did you shut those little girls up in the cave?"

"Would you take young'uns to the Wal-Mart?" she countered irritably. "Biggest pest in the world, young'uns, when you want to do your trading. I had to git a cuttlebone for my mynah bird, so I told them to play nice till I got back."

"But you shut that door and put the bar on it," pointed out the sheriff. "They couldn't get out that way and so they tried to climb to the top. That's where they are now and they are trapped, Addie. You know, you have committed a crime."

"I declare," murmured Addie with mild interest, turning her backside to the fire and hoisting her flowered skirt.

Kate wanted to say, *You old monster. You lied to them and you have terrified them and endangered their lives.* But she felt so much blame on herself for leaving them with a stranger and she thought it might be an exaggeration to say the Gandys were terrified. Inconvenienced, yes. Endangered and disappointed, of course. With dark settling on the mountain they would be cold and scared, but not terrified. The sturdy, self-possessed young Gandys didn't terrify easily.

All thought of the missing Return Pickett had slipped from Kate's mind. She wondered impatiently where those premier cavers, Jim and Smokey, were.

Suddenly they were there in their hard hats and boots, exuding confidence. They nodded to her and went directly to the sheriff.

"No trace of Turn," said Smokey.

"What do we have here?" asked Jim.

"It's Addie's cave," explained the sheriff. "She locked the two little girls in it and went to town. They must have seen a rock in the ceiling that they thought they could move.

It's one of those chimney-shaped caves, you know. They pushed the rock aside and started climbing and I reckon it fell back in place, shutting them off from the bottom and then another one fell. Sounds like they are near the top but there's a big rock there and we are fearful of trying to move it. What do you think?"

The two men climbed the mountainside the way Kate had but were more surefooted and nimble. At the top Kate heard them talking to the girls. Were they getting plenty of air? Could they see light? Air blew in from somewhere but it was very dark.

"I think we'll move this one, fellers," Jim called down the hill. "Need muscle, you all. Come on up but take it easy and slow."

The sheriff and PawPaw and two men from the fire truck obeyed. Jim deployed them around the great sandstone "floater," a boulder which was not anchored in the earth. "Grab the come-along. It's in the Jeep," he directed Kate.

In her haste to do something constructive Kate stumbled, scrambled to her feet and stumbled again. Smokey met her halfway down the slope and took the tool from her hands.

Jim was busy tying a rope around the boulder. If it fell, she thought anxiously, it might jar loose more rocks inside the cave. It might even crush the girls who waited on the other side.

*Oh, God, let it work,* she prayed soundlessly. *Let them out.*

The idea, Jim told his helpers, was not to try to lift the rock, but to ease it off to one side, shifting it away from the opening to the cave. He and Smokey manned the ropes. The others laid hands on the boulder and waited for the signal.

"All together, now," said Jim. "Push! Push!"

"Heave ho!" shouted Addie from her place by the fire.

"Shut up," muttered Kate between clenched teeth.

The giant "floater," which had not floated in a couple of thousand years, did not float now, but there was a barely perceptible movement.

"Again," said Smokey, pumping the come-along. "All together . . . *push*!"

An inch or two at a time, agonizingly, slowly, they edged the monster from its resting place. Once in a while they caught their breath. Jim used the pick to clear a path for the big rock, pulling away smaller rocks and bushes.

"Now again!" he cried, and they pushed.

Suddenly there was sound from the shaft.

"We see light!" yelled Sheena.

"Kin we git out now?" importuned Kim Sue.

"Not yet," said Jim. "Not quite yet. Be very

still and we'll have you on the ground in no time." He eased his hand into the little aperture that moving the rock had opened up, to make sure there were no other rocks that might turn loose from the cave wall and further trap the girls.

At that moment a wrecker with its roof light blazing pulled up in the yard. The sheriff's call for help had been heard. The driver got out and strode to the foot of the mountain.

"I got a cable and a hoist, Jim. Want 'em?"

"Can you reach this far?" asked Jim. "Give it a try, Bud. Be easy backing up."

Bud nodded and returned to the wrecker, backing it slowly over the rough grass and bushes and rocks that edged the little path to the cave. Suddenly there was a roar on the road and a big yellow piece of earth-moving machinery appeared.

The young volunteer firemen, blowing on their cold, skinned hands, smiled broadly.

"Hot damn!" said one. "A bulldozer!"

Edie, wearing a jumpsuit and a fleece-lined denim jacket, jumped out of the bulldozer cab and ran across the yard. "More coming," she said. "Trucks with chains and shovels. Lot of manpower from Pearlie's. Ambulance, just in case."

Kate watched the procession of vehicles on the little dirt road and choked back tears.

"Bless them! Bless them!" she murmured. "So many of them coming to help!"

"The legislators aren't coming," Edie told them. "They still haven't found Turn, and that big talky man who was with them—Representative Banks, I think—is also missing. He was with them when they started checking Running Water Creek and then he wasn't."

"How long ago?" asked Kate.

"About noon, I think. Just after we came over here."

Suddenly the big boulder, like a sleeping animal, seemed to breathe . . . and stir.

"Rock! Look out below!" shouted Jim. He and Smokey tried to hold back on the ropes, but the ropes snapped and the big boulder began to move. "Get outa the way, Bud!" Jim hollered at the wrecker driver. "Run, evvabody!"

Everybody did run, and the wrecker, which fortunately still had its motor going, skidded across the yard just in time. Kate couldn't be sure what had happened. She was scrambling up the hillside toward the top of the cave just out of the path of the sliding rock. Jim was ahead of her. He lifted Kim Sue out first and handed her to Kate and then he got Sheena.

"You're good girls," he said huskily. "Brave girls."

Squatting precariously on the steep slope, Kate tried to hug them both at once and fight the tears that seemed to keep blurring her vision.

The boulder, sliding ominously out of control, had stopped short of the bonfire, and there was a compulsion among them all to touch it as if they were patting a wild animal that was suddenly domesticated. Even Addie patted it and smiled a merry, crinkly smile at the group.

"How 'bout some of my fried pies, you all?" she asked.

Kate, examining scratches and scrapes on the girls' legs and a cut on Kim Sue's cheek, said, "I'm gon' get you all bathed and in bed." Then she stopped.

What bed? She certainly didn't intend to let them spend the night in that silver cabin within range of crazy Addie.

"I'm gon' take Addie into protective custody, if it's any help," said the sheriff. "Lorena's neighbor is my matron and she has a secure place for women prisoners in her house."

"Good," said Addie. "I'll feed my bird and be ready. Lucy's house is just one block from Wal-Mart. I'll take my list."

"I'm gon' take Kate and these girls into protective custody, too," said Edie. "Mama and I have plenty of room and plenty of hot water and maybe some hot soup."

Kate smiled at her gratefully. She looked around at all the people who had come out in the cold rainy twilight to help rescue the two girls—Jim and Smokey, the firemen, the wrecker driver, the bulldozer operator, the sheriff, PawPaw, and the whole colorful procession of townspeople in trucks and cars on the road.

"I wish I could do something to say thank you to you all," she said. "If you go to Pearlie's, I'll treat you to a hot supper."

PawPaw lifted an eyebrow and Lorena said, "I bet a cold drink would suit better."

Kate gulped. "Yes! But where? Is there a pub or a bar or something in town?"

"How about a couple of six-packs at the fire station?" one of the firemen said. "We'll send the bill to you."

"I wish I could go with you," said Kate, "but . . . " She looked at the girls, who were leaning against her sleepily, and it moved her that Kim Sue, although a big girl, was clinging tight to her skirt. "I'm a little tied down now," she said.

They did stop by the jail to see if there was any word from the search party looking for Return. There was none. But the photographer Shell had sent was there, and Kate's heart sank when she saw him tilted back in the sheriff's chair with the sheriff's phone tucked between his shoulder and his ear and his feet on the sheriff's desk. She liked photographers almost better than anybody she had to work with, having had decades of happy association with them. But this one, an import from some Ivy League school in the East, thought himself far too good for the job and the region, a totally arrogant and pompous fraud. His pictures were far from exceptional; his attitude was infuriating. He never said he came from New York but always from Westchester County, which, Kate assumed, was a far more elegant reach of the city. He didn't plan to stay long—only till his "old man" returned from business commitments around the world and fixed him up with network television.

Meanwhile, his L. L. Bean all-weather boots remained on the sheriff's desk and his hand-knit virgin wool cap remained on his silken blond head. He waved at Kate and the sheriff imperiously and brought his conversation to a leisurely end. Then he got to his feet.

"Glad you could make it, Kate," he said, as if she were the tardy arrival. "Couldn't find you at that Blue Hole the assignment mentioned, so I went out on my own. Shot some of the scenery.

"The mountains up here aren't bad, are they? I got a few shots of the legislators and cavers along that bleak briar patch they call Scratch Ankle. That about wind it up? Not much happening, is there? I'd like to shove off."

"Not much happening!" Kate wanted to hit him. "Just murder and lost people and blood and . . . and . . . " She grasped the corner of the desk to try to pull herself together and tell him about Representative Pickett's bloody trailer.

Finally she said in disgust, "Go back and shoot that trailer." And then, realizing there had been no introductions, she said, "Sheriff Atkins, this is Chris Mallory of our staff. Are the tapes still up at the scene or can Chris take a picture in the trailer?"

The sheriff, who had better manners than the elegant import from the East, shook hands and said, "The tapes are still up, Kate, but I could let him shoot from the door as long as he doesn't touch anything. I think the crew from the crime lab finished, but I don't want to risk disturbing anything."

"You heard that, Chris," Kate said severely. "You will photograph, not touch."

"Gotcha," said the boy with a smile so charming it was hard to believe it was on the face of an incompetent jerk. "Sheriff, how about being a good scout and taking me to the scene?" he asked patronizingly.

Kate grimaced in embarrassment, but the sheriff smiled.

"I'll ask my deputy, Mr. King, to accompany you," he said with unaccustomed formality.

"I think you'd better plan to stay tonight," Kate said. "If they find Representative Pickett or his body, the other newspapers and television will be jumping on the story. We should have a photographer here."

"Okay, so while I'm gone get me a room, will you?"

Kate's smile was warm. "I'll be glad to. There's a charming motel called 'Home in the Pines' down there on Scratch Ankle Road. I already have a room paid for there, a pretty silver one, but I have other plans. You may have it."

Edie was smiling, too, visualizing this foppish fellow in the unheated silver shack on this cold night trying to cope with the woodstove. "I'll get you a key," she said.

As they were leaving, Kate asked curiously, "Chris, how did you happen to get this assignment?"

"Small Sunday staff and everybody out but me. Besides, this is probably page one and they kind of like to have me on the good stuff."

"In a pig's eye," Kate muttered to herself.

She collected the little girls, who were lumped together and dozing on the sheriff's sofa, and propelled them toward her car. Edie had pointed out the house she shared with her mother two blocks away. Its lighted windows looked warm and welcoming.

Kate did like photographers; she apologized to herself for her scornful attitude toward this one. Some of them were very brave, risking their lives at fires and shootouts and tornadoes and hurricanes and wrecks. They worked hard, not complaining about long hours and bad weather, and were usually fun, good company. Why did she have to have a gruesome one on this gruesome assignment?

Edie's house, an old-fashioned, vaguely Victorian white frame, was really her mother's and it almost made up for the rigors of the day. Mrs. Putnam, herself a retired teacher, received them with old-fashioned courtesy, offering her hand to Kate and to each of the girls—a grown-up attention they enjoyed in spite of being exhausted, hungry, and pinched with cold.

"I'm gon' show you your beds and the bathroom and give you a chance to freshen up," she said, using Kate's favorite genteelism for going to the bathroom. "Then I want you to come straight to the kitchen and have some of my soup." She leaned toward the girls and in a conspiratorial whisper said, "I made brownies this afternoon."

Kim Sue promptly burst into tears and clutched at Kate. In a second Sheena, although avowedly too big to cry, swallowed hard and tears came in her eyes.

"Oh, Mrs. Putnam," Kate began an awkward apology, but Edie interrupted. "I'll explain to Mother, Kate. The girls have gone through a thoroughly traumatic experience and it all began when that crazy Addie Armentrout told them she had some fried pies. They'll probably never want another goodie as long as they live."

"Yes, they will," said Kate, using her shirttail to wipe their faces and smiling at them. "That turned out bad, but they know they're safe now. They're just real tired. I can't wait to try some of Mrs. Putnam's soup."

The girls followed Kate into the bedroom, crowding close to her, but Kim Sue turned at the door and ventured a forgiving smile in Mrs. Putnam's direction.

The rooms in this house were big and the guest room assigned to Kate and the girls had wide matching spool beds, three-quarter in size, if not double. They were covered with crocheted counterpanes over flowered chintz dust ruffles, which matched draperies over white nylon curtains at the windows. There was a dressing table with a flouncy flowered skirt and a mirror encircled in dried corsages, spoils of Edie's teenage years, Kate thought.

Edie saw and interpreted Kate's look at the corsages and shook her head.

"My niece. I never got enough flowers to frame a compact mirror. Ugly duckling."

"Well, you're not that now," said Kate, steering the girls toward the connecting bathroom and a vast legged tub which somebody was filling with hot water foaming with bubble bath.

"That's how Turn felt," said Edie softly.

Kate busied herself pulling T-shirts over the girls' heads.

"I should have guessed," she said. "You were in love."

"The term, Kate, is lovers."

"Did anybody know?"

"In these small towns? Rising Fawn and Pudding Hill?"

"And Scratch Ankle and New Salem and Hog Jowl Road?" threw in Kate, grinning. "You mean privacy was nonexistent. Except from your mother, I suppose. She doesn't know."

"Unwritten code," said Edie. "Nobody tells anybody's mother. They find out sometimes—by osmosis, I reckon. Mother liked Turn and would have been proud to have Cherokee grandchildren, but we hadn't come to that point yet. He had this obsession about his ancestors and that land and I'm not even sure he would want to marry anybody but some dusky Minnehaha."

"I can't believe that," Kate said. "I don't suppose I dare say he's so thoroughly American. That's considered chauvinistic now and of course everybody makes a point of the fact that his ancestors got here first. But I did have a couple of beers with him after the legislature one afternoon and I didn't feel any prejudice against . . . the rest of us."

They both smiled wryly at Kate's inability to simply say "white people." But Edie's freckled face was shadowed with unhappiness. She turned to her room across the wide hall and returned with nightdresses for Kate and the girls, the little ones her own, the bigger one her mother's.

When the girls were clean and dry and enveloped in the only-slightly-too-big gowns, they filed into the big bright kitchen where an enormous oil burner sent out heat and an iron Dutch oven on the stove sent out the fragrance of beef and vegetable soup. Places were set at a round oak table in the middle of the room.

"Sit down, sit down," urged Mrs. Putnam. "The corn bread is ready to come out of the oven. You girls want milk? Kate—may I call you Kate? I read your column!—you may have coffee, tea, buttermilk, or some of my muscadine wine with your dinner. It's nice and dry."

Sleet lashed against the big kitchen windows and Kate could hear a chill north wind slicing at the roof.

"Wine," she said promptly.

The soup was good, the kind only a meaty knuckle bone simmered for days and home-grown vegetables could make, and the brownies were well filled with pecans, which the girls couldn't pass up.

The girls went off to bed content and were sound asleep within moments. Kate, wrapped in one of Mrs. Putnam's robes over the borrowed nightgown, went to sit in the living room with the other two women, thinking there might be something on the news about Pickett and probably a mention that Representative Banks was missing, if that was still true. The sheriff had an idea that he had wandered away from the search party and was only temporarily lost. Listening to the wind and the crackle of the sleet, Kate hoped he had been found or had found shelter in one of the many caves.

"Could the cavers possibly be out there still looking in this weather?" she asked.

"If there's a chance of finding either of them dead or alive, they're out there," said Edie. "I saw Jim rescue a girl when the temperature was seven degrees. Rescue work is one of the important things about being a caver."

The recital of humdrum television news by a handsome young man with an unctuous chocolate-flavored delivery was suddenly interrupted for a bulletin. Two legislators were missing in the Scratch Ankle area tonight, one of them believed to be dead, since there were bloodstains and evidence of a struggle in his trailer home. The other disappeared while a member of the search party.

It went on from there.

"Chris better get his pictures to the office right away," said Kate, standing up. "I need to find him and tell him the competition has come to life."

"You can't get him on Addie's phone, you know," said Edie. "She's a sort of prisoner at Lucy's. Her office is locked up tight except for that window I broke. He wouldn't hear or answer the phone anyway, would he?"

"Probably not," said Kate. "I'll have to go find him. He can transmit from Chattanooga, I suppose."

"Let me go," said Edie. "You better stay with the girls. They'll be frightened if they wake up and you aren't here."

Kate paused.

"I know, but I don't want you prowling around out there in that weather looking for our photographer. It's my job. The girls know you and I think they'll feel safe with you and your mother. Besides, they're so tired I don't believe they'll wake up."

"Child, you can't go," Mrs. Putnam spoke up unexpectedly from her recliner close to the television set. "I put yours and the children's clothes in the washing machine."

"Well, thank you," said Kate, "but . . . "

The three of them gave way to helpless laughter.

"There must be something I can wear," Kate said, looking distractedly around the room.

"Don't look at our green velvet drapes, Scarlett," said Edie.

They laughed again and Mrs. Putnam got to her feet. "I have a hunting suit that belonged to my husband. I bet it will fit you."

And it did, loosely enough to be comfortable over the long underwear, which was Mrs. Putnam's.

"Now my jacket," said Kate.

"Oh, it's washable, too," said Mrs. Putnam. "I read the label. You know how muddy it was."

Kate wanted to shake her for a meddlesome

old lady, but she looked at the distress on the soft pink face and she hugged her instead.

"I'll be fine without it. My car has a heater, and besides, this is a pretty warm outfit."

"Not warm enough," said Mrs. Putnam. "Wait a minute. I have something that will be plenty big."

She returned with a fur coat.

"Oh, no!" gasped Kate. "I can't take your nice coat."

"You certainly can," said Mrs. Putnam. "I don't wear it much anymore since Edie came home with one of those signs about killing helpless animals. Here."

She draped it over Kate's shoulders and Kate reluctantly shoved her arms into the satin-lined, lavender-smelling sleeves.

The sleet on the roof was making staccato Krupa-on-drums sounds as Kate reached the porch.

"Here's Papa's cap," said Edie, running out with a khaki hunting cap. "It has earflaps. Warmer than a head scarf and will turn the rain."

Gratefully Kate pushed her hair up under the cap, saluted, and ran for her car. In spite of the sleet beating against the windshield, she had no trouble finding Scratch Ankle Road and the sad little tourist court, although there were no streetlights and certainly no lighted sign to advertise its presence. But to her surprise, when she drove in the yard one of the cabins had a light in the window and smoke pluming out of its small chimney. It was not the silver one she had rented but one farther down the line—the purple one, for goodness' sake!

Kate smiled to herself, thinking how hath the mighty Westchester County boy fallen. She touched the horn and opened the door, preparing to slide out into the sleety night.

The cabin door opened and a man's voice—but not Chris's—called out gruffly, "You sure took your time!"

"What?" said Kate, fighting a creepy feeling that the cabins were haunted.

"Git on in here," said the voice, "and git off that coat."

"Not on your life!" yelled Kate. "Not on a night like this!"

She slammed the car door, started the engine, and skidded out of the driveway. A mile down the road she slowed down and watched the rearview mirror. No following lights. There had been something familiar about that voice and she felt that the meeting in the purple cabin was to have been more than a lovers' tryst. On impulse she turned into a rocky weed-grown clearing off the road and doused her lights. She didn't know what kind of car she was expecting, because Addie or some other owner when it was the No Tell Inn had obligingly arranged hidden parking spaces back of the cabins to protect the customers from the eyes of the curious, especially curious spouses. She had not seen a car.

If she had had time, she would have backed the car into the briar patch instead of nosing it in, so she would have been in position to follow speedily when the car appeared. But she never had been good at backing up and that rocky spot was less road than ledge, with a steep fall on either side. Better to wait as she was, damning her capricious heater for quitting so promptly when the engine was off, and drawing the collar of Mrs. Putnam's coat closer around her neck.

After twenty minutes no car had appeared and Kate started trying to remember the way the old road wound down the mountain. Was there an exit at the other end? She seemed to recall a narrow dirt road past a collection of little houses which had been occupied by miners up until the mines went out of business in the 1920s or '30s. They were sad little houses but probably no sadder now than in the days when the mines operated and living was hard and dirty.

The man in the purple cabin had either gone back to bed or taken the road to the shoddy little mining shacks or beyond. Kate started the car, wondering why she had waited anyhow. The tailing technique might be good for catching murderers, but she suspected all she would be catching would be some married man who picked the worst night of the year for his philandering.

Meanwhile, where was Chris, that photographer?

She had not checked the silver cabin, but it was obviously untenanted—closed up, unlighted, unheated.

She drove to the sheriff's office. It was brightly lighted. She could see through the window a number of people standing around. In a town which numbered among its charms the fact that motorists could always find a parking space, she couldn't find one near the jail. She drove around the block and came up on a side street, relieved to make out—in spite of the darkness and the sleet, which seemed to be turning to snow—a white car with her newspaper's logo on the door.

*Praise be,* she thought, *home and mother! Somebody will be here—Chris, if all else fails—but possibly another reporter and a* good *photographer.* She reached the corner of the building and was about to turn toward the main street when something grazed the collar of Mrs. Putnam's coat—something hard, moving fast and so hot it scorched the fur.

It struck the building beyond her and Kate started running. She had been shot at!

As she mounted the steps, she heard a car roar off.

The door to the sheriff's office was standing open and she barely made it in, collapsing on the old sofa in speechless shock.

Sheriff Atkins was standing back of his desk with a coffee cup in his hand. He took one look at Kate and strode over to her.

"You're white as a sheet—" he began.

Kate nodded. "Been shot at. Somebody just shot at me," she quavered.

"Where? How long ago?"

"A minute ago. Right outside."

"Come on," the sheriff said to the others, grabbing his jacket and running for the door.

"Too late," said Kate. "He's gone. The car raced off before I even got to the steps outside. You'd never catch it."

The sheriff turned back. "Anybody hear whose car that was?"

"I did," said Lorena morosely, leaning into her covered typewriter. "But I don't know whose car it was. Not for sure."

KATE STARTED OUT THE DOOR with the sheriff and his deputy, followed by a gallery of cavers and Chris, the photographer. Too late to find the gunman, they were hoping to find the bullet and perchance where it hit the courthouse wall. Kate wanted to see, too, but the smell of scorched hair around her neck stopped her. She had indeed been shot at, crazy as it seemed. She had been shot at and the bullet had come close!

She took off Mrs. Putnam's coat and draped it over the sheriff's desk. Lorena was enabled by a sudden surge of energy to get to her feet and come and look over Kate's shoulder.

"You wasn't kidding," she muttered. "Come close."

"And whoever shot at me," Kate said, managing a grin, "wasn't kidding, either. But why? Why?"

"Maybe you hurt somebody's feelings," Lorena suggested idly, returning to her chair back of the typewriter."

Kate stared at her. "Is that the Rising Fawn way, to shoot anybody who hurts your feelings?"

Lorena shrugged and resumed her seat.

The sheriff came in with an envelope in his hand. "Thirty-eight pistol," he said. "We got the bullet."

"The kind everybody in Dade County has," said one of the cavers.

"I think it had a silencer," said Kate. "At least I didn't hear it."

"Not many folks have silencers," the same caver said.

The sheriff saw Mrs. Putnam's coat laid out damply on his desk. "I'm gon' have to ask you to leave your coat with us," he said. "I know it's a cold night, but this is evidence."

Kate nodded. "I know, but it isn't my coat. I borrowed it from Edie's mother. I was going—" Suddenly she remembered where she had been going. "To find you, Chris," she said to the photographer, who was hovering in the doorway, his camera trained on the coat.

"Put it back on, Kate," he said. "Let me get a picture."

Kate started to protest. She hated pictures of herself. But this was news, she knew, and it would be unfair for her to ask other people in the news to do what she wouldn't do herself.

"Okay, Sheriff?" asked Chris with a new turn toward manners.

"Go ahead, but be careful of the collar." He held the coat out to Kate to slip her arms in, and carefully spread the collar so the photographer could get the brown runnel of scorched fur across the middle.

"I was looking for you, Chris, to tell you that this story is already on television and up for grabs and to be sure you knew so you could rush your pictures back to the office. Did you get anything at the trailer?"

The young photographer looked smug. "Everything. Pretty gory, huh?"

"Next question. Did you bring a portable so you can transmit from here, or do you have to go to Chattanooga?"

"I guess it's Chattanooga. AP bureau? And Kate, is it okay if I get a room there somewhere? I saw that silver junk you paid for . . . honestly, kid!"

"You did?" said Kate eagerly. "What time were you there? Did you see anybody else there?"

"Nope. The place was a graveyard."

Kate turned to the sheriff. "I went there

looking for Chris and a man came out of the purple cabin and snarled at me, ordering me to take off my coat and come in. I left."

The sheriff looked unimpressed. "It's been that kind of place where ladies and gentlemen meet."

Turning to the cavers, he said, "Boys, why don't you call it a day? It's too wet and too dark to keep searching tonight. Anybody lost on the mountain has likely found a cave by now."

Kate thought of the cave Kim Sue and Sheena had "found" and stirred restively. "I'd better go," she said, taking off the coat and handing it to the sheriff.

"Lorena," said the sheriff, "get a blanket from the jail and let Kate wrap up in it for the trip to Mrs. Putnam's."

Lorena was slow to get up and Kate said her car was close and she would be warm enough for the short trip. It was enough for Lorena, who had started to rise and then settled back, looking, Kate thought, like some primitive household god, who sat motionless, unwinking in the corner. And the sheriff had said she "ran" the office!

Chris walked to the staff car as Kate headed toward her car. She prided herself on never asking for special care or consideration from her male colleagues, but she turned down the dark street wishing that some able-bodied man was along to be sure no .38-toting strangers were waiting for her. She wished fleetingly for the screwdriver and pliers she habitually carried in her pocket when she was investigating a crime. They had on occasion fooled some street slicker into thinking she packed a gun. But how did she know to prepare for crime here? And how did she know she was the intended victim of a crime?

The backseat of her car was dark but blessedly unoccupied and she hurried to start the engine and pull out into the lighted street. There was space for her car in the driveway back of Mrs. Putnam's house, but she stopped at the curb thinking it looked very dark back there. While she hesitated, a floodlight went on in the backyard and she gratefully pulled in off the street and parked next to Edie's red Blazer and her mother's sedate blue Oldsmobile. Both Edie and her mother met her at the kitchen door, holding it open so the warm, food-fragrant air rushed out to meet her.

Kate stumbled tiredly up the back steps and to the welcoming arms of the two women.

"We worried, honey," said Mrs. Putnam. "You were gone a long time for a trip to Addie's place."

"Oh, it was more complicated than that,"

said Kate, "and how nice of you to worry about me and not about your coat. You see I'm not wearing it."

"You had to hide it in a cave to keep animal lovers from spraying it with yellow paint, didn't you?" joked Edie.

"It's all right," said Mrs. Putnam. "Whatever happened, I don't care. Just so long as you are safe. Those precious girls haven't even turned over once since they went to bed. Come on and let me fix you a snack or something."

"Let me fix you a drink," said Edie, helping to unzip the khaki hunting suit and lifting the rain- and sleet-soggy hunting cap from Kate's head. "I don't mean Mother's muscadine wine, either. Something stronger. What do you normally drink in fiendish weather?"

"Oh, a cup of tea will be fine," said Kate, stepping out of her wet shoes.

"Good girl," said Mrs. Putnam, collecting the wet clothes. "We'll put a little rum and honey in it."

In the living room the television still hadn't revealed the full extent of the dire happenings at Scratch Ankle. Edie said they had mentioned the missing legislators—but perfunctorily—and gone ahead with an old movie starring Alice Faye, Don Ameche, and Tyrone Power.

"Good, too," said Mrs. Putnam, spreading an afghan over Kate's shoulders as Edie handed her a steaming mug which telegraphed its contents with the fine smell of honey and rum.

Kate told them of the man at the motel and the shooting just outside the country courthouse, attempting to apologize for the damage to Mrs. Putnam's coat and the fact that it might be months before she saw it again.

"Don't you give it a thought, child," the older woman said. "I feel guilty every time I put that thing on and now that it's been shot at I can wear it with pride."

Kate tried to insist that when the sheriff released it she would take it to a furrier and have the collar replaced.

"You'll do nothing of the kind," said Mrs. Putnam, standing up. "Now I'm going to bed and you and Edie can talk."

Kate was so tired she didn't think she was up to more talk, but one look at the pain on Edie's freckled face was sufficient to keep her up and trying.

"Have you heard anything more from the search?" she asked.

Edie shook her head. "Jim and Smokey are still out there. They've looked in all the big well-known caves. Jim called from some farmer's house up on Sand Mountain. They alerted everybody up there. Even checked out some abandoned buildings, including a church. But they were going back into the wilds where they may have overlooked some of the smaller caves and some of the places like Shelter Rock where hunters sometimes get in out of the weather and build campfires. I don't think there's any hope of finding Turn, do you, Kate?"

Kate hadn't thought there was any hope of finding Turn alive since she saw his trailer and especially that scuffed-up section of trail where the leaves bore evidence of a bloody struggle. She couldn't say that to Edie. Instead she asked who would want the young legislator dead.

"I can't think of anybody," Edie said. "I've racked my brain all day. He was popular enough to win the race for the legislature—almost overwhelmingly. He was friends with all the cavers, and people in town thought a lot of him. He supported all our good causes like the historical society and the library. He didn't go to church—but have you ever heard of killing somebody because they didn't go to church?"

"Maybe some places in the world, but not in the Georgia mountains," Kate said.

"I've even thought of other women," Edie said softly. "It was presumptuous of me to assume I was the only one, I guess. I thought maybe in Atlanta or somewhere else there might be a girl. But I can't believe that, really. We were so close . . . so much in love!" Her voice broke and she ducked her head and pushed at her eyes with the backs of her hands.

"Oh, it's absurd to even think he had a relationship with a woman that would come to this horrible pass," said Kate with more conviction than she felt.

Edie smiled tremulously. "You know that's what I want to believe. I don't know how I can go on without him. He was interested in so many things and taught me so much. We hiked a lot and camped out and he knew all kinds of woodlore I never dreamed of in all the years I've lived in the mountains. Besides that . . . " She paused and bit her lip and her eyes filled with tears, "he was so gentle and sweet."

Kate wanted to cry for her, this kind little schoolteacher who had met a good man and fallen in love and lost it all so fast. Kate had known Benjy Mulcay most of her life, since their fathers were on the Atlanta police force together and they went as children to department picnics in Grant Park. They had had time to fight and squabble and hate each other and grow up and fall in love and embark on an adventurous twenty-year marriage. This girl—this nice brave generous girl—had had, what, two years? Kate felt guilty to have had so much.

Edie sat next to her on the sofa and Kate put an arm around her. "I'm sorry, honey," was all she could think to say.

"I keep thinking," said Edie, "that if he's alive, he's in terrible pain somewhere out there on the mountain. I just hope that you will help us find whoever did this awful thing. I know you have had experience in catching killers."

"Nothing like this, not ever," said Kate. "You've got better people—experts in Jim and Smokey. But if there's anything I can do . . . "

"I know," said Edie. "And I love you for it." She blew her nose and stood up. "You go to bed. It's been a long day and you must be dead on your feet."

Kate was tired, so shaky from weariness she staggered a bit as she walked toward the guest room. At the door she turned. Edie was locking the front door.

"We never do this," she said. "As long as I can remember, I've thought that key was for decoration. But tonight. . . "

"Lock it," said Kate. "How about the back door?"

"I'll get it, too."

Kate stood in the hall and watched as Edie turned keys and extinguished lights.

"How about Representative Banks? Any word on him?"

Edie shook her head. She paused in the dim light of the hall. "I wonder," she said, "if he and Turn were together on anything down at the capitol? Could it be the same people were after both of them?"

Kate looked at her reflectively. It was something she hadn't thought of. Tomorrow . . . if she could only sleep a bit she'd think about it.

"Go on," said Edie. "The covers are turned back. There's a comforter at the foot if you need it. Sleep as late as you like. Mother and I go to church, but you'll find breakfast makings in the kitchen."

Kate meant to think about the question Edie had raised, but she only had time to appreciate the silky feel of Mrs. Putnam's percale sheets and the softness of real down pillows before she slept.

Kate awakened to the sound of church bells. The girls had retrieved from the car their zipper bag, which Kate had forgotten about, and were dressed in their Sunday best—flowered nylon, over which they wore their red and blue zipper jackets and beneath which they wore the mud-stained running shoes of the day before.

The effect was ludicrous, but Mrs. Putnam

winked at Kate and said they looked fine and were going to church with her.

"The Pepper family belongs to our church and they're going to be singing today. I knew the girls would want to hear them. How about you? Would you like to go?"

"Mother, let her rest," put in Edie, also dressed for church. "I bet Kate never heard of the Pepper family and would rather have a leisurely cup of coffee, no matter how pretty they sing."

Kate, wrapped in Mrs. Putnam's robe, grinned gratefully. "I would, Edie, I really would like to go with you all, but it would be wonderful to take my time over a cup of coffee. If you'll excuse me, Mrs. Putnam?"

"Of course, honey," said Mrs. Putnam over a mouthful of pins she was using to pull Kim Sue's hair into a semblance of Sunday smoothness. "Coffee's on the stove, biscuits in the oven, and your clean clothes are on that table in the bathroom. Take your time and we'll see you in about an hour."

Kate thought of a leisurely soak in the big tub but gave coffee priority. She took her cup to the living room and looked first for the Atlanta newspaper. The Putnams subscribed to the *Chattanooga Times*. It was open to the front page and there was a five-paragraph story about the two missing legislators. No mention of blood and possible murder. Apparently lost campers and hikers were routine weekend happenings on Lookout Mountain and the supposition was that they would turn up sooner or later, safe and happy to have had a taste of exceptional scenery.

Kate was on her second cup of coffee when she heard a thud on the front porch and peered out the hall window to see the Atlanta paper.

Bless the Putnams, she thought, they have taste. No polyester sheets on their beds, no day without their capital city newspaper. She pulled the paper out of its plastic case and opened it to find her story and Chris's pictures on page one.

The rain and sleet had let up. The sun was shining outside and Kate felt the inner lightness and brightness which came from having scooped another newspaper with a page one story.

But the feeling speedily passed. It was a superficial attitude from her competitive youth. Now she faced a far more serious—remembering Edie—tragic situation. She took her cup to the kitchen and washed and dried it and hurried to the bathroom, not for the leisurely soak she had wanted, but for a quick wash, tooth brushing, and hair combing. Dressed in the slacks and shirt Mrs. Putnam had washed for her, she sought the kitchen telephone. There was another one in the hall, but she had developed an affection for the big warm kitchen with its cushioned ladder-back chairs and big rocker. It now smelled enticingly of Sunday roast and under a clean towel on the counter there was an apple pie Mrs. Putnam must have made before dawn.

She dialed the sheriff's office.

"You brought them down on us, Kate," the sheriff said. "Two television crews and Lord knows how many reporters are here. I sent a batch of them over to Pearlie's for breakfast. I expect there'll be more as the day goes along."

"Did our photographer, Chris, make it back or call in?" Kate asked.

"He was asleep on my sofa when I left home at five o'clock. Said there wasn't a thing in Chattanooga. We got that boy broke in. He would have been glad to spend the night in a jail cell if I hadn't taken him home with me."

Kate laughed. "A little murder makes troupers out of the worst of us."

"Speaking of which"—the sheriff's tone turned serious—"you're some trouper yourself. We haven't got the first line on whoever that was shot at you. We got to figure he was either a poor shot or was just trying to scare you."

"Well, it was dark back there in your alley," Kate said thoughtfully. "I'm not even sure where it came from. There were a lot of cars parked back there."

"My guess is he thought you were somebody else."

Kate heard the voices of arriving reporters and television crews. She didn't want to share what she was thinking with anybody else. She got up, put on her jacket, and headed for her car in the backyard. The churchgoers were just arriving in Mrs. Putnam's blue Oldsmobile.

The girls were singing melodiously, not one of the Pepper family's stellar hymns but the sweet ballad "Fair and Tender Ladies." The place was exercising charm on them in spite of the dire happenings.

Edie and Mrs. Putnam shepherded them toward the back steps. Kate pulled Edie aside.

"Where does Lorena live?"

"Just down the street," said Edie. "Why?"

"Something I need to ask her," Kate said.

"Go ahead," said Mrs. Putnam. "The girls are going to change their clothes and help me put out seed for my birds. That rain last night washed away every grain I had on the feeders and the birds are hungry. Then we gon' put dinner on the table and we want you to be back for that, hear?"

"Yes, ma'am" Kate said meekly. "You girls all right? Did you enjoy church?"

"Yes, *ma'am*!" they said together. "Mommer ain't gon' believe we got to see the Peppers in person. We even got autographs!" They held up church programs to show her.

"Well, I'm gon' run down the street and see Miss Lorena. You know, from the sheriff's office? You'll be okay here with Mrs. Putnam till I get back?"

Sheena looked accepting but uncertain. They had had enough of being left behind after their experience with Addie Armentrout. Still, they recognized, as Kate herself did, how seductive comfort and food were and the charms of putting sunflower seeds out for all the birds which gathered around the colorful assemblage of birdhouses and bird feeders encircling Mrs. Putnam's backyard.

"We'll wait for you," Sheena finally said. "Just so you don't be too long."

Amused at having obtained permission, Kate walked up the street toward the brick ranch house Edie had pointed out as Lorena's. It had aluminum awnings in morose dirt-smudged stripes of maroon sheltering the doorway and front windows. Last night's rainwater and melted sleet dripped sibilantly from the scallops. A little dog barked hysterically as Kate mounted the steps. She rang the bell and after an interminable wait the door opened and Lorena stood there naked, clutching a purple satin gown to her chest in a pitiful attempt at cover. Her blue-black hair, pulled from its glued cone, sprangled out in all directions. Her sagging breasts, her face, and her arms were a mass of lacerations rapidly turning the same blue-black color of her hair. A little white dog circled her bare feet and leaped at her frantically before racing out the open door.

"Lorena!" cried Kate. "What on earth happened to you?"

The battered woman swayed and grabbed at the door for support.

"It was me, not you, he was after," she whispered. "I told him I wouldn't tell."

"Who?" demanded Kate. "Tell what?"

But Lorena swayed again and toppled to the floor.

Oh, let it be a faint, Kate prayed silently, kneeling to feel her pulse. She couldn't find it. She never could seem to find her own pulse, much less anybody else's. She looked around distractedly for a telephone. There was one beside a badly tumbled bed in the front room. She tried to reach it and punch in 911 without touching anything. Obviously somebody had pulled Lorena out of her bed and beaten her viciously. Maybe fatally. The sheriff answered the emergency number himself, now that he didn't have Lorena there to do it for him.

"I'll be right there," he said. "Do we need an ambulance?"

"I don't know," Kate faltered. "I'm afraid so. A doctor anyway."

The fire department's rescue service arrived almost as fast as the sheriff did and had lifted Lorena to a stretcher and were taking her out the door in a matter of minutes. The sheriff followed along, holding Lorena's hand and chafing it anxiously.

"What is it, Lo? What happened? Who hurt you?"

The snarl of blue-black hair turned restlessly. The eyes back of the swollen blue-black pouches did not open.

Kate stood in the doorway looking after them. If she had only thought, she would have put a robe or something on Lorena. It was awful sending the bruised flesh off uncovered for all to see when they lifted the ambulance sheet and blanket.

The sheriff turned and came back up the walk. "What happened?"

"I don't know," said Kate. "I came to ask her. She said the shot aimed at me was intended for her. And then she fainted."

The young sheriff sighed deeply. "It doesn't let up, does it? Well, I'm gon' have to lock the door and call the experts again. There's bound to be something. What did he hit her with? He must have touched something. Fingerprints. Tracks. We better get out of here."

Kate stood in the bedroom door looking at the mess a beating made: tangled sheets, blanket on the floor, a lamp shaped like a rooster dangling from a cord over the bed, a SEE ROCK CITY shag rug pushed to one side.

"Sheriff," she asked, "who was Lorena seeing? Who gave her that fur coat?"

The young man turned from an inspection of the kitchen. "You know, I don't know. We kidded her about it, but she never would say. When she was younger Lorena wasn't bad-looking and she got around quite a bit. Some thought she was . . . " he fumbled for a word and came out with an old-fashioned one, "fast. She had to help a bunch of relatives. Used to live out Scratch Ankle Road and I thought what she did on her own time was none of my business."

"Let me ask a favor," said Kate. "Let me look at her fur coat."

The sheriff looked puzzled and reluctant, but after a pause he said, "I reckon it's all right. See if it's in her closet. And don't touch it any more than you can help."

Kate didn't know if the plastic cleaner's bag would hold fingerprints, so she slipped her hand up under it without touching the outside. The label was what she wanted to see and after a moment she was able to pull it to the edge of the plastic.

The sheriff, watching, said suddenly, "I see what you're looking for. You had on that fur coat and whoever shot that pistol thought you were Lorena in hers. What does the label tell you?"

"I hope the name of the store where he bought the coat," Kate said. "Do you know Isaacson, Furriers?"

The sheriff shook his head. "But we can sure find out."

They left together, the sheriff to go to the hospital and check on Lorena and once again activate the scene-of-the-crime crew from Atlanta. Kate turned back to Mrs. Putnam's to check on Kim Sue and Sheena. Edie had packed a lunch to take to the searching party at Blue Hole and the girls, back in their jeans and T-shirts, were eager to get to the mountain and resume their search for Smokey the Bear. Mrs. Putnam had put a plate of Sunday dinner in the oven for Kate and gone to take a nap.

Kate sat at the kitchen table, but she had no appetite for the excellent roast and vegetables. She kept thinking about poor gaudy Lorena, who either cared too much about some man or was too afraid of him to name him and solve the whole bitter mess. Kate only belatedly remembered the little white dog and wondered if she should go find him.

When she told Edie about Lorena and the dog, Edie said, "Aw, we'll look later. Lorena is crazy about that pooch, but she lets her-him run outside a lot."

"You know, you said in a small town everybody knows everything about each other," Kate said. "Who was Lorena seeing? Who gave her that fur coat?"

Edie, busy at the sink filling a big Thermos jug with hot coffee, shook her head. "She used to be a rounder, going with anybody who would give her the time of day. But . . . well, you saw how she looks. Older and no longer pretty and I guess the whole town was amazed when she stepped out in that fur coat. But I don't think anybody knows where it came from. Lorena wasn't saying and the man, if he was from around here, sure kept a low profile."

"I guess we can find out tomorrow," Kate said. "I looked at the label and the coat came from Isaacson's. Would that be Chattanooga or Memphis or Atlanta?"

"It was Chattanooga," said Edie, "but they sold the store last summer. I don't know who the buyer was."

"Makes it harder," said Kate. "But not

impossible. When the stores open tomorrow, we'll start trying."

Edie was gathering her gear for the trip back to the mountain and the girls couldn't tear themselves away from watching and inspecting it.

"You gon' plumb jump off the mountain, Miss Edie?" asked Sheena.

"Only after I have myself safe with these things," said Edie, smiling at them. "You see, you have this nice strong rope and you tie it to a tree—or two good stout trees if you can find them close. That's what we call 'anchoring it.' And then I have this seat sling made out of webbing and this rack and carabiner made out of steel. I'll weave the rope through these bars, over and under." She demonstrated. "That will let me down gradually."

The girls were losing interest.

"That rope don't look like nothing but a piece of clothesline to me," observed Sheena. "Mommer's got one runs between the corncrib and the chinaberry tree. I could git that and jump, couldn't I?"

"You certainly could not!" said Edie emphatically. "You could hurt yourself—break bones, even kill yourself. You wait, and when you are a little older you and Kim Sue can come up here and we'll teach you how to rappel. This is very special rope, made in only two counties in Georgia and used by fire departments and police departments and the Army and Navy and us. We'll get you some when you get bigger."

"Shit," said Kim Sue, and then recovered quickly. "I mean—"

"I know what you mean," Edie said. "And don't you let my mama hear you say that word. She'd wash your mouth out with soap."

"Yes'm," said Kim Sue. "But don't you git tard of having everything you want to do put off till you git old?"

Edie put down a seat sling she was preparing to pack in a nylon carryall and put an arm around the little girl.

"No, honey, when you are young you get to do things you can't do when you get old. The best thing is to enjoy everything as you go along."

Kim Sue sniffed and Kate turned away to keep from smiling. Kate's little neighbors were far more cynical and worldly than Edie. They most certainly had never heard of the scholar who said "Carpe diem" or "Seize the day," but they were natural believers in the rest of the line: "Put no trust in the morrow." They were born doubting.

With the picnic and rappelling gear loaded in the Blazer, they were ready to go until Mrs. Putnam hurried out on the porch in her housecoat. She motioned urgently for Edie and held her a moment in whispered conversation.

Edie laughed, bobbed her head, and rejoined Kate and the girls in her car.

"Something funny?" Kate asked.

Edie nodded. "Mama's funny. For an educated woman she's full of superstition and hocus-pocus. She'd die if she knew I told you, but she wanted me to go see Dr. Poultice."

"Poultice?" Kate repeated the name. "Polish, maybe?"

Edie shook her head. "Gosh, no! He was Georgia planter aristocracy originally, but he's been in these mountains eighty years or more. I forget what his real name is. Everybody calls him Dr. Poultice because he's an herb doctor and treats everything with poultices. He's also a sort of jackleg mystic. Finds lost dogs and cows and advises people about the phases of the moon. Mama thinks—"

"He might find Turn?" Kate interjected. "Let's go see him!"

Edie smiled and made a sharp left turn in the street. "Okay. If you want to. The cavers are probably already on the job, so I reckon we have time. Besides, he lives on the way."

"Here in town?"

"Certainly not! If you were into herbs and poultices would you live in this urban center?"

Kate looked at the little houses lining the

main street, Pearlie's Café, the one grocery store, the neat little post office, the faded beauty of the Victorian courthouse with its small square of grass and borders of indefatigable pansies.

"T'wouldn't be fitting," she admitted.

"I hate to tell you where he lives," said Edie. "He didn't name it that, but he didn't try to change it. The name stuck. Sweet Love settlement. Out from, really. His house is not in metropolitan Sweet Love but beyond on a ridge."

"Sweet Love," marveled Kate, giggling. "I bet I know the origin. Beautiful Indian maiden, brave from another tribe. Sweet forbidden love."

Edie made a face. "You got us wrong. We may not be Yellowstone National Park, but we're not banal. There's not a Lover's Leap in the entire county."

At that moment a siren bleated behind them and Edie looked in her rearview mirror to see the sheriff's car. She pulled over to the curb.

The lanky young sheriff, his face troubled, walked toward them.

Edie rolled down her window. "You want us to get out with our hands up, Jeff?"

He smiled briefly, but the creases of care and unaccustomed responsibility remained on his sun-browned brow.

"Thought you'd want to know," he said. "Lorena's pretty bad. Damage to her kidneys and spleen. She's in intensive care. Can't see anybody."

Kate had a sudden thought. "Sheriff, have you got somebody who can stand guard at the hospital? You know nurses would probably let anybody who claimed to be kin get to her."

The sheriff looked thoughtful. "See what you mean," he said. "As you know, I only got one deputy and he's up yonder." He nodded toward the blue mountains which cupped the valley. "I reckon I could deputize somebody else."

"I would," said Kate. "Somebody big and strong who won't listen to any lies."

The sheriff gave a little salute and turned to his car. Edie turned into a narrow road that climbed toward the mountains.

"Tell me about this Dr. Poultice," said Kate.

"Doctor?" squeaked Kim Sue from the backseat. "We ain't going to no doctor, are we?"

"Not your kind of doctor," said Edie soothingly. "In fact, you don't need to see him at all. You all can wait in the car."

"We'll see," said Sheena, not wanting to lose any options.

Kate wanted to sort out the details of the crimes, which seemed to have multiplied with terrifying rapidity, but the beauty of the countryside distracted her. The road climbed steeply with a confusion of sharp curves. Sheer walls of sandstone rose on one side, and between the trees there was a panoramic view of the valley and, beyond it, another blue mountain. On any other day she would have wanted to park and get out and look, but today the press of the pains and the loss of the good people in this beautiful spot weighed on her. They had called it the "lost county" once, and now it seemed to be lost in troubles too big to handle. The boy sheriff, serving his first term and untrained for the complexities facing him, particularly moved her. And she had developed a real affection for Edie and her mother. Even Lorena, garish and bitter, living in her overstuffed, pretentious bungalow which reflected the neglect she felt applied to herself, had been kind enough to be concerned when the girls were locked in the cave. She had found Addie Armentrout and brought her to the scene with . . .

"Edie," Kate asked suddenly, "that man who came with Lorena to the Armentrout cabins—was that one of her lovers?"

"PawPaw?" said Edie. "Probably. He's the richest man in town and doesn't have to make do with the local product, but he's not choosy. He's even made passes at me."

"Well, that shows taste," said Kate, grinning. "Hasn't he a family? Where did he come from?"

"I don't know where he came from. It was a while back when I was at the university. He must have been married because he refers to somebody as 'the late Mrs.' Doesn't that sound like a wife? I don't believe he has had any visitors like sons and daughters, but he's right friendly with all the local people. Even made a start on caving, but he's not very good at it. Too fat, I think."

"What's his business?" Kate asked.

"Oh, everything," said Edie. "Lumber, textiles, the bank, even an automobile agency in the next county. He's into everything. Bought a big house on Lookout Mountain just outside Chattanooga but seems to spend all his time in Rising Fawn."

The road took a sudden turn and they were on top of the mountain.

"Oh, Edie, can we look?" cried Kate.

"Oooh, yes, ma'am!" said a voice from the backseat.

Edie obligingly pulled over to the side of the road. Kate and the children piled out and stood on the edge of the slope where trees had been thinned to give a clear view of the valley with its little towns, the toy-sized railroad train puffing along, and the vast blue mountain beyond.

"Ain't it somepin?" murmured Sheena. "Ain't it really somepin?"

Edie smiled at her. "We like it a lot. But prepare yourself to see something totally different. The community of Sweet Love, Georgia!"

Half a mile down the road, almost hidden by trees and titanic boulders, there was a niche in the mountainside like an enormous room. Gray granite walls, silvered by spray from a waterfall, enclosed it on three sides. Small pointed cedars like Christmas trees grew at the base of the walls and here and there out of the rock itself.

"Sweet Love Quarry," said Edie. "Sandstone was quarried out years ago and some of the limestone. You see the white rock, girls? That's limestone and that's the reason for all the pretty cedar trees. They love limestone."

She had pulled to a stop in the road and Kate and the girls gazed upward in awe for several minutes before they saw what Edie called Sweet Love Village. Scattered over the enclosure, where they were probably sheltered from everything but the south wind, was an assortment of trailers and shacks in the most appalling state of dilapidation Kate had seen outside a city dump. Junked cars and tractors were piled high with kitchen garbage and old rags. The waterfall was crisscrossed with lines on which jeans and shirts and diapers flapped.

"Look, girls," said Edie, laughing. "That's some lady's washing machine. Just hang your clothes under the falling water and let nature do the rest!"

Kate got over her astonishment in time to ask, "Does Dr. Poultice live in this place?"

"Oh, no," said Edie. "He's close—around the bend. But Sweet Lovers are his friends and he discourages any effort by environmentalists to disturb them. They live as they can, he says, and they aren't hurting anybody."

Around the bend on a shelf overlooking the valley was a small stone house surrounded by fruit trees and tidy cultivated beds of wild plants. It was neat and lovingly kept. Edie pulled into the gravel driveway beside a battered rust-raddled 1950 pickup truck.

"This is it," she said. "The domicile and the office of Dr. Poultice!"

As if the mention of his name had summoned him, a small white-bearded man in old Army fatigues stepped out the door. He was scrupulously clean but so old both he and his clothes looked as if they might have been faded in the wash.

"Ladies?" he said politely.

Edie got out of the car and introduced them all, including Sheena and Kim Sue.

"What can I do for you?" the old man asked. "Warts? Stomach upset? Lost property?"

"Lost people," Edie said. "And maybe murder. My mother, Edith Putnam, thinks you might solve it all."

"I know Mrs. Putnam very pleasantly," Dr. Poultice said. "She graciously invited me to speak to her students when she taught at the high school. Won't you come in?"

They started toward the back door, but he stopped them. "No. Come. You are front-door visitors and I want to show you my most precious possession."

He stopped at the corner of the stone house and pointed to the view. Tall pines and spruce framed the vista of mountain and valley. Nothing seemed to keep his little house from tumbling over the precipice except two great boulders thrusting out from the earth at either end of what appeared to be his dooryard. Beside one of these he had contrived a bench with a slab of slate, where Kate envisioned him watching the sunrise and sunset.

The old man looked at it with undiminished pride and affection.

"'Ah, the indescribable innocence and beneficence of nature!'" he murmured. "Do you know Thoreau? How I wish he had had the advantage of living in a spot like this! 'Of sun and wind and rain, of summer and winter,'" he went on, "'such health, such cheer, they afford forever!'"

"Thoreau again?" asked Kate.

"Still," the old man said. "It's part of the same passage. You know Henry David, too?"

"Not well," said Kate. "But I live in the country and I do enjoy him."

The faded blue eyes back of steel-rimmed glasses regarded her with approval.

"Well, do come in, please."

The smells of the little house were palpable—a grassy, weedy compound of herb and leaf scents, and something else Kate hadn't smelled in years, a coal fire burning on the hearth. Bunches of dried plants Kate couldn't identify hung from the rough boards overhead. It was one room, with bookshelves from floor to ceiling. Even at the end where there was a sink and a row of apothecary jars filled with colored liquid, there were more shelves of books.

"It's so nice and warm," Kate said. "I haven't seen a coal fire in a long, long time."

The old man pointed to a bucket full of coal at the edge of the hearth. "See, I pick up coal more easily than wood, which has to be sawed. These mountains are full of coal, the leavings of miners who brutalized our land and were themselves brutalized. Ten or twelve hours a day in the bowels of the earth and they coughed and spat their lungs away. Even the deer and foxes and quail vanished. There was no redbud on the hills. Until . . . until the owners thought the supply of coal had diminished and they moved away, leaving our people hungry and broken. Then . . . " he paused and smiled, "the bats returned."

It was an old theme with him, Kate realized, but looking at Edie's face, she knew they hadn't time for it. To change the subject, she inspected his room again admiringly but covertly for a door to a bedroom and possibly a bathroom. The old man's eyes were on her.

"This is all there is," he said. "I have a bedroll in front of the fireplace for my sleeping chamber and an outhouse in the backyard for other purposes. I bathe under a waterfall nature provides over yonder." He pointed to a small stream trickling off the mountain.

"Gollee, really?" gasped Sheena. "I wish we had a waterfall!"

"But ain't it cold?" demanded Kim Sue.

"Some days it is," said Dr. Poultice. "Then I postpone my ablutions."

The little girls weren't sure what he postponed, but if it happened to be baths, they were on his side.

"Please be seated," directed the old man. "I will bring refreshments. And we will talk."

Since his water supply was outside, Kate felt

sure the glasses wouldn't be sparklingly clean, but it was not glasses he brought but a tray of small stoneware cups in a deep blue-gray. Lifting one, Kate remarked on their beauty.

"One of the lovely things our mountains produce," said the old man, gratified. "There is a pottery down in the valley run by a young woman who gave me these cups in exchange for some wild ferns. The juice of the male fern, you know, is efficacious against burns."

"No, I didn't know," said Kate. "I'm glad to learn it."

"I think I did know," said Edie. "I think my mother uses that remedy. Did you teach her?"

"Perhaps," said the old man, passing around his cups. "This is sassafras, sweetened with sourwood honey. I have some hives up the hill there."

His chairs were old mule-ear straight chairs with seats of woven white-oak splits. He made sure his visitors had one each and then he took one for himself.

"You are interested in botanic medicine?" he asked Kate.

"Oh, yes," she said, not wishing to seem impolite by getting directly to the purpose of their visit. "They tell me you are able to cure so many things."

"I try," he said modestly. "Fortunately, if I fail my patients can seek other physicians who will deplete their bodies with more drastic measures. It was not so for the Cherokees. If they failed, they failed. Today"—his eyes went to the iron pot he had simmering very slowly on the hearth—"I am working with yarrow leaves for poultices for spider bites. Do you have yarrow in your yard?"

"Oh, yes," said Kate, "and spiders, too."

"You should keep the ingredients for poultices handy. Here in the mountains we have many caves and many people who like to explore them." He looked at Edie and smiled. "Caves have few snakes—too chilly—but many spiders. I like to be ready."

They were all silent, even the little girls, sipping their tea. Edie, Kate realized, dreaded to hear what this man might have to tell them about Return. She delayed for her benefit.

"What are all these herbs you have hanging from the ceiling?"

He stood up and touched each dried bunch with pride. "Willow leaves for infusions for rheumatism, wormwood to revive a comatose patient, wild cherry to make a syrup for colds, peach leaves to combine with cornmeal to make a poultice for risings, tobacco to fry with elder leaves to kill the insects that infest the ears and dry up the brain."

The little girls shivered and Kate thought she might have had enough, too, although there were dozens of other shriveled and sere plants hanging there.

The old gentleman, sensing their flagging interest, put down his cup and turned his chair to face them.

"It's Return you want to know about, isn't it?"

"Yes, sir, if you please," said Edie.

"I don't know," he said. "I can only tell you that he's deep in the ground. Bad, very bad."

"Where?" asked Edie desperately. "Tell us where."

"Can we save him?" asked Kate.

"You cannot. But make haste. He deserves a better grave. You will find him, I can't say where. Somewhere beyond Scratch Ankle Road. The other one, too. A spot very jeopardous."

"But we've been all up and down Scratch Ankle," protested Edie. "We've looked everywhere—everywhere!"

"Look again," whispered the old man. "Deep. Deep." He stood up by way of dismissal.

"Can't you tell us any more?" pleaded Edie. "Who hurt him?"

The old man reached up and pulled a shriveled leaf from a bunch in the ceiling and made no answer.

"The other man missing, a man named Banks. Can you tell us where he is?" asked Kate.

"Alive. In little trouble," said the old man.

"Let's go." Edie sighed, pushing her handkerchief into her mouth to keep from sobbing. "Jim and Smokey . . . let's get them. They'll keep trying," she said as she reached the car.

Kate and the girls hurried to get in, pausing only briefly to thank Dr. Poultice, who offered them a limp hand and hardly seemed to pay attention to what they were saying.

"Would you say we learned anything?" Kate asked as they attained the road.

Edie shook her head. "Only what we knew. It's too late for Turn."

As they reached the paved road, the sheriff's car appeared. He forgot blue light and siren and flapped an arm out the open window to stop them. His young face looked stunned and more unhappy than ever.

"I need you, Edie," he said. "Lorena's dying. May not last the day. She should have somebody with her. Do you mind? I'll try to find some of her relatives. But in the meantime . . . "

"I'll go," Edie said promptly. "Here, Kate, take my car and get the food to Blue Hole. I'll ride with Jeff. See you back in town or the hospital . . . whatever . . . later."

"Sheriff!" Kate called suddenly. "Did you find somebody to stand guard outside Lorena's room at the hospital?"

For the first time the young sheriff's face lightened in a smile.

"Sure did," he said. "Your photographer. He didn't have to have a gun and a badge. He had his camera and he told anybody who tried to get in that they were violating the law and he would take their picture. Worked!"

What a wonderful use of Chris Mallory, Kate thought as she slid into the driver's seat and waited while the sheriff turned around and headed back to town.

By now she knew how to find Blue Hole and she pushed the little Blazer to get there. It was well past midday and the searchers, if they had been depending on Edie's basket of food, would be starving. The tents brought by the legislators were still standing on the greensward that by now was mostly mud, and only one of the lawmakers remained. He sat on a camp stool glancing nervously at the water flowing into the Blue Hole and alternately at the sky.

Kate and the girls hauled the picnic basket and Thermos jug across the little footlog to his campsite.

"Hi, Mr. Hawkins," Kate said. "Are you keeping the campfires burning? Did you have a miserable night out here in the weather?"

"Not too bad for me," the representative

said. "After we got down from the mountain I crawled in my sleeping bag and went to sleep. The other boys had a bad scare and took off. I haven't seen them since."

"What on earth?" asked Kate.

"Well, it was kind of funny," the legislator said sheepishly. "They were sitting by the campfire having a few drinks to ward off the cold and this . . . er . . . thing came up out of the hole and swum straight for them! It was all black and shiny with a mask over its face and I reckon they thought it was some creature from the black lagoon."

"And they ran off and left you?" Kate asked.

"Well, I was asleep and I don't wake easy. By the time I came to, the creature was standing here by our campfire warming himself. He was one of them cavers in a wet suit. I laughed a-plenty."

Kate laughed, too. "I bet that was scary."

The legislator wiped his eyes. "Spooky, but funny after the fellow explained it. You can't see it, but there's a stream over yonder flowing into the Blue Hole that comes out of a right big cave. The only way you can get to it from here is to swim, and the ceiling on the passage is so low you have to have scuba gear. Anybody would recognize that in daylight, but it was after midnight and raining and the firelight made it look eerie. That slick black suit, that mask."

"I'd a been sure 'nough scared," said Sheena, speaking for the first time.

"Not me," said Kim Sue. "I'd a shot him."

Representative Hawkins was eyeing the picnic basket hungrily.

"Oh, I'm sorry," said Kate. "Edie Putnam sent you and the others some lunch. There's coffee in the Thermos. She thought the cavers might be coming down off the mountain and she put in plenty of food. Why don't you go ahead and eat? And if you're here when they get back, you can share."

"I'll be here, I reckon. I have to wait for the state helicopter to come back for us. And I should go on and break camp, looks like. They haven't found any sign of Turn or Motley Banks, have they? Don't seem much point in hanging around. Except"—he grinned ruefully—"how do you get away from here?"

"I could offer you a ride," Kate said, "but I planned to go back up to Scratch Ankle and look around a little more. Would you want to go along?"

"No, much obliged. I better wait here for the others, in case they get brave enough to come back."

Kate found Scratch Ankle without too much

trouble. The upper end of the road was paved, with a few pretty houses and well-kept yards on either side. It seemed to have nothing to do with the sad trail the miners had known, especially those who had been mistreated convicts dragging their shackles and chains underground every day. Someone had told her there was a hill just off the road where convicts were buried. She decided to stop there first.

It was a good-sized cemetery with plain flat headstones which carried no names. Was it because the dead did not deserve the stigma of their names engraved in a convict cemetery? Or was it because those who had abused them did not care to go to the trouble and expense of markers? She wandered among them, pausing to admire, in a sheltered corner, a stand of blooming daffodils. Someone had cared enough to plant them there. She brooded sadly about the men, black and white, who had been victims of the vicious convict lease system. Even Scarlett's friends in *Gone With the Wind* had been horrified that she would use convict labor in her sawmill. The operators of the coal mines in these mountains had no such scruples.

Kate turned to show the girls the flowers and tell them something about the people who were buried there, but they were nowhere in sight. She walked to the Blazer, thinking they may have gotten back in. After all, children had little interest in cemeteries. They were not in the car.

She leaned in and blew the horn and then she started calling their names. The woods around the cemetery were not particularly thick. The mountain slope behind it was only moderately steep. There was no dangerous cliff close by.

She walked to the back of the little graveyard, calling as she walked. There was a rustle in the bushes and Kim Sue appeared, crying.

Kate ran to meet her. "What's the matter? Where's Sheena? Where did you all go?"

"Miss Kate, somebody's in a big old well back there crying for help. Sheena was trying to poke a stick down for him to get hold of! I come to tell you!"

"Well, you shouldn't have wandered off. Now show me where Sheena is!"

"We didn't have time to tell you. We saw Smokey the Bear, and we wanted to catch up with him!"

"Oh, for goodness' sake!" snapped Kate. "You saw a shadow or something."

She was walking so fast Kim Sue had trouble keeping up with her. She was clawing at her blue-jeaned legs where heavy briars had taken hold.

"No, ma'am, it was Smokey the Bear. He had

on the hat and the brown suit. He waved his paw at us to come on and then run into the forest. We wanted to catch up with him, but—"

"Never mind," said Kate. "Show me where Sheena is."

Down a briar-thick slope and up a hill, she saw the tall masonry coping of an air shaft, the kind that reaches deep into the coal mines. The rocks, laid in a beautiful pattern, made a tower twenty feet tall and eight or ten feet in circumference. She saw no sign of Sheena, but then she heard her.

"Shut up that hollering," she was saying to somebody deep within the shaft as she leaned through a rectangular opening on the side. "Miss Kate will git you out. So be quiet. You're gittin' on my nerves."

Kate pushed her out of the way and leaned into the window-sized opening near the base of the shaft. Daylight struck the upper half of it, illuminating walls covered with green moss and small ferns. At intervals narrow rock shelves projected from the sides, maybe enough to serve as steps if they weren't too slippery and the climber had a rope. She could not see anybody, but she called out anyhow.

"How far down are you? If I dropped a rope to you, could you climb out?"

"No! Arm broken!" a man's voice she didn't quite recognize answered.

"Are you at the bottom of the well?"

"*No!* Hanging on a tree branch. Halfway, maybe. For God's sake, hurry. I can't hang on much longer!"

Kate pulled her head out and squatted on the briar-thick well sweep. She needed a caver and it might be an hour before she could get anybody. These air shafts were very deep, she knew. She remembered hearing that some of them plunged seventy feet into the mines. Nobody could fall that far and live.

She stood up. "Girls, I want you to go out there on the paved road and stop anybody who comes along. If there are no cars passing, go as fast as you can to those houses we passed back there about a mile and tell them we need help. I'm gon' get Edie's rappelling gear and go into that shaft."

"Miss Kate, you don't know how to rappel!" cried Sheena, grabbing her arm. The little girl was white and trembling, and Kate hugged her briefly and made herself smile reassuringly before striking out for the Blazer and Edie's gear.

"I'm like Brer Rabbit. Remember? He climbed a tree and he didn't know how. He did it because he was 'obleeged' to. Remember? Now, run!"

KATE RAN THROUGH THE little graveyard, sidestepping the tombstones when she could, but not slowing down. From the back of the Blazer she snatched the nylon bag with Edie's rappelling gear, then reached back in and grabbed the hard hat and plopped it on her head. She had no idea why she would need it, if indeed she was going to need it. The neatly coiled rope was the only thing she thought she understood, and that not too well. She had flunked knots in the Girl Scouts and the idea of tying one that would support her weight, much less the weight of whatever man clung to a tree branch in that pit, was the most frightening thing she had ever faced. The day was chilly, but sweat poured off her brow and her hands were wet as she fumbled with the bag's zipper.

The girls had made it through the graveyard and disappeared down the little dirt road, but there was only a remote chance they would find any passerby who would take seriously their plea for help.

And that man in the well . . . Kate wished it would be Return, still able to cling to a fallen tree trunk and ask for help. But Banks, poor fellow—had he stumbled in while searching for Turn? It didn't seem likely that you could accidentally pitch into that shaft, but how else would he have gotten in there?

These thoughts raced through Kate's head as she galloped back through the graveyard, out of breath and unsteady on her legs. She was a walker, not a runner, especially with a hard hat banging about her ears and a bag full of rope and little metal thingamajigs bumping against her knees.

*Oh, let him hang on till I get there,* she prayed. *Keep that tree branch strong enough to hold him!*

The sun had moved when she got back to the shaft and the interior was not as light. She could make out the edges of the rock protruding along the sides near the top, but she couldn't see the human being below.

"Are you there?" she called into the shaft.

"Help! Help me!" cried a weak voice.

"Help is here," said Kate with what she recognized as insane confidence. "Hang on, I'm coming!"

She knew nothing about rappelling except what she had heard Edie explaining to the girls, but she knew she had to do something. No human being could be allowed to plunge to his death if a rope tied to a tree would save him.

Her hands trembled as she unwound two neatly coiled ropes. She looked around for a tree to tie them to. Two trees, Edie had said. But there was only one tree close by and it was a small cedar. Would it hold? It had to, she decided. The rope wouldn't extend up the hill to the old broad-beamed oak there, which was what she needed.

She quickly wrapped one of the two ropes around the broadest part of the cedar trunk and tied it with many knots, none they had tried to teach her in Girl Scouts but the only ones she knew—from tying shoestrings or Christmas packages or affixing a new piece of yarn to her knitting. Grabbing the free end of the rope, she ran to the window in the rock coping and called down.

"I'm dropping you a rope! Can you grab it and hold on till I get there?"

For response she got a faint moan.

If only she could see, but the lights Edie had—a bunch of them, because she never entered a cave without at least three—were back in the Blazer. She dared not make that run across the graveyard again—the man in the shaft might not last, and she wasn't sure her own legs were up to it. If only the sun had stayed put. It had given plenty of light when she first peered down into that hole in the ground.

Now only the first few feet of damp and mossy wall were visible.

She spread the second rope out on the ground. The seat sling she recognized. The rest she wasn't sure about. Steel rings—maybe to attach the seat? Swiftly, because she didn't know what else to do, she wrapped the rope around her waist and between her legs and then around each leg separately, tying everything together with lumpy, cumbersome knots. She was glad the girls weren't there to see her. They had paid attention when Edie explained the gear. She had only half listened and like everything else in her life, she reflected, what she had not learned was what she needed.

Within moments she had built herself a cage of rope and taken a seat on the ground beside the little opening. All she had to do was slide into the pit, and suddenly her resolution failed her. She hated dark holes in the ground. She was terrified that the rocks jutting from the wall harbored snakes. She had no hope that the snarl of rope would hold her. And if she had misjudged the distance to the injured man, she would probably go catapulting to the bottom of the shaft. She had no way of judging how far she had to go to reach him, and so she guessed—as many feet, she supposed, as the distance from her back door to the little log corncrib at the edge of her garden. Twenty feet? Thirty feet?

Hopefully, she called to the man.

"Did you get the rope? Are you holding on?"

There was no answer.

If only he had grabbed the rope and somehow wound it around himself, but he said he had a broken arm and if he had been hanging there in the shaft long, he was probably too weak and dazed to help himself.

Before she made herself swing out into the hole, Kate took a look around. Maybe the girls had found help and she wouldn't have to go down there. Already her hands on the rope hurt and she remembered Edie wore heavy gloves.

Well, she couldn't get out now and go look for them. This was one case when you couldn't say, *Excuse me, I forgot my gloves.*

There was a noise in the shaft, a creaking like cracking wood. The tree branch he held to!

"Hang on!" Kate called. "I'm coming!"

She knew that rappellers had ways of pacing themselves, dropping slowly a little at the time. She supposed it was done by hanging on to the rope and sliding gradually. She made a loop around her wrist and as she eased into the shaft, it pulled tight.

*Wrong,* she thought. *It'll pull my arm out of its socket.* Clutching at a rock on the shaft wall, she disentangled her wrist. If only she knew how to play out the rope gradually . . . if only somebody would come and get her out of that hole! Holding tight to the first thing her hand found, she made a decision. She would not rappel. She would emulate old-time well diggers in the country who dug themselves toeholds in the clay walls and ascended and descended like they were on a ladder. She would not swing free but would hang on to the rocks and set her feet onto those rocky shelves one at the time and not even think about snakes. Edie had boots. She herself wore sneakers, slippery on the bottom and low-cut. If only . . .

*I won't think,* she told herself firmly. *I'll just do it.*

"Hang on!" she called into the shaft. "I'm coming!"

Everything she touched was slippery and twice her feet slipped off the rocks and she swung free into the shaft, hanging on only by gripping the rope with both hands, which by now were bruised and bleeding. Her eyes didn't seem to get accustomed to the darkness, as she had hoped, but she could see far, far below the shimmer of water and silhouetted against it a human body crumpled across a heavy tree branch which could have blown into the shaft or pushed through the rock coping or the earth below it. Was it breaking? How was it supported? She dared not think about it. All she had strength for was to brace herself against the slick wall with one hand, hold on to the rope with the other, and put one foot at a time on the next lower jutting rock. She prayed the toeholds would last. If the rocks started slipping out, she and the man below her had no hope of climbing out.

Kate had no idea how they would get out. She had not thought beyond saving him from falling. She supposed something would occur to her when she got there. Rappellers and cavers got people out of hazardous places all the time. If the victims were dead, it was called "body recovery."

*Oh, don't let this one be dead,* she prayed as she alternately pushed her feet into the niches along the wall and fought to keep from swinging free and falling.

Suddenly she was there! Her foot struck

something soft. The tendency of the rope to carry her downward was halted.

"Oohh!" moaned a voice. "You're standing on my arm. It's broken! Ooohh!"

"Sorry," said Kate, trying to pull herself a little to the side by clutching at the rope and bracing herself against the wall. She was afraid the tree trunk wasn't strong enough to hold them both, but as long as she could hang on to it she wouldn't fall any farther.

"I'm gon' see if I can help you," she said to the lump beside her. He smelled of whiskey and cigars and fear and she couldn't see his face, but it didn't matter.

"Did you get that rope I threw down?"

"Yeah, but I can't tie it. Only one hand—and that's holding on."

"Okay," said Kate. "I think I can loop it around you and tie it so you won't fall all the way."

"Who are you?" the voice asked.

"Hush, now, and let me think. Try to raise up a little bit so I can get this thing around you." Then, as an afterthought, "I'm Kate Mulcay."

"Oh, God," moaned the man. "Wasn't there anybody else that could come?"

"No," said Kate. "We got to make do. Who are you?"

"PawPaw," he croaked. And then, quaveringly, "Don't . . . let . . . me . . . fall!"

"We both may fall if you don't shut up and lie still," Kate said grimly. And to herself she thought, *It's true. I can't get him or myself out of here. And he may try to kill me again if he's the one who shot at me.*

Sheena and Kim Sue stood by the paved road long moments before a car came by. They waved frantically and the people in the car waved back and drove on.

"Miss Kate said if no cars come to start walking toward them houses we saw," Sheena said. "You go. I got a better idea. I'm going back to the Blazer."

"Sheena, you cain't drive airy car!" cried Kim Sue. "You know you cain't. Them cliffs and curves! You know you cain't!"

"Hush up and listen," said Sheena. "I ain't gon' try to drive. I think Miss Edie's got a CB in there. I'm gon' holler for help. But just in case, you keep a-going and stop somebody, if you have to jump in the road."

Kim Sue burst into tears.

Sheena viewed her without compassion. "That's good. Keep a-bawling," she said. "Anybody seeing you cry will stop to help. But run! Run fast as you can!"

She turned and loped down the cemetery

road, thinking all the time that maybe it wasn't a CB radio she saw in Miss Edie's van. Maybe it was a weather radio or something like that. People in the mountains seemed crazy about the weather. If there was no CB, she knew what she would have to do, in spite of what Kim Sue said and what she herself knew. She couldn't drive airy car, but like Miss Kate said about going in that hole, maybe she'd be obleeged to.

The Blazer was not locked and the key was in the ignition. Just like Miss Kate, Sheena thought disapprovingly. Never locked nothing. Never thought anybody would do her bad—and look at her now, in the bottom of a mine. Sheena got in the car and turned on the switch. There was a CB! Her young heart lifted.

She grabbed it with both hands and pressed the button she had learned about years before when CB radios were the rage and two of her truck-driving uncles had let the children play with them.

"Breaker! Breaker!" she yelled. "Anybody! Anybody anywhere! I need help! Miss Kate's in the air shaft. Help! Somebody help us!" And then she burst into tears.

"Little girl, are you playing?" a querulous old voice asked. "Because it's against the law to play with these radios!"

Sheena responded by wailing, "We need help! We need the sheriff! Oh, somebody please come before Miss Kate gits kilt in the air shaft!"

She leaned into the windshield, looking at the contraption in her hand. Had she pushed the button for sending or the one for receiving? She couldn't remember, so she did it all over again.

"Child," a weak voice said, "punch nine. That's the emergency channel."

Sheena obediently punched nine and shouted, "Help! This is Sheena and Miss Kate's in the well! She'll die. Somebody come quick!" The radio crackled and several voices spoke at once. One of them she recognized as the sheriff's.

"Sheena, this is Sheriff Atkins," he said. And the other voices were suddenly silent. "Tell me what your trouble is and where you are!"

"My trouble is Miss Kate going in that big well where a man is. She went to get him out. And Sheriff . . . " she started crying again, "Miss Kate don't know how to rappel!"

"I know, honey," said the sheriff soothingly. "Tell me which big well."

"The one by the convict cemetery."

"Near Scratch Ankle Road?" another voice put in.

"Un-huh," said Sheena uncertainly. "I think."

"Sheena," said the sheriff. "Hang on and don't worry. We'll be there to get Miss Kate out in a few minutes."

Sheena put the hand-held microphone down on the seat and started across the cemetery. Then she turned back and picked it up and pushed the button.

"Ten Four, good buddy," she said in the timeless patois of CBers.

By the time Sheena had crossed the cemetery and was approaching the big air shaft, pickup trucks had started arriving from all directions; six cavers who had been close by on the mountain, wearing walkie-talkies, had gotten the word and passed it along. They were there with their ropes and lights, striding confidently across the field in sturdy boots and with well-gloved hands.

Sheena saw them and suddenly remembered Kim Sue.

"My little sister," she quavered. "Did anybody see her on the road?"

"Don't tell me your sister is in the air shaft too!" snapped a caver.

"No, sir," said Sheena humbly. "She went down the paved road looking for help. She ain't but eleven year old."

At that moment the sheriff wheeled up, his

blue dome light whirling. Kim Sue was with him.

Sheena rushed to her side and, lest somebody think she loved her sister and had worried about her, she said accusingly, "Ain't Mommer told you not to ride with strange men?"

Kim Sue got out of the car, her jeans mud-stained at the knee, where she had stumbled and fallen in the road, her face tear-smudged and dirty. She lifted her chin and said loftily, "The sheriff ain't strange."

Kate was lifted out of the shaft first, to make room for one of the cavers who was a doctor to go down with splints and bandages and painkiller to prepare the injured man to be moved. Somebody had wrapped Kate in a blanket and handed her a cup of coffee and she sat on the ground, leaning against a rock, and watched the rescue operation. The Gandy sisters crawled as close to her as they could get. One of them held one of her rope-burned, rock-cut hands, which somebody had smeared with ointment and bandaged. The other dug a chin into her shoulder. She smiled at them, but her mind was busy trying to retrieve some detail she had seen. She had been so engrossed with that slippery rope and those knots, she hadn't paid enough attention.

Suddenly she knew what she had seen. Blood.

There were smears of dark brown blood on rocks near the top of the shaft. Her hands, although cut, had not bled that much. Besides, fresh blood was red, not brown. PawPaw? She didn't think a broken arm bled.

She called to the sheriff.

He had been standing by, watching the cavers work, but he came to her side.

"You okay, Kate?"

"All right, but Sheriff, I think Turn Pickett is at the bottom of the well!"

The sheriff turned swiftly and called Smokey.

Within minutes a floodlight was rigged up and Smokey himself waited to descend to the bottom of the shaft.

The girls stirred restlessly against her, and Kim Sue, her chin in Kate's shoulder, whispered, "What happened to Smokey the Bear? We saw him. We really did, Miss Kate."

Kate threw off the blanket and stood up. Horace Waters, a Georgia Bureau of Investigation agent she had met years before on a serial murder case in Columbus, was standing by the sheriff and she went over and touched him on the shoulder. He turned to greet her, but she brushed aside cordiality to whisper urgently.

"A man wearing one of those state patrol Sergeant York hats, looking like Smokey the Bear, was here a few minutes before I got here. My girls saw him and he ran off into the woods. He beckoned to them to follow him, but they heard the groans in the well and didn't go."

"Oh, good God!" he said. "A child molester."

"Almost as bad," Kate said. "A murderer."

The sheriff crouched over the side of the well and stared in disbelief as the makeshift gurney swung to the surface bearing the mud-stained groaning hulk that was PawPaw. In the excitement of her own rescue, Kate had not thought to mention the identity of the man halfway down the shaft. The sheriff was slow to believe that stout, potbellied PawPaw, the town's richest man, was a victim. As they wrapped PawPaw in a blanket and prepared to put him in the rescue vehicle, the young sheriff stuck by his side.

"Who did it, PawPaw?" he asked. "Who put you in the shaft?"

PawPaw closed his eyes and shook his head.

The caver who was a doctor checked the splint he had contrived below ground and said, "Better take him in to the emergency room, Sheriff, and talk to him later."

"Go ahead," the sheriff said, diverted by a

muffled shout from the bottom of the shaft.

"Here!" called Jim hoarsely. "Body! It's Turn!"

There was no need to ask if he was alive. They all knew he couldn't have survived both the bloody struggle and the fall, much less twenty-four hours of exposure. So the business of body retrieval began.

Kate didn't want the girls to be there when poor Turn's tortured body reached the surface. She murmured to the sheriff that she was taking Edie's car back to her and needed to call the newspaper.

The girls walked along beside her, sedate and subdued. The afternoon's experience had drained them as well as Kate herself. Before they reached the Blazer, Sheena said hesitantly, "Miss Kate. It may not start. I think I forgot and left the switch on."

Kate looked at the troubled little face and smiled reassuringly. "Plenty of people here to jump us off, if need be," she said. "What you did, what you both did"—she looked at the drying tear paths on Kim Sue's dirty face—"was perfectly wonderful! You were smart to think of it. I should have remembered the CB and saved myself the trip down in that hole."

"Was you skeered down there?" asked Kim Sue.

"Oh, yeah," said Kate cheerfully. "I was plenty scared. I'd never done anything like that before. We've got to get lessons, all three of us. Might come in handy someday when somebody else needs help."

The young faces brightened. "We could start tomorrow," offered Sheena.

"Yeah!" put in Kim Sue. "I'll learn to fly off that mountain like a big old red-tailed hawk!" She stretched her arms and loped ahead, giving an imitation of a red-tailed hawk in full flight.

"I hate to put a damper on your spirits," said Kate, "but we've got to get you back home. School tomorrow."

"Sez you," said Sheena. "Teacher's workday. We got a holiday."

"We gon' stay and hep you ketch a killer," said Kim Sue.

Kate sighed—she didn't know whether from relief at not having to drive back to Atlanta tonight or at the prospect of the unalloyed presence of two such aides. They were capricious about taking orders. They were incorrigible about wandering off on their own.

Their wandering, she suddenly remembered, was what found PawPaw and the big hole in the ground. She hadn't planned to go that way, but they went in pursuit of a man dressed like Smokey the Bear, and they heard the cries for help from the air shaft.

Instead of scolding them for Sheena's impertinent "Sez you," she hugged them and opened the door to the Blazer. The switch was still on, but by a miracle it had not drained the battery. Perhaps they had not been gone as long as Kate felt. Seeping fatigue seemed to start in the bottoms of her sore feet and rise up in her body, making her arms and shoulders ache and feel limp. Her hands, burned by the rope and cut by the rocks, really hurt. She couldn't complain to Edie because she didn't feel like a lecture on proper preparation. Where were your gloves?

Where would Edie be anyhow? Hospital? Home? And what of poor Lorena? She stopped at the sheriff's office to use the phone. Luckily, Chris the photographer was there, again ensconced in the sheriff's chair with his feet on the sheriff's desk.

"Hi, babe," he greeted Kate and the girls cordially. "Where you been?"

"Down in a hole in the ground trying to help a man who was thrown down there," said Kate sourly. "Did you get pictures?"

"Well, not of that," said the young man defensively. "Nobody told me. They had me doing guard duty at the hospital for that old broad, Lorena. I stood 'em off, too, until her cousin or aunt or somebody took over."

"Are you sure they were her relatives and

not somebody who might hurt her? Did Edie see them? Where is Edie?"

"They called her to the hospital office to make financial arrangements. You know how they are: Where's the money coming from? While she was there Lorena's Aunt Somebody showed up—old biddy with a walking stick and a weird hat you wouldn't believe."

"Did you get a picture of her?"

"As a matter of fact"—he looked chagrined—"I didn't. She said she was of a religion that was against pictures, believed the devil would get you if you let your likeness be committed to film. I said what the hell and let her go on in."

Kate grabbed the phone and called the hospital. She asked for the administrator and found Edie in his office crying.

"Lorena . . ." she said in a queer strained voice. "They called me out of the room and . . . cut her throat! She's dying! I heard her scream! Oh, Kate!"

Kate ran for Edie's car where the Gandys waited and raced to the hospital. Chris followed and got out of the staff car with his camera in hand, for once looking chastened. At the same time, an ambulance was pulling into the emergency entrance with PawPaw. The sheriff followed.

Lorena was dead. A doctor and a nurse

escorted Kate and the sheriff into a little waiting room, where Edie and her mother sat silent and blank-faced. Kate recognized the room as one of those little parlors hospitals reserve for grieving families, a place to put them when the shock of a loved one's death was fresh on them and they were likely to make noises of grief or outraged suggestions that the hospital was somehow to blame, all upsetting to staff and other patients. Close a door on them and call it privacy. But where was Lorena's family?

"I couldn't find anybody kin to her around here," the sheriff said.

"I think the last of her aunts died last year," offered Mrs. Putnam.

"But what about the woman who came to see her? She told Chris, our photographer, she was an aunt."

The moment she said it, Kate knew it was a false assumption. The person with the walking stick and the weird hat . . . where did she go? Who had seen her besides Chris?

THE SAME AMBULANCE that brought PawPaw to the hospital apparently brought the body of Turn Pickett in a plastic bag, and forensic experts from the state crime lab in Atlanta were at the back door to meet it.

Edie started for the stairs and her mother rose to follow her.

The young hospital administrator threw Kate an agonized look. "Don't let her . . . " he began. "It's not . . . She shouldn't see him yet. Can you stop her?"

Kate stopped both Edie and her mother on the stairs. "Let's wait," she said, taking hold of each of them by the arm. "Let's give them time for their examination—the crime lab people. Then—"

"Then we'll see him, honey," Mrs. Putnam said gently. "Plenty of time."

Ah, yes, Kate thought to herself. Plenty of time for Turn, for whom time had stopped, and plenty of time for no telling how many more murders in this serene little valley. She had already seen the cart go toward the elevator bearing the body of Lorena covered by not one but several sheets to cover the scarlet tide of the poor woman's blood. Whatever the hospital used to stanch the blood had not been effective until death itself dammed the red stream.

Edie, white-faced and trembling, turned back and her mother guided her toward the elevator. "We'll go home," she murmured to Kate. "That'll be best, won't it?"

Kate nodded. "I'll see you all later."

"Look, chick, I want to go home, too," said Chris, appearing suddenly in the stairwell. "I'm sick." He retched.

His face was in fact pale green and his golden hair was dark with sweat. For a second Kate wondered if murder was reaching out and touching her photographer friend.

"What happened?" Before he could answer, she knew. "You didn't try to get a picture of Lorena, did you?"

He nodded mutely. "They left the room and—"

"Aw, Chris," Kate said sympathetically, "you know we don't use pictures of dead bodies, especially mutilated ones."

He gulped. "I got both of them, Pickett and Lorena, and the man that was down in the well, too. Kate, I've had it! There are some rooms available at the Big Rock Motel. People start checking out on Sunday. Somebody called while I was in the sheriff's office and I told them we'd take them. You mind if I hole up there for a little while?"

Kate couldn't think of anything else he could do if he had gotten a good picture of PawPaw. The mining shaft might make a good one, but clearly he was in no condition to go looking for it, if he was vomiting.

"Go ahead," she said. "Tell the motel people I'll take the other room and be checking in later."

She wanted to see PawPaw, but he was sitting in the sheriff's car surrounded by reporters and television crews. His arm was in a cast and there were patches of tape and bandage over his face and neck. He was plainly refusing to answer questions.

Kate decided to hold back till her competitors had given up and she could get the help of the sheriff for a quiet exclusive interview with PawPaw. After all, she had risked her life—butt, anyhow—to get him out of that well. He owed her some answers.

Meanwhile, Sheena and Kim Sue had gone to sleep on the waiting room sofa. Sleeping, they wouldn't be a nuisance, Kate thought, but she really should get them home. With all the people she needed to talk to, all the things she wanted to follow up, she didn't need even such peerless help as the Gandy sisters. She took the phone to the corner farthest from the sofa sleepers and dialed the Gandys' home as quietly as possible.

Their mother answered.

"Lordamercy, Kate!" she cried. "I'm glad you called!"

"Did the baby come?" Kate asked out of politeness.

"By the hardest," Mrs. Gandy said. "A fine baby girl, weighed nine pounds. Her water broke about ten o'clock and . . ."

Kate sighed. The last thing she wanted was a blow-by-blow account of the delivery. Country women of the old school, before the city came out to give them something else to think about, savored the details of birth and left no fecund particular unexplored.

To sidetrack Mommer, she asked the new baby's name.

Mrs. Gandy laughed proudly. "My sister's got a hand for names," she said. "She named Sheena and Kim Sue for me, did you know that? Well, I let her because I didn't know she was gon' keep on having young'uns of her own to name. She come up with a good one this time: Michael Madonna!"

"Oh, my," murmured Kate, choking a little. "Goodness."

"A name like that stands for something, you know," young Mrs. Gandy said ponderously.

"It does?" said Kate, and then hastily, "It does! Well, I know the girls are going to be thrilled to see their new cousin, and since we have run into some problems up here on Lookout Mountain and I'm gon' have to stay over awhile, I wonder if you could come and get them? I'll give you directions."

"Oh, Kate, I ain't got no way!" Mrs. Gandy said. "You know his car is on the blink." (Kate noted that she never called her husband by his name but simply "he-him-his," as if he were the only man in the world.) "And mine"—she giggled—"while I was at my sister's he drove it to the VFW club and . . . well, he took on . . . " Kate joined her in finishing it: "a little too much." She knew the rest. He wrecked it.

"Well, yes. Pretty bad. So we ain't got no way. Just let the girls stay with you. I read in this morning's paper that you was involved in a murder and I told him, 'Lord, the girls will be tickled with that.'"

Kate made sounds of resignation and hung up. The Gandys spoke of murder as if it were something designed for the edification of the young. She wanted to cry, *Why don't you get ballet lessons for them or enroll them in aerobics?* Fools, she raged inwardly, to turn their fragile offspring over to an old police reporter!

But the fragile offspring were stirring on the hospital's sofa and they threw such beatific smiles at Kate that she felt her annoyance melting. In spite of fools for parents, they were remarkably nice, smart children and she would think of something to do with them while she worked. She remembered the Big Rock Motel. Television! That would occupy them for hours.

On the way out of the hospital Kate paused to see if PawPaw and the sheriff were still at the ambulance entrance. They had gone and so had the covey of reporters and photographers from other papers and television stations.

She would drop by the sheriff's office and see if PawPaw had told him anything that would solve the deaths of Turn and Lorena and at least explain the attempt on herself.

The sheriff wasn't just noncommittal. He was uninformed.

"Kate, he was the most shut-mouthed, say-nothing feller that's ever been in this office—at least since I been here," he said.

Kate smiled, figuring he had been there

roughly a month. Not a Guinness record for shut-mouth, say-nothing, to say the least.

"First, may I use your phone? I need to call the office," she said.

The sheriff nodded, then stood up and walked to the window so she could use his desk and chair. The details of Lorena's death were easy to dictate and the retrieval of Representative Pickett's body she could handle in a few brief paragraphs, but the presence of PawPaw in the well and her own part in it gave her trouble. If she described her rescue effort, she would be making some kind of heroine of herself and that was not allowed. The newspaper frowned on valor in staffers. Sometimes they unwittingly committed it, as Kate herself had done with PawPaw, but it was considered self-serving to put it in the paper.

The rewrite man, a veteran who was good at his job, helped her muddle through. She hung up the phone and turned back to the sheriff.

"Well, where is he? PawPaw, I mean. Maybe I could talk to him. After all—"

"Yeah," said the sheriff, suddenly seeing the point she was going to try not to make. "He sure ought to talk to you! If it hadn't been for you, he'd be in the bottom of that shaft—dead. That was mighty nice of you,

Kate, to go down there and keep a hold on him till help came."

Kate smiled at the embroidered-doily, tea-party word "nice." She hadn't been "nice"; she'd been dirty and incompetent and scared. But if the sheriff was paying her a useful compliment, she would accept it.

"Where did you say he is?"

"Oh, he wanted to go home and go to bed and there was no way I could keep him. It's not against the law to fall in a well."

"Did he fall or was he pushed?"

The sheriff, back in his swivel chair, looked out the window. "That I don't know."

"How about Lorena? Did he know who killed her?"

The young sheriff looked at her wearily. "Said he didn't."

"Did he shoot at me?"

The sheriff looked surprised and then chagrined. "Kate, so much has happened I plumb forgot to ask him. But I don't think he would have done that to Lorena—I think whoever shot at you thought you was her—and we know he didn't cut her throat. He wasn't hardly out of the well when that happened."

"Well, who did? Did you find any prints or the murder weapon?"

"Not the sign of one. Of course, the boys from the crime lab might come up with something. They gon' take over on PawPaw when they get through with Turn and the fingerprints at the air shaft and all like that. They told me they wanted the clothes he was wearing for testing and he promised me soon as he got home he would change and put them in a plastic bag."

"And the murder weapon?"

"Knives. Some kind of thin-bladed knife that would be easy to hide coming into the hospital. Of course, an ax would have worked at Turn's trailer."

Kate sighed and stood up.

"How about Representative Banks? Any word on him?"

The sheriff stood up. "Kate, you're a gadfly, showing me my duty. I forgot about Banks. I'll go now and see if there's any word at the Blue Hole. Why don't you . . . " He looked at her muddy, moss-stained, blood-spotted clothes and smiled. "Why don't you go somewhere and get a bath?"

"Sure, Sheriff," she said crisply. "I'll get out of your hair. I think I have a room at the Big Rock Motel. Call me there if you decide to let the press in on your investigation."

For once the sheriff was decisive. "I'll do that, Kate," he said, walking her toward the door.

On the way to the Big Rock, Kate looked at

her slacks and shirt and the clothes of the girls and shuddered. It would be wonderful if the motel provided a washer-dryer and she could do a spot of laundry for herself and the girls while she took a nap. But mindful of the unanswered questions that were piling up, she decided not to count on it. If need be she would seek out Mrs. Armentrout's Wal-Mart and buy a change of clothes.

Dusk was settling in as she drove into the Big Rock parking lot, a very ugly flat-topped yellow brick structure. With the plentiful native materials, beautiful stone, and timber, it could have been more inviting, Kate thought. But it was laid out in the usual rectangle, with no trees and with empty concrete flower boxes, ornamented occasionally with paper cups from Shoney's restaurant. However, the elderly woman at the desk was decorative enough in her David Dow tweed suit and pearls with smoothly coiffed white hair and pink cheeks. And she was welcoming.

"We've had a swift turnover this weekend," she said. "Conventioneers. They came, complained loudly and constantly, left their rooms in a hurrah's nest, and checked out, taking our best towels with them," she said good-humoredly, as if sharing a joke with Kate and the girls. "And I'm temporary manager, Mrs. Charles Land."

"Oh, we won't do nothing like that, ma'am," said Sheena earnestly.

"I know you won't," the woman said. "I know who Kate Mulcay is and I am very glad to have you all here in my motel. It's not really mine. I just work here, but I do like a nice clientele."

Kate, signing the register, knew the girls were considering that word, "clientele," and she was back to "nice." People did expect you to be nice in this funny, murder-assailed county, she thought.

"The rooms do have telephones?" she asked.

"And teevees?" put in Kim Sue.

"Both," said the proprietor. And looking at their dirty faces and clothes, she added, "*And* hot water and soap!"

Kate laughed. "We need it. Unfortunately, we didn't come prepared to stay and we didn't bring enough clothes. When the stores open we might go find something."

"Murder is always so sudden, isn't it?" Mrs. Land said reflectively.

Kate looked at her in surprise. This elegant lady in her fine clothes didn't seem to be a person who would be privy to violence and homicide.

"Oh, you've read about it," Kate said, wondering if she could pick up an afternoon newspaper somewhere there in the lobby.

"Yes, but I expected it was going to come to that," Mrs. Land said, handing Kate a key. "I could almost have predicted that young Return Pickett would meet an untimely end."

Before Kate could pursue that line, Mrs. Land reached behind her and took a coat off a coatrack. "I see my family is here to gather me up," she said. "I'll probably see you tomorrow. The regular manager, Mr. Goodman, will be here shortly and if you need anything call him. Have a pleasant night."

Gracefully, moving swiftly on her pretty high-heeled pumps and leaving behind a whiff of some expensive fragrance, Mrs. Land was gone.

Thoughtfully, Kate picked up the room key and led the girls down the outside walk beside the building to their room. The room was clean with its plastic-shrouded glasses and tape across the toilet, but no more cheerful than any modern motel swathed in chocolate-colored draperies with matching bedspreads and carpet. Kate thought fleetingly that as far as decor was concerned, she preferred Addie Armentrout's "Home in the Pines." The little silver cabin at least had a woodstove, and it would have been cheerful to sit by it on a winter night if you weren't out looking for murderers. She ran the girls through the shower and took a slow soak herself. Before she set off for Edie's, she settled them in front of the television.

"You stay in this room," she said. "Keep the door locked and if anybody asks for me—or your mother or any other grown-up—say, 'She's outside, she'll be back in a minute.' Don't let anybody inside. I'm going to run over to Miss Edie's and exchange cars with her and get our bags. I'll be right back before you've even looked at one program."

The novelty of motel television pleased the girls, and they waved Kate off with newly scrubbed paws.

"If you see any food . . . " began Sheena tentatively.

"Oh, my goodness!" Kate turned at the door and looked at them. "I forgot. You haven't had anything since dinner at Mrs. Putnam's. How about hamburgers and milkshakes?"

Their smiles assured her it would be acceptable fare.

"I'll be right back!"

Outside the door Kate thought of Chris and wondered if he had recovered sufficiently to eat something and talk to her. The company car was not in that area of the parking lot, but he might have stowed it somewhere in the back. She stopped by the motel office to get his room number.

The office was empty, the front desk unmanned. There was a little bell by the cash register and she punched it. Nothing happened, and after a few minutes she rang the bell again. Down the hallway back of the desk a door opened and a tall, heavyset man came lumbering out, digging at his eyes with his fingers and stumbling blindly. He had a frowsy beard and long uncombed hair and he wore a dirty shirt, its tails hanging loosely over khaki pants.

"Whatcha want?" he said brusquely.

"I'm Mrs. Mulcay," Kate said stiffly, suddenly needing to be formal. "I'm looking for my associate, Mr. Christopher Mallory. Will you give me his room number, please."

The man yawned, scratched his belly, and stood looking at her with a grin on his face.

"You that newspaper woman, ain't you?"

"Yes," Kate said.

"Well, you all know so much down in Atlanta, always running everybody's business. You ought to know we can't give out room numbers of our guests. They may not want to be bothered by company barging in. Besides," he leered, "this ain't the kind of motel that has women going to the rooms of men."

Kate fought an impulse to reach across the

desk and slap his face. Instead, she said pleasantly, "Oh, you mean it's not a whorehouse? Well, in that case I'll just phone him." She reached for the phone on the desk but he came out of his lethargy and grabbed it first.

"Pay station outside," he said. "This here is a business phone."

Angrily Kate stalked out the door, digging into her bag for a quarter. In front of the plastic pay phone shell on the side of the building she paused. Mrs. Land had said her relief at the front desk would be a Mr. Goodman. Kate smiled.

Expecting the oaf to bark an answer into the motel phone, she was startled when he said in a mincing falsetto, "Big Rock Moo-tell!"

"Mr. Goodman," she said softly, "please ring Chris Mallory's room . . . or I'm gon' tell your daddy, the distinguished legislator!"

He coughed and cleared his throat—or was he retching? Then he said squeakily, "That's room 275. I'll ring."

The room didn't answer and Kate turned from the phone thoughtfully. Chris might be out looking for food and she should get on to a take-out window, but Mr. Goodman . . . could it be that he was the flowery oratorical lawmaker's son? Such a slob? The khaki pants . . . surely he wasn't a military type. More likely a hunter.

She gave up and hurried to McDonald's to stock up on cheeseburgers and chocolate milkshakes for the girls. There was nothing that she could think of for herself after what her digestive system had been through that day. She settled for a cup of coffee to go and hurried back to the motel.

"Don't eat in bed," she admonished the girls, and then she withdrew the order. Crumbs and grease on the dark brown, cigarette-smelling bedspreads wouldn't make much difference.

The Putnams' house was dark except for a light in the kitchen. Kate parked on the street and went to the front door. She could hear the doorbell resounding in the back of the house, but it was a long time before Mrs. Putnam came to the door. Even as she opened it and invited her in, Kate heard the back door closing and a car start up in the backyard.

Mrs. Putnam looked flustered.

"Come in, dear," she said. "Sit down. Edie isn't here. She went out to the Blue Hole with some of the cavers."

"Oh, I can't stay," Kate said. "I left the girls at the Big Rock Motel. We got a room there and we won't impose on your hospitality tonight. I just thought . . . "

A car was coming down the driveway out

of the backyard. She couldn't see any headlights. On impulse she ran to the door and looked out. The porch light caught the driver in its beam. PawPaw and somebody else. Kate couldn't see who before the big Lincoln picked up speed and turned into the street.

Kate watched its taillights disappear in the distance before she moved back toward the living room.

Mrs. Putnam waited impassively.

"You're curious about my other guests," she said stonily.

Kate studied the pink face under the soft gray hair. Something had happened to the "nice" Mrs. Putnam, maker of brownies, washer of clothes, source of comfort and gracious hospitality.

"I don't know," she said uncertainly. "I've been looking for PawPaw. I wish I had known he was here. I need to talk to him."

"Your bags are in the hall," Mrs. Putnam said.

"What?" Kate said. And then, "Oh, thank you." She started toward the two little nylon zipper bags by the guest-room door and turned suddenly. "Mrs. Putnam, something is wrong. Tell me what it is. I can't go with you acting so angry and mysterious. Why was PawPaw here? Who was that with him? What's going on?"

Mrs. Putnam attempted a smile that didn't come off.

"I think you'd better get back to the little girls," she said. "Our nice little town is brimming with evil. You don't want to leave them alone too long."

She had struck a sensitive chord. Kate felt a sudden compulsion to get out of this pleasant comfortable house and back to Sheena and Kim Sue before something did happen to them. She grabbed the bags and strode to the door.

"Your key is in your car," Mrs. Putnam called after her. "Leave Edie's on the table there."

Kate looked back at her and surprised a look of pain on her face.

Chris was taking his camera out of his car in front of his motel room when Kate got back to the Big Rock.

"Where you been?" asked Kate. "Feeling better?"

"Aw, I'm okay," he said. "Ran over to Chattanooga to transmit my pictures."

"Good," said Kate, unlocking the door to her room and looking at the girls, both of them safely asleep on top of the ugly bedspreads, chocolate-shake smears on their faces.

She closed the door and turned back to the

photographer. "I need to talk to you," she said.

"My place or yours?" He strove for jocularity.

"Yours," said Kate shortly. "I don't want to wake up the girls."

He unlocked his door and held it open for her.

"Tell me," Kate said, taking a seat in the chair by the window, "what did that person who claimed to be Lorena's aunt look like?"

"Well, she wasn't Jackie Onassis," said Chris. "Tall, hefty. The southern word: tacky."

"Are you sure it was a woman?"

Chris, sitting on one of the beds, turned restively. "No, I'm not sure. I'm not sure at all. I did think her voice was kind of hoarse for a woman's, but she had that walking stick and I figured the old biddy might have been down sick with something."

"Walking stick," Kate said thoughtfully. "Walking stick! Chris, that's where the blade was! You know those trick walking sticks where they conceal things—little vials of whiskey and rapiers! That's what she-he had!"

Excited, Chris jumped to his feet. "That's it! That's it exactly! The old bastard!"

"Now tell me," said Kate, reaching for a piece of motel stationery and a pen, "what did she look like? What was she wearing? Exactly what did she-he say to you?"

Chris sat back down and closed his eyes in an effort to re-create the encounter. "Clothes? Droopy, saggy. No color."

"Hat? Shoes?" prompted Kate.

"Shoes I think were high-topped sneakers. Hat . . . boy, that was really something! Had a bunch of stuff on it and hung down around her-his ears."

"What kind of stuff?"

"Aw, Kate, I don't know. Fur-like mice all around the crown."

Kate stood up. "Chris, you underwhelm me. So precise. Can you tell me what she-he said?"

He pondered. "Well, she went marching up to the room door, but I stopped her. I said, 'Hold on, no visitors,' or something sharp like that. She said she was the patient's blood kin and she had a right. I said 'Doctor's orders' or something. She still had a hold on the doorknob. So I aimed my camera and said anybody going in that room had to be photographed. That stopped her."

"But not long enough," said Kate. "What did she say?"

"I told you. All about her religion that holds it a sin to have your image on film. I didn't want her sinning, bad shape as she was in already."

"Nice of you," Kate said grimly. "So you let her go in?"

"Yeah. I walked down the hall to the drink machine and then all hell broke loose. Screaming and everybody running."

"Did you see her-him?"

"Yeah, the old broad in the hat came catapulting out of that room and headed for the stairs. Nurses and doctors and people went right past her on the run. Code Blue, a lady in a pink smock told me."

"I guess so," said Kate. "It's what they call it when a patient's heart stops or something."

Kate folded her notes, lifted a hand to tell Chris good night, and went back to her own room. For long moments she sat at the little desk the Big Rock afforded, looking with unseeing eyes at the nearly blank piece of paper. She began a list of people who might have somehow had something to do with the murders: starting with the people whose names she remembered at Pearlie's, going to Addie Armentrout, the state house quartet, the sheriff and his deputy, and finally even Mrs. Charles Land and Mr. Goodman there at the motel. *Goodman,* she thought, staring at the name. What did she know about that name? Suddenly she remembered. Representative Goodman, the verbose fellow from the peach belt, one of those who had fled when the wet-suited apparition had come up out of the Blue Hole. She wrote down by his name the well-worn southern question: *Any kin?*

She thought of the list as she divested the girls of their dirty blue jeans and pulled blankets over them. She was pulling off her own when she thought she and Edie and Edie's mother were the only people in town who hadn't made the list. She went back to the desk and wrote down Mrs. Putnam's name.

On Monday morning Kate and the girls, showered and shampooed but still wearing jeans and shirts with the evidence of Sunday's dire happenings on them, approached the desk to check out. Mrs. Land was back, this time wearing a hand-knit powder-blue skirt with a matching sweater, and silver earrings and necklace instead of pearls.

She greeted them cordially. "On your way back to Atlanta, are you?"

"Not quite yet," Kate said. "I want to run over to Chattanooga to the courthouse first."

"Ah, of course. You think land sales and transfers will help you solve murders."

Kate hesitated. "I don't know. Do you think so?"

"What do I know?" Mrs. Land asked, rolling her pretty blue eyes. "I just work here.

What have you got for a motive? If it isn't sex or power it is usually money, I find from reading my murder mysteries. And around here land is about all the money that's left."

Kate brightened. "You could tell me things, I know. I'd appreciate help."

"Why don't you call Edith Putnam—mother, not daughter—and ask her to ride over to Chattanooga with you? I bet she'd like to get away."

Kate was about to explain that Mrs. Putnam had practially thrown her out of the house the night before, but Mrs. Land had dialed the number and was handing her the phone. No mention of a five-minute limit from this desk clerk.

Mrs. Putnam answered promptly, accepted promptly, and asked Kate to pick her up back of the high school. She would, she said, be waiting inside the back door.

"How funny," Kate said, handing the phone back.

Mrs. Land quirked a dark eyebrow.

"I just didn't think she'd go," Kate said, shrugging. She decided not to mention the high school as a pickup place and she really didn't know why. Instead, she said, "Mr. Goodman who works here, is he related to Representative Trent Goodman?"

"Son," Mrs. Land said. "Trent owns this elegant hostelry. Junior is supposed to look after it and I'm supposed to look after him." She grinned and added, "Don't tell anybody I said that. I need this job."

"I won't," Kate said, collecting the girls from the lobby drink machine and marshaling them toward the parking lot.

The Mrs. Putnam who waited inside the high school hall for her was a different person from the warm assured woman who had been so welcoming on Saturday night. She seemed smaller and pale and very nervous. She got in Kate's car and locked the door, forgetting to speak to the little girls until they patted her shoulder and spoke to her.

"Oh, hi, honey," she said. And then to Kate, "Take off, let's go. I hate wasting time."

"Me, too," said Kate, whipping out of the school parking lot and onto the highway. When she felt well under way she said conversationally, "Who's after us? Who are we running from?"

"I'll tell you, but wait . . . don't turn here. Keep on up the mountain!"

"That's the Chattanooga turn," said Kate. "You don't want to go there?"

"No-o! And you don't need to. I'll tell you all you need to know."

Kate wanted to snap, *Start telling me, then!* but the frightened face of the little woman stopped her. She said gently, "When you get your breath."

"Thank you," said Mrs. Putnam. "When we get there—"

"Where?" asked Kate.

"Up to Dr. Polgrim's. I'll show you."

"You mean Dr. Poultice? I know the way there."

Mrs. Putnam sighed and settled back in the seat and closed her eyes.

Kate passed the Sweet Love community and found Dr. Poultice's neat little house with no trouble. He heard them drive in and came out in the yard to meet them. His old face was troubled and he offered none of the usual pleasantries but opened the door on Mrs. Putnam's side and said quietly, "Go on in the house." To Kate he said, "Pull over there back of the shed. Close. It won't be seen from the road."

"Why we hiding, Miss Kate?" asked Sheena.

"Beats me," said Kate. "I hope we'll soon find out. You girls be very quiet."

"Then will we go to Rock City?" asked Kim Sue.

"We'll see," said Kate, still thinking of going on to Chattanooga.

The old man had settled Mrs. Putnam by his coal fire with a cup of herb tea, and he got out cups and a pot of tea for Kate and the girls.

"You tell her, Doctor," Mrs. Putnam said respectfully. "You know the story."

"Yes." The old man sighed. "Only too well. I told you, I believe, that this country is still rich in every kind of mineral, in coal and in lead. Many entrepreneurs have thought to resume mining through the years and for one reason or another given it up. But in the last few months a Tennessee company has been very active buying up land, first across the state line and then on our side. We heard they were going to try strip-mining and that's when Turn Pickett got busy. But it wasn't just that he feared his ancestors' old lands would be ruined again, it was worse than that."

"They started buying up everything in town," Mrs. Putnam said. "I don't even own my own home anymore. They said they needed it for some kind of big church they were planning. They offered me quite a lot of money and told me I could stay there till they were ready to build. I didn't tell Edie. I thought she was probably going to marry Turn and I was hoping to surprise her with a nice chunk of money."

"You signed papers?" Kate asked.

"Oh, yes, all notarized and everything."

"But you haven't collected any money yet?"

"Oh, no." Mrs. Putnam looked as if she might cry. "After Turn's death I changed my mind and told them so—but they wouldn't let me out of it!"

"Who wouldn't?" asked Kate.

"PawPaw," Mrs. Putnam whispered. "That's why he was at my house last night."

"He and . . . ?"

"Trent Goodman, Jr."

"They're in this together?"

"PawPaw is a resident of Tennessee with a home there," Dr. Poultice put in. "He's the one who formed this mysterious company north of the line and started buying up property. Trent Goodman is the leader in some strange religious cult. He wants to build a big church complex in the valley, which would take in most of Rising Fawn." The old doctor made a face. "I think he had in mind something like that one in Waco, Texas, until the FBI wiped that out."

"But the mines?" put in Kate. "Why would he want all that country?"

"I'm going to tell you," the old man said. "That's why they killed Turn Pickett. Those underground tunnels and passages were going to be connected to the church. We didn't know that until some of my friends up at Sweet Love came to see me. They don't seem very energetic people"—he allowed himself a wry smile—"but they get around a lot at night and some of the underground passages lend themselves admirably to whiskey making. One night a couple of my friends found a very large cache of rifles, machine guns, and boxes of ammunition and other explosives. They didn't know what to do with it, so they came to see me."

"Church supplies?" Kate said sarcastically.

Dr. Poultice nodded. "More useful than hymnbooks and missals," he said. "Anyhow, to continue, I wanted Turn's help, but he was in Atlanta and I didn't think we should take a chance on waiting. My friends from Sweet Love and I took my truck and theirs and went into the mine late at night and hauled everything out and brought it here and secured it in a cave back of their waterfall."

Kate had a mental picture of that hideaway, with dirty clothes a-washing under the falling water and concealing the mouth of the cave. Edie had called it the Sweet Love community's Laundromat, but it seemed to be much, much more.

"When did you tell Turn?"

The old man sighed and was silent. Tears came to his eyes and he wiped them on the sleeve of his work shirt.

"The night he got home from Atlanta. He often brought me supplies from town and if it was late he would leave them inside the door and go on. That night I was awake waiting for him. He must have called and confronted one of them with that information."

"They didn't need to kill him!" Kate cried.

"They may have thought he would report their arsenal or that he knew where it was hidden and wouldn't tell," Dr. Poultice said. "I don't know any more about it than that which I have told you."

That which, Kate wanted to tell him, left a lot of unanswered questions.

"You see, my dear," said Mrs. Putnam, looking very sad, "you won't get any information at the courthouse. I don't think there's a record there yet of a single of these land transactions, and they were many, including the Big Rock Motel, among others."

"If it isn't recorded and you haven't been paid anything, I think you can get your house back," Kate said. "Do you have a lawyer? Let's go see him!"

Mrs. Putnam's lawyer had an office in the neighboring town of Summerville. Kate drove her there, wishing she could cut loose and go seek some answers on her own. But the little woman had been kind to her and Kim Sue and Sheena, and Kate couldn't cut her loose until Edie got home from school and could look after her.

"Is it PawPaw you're afraid of?" Kate asked as they entered the lawyer's office.

"Not so much PawPaw himself," Mrs. Putnam said. "It's the people he can round up to do his meanness. Last night he brought Trent Goodman, Jr., to my house. I've known that boy several years and he's always had a streak of violence in him. I think he would have hurt me if PawPaw had told him to."

"How about Lorena?" Kate asked. "Who killed her, and why?"

"I don't know," Mrs. Putnam said. "She was close to them. Typed all their papers and served as their notary public. I always thought they gave her that fur coat as a kind of payoff."

"That reminds me of something else I was going to do in Chattanooga," Kate said. "I had the name of the furrier from the label in Lorena's coat and I was going to call and see if there was a record of the sale. I'll find a phone and call while you're talking to your lawyer."

It didn't take the young lawyer long to tell Mrs. Putnam she and half a dozen other people in Rising Fawn had been victims of fraud. And it didn't take Kate long to trace the former well-respected Chattanooga furrier. He had retired and gone out of business, selling some of his leftover stock to a costume company.

Mrs. Putnam came out of the lawyer's office smiling and Kate came out of the telephone booth in the lobby laughing.

"Lorena's coat was rented!" she cried.

By the time they got back to Rising Fawn, Edie was home from school, and Kate dropped off her mother at their house. Sheena and Kim Sue were clamoring for lunch, and Kate thought she had figured out most of the Scratch Ankle happenings. She picked up hamburgers for the girls and drove straight to the sheriff's office.

He was in conference with PawPaw once more. This time he insisted that the big man stay in his office while he went out to speak to Kate, who left the girls reading old comic books in the outer office.

"I have him for you if you want to ask him some questions," he murmured to Kate. "I can't make him answer you, but you can give it a try."

"Thanks, Sheriff," Kate said, smiling at him. "I think I have some answers for him instead of questions."

She entered the office, took a chair opposite PawPaw, and began pleasantly enough. "How are you feeling after your ordeal in the well?"

"Aw, great! Great!" he said. "You can't keep

a good man down. Or, as somebody up at Pearlie's said this morning, you can't shaft a shafter!" He laughed immoderately.

Kate waited for the sheriff to come in and take a seat. Then she said, "I guess we know about your dealings with Mr. Goodman, the land, the proposed church, and all those guns you all were stockpiling in the mines!"

PawPaw's red face went white. The sheriff was very quiet.

"When Turn told you he had found the arsenal and was going to report it to the authorities, you decided to kill him. Why?"

"Oh, I didn't . . . I wouldn't a done that!" cried PawPaw. "It was Junior, Goodman's boy." His eyes appealed to the sheriff. "You know how wild he gets. We just told him—"

Suddenly Kate remembered the motel clerk's khaki pants. *Smokey the Bear wears khaki,* she remembered, and she said quickly, "Sheriff, Representative Goodman's son . . . I think he's the one who has been playing Smokey in the woods. I bet if you searched his room at the motel you'd find a ranger's broad-brimmed hat and other Smokey stuff."

"Yeah," said PawPaw eagerly. "You know Junior. He likes to play games."

"Wait a minute, PawPaw," the sheriff said. "We want to get this down right. Byron, bring a notebook."

The deputy came in with a notebook and a tape recorder.

"Raise your hand, PawPaw."

"I ain't gon' do this, Jeff," PawPaw protested. "I'm a innocent party. Trent got me into this and he's a powerful legislator and I'm gon' be stuck with it. You know I wouldn't a hurt Lorena, not for the world!"

"When she found out that fur coat you gave her was rented . . . " Kate said softly.

PawPaw attempted a laugh. "It was a joke."

"Is that when she told you she wasn't gon' give back the bills of sale for that real estate you were acquiring?"

"Well, she did act unreasonable about that. Made Trent and Junior pretty mad."

"And so they beat her up and still didn't get the papers, so Junior decided to finish the job with a rapier in a walking cane at the hospital."

The sheriff stood up suddenly and walked to the big iron safe in the corner of the room. He fumbled with the combination and finally the tumblers fell into place with a satisfactory bump and he opened the heavy iron door. When he turned again, he had a big folder in his hand. He sat down and showed it to Kate.

"'Private, Personal Property of Lorena Cumby. Do not open.'"

Kate waited while he opened it. A dozen

agreements to sell—little houses, farmland, the motel, one church, all signed and notarized.

"Well, good God-amighty!" cried PawPaw.

"Nifty hiding place," said Kate.

The sheriff smiled at her and said, "Byron, show PawPaw to the guest room."

Kate took the little girls shopping for clean clothes and then to see Rock City. When they swung back by Rising Fawn, both Trent and his son had been arrested and FBI agents had been introduced to the arsenal back of Sweet Love's waterfall.

Representative Banks had come walking in from a warm and congenial evening spent with some of the young ladies from Pearlie's Café. And Addie Armentrout was in the sheriff's office crying her head off.

"I know Trent Junior done it! I know!" she cried. "When he gits mad he kills things." She held up an embroidered doily that enclosed the body of her mynah bird, its neck wrung. "That night I let him use one of my cabins to meet a lady friend and . . . " her eyes fell on Kate, "*she* come instid! Hit made him mad!"

"And rightfully so," Kate murmured.

The sheriff walked Kate to the front steps, where he thanked her warmly for her help, promised to keep her informed about the case, and hugged each of the Gandy sisters. "If they let me keep this office," he said, "I'm gon' make deputies out of all three of you."

Kate started to say it was an honor she thought she could forgo, but she thought of something else.

"Sheriff, that hat Junior wore to get in the hospital . . . if you can find it, save it for evidence. I think he may have decorated it with stuffed mice that were killed the same way he killed Addie's mynah bird."

Celestine Sibley has written for the *Atlanta Constitution* for more than forty years. Her first book, *The Malignant Heart*, a mystery, was published in 1958. She has since written seventeen books, including her recent memoirs, *Turned Funny*. *Dire Happenings at Scratch Ankle* is her third Kate Mulcay mystery, following *Ah, Sweet Mystery* and *Straight as an Arrow*.

# HarperPaperbacks *By Mail*

## A ROARING FIRE, A CUP OF TEA, AND A GOOD MYSTERY...

### AH, SWEET MYSTERY
by Celestine Sibley

A lot of people hated Garney Wilcox. Just about the only person who had anything good to say about the ornery real estate developer was the woman whose land was making him rich—his mama. But when Garney is found dead, it is his mama, Miss Willie, who confesses to the murder. Unable to believe that her sweet neighbor could be capable of such a crime, Kate Mulcay, local newspaper columnist cum sleuth, sets out to clear Miss Willie's name without becoming a murder victim herself.

### PRIVATE LIES by Carol Cail

When small town reporter Maxey Burnell's boss is killed in a fiery explosion, she's determined to pull her best investigative skills and dig for some real answers. What she finds is a whole lot of trouble, and a very handsome detective with whom she'd like to spend the rest of her life—if she has one left to live.

### SOMETHING'S COOKING
by Joanne Pence

For sassy food columnist Angelina Amalfi, life's a banquet—until the man who's been contributing unusual recipes for her column is found dead. Not one to whimper in fear, Angelina insists on helping the tall, dark and handsome police inspector who's assigned to the case. What follows is a spicy smorgasbord filled with danger and romance that's sure to whet your appetite.

# MYSTERIES TO DIE FOR

## THE WOLF PATH
### by Judith Van Gieson

Low-rent, downtown Albuquerque lawyer Neil Hamel has a taste for tequila and a penchant for clients who get her into deadly trouble. *Entertainment Weekly* calls Hamel's fourth outing "Van Gieson's best book yet — crisp, taut and utterly compelling."

## THE RED, WHITE, AND BLUES
### by Rob Kantner

From the Shamus Award-winning author of THE QUICK AND THE DEAD. P.I. Ben Perkins takes on a case that strikes too close to home. When babies begin to mysteriously disappear from the very hospital where his own daughter was born, Ben embarks on a macabre trail of corruption, conspiracy and horror.

## PORTRAIT IN SMOKE/ THE TOOTH AND THE NAIL
### by Bill S. Ballinger

HarperPaperbacks is proud to bring back into print, after thirty years, a special two-in-one edition from the Edgar Allan Poe Award-winning author the *New York Times* dubbed "a major virtuoso of mystery technique." In PORTRAIT IN SMOKE, second-rate businessman Danny April is haunted by a beautiful woman. So is magician Lew Mountain in THE TOOTH AND THE NAIL. And both are involved in mysteries that seem impossible to solve.

## RUNNING MATES
### by John Feinstein

From the *New York Times* bestselling author. Investigative reporter Bobby Kelleher has just about given up the hope of ever landing the "big hit"—the story that will make him a star. Then the governor of Maryland is assassinated and things start to change—quickly and violently.

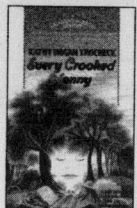

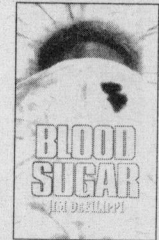

# DAY BY DAY

# DAY BY DAY

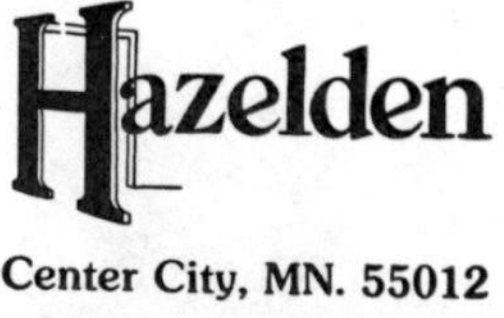


Center City, MN. 55012

ISBN: 0-89486-016-X

**Printed in the United States of America**

# PREFACE

A key fact about this book is that it was written by The Young People's Group in Denver, Colorado. *Day By Day* is the product of their effort to speak directly to young alcoholics and addicts. The result is an eloquent message about living one day at a time which speaks in a very meaningful way to all generations. It contains a helpful lesson for living every day of the year. It is a book which deals in a profound, yet simple, way with getting to know our Creator, sharing ourselves fully with one another, and the difficult but rewarding process of growing as a person.

Hazelden is proud to present *Day By Day* as a worthy companion to its *Twenty-Four Hours A Day*. The two books augment and reinforce one another in their inspirational thoughts and meditations designed to aid alcoholics and addicts everywhere in coping with life's problems. And just as *Twenty-Four Hours A Day* has brought meaning and inspiration to the lives of many persons who do not suffer from chemical dependency, *Day By Day* carries a universal message for anyone concerned with putting the most life into today—and getting the most life out of it.

To the young people out in Denver we say "Shalom! God's Peace Be With You!", and thank you for sharing yourselves with us.

**HAZELDEN**

*Lord, make me an instrument of*
*Your peace!*

*Where there is hatred—let me sow love*
*Where there is injury—pardon*
*Where there is doubt—faith*
*Where there is despair—hope*
*Where there is darkness—light*
*Where there is sadness—joy*

*O Divine Master, grant that I*
*may not so much seek*

*To be consoled—as to console*
*To be understood—as to understand*
*To be loved—as to love*
*for*
*It is in giving—that we receive*
*It is in pardoning—that we are pardoned*
*It is in dying—that we are born to*
*eternal life.*

*Prayer of St. Francis*

# TABLE OF CONTENTS

February 1 – Doing Our Best
February 2 – Learning Patience
February 3 – Practicing What We Know
February 4 – Carrying The Message
February 5 – Imitating
February 6 – Seeing The Good
February 7 – Avoiding Compulsiveness
February 8 – Expressing Love
February 9 – Recalling Powerlessness
February 10 – Praying For Things
February 11 – Avoiding Procrastination
February 12 – Living Today
February 13 – Solving Problems
February 14 – Knowing God Is Love
February 15 – Overcoming Barriers
February 16 – Being Kind
February 17 – Mastering Today
February 18 – Praying By Acting
February 19 – Practicing HALT
February 20 – Expecting Too Much
February 21 – Finding Freedom
February 22 – Taking The Steps
February 23 – Being Sick And Tired
February 24 – Being Grateful
February 25 – Hanging On
February 26 – Learning To Live
February 27 – Fighting Not
February 28 – Being Open-Minded

March 1 – Being Vulnerable
March 2 – Trusting God
March 3 – Experiencing Growth
March 4 – Reaching A Balance With Sex
March 5 – Finding Happiness Within
March 6 – Feeling Desperate
March 7 – Accepting God's Love
March 8 – Going To Any Lengths
March 9 – Having A Sponsor
March 10 – Exercising Patience
March 11 – Finding Happiness
March 12 – Believing In Abstinence
March 13 – Changing Our Ways
March 14 – Making Amends
March 15 – Living Honestly
March 16 – Giving Up Possessiveness
March 17 – Showing Our Feelings
March 18 – Judging Others
March 19 – Removing Defects
March 20 – Getting Rid Of False Pride
March 21 – Nurturing New Growth
March 22 – Being Honest Inside
March 23 – Getting Well
March 24 – Forming New Habits
March 25 – Experiencing Change
March 26 – Worshiping
March 27 – Being Free To Be Me
March 28 – Growing Up
March 29 – Smiling
March 30 – Debating The Program
March 31 – Handling The Little Things

April 1 – Changing Our Fate
April 2 – Competing
April 3 – Rediscovering Love
April 4 – Working For Peace Of Mind
April 5 – Unlearning Old Ways
April 6 – Working The Steps
April 7 – Turning It Over
April 8 – Keeping It Simple
April 9 – Rewriting The Program
April 10 – Changing Our Emotions
April 11 – Being Free
April 12 – Accepting God's Will
April 13 – Growing
April 14 – Discovering Reality
April 15 – Relying On Faith
April 16 – Practicing Our Ideals
April 17 – Struggling Alone
April 18 – Doing The Little Things
April 19 – Using Today's Tools
April 20 – Being Willing
April 21 – Reflecting Kindness And Love
April 22 – Repairing The Damage
April 23 – Overcoming The Urge
April 24 – Dealing With Problems
April 25 – Turning On To Life
April 26 – Doing What It Takes
April 27 – Developing Ourselves
April 28 – Deflating Our Egos
April 29 – Being Forgiving
April 30 – Changing Our Thinking

May 1 – Loving Ourselves
May 2 – Helping Others
May 3 – Losing Self-Centeredness
May 4 – Expressing Love
May 5 – Cunning, Baffling And Powerful
May 6 – Being Humble
May 7 – Returning To Sanity
May 8 – Sticking To Basics
May 9 – Knowing Our Limitations
May 10 – Relating To God
May 11 – Conquering Indecision
May 12 – Measuring Success
May 13 – Befriending Others
May 14 – Staying Clean And Sober
May 15 – Giving It Away Each Day
May 16 – Accepting Our Condition
May 17 – Overreacting
May 18 – Handling Stress
May 19 – Living Harmoniously
May 20 – Tuning In To God
May 21 – Growing By Sharing
May 22 – Accepting Tragedy
May 23 – Listening
May 24 – Accepting Our Addiction
May 25 – Living In The Now
May 26 – Hanging On Days
May 27 – Waiting For Answers
May 28 – Being Honest
May 29 – Sharing In The Fellowship
May 30 – Paying Attention
May 31 – Living Well Today

July 1 – Seeking Freedom
July 2 – Overcoming Worry
July 3 – Sharing Our Program
July 4 – Needing To Escape
July 5 – Praying For Direction
July 6 – Putting The Program First
July 7 – Being A Good Twelfth Stepper
July 8 – Getting Rid Of Anger
July 9 – Working On Problems
July 10 – Criticizing Not
July 11 – Showing Mercy
July 12 – Knowing Our Higher Power
July 13 – Lacking Power Over Others
July 14 – Paying For Freedom
July 15 – Recognizing Opportunities
July 16 – Being Paranoid
July 17 – Being Willing To Act
July 18 – Practicing Sane Living
July 19 – Taking Just One
July 20 – Making A Decision
July 21 – Judging Other Addicts
July 22 – Being Reasonable
July 23 – Babysitting
July 24 – Sharing A Common Goal
July 25 – Practicing These Principles
July 26 – Pitying Not
July 27 – Making Progress
July 28 – Testing The Fellowship
July 29 – Changing Locations
July 30 – Realizing The Consequences
July 31 – Using The Phone

September 1 – Believing
September 2 – Living Spiritually
September 3 – Giving Truth
September 4 – Coping With Fear
September 5 – Practicing Abstinence
September 6 – Dealing With Now
September 7 – Meshing Smoothly
September 8 – Spreading Joy
September 9 – Reflecting The Good
September 10 – Diagnosing Others
September 11 – Working With God
September 12 – Intellectualizing
September 13 – Laughing
September 14 – Desiring The Good
September 15 – Knowing How To Pray
September 16 – Getting Rid Of Guilt
September 17 – Mastering Ourselves
September 18 – Working On Sobriety
September 19 – Being Human
September 20 – Desiring To Change
September 21 – Choosing The Spiritual
September 22 – Seeking Truth
September 23 – Wasting Life
September 24 – Becoming Mature
September 25 – Overcoming Passion
September 26 – Thinking Now
September 27 – Thinking Positive
September 28 – Keeping The Faith
September 29 – Overcoming Self
September 30 – Praying Well

November 1 – Being Inspired
November 2 – Becoming Selfless
November 3 – Expressing Gratitude
November 4 – Expressing Love
November 5 – Giving Joy
November 6 – Welcoming New Ideas
November 7 – Pleasing Ourselves
November 8 – Growing Opportunities
November 9 – Dropping Our Delusions
November 10 – Helping The Hopeless
November 11 – Trusting God's Love
November 12 – Working The Program
November 13 – Gaining Peace Of Mind
November 14 – Practicing Principles
November 15 – Seeking Spirituality
November 16 – Finding The Real World
November 17 – Finding Happiness
November 18 – Striving For Progress
November 19 – Loosing The Bonds
November 20 – Living In Fellowship
November 21 – Practicing NOW
November 22 – Counting Our Blessings
November 23 – Being Consistent
November 24 – Looking For Substitutes
November 25 – Feeling Alive
November 26 – Sharing Opinions
November 27 – Knowing Our Author
November 28 – Growing As Individuals
November 29 – Finding Friendship
November 30 – Lives Worth Saving

The beginning of the New Year will often bring sad memories back to us. This has been the big day for hangovers, coming down, remorse, guilt and shame. But if we stay with our new purpose, staying clean and close to our Higher Power, we need have no fears for the New Year. God has forgiven us our past mistakes and tomorrow is not yet here. If we do what we know is right today, all else will be taken care of.

It is not always easy to do what is necessary today, but it is *impossible* to change yesterday or guarantee what tomorrow will bring. Our year will unfold better by living each day as it comes than it will by regretting the past or anticipating the future. Have I learned to live one day at a time?

Father grant me the willingness to deal with today–instead of being obsessed with the past or the future.

My plan for living today is:

There is a saying that most of us are familiar with, "Plan plans, not results." For those of us with addictive-compulsive personalities this is a very important message. Our heads can spin so much with the results we plan for tomorrow that we forget what to do for a good life today.

If we plan to have a devastating partner, $5,000 in the bank, and a new home by this time next year, chances are we will blow it. We know from experience that if we take that first fix, pill or drink we will have nothing at this time next year. Do I know how to plan well?

Lord, may I do the footwork necessary today and leave the results with you.

The results I will leave to God today are:

Many days we are tempted to ask "Why?"—*Why* did this happen to me? *Why* was I singled out? *Why* am I not a different person? But the "whys" only lead to clever explanations and rationalizations of what we do or what we are. The question for us is not "why," but "how!"

The "how" can give us a deeper understanding of the program; we ask how to do, listen to and learn the program of recovery. We ask God how and He provides the strength and guidance needed. "How" will lead to everything needed for recovery and personal growth. "Why" is irrelevant. Have I learned how to live?

Father, teach me how to live, love and learn.

Today I will ask how to:

Once we achieve a consciousness of God, a connection with our Higher Power, the abiding problem is to hold on to it. Repeatedly we slip into the old ways, habit patterns and modes of thinking. These will eventually lead us back to the first fix, pill or drink if they are not curtailed. We need only a word, thought or familiar situation to be caught up again in a habit from the past.

We have to discover and rediscover that the old way of life has become impossible and the new one essential. This we achieve and maintain by praying, meditating and working the twelve steps of recovery. Do I live the program?

Lord, with Thy help may I avoid being smug and complacent in my new life. Constantly remind me that old ways of living have become impossible for me.

The new ways I will cultivate today are:

**God help me to stay clean and sober today!**

We need to compete with everyone, sometimes subtly, sometimes less so. We always had to be right, for to be wrong felt unbearable. We could never seem to bring ourselves to say simply, "I was wrong." We were afraid of what would happen to us if we did. Our egos were very fragile things; we weren't ever as strong as we had led ourselves to believe.

We came to discover that real strength comes from being able to be wrong, and being willing to change our ways of thinking and living. Can I face being wrong and learn from it?

Lord, help me realize each day that it is okay to be wrong; that real communication with other people depends on my being willing to see other points of view; and that being teachable is a Divine quality.

I will handle being wrong today by:

There is nothing negative in the first step of the program, wherein we admit that we are powerless over our addiction and over our lives. Powerlessness is not weakness. It is simply a recognition of the fact that power is an attribute of God, not of man.

We are powerless in and of ourselves. But when we look to the One who has all power, we can be set free—no longer bound by an addiction that does not love us. Have I tapped the Source of all power?

Lord, help me to joyfully accept my powerlessness over my addiction, knowing that this will set me free.

I will accept my powerlessness today by:

Let us not forget to play. Our new way of life is a serious matter, true enough. But it is not intended as a punishment, or that we should repent and suffer for the rest of our lives. It is intended to produce growth.

Achieving growth should be a joy. We require balance. If we forget to play and be joyful, our life will become unbalanced and we will suffer needlessly. Have I found a balance?

Lord, help me to remember that all living things need balance in their existence. Let me laugh; let me play; let me grow.

My plan for playing today is:

Anger may have its place in human affairs, but chemically dependent people have a knack for letting anger run away with them. "Be angry, but sin not," is an old saying and a tall order for us. The three sins of anger are retaliation, revenge and resentment. Any of these mixed with anger has its own way of poisoning the angry one, mentally and spiritually.

We should always let God handle the situations and people we are angry with, for only our Higher Power can judge the situation objectively. Since retaliation, revenge and resentment are killers for us, it is best to leave them in the Divine Hands. How do I deal with anger?

Lord, when I feel angry, justifiably or unjustifiably, may I not yield to the poisoning expressions of it.

Today I will deal with my anger constructively by:

You cannot build a house on sand nor can you build a life without some foundation. While we were still drinking or using drugs our lives did not seem to be improvable. But there was no foundation to build on. We had no real working principles in our lives. We discovered that we were not able to be the good things we wanted to be.

We didn't know, until we quit drinking or using, that there was a way we could build ourselves, one day at a time, into the kind of person we could accept. The steps and the fellowship make personality changes possible. Have I changed?

Lord, let me be willing to love myself and live myself into a new life, one day at a time, based on honesty, open-mindedness and willingness.

I will seek change today by:

We should realize that we are where we are for a reason, and as long as that reason remains we will remain there. If we are not where we think we should be, working the steps will clear the way for us to get to where our deepest self longs to be.

Growth is a joyful thing. We must be willing to do the very simple things that our new understanding asks of us. We are never given more than we can handle, and we are given all the loving help we need along the way. But we never get this help in advance, only as we need it. Am I seeking growth?

Father, help me want to grow and be willing to do those simple things, day by day, which add up to big changes.

Today I will seek growth by:

The joys and beauty of a clean life are not comparable to Cloud Nine. Cloud Nine is actually opposed to our new way of life. Cloud Nine is a fantasy, a trip, a high, and we know very well how to do that with the first drink, fix or pill.

Now we are dealing with and living with reality, which is a beautiful place instead of a fanciful dream. Each day can be a journey with God, beyond pain, beyond suffering, beyond Cloud Nine, into a wonderful here and now. Have I learned to enjoy today?

God guide me through all aspects of growing, so I don't get stuck and stagnate in any one place.

The real things I will enjoy today are:

Our prayer is, "God grant me the serenity to accept the things I cannot change, the courage to change the things I can, and the wisdom to know the difference." This is a daily prayer, for the things we cannot change today must be accepted today. But tomorrow they may be changeable.

What explains the apparent paradox is that once we have really and fully accepted something, it begins to change. The objective fact may remain unchanged, but our attitude toward it or our relationship to it has changed.

It is with our attitudes and our relationships to people and things that we must learn to live. Have I changed my attitudes?

God, help me live fully in this day, neither forward nor backward, but here and now.

The attitudes I will change today are:

God help me to stay clean and sober today!

God has put so many beautiful things in this world to see His face in: the reflection of light in the running brook, the spectrum of colors in the oil spot in the street, the stubbly grass peeking up out of the snow like morning whiskers, the hail jumping like popcorn on the ground, the musical sound of morning rain.

Some of us see Him most clearly in the light of each other's eyes, and in the kind, patient acts of others being true to God as they understand Him. We can see beauty and know ourselves to be part of that beauty through clean, sober eyes. Do I see beauty all around me?

Father, help me see the beauty that surrounds me today, and to know that I, too, am beautiful in Your eyes.

Today I will look for the beauty in:

We feel we can become beautiful, addiction free people. With the program, belief in a Higher Power and the fellowship, we don't have to stay where we were. Our purpose in life is to stay sober and clean.

God knows our true purpose in life and He will help us. God knows what we are capable of becoming, even though others may misjudge us. Am I staying true to my purpose?

Lord, I pray that I may see the good within and remain true to my purpose.

I will fulfill my true purpose today by:

Many of us did "what other people do." It was the way we did it, and how totally unfulfilling it was for us, that made us feel we differed from "normal" people. It is a joke among us recovering addicts how hard we tried to appear normal.

The non-addicts didn't know our torment, how we lived in another world because theirs did not meet our needs. While high we experienced moments of euphoria and false well-being. When the drugs wore off we suffered centuries of misery. These were feelings that normal people did not experience.

In our fellowship we share all of our feelings and know that we are among friends and finally home. Do I share my true feelings with others?

Lord, help me be willing to see more clearly my true feelings and to share myself with my fellow addicts.

The feelings I will share today are:

We cannot give away something we haven't got. Most of us resented the people closest to us; they forced us to see our inadequacy, our inability to love. Although we were intellectually aware of this, we hated having it proven to us regularly. We were empty and scared, and there was no hope in sight. We blamed our problems on those around us.

Coming into the program we get hope, then strength and experience to share with other alcoholics and non-alcoholics. We learn that in order to keep what we've been given so freely in the program, we have to give it away. Do I share my sobriety with others?

Lord, let me be ever mindful of the Source of all the good things I've been given, and show me daily how to share them with others.

Today I will share my sobriety with:

Helen Keller said, "Life is a banquet and most of us are starving to death." Today, most of us can get higher on love and the real things than we did when we drank and used. God provides for all our needs.

Those of us who appear to others to be successful in relationship areas are so, because, at some point, we learned to live with more failure than most. Have I learned to accept my limitations?

Lord, help me accept myself as I am today, with all my defects, in the knowledge that in Your time I will be changed gradually for the better.

The personal limitations I will accept today are:

God help me to stay clean and sober today!

Learning to really listen to another human being, to listen to what he is saying beyond just his words, is good practice in learning to listen to God. Constant thoughts running through our minds represent a form of talking; we can't listen to another person while we are still talking.

Valuable exchanges between human beings can only occur when each listens to the other and makes a sincere effort to understand what he means. Most of our anger and frustration with each other could be avoided, if we really understood each other's motives. Do I really listen?

Father, help me be quiet enough within to listen to someone else today; let me learn something about myself today by trying to understand another.

Today I will hush my inner voice and really listen to:

God help me to stay clean and sober today!

"Easy does it." Pushing does not help our program; it causes more pressure within us. Many of us lived with the philosophy of: "if it doesn't work, get a bigger hammer." We are given the opportunity to work out each of our difficulties, if we will only wait for the opportunity.

It is sometimes better to overcome our difficulty in a two steps forward and one step backward fashion, than to blow up in the middle of our effort and leave it all behind. We are never given more than we can handle one day at a time. Have I learned to take it easy?

Father, by myself I cannot be alive at all, for I am dependent on You for my very breath; help me realize that the greater my dependency on You, the more "I" can handle.

I will take it easy in the following ways today:

God help me to stay clean and sober today!

Someone in our group is always wailing, "why do these things always happen to me?" The obvious answer, if these things *always* happen to us, is that we put ourselves in the position to have them happen. We are largely unconscious of our motives until, one by one, we uncover ourselves from beneath them. It seems incredible to believe that we actually seek to be hurt, but many of us do, with regularity.

It's a selfish program; we desire to be free of resentment and anger because of the peace it brings us. Am I completely rid of anger and resentments?

Lord, let me be willing to turn the other cheek, knowing that anger and resentment will only hurt me in the end.

Today I will avoid anger and resentment by:

It is our motives that are important in dealing with others. Sometimes we think other people can't handle our honesty, when it is usually we ourselves who can't handle our honesty. We must be willing to bear the consequences of our honesty, the bad as well as the good.

Many of us were afraid to say, "I love you," because we didn't know what to do next. In this program we learn what to do next, and next, and next. Our progress can be as unlimited as God is infinite. Honesty without love has been defined as brutal frankness. Honesty with love is from God. Are my motives always honest?

Please show me, Lord, where my motives are selfish or mean or petty, so that I will not confuse brutal frankness with honesty.

Today I will examine my motives concerning:

God help me to stay clean and sober today!

Carl Jung, noted psychiatrist, once said, "If one can accept one's sin, one can live with it. If one cannot accept it, one has to suffer the inevitable consequences." We must come to accept the acts of our past before they will cease to cause us pain.

All of the steps help us to do this, but in particular, the fourth and fifth "inventory" steps and the eighth and ninth "amends" steps. If we attend to these steps properly, we will no longer regret the past nor wish to shut the door on it. Have I accepted myself?

Father, help me accept the ways I have been and the ways I am which cause me pain, so that in Your time I may be freed.

I will work on self-acceptance today by:

Our new way of life is a self-development program. We cannot heal the whole world of addiction. Each must do it for himself. How many times have we seen eager newcomers drop away when they discover there are no magic wands, only hard work in getting right with our Father?

We can't shove our new ideals down anyone's throat, but we can hold out a hand when they decide they want to get well too. Do I let others do it for themselves?

Lord, may I realize that it took what it took for me and it will be the same for others.

Today I will let others do it for themselves by:

Most of us tried to con ourselves into believing that maybe it wasn't good for us not to use drugs, because we needed an occasional tension reliever. When we said that, we were still considering drugs as our higher power.

We approached the question of "why not?" use drugs from every direction in the hope that we could win the argument and rationalize using. When we get honest about "why not?" we begin to accept our condition. Am I honest about my true condition?

Lord, help me accept that I am mentally and physically different from non-addicts, so that I will be free of the desire to use chemicals.

I will be honest about my condition today by:

Sometimes we get the mistaken impression that we have to pretend to be at places in the program that we really have not reached. We may feel that we have to impress our fellows with how well we are doing in staying off mind altering chemicals. It may be that we are really only trying to convince ourselves. We know how difficult it is, and surely our Higher Power is not fooled by our "act" of well-being.

If we try to hide our disappointment and problems, we cannot be helped with them. We must remember that we have to tell people where we're really at to make it possible for them to help. No one can read a closed book. Am I open with others?

Father, let me believe that Your words are true, "Ask and ye shall receive."

Today I will open up about:

God help me to stay clean and sober today!

Because of our addiction, what we have done and not done has fostered attitudes of cynicism, futility and distrust. How could we ever have hoped to succeed with that in our midst?

Now we are learning to cultivate the attributes of understanding, love and patience. It is difficult and often slow. We must know that our Father loves us and will lead us by the hand, if we only hold it out. Have I developed new attitudes?

God take my hand and lead me this day toward my new attributes and away from the old attitudes.

I will work on the following attitudes today:

There should be gladness and joy in our activities. Not highs from booze, pills or junk, but joy in the revelation of life! Our first joy is usually the very fact that we are alive. Next, we find little joys from our daily accomplishments.

Soon we find joy in service to others. Later our scope of happiness is widened when we learn to share the joys of our brothers. And finally we find joy in our Creator, our Giver of Light. Have I found joy?

Lord, may I experience joy in the world around me. May I experience joy in my Creator. May I experience joy in being myself today!

Today I will try to see the joy in:

Some of us didn't "look like" addicts, but we were; some of us, on the other hand, did look like addicts. At first, drugs or booze turned us on; but later they turned on us.

We couldn't find any peace anywhere. We began to turn into the kind of person we didn't want to be. But we didn't know what was happening to us or how to change it.

When we came to believe that our lives could and would turn around if we would quit drinking or using drugs, things began to get better. Do I believe I can change?

Lord, help me to be open-minded and humble enough to believe that what has worked to change the lives of others will work to change mine.

I will seek change in the following ways today:

God help me to stay clean and sober today!

Those of us who have been sober and clean for a period of time share the newcomer's concern for the future; but we do not share his fear. We know how safe the newcomer is; we know also how unsafe he feels. The richness of life is often overlooked by giving mundane occurrences undue attention when they have little quality.

But by working the steps, going to meetings and sharing in the fellowship—the newcomer will learn to relax. He will feel the richness of life and lose his fear as a result of working the program and staying clean and sober. Have I lost my fear?

Father, help me to lose my fear today, that I may be ready to experience the richness of life as it comes my way.

Today I will combat my fear by:

Let's not make haste and demand our perfection at once. To try to gain all at once will only blind us. If we are impatient, it is impossible to work a daily program. In exercising patience we learn to recognize our daily opportunities to grow.

Our new relationship with the Divine cannot be acquired overnight. It is worth waiting, striving and working to develop this relationship. Let us not go too fast, but count each day as a new opportunity. Have I learned to take it slowly?

Father, I pray that I may meet each day with patience, and as an opportunity to grow closer to You.

Today I will take it easy in the following ways:

God help me to stay clean and sober today!

If we will thank our Higher Power each day for the problems in our life, we will find that we can live and cope with them. And if it be God's will, He will transform them in ways we cannot comprehend. We do not understand our lives.

If we will become willing to let God handle each of our situations in His way, we will find ourselves living ourselves into new ways of being. We will experience a freedom and joy which we could not have comprehended in our old ways of thinking and being.

We cannot think ourselves into a better life; we must live ourselves each day into better thinking. Have I lived myself into a new life?

God, I thank You today for the problems in my life, that I may use them to change myself into a new being.

Today I will live myself into a new way of thinking about:

**God help me to stay clean and sober today!**

Often we find ourselves saving our best efforts for the "big break." "When such and such happens then I'll give it my all." But we don't realize that the big breaks consist of a lot of little things well done. Learning to live is learning to take care of all the daily responsibilities.

If we can't handle housework, getting up on time and petty irritations, how can we expect to take care of promotions, marriages and crisis situations? The daily growths may seem thankless, but our "big breaks" are the result of all our todays well lived. Do I always give my best efforts?

Lord, help me not to "save" my efforts, but take care of all things as they arise.

I will try my very best today to:

God help me to stay clean and sober today!

Many of us spent a long time getting sick and we cannot expect to get well overnight. We have to want to get well; we have to have patience. If we lose control of ourselves through lack of patience, we can lose all we have gained.

Patience is a virtue that has to be developed, slowly, through daily effort. It requires the daily practice of watching ourselves, and using prayer in trying times. Selfishness retards our progress in gaining patience. Do I have patience?

Oh Lord, be my Guide, that I, with patience, may learn to live the life that is set before me.

Today I will cultivate patience by:

God help me to stay clean and sober today!

God does not expect us to live what we do not know or understand yet. We can gain understanding by applying what we know day by day. It is only when we turn our backs on what we already know that we stumble.

We already know that drinking and using will only block the way. When should we begin applying what we already know? Today, for today is the only day we have. Do I practice what I know?

Lord, I pray that I may be guided in applying what I know, and that I may not turn my back on You.

I will practice what I know today by:

God help me to stay clean and sober today!

When first we experience the joys and blessings of this program, we get filled with a fever to carry the message and do God's work. We start glimpsing some spiritual principles and elation takes over at the prospect of our do-gooding! When we reach this point vanity becomes a danger to us all. We may suddenly feel that we, above others, are true messengers of God.

We may be tempted to start preaching THE way to spiritual growth. What vanity! God works through everyone–not just a select few. Doesn't He even work through the failure of others, so that we may be reminded of our own past? No one of us knows THE way, for God has provided many ways. How do I carry the message?

As I do my work today, may I know that all of us are from God and are returning to God, and no one of His children is more beautiful than the next.

I will try to show others the way humbly today by:

**God help me to stay clean and sober today!**

We don't need to imitate anyone. If we admire people, we can strive for their qualities and virtues, but we need not imitate their every gesture and word. The gifts of each are a culmination of his own experiences, and we can't adopt the talent of another. We don't need to! Only our Creator can teach us what we have to offer.

We or others don't know our best capabilities until we have exhibited them. When we do what is assigned us, to the best of our ability, there is at that time the greatest moment of joy and fulfillment. We are then rich in the eyes of God no matter how small the task. Have I stopped imitating?

Lord, dwell in all regions of my life and put the Divine touch into all I do.

I will do my own thing today by:

There are many channels by which the beauty of our souls may shine forth from our Creator. Above all is love. To love, and to love purely, means that every day a little ugliness is removed. The pettiness of our lives becomes less and less pronounced through the eyes of love.

When we offer our love to God, our lives become fresher and our souls humbler. Evil seems to disappear in love's eyes, and we learn to distinguish the sinner from the sin. Do I see the good in people?

Father, let me walk in Your love to more beautiful and loving things.

I will look for the good today in:

Being compulsive people, once we leave the drugs behind we want our dreams to be fulfilled immediately. However, in the beginning, we have only the potentiality of having our promises fulfilled. The fulfillment is something we build toward, not to be realized immediately.

Each day we have to work on our lives with what we know now, and gradually we will grow closer toward our ideal. We won't get anywhere if we try to force ourselves into situations that we are not ready for. God sets the pace. Have I stopped being compulsive?

Lord, I pray for the patience to live today with what I have been given to see and do.

Today I will avoid being compulsive by:

As we get better, we come to realize the presence of the Father. And we become aware that progress with our addictive problems comes through Him. This is made perfect in love.

To love is the noblest expression of man. We cannot love mankind until we love our God, and paradoxically, we cannot love our God until we love each other. As we manifest love, we manifest the God force that is in all of us.

All that is good is part of us, as we seek to express love for our fellow man. Thoughts, words and actions are opportunities for us to express this God force in our daily lives. Do I express my love for others?

I pray that I may love my God. I pray that He may enter my heart and be with me always.

I will show my love for others today by:

**God help me to stay clean and sober today!**

If we've been around so long that we think our "bad times" are over and we can't get "crazy" again, then we probably have already gotten "crazy" in the head. None of us are so spiritual that we don't have room for improvement. And none of us are immune to getting stoned. If we think we no longer need help, we may already be in trouble.

Our lives will always be unmanageable, but properly guided they can be productive and fulfilling. If we have forgotten our powerlessness, we may have to learn it all over again. Do I realize how powerless and unmanageable I really am?

Lord, I want to take joy and pride in my sobriety and cleanness, but protect me from smugness or untouchableness.

I will remind myself of my powerlessness today by:

It seems that in our selfishness we're always praying for the things that we want and not the things that we need. If we're praying for material luxuries, sex partners and an easy life, what do we gain? Certainly not strength, wisdom and love.

To gain strength we must carry burdens; to gain wisdom we have to get honest with ourselves; and to gain love we must learn to be loving. These things are not accomplished through material things, through sex, or through a soft life. Do I pray for the right things?

Lord, I pray for Your guidance, that I may trust and know You'll give me what I need and not necessarily what I want.

Today I will pray for:

Is our standard the best we can reach today? Or are we putting things off for tomorrow? When we were in the midst of our addiction everything could be put off, including people—we had to have our stuff.

Now that we have the business of life to tend to, now that we have a life—are we doing our best or are we still putting off? If we don't try to the best of our ability today, we may lose what we have gained from the twelve steps and the fellowship. Have I stopped procrastinating?

Lord, I pray that I may reach for the highest standard possible for me today. I pray that You will help keep me from procrastinating, so that I don't lose what I have gained.

I will do the following things that I have been putting off, *today:*

God help me to stay clean and sober today!

We often expect so much so fast that we soon become nervous wrecks. Expecting answers for tomorrow's or next week's problems is not living today. If we have a problem today, let us offer it to God for an answer.

However, if we are demanding an answer today for next week's problem, we are being immature and impatient. Let us retake our third step today and not fret over the future. Am I working on today's problems?

God, give me the strength to accept what You send me when You send it.

My plan for working on today's problems is:

If we arise in the morning with a feeling of hopelessness, our day doesn't stand a chance. However, we can meet God in the morning and ask Him to "take over." If we ask God for help in the morning, then accept His help through the day, we won't have to solve anything alone.

We will realize that problems aren't unsolvable, and that God is responsible for solutions. We are only responsible to Him for our efforts, not for finding the solutions to all our problems. Do I let the solutions to God?

God let me meet You today, so that I'll never be alone.

Today I will work on the following problems, and let the solutions to God:

"God is Love." It is in these three words that all can be realized. It is through love that our life can be perfected. If we really loved ourselves, would we abuse our bodies with alcohol or drugs? Would we abuse our minds with hate? Would we abuse our fellows with unkindness?

Divine Love is universal, pure and from the Giver of Light. When we truly know that God is Love, we need never be alone in despair again. "God is Love," is not a shallow or trite statement; it is rich and full, and includes suffering and pain as well as splendor and light. Do I know God is Love?

Lord I pray that I may know the Love that passes all understanding, which is found in consciousness of You.

I will seek to know God's love today by:

When situations seem the darkest for us, the storm may be about to break and let the sun shine through. Just a little more persistence, just a bit more effort, and the emotions that seemed so hopeless may turn into an exciting growth process. The only battles we lose are within and the only battles we win are within.

God never places insurmountable barriers in front of us and our only barriers are those we create for ourselves out of our own intrinsic weaknesses. Have I stopped erecting barriers to impede my own progress?

Lord help me recognize the glory that can be won within.

I will avoid blocking myself today by:

We should strive to be kind to others, even to those who don't seem to appreciate it. An unkind word to another may not hurt him the rest of his life, but what does it do to us? It puts us out of fellowship with the Father, which we cannot afford.

It is when we are out of step, out of harmony, that we are vulnerable to taking that first fix, drink or pill. Can we really afford to be unkind to others? Am I kind to others?

Father, help me show kindness to my brothers, even when it is hard, as you have shown kindness to me.

I will show kindness today by:

If a chemical-free condition is our aim, then we must begin right where we are today. Idly wishing for the past to be removed or the future to come closer will bring us nothing. We must master today to make a better tomorrow possible.

This requires a clear understanding of our capacities and abilities today. Let us not distress ourselves by dwelling in the past or future, but let us express ourselves to the fullest today. Have I learned to master today?

God guide me in my activities today, and keep me from idly dwelling on yesterdays or tomorrows.

I will work to master today by:

God help me to stay clean and sober today!

There is more to prayer than kneeling at night and folding our hands. Thoughts of love and creation are prayers. Feelings of gratitude are prayers. Prayers can be seen in a kindly smile, a friendly gesture or even in a negative movement not made.

Bursts of joy surging through our bodies are prayers. Caring for and comforting a child is a form of prayer in God's eyes. There are many times when whatever the position of our bodies, our soul is on its knees. Do I express prayer in all that I do?

Lord, help me pray throughout the day, knowing that Your goodness constantly abounds in me.

Today my actions will express prayer in the following ways:

There is a mini-program in our larger program called HALT. It means never get too Hungry, too Angry, too Lonely, or too Tired. Any of these conditions can fog our minds so we lose sight of our true purpose. Soon we can begin to wallow in self-pity, and the next step may be to get loaded.

If we pause long enough to follow the suggestions of our more successful predecessors, we may avoid joining the ranks of the constant "slippers." HALT is a program to remember. Do I practice HALT?

Lord, let me be aware of those times when I am in danger of losing my connection with You, and keep me from falling into the trap of self-pity.

If I feel hungry, angry, lonely, or tired today, I will:

God help me to stay clean and sober today!

We should try to be honest with ourselves about judging the merits of being clean and sober. If we judge a pair of hosiery after they get a run, or a razor blade after it becomes dull, we are going to be perpetually displeased. Things have their limitations. It's the same with the program, if we judge its effectiveness by whether or not we are happy all the time.

The program will only be perfect when we are perfect. We must let go of our childish "all or nothing" attitude and apply realistic standards. After all, when in our lives were we ever happy *all* the time? Do I expect too much?

Lord, help me to be honest with myself about where the problem lies, when I am unhappy with the program.

Today I will have reasonable expectations about:

Many of us have said repeatedly, "I want to be free." Do we realize that there is a one to one correspondence between how much freedom we allow others and how much we can have for ourselves? We are judged as we judge others.

If we judge that another cannot have his freedom of will, then we will be bound also. Others are mirrors for us. But more than that, they can be windows through whom we can find our freedom. Have I found my freedom?

Help me learn, Father, from the valuable differences I see in people that it takes all kinds to keep this world spinning.

I will search for my freedom today by allowing freedom to:

God help me to stay clean and sober today!

We used drugs for many reasons. Often it was to take the edge off life. In the beginning drugs made the world more beautiful, more satisfying to us. Toward the end we used chemicals to turn off our guilt, our fear and our loneliness. It was hard to see when we passed over the line where using began to be more the cause of conditions than the cure. Finally, our using met none of our needs at all.

However, by taking the steps, we can relearn how to meet our needs in constructive rather than destructive ways. Am I taking all the steps necessary to meet my needs without chemicals?

Lord, help me seek out those things in life, sober and clean, that I was trying to find by using drugs.

Today I will take the following steps:

"We are sick and tired of being sick and tired." There comes a point when the drain of game playing, dishonesty and ego building gets to be too much. Then we are ready to turn it over to our Higher Power. We have to make many decisions about being "sick and tired."

We get sick and tired of blaming others for our faults. We get sick and tired of running the show. We get sick and tired of trying to impress people. We only need remember that when we get sick and tired of anything, God is always ready to take it from us. Have I stopped feeling sick and tired?

Lord, may I not always wait for that sick and tired feeling before turning things over.

Today I will ask my Higher Power to take over the following problems:

We grow in gratitude for the gift of being sober and clean. Ultimately, we become grateful that this gift comes free, with no strings attached. Also, we come to be grateful for the other benefits of our sobriety and cleanness.

Our reasons for gratitude are many: the ability to sustain honest relationships with friends, the awareness and appreciation of our being, our health, the ability to help others, the ability to ask for help when needed, the mended relationships with family and others, and many more changes. Am I grateful?

Lord, help me to be grateful daily for the many blessings which come from being clean and sober, and especially for the blessing of just being sober and clean.

I will express my gratitude today by:

We had a great deal of sticking power. The only problem was that we were hanging on, for dear life, to those things that were destroying us: our resentments, self-pity, bad habits and drugs.

We must transfer this tremendous sticking power to the things in life that are possible and good for us to hold, then hold on very carefully. Someone once said that a loving spirit holds another in an open hand, as if the other were a very fragile baby duckling. Am I holding on to the good things?

Lord, remove that fear from me which prevents me from letting go of my defects. fects.

The good things I will hang on to today are:

God help me to stay clean and sober today!

We must learn to live, day by day, just as we learn to walk or talk or to develop any physical attribute. When we stopped our addiction, we had to start all over on how to live. Obviously, judging by our past we had not done so well in this area.

If our desire is strong enough, God will take our hand and lead us step by step, day by day, into our new life. Eventually we will become the loving, mature adults which we were unable to be for so many years before. Have I learned to live?

Lord, I pray that I may let You take my hand today to lead me through Your will and not my own.

I will work on learning to live today by:

God help me to stay clean and sober today!

An important part of our program is to stop fighting anybody or anything. Joining in any battle will only blur our principles and weaken our minds so we can't do what we know is right. In fighting, our center of authority is anywhere but with God.

We work more effectively by being examples to other people rather than soldiers. God will show us how to handle all situations. We can praise, petition, supplicate, intercede—but we cannot fight. Have I stopped fighting?

Lord, as an example I am an effective messenger of Your will, as a fighter I may lose sight of Your principles.

The things I will stop fighting today are:

Many of us said when we came into this beloved fellowship, "these people are very narrow-minded. If I get hooked up with this crowd my friendship opportunities will be very limited." That was our tricky mind talking. How many other fellowships include people of such varied economic, social, occupational, and age backgrounds?

Most of us were much more limited in our contacts with others before we joined the fellowship. As we ourselves become less narrow-minded, we discover some of the most open-minded people in the world in this fellowship. Have I stopped being narrow-minded?

Father, help me to be honest enough with myself to realize that I was guided to this fellowship for no other reason than that I needed help.

Today I will be open-minded about:

**God help me to stay clean and sober today!**

When we choose not to escape through that first fix, drink or pill, we are refusing to choose death. We are challenging life to be interesting, to be worthwhile, to be more than it ever was before. If we had no hope of this, we would have never stopped using.

We have been losers, failures, escapists, and to finally give life an honest try is to become vulnerable. Will the program really work? Am I taking too big a risk? Does God really love me? Is He really there?

Through thousands of clean and sober people we know the program works. What we don't know is whether we are willing to take the risk of working the program. It is only through taking this risk and being vulnerable that our life will ever "open up." Do I dare to be vulnerable?

God grant me the courage to risk being one of Your children come home.

I will risk being vulnerable today by:

**God help me to stay clean and sober today!**

Let us become as little children and put our trust in the Giver of all good and perfect gifts. We know that other people, jobs and places failed to relieve us of our addiction. Where then does our hope lie?

God, as we understand Him, can give us freedom from drugs if we will only open up and let Him. Let nothing stand between us and our Father, and let us cast aside the things from the past that have hindered us. Do I trust God?

Lord, let nothing from the past hinder me from placing my trust in You, my God.

Today I will seek to deepen my trust in God by:

God help me to stay clean and sober today!

It is not easy to stay clean and sober. It takes every bit of guts we have inside. We may suffer much mentally or physically, but now we can learn from our experiences. In our using days, we could go through the same suffering many times but never learn a thing.

Now we are facing life for the first time and we have a chance to grow through our experiences. If we take that first pill, fix or drink, our chances of growing are dead. Do I grow from each new experience?

May I trust in the Divine Will for the strength to endure, and the ability to grow through each life experience without that first fix, pill or drink.

I will look for opportunities to grow today by:

**God help me to stay clean and sober today!**

## March 4 Reaching A Balance With Sex

Sex has always been a problem to us in one way or another. Either we had too much or too little; either we were outlandishly immoral or we were real prigs about the whole thing. As with other areas of our life, we need to be realistic about sex and learn to reach a balance with ourselves.

Taking "chastity vows" or "letting it all hang out" are a little ridiculous. And we find that the balance has to be ours—not an institution's or another's views. Have I found my balance with sex?

Lord, let me know that my conclusions on sex are between my Creator and me—not based on the views of others.

Today I will seek a better balance with sex by:

**God help me to stay clean and sober today!**

When we were taking drugs we were looking for fulfillment and happiness. We couldn't face the reality of life, so we tried to create a world that we could feel comfortable in. We searched for our pleasures in sources outside ourselves—in people, places and things.

In working our spiritual program we come to realize that happiness and contentment are to be found inside ourselves. We gradually become aware of our achievement, and the beginning of gratitude slowly sets in. Little by little, the peace, pleasure and happiness within grow, and then we are able to reach out and say "Hey life, here I am!" Am I full of inner peace and happiness?

Lord, I pray I may always remember that peace and happiness come from You, and may I be grateful for it.

Today I will express my gratitude for inner peace and happiness by:

**God help me to stay clean and sober today!**

When we were drinking and using chemicals, we became accustomed to waking up to a feeling of impending doom. The indescribable desperate feeling of "What did I do or say yesterday and what did people think?"

Sometimes following a good day, many of us continue to experience this feeling even after we have quit using drugs or alcohol. It is a bad habit pattern which is gradually eliminated by time itself and by rationally thinking over the previous day. Have I learned to handle feelings of desperation?

Lord, on paranoid days, grant me peace of mind to look at things rationally, and let me avoid being led into feelings of desperation by old habit patterns.

If I feel desperate today, I will handle it by:

**God help me to stay clean and sober today!**

God's love is so encompassing, so all powerful, that it surpasses our understanding. Doubtless, the reason many have turned away from our fellowship is an inability to accept that love. "What's in it for them? Why do they want to love me?"

Maybe these words were once ours. But as we apply our new found principles, we learn to understand love, not in our intellect, but in our being. It is through the love and grace of our Lord that we have gained so much. Do I accept God's love?

Lord, may I come to know the influence of Your love, helping me day by day, hour by hour.

Today I will accept God's love from:

Before we sought help we became physically, mentally and spiritually very ill. We couldn't stand to look at ourselves in a mirror. We had to hit bottom. We had to be ready to try anything, to go to any lengths, to help ourselves.

We must never forget where we came from and in what condition we arrived here. It is important not to forget that we are pill heads, drunks and junkies, because if we do forget, our willingness to "go to any lengths" fades away. Am I still willing to go to any lengths?

Lord, I pray that I may never forget where I was at and in what condition I came to this program.

The lengths I will go to today are:

**God help me to stay clean and sober today!**

Why are people in this program always suggesting we get a sponsor? Doubtful people ask, "If I have the whole fellowship to turn to, why do I need a sponsor?" Considering the fact that we have tricky minds, the whole fellowship would give us too many answers.

If we didn't like one answer, we would go to another and another until we got the answer we wanted. This would be self-will run riot and contrary to turning our will over to the care of God. A sponsor can put a check on our self-will. Do I have a sponsor?

Lord, may I learn not to operate on self-will, and may my mind stay clear so that I don't play games with my life.

Today I will see my sponsor about:

God help me to stay clean and sober today!

Patience is much more than just a "hide and watch" attitude. It is sustained trying. We must be willing to wait for fulfillment. We can head straight for our goal of sobriety and cleanness, if we will only pause for the stop-lights along the way and wait.

If we insist on plunging ahead, refusing to wait, we are sure to go the long way around, and we lose sight of our objective in the roundabout journey. We need to keep in mind always that our objective is a sober, clean way of thinking and living. Yes, we have to have patience or our objective will slip away. Do I exercise patience?

Lord, help me to do the things today that will make me ready. Help me to be willing to wait for the right things.

I will exercise patience today in the following ways:

**God help me to stay clean and sober today!**

Happiness is not a goal for us, it is the result of following the twelve steps. If we make it an object of pursuit, it will only lead us on a wild goose chase. This we know because whenever we sought happiness out of a bottle, a needle, a pill or whatever, it always eluded us.

When we are following our true purpose, we often find happiness we never dreamed possible staring us in the face. When we work the steps, help others and go to meetings, we can't help but have happiness presented to us. It is a result.

The sooner we learn not to seek happiness for itself, the sooner we will realize it is the by-product of our new life. Have I stopped chasing rainbows?

Lord help me see happiness as the result of the way I live, and not as life itself.

Today I will practice the program in the following ways:

Some of us said that we didn't know if we were "addicts" or not when we came to the fellowship. We knew we were unhappy and that we drank and used drugs too much. But we hadn't resolved whether we were unhappy because we used chemicals too much, or used chemicals too much because we were unhappy.

It was suggested to us that we try changing the pattern by not using drugs and working the twelve steps to see if our lives didn't change. They did! We have come to believe that there is no problem that taking a drink, fix or pill will not make worse. Am I convinced that abstinence is the only way?

Lord help me carry the message that if we simply don't take a drink, pill or fix, our lives will change for the better.

Today I will carry the message of abstinence to:

We must be willing to grow in understanding. We understood everything when we were using chemicals in one way. A way which caused us pain and grief and misery. When we quit drinking or using other drugs we began to see things in another way.

Sometimes the new way of seeing things meant we had to make some changes in our way of living. Any new way of thinking requires new ways of being. Are we willing to make the changes in our living that correspond with our new ways of thinking? Have I changed my ways of living?

Father, give me the courage, belief, strength and willingness I need to allow changes to take place in my life.

The ways of living I will change today are:

God help me to stay clean and sober today!

In the amends steps, first we must become willing to make amends. There will be no benefit in trying to make amends until we are entirely willing. We have to be ready to make our amends with no preconceived requirements as to how the other party involved will receive them.

The success of these steps does not depend on the acceptance of the other party, but merely on our total willingness to admit where we were wrong. There is magic in working the amends steps; magic we can never believe in unless we work them. Have I made all of my amends?

Father, help me to be willing to ask forgiveness of You, and to admit to those I have wronged that I have done so. Please remove my fear of doing so.

Today I will make amends to:

We can live ourselves into being new people as we act honestly in each situation, one by one. Each day, honestly lived, to the depth of our ability, will result in a day full of new experiences, richer and fuller than the day before.

Being honest with ourselves and others creates a multitude of new opportunities for us. Unless we live our honesty, we are destined to stay in our old ruts. Do I practice honesty in all of my affairs?

God, grant me the humility to be honest with others today, and the light to be honest with myself.

I will cultivate self-honesty today by:

Gradually we begin to know that everything belongs to God. As long as we seek to possess, we are not free. There is a way of using all things for good, without possessing or feeling possession of anything. Ownership is merely stewardship, and we need to see that what is in our care is used for good.

Do not think that this leaves us without in any way. We will find that if we "seek first the kingdom of heaven, all things will be added unto (us)." Have I given up my possessiveness?

Lord, I pray to remember that even the air I breathe, upon which my life is dependent today, is only mine to use as I need it.

Today I will share what I have with:

When we were drinking and using drugs, our dilemma was that nothing seemed real, neither the good nor the bad. It caused us a lot of anguish to know we really felt one way but were acting as if we felt another. We were so confused that even we came to wonder how we really felt.

No wonder we weren't understood; there simply wasn't any consistent part of us to hold on to. When we come into the program, we begin to build on that little honest part. After a time, those around us begin at last to feel they can trust and depend on us. Do I reveal my true feelings?

God, give me the courage to be honest with others about how I feel, even if it's not how I wish I felt.

The true feelings I will disclose today are:

We must free ourselves from judgements. We usually condemn in others what we dislike in ourselves. Whatever we express is reflected back to us, so love should be our expression.

When we judge, condemn and misunderstand, we invite the same things for ourselves. Why should we express what we do not want for ourselves? Have I stopped judging others?

Lord, let me express today all the love that I am capable of giving, and so achieve all the love I am capable of receiving.

Today I will express love to:

We can discover, through working the steps, which parts of us are valuable and which parts are useless and outdated. And very, very gradually, as we grow in the program, the useless parts of us can be discarded. We have been allowed to live in spite of how we have been.

But we have suffered much because of our imperfection. When we truly want to quit suffering, we will be willing to ask that our defects be removed, one at a time. As soon as we are willing to work at it a day at a time, we will discover miraculous changes beginning to take place in ourselves. Have I discarded all of my defects?

Lord, I want my resentments and defects to be removed in Your time, not in mine, when I am entirely ready and willing.

I will work at removing the following defects today:

Who do we think we are when we say some things are not good enough for us? Like jobs. Some people feel that if they can't beat the top guy they won't take the job, not that they earned any money in the meantime. This is called pride, false pride.

If we are operating with false pride, we'll also refuse help from others, the very help that might save our lives. We should practice waylaying false pride by accepting little things from others. If we can't accept anything from anybody, how do we expect to be sufficient vessels to accept God's big gifts for us? Am I completely rid of false pride?

Open me up, God, that I may be able to accept things from others, be they simple or grand.

Today I will purge myself of false pride by:

**God help me to stay clean and sober today!**

Spring is a time of new and beautiful growth. For us, too, there can be growth. We have spent too long in the fall and winter of our lives, fading away the flowering and filtering the sunshine with mind altering chemicals. Finally, our lives appeared to be empty and dead.

But like earth, there is still life within. And when we make the conditions suitable, our lives will again bring forth new growth and beauty. This requires patience, abstinence, kindness and love. Do I show a lot of new growth?

Lord, may I feel the sunshine of Love shine down on me that I may have the opportunity always to grow.

Today I will prepare for new growth by:

Fortunately, all the answers we will ever need are available to us. Although answers seem to come from outside us, such as through other people, actually the answers are already inside us. We need only to recognize them when they emerge. Something inside us hears the truth. We try for a long time to pretend that we don't notice or hear, but one day we decide to get honest about how things really are with us.

At that point we acquire a new bit of freedom. When we begin to get honest about how we really feel, we begin to get somewhere. God can change how we feel, but only if we come to Him, just as we are, just as we really are. Am I honest with myself about how I really feel inside?

Lord, allow me to really feel today, even though I risk being vulnerable.

Today I will examine my true feelings about:

Let us remember that physically, mentally, and spiritually we have been defunct. It is all these areas that have to be worked on to get well. Just stopping our addiction is not enough. Stopping addiction is only the first step, because it is a symptom of what is really wrong in all areas.

From there we have to learn how to live, and then how to be aware of God's presence. Let us work on all these things, day by day. In so doing the light of His presence will shine forth in our lives. Am I completely well mentally, physically and spiritually?

Lord, let me remember that my addiction is a symptom of what is wrong physically, mentally and spiritually.

I will work on getting well physically, mentally and spiritually today by:

God help me to stay clean and sober today!

We begin to form habits and then habits begin to form us. For so long our habits were self-destructive. We were self-centered, angry, critical people. This is how we behaved and how our destructive tendencies were formed.

To stay clean and sober we have to form new habits. We must give up many old hangouts, friends, attitudes and ideas. We find that this is the only way we can form new habits. Habits of kindness, love and honesty are what our program is based on. What do my habits tell about me?

God help me to form new habits from Your consciousness to replace the old habits that almost destroyed my life.

Today I will work at discarding the following old habit:

**God help me to stay clean and sober today!**

As we seek to know God, great upheavals will occur in our lives. As our whole drug world had to be replaced, so will our old ideas have to be replaced. Ideas that we thought had a strong foundation will crumble within us. Many premises for our lives will prove to be false.

The only thing unchangeable is God. Experiencing change may be difficult to endure, but God loves us and will guide us through if we only let Him. Have I experienced a great upheaval?

God grant me the strength that I don't turn away before I have met You face to face.

The areas of my life in which I will seek change today are:

God help me to stay clean and sober today!

Our lives reflect what we worship. When we were young we worshipped ourselves, demanding candy, toys, and whatever our fancies desired. Later in life we worshipped our addiction–going to any length to get loaded and stay loaded. In our new life we learn what it means to worship God.

Let us work our program in all areas to make ourselves worthy of our Higher Power. By looking at the activities of others we can see what attitudes they have developed toward God. By our own example we show others how we look upon our Higher Power. What do my actions show?

God, guide me to express my beliefs in words, thoughts, deeds and attitudes.

Today I will express my love of God by:

Being free from fear, living naturally, means being able to say, "I don't know," if that is true. It means not being bound by the need to impress others. It means living in simple honesty and sincerity. Freedom means not having to be famous, rich, powerful or even "good."

We can just be radiant in health, love, patience, kindness and gentleness. To be free from fear means that we can live as we choose, without having to be approved by anyone save our Higher Power. Do I feel free to be me?

Lord, the supreme prayer of my heart is simply to be me, with the loving guidance of my Higher Power.

Today I will be natural in the following ways:

Most of us, agewise, are something like 15 going on 30 or 40 or 50. People in the program have observed that we stop growing emotionally at about the age we start using mind altering chemicals. It may sound funny, but these observations appear accurate. If we look around us the newer members do seem stuck in their teenage years.

But abstinence, patience and working the program help us mature to our proper ages. Given time, we can become the adults we pretended to be for so many years. Have I grown up?

Lord, allow me to grow emotionally so that I'll no longer have to pretend maturity.

Today I will act maturely by:

It is not uncommon for people addicted to chemicals to want to "get back" at all those who rejected or hurt them. For many years, we may have operated on the law of revenge, and there was no bad situation that we couldn't make worse. What is our guide now? What is our light?

Have we tried to operate on the law of kindness and to see how this affects our neighbor? A smile can raise hope, and hope can make a haven for some discouraged, disheartened soul. Let us smile to bring hope and leave revenge in the old world of selfishness. Am I smiling?

May we rejoice in His light and may our smiles show forth His joy.

I will smile today to all I meet and especially to:

**God help me to stay clean and sober today!**

When we were in school we often joined in the great debates . . . they went on and on and nobody ever gave any answers, if anyone even knew the answers. In our personal training grounds (the world of the streets) we often heard or participated in lengthy debates about the evils of our society.

Sometimes people get clean and sober and begin debating the values of the twelve steps. Nobody knows the answers except those who live the program. No amount of debate will give us the answers, only action and action now. Am I living the program?

God, grant me the courage to take action now and let my action be guided by Your Divine Will.

Today I will act the steps out in the following ways:

God help me to stay clean and sober today!

It is not the big tragedies in life that cause us trouble–it's the irritating and petty daily things that get to us. There is merit and glory in handling big crises, but who notices how we handle the little things? (We will notice it if we get stoned!)

There is no glory in getting rid of petty irritations, but there is peace and serenity. It is only when peace and serenity dominate our daily lives that we appreciate the real gift of this program, the gift of daily living. Have I learned to handle the little things?

God, grant me the serenity to handle all the little things today without irritation or annoyance.

I will handle any irritations or annoyances today by:

Sometimes we feel that life has played a trick on us. Fate made us different from our fellows because we are chemically dependent people. We feel like life has made fools out of us. But if we really examine ourselves, we find that it is not life but our self will that got us into trouble.

Our problems were really of our own making, not something fate dealt out. The only way we know to remedy this is to make our will one with the Father's. We can choose not to be fools of fate, but children of God. Have I stopped playing the fool?

Father, I pray that I may see myself not as a fool, but as Your child, loved and cared for.

Today I will conform my will to God's will by:

God help me to stay clean and sober today!

Learning to turn our lives over to God is not a spiritual contest. In our chemically dependent days, we demanded to know who did more of what, who made more than whom, and so on. Hopefully we have left all that behind.

Our spiritual quest should be with the desire that His will be done in all things: never to override, outwit or outdistance others in the same quest. God knows our possibilities and gives us a place that we can fill acceptably.

We do not know what others have learned, so how can we judge or take part in a contest? Have I stopped competing?

May I stop competing and leave the measurement of this day to my Higher Power.

I will avoid competing today by:

We know that in each of us there is a buried treasure of love, just waiting to be discovered. From the history of our past we often think of it as a hidden treasure. If we practice our new found principles and continue searching, little by little, we'll uncover our treasure. It is buried deep under our resentments, unclean living and shame.

But, God, as we understand Him, gives us the guidance and strength necessary to uncover it. And the program provides all the tools we need to find and uncover our lost treasure of love. Have I found love?

Lord, I pray that I may use the tools You constantly give me so that I may find my lost treasure of love.

Today I will search for love by:

**God help me to stay clean and sober today!**

## Working For Peace Of Mind

To stay clean and away from mind altering chemicals, we must keep our thoughts always close to God–knowing that nothing can prevent us from staying clean and sober. God promises peace if we stay close, but He does not promise leisure.

Our work is hard, but our rewards are many. They are much more lasting than those immediate gratifications we sought in the past. For our daily struggles, He promises inner peace and serenity. Have I found peace of mind?

Lord, I pray that I may stay close to You and remember why I must work.

I will work for peace of mind today by:

In this program we are not asked so much to learn new ways as we are asked to unlearn the old ones. We are not pressed to follow new values so much as to see the folly of the values we came in with. What we determine for our new lives is between us and our Higher Power, and surely there is great diversity among us.

We are not asked to adopt the lifestyles or thinking of fellow addicts, we are only asked to live with honesty, open-mindedness and willingness to learn. Our solution to problems is the same, but what that solution leads to is up to us. Have I unlearned all the futile old ways?

Lord, may the way of life I am now practicing lead me into a more perfect union with You my Creator.

Today I will work at changing the following old habit pattern:

In the beginning, the steps were just a theory to us. A beautiful, but remote, ideal. "That's how I'm to stay clean and sober!" we might have exclaimed. Some of us probably thought we couldn't possibly work these steps. Some may have been arrogant and worked them all in three days.

The steps *are* only a theory until we work them! They can never change from a theory to reality unless we apply them. Then the results of this program become manifest in our lives. We don't get the results and then work the steps; we work the steps, then get results. Am I satisfied with the results I see?

Lord when I want results, let me know that they come from working the steps and staying close to You.

I will work especially hard on the following step today:

God help me to stay clean and sober today!

It is a truth that if we turn our lives over to God all our problems will be lifted from us. But it is easier to speak this truth, than to live it. If we only come to realize that of ourselves we are nothing, can accomplish nothing, then what choice do we have?

Through our own wills we misuse God's gifts to us, causing only pain and destruction in the end. If we turn our wills over to the Father, he will guide us with His will. We must pray, meditate, listen and believe. Have I turned it over?

God, let me live this day to the fullest and be as One with You.

Today I will turn my will in the following matters over to God:

**God help me to stay clean and sober today!**

Keep it simple. The complexities of our minds are not reality. We are not really in the mess we think we are. We can have total peace today, if we will accept today as it is, without anxieties over tomorrow or worries over yesterday. If we do what is given us to do this day, we will be doing God's will for us.

God's will is not something "out there." It is right here, right now, as close as the telephone, our children, our job or our fellow addicts. If we will keep it simple today, perhaps tomorrow we will be given something more. Do I keep it simple?

Lord, help me let go of everything that interferes with doing Your will for me today.

I will simplify my life today by:

People abusing mind-altering chemicals have been placed in three categories in relation to our program; those who neglect it entirely; those who try to put it right; and those who want it to put them right. Needless to say, those in the first two categories will do themselves little good.

If we expect to rewrite the steps or do it our own way, self-centeredness and arrogance will block us every time. But when we admit that something bigger than us is our only help, we are half-way on the road to recovery. Do I live the program as prescribed?

Lord, truly in my heart I want to know that if I can't, You can, and You will if I let You.

I will submit to the program today by:

It is difficult to see that no emotions can exist in us without our first laying the groundwork for that emotion. We always want to blame our hurt on anything or anyone else. That way all responsibility is placed outside of ourselves and we are not accountable for it.

But we ourselves are at the base of most of our troubles. We also can be at the base of our happiness. If we make conditions inside ourselves conducive to joy and happiness, they too will be a part of us. Through God, we can change conditions inside ourselves. How do I feel inside?

Lord, with Your Grace may I change conditions inside myself to make a place for good things rather than troubles.

I will improve the way I feel today by:

God help me to stay clean and sober today!

Many psychologists insist that people today don't want to be free. When we were in the middle of our addiction, we certainly had no freedom at all. We lost our freedom by the call of that fix, pill or drink. We lost our freedom because we lost our power of decision in how we wanted to behave. We had no choice.

Now we have a choice. We can never be free from our addiction, but we can be free *in* our addiction! We can never be a former alcholic or an ex-addict, but we never again have to take those chemicals and destroy our being. We have a choice of freedom and a freedom of choice. Am I free?

May I realize that if I let go and let God, I will be free.

Today I will enjoy my freedom by:

**God help me to stay clean and sober today!**

"Praying only for knowledge of His will for us and the power to carry that out." When we pray for "whatever's right," that which is best for all concerned (including ourselves) will happen. We may find ourselves given something better than we asked for.

In times of crisis, when we feel as if things must go our way or we will refuse to believe that God is good, do we stop to remember that God works in mysterious ways his wonders to perform. Nothing, not death nor disfigurement, nor any other seeming disaster is without a purpose. Accepting it as God's will brings God's grace and glory to all concerned. Have I learned acceptance?

Lord, let me understand that disasters can make clear Your purposes and that they are not punishments.

I will practice acceptance today by:

All of us have two stages that we perform on. One stage is public—what we do and what we say. The other stage is private—what we think and what we rehearse in our minds to do on the public stage. What we rehearse in our mind helps to mold our character and guide our actions.

Are we rehearsing anger, fights, and what we are going to tell that S.O.B. next time? Are we rehearsing the use of drugs, the old ways of living? If so, we are putting ourselves in danger of losing any good we have achieved.

To keep growing and building our character, we need to rehearse kindness, patience and love. We need to rehearse God consciousness in our lives. Am I growing?

May I rehearse God consciousness in all my affairs today.

Today I will seek to grow by:

When we were stoned we had only artificial seasons. We cared not how beautiful life could be around us, but only if we could get high and stay high. As we grow in awareness we are like little children discovering the world all over again.

There is more excitement around each discovery we make than there ever was in any high, and it is real and cannot be taken from us. Am I rediscovering the world around me?

Lord, I pray that I will continue to discover all that You have put here for me.

I will look for the beauty today in:

With our new outlook on life, we find that we are facing new situations with confidence. But are we mistaking confidence for faith? Confidence is from the physical world and faith is from God.

When trials and disasters arise, we realize how powerless we are and our confidence crumbles. Only faith can rescue us. Let us examine ourselves and see whether we are relying on confidence or faith. Do I have enough faith?

God, increase my faith and keep me from mistaking confidence for faith, so that I may face life's trials with courage from You.

I will seek deeper faith today by:

Our ideal, staying clean and sober, is good. But our ideal has to be made practical and must be put to work. At the spiritual level our ideal is very clear, but at the practical level many of us lack commitment to it. Unfortunately, some of us may even believe that the program won't work for us.

Such a belief only serves to give us an excuse not to build our ideals into reality. Fear and selfishness always stand in our way. We must work hard to hold to our ideals when lack of belief, fear and selfishness stand in our way. Do I practice my ideals?

Lord, help my unbelief so that I may understand you on a practical level as well as on a spiritual level.

The ideals I will practice today are:

Each of us is a struggling soul. It seems we had to struggle through our addictions before we found this program. And each struggling soul must eventually face the realities of life. If we face the trials of life alone we must fall.

But if we make our will one with the Divine Will in the third step, nothing will be too much to bear. After taking this step, we will realize that we are one with God and need struggle alone no longer. Am I still struggling alone?

May I attune my will to the Will of the Father; may I turn my life over to Him.

Today I will seek God's help in my struggles by:

Commonplace acts of kindness are a way to God even more than grand and glorious acts. It is the everyday observance of what we know to be right that will lead us to our Father. We must measure up to that which we know will sustain us in our drug-free life.

With our smiles, friendly words, and patience during trying times, we will slowly climb the steps of growth. It is harder to do the little things everyday than to shine forth in a crisis—and nothing that we do or don't do goes unnoticed by our Higher Power. Do I tend to the little things every day?

Lord, let me find satisfaction in doing the simple, common tasks.

The little things I will tend to today are:

Are we falling subject to the "if onlys?" ("if only I had more money," "if only I were more attractive," "if only my parents had listened to Dr. Spock," etc.). The "if onlys" will get us absolutely nowhere. What do we have to work with today?

Do we remember that we are fortunate just to be alive? When we are willing to learn, God will surely disclose many things to us. But when we dwell in the "if onlys," we get stuck in yesterday. What we have to work with today are today's tools, and if we use them we will have no need for the "if onlys." Do I use the tools I have today?

God show me today's tools and make me willing to use them.

The tools I will use today are:

God help me to stay clean and sober today!

The question is often asked, "How does the program work?" The HOW of this program is Honesty, Open-mindedness and Willingness. Often we have to pray for willingness; sometimes we even have to pray to be willing to be willing!

We have very stubborn wills, but surrendered on a daily basis, they can accomplish much good for us and for others. Surely those who say, "I will, I will," and don't, are not as close to the heart of God as those who say, "I will not," but do! Am I really willing?

God, help me realize that to accomplish Your Will for me today, in however small a way, I must let go of my own conflicting will.

I will practice willingness today by:

God help me to stay clean and sober today!

## April 21 Reflecting Kindness and Love

Alcoholics and addicts can be very sensitive to the remarks of friends and loved ones because they seem to be so unkind to them. But if we alcoholics and addicts examine ourselves, we will see that it is we who are out of tune. We may have turned from the Light and are probably not working our programs.

What we see in others is only a reflection of what is within ourselves. When we come to understand that living today means turning to the Source of Light, then our reflection will be a beautiful one of kindness and love. What does my reflection look like?

Lord, allow me to reflect the true nature of Your Divine Love.

Today I will reflect kindness and love by:

It really does not matter how much we used or drank. The important thing is what was it doing to us? How was it affecting our lives? The biggest cop-out for addictive people has always been, "I'm not using as much as the next guy, so maybe I'm not chemically dependent."

We didn't want to admit what using was doing to our lives, our families, our friends and ourselves. It literally destroyed us in all areas. But now we have a chance to repair the damage. If we are willing to face ourselves and give all to God, we can truly restore our lives. Do I see clearly the destruction my using caused?

Lord, help me today to face what I really am and to stop using excuses to avoid the task of learning.

I will repair the damage caused by my using today by:

God help me to stay clean and sober today!

When you feel the urge to take, think the drink, ponder the pill and figure the fix all the way through. This is an important step in staying away from the first one. Sometimes we are confronted with situations in which it seems we have no defense against the first one. In a panic, we then ask, "What did my fellow addicts say to do?"

*Think it through,* to its logical conclusion. For us it can mean nothing but wreckage and despair. And with such thought to the consequences, we will gain the courage to turn the urge away. Do I know how to overcome the urge?

Lord, when my defenses are down, grant me the presence of mind to think the drugs all the way through.

If I feel the urge today, the consequences I will reflect on are:

For many of us, chemicals were an escape from the trials of the world. We deeply resented all the trials of the world, and earnestly sought escape. Being clean and sober now, all of our problems do not disappear. But we now have an opportunity to deal with them constructively.

If we do not take that first pill, drink or fix, our problems can be solved, and stumbling blocks can become stepping stones to the good life. Have I learned how to handle daily problems?

Lord, I pray that I do not try to escape daily problems, but face them with You and walk more in Your ways.

I will deal effectively with my problems today by:

Everything is grounded in awareness. While drinking or shooting we tried to dull our awareness. Possibly we used some drugs with the excuse that we were heightening our awareness. But in every way we ended up with little awareness of anything but pain. We were turned off.

Communication is also based on awareness. We make others aware of ourselves and are made aware of those around us. Without communication with God there is no awareness of God working in our lives. If we want to turn on to life, we can begin by turning on to God. Am I turned on?

God, let me turn on with You, so that I may be aware of Your presence in my life.

Today I will turn on by:

This Universe can be so beautiful, but that doesn't mean the Universe owes us a living. We can't ask for results before we put forth the effort. We can't be using mind altering chemicals and say we'll straighten up when we get a job. It doesn't work that way.

We have to be willing to do what it takes to straighten up first, and then we will get the benefits. We have to be willing to do it His way, not ours. Am I willing to do what it takes?

Father, grant me the willingness to put forth the effort today, to work the steps, to stay sober and clean.

I will do what it takes today to:

We have to know in our own hearts that we are building a better us. It requires that we apply our highest ideals and efforts. The way we apply these is by turning our lives over to God. He will guide us if we sincerely ask.

As we develop our personalities, we find that our contribution to life is much more than just staying away from mind altering chemicals. We love and help others, by thinking, feeling and acting maturely in all situations. Am I developing into a better person?

Lord, I pray that I may realize my new life is not just coming from the past, but developing into the future.

Today my plan for self-development is:

God help me to stay clean and sober today!

So often we want to puff up our egos, saying "I'm overcoming this terrible addiction so I must have a great deal of wisdom." It is not in self or in our own wisdom that we overcome our addiction. It is through the guidance and love of our Father in Heaven that we find hope.

If we continue to remember who and what we are and where our hope came from, we can grow closer and closer to God. If we forget these basics and operate from our own egos, we grow closer to the streets and to despair. Is my ego deflated?

I pray that I glory in God, not in self and intellectual "wisdom."

I will deflate my ego today by:

One thing which is harmful to our spiritual progress is the lack of a forgiving spirit. In being unforgiving we cause resentment, which is always dangerous to our new way of life.

Our Lord has told us that if we forgive, then we will be forgiven; but that if we do not forgive, we will not experience forgiveness. So aren't we just hurting ourselves by not forgiving others? Am I forgiving?

Lord, I pray that I may forgive each person whom I need to forgive today.

Today I will forgive:

Sometimes it seems like we need to have the stubborn places in our minds pounded on with a sledge hammer in order to reset our thinking. We are not flabby minded people! We have to learn to accept the *good* without falling apart as well as accepting the bad.

Our old reasons for doing or not doing some things no longer work, no longer make sense. Yet, many of the things that we were formerly convinced were right or wrong are still right or wrong for us. Only our reasons for believing so have changed. Has my thinking changed?

Father, make me willing to not have to understand everything anymore, if waiting to understand prevents my working the program today.

I will examine my thinking today about:

God help me to stay clean and sober today!

Our fellowship tells us to take care of ourselves first, that life and program come before anyone or anything else. But it is easy to confuse this with narcissism. Taking care of ourself does not mean being selfish, wantonly hurting for the sake of our own needs. What is intended is for us to learn to love and care for ourselves, for we are the objects of our own feelings and attitudes.

Fromm says that if an individual is able to love productively, he loves himself too; if he can love *only* others he cannot love at all. Consequently, we need to love and care for ourselves to be able to love others. Have I learned to love myself?

Lord, let me learn to love myself so that I may love You and others.

Today I will seek to improve my feelings about myself by:

It is only through countless other people who searched for a solution that we have been given so much help in our addiction. If others hadn't searched and found, who would have been there to offer us a helping hand? The ones who come after us can help us best by letting us help them.

And the very newest people seeking freedom from their addiction are a constant reminder and a source of joy to us. We're together on this path and we should never forget to be grateful for our fellow addicts. Do I help others?

Lord, let me always be grateful for the ones who have helped me and let me offer my hand to others.

Today I will help my fellow addicts by:

The inventory is used to disclose our character defects. By evaluating why we resented others our self-centeredness jumps right out at us. We tried in the past to set up situations that were beneficial only to ourselves. Then, when things did not go our way, we started resenting people, places and things.

It is that kind of self-centeredness that nearly killed us, but we persisted in spite of it all. If we apply that same persistence to finding and removing our character defects, our self-centeredness will diminish and make way for the progress and growth promised to us all. Am I rid of self-centeredness?

God, steady me so that I am able to do my full stint of work today as well as I can.

Today I will forget myself by helping:

God help me to stay clean and sober today!

Love is the answer to our problem. For a thousand ages we have reached and reached for God. He has been there, here, in all of every moment—available, willing, desiring, yearning to share His love. In sobriety and cleanness we are at the very beginning, finally admitting that alone we are powerless.

But with love, with God, all things can be changed. Love seems to be such a hard, hard lesson to learn! We deny love, deprive each other of love that should be expressed. Each expression of love is a Divine thing, for "God is Love." Do I show my love for others?

Lord, help me to recognize within myself as well as all men a true and loving God, and help me learn to express Him.

I will express the love within me today by:

## May 5 Cunning, Baffling and Powerful

We say that mind altering chemicals are cunning, baffling, and powerful. There are a number of subtle ways in which we try to set ourselves up to use again. If we preferred one drug we might try to convince ourselves that it is OK to use a different one. Some of us continue to hang around our using "friends" until we just can't hold out any longer.

There are many insidious plans that we devise so that we can go back to using and say, "well, I just didn't know it was so dangerous." We know these things are dangerous, and continuing to set ourselves up will only succeed in destroying our program. Have I stopped setting myself up?

Lord, look out for my fool self when I'm not capable of doing so.

Today I will be on guard by:

We are servants of our groups, never authorities or presidents. Responsibilities should be shared by all of us doing God's work. When any of us takes on more than we can handle, the outcome is martyrdom or simply dropping out. These are not natural outcomes of God's work. When we share of ourselves, in the true spirit of service, we will never fall victim to martyrdom or dropping out.

If we truly carry the spirit of humility, picking up ash trays and washing dishes will never be too low a task for us. And being a committee member will never be too exalted a task for us. Is humility a part of me?

Lord, show me how to serve, in any capacity, for my group today.

I will practice humility in serving my brothers today by:

For most of us staying straight was always a life and death matter. For some it took longer for this realization to sink in than for others. But the highlight of our insanity was trying to prove that we were different. We wanted to prove that somehow we could get out of the work that was required. We tried to prove that somehow this program wasn't the only way out for us.

We tried all this while our lives layed on the line. Our insanity does run to the extreme at times, and nothing short of a spiritual awakening and guidance from our Higher Power will restore our sanity. Is my insanity behind me?

Lord, teach me how I can return to sanity: teach me how to live in a drug-free world.

Today I will work the program in the following ways:

**God help me to stay clean and sober today!**

We need to stick to the basics or we lose sight of who we are and where we came from. We are not perfect, spiritual giants. We are drunks, junkies and pill heads who have found a solution to our living problem. It is a practical solution to an impractical life style.

And if we forget the basics, where we came from, working the steps and attending meetings, then we are exposed to many sorts of lofty ideals and unrealistic illusions. These can get in the way of our recovery. Do I keep it simple?

Lord, help me to keep it simple and remember the basics.

I will stick to the basics today by:

If we are asked for information or spiritual guidance, we should be sure that we have it before we try to give it away. We shouldn't assume that just because we are clean and sober anything we suggest is correct. There is nothing degrading about saying, "I don't know," or suggesting a more appropriate source of help.

It takes great courage to recognize and admit our limitations. When we ask for guidance in helping others, we should listen for that "still small voice within" to tell us whether to go on or to hold back. Do I know my limitations?

God, make my directions so clear that I will be of real service to You and Your children.

Today I will seek spiritual guidance in helping others by:

God help me to stay clean and sober today!

The relation of our souls to the Divine Spirit is so pure that it is vain to think that we can separate it from any of our being. When God speaks in our life, He speaks to all of our life. There isn't one part that belongs to our Higher Power, and other parts that belong to a job, family, friends, interests and so on.

Our relationship to our Creator is sacred, and so all of our life is sacred. God loves beyond all things, and His love and purity enter into all our life. We need but recognize and live by this. How do I relate to God?

God, I know that you see me, hear me, and know all my thoughts and desires, even the innermost secrets of my heart!

I will improve my relationship with my Higher Power today by:

God help me to stay clean and sober today!

We often find it difficult to make simple decisions in our everyday lives. The major decisions are sometimes easier to make than are the simple ones. We must ask for guidance on all issues that we need help with, simple or complex.

God, as we understand Him, will help us see life situations with increasing clarity, as they really are. Daily decisions will become easier to make, and everyday irritations will cease to paralyze our thinking. Have I conquered indecision?

Lord, I pray that I may gain more of Your consciousness and that I may turn everyday indecisiveness over to You.

Today I will be decisive about:

Success and happiness in working our program are subjective matters. They have to be. Personal satisfaction or success in anything depends on how the individual perceives it for himself. Members will comment on what makes for happiness or success in the program, but we can only measure it for ourselves. To judge our success by someone else's standards is not being true to ourselves.

Some judge success in terms of the material, some in terms of the body, others in terms of emotional adjustments or spiritual or mental growth. It depends on us and our Higher Power, not on family, friends or therapists. Our success is measured by ourselves alone. How do I measure my success?

God, grant that today all my thoughts, words, actions, and successes will be directed by Your powerful assistance.

I will examine my standards today by:

If we would be miserable, let us think only of ourselves. "I'm not getting what I want—that person doesn't treat me right—I don't deserve to have misfortunes." It's easy to be miserable. But if we would have happiness, let us be a friend to someone.

Let us share our experience, strength and hope. If we would know the love of God, let us show love to those who seek it. God will always bring contentment and joy to those of us who choose to walk and talk with Him. Do I bring happiness to others?

Lord, let me know that to seek redemption I have to be led by Your Spirit, today and everyday.

Today I will be a friend to:

We all know that our skills will deteriorate in any area without practice. To stay drug-free is a skill that we develop through practice. We need to determine what our skills are in working our program. How do we keep ourselves drug-free?

Do we pray? Do we take daily inventory? Do we admit when we're wrong? Do we work with others? If not . . . we are getting complacent and complacency will erode our skills. And if we're deprived of our skills, soon we will be deprived of our sobriety and cleanness. Do I practice the steps daily?

God, help me to develop the skills necessary to keep me clean and sober today.

I will avoid complacency today by action in the following ways:

Heroic qualities, shining beauty, and natural talents that seem to impress most of society are but little in comparison to our all important twelfth step work. Twelfth step work brings our every faculty, intuition and gift into play, but in very different ways than those of the "professional."

Through God we acquire the power to sooth, to empathize, to suggest, to endure, to relate and to love. These daily encounters far outweigh the work of the statesman or hero. It is by this giving that our program exists and is perpetuated. Do I give it away every day?

Lord, reveal to me the joy of being loving and self-sacrificing.

Today I will practice giving by:

There is an important precept in the awareness that we *are* alcoholic and addicts and *not* ex-alcoholics and ex-addicts. We accept the fact that we have a chronic illness, and no amount of "discipline" or magic cures are going to make us normal again.

It is when we delude ourselves about being able to handle "just a little," that we start rationalizing like crazy. If we say, "I used to be a drug addict or an alcoholic," then we are inferring we can drink or take and be in control. That is the route to despair, disgust and death for us. Do I accept being incurable?

Lord, let me never forget who I am, what I am and where my salvation lies.

I will practice acceptance today by:

The toxin of fatigue and hunger has been well demonstrated by us addicted to mind altering chemicals. And in the same way the poisons fermented by resentment and temper have been demonstrated by us. Ironically, our outbursts often occur over non-essentials. And that is a real killer for us.

Our panic over misfortune, needless fears and emotional turmoils is merely a bad habit. When we air our minds spiritually and let our Creator flow through, it is possible to achieve more comfortable habits of patience, tolerance and love. Have I stopped overreacting?

May my mind be ventilated by the Spirit so that my soul may be fresh and clean.

Today I will deal with negative emotions constructively by:

God help me to stay clean and sober today!

Sometimes we feel as if we have to find our way through a labyrinth of old ideas. We have to keep it simple. Stick to the things that work. Mountains are made to establish an equilibrium in the universe. Before they have taken visible form, their being is contained in the stresses within the earth.

In a very like way, when we are being changed, before the change is visible in us, we feel it as stress. If we continue to work the steps, work with others and attend meetings, we will one day find something in us has changed for the better. Have I learned to handle stress?

Lord, help keep the vision before me of that which I would be; help to keep me faithful during the stressful times.

I will deal with stress effectively today by:

**God help me to stay clean and sober today!**

Harmony in our lives is produced by living according to principle. This principle is always Divine principle and is the way that produces happiness for us. Our happiness is destroyed by our own mistakes.

But principles are not destroyed by our mistakes. After recognizing our mistakes, we need only reapply the principles we have learned and harmony will be returned to us. Is my life full of harmony?

God, please help me to recognize and live according to principle.

Today I will apply my principles by:

In order to stay away from mind altering chemicals we must try to tune in to the One. However, we cannot necessarily go by someone else's attunement. The attunement on any radio may be near to the point of another, but even if they are side by side it is not exactly the same.

Each of us must tune in according to his own development. Even as our stories of the past will not be exactly like one another, neither will our attunement to our Higher Power be precisely the same. Have I found my proper attunement to God?

I pray that I may find my own attunement to God, for I am God's child. I must have my own personal relationship with Him, not another's.

Today I will tune in to God by:

Life is growth. Never can we fully channel blessings to others unless we experience and live through the same things we would help others with. If we truly know the pain and misery of chemical addiction, and desire to change, then we have grown.

With our new understanding we can surely plant the seeds for our brothers still out there. As others have helped us to grow, we can turn around and help others to grow and experience God's love. Am I still growing?

Lord, may I know that it is through Your love that I grow, and by sharing Your love with others that they grow.

Today I will share my growth with:

There are tragic experiences in our lives, even clean and sober. There often seems to be no logical or compassionate answer. The unexplained misery of the faithful sometimes seems so cruel that we wonder how God can do this to His children. We do *not* know the answers.

We know that our problems are of our own making, but what about the acts of God? It is said that our greatest burdens are also our greatest gifts. The most tragic experiences can help us really learn to be of service and at one with our Creator. Can I accept tragedy?

**I can't, God can, and He will if I let Him.**

**I will practice acceptance today by:**

**God help me to stay clean and sober today!**

"If you don't like what you hear at this meeting, leave it here," is a common saying in our program. Many people do just that, they leave *everything* at the meetings. Most of us did not get better by listening to what we wanted to hear.

What helped us was listening to things we didn't like, such as "Work steps, you're not better than anyone else," and, "Don't take the first fix, pill or drink." The hard work, things we don't like, are usually the very things that make it possible for us to arrest our disease. Do I listen to what I need to hear?

God, grant me the courage to listen to the hard things and apply them in my program today.

Today I will listen to:

"I can't be a drug addict or an alcoholic—because I can quit anytime, because I only use weekends, because I never drink anything but beer or use anything but grass, because I am too young." Many times we have heard these excuses or perhaps we used them ourselves. But ignorance and stubbornness can kill us.

Only honest acceptance of the truth can free us from our addiction. Many old timers are fond of saying that people don't get to this program by mistake. If we are reading this page today, let's hope all these excuses are behind us. Have I stopped denying it?

God grant me the courage to leave the excuses behind and accept the truth about myself today.

I will accept my addiction today by:

Just for Today. Live in the Now. It's a 24-hour program. Ask for sobriety and cleanness each day upon arising. Take a daily inventory.

Such expressions show that the ones before us considered the 24-hour concept pretty important. Do we know that this is true? Do I practice living a day at a time?

God, grant me the patience to live in today and give me the insight for a greater tomorrow.

Today I will work at living in the now by:

There are some days in this program that are just "hanging on" days. Somehow we break contact with our Higher Power and we feel right about nothing. God loves us always—but somehow we have lost contact. So we have to know that it will get better if we do the right things.

Pray. Meditate. Keep in touch with fellow addicts. Work the steps. Call your sponsor. Then just hang on. Time will take away most of our greatest fears, but we should expect and be prepared for some days of just "hanging on." Do I have something to hang on to?

Father, when I "hang on," let me hang on to the love You have for me always.

I will improve my hold on sobriety today by:

We are filled with questions and desire so many answers that aren't available to us. The only real answers will be given by the Giver of opportunities as we are able to handle them, not before. If we try to manufacture our own answers we will be operating on self-will, and we will create even more questions.

Our associations, our desires and our answers are given and guided by our Higher Power–provided we have kept close enough to Him to be prepared and ready for such answers. Am I willing to wait for the right answers?

Not my will but Thine, O Lord, be done in and through me.

Today I will prepare myself for answers to my problems by:

**God help me to stay clean and sober today!**

While we search for ourselves in the twelve steps we often forget to be gut-level honest. We have said for a long time, "Sure I'm aware of my defects." But we don't always face our newly revealed defects.

As we seek honesty from the God of our understanding, we have to ask Him for insight so that our buried defects can be revealed. It is only through continuing honesty that we can maintain continuing sobriety and cleanness. Am I honest with myself?

Lord, I pray that from day to day I can honestly turn over my faults and fears to You.

I will cultivate self-honesty today by:

People say that you can always tell a room full of recovering addicts because the room is filled with smoke, everyone has coffee, and everyone is talking at the same time. This is a humorous aspect of our fellowship and sharing. But underneath it is serious business.

The program, slogans and suggestions are talked to death so that no one can possibly miss any aspect of recovery. Daily problems of individuals are hashed out by anyone within hearing distance—and it works! Our big mouths that kept us sick for so long are now flapping to keep us well.

So our smoke filled, coffee filled and talk filled clubs, meetings, and social gatherings are the basis for a lot more than laughter—they portray a major part of our recovery. Do I contribute to the fellowship?

Lord, show me what I can contribute to the social aspect of someone's recovery today.

Today I will participate in the fellow ship by:

God help me to stay clean and sober today!

Planning our own speech during a discussion meeting is not conducive to listening. If we spend the major part of any meeting planning our own words of wisdom, how are we going to hear?

Sometime, somewhere, something we've heard in a meeting may come to mind just when we need it. But if we sit at meetings engrossed in our own thoughts, the suggestions we may need in times of danger will not be there. Do I pay attention at meetings?

Lord, help me to open my ears and close my mouth just a little more today.

I will avoid preoccupation today by:

God's will for us is always better than our will for ourselves. However, we can never discover this unless we let go enough to be willing to venture into the new areas we are being led into. All growth comes at the expense of letting go of old ideas. Our old ideas only fit our drug world.

Each day, well lived, moves us closer to what we are seeking. We have to learn new ways of being less selfish and more willing to use what we have today, for today's good, Am I living today well?

Father, help me to want Your will for me today, and to know that it is what I really want for myself.

Today I will live well by:

We have to study ourselves so that we truly know we are on God's path. We need to be positive, but not rigid. All positive points can become handicaps if we apply them wrongly. Honesty, justice, patience, love and kindness are the ways to God.

However, honesty applied wrongly turns into brutal frankness; justice into cold facts; patience into irritable silence; love into sullen possessiveness; and kindness into a gooey habit. In studying ourselves, we should see that we have not misapplied our virtues so they have become destructive. Do I practice virtue constructively?

Lord, in my pursuit of virtue, help me not be so zealous that virtues turn into defects.

Today I will practice virtue humbly by:

God help me to stay clean and sober today!

Absolute statements are almost always wrong. "All blacks are this; all whites are that; all addicts are (whatever); no straight person ever understands (whatever)." But here's one that holds up under examination: "We are all stumbling human beings."

As such we should cultivate understanding to the best of our ability. Without understanding, we do not grant others their right to be "human!" Do I overlook the shortcomings of others?

Whenever I say "Our Father," make me aware that calling You Father makes every man my brother and every woman my sister.

I will seek greater understanding of my fellows today by:

**God help me to stay clean and sober today!**

Many of us used to think, "God hates this" and "God hates that," about ourselves or others. But God, as we've come to know Him, doesn't "hate" at all. He accepts and loves us no matter how we have lived. He understands that we are capable of changing only to the extent that we are given the light and the strength from Him to do so.

We only come to know God in this way as we begin to accept ourselves and others. The ability to accept ourselves in growing measure is a gift from God, as we build upon the strong, valuable parts of ourselves. Have I learned to accept myself?

Father, help me to be open-minded about what You are like; help me to be willing to see myself in a new way.

Today I will work on self-acceptance by:

Such egos we possess! Even when talking about our past, it often amounts to something close to bragging. We build up our stories, take pride in the amount of drugs we used and the way we used them, and often try to top the other guy's drug-alog. It sometimes looks like we were really saying, "See how good I am, I don't do those things anymore."

Then we confidently pat ourselves on the back for not doing what we shouldn't have been doing in the first place! But now that we have a choice in our behavior, trying to impress others with our past doesn't show a loving, kind person–it shows a braggadocio. Am I a story teller?

Lord, keep me from glorifying my story to impress myself and others.

I will keep my story straight today by mentioning:

**God help me to stay clean and sober today!**

It is very easy, when talking in general terms, to sweep away our past and say we want forgiveness and understanding of the nature of our wrongs. But this should not be confused with the fourth step. In the fourth step we aren't asked to generalize or simplify the nature of our wrongs. We are asked to individualize every situation. When we put these things on a personal level, we begin to see how difficult the inventory steps are.

The willingness to go on often has to be prayed for. But as we are willing, God provides the opportunities for working the steps. Being willing to be specific may be the hardest thing we have ever had to do. But seeing the living miracles around us testifies to the fact that the rewards are great. Have I stopped generalizing about my defects?

Lord, please show me the value of working the steps specifically, not generally.

Today I will be specific about the following specific defects:

**God help me to stay clean and sober today!**

The pity game, if we are playing it, is hard to reverse. Our mixed up emotions and wrecked lives can easily elicit pity from those who try to help us. Besides the real damage in our lives, we sometimes exaggerate and even produce a few goodies to get more pity if we need it. In our program we share feelings because we've been there. But we know how destructive pity is.

When we say, "this too shall pass," we are not giving our fellows the brush-off. We are saying, "Don't wallow in self-pity, it's a killer. we've all experienced similar situations. God loves you and it *will* pass!" Have I stopped pitying myself?

Lord, help me to remember that pity leads to self-pity, and I want to stop that game.

Today I will avoid self-pity by:

Most of us have had spiritual experiences and spiritual awakenings as a result of this program. Some have had visions while others have heard voices. Some people had these when they first arrived, some before they arrived, others some years after they arrived. But we need not hear a voice booming from the heavens saying, "You are a damn junkie—straighten up!" before we come to realize our powerlessness.

The spiritual experience most of us have is a quiet realization that God has given us our lives. What greater, more wonderful experience can we ask for? Have I had a spiritual awakening?

Lord, thank You for the gift of my life.

I will show how spiritually alive I am today by:

Why do they have to suffer? Why is it that we have found and accepted this fellowship while some seem incapable or have to experience untold hardships before they can accept? Many times our hearts have ached at the seeming failure of twelfth step work.

We watch others suffer needlessly and we watch some die. We watch others repeatedly slip and our hearts cry out to them. Those of us who make it must never give up on the ones who don't... they need us desperately and we need them. If truly they can't make it, they are in God's hands and he loves them all. Do I let the results of twelfth step work with God?

All God's children are in His hands. Thank You for the way You are holding me!

Today I will try to help a slipper by:

When people constantly abuse alcohol and drugs, it seems that only a miracle can take them out of the depths of despair. It is a miracle when this happens. But it is not necessary to have a great vision or experience, if we just do each task asked of us daily.

Amidst all the turmoil of the day, if we exercise patience, faith and love, we will have the greatest opportunity to gain a clean, joyful life. If we practice the things of the spirit, we will become our own living miracles. Am I living spiritually?

Lord, day by day, may I see more of Your spirit in what I do in the miracle of life.

I will practice spiritual living today by:

God help me to stay clean and sober today!

It is not unusual for us to say that we have gained everything from this program in spite of ourselves. We get in our own way, blocking ourselves from our Father and fellow addicts. We do stupid things in the beginning, like going to bars—pot parties—deliberately setting ourselves up to take that first fix, pill or drink.

But even when we are so stupid, God still holds out His hand. We still have the choice to pray and ask His help. Even with our stupid moments, in spite of ourselves, God will help if we but ask. Have I stopped being stupid?

Father, save me from myself—protect me from the disaster of my own thinking.

Today I will try to stay out of my own way by:

Sometimes people feel more qualified as members of our program because it seems they have suffered more on the skids or in the slums. But whatever end of the physical spectrum we may have been on, an addict is an addict.

We can view it this way: when a man is on the skids, with holes in his pants, no shoes and hungry, he may be able to kid himself that a new pair of pants, some shoes and a juicy steak will make him happy.

However, when a person is well off and has all his physical comforts and is still miserable, there is no doubt in his mind that he is *truly* miserable. Do I recognize that skid row is a state of mind?

God, it is not my place to judge–show me that pain is pain and I don't know the degrees for anyone.

I will help those who still suffer today by:

**God help me to stay clean and sober today!**

We're not exactly garden variety personalities. We constantly demand and require attention and would die if we discovered we were not the center of a few lives. Often we want reassurances that we are coming across as the generous, honorable people we are striving to become. But we soon realize that our character defects and self-centeredness still plague us.

When we occasionally get a glimpse of how others truly see us, it is a dreadful and painful experience. Were it not for the loving attitude of our fellow addicts, many of us could not endure it. But the growth process is worth the pain as we find out we are gradually becoming the generous, honorable people that we want to be. Am I rid of my defects?

As the pain produces growth, I thank You, Lord, for the love that shines from my fellow addicts.

Today I will work on self-centeredness by:

Making our lives into a series of rainbows is an all-out effort to put the best into everything we do. The rainbow is the glow that crowns our best effort to do a job, any job. It takes more time and more energy, but the rewards for this are high. In sobriety and cleanness it may be the difference between peace of mind and confusion.

Often the fear of failure keeps us from putting everything we have into living. This way we prepare our excuse in advance, "I wasn't really trying." The more we give to anything, the more we have to give, and the more rainbows we create in our lives. Do I always exert my best efforts?

Teach me to give, today, everything I am capable of.

I will try my best today, without fear, to:

Meetings are not just something we attend in our spare time. They are a way of finding answers, support and maintenance. We may have many problems, financial, legal and emotional. And when we ask someone for advice they say "Go to a meeting."

It's crazy; what kind of advice is that for practical problems? But what's even crazier is that it works! For any straight person that would be silly and impractical, but for us it is the beginning of solutions. Meetings are not spare time, but important life time. Do I get the most out of meetings?

God grant me faith in our fellowship.

Today I will go to the meeting at:

We often feel that we are so unique that no person or group can help us or understand us. We feel alone and different. But any differences from one another can be reconciled by emphasizing the purpose which is common to all. For us it is learning to live a drug-free life by reunion in consciousness with our Divine Source.

God would not let us be alone if we would but recognize His love in our brothers. Are we looking for what we have in common or are we forcing ourselves to be alone and different? Do I realize that our common purpose outweighs all differences?

May I see the love of God shining through my brothers that I may never have to be alone.

I will overlook all differences today in:

**God help me to stay clean and sober today!**

Our personality "types" don't differ much from the rest of society, except that we couldn't stop abusing mind-altering chemicals. We were the power people, intellectuals, lives of the party, the spenders, the flower children, the parent figures, the experts, revolutionists, or anything else that seemed to get us our way. The masks we wore were defenses, and because of our defenses we were only living partially.

By working the program our defenses cease to be so important to us. Step by step we become full people, living full lives, no longer bound to society, defenses, or mind-altering chemicals. Then we can enjoy living rather than just masquerading. Have I stopped wearing masks?

Lord, deliver me from a partial existence by my own frailty, and let me live fully through Your divine will.

Today I will drop my defenses and be myself with:

All of us are only one drink, pill or fix away from a drunk. But we should never discount the credibility that increases steadily by continuance in one direction. We who strive for spiritual progress over any length of time become familiar with our resistances and with our strengths.

Emerson wrote that "this kind of person increases his skill and strength and learns the favorable moments and the favorable accidents. He is his own apprentice, and more time gives a great addition of power, just as a falling body acquires momentum with every foot of the fall." Has my sobriety grown steady and strong?

Lord, may my striving for spiritual growth bring momentum and strength to my sobriety and cleanness.

I will bolster my sobriety today by:

Will is an attribute of the soul. We must realize that we can either make it one with our Maker or separate ourselves from Him. When we exercise uncontrolled self-will, things crumble before us and we more often than not find ourselves in the streets again. This is not necessary, for now we have a choice.

We can be channels through which our Higher Power flows. When we make our will one with our Maker's, we will have no trouble staying away from mind-altering chemicals. Have I turned my will over?

I pray that I will let my will be one with my Maker. I pray that I will walk with Him today.

Today I will restrain my self-will by:

Many times we ask God for "gifts" of spiritual assets, but we leave out the work involved in acquiring these. To be strong, we must learn to carry burdens; to gain patience, we must learn to work under stress; to follow God's will, we must be willing to squelch our own when it conflicts with His.

If we would not be afraid, we must practice faith in the presence of fear; if we would be right, we must learn to admit our wrongs; if we would be loved, we must learn to be loving. The footwork is up to us, God presents the opportunities for us to grow. Do I do my part?

Let my eyes see Your gracious hand in all Your works and help me rejoice in Your creations.

I will do the footwork necessary today to:

God help me to stay clean and sober today!

Beauty is simply reality seen through the eyes of love. We should learn to see the sentences and paragraphs of love made visible to us in each day. On loving days, the leaves are greener, the sky is bluer.

We can see beauty even amid squalor if we look closely, for the brilliance of yellows and the cheerfulness of reds cannot be confined to any limited locations.

We can see love in the wrinkles of faces and in the small, heroic acts of trying human beings which we can observe on any day. Do I realize that beauty lies in the eyes of the beholder?

Father, let me notice how things look on the days I am loving, so that I may have a color photo to look at on gray days.

Today I will look for all the beauty in:

We reach a point in this program where one trying incident doesn't have to ruin our whole day. We reach a point where we don't have to be strung out on emotional binges anymore. We eventually learn to take each day with everything in it. We learn to take today with humor, with acceptance, and with love.

This is not to say we become doormats to be used as anyone chooses. It just means we're not going to complicate existing situations with emotional excesses. Just for today, let's leave all the trials and complications for our Higher Power to handle. Have I learned to avoid emotional binges?

When I start to feel the pressure of today's tribulations let me know that God can handle anything.

My plan for handling problems today is:

**God help me to stay clean and sober today!**

Most of us described ourselves as loners when we came into the program. Some of us had divided the world into people who hated us and people who didn't like us very much! Others of us experienced the miserable feeling of being alone even though people liked us.

We never have to be alone again. Those walls we built around ourselves gradually come down as we stay sober and clean. Have I stopped being a loner?

Lord, help me realize that I need never be alone again.

I will avoid loneliness today by:

Let us not make haste and demand our perfection all at once. To try to gain it all at once will only blind us. If we are impatient, it is impossible to work a daily program, but in exercising patience we learn to recognize our daily opportunities to grow.

Our new relationship with the Divine cannot be acquired overnight. It is worth waiting, striving, and working to develop this relationship. Let us not go too fast, but count each day as an opportunity. Have I learned patience?

Father, I pray that I meet each day with patience as an opportunity to grow closer to You.

Today I will be patient about:

Because we are recovering addicts there is an intuitive understanding between the clean addict and the new member. We know the games we've played for so long and recognize newcomers' first attempts to play these games too. The newcomer is not asked what he is thinking, he is told what he is thinking! We don't have to trap a new member into lies–we tell him the lies he is about to tell.

In the beginning we start to get honest because we hardly have a choice. Thus we give up on the game playing because there are no more tricks left in the bag. We can be grateful for our intuitiveness. By being confronted by others we have to get honest–honest enough to save our lives. Have I stopped playing games?

Lord, let me be grateful for the sharp eye and the quick tongue that can halt my game playing, that I may get honest.

I will cultivate honesty today by:

God help me to stay clean and sober today!

Our incessant analyzing could mean our failure at the steps and eventually cost us our lives. It's as if we were standing in a burning fire trying to understand the principles of oxidation, and why or why not the fire might have started, before we make plans for escape.

What we need to do is get out of the fire first and try to understand later. For a long time we still stand on the fringes of our addiction and ponder on our choice to go back. Have I made a clear choice?

Lord may I learn how to relate to my Higher Power rather than my analytical mind.

Today I will stop analyzing and act in the following ways:

God help me to stay clean and sober today!

If we don't listen to drug-free members of the program, we may not hear what it takes to stay clean and sober. "Listening" is not just confined to meetings. There is lots of literature that discusses our program and how to work it more effectively.

The reading of books, magazines and pamphlets can all be considered ways of listening. It is a real gift from our fellow addicts that so much "listening" is available to us. It is wise when we first come into the program to learn to keep our mouths shut and eyes and ears open. Am I well read on the program?

Lord help me learn to "listen" in all the ways made available to me today.

I will read the following today:

Since addiction is no respecter of persons, neither should our program be a respecter of persons. Whatever our beliefs before we found this solution, we should not let them interfere with our twelfth step work. There are few enough places where people are accepted regardless of status, religion, nationality or appearance.

We all need each other in our fellowship. Whether a person is a laborer or a judge, black or white, alcoholic or addict, if he can bring you the message of cleanness and sobriety he can save your life. Am I rid of all bias?

Lord any biases that I may have carried before, let them drop when we speak of saving lives.

Today I will be totally unbiased by:

God help me to stay clean and sober today!

What good is happiness if we allow it to become complacency, and lose it? What good is our reason if we don't use it, and it becomes dull? What good is our virtue if we don't love, and it vanishes?

What good is justice if we moralize and judge, and lose our ability to be just any longer? What good is our sobriety and cleanness if we don't carry the message, and stay straight any longer? Have I stopped being complacent?

Lord help me to use the qualities that I have for Your purposes lest I should lose them from misuse.

I will take action today on:

We must understand from the very beginning that we learn to live day by day. We learn not to take that first fix, pill or drink TODAY. It is much too hard for us to bear thinking of abstaining for years or a lifetime.

But the point we most often miss is that the TODAY program applies to all areas of our life, not just abstinence. Honesty, resentment, sex, tragedy, love, all have to be dealt with on a daily basis. God expects no more of us than to do the things we are able TODAY. Am I living TODAY today?

God grant me TODAY in every area of my life.

Today I will apply TODAY to:

Being clean and sober is more, much more, than just being dry. It is a state of mind. Simply staying away from the first fix, pill or drink is not our only goal. If we are just dry and have not received the spiritual gifts, we will still have unreasonable cravings for alcohol or drugs.

But "straight" for us is a whole new way of life–not just abstinence. We try to become better people and in the process no longer *need* to take that first fix, pill or drink. This is the difference between just being dry or being clean and sober by the grace of God. Have I stopped being just dry?

Lord I am thankful that I can learn how to live, and no longer crave the very things that were destroying me.

I will cultivate my sobriety today by:

God help me to stay clean and sober today!

Those who want truth and freedom from their addiction have to make the initial effort to get it. In order to be free we must approach the solution ourselves. We must take the help and follow the indications available through God. Knowledge cannot come to us without effort on our part.

At first we seek to gain sobriety and cleanness. But later, there are greater things we need and seek in order to participate in the joys of living. It often takes months, years, even a lifetime to grasp the principles that will set us free.

Free of what? At first freedom from drugs, then freedom from fear, freedom from anything that binds us. We can be set free by starting today to seek our principles, our truth, our freedom. Am I free?

Lord set me free, set me free, set me free!

Today I will work for freedom from:

Worrying will only succeed in ruining our days, weeks, and months, and driving us nuts. It's better for us if we do not burden ourselves with conditions to be met, until the time arises. Worry kills, but labor strengthens. If we throw ourselves into helping others, we have no time to worry.

God knows what we have need of and it will be provided, so there is no need to worry. God will give us all the knowledge and power we need, as well as love and peace, if we trust wholly in Him. Why worry when we can pray. Do I let God handle all the worries?

Here, Lord, am I. Use me as a channel of Your blessing to others that I may not worry, but carry Your faith.

I will avoid all worry today by:

God help me to stay clean and sober today!

Are we truly remembering the importance and value of sharing? Sharing is not just helping the other guy, it is specifically designed to aid us. By sharing how our program is working, we can get the positive or negative feedback we need to see clearly. It is an advantage for us to know more immediately how we are doing.

We can spare ourselves unnecessary heartache if we carry our experience to the meetings for feedback. As we develop our lives, it helps to know what others are doing to develop their lives. Do I share my problems and progress with others?

Lord may I truly share what I am doing, thereby helping myself and others.

Today I will share my program with:

Holidays have always been the time when getting stoned was easiest to justify. We could use festivities and the need to escape as a handy excuse. When at first we are clean and sober we realize that on holidays we don't have to escape anymore. Now we have a choice. Then the glorious time comes when the question of escape is no longer an issue.

We no longer wake up in the morning saying, "I don't have to escape because it is a holiday." We wake up appreciating our sobriety and cleanness, and just live the day to the best of our ability. We experience no more fear of the escapes, festivities, free time or pressures. Have I overcome the need to escape?

Thank You God for this time as well as any other; thank You for Your grace.

I will avoid the need to escape today by:

Our prayers are always answered, but sometimes the answer is "No". Many times our prayers are answered in ways we can't possibly understand. How could we know the incredible plans of our Higher Power? All we can do is the best we are able to do on a daily basis. If we have faith that God can keep us clean and sober, we also need faith that God will direct every area of our lives.

There is another saying in our program that makes a lot of sense to us, "We should work every day as if everything depended on us, and pray every day as if everything depended on God." Do I pray well every day?

Lord I may not have lived up to my capabilities in the past, but I can start now with Your help.

Today I will spend at least ten minutes praying for:

There is no substitute for our program, but that doesn't exclude other forms of help. In the beginning other therapies or activities lead only to confusion. However, after a firm foundation has been established, our program can be usefully combined with other forms of aid.

Our stories are filled with other interests and mutually beneficial therapies, but they only seem to help when they work in conjunction with our program. The only danger in other forms of help is when we presume that they precede the program that saved our lives. Do I remember "First Things First"?

Lord may I not find it necessary to excuse myself out of my program, and possibly out of my sobriety and cleanness.

I will give my program priority today by:

## Being A Good Twelfth Stepper

None of us is Mr. or Ms. twelfth stepper. Twelfth stepping is one of the most important aspects of our recovery, but it can become dangerous. The danger is when we try to impress rather than carry the message, and when we get grandiose or mysterious.

It is not our power or shining personalities that aid people on our twelfth step calls. God's love and beauty shining through us provides the real help. It is our steady hands, clear minds, and God's works that others respond to. No, none of us is Mr. or Ms. twelfth stepper. We only carry the message–God delivers it. Am I a good twelfth stepper?

Lord Your work is not my power or my glory–Let me be grateful to be one of Your instruments.

Today I will carry the message truly to:

As long as anger dominates any of us, it is difficult to progress. Some of the masks that anger hides behind are gossip, slander, backstabbing, profanity, fault finding, resentment, quarrelsomeness, impatience, mockery and irritability. We are all guilty of these things, probably a little every day.

Anger is an old pattern that we need to break to make any progress. It has probably caused more grief than any of our other character defects. This program will yield little results when we are dominated by any form of anger. We shed anger by inventorying it, praying to be rid of it and practicing not to get angry. Have I removed all my masks of anger?

God help me today to practice the virtues of patience and love, for if I am loving I cannot be angry.

Today I will search out any remaining signs of anger and will:

God help me to stay clean and sober today!

We often complain about all the problems we have being clean and sober. We have bills, we want a job, we want sex, we want more clothes, and on and on. We usually are told not to worry about the problems, just work the program! It is hard to believe that these problems will solve themselves as we work our program, but they do.

We have promises in this program: freedom from fear, peace of mind, and many more. Our Higher Power will fulfill these promises provided we do the necessary footwork. But the footwork doesn't mean complaining about problems, it means working the steps. The problems will be taken care of as a result of our work. Have I stopped complaining?

Lord as I work the program, let me know in my heart that all Your promises will be fulfilled for me.

Instead of complaining, I will work on the following problems today:

**God help me to stay clean and sober today!**

Criticism is a hard thing to take. But if we would not be criticized, we should not criticize others. This does not mean that we become social vegetables, mute carrots. Expressing concern in a loving manner does not mean we are criticizing.

We are entitled to our opinions, but we are not entitled to lay traps on those around us. The sharing of our experience, strength and hope is a way to help others —not needless and biting criticism. Have I begun to share instead of criticize?

Lord let me not belittle others knowing that You are with me and everyone until the end of the earth.

Today I will praise:

Some of us have to learn to be quiet so we can hear God. "Be still and know I am the Lord." There is strength in quietness if it is developed. Mercy, also, can be found in quietness.

Mercy is a quality of strong people, even as God demonstrates a multitude of mercies to us. Many of us know the truth of the statement, "God hath tempered the winds for the shorn lamb." Do I show mercy to others?

Father, give me the strength to be merciful to my brothers and sisters, as you have been merciful to me.

Today I will show mercy to:

## Knowing Our Higher Power

A clear understanding of our Higher Power may be necessary for some, but we needn't get hung up on any image. All we have to do is become willing to believe that a source of energy outside of ourselves is going to help us toward sobriety and cleanness. Electricity works just the same after an electronics course as it does before one understands the nature of electricity.

Our Higher Power works just the same for us before we understand how He operates, too. It amounts to this simple statement: We needn't care if we understand God, we just need to believe that He understands us. Do I have complete faith in my Higher Power?

Lord show me that to understand Your ways is not as important as believing that You are present in my life, today.

Today I will apply my faith in my Higher Power by:

If we examine our lives it may become clear that we do not have much power over others, as shocking as that may seem. But often our arrogance gets so blown out of proportion that we think our actions can get someone stoned or keep him straight! Think of that!

Of such importance we are to ourselves, we begin to think that we are so with others. Seldom do we make the obvious reflection that our affairs have about as much weight with others as theirs do with us, and this is often little enough. Do I know I am able to manage no one?

Lord, help me realize that my power over others is actually very little, and protect me from my own arrogance.

If I find myself trying to manage others today, I will:

Thoreau has said, "The cost of a thing is the amount of what I will call life which is required to be exchanged for it, immediately or in the long run." The price that we paid for drug behavior was our freedom. We finally came to the realization that we had to pay too dearly in order to feel the oblivion take over. Our price became so high that we could no longer barter with mind-altering chemicals for our time and freedom. They had absolute control.

Unless we somehow wake up and pay the price for freedom (spiritual growth), we will be a slave 'til death. But by turning our lives over to God, all the liberty we need is made available to us. Am I paying a fair price for my freedom?

Lord let me be free!

Today I will pay for greater freedom by:

Today is a day of opportunity. Any experiences, good or bad, that are brought to us today can be looked upon as opportunities.

Bad experiences are not good excuses to take that first pill, fix or drink. They can be used as opportunities to grow closer to God.

As bread is food for the body, opportunities are food for the soul. Do I see all the opportunities in my daily life?

I pray that I may use every experience as an opportunity to grow closer to God.

Today I will look for opportunities by:

God help me to stay clean and sober today!

Elbert Hubbard has described paranoiacs as "people who are suffering from fatty enlargement of the ego." Paranoiacs, today, are people full of fear. Could it be that our overstuffed egos are the main cause of our fears? Paranoiacs demand attention, compliments, obedience, and anything else that will "prove" they have control over others.

We do this out of fear, and out of fear we imagine that we are being wronged, that others have it in for us, and that society is down on us. Our ego problems, connected with fear problems, cause us to act strangely and peculiarly, and often irrationally and erratically. Have I stopped being paranoid?

God help me to do my own work and not worry about controlling others.

Today I will work on ego reduction by:

The miracles in our program do not simply "rub off" at meetings. The key to sobriety and cleanness is willingness to act. Just sitting at meetings waiting for something to "rub off" is not going to produce results. So the something that we hope will "rub off" is not a miracle, but a willingness to act.

Once the willingness to do something appears, the miracles come. "Action is the Magic Word." We must not wait for the "rub off" but act as soon as possible. Have I learned to act myself into better ways?

Lord help me become willing to act so that mental, spiritual, and physical "rigor mortis" doesn't set in.

I will take action today on the following problems:

God help me to stay clean and sober today!

Practicing anything will eventually make us pretty good at it. When we were getting high we were practicing insanity, and at first it was a lot of fun. However, we got so good at insanity that we couldn't tell if we were playing or serious any longer. Whether we were straight or high, insanity seemed to take over.

Now we can practice sanity on a daily basis. With the grace of God we can get pretty good at sanity too. Have I left my insane behavior behind me?

God give me faith, that I may know sanity is possible with Your grace.

Today I will live sanely, especially in the following areas:

It is the first fix, pill or drink that gets us stoned. It is not the third or fourth one, or the second day, or the third week of using that gets us into trouble. It is the first one, the first time we take it. Until we understand this concept, we will constantly try in vain to gain control over our drug taking behavior.

For us, control no longer exists and never will. When we start thinking in terms of "well, just one won't hurt me," we are on our way back to that same pain and discouragement of a drug-induced life. Have I learned that just one is too many?

God, please keep me from the self-deception that I might gain control again.

I will avoid taking that first one today by:

We made a decision. We made a decision to try this program because all else failed. We doubted it would work, but we were desperate. This decision was made mostly on hope and a belief. Not, at first, a belief in God, but a belief in other people. If we make a decision to do whatever is necessary, then our belief grows.

It grows to a point where no power on earth can shake our foundation. And from this foundation, we can turn to others in need and give them some hope. We can precipitate in them that same belief that made our cleanness and sobriety possible. Is my belief unshakeable?

Lord, as my belief in myself and my Higher Power grows, let others in need see and gain hope from my belief.

Today I will decide to:

Sometimes we had a tendency to place people in a caste system so that we might appear superior. Alcoholics looked down on junkies; junkies looked down on speed freaks; speed freaks looked down on drug store addicts; everyone looked down on glue-sniffers. But there comes a time when "war stories" need to be set aside, and we have to pull together.

We are dealing with the lives of every one of us, and making value judgements on the severity of another's habit is a childish, dangerous game. Taking any mind-altering chemical means taking our lives in our hands. "I did more and worse than you did," kinds of games are better left to children. Have I stopped looking down on other addicts?

Lord, may I need not "prove" my illness, but know that we all have paid a heavy toll for our membership.

I will help someone addicted to another chemical today by:

God help me to stay clean and sober today!

Our spiritual experiences are valuable and exciting. But we can get carried away with "messages" from God. If spirituality does not contain reason, there is good question as to its validity. God would not have us being unreasonable, since reason is a faculty He bestowed on us.

If what we are doing is not a reasonable thing, it could easily be just another "trip." It is easy for us to get out of tune with what is real, and get carried away with "messages." If our actions don't hold up under the light of reason, we should reexamine the source of our "message." Have I learned to apply the test of reason to my actions?

Lord, I may not have good reasons for everything, but please let me be reasonable.

Today I will look at my unreasonableness about:

Being responsible to those who reach out for help doesn't mean going to extremes. Babysitting while a person continues using may not be helping him at all. Racing through the streets demanding that addicts accept our help probably does more harm than good. However, if someone truly desires help to stop using mind-altering chemicals, we have a responsibility to do all we can.

Intuitively, we know if a person is sincerely seeking help or just a shoulder to cry on. We should always carry the message, but we need not spend hours or days sitting those not yet ready to quit. Have I learned to spot those who really want help?

Lord as I apply myself in Your service, may You grant me strength and wisdom to help others.

I will fulfill my responsibility today by helping:

We're going the same way so let us go hand in hand. You help me and I'll help you. We may have some differences, but in the end we are reaching for the same goal. Rather than compete, let us work out our differences and respect each other's opinions.

But never let us withhold love as a weapon against each other. It is unnecessary for us to hurt each other, or cause suffering, or increase pain, for we are held together by the common bond of our solution. Have I learned to share in our common purpose?

Lord, show me how to be a soldier of the common good and walk hand in hand with my brother, homeward!

Today I will advance our common cause by:

Our principles and our program must apply to every area of our life. People sometimes say that they would lose their jobs or their businesses would go broke if they applied the principles to such areas. This is a bunch of garbage. If we have to lie or be hypocritical in *any* area of our life, then we are *not* applying the principles.

Once we come to realize that it is rewarding and reassuring, not threatening, to let God work through us all the time, peace of mind becomes a reality for us. And gaining peace of mind is a result of applying the principles to *all* areas of our new life. Do I practice these principles in *all* my affairs?

Lord, if any area of my life is operated without Your principles, may it be revealed to me today.

My plan for practicing these principles in *all* my affairs today is:

God help me to stay clean and sober today!

Coming into the fellowship, the newcomer may feel as if the older members are rather impolite. They tell newcomers to go back out and try some more if they haven't had enough. Older members don't pity the newcomers. They know that pity will kill, because it leads to self-pity and eventually back to the streets.

Longtimers do understand the fear and pain, but they know also that the "poor me's" will not help the recovery. So they may seem impolite and unsympathetic, but they act as they do from a loving, knowing heart. Have I stopped pitying myself and others?

Lord, when I feel as if another addict is harsh with me, may I know that he's doing what he thinks will help.

Today I will tell it like it is to:

Even though we are sick people our progress needs to be visible to us. It is important for us to know that we are getting better, or our sobriety and cleanness would mean little to us. To see improvements, knowing we are still sick, is an exciting experience.

It used to be every time something went wrong we *had* to run. Now we just *want* to run. The running feeling is still there, but now we have a choice. Later, with the grace of God, we may not even want to run. We are sick people, but we are making progress. Can I see the progress I have made?

Lord show me today's progress, and show me also that there is always room for more improvement.

I will seek to improve myself in the following ways today by:

As wonderful as our fellowship is, there is nothing irrevocable about it. Our bonds are not chains that will hold up against incessant demands and assaults. Sometimes, in our foolishness, we find it necessary to "test" our fellowship to see how much others will respond to us.

When people have had enough and realize we're playing an attention game, they frankly tell us what they think. Unfortunately, we may then judge the fellowship unworthy. But our fellowship needs as much respect and care as any other relationship. Do I respect the fellowship?

Lord, help me know Your children as You know them, and let me contribute as much as I am capable of.

Today I will show my respect for the fellowship by:

Our souls are not travelers. Just as we learned that the geographical cure did not change our addiction, we learn that location does not insure our sobriety and cleanness. If we are at all wise, we know that it is better to look for the answers in ourselves and our program, and not in a certain city, town or country.

No person, place or thing will secure our sobriety and cleanness. It is in our program, in our hearts, in the "still small voice within" that we find peace. Our soul does not need to go to glamorous places to find peace, it is within. Do I know where to look for answers?

Lord, show me that I will find peace here in my soul, not in the far off distant places that lead to dead ends.

My plan for changing myself today is:

God help me to stay clean and sober today!

We can all be as different as we like, straight or stoned, but it always amounts to the same thing in the end. We bear the consequences of our lifestyle and actions. Stoned, our consequences are pain, suffering, and grief, eventually ending up in insanity, suicide or other premature death. Clean and sober, we can have rewarding lives.

To be clean from drugs does not mean that we have to be middle class Americans. We can all find our own niche. But our niche must include patience, kindness, tolerance and love. The consequences of these will be meaningful lives that reach far beyond any previous dreams of happiness. Am I fully aware of the consequences?

Lord, let my effort for growth not be blind pleasure seeking, but in the long run yield patience, kindness, tolerance and love.

Today I will work for favorable consequences by:

An important tool to use in staying off of mind-altering chemicals is the phone. There are times when it seems nothing is going to stop us from reaching for the first fix, pill or drink.

At times like these we should call our sponsor or at least another addict—regardless of the time, day or night. We should call them before, not after, we make that move. Many are the times that a call before has saved all we have gained in the program. Do I use the phone?

Lord, may I not feel too foolish or embarrassed to use the phone when I am in real need.

Today I will call:

God help me to stay clean and sober today!

Any leader that we may have is only an instrument, whether it is a leader in the program, in our country, in a church, or any other organization. Upon the death of any of these leaders, our true Leader is never gone. If we allow the absence of a person, any person, to dim the lights from the love of God, we don't know who our real Leader is.

If we allow the absence of any person to halt our progress or what we know is right, we are not following our true Leader. Our Higher Power is our Leader, all others are only instruments in the plan of life. Do I follow my true Leader faithfully?

Lord, let me know that my Leader is always on my case; He will never be absent; only I can pull away.

I will share my faith in God today by:

No human power could have relieved our addiction. That includes our spouse, the law, the clergy, counselors, friends, or even ourselves. Through trial and error and many, many failures, we come to know that another human being is not our way to recovery. A spiritual program is our only way to recovery, and it must be based on a Power greater than ourselves.

Not only our program is spiritual, but our life must be spiritual. Dependency, expectations and living cannot be based on our fellow humans. Our life must be based on the spiritual, which is developed by our twelve steps. Have I grown up spiritually?

Lord, I pray that my life is based on Your way and not others' conceptions of right or wrong.

Today I will work on my spiritual program in the following ways:

## Following A Positive Path

There are obviously positive points to using mind-altering chemicals or so many people would not be doing it. The positive points may be fine for others, but for us they are exaggerated into negative points. Drugs make other people feel good—they bring us to oblivion. Drugs make other people feel free—they make us so free we're liable to stop at nothing. Drugs relax other people—they paralyze us.

Those of us who abused mind-altering chemicals have lost our privilege to use them. Now our positive path is the program, not the negative way of drugs. Am I on the positive path?

God help me to seek the positive path in the program.

I will work my program today by:

Many people refer to luck as the reason for success in their lives. But we might reflect for a moment on luck. Luck means the suffering and the pain that we have not hesitated to endure. Luck represents the opportunities for growth that we have embraced. Luck includes the hours we have devoted to working. Luck reflects all the gentleness, kindness, and humor that we have shown to others.

Luck means the appointments we have kept, and the thanks we have expressed to others for their kindness to us. All of these things have been made possible through our communication with our Higher Power. So it seems that luck is actually the Grace of God. Do I realize what a lucky person I am?

Lord, keep Your blessings with me always, and help me know that my luck is actually Your grace.

Today I will thank God for my luck by:

There is much work to be done and many lessons to be learned as we mend our ways, through love, in the fellowship we find. Each time God changes us so that we are freer to love another human being, we have learned another lesson.

Our responsibility is to desire the changes that free us, and to be willing to let them happen when the time is right. Often we are so attached to our defects and dependencies that we are afraid of change, even good change. Am I a changed person?

God give me the power to view the world today through loved filled eyes, so that through Your love I will not be afraid to change.

I am willing to change in the following ways today:

Our addictive-type personalities often produce strange twists in our character. There are many of us who can't stand practicing drunks, pill heads or junkies. It's an eerie feeling to twelfth step someone that reminds us of where we came from. Who really wants to get up at 3:00 o'clock in the morning to twelfth step someone who's going to throw up on you and probably won't remember what you've said anyway?

We are tempted to ask. "what's the use?" We're the use! We're here and even though there are things we have to do to stay straight that we don't like, we are clean and need to continue to do these things to keep growing. Am I always willing to carry the message to those who still suffer?

God give me the strength, patience, and love it requires to twelfth step the people I have a hard time liking.

Today I will twelfth-step:

The program is not a religious affair, but a beloved spiritual fellowship. Spirituality is a manifestation of the living God. If we take explicit directions from the emotion-divorced voice within ourselves, we find freedom.

Many of us discovered that our former "trip" experiences left us with a residue of wreckage. Having exposed ourselves to their effects for several years, we found ourselves having to scrape the mire off our souls to let in the sunshine of the spirit.

When we line ourselves up with the spirit of love, we find that it leaves no residue. Do I have the spirit of love?

Father, let me make each of my decisions today in accordance with the direction that is coming to me through love's eyes.

I will express love today by:

Our Higher Power has always loved us and always will. Our major problem is learning to accept and believe that. While using mind-altering chemicals we were unable to accept God's love. Later we found we could not even believe in God's love. We found we could not accept the idea that God's love was perfect.

We soon learn it is we who suffer from imperfection. If we desire to know God's perfect love, we cannot come to Him with our own preconceived ideas. God will teach us about His perfect love when we clear ourselves out of the way. Eventually we will know always that God is loving us now. Am I absolutely sure that God loves me?

God may I know You are loving me now.

Today I will open myself up to God's love by:

**God help me to stay clean and sober today!**

"What do you mean, unmanageable?", we often ask when we first come in. And we are surprised to see the smiling faces and suppressed chuckles. For so long we have been living with our delusions. We really believe everything is OK, or will be OK next week. We simply can't see how unmanageable everything really is—like unbalanced finances, emotionally unstable children, wrecked spouses or companions, and everything else.

These situations seem hard to believe after a period on the program. Some were ridiculous, others were tragic, and still we lived in our fantasy of manageability. If we have a problem recognizing this, we can sincerely ask God to reveal the facts and help us face our "tomorrow will be better" syndrome. Have I turned the management over to God?

Lord, if I have not yet accepted step one, please clear my eyes, my mind, my ego—that I may accept it now.

I will examine my unmanageability today by:

"Live only in today. Don't feel guilt about yesterday or worry over tomorrow." That's a fine ambition, we may think, but just how does one live in today? It means dealing only with what is presented to us now, and the courses of action which are possible to take now. We don't need to worry about all the other possibilities, and the numerous if's, and's and but's.

We simply have to deal with what is at hand. If the possibilities we are considering are not at hand, or are out of our realm, we need to disengage ourselves from them. No lifestyle or scheme can adapt the world to our will. Have I learned to fit myself to the world?

God help me remember, "Conquer yourself rather than the world."

Today I will adapt myself to whatever happens by:

We little realize that our true desires are our never ending prayers. Not our head prayers, but the ones from our heart. God takes for granted what we truly desire, and He aids us in accomplishing it. Many of us have no doubt but that being an alcoholic and drug addict was an answer to our search. Else how would we have discovered this way of life.

Many of us feel that we would have been hopeless neurotics were it not for our addiction and this solution. Thus we know that our true hearts' desires were answered, and not our ego-tripping head prayers. Has God answered my true prayers in spite of myself?

Father, please answer my true urge to be one with You, and not the ego-pleasure prayers that I so easily fall prone to.

I will seek to know His will for me today by:

Virtue for us is a subordination of our actions and passions to a Higher Will. Virtue is any action we take in accordance with our highest convictions. It is not necessarily in accordance with the doctrine of any church.

Virtue need not conform to the things drummed into our heads during childhood, although it may. And virtue is not a result of believing or associating with the virtuous, it consists simply in the doing, in the action. Do I act out my virtue?

God show me how to live in accordance with Your Will.

Today I will live my virtue by doing:

Anonymity means much more to our way of living than just the protection of the members from exposure and shame. With the increasing popularity of the recovering addict, it may even become a temptation to use our recovery as a prestige point. This type of self-seeking can be a real spiritual danger to us.

It is our duty to avoid such destructive self-seeking so that our organizations are not endangered either. Anonymity is also a reminder to place principles above personalties. Do I remain anonymous at the public level?

God help me to not seek personal prestige in daily recovery, remembering always that I am one drug away from disaster.

I will look at my anonymity today and safeguard it by:

When the summer is hot and tempers are short, it can be hard to remember that we have meetings to attend and a program to work. But it is at times like these that it is so important to remember what keeps us straight. It will do us no good to have a cool drink of wine, or to lose our tempers as others may be doing.

When we think we are too busy to make meetings or to work steps, our minds are beginning to slip. That old call of mind-altering chemicals is tricky, and can creep up from laziness, boredom or uncomfortable circumstances. Do I remember my program at all times and under all circumstances?

Lord, may nothing in my lifestyle interfere with my program of sobriety and cleanness.

Today I will practice my program in the following ways:

We must be more aware that we should not, cannot, need not, fear the crosses of life. Our Creator has given us examples, promises and friends as sharers of all our crosses. We used to be disappointed in ourselves when we could not rise above the situations that enveloped us. We felt discouraged with those around us who seemed indifferent to our suffering.

But coming to the program, we find that our Creator did leave us a way out. With understanding people we find that we need never be alone again. Do I share all my crosses with my fellows and with my Creator?

Lord, as I follow my Creator, let me know there are others on the same path!

The crosses I will share today are:

**God help me to stay clean and sober today!**

This is a program of attraction and not promotion. We do not have to persuade people to see things our way. If our existence, being clean, sober, and at peace, is not enough to convince others, then they have not yet gone far enough in their own misery to want help.

God will place us in a position to help others and He will place them in a position to be helped. From there it is their choice, they either want help and will reach out for it, or they will decide to turn away.

God tells us to carry the message, but he doesn't say anything about delivering it. Do I know I can't help anyone unless they want help?

Lord, while I try to carry the message, help me remember that all will not hear or see, and they have to learn as I had to learn.

Today I will try to carry the message to:

There is a mini program called HALT. It tells us never to get too hungry, too angry, too lonely or too tired. When we allow any one or combination of these simple conditions to exist for too prolonged a period, our resistance to the state of mind which will take us back to alcohol or drugs is very low.

We learn to take care of our bodies as well as our minds, by pausing when we feel too hungry, angry, lonely or tired. And we find it possible to live within these suggestions without becoming fanatical. Do I pause when I feel HALT?

Lord, help me be willing to be good to my body, which is the temple of Your spirit.

If I feel hungry, angry, lonely or tired today, I will pause and:

**God help me to stay clean and sober today!**

Adjusting and coping are two words not well liked by recovering addicts. We have tried for so long to be the director of our lives, that it is hard to learn that the world does not revolve around us. But it doesn't. We share this planet with billions of others, and it is certainly going to take a bit of adjusting and coping to get along smoothly.

Trying to force each situation to suit ourselves is going to leave a lot of other people unsuited by the same situation. But we can remember that we don't have to adjust and cope for the rest of our lives, we need only do it today. Do I cope well?

Lord, if I cannot have what I want, help me want what I have—today.

Today I will adjust myself to others in the following ways:

After being in the program awhile, some of us feel that we know much more than the average member. But God is not a respecter of persons, and anyone can play the fool by appearing to be important. The greatest among us are the ones who serve the most, not boast the most.

It is an easy trap to fall into, thinking we know so much more than others because we have been clean and sober a little while. We shouldn't try to appear more important than the next guy, especially when he's sincerely trying to stay straight. After all, he may be more sincere than we are.

Let us offer a helping hand and carry the message, but let us not set ourselves above and apart. Let's not play the fool. Am I rid of self-importance?

Lord, let me know deep within myself why I should not place myself above others.

I will humble myself today by:

God help me to stay clean and sober today!

There is a Divine plan for each of us. However, it may take awhile for us to understand our place in it. Often we do not know what we are supposed to do at all. We simply know things we are not supposed to do at all. We may experience empty feelings at times. If we can learn to become expectant during these very slow, sometimes painfully slow times, we can learn to endure the necessary uncertain times with less difficulty and less fear.

It seems to us during these times that nothing is happening. But just as surely as one day mountains emerge from the stress of restless terrain, so does growth emerge in our lives after a period of stress. Growth can only emerge if we have been willing to wait for the right time. Is my growth slow but sure?

Lord, help me to be patient in my wait for Your plan to be fulfilled in my life.

Today I will be patient, but expectant, about:

Other people's bigotry should not worry us unduly. We cannot help what others feel, and we are not responsible for their actions. We are responsible to ourselves and our Higher Power, and to no one else. When people oppose us, even though we know we're right, we should try not to be angry.

No one can oppose the order of Nature or God's will. Our personal plans or self-will may be upset, but we should try to understand that there are much greater plans. Am I tolerant even of those who oppose me?

God, please help me keep You in my heart, and know that I am building that which can never be pulled down.

I will cultivate tolerance today by:

The reality of staying clean and sober seems very strange to men of great minds. But there is something we've noticed about reality. It's odd. It isn't neat, or what we expect it to be.

It's like once we've grasped that planets go around the sun, we expect it to follow some sort of symmetry. But the planets are not equally spaced according to size and weight. The reality is different than we expect. Reality is always something we couldn't have guessed.

Our program is something we couldn't have guessed. No pledges, no money, just the twelve steps. If we had found just what we thought we wanted, we would have felt we had made it up. But in fact we haven't made it up. It works! Do I like the reality I have found?

Lord, let me not keep expecting sobriety and cleanness to be my way, but let me accept it with that strange twist of reality that it has.

Today I will explore the reality I have found by:

God help me to stay clean and sober today!

It has been said that the harder the conflict, the more beautiful the triumph. Some of us may feel that we would gladly have passed the conflict along with our triumph. If so, we have not fully experienced the triumph, or that kind of thought would be far from our minds.

What is bought too cheaply, we regard too lightly. But the prices we paid for our lives make them the dearest treasures we have. Our freedom is highly rated, dearly bought. And it is also said that heaven knows the proper price for its goods. Do I appreciate the full value of what I have won?

Lord, help me realize that Your plans are Divine, even though they may often seem severe.

I will express my gratitude for my sobriety today by:

God help me to stay clean and sober today!

The savage worships a God who will bring rain and protect him from storms. The philosopher seeks a God who will give him peace of mind. The drug abuser begs a God to get him out of jams. Do we know in whom we believe?

It is from a God of our understanding that we will gain guidance and freedom. Then we can cultivate the blessings we have received, and sow them in the lives of others. Have I found God?

May I know my Father in heaven and seek a constant reinforcement from His spirit that gives me life.

Today I will seek God by:

In the beginning it is hard to realize that trouble is not second nature to us. Trouble is not a part of our personality. Many of us have had numerous encounters with police and jails, quarrels with our families and friends, losses of jobs and failures in school. We began to feel that we were jinxed.

But then we came to realize that we didn't have to live that way. We didn't have to be jinxed. We were finally able to see what was meant by peace of mind. Have I left all my troubles behind me?

Lord, with You in my heart and this fellowship in my life, I have a choice in how I want to live today.

Today I will enhance my peace of mind by:

God help me to stay clean and sober today!

Some people have described what they call the Four Horsemen of drugs. They are Terror, Bewilderment, Frustration and Despair. The Four Horsemen have a Group Leader, Fear, and there are 100,000 forms of fear with the horsemen to command.

The only way to combat these is by abstinence, honesty and turning it over. It has been said that fear cannot exist where there is faith. Have I lost all my fear?

Lord, when I fight too hard, the battle itself perpetuates the problem, so help me to let go easily.

If I feel afraid about anything today, I will:

God help me to stay clean and sober today!

When we found ourselves falling into the depths of depression, we often remedied this by seeking the quickest escape route. This in our weakened condition was often getting high or drunk. At these times we forget the strength and power of the God of our understanding.

If we only let go of our self-will and give it over to our Higher Power, we will avoid the depths of depression. We will find this a much easier, safer escape route. Have I learned how to deal with depression?

Lord, I pray that when depression tries to destroy me, I will have the strength to go to You in heaven and not be ashamed to ask for help.

Today I will avoid the depths of depression by:

When we go to meetings, it is fairly easy to work the program and say the right words. But the other hours of the day are another matter. And these hours are the most important, for this is when we are faced with the situations that have always been our downfall. The only way to work the program through the day is to keep in conscious contact with the Father.

Many of us use the Serenity Prayer. Others use other prayers or simple moments taken aside for quietness during the day. The Serenity Paryer has been called the number for the hotline to God. Are we hooked up to our Higher Power? Do we have a method for hooking up?

Lord, may I devote my working hours to improving my conscious contact with You.

I will improve my conscious contact with God today by:

There is a good reason why the twelve steps are numbered from one to twelve. They are meant to be taken in order. For instance, in step one we have to know we are powerless over our addiction and the world before the other steps will benefit us.

Likewise, the fourth step would be too painful had we not turned our wills and our lives over to the care of God in step three. And how can we make amends in steps eight and nine, unless we find out who we have hurt by taking the fourth and fifth steps?

Step twelve, of course, only comes as a result of taking all the other steps. The hop-skip-jump method is not reliable, and might hop-skip-jump us right back into our addiction. Do I practice all twelve steps of the program?

Lord, let me know that I will only find the answers I need when I begin to take all of the steps, as they were meant to be taken.

Today I will review my progress with each of the twelve steps, and:

God help me to stay clean and sober today!

We should try each day to be on guard against judging other human beings, for as we judge so are we judged. This means that if we are continually assessing that others will slip, we are likely condemning ourselves.

We unconsciously seek relief from our own character defects by projecting them onto others. The only way to accept ourselves today is to try to accept others, including those with qualities we may find undesirable in ourselves.

We can do this by realizing that our defects will be removed in God's time, if we desire and pray that they be removed. In the meantime, we should realize that we are God's children and needful of love. Do I fully accept myself and others?

Father, show me the path of personal freedom today by letting me not pass judgement on another human being.

I will look closely at those I find difficult to accept today, and:

God help me to stay clean and sober today!

Tragedy is a part of life. If we are not faced with it right now, there always seems to be some tragedy imminent, whether great or small. But the effect of tragedy is blended with victory and defeat.

The defeat is in knowing that we can't change the physical circumstances of the situation. The victory is in knowing that it is not our burden alone to carry, but also the burden of a loving God as we understand Him.

There is a Higher Power at work, and through any tragedy there is the power of love seeking to express itself in the situation and in us. The nobility of this life only fails when we are insufficient in leaving the results with God. Can I handle tragedy?

Lord help me recognize that being finite, I cannot understand the Divine plan of the infinite.

Today I will work at preparing myself to handle tragedy by:

God help me to stay clean and sober today!

There are many who come to our program with little or no belief in a Higher Power. These people are not to be condemned or turned away. They are to be helped along until they can take step two. There are many reasons why we turned from God. Perhaps we tried religion and it didn't help, or maybe we were too scientifically minded.

But if lack of belief in God has driven us away from this program, drugs will drive us back. It's very hard to clear out the junk in our heads long enough to see that God is really here, and our troubles are of our own making–not God's. It's very hard, but never too hard. Do I have a firm belief?

Lord, please add the blessing of faith to my daily program.

I will seek to establish contact with my Higher Power today by:

Just exactly what can we do to put spiritual principles into our lives?

We can say people when others say money. We can speak when others are silent. We can give help when others give up. We can recognize true meanings when others see little meaning in life.

We can say love when others say hate. We can take God's path while others search for a softer way. We can give ourselves in service to God when others deny themselves His love. How is my spiritual life?

Lord, inspire me with the courage to follow Your path and do what I know is right.

Today I will give myself wholly to spiritual living by:

For us to give sympathy and weep foolishly with the ones still sick is to give them little. What they need is truth. The truth will shock and jolt them back into communication with the soul. We can give them joy and hope by imparting the truth.

The truth being that we have a choice, that with God in our lives we need never be alone again, that today we can start recovering. Yes, we can give them the truth, instead of just a shoulder. And with the truth will come the hope and the glory. Do I tell it like it is?

Lord, give me the truth that I may impart it to others.

I will tell the truth today to:

After cleaning up, we become aware of many fears. Situations that never fazed us in our using days suddenly loom up at us. Many of us experience terror when we ride with a careless driver. We might panic at the prospect of some maniac breaking into our house. Some of us go to the extreme of fearing evil spirits gaining control of our bodies.

After the long process of withdrawal, regaining our sanity may produce an exaggerated value on our lives. These fears need to be turned over as the other areas of our life are. When we trust the will of our Father and believe in His wisdom for us, these fears will recede into their normal place in a reasonable lifestyle. Have I learned to handle fear?

Lord, lift me to Your Spirit that I may know peace.

Today I will deal with fear by:

We must always remember that *absolute* abstinence is the keystone to our recovery. Any mind-altering chemical will prevent us from working the program effectively. Mind-altering chemicals flip our thinking back into old patterns, and eventually they will con us back into full-fledged addiction.

There are a lot of products we have to be careful of: antihistamines, cough syrups, over-the-counter sleeping and non-sleep pills, and many more. If we are addictive-compulsive people, we have to be extremely careful about what we pop into our mouths. Do I stay absolutely clean?

Lord, may I accept the fact that I have lost the dubious privilege of taking mind-altering chemicals.

I will examine the state of my abstinence today by:

God help me to stay clean and sober today!

We can look at the program and ourselves in many different ways. But we always return to the fact that we must work the steps. And we must work them on a daily basis. Life is an infinite succession of nows. Therefore, we have to deal with what is happening now.

How can we use the program now? What will keep our sobriety and cleanness now? How do we live the way we want to now? The now is the basis of applying these steps, and although it is difficult, if we keep reminding each other, we may catch on to the concept. Do I live in the now?

Lord, show me what I can do now to work my program to the best of my ability.

Today I will practice living now by:

The fellowship of man is comprised of many whirling little gears meshing together to produce love. If each of us would find the place in which we could offer the greatest service to others, we would have a smoother running operation.

As each of us spin through life we come into contact with others, also spinning, to offer or be offered comfort, strength, experience or hope when we mesh together. Sometimes we just need to see another spinning gear of light to remember what we are, and not get turned off by self-pity or resentment. Do I mesh well?

Lord, help me realize today that I am simply one among many, and help me to find where I can be of the greatest service to others.

I will try to mesh more smoothly today by:

With this program we learn to live, laugh, and express pure JOY. We learn to work and play with people, to love them, to fight fairly with them, to give and take. We learn to be happy with people or happy in solitude.

This joy in living sets us free to lead or follow. It sets us free to create or admire. So many things that before were out of our reach, are now coming within our grasp.

And, always, part of carrying our message is carrying and spreading the JOY. How much joy do I spread?

Today, Father, may I spread some joy to those around me.

Today I will bring joy to:

God help me to stay clean and sober today!

If we fill our thoughts with truth and love, then resentments, fears, and self-centeredness cannot affect us. When our minds are filled with positive thoughts, negative thoughts have a difficult time entering. Good thoughts are like shining armor, and they not only protect us but benefit others.

The self-seeking pride of the negative thinker eventually just hurts himself, and inevitably harms others too. When we practice living truth and love, the light of our Higher Power will shine through and reflect on those around us. How well do I reflect truth and love?

Lord make me a mirror of Your truth and love.

I will seek truth and love today by:

We often remind ourselves that sex, age, race, status or religious preference do not affect anyone's joining the program to get straight. We take great pride in this. But do we forget that we do not diagnose other abusers? If someone says they are addict, alcoholic, pill head, do we take them at their word?

It is not for us to say, "I spilled more on my tie than you ever drank," or "My habit cost more in one day than yours did in a year." We don't know if others are addicts or not, but if someone says they are we take them at their word. Do I diagnose anyone but myself?

Lord, help me understand that I am not a doctor or demigod, and although I have opinions I cannot honestly diagnose others.

Today I will express my acceptance of all fellow addicts by:

We are all as cells in the body of God. As such, we are all endowed with free will and are co-creators with God. But with our limited knowledge, unless we desire to make our will one with the Father's, we will generally mess up.

In order to come into full awareness of our greater abilities, we must experience and learn from all our situations, both good and bad. Each situation is an opportunity presented by the Grace of God. It is for our learning, a learning to make our will one with the Father's. Am I working with God right now?

Lord, just the awareness of myself gives me assurance that You are mindful of me now, today.

I will work with God today in the following ways:

Intellectual pride is often a great downfall of addicts and alcoholics. We should not think that our program guidelines apply only to the mediocre mind or only to those with a certain faith. They apply to all of us. We were not smart enough to avoid ending up here in the first place!

All aspects of this program apply, whether we shine shoes, wait tables, or are president of a bank. Until we realize that our common bond is our solution—not our position or lifestyle—we will not make much progress. As our problem is no respecter of persons, neither is our solution. Have I stopped intellectualizing?

Lord, help me realize that my solution is my common bond with my fellow addicts, and intellectual pride is only another barrier to working my program.

Today I will look at my intellectual pride by:

It is well for us to remember that life isn't all that serious. We should always look at the humorous side of things. A sense of humor has saved many of us from the effects of tragic experiences. To be able to laugh with ourselves and others is to be able to forgive. For if we are not forgiving, we can never laugh.

There is joy in sobriety and cleanness, and there is joy in laughing. When we go parading around under a veil of tragedy, we are cheating ourselves from one of the joys that this program brings to us: laughter. Have I laughed today?

Lord, may laughter be as much a part of me as my seriousness.

Today I will cultivate my sense of humor by:

We will find what we are looking for in this program. If we come seeking a better way of life, we will find that. Those of us who merely want out of the pain will find relief. If we want to be loved, we will learn how to love and how to accept love.

If we desire freedom, we will learn how to turn loose and be free of resentment. Desire is the keystone of this program. We will find our heart's desires! Do I desire the right things?

Father, help me desire those things which are best for all concerned.

I will examine my desires today by:

The eleventh step gives many of us unnecessary concern. "I haven't prayed in so many years! What do I do? I really don't know where to begin." These might have been the cries of all of us at one time or another.

But we should remember that God didn't make the rituals—man did. Talking to God in prayer can be just saying our feelings, asking for forgiveness or reviewing the day. It is as simple as that.

Good thoughts are also prayers. We need not worry about doing it right, because we are always acceptable to God. Do I pray every day?

God, whatever happens today, I know Your will for me is good. Bless us all.

Today I will pray especially for:

Once in the grips of our disease, we were using mind-altering chemicals not because we wanted them, but because we knew no other way. We hurt other people, not wanting to, but knowing no other way. As our disease progressed, we became overburdened with guilt. This guilt carries over into our sobriety and cleanness, and must be eliminated along with our insane past.

The fourth and fifth steps are the ones that clean house for us. Until they are taken, we continue to operate from the crippling effects of guilt. As these soul-searching and cleansing steps are taken, as they were intended, we become capable of genuinely loving ourselves. And then we can become capable of loving others. Have I rid myself of all guilt?

Lord, help me to willingly work the steps, and release the guilt that is now crippling me.

If I feel guilty about anything today, I will:

Many people who abuse mind-altering chemicals are urged by friends and relatives to use "will power" or "resist temptation." It is never very clear as to what they mean by this, but the addicted person numbly nods his head and agrees with them. It's a common misconception that we should be masters of our souls.

But it is not until we truly realize that we don't know how to be masters, that we can progress. There is only one Master who has the wisdom and knowledge to guide our souls. If we ourselves were capable of being masters of our souls, how did we end up here in the first place? Have I turned my life and my will over?

May my soul be guided by the only Master that truly knows what is best for me.

Today I will look at my unmanageability and seek guidance by:

God help me to stay clean and sober today!

Ninety meetings in ninety days. It makes sense when we first dry out and come clean. Our minds are still in a haze, and we need extra support and extra meetings in the beginning. Making the effort to go to ninety meetings in the first ninety days gives insurance that we won't trip our minds up in this haze.

It took a lot of work and effort to get where we were at. Similarly, it will take a lot of work and effort to stay clean and sober now. Am I working hard on my sobriety?

Lord, may I channel as much energy into staying clean and sober as I used to put into getting stoned.

I will work on my sobriety today in the following ways:

God help me to stay clean and sober today!

We are spirits. It appears that God lent us these bodies that we might learn about pleasure, have a way of acquiring knowledge and be of aid to our fellow man. We learn about the proper use of these qualities by misusing them, and suffering as a result. Misusing our gifts is a large part of being spirit in the human form.

Obviously God has a plan for us. So when we do very human things we should not punish ourselves, but accept our humanness. For if God wanted us to be purely spirit, He would have dispensed with our bodies and made us so. Have I learned to accept my humanness?

Lord, show me that my humanness is not to be despaired of, but loved as a very real path back to You my Creator.

Today I will rejoice in my humanness by:

It is not faith that keeps us straight but a desire to change that is our key. Well-meaning people with a superfluous zeal will shout to those who aren't making it, "You lack faith." They are speaking from a lack of spiritual knowledge.

Once we have the true desire, God's promises will not and cannot be denied us. Faith is a gift, granted from our desire to change. Those of us lucky enough to receive it should never condemn another's lack of it. Do I still have desire?

Lord, let my eyes see Your gracious hand in all Your works and let me rejoice in Your creations.

I will work on change today in the following ways:

God help me to stay clean and sober today!

Working our program, we all have a choice of gaining freedom via the twelve steps or becoming part of the crowd that believes in materialistic miracles. We have a choice of living in an illusory world, or living vitally through the Spirit.

Through ignorance we can fall into the trap of living in fear of public opinion. Or we might elect to live the life of a hypocrite playing the "cool" role. Our true spiritual life consists of living to the fullest, and developing our contact with our Higher Power so that we need never fear again. Have I chosen wisely?

Lord, today when I am faced with choices, may I choose to follow You, as I understand You, and not be swayed by public opinion.

Today I will choose spiritual living in the following ways:

God help me to stay clean and sober today!

We cannot pretend to know all that Truth is. We cannot pretend to have crossed the abyss and to have reached an ultimate knowledge of good and evil, right and wrong. We cannot try to tell the world about immediate enlightenment. All we can ask for, for ourselves, is freedom. We want to break our chains, free our limbs, and release our wills to God.

When we are bound by fear, resentment and self-centeredness, any truth is helpless to enter our lives. In our quest we can only find our own truths, not others' truths. Our new life will be enriched mostly by our own honest thoughts. Do I still seek truth in all my affairs?

Lord, may I not pretend to know all truth, but find from my own honest thinking Your truth for me.

I will live truthfully today by:

It is so easy for us to fall into a pattern of self-pity that we sometimes waste the best parts of our lives. The waste of life lies in the love we have not given, the experiences we have not used, the selfishness that will risk nothing, and the fear that blocks us from other people.

Trying to avoid pain often implies that we misuse happiness too. Now that we finally have a life, it seems a shame to throw the most beautiful and giving parts of it away. Have I stopped wasting my life?

Lord, may I know that I will never be any poorer for giving of myself to others.

Today I will live life to the fullest by:

It seems like addicts, alcoholics and pill-heads are particularly immature people, especially in the early stages of recovery. When we really got into drugs, the painful process of problem-solving was bypassed. When we got into difficult relationships, we got stoned. When responsibility was demanded of us, we got stoned. When we were threatened by life, we got stoned. Drugs became a substitute for learning encounters, instead of resolving or enduring those encounters.

Now that we can learn, it is still difficult for us to solve what before we evaded, but it is the process of maturing. And it is much more rewarding to be mature adults than childish alkies, junkies, speed freaks, red freaks or glue sniffers. Do I think, feel and act maturely?

Lord, show me that though maturing may be painful, dealing with childish emotions is more painful still.

I will cultivate maturity today by:

Passion is a kind of fever of the mind. It always seems to place us in a weaker position than it found us. It does not necessarily mean sex or desire for another person. It could be passion for money, for power, for prestige or for mind-altering chemicals. When we become overwhelmed with passion for a particular goal, our minds operate out of a kind of haze.

This mind-haze deprives us of good use of judgment. Passion placed above our program, our Higher Power, and our sobriety and cleanness, leaves us without reason. We need no more riots upon our reason than we've already had to deal with. Have I overcome all passion?

Lord, help me to release any passions that might keep me from reason and judgment in my life.

Today I will deal with my passion by:

It is sometimes very wise to listen to the words that have come before us. We might read ancient works and find comfort and wisdom in their thoughts. But we should never narrow our minds so that all we read are old works and all we think are old thoughts.

We are sure that God spoke to those before us but we are also sure that God speaks to us now also. We should never forget that God directs us now, and to follow other thoughts before those from God is not living God's will for us today. Am I receptive to new ideas?

Lord, release me from the bondage of old ideas and aid me in following Your will for me today.

I will formulate new ideas today about:

So often when we think bad thoughts we get ourselves into trouble. We used to think about all the bad breaks the world had given us, and we used to hold our fellow man in contempt.

Are we thinking about our soul development? It is a privilege to think, providing it is in accord with our Higher Power, which is positive and not negative. Do I think positive?

I pray that I may use my thinking ability in accord with my Higher Power.

Today I will think positive about:

Nothing can have much meaning or seem like it is worthwhile unless we have faith in God's wisdom. Tragedies would not make sense. Aborted plans would make life seem pointless. Working to be one with God might appear fruitless. But our Higher Power is the Wisdom that guides us.

God is our Guide and the events outside our realm are under God's jurisdiction too. We may not understand, but we need the faith to continue to turn life over. God has the wisdom, we do not. But if we can have faith in His widsom, then we don't need that all-powerful wisdom ourselves. Is my faith unshakeable?

Lord, may I have faith in Your wisdom to save me from my own false choices, doubts and uncertainties.

I will express my faith today by:

It is a shock to realize how false we often appear to others. We try so laboriously to impress them that it is difficult to see how we really look. It is easy to confuse the issues. Often we start experiencing God in our lives and use this for our own self-esteem. At meetings we may sound as if God is doing wonderful things for us and not for others.

Of course this attitude puts us back into the bag of self-centeredness. As long as we try to remain honest in all areas, these bags of self-centeredness will remain empty. We won't have to try to impress others because our realness will be enough. Have I lost all self-centeredness?

Lord keep me honest; keep me clean, keep me sober.

Today I will be my real self by:

What kind of prayers do we allow ourselves to pray? Are we selfishly seeking material gains for ourselves? Are we craving a particular thing from outside ourselves to be added on to us, instead of developing it inside ourselves?

Prayers are the highest realization of life and living. They shine forth from a loving and joyful soul. Prayers are the Spirit of God showing His works through man. However, prayers that try to get at private ends rather than good are a form of thievery.

But when we are one with the Father, we don't have to petition and beg, we will see prayer in the actions of our lives, in our very existence. How do I pray?

Lord, teach me to pray well.

I will pray today by doing:

Despite all the facts that we can arm ourselves with about mind-altering chemicals, there are going to be real addicts who will not consider themselves such. We cannot prance around diagnosing people as addicts. But we can make suggestions so that they can diagnose themselves.

There is the "controlled" using for thirty days test, or we could suggest several of the written self-tests. If the tests are successful, then their problem is probably not like ours. We are not doctors or demi-gods, but we can carry the message. And when God sees fit, there are those we can aid. Do I try to help others diagnose themselves?

Lord may Your love and light shine forth through me, but may I not set myself up to do Your job.

Today I will carry the message to:

Now, being straight, we are discovering the joys of this old concept, love. But our old ideas about love have to be changed, as our old ideas about living had to be changed. Love can't always be measured by self-sacrifice or generosity. We can self-sacrifice ourselves into martyrdom or generosity ourselves into directing and managing others' lives.

Love doesn't stipulate or limit. Does God limit us? He loves us so much that He will even let us destroy ourselves. Few of us know anything about the true nature of love. But God will reveal Himself to us, and show us about love as we are ready. Have I learned all about love?

May I know with all my heart that God is Love.

I will make myself ready to learn about love today by:

**God help me to stay clean and sober today!**

We can't give away what we don't have. But what can we give away? What anyone shares is himself. What we give away is ourselves. We do this by sharing our experience, strength and hope. Whether it is a personal sharing or a social one, we are walking, talking miracles of what our program can do.

But this program works only through our Higher Power, and only through our Higher Power can we have the joy of sharing with others. Do I share myself wholly with my fellows?

Lord, meet and defeat the hostile forces in me that I may bring Your glory to others.

Today I will share myself wholeheartedly with:

**God help me to stay clean and sober today!**

Many of us tried the geographic escape in an attempt to get out of the box we found ourselves in. We moved from place to place, but invariably found ourselves in pretty much the same situation, if not worse.

We knew we had real problems, but we weren't aware that using chemicals was actually causing many of our emotional and material problems. The state of mind the chemicals induced led to patterns of behavior that would not have occurred had we not been "out of our minds." Have I stopped trying to escape?

Lord, help me to know that it's not my location that makes the difference in my life–it's what I'm working with inside.

Instead of seeking escape, I will try to improve my situation today by:

God help me to stay clean and sober today!

It seems that in our need to become a whole person we sometimes find it necessary to project an environment we imagine to be more satisfactory than our present situation: a town, a position or a goal. But this can sometimes become a pitfall if we don't remember the fact that we have absolutely no power over our own life.

If we forget our powerlessness and start searching frantically for this kind of goal or place, we let ourselves open to discouragement and disillusionment. But, if we truly turn our wills and our lives over to God's care, we will surely end up in a place containing security and real happiness in God's love. Do I let the future with God?

Lord, I pray that when I look further ahead than today, You will help me to be where it is best for me.

Today I will reappraise my goals and aspirations and:

God help me to stay clean and sober today!

It is difficult to draw away from mind-altering chemicals when we have spent so much time in that environment. We are the result of what we have applied. Now we have a chance to apply new principles to our life. In doing so, we are able to slowly pull away from our old habits and ideas.

Cleaning house is a necessary beginning for our new way of life. Every day we can practice new thoughts and habits that follow the plan of our Creator instead of our own childish self-will. Have I become what I want to be?

Lord, today may I begin practicing, thinking and living according to Your plan for me.

I will act myself into a new way of living today by:

Some of us come into the program and are gung-ho for the first three to six weeks. We're like a quarter horse, good for a short run but can't finish the stretch. After we come down from our first run, reality and responsibility seep in and we step out, possibly give up.

So something has to carry us through and that will be our Higher Power, providing we let Him. Then, as time passes, we find we no longer feel the need to get stoned. And our Higher Power is what guides us through. Am I good for the long stretch?

Lord guide me with Your loving light for the whole race.

Today I will improve my stamina by practicing:

Because most of us who have been around the program awhile like it here, the newcomer makes the mistake of thinking that we wanted to be here. They think we were so eager and anxious we just couldn't wait to dash into the promised land.

Ha! None of us wanted to come here at first. But how can we help it if we love it here now that we've found a way to solve our problems of living? Do I like it here?

Lord, let me be grateful always for having found this new way of life, but help me remember how the newcomer feels.

I will enjoy the program today by:

A common rationalization about not making the program goes like this: "Harry over there slipped 10 times before he made it, so what if I slip a few times?"

What is overlooked is the last time Jack slipped–he slipped into a coffin; the last time Bob slipped–his baby son burned to death in a crib because of his negligence; the last time Ann slipped–she got strychnine poisoning and is blind; and the last time Jim slipped–he tried to kill his wife and nearly did.

We're not playing games here–this is a matter of life and death. Have I stopped slipping?

Lord, let me know that it is not only my life, but the lives of others that I endanger by playing loaded games.

I will avoid slipping today by:

The physical part of our addiction is not the main factor of our illness. Many of us have had allergies to things like milk, but we didn't have to join Milk Drinkers Anonymous because we couldn't stop. The physical part would be of little consequence if it weren't accompanied by an equally progressive spiritual deterioration.

Since the major contributing factor is spiritual deterioration, the emphasis in recovery should be on the spiritual. That is why only two steps mention the alcoholic and ten talk about spiritual growth. Is my spiritual progress evident in all my actions?

Lord may the spiritual illumination of the twelve steps become a reality for me and help me grow today.

My plan for living spiritually today is:

Sometimes, straight people "accuse" us of using our program as a crutch. Obviously they have little understanding and are quick to "put down" what they don't understand. But looking at this reasoning realistically, is a job a crutch?

People have to work to earn a living—we have to work our program to live. A job is a form of support, and our fellowship is also a form of support. We need never be ashamed of our glorious fellowship that has brought so much joy into so many lives. Do I use the program to the fullest?

Lord, may I know that I do not have to justify my program, my addiction or my existence.

I will use the program in the following ways today:

**God help me to stay clean and sober today!**

When we have loved ones also in the program we must constantly remind ourselves where our priorities lie. We are told constantly not to interfere in family members' programs. We have to take care of our own addiction first, then tend to other affairs.

The same holds for loved ones; we must respond to the addict in them first, and then tend to other matters. Our responsibility to the addict in people must come first, or we may lose sight of our true priorities and mess up our own lives as well as theirs. Do I put first things first?

My messages come from my Father first, they flow through me and then spread to loved ones and to all other areas of my life.

I will reassess my priorities today and:

God help me to stay clean and sober today!

People pleasing! Why do we spend so much time and energy trying to please other people? We sometimes find ourselves saying "yes" to every request made of us. Perhaps we look to other people because we feel guilty about our past and want to make up for it. Or possibly we just need to be in the limelight.

However, people-pleasing or being a yes-man really only hurts us. What is not coming from our hearts and is not done in the true spirit of loving, is only another game of martyrism or egoism. Hopefully we are learning not to play games any longer. Do I truly serve others from the heart?

Lord I need not "please" those around me to be a nice guy, but I do need to serve You and my fellowman in the true spirit of love.

Today I will examine my true feelings about:

God help me to stay clean and sober today!

It is easy for friends and associates to see us as people who are super-sober, super-clean. They often think that we have the problem licked, that we're cured. This is shown by their uneasiness when we say, "I am an alcoholic, I am an addict." They would prefer us to say "I was."

We would like to listen to them. But in our hearts we know that it is not possible to drink or use any longer. By saying we are addicted, we are continually reminding ourselves who we are and where we came from. Am I grateful for being clean and sober, even though I can never be cured?

God grant me the acceptance to understand that I am not "cured," and help to relieve my temptation to believe well meaning people when they insist I am.

I will enjoy being clean and sober today by:

For us to grow and develop spiritually, it is important to start noticing what we think and what we really believe. To know and believe the truth generates power for day to day victorious life.

Negative thinking produces negative ways and weak living. It undermines our morals so that we develop a "what's the difference" attitude. But a positive faith in God, as each of us understands Him, give strength to the body and courage to the soul. Do I have positive beliefs?

Lord, may positive thoughts and beliefs be the guiding forces for my life instead of undermining negative attitudes.

I will cultivate positive beliefs today by:

God help me to stay clean and sober today!

A concept of right and wrong, good and evil, is reintroduced into our lives by the program. Some people ask in panic, "Do you really mean at this time in history, to reintroduce the devil, hooves, horns and all?" Well, we really don't know what this time in history has to do with it. The hooves and horns are important only because we wear them ourselves.

So our answer is yes, the devil in us, the cause of our troubles, must be reintroduced and understood to be conquered. We are at the root of our own troubles, we are our own devils. And until we act to release ourselves of our selves, we will continue to slip and suffer. Have I conquered myself?

Lord, with Your grace may I recognize my own devil and turn it over to You so that with Your help it may be conquered.

I will restrain myself today in the following ways:

Whether or not we now have an awareness of our Higher Power, our program is spiritual and knowledge of our Higher Power has to be gained to work the program. New knowledge becomes available through new instruments. We did not have much knowledge of the stars until the telescope, or much knowledge of germs until the microscope.

When we want to explore things that lie beyond our senses, we have to use instruments that reach beyond our senses. When we sincerely ask God He will show us. Maybe not with the writing on the wall, but there will be guidance. After all, how did we get to this program? Am I in touch with my Higher Power?

God, help me to use these steps as an instrument to gain knowledge of Your presence in my life.

Today I will improve my conscious contact with God by:

Our new life is deeply moved by powerful ideals. There is no perfectly clean and sober person among us. The virtues and wisdom of many of our pursuits must split apart and come together again, perhaps many times, before they begin to grow toward a perfect program and ideal spiritual values.

The speakers at our meetings are not saints or prophets, but always some nameless ones who present God's messages better than they could have been staged. Together our unknown names and our new lives emerge from the old ruins, and we form a body of God's beautiful children. Do my actions reflect the highest ideals?

Lord, even though ideals may try my faith, let me know that nothing is too good to be true.

I will strive toward the following ideal today:

**God help me to stay clean and sober today!**

Being ungrateful and feeling sorry for ourselves is a great self-destroyer. Often we feel that we know all the reasons to be grateful and *not* feel sorry for ourselves, but we don't know how to be reasonable about our feelings. Being reasonable is not a strong virtue of alcoholics and addicts.

Quite often we find we have to pray for reasonableness, then simply cling to the program and the fellowship when feelings of ungratefulness overtake us. Am I a more reasonable person than I was before?

Lord, even though I know all the reasons, I am not always reasonable. Help me to become more reasonable.

Today I will try to be reasonable about:

God help me to stay clean and sober today!

Emerson once wrote, "No change of circumstances can repair a defect of character." For us, this is true. If we are impossible to live with, getting another spouse will not change our disagreeableness. If we constantly bum from friends, changing our friends will not make us less of a bum. If we are basically inconsiderate, moving to another state will not make us more considerate.

But working our character defect steps *can* remove our undesirable characteristics. In fact, working these steps will help us *want* to give up our faults. Am I rid of all my defects of character?

Lord, help me realize that the only way to change my character defects is to change my character defects.

The defects I will work on today are:

Often we find ourselves thinking that it is important to complete a good number of human tasks, rather than how much good we can express. If our tasks are interrupted or thwarted, these should not be seen as frustrating delays in completing human plans, but as opportunities to glorify God.

Our primary task each day is to express the nature of Infinite Spirit. A day can be considered fruitful if its spiritual demands are recognized and fulfilled. Responding to setbacks with peace and love is much easier when we recognize that our main job in this life is to express good. How much good have I expressed today?

Father, help me to remember throughout this day that there is no task or plan more important than expressing Your love.

Today I will express good in the following ways:

The less there is said about the physical nature of our disease, the more will be said about our moral and spiritual principles. Our program is a set of suggestions for spiritual health that has worked to get many well. We have found that attending to our physical needs only does not really go far enough, and we must tend to our spiritual needs as well.

We have a firm foundation for spiritual health when we are able to remove ourselves from the trickiness, cunningness and stupidity of our limited minds. As confident as we may be of our own thinking, we can hardly guide ourselves alone. Only spiritual principles and a Higher Power can make a lasting difference in our lives. How is my spiritual health?

Lord, help me to bring my life nearer and nearer to Your eternal, immortal, Higher Power.

I will enhance my spiritual health today by:

If we are trying to stay clean and sober while drinking a little beer or smoking a little weed, we are missing the mark. We can never know sobriety and cleanness under those conditions. Our programs cannot be effective or honest while using any type of mind-altering chemical.

If you sincerely want the freedom, serenity and joy of a drug-free existence, just doing "a little" will never get it for you. Have I learned that taking just a little invariably ends up in taking way too much?

Lord, show me the ways that I try to trick myself into using mind-altering chemicals, and keep me from them.

I will remember my powerlessness today by:

There are as many types of meditations as there are individuals. We were so busy in our old lives giving orders, demanding things, and trying to direct others, that we find it is now time for us to try to listen.

Prayer is talking to God; meditation is listening to God. We find that meditation is invaluable to us in working our daily program. Have I learned to meditate?

I pray that I may learn to listen to God, so that I may be in harmony with the Higher Forces.

Today I will listen to God by meditating about:

Do we remember how important preventive talk is for our fellowship and our program? Drug- a-logues and drunk- a-logues are fine for identification in open meetings. But if we constantly sit around in social groups expounding on the "good times"—when we were abusing drugs and booze—what are we really doing?

Are we trying to tell ourselves drugs are really beneficial? Are we forgetting the pain and disaster? Are we ignoring the new beauty we have found? Preventive talk is discussing the solution, pointing out the tendency when other people are tempted to expound on the "good old days." Preventive talk is necessary to keep our heads straight. Do I remember the consequences well?

Lord, when I am tempted to talk or think about the "good old days," let me never forget the "bad old days" as well.

Today I will look back at:

Greed will totally enslave us to material things and divert our values from the spiritual. As lust binds us to the animal plane, greed binds us to the material plane. We start to worship many valuable and precious possessions. We begin to place love for the material before love for our brothers or our Father in heaven. Greed can harden our conscience and become the greatest of slave-drivers.

As we work to be free from drugs, we must work to be free from greed or we will always be slaves. Greed will make us into liars, hypocrites, robbers, bribers and extorters. We cannot live like that and stay clean and sober for long. Have I stopped being so materialistic?

Lord in Your infinite mercy show me that material greed will only enslave me. Set me free.

I will give the following material thing away today:

## October 27 Affecting Those Around Us

Addiction is not a lone disease; it is surrounded by people who play a part in keeping the cycle going. These people are usually family, peers and co-workers, and sometimes even therapists. A person gets stoned, those around him react to his drug taking, and then the addict reacts to their reaction and probably gets stoned again.

So the cycle is continued in the downward spiral that always characterizes abuse of mind-altering chemicals. We should be aware that the loved ones around us may be in need of help also. They become a part of our illness and need a way out just as much as we do. Do I try to empathize with those close to me?

Lord, may I not expect my abstinence to make the ones around me "shape up," because they have been a part of my illness for a long, long time.

Today I will examine my impact on those around me and:

God help me to stay clean and sober today!

Many doubts and conflicts that we encounter are strong reminders that we are not living harmoniously with God's will for us. These conflicts grow out of our own attempt to give meaning and significance to our lives, rather than letting God fill our lives with meaning and significance. Our own meaning is usually based on ego, money and pleasure.

God's meaning is love, patience and kindness which we often resist practicing in our lives. If we did live according to our Higher Power's will, doubts and conflicts would not exist. We have gauges to measure our conscious contact. Harmony in our lives is striving toward and conflict is straying from our Father. Is my life full of harmony?

God, keep me on course; keep me from drifting away from Your will for me today.

I will work at resolving the following conflict today by:

With most people addicted to mind-altering chemicals there are many sex problems. An erotic desire is often confused with the love of our brothers in this fellowship. When men or women grab the newcomer to attempt to fulfill their own sexual desires, this has been called thirteenth stepping.

For the newcomer, who is feeling ashamed, helpless and lonely, he is only too glad to grab on to someone for a little security. But the newcomer needs, above all, to learn how to stay clean and sober. To thirteenth step someone only confuses him and makes him concentrate on the relationship rather than the program. Do I know how to twelfth step without getting too involved?

Lord, help me to keep my twelfth stepping from progressing to thirteenth stepping.

Today I will look at my sex problems and:

God help me to stay clean and sober today!

There are times when we are so squirrelly that nothing seems to make much sense to us. This is not an unusual predicament for people who abuse drugs. At times like these we should follow the suggestions of fellow addicts whether they seem to make sense or not.

We have proved that our own judgment is not what it should be, and we have nothing to lose by following directions from those who love us and have experienced similar patterns. During our confused times, we must take our bodies to meetings and our heads will follow. Am I receptive to the suggestions of others?

Lord, may I learn to turn to others to ask for help when I know my own head is shot!

I will seek help today from:

We can use; God won't stop us. He won't take a joint out of our hand, tell the doctor not to give us tranquilizers or pain pills, or close the door to the corner bar. But God will give us the power to refuse that first fix, pill or drink. It is only necessary for us to practice that refusal.

NO, is an excellent word to use. Other fancy refusals will work, but NO works best of all. After we have been given the power to refuse mind-altering chemicals, we are given the power to work the steps. God gives us this power, but we have to exercise it ourselves. Do I exercise my God given power wisely?

Lord, help me to exercise the power You have already given me.

Today I will ask God for power to:

There is no complexity that could arise today that cannot find its solution in spiritual inspiration. If we stay clean and sober, His promises are sure. With every fear, that voice from within will still our troubled minds.

We have to hold fast to our intent to stay away from all mind-altering chemicals. Then we will know His promises are sure. Do I feel inspired?

I pray that I may do all I know how to do, with love, and leave the results with God.

I will seek inspiration today by:

We know that only through the grace of God can we feel peace and serenity and have our problems removed. We know that self and self-based decisions have always ended in pain. We have to replace self with God. If our hearts are full of self there is no room for God.

We become selfless when we recognize that we need God in our lives. We have learned from experience that no other way works for us. This does! The only point in talking about self is to know what we're trying to be free of—what we're trying to replace with God. Am I a selfless person now?

Lord, let me put a little more of You into a place where I still have much self.

Today I will do the following things for others:

God help me to stay clean and sober today!

Gratitude is more than just being thankful. The *principle* of gratitude is a moral responsibility. If we are truly grateful we will help others achieve what we have achieved. Next is the *priority* of gratitude. As soon as we know that God has changed our lives, we must let nothing interfere with what we know is right.

The *propriety* of gratitude shows us that God is not a respecter of persons, and we deserve His grace as do all people. Then the *purpose* of our gratitude is not for the one blessed, but to shed light on the ONE who blessed us. Do my actions reflect my gratitude?

Lord, give me a grateful heart for what I have been blessed with, and let me fully understand the magnitude of gratitude.

I will show my gratitude today by:

Our fellowship is saturated with love and caring. We can touch one another and know that it comes from the love of the Spirit. In the beginning some confuse this love with sexual desires. A man may cringe when first embraced by another man. But the love we receive from God is pure and needs no justification.

An embrace is an embrace of love in the true sense of brotherhood. We can, now, freely express our love for each other. It is the same love which flows from our Father. All true expression of love is good. Do I know how to express my love outwardly?

Lord, let me express love from You in some way today, if only touching another's hand.

Today I will openly express my love to:

We deserve to have beautiful things and need not continue disparaging and punishing ourselves for our past behavior. If someone wants to give us something, we should accept it! They have a right to the joy of giving, and we have a right to the joy of receiving.

We also have a right to the joy of giving so others may receive. We can give material things, we can give moral support, we can give a friendly ear and, best of all, we can give love. These are the beautiful things. Have I learned to give?

God help me to be able to give and receive in a true and loving spirit today.

I will give something of value today to:

## Welcoming New Ideas

No group has a harness on the program or a harness on God's will for us. The emergence of new ideas and groups is wonderful, providing our main purpose is never forgotten. Employing new methods of identification with and help for the persons still sick is the creative, expansive part of our recovery.

We must never too narrowly define our work. Book-thumpers, hardnosers, do-it-on-your-own-timers . . . . all of us contribute. And those who need our particular brand of help will be brought to us by God. Am I receptive to new and different ways?

Today I will look for new ideas by:

God help me to stay clean and sober today!

Many of our character defects stem from social acceptance motives. We worry about our popularity, career prospects, financial future, reputation and so on. By trying to please people we often exaggerate our real capabilities and may even resort to lying to impress others.

We may say that we will do things for others, when we really can't or don't want to. This causes resentment on our part and resentment from others when we don't live up to our promises. But we don't need or have to "people please," only "God please." Knowing this, many defects no longer exist. Do I know it is not necessary to please everybody all the time?

Please, Father, show me how to please You and me, and stop worrying about others.

I will try to please myself today by:

Any time and all of the time that we spend in growing spiritually becomes a sacred experience in life. It is an opportunity for us to change the quality of our existence. When we were drinking or using drugs, we may have had a lot of quantity in living, but our quality was shot.

We have many opportunities for spiritual growth today, and more will come later. But we've already let many opportunities slip away unused. Now we can little afford to be hesitant or lazy, wasting our remaining opportunities for growth. Do I recognize the opportunities all around me?

Lord, show me what I can do today to make myself more worthy of the precious time given to me.

Today I will look for opportunities to grow in the following ways:

God help me to stay clean and sober today!

## Dropping Our Delusions

While using mind-altering chemicals, we often operated under delusions of grandeur. We thought we didn't have to take anything from anybody. We were confident that we could really handle everything. But if we remember correctly, when the landlady said, "Get out," we got out. When the police said, "Get in," we got in.

Actually, we were pushed around a lot even in our delusions of pride. And it is the destruction of these delusions that clears the way for real confidence. Have I grown out of my delusions?

Lord, I am grateful for the freedom that comes simply because I don't have to behave like a deviant.

I will cultivate humility today by:

There is often talk in our fellowship of the so-called hopeless ones. Included on this list are people who seem different from ourselves. Sometimes our minds like to twist the facts so that we feel superior and feel our chances of recovery are better than theirs.

Do we forget that we **all** have abused mind-altering chemicals? Do we forget that our common bond is our solution and a loving God, as we understand Him, **not** our backgrounds, sexual preferences, age, or mental states? Our life situations are many and varied. However, if we have a desire to stay clean and sober, and start with honesty, those that may seem the most hopeless to us can make it.

God loves all His children and we all have equal chances.

Do I extend my hand to all, even those I see as different from myself?

Today I will work on my prejudices by:

**God help me to stay clean and sober today!**

Trusting that our Higher Power wants the best for us also means trusting that He wants the best for our loved ones. God works in the lives of all. We can't believe that God has led us through rebellion, pain, and suffering to this fellowship, without believing He will also help everyone else.

It is just in different ways that God reaches all people, and we find it difficult to understand the wisdom behind all this. All we can do is carry the message by being an example–the rest is in God's hands. Do I feel secure knowing we are all in God's hands?

Lord, I entrust all those who are dear to me to Your never failing care and love.

I will express my trust in God's love today by:

Who can adequately describe the serenity and fulfillment of working our program through the years, through hard times, good times, gentle times, rocky times? Who can fully express the feelings of acceptance and peace in the midst of close and noisy places? How can we share the joy engrained deeply into our lives by our spiritual growth?

For men who have lived in the depths of despair and suffering, it is truly a miracle to pass into this new state of being. And we know surely that this is available to all who are willing to work for it. Am I willing to work the program wholeheartedly at all times?

Lord, help me remember always that working my program is the only way for me.

Today I will work the program especially hard in the following ways:

Even though many of us were certainly ready to admit that we were addicts, we balked at taking the eleven steps after step one. We felt it was too much work, or ridiculous work, or we disclaimed a belief in a Higher Power so that it seemed unnecessary.

But we forgot the promise of peace of mind contained in those steps. It was not until we hurt bad, or almost reached for that first fix, pill or drink that we woke up. The PROMISE! Then we made a decision to work these steps and gain that promise. Do I have peace of mind?

The plan is up to God; the decision is up to me.

My plan for working all of the steps today is:

God help me to stay clean and sober today!

We come to understand that we don't find God through reading, discussing, studying, thinking, or any other form of intellectual pursuit. God is found as we put principles into action. When we practice our principles, we set ourselves free, so that our ignorance does not stand between us and God.

We may gain insights by reading, discussing, studying, thinking, and so on. But we can never gain the freedom that truly comes from finding God, except through practicing the principles. Have I stopped intellectualizing about God?

Lord, remind me that insight is not freedom, and help me to do the things necessary for finding and knowing my Higher Power completely.

Today I will put my principles into action in the following ways:

Spiritual growth is an urge and also a quest. The urge is from within and the quest is manifested outwardly. Our quest suffers considerably when we make mind-altering chemicals our higher power. The urge for spiritual growth is still within us, but we have either lost sight of or never found our true purpose if we are still chained to our addiction.

For us the true quest is our program. While the urge for spiritual growth is always an individual one, we are privileged to share the same quest in our fellowship. Have I joined the common quest?

Father, let my quest for spiritual growth be in keeping with my true purpose.

I will seek to fulfill my urge for spiritual growth today by:

Our old ideas were often based on misconceptions of how the world was mistreating us. These misconceptions don't die easily, and it's hard to realize that the evils of the world were not what made us suffer. We made ourselves suffer. Our aimless rebellion only led us further down the road of destruction.

There can be no denying that our lifestyle contributed greatly to all the evils. It reminds us of the comic character who said, "I have found the enemy establishment pig, and he is me!" When we come to this realization, we suddenly become aware of how beautiful a world we really live in—because we let it be! Have I found the real world?

Lord, the world reflects what I see in myself—let me see love, beauty and kindness.

Today I will explore the real world by:

How often we mistake pleasure for happiness! Yet we can see many people enjoying every pleasure that the earth can provide, and despite this they are sad and lonely. Pleasure comes from the world, something outside of us. It can be deceiving and unsatisfying as we learned from our drug experiences. Pleasure left us no rewards and exacted a heavy toll as we sought our unrealized and unfulfilled dreams.

Happiness comes from within, from being secure in the knowledge of God's love for us. And we may truly know happiness when we have lost sight of ourselves in love for the Creative Force. Have I found happiness?

Lord, show me that happiness comes from actively experiencing You in my life.

I will express God's love today by:

We are not perfect. And because we are not perfect, we cannot expect to work the program perfectly. Some people sit around and feel sorry for themselves because they can't work the steps to perfection. But what they overlook is that they have not put forth enough effort.

All that is necessary is that we honestly try. Instead of feeling overwhelmed by all that we have to do—we just have to be willing to do it. We are not perfect; we only strive for progress. Am I still trying?

Lord, let me be satisfied with my progress, and not expect perfection from an imperfect being.

Today I will strive for spiritual progress by:

**God help me to stay clean and sober today!**

Our self-centeredness and resentments are the chains that bind us. It makes little difference whether these faults are outstanding or subtle, whether they are justified or unjustified. We are still in a bind.

It matters little whether we are held by a slender thread or by a heavy rope. If we are anchored we can't be freed until the bond that holds us is broken. A thin thread is more easily broken, but still it must be broken for us to be free.

Unless our attachments to negative things are broken, our union with the Divine Source is hindered. Have I broken free of my bonds?

Lord, help me discover and release all the character defects which hold me back from union with You.

I will try to break free of self-centeredness today by:

**God help me to stay clean and sober today!**

Without our fellowship, many people would not be able to cross the line to sanity. For those who are far from meeting places, letters and visits keep us close to one another. The fellowship is a pleasure and necessity, and many of us believe that it is a Divine gift from God.

There is perhaps nothing else that can so completely multiply all our joys and divide all our griefs. Have I given what I can to the fellowship today?

Lord, may I do one deed today that will increase the beauty of our fellowship.

Today I will enjoy the fellowship by sharing:

God help me to stay clean and sober today!

Principles, principles, principles. We talk so much about the principles of the twelve steps. But exactly what are the principles? HOW – Honesty, Open-mindedness, and Willingness are surely key ones.

If we can strive to live with these, we will be living according to important principles of our program. And working the twelve steps is the process of applying all of the principles. Do I practice honesty, open-mindedness and willingness at all times?

Lord, help me to apply honesty, open-mindedness, and willingness to every hour of this day.

I will practice honesty, open-mindedness and willingness today by:

We have passed from death into life. We know that a new life flows through us, and a new and beautiful serenity is ours. What we once despised, we now cherish. Our old drug world ceases to attract.

This is a blessing and a miracle, for we were considered the hopeless ones. Let us give thanks to God for our spiritual understanding and the blessings of a clean and sober life. Do I count my blessings each day?

Lord, I give thanks from the depths of my soul for the blessing of my new life.

Today I will look at my blessings, one by one, and:

**God help me to stay clean and sober today!**

What we believe today is always subject to change tomorrow. We change and grow in many ways. We don't have to adhere to yesterday's words just because we said them in public. We may have received new data for today's opinion! We don't have to grapple with our memories so that we won't say something that contradicts past words. We live always in a new day.

We can trust ourselves and our Higher Power if our words and messages are coming from "the still small voice within." We must remember that what was necessary for us yesterday may not be what we need today. Am I always open to growth, change and new ideas?

Lord, help me understand that I need not be rigidly consistent in what I think or say, but that I need to be consistent in continuing to grow.

I will question my beliefs today about:

Therapy is no substitute for the program. Religious doctrine is no substitute for the program. Words are no substitute for the program. Intelligence is no substitute for the program. Heroic acts are no substitute for the program. "Easy does it" is no substitute for the program. Education is no substitute for the program.

Sex is no substitute for the program. A warm heart is no substitute for the program. A job is no substitute for the program. Only action, only the steps are going to get it for us. There are no substitutes. Do I realize there are no quick and easy ways?

Lord, may I stop playing games, may I stop using excuses, and may I do what I can in my program today.

Today I will work the program extra hard by:

Not one of us has tasted the success of our sobriety and cleanness until we have awakened to a glorious day. It is made up of boundless energy, limitless joy, and knowing that whatever God's will for us, it is good.

It tastes of spring to meet the day with the thrill of being alive. On these days we can feel a true spiritual joy that comes from feeling like a corpuscle in the body of God. Do I savor life?

Thank You, Father, for this day. Whatever Your will is for me, I know it is good.

I will enjoy being alive today by:

At first, *really hearing* fellow addicts is an exciting experience. We may charge off explaining our insights at meetings and social gatherings. We truly need to share in this manner, but it should not affect us too much when other people don't accept our pearls of wisdom. What may be a gem for us could be a mere pebble for another.

So when others "shoot us down" for something we've said, we needn't take it too personally. What is right for one may not be right for another. However, we all have the right to express our opinions. Do I share my views freely with others?

Lord, may my sharing not turn into imposing, and may I not take opinions as personal insults or rejections.

Today I will share my deepest insights with:

It is well for us to know the Author of our hopes and desires. If we do not know who we follow, and why we follow Him, anything can lead us anywhere. The steps are helpful tools in learning to know our true Author. They are a personal path to God and give us guidance beyond anything we have experienced before.

Our lives can only be written for us *now*. The past cannot be erased nor the future written before it happens. Only today's activities are recorded today. Who is the Author of my life?

May today be written by the Supreme Author.

I will try to make today's page beautiful by:

God help me to stay clean and sober today!

By joining a program of this nature, going to meetings, working steps, associating with fellow addicts—we might begin to wonder about our personalities and individuality. Personality is what we wish others to think and see. Individuality is what our soul prays and hopes for. One is desire for personal recognition and the other is universal consciousness.

Our program is designed so that we may learn how to meet our conditions from our individuality and not our worldly personalities. It is not necessary to worry about personality when we are meeting our life conditions, individually, with God, because personality grows as a result of this. Am I a true individual?

Lord, may I get past my personality so I may meet You face to face, as an individual.

Today I will express my individuality by:

There are friends we play with as in sports and dancing–this is purely a pleasure plane. Then we have friends in our professions and jobs–this is a slightly higher plane of common interests. Next is the identity and intellectual plane where we share each others favorite topics. But the highest and most beautiful plane of friendship is one on which we share the same spiritual quest.

We have the glory, through this fellowship, of experiencing immediate communion and intimacy with our people wherever we go. Such friendships last as long as the solution which is our common bond. Have I found a multitude of friends?

Lord, thank You for the blessing of a world full of friends who share my spiritual purpose.

I will offer my friendship today to:

For many of us the prospect of death was not a big thing. In fact, there were many times while drinking or using drugs that we would have preferred to die. So it may not have seemed much of a favor to have our lives saved by God.

But what God also did was to show us that our lives were *worth* saving. This was the big step for us. We deserved to live!

We were worth saving! We were not such wretches as we had led ourselves to believe! How glorious to have our Higher Power show us where we could do His work, carry the message, and be worth something to ourselves, to Him, and to countless others! Do I value my life highly?

Thank You, Lord, for showing me that, after all, I am worth saving.

Today I will enhance my self-worth by:

## December 1 A Rewarding Way Of Life

Let us pause today and ask ourselves this question, "Why have I chosen this new way of life?" To the sick and weary, it seems a long, hard road to travel. We often would like an easier, softer path, but we know it would not satisfy us. Mind-altering chemicals ceased to satisfy us, and we had no choice left but this fellowship.

We come to realize that there is no other way to stay clean and sober, than to reach an understanding and oneness with our Higher Power. Yes, the way is sometimes hard, but the rewards are great. Do I relish my new way of life?

Lord, may I not falter because the way is hard, but rejoice because the rewards are great.

I will enjoy my new way of life today by:

God help me to stay clean and sober today!

Those with seemingly the greatest burdens may be the most blessed, if they recognize the challenge of the burdens. The richness of joy is somehow in direct proportion to the experience of suffering. Each of us has known a sense of achievement, and the depth of that feeling has been influenced by the failures we have known.

Before the blooms appear so hopefully in spring, the barren winter must come and go. To bring out the best in us, we have to overcome the obstacles of life, ask for strength to deal with them, and learn to accept them on a daily basis. Have I grown as a result of my difficulties?

Lord, help me accept my problems as opportunities to have Your power demonstrated in my life.

Today I will shoulder my heaviest burden and:

God help me to stay clean and sober today!

We are all fellow travelers on our way to God, whatever our conception of God is. There are many paths and modes of transportation for us to choose from. There are many teachers to help guide the way.

But we should never forget that no one can show the whole way but Him. So we must open our hearts and minds to our Higher Power, that He may work through us and show us the way. Am I on the way?

Lord, may I begin to know the way, and as I go along may more be revealed to me.

I will seek to find the way today by:

Under the influence of drugs our thinking and our behavior changed. This is one of the hallmarks of an addict. Under the influence, nothing was real. A good day wasn't really much more satisfying than a terrible one, because we always had the feeling of being on the periphery, on the outside looking in.

The good days provided no joy; they were unfulfilling. We often played a sadistic game, sickeningly aware at the time that we were hurting ourselves as well as others involved. But at the same time we felt very misunderstood, like, "don't they know we don't want to be this way?" Am I under a new influence now?

Lord, help me slow down today and have courage to live in the now.

Today I will savor life by:

When we talk about being clean and sober, we are not talking about any kind of trance, ecstasy or high. We are not talking about the aloof, alienated thinker who withdraws from society. Nor are we talking about the rigid, unbending one who screams for temperance. The sobriety and cleanness we are talking about is living today well.

We enjoy our children and friends, live life to the fullest, and are engaged in many activities. Some of us are great lovers, husbands, wives or leaders. We all, at times, suffer anguish and doubt. No, we are not drawn away from life, but to it. Am I living today well?

Lord, let my love of the world shine forth from the irresistible burning love of God.

My plan for living today well is:

There are many times in our drug free lives that we experience great joy and happiness. Because of our past lives we often feel so guilty that it is difficult for us to accept this happiness. Often we will create new problems to avoid being happy.

Because we are familiar with past problems, we feel more comfortable in that type of situation. However, we must try to accept God's gifts of joy to us, and we must try to learn that we are acceptable to God. Have I learned how to accept joy and happiness?

Lord, may I truly know in my heart that You love me, and that I am acceptable in Your eyes.

Today I will savor the joy of living by:

Troubles we find are of our own making. At first it is hard to understand that trials and suffering are our own fault. Sometimes we find ourselves asking, "Why does God let these things happen to me?" But this is God's way of letting us come to the realization that we are on the wrong path.

The longer we fail to accept responsibility for our own actions, the longer it takes to have a full relationship with our Creator. We have to acknowledge that our failures and hardships are ours, not our parents', society's or God's. Do I accept full responsibility for all my actions?

Lord, may my desire be such that I turn to You for guidance, and stop blaming others for my misfortunes.

I will look at my personal responsibility today in relation to the following problems:

God help me to stay clean and sober today!

Our lives have not come to a standstill. Once we have decided not to take that first fix, pill or drink, our lives have just begun. This program isn't a big punishment, but a glorious gift from God.

When things are bad, we can change them to good. When things are good, we can improve them. There are many things we must do to go forward, for if we stay at a standstill, what is it worth? With God's guidance we can go forward, and not get stuck in a rut. Am I out of all the old ruts?

Lord, may I realize that this program is not a punishment but a step forward with You.

Today I will take a step forward by improving:

God help me to stay clean and sober today!

Once we are clean and sober, there are many things we have to face that we rationalized away before. Often we find that we are not only mentally sick, but have harmed our bodies as well. It is important that we do what we can for our bodies, then turn it over to our Higher Power.

After years of mistreatment of ourselves, we cannot expect perfect health immediately. Some conditions may even be permanent. The next time we start to feel sorry for ourselves because our bodies are not perfect, let us breathe in and out and listen to our heartbeat. Can we say our Father is not good to us? How is my spiritual health?

Father, let me be grateful for my daily breath, and although I may not be perfect of body, let me strive for perfection of soul.

I will enhance my spiritual health today by:

Many of us thought of ourselves at some point as loving persons. That is why we reproached ourselves so when we observed that we could not "love" someone as we thought we should. We knew we couldn't love the person, but we presumed that it was our "fault." We didn't realize that love is a gift from God.

We didn't know that to find love we needed only to ask for it. It is when love occurs between us and our enemies that we know beyond a shadow of a doubt that God is with us. We know in such situations that we could not love of ourselves. Do I have the gift of love?

Father, help me be willing today to love any person you set in my path.

Today I will ask God for love in my relationship with:

Do we remember the "geographical cure?" Remember the days when we were using and we felt "if only we could just change our location our problems would melt away." Some of us left the city. Some left the state. Others thought the communes had the answer. Some even sought the answer in other countries.

But we found that our program was the only answer for us. Wherever we went we always brought our selves along. Unless we changed ourselves, we learned, the whole universe could not provide the answer. Has there been a change within?

Lord, let me hear the "still small voice within" and know that change begins within me.

I will analyze what has changed today by:

God help me to stay clean and sober today!

We find that our turmoils and strife are caused by emotions within ourselves. Other people are not going to subvert us or make life unbearable. Whatever happens, the turmoil will not be in the event, but in our reaction to it.

If a friend slips and falls, will we react with, "Look what you have done to me?," or will we offer patience and love? Will our hearts be torn with turmoil and conflict when we are frustrated in our dealings with others, or will they be filled with understanding and the spirit of God's love? Have I stopped reacting?

Lord, I pray that I may gain strength in Your love, and turn away the strife caused by unbelief and fear.

Today I will handle any frustration placidly by:

**God help me to stay clean and sober today!**

We believe that God can restore us to sanity. If we work on getting spiritually fit, we know our mental and physical problems will straighten out.

God can and will heal us. God can and will guide us. We believe in our Higher Power. Have I been restored to sane living?

Father, teach me to be willing to believe that you can and will restore me to sanity.

I will work on sane behavior today regarding the following problems:

What we don't possess, we cannot give away. What we don't live, we cannot teach others to live. As when we were using, our very acts condemn us. Before we can tell others about the joys of a chemical-free existence, we must be living that chemical-free existence.

Only through God's guidance can we really carry the message to others. Only through God's guidance will we be led to the right people to help. Do I give it away every day?

Lord, I pray that I may be a channel of Your blessing to others.

Today I will give it away to:

There are many bad things that happen to us that we do not understand. Many things we will never understand and do not need to understand. It is a matter of scale. We do not need to know the city in the same detail that we know our neighborhood, and certainly not in the same detail that we know our own homes.

It is the recurrent bad things that we need to understand. We can gain understanding from the fellowship, from the steps and from our sponsors. The cycle can be broken by uncovering the old ideas and habits that initiate the recurrent bad things. How well do I understand myself?

Father, help me be willing to give up those old ideas and habits of mine that cause bad things to happen.

I will look at the bad things in my life today and seek to understand them by:

We have to learn to be more and more rigorously honest with ourselves. If we can't be honest with ourselves, we can't be honest with others, we can't be honest with God, and we certainly can't expect to change.

If we call a cab to one address, and we are, in fact, at another, we cannot say that the cab failed to pick us up. So it is with God. If we ask for healing of one thing and our malady is something else, we cannot expect the change we hoped for.

We have to begin noticing how we really feel and how our guts react. Most of us have very tricky heads but very honest guts! Do I have gut-level honesty?

Lord, help me not feed my dishonesty with myself today. Help me to observe where I'm really at today and to accept it.

Today I will explore my gut reactions to things by:

God help me to stay clean and sober today!

We are the survivors! We are the ones that lived long enough to be able to let God save our lives. We managed not to O.D., die of cirrhosis, die in a car accident, die in jail, get shot, or meet any of the other horrible ends associated with our disease.

By the grace of God, we may never have to live in that world again. If we tend to forget where we came from, let us visit the detox units of our local hospitals. We will be reminded by observing victims of D.T.'s, brain damage, and many other injuries resulting from the abuse of mind-altering chemicals. Do I remember where I came from?

Father, let me never forget where I came from, and where I could go back to if I don't learn to live by Your principles.

I will recall the past today by:

There are many slogans in our fellowship that might appear trite to the uninitiated. "Easy Does It." "First Things First." "Live and Let Live." "One day at a Time." "Keep It Simple."

These slogans were developed from the experiences of many others, and are anything but trite. Next time we hear them, let's consider if they're working in our lives. It may be the difference between a good program or just staying off the stuff. Do I appreciate the full meaning in our slogans?

Lord, let me be able to hear the things others have done, so they may be able to aid me today.

Today I will coin the following new slogan:

**God help me to stay clean and sober today!**

It is not knowledge or understanding that leads us to the new life. If that were so, psychiatrists and psychologists would have a better success rate with us. But they admit defeat. So what is the source of our success? It is the application of the opportunities that God presents to us each day.

Let us follow the promptings that come to us from our Higher Power—that we may better learn what it means to live in His glory. What originates from the soul will be expressed in our daily dealings with our fellows. And it is not only the knowledge of God, but the application of what we learn from Him, that makes for success. How well do I express my soul in daily living?

Lord, through the power You have given me, may I make known Your beauty and love to others.

I will follow my Higher Power today by:

Leaving the life of mind-altering chemicals and turning to our Creator in this fellowship does not infer that we will become mindless, spiritless, sexless robots. It doesn't mean all fun will be taken from us.

Being one with God gives us life; it doesn't take life away. It means we have the opportunity to gain more abundant life. We become able to think, feel, and breathe with more perception and depth than we ever could have imagined in our addiction. Is my life full and rich?

Lord, let my eyes see the beauty, let my ears hear the happiness, let my body feel the joy, and let my words spread the hope.

Today I will enrich my life by:

No matter how long we abused mind-altering drugs, no matter how desperately we led our lives, we should never think that our opportunity has passed. God's grace is without limit. We can make our choice at any time and finally come to realize that TODAY is always acceptable to our Lord.

We must never feel that it is too late or that we have failed too often to be acceptable to God. He loves us and He is loving us NOW, TODAY, ALWAYS. All things are possible with our Father, and He will always give us life and love unless we choose otherwise. Can I feel God's love now?

May I know that today is always the acceptable day to my Father.

I will choose God's love today by:

The way is simple, and the way is through our Higher Power. Those who seek through mysterious cults, strange manifestations of the earth, or friends and neighbors will become troubled and confused.

For the voice and guidance is within, and only we can know what God has to say to us—not others. We should always remember that God abides within us—not in strange places around the world. Do I follow my conscience in all things?

Lord, today I will know and listen to the "still, small voice within."

Today I will seek inner guidance by:

Our activities are our voluntary choices. What we choose to work on and live with will show in our lives. If we choose to go to drinking or pot parties, or to have practicing addicts in our social life—then we will probably head back to our old environment.

If we choose to associate with clean and sober people and surround ourselves with people on the path to God, then we are more likely to grow to be beautiful, clean people. We can be shown the way if we are willing to choose the activities that make for growth. Our Higher Power will constantly disclose these activities to us. Do I always choose wisely?

Lord, may I learn to choose the activities that will lead to growth, not despair.

I will choose the good today by:

Often we find that it is very difficult to accept things from other people. We don't want to be obligated to them for loving us, giving us money, or helping us in any way. We feel that we may have to do or be things in return for their help. But let us remember that all of their help comes from God, and God works through people.

As long as we remain true to our God, all things are right. It's only when we deviate from our true purpose that we make mistakes in accepting things. God loves us and will provide all things if we remain true to His Purpose. Have I learned to accept help from others?

Lord, I want to accept all gifts from Thee, be they mental, emotional or material.

Today I will help:

Giving is the spirit of Christmas, and we need not suffer because we don't understand the nature of giving. Many of us suffer from feelings of inadequacy on this day, but for a reason a little more subtle than our usual egotism. Though we don't know it, we suffer from feeling inadequate to the magnificence of the true Christmas spirit.

We are all God's children. We should joyfully accept His gifts of love, peace, fellowship, sobriety and cleanness that He showers on each of us who desires them on this day and forever. Do I have the true Christmas spirit?

Thank you, Lord, for Your gifts to me today and every day.

I will share in the true Christmas spirit today by:

Our reaction after the Christmas holidays can be discouraging because the excitement is over, but also because we approach a new year. This can lead us to feel fear and get us into a bag of looking at the past and worrying about the future.

But if we remember we only have today, we can work today to make that future better. We have found true friends in our fellowship and this is a time to be together. Am I insuring the future by working with all I've got today?

Lord, I pray for guidance and help for today, and freedom from worry about tomorrow.

Today I will work for the fellowship by:

God help me to stay clean and sober today!

There is certainly a thing called danger for us. The biggest danger is that of delusion. Delusion, once started, is unable to check itself. Once we lost sight of honesty, we get caught up in a world of delusion and can lose sight of all that is good for us.

But there is a guide for us, a knowing Guide who will always help the wanderer. If that Guide is not heeded, it is only because we are caught up in the midst of our delusion—but sincere petition will always bring our Guide to our aid. Do I follow my true Guide?

May I be able to call upon my Guide whenever I get caught up in my delusions.

I will check myself for delusions today by:

Slowly we have to change the attitudes of the mind, and put away hate, resentment, anxiety and jealousy. These can be replaced with love of the Spirit, patience, mercy, kindness and gentleness.

When we practice these new attitudes, we will break down old barriers. Our outlook on life will cease to consist of finding fault because someone forgot something, someone's judgement was bad, or someone acted selfishly. These things can be overlooked, just as He does with us. Have I changed my attitudes?

Lord, may the desire of my heart be to change my attitudes, and to see and reflect the glory of God in man.

Today I will appraise my current attitudes by:

**God help me to stay clean and sober today!**

We find in our daily lives that there are people who have no Higher Power or God. Some of these people may ridicule us for our belief. But we *need* faith to get better.

It is important to rely on God, as He is the only One who can save us from drugs and alcohol. We must remember to practice faith and belief, and not to be swayed by contrary opinions. Am I a true believer?

Lord, I pray that I may have the patience to love my fellow man no matter what his beliefs.

I will express my faith today by:

When we were in the streets we acquired many social friends. They were our friends until the bad times came, and then where were they? With our new understanding, friends take on a new meaning. Are we ready to have friends? Like begets like. If we show ourselves friendly, there will be friends.

We needn't impose ourselves on friends, but rather create hope and help in their lives. A kind word here, a brotherly act there–not great deeds, just availability is all that is really necessary. This is how we can show ourselves worthy of being called friend. Am I a true friend?

Lord, may I be able to offer hope and help and acts of kindness to the ones I call friends.

Today I will befriend:

**God help me to stay clean and sober today!**

It was not a perfect year. But is there ever a perfect year? Being clean and sober does not purport to offer perfection. What it does is give us a chance to strive for progress. When we are keeping God in our thoughts and actions, we come closer to perfection all the time.

Despite the disappointments of our complex lives, we are finally beginning to learn how to live. We are finally making progress. Am I content to be less than perfect?

Lord, I pray that I may continue to strive for progress, and be satisfied to be an imperfect human.

I will enjoy my humanity today by:

*Other daily meditation books that will interest you . . .*

**Each Day a New Beginning**

The first daily meditation guide created by and for women involved in Twelve Step recovery programs. Hundreds of thousands of women have found help in this collection of thoughts and reflections that offers hope, strength, and guidance every day of the year. 400 pp.
Order No. 1076

**Touchstones**

As recovering men, becoming more open about our feelings, becoming whole people, and finding spiritual enlightenment are important paths in our new lives. These ideas are at the heart of *Touchstones,* a book of daily meditations for recovering men seeking support in dealing with contemporary issues. 400 pp.
Order No. 5029

---

Enid Blyton's

# THE MYSTERY OF THE STRANGE MESSAGES

## *Also in the* Mystery *series*

The Mystery of the Burnt Cottage
The Mystery of the Disappearing Cat
The Mystery of the Secret Room
The Mystery of the Spiteful Letters
The Mystery of the Missing Necklace
The Mystery of the Hidden House
The Mystery of the Pantomime Cat
The Mystery of the Invisible Thief
The Mystery of the Vanished Prince
The Mystery of the Strange Bundle
The Mystery of Holly Lane
The Mystery of Tally-Ho Cottage
The Mystery of the Missing Man
The Mystery of the Strange Messages
The Mystery of Banshee Towers

Neha Baporikar

Enid Blyton's

# THE MYSTERY OF THE STRANGE MESSAGES

MAMMOTH

First published in Great Britain 1957
by Methuen & Co Ltd
This edition first published 1991 by Dean
an imprint of the Hamlyn Publishing Group
Published 1996 by Mammoth
an imprint of Reed International Books Limited
Michelin House, 81 Fulham Road, London SW3 6RB
and Auckland and Melbourne

Reprinted 1997 (three times)



ISBN 0 7497 1981 8

A CIP catalogue record for this title
is available from the British Library

# CONTENTS

# 1 MR. GOON IS ANGRY

MR. GOON, the village policeman, was in a very bad temper. He sat at his desk, and stared at three pieces of paper there, spread out before him. Beside them were three cheap envelopes.

On each sheet of paper separate words were pasted in uneven lines. 'They're all words cut out of some newspaper,' said Mr. Goon. 'So's the writer's handwriting wouldn't give him away, I suppose! And what nonsense they make—look at this one now— "TURN HIM OUT OF THE IVIES!" What does *that* mean, I'd like to know. And this one— "ASK SMITH WHAT HIS REAL NAME IS". Who's Smith?'

He stared at the last piece of paper. 'CALL YOURSELF A POLICEMAN? BETTER GO AND SEE SMITH.'

'Gah!' said Mr. Goon. 'Better put them all into the waste-paper basket!' He took one of the envelopes and looked at it. It was a very cheap one, square in shape, and on each one was pasted two words only.

Mr. goon.

Each word was pasted separately, as if cut from a newspaper. Goon's surname had no capital letter, and he nodded his head at that.

'Must be a fellow with no education that put my

name with a small letter,' he said. 'What's he mean—all this business about some place called The Ivies, and a fellow called Smith? Must be mad! Rude too— "Call myself a policeman!" I'll tell him a few things when I see him.'

He gave a sudden shout. 'Mrs. Hicks! Come here a minute, will you?'

Mrs. Hicks, the woman who came in to clean for Mr. Goon, shouted back, 'Let me wipe me hands and I'll be there!'

Mr. Goon frowned. Mrs. Hicks treated him as if he were an ordinary man, not a policeman, whose frown ought to send her scuttling, and whose voice ought to bring her in at top speed. After a minute or two she arrived, panting as if she had run for miles.

'Just in the middle of washing-up,' she began. 'And I think I'd better tell you, Mr. Goon, you want a couple of new cups, and a . . .'

'I've no time to talk about crockery,' said Mr. Goon, snappily. 'Now see here . . .'

'And me tea-cloth is just about in rags,' went on Mrs. Hicks. 'How I'm supposed to wash up with . . .'

'MRS. HICKS! I called you in on an official matter,' said the policeman, sternly.

'All right, all right,' said Mrs. Hicks, in a huff. 'What's up? If you want my advice on that fellow who goes round stealing the vegetables off our allotments, well, I can give a good guess. I . . .'

'Be quiet, woman,' said Mr. Goon, fiercely, wishing he could clap her into a cell for an hour or two. 'I merely want to ask you a few questions.'

'What about? I've done nothing wrong,' said Mrs. Hicks, a little alarmed at Goon's angry face.

'Look—see these three letters you brought in to me?' said Goon, pushing the envelopes over towards Mrs. Hicks. 'Well, where exactly did you find them? You said one was in the coal-shed, on the shovel.'

'That's right,' said Mrs. Hicks, 'set right in the middle of the shovel it was. And all it said on the envelope was "Mr goon" and I brought it straight into you today.'

'And where did you say the others were?' asked Mr. Goon, in his most official manner.

'Well, one come in through the letter-box some time,' said Mrs. Hicks, 'and you weren't in so I put it on your desk. And the second one was on the dustbin lid, sir—stuck there with a bit of sticky paper. Couldn't help but see it when I went to empty the dustpan. And what I say is, it's pretty queer to have notes all . . .'

'Yes, yes,' said Mr. Goon. 'Have you seen anyone sneaking about round the back? Somebody must have climbed over the fence to put the notes in the coal-shed and on the dustbin.'

'I haven't seen no one,' said Mrs. Hicks, 'and what's more if I had, I'd have taken my broom and given him a whack on the head. What's in the notes, sir—anything important?'

'No,' said Mr. Goon. 'It's probably all just a silly joke—you don't know of any place here called The Ivies, do you?'

'The Ivies?' said Mrs. Hicks, considering. 'No, I don't.

Sure you don't mean "The Poplars," sir? Now, a nice gentleman lives there, sir, I do for him each Friday when I don't come to you, and he's ever so nice to me, he. . .'

'I said The *Ivies*, not The Poplars,' said Mr. Goon. 'All right. You can go, Mrs. Hicks. But keep an eye on the back garden, will you? I'd like to get a description of whoever it is leaving these notes about the place.'

'I will that, sir,' said Mrs. Hicks. 'And what about me getting you a couple more cups, sir—one broke in my hand, and . . .'

'Oh, *get* the cups,' said Mr. Goon. 'And I don't want to be disturbed for the next hour. I've important work to do!'

'So've I,' said Mrs. Hicks. 'That kitchen stove of yours is just crying out for a good clean and . . .'

'Well, go and stop it crying,' snapped Mr. Goon, and heaved a sigh of relief as Mrs. Hicks disappeared in a huff.

He studied the three notes again, puzzling over the cut-out, pasted on words. What newspaper had they been cut from? It would be a help to find out, but Goon could see no way of discovering that. Who had sent them—and why? There wasn't any place called 'The Ivies' in Peterswood.

He took up a local directory of roads and houses again, and went through it carefully. Then he picked up the telephone receiver.

When the exchange answered he asked for the postmaster. 'P. C. Goon here,' he said, importantly, and at once he was put through to the right department.

'Er—Postmaster,' said Goon, 'I want a little

information, please. 'Is there a house—possibly a new one—called The Ivies here in Peterswood?'

'The Ivies?' said the Postmaster. 'Let me think—Ivies. No, there isn't, Mr. Goon. There's The Poplars, though, that might be . . .'

'It is *not* The Poplars,' said Goon. 'I'm also looking for someone called Smith, who . . .'

'Smith? Oh, I can give you the addresses of at least fifteen Smiths in Peterswood,' said the Postmaster. 'Do you want them now?'

'No, I don't,' said Mr. Goon, desperately, and put down the receiver with a bang. He gazed at the three notes again. No address on them. No name at the bottom. Where did they come from? Who had sent them? Did they mean anything—or was it a fat-headed joke?

A joke? Who would dare to play a joke like that on *him*, P. C. Goon, representative of the law for Peterswood? An uneasy feeling crept over Mr. Goon, as a vision of a plump boy with a broad grin on his face came into his mind.

'That fat boy! Frederick Trotteville!' he said, out loud. 'He's home for the holidays—and he won't have gone back to school yet. Gah! That toad of a boy! He'd think it was clever to send me notes like this—sending me off on a false trail—putting me on a wrong scent—deceiving me and making me look for houses called The Ivies. GAH!'

He sat down to do some work, but at the back of his mind was the continual thought that it might be Fatty Trotteville playing a joke, and he found himself unusually slow with the making out of his reports. In the middle of his second report Mrs. Hicks came running in, breathless as usual.

'Mr. Goon, sir—here's another of them notes!' she said, panting as if she had run a mile, and putting another of the familiar square envelopes down on Mr. Goon's desk. He stared at it. Yes—his name was there as usual, pasted on the envelope. 'Mr. goon'. No capital letter for his surname—so it was obviously from the same sender.

'Did you see anyone? Where did you find it?' demanded Mr. Goon, slitting it open very carefully.

'Well, I went to hang out my dish-cloth—and a real rag it is too,' said Mrs. Hicks. 'And when I put my hand into the peg-bag, there was this letter—on top of the pegs!'

'Was anyone about?' asked Mr. Goon.

'No—the only person who's been this morning is the butcher-boy with your chops, sir,' said Mrs. Hicks.

'BUTCHER-boy !' said Goon, starting up, and making Mrs. Hicks step backwards in fright. 'HO! Now we know where we are! Butcher-boy! Did you see this boy?'

'No, sir. I was upstairs making your bed,' said Mrs. Hicks, alarmed at Goon's purple face. 'I just called out to him to leave the meat on the table, and he did, because I found it there, and he went off whistling, and . . .'

'All right. That's enough. I know all I want to know now,' said Goon. 'I'm going out, Mrs. Hicks, so answer the telephone for me till I'm back. And you'll be glad to know that's the last of these notes you'll find. Butcher-boy! *I'll* butcher-boy him! I'll . . .'

'But Charlie Jones is a *good* lad!' said Mrs. Hicks. 'He's

the best boy the butcher ever had, he told me so. He . . .'

'I'm not thinking of Charlie Jones,' said Mr. Goon, putting on his helmet, and adjusting the strap. 'Ho no—I'm thinking of someone else! And that someone else is going to get a Nasty Shock.'

Mrs. Hicks was puzzled and curious, but not another word would Mr. Goon say. He strode out of his office, fetched his bicycle and rode off. In his pocket were the four notes he had received. He thought over the fourth one as he rode down the street. Ten words, cut out from newspapers again, and pasted on the sheet. 'You'll be sorry if you don't go and see Smith.'

'It's that fat boy, Frederick Trotteville, I'm certain it is,' thought Goon, pedalling fast. 'Ha—he disguised himself as a butcher-boy again, did he? Well, he's done that before, and he's made a great mistake doing it again! I can see through you, you toad of a boy! Wasting my time with idiotic notes! I've got you this time. You just wait!'

He turned in at Fatty's gate, and rode up the drive to the house. At once a small Scottie raced out of the bushes, barking gleefully at the policeman's ankles.

'You clear orf!' shouted Mr. Goon, and kicked out at the delighted dog. 'Bad as your master you are! Clear orf, I say!'

'Hallo, Mr. Goon!' said Fatty's voice. 'Come here, Buster. You can't treat your best friend like that! You seem in a hurry, Mr. Goon.'

The policeman dismounted, his face red with pedalling so furiously. 'You keep that dog off me,' he said.

'I want a word with you, Master Frederick Trotteville. In fact, I want a Long Talk. Ha—you thought you were very clever, didn't you, sending all those notes?'

'I really don't know what you're talking about,' said Fatty, puzzled. 'But do come in. We'll have a nice cosy chat together!'

## 2. A NEW MYSTERY, PERHAPS?

FATTY took Mr. Goon in at the side door and then into the sitting-room. 'Is your mother in—or your father?' asked Goon, thinking that it would be good for them to see their wonderful son properly ticked off by him.

'No, they're out,' said Fatty. 'But Larry and the others are here. I'm sure they would be interested to hear your little tale, whatever it is. We've been a bit dull these holidays, so far—no mystery to solve, Mr. Goon. I suppose you haven't one that you want any help with?'

'You'd talk the hind leg off a donkey, you would,' said Mr. Goon, glad to get a word in. 'So those friends of yours are here, are they? Yes, you bring them in. Do them good to hear what I've got to say!'

Fatty went to the door and gave such a loud shout that Mr. Goon almost jumped out of his skin. It made Buster come out from under a chair and bark madly. Mr. Goon glared at him.

'You keep away from me, you pest of a dog,' he said. 'Master Frederick, can't you send that animal out of the room? If he comes near me I'll give him such a kick.'

'No, you won't,' said Fatty. 'You wouldn't want me to report you to the police for cruelty to an animal, would you, Mr. Goon? Buster, sit!'

There was the sound of feet coming down the stairs,

and Larry, Daisy, Pip and Bets rushed in, eager to know why Fatty had yelled so loudly. They stopped short when they saw the stout policeman.

'Oh—hallo, Mr. Goon,' said Larry, surprised. 'What a pleasant surprise!'

'So you're all here, are you?' said Mr. Goon, glaring round. 'Hatching mischief as usual, I suppose?'

'Well, not exactly,' said Pip. 'Fatty's mother is having a jumble sale, and we're turning out the attic for her to see what we can find. Have *you* got any jumble to spare, Mr. Goon—a couple of old helmets that don't fit you, perhaps—they'd sell like hot cakes.'

Bets gave a sudden giggle, and then retreated hurriedly behind Fatty as Goon looked sternly at her.

'Sit down, all of you,' commanded Mr. Goon. 'I've come here about a serious matter. I thought I'd see what you've got to say about it before I report it to Headquarters.'

'This sounds very very interesting,' said Fatty, sitting on the couch. 'Do sit down too, Mr. Goon. Let's all be comfortable and listen to your bedtime story.'

'It won't do you any good to be cheeky, Master Frederick, I can tell you that,' said Mr. Goon, seating himself majestically in the biggest arm-chair in the room. 'No, that it won't. First of all—why weren't you upstairs in the attics with the others?'

Fatty looked astonished. 'I brought some jumble downstairs to stack in the garage,' he said. 'Then I heard old Buster barking and came to see who the visitor was. Why?'

'Ho! Well, let me tell you that *I* know what you've

been doing this morning!' said Goon. 'You've been putting on that butcher-boy disguise of yours, haven't you? Oh yes, I know all about it! You got out your striped butcher-boy apron, didn't you—and you put on that red wig—and . . .'

'I'm sorry to say that I didn't,' said Fatty. 'I agree that it would have been much more exciting to parade round as a butcher-boy, than to stagger downstairs with smelly old jumble—but I must be truthful, Mr. Goon. You wouldn't like me to tell a lie, just to please you, would you? I'm afraid I *haven't* been a butcher-boy this morning!'

'Ho! You haven't—so you *say*!' said Mr. Goon, raising his voice. 'And I suppose you didn't leave a note in my peg-bag when you came to my house? And you didn't leave one on my coal-shovel and. . .'

Fatty was too astonished for words. So were the others. They looked at one another, wondering uneasily if Mr. Goon had gone mad. Peg-bags? Coal-shovels? What next?

'And I suppose you thought it was *very* clever to stick a note on my dustbin lid?' went on Mr. Goon, his voice growing louder still. He stared round at the silent children, who were all gazing at him, astounded.

'Where will you put the notes next?' he said sarcastically. 'Go on, tell me. Where? I'd like to know, then I could look there.'

'Well, let's see,' said Fatty, frowning hard. 'What about inside a watering-can—if you've got one, have you, Mr. Goon. Or in your shopping-basket . . .'

'Or on his dressing-table,' said Larry, joining in. 'He wouldn't have to go and look for a note there. It would be right under his nose.'

Mr. Goon had gone purple. He looked round threateningly, and Bets half-thought she would make a dash out of the door. She didn't like Mr. Goon when he looked like that!

'That's not funny,' said Mr. Goon, angrily. 'Not at all funny. It only makes me more certain than ever that you've planned those silly notes together.'

'Mr. Goon, we haven't the least idea what you're talking about,' said Fatty, seeing that the policeman really had some serious complaint to do with notes sent to him. 'Suppose you tell us what you've come about—and we'll tell you quite honestly whether we know anything about it or not.'

'Well, I *know* you're mixed up in it, Master Frederick,' said Goon. 'It—it *smells* of you. Just the sort of thing you'd do, to make a bit of fun for the others. But sending anonymous notes isn't funny. It's wrong.'

'What are *anonymous* notes? asked Bets. 'I don't quite know.'

'They're letters sent by someone who is afraid to put his name at the end,' explained Fatty. 'Usually anonymous notes have no address and no signature—and they're only sent by mean, cowardly people. Isn't that so, Mr. Goon?'

'That is so,' said the policeman. 'And I tell you straight, Master Frederick, that you've described yourself good and proper, if you sent those notes!'

'Well, I didn't,' said Fatty, beginning to lose patience. 'For goodness' sake, Mr. Goon, come to the point, and tell us what's happened. We're completely in the dark.'

'Oh no, you're not,' said Goon, and took the four notes from his pocket, each in their envelopes. He handed them to Fatty, who slid the notes out of their envelopes, one by one, and read them out loud.

'Here's the first note. All it says is "Ask Smith what his real name is." And here's the second. "Turn him out of the Ivies." And this one says "Call yourself a policeman? Go and see Smith!" And the last one says "You'll be sorry if you don't go and see Smith!" Well—what queer notes! Look, all of you—they're not even handwritten!'

He passed them round. 'Whoever wrote them cut the words out of newspapers—and then pasted them on the sheets of writing-paper,' said Larry. 'That's a common trick with people who don't want their writing recognized.'

'This is really rather peculiar,' said Fatty, most interested. 'Who's Smith? And where is the house called "The Ivies"?'

'Don't know one,' said Daisy. 'But there's "The Poplars"—it's in our road.'

'Gah!' said Mr. Goon, aggravated to hear 'The Poplars' suggested once more. Nobody took any notice of him.

'And there's "The Firs",' said Bets, 'and "The Chestnuts". But I can't think of any house called "The Ivies".'

'And this Mr. Smith,' said Fatty, staring at one of the notes. 'Why should he have to be turned out of the Ivies, wherever it is? And why should Mr. Goon ask him what his *real* name is? It must be someone going under a false name for some purpose. Most peculiar.'

'It *really* sounds like a mystery!' said Pip, hopefully. 'We haven't had one this hols. This is exciting.'

'And the notes were put into a peg-bag—and on a coal-shovel—and stuck to the dustbin,' said Fatty, frowning. 'Isn't that what you said, Mr. Goon? Where was the fourth one?'

'*You* know that as well as I do,' growled the policeman. 'It came through the letter-box. My daily woman, Mrs. Hicks, found them all. And when she told me that the butcher-boy arrived this morning at the same time as the last note—well, I guessed who was at the bottom of all this.'

'Well, as *I* wasn't that butcher-boy, why don't you go and question the *real* butcher-boy,' said Fatty. 'Or shall I? This is jolly interesting, Mr. Goon. I think there's something behind all this!'

'So do I. *You* are, Master Frederick Trotteville !' said Mr. Goon. 'No—don't you keep telling me it wasn't you. I know you well enough by now. You'll come to a bad end, you will—telling me fibs like this!'

'I think we'll bring this meeting to an end,' said Fatty, 'I never tell lies, Mr. Goon, never. You ought to know that by now. I've had my jokes, yes—and played a good many tricks. But I—do—NOT—tell lies! Here—take the letters, and get your bicycle.'

Mr. Goon rose up majestically from his arm-chair. He took the letters from Fatty and then threw them violently on the floor.

*'This is jolly interesting, Mr. Goon'*

'You can have them back!' he said, 'You sent them, and you can keep them. But mind you—if ONE MORE of those notes arrives at my police-station, I go straight to Superintendent Jenks and report the whole lot.'

'I really do think you'd better do that anyhow,' said Fatty. 'There may be something *serious* behind all this, you know. You've got a bee in your bonnet about me — I don't know a thing about these anonymous letters. Now please go.'

'Why didn't you have the envelopes and the writing-paper inside tested for finger-prints, Mr. Goon?' said Pip, suddenly. 'Then you'd have known if Fatty's were there, or not. You could have taken his too, to prove it.'

'As it is, we've all handled the notes, and must have messed up any finger-prints that were there already,' said Fatty. 'Blow!'

'Finger-prints! Bah!' said Goon. 'You'd be clever enough to wear *gloves* if you sent anonymous notes, Master Frederick Trotteville. Well, I've said my say, and I'm going. But just you mind my words—ONE MORE NOTE, and you'll get into such trouble that you'll wish you'd never been born. And I should burn that butcher-boy rig-out of yours, if I were you—if it hadn't been for you acting the butcher-boy this morning I'd never have guessed it was you leaving those notes.'

He went out of the room and banged the door so violently that Buster barked in astonishment, and ran to the door, scratching at it eagerly.

'Be quiet, Buster,' said Fatty, sitting down on the couch

again. 'I say, you others—what do you think about these notes? A bit queer, aren't they?'

Larry had picked them all up and put them on the table. The five looked at them.

'Do we do a little detective work?' said Larry, eagerly. 'Goon's given it up, obviously—shall we take it on?'

'Rather!' said Fatty. 'Our next mystery is now beginning!'

## 3 MR. GOON IS WORRIED

MR. GOON cycled home, very angry indeed. Fatty always seemed to get the best of him somehow—and yet the policeman felt that he, Goon, had been in the right all the time. That fat boy had given himself away properly by disguising himself as the butcher-boy again. He'd done it once too often this time! Ah well—he could tell Mrs. Hicks that he had solved the business of those notes, and given someone a good ticking-off!

He flung his bicycle against the fence, and went into his house. He found Mrs. Hicks scrubbing the kitchen floor, a soapy mess all round her.

'Oh, there you are, sir,' she began, 'Look, I'll have to have a new scrubbing-brush, this here one's got no bristles left, and I can't. . .'

'Mrs. Hicks—about those notes,' interrupted Mr. Goon. 'There won't be any more, you'll be glad to know. I've been to talk to the one who wrote them—frightened him almost to death, I did—he admitted everything, but I've taken a kindly view of the whole matter, and let him off, this time. so there won't be any more.'

'Oh, but you're quite wrong, sir,' said Mrs. Hicks, rising up from her knees with difficulty, and standing before him with the dripping scrubbing-brush still in her hand. 'You're quite wrong. I found another note, sir, as soon as you'd gone!'

'You couldn't have,' said Mr. Goon, taken aback.

'Oh, but I did, sir,' said Mrs. Hicks. 'And a funny place it was in too. I wouldn't have noticed it if the milkman hadn't pointed it out.'

'The milkman? Why, did *he* find it?' said Mr. Goon, astonished. 'Where was it?'

'Well, sir, it was tucked into the empty milk-bottle, stood outside the back-door,' said Mrs. Hicks, enjoying the policeman's surprise. 'The milkman picked up the bottle and of course he saw the note at once—it was sticking out of the bottle-neck, sir.'

Mr. Goon sat down heavily on a kitchen chair. 'When was the note put there?' he asked. 'Could it have been slipped in some time ago—say when the butcher-boy was here?'

'Oh no, sir. Why, I'd only put out the milk-bottle a few minutes before the milkman came,' said Mrs. Hicks. 'I washed it out, sir—I always do wash my milk-bottles out, I don't hand them dirty to the milkman, like *some* folks—and I put it out nice and clean. And about three minutes later along came Joe—that's the milkman, sir—and puts down your quart, sir, and picks up the empty bottle.'

'And was the note in it then?' asked Mr. Goon, hardly able to believe it.

'Yes, sir. And the milkman, he says to me, "Hey, what's this note for? It's addressed to Mr. Goon!" and he gave it to me, sir, and it's on your desk this very minute.'

'Exactly when did the milkman hand you the note?'

asked poor Mr. Goon.

'About twenty minutes ago, sir,' said Mrs. Hicks. Goon groaned. Twenty minutes ago he had been with all five children—so it was plain that not one of them could have been stuffing a note into his empty milk-bottle then. Certainly not Fatty.

'You look upset, sir,' said Mrs. Hicks. 'Shall I make you a nice hot cup of tea. The kettle's boiling.'

'Yes. Yes, I think I could do with one,' said Goon, and walked off heavily to his little office. He sat down in his chair.

*Now* what was he to do? It couldn't have been Fatty after all. There was someone else snooping about, hiding notes here and there when no one was around. And good gracious—he had left all the notes with those five kids! What a thing to do! Mr. Goon brooded for a few minutes and was glad to see Mrs. Hicks coming in with an enormous cup of hot tea.

'I put in four lumps,' said Mrs. Hicks. 'And there's another in the saucer. You've got a sweet tooth, haven't you, sir? What about me getting a new scrubbing-brush, now we're on the subject, and . . .'

'We're *not* on the subject,' said Mr. Goon, shortly. 'Put the cup down, Mrs. Hicks. I've something difficult to work out, so don't disturb me till my dinner-time.'

Mrs. Hicks went out, offended, and shut the door loudly. Goon called her as she went down the passage.

'Hey, Mrs. Hicks. Half a minute. I want to ask you a question.'

Mrs. Hicks came back, still looking offended. 'And what might you be wanting to know?' she said.

'That butcher-boy—what was he like?' asked Goon, still vainly hoping that he might have been Fatty in disguise. 'And did he really bring some meat—the meat you ordered?'

'Of course he did!' said Mrs. Hicks. 'Two very nice lean chops, sir, the kind you like. I told you before. And I told you I didn't *see* the butcher-boy, I was upstairs. But it was him all right. I know his whistle. And I heard him calling over the fence to the next-door kid. It was Charlie Jones all right. What's all the mystery, sir?'

'Nothing, nothing, nothing!' said Mr. Goon, feeling very down-hearted. It couldn't have been Fatty after all; it *must* have been the real butcher-boy. He might have guessed that, when Mrs. Hicks told him that his chops had come. Fatty wouldn't have known that chops were ordered. Oh, what an ass he had been!

He caught sight of the note on his desk. Same square, cheap envelope. Same pasted-on bit of paper, with 'Mr. goon' on, in cut-out letters. What was inside this time?

He slit the envelope open. He paused before he took out the note. He remembered what Larry had said about finger-prints. There *might* be some on the writing paper inside. Goon fetched his own gloves and put them on. They were thick leather ones, and he found it very difficult to get the thin sheet of paper out of the envelope, while wearing such bulky gloves.

At last it was out, and he unfolded it to read. He saw the usual cut-out words and letters, all pasted on a strip of paper, which itself was stuck on the sheet of writing-paper.

'Why don't you do what you are told, egg-head', he read, and grew crimson in the face. WHO was writing these rude notes? Just wait till he got his hands on him!

He forgot all about his cup of tea, and it grew cold. Poor Goon. He simply could *not* make up his mind what to do! Why, oh why had he gone to see Fatty that morning, and left behind all the other notes?

'I can't go and report things to the Super now,' he thought. 'If I do, I'll have to tell him I went and told everything to that Trotteville boy—and he'll telephone to him and tell *him* to take over. He's always in the middle of things, that boy—always doing me down. What am I to do?'

Goon sat and worried for a long time. If only he could catch whoever it was delivering these notes! That would be the thing to do! He would soon solve everything then, once he got his hands on the fellow! Yes, that was certainly the thing to do. But how could he watch for him every minute of the day? It was impossible.

Then a sudden thought came to him, and he brightened. What about his nephew Ern? What about asking him to stay with him for a while, and give some pocket-money to keep a watch for him? Ern was smart.

Leaving his cold tea, he went out to Mrs. Hicks, who was sitting down enjoying her second cup of tea.

I've got to go out,' he said. 'Be back by tea-time. Keep a look-out in case anyone else comes with a note.'

'But your chops, sir,' began Mrs. Hicks. It was no good—Goon was off on his bicycle, riding at top speed to Ern's home. Mrs. Hicks sighed and poured herself out a third cup of tea. Well, if he wasn't back by dinner-time she would have those chops herself!

Meantime Fatty and the others had been busy discussing what seemed like a new, and rather sudden, mystery. They were in the middle of it when Mrs. Trotteville came home from her shopping, hoping to find that all the jumble had been taken from the attics, and neatly stacked into the garage. She was not very pleased to find so little done.

'Well! You said you could get everything downstairs for me by the time I came back, so that I could look over it,' she said. 'Whatever have you been doing?'

Nobody said a word about Mr. Goon's visit. Mrs. Trotteville was always displeased if she thought that Fatty had been 'meddling in mysteries' again. She was tired of Mr. Goon coming along with complaints of his doings.

'Sorry, Mother! We'll finish everything this afternoon,' said Fatty. 'Larry and the rest can easily come along again. Anyway, we've got quite a few things out in the garage already.'

'I should hope so!' said his mother. 'I've got to look over everything, mend what can be mended, and price each thing. And by the way, Frederick, I've the names and addresses of a few people in Peterswood who have said that they will be pleased to give some jumble for the sale, if you go and collect it on a barrow.'

'A *barrow*!' said Fatty. 'Do you mean I'm to borrow the gardener's old barrow and trundle it through the streets? No, thank you!'

'I've arranged with the builder to lend you *his* barrow,' said his mother. 'Well, I suppose it's a hand-cart, really, not a barrow. Larry can go with you to help you. It's for a good cause, so you can do your bit, surely.'

'You have an awful lot of good causes, Mother,' said Fatty. 'Still, I'd rather have a mother with too many, than one with none at all! All right—I'll do some collecting round and about for you. Larry and Pip can both help me.'

'We'll come this afternoon and clear out the attics properly,' promised Larry. 'What time? Half-past two?'

'Yes,' said Fatty. 'And I vote we all go out to tea at the best tea-shop in the village. We'll be hungry after our hard work.'

'Well, I'll pay for a good tea,' said his mother, laughing. 'I see you've forgotten that you want to take off some of your fat, Frederick.'

'Don't remind me of that, Mother, just when I'm looking forward to meringues and chocolate eclairs,' groaned Fatty.

That afternoon the five, with Buster continually getting in their way at awkward moments, carried down an enormous amount of jumble from the big attics—and, just as they were in the very middle of it, a piercing whistle was heard coming up the attic stairs.

'Whoever's that?' said Fatty, startled. He looked down the steep little flight of stairs. 'Gosh! It's ERN! Ern, what on earth are you doing here?'

'Come on down,' said Ern. 'I got something to tell you. I'm staying with my uncle—he fetched me this morning.'

'Staying with *Goon*!' said Fatty, disbelievingly. 'But you detest him! Half a mo—we'll all be down and hear what you've got to say. My word, Ern—this *is* a surprise! We'll be down in a tick.'

## 4 ERN'S NEW JOB

EVERYONE was amazed to hear that Ern had suddenly come to stay with Mr. Goon. They hurried down the attic stairs at top speed. Ern was delighted to see them.

'Well,' said Fatty, clapping the boy on the back. 'Still the same old Ern!'

And, indeed, Em looked exactly the same as he had always looked, though he had grown a little. He was still rather plump, and his cheeks were as brilliant red as ever. His eyes bulged a little, just like his uncle's. He grinned happily at everyone.

'Coo! You're all here. That's a bit of luck,' he said.

'Let's go down to my shed,' said Fatty. 'We can talk without being heard there. Do you think we've got enough stuff out of the attic to satisfy my mother? The garage will soon be so full that it won't take Dad's car!'

'Yes, we've done enough,' said Larry, who was feeling really tired after carrying so many heavy, awkward articles down the steep attic stairs. 'I want a rest.'

So off they all went, out of the side door, down the garden path, to Fatty's secluded little shed at the bottom of the garden, well-hidden among shrubs and trees.

The winter afternoon was now getting dark, and Fatty lighted a lantern, and also an oil stove, for the shed felt very chilly. Soon the glow spread over the six children and Buster, as they sat together, glad of a rest after so much hard work.

'I won't offer anyone anything to eat,' said Fatty, 'because we're all going out to tea, Ern—and my mother's paying, so we can have what we like. You can come with us.'

'Coo!' said Ern, delighted. 'Thanks a lot.'

'What's all this about your uncle asking you to stay with him so suddenly?' asked Fatty.

'Well, I was just eating my dinner with Mum and my twin brothers, Sid and Perce, when my uncle comes sailing up on his bicycle,' began Ern, thoroughly enjoying all the attention he was getting. 'And Mum says, "Look who's here!" And we looked, and it was Uncle Theophilus . . .'

'Oh! I'd forgotten that was Mr. Goon's name,' said Bets, with a squeal of delight.

'Well, Sid and Perce, they bolted upstairs straightaway,' said Ern. 'They're scared stiff of Uncle because he's a policeman—and I was going, too, when Uncle yelled at me and said, "You stay here, young Ern. I got a job for you to do. I want you to help the law".'

'Go on, Ern,' said Fatty, enjoying the way Ern imitated Goon.

'Well, Uncle was sort of pally and slapped me on the back, and said, "Well, how's the smart boy of the family," and that made me and Mum proper suspicious,' said Ern. 'And then he said he wanted me to come and stay with him, and do a bit of snooping round for him —and I was going to say No, that I wouldn't, straight off like that—when he said he'd pay me proper wages!'

'Did he, now?' said Fatty. 'What did he offer you?'

'Half a crown a day!' said Ern. 'Loveaduck, I've never had so much money in my life! But I was smart, I was. I said, "Done, Uncle—if you throw in an ice-cream a day as well!" And he said "Right—if you come along with me now".'

'So you came?' said Bets. 'Did your mother mind?'

'Oooh no—she's glad to get rid of one or other of us for a few days,' said Ern. 'She just said; "What sort of a job is this?" And my uncle said, "Can't tell you—it's secret. But Ern here's smart, and he'll be able to do it all right." Coo—I never knew my uncle thought so much of me.'

'I hope he'll be kind to you,' said Daisy, remembering how unkind Goon had been to the boy on other occasions when he had stayed with him.

'Well, I've told him straight, I'll go back home if the job don't please me,' said Ern, boastfully. 'Job! Funny business it is, really. It's just to keep a look-out for anyone snooping about the house, hiding notes anywhere, when Uncle's out and can't keep watch himself. And if I do see anyone and describe him good and proper, I'm to get an extra five shillings.'

'So Goon has made up his mind I'm *not* the guilty one!' said Fatty. 'Did he tell you anything else, Ern?'

'No,' said Ern. 'But he said I could skip along here this afternoon, and you'd tell me anything you wanted to—and I was to say he'd made a mistake. He says you can burn those notes he left, and don't you bother about them any more. He can manage all right.'

'He thinks we'll give up solving the mystery of the notes, I suppose,' said Pip. 'Well, we shan't, shall we, Fatty?'

'No,' said Fatty. 'There certainly is something decidedly queer about those notes. We won't burn them. We'll hang on to them. I vote we have a meeting down here tomorrow morning, and consider them carefully.'

'Can I have a look at them?' asked Ern, filled with curiosity.

'They're indoors,' said Fatty. 'Anyway, it's almost time we went out to have our tea. Got your bike, Ern?'

'You bet,' said Ern. 'I say, it's a bit of good luck for me, isn't it—getting so much money! I can stand you all ice-creams in a day or two—pay you back a bit for the ones you've bought me so many times.'

He grinned round at the five children, and they smiled back pleased with his good-natured suggestion. That was so like Ern.

'How are Sid and Perce, your two brothers?' asked Pip. 'Does Sid still suck that awful toffee?'

'No. He's on to chewing-gum now,' said Ern, seriously. 'He got into trouble at school over that toffee—couldn't spit it out soon enough when the teacher got on to him about it. So now he buys chewing-gum. It's easier to manage, he says. Perce is all right too. You should have seen him and Sid scoot upstairs when Uncle arrived this morning. Atom-bombs couldn't have got them up quicker!'

They all laughed. Fatty stood up. 'Well let's go,' he said. 'Ern, if your uncle is at home tomorrow morning, you come and join our meeting. You may as well listen to our plans, seeing you're more or less in this affair too.'

'Oooh, I'd love to,' said Ern overjoyed. 'I might bring my latest pome to read to you. It's not quite finished, but

I'll try and think of the ending tonight.'

Everyone smiled. Ern and his poems! He did try so hard to write them, but nearly always got stuck in the middle. They all went out of Fatty's shed, and he locked it behind him carefully. No grown-up was allowed to see what treasures he had there! All his many disguises. His make-up. His false teeth and moustaches and whiskers. Mr. Goon's eyes would have fallen out of his head if he had seen them.

They lighted their bicycle lamps and rode off to the tea-shop, Buster in Fatty's bicycle basket. They left their bicycles outside the shop, and went in, Buster keeping close to heel. 'A table for six, please,' said Fatty, politely.

Soon they were all sitting down enjoying a truly marvellous tea. Fatty's mother had handed out ten shillings as a reward for their hard work, and that bought a very fine tea indeed—but wasn't quite enough to pay for ice creams each as well, so Fatty delved into his own pocket as usual.

'I vote for scones and honey to begin with, macaroons to follow, and either éclairs or meringues after that, with ice-creams to end with,' suggested Fatty.

'Loveaduck!' said Ern, overcome. 'I wish I hadn't eaten so much dinner. What about Buster?

'Oh, Buster can have his usual tit-bits,' said Fatty, and gave the order to a most amused waitress.

'Are you sure that all this will be enough?' she said, smiling.

'Well, no, I'm not quite sure,' said Fatty. 'But that will do to start with!'

It was a hilarious meal, and Ern made them all laugh

till they cried by telling them of Sid's mistake over his chewing-gum the day before.

'You see, Perce had got out his clay-modelling set,' began Ern, 'and he was flattening out some of the clay to work it up properly, like. And Mum called him, and off he went. Then Sid came in, and what does Sid think but that them flat pieces is some of his chewing-gum! So into his mouth they went. He didn't half complain about the taste—said he'd take it back to the shop—but he wouldn't spit it out, he said he couldn't waste it. And then Perce came back, and there was an awful shindy because Sid was chewing up his bits of clay!'

Everyone roared with laughter at Ern's peculiar story. 'Quite revolting,' said Fatty. 'Simply horrible, But very funny, the way you tell it, Ern. Don't, for pity's sake, repeat the story in front of my mother, will you?'

'I'd never *dare* to open my mouth to your mother,' said Ern, looking quite scared at the thought of telling a story about Sid and Perce to Mrs. Trotteville. 'Coo—even my uncle's scared of your mother, Fatty. What's the time? I've got to get back to my job sharp on halfpast five, because Uncle's going out then.'

'Well, you'd better scoot off,' said Fatty, looking at his watch. 'When you're paid to do a job, young Ern, it's better to give a few minutes more to it, than a few minutes less. That's one of the differences between doing a job honestly, and doing it dishonestly! See?'

'Right-o, Fatty,' said Ern, slipping out of his chair. 'I'll do anything you say. So long! See you tomorrow if I can.'

'Good old Ern,' said Pip, watching the boy make his

way to the door of the tea-shop. 'I hope old Goon will treat him all right. And if he doesn't pay him as he promised, *we'll* have something to say about that!'

'Can anyone eat any more?' said Fatty. 'No? Sorry, Buster, but everyone says no, so it's no use wagging your tail like that! Well, I feel decidedly better now, if rather plumper. If *only* I could get thinner! I'll have to try some cross-country racing again.'

'What! In this cold weather!' said Pip. 'It would make you so hungry, you'd eat twice as much as usual—so what would be the good?'

'I hoped you'd say that, Pip, old thing,' said Fatty, with a chuckle. 'Well, we'll get home. Tomorrow at half-past ten, all of you. I've got a little job to do tonight, before I go to bed.

'What's that?' asked the others.

'I'm going to use my finger-printing powder, and see if I can find any unusual prints on the sheets of paper those messages were pasted on,' said Fatty.

And so, all by himself in his shed, Fatty tested the sheets for strange finger-prints, feeling very professional indeed. But it was no use—the sheets were such a mass—of prints, that it would have been quite impossible to decipher a strange one!

'There are Goon's prints—and all of ours,' groaned Fatty. 'I do hope Goon doesn't mess up any new notes. He *ought* to test for prints as soon as he gets one. Well, I hope this *is* a mystery boiling up. It certainly has the smell of one!'

## 5 A MEETING—AND THE FIRST CLUE

NEXT morning Fatty was waiting for the others down in his shed. He had biscuits in a tin, and lemonade in a bottle. He also had the four notes set out in their envelopes.

Larry and Daisy were the first to arrive. 'Hallo, Fatty! Solved the mystery yet?' said Daisy.

'I don't somehow think it's going to be very easy,' said Fatty. 'That box is for you to sit on, Daisy. I've put a cushion on it—and there's a cushion for Bets too.'

Pip and Bets arrived almost immediately, and then Ern came running down the path. Buster greeted him loudly, leaping round his ankles. He liked Ern.

'Hallo, everybody,' said Ern, panting. 'Am I late? I thought I wouldn't be able to come, but Uncle said he'd be in all morning, so here I am. I'm on duty this afternoon.'

'Has he paid you anything yet?' asked Bets.

'No. He says he'll pay me each dinner-time,' said Ern. 'I asked him for a bit in advance, but he wouldn't give me any. If he had I'd have bought some sweets and brought them along for us all, but I'll do that tomorrow.

'Thanks, Ern,' said Fatty. 'Tell us—did you have any luck in seeing anyone snooping around, placing notes anywhere?'

'No. No luck at all,' said Ern. 'Uncle's quite disappointed there's no more notes. I watched him testing the one he got yesterday morning for finger-prints. All that powder and stuff! Beats me how it fetches up finger-prints!'

'Oh! Did Goon test for finger-prints too?' said Fatty, interested. 'Did he find any? The note he had wouldn't have any prints of ours on it—it would show up a strange print at once.'

'Well, it didn't show *any*thing,' said Ern. 'Not a thing. Uncle said the writer must have worn gloves. Didn't mean to be found out, did he?'

'No, he didn't,' said Fatty, looking thoughtful. 'It rather looks as if he was afraid that his finger-prints would be recognized . . .'

'And *that* would mean that he'd had them taken already for some reason,' said Larry, at once. 'So he might be a bad lot—might have been in prison.'

'Yes, that's true,' said Fatty. 'I wonder if the man who writes the notes is the one who's putting them all about Goon's garden. No wonder Goon wants to spot him, if so.'

'Coo,' said Ern, looking startled. 'Do you think he might be dangerous? Do you think he'd shoot me if he saw me spying for him?'

'Oh no—I shouldn't think so!' said Fatty. 'I don't think you *will* spot him, Ern. He'd be very careful indeed. I wish I knew what he meant by these notes, though. And why does he go to so much trouble cutting out letters and words from the newspapers, and putting them laboriously on strips of paper, and then sticking the strips on writing-paper. Why couldn't he just disguise his writing? It's easy enough to do!'

'It might be easy for you, Fatty, but not for most people,' said Daisy.

'You say you saw and heard nothing at all to make you think anyone was around, and that no note was found this morning?' said Fatty to Ern. 'I wonder if that was because you were there? Who is in the house when Goon is out?'

'Only Mrs. Hicks, the woman who comes in to clean,' said Ern. 'She's not there all the time, anyway. And I don't believe she'd notice anyone around unless they rang the bell or banged on the knocker. Why, she never even noticed the boy next door when he hopped over the fence to get his ball.'

'The boy next door? Did *he* come over? said Fatty, at once. 'It's possible someone might pay him to slip the notes here and there.'

'Well, I watched him like anything,' said Ern. 'I was peeping out of the bedroom window, see—and I saw two kids playing ball next door—and suddenly their ball came over the fence. And then the boy climbed over, got his ball and went back, looking all round in case my uncle came rushing out. He didn't have any note—he just picked up his ball and ran for his life.'

'He doesn't *sound* suspicious,' said Fatty, and the others nodded in agreement. 'Still—you've got to suspect *any*one who comes, Ern.'

'Right-o. I'll even give the next door cat the once-over if he comes,' said Ern, grinning.

'Now let's consider these notes carefully,' said Fatty, and spread them out in a row on the table. 'I'll read them all out again. Listen, everyone, you too, Ern, because you haven't heard them before.'

Fatty picked up the first one. 'Number one—"Ask Smith what his real name is". Number two—"Turn him out of the Ivies". Number three—"Call yourself a policeman? Go and see Smith !" Number four—"You'll be sorry if you *don't* go and see Smith".'

'And I can tell you Number five,' said Ern, eagerly. 'It was on Uncle's desk when he was doing the finger-print test, and I saw it. It said, "Why don't you do what you're told, egghead?" '

Everyone laughed. Ern grinned. 'Uncle didn't like that,' he said.

'Well,' said Fatty, 'what does anyone gather from these notes?'

'There's a house called The Ivies somewhere,' said Bets.

'And a man called Smith lives in it,' said Daisy.

'And it's not his real name, it's a false one,' said Larry.

'And if he's using a false name there must be some reason for it,' added Pip, 'and possibly it means that at one time or another he's been in trouble—and doesn't want people to know his real name now.'

'But why should the writer of these notes want him turned out of the Ivies?' said Fatty, frowning. 'And what reason would there *be* to turn him out? Well—until we find the Ivies, it's impossible to do anything. To find a

*'Now let's consider these notes carefully,' said Fatty*

house called The Ivies must be our very first step.'

'I suppose we can't find the writer of the notes, can we?' suggested Daisy. 'It might be a help if we knew who *he* was!'

'How can we?' asked Larry. 'He doesn't give a thing away, not a thing—not his handwriting, not his fingerprints, nothing! He's so jolly careful that he's spent ages and ages snipping printed letters or words out of newspapers and pasting them on the sheet!'

'I wonder if we could find anything out about him from these little snippings,' said Fatty, gazing at them. 'Newspapers are printed on both sides. There might be a guide to us in something on the *other* side of the snippings. I rather think the man is using only *one* newspaper. The letters all seem to be the same type of printing.'

'But goodness me—we can't *un*paste the letters from the sheets,' said Bets.

'I could,' said Fatty. 'It would be a very tricky job, but I think I could. I've got some special stuff somewhere for that very purpose, but I've never yet used it. I'd forgotten about it. I might be able to do something tonight. It's worth trying, anyhow.'

'Yes. And surely we *ought* to be able to find the house called The Ivies?' said Daisy.

'I've looked in the street directory and examined the names there of every house in Peterswood, and I'm sure Goon has too,' said Fatty, gloomily. 'There isn't a single one called "The Ivies", not a single one.'

'What about Marlow? said Daisy. 'There might be a

house called "The Ivies" there.'

'There might. And there might be one in Maidenhead and one in Taplow,' said Fatty. 'But it would take absolutely ages to look up all the houses in the directory.'

'What a pity the man took the name of Smith—the man who apparently lives at The Ivies,' said Pip. 'There are so many Smiths.'

'Yes. I looked them up in the telephone directory to start with,' said Fatty. 'There are dozens there—and this man may not even be on the telephone. We can't go ringing up all the Smiths in the neighbourhood to find out if any of them have a false name!'

'No. Of course not,' said Pip.

'Well, I simply do not see how we can even make a start,' said Larry. 'Have you any ideas, Fatty?'

'None,' said Fatty. 'Ern—what about you?

Ern looked startled. 'Well—if *you* haven't got any ideas, 'tisn't likely I would,' he said. 'You're the cleverest of us all, Fatty, you know you are.'

'Let's have a biscuit and some lemonade,' said Fatty. And Ern—what about that poem of yours? Did you bring it along?'

'Er—well, yes, I did,' said Ern, blushing, and dived into deep recesses of his clothing. He brought out a little black notebook, and opened it.

'Read away,' said Fatty, handing round the biscuits 'We're waiting, Ern.'

So Ern, looking very serious, read out his newest 'Pome' as he called it.

'The Old Old House

by Ern Goon

*There was a poor old house*
*That once was full of folk,*
*But now was sad and empty,*
*And to me it spoke.*
*It said, "They all have left me,*
*The rooms are cold and bare,*
*The front door's locked and bolted . . ."*'

Ern stopped, and looked at the others. 'Well, go on, Ern—it's very good,' said Fatty, encouragingly.

'I'm stuck there,' said Ern, looking miserable. 'It took me six months to write those lines—and now I can't go on. I suppose you can't help me, Fatty? You're so good at making up poetry.'

Fatty laughed. 'Yes—I can tell you how your poem goes on, Ern. Here, let me read what you've written—and when I come to the end of it, I'll let my tongue go loose, and maybe we'll see what the end of the verse is. Here goes!'

And Fatty began to read Ern's poem out again. He didn't stop when he came to where Ern had finished. No—he went straight on, just as though he was reading more and more lines! No wonder Ern stared in the greatest astonishment!

*'There was a poor old house*
*That once was full of folk,*
*But now was sad and empty,*
*And to me it spoke.*
*It said, "They all have fled,*

*My rooms are cold and bare,*
*The front door's locked and bolted,*
*And all the windows stare.*
*No smoke comes from my chimneys,*
*No rose grows up my wall,*
*But only ivy shrouds me,*
*In green and shining shawl!*
*No postman brings me letters,*
*No name is on my gate,*
*I once was called The Ivies,*
*But now I'm out of date,*
*The garden's poor and weedy,*
*The trees won't leaf again,*
*But though I fall to ruin,*
*The ivy—will—remain!'*

There was a silence after this. Everyone stared at Fatty in astonishment and admiration. Ern hadn't a word to say. He sat open-mouthed. How DID Fatty do it? He, Em, had slaved for six months over the first few lines—and then Fatty had stood up and recited the rest. Without even THINKING! And Ern sorrowfully confessed to himself that Fatty's lines were much better than his.

He found his tongue at last. 'Well, it's what I thought. You're a genius, Fatty, and I'm not. That's your pome, not mine.'

'No, Ern. It's yours. You *began* it, and I expect that's how it was meant to go,' said Fatty, smiling. 'I shouldn't have been able to think of the ending, if you hadn't thought of the beginning.'

'It beats me. It really does,' said Em. 'I say—fancy you

putting in that bit about The Ivies, too—and the ivy growing up the wall. Well—even if it had no name on the gate, like you said, anyone would know it was still The Ivies, because of its "green and shining shawl" that's a lovely line, Fatty. You're a real poet, you are.'

But Fatty wasn't listening to Ern's last few words. He stood still, staring into space, and Bets felt quite alarmed. Was Fatty ill?

'What's the matter, Fatty?' she said.

'Well—don't you *see?*' said Fatty, coming to himself again. 'What I said in the verses—even if there's no name on the gate, even if the house hasn't *got* a name, it must still have got the *ivy* that gave it its old name. Why don't we go out and look for a house *covered with* ivy? We can easily cycle all round and about. We might find the very house we want!'

'Loveaduck !' said Em, in awe. 'You're a One, Fatty. You really are. You make up a pome—and it gives us the first clue! I never knew anyone like you—honest I didn't!'

# 6 LOOKING FOR IVY!

THE six children began to talk about Fatty's sudden brain-wave. Of course! Any house once called 'The Ivies' must certainly be covered with ivy, or there would be no point in giving it such a name!

'But why wouldn't it *still* be called "The Ivies"?' asked Daisy.

'It's an old-fashioned sort of name,' said Larry. 'Maybe it's owned now by someone who just prefers a number for their house. Some people do. The house opposite ours used to be called "Four Towers" but now it's simply "Number Seventeen" with the "seventeen" written out in full.'

'I think you're probably right, Larry,' said Fatty. 'Well, the thing to do is to go round looking for houses covered with ivy. I don't imagine that anyone would have the ivy pulled up, if they bought the house, because it clings to the wall so tightly, and sends its tiny rootlets into every nook and cranny. The ivy will still be there.'

'A green and shining shawl,' quoted Ern, who still hadn't recovered from Fatty's ending to his poem. 'Coo, Fatty, you're a wonder ! To think of you standing up there, and . . .'

'Forget it, Ern,' said Fatty. 'You could do it too if you

let your tongue just go loose. Practice is all you need. Now, let's go on with the discussion. We're all agreed, then, that the next thing to do is to search for an ivy-covered house, with just a number, since we know there isn't a single house in Peterswood called "The Ivies".'

'It might have another *name,'* said Bets.

'Yes—you're right, Bets,' said Fatty. 'It might. The people who called it "The Ivies" might not be there now. They might have moved.'

'Still, we know that people called Smith live there—if what those peculiar notes say is true,' said Daisy.

'So, whenever we find a house covered with ivy, we have to try and find out if the people in it are called Smith,' said Larry, triumphantly. 'I really feel as if we're getting somewhere now.'

'I bet my uncle won't think up anything as clever as this,' said Ern, thoroughly enjoying himself.

'He didn't hear Fatty's verses,' said Pip. 'If we hadn't heard them either, we'd not have thought of that clue—looking for an ivy-covered house that wasn't *called* "The Ivies". Fatty, when can we go and look for this house?'

'No time like the present,' said Fatty. 'Got your bike, young Ern? Then you can come with us.'

'Suppose my uncle asks me what I've been up to this morning?' said Ern. 'Shall I tell him I haven't seen you?'

'Certainly *not,'* said Fatty, shocked. 'Any fibs of that sort from you, Ern, and you don't come to any more meetings. You ought to know by now what we think of people who don't tell the truth.'

'I'm sorry, Fatty,' said Ern, humbly. 'But I just didn't

want to give anything away. My uncle's bound to ask me to tell him everything we said—and I don't want him to worm things out of me. I just thought it would make it easy, like, to say I hadn't seen you.'

'Never you take the easy way out if it means being dishonest or untruthful,' said Fatty. 'You've got a lot of things to learn, young Ern, and that's one of them.'

'I'll do anything you say, Fatty,' said Ern. 'Am I to tell Uncle what we've decided then?'

Fatty considered. 'Well—I can see it's difficult for you, Ern. If you refuse to say anything, your uncle may be beastly to you. You can tell him we're all going out to look for houses covered with ivy. Let him make what he likes of that.'

'But *he'll* go out and look for them too,' objected Ern.

'Well, there's no law against anyone looking for ivy-covered houses,' said Fatty, going out of the shed. 'Come on, everyone. Let's go. Brrrrr ! It's cold out here. Buster, are you coming?'

Buster certainly *was* coming. He tore out after the others, barking, and Fatty locked the door carefully behind them.

Soon they were all on their bicycles, and rode to the end of Fatty's lane. There they dismounted at Fatty's command.

'It would be a waste of time for us all to go together,' said Fatty. 'We'll go in pairs, and try to examine every road in Peterswood. Got your notebooks, everyone? As soon as you see an ivy-covered house, stop. Note if it has a name, or a number, and the street it's in. Don't bother about *new* houses anywhere—ivy takes years to grow. We must look out for an *old* house. Bets and I will go this way—you others decide which street you'll explore.'

Bets went off with Fatty, Ern cycled away with Pip, and Daisy and Larry rode off together. 'Meet at this corner in an hour's time!' yelled Fatty, as they parted.

Fatty and Bets rode slowly up the first road. 'You examine the houses on one side of the road, and I'll watch the ones on the other,' said Fatty.

They cycled along together, but to their disappointment not one house had any ivy at all growing up the walls. They turned down another road, and Bets suddenly gave an exclamation. 'Here's a house: that's green from top to bottom, Fatty.'

'But not with ivy, Bets, old thing,' said Fatty. 'That's creeper—ordinary Virginia creeper. At least, that's what our gardener calls it. Bad luck!'

Down another road, riding very slowly this time, as there were big houses here, standing right back from the road, and difficult to see because of trees in the front gardens.

'Here's one covered with ivy!' said Fatty at last. 'Look, Bets!'

'Yes. But it's got a name on the gate,' said Bets. . 'See—Barton House.'

'Well, we know we shan't find a house called "The Ivies",' said Fatty, 'because there's none in the directory. We'll have to put this down, Bets. Now wait while I get my notebook.'

He took it from his pocket and wrote quickly, Bets peeping over his shoulder. 'Barton Grange. Old house, with ivy almost up to roof. In Hollins Road.'

He shut his notebook. 'Good. That's one ivy-covered

house, anyway. I wonder if anyone called Smith lives there. We'll have to find out.'

They only found one more ivy-covered house and that was quite a small one, in Jordans Road. It had obviously once been a cottage belonging to the big house nearby, but had been sold, and now had its own little garden, and a hedge round it.

'What's it called?' said Fatty. 'Oh—it hasn't a name — just a number. Number 29, Jordans Road. It looks well-kept—nice curtains at the windows, neat garden. I say, Bets—what about going to ask if people called Smith live here? You just never know your luck!'

'You go, Fatty,' said Bets, who was always shy of strange people.

'Right,' said Fatty, and leaned his bicycle against the trim little hedge. With Buster at his heels he went in at the gate. 'I bet someone called Cholmondley or Montague-Paget lives here,' he thought, just when I'm looking for a nice short, straightforward Smith!'

He rang the brightly-polished bell. At once a dog began to bark inside the house, and Buster stiffened. Fatty picked him up immediately. He didn't want a dog-fight on the door-step!

Someone came up the passage to the front door, and it opened. At once a Pekinese flew out, dancing round excitedly, barking at the top of its voice. Buster wriggled in Fatty's arms, and began barking too.

'Come here, Ming !' said the little old woman at the door, and Ming obeyed, still barking. 'What is it you want?'

'Er —I'm looking for someone called Smith,' said Fatty,

politely. 'I don't know if you can help me.'

'Smith? Well, that's *our* name,' said the old lady. 'Who are you? And which of us do you want—me, or my husband?'

For once in a way Fatty was taken aback. He hadn't for one moment imagined that he would find a Smith in an ivy-covered house so quickly, and he hardly knew what to say ! But Fatty was never at a loss for long.

'Er—I'd like to see Miss Annabella-Mary Smith,' he said. 'That's if she's here, of course.'

'Oh, you've got the *wrong* Smith,' said the old lady, briskly. 'There's no *Miss* Smith here, only a Mr. and Mrs. Smith—my husband and myself. Wait—my husband's here. He may know of another Smith somewhere near. John! Come here a minute, will you, dear?'

A nice old man appeared, with a wrinkled, kindly face, and twinkling eyes. Fatty liked him at once. His wife repeated what Fatty had said.

'Miss Annabella-Mary Smith?' he said. 'No, I don't know anyone of that name in this road, anyway. We used to live in the big house next door, you know, and knew everyone in the district—but the place was too big for us and we moved into this little place—used to be our gardener's cottage, and very cosy it is too!'

'Was it ever called "The Ivies" asked Fatty, hopefully. Mr. Smith shook his head.

'No. It was just called "The Cottage", he said. 'Sorry I can't help you.'

'I'm very sorry to have bothered you," said Fatty, and he raised his cap politely, pleased to have met with such a nice old couple. He went back to Bets and told her what had happened.

'I felt rather mean, bothering such nice people,' he said, putting Buster down. 'Well—although their name is Smith and they live in an ivy-covered house, they can't be anything to do with the Smith in those notes. That little place used to be called "The Cottage" not "The Ivies". Come along—on with the search, Bets. I wonder how the others are getting on!'

Bets and Fatty were astonished to discover that there were no more houses with ivy in the roads they rode along. 'Ivy must have gone out of fashion,' said Bets. 'There are plenty of houses with roses on the wall, and clematis and wisteria, and creeper—but no ivy! Well—I must say ivy is a dark, rather ugly thing to cover a house with, when you can get so much prettier things to grow up the walls. What's the time, Fatty?'

'Time to meet the others,' said Fatty, looking at his watch. 'Come on—let's see how they've got on. Better than we have, I hope. Certainly we found an ivy-covered house, and people called Smith—but not the ones we want!'

They cycled off to the corner where they were to meet the others. Larry and Daisy were there already, waiting patiently. Ern and Pip arrived soon after, Ern grinning all over his face as usual.

'Any luck?' asked Fatty.

'We're not quite sure,' said Pip. 'Let's go to your shed, Fatty. We can't talk here. We'll all compare notes, and see if we've got anything useful!'

# 7 PIP AND ERN HAVE SOME NEWS

SOON all six, with Buster running round busily,were sitting once more in Fatty's shed. He produced some chocolate biscuits, and Buster sat up and begged at once.

'No, Buster. Think of your figure,' said Fatty, solemnly. Buster barked loudly.

'He says— "You jolly well think of *yours*, Fatty!" ' said Bets, with a chuckle. 'I'll only have one, thank you. It's getting near dinner-time, and we're having steak and kidney pudding—I don't want not to be hungry for that!'

'Well—any news?' asked Fatty, producing his note-book.

'You tell yours first,' said Pip.

'There's not much,' said Fatty. 'Bets and I found one big ivy-covered house called Barton Grange, in Hollins Road. Ivy almost up to the roof. We'll have to find out if it was ever called "The Ivies". And we found a nice little cottage, with no name in Jordans Road, No. 29 —AND the people who live there are called Smith.'

Everyone sat up in surprise. 'Goodness—you don't mean to say you've hit on the right house and people straightaway!' said Larry, astonished.

'No. Apparently the house once belonged to the gardener of the big place next to it, and was called "The *Cottage*"—not "The Ivies",' said Fatty. 'And the Smiths weren't the right Smiths either. Most disappointing! We'll have to rule it out, I'm afraid. Well, what about you, Larry and Daisy?'

'Absolutely nothing to report,' said Larry. 'We did see one old ivy-covered house—ivy right up to the roof, so it must have been quite an old house.'

'But its name was Fairlin Hall,' said Daisy. 'And it was empty. We rode in at the drive, because we couldn't see the house properly from the front gates. We guessed it would be empty because there was a big board up outside "To be Sold".'

'It looked a dreadful old place,' said Larry. 'Old-fashioned, with great pillars at the front door, and heavy balconies jutting out everywhere. I wonder if people ever sat out on those stone balconies in the old days.'

'It looked so lonely and dismal,' said Daisy. 'It really gave me the shivers. It reminded me of the line in that poem, Fatty—"All my windows stare". They did seem to stare at us, as if they were hoping we might be coming to live there, and put up curtains and light fires.'

'But we ruled it out because it was called Fairlin Hall, and was *empty*,' said Larry. 'No Smith there!'

'Quite right,' said Fatty. 'What about you and Ern, Pip?'

'We found *two* ivy-covered houses,' said Pip. 'And one really might be worth while looking into, Fatty. Ern and I agreed that it *might* be the one!'

'Ah—this is better news,' said Fatty. 'Out with it, Pip.'

'Well, Ern found the first one,' said Pip, seeing that Ern had taken out his notebook, and was looking hopefully at him, eager to enter into the debate.

'It was called "Dean Lodge", and was in Bolton Road,' said Ern, in a very business-like voice, flicking over the pages of his notebook, as he had seen his uncle do. 'Ivy-covered to the roof—well, almost to the roof. And it wasn't empty, like the one Pip talked about. It had people in it.'

'Called Smith? said Bets.

'No. Afraid not,' said Ern, looking hard at his notebook as if he needed to refer to a list of names. 'Me and Pip decided it might be a likely place, as the people who lived in it first *might* have called it "The Ivies". So we decided to ask if anyone called Smith lived there now.'

'And was there?' asked Fatty.

'No. The milkman came up just as we were looking at it, and I asked him,' said Ern. 'I said, 'Anyone called Smith live here, mate?" And he said no, it was the Willoughby-Jenkins, or some such name, and they'd been there sixteen years, and he'd brought them their milk every single morning on those sixteen years, except the two days he got married.'

Everyone laughed at Ern's way of telling his little tale. 'Now you, Pip,' he said, shutting his notebook.

'Well, the house I spotted was in Haylings Lane,' said Pip, referring to *his* notebook. 'Not a very big one, and not very old. Actually it isn't really a house now, it's been made into half-shop, half-house, and over the front gate is a notice. It said "Smith and Harris, Nursery-Men. Plants and shrubs for sale. Apply at house".'

'*Smith* and Harris!' said Fatty, interested at once. 'And

you say the house is ivy-covered?'

'Well—not exactly *covered,'* said Pip. 'It had a kind of variegated ivy growing halfway up the whitewashed walls, the leaves were half-yellow and half-green—rather unusual, really. We thought perhaps as Smith and Harris grew shrubs and things, they probably planted one of their own ivies there, to cover the house. But the place wasn't called "The Ivies". It was just called "Haylings Nursery"—after the lane, I suppose. I told you it was in Haylings Lane.'

'Yes,' said Fatty, thoughtfully, 'I can't help thinking that your house is the most likely one, Pip. Ivy up the walls—owned by *Smith* and Harris—and it *might* have been called "The Ivies" before they took it over.'

'Well—what shall we do next?' said Ern, eagerly. 'Loveaduck—whatever would my uncle say if he knew all we'd been doing this morning!'

'Let's quickly run over the ivy-covered houses we've all discovered,' said Fatty, 'and make up our minds which are definitely no good, and which are worth enquiring into. I'll take Bets' and mine first.'

He ran over them quickly. 'Barton Grange, Hollins Road. Ivy-covered. Well, I suppose we'd better find out if people called Smith lived there, and if it was ever named "The Ivies". Then there was the house we found in Jordans Road, but we've ruled that out already, because it never *was* called The Ivies. Then there's the house called Fairlin Hall, that Larry and Daisy found but it's empty, so that's no good.'

'So that only leaves Haylings Nursery, owned by Smith and Harris,' said Pip. 'I vote we enquire into that! If that's no good, we'll find out a bit more about Barton Grange in Hollins Road, the one you and Bets found, Fatty.'

'I wonder if my mother knows who lives in Barton Grange,' said Fatty. 'She's lived in Peterswood so long, she knows practically everybody. I'll ask her. Gosh, look at the time! And there's our dinner-bell! Buck up, all of you, you'll get into a row!'

'Oh my goodness!' said Ern, in a panic. 'What will Uncle say if I'm late! And he's supposed to pay me my first half-crown at dinner-time. Goodbye, all!'

He raced off to get his bicycle, and Larry and the others rode away at top speed too.

'I'll telephone you later!' Fatty shouted after them, and ran indoors to his own lunch. How the time flew when there was detective work to be done! He washed his hands, slicked back his hair and went into the dining room, to find his mother just about to sit down herself.

'So sorry I'm a bit late, Mother,' said Fatty, sliding into his seat.

'It will be a nice surprise for me when you decide to be punctual, Frederick,' said his mother. 'What have you been doing this morning?'

'Oh—just messing about with the others,' said Fatty, truthfully. 'We did a bit of cycling. Mother, can you tell me something? Who lives at Barton Grange—the big house in Hollins Road?'

'Barton Grange—let me think now,' said his mother. 'First the Fords lived there—then the old man died and his widow went to live with her daughter. Then the Jenkins came there—but they lost all their money and left. Then the Georges came—now what happened to them? I know they left very hurriedly indeed—there was some trouble . . .'

'And then did the Smiths come?' asked Fatty, hopefully.

'The Smiths? What Smiths?' said his mother, in surprise.

'Oh—I don't really know,' said Fatty. 'Anyway who's there now? It wouldn't *be* people called Smith, would it?'

'No. Nothing *like* Smith,' said his mother, decidedly. 'Yes—I remember now—it's old Lady Hammerlit. I don't know her at all—she's bedridden, poor old thing. But why are you so interested in Barton Grange, Frederick?'

'Well, I was—but I'm not now,' said Fatty, disappointed to find that no Smiths lived there. 'Mother, I suppose you don't know any place that was once called "The Ivies", do you?'

'Frederick, what *is* all this?' asked his mother, suspiciously. 'You're not getting mixed up in anything peculiar again, are you? I don't want that unpleasant Mr. Goon here again, complaining about you.'

'Mother, he's got *nothing* to complain about,' said Fatty, impatiently. 'And you haven't answered my question. Was there *ever* any house called "The Ivies" in Peterswood—its name will have been changed by now. We've heard of one—but nobody seems to know of it now.'

'The Ivies?' said Mrs. Trotteville. 'No—I don't think I've ever heard of it. I've lived in Peterswood for nineteen years, and as far as I remember there never *has* been any place called "The Ivies". Why do you want to know?'

Fatty didn't like the way his mother was questioning him. He wasn't going to tell any fibs, and yet he couldn't give away the reason for his questions, or his mother would at once complain that he was 'getting mixed up in something peculiar again'.

He reached out for the salt—and upset his glass of water. 'Oh *Frederick!*' said his mother, vexed. 'You really are careless. Dab it with your table-napkin, quick.'

Fatty heaved a sigh of relief. The subject was certainly changed now! 'Sorry, Mother,' he said. 'I say—what was that story you used to tell about the man who sat next to you at a big dinner-party one night—and told you what a big fish he had caught, and . . .'

'Oh yes,' said his mother, and laughed. 'He stretched out his arms to show me how big it was, and said, "You should have *seen* the fish—" and knocked a whole dish of fish out of the waiter's hand all over himself. He certainly saw a lot of fish then!'

Clever old Fatty! No more awkward questions were asked about "The Ivies" after that. His mother happily related a few more amusing stories, to which Fatty listened with great enjoyment. In the middle of them, the telephone bell rang.

'You answer it,' said his mother. 'It's probably your father to say he'll be late tonight.'

But it wasn't. It was Ern, and he sounded very upset indeed.

'That you, Fatty? I say, my uncle's in an awful temper with me, because I wouldn't tell him all we did this morning. He won't pay me my wages. And he says I'm not to go home, I've got to stay here. What shall I do? Shall I scoot off home? I don't want to, because it's so nice to be in the middle of a mystery with all of you.'

'I'll come up and see Mr. Goon,' said Fatty, sorry for poor old Ern. 'You stay put. I'll be up in half an hour's time!'

# 8 FATTY PAYS A CALL ON MR. GOON

FTY kept his promise to Ern. As soon as he had finished his lunch, he put Buster in his bedroom and told him to stay there.

'I'm going to see your enemy, old Goon,' he told Buster, 'and much as you would like to go with me and snap at his ankles, I don't feel that it would be wise this afternoon, Buster. I've got to get poor old Ern his wages !'

Fatty fetched his bicycle and rode off; pondering as he went what to tell Mr. Goon. He decided to tell him everything that had happened that morning, even about Smith and Harris.

'If the Smith of Smith and Harris *is* the man written of in those notes, and he's using a false name to cover up some misdeed or other, I suppose it would sooner or later be a job for Goon to take over,' Fatty thought. 'He'd have to find out what the fellow had done—and why he should be turned out of "The Ivies" —if that's the place that is now called "Haylings Nursery". Anyway, I can't let poor old Ern get into trouble.'

He arrived at Goon's house, and knocked vigorously at the door. Mrs. Hicks arrived in her usual breathless manner.

'There now!' she said. 'I've just bin reading the tea-leaves in my after-dinner cup of tea—and they *said* there would be a stranger coming to the house!'

'How remarkable,' said Fatty, politely. 'Tell Mr. Goon that Frederick Trotteville wishes to see him, please.'

Mrs. Hicks left him standing in the hall, and went into the policeman's office. He scowled at her. 'Bring that boy in,' he said, before she could speak. 'I saw him through the window. I've got something to SAY to him!'

Fatty walked in and nodded to Mr. Goon. He knew that the policeman would not ask him to sit down, so he sat down at once, without being asked. He wasn't going to stand in front of Mr. Goon like a schoolboy called in for a talking to!

'Ah, Mr. Goon,' he said, in an amiable voice. 'I felt I should like to see you for a few minutes. About Ern.'

'Ern! I'm *tired* of Ern !' said Mr. Goon. 'Thinks he can come here and eat me out of house and home, go out when he wants to, solve mysteries, and cheek me into the bargain. *And* expects me to pay him for all that!'

'But didn't you promise to pay him?' asked Fatty, in a surprised voice. 'I must say that Ern has done very well, so far. Where is he?'

'Upstairs. Locked into his room,' said Mr. Goon, in a surly voice. 'And I'd like to tell you this, Master Frederick Trotteville—I haven't time to waste on you. I've business to do this afternoon, see?'

'Right, Mr. Goon,' said Fatty, standing up at once. 'I only came to tell you what Ern and the rest of us had been doing this morning. I thought you'd like to know.'

'But that's what I *asked* Ern! And all he said was that

you'd gone hunting for houses covered with ivy!' said Mr. Goon, almost exploding with wrath. 'Telling me tales like that! Making fun of me! I ticked him off properly for telling me untruths. Then he had the cheek to ask me for half a crown!'

Fatty looked sternly at Mr. Goon. 'Ern was quite right, Mr. Goon. He told you the absolute truth. We *did* go searching for ivy-covered houses—and if you were half as cute as that young nephew of yours, you'd guess at once *why* we decided to do such a thing.'

Mr. Goon stared at Fatty in surprise. Ern had told him the truth, had he? But why go after ivy-covered houses? Then it all dawned on poor Mr. Goon at once. Of course—they were looking for houses that *might* have been called 'The Ivies' at some time or another! Why hadn't *he* thought of that?

'Well, I'll go now,' said Fatty, politely. 'I shouldn't punish Ern, Mr. Goon. He was telling you the truth. But obviously you don't want to hear any more about the matter, so I'll go.'

'No! No, sit down,' almost shouted Mr. Goon. 'You tell me about these here ivy-covered houses.'

'I wouldn't dream of holding up your work,' said Fatty, and began to walk out of the room.

Mr. Goon knew when he was beaten. 'Here! You come back, Master Frederick,' he called. 'I've made a mistake, I see it all now. I'd like to hear anything you've got to say.'

'Fetch Ern down, then,' said Fatty. 'He's on this. He did some very good work this morning. You ought to be proud of Ern, not disbelieve him, and lock him up and refuse to pay him. The work he did this morning was worth a lot!'

Mr. Goon began to wonder if he had made a great mistake about Ern. According to Fatty Ern was much cleverer than he had thought him. Oh, Ern *could* be smart,—he knew that—but to hear this boy Frederick Trotteville talking about him, you'd think Ern was really *brainy*.

'Well—I'll get Ern down,' he said, and got up heavily from his chair. He went upstairs and Fatty could hear him unlocking Ern's door. Ern shot out at once, dodging round his uncle as if he expected a cuff. He came down the stairs two at a time, and ran into the office.

'I heard your voice, Fatty!' he said, gladly. 'Coo you're a real brick to come. How did you make my uncle let me out?'

'Listen, Ern—I'm going to tell him quite shortly about this morning,' said Fatty, quickly, hearing Mr. Goon treading heavily down the stairs. 'But I want *you* to tell him about the house that you and Pip discovered — Haylings Nursery, run by Smith and Harris, see? I've decided that he'd better know about it.'

Ern just had time to nod before Mr. Goon came into the room. He sat down and cleared his throat.

'Well,' he said, 'I hear that the tale you told me wasn't far off the mark, young Ern. If you'd told me a bit more, I'd have listened.'

'But you *wouldn't* listen, Uncle,' said Ern. 'You just roared at me when I asked for my half-crown, and rushed me upstairs and . . .'

'Well, I'm sure your uncle is quite willing to pay you now,' said Fatty. 'I've told him you were a great help this morning. In fact I think he should pay you five shillings, not half a crown. You and Pip were the most successful of us all.'

'Here! I'm not paying Ern any five shillings,' said Mr. Goon at once.

'In that case I shall not say any more,' said Fatty, and stood up. 'You've been unfair to Ern, Mr. Goon, and I should have thought you'd have liked to make it up to him a bit. My word, he did some good work this morning. He and Pip may have put us on to the track of Mr. Smith.'

'What! The Smith mentioned in those notes?' said Goon astonished.

Fatty nodded. 'Maybe. We don't know for certain, of course. You'll be able to judge if you hear what Ern has to say. But as I consider the information is worth five shillings, I shan't give Ern permission to tell you unless you pay him—and pay him now, in front of me.'

Ern's rather bulging eyes bulged even more when he heard Fatty talking to his dreaded uncle in such a cool, determined voice. He gazed at Fatty in awe and admiration. What a friend to have!

Mr. Goon's eyes bulged too—not with admiration, but with wrath and annoyance. He glared at Ern and Fatty. But again he knew he was beaten. That toad of a boy! He was somehow always just a little bit ahead of him. Mr. Goon heaved a great sigh, and delved into his trousers pocket. Ern's eyes brightened as he heard the clink of coins.

Goon brought out two half-crowns. He put them on be table beside Ern. 'Here you are, he said. 'But mind—if I think you don't deserve it, back it comes!'

'You keep it for me, Fatty,' said Ern, hurriedly passing it to Fatty. 'So's I don't spend it all at once, see?'

Fatty laughed and pocketed the money. He didn't trust Goon any more than Ern did. 'Well, now you can tell him what we did this morning, Ern,' he said. 'He knows that we went out hunting for ivy-covered houses —you told him that, and he didn't believe you. But he knows it's true now, and he knows *why* we went. I'll just say, Mr. Goon, that we found a fair number of ivy-covered houses, not one of them called "The Ivies" of course, or it would be in the directory—but that we decided that the only one worth looking into was the one that Ern and Pip found together. Now you do the talking, Ern.'

Ern told his story well. He described Haylings Nursery, half-shop, half-house, well covered with variegated ivy, and told about the board outside, 'Smith and Harris'.

'And we were going to find out if the Mr. Smith was the one mentioned in the notes,' finished Ern.

'But I decided that perhaps that was *your* job, not ours, Mr. Goon,' said Fatty. 'If it *is* the Mr. Smith, then, according to the notes, it's a false name—and you can probably easily find out what his real name is, by making a few enquiries into his past.'

'H'm! said Goon, most interested. 'Yes—yes, I can. And you've been wise to come to me about this, Master Frederick. This is a job for the police, as you said. *I'll* take this over now. You keep out of it. I think there's no doubt that the Smith in "Smith and Harris" is the man who is going under a false name—a criminal who's been in prison, probably. Well, if so, there will be a record of his finger-prints, and we'll soon find his name.'

'How will you get his finger-prints?' asked Fatty, with much interest.

'Oh, I have my own ways of doing that,' said Goon, putting on a very cunning expression, which Fatty didn't like at all.

'Well—it isn't by any means certain that this fellow Smith is anything to do with those notes, you know,' said Fatty, getting up. 'Better be a bit careful, in case he isn't, Mr. Goon.'

'You don't need to give *me* any instructions,' said Goon, annoyed. 'I've been in the police force long enough to know my way about.'

Fatty said goodbye and went. Ern was told to go and keep his usual watch from his bedroom window, in case anyone turned up with another note. Goon finished some reports and then decided to go and interview Mr. Smith of Smith and Harris. Ha—good thing that fat boy had had the sense to tell him about it. And fancy young Ern discovering the house! Goon brooded for a while over the five shillings he had parted with.

'Good mind to go and get it off him,' he thought. No, I can't—he's given it to that fat boy. Well—I'd better get down to Haylings Lane, and see this Mr. Smith.'

He went to get his bicycle, passing through the kitchen where Mrs. Hicks was reading the tea-leaves in her cup again. Mr. Goon shouted.

'You and your tea-leaves!' he said. 'Waste of time!'

He went out of the kitchen door and shut it with a bang. Lazy, careless woman—always breaking things, always having cups of tea, always . . . Mr. Goon's thoughts stopped suddenly as he saw something that gave him a real shock.

One of those anonymous notes! Yes, it must be. It lay on the kitchen window-sill—a cheap square envelope, and on it was 'Mr. goon' just as before, with a small letter for his surname. He stared at it in amazement.

Well, *Ern* must have seen who put it there—and so must Mrs. Hicks! No one could have come across the garden to the kitchen window-sill without being seen! He strode indoors with the letter.

'ERN!' he yelled. 'ERN! Come down here. And you, Mrs. Hicks, you sit still. I've got a few questions to ask you both. Ho yes—I certainly have!'

# 9 ERN GETS INTO TROUBLE—AND SO DOES MR. GOON!

ERN had heard his uncle's stentorian call, and leapt up, scared. *Now* what was the matter? Thank goodness he had handed that five shillings to Fatty.

He tore down the stairs, two steps at a time., 'What is it, Uncle? What's the matter.?'

Mrs. Hicks was sitting in her chair, looking very startled, staring at Mr. Goon.

'See here, Ern,' said Mr. Goon, in a voice of thunder. 'See here—another of those notes I told you about. Put on the window-sill outside the kitchen here! Mrs. Hicks! How long have you been sitting here, facing the window?'

'About three minutes,' said Mrs. Hicks, looking quite taken aback. 'I did my washing-up, and then sat down for my second cup of tea. Not more than three minutes ago.'

'Did you see anyone come into the garden?' demanded Goon.

'Not a soul,' answered Mrs.Hicks. 'Well, bless us all, is that really another of them ominous letters, sir—or whatever you call them? And left on the window-sill too! What a nerve!'

'You *must* have seen someone put it there,' said Goon, exasperated.

'Well, it wasn't there ten minutes ago, that I do know,' said Mrs. Hicks. 'Because I opened the window to throw out some bread to the birds, Mr. Goon, and I'd have noticed at once if that letter was there. I'm not blind. And don't you glare at me like that, Mr. Goon, you make me feel right down queer!'

'Well—someone must have come over the fence, crossed the garden, and actually placed the note on the sill within the last ten minutes,' said Goon. 'Ernie *must* have seen them, even if you didn't. Ern, did you see anyone?'

'No, no one,' answered Ern, puzzled. 'No one at all.'

'Then you couldn't have been watching,' said Goon, losing his temper.

'I *was* watching. I was sitting at my window all the time,' said Ern, indignantly. 'I tell you, nobody came into the yard, NOBODY!'

'Then how did this note get here?' shouted Goon. 'There's Mrs. Hicks here in the kitchen, and you upstairs at the window—and yet someone steals into the yard under your very eyes, leaves the note on the sill and goes away again.'

'Well, I dunno!' said Ern, bewildered. 'If I didn't see anyone, and Mrs. Hicks didn't either, there couldn't have *been* anybody. Unless he was invisible!'

'Now don't you cheek me,' said Mr. Goon. 'Invisible indeed! I don't suppose Mrs. Hicks would see anything under her nose except tea-leaves, and . . .'

'Don't you sauce *me*!' said Mrs. Hicks, annoyed.

'And as for Ern, here, he must have been reading one

of those comics of his!' said Goon. 'Ern—speak the truth. YOU WERENT WATCHING!'

'I was, Uncle, I was,' said poor Ern, retreating as his uncle came forward towards him. 'I do honest work. You paid me to watch, and I do watch when I'm up there. I tell you nobody came into that garden since you sent me upstairs.'

Goon aimed his hand at him, but Ern ducked and the policeman's fingers caught the edge of a table. He danced round in pain. Ern tore out of the house at top speed. He snatched up his bicycle and rode off on it. He wouldn't stay with his uncle one more hour! Disbelieving him like that! Trying to cuff him when he'd done nothing wrong! Mrs. Hicks hadn't seen, anyone. Well, if *she* hadn't, how could *he* have seen anybody!

Mr. Goon tore open the square envelope, then saw Mrs. Hicks staring open-mouthed, and stamped back into his office. The note was in message-form again, made with cut-out letters as before. Goon read it. It was even more puzzling than the others.

'When you see Smith, say SECRETS to him. Then watch him show his heels.'

'Gah!' said Mr. Goon, in disgust. 'What's it all mean? *Secrets,* now! What secrets? All right, I'll say "secrets" to this Mr. Smith at Haylings Nursery when I see him! I'm getting tired of this. That boy Ern! Sitting upstairs like that and letting the fellow who writes these notes come and put one on the window-sill under his very nose—and I paid him five shillings!'

He was just going out again to get his bicycle when he

stopped. Hadn't he better telephone to that fat boy and say another note had arrived—and tell him how badly Ern had behaved? Right down dishonest of Ern it was, to take his five shillings, and then not do his job. And most ungrateful too.

So Goon telephoned to a rather surprised Fatty and told him about the new letter, and what it contained. Fatty noted it down at once 'When you see Smith, say "SECRETS" to him. Then watch him show his heels.'

Goon went on to tell about Ern, and how he had failed to spot anyone coming into the garden with the note. 'Reading his comics, that's what he was doing, instead of paying attention to his job, as he was paid to do,' grumbled Goon. 'Can't let Ern get away with behaviour like that, you know—taking money for what he doesn't do. You'd better let me have that five bob back.'

'Sorry, Mr. Goon, but you paid Ern for what he'd *already* done, not for what he was *going* to do,' said Fatty. 'That five shillings is Ern's. What are you going to do now? Go to see Smith and Harris?'

'Yes,' said Goon. 'But about that five bob. If Ernie comes up to you, you tell him I want half-a-crown back, see?'

Fatty put down the receiver, cutting off any more remarks from the angry Goon. He felt sorry that Ern had failed to see anyone coming into the garden with another note—in full daylight too. The messenger certainly had a nerve to do a thing like that!

He heard the sound of a bicycle bell outside in the drive and looked out of the window. It was Ern, panting with his exertions to reach Fatty's house at the first possible moment.

'Hallo, Ern,' said Fatty. 'Your uncle's just been on the phone. I hear there's another anonymous note—put on the window-sill under everyone's nose, apparently. How on earth was it that you didn't spot whoever brought it? Apparently it happened while you were supposed to be watching.'

'I *was* watching,' said Ern, indignantly. You told me to do my job honestly, and I did. I tell you, Fatty, as soon as Uncle sent me upstairs to watch, I sat at my window and glued my eyes on the yard. I did, really. I saw some bread dropping into the yard, and I guessed it was Mrs. Hicks throwing some out to the birds. She says the note wasn't on the window-sill when she threw out the bread.'

'And after she threw it out, you still kept our eyes glued on the yard below?' asked Fatty, doubtfully. 'Didn't Mrs. Hicks see anyone either?'

'No. No one. Well, if *she* had, I'd have seen him too, wouldn't I?' said Ern, half-angry. 'She was sitting opposite the window—she could almost have reached out and touched it! Well, if *she* didn't see anyone, how could *I*? I just don't understand it, Fatty. The note *must* have been there when Mrs. Hicks threw out the bread —and she didn't see it—that's the only explanation.'

'I suppose it is,' said Fatty. 'There's something really queer about it though, I can't just put my finger on it. Well, I expect your uncle will cool down again, Ern. You can stay here for tea though, if you like. I shouldn't think there's much point in your going back to do any more

*'Look where you're going,' shouted the man*

watching—there isn't likely to be another note today!'

'Oh thanks, Fatty. I'd like to stay here,' said Ern. 'Can I help you with anything?'

'Yes. I'm going to pack up some of the jumble to take to the Village Hall some time,' said Fatty. 'You can help me with that. I wonder how your uncle will get on with Smith and Harris. It's *possible* that Smith may be the man mentioned in the notes. Well, we shall soon know.'

Mr. Goon was not getting on very well in his afternoon's work. In fact, he was having rather a bad time. He had arrived at the Nursery in a bad temper, owing to Ern's failure to spot the messenger who brought the last anonymous note. He rode in at the gate at top speed and almost knocked down a man coming up the path wheeling a barrow.

'Look where you're going!' shouted the man, as a flower-pot crashed to the ground. Goon dismounted, and spoke in his most official manner.

'I want to see Smith and Harris.'

'Well, you're speaking to half of them,' said the man, setting the barrow legs down on the path. 'I'm Harris. What do you want? I've got a licence for my dog, and one for my radio, and one for my van, and . . .'

'I haven't come about licences,' said Goon, with a feeling that the man was making fun of him. 'I want to see Mr. Smith.'

'Oh now—that's rather difficult,' said Mr. Harris, rubbing his chin, and making a rasping noise as he did so. 'Yes, rather difficult.'

'Is he in the house? said Mr. Goon, impatiently. 'Or

out in the nursery gardens?'

'No, no. You won't find him there,' said Mr. Harris, who had taken a real dislike to the bumptious policeman. 'I couldn't rightly put my finger on him at the moment.'

'Well, I *must* see him,' said Goon. 'It's important. Don't put me off, please. Take me to him.'

'Oh, I haven't time to do that,' said Mr. Harris. 'It's too far to take you when I'm busy, like. I've only one man working for me, and time's precious.'

Mr. Goon began to feel exasperated. Where was this elusive Mr. Smith? He decided to put a leading question.

'Is Mr. Smith his real name?' he asked, bluntly. Mr. Harris looked very startled indeed. He stared at Mr. Goon and rasped his rough chin again.

'Far as I know it is,' he said. 'Known him all my life I have, and he always went by the name of Smith, since he was a tiddler. You being funny?'

'No,' said Mr. Goon, shortly, disappointed to hear that Smith's name was apparently correct. 'Er—can you tell me if this place was ever called "The Ivies"?'

'And why for should it be?' demanded Mr. Harris. 'It was Haylings Nursery when I bought it, and Haylings Nursery afore that, and probably Haylings Nursery afore you were born, Mr. Nosey Policeman. What's this about The Ivies?'

'Well—you've got ivy growing up the wall,' said Mr. Goon, beginning to feel very foolish, and wishing he had looked up how old the Haylings Nursery was.

'Now please—I want you to show me where Mr. Smith is.'

'All right. Seeing as you insist,' said Mr. Harris, and leaving his barrow on the path, he took Mr. Goon indoors. He led him to a big round globe of the world, and swung it a little, so that South America came into view. Mr. Harris then pointed to a town marked there.

'See that place Rio de Janeiro? Well, *that's* where he is. Retired there twenty years ago, he did, and I carried on by myself—but I still keep the old name going Smith and Harris. You catch the next plane there, Mister, and ask him if his name's Smith. He won't mind telling you.'

And with that he burst into such a roar of laughter that Goon was almost deafened. Very angry at the joke played on him, the policeman departed, looking as dignified as he could. But right to the end of the lane he could hear Mr. Harris's delighted guffaws.

Why hadn't he let that fat boy interview Mr. Harris? It would have done him good to have that silly joke played on *him*. Policemen should be treated with more respect! Mr. Goon was Very Annoyed Indeed.

## 10 FATTY COMES TO A FULL STOP

MR. GOON never told anyone all that had happened at Haylings Nursery. When Fatty telephoned him that evening to ask if he had had any success, Mr. Goon said very little.

'There is no Mr. Smith there now,' he said. 'He left the firm twenty years ago. It was a waste of my time to go there. Is Ern with you, Master Frederick?'

'Yes. I'm just sending him back to you,' said Fatty. 'He's been a great help to me this afternoon—nice of you to send him up, Mr. Goon. Thanks very much.'

Goon was astonished. Hadn't Ern told Fatty how angry he had been with Ern, then—and that he had tried to hit him? Well, Ern could stay another night with him, and then he could go home. He wasn't much good as a watcher, and as for paying him another penny, he wasn't even going to *think* of it!

Ern arrived, wondering how Goon was going to treat him. He sent him out to have his supper with Mrs. Hicks in the kitchen. 'Got some work to do,' he said, and Ern fled thankfully to the warm kitchen.

He sat down by the fire, and watched Mrs. Hicks making some pastry. 'Funny how neither of us saw that fellow, whoever he was, bringing that note this afternoon,' said Ern.

'Well, I wasn't really looking,' said Mrs. Hicks. 'I was just sitting here with my teacup, reading the tea-leaves, like I always do. *You* couldn't have been looking either, young man. You can tell fibs to your uncle, if you like, but you needn't tell them to me. You just wasn't looking!'

'Oooh, I *was*,' said Ern. 'I tell you I never took my eyes off that yard. Never once. When I'm paid to do thing I do it, see? And I never saw anyone—all I saw were the birds flying down to peck at the bread you threw out.'

'Oh—you saw me doing that, did you?' said Mrs. Hicks. 'Well, it's funny you didn't see who brought that note then, because he must have come along just after that—as I was telling your uncle.'

'He *couldn't* have come then,' said Ern. 'I tell you I was watching all the time, Mrs. Hicks. *I'm* not making a mistake, I know I'm not.'

'Are you telling me that *I* am, then?' said Mrs. Hicks, looking so fierce that Ern felt quite alarmed. 'You just be careful of that tongue of yours, young Ern, else not a mite of supper do you get.'

Ern subsided, feeling puzzled. Everyone was cross with him just now—but on the whole it was safer to sit with Mrs. Hicks in the kitchen rather than with his uncle in the office. He wondered if Mrs. Hicks would like to hear his 'pome'. It might put her into a better temper.

'I write portry, Mrs. Hicks,' he said.

'Well, I shouldn't think that's very difficult, is it?' said Mrs. Hicks. 'I'd write it myself if I had time.'

This was rather damping. Ern tried again. 'I'd like to

know what you think of my last pome,' he said. 'Can I say it to you?'

'If you like,' said Mrs. Hicks, still rolling the pastry vigorously. 'Silly stuff really. I used to do reciting at school meself.'

'But this is something I made up,' said Ern. 'At least —I made up some of it, and a friend of mine made up the other half.' And with that he stood up and recited his verses—and Fatty's—about the 'Poor Old House'. He didn't see Mr. Goon at the kitchen door, standing amazed at Ern's recital. He almost jumped out of his skin when he heard his uncle's voice at the end.

'Have you taken to poetry writing again, Ern?' said Mr. Goon. 'How many times have I told you it's a waste of time? Do you remember that rude poem you wrote about me, once? Well, *I* haven't forgotten it, see? And what's all that about "The Ivies" in that poem? Don't you go putting secret information like that into your poem. You give me that notebook of yours and let me see what other poems you've got there.'

'No, Uncle. My notebook's private,' said Ern, remembering that he had put into it notes of the meetings he had had with Fatty and the others.

'Now, look here, young Ern,' said Goon, advancing on him, and Ern promptly fled out of the back-door. He saw a black shadow moving before him, and yelled.

'Uncle! There's someone out here! Quick, uncle!'

Mr. Goon rushed out at once—and ran straight into Mrs. Hicks' washing-line, which was hung with overalls, two sheets and a dark blanket. The line broke, and Mr.

Goon gave a yell as the blanket folded itself round him.

Poor Ern! He really had thought that the washing blowing in the darkness on the line was somebody in the yard. When he saw his uncle staggering into the kitchen with the washing dragging behind him on the broken line, he knew there was only one thing to do—and that was to rush up to his bedroom and lock himself in!

That meant going without his supper—but at least he still had his precious notebook and at least he was safe from his uncle's anger. Judging from the noise downstairs he was lucky to have escaped in time. Why, oh why had he ever said he would come and help his uncle? Never again, thought poor Ern. Never again!

Meantime Fatty was feeling that he had come to a full stop where the mysterious notes were concerned. They hadn't found a house called The Ivies, or even one with ivy growing up it that *had* been called The Ivies. Neither had they found the right Smith. Was there anything else to do?

'Only one thing,' thought Fatty. 'And that will be a terribly fiddling job. I'd better try and get the letters and words off, that are stuck on to the sheet of writing-paper. I might find something printed on the other side to help me—I might even find out what newspaper they come from. If it was, say, a Bristol paper, the odds are that the writer of the notes comes from Bristol—or if it turns out to be a Manchester paper, maybe he comes from Manchester. Not that that will be much help.'

So he went down to his shed that evening and set to work. It was indeed a horribly fiddling job. In the middle of it, his lamp flickered and went out.

'Blow!' said Fatty, and gathered up his things by the light of a candle and went indoors. He sat himself down in his bedroom to finish the job.

He found a few interesting things as he tried to get the pasted-on letters off the strips they were stuck on. The word 'goon' for instance, which was, in every case, apparently part of a whole word—it was not made of four separate letters. Fatty stared at it. 'goon'. It must be part of a whole word. But what word had 'goon' in it. He couldn't think of any.

As he went on with his work, a tap came at the door, and his mother came in. 'Frederick, have you taken my library book?' she asked. 'Good gracious, whatever are you doing? What a mess!'

'I'm just solving a—well, a kind of puzzle really,' said Fatty. His mother picked up the cut-out piece of paper he had just put down—the bit with 'goon' on.

'Goon,' she said. 'What a funny puzzle, Frederick. Is this part of "Rangoon" or something?'

'*Rangoon*!' said Fatty. 'I never thought of Rangoon. It's about the only word ending in "goon", isn't it, Mother? Has Rangoon been in the papers much lately? Has anything happened there? Would the name be printed a lot in our papers?'

'Well no—I can't remember seeing anything about Rangoon,' said his mother. 'Oh Frederick—you *have* got my library book! Really, that's too bad of you.'

'Gosh, sorry, Mother—I must have brought it up by mistake,' said Fatty. 'It's almost exactly like mine, look.'

'Would you like me to stay and help you to sort out this queer puzzle?' asked his mother. 'I like puzzles, as you know.'

'Oh no, Mother, thank you, I wouldn't dream of bothering you,' said Fatty, hastily, afraid of some awkward questions as to where he had got the 'puzzle' from. 'It's hopeless, really. I expect I'll have to give it up.'

And that is exactly what poor Fatty had to do, after struggling with it for at least two hours. There was nothing on the other side of the pasted-on letters that could help him to identify any newspapers—only odd letters that might have come from any part of any paper. It was very disappointing.

'*That* idea's no good then,' said Fatty, putting the bits and pieces back into the envelope. 'Waste of two hours! I'm at a dead-end. Can't find any clues at all—and even when there was a chance of actually *seeing* that fellow who delivers the notes, Ern doesn't see him. He must have had forty winks—he couldn't have failed to see him if he was really awake. Blow! Where do we go from here? I'll call a meeting tomorrow morning, and we'll see if anyone has any ideas.'

So next morning, at ten o'clock sharp, everyone was at Fatty's, including Ern. Ern was feeling a bit happier. His uncle had had a nice letter from Superintendent Jenks that morning, about some small case that Goon had apparently handled quite well—and the big police-man had beamed all through breakfast. He read the letter to Ern three times, very solemnly.

'Now if *I* had done what *you* did yesterday, and sat

looking out of that window of yours, keeping watch, and hadn't even *seen* something going on under my very nose, I wouldn't be getting letters like this,' said Goon.

Ern didn't argue. He nodded his head and helped himself to more bread and butter and marmalade. He made up his mind to go up to Fatty's immediately after breakfast and tell him he was going home. He was sure that his uncle wouldn't pay him any more wages, and he wasn't going to stop with him for nothing!

So Ern was at the meeting too. When they were all in the shed, Fatty told them of his failure the night before. 'Mother came up and offered to help me,' he said. 'But I was afraid she'd ask me awkward questions. She did say that she thought the word "goon" with the small letter instead of the capital one, night be part of *Rangoon.* And it *might*, though I can't think how it could help us! I gave up trying to find a clue by unpasting the letters in the messages. And now I don't really see what else we can do.'

'Well, there's only one thing left,' said Daisy, 'and that's that place that Larry and I found. What was it called now—Fairlin Hall. The place that was empty. I just wondered if it might be worth while finding out if it had *ever* been called "The Ivies"..'

'But you said it was empty,' said Fatty. 'You saw a notice-board up, saying that it was for sale.'

'Yes, I know,' said Daisy. 'But I went by it today—just out of curiosity, you know—and I saw something queer.'

'What?' asked everyone at once.

'Well—I'm sure there was smoke coming out of a chimney at the back,' said Daisy. 'I couldn't be *quite* certain—the chimney might have belonged to a house I couldn't see. But it did *look* as if a chimney belonging to Fairlin Hall itself was smoking.'

'Well! This certainly needs investigating,' said Fatty, cheering up at once. 'There might be someone hiding there—Smith perhaps! I vote we all cycle down straightaway and have a snoop round. What about it, everyone? Come on!'

And out they all rushed to get their bicycles, with Buster barking madly round them. Was this a clue to the mystery–or wasn't it? A smoking chimney! If only it *did* belong to Fairlin Hall!

# 11 THE CARETAKERS AT FAIRLIN HALL

THE six cyclists, with Buster panting behind, rode through Peterswood at top speed. It was most unfortunate that they should meet Mr. Goon round a corner. He was on his bicycle too, and Ern, being on the middle of the road, almost ran into him.

'Ern!' yelled Mr. Goon, wobbling dangerously. 'I'll teach you to—here, where are you going, Ern ! ERN!'

But Ern, and the others too, were away up the road, Ern looking scared. 'Hope he won't come after me,' he said. He looked round, and to his horror saw that Mr. Goon had swung round and was pedalling furiously some way behind them.

'Can't let him see us going into Fairlin Hall,' panted Fatty. 'We'll go right past it, and up Cockers Hill. Goon will soon be left behind then.'

So they swept past Fairlin Hall, each trying to see whether smoke was coming from any chimney, turned the corner and made for the steep Cockers Hill. Up they went, more slowly now, hearing Mr. Goon's shouts for Ern faintly behind them. Bets began to giggle.

'Oh dear! Mr. Goon will be as red as a beetroot when he's half-way up this hill ! It's rather a shame, Fatty.'

'He doesn't *need* to follow us up it,' panted Fatty, who was a good deal too plump for such violent exercise.

'Look behind, Bets. Has he dismounted yet?'

Bets glanced behind. 'Yes, he has. He's standing still, mopping his head. Poor Goon! We'll soon shake him off.'

They came to the top of Cockers Hill, sailed down it thankfully, and then made their way back to the road in which Fairlin Hall stood. There was no sign of Goon anywhere. They put their bicycles against the wall, and stood at the gate entrance, looking into the drive.

'See what I mean,' said Daisy, eagerly. 'Isn't that smoke from one of the chimneys right at the back of the house?'

'Yes. I rather think it is,' said Fatty. 'What an ugly old place! Look at those great pillars at the front door—and those heavy stone balconies. It must have been empty for years.'

He went to look at the 'For Sale' board, and noted the House Agent's name on it. 'Paul and Ticking,' he said. 'It wouldn't be a bad idea to go and ask them for particulars of this place—we might find out if it had ever been called "The Ivies".'

'Yes. That's a good idea!' said Pip. 'Well—shall we snoop round the place and see if anyone's about? We must find out if that smoking chimney belongs to the house.'

'Yes,' said Fatty. 'I'll go with Bets. You stay here, you three, out of sight, with Buster. Bets and I will go round to the back of the house, calling Buster, as if we'd lost him, and if anyone *is* there, they'll probably come out to us. When we've stopped yelling for Buster, you can let him go, and he'll come to us.'

'Right,' said Larry, catching hold of the little Scottie

*An oldish woman came out of the kitchen door*

by the collar. Fatty and Bets made their way down the overgrown drive, Fatty calling : 'Buster, Buster, where are you?' at the top of his voice. Buster nearly went mad trying to follow, and was extremely angry with Larry for hanging on to his collar. He almost choked himself, trying to get away.

Fatty peeped into the windows he passed. The house was as dismal inside as it was outside. Great empty rooms, dirty and dreary, with filthy windows, and faded paint—Bets shivered, and turned her face away.

They rounded a corner and came to the kitchen end. There was a line across a yard, with clothes blowing on it—aha, there was certainly someone here, then! Fatty nudged Bets and glanced upwards. Bets did the same and saw a chimney above, smoking. Daisy had been right.

'Buster, Buster, where are you, you naughty dog!' shouted Fatty, and whistled piercingly.

An oldish woman came out of the kitchen door, thin and sad-looking, but with a kindly, rather sweet old face. 'Have you lost your dog? she said.

'He's somewhere about,' said Fatty truthfully. 'I do hope I didn't disturb you. Isn't this place empty? I saw a "For Sale" notice outside.'

'That's right,' said the woman, pulling her shawl round her. 'We're caretakers. The house was left quite empty for years, but tramps kept breaking in—so the agents put in caretakers. We've been here for fifteen years now-and we hope the place *won't* be sold, because we don't want to be turned out!'

Buster suddenly came rushing round the comer, and

barked madly when he saw Fatty. He was most indignant at being held so long by Larry, who, of course, had let him go as soon as Fatty had stopped calling him.

'Ah—there's your dog,' said the old woman. 'He couldn't have been far away. I sometimes wish *we* had a dog. Three times since we've been here there's been burglars—though what they expect to find in an empty house, *I don't* know!'

A voice called her from indoors, and then someone coughed long and painfully. 'That's my poor husband,' said the old woman. 'He's ill. I suppose you aren't going back to the village, are you? I ought to go to the chemist and get him some more medicine, but I don't really like leaving him.'

'Of course we'll leave a message at the chemist for you—or better still we'll pop down and get the medicine ourselves and bring it back!' said Fatty. 'We've got our bicycles.'

'Well, that would be real kind of you,' said the old lady. 'I'll just get the bottle,' and she hurried indoors.

'Wonder if their name is Smith,' said Fatty, in a low voice. 'Shouldn't think so. Obviously they're just caretakers who've been here for years. Ah—here she comes.'

'Here's the bottle,' said the old woman. 'And here's the shilling for the medicine. Ask for the same prescription as before, please.'

'Er—what name shall I say?' asked Fatty.

'Smith,' said the old lady. 'Mr. John Smith. The chemist will know.

'Right,' said Fatty, startled to hear that there *was* a Mr. Smith in this ivy-covered place. He glanced at Bets, and saw that she was astonished too. 'Come on, Buster, old thing. We'll be back in about ten minutes, Mrs. Smith.'

'You're kind, real kind,' she said, and gave them a smile that made her old face quite beautiful.

Fatty and Bets ran back up the drive with Buster at their heels. Fatty's thoughts were in a whirl. Was this another wrong Smith—or could it be—could it possibly be the right one?

'What an awfully long time you were,' said Larry. 'What happened?'

Fatty told the others briefly, as they wheeled their bicycles into the road. 'Two caretakers there—been in charge of the house for fifteen years. And the name is SMITH! What do you think of that?'

'Come on—we're going to the chemist,' said Bets.

'What on earth for?' demanded Pip.

'Tell you as we go,' said Fatty, which was really rather a dangerous thing to do, as the other four were so keen to hear Fatty's tale that they rode in a close bunch as near to him as possible, their pedals almost touching! However, they arrived at the chemist's safely, and Fatty went in with the bottle, planning to get a little more information about the Smiths if he could.

'For Mr. Smith?' said the chemist, who knew Fatty. 'How's the old fellow? He's been ailing for the past year. He really ought to get out of that damp old place, and go and live by the sea—but they're as poor as church mice.'

'Mrs. Smith seemed very nice,' said Fatty. 'I don't know her husband.'

'He's a queer fellow,' said the chemist, writing out a label. 'Sort of scared. Hardly ever goes out, and when his wife was ill, and he had to come in to get medicine for her, he hardly opened his mouth. I guess they don't want that old place to be sold—they'd have to look for somewhere else to go to, and that's not easy these days, when you're old and poor.'

'Who used to own Fairlin Hall?' asked Fatty.

'I've no idea,' said the chemist. 'It's been empty for years—long before *I* came here. Falling to pieces, I should think. It's a dismal place. Well, there you are. One shilling, please, and give my kind regards to the old lady. She's a pet, and simply worships the old man.'

'Thanks,' said Fatty, and went out with Bets. 'We'll go straight back to Fairlin Hall,' he said to the others, who were waiting outside. 'I'll see if I can ge to any more information out of Mrs. Smith. Then we'll go to the House Agent. We simply MUST find out if that house was ever called The Ivies—if it was, we're really on the track of the mystery!'

They all went back to Fairlin Hall, and Fatty and Bets once more went round to the back door, this time with Buster free, dancing round them. The kitchen door was shut, and they knocked.

'If that's the medicine, would you leave it on the doorstep?' called the old woman's voice. 'I'm just seeing to my husband. He's had a nasty coughing attack. Thank you very much.'

Fatty put the bottle down on the step, rather disappointed at not being able to get any more information. He took a quick look round. The yard was very clean and tidy. Spotless, well-mended curtains hung at the windows—the only clean windows in the house! The door-step was well-scrubbed. A washed milk-bottle stood there, waiting for the milkman.

'Well—Mr. Smith *may* be a man with a false name and a queer past of some sort,' said Fatty, as they went back to the others. 'But there's nothing wrong with the old lady. Even the chemist said she was a pet. I liked her, didn't you, Bets?

'Yes, I did,' said Bets. 'Oh dear—I do hope nothing horrid will happen to Mr. Smith, it would make his wife so unhappy. The man who wrote those notes didn't seem to like him at all, did he? I wonder what he meant by telling Mr. Goon to say SECRETS to him.'

'Can't imagine,' said Fatty. 'Well now—off we go to the House Agent's. Hallo—what's all the noise going on outside the front gates?'

Fatty soon found out! Mr. Goon had come cycling by and had suddenly seen Larry, Daisy, Pip—and Ern! He also saw Fatty's bicycle and Bets', leaning against the wall, and felt very curious indeed. He had dismounted heavily from his own bicycle; after making sure that Buster was nowhere around, and demanded to know what they were all doing there.

'Just having a bit of a rest,' said Pip. 'Going up Cockers Hill at top speed was tiring, Mr. Goon. I expect you found it so, too.'

'I don't want any cheek,' said Mr. Goon, glaring at Pip. 'Where's that fat boy gone? What's he here for? Ho—another ivy-covered house! Snooping round again, I suppose. Well, you won't find much there—it's empty, see? Ern—you come here.'

Just at that moment Fatty and Bets and Buster came out of the gate, and Buster ran barking in delight towards his old enemy. Goon leapt on his bicycle at once, and rode off quickly, shouting to Ern.

'You come back with me, young Ern. I've got a job for you, delivering messages. You come at once, Ern.'

'Better go, Ern,' said Fatty. 'Who knows—he may give you some more wages at dinner-time, if you do some work for him this morning!'

'What a hope!' said Ern, in disgust. 'All right, Fatty. I'll go, if you say so. I'll be down at your place as soon as I can to hear your news. So long!'

And away he went after his uncle, looking so doleful that the others couldn't help laughing. 'Now to the House Agent's,' said Fatty, mounting his bicycle too. 'I feel we're getting somewhere now!'

# 12 MR. GRIMBLE TALKS

THE House Agent's office was in the middle of the High Street, and its window was set out with all kinds of very dull particulars of houses for sale.

'I hope you won't be too long, Fatty,' said Pip. 'It's a bit boring for the rest of us, waiting about while you and Bets do the work.'

'Sorry!' said Fatty. 'Yes, you're right—I've been making you wait about half the morning. Look, go into the dairy, and order what you like. It's gone eleven o'clock, I should think. I'll pay. I've still got heaps left from my Christmas money. Bets, you go too, and order me two macaroons and an ice-cream.'

'Oh *Fatty*—didn't you have any breakfast!' said Bets. But Fatty had already disappeared into the House Agent's office. A young man was there, very busy at a big desk. In a corner, at a much smaller desk, sat a clerk, an older man, round-shouldered and shabby.

'Well—what can I do for *you*?' said the young man. 'Have you any particulars about Fairlin Hall?' asked Fatty, politely. The young man stared at him.

'That old place! You're not thinking of buying it, by any chance, are you?' he said, and laughed,

'Well, no,' said Fatty. 'I'm—er—interested in its

history, to tell you the truth.'

'Well, I'm sorry—but I haven't time to give you a history lesson,' said the young man rudely. 'The place has been empty as long as I can remember—since before I was born. We're hoping to sell it as a school of some sort, but it's in such bad condition, nobody will buy. It's got no history as far as *I* know!'

The telephone bell rang at that moment, and the young man picked up the receiver. 'Mr. Paul here,' he said. 'Oh *yes*, Mrs. Donning. Yes, yes, yes. Of course, of course. No trouble at all. Do give me all the particulars.'

It was quite plain to Fatty that he wasn't going to get any help from the bumptious Mr. Paul, who was evidently one of the partners in the business of Paul and Ticking. He turned and made for the door.

But as he passed the old clerk in the corner, he heard a few quiet words. 'I can tell you something about the house if you like, sir.'

Fatty turned and saw that the old man was trying to make up for Mr. Paul's rudeness. He went over to his desk.

'Do you know anything about the place?' he said, eagerly. 'You know it, don't you—covered with ivy from top to bottom.'

'Oh yes. I sold it to its present owners twenty-one years ago,' said the clerk. 'It was a lovely place then. I and my wife used to know the old lady who lived there. Ah, Fairlin Hall was well-kept then—it had four gardeners, and you should have seen the rose-garden! I was talking about it to old Grimble only the other day. He was head gardener there, and knew every corner of it.'

Fatty pricked up his ears at once. Surely an old gardener would know far more about Fairlin Hall than anyone else. He might be pleased to talk about the old place, too.

'Perhaps you could give me Grimble's address,' he said. 'Does he still work?'

'Oh no—he's retired. Just potters about his own garden,' said the old clerk. 'I'll scribble down his address for you.'

'Er—was Fairlin Hall ever called anything else? asked Fatty, hopefully.

'I believe it was—but I can't remember,' said the old man. 'But perhaps I can look it up for you.'

'Potter!' said Mr. Paul, putting down the telephone receiver, 'it's very difficult for me to telephone, with you jabbering in the corner.'

'Sorry, Mr. Paul,' said poor old Potter, and hastily pushed a piece of paper over to Fatty, who shot out of the office before the rude Mr. Paul could admonish him too. Ugh! Fancy that old clerk having to put up with young Mr. Paul's rudeness all the time! Fatty glanced down at the piece of paper he had been given.

'Donald Grimble,' he read. 'Primrose Cot, Burling Meadows. Gardener.'

He ran across the road to the dairy, where all the others were now sitting round a table, eating macaroons. Buster greeted him loudly as usual, barking as if he hadn't seen Fatty for at least a month.

'You haven't been long, Fatty,' said Bets. 'I've only taken

two bites at my macaroon. Have one—they're lovely and fresh. All gooey.'

'Did you find out anything?' asked Larry.

Fatty told them about the rude Mr. Paul and the nice old man in the corner who seemed so scared of him. Then he showed them the piece of paper. 'Donald Grimble used to be head gardener at Fairlin Hall,' he said, 'and apparently knew every corner of the place. He's retired now—but I bet he can tell us plenty about it. If ONLY we could find out if it has ever been called "The Ivies"! I can't help thinking that old Mr. Smith, whose medicine we got this morning, *must* be the Smith referred to in those anonymous notes.'

'We've got time to go and see Grimble this morning,' said Bets. 'But what excuse can we make? He'll wonder why we're so interested in the old place. He might think we were making fun of him, or something.'

'I know! Let's buy a pot with some queer plant in at the florist's,' said Daisy, 'and go and ask him to tell us what it is! Then we can get talking.'

'Daisy, that's a very bright idea,' said Fatty, approvingly, and Daisy went red with pleasure. 'That will mean we can all go, instead of most of you waiting about outside. I'll have another macaroon, please.'

'I suppose you're counting, Fatty?' said Pip, handing him the plate. 'You've had three already, and they're expensive, you know. Even *your* Christmas money won't last long if you empty plates of macaroons at this rate.'

'Have an ice-cream, Pip,' said Fatty, 'and stop counting how many macaroons I eat. Bets, aren't *you* going to have an ice-cream? You'd better feed yourself up, because I'm going to make *you* take the pot-plant in to old Mr. Grimble!'

'Oh *no*!' said Bets. 'Why can't one of the others?'

'Because you have a very nice smile, Bets, enough to melt the crabbed old heart of even a fierce head gardener!' said Fatty.

Bets laughed. 'You might be Irish, Fatty, with all your blarney!' she said. 'All right, I'll do it for you. Shall Daisy and I go and buy the plant now, while you others are finishing? We can't eat another thing.'

'Yes. Here's the money,' said Fatty, but Daisy pushed it away. 'Oddly enough, *I* have, some Christmas money left too!' she said. 'Come on, Bets—let's leave these guzzlers, and go to the flower shop.'.

They were back again with a small plant just as the three boys and Buster came out of the dairy, looking rather well-fed.

'Please, Mr. Grimble,' said Bet, looking up at Fatty with a smile, 'could you tell me what this plant is?'

Fatty laughed. 'Fine, Bets! But be sure to get *us* into the picture somehow, so that we can come and listen — and so that I can ask questions!'

They went off to Burling Meadows on their bicycles. Primrose Cot was a small cottage standing by itself in a beautiful little garden. Not a weed showed in the smooth grass lawn. Nor was there a weed in any of the beds, either. The hedges were trim and neat. Early snowdrops showed their little white bonnets under a tree, and yellow aconites wore their pretty green frills just beside them.

*'Please, Mr. Grimble,' said Bets... 'could you tell me what this plant is?'*

'That must be old Grimble sawing logs at the bottom of the garden,' said Fatty, seeing a sturdy old man there, a battered hat at the back of his head, and the dark blue apron of a head gardner over his corduroy trousers. 'Let's go into the field nearby and speak to him over the hedge.'

So they went down a side-path into the field that skirted the bottom of Grimble's garden. Bets called to him over the hedge. 'Please, are you Mr. Grimble?'

'Yes, I am,' answered the old fellow, peering over at Bets. 'What do you want with me?'

'Oh please, could you tell me what this plant is?' asked Bets, with her sweetest smile, and handed up the pot. 'It's got such pretty leaves, and I do want to know its name. You know the names of every plant, don't you, Mr. Grimble?'

Grimble beamed down at her. 'Well, I know a tidy few, Missie. This here plant is a young Coleus—but you want to take it home and keep it in the warm. It don't like cold air.'

'Have you ever grown Coleuses?' asked Bets.

'Oh aye! Thousands,' said old Grimble. 'I used to work at that old place, Fairlin Hall—I were head gardener there for years—and I always kept one corner of the heated greenhouse for them Coleus. Pretty things they are, with their patterned leaves—all colours!'

'Oh, Fatty—he used to work at Fairlin Hall,' called Bets, anxious to bring the others into the conversation. 'Wasn't that the place we saw this morning—you know, where that old woman lives, whose husband we fetched medicine for.'

Fatty came up at once, pleased with Bets. The others followed, amused at her little performance.

'Good morning,' said Fatty, politely. 'Yes, we did go into the front drive and round to the back this morning. We didn't see much of the garden though.'

'Ah, it's a terrible place now,' said Grimble, sadly. 'I worked there, man and boy, for years, young sir, and was made head gardener. You should have seen my roses—'twas a show place, my rose garden. 1 never go down that road now—can't bear to see my old garden gone to ruin.

'The house is absolutely *covered* with ivy now,' said Pip, putting in a word himself. 'Even the chimneys are green with it. Was it covered with ivy when you were there, Mr. Grimble?'

'Oh yes—but not as thick as it is now,' said Grimble. 'My father planted that ivy, so he told me. It weren't called Fairlin Hall then, you know. It were called The Ivies.'

This welcome bit of news came so suddenly that all the children had quite a shock. So they were right! Fairlin Hall *was* once The Ivies! It *was* the house spoken of in those anonymous notes. But how strange that the writer didn't know that it had a different name now—it had been called Fairlin Hall for years and years!

'Why was the name changed?' asked Fatty.

Grimble looked at him and said nothing for some twenty seconds. Then he spoke in a curiously sad voice. 'The Ivies got a bad name,' he said. 'Something happened there. My master and mistress, Colonel and Mrs.

Hasterley, couldn't abear their home to be pointed at—it were in all the papers, you see—and they sold up and went. And when new people bought the place, they changed the name. Yes—it were once The Ivies—but that's a long time since.'

The children were silent for a minute or two, and the old gardener began his sawing again, looking sad and far-away.

'What happened? ventured Fatty, at last: 'Was it—was it something bad that your master did?'

'Nay—he were as good a man as ever lived,' said old Grimble. 'It were his son, Master Wilfrid, that brought shame on the old place, and on his parents too.' And to the children's horror, tears gathered in the old man's eyes, and dripped on to his saw!

'Let's go,' said Fatty, at once. 'Come on—let's go.'

# 13 MR. GOON IS PLEASED WITH HIMSELF

THE five murmured a quiet goodbye to old Grimble, who took no notice at all. He was evidently lost in far-off memories, which were still powerful enough to upset him. They all felt very sorry to have made the old fellow weep. Bets felt tears in her own eyes.

'We shouldn't have asked him questions, Fatty,' she said. 'I feel dreadful about it.'

'Well, we couldn't tell that he would take it like that,' said Fatty, feeling rather uncomfortable himself. 'My word, though—we were right. Fairlin Hall *was* The Ivies. I wonder what dreadful thing Wilfrid Hasterley did to bring the house such shame and notoriety—enough to make its name known all over the country, and force his parents to sell it.'

'We'd better find out,' said Larry. 'How can we?'

'I almost think I'd better ask Superintendent Jenks about it,' said Fatty. 'If he can tell us what the shocking happening was, it might make all this business of the anonymous notes a bit clearer. It's plain that the writer wants old Smith to be cleared out of Fairlin Hall—and it's also plain that he, the writer, must have been away for a good long time, if he doesn't know that the name has been changed for twenty years or more. It's a proper mystery, this!'

'You'd better telephone the Super when you get home, Fatty,' said Larry. 'Gosh, it's almost one o'clock! Daisy, come on—we'll be late for lunch!'

Fatty went home thinking hard. There were a great many questions in this mystery that had no answers. Who was the writer of the notes? How did he keep putting them where Goon could find them, and yet never be seen himself? Why didn't he know that The Ivies was now Fairlin Hall, and had been for years? Why did he want Smith sent out of Fairlin Hall—and why did Smith apparently have a false name?

'Too *many* mysteries this time,' said Fatty, cycling home fast. 'Well—the time has come to tackle the Super about it. I'll telephone immediately after my lunch.'

He went to the telephone at two o'clock, hoping that The Super might have finished his own lunch. Alas, he was away in the north of England. His deputy, who knew a little about Fatty's amateur detective work, was sympathetic, but not very helpful.

'You could go and see Mr. Goon, the constable in your village,' he suggested. 'He might be able to help you. In fact, Master Frederick, I think that is the thing you *should* do. I believe we have had information from Mr. Goon that some rather peculiar anonymous notes have been arriving at his house, and if you know anything that ties up with those, it's your duty to inform him. I'll tell the Super when he comes back—but I don't expect him for some days.'

This was extremely disappointing. Fatty put down the telephone with a groan. Blow! Now he'd *have* to go to Goon! The Super would not be at all pleased with him if he held up his information just because he wasn't friendly with Goon. He sat down and considered the matter.

'Well—it's no good. I'd better get it over,' thought Fatty. 'I'll cycle down to Goon's house now. How cock-a-hoop he'll be to think I'm passing on my information to him. Well—I jolly well shan't tell him HOW I got it!'

Fatty fetched his bicycle and went off to Goon's, feeling decidedly down in the dumps. He knew quite well that Goon would pretend to the Super that *he* had found out most of the information himself, and give no credit to Fatty and the others. He came to Goon's house and knocked at the door. Mrs. Hicks opened it, breathless and panting, as if she had been running a mile.

'Mr. Goon's not in,' she told him. 'But Ern is. Do you want to see him? He's up in his room, watching out of the window. We had another of them ominous notes this morning.'

Fatty was interested. He went up to Ern's room, and found the boy sitting close to his window, his eyes glued on the yard below. 'I heard your voice, Fatty,' he said, without turning round. 'I'm on the watch again. We've had another note this morning—pegged to the washing line it was!'

'What—right in the middle of the yard!' said Fatty, astonished. 'I must say the writer's bold. Nobody saw him, I suppose?

'No,' said Ern. 'But nobody was watching. Funny note

it was. It didn't say "The Ivies" this time. It said Fairlin Hall. "Ask Smith at Fairlin Hall what his real name is," that's what it said.'

'Oho! So the writer has at last found out that The Ivies has changed its name,' said Fatty. 'I suppose this means that your uncle has gone racing round to Fairlin Hall, Ern?'

'Yes,' said Ern. 'He wasn't half pleased about it, either—getting in on Mr. Smith like that. He doesn't know that you saw old Mrs. Smith this morning, and found out so much.'

'Poor old Smith,' said Fatty. 'I wouldn't like to be in *his* shoes when old Goon asks him questions. He'll be pretty beastly to the poor fellow. I think I'll stay here till he comes back, Ern. He may have some news. Gosh—to think we've all been working so hard to find out if Fairlin Hall was once The Ivies—and now Goon's been lucky enough to have the information handed to him in one of those notes!'

A scream came suddenly from downstairs, and made Fatty and Ern jump. 'That's Mrs. Hicks,' said Ern, and they both ran downstairs. Mrs. Hicks was lying back in the kitchen arm-chair, fanning herself with the dish-cloth.

'What's the matter?' cried Ern.

'Another note!' wailed Mrs. Hicks. 'I went to my larder just now—and there was a note, pushed in through the larder window—on top of the fish, it was. It give me such a turn, seeing it there. You go and get it, Ern. I'm getting so as I don't want to touch the things. Horrible ominous notes!'

Fatty went to the larder before Ern. He looked in at the open door, and saw the square envelope lying on top of a plate of fish, just beside the open larder window. He took it and tore it open, though he knew he ought to wait for Mr. Goon.

'Found out about Smith yet, you dunder-head?' said the note, in the familiar cut-out, pasted letters.

'When did you go to the larder last, Mrs. Hicks?' demanded Fatty.

'About twenty minutes ago,' said Mrs. Hicks. 'The note wasn't there then, I'll swear it wasn't. I got some fish for the cat, off that dish—and put it back again on the shelf.'

'It *couldn't* have been put there in the last twenty minutes,' said Ern, at once. 'Haven't I been watching out of that window for the last half-hour? You know I have!'

'Ah, but your friend went up to see you,' said Mrs. Hicks. 'The note must have come then, when you were talking to him and not keeping a watch.'

'I *was* watching,' said Ern, angrily. 'I never took my eyes off the yard. Did I, Fatty?

'Well, *I* heard you talking all right,' said Mrs. Hicks. 'And when people talk, they can't watch too. *You'll* catch it from that uncle of yours!'

'I don't know how the messenger has the nerve to walk across the yard and back like that,' said Fatty. 'He must know that Ern was watching—he could easily see him at the bedroom window. It must mean that the messenger hides himself somewhere very near, and watches his chance.'

'That's it, sir,' said Mrs. Hicks. 'Artful as a bagful of monkeys he is. I've never seen him—though once or twice I've thought I heard him. It scares me proper, it does.'

'There's Uncle,' said Ern, looking suddenly anxious.

'Loveaduck—won't he be angry with me when he hears there's another note, left under our noses—me watching and all!'

Mr. Goon came in, whistling softly. 'Pleased with himself!' said Ern, looking at Fatty. Goon walked into the kitchen, calling to Mrs. Hicks.

'A cup of tea, please, Mrs. Hicks. Hallo—you here, Master Frederick? And why aren't you watching at your window, Ern?'

'Er—well, Mrs. Hicks found another note, Uncle,' said Ern, warily. 'And she screamed, and me and Fatty, we shot down to see what was the matter.'

'Well—there won't be any more notes,' said Goon. 'Not as soon as the writer of them hears that old Smith has gone from Fairlin Hall. I sent him packing!'

'But why, Mr. Goon?' asked Fatty, troubled to think that poor old Mrs. Smith should have had to turn out with her sick husband.

'Come into the office,' said Goon, who was looking very pleased with himself. 'Do you good, Master Fredrick, to hear how the police can get to work and settle things.' Fatty and Ern followed him, leaving Mrs. Hicks alone in the kitchen, looking annoyed at being left out.

'Sit down,' ordered Goon, and Ern and Fatty obediently sat down. Goon leaned back and put his finger-tips together, looking at the two boys in a most irritating way.

'Well, acting on information received, I went round to Fairlin Hall—you probably don't know, but it was once called The Ivies,' began Goon. 'And there I found this fellow Smith, talked about in those notes. His wife was most obstructive—said he was ill, and I wasn't to disturb him—such nerve to tell *me* that,' frowned Goon. 'Well, I soon told her I wasn't standing any nonsense, and pushed her aside . . .'

'Not really *pushed!*' said Fatty, horrified to think of the gentle old lady being roughly handled by the big policeman.

'Well, shoved, if you want a better word,' grinned Goon. 'And there was Smith, in bed *pretending* to be ill, of course. Well, I made him get out—couldn't let him get away with a lot of humbug like that—and I said to him, 'Now then! What are you masquerading round under a false name for? You tell me *that!*'

There was a pause, presumably for Ern and Fatty to exclaim in admiration of Goon's behaviour with the Smiths. As neither of them said a word, he went on, not at all taken aback.

'Well, the old woman got hold of my arm, and began to sob—all put on, of course. She said their name wasn't Smith, it was Canley—and that rang a bell with me, that did! *Canley!* He was a bad lot, he was—he sold the secrets of a new war-plane of ours to the enemy, and he went to jail for years. Ha—and when he came out, he had to report to the police every so often, but he didn't-he just took a false name and disappeared! Helped by that wife of his, of course. She waited for him all the time he was in jail.'

'So that was what the word "SECRETS" meant, in that note,' said Fatty, quite disgusted with Goon's hardhearted narrative. 'Smith—or Canley—would react to that word at once, be afraid—and pack up and go.'

'That's right,' said Goon. 'And that's just what I told

him to do—pack up and go! Can't have a man like that in a responsible position as caretaker.'

'But he was ill,' said Fatty, 'and his wife is old. Poor things.'

'I'll! No, he was putting that on,' snorted Goon. 'He might deceive you, but he couldn't deceive *me*. I told him he's got to report to me here tomorrow morning, then we'll go into all this. Then I left. Now we know what all those notes meant!'

'We don't,' said Fatty, shaking his head. 'All we know is that someone had a spite against old Smith and wanted him out of Fairlin Hall. We don't know what the real reason was. There must be *some* reason!'

'You'll wear your brains out, you will,' said Goon. 'There's no mystery left, so don't pretend there is. Think yourself lucky that I've told you the end of it —fiddling about with Ivies and Smiths and Secrets. It's all plain as the nose on your face. I've settled it!'

He turned to Ern. 'You can go home, Ern. There's no more watching to do. I don't know who sent those notes and I don't care. He put me on to a man the police want to keep their, eyes on—and the Super will be pleased about *that!* I'll get another Letter of Commendation, you see if I don't!'

'Well, you wouldn't get one from *me*,' said Fatty, standing up. 'You'd no right to treat a poor old woman and an ill man so roughly. And let me tell you this—you think you've washed out this mystery—but you haven't! You'll never wear *your* brains out, Mr. Goon—you don't use them enough!'

# 14 FATTY IS A GREAT HELP

FATTY stalked out of Goon's office, paying no attention to his snorts of anger. 'Go and get your things, Ern,' he said. 'You needn't go home just yet. You can come with me. Whatever Goon says, this mystery isn't settled. There's a lot more to it than hounding old Smith out of Fairlin Hall!'

'Coo, Fatty! Can I really come with you?' said Ern, overjoyed. He shot upstairs, and was soon down again with his small bag. He didn't even say goodbye to his uncle.

'We'll call a meeting at once,' said Fatty. 'I'll telephone to . . . no . . . I don't think I will. There's something else more urgent. Ern, the Smiths may still be at Fairlin Hall, packing up to go—arranging for their bits and pieces of furniture to be moved. Let's go down there and see.'

'Right. Anything you say,' said Ern, giving Fatty a worshipping look. Loveaduck! Fatty was worth ten Mr. Goons any day, the way he always knew what to do!

In a few minutes they had cycled to Fairlin Hall, and went round the back to the kitchen quarters. As Fatty had thought, the Smiths were still there. But they were not packing!

Mr. Smith was lying on the floor, and the old lady was

kneeling beside him, weeping, and wiping his forehead with a damp cloth. 'John!' she was saying. 'John, I'm here. I'm going to get the doctor, dearie. Open your eyes! I'm going to get the doctor.'

She didn't even hear the two boys open the door and come in. Fatty had looked through the window, and had seen what was happening. She jumped violently when he touched her gently on the arm.

'Mrs. Smith,' he said. 'I'll get the doctor for you. Let Ern and I lift your husband back into bed. He seems very ill.'

'Oh, he is, he is,' wept the old lady, recognizing Fatty as the boy who had gone to the chemist for her. 'He's just had a terrible shock too—I can't tell you what it was—and we've been told to go. But where *can* we go, young sir—and him as ill as that?'

'Now listen,' said Fatty, gently. 'Let us get your husband back into bed. We'll get the doctor—and probably an ambulance, because I'm sure your husband ought to be in hospital. That's the first thing to do.'

He and Ern managed to get the old man back into bed. He murmured something and half opened his eyes, then began to cough in a terrible manner. His old wife wiped his face with the damp cloth, and comforted him. Ern's eyes filled with tears, and he looked desperately at Fatty.

'Don't worry, Ern,' said Fatty. 'We'll soon put this right. Stay here and do what you can to help Mrs. Smith. I'm going to telephone the doctor. Who is your doctor, Mrs. Smith?'

She told him, and Fatty nodded. 'He's mine too—so that's fine. I'll be back soon.'

Fatty ran to the nearest kiosk to telephone, and Dr. Rainy listened in surprise to what he had to say.

'Well, well—the poor old fellow! I saw him yesterday and told Mrs. Smith I'd send an ambulance to take him to hospital, but she wouldn't hear of it. I'll get one along at once and arrange for a bed for him in the Cottage Hospital here. See you later!'

Fatty raced back to Fairlin Hall. The old fellow looked a little better, now that he was in bed again. 'But where shall we go?' he kept saying to his wife, who was fondling his hands. 'Mary, where shall we go? Oh, what a lot of trouble I've brought on you. I've always been a trouble to you, always.'

'No, no, you haven't,' said the old woman. 'It's I that's been the trouble—having that dreadful illness all those years ago, and being such an expense. You'd never have sold those secrets to pay the doctors, never have gone to prison if it hadn't been for me!' She turned to Fatty, and touched his sleeve.

'You're kind,' she said. 'Don't judge my old man hardly, whatever he says to you. He's paid for what he did, paid over and over again. But I was so ill, you see, and we needed money to get me better—and it was because he loved me that he did wrong.'

'Don't worry about anything,' said Fatty, touched by the old woman's confidence in him. 'He'll soon get better in hospital. The ambulance will be here in a few minutes.'

'When he came out of prison we changed our name,

you see,' said Mrs. Smith, weeping again. 'People point their fingers so when you've done something wrong. We tried to hide ourselves away, but always somebody found out who we were. And then kind old Mrs. Hasterley let us come here to caretake the house.'

'Mrs. Hasterley?' said Fatty, surprised. 'Is she still alive? She owned this place when it was The Ivies, didn't she?'

'Yes. She's an old old woman now,' said Mrs. Smith. 'Older than I am. You've heard of Wilfrid Hasterley, her son, haven't you—he planned the biggest diamond robbery ever heard of—and got away with it too—though nobody ever knew where he hid the diamonds. He went to prison for it, and died there—and broke his father's heart. His mother never got over it either, and she sold this house at once. My, my—every newspaper in the kingdom had a picture of this house in it then—The Ivies, it was called . . .'

'It was changed to Fairlin Hall after that, wasn't it,' said Fatty, listening with great interest.

'Yes. But somehow it never got sold,' said Mrs. Smith. 'It had a bad name, you see. Poor Mr. Wilfrid. He had some wicked friends. He wasn't really the bad one, he was just weak and easy-going. The other two were the clever ones. One went to prison with Mr. Wilfrid—and the other was never caught. He fled away abroad somewhere—to Burma, I did hear say. Prison's a dreadful place, young sir—see what it's done to my poor old husband.'

'I think I can hear the ambulance, Ern,' said Fatty, raising his head. 'Go and see, will you? Ask them to come as far down the drive as they can.'

The old fellow opened his eyes. 'Mary,' he said, hoarsely. 'Mary. What will you do? Where will you go?'

'I don't know, John, I don't know,' said his old wife. 'I'll be all right. I'll come and see you in hospital.'

Ern came in at the door. 'There's two men and a stretcher,' he said, importantly. 'And an awfully nice nurse. The doctor couldn't come after all, but the nurse knows all about it.'

A rosy-cheeked nurse looked in at the door and took everything in at a glance. 'Is that my patient? she said in a cheery voice to Mrs. Smith. 'Don't you worry, dear—we'll look after him for you. Here, Potts—bring the stretcher right inside.'

Everything was done very swiftly indeed. It took less than a minute to get Mr. Smith into the ambulance. He couldn't say goodbye, because he had another fit of coughing, but his old wife held his hand to the very last moment. Then the ambulance door was shut and the big van trundled up the drive and out of the gate.

'I can't pack and go tonight,' said Mrs. Smith, looking dazed. 'I feel queer. And I've got nowhere to go.'

'Stay here tonight then,' said Fatty, 'I'll arrange something for you tomorrow. My mother will know what to do. But you're too upset and tired to bother about anything. The only thing is, I don't like to think of you staying here all alone at night, Mrs. Smith.'

'I'll stay here with her,' said Ern, suddenly. The whole affair had touched him as nothing else in his life had done. Ern longed to do something to help, he didn't care what it was—but he had Got To Do Something, as he put it to himself. And to stay and look after the sad old woman was the only thing he could think of.

'You're a good-hearted fellow, Ern,' said Fatty, touched. 'Thanks awfully. I was going to offer you a bed up at my house, as your uncle had sent you off —but if you'll shake down here, I'm sure Mrs. Smith would be glad.'

'Oh, I would,' said Mrs. Smith, and actually gave Ern, a little smile. 'There's a sofa in the next room he can have. What's your name, now—Ern? That's a kind thought of yours, my boy. I'll cook you a nice little supper, you see if I don't.'

'Well, I'll go home now, and see my mother, and get her to fix up something for you, Mrs. Smith,' said Fatty.

'I can work, you know,' said the old lady, eagerly. 'I kept this little place spotless. I can sew, too. I'll earn my keep, young sir, don't you be afraid of that.'

'I'm not,' said Fatty, marvelling at the brave old lady. 'Now I know Ern will look after you well. Ern, what about making a pot of tea for Mrs. Smith?'

'I'll do that,' said Ern. He went beaming to the door with Fatty. Then he pulled at his arm, and spoke in a low voice. 'Fatty—what shall I talk to her about? To keep her from worrying, you know?'

'Well, Ern—have you got your notebook with you?' said Fatty. 'What about reading her some of your poetry? I'm sure she'd like that. She'd be very surprised to think you could write poetry.'

'Loveaduck! I never thought of that,' said Ern, delighted. 'It might keep her amused, mightn't it? So long, Fatty. See you tomorrow.'

'So long, Ern-and thanks for all your help,' said Fatty, making Ern beam all over his red-cheeked face. He gazed proudly after Fatty as he disappeared into the darkness of the January afternoon. Ern was absolutely certain there was no one in the whole world to equal Fatty!

Fatty surprised his mother very much when he got home, just in time for tea. He looked so serious that she was quite concerned.

'Mother, can you spare a few minutes for me to tell you something?' said Fatty. 'I simply must have your help.'

'Oh, Frederick dear—you haven't got into any trouble, have you?' said his mother at once.

'Not more than usual,' said Fatty, with a grin that reassured his mother at once. 'Listen, Mother—it's rather a long story.' And he plunged into the tale of the anonymous notes, the search for ivy-covered houses, Mr. Grimble's tale, the Smiths, and Goon's treatment of them. His mother listened in amazed silence. What in the world would Frederick get mixed up in next?

Finally Fatty came to his main point. 'Mother, as old Mr. Smith has gone to hospital, and Mrs. Smith's alone, and has nowhere to go, could one of your Good Causes help her?' he said. 'She can do housework, and she can sew.'

'Why, she can come *here!*' said his mother at once. 'She can help me to make the new curtains. I'd love to have the poor old thing—and Cook's so kind she will make her really welcome in the kitchen. We're not far from the hospital too, so she can visit her husband easily, every day. She can come here, Fatty.'

Fatty got up and kissed his mother. 'I *knew* you'd think of something, Mother,' he said. 'You always do. I'm glad I own a mother like you!'

'Well, Frederick—what a nice thing to say!' said Mrs. Trotteville, pleased. 'I only wish the old lady had come here tonight. I don't like to think of her there in that big empty house, all alone.'

'Oh, Ern's staying there to look after her,' said Fatty. 'He's going to read old Mrs. Smith his poetry. Ern will have a very pleasant night, Mother!'

But he was wrong! Ern didn't have a pleasant night at all. Quite the opposite. Ern had a very disturbed night indeed!

## 15 FATTY HAS A PLAN

'FATTY, you won't forget that you promised to fetch jumble for me from one or two of my friends, will you, for the Sale next week,' said Mrs. Trotteville next day at breakfast. 'I told you I'd borrowed a hand-cart for you to fetch it, didn't I?'

'Oh yes—I *had* forgotten,' said Fatty. 'But I'll do it, of course. You just give me the addresses and I'll see if I've time to go today. I'm just off down to Fairlin Hall now to get old Mrs. Smith up here. I should think she could leave her bits and pieces of furniture down there, couldn't she, Mother? Just till she knows when her husband's coming out of hospital, and where they're going?'

'I don't see why not,' said Mrs. Trotteville. 'If old Mrs. Hasterley gave her the job of caretaking, that fat policeman has no right to turn her furniture out. If he does, tell me. I'll go and see him about it.'

'Gosh—I'd like to be at the interview,' said Fatty, longingly. 'Are you afraid of *anyone,* Mother?'

'Don't be silly, Frederick,' said Mrs. Trotteville. 'I'm certainly not afraid of Mr. Goon. Get a taxi for old Mrs. Smith, and bring her up here in it with her bags. Leave all the other stuff behind and lock the door. I could perhaps write to old Mrs. Hasterley, and tell her what's happened.'

'Right,' said Fatty, and got up. 'I'll just phone for a taxi now—and tell the man to arrive at Fairlin Hall in an hour's time. That will give me time to scoot down and make sure she's ready.'

'I've told Cook about her,' said his mother. 'And she's going to put up a bed in her room for her. Now DON'T forget about my jumble, Frederick. I've given you the addresses.'

'Yes. I've got them in my pocket,' said Fatty. He went out of the room and telephoned for the taxi and then fetched his bicycle. He debated whether or not to telephone to Larry and the others, to tell them the latest news, but decided he hadn't time.

He was soon cycling down to Fairlin Hall. It was a frosty morning and rather slippery, so he was careful as he rode round the corners. He hoped Goon was out on *his* bicycle too, 'slipping about all over the place!' thought Fatty. 'Serve him right if he fell on that big nose of his. Scaring those poor Smiths out of their lives!'

He rang his bicycle bell as he went down the drive, with Buster panting after him. He was most surprised to find the kitchen door locked when he tried to open it. Surely Ern and Mrs. Smith were up! He banged loudly on it.

Ern's face peeped cautiously from behind the window curtain, making Fatty feel still more astonished! 'Come on, Ern—open the door!' he shouted. Almost at once he heard the key turned and the door opened. Ern stood there, looking pleased.

'Coo, Fatty—I'm glad you've come!' he said. 'We've had such a night!'

'Whatever do you mean?' asked Fatty, surprised. 'What happened?'

'Well—footsteps round the place. And someone trying to open the kitchen door. And noises, and people on the balcony, and goodness knows what,' said Ern. 'I was real scared. So was old Mrs. Smith. Good thing I stayed to look after her.'

Fatty walked into the warm little kitchen. 'Good morning, Mrs. Smith,' he said, 'I'm sorry you had a disturbed night.'

'It was those burglars again,' she said. 'My old man and me, we've often heard them trying to get in. Once they did get in, too, over one of the balconies—but there's nothing to steal in this empty old place. All they took was a mirror off one of the walls in the dining-room! I was glad of Ern here, last night, I can tell you. Real brave he was.'

'They did all they could to get in,' said Ern. 'Mrs. Smith says the house is pretty well burglar-proof now—except the kitchen part, but as she and Mr. Smith were living in these few rooms, the burglars avoided them. Not last night, though! Look, they broke this window—but they couldn't undo the catch!'

'Good thing you were here, Ern, or they might have bashed the door in, and wrecked the place,' said Fatty. 'Perhaps it was tramps looking for shelter. It was a cold, bitter night.'

'They went when I shouted,' said Ern, proudly. 'And I pretended there was a dog here, didn't I, Mrs. Smith? You should have heard me yapping. Like this!' And Ern broke into such realistic yaps that Buster looked at him, startled, and then began to bark himself.

'That was a jolly good idea, Ern, to pretend there was a dog here,' said Fatty, and Ern beamed. 'Well, Mrs. Smith, do you think you could get your bits and pieces together? My mother says she would be very glad if you could come and help her with her new curtains —you said you could sew, didn't you? We've put up a bed for you already.'

'I never knew there were such kind folk in the world,' said Mrs. Smith. 'Never. I've packed already, sir. I can't do anything about my furniture. It'll have to stay here till I can send someone for it. I don't think Mrs. Hasterley will mind. I'd be glad to help your mother—if she's anything like you, it'll be a pleasure to work for her. I'll be able to see my old man, won't I, though?'

'Oh yes—the Cottage Hospital is quite near,' said Fatty. 'You'll be able to go every day. My mother will ring up the hospital when you arrive, and get the nurse to tell you how Mr. Smith is.'

'Such kindness!' said the old lady, overcome. 'And this boy Ern here—he was such a comfort last night. And the poetry he read me! Well, I reckon he's a genius, I do really.'

Ern blushed. He knew he was no genius, but it was very very pleasant to be thought one! He helped Mrs. Smith out with her things, ready for the taxi. 'You go with Mrs. Smith in the taxi, Ern,' said Fatty. 'I've got my bicycle and Buster. Go down to my shed and wait for me, when you get there. You'll find some biscuits in the tin.'

'Oooh, thanks, Fatty,' said Ern. He had been afraid that he would be sent home. Perhaps he would have yet one more day with Fatty?

The taxi came, and Ern put all Mrs. Smith's things into it. He helped her in and then climbed in himself. He felt rather important. 'First time I've been in a taxi!' he said. 'Loveaduck, I'm getting grand!'

'I'll lock the back door and take the key,' said Fatty. 'I'd better return it to the house agent and I'll warn them that burglars came again.'

He went back into the kitchen. It still had the Smith's things there—rather poor bits of furniture, a carpet, worn and old, the curtains. 'They could really go on a handcart,' thought Fatty, and suddenly remembered that he had promised his mother to fetch her jumble.

He locked the door and walked to where he had left his bicycle. Then he and Buster went to the front gate. A man was standing there, hands in pocket. Buster barked at him and he kicked out.

Fatty felt rather suspicious. Why should the man be hanging about outside an empty house? Was he one of the men who had tried to break in the night before? Had he watched Mrs. Smith and Ern leaving in a taxi? Fatty rode off to the House Agent's, wondering.

He walked into the office and was relieved to find that the young and conceited Mr. Paul was not there.

Only the older man was present, sitting in his corner. He recognized Fatty at once and smiled.

'I've brought you the back-door key of Fairlin Hall,' said Fatty. 'There were caretakers there, as you probably know, and they've left. Their furniture is still there, though.'

'Well, that's nice of you,' said the old clerk. 'But you'd better keep the key in case the Smiths want to fetch their things. Were they given notice, or something? We haven't heard anything from Mrs. Hasterley.'

'Er—Mr. Smith fell ill and has gone to hospital,' said Fatty, thinking that was the best, thing to say. 'And by the way, burglars tried to break in there again last night.'

The old clerk tut-tutted, and shook his head. 'Bound to get tramps and rogues trying to get in, when a house has stood empty for years,' he said. 'We've tried to make it burglar proof—but what it wants is people living in it, filling the house! By the way, it's a funny thing—but some people came in to enquire about it this morning. Two men. Said they might like to buy it for a boys' prep school.'

'Did you give them keys?' asked Fatty, at once.

'Yes. And I told them that a couple of old folk were there, caretaking,' said the man. 'I didn't know they'd gone.'

Mr. Paul arrived at that moment and Fatty at once went, in case the old fellow should be admonished for wasting his time talking to him again! Fatty was very thoughtful as he rode home. People enquiring about Fairlin Hall—so soon after the Smiths had gone? Could it be someone who had tried to force a way in last night—and now, knowing that the house had no caretakers, had got the keys so that they would have the house to themselves? But what was the point of that?

'I rather think I'd better keep some kind of watch on Fairlin Hall,' thought Fatty, and at once his mind flew to a possible disguise. How could he watch the house without anyone guessing?

'Of course!' he said, aloud, making the panting duster look up at hum in surprise. 'Of course! I'll be a rag-and-bone man! I'll get that hand-cart, and go and collect jumble! And I'll park my cart outside Fairlin Hall, and keep my eye on anyone going in and out!'

He cycled even more quickly and went down the drive to his own house at top speed, almost running down the baker. He went straight to his shed, and found Ern there, patiently waiting.

'Ern I'm going to disguise myself,' said Fatty. 'Look, you go up to the house and telephone the others. Tell them to come here at once, if they can. I'll talk to them while I'm disguising myself.'

'Right,' said Ern, thrilled, and sped off to telephone. He wasn't very sure about it, because he had rarely used the telephone—but Mrs. Trotteville, amused by Ern's serious face, got the numbers for him, and he delivered his message faithfully, saying every word so distinctly that it sounded as if he were reciting!

Meantime Fatty was swiftly disguising himself: 'Dirty old, rag-and-bone man,' he thought. 'Those old corduroy trousers. That torn shirt. No tie. Scarf round my neck—

that filthy white one will do. Awful old boots, now where did I put them? A cap—and that frightful overcoat I found left behind a hedge one day!'

He got out his make-up box, and in ten minutes had transformed himself from a boy in his teens, to a wrinkled, dirty, slouching fellow, with protruding teeth, shaggy eyebrows and a ragged moustache.

Ern watched in unbounded admiration. 'Loveaduck!' he kept saying. 'Loveaduck, Fatty! How do you do it? You are a one, you are! My word, my uncle will chase you out of Peterswood, if he sees you!'

Fatty laughed. 'Here come the others,' he said, as Buster barked. 'Let them in!' And in they all trooped—to stop in astonishment at the sight of the dirty old rag-and-bone man.

'FATTY!' squealed Bets. 'It's you! Fatty, you look *awful!* What are you going to do? Quick, tell us! What's up? Has something happened?'

## 16 RAG-A'-BONES! RAG-A'-BONES!

EVERYONE crowded round the dirty old rag-and-bone man, thrilled. How did Fatty do it? Except for his twinkling eyes and too-clean hands nobody would know he was anything but what he looked!

'Your hands—and your nails, Fatty,' said Bets. 'Don't forget those.'

'Go and fill this plant pot with some wettish earth, Bets,' said Fatty, re-tying his filthy neck-scarf. 'I think our gardener's out there, and if he sees me he'll chase me off the premises.'

Bets rushed out with the pot and a trowel and filled it with damp earth. Fatty put his hands into it and made them really dirty. The dirt got into his nails too.

'You look simply frightful,' said Larry. 'And you smell a bit, Fatty. Must be that horrible overcoat.'

'Yes. It does smell,' said Fatty, sniffing at a sleeve. 'Still, it's all in a good cause, as Mother would say. Listen, and I'll tell you quickly what's happened this morning and yesterday.'

He swiftly outlined all the events, and Ern nodded in approval. That was the way to tell things—no 'ers' or 'ums', or stammerings—but everything set out absolutely clearly. Lovely to listen to! Everyone sat enthralled as Fatty related his tale at top speed.

'There's a few things *I can't* understand,' finished Fatty, 'and one is why the writer of those "ominous" notes as Mrs. Hicks calls them, is so set on getting old Smith out—I suppose he's got some kind of spite against him—and the other is how on earth do those notes get put all over the place at old Goon's without anyone seeing them?'

'Right under my nose again, yesterday!' said Ern. 'I was watching like anything, never took my eyes off the back yard, never once, not even when Fatty came into my room and spoke to me. And Mrs. Hicks was down in the kitchen too, in full view of the window —and yet there was the note, sitting on top of the plate of fish in the larder! And *neither* of us saw anyone come into the yard, or creep over to the larder window and pop the note on the fish! Beats me! Must have got an invisible cloak or something!'

'Do you know what *I* think?' said Daisy, suddenly. '*I* think it's Mrs. Hicks who's putting the notes there! Putting them there herself! We once had a gardener who complained that someone was slipping into the garden and taking the strawberries, and there wasn't—Daddy caught *him* taking them himself! I bet it was *Mrs. Hicks* with those notes, pretending it was someone else all the time!'

There was a silence after this speech of Daisy's. Fatty stared at her—and then smacked his hand in delight on the chest beside him, making Buster jump in fright.

'*Daisy!* What an ass I've been! Of course—that's the only possible explanation! Mrs. Hicks is being paid by someone to hide those notes at Goon's—someone who doesn't want to be seen for some reason. I wonder who's paying her. Where does she live, Ern?'

'With her sister and little niece,' said Ern. 'To think she got me into all that trouble with my uncle! How *could* I see anyone delivering notes when all the time she must have had them hidden in her apron pocket? Just wait till I see that Mrs. Hicks again.'

'No. Don't you say a word to her if you do see her,' warned Fatty. 'Let her think she isn't suspected at all. There won't be any more notes, of course, because old Mr. Smith has been got rid of.'

'Maybe that's the end of the whole thing, then,' said Pip.

'I don't think so,' said Fatty. 'No, I *certainly* don't think so, though Goon does, of course. There's something more behind those notes than just spite against an old man. Well, I must go. Ern, you go and see how Mrs. Hicks is getting on, and ask my mother if you can do any jobs. She'll like that.'

'Can we come with you, Fatty?' asked Bets, longingly. 'Could we walk a little way behind you just to watch you being a rag-and-bone man? You do look exactly like one—in fact you look so awful that I'm sure Mother would send you of at once if you came to *our* house!'

'I say—I haven't overdone it, have I? said Fatty, anxiously, and looked at himself in the glass. 'Do these false teeth that I've put on over my own stick out too much?'

'Oh no. They're fine,' said Larry. 'And I love the way your shaggy eyebrows go up and down. I do hope you meet Goon.'

'Well, I don't,' said Fatty. 'if I do I shall put on a foreign accent—or stammer or something, so that Goon can't get any sense out of me. Well, so-long. I'm going to get the hand-cart now.'

He looked out of the shed window to make sure that the gardener was nowhere near, and then went rapidly to the garage. The hand-cart was there, together with a good deal of jumble taken from the attics. Fatty piled some on, and then set off to Fairlin Hall. Perhaps he could catch sight of those men who had got the keys.

He sang out the usual rag-and-bone ditty. 'Rag-a'-bones!· Rag-a'-bo-o-o-ones ! Bring out your rag-a'-bo-o-o-nes !'

He hoped that nobody would, because he hadn't much money in his pocket, and didn't really want to pay anyone for jumble! He came safely to Fairlin Hall, and set down the hand-cart. He took an old pipe out of his pocket and began to fiddle with it, keeping a watch on the house, trying to make out if anyone was there.

He couldn't see anyone, and decided to wheel his cart right into the drive. Perhaps he would be able to spot the two men who had gone to the House Agent's for the keys, if he went down the drive. He decided not to shout his rag-a'-bone cry, but to go very quietly.

Ah—the men must be in the house, there was a small car at the front door. Fatty noted the number swiftly, and the make and colour. 'Brown Riley, AJK 6660.' Then he went on cautiously, wheeling his hand-cart, making his way to the back door.

*''Ere, mate, I've come to see me frens'*

He stood in a corner, pretending to arrange the things on the cart, but keeping his ears open for any sound that might tell him where the men were, and what they were doing. He couldn't hear or see a sign of them.

He decided to go to the back door and knock, pretending that he had come to see the Smiths. But as he passed the window of the kitchen, he caught sight of a movement inside, and stopped. He peered through the window.

Two men were inside, one opening the cupboard doors, the other taking up the carpet, rolling it to one side. Fatty felt angry. What did they think they were doing? Robbing the poor old Smiths of the few things they had left behind?

Fatty went to the door and banged on it violently. There was an exclamation from inside and one of the men went to the window and peered out. He said something to the other man, and then opened the window. Apparently he hadn't a key to open the kitchen door.

The window swung wide open, and a thin-faced elderly man looked out, and shouted at Fatty.

'What are you doing here? Clear out!'

Fatty put on a real Cockney voice. "Ere, mate, I've come to see me frens, the Smiffs,' he said. 'What you a-doin' of, messin' abart in their rooms? You ain't up to no good. I'll git the police in, see if I don't.'

'The Smiths have gone,' said the man, curtly. 'We're probably going to buy the house; we've got the keys to look over the place. Clear out, now, your friends have gone.

'Well, what you a-doin' of then, wiv their things?' shouted Fatty. 'What you rollin' up that bit of carpet for? What you. . .'

'Now, now, now; what's all this?' said a familiar voice, and to Fatty's surprise and annoyance Mr. Goon marched up to the window. 'That your cart in the drive, fellow? Take it out then. And who's this in the house?'

'Constable, remove this man,' said one of the men indoors. 'He says he's a friend of someone called Smith, but it's my belief he knew they were gone, and came to steal their bits of furniture. We've got the keys to look over the house, and suddenly saw this fellow at the back door.'

'Ho! So that's it, is it?' said Goon, roughly, and turned on Fatty. 'You clear orf, my man, or I'll march you off to the police-station. What's your name?'

Fatty pretended to be scared. 'F-f-f-f- f,' he stammered, while Goon still glared at him. 'F-f-f-f-f . . .'

'Well, go on—get it out,' commanded Goon, taking out his notebook. 'Name *and* address.'

'F-f-f f-Fred,' said Fatty, 'T-t-t-t-t . . .'

'Fred,' said Goon, writing it down. 'Fred what?'

'T-t-t-t-t,' stammered Fatty, looking absolutely agonized. 'T-t-t.'

'All right, all right,' said Goon, shutting his notebook. 'I've got more important things to do than to stand here and listen to a stutterer. You go and get your tongue seen to—and take that cart out of this drive. If I set eyes on you again today, I'll run you in.'

'R-r-right,' said Fatty, and shot out of the drive with

his cart, grinning. He stood at the front gate, wondering what to do. He had seen those two men, and noted what they looked like—he had got particulars of their car—he had watched them examining the Smith's kitchen and the things in it, goodness knew what for ... and he had had a successful few minutes with Goon. What next?

He moved on down the road, shouting 'Rag-a'-bones' at intervals—and then he saw someone he knew, hurrying along on the pavement.

'It's Mrs. Hicks,' he thought, and his interest quickened. 'I suppose she's got the morning off. Where's she going in such a hurry?'

He decided to follow her. If she had really been the one to hide those notes, then someone must have given them to her, and presumably she was being paid for hiding them at Goon's. Goon, of course, was the only person who had the power to turn the Smiths out, so that was why the notes had been sent to him. It would be very very interesting to find out who the sender was. It might throw quite a lot of light on the mystery.

Fatty trundled his hand-cart after Mrs. Hicks. Round the corner she went and round the corner went Fatty. Down a little hill and round another corner. And ah Mrs. Hicks turned in at a gateway and vanished.

Fatty trundled his cart along the gutter, and came to a stop outside the gate. He pretended to fiddle with his pipe again, examining the house as he did so. It was a fairly big one, well-kept, and looked comfortable. From between the curtains he could see what looked like a gleaming brass ornament.

The name on the house was 'KUNTAN'. Who lived there? Was it someone who had given those notes to Mrs. Hicks? He decided to go to the back door and ask for anything old and done for. Even if he had to give up all his money for junk, it would be worth it, if he could find the sender of those anonymous notes.

He went cautiously down the side-entrance, and came to the back door. Beside it were piled wooden crates, with foreign words printed across them-empty crates, evidently unpacked, and then thrown out for firewood. One was already half-chopped up.

Fatty looked at them—and then one word made him stare in excitement. Just one word, stamped across each crate in big black letters—the name of the place the crate had come from.

'RANGOON'

## 17 A VERY LUCKY FIND

FATTY stared at the name on the crate, remembering how hard he had tried to think of a word with 'goon' as part of it, when he had tried to fathom why Mr. Goon's name should have been spelt each time with a small letter g. 'Mr. goon', not 'Mr. Goon' had been on each of the envelopes containing those anonymous notes.

'When I asked Mother if she knew of any word with the four letters "goon" in it, she suggested "Rangoon",' thought Fatty, remembering. 'And here's a crate with "Rangoon" stamped across it. Can it be just chance—just a coincidence? Or is it a real clue—a clue pointing to the man who sent those letters to Goon?

He stared at the crate again. 'A man lives here who has friends in Rangoon, that's certain—friends who send him crates of something. Well, he might have Rangoon *newspapers* sent to him too—he might have cut out words and letters from them, and taken "goon" from the title of the newspaper—*Rangoon Times,* it might be, or something like that. Gosh—I think I'm on to something here!'

He was still staring at the crate, when the back door suddenly opened and made him jump. He turned in fright, and saw Mrs. Hicks there, being ushered out by a small, foreign-looking man.

'Burmese!' thought Fatty, at once, recognizing the slanting Burmese eyes, the brown complexion and black

*He turned in fright, and saw Mrs. Hicks there*

hair. 'And Rangoon is in Burma! Is this the fellow who sent those notes?'

Mrs. Hicks caught sight of him at once and frowned.

'Rag-a'-bones, rubbish, jumble, anythink bought!' said Fatty at once. 'Good price paid!'

'Do you want to get rid of any rubbish, sir? asked Mrs. Hicks, turning to the Burmese. 'This fellow will take it for you. Your yard looks pretty cluttered up. I can deal with him for you, if you like. What about those crates—he'd buy them for firewood—I see you've already got plenty chopped up.'

'Yes, Meesees Icks,' said the Burmese, and nodded. 'You do beesinees wiz zis man. Much much rubbish here!'

And with that he shut the door. Mrs. Hicks beamed. What a bit of luck! Now she could sell these crates and keep the money herself!

'You can have the crates,' she said. 'And I'll have a peep in the shed and see if there's any rubbish there.'

She disappeared into a small shed, and Fatty followed her. It was stacked with old junk, just as his mother's attic had been—but Burmese junk! A big brass tray, green with neglect, stood on its side in one corner. A broken gong was near it, and a pair of small Burmese idols in brass. Other curiously-shaped ornaments were thrown here and there.

'You could have some of these if you liked,' said Mrs. Hicks. 'Cheap too—you could sell them for a good bit to a dealer. Take what you like.'

'Nobody wants junk like that,' said Fatty, knowing that he must bargain. 'Funny stuff, this—where's it come from?

It's all foreign-like! Does it belong to that gentleman there? and he nodded his head towards the house.

'Yes,' said Mrs. Hicks. 'Burmese, he is, but he married an English wife. I do sewing for her, but she's too stuckup for me. Her husband's all right, though, and so are his two friends. Free with their money, and that's what I like.'

'What are the friends like? asked Fatty, poking about among the junk. 'Burmese too?'

'No! English,' said Mrs. Hicks. 'One's been in Burma for years, but the other's a close one—don't know where he's from, I'm sure. Never opens his mouth! Well, what about this stuff? Give me a good price and you can take what you like.'

'I can't sell trays and gongs,' said Fatty, giving the tray a kick with his foot. 'Now those crates out there—I could take some of those. And newspapers—old newspapers if you've got any. I can sell those to fishmongers and butchers. But this brass stuff—no, I wouldn't get a penny for it!'

'Go on!' said Mrs. Hicks, disbelievingly.

'Well, I'll give you sixpence for this ornament,' said Fatty, picking up a hideous little brass figure, 'and sixpence each for four of those crates—and a shilling a bundle for any old newspapers you've got.'

'What—a shilling for newspapers, and only sixpence for that there lovely brass ornament!' said Mrs. Hicks. 'You're crazy!'

'No, I'm not. I know what I can sell and what I can't,' said Fatty, fingering the ornament with his dirty hands. He looked at Mrs. Hicks from under his shaggy false eyebrows, and smiled, showing his awful protruding teeth.

'Go on, Missus. You let me buy what I can sell—four of those crates, and as many old newspapers as you've got—and one ornament.

'All right,' said Mrs. Hicks. 'You put four of those crates on to your barrow, while I fetch the newspapers. There's plenty stacked in the kitchen cupboard!'

Fatty grinned at her, showing his revolting false teeth again, and took the little ornament and the crates to his hand-cart. He waited there for Mrs. Hicks. Out she came with a vast number of newspapers, which she dumped in the cart.

'There you are,' she said: 'How much are you giving me for all that?'

'Five shillings,' said Fatty. 'And not a penny more.'

'That's robbery,' said Mrs. Hicks.

'All right, take the things back,' said Fatty, and handed her a crate.

'No. Give me the five bob,' said Mrs. Hicks. 'But you're a robber, that's what you are.' She took the five shillings, and put it into her pocket. Just as she did so, a car drew up at the house, and two men got out, the very two that Fatty had seen at Fairlin Hall! Fatty noted the car at once—aha—Brown Riley, AJK 6660. So those two men were staying here—they must be the two friends that Mrs. Hicks spoke of—one who had come from Burma, and the other whom she said 'never opened his mouth.' Fatty took a good look at them.

Things were beginning to fit together nicely! Rangoon. Mrs. Hicks and the notes. The two men who were staying here—was it one of them who had paid her to put the notes round and about Goon's house and yard? And now they had been to Fairlin Hall!

'They wanted to get the Smiths out because *they* want to take it—or to find something there,' thought Fatty, with a surge of excitement. 'And what do they want to find there? Could it be—could it *possibly* be—the diamonds that were never found after the robbery? Whew! Everything's boiling up at once! My word!

He wheeled his cart away slowly, gazing at the men as they walked up to the front door of the house. He was longing to get out his notebook, and write down their descriptions!

He set off down the road with his hand-cart, feeling quite in a daze. He suddenly caught sight of the name of a house on the other side of the road.

'Gosh! That's one of the houses that Mother asked me to collect jumble from,' he thought. 'Well, as I'm so near, I'd better collect it. Let's see—it was Mrs. Henry's, wasn't it.'

Still in rather a daze, trying to sort out everything in his mind, Fatty pushed his hand-cart up the drive of the house. He went to the front door, quite forgetting that he was disguised as a dirty old rag-and-bone man. He rang the bell.

Mrs. Henry came to the door and stared. 'The back door is round there,' she said, pointing. 'But we've nothing for you today, Nothing at all.'

'Er—well, my mother said 'you'd have some old clothes, Mrs. Henry,' said Fatty, politely. 'For her Jumble Sale you know.'

'Your *mother,'* said Mrs. Henry, staring in amazement at this awful, dirty old fellow, with his shaggy grey, eyebrows and filthy overcoat. '*I* don't know your mother. Who is she?'

'She's Mrs. Trotteville,' said Fatty, and was most astonished when the door was banged in his face. Then he suddenly realized that he was in disguise, and rushed off down the drive with his cart. Good gracious! How *could* he have forgotten he was a rag-and-bone man—whatever must Mrs. Henry have thought?

'Why did I mention Mother's name?' thought Fatty, with a groan. 'She's bound to ring her up—and Mother won't be at all pleased. Well, I'll get home quickly. I'm longing to have a look through these newspapers and see if there are any from Rangoon. Mother didn't know how clever she was when she mentioned *Rangoon* to me!'

He was soon back at his house and pushed the handcart into the garage. He took one of the crates, with RANGOON stamped on it, and also the little brass ornament, and all the newspapers, down to his shed, keeping a sharp look-out for the gardener as he went.

The others had all gone. Not even Ern was there. 'I bet they're having macaroons at the dairy again,' thought Fatty, feeling suddenly hungry. 'Now to have a look through these newspapers!'

He took them up one by one, and laid them down again, disappointed. '*The Daily Telegraph*—heaps of those. *The Daily Mail, Daily Express, Evening Standard* —wait now—what's this!'

He had come to a magazine, printed on cheap paper.

He looked at the title. *'The Rangoon Weekly'.* He scrutinized the type carefully—was it the same type as the letters and words in. those notes? It really did look like it!

'I'll get that anonymous note I have, in a minute,' thought Fatty. 'I'll just look through a few more papers. Ah—here's another of those magazines—another *Rangoon Weekly,* but still in its wrapper. And here's another—but wait a minute, wait a minute! This one's all cut up! My word, *what* a bit of luck! I do believe this is one of the papers that the sender of those notes cut the letters from, that he stuck on to the note-paper! IT IS!'

Fatty stared at the magazine he was holding. Bits had been cut from it. The 'goon' had been cut from the words *Rangoon Weekly!* Yes, not only on this page, but on the next one too! Only the 'Ran' was left in the word 'Rangoon'—the 'goon' had been neatly snipped away!

Fatty found that his hands were trembling. The jigsaw of the mystery was fitting together now. Fatty had quite a lot of the pieces. Not many were missing! He went swiftly through the rest of the papers he had bought.

He found two more of the *Rangoon Weekly* magazines with letters and words snipped from them. He gazed at them in rapture. What a *wonderful* piece of luck!

He stood up and put the three snipped magazines into an envelope, opened a drawer and put them carefully inside. Then he locked the drawer.

'Very valuable evidence!' said Fatty. 'But evidence of *what,* I don't quite know. Funny mystery this—all made up bits and pieces—but I'll make a proper picture of them soon, and then we'll see what it shows! Whew! I wish the others were here. Oh my goodness, there's Mother calling! AND she's coming down to the shed. Whatever will she say when she sees an old rag-and-bone man here!'

# 18 FATTY REPORTS HIS DOINGS

FATTY hadn't time even to take out his horrible false teeth, before his mother opened the shed-door. She looked inside. 'Frederick—are you here?'

Fatty stood with his back to her, in the darkest comer of the shed. 'Yes, Mother. Did you want me?'

'Frederick, Mrs. Henry has just telephoned, me,' began his mother. 'Do turn round, dear, I'm speaking to you. . .'

'Er—I'm in disguise, Mother,' said Fatty, embarrassed.

'Turn *round*,' said his mother, and Fatty reluctantly faced her. She gave a horrified scream.

'FREDERICK! Come here! Into the light. How *can* you dress like that? Disguise indeed! Oh Frederick—*don't* tell me that you were the horrible rag-and-bone man that Mrs. Henry just rang me up about. Surely, surely, you didn't really go there and say that your mother had sent you—that *I* had sent you.'

'Well, Mother—it was a bit of a mistake,' began Fatty, his dirty face as red as a beetroot. 'I forgot I was in disguise, you see, and . . .'

'Don't talk such rubbish,' said his mother, really angry. 'How could you *possibly* forget you were in that horrible, revolting get-up? I'm absolutely ashamed of you,

Frederick. To go to Mrs. Henry's like that! Please don't bother about collecting any more jumble for me. If you're just going to make it a joke, and deceive my friends like that, and . , .'

'But, *Mother*—I tell you I *forgot* for just a minute or two,' said poor Fatty. 'I'm most terribly sorry. I'll go and apologize to Mrs. Henry. You see, I'd just discovered a few amazing things, and I was a bit dazed, thinking them out, but when *you* hear what's been happening, you'll be just as astonished, and you'll . . .'

'Stop all this rigmarole,' said Mrs. Trotteville, angrier than Fatty had ever seen her. 'I don't wonder that Mr. Goon gets annoyed with you if you wander about like that. Has *he* seen you in that get-up too? He has? Well, I suppose he'll soon be along here then, complaining as usual. I only hope your father doesn't hear about this.'

And away she went up the garden path, her skirts whisking angrily over the edges of the border. Fatty stared after her, quite shocked. *Now* he was in a fix! His mother would continue to be very upset with him—and yet he couldn't very well explain to her what had been happening. Life was going to be very uncomfortable indeed.

Fatty groaned heavily, and began to remove his make-up and various pieces of disguise. Out came the awful teeth, and off came the shaggy grey eyebrows. He stripped off the smelly overcoat and hung it up, and bit by bit became himself again.

He looked at himself in the glass. Yes, his face was clean now. Should he take the hand-cart out and go and collect the jumble his mother had asked him to? Should he go and apologize first of all to Mrs. Henry and get *her* jumble?

No, Fatty thought *not*. Let it all blow over for a day. He would sit down now and write out a report of the morning's happenings. Nothing like writing everything down, to get it straight in his mind! Fatty found his pen, and took out his notebook. He wrote rapidly.

About half-past twelve he heard the sound of voices. It was the others coming to see if he were back again. Fatty shut his notebook and went to the shed-door.

'Oh, you're back, Fatty!' said Bets, pleased. 'Any luck this morning?'

'Plenty,' said Fatty, grinning. 'Some good and some bad.'

'Oh—what was the bad? asked Daisy, anxiously. 'Well, in a fit of absent-mindedness, I went to Mrs. Henry's front door to collect her jumble while I was in my rag-and-bone man get-up,' said Fatty. 'And, also absent-mindedly, I told her that my mother had sent me to her!'

There was laughter at this and horrified exclamations. 'I *say*—you surely didn't say that your mother was *Mrs. Trotteville,* did you? said Pip. 'Well, *Fatty*—I never thought you could be such a prize ass! She'll telephone to your mother, and you'll get into an awful row.'

'She did, and I have,' said Fatty, soberly. 'My mother is not on speaking terms with me now.'

'Loveaduck!' said Ern. 'The things you do, Fatty. What was the good luck?'

'Well, I've just written a sort of report on what happened,' said Fatty. 'To get things straight in my mind, really. I'll read it to you.'

He opened his notebook and read from it. 'Dressed up as rag-and-bone man. Went to watch Fairlin Hall. Saw car there, Brown Riley, AJK 6660. Guessed it had brought the two men who had got the keys of the place from the Agent's. Went to back door and saw men in kitchen, peering into cupboards, taking up carpets, etc. They saw me, and told me to clear out. Then Goon arrived. . .'

'Oh *no*!' said Bets. 'Oh dear!'

'Goon arrived and the men told him to send me off: He asked my name, and . . .'

'Oh, you didn't give it!' cried Daisy.

'No. I said it was F-f-f-f-f,' said Fatty, stammering. 'T-t- t-t-t ... well, he just couldn't be bothered with stutterers, he said, so that was all right!'

The others laughed. Fatty turned to his notebook, and went on. 'I then left Fairlin Hall and went out, shouting like a rag-and-bone man. Saw Mrs. Hicks coming along in a hurry and decided to follow her. I thought she might be going to the sender of the notes, to be paid. So I followed and she went into a house called Kuntan. I went to the back door, thinking I'd ask if they'd any rubbish.'

'Oh Fatty—how exciting!' said Bets. 'Is this the good luck part?

Fatty nodded, and went on reading. 'Outside the door were crates with RANGOON stamped across them, evidently sent from Burma. Then the back door opened and out came Mrs. Hicks, and behind her was a Burmese—and he said she could sell me any junk she liked out of the shed. She told me she did sewing for the Burmese fellow's wife, and she also said there were two other men staying there—one from Burma, an Englishman, and another man, very quiet, that she knew nothing about.'

'Two men! Were they the two you saw at Fairlin Hall, Fatty?' asked Larry.

Fatty nodded, and went on reading. 'Mrs. Hicks sold me a brass ornament, four of the Rangoon-stamped crates and a great bundle of newspapers. I brought them here and examined them. Among them were some magazines, printed on cheap paper, called *The Rangoon Weekly*. Three of these were cut about—letters and words had been snipped from them, especially from the word Rangoon, which, in several cases had had the four letters "goon" cut from it.'

'Fatty!' shouted Pip. 'That's where the "goon" came from on those envelopes! Gosh—fancy you getting the very papers they were cut from!'

'Sheer luck,' said Fatty. 'Well, there you are—we know a lot now, don't we! The only thing we *don't* know for certain is—why did those men want to turn old Smith out of Fairlin Hall? Anyone any ideas?'

'Yes. What about that diamond robbery? The diamonds were never found!' said Pip, in excitement. 'Fatty, they must be hidden in Fairlin Hall somewhere! Wilfrid Hasterley must have hidden them there himself, and then gone to prison hoping that when he came out, he could get them again, and be rich!'

'Yes—and those two men you saw this morning must have been the ones who planned the robbery with him!'

cried Daisy. 'We know they didn't both go to prison ... one went and hid himself abroad . . .'

'In Burma!' said Pip.

'And the other one, the one who was in prison with Wilfrid, must have some time been told by him that the diamonds were hidden at Fairlin Hall,' said Larry. 'Gosh—what a thing to happen! Fatty, what do you think about it all?'

'I agree with you absolutely,' said Fatty. 'And I'm sure that's why those fellows sent those notes about Smith to Goon, having first found out that he had a shady past. The thing is, having been away so long, they didn't know that the name of The Ivies had been changed to Fairlin Hall!'

'It all begins to fit, doesn't it,' said Larry. 'Gosh, to think how we rushed round looking for ivy-covered houses! If only we'd known it was Fairlin Hall from the beginning, we could have got going much more quickly!'

'Fatty,' said Bets, earnestly. 'What about those hidden diamonds? Oughtn't you to tell Superintendent Jenks all this?'

'He's away up north,' said Fatty. 'I telephoned—only to be told to report everything to Goon! Goon, who thinks that he's settled the whole affair—why, we're still right in the very middle of it! I wish I *could* tell the Super.'

'Can't you wait till he comes back, before you do anything else? said Bets.

'What! And let those two men find the hidden diamonds!' said Ern, entering into the discussion for the first time. 'Coo, Fatty—let's you and me go and hunt for them! I bet those men will be there as often as they can, searching everywhere.'

'I rather think the diamonds must be in the kitchen quarters,' said Fatty. 'Otherwise, why try so hard to turn out the poor old Smiths?'

'I suppose the Smiths wouldn't know anything about the diamonds, would they?' said Pip. 'No, of course they wouldn't. But would they know of any secret place, Fatty, do you think? You know—a trap-door leading downwards—a secret cavity in a cupboard? Mrs. Smith kept the place jolly clean, you said, and she probably knows every corner of it.'

'That's quite an idea, Pip,' said Fatty, considering it. 'She's here, you know, helping my mother with the new curtains. I could easily have a word with her. She might let something drop that would help us. Yes, that's quite an idea. But we've got to be quick, if we're going to do any hunting ourselves, because now that the Smiths are out of the way, those two men will lose no time in getting the diamonds if they can.'

'When do you think of going, then, Fatty?' asked Larry, feeling excited. 'This afternoon?'

'I don't see why not,' said Fatty. 'I've got the back door key. Yes, let's. But we'll have to keep a good look-out for the men. Gosh, there's the lunch-gong! I must go, because I don't want my mother to be any more annoyed with me than she already is. Look—will you all be at the corner with your bikes, at three o'clock?'

'You bet!' said Pip, thrilled. 'What about Ern?'

'Fatty's cook has asked me to the kitchen for dinner,' said Ern, proudly. 'Mrs. Smith said some nice things about me, that's why. I'll be there at three too, with Fatty.'

'So long!' said Fatty, shooing them all out, and locking his shed hurriedly. 'Look here, Ern, as you'll be chatting with Mrs. Smith over your dinner, you try to get a few hints about possible hiding-places, see?'

'Coo, yes, Fatty!' said Ern, delighted. 'I'll do my very very best. Loveaduck—this isn't half a lark, is it!'

# 19 A DISAPPOINTING AFTERNOON

FATTY and Ern were at the corner before the others, waiting there with their bicyles. Buster was safely shut up in Fatty's bedroom.

'Well, did you enjoy your dinner, Ern?' asked Fatty.

'Oooh yes.' said Ern happily. 'Made quite a fuss of me they did. Especially Mrs. Smith. She told your cook and Jane all about my portry.'

'You don't mean to say you read them any?' said Fatty, amused. Ern went red.

'Well—they kept on and on about it,' he said. 'So I read them one or two pomes. They liked the one about the Ivies, Fatty—but I told them you wrote half of it. I wasn't going to let them think I'd written those *good* lines. Coo, Fatty, I don't know how you let your tongue go loose, like you say, and spout out portry by the yard, rhymes and all.'

'You do it like this, Ern, as I've told you before,' said fatty, and rested his bicycle against the fence. He stood up and opened his mouth. Ern waited breathlessly. Fatty began to declaim at top speed.

*'Oh every time*
*You want a rhyme,*
*Then let your tongue go loose,*
*Don't hold it tight,*
*Or try to bite,*

*That won't be any use!*
*just let it go*
*And words will flow*
*From off your eager tongue,*
*And rhymes and all*
*Will lightly fall*
*To make a little song!'*

'There you are, Ern, that's how you do it,' said Fatty, with a chuckle. 'You try it when you're alone. Just think of the first line, that's all—then let your tongue go loose.'

'I don't think I've got your sort of tongue,' sighed Ern, half-inclined to try it there and then. 'Coo, Fatty, it's queer, you know—you don't really care about writing portry, and I do, but I can't. And *I'd* give anything to write it, and you wouldn't, but you can.'

'You're muddling me, Ern,' said Fatty. 'Ah, here are the others. Good.'

Soon all six of them were cycling to Fairlin Hall. They sent Ern in to make sure the coast was clear. He came back very quickly.

'Okay!' he said. 'No car at the front door. Nobody about at all, as far as I can see.'

'Come on, then,' said Fatty. 'We'll hide our bikes in some thick bushes round the back, so that they can't be seen. We'll take it in turns to keep a watch out. Pip, you keep first watch.'

'Right,' said Pip, at once, though he was longing to go in with the others. 'If you hear me whistling "Over the Seas to Skye", you'll know there's something up.'

They put their bicycles behind a thickly-growing bush and went to the kitchen door. Fatty unlocked it, and looked round. 'I think we'll keep to the kitchen quarters,' he said. 'Let's see—there's the kitchen—a small scullery—and a room the Smiths had for a bedroom. Oh, and there's a tiny bathroom here as well, leading off the bedroom.'

'Where exactly do we look?' asked Bets. 'I've been trying to think where I'd hide diamonds away in these rooms, if I had to—and except for silly places like at the back of a drawer, or on the very top of a cupboard, I can't think of any.'

'Well—the hiding-place is sure to be pretty good,' said Fatty. 'A prepared one, perhaps—you know, a hole knocked in the wall behind a cupboard, and then the cupboard put back again.'

'Oh,' said Bets. 'Well, I'm pretty sure I shouldn't find *that*.'

The five began to hunt carefully. Every mat, every scrap of carpet was turned back. Every bit of furniture was moved. Then Bets went to a chest of drawers.

'No good looking in the drawers of that chest, Bets, old thing,' said Fatty. 'The furniture belongs to the Smiths, you know. Hallo, what's this?'

Everyone turned at once. Fatty was down on his knees, trying to peer into a hole that was at the bottom of one corner of the kitchen wall. 'It seems to go back a little way,' he said. 'Gosh, I can see something there! Bets, can you get your tiny hand in and feel?'

Bets knelt down and tried to put her hand in at the hole. 'I can feel something!' she said excitedly. She stretched her fingers to the utmost and tried to get hold of whatever it was, with the very ends of her fingers. There was a sudden SNAP! and Bets screamed.

'Oh! My finger! Something caught it!'

'It's a mouse-trap, isn't it!' said Pip, with a squeal of laughter. 'I know that SNAP Mother put a trap in my bedroom last night, and it went SNAP and caught a mouse.'

'Oh, Bets—did it trap your fingers? said Fatty, in concern, as Bets stood up, squeezing the fingers of her right hand.

'No. Not quite. The trap part just missed them,' said Bets. 'Oh, Fatty—and I thought I was reaching out for a bag of diamonds! and it was only just a mouse-trap that the Smiths must have put into the hole!'

Fatty took his torch from his pocket and bent down to make sure, his check against the ground, as. he flashed the light of his torch into the hole. 'You're right, Bets,' he said. 'It's a trap. What a disappointment. Still—a bag of diamonds wouldn't be pushed into a mouse-hole, of course! The hiding-place will be very much cleverer than that! Call Pip in, Ern, and take his place.'

Pip came in, rubbing his hands. 'Jolly cold out there,' he said, stamping his feet. 'Shouldn't be surprised if it's going to snow. Found anything?'

'Not a thing,' said Bets. 'Except a mouse-trap.'

The hunt was a complete failure. Fatty gave it up after a whole hour's search. It was getting dark, and he was the only one with a torch.

'No go,' said Fatty. 'I think probably only professional police searchers could find the diamonds. They may even be embedded in one of the walls—a hole could have been made, the plaster put back, and painted over. Short of pulling the walls to pieces, and taking up the floor, I don't see that we can do anything else! I vote we go and have tea somewhere.'

'You can come and have it at our house,' said Pip. 'Mother's gone out, and she said if we cleared away ourselves and washed up, she would leave a smashing tea on the table. And if we break anything, we've got to replace it.'

'Jolly nice of your mother,' said Larry. 'Shall we go to Pip's, Fatty?'

'Yes. Splendid idea,' said Fatty. 'I'd have liked you all to come to my house for tea, but Mother is Very Very Distant to me at the moment. I really might be some third cousin she hasn't seen for years, and doesn't want to know. Poor Mother—she'll never get over my going to Mrs. Henry's disguised as a smelly rag-and-bone man. That overcoat did smell, you know.'

'My word it did,' said Pip. 'You smell of it a bit still, Fatty. Ern, you can come to tea, too, of course.'

Ern beamed. He had been afraid that he might not be asked. What would Sid and Perce say when he told them how he'd been here, there and everywhere? He was very happy indeed as he cycled up to Pip's with the others—but quite horrified when he suddenly met his uncle round a corner! Goon saw him at once and leapt off his bicycle. He caught hold of Ern's handle-bars and Ern wobbled and fell off.

'What you doing here in Peterswood, Ern?' he

demanded. 'Didn't I tell you to go home? What you been doing all this time?'

'I asked him to stay with me,' said Fatty, in what Goon called his 'high and mighty voice.' 'Don't you want to know what happened to those poor old Smiths, Mr. Goon—the ones you tried to turn out of their caretaking job?'

'All I know is they've gone, and good riddance to them,' said Goon. 'Smith was a traitor—didn't ought to be in any responsible job. The man that wrote those notes to warn me, was quite right.'

'Well, Mrs Smith is staying up at our house, helping my mother,' said Fatty. 'And Mr. Smith is in the cottage hospital, very ill, but Mrs. Smith can see him every day, you'll be pleased to know. At least I hope you *will* be pleased to know. You were very unkind to her, Goon.'

'Don't you talk to me like that, you—you pest of a boy!' said Goon, furious at being ticked off by Fatty in front of Ern, whose eyes were nearly falling out of his head. 'And let me tell you this—Fairlin Hall's bin bought, see—and anyone going there will be TRESPASSING, and will be PROSECUTED. Those are the new owner's orders. Two gentlemen have bought it—very nice too, they are, and very friendly. So you be careful, Master Frederick Trotteville.'

'Thank you for the news, Goon,' said Fatty, 'I was rather expecting it. But why should you think I'd want to go there?'

'Oh, I wouldn't put it past you to go and move out all the Smith's furniture,' said goon. 'Always interfering in everything! Ern, you come with me.'

'I've been asked out to tea, Uncle,' said Ern, edging away. He leapt suddenly on his bicycle and rode away at top speed.

'Gah !' said Goon, in disgust. 'You've made Ern as bad as you are. Just wait till I get my hands on him!'

Goon rode away angrily. That Frederick Trotteville! Was he up to anything? Goon couldn't help feeling that there was still something going on that he didn't know about. Gah !

The others laughed and rode off again. They arrived at Pip's to find Ern waiting for them behind a bush. Soon they were sitting round a loaded tea-table. Fatty wished he had gone to fetch Buster, because Mrs. Hilton, Pip's mother had Ieft a plate of dog-biscuits for him, smeared with potted meat, a meal that old Buster simply loved!

'Will the Smiths be able to get their furniture out before those men move in?' asked Ern. 'Mrs. Smith was very worried about it at dinner-time. And she said that lots of things ought to be done before anyone else uses that kitchen. She said the kitchen-range was right down dangerous. And she said the sink smelt something awful. I did try to find out if there were any possible hidingplaces, Fatty—but the only things she said were about the kitchen-range, and the sink, and the coal-cellar,the cold pipe in the bathroom, and the mouse-hole in the wall.'

'What did she say about the coal-cellar?' asked 'We never examined that, now I come to think of it.'

'She said the steps down were so rickety she was afraid of breaking her leg,' said Ern. 'And she said the cold pipe in the bathroom ran so slowly that their baths were always too hot. It had a leak too, she said, and the sink . . .'

'Smelt something awful,' said Fatty. 'Hm. Nothing very helpful there—though I think we *ought* to have looked in the coal-cellar. I've a good mind to go there tonight, as a matter of fact. It'll be my only chance if those men are going to move in. Yes, I think I *ought* to have a squint at that coal-cellar.'

'I'll come with you, Fatty,' said Ern, eagerly. 'Do, say I can.'

'No,' said Fatty. 'I shall go alone, if I do go, but I'm not certain yet. If only Superintendent Jenks was back I'd go and see him, and ask for a couple of men to search those kitchen quarters. No, no more jam tarts, thank you, Pip! Ern, you'll go pop if you have any more. Try Buster's dog-biscuits smeared with potted meat!'

'Well, they don't look half bad,' said Ern, and made everyone laugh. 'I've a good mind to try one!'

There wasn't much left on the table when they had all finished. 'Let's play cards now, Fatty,' said Pip. But Fatty shook his head.

'No. I want to go to the flower-shop before it shuts,' he said.

'Why? To buy another Coleus plant?' said Bets, with a laugh.

'No—to buy a very expensive bunch of red roses for someone I've mortally offended,' said Fatty, solemnly. 'My mother! I simply cannot bear to go home and be treated like a bad smell—and Mother really is Very Very Annoyed with me. I feel rather bad about it, actually, she's such a dear. See you tomorrow! Mind you don't break anything when you wash up!'

## 20 FATTY INVESTIGATES

ERN had been told that he could sleep the night in Fatty's shed, if he didn't want to go home. He decided that he certainly would—and Ern had strong reason for his decision.

If Fatty was going down to Fairlin Hall that night, then he, Ern, was going too. Not *with* Fatty, because he might be sent back. He was just going to follow him, and make sure nothing happened to him.

'Just suppose those men have moved in,' thought Ern, anxiously. 'Fatty would be no match for them. I won't let him see me—but I'll keep watch, in case those men are there and hear him.'

So, as he cycled back to Fatty's after Pip's tea-party; Ern made his plans. He would leave his bicycle in a bush down the drive, at Fatty's house, so that as soon as Fatty went off, he could follow him. And if Fatty walked, well, Ern would walk too. He felt in his pocket to see if his torch was there. Yes, it was.

Fatty was down in his shed when Ern arrived, looking through his notes. 'Hallo, Ern!' he said. 'Did you break anything when you all washed up?'

'Not a thing,' said Ern. 'You ought to have stayed, Fatty. We played cards, and little Bets won the lot. Did you get some flowers for your mother?

'I did,' said Fatty. 'And Mother was very pleased. So that's settled. I'm not a nasty smell any more.'

'Are you really going down to Fairlin Hall tonight, Fatty?' asked Ern.

'I am—and you are *not* coming, so don't ask me again,' said Fatty. 'I shall creep down the stairs when the household is in bed. Ern, if you're sleeping down in this shed, I think you'd better have Buster, if you don't mind. He might bark the place down if I go without him.'

'Oooh, I will. I'd like to,' said Ern, who was very fond of the lively little Scottie. 'He'll be company.'

'Well, I must go in and make myself respectable,' said Fatty. 'They're expecting you to supper in the kitchen, Ern. You'd better write a bit more poetry to recite to them.'

'Oooh, I couldn't write it in such a hurry,' said Ern. 'It takes me weeks to write two lines, Fatty.'

'Rubbish,' said Fatty. 'Remember what I told you. Just let your tongue go loose, and it comes—it comes! Think of a good line to begin with, Ern—then let your tongue wag away as it likes.'

Fatty left him, and Ern opened his notebook. He looked at his 'portry'. If only he could think of it easily, like Fatty ! It would be so very very nice to stand up in the kitchen tonight and recite a new 'pome'.

'Well, I'll have another try,' said Ern, valiantly, and stood up. He worked his tongue about a little to 'loose' and then delivered himself of one line.

'There was a pore old mouse . . .'

He waggled his tongue desperately, hoping the next

line would come spouting forth, just as it did when Fatty made up verses. 'There was a pore old mouse. . . mouse. There was a pore old mouse . . .'

'Snogood,' said Ern, flopping down again. 'Fatty's tongue must be different from mine. I wonder what's for supper tonight.'

At ten o'clock Fatty said goodnight to his mother and father and went up to bed. He waited for half an hour and then he heard his parents come up, and the lights click off. He quickly put on his overcoat and slipped downstairs again, with a very quiet Buster at his heels. Buster's tail was wagging hard. A walk ! At this time of night too !

It was snowing a little as Fatty walked down to his shed. He knocked quietly. Ern opened the door at once.

'Goodness—aren't you going to get undressed, Ern?' said Fatty, in surprise. 'I left you an old pair of pyjamas, didn't I?'

'I'm not sleepy yet,' said Ern, truthfully. 'Hullo, Buster. Come on in. Well, good luck, Fatty.'

'Thanks. I'll be off,' said Fatty, and went down the path, the snowflakes shining white in the light of his torch. Ern waited a few seconds and then slipped out himself, pulling on his overcoat. Buster began to bark frantically as Ern shut the door. He leapt up and down at it, flinging himself against it. He was furious at being deserted by both Fatty *and* Ern.

'Blow!' thought Ern. 'I hope he won't wake everyone. Still, the shed's pretty far away from the house!'

He hurried along down the garden-path, into the drive

and out of the front gate. He could just see Fatty passing under a street-lamp some way off. He followed quickly, his feet making no noise on the snow-covered path.

Fatty had no idea that Ern was following him. He went along quickly, feeling the key of the kitchen door of Fairlin Hall in his pocket. His mind went over what Ern had related to him. Kitchen-range. Smelly sink. Leaking pipe. Coal-cellar. Yes—he'd certainly better examine that coal-cellar. It might make a splendid hiding-place.

Behind him plodded Ern. Fatty came to the drive of Fairlin Hall and turned down it cautiously, looking for lights in the house. Ern turned in after him, keeping Fatty in sight as best he could, a dark shadow in the distance.

Fatty could see no lights anywhere, but of course the electricity would not be connected yet. If the two men came, they would have to use torches. The Smiths had had an oil lamp in their kitchen, because no gas or electricity was on.

'Those men will have to come pretty soon, certainly within the next week, I suppose,' thought Fatty. 'I don't expect they *really* mean to buy it—all they want is to find the hoard of diamonds they stole so many years ago, and take them. Anyway, they've got the keys, so they can get in at any time.'

He let himself in quietly at the kitchen door, and left it open, in case he had to run out quickly. He slipped through the scullery and kitchen, and went to the door that led from the kitchen to the hall. He opened it and stood there listening. He could hear nothing at all.

Slipping off his shoes he padded into the dark hall and went to the bottom of the stairs. There was no light to be seen anywhere, and the whole house was heavy with silence. 'Almost as if it were listening, too!' thought Fatty. 'Well, as there's absolutely no one about, I'll just examine that coal-cellar. I suppose it's outside, because I don't remember seeing a cellar indoors.'

He put on his shoes again and slipped through the kitchen and out into the little yard. He didn't see Ern standing like a statue in the shadow of some bushes not far off; but Ern saw the light from Fatty's torch, and knew that he was going to examine the coal-cellar.

The Fairlin Hall coal-cellar was a truly enormous one. A large, heavy grating covered the entrance hole, and Fatty lifted it off, and peered down. A steep wooden ladder led downwards to what looked more like an underground room than a coal-hole. The ladder was rickety, as Mrs. Smith had related to Ern, and Fatty didn't really fancy going down it.

He flashed his torch down the ladder, and came to the conclusion that if any diamonds had been hidden in the cellar they would have been discovered, for there was very very little coal left—only a sprinkling over the stone floor.

Fatty went back to the house, and flashed his torch over the kitchen-range. Was there any hiding-place at the back? No, not possibly. He went round the rooms methodically, trying to think of somewhere he hadn't examined that afternoon.

He suddenly heard a small sound, and stood still, listening. There it was again. What was it?

Was it someone opening the front door and shutting it? Fatty's heart began to thump a little. If it were the two men they would probably come into the kitchen quarters to search. He switched off his torch and stood in the tiny bathroom listening intently.

Suddenly he felt a soft touch on the top of his head, and he stiffened in fright. It felt like a moth settling on his hair—but no moths were about in January.

There it was again—just a soft touch on his hair. Fatty put up his hand and felt the spot—and it was damp! He heaved a sigh of relief. Just a little drip of water from somewhere—probably from the leaking water-pipe that Mrs. Smith had told Ern about!

He stood there in the dark, listening for any further sound, but none came. He must have been mistaken. He took a step forward and switched on his torch again, looking up at the water-pipe to see where the drip had come from.

'It's from that loose joint,' thought Fatty, seeing a place where two pipes had been joined together. 'Gosh, it made me jump.'

He reached up his hand and touched the joint. It was rather loose, so no wonder the water leaked out. A sudden idea flashed into Fatty's mind—an idea that made him catch his breath. Could it be—no, it *couldn't* be what he was thinking!

His hand shook a little as he held the torch up to the joint of the pipes. Why should there be a join there, held together by an iron band round the pipe? Could the pipe have been deliberately cut—could something have been slid into it—then the cut ends fixed together by the joint, hiding whatever had been forced into the pipe?

Fatty stood below the narrow little pipe, hearing the small noise that the tiny drip made every now and again. Mrs. Smith had said that the flow in the cold water-pipe was very poor—very slow—so slow that they couldn't make their hot baths cool! Was that because the pipe had been stuffed with something that impeded the flow of the water-stuffed with *diamonds,* perhaps!

Fatty flashed his torch on the joint again. It didn't look as neat a job as the other joints he could see. A surge of excitement made his heart begin to beat fast.

'I believe I've got it!' thought Fatty to himself. 'I really believe I have! My word—if Wilfrid Hasterley really did push all his diamonds into a water-pipe and then sealed it up, he was a wizard at hiding things! I bet he put a few big ones in first, hoping they would jam together, and not be taken down to the outlet. Whew!'

He had heard no more noises, and felt certain he was mistaken in thinking anyone had come into the house. He would surely have heard something more by now! He debated whether he should find the main water-cock and turn off the water. Then he might be able to back off the pipe-joint, force the two ends of the little pipe apart, aid peer into them.

But where *was* the water-cock? He hadn't the faintest idea. 'No good messing about,' thought Fatty. 'I'll get back home—and tomorrow I simply MUST get into touch with the Superintendent, even if I have to telephone to the back of beyond!'

He crept silently out of the little bathroom, shining his torch in front of him—and then he had the shock of his life! Someone pounced on him from a corner and gripped him so tightly that he couldn't even struggle!

Then a torch was shone into his face, and a voice exclaimed: 'Oh—so it's that fat boy, is it? Why are you here again? What are you looking for? Go on, tell us, or we'll make you!'

Fatty saw two men—yes, the two he had been on guard against, and listening for ! So he *had* heard something! What an ass he had been not to go and investigate.

He began to shout at the top of his voice. 'Let me go! Let me go! Help! Let me go?'

'There's nobody to hear you!' said one of the men. 'Shout all you like! Go on—shout!'

# 21 ERN HAS A REALLY EXCITING TIME!

BUT there was somebody to hear Fatty, of course. Ern was still outside, shivering in the shelter of the bush he was hiding in. He almost jumped out of his skin when he heard Fatty's shouts.

'They've got him—somebody in the house has caught him!' thought Ern, shaking at the knees. 'What shall I do? I daren't go in—I'll be caught too if I do. Oh Fatty—what can I do to help?'

He stole from the shelter of his bush and crept nearer to the kitchen door. He could hear a struggle going on as Fatty tried to kick the men on the shins. He heard Fatty yell in pain at some blow given him.

'You let me go! Oh ! You brute ! Let go!'

Ern listened in anguish. He longed to go to Fatty's help, but what *would* be the sense of two of them being caught? Oh, poor Fatty! Ern strained his ears to hear what the men were saying.

"Lock him in this cupboard,' panted one of them. 'My word, he's strong. Knock him over the head.'

'No. Be careful. I don't want a spell in prison again,' said the second man. 'Shove him in!"

Ern heard a crash as Fatty was pushed violently into the big cupboard, where the Smith's brooms and brushes and pans still stood. Then there was a short silence. Not another sound from Fatty!

'Lock the door on him,' said a voice. 'He's knocked out for a bit, at any rate. My word, he gave me a kick that almost took off my knee-cap! Now come on—we've got to find those stones! We know they're here somewhere!'

Ern, his heart thumping so loudly that he felt the men must hear it, stood watching their torches flashing here and there, as they made their search for the hidden diamond haul. There was no sound to be heard from Fatty, not even a groan. Em began to feel very anxious.

'I must get help!' he thought. 'I really must. But how? He stood and thought hard.

'I'll go and stand at the front gate and stop the first person coming by,' he decided at last, and he crept through the falling snow up to the gate. He waited, shivering, for a few minutes, and then, to his delight, saw someone coming. It was a small man, hurrying along. Ern ran to him.

'Please will you help! Two men have got hold of a friend of mine in that empty house there. They've hurt him and locked him in a cupboard. Please come and help him.'

The little man looked quite scared. 'That's a matter for the police!' he said.

'Oh *no*!' said Em, thinking of his uncle at once. 'No, I don't want the police here.'

'Well, all I can do is to telephone them for you,' said the man, and hurried off. 'It's the police you need!'

Ern was in despair. The last person he wanted to see was his uncle, the very *last*! He hurried back to the house, his feet making no noise over the snow. He peeped through the kitchen window. No sign or sound of poor old Fatty—but the men were obviously still there, for Ern could see the flash of their torches from the little bedroom.

He debated whether he dared to go in and unlock the cupboard door: No, he daren't. He couldn't possibly get Fatty out without making a noise. Ern's heart sank down into his shoes. 'I'm no good when there's trouble about,' he thought, sorrowfully. 'No good at all. Fatty would know what to do at once. I wish I had better brains.'

And then he jumped violently as something brushed against his leg, and then planted a wet lick on his hand. 'Oooh ! What's that! Oh, it's you, Buster! Sh! How in the world did you get out?'

Buster wagged his tail. He knew quite well how he had got out! He had leapt up on to the chest of drawers in Fatty's shed, and had found the window open a little, He had squeezed himself through the opening and jumped to the ground. Then he had nosed his way after Ern's tracks and Fatty's, sniffing them easily all along the roads to Fairlin Hall.

But now Buster sensed trouble, and that was why he hadn't barked when he saw Ern! He put his paws up on the boy's knees and whined a very small whine, as if to say, 'Where's Fatty? Please tell me what's up?'

Then Buster heard the men inside the house and his ears pricked up at once. He ran to the door. He smelt Fatty's tracks, he smelt Fatty himself! Where was his master? What had happened to him? He ran to the cupboard and pawed at it. He knew Fatty was in there!

The men heard him and ran out of the bedroom. They flashed their torches on the little Scottie—and at the same moment he leapt at them. One man felt a nip on his ankle—then the other felt a glancing bite on his hand. He hit out at the excited dog, who bounded all round them like a mad thing, barking, and nipping them whenever he could.

One man ran out of the kitchen into the hall, and the other followed. Buster went too, and Ern heard him chasing them all the way up the stairs. Ern was almost weeping in relief. He raced to the locked cupboard and turned the key.

'Fatty! Quick! Come out!', he said.

Fatty was lying back on a collection of pails, pans and brushes. He stared up at Ern, still half-dazed.

'Ern!' he said, in a weak voice. 'What's up?'

'Oh Fatty—you've an awful bruise on your head,' said Ern, in distress. 'Quick, I want to get you out of here. Can you stand? Let me help you.'

Fatty stood up with difficulty. Evidently the blow on his head had quite dazed him. Ern helped him anxiously out into the air.

'Let me sit down,' said Fatty. 'This cold air is making me feel better. I don't feel quite so dazed. Gosh, what happened? I'm just remembering! Ern, what on earth are *you* doing here? And is that Buster I can hear barking?

'Fatty, don't bother about anything now,' said Ern, as the boy sat down heavily beside a bush. 'Old Buster is chasing the men who knocked you out. Stay here a minute and I'll just go and see what's happened to him.'

Ern went back cautiously to the kitchen. But before he could even look inside, he saw a lamp coming waveringly round the corner of the house, and stared at it in amazement. Who was this coming now? Then a loud and angry voice hailed him.

'ERN! What you doing here? Some fellow phoned me and said there was a boy here who wanted help Ern, if it was *you* playing a joke like that on me, I'll—I'll. . . '

It was Goon! He leapt off his bicycle and strode towards the terrified Ern, who promptly fled into the kitchen. Goon padded after him, quite convinced that Ern had got him out here in the snowy night just for fun.

And then Buster appeared at top speed! He had heard Goon's voice, and had come to investigate. He leapt at the policeman in delight and nipped his trousers at the ankle.

'What—that dog's here too! Is that fat boy here as well?' thundered Goon. 'What's going on? I never heard of such doings in my life. Oh get off, you horrible little dog! Clear orf, I say! Ern, get him off, or I'll pull every hair out of your head! WILL you get away, dog?'

But Buster was having the time of his life. No Fatty to call him off, nobody to stop him from harrying his old enemy all he liked. It was too good to be true! He chased Mr. Goon all round the kitchen, and then into the broom cupboard, where the angry policeman subsided among the same pails and brooms that Fatty had fallen on.

And then Ern suddenly saw the two men peeping round

the door, and he crouched in a corner in terror, praying that they would not see him. One flashed his torch into the cupboard and saw the policeman there, with Buster on top of him.

'Look there—the police!' he cried in alarm, and slammed the cupboard door at once. He turned the key, locking the door. 'Well, thank goodness we've got rid of the dog, and locked up the policeman' he said, in a shaky voice. 'I can't understand all this. Where's that boy gone that we knocked out?'

'He's lying under the bobby, I expect,' said the second man. 'He was quite knocked out. The policeman must have fallen on top of him, trying to get away from that vicious little dog. Phew! What a night! Do we search any more—or what??

'No. We get back to Kuntan,' said the second man. 'My ankles are bitten all over! I must put some iodine on them. I'd like to have killed that dog!'

'Well, he can keep the policeman and the boy company till morning,' said his companion. Then he turned sharply. 'Hallo—who's this? he said, and he flashed his torch on to the corner where Ern was crouching.

And then Ern behaved magnificently. He reached up a hand and swept a whole row of kettles and pans off the shelf just above him. They clattered to the floor with an awful din, and startled the two men out of their wits. Then Ern leapt up into the air, hands above his head, and moaned in a horrible, hollow voice, 'I'm coming! I'm coming!'

The two men took to their heels and raced out of the

*They clattered to the floor with an awful din*

kitchen door. This was absolutely the last straw—what with boys and policemen and dogs roaming about—and now this awful creature, whatever it was, clattering pans everywhere! The men were really terrified.

Ern looked out of the door after them, hardly able to believe that his sudden mad idea had acted so well. Then he heard a loud shriek, and wondered what had happened. Then came a crash, and angry voices.

'What's up now?' wondered Ern, uneasily. As the voices came no nearer he tiptoed out of the kitchen door and went cautiously towards them.

'Coo—lovaduck! They've fallen down the coal-cellar!' he said. 'Fatty must have forgotten to put the grating back over it—and down they've gone! They must be hurt or they'd try getting up the ladder. Quick, Ern, my lad, you can do something here!'

And Ern flew to where the big heavy grating lay on the snow-covered ground. He dragged and pulled, pulled and dragged, panting hard. At last he got it half across the cellar-opening, and the men, who had been quite silent, hoping that perhaps their hiding-place would not be discovered, suddenly realized what was happening.

One gave a yell and began to climb the ladder—but the rickety rungs broke under his weight and he fell back into the cellar again. Ern at last pulled the grating right across. Then he flashed his torch down at the two angry, frightened men.

'You can stay there till you're fetched!' he said, and looked about for something else heavy enough to drag over the grating, to keep it down. He found the dustbin, and dragged it there, and then filled it with stones from a nearby rockery. He was very hot and tired when he had finished. The men yelled and threatened him with all kinds of terrible things—but Ern was feeling on top of the world, and took no notice.

'Loveaduck—there's the men down the coal-cellar—and uncle in the cupboard with Buster on top of him—I've done a good night's work,' thought Ern, hurrying back to where he had left Fatty. 'If only poor old Fatty is feeling better!'

Fatty was decidedly better. He was standing up wondering whether to go and join the row he could hear going on not far off. He didn't know that it was Ern well and truly imprisoning the men in the coal-cellar!

'Hallo, Fatty,' said Ern's voice. 'You better? Come on, I'll take you home. You lean on me. No, don't ask any questions now—you'll be all right tomorrow. I'll answer them then.'

And so the still-dazed Fatty, frowning with an enormous headache, went slowly home, leaning on Ern's shoulder. His head was in a muddle. All he wanted was to lie down and rest in bed. Good old Ern—he'd explain everything to him tomorrow! Fatty simply couldn't be bothered to worry about anything just then!

## 22 A MOST SURPRISING FINISH

ERN slept the night in Fatty's room, so that if the boy wanted anything in the night he could get it for him. He curled himself up in a chair, dressed as he was, meaning to keep awake and think over the exciting happenings of the night. Coo—think of Uncle in that cupboard with Buster barking in his ear. A very very pleasant thought for Ern!

He fell asleep—and as for Fatty, once his headache had eased, he too slept like a log. He sat up in bed at halfpast seven next morning as lively as a cricket, and was most amazed to see Ern asleep in his arm-chair. His mind groped back to the evening before. What had happened?

'I can remember as far as being attacked by those men—and being thrown into the cupboard—but all the rest is hazy,' thought Fatty, and gently felt the bump on his head. 'I suppose they knocked me out. How did I get here? Ern! Wake up, Ern!'

Ern awoke with a jump and uncurled himself. He went to Fatty's bed. 'Coo, Fatty—you've got an awful bruise on your head,' he said. 'How do you feel?'

'Fine,' said Fatty, getting out of bed. 'Ern, how did I get back here? What on earth happened last night? How did *you* come into it? You weren't even there!'

'Oh yes I was, Fatty,' said Ern. 'You just listen. Get

back into bed and I'll tell you the best story you ever heard in your life.'

'Well, make it short,' said Fatty. 'I've simply *got* to phone the Superintendent now!'

'Yes, you have. But there's no hurry,' said Ern, grinning. 'I've got everyone nicely in the bag for you.'

'What do you mean, young Ern?' demanded Fatty. 'Don't sit there grinning—tell me everything.'

'Well—my uncle's locked up in the cupboard where *you* were,' said Ern, 'and Buster's with him, and the two men are imprisoned in the coal-cellar. I scared them and they ran out and didn't see the opening—and fell down it. Good thing you didn't put the grating back, Fatty. I pulled it across the hole, and my word, it was heavy, and I stood the dustbin on top as well and filled it with big stones from the rockery.'

Fatty was too astonished to say a word. He stared at Ern as if he couldn't believe his ears. 'Is this true?' he said at last. 'How was it you were there?'

'I followed you,' said Ern. 'I was afraid something might happen to you. I left Buster in the shed, but he must have got out somehow. He chased those men all over the place.'

'Ern—thank you,' said Fatty. 'Thank you more than I can say. I made a mess of things—and you didn't. You—you did magnificently. My word, Ern, what a time you had!'

'Coo, I did!' said Ern. 'I dragged you out of that cupboard, Fatty, and put you outside in the drive—you did look awful. I was that upset and scared. Then suddenly

I wasn't scared any more, and, well—I suppose I sort of went mad, and swept all the pans off the shelf, clitter-clatter, and booed at those men at the top of my voice, and chased them!' Ern began to laugh as he remembered. 'Honest, I didn't know I could do it.'

'You'll have to write a poem about it, Ern,' said Fatty, getting out of bed again. 'Well, I can see there's a lot of loose ends to tie up this morning! My word—fancy old Goon having to spend the night in a cupboard with Buster—I bet he didn't enjoy that.'

Fatty was soon very busy indeed. He felt perfectly all right now, though the bruise on his head was sore. He telephoned immediately to the Superintendent's office, and oh, what a relief, he was there! Fatty was put through to him at once.

'This is an early call, Frederick,' said the Superintendent's crisp voice. 'What's up?'

'Plenty,' said Fatty. 'Superintendent, will you turn up details of a big diamond robbery over twenty years ago, when a Wilfrid Hasterley of The Ivies, Peterswood, and two friends, got away with an enormous haul of diamonds.'

'I don't need to turn it up,' said the Superintendent 'I was a young man then, and happened to be one of the men put on the job. Wilfrid got a jail sentence and died in prison. One man fled abroad, and we never heard of him again. The other man went to jail, and came out a few months ago. We meant to watch him, hoping he'd know where Wilfrid had hidden the diamonds, but he was too wily and went to ground. What about it? It's a very old case now.'

'I know. But two of the men came back to Peterswood-to The Ivies, which is now called Fairlin Hall,' said Fatty. 'And. . .'

'Frederick! You don't mean this!' said the Superintendent's voice, sounding amazed. 'Where are they?'

'Well, at the moment they're imprisoned in a coal-cellar at Fairlin Hall,' said Fatty, chuckling. 'And you'll be surprised to know that that was the work of young Ern, Superintendent—Goon's nephew, you know.'

'Good heavens!' said the Superintendent, sounding more astonished than ever. 'What about Goon? Is he in on this too?'

'Well—he was at the beginning,' said Fatty. 'But he didn't last till the end, I fear. He gave up half-way. At the moment, I regret to say, he's locked up in a broom cupboard at Fairlin Hall, with Buster, He's been there all night.'

There was a dead silence, then the Superintendent spoke again. 'This isn't a joke, is it, Frederick? he said.

'Oh no. It's all absolutely true,' said Fatty, earnestly. 'Can you come over? We could go down to Fairlin Hall and you can examine the various people there who are imprisoned in one way or another!'

'Right. I'll be along in twenty minutes,' said the Superintendent, briskly. 'With a few men. Meet me there, Frederick. Good heavens—this all sounds *quite* impossible!'

Fatty put down the telephone and turned to Ern, who

was listening nearby. 'Ring up the others for me, Ern,' he said. 'Tell them to meet us at Fairlin Hall quickly—even if they're in the middle of breakfast. This is going to be exciting. I'm going to get some biscuits for poor old Buster—he'll be starving!'

In fifteen minutes' time Larry, Daisy, Pip, Bets and Ern were all in the drive of Fairlin Hall, in a state of the greatest excitement. Fatty was at the gate waiting for the Superintendent and his men. Ah—here they came in two black police cars. The Superintendent jumped out and said a few words to the man with him. Then he strode toward Fatty.

'Now let's get down to business,' he said, clapping Fatty on the back. 'Lead on!'

'We'd better rescue poor Mr. Goon first,' said Fatty. 'And Buster too. I'm afraid Mr. Goon will be in a fearful temper, sir.'

'That won't matter,' said the Superintendent hardheartedly, 'Hallo, Bets! You here! And all the others too! Well, I'm blessed!'

They all went to the kitchen door and Fatty pushed it open. A loud barking was coming from the locked cupboard. Fatty went over and unlocked it. Out leapt Buster, mad with joy at seeing Fatty again, and being free once more.

'Steady, Buster, steady,' said Fatty. There came a noise from the cupboard and Mr. Goon walked out, looking as if he was about to burst with rage! He advanced on Fatty.

'*You're* at the bottom of this!' he roared. 'Toad of a

boy! And you, Ern, what do you mean by getting me here in the middle of the night, and ... oh ... er ... good morning, Superintendent. Didn't see you, I'm afraid. I've got a complaint to lay against this Frederick Trotteville. Always interfering with the law, he is, sir. After I'd settled a case, he goes on with it, poking his nose in, and . . .'

'That's enough, Goon, for the moment,' said the Superintendent. 'Where are these other men, did you say, Frederick?

Goon looked astounded. Other men? What did the Superintendent mean? He followed Fatty and the others out into the yard. A voice came from the coal-cellar.

'Let us out! One of us has a broken ankle. We give up!'

Goon stared in surprise at the dustbin full of big stones, as one of the policemen heaved it off the grating. He stared even more when the grating was taken off too, and a constable shouted down into the cellar.

'Come on up—you're wanted for questioning. We know you're the fellows in that Diamond Case years ago.'

The men had to be dragged up, because the ladder had broken in half. Goon was overcome with astonishment. What *was* all this?

'We can explain everything,' said one of the men. 'You've got nothing on us. We only came back here to visit the old place—to see old Mrs. Hasterley.'

'People don't live in empty houses,' said the Superintendent curtly. 'Frederick—we'll all go somewhere and talk over this, I think.'

'There's nothing to talk about,' interrupted Goon. 'It's

just a case I cleared up myself. These fellows sent notes to me, telling me about a caretaker here—man run in for being a traitor—and . . .'

'Sir—could we go into Fairlin Hall for a few minutes?' said Fatty. 'There's still a little matter to be cleared up there, if you don't mind. We could go into the kitchen.'

'Very well,' said the Superintendent, and he and Goon, and all the children filed in. The Superintendent sat down in the old arm-chair.

'You know all about that long ago diamond affair, sir,' began Fatty. 'Well, as soon as those two fellows you caught just now got together, when one of them came out of prison, they decided to come back here and find the diamond haul, which Wilfrid Hasterley had hidden safely away. They found caretakers in the kitchen quarters, so they couldn't search. They then discovered that Mr. Smith, the caretaker, had a shady past—had sold some secret papers to a foreign government . . .'

'And I turned them out of here!' said Goon. 'Quite right, too. Couldn't have a fellow . . .'

'Quiet, Goon,' said the Superintendent. 'Go on, Frederick.'

'Well, as Mr. Goon said, he turned them out—and so left the place clear for the two thieves to search,' said Fatty, 'which is exactly what they wanted! Well, *we* were on the trail, as well—we knew about the messages to Goon, you see—and we guessed the two fellows were after the hidden diamonds. So we came to search too!'

'Gah !' said Goon, in disgust.

'Well, we didn't find them. But last night I came back

here again, and the men were here too—and to cut a long story short, sir, Ern here imprisoned the two men in the coal-cellar, got me out of a cupboard where I'd been locked, and . . .'

'But how did *Goon* get locked in? said the Superintendent, looking suspiciously at Ern.

'Oooh, *I* didn't lock my uncle in,' said Ern, hastily. 'I wouldn't do such a thing. The *men* locked him in, sir.'

'And did those fellows give you any hint as to where the diamonds were?' asked the Superintendent, looking at Fatty expectantly.

'No, sir,' said Fatty. Everyone groaned—what a pity! No diamonds after all!

'Well—that's rather an anti-climax,' said the Superintendent, looking disappointed. '*Sure* you don't know where they are, Frederick?'

'Well—yes, sir, I think I *do* know where they are—though I haven't *seen* them!' said Fatty.

WHAT a sensation that made! Everyone gaped at Fatty, and the Superintendent stood up at once.

'You *know* where they're hidden!' he said. 'You actually *know*?'

'Well—I can make a jolly good guess,' said Fatty. 'If I were a plumber I could find out at once.'

'A *plumber?* What do you mean?' said the Superintendent. 'Come on, Frederick—no more mystery, please!'

'Well, sir—come into the bathroom,' said Fatty, and everyone squeezed into the tiny bathroom, even Goon. Fatty tapped the cold-water pipe, that still sent out a tiny drip at the loose joint.

'I think the diamonds are all jammed into this pipe, sir,' he said. 'It was Mrs. Smith who first mentioned the pipe to me—she said the flow of water was very poor indeed. Then when I examined it, I saw that the joint was loose—it's been badly done, sir, if you look—not a professional job at all. And I just put two and two together, sir, and thought. 'Well, this is about the only place where nobody's looked! They must be here!'

'Can't be!' said the Superintendent, staring at the pipe. 'What an idea! But what a hiding-place! What do *you* think Goon?'

'Diamonds in a water-pipe?' said Goon, scornfully, delighted at being asked his advice. 'Never heard of such a thing in my life. You have that pipe cut, sir—we'll flood the bathroom, but that's about all we'll do!'

The Superintendent went to the door and called out to one of his men. 'Get that hack-saw of yours, Sergeant!'

'Right, sir!' And in half a minute in came the Sergeant with an efficient-looking little saw.

'I want that pipe cut,' said the Superintendent, nodding his head at the little water-pipe. 'The water's turned off, so there's only what's in the pipes. Cut below that loose joint, where the water's dripping a little.'

Everyone watched while the Sergeant did a little sawing—then water spurted out—and with it came two small sparkling things that fell to the ground, and lay there, glittering. Fatty pounced on them at once, and dropped them into the Superintendent's hand.

'Whew! Yes—they're diamonds all right,' he said. 'The

pipe must be crammed with them! No wonder the water wouldn't flow through properly. Cut another place, Sergeant.'

The man obeyed—and there was no doubt of it, the pipe was full of diamonds—some big, some small, none of them any the worse for having lain in water for so many years.

'Sergeant—take a couple of men and empty the pipe,' ordered the Superintendent, looking extremely pleased. 'Frederick—you deserve a medal for this! Good work, my boy—as good as any you've ever done. Don't you think so, Goon?'

Goon didn't think so. Goon was busy blowing his nose loudly. Goon didn't want to answer *any* questions about Fatty at all. He was tired to death of Fatty and Ern, and all he wanted to do was to go home and have a Nice Hot Cup of Tea.

'I'll have to come and take a report about all this from you, Frederick, some time or other,' said the Superintendent, his hand on Fatty's shoulder. 'But now I must go and question those two men. My warm congratulations—and if I were you, I'd go and put something on that frightful bruise. One of the men did that, I suppose?'

'Yes. But I don't mind!' said Fatty. 'I gave as good as I got. Gosh—it *was* a night and a half, sir—and Ern here did as much as I did. More!'

'My congratulations to you too, Ern,' said the Superintendent. 'I shouldn't be surprised if you didn't have a little Something coming to you as a reward for your good work.'

Ern blushed all over his face in surprise and delight. How he longed to be like Fatty, and let his 'tongue go loose'. What a 'pome' he would recite to the Superintendent! But all he could say was, 'I'm going to be a policeman some day, sir—and I'll be a Sergeant in no time at all—you see if I don't!'

'Gah!' said Goon, before he could stop himself, and marched off angrily. That Ern ! And to think he'd given him five shillings for helping him. What a waste!

'Let's all go back and have breakfast at my house,' said Fatty. 'I'm starving. Mother will have a fit when she sees my bruise! Gosh, I do hope it doesn't go down before I'm back at school—I'll be the envy of everyone when I tell them how I got it. Well, Ern—how did you enjoy *this* Mystery?'

'Loveaduck !' said Ern, beaming. 'It was Smashing, Fatty. Thanks a lot for letting me in on it. Never enjoyed myself so much in my life. And don't forget—I've still got that five shillings left that my uncle gave me. I'll stand you all ice-creams this morning, and that goes for Buster too!'

'Good old Ern,' said Fatty, and clapped him on the shoulder. And the others all said the same, making the boy blush as red as a beetroot. 'Good Old Ern.'

THE END

W9-ARN-502

COLLECTION FOLIO

Jean-Paul Sartre

# Le mur

Gallimard

Né le 21 juin 1905 à Paris, Jean-Paul Sartre, avec ses condisciples de l'École normale supérieure, critique très jeune les valeurs et les traditions de sa classe sociale, la bourgeoisie. Il enseigne quelque temps au lycée du Havre, puis poursuit sa formation philosophique à l'Institut français de Berlin. Dès ses premiers textes philosophiques, *L'imagination* (1936), *Esquisse d'une théorie des émotions* (1939), *L'imaginaire* (1940), apparaît l'originalité d'une pensée qui le conduit à l'existentialisme, dont les thèses sont développées dans *L'être et le néant* (1943) et dans *L'existentialisme est un humanisme* (1946).

Sartre s'est surtout fait connaître du grand public par ses récits, nouvelles et romans — *La nausée* (1938), *Le mur* (1939), *Les chemins de la liberté* (1943-1949) — et ses textes de critique littéraire et politique — *Réflexions sur la question juive* (1946), *Baudelaire* (1947), *Saint Genet, comédien et martyr* (1952), *Situations* (1947-1976), *L'Idiot de la famille* (1972). Son théâtre a un plus vaste public encore : *Les mouches* (1943), *Huis clos* (1945), *La putain respectueuse* (1946), *Les mains sales* (1948), *Le diable et le bon dieu* (1951) ; il a pu y développer ses idées en en imprégnant ses personnages.

Soucieux d'aborder les problèmes de son temps, Sartre a mené jusqu'à la fin de sa vie une intense activité politique (participation au Tribunal Russell, refus du prix Nobel de littérature en 1964, direction de *La cause du peuple* puis de *Libération*). Il est mort à Paris le 15 avril 1980.

*A Olga Kosakiewicz*

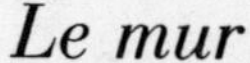

# *Le mur*

On nous poussa dans une grande salle blanche, et mes yeux se mirent à cligner parce que la lumière leur faisait mal. Ensuite, je vis une table et quatre types derrière la table, des civils, qui regardaient des papiers. On avait massé les autres prisonniers dans le fond et il nous fallut traverser toute la pièce pour les rejoindre. Il y en avait plusieurs que je connaissais et d'autres qui devaient être étrangers. Les deux qui étaient devant moi étaient blonds avec des crânes ronds, ils se ressemblaient : des Français, j'imagine. Le plus petit remontait tout le temps son pantalon : c'était nerveux.

Ça dura près de trois heures ; j'étais abruti et j'avais la tête vide mais la pièce était bien chauffée et je trouvais ça plutôt agréable : depuis vingt-quatre heures, nous n'avions pas cessé de grelotter. Les gardiens amenaient les prisonniers l'un après l'autre devant la table. Les quatre types leur demandaient alors leur nom et leur profession. La plupart du temps ils n'allaient pas plus loin — ou bien alors ils posaient une question par-ci par-là : « As-tu pris part au sabotage des munitions ? » Ou bien : « Où étais-tu le matin du 9 et que faisais-tu ? » Ils n'écoutaient pas les réponses ou du moins ils n'en avaient pas l'air : ils se taisaient un moment et regardaient droit devant eux puis ils se mettaient à écrire. Ils demandèrent à Tom si c'était vrai qu'il servait dans la Brigade internationale : Tom ne pouvait pas dire le contraire à cause des papiers qu'on avait trouvés dans sa veste. A Juan ils ne demandèrent rien, mais, après qu'il eut dit son nom, ils écrivirent longtemps.

— C'est mon frère José qui est anarchiste, dit Juan. Vous savez bien qu'il n'est plus ici. Moi je ne suis d'aucun parti, je n'ai jamais fait de politique.

Ils ne répondirent pas. Juan dit encore :

— Je n'ai rien fait. Je ne veux pas payer pour les autres.

Ses lèvres tremblaient. Un gardien le fit taire et l'emmena. C'était mon tour :

— Vous vous appelez Pablo Ibbieta ?

Je dis que oui.

Le type regarda ses papiers et me dit :

— Où est Ramon Gris ?

— Je ne sais pas.

— Vous l'avez caché dans votre maison du 6 au 19.

— Non.

Ils écrivirent un moment et les gardiens me firent sortir. Dans le couloir Tom et Juan attendaient entre deux gardiens. Nous nous mîmes en marche. Tom demanda à un des gardiens.

— Et alors ?

— Quoi ? dit le gardien.

— C'est un interrogatoire ou un jugement ?

— C'était le jugement, dit le gardien.

— Eh bien ? Qu'est-ce qu'ils vont faire de nous ?

Le gardien répondit sèchement :

— On vous communiquera la sentence dans vos cellules.

En fait, ce qui nous servait de cellule c'était une des caves de l'hôpital. Il y faisait terriblement froid à cause des courants d'air. Toute la nuit nous avions grelotté et pendant la journée ça n'avait guère mieux été. Les cinq jours précédents je les avais passés dans un cachot de l'archevêché, une espèce d'oubliette qui devait dater du Moyen Age : comme il y avait beaucoup de prisonniers et peu de place, on les casait n'importe où. Je ne regrettais pas mon cachot : je n'y avais pas souffert du froid mais j'y étais seul ; à la longue c'est irritant. Dans la cave j'avais de la compagnie. Juan ne parlait guère : il avait peur et puis il était trop jeune pour avoir son mot à dire. Mais Tom était beau parleur et il savait très bien l'espagnol.

Dans la cave il y avait un banc et quatre paillasses. Quand ils nous eurent ramenés, nous nous assîmes et nous attendîmes en silence. Tom dit, au bout d'un moment :

— Nous sommes foutus.

— Je le pense aussi, dis-je, mais je crois qu'ils ne feront rien au petit.

— Ils n'ont rien à lui reprocher, dit Tom. C'est le frère d'un militant, voilà tout.

Je regardai Juan : il n'avait pas l'air d'entendre. Tom reprit :

— Tu sais ce qu'ils font à Saragosse ? Ils couchent les types sur la route et ils leur passent dessus avec des camions. C'est un Marocain déserteur qui nous l'a dit. Ils disent que c'est pour économiser les munitions.

— Ça n'économise pas l'essence, dis-je.

J'étais irrité contre Tom : il n'aurait pas dû dire ça.

— Il y a des officiers qui se promènent sur la route, poursuivit-il, et qui surveillent ça, les mains dans les poches, en fumant des cigarettes. Tu crois qu'ils achèveraient les types ? Je t'en fous. Ils les laissent gueuler. Des fois pendant une heure. Le Marocain disait que, la première fois, il a manqué dégueuler.

— Je ne crois pas qu'ils fassent ça ici, dis-je. A moins qu'ils ne manquent vraiment de munitions.

Le jour entrait par quatre soupiraux et par une ouverture ronde qu'on avait pratiquée au plafond, sur la gauche, et qui donnait sur le ciel. C'est par ce trou rond ordinairement fermé par une trappe, qu'on déchargeait le charbon dans la cave. Juste au-dessous du trou il y avait un gros tas de poussier ; il avait été destiné à chauffer l'hôpital, mais, dès le début de la guerre, on avait évacué les malades et le charbon restait là, inutilisé ; il pleuvait même dessus, à l'occasion, parce qu'on avait oublié de baisser la trappe.

Tom se mit à grelotter :

— Sacré nom de Dieu, je grelotte, dit-il, voilà que ça recommence.

Il se leva et se mit à faire de la gymnastique. A chaque mouvement sa chemise s'ouvrait sur sa poitrine blanche et velue. Il s'étendit sur le dos, leva les jambes en l'air et fit les ciseaux : je voyais trembler sa grosse croupe. Tom était costaud mais il avait trop de graisse. Je pensais que des balles de fusil ou des pointes de baïonnettes allaient bientôt s'enfoncer dans cette masse de chair tendre comme dans une motte de beurre. Ça ne me faisait pas le même effet que s'il avait été maigre.

Je n'avais pas exactement froid, mais je ne sentais plus mes épaules ni mes bras. De temps en temps, j'avais l'impression qu'il me manquait quelque chose et je commençais à chercher ma veste autour de moi, et puis je me rappelais brusquement qu'ils ne m'avaient pas donné de veste. C'était plutôt pénible. Ils avaient pris nos vêtements pour les donner à leurs soldats et ils ne nous avaient laissé que nos chemises — et ces pantalons de toile que les malades hospitalisés portaient au gros de l'été. Au bout d'un moment, Tom se releva et s'assit près de moi en soufflant.

— Tu es réchauffé ?

— Sacré nom de Dieu, non. Mais je suis essoufflé.

Vers huit heures du soir, un commandant entra avec deux phalangistes. Il avait une feuille de papier à la main. Il demanda au gardien :

— Comment s'appellent-ils, ces trois-là ?

— Steinbock, Ibbieta et Mirbal, dit le gardien.

Le commandant mit ses lorgnons et regarda sa liste :

— Steinbock... Steinbock... Voilà. Vous êtes condamné à mort. Vous serez fusillé demain matin.

Il regarda encore :

— Les deux autres aussi, dit-il.

— C'est pas possible, dit Juan. Pas moi.

Le commandant le regarda d'un air étonné :

— Comment vous appelez-vous ?

— Juan Mirbal, dit-il.

— Eh bien, votre nom est là, dit le commandant, vous êtes condamné.

— Je n'ai rien fait, dit Juan.

Le commandant haussa les épaules et se tourna vers Tom et vers moi.

— Vous êtes Basques ?

— Personne n'est Basque.

Il eut l'air agacé.

— On m'a dit qu'il y avait trois Basques. Je ne vais pas perdre mon temps à leur courir après. Alors naturellement vous ne voulez pas de prêtre ?

Nous ne répondîmes même pas. Il dit :

— Un médecin belge viendra tout à l'heure. Il a l'autorisation de passer la nuit avec vous.

Il fit le salut militaire et sortit.

— Qu'est-ce que je te disais, dit Tom. On est bons.

— Oui, dis-je, c'est vache pour le petit.

Je disais ça pour être juste mais je n'aimais pas le petit. Il avait un visage trop fin et la peur, la souffrance l'avaient défiguré, elles avaient tordu tous ses traits. Trois jours auparavant, c'était un môme dans le genre mièvre, ça peut plaire ; mais maintenant il avait l'air d'une vieille tapette, et je pensais qu'il ne redeviendrait plus jamais jeune, même si on le relâchait. Ça n'aurait pas été mauvais d'avoir un peu de pitié à lui offrir, mais la pitié me dégoûte, il me faisait plutôt horreur.

Il n'avait plus rien dit mais il était devenu gris : son visage et ses mains étaient gris. Il se rassit et regarda le sol avec des yeux ronds. Tom était une bonne âme, il voulut lui prendre le bras, mais le petit se dégagea violemment en faisant une grimace.

— Laisse-le, dis-je à voix basse, tu vois bien qu'il va se mettre à chialer.

Tom obéit à regret ; il aurait aimé consoler le petit : ça l'aurait occupé et il n'aurait pas été tenté de penser à lui-même. Mais ça m'agaçait : je n'avais jamais pensé à la mort parce que l'occasion ne s'en était pas présentée, mais maintenant l'occasion était là et il n'y avait pas autre chose à faire que de penser à ça.

Tom se mit à parler :

— Tu as bousillé des types, toi ? me demanda-t-il.

Je ne répondis pas. Il commença à m'expliquer qu'il en avait bousillé six depuis le début du mois d'août ; il ne se rendait pas compte de la situation, et je voyais bien qu'il ne *voulait* pas s'en rendre compte. Moi-même je ne réalisais pas encore tout à fait, je me demandais si on souffrait beaucoup, je pensais aux balles, j'imaginais leur grêle brûlante à travers mon corps. Tout ça c'était en dehors de la véritable question ; mais j'étais tranquille : nous avions toute la nuit pour comprendre. Au bout d'un moment Tom cessa de parler et je le regardai du coin de l'œil ; je vis qu'il était devenu gris, lui aussi, et qu'il avait l'air misérable, je me dis : « Ça commence. » Il faisait presque nuit, une lueur terne filtrait à travers les soupiraux et le tas de charbon, et faisait une grosse tache sous le ciel ; par le trou du plafond je voyais déjà une étoile : la nuit serait pure et glacée.

La porte s'ouvrit, et deux gardiens entrèrent. Ils étaient suivis d'un homme blond qui portait un uniforme belge. Il nous salua :

— Je suis médecin, dit-il. J'ai l'autorisation de vous assister en ces pénibles circonstances.

Il avait une voix agréable et distinguée. Je lui dis :

— Qu'est-ce que vous venez faire ici ?

— Je me mets à votre disposition. Je ferai tout mon possible pour que ces quelques heures vous soient moins lourdes.

— Pourquoi êtes-vous venu chez nous ? Il y a d'autres types, l'hôpital en est plein.

— On m'a envoyé ici, répondit-il d'un air vague.

« Ah ! vous aimeriez fumer, hein ? ajouta-t-il précipitamment. J'ai des cigarettes et même des cigares. »

Il nous offrit des cigarettes anglaises et des puros, mais nous refusâmes. Je le regardai dans les yeux, et il parut gêné. Je lui dis :

— Vous ne venez pas ici par compassion. D'ailleurs je vous connais. Je vous ai vu avec des fascistes dans la cour de la caserne, le jour où on m'a arrêté.

J'allais continuer, mais tout d'un coup il m'arriva quelque chose qui me surprit : la présence de ce médecin cessa brusquement de m'intéresser. D'ordinaire, quand je suis sur un homme je ne le lâche pas. Et pourtant l'envie de parler me quitta ; je haussai les épaules et je détournai les yeux. Un peu plus tard, je levai la tête : il m'observait d'un air curieux. Les gardiens s'étaient assis sur une paillasse. Pedro, le grand maigre, se tournait les pouces, l'autre agitait de temps en temps la tête pour s'empêcher de dormir.

— Voulez-vous de la lumière ? dit soudain Pedro au médecin.

L'autre fit « oui » de la tête : je pense qu'il avait à peu près autant d'intelligence qu'une bûche, mais sans doute n'était-il pas méchant. A regarder ses gros yeux bleus et froids, il me sembla qu'il péchait surtout par défaut d'imagination. Pedro sortit et revint avec une lampe à pétrole qu'il posa sur le coin du banc. Elle éclairait mal, mais c'était mieux que rien : la veille on nous avait laissés dans le noir. Je regardai un bon moment le rond de lumière que la lampe faisait au plafond. J'étais fasciné. Et puis, brusquement, je me réveillai, le rond de lumière s'effaça, et je me sentis écrasé sous un poids énorme. Ce n'était pas la pensée de la mort, ni la crainte : c'était anonyme. Les pommettes me brûlaient et j'avais mal au crâne.

Je me secouai et regardai mes deux compagnons. Tom avait enfoui sa tête dans ses mains, je ne voyais que sa nuque grasse et blanche. Le petit Juan était de beaucoup le plus mal en point, il avait la bouche ouverte et ses narines tremblaient. Le médecin s'approcha de lui et lui posa la main sur l'épaule comme pour le réconforter : mais ses yeux restaient froids. Puis je vis la main du Belge descendre sournoisement le long du bras de Juan jusqu'au poignet. Juan se laissait faire avec indifférence. Le Belge lui prit le poignet entre trois doigts, avec un air distrait, en même temps il recula un peu et s'arrangea pour me tourner le dos. Mais je me penchai en arrière et je le vis tirer sa montre et la consulter un instant sans lâcher le poignet du petit. Au bout d'un moment, il laissa retomber la main inerte et alla s'adosser au mur, puis, comme s'il se rappelait soudain quelque chose de très important qu'il fallait noter sur-le-champ, il prit un carnet dans sa poche et y inscrivit quelques lignes. « Le salaud, pensai-je avec colère, qu'il ne vienne pas me tâter le pouls, je lui enverrai mon poing dans sa sale gueule. »

Il ne vint pas, mais je sentis qu'il me regardait. Je levai la tête et lui rendis son regard. Il me dit d'une voix impersonnelle :

— Vous ne trouvez pas qu'on grelotte ici ?

Il avait l'air d'avoir froid ; il était violet.

— Je n'ai pas froid, lui répondis-je.

Il ne cessait pas de me regarder, d'un œil dur. Brusquement je compris et je portai mes mains à ma figure : j'étais trempé de sueur. Dans cette cave, au gros de l'hiver, en plein courant d'air, je suais. Je passai les doigts dans mes cheveux qui étaient feutrés par la transpiration ; en même temps, je m'aperçus que ma chemise était humide et collait à ma peau : je ruisselais depuis une heure au moins et je n'avais rien senti. Mais ça n'avait pas échappé au cochon de Belge ; il avait vu les gouttes rouler sur mes joues et il avait pensé : c'est la manifestation d'un état de terreur quasi pathologique ; et il s'était senti normal et fier de l'être parce qu'il avait froid. Je voulus me lever pour aller lui casser la figure, mais à peine avais-je ébauché un geste que ma honte et ma colère furent effacées ; je retombai sur le banc avec indifférence.

Je me contentai de me frictionner le cou avec mon mouchoir parce que, maintenant, je sentais la sueur qui gouttait de mes cheveux sur ma nuque et c'était désagréable. Je renonçai d'ailleurs bientôt à me frictionner, c'était inutile : déjà mon mouchoir était bon à tordre, et je suais toujours. Je suais aussi des fesses et mon pantalon humide adhérait au banc.

Le petit Juan parla tout à coup.

— Vous êtes médecin ?

— Oui, dit le Belge.

— Est-ce qu'on souffre... longtemps ?

— Oh ! Quand... ? Mais non, dit le Belge d'une voix paternelle, c'est vite fini.

Il avait l'air de rassurer un malade payant.

— Mais je... on m'avait dit... qu'il fallait souvent deux salves.

— Quelquefois, dit le Belge en hochant la tête. Il peut se faire que la première salve n'atteigne aucun des organes vitaux.

— Alors il faut qu'ils rechargent les fusils et qu'ils visent de nouveau ?

Il réfléchit et ajouta d'une voix enrouée :

— Ça prend du temps !

Il avait une peur affreuse de souffrir, il ne pensait qu'à ça : c'était de son âge. Moi je n'y pensais plus beaucoup et ce n'était pas la crainte de souffrir qui me faisait transpirer.

Je me levai et je marchai jusqu'au tas de poussier. Tom sursauta et me jeta un regard haineux : je l'agaçais parce que mes souliers craquaient. Je me demandais si j'avais le visage aussi terreux que lui : je vis qu'il suait aussi. Le ciel était superbe, aucune lumière ne se glissait dans ce coin sombre, et je n'avais qu'à lever la tête pour apercevoir la Grande Ourse. Mais ça n'était plus comme auparavant : l'avant-veille, de mon cachot de l'archevêché, je pouvais voir un grand morceau de ciel et chaque heure du jour me rappelait un souvenir différent. Le matin quand le ciel était d'un bleu dur et léger, je pensais à des plages au bord de l'Atlantique ; à midi je voyais le soleil et je me rappelais un bar de Séville, où je buvais du manzanilla en mangeant des anchois et des olives ; l'après-midi j'étais à l'ombre et je pensais à l'ombre profonde qui s'étend sur la moitié des arènes pendant que l'autre moitié scintille au soleil : c'était vraiment pénible de voir ainsi toute la terre se refléter dans le ciel. Mais à présent je pouvais regarder en l'air tant que je voulais, le ciel ne m'évoquait plus rien. J'aimais mieux ça. Je revins m'asseoir près de Tom. Un long moment passa.

Tom se mit à parler, d'une voix basse. Il fallait toujours qu'il parlât, sans ça il ne se reconnaissait pas bien dans ses pensées. Je pense que c'était à moi qu'il s'adressait mais il ne me regardait pas. Sans doute avait-il peur de me voir comme j'étais, gris et suant : nous étions pareils et pires que des miroirs l'un pour l'autre. Il regardait le Belge, le vivant.

— Tu comprends, toi ? disait-il. Moi, je comprends pas.

Je me mis aussi à parler à voix basse. Je regardais le Belge.

— Quoi, qu'est-ce qu'il y a ?

— Il va nous arriver quelque chose que je ne peux pas comprendre.

Il y avait une étrange odeur autour de Tom. Il me sembla que j'étais plus sensible aux odeurs qu'à l'ordinaire. Je ricanai :

— Tu comprendras tout à l'heure.

— Ça n'est pas clair, dit-il d'un air obstiné. Je veux bien avoir du courage, mais il faudrait au moins que je sache... Écoute, on va nous amener dans la cour. Les types vont se ranger devant nous. Combien seront-ils ?

— Je ne sais pas. Cinq ou huit. Pas plus.

— Ça va. Ils seront huit. On leur criera : « En joue », et je verrai les huit fusils braqués sur moi. Je pense que je voudrai rentrer dans le mur, je pousserai le mur avec le dos de toutes mes forces, et le mur résistera, comme dans les cauchemars. Tout ça je peux me l'imaginer. Ah ! si tu savais comme je peux me l'imaginer.

— Ça va ! lui dis-je, je me l'imagine aussi.

— Ça doit faire un mal de chien. Tu sais qu'ils visent les yeux et la bouche pour défigurer, ajouta-t-il méchamment. Je sens déjà les blessures ; depuis une heure j'ai des douleurs dans la tête et dans le cou. Pas de vraies douleurs ; c'est pis : ce sont les douleurs que je sentirai demain matin. Mais après ?

Je comprenais très bien ce qu'il voulait dire, mais je ne voulais pas en avoir l'air. Quant aux douleurs, moi aussi je les portais dans mon corps, comme une foule de petites balafres. Je ne pouvais pas m'y faire, mais j'étais comme lui, je n'y attachais pas d'importance.

— Après, dis-je rudement, tu boufferas du pissenlit.

Il se mit à parler pour lui seul : il ne lâchait pas des yeux le Belge. Celui-ci n'avait pas l'air d'écouter. Je savais ce qu'il était venu faire ; ce que nous pensions ne l'intéressait pas ; il était venu regarder nos corps, des corps qui agonisaient tout vifs.

— C'est comme dans les cauchemars, disait Tom. On veut penser à quelque chose, on a tout le temps l'impression que ça y est, qu'on va comprendre et puis ça glisse, ça vous échappe et ça retombe. Je me dis : après, il n'y aura plus rien. Mais je ne comprends pas ce que ça veut dire. Il y a des moments où j'y arrive presque... et puis ça retombe, je recommence à penser aux douleurs, aux balles, aux détonations. Je suis matérialiste, je te le jure ; je ne deviens pas fou. Mais il y a quelque chose qui ne va pas. Je vois mon cadavre : ça n'est pas difficile mais c'est *moi* qui le vois, avec *mes* yeux. Il faudrait que j'arrive à penser... à penser que je ne verrai plus rien, que je n'entendrai plus rien et que le monde continuera pour les autres. On n'est pas faits pour penser ça, Pablo. Tu peux me croire : ça m'est déjà arrivé de veiller toute une nuit en attendant quelque chose. Mais cette chose-là, ça n'est pas pareil : ça nous prendra par-derrière, Pablo, et nous n'aurons pas pu nous y préparer.

— La ferme, lui dis-je, veux-tu que j'appelle un confesseur ?

Il ne répondit pas. J'avais déjà remarqué qu'il avait tendance à faire le prophète et à m'appeler Pablo en parlant d'une voix blanche. Je n'aimais pas beaucoup ça ; mais il paraît que tous les Irlandais sont ainsi. J'avais l'impression vague qu'il sentait l'urine. Au fond je n'avais pas beaucoup de sympathie pour Tom et je ne voyais pas pourquoi, sous prétexte que nous allions mourir ensemble, j'aurais dû en avoir davantage. Il y a des types avec qui ç'aurait été différent. Avec Ramon Gris, par exemple. Mais, entre Tom et Juan, je me sentais seul. D'ailleurs, j'aimais mieux ça : avec Ramon je me serais peut-être attendri. Mais j'étais terriblement dur, à ce moment-là, et je voulais rester dur.

Il continua à mâchonner des mots, avec une espèce de distraction. Il parlait sûrement pour s'empêcher de penser. Il sentait l'urine à plein nez comme les vieux prostatiques. Naturellement j'étais de son avis, tout ce qu'il disait j'aurais pu le dire : ça n'est pas *naturel* de mourir. Et, depuis que j'allais mourir, plus rien ne me semblait naturel, ni ce tas de poussier, ni le banc, ni la sale gueule de Pedro. Seulement, ça me déplaisait de penser les mêmes choses que Tom. Et je savais bien que, tout au long de la nuit, à cinq minutes près, nous continuerions à penser les choses en même temps, à suer ou à frissonner en même temps. Je le regardai de côté et, pour la première fois, il me parut étrange : il portait sa mort sur sa figure. J'étais blessé dans mon orgueil : pendant vingt-quatre heures, j'avais vécu aux côtés de Tom, je l'avais écouté, je lui avais parlé, et je savais que nous n'avions rien de commun. Et maintenant nous nous ressemblions comme des frères jumeaux, simplement parce que nous allions crever ensemble. Tom me prit la main sans me regarder :

— Pablo, je me demande... je me demande si c'est bien vrai qu'on s'anéantit.

Je dégageai ma main, je lui dis :

— Regarde entre tes pieds, salaud.

Il y avait une flaque entre ses pieds, et des gouttes tombaient de son pantalon.

— Qu'est-ce que c'est ? dit-il avec effarement.

— Tu pisses dans ta culotte, lui dis-je.

— C'est pas vrai, dit-il furieux, je ne pisse pas, je ne sens rien.

Le Belge s'était approché. Il demanda avec une fausse sollicitude :

— Vous vous sentez souffrant ?

Tom ne répondit pas. Le Belge regarda la flaque sans rien dire.

— Je ne sais pas ce que c'est, dit Tom d'un ton farouche, mais je n'ai pas peur. Je vous jure que je n'ai pas peur.

Le Belge ne répondit pas. Tom se leva et alla pisser dans un coin. Il revint en boutonnant sa braguette, se rassit et ne souffla plus mot. Le Belge prenait des notes.

Nous le regardions tous les trois parce qu'il était vivant. Il avait les gestes d'un vivant, les soucis d'un vivant ; il grelottait dans cette cave, comme devaient grelotter les vivants ; il avait un corps obéissant et bien nourri. Nous autres nous ne sentions plus guère nos corps — plus de la même façon, en tout cas. J'avais envie de tâter mon pantalon, entre mes jambes, mais je n'osais pas ; je regardais le Belge, arqué sur ses jambes, maître de ses muscles — et qui pouvait penser à demain. Nous étions là, trois ombres privées de sang ; nous le regardions et nous sucions sa vie comme des vampires.

Il finit par s'approcher du petit Juan. Voulut-il lui tâter la nuque pour quelque motif professionnel ou bien obéit-il à une impulsion charitable ? S'il agit par charité ce fut la seule et unique fois de toute la nuit. Il caressa le crâne et le cou du petit Juan. Le petit se laissait faire, sans le quitter des yeux, puis, tout à coup, il lui saisit la main et la regarda d'un drôle d'air. Il tenait la main du Belge entre les deux siennes, et elles n'avaient rien de plaisant, les deux pinces grises qui serraient cette main grasse et rougeaude. Je me doutais bien de ce qui allait arriver et Tom devait s'en douter aussi : mais le Belge n'y voyait que du feu, il souriait paternellement. Au bout d'un moment, le petit porta la grosse patte rouge à sa bouche et voulut la mordre. Le Belge se dégagea vivement et recula jusqu'au mur en trébuchant. Pendant une seconde il nous regarda avec horreur, il devait comprendre tout d'un coup que nous n'étions pas des hommes comme lui. Je me mis à rire, et l'un des gardiens sursauta. L'autre s'était endormi, ses yeux, grands ouverts, étaient blancs.

Je me sentais las et surexcité, à la fois. Je ne voulais plus penser à ce qui arriverait à l'aube, à la mort. Ça ne rimait à rien, je ne rencontrais que des mots ou du vide. Mais dès que j'essayais de penser à autre chose je voyais des canons de fusil braqués sur moi. J'ai peut-être vécu vingt fois de suite mon exécution ; une fois même, j'ai cru que ça y était pour de bon : j'avais dû m'endormir une minute. Ils me traînaient vers le mur, et je me débattais ; je leur demandais pardon. Je me réveillai en sursaut et je regardai le Belge : j'avais peur d'avoir crié dans mon sommeil. Mais il se lissait la moustache, il n'avait rien remarqué. Si j'avais voulu, je crois que j'aurais pu dormir un moment : je veillais depuis quarante-huit heures, j'étais à bout. Mais je n'avais pas envie de perdre deux heures de vie : ils seraient venus me réveiller à l'aube, je les aurais suivis, hébété de sommeil, et j'aurais clamecé sans faire « ouf » ; je ne voulais pas de ça, je ne voulais pas mourir comme une bête, je voulais comprendre. Et puis je craignais d'avoir des cauchemars. Je me levai, je me promenai de long en large et, pour me changer les idées, je me mis à penser à ma vie passée. Une foule de souvenirs me revinrent, pêle-mêle. Il y en avait de bons et de mauvais — ou du moins je les appelais comme ça *avant.* Il y avait des visages et des histoires. Je revis le visage d'un petit novillero qui s'était fait encorner à Valence pendant la Feria, celui d'un de mes oncles, celui de Ramon Gris. Je me rappelai des histoires : comment j'avais chômé pendant trois mois en 1926, comment j'avais manqué crever de faim. Je me souvins d'une nuit que j'avais passée sur un banc à Grenade : je n'avais pas mangé depuis trois jours, j'étais enragé, je ne voulais pas crever. Ça me fit sourire. Avec quelle âpreté, je courais après le bonheur, après les femmes, après la liberté. Pour quoi faire ? J'avais voulu libérer l'Espagne, j'admirais Pi y Margall, j'avais adhéré au mouvement anarchiste, j'avais parlé dans des réunions publiques : je prenais tout au sérieux, comme si j'avais été immortel.

A ce moment-là, j'eus l'impression que je tenais toute ma vie devant moi et je pensai : « C'est un sacré mensonge. » Elle ne valait rien puisqu'elle était finie. Je me demandai comment j'avais pu me promener, rigoler avec des filles : je n'aurais pas remué le petit doigt si seulement j'avais imaginé que je mourrais comme ça. Ma vie était devant moi, close, fermée, comme un sac, et pourtant tout ce qu'il y avait dedans était inachevé. Un instant, j'essayai de la juger. J'aurais voulu me dire : c'est une belle vie. Mais on ne pouvait pas porter de jugement sur elle, c'était une ébauche ; j'avais passé mon temps à tirer des traites pour l'éternité, je n'avais rien compris. Je ne regrettais rien : il y avait des tas de choses que j'aurais pu regretter, le goût du manzanilla ou bien les bains que je prenais en été dans une petite crique près de Cadix ; mais la mort avait tout désenchanté.

Le Belge eut une fameuse idée, soudain.

— Mes amis, nous dit-il, je puis me charger — sous réserve que l'administration militaire y consentira — de porter un mot de vous, un souvenir aux gens qui vous aiment...

Tom grogna :

— J'ai personne.

Je ne répondis rien. Tom attendit un instant, puis me considéra avec curiosité :

— Tu ne fais rien dire à Concha ?

— Non.

Je détestais cette complicité tendre : c'était ma faute, j'avais parlé de Concha la nuit précédente, j'aurais dû me retenir. J'étais avec elle depuis un an. La veille encore, je me serais coupé un bras à coups de hache pour la revoir cinq minutes. C'est pour ça que j'en avais parlé, c'était plus fort que moi. A présent je n'avais plus envie de la revoir, je n'avais plus rien à lui dire. Je n'aurais même pas voulu la serrer dans mes bras : j'avais horreur de mon corps parce qu'il était devenu gris et qu'il suait — et je n'étais pas sûr de ne pas avoir horreur du sien. Concha pleurerait quand elle apprendrait ma mort ; pendant des mois, elle n'aurait plus de goût à vivre. Mais tout de même c'était moi qui allais mourir. Je pensai à ses beaux yeux tendres. Quand elle me regardait, quelque chose passait d'elle à moi. Mais je pensai que c'était fini : si elle me regardait *à présent* son regard resterait dans ses yeux, il n'irait pas jusqu'à moi. J'étais seul.

Tom aussi était seul, mais pas de la même manière. Il s'était assis à califourchon et il s'était mis à regarder le banc avec une espèce de sourire, il avait l'air étonné. Il avança la main et toucha le bois avec précaution, comme s'il avait peur de casser quelque chose, ensuite il retira vivement sa main et frissonna. Je ne me serais pas amusé à toucher le banc, si j'avais été Tom ; c'était encore de la comédie d'Irlandais, mais je trouvais aussi que les objets avaient un drôle d'air : ils étaient plus effacés, moins denses qu'à l'ordinaire. Il suffisait que je regarde le banc, la lampe, le tas de poussier, pour que je sente que j'allais mourir. Naturellement, je ne pouvais pas clairement penser ma mort, mais je la voyais partout, sur les choses, dans la façon dont les choses avaient reculé et se tenaient à distance, discrètement, comme des gens qui parlent bas au chevet d'un mourant. C'était *sa* mort que Tom venait de toucher sur le banc.

Dans l'état où j'étais, si l'on était venu m'annoncer que je pouvais rentrer tranquillement chez moi, qu'on me laissait la vie sauve, ça m'aurait laissé froid : quelques heures ou quelques années d'attente c'est tout pareil, quand on a perdu l'illusion d'être éternel. Je ne tenais plus à rien, en un sens, j'étais calme. Mais c'était un calme horrible — à cause de mon corps : mon corps, je voyais avec ses yeux, j'entendais avec ses oreilles, mais ça n'était plus moi ; il suait et tremblait tout seul, et je ne le reconnaissais plus. J'étais obligé de le toucher et de le regarder pour savoir ce qu'il devenait, comme si ç'avait été le corps d'un autre. Par moments, je le sentais encore, je sentais des glissements, des espèces de dégringolades, comme lorsqu'on est dans un avion qui pique du nez, ou bien je sentais battre mon cœur. Mais ça ne me rassurait pas : tout ce qui venait de mon corps avait un sale air louche. La plupart du temps, il se taisait, il se tenait coi, et je ne sentais plus rien qu'une espèce de pesanteur, une présence immonde contre moi ; j'avais l'impression d'être lié à une vermine énorme. A un moment, je tâtai mon pantalon et je sentis qu'il était humide ; je ne savais pas s'il était mouillé de sueur ou d'urine, mais j'allai pisser sur le tas de charbon, par précaution.

Le Belge tira sa montre et la regarda. Il dit :

— Il est trois heures et demie.

Le salaud ! Il avait dû le faire exprès. Tom sauta en l'air ; nous ne nous étions pas encore aperçus que le temps s'écoulait ; la nuit nous entourait comme une masse informe et sombre, je ne me rappelais même plus qu'elle avait commencé.

Le petit Juan se mit à crier. Il se tordait les mains, il suppliait :

— Je ne veux pas mourir, je ne veux pas mourir.

Il courut à travers toute la cave en levant les bras en l'air, puis il s'abattit sur une des paillasses et sanglota. Tom le regardait avec des yeux mornes et n'avait même plus envie de le consoler. Par le fait ce n'était pas la peine : le petit faisait plus de bruit que nous, mais il était moins atteint : il était comme un malade qui se défend contre son mal par de la fièvre. Quand il n'y a même plus de fièvre, c'est beaucoup plus grave.

Il pleurait : je voyais bien qu'il avait pitié de lui-même ; il ne pensait pas à la mort. Une seconde, une seule seconde, j'eus envie de pleurer moi aussi, de pleurer de pitié sur moi. Mais ce fut le contraire qui arriva : je jetai un coup d'œil sur le petit, je vis ses maigres épaules sanglotantes et je me sentis inhumain : je ne pouvais avoir pitié ni des autres ni de moi-même. Je me dis : « Je veux mourir proprement. »

Tom s'était levé, il se plaça juste en dessous de l'ouverture ronde et se mit à guetter le jour. Moi j'étais buté, je voulais mourir proprement et je ne pensais qu'à ça. Mais, par en dessous, depuis que le médecin nous avait dit l'heure, je sentais le temps qui filait, qui coulait goutte à goutte.

Il faisait encore noir quand j'entendis la voix de Tom :

— Tu les entends.

— Oui.

Des types marchaient dans la cour.

— Qu'est-ce qu'ils viennent foutre ? Ils ne peuvent pourtant pas tirer dans le noir.

Au bout d'un moment nous n'entendîmes plus rien. Je dis à Tom :

— Voilà le jour.

Pedro se leva en bâillant et vint souffler la lampe. Il dit à son copain.

— Mince de froid.

La cave était devenue toute grise. Nous entendîmes des coups de feu dans le lointain.

— Ça commence, dis-je à Tom, ils doivent faire ça dans la cour de derrière.

Tom demanda au médecin de lui donner une

cigarette. Moi je n'en voulais pas ; je ne voulais ni cigarettes ni alcool. A partir de cet instant, ils ne cessèrent pas de tirer.

— Tu te rends compte ? dit Tom.

Il voulait ajouter quelque chose mais il se tut, il regardait la porte. La porte s'ouvrit, et un lieutenant entra avec quatre soldats. Tom laissa tomber sa cigarette.

— Steinbock ?

Tom ne répondit pas. Ce fut Pedro qui le désigna.

— Juan Mirbal ?

— C'est celui qui est sur la paillasse.

— Levez-vous, dit le lieutenant.

Juan ne bougea pas. Deux soldats le prirent aux aisselles et le mirent sur ses pieds. Mais dès qu'ils l'eurent lâché il retomba.

Les soldats hésitèrent.

— Ce n'est pas le premier qui se trouve mal, dit le lieutenant, vous n'avez qu'à le porter, vous deux ; on s'arrangera là-bas.

Il se tourna vers Tom :

— Allons, venez.

Tom sortit entre deux soldats. Deux autres soldats suivaient, ils portaient le petit par les aisselles et par les jarrets. Il n'était pas évanoui ; il avait les yeux grands ouverts, et des larmes coulaient le long de ses joues. Quand je voulus sortir, le lieutenant m'arrêta :

— C'est vous, Ibbieta ?

— Oui.

— Vous allez attendre ici : on viendra vous chercher tout à l'heure.

Ils sortirent. Le Belge et les deux geôliers sortirent aussi ; je restai seul. Je ne comprenais pas ce qui m'arrivait, mais j'aurais mieux aimé qu'ils en finissent tout de suite. J'entendais les salves à intervalles presque réguliers ; à chacune d'elles, je tressaillais. J'avais envie de hurler et de m'arracher les cheveux. Mais je serrais les dents et j'enfonçais les mains dans mes poches parce que je voulais rester propre.

Au bout d'une heure, on vint me chercher et on me conduisit au premier étage, dans une petite pièce qui sentait le cigare et dont la chaleur me parut suffocante. Il y avait là deux officiers qui fumaient assis dans des fauteuils, avec des papiers sur leurs genoux.

— Tu t'appelles Ibbieta ?

— Oui.

— Où est Ramon Gris ?

— Je ne sais pas.

Celui qui m'interrogeait était petit et gros. Il avait des yeux durs derrière ses lorgnons. Il me dit :

— Approche.

Je m'approchai. Il se leva et me prit par les bras en me regardant d'un air à me faire rentrer sous terre. En même temps, il me pinçait les biceps de toutes ses forces. Ça n'était pas pour me faire mal, c'était le grand jeu : il voulait me dominer. Il jugeait nécessaire aussi de m'envoyer son souffle pourri en pleine figure. Nous restâmes un moment comme ça, moi ça me donnait plutôt envie de rire. Il en faut beaucoup plus pour intimider un homme qui va mourir : ça ne prenait pas. Il me repoussa violemment et se rassit. Il dit :

— C'est ta vie contre la sienne. On te laisse la vie sauve si tu nous dis où il est.

Ces deux types chamarrés avec leurs cravaches et leurs bottes, c'étaient tout de même des hommes qui allaient mourir. Un peu plus tard que moi, mais pas beaucoup plus. Et ils s'occupaient à chercher des noms sur leurs paperasses, ils couraient après d'autres hommes pour les emprisonner ou les supprimer ; ils avaient des opinions sur l'avenir de l'Espagne et sur d'autres sujets. Leurs petites activités me paraissaient choquantes et burlesques : je n'arrivais plus à me mettre à leur place, il me semblait qu'ils étaient fous.

Le petit gros me regardait toujours, en fouettant ses bottes de sa cravache. Tous ses gestes étaient calculés pour lui donner l'allure d'une bête vive et féroce.

— Alors ? C'est compris ?

— Je ne sais pas où est Gris, répondis-je. Je croyais qu'il était à Madrid.

L'autre officier leva sa main pâle avec indolence. Cette indolence aussi était calculée. Je voyais tous leurs petits manèges et j'étais stupéfait qu'il se trouvât des hommes pour s'amuser à ça.

— Vous avez un quart d'heure pour réfléchir, dit-il lentement. Emmenez-le à la lingerie, vous le ramènerez dans un quart d'heure. S'il persiste à refuser, on l'exécutera sur-le-champ.

Ils savaient ce qu'ils faisaient : j'avais passé la nuit dans l'attente ; après ça, ils m'avaient encore fait attendre une heure dans la cave, pendant qu'on fusillait Tom et Juan, et maintenant ils m'enfermaient dans la lingerie ; ils avaient dû préparer leur coup depuis la veille. Ils se disaient que les nerfs s'usent à la longue et ils espéraient m'avoir comme ça.

Ils se trompaient bien. Dans la lingerie, je m'assis sur un escabeau, parce que je me sentais très faible et je me mis à réfléchir. Mais pas à leur proposition. Naturellement, je savais où était Gris : il se cachait chez ses cousins, à quatre kilomètres de la ville. Je savais aussi que je ne révélerais pas sa cachette, sauf s'ils me torturaient (mais ils n'avaient pas l'air d'y songer). Tout cela était parfaitement réglé, définitif et ne m'intéressait nullement. Seulement j'aurais voulu comprendre les raisons de ma conduite. Je préférais plutôt crever que de livrer Gris. Pourquoi ? Je n'aimais plus Ramon Gris. Mon amitié pour lui était morte un peu avant l'aube en même temps que mon amour pour Concha, en même temps que mon désir de vivre. Sans doute je l'estimais toujours ; c'était un dur. Mais ça n'était pas pour cette raison que j'acceptais de mourir à sa place ; sa vie n'avait pas plus de valeur que la mienne ; aucune vie n'avait de valeur. On allait coller un homme contre un mur et lui tirer dessus jusqu'à ce qu'il en crève : que ce fût moi ou Gris ou un autre c'était pareil. Je savais bien qu'il était plus utile que moi à la cause de l'Espagne, mais je me foutais de l'Espagne et de l'anarchie : rien n'avait plus d'importance. Et pourtant j'étais là, je pouvais sauver ma peau en livrant Gris et je me refusais à le faire. Je trouvais ça plutôt comique : c'était de l'obstination. Je pensai : « Faut-il être têtu ! » Et une drôle de gaieté m'envahit.

Ils vinrent me chercher et me ramenèrent auprès des deux officiers. Un rat partit sous nos pieds et ça m'amusa. Je me tournai vers un des phalangistes et je lui dis :

— Vous avez vu le rat ?

Il ne répondit pas. Il était sombre, il se prenait au sérieux. Moi j'avais envie de rire mais je me retenais parce que j'avais peur, si je commençais, de ne plus pouvoir m'arrêter. Le phalangiste portait des moustaches. Je lui dis encore :

— Il faut couper tes moustaches, ballot.

Je trouvais drôle qu'il laissât de son vivant les poils envahir sa figure. Il me donna un coup de pied sans grande conviction, et je me tus.

— Eh bien, dit le gros officier, tu as réfléchi ?

Je les regardai avec curiosité comme des insectes d'une espèce très rare. Je leur dis :

— Je sais où il est. Il est caché dans le cimetière. Dans un caveau ou dans la cabane des fossoyeurs.

C'était pour leur faire une farce. Je voulais les voir se lever, boucler leurs ceinturons et donner des ordres d'un air affairé.

Ils sautèrent sur leurs pieds.

— Allons-y. Moles, allez demander quinze hommes au lieutenant Lopez. Toi, me dit le petit gros, si tu as dit la vérité, je n'ai qu'une parole. Mais tu le paieras cher si tu t'es fichu de nous.

Ils partirent dans un brouhaha, et j'attendis paisiblement sous la garde des phalangistes. De temps en temps, je souriais parce que je pensais à la tête qu'ils allaient faire. Je me sentais abruti et malicieux. Je les imaginais, soulevant les pierres tombales, ouvrant une à une les portes des caveaux. Je me représentais la situation comme si j'avais été un autre : ce prisonnier obstiné à faire le héros, ces graves phalangistes avec leurs moustaches et ces hommes en uniforme qui couraient entre les tombes ; c'était d'un comique irrésistible.

Au bout d'une demi-heure le petit gros revint seul. Je pensai qu'il venait donner l'ordre de m'exécuter. Les autres devaient être restés au cimetière.

L'officier me regarda. Il n'avait pas du tout l'air penaud.

— Emmenez-le dans la grande cour avec les autres, dit-il. A la fin des opérations militaires, un tribunal régulier décidera de son sort.

Je crus que je n'avais pas compris. Je lui demandai :

— Alors on ne me... on ne me fusillera pas ?...

— Pas maintenant en tout cas. Après, ça ne me regarde plus.

Je ne comprenais toujours pas. Je lui dis :

— Mais pourquoi ?

Il haussa les épaules sans répondre, et les soldats m'emmenèrent. Dans la grande cour il y avait une centaine de prisonniers, des femmes, des enfants, quelques vieillards. Je me mis à tourner autour de la pelouse centrale, j'étais hébété. A midi, on nous fit manger au réfectoire. Deux ou trois types m'interpellèrent. Je devais les connaître, mais je ne leur répondis pas : je ne savais même plus où j'étais.

Vers le soir, on poussa dans la cour une dizaine de prisonniers nouveaux. Je reconnus Garcia, le boulanger. Il me dit :

— Sacré veinard ! Je ne pensais pas te revoir vivant.

— Ils m'avaient condamné à mort, dis-je, et puis ils ont changé d'idée. Je ne sais pas pourquoi.

— Ils m'ont arrêté à deux heures, dit Garcia.

— Pourquoi ?

Garcia ne faisait pas de politique.

— Je ne sais pas, dit-il. Ils arrêtent tous ceux qui ne pensent pas comme eux.

Il baissa la voix.

— Ils ont eu Gris.

Je me mis à trembler.

— Quand ?

— Ce matin. Il avait fait le con. Il a quitté son cousin mardi parce qu'ils avaient eu des mots. Il ne manquait pas de types qui l'auraient caché, mais il ne voulait plus rien devoir à personne. Il a dit : « Je me serais caché chez Ibbieta, mais puisqu'ils l'ont pris j'irai me cacher au cimetière. »

— Au cimetière ?

— Oui. C'était con. Naturellement, ils y ont passé ce matin, ça devait arriver. Ils l'ont trouvé dans la cabane des fossoyeurs. Il leur a tiré dessus, et ils l'ont descendu.

— Au cimetière !

Tout se mit à tourner et je me retrouvai assis par terre : je riais si fort que les larmes me vinrent aux yeux.

*La chambre*

## I

M$^{me}$ Darbédat tenait un rahat-loukoum entre ses doigts. Elle l'approcha de ses lèvres avec précaution et retint sa respiration de peur que ne s'envolât à son souffle la fine poussière de sucre dont il était saupoudré : « Il est à la rose », se dit-elle. Elle mordit brusquement dans cette chair vitreuse, et un parfum de croupi lui emplit la bouche. « C'est curieux comme la maladie affine les sensations. » Elle se mit à penser à des mosquées, à des Orientaux obséquieux (elle avait été à Alger pendant son voyage de noces) et ses lèvres pâles ébauchèrent un sourire : le rahat-loukoum aussi était obséquieux.

Il fallut qu'elle passât, à plusieurs reprises, le plat de la main sur les pages de son livre, parce qu'elles s'étaient, malgré ses précautions, recouvertes d'une mince couche de poudre blanche. Ses mains faisaient glisser, rouler, crisser les petits grains de sucre sur le papier lisse : « Ça me rappelle Arcachon, quand je lisais sur la plage... » Elle avait passé l'été de 1907 au bord de la mer. Elle portait alors un grand chapeau de paille avec un ruban vert ; elle s'installait tout près de la jetée, avec un roman de Gyp ou de Colette Yver. Le vent faisait pleuvoir sur ses genoux des tourbillons de sable, et, de temps à autre, elle secouait son livre en le tenant par les coins. C'était bien la même sensation : seulement les grains de sable étaient tout secs, tandis que ces petits graviers de sucre collaient un peu au bout de ses doigts. Elle revit une bande de ciel gris perle au-dessus d'une mer noire. « Ève n'était pas encore née. » Elle se sentait tout alourdie de souvenirs et précieuse comme un coffret de santal. Le nom du roman qu'elle lisait alors lui revint tout à coup à la mémoire : il s'appelait *Petite Madame*, il n'était pas ennuyeux. Mais depuis qu'un mal inconnu la retenait dans sa chambre, Mme Darbédat préférait les mémoires et les ouvrages historiques. Elle souhaitait que la souffrance, des lectures graves, une attention vigilante et tournée vers ses souvenirs, vers ses sensations les plus exquises, la mûrissent comme un beau fruit de serre.

Elle pensa, avec un peu d'énervement, que son mari allait bientôt frapper à sa porte. Les autres jours de la semaine il venait seulement vers le soir, il la baisait au front en silence et lisait *Le Temps* en face d'elle, dans la bergère. Mais, le jeudi, c'était « le jour » de M. Darbédat : il allait passer une heure chez sa fille, en général de trois à quatre. Avant de sortir, il entrait chez sa femme et tous deux s'entretenaient de leur gendre avec amertume. Ces conversations du jeudi, prévisibles jusqu'en leurs moindres détails, épuisaient Mme Darbédat. M. Darbédat remplissait la calme chambre de sa présence. Il ne s'asseyait pas, marchait de long en large, tournait sur lui-même. Chacun de ses emportements blessait Mme Darbédat comme un éclat de verre. Ce jeudi-là, c'était pis encore que de coutume : à la pensée qu'il faudrait, tout à l'heure, répéter à son mari les aveux d'Ève et voir ce grand corps terrifiant bondir de fureur, Mme Darbédat avait des sueurs. Elle prit un loukoum dans la soucoupe, le considéra quelques instants avec hésitation, puis elle le reposa tristement : elle n'aimait pas que son mari la vît manger des loukoums.

Elle sursauta en entendant frapper.

— Entre, dit-elle d'une voix faible.

M. Darbédat entra sur la pointe des pieds.

— Je vais voir Ève, dit-il comme chaque jeudi.

M$^{me}$ Darbédat lui sourit.

— Tu l'embrasseras pour moi.

M. Darbédat ne répondit pas et plissa le front d'un air soucieux : tous les jeudis à la même heure, une irritation sourde se mêlait aux pesanteurs de la digestion.

— Je passerai voir Franchot en sortant de chez elle, je voudrais qu'il lui parle sérieusement et qu'il tâche de la convaincre.

Il faisait des visites fréquentes au docteur Franchot. Mais en vain. M$^{me}$ Darbédat haussa les sourcils. Autrefois, quand elle était bien portante, elle haussait volontiers les épaules. Mais depuis que la maladie avait alourdi son corps, elle remplaçait les gestes, qui l'eussent trop fatiguée, par des jeux de physionomie : elle disait oui avec les yeux, non avec les coins de la bouche ; elle levait les sourcils au lieu des épaules.

— Il faudrait pouvoir le lui enlever de force.

— Je t'ai déjà dit que c'était impossible. D'ailleurs la loi est très mal faite. Franchot me disait l'autre jour qu'ils ont des ennuis inimaginables avec les familles : des gens qui ne se décident pas, qui veulent garder le malade chez eux ; les médecins ont les mains liées, ils peuvent donner leur avis, un point c'est tout. Il faudrait, reprit-il, qu'il fasse un scandale public ou alors qu'elle demande elle-même son internement.

— Et ça, dit M$^{me}$ Darbédat, ça n'est pas pour demain.

— Non.

Il se tourna vers le miroir et, plongeant ses doigts dans sa barbe, il se mit à la peigner. M^me^ Darbédat regardait sans affection la nuque rouge et puissante de son mari.

— Si elle continue, dit M. Darbédat, elle deviendra plus toquée que lui, c'est affreusement malsain. Elle ne le quitte pas d'une semelle, elle ne sort jamais sauf pour aller te voir, elle ne reçoit personne. L'atmosphère de leur chambre est tout simplement irrespirable. Elle n'ouvre jamais la fenêtre parce que Pierre ne veut pas. Comme si on devait consulter un malade. Ils font brûler des parfums, je crois, une saleté dans une cassolette, on se croirait à l'église. Ma parole, je me demande quelquefois... elle a des yeux bizarres tu sais.

— Je n'ai pas remarqué, dit M^me^ Darbédat. Je lui trouve l'air naturel. Elle a l'air triste, évidemment.

— Elle a une mine de déterrée. Dort-elle ? Mange-t-elle ? Il ne faut pas l'interroger sur ces sujets-là. Mais je pense qu'avec un gaillard comme Pierre à ses côtés, elle ne doit pas fermer l'œil de la nuit. — Il haussa les épaules : Ce que je trouve fabuleux, c'est que nous, ses parents, nous n'ayons pas le droit de la protéger contre elle-même. Note bien que Pierre serait mieux soigné chez Franchot. Il y a un grand parc. Et puis je pense, ajouta-t-il en souriant un peu, qu'il s'entendrait mieux avec des gens de son espèce. Ces êtres-là sont comme les enfants, il faut les laisser entre eux ; ils forment une espèce de franc-maçonnerie. C'est là qu'on aurait dû le mettre dès le premier jour et je dis : pour lui-même. C'était son intérêt bien entendu.

Il ajouta au bout d'un instant :

— Je te dirai que je n'aime pas la savoir seule avec Pierre, surtout la nuit. Imagine qu'il arrive quelque chose. Pierre a l'air terriblement sournois.

— Je ne sais pas, dit M^me^ Darbédat, s'il y a lieu de beaucoup s'inquiéter, attendu que c'est un air qu'il a toujours eu. Il donnait l'impression de se moquer du monde. Pauvre garçon, reprit-elle en soupirant, avoir eu son orgueil et en être venu là. Il se croyait plus intelligent que nous tous. Il avait une façon de te dire : « Vous avez raison » pour clore les discussions... C'est une bénédiction pour lui qu'il ne puisse pas voir son état.

Elle se rappelait avec déplaisir ce long visage ironique, toujours un peu penché de côté. Pendant les premiers temps du mariage d'Ève, M^me^ Darbédat n'eût pas demandé mieux que d'avoir un peu d'intimité avec son gendre. Mais il avait découragé ses efforts : il ne parlait presque pas, il approuvait toujours avec précipitation et d'un air absent.

M. Darbédat suivait son idée :

— Franchot m'a fait visiter son installation, dit-il, c'est superbe. Les malades ont des chambres particulières, avec des fauteuils de cuir, s'il te plaît, et des lits-divans. Il y a un tennis, tu sais, et ils vont faire construire une piscine.

Il s'était planté devant la fenêtre et regardait à travers la vitre en se dandinant un peu sur ses jambes arquées. Soudain, il pivota sur ses talons, les épaules basses, les mains dans les poches, en souplesse. M^me^ Darbédat sentit qu'elle allait se mettre à transpirer : toutes les fois c'était la même chose ; à présent il allait marcher de long en large comme un ours en cage, et, à chaque pas, ses souliers craqueraient.

— Mon ami, dit-elle, je t'en supplie, assieds-toi, tu me fatigues. — Elle ajouta en hésitant : J'ai quelque chose de grave à te dire.

M. Darbédat s'assit dans la bergère et posa ses mains sur ses genoux ; un léger frisson parcourut l'échine de M^me^ Darbédat : le moment était venu, il fallait qu'elle parlât.

— Tu sais, dit-elle avec une toux d'embarras, que j'ai vu Ève mardi.

— Oui.

— Nous avons bavardé sur un tas de choses, elle était très gentille, il y a longtemps que je ne l'avais vue si en confiance. Alors je l'ai un peu questionnée, je l'ai fait parler sur Pierre. Eh bien, j'ai appris, ajouta-t-elle, embarrassée de nouveau, qu'elle tient *beaucoup* à lui.

— Je le sais parbleu bien, dit M. Darbédat.

Il agaçait un peu M^me^ Darbédat : il fallait toujours lui expliquer minutieusement les choses, en mettant les points sur les *i*. M^me^ Darbédat rêvait de vivre dans le commerce de personnes fines et sensibles qui l'eussent toujours comprise à demi-mot.

— Mais je veux dire, reprit-elle, qu'elle y tient *autrement* que nous ne nous l'imaginions.

M. Darbédat roula des yeux furieux et inquiets, comme chaque fois qu'il ne saisissait pas très bien le sens d'une allusion ou d'une nouvelle :

— Qu'est-ce que ça veut dire ?

— Charles, dit M^me^ Darbédat, ne me fatigue pas. Tu devrais comprendre qu'une mère peut avoir de la peine à dire certaines choses.

— Je ne comprends pas un traître mot à tout ce que tu me racontes, dit M. Darbédat avec irritation. Tu ne veux tout de même pas dire ?...

— Eh bien si ! dit-elle.

— Ils ont encore... encore à présent ?

— Oui ! Oui ! Oui ! fit-elle agacée en trois petits coups secs.

M. Darbédat écarta les bras, baissa la tête et se tut.

— Charles, dit sa femme inquiète, je n'aurais pas

dû te le dire. Mais je ne pouvais pas garder ça pour moi.

— Notre enfant ! dit-il d'une voix lente. Avec ce fou ! Il ne la reconnaît même plus, il l'appelle Agathe. Il faut qu'elle ait perdu le sens de ce qu'elle se doit.

Il releva la tête et regarda sa femme avec sévérité.

— Tu es sûre d'avoir bien compris ?

— Il n'y avait pas de doute possible. Je suis comme toi, ajouta-t-elle vivement ; je ne pouvais pas la croire et d'ailleurs je ne la comprends pas. Moi, rien qu'à l'idée d'être touchée par ce pauvre malheureux... Enfin, soupira-t-elle, je suppose qu'il la tient par là.

— Hélas ! dit M. Darbédat. Tu te souviens de ce que je t'avais dit quand il est venu nous demander sa main ? Je t'ai dit : « Je crois qu'il plaît *trop* à Ève. » Tu n'avais pas voulu me croire.

Il frappa soudain sur la table et rougit violemment :

— C'est de la perversité ! Il la prend dans ses bras et il l'embrasse en l'appelant Agathe et en lui débitant toutes ses calembredaines sur les statues qui volent et je ne sais quoi ! Et elle se laisse faire ! Mais qu'est-ce qu'il y a donc entre eux ? Qu'elle le plaigne de tout son cœur, qu'elle le mette dans une maison de repos où elle puisse le voir tous les jours, à la bonne heure. Mais je n'aurais jamais pensé... Je la considérais comme veuve. Écoute, Jeannette, dit-il d'une voix grave, je vais te parler franchement ; eh bien, si elle a des sens, j'aimerais encore mieux qu'elle prenne un amant !

— Charles, tais-toi ! cria Mme Darbédat.

M. Darbédat prit d'un air las le chapeau et la canne qu'il avait déposés en entrant, sur un guéridon.

— Après ce que tu viens de me dire, conclut-il, il ne me reste pas beaucoup d'espoir. Enfin, je lui parlerai tout de même parce que c'est mon devoir.

Mme Darbédat avait hâte qu'il s'en allât.

— Tu sais, dit-elle pour l'encourager, je crois qu'il y a malgré tout chez Ève plus d'entêtement que... d'autre chose. Elle sait qu'il est incurable mais elle s'obstine, elle ne veut pas en avoir le démenti.

M. Darbédat se flattait rêveusement la barbe.

— De l'entêtement ? Oui, peut-être. Eh bien, si tu as raison, elle finira par se lasser. Il n'est pas commode tous les jours et puis il manque de conversation. Quand je lui dis bonjour, il me tend une main molle et il ne parle pas. Dès qu'ils sont seuls, je pense qu'il revient sur ses idées fixes : elle me dit qu'il lui arrive de crier comme un égorgé parce qu'il a des hallucinations. Des statues. Elles lui font peur parce qu'elles bourdonnent. Il dit qu'elles volent autour de lui et qu'elles lui font des yeux blancs.

Il mettait ses gants ; il reprit :

— Elle se lassera, je ne te dis pas. Mais si elle se détraque auparavant ? Je voudrais qu'elle sorte un peu, qu'elle voie du monde : elle rencontrerait quelque gentil garçon — tiens, un type comme Schröder qui est ingénieur chez Simplon, quelqu'un d'avenir, elle le reverrait un petit peu chez les uns, chez les autres, et elle s'habituerait tout doucement à l'idée de refaire sa vie.

M^me^ Darbédat ne répondit point, par crainte de faire rebondir la conversation. Son mari se pencha sur elle.

— Allons, dit-il, il faut que je parte.

— Adieu, papa, dit M^me^ Darbédat en lui tendant le front. Embrasse-la bien et dis-lui de ma part qu'elle est une pauvre chérie.

Quand son mari fut parti, M^me^ Darbédat se laissa aller au fond de son fauteuil et ferma les yeux, épuisée. « Quelle vitalité », pensa-t-elle avec reproche. Dès qu'elle eut retrouvé un peu de force, elle allongea doucement sa main pâle et prit un loukoum dans la soucoupe, à tâtons et sans ouvrir les yeux.

Ève habitait avec son mari au cinquième étage d'un vieil immeuble, rue du Bac. M. Darbédat grimpa lestement les cent douze marches de l'escalier. Quand il appuya sur le bouton de la sonnette, il n'était même pas essoufflé. Il se rappela avec satisfaction le mot de M^lle^ Dormoy : « Pour votre âge, Charles, vous êtes tout simplement merveilleux. » Jamais il ne se sentait plus fort ni plus sain que le jeudi, surtout après ces alertes escalades.

Ce fut Ève qui vint lui ouvrir : « C'est vrai, elle n'a pas de bonne. Ces filles *ne peuvent pas* rester chez elle : je me mets à leur place. » Il l'embrassa : « Bonjour, la pauvre chérie. »

Ève lui dit bonjour avec une certaine froideur.

— Tu es un peu pâlotte, dit M. Darbédat en lui touchant la joue, tu ne prends pas assez d'exercice.

Il y eut un silence.

— Maman va bien ? demanda Ève.

— Couci-couça. Tu l'as vue mardi ? Eh bien, c'est comme toujours. Ta tante Louise est venue la voir hier, ça lui a fait plaisir. Elle aime bien recevoir des visites, mais il ne faut pas qu'elles restent longtemps. Ta tante Louise venait à Paris avec les petits pour cette histoire d'hypothèques. Je t'en ai parlé, je crois, c'est une drôle d'histoire. Elle est passée à mon bureau pour me demander conseil. Je lui ai dit qu'il n'y avait pas deux partis à prendre : il faut qu'elle vende. Elle a trouvé preneur, d'ailleurs : c'est Bretonnel. Tu te rappelles Bretonnel ? Il s'est retiré des affaires à présent.

Il s'arrêta brusquement : Ève l'écoutait à peine. Il songea avec tristesse qu'elle ne s'intéressait plus à rien. « C'est comme les livres. Autrefois, il fallait les lui arracher. A présent elle ne lit même plus. »

— Comment va Pierre ?

— Bien, dit Ève. Veux-tu le voir ?

— Mais certainement, dit M. Darbédat avec gaieté, je vais lui faire une petite visite.

Il était plein de compassion pour ce malheureux garçon, mais il ne pouvait le voir sans répugnance. « J'ai horreur des êtres malsains. » Évidemment, ce n'était pas la faute de Pierre : il avait une hérédité terriblement chargée. M. Darbédat soupirait : « On a beau prendre des précautions, ces choses-là se savent toujours trop tard. » Non, Pierre n'était pas responsable. Mais, tout de même, il avait toujours porté cette tare en lui ; elle formait le fond de son caractère ; ça n'était pas comme un cancer ou la tuberculose, dont on peut toujours faire abstraction quand on veut juger l'homme tel qu'il est en lui-même. Cette grâce nerveuse et cette subtilité qui avaient tant plu à Ève, quand il faisait sa cour, c'étaient des fleurs de folie. « Il était déjà fou quand il l'a épousée ; seulement ça ne se voyait pas. On se demande, pensa M. Darbédat, où commence la responsabilité, ou, plutôt, où elle s'arrête. En tout cas, il s'analysait trop, il était tout le temps tourné vers lui-même. Mais, est-ce la cause ou l'effet de son mal ? » Il suivait sa fille à travers un long corridor sombre :

— Cet appartement est trop grand pour vous, dit-il, vous devriez déménager.

— Tu me dis ça toutes les fois, papa, répondit Ève, mais je t'ai déjà répondu que Pierre ne veut pas quitter sa chambre.

Ève était étonnante : c'était à se demander si elle se rendait bien compte de l'état de son mari. Il était fou à lier, et elle respectait ses décisions et ses avis comme s'il avait tout son bon sens.

— Ce que j'en dis, c'est pour toi, reprit M. Darbédat légèrement agacé. Il me semble que, si j'étais femme, j'aurais peur dans ces vieilles pièces mal éclairées. Je souhaiterais pour toi un appartement lumineux, comme on en a construit, ces dernières années, du côté d'Auteuil, trois petites pièces bien aérées. Ils ont baissé le prix de leurs loyers parce qu'ils ne trouvent pas de locataires ; ce serait le moment.

Ève tourna doucement le loquet de la porte, et ils entrèrent dans la chambre. M. Darbédat fut pris à la gorge par une lourde odeur d'encens. Les rideaux étaient tirés. Il distingua, dans la pénombre, une nuque maigre au-dessus du dossier d'un fauteuil : Pierre leur tournait le dos : il mangeait.

— Bonjour, Pierre, dit M. Darbédat en élevant la voix. Eh bien, comment allons-nous aujourd'hui ?

M. Darbédat s'approcha : le malade était assis devant une petite table ; il avait l'air sournois.

— Nous avons mangé des œufs à la coque, dit M. Darbédat en haussant encore le ton. C'est bon, ça !

— Je ne suis pas sourd, dit Pierre d'une voix douce.

M. Darbédat, irrité, tourna les yeux vers Ève pour la prendre à témoin. Mais Ève lui rendit un regard dur et se tut. M. Darbédat comprit qu'il l'avait blessée. « Eh bien, tant pis pour elle. » Il était impossible de trouver le ton juste avec ce malheureux garçon : il avait moins de raison qu'un enfant de quatre ans, et Ève aurait voulu qu'on le traitât comme un homme. M. Darbédat ne pouvait se défendre d'attendre avec impatience le moment où tous ces égards ridicules ne seraient plus de saison. Les malades l'agaçaient toujours un peu — et tout particulièrement les fous parce qu'ils avaient tort. Le pauvre Pierre, par exemple, avait tort sur toute la ligne, il ne pouvait souffler mot sans déraisonner, et cependant il eût été vain de lui demander la moindre humilité, ou même une reconnaissance passagère de ses erreurs.

Ève ôta les coquilles d'œuf et le coquetier. Elle mit devant Pierre un couvert avec une fourchette et un couteau.

— Qu'est-ce qu'il va manger, à présent ? dit M. Darbédat, jovial.

— Un bifteck.

Pierre avait pris la fourchette et la tenait au bout de ses longs doigts pâles. Il l'inspecta minutieusement puis il eut un rire léger :

— Ce ne sera pas pour cette fois, murmura-t-il en la reposant ; j'étais prévenu.

Ève s'approcha et regarda la fourchette avec un intérêt passionné.

— Agathe, dit Pierre, donne-m'en une autre.

Ève obéit, et Pierre se mit à manger. Elle avait pris la fourchette suspecte et la tenait serrée dans ses mains sans la quitter des yeux : elle semblait faire un violent effort. « Comme tous leurs gestes et tous leurs rapports sont louches ! » pensa M. Darbédat.

Il était mal à l'aise.

— Attention, dit Pierre, prends-la par le milieu du dos à cause des pinces.

Ève soupira et reposa la fourchette sur la desserte. M. Darbédat sentit la moutarde lui monter au nez. Il ne pensait pas qu'il fût bon de céder à toutes les fantaisies de ce malheureux — même du point de vue de Pierre, c'était pernicieux. Franchot l'avait bien dit : « On ne doit jamais entrer dans le délire d'un malade. » Au lieu de lui donner une autre fourchette, il aurait mieux valu le raisonner doucement et lui faire comprendre que la première était toute pareille aux autres. Il s'avança vers la desserte, prit ostensiblement la fourchette et en effleura les dents d'un doigt léger. Puis il se tourna vers Pierre. Mais celui-ci découpait sa viande d'un air paisible ; il leva sur son beau-père un regard doux et inexpressif.

— Je voudrais bavarder un peu avec toi, dit M. Darbédat à Ève.

Ève le suivit docilement au salon. En s'asseyant sur le canapé, M. Darbédat s'aperçut qu'il avait gardé la fourchette dans sa main. Il la jeta avec humeur sur une console.

— Il fait meilleur ici, dit-il.

— Je n'y viens jamais.

— Je peux fumer ?

— Mais oui, papa, dit Ève avec empressement. Veux-tu un cigare ?

M. Darbédat préféra rouler une cigarette. Il pensait sans ennui à la discussion qu'il allait entamer. En parlant à Pierre, il se sentait embarrassé de sa raison comme un géant peut l'être de sa force quand il joue avec un enfant. Toutes ses qualités de clarté, de netteté, de précision se retournaient contre lui. « Avec ma pauvre Jeannette, il faut bien l'avouer, c'est un peu la même chose. » Certes, M^me^ Darbédat n'était pas folle, mais la maladie l'avait... assoupie. Ève, au contraire, tenait de son père, c'était une nature droite et logique ; avec elle, la discussion devenait un plaisir. « C'est pour cela que je ne veux pas qu'on me l'abîme. » M. Darbédat leva les yeux ; il voulait revoir les traits intelligents et fins de sa fille. Il fut déçu : dans ce visage autrefois si raisonnable et transparent, il y avait maintenant quelque chose de brouillé et d'opaque. Ève était toujours très belle. M. Darbédat remarqua qu'elle s'était fardée avec grand soin, presque avec pompe. Elle avait bleui ses paupières et passé du rimmel sur ses longs cils. Ce maquillage parfait et violent fit une impression pénible à son père :

— Tu es verte sous ton fard, lui dit-il, j'ai peur que tu ne tombes malade. Et comme tu te fardes à présent ! Toi qui étais si discrète.

Ève ne répondit pas et M. Darbédat considéra un instant avec embarras ce visage éclatant et usé, sous la lourde masse des cheveux noirs. Il pensa qu'elle avait l'air d'une tragédienne. « Je sais même exactement à qui elle ressemble. A cette femme, cette Roumaine qui a joué *Phèdre* en français au mur d'Orange. » Il regrettait de lui avoir fait cette remarque désagréable : « Cela m'a échappé ! Il vaudrait mieux ne pas l'indisposer pour de petites choses. »

— Excuse-moi, dit-il en souriant, tu sais que je suis un vieux naturiste. Je n'aime pas beaucoup toutes ces pommades que les femmes d'aujourd'hui se collent sur la figure. Mais c'est moi qui ai tort, il faut vivre avec son temps.

Ève lui sourit aimablement. M. Darbédat alluma sa cigarette et en tira quelques bouffées.

— Ma petite enfant, commença-t-il, je voulais justement te dire : nous allons bavarder, nous deux, comme autrefois. Allons, assieds-toi et écoute-moi gentiment ; il faut avoir confiance en son vieux papa.

— J'aime mieux rester debout, dit Ève. Qu'est-ce que tu as à me dire ?

— Je vais te poser une simple question, dit M. Darbédat un peu plus sèchement. A quoi tout cela te mènera-t-il ?

— Tout cela ? répéta Ève étonnée.

— Eh bien oui, tout, toute cette vie que tu t'es faite. Écoute, reprit-il, il ne faut pas croire que je ne te comprenne pas (il avait eu une illumination soudaine). Mais ce que tu veux faire est au-dessus des forces humaines. Tu veux vivre uniquement par l'imagination, n'est-ce pas ? Tu ne veux pas admettre qu'il est malade ? Tu ne veux pas voir le Pierre d'aujourd'hui, c'est bien cela ? Tu n'as d'yeux que pour le Pierre d'autrefois. Ma petite chérie, ma petite fille, c'est une gageure impossible à tenir, reprit M. Darbédat. Tiens, je vais te raconter une histoire que tu ne connais peut-être pas : quand nous étions aux Sables-d'Olonne, tu avais trois ans, ta mère a fait la connaissance d'une jeune femme charmante qui avait un petit garçon superbe. Tu jouais sur la plage avec ce petit garçon, vous étiez hauts comme trois pommes, tu étais sa fiancée. Quelque temps plus tard, à Paris, ta mère a voulu revoir cette jeune femme ; on lui a appris qu'elle avait eu un affreux malheur : son bel enfant avait été décapité par l'aile avant d'une automobile. On a dit à ta mère : « Allez la voir mais ne lui parlez surtout pas de la mort de son petit, elle *ne veut pas* croire qu'il est mort. » Ta mère y est allée, elle a trouvé une créature à moitié timbrée : elle vivait comme si son gamin existait encore ; elle lui parlait, elle mettait son couvert à table. Eh bien, elle a vécu dans un tel état de tension nerveuse qu'il a fallu, au bout de six mois, qu'on l'emmène de force dans une maison de repos où elle a dû rester trois ans. Non, mon petit, dit M. Darbédat en secouant la tête, ces choses-là sont impossibles. Il aurait bien mieux valu qu'elle reconnaisse courageusement la vérité. Elle aurait souffert une bonne fois et puis le temps aurait passé l'éponge. Il n'y a rien de tel que de regarder les choses en face, crois-moi.

— Tu te trompes, dit Ève avec effort, je sais très bien que Pierre est...

Le mot ne passa pas. Elle se tenait très droite, elle posait les mains sur le dossier d'un fauteuil : il y avait quelque chose d'aride et de laid dans le bas de son visage.

— Eh bien... alors ? déclara M. Darbédat étonné.

— Alors quoi ?

— Tu... ?

— Je l'aime comme il est, dit Ève rapidement et d'un air ennuyé.

— Ce n'est pas vrai, dit M. Darbédat avec force. Ce n'est pas vrai : tu ne l'aimes pas ; tu ne peux pas l'aimer. On ne peut éprouver de tels sentiments que pour un être sain et normal. Pour Pierre, tu as de la compassion, je n'en doute pas, et sans doute aussi tu gardes le souvenir des trois années de bonheur que tu lui dois. Mais ne me dis pas que tu l'aimes, je ne te croirai pas.

Ève restait muette et fixait le tapis d'un air absent.

— Tu pourrais me répondre, dit M. Darbédat avec froideur. Ne crois pas que cette conversation me soit moins pénible qu'à toi.

— Puisque tu ne me croiras pas.

— Eh bien, si tu l'aimes, s'écria-t-il exaspéré, c'est un grand malheur pour toi, pour moi et pour ta pauvre mère parce que je vais te dire quelque chose que j'aurais préféré te cacher : avant trois ans, Pierre aura sombré dans la démence la plus complète, il sera comme une bête.

Il regarda sa fille avec des yeux durs : il lui en voulait de l'avoir contraint, par son entêtement, à lui faire cette pénible révélation.

Ève ne broncha pas ; elle ne leva même pas les yeux.

— Je le savais.

— Qui te l'a dit ? demanda-t-il stupéfait.

— Franchot. Il y a six mois que je le sais.

— Et moi qui lui avais recommandé de te ménager, dit M. Darbédat avec amertume. Enfin, peut-être cela vaut-il mieux. Mais dans ces conditions tu dois comprendre qu'il serait impardonnable de garder Pierre chez toi. La lutte que tu as entreprise est vouée à l'échec, sa maladie ne pardonne pas. S'il y avait quelque chose à faire, si on pouvait le sauver à force de soins, je ne dis pas. Mais regarde un peu : tu étais jolie, intelligente et gaie, tu te détruis par plaisir et sans profit. Eh bien, c'est entendu, tu as été admirable, mais voilà, c'est fini, tu as fait tout ton devoir, plus que ton devoir ; à présent, il serait immoral d'insister. On a aussi des devoirs envers soi-même, mon enfant. Et puis tu ne penses pas à nous. *Il faut*, répéta-t-il en martelant les mots, que tu envoies Pierre à la clinique de Franchot. Tu abandonneras cet appartement où tu n'as eu que du malheur et tu reviendras chez nous. Si tu as envie de te rendre utile et de soulager les souffrances d'autrui, eh bien, tu as ta mère. La pauvre femme est soignée par des infirmières, elle aurait bien besoin d'être un peu entourée. Et *elle*, ajouta-t-il, elle pourra apprécier ce que tu feras pour elle et t'en être reconnaissante.

Il y eut un long silence. M. Darbédat entendit Pierre chanter dans la chambre voisine. C'était à peine un chant, du reste ; plutôt une sorte de récitatif aigu et précipité. M. Darbédat leva les yeux sur sa fille :

— Alors, c'est non ?

— Pierre restera avec moi, dit-elle doucement, je m'entends bien avec lui.

— A condition de bêtifier toute la journée.

Ève sourit et lança à son père un étrange regard moqueur et presque gai. « C'est vrai, pensa M. Darbédat, furieux, ils ne font pas que ça ; ils couchent ensemble. »

— Tu es complètement folle, dit-il en se levant.

Ève sourit tristement et murmura, comme pour elle-même :

— Pas assez.

— Pas assez ? Je ne peux te dire qu'une chose, mon enfant, tu me fais peur.

Il l'embrassa hâtivement et sortit. « Il faudrait, pensa-t-il en descendant l'escalier, lui envoyer deux solides gaillards qui emmèneraient de force ce pauvre déchet et qui le colleraient sous la douche sans lui demander son avis. »

C'était un beau jour d'automne, calme et sans mystère ; le soleil dorait les visages des passants. M. Darbédat fut frappé par la simplicité de ces visages : il y en avait de tannés et d'autres étaient lisses, mais ils reflétaient tous des bonheurs et des soucis qui lui étaient familiers.

« Je sais très exactement ce que je reproche à Ève, se dit-il en s'engageant sur le boulevard Saint-Germain. Je lui reproche de vivre en dehors de l'humain. Pierre n'est plus un être humain : tous les soins, tout l'amour qu'elle lui donne, elle en prive un peu tous ces gens-là. On n'a pas le droit de se refuser aux hommes ; quand le diable y serait, nous vivons en société. »

Il dévisageait les passants avec sympathie ; il aimait leurs regards graves et limpides. Dans ces rues ensoleillées, parmi les hommes, on se sentait en sécurité, comme au milieu d'une grande famille.

Une femme en cheveux s'était arrêtée devant un étalage en plein air. Elle tenait une petite fille par la main.

— Qu'est-ce que c'est ? demanda la petite fille en désignant un appareil de T.S.F.

— Touche à rien, dit sa mère, c'est un appareil ; ça fait de la musique.

Elles restèrent un moment sans parler, en extase. M. Darbédat, attendri, se pencha vers la petite fille et lui sourit.

## II

« Il est parti. » La porte d'entrée s'était refermée avec un claquement sec ; Ève était seule dans le salon : « Je voudrais qu'il meure. »

Elle crispa ses mains sur le dossier du fauteuil : elle venait de se rappeler les yeux de son père. M. Darbédat s'était penché sur Pierre d'un air compétent ; il lui avait dit : « C'est bon, ça ! » comme quelqu'un qui sait parler aux malades ; il l'avait regardé, et le visage de Pierre s'était peint au fond de ses gros yeux prestes. « Je le hais quand il le regarde, quand je pense qu'il le *voit.* »

Les mains d'Ève glissèrent le long du fauteuil, et elle se tourna vers la fenêtre. Elle était éblouie. La pièce était remplie de soleil, il y en avait partout : sur le tapis en ronds pâles, dans l'air, comme une poussière aveuglante. Ève avait perdu l'habitude de cette lumière indiscrète et diligente, qui furetait partout, récurait tous les coins, qui frottait les meubles et les faisait reluire comme une bonne ménagère. Elle s'avança pourtant jusqu'à la fenêtre et souleva le rideau de mousseline qui pendait contre la vitre. Au même instant, M. Darbédat sortait de l'immeuble ; Ève aperçut tout à coup ses larges épaules. Il leva la tête et regarda le ciel en clignant des yeux puis il s'éloigna à grandes enjambées, comme un jeune homme. « Il se force, pensa Ève, tout à l'heure il aura son point de côté. » Elle ne le haïssait plus guère : il y avait si peu de chose dans cette tête ; à peine le minuscule souci de paraître jeune. Pourtant la colère la reprit quand elle le vit tourner au coin du boulevard Saint-Germain et disparaître. « Il pense à Pierre. » Un peu de leur vie s'était échappée de la chambre close et traînait dans les rues, au soleil, parmi les gens. « Est-ce qu'on ne pourra donc jamais nous oublier ? »

La rue du Bac était presque déserte. Une vieille dame traversait la chaussée à petits pas ; trois jeunes filles passèrent en riant. Et puis des hommes, des hommes forts et graves qui portaient des serviettes et qui parlaient entre eux. « Les gens normaux », pensa Ève, étonnée de trouver en elle-même une telle puissance de haine. Une belle femme grasse courut au-devant d'un monsieur élégant. Il l'entoura de ses bras et l'embrassa sur la bouche. Ève eut un rire dur et laissa tomber le rideau.

Pierre ne chantait plus, mais la jeune femme du troisième s'était mise au piano ; elle jouait une *Étude* de Chopin. Ève se sentait plus calme ; elle fit un pas vers la chambre de Pierre, mais elle s'arrêta aussitôt et s'adossa au mur avec un peu d'angoisse : comme chaque fois qu'elle avait quitté la chambre, elle était prise de panique à l'idée qu'il lui fallait y rentrer. Pourtant elle savait bien qu'elle n'aurait pas pu vivre ailleurs : elle aimait la chambre. Elle parcourut du regard avec une curiosité froide, comme pour gagner un peu de temps, cette pièce sans ombres et sans odeur où elle attendait que son courage revînt. « On dirait le salon d'un dentiste. » Les fauteuils de soie rose, le divan, les tabourets étaient sobres et discrets, un peu paternels ; de bons amis de l'homme. Ève imagina que des messieurs graves et vêtus d'étoffes claires, tout pareils à ceux qu'elle avait vus de la fenêtre, entraient dans le salon en poursuivant une conversation commencée. Ils ne prenaient même pas le temps de reconnaître les lieux ; ils avançaient d'un pas ferme jusqu'au milieu de la pièce ; l'un d'eux, qui laissait traîner sa main derrière lui comme un sillage, frôlait au passage des coussins, des objets, sur les tables, et ne sursautait même pas à ces contacts. Et quand un meuble se trouvait sur leur chemin, ces hommes posés, loin de faire un détour pour l'éviter, le changeaient tranquillement de place. Ils s'asseyaient enfin, toujours plongés dans leur entretien, sans même jeter un coup d'œil derrière eux. « Un salon pour gens normaux », pensa Ève. Elle fixait le bouton de la porte close et l'angoisse lui serrait la gorge : « Il faut que j'y aille. Je ne le laisse jamais seul si longtemps. » Il faudrait ouvrir cette porte ; ensuite Ève se tiendrait sur le seuil, en tâchant d'habituer ses yeux à la pénombre, et la chambre la repousserait de toutes ses forces. Il faudrait qu'Ève triomphât de cette résistance et qu'elle s'enfonçât jusqu'au cœur de la pièce. Elle eut soudain une envie violente de voir Pierre ; elle eût aimé se moquer avec lui de M. Darbédat. Mais Pierre n'avait pas besoin d'elle ; Ève ne pouvait pas prévoir l'accueil qu'il lui réservait. Elle pensa soudain avec une sorte d'orgueil qu'elle n'avait plus de place nulle part. « Les normaux croient encore que je suis des leurs. Mais je ne pourrais pas rester une heure au milieu d'eux. J'ai besoin de vivre là-bas, de l'autre côté de ce mur. Mais là-bas, on ne veut pas de moi. »

Un changement profond s'était fait autour d'elle. La lumière avait vieilli, elle grisonnait : elle s'était alourdie, comme l'eau d'un vase de fleurs, quand on ne l'a pas renouvelée depuis la veille. Sur les objets, dans cette lumière veillie, Ève retrouvait une mélancolie qu'elle avait depuis longtemps oubliée : celle d'un après-midi d'automne qui finit. Elle regardait autour d'elle, hésitante, presque timide : tout cela était si loin : dans la chambre il n'y avait ni jour, ni nuit, ni saison, ni mélancolie. Elle se rappela vaguement des automnes très anciens, des automnes de son enfance puis, soudain, elle se raidit : elle avait peur des souvenirs.

Elle entendit la voix de Pierre.

— Agathe ! Où es-tu ?

— Je viens, cria-t-elle.

Elle ouvrit la porte et pénétra dans la chambre.

L'épaisse odeur de l'encens lui emplit les narines et la bouche, tandis qu'elle écarquillait les yeux et tendait les mains en avant — le parfum et la pénombre ne faisaient plus pour elle depuis longtemps qu'un seul élément, âcre et ouaté, aussi simple, aussi familier que l'eau, l'air ou le feu — et elle s'avança prudemment vers une tache pâle qui semblait flotter dans la brume. C'était le visage de Pierre : le vêtement de Pierre (depuis qu'il était malade, il s'habillait de noir) s'était fondu dans l'obscurité. Pierre avait renversé sa tête en arrière et fermé les yeux. Il était beau. Ève regarda ses longs cils recourbés, puis elle s'assit près de lui sur la chaise basse. « Il a l'air de souffrir », pensa-t-elle. Ses yeux s'habituaient peu à peu à la pénombre. Le bureau émergea le premier, puis le lit, puis les objets personnels de Pierre, les ciseaux, le pot de colle, les livres, l'herbier, qui jonchaient le tapis près du fauteuil.

— Agathe ?

Pierre avait ouvert les yeux, il la regardait en souriant.

— Tu sais, la fourchette ? dit-il. J'ai fait ça pour effrayer le type. Elle n'avait *presque* rien.

Les appréhensions d'Ève s'évanouirent et elle eut un rire léger.

— Tu as très bien réussi, dit-elle, tu l'as complètement affolé.

Pierre sourit.

— As-tu vu ? Il l'a tripotée un bon moment, il la tenait à pleines mains. Ce qu'il y a, dit-il, c'est qu'ils ne savent pas prendre les choses ; ils les empoignent.

— C'est vrai, dit Ève.

Pierre frappa légèrement sur la paume de sa main gauche avec l'index de sa main droite.

— C'est avec ça qu'ils prennent. Ils approchent leurs doigts et quand ils ont attrapé l'objet, ils plaquent leur paume dessus pour l'assommer.

Il parlait d'une voix rapide et du bout des lèvres : il avait l'air perplexe.

— Je me demande ce qu'ils veulent, dit-il enfin. Ce type est déjà venu. Pourquoi me l'ont-ils envoyé ? S'ils veulent savoir ce que je fais, ils n'ont qu'à le lire sur l'écran, ils n'ont même pas besoin de bouger de chez eux. Ils font des fautes. Ils ont le pouvoir mais ils font des fautes. Moi je n'en fais jamais, c'est mon atout. Hoffka, dit-il, hoffka. — Il agitait ses longues mains devant son front : La garce ! Hoffka paffka suffka. En veux-tu davantage ?

— C'est la cloche ? demanda Ève.

— Oui. Elle est partie. — Il reprit avec sévérité : Ce type, c'est un subalterne. Tu le connais, tu es allée avec lui au salon.

Ève ne répondit pas.

— Qu'est-ce qu'il voulait ? demanda Pierre. Il a dû te le dire.

Elle hésita un instant puis répondit brutalement :

— Il voulait qu'on t'enferme.

Quand on disait doucement la vérité à Pierre, il se méfiait, il fallait la lui assener avec violence, pour étourdir et paralyser les soupçons. Ève aimait encore mieux le brutaliser que lui mentir : quand elle mentait et qu'il avait l'air de la croire, elle ne pouvait se défendre d'une très légère impression de supériorité qui lui donnait horreur d'elle-même.

— M'enfermer ! répéta Pierre avec ironie. Ils déraillent. Qu'est-ce que ça peut me faire, des murs ? Ils croient peut-être que ça va m'arrêter. Je me demande quelquefois s'il n'y a pas deux bandes. La vraie, celle du nègre. Et puis une bande de brouillons qui cherche à fourrer son nez là-dedans et qui fait sottise sur sottise.

Il fit sauter sa main sur le bras du fauteuil et la considéra d'un air réjoui :

— Les murs, ça se traverse. Qu'est-ce que tu lui as répondu ? demanda-t-il en se tournant vers Ève avec curiosité.

— Qu'on ne t'enfermerait pas.

Il haussa les épaules.

— Il ne fallait pas dire ça. Toi aussi tu as fait une faute à moins que tu ne l'aies fait exprès. Il faut les laisser abattre leur jeu.

Il se tut. Ève baissa tristement la tête : « Ils les empoignent ! » De quel ton méprisant il avait dit ça — et comme c'était juste. « Est-ce que moi aussi j'empoigne les objets ? J'ai beau m'observer, je crois que la plupart de mes gestes l'agacent. Mais il ne le dit pas. » Elle se sentit soudain misérable, comme lorsqu'elle avait quatorze ans et que M$^{me}$ Darbédat, vive et légère, lui disait : « On croirait que tu ne sais pas quoi faire de tes mains. » Elle n'osait pas faire un mouvement et, juste à ce moment, elle eut une envie irrésistible de changer de position. Elle ramena doucement ses pieds sous sa chaise, effleurant à peine le tapis. Elle regardait la lampe sur la table — la lampe dont Pierre avait peint le socle en noir — et le jeu d'échecs. Sur le damier, Pierre n'avait laissé que les pions noirs. Quelquefois il se levait, il allait jusqu'à la table et il prenait les pions un à un dans ses mains. Il leur parlait, il les appelait Robots, et ils paraissaient s'animer d'une vie sourde entre ses doigts. Quand il les avait reposés, Ève allait les toucher à son tour (elle avait l'impression d'être un peu ridicule) : ils étaient redevenus de petits bouts de bois mort mais il restait sur eux quelque chose de vague et d'insaisissable, quelque chose comme un sens. « Ce sont *ses* objets, pensa-t-elle. Il n'y a plus rien à moi dans la chambre. » Elle avait possédé quelques meubles, autrefois. La glace et la petite coiffeuse en marqueterie qui venait de sa grand-mère et que Pierre appelait par plaisanterie : *ta* coiffeuse. Pierre les avait entraînés avec lui : à Pierre seul les choses montraient leur vrai visage. Ève pouvait les regarder pendant des heures : elles mettaient un entêtement inlassable et mauvais à la décevoir, à ne lui offrir jamais que leur apparence — comme au docteur Franchot et à M. Darbédat. « Pourtant, se dit-elle avec angoisse, je ne les vois plus tout à fait comme mon père. Ce n'est pas possible que je les voie tout à fait comme lui. »

Elle remua un peu les genoux : elle avait des fourmis dans les jambes. Son corps était raide et tendu, il lui faisait mal ; elle le sentait trop vivant, indiscret : « Je voudrais être invisible et rester là ; le voir sans qu'il me voie. Il n'a pas besoin de moi ; je suis de trop dans la chambre. » Elle tourna un peu la tête et regarda le mur au-dessus de Pierre. Sur le mur, des menaces étaient écrites. Ève le savait mais elle ne pouvait pas les lire. Elle regardait souvent les grosses roses rouges de la tenture murale, jusqu'à ce qu'elles se missent à danser sous ses yeux. Les roses flamboyaient dans la pénombre. La menace était, la plupart du temps, inscrite près du plafond, à gauche au-dessus du lit : mais elle se déplaçait, quelquefois. « Il faut que je me lève. Je ne peux pas — je ne peux pas rester assise plus longtemps. » Il y avait aussi, sur le mur, des disques blancs qui ressemblaient à des tranches d'oignon. Les disques tournèrent sur eux-mêmes et les mains d'Ève se mirent à trembler : « Il y a des moments où je deviens folle. Mais non, pensa-t-elle avec amertume, je ne *peux pas* devenir folle. Je m'énerve, tout simplement. »

Soudain, elle sentit la main de Pierre sur la sienne.

— Agathe, dit Pierre avec tendresse.

Il lui souriait mais il lui tenait la main du bout des doigts avec une espèce de répulsion, comme s'il avait pris un crabe par le dos et qu'il eût voulu éviter ses pinces.

— Agathe, dit-il, je voudrais tant avoir confiance en toi.

Ève ferma les yeux, et sa poitrine se souleva : « Il ne faut rien répondre, sans cela il va se défier, il ne dira plus rien. »

Pierre avait lâché sa main :

— Je t'aime bien, Agathe, lui dit-il. Mais je ne peux pas te comprendre. Pourquoi restes-tu tout le temps dans la chambre ?

Ève ne répondit pas.

— Dis-moi pourquoi.

— Tu sais bien que je t'aime, dit-elle avec sécheresse.

— Je ne te crois pas, dit Pierre. Pourquoi m'aimerais-tu ? Je dois te faire horreur : je suis hanté.

Il sourit mais il devint grave tout d'un coup :

— Il y a un mur entre toi et moi. Je te vois, je te parle, mais tu es de l'autre côté. Qu'est-ce qui nous empêche de nous aimer ? Il me semble que c'était plus facile autrefois. A Hambourg.

— Oui, dit Ève tristement. Toujours Hambourg.

Jamais il ne parlait de leur vrai passé. Ni Ève ni lui n'avaient été à Hambourg.

— Nous nous promenions le long des canaux. Il y avait un chaland, tu te rappelles ? Le chaland était noir ; il y avait un chien sur le pont.

Il inventait à mesure ; il avait l'air faux.

— Je te tenais par la main, tu avais une autre peau. Je croyais tout ce que tu me disais. Taisez-vous, cria-t-il.

Il écouta un moment :

— Elles vont venir, dit-il d'une voix morne.

Ève sursauta :

— Elles vont venir ? Je croyais déjà qu'elles ne viendraient plus jamais.

Depuis trois jours, Pierre était plus calme ; les statues n'étaient pas venues. Pierre avait une peur horrible des statues, quoiqu'il n'en convînt jamais. Ève n'en avait pas peur : mais quand elles se mettaient à voler dans la chambre, en bourdonnant, elle avait peur de Pierre.

— Donne-moi le ziuthre, dit Pierre.

Ève se leva et prit le ziuthre : c'était un assemblage de morceaux de carton que Pierre avait collés lui-même : il s'en servait pour conjurer les statues. Le ziuthre ressemblait à une araignée. Sur un des cartons

Pierre avait écrit : « Pouvoir sur l'embûche » et sur un autre « Noir ». Sur un troisième il avait dessiné une tête rieuse avec des yeux plissés : c'était Voltaire. Pierre saisit le ziuthre par une patte et le considéra d'un air sombre.

— Il ne peut plus me servir, dit-il.

— Pourquoi ?

— Ils l'ont inversé.

— Tu en feras un autre ?

Il la regarda longuement.

— Tu le voudrais bien, dit-il entre ses dents.

Ève était irritée contre Pierre. « Chaque fois qu'elles viennent, il est averti ; comment fait-il : il ne se trompe jamais. »

Le ziuthre pendait piteusement au bout des doigts de Pierre : « Il trouve toujours de bonnes raisons pour ne pas s'en servir. Dimanche, quand elles sont venues, il prétendait l'avoir égaré mais je le voyais, moi, derrière le pot de colle et il ne pouvait pas ne pas le voir. Je me demande si ça n'est pas *lui* qui les attire. » On ne pouvait jamais savoir s'il était tout à fait sincère. A certains moments, Ève avait l'impression que Pierre était envahi malgré lui par un foisonnement malsain de pensées et de visions. Mais, à d'autres moments, Pierre avait l'air d'inventer. « Il souffre. Mais jusqu'à quel point *croit-il* aux statues et au nègre ? Les statues, en tout cas, je sais qu'il ne les voit pas, il les entend seulement : quand elles passent, il détourne la tête ; il dit tout de même qu'il les voit ; il les décrit. » Elle se rappela le visage rougeaud du docteur Franchot : « Mais, chère madame, tous les aliénés sont des menteurs ; vous perdriez votre temps si vous vouliez distinguer ce qu'ils ressentent réellement de ce qu'ils prétendent ressentir. » Elle sursauta : « Qu'est-ce que Franchot vient faire là-dedans ? Je ne vais pas me mettre à penser comme lui. »

Pierre s'était levé, il alla jeter le ziuthre dans la corbeille à papiers : « C'est comme *toi* que je voudrais penser », murmura-t-elle. Il marchait à petits pas, sur la pointe des pieds, en serrant les coudes contre ses hanches, pour occuper le moins de place possible. Il revint s'asseoir et regarda Ève d'un air fermé.

— Il faudra mettre des tentures noires, dit-il, il n'y a pas assez de noir dans cette chambre.

Il s'était tassé dans le fauteuil. Ève regarda tristement ce corps avare, toujours prêt à se retirer, à se recroqueviller : les bras, les jambes, la tête avaient l'air d'organes rétractiles. Six heures sonnèrent à la pendule ; le piano s'était tu. Ève soupira : les statues ne viendraient pas tout de suite ; il fallait les attendre.

— Veux-tu que j'allume ?

Elle aimait mieux ne pas les attendre dans l'obscurité.

— Fais ce que tu veux, dit Pierre.

Ève alluma la petite lampe du bureau, et un brouillard rouge envahit la pièce. Pierre aussi attendait.

Il ne parlait pas mais ses lèvres remuaient, elles faisaient deux taches sombres dans le brouillard rouge. Ève aimait les lèvres de Pierre. Elles avaient été, autrefois, émouvantes et sensuelles ; mais elles avaient perdu leur sensualité. Elles s'écartaient l'une de l'autre en frémissant un peu et se rejoignaient sans cesse, s'écrasaient l'une contre l'autre pour se séparer de nouveau. Seules, dans ce visage muré, elles vivaient ; elles avaient l'air de deux bêtes peureuses. Pierre pouvait marmotter ainsi pendant des heures sans qu'un son sortît de sa bouche, et, souvent, Ève se laissait fasciner par ce petit mouvement obstiné.

« J'aime sa bouche. » Il ne l'embrassait plus jamais ; il avait horreur des contacts : la nuit on le touchait, des mains d'hommes, dures et sèches, le pinçaient par tout le corps ; des mains de femmes, aux ongles très longs, lui faisaient de sales caresses. Souvent, il se couchait tout habillé, mais les mains se glissaient sous ses vêtements et tiraient sur sa chemise. Une fois, il avait entendu rire et des lèvres bouffies s'étaient posées sur ses lèvres. C'était depuis cette nuit-là qu'il n'embrassait plus Ève.

— Agathe, dit Pierre, ne regarde pas ma bouche !

Ève baissa les yeux.

— Je n'ignore pas qu'on peut apprendre à lire sur les lèvres, poursuivit-il avec insolence.

Sa main tremblait sur le bras du fauteuil. L'index se tendit, vint frapper trois fois sur le pouce et les autres doigts se crispèrent : c'était une conjuration. « Ça va commencer », pensa-t-elle. Elle avait envie de prendre Pierre dans ses bras.

Pierre se mit à parler très haut, sur un ton très mondain :

— Te souviens-tu de Sankt Pauli ?

Ne pas répondre. C'était peut-être un piège.

— C'est là que je t'ai connue, dit-il d'un air satisfait. Je t'ai soulevée à un marin danois. Nous avons failli nous battre, mais j'ai payé la tournée et il m'a laissé t'emmener. Tout cela n'était que comédie.

« Il ment, il ne croit pas un mot de ce qu'il dit. Il sait que je ne m'appelle pas Agathe. Je le hais quand il ment. » Mais elle vit ses yeux fixes, et sa colère fondit. « Il ne ment pas, pensa-t-elle, il est à bout. Il sent qu'elles approchent ; il parle pour s'empêcher d'entendre. » Pierre se cramponnait des deux mains au bras du fauteuil. Son visage était blafard ; il souriait.

— Ces rencontres sont souvent étranges, dit-il,

mais je ne crois pas au hasard. Je ne te demande pas qui t'avait envoyée, je sais que tu ne répondrais pas. En tout cas, tu as été assez habile pour m'éclabousser.

Il parlait péniblement, d'une voix aiguë et pressée. Il y avait des mots qu'il ne pouvait prononcer et qui sortaient de sa bouche comme une substance molle et informe.

— Tu m'as entraîné en pleine fête, entre des manèges d'automobiles noires, mais derrière les autos il y avait une armée d'yeux rouges qui luisaient dès que j'avais le dos tourné. Je pense que tu leur faisais des signes, tout en te pendant à mon bras, mais je ne voyais rien. J'étais trop absorbé par les grandes cérémonies du Couronnement.

Il regardait droit devant lui, les yeux grands ouverts. Il se passa la main sur le front, très vite, d'un geste étriqué et sans cesser de parler : il ne voulait pas cesser de parler.

— C'était le Couronnement de la République, dit-il d'une voix stridente, un spectacle impressionnant dans son genre à cause des animaux de toute espèce qu'envoyaient les colonies pour la cérémonie. Tu craignais de t'égarer parmi les singes. J'ai dit parmi les singes, répéta-t-il d'un air arrogant, en regardant autour de lui. *Je pourrais dire parmi les nègres !* Les avortons qui se glissent sous les tables et croient passer inaperçus sont découverts et cloués sur-le-champ par mon Regard. La consigne est de se taire, cria-t-il. De se taire. Tous en place et garde à vous pour l'entrée des statues, c'est l'ordre. Tralala — il hurlait et mettait ses mains en cornet devant sa bouche — tralalala, tralalalala.

Il se tut, et Ève sut que les statues venaient d'entrer dans la chambre. Il se tenait tout raide, pâle et méprisant. Ève se raidit aussi et tous deux attendirent en silence. Quelqu'un marchait dans le corridor : c'était Marie, la femme de ménage, elle venait sans doute d'arriver. Elle pensa : « Il faudra que je lui donne de l'argent pour le gaz. » Et puis les statues se mirent à voler ; elles passaient entre Ève et Pierre.

Pierre fit « Han » et se blottit dans le fauteuil en ramenant ses jambes sous lui. Il détournait la tête ; de temps à autre, il ricanait mais des gouttes de sueur perlaient à son front. Ève ne put supporter la vue de cette joue pâle, de cette bouche qu'une moue tremblante déformait : elle ferma les yeux. Des fils dorés se mirent à danser sur le fond rouge de ses paupières ; elle se sentait vieille et pesante. Pas très loin d'elle, Pierre soufflait bruyamment. « Elles volent, elles bourdonnent ; elles se penchent sur lui... » Elle sentit un chatouillement léger, une gêne à l'épaule et au flanc droit. Instinctivement, son corps s'inclina vers la gauche comme pour éviter un contact désagréable, comme pour laisser passer un objet lourd et maladroit. Soudain, le plancher craqua, et elle eut une envie folle d'ouvrir les yeux, de regarder sur sa droite en balayant l'air de sa main.

Elle n'en fit rien ; elle garda les yeux clos, et une joie âcre la fit frissonner : « *Moi aussi* j'ai peur », pensa-t-elle. Toute sa vie s'était réfugiée dans son côté droit. Elle se pencha vers Pierre, sans ouvrir les yeux. Il lui suffirait d'un tout petit effort et, pour la première fois, elle entrerait dans ce monde tragique. « J'ai peur des statues », pensa-t-elle. C'était une affirmation violente et aveugle, une incantation : de toutes ses forces, elle voulait croire à leur présence ; l'angoisse qui paralysait son côté droit, elle essayait d'en faire un sens nouveau, un toucher. Dans son bras, dans son flanc et son épaule, elle *sentait* leur passage.

Les statues volaient bas et doucement ; elles bourdonnaient. Ève savait qu'elles avaient l'air malicieux et que des cils sortaient de la pierre autour de leurs yeux ; mais elle se les représentait mal. Elle savait aussi qu'elles n'étaient pas encore tout à fait vivantes, mais que des plaques de chair, des écailles tièdes, apparaissaient sur leurs grands corps ; au bout de leurs doigts, la pierre pelait, et leurs paumes les démangeaient. Ève ne pouvait pas *voir* tout cela : elle pensait simplement que d'énormes femmes glissaient tout contre elle, solennelles et grotesques, avec un air humain et l'entêtement compact de la pierre. « Elles se penchent sur Pierre. » Ève faisait un effort si violent que ses mains se mirent à trembler. « Elles se penchent vers moi... » Un cri horrible la glaça tout à coup. « Elles l'ont touché. » Elle ouvrit les yeux : Pierre avait la tête dans ses mains, il haletait. Ève se sentit épuisée : « Un jeu, pensa-t-elle avec remords ; ce n'était qu'un jeu, pas un instant je n'y ai cru sincèrement. Et pendant ce temps-là, il souffrait pour de vrai. »

Pierre se détendit et respira fortement. Mais ses pupilles restaient étrangement dilatées ; il transpirait.

— Tu les as vues ? demanda-t-il.

— Je ne peux pas les voir.

— Ça vaut mieux pour toi, elles te feraient peur. Moi, dit-il, j'ai l'habitude.

Les mains d'Ève tremblaient toujours, elle avait le sang à la tête. Pierre prit une cigarette dans sa poche et la porta à sa bouche. Mais il ne l'alluma pas :

— Ça m'est égal de les voir, dit-il, mais je ne veux pas qu'elles me touchent : j'ai peur qu'elles ne me donnent des boutons.

Il réfléchit un instant et demanda :

— Est-ce que tu les as entendues ?

— Oui, dit Ève, c'est comme un moteur d'avion.

(Pierre le lui avait dit en propres termes, le dimanche précédent.)

Pierre sourit avec un peu de condescendance.

— Tu exagères, dit-il. — Mais il restait blême. Il regarda les mains d'Ève. — Tes mains tremblent. Ça t'a impressionnée, ma pauvre Agathe. Mais tu n'as pas besoin de te faire du mauvais sang : elles ne reviendront plus avant demain.

Ève ne pouvait pas parler, elle claquait des dents et elle craignait que Pierre ne s'en aperçût. Pierre la considéra longuement.

— Tu es rudement belle, dit-il en hochant la tête. C'est dommage, c'est vraiment dommage.

Il avança rapidement la main et lui effleura l'oreille.

— Ma belle démone ! Tu me gênes un peu, tu es trop belle : ça me distrait. S'il ne s'agissait pas de récapitulation...

Il s'arrêta et regarda Ève avec surprise :

— Ce n'est pas de ce mot-là... Il est venu... il est venu, dit-il en souriant d'un air vague. J'avais l'autre sur le bout de la langue... et celui-là... s'est mis à sa place. J'ai oublié ce que je te disais.

Il réfléchit un instant et secoua la tête :

— Allons, dit-il, je vais dormir. — Il ajouta d'une voix enfantine : Tu sais, Agathe, je suis fatigué. Je ne trouve plus mes idées.

Il jeta sa cigarette et regarda le tapis d'un air inquiet. Ève lui glissa un oreiller sous la tête.

— Tu peux dormir aussi, lui dit-il en fermant les yeux, elles ne reviendront pas.

« Récapitulation. » Pierre dormait, il avait un demi-sourire candide ; il penchait la tête : on aurait dit qu'il voulait caresser sa joue à son épaule. Ève n'avait pas sommeil, elle pensait : « Récapitulation. » Pierre avait pris soudain l'air bête, et le mot avait coulé hors de sa bouche, long et blanchâtre. Pierre avait regardé devant lui avec étonnement comme s'il voyait le mot et ne le reconnaissait pas ; sa bouche était ouverte, molle ; quelque chose semblait s'être cassé en lui. « Il a bredouillé. C'est la première fois que ça lui arrive : il s'en est aperçu, d'ailleurs. Il a dit qu'il ne trouvait plus ses idées. » Pierre poussa un petit gémissement voluptueux, et sa main fit un geste léger. Ève le regarda durement : « Comment va-t-il se réveiller ? » Ça la rongeait. Dès que Pierre dormait, il fallait qu'elle y pensât, elle ne pouvait pas s'en empêcher. Elle avait peur qu'il ne se réveillât avec les yeux troubles et qu'il ne se mît à bredouiller. « Je suis stupide, pensa-t-elle, ça ne doit pas commencer avant un an ; Franchot l'a dit. » Mais l'angoisse ne la quittait pas ; un an ; un hiver, un printemps, un été, le début d'un autre automne. Un jour, ces traits se brouilleraient, il laisserait pendre sa mâchoire, il ouvrirait à demi des yeux larmoyants. Ève se pencha sur la main de Pierre et y posa ses lèvres : « Je te tuerai avant. »

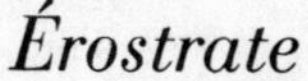

# *Érostrate*

Les hommes, il faut les voir d'en haut. J'éteignais la lumière et je me mettais à la fenêtre : ils ne soupçonnaient même pas qu'on pût les observer d'en dessus. Ils soignent la façade, quelquefois les derrières, mais tous leurs effets sont calculés pour des spectateurs d'un mètre soixante-dix. Qui donc a jamais réfléchi à la forme d'un chapeau melon vu d'un sixième étage ? Ils négligent de défendre leurs épaules et leurs crânes par des couleurs vives et des étoffes voyantes, ils ne savent pas combattre ce grand ennemi de l'Humain : la perspective plongeante. Je me penchais et je me mettais à rire : où donc était-elle, cette fameuse « station debout » dont ils étaient si fiers : ils s'écrasaient contre le trottoir et deux longues jambes à demi rampantes sortaient de dessous leurs épaules.

Au balcon d'un sixième : c'est là que j'aurais dû passer toute ma vie. Il faut étayer les supériorités morales par des symboles matériels, sans quoi elles retombent. Or, précisément, quelle est ma supériorité sur les hommes ? Une supériorité de position, rien d'autre : je me suis placé au-dessus de l'humain qui est en moi et je le contemple. Voilà pourquoi j'aimais les tours de Notre-Dame, les plates-formes de la tour

Eiffel, le Sacré-Cœur, mon sixième de la rue Delambre. Ce sont d'excellents symboles.

Il fallait quelquefois redescendre dans les rues. Pour aller au bureau, par exemple. J'étouffais. Quand on est de plain-pied avec les hommes, il est beaucoup plus difficile de les considérer comme des fourmis : ils *touchent.* Une fois, j'ai vu un type mort dans la rue. Il était tombé sur le nez. On l'a retourné, il saignait. J'ai vu ses yeux ouverts, et son air louche, et tout ce sang. Je me disais : « Ce n'est rien, ça n'est pas plus émouvant que de la peinture fraîche. On lui a badigeonné le nez en rouge, voilà tout. » Mais j'ai senti une sale douceur qui me prenait aux jambes et à la nuque, je me suis évanoui. Ils m'ont emmené dans une pharmacie, m'ont donné des claques sur les épaules et fait boire de l'alcool. Je les aurais tués.

Je savais qu'ils étaient mes ennemis, mais eux ne le savaient pas. Ils s'aimaient entre eux, ils se serraient les coudes ; et moi, ils m'auraient bien donné un coup de main par-ci, par-là, parce qu'ils me croyaient leur semblable. Mais s'ils avaient pu deviner la plus infime partie de la vérité, ils m'auraient battu. D'ailleurs, ils l'ont fait plus tard. Quand ils m'eurent pris et qu'ils ont su *qui* j'étais, ils m'ont passé à tabac, ils m'ont tapé dessus pendant deux heures, au commissariat, ils m'ont donné des gifles et des coups de poing, ils m'ont tordu les bras, ils m'ont arraché mon pantalon et puis, pour finir, ils ont jeté mon lorgnon par terre et pendant que je le cherchais, à quatre pattes, ils m'envoyaient en riant des coups de pied dans le derrière. J'ai toujours prévu qu'ils finiraient par me battre : je ne suis pas fort et je ne peux pas me défendre. Il y en a qui me guettaient depuis longtemps : les grands. Ils me bousculaient dans la rue, pour rire, pour voir ce que je ferais. Je ne disais rien. Je faisais semblant de n'avoir pas compris. Et pourtant, ils m'ont eu. J'avais peur d'eux : c'était un pressentiment. Mais vous pensez bien que j'avais des raisons plus sérieuses pour les haïr.

De ce point de vue, tout est allé beaucoup mieux à dater du jour où je me suis acheté un revolver. On se sent fort quand on porte assidûment sur soi une de ces choses qui peuvent exploser et faire du bruit. Je le prenais le dimanche, je le mettais tout simplement dans la poche de mon pantalon et puis j'allais me promener — en général sur les boulevards. Je le sentais qui tirait sur mon pantalon comme un crabe, je le sentais contre ma cuisse, tout froid. Mais peu à peu, il se réchauffait au contact de mon corps. Je marchais avec une certaine raideur, j'avais l'allure du type qui est en train de bander et que sa verge freine à chaque pas. Je glissais ma main dans ma poche et je tâtais l'*objet*. De temps en temps, j'entrais dans un urinoir — même là-dedans je faisais bien attention parce qu'on a souvent des voisins —, je sortais mon revolver, je le soupesais, je regardais sa crosse aux quadrillages noirs et sa gâchette noire qui ressemble à une paupière demi-close. Les autres, ceux qui voyaient, du dehors, mes pieds écartés et le bas de mon pantalon, croyaient que je pissais. Mais je ne pisse jamais dans les urinoirs.

Un soir, l'idée m'est venue de tirer sur des hommes. C'était un samedi soir, j'étais sorti pour chercher Léa, une blonde qui fait le quart devant un hôtel de la rue du Montparnasse. Je n'ai jamais eu de commerce intime avec une femme : je me serais senti volé. On leur monte dessus, c'est entendu, mais elles vous dévorent le bas-ventre avec leur grande bouche poilue et, à ce que j'ai entendu dire, ce sont elles — et de loin — qui gagnent à cet échange. Moi je ne demande rien à personne, mais je ne veux rien donner non plus. Ou alors il m'aurait fallu une femme froide et pieuse qui me subisse avec dégoût. Le premier samedi de chaque mois, je montais avec Léa dans une chambre de l'hôtel Duquesne. Elle se déshabillait, et je la regardais sans la toucher. Quelquefois, ça partait tout seul dans mon pantalon ; d'autres fois, j'avais le temps de rentrer chez moi pour me finir. Ce soir-là, je ne la trouvai pas à son poste. J'attendis un moment et comme je ne la voyais pas venir, je supposai qu'elle était grippée. C'était au début de janvier et il faisait très froid. J'étais désolé : je suis un imaginatif et je m'étais vivement représenté le plaisir que je comptais tirer de cette soirée. Il y avait bien, dans la rue d'Odessa, une brune que j'avais souvent remarquée, un peu mûre mais ferme et potelée : je ne déteste pas les femmes mûres : quand elles sont dévêtues, elles ont l'air plus nues que les autres. Mais elle n'était pas au courant de mes convenances, et ça m'intimidait un peu de lui exposer ça de but en blanc. Et puis je me défie des nouvelles connaissances : ces femmes-là peuvent très bien cacher un voyou derrière une porte, et, après ça, le type s'amène tout d'un coup et vous prend votre argent. Bien heureux s'il ne vous donne pas des coups de poing. Pourtant, ce soir-là, j'avais je ne sais quelle hardiesse, je décidai de passer chez moi pour prendre mon revolver et de tenter l'aventure.

Quand j'abordai la femme, un quart d'heure plus tard, mon arme était dans ma poche, et je ne craignais plus rien. A la regarder de près, elle avait plutôt l'air misérable. Elle ressemblait à ma voisine d'en face, la femme de l'adjudant, et j'en fus très satisfait parce qu'il y avait longtemps que j'avais envie de la voir à poil, celle-là. Elle s'habillait la fenêtre ouverte, quand l'adjudant était parti, et j'étais resté souvent derrière mon rideau pour la surprendre. Mais elle faisait sa toilette au fond de la pièce.

A l'hôtel Stella, il ne restait qu'une chambre libre, au quatrième. Nous montâmes. La femme était assez lourde et s'arrêtait à chaque marche, pour souffler. J'étais très à l'aise : j'ai un corps sec, malgré mon ventre et il faudrait plus de quatre étages pour me faire perdre haleine. Sur le palier du quatrième, elle s'arrêta et mit sa main droite sur son cœur en respirant très fort. De la main gauche elle tenait la clef de la chambre.

— C'est haut, dit-elle en essayant de me sourire.

Je lui pris la clef sans répondre et j'ouvris la porte. Je tenais mon revolver de la main gauche, braqué droit devant moi à travers la poche et je ne le lâchai qu'après avoir tourné le commutateur. La chambre était vide. Sur le lavabo, ils avaient mis un petit carré de savon vert, pour la passe. Je souris : avec moi ni les bidets ni les petits carrés de savon n'ont fort à faire. La femme soufflait toujours, derrière moi, et ça m'excitait. Je me retournai ; elle me tendit ses lèvres. Je la repoussai.

— Déshabille-toi, lui dis-je.

Il y avait un fauteuil en tapisserie ; je m'assis confortablement. C'est dans ces cas-là que je regrette de ne pas fumer. La femme ôta sa robe puis s'arrêta en me jetant un regard méfiant.

— Comment t'appelles-tu ? lui dis-je en me renversant en arrière.

— Renée.

— Eh bien, Renée, presse-toi, j'attends.

— Tu ne te déshabilles pas ?

— Va, va, lui dis-je, ne t'occupe pas de moi.

Elle fit tomber son pantalon à ses pieds puis le

ramassa et le posa soigneusement sur sa robe avec son soutien-gorge.

— Tu es donc un petit vicieux, mon chéri, un petit paresseux ? me demanda-t-elle ; tu veux que ce soit ta petite femme qui fasse tout le travail ?

En même temps elle fit un pas vers moi et, s'appuyant avec les mains sur les accoudoirs de mon fauteuil, elle essaya lourdement de s'agenouiller entre mes jambes. Mais je la relevai avec rudesse :

— Pas de ça, pas de ça, lui dis-je.

Elle me regarda avec surprise.

— Mais qu'est-ce que tu veux que je te fasse ?

— Rien. Marche, promène-toi, je ne t'en demande pas plus.

Elle se mit à marcher de long en large, d'un air gauche. Rien n'embête plus les femmes que de marcher quand elles sont nues. Elles n'ont pas l'habitude de poser les talons à plat. La putain voûtait le dos et laissait pendre ses bras. Pour moi, j'étais aux anges : j'étais là, tranquillement assis dans un fauteuil, vêtu jusqu'au cou, j'avais gardé jusqu'à mes gants, et cette dame mûre s'était mise toute nue sur mon ordre et virevoltait autour de moi.

Elle tourna la tête vers moi et, pour sauver les apparences, me sourit coquettement :

— Tu me trouves belle ? Tu te rinces l'œil ?

— T'occupe pas de ça.

— Dis donc, me demanda-t-elle avec une indignation subite, t'as l'intention de me faire marcher longtemps comme ça ?

— Assieds-toi.

Elle s'assit sur le lit, et nous nous regardâmes en silence. Elle avait la chair de poule. On entendait le tic-tac d'un réveil, de l'autre côté du mur. Tout à coup je lui dis :

— Écarte les jambes.

Elle hésita un quart de seconde, puis elle obéit. Je regardai entre ses jambes et je reniflai. Puis je me mis à rire si fort que les larmes me vinrent aux yeux. Je lui dis simplement :

— Tu te rends compte ?

Et je repartis à rire.

Elle me regarda avec stupeur, puis rougit violemment et referma les jambes.

— Salaud, dit-elle entre ses dents.

Mais je ris de plus belle, alors elle se leva d'un bond et prit son soutien-gorge sur la chaise.

— Hé là, lui dis-je, ça n'est pas fini. Je te donnerai cinquante francs tout à l'heure, mais j'en veux pour mon argent.

Elle prit nerveusement son pantalon.

— J'en ai marre, tu comprends. Je ne sais pas ce que tu veux. Et si tu m'as fait monter pour te fiche de moi...

Alors j'ai sorti mon revolver et je le lui ai montré. Elle m'a regardé d'un air sérieux et elle a laissé tomber son pantalon sans rien dire.

— Marche, lui dis-je, promène-toi.

Elle s'est promenée encore cinq minutes. Puis je lui ai donné ma canne et je lui ai fait faire l'exercice. Quand j'ai senti que mon caleçon était mouillé, je me suis levé et je lui ai tendu un billet de cinquante francs. Elle l'a pris.

— Au revoir, ajoutai-je, je ne t'aurai pas beaucoup fatiguée pour le prix.

Je suis parti, je l'ai laissée toute nue au milieu de la chambre, son soutien-gorge dans une main, le billet de cinquante francs dans l'autre. Je ne regrettais pas mon argent : je l'avais ahurie et ça ne s'étonne pas facilement, une putain. J'ai pensé en descendant l'escalier :

« Voilà ce que je voudrais, les étonner tous. » J'étais joyeux comme un enfant. J'avais emporté le savon vert et, rentré chez moi, je le frottai longtemps sous l'eau chaude jusqu'à ce qu'il ne fût plus qu'une mince pellicule entre mes doigts et qu'il ressemblât à un bonbon à la menthe sucé très longtemps.

Mais, la nuit, je me réveillai en sursaut et je revis son visage, les yeux qu'elle faisait quand je lui ai montré mon feu, et son ventre gras qui sautait à chacun de ses pas.

Que j'ai été bête, me dis-je. Et je sentis un remords amer : j'aurais dû tirer pendant que j'y étais, crever ce ventre comme une écumoire. Cette nuit-là et les trois nuits suivantes, je rêvai de six petits trous rouges groupés en cercle autour du nombril.

Par la suite je ne sortis plus sans mon revolver. Je regardais le dos des gens et j'imaginais, d'après leur démarche, la façon dont ils tomberaient si je leur tirais dessus. Le dimanche, je pris l'habitude d'aller me poster devant le Châtelet, à la sortie des concerts classiques. Vers six heures, j'entendais une sonnerie, et les ouvreuses venaient assujettir les portes vitrées avec des crochets. C'était le commencement : la foule sortait lentement ; les gens marchaient d'un pas flottant, les yeux encore pleins de rêve, le cœur encore plein de jolis sentiments. Il y en avait beaucoup qui regardaient autour d'eux d'un air étonné : la rue devait leur paraître toute bleue. Alors, ils souriaient avec mystère : ils passaient d'un monde à l'autre. C'est dans l'autre que je les attendais, moi. J'avais glissé ma main droite dans ma poche et je serrais de toutes mes forces la crosse de mon arme. Au bout d'un moment, je me *voyais* en train de leur tirer dessus. Je les dégringolais comme des pipes, ils tombaient les uns sur les autres, et les survivants, pris de panique, refluaient dans le théâtre en brisant les vitres des portes. C'était un jeu très énervant : mes mains tremblaient, à la fin, et j'étais obligé d'aller boire un cognac chez Dreher pour me remettre.

Les femmes je ne les aurais pas tuées. Je leur aurais tiré dans les reins. Ou alors dans les mollets, pour les faire danser.

Je n'avais rien décidé encore. Mais je pris le parti de tout faire comme si ma décision était arrêtée. J'ai commencé par régler des détails accessoires. J'ai été m'exercer dans un stand, à la foire de Denfert-Rochereau. Mes cartons n'étaient pas fameux mais les hommes offrent des cibles larges, surtout quand on tire à bout portant. Ensuite, je me suis occupé de ma publicité. J'ai choisi un jour où tous mes collègues étaient réunis au bureau. Un lundi matin. J'étais très aimable avec eux, par principe, bien que j'eusse horreur de leur serrer la main. Ils ôtaient leurs gants pour dire bonjour, ils avaient une façon obscène de déculotter leur main, de rabattre leur gant et de le faire glisser lentement le long des doigts en dévoilant la nudité grasse et chiffonnée de la paume. Moi, je gardais toujours mes gants.

Le lundi matin, on ne fait pas grand-chose. La dactylo du service commercial venait de nous apporter les quittances. Lemercier la plaisanta gentiment, et, quand elle fut sortie, ils détaillèrent ses charmes avec une compétence blasée. Puis ils parlèrent de Lindbergh. Ils aimaient bien Lindbergh. Je leur dis :

— Moi j'aime les héros noirs.

— Les nègres ? demanda Massé.

— Non, noirs comme on dit Magie noire. Lindbergh est un héros blanc. Il ne m'intéresse pas.

— Allez voir si c'est facile de traverser l'Atlantique, dit aigrement Bouxin.

Je leur exposai ma conception du héros noir :

— Un anarchiste, résuma Lemercier.

— Non, dis-je doucement, les anarchistes aiment les hommes à leur façon.

— Alors, ce serait un détraqué.

Mais Massé, qui avait des lettres, intervint à ce moment :

— Je le connais votre type, me dit-il. Il s'appelle Érostrate. Il voulait devenir illustre et il n'a rien trouvé de mieux que de brûler le temple d'Éphèse, une des sept merveilles du monde.

— Et comment s'appelait l'architecte de ce temple ?

— Je ne me rappelle plus, confessa-t-il, je crois même qu'on ne sait pas son nom.

— Vraiment ? Et vous vous rappelez le nom d'Érostrate ? Vous voyez qu'il n'avait pas fait un si mauvais calcul.

La conversation prit fin sur ces mots, mais j'étais bien tranquille ; ils se la rappelleraient au bon moment. Pour moi, qui, jusqu'alors, n'avais jamais entendu parler d'Érostrate, son histoire m'encouragea. Il y avait plus de deux mille ans qu'il était mort, et son acte brillait encore, comme un diamant noir. Je commençais à croire que mon destin serait court et tragique. Cela me fit peur tout d'abord, et puis je m'y habituai. Si on prend ça d'une certaine façon, c'est atroce, mais, d'un autre côté, ça donne à l'instant qui passe une force et une beauté considérables. Quand je descendais dans la rue, je sentais en mon corps une puissance étrange. J'avais sur moi mon revolver, cette chose qui éclate et qui fait du bruit. Mais ce n'était plus de lui que je tirais mon assurance, c'était de moi : j'étais un être de l'espèce des revolvers, des pétards et des bombes. Moi aussi, un jour, au terme de ma sombre vie, j'exploserais et j'illuminerais le monde d'une flamme violente et brève comme un éclair de magnésium. Il m'arriva, vers cette époque, de faire plusieurs nuits le même rêve. J'étais un anarchiste, je m'étais placé sur le passage du tsar et je portais sur moi une machine infernale. A l'heure dite, le cortège passait, la bombe éclatait, et nous sautions en l'air, moi, le tsar et trois officiers chamarrés d'or, sous les yeux de la foule.

Je restais maintenant des semaines entières sans paraître au bureau. Je me promenais sur les boulevards, au milieu de mes futures victimes, ou bien je m'enfermais dans ma chambre et je tirais des plans. On me congédia au début d'octobre. J'occupai alors mes loisirs en rédigeant la lettre suivante, que je copiai en cent deux exemplaires :

« Monsieur,

« Vous êtes célèbre et vos ouvrages tirent à trente mille. Je vais vous dire pourquoi : c'est que vous aimez les hommes. Vous avez l'humanisme dans le sang : c'est bien de la chance. Vous vous épanouissez quand vous êtes en compagnie ; dès que vous voyez un de vos semblables, sans même le connaître, vous vous sentez de la sympathie pour lui. Vous avez du goût pour son corps, pour la façon dont il est articulé, pour ses jambes qui s'ouvrent et se ferment à volonté, pour ses mains surtout : ça vous plaît qu'il ait cinq doigts à chaque main et qu'il puisse opposer le pouce aux autres doigts. Vous vous délectez, quand votre voisin prend une tasse sur la table, parce qu'il y a une manière de prendre qui est proprement humaine et que vous avez souvent décrite dans vos ouvrages, moins souple, moins rapide que celle du singe, mais, n'est-ce pas ? tellement plus intelligente. Vous aimez aussi la chair de l'homme, son allure de grand blessé en rééducation, son air de réinventer la marche à chaque pas et son fameux regard que les fauves ne peuvent supporter. Il vous a donc été facile de trouver l'accent qui convient pour parler à l'homme de lui-même ; un accent pudique mais éperdu. Les gens se jettent sur vos livres avec gourmandise, ils les lisent dans un bon fauteuil, ils pensent au grand amour malheureux et discret que vous leur portez et ça les console de bien des choses, d'être laids, d'être lâches, d'être cocus, de n'avoir pas reçu d'augmentation au premier janvier. Et l'on dit volontiers de votre dernier roman : c'est une bonne action.

« Vous serez curieux de savoir, je suppose, ce que peut être un homme qui n'aime pas les hommes. Eh bien, c'est moi, et je les aime si peu que je vais tout à l'heure en tuer une demi-douzaine ; peut-être vous demanderez-vous : pourquoi *seulement* une demi-douzaine ? Parce que mon revolver n'a que six cartouches. Voilà une monstruosité, n'est-ce pas ? Et, de plus, un acte proprement impolitique ? Mais je vous dis que je ne *peux pas* les aimer. Je comprends fort bien ce que vous ressentez. Mais ce qui vous attire en eux me dégoûte. J'ai vu comme vous des hommes mastiquer avec mesure en gardant l'œil pertinent, en feuilletant de la main gauche une revue économique. Est-ce ma faute si je préfère assister au repas des phoques ? L'homme ne peut rien faire de son visage sans que ça tourne au jeu de physionomie. Quand il mâche en gardant la bouche close, les coins de sa bouche montent et descendent, il a l'air de passer sans relâche de la sérénité à la surprise pleurarde. Vous aimez ça, je le sais, vous appelez ça la vigilance de l'Esprit. Mais moi ça m'écœure : je ne sais pas pourquoi ; je suis né ainsi.

« S'il n'y avait entre nous qu'une différence de goût, je ne vous importunerais pas. Mais tout se passe comme si vous aviez la grâce et que je ne l'aie point. Je suis libre d'aimer ou non le homard à l'américaine, mais si je n'aime pas les hommes, je suis un misérable et je ne puis trouver de place au soleil. Ils ont accaparé le sens de la vie. J'espère que vous comprenez ce que je veux dire. Voilà trente-trois ans que je me heurte à des portes closes au-dessus desquelles on a écrit : “ Nul n'entre ici s'il n'est humaniste. ” Tout ce que j'ai entrepris j'ai dû l'abandonner ; il fallait choisir : ou bien c'était une tentative absurde et condamnée ou bien il fallait qu'elle tournât tôt ou tard à leur profit. Les pensées que je ne leur destinais pas expressément, je n'arrivais pas à les détacher de moi, à les formuler : elles demeuraient en moi comme de légers mouvements organiques. Les outils mêmes dont je me servais, je sentais qu'ils étaient à eux ; les mots par exemple : j'aurais voulu des mots *à moi.* Mais ceux dont je dispose ont traîné dans je ne sais combien de consciences ; ils s'arrangent tout seuls dans ma tête en vertu d'habitudes qu'ils ont prises chez les autres et ça n'est pas sans répugnance que je les utilise en vous écrivant. Mais c'est pour la dernière fois. Je vous le dis : il faut aimer les hommes ou bien c'est tout juste s'ils vous permettent de bricoler. Eh bien, moi, je ne veux pas bricoler. Je vais prendre, tout à l'heure, mon revolver, je descendrai dans la rue et je verrai si l'on peut réussir quelque chose *contre eux.* Adieu, monsieur, peut-être est-ce vous que je vais rencontrer. Vous ne saurez jamais alors avec quel plaisir je vous ferai sauter la cervelle. Sinon — et c'est le cas le plus probable — lisez les journaux de demain. Vous y verrez qu'un individu nommé Paul Hilbert a descendu, dans une crise de fureur, cinq passants sur le boulevard Edgar-Quinet. Vous savez mieux que personne ce que vaut la prose des grands quotidiens. Vous comprendrez donc que je ne suis pas “ furieux ”. Je suis très calme au contraire et je vous prie d'accepter, Monsieur, l'assurance de mes sentiments distingués.

« Paul HILBERT. »

Je glissai les cent deux lettres dans cent deux enveloppes et j'écrivis sur les enveloppes les adresses de cent deux écrivains français. Puis je mis le tout dans un tiroir de ma table avec six carnets de timbres.

Pendant les quinze jours qui suivirent, je sortis fort peu, je me laissais occuper lentement par mon crime. Dans la glace, où j'allais parfois me regarder, je constatais avec plaisir les changements de mon visage. Les yeux s'étaient agrandis, ils mangeaient toute la face. Ils étaient noirs et tendres sous les lorgnons, et je les faisais rouler comme des planètes. De beaux yeux d'artiste et d'assassin. Mais je comptais changer bien plus profondément encore après l'accomplissement du massacre. J'ai vu les photos de ces deux belles filles, ces servantes qui tuèrent et saccagèrent leurs maîtresses. J'ai vu leurs photos d'*avant* et d'*après*. *Avant*, leurs visages se balançaient comme des fleurs sages au-dessus de cols de piqué. Elles respiraient l'hygiène et l'honnêteté appétissante. Un fer discret avait ondulé pareillement leurs cheveux. Et, plus rassurante encore que leurs cheveux frisés, que leurs cols et que leur air d'être en visite chez le photographe, il y avait leur ressemblance de sœurs, leur ressemblance si bien pensante, qui mettait tout de suite en avant les liens du sang et les racines naturelles du groupe familial. *Après*, leurs faces resplendissaient comme des incendies. Elles avaient le cou nu des futures décapitées. Des rides partout, d'horribles rides de peur et de haine, des plis, des trous dans la chair comme si une bête avec des griffes avait tourné en rond sur leurs visages. Et ces yeux, toujours ces grands yeux noirs et sans fond — comme les miens. Pourtant elles ne se ressemblaient plus. Chacune portait à sa manière le souvenir de leur crime commun. « S'il suffit, me disais-je, d'un forfait où le hasard a la plus grande part pour transformer ainsi ces têtes d'orphelinat, que ne puis-je espérer d'un crime entièrement conçu et organisé par moi ? » Il s'emparerait de moi, bouleverserait ma laideur trop humaine... un crime, ça coupe en deux la vie de celui qui le commet. Il devait y avoir des moments où l'on souhaiterait revenir en arrière, mais il est là, derrière vous, il vous barre le passage, ce minéral étincelant. Je ne demandais qu'une heure pour jouir du mien, pour sentir son poids écrasant. Cette heure, j'arrangerai tout pour l'avoir à moi : je décidai de faire l'exécution dans le haut de la rue d'Odessa. Je profiterais de l'affolement pour m'enfuir en les laissant ramasser leurs morts. Je courrais, je traverserais le boulevard Edgar-Quinet et tournerais rapidement dans la rue Delambre. Je n'aurais besoin que de trente secondes pour atteindre la porte de l'immeuble où j'habite. A ce moment-là, mes poursuivants seraient encore sur le boulevard Edgar-Quinet, ils perdraient ma trace et il leur faudrait sûrement plus d'une heure pour la retrouver. Je les attendrais chez moi et, quand je les entendrais frapper à ma porte, je rechargerais mon revolver et je me tirerais dans la bouche.

Je vivais plus largement ; je m'étais entendu avec un traiteur de la rue Vavin qui me faisait porter, matin et soir, de bons petits plats. Le commis sonnait, je n'ouvrais pas, j'attendais quelques minutes puis j'entrebâillais ma porte et je voyais, dans un long panier posé sur le sol, des assiettes pleines qui fumaient.

Le 27 octobre, à six heures du soir, il me restait dix-sept francs cinquante. Je pris mon revolver et le paquet de lettres, je descendis. J'eus soin de ne pas fermer la porte, pour pouvoir rentrer plus vite quand j'aurais fait mon coup. Je ne me sentais pas bien, j'avais les mains froides et le sang à la tête, les yeux me chatouillaient. Je regardai les magasins, l'hôtel des Écoles, la papeterie où j'achète mes crayons et je ne les reconnus pas. Je me disais : « Qu'est-ce que c'est que cette rue ? » Le boulevard du Montparnasse était plein de gens. Ils me bousculaient, me repoussaient, me frappaient de leurs coudes ou de leurs épaules. Je me laissais ballotter, la force me manquait pour me glisser entre eux. Je me vis soudain au cœur de cette foule, horriblement seul et petit. Comme ils auraient pu me faire mal, s'ils l'avaient voulu ! J'avais peur à cause de l'arme, dans ma poche. Il me semblait qu'ils allaient deviner qu'elle était là. Ils me regarderaient de leurs yeux durs, ils diraient : « Hé mais... mais... » avec une indignation joyeuse, en me harponnant de leurs pattes d'hommes. Lynché ! Ils me jetteraient au-dessus de leurs têtes, et je retomberais dans leurs bras comme une marionnette. Je jugeai plus sage de remettre au lendemain l'exécution de mon projet. J'allai dîner à *La Coupole* pour seize francs quatre-vingts. Il me restait soixante-dix centimes que je jetai dans le ruisseau.

Je suis resté trois jours dans ma chambre, sans manger, sans dormir. J'avais fermé les persiennes et je n'osais ni m'approcher de la fenêtre ni faire de la lumière. Le lundi, quelqu'un carillonna à ma porte. Je retins mon souffle et j'attendis. Au bout d'une minute, on sonna encore. J'allai sur la pointe des pieds coller mon œil au trou de la serrure. Je ne vis qu'un morceau d'étoffe noire et un bouton. Le type sonna encore puis redescendit : je ne sais pas qui c'était. Dans la nuit, j'eus des visions fraîches, des palmiers, de l'eau qui coulait, un ciel violet au-dessus d'une coupole. Je n'avais pas soif parce que, d'heure en heure, j'allais boire au robinet de l'évier. Mais j'avais faim. J'ai revu aussi la putain brune. C'était dans un château que j'avais fait construire sur les Causses Noires à vingt lieues de tout village. Elle était nue et seule avec moi. Je l'ai forcée à se mettre à genoux sous la menace de mon revolver, à courir à quatre pattes ; puis je l'ai attachée à un pilier et, après lui avoir longuement expliqué ce que j'allais faire, je l'ai criblée de balles. Ces images m'avaient tellement troublé que j'ai dû me contenter. Après, je suis resté immobile dans le noir, la tête absolument vide. Les meubles se sont mis à craquer. Il était cinq heures du matin. J'aurais donné n'importe quoi pour quitter ma chambre, mais je ne pouvais pas descendre à cause des gens qui marchaient dans les rues.

Le jour est venu. Je ne sentais plus ma faim, mais je me suis mis à suer : j'ai trempé ma chemise. Dehors, il y avait du soleil. Alors j'ai pensé : « Dans une chambre close, dans le noir Il est tapi. Depuis trois jours, Il n'a ni mangé ni dormi. On a sonné, et Il n'a pas ouvert. Tout à l'heure, Il va descendre dans la rue et Il tuera. » Je me faisais peur. A six heures du soir, la faim m'a repris. J'étais fou de colère. Je me suis cogné un moment dans les meubles, puis j'ai allumé l'électricité dans les chambres, à la cuisine, aux cabinets. Je me suis mis à chanter à tue-tête, j'ai lavé mes mains et je suis sorti. Il m'a fallu deux bonnes minutes pour mettre toutes mes lettres à la boîte. Je les enfonçais par paquets de dix. J'ai dû friper quelques enveloppes. Puis, j'ai suivi le boulevard du Montparnasse jusqu'à la rue d'Odessa. Je me suis arrêté devant la glace d'une chemiserie et, quand j'y ai vu mon visage, j'ai pensé : « C'est pour ce soir. »

Je me postai dans le haut de la rue d'Odessa, non loin du bec de gaz, et j'attendis. Deux femmes passèrent. Elles se donnaient le bras, la blonde disant :

— Ils avaient mis des tapis à toutes les fenêtres et c'étaient les nobles du pays qui faisaient la figuration.

— Ils sont panés ? demanda l'autre.

— Il n'y a pas besoin d'être pané pour accepter un travail qui rapporte cinq louis par jour.

— Cinq louis ! dit la brune, éblouie. — Elle ajouta, en passant près de moi : Et puis je me figure que ça devait les amuser de mettre les costumes de leurs ancêtres.

Elles s'éloignèrent. J'avais froid, mais je suais abondamment. Au bout d'un moment, je vis arriver trois hommes ; je les laissai passer : il m'en fallait six. Celui de gauche me regarda et fit claquer sa langue. Je détournai les yeux.

A sept heures cinq, deux groupes qui se suivaient de près débouchèrent du boulevard Edgar-Quinet. Il y avait un homme et une femme avec deux enfants. Derrière eux venaient trois vieilles femmes. Je fis un pas en avant. La femme avait l'air en colère et secouait le petit garçon par le bras. L'homme dit d'une voix traînante :

— Il est emmerdant, aussi, ce morpion.

Le cœur me battait si fort que j'en avais mal dans les bras. Je m'avançai et me tins devant eux, immobile. Mes doigts, dans ma poche, étaient tout mous autour de la gâchette.

— Pardon, dit l'homme en me bousculant.

Je me rappelai que j'avais fermé la porte de mon appartement et cela me contraria : il me faudrait perdre un temps précieux à l'ouvrir. Les gens s'éloignèrent. Je fis volte-face et je les suivis machinale ment. Mais je n'avais plus envie de tirer sur eux. Ils se perdirent dans la foule du boulevard. Moi, je m'appuyai contre le mur. J'entendis sonner huit heures et neuf heures. Je me répétais : « Pourquoi faut-il tuer tous ces gens qui sont déjà *morts* », et j'avais envie de rire. Un chien vint flairer mes pieds.

Quand le gros homme me dépassa, je sursautai et je lui emboîtai le pas. Je voyais le pli de sa nuque rouge entre son melon et le col de son pardessus. Il se dandinait un peu et respirait fort, il avait l'air costaud. Je sortis mon revolver : il était brillant et froid, il me dégoûtait, je ne me rappelai pas très bien ce que je devais en faire. Tantôt je le regardais et tantôt je regardais la nuque du type. Le pli de la nuque me souriait, comme une bouche souriante et amère. Je me demandais si je n'allais pas jeter mon revolver dans un égout.

Tout d'un coup le type se retourna et me regarda d'un air irrité. Je fis un pas en arrière.

— C'est pour vous... demander...

Il n'avait pas l'air d'écouter, il regardait mes mains. J'achevai péniblement.

— Pouvez-vous me dire où est la rue de la Gaîté ?

Son visage était gros, et ses lèvres tremblaient. Il ne dit rien, il allongea la main. Je reculai encore et je lui dis :

— Je voudrais...

A ce moment je *sus* que j'allais me mettre à hurler. Je ne voulais pas : je lui lâchai trois balles dans le ventre. Il tomba d'un air idiot, sur les genoux, et sa tête roula sur son épaule gauche.

— Salaud, lui dis-je, sacré salaud !

Je m'enfuis. Je l'entendis tousser. J'entendis aussi

des cris et une galopade derrière moi. Quelqu'un demanda : « Qu'est-ce que c'est, ils se battent ? » puis tout de suite après on cria : « A l'assassin ! A l'assassin ! » Je ne pensais pas que ces cris me concernaient. Mais ils me semblaient sinistres, comme la sirène des pompiers quand j'étais enfant. Sinistres et légèrement ridicules. Je courais de toute la force de mes jambes.

Seulement j'avais commis une erreur impardonnable : au lieu de remonter la rue d'Odessa vers le boulevard Edgar-Quinet, *je la descendais vers le boulevard du Montparnasse.* Quand je m'en aperçus, il était trop tard : j'étais déjà au beau milieu de la foule, des visages étonnés se tournaient vers moi (je me rappelle celui d'une femme très fardée qui portait un chapeau vert avec une aigrette), et j'entendais les imbéciles de la rue d'Odessa crier à l'assassin derrière mon dos. Une main se posa sur mon épaule. Alors je perdis la tête : je ne voulais pas mourir étouffé par cette foule. Je tirai encore deux coups de revolver. Les gens se mirent à piailler et s'écartèrent. J'entrai en courant dans un café. Les consommateurs se levèrent sur mon passage mais ils n'essayèrent pas de m'arrêter, je traversai le café dans toute sa longueur et je m'enfermai dans les lavabos. Il restait encore une balle dans mon revolver.

Un moment s'écoula. J'étais essoufflé et je haletais. Tout était d'un silence extraordinaire, comme si les gens faisaient exprès de se taire. J'élevai mon arme jusqu'à mes yeux et je vis son petit trou noir et rond : la balle sortirait par là ; la poudre me brûlerait le visage. Je laissai retomber mon bras et j'attendis. Au bout d'un instant, ils s'amenèrent à pas de loup ; ils devaient être toute une troupe, à en juger par le frôlement des pieds sur le plancher. Ils chuchotèrent un peu puis se turent. Moi, je soufflais toujours et je pensais qu'ils m'entendaient souffler, de l'autre côté de la cloison. Quelqu'un s'avança doucement et secoua la poignée de la porte. Il devait s'être plaqué de côté contre le mur, pour éviter mes balles. J'eus tout de même envie de tirer — mais la dernière balle était pour moi.

« Qu'est-ce qu'ils attendent ? me demandai-je. S'ils se jetaient sur la porte et s'ils la défonçaient *tout de suite*, je n'aurais pas le temps de me tuer, et ils me prendraient vivant. » Mais ils ne se pressaient pas, ils me laissaient tout le loisir de mourir. Les salauds, ils avaient peur.

Au bout d'un instant, une voix s'éleva.

— Allons, ouvrez, on ne vous fera pas de mal.

Il y eut un silence, et la même voix reprit :

— Vous savez bien que vous ne pouvez pas vous échapper.

Je ne répondis pas, je haletais toujours. Pour m'encourager à tirer, je me disais : « S'ils me prennent, ils vont me battre, me casser des dents, ils me crèveront peut-être un œil. » J'aurais voulu savoir si le gros type était mort. Peut-être que je l'avais seulement blessé... et les deux autres balles, peut-être qu'elles n'avaient atteint personne... Ils préparaient quelque chose, ils étaient en train de tirer un objet lourd sur le plancher ? Je me hâtai de mettre le canon de mon arme dans ma bouche et je le mordis très fort. Mais je ne pouvais pas tirer, pas même poser le doigt sur la gâchette. Tout était retombé dans le silence.

Alors j'ai jeté le revolver et je leur ai ouvert la porte.

# *Intimité*

# I

Lulu couchait nue parce qu'elle aimait se caresser aux draps et que le blanchissage coûte cher. Henri avait protesté au début : on ne se met pas toute nue dans un lit, ça ne se fait pas, c'est sale. Il avait tout de même fini par suivre l'exemple de sa femme mais chez lui c'était du laisser-aller ; il était raide comme un piquet quand il y avait du monde, par genre (il admirait les Suisses et tout particulièrement les Genevois, il leur trouvait grand air parce qu'ils étaient en bois), mais il se négligeait dans les petites choses, par exemple il n'était pas très propre, il ne changeait pas assez souvent de caleçon ; quand Lulu les mettait au sale, elle ne pouvait pas s'empêcher de remarquer qu'ils avaient le fond jaune à force de frotter contre l'entrejambe. Personnellement, Lulu ne détestait pas la saleté : ça fait plus intime, ça donne des ombres tendres ; au creux des coudes par exemple ; elle n'aimait guère ces Anglais, ces corps impersonnels qui ne sentent rien. Mais elle avait horreur des négligences de son mari, parce que c'étaient des façons de se dorloter. Le matin, à son lever, il était toujours très tendre pour lui-même, la tête pleine de rêves, et le grand jour, l'eau froide, le crin des brosses lui faisaient l'effet d'injustices brutales.

Lulu était couchée sur le dos, elle avait introduit le gros orteil de son pied gauche dans une fente du drap ; ce n'était pas une fente, c'était un décousu. Ça l'embêtait ; il faut que je raccommode ça demain, mais elle tirait tout de même un peu sur les fils pour les sentir casser. Henri ne dormait pas encore, mais il ne gênait plus. Il l'avait souvent dit à Lulu : dès qu'il fermait les yeux il se sentait ligoté par des liens ténus et résistants, il ne pouvait même plus lever le petit doigt. Une grosse mouche embobinée dans une toile d'araignée. Lulu aimait sentir contre elle ce grand corps captif. S'il pouvait rester comme ça paralysé, c'est moi qui le soignerais, qui le nettoierais comme un enfant et quelquefois je le retournerais sur le ventre et je lui donnerais la fessée, et d'autres fois quand sa mère viendrait le voir, je le découvrirais sous un prétexte, je rabattrais les draps et sa mère le verrait tout nu. Je pense qu'elle en tomberait raide, il doit y avoir quinze ans qu'elle ne l'a pas vu comme ça. Lulu passa une main légère sur la hanche de son mari et le pinça un peu à l'aine. Henri grogna mais ne fit pas un mouvement. Réduit à l'impuissance. Lulu sourit : le mot « impuissance » la faisait toujours sourire. Quand elle aimait encore Henri et qu'il reposait, ainsi paralysé, à côté d'elle, elle se plaisait à imaginer qu'il avait été patiemment saucissonné par de tout petits hommes dans le genre de ceux qu'elle avait vus sur une image quand elle était petite et qu'elle lisait l'histoire de Gulliver. Elle appelait souvent Henri « Gulliver », et Henri aimait bien ça parce que c'était un nom anglais et que Lulu avait l'air instruite, mais il aurait préféré que Lulu le prononçât avec l'accent. Ce qu'ils ont pu m'embêter : s'il voulait quelqu'un d'instruit il n'avait qu'à épouser Jeanne Beder, elle a des seins en cor de chasse mais elle sait cinq langues. Quand on allait encore à Sceaux, le dimanche, je m'embêtais tellement dans sa famille que je prenais un livre, n'importe quoi ; il y avait toujours quelqu'un qui venait regarder ce que je lisais et sa petite sœur me demandait : « Vous comprenez, Lucie ?... » Ce qu'il y a, c'est qu'il ne me trouve pas distinguée. Les Suisses, oui, ça c'est des gens distingués parce que sa sœur aînée a épousé un Suisse qui lui a fait cinq enfants et puis ils lui en imposent avec leurs montagnes. Moi je ne peux pas avoir d'enfant, c'est constitutionnel, mais je n'ai jamais pensé que c'était distingué ce qu'il fait, quand il sort avec moi, d'aller tout le temps dans les urinoirs et je suis obligée de regarder les devantures en l'attendant, j'ai l'air de quoi ? et il ressort en tirant sur son pantalon et en arquant les jambes comme un vieux.

Lulu retira son orteil de la fente du drap et agita un peu les pieds, pour le plaisir de se sentir alerte auprès de cette chair molle et captive. Elle entendit un gargouillis : un ventre qui chante, ça m'agace, je ne peux jamais savoir si c'est son ventre ou le mien. Elle ferma les yeux : ce sont des liquides qui glougloutent dans des paquets de tuyaux mous, il y en a comme ça chez tout le monde, chez Rirette, chez moi (je n'aime pas y penser, ça me donne mal au ventre). Il m'aime, il n'aime pas mes boyaux, si on lui montrait mon appendice dans un bocal, il ne le reconnaîtrait pas, il est tout le temps à me tripoter mais si on lui mettait le bocal dans les mains il ne sentirait rien, au-dedans, il ne penserait pas « c'est à elle », on devrait pouvoir aimer tout d'une personne, l'œsophage, et le foie, et les intestins. Peut-être qu'on ne les aime pas par manque d'habitude, si on les voyait comme ils voient nos mains et nos bras peut-être qu'on les aimerait ; alors les étoiles de mer doivent s'aimer mieux que nous, elles s'étendent sur la plage quand il fait soleil et elles sortent leur estomac pour lui faire prendre l'air, et tout le monde peut le voir ; je me demande par où nous ferions sortir le nôtre, par le nombril ? Elle avait fermé les yeux, et des disques bleus se mirent à tourner, comme à la foire, hier, je tirais sur les disques avec des flèches de caoutchouc, et il y avait des lettres qui s'allumaient, une à chaque coup, et elles formaient un nom de ville, il m'a empêchée d'avoir Dijon au complet avec sa manie de se coller contre moi par-derrière, je déteste qu'on me touche par-derrière, je voudrais n'avoir pas de dos, je n'aime pas que les gens me fassent des trucs quand je les vois pas, ils peuvent s'en payer et puis on ne voit pas leurs mains, on les sent qui descendent ou qui montent, on ne peut pas prévoir où elles vont, ils vous regardent de tous leurs yeux, et vous ne les voyez pas, il adore ça ; jamais Henri n'y aurait songé, mais lui il ne pense qu'à se mettre derrière moi, et je suis sûre qu'il fait exprès de me toucher le derrière parce qu'il sait que je meurs de honte d'en avoir un, quand j'ai honte ça l'excite mais je ne veux pas penser à lui (elle avait peur), je veux penser à Rirette. Elle pensait à Rirette tous les soirs à la même heure, juste au moment où Henri commençait à bredouiller et à gémir. Mais il y eut de la résistance, l'autre voulait se montrer, elle vit même un instant des cheveux noirs et crépus et elle crut que ça y était, et elle frissonna parce qu'on ne sait jamais ce qui va venir, si c'est le visage ça va, ça passe encore, mais il y a des nuits qu'elle avait passées sans fermer l'œil à cause des sales souvenirs qui étaient remontés à la surface, c'est affreux quand on connaît tout d'un homme et surtout *ça*. Henri, ça n'est pas la même chose, je peux l'imaginer de la tête aux pieds, ça m'attendrit, parce qu'il est mou, avec une chair toute grise sauf le ventre qui est rose, il dit qu'un homme bien fait, quand il est assis, son ventre fait trois plis mais le sien en a six, seulement il les compte de deux en deux et il ne veut pas voir les autres. Elle éprouva de l'agacement en pensant à Rirette : « Lulu, vous ne savez pas ce que c'est qu'un beau corps d'homme. » C'est ridicule, naturellement si, je sais ce que c'est, elle veut dire un corps dur comme la pierre, avec des muscles, j'aime pas ça, Patterson avait un corps comme ça, et moi je me sentais molle comme une chenille quand il me serrait contre lui ; Henri, je l'ai épousé parce qu'il était mou, parce qu'il ressemblait à un curé. Les curés c'est doux comme les femmes avec leurs soutanes et il paraît qu'ils ont des bas. Quand j'avais quinze ans, j'aurais voulu relever doucement leur robe et voir leurs genoux d'hommes et leurs caleçons, ça me faisait drôle qu'ils aient quelque chose entre les jambes ; dans une main j'aurais pris la robe et l'autre main je l'aurais glissée le long de leurs jambes, en remontant jusque-là où je pense, c'est pas que j'aime tellement les femmes, mais un machin d'homme, quand c'est sous une robe, c'est douillet, c'est comme une grosse fleur. Ce qu'il y a c'est qu'en réalité on ne peut jamais prendre ça dans ses mains, si seulement ça pouvait rester tranquille, mais ça se met à bouger comme une bête, ça durcit, ça me fait peur, quand c'est dur et tout droit en l'air c'est brutal ; ce que c'est sale, l'amour. Moi j'aimais Henri parce que sa petite affaire ne durcissait jamais, ne levait jamais la tête, je riais, je l'embrassais quelquefois, je n'en avais pas plus peur que de celle d'un enfant ; le soir, je prenais sa douce petite chose entre mes doigts, il rougissait et il tournait la tête de côté en soupirant, mais ça ne bougeait pas, ça restait bien sage dans ma main, je ne serrais pas, nous restions longtemps ainsi et il s'endormait. Alors je m'étendais sur le dos et je pensais à des curés, à des choses pures, à des femmes, et je me caressais le ventre d'abord, mon beau ventre plat, je descendais les mains, je descendais et c'était le plaisir ; le plaisir il n'y a que moi qui sache me le donner.

Les cheveux crépus, les cheveux de nègre. Et l'angoisse dans la gorge comme une boule. Mais elle serra fortement les paupières et, finalement, ce fut l'oreille de Rirette qui apparut, une petite oreille cramoisie et dorée qui avait l'air en sucre candi. Lulu, à la voir, n'eut pas autant de plaisir que d'ordinaire parce qu'elle entendait la voix de Rirette, en même temps. C'était une voix aiguë et précise que Lulu n'aimait pas. « Vous *devez* partir avec Pierre, ma petite Lulu ; c'est la seule chose intelligente à faire. » J'ai beaucoup d'affection pour Rirette, mais elle m'agace un tout petit peu quand elle fait l'importante et qu'elle s'enchante de ce qu'elle dit. La veille, à la Coupole, Rirette s'était penchée avec des airs raisonnables et un peu hagards : « Vous ne *pouvez* pas rester avec Henri, puisque vous ne l'aimez plus, ce serait un crime. » Elle ne perd pas une occasion de dire du mal de lui, je trouve que ce n'est pas très gentil, il a toujours été parfait avec elle, je ne l'aime plus, c'est possible, mais ça n'est pas à Rirette de me le dire ; avec elle tout paraît simple et facile ; on aime ou on n'aime plus ; mais moi je ne suis pas simple. D'abord, j'ai mes habitudes ici et puis je l'aime bien, c'est mon mari. J'aurais voulu la battre, j'ai toujours envie de lui faire mal parce qu'elle est grasse. « Ce serait un crime. » Elle a levé le bras, j'ai vu son aisselle, je l'aime toujours mieux quand elle a les bras nus. L'aisselle. Elle s'entrouvrit, on aurait dit une bouche, et Lulu vit une chair mauve, un peu ridée, sous des poils frisés qui ressemblaient à des cheveux ; Pierre l'appelle « Minerve potelée », elle n'aime pas ça du tout. Lulu sourit parce qu'elle pensait à son petit frère Robert qui lui avait dit un jour qu'elle était en combinaison : « Pourquoi que tu as des cheveux sous les bras ? » et elle avait répondu : « C'est une maladie. » Elle aimait bien s'habiller devant son petit frère parce qu'il avait toujours des réflexions drôles, on se demande où il va chercher ça. Et il touchait à toutes les affaires de Lulu, il pliait les robes soigneusement, il a les mains si prestes, plus tard ce sera un grand couturier. C'est un métier charmant, et moi, je dessinerai des tissus pour lui. C'est curieux qu'un enfant songe à devenir couturier ; si j'avais été garçon, il me semble que j'aurais voulu être explorateur ou acteur, mais pas couturier ; mais il a toujours été rêveur, il ne parle pas assez, il suit son idée ; moi, je voulais être bonne sœur pour aller quêter dans les beaux immeubles. Je sens mes yeux tout doux, tout doux comme de la chair, je vais m'endormir. Mon beau visage pâle sous la cornette, j'aurais eu l'air distingué. J'aurais vu des centaines d'antichambres sombres. Mais la bonne aurait allumé presque tout de suite ; alors j'aurais aperçu des tableaux de famille, des bronzes d'art sur des consoles. Et des portemanteaux. La dame vient avec un petit carnet et un billet de cinquante francs : « Voici, ma sœur. — Merci, madame, Dieu vous bénisse. A la prochaine fois. » Mais je n'aurais pas été une vraie sœur. Dans l'autobus, quelquefois, j'aurais fait de l'œil à un type, il aurait été ahuri d'abord, ensuite il m'aurait suivie en me racontant des trucs et je l'aurais fait coffrer par un agent. L'argent de la quête je l'aurais gardé pour moi. Qu'est-ce que je me serais acheté ? DE L'ANTIDOTE. C'est idiot. Mes yeux s'amollissent, ça me plaît, on dirait qu'on les a trempés dans l'eau et tout mon corps est confortable. La belle tiare verte, avec les émeraudes et les lapis-lazuli. La tiare tourna, tourna, et c'était une horrible tête de bœuf, mais Lulu n'avait pas peur, elle dit : « Secourge. Les oiseaux du Cantal. Fixe. » Un long fleuve rouge se traînait à travers d'arides campagnes. Lulu pensait à son hachoir mécanique puis à de la gomina.

« Ce serait un crime ! » Elle sursauta et se dressa dans sa nuit, les yeux durs. Ils me torturent, ils ne s'en aperçoivent donc pas ? Rirette, je sais bien qu'elle le fait dans une bonne intention, mais elle qui est si raisonnable pour les autres, elle devrait comprendre que j'ai besoin de réfléchir. Il m'a dit : « Tu viendras ! » en faisant des yeux de braise. « Tu viendras dans ma maison à moi, je te veux toute à moi. » J'ai horreur de ses yeux quand il veut faire l'hypnotiseur, il me pétrissait le bras ; quand je lui vois ces yeux-là, je pense toujours aux poils qu'il a sur la poitrine. Tu viendras, je te veux toute à moi ; comment peut-on dire des choses pareilles ? Je ne suis pas un chien.

Quand je me suis assise, je lui ai souri, j'avais changé ma poudre pour lui et j'avais fait mes yeux parce qu'il aime ça, mais il n'a rien vu, il ne regarde pas mon visage, il regardait mes seins, et j'aurais voulu qu'ils sèchent sur ma poitrine, pour l'embêter, pourtant je n'en ai pas beaucoup, ils sont tout petits. Tu viendras dans ma villa de Nice. Il a dit qu'elle était blanche avec un escalier de marbre et qu'elle donne sur la mer, et que nous vivrons tout nus toute la journée, ça doit faire drôle de monter un escalier quand on est nue ; je l'obligerai à monter devant moi, pour qu'il ne me regarde pas ; sans ça, je ne pourrais même pas lever le pied, je resterais immobile en souhaitant de tout mon cœur qu'il devienne aveugle ; d'ailleurs ça ne me changera guère ; quand il est là, je crois toujours que je suis nue. Il m'a prise par les bras, il avait l'air méchant, il m'a dit : « Tu m'as dans la peau ! » et moi j'avais peur, j'ai dit : « Oui » ; je veux faire ton bonheur, nous irons nous promener en auto, en bateau, nous irons en Italie et je te donnerai tout ce que tu voudras. Mais sa villa n'est presque pas meublée, et nous coucherons par terre sur un matelas. Il veut que je dorme dans ses bras, et je sentirai son odeur ; j'aimerais bien sa poitrine parce qu'elle est brune et large, mais il y a un tas de poils dessus, je voudrais que les hommes soient sans poils, les siens sont noirs et doux comme de la mousse, des fois je les caresse et des fois j'en ai horreur, je me recule le plus loin possible, mais il me plaque contre lui. Il voudra que je dorme dans ses bras, il me serrera dans ses bras, et je sentirai son odeur ; et quand il fera noir nous entendrons le bruit de la mer, et il est capable de me réveiller au milieu de la nuit s'il a envie de faire cela : je ne pourrai jamais m'endormir tranquille sauf quand j'aurai mes affaires, parce que là, tout de même, il me fichera la paix, et encore il paraît qu'il y a des hommes qui font cela avec les femmes indisposées et après ils ont du sang sur le ventre, du sang qui n'est pas à eux, et il doit y en avoir sur les draps, partout, c'est dégoûtant, pourquoi faut-il que nous ayons des corps ?

Lulu ouvrit les yeux, les rideaux étaient colorés en rouge par une lumière qui venait de la rue, il y avait un reflet rouge dans la glace ; Lulu aimait cette lumière rouge, et il y avait un fauteuil qui se découpait en ombre chinoise contre la fenêtre. Sur les bras du fauteuil, Henri avait déposé son pantalon, ses bretelles pendaient dans le vide. Il faut que je lui achète des tirants de bretelles. Oh ! je ne veux pas, je ne veux pas partir. Il m'embrassera toute la journée, et je serai *à lui*, je ferai son plaisir, il me regardera ; il pensera « c'est mon plaisir, je l'ai touchée là et là, et je peux recommencer quand ça me plaira ». A Port-Royal.

Lulu donna des coups de pied dans les draps, elle détestait Pierre quand elle se rappelait ce qui s'était passé à Port-Royal. Elle était derrière la haie, elle croyait qu'il était resté dans l'auto, qu'il consultait la carte, et tout d'un coup elle l'avait vu, il était venu à pas de loup derrière elle, il la regardait. Lulu donna un coup de pied à Henri ; il va se réveiller, celui-là. Mais Henri fit « Homphph » et ne se réveilla pas. Je voudrais connaître un beau jeune homme, pur comme une fille, et nous ne nous toucherions pas, nous nous promènerions au bord de la mer et nous nous tiendrions par la main et la nuit nous coucherions dans deux lits jumeaux, nous resterions comme frère et sœur et nous parlerions jusqu'au matin. Ou alors j'aimerais bien vivre avec Rirette, c'est si charmant les femmes entre elles ; elle a des épaules grasses et polies ; j'étais bien malheureuse quand elle aimait Fresnel, mais ça me troublait de penser qu'il la caressait, qu'il passait lentement les mains sur ses épaules et sur ses flancs, et qu'elle soupirait. Je me demande comment peut être son visage quand elle est étendue comme ça, toute nue, sous un homme, et qu'elle sent des mains qui se promènent sur sa chair. Je ne la toucherais pas pour tout l'or du monde, je ne saurais que faire d'elle, même si elle voulait bien, si elle me disait : « Je veux bien », je ne saurais pas, mais si j'étais invisible, je voudrais être là pendant qu'on lui fait ça et regarder son visage (ça m'étonnerait qu'elle ait encore l'air d'une Minerve), et caresser d'une main légère ses genoux écartés, ses genoux roses, et l'entendre gémir. Lulu, la gorge sèche, eut un rire bref : on a quelquefois de ces idées. Une fois, elle avait inventé que Pierre voulait violer Rirette. Et je l'aidais, je tenais Rirette dans mes bras. Hier. Elle avait le feu aux joues, nous étions assises, sur son divan, l'une contre l'autre, elle avait les jambes serrées, mais nous n'avons rien dit, nous ne dirons jamais rien. Henri se mit à ronfler, et Lulu siffla. Je suis là, je ne peux pas dormir, je me fais du mauvais sang, et lui il ronfle, l'imbécile. S'il me prenait dans ses bras, s'il me suppliait, s'il me disait : « Tu es tout pour moi, Lulu, je t'aime, ne pars pas ! » je lui ferais ce sacrifice, je resterais, oui, je resterais avec lui, toute ma vie, pour lui faire plaisir.

## II

Rirette s'assit à la terrasse du Dôme et commanda un porto. Elle se sentait lasse, elle était irritée contre Lulu :

« ... et leur porto a le goût de bouchon. Lulu s'en moque parce qu'elle prend des cafés, mais on ne peut tout de même pas prendre un café à l'heure de l'apéritif ; ici ils prennent des cafés toute la journée ou bien des cafés-crème parce qu'ils n'ont pas le sou, ce que ça doit les énerver, moi je ne pourrais pas, je flanquerais toute la boutique au nez des clients, ce sont des gens qui n'ont pas besoin de se tenir. Je ne comprends pas pourquoi elle me donne toujours ses rendez-vous à Montparnasse, finalement ça serait aussi près de chez elle si elle me retrouvait au Café de la Paix ou au Pam-Pam, et moi ça m'éloignerait moins de mon travail ; je ne peux pas dire comme ça m'attriste de voir toujours ces têtes-là, dès que j'ai une minute il faut que je vienne ici, sur la terrasse encore ça peut aller, mais dedans, ça sent le linge sale, je n'aime pas les ratés. Et même sur la terrasse je me sens déplacée parce que je suis un peu propre sur moi, ça doit étonner les gens qui passent de me voir au milieu des gens d'ici qui ne se rasent même pas et les femmes qui ont l'air de je ne sais quoi. On doit se dire :

“ Qu’est-ce qu’elle fait là ? ” Je sais bien qu’il vient quelquefois des Américaines assez riches quand c’est l’été, mais il paraît qu’elles s’arrêtent maintenant en Angleterre avec le gouvernement que nous avons, c’est pour ça que le commerce de luxe ne marche pas, j’ai vendu moitié moins que l’an dernier à pareille époque, et je me demande comment font les autres, puisque c’est moi la meilleure vendeuse, M^me^ Dubech me l’a dit, je plains la petite Yonnel, elle ne sait pas vendre, elle n’a pas dû se faire un sou de plus que son fixe, ce mois-ci ; et quand on est restée sur ses pieds toute la journée on voudrait se détendre un peu dans un endroit agréable, avec un peu de luxe, un peu d’art et un personnel bien stylé, on voudrait fermer les yeux et se laisser aller, et puis il faudrait de la musique en sourdine, ça ne coûterait pas tellement cher d’aller de temps en temps au dancing des Ambassadeurs ; mais les garçons d’ici sont tellement insolents, on voit qu’ils ont affaire à du petit monde, sauf le petit brun qui me sert, il est gentil ; je crois que ça plaît à Lulu de se sentir entourée par tous ces types-là, ça lui ferait peur d’aller dans un endroit un peu chic, au fond elle n’est pas sûre d’elle, ça l’intimide dès qu’un homme a de belles manières, elle n’aimait pas Louis ; eh bien, je pense qu’ici elle peut se sentir à son aise, il y en a qui n’ont même pas de faux cols, avec leur air de pauvres et leurs pipes, et ces yeux qu’ils vous jettent, ils n’essaient même pas de dissimuler, on voit qu’ils n’ont pas d’argent pour se payer des femmes, ça n’est pourtant pas ce qui manque dans le quartier, c’en est même dégoûtant ; on dirait qu’ils vont vous manger, et ils ne seraient même pas capables de vous dire un peu gentiment qu’ils ont envie de vous, de tourner la chose de manière à vous faire plaisir. »

Le garçon s’approche :

— Sec, votre porto, mademoiselle ?

— Oui, merci.

Il dit encore, d'un air aimable :

— Quel beau temps !

— Ça n'est pas trop tôt, dit Rirette.

— C'est vrai, on aurait cru que l'hiver n'aurait jamais fini.

Il s'en alla, et Rirette le suivit des yeux. « J'aime bien ce garçon, pensa-t-elle, il sait se tenir à sa place, il n'est pas familier, mais il a toujours un mot pour moi, une petite attention particulière. »

Un jeune homme maigre et voûté la regardait avec insistance ; Rirette haussa les épaules et lui tourna le dos : « Quand on veut faire de l'œil aux femmes, on pourrait au moins avoir du linge propre. Je lui répondrai ça, s'il m'adresse la parole. Je me demande pourquoi elle ne part pas. Elle ne veut pas faire de peine à Henri, je trouve ça trop joli : une femme n'a tout de même pas le droit de gâcher sa vie pour un impuissant. » Rirette détestait les impuissants, c'était physique. « Elle doit partir, décida-t-elle, c'est son bonheur qui est en jeu, je lui dirai qu'on ne doit pas jouer avec son bonheur. Lulu, vous n'avez pas le droit de jouer avec votre bonheur. Je ne lui dirai rien du tout, c'est fini, je lui ai dit cent fois, on ne peut pas faire le bonheur des gens malgré eux. » Rirette sentit un grand vide dans sa tête, parce qu'elle était si fatiguée, elle regardait le porto, tout visqueux dans son verre, comme un caramel liquide, et une voix répétait en elle : « Le bonheur, le bonheur », et c'était un beau mot attendrissant et grave, et elle pensait que, si on lui avait demandé son avis au concours de *Paris-Soir*, elle aurait dit que c'était le plus beau mot de la langue française. « Est-ce que quelqu'un y a pensé ? Ils ont dit : énergie, courage, mais c'est parce que ce sont des hommes, il aurait fallu que ce soit une femme, ce sont les femmes qui peuvent trouver ça, il aurait fallu deux prix, un pour les hommes, et le plus beau nom ç'aurait été Honneur ; un pour les femmes, et j'aurais gagné, j'aurais dit Bonheur ; Honneur et Bonheur ça rime, c'est amusant. Je lui dirai : " Lulu, vous n'avez pas le droit de manquer votre bonheur. Votre Bonheur, Lulu, votre Bonheur. " Personnellement, je trouve Pierre très bien, d'abord c'est un homme pour de bon, et puis il est intelligent, ce qui ne gâte rien, il a de l'argent, il sera aux petits soins pour elle. Il est de ces hommes qui savent aplanir les petites difficultés de la vie, c'est agréable pour une femme ; j'aime bien qu'on sache commander, c'est une nuance, mais il sait parler, aux garçons, aux maîtres d'hôtel ; on lui obéit, moi j'appelle ça avoir de la carrure. C'est peut-être ce qui manque le plus à Henri. Et puis il y a des considérations de santé, avec le père qu'elle a eu, elle ferait bien de faire attention, c'est charmant d'être mince et diaphane et de n'avoir jamais ni faim, ni sommeil, de dormir quatre heures par nuit et de courir Paris toute la journée pour placer des projets de tissus, mais c'est de l'inconscience, elle aurait besoin de suivre un régime rationnel, manger peu à la fois, je veux bien, mais souvent et à heures fixes. Elle sera bien avancée quand on l'enverra pour dix ans dans un sanatorium. »

Elle fixa d'un air perplexe l'horloge du carrefour Montparnasse dont les aiguilles marquaient onze heures vingt. « Je ne comprends pas Lulu, c'est un drôle de tempérament, je n'ai jamais pu savoir si elle aimait les hommes, ou s'ils la dégoûtaient : pourtant avec Pierre elle devrait être contente, ça la change tout de même un peu de son type de l'an dernier, de son Rabut, Rebut comme je l'appelais. » Ce souvenir l'amusa, mais elle retint son sourire parce que le jeune homme maigre la regardait toujours, elle avait surpris son regard en tournant la tête. Rabut avait la figure criblée de points noirs, et Lulu s'amusait à les lui ôter en pressant sur la peau avec les ongles : « C'est écœurant, mais ça n'est pas sa faute, Lulu ne sait pas ce que c'est qu'un bel homme, moi j'adore les hommes coquets, d'abord c'est si joli de belles affaires d'hommes, leurs chemises, leurs souliers, les belles cravates chatoyantes, c'est rude si l'on veut mais c'est si doux, c'est fort, une force douce, c'est comme leur odeur de tabac anglais et d'eau de Cologne et leur peau quand ils sont bien rasés, ça n'est pas... ça n'est pas de la peau de femme, on dirait du cuir de Cordoue, leurs bras forts se ferment sur vous, on met la tête sur leur poitrine, on sent leur douce odeur forte d'hommes soignés, ils vous murmurent des mots doux ; ils ont de belles affaires, de beaux souliers rudes en cuir de vache, ils vous murmurent " Ma chérie, ma douce chérie ", et on se sent défaillir », Rirette pensa à Louis qui l'avait quittée l'an dernier, et son cœur se serra : « Un homme qui s'aime et qui a des tas de petites manières, une chevalière, un étui à cigarettes en or et des petites manies..., seulement ceux-là, ce qu'ils peuvent être rosses, quelquefois, c'est pis que des femmes. Ce qui serait le mieux ce serait un homme de quarante ans, quelqu'un qui se soignerait encore avec des cheveux grisonnants aux tempes et rejetés en arrière, très sec avec de larges épaules, très sportif, mais qui connaîtrait la vie et qui serait bon parce qu'il aurait souffert. Lulu n'est qu'une gamine, elle a de la chance d'avoir une amie comme moi, parce que Pierre commence à se lasser, et il y en a qui en profiteraient au lieu que moi je lui dis toujours de prendre patience, et, quand il est un peu tendre avec moi, je n'ai pas l'air d'y faire attention, je me mets à parler de Lulu et je trouve toujours un mot pour la faire valoir, mais elle ne mérite pas la chance qu'elle a, elle ne se rend pas compte, je lui souhaite de vivre un peu seule comme moi depuis que Louis est parti, elle verrait ce que c'est de rentrer seule dans sa chambre le soir, quand on a travaillé toute la journée, et de trouver la chambre vide, et de mourir d'envie de poser sa tête sur une épaule. On se demande où on trouve le courage de se lever le lendemain matin et de retourner au travail, et d'être séduisante et gaie, et de donner du courage à tout le monde alors qu'on voudrait plutôt mourir que de continuer cette vie-là. »

L'horloge sonna la demie de onze heures. Rirette pensait au bonheur, à l'oiseau bleu, à l'oiseau du bonheur, à l'oiseau rebelle de l'amour. Elle sursauta : « Lulu a trente minutes de retard, c'est normal. Elle ne quittera jamais son mari, elle n'a pas assez de volonté pour ça. Au fond, c'est surtout par respectabilité qu'elle reste avec Henri : elle le trompe mais tant qu'on lui dit " Madame ", elle pense que ça ne compte pas. Elle dit pis que pendre de lui mais il ne faudrait pas qu'on lui répète le lendemain ce qu'elle a dit, elle se fâcherait tout rouge. J'ai fait tout ce que je pouvais et je lui ai dit ce que j'avais à lui dire, tant pis pour elle. »

Un taxi s'arrêta devant le Dôme, et Lulu en descendit. Elle portait une grosse valise, et son visage était un peu solennel.

— J'ai quitté Henri, cria-t-elle de loin.

Elle s'approcha, courbée sous le poids de sa valise. Elle souriait.

— Comment, Lulu? dit Rirette saisie, vous ne voulez pas dire... ?

— Oui, dit Lulu, c'est fini, je l'ai laissé tomber.

Rirette était encore incrédule :

— Il le sait ? Vous le lui avez dit ?

Les yeux de Lulu devinrent orageux :

— Et comment ! dit-elle.

— Eh bien, ma petite Lulu !

Rirette ne savait trop que penser mais, en tout état de cause, elle supposa que Lulu avait besoin d'encouragements :

— Comme c'est bien, dit-elle, comme vous avez été courageuse.

Elle eut envie d'ajouter : vous voyez que ça n'était pas bien difficile. Mais elle se retint. Lulu se laissait admirer : elle avait le rouge aux joues, et ses yeux flamboyaient. Elle s'assit et posa sa valise près d'elle. Elle portait un manteau de laine grise avec une ceinture de cuir et un pull-over jaune clair au col roulé. Elle était tête nue. Rirette n'aimait pas que Lulu se promenât tête nue : elle reconnut tout de suite le curieux mélange de blâme et d'amusement où elle était plongée ; Lulu lui produisait toujours cet effet-là. « Ce que j'aime en elle, décida Rirette, c'est sa vitalité. »

— En cinq sec, dit Lulu. Et je lui ai dit ce que j'avais sur le cœur. Il était sonné.

— Je n'en reviens pas, dit Rirette. Mais qu'est-ce qui vous a pris, ma petite Lulu ? Vous avez mangé du lion. Hier soir, j'aurais donné ma tête à couper que vous ne le quitteriez pas.

— C'est à cause de mon petit frère. Avec moi je veux bien qu'il fasse le supérieur, mais je ne peux pas souffrir qu'il touche à ma famille.

— Mais comment ça s'est-il passé ?

— Où est le garçon ? dit Lulu en s'agitant sur sa chaise. Les garçons du Dôme ne sont jamais là quand on les appelle. C'est le petit brun qui nous sert ?

— Oui, dit Rirette. Vous savez que j'ai fait sa conquête ?

— Ah ? Eh bien alors méfiez-vous de la dame du lavabo, il est tout le temps fourré avec elle. Il lui fait la cour, mais je crois que c'est un prétexte pour voir les dames entrer aux cabinets ; quand elles sortent, il les regarde dans les yeux pour les faire rougir. A propos, je vous laisse une minute, il faut que je descende téléphoner à Pierre, il va faire une tête ! Si vous voyez le garçon, commandez-moi un café-crème ; j'en ai pour une minute et je vous raconterai tout.

Elle se leva, fit quelques pas et revint vers Rirette.

— Je suis bien heureuse, ma petite Rirette.

— Chère Lulu, dit Rirette en lui prenant les mains.

Lulu se dégagea et traversa la terrasse d'un pas léger. Rirette la regarda s'éloigner. « Je ne l'aurais jamais crue capable de ça. Comme elle est gaie, pensa-t-elle, un peu scandalisée, ça lui réussit de plaquer son mari. Si elle m'avait écoutée, ce serait fait depuis longtemps. De toute façon c'est grâce à moi ; au fond, j'ai beaucoup d'influence sur elle. »

Lulu revint au bout de quelques instants :

— Pierre en était assis, dit-elle. Il voulait des détails, mais je les lui donnerai tout à l'heure, je déjeune avec lui. Il dit qu'on pourra peut-être partir demain soir.

— Comme je suis heureuse, Lulu, dit Rirette. Racontez-moi vite. C'est cette nuit que vous avez décidé ça ?

— Vous savez, je n'ai rien décidé, dit Lulu modestement, ça s'est décidé tout seul. Elle tapa nerveusement sur la table : « Garçon ! Garçon ! Il m'embête ce garçon, je voudrais un café-crème. »

Rirette était choquée : à la place de Lulu et dans des circonstances aussi graves, elle n'aurait pas perdu son temps à courir après un café-crème. Lulu est quelqu'un de charmant, mais c'est étonnant comme elle peut être futile, c'est un oiseau.

Lulu pouffa de rire :

— Si vous aviez vu la tête d'Henri !

— Je me demande ce que va dire votre mère, dit Rirette avec sérieux.

— Ma mère ? Elle sera en-chan-tée, dit Lulu d'un air assuré. Il était malpoli avec elle, vous savez, elle en avait jusque-là. Toujours à lui reprocher de m'avoir mal élevée, que j'étais ci, que j'étais ça, qu'on voyait bien que j'avais reçu une éducation d'arrière-boutique. Vous savez, ce que j'en ai fait c'est un peu à cause d'elle.

— Mais que s'est-il passé ?

— Eh bien, il a giflé Robert.

— Mais Robert est donc venu chez vous ?

— Oui, en passant ce matin, parce que maman veut le mettre en apprentissage chez Gompez. Je crois que je vous l'ai dit. Alors il est passé chez nous pendant que nous prenions notre petit déjeuner, et Henri l'a giflé.

— Mais pourquoi ? demanda Rirette légèrement agacée. Elle détestait la façon dont Lulu racontait les histoires.

— Ils ont eu des mots, dit Lulu vaguement, et le petit ne s'est pas laissé faire. Il lui tient tête. « Vieux cul » qu'il lui a fait, en pleine figure, parce qu'Henri l'a appelé mal élevé, naturellement, il ne sait dire que ça ; je me tordais. Alors Henri s'est levé, nous déjeunions dans le studio, et il lui a flanqué une gifle, je l'aurais tué !

— Alors vous êtes partie ?

— Parti ? dit Lulu étonnée, où ?

— Je croyais que c'était à ce moment-là que vous l'aviez quitté. Écoutez, ma petite Lulu, il faut me raconter ça en ordre, sans ça je n'y comprends rien. Dites-moi, ajouta-t-elle, prise d'un soupçon, vous l'avez bien quitté, c'est bien vrai ?

— Mais oui, voilà une heure que je vous l'explique.

— Bon. Alors Henri a giflé Robert. Et après ?

— Après, dit Lulu, je l'ai enfermé sur le balcon, c'était trop drôle ! Il était encore en pyjama, il tapait à la vitre mais il n'osait pas casser les carreaux parce qu'il est avare comme un pou. Moi, à sa place, j'aurais tout bousillé, même si j'avais dû me mettre les mains en sang. Et puis les Texier se sont amenés. Alors il m'a fait des sourires à travers la fenêtre, il faisait semblant que c'était une plaisanterie.

Le garçon passait ; Lulu le saisit par le bras :

— Alors, vous voilà, garçon ? Est-ce que ça vous dérangerait de me servir un café-crème ?

Rirette se sentit gênée et elle fit au garçon un sourire un peu complice, mais le garçon resta sombre et s'inclina avec une obséquiosité pleine de blâme. Rirette en voulut un peu à Lulu : elle ne savait jamais prendre le ton juste avec les inférieurs, elle était tantôt trop familière, tantôt trop exigeante et trop sèche.

Lulu se mit à rire.

— Je ris parce que je revois Henri en pyjama sur le balcon ; il tremblait de froid. Vous savez comment je m'y suis prise pour l'enfermer ? Il était au fond du studio, Robert pleurait, et il faisait des sermons. J'ai ouvert la fenêtre et j'ai fait : « Regarde Henri ! il y a un taxi qui a renversé la marchande de fleurs. » Il est venu à côté de moi : il aime bien la marchande de fleurs parce qu'elle lui a dit qu'elle était Suisse et il croit qu'elle est amoureuse de lui. « Où ça ? Où ça ? » qu'il disait. Moi je me suis retirée en douce, je suis rentrée dans la chambre et j'ai refermé la fenêtre. Je lui ai crié à travers la vitre : « Ça t'apprendra à faire la brute avec mon frère. » Je l'ai laissé plus d'une heure sur le balcon, il nous regardait avec des yeux ronds, il était bleu de colère. Moi je lui tirais la langue et je donnais des bonbons à Robert ; après ça, j'ai apporté mes affaires dans le studio et je me suis habillée devant Robert parce que je sais qu'Henri déteste ça : Robert m'embrassait les bras et dans le cou comme un petit homme, il est charmant ; nous faisions comme si Henri n'était pas là. De l'affaire, j'ai oublié de me laver.

— Et l'autre qui était là derrière la fenêtre. C'est trop comique, dit Rirette en riant aux éclats.

Lulu cessa de rire :

— J'ai peur qu'il n'ait pris froid, dit-elle sérieusement ; dans la colère on ne réfléchit pas. Elle reprit avec gaieté : « Il nous tendait le poing et il parlait tout le temps, mais je ne comprenais pas la moitié de ce qu'il disait. Puis Robert est parti, et là-dessus les Texier ont sonné, et je les ai fait entrer. Quand il les a vus, il est devenu tout sourire, il a fait des courbettes sur le balcon et moi je leur disais : " Regardez mon mari, mon grand chéri, s'il ne ressemble pas à un poisson dans un aquarium ? " Les Texier le saluaient à travers la vitre, ils étaient légèrement ahuris mais ils savent se tenir.

— Je vois ça d'ici, dit Rirette en riant. Haha ! Votre mari sur le balcon et les Texier dans le studio ! » Elle répéta plusieurs fois « votre mari sur le balcon et les Texier dans le studio... ». Elle aurait voulu trouver des mots drôles et pittoresques pour décrire la scène à Lulu, elle pensait que Lulu n'avait pas le sens du comique. Mais les mots ne vinrent pas.

— J'ai ouvert la fenêtre, dit Lulu, et Henri est rentré. Il m'a embrassée devant les Texier et il m'a appelée petite friponne. « La petite friponne, qu'il faisait, elle a voulu me jouer un tour. » Et je souriais, et les Texier souriaient poliment, tout le monde souriait. Mais quand ils ont été partis, il m'a lancé un coup de poing sur l'oreille. Alors j'ai pris une brosse et je la lui ai envoyée sur le coin de la bouche : je lui ai fendu les deux lèvres.

— Ma pauvre Lulu, dit Rirette avec tendresse.

Mais Lulu repoussa du geste toute compassion. Elle se tenait droite en secouant ses boucles brunes d'un air combatif, et ses yeux lançaient des éclairs.

— C'est là qu'on s'est expliqué : je lui ai lavé les lèvres avec une serviette et je lui ai dit que j'en avais marre, que je ne l'aimais plus, et que je partirais. Il s'est mis à pleurer, il a dit qu'il se tuerait. Mais ça ne prend plus : vous vous rappelez, Rirette, l'année dernière, au moment de ces histoires avec la Rhénanie, il me chantait ça tous les jours : il va y avoir la guerre. Lulu, je vais partir et je serai tué, et tu me regretteras, tu auras du remords pour toutes les peines que tu m'as faites. « Ça va, que je lui répondais, tu es impuissant, c'est un cas de réforme. » Tout de même je l'ai calmé, parce qu'il parlait de m'enfermer à clef dans le studio, je lui ai juré que je ne partirais pas avant un mois. Après ça, il a été à son bureau, il avait les yeux rouges et un bout de taffetas gommé sur la lèvre, il n'était pas beau. Moi, j'ai fait le ménage, j'ai mis les lentilles sur le feu et j'ai fait ma valise. Je lui ai laissé un mot sur la table de la cuisine.

— Qu'est-ce que vous lui écriviez ?

— Je lui mettais, dit Lulu fièrement : « Les lentilles sont sur le feu. Sers-toi et éteins le gaz. Il y a du jambon dans le frigidaire. Moi j'en ai marre et je les mets. Adieu. »

Elles rirent toutes deux et des passants se retournèrent. Rirette pensa qu'elles devaient offrir un spectacle charmant et elle regretta de ne pas être assise à la terrasse de Viel ou du Café de la Paix. Quand elles eurent fini de rire, elles se turent, et Rirette s'aperçut qu'elles n'avaient plus rien à se dire. Elle était un peu déçue.

— Il faut que je me sauve, dit Lulu en se levant ; je retrouve Pierre à midi. Qu'est-ce que je vais faire de ma valise ?

— Laissez-la-moi, dit Rirette, je la confierai tout à l'heure à la dame des lavabos. Quand est-ce que je vous revois ?

— Je viendrai vous prendre chez vous à deux heures, j'ai un tas de courses à faire avec vous : je n'ai pas pris la moitié de mes affaires, il faudra que Pierre me donne de l'argent.

Lulu partit, et Rirette appela le garçon. Elle se sentait grave et triste pour deux. Le garçon accourut : Rirette avait déjà remarqué qu'il s'empressait toujours de venir quand c'était elle qui l'appelait.

— C'est cinq francs, dit-il. Il ajouta d'un air un peu sec : vous étiez bien gaies toutes les deux, on vous entendait rire d'en bas.

Lulu l'a blessé, pensa Rirette avec dépit. Elle dit en rougissant :

— Mon amie est un peu nerveuse ce matin.

— Elle est charmante, dit le garçon avec âme. Je vous remercie, mademoiselle.

Il empocha les six francs et s'en fut. Rirette était un peu étonnée mais midi sonna et elle pensa qu'Henri allait rentrer chez lui et trouver le mot de Lulu : ce fut pour elle un moment plein de douceur.

— Je voudrais qu'on envoie tout ça *avant demain soir,* à l'hôtel du Théâtre, rue Vandamme, dit Lulu à la caissière, d'un air de dame. Elle se tourna vers Rirette :

— C'est fini, Rirette, on les met.

— Quel nom ? dit la caissière.

— M^me^ Lucienne Crispin.

Lulu jeta son manteau sur son bras et se mit à courir ; elle descendit en courant le grand escalier de la Samaritaine. Rirette la suivait, faillit plusieurs fois tomber parce qu'elle ne regardait pas ses pieds : Elle n'avait d'yeux que pour la mince silhouette bleue et jaune serin qui dansait devant elle ! « C'est pourtant vrai qu'elle a un corps obscène... » Chaque fois que rirette voyait Lulu de dos ou de profil, elle était frappée par l'obscénité de ses formes mais elle ne s'expliquait pas pourquoi : c'était une impression. « Elle est souple et mince, mais elle a quelque chose d'indécent, je ne sors pas de là. Elle fait tout ce qu'elle peut pour se mouler, ça doit être ça. Elle dit qu'elle a honte de son derrière et elle met des jupes qui lui collent aux fesses. Il est petit, son derrière, je veux bien, bien plus petit que le mien, mais il se voit davantage. Il est tout rond, au-dessous de ses reins maigres, il remplit bien la jupe, on dirait qu'on l'a coulé dedans ; et puis il danse. »

Lulu se retourna, et elles se sourirent. Rirette pensait au corps indiscret de son amie avec un mélange de réprobation et de langueur : de petits seins retroussés, une chair polie, toute jaune — quand on la touchait on aurait juré du caoutchouc — de longues cuisses, un long corps canaille, aux membres longs : « Un corps de négresse, pensa Rirette, elle a l'air d'une négresse qui danse la rumba. » Près de la porte-tambour, une glace renvoya à Rirette le reflet de ses formes pleines : « Je suis plus sportive, pensa-t-elle en prenant le bras de Lulu, elle fait plus d'effet que moi quand nous sommes habillées, mais, toute nue, je suis sûrement mieux qu'elle. »

Elles restèrent un moment silencieuses, puis Lulu dit :

— Pierre a été charmant. Vous aussi vous avez été charmante, Rirette, je vous suis bien reconnaissante à tous les deux.

Elle avait dit ça d'un air contraint, mais Rirette n'y fit pas attention : Lulu n'avait jamais su remercier, elle était trop timide.

— Ça m'embête, dit soudain Lulu, mais il faut que je m'achète un soutien-gorge.

— Ici ? dit Rirette. Elles passaient justement devant un magasin de lingerie.

— Non. Mais c'est parce que j'en voyais que j'y ai pensé. Pour les soutiens-gorge, je vais chez Fischer.

— Boulevard du Montparnasse ? s'écria Rirette. Faites bien attention, Lulu, reprit-elle gravement, il vaudrait mieux ne pas trop hanter le boulevard du Montparnasse, surtout à cette heure-ci : nous allons tomber sur Henri, ce sera infiniment désagréable.

— Sur Henri ? dit Lulu en haussant les épaules ; mais non, pourquoi ?

L'indignation empourpra les joues et les tempes de Rirette.

— Vous êtes bien toujours la même, ma petite Lulu, quand une chose vous déplaît, vous la niez, purement et simplement. Vous avez envie d'aller chez Fischer, alors vous me soutenez qu'Henri ne passe pas sur le boulevard du Montparnasse. Vous savez très bien qu'il y passe tous les jours à six heures, c'est son chemin. Vous me l'avez dit vous-même : il remonte la rue de Rennes et il va attendre l'AE à l'angle du boulevard Raspail.

— D'abord il n'est que cinq heures, dit Lulu, et

puis il n'a peut-être pas été au bureau : après le mot que je lui ai écrit, il a dû s'étendre.

— Mais Lulu, dit soudain Rirette, il y a un autre Fischer, vous savez bien, pas loin de l'Opéra, dans la rue du Quatre-Septembre.

— Oui, dit Lulu d'un air veule, mais il faudra y aller.

— Ah ! je vous aime bien, ma petite Lulu ! Il faudra y aller ! Mais c'est à deux pas, c'est bien plus près que le carrefour Montparnasse.

— J'aime pas ce qu'ils vendent.

Rirette pensa avec amusement que tous les Fischer vendaient les mêmes articles. Mais Lulu avait des obstinations incompréhensibles : Henri était incontestablement la personne qu'elle avait le moins envie de rencontrer en ce moment, et on aurait dit qu'elle faisait exprès de se jeter dans ses jambes.

— Eh bien, dit-elle avec indulgence, allons à Montparnasse, d'ailleurs Henri est si grand que nous l'apercevrons avant qu'il ne nous voie.

— Et puis, quoi ? dit Lulu, si on le rencontre, on le rencontrera, c'est tout. Il ne va pas nous manger.

Lulu tint à gagner Montparnasse à pied ; elle dit qu'elle avait besoin d'air. Elles suivirent la rue de Seine, puis la rue de l'Odéon et la rue de Vaugirard. Rirette fit l'éloge de Pierre et montra à Lulu combien il avait été parfait dans cette circonstance.

— Ce que j'aime Paris, dit Lulu, ce que je vais avoir de regrets !

— Taisez-vous donc, Lulu. Quand je pense que vous avez la chance d'aller à Nice et que vous regrettez Paris.

Lulu ne répondit pas, elle se mit à regarder à droite et à gauche d'un air triste et chercheur.

Lorsqu'elles sortirent de chez Fischer elles entendirent sonner six heures. Rirette prit Lulu par le coude et voulut l'emmener au plus vite. Mais Lulu s'arrêta devant Baumann le fleuriste.

— Regardez ces azalées, ma petite Rirette. Si j'avais un beau salon, j'en mettrais partout.

— Je n'aime pas les fleurs en pot, dit Rirette.

Elle était exaspérée. Elle tourna la tête du côté de la rue de Rennes et, naturellement, au bout d'une minute elle vit apparaître la grande silhouette stupide d'Henri. Il était nu-tête et portait un veston de sport en tweed marron. Rirette détestait le marron :

— Le voilà, Lulu, le voilà, dit-elle précipitamment.

— Où ? dit Lulu, où est-il ?

Elle n'était guère plus calme que Rirette.

— Derrière nous, sur l'autre trottoir. Filons, et ne vous retournez pas.

Lulu se retourna tout de même.

— Je le vois, dit-elle.

Rirette chercha à l'entraîner mais Lulu se raidit, elle regardait fixement Henri. Elle dit enfin :

— Je crois qu'il nous a vues.

Elle paraissait effrayée, elle céda d'un seul coup à Rirette et se laissa docilement emmener.

— Maintenant, pour l'amour du Ciel, Lulu, ne vous retournez plus, dit Rirette un peu essoufflée. Nous allons tourner dans la prochaine rue à droite, c'est la rue Delambre.

Elles marchaient très vite et bousculaient les passants. Par moments, Lulu se faisait un peu traîner, à d'autres moments c'était elle qui tirait Rirette en avant. Mais elles n'avaient pas atteint le coin de la rue Delambre quand Rirette vit une grande ombre brune un peu en arrière de Lulu ; elle comprit que c'était Henri et se mit à trembler de colère. Lulu gardait les paupières baissées, elle avait l'air sournois et buté.

« Elle regrette son imprudence mais il est trop tard, tant pis pour elle. »

Elles pressèrent le pas ; Henri les suivait sans dire un mot. Elles dépassèrent la rue Delambre et continuèrent à marcher dans la direction de l'Observatoire. Rirette entendait craquer les souliers d'Henri ; il y avait aussi une sorte de râle léger et régulier qui scandait leur marche : c'était le souffle d'Henri (Henri avait toujours eu le souffle fort, mais jamais à ce point-là : il avait dû courir pour les rejoindre, ou bien c'était l'émotion).

« Il faut faire comme s'il n'était pas là, pensa Rirette. Ne pas avoir l'air de s'apercevoir de son existence. » Mais elle ne put s'empêcher de le regarder du coin de l'œil. Il était blanc comme un linge et baissait tellement les paupières que ses yeux semblaient clos. « On dirait un somnambule », pensa Rirette avec une espèce d'horreur. Les lèvres d'Henri tremblaient, et sur la lèvre inférieure, un petit bout de taffetas rose, à moitié décollé, s'était mis à trembler aussi. Et le souffle ; toujours le souffle égal et rauque qui se terminait à présent par une petite musique nasillarde. Rirette se sentait mal à l'aise : elle ne craignait pas Henri mais la maladie et la passion lui faisaient toujours un peu peur. Au bout d'un moment, Henri avança doucement la main, sans regarder, et saisit le bras de Lulu. Lulu tordit la bouche comme si elle allait pleurer et se dégagea en frissonnant.

— Pfffouh ! fit Henri.

Rirette avait une envie folle de s'arrêter : elle avait un point de côté, et ses oreilles bourdonnaient. Mais Lulu courait presque ; elle aussi, elle avait l'air d'une somnambule. Rirette eut l'impression que, si elle lâchait le bras de Lulu et si elle s'arrêtait, ils continueraient tous deux à courir côte à côte, muets, pâles comme des morts et les yeux clos.

Henri se mit à parler. Il dit d'une drôle de voix enrouée :

— Rentre avec moi.

Lulu ne répondit pas. Henri reprit, de la même voix rauque et sans intonation :

— Tu es ma femme. Rentre avec moi.

— Vous voyez bien qu'elle ne veut pas rentrer, répondit Rirette les dents serrées. Laissez-la tranquille.

Il n'eut pas l'air de l'entendre. Il répétait :

— Je suis ton mari, je veux que tu rentres avec moi.

— Je vous prie de la laisser tranquille, dit Rirette sur un ton aigu, vous ne gagnerez rien à l'embêter comme ça, fichez-nous la paix.

Il tourna vers Rirette un visage étonné :

— C'est ma femme, dit-il ; elle est à moi ; je veux qu'elle rentre avec moi.

Il avait pris le bras de Lulu, et cette fois Lulu ne se dégagea pas :

— Allez-vous-en, dit Rirette.

— Je ne m'en irai pas, je la suivrai partout, je veux qu'elle rentre à la maison.

Il parlait avec effort. Tout à coup, il fit une grimace qui découvrit ses dents et il cria de toutes ses forces ·

— Tu es à moi !

Des gens se retournèrent en riant. Henri secouait le bras de Lulu et grondait comme une bête en retroussant les lèvres. Par bonheur, un taxi vide vint à passer. Rirette lui fit signe et s'arrêta. Henri s'arrêta aussi. Lulu voulut poursuivre sa marche mais ils la maintinrent solidement, chacun par un bras.

— Vous devriez comprendre, dit Rirette en tirant

Lulu vers la chaussée, que vous ne la ramènerez jamais à vous par ces violences.

— Laissez-la, laissez ma femme, dit Henri en tirant en sens inverse.

Lulu était molle comme un paquet de linge.

— Vous montez ou vous ne montez pas ? cria le chauffeur impatienté.

Rirette lâcha le bras de Lulu et fit pleuvoir une grêle de coups sur les mains d'Henri. Mais il ne paraissait pas les sentir. Au bout d'un moment, il lâcha prise et se mit à regarder Rirette d'un air stupide. Rirette le regarda aussi. Elle avait peine à rassembler ses idées, un immense écœurement l'avait envahie. Ils restèrent ainsi les yeux dans les yeux pendant quelques secondes ; ils soufflaient tous les deux. Puis Rirette se reprit, elle saisit Lulu par la taille et la traîna jusqu'au taxi.

— Où va-t-on ? dit le chauffeur.

Henri les avait suivies, il voulait monter avec elles. Mais Rirette le repoussa de toutes ses forces et referma précipitamment la portière.

— Oh ! partez, partez, fit-elle au chauffeur. On vous dira l'adresse après.

Le taxi démarra, et Rirette se laissa aller au fond de la voiture. « Comme tout cela était vulgaire », pensa-t-elle. Elle haïssait Lulu.

— Où voulez-vous aller, ma petite Lulu ? demanda-t-elle doucement.

Lulu ne répondit pas. Rirette l'entoura de ses bras et se fit persuasive :

— Il faut me répondre. Voulez-vous que je vous dépose chez Pierre ?

Lulu fit un mouvement que Rirette prit pour un acquiescement. Elle se pencha en avant :

— 11, rue de Messine.

Quand Rirette se retourna, Lulu la regardait d'un drôle d'air.

— Qu'est-ce qu'il..., commença Rirette.

— Je vous déteste, hurla Lulu, je déteste Pierre, je déteste Henri. Qu'est-ce que vous avez tous après moi ? Vous me torturez.

Elle s'arrêta net, et tous ses traits se brouillèrent.

— Pleurez, dit Rirette avec une dignité calme, pleurez, ça vous fera du bien.

Lulu se plia en deux et se mit à sangloter. Rirette la prit dans ses bras et la serra contre elle. De temps à autre, elle lui caressait les cheveux. Mais, au-dedans, elle se sentait froide et méprisante. Quand la voiture s'arrêta, Lulu s'était calmée. Elle s'essuya les yeux et se poudra.

— Excusez-moi, dit-elle gentiment, c'était nerveux. Je n'ai pas pu supporter de le voir dans cet état, il me faisait mal.

— Il avait l'air d'un orang-outang, dit Rirette rassérénée.

Lulu sourit.

— Quand est-ce que je vous revois ? demanda Rirette.

— Oh ! pas avant demain. Vous savez que Pierre ne peut pas me loger à cause de sa mère ? Je suis à l'hôtel du Théâtre. Vous pourriez venir assez tôt, vers les neuf heures, si ça ne vous dérange pas, parce qu'ensuite j'irai voir maman.

Elle était blafarde, et Rirette pensa avec tristesse que c'était terrible la facilité avec laquelle Lulu pouvait se décomposer.

— N'en faites pas trop, ce soir, dit-elle.

— Je suis terriblement fatiguée, dit Lulu, j'espère que Pierre me laissera rentrer de bonne heure, mais il ne comprend jamais ces choses-là.

Rirette garda le taxi et se fit conduire chez elle. Elle avait pensé un moment qu'elle irait au cinéma mais elle n'en avait plus le cœur. Elle jeta son chapeau sur une chaise et fit un pas vers la fenêtre. Mais le lit l'attirait, tout blanc, tout doux, tout moite dans son creux d'ombre. S'y jeter, sentir la caresse de l'oreiller contre ses joues brûlantes. « Je suis forte, c'est moi qui ai tout fait pour Lulu et maintenant je suis seule et personne ne fait rien pour moi. » Elle avait tant de pitié pour elle-même qu'elle sentit une houle de sanglots monter jusqu'à sa gorge. « Ils vont partir pour Nice, et je ne les verrai plus. C'est moi qui aurai fait leur bonheur, mais ils ne penseront plus à moi. Et moi je resterai ici à travailler huit heures par jour, à vendre des perles fausses chez Burma. » Quand les premières larmes roulèrent sur ses joues, elle se laissa tomber doucement sur son lit. « A Nice... répétait-elle en pleurant amèrement, à Nice... au soleil... sur la Riviera... »

## III

« Pouah ! »

Nuit noire. On aurait dit que quelqu'un marchait dans la chambre : un homme avec des pantoufles. Il avançait avec précaution un pied, puis l'autre, sans pouvoir éviter un léger craquement du plancher. Il s'arrêtait, il y avait un moment de silence, puis, transporté soudain à l'autre bout de la chambre, il reprenait, comme un maniaque, sa marche sans but. Lulu avait froid, les couvertures étaient beaucoup trop légères. Elle avait dit : « Pouah ! » à voix haute et le son de sa voix lui avait fait peur.

Pouah ! Je suis sûre qu'à présent il regarde le ciel et les étoiles, il allume une cigarette, il est dehors, il a dit qu'il aimait la teinte mauve du ciel de Paris. A petits pas, il rentre chez lui, à petits pas : il se sent poétique quand il vient de faire ça, il me l'a dit, et léger comme une vache qu'on vient de traire, il n'y pense plus — et moi je suis souillée. Ça ne m'étonne pas qu'il soit pur en ce moment, il a laissé son ordure ici, dans le noir, il y a un essuie-main qui en est rempli, et le drap est humide au milieu du lit, je ne peux pas étendre mes jambes parce que je sentirais le mouillé sous ma peau, quelle ordure, et lui il est tout sec, je l'ai entendu qui sifflotait sous ma fenêtre quand il est sorti ; il était là en dessous, sec et frais dans ses beaux habits, dans son pardessus de demi-saison, il faut reconnaître qu'il sait s'habiller, une femme peut être fière de sortir avec lui, il était sous ma fenêtre, et moi j'étais nue dans le noir, et j'avais froid, et je me frottais le ventre avec les mains parce que je me croyais encore toute mouillée. « Je monte une minute, qu'il avait fait, juste pour voir ta chambre. » Il est resté deux heures, et le lit grinçait — ce sale petit lit de fer. Je me demande où il a été chercher cet hôtel, il m'avait dit qu'il y avait passé quinze jours autrefois, que j'y serais très bien, ce sont de drôles de chambres, j'en ai vu deux, je n'ai jamais vu de chambres si petites, et elles sont encombrées de meubles, il y a des poufs et des canapés et des petites tables, ça pue l'amour, je ne sais pas s'il y a passé quinze jours mais il ne les a sûrement pas passés seul; il faut qu'il me respecte bien peu pour m'avoir collée là-dedans. Le garçon de l'hôtel rigolait quand nous sommes montés, c'est un Algérien, je déteste ces types-là, j'en ai peur, il m'a regardé les jambes, après ça il est entré dans le bureau, il a dû se dire : « Ça y est, ils font ça » et il s'est imaginé des choses sales, il paraît que c'est effrayant ce qu'ils font là-bas, aux femmes ; s'il y en a une qui leur tombe sous la main, elle reste boiteuse pour la vie ; et tout le temps que Pierre m'embêtait je pensais à cet Algérien qui pensait à ce que je faisais et qui se figurait des ordures pires encore que ça n'était. Il y a quelqu'un dans la chambre !

Lulu retint son souffle, mais les craquements cessèrent presque aussitôt. J'ai mal entre les cuisses, ça me démange et ça me cuit, j'ai envie de pleurer, et ce sera ainsi toutes les nuits sauf la nuit prochaine parce que nous serons dans le train. Lulu se mordit la lèvre et frissonna parce qu'elle se rappelait qu'elle avait gémi. C'est pas vrai, je n'ai pas gémi, j'ai seulement respiré un peu fort, parce qu'il est si lourd, que quand il est sur moi il me coupe le souffle. Il m'a dit : « Tu gémis, tu jouis », j'ai horreur qu'on parle en faisant ça, je voudrais qu'on s'oublie, mais lui il n'arrête pas de dire des cochonneries. Je n'ai pas gémi, d'abord, je ne peux pas prendre de plaisir, c'est un fait, le médecin l'a dit, à moins que je ne me le donne moi-même. Il ne veut pas le croire, ils n'ont jamais voulu le croire, ils disaient tous : « C'est parce qu'on t'a mal commencée, moi je t'apprendrai le plaisir » ; je les laissais dire, je savais bien ce qui en était, c'est médical ; mais ça les vexe.

Quelqu'un montait l'escalier. C'est quelqu'un qui rentre. A moins, mon Dieu, que ce soit lui qui revienne. Il en est bien capable, si l'envie l'a repris. Ce n'est pas lui, ce sont des pas lourds — ou alors — le cœur de Lulu sauta dans sa poitrine — si c'était l'Algérien, il sait que je suis seule, il va venir cogner à la porte, je ne peux pas, je ne peux pas supporter ça, non, c'est à l'étage d'en dessous, c'est un type qui rentre, il met sa clef dans la serrure, il lui faut du temps, il est soûl, je me demande qui loge dans cet hôtel, ça doit être du propre ; j'ai rencontré une rousse, cet après-midi, dans l'escalier, elle avait des yeux de droguée. Je n'ai pas gémi ! Mais naturellement il a fini par me troubler avec tous ses tripotages, il sait faire ; j'ai horreur des types qui savent faire, j'aimerais mieux coucher avec un vierge. Ces mains qui vont tout droit où il faut, qui frôlent, qui appuient un peu, pas trop... ils vous prennent pour un instrument dont ils sont fiers de savoir jouer. Je déteste qu'on me trouble, j'ai la gorge sèche, j'ai peur et j'ai un goût dans la bouche, et je suis humiliée parce qu'ils croient qu'ils me dominent ; Pierre, je le giflerais quand il prend son air fat et qu'il dit : « J'ai la technique. » Mon Dieu, dire que la vie c'est ça, c'est pour ça qu'on s'habille et qu'on se lave, et qu'on se fait belle, et tous les romans sont écrits sur ça, et on y pense tout le temps, et finalement voilà ce que c'est, on s'en va dans une chambre avec un type qui vous étouffe à moitié et qui vous mouille le ventre pour finir. Je veux dormir, oh ! si je pouvais seulement un peu dormir, demain je voyagerai toute la nuit, je serai brisée. Je voudrais tout de même être un peu fraîche pour me balader dans Nice ; il paraît que c'est si beau, il y a des petites rues italiennes et des linges de couleur qui sèchent au soleil, je m'installerai avec mon chevalet et je peindrai, et des petites filles viendront regarder ce que je fais. Saloperie ! (elle s'était un peu avancée et sa hanche avait touché la tache humide du drap). C'est pour faire ça qu'il m'emmène. Personne, personne ne m'aime. Il marchait à côté de moi, et je défaillais presque et j'attendais un mot de tendresse, il aurait dit : « Je t'aime » je ne serais pas revenue chez lui bien sûr, mais je lui aurais dit quelque chose de gentil, on se serait quittés bons amis, j'attendais, j'attendais, il m'a pris le bras et je lui ai laissé mon bras, Rirette était furieuse, ça n'est pas vrai qu'il avait l'air d'un orang-outang, mais je savais qu'elle pensait quelque chose comme ça, elle le regardait de côté avec de sales yeux, c'est étonnant comme elle peut être mauvaise, eh bien, malgré ça quand il m'a pris le bras je n'ai pas résisté mais ça n'est pas *moi* qu'il voulait, il voulait *sa femme* parce qu'il m'a épousée et qu'il est mon mari ; il me rabaissait toujours, il disait qu'il était plus intelligent que moi, et tout ce qui est arrivé, c'est sa faute, il n'avait qu'à ne pas me traiter de son haut, je serais encore avec lui. Je suis sûre qu'il ne me regrette pas en ce moment, il ne pleure pas, il râle, voilà ce qu'il fait et il est bien content parce qu'il a le lit pour lui tout seul et qu'il peut étendre ses grandes jambes. Je voudrais mourir. J'ai si peur qu'il ne pense du mal de moi ; je ne pouvais rien lui expliquer parce que Rirette était entre nous, elle parlait, elle parlait, elle avait l'air hystérique. Elle est contente à présent, elle se complimente sur son courage, comme c'est malin avec Henri qui est doux comme un mouton. J'irai. Ils ne peuvent tout de même pas me forcer à le quitter comme un chien. Elle sauta hors du lit et tourna le commutateur. Mes bas et une combinaison ça suffit. Elle ne prit même pas la peine de se peigner, tant elle était pressée, et les gens qui me verront ne sauront pas que je suis nue sous mon grand manteau gris, il me tombe jusqu'aux pieds. L'Algérien — elle s'arrêta le cœur battant — il va falloir que je le réveille pour qu'il m'ouvre la porte. Elle descendit à pas de loup — mais les marches craquaient une à une ; elle frappa contre la vitre du bureau.

— Qu'est-ce que c'est ? dit l'Algérien.

Ses yeux étaient roses et ses cheveux embroussaillés, il n'avait pas l'air bien redoutable.

— Ouvrez-moi la porte, dit Lulu avec sécheresse.

Un quart d'heure plus tard, elle sonnait chez Henri.

— Qui est là ? demanda Henri à travers la porte.

— C'est moi.

Il ne répond rien, il ne veut pas me laisser rentrer chez moi. Mais je taperai sur la porte jusqu'à ce qu'il ouvre, il cédera à cause des voisins. Au bout d'une minute la porte s'entrebâilla et Henri apparut, blafard avec un bouton sur le nez ; il était en pyjama. « Il n'a pas dormi », pensa Lulu avec tendresse.

— Je ne voulais pas partir comme ça ; je voulais te revoir.

Henri ne disait toujours rien. Lulu entra en le

poussant un peu. Qu'il est donc emprunté, on le trouve toujours sur son passage, il me regarde avec des yeux ronds, il a les bras ballants, il ne sait que faire de son corps. Tais-toi, va, tais-toi, je vois bien que tu es ému et que tu ne peux pas parler. Il faisait effort pour avaler sa salive, et ce fut Lulu qui dut fermer la porte.

— Je veux qu'on se quitte bons amis, dit-elle.

Il ouvrit la bouche comme s'il voulait parler, tourna précipitamment sur lui-même et s'enfuit. Qu'est-ce qu'il fait ? Elle n'osait le suivre. Est-ce qu'il pleure ? Elle l'entendit soudain tousser : il est aux cabinets. Quand il revint, elle se pendit à son cou et colla sa bouche contre la sienne : il sentait le vomi. Lulu éclata en sanglots :

— J'ai froid, dit Henri.

— Couchons-nous, proposa-t-elle en pleurant, je peux rester jusqu'à demain matin.

Ils se couchèrent, et Lulu fut secouée d'énormes sanglots parce qu'elle retrouvait sa chambre et son beau lit propre et la lueur rouge dans la vitre. Elle pensait que Henri la prendrait dans ses bras, mais il n'en fit rien : il était couché tout de son long, comme si on avait mis un piquet dans le lit. Il est aussi raide que quand il parle avec un Suisse. Elle lui prit la tête à deux mains et le regarda fixement. « Tu es pur, toi, tu es pur. » Il se mit à pleurer.

— Que je suis malheureux, dit-il, je n'ai jamais été aussi malheureux.

— Moi non plus, dit Lulu.

Ils pleurèrent longtemps. Au bout d'un moment, elle éteignit et mit la tête sur son épaule. Si on pouvait rester comme ça toujours : purs et tristes comme deux orphelins ; mais ça n'est pas possible, ça n'arrive pas dans la vie. La vie était une énorme vague qui allait fondre sur Lulu et l'arracher aux bras de Henri. Ta main, ta grande main. Il en est fier parce qu'elles sont grandes, il dit que les descendants de vieille famille ont toujours de grandes extrémités. Il ne me prendra plus la taille entre ses mains — il me chatouillait un peu mais j'étais fière parce qu'il pouvait presque joindre ses doigts. Ce n'est pas vrai qu'il est impuissant, il est pur, pur — et un peu paresseux. Elle sourit à travers ses larmes et l'embrassa sous le menton.

— Qu'est-ce que je vais dire, à mes parents ? fit Henri. Ma mère en mourra.

M$^{me}$ Crispin ne mourrait pas, elle triompherait au contraire. Ils parleront de moi, au repas, tous les cinq, avec des airs de blâme, comme des gens qui en savent long mais qui ne veulent pas tout dire à cause de la petite qui a seize ans, qui est trop jeune pour qu'on parle de certaines choses devant elle. Elle rigolera au-dedans parce qu'elle saura tout, elle sait toujours tout et elle me déteste. Toute cette boue ! Et les apparences sont contre moi.

— Ne leur dis pas tout de suite, supplia-t-elle, dis que je suis à Nice pour ma santé.

— Ils ne me croiront pas.

Elle embrassa Henri à petits coups rapides sur tout le visage.

— Henri, tu n'étais pas assez gentil avec moi.

— C'est vrai, dit Henri, je n'étais pas assez gentil. Mais toi non plus, dit-il à la réflexion, tu n'étais pas assez gentille.

— Moi non plus. Hou ! dit Lulu, que nous sommes malheureux !

Elle pleurait si fort qu'elle pensa suffoquer : bientôt le jour allait paraître, et elle partirait. On ne fait jamais, jamais ce qu'on veut, on est emporté.

— Tu n'aurais pas dû partir comme ça, dit Henri.

Lulu soupira.

— Je t'aimais bien, Henri.

— Et maintenant, tu ne m'aimes plus ?

— Ce n'est pas la même chose.

— Avec qui pars-tu ?

— Avec des gens que tu ne connais pas.

— Comment connais-tu des gens que je ne connais pas, dit Henri avec colère, où les as-tu vus ?

— Laisse ça, mon chéri, mon petit Gulliver, tu ne vas pas faire le mari en ce moment ?

— Tu pars avec un homme ! dit Henri en pleurant.

— Écoute, Henri, je te jure que non, je te le jure sur la tête de maman, les hommes me dégoûtent trop en ce moment. Je pars avec un ménage, des amis de Rirette, des gens âgés. Je veux vivre seule, ils me trouveront du travail ; oh ! Henri, si tu savais comme j'ai besoin de vivre seule, comme tout ça me dégoûte.

— Quoi ? dit Henri, qu'est-ce qui te dégoûte ?

— Tout ! elle l'embrassa — il n'y a que toi qui ne me dégoûtes pas, mon chéri.

Elle passa ses mains sous le pyjama de Henri et le caressa longuement par tout le corps. Il frissonna sous ces mains glacées mais il se laissa faire, il dit seulement :

— Je vais prendre mal.

Il y avait en lui, sûrement, quelque chose de brisé.

A sept heures, Lulu se leva, les yeux gonflés de larmes, elle dit avec lassitude.

— Il faut que je retourne là-bas.

— Où là-bas ?

— Je suis à l'hôtel du Théâtre, rue Vandamme. C'est un sale hôtel.

— Reste avec moi.

— Non, Henri, je t'en prie, n'insiste pas, je t'ai dit que c'était impossible.

« C'est le flot qui vous emporte, c'est la vie ; on ne peut pas juger, ni comprendre, il n'y a qu'à se laisser aller. Demain je serai à Nice. » Elle passa dans le cabinet de toilette pour baigner ses yeux dans l'eau tiède. Elle remit son manteau en grelottant. « C'est comme une fatalité. Pourvu que je puisse dormir dans le train, cette nuit, sans ça je serai claquée en arrivant à Nice. J'espère qu'il a pris des premières ; ce sera la première fois que je voyagerai en première. Tout est toujours comme ça : voilà des années que j'ai envie de faire un long voyage en première classe et le jour où ça m'arrive les choses s'arrangent de telle façon que ça ne me fait presque plus de plaisir. » Elle avait hâte de partir, à présent, parce que ces derniers moments avaient quelque chose d'insupportable.

— Qu'est-ce que tu vas faire avec ce Gallois ? demanda-t-elle.

Gallois avait commandé une affiche à Henri, Henri l'avait faite et, à présent, Gallois n'en voulait plus.

— Je ne sais pas, dit Henri.

Il s'était blotti sous les couvertures, on ne voyait plus que ses cheveux et un bout d'oreille. Il dit d'une voix lente et molle :

— Je voudrais dormir pendant huit jours.

— Adieu, mon chéri, dit Lulu.

— Adieu.

Elle se pencha sur lui, écarta un peu les couvertures et l'embrassa sur le front. Elle demeura longtemps sur le palier, sans se décider à fermer la porte de l'appartement. Au bout d'un moment, elle détourna les yeux et tira violemment sur la poignée. Elle entendit un bruit sec et crut qu'elle allait s'évanouir : elle avait connu une impression semblable quand on avait jeté la première pelletée de terre sur le cercueil de son père.

« Henri n'a pas été très gentil. Il aurait pu se lever pour m'accompagner jusqu'à la porte. Il me semble que j'aurais eu moins de chagrin si c'était lui qui l'avait refermée. »

## IV

— Elle a fait ça ! dit Rirette le regard au loin, elle a fait ça !

C'était le soir. Vers six heures, Pierre avait téléphoné à Rirette, et elle était venue le rejoindre au Dôme.

— Mais vous, dit Pierre, est-ce que vous ne deviez pas la voir ce matin vers neuf heures ?

— Je l'ai vue.

— Elle n'avait pas l'air drôle ?

— Mais non, dit Rirette, je n'ai rien remarqué. Elle était un peu fatiguée, mais elle m'a dit qu'elle avait mal dormi après votre départ parce qu'elle était très excitée à l'idée de voir Nice et parce qu'elle avait un peu peur du garçon algérien... Tenez, elle m'a même demandé si je croyais que vous aviez pris des premières dans le train, elle a dit que c'était le rêve de sa vie de voyager en première. Non, décida Rirette, je suis sûre qu'elle n'avait rien de semblable en tête ; du moins pas tant que j'étais là. Je suis restée deux heures avec elle, et, pour ces choses-là, je suis assez observatrice, ça m'étonnerait si quelque chose m'avait échappé. Vous me direz qu'elle est très dissimulée, mais je la connais depuis quatre ans et je l'ai vue dans des masses de circonstances, je possède ma Lulu sur le bout du doigt.

— Alors ce sont les Texier qui l'auront décidée. C'est drôle... — Il rêva quelques instants et reprit soudain : Je me demande qui leur a donné l'adresse de Lulu. C'est moi qui ai choisi l'hôtel et elle n'en avait jamais entendu parler auparavant.

Il jouait distraitement avec la lettre de Lulu, et Rirette était agacée parce qu'elle aurait voulu la lire et qu'il ne le lui proposait pas.

— Quand l'avez-vous reçue ? demanda-t-elle enfin.

— La lettre ?... Il la lui tendit avec simplicité.

— Tenez, vous pouvez lire. On a dû la poser chez la concierge vers une heure.

C'était une mince feuille violette, comme on en vend, dans les bureaux de tabac :

« Mon grand chéri,

« Les Texier sont venus (je ne sais pas qui leur a donné l'adresse), et je vais te faire beaucoup de peine, mais je ne pars pas, mon amour, mon Pierre chéri ; je reste avec Henri parce qu'il est trop malheureux. Ils ont été le voir ce matin, il ne voulait pas ouvrir, et M$^{me}$ Texier a dit qu'il n'avait plus figure humaine. Ils ont été très gentils et ils ont compris mes raisons, elle dit que tous les torts sont de son côté, que c'est un ours mais qu'il n'est pas mauvais dans le fond. Elle dit qu'il lui a fallu ça pour qu'il comprenne combien il tenait à moi. Je ne sais pas qui leur a donné mon adresse, ils ne l'ont pas dit, ils ont dû me voir par hasard quand je suis sortie de l'hôtel ce matin avec Rirette. M$^{me}$ Texier m'a dit qu'elle savait bien qu'elle me demandait un énorme sacrifice mais qu'elle me connaissait assez pour savoir que je ne m'y déroberai pas. Je regrette bien fort notre beau voyage à Nice, mon amour, mais j'ai pensé que tu serais le moins malheureux parce que tu m'as toujours. Je suis à toi de tout mon cœur et de tout mon corps, et nous nous verrons aussi souvent que par le passé. Mais Henri se tuerait s'il ne m'avait plus, je lui suis indispensable ; je t'assure que ça ne m'amuse pas de me sentir une pareille responsabilité. J'espère que tu ne feras pas ta vilaine petite gueule qui me fait si peur, tu ne voudrais pas que j'aie des remords, dis. Je rentre chez Henri tout à l'heure, je suis un peu révulsée quand je pense que je vais le revoir dans cet état mais j'aurai le courage de poser mes conditions. D'abord je veux plus de liberté parce que je t'aime et je veux qu'il laisse Robert tranquille, et qu'il ne dise plus jamais de mal de maman. Mon chéri, je suis bien triste, je voudrais que tu sois là, j'ai envie de toi, je me serre contre toi et je sens tes caresses par tout mon corps. Je serai demain à cinq heures au Dôme. — Lulu. »

— Mon pauvre Pierre !

Rirette lui avait pris la main.

— Je vous dirai, dit Pierre, que c'est pour elle surtout que j'ai des regrets ! Elle avait besoin d'air et de soleil. Mais puisqu'elle en a décidé ainsi... Ma mère me faisait des scènes épouvantables, reprit-il. La villa est à elle, elle ne voulait pas que j'y amène une femme.

— Ah ? dit Rirette d'une voix entrecoupée. Ah ? C'est très bien alors, alors tout le monde est content !

Elle laissa retomber la main de Pierre : elle se sentait, sans savoir pourquoi, envahie par un amer regret.

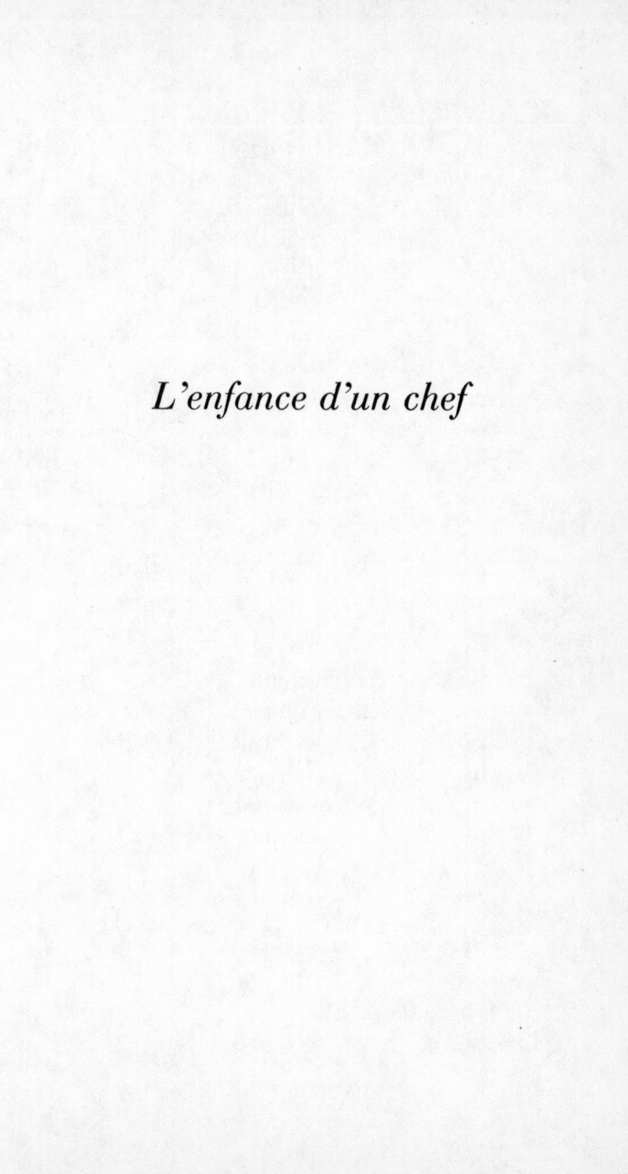

# *L'enfance d'un chef*

« Je suis adorable dans mon petit costume d'ange. » M$^{me}$ Portier avait dit à maman : « Votre petit garçon est gentil à croquer. Il est adorable dans son petit costume d'ange. » M. Bouffardier attira Lucien entre ses genoux et lui caressa les bras : « C'est une vraie petite fille, dit-il en souriant. Comment t'appelles-tu ? Jacqueline, Lucienne, Margot ? » Lucien devint tout rouge et dit : « Je m'appelle Lucien. » Il n'était plus tout à fait sûr de ne pas être une petite fille : beaucoup de personnes l'avaient embrassé en l'appelant mademoiselle, tout le monde trouvait qu'il était si charmant avec ses ailes de gaze, sa longue robe bleue, ses petits bras nus et ses boucles blondes ; il avait peur que les gens ne décident tout d'un coup qu'il n'était plus un petit garçon ; il aurait beau protester, personne ne l'écouterait, on ne lui permettrait plus de quitter sa robe sauf pour dormir, et le matin en se réveillant il la trouverait au pied de son lit et quand il voudrait faire pipi, au cours de la journée, il faudrait qu'il la relève, comme Nénette et qu'il s'asseye sur ses talons. Tout le monde lui dirait : ma jolie petite chérie ; peut-être que ça y est déjà, que je *suis* une petite fille ; il se sentait si doux en dedans, que c'en était un petit peu écœurant, et sa voix sortait toute flûtée de ses lèvres, et il offrit des fleurs à tout le monde avec des gestes arrondis ; il avait envie de s'embrasser la saignée du bras. Il pensa : ça n'est pas pour de vrai. Il aimait bien quand ça n'était pas pour de vrai mais il s'était amusé davantage le jour du Mardi gras : on l'avait costumé en Pierrot, il avait couru et sauté en criant, avec Riri, et ils s'étaient cachés sous les tables. Sa maman lui donna un coup léger de son face-à-main. « Je suis fière de mon petit garçon. » Elle était imposante et belle, c'était la plus grasse et la plus grande de toutes ces dames. Quand il passa devant le long buffet couvert d'une nappe blanche, son papa qui buvait une coupe de champagne le souleva de terre en lui disant : « Bonhomme ! » Lucien avait envie de pleurer et de dire : « Na ! » Il demanda de l'orangeade parce qu'elle était glacée et qu'on lui avait défendu d'en boire. Mais on lui en versa deux doigts dans un tout petit verre. Elle avait un goût poisseux et n'était pas du tout si glacée que ça : Lucien se mit à penser aux orangeades à l'huile de ricin qu'il avalait quand il était si malade. Il éclata en sanglots et trouva bien consolant d'être assis entre papa et maman dans l'automobile. Maman serrait Lucien contre elle, elle était chaude et parfumée, toute en soie. De temps à autre, l'intérieur de l'auto devenait blanc comme de la craie, Lucien clignait des yeux, les violettes que maman portait à son corsage sortaient de l'ombre et Lucien respirait tout à coup leur odeur. Il sanglotait encore un peu mais il se sentait moite et chatouillé, à peine un peu poisseux, comme l'orangeade ; il aurait aimé barboter dans sa petite baignoire et que maman le lavât avec l'éponge de caoutchouc. On lui permit de se coucher dans la chambre de papa et de maman, comme lorsqu'il était bébé ; il rit et fit grincer les ressorts de son petit lit, et papa dit : « Cet enfant est surexcité. » Il but un peu d'eau de fleurs d'oranger et vit papa en bras de chemise.

Le lendemain Lucien était sûr d'avoir oublié quelque chose. Il se rappelait très bien le rêve qu'il avait fait : papa et maman portaient des robes d'anges, Lucien était assis tout nu sur son pot, il jouait du tambour, papa et maman voletaient autour de lui ; c'était un cauchemar. Mais, avant le rêve, il y avait eu quelque chose, Lucien avait dû se réveiller. Quand il essayait de se rappeler, il voyait un long tunnel noir éclairé par une petite lampe bleue toute pareille à la veilleuse qu'on allumait le soir, dans la chambre de ses parents. Tout au fond de cette nuit sombre et bleue quelque chose s'était passé — quelque chose de blanc. Il s'assit par terre aux pieds de maman et prit son tambour. Maman lui dit : « Pourquoi me fais-tu ces yeux-là, mon bijou ? » Il baissa les yeux et tapa sur son tambour en criant : « Boum, boum, tararaboum. » Mais quand elle eut tourné la tête il se mit à la regarder minutieusement, comme s'il la voyait pour la première fois. La robe bleue avec la rose en étoffe, il la reconnaissait bien, le visage aussi. Pourtant ça n'était plus pareil. Tout à coup il crut que ça y était ; s'il y pensait encore un tout petit peu, il allait retrouver ce qu'il cherchait. Le tunnel s'éclaira d'un pâle jour gris, et on voyait remuer quelque chose. Lucien eut peur et poussa un cri : le tunnel disparut. « Qu'est-ce que tu as, mon petit chéri ? » dit maman. Elle s'était agenouillée près de lui et avait l'air inquiet. « Je m'amuse », dit Lucien. Maman sentait bon, mais il avait peur qu'elle ne le touchât : elle lui paraissait drôle, papa aussi, du reste. Il décida qu'il n'irait plus jamais dormir dans leur chambre.

Les jours suivants, maman ne s'aperçut de rien. Lucien était tout le temps dans ses jupes, comme à l'ordinaire, et il bavardait avec elle en vrai petit homme. Il lui demanda de lui raconter *Le Petit Chaperon Rouge*, et maman le prit sur ses genoux. Elle lui parla du loup et de la grand-mère du Chaperon Rouge, un doigt levé, souriante et grave. Lucien la regardait, il lui disait : « Et alors ? » et quelquefois, il lui touchait les frisons qu'elle avait dans le cou ; mais il ne l'écoutait pas, il se demandait si c'était bien sa vraie maman. Quand elle eut fini son histoire, il lui dit : « Maman, raconte-moi quand tu étais petite fille. » Et maman raconta : mais peut-être qu'elle mentait. Peut-être qu'elle était autrefois un petit garçon et qu'on lui avait mis des robes — comme à Lucien, l'autre soir — et qu'elle avait continué à en porter pour faire semblant d'être une fille. Il tâta gentiment ses beaux bras qui, sous la soie, étaient doux comme du beurre. Qu'est-ce qui arriverait si on ôtait la robe de maman, et si elle mettait les pantalons de papa ? Peut-être qu'il lui pousserait tout de suite une moustache noire. Il serra les bras de maman de toutes ses forces ; il avait l'impression qu'elle allait se transformer sous ses yeux en une bête horrible — ou peut-être devenir une femme à barbe comme celle de la foire. Elle rit en ouvrant la bouche toute grande, et Lucien vit sa langue rose et le fond de sa gorge : c'était sale, il avait envie de cracher dedans. « Hahaha ! disait maman, comme tu me serres, mon petit homme ! Serre-moi bien fort. Aussi fort que tu m'aimes. » Lucien prit une des belles mains aux bagues d'argent et la couvrit de baisers. Mais le lendemain, comme elle était assise près de lui et qu'elle lui tenait les mains pendant qu'il était sur son pot et qu'elle lui disait : « Pousse, Lucien, pousse, mon petit bijou, je t'en supplie », il s'arrêta soudain de pousser et lui demanda, un peu essoufflé : « Mais tu es bien ma vraie maman, au moins ? » Elle lui dit : « Petit sot » et lui demanda si ça n'allait pas bientôt venir. A partir de ce jour Lucien fut persuadé qu'elle jouait la comédie et il ne lui dit plus jamais qu'il l'épouserait quand il serait grand. Mais il ne savait pas trop quelle était cette comédie : il se pouvait que des voleurs, la nuit du tunnel, soient venus prendre papa et maman dans leur lit et qu'ils aient mis ces deux-là à leur place. Ou bien alors c'étaient bien papa et maman pour de vrai, mais dans la journée ils jouaient un rôle et, la nuit, ils étaient tout différents. Lucien fut à peine surpris, la nuit de Noël, quand il se réveilla en sursaut et qu'il les vit mettre les jouets dans la cheminée. Le lendemain, ils parlèrent du père Noël, et Lucien fit semblant de les croire : il pensait que c'était dans leur rôle ; ils avaient dû voler les jouets. Au mois de février, il eut la scarlatine et s'amusa beaucoup.

Quand il fut guéri, il prit l'habitude de jouer à l'orphelin. Il s'asseyait au milieu de la pelouse, sous le marronnier, remplissait ses mains de terre et pensait : « Je serais un orphelin, je m'appellerais Louis. Je n'aurais pas mangé depuis six jours. » La bonne, Germaine, l'appela pour le déjeuner, et, à table, il continua de jouer ; papa et maman ne s'apercevaient de rien. Il avait été recueilli par des voleurs qui voulaient faire de lui un pickpocket. Quand il aurait déjeuné, il s'enfuirait et il irait les dénoncer. Il mangea et but très peu ; il avait lu dans *L'Auberge de l'Ange Gardien* que le premier repas d'un homme affamé devait être léger. C'était amusant parce que tout le monde jouait. Papa et maman jouaient à être papa et maman ; maman jouait à se tourmenter parce que son petit bijou mangeait si peu, papa jouait à lire le journal et à agiter, de temps en temps, son doigt devant la figure de Lucien en disant : « Badaboum, bonhomme ! » Et Lucien jouait aussi, mais il finit par ne plus très bien savoir à quoi. A l'orphelin ? Ou à être Lucien ? Il regarda la carafe. Il y avait une petite lumière rouge qui dansait au fond de l'eau et on aurait juré que la main de papa était dans la carafe, énorme et lumineuse, avec de petits poils noirs sur les doigts. Lucien eut soudain l'impression que la carafe aussi jouait à être une carafe. Finalement il toucha à peine aux plats et il eut si faim, l'après-midi, qu'il dut voler une douzaine de prunes et faillit avoir une indigestion. Il pensa qu'il en avait assez de jouer à être Lucien.

Il ne pouvait pourtant pas s'en empêcher et il lui semblait tout le temps qu'il jouait. Il aurait voulu être comme M. Bouffardier qui était si laid et si sérieux. M. Bouffardier, quand il venait dîner, se penchait sur la main de maman en disant : « Mes hommages, chère madame » et Lucien se plantait au milieu du salon et le regardait avec admiration. Mais rien de ce qui arrivait à Lucien n'était sérieux. Quand il tombait et se faisait une bosse, il s'arrêtait parfois de pleurer et se demandait : « Est-ce que j'ai vraiment bobo ? » Alors, il se sentait encore plus triste, et ses pleurs reprenaient de plus belle. Lorsqu'il embrassa la main de maman en lui disant : « Mes hommages, chère madame », maman lui ébouriffa les cheveux en lui disant : « Ce n'est pas bien, ma petite souris, tu ne dois pas te moquer des grandes personnes », et il se sentit tout découragé. Il ne parvenait à se trouver quelque importance que le premier et le troisième vendredi du mois. Ces jours-là, beaucoup de dames venaient voir maman et il y en avait toujours deux ou trois qui étaient en deuil ; Lucien aimait les dames en deuil surtout quand elles avaient de grands pieds. D'une manière générale, il se plaisait avec les grandes personnes parce qu'elles étaient si respectables — et jamais on n'a envie de penser qu'elles s'oublient au lit à toutes ces choses que font les petits garçons ; parce qu'elles ont tellement d'habits sur le corps et si sombres, on ne peut pas s'imaginer ce qu'il y a dessous. Quand elles sont ensemble, elles mangent de tout et elles parlent, et leurs rires même sont graves, c'est beau comme à la messe. Elles traitaient Lucien comme un personnage. M^me^ Couffin prenait Lucien sur ses genoux et lui tâtait les mollets en déclarant : « C'est le plus joli petit mignon que j'aie vu. » Alors, elle l'interrogeait sur ses goûts, elle l'embrassait et elle lui demandait ce qu'il ferait plus tard. Et tantôt il répondait qu'il serait un grand général comme Jeanne d'Arc et qu'il reprendrait l'Alsace-Lorraine aux Allemands, tantôt qu'il voulait être missionnaire. Tout le temps qu'il parlait, il croyait ce qu'il disait. M^me^ Besse était une grande et forte femme avec une petite moustache. Elle renversait Lucien, elle le chatouillait en disant : « Ma petite poupée. » Lucien était ravi, il riait d'aise et se tortillait sous les chatouilles ; il pensait qu'il était une petite poupée, une charmante petite poupée pour grandes personnes et il aurait aimé que M^me^ Besse le déshabille, et le lave, et le mette au dodo dans un tout petit berceau comme un poupon de caoutchouc. Et parfois M^me^ Besse disait : « Est-ce qu'elle parle, ma poupée ? » et elle lui pressait tout à coup l'estomac. Alors, Lucien faisait semblant d'être une poupée mécanique, il disait : « Couic » d'une voix étranglée, et ils riaient tous les deux.

M. le curé, qui venait déjeuner à la maison tous les samedis, lui demanda s'il aimait bien sa maman. Lucien adorait sa jolie maman et son papa qui était si fort et si bon. Il répondit : « Oui » en regardant M. le curé dans les yeux, d'un petit air crâne, qui fit rire tout le monde. M. le curé avait une tête comme une framboise, rouge et grumeleuse, avec un poil sur chaque grumeau. Il dit à Lucien que c'était bien et qu'il fallait toujours bien aimer sa maman ; et puis il demanda qui Lucien préférait de sa maman ou du Bon Dieu. Lucien ne put deviner sur-le-champ la réponse et il se mit à secouer ses boucles et à donner des coups de pied dans le vide en criant : « Baoum, tararaboum », et les grandes personnes reprirent leur conversation comme s'il n'existait pas. Il courut au jardin et se glissa au-dehors par la porte de derrière, il avait emporté sa petite canne de jonc. Naturellement, Lucien ne devait jamais sortir du jardin, c'était défendu ; d'ordinaire, Lucien était un petit garçon très sage mais ce jour-là il avait envie de désobéir. Il regarda le gros buisson d'orties avec défiance ; on voyait bien que c'était un endroit défendu ; le mur était noirâtre, les orties étaient de méchantes plantes nuisibles, un chien avait fait sa commission juste au pied des orties ; ça sentait la plante, la crotte de chien et le vin chaud. Lucien fouetta les orties de sa canne en criant : « J'aime ma maman, j'aime ma maman. » Il voyait les orties brisées, qui pendaient minablement en jutant blanc, leurs cous blanchâtres et duveteux s'étaient effilochés en se cassant, il entendait une petite voix solitaire qui criait : « J'aime ma maman, j'aime ma maman » ; il y avait une grosse mouche bleue qui bourdonnait : c'était une mouche à caca, Lucien en avait peur — et une odeur de défendu, puissante, putride et tranquille lui emplissait les narines. Il répéta : « J'aime ma maman », mais sa voix lui parut étrange, il eut une peur épouvantable et s'enfuit d'une traite jusqu'au salon. De ce jour, Lucien comprit qu'il n'aimait pas sa maman. Il ne se sentait pas coupable, mais il redoubla de gentillesse parce qu'il pensait qu'on devait faire semblant toute sa vie d'aimer ses parents, sinon on était un méchant petit garçon. M^me^ Fleurier trouvait Lucien de plus en plus tendre, et justement il y eut la guerre cet été-là, et papa partit se battre, et maman était heureuse, dans son chagrin, que Lucien fût tellement attentionné ; l'après-midi, quand elle reposait au jardin dans son transatlantique parce qu'elle avait tant de peine, il courait lui chercher un coussin et le lui glissait sous la tête ou bien il lui mettait une couverture sur les jambes, et elle se défendait en riant : « Mais j'aurai trop chaud, mon petit homme, que tu es donc gentil ! » Il l'embrassait fougueusement, tout hors d'haleine, en lui disant : « Ma maman à moi ! » et il allait s'asseoir au pied du marronnier.

Il dit « marronnier ! » et il attendit. Mais rien ne se produisit. Maman était étendue sous la véranda, toute petite au fond d'un lourd silence étouffant. Ça sentait l'herbe chaude, on aurait pu jouer à être un explorateur dans la forêt vierge : mais Lucien n'avait plus de goût à jouer. L'air tremblait au-dessus de la crête rouge du mur, et le soleil faisait des taches brûlantes sur la terre et sur les mains de Lucien. « Marronnier ! » C'était choquant : quand Lucien disait à maman : « Ma jolie maman à moi », maman souriait et quand il avait appelé Germaine : arquebuse, Germaine avait pleuré et s'était plainte à maman. Mais quand on disait : marronnier, il n'arrivait rien du tout. Il marmotta entre ses dents : « Sale arbre » et il n'était pas rassuré, mais, comme l'arbre ne bougeait pas, il répéta plus fort : « Sale arbre, sale marronnier ! attends voir, attends un peu ! » et il lui donna des coups de pied. Mais l'arbre resta tranquille, tranquille — comme s'il était en bois. Le soir à dîner, Lucien dit à maman : « Tu sais, maman, les arbres, eh bien, ils sont en bois » en faisant une petite mine étonnée que maman aimait bien. Mais M$^{me}$ Fleurier n'avait pas reçu de lettre au courrier de midi. Elle dit sèchement : « Ne fais pas l'imbécile. » Lucien devint un petit brise-tout. Il cassait tous ses jouets pour voir comment ils étaient faits, il taillada les bras d'un fauteuil avec un vieux rasoir de papa, il fit tomber la tanagra du salon pour savoir si elle était creuse et s'il y avait quelque chose dedans ; quand il se promenait il décapitait les plantes et les fleurs avec sa canne : chaque fois il était profondément déçu, les choses c'était bête, ça n'existait pas pour de vrai. Maman lui demandait souvent en lui montrant des fleurs ou des arbres : « Comment ça s'appelle, ça ? » Mais Lucien secouait la tête et répondait : « Ça c'est rien du tout, ça n'a pas de nom. » Tout cela ne valait pas la peine qu'on y fît attention. Il était beaucoup plus amusant d'arracher les pattes d'une sauterelle parce qu'elle vous vibrait entre les doigts comme une toupie et, quand on lui pressait sur le ventre, il en sortait une crème jaune. Mais tout de même les sauterelles ne criaient pas. Lucien aurait bien voulu faire souffrir une de ces bêtes qui crient quand elles ont mal, une poule, par exemple, mais il n'osait pas les approcher. M. Fleurier revint au mois de mars parce que c'était un chef et le général lui avait dit qu'il serait plus utile à la tête de son usine que dans les tranchées comme n'importe qui. Il trouva Lucien très changé et il dit qu'il ne reconnaissait plus son petit bonhomme. Lucien était tombé dans une sorte de somnolence ; il répondait mollement, il avait toujours un doigt dans le nez ou bien il soufflait sur ses doigts et se mettait à les sentir, et il fallait le supplier pour qu'il fît sa commission. A présent, il allait tout seul au petit endroit ; il fallait simplement qu'il laissât sa porte entrebâillée et, de temps à autre, maman ou Germaine venaient l'encourager. Il restait des heures entières sur le trône et, une fois, il s'ennuya tellement qu'il s'endormit. Le médecin dit qu'il grandissait trop vite et prescrivit un reconstituant. Maman voulut enseigner à Lucien de nouveaux jeux mais Lucien trouvait qu'il jouait bien assez comme cela et que finalement tous les jeux se valaient, c'était toujours la même chose. Il boudait souvent : c'était aussi un jeu mais plutôt amusant. On faisait de la peine à maman, on se sentait tout triste et rancuneux, on devenait un peu sourd avec la bouche cousue et les yeux brumeux, au-dedans il faisait tiède et douillet comme quand on est sous les draps le soir et qu'on sent sa propre odeur ; on était seul au monde. Lucien ne pouvait plus sortir de ses bouderies, et, quand papa prenait sa voix moqueuse pour lui dire : « Tu fais du boudin », Lucien se roulait par terre en sanglotant. Il allait encore assez souvent au salon quand sa maman recevait, mais, depuis qu'on lui avait coupé ses boucles, les grandes personnes s'occupaient moins de lui ou alors c'était pour lui faire la morale et lui raconter des histoires instructives. Quand son cousin Riri vint à Férolles à cause des bombardements avec la tante Berthe, sa jolie maman, Lucien fut très content et il essaya de lui apprendre à jouer. Mais Riri était trop occupé à détester les Boches et puis il sentait encore le bébé quoiqu'il eût six mois de plus que Lucien ; il avait des taches de son sur la figure et il ne comprenait pas toujours très bien. Ce fut à lui pourtant que Lucien confia qu'il était somnambule. Certaines personnes se lèvent la nuit et parlent, et se promènent en dormant : Lucien l'avait lu dans *Le Petit Explorateur* et il avait pensé qu'il devait y avoir un vrai Lucien qui marchait, parlait et aimait ses parents pour de vrai pendant la nuit ; seulement, le matin venu, il oubliait tout et il recommençait à faire semblant d'être Lucien. Au début, Lucien ne croyait qu'à moitié à cette histoire mais un jour ils allèrent près des orties, et Riri montra son pipi à Lucien et lui dit : « Regarde comme il est grand, je suis un grand garçon. Quand il sera tout à fait grand, je serai un homme et j'irai me battre contre les Boches, dans les tranchées. » Lucien trouva Riri tout drôle et il eut une crise de fou rire. « Fais voir le tien », dit Riri. Ils comparèrent et celui de Lucien était le plus petit, mais Riri trichait : il tirait sur le sien pour l'allonger. « C'est moi qui ai le plus grand, dit Riri. — Oui, mais moi je suis somnambule », dit Lucien tranquillement. Riri ne savait pas ce que c'était qu'un somnambule, et Lucien dut le lui expliquer. Quand il eut fini il pensa : « C'est donc vrai que je suis somnambule » et il eut une terrible envie de pleurer. Comme ils couchaient dans le même lit, ils convinrent que Riri resterait éveillé la nuit suivante, et qu'il observerait bien Lucien quand Lucien se lèverait, et qu'il retiendrait tout ce que Lucien dirait : « Tu me réveilleras au bout d'un moment, dit Lucien, pour voir si je me rappellerai tout ce que j'ai fait. » Le soir, Lucien, qui ne pouvait s'endormir, entendit des ronflements aigus et dut réveiller Riri. « Zanzibar ! » dit Riri. « Réveille-toi, Riri, tu dois me regarder quand je me lèverai. — Laisse-moi dormir », dit Riri d'une voix pâteuse. Lucien le secoua et le pinça sous sa chemise, et Riri se mit à gigoter et il demeura éveillé, les yeux ouverts, avec un drôle de sourire. Lucien pensa à une bicyclette que son papa devait lui acheter, il entendit le sifflement d'une locomotive, et puis, tout d'un coup, la bonne entra et tira les rideaux, il était huit heures du matin. Lucien ne sut jamais ce qu'il avait fait pendant la nuit. Le Bon Dieu le savait, lui, parce que le Bon Dieu voyait tout. Lucien s'agenouillait sur le prie-Dieu et s'efforçait d'être sage pour que sa maman le félicite à la sortie de la messe, mais il détestait le Bon Dieu : le Bon Dieu était plus renseigné sur Lucien que Lucien lui-même. Il savait que Lucien n'aimait pas sa maman ni son papa, et qu'il faisait semblant d'être sage, et qu'il touchait son pipi le soir dans son lit. Heureusement, le Bon Dieu ne pouvait pas tout se rappeler, parce qu'il y avait tant de petits garçons au monde. Quand Lucien se frappait le front en disant : « Picotin », le Bon Dieu oubliait tout de suite ce qu'il avait vu. Lucien entreprit aussi de persuader au Bon Dieu qu'il aimait sa maman. De temps à autre, il disait dans sa tête : « Comme j'aime ma chère maman ! » Il y avait toujours un petit coin en lui qui n'en était pas très persuadé, et le Bon Dieu naturellement voyait ce petit coin. Dans ce cas-là, c'était Lui qui gagnait. Mais quelquefois on pouvait s'absorber complètement dans ce qu'on disait. On prononçait très vite « oh ! que j'aime ma maman », en articulant bien, et on revoyait le visage de maman, et on se sentait tout attendri, on pensait vaguement, vaguement que le Bon Dieu vous regardait et puis après on n'y pensait même plus, on était tout crémeux de tendresse, et puis il y avait les mots qui dansaient dans vos oreilles : maman, *maman*, MAMAN. Cela ne durait qu'un instant, bien entendu, c'était comme lorsque Lucien essayait de faire tenir une chaise en équilibre sur deux pieds. Mais si, juste à ce moment-là, on prononçait « Pacota », le Bon Dieu était refait : il n'avait vu que du Bien, et ce qu'il avait vu se gravait pour toujours dans Sa mémoire. Mais Lucien se lassa de ce jeu parce qu'il fallait faire de trop gros efforts et puis finalement on ne savait jamais si le Bon Dieu avait gagné ou perdu. Lucien ne s'occupa plus de Dieu. Quand il fit sa première communion, M. le curé dit que c'était le petit garçon le plus sage et le plus pieux de tout le catéchisme. Lucien comprenait vite et il avait une bonne mémoire, mais sa tête était remplie de brouillards.

Le dimanche était une éclaircie. Les brouillards se déchiraient quand Lucien se promenait avec papa sur la route de Paris. Il avait son beau petit costume marin, et on rencontrait des ouvriers de papa qui saluaient papa et Lucien. Papa s'approchait d'eux, et ils disaient : « Bonjour, monsieur Fleurier », et aussi « Bonjour, mon petit monsieur ». Lucien aimait bien les ouvriers parce que c'étaient des grandes personnes mais pas comme les autres. D'abord, ils l'appelaient : monsieur. Et puis ils portaient des casquettes et ils avaient de grosses mains aux ongles ras qui avaient toujours l'air souffrantes et gercées. Ils étaient responsables et respectueux. Il n'aurait pas fallu tirer la moustache du père Bouligaud : papa aurait grondé Lucien. Mais le père Bouligaud, pour parler à papa, ôtait sa casquette, et papa et Lucien gardaient leurs chapeaux sur leurs têtes et papa parlait d'une grosse voix souriante et bourrue : « Eh bien, père Bouligaud, on attend son fiston, quand est-ce qu'il aura sa permission ? — A la fin du mois, monsieur Fleurier, merci, monsieur Fleurier. » Le père Bouligaud avait l'air tout heureux et il ne se serait pas permis de donner une tape sur le derrière de Lucien en l'appelant Crapaud, comme M. Bouffardier. Lucien détestait M. Bouffardier, parce qu'il était si laid. Mais quand il voyait le père Bouligaud, il se sentait attendri et il avait envie d'être bon. Une fois, au retour de la promenade, papa prit Lucien sur ses genoux et lui expliqua ce que c'était qu'un chef. Lucien voulut savoir comment papa parlait aux ouvriers quand il était à l'usine, et papa lui montra comment il fallait s'y prendre, et sa voix était toute changée. « Est-ce que je deviendrai aussi un chef ? demanda Lucien. — Mais bien sûr, mon bonhomme, c'est pour cela que je t'ai fait. — Et à qui est-ce que je commanderai ? — Eh bien, quand je serai mort, tu seras le patron de mon usine et tu commanderas à mes ouvriers. — Mais ils seront morts aussi. — Eh bien, tu commanderas à leurs enfants et il faudra que tu saches te faire obéir et te faire aimer. — Et comment est-ce que je me ferai aimer, papa ? » Papa réfléchit un peu et dit : « D'abord, il faudra que tu les connaisses tous par leur nom. » Lucien fut profondément remué, et, quand le fils du contremaître Morel vint à la maison annoncer que son père avait eu deux doigts coupés, Lucien lui parla sérieusement et doucement, en le regardant tout droit dans les yeux et en l'appelant Morel. Maman dit qu'elle était fière d'avoir un petit garçon si bon et si sensible. Après cela, ce fut l'armistice, papa lisait le journal à haute voix tous les soirs, tout le monde parlait des Russes, et du gouvernement allemand, et des réparations, et papa montrait à Lucien des pays sur une carte : Lucien passa l'année la plus ennuyeuse de sa vie, il aimait encore mieux quand c'était la guerre ; à présent tout le monde avait l'air désœuvré, et les lumières qu'on voyait dans les yeux de M^me^ Coffin s'étaient éteintes. En octobre 1919, M^me^ Fleurier lui fit suivre les cours de l'école Saint-Joseph en qualité d'externe.

Il faisait chaud dans le cabinet de l'abbé Gerromet. Lucien était debout près du fauteuil de M. l'abbé, il avait mis ses mains derrière son dos et s'ennuyait ferme. « Est-ce que maman ne va pas bientôt s'en aller ? » Mais M^me^ Fleurier ne songeait pas encore à partir. Elle était assise sur l'extrême bord d'un fauteuil vert et tendait son ample poitrine vers M. l'abbé ; elle parlait très vite et elle avait sa voix musicale, comme quand elle était en colère et qu'elle ne voulait pas le montrer. M. l'abbé parlait lentement, et les mots avaient l'air beaucoup plus longs dans sa bouche que dans celle des autres personnes, on aurait dit qu'il les suçait un peu comme des sucres d'orge, avant de les laisser passer. Il expliquait à maman que Lucien était un bon petit garçon poli et travailleur mais si terriblement indifférent à tout, et M^me^ Fleurier dit qu'elle était très déçue parce qu'elle avait pensé qu'un changement de milieu lui ferait du bien. Elle demanda s'il jouait, au moins, pendant les récréations. « Hélas ! madame, répondit le bon père, les jeux même ne semblent pas l'intéresser beaucoup. Il est quelquefois turbulent et même violent mais il se lasse vite ; je crois qu'il manque de persévérance. » Lucien pensa : « C'est de moi qu'ils parlent. » C'étaient deux grandes personnes et il faisait le sujet de leur conversation, tout comme la guerre, le gouvernement allemand ou M. Poincaré ; elles avaient l'air grave et elles raisonnaient sur son cas. Mais cette pensée ne lui fit même pas plaisir. Ses oreilles étaient pleines des petits mots chantants de sa mère, des mots sucés et collants de M. l'abbé, il avait envie de pleurer. Heureusement la cloche sonna, et on lui rendit sa liberté. Mais pendant la classe de géographie, il resta très énervé et il demanda à l'abbé Jacquin la permission d'aller au petit coin parce qu'il avait besoin de bouger.

Tout d'abord, la fraîcheur, la solitude et la bonne odeur du petit coin le calmèrent. Il s'était accroupi par acquit de conscience mais il n'avait pas envie ; il leva la tête et se mit à lire les inscriptions dont la porte était couverte. On avait écrit au crayon bleu : « Barataud est une punaise. » Lucien sourit : c'était vrai, Barataud était une punaise, il était minuscule, et on disait qu'il grandirait un peu mais presque pas, parce que son papa était tout petit, presque un nain. Lucien se demanda si Barataud avait lu cette inscription et il pensa que non : autrement elle serait effacée. Barataud aurait sucé son doigt et aurait frotté les lettres jusqu'à ce qu'elles disparaissent. Lucien se réjouit un peu en imaginant que Barataud irait au petit coin à quatre heures et qu'il baisserait sa petite culotte de velours et qu'il lirait : « Barataud est une punaise. » Peut-être n'avait-il jamais pensé qu'il était si petit. Lucien se promit de l'appeler punaise, dès le lendemain matin à la récréation. Il se releva et lut sur le mur de droite une autre inscription tracée de la même écriture bleue : « Lucien Fleurier est une grande asperche. » Il l'effaça soigneusement et revint en classe. « C'est vrai, pensa-t-il en regardant ses camarades, ils sont tous plus petits que moi. » Et il se sentit mal à l'aise. « Grande asperche. » Il était assis à son petit bureau en bois des Iles. Germaine était à la cuisine, maman n'était pas encore rentrée. Il écrivit « grande asperge » sur une feuille blanche pour rétablir l'orthographe. Mais les mots lui parurent trop connus et ne lui firent plus aucun effet. Il appela : « Germaine, ma bonne Germaine ! — Qu'est-ce que vous voulez encore ? demanda Germaine. — Germaine, je voudrais que vous écriviez sur ce papier : « Lucien Fleurier est une grande asperge. » — Vous êtes fou, monsieur Lucien ? » Il lui entoura le cou de ses bras. « Germaine, ma petite Germaine, soyez gentille. » Germaine se mit à rire et essuya ses doigts gras à son tablier. Pendant qu'elle écrivait, il ne la regarda pas, mais, ensuite, il emporta la feuille dans sa chambre et la contempla longuement. L'écriture de Germaine était pointue, Lucien croyait entendre une voix sèche qui lui disait à l'oreille : « Grande asperge. » Il pensa : « Je suis grand. » Il était écrasé de honte : grand comme Barataud était petit — et les autres ricanaient derrière son dos. C'était comme si on lui avait jeté un sort : jusque-là, ça lui paraissait naturel de voir ses camarades de haut en bas. Mais à présent, il lui semblait qu'on l'avait condamné tout d'un coup à être grand pour le reste de sa vie. Le soir, il demanda à son père si on pouvait rapetisser quand on le voulait de toutes ses forces. M. Fleurier dit que non : tous les Fleurier avaient été grands et forts, et Lucien grandirait encore. Lucien fut désespéré. Quand sa mère l'eut bordé, il se releva et il alla se regarder dans la glace. « Je suis grand. » Mais il avait beau se regarder, ça ne se voyait pas, il n'avait l'air ni grand ni petit. Il releva un peu sa chemise et vit ses jambes ; alors il imagina que Costil disait à Hébrard : « Dis donc, regarde les longues jambes de l'asperge » et ça lui faisait tout drôle. Il faisait froid, Lucien frissonna et quelqu'un dit : « L'asperge a la chair de poule ! » Lucien releva très haut le pantet de sa chemise, et ils virent tous son nombril et toute sa boutique, et puis, il courut à son lit et s'y glissa. Quand il mit la main sous sa chemise il pensa que Costil le voyait et qu'il disait : « Regardez donc un peu ce qu'elle fait, la grande asperge ! » Il s'agita et tourna dans son lit en soufflant : « Grande asperge ! grande asperge ! » jusqu'à ce qu'il ait fait naître sous ses doigts une petite démangeaison acidulée.

Les jours suivants, il eut envie de demander à M. l'abbé la permission d'aller s'asseoir au fond de la classe. C'était à cause de Boisset, de Winckelmann et de Costil qui étaient derrière lui et qui pouvaient regarder sa nuque. Lucien sentait sa nuque mais il ne la voyait pas et même il l'oubliait souvent. Mais pendant qu'il répondait de son mieux à M. l'abbé, et qu'il récitait la tirade de Don Diègue, les autres étaient derrière lui et regardaient sa nuque, et ils pouvaient ricaner en pensant : « Qu'elle est maigre, il a deux cordes dans le cou. » Lucien s'efforçait de gonfler sa voix et d'exprimer l'humiliation de Don Diègue. Avec sa voix, il faisait ce qu'il voulait ; mais la nuque était toujours là, paisible et inexpressive, comme quelqu'un qui se repose, et Basset la voyait. Il n'osa pas changer de place, parce que le dernier banc était réservé aux cancres, mais la nuque et les omoplates lui démangeaient tout le temps, et il était obligé de se gratter sans cesse. Lucien inventa un jeu nouveau : le matin, quand il prenait son tub tout seul dans le cabinet de toilette comme un grand, il imaginait que quelqu'un le regardait par le trou de la serrure, tantôt Costil, tantôt le père Bouligaud, tantôt Germaine. Alors, il se tournait de tous côtés pour qu'ils le vissent sous toutes ses faces et parfois il tournait son derrière vers la porte et se mettait à quatre pattes pour qu'il fût bien bombé et bien ridicule ; M. Bouffardier s'approchait à pas de loup pour lui donner un lavement. Un jour qu'il était au petit endroit, il entendit des craquements ; c'était Gertrude qui frottait à l'encaustique le buffet du couloir. Son cœur s'arrêta de battre, il ouvrit tout doucement la porte et sortit, la culotte sur les talons, la chemise roulée autour des reins. Il était obligé de faire de petits bonds, pour avancer sans perdre l'équilibre. Germaine leva sur lui un œil placide : « C'est-il que vous faites la course en sac ? » demanda-t-elle. Il remonta rageusement son pantalon et courut se jeter sur son lit. Mme Fleurier était désolée, elle disait souvent à son mari : « Lui qui était si gracieux quand il était petit, regarde comme il a l'air gauche ; si ça n'est pas dommage ! » M. Fleurier jetait un regard distrait sur Lucien et répondait : « C'est l'âge ! » Lucien ne savait que faire de son corps ; quoi qu'il entreprît, il avait toujours l'impression que ce corps était en train d'exister de tous les côtés à la fois, sans lui demander son avis. Lucien se complut à imaginer qu'il était invisible puis il prit l'habitude de regarder par les trous de serrure pour se venger et pour voir comment les autres étaient faits sans le savoir. Il vit sa mère pendant qu'elle se lavait. Elle était assise sur le bidet, elle avait l'air endormi et elle avait sûrement tout à fait oublié son corps et même son visage, parce qu'elle pensait que personne ne la voyait. L'éponge allait et venait toute seule sur cette chair abandonnée ; elle avait des mouvements paresseux, et on avait l'impression qu'elle allait s'arrêter en cours de route. Maman frotta une lavette avec un morceau de savon, et sa main disparut entre ses jambes. Son visage était reposé, presque triste, sûrement elle pensait à autre chose, à l'éducation de Lucien ou à M. Poincaré. Mais pendant ce temps-là, elle *était* cette grosse masse rose, ce corps volumineux qui s'affalait sur la faïence du bidet. Lucien, une autre fois, ôta ses souliers et grimpa jusqu'aux mansardes. Il vit Germaine. Elle avait une longue chemise verte qui lui tombait jusqu'aux pieds, elle se peignait devant une petite glace ronde et elle souriait mollement à son image. Lucien fut pris de fou rire et dut redescendre précipitamment. Après cela, il se faisait des sourires et même des grimaces devant la psyché du salon et, au bout d'un moment, il était pris de peurs épouvantables.

Lucien finit par s'endormir tout à fait mais personne ne s'en aperçut sauf M^me^ Coffin qui l'appelait son bel-au-bois dormant ; une grosse boule d'air qu'il ne pouvait ni avaler ni cracher lui tenait toujours la bouche entrouverte : c'était son *bâillement* ; quand il était seul, la boule grossissait en lui caressant doucement le palais et la langue ; sa bouche s'ouvrait toute grande, et les larmes roulaient sur ses joues : c'étaient des moments très agréables. Il ne s'amusait plus autant quand il était aux cabinets mais en revanche il aimait beaucoup éternuer, ça le réveillait et, pendant un instant, il regardait autour de lui d'un air émoustillé, et puis il s'assoupissait de nouveau. Il apprit à reconnaître les diverses sortes de sommeil : l'hiver, il s'asseyait devant la cheminée et tendait sa tête vers le feu ; quand elle était rouge et bien rissolée, elle se vidait d'un seul coup ; il appelait ça « s'endormir par la tête ». Le matin du dimanche, au contraire, il s'endormait par les pieds : il entrait dans son bain, il se baissait lentement et le sommeil montait le long de ses jambes et de ses flancs en clapotant. Au-dessus du corps endormi, tout blanc, et ballonné au fond de l'eau, et qui avait l'air d'une poule bouillie, une petite tête blonde trônait, pleine de mots savants, templum, templi, templo, séisme, iconoclastes. En classe le sommeil était blanc, troué d'éclairs : « Que vouliez-vous qu'il fît contre trois ? » Premier : Lucien Fleurier « Qu'est-ce que le Tiers État : rien. » Premier : Lucien Fleurier, second Winckelmann. Pellereau fut premier en algèbre ; il n'avait qu'un testicule, l'autre n'était pas descendu ; il faisait payer deux sous pour voir et dix pour toucher. Lucien donna les dix sous, hésita, tendit la main et s'en alla sans toucher, mais ensuite ses regrets étaient si vifs qu'ils le tenaient parfois éveillé plus d'une heure. Il était moins bon en géologie qu'en histoire, premier Winckelmann, second Fleurier. Le dimanche, il allait se promener à bicyclette, avec Costil et Winckelmann. A travers de rousses campagnes que la chaleur écrasait, les bicyclettes glissaient sur la moelleuse poussière ; les jambes de Lucien étaient vivaces et musclées mais l'odeur sommeilleuse des routes lui montait à la tête, il se courbait sur son guidon, ses yeux devenaient roses et se fermaient à demi. Il eut trois fois de suite le prix d'excellence. On lui donna *Fabiola ou l'Église des Catacombes*, *Le Génie du Christianisme* et la *Vie du Cardinal Lavigerie.* Costil au retour des grandes vacances leur apprit à tous le *De Profundis Morpionibus* et l'*Artilleur de Metz.* Lucien décida de faire mieux et consulta le Larousse médical de son père à l'article « Utérus », ensuite il leur expliqua comment les femmes étaient faites, il leur fit même un croquis au tableau et Costil déclara que c'était dégueulasse ; mais après cela ils ne pouvaient plus entendre parler de trompes sans éclater de rire, et Lucien pensait avec satisfaction qu'on ne trouverait pas dans la France entière un élève de seconde et peut-être même de rhétorique qui connût aussi bien que lui les organes féminins.

Quand les Fleurier s'installèrent à Paris, ce fut un éclair de magnésium. Lucien ne pouvait plus dormir à cause des cinémas, des autos et des rues. Il apprit à distinguer une Voisin d'une Packard, une Hispano-Suiza d'une Rolls et il parlait à l'occasion de voitures surbaissées ; depuis plus d'un an, il portait des culottes longues. Pour le récompenser de son succès à la première partie du baccalauréat, son père l'envoya en Angleterre ; Lucien vit des prairies gonflées d'eau et des falaises blanches, il fit de la boxe avec John Latimer et il apprit l'over-arm-stroke, mais, un beau matin, il se réveilla endormi, ça l'avait repris ; il revint tout somnolent à Paris. La classe de Mathématiques-Élémentaires du lycée Condorcet comptait trente-sept élèves. Huit de ces élèves disaient qu'ils étaient dessalés et traitaient les autres de puceaux. Les dessalés méprisèrent Lucien jusqu'au 1^er^ novembre, mais, le jour de la Toussaint, Lucien alla se promener avec Garry, le plus dessalé de tous et il fit preuve, négligemment, de connaissances anatomiques si précises que Garry fut ébloui. Lucien n'entra pas dans le groupe des dessalés parce que ses parents ne le laissaient pas sortir le soir, mais il eut avec eux des rapports de puissance à puissance.

Le jeudi, tante Berthe venait déjeuner rue Raynouard, avec Riri. Elle était devenue énorme et triste et passait son temps à soupirer ; mais comme sa peau était restée très fine et très blanche, Lucien aurait aimé la voir toute nue. Il y pensait le soir dans son lit : ça serait par un jour d'hiver, au bois de Boulogne, on la découvrirait nue dans un taillis, les bras croisés sur sa poitrine, frissonnante avec la chair de poule. Il imaginait qu'un passant myope la touchait du bout de sa canne en disant : « Mais qu'est-ce que c'est que cela ? » Lucien ne s'entendait pas très bien avec son cousin : Riri était devenu un joli jeune homme un peu trop élégant, il faisait sa philosophie à Lakanal et ne comprenait rien aux mathématiques. Lucien ne pouvait s'empêcher de penser que Riri, à sept ans passés, faisait encore son gros dans sa culotte, et qu'alors il marchait les jambes écartées comme un canard, et qu'il regardait sa maman avec des yeux candides en disant : « Mais non, maman, j'ai pas fait, je te promets. » Et il avait quelque répugnance à toucher la main de Riri. Pourtant, il était très gentil avec lui et lui expliquait ses cours de mathématiques ; il fallait qu'il fasse souvent un gros effort sur lui-même pour ne pas s'impatienter, parce que Riri n'était pas très intelligent. Mais il ne s'emporta jamais et il gardait toujours une voix posée et très calme M^me^ Fleurier trouvait que Lucien avait beaucoup de tact, mais tante Berthe ne lui marquait aucune gratitude. Quand Lucien proposait à Riri de lui donner une leçon, elle rougissait un peu et s'agitait sur sa chaise en disant : « Mais non, tu es bien gentil, mon petit Lucien, mais Riri est trop grand garçon. Il pourrait s'il voulait ; il ne faut pas l'habituer à compter sur les autres. » Un soir, M^me^ Fleurier dit brusquement à Lucien : « Tu crois peut-être que Riri t'est reconnaissant de ce que tu fais pour lui ? Eh bien, détrompe-toi, mon petit garçon : il prétend que tu te gobes, c'est ta tante Berthe qui me l'a dit. » Elle avait pris sa voix musicale et un air bonhomme ; Lucien comprit qu'elle était folle de colère. Il se sentait vaguement intrigué et ne trouva rien à répondre. Le lendemain et le surlendemain, il eut beaucoup de travail et toute cette histoire lui sortit de l'esprit.

Le dimanche matin, il posa brusquement sa plume et se demanda : « Est-ce que je me gobe ? » Il était onze heures ; Lucien, assis à son bureau, regardait les personnages roses de la cretonne qui tapissait les murs ; il sentait sur sa joue gauche la chaleur sèche et poussiéreuse du premier soleil d'avril, sur sa joue droite la lourde chaleur touffue du radiateur. « Est-ce que je me gobe ? » Il était difficile de répondre. Lucien essaya d'abord de se rappeler son dernier entretien avec Riri et de juger impartialement sa propre attitude. Il s'était penché sur Riri et lui avait souri en disant : « Tu piges ? Si tu ne piges pas, mon vieux Riri, n'aie pas peur de le dire : on remettra ça. » Un peu plus tard, il avait fait une erreur dans un raisonnement délicat et il avait dit gaiement : « Au temps pour moi. » C'était une expression qu'il tenait de M. Fleurier et qui l'amusait. Il n'y avait pas de quoi fouetter un chat : « Mais est-ce que je me gobais, pendant que je disais ça ? » A force de chercher, il fit soudain réapparaître quelque chose de blanc, de rond, de doux comme un morceau de nuage : c'était sa pensée de l'autre jour : il avait dit : « Tu piges ? » et il y avait eu ça dans sa tête, mais ça ne pouvait pas se décrire.

Lucien fit des efforts désespérés pour *regarder* ce bout de nuage et il sentit tout à coup qu'il tombait dedans, la tête la première, il se trouva en pleine buée et devint lui-même de la buée, il n'était plus qu'une chaleur blanche et humide qui sentait le linge. Il voulut s'arracher à cette buée et reprendre du recul, mais elle venait avec lui. Il pensa : « C'est moi, Lucien Fleurier, je suis dans ma chambre, je fais un problème de physique, c'est dimanche. » Mais ses pensées fondaient en brouillard, blanc sur blanc. Il se secoua et se mit à détailler les personnages de la cretonne, deux bergères, deux bergers et l'Amour. Puis tout à coup il se dit : « Moi, je suis... » et un léger déclic se produisit : il s'était réveillé de sa longue somnolence.

Ça n'était pas agréable : les bergers avaient sauté en arrière, il semblait à Lucien qu'il les regardait par le gros bout d'une lorgnette. A la place de cette stupeur qui lui était si douce et qui se perdait voluptueusement dans ses propres replis, il y avait maintenant une petite perplexité très réveillée qui se demandait : « Qui suis-je ? »

« Qui suis-je ? Je regarde le bureau, je regarde le cahier. Je m'appelle Lucien Fleurier mais ça n'est qu'un nom. Je me gobe. Je ne me gobe pas. Je ne sais pas, ça n'a pas de sens.

« Je suis un bon élève. Non. C'est de la frime : un bon élève aime travailler — moi pas. J'ai de bonnes notes, mais je n'aime pas travailler. Je ne déteste pas ça non plus, je m'en fous. Je me fous de tout. Je ne serai jamais un chef. » Il pensa avec angoisse : « Mais qu'est-ce que je vais devenir ? » Un moment passa ; il se gratta la joue et cligna de l'œil gauche parce que le soleil l'éblouissait : « Qu'est-ce que je suis, *moi* ? » Il y avait cette brume, enroulée sur elle-même, indéfinie. « Moi ! » Il regarda au loin ; le mot sonnait dans sa tête et puis peut-être qu'on pouvait deviner quelque chose comme la pointe sombre d'une pyramide dont les côtés fuyaient, au loin, dans la brume. Lucien frissonna et ses mains tremblaient : « Ça y est, pensa-t-il, ça y est ! J'en étais sûr : *je n'existe pas.* »

Pendant les mois qui suivirent, Lucien essaya souvent de se rendormir mais il n'y réussit pas : il dormait bien régulièrement neuf heures par nuit et, le reste du temps, il était tout vif et de plus en plus perplexe : ses parents disaient qu'il ne s'était jamais si bien porté. Quand il lui arrivait de penser qu'il n'avait pas l'étoffe d'un chef, il se sentait romantique et il avait envie de marcher pendant des heures sous la lune ; mais ses parents ne l'autorisaient pas encore à sortir le soir. Alors souvent, il s'allongeait sur son lit et prenait sa température : le thermomètre marquait 37-5 ou 37-6 et Lucien pensait avec un plaisir amer que ses parents lui trouvaient bonne mine. « Je n'existe pas. » Il fermait les yeux et se laissait aller : l'existence est une illusion ; puisque je *sais* que je n'existe pas, je n'ai qu'à me boucher les oreilles, à ne plus penser à rien, et je vais m'anéantir. Mais l'illusion était tenace. Au moins avait-il sur les autres gens la supériorité très malicieuse de posséder un secret : Garry, par exemple, n'existait pas plus que Lucien. Mais il suffisait de le voir s'ébrouer tumultueusement au milieu de ses admirateurs : on comprenait tout de suite qu'il croyait dur comme fer à sa propre existence. M. Fleurier non plus n'existait pas — ni Riri ni personne — le monde était une comédie sans acteurs. Lucien, qui avait obtenu la note 15 pour sa dissertation sur « la Morale et la Science », songea à écrire un *Traité du Néant* et il imaginait que les gens, en le lisant, se résorberaient les uns après les autres, comme les vampires au chant du coq. Avant de commencer la rédaction de son traité, il voulut prendre l'avis du Babouin, son prof de philo. « Pardon, monsieur, lui dit-il à la fin d'une classe, est-ce qu'on peut soutenir que nous n'existons pas ? » Le Babouin dit que non. « Goghito, dit-il, ergo çoum. Vous existez puisque vous doutez de votre existence. » Lucien n'était pas convaincu mais il renonça à écrire son ouvrage. En juillet, il fut reçu sans éclat à son baccalauréat de mathématiques et partit pour Férolles avec ses parents. La perplexité ne passait toujours pas : c'était comme une envie d'éternuer.

Le père Bouligaud était mort, et la mentalité des ouvriers de M. Fleurier avait beaucoup changé. Ils touchaient à présent de gros salaires, et leurs femmes s'achetaient des bas de soie. Mme Bouffardier citait des détails effarants à Mme Fleurier : « Ma bonne me racontait qu'elle voyait hier chez le rôtisseur la petite Ansiaume, qui est la fille d'un bon ouvrier de votre mari et dont nous nous sommes occupées quand elle a perdu sa mère. Elle a épousé un ajusteur de Beaupertuis. Eh bien, elle commandait un poulet de vingt francs ! Et d'une arrogance ! Rien n'est assez bon pour elles ; elles veulent avoir tout ce que nous avons. » A présent, quand Lucien faisait, le dimanche, un petit tour de promenade avec son père, les ouvriers touchaient à peine leurs casquettes en les voyant et il y en avait même qui traversaient pour n'avoir pas à saluer. Un jour, Lucien rencontra le fils Bouligaud qui n'eut même pas l'air de le reconnaître. Lucien en fut un peu excité : c'était l'occasion de se prouver qu'il était un chef. Il fit peser sur Jules Bouligaud un regard d'aigle et s'avança vers lui, les mains derrière le dos. Mais Bouligaud ne sembla pas intimidé : il tourna vers Lucien des yeux vides et le croisa en sifflotant.

« Il ne m'a pas reconnu », se dit Lucien. Mais il était profondément déçu et, les jours qui suivirent, il pensa plus que jamais que le monde n'existait pas.

Le petit revolver de M$^{me}$ Fleurier était rangé dans le tiroir de gauche de sa commode. Son mari lui en avait fait cadeau en septembre 1914 avant de partir au front. Lucien le prit et le tourna longtemps entre ses doigts : c'était un petit bijou, avec un canon doré et une crosse plaquée de nacre. On ne pouvait pas compter sur un traité de philosophie pour persuader aux gens qu'ils n'existaient pas. Ce qu'il fallait c'était un acte, un acte vraiment désespéré qui dissipât les apparences et montrât en pleine lumière le néant du monde. Une dénotation, un jeune corps saignant sur un tapis, quelques mots griffonnés sur une feuille : « Je me tue parce que je n'existe pas. Et vous aussi, mes frères, vous êtes néant ! » Les gens liraient leur journal le matin ; ils verraient : « Un adolescent a osé ! » Et chacun se sentirait terriblement troublé et se demanderait : « Et moi ? Est-ce que j'existe ? » On avait connu dans l'histoire, entre autres lors de la publication de *Werther*, de semblables épidémies de suicides ; Lucien pensa que « martyr » en grec veut dire « témoin ». Il était trop sensible pour faire un chef mais non pour faire un martyr. Par la suite, il entra souvent dans le boudoir de sa mère, et il regardait le revolver, et il entrait en agonie. Il lui arriva même de mordre le canon doré en serrant fortement ses doigts contre la crosse. Le reste du temps, il était plutôt gai parce qu'il pensait que tous les vrais chefs avaient connu la tentation du suicide. Par exemple, Napoléon. Lucien ne se dissimulait pas qu'il touchait le fond du désespoir mais il espérait sortir de cette crise avec une âme trempée et il lut avec intérêt le *Mémorial de Sainte-Hélène*. Il fallait pourtant prendre une décision : Lucien se fixa le 30 septembre comme terme ultime de ses hésitations. Les derniers jours furent extrêmement pénibles : certes la crise était salutaire, mais elle exigeait de Lucien une tension si forte qu'il craignait de se briser, un jour, comme du verre. Il n'osait plus toucher au revolver ; il se contentait d'ouvrir le tiroir, il soulevait un peu les combinaisons de sa mère et contemplait longuement le petit monstre glacial et têtu qui se tassait au creux de la soie rose. Pourtant lorsqu'il eut accepté de vivre, il ressentit un vif désappointement et se trouva tout désœuvré. Heureusement, les multiples soucis de la rentrée l'absorbèrent : ses parents l'envoyèrent au lycée Saint-Louis suivre les cours préparatoires à l'École centrale. Il portait un beau calot à liséré rouge avec un insigne et chantait :

*C'est le piston qui fait marcher les machines*
*C'est le piston qui fait marcher les wagons...*

Cette dignité nouvelle de « piston » comblait Lucien de fierté ; et puis sa classe ne ressemblait pas aux autres : elle avait des traditions et un cérémonial ; c'était une force. Par exemple, il était d'usage qu'une voix demandât, un quart d'heure avant la fin du cours de français : « Qu'est-ce qu'un cyrard ? » et tout le monde répondait en sourdine : « C'est un con ! » Sur quoi la voix reprenait : « Qu'est-ce qu'un agro ? » et on répondait un peu plus fort : « C'est un con ! » Alors M. Béthune qui était presque aveugle et portait des lunettes noires, disait avec lassitude : « Je vous en prie, messieurs ! » Il y avait quelques instants de silence absolu, et les élèves se regardaient avec des sourires d'intelligence, puis quelqu'un criait : « Qu'est-ce qu'un piston ? » et ils rugissaient tous ensemble :

« C'est un type énorme ! » A ces moments-là, Lucien se sentait galvanisé. Le soir, il relatait minutieusement à ses parents les divers incidents de la journée et quand il disait : « Alors toute la classe s'est mise à rigoler... » ou bien « toute la classe a décidé de mettre Meyrinez en quarantaine », les mots, en passant, lui chauffaient la bouche comme une gorgée d'alcool. Pourtant les premiers mois furent très durs : Lucien manqua ses compositions de mathématiques et de physique et puis, individuellement, ses camarades n'étaient pas trop sympathiques : c'étaient des boursiers, pour la plupart bûcheurs et malpropres avec de mauvaises manières. « Il n'y en a pas un, dit-il à son père, dont je voudrais me faire un ami. — Les boursiers, dit rêveusement M. Fleurier, représentent une élite intellectuelle et pourtant ils font de mauvais chefs : ils ont brûlé une étape. » Lucien, en entendant parler de « mauvais chefs », sentit un pincement désagréable à son cœur et il pensa de nouveau à se tuer pendant les semaines qui suivirent ; mais il n'avait plus le même enthousiasme qu'aux vacances. Au mois de janvier, un nouvel élève nommé Berliac scandalisa toute la classe : il portait des vestons cintrés verts ou mauves, à la dernière mode, de petits cols ronds et des pantalons comme on en voyait sur les gravures de tailleurs, si étroits qu'on se demandait comment il pouvait les enfiler. D'emblée, il se classa dernier en mathématiques. « Je m'en fous, déclara-t-il, je suis un littéraire, je fais des maths pour me mortifier. » Au bout d'un mois, il avait séduit tout le monde : il distribuait des cigarettes de contrebande et il leur dit qu'il avait des femmes et leur montra les lettres qu'elles lui envoyaient. Toute la classe décida que c'était un chic type et qu'il fallait lui ficher la paix. Lucien admirait beaucoup son élégance et ses manières, mais Berliac traitait Lucien avec condescendance et l'appelait « gosse de riches ». « Après tout, dit un jour Lucien, ça vaut mieux que si j'étais gosse de pauvres. » Berliac sourit « Tu es un petit cynique ! » lui dit-il, et le lendemain, il lui fit lire un de ses poèmes : « Caruso gobait des yeux crus tous les soirs, à part ça sobre comme un chameau. Une dame fit un bouquet avec les yeux de sa famille et les lança sur la scène. Chacun s'incline devant ce geste exemplaire. Mais n'oubliez pas que son heure de gloire dura trente-sept minutes : exactement depuis le premier bravo jusqu'à l'extinction du grand lustre de l'Opéra (par la suite il fallait qu'elle tînt en laisse son mari, lauréat de plusieurs concours, qui bouchait avec deux croix de guerre les cavités roses de ses orbites). Et notez bien ceci : tous ceux d'entre nous qui mangeront trop de chair humaine en conserve périront par le scorbut. » « C'est très bien, dit Lucien décontenancé. — Je les obtiens, dit Berliac avec nonchalance, par une technique nouvelle, ça s'appelle l'écriture automatique. » A quelque temps de là, Lucien eut une violente envie de se tuer et décida de demander conseil à Berliac. « Qu'est-ce que je dois faire ? » demanda-t-il quand il eut exposé son cas. Berliac l'avait écouté avec attention ; il avait l'habitude de sucer ses doigts et d'enduire ensuite de salive les boutons qu'il avait sur la figure, de sorte que sa peau brillait par places comme un chemin après la pluie. « Fais comme tu voudras, dit-il enfin, ça n'a aucune importance. » Il réfléchit un peu et ajouta en appuyant sur les mots : « *Rien* n'a *jamais* aucune importance. » Lucien fut un peu déçu, mais il comprit que Berliac avait été profondément frappé quand celui-ci, le jeudi suivant, l'invita à goûter chez sa mère. M^me^ Berliac fut très aimable ; elle avait des verrues et une tache de lie de vin sur la joue gauche : « Vois-tu, dit Berliac à Lucien, les vraies victimes de la guerre c'est nous. » C'était bien l'avis de Lucien, et ils convinrent qu'ils appartenaient tous les deux à une génération sacrifiée. Le jour tombait, Berliac s'était couché sur son lit, les mains nouées derrière la nuque. Ils fumèrent des cigarettes anglaises, firent tourner des disques au gramophone, et Lucien entendit la voix de Sophie Tucker et celle d'Al Johnson. Ils devinrent tout mélancoliques et Lucien pensa que Berliac était son meilleur ami. Berliac lui demanda s'il connaissait la psychanalyse ; sa voix était sérieuse et il regardait Lucien avec gravité. « J'ai désiré ma mère jusqu'à l'âge de quinze ans », lui confia-t-il. Lucien se sentit mal à l'aise ; il avait peur de rougir et puis il se rappelait les verrues de M$^{me}$ Berliac et ne comprenait pas bien qu'on pût la désirer. Pourtant lorsqu'elle entra pour leur apporter des toasts, il fut vaguement troublé et essaya de deviner sa poitrine à travers le chandail jaune qu'elle portait. Quand elle fut sortie, Berliac dit d'une voix positive : « Toi aussi, naturellement, tu as eu envie de coucher avec ta mère. » Il n'interrogeait pas, il affirmait. Lucien haussa les épaules : « Naturellement », dit-il. Le lendemain, il était inquiet, il avait peur que Berliac ne répétât leur conversation. Mais il se rassura vite : « Après tout, pensa-t-il, il s'est plus compromis que moi. » Il était très séduit par le tour scientifique qu'avaient pris leurs confidences et, le jeudi suivant, il lut un ouvrage de Freud sur le rêve à la bibliothèque Sainte-Geneviève. Ce fut une révélation. « C'est donc ça, se répétait Lucien en marchant au hasard par les rues, c'est donc ça ! » Il acheta par la suite l'*Introduction à la Psychanalyse* et la *Psychopathologie de la vie quotidienne*, tout devint clair pour lui. Cette impression étrange de ne pas exister, ce vide qu'il y avait eu longtemps dans sa conscience, ses somnolences, ses perplexités, ses efforts vains pour se connaître, qui ne rencontraient jamais qu'un rideau de brouillard... « Parbleu, pensa-t-il, j'ai un complexe. » Il raconta à Berliac comment il s'était, dans son enfance, figuré qu'il était somnambule et comment les objets ne lui paraissaient jamais tout à fait réels : « Je dois avoir, conclut-il, un complexe de derrière les fagots. — Tout comme moi, dit Berliac, nous avons des complexes maison ! » Ils prirent l'habitude d'interpréter leurs rêves et jusqu'à leurs moindres gestes ; Berliac avait toujours tant d'histoires à raconter que Lucien le soupçonnait un peu de les inventer ou, tout au moins, de les embellir. Mais ils s'entendaient très bien et ils abordaient les sujets les plus délicats avec objectivité ; ils s'avouèrent qu'ils portaient un masque de gaieté pour tromper leur entourage mais qu'ils étaient au fond terriblement tourmentés. Lucien était délivré de ses inquiétudes. Il s'était jeté avec avidité sur la psychanalyse parce qu'il avait compris que c'était ce qui lui convenait et, à présent, il se sentait raffermi, il n'avait plus besoin de se faire du mauvais sang et d'être toujours à chercher dans sa conscience les manifestations palpables de son caractère. Le véritable Lucien était profondément enfoui dans l'inconscient ; il fallait rêver à lui sans jamais le voir, comme à un cher absent. Lucien pensait tout le jour à ses complexes et il imaginait avec une certaine fierté le monde obscur, cruel et violent qui grouillait sous les vapeurs de sa conscience. « Tu comprends, disait-il à Berliac, en apparence j'étais un gosse endormi et indifférent à tout, quelqu'un de pas très intéressant. Et même du dedans, tu sais, ça avait tellement l'air d'être ça, que j'ai failli m'y laisser prendre. Mais je savais bien qu'il y avait autre chose. — Il y a *toujours* autre chose », répondait Berliac. Et ils se souriaient avec orgueil. Lucien fit un poème intitulé *Quand la brume se déchirera* et Berliac le trouva fameux, mais il reprocha à Lucien de l'avoir écrit en vers réguliers. Ils l'apprirent tout de même par cœur et quand ils voulaient parler de leurs libidos ils disaient volontiers :

« Les grands crabes tapis sous le manteau de brume » puis, tout simplement, « les crabes » en clignant de l'œil. Mais au bout de quelque temps, Lucien, quand il était seul et surtout le soir, commença à trouver tout cela un peu effrayant. Il n'osait plus regarder sa mère en face, et quand il l'embrassait avant d'aller se coucher, il craignait qu'une puissance ténébreuse ne déviât son baiser et ne le fît tomber sur la bouche de Mme Fleurier, c'était comme s'il avait porté en lui-même un volcan. Lucien se traita avec précaution, pour ne pas violenter l'âme somptueuse et sinistre qu'il s'était découverte. Il en connaissait à présent tout le prix et il en redoutait les terribles réveils. « J'ai peur de moi », se disait-il. Il avait renoncé depuis six mois aux pratiques solitaires parce qu'elles l'ennuyaient et qu'il avait trop de travail mais il y revint : il fallait que chacun suivît sa pente, les livres de Freud étaient remplis par les histoires de malheureux jeunes gens qui avaient eu des poussées de névrose pour avoir rompu trop brusquement avec leurs habitudes. « Est-ce que nous n'allons pas devenir fous ? » demandait-il à Berliac. Et de fait, certains jeudis, ils se sentaient étranges : la pénombre s'était sournoisement glissée dans la chambre de Berliac, ils avaient fumé des paquets entiers de cigarettes opiacées, leurs mains tremblaient. Alors l'un d'eux se levait sans mot dire, marchait à pas de loup jusqu'à la porte et tournait le commutateur. Une lumière jaune envahissait la pièce, et ils se regardaient avec défiance.

Lucien ne tarda pas à remarquer que son amitié avec Berliac reposait sur un malentendu : nul plus que lui, certes, n'était sensible à la beauté pathétique du complexe d'Œdipe, mais il y voyait surtout le signe d'une puissance de passion qu'il souhaitait dériver plus tard vers d'autres fins. Berliac, au contraire, semblait se complaire dans son état et n'en voulait pas sortir. « Nous sommes des types foutus, disait-il avec orgueil, des ratés. Nous ne ferons jamais rien. — Jamais rien », répondait Lucien en écho. Mais il était furieux. Au retour des vacances de Pâques, Berliac lui raconta qu'il avait partagé la chambre de sa mère dans un hôtel de Dijon : il s'était levé au petit matin, s'était approché du lit où sa mère dormait encore et avait rabattu doucement les couvertures. « Sa chemise était relevée », dit-il en ricanant. En entendant ces mots, Lucien ne put se défendre de mépriser un peu Berliac et il se sentit très seul. C'était bien joli d'avoir des complexes mais il fallait savoir les liquider à temps : comment un homme fait pourrait-il assumer des responsabilités, et prendre un commandement, s'il avait gardé une sexualité infantile ? Lucien commença à s'inquiéter sérieusement : il aurait aimé prendre le conseil d'une personne autorisée, mais il ne savait à qui s'adresser. Berliac lui parlait souvent d'un surréa liste nommé Bergère qui était très versé dans la psychanalyse et qui semblait avoir pris un grand ascendant sur lui ; mais jamais il n'avait proposé à Lucien de le lui faire connaître. Lucien fut aussi très déçu parce qu'il avait compté sur Berliac pour lui procurer des femmes ; il pensait que la possession d'une jolie maîtresse changerait tout naturellement le cours de ses idées. Mais Berliac ne parlait plus jamais de ses belles amies. Ils allaient quelquefois sur les grands boulevards et suivaient des typesses mais ils n'osaient pas leur parler : « Que veux-tu, mon pauvre vieux, disait Berliac, nous ne sommes pas de la race qui plaît. Les femmes sentent en nous quelque chose qui les effraie. » Lucien ne répondait pas ; Berliac commençait à l'agacer. Il faisait souvent des plaisanteries de très mauvais goût sur les parents de Lucien, il les appelait monsieur et madame Dumollet. Lucien comprenait fort bien qu'un surréaliste méprisât la bourgeoisie en général, mais Berliac avait été invité plusieurs fois par M^me^ Fleurier qui l'avait traité avec confiance et amitié : à défaut de gratitude, un simple souci de décence aurait dû l'empêcher de parler d'elle sur ce ton. Et puis Berliac était terrible avec sa manie d'emprunter de l'argent qu'il ne rendait pas : dans l'autobus il n'avait jamais de monnaie, et il fallait payer pour lui ; dans les cafés, il ne proposait qu'une fois sur cinq de régler les consommations. Lucien lui dit tout net, un jour, qu'il ne comprenait pas cela, et qu'on devait, entre camarades, partager tous les frais des sorties. Berliac le regarda avec profondeur et lui dit : « Je m'en doutais : tu es un anal » et il lui expliqua le rapport freudien : fèces = or et la théorie freudienne de l'avarice. « Je voudrais savoir une chose, dit-il ; jusqu'à quel âge ta mère t'a-t-elle essuyé ? » Ils faillirent se brouiller.

Dès le début du mois de mai, Berliac se mit à sécher le lycée : Lucien allait le rejoindre, après la classe, dans un bar de la rue des Petits-Champs où ils buvaient des vermouths Crucifix. Un mardi après-midi, Lucien trouva Berliac attablé devant un verre vide. « Te voilà, dit Berliac. Écoute, il faut que je les mette, j'ai rendez-vous à cinq heures avec mon dentiste. Attends-moi, il habite à côté, et j'en ai pour une demi-heure. — O. K., répondit Lucien en se laissant tomber sur une chaise. François, donnez-moi un vermouth blanc. » A ce moment un homme entra dans le bar et sourit d'un air étonné en les apercevant. Berliac rougit et se leva précipitamment. « Qui ça peut-il être ? » se demanda Lucien. Berliac, en serrant la main de l'inconnu, s'était arrangé pour lui masquer Lucien ; il parlait d'une voix basse et rapide, l'autre répondit d'une voix claire. « Mais non, mon petit, mais non, tu ne seras jamais qu'un pitre. » En même temps, il se haussait sur la pointe des pieds et dévisageait Lucien par-dessus le crâne de Berliac, avec une tranquille assurance. Il pouvait avoir trente-cinq ans ; il avait un visage pâle et de magnifiques cheveux blancs : « C'est sûrement Bergère, pensa Lucien le cœur battant, ce qu'il est beau ! »

Berliac avait pris l'homme aux cheveux blancs par le coude d'un geste timidement autoritaire :

— Venez avec moi, dit-il, je vais chez mon dentiste, c'est à deux pas.

— Mais tu étais avec un ami, je crois, répondit l'autre sans quitter Lucien des yeux, tu devrais nous présenter l'un à l'autre.

Lucien se leva en souriant. « Attrape ! » pensait-il ; il avait les joues en feu. Le cou de Berliac rentra dans ses épaules, et Lucien crut une seconde qu'il allait refuser. « Eh bien, présente-moi donc », fit-il d'une voix gaie. Mais à peine avait-il parlé que le sang afflua à ses tempes ; il aurait voulu rentrer sous terre. Berliac fit volte-face et marmotta sans regarder personne :

— Lucien Fleurier, un camarade de lycée, monsieur Achille Bergère.

— Monsieur, j'admire vos œuvres, dit Lucien d'une voix faible. Bergère lui prit la main dans ses longues mains fines et l'obligea à se rasseoir. Il y eut un silence ; Bergère enveloppait Lucien d'un chaud regard tendre ; il lui tenait toujours la main : « Êtes-vous inquiet ? » demanda-t-il avec douceur.

Lucien s'éclaircit la voix et rendit à Bergère un ferme regard :

— Je suis inquiet ! répondit-il distinctement. Il lui semblait qu'il venait de subir les épreuves d'une initiation. Berliac hésita un instant puis vint rageusement reprendre sa place en jetant son chapeau sur la table. Lucien brûlait d'envie de raconter à Bergère sa tentative de suicide ; c'était quelqu'un avec qui il fallait parler des choses abruptement et sans préparation. Il n'osa rien dire à cause de Berliac ; il haïssait Berliac.

— Avez-vous du raki ? demanda Bergère au garçon.

— Non, ils n'en ont pas, dit Berliac avec empressement ; c'est une petite boîte charmante mais il n'y a rien à boire que du vermouth.

— Qu'est-ce que c'est que cette chose jaune que vous avez là-bas dans une carafe ? demanda Bergère avec une aisance pleine de mollesse.

— C'est du crucifix blanc, répondit le garçon.

— Eh bien, donnez-moi de ça.

Berliac se tortillait sur sa chaise : il semblait partagé entre le désir de vanter ses amis et la crainte de faire briller Lucien à ses dépens. Il finit par dire, d'une voix morne et fière :

— Il a voulu se tuer.

— Parbleu ! dit Bergère, je l'espère bien.

Il y eut un nouveau silence : Lucien avait baissé les yeux d'un air modeste mais il se demandait si Berliac n'allait pas bientôt foutre le camp. Bergère regarda tout à coup sa montre.

— Et ton dentiste ? demanda-t-il.

Berliac se leva de mauvaise grâce.

— Accompagnez-moi, Bergère, supplia-t-il, c'est à deux pas.

— Mais non, puisque tu reviens. Je tiendrai compagnie à ton camarade.

Berliac demeura encore un moment, il sautait d'un pied sur l'autre.

— Allez, file, dit Bergère, d'une voix impérieuse, tu nous retrouveras ici.

Lorsque Berliac fut parti, Bergère se leva et vint s'asseoir sans façon à côté de Lucien. Lucien lui raconta longuement son suicide ; il lui expliqua aussi qu'il avait désiré sa mère, et qu'il était un sadico-anal, et qu'il n'aimait rien au fond, et que tout en lui était comédie. Bergère l'écoutait sans mot dire en le regardant profondément, et Lucien trouvait délicieux d'être compris. Quand il eut fini, Bergère lui passa familièrement le bras autour des épaules, et Lucien respira une odeur d'eau de Cologne et de tabac anglais.

— Savez-vous, Lucien, comment j'appelle votre état ? Lucien regarda Bergère avec espoir ; il ne fut pas déçu.

— Je l'appelle, dit Bergère, le Désarroi.

Désarroi : le mot avait commencé tendre et blanc comme un clair de lune, mais le « oi » final avait l'éclat cuivré d'un cor.

— Désarroi..., dit Lucien.

Il se sentait grave et inquiet comme lorsqu'il avait dit à Riri qu'il était somnambule. Le bar était sombre, mais la porte s'ouvrait toute grande sur la rue, sur le lumineux brouillard blond du printemps ; sous le parfum soigné que dégageait Bergère, Lucien percevait la lourde odeur de la salle obscure, une odeur de vin rouge et de bois humide. « Désarroi... pensait-il ; à quoi est-ce que ça va m'engager ? » Il ne savait pas bien si on lui avait découvert une dignité ou une maladie nouvelle ; il voyait près de ses yeux les lèvres agiles de Bergère qui voilaient et dévoilaient sans répit l'éclat d'une dent d'or.

— J'aime les êtres qui sont en désarroi, disait Bergère, et je trouve que vous avez une chance extraordinaire. Car enfin, cela vous a été donné. Vous voyez tous ces porcs ? Ce sont des assis. Il faudrait les donner aux fourmis rouges, pour les asticoter un peu. Vous savez ce qu'elles font ces consciencieuses bestioles ?

— Elles mangent de l'homme, dit Lucien.

— Oui, elles débarrassent les squelettes de leur viande humaine.

— Je vois, dit Lucien. — Il ajouta : Et moi ? Qu'est-ce qu'il faut que je fasse ?

— Rien, pour l'amour de Dieu, dit Bergère avec un effarement comique. Et surtout ne pas vous asseoir. A moins, dit-il en riant, que ce ne soit sur un pal. Avez-vous lu Rimbaud ?

— Nnnnon, dit Lucien.

— Je vous prêterai *Les Illuminations.* Écoutez, il faut que nous nous revoyions. Si vous êtes libre jeudi, passez donc chez moi vers trois heures, j'habite à Montparnasse, 9, rue Campagne-Première.

Le jeudi suivant, Lucien alla chez Bergère et il y retourna presque tous les jours du mois de mai. Ils avaient convenu de dire à Berliac qu'ils se voyaient une fois par semaine, parce qu'ils voulaient être francs avec lui tout en évitant de lui faire de la peine. Berliac s'était montré parfaitement déplacé ; il avait dit à Lucien en ricanant : « Alors, c'est le béguin ? Il t'a fait le coup de l'inquiétude, et tu lui as fait le coup du suicide : le grand jeu, quoi ! » Lucien protesta : « Je te ferai remarquer, dit-il en rougissant, que c'est toi qui as parlé le premier de mon suicide. — Oh ! dit Berliac, c'était seulement pour t'éviter ıa honte de le faire toi-même. » Ils espacèrent leurs rendez-vous. « Tout ce qui me plaisait en lui, dit un jour Lucien à Bergère, c'est à vous qu'il l'empruntait, je m'en rends compte à présent. — Berliac est un singe, dit Bergère en riant, c'est ce qui m'a toujours attiré vers lui. Vous savez que sa grand-mère maternelle est juive ? Cela explique bien des choses. — En effet », répondit Lucien. Il ajouta au bout d'un instant : « D'ailleurs, c'est quelqu'un de charmant. » L'appartement de Bergère était encombré d'objets étranges et comiques : des poufs dont le siège de velours rouge reposait sur des jambes de femmes en bois peint, des statuettes nègres, une ceinture de chasteté en fer forgé avec des piquants, des seins en plâtre dans lesquels on avait planté de petites cuillers ; sur le bureau, un gigantesque pou de bronze et un crâne de moine volé dans un ossuaire de Mistra servaient de presse-papiers. Les murs étaient tapissés de lettres de faire-part qui annonçaient la mort du surréaliste Bergère. Malgré tout, l'appartement donnait une impression de confort intelligent, et Lucien aimait à s'étendre sur le divan profond du fumoir. Ce qui l'étonnait particulièrement c'était l'énorme quantité de farces et d'attrapes que Bergère avait accumulées sur une étagère : fluide glacial, poudre à éternuer, poil à gratter, sucre flottant, étron diabolique, jarretelle de la mariée. Bergère prenait, tout en parlant, l'étron diabolique entre ses doigts et le considérait avec gravité : « Ces attrapes, disait-il, ont une valeur révolutionnaire ; elles inquiètent. Il y a plus de puissance destructrice en elles que dans les œuvres complètes de Lénine. » Lucien, surpris et charmé, regardait tour à tour ce beau visage tourmenté aux yeux caves et ces longs doigts fins qui tenaient avec grâce un excrément parfaitement imité. Bergère lui parlait souvent de

Rimbaud et du « dérèglement systématique de tous les sens ». « Quand vous pourrez, en passant sur la place de la Concorde, voir distinctement et à volonté une négresse à genoux en train de sucer l'obélisque, vous pourrez vous dire que vous avez crevé le décor et que vous êtes sauvé. » Il lui prêta *Les Illuminations*, les *Chants de Maldoror*, et les œuvres du marquis de Sade. Lucien essayait consciencieusement de comprendre, mais beaucoup de choses lui échappaient et il était choqué parce que Rimbaud était pédéraste. Il le dit à Bergère qui se mit à rire : « Mais pourquoi, mon petit ? » Lucien fut très embarrassé. Il rougit et pendant une minute il se mit à haïr Bergère de toutes ses forces ; mais il se domina, releva la tête et dit avec une franchise simple : « J'ai dit une connerie. » Bergère lui caressa les cheveux : il paraissait attendri : « Ces grands yeux pleins de trouble, dit-il, ces yeux de biche... Oui, Lucien, vous avez dit une connerie. La pédérastie de Rimbaud, c'est le dérèglement premier et génial de sa sensibilité. C'est à elle que nous devons ses poèmes. Croire qu'il y a des objets spécifiques du désir sexuel et que ces objets sont les femmes, parce qu'elles ont un trou entre les jambes, c'est la hideuse et volontaire erreur des assis. Regardez ! » Il tira de son bureau une douzaine de photos jaunies et les jeta sur les genoux de Lucien. Lucien vit d'horribles putains nues, riant de leurs bouches édentées, écartant leurs jambes comme des lèvres et dardant entre leurs cuisses quelque chose comme une langue moussue. « J'ai eu la collection pour trois francs à Bou-Saada, dit Bergère. Si vous embrassez le derrière de ces femmes-là, vous êtes un fils de famille et tout le monde dira que vous menez la vie de garçon. Parce que ce sont des femmes, comprenez-vous ? Moi je vous dis que la première chose à faire c'est de vous persuader que *tout* peut être objet de désir sexuel, une machine à coudre, une éprouvette, un cheval ou un soulier. Moi, dit-il en riant, j'ai fait l'amour avec des mouches. J'ai connu un fusilier marin qui couchait avec des canards. Il leur mettait la tête dans un tiroir, les tenait solidement par les pattes et allez donc ! » Bergère pinça distraitement l'oreille de Lucien et conclut : « Le canard en mourait, et le bataillon le mangeait. » Lucien sortait de ces entretiens, la tête en feu, il pensait que Bergère était un génie, mais il lui arrivait de se réveiller la nuit, trempé de sueur, la tête remplie de visions monstrueuses et obscènes, et il se demandait si Bergère exerçait sur lui une bonne influence : « Être seul ! gémissait-il en se tordant les mains, n'avoir personne pour me conseiller, pour me dire si je suis dans le droit chemin ! » S'il allait jusqu'au bout, s'il pratiquait pour de bon le dérèglement de tous ses sens, est-ce qu'il n'allait pas perdre pied et se noyer ! Un jour que Bergère lui avait longtemps parlé d'André Breton, Lucien murmura comme dans un rêve : « Oui, mais si, après ça, je ne peux plus revenir en arrière ? » Bergère sursauta : « Revenir en arrière ? Qui parle de revenir en arrière ? Si vous devenez fou, c'est tant mieux. Après, comme dit Rimbaud, " viendront d'autres horribles travailleurs ". — C'est bien ce que je pensais », dit Lucien tristement. Il avait remarqué que ces longues causeries avaient un résultat opposé à celui que souhaitait Bergère : dès que Lucien se surprenait à éprouver une sensation un peu fine, une impression originale, il se mettait à trembler : « Ça commence » pensait-il. Il aurait volontiers souhaité n'avoir plus que les perceptions les plus banales et les plus épaisses ; il ne se sentait à l'aise que le soir avec ses parents : c'était son refuge. Ils parlaient de Briand, de la mauvaise volonté des Allemands, des couches de la cousine Jeanne et du prix de la vie : Lucien échangeait voluptueusement avec eux des propos d'un grossier bon sens. Un jour, comme il rentrait dans sa chambre après avoir quitté Bergère, il ferma machinalement la porte à clef et poussa la targette. Quand il s'aperçut de son geste, il s'efforça d'en rire, mais il ne put dormir de la nuit : il venait de comprendre qu'il avait peur.

Cependant, il n'aurait cessé pour rien au monde de fréquenter Bergère. « Il me fascine », se disait-il. Et puis il appréciait vivement la camaraderie si délicate et d'un genre si particulier que Bergère avait su établir entre eux. Sans quitter un ton viril et presque rude, Bergère avait l'art de faire sentir et, pour ainsi dire, toucher à Lucien sa tendresse : par exemple, il lui refaisait le nœud de sa cravate en le grondant d'être si mal fagoté, il le peignait avec un peigne d'or qui venait du Cambodge. Il fit découvrir à Lucien son propre corps et lui expliqua la beauté âpre et pathétique de la jeunesse : « Vous êtes Rimbaud, lui disait-il, il avait vos grandes mains quand il est venu à Paris pour voir Verlaine, il avait ce visage rose de jeune paysan bien portant et ce long corps grêle de fillette blonde. » Il obligeait Lucien à défaire son col et à ouvrir sa chemise, puis il le conduisait, tout confus, devant une glace et lui faisait admirer l'harmonie charmante de ses joues rouges et de sa gorge blanche ; alors il effleurait d'une main légère les hanches de Lucien et ajoutait tristement : « On devrait se tuer à vingt ans. » Souvent, à présent, Lucien se regardait dans les miroirs, et il apprenait à jouir de sa jeune grâce pleine de gaucherie. « Je suis Rimbaud », pensait-il, le soir, en ôtant ses vêtements avec des gestes pleins de douceur et il commençait à croire qu'il aurait la vie brève et tragique d'une fleur trop belle. A ces moments-là, il lui paraissait qu'il avait connu, très longtemps auparavant, des impressions analogues et une image absurde lui revenait à l'esprit : il se revoyait tout petit, avec une longue robe bleue et des ailes d'ange, distribuant des fleurs dans une vente de charité. Il regardait ses longues jambes. « Est-ce que c'est vrai que j'ai la peau si douce ? » pensait-il avec amusement. Et une fois il promena ses lèvres sur son avant-bras, du poignet à la saignée du coude, le long d'une charmante petite veine bleue.

Un jour, en entrant chez Bergère, il eut une surprise désagréable : Berliac était là, il s'occupait à détacher avec un couteau des fragments d'une substance noirâtre qui avait l'aspect d'une motte de terre. Les deux jeunes gens ne s'étaient pas revus depuis dix jours : ils se serrèrent la main avec froideur. « Tu vois ça, dit Berliac, c'est du haschich. Nous allons en mettre dans ces pipes entre deux couches de tabac blond, ça fait un effet étonnant. Il y en a pour toi, ajouta-t-il. — Merci, dit Lucien, je n'y tiens pas. » Les deux autres se mirent à rire, et Berliac insista, l'œil mauvais : « Mais tu es idiot, mon vieux, tu vas en prendre : tu ne peux pas te figurer comme c'est agréable. — Je t'ai dit que non ! » dit Lucien. Berliac ne répondit plus rien, il se borna à sourire d'un air supérieur, et Lucien vit que Bergère souriait aussi. Il tapa du pied et dit : « Je n'en veux pas, je ne veux pas m'esquinter, je trouve idiot de prendre de ces machins-là qui vous abrutissent. » Il avait lâché ça malgré lui, mais quand il comprit la portée de ce qu'il venait de dire et qu'il imagina ce que Bergère pouvait penser de lui, il eut envie de tuer Berliac, et les larmes lui vinrent aux yeux. « Tu es un bourgeois, dit Berliac en haussant les épaules, tu fais semblant de nager, mais tu as bien trop peur de perdre pied. — Je ne veux pas prendre l'habitude des stupéfiants, dit Lucien d'une voix plus calme ; c'est un esclavage comme un autre et je veux rester disponible. — Dis que tu as peur de t'engager », répondit violemment Berliac. Lucien allait lui donner une paire de gifles quand il entendit la voix impérieuse de Bergère. « Laisse-le, Charles, disait-il à Berliac, c'est lui qui a raison. Sa peur de s'engager c'est aussi du désarroi. » Ils fumèrent tous deux, étendus sur le divan, et une odeur de papier d'Arménie se répandit dans la pièce. Lucien s'était assis sur un pouf en velours rouge et les contemplait en silence. Berliac, au bout d'un moment, laissa aller sa tête en arrière et battit des paupières avec un sourire mouillé. Lucien le regardait avec rancune et se sentait humilié. Enfin Berliac se leva et quitta la pièce d'un pas hésitant : il avait gardé jusqu'au bout sur ses lèvres ce drôle de sourire endormi et voluptueux. « Donnez-moi une pipe », dit Lucien d'une voix rauque. Bergère se mit à rire. « Pas la peine, dit-il. Ne t'en fais pas pour Berliac. Tu ne sais pas ce qu'il fait en ce moment ! — Je m'en fous, dit Lucien. — Eh bien, sache tout de même qu'il vomit, dit tranquillement Bergère. C'est le seul effet que le haschich lui ait jamais produit. Le reste n'est qu'une comédie, mais je lui en fais fumer quelquefois parce qu'il veut m'épater et que ça m'amuse. » Le lendemain Berliac vint au lycée et il voulut le prendre de haut avec Lucien. « Tu montes dans les trains, dit-il, mais tu choisis soigneusement ceux qui restent en gare. » Mais il trouva à qui parler. « Tu es un bonimenteur, lui répondit Lucien, tu crois peut-être que je ne sais pas ce que tu faisais hier dans la salle de bains ? Tu dégueulais, mon vieux ! » Berliac devint blême. « C'est Bergère qui te l'a dit ? — Qui veux-tu que ça soit ? — C'est bien, balbutia Berliac, mais je n'aurais pas cru que Bergère fût un type à se foutre de ses anciens copains avec les nouveaux. » Lucien était un peu inquiet : il avait promis à Bergère de ne rien répéter. « Allez, ça va ! dit-il, il ne s'est pas foutu de toi, il a simplement voulu me montrer que ça ne prenait pas. » Mais Berliac lui tourna le dos et partit sans lui serrer la main. Lucien n'était pas trop fier quand il retrouva Bergère. « Qu'est-ce que vous avez dit à Berliac ? » demanda Bergère d'un air neutre. Lucien baissa la tête sans répondre : il était accablé. Mais il sentit soudain la main de Bergère sur sa nuque : « Ça ne fait rien du tout, mon petit. De toute façon, il fallait que ça finisse : les comédiens ne m'amusent jamais longtemps. » Lucien reprit un peu de courage : il releva la tête et sourit : « Mais moi aussi je suis un comédien, dit-il en battant des paupières. — Oui, mais toi, tu es joli », répondit Bergère en l'attirant contre lui. Lucien se laissa aller ; il se sentait doux comme une fille et il avait les larmes aux yeux. Bergère l'embrassa sur les joues et lui mordilla l'oreille en l'appelant tantôt « ma belle petite canaille » et tantôt « mon petit frère », et Lucien pensait qu'il était bien agréable d'avoir un grand frère si indulgent et si compréhensif.

M. et Mme Fleurier voulurent connaître ce Bergère dont Lucien parlait tant et ils l'invitèrent à dîner. Tout le monde le trouva charmant, jusqu'à Germaine, qui n'avait jamais vu un si bel homme. M. Fleurier avait connu le général Nizan qui était l'oncle de Bergère et il en parla longuement. Aussi Mme Fleurier fut-elle trop heureuse de confier Lucien à Bergère pour les vacances de la Pentecôte. Ils allèrent à Rouen, en auto ; Lucien voulait voir la cathédrale et l'hôtel de ville, mais Bergère refusa tout net : « Ces ordures ? » demanda-t-il avec insolence. Finalement ils allèrent passer deux heures dans un bordel de la rue des Cordeliers, et Bergère fut marrant : il appelait toutes les poufiasses « Mademoiselle » en donnant des coups de genou à

Lucien sous la table, puis il accepta de monter avec l'une d'elles, mais revint au bout de cinq minutes : « Foutons le camp, souffla-t-il, sans quoi, ça va barder. » Ils payèrent rapidement et sortirent. Dans la rue, Bergère raconta ce qui s'était passé ; il avait profité de ce que la femme avait le dos tourné pour jeter dans le lit une pleine poignée de poil à gratter, puis il avait déclaré qu'il était impuissant et il était redescendu. Lucien avait bu deux whiskies et il était un peu parti ; il chanta l'*Artilleur de Metz* et le *De Profundis Morpionibus* ; il trouvait admirable que Bergère fût à la fois si profond et si gamin.

« Je n'ai retenu qu'une chambre, dit Bergère quand ils arrivèrent à l'hôtel, mais il y a une grande salle de bains. » Lucien ne fut pas surpris : il avait vaguement pensé pendant le voyage qu'il partagerait la chambre de Bergère mais sans jamais s'arrêter bien longtemps sur cette idée. A présent qu'il ne pouvait plus reculer, il trouvait la chose un peu désagréable, surtout parce qu'il n'avait pas les pieds propres. Il imagina, pendant qu'on montait les valises, que Bergère lui dirait : « Comme tu es sale, tu vas noircir les draps », et il lui répondrait avec insolence : « Vous avez des idées bien bourgeoises sur la propreté. » Mais Bergère le poussa dans la salle de bains avec sa valise en lui disant : « Arrange-toi là-dedans, moi je vais me déshabiller dans la chambre. » Lucien prit un bain de pieds et un bain de siège. Il avait envie d'aller aux cabinets mais il n'osa pas et se contenta d'uriner dans le lavabo ; puis il revêtit sa chemise de nuit, mit des pantoufles que sa mère lui avait prêtées (les siennes étaient toutes trouées) et frappa : « Êtes-vous prêt ? demanda-t-il. — Oui, oui, entre. » Bergère avait enfilé une robe de chambre noire sur un pyjama bleu ciel. La chambre sentait l'eau de Cologne. « Il n'y a qu'un lit ? »

demanda Lucien. Bergère ne répondit pas : il regardait Lucien avec une stupeur qui s'acheva en un formidable éclat de rire : « Mais tu es en bannière ! dit-il en riant. Qu'as-tu fait de ton bonnet de nuit ? Ah ! non, tu es trop drôle, je voudrais que tu te voies. — Voilà deux ans, dit Lucien très vexé, que je demande à ma mère de m'acheter des pyjamas. » Bergère vint vers lui : « Allez, ôte ça, dit-il d'un ton sans réplique, je vais t'en donner un des miens. Il va être un peu grand, mais ça t'ira toujours mieux que ça. » Lucien demeura cloué au milieu de la pièce, les yeux rivés sur les losanges rouges et verts de la tapisserie. Il aurait préféré retourner dans la salle de bains mais il eut peur de passer pour un imbécile, et d'un mouvement sec il envoya promener sa chemise par-dessus sa tête. Il y eut un instant de silence : Bergère regardait Lucien en souriant, et Lucien comprit soudain qu'il était tout nu au milieu de la chambre et qu'il portait à ses pieds les pantoufles à pompon de sa mère. Il regarda ses mains — les grandes mains de Rimbaud — il aurait voulu les plaquer contre son ventre et cacher au moins ça, mais il se reprit et les mit bravement derrière son dos. Sur les murs, entre deux rangs de losanges, il y avait de loin en loin un petit carré violet. « Ma parole, dit Bergère, il est aussi chaste qu'une pucelle : regarde-toi dans une glace, Lucien, tu as rougi jusqu'à la poitrine. Tu es pourtant mieux comme ça qu'en bannière. — Oui, dit Lucien avec effort, mais on n'a jamais l'air fin quand on est à poil. Passez-moi vite le pyjama. » Bergère lui jeta un pyjama de soie qui sentait la lavande, et ils se mirent au lit. Il y eut un lourd silence : « Ça va mal, dit Lucien ; j'ai envie de dégueuler. » Bergère ne répondit pas et Lucien eut un renvoi de whisky. « Il va coucher avec moi », se dit-il. Et les losanges de la tapisserie se mirent à tourner pendant que l'étouffante odeur d'eau de Cologne le saisissait à la gorge. « Je n'aurais pas dû accepter de faire ce voyage. » Il n'avait pas eu de chance ; vingt fois, ces derniers temps, il avait été à deux doigts de découvrir ce que Bergère voulait de lui et puis chaque fois, comme par un fait exprès, un incident était survenu qui avait détourné sa pensée. Et à présent, il était là, dans le lit de ce type, et il attendait son bon plaisir. « Je vais prendre mon oreiller et aller coucher dans la salle de bains. » Mais il n'osa pas ; il pensait au regard ironique de Bergère. Il se mit à rire : « Je pense à la putain de tout à l'heure, dit-il, elle doit être en train de se gratter. » Bergère ne répondait toujours pas. Lucien le regarda du coin de l'œil : il était étendu, sur le dos, l'air innocent, les mains sous la nuque. Alors une fureur violente s'empara de Lucien, il se dressa sur un coude et lui dit : « Eh bien, qu'est-ce que vous attendez ? C'est pour enfiler des perles que vous m'avez amené ici ? »

Il était trop tard pour regretter sa phrase : Bergère s'était tourné vers lui et le considérait d'un œil amusé : « Voyez-moi cette petite grue avec son visage d'ange. Alors, mon bébé, je ne te l'ai pas fait dire : c'est sur moi que tu comptes pour les dérégler, tes petits sens. » Il le regarda encore un instant, leurs visages se touchaient presque, puis il prit Lucien dans ses bras et lui caressa la poitrine sous la veste du pyjama. Ça n'était pas désagréable, ça chatouillait un peu, seulement Bergère était effrayant : il avait pris un air idiot et répétait avec effort : « Tu n'as pas honte, petit cochon, tu n'as pas honte, petit cochon ! » comme les disques de phono qui annoncent dans les gares le départ des trains. La main de Bergère au contraire, vive et légère, semblait une personne. Elle frôlait doucement la pointe des seins de Lucien, on aurait dit la caresse de l'eau tiède quand on entre dans le bain. Lucien aurait voulu attraper cette main, l'arracher de lui et la tordre, mais Bergère aurait rigolé : voyez-moi ce puceau. La main glissa lentement le long de son ventre et s'attarda à défaire le nœud de la cordelière qui retenait son pantalon. Il la laissa faire : il était lourd et mou comme une éponge mouillée et il avait une frousse épouvantable. Bergère avait rabattu les couvertures, il avait posé la tête sur la poitrine de Lucien et il avait l'air de l'ausculter. Lucien eut coup sur coup deux renvois aigres et il eut peur de dégueuler sur les beaux cheveux argentés qui étaient si dignes. « Vous me pressez sur l'estomac », dit-il. Bergère se souleva un peu et passa une main sous les reins de Lucien ; l'autre main ne caressait plus, elle tiraillait. « Tu as de belles petites fesses », dit soudain Bergère. Lucien croyait faire un cauchemar : « Elles vous plaisent ? » demanda-t-il avec coquetterie. Mais Bergère le lâcha soudain et releva la tête d'un air dépité. « Sacré petit bluffeur, dit-il rageusement, ça veut jouer les Rimbaud et voilà plus d'une heure que je m'escrime sur lui sans parvenir à l'exciter. » Des larmes d'énervement montèrent aux yeux de Lucien, et il repoussa Bergère de toutes ses forces : « Ça n'est pas ma faute, dit-il d'une voix sifflante, vous m'avez fait trop boire, j'ai envie de dégueuler. — Eh bien, va ! va ! dit Bergère, et prends ton temps. » Il ajouta entre ses dents : « Charmante soirée. » Lucien remonta son pantalon, enfila la robe de chambre noire et sortit. Quand il eut refermé la porte des cabinets, il se sentit si seul et si désemparé qu'il éclata en sanglots. Il n'y avait pas de mouchoirs dans les poches de la robe de chambre et il s'essuya les yeux et le nez avec le papier hygiénique. Il eut beau se mettre deux doigts dans le gosier, il n'arriva pas à vomir. Alors il fit machinalement tomber son pantalon et s'assit sur le trône en grelottant. « Le salaud, pensait-il, le salaud ! » Il était atrocement humilié, mais il ne savait pas s'il avait honte d'avoir subi les caresses de Bergère ou de n'avoir pas été troublé. Le couloir craquait de l'autre côté de la porte, et Lucien sursautait à chaque craquement, mais il ne pouvait se décider à rentrer dans la chambre : « Il faut pourtant que j'y aille, pensait-il, il le faut, sans quoi il se foutra de moi — avec Berliac ! » et il se levait à demi, mais aussitôt il revoyait le visage de Bergère et son air bête, il l'entendait dire : « Tu n'as pas honte, petit cochon ! » Il retombait sur le siège, désespéré ! Au bout d'un moment, il fut pris d'une violente diarrhée qui le soulagea un peu : « Ça s'en va par le bas, pensa-t-il, j'aime mieux ça. » De fait, il n'avait plus envie de vomir. « Il va me faire mal », pensa-t-il brusquement, et il crut qu'il allait s'évanouir. Lucien finit par avoir si froid qu'il se mit à claquer des dents : il pensa qu'il allait tomber malade et se leva brusquement. Quand il rentra, Bergère le regarda d'un air contraint ; il fumait une cigarette, son pyjama était ouvert et on voyait son torse maigre. Lucien ôta lentement ses pantoufles et sa robe de chambre, et se glissa sans mot dire sous la couverture : « Ça va ? » demanda Bergère. Lucien haussa les épaules : « J'ai froid ! — Tu veux que je te réchauffe ? — Essayez toujours », dit Lucien. A l'instant il se sentit écrasé par un poids énorme. Une bouche tiède et molle se colla contre la sienne, on aurait dit un bifteck cru. Lucien ne comprenait plus rien, il ne savait plus où il était et il étouffait à demi, mais il était content parce qu'il avait chaud. Il pensa à Mme Besse qui lui appuyait sa main sur le ventre en l'appelant « ma petite poupée », et à Hébrard qui l'appelait « grande asperche », et aux tubs qu'il prenait le matin, en s'imaginant que M. Bouffardier allait rentrer pour lui donner un lavement, et il se dit : « Je suis sa petite poupée ! » A ce moment, Bergère poussa un cri de triomphe. « Enfin ! dit-il, tu te décides. Allons, ajouta-t-il en soufflant, on fera quelque chose de toi. » Lucien tint à ôter lui-même son pyjama.

Le lendemain, ils se réveillèrent à midi. Le garçon leur porta leur petit déjeuner au lit, et Lucien trouva qu'il avait l'air rogue. « Il me prend pour une lope », pensa-t-il avec un frisson de désagrément. Bergère fut très gentil, il s'habilla le premier et alla fumer une cigarette sur la place du Vieux-Marché pendant que Lucien prenait son bain. « Ce qu'il y a, pensa Lucien en se frottant soigneusement au gant de crin, c'est que c'est ennuyeux. » Le premier moment de terreur passé, et quand il s'était aperçu que ça n'était pas si douloureux qu'il croyait, il avait sombré dans un morne ennui. Il espérait toujours que c'était fini et qu'il allait pouvoir dormir, mais Bergère ne l'avait pas laissé tranquille avant quatre heures du matin. « Il faudra tout de même que je finisse mon problème de trigo », se dit-il. Et il s'efforça de ne plus penser qu'à son travail. La journée fut longue. Bergère lui raconta la vie de Lautréamont, mais Lucien ne l'écouta pas très attentivement ; Bergère l'agaçait un peu. Le soir, ils couchèrent à Caudebec et naturellement Bergère embêta Lucien pendant un bon moment, mais, vers une heure du matin, Lucien lui dit tout net qu'il avait sommeil et Bergère sans se fâcher lui ficha la paix. Ils rentrèrent à Paris vers la fin de l'après-midi. Somme toute Lucien n'était pas mécontent de lui-même.

Ses parents l'accueillirent à bras ouverts : « As-tu bien remercié M. Bergère au moins ? » demanda sa mère. Il resta un moment à bavarder avec eux sur la campagne normande et se coucha de bonne heure. Il dormit comme un ange, mais le lendemain, à son réveil, il lui sembla qu'il grelottait en dedans. Il se leva et se contempla longtemps dans la glace. « Je suis un pédéraste », se dit-il. Et il s'effondra. « Lève-toi, Lucien, cria sa mère à travers la porte, tu vas au lycée ce matin. — Oui, maman », répondit Lucien avec docilité, mais il se laissa tomber sur son lit et se mit à regarder ses orteils. « C'est trop injuste, je ne me rendais pas compte, moi, je n'ai pas d'expérience. » Ces orteils, un homme les avait sucés l'un après l'autre. Lucien détourna la tête avec violence : « Il savait, lui. Ce qu'il m'a fait faire porte un nom, ça s'appelle coucher avec un homme et il le savait. » C'était marrant — Lucien sourit avec amertume —, on pouvait, pendant des journées entières, se demander : suis-je intelligent, est-ce que je me gobe, on n'arrivait jamais à décider. Et à côté de ça, il y avait des étiquettes qui s'accrochaient à vous un beau matin et il fallait les porter toute sa vie : par exemple, Lucien était grand et blond, il ressemblait à son père, il était fils unique et, depuis hier, il était pédéraste. On dirait de lui : « Fleurier, vous savez bien, ce grand blond qui aime les hommes ? » Et les gens répondraient : « Ah ! oui. La grande tantouse ? Très bien, je sais qui c'est. »

Il s'habilla et sortit, mais il n'eut pas le cœur d'aller au lycée. Il descendit l'avenue de Lamballe jusqu'à la Seine et suivit les quais. Le ciel était pur, les rues sentaient la feuille verte, le goudron et le tabac anglais. Un temps rêvé pour porter des vêtements propres sur un corps bien lavé avec une âme toute neuve. Les gens avaient tous un air moral ; Lucien, seul, se sentait louche et insolite dans ce printemps. « C'est la pente fatale, songeait-il, j'ai commencé par le complexe d'Œdipe, après ça je suis devenu sadico-anal et maintenant, c'est le bouquet, je suis pédéraste ; où est-ce que je vais m'arrêter ? » Évidemment, son cas n'était pas encore très grave ; il n'avait pas eu grand plaisir aux caresses de Bergère. « Mais si j'en prends l'habitude ? pensa-t-il avec angoisse. Je ne pourrai plus m'en passer, ça sera comme la morphine ! » Il deviendrait un homme taré, personne ne voudrait plus le recevoir, les ouvriers de son père rigoleraient quand il leur donnerait un ordre. Lucien imagina avec complaisance son épouvantable destin. Il se voyait à trente-cinq ans, mignard et fardé, et déjà un monsieur à moustache avec la Légion d'honneur, levait sa canne d'un air terrible. « Votre présence ici, monsieur, est une insulte pour mes filles. » Lorsque soudain, il chancela et cessa brusquement de jouer : il venait de se rappeler une phrase de Bergère. C'était à Caudebec pendant la nuit. Bergère avait dit : « Eh mais dis donc ! tu y prends goût ! » Qu'avait-il voulu dire ? Naturellement, Lucien n'était pas de bois et à force d'être tripoté... « Ça ne prouve rien », se dit-il avec inquiétude. Mais on prétendait que ces gens-là étaient extraordinaires pour repérer leurs pareils, c'était comme un sixième sens. Lucien regarda longuement un sergent de ville qui réglait la circulation devant le pont d'Iéna. « Est-ce que cet agent pourrait m'exciter ? » Il fixait le pantalon bleu de l'agent, il imaginait des cuisses musculeuses et velues : « Est-ce que ça me fait quelque chose ? » Il repartit très soulagé. « Ça n'est pas si grave, pensa-t-il, je peux encore me sauver Il a abusé de mon désarroi, mais je ne suis pas *vraiment* pédéraste. » Il recommença l'expérience avec tous les hommes qui le croisèrent, et chaque fois le résultat était négatif. « Ouf ! pensa-t-il, eh bien, j'ai eu chaud ! » C'était un avertissement, voilà tout. Il ne fallait plus recommencer, parce qu'une mauvaise habitude est vite prise et puis il fallait de toute urgence qu'il se guérît de ses complexes. Il résolut de se faire psychanalyser par un spécialiste sans le dire à ses parents. Ensuite, il prendrait une maîtresse et deviendrait un homme comme les autres.

Lucien commençait à se rassurer lorsqu'il pensa tout à coup à Bergère : à ce moment même, Bergère existait quelque part dans Paris, enchanté de lui-même et la tête pleine de souvenirs : « Il sait comment je suis fait, il connaît ma bouche, il m'a dit : “ Tu as une odeur que je n'oublierai pas ” ; il ira se vanter à ses amis, en disant : “ Je l'ai eu ” comme si j'étais une gonzesse. A l'instant même, il est peut-être en train de raconter ses nuits à... — le cœur de Lucien cessa de battre — à Berliac ! S'il fait ça, je le tue : Berliac me déteste, il le racontera à toute la classe, je suis un type coulé, les copains refuseront de me serrer la main. Je dirai que ça n'est pas vrai, se dit Lucien avec égarement, je porterai plainte, je dirai qu'il m'a violé ! » Lucien haïssait Bergère de toutes ses forces : sans lui, sans cette conscience scandaleuse et irrémédiable, tout aurait pu s'arranger, personne n'aurait rien su et Lucien lui-même aurait fini par l'oublier. « S'il pouvait mourir subitement ! Mon Dieu, je vous en prie, faites qu'il soit mort cette nuit avant d'avoir rien dit à personne. Mon Dieu, faites que cette histoire soit enterrée, vous ne pouvez pas vouloir que je devienne un pédéraste ! En tout cas, il me tient ! pensa Lucien avec rage. Il va falloir que je retourne chez lui et que je fasse tout ce qu'il veut et que je lui dise que j'aime ça, sinon je suis perdu ! » Il fit encore quelques pas et ajouta, par mesure de précaution : « Mon Dieu, faites que Berliac meure aussi. »

Lucien ne put prendre sur lui de retourner chez Bergère. Pendant les semaines qui suivirent, il croyait le rencontrer à chaque pas et, quand il travaillait dans sa chambre, il sursautait aux coups de sonnette ; la nuit, il avait des cauchemars épouvantables : Bergère le prenait de force au milieu de la cour du lycée Saint-Louis, tous les pistons étaient là et ils regardaient en rigolant. Mais Bergère ne fit aucune tentative pour le revoir et ne donna pas signe de vie. « Il n'en voulait qu'à ma peau », pensa Lucien, vexé. Berliac avait disparu, lui aussi et Guigard qui allait parfois aux courses avec lui le dimanche, affirmait qu'il avait quitté Paris à la suite d'une crise de dépression nerveuse. Lucien se calma peu à peu : son voyage à Rouen lui faisait l'effet d'un rêve obscur et grotesque qui ne se rattachait à rien ; il en avait oublié presque tous les détails, il gardait seulement l'impression d'une morne odeur de chair et d'eau de Cologne et d'un intolérable ennui. M. Fleurier demanda plusieurs fois ce que devenait l'ami Bergère : « Il faudra que nous l'invitions à Férolles pour le remercier. — Il est parti pour New York », finit par répondre Lucien. Il alla plusieurs fois canoter sur la Marne avec Guigard et sa sœur, et Guigard lui apprit à danser. « Je me réveille, pensait-il, je renais. » Mais il sentait encore assez souvent quelque chose qui pesait sur son dos comme une besace : c'étaient ses complexes ; il se demanda s'il ne devrait pas aller trouver Freud à Vienne : « Je partirai sans argent, à pied s'il le faut, je lui dirai : je n'ai pas le sou mais je suis un cas. » Par un chaud après-midi de juin, il rencontra sur le boulevard Saint-Michel, le Babouin, son ancien prof de philo. « Alors, Fleurier, dit le Babouin, vous préparez Centrale ? — Oui, monsieur, dit Lucien. — Vous auriez pu, dit le Babouin, vous orienter vers les études littéraires. Vous étiez bon en philosophie. — Je n'ai pas abandonné la philo, dit Lucien. J'ai fait des lectures cette année. Freud, par exemple. A propos, ajouta-t-il, pris d'une inspiration, je voulais vous demander, monsieur : que pensez-vous de la psychanalyse ? » Le Babouin se mit à rire : « C'est une mode, dit-il, qui passera. Ce qu'il y a de meilleur chez Freud, vous le trouvez déjà chez Platon. Pour le reste, ajouta-t-il d'un ton sans réplique, je vous dirai que je ne coupe pas dans ces fariboles. Vous feriez mieux de lire Spinoza. » Lucien se sentit délivré d'un fardeau énorme et il rentra chez lui à pied, en sifflotant : « C'était un cauchemar, pensa-t-il, mais il n'en reste plus rien ! » Le soleil était dur et chaud ce jour-là, mais Lucien leva la tête et le fixa sans cligner des yeux : c'était le soleil de tout le monde et Lucien avait le droit de le regarder en face ; il était sauvé ! « Des fariboles ! pensait-il, c'étaient des fariboles ! Ils ont essayé de me détraquer, mais ils ne m'ont pas eu. » En fait, il n'avait cessé de résister : Bergère l'avait emberlificoté dans ses raisonnements, mais Lucien avait bien senti par exemple, que la pédérastie de Rimbaud était une tare, et, quand cette petite crevette de Berliac avait voulu lui faire fumer du haschich, Lucien l'avait proprement envoyé promener : « J'ai failli me perdre, pensa-t-il, mais ce qui m'a protégé c'est ma santé morale ! » Le soir, au dîner, il regarda son père avec sympathie. M. Fleurier était carré d'épaules, il avait les gestes lourds et lents d'un paysan, avec quelque chose de racé et les yeux gris, métalliques et froids d'un chef. « Je lui ressemble », pensa Lucien. Il se rappela que les Fleurier de père en fils, étaient chefs d'industrie depuis quatre générations : « On a beau dire, la famille ça existe ! » Et il pensa avec orgueil à la santé morale des Fleurier.

Lucien ne se présenta pas, cette année-là, au concours de l'École centrale, et les Fleurier partirent très tôt pour Férolles. Il fut enchanté de retrouver la maison, le jardin, l'usine, la petite ville calme et équilibrée. C'était un autre monde : il décida de se lever de bon matin pour faire de grandes promenades dans la région. « Je veux, dit-il à son père, m'emplir les poumons d'air pur et faire provision de santé pour l'an prochain, avant le grand coup de collier. » Il accompagna sa mère chez les Bouffardier et chez les Besse, et tout le monde trouva qu'il était devenu un grand garçon raisonnable et posé. Hébard et Winckelmann qui suivaient des cours de droit à Paris, étaient revenus à Férolles pour les vacances. Lucien sortit plusieurs fois avec eux, et ils parlèrent des farces qu'ils faisaient à l'abbé Jacquemart, de leurs bonnes balades en vélo et chantèrent l'*Artilleur de Metz* à trois voix. Lucien appréciait vivement la franchise rude et la solidité de ses anciens camarades, et il se reprocha de les avoir négligés. Il avoua à Hébrard qu'il n'aimait guère Paris, mais Hébrard ne pouvait pas le comprendre : ses parents l'avaient confié à un abbé et il était très tenu ; il restait encore ébloui de ses visites au musée du Louvre et de la soirée qu'il avait passée à l'Opéra. Lucien fut attendri par cette simplicité ; il se sentait le frère aîné d'Hébrard et de Winckelmann, et il commença à se dire qu'il ne regrettait pas d'avoir eu une vie si tourmentée : il y avait gagné de l'expérience. Il leur parla de Freud et de la psychanalyse, et s'amusa un peu à les scandaliser. Ils critiquèrent violemment la théorie des complexes mais leurs objections étaient naïves, et Lucien le leur montra, puis il ajouta qu'en se plaçant à un point de vue philosophique on pouvait aisément réfuter les erreurs de Freud. Ils l'admirèrent beaucoup, mais Lucien fit semblant de ne pas s'en apercevoir.

M. Fleurier expliqua à Lucien le mécanisme de l'usine. Il l'emmena visiter les bâtiments centraux, et Lucien observa longuement le travail des ouvriers. « Si je mourais, dit M. Fleurier, il faudrait que tu puisses prendre du jour au lendemain toutes les commandes de l'usine. » Lucien le gronda et lui dit : « Mon vieux papa, veux-tu bien ne pas parler de cela ! » Mais il fut grave plusieurs jours de suite en pensant aux responsabilités qui lui incomberaient tôt ou tard. Ils eurent de longues conversations sur les devoirs du patron, et M. Fleurier lui montra que la propriété n'était pas un droit mais un devoir : « Qu'est-ce qu'ils viennent nous embêter avec leur lutte de classes, dit-il, comme si les intérêts des patrons et des ouvriers étaient opposés ! Prends mon cas, Lucien. Je suis un petit patron, ce qu'on appelle un margoulin dans l'argot parisien. Eh bien, je fais vivre cent ouvriers avec leur famille. Si je fais de bonnes affaires, ils sont les premiers à en profiter. Mais si je suis obligé de fermer l'usine, les voilà sur le pavé. *Je n'ai pas le droit*, dit-il avec force, de faire de mauvaises affaires. Voilà ce que j'appelle, moi, la solidarité des classes. »

Pendant plus de trois semaines, tout alla bien ; il ne pensait presque plus jamais à Bergère ; il lui avait pardonné : il espérait simplement ne plus le revoir de sa vie. Quelquefois, quand il changeait de chemise, il s'approchait de la glace et s'y regardait avec étonnement : « Un homme a désiré ce corps », pensait-il. Il promenait lentement les mains sur ses jambes et pensait : « Un homme a été troublé par ces jambes. » Il touchait ses reins et regrettait de ne pas être un autre pour pouvoir se caresser à sa propre chair comme à une étoffe de soie. Il lui arrivait parfois de regretter ses complexes : ils étaient solides, ils pesaient lourd, leur énorme masse sombre le lestait. A présent, c'était fini, Lucien n'y croyait plus et il se sentait d'une légèreté pénible. Ça n'était pas tellement désagréable, d'ailleurs, c'était plutôt une sorte de désenchantement très supportable, un peu écœurant, qui pouvait, à la rigueur, passer pour de l'ennui. « Je ne suis rien, pensait-il, mais c'est parce que rien ne m'a sali. Berliac, lui, est salement engagé. Je peux bien supporter un peu d'incertitude : c'est la rançon de la pureté. »

Au cours d'une promenade, il s'assit sur un talus et pensa : « J'ai dormi six ans et puis, un beau jour, je suis sorti de mon cocon. » Il était tout animé et regarda le paysage d'un air affable. « Je suis fait pour l'action ! » se dit-il. Mais à l'instant ses pensées de gloire tournèrent au fade. Il dit à mi-voix : « Qu'ils attendent un peu et ils verront ce que je vaux. » Il avait parlé avec force, mais les mots roulèrent hors de lui comme des coquilles vides. « Qu'est-ce que j'ai ? » Cette drôle d'inquiétude il ne *voulait* pas la reconnaître, elle lui avait fait trop de mal, autrefois. Il pensa : « C'est ce silence... ce pays... » Pas un être vivant, sauf des grillons qui traînaient péniblement dans la poussière leurs abdomens jaune et noir. Lucien détestait les grillons parce qu'ils avaient toujours l'air à moitié crevés. De l'autre côté de la route, une lande grisâtre, accablée, crevassée se laissait glisser jusqu'à la rivière. Personne ne voyait Lucien, personne ne l'entendait ; il sauta sur ses pieds et il eut l'impression que ses mouvements ne rencontraient aucune résistance, pas même celle de la pesanteur. A présent, il était debout, sous un rideau de nuages gris ; c'était comme s'il existait dans le vide. « Ce silence... », pensa-t-il C'était plus que du silence, c'était du néant. Autour de Lucien, la campagne était extraordinairement tranquille et molle, inhumaine : il semblait qu'elle se faisait toute petite et retenait son souffle pour ne pas le déranger. « Quand l'artilleur de Metz revint en garnison... » Le son s'éteignit sur ses lèvres comme une flamme dans le vide : Lucien était seul, sans ombre, sans écho, au milieu de cette nature trop discrète, qui ne pesait pas. Il se secoua et tenta de reprendre le fil de ses pensées. « Je suis fait pour l'action. D'abord j'ai du ressort : je peux faire des sottises, mais ça ne va pas loin parce que je me reprends. » Il pensa : « J'ai de la santé morale. » Mais il s'arrêta en faisant une grimace de dégoût, tant ça lui paraissait absurde de parler de « santé morale » sur cette route blanche que traversaient des bêtes agonisantes. De colère, Lucien marcha sur un grillon ; il sentit sous sa semelle une petite boulette élastique, et, quand il leva le pied, le grillon vivait encore : Lucien lui cracha dessus. « Je suis perplexe. Je suis perplexe. C'est comme l'an dernier. » Il se mit à penser à Winckelmann qui l'appelait « l'as des as », à M. Fleurier qui le traitait en homme, à Mme Besse qui lui avait dit : « C'est ce grand garçon-là que j'appelais ma petite poupée, je n'oserais plus le tutoyer à présent, il m'intimide. » Mais ils étaient loin, très loin, et il lui sembla que le vrai Lucien était perdu, il n'y avait qu'une larve blanche et perplexe. « Qu'est-ce que je suis ? » Des kilomètres et des kilomètres de lande, un sol plat et gercé, sans herbes, sans odeurs et puis, tout d'un coup, sortant droite de cette croûte grise, l'asperge, tellement insolite qu'il n'y avait même pas d'ombre derrière elle. « Qu'est-ce que je suis ? » La question n'avait pas changé depuis les vacances précédentes, on aurait dit qu'elle attendait Lucien à l'endroit même où il l'avait laissée ; ou plutôt ça n'était pas une question, c'était un état. Lucien haussa les épaules. « Je suis trop scrupuleux, pensa-t-il, je m'analyse trop. »

Les jours suivants, il s'efforça de ne plus s'analyser : il aurait voulu se fasciner sur les choses, il contemplait longuement les coquetiers, les ronds de serviette, les arbres, les devantures ; il flatta beaucoup sa mère en lui demandant si elle voulait bien lui montrer son argenterie. Mais pendant qu'il regardait l'argenterie, il pensait qu'il regardait l'argenterie et, derrière son regard, un petit brouillard vivant palpitait. Et Lucien avait beau s'absorber dans une conversation avec M. Fleurier, ce brouillard abondant et ténu, dont l'inconsistance opaque ressemblait faussement à de la lumière, se glissait *derrière* l'attention qu'il prêtait aux paroles de son père : ce brouillard, c'était lui-même. De temps à autre, agacé, Lucien cessait d'écouter, il se retournait, essayait d'attraper le brouillard et de le regarder en face : il ne rencontrait que le vide, le brouillard était encore *derrière.*

Germaine vint trouver M^me^ Fleurier, en larmes : son frère avait une broncho-pneumonie. « Ma pauvre Germaine, dit M^me^ Fleurier, vous qui disiez toujours qu'il était si solide ! » Elle lui accorda un mois de vacances et fit venir, pour la remplacer, la fille d'un ouvrier de l'usine, la petite Berthe Mozelle, qui avait dix-sept ans. Elle était petite avec des nattes blondes enroulées autour de la tête ; elle boitait légèrement. Comme elle venait de Concarneau, M^me^ Fleurier la pria de porter une coiffe de dentelles : « ça sera plus gentil ». Dès les premiers jours, ses grands yeux bleus chaque fois qu'elle rencontrait Lucien, reflétaient une admiration humble et passionnée, et Lucien comprit qu'elle l'adorait. Il lui parla familièrement et lui demanda plusieurs fois : « Est-ce que vous vous plaisez chez nous ? » Dans les couloirs il s'amusait à la frôler pour voir si ça lui faisait de l'effet. Mais elle l'attendrissait, et il puisa dans cet amour un précieux réconfort ; il pensait souvent avec une pointe d'émotion à l'image que Berthe devait se faire de lui. « Par le fait je ne ressemble guère aux jeunes ouvriers qu'elle fréquente. » Il fit entrer Winckelmann à l'office sous un prétexte, et Winckelmann trouva qu'elle était bien roulée : « Tu es un petit veinard, conclut-il, à ta place je me l'enverrais. » Mais Lucien hésitait : elle sentait la sueur, et sa chemisette noire était rongée sous les bras. Par un pluvieux après-midi de septembre, Mme Fleurier se fit conduire à Paris en auto, et Lucien resta seul dans sa chambre. Il se coucha sur son lit et se mit à bâiller. Il lui semblait être un nuage capricieux et fugace, toujours le même et toujours autre, toujours en train de se diluer dans les airs par les bords. « Je me demande pourquoi j'existe ? » Il était là, il digérait, il bâillait, il entendait la pluie qui tapait contre les vitres, il y avait cette brume blanche qui s'effilochait dans sa tête : et puis après ? Son existence était un scandale et les responsabilités qu'il assumerait plus tard suffiraient à peine à la justifier. « Après tout, je n'ai pas demandé à naître », se dit-il. Et il eut un mouvement de pitié pour lui-même. Il se rappela ses inquiétudes d'enfant, sa longue somnolence, et elles lui apparurent sous un jour neuf : au fond, il n'avait cessé d'être embarrassé de sa vie, de ce cadeau volumineux et inutile, et il l'avait portée dans ses bras sans savoir qu'en faire ni où la déposer. « J'ai passé mon temps à regretter d'être né. » Mais il était trop déprimé pour pousser plus loin ses pensées : il se leva, alluma une cigarette et descendit à la cuisine pour demander à Berthe de faire un peu de thé.

Elle ne le vit pas entrer. Il lui toucha l'épaule, et elle sursauta violemment. « Je vous ai fait peur ? » demanda-t-il. Elle le regardait d'un air épouvanté en s'appuyant des deux mains à la table, et sa poitrine se soulevait : au bout d'un moment, elle sourit et dit : « Ça m'a fait un coup, je ne croyais pas qu'il y avait personne. » Lucien lui rendit son sourire avec indulgence et lui dit : « Vous seriez bien gentille de me préparer un peu de thé. — Tout de suite, monsieur Lucien », répondit la petite, et elle s'enfuit vers son fourneau : la présence de Lucien semblait lui être pénible. Lucien demeurait sur le pas de la porte, incertain. « Eh bien, demanda-t-il paternellement, est-ce que vous vous plaisez chez nous ? » Berthe lui tournait le dos et remplissait une casserole au robinet. Le bruit de l'eau couvrit sa réponse. Lucien attendit un moment et, quand elle eut posé la casserole sur le fourneau à gaz, il reprit : « Avez-vous déjà fumé ? — Des fois », répondit la petite avec méfiance. Il ouvrit son paquet de Craven et le lui tendit. Il n'était pas trop content : il lui semblait qu'il se compromettait, il n'aurait pas dû la faire fumer. « Vous voulez... que je fume ? dit-elle surprise. — Pourquoi pas ? — Madame va me disputer. » Lucien eut une impression désagréable de complicité. Il se mit à rire et dit : « Nous ne lui dirons pas. » Berthe rougit, prit une cigarette du bout des doigts et la planta dans sa bouche. « Dois-je lui offrir du feu ? Ce serait incorrect » Il lui dit : « Eh bien, vous ne l'allumez pas ? » Elle l'agaçait ; elle restait là, les bras raides, rouge et docile, les lèvres en cul de poule autour de la cigarette : on aurait dit qu'elle s'était enfoncé un thermomètre dans la bouche. Elle finit par prendre une allumette soufrée dans une boîte de fer-blanc, la gratta, fuma quelques bouffées en clignant des yeux et dit : « C'est doux », puis elle sortit précipitamment la cigarette de sa bouche et la serra gauchement entre les cinq doigts « C'est une victime-née », pensa Lucien Pourtant, elle se dégela un peu quand il lui demanda si elle aimait sa Bretagne, elle lui décrivit les différentes sortes de coiffes bretonnes et même elle chanta d'une voix douce et fausse une chanson de Rosporden. Lucien la taquina gentiment, mais elle ne comprenait pas la plaisanterie et le regardait d'un air effaré : à ces moments-là, elle ressemblait à un lapin. Il s'était assis sur un escabeau et se sentait tout à fait à l'aise : « Asseyez-vous donc », lui dit-il. « Oh ! non, monsieur Lucien, pas devant monsieur Lucien. » Il la prit par les aisselles et l'attira sur ses genoux : « Et comme ça ? » lui demanda-t-il. Elle se laissa faire en murmurant : « Sur vos genoux ! » d'un air d'extase et de reproche avec un drôle d'accent, et Lucien pensa avec ennui : « Je m'engage trop, je n'aurais jamais dû aller si loin. » Il se tut : elle restait sur ses genoux, toute chaude, bien tranquille, mais Lucien sentait son cœur battre. « Elle est ma chose, pensa-t-il, je peux en faire tout ce que je veux. » Il la lâcha, prit la théière et remonta dans sa chambre : Berthe ne fit pas un geste pour le retenir. Avant de boire son thé, Lucien se lava les mains avec le savon parfumé de sa mère, parce qu'elles sentaient les aisselles.

« Est-ce que je vais coucher avec elle ? » Lucien fut très absorbé, les jours suivants, par ce petit problème ; Berthe se mettait tout le temps sur son passage et le regardait avec de grands yeux tristes d'épagneul. La morale l'emporta : Lucien comprit qu'il risquait de la rendre enceinte parce qu'il n'avait pas assez d'expérience (impossible d'acheter des préservatifs à Férolles, il était trop connu) et qu'il attirerait de gros ennuis à M. Fleurier. Il se dit aussi qu'il aurait, plus tard, moins d'autorité dans l'usine si la fille d'un de ses ouvriers pouvait se vanter d'avoir couché avec lui. « Je n'ai pas le droit de la toucher. » Il évita de se trouver seul avec Berthe pendant les derniers jours de septembre. « Alors, lui dit Winckelmann, qu'est-ce que tu attends ? — Je ne marche pas, répondit sèchement Lucien, j'aime pas les amours ancillaires. » Winckelmann, qui entendait parler d'amours ancillaires pour la première fois, émit un léger sifflement et se tut.

Lucien était très satisfait de lui-même : il s'était conduit comme un chic type, et cela rachetait bien des erreurs. « Elle était à cueillir », se disait-il avec un peu de regret. Mais, à la réflexion, il pensa : « C'est comme si je l'avais eue : elle s'est offerte et je n'en ai pas voulu. » Et il considéra désormais qu'il n'était plus vierge. Ces légères satisfactions l'occupèrent quelques jours puis elles fondirent en brume elles aussi. A la rentrée d'octobre, il se sentait aussi morne qu'au début de la précédente année scolaire.

Berliac n'était pas revenu, et personne n'avait de ses nouvelles. Lucien remarqua plusieurs visages inconnus : son voisin de droite qui s'appelait Lemordant avait fait une année de mathématiques spéciales à Poitiers. Il était encore plus grand que Lucien et, avec sa moustache noire, avait déjà l'allure d'un homme. Lucien retrouva sans plaisir ses camarades, ils lui semblèrent puérils et innocemment bruyants : des séminaristes. Il s'associait encore à leurs manifestations collectives mais avec nonchalance, comme le lui permettait d'ailleurs sa qualité de « carré ». Lemordant l'aurait attiré davantage parce qu'il était mûr ; mais il ne paraissait pas avoir acquis, comme Lucien, cette maturité à travers de multiples et pénibles expériences : c'était un adulte de naissance. Lucien contemplait souvent avec une pleine satisfaction cette tête volumineuse et pensive, sans cou, plantée de biais dans les épaules : il semblait impossible d'y faire rien entrer, ni par les oreilles, ni par ses petits yeux chinois, roses et vitreux : « C'est un type qui a des convictions », pensait Lucien avec respect ; et il se demandait non sans jalousie quelle pouvait être cette certitude qui donnait à Lemordant une si pleine conscience de soi. « Voilà comme je devrais être : un roc. » Il était tout de même un peu surpris que Lemordant fût accessible aux raisons mathématiques ; mais M. Husson le rassura quand il rendit les premiers devoirs : Lucien était septième et Lemordant avait obtenu la note cinq et le soixante-dix-huitième rang ; tout était dans l'ordre. Lemordant ne s'émut pas ; il semblait s'attendre au pis, et sa bouche minuscule, ses grosses joues jaunes et lisses n'étaient pas faites pour exprimer des sentiments ; c'était un Bouddha. On ne le vit en colère qu'une fois, ce jour où Loewy l'avait bousculé dans le vestiaire. Il émit d'abord une dizaine de petits grognements aigus, en battant des paupières : « En Pologne ! dit-il enfin, en Pologne ! sale Youpin et ne viens pas nous emmerder chez nous. » Il dominait Loewy de toute sa taille, et son buste massif vacillait sur ses longues jambes. Il finit par lui donner une paire de gifles, et le petit Loewy fit des excuses : l'affaire en resta là.

Le jeudi, Lucien sortait avec Guigard qui l'emmenait danser chez les amies de sa sœur. Mais Guigard finit par avouer que ces sauteries l'ennuyaient. « J'ai une amie, lui confia-t-il, elle est première chez Plisnier, rue Royale. Justement elle a une copine qui n'a personne : tu devrais venir avec nous samedi soir. » Lucien fit une scène à ses parents et obtint la permission de sortir tous les samedis ; on lui laisserait la clef sous le paillasson. Il rejoignit Guigard vers neuf heures dans un bar de la rue Saint-Honoré. « Tu verras, dit Guigard, Fanny est charmante et puis ce qu'elle a de bien, c'est qu'elle sait s'habiller. — Et la mienne ? — Je ne la connais pas ; je sais qu'elle est petite main et qu'elle vient d'arriver à Paris, elle est d'Angoulême. A propos, ajouta-t-il, ne fais pas de gaffe. Je suis Pierre Daurat. Toi, comme tu es blond, j'ai dit que tu avais du sang anglais, c'est mieux. Tu t'appelles Lucien Bonnières. — Mais pourquoi ?

demanda Lucien intrigué. — Mon vieux, répondit Guigard, c'est un principe. Tu peux faire ce que tu veux avec ces femmes-là, mais il ne faut jamais dire ton nom. — Bon, bon ! dit Lucien et qu'est-ce que je fais, dans la vie ? — Tu peux dire que tu es étudiant, ça vaut mieux, tu comprends, ça les flatte, et puis tu n'es pas obligé de les sortir coûteusement. Pour les frais, on partage, naturellement ; mais, ce soir, tu me laisseras payer, j'ai l'habitude : je te dirai lundi ce que tu me dois. » Lucien pensa tout de suite que Guigard cherchait à faire de petits bénéfices : « Ce que je suis devenu méfiant ! » pensa-t-il avec amusement. Fanny entra presque aussitôt : c'était une grande fille brune et maigre, avec de longues cuisses et un visage très fardé. Lucien la trouva intimidante. « Voilà Bonnières, dont je t'ai parlé, dit Guigard. — Enchantée, dit Fanny d'un air myope. Voilà Maud, ma petite amie. » Lucien vit une petite bonne femme sans âge coiffée d'un pot de fleurs renversé. Elle n'était pas fardée et paraissait grisâtre auprès de l'éclatante Fanny. Lucien fut amèrement déçu, mais il s'aperçut qu'elle avait une jolie bouche — et puis, avec elle, il n'aurait pas besoin de faire d'embarras. Guigard avait pris soin de régler les bocks à l'avance, de sorte qu'il put profiter du brouhaha de l'arrivée pour pousser gaiement les deux jeunes filles vers la porte, sans leur laisser le temps de consommer. Lucien lui en sut gré : M. Fleurier ne lui donnait que cent vingt-cinq francs par semaine et, avec cet argent, il fallait encore qu'il payât ses communications. La soirée fut très amusante ; ils allèrent danser au Quartier latin, dans une petite salle chaude et rose avec des coins d'ombre et où le cocktail coûtait cent sous. Il y avait beaucoup d'étudiants avec des femmes dans le genre de Fanny mais moins bien. Fanny fut superbe : elle regarda dans les yeux un gros barbu qui fumait la pipe et elle dit très haut : « J'ai horreur des gens qui fument la pipe au dancing. » Le type devint cramoisi et remit sa pipe tout allumée dans sa poche. Elle traitait Guigard et Lucien avec un peu de condescendance et leur dit plusieurs fois : « Vous êtes de sales gosses », d'un air maternel et gentil. Lucien se sentait plein d'aisance et tout sucre ; il dit à Fanny plusieurs petites choses amusantes et il souriait en les disant. Finalement, le sourire ne quitta plus son visage et il sut trouver une voix raffinée avec un rien de laisser-aller et de courtoise tendresse nuancée d'ironie. Mais Fanny lui parlait peu : elle prenait le menton de Guigard dans sa main et tirait sur les bajoues pour faire saillir la bouche ; quand les lèvres étaient toutes grosses et un peu baveuses, comme des fruits gonflés de jus ou comme des limaces, elle les léchait à petits coups en disant « Baby ». Lucien était horriblement gêné et il trouvait Guigard ridicule : Guigard avait du rouge à côté des lèvres et des traces de doigts sur les joues. Mais la tenue des autres couples était encore plus négligée : tout le monde s'embrassait ; de temps à autre, la dame du vestiaire passait avec un petit panier et elle jetait des serpentins et des boules multicolores en criant : « Olé, les enfants, amusez-vous, riez, olé, olé ! » et tout le monde riait. Lucien finit par se rappeler l'existence de Maud et il lui dit en souriant : « Regardez ces tourtereaux. » Il désignait Guigard et Fanny et ajouta : « Nous autres, nobles vieillards... » Il n'acheva pas sa phrase, mais sourit si drôlement que Maud sourit aussi. Elle ôta son chapeau, et Lucien vit avec plaisir qu'elle était plutôt mieux que les autres femmes du dancing ; alors il l'invita à danser et lui raconta les chahuts qu'il faisait à ses professeurs, l'année de son baccalauréat. Elle dansait bien, elle avait des yeux noirs et sérieux et un air averti. Lucien lui parla de Berthe et lui dit qu'il avait des remords. « Mais, ajouta-t-il, cela valait mieux pour elle. » Maud trouva l'histoire de Berthe poétique et triste, elle demanda combien Berthe gagnait chez les parents de Lucien. « Ça n'est pas toujours drôle pour une jeune fille, ajouta-t-elle, d'être en condition. » Guigard et Fanny ne s'occupaient plus d'eux, ils se caressaient, et le visage de Guigard était tout mouillé. Lucien répétait de temps en temps : « Regardez les tourtereaux, mais regardez-les ! » et il avait sa phrase prête. « Ils me donneraient envie d'en faire autant. » Mais il n'osait pas la placer et se contentait de sourire, puis il feignit que Maud et lui fussent de vieux copains, dédaigneux de l'amour et il l'appela « vieux frère » et fit le geste de lui frapper sur l'épaule. Fanny tourna soudain la tête et les regarda avec surprise. « Alors, dit-elle, la petite classe, qu'est-ce que vous faites ? Embrassez-vous donc, vous en mourez d'envie. » Lucien prit Maud dans ses bras ; il était un peu gêné parce que Fanny les regardait : il aurait voulu que le baiser fût long et réussi, mais il se demandait comment les gens faisaient pour respirer. Finalement, ça n'était pas si difficile qu'il pensait, il suffisait d'embrasser de biais, pour dégager les narines. Il entendait Guigard qui comptait « un, deux..., trois..., quatre... » et il lâcha Maud à cinquante-deux. « Pas mal pour un début, dit Guigard ; mais je ferai mieux. » Lucien regarda son bracelet-montre et dut compter à son tour : Guigard lâcha la bouche de Fanny à la cent cinquante-neuvième seconde. Lucien était furieux et trouvait ce concours stupide. « J'ai lâché Maud par discrétion, pensa-t-il, mais ça n'est pas malin, une fois qu'on sait respirer on peut continuer indéfiniment. » Il proposa une seconde manche et la gagna. Quand ils eurent tous fini, Maud regarda Lucien et lui dit sérieusement :

« Vous embrassez bien. » Lucien rougit de plaisir. « A votre service », répondit-il en s'inclinant. Mais il aurait tout de même préféré embrasser Fanny. Ils se quittèrent vers minuit et demi à cause du dernier métro. Lucien était tout joyeux ; il sauta et dansa dans la rue Raynouard, et il pensa : « L'affaire est dans le sac. » Les coins de sa bouche lui faisaient mal parce qu'il avait tant souri.

Il prit l'habitude de voir Maud le jeudi à six heures et le samedi soir. Elle se laissait embrasser, mais ne voulait pas se donner à lui. Lucien se plaignit à Guigard qui le rassura : « Ne t'en fais pas, dit Guigard, Fanny est sûre qu'elle couchera ; seulement elle est jeune et elle n'a eu que deux amants ; Fanny te recommande d'être très tendre avec elle. — Tendre ? dit Lucien. Tu te rends compte ? » Ils rirent tous deux, et Guigard conclut : « Faut ce qu'il faut, mon vieux. » Lucien fut très tendre. Il embrassait beaucoup Maud et lui disait qu'il l'aimait, mais à la longue c'était un peu monotone, et puis il n'était pas très fier de sortir avec elle : il aurait aimé lui donner des conseils sur ses toilettes, mais elle était pleine de préjugés et se mettait très vite en colère. Entre leurs baisers, ils demeuraient silencieux, les yeux fixes en se tenant par la main. « Dieu sait à quoi elle pense, avec des yeux si sévères. » Lucien, lui, pensait toujours à la même chose : à cette petite existence triste et vague qui était la sienne, il se disait : « Je voudrais être Lemordant, en voilà un qui a trouvé sa voie ! » A ces moments-là, il se voyait comme s'il était un autre : assis près d'une femme qui l'aimait, la main dans sa main, les lèvres encore humides de ses baisers et refusant l'humble bonheur qu'elle lui offrait : seul. Alors il serrait fortement les doigts de la petite Maud et les larmes lui venaient aux yeux : il aurait voulu la rendre heureuse.

Un matin de décembre, Lemordant s'approcha de Lucien ; il tenait un papier. « Veux-tu signer ? demanda-t-il. — Qu'est-ce que c'est ? — C'est à cause des youtres de Normale Sup ; ils ont envoyé à *L'Œuvre* un torchon contre la préparation militaire obligatoire avec deux cents signatures. Alors nous protestons ; il nous faut au moins mille noms : on va faire donner les cyrards, les flottards, les agro, les X, tout le gratin. » Lucien se sentit flatté ; il demanda : « Ça va paraître ? — Dans *L'Action*, sûrement. Peut-être aussi dans *L'Écho de Paris.* » Lucien avait envie de signer sur-le-champ, mais il pensa que ce ne serait pas sérieux. Il prit le papier et le lut attentivement. Lemordant ajouta : « Tu ne fais pas de politique, je crois ; c'est ton affaire. Mais tu es Français, tu as le droit de dire ton mot. » Quand il entendit « tu as le droit de dire ton mot », Lucien fut traversé par une inexplicable et rapide jouissance. Il signa. Le lendemain il acheta *L'Action Française*, mais la proclamation n'y figurait pas. Elle ne parut que le jeudi Lucien la trouva en seconde page sous ce titre : *La jeunesse de France donne un bon direct dans les gencives de la Juiverie internationale.* Son nom était là, condensé, définitif, pas très loin de celui de Lemordant, presque aussi étranger que ceux de Flèche et de Flipot qui l'entouraient ; il avait l'air habillé. « Lucien Fleurier, pensa-t-il, un nom de paysan, un nom bien français. » Il lut à haute voix toute la série des noms qui commençaient par F, et quand ce fut le tour du sien, il le prononça en faisant semblant de ne pas le reconnaître. Puis il fourra le journal dans sa poche et rentra chez lui tout joyeux.

Ce fut lui qui alla, quelques jours plus tard, trouver Lemordant. « Tu fais de la politique ? lui demanda-t-il. — Je suis ligueur, dit Lemordant, est-ce que tu lis quelquefois *L'Action* ? — Pas souvent, avoua Lucien, jusqu'ici ça ne m'intéressait pas, mais je crois que je suis en train de changer. » Lemordant le regardait sans curiosité, de son air imperméable. Lucien lui raconta, tout à fait en gros, ce que Bergère avait appelé son « désarroi ». « D'où es-tu ? demanda Lemordant. — De Férolles. Mon père y a une usine. — Combien de temps es-tu resté là-bas ? — Jusqu'en seconde. — Je vois, dit Lemordant, eh bien, c'est simple, tu es un déraciné. As-tu lu Barrès ? — J'ai lu *Colette Baudoche*. — Ce n'est pas cela, dit Lemordant avec impatience. Je vais t'apporter *Les Déracinés*, cet après-midi : c'est ton histoire. Tu trouveras là le mal et son remède. » Le livre était relié en cuir vert. Sur la première page un « ex-libris André Lemordant » se détachait en lettres gothiques. Lucien fut surpris : il n'avait jamais songé que Lemordant pût avoir un petit nom.

Il commença sa lecture avec beaucoup de méfiance : tant de fois déjà on avait voulu l'expliquer ; tant de fois on lui avait prêté des livres en lui disant : « Lis ça, c'est tout à fait toi. » Lucien pensa, avec un sourire un peu triste, qu'il n'était pas quelqu'un qu'on pût démonter ainsi en quelques phrases. Le complexe d'Œdipe, le Désarroi : quels enfantillages et comme c'était loin, tout ça ! Mais, dès les premières pages, il fut séduit : d'abord ça n'était pas de la psychologie — Lucien en avait par-dessus la tête, de la psychologie — les jeunes gens dont parlait Barrès n'étaient pas des individus abstraits, des déclassés comme Rimbaud ou Verlaine, ni des malades comme toutes ces Viennoises désœuvrées qui se faisaient psychanalyser par Freud. Barrès commençait par les placer dans leur milieu, dans leur famille : ils avaient été bien élevés, en province, dans de solides traditions ; Lucien trouva que Sturel lui ressemblait. « C'est pourtant vrai, se dit-il, je suis un déraciné. » Il pensa à la santé morale des Fleurier, une santé qui ne s'acquiert qu'à la campagne, à leur force physique (son grand-père tordait un sou de bronze entre ses doigts) ; il se rappela avec émotion les aubes de Férolles : il se levait, il descendait à pas de loup pour ne pas réveiller ses parents, il enfourchait sa bicyclette et le doux paysage d'Ile-de-France l'enveloppait de sa discrète caresse. « J'ai toujours détesté Paris », pensa-t-il avec force. Il lut aussi *Le Jardin de Bérénice* et, de temps à autre, il interrompait sa lecture et se mettait à réfléchir, les yeux dans le vague : voilà donc que, de nouveau, on lui offrait un caractère et un destin, un moyen d'échapper aux bavardages intarissables de sa conscience, une méthode pour se définir et s'apprécier. Mais combien il préférait aux bêtes immondes et lubriques de Freud, l'inconscient plein d'odeurs agrestes dont Barrès lui faisait cadeau. Pour le saisir, Lucien n'avait qu'à se détourner d'une stérile et dangereuse contemplation de soi-même : il fallait qu'il étudiât le sol et le sous-sol de Férolles, qu'il déchiffrât le sens des collines onduleuses qui descendent jusqu'à la Sernette, qu'il s'adressât à la géographie humaine et à l'histoire. Ou bien, tout simplement, il devait retourner à Férolles, y vivre : il le trouverait à ses pieds, inoffensif et fertile, étendu à travers la campagne férollienne, mêlé aux bois, aux sources, à l'herbe, comme un humus nourrissant où Lucien puiserait enfin la force de devenir un chef. Lucien sortait très exalté de ces longues songeries et même, de temps à autre, il avait l'impression d'avoir trouvé sa voie. A présent, quand il demeurait silencieux près de Maud, un bras passé autour de sa taille, des mots, des bribes de phrases résonnaient en lui : « renouer la tradition », « la terre et les morts » ; mots profonds et opaques, inépuisables. « Comme c'est tentant », pensait-il. Pourtant, il n'osait y croire : trop souvent déjà, on l'avait déçu. Il s'ouvrit de ses craintes à Lemordant : « Ce serait trop beau. — Mon cher, répondit Lemordant, on ne croit pas tout de suite ce qu'on veut : il faut des pratiques. » Il réfléchit un peu et dit : « Tu devrais venir avec nous. » Lucien accepta de grand cœur, mais il tint à préciser qu'il gardait sa liberté : « Je viens, dit-il, mais ça ne m'engage pas. Je veux voir et réfléchir. »

Lucien fut charmé par la camaraderie des jeunes camelots ; ils lui firent un accueil cordial et simple, et, tout de suite, il se sentit à l'aise au milieu d'eux. Il connut bientôt la « bande » de Lemordant, une vingtaine d'étudiants qui portaient presque tous le béret de velours. Ils tenaient leurs assises au premier étage de la brasserie *Polder* où ils jouaient au bridge et au billard. Lucien allait souvent les y retrouver et bientôt il comprit qu'ils l'avaient adopté, car il était toujours reçu aux cris de : « Voilà le plus beau ! » ou « C'est notre Fleurier national ! ». Mais c'était leur bonne humeur qui séduisait surtout Lucien : rien de pédant ni d'austère ; peu de conversations politiques. On riait, et on chantait, voilà tout, on poussait des gueulantes ou bien on battait des bans en l'honneur de la jeunesse estudiantine. Lemordant lui-même, sans se départir d'une autorité que personne n'aurait osé lui contester, se détendait un peu, se laissait aller à sourire. Lucien, le plus souvent, se taisait, son regard errait sur ces jeunes gens bruyants et musclés : « C'est une force », pensait-il. Au milieu d'eux il découvrait peu à peu le véritable sens de la jeunesse : il ne résidait plus dans la grâce affectée qu'appréciait un Bergère ; la jeunesse, c'était l'avenir de la France. Les camarades de Lemordant, d'ailleurs, n'avaient pas le charme trouble de l'adolescence : c'étaient des adultes et plusieurs portaient la barbe. A les bien regarder, on trouvait en eux tous un air de parenté : ils en avaient fini avec les errements et les incertitudes de leur âge, ils n'avaient plus rien à apprendre, ils étaient faits. Au début, leurs plaisanteries légères et féroces scandalisaient un peu Lucien : on aurait pu les croire inconscients. Quand Rémy vint annoncer que Mme Dubus, la femme du leader radical, avait eu les jambes coupées par un camion, Lucien s'attendait d'abord a ce qu'ils rendissent un bref hommage à un adversaire malheureux. Mais ils éclatèrent tous de rire et se frappèrent sur les cuisses en disant : « La vieille charogne ! » et « Estimable camionneur ! » Lucien fut un peu contraint mais il comprit tout à coup que ce grand rire purificateur était un refus : ils avaient flairé un danger, ils n'avaient pas voulu d'un lâche apitoiement et ils s'étaient fermés. Lucien se mit à rire aussi. Peu à peu, leur espièglerie lui apparut sous son véritable jour : elle n'avait que les dehors de la frivolité ; au fond, c'était l'affirmation d'un droit : leur conviction était si profonde, si religieuse, qu'elle leur donnait le droit de paraître frivole, d'envoyer promener d'une boutade, d'une pirouette, tout ce qui n'était pas l'essentiel. Entre l'humour glacé de Charles Maurras et les plaisanteries de Desperreau, par exemple (il traînait dans sa poche un vieux bout de capote anglaise qu'il appelait le prépuce à Blum), il n'y avait qu'une différence de degré. Au mois de janvier, l'Université annonça une séance solennelle au cours de laquelle le grade de « doctor honoris causa » devait être conféré à deux minéralogistes suédois. « Tu vas voir un beau chahut », dit Lemordant à Lucien en lui remettant une carte d'invitation. Le grand Amphithéâtre était bondé. Quand Lucien vit entrer, aux sons de *La Marseillaise*, le président de la République et le recteur, son cœur se mit à battre, il eut peur pour ses amis. Presque aussitôt, quelques jeunes gens se dressèrent dans les tribunes et se mirent à crier. Lucien reconnut avec sympathie Rémy, rouge comme une tomate, se débattant entre deux hommes qui le tiraient par son veston et criant : « La France aux Français. » Mais il se plut tout particulièrement à voir un monsieur âgé qui soufflait, d'un air d'enfant terrible, dans une petite trompette, « comme c'est sain », pensa-t-il. Il goûtait vivement ce mélange original de gravité têtue et de turbulence qui donnait aux plus jeunes cet air mûr et aux plus âgés cette allure de diablotins. Lucien s'essaya bientôt, lui aussi, à plaisanter. Il eut quelques succès et quand il disait d'Herriot : « S'il meurt dans son lit, celui-là, il n'y a plus de Bon Dieu », il sentait naître en lui une fureur sacrée. Alors il serrait les mâchoires et, pendant un moment, il se sentait aussi convaincu, aussi étroit, aussi puissant que Rémy ou que Desperreau. « Lemordant a raison, pensa-t-il, il faut des pratiques, tout est là. » Il apprit aussi à refuser la discussion : Guigard, qui n'était qu'un républicain, l'accablait d'objections. Lucien l'écoutait de bonne grâce, mais, au bout d'un moment, il se fermait. Guigard parlait toujours, mais Lucien ne le regardait même plus : il lissait le pli de son pantalon et s'amusait à faire des ronds avec la fumée de sa cigarette en dévisageant les femmes. Il entendait un peu, malgré tout, les objections de Guigard, mais elles perdaient brusquement leur poids et glissaient sur lui, légères et futiles. Guigard finissait par se taire, très impressionné. Lucien parla à ses parents de ses nouveaux amis, et M. Fleurier lui demanda s'il allait devenir camelot. Lucien hésita et dit gravement : « Je suis tenté, je suis vraiment tenté — Lucien, je t'en prie, ne fais pas ça, dit sa mère, ils sont très agités, et un malheur est vite arrivé. Vois-tu qu'on te passe à tabac ou qu'on te mette en prison ? Et puis tu es beaucoup trop jeune pour faire de la politique. » Lucien ne lui répondit que par un sourire ferme, et M. Fleurier intervint : « Laisse-le faire, ma chérie, dit-il avec douceur, laisse-le suivre son idée ; il faut en avoir passé par là. » A dater de ce jour, il sembla à Lucien que ses parents le traitaient avec une certaine considération. Pourtant, il ne se décidait pas ; ces quelques semaines lui avaient beaucoup appris : il se représentait tour à tour la curiosité bienveillante de son père, les inquiétudes de Mme Fleurier, le respect naissant de Guigard, l'insistance de Lemordant, l'impatience de Rémy et il se disait en hochant la tête : « Ce n'est pas une petite affaire. » Il eut une longue conversation avec Lemordant, et Lemordant comprit très bien ses raisons, et lui dit de ne pas se presser. Lucien avait encore des crises de cafard : il avait l'impression de n'être qu'une petite transparence gélatineuse qui tremblotait sur la banquette d'un café, et l'agitation bruyante des camelots lui paraissait absurde. Mais, à d'autres moments, il se sentait dur et lourd comme une pierre et il était presque heureux.

Il était de mieux en mieux avec toute la bande. Il leur chanta *La Noce à Rebecca* que Hébrard lui avait apprise aux vacances précédentes, et tout le monde déclara qu'il avait été fort amusant. Lucien mis en verve fit plusieurs réflexions mordantes sur les juifs et parla de Berliac qui était si avare : « Je me disais toujours : mais pourquoi est-il si radin, ça n'est pas possible d'être aussi radin. Et puis un beau jour j'ai compris : il était de la tribu. » Tout le monde se mit à rire et une sorte d'exaltation s'empara de Lucien : il se sentait vraiment furieux contre les juifs et le souvenir de Berliac lui était profondément désagréable. Lemordant le regarda dans les yeux et lui dit : « Toi, tu es un pur. » Par la suite, on demandait souvent à Lucien : « Fleurier, dis-nous-en une bien bonne sur les youtres », et Lucien racontait des histoires juives qu'il tenait de son père ; il n'avait qu'à commencer sur un certain ton « un chour Léfy rengontre Plum... » pour mettre ses amis en joie. Un jour, Rémy et Patenôtre dirent qu'ils avaient croisé un juif algérien sur les bords de la Seine et qu'ils lui avaient fait une peur affreuse en s'avançant sur lui comme s'ils voulaient le jeter à l'eau : « Je me disais, conclut Rémy : quel dommage que Fleurier ne soit pas avec nous. — Ça vaut peut-être mieux, qu'il n'ait pas été là, interrompit Desperreau, parce que, lui, il aurait foutu le juif à l'eau pour de bon ! » Lucien n'avait pas son pareil pour reconnaître un juif à vue de nez. Quand il sortait avec Guigard, il lui poussait le coude : « Ne te retourne pas tout de suite : le petit gros, derrière nous, c'en est un ! — Pour ça, disait Guigard, tu as du flair ! » Fanny, elle non plus, ne pouvait pas sentir les juifs ; ils montèrent tous les quatre dans la chambre de Maud un jeudi, et Lucien chanta *La Noce à Rebecca.* Fanny n'en pouvait plus, elle disait : « Arrêtez, arrêtez, je vais faire pipi dans mon pantalon » et, quand il eut fini, elle lui lança un regard heureux, presque tendre. A la brasserie *Polder*, on finit par monter un bateau à Lucien. Il se trouvait toujours quelqu'un pour dire négligemment : « Fleurier qui aime tant les juifs... » ou bien « Léon Blum, le grand ami de Fleurier... » et les autres attendaient dans le ravissement, en retenant leur souffle, la bouche ouverte. Lucien devenait rouge, il frappait sur la table en criant : « Sacré nom... ! » et ils éclataient de rire, ils disaient : « Il a marché ! il a marché ! Il n'a pas marché : il a couru ! »

Il les accompagnait souvent à des réunions politiques et il entendit le professeur Claude et Maxime Real del Sarte. Son travail souffrait un peu de ces obligations nouvelles, mais comme, en tout état de cause, Lucien ne pouvait compter, cette année-là, sur un succès au concours de Centrale, M. Fleurier se montra indulgent : « Il faut bien, dit-il à sa femme, que Lucien apprenne son métier d'homme. » Au sortir de ces réunions, Lucien et ses amis avaient la tête en feu et ils faisaient des gamineries. Une fois, ils étaient une dizaine et ils rencontrèrent un petit bonhomme olivâtre qui traversait la rue Saint-André-des-Arts en lisant *L'Humanité*. Ils le coincèrent contre un mur, et Rémy lui ordonna : « Jette ce journal. » Le petit type voulait faire des manières, mais Desperreau se glissa derrière lui et le ceintura pendant que Lemordant, de sa poigne puissante, lui arrachait le journal. C'était très amusant. Le petit homme, furibond, donnait des coups de pied dans le vide en criant : « Lâchez-moi, lâchez-moi » avec un drôle d'accent et Lemordant, très calme, déchirait le journal. Mais quand Desperreau voulut lâcher son bonhomme, les choses commencèrent à se gâter : l'autre se jeta sur Lemordant et l'aurait frappé si Rémy ne lui avait décoché à temps un bon coup de poing derrière l'oreille. Le type alla dinguer contre le mur et les regarda tous d'un air mauvais en disant : « Sales Français ! — Répète ce que tu as dit », demanda froidement Marchesseau. Lucien comprit qu'il allait y avoir du vilain : Marchesseau n'entendait pas la plaisanterie quand il s'agissait de la France. « Sales Français ! » dit le métèque. Il reçut une claque formidable et se jeta en avant, tête baissée en hurlant : « Sales Français, sales bourgeois, je vous déteste, je voudrais que vous creviez tous, tous, tous ! » et un flot d'autres injures immondes et d'une violence que Lucien n'aurait même pas pu imaginer. Alors ils perdirent patience et furent obligés de s'y mettre un peu tous, et de lui donner une bonne correction. Au bout d'un moment, ils le lâchèrent, et le type se laissa aller contre le mur ; il flageolait, un coup de poing lui avait fermé l'œil droit, et ils étaient tous autour de lui, fatigués de frapper, attendant qu'il tombe. Le type tordit la bouche et cracha : « Sales Français ! — Tu veux qu'on recommence », demanda Desperreau, tout essoufflé. Le type ne parut pas entendre : il les regardait avec défi de son œil gauche et répétait : « Sales Français, sales Français ! » Il y eut un moment d'hésitation, et Lucien comprit que ses copains allaient abandonner la partie. Alors ce fut plus fort que lui, il bondit en avant et frappa de toutes ses forces. Il entendit quelque chose qui craquait, et le petit bonhomme le regarda d'un air veule et surpris : « Sales... » bafouilla-t-il. Mais son œil poché se mit à béer sur un globe rouge et sans prunelle ; il tomba sur les genoux et ne dit plus rien. « Foutons le camp », souffla Rémy. Ils coururent et ne s'arrêtèrent que sur la place Saint-Michel : personne ne les poursuivait. Ils arrangèrent leurs cravates et se brossèrent les uns les autres, du plat de la main.

La soirée s'écoula sans que les jeunes gens fissent allusion à leur aventure, et ils se montrèrent particulièrement gentils les uns pour les autres : ils avaient délaissé cette brutalité pudique qui leur servait, d'ordinaire, à voiler leurs sentiments. Ils se parlaient avec politesse, et Lucien pensa qu'ils se montraient, pour la première fois, tels qu'ils devaient être dans leurs familles ; mais il était lui-même très énervé : il n'avait pas l'habitude de se battre en pleine rue contre des voyous. Il pensa à Maud et à Fanny avec tendresse.

Il ne put trouver le sommeil. « Je ne peux pas continuer, pensa-t-il, à les suivre dans leurs équipées en amateur. A présent, tout est bien pesé, il *faut* que je m'engage ! » Il se sentait grave et presque religieux quand il annonça la bonne nouvelle à Lemordant. « C'est décidé, lui dit-il, je suis avec vous. » Lemordant lui frappa sur l'épaule, et la bande fêta l'événement en buvant quelques bonnes bouteilles. Ils avaient repris leur ton brutal et gai et ne parlèrent pas de l'incident de la veille. Comme ils allaient se quitter, Marchesseau dit simplement à Lucien : « Tu as un fameux punch ! » et Lucien répondit : « C'était un juif ! »

Le surlendemain, Lucien vint trouver Maud avec une grosse canne de jonc qu'il avait achetée dans un magasin du boulevard Saint-Michel. Maud comprit tout de suite : elle regarda la canne et dit : « Alors, ça y est ? — Ça y est », dit Lucien en souriant. Maud parut flattée ; personnellement, elle était plutôt favorable aux idées de gauche, mais elle avait l'esprit large. « Je trouve, disait-elle, qu'il y a du bon dans tous les partis. » Au cours de la soirée, elle lui gratta plusieurs fois la nuque en l'appelant son petit camelot. A peu de temps de là, un samedi soir, Maud se sentit fatiguée : « Je crois que je vais rentrer, dit-elle, mais tu peux monter avec moi, si tu es sage : tu me tiendras la main et tu seras bien gentil avec ta petite Maud qui a si mal, tu lui raconteras des histoires. » Lucien n'était guère enthousiaste : la chambre de Maud l'attristait par sa pauvreté soigneuse ; on aurait dit une chambre de bonne. Mais il aurait été criminel de laisser passer une si belle occasion. A peine entrée, Maud se jeta sur son lit en disant : « Houff ! comme je suis bien », puis elle se tut et fixa Lucien dans les yeux en retroussant les lèvres. Il vint s'étendre près d'elle, et elle se mit la main sur les yeux en écartant les doigts et en disant d'une voix enfantine : « Coucou, je te vois, tu sais, Lucien, je te vois ! » Il se sentait lourd et mou, elle lui mit les doigts dans la bouche et il les suça, puis il lui parla tendrement, il lui dit : « La petite Maud est malade, qu'elle a donc du malheur, la pauvre petite Maud ! » et il la caressa par tout le corps ; elle avait fermé les yeux et elle souriait mystérieusement. Au bout d'un moment, il avait relevé la jupe de Maud et il se trouva qu'ils faisaient l'amour ; Lucien pensa : « Je suis doué. » « Eh bien, dit Maud quand ils eurent fini, si je m'attendais à ça ! » Elle regarda Lucien avec un tendre reproche : « Grand vilain, je croyais que tu serais sage ! » Lucien dit qu'il avait été aussi surpris qu'elle. « Ça s'est fait comme ça », dit-il. Elle réfléchit un peu et lui dit sérieusement : « Je ne regrette rien. Avant c'était peut-être plus pur, mais c'était moins complet. »

« J'ai une maîtresse », pensa Lucien dans le métro. Il était vide et las, imprégné d'une odeur d'absinthe et de poisson frais ; il alla s'asseoir en se tenant raide pour éviter le contact de sa chemise trempée de sueur ; il lui semblait que son corps était en lait caillé. Il se répéta avec force : « J'ai une maîtresse », mais il se sentait frustré : ce qu'il avait désiré de Maud, la veille encore, c'était son visage étroit et fermé, qui avait l'air habillé, sa mince silhouette, son allure de dignité, sa réputation de fille sérieuse, son mépris du sexe masculin, tout ce qui faisait d'elle une personne étrangère, vraiment *une autre*, dure et définitive, toujours hors d'atteinte, avec ses petites pensées propres, ses pudeurs, ses bas de soie, sa robe de crêpe, sa permanente. Et tout ce vernis avait fondu sous son étreinte, il était resté de la chair, il avait approché ses lèvres d'un visage sans yeux, nu comme un ventre, il avait possédé une grosse fleur de chair mouillée. Il revit la bête aveugle qui palpitait dans les draps avec des clapotis et des bâillements velus et il pensa : c'était *nous deux*. Ils n'avaient fait qu'un, il ne pouvait plus distinguer sa chair de celle de Maud, personne ne lui avait jamais donné cette impression d'écœurante intimité, sauf peut-être Riri, quand Riri montrait son pipi derrière un buisson ou quand il s'était oublié et qu'il restait couché sur le ventre et gigotait, le derrière nu, pendant qu'on faisait sécher son pantalon. Lucien éprouva quelque soulagement en pensant à Guigard : il lui dirait demain : « J'ai couché avec Maud, c'est une petite femme épatante, mon vieux : elle a ça dans le sang. » Mais il était mal à l'aise : il se sentait nu dans la chaleur poussiéreuse du métro, nu sous une mince pellicule de vêtements, raide et nu à côté d'un prêtre, en face de deux dames mûres, comme une grande asperge souillée.

Guigard le félicita vivement. Il en avait un peu assez de Fanny : « Elle a vraiment trop mauvais caractère. Hier elle m'a fait la tête toute la soirée. » Ils tombèrent d'accord tous les deux : des femmes comme ça, il fallait bien qu'il y en eût, parce qu'on ne pouvait tout de même pas rester chaste jusqu'au mariage et puis elles n'étaient pas intéressées, ni malades, mais ç'aurait été une erreur de s'attacher à elles. Guigard parla de vraies jeunes filles avec beaucoup de délicatesse et Lucien lui demanda des nouvelles de sa sœur. « Elle va bien, mon vieux, dit Guigard, elle dit que tu es un lâcheur. Tu comprends, ajouta-t-il avec un peu d'abandon, je ne suis pas mécontent d'avoir une sœur : sans ça, il y a des choses dont on ne peut pas se rendre compte. » Lucien le comprenait parfaitement. Par la suite, ils parlèrent souvent des jeunes filles et ils se sentaient pleins de poésie, et Guigard aimait à citer les paroles d'un de ses oncles, qui avait eu beaucoup de succès féminins : « Je n'ai peut-être pas toujours fait le bien, dans ma chienne de vie, mais il y a une chose dont le Bon Dieu me tiendra compte ; je me serais plutôt tranché les mains que de toucher à une jeune fille. » Ils retournèrent quelquefois chez les amies de Pierrette Guigard. Lucien aimait beaucoup Pierrette, il lui parlait comme un grand frère un peu taquin et il lui était reconnaissant parce qu'elle ne s'était pas fait couper les cheveux. Il était très absorbé par ses activités politiques ; tous les dimanches matin, il allait vendre *L'Action Française* devant l'église de Neuilly. Pendant plus de deux heures, Lucien se promenait de long en large, le visage durci. Les jeunes filles qui sortaient de la messe levaient parfois vers lui leurs beaux yeux francs ; alors Lucien se détendait un peu, il se sentait pur et fort ; il leur souriait. Il expliqua à la bande qu'il respectait les femmes et il fut heureux de trouver chez eux la compréhension qu'il avait souhaitée. D'ailleurs, ils avaient presque tous des sœurs.

Le 17 avril, les Guigard donnèrent une sauterie pour les dix-huit ans de Pierrette, et, naturellement, Lucien fut invité. Il était déjà très ami avec Pierrette, elle l'appelait son danseur, et il la soupçonnait d'être un peu amoureuse de lui. M$^{me}$ Guigard avait fait venir une tapeuse, et l'après-midi promettait d'être fort gai. Lucien dansa plusieurs fois avec Pierrette puis il alla retrouver Guigard qui recevait ses amis dans le fumoir. « Salut, dit Guigard, je crois que vous vous connaissez tous : Fleurier, Simon, Vanusse, Ledoux. » Pendant que Guigard nommait ses camarades, Lucien vit qu'un grand jeune homme roux et frisé, à la peau laiteuse et aux durs sourcils noirs s'approchait d'eux en hésitant, et la colère le bouleversa. « Qu'est-ce que ce type fait ici ? se demanda-t-il, Guigard sait pourtant bien que je ne peux pas sentir les juifs ! » Il pirouetta sur ses talons et s'éloigna rapidement pour éviter les présentations.

« Qu'est-ce que ce juif ? demanda-t-il un moment plus tard à Pierrette. — C'est Weill, il est aux Hautes Études Commerciales ; mon frère l'a connu à la salle d'armes. — J'ai horreur des juifs », dit Lucien. Pierrette eut un rire léger. « Celui-là est plutôt bon garçon, dit-elle. Menez-moi donc au buffet. » Lucien prit une coupe de champagne et n'eut que le temps de la reposer : il se trouvait nez à nez avec Guigard et Weill. Il foudroya Guigard des yeux et fit volte-face. Mais Pierrette le saisit par le bras, et Guigard l'aborda d'un air ouvert : « Mon ami Fleurier, mon ami Weill, dit-il avec aisance, voilà : les présentations sont faites. » Weill tendit la main, et Lucien se sentit très malheureux. Heureusement, il se rappela tout à coup Despereau : « Fleurier aurait foutu le juif à l'eau pour de bon. » Il enfonça ses mains dans ses poches, tourna le dos à Guigard et s'en fut. « Je ne pourrai plus remettre les pieds dans cette maison », songea-t-il, en demandant son vestiaire. Il ressentait un orgueil amer. « Voilà ce que c'est que de tenir fortement à ses opinions ; on ne peut plus vivre en société. » Mais dans la rue son orgueil fondit et Lucien devint très inquiet. « Guigard doit être furieux ! » Il hocha la tête et tenta de se dire avec conviction : « Il n'avait pas le droit d'inviter un juif s'il m'invitait ! » Mais sa colère était tombée ; il revoyait avec une sorte de malaise la tête étonnée de Weill, sa main tendue, et il se sentait enclin à la conciliation : « Pierrette pense sûrement que je suis un mufle. J'aurais dû serrer cette main. Après tout, ça ne m'engageait pas. Faire un salut réservé et m'éloigner tout de suite après : voilà ce qu'il fallait faire. » Il se demanda s'il était encore temps de retourner chez les Guigard. Il s'approcherait de Weill et lui dirait : « Excusez-moi, j'ai eu un malaise », il lui serrerait la main et lui ferait un bout de conversation gentille. Mais non : c'était trop tard, son geste était irréparable. « Qu'avais-je besoin, pensa-t-il avec irritation, de montrer mes opinions à des gens qui ne peuvent pas les comprendre ! » Il haussa nerveusement les épaules : c'était un désastre. A cet instant même, Guigard et Pierrette commentaient sa conduite, Guigard disait : « Il est complètement fou ! » Lucien serra les poings. « Oh ! pensa-t-il avec désespoir, ce que je les hais ! Ce que je hais les juifs ! » et il essaya de puiser un peu de force dans la contemplation de cette haine immense. Mais elle fondit sous son regard, il avait beau penser à Léon Blum qui recevait de l'argent de l'Allemagne et haïssait les Français, il ne ressentait plus rien qu'une morne indifférence. Lucien eut la chance de trouver Maud chez elle. Il lui dit qu'il l'aimait et la posséda plusieurs fois, avec une sorte de rage. « Tout est foutu, se disait-il, je ne serai jamais *quelqu'un.* » « Non, non ! disait Maud, arrête, mon grand chéri, pas ça, c'est défendu ! » Mais elle finit par se laisser faire : Lucien voulut l'embrasser partout. Il se sentait enfantin et pervers ; il avait envie de pleurer.

Le lendemain matin, au lycée, Lucien eut un serrement de cœur en apercevant Guigard. Guigard avait l'air sournois et fit semblant de ne pas le voir. Lucien rageait si fort qu'il ne put prendre des notes : « Le salaud ! pensait-il, le salaud ! » A la fin du cours, Guigard s'approcha de lui, il était blême. « S'il rouspète, pensa Lucien, terrorisé, je lui fous des claques. » Ils demeurèrent un instant côte à côte, chacun regardant la pointe de ses souliers. Enfin Guigard dit, d'une voix altérée : « Excuse-moi, mon vieux, je n'aurais pas dû te faire ce coup-là. » Lucien sursauta et le regarda avec méfiance. Mais Guigard continua péniblement : « Je le rencontre à la salle, tu comprends, alors j'ai voulu... nous faisons des assauts ensemble, et il m'avait invité chez lui, mais je comprends, tu sais, je n'aurais pas dû, je ne sais pas comment ça se fait, mais, quand j'ai écrit les invitations, je n'y ai pas pensé une seconde... » Lucien ne disait toujours rien parce que les mots ne passaient pas, mais il se sentait porté à l'indulgence. Guigard ajouta, la tête basse : « Eh bien, pour une gaffe... — Espèce d'andouille, dit Lucien, en lui frappant sur l'épaule, je sais bien que tu ne l'as pas fait exprès. » Il dit avec générosité : « J'ai eu mes torts, d'ailleurs. Je me suis conduit comme un mufle. Mais qu'est-ce que tu veux, c'est plus fort que moi, je ne peux pas les toucher, c'est physique, j'ai l'impression qu'ils ont des écailles sur les mains. Qu'a dit Pierrette ? — Elle a ri comme une folle, dit Guigard piteusement. — Et le type ? — Il a compris. J'ai dit ce que j'ai pu, mais il a mis les voiles au bout d'un quart d'heure. » Il ajouta, toujours penaud : « Mes parents disent que tu as eu raison, que tu ne pouvais agir autrement du moment que tu as une conviction. » Lucien dégusta le mot de « conviction » ; il avait envie de serrer Guigard dans ses bras : « C'est rien, mon vieux, lui dit-il ; c'est rien, du moment qu'on reste copains. » Il descendit le boulevard Saint-Michel dans un état d'exaltation extraordinaire : il lui semblait qu'il n'était plus lui-même.

Il se dit : « C'est drôle, ça n'est plus moi, je ne me reconnais pas ! » Il faisait chaud et doux : les gens flânaient, portant sur leurs visages le premier sourire étonné du printemps ; dans cette foule molle, Lucien s'enfonçait comme un coin d'acier, il pensait : « Ça n'est plus moi. » Moi, la veille encore, c'était un gros insecte ballonné, pareil aux grillons de Férolles ; à présent, Lucien se sentait propre et net comme un chronomètre. Il entra à *La Source* et commanda un pernod. La bande ne fréquentait pas *La Source* parce que les métèques y pullulaient ; mais, ce jour-là, les métèques et les juifs n'incommodaient pas Lucien. Au milieu de ces corps olivâtres, qui bruissaient légèrement, comme un champ d'avoine sous le vent, il se sentait insolite et menaçant, une monstrueuse horloge accotée contre la banquette et qui rutilait. Il reconnut avec amusement un petit juif que les J. P. avaient rossé, au trimestre précédent, dans les couloirs de la faculté de droit. Le petit monstre, gras et pensif, n'avait pas gardé la trace des coups, il avait dû rester cabossé quelque temps et puis il avait repris sa forme ronde ; mais il y avait en lui une sorte de résignation obscène.

Pour le moment, il avait l'air heureux : il bâilla voluptueusement ; un rayon de soleil lui chatouillait les narines ; il se gratta le nez et sourit. Était-ce un sourire ? ou plutôt une petite oscillation qui avait pris naissance au-dehors, quelque part dans un coin de la salle, et qui était venue mourir sur sa bouche ? Tous ces métèques flottaient dans une eau sombre et lourde dont les remous ébranlaient leurs chairs molles, soulevant leurs bras, agitant leurs doigts, jouant un peu avec leurs lèvres. Les pauvres types ! Lucien avait presque pitié d'eux. Qu'est-ce qu'ils venaient faire en France ? Quels courants marins les avaient apportés et déposés ici ? Ils avaient beau s'habiller décemment, chez des tailleurs du boulevard Saint-Michel, ils n'étaient guère plus que des méduses. Lucien pensa qu'il n'était pas une méduse, qu'il n'appartenait pas à cette faune humiliée, il se dit : « Je suis en plongée ! » Et puis, tout à coup, il oublia *La Source* et les métèques, il ne vit plus qu'un dos, un large dos bossué par les muscles, qui s'éloignait avec une force tranquille, qui se perdait, implacable, dans la brume. Il vit aussi Guigard : Guigard était pâle, il suivait des yeux ce dos, il disait à Pierrette invisible : « Eh bien, pour une gaffe !... » Lucien fut envahi par une joie presque intolérable : ce dos puissant et solitaire, c'était le *sien* ! Et la scène s'était passée hier ! Pendant un instant, au prix d'un violent effort, il fut Guigard, il suivit son propre dos avec les yeux de Guigard, il éprouva devant lui-même l'humilité de Guigard et se sentit délicieusement terrorisé. « Ça leur servira de leçon ! » pensa-t-il. Le décor changea : c'était le boudoir de Pierrette, ça se passait dans l'avenir. Pierrette et Guigard désignaient, d'un air un peu confit, un nom sur une liste d'invitations. Lucien n'était pas présent, mais sa puissance était sur eux. Guigard disait : « Ah ! non, pas celui-là ! Eh bien, avec Lucien, ça ferait du joli ; Lucien qui ne peut pas souffrir les juifs ! » Lucien se contempla encore une fois, il pensa : « Lucien, c'est moi ! Quelqu'un qui ne peut pas souffrir les juifs. » Cette phrase, il l'avait souvent prononcée, mais aujourd'hui ça n'était pas pareil aux autres fois. Pas du tout. Bien sûr, en apparence, c'était une simple constatation, comme si on avait dit : « Lucien n'aime pas les huîtres », ou bien : « Lucien aime la danse. » Mais il ne fallait pas s'y tromper : l'amour de la danse, peut-être qu'on aurait pu le découvrir aussi chez le petit juif, ça ne comptait pas plus qu'un frisson de méduse ; il n'y avait qu'à regarder ce sacré youtre pour comprendre que ses goûts et ses dégoûts restaient collés à lui comme son odeur, comme les reflets de sa peau, qu'ils disparaîtraient avec lui comme les clignotements de ses lourdes paupières, comme ses sourires gluants de volupté. Mais l'antisémitisme de Lucien était d'une autre sorte : impitoyable et pur, il pointait hors de lui comme une lame d'acier, menaçant d'autres poitrines. « Ça, pensa-t-il, c'est... c'est sacré ! » Il se rappela que sa mère, quand il était petit, lui disait parfois d'un certain ton : « Papa travaille dans son bureau. » Et cette phrase lui semblait une formule sacramentelle qui lui conférait soudain une nuée d'obligations religieuses, comme de ne pas jouer avec sa carabine à air comprimé, de ne pas crier « Tararaboum » ; il marchait dans les couloirs sur la pointe des pieds, comme s'il avait été dans une cathédrale. « A présent, c'est mon tour », pensa-t-il avec satisfaction. On disait en baissant la voix : « Lucien n'aime pas les juifs », et les gens se sentaient paralysés, les membres transpercés d'une nuée de petites fléchettes douloureuses. « Guigard et Pierrette, se dit-il avec attendrissement, sont des enfants. » Ils avaient été très coupables, mais il avait suffi que Lucien leur montrât un peu les dents, et, aussitôt, ils avaient eu du remords, ils avaient parlé à voix basse et s'étaient mis à marcher sur la pointe des pieds.

Lucien, pour la seconde fois, se sentit plein de respect pour lui-même. Mais, cette fois-ci, il n'avait plus besoin des yeux de Guigard : c'était à ses propres yeux qu'il paraissait respectable — à ses yeux qui perçaient enfin son enveloppe de chair, de goûts et de dégoûts, d'habitudes et d'humeurs. « Là où je me cherchais, pensa-t-il, je ne pouvais pas me trouver. » Il avait fait, de bonne foi, le recensement minutieux de tout ce qu'il *était.* « Mais si je ne devais être que ce que je suis, je ne vaudrais pas plus que ce petit youtre. » En fouillant ainsi dans cette intimité de muqueuse, que pouvait-on découvrir, sinon la tristesse de la chair, l'ignoble mensonge de l'égalité, le désordre ? « Première maxime, se dit Lucien, ne pas chercher à voir en soi ; il n'y a pas d'erreur plus dangereuse. » Le vrai Lucien — il le savait à présent —, il fallait le chercher dans les yeux des autres, dans l'obéissance craintive de Pierrette et de Guigard, dans l'attente pleine d'espoir de tous ces êtres qui grandissaient et mûrissaient pour lui, de ces jeunes apprentis qui deviendraient *ses* ouvriers, des Férolliens grands et petits, dont il serait un jour le maire. Lucien avait presque peur, il se sentait presque trop grand pour lui. Tant de gens l'attendaient, au port d'armes : et lui il était, il serait toujours cette immense attente des autres. « C'est ça, un chef », pensa-t-il. Et il vit réapparaître un dos musculeux et bossué, et puis, tout de suite après, une cathédrale. Il était dedans, il s'y promenait à pas de loup sous la lumière tamisée qui tombait des vitraux. « Seulement, ce coup-ci, c'est moi la cathédrale ! » Il fixa son regard avec intensité sur son voisin, un long Cubain brun et doux comme un cigare. Il fallait absolument trouver des mots pour exprimer son extraordinaire découverte. Il éleva doucement, précautionneusement sa main jusqu'à son front, comme un cierge allumé, puis il se recueillit un instant, pensif et sacré, et les mots vinrent d'eux-mêmes, il murmura : « J'AI DES DROITS ! » Des droits ! Quelque chose dans le genre des triangles et des cercles : c'était si parfait que ça n'existait pas, on avait beau tracer des milliers de ronds avec des compas, on n'arrivait pas à réaliser un seul cercle. Des générations d'ouvriers pourraient, de même, obéir scrupuleusement aux ordres de Lucien, ils n'épuiseraient jamais son droit à commander; les droits, c'était, par-delà l'existence, comme les objets mathématiques et les dogmes religieux. Et voilà que Lucien, justement, c'était ça : un énorme bouquet de responsabilités et de droits. Il avait longtemps cru qu'il existait par hasard, à la dérive : mais c'était faute d'avoir assez réfléchi. Bien avant sa naissance, sa place était marquée au soleil, à Férolles. Déjà — bien avant, même, le mariage de son père — on l'*attendait*; s'il était venu au monde, c'était pour occuper cette place : « J'existe, pensa-t-il, parce que j'ai le droit d'exister. » Et, pour la première fois, peut-être, il eut une vision fulgurante et glorieuse de son destin. Il serait reçu à Centrale, tôt ou tard (ça n'avait d'ailleurs aucune importance). Alors, il laisserait tomber Maud (elle voulait tout le temps coucher avec lui, c'était assommant ; leurs chairs confondues dégageaient à la chaleur torride de ce début de printemps une odeur de gibelotte un peu roussie. « Et puis Maud est à tout le monde, aujourd'hui à moi, demain à un autre, tout ça n'a aucun sens ») ; il irait habiter à Férolles. Quelque part en France, il y avait une jeune fille claire dans le genre de Pierrette, une provinciale aux yeux de fleur, qui se gardait chaste pour lui : elle essayait parfois d'imaginer son maître futur, cet homme terrible et doux ; mais elle n'y parvenait pas. Elle était vierge ; elle reconnaissait au plus secret de son corps le droit de Lucien à la posséder seul. Il l'épouserait, elle serait *sa* femme, le plus tendre de ses droits. Lorsqu'elle se dévêtirait le soir, à menus gestes sacrés, ce serait comme un holocauste. Il la prendrait dans ses bras avec l'approbation de tous, il lui dirait : « Tu es à moi ! » Ce qu'elle lui montrerait, elle aurait le devoir de ne le montrer qu'à lui, et l'acte d'amour serait pour lui le recensement voluptueux de ses biens. Son plus tendre droit ; son droit le plus intime : le droit d'être respecté jusque dans sa chair, obéi jusque dans son lit. « Je me marierai jeune », pensa-t-il. Il se dit aussi qu'il aurait beaucoup d'enfants ; puis il pensa à l'œuvre de son père ; il était impatient de la continuer et il se demanda si M. Fleurier n'allait pas bientôt mourir.

Une horloge sonna midi ; Lucien se leva. La métamorphose était achevée : dans ce café, une heure plus tôt, un adolescent gracieux et incertain était entré ; c'était un homme qui en sortait, un chef parmi les

Français. Lucien fit quelques pas dans la glorieuse lumière d'un matin de France. Au coin de la rue des Écoles et du boulevard Saint-Michel, il s'approcha d'une papeterie et se mira dans la glace : il aurait voulu retrouver sur son visage l'air imperméable qu'il admirait sur celui de Lemordant. Mais la glace ne lui renvoya qu'une jolie petite figure butée, qui n'était pas encore assez terrible : « Je vais laisser pousser ma moustache », décida-t-il.

## DU MÊME AUTEUR

*Aux Éditions Gallimard*

*Romans*

LA NAUSÉE (Folio).

LES CHEMINS DE LA LIBERTÉ, I : L'ÂGE DE RAISON (Folio).

LES CHEMINS DE LA LIBERTÉ, II : LE SURSIS (Folio).

LES CHEMINS DE LA LIBERTÉ, III : LA MORT DANS L'ÂME (Folio).

ŒUVRES ROMANESQUES (Bibliothèque de la Pléiade).

*Nouvelles*

LE MUR *(Le mur — La chambre — Érostrate — Intimité — L'enfance d'un chef)* (Folio).

*Théâtre*

THÉÂTRE, I : *Les mouches — Huis clos — Morts sans sépulture — La putain respectueuse.*

LES MAINS SALES (Folio).

LE DIABLE ET LE BON DIEU (Folio)

KEAN, d'après Alexandre Dumas.

NEKRASSOV (Folio).

LES SÉQUESTRÉS D'ALTONA (Folio).

LES TROYENNES, d'après Euripide.

*Littérature*

SITUATIONS, I, II, III, IV, V, VI, VII, VIII, IX, X.

BAUDELAIRE (Folio Essais).

CRITIQUES LITTÉRAIRES (Folio Essais).

QU'EST-CE QUE LA LITTÉRATURE ? (Folio Essais).

SAINT GENET, COMÉDIEN ET MARTYR (Les Œuvres complètes de Jean Genet, tome I).

LES MOTS (Folio).

LES ÉCRITS DE SARTRE, de Michel Contat et Michel Rybalka.

L'IDIOT DE LA FAMILLE, *Gustave Flaubert de 1821 à 1857*, I, II et III *(nouvelle édition revue et augmentée).*

PLAIDOYER POUR LES INTELLECTUELS.

UN THÉÂTRE DE SITUATIONS (Folio).

CARNETS DE LA DRÔLE DE GUERRE (septembre 1939-mars 1940).

LETTRES AU CASTOR et à quelques autres :
I. 1926-1939.
II. 1940-1963.

MALLARMÉ, *La lucidité et sa face d'ombre.*

ÉCRITS DE JEUNESSE.

LA REINE ALBEMARLE OU LE DERNIER TOURISTE.

*Philosophie*

L'IMAGINAIRE, *Psychologie phénoménologique de l'imagination* (Folio Essais).

L'ÊTRE ET LE NÉANT, *Essai d'ontologie phénoménologique.*

L'EXISTENTIALISME EST UN HUMANISME (Folio Essais).

CAHIERS POUR UNE MORALE.

CRITIQUE DE LA RAISON DIALECTIQUE (*précédé de* QUESTIONS DE MÉTHODE), I : *Théorie des ensembles pratiques.*

CRITIQUE DE LA RAISON DIALECTIQUE, II : *L'intelligibilité de l'Histoire.*

QUESTIONS DE MÉTHODE (collection « Tel »).

VÉRITÉ ET EXISTENCE.

SITUATIONS PHILOSOPHIQUES (collection « Tel »).

*Essais politiques*

RÉFLEXIONS SUR LA QUESTION JUIVE.

ENTRETIENS SUR LA POLITIQUE, avec David Rousset et Gérard Rosenthal.

L'AFFAIRE HENRI MARTIN, textes commentés par Jean-Paul Sartre.

ON A RAISON DE SE RÉVOLTER, avec Philippe Gavi et Pierre Victor.

*Scénarios*

LES JEUX SONT FAITS (Folio).

L'ENGRENAGE (Folio).

LE SCÉNARIO FREUD.

SARTRE, *un film réalisé par Alexandre Astruc et Michel Contat.*

*Entretiens*

Entretiens avec Simone de Beauvoir, *in* LA CÉRÉMONIE DES ADIEUX de Simone de Beauvoir.

*Iconographie*

SARTRE, IMAGES D'UNE VIE, album préparé par L. Sendyk-Siegel, commentaire de Simone de Beauvoir.

ALBUM SARTRE. Iconographie choisie et commentée par Annie Cohen-Solal.

*Impression Bussière Camedan Imprimeries*
*à Saint-Amand (Cher),*
*le 3 juin 1998.*
*Dépôt légal : juin 1998.*
*1er dépôt légal dans la collection : mars 1972.*
*Numéro d'imprimeur : 983020/1.*
ISBN 2-07-036878-5./Imprimé en France.

87223

# On Appreciating Congress

# On Politics

*L. Sandy Maisel, Series Editor*

On Politics is a new series of short reflections by major scholars on key subfields within political science. Books in the series are personal and practical as well as informed by years of scholarship and deliberation. General readers who want a considered overview of a field as well as students who need a launching platform for new research will find these books a good place to start. Designed for personal libraries as well as student backpacks, these smart books are small format, easy reading, aesthetically pleasing, and affordable.

**Books in the Series**

*On the Presidency,* Thomas E. Cronin
*On Foreign Policy,* Alexander L. George
*On Appreciating Congress,* Louis Fisher
*On Media and Making Sense of Politics,* Doris A. Graber
*On Thinking Institutionally,* Hugh Heclo
*On Legislatures,* Gerhard Loewenberg
*On Ordinary Heroes and American Democracy,*
Gerald M. Pomper

Louis Fisher

# On Appreciating Congress

## *The People's Branch*

*Paradigm Publishers*
Boulder • London

To Mickey Edwards and David Skaggs



Published in the United States by Paradigm Publishers, 3360 Mitchell Lane, Suite E, Boulder, CO 80301 USA.

Paradigm Publishers is the trade name of Birkenkamp & Company, LLC, Dean Birkenkamp, President and Publisher.

Library of Congress Cataloging-in-Publication Data

Fisher, Louis.
On appreciating Congress / Louis Fisher.
p. cm. — (On politics)
Includes bibliographical references and index.
ISBN 978-1-59451-794-5 (hardcover : alk paper)
ISBN 978-1-59451-795-2 (paperback : alk paper)
1. United States. Congress. 2. Legislative power—United States. 3. Separation of powers—United States. I. Title.
JK1041.F57 2009
328.73—dc22

2009027138

Printed and bound in the United States of America on acid-free paper that meets the standards of the American National Standard for Permanence of Paper for Printed Library Materials.

Designed and Typeset by Cheryl Hoffman.

14 13 12 11 10 1 2 3 4 5

# Contents

# Preface

This book explains why Congress is the indispensable institution for safeguarding popular, democratic, and constitutional government. No doubt its record over the past two centuries presents a mixed picture, with many plusses and minuses. Having worked for Congress for the past four decades, I am well aware of its shortcomings. The records of the other two branches are also decidedly mixed, and yet they escape much of the public wrath. Portraying Congress as so inherently inept that it must be kept subordinate to presidential and judicial power is misguided and uninformed.

The virtues widely attributed to the president and the Supreme Court are greatly exaggerated. This book spells out why. Second, the framers looked to Congress as the first branch because it is the institution through which citizens at the local and state levels engage in self-government. Although presidents claim to be the "national representative," they cannot substitute for the knowledge and legitimacy brought by members of Congress. Third, weaken or downgrade Congress and you undercut the hope and future of democracy. The eventual result: a system where citizens vote for lawmakers but the important decisions of public policy are left primarily to nonelected executive officials and federal judges. In other words, citizens are asked to return to their lowly category as "subjects."

Chapter 1 traces the slow and uneven growth of democracy. After much bloodshed, citizens gained the right to exercise control over their lives by voting for public officials to represent and protect their interests. Democratic government affirms the worth and dignity of individuals by recognizing their right to participate in public policy, not only during elections but throughout the year. In tension with this model at all times is the persistent belief that monarchs, aristocrats, and experts are the natural and superior wielders of power.

Chapter 2 explores the sources and limits of presidential power, beginning with powers expressly stated in the Constitution and reasonably implied in those powers. From those core powers are added, over the years, other prerogatives variously called emergency, inherent, and residual, converting the president into a political force never imagined by the framers and an ever-present threat to democratic government. Although Americans broke with the British model of monarchy, claims have been made over the years that the U.S. president incorporates many of the powers formerly vested in the British king. Those models undermine republican government and congressional power. The idolatry of the presidency, so popular after World War II, is being challenged today by some scholars, both liberal and conservative.

Chapter 3 examines the role of Congress in shaping and deciding constitutional issues. Unfortunately, it is commonplace today to accept the Supreme Court as the final word on the meaning of the Constitution. Even worse, many members of Congress increasingly take the view that they have no say, and should have no say, on constitutional interpretation. That was never the framers' expectation and was not even the position of Chief Justice John Marshall when he wrote *Marbury v. Madison* (1803). Congress and the president have at various times functioned as coequal (if not superior) interpreters of the Constitution. Genuflection to the judiciary is no less damaging to republican government than obeisance to presidents and their aides. Many pivotal decisions about constitutional values occur outside all three branches of government, giving life to republican principles.

Another common belief is that Congress cannot possibly protect the rights of minorities because it operates by majority vote. For that reason, safeguarding minority rights must be left to the judiciary. That position might seem logical, even unassailable, but Chapter 4 offers repeated examples of Congress protecting the rights of women, blacks, religious minorities, and other groups far better than the courts. Throughout its history, the Supreme Court spent most of its time protecting government or private corporations. Whatever relief it has brought to individuals and minorities is very much a modern development.

Chapter 5 focuses on the weaknesses of Congress, and there are many. Particularly troublesome since World War II is the failure of Congress to protect its core powers over war and spending. Not only has it been unwilling or unable to fight off encroachments from other branches, at times it takes the initiative to surrender its powers to the president and the courts. When it acts in this manner, it weakens its institutional powers and undermines its capacity to protect constituents in congressional districts and the states. Members of Congress take an oath to support and defend the Constitution, not presidents or the Supreme Court.

A concluding chapter, Chapter 6, offers suggestions on what members of Congress might do if they want to function as part of a coequal branch. For a variety of reasons, lawmakers are unlikely to take those steps on their own. Invigorating democracy depends on the willingness of constituents, scholars, the media, and other parts of society to insist that Congress protect itself and check the other branches. Our liberties depend on a confident and independent Congress. As noted in a recent work, the "path to a healthy democracy, in the American context, leads through a robust Congress." Unfortunately, political leaders and news commentators in their critiques of Congress "rarely take stock of Congress as an institution of democracy. Regrettably, neither do scholars."[1] In a separate study, Julian Zelizer describes Congress as "the heart and soul of democracy, the arena where politicians and citizens most directly interact over pressing concerns."[2] This book is written in that spirit.

I began to think about this book after sitting down with political scientist Sandy Maisel and Paradigm vice president Jennifer Knerr. Congress regularly takes a pounding from all sides. I wanted to do a fair treatment, acknowledging the serious problems of the legislative branch but also calling attention to its contributions and its vital role in protecting democracy. Sandy and Jennifer offered many constructive comments at each stage of the project. My thanks to Lauren Arnest for her careful and thoughtful editing.

Reb Brownell, an attorney and congressional staffer, shares my interest in institutional and constitutional issues. His review of the manuscript offered many thoughtful suggestions on how to clarify and deepen the principal themes. My brother, Lee, read the full manuscript and gave me the benefit of a citizen who follows government and is greatly disappointed with what he sees. It was healthy for me to keep in mind his harsh appraisal of Congress. After I finished the manuscript I received from *Boston University Law Review* its symposium issue of April 2009 entitled "The Most Disparaged Branch: The Role of Congress in the Twenty-First Century." I had long ago realized that writing anything complimentary about Congress is an uphill climb.

Friends and colleagues read portions of the manuscript. I sought advice from House and Senate staffers, Democrats and Republicans, current staff and retirees. For congressional staff let me thank Jeff Biggs, Bill Ellis, David Lachmann, Daniel McAdams, Bob Schiff, and Don Wolfensberger. For my valued colleagues at the Library of Congress, my thanks to Rick Beth, Clint Brass, Henry Hogue, Kevin Kosar, Walter Oleszek, Harold Relyea, Mort Rosenberg, and Stephen Stathis. For friends in the academic community, appreciation goes to Dave Adler, Dick Pious, Chris Pyle, Mark Rozell, Mitch Sollenberger, Bob Spitzer, and Charles Tiefer for their comments.

With great pleasure I dedicate the book to Mickey Edwards and David Skaggs. Edwards served for many years as a Republican member of the U.S. House of Representatives from Oklahoma, rising in the party leadership. Skaggs served for years as a Democratic member of the House from Colorado, assigned to such committees as Appropriations and Intelligence. I admired both for the way they defended constitutional values (especially structural checks) and protected the powers of Congress. They were institutionalists then and institutionalists now. After leaving Congress they continue to be active in public service, including with the Constitution Project, where it is my delight to work with them. The country depends on such individuals with their steady, informed, and articulate commitment to a constitutional republic.

—Louis Fisher

# Chapter One
# Popular Government

Sovereignty was long associated exclusively with royal power. Only in recent centuries has it come to mean government by the people. The U.S. Constitution begins with three powerful words that astonished previous rulers and all of Europe: "We the People." For most of recorded history, men and women accepted that political decisions about their lives were assigned to a select few, either a monarch assisted by courtiers or an aristocracy. The general public was considered too ignorant, incompetent, and socially inferior to participate in public affairs. Like children, they were expected to submit to the direction and control of those who knew best.

## Divine Right

To shore up the political power and legitimacy of a monarchy, kings claimed to rule by divine right. No earthly force or authority could constrain the king. Policies and decisions descended from Heaven, even when the results for the country were calamitous. An associated principle held that the king could do no wrong, and therefore no action at law could ever be brought against him. England discovered ways to allow legitimate grievances to be settled by lesser officials.[1] Countries found it convenient to recognize the divine right of the king to offset the same claim of divine right by the pope.[2] The crown represented the headdress or cap of sovereignty. In some political systems the monarch was above the community, but the law was above the monarch.[3]

It would take centuries of political struggle for the system of monarchy and divine right to give way to elected representatives serving in an assembly to protect the general public and check executive power. In Great Britain, Parliament emerged as a separate institution to challenge royal power. The growth of self-government in England led to costly and bloody civil wars, eventually reducing the monarch to a figurehead without political power. The appeal of popular government in the American colonies prompted the Continental Congress to meet in 1774. With the Declaration of Independence two years later, Americans were determined to cast off monarchy and embrace broad public participation.

## Monarchy on the Defensive

Royal government in England faced repeated challenges. With the Magna Carta of 1215, King John at Runnymede promised not to capture or imprison a freeman "except by the lawful judgment of his peers or by the law of the land." Royal power now had a secular competitor, at least for the upper class. They were entitled to a legal process that assured fair and public trials. The Magna Carta, marking a concession to barons, was reissued several times by subsequent kings, serving as an initial check on arbitrary and unjust rule. In later years, English kings were often successful in placing the Crown and personal interests above the law and the interests of the country.

Another curb on royal power took the form of the Petition of Right in 1628. Members of the House of Commons drafted language to place limits on arbitrary arrest, imprisonment without cause, forced loans by the king, and martial law. Charles I struggled with financial burdens after embarking on wars against both France and Spain. One remedy was forced loans. Anyone who protested and refused to lend money to the government could face imprisonment. Upon examining draft language of the petition, Charles I offered to grant certain benefits by divine grace. That did not sit well with Parliament. It insisted that new privileges be grounded not in royal grace but as a matter of right.[4]

The existence of natural rights was no more grounded in fact and evidence than the divine right of kings. Each rested on an assumption, a premise, an ideal system. Each claimed to operate on first principles. Over time, in Anglo-American society, individual rights took hold: the right of conscience, the right to hold political and religious opinions without fear of persecution, the right to participate in government. The Declaration of Independence in 1776 would claim: "We hold these truths to be self-evident, that all men are created equal, that they are endowed by their Creator with certain unalienable Rights." Carl Becker observed that the eighteenth century "deified Nature and denatured God."[5]

After Parliament passed the Petition of Right, Charles I decided to rule the country without Parliament and did so from 1629 to 1640. Parliament returned to pass the Triennial Act, requiring the legislative branch to sit every three years whether the king called lawmakers or not. Conflicts between the royalists and Parliament grew worse, leading to years of civil war between the two sides. Charles I was captured and later beheaded, in 1649. During that period, opponents of royal power looked for ways to strengthen popular sovereignty by having Parliament meet on a regular basis and enlarge the right of suffrage.

Ever so slowly, popular rule began to displace monarchical edicts.[6] When Oliver Cromwell took power after Charles I, his military dictatorship and replacement of a king snapped the pretense of divine right. England restored the monarchy with Charles II, followed by James II. As part of the "Bloodless Revolution," James II was expelled and replaced in 1688 by Princess Mary and her husband, William of Orange. Their rule marked another decisive break with divine right. John Locke wrote *Two Treatises of Government* (1690) in part to reject the doctrine of absolute monarchy and divine right. However, once ideas and concepts come on the scene, they rarely disappear entirely. The divine right of kings would later assume new forms of authority called "executive prerogative" and "inherent" presidential power, examined in the next chapter.

## Colonial America

Those who settled in American colonies in the 1600s functioned under the jurisdiction and control of British kings and the Parliament. The notion of a monarch governing by divine right was far too abstract for the hardy souls who arrived on the eastern seaboard to eke out an existence under harsh conditions. Survival depended on individual effort, not heavenly assistance or guidance. London, trying to govern the colonies from 3,000 miles away, inevitably exercised less control than it could at home. Popular sovereignty in America took root more than it did in England.

To sustain themselves in the new wilderness, settlers drafted and agreed to abide by social contracts and compacts. Through initiative and adaptation they learned how to build effective government and manage their affairs. Representative assemblies in the colonies met to pass laws more informed and constructive than the broad orders adopted in England could ever assure. Colonists participating in these assemblies produced public policies more acceptable and easier to enforce. Under the press of daily demands, representative assemblies emerged in the colonies to safeguard the people.

Popular consent and a spirit of independence were less political theory than a practical demand. Colonies continued to operate under the king's grant, but royal control was distant and tenuous. To settle problems within their communities, Americans learned skills by meeting in town halls to debate and decide social and political issues. They mastered parliamentary rules and took conscious and sometimes unconscious steps toward self-government. In discovering how to govern themselves and find solutions, they developed confidence, personal integrity, and responsibility.

British difficulty in controlling the colonies was highlighted by the Stamp Act crisis. The exertion of royal power triggered popular resentment and resistance. The French and Indian War, lasting from 1754 to 1763, prompted military operations from the Ohio Valley to Canada and placed great financial burdens on Great Britain. It seemed reasonable to ask Americans to help pay the cost. After England and France signed a peace treaty, the British Parliament passed the Sugar Act, adding a three-penny tax on molasses. The statute proved difficult to administer and enforce, in part because colonists objected to being taxed from London and learned ingenious methods of evasion. In frustration, Parliament searched for other ways to attract much needed revenue.

England turned to the Stamp Act of 1765, placing an excise tax on all documents and articles made of paper. Swept within this statute were such items as court documents, college diplomas, mortgages, pamphlets, newspapers, and even playing cards. Those documents and others had to be printed on paper carrying a stamp embossed by the Treasury Office. Taxes were imposed in varying amounts. How should the statute be administered? From distant London? Parliament decided to ask colonists to enforce the law. Once again there would be taxation without consent.

Americans sent petitions to London to detail their opposition. Resolutions at home declared that colonists were entitled to all the liberties and privileges of people living in England. Constitutional principles, argued these resolutions, required that taxation be decided by representatives chosen by the people. Only in that manner would representatives know "what

Taxes the People are able to bear, or the easiest Method of raising them, and must themselves be affected by every Tax laid on the People."[7]

These initial verbal protests were followed by action. In Boston, an organization later called the Sons of Liberty decided on concrete steps. Initially they hung in effigy the figure of Andrew Oliver, who had been appointed distributor of stamps for Massachusetts. A mob leveled the building he planned to use to distribute the stamps, beheaded his effigy, and threw stones through the windows of his home. The rest of the effigy disappeared in a bonfire. The mob returned to break into his house and wreck furniture and other possessions. By that time Oliver had fled. Although he had yet to receive his commission from London, he promised a group of visitors he would do nothing to carry out the Stamp Act. When the commission arrived, Oliver, under great public pressure, read his resignation.

Whoever seemed willing to enforce the statute in Massachusetts had their homes attacked, including Lieutenant-Governor Thomas Hutchinson. After the instigator of the violence was seized and faced prosecution, a threat by his supporters to destroy the custom-house provided sufficient cause to release him and drop all charges. Later, the stamped papers arrived from London to permit enforcement, but Governor Francis Barnard publicly announced that the papers would not be distributed. On the day the statute formally took effect, November 1, 1765, the courts and other institutions agreed to meet and function without stamps. If courts were crippled because of a lack of stamped paper, creditors and other litigants would be unable to litigate their interests.

Opposition to the Stamp Act spread to other colonies. Warned that a mob would destroy his house, the distributor of stamps in Rhode Island publicly resigned. The distributor in Maryland refused to resign, but after his house was pulled down he had to flee for his life. He later gave up his post, as did distributors in New Hampshire, North Carolina, and Virginia. Individuals in Connecticut, Delaware, and Pennsylvania appointed to implement the statute agreed not to. The distributor for Georgia pledged to enforce the law until his safety was so threatened that within two weeks he left the area. Colonial activities proceeded with unstamped paper. In areas where England closed ports to force compliance with the statute, the economic interests of both colonial and English merchants suffered.

Members of Parliament were deeply offended by mob opposition to law. They debated sending British troops to compel compliance, forcing the Sons of Liberty in various states to prepare for armed resistance. The Stamp Act served to unite Americans around a common cause of shared interests and loyalty, years before the decision to break with England. London merchants pressured Parliament to repeal the statute, which it finally did in February 1766. Americans had tasted freedom from British rule and dominance. Just as they had begun to deny the power of Parliament, they "were beginning to take stronger ground against the authority of the royal prerogative."[8] A small colony confronted a great power and watched England stand down.

Bloodshed would come soon with Lexington and Concord and the War of Independence, yet the Stamp Act helped discredit many American political leaders who supported continuation of British rule. At the same time it elevated the political careers of those willing to fight for independence, individual freedom, self-government, and the repudiation of monarchy. Service in the French and Indian War from 1754 to 1763 gave military experience to many Americans, including George Washington.

## Making the Break

On January 10, 1776, Thomas Paine published *Common Sense*, justifying independence from England. He leveled contempt at the existing process of Americans carrying their grievances to London: "To be always running three or four thousand miles with a tale or a petition, waiting four or five months for an answer, which, when obtained, requires five or six more to explain it in, will in a few years be looked upon as folly and childishness. There was a time when it was proper, and there is a proper time for it to cease." He urged Americans to send delegates from each colony to form a congress for the purpose of deliberating and making law. By rejecting monarchy, in America "*the law is king*. For as in absolute governments the king is law, so in free countries the law *ought* to be king; and there ought to be no other."[9]

Paine explained that monarchies were regularly involved in wars outside the country and civil wars inside. In contrast, republican forms of government in Switzerland and Holland were largely spared military conflicts. Many of the framers reached the same conclusion. When the *Federalist Papers* were published in 1788 to promote ratification of the Constitution, John Jay in Federalist No. 4 warned about the pattern of monarchs and single executives taking their countries into costly and painful wars. Absolute monarchs "will often make war when their nations are to get nothing by it, but for purposes and objects merely personal, such as a thirst for military glory, revenge for personal affronts, ambition, or private compacts to aggrandize or support their particular families or partisans." Executive leaders often engaged in wars "not sanctified by justice or the voice and interests of his people."

To prepare for independence from England, America created the Continental Congress in 1774. Delegates from the colonies met at Philadelphia to protest recent actions by Parliament and petition for a redress of grievances. War began with the battles of Lexington and Concord in April 1775, and two months later Congress created the Continental Army and issued the Declaration of Independence in July 1776. Congress also drafted the Articles of Confederation to define the powers of the new national government.

Throughout this period, there was only one branch of government: the Continental Congress. There was a president of Congress, but he functioned merely as a presiding officer of the legislature, lacking any executive power. There was no separate judiciary. The delegates at the Congress sat on committees to handle administrative questions and judicial disputes. In November 1777, Congress experimented with a board of three commissioners to execute the business of the navy, subject to the direction of the Marine Committee. Congress found the system of boards frustrating because work was too slow and no single officer could be held responsible. The next step came in 1781: the creation of single executives to handle the positions of superintendent of finance, the secretary at war, and the secretary of marine. In that same year, Congress created the office of attorney general to prosecute all suits on behalf of the Confederation of States and to advise Congress on all legal matters submitted to him. These executive officers were purely agents of Congress. They had no independent or separate status.

Much has been written about the framers' dependence on political theories borrowed from foreign writers, such as Montesquieu. What we see in this period with the Continental Congress is less theory and more practice. Year by year the delegates learned which systems of government worked and which did not. Executive and judicial powers originally placed in Congress were spun out with limited autonomy at first and greater discretion later. Congress also established a Court of Appeals in Cases of Capture. The historian Francis Wharton put it very well: The Constitution of 1787 "did not make this distribution of power. It would be more proper to say that this distribution of power made the Constitution of the United States."[10]

## Drafting the Constitution

When delegates met at the Philadelphia Convention in 1787, they agreed that the new national government would consist of three separate branches. How separate no one was prepared to say. The Virginia Plan presented on May 29 provided for three branches but made no reference to "separate and distinct" or any other formulation of the separation doctrine. In fact, Congress was to choose the president, and members of Congress were to be joined with the judiciary to form a council of revision, charged with reviewing the constitutionality of legislation. Those ideas did not survive.

Late in July, the Convention adopted a resolution affirming the separation doctrine. The three branches were to be kept distinct and independent, except in specified cases. The version presented on August 6 by the Committee on Detail made no mention of the separation clause and the Constitution was adopted in September and ratified the next year without specific reference to the separation doctrine. The relationships between the branches would have to be worked out in practice. There should be no doubt that the framers rejected the British model that placed all of external affairs, foreign policy, and the war power with the executive. As explained in Chapter 2, not a single one of those powers was granted to the president. They were vested entirely in Congress or shared between the president and the Senate.

In the *Federalist Papers*, James Madison defended the overlapping of powers found in the Constitution. He was a fine writer and political analyst, but in Federalist No. 37 he confessed that words often failed. Just as naturalists had difficulty in defining the precise line between vegetable life and the animal world, so was it impossible to draw the boundary between the three branches of government or "even the privileges and powers of the different legislative branches. Questions daily occur in the course of practice, which prove the obscurity which reigns in these subjects, and which puzzle the greatest adepts in political science."

Much of Madison's analysis of the separation doctrine appears in Federalist No. 47. He acknowledged that tyranny results whenever three branches are concentrated in the same hands, but cautioned that the maxim had been "totally misconceived and misapplied," especially by those who insisted that the three branches had to be totally separate. Montesquieu, he said, could not have intended such separation. In England, the executive magistrate formed a part of the legislative power by making treaties. It shared part of the judicial power by appointing judges. One chamber of Parliament formed a constitutional council for the executive, possessed judicial power in the impeachment process, and exercised supreme appellate jurisdiction in all other cases.

At the state level, Madison could find no instance in which the departments of power had been kept absolutely separate and distinct. What Montesquieu intended, he said, could be no more than this: "that where the *whole* power of one department is exercised by the same hands which possess the *whole* power of another department, the fundamental principles of a free constitution are subverted." During the period when Madison wrote, the strict theory of separation of powers had been replaced by the more practical system of checks and balances. One contemporary pamphleteer referred to the separation doctrine as a "hackneyed principle" and a "trite maxim."[11]

Critics of the draft Constitution attacked the impeachment process because it combined legislative and judicial powers in the same department (the Senate). In Federalist No. 66, Alexander Hamilton dismissed this objection by pointing out that the true meaning of the separation maxim was "entirely compatible with a partial intermixture" and that overlapping was not only "proper, but necessary to the mutual defence of the several members of the government, against each other." To those who complained that the treaty process mixed the president with the Senate, he could only respond wearily in Federalist No. 75 to "the trite topic of the intermixture of powers."

Three states (North Carolina, Pennsylvania, and Virginia) insisted at their ratification conventions that the powers of government be kept separate. They wanted that principle added to the Bill of Rights. After the new government began in 1789, Congress compiled a list of amendments to the Constitution, including this provision: "The powers delegated by this constitution are appropriated to the departments to which they are respectively distributed: so that the legislative department shall never exercise the powers vested in the executive or judicial, nor the executive exercise the powers vested in the legislative or judicial, nor the judicial exercise the powers vested in the legislative or executive departments."[12]

Had this language been adopted, it would not have affected the overlapping of powers already sanctioned by the Constitution. It would not have altered the essential dependence on checks and balances. The separation clause was among 17 amendments sent by the House to the Senate, where it was struck from the list on September 7, 1789. A substitute amendment (to make the three departments "separate and distinct" and to assure that the legislative and executive departments would be restrained from oppression by "feeling and participating the public burthens" through regular elections) failed also. The House and the Senate met in conference to reconcile their two versions. The conferees reduced the list from 17 to 12. Among the deleted amendments was the separation clause.

What would keep the three branches separate and remain faithful to the powers defined in the Constitution? Each branch could be expected to push the limits of their assigned powers and encroach on others. Madison explained in Federalist No. 48 that "a mere demarcation on parchment of the constitutional limits of the several departments is not a sufficient guard against those encroachments which lead to a tyrannical concentration of all the powers of government in the same hands."

Madison held firm to certain constitutional principles. He noted in Federalist No. 49 that "the people are the only legitimate foundation of power." Although he expressed concern about the tendency of republican governments to permit aggrandizement by the legislative department, he did not hesitate in Federalist No. 51 to conclude that in republican government "the legislative authority necessarily predominates." Legislative abuse, he said, would be checked initially to some degree by dividing Congress into two chambers.

As to the future of the republic, Madison left it to the three branches to protect their powers. He advised in Federalist No.

51 that the great safeguard against a gradual concentration of power in a single department "consists in giving those who administer each department the necessary constitutional means and personal motives to resist encroachments of the others. . . . Ambition must be made to counteract ambition. The interest of the man must be connected with the constitutional rights of the place." Over the last 200 years, the presidency and the judiciary have been effective not only in protecting their branches but in extending their powers. Congress was coequal over most of that period, but in the last seven decades it has in large part allowed its powers to decline, partly for refusing to fight off encroachments and in some cases by taking the initiative to surrender power. That pattern will be explored in Chapter 5.

It is tempting to say that if Congress does not protect itself, the fault is its own and it deserves no sympathy or support. The deeper problem is that a decline in the power of Congress is a decline in the power of the people that the legislative branch represents. What is meant by republican government or a "republic"? If you asked that question today you would likely receive puzzled expressions. The framers knew the meaning of a republic and were willing to fight and die for it. A republic is a form of government in which the supreme power rests with the people, exercised through representatives. The value of a republic appears in the Pledge of Allegiance: "I pledge allegiance to the flag of the United States of America and to the Republic for which it stands." The overriding value is not the flag. It is the republic. If the republic disappears, the flag stands for nothing.

## Democracy on Trial

The first decade of the new government, beginning in 1789, put democracy and popular control (with a limited franchise) to a severe test. The struggles during this period reaffirm Madison's insight that one should put modest faith in a written constitution. Words can be high sounding and inspiring but meaningless in practice. What matters is the willingness of citizens to defend their rights, often at great cost to themselves. What happens in a democracy when a group uses its power to subjugate others?

Madison anticipated that problem in Federalist No. 10 when he spoke about factions. By that term he meant a number of citizens "united and actuated by some common impulse of passion, or of interest, adverse to the rights of other citizens, or to the permanent and aggregate interests of the community." One remedy would be to destroy the liberty of factions to exist and operate. To Madison, that prescription was "worse than the disease." It would be like abolishing oxygen to eliminate the threat of fires. A republic exists to protect liberty, not to crush it. Nor was there any possibility of controlling factions by giving each citizen the same set of opinions. Beyond its impracticality, it too would destroy liberty and individual choice. In a democracy, citizens naturally had different interests and values.

Madison said that if a faction were less than a majority it could be controlled through the regular political process. Suppose the faction formed a majority? If it existed in a small republic, it could use its political power to suppress the rights and liberties of those in the minority. But Madison looked to a country so large that it would contain hundreds of factions, with one neutralizing the other. Also, the popular passion of a faction would be filtered to some extent through elected representatives and the compromises and accommodations that are part of the political process. The danger of factions could thus be controlled without resorting to punishment, suppression, or expulsion of an unpopular faction. Madison's model worked well in some cases but failed in 1798 when Congress passed the Alien and Sedition Acts, discussed later in this chapter.

In 1792, Congress passed legislation to create a uniform militia drawn from the states. The purpose was to give the country a capacity to suppress insurrections and repel invasions, but lawmakers understood that an abusive militia could also turn itself against the community and threaten individual rights. To guard against ill-use, Congress authorized the president to call up the militia, subject to two checks: the state legislature or the governor had to request assistance, and a Supreme Court justice or district judge had to notify the president.

President George Washington followed those statutory procedures in 1794 when he called up the militia to put down what became known as the Whiskey Rebellion. In 1791, Congress had enacted a federal excise tax on spirits distilled within the United States. Farmers in western Pennsylvania wondered why converting grain into alcohol was taxable and converting grain into flour was not. Federal agents who attempted to collect revenue were tarred and feathered and stripped of horse and money. Opposition to the tax resulted in several deaths, the capture of a federal marshal, and the destruction of property by fire. Justice James Wilson presented to President Washington a certification that state officials were unable to control the rebellion. Washington called up the militias from four states to put down the resisters. Several were tried and convicted.

Washington learned that citizens were holding "certain irregular meetings" to discuss government policies. In Pennsylvania and in other states, citizens formed political clubs and "democratic societies" to meet regularly and debate public issues. Today we would be pleased when citizens take an active interest in government and are willing to attend meetings to express their views. Washington, however, found the meetings offensive and dangerous. He asked: "can any thing be more absurd, more arrogant, or more pernicious to the peace of Society, than for self-created bodies, forming themselves into *permanent* Censors, and under the shade of Night in a concave," especially when they met to criticize statutes that Congress had passed.[13]

In Madison's framework, Washington viewed these self-created societies as "factions" intent on doing harm to the community. Unlike Madison, Washington was not willing to wait for factions to neutralize one another or be curbed by the majority. Washington recognized that all citizens had a constitutional right to petition the government, but he thought that meeting in secret and quite likely without accurate information posed a threat to society. Unless government was willing to intervene and control these meetings, "there is an end of and we may bid adieu to all government in this Country, except Mob and Club Govt. from whence nothing but anarchy and confusion can ensue."[14]

Critics of political clubs saw them as the type of Jacobin societies in Paris that had helped foment the French Revolution. Some members of Washington's cabinet agreed that prompt and decisive action was needed to suppress these organizations. Secretary of State Edmund Randolph advised Washington that he "never did see an opportunity of destroying these self-constituted bodies, until the fruit of their operations was discharged in the insurrection."[15] Now was the time for them to "be crushed."

It was the practice of early presidents to submit an annual message. On November 19, 1794, Washington reviewed the Whiskey Rebellion and the steps he had taken to bring it under control. He singled out for criticism "certain self-created societies" and urged Congress "to turn the machinations of the wicked to the confirming of our constitution: to enable us at all times to root out internal sedition, and put invasion to flight."[16] A very heavy word: *sedition*. For Washington, anyone who attended a meeting and criticized government policy was guilty of sedition, which generally meant open resistance to government authority. A sedition law with criminal penalties appeared four years later.

The Senate quickly praised Washington for his condemnation of self-created societies. In contrast, the House of Representatives spent five full days debating that part of his message. William Smith warned that if the House failed to rush to Washington's defense it "would be an avowed desertion of the Executive."[17] This was an extraordinary argument. If a president made a public statement, each chamber of Congress had a bounden duty to announce its support; otherwise it would be "desertion." The Constitution does not require Congress to walk in lockstep with the president. Each lawmaker is expected to exercise independent thought, as are constituents.

Several members denied they had any obligation to salute whatever a president said. John Nichols asked whether he was expected to "abandon my independence for the sake of the president."[18] If Washington's advisers put him in this dilemma, it was their problem (and Washington's), not Congress's. Josiah Parker of Virginia agreed, pointing out that Washington seemed "misinformed." There was no obligation for a lawmaker "to give up his opinions for the sake of any man." Parker knew of self-created societies in his district and defended them. His constituents "love your Government much, but they love their independence more."[19] Here was a ringing endorsement of government by the people, not government over the people.

William Giles, also of Virginia, wondered what benefit could possibly come from rebuking such abstractions as "self-created societies." What was Washington talking about? People who met in the evening to discuss philosophy, religion, or their stamp collection? What possible constitutional authority did the government have to suppress such meetings? For Giles, Congress had no business trying to restrain or direct public opinion. Citizens had every right to discuss whatever they wanted. If a self-created society violated the law, they could be prosecuted. Otherwise, they were at liberty to function as they liked. Citizens had a right to censure government; government did not have a right to censure citizens.

Madison drove home the same points: "When the people have formed a Constitution, they retain those rights which they have not expressly delegated. It is a question whether what is thus retained can be legislated upon."[20] To Madison, Congress had no authority to legislate on personal opinions or the liberties of speech and press. It was false to say that censure by the government is no punishment: "If it falls on classes of individuals, it will be severe punishment." If Congress were to be faithful to the nature of republican government, "we shall find that the censorial power is in the people over the Government and not in the Government over the people."[21]

After lengthy and thoughtful debate, the House decided against a general attack on self-created societies and limited its remarks to the actions of political clubs in four western counties of Pennsylvania. The House expressed its concern about "misrepresentations" by individuals "or combinations of men" that might have provoked the rebellion and regretted that the public order had "suffered so flagrant a violation." The effort by President Washington to single out political societies for wholesale condemnation and to restrict a citizen's right to express opinions about public policy was soundly rejected.

## Individual Conscience

Congressional pushback on Washington's attempt to discredit political clubs depended on lawmakers exercising their independent judgment. Government by the people in these early decades assumed that individuals had the capacity to participate actively and independently in public affairs. Consistent with that philosophy were principles derived from the Enlightenment. A successful government nurtured the liberty of the individual to pursue employment, self-education, and the "pursuit of happiness." The emphasis was on pursuit, not attainment. Individuals needed freedom to develop personal thoughts, beliefs, and talents.

Those principles are captured in an essay that Madison published in *The National Gazette*, March 29, 1792. Entitled "Property," it has nothing to do with modern notions of physical property, including homes, cars, and money. Property in its original meaning derived from the Latin *proprius*: that which is one's own. Madison had talked about this form of property in Federalist No. 10, where he spoke of the "diversity in the faculties of men, from which the rights of property originate." The fundamental value was not physical property but the faculties that individuals use in creating property. For that reason the most important function of government was not to protect property. Rather, the "protection of these faculties is the first object of government."

The 1792 essay explains the personal liberties that individuals need to develop to contribute to the larger community. To Madison, property "embraces every thing to which a man may attach a value and have a right; and *which leaves to every one else the like advantage*."[22] One's conscience existed as a natural right, subject to no restrictions. Madison and Jefferson had helped draft the Virginia Statute for Establishing Religious Freedom. Religion and its free exercise was a fundamental human right over which the state could not intrude: "Our rulers can have authority over such natural rights, only as we have submitted them. The rights of conscience we never submitted, we could not submit."[23]

A century earlier, the Dutch philosopher Spinoza had defended the same values. Individuals had the right to think and reason independently. No man's mind, he wrote, "can possibly lie wholly at the disposition of another, for no one can willingly transfer his natural right of free reason and judgment, or be compelled so to do." Any government that attempted to control minds was, by definition, tyrannical. No government could prescribe what was true or false or what opinions were legitimate or not. "All these questions fall within a man's natural right, which he cannot abdicate even with his own consent."[24]

Those themes emerge clearly in Madison's 1792 essay. A man has a property "in his opinions and the free communication of them." He has a property "in his religious opinions, and in the profession and practice dictated by them." He has a property "in the safety and liberty of his person." He has a property "in the free use of his faculties and free choice of the objects on which to employ them. In a word, as a man is said to have a right to his property, he may be equally said to have a property in his rights."

In a concurrence in 1927, Justice Louis Brandeis restated the basic values that make America special. The framers who won independence from England believed that "the final end of the State was to make men free to develop their faculties; and that in its government the deliberative forces should prevail over the arbitrary."[25] The purpose of government was not to crush independent thought but to encourage it. The framers valued liberty "both as an end and as a means. They believed liberty to be the secret of happiness and courage to be the secret of liberty. They believed that freedom to think as you will and to speak as you think are indispensable to the discovery and spread of political truth; that without free speech and assembly discussion would be futile; that with them, discussion affords ordinarily adequate protection against the dissemination of noxious doctrine; that the greatest menace to freedom is an inert people; that public discussion is a political duty; and that this should be a fundamental principle of the American government."[26]

## Sedition and Democracy

Washington's suspicion about "disloyal" members of the political community took root a few years later when President John Adams signed the Alien and Sedition Acts. In 1798, pressures mounted for going to war against France. A similar intolerance of individual opinions and independent thought after the terrorist attacks of September 11, 2001, were present during the Adams administration. On September 20, 2001, President George W. Bush said in a message to Congress: "Every nation, in every region, now has a decision to make: Either you are with us, or you are with the terrorists." In 1798, the nation's leading periodical for the Federalist Party, Philadelphia's *Gazette of the United States*, warned: "He that is not for us, is against us."[27] Those who faced repression in 1798 were the foreign born: "enemy aliens" and "alien friends." Individuals subjected to repression after 9/11 were aliens and "enemy combatants," although there was no effort to punish or prosecute general criticism of the war against terrorism.

In 1798, Congress first passed legislation to extend the waiting period for citizenship from 5 years to 14 years. Part of the motivating force was hostility toward foreigners (even if the lawmakers voting for the legislation were from families born abroad!). Much of the incentive behind this legislation consisted of partisan calculation. The Federalists believed that immigrants were more likely to vote for the Republican-Jeffersonian Party.

After enacting the naturalization bill, Congress passed the Alien Friends Act. It made it lawful for the president to deport any alien "he shall judge dangerous to the peace and safety of the United States." Deportation was also justified if the president had "reasonable grounds" to believe that an alien was involved "in any treasonable or secret machinations" against the federal government. Opponents of the bill objected that existing laws were sufficient to deal with anyone who threatened the government. They objected to vague words like "dangerous" and "machinations." They warned that the bill created a despotic political system, placing all legislative, executive, and judicial powers in a single person: the president. Individuals targeted by this legislation had no right to a public trial to be heard by a jury, confrontation with witnesses, or other procedural safeguards.

A separate statute was aimed at "alien enemies." Whenever there was a declared war between the United States and a foreign nation or any threat of military force by that nation, all noncitizen males 14 years or older were subject to removal from the country. There was no need for evidence about disloyalty or improper conduct. Mere identification with an enemy nation was sufficient. The alien had to appear before a federal court. If the court found "sufficient cause" it would order deportation.

The fourth repressive statute was the Sedition Act. Unlike the two alien bills, penalties for seditious activity applied to both aliens and citizens. Individuals could be fined and imprisoned if they wrote or said anything about Congress or the president deemed to be "false, scandalous and malicious," had the intent to "defame" those political institutions or bring them into "contempt or disrepute," "excite" any hatred against them, or "stir up" sedition or act in combination to oppose or resist federal laws or any presidential act to implement those laws. Any criticism of the government could lead to prosecution. The principle of popular government changed to government threatening the sovereign people. The debate on "self-created societies" in 1794, momentarily turned aside, now took the form of federal law. People were not at liberty to censure government; government was free to censure (and imprison) the people.

The Sedition Act authorized individuals to present as part of their defense "the truth of the matter contained in the publication as a libel." In the end, the government would decide what was true and false. The Adams administration, backed by congressional legislation, began to prosecute and intimidate newspapers that were critical of the Federalist Party and its policies. Because of that policy, many people saw government not as the defender of liberty but its enemy. Moreover, most of the newspapers in the country favored the Federalists, not the Jeffersonians. "Friendly" periodicals got a free pass. Their political opinions of support for the Adams administration were safe and protected.

When Thomas Jefferson was elected president, he used his pardon power to relieve those who had been prosecuted and convicted under the Sedition Act. Years later, Congress passed legislation to appropriate funds to reimburse individuals who had been fined under the statute. A congressional committee denounced the statute as "unconstitutional, null, and void."[28] In *New York Times Co. v. Sullivan* (1964), the Supreme Court acknowledged that the Sedition Act was not struck down by a court of law but by the "court of history." The decisive judgment came not from the judiciary but from a newly elected administration and the general public.

One of the casualties of the war against France in 1798 was John Fries. In order to finance the war, the Federalists enacted a direct tax against homes and improved farmlands. Just as rebels in western Pennsylvania had opposed the excise tax on alcohol, so did Fries and his supporters in eastern Pennsylvania decide they had an obligation and a freedom as citizens to oppose the war tax imposed by the Federalists. Thousands of German American citizens interpreted the tax as a measure designed to drive them into poverty. Believing that resistance to the tax was part of popular sovereignty, they raised "liberty poles" to highlight their opposition. Although John Fries had joined the militia to fight against the Whiskey Rebellion, he now decided to take a stand against his government.

Fries and several hundred supporters marched into Bethlehem, Pennsylvania, to demand the release of men jailed for resisting the tax. They thought the march was consistent with the spirit of the American Revolution and the Constitution, even though they used the threat of force to free the prisoners. To them it was a modest rebellion, at most punishable for inciting a riot or kidnapping federal prisoners. To the Federalists it smacked of sedition and an act of war against the government that satisfied the constitutional language on treason: "Treason against the United States shall consist only in Levying War against them, or in adhering to their Enemies, giving them Aid and Comfort. No Person shall be convicted of Treason unless on the Testimony of two Witnesses to the same overt Act, or in Confession in open Court."

A number of the marchers were found guilty of lesser crimes, fined, and given prison sentences. Fries and two of his colleagues were found guilty of treason ("levying war") and sentenced to be hanged. Gallows were constructed. Shortly before the planned execution President Adams pardoned all three.[29] Enactment of the alien and sedition legislation, the prosecution of Fries and his colleagues, and other national policies helped cripple the Federalist Party. It became identified with elitism and hostility to popular government, public debate, free press, dissent, and civil liberties. After the Jeffersonians won the 1800 elections, the Federalists never again controlled the presidency or Congress. Gradually, the Federalist Party disappeared as a political force.

## Free Speech in Wartime

Writing in 1927, Justice Brandeis warned that political order could not be secured "merely through fear of punishment for its infraction; that it is hazardous to discourage thought, hope and imagination; that fear breeds repression; that repression breeds hate; that hate menaces stable government; that the path to safety lies in the opportunity to discuss supposed grievances and proposed remedies."[30] Democracy depended on the power of reason and public discussion. As Brandeis noted, the framers "eschewed silence coerced by law—the argument of force in its worst form."

Yet America has several times passed sedition laws to intimidate and punish citizens who thought in ways the government disliked. It is remarkable in a system of self-government that there should ever be a law of sedition. Citizens go to the polls to elect representatives to protect their rights. At times these representatives have passed laws to imprison individuals who speak or write in a manner objectionable to the government. Criticism of government, no matter how informed and responsible, is equated with "disloyalty." Understandably, attempts to overthrow government must be met by force. No such threat comes from those who simply criticize government. The threat comes in trying to repress them.

Under royal government, citizens had no right to say the king was wrong or utter any misgivings, no matter how mildly or cautiously expressed. Similarly, a sedition statute makes it a crime to find fault with the president, Congress, or the Supreme Court. Under either system, the individual is subordinate to those who exercise power. Patriots often say: "my country, right or wrong." During congressional debate in 1872, Senator Carl Schurz presented a more thoughtful and independent position: "My country, right or wrong; if right, to be kept right; and if wrong, to be set right."[31]

At hearings in 1987, Senator George Mitchell reflected on his service as a federal judge. He asked immigrants, about to take their oath to become U.S. citizens, why they came to America. Those who fled from totalitarian or repressive systems said, "We came here because here in America you can criticize the government without looking over your shoulder." They valued the individual freedom to disagree with public authorities. Mitchell emphasized that disagreement with government "was not evidence of lack of patriotism."[32] More recently, when critics of the Iraq War were attacked as unpatriotic in 2005, Senator Chuck Hagel advised: "[t]o question your government is not unpatriotic—to *not* question your government is unpatriotic."[33]

As with the Quasi-War against France in 1798, sedition laws generally appear when the nation faces an outside enemy or the government decides that prosecuting "seditionists" will yield partisan benefits. During the War of 1812, Jeffersonians did not enact a federal sedition law but nevertheless were willing to prosecute newspapers owned by Federalists. Jeffersonians relied not on a sedition statute but on the law of "seditious libel" borrowed from British law. This period is described in greater detail in Chapter 3.

In 1917, after the United States had entered into World War I, several states passed sedition legislation. One individual was prosecuted and convicted under a Minnesota law for remarking in public: "We were stampeded into this war by newspaper rot to pull England's chestnuts out of the fire."[34] Congress used the Montana sedition act as a model. With only the change of three words it became the federal sedition statute of 1918. It covered anyone who "shall willfully utter, print, write, or publish any disloyal, profane, scurrilous, or abusive language" about the form of the U.S. government, the U.S. Constitution, military or naval forces, the U.S. flag, or the uniform of the army or the navy, or use any language intended to bring the U.S. government, the Constitution, or U.S. armed forces "into contempt, scorn, contumely, or disrepute." The penalties: a fine of $10,000 and 20 years in prison, or both. How could prosecutors and judges possibly understand and apply such words as "scurrilous"? In the 1940 Smith Act, Congress adopted legislation to punish seditious utterances. The statute did not use the word *sedition*, but the government nonetheless proceeded to hold sedition trials.[35]

Should free speech be permitted in time of war? May citizens in a republic express their views? During World War I, justices of the Supreme Court reasoned that whatever rights of free speech and free press exist during peacetime, those freedoms are properly circumscribed when the country is at war. In a major case in 1919, Justice Oliver Wendell Holmes offered a famous analogy: "The most stringent protection of free speech would not protect a man in falsely shouting fire in a theater and causing a panic."[36] At issue in this case was the conviction of opponents of the war who mailed printed circulars intended to obstruct the recruitment of U.S. soldiers. What does shouting fire in a crowded theater have to do with circulating a leaflet that expresses an *opinion*? Citizens in a democratic country should be at liberty to express their views about the nation's commitment to war. They pay for it and provide the soldiers.

In the June 1919 issue of *Harvard Law Review*, Professor Zechariah Chafee Jr. rejected the theory that individual rights to speak and write about government policies are restricted in time of war. Under his analysis, the First Amendment applies in time of peace and war. Citizens are entitled to engage in broad debate about national policies. Chafee defended two interests: the right of an individual to express opinions and the need of society to hear and consider criticism. Raising objections is not seditious; it is a citizen's duty. Chafee noted that the framers who drafted the Bill of Rights, including the First Amendment, had just been through a war. It was especially in time of military emergencies that citizens need to speak out freely, because it is during such periods that government can inflict the greatest damage on constitutional rights. War brings burdens and sacrifices, including financial costs, military service, combat deaths, and casualties. The rights of speech and press during that period should be unimpaired.

To defend the American value of popular sovereignty and the system of checks and balances, Congress needs to assert its ample powers. Our liberties depend on independent lawmakers able and willing to correct presidential and judicial mistakes. The next two chapters examine the record of Congress in pushing back against the other branches and protecting the rights of citizens.

# Chapter Two
# Facing Executive Power

The framers looked to Congress as the first branch of government. Its powers appear in Article I of the Constitution. By contrast, reading the debates at the Philadelphia Convention provides little insight into what the delegates expected of presidential power. Beyond the executive powers listed in Article II, there is barely a glimpse of how the office of the president might evolve. The only express presidential power associated with the British king is the power to pardon, an act of grace and mercy that emerged centuries ago. Other presidential duties have British precedents: receiving ambassadors and serving as commander in chief.

Presidents have over the years claimed "emergency" and "inherent" powers that seem close cousin to monarchical powers. Unfortunately, some scholars have encouraged this trend, even if they later expressed regret for giving encouragement to illegal and abusive executive actions. For its part, Congress has failed to consistently check presidential excesses that threaten constitutional government and the rights and liberties of individuals. What are the legitimate sources of presidential power? Where does danger lie?

## Enumerated Powers Only?

On several occasions the Supreme Court has announced that the authority of the national government is defined by enumerated powers. Consider the Court's claim in 1995: "We start with first principles. The Constitution creates a Federal Government of enumerated powers." Two years later the Court stated: "Under our Constitution, the Federal Government is one of enumerated powers."[1] It is doubtful that a single framer had that understanding of the Constitution. If each branch possessed only powers specifically enumerated, the Court would have no power of judicial review, a power that is not expressly stated in the Constitution. Many other federal powers routinely exercised today (and even from the start) are not expressly stated in that document.

The Articles of Confederation attempted to confine government to enumerated powers. The states retained all powers except those "expressly delegated" to the national government. In 1791, during debate on the Tenth Amendment, it was proposed that the same language be used to limit the national government. Powers not "expressly delegated" to the national government would be reserved to the states or to the people. Madison strongly objected to limiting the federal government to express powers. He said the functions and responsibilities of government could not be delineated with such precision. It was impossible to confine a government to the exercise of express powers, for there "must necessarily be admitted powers by implication, unless the Constitution descended to recount every minutia."[2] Congress deleted "expressly" from the Tenth Amendment.

It is often claimed that Congress is restricted to enumerated powers but the president is not. Here is the argument. Article I of the Constitution begins: "All legislative Powers herein granted shall be vested in a Congress of the United States, which shall consist of a Senate and House of Representatives." The words "herein granted" do not appear in Article II: "The executive Power shall be vested in a President." From that language it is reasoned that Congress possesses only those powers specifically granted, whereas the president has the whole of the "executive Power" (powers specifically stated plus unnamed powers customarily associated with the executive).

As explained in one study, the president's powers "go beyond those specifically enumerated in Article II, Sections 2 and 3, and include at least some implied, residual executive powers, like the removal power, as well."[3] It is quite true that presidents have implied powers that can be reasonably drawn from express powers. Presidents have the express duty under the Constitution to see that the laws are faithfully executed and may therefore remove an executive official (including a department head) who interferes with the execution of a law. But implied powers are not unique to the president. They are available to the other branches. Congress has the express power to legislate. To legislate in an informed manner, it has the implied power to investigate, issue subpoenas, and hold executive officials and private citizens in contempt. To assure that statutes are being properly implemented, Congress has the implied power to conduct oversight of executive agencies and seek agency documents and testimony.

There is a second reason why congressional powers are not confined to powers expressly stated in Article I. It is what is called the Necessary and Proper Clause. Consider the breadth of this constitutional grant of power to Congress: "To make all Laws which shall be necessary and proper for carrying into Execution the foregoing [express] Powers, and all other Powers vested by this Constitution in the Government of the United States, or in any Department or Officer thereof." This provision has been interpreted over the years to grant Congress broad authority, not only over its own powers but extending to powers vested in "any Department or Officer thereof." In the celebrated case of *McCulloch v. Maryland* (1819), Chief Justice John Marshall offered a generous interpretation of congressional power under the clause: "Let the end be legitimate, let it be within the scope of the constitution, and all means which are appropriate, which are plainly adapted to that end, which are not prohibited, but consist with the letter and spirit of the constitution, are constitutional."[4]

## Operating Under the Prerogative

Beyond express and implied powers, presidents have exercised what has been called the "prerogative." In his *Second Treatise on Government* (1690), the British philosopher John Locke anticipated situations in which an executive must be at liberty to protect the community, with or without law. The power to act "according to discretion for the public good, without the prescription of the law and sometimes against it, is that which is called prerogative." The only limit placed by Locke on executive discretion was to act for the good of the people and not against it. In cases where the legislature or the people questioned the necessity or propriety of executive action, "there can be no judge on earth." The sole remedy: an "appeal to Heaven."

The American framers did not look to the skies to control executive abuse. If presidents decided to act in the absence of law or against it, they had to come to Congress and seek legislative authority, even if applied retroactively. After Congress had recessed in 1807, a British vessel fired on the American ship Chesapeake. Jefferson responded by ordering military purchases and reported his actions to Congress. He reasoned: "To have awaited a previous and special sanction by law would have lost occasions which might not be retrieved."[5] Congressional adjournments at that time were for much longer periods than today, especially in the second session. If Congress decided that Jefferson's initiative violated law or was abusive, it could act against him by withholding funds or setting in motion an impeachment trial. The president acts outside the law at risk. In Jefferson's case (and others), the remedy is secular, not celestial.

In his years of retirement, Jefferson remarked that observance of the written law is a high duty of a public official but not the highest. A higher priority is the law of self-preservation: "To lose our country by a scrupulous adherence to written law, would be to lose the law itself, with life, liberty, property and all those who are enjoying them with us; thus absurdly sacrificing the end to the means."[6] This version of the prerogative aims at national survival. Under this interpretation, the president's express power to see that the laws are faithfully executed might be waived in an emergency.

That precise condition faced President Abraham Lincoln in April 1861, when Congress was out of session. Responding to confederate attacks on Ft. Sumter in South Carolina, he issued proclamations calling forth the militia, withdrawing funds from the treasury without an appropriation, placing a blockade on the rebellious states, and suspending the writ of habeas corpus. In taking those emergency actions, he never claimed to possess authority to do what he did. He explained to Congress when it returned that his actions "whether strictly legal or not" were undertaken as a public necessity, "trusting then, as now, that Congress would readily ratify them."[7]

In other public messages Lincoln said he exercised the "war power," by which he meant whatever he had under Article II plus whatever legislative powers Congress had under Article I. As noted in his message, he believed his actions were not "beyond the constitutional competency of Congress." He therefore admitted to using congressional powers and understood he had to come to Congress, present his case, and ask for a statute to approve and legalize his actions, as though they had been done under the express authority and direction of Congress. In debating his request, lawmakers voted with the understanding that Lincoln exceeded his constitutional authority. Congress passed the bill and presented it to Lincoln for his signature. Through this conduct Lincoln preserved both the Union and the Constitution.

Those who believe the president may go to war without seeking authority from Congress frequently cite the Supreme Court's decision in *The Prize Cases* (1863), which upheld Lincoln's blockade in the South. However, Lincoln and his advisers never argued that he could take unilateral military actions against other nations without first coming to Congress for approval. In the 1863 case, Justice Robert Grier specifically denied that the president as commander in chief had any authority to initiate war against another country. What was at stake in the case was a domestic matter: civil war. It was internal, not external. Lincoln acted defensively, not offensively. Grier plainly stated that the president "has no power to initiate or declare a war either against a foreign nation or a domestic State." The executive branch agreed. During oral argument, the attorney representing the president acknowledged that Lincoln's actions had nothing to do with "the right *to initiate a war, as a voluntary act of sovereignty*. That is vested only in Congress."[8]

## Upping the Ante: Inherent Powers

Beyond implied powers and the prerogative (yet often confused with each) is the claim that the president possesses certain "inherent powers." Here one needs to repair to the dictionary to understand terms. The fifth edition of *Black's Law Dictionary* gives this account of *inherent*: "An authority possessed without its being derived from another. . . . Powers over and beyond those explicitly granted in the Constitution or reasonably to be implied from express powers." Inherent is clearly set apart from express and implied powers. That definition remained in the sixth edition. The eighth edition, published in 2004, contains different language: "A power that necessarily derives from an office, position, or status." Again, the authority is not express or implied. It exists somewhere in the nature of the office or person.

The purpose of a constitution is to limit government to preserve a realm of individual freedom. Express and implied powers serve that objective. Inherent powers do not. They are too open-ended. What "inheres" in the president? The standard collegiate dictionary explains that *inherent* covers the "essential character of something: belonging by nature or habit."That is much too vague and uncertain for a constitutional system. Who knows what is essential or belongs to nature? Dictionaries cross-reference *inherent* to *intrinsic*, which means something within a body (as distinct from extrinsic). It belongs "to the essential nature or constitution of a thing." Such words as *inherent*, *essential*, *nature*, and *intrinsic* open the door to broad executive powers that are destructive of a constitutional order and threaten individual liberties.

Also falling within the category of inherent power is the claim that the president functions as "sole organ" in foreign affairs. In *United States v. Curtiss-Wright* (1936),[9] the Supreme Court upheld a congressional grant of power to the president in international relations. The power delegated was exclusively legislative, not executive, yet Justice George Sutherland devoted pages of dicta (extraneous matter) to claim that the president possesses plenary and unchecked powers in foreign affairs. He cited this statement by John Marshall when he served as a member of the House of Representatives in 1800: "The President is the sole organ of the nation in its external relations, and its sole representative with foreign nations."[10]

The "sole organ" doctrine has been cited ever since to justify presidential actions even when they violate statutes and treaties. A recent example of invoking that doctrine is the defense of secret surveillance by the National Security Agency (NSA) after 9/11, despite enactment of the Foreign Intelligence Surveillance Act (FISA) that requires warrants from a court. The Justice Department concluded that the NSA program was constitutional because the president may exercise "well-recognized inherent constitutional authority as Commander in Chief and sole organ for the Nation in foreign affairs to conduct warrantless surveillance of enemy forces for intelligence purposes to detect and disrupt armed attacks on the United States."[11] Some case law can be read to support presidential action outside of FISA, but the argument is strained and unpersuasive.[12]

When one reads the congressional debate in 1800 it is obvious that Marshall never claimed for the president any authority to act outside the law. At no time in his lengthy public service as secretary of state, member of Congress, or chief justice of the United States, did he ever come close to supporting such a doctrine. What was debated in 1800 was whether Congress should censure or impeach President John Adams for handing over to England a person charged with murder. Some lawmakers condemned Adams for invading the powers of the judiciary.

It was at that point that Marshall took the floor to argue that there were no grounds for taking any punitive action against the president. What Adams had done was to fulfill his constitutional duty to see that the laws be faithfully executed. The law was the Jay Treaty. Article 27 provided that the United States and Great Britain would deliver up to each other "all persons" charged with murder or forgery. Marshall was not arguing for any kind of inherent or exclusive executive power, much less a power that found its existence outside the Constitution. Adams was simply carrying out a treaty. He was not the sole organ in formulating the treaty. He was the sole organ in *implementing* it. Article II states that it is the president's duty to "take Care that the Laws be faithfully executed." Article VI provides that all treaties "shall be the supreme Law of the Land." Only after government policy had been established through the collective action of the executive and legislative branches, either by treaty or statute, did the president emerge as the sole organ in implementing national policy.

Later, as chief justice of the Supreme Court, Marshall held firm to his position that the making of foreign policy is a joint exercise by the executive and legislative branches. Unlike England and the British royal prerogative, as set forth by William Blackstone in his *Commentaries*, the U.S. president did not enjoy plenary and exclusive power over foreign affairs and the war power. With the war power, Marshall looked solely to Congress—not the president—for authority to take the country to war: "The whole powers of war being, by the constitution of the United States, vested in congress, the acts of that body can alone be resorted to as our guides in this enquiry."[13]

An 1804 opinion by Marshall underscores the degree to which the United States had broken free of royal authority over foreign affairs and war. At the start of the Quasi-War against France, Congress passed legislation to authorize the president to seize vessels sailing *to* French ports. President Adams exceeded the statute by ordering American ships to capture vessels sailing *to or from* French ports. A U.S. naval captain was sued for violating the statute. Initially, Marshall thought that the captain's action was appropriate because he had followed the instructions of his superior, the president. Marshall, however, concluded that the president "cannot change the nature of the transaction, or legalize an act which, without those instructions, would have been a plain trespass."[14] Even when a president issues an order as commander in chief in time of war, an action contrary to statutory policy is invalid under the Constitution.

## Exercising Inherent Powers

Anyone who studies the use of inherent presidential power will find that these claims of plenary and exclusive authority are regularly met and defeated by congressional and judicial action. One example is the decision by President Harry Truman to seize steel mills in 1952 to prosecute the war in Korea. By that time the war was extremely unpopular in the United States because of lives lost, fortunes spent, and little hope of military victory. Americans did not "rally round the president." Instead of exercising existing statutory authority to place an 80-day cooling-off period on the pending strike by labor unions, Truman chose to act independently by invoking broad emergency authority.

The Justice Department made things worse in court by defending his action solely on the basis of inherent executive power. The attorney handling the case for the administration told the trial judge that courts were powerless to control this exercise of presidential power. To the attorney, only two limits on presidential power existed: the ballot box and impeachment.

The trial judge inquired whether when the sovereign people ratified the Constitution "it limited Congress, it limited the judiciary, but did not limit the executive." Unfazed, the attorney responded: "That's our conception, Your Honor." The judge probed further, asking whether once the president determines that an emergency exists, "the courts cannot even review whether it is an emergency." Back came the confident reply: "That is correct."[15]

This theory of presidential power backfired. Reporters asked Truman, if he could seize steel mills, could he also seize newspapers and radio stations? He said that under the Constitution the president could do whatever he thought best for the country. Editorials around the country condemned him for acting unconstitutionally and for trying to wield dictatorial powers. The trial judge issued an injunction to stop the steel seizure, releasing a blistering opinion that shredded the administration's claim of inherent and emergency powers for the president. The administration had proposed a form of government "alien to our Constitutional government of limited powers."[16] The judge acknowledged that a nationwide strike could do extensive damage to the country, but concluded that a strike "would be less injurious to the public than the injury which would flow from a timorous judicial recognition that there is some basis for this claim to unlimited and unrestrained Executive power, which would be implicit in a failure to grant the injunction."[17] The Supreme Court, divided six to three, upheld the trial court.[18]

The Nixon administration argued that the president had inherent authority not to spend appropriated funds. In what became known as the impoundment dispute, President Nixon proceeded to cut programs in half and even eliminate them. Congress held hearings to explore the legal basis for this theory. Litigation led to about 80 cases, with the administration losing all but 2 or 3 and losing the 1 case that reached the Supreme Court. After several years of confrontation, Nixon agreed to sign the Impoundment Control Act of 1974, establishing restrictions on efforts to temporarily slow down a program or terminate funding entirely. What began as a claim of unlimited presidential power ended with the acceptance of statutory restraints.

I was fortunate to have a front-row seat to this battle. Because of two articles I had published on the impoundment issue, Senator Sam J. Ervin Jr. invited me to work with his Subcommittee on Separation of Powers. I sat behind him at hearings to provide professional counsel, sat next to him at committee markup to offer views on amendments submitted to the draft bill, wrote the conference report, and prepared a "dialogue" between Senator Ervin and Senator Hubert Humphrey that went into the *Congressional Record* to explain the intent of the bill. I received a letter from President Nixon, dated July 22, 1974, because of my "special interest in this legislation." The package included a ceremonial signing pen.[19]

Nixon also claimed inherent authority to conduct warrantless domestic surveillance. He lost in court at every level: federal district court, the Court of Appeals for the Sixth Circuit, and the Supreme Court. The Sixth Circuit, in *United States v. United States District Court* (1971), remarked: "It is strange, indeed, that in this case the traditional power of sovereigns like King George III should be invoked on behalf of an American President to defeat one of the fundamental freedoms for which the founders of this country overthrew King George's reign."[20] Unanimously, the Supreme Court affirmed the Sixth Circuit. This litigation focused on domestic surveillance. Congress later passed legislation to limit presidential authority in the field of national security surveillance (the Foreign Intelligence Surveillance Act of 1978).

Following the terrorist attacks of 9/11, President George W. Bush invoked inherent powers in several areas. He issued a military order on November 13, 2001, to authorize military tribunals for noncitizens who belonged to al Qaeda, engaged in international terrorism, or harbored such individuals. The Justice Department pointed to statutory authority to justify his action but also insisted that the president had inherent authority to convene the tribunals, even in the absence of specific congressional authority. Bush's initiative represented a "core exercise of the president's commander-in-chief and foreign affairs powers during wartime and is entitled to be given effect by the courts."[21] In 2006, the Supreme Court in *Hamdan v. Rumsfeld* found that argument without merit. No such inherent, Article II authority existed. It was necessary for President Bush to seek legislation, which passed in the form of the Military Commissions Act.[22]

Similarly, the administration argued that President Bush possessed constitutional authority to designate U.S. citizens (Yaser Esam Hamdi and Jose Padilla) as "enemy combatants" and hold them incommunicado year after year without access to an attorney or trial. The Justice Department advised courts not to interfere with presidential decisions in this area, insisting that the Constitution vests the president "with exclusive authority to act as commander in chief and as the nation's sole organ in foreign affairs."[23] Courts should not try to "second-guess" presidential judgments and intrude upon "the constitutional prerogative of the commander in chief." In 2004, eight justices of the Supreme Court rejected the administration's central argument that the detention of a U.S. citizen was quintessentially a presidential decision. Justice O'Connor announced in *Hamdi v. Rumsfeld*: "We necessarily reject the Government's assertion that separation of powers principles mandate a heavily circumscribed role for the courts in such circumstances. . . . Whatever power the United States Constitution envisions for the Executive in its exchanges with other nations or with enemy organizations in times of conflict, it most assuredly envisions a role for all three branches when individual liberties are at stake."[24]

Legal memos produced in the Bush administration concluded that terrorist suspects picked up in Afghanistan, Pakistan, and other countries could be held indefinitely at the U.S. naval base at Guantánamo Bay, Cuba, without interference by the judiciary. The naval base, according to the administration, was outside the United States and therefore beyond the jurisdiction of federal judges. The United States occupies the base under a lease entered into with the Cuban government in 1903 and exercises complete jurisdiction and control over the property. In court, the administration argued that the base was nonetheless beyond the jurisdiction of courts because the United States did not possess "sovereignty" over the area. Cuba did. That defense of presidential discretion was rejected by the Supreme Court in *Rasul v. Bush* (2004).[25] Four years later, in *Boumediene v. Bush*,[26] the Court again insisted that federal courts had a role to play in resolving the issues of detainees held at the naval base.

Finally, the Bush administration decided to violate FISA and secretly conduct warrantless surveillance. A primary part of the FISA statute is the requirement that executive officials must first obtain a warrant from a specially created court. When the project was revealed by the *New York Times* in December 2005, the administration relied in part on inherent presidential powers in its defense. Private parties filed many court cases to challenge NSA surveillance. After much activity by all three branches, the administration came to Congress and obtained statutory authority.[27]

## Championing the Imperial Presidency

The framers understood that all three branches would attempt to expand their powers. Checks and balances were available to fight off encroachments. It is unlikely that any framer could have anticipated that scholars would later throw their weight wholly behind presidential power and dismiss legislative and judicial constraints. Especially after World War II, historians, political scientists, and law professors placed the president on a pedestal and attributed to that office a host of wondrous qualities. Scholars expected occupants of the Oval Office to act invariably for the "national interest" on the basis of unrivaled expertise and benevolent intentions. Political idolatry of any stripe, including the divine right of kings or waiting for a Great Man, found no support among the framers. They did not put their faith in a single person. Fearing concentrated power, they believed in process and structural checks.

The framers were well aware that British precedents assigned all of external affairs, including the war power, to the king. William Blackstone in his *Commentaries* treated all of foreign affairs and the war power as monarchical: the power to declare war, make treaties, appoint ambassadors, order reprisals (small wars), and issue letters of marque (authorizing private citizens to contribute ships and other property for military operations). Under the U.S. Constitution, those powers were either given expressly to Congress in Article I or shared between the president and the Senate (treaties and appointments). Not one of those powers was vested exclusively with the president. The framers broke decisively with the English and Blackstone model.

In June 1950, President Truman went to war against North Korea without ever coming to Congress for authority. It was the first time that a president had ever unilaterally committed the nation to a major war without first seeking legislative authority. For 160 years presidents regularly came to Congress to request either a declaration or authorization for significant military commitments. The academic community in 1950 had an opportunity to challenge Truman's actions and remind him and the public of fundamental constitutional values. Instead, prominent scholars and professors rushed to his defense and concocted feeble arguments they would later regret and retract.

The historian Henry Steele Commager rebuked the critics of Truman's intervention in Korea, briskly stating that their objections "have no support in law or in history." Supremely confident of his understanding, the matter seemed "so hackneyed a theme that even politicians might reasonably be expected to be familiar with it."[28] Commager cited precedents from a number of presidents but not a single one came close to justifying Truman's action. Commager believed that strong presidents may act boldly without any threat to democracy or the constitutional system. There were no grounds, he advised, for distrusting executive authority. What had happened to scholarly appreciation for separation of powers, checks and balances, and concerns about political mistakes and abuse?

Less than two decades later, with the country mired in a bitter war in Southeast Asia, Commager publicly apologized for his earlier unrestrained enthusiasm for presidential power. In testimony before the Senate Foreign Relations Committee in 1967 he urged a reconsideration of executive-legislative relations in the field of foreign affairs and the war power. Four years later he told the committee that "it is very dangerous to allow the president to, in effect, commit us to a war from which we cannot withdraw, because the war-making power is lodged and was intended to be lodged in the Congress." Had he just learned that? Probably not. More likely he decided in 1950 to remove his academic hat and don a partisan one.

Another major supporter of Truman's military action in Korea was the historian Arthur M. Schlesinger Jr. In the past he had written a number of books extolling the virtues and strengths of such presidents as Andrew Jackson and Franklin D. Roosevelt. He wrote another glowing tribute to John F. Kennedy. He remained a presidency man with little regard for or understanding of constitutional limits and checks. The more power concentrated in the president, the better. Ironically, after this pattern of hagiographic studies about executive power he would publish a critique in 1973 called *The Imperial Presidency*. He had done much to defend imperial pretensions.

In 1950, at the start of the Korean War, Schlesinger issued a public attack on Senator Robert Taft for saying that Truman "had no authority whatever to commit American troops to Korea without consulting Congress and without congressional approval."[29] Taft charged that Truman had usurped authority and violated statutes and the Constitution. Schlesinger dismissed Taft's analysis as "demonstrably irresponsible." He issued a stern rebuke: "Until Senator Taft and his friends succeed in rewriting American history according to their own specifications these facts must stand as obstacles to their efforts to foist off their current political prejudices as eternal American verities."[30]

There were indeed demonstrably irresponsible statements and foisting off of political prejudices, but they were by Schlesinger—not Taft. The historical examples Schlesinger identified had zero bearing on Truman's claim that he could go to war against another country without first coming to Congress for authority. Presidential scholar Edward S. Corwin reacted to Commager and Schlesinger by criticizing the "course of constitutional development, practical and polemical, which ascribes to the President a truly royal prerogative in the field of foreign relations, and does so without indicating any correlative legal or constitutional control to which he is answerable." Corwin warned: "Our high-flying prerogative men appear to resent the very idea that the only possible source of such control, Congress to wit, has any effective power in the premises at all."[31]

After witnessing the abuse of presidential power in the Vietnam War and the Watergate scandal, Schlesinger publicly apologized in his book, *The Imperial Presidency*, for calling Taft's statement "demonstrably irresponsible." He said that he had responded with "a flourish of historical documentation and, also, hyperbole." His errors went beyond flourishes and hyperbole. The historical documentation he offered had nothing to do with Truman's war in Korea. Unlike Taft, Schlesinger had no constitutional model other than a slavish devotion to presidential power, in this case a convenient one. Truman was a Democrat and Schlesinger remained a party loyalist.

In a book he coauthored with Alfred de Grazia, *Congress and the Presidency* (1967), Schlesinger counseled that "something must be done to assure the Congress a more authoritative and continuing voice in fundamental decisions in foreign policy." In *The Imperial Presidency*, Schlesinger analyzed the domestic and international pressures that helped push power to the presidency: "It must be said that historians and political scientists, this writer among them, contributed to the presidential mystique."[32] Why would a scholar, devoted to his craft, engage in mystery-making? Corwin and other scholars chose not to. It is important for every individual, including famous scholars, to reevaluate and rethink what they have said and written. But independent scholarly analysis is needed at the time of constitutional violations, not two decades later.

Probably no presidential study has been as influential as Richard Neustadt's *Presidential Power* (1960). The book was popular with professors and students because it offered lively case studies and put an emphasis on practical politics. However, entirely missing from the book was anything to do with institutional, legal, or constitutional values. Although the book is often remembered for defining presidential power as "the power to persuade," Neustadt clearly urged presidents to take power, not share it. Political power was something to be acquired and concentrated in the presidency. The power was to be used for *personal* use, not for something more general. He urged presidents to practice the "politics of self-aggrandizement." Because President Dwight D. Eisenhower appeared to care more about national unity than personal power, Neustadt dismissed him as an "amateur."

Among the case studies in the book is the Korean War, including Truman's dismissal of General Douglas MacArthur and the Supreme Court's action in striking down the steel seizure. Not one word was devoted to analyzing Truman's legal and constitutional authority to initiate the war without congressional approval. No attention was given to Truman's inflated definition of emergency power. Certainly he did not practice the politics of "persuasion" to convince Congress and the people about the war. To Neustadt, those issues did not matter. What counted was Truman's intention to make decisions, take initiatives, and be the "man-in-charge." Neustadt's advice: "The more determinedly a President seeks power, the more he will be likely to bring vigor to his clerkship. As he does so he contributes to the energy of government."[33]

Alexander Hamilton and other framers saw the need for "energy" in the executive, but it was energy within the law, not outside it. Otherwise, why would the Constitution direct the president to take care that the laws be faithfully executed? Executive power under the Constitution is more than making decisions, taking initiatives, and bringing vigor and energy to the office. Neustadt provided advice for "a man who seeks to maximize his power." Such a framework describes the administrations of Franklin Roosevelt and Winston Churchill but fits equally well the careers of Adolf Hitler, Benito Mussolini, and Joseph Stalin. One system is constitutional, limited by checks and balances; the other is dictatorial. By wholly ignoring law and the Constitution, Neustadt never distinguished between these competing models of government.[34]

## Defenders of Congress

Commager, Schlesinger, and Neustadt wrote and spoke as academic liberals, putting their weight fully behind presidential power. Conservatives in early periods of American history had also supported central power, especially in the executive, to guard against possible dangers and risks from what they feared would be mob democracy. But later they were more likely to endorse an independent Congress and the system of checks and balances, finding safety and protection in decentralized government and the deliberative process. Placing trust in a single official to guide the country did violence to their principles.

Over the past seven decades, critiques of presidential power came typically from scholars who touted conservative or Whiggish views (supportive of legislative power). They were the ones who kept alive the values of republican government. In his classic *The Road to Serfdom* (1944), Friedrich A. Hayek warned about the transfer of legislative power to "experts" in the executive branch. He said the shift posed a threat to democracy and would produce arbitrary power and dictatorship. Conservatives counted Hayek among their ranks, but in a thoughtful article he declined full membership, preferring to classify himself as "an unrepentant Old Whig—with the stress on the 'old.'"[35]

Another conservative, James Burnham, published a full-fledged defense of congressional prerogatives in *Congress and the American Tradition* (1959). He said the framers believed that "in a republican and representative governmental system the preponderating share of power was held and exercised by the legislature."[36] He explained that conservatives favored the relative power of Congress "within the diffused power equilibrium." Liberals tended to distrust Congress and prefer executive power. As to the war power, Burnham concluded that by "the intent of the Founding Fathers and the letter and tradition of the Constitution, the bulk of the sovereign war power was assigned to Congress."[37] Preserving liberty and strengthening a strong legislature were closely linked: "If Congress ceases to be an actively functioning political institution, then political liberty in the United States will soon come to an end."[38]

In 1960, an article by Willmoore Kendall placed a conservative imprimatur on the role of Congress in safeguarding republican government and individual liberties. He listed some conventional generalizations about the virtues of the president and Congress, with the president representing "high principle" and Congress associated with low principle, no principle at all, reaction, and unintelligence. Kendall found those stereotypes not only trite and inaccurate but destructive of the system of checks and balances and constitutional principles.[39]

The conservative American Enterprise Institute sponsored a series of studies edited by Alfred de Grazia and published in 1967. The title left no doubt about the commitment to republican government: *Congress: The First Branch of Government.* De Grazia described Congress as "the central institution of the American democratic republic. Unless it functions well and powerfully, much more so than it has in the past, the road to a bureaucratic state and kind of monarchic government will be opened up."[40] To those who rhapsodized about the coherence, unity, harmony, and rationality of the president, de Grazia reminded them that the president is "a Congress with a skin thrown over him."[41] If you look carefully within the executive branch you will see fragmentation, divisions, compromise, and various interests fighting for control. The difference is that the legislative process is largely visible; the executive process is not.

Ronald Moe published a book of readings in 1971 called *Congress and the President: Allies and Adversaries.* His selections underscored the vital importance of Congress in a constitutional order. He described what seemed to him as the liberals' attraction to the presidency: "Historically, there has been a tendency for intellectuals to be wary of democratic legislatures, and hesitant about the ability of people to completely run their affairs, especially the affairs of state."[42] He noted that liberals concluded that their influence within the executive branch would be greater than in Congress.

## Switching Sides

In recent decades, political scientists, historians, and law professors have begun to rethink the scholarly fascination with the presidency. In a paper delivered at the 1970 American Political Science Association annual meeting, Thomas Cronin criticized existing textbooks for promoting "inflated and unrealistic interpretations of presidential competence and beneficence." Scholarly works inclined toward "exaggerations about past and future presidential performance." Infatuation with the presidency necessarily diminishes the importance of Congress, the judiciary, the Constitution, the rule of law, and the democratic process.

Having nourished the "textbook presidency," liberals turned against it for a time because of the Vietnam War and Watergate. Yet some scholars see those periods as mere aberrations, attributable to poor misjudgments by a few occupants of the White House. Taking Vietnam and Watergate as the exception, not the rule, they continued to endorse and teach Neustadt's model of presidential power. Students were taught that American foreign policy and military commitments are dominated by presidents and their advisors, giving little attention to constitutional principles.[43] Admissions of error by Commager and Schlesinger appeared to be mere mid-course corrections of no lasting value.

With liberals reconsidering their views, some conservatives switched course and defended a strong presidency. An article in the *Wall Street Journal* on September 20, 1974, by Irving Kristol was called "The Inexorable Rise of the Executive." Especially in the area of foreign affairs he wanted a strong president. The "imperial presidency," in one form or another, was "here to stay." Conservatives like Kristol looked to threats from the Soviet Union and placed their bets with presidential power. Constitutional values did not matter. To Norman Podhoretz, editor of the conservative magazine *Commentary*, the attacks on the presidency after Vietnam and Watergate damaged "the main institutional capability the United States possesses for conducting an overt fight against the spread of Communist power in the world."[44] For Podhoretz and others, the outside threat of communism justified the abandonment or diminishment of constitutional checks.

Essentially, Kristol, Podhoretz, and other conservatives (later called "neoconservatives") adopted the same position as the liberal trio of Commager, Schlesinger, and Neustadt. Each side calculated which branch would better serve its political agenda or national needs. Neither side paid attention to the Constitution, separation of powers, checks and balances, or the structural principles that provide fundamental safeguards for protecting individual rights. These liberals and conservatives were willing to move the United States toward a centralized political system to counter the power of the Soviet Union.

Conservative scholars in recent decades gave little attention to Congress, other than to write derogatory studies. One example is a book edited by Gordon S. Jones and John A. Marini entitled *The Imperial Congress* (1988). Fortunately, there were exceptions to this pattern, including the works of Joseph Bessette and a volume he edited with Jeffrey Tulis.[45] It was their purpose to assure that the president operates within the constraints of public law, and to that extent they broke decisively with Neustadt, David Barber, and other presidential scholars. Mickey Edwards, former Republican member of the House of Representatives from Oklahoma, has been active in promoting checks and balances and an independent Congress. In *Reclaiming Conservatism* (2008), he criticizes Republicans after 9/11 for "failing to scrutinize President Bush's determination to go to war in Iraq." Decisions of war, he said, "rest with the people, not an imperial 'decider-in-chief.'" Restraint of power and the division between the three branches "are at the core not only of America but of American conservatism."[46]

## Defender of National Security

Over the last decade, a prominent voice promoting broad presidential powers in foreign affairs and national security is a conservative, John Yoo. Long active with the Federalist Society, he served as one of the deputies in the Office of Legal Counsel in the administration of George W. Bush. Later he returned to his position as professor of law at the University of California at Berkeley.

The framers consciously and deliberately broke with the British models of John Locke and William Blackstone, who placed all of external power and military decisions with the executive. At the Philadelphia Convention, Pierce Butler was the only delegate who wanted to vest the war power with the president, "who will have all the requisite qualities, and will not make war but when the Nation will support it."[47] Every other delegate spoke against Butler at Philadelphia and in the state ratification debates. Elbridge Gerry told his colleagues at Philadelphia that he "never expected to hear in a republic a motion to empower the Executive alone to declare war."[48]

That settled consensus was challenged by John Yoo in a lengthy article in the *California Law Review* in 1996. Relying on English history, he concluded that "the Framers created a framework designed to encourage presidential initiatives in war." Congress was given a role in war-making decisions, he argued, but not because of its authority to declare war. Legislative constraints came from powers over funding and impeachment. To Yoo, the Declare War Clause did not give Congress the power to initiate war. Instead, its purpose was to announce to other nations that America was at war, even if started by the president. In Yoo's words: "A declaration did not create or authorize; it recognized." The clause did not "add to Congress' store of war powers at the expense of the President." Rather, it gave Congress "a judicial role in declaring that a state of war exists between the United States and another nation."[49] In matters of war, Yoo wrote, federal courts "were to have no role at all."

Most law reviews are not peer-edited by experts. Second- and third-year students look for manuscripts that present original themes, are likely to stimulate debate, and be cited by other authorities and the courts. Yoo's article met those standards. In its published form it ran 139 pages and contained 625 footnotes. Even if student editors are no match for the intellectual depth and experience of authors who submit articles for consideration, it should have been within the capacity of students at the *California Law Review* to ask Yoo four fundamental questions.

First, if the framers created a constitution to encourage presidents to initiate war, why is the Constitution written the way it is? All of Blackstone's foreign policy prerogatives are vested either solely in Congress by Article I or shared between the president and the Senate. Not one of those prerogatives appears in Article II exclusively for the president. The president is commander in chief, but only one delegate (Pierce Butler) thought that the president could be safely entrusted to initiate war.

Second, if the constitutional design is intended to encourage presidents to initiate war, why did such prominent framers as John Jay, James Madison, and James Wilson consistently warn about the dangers of executive wars? Why did they assure voters in the ratification debates that the Constitution took the power of war away from the executive and placed it safely in Congress, the people's branch? Those framers viewed that constitutional principle as crucial and fundamental.

Third, if the Constitution authorizes presidents to initiate wars against other countries, why did every president from George Washington to Franklin D. Roosevelt, who decided it was necessary to engage in offensive war, come to Congress to request either a legislative declaration or authorization? No president before Truman ever claimed he could unilaterally take the country to war. Even President James Polk, having placed American soldiers in a disputed region near the Mexican border, did not believe he had the right to go to war on his own. After hostilities broke out he said that "war exists" but nevertheless came to Congress to request a declaration. Polk and Congress understood that the legislative branch needed to exercise an independent decision to authorize war, not merely bless a president's initiative.

Fourth, if courts have "no role" in questions of war, why did the Supreme Court decide such war power cases as *Bas v. Tingy* (1800), *Talbot v. Seeman* (1801), and *Little v. Barreme* (1804)? The students at the law review might have even found *United States v. Smith* (1806), a war power case decided by a federal circuit court.[50] In all of those cases the courts looked not to the president for deciding war power issues but to Congress alone. From 1789 to 1950 all three branches understood that offensive wars against other countries could be authorized solely by Congress.[51]

The scope and authority of the war power will be examined more closely in Chapter 5. Here it is sufficient to recall the congressional debate in 1917 to declare war against Germany. President Woodrow Wilson had promised in the election of 1916 to "keep the country out of war." Once returned to the White House, he decided it was time to join the bloody conflagration that became known as World War I. There was no claim on his part that the decision was his alone. He knew he had to come to Congress for statutory authority. For some members of Congress it was enough that the president had made his move and it was their duty to stand with him. Lawmakers exhausted every stale phrase possible to defend a declaration of war, including "wherever the flag leads we must follow," "America first," and the "command is 'Forward!'" Another shallow argument frequently repeated: "Stand by the president." Representative Ernest Lundeen, Republican from Minnesota, took dead aim at that platitude:

> There are those who insist on the slogan, "Stand by the President." Stand by the President! Which one—the one that "kept us out of war" or the one that plunged us in? You might as well say, "Stand by Congress." Its duties are just as important and its rights just as sacred as those of the Chief Executive. A better slogan would be, Stand by the Government. . . . But why not have a still better and a still greater slogan and sentiment that comes out of the great American heart: Stand by the people. . . . I refuse to crown the President with kingly powers. I am standing by Congress in the performance of its constitutional duties. The mandate of the people is the only command I recognize, and no one can swerve me from that position.[52]

Today, both conservative and liberal scholars are busy rethinking presidential power. The halo has been removed somewhat and in its place is a more realistic attitude about the capacities of those who sit in the Oval Office. One of the curious patterns is the extent to which presidential scholars over the years have developed elaborate theories and models of an informed, responsible, and enlightened president, and how those models have scant bearing on those elected as president. From Truman to the present, occupants of the White House fall far short of the glamorous and idealized models fashioned by scholars and widely accepted by the voters.

## Who Represents the National Interest?

One healthy step would be to discard the facile doctrine that associates the president with the "national interest" and lawmakers with "local" or "special interests." There is nothing automatically negative about local or special interests and certainly nothing automatically virtuous about the national interest. Every nation has a right to preserve its sovereignty and fight off invaders. There is a national interest in preserving and protecting the Constitution. There is a national interest for each branch to check each other. It is in the country's interest to have citizens criticize government, both for reasons of free speech and to limit the damage that government can do, especially in times of emergency.

It is not in the national interest to pass sedition laws, although advocates of such bills defend them precisely for that reason. The country and the Constitution are weakened by sending men and women to prison for speaking their minds. It is not in the national interest to have lawmakers spend so much time raising money for their reelection, time needed to devote to their constitutional and institutional duties. It was not in the national interest for the United States to intervene in Vietnam, even if President Johnson said it was. In his private moments he and his advisers knew it was foolhardy to commit troops to Southeast Asia. He escalated the war in Vietnam for personal and partisan reasons, not for the national interest.[53]

The Soviet Union considered it was in their national interest to spread world communism. To promote that cause, individual rights had to be suppressed. Nazi Germany concluded it was in their national interest to occupy the Sudetenland, Austria, Czechoslovakia, Poland, and the rest of Europe. Individual rights had to be subordinated to pursue this collective effort. If the national interest dominates, minorities and the politics of pluralism have no freedom to operate. The state will always trump the individual.

The perils of promoting the "national interest" have been well described by J. David Singer, who referred to it as "a smokescreen by which we all too often oversimplify the world, denigrate our rivals, enthrall our citizens, and justify acts of dubious morality and efficacy." The overriding danger is that when presidents or politicians invoke the national interest, the general public will "snap to attention, do their duty and turn off their ethical and intellectual equipment."[54] A republican form of government depends on individuals (and members of Congress) willing to exercise independent judgment.

On April 15, 1834, President Andrew Jackson in his protest of the Senate's vote to censure him described the president as "the direct representative of the American people." Presidents have a representative function, but they are elected by a portion of the country. Because of third parties, they often take office with less than 50 percent of the popular vote. Generally they have a narrow margin over defeated candidates. Members of Congress represent smaller territories, but to pass a bill these local and state interests must form a consensus. Why shouldn't the final product represent the national interest as well as, or better than, a president's proposal? Moreover, what emerges from the legislative branch reflects the agreement of *elected* officials. Other than the president and the vice president, the executive branch consists of careerists and political appointees.

Presidents cannot govern effectively by focusing exclusively on the national interest. To prevail, they necessarily seek the support of local, special, and sectional interests. Satisfying special interests can be in the national interest. Otherwise, we would never have congressionally funded bridges, roads, reclamation projects, housing assistance, government buildings, disaster relief, Pell education grants, food stamps, child nutrition, and much else that is regularly included in the federal budget.

## Reconsidering Presidential Power

Presidents have injured themselves, their parties, and the country by embarking on policies claimed to be in the national interest. What is announced as national interest is often a broad cloak that conceals personal and party interests. In the 1980s, Larry Berman published a number of probing works on the miscalculations of President Lyndon Johnson in widening the Vietnam War. Using declassified documents Berman spotlighted deliberate manipulations and the steady reliance on illusions that eventually discredited Johnson, his senior advisers, and the Democratic Party. Berman's books include *Planning a Tragedy: The Americanization of the War in Vietnam* (1982) and *Lyndon Johnson's War: The Road to Stalemate in Vietnam* (1989). John Burke and Fred Greenstein, in *How Presidents Test Reality: Decisions on Vietnam, 1954 and 1965*

(1989), explained how Johnson's style of leadership (compared unfavorably with Eisenhower's) undermined the reality, feasibility, and constitutionality of U.S. national security policy.

H. R. McMaster, an air force major, published *Dereliction of Duty: Lyndon Johnson, Robert McNamara, the Joint Chiefs of Staff, and the Lies That Led to Vietnam* (1998), a scathing attack on the decisions that precipitated failures in Vietnam. In biting prose he captures Johnson's partisan calculations, poor judgments by Secretary of Defense McNamara, the timidity of the joint chiefs for failing to offer realistic options, the arrogance of Pentagon planners, and a persistent record of stealth and deception by executive officials.

Political scientist George Edwards, in an article published in 1991, described the broad constitutional role for Congress in matters of war: "There is little question that the Constitution allocates to Congress a central role in determining the major elements of national security policy if Congress chooses to do so."[55] He sharply questioned the conventional models that assigned to the president and executive officials a decided superiority in providing competent, coherent, and rational policy analysis. He found little evidence that the executive branch possessed any monopoly on wisdom that could not benefit from the regular deliberative process offered by Congress.

The University Press of Kansas regularly publishes books that analyze the importance of congressional and judicial checks on presidential military decisions. In *The Constitution and the Conduct of American Foreign Policy* (1996), David Gray Adler and Larry George edited a collection of 14 articles that looked in depth at interbranch relations in formulating national security policy. Six years later, in *The Presidency and the Law: The Clinton Legacy*, Adler teamed with Michael Genovese to explore the legal and constitutional controversies of President Bill Clinton.

Alexander DeConde, in *Presidential Machismo* (2000), released a trenchant analysis of the costs of presidential wars. He noted that presidential scholars had given the office "fictitious qualities that defied reality." He found no substantial body of evidence that in matters of war "one man can decide better than many or that the presidency ennobles the incumbent." The great danger to constitutional government, he advised, "lurks in executive machismo in the conduct of foreign affairs because it breeds contempt for law, can subvert democratic institutions, and could lead to tyranny."[56]

In an article published in 2002, Richard Pious urged a reconsideration of Neustadt's formulations, such as his distinction between the amateur (Eisenhower) who thinks first of the public interest and then of the political stakes, compared to the professional (Franklin Roosevelt) who defines the public interest in terms of his political advantage. Pious noted that the distinctions by Neustadt "have been at the core of our theoretical understanding of presidential power, but they cannot account for the spectacular failures of presidents such as Nixon, Johnson, or Clinton, all of whom understood and acted on their power stakes and showed no signs of being willing to sacrifice their political interests for any abstract conceptions of the public interest."[57]

That essay, enriched by other research, led to Pious's book *Why Presidents Fail* (2008). He explains why the neglect of law and constitutional boundaries increases the risk of presidential error. That danger expands with confidential and covert operations: "When policies are inverted and operations privatized, they attract lowlifes as middlemen and brokers, as in the Iran-Contra arms sales." A president's effort to hide his involvement adds to the risk, "because inexperienced, overly eager, or unstable operatives are recruited to do the work. They may go off the deep end or decide they have been poorly treated and betray their handlers." Blackmail, Pious warns, "is always a possibility, because if these operatives are ever caught in any illegality, their ace in the hole is to give up their White House sponsors."[58]

Pious punctures the belief that presidents enjoy a unique advantage over Congress in terms of expertise and reliable information. Despite the presence of tens of thousands of experts within executive agencies, presidents are regularly unable to obtain accurate or even semiaccurate projections about the economy, the national budget, and the military strengths or weaknesses of other nations. Administrations have failed to predict missile gaps, the collapse of the Soviet Union, and weapons of mass destruction in Iraq. The ill-conceived military initiatives with the Bay of Pigs and the war in Vietnam inflicted great damage on the country. Presidential actions with U-2 flights (Eisenhower), the Cuban Missile Crisis (Kennedy), and rescuing the American merchant ship *Mayaguez* (Ford) were all accompanied by false and deceptive executive announcements.

James P. Pfiffner and Eric Alterman have turned our attention to presidential lies, big and small.[59] In recent years, scholars have published a number of works sharply criticizing presidential claims of power and urging a return to a constitutional system of checks and balances.[60] It is too early to tell if these studies mark a permanent appreciation for constitutional values and the rule of law or whether they were largely triggered by the excesses and abuses that emerged during the administration of George W. Bush. One test will come with the Obama administration. Will the United States once again fall prey to romances about a personal presidency and ignore the structural safeguards intended by the framers?

Those who teach, write for newspapers, and opine on television can help educate the public that strong presidents are not always good presidents, there is nothing automatically superior about the "national interest," executive decisiveness is not the same as sound judgment, unleashing military might can weaken national security, and opposition to misguided and illegal presidential action is the highest form of patriotism. All of those lessons underscore the need for a strong and independent Congress to check presidential power.

# Chapter Three
# Interpreting the Constitution

From elementary school to law school to graduate school, students are likely to be taught that the U.S. Supreme Court is the dominant and final voice on the meaning of the Constitution. How did we go from popular sovereignty, with Congress as the first branch, to a system of government that places such vast power in the hands of nine justices? More precisely: in the hands of five justices who form the majority? When, why, and how was self-government shoved aside by a small elite of non-elected judges? Justice Robert Jackson offered this claim in *Brown v. Allen* (1953): "We are not final because we are infallible, but we are infallible only because we are final."[1] No one even vaguely familiar with American history could believe that the Court has been either infallible or final.

This chapter explains that judicial supremacy was never the framers' intent or aspiration. For most of its career, the Supreme Court understood that it shared constitutional interpretation with the other two federal branches, the independent states, and the general public. Only in the last half-century has the Court pretended to be the Final Word. That claim is regularly exploded when one follows how judicial rulings are actually implemented. Congress has always played a significant role in constitutional interpretation, often substituting its judgment for the rulings of courts.

## The Misunderstood *Marbury* Case

Judicial review is the power of courts to declare the acts of other branches and the states unconstitutional. Although not expressly provided for in the Constitution, judicial review is implied at least in a limited sense. Were Congress to reduce the salaries of federal courts, judges would properly strike down the legislation as a violation of express language in Article III: Federal judges shall receive a compensation "which shall not be diminished during their Continuance in Office." As with other branches, the judiciary has every right to protect its independence and fight off encroachments. The Constitution states that Congress shall not pass a "bill of attainder" (legislative punishment without trial). Were Congress to use its appropriations power to deny salaries to executive officials because of their political views and opinions, the Supreme Court would be justified in nullifying the statutory language, as it did in *United States v. Lovett* (1946).[2]

Beyond clear cases grounded in constitutional text lies a much larger universe of complex questions presented to the Court. If the lawsuit is a "case or controversy," the Court has jurisdiction to hear the dispute and decide it. Does the Court's ruling then become binding, conclusive, and irreversible? Or may other branches, the 50 states, and the general public reenter the field and participate again, leading to a different result? The history of the United States is very much the latter.

Judicial review dates from the famous case of *Marbury v. Madison* (1803).[3] Before that decision, justices were uncertain whether they had authority to strike down the actions of Congress or the executive branch. In *Hylton v. United States* (1796), the Court upheld a congressional statute that imposed a tax on carriages. If justices had authority to uphold a statute, did that mean they could invalidate one? Apparently so. In *Hylton*, Justice

Samuel Chase tiptoed around the question, saying it was unnecessary "*at this time*, for me to determine, whether this court, *constitutionally* possesses the power to declare an act of Congress void. . . . [B]ut if the court have such power, I am free to declare, that I will never exercise it, *but in a very clear case*."[4]

Two years later, in *Hollingsworth v. Virginia*, the Court upheld the process Congress used for constitutional amendments.[5] In a case also decided in 1798, *Calder v. Bull*, Justice James Iredell echoed the sentiments of Justice Chase. If a statute passed by Congress or one of the states violated the express constitutional provision on ex post facto laws, "it is unquestionably void; though, I admit, that as the authority to declare it void is of delicate and awful nature, the Court will never resort to that authority, but in a clear and urgent case."[6]

In *Marbury v. Madison*, the Court for the first time invalidated a section of a congressional statute. That decision is regularly cited by justices today to defend the proposition that the judiciary is supreme and final on fixing the meaning of the Constitution. Such an interpretation was never on the mind of the author of *Marbury*, Chief Justice John Marshall. The Court in 1803 was in far too weak a position, politically and institutionally, to claim supremacy over the other two branches. The Jeffersonians had taken control of the White House and both chambers of Congress. Muscle-flexing by the Court would have been disastrous for the judiciary, the one branch the Federalist Party still controlled.

Here was Marshall's predicament. William Marbury and several other individuals had received judicial appointments during the final days of the administration of John Adams. Some of the commissions were not delivered. Marbury took his case directly to the Supreme Court, asking that it exercise its power under Section 13 of the Judiciary Act of 1789 and issue a writ of mandamus, compelling Secretary of State James Madison to deliver his commission. Marshall knew that any order he issued would be ignored by Madison and President Jefferson. Marshall saw no point in provoking a confrontation he could not possibly win. Instead, he ruled that the mandamus provision was unconstitutional. His reasoning (distinguishing between appellate and original jurisdiction) was not very persuasive but it saved the Court from a humiliating defeat. There was nothing in Marshall's decision to imply judicial superiority over constitutional interpretation.

Take a look at the sentence in *Marbury* that is regularly cited to defend judiciary supremacy: "It is emphatically the province and duty of the judicial department to say what the law is."[7] Read that language with care. It contains nothing about judiciary supremacy. It says that courts decide cases, which is of course true. That is why we have courts. But it would be just as true to write: "It is emphatically the province and duty of the legislative department to say what the law is." No one could disagree with that sentence, and yet it would be misleading to claim that Congress held final authority to say what the law is. Presidents may exercise their veto power and courts can review congressional statutes both for meaning and constitutionality. All three branches are deeply involved in deciding what the law is. So are the 50 states, jurors, and citizens at large. Examples of this rich and ongoing constitutional dialogue are provided in this chapter and the next.

John Marshall had another reason not to claim that the Court was superior to the other branches. He decided *Marbury* on February 24, 1803. The House impeached District Judge John Pickering on March 2, 1803, and the Senate removed him on March 12, 1804. The House then impeached Justice Samuel Chase, in large part for his partisan conduct toward opponents of the John Adams administration. Had he been removed by the Senate, the House might have next turned the impeachment machinery against Marshall. It was in this tense political climate that Marshall wrote to Chase on January 23, 1805, offering private views about the legislative threat. Marshall advised that if Congress disliked a judicial opinion it could simply pass legislation to reverse the ruling. There was no need to impeach judges. Far from boasting about judiciary supremacy, Marshall referred to the "mildness of our character." Here is what Marshall wrote to Chase: "I think the modern doctrine of impeachment should yield to an appellate jurisdiction in the legislature. A reversal of those legal opinions deemed unsound by the legislature would certainly better comport with the mildness of our character than [would] a removal of the judge who has rendered them unknowing of his fault."[8]

Judges and scholars who treat *Marbury* as the source of judicial supremacy ignore what happened during Marshall's tenure from 1801 to 1835. *Marbury* was the one and only time that Marshall invalidated a statute passed by Congress. He used judicial review primarily to *uphold* congressional power and federal regulation over the states. He consistently found ways to support legislation that Congress passed to create the U.S. Bank and exercise the commerce power. Judicial review was not wielded as a nay-saying axe against Congress—against state action on occasion, yes, but not against the coequal national branches. Judicial review was used affirmatively to justify and legitimate what they decided to do. Members of Congress took the lead in determining how they could exercise their express and implied powers. The Court then sanctioned the legislative judgment.

## Early Constitutional Disputes

In the early decades, Congress and the president necessarily made independent judgments about the meaning of the Constitution. Few decisions of the Supreme Court or the lower courts provided much guidance on these issues. The two elected branches debated and reached agreement on the constitutionality of the U.S. Bank, the congressional investigative power, the president's power to remove top executive officials, the principle of federalism, internal improvements, the war-making power, treaties and foreign relations, and the scope of the commerce power. It was in the elected branches, "not in the courts, that the original understanding of the Constitution was forged."[9]

Private citizens also helped determine what was constitutional. In 1793, President George Washington issued what has come to be known as the Neutrality Proclamation. He directed Americans not to take sides in the war between England and France. Individuals who defied the proclamation were prosecuted. However, the constitutionality of the proclamation was not decided in the courts by federal judges. Ordinary citizens, serving as jurors, put a check on Washington. They advised federal prosecutors that proclamations issued by British kings might have been treated as law, but in America the only way to create criminal law was action by Congress by statute. The message from jurors was clear: If you bring a prosecution based solely on the proclamation we will acquit. President Washington heard the communication clearly and came to Congress to seek legislation. The result was the Neutrality Act of 1794, providing legal authority to prosecute and punish individuals who violated federal law.[10] Jurors sitting on trials directed the administration to respect and follow the principles of self-government.

Another constitutional issue decided largely outside the courts was whether the government could punish citizens for what they said or wrote. At times prosecution was based on a statute, such as the Sedition Act of 1798, discussed in the first chapter. Another option was the doctrine of "seditious libel," drawn from British common law. Once in power, the Jeffersonians were willing to use seditious libel to punish Federalist newspapers that criticized the administration. Many of these cases were brought at the state level. The case that reached the Supreme Court in 1812 was a federal, not a state, case. The individuals prosecuted were editors of a Federalist newspaper in Connecticut. The Court noted that it was the first time that it had been faced with the question whether federal courts had jurisdiction over seditious libel. It concluded that the issue had "been long since settled in public opinion." It meant that Congress had yet to establish by law that criticism of the national government was a criminal act. In short, constitutional law was decided by the people, working through their representatives, not by the courts. Whatever the law in England, the exercise of criminal jurisdiction in common law cases was not within the implied powers of federal courts.[11]

The Supreme Court learned that its decisions were anything but final. During the 1850s, the Court held that the height of a bridge over the Ohio River, constructed under state law, was a "nuisance" because it obstructed navigation. Congress passed a law a few months later declaring that bridge and a second one to be "lawful structures." Which branch should be supreme on this question? The Court had first held the bridge was to be illegal. Now, because of congressional action, it decided the structures were legal. Three justices, writing in dissent, were dumbfounded. They thought that when the Court initially held the bridge to be obstructive, that was the end of the matter. How could Congress come along and reach an opposite judgment? What did this do to the finality of judicial decisions or the dignity of the Court? Their objections have remained very much a minority position. The Court frequently acknowledges in this type of case on state power that if Congress by statute contradicts a Court opinion, the Court will acquiesce to the legislative judgment.[12]

In the decades leading up to the Civil War, the political engine for eliminating slavery came not from the three branches of government but from private citizens. Large numbers of Americans, regarding slavery as a violation of the principles stated in the Declaration of Independence, pressed for abolition. "All men are created equal" left no room for slavery. Americans during that period "were not inclined to leave to private lawyers any more than to public men the conception, execution, and interpretation of public law. The conviction was general that no aristocracy existed with respect to the Constitution. Like politics, with which it was inextricably joined, the Constitution was everyone's business."[13]

By the time the slavery issue reached the national government in the late 1850s, all three branches had failed in their public duties. President James Buchanan, who wanted to mention slavery in his inaugural address in March 1857, learned from several justices that the Supreme Court was about to decide the pending case of *Dred Scott v. Sandford*.[14] Buchanan proceeded to tell the country that the controversy over slavery was "a judicial question, which legitimately belongs to the Supreme Court of the United States, before whom it is now pending, and will, it is understood, be speedily and finally settled. To their decision, in common with all good citizens, I shall cheerfully submit, whatever this may be, . . ." He might have been willing to defer to the Court; the country did not.

In *Dred Scott*, the Court held that the "enslaved African race" could not be citizens of the United States and could not sue in federal court. It also ruled that Congress lacked authority to prevent the spread of slavery to the territories in the West and that therefore the Missouri Compromise statute was unconstitutional. Newspapers differed in their views about the "finality" of this decision. To the *New York Tribune* the Court's action "we need hardly say, is entitled to just as much moral weight as would be the judgment of a majority of those congregated in any Washington bar-room."[15] Newspapers in the South joined with President Buchanan in accepting the ruling as the final word.

During the campaign of 1858, Senator Stephen Douglas treated *Dred Scott* as conclusive and binding. His opponent, Abraham Lincoln, accepted the decision only to the extent that it affected the particular litigants. He refused to accept the decision as national policy.[16] In his first inaugural address, Lincoln explained the conditions under which a decision of the Court is binding:

> I do not forget the position assumed by some that constitutional questions are to be decided by the Supreme Court, nor do I deny that such decisions must be binding in any case upon the parties to a suit as to the object of that suit, while they are also entitled to a very high respect and consideration in all parallel cases by all other departments of the Government. . . . At the same time, the candid citizen must confess that if the policy of the Government upon vital questions affecting the whole people is to be irrevoca-

> bly fixed by decisions of the Supreme Court, the instant they are made in ordinary litigation between parties in personal actions the people will have ceased to be their own rulers, having to that extent practically resigned their Government into the hands of that eminent tribunal.

On November 29, 1862, Attorney General Edward Bates released a legal opinion that repudiated the reasoning of *Dred Scott*. He concluded that men of color, if born in the United States, are citizens of the United States. The rest of the Court's decision was rejected in 1862 when Congress passed legislation prohibiting slavery in the territories. During legislative debate, no member of Congress even referred to the Court's decision or felt in any way bound by it. Lawmakers decided they were free to exercise independent judgment on the constitutional issue, with or without the Court. The Thirteenth Amendment, adopted in 1865, abolished the institution of slavery. The Fourteenth Amendment, ratified in 1868, provided for the equality of blacks before the law. It specifically provides that all persons born in the United States are American citizens and of the state in which they reside. The Fifteenth Amendment, which became effective in 1870, gave blacks the right to vote. In other areas of public policy, Congress would continue to press its understanding of the Constitution in the face of contrary positions by the Court.

## Efforts to Regulate the Economy

Many of the constitutional disputes after the Civil War, pitting Congress against the Supreme Court, involved economic issues of federal currency, taxation, and government regulation. Judicial decisions at times blocked congressional legislation but only temporarily. Either by a change in membership on the Court, constitutional amendments, or subsequent statutory action, Congress regularly prevailed. The dominant branch in these struggles was Congress, not the judiciary. The Court conceded in 1946: "The history of judicial limitation of congressional power over commerce, when exercised affirmatively, has been more largely one of retreat than of ultimate victory."[17] In 1951, Justice Owen Roberts reached a similar conclusion: "Looking back, it is difficult to see how the Court could have resisted the popular urge for uniform standards throughout the country—for what in effect was a unified economy."[18] Justice Robert Jackson observed in a 1951 speech: "The practical play of the forces of politics is such that judicial power has often delayed but never permanently defeated the persistent will of a substantial majority."[19]

An early collision between Congress and the Court after the Civil War involved the issue of "greenbacks." When President Lincoln entered the White House in March 1861 he discovered that the U.S. Treasury had hardly any money and little in the way of precious metals (gold and silver) to support money that circulated as legal tender. On February 25, 1862, Congress enacted a bill that authorized the issuance of paper notes to be accepted as legal tender to pay debts and other obligations. The notes, printed on one side in black and green, became known as "greenbacks." There was no dispute about the legality of the bills for present and future use, but were they legal to settle prior debts?

That question reached the Supreme Court in *Hepburn v. Griswold* (1870).[20] At that time, the Court consisted of eight justices. A narrow majority of 4 to 3 decided that the statute was unconstitutional because debts entered into before passage of the law had to be repaid in gold and silver. In earlier decisions, from 1863 to 1869, 15 state courts of last resort had upheld the Legal Tender Act of 1862. One court, from Kentucky, found the statute unconstitutional, and it was that case that reached the Supreme Court in *Hepburn v. Griswold*. Initially it looked like the eight justices on the Court were equally divided, but Justice Robert Grier switched his vote and the majority seemed to be five to three against the statute.

Changing votes did much to discredit the Court. It planned to issue a decision on January 31, 1870, one day before Grier's resignation. However, Justice Samuel Miller asked for an additional week to finish his dissenting opinion, delaying the release of the opinion until February 7. By that time Grier had resigned, putting the majority at four to three. There was little reason to think that the slim majority would survive. President Ulysses S. Grant appointed two new justices, one to replace Grier and a second to fill a new position created by Congress.

The two nominees, William Strong of Pennsylvania and Joseph P. Bradley of New Jersey, appeared likely to uphold the Legal Tender Act. Strong, as a member of the Pennsylvania Supreme Court, had already upheld the statute, and Bradley seemed likely to vote the same way. In the *Legal Tender Cases* (1871), the Court five to four reversed *Hepburn v. Griswold* and ruled that the statute of 1862 was constitutional.[21] The one-year turnaround highlighted that the meaning of the Constitution does not depend on fixed and eternal principles discovered by the judiciary but rather in no small part on the Court's membership and new appointments.

Over the years, federal courts tried to carve out exclusive jurisdictions for the national government and the states. The Supreme Court remarked in *United States v. Cruikshank* (1876): "The powers which one possesses, the other does not."[22] But national and state powers were not that precise, especially in the field of commerce. In *Leisy v. Hardin* (1890), the Court held that the power of Congress over interstate commerce trumped state powers and local options.[23] If a state prohibited intoxicating liquors from entering its territory, the prohibition could not apply to incoming original packages or kegs. The state could regulate the material only after the original packages had been broken into smaller units. In so deciding, the Court added an important qualifier: States could not exclude the incoming articles "without congressional permission."

The constitutional meaning of interstate commerce therefore depended on what members of Congress decided to do. Less than a month after the Court's decision, Congress began debate on legislation to give the states independent authority to regulate incoming liquor. The determination of lawmakers to exercise independent judgment is reflected in comments from Senator George Edmunds of Vermont. He said the opinions of the Court regarding Congress "are of no more value to us than ours are to it. We are just as independent of the Supreme Court of the United States as it is of us, and every judge will admit it." If members of Congress concluded that the Court had made an error, "are we to stop and say that is the end of the law and the mission of civilization in the United States for that reason? I take it not." Further deliberation by the Court might produce a different result: "[A]s they have often done, it may be their mission next year to change their opinion and say that the rule ought to be the other way."[24]

The decision in *Leisy* is dated April 28, 1890. Less than four months later, on August 8, Congress enacted legislation overriding the Court. The law provided that all fermented, distilled, or other intoxicating liquors or liquids transported into any state or territory for use, consumption, or sale "shall upon arrival in such State or Territory be subject to the operation and effect of the laws of such State or Territory enacted in the exercise of its police powers to the same extent and in the same manner as though such liquids or liquors had been produced in such State or Territory, and shall not be exempt therefrom by reason of being introduced in original packages or otherwise." A year later, in a ruling called *In re Rahrer* (1891), the Court decided that Congress was authorized to act as it did.[25]

National debate over a federal income tax produced a pitched battle between Congress and the Court that had to be resolved by a constitutional amendment. The Court's performance damaged its prestige. The Constitution speaks clearly only about one aspect of the taxing power: "No Tax or Duty shall be laid on Articles exported from any State" (Article I, Section 9). The Constitution refers to "direct taxes" and "indirect taxes" and requires the latter to adhere to the rule of uniformity: "The Congress shall have Power to lay and collect Taxes, Duties, Imposts, and Excises, to pay the Debts and provide for the common Defence and general Welfare of the United States; but all

Duties, Imposts and Excises shall be uniform throughout the United States" (Article I, Section 8). The purpose of this language is to protect states from discriminatory actions by the national government.

The problem is that there was no clear understanding about direct taxes. The Constitution states: "No Capitation, or other direct, Tax shall be laid, unless in Proportion to the Census or Enumeration herein before directed to be taken." Congress has never relied on capitation taxes or "head taxes," which would levy a fixed rate on each person regardless of income or worth. Must all other direct taxes be levied among the states in accordance with the rule of apportionment? The Court's decision in *Hylton v. United States* (1796), involving a carriage tax, provided some guidance for constitutional analysis.[26] Further direction came from a congressional enactment in 1861 for a direct tax of $20,000,000 to be apportioned among the states. The same statute included an income tax of 3 percent for those whose annual income exceeded $800. That tax was not apportioned among the states. A decision by the Court in *Veazie Bank v. Fenno* (1869) supplied additional clues.[27] The Court, holding that a federal tax on circulation bank notes was not a direct tax, drew attention to the debates at the 1787 Philadelphia Constitutional Convention. When Massachusetts delegate Rufus King asked his colleagues for the meaning of direct taxation, "no one answered."

In *Springer v. United States* (1881), a unanimous Court decided that direct taxes meant capitation taxes and taxes on real estate.[28] To the Court, a federal income tax enacted in 1864 and amended the next year was an indirect tax. To the extent the tax inflicted "any wrong or unnecessary harshness, it was for Congress, or the people who make congresses, to see that the evil was corrected. The remedy does not lie with the judicial branch of the government."[29] Here the Court appeared to come down strongly on the side of popular sovereignty and the capacity of Congress to determine for itself the meaning of the Constitution. As with *Veazie*, the Court pointed to the debates at the

Philadelphia Convention to underscore the vague meaning of "direct taxes." After reviewing tax laws from 1789 to 1861, the Court concluded that whenever the federal government imposed a direct tax it was only on real estate and slaves. How would those precedents bear on the constitutionality of a federal income tax?

In 1894, Congress enacted a tax on individual and corporate incomes, to be effective January 1, 1895. The constitutional issue was taken quickly to the Supreme Court, which decided in *Pollock v. Farmers' Loan & Trust Co.* (1895) that the tax on rents or income from real estate was a direct tax and violated the Constitution by not adhering to the apportionment rule.[30] A second decision, under the same case name, struck down the income tax. Flavoring the decision and the legal analysis were fears of socialism and communism. During oral argument in the first case, private attorney Joseph H. Choate warned the Court that the income tax was "communistic in its purposes and tendencies."[31] Writing as part of the majority in this case, Justice Stephen Field predicted that the "present assault upon capital is but the beginning," leading to "a war of the poor against the rich; a war constantly growing in intensity and bitterness."[32]

The second decision was subject to special criticism. The Court split five to four, and one justice evidently switched sides. When the question of the income tax was addressed in the first case, the justices divided four to four. Not participating in that case was Justice Howell Jackson, but in the second case he voted to *uphold* the income tax. That should have produced a majority of five justices in support of the federal income tax, yet it went the other way. Someone changed his position. Exactly which justice moved over has never been revealed. Because of the narrow five-to-four majority and the vote switch, this decision has been called one of three "self-inflicted wounds" on the Court, the other two being *Dred Scott* and the *Legal Tender Cases*.[33]

Each chamber of Congress passed a resolution to set in motion an amendment to the Constitution to authorize a federal income tax. The Sixteenth Amendment, ratified in 1913, provides: "The Congress shall have power to lay and collect taxes on incomes, from whatever source derived, without apportionment among the several States, and without regard to any census or enumeration."

## Regulating Child Labor

An especially bitter and protracted legislative-judicial clash involved efforts by the national government to place statutory constraints on child labor. Repeatedly the Supreme Court struck down congressional initiatives to regulate this area. At first lawmakers relied on the Commerce Clause and later turned to the taxing power. Blocked each time by the Court, Congress passed a constitutional amendment but could not attract sufficient states to have it ratified. Eventually the composition of the Court changed to assure not only judicial acceptance of the legislative judgment but validation by a unanimous opinion.

In 1916, Congress passed legislation to prevent the products of child labor from being shipped interstate. The legislative history explained the dangers facing young workers under age 16 in hazardous and burdensome occupations, including factories, mines, and quarries. Some children worked 11-hour days 6 days a week. Children as young as 12 worked 11 hours a day. Congress concluded that it had ample constitutional authority under the Commerce Clause to regulate public health and morals. The Supreme Court disagreed. A five-to-four majority in *Hammer v. Dagenhart* (1918) struck down the law as beyond the scope of the commerce power and an invasion of powers reserved to the states.[34] The Court reasoned that although child labor might have harmful effects on the children employed, the "goods shipped are of themselves harmless." Whatever might be necessary to regulate child labor, said the Court, had to be left to the states operating under their police powers.

Members of Congress refused to accept the Court's ruling as the last word on regulating child labor. To them, the superior body to decide national policy was Congress, not the judiciary. During debate on a bill to replace the one the Court declared invalid, Senator Robert Owen of Oklahoma rejected the argument that federal judges are somehow better able to interpret the Constitution than members of Congress:

> It is said by some that the judges are much more learned and wiser than Congress in construing the Constitution. I can not concede to this whimsical notion. They are not more learned; they are not wiser; they are not more patriotic; and what is the fatal weakness if they make their mistakes there is no adequate means of correcting their judicial errors, while if Congress should err the people have an immediate redress; they can change the House of Representatives almost immediately and can change two-thirds of the Senate within four years, while the judges are appointed for life and are removable only by impeachment.[35]

A new child labor bill enacted in 1919 rested wholly on the taxing power. The bill imposed an excise tax of 10 percent on any company operating a mine, quarry, mill, cannery, workshop, or factory that employed children of certain ages working at hours prohibited by Congress. Some lawmakers, reluctant to use the power of the national government to regulate the states, made an exception to deal with what they considered to be the evils of child labor. After a lower court ruled the statute invalid, the matter came once again to the Supreme Court.

In defending the authority of Congress to regulate child labor, Solicitor General James Beck urged the Court to respect the judgment of the people and their representatives to decide national policy. During oral argument, he warned that any action by the judiciary to invalidate the child labor law would weaken public support and acceptance of the Constitution. The "erroneous" idea that the Court is the "sole guardian and protector of our constitutional form of government has inevitably led to an impairment, both with the people and with their representatives, of what may be called the constitutional conscience."[36] It was healthy in a system of popular sovereignty to have constitutional issues debated and resolved by the general public instead of shifting those questions to the courts.

In *Bailey v. Drexel Furniture Co.* (1922), the Court mounted a majority of eight to one in striking down the child labor statute.[37] The new legislative strategy did not persuade the Court, which said it would have to "be blind not to see that the so-called tax is imposed to stop the employment of children within the age limits prescribed." The prohibited and regulatory effect and purpose seemed obvious to the Court: "All others can see and understand this. How can we properly shut our minds to it?" The subject of child labor, said the Court, had to be left to the states to regulate. To permit Congress to tax child labor "would be to break down all constitutional limitation of the powers of Congress and completely wipe out the sovereignty of the States."[38]

Even with this lopsided defeat, Congress refused to accept the Court's ruling as the final word on child labor. In 1924, both chambers of Congress passed a constitutional amendment to give Congress the power to "limit, regulate and prohibit the labor of persons under 18 years of age." Twenty-eight states ultimately ratified the amendment but 36 were needed.

Tension between the judiciary and the elected branches led to a court-packing plan offered by President Franklin D. Roosevelt in 1937. It authorized the president to nominate justices to the Supreme Court whenever an incumbent over the age of 70 declined to resign or retire. Had his plan been adopted, Roosevelt could have named as many as 6 new justices. He wanted the same authority for the lower courts, opening the possibility of 50 new judgeships.

Congress rejected the plan, but the confrontation appeared to persuade some justices to be more accepting of national regulation. By 1935, the Court was already moving in a direction to accommodate federal legislation.[39] Early in 1937 Congress passed legislation to provide full judicial pay during retirement. Perhaps because of that benefit, the conservative justice Willis

Van Devanter retired on June 2, 1937, giving Roosevelt his first opportunity in more than four years to nominate someone to the Court. Other justices retired, allowing Roosevelt to nominate Felix Frankfurter, James Byrnes, William O. Douglas, Frank Murphy, Stanley Reed, and Robert Jackson. The Court was now fundamentally restructured.

In 1938, Congress attached a child labor section to the Fair Labor Standards Act. Far from acquiescing to the judicial reasoning in *Hammer v. Dagenhart*, Congress once again based its authority to regulate child labor on its commerce power. In *United States v. Darby* (1941), a reconstituted Court upheld the child labor provision. Strikingly, the vote was unanimous.[40] The Court conceded that *Dagenhart* had been repudiated over the years and that congressional regulation of child labor was not "a forbidden invasion of state power." It found the conclusion "inescapable" that *Dagenhart* "was a departure from the principles which have prevailed in the interpretation of the Commerce Clause both before and since the decision"[41] and therefore overruled *Dagenhart*. Congress and the country, going head to head against the Court in interpreting the Constitution, had prevailed.

## A Judicial Option: Someone Else Do It

Many constitutional issues do not reach the courts. Even when they do, they are regularly turned aside by the judiciary and sent back to the elected branches and the general public for resolution. An example is what is called the Statement and Account Clause. Article I, Section 9, Clause 7 of the Constitution provides: "A regular Statement and Account of the Receipts and Expenditures of all public Money shall be published from time to time." It was deemed essential in republican government that citizens know how public funds are received and spent. Accountability to the people by federal representatives is a fundamental value. The language "from time to time" gave the government some discretion over the release of financial data. At the

Virginia ratifying convention in 1788, George Mason said that the words "from time to time" were added because "there might be some matters which might require secrecy."[42] He did not mean that that information could be withheld permanently. Some delay might be justified.

In 1790, Congress began to authorize a very selective and limited use of secret expenditures. It gave the president a $40,000 account to be used for foreign intercourse, reserving to the president the discretion to decide the degree to which the expenditures should be made public. He could provide public vouchers, explaining how the money was used, or resort to unvouchered expenditures. Other confidential and unvouchered accounts appeared over the years. From 1789 to 1935, Congress departed from the Statement and Account Clause on rare occasions to permit unvouchered expenditures by the president, the secretary of the navy, and the Federal Bureau of Investigation. In each case the amounts were modest: in the range of $70,000 or less.[43]

World War II provoked greater recourse to secret funding, especially the appropriation of billions of dollars to fund development of the atomic bomb (the Manhattan Project). Many agencies began to receive authority to spend money without vouchers, including the White House, the Defense Department, the District of Columbia, the attorney general, the Bureau of Narcotics and Dangerous Drugs, the Secret Service, the Coast Guard, the Bureau of Customs, and the Immigration and Naturalization Service. Typically these were for small amounts.

Far greater in magnitude are the secret expenditures of the U.S. intelligence community, consisting of the Central Intelligence Agency, the National Security Agency, the Defense Intelligence Agency, and more than a dozen other agencies. Tens of billions are spent for these purposes, creating two major problems. One is the integrity of the Statement and Account Clause, designed to protect republican government. The other is deceptive budgeting. In order to provide the intelligence community with undisclosed amounts, it is necessary to pad the appropriation accounts that are made public. To do that, members of

Congress end up voting on statutory language that is not what it appears to be.

William B. Richardson, at attorney in Pennsylvania, decided to take the constitutional issue to the courts in the 1960s. He wanted the judiciary to declare secret funding for the CIA a violation of the Statement and Account Clause. A district court held that he lacked standing to bring the lawsuit because he could not point to a sufficient injury to himself. An appellate court held that the district court lacked jurisdiction to even hear the case. The Supreme Court refused to take this case, but several years later Richardson was again in the courts, asking that the secretary of the treasury be compelled to make a public account of CIA receipts and expenditures. This time an appellate court held that he had standing and that the government had to publish the figures.

In *United States v. Richardson* (1974), the Supreme Court threw the case out on the ground of standing.[44] Divided five to four, it concluded that the subject matter of the lawsuit demanded that the issue be left "to the surveillance of Congress, and ultimately to the political process." In one of the dissents, Justice William O. Douglas objected that standing should not be invoked to read the Statement and Account Clause "out of the Constitution" when it comes to certain intelligence agencies. Such a proposition, he said, was "astounding."[45] Justices William J. Brennan, Potter Stewart, and Thurgood Marshall wrote separate dissents.

Congress held hearings on disclosing the aggregate amount of the budget for the intelligence community. I testified before the House Intelligence Committee in 1994, urging that the aggregate amount be made public, both to comply with the Statement and Account Clause and to eliminate deceptive budgeting practices. Sometimes one chamber would support disclosure, and at other times the second chamber, but never both in the same Congress. Although a presidential commission in 1996 recommended disclosure of the aggregate, no legislation resulted.

Inadvertently, the commission publicly released the budgets of the National Reconnaissance Office ($6.2 billion), the National Security Agency ($3.7 billion), the Central Intelligence Agency ($3.1 billion), and the Defense Intelligence Agency ($2 billion).[46]

Litigation in the 1990s by Steven Aftergood of the Federation of American Scientists prompted the CIA in 1997 to release the aggregate figure of $26.7 billion (of which the CIA represented $3 billion). The aggregate for the next year: $26.7 billion.[47] After that point the CIA refused to release the figures. In 2004, the 9/11 Commission recommended public disclosure of the aggregate amount. Three years later Congress passed legislation to implement the recommendation. The intelligence community released the aggregate amount of $43.5 billion for fiscal year 2007. After adding the amounts spent by the military services for intelligence operations, the total exceeds $50 billion.[48] A constitutional dispute that could not be resolved in the courts was settled through the regular political process.

Another constitutional issue involving the CIA arose in 1997. The Senate Intelligence Committee drafted legislation to authorize employees within the intelligence community to report directly to the intelligence committees when they learned of illegality, gross mismanagement, gross waste of funds, and other agency misconduct. The Justice Department regarded this type of legislation as an unconstitutional encroachment of the president's authority over the executive branch. Asked to testify before the committee in February 1998, I defended the constitutional right of Congress to gain access to disclosures by lower-level employees about agency wrongdoing. I was asked to testify a week later, this time sitting next to an attorney from the Justice Department, who continued to raise constitutional objections. Two hours after the hearing, the committee unanimously voted (19 to 0) to report the bill. I testified in favor of the legislation before the House Intelligence Committee. With some changes made to reconcile the Senate and House bills, the legislation was signed into law.[49]

## The Durable Legislative Veto

In the 1800s, Congress began to use legislative vehicles short of a public law to control executive agencies. At times Congress relied on simple resolutions (passed by one chamber) and at other times adopted concurrent resolutions (passed by both chambers but not presented to the president for his signature or veto). Although those procedures lacked the force of law, agencies generally found it prudent to comply with one-house and two-house legislative vetoes.

What if this process had been sanctioned by a public law? Would they be legally binding? In 1854, Attorney General Caleb Cushing reasoned that simple resolutions could compel a department head to act if they had been recognized by a previous law.[50] By the early 1900s, Congress was using simple and concurrent resolutions to control certain operations within the executive branch, such as directing the secretary of war to investigate matters relating to rivers and harbors.

President Woodrow Wilson issued constitutional objections to legislative vetoes. In one veto message, he told Congress it could not use a concurrent resolution to remove the comptroller general and the assistant comptroller general. Congress responded by replacing the concurrent resolution with a joint resolution, which passes both chambers and is submitted to the president. Wilson also objected to a process that allowed the Joint Committee on Printing to issue regulations controlling what would be printed and what would be discontinued.

Some presidents recognized the benefit of a legislative veto. President Herbert Hoover wanted to reorganize the executive branch to save money but understood that if he submitted a bill to Congress it could either be ignored or so amended that he would not like the final product. In his first annual message to Congress in 1929, he recommended that Congress delegate reorganization powers to him, subject to some form of legislative veto, including even a committee veto. Congress would have to disapprove within a set period of time, acting up or down on his proposal without any amendments. Congress agreed to that process in 1932, reserving for itself a one-house legislative veto within 60 days. By the time Hoover submitted a reorganization plan, he had been defeated for reelection. On January 19, 1933, the House of Representatives passed a resolution disapproving all of his proposals, preferring to leave agency restructuring to his successor, Franklin D. Roosevelt.[51]

Roosevelt struggled with the merits of the legislative veto, finding it unconstitutional on some occasions but embracing it when it offered important advantages. His arguments had less to do with strict constitutional principles than with his desire for additional authority and flexibility. If he needed to swallow a legislative veto to get authority he wanted, he would do so. The record of subsequent presidents has also been inconsistent. President Dwight D. Eisenhower opposed committee vetoes in one form, yet consented to others. Over the decades, the legislative veto spread from executive reorganization to cover federal salaries, impoundment of funds, war powers, national emergencies, presidential papers, and agency regulations.

Whatever advantages presidents had found over the years, by the time of President Jimmy Carter it was decided to take a stand against all legislative vetoes. In 1978, Carter issued a major critique of the process. Nevertheless, White House aides and the Justice Department gave some ground and announced an accommodation for certain kinds of legislative vetoes, particularly over executive reorganization and war powers. Litigation produced many conflicting positions by federal courts. It appeared to some observers that the constitutionality of the legislative veto would be settled once and for all with the 1983 case of *INS v. Chadha*.[52]

With *Chadha* heading to the Supreme Court, I wrote an article predicting that the legislative veto would survive even if the justices found it unconstitutional. My work with the appropriations committees convinced me that Congress and executive agencies were satisfied with a process they had perfected over the decades. It involved "reprogramming of funds"—moving funds within an appropriations account to satisfy new needs. Once a fiscal year begins, it becomes evident that Congress and the agencies failed to anticipate certain budgetary needs. Legal and technical developments can play havoc with agency projections. For whatever reason, it was often important to shift money from a program of lesser priority to one of greater priority.

Congress was not about to leave those decisions entirely to the agencies. The two branches worked out detailed agreements on how to handle reprogramming. In some cases the agencies need only notify the committees of jurisdiction. For other reprogramming actions, the agencies would have to seek and obtain prior approval from those committees. Nothing the Supreme Court would decide about the legislative veto, at some abstract level of constitutional principle, would eliminate the effectiveness, attractiveness, and continuity of this agency-committee process.[53]

In *INS v. Chadha* (1983), the Supreme Court held the legislative veto to be unconstitutional. The procedure challenged in the lawsuit was a one-house veto over deportation decisions, but the Court swept broadly (too broadly), insisting that whenever Congress intends to control activities outside the legislative branch, it must comply with two requirements: bicameralism (action by both chambers) and presentment (submitting a bill to the president for his signature or veto). This analysis invalidated every form of legislative veto: one-house, two-house, committee, and subcommittee. The Court wrote: "the fact that a given law or procedure is efficient, convenient, and useful in facilitating functions of government, standing alone, will not save it if it is contrary to the Constitution. Convenience and efficiency are not the primary objectives—or the hallmarks—of democratic government."[54]

This lofty language masked a failure to understand how the legislative veto began and why it flourished. For the Court, the legislative veto seemed to originate from lawmakers determined to meddle in executive decisions. Yet it was President Hoover who asked for the legislative veto, and other presidents tolerated the process because it brought with it tangible benefits, including broad delegations of legislative power. At no point in the Court's decision did it attempt to analyze and comprehend the complex negotiations that allowed agencies and congressional committees to reach agreement on reprogramming actions.

Committee vetoes retained their vitality after *Chadha*. Between 1983 and 2009, the number of new legislative vetoes enacted has exceeded 1,000. Unlike earlier versions that operated in plain sight (one-house and two-house vetoes), committee and subcommittee controls over reprogramming are largely subterranean and invisible. Presidents regularly condemn these provisions when they sign bills, suggesting that agencies need only notify committees of executive decisions. But it does not work that way. Agencies in the decades after *Chadha* continue to spell out in their budget manuals the reprogramming actions that need notification and those that require prior approval. The particular committees involved in this process are identified in the budget manuals. The appropriations committees are centrally involved, but authorizing committees are frequently included. Depending on the agreement fashioned, agencies seek prior approval from a committee or subcommittee.

The complicated history of the legislative veto offers several lessons. It originated and developed for decades by the elected branches without any judicial involvement. When courts became entangled, they could resolve only part of the dispute. If the elected branches valued the advantages of the process before the Court's decision in 1983, they would protect those benefits after the decision. Presidential condemnation of the legislative veto after *Chadha* underscores that the executive branch consists of two separate worlds. One is the macro part (including the White House and the Justice Department) that may find it useful to denounce legislative vetoes as unconstitutional and nonbinding. The other part of government consists of agencies trying to get through the fiscal year as best they can, seeking committee and subcommittee approval whenever they have to.

If presidents, White House aides, and Justice Department officials wanted to push their doctrine of a unitary executive, which places all agencies directly under the president and subject to his orders, executive officials could draft a memorandum and have the president sign it. It would be sent to all agencies, directing them to remove from their budget manuals any language about committee approval. The consequences could be several. Agencies could delete the language but continue to seek committee and subcommittee approval on an informal basis. The result would be some kind of sophisticated game, with the executive branch pretending to honor one model while following another.

There is another possibility. Congress could tell the agencies that if they want spending discretion in the middle of a fiscal year and refuse to seek committee approval, they may adopt the constitutional principles of *Chadha*: comply with bicameralism and presentment. In other words, send your requests to Congress in bill form, get both chambers to pass them, and if the two houses differ in their versions, iron out the differences in conference committee. Then submit the bill to the president for his signature. The frightening uncertainties and burdens of that process have convinced the macro part of the executive branch to limit itself to occasional rhetorical flourishes and leave the agencies alone.

## An Open-Ended Process

In a democratic republic, constitutional disputes are necessarily shared between elected and nonelected officials. Yet professors have fallen into the habit of teaching students that the meaning of the Constitution is left to the Supreme Court, which supposedly has unrivaled expertise and authority. For the past half-century the judiciary has promoted that model as well. Government has not functioned that way and should not function that way. It may go in that direction, however, if presidents and members of Congress routinely salute whatever the Court decides. It is remarkable how often presidents and lawmakers criticize a decision, announce that it was wrongly reasoned, and nevertheless accept the result as final. This type of subservient attitude is not healthy for democracy or the courts.

William Howard Taft served in many positions of public office: assistant prosecuting attorney, Ohio superior judge, U.S. solicitor general, federal appellate judge, civil governor of the Philippines, secretary of war, president of the United States, and chief justice of the Supreme Court. In all those positions he saw constitutional law develop at various levels and came to appreciate the virtues and limits of judicial experts. He discovered that often the untutored general public had a better understanding of constitutional law than officials trained in law and assigned to positions of authority.

During his service as a federal appellate judge, Taft wanted courts exposed to unflinching criticism. The right to publicly criticize judicial rulings is "of vastly more importance to the body politic than the immunity of courts and judges from unjust aspirations and attack." Judges would be more careful in their decisions if they understood that each ruling would be subject to candid evaluation, not only by legal practitioners, but by the general public. Taft concluded that if the law "is but the essence of common sense, the protest of many average men may evidence a defect in a judicial conclusion though based on the nicest legal reasoning and profoundest learning."[55]

Writing in 2003, Justice Sandra Day O'Connor observed that if one looks at the history of the Supreme Court and the country over a long period of time, "the relationship appears to be more of a dialogue than a series of commands." Although courts shape the elected branches and the public, the elected branches and the public shape the judiciary. No one should have believed, she said, that the Court's decision in *Roe* v. *Wade* (1973) would have settled the abortion issue "for all time." The ruling triggered violent protests across the country, which O'Connor said was appropriate and expected. She advised that a nation that "docilely and unthinkingly approved every Supreme Court decision as infallible and immutable would, I believe, have severely disappointed our founders." The U.S. Constitution "is not—and could never be—defended only by a group of judges."[56]

For more than two centuries, Congress has played a vital and continuing role in interpreting the Constitution and protecting individual rights. In recent years, however, members of Congress have been too deferential toward court rulings. They need to reassert themselves as a coequal and independent branch of government. Institutional assertion would be healthy for Congress, citizens, and the judiciary.

# Chapter Four
# Protecting Minority Rights

The public understands that Congress legislates on policies for the entire country. There is less appreciation for how it protects the rights of minorities and individuals. To many, it may seem inconceivable that a legislative body voting by majority could ever defend minorities and individuals. How could a majoritarian institution protect isolated and politically weak minorities? The record shows that Congress over the past two centuries has done precisely that. Federal courts, supposedly the "guardians" of individual rights, have not performed as well.

## Judicial Guardians?

From James Madison to the present, it has been widely assumed that the judiciary stands as a sturdy sentinel in shielding individuals and minorities from majoritarian abuse. Madison believed that by adding the Bill of Rights to the Constitution, "independent tribunals of justice will consider themselves in a peculiar manner the guardians of those rights."[1] All three branches failed that test by passing and supporting the Sedition Act of 1798. As discussed at the end of the first chapter, the Adams administration and Congress agreed to punish individuals for their criticism of government. Some members of Congress regarded the statute as a blatant violation of the individual right to express personal opinions. Representative Nathanial Macon of North Carolina "could only hope that the Judges would exercise the power placed in them of determining the law an unconstitutional law, if, upon scrutiny, they find it to be so."[2]

Thomas Jefferson wanted federal courts to declare the Sedition Act unconstitutional: "The laws of the land, administered by upright judges, would protect you from any exercise of power unauthorized by the Constitution of the United States."[3] Federalist judges were unlikely to strike down a statute passed by a Federalist Congress and a Federalist administration. The judicial relief desired by Macon and Jefferson never materialized.

For the first century and a half, individual rights were protected almost exclusively by states, Congress, and the president. Nonjudicial institutions were more reliable than the courts. On the rare occasions that issues of individual or minority rights came to a federal court, judges were more likely to side with government and corporations than with individuals seeking justice.[4] In 1937, when the Senate Judiciary Committee rejected a court-packing plan submitted by President Roosevelt, it warned that the proposal "undermines the protection our constitutional system gives to minorities and is subversive of the rights of individuals."

The committee report claimed that the framers "never wavered in their belief that an independent judiciary and a Constitution defining with clarity the rights of the people, were the only safeguards of the citizens." The committee report lapsed into romantic hyperbole: "Minority political groups, no less than religious and racial groups, have never failed, when forced to appeal to the Supreme Court of the United States, to find in its opinions the reassurance and protection of their constitutional rights." The independence of the judiciary was "the only certain shield of individual rights."[5] The record offers scant evidence to support this confidence in the courts.

The performance of federal courts after 1937 has improved, but contemporary studies continue to exaggerate the capacity of courts to protect individual and minority rights. In a famous footnote in 1938, Justice Stone observed that a "more searching judicial inquiry" might be required to protect "discrete and insular minorities."[6] He must have been looking expectantly forward, not backward. For the first century and a half, the process of protecting individual rights was left largely to the regular political process operating outside the courts.

It should not be too surprising that individual liberties would depend on the elected branches. Congress, the president, and state governments have major institutional strengths and responsibilities and are frequently driven by private groups that are well organized and effective in advancing their values, preferences, and agendas. Scholars conclude that the Supreme Court "has not been behaving as the counter-majoritarian force of its textbook description." Instead, it often heeds "quite carefully the policies endorsed by the majoritarian branches of government."[7] Throughout American history, citizens have interacted closely with the elected branches to safeguard individual and minority rights.[8]

In the protection of individual rights, too much attention is directed toward the national government and federal courts. Liberties and rights depend to a great extent on local and state governments. In 1854, the Supreme Court of Indiana held that a "civilized community" could not put a citizen in jeopardy and withhold counsel from the poor. Five years later, the Wisconsin Supreme Court called it a "mockery" to promise a pauper a fair trial and tell him to hire his own counsel. One juror told a judge: "Until the state provided a public defender, he would let everyone go free."[9] The states were far ahead of the national government, including the president and Congress. The U.S. Supreme Court did not recognize those elementary rights until 1963.[10]

During the nineteenth century, jurors provided steady feedback to state legislatures. If jurors considered penalties (especially the sentence of death) too severe for certain crimes, they would simply vote to acquit. State lawmakers were then forced to write new laws to reduce penalties and add sentencing discretion to the criminal process. Otherwise, no matter how much evidence prosecutors could assemble in court, the accused would go free. Citizens checked heavy-handed legislation.

By exercising independent judgment, jurors help redirect government policy, no matter what legislatures enact, prosecutors bring, or courts decide. In the case of obscenity and pornography, the Supreme Court issues very general guidelines about "contemporary community standards." It asks whether something is of "prurient interest," patently offensive, and lacks serious literary, artistic, political, or scientific value. It is up to jurors in various communities to apply those general standards to particular cases involving books, movies, art exhibits, or music performances. The final word is not with legislatures, prosecutors, or judges but with citizens sitting on juries and reaching personal judgments. As explained in the next section, Congress must take into account the values of the community when it legislates.

## Conscientious Objectors

The first governmental institution in America to recognize the rights of conscientious objectors was the legislature, not the courts. Lawmakers responded to social needs when they carved out exemptions for those who refused, for religious or ethical reasons, to bear arms. Judges came late to this constitutional issue. In requiring citizens to serve in the militia, colonies and early state governments made exceptions for individuals who expressed religious objections. A Pennsylvania law in 1757 provided that all "Quakers, Mennonites, Moravians, and other conscientiously scrupulous of bearing arms" were entitled, upon the call to arms, to assist in nonviolent ways by extinguishing fires, suppressing the insurrection of slaves and other persons, caring for the wounded, and performing other services. When the Assembly of Pennsylvania passed legislation to create a militia in 1775, it recognized that "many of the good people of this Province are conscientiously scrupulous of bearing of arms," and counseled those willing to join to "bear a tender and brotherly regard toward this class of their fellow-subjects and Countrymen."

On July 18, 1775, the Continental Congress debated proposals to create a militia. It recognized that some people, for religious principles, "cannot bear arms in any case." It asked those individuals to assist "their distressed brethren" by providing assistance "consistently with their religious principles." After the Declaration of Independence, a number of state constitutions, including those of Pennsylvania, Vermont, New Hampshire, and Maine, recognized the rights of conscientious objectors.[11]

During the Civil War, several efforts were made to accommodate individuals who cited religious reasons for refusing to kill. Some Quakers, as a substitute for military service, agreed to serve as chaplains and nurses.[12] Secretary of War Edwin Stanton offered a compromise designed to satisfy both the government and the Quakers. He proposed the creation of a special fund to benefit freed slaves. Any Quaker who paid $300 into that fund would be exempt from military service.[13] That kind of creative proposal could not have come from a court. Congress passed legislation in 1864 to provide that members of religious denominations who, by oath or affirmation, declared they were conscientiously opposed to bearing arms, could be assigned to "duty in the hospitals, or to the care of freedmen."[14]

After the United States entered World War I in April 1917, Congress passed legislation creating a military establishment but stated that nothing in the statute was to be construed to compel any person to serve in the military services who belonged to "any well-recognized religious sect or organization" whose principles forbid its members to participate in war in any form. Implementation of the statute was left to regulations drawn up by the president. An executive order issued by President Woodrow Wilson set forth guidelines on the type of noncombatant service that could be performed by conscientious objectors, including service in the Medical Corps, the Quartermaster Corps, and the engineer service.[15]

When Congress considered similar legislation for World War II, it was understood by that time that individuals could be considered legitimate conscientious objectors who were not members of a religious organization. Initially, House and Senate bills restricted conscientious objectors to members of a "well-recognized religious sect." Two Quakers intervened to insist that the status of conscientious objector depended on individual conscience, not membership in a group. Congress amended the statute to exempt anyone who, "by reason of religious training and belief, is conscientiously opposed to participation in war in any form."[16] That language remains part of current law.

## Equal Accommodations

In 1875, Congress passed legislation giving blacks equal access to such public accommodations as inns, land or water transportation, theaters, "and other places of public amusement." Some lawmakers objected that the measure was an effort to make blacks and whites socially equal. Supporters of the bill denied they had that objective. No legislation, they said, could ever direct social relationships. Individuals would associate with the friends they chose. The purpose of the bill was legal, not social. It was designed to give blacks the same legal access to public facilities that whites enjoyed. During House debate, Representative Benjamin Butler of Massachusetts pointed out that the Fourteenth Amendment made blacks citizens of the United States, giving them "a political and legal equality with every other citizen." Nothing in the bill provided for social equality, which continued to "come from the voluntary will of each person." As in the past, each person would select his or her friends and associates. He then moved to the substance of the bill:

> But it is said we put them into the [railroad] cars. The men that are put into the cars and the women that are put into the cars I trust are not my associates. There are many white men and white

> women, whom I should prefer not to associate with who have a right to ride in the cars. That is not a question of society at all; it is a question of a common right in public conveyance.
>
> And so in regard to places of amusement, in regard to theaters. I do not understand that a theater is a social gathering. I do not understand that men gather there for society, except the society they choose to make each for himself. So in regard to inns. Inns or taverns are for all classes of people; and every man, high or low, rich and poor, learned or ignorant, clean or dirty, has a right to go into an inn and have such accommodations exactly as he will pay for. . . . I am not obliged to speak to any man or associate with him that I meet at an inn. . . .
>
> The bill is necessary because there is an illogical, unjust, ungentlemanly, and foolish prejudice upon this matter. There is not a white man [in] the South that would not associate with the negro—all that is required by this bill—if that negro were his servant. He would eat with him, suckle from her, play with her or him as children, be together with them in every way, provided they were slaves. ...[17]

After clearing Congress and becoming law, the bill was challenged in the courts as unconstitutional. In the *Civil Rights Cases* (1883),[18] the Supreme Court struck down the equal accommodation provision. It held that Section 5 of the Fourteenth Amendment empowered Congress to enforce only the prohibitions placed upon the states. It could regulate "state action," but not discriminatory actions by private parties. Dissenting in the case, Justice John Harlan explained that for centuries the common law had prohibited private parties from discriminating against travelers who stopped at inns and restaurants. Railroads were regarded as public, not private, highways. Government authorized them for public use even if private corporations owned and operated them. To Harlan, the rights established by Congress in the 1875 legislation "are legal, not social rights." The right of a black to use the accommodations of a public highway was no more "a social right than his right, under the law, to use the public streets of a city or a town, or a turnpike road, or a public market, or a post office, or his right to sit in a public building."[19] Because of the Court's decision in the

*Civil Rights Cases*, equal access to public accommodations had to await the Civil Rights Act of 1964.

## Women and the Practice of Law

In the years following the Civil War, women entered universities in large numbers to pursue careers in medicine, law, and other professions. Women who possessed a law degree had to seek the approval of a panel of judges (all male) in order to practice law. Routinely they were denied permission. The Illinois Supreme Court refused to grant Myra Bradwell a license to practice law, even though it did not doubt her qualifications. It anticipated that engaging in "the hot strifes of the bar" might tend to destroy "the deference and delicacy with which it is the pride of our ruder sex to treat her."[20] Moreover, the state legislature had not acted to authorize women to practice law. Courts of justice "were not intended to be made the instruments of pushing forward measures of popular reform.[21]

The message was clear. There would be no relief from the courts. Women had to seek rights from legislative bodies. On March 22, 1872, the Illinois legislature passed a bill stating that "no person shall be precluded or debarred from any occupation, profession or employment (except military) on account of sex: Provided that this act shall not be construed to affect the eligibility of any person to an elective office." Also, nothing in the legislation was to be construed "as requiring any female to work on streets or roads, or serve on juries." All laws inconsistent with the 1872 law were "hereby repealed."[22]

Successful at the state level, Bradwell attempted to give women a national right to practice law. Taking her case to the U.S. Supreme Court, she argued that rejection by the judiciary of her application to practice law violated the Privileges and Immunities Clause of the Fourteenth Amendment, which reads: "No State shall make or enforce any law which shall abridge the privileges or immunities of citizens of the United States."

Although the Court in *Bradwell v. State* (1873) agreed that there are privileges and immunities belonging to citizens of the United States, "the right to admission to practice in the courts of a State is not one of them."[23] The right to control and regulate the granting of licenses to practice law in state courts "is one of those powers which are not transferred for its protection to the Federal Government." To that extent, the Court shifted the issue away from the national government and returned it to the states, especially to state legislatures. The right of women to practice law before the U.S. Supreme Court would soon provoke legislation by Congress.

In a concurrence in Bradwell's case, Justice Joseph Bradley expressed some views that were typical of the judiciary (but not for legislative bodies). He argued that the civil law, "as well as nature herself, has always recognized a wide difference in the respective spheres and destinies of man and woman." Man is, "or should be, woman's protector and defender." The "natural and proper timidity and delicacy which belongs to the female sex evidently unfits it for many of the occupations of civil life." He did not point to evidence, unless it was something in nature itself. The family organization, founded in "the divine ordinance, as well as in the nature of things, indicates the domestic sphere as that which properly belongs to the domain and functions of womanhood." This duty to the family "is repugnant to the idea of a woman adopting a distinct and independent career from that of her husband." Bradley observed that it was a maxim of common law that a woman had no legal existence separate from her husband, and that a married woman was incapable, without her husband's consent, of making contracts that would be binding on her or him. He conceded that some women are unmarried but they were exceptions to the general rule. He continued:

> The paramount destiny and mission of woman are to fulfill the noble and benign offices of wife and mother. This is the law of the Creator. And the rule of civil society must be adapted to the general constitution of things, and cannot be based upon exceptional cases.

> The humane movements of modern society, which have for their object the multiplication of avenues for woman's advancement, and of occupations adapted to her condition and sex, have my heartiest concurrence. But I am not prepared to say that it is one of her fundamental rights and privileges to be admitted into every office and position, including those which require highly special qualifications and demanding special responsibilities. ... [I]n my opinion, in view of the peculiar characteristics, destiny, and mission of woman, it is within the province of the legislature to ordain what offices, positions, and callings shall be filled and discharged by men, and shall receive the benefit of those energies and responsibilities, and that decision and firmness which are presumed to predominate in the sterner sex.[24]

Whatever one might say about a divine ordinance or the nature of the female sex, Justice Bradley understood that the decision regarding the right of women to practice law would be left in the hands of legislative bodies. Just as the Illinois legislature opened the legal profession to women, so did Congress. In 1878, Congress began consideration of a bill to allow women to practice before the U.S. Supreme Court. Belva Lockwood, who had been admitted to the Washington, D.C., bar in 1873, drafted legislation and worked closely with members of Congress to move the bill through both chambers. The bill provided that when any woman had been admitted to the bar of the highest court of a state, or of the supreme court of the District of Columbia, and was otherwise qualified as set forth in the bill (three years of practice and a person of good moral character, as with male attorneys) she may be admitted to practice before the U.S. Supreme Court. The bill came out of the House Judiciary Committee unanimously and passed the House, 169 to 87, on February 21, 1878.[25]

The Senate Judiciary Committee reported the bill adversely after concluding that it would interfere with the rules of the U.S. Supreme Court, which prohibited women from practicing there. A floor statement on March 18 explained that the committee believed that each federal court had full discretion on the admission of lawyers and that the bill appeared in some cases to favor women over men. Senator Aaron Sargent (R-CA) offered an amendment to delete the text of the bill and replace it with: "That, no person shall be excluded from practicing as an attorney and counselor at law from any court of the United States on account of sex." He pointed out that the District of Columbia and many states had admitted women to the bar. The states included California, Illinois, Michigan, Minnesota, Missouri, North Carolina, Utah, and Wyoming. He thought it was absurd to have female lawyers handle a case in state court and then, if the dispute moved on appeal to a federal court, be forced to transfer the case to a male lawyer.

Sargent recalled that in Shakespeare's time it was impermissible for a woman to appear on stage as an actress. Those parts were performed by men. To have a chance at publication, female writers of great talent had to submit their manuscripts with a male name. He thought it unfortunate for the Court in *Bradwell* to require action by legislatures, "but they seem to have done so, and that makes the necessity for this legislation which I have now offered." The bill was returned to the committee with instructions to report it soon to the floor for debate. Instead, the committee concluded there was no need for the bill and recommended that it be postponed indefinitely. On May 29, Senator Sargent asked that his amendment be reported. He wanted his colleagues to vote, up or down. The initial vote was 26 to 26. Twenty-four Senators were absent. Therefore, the motion to take up the bill was not agreed to.

The bill returned to the Senate floor on February 7, 1879. Once again the Judiciary Committee reported the bill adversely, without written report. Senator Joseph McDonald acknowledged that the Supreme Court might resolve the controversy by a different construction of its rule or by amending it, but "does not seem inclined to do so." Senator Sargent reviewed the progress made by women in entering professions, including medicine and surgery. "No man," he said, "has a right to put a limit to the exertions or the sphere of woman. That is a right which only can be possessed by that sex itself." He then drew a comparison between the rights recently granted to black slaves and the rights still to be recognized for women:

> I say again, men have not the right, in contradiction to the intentions, the wishes, the ambition, of women, to say that their sphere shall be circumscribed, that bounds be set which they cannot pass. The enjoyment of liberty, the pursuit of happiness in her own way, is as much the birthright of woman as of man. In this land man has ceased to dominate over his fellow—let him cease to dominate over his sister; for he has no higher right to do the latter than the former. It is mere oppression to say to the bread-seeking woman, you shall labor only in certain narrow ways for your living, we will hedge you out by law from profitable employments, and monopolize them for ourselves.
>
> Who fears the competition of women? Who pleads for a law to help him hold his medical or legal practice? Let him step down and out. It would be as well to enact that women should not mount the rostrum or pulpit, or engage in writing books in competition with men.[26]

Lawmakers debated what degree of deference should be extended to the Supreme Court to decide its own rules and who should be admitted to practice. Senator George Hoar (R-MA) remarked: "Now, with the greatest respect for that tribunal, I conceive that the law-making and not the law-expounding power in the Government ought to determine the question what class of citizens shall be clothed with the office of the advocate."[27] Suppose, he asked, that the Court decided to prohibit black lawyers from practicing before it, notwithstanding the Civil War amendments. Would there be any doubt that Congress could intercede and pass legislation to reverse the Court? The bill passed the Senate, 39 to 20, and became law. On March 3, 1879, Belva Lockwood was admitted to the Supreme Court bar. A year later she sponsored Samuel R. Lowery, the first southern black to practice before the Court.[28]

The issue of women practicing law was not an isolated and rare example of judicial shortcoming. Not until 1971, in *Reed v. Reed*, did the Supreme Court strike down a law that discriminated against women.[29] The statute invalidated was an Idaho law that preferred men over women in administering estates. In the early decades of the twentieth century, the Court upheld state laws that adopted maximum hours and minimum wages for women, or prohibited women in large cities from working between 10 p.m. and 6 a.m., but this period of "protective legislation" perpetuated the stereotype of delicate women advanced in *Bradwell*.

In *Goeseart v. Cleary* (1948), the Court upheld a Michigan law that prohibited female bartenders unless they were the wife or daughter of the male owner.[30] Writing for the majority, Justice Frankfurter made short work of the legal dispute: "Beguiling as the subject is, it need not detain us for long. To ask whether or not the Equal Protection of the Laws Clause of the Fourteenth Amendment barred Michigan from making the classification the State has made between wives and daughters of owners of liquor places and wives of daughters of nonowners, is one of those rare instances where to state the question is in effect to answer it."[31] In *Hoyt v. Florida* (1961), a unanimous Court agreed that women could be largely exempted from jury service because (echoing *Bradwell*) they are "still regarded as the center of home and family life."[32]

Throughout this period, legal rights for women were advanced by Congress and state legislatures, not the courts. Congress passed the Equal Pay Act in 1963 to prohibit employers in the private sector from discriminating on the basis of sex. Title VII of the Civil Rights Act of 1964 made it illegal for any employer to discriminate against anyone with respect to "compensation, terms, conditions, or privileges of employment" because of the person's sex. Congress passed Title IX of the Education Amendments of 1972 to withdraw federal financial assistance from any educational institution that practices sex discrimination. By the time the Court decided the *Reed* case in 1971, scholarly studies regarded the judicial record as deplorable. According to one study published that year: "Our conclusion, independently reached, but completely shared, is that by and large the performance of American judges in the area of sex discrimination can be succinctly described as ranging from poor to abominable."[33]

Frustration with judicial attitudes reached the point in 1970 when the House of Representatives passed the Equal Rights Amendment by the margin of 350 to 15. After Senate approval, the language submitted to the states for ratification read: "Equality of rights under the law shall not be denied or abridged by the United States or by any State on account of sex." A major advocate of the ERA, Representative Martha Griffiths (D-MI), had this to say during debate in October 1971: "Mr. Chairman, what the equal rights amendment seeks to do, and all that it seeks to do, is to say to the Supreme Court of the United States, 'Wake up! This is the 20th century. Before it is over, judge women as individual human beings.'"[34] A month later the Court decided *Reed*, invalidating a state law that gave preferences to men in administering estates.

## Compulsory Flag Salutes

As with other constitutional rights, religious liberty generally depends more on community attitudes and legislative action than it does on court decisions. In *Minersville School District v. Gobitis* (1940), the Supreme Court reviewed a Pennsylvania statute that compelled public school children to salute the American flag.[35] Jehovah's Witnesses adopted a literal interpretation of the biblical injunction against saluting secular symbols: "Thou shalt not make unto thee any graven image, or any likeness of anything that is in heaven above, or that is in the earth beneath, or that is in the water under the earth. Thou shalt not bow down thyself to them, nor serve them" (Exodus 2:4–5). Witnesses regarded the flag salute (extending the right hand, palm upward, toward the flag) as religiously repugnant and saw the gesture as similar to the Nazi salute in Germany. Lower federal courts, drawing attention to the history of religious freedom in Pennsylvania, struck down the compulsory flag salute. The state constitution provided that "[a]ll men have a natural and indefeasible right to worship Almighty God according to the dictates of their own consciences; . . . no human authority can, in any case whatsoever, control or interfere with the rights of conscience."[36]

Yet the Supreme Court in an eight-to-one opinion reversed the lower courts. The decision was issued on June 3, 1940, a time when Nazi Germany was extending its control over Europe. Writing for the majority, Justice Frankfurter appeared to conclude that at such times individual rights must be subordinated to national needs. He argued that individual liberty and national survival required such unifying sentiments as a flag salute. The only dissent came from Justice Harlan Fiske Stone. The top-heavy majority, delivered when the country was on the verge of world war, seemed to be the last word. But several developments made the decision exceedingly fragile.

When the justices returned to the Court after the summer recess, William O. Douglas advised Frankfurter that Hugo Black was having second thoughts about the compulsory flag salute decision. Sarcastically, Frankfurter asked whether Black had been reading the Constitution. "No," Douglas explained, "he has been reading the papers."[37] In addition to Black, Douglas and Frank Murphy had begun to regret joining with Frankfurter. All three had recently come to the Court and looked to Frankfurter for guidance, especially on matters of civil liberties. Within two years they would desert him on this case.

Similar to the Court in *Bradwell,* Frankfurter advised the Jehovah's Witnesses that the relief they sought could come not from the judiciary but from "the forum of public opinion and before legislative assemblies." What Black and the other justices learned over the summer was that newspapers, law reviews, the press, and religious organizations strongly condemned the Court. They accused the Court of violating constitutional rights and buckling to popular hysteria. Frankfurter and his seven colleagues seemed to be adopting oppressive policies from the

Nazis. Of 39 law reviews that analyzed the decision, 31 did so critically. Editorials in 171 newspapers ripped Frankfurter's decision and his reasoning.[38]

This national dialogue had an impact on Black, Douglas, and Murphy. In *Jones v. Opelika* (1942), they recanted from their earlier support for the compulsory flag salute and announced that the 1940 decision had been "wrongly decided."[39] What seemed like an insurmountable eight-to-one majority was now five to four. A change in the Court's composition further undercut Frankfurter's position. Two new justices joined the Court (Wiley Rutledge and Robert H. Jackson) and they joined with Stone, Black, Douglas, and Murphy. Congress also helped undermine the 1940 decision. Legislation passed in 1942 did not support flag salutes. Instead, it provided that "civilians will always show full respect to the flag when the pledge is given by merely standing at attention, men removing the headdress." To the Justice Department, the statute represented a rebuttal of the 1940 decision. The department directed U.S. attorneys to advise local authorities of this new statutory standard.[40]

With *West Virginia State Board of Education v. Barnette* (1943), the Supreme Court had an opportunity to revisit the compulsory flag salute. A six-to-three Court reversed Frankfurter's 1940 ruling.[41] Writing for the majority, Justice Jackson issued a memorable and stirring defense of religious liberty. In striking down the compulsory flag salute, he declared that the "very purpose of a Bill of Rights was to withdraw certain subjects from the vicissitudes of political controversy, to place them beyond the reach of majorities and officials and to establish them as legal principles to be applied by the courts." Powerful sentiments, but much of the credit for changing constitutional doctrine belonged to private citizens, newspapers, law reviews, members of Congress, and attorneys in the Justice Department who recognized that a compulsory flag salute for children was deeply offensive. They did not defer to the Court, even with its imposing eight-to-one majority. In other cases brought in the early 1940s, the Court was more protective of the religious opinions and liberties of minorities, including Jehovah's Witnesses.[42]

## The Yarmulke Case

In the 1980s, Congress played a more central role in reversing a restrictive ruling by the Supreme Court on religious liberty. Captain Simcha Goldman of the U.S. Air Force wore his yarmulke indoors on duty for years. An Orthodox Jew and ordained rabbi, he was assigned to a mental health clinic and worked as a clinical psychologist. There was no dispute about wearing a yarmulke until he testified at a court-martial and took a position at odds with the air force. A month later, on May 8, 1981, the air force told him that wearing a yarmulke indoors violated the military dress code.

His first recourse was with the air force, asking it to reconsider its application of the military regulation or rewrite it in a manner that permitted continued use of the yarmulke indoors. The air force declined to provide that relief. He then went to court, asking that a preliminary injunction be issued against the secretary of defense and the secretary of the air force. The district court held that the air force regulation violated his free exercise rights under the First Amendment. The court dismissed the military's claim that allowing Goldman to wear his yarmulke "will crush the spirit of uniformity, which in turn will weaken the will and fighting spirit of the Air Force." A year later, in a separate yarmulke case involving the military, a district court seemed to accept the military's argument that departures from uniformity would adversely affect "the promotion of teamwork, counteract pride and motivation, and undermine discipline and morale, all to the detriment of the substantial compelling governmental interest of maintaining an efficient Air Force."[43]

At the appellate level, all three judges of a D.C. Circuit panel agreed in 1984 that the air force regulation was justified. The military warned that allowing Goldman to wear his yarmulke would trigger religious liberty claims from other military personnel, with soldiers insisting on the right to wear turbans, robes, face and body paint, shorn hair, unshorn hair, badges, rings, amulets, bracelets, jodhpurs, and symbolic daggers. A motion to rehear the case was denied. The case now moved to the Supreme Court.

The rulings by the D.C. Circuit prompted Representative Stephen Solarz (D-NY) to introduce legislation to permit military personnel to wear unobtrusive religious headgear, such as a skullcap, if required for religious reasons. Under his legislation, the secretary of defense could prohibit any religious apparel that interfered with a military duty. The House agreed to the Solarz amendment, even though Representative William Dickinson (R-AL) warned that "we are flying in the face of a court decision just made." Had he looked at the Constitution, Article I expressly empowers Congress to "make rules for the Government and Regulation of the land and naval Forces." The superior judge in this area is Congress, not the judiciary. The Solarz amendment was later removed from the defense authorization bill that became law in 1984.

At the Supreme Court, the brief for the Justice Department defended the air force and argued that support for Captain Goldman would compel the military to choose between "virtual abandonment of its uniform regulations and constitutionally impermissible line drawing." The entire purpose of uniform standards "would be defeated if individuals were allowed exemptions." To disregard the government's interest and permit exceptions "would make a mockery of the military's compelling interest in uniformity." High-flying language, but in fact the military did not insist on total conformity. Without incident, individuals wore a crucifix, Star of David, or other religious symbols on chains placed around their necks.

During oral argument, some justices seemed uncomfortable about telling the Defense Department to rewrite its regulations. Kathryn Oberly of the Justice Department advised them to leave the issue to the elected branches: "If Congress thinks that further accommodation is either required or desirable it can legislate it." If Congress wrote legislation that turned out to be impractical or unwise, it could offer amendments in the future. The Court was not so flexible. Once it recognized a constitutional basis for Goldman's religious liberty it would be awkward in future rulings to redirect court doctrine.

In *Goldman v. Weinberger* (1986), the Court held five to four that the First Amendment did not prohibit the air force regulation.[44] It accepted the military's argument that the outfitting of military personnel in standardized uniforms "encourages the subordination of personal preferences and identities in favor of the overall group mission." Goldman's interests were therefore inferior to the values of uniformity, hierarchy, unity, discipline, and obedience. Justice Brennan, joined by Justice Marshall, wrote a dissent with two conflicting messages. On the one hand he chided the majority for abdicating the judiciary's role "as principal expositor of the Constitution and protector of individual liberties in favor of credulous deference to unsupported assertions of military necessity."[45] He then conceded that the judiciary was not the only institution capable of protecting religious freedom: "Guardianship of this precious liberty is not the exclusive domain of federal courts. It is the responsibility as well of the states and of the other branches of the Federal Government." Having concluded that the Court and the military had refused to grant servicemen their constitutional rights, he identified the remedy: "we must hope that Congress will correct this wrong."[46]

Within two weeks of the Court's decision, legislation was introduced in Congress to permit members of the armed forces to wear items of apparel not part of the official uniform. They could wear any "neat, conservative, and unobtrusive" item that satisfied the tenets of a religious belief. The armed services would retain authority to prohibit the wearing of an item after determining that "it significantly interferes with the performance of the member's military duties." For those who might regard "neat and conservative" as far too vague a standard, those words appeared in existing military regulations.

The House passed the legislation, but the Senate balked. The language was initially tabled, 51 to 49. Senator Barry Goldwater (R-AZ), chairman of the Armed Services Committee, warned that Native Americans would want to wear feather headdresses. He advised soldiers who disliked uniforms to get out of them and join something else.[47] In conference committee, the House provision was eliminated.

Debate continued the next year. Once again the House adopted its amendment. No one spoke against it. Between 1986 and 1987, some of the senators switched their votes. Six senators who had supported the tabling motion (Boschwitz, Burdick, Danforth, Domenici, Harkin, and Rockefeller) now favored the House language. Eight newly elected senators (Adams, Breaux, Daschle, Graham, Karnes, Mikulski, Reid, and Wirth) offered their support. The final vote in the Senate was 55 to 42 for the House amendment.

The comfortable majority in the Senate is remarkable in view of intense opposition around the country. The American Legion, with over 2.5 million members, and the Military Coalition, representing 16 of the largest organizations for military personnel, strongly denounced the House amendment. Secretary of Defense Caspar Weinberger opposed it. A document called a "twenty-star letter" registered intense disagreement. It was signed by five military officers, each wearing four stars: the chairman of the Joint Chiefs of Staff and the other four members representing the army, air force, marine corps, and navy. Congress ignored these grave warnings. The bill protecting the religious liberties of members of the military became law.

## Civil Rights Made Real

Those who regard the Supreme Court as the principal guardian of civil rights and civil liberties will think first of the Court's ruling in *Brown v. Board of Education* (1954).[48] A unanimous Court struck down the "separate but equal" doctrine that emerged in 1896 with *Plessy v. Ferguson*.[49] With only one justice dissenting, the Court in *Plessy* upheld a Louisiana law that required railroads to provide equal, but separate, accommodations for white and black passengers. The Court for decades had resisted congressional efforts to secure the rights of black Americans. No doubt *Brown* marked a major breakthrough in race relations. An important question: How effective was it in producing social and political change?

The unanimity of *Brown* cloaked a deeply divided Court. In 1952 and 1953 the justices appeared to be evenly split on what to do about *Plessy*. Four Justices (Hugo Black, William Douglas, Harold Burton, and Sherman Minton) were ready to overturn the 1896 precedent. Five Justices (Fred Vinson, Stanley Reed, Felix Frankfurter, Robert Jackson, and Tom Clark) did not support overruling *Plessy*. When Chief Justice Vinson died on September 8, 1953, and Earl Warren was confirmed as his successor, the five-to-four majority now seemed to swing in the direction of change.[50] For political reasons, reversing a precedent that had lasted for a half century needed, if possible, a unanimous Court. What could Warren do to convince four justices to join the other five?

The strategy was to announce the Court's position not in one decision but two. In 1954 a unanimous Court declared racial discrimination in public schools unconstitutional. In stirring language, Chief Justice Warren announced that segregating children in public schools solely on the basis of race, even if the physical facilities and other factors were equal, deprived black children of equal educational opportunities. He concluded that "in the field of public education the doctrine of 'separate but equal' has no place. Separate educational facilities are inherently unequal."[51] Segregation marked a denial of the equal protection of the laws.

How to implement this new constitutional principle was pushed to the future. Four justices convinced the majority of five to give local school districts substantial discretion in putting *Brown* into effect. The Court's ruling a year later, *Brown v. Board of Education* (1955)—referred to as *Brown II*—explained in the opening paragraph: "There remains for consideration the manner in which relief is to be accorded."[52] Full implementation of the principles announced in *Brown I* "may require solution of varied local school problems." School authorities had the primary responsibility for solving the problems and federal courts would have to consider whether their response "constitutes good faith implementation of the governing constitutional principles."[53]

Language in *Brown II* invited substantial delays in putting *Brown I* into effect. A federal judge should consider "a practical flexibility in shaping its remedies and by a facility for adjusting and reconciling public and private needs." Black children should be admitted to public schools "as soon as practicable." The vitality of the constitutional principles put forth in *Brown I*, the Court cautioned, "cannot be allowed to yield simply because of disagreement with them." Yet in directing segregated schools to make "a prompt and reasonable start" in complying with *Brown I*, federal courts "may find that additional time is necessary to carry out the ruling in an effective manner."[54] Courts would have to weigh many factors, including the physical condition of schools, the school transportation system, personnel, and revising school districts and local regulations. The Court directed district courts to implement *Brown I* "with all deliberate speed." Many of the states placed the priority on deliberation, not speed.

Through its language in the implementing decision, the Court encouraged resistance, obstruction, and procrastination. In the decade following *Brown I*, there was little progress in desegregating public schools. As late as 1964, the Court complained that there "has been entirely too much deliberation and not enough speed."[55] In 1964, only 2 percent of black children attended biracial schools in the 11 Southern states. Two years later a federal appellate court remarked: "A national effort, bringing together Congress, the executive and the judiciary may be able to make meaningful the right of Negro children to equal educational opportunities. *The courts acting alone have failed*."[56] Securing constitutional rights required action by all three branches.

Much of the progress that *Brown I* promised awaited congressional action on the Civil Rights Act of 1964, the most far-reaching statute in this area since the decades following the Civil War. Consistent with public pressures on other constitutional issues, passage of the statute demanded citizens to intervene with years of sit-ins, demonstrations, picketing, and boycotts. The media gave close coverage to harsh police actions against peaceful protesters. The world watched to see if America could reconcile its principles of democracy and equal rights with its practices.

Unlike the limited leverage of a Supreme Court decision, congressional action combined with broad public support could change national policy. Members of Congress held lengthy hearings to explain the need for the legislation. Private citizens testified at those hearings to help inform lawmakers. What emerged from Congress had a legitimacy, solidity, and public understanding that could never come from a judicial ruling. The civil rights bill attracted broad bipartisan support. The House voted 289 to 126 for the legislation; the Senate majority was 73 to 27. Democrats in the House supported the bill 153 to 91. Republican support was even stronger, 136 to 35. The party split in the Senate: 46 to 21 for Democrats and 27 to 6 for Republicans.

Among other features, the Civil Rights Act of 1964 covered public accommodations, the issue that had preoccupied Congress after the Civil War. It prohibited discrimination on grounds of race, color, religion, or national origin if the activity affected interstate commerce or the discrimination was supported by state policy. The activities covered by Congress included restaurants, cafeterias, lunchrooms, lunch counters, soda fountains, gas stations, movies, theaters, concert halls, sports arenas, stadiums, and any inn, hotel, motel, or lodging house open for transient guests. Exempted from the statute were units with five or fewer rooms. Also outside the reach of the statute were private clubs.

The Supreme Court had never overruled the *Civil Rights Cases* of 1883, which invalidated the equal accommodation provision in an 1875 statute. Congress in 1964 offered the Court two justifications: the Fourteenth Amendment and the Commerce Clause. In two unanimous rulings the Court sustained the equal accommodations section.[57] Persistent pressure from the public and Congress eventually prevailed over a nearly century-old judicial ruling. Once again Congress overcame judicial obstacles to protect minorities.

After Congress passed the Civil Rights Act with strong bipartisan support, the Court decided to return to an issue it had earlier ducked. One year after deciding *Brown I*, a mixed marriage case came to the Court. Virginia had passed legislation forbidding miscegenation: marriage or cohabitation between a white person and a member of another race. Given the political climate in 1955 and the uproar in some states to the desegregation decision, the Court decided to sidestep a socially explosive issue. Opponents of *Brown I* predicted that integrated schools would lead to "mongrelization" of the white race. A lower court, in upholding the Virginia statute, said it was necessary for the state to forbid interracial marriages "so that it shall not have a mongrel breed of citizens."[58] Rather than risk further attacks, the Court decided to send the case back to Virginia by citing the "inadequacy of the record."[59] A year later the Court declined to take the case because it was "devoid of a properly presented federal question."[60] In essence the Court decided to buy some time.

The public debate and education that came from congressional action on the Civil Rights Act did much to change attitudes in the country about race. In this new climate, the Court was ready to strike down Virginia's statute and did so in *Loving v. Virginia* (1967).[61] The Court noted that 14 states in the previous 15 years had repealed laws prohibiting interracial marriages. Contemporary public opinion encouraged the Court to accept the case this time and decide it. The Court rejected the argument that Virginia's law should be upheld because the framers of the Fourteenth Amendment did not intend to prohibit miscegenation laws. Under the Constitution, said the Court, "the freedom to marry, or not marry, a person of another race resides with the individual and cannot be infringed by the States." A bold ruling, but the Court would not have issued that decision in 1955. It took political action by Congress, President Johnson, a number of states, and the general public to prepare the groundwork for invalidating racial restrictions on marriage.

In an article in 1962, Chief Justice Earl Warren drew attention to the need for the general public to protect constitutional values and minority rights. Although remembered as an "activist" member of the judiciary, he took care to explain the limits of the courts. In times of emergencies and external threats, the courts may acquiesce to executive and legislative abuses. In particular, he had in mind what happened after World War II with the detention of Japanese Americans, most of them U.S. citizens. Interestingly, he said the fact that the Court held that the actions by President Roosevelt and Congress were constitutional, did "not necessarily answer the question whether, in a broader sense, it actually is." The plain message: The Supreme Court can acquiesce to unconstitutional actions. To Warren, it was a mistake to place too much expectation on the courts: "In our democracy it is still the Legislature and the elected Executive who have the primary responsibility for fashioning and executing policy consistent with the Constitution." The day-to-day job of defending the Constitution also "lies elsewhere. It rests, realistically, on the shoulders of every citizen."[62]

Constitutional law develops not only through the courts but as a result of individuals and groups operating through the executive and legislative branches. Many constitutional disputes are resolved without a lawsuit, although that may be difficult to imagine in our litigious society. Even when an issue is brought before a court there is no assurance it will be decided or resolved there. The judiciary can avoid a constitutional issue, including matters of individual and minority rights, by invoking such threshold tests as standing, ripeness, mootness, and the political question doctrine. If the Supreme Court actually issues a ruling, it must rely on legislative bodies, executive agencies, jurors, and the general public to decide how the new policy will be given effect. At each of these stages Congress plays a central role.

# Chapter Five
# Congress at Risk

To preserve separation of powers and constitutional checks, the framers understood that each branch is responsible for fighting off encroachments and safeguarding its institutional prerogatives. Only through that effort could individual rights and liberties be protected. Maintaining institutional independence is especially crucial for members of Congress. They represent constituents who vote them into office and give meaning to democratic and republican government. For most of its history Congress honored that purpose. In the six decades after World War II, members of Congress began to reveal a lack of confidence, willingness, and interest in defending their institution. Far from being a coequal or even a superior branch, Congress seemed on a downward slide. When Congress does not protect itself, it fails to protect private citizens, democratic values, individual rights, and the system of checks and balances.

## The Pendulum Stops Swinging

For most of American history, political power swung back and forth between the executive and legislative branches. Strong presidents were routinely replaced by weak presidents. Congress became ascendant in some periods, weaker in others. This cycle of power changed fundamentally during the Great Depression of the 1930s and World War II. Congress found itself ceding large portions of national policy to the president and executive agencies, shifting the balance not temporarily but permanently. Congress recognized the seriousness of the problem and took steps to reassert itself. Ironically, some of those reforms made Congress weaker.

Massive delegations of legislative power to the executive branch were part of the policies adopted in the 1930s to combat the Great Depression. Congress created new federal agencies and committed billions of dollars to them, offering few details or guidelines. The Emergency Relief Appropriations Act of 1935 appropriated $4,880,000,000 to be used "in the discretion and under the direction of the President." During debate, Senator Arthur Vandenberg (R-MI) expressed his frustration and dismay about the scope of the delegation. The original resolution provided funds for such vague objectives as "relieving economic maladjustment" and "alleviating distress." Vandenberg suggested it would be easier to eliminate even those general purposes and simply enact two sections. The first: "Congress hereby appropriates $4,880,000,000 to the President of the United States to use as he pleases." The second: "Anybody who does not like it is fined $1,000."[1]

A study published in 1937 estimated that Congress, over the previous four years, had given President Roosevelt discretionary authority over the sum of $15,428,498,815. That aggregate compared to a total of $1.6 billion in discretionary spending authority granted to all previous presidents.[2] During his first six years in office, Roosevelt declared 39 emergencies. Representative Bruce Barton (R-NY) remarked: "Any national administration is entitled to one or two emergencies in a term of six years. But an emergency every six weeks means plain bad management."[3]

Congress resorted to secret funding during World War II to develop and produce an atomic bomb. Billions were directed to the "Manhattan Project" to further that objective, with few lawmakers informed of how the money would be spent. Appropriated funds were placed in such general accounts as "Engineer Service, Army" and "Expediting Production."[4] There had been confidential spending in the past, but in small amounts. Congress now took steps in authorizing vast amounts of covert spending and covert operations by the intelligence agencies.

Roosevelt was generally successful in persuading Congress to transfer to him broad legislative and spending authority. If Congress delayed or resisted, he threatened to act without it. He warned lawmakers in 1942 that if they "should fail to act, and act adequately, I shall accept the responsibility, and I will act." In that same announcement he predicted that when "the war is won, the powers under which I act automatically revert to the people—to whom they belong."[5] If the power belonged to the people, and therefore to the people's representatives in Congress, what authority did he possess to act with such independence? Moreover, it was not true that the power reverted to the people after the war. Power remained lodged in the executive branch.

With World War II winding down, Congress began to take stock of itself, especially its constitutional powers over public spending and military commitments. Concern was heightened by the rise of fascism in Europe and Asia and the loss of democratic institutions. At stake, worldwide, was the fate of representative government. Congress understood that it was no longer coequal with the executive branch and had become a second-class, second-rate institution. The Joint Committee on the Organization of Congress, established in 1944, bluntly voiced its concerns:

> Under the Constitution, Congress is the policy-making branch of government. There are manifest growing tendencies in recent times toward the shift of policy-making to the Executive, partly because of the comparative lack of effective instrumentalities and the less adequate facilities of the legislative branch. To redress the balance and recover its rightful position in our governmental structure, Congress, many Members feel, must modernize its machinery, coordinate its various parts, and establish the research facilities that can provide it with the knowledge that is power.

Emerging from the committee's study was the Legislative Reorganization Act of 1946, which restructured congressional committees and offered new analytical tools to lawmakers. The statute directed standing committees of Congress to exercise "continuous watchfulness" over executive agencies. In 1947, Congress terminated 175 statutory grants of emergency and war powers. Some of those provisions dated back to World War I. A number of emergency and war statutes remained in place. In attempting to dial back executive power, Congress inadvertently opened the door to greater presidential power by adopting the United Nations Charter and various mutual security pacts, including NATO. Few people at the time understood that these international and regional compacts would (or could) be used by presidents to initiate war without seeking authority from Congress.

## The Impact of the U.N. Charter and NATO

The terrible destruction of World War I brought nations together to form an international body: the League of Nations. Countries joining this organization agreed to submit to it all disputes threatening war and to use military and economic sanctions against nations that practiced aggression. President Woodrow Wilson submitted the plan to the Senate as the Versailles Treaty. A Senate "reservation" to the treaty stated that nothing in the League of Nations could take from Congress its "sole power" under the Constitution to declare or authorize the use of military force against other nations. Wilson's advisers urged him to accept the reservation. He admitted, in a letter to a senator, that no principled objection could be raised against the language. Yet Wilson chose to emotionally confront the Senate, insisting that the reservation "cut the heart" of the treaty and rendered it a nullity.[6] As a result of his stubbornness and rigidity, the United States never joined the League of Nations.

In the middle of World War II, allied nations began to plan for a more effective world organization. Participants in the United States recalled Wilson's failed campaign to join the League of Nations and understood that any commitment of U.S. forces to a world body would require prior authorization by both chambers of Congress. Procedures were drafted to permit the United Nations to use military force against threats to the peace or breaches of the peace. United Nations members would make available to the Security Council, "on its call and in accordance with a special agreement," armed forces and other military assistance. Special agreements would be entered into in accordance with the respective "constitutional processes" of each country.

In a cable from Potsdam, President Truman advised the Senate in 1945 that when any of these agreements were negotiated "it will be my purpose to ask the Congress for appropriate legislation to approve them."[7] There would be no circumvention of the legislative branch. With that assurance, the Senate supported the U.N. Charter by a vote of 89 to 2. To avoid any uncertainty about constitutional principles, Congress passed the U.N. Participation Act of 1945, specifically stating that the agreements "shall be subject to the approval of the Congress by appropriate Act or joint resolution." Statutory language could not be expressed with greater clarity.[8]

Nonetheless, five years later President Truman used military force against North Korea without ever seeking authority from Congress. Never before had a president engaged in a major military commitment without first receiving either a declaration or authorization from Congress. Truman claimed to receive "authority" from two resolutions passed by the Security Council. He told reporters that the military action was not "war" but a U.N. "police action."[9]

This method of circumventing Congress would be used several times. In November 1990, President George H. W. Bush obtained a Security Council resolution to use military force against Iraq, claiming that the resolution made it unnecessary to seek authorization from Congress. Congress passed legislation in January 1991 to support the military action, but Bush in a signing statement argued that he had sought only legislative support, not authority. President Bill Clinton received Security Council support in 1994 to invade Haiti and in 1995 to send U.S. forces into Bosnia. Not once did he seek congressional authority for his military actions.[10]

In the case of the Korean War in 1950, Congress could have defended its prerogatives over war and spending. It chose not to. Instead of fulfilling their oaths to defend the Constitution, lawmakers opted for a different priority: fighting world communism. That choice was not necessary. Members could have resisted aggression in Korea while at the same time protecting the Constitution by telling Truman he needed to come to Congress for authority. Failing to do that, they widened the door for unilateral presidential action and diminished their own institution. This was not the first time that an outside threat was used to place the Constitution in a subordinate position. That pattern began with the Alien and Sedition Act of 1798 and often resurfaces. Violating the Constitution comes with a political price. Just as the 1798 legislation did much to discredit the Federalist Party, U.S. soldiers in Korea became mired in a costly conflict that showed no hope of military victory. The public turned against Truman and elected the Republican candidate, Dwight D. Eisenhower. Having controlled the White House for the last two decades, the Democrats lost the presidential election in large part because of the Korean War.

Another step toward independent, unchecked presidential power came with the adoption of mutual security treaties after World War II. The Rio Treaty of 1947, signed by the United States and 18 countries in Central America, South America, and the Caribbean, promised joint action in the event of military threats. An armed attack against one state was considered an attack against all. The NATO treaty, signed in 1949, represented a pact between the United States, Canada, and 10 European countries. It provided that an armed attack "against one or more of them in Europe or North America shall be considered an attack against them all." In the event of an attack, NATO countries could exercise the right of self-defense. Consistent with the U.N. Charter, the treaty was to be carried out by the parties in accordance with "their respective constitutional processes."

Nothing in the legislative history of NATO anticipated that the mutual security pact would become a substitute for congressional authority, especially for offensive wars. The treaty was explicitly designed for defensive purposes. Under the terms of the treaty, any use of military force would be carried out in accordance with the constitutional processes of the United States, requiring congressional approval by declaration or authorization for offensive actions and any military operations beyond an initial effort to repel sudden attacks.[11] Yet, similar to the misuse of the U.N. Charter, NATO offered another unilateral war-power tool for the president. In 1999, when President Clinton was unable to get the Security Council to support military action against Kosovo, and when Congress refused to provide authority, Clinton circumvented both institutions and used NATO. Instead of seeking approval from elected members of Congress, he sought approval from each of the NATO countries: Belgium, Germany, Italy, etc. The military operation in Kosovo had nothing to do with self-defense.

## Congressional "Reassertion"

Truman's military initiative in Korea provoked Congress to reconsider its constitutional role. A report by the House Foreign Affairs Committee in 1951 underscored the profound impact of the Korean War: "The action of the United States in Korea is in one sense unprecedented. For the first time the United States has committed large military forces in a foreign country in response to the action of an international organization. United States forces were committed in Korea by Presidential action."[12] Five years later another House study expressed concern about the growth of presidential war power. Looking back over the past two decades, the study concluded that in no other period "have so many different presidents been called on to exercise this constitutional power [of commander in chief] in so many different kinds of situations, each one of major importance."[13]

President Eisenhower thought that Truman had made a mistake, politically and constitutionally, by going to war against North Korea without seeking authority from Congress. Eisenhower reasoned that joint action by the president and Congress would send the strongest possible message to both allies and enemies. America would be making a military commitment with the support of the legislative and executive branches, not by unilateral presidential action. On New Year's Day in 1957, he met with congressional leaders of both parties to discuss what to do about tensions in the Middle East. House Majority Leader John McCormack (D-MA) asked Eisenhower whether he, as commander in chief, already possessed sufficient authority over military troops without coming to Congress. Eisenhower reminded the lawmakers "that the Constitution assumes that our two branches of government should get along together."[14]

In August 1964, President Lyndon Johnson came to Congress to request the Gulf of Tonkin Resolution to use military force against North Vietnam. He reported that North Vietnam had made unprovoked attacks on American ships, not once but twice. Coming as it did in the middle of a presidential election, no member of the House voted against the resolution. Only two Senators dared oppose it. As with Korea, the overriding value was to unite both branches and both political parties against an outside threat. By demonstrating "resolve" and a common front to an enemy, Congress abandoned any independent role for itself, even to take the time to investigate whether the second attack in the Tonkin Gulf actually occurred (which we now know it did not).

Lawmakers of both parties assumed that passage of the resolution would send an effective warning to North Vietnam, eliminating the need for further military action. A firm stance against aggression, they thought, would prevent a large-scale war. Yet early the next year, after his reelection, President Johnson began to escalate the war in Southeast Asia, eventually placing over 500,000 American soldiers in that region. A huge increase in combat deaths and casualties, joined by massive financial costs and reports of executive branch stealth and deception, turned the country against the war, Johnson, and the Democrats. Like Eisenhower in 1952, Richard Nixon was elected president in 1968 to end an unpopular war. Misguided presidential wars had twice driven Democrats from the White House. 

Senator J. William Fulbright (D-AR), who managed the Tonkin Gulf Resolution in the Senate, had written in 1961 that "for the existing requirements of American foreign policy we have hobbled the president by too niggardly a grant of power."[15] Watching with dismay at the widening Vietnam War, by 1967 he could see "great merit in the checks and balances of our 18th-century Constitution."[16] The panel he chaired, the Senate Foreign Relations Committee, released a thoughtful report on the alarming decline of Congress as a separate branch of government. The committee said that if blame is to be apportioned for the expansion of presidential war power "a fair share belongs to the Congress" because of its acquiescence and passivity.[17] The report noted that the United States was unfamiliar with its new role as a world power after 1900. Legislative action was often taken in an atmosphere of urgency, both real and contrived. Members of Congress might have been "overawed by the cult of executive expertise." However, any lawmaker paying attention should have recognized that this pretense of expertise was regularly undermined by a record of executive uncertainty, incompetence, and deception.

Oddly, the committee report claimed that the Senate's rejection of the Covenant of the League of Nations might have created in Congress "a kind of penance for its prewar isolationism, and that penance has sometimes taken the form of overly hasty acquiescence in proposals for the acceptance of one form or another of international responsibility."[18] That analysis was flawed. The failure to join the League of Nations had more to do with President Wilson's stubborn and groundless refusal to accept the Senate reservations. Also, if any branch should be inclined toward "penance" and confess to past errors, it would be the executive branch for entering into wars in Korea and Vietnam without first calculating the costs and the likelihood of failure.

The Senate report stood on firmer ground when it criticized lawmakers for "making a *personal* judgment as to how President Johnson would implement the [Tonkin Gulf] resolution when it had a responsibility to make an *institutional* judgment, first, as to what *any* president would do with so great an acknowledgment of power, and, second, as to whether, under the Constitution, Congress had a right to grant or concede the authority in question."[19] In short, lawmakers forgot what was

elementary to the framers: Do not trust people with power. Especially do not trust presidents with the war power, even when they belong to your party. Republicans under George W. Bush would make the same mistake.

Congressional studies led to the drafting of a War Powers Resolution of 1973, intended to give a statutory structure to the commitment of U.S. forces abroad. The House was reluctant to place any advance restrictions on the president. It was willing to recognize that the president "in certain extraordinary and emergency circumstances has the authority to defend the United States and its citizens without specific prior authorization by the Congress."[20] Under the House bill, the president would be required, "whenever feasible," to consult with Congress before sending American troops into combat. He would report the circumstances that necessitated his initiative and why he had not sought prior legislative authority. The House bill allowed presidential military commitments without seeking advance legislative authority.

The Senate regarded the House bill as too permissive and insufficiently protective of legislative and public interests. It decided to identify the precise conditions that would justify unilateral presidential action: a need (1) to repel an armed attack upon the United States and its territories and possessions, retaliate in the event of such an attack, and forestall the direct and imminent threat of such an attack; (2) to repel an armed attack against U.S. armed forces located outside the United States and its territories and possessions and forestall the direct and imminent threat of such an attack; and (3) to rescue endangered American citizens and nationals in foreign countries or at sea. The first situation (except for the final clause) conforms to the understanding of the delegates at the Philadelphia Convention that the president could "repel sudden attacks." The second and third situations reflect later developments of defensive war and protecting American lives and property. The Senate bill required the president to cease military operations within 30 days unless Congress specifically authorized the action.

The bill that came out of conference committee tilted very much toward presidential power. Senator Tom Eagleton (D-MO), who had helped draft the Senate bill, protested that the compromise version gave the president "carte blanche" authority to use military force for up to ninety days. He called it a surrender, a sellout, and "horribly bastardized to the point of being a menace."[21] Nevertheless, the bill passed each chamber. President Nixon vetoed it, but each house had sufficient votes for an override. Many lawmakers interpreted the override as a great triumph for congressional power. They did not read the bill with care to know what they had given away.

The statute has little to commend it. Much of it is dishonest and ineffective. Section 2(a) claims that the purpose of the resolution is to "fulfill the intent of the framers" and "insure the collective judgment" of both branches when U.S. forces are introduced into hostilities. The statute satisfies neither purpose. The framers would have never recognized the authority of the president to use military force against another country for up to 90 days without prior congressional authority. Also, nothing in the resolution "insures the collective judgment." The initiation of military force under the statute is solely by the president. He need only consult with Congress "in every possible instance" before introducing U.S. troops into combat, followed by regular reports.

It is not even clear when the clock starts. According to the resolution, the clock does not start ticking unless the president reports under a very specific section: Section 4(a)(1). No president has reported under that section except Gerald Ford, but by the time he reported to Congress on the *Mayaguez* incident in 1975, the military operation had ceased. Congress could start the clock by passing a statute, as it did in 1983 with the crisis in Lebanon, but it makes little sense to pass a statute to trigger the clock. It simply underscores the weakness of the War Powers Resolution.

A recent effort to replace the War Powers Resolution appears in a 2008 proposal by a war power commission chaired by former secretaries of state James Baker (Republican) and Warren Christopher (Democrat). The study recommends the creation of a 20-person congressional committee, consisting of party leaders, committee chairmen, and ranking members. Except in emergency situations, the president would consult with this select group. That mechanism is unconstitutional. The framers placed the war power with the whole of Congress, from senior lawmakers to junior members, not with some subgroup limited to a consultative function.

If within thirty days Congress has not authorized the military action, the Baker-Christopher proposal calls for two legislative votes. The first would be a nonbinding resolution of approval. That is, Congress would not be called upon to provide legal authority for going to war, just some kind of nonbinding measure. If Congress failed to pass that, it would be required to vote on a binding joint resolution of disapproval. The resolution would go to the president for his signature. If he vetoed it, as expected, Congress would need a two-thirds majority in each chamber to maintain control. In other words, the president could initiate war and continue it provided he had one-third plus one in a single chamber. This proposal, supposedly designed to balance the interests of the two branches, clearly favors the president.[22]

## The Impoundment Fight

For the framers, the power of the purse was a fundamental prerogative of Congress. In Federalist No. 58, James Madison said that this power represents the "most complete and effectual weapon with which any constitution can arm the immediate representatives of the people, for obtaining a redress of every grievance, and for carrying into effect every just and salutary measure." Article I, Section 9, of the Constitution vests that power exclusively in the hands of Congress: "No Money shall be drawn from the Treasury, but in Consequence of Appropriations made by Law." In Federalist No. 48, Madison remarked that "the legislative department alone has access to the pockets of the people."

In the years following World War II, members of Congress recognized that great harm had been done to its power of the purse, especially after appropriating vast sums to President Roosevelt with few details to guide actual use. To the extent that presidents took the initiative in war-making as with Korea, or expanded statutory authority as with Vietnam, congressional control over the power of the purse was further diminished. By the early 1970s, Congress faced another challenge from the executive branch. The Nixon administration claimed that the president had no obligation to spend money that Congress appropriated. According to the administration's reasoning, the president could reduce the funds as he liked and even zero out a program. There was nothing new about this dispute over impounding funds. Presidents over the years had often asserted the right not to spend funds. What was new about the Nixon years was the legal theory. The impoundment power was now described as "inherent" in the presidency and thus beyond legislative or judicial checks. Also, no president in the past had claimed such sweeping powers over every facet of the budget, domestic and military.

No one in Congress questioned the right of the president to spend less if the legislative purpose could be fulfilled with less money. But if the power is wielded to cripple or obliterate a statutory project, the president is no longer carrying out his constitutional duty to "take Care that the Laws be faithfully executed." Through this asserted authority, the president in effect exercises an item-veto authority. He could fully fund some programs, drastically retrench others, and cancel programs in their entirety. The question for Congress and the courts was whether appropriations were merely permissive, to be spent entirely under the discretion of the president, or mandatory. About 80 cases went to court. The administration lost almost all of them, including the one that reached the Supreme Court, *Train v. City of New York* (1975).[23] The Court held that Congress in the Clean Water Act had made a deliberate commitment to spend the full amount.

Nixon's claim of inherent impoundment power struck so deeply at the prerogatives of Congress, to both legislate and appropriate, that both chambers fought back strongly. As part of an omnibus budget reform bill, Congress passed legislation in 1974 to limit the president's power. The Impoundment Control Act requires the president to submit two kinds of special messages to Congress when he decides to withhold funds. If he wants to withhold funds permanently and terminate a program, he must submit a "rescission" message. To rescind funds, both houses must complete action on a bill or a joint resolution within 45 days. The burden is entirely on the president to seek support for that legislation. Congress may prevail by doing nothing.

If the president wants to withhold funds temporarily, he must submit a "deferral" message. Deferrals would remain in effect unless one house passed a resolution of disapproval. That type of legislative veto was invalidated by the Supreme Court in *INS v. Chadha* (1983). The Court reasoned that legislative disapproval could not come from a single chamber. Both houses had to disapprove in a bill or joint resolution that went to the president for his signature or disapproval. Federal courts later decided that the one-house veto could not be severed from the deferral authority. If the first was invalid, as a result of *Chadha,* so was the second. Congress in 1987 quickly converted that judicial ruling into statutory law.

## Budget Reforms of 1974

After deciding to restrict impoundment, some lawmakers feared that voters would interpret legislative action to mean that Congress was "pro-spending" and thus fiscally irresponsible. To offset that impression, Congress began to look at its budget process. A joint committee on budget control in 1973 associated the growth of budget deficits to procedural inadequacies within Congress: "The constant continuation of deficits plus their increasing size illustrates the need for Congress to obtain better control over the budget."[24] It blamed Congress for its highly decentralized system of committees and subcommittees, with no committee responsible for aggregate numbers and no committee able to match projected spending to projected revenues. It became fashionable to condemn the legislative process for being fragmented, incoherent, and irresponsible.

Those arguments played on stereotypes. The president was considered "responsible" because he headed a centralized and unified branch. The process in Congress was condemned as "splintered": two separate chambers acting on an array of tax, appropriation, and authorizing bills. Part of that fragmented process (two chambers) was constitutional in nature. The framers adopted two chambers as an important check on legislative excesses. It was also a way of reconciling democratic principles (citizens voting directly for House members) with federalism (the Senate protecting the states). The decentralization of Congress also made it more difficult for a president to capture and control all of its parts.

It is a serious misconception to say that Congress in the early 1970s was institutionally unable to comprehend how its separate actions fit into an aggregate budget picture. During that period, the Joint Committee on Reduction of Federal

Expenditures prepared "scorekeeping reports" and circulated them on a regular basis. Legislators knew how congressional action compared to a presidential proposal. Congress took seriously its duty to live within the aggregate amounts of the president's budget. It stayed within the ballpark of those totals while making major changes on individual programs and national priorities. Legislative spending and annual deficits did not spin wildly out of control because of the way Congress was structured before 1974.

Nevertheless, the politics of the early 1970s put pressure on lawmakers to reject "piecemeal" action on tax, appropriation, and authorization bills. The popular catchphrases called for "coordination," "coherence," "comprehensiveness," and a "unified" budget process. To many lawmakers, congressional procedures seemed inferior to the executive process. The Budget and Accounting Act of 1921 had made the president personally responsible for presenting a budget. The statute created a new Bureau of the Budget (now the Office of Management and Budget). The executive budget came nicely bound, unlike the scattered pieces of the congressional process. By 1974, lawmakers assumed that if the president performed better with a centralized process, so would Congress. Yet it was neither wise nor necessary for Congress, functioning as a separate branch with unique institutional qualities, to emulate the president. What were the likely benefits, other than "looking better"? What were the risks?

With the Budget Act of 1974 Congress took the plunge, for better or for worse. The statute created new budget committees and established the Congressional Budget Office to provide the kind of analytical skills that OMB offered to the president. Congress would now pass "budget resolutions" that contained five aggregates: total budget authority, total outlays, total revenues, the surplus or deficit, and the public debt. Outlays and budget authority would be organized by major "functional categories" (such as national defense, transportation, and agriculture) to permit legislative debate on budget priorities. With this legislation, it appeared that Congress had joined the modern world.

Appearances are always complex and certainly that is true of federal budgeting. Increasing the size of a legislative vehicle—from individual tax, appropriation, and authorizing bills to a budget resolution—was of high risk. Why would passing a comprehensive budget resolution automatically usher in responsible action? Why would it protect congressional (or constituent) interests? Operating under the 1974 law, the appropriations committees encountered new problems. Previously, it was in their institutional and political interest to stay below the president's spending proposals to demonstrate that Congress is the more responsible branch.

Under the new system, if the appropriations committees proposed less than the amount allocated to them by the budget resolution, pressures mounted for amendments to bring the total up to the ceiling. Any gap between the total recommended by the appropriations committees and the total allowed by the budget resolution would be quickly filled with projects offered by lawmakers. The Budget Act of 1974 began to legitimize spending that would not have occurred before.

Constituents found it hard to follow the new process. Previously, it was easy. Beginning in 1921, the president proposed a specified amount. Congressional action could be compared to that target. It was either below, above, or the same. Now there are two competing budgets: the president's budget plus the budget resolution. Although the latter might be higher than the president's budget, lawmakers could vote for the amount in the budget resolution and announce that they had "stayed within the budget" (i.e., the congressional budget). In 1979, the chairman of the House Budget Committee, Bob Giaimo (D-CT), admitted that budget resolutions had sanctioned sizable funding increases for program after program, "almost regardless of its effectiveness."[25]

## The Era of Deficits

Another unintended consequence of the 1974 budget act materialized in 1981. President Reagan was able to attract a majority of votes from Republicans and conservative Democrats to gain control of the budget resolution in both the House and the Senate. Through that action he possessed a budget tool that enabled him to enforce his priorities: a major tax cut, a large defense buildup, and some cutbacks in domestic programs. The budget resolution was no longer a congressional instrument of control. It was solidly in the hands of the president. Congress had worried about annual budget deficits in the range of $25 billion in the early 1970s. That number was about to explode.

When Reagan entered office, the total national debt (accumulated from 1789 to January 1981) stood at approximately $1 trillion. Much of that amount reflected deficits created by various wars. The result of Reagan's fiscal experiment in 1981 drove annual deficits to several hundred billion a year. By the end of his first term in office, the national debt had doubled from $1 trillion to $2 trillion. By the time he left office four years later, it had tripled to $3 trillion.[26]

It is highly doubtful that this ballooning of budget deficits could have occurred under the previous budget process. Every step of Reagan's proposal in 1981 would have been scrutinized and modified by the tax, appropriation, and authorizing committees. His aggregate policy would have been chopped to bits and radically transformed through this decentralized system of committees and subcommittees. Gaining control of the budget resolution, however, allowed Reagan to achieve his major budget objectives: deep tax cuts and major increases in military spending. There was never a chance that domestic programs could be reduced in size to prevent the deficit from spinning out of control. The politics of 1981 combined with the budget process of 1974 made Congress subordinate to the president. He set the direction, and lawmakers marched to it.

David Stockman, Reagan's OMB director from 1981 to 1985, appreciated how the new congressional budget process promoted White House goals. His book *The Triumph of Politics* (1986) explained that the constitutional powers of Congress "would have to be, in effect, suspended. Enacting the Reagan administration's economic program meant rubber-stamp approval, nothing less. The world's so-called greatest deliberative body would have to be reduced to the status of a ministerial arm of the White House."[27] For the president's plan to work, Congress had to "forfeit its independence."

Reagan's victory over budgeting led to record deficits. After leaving office, Stockman admitted that "a plan for radical and abrupt change required deep comprehension—and we had none of it."[28] All of the confident executive branch predictions of soaring revenues under Reagan's plan fell far short of expectations. Instead of balanced budgets or surpluses, huge deficits appeared. Instead of Congress relying on budget projections from its own CBO, it regularly accepted the administration's flawed and false premises.

## Attempts at Deficit Control

Faced with deficits of stunning size, Congress and the administration created a new budget process called the Gramm-Rudman-Hollings (GRH) Act of 1985. The statute publicly admitted that the supposedly superior budget process of 1974 was helpless in dealing with deficits in the range of $200 billion a year. Gramm-Rudman promised to eliminate deficits by fiscal 1991. Starting with a deficit of $171.9 billion for fiscal 1986, the statute commanded a decrease in that level by $36 billion each year over a five-year period. Presto. Under this formula deficits would disappear. The statute further directed the president's budget and the congressional budget resolution to adhere faithfully to those targets. If in any fiscal year a projected deficit exceeded what was allowed in the statute by more than $10 billion, a "sequestration" process would force across-the-board cuts to stay on course. The Senate did not hold hearings on the bill. In the House, four people testified, but I was the only one to analyze the constitutionality of Gramm-Rudman. I told the House panel that Congress could not vest executive duties (sequestration) in a legislative officer (the Comptroller General).

All of the political judgments expected of presidents and members of Congress were now replaced by an abstract, mechanical process designed to achieve deficit control. Gramm-Rudman merely invited further irresponsibility. Costs could be shifted from one year to the next; items were moved off-budget; both sides could invent improbable revenue estimates. Allen Schick, a noted budget expert, correctly observed that Gramm-Rudman "started out as a process for reducing deficits and has become a means of hiding the deficit and running away from responsibility."[29] Both branches routinely practiced deceit in "adhering" to statutory targets. If the president submitted a budget with entirely unrealistic estimates about spending constraints and revenues, Congress was likely to adopt the same phony numbers. Honest and professional estimates would have made Congress look like the "big spender." If the president offered a disingenuous budget, lawmakers eagerly embraced it.

Gramm-Rudman never fulfilled any of its objectives. When it became obvious that deficit targets would not be met by the end of the five-year period, the two branches kicked the can down the road. A new statute, Gramm-Rudman II of 1987, pushed the fantasy forward by two years. By that time, the Supreme Court in *Bowsher v. Synar* (1986) had struck down the procedure used for spending cuts (sequestration).[30] Under Gramm-Rudman II, the deficit for fiscal 1993 was supposed to be zero. It turned out to be $255 billion.[31]

In 1990, former CBO director Rudolph Penner made an interesting observation. He was struck by the fact that in looking at the history of the congressional budget process in the late nineteenth and early twentieth centuries, it appeared to be "chaotic" and yet yielded "balanced budgets or surpluses most of the time, unless there was really a good reason to run a deficit." The budget process in place after 1974 "looks very elegant on paper, but it is leading to very dishonest and disorderly results."[32]

## Item Vetoes and Balanced Budgets

Some members of Congress began to regard the rescission procedure of 1974 as too restrictive on the president. As a means of gaining better control over the budget deficits of the Reagan years, they wanted to authorize some type of item-veto authority for the president. Strangely, presidential irresponsibility was to be rewarded with new budget powers. Different proposals emerged. One approach was called "expedited rescission." It required Congress to vote on a president's proposal to rescind funds. Lawmakers could no longer sit on their hands when the president recommended rescissions (as the 1974 statute permitted). Under expedited rescission, if one house took a vote and disapproved, obviously that would be the end of it. There would be no purpose for the other house to act. Approval of both houses would be necessary. The House of Representatives passed bills for expedited rescission in 1992, 1993, and 1994. The Senate did not act on those proposals.

In 1995, Republicans gained control of the House of Representatives and began to push an alternative more favorable to presidential power. It was called "enhanced rescission." Instead of the burden being on the president to get both houses to support a rescission proposal, the burden would be reversed. Presidential proposals would become law unless Congress passed a resolution of disapproval within a fixed number of days. If Congress failed to act during that period, the rescissions would take effect. If Congress passed a resolution of disapproval, it would go to the president and face a likely veto. If vetoed, it would take two-thirds of the members of each house to restore the funds.

The House passed the enhanced rescission bill in 1995. The Senate agreed to pass a different measure and the two chambers settled, the next year, on a modified form of enhanced rescission. Before a Senate committee, I testified that Congress should not surrender its power of the purse to the president. Under the new law, the Line Item Veto Act of 1996, the burden was on Congress to disapprove presidential rescission requests during a 30-day period. In addition to rescissions of discretionary appropriations, the president could also cancel any new item of direct spending (entitlements) and certain limited tax benefits.

The shift of constitutional authority seemed quite extraordinary. However, in terms of presidential cuts and deficit control, the statute had minimal effects. The total savings achieved by President Bill Clinton, over a five-year period, came to less than $600 million. His cancellations for fiscal year 1998 represented about $355 million out of a total budget of $1.7 trillion. Although the budgetary reductions were minor, the damage done to Congress as a coequal branch was substantial. The statute basically announced: "Lawmakers are irresponsible and unable to control their appetite for spending. We need the leadership and fiscal responsibility of the president to protect the national interest." In 1998, in *Clinton v. City of New York*, the Supreme Court struck down the Line Item Veto Act as a violation of the legislative procedures set forth in the Constitution.[33]

Anyone familiar with budgetary policy over the last two centuries would be surprised at lawmakers championing the president as a fiscal guardian. The driving force behind large increases in federal spending has generally been the president, certainly from the 1930s to the present. To a great extent that is because of presidential wars in Korea, Vietnam, and Iraq. But presidents have also been behind such initiatives as Eisenhower's federal highway program, Kennedy's plan to send a man to the moon, Johnson's "Great Society" programs, and Reagan's defense buildup.

Over his eight years in office, George W. Bush allowed federal spending to rise dramatically, fueled in part by the Iraq war but also reflecting generous increases in domestic and international programs. Mickey Edwards, former House Republican from Oklahoma, wrote a book in 2008 entitled *Reclaiming Conservatism*. He expressed dismay at the lack of fiscal discipline during the Bush years. The federal deficit, he pointed out, "mushroomed, and not only because of the wars in Afghanistan and Iraq."[34] Republicans have attributed their defeats in the 2006 and 2008 elections in large part to their failure to exercise fiscal discipline. Democrats may suffer the same kind of losses in the 2010 and 2012 elections if they acquiesce to heavy spending and large deficits by the Obama administration.

## Some Reform Proposals

Congress has successfully blocked action on some proposals that would have weakened budgetary control. Throughout the 1980s and 1990s, members of Congress debated a constitutional amendment to require a "balanced budget." In 1984, President Reagan claimed that a balanced budget amendment "would force the Federal Government to do what so many States and municipalities and all average Americans are forced to do—to live within its means and stop mortgaging our children's future."[35] His claim of fiscal responsibility by states and municipalities was extremely misleading.

There are several drawbacks to a balanced budget amendment. As with line-item proposals, congressional efforts to pass an amendment and send it to the states for ratification would send a clear message to the public that lawmakers are unable, or unwilling, to control federal spending. In 1995, Representative Gerald Solomon (R-NY) told the House: "Madame Speaker, Congress has repeatedly shown that it is not prepared to deal responsibly with the problems without some kind of a prod. The enactment of a balanced budget amendment will help to give Congress—and this is the point—it will help to give Congress that prod, that spine, that backbone and, for some who need it, the excuse to do what the American people have to do, and that is to live within means."[36]

However appealing a constitutional amendment might seem, it is easy to predict that a balanced budget requirement would not produce a balanced budget. In testifying before a House committee in 1992 and a Senate committee in 1994, I urged lawmakers to look at the states and their history of balancing budgets. What states have done over the years is to spawn two budgets: an operating budget (balanced) and a capital budget (authorizing indebtedness). If states actually balanced their budgets by limiting expenditures to available or projected revenues, we would not hear of state and municipal bond offerings or states worrying about their bond ratings. Much of the borrowing by state and local governments goes for capital expenditures for roads, education, sewerage, housing, and urban renewal.

Congress would have little trouble coming up with an "operating budget" that is in balance while transferring many expenditures to a "capital" budget. States have the advantage in relying on the federal government for much of their budgetary needs, ranging from federal grants each year (about one-fifth of state revenues) to extra federal assistance in time of natural disasters. In 2009, states gratefully received billions in federal funds as part of the economic stimulus package. Were Congress to adopt a "balanced budget," its power and prestige would suffer when citizens discovered that lawmakers (assisted by executive officials) had performed a cynical accounting trick.

After the Supreme Court invalidated the Line Item Veto Act, Congress debated substitute proposals. One idea, explored at a House subcommittee hearing in 2000, was to amend the Constitution. Under consideration was language adopted from a state constitution to authorize the president to item veto "any appropriation or provision." I pointed out that at the state level that kind of language is effective because appropriations are made for discrete amounts. It is not unusual to see state bills with amounts as small as $2,000. But the federal government does not appropriate with that detail. Appropriations accounts typically provide lump-sums in the billions. If the language above were added to the U.S. Constitution, presidents would not find any appropriation "items" in the bills submitted to them.

The proposal submitted to the House subcommittee in 2000 did not define "provision." Would it apply to conditions placed on appropriations and other nondollar language? In exercising this type of item veto, could a president convert a conditional appropriation into an unconditional appropriation and eliminate the restriction that Congress had all along intended? Borrowing language from state constitutions is often misleading. Part of the reason for giving governors an item veto was that most legislatures were part-time institutions. They met every other year and when they did assemble it was for a few months. Those conditions forced state legislatures to delegate to the governor substantial discretion, including the power of an item veto. Congress has met in annual session ever since 1789 and its sessions in the modern era are almost year-round.

In 2006, the House and Senate Budget Committees held hearings to consider an item-veto bill designed to satisfy the Supreme Court's ruling in *Clinton v. City of New York*. The legislation would authorize the president to propose the rescission of any dollar amount of discretionary budget authority or rescind, "in whole or in part," any item of direct spending (entitlements). Once those proposals were submitted to Congress, an expedited process would require lawmakers to vote up or down within a fixed period of time. No amendments by lawmakers would be permitted, either in committee or on the floor. The essence of legislative authority is the capacity to shape a product. Under this item-veto proposal, the president could do that. Congress could not. Also, the rescission legislation would give presidents substantial control in driving and dictating the congressional schedule.

In testifying at these hearings, I concluded that the procedure mapped out above would probably satisfy *Clinton*, but lawmakers have a duty that goes beyond drafting bills acceptable to the Supreme Court. They need to ask: Does the legislation protect the powers and reputation of Congress as a coequal branch?

The answer does not come solely from court rulings. It lies in the willingness of each lawmaker to determine what Congress must do to preserve its place in a system of coordinate branches. The true expert here is the lawmaker, not the judge. No one outside the legislative branch has the requisite understanding of congressional needs or can be entrusted to safeguard legislative or national interests.

A lawmaker need not be an attorney to decide such questions. Someone without a law degree is just as able and experienced in judging what Congress must do to protect representative democracy and the rights of citizens and constituents. Just as Congress should not consciously pass an unconstitutional bill, so should it not pass legislation that damages itself. The item-veto legislation considered in 2006 would have damaged the institutional interests of Congress in several ways.

First, it sent a clear message to the public that Congress has been irresponsible with its legislative work, both in the level of spending and the particular provisions it placed in bills. To correct those supposed defects, Congress would sanction a fast-track procedure that enables a president to publicly identify wasteful projects and force congressional votes. By selecting that process lawmakers advertise their incompetence to perform constitutional duties. That is Damage No. 1.

On what grounds can it be said that the president has a unique and superior capacity to look at bills presented to him and judge which items lack merit? Would those judgments be actually made by the president or by aides and even private individuals and groups who want to reverse a congressional decision? Are they more qualified than lawmakers to determine what should be allocated to particular districts and states? No. Would their judgments be based on nonpartisan, rational analysis or strongly tilted by political and partisan objectives? Generally the latter. It is unclear how a president would credibly put together a list of proposed rescissions.

Whatever the merits or demerits of the president's selections, he would probably receive public credit for "fighting against waste." Few voters and constituents would have the time or expertise to examine each item on the president's list. It is difficult to distinguish between "justified" and "unjustified" programs. The president may win on image alone, not on substance or convincing analysis. At the same time, Congress would receive a public rebuke for having enacted the supposedly wasteful items (Damage No. 2).

What of the next stage? If Congress were to disapprove the rescission proposals, it would be criticized for not supporting the good-faith efforts of the president. It would be an easy matter for the president to condemn Congress for establishing a fast-track procedure to correct for its deficiencies and then refuse to delete unwanted and unneeded funds (Damage No. 3). If Congress has an interest in building public support and credibility, this is a process to avoid.

Finally, consider the politics of this form of line-item veto authority. The president would have a new tool to coerce lawmakers and limit their independence. He or his aides could call members of Congress to alert them that a particular project in their district or state might be on a list of programs scheduled for the rescission list. During the phone conversation, the member would be told that the administration actually thinks the project is a good one and should be preserved. The member is assured that the administration will do everything in its power to see that the project is kept off the list. At that point the conversation shifts ever so slightly to another topic. The member is asked whether he or she is willing to support a bill, treaty, or nomination desired by the president. The lawmaker is at a distinct disadvantage. To preserve the project in a state or district, it may be necessary to support a presidential program that lacks merit. Perhaps both sides sign off to this deal, pushing spending higher (without the public ever knowing). The political leverage of this process diminishes the constitutional independence of Congress (Damage No. 4).

Of course one final action would further degrade Congress as an institution: voting in favor of the president's rescission list.

The president would receive full credit for guarding the purse. Congress gets a pounding for having ever included the items. It's possible that the projects were more than justified, but lawmakers chose to capitulate to an angry public. These events would be costly sideshows, highly damaging to Congress and bringing insignificant relief to budgetary problems.

To control budgets and deficits, Congress has more effective ways than enacting line-item veto authority or passing balanced budget amendments. Much more profound would be a refusal to authorize military commitments unless the need is clearly urgent, supported by reliable information, and subject to independent investigation by Congress and outside parties. The Vietnam War and the current Iraq War caused profound damage to the national budget. Congress should have insisted that UN inspectors be sent to Iraq before it acted on authorizing legislation. Strategic errors of that magnitude require generations for recovery.

Presidents have sufficient constitutional powers over the budget. Through the regular veto power, presidents can tell Congress that unless it strips certain items from a bill that is in conference committee, they will exercise the veto. Threats of that nature are regularly employed to shape the contents of legislation. The president may announce that if a bill exceeds a particular total he will veto it, again putting pressures on lawmakers to modify the bill to meet the president's satisfaction.

More important than the veto power is the budget the president submits. Under the 1921 statute, he is supposed to submit a "responsible" budget. It is within the president's power to recommend a bill that balances expenditures and revenues. The historical record provides strong evidence that the aggregate numbers submitted by presidents (total spending, deficits and surpluses, etc.) are generally followed by Congress, and that legislative changes have more to do with priorities than totals. The key to fiscal discipline is a president who submits a responsible budget. Without that leadership, all other reform proposals are superficial diversions.

Congress effectively challenged the Nixon impoundments and has, fortunately, decided against a balanced budget amendment and recent item-veto proposals. The experience with the Gramm-Rudman bills was a healthy reminder that statutory mechanisms, no matter how ingenious, are no substitute for the individual and collective judgments required of elected officials.

# Chapter Six
# Safeguarding Democracy

From World War II to the present, Congress has lost much of its independent capacity to legislate, monitor executive agencies, and protect its powers. Parliamentary bodies around the globe have experienced similar declines. The damage is not merely to one branch of government but to the entire democratic system. When Congress is weak, so are constituents and so is their trust in government. If members of Congress want to restore their institution to coequal status and gain the respect of other branches and constituents, constructive steps are available.

## A Separate Branch

Little can be accomplished unless a basic shift occurs in legislative attitudes. Members of Congress and their staffs must view themselves as part of a separate branch with distinct and nondelegable duties, procedures, and customs. Without that basic understanding there can be no system of checks and balances. The structural safeguards intended to protect individual rights and liberties disappear. Lee Hamilton, drawing on thirty-four years of public service in the House of Representatives as a Democrat from Indiana, observed: "It is one of the American system's marks of genius that we always have one branch keeping an eye on the other."[1] Much of Congress's decline over the last six decades is rooted in lawmakers identifying themselves not with their own branch but in deferring to the president and the judiciary. Being coequal requires independent judgment, not acquiescence and submission. As noted by political scientists Thomas Mann and Norman Ornstein, contemporary lawmakers "simply do not identify strongly as members of the first branch of government."[2]

## Independent Spirit

When members of Congress take the oath of office to defend the Constitution, it is as they see the Constitution, drawing on their personal analysis and the understandings they bring to public office. They come to Congress as former governors, mayors, state lawmakers, physicians, farmers, engineers, and other professions. Their view of government and public affairs is unmatched by the other branches. It is appropriate for lawmakers to be guided and informed by the Supreme Court and the president, but not to the point of losing capacity for independent judgment and action. Otherwise, we would still be stuck with the Court's reasoning in *Dred Scott* and its cramped constitutional rulings on child labor, the right of women to practice law, the legislative veto, religious liberty in the military, and other issues. Without institutional autonomy, lawmakers would bow to overblown claims by presidents and federal courts about their "plenary" powers. No doubt there are personal risks for lawmakers who publicly object to presidential and judicial positions, but the risk is far greater when Congress capitulates and falls silent.

## Institutional Pride

A spirit of independent inquiry must originate with lawmakers. They need to communicate that value to aides who serve in personal offices and committees. Some years ago I listened to a talk on congressional oversight by David Skaggs, former Democratic House member from Colorado. He asked the audience: "How many of you work in a member's office?" A number of hands shot up. Next: "How many work on committees?" A show of more hands. Third question: "How many of you are proud to work for Congress?" After a pause, a few uncomfortable hands appeared. I became a congressional staffer in September 1970. If anyone had asked the third question to a room of staffers then, the response would have been quick and positive. We understood that whatever the faults of Congress, we supported the legislative branch and the system of checks and balances.

## Outside Help Needed

Strengthening Congress will require the combined efforts of scholars, private organizations, the media, and other participants. Justice Brandeis in 1927 reminded us that the "greatest menace to freedom is an inert people."[3] Self-government requires continued participation by the public. It is easy for citizens to poke fun at Congress; most of its actions are in public view. If the process of reaching decisions in the other branches were more visible, we would have a far less favorable opinion of presidents, executive officials, and federal judges.

Citizens need to do more than turn out for elections. Working individually and with others, they can press for change and are often successful.[4] Private organizations, through litigation, congressional testimony, and independent investigations, can provide a type of checks and balances that one would expect to come from collisions among the three branches. If political institutions fail to do that job, because of passivity or deference, the burden on private citizens and groups is all the greater.

The goal is to restore not merely Congress as an institution but democratic values and the principle of self-government. Moving away from the current concentration of power in the presidency and the Supreme Court is a necessary structural step to protect individual rights and liberties. At town hall meetings, constituents can ask lawmakers if they are fulfilling their oath to the Constitution by exercising independent judgment or simply taking direction from other branches. In their recent book, Frederick Schwarz and Aziz Huq correctly advise: "Voters, both Democratic and Republican, must ask their candidates whether they are willing to fulfill their constitutional responsibilities."[5]

Congressional action is easier when assisted and spurred by a national consensus. Individuals throughout the country are part of the process that debates issues and demands change. At times Congress and the president get credit for enacting a federal program when the origin was rooted in pressure that began in local communities, spread to the states, and exerted such national force that elected officials responded with public laws and effective oversight.

## What the Party Asks

The willingness of individual members of Congress to think and act independently depends on how their institution is structured and organized. If the Speaker of the House gains effective control over the legislative agenda, lawmakers may be asked to suspend individual views to support "party unity" or the "interests of the president." Congress is weakened as an institution when party unity becomes the dominant value, both in supporting a president's program or in opposing it. Individual doubts and judgments are put to the side. Majority leaders in Congress may insist that the president's program "trump everything."[6] The all-inclusive "everything" can include the Constitution. At that point the legislative branch loses its separate character and functions as an arm of the executive branch, unable or unwilling to exercise checks and balances.

If the president's agenda is seriously misguided (e.g., Lyndon Johnson's war in Vietnam and George W. Bush's intervention in Iraq), the price is heavy. Not only do the president and the nation suffer but so does the president's party in Congress and so do the reelection chances of the members of that party. Roy Blunt (R-MO), who served as House Republican Whip from 2006 to 2008, later reflected: "I think you can argue that our leadership was too close to President Bush."[7] Party leaders, preoccupied with strategic interests, can lose touch with their party base and even their own leadership team.[8] A member of Congress takes a solemn oath to the Constitution, not to the president, the Supreme Court, or a political party. The oath is informed and directed by personal values and one's conscience. The oath is inescapably individual, not part of a group exercise.

On one occasion I met with seven House members after their party won the presidency. Because they also controlled Congress, I said they needed to provide close oversight of the executive branch. If they did not, the White House would get in trouble and eventually so would their party and their colleagues in Congress. If the other party controlled both branches, I would have offered the same advice. The seven members and their party colleagues chose to put their trust and loyalty in the president. Several years later, after the president had gotten in trouble and their party suffered at the polls, we met again. They shook their heads at their failure to exercise institutional checks. Heedless loyalty to a president runs against the Constitution, legislative powers, party interests, and the chances for reelection by members of that party. If members of Congress mechanically salute to whatever a president wants, they stop being representatives and become White House aides.

## What We Owe the President

Representative Jim Wright recalls how he and Speaker Tip O'Neill helped President Ronald Reagan on matters of foreign affairs: "He was our President. We owed him that."[9] Lawmakers owe the president independent and informed judgment, not deferential loyalty. No president says: "This is my Congress. I owe it that." Members of Congress weaken their institution and democratic government when they decide to "close ranks" on issues of foreign affairs and national security. Another platitude guaranteed to enfeeble Congress: "Politics stops at the water's edge." No. Politics—in the sense of exercising informed judgment—continues. O'Neill initially advised that "when it comes to foreign policy, you support your president."[10] By September 1967 he turned against President Johnson and the Vietnam War.[11]

During the Cuban Missile Crisis of 1962, President Kennedy sought and received congressional support. Speaker Carl Albert agreed with that legislative attitude: "He was our president."[12] No matter what misgivings might have surfaced privately, lawmakers remained loyal. Two years later, Albert began to learn the costs of automatically uniting behind presidential military action. In response to two reported attacks by North Vietnam in the Gulf of Tonkin (the second "attack" never occurred), the House unanimously and the Senate with only two negative votes passed a resolution giving President Johnson broad authority to use military force. The costs were military,  constitutional, political, and economic. Funds planned for the War on Poverty went to Vietnam, Republicans picked up 47 House seats in 1966, and the war created bitter divisions among Democrats, helping Richard Nixon win the presidency in 1968.[13]

On December 12, 2000, the Supreme Court in *Bush v. Gore* put an end to recounts in Florida and helped usher George W. Bush into the White House.[14] Few Democrats, Republicans, liberals, or conservatives can view the Court's reasoning as anything other than unprincipled and ad hoc, but the country "united" behind the Court and the new president.[15] In his concession speech the next day, Al Gore announced: "Now the U.S. Supreme Court has spoken. Let there be no doubt, while I strongly disagree with the Court's decision, I accept it. I accept the finality of this outcome."[16] He added: "This is America and we put country before party. We will stand together behind our new president."[17]

Perhaps the effort to place country over party seemed patriotic, but the country, democracy, and the Constitution all suffer by mindlessly saluting a Supreme Court ruling regardless of its merits. It is also pointless to "stand together" behind a new president. Stand lockstep without offering independent judgment or exercising necessary checks and balances? Keep criticism and doubts to oneself? Such conduct converts the president into an imperial force. That kind of attitude was present in October 2002 when Congress passed a resolution authorizing military action against Iraq without any reliable evidence that Iraq possessed weapons of mass destruction or presented any sort of national security threat to the United States.

## Campaign Finance

For lawmakers to act independently and exercise checks and balances, fundamental changes in campaign financing are required. The time needed for effective legislation and oversight is consumed by each member raising money for his or her race or party. Fund-raising becomes a part of every day spent at home and every day in the nation's capital. In a floor statement on January 6, 2009, Senator Robert C. Byrd (D-WV) recalled the dramatic shifts in money needed for election and reelection. In 1958, he and Jennings Randolph (D-WV) spent a combined $50,000 to win their Senate seats in West Virginia. Today, driven by the costs of radio and television ads, Senator Byrd estimated that senators "can expect to spend about $7 million."[18] Members tell me that half of their time, and even more, is spent raising money. In the chase for dollars, some lawmakers step over the line and land in prison. For the great majority who avoid illegal conduct, precious hours needed to fulfill constitutional duties are lost.

Congressional efforts to control campaign expenditures are limited by the Supreme Court's decision in *Buckley v. Valeo* (1976), which concluded that money is "speech" and therefore entitled to constitutional protection.[19] Several justices at the time rejected the Court's analysis, and justices ever since have sharply repudiated the supposed link between money and First Amendment interests. They recommend that national policies over campaign funding be left to the elected branches. Congress has every right to hold extensive hearings to determine whether *Buckley* needs to be overruled, especially in light of more than three decades of experience. Congress has more competence, authority, and legitimacy in this area than the Court. Independent analysis by Congress can justify lawmakers telling the Court: "With all respect, you got it wrong. We are passing new legislation to regulate political campaigns. The level of spending is corrupting our political system and weakening Congress as an independent branch."

## Legislative Staff

Congress needs to take a fresh look at the salaries and incentives of congressional staff. Many of the top positions in the offices of representatives and senators and on legislative committees receive adequate pay. Other staff salaries are much too low, especially in a city as expensive as Washington, D.C. Pressures are intense and hours are long.[20] The temptation is great to work a few years, add the congressional job to one's resume, and move on. Congress needs to retain these talented staffers and the skills they have acquired. A half-century ago it was not unusual to see staffers devote their professional careers to a congressional committee. That is less the case today.

## Hackneyed Debates

Much of the criticism aimed at Congress is preoccupied with trite complaints. There is nothing wrong with "lobbyists" and "special interests" trying to influence government. From 1789 forward, they have exercised pressure on all three branches. It is their constitutional right to participate and bring information and perspective to the political process. Individuals who strongly condemn lobbyists and special interests will inevitably make exceptions for their own favorite organizations. Broadsides against lobbyists and special interests have little meaning and are not helpful in shaping or debating public policy. The remedy comes not from eliminating this type of public participation but making it visible and avoiding the corruption that can occur.

It is similarly unhelpful to condemn Congress for "pork-barrel" spending or for engaging in "earmarks." Some projects are wasteful and damage the reputation of Congress, as with Alaska's famed "bridge to nowhere." Certain earmarks should be prohibited, such as funneling money to a company that contributes to a lawmaker's campaign or sending public funds to a lawmaker's family.[21] Informed criticism of earmarks would require a detailed analysis of each project in each district and state. That effort would find merit in many projects.

Lawmakers have every right to direct spending to their districts or states. There is no reason in a system of representative government to shift those decisions from elected officials to executive officials. Nor are there any grounds to think that agency employees, in allocating funds, will be more expert or less immune from partisan and political pressures. The remedy, as with lobbying and special interests, is to assure full visibility before projects are authorized and funded.

Earmarks are commonly defined as "congressionally directed spending." The public and the press should pay comparable attention to "presidentially directed spending." Newspaper stories will highlight a congressional earmark of $50,000 to construct a National Mule and Packers Museum in Bishop, California. Take a look at presidential spending and you will see some really huge figures, such as $13 billion for 28 presidential helicopters.[22] Some reformers insist that each congressional earmark be not only funded but specifically authorized. Much of executive spending, such as foreign assistance, does not receive regular authorizations.

Public outrage at lobbyists, special interests, earmarks, and special projects takes the focus off of significant issues and obsesses on minor ones. In 2009, lawmakers rebuked AIG for giving $165 million in retention bonuses to its employees. Additional criticism was leveled at the approximately $7.7 billion covering 8,500 earmarks in the omnibus spending bill enacted in March 2009. Those were legitimate targets for public debate. Yet a story in the *New York Times* that same month described phenomenal sums wasted in the Defense Department for weapons programs. Nearly 70 percent of the programs were over budget for a combined total of $296 billion.[23] That problem persists decade after decade with little improvement. Fewer cases of fraud and corruption involving military contracts are sent to the Justice Department for prosecution. The number of employees in the Defense Department tasked with identifying and correcting fraud and corruption has been cut substantially in recent decades.[24] If constituents want Congress to take action to eliminate waste, that is one area of opportunity. Many others deserve close and continuing scrutiny.

## Using Legislative Weapons

Members of Congress have many powerful tools to protect their prerogatives, but they have to use them. In 1986, President Reagan nominated William Rehnquist to move from associate justice of the Supreme Court to chief justice. The Senate Judiciary Committee asked the administration for certain memos that Rehnquist had written when he headed the Office of Legal Counsel in the Justice Department. As expected, the administration told the committee that the memos could not be released because they were part of the internal deliberative process. That marked step one in the confrontation. The committee then played its card, announcing that Rehnquist would not be reported from committee until it received the documents. Not only would there be no floor vote on Rehnquist but no floor vote on Antonin Scalia as associate justice. The Senate planned to take up the two together. The administration understood the committee's leverage and released enough memos to satisfy Senate needs.[25]

During the Reagan years, the two branches collided over the president's power to "reinterpret" a treaty. Could the administration arrive at a meaning of a treaty contrary to what the Senate understood at the time it granted approval? The Reagan administration promoted an expensive antimissile shield consisting of satellites armed with laser weapons. Executive officials referred to it as the Strategic Defense Initiative (SDI). The press called it "Star Wars." Some members of Congress objected that deployment or even testing of SDI would violate the Antiballistic Missile (ABM) treaty with the Soviet Union. The complex debate about treaty interpretation came to an abrupt halt when Congress enacted legislative language prohibiting the secretary of defense from deploying any ABM system "unless such deployment is specifically authorized by law after the date of the enactment of this Act."[26]

A similar story of congressional hardball occurred in 1992. In the midst of his reelection campaign, President George H. W. Bush decided to put Congress on the defensive by sending up a list of programs to be eliminated. He would get credit for being a "fiscal guardian." If Congress didn't approve his proposals, it would be condemned for wasteful spending. He planned to submit new lists each month. To strengthen his position, Bush identified a number of seemingly frivolous programs, including asparagus research, celery research, prickly pear research, Vidalia onion storage, and manure disposal. His total came to $7.9 billion.

Senator Byrd was more than ready to play this game. He produced an even larger package of cuts: ($8.2 billion), but his list would demonstrate that there "is plenty of 'pork' . . . at the other end of Pennsylvania Avenue."[27] The congressional substitute included plans by the executive branch to study the significance of holism in German-speaking society and a $94,000 study of why people feared going to the dentist. To Byrd the reason was obvious: "Any child who has to go to the dentist will tell you why he fears the dentist. It hurts."[28] Other executive branch programs to be terminated by the congressional list: research grants for monogamy and aggression in fish in Nicaragua, the well-being of middle-class lawyers, sexual mimicry of swallowtail butterflies, and song production in freely behaving birds. Bush was in a spot. Having gone public on his pledge to cut federal spending, he had little choice but to sign the congressional substitute. He did not send up future lists.[29]

## Constitutional Checks

The initiatives on SDI testing, Rehnquist's nomination, and Bush's rescission strategy came from lawmakers determined to protect institutional interests. They did what Madison hoped for in Federalist No. 51, using "personal motives to resist encroachments of the others." When Tom Foley (D-WA) became a member of the House of Representatives in 1965, he had no idea he would rise in the ranks to become Speaker in 1989. What he did know, from the start, was the importance of thinking for himself. Lawmakers had to understand that they represented a separate branch with separate duties: "The members of Congress must be independent. The Congress is designed to be a separate entity from the president, not to be the instrument of presidential power, but to be a separate check and balance to the president, not to oppose him all the time, not to support him all the time, but to have a different viewpoint."[30]

Foley also understood that when lawmakers represent their states and districts they must remain free to exercise independent judgment, even when they disappoint some constituents. Members of Congress have a representative function but not to the point of trying at every step to simply reflect what local public polls indicate. Foley remarked: "Throughout my career one of my own unspoken standards was that if I didn't take at least one vote a term that jeopardized my job, then I was maybe going down a slippery slope."[31]

The search for common ground by lawmakers is a necessary part of the political process. Surrendering institutional interests to other branches is not. An active system of checks and balances is not only consistent with constitutional principles but produces better policies and smarter, safer politics. That lesson, driven home many times, must be rediscovered and practiced regularly.

# NOTES

## Preface

1. Paul J. Quirk and Sarah A. Binder, eds., *The Legislative Branch* (New York: Oxford University Press, 2005), xx, 525.

2. Julian E. Zelizer, ed., *The American Congress: The Building of Democracy* (Boston: Houghton Mifflin, 2004), xiv.

## Chapter 1

1. Louis Fisher, *In the Name of National Security: Unchecked Presidential Power and the* Reynolds *Case* (Lawrence: University Press of Kansas, 2006), 4–5.

2. John Nevill Figgis, *The Theory of the Divine Right of Kings* (Cambridge, UK: At the University Press, 1896). His second edition was published in 1914 under the title *The Divine Right of Kings* and reprinted in 1994 as a paperback by Thoemmes Press.

3. Fritz Kern, *Kingship and Law in the Middle Ages*, translated by S. B. Chrimes (New York: Harper Torchbook, 1970), 140.

4. Stephen D. White, *Sir Edward Cook and "the Grievances of the Commonwealth," 1621–1628* (Chapel Hill: University of North Carolina Press, 1979).

5. Carl L. Becker, *The Declaration of Independence* (New York: Vintage Books, 1959), 51.

6. Among the many fine studies of political reforms in England and America, see Carl Ubbelohde, *The American Colonies and the British Empire, 1607–1763* (New York: Thomas Y. Crowell, 1968); Edmund S.

Morgan, *Inventing the People: The Rise of Popular Sovereignty in England and America* (New York: Norton, 1988); and Alan Taylor, *American Colonies: The Settling of North America* (New York: Penguin, 2001).

7. Edmund S. Morgan and Helen M. Morgan, *The Stamp Act Crisis: Prologue to Revolution* (Chapel Hill: University of North Carolina Press, 1995 ed.), 95. This is an excellent study of the problems of administering this law and the growing spirit of self-government and independence in America.

8. Charles Andrews, *The Colonial Background of the American Revolution* (New Haven, CT: Yale University Press, 1961 ed.), 63.

9. Thomas Paine, *Common Sense and Other Political Writings* (New York: The Liberal Arts Press, 1953), 32 (italics in original).

10. Francis Wharton, *The Revolutionary Correspondence of the United States* (Washington, DC: Government Printing Office, 1889), vol. 1, 663. For additional details on the influence of Montesquieu and other writers and the creation of boards, single executives, and a separate court by the Continental Congress, see Louis Fisher, *President and Congress: Power and Policy* (New York: Free Press, 1972), 1–17, 241–270, 273–278, 329–334.

11. M. J. C. Vile, *Constitutionalism and the Separation of Powers* (Oxford: Oxford University Press, 1967), 153.

12. *Annals of Congress*, vol. 1, 453 (June 8, 1789).

13. George Washington, *The Writings of George Washington*, vol. 1, ed. John C. Fitzpatrick (Washington, DC: Government Printing Office), 506 (emphasis in original). For background on this issue, see Louis Fisher, *The Constitution and 9/11: Recurring Threats to America's Freedoms* (Lawrence: University Press of Kansas, 2008), 60–68; Robert M. Chesney, "Democratic-Republican Societies, Subversion, and the Limits of Legitimate Dissent in the Early Republic," *North Carolina Law Review*, vol. 82, 1525 (2004); and Eugene Perry Link, *Democratic-Republican Societies, 1790–1800* (New York: Columbia University Press, 1942). For a collection of documents on these political clubs, see Philip S. Foner, ed., *The Democratic-Republican Societies, 1790–1800* (Westport, CT: Greenwood, 1976).

14. Washington, *The Writings of George Washington*, vol. 33, 523.

15. Letter of Edmund Randolph to George Washington, October 11, 1794, George Washington Papers, Series 4, Reel 106, Library of Congress Manuscript Division.

16. Washington, *The Writings of George Washington*, vol. 34, 37.

17. *Annals of Congress*, 3d Cong., 1–2 Sess. 901 (1794).

18. Ibid., 910.

19. Ibid., 913–914.

20. Ibid., 934.

21. Ibid.

22. Madison's essay is reprinted in James Madison, *The Writings of James Madison*, ed. Gaillard Hunt, vol. 6, 101–103.

23. Jefferson, *The Writings of Thomas Jefferson*, vol. 3, 263.

24. Benedict de Spinoza, *A Theological-Political Treatise* (Mineola, NY: Dover Publications, 2004), 257.

25. *Whitney v. California*, 274 U.S. 357, 375 (1927) (Brandeis, J., concurring).

26. Ibid.

27. James Morton Smith, *Freedom's Fetters: The Alien and Sedition Laws and American Civil Liberties* (Ithaca, NY: Cornell University Press, 1956), 15.

28. H. Rept. No. 86, 26th Cong., 1st Sess. (1840), 2; 6 Stat. 802, ch. 45 (1840).

29. Paul Douglas Newman, *Fries's Rebellion: The Enduring Struggle for the American Revolution* (Philadelphia: University of Pennsylvania Press, 2004).

30. *Whitney v. California*, 375–376.

31. *Congressional Globe*, 42d Cong., 2d Sess., 1287 (February 29, 1872).

32. "Iran-Contra Investigation," joint hearings before the Senate Select Committee on Secret Military Assistance to Iran and the Nicaraguan Opposition and the House Select Committee to Investigate Covert Arms Transactions with Iran, 100th Cong., 1st Sess., vol. 100–107 (Part II), 45–46.

33. Glenn Kessler, "Hagel Defends Criticism of Iraq Policy," *Washington Post*, November 16, 2005, A6 (emphasis added).

34. Geoffrey R. Stone, *Perilous Times: Free Speech in Wartime* (New York: Norton, 2004), 211.

35. Fisher, *The Constitution and 9/11*, 131–138.

36. *Schenck v. United States,* 249 U.S. 47, 52 (1919).

## Chapter 2

1. *United States v. Lopez,* 514 U.S. 549, 552 (1995); *City of Boerne v. Flores,* 521 U.S 507, 516 (1997).

2. *Annals of Congress,* vol. 1, 761 (August 18, 1789).

3. Steven G. Calabresi and Christopher S. Yoo, *The Unitary Executive: Presidential Power from Washington to Bush* (New Haven, CT: Yale University Press, 2008), 4.

4. 17 U.S. (4 Wheat.) 315, 420 (1819).

5. James D. Richardson, ed., *A Compilation of the Messages and Papers of the Presidents,* 20 vols. (New York: Bureau of National Literature, 1897–1925), vol. 1, 416 (October 27, 1807) (hereafter "Richardson").

6. Thomas Jefferson, *The Writings of Thomas Jefferson,* ed. H. A. Washington (9 vols., New York: H. W. Derby, 1861), vol. 5, 542–545.

7. Richardson, vol. 7, 3225.

8. *The Prize Cases,* 67 U.S. 635, 660 (emphasis in original). Justice Grier's comment appears on 668.

9. *United States v. Curtiss-Wright,* 299 U.S. 304, 319 (1936).

10. Ibid.

11. Quoted in Louis Fisher, *The Constitution and 9/11: Recurring Threats to America's Freedoms* (Lawrence: University Press of Kansas, 2008), 294.

12. In 2002 the FISA Court of Review stated: "We take it for granted that the President does have that authority [to conduct warrantless searches to obtain foreign intelligence information] and, assuming that is so, FISA could not encroach on the President's constitutional power." *In re Sealed Case,* 310 F.3d 717, 742 (Foreign Int.Surv.Ct. Rev. 2002). "Taking it for granted" and "assuming that is so" falls short of legal analysis. Moreover, the FISA Court is a secret court without any adversary process for determining the truth or settling constitutional questions.

13. *Talbot v. Seeman,* 5 U.S. 1, 28 (1801); see also *Bas v. Tingy,* 4 U.S. 37 (1800).

14. *Little v. Barreme,* 6 U.S. (2 Cr.) 169, 179 (1804). For further analysis of the "sole organ" doctrine, see Louis Fisher, "Presidential Inherent Power: The 'Sole Organ Doctrine,'" *Presidential Studies Quarterly,* vol. 37, no. 1, 139–152 (March 2007).

15. U.S. Congress, H. Doc. No. 534 (part 1), 82d Cong., 2d Sess., 371–372 (1952).

16. *Youngstown Sheet & Tube Co. v. Sawyer,* 103 F. Supp. 569 (D.D.C. 1952), aff'd 343 U.S. 579 (1952).

17. Ibid.

18. Ibid. See Maeva Marcus, *Truman and the* Steel Seizure Case: *The Limits of Presidential Power* (Durham, NC: Duke University Press, 1994).

19. For impoundment, see James P. Pfiffner, *President, the Budget and Congress: Impoundment and the 1974 Budget Act* (Boulder, CO: West-

view Press, 1979); and Louis Fisher, *Presidential Spending Power* (Princeton, NJ: Princeton University Press, 1975), 147–201. For litigation striking down domestic surveillance, see *United States v. United States District Court*, 407 U.S. 297 (1972); and Fisher, *The Constitution and 9/11*, 285–290.

20. *United States v. United States District Court for the Eastern District of Michigan*, 444 F.2d 651, 665 (6th Cir. 1971).

21. Brief for Respondents, *Hamdan v. Rumsfeld*, on writ of certiorari to the United States Court of Appeals for the District of Columbia Circuit, U.S. Supreme Court, No. 05-184, February 2006, 9.

22. *Hamdan v. Rumsfeld*, 548 U.S. 557 (2006); Military Commissions Act of 2006, P.L. 109–366, 120 Stat. 2600.

23. Brief for Respondents-Appellants, *Hamdi v. Rumsfeld*, No. 02–6895 (4th Cir. 2002), 14.

24. *Hamdi v. Rumsfeld*, 542 U.S. 507, 535–536 (2004).

25. *Rasul v. Bush*, 542 U.S. 466 (2004).

26. *Boumediene v. Bush*, 553 U.S. ___ (2008).

27. Fisher, *The Constitution and 9/11*, 285–320.

28. Henry Steele Commager, "Presidential Power: The Issue Analyzed," *New York Times Magazine* (January 14, 1951): 11. See also his article "Does the President Have Too Much Power?" *New York Times Magazine* (April 1, 1951): 15.

29. Arthur M. Schlesinger Jr., "Presidential Powers: Taft Statement on Troops Opposed, Actions of Past Precedents Cited," *New York Times*, January 9, 1951, 28.

30. Ibid.

31. Edward S. Corwin, "The President's Power," *New Republic*, January 29, 1951, 15.

32. Arthur M. Schlesinger Jr., *The Imperial Presidency* (Boston: Houghton Mifflin, 1973), ix.

33. Richard E. Neustadt, *Presidential Power* (New York: Signet, 1964), 174.

34. For further details on Commager, Schlesinger, and Neustadt, see Louis Fisher, "Scholarly Support for Presidential Wars," *Presidential Studies Quarterly*, vol. 35, no. 3 (September 2005), 590–607.

35. Friedrich A. Hayek, "Why I Am Not a Conservative," in *What Is Conservatism?* ed. Frank S. Meyers (New York: Holt, Rinehart and Winston, 1964), 100.

36. James Burnham, *Congress and the American Tradition* (Chicago: Regnery, 1959), 92.

37. Ibid., 184.

38. Ibid., 344.

39. Willmoore Kendall, "The Two Majorities," *Midwest Journal of Political Science*, vol. 4 (1960), 317–345.

40. Alfred de Grazia, *Republic in Crisis: Congress Against the Executive Force* (New York: Federal Legal Publications, 1965), 72.

41. Ibid.

42. Ronald C. Moe, ed., *Congress and the President: Allies and Adversaries* (Pacific Palisades, CA: Goodyear, 1971), 3.

43. John Hart, "Presidential Power Revisited," *Political Studies*, vol. 25 (1977), 48–61; David Gray Adler, "Textbooks and the President's Constitutional Powers," *Presidential Studies Quarterly*, vol. 35 (2005), 376–388.

44. Norman Podhoretz, "Making the World Safe for Communism," *Commentary*, April 1976, 35.

45. Joseph M. Bessette and Jeffrey Tulis, eds., *The Presidency in the Constitutional Order* (Baton Rouge: Louisiana State University Press, 1981); see also Joseph M. Bessette, *The Mild Voice of Reason: Deliberative Democracy and American National Government* (Chicago: University Press of Chicago, 1994).

46. Mickey Edwards, *Reclaiming Conservatism* (New York: Oxford University Press, 2008), 185.

47. Max Farrand, ed., *The Records of the Federal Convention of 1787* (New Haven, CT: Yale University Press, 1937), vol. 2, 318.

48. Ibid.

49. John C. Yoo, "The Continuation of Politics by Other Means: The Original Understanding of War Powers," *California Law Review*, vol. 84, no. 2 (March 1996), 167–305. Many of these arguments appear in Yoo's book, *The Powers of War and Peace: The Constitution and Foreign Affairs After 9/11* (Chicago: University of Chicago Press, 2005).

50. *United States v. Smith*, 27 Fed. Cas. 1192 (C.C.N.Y. 1806) (No. 16, 342).

51. For some evaluations of John Yoo's scholarship, see Louis Fisher, "Unchecked Presidential Wars," *University of Pennsylvania Law Review*, vol. 148 (2000), 1637–1672; David Cole, "What Bush Wants to Hear," *New York Review of Books*, November 17, 2005, 8–12; Gordon Silverstein, "All Power to the President," *The American Prospect*, vol. 17, no. 3 (March 2006), 1–6; David Luban, "The Defense of Torture," *New York Review of Books*, March 15, 2007, 37–40; Robert F. Turner, "An Insider's Look at the War on Terrorism," *Cornell Law Review*, vol. 93 (2008), 471–500; Stuart Streichler, "Mad About Yoo, or, Why Worry About the Next Unconstitutional War?" *Journal of Law & Politics*, vol. 24 (2008), 93–128.

52. *Congressional Record*, vol. 55, 363 (1917).

53. Louis Fisher, *Presidential War Power* (Lawrence: University Press of Kansas, 2d ed., 2004), 133–135.

54. Singer's remarks appear in David W. Clinton, *The Two Faces of National Interest* (Baton Rouge: Louisiana State University Press, 1994), x.

55. George S. Edwards III, "Congress and National Strategy: The Appropriate Role?" in *U.S. National Security Strategy for the 1990s*, ed. Daniel J. Kaufman, David S. Clark, and Kevin P. Sheehan (Baltimore, MD: Johns Hopkins University Press, 1991), 82.

56. Alexander DeConde, *Presidential Machismo: Executive Authority, Military Intervention, and Foreign Relations* (Boston: Northeastern University Press, 2000), 294.

57. Richard M. Pious, "Why Do Presidents Fail?," *Presidential Studies Quarterly*, vol. 32 (2002), 727.

58. Richard M. Pious, *Why Presidents Fail* (Lanham, MD: Rowman and Littlefield, 2008), 247.

59. James P. Pfiffner, *The Character Factor: How We Judge America's Presidents* (College Station: Texas A&M University Press, 2004); Eric Alterman, *Why Presidents Lie: A History of Official Deception and Its Consequences* (New York: Viking, 2004). For a string of false and deceptive claims about weapons of mass destruction held by Iraq in 2002, see Louis Fisher, "Justifying War Against Iraq," in *Rivals for Power: Presidential-Congressional Relations*, ed. James A. Thurber (Lanham, MD: Rowman and Littlefield, 2006), 289–313.

60. E.g., Gene Healy, *The Cult of the Presidency: America's Dangerous Devotion to Executive Power* (Washington, DC: Cato Institute, 2008); Dana D. Nelson, *Bad for Democracy: How the Presidency Undermines the Power of the People* (Minneapolis: University of Minnesota Press, 2008); James P. Pfiffner, *Power Play: The Bush Presidency and the Constitution* (Washington, DC: Brookings Institution Press, 2008); Matthew Crenson and Benjamin Ginsberg, *Presidential Power: Unchecked and Unbalanced* (New York: W. W. Norton, 2007); Charlie Savage, *Takeover: The Return of the Imperial Presidency and the Subversion of American Democracy* (New York: Little, Brown, 2007); Andrew Rudalevige, *The New Imperial Presidency: Renewing Presidential Power After Watergate* (Ann Arbor: University of Michigan Press, 2005).

## Chapter 3

1. *Brown v. Allen,* 344 U.S. 443, 540 (1953) (Jackson, J., concurring).

2. *United States v. Lovett,* 328 U.S. 303 (1946).

3. *Marbury v. Madison,* 5 U.S. (1 Cr.) 137 (1803).

4. *Hylton v. United States,* 3 Dall. 171, 175 (1796), emphasis in original.

5. *Hollingsworth v. Virginia,* 3 Dall. 378 (1798).

6. *Calder v. Bull,* 3 Dall. 386, 399 (1798) (Iredell, J., concurring).

7. *Marbury v. Madison,* 177.

8. Louis Fisher and Katy J. Harriger, *American Constitutional Law,* 8th ed. (Durham, NC: Carolina Academic Press, 2009), 43.

9. David P. Currie, *The Constitution in Congress* (Chicago: University of Chicago Press, 1997), 296.

10. Francis Wharton, *State Trials of the United States During the Administration of Washington and Adams* (Philadelphia: Carey and Hart, 1849), 84–85, 88; Henfield's Case, 11 F. Cas. 1099 (C.C. Pa. 1793) (No. 6,360).

11. *United States v. Hudson and Goodwin,* 11 U.S. (7 Cr.) 32 (1812); *United States v. Coolidge,* 14 U.S. (1 Wheat.) 415 (1816); Leonard W. Levy, *Jefferson and Civil Liberties: The Darker Side* (New York: Quadrangle, 1973), chap. 3; Herbert A. Johnson, *History of the Supreme Court of the United States: Foundations of Power: John Marshall, 1801–1815* (New York: Macmillan, 1981), 633–646; Richard Buel Jr., *America on the Brink: How the Political Struggle over the War of 1812 Almost Destroyed the Young Republic* (New York: Palgrave Macmillan, 2005), 147, 162, 196.

12. *Pennsylvania v. Wheeling &c. Bridge Co.,* 54 U.S. (13 How.) 518 (1852); 10 Stat. 110, 112, sec. 6 (1852); *Pennsylvania v. Wheeling and Belmont Bridge Co.,* 59 U.S. (18 How.) 421 (1856). See also *Prudential Ins. Co. v. Benjamin,* 326 U.S. 408, 425 (1946); *United States v. Lopez,* 514 U.S. 549, 580 (1995).

13. Harold M. Hyman, *A More Perfect Union* (Boston: Houghton Mifflin, 1975), 6.

14. *Dred Scott v. Sandford,* 60 U.S. (19 How.) 393 (1857).

15. Quoted in Stanley I. Kutner, *The* Dred Scott *Decision: Law or Politics?* (Boston: Houghton Mifflin, 1967), 47.

16. *Political Debates Between Abraham Lincoln and Stephen A. Douglas* (Cleveland, OH: The Burrows Brothers Co., 1894), 70–71, 76–77, 78–79.

17. *Prudential Ins. Co. v. Benjamin,* 328 U.S. 408, 415 (1946).

18. Owen J. Roberts, *The Court and the Constitution* (Cambridge, MA: Harvard University Press, 1951), 61.

19. Robert H. Jackson, "Maintaining Our Freedoms: The Role of the Judiciary," *Vital Speeches*, no. 24, vol. XIX, October 1, 1951, 761.

20. *Hepburn v. Griswold,* 8 Wall. (75 U.S.) 603 (1870).

21. *Legal Tender Cases,* 12 Wall. (79 U.S.) 457 (1871).

22. *United States v. Cruikshank,* 92 U.S. (2 Otto.) 542, 550 (1876).

23. *Leisy v. Hardin,* 135 U.S. 100 (1890).

24. Quoted in Fisher and Harriger, *American Constitutional Law*, 323.

25. *In re Rahrer,* 140 U.S. 545 (1891).

26. *Hylton v. United States*, 3 Dall. at 171.

27. *Veazie Bank v. Fenno,* 75 U.S. (8 Wall.) 533 (1869).

28. *Springer v. United States,* 102 U.S. 586 (1881).

29. Ibid., 594.

30. *Pollock v. Farmers' Loan & Trust Co.,* 157 U.S. 429 (1895).

31. Ibid., 532.

32. Ibid., 607.

33. Charles Evans Hughes, *The Supreme Court of the United States* (New York: Columbia University Press, 1928), 54.

34. *Hammer v. Dagenhart,* 247 U.S. 251 (1918).

35. *Congressional Record*, vol. 56, 7433 (1918).

36. "Brief on Behalf of Appellants and Plaintiff in Error," *J. W. Bailey and J. W. Bailey, Collector of Internal Revenue for the District of North Carolina v. Drexel Furniture Co.*, in *Landmark Briefs and Arguments of the Supreme Court of the United States: Constitutional Law* (Arlington, VA: University Publications of America, 1975), 59.

37. *Bailey v. Drexel Furniture Co.,* 259 U.S. 20 (1922).

38. Ibid., 38.

39. Fisher and Harriger, *American Constitutional Law*, 442–445.

40. *United States v. Darby,* 312 U.S. 100 (1941).

41. Ibid., 116–117.

42. Jonathan Elliot, ed., *The Debates in the Several State Conventions on the Adoption of the Federal Constitution*, vol. 3 (Philadelphia, PA: Lippincott, 1937), 459.

43. Louis Fisher, "Confidential Spending and Government Accountability." *George Washington Law Review*, vol. 47 (1979), 347.

44. *United States v. Richardson,* 418 U.S. 166, 179 (1974).

45. Ibid., 200–201.

46. "Making Connections with Dots to Decipher U.S. Spy Spending," *Washington Post*, March 12, 1996, A11.

47. Louis Fisher, *Constitutional Conflicts Between Congress and the President* (Lawrence, KS: University Press of Kansas, 2007), 213–214.

48. Mark Mazzetti, "$43.5 Billion Spying Budget for Year, Not Including Military," *New York Times*, October 31, 2007, A16; Walter Pincus, "2007 Spying Said to Cost $50 Billion," *Washington Post*, October 30, 2007, A4.

49. Louis Fisher, *The Politics of Executive Privilege* (Durham, NC: Carolina Academic Press, 2004), 254–255.

50. *Opinions of the Attorney General*, vol. 6 (1854), 680.

51. For details on the experience with the legislative veto, see Fisher, *Constitutional Conflicts Between Congress and the President*, 137–154.

52. *INS v. Chadha,* 462 U.S. 919 (1983).

53. Louis Fisher, "Congress Can't Lose on Its Veto Power," *Washington Post*, February 21, 1982, D1, D5.

54. *Chadha*, 462 U.S. at 944.

55. William Howard Taft, "Criticisms of the Federal Judiciary," *American Law Review*, vol. 29 (1895), 643.

56. Sandra Day O'Connor, *The Majesty of the Law: Reflections of a Supreme Court Justice* (New York: Random House, 2003), 44, 45.

## Chapter 4

1. *Annals of Congress*, vol. 1, 439 (1789).

2. *Annals of Congress*, 5th Cong., 2d and 3d Sessions, vol. 9 (1798), 2152.

3. *The Writings of Thomas Jefferson*, memorial ed., vol. 10 (Washington, DC: Thomas Jefferson Memorial Association, 1903–1904), 61.

4. Henry W. Edgerton, "The Incidence of Judicial Control over Congress," *Cornell Law Quarterly*, vol. 22 (1937), 299.

5. S. Rept. No. 711, 75th Cong., 1st Session (1937), 3, 19, 20, 23.

6. *United States v. Carolene Products Co.*, 304 U.S. 144, 152–153 n.4 (1938).

7. Leslie Friedman Goldstein, "The ERA and the U.S. Supreme Court," *Research in Law and Policy Studies*, vol. 1 (1987), 154–155.

8. John J. Dinan, *Keeping the People's Liberties: Legislators, Citizens, and Judges as Guardians of Rights* (Lawrence: University Press of Kansas, 1998). See also Larry D. Kramer, *The People Themselves: Popular Constitutionalism and Judicial Review* (New York: Oxford University Press,

2004) and Kramer, *"Here, the People Rule": A Constitutional Populist Manifesto* (Cambridge, MA: Harvard University Press, 1994).

9. Harry Kalven Jr. and Hans Zeisel, *The American Jury* (Boston: Little, Brown, 1966), 319.

10. *Webb, Auditor & Co. v. Bird*, 6 Ind. 11, 15 (1854); *Carpenter & Sprague v. Dane County*, 9 Wis. 274, 276 (1859); *Gideon v. Wainwright*, 372 U.S. 335 (1963).

11. For recognition of the rights of conscientious objectors by communities and legislatures, see Louis Fisher, *Religious Liberty in America: Political Safeguards* (Lawrence: University Press of Kansas, 2002), 82–104.

12. Edward Needles Wright, *Conscientious Objectors in the Civil War* (Philadelphia: University of Pennsylvania Press, 1931), 70–71.

13. Ibid., 72.

14. 13 Stat. 6, 9 (1864).

15. 40 Stat. 40, 68 (1917); Executive Order 2823 (March 20, 1918).

16. 54 Stat. 885, 889 (1940).

17. *Congressional Record*, 43d Cong., 2d Session, vol. 3, 940 (1875).

18. *Civil Rights Cases,* 109 U.S. 3 (1883).

19. Ibid., 59–60.

20. *In re Bradwell*, 55 Ill. 535, 542 (1869).

21. Ibid., 540.

22. Illinois Laws, 1871–1872, 578.

23. 16 Wall. (83 U.S.) 130, 139 (1873).

24. Ibid., 141–142.

25. *Congressional Record*, vol. 7, 1235 (1878).

26. *Congressional Record*, vol. 8, 1084 (1879).

27. Ibid.

28. Edward T. James, ed., *Notable American Women, 1607–1950* (Cambridge, MA: Harvard University Press, 1971), 414.

29. *Reed v. Reed,* 404 U.S. 71 (1971).

30. *Goeseart v. Cleary,* 335 U.S. 464 (1948).

31. Ibid., 465.

32. *Hoyt v. Florida,* 368 U.S. 57, 62 (1961).

33. John D. Johnston Jr. and Charles L. Knapp, "Sex Discrimination by Law: A Study in Judicial Perspective," *New York University Law Review*, vol. 46 (1971), 676.

34. *Congressional Record*, 91st Cong., 2d Sess., vol. 117, 35323 (1971).

35. *Minersville School District v. Gobitis,* 310 U.S. 586 (1940).

36. Cited in *Minersville School District v. Gobitis*, 21 F. Supp. 581, 584 (E.D. Pa. 1937).

37. H. N. Hirsch, *The Enigma of Felix Frankfurter* (New York: Basic Books, 1981), 152.

38. Fisher, *Religious Liberty in America,* 109.

39. *Jones v. Opelika,* 316 U.S. 584 (1942).

40. Fisher, *Religious Liberty in America*, 112–113; 46 Stat. 380, sec. 7 (1942).

41. *West Virginia State Board of Education v. Barnette,* 319 U.S. 624, 638 (1943).

42. E.g., *Cantwell v. Connecticut*, 310 U.S. 296 (1940) (upholding the right of a Jehovah's Witness to solicit money and sell books); *Largent v. Texas*, 318 U.S. 418 (1943) (striking down an ordinance that required a permit to solicit orders and sell books); and *Murdoch v. Pennsylvania*, 319 U.S. 105 (1943) (striking down a license tax applied to Jehovah's Witnesses who engaged in missionary evangelism).

43. *Goldman v. Secretary of Defense*, 530 F. Supp. 12, 15, 16 (D.D.C. 1981); *Bitterman v. Secretary of Defense*, 553 F. Supp. 719, 725 (D.D.C. 1982).

44. *Goldman v. Weinberger,* 475 U.S. 503 (1986).

45. Ibid., 514.

46. Ibid., 523, 524.

47. *Congressional Record*, 99th Cong., 2d Sess., vol. 132, 19803 (1986).

48. *Brown v. Board of Education,* 347 U.S. 483 (1954).

49. *Plessy v. Ferguson,* 163 U.S. 537 (1896).

50. For divisions within the Court prior to *Brown*, see the box in Fisher and Harriger, *American Constitutional Law*, 771.

51. *Brown v. Board of Education*, 357 U.S. 483, 495 (1954).

52. *Brown v. Board of Education*, 349 U.S. 294, 298 (1955).

53. Ibid., 299.

54. Ibid., 300.

55. *Griffin v. School Bd.*, 377 U.S. 218, 229 (1964) (emphasis in original).

56. *United States v. Jefferson County Board of Education*, 372 F.2d 836, 837 (5th Cir. 1966) (emphasis in original).

57. *Heart of Atlanta Motel v. United States*, 379 U.S. 241 (1964); *Katzenbach v. McClung*, 379 U.S. 294 (1964).

58. *Naim v. Naim*, 87 S.E.2d 749, 756 (Va. 1955).

59. *Naim v. Naim*, 350 U.S. 891 (1955).

60. *Naim v. Naim*, 350 U.S. 985 (1956).

61. *Loving v. Virginia,* 388 U.S. 1 (1967).

62. Earl Warren, "The Bill of Rights and the Military," *New York University Law Review,* vol. 37 (1962), 181.

## Chapter 5

1. *Congressional Record*, vol. 79, 2014 (1935).

2. *Congressional Digest*, vol. xvi, 172 (June-July 1937).

3. *Congressional Record*, vol. 84, 2854 (1939).

4. Louis Fisher, *Presidential Spending Power* (Princeton, NJ: Princeton University Press, 1975), 214.

5. *Public Papers and Addresses of Franklin D. Roosevelt*, vol. 11, 364–365 (New York: Random House, 1950).

6. Woodrow Wilson, *The Papers of Woodrow Wilson*, ed. Arthur S. Link (Princeton, NJ: Princeton University Press), vol. 63, 451, and vol. 64, 47, 51; Louis Fisher, *Presidential War Power* (Lawrence: University Press of Kansas, 2d ed., 2004), 81–83.

7. *Congressional Record*, vol. 91, 8185 (1945).

8. Fisher, *Presidential War Power*, 84–95.

9. *Public Papers of the Presidents* (Washington, DC: Government Printing Office), vol. 1950, 504.

10. Fisher, *Presidential War Power*, 169–172, 180–192.

11. Ibid., 105–115.

12. "Background Information on the Use of United States Armed Forces in Foreign Countries," printed for the use of the House Committee on Foreign Affairs, 82d Cong., 1st Sess. (Comm. Print, 1951), 1.

13. H. Doc. No. 443, 84th Cong., 2d Sess. (1956), viii.

14. Dwight D. Eisenhower, *Waging Peace* (Garden City, NY: Doubleday, 1965), 179.

15. J. William Fulbright, "American Foreign Policy in the Twentieth Century under an Eighteenth-Century Constitution," *Cornell Law Quarterly* 47 (1961): 2.

16. U.S. Commitments to Foreign Powers," hearings before the Senate Foreign Relations Committee, 90th Cong., 1st Session (1967), 3.

17. S. Rept. No. 129, 91st Cong., 1st Session (1969), 8.

18. Ibid., 16.

19. Ibid., 23 (emphasis in original).

20. Fisher, *Presidential War Power*, 145.

21. Ibid., 148.

22. Louis Fisher, "The Baker-Christopher War Power Commission," *Presidential Studies Quarterly*, vol. 39, no. 1 (March 2009), 128–140.

23. *Train v. City of New York,* 420 U.S. 35 (1975).

24. H. Rept. No. 147, 93d Cong., 1st Session (1973), 1.

25. *Congressional Record,* vol. 125, 9028 (1979).

26. Louis Fisher, *The Politics of Shared Power: Congress and the Executive*, 4th ed. (College Station, Texas A&M University Press, 1998), 234.

27. David A. Stockman, *The Triumph of Politics* (New York: Harper and Row, 1986), 159.

28. Ibid., 91.

29. Allen Schick, *The Capacity to Budget* (Washington, DC: Urban Institute Press, 1990), 204.

30. *Bowsher v. Synar,* 478 U.S. 714 (1986).

31. Fisher, *The Politics of Shared Power,* 240 (Table 7-3).

32. "Budget Process Reform," hearing before the House Committee on the Budget, 101st Cong., 2d Session (1990), 20–21.

33. *Clinton v. City of New York,* 524 U.S. 417 (1998).

34. Mickey Edwards, *Reclaiming Conservatism* (New York: Oxford University Press, 2008), 174.

35. *Public Papers of the Presidents* (Washington, DC: Government Printing Office, 1984), 1228.

36. *Congressional Record,* vol. 141, 2361 (1995), 135.

## Chapter 6

1. Lee Hamilton, *How Congress Works and Why You Should Care* (Bloomington: Indiana University Press, 2004), 23. A very thoughtful analysis of the many virtues of Congress and a frank, informed assessment of its weaknesses.

2. Thomas E. Mann and Norman J. Ornstein, *The Broken Branch: How Congress Is Failing America and How to Get It Back on Track* (New York: Oxford University Press, 2006), 215.

3. *Whitney v. California,* 274 U.S. 357, 375 (1927) (Brandeis, J., concurring).

4. Specific examples of individuals who made a difference are listed in Lee Hamilton's book, 138–140.

5. Frederick A. O. Schwarz Jr. and Aziz S. Huq, *Unchecked and Unbalanced: Presidential Power in a Time of Terror* (New York: New Press, 2007), 204.

6. Mann and Ornstein, *The Broken Branch,* xi.

7. *Congressional Quarterly Weekly Report*, March 30, 2009, 707.

8. Newt Gingrich, *Lessons Learned the Hard Way* (New York: HarperCollins, 1998), 144–147, 149–152.

9. Jim Wright, *Balance of Power: Presidents and Congress from the Era of McCarthy to the Age of Gingrich* (Atlanta, GA: Turner, 1996), 382.

10. Tip O'Neill, *Man of the House: The Life and Political Memoirs of Speaker Tip O'Neill* (New York: Random House, 1987), 190.

11. Ibid., 194–195.

12. Carl Albert, *Little Giant: The Life and Times of Speaker Carl Albert* (Norman: University of Oklahoma Press, 1990), 165.

13. Ibid., 294–301.

14. *Bush v. Gore,* 531 U.S. 98 (2000).

15. The literature on *Bush* v. *Gore* is vast, but a good analysis appears in Charles L. Zelden, Bush v. Gore: *Exposing the Hidden Crisis in American Democracy* (Lawrence: University Press of Kansas, 2008).

16. Gore's concession speech of December 13, 2000, http://abcnews.go.com/print?id=122220.

17. Ibid.

18. *Congressional Record*, vol. 155, S12 (daily ed. January 6, 2009).

19. *Buckley v. Valeo,* 424 U.S. 1 (1976).

20. Legistorm, "About Congressional Staff Salaries," http://www.legistorm.com/salaries/aboutcs.html, accessed June 27, 2009.

21. Other possible reforms are explored in Susan Crabtree, "Obey Tackles Earmarks, but Colleagues Skeptical," *The Hill*, June 18, 2009, 6.

22. Christopher Drew, "Work Halted on Helicopter for President," *New York Times*, May 16, 2009, B1.

23. Christopher Drew, "$296 Billion in Overruns in U.S. Weapons Programs," *New York Times*, March 31, 2009, B8.

24. Nick Schwellenbach, "Fraud Cases Fell While Pentagon Contracts Surged," April 1, 2009, available at Center for Public Integrity website, http:www.publicintegrity.org/articles/entry/1243, accessed June 27, 2009.

25. Louis Fisher, *The Politics of Executive Privilege* (Durham, NC: Carolina Academic Press, 2004), 76–77.

26. 101 Stat. 1057, sec. 226 (1987).

27. *Congressional Record*, vol. 138, 6807 (1992).

28. "House Rearranges Bush's Budget Cuts," *Washington Post*, May 8, 1992, A8.

29. Louis Fisher, *Congressional Abdication on War and Spending* (College Station: Texas A&M University Press, 2000), 145–146.

30. Tom Foley, *Honor in the House* (Pullman: Washington State University Press, 1999), 32–33.

31. Ibid., 224, 243.

# Index

# About the Author

Louis Fisher is a specialist in constitutional law at the Law Library of the Library of Congress, after working with the Congressional Research Service from 1970 to March 2006. The views expressed in this book are personal, not institutional. During his service with CRS, Fisher was research director of the House Iran-Contra Committee in 1987, writing major sections of the final report. He is the author of nineteen books, including *The Constitution and 9/11: Recurring Threats to America's Freedoms* (2008), *In the Name of National Security: Unchecked Presidential Power and the* Reynolds *Case* (2006), *Military Tribunals and Presidential Power: American Revolution to the War on Terrorism* (2005), *The Politics of Executive Privilege* (2004), *Presidential War Power* (2d ed. 2004), *Constitutional Conflicts between Congress and the President* (5th ed. 2007), and *American Constitutional Law* (with Katy J. Harriger, 8th ed., 2009). He has received the Dartmouth Book Award, the Neustadt Book Award, and has twice received the Louis Brownlow Book Award.

He received his doctorate in political science from the New School for Social Research (1967) and has taught at Queens College, Georgetown University, American University, Catholic University, Indiana University, Johns Hopkins University, and the law schools of William and Mary and Catholic University. He has testified before congressional committees on such issues as state secrets, war powers, NSA surveillance, executive privilege, executive lobbying, presidential reorganization authority, national security whistleblowing, covert spending, legislative vetoes, item vetoes, pocket vetoes, recess appointments, Congress and the Constitution, the Gramm-Rudman-Hollings Act, biennial budgeting, and the balanced budget amendment.

Fisher's specialties include constitutional law, national security law, budget policy, executive-legislative relations, and judicial-congressional relations. He is the author of more than four hundred articles in law reviews, political science journals, encyclopedias, books, magazines, and newspapers, and has been invited to speak in several dozen countries.

**"Do you have any other weapons?"**

"If I did, I'd have used them already," Esme said.

"Mind if I check? Just to be sure?"

"Yes. I do."

"I'm going to have to do it anyway. You could make it easier by not struggling."

"You could make it easier by letting me go."

"That would defeat the purpose of me and King spending the last three days hanging around Long Pine Key Campground searching for you."

"Is that Cujo's name? King?"

"Yeah. Why?" Ian patted her down one-handed, refusing to release his hold. No matter how small she seemed, no matter how harmless, she was part of the crime family that had killed his parents.

* * *

**CLASSIFIED K-9 UNIT:**
**These lawmen solve the toughest cases with the help of their brave canine partners**

*Guardian*–Terri Reed, April 2017
*Sheriff*–Laura Scott, May 2017
*Special Agent*–Valerie Hansen, June 2017
*Bounty Hunter*–Lynette Eason, July 2017
*Bodyguard*–Shirlee McCoy, August 2017
*Tracker*–Lenora Worth, September 2017
*Classified K-9 Unit Christmas*–Terri Reed and Lenora Worth, December 2017

Aside from her faith and her family, there's not much **Shirlee McCoy** enjoys more than a good book! When she's not teaching or chauffeuring her five kids, she can usually be found plotting her next Love Inspired Suspense story or wandering around the beautiful Inland Northwest in search of inspiration. Shirlee loves to hear from readers. If you have time, drop her a line at shirlee@shirleemccoy.com.

**Books by Shirlee McCoy**

**Love Inspired Suspense**

***Classified K-9 Unit***

*Bodyguard*

***Mission: Rescue***

*Protective Instincts*
*Her Christmas Guardian*
*Exit Strategy*
*Deadly Christmas Secrets*
*Mystery Child*
*The Christmas Target*
*Mistaken Identity*

***Rookie K-9 Unit***

*Secrets and Lies*

***Capitol K-9 Unit***

*Protection Detail*
*Capitol K-9 Unit Christmas*
"Protecting Virginia"

Visit the Author Profile page
at Harlequin.com for more titles.

# BODYGUARD

SHIRLEE McCOY

HARLEQUIN® LOVE INSPIRED® SUSPENSE

Special thanks and acknowledgment to Shirlee McCoy for her participation in the Classified K-9 Unit miniseries.

Recycling programs for this product may not exist in your area.

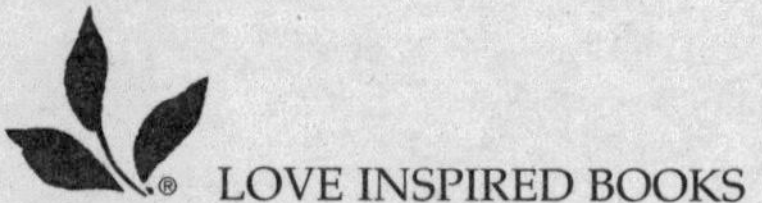


ISBN-13: 978-0-373-67839-6

Bodyguard



This edition published by arrangement with Love Inspired Books.



www.Harlequin.com

**Printed in U.S.A.**

Have I not commanded you? Be strong and courageous.
Do not be afraid, do not be discouraged. For the
Lord your God will be with you wherever you go.

–*Joshua* 1:9

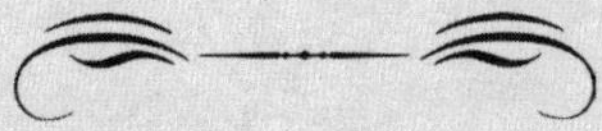

To my beautiful and brave niece, Aaliyah Parker.
The strongest young lady I know. I am so proud of you
and so blessed to call you family! Keep smiling, sweetie.
And, I will keep praying! I love you dearly!

# ONE

If the Everglades didn't kill her, her uncle would.

Either way, Esme Dupree was going to die.

The thought of that—of all the things she'd leave behind, all the dreams she'd never fulfill—had kept her moving through the Florida wetland for three days, but she was tiring. Even the most determined person in the world couldn't keep running forever. And she'd been running for what seemed like nearly that long. First, she'd fled witness protection, crisscrossing states to try to stay a step ahead of her uncle's henchmen. She'd finally found her way to Florida, to the thick vegetation and quiet waterways that her parents had loved.

Esme wasn't as keen. Her family had spent every summer of her childhood here, exploring the wetland, documenting flora and fauna as part of Esme's homeschool experience. She preferred open fields and prairie grass, but her parents had loved the shallow green water of the Everglades. She'd never had the heart to tell them that she didn't. By that time, her older siblings were grown and gone, and it was just the three of them, exploring the world together.

Funny that she'd come back here when her life was falling apart; when everything she'd worked for had been shot to smithereens by her brother's and uncle's crimes, Esme had returned to a place filled with fond memories.

It was also filled with lots of things that could kill a person. Alligators. Crocodiles. Snakes. Panthers. She wasn't as worried about those as she was about human predators.

Her uncle and the people he'd hired.

The FBI, too. If they tracked her down, they wouldn't kill her, but she'd put her hope in them before, trusted them for her safety. She'd almost died because of it.

She wiped sweat from her brow and sipped water from her canteen. Better to go it alone than to count on people who couldn't be depended on. She'd been learning that the hard way these past few months.

Bugs dive-bombed every inch of her exposed flesh, the insect repellant sweating off almost as quickly as she could spray it on. Things hadn't been so bad when she'd been renting a little trailer at the edge of the national park. She'd had shelter from the bugs and the critters. But

Uncle Angus had tracked her down and nearly killed her. He would have killed her if she hadn't smashed his head with a snow globe and called the police. They'd come quickly.

Of course they had.

They were as eager to get their hands on her as Uncle Angus had been. It seemed like every law enforcement office in the United States was keeping its eyes out for her.

Thanks to the feds, the organization that had sworn to protect her. Witness protection was supposed to be her ticket out of the mess she'd found herself in. She'd hoped it would be. She'd probably even believed it would. She'd entered the program because she'd seen her brother murder a man in cold blood. She'd seen the look in his eyes, and she'd known that he was capable of anything. Even killing her to keep her quiet. What she'd learned since then was that there was no panacea to her trouble. No easy way out. No certain solution. Her best hope was in herself and her ability to keep a step ahead of her uncle until the trial.

"That might have been easier if you'd stayed with the police," she muttered, using a long wooden pole to move the canoe through shallow water.

There was no sense beating herself up over the decision to run again. Uncle Angus's hired guns had firebombed the tiny police station she'd been taken to after she'd been attacked. During the chaos that had followed, she'd seen the opportunity and she'd run.

It had seemed like the right decision at the time.

Now she wasn't so sure. The sun had nearly set, its golden glow still lingering on the horizon. Mosquitoes buzzed around her head. She didn't bother slapping at them. Her arms ached. Her head throbbed. Her body felt leaden. All she wanted was to get out of the Glades and back to civilization. She'd make different decisions this time. Head for a place she'd never been before. She'd buy colored contacts to change the bright green eyes she'd inherited from her mother. The reading glasses she'd bought and worn hadn't hidden them well enough, and Uncle Angus had told her that was how she'd been found.

"Those eyes, kid," he'd growled. "You can't hide them."

He was wrong. She could, and she would.

No more living in her delusions, telling herself that everything was going to be okay because she was a good person with a good heart who wanted only what was best for the people she loved.

*A fool.*

Because she really wanted to believe that

good begat good and that the happily-ever-after she'd planned for so many clients would happen for her one day.

She might be a fool, but she wasn't stupid.

If she was found again, she *would* die.

But she wasn't going to be found. She'd sleep in the canoe again. Just like she had the past three nights, covered by mosquito netting, listening to things slither in and out of the water. By tomorrow afternoon, she should reach her destination—Long Pine Key Campground. She eyed the compass she'd bought before she'd left Wyoming, using a small Mag light to study the map she'd grabbed from the Everglades National Park information center.

She'd had a feeling she was going to need both.

As a matter of fact, she'd put together a survival pack, and she'd hidden it in the crumbling loft of one of the boat sheds that dotted the trailer park where she'd been staying.

She'd been able to grab it after she'd escaped the police.

Maybe she wasn't as much of a fool as her ex-fiancé, Brent, had said she was when she'd told him she was going to testify against her brother. She *was* tired, though. Tired people made mistakes. Like coming to the Everglades instead of heading for Texas or California or somewhere else where no one would think to look for her.

Death.

It had been stalking her for months, but now…

Now she could feel it breathing down her neck.

She shuddered, watching the edges of the murky water for a place to pull onto the shore. She needed a spot clear of vegetation. One that would allow her to drag the canoe far away from the edge of the water.

Tomorrow she'd be away from the slithering, slapping, plopping sounds of things moving through the water. She'd leave the canoe behind and make her way out of Florida. She still had money. Not much, but enough to get her to another state. She'd start fresh, build a new business. Nothing to do with weddings or brides. Nothing that anyone she knew would connect her with.

Not even Violetta.

Her eyes burned at the thought of never seeing her older sister again, her heart heavy with what that would mean—no family, no connections, no one who shared all her childhood memories.

If she could have, she'd have contacted her sister. But she didn't dare. Their brother, Reginald, would use Violetta's knowledge about Esme to his advantage. He'd probably been doing it all along. As much as she loved her sister, she also knew Violetta's weakness—greed. She liked the good things in life, and she was happy to let their brother, Reginald, give them to her. Even if his means to those ends was murder.

Esme winced at the thought, pushing aside the memory that was always at the back of her mind. She'd witnessed a murder. Her brother had been the murderer. She'd watched the victim die, and she'd known that she couldn't keep quiet.

She'd turned on her family, betraying the deepest of all bonds.

That was what Uncle Angus had said when he'd broken into the trailer.

*Turned on family, and that makes you the lowest of low. You have to die, Esme. Because family is everything.*

It *was* a lot, but there was more to life. There was integrity, there was honor, there was faith. The last was what had enabled her to offer herself as a witness to her brother's crimes. She had what no one else in her family did—a certainty that God was in control, that He'd work everything out for His good.

She just hoped His good didn't involve her dying in the middle of the Florida wetland.

Esme flashed her light along the edges of the water, ready to stop for the night, to try to shut off her thoughts and get some sleep. Somewhere in the distance, a dog barked, the sound both alarming and comforting. She had to be on the right track, moving closer to civilization. The map and the compass hadn't steered her wrong, but civilization meant people, and that meant more danger.

Her light shone on marshy land. Eyes peered out from thick foliage, and she tried not to let herself think about what was watching her. She didn't mind the mammals. Mice, marsh rats, deer. Even thinking about panthers and bears didn't bother her. It was the reptiles that made her skin crawl—alligators, crocodiles, snakes.

"Cut it out!" she whispered, her voice filled with the fear she'd been working hard not to acknowledge. Oh, what she wouldn't give to be back in her cute little Chicago apartment, making dinner after a long day planning weddings.

Esme sighed. She did not want to be in a place where predators were waiting to do what they did best.

The dog barked again—a quick sharp sound that made her wonder if she were even closer to civilization than she'd originally thought. She'd already planned her escape route and knew—in theory—how to get from the dock at the trailer park to the closest Everglade car-accessible campground. If cars could get in, she could walk out. And that was what she planned to do.

Her light glanced off what looked like a tiny boathouse, the old wood structure gray against the lush vegetation. She checked her map, circling the camping area she thought she'd arrived at. The glades were dotted with little places like this—areas where a couple of campers could bed down for the night. This time of year, though, the water was high and the risk was greater. There weren't as many campers. Just die-hard naturalists and explorers who wanted adventure.

Esme was neither of those things.

She liked home and books and routine.

She hated scary movies, danger, intrigue.

All she'd wanted was to plan weddings, marry her college sweetheart, have the nice life she'd been dreaming of for years.

But here she was.

Ready to bed down for another night in a place that she'd rather not be.

She steered toward the wood structure, saw the clearing beyond it. There were lights in the distance—unexpected signs that she really was closer to civilization than she thought.

Esme dragged the canoe out of the water, her waders sucked in by the muddy ground. Behind her, something splashed, and she imagined a crocodile or giant snapping turtle moving toward her.

There were no other boats, no campers, nothing human that she could see. Whatever the light had been, it was gone now. Twilight turned the world deep purple, casting long shadows across the wet ground.

She climbed into the boat, traced the route she'd highlighted on the map, double-and triple-checking her coordinates. Two more camping spots before she reached her destination. Unless she'd missed a couple on the journey.

That was a possibility.

If she had, she might be at the last stop before the road-accessible campground. Something rustled in the brush, and she jumped, scanning the area, looking for whatever had made the noise. Not a mouse or rat. This had sounded large. A panther? A bear? Her heart thudded in her chest as she pulled the bowie knife from the sheath she'd strapped to her thigh. It glinted in the last rays of the setting sun, the blade new and wicked-looking. A great weapon for fighting something close-up, but she'd prefer to keep far from whatever was lurking in the shadows. In hindsight, a gun would have been a better idea. Purchasing a firearm would have been a problem, but she could have gotten her hands on one if she'd tried hard enough.

It wasn't like she didn't know how to use one. Her parents had taught her, and Reginald had reiterated the importance of knowing how to defend herself. Probably because he'd been afraid that his crimes would catch up to him, that the people he'd hurt would come back to hurt his family.

Family was everything, but he hadn't loved his enough to keep them out of harm's way. The irony of that wasn't lost on her.

The bushes rustled again—closer this time. Whatever it was, it was stalking her. She could feel it coming closer, see leaves shifting and plants shivering as something moved past.

"Please, God," she whispered, her fingers so tight around the knife hilt they ached. "Please."

And then it was on her, springing out from the brush in a flash of dark fur and dark eyes, her light following the movement as she scrambled back. Her knife hand moving as her brain screamed the truth—

A dog!

The *thing* was a dog, bounding across the open ground and stopping beside her. Sniffing at the air, at the boat, its nose so close she could have touched it.

"Hello," she said, her voice shaking, but the dog was already bounding away, barking wildly, the bright orange vest it was wearing glowing in the beam of Esme's light.

It took a second for that to register.

The vest.

The dog.

A search team. Either her uncle's henchmen or the police.

Looking for her.

She jumped out of the canoe, dragged it back toward the water, her heart slamming against her ribs as she tried desperately to escape whoever was on her trail.

The lady was back in the water, tugging the canoe out of the shallows. She probably thought she could escape again, but Esme Dupree was about to be disappointed.

Ian Slade sprinted the last few yards that separated him from his quarry, his K-9 partner, King, barking ferociously beside him. Esme had to know they were coming, but she didn't glance back, didn't stop, she just kept dragging the canoe, splashing through the green water, alerting every predator in the area that prey was moving through.

He grabbed her arm, was surprised when she swung around, a bowie knife clutched in her free hand.

King growled low in his throat, a warning that Esme would be wise to heed. The Belgian Malinois was trained in protection. Smart, agile and strong, King had a bite as vicious as his bark.

"My partner," Ian warned, "doesn't like when people threaten me."

"Is that what I'm doing?" She tried to pull away, but after three days of tracking her, there was no way Ian planned to let her go.

"What would you call it?" he replied, dragging her back a few steps.

"Defending myself."

King growled again, and Esme's gaze shifted, her attention caught just long enough for Ian to make his move.

He disarmed her with ease, grabbing her knife arm and twisting it until she dropped the weapon. Even then, he didn't release his hold.

Sure, her record was clean. She made a living planning weddings…pretty aboveboard, from the looks of it. But Esme was a member of the Dupree crime family, cut from the same cloth as her brother—a man who killed first and asked questions later.

Ian knew that more than most.

She yanked against his hold, forcing her arm into an angle that had to be painful. He might not trust her, but he didn't want to hurt her.

"Calm down," he said, shifting his grip. "I'm Agent Ian Slade. With the FBI."'

"And that's supposed to be comforting?" Esme ground out as she continued to tug against his hold.

"More comforting than staying out in the middle of nowhere with your uncle still on the loose."

"He wouldn't be loose if your team would focus on apprehending him rather than me." She yanked hard, her boots slipping in the muck.

She'd have gone down if he weren't holding on to her.

She didn't seem to realize that there was no way she was going to escape. Ian was a well-trained federal officer, part of an elite group of agents. He was also a head taller than she was and seventy pounds heavier. Maybe more. Her bones were small, her wrist tiny, his hand circling it with ease.

As battles went, this wasn't a fair one, and he almost felt bad for restraining her.

*Almost.*

He knew what her family was capable of.

Until she proved differently, he had to assume she was capable of the same. Even if he'd been one-hundred-percent certain that she wasn't, he wouldn't have let her go. Protecting her was his assignment. Keeping her alive until the case against her brother went to trial was what he'd agreed to do.

Despite the fact that she was a Dupree.

"Do you have any other weapons on you?" he asked, his fingers curved around her wrist.

She'd stopped tugging. Maybe she'd finally realized she couldn't get away.

"If I did, I'd have used them already," she spat.

"On a federal officer?" he asked.

"I didn't realize you were a federal officer at first. If I had, I wouldn't have pulled the knife."

"Good to know. Mind if I make sure you're telling the truth about weapons?"

"Yes. I do."

He could have forced the issue, but there wasn't any point. She might try to run, but he didn't think she'd attack him to do it. She had a clean record, no history of violence or trouble.

"All right," he said, releasing her.

"Thanks." She started walking to the canoe as if she thought he'd let her leave.

"I'm not checking for a weapon, but I'm not letting you leave, either."

"It would be easier on both of us if you did." She turned to face him, the darkening evening wrapping her in shadows. He couldn't see her expression through the gloom, but he could see the pale oval of her face, the tension in her shoulders.

"That would defeat the purpose of me and King spending the last three days hanging around Long Pine Key Campground waiting for you to show up."

"I didn't ask you to come looking for me. As

a matter of fact, I would have preferred that you didn't, Agent Slade," she responded.

"Ian. We'll be spending a lot of time together. We might as well be on a first-name basis."

"I'm not going back into witness protection."

"That's fine. We'll work something else out."

"I guess I should have been more clear. I'm not going back into any kind of federal protection. I've been on my own for a few months now, and I've been doing just fine."

"Until your uncle tracked you down," he pointed out, and she stiffened.

"I was tracked down long before I came to Florida," she responded. "Or have you forgotten that poor woman who was murdered because she was in the same state you'd hidden me in?"

He hadn't forgotten.

None of the members of the team had.

Information about Esme's location had been leaked to the Dupree crime family, and a woman who'd looked a lot like her had been killed. "I'm sorry that happened. More than I can express, but I'm not part of the witness protection unit. I work for the FBI Tactical K-9 Unit."

"It doesn't matter who you work for. I'm not spending any more time with you."

"I wish that was how things worked, but it isn't. You agreed to testify against your brother."

"And I plan to."

"That will be really difficult to do if you're dead."

"If I'd stayed in Wyoming, I probably would be. Then we wouldn't be having this conversation."

She had a point. A good one. Esme was the sole witness to a murder her brother had committed. Her brother, Reginald, and Angus would do anything to keep her from testifying.

"We had a security breach," he explained, snagging her backpack from the bottom of the canoe. "It won't happen again."

"It won't happen again because I'm not going back into protective custody."

"I'm afraid you are."

She narrowed her eyes at him. "Have you ever been wrong before?"

"More than I'd like to be."

"Good," she retorted. "Then you won't be upset that you're wrong this time." She whirled around and would have walked away, but King blocked her path, pressing in close to her legs.

She shot a look in Ian's direction, her eyes still flashing with anger. "Call off your dog."

"Release," he said, and King pranced back to his side.

"Thanks." She probably would have walked away, but he held up her pack.

"Forgetting something?"

She reached for it and King growled.

"He doesn't like people taking things from me."

"I don't like people touching my things," she responded, her focus on King. She looked scared. He didn't blame her. At home, King was goofy and friendly, funny and entertaining. On the job, he was intimidating, his tan face and dark muzzle giving him a wolflike appearance.

"Sorry. I've got to check the contents before we move out."

"I think I made it clear that—"

"You plan on going it alone. You've made it very clear. Unfortunately, my job is to get you to trial safely. I can't do that if we're not together."

"We're at cross purposes, then, and I don't see us finding common ground." She stepped back, and he thought she might be looking for an escape route. One that King wouldn't be able to follow.

"The common ground is this—we both want to keep you alive. How about you let me do what I'm trained to do?"

"Which is?"

"Protecting people like you."

King growled, the sound low and mean.

Esme froze, but Ian could have told her the growl wasn't directed at her. It was a warning.

One that sent adrenaline shooting through Ian's bloodstream. He grabbed Esme's wrist, dragging her close.

"What—" she began, but Ian held up his hand, silencing her so that he could listen. The evening had gone eerily quiet, King's rumbling growl the only sound.

He pulled Esme to the thick brush that surrounded the campsite, motioning for her to drop down into the cover it offered. She slipped into the summer-soft leaves silently, folding herself down so that even he could barely see her.

King swiveled, tracking something that Ian could neither see nor hear. He wanted to think that it was a panther, a bear, an alligator, but King was trained to differentiate between human and animal threats. Besides, thanks to former team member Jake Morrow, the Dupree crime family seemed to always be just one step behind the K-9 team. There was every possibility that one or more of Angus's henchmen was wandering through the Everglades.

He thrust Esme's backpack into her arms, leaning close to whisper in her ear. "Stay down. Stay quiet. Don't move."

She nodded, clutching the backpack to her chest.

King's growl changed pitch. Whoever was coming was getting closer. It wasn't local law enforcement, and it wasn't a member of the K-9 team. They were back at headquarters waiting for word that Ian had finally found Esme's trail.

That left only one other option.

Angus Dupree or his hired guns.

Ian acted quickly, shoving the canoe into the water with just enough force to keep it moving. He gave King the signal to heel and went with him into the shelter of thick vegetation. Mosquitoes and flies buzzed around King's head, but the dog didn't move; his attention was fixed on a spot just beyond the clearing. Ian knew the area. He'd walked it several times the past few days, certain that Esme would arrive there eventually.

She was smart.

There was no doubt about that.

Ian had done his research. He knew as much as there was to know about her childhood, her schooling, her college years. He knew she'd built her business without the help of her older sister, that she'd never taken a dime from her brother. Everything she had, she'd earned on the right side of the law by using the brain God had given her.

The fact that she'd escaped witness protection and had stayed under the radar for months was even more proof of her keen intelligence. Smart people didn't go into situations without a plan. Ian had visited the trailer she'd been renting at the edge of the Everglades. He'd seen the old boathouse and the dock, and he'd known she'd had an escape route in mind when she'd chosen to rent the place.

All he'd needed was a map and a highlighter. He'd done some calculations, tried to think of how far someone like Esme would be willing to travel in a hostile environment. It hadn't taken any time at all to figure out that the quickest, most direct route out of the Everglades brought her here.

He'd staked out the area, walking a grid pattern every day, waiting for her to show.

Apparently, he wasn't the only one who'd been haunting this place looking for her. She was smart, but she'd have been better off leaving the area. She hadn't had the backpack with her while she was in protective custody with the local police, and she hadn't visited any of the local outdoor supply stores, either. He had to assume that she'd returned to the rental to retrieve the pack. Which meant there was something she needed in it. Money seemed more likely than anything.

King's growl had become a deep rumble of unease. Scruff standing on end, muscles taut, he waited for the signal to go in. Ian waited, too. He didn't know how many people were approaching or what kind of firepower they'd brought.

Backup was already on the way. He'd called in to headquarters as soon as he'd seen Esme paddling toward the campsite.

A shadow appeared a hundred yards out, and King crouched, ready to bound toward it. Ian gave him the signal to hold, watching as two more people stepped into view. A posse of three hunting a lone woman. If Esme had been bedded down for the night, they'd have been on her before she'd realized what was happening.

An unfair fight, but that was the way the Duprees did things.

One of the men turned on a flashlight, the beam bouncing across the camping area and flashing on the water. Twenty feet from the shore, the canoe floated languidly.

"There!" the man hollered, pulling a gun, the world exploding in a hail of gunfire.

# TWO

If she'd been in the campground, she'd be dead.

Every bullet fired, every ping of metal against metal, reminded Esme that her family—the one she had loved and admired and been so proud of—wanted her dead.

*Traitor. Benedict Arnold. Turn-tail. Judas.*

Uncle Angus had whispered all those names as he tried to choke the life out of her four nights ago. The words were still ringing in her head and in her heart, mixing with the echoing sound of the automatic weapon Angus's hit men were using.

She wasn't sure what had happened to Ian and King. Either they'd run or they were biding their time, waiting for an opportunity to strike. One man against three didn't seem like good odds, and it was possible Ian was waiting for backup.

He could wait until the cows came home.

Esme was leaving.

She slithered through muddy grass and damp leaves, praying the sound of her retreat was covered by gunfire. Eventually, they'd stop shooting. When they did, her chance of escaping undetected would go from slim to none.

Who was she kidding?

It was already that. She might get out of the Everglades. She might get out of Florida. Eventually, though, Uncle Angus would find her. He had money backing him, and he had a lot riding on his ability to silence her. If she testified against Reginald, everything the two men had built—the entire crime family they'd grown—would collapse. He'd been chasing her for months, and he wouldn't give up now. Not with the trial date approaching. A few weeks, and she'd be in the courtroom, looking at her brother as she told the jury and judge what she'd seen him do.

She shuddered, sliding deeper into the foliage.

She wasn't going to give up on life, and she couldn't give up on saving the one remaining bright spot in her very dark family tree.

Violetta.

They hadn't seen or spoken to each other since Esme had gone into witness protection, but they were sisters, bound by blood and by genuine affection for each other. As far as Esme knew, Violetta hadn't been involved in any of Reginald's and Angus's crimes. Whether or not she'd known about them, however, was a question Esme needed to ask.

After she testified and shut her brother's operations down for good.

The gunfire stopped, and she froze, her belly pressed into damp earth, her heart thundering. They'd check the canoe, find it empty, realize she'd escaped.

She had to get farther away before that happened.

Taking a deep breath, she slithered forward, her pack slung over her shoulder, the soft rustle of leaves making her heart beat harder. A man called out, and someone splashed into the water, cursing loudly as he went.

She used the commotion as cover, moving quickly, trying to put as much distance between herself and the campsite as possible.

"FBI, K-9 unit. Put your weapons down or I'll release my dog," a man called, his voice carrying above the chaos.

She froze again. Ian *was* still there. She hadn't intended on spending much time with him. The entire time they'd been talking, she'd been planning her escape, trying to work out a solution to the newest problem. Just like she did when she'd planned a wedding and there was a hiccup on the big day.

"I said, drop your weapons," he repeated sharply.

A single shot rang out, and someone shouted. A dog growled, and Esme could picture the dark-eyed, dark-faced K-9 racing into danger.

Two against three.

One weapon against many.

She couldn't leave.

No matter how much she wanted to.

She couldn't abandon a man to almost certain death.

Esme didn't have a gun, but she had surprise on her side. She scooted back the way she'd come, the dog growling and barking, men shouting, chaos filling the darkness. She was heading right toward it, because she didn't know when to quit. Another thing Brent had said to her.

He'd been right.

She never quit.

Not even when the odds were stacked against her. Hopefully, this time, it wouldn't get her killed.

She crawled closer to the edge of the campsite, dropping her pack and grabbing a fist-sized rock from the mud. Reginald had taught her to play ball when they were kids. He'd shown her how to throw a mean right hook, to take a man down with a well-placed kick. She'd loved him as much as she'd loved Violetta, and she'd soaked up everything he'd had to offer. Until she'd realized that the road he'd chosen was one she had no intention of traveling. Then she'd distanced herself from her brother and, to a lesser extent, Violetta. That had been eight years ago. Even after all that time and all the years away from Reginald's coaching, she still knew how to fight.

She stopped at the edge of the clearing, her heart pounding as she waited. The campsite had gone silent. No gunfire. No barking dog. Sirens were blaring in the distance, the sound muted by the thick foliage.

Somewhere nearby, a branch snapped, the sound breaking the eerie quiet. King barked again, and someone crashed through the brush just steps from where Esme lay.

She levered up, would have lobbed the rock at the fleeing man, but King was there, a shadowy blur, so close she could feel his fur as he raced past.

Surprised, she jerked back, her knees slipping in the layer of wet earth, her elbows sliding out from under her. She would have face-planted, but someone grabbed the back of her shirt, yanking her up.

"Hey!" She turned, the rock still in her hand.

"I told you to stay where you were," Ian growled.

"I was trying to help."

"Since when is getting in the way helping?" he retorted, King's wild barking nearly covering his words.

Esme didn't think he expected a response, and she didn't bother giving one. He was already moving again, sprinting toward his dog.

She followed, keeping a few steps behind him. Despite his sarcastic comment, she had no intention of getting in the way. The more gunmen he could take out, the safer they'd be. Once they were safe, she could go back to her plan. Get out of the Everglades and out of Florida.

Alone.

"Federal agent! Freeze!" Ian shouted, and she froze before she realized he hadn't shouted the command at her.

"Call off your dog!" a man replied, his voice tinged with a hint of panic.

"You want me to call off the dog, you freeze."

"This is all a mistake!" the man whined. "I was out here hunting gators and—"

"One command, and his teeth will go straight to the bone," Ian cut in.

The man must have stopped moving, because Ian stepped forward, gun trained toward something Esme couldn't see.

"Keep your hands where I can see them," he commanded, King still growling beside him.

"And you," he continued, and even though he hadn't turned to look at her, Esme was certain he was talking to her. "Stay where you are. The guy ditched his gun back at the campsite, but that doesn't mean he's not armed."

"I ditched my gun because your crazy dog was trying to kill me."

"You can explain it all to the judge."

"What judge? I was hunting gators. I can't help it if I got in the middle of your shoot-out."

"Like I said, you can explain it all to the judge. I'm sure he'll be really interested in your version. He'll also be interested in what your friend has to say. If he survives."

"I didn't come with a friend. Never seen either of those men before in my life."

Ian didn't respond.

Esme could hear the men walking toward her, their feet slapping against wet grass and soggy leaves. They reached her seconds later, Ian taller and broader than the man he'd apprehended. He looked fit and strong. The perfect bodyguard. If she were looking for one. She wasn't. What she was looking for was some peace. She wouldn't get that until her uncle was apprehended and he and her brother were convicted of their crimes.

"What now?" she asked, trying to think ahead, to figure out the best way to separate herself from the situation. Once she knew his plans, it would be easier to make hers.

"We're heading back to the camp. I've got one man down and cuffed there. The other ran off."

"He could return," she pointed out.

"Local law enforcement is close. Hopefully, one of them will pick him up."

"I stopped hoping for safety right around the time my uncle tried to murder me," she muttered.

He eyed her through the evening gloom, his expression unreadable. For a moment, she thought he wouldn't respond. When he did, his tone was gruff. "I hope you're not living in the delusion that your uncle is the one responsible for all of this."

"Who else would it be?"

"Your uncle might have tracked you to Florida, but your brother is calling the shots from prison."

"Maybe." Probably.

She didn't want to admit that.

Not even to herself.

She and her uncle had never been close. She could almost pretend they weren't family.

She and Reginald, though…

They were siblings. Sure, he was much older, but they'd been raised by the same parents with the same values.

Somehow they'd taken completely different paths, found value in completely different things.

She'd watched him kill a man.

She would never forget that. She *would* testify against him.

But this was by far the most difficult thing she'd ever done.

It was the right thing, but that didn't make her feel good about it. It sure didn't make her safe. Her family would do anything to keep her from testifying. She still couldn't wrap her mind around that.

The proof was here, though—the cuffed man walking beside a federal agent who had come to track her down. Both of them wanted Esme for different purposes. One wanted her dead. The other wanted her to stay alive. At least until her brother's trial.

The sirens had grown louder, and she could see flashing lights through the mangroves. Help had arrived. It didn't seem like Ian needed it. He motioned for his prisoner to sit on the raised sleeping platform.

"Guard," he commanded, and King snapped to attention, his eyes trained on the cuffed man.

"He's guarding you, too," Ian said, meeting Esme's eyes.

"It's not like I have anywhere to go," she responded. She could see the canoe, a dozen yards out, listing heavily to the right. Enough bullets had been fired to cause it to sink. If she'd been in it, she'd be dead. She shivered, suddenly chilled despite the warmth and humidity.

"There are plenty of places to go. You've proved that several times." He turned and walked away, moving across the clearing and crouching next to a man who lay near the water.

She thought he was checking the guy's pulse and rendering first aid, but it was hard to see through the deepening gloom. This would have been her third night out in the Glades. She should be used to how quickly darkness descended After so many months running from people who wanted her dead, she should also be used to skin-crawling, heart-stopping fear.

The cuffed gunman shifted position, and King growled, flashing teeth that looked as deadly as any gun or knife Esme had ever seen. He was focused on the prisoner. If she were going to try to escape, now would be the time to do it. She could see the emergency vehicles, hear people moving through the mangroves. She scanned the clearing and spotted her backpack abandoned near the edge of the campsite.

It would take seconds to grab it and just a little bit longer than that to disappear. She'd done it before. She could do it again.

But she was exhausted from endless running, tired from months of being on guard. She didn't trust the police or the FBI to keep her safe, but she wasn't sure she had the stamina to keep trying to do the job herself. Not that she had any choice.

The trial was just a month away. That seemed like forever, but it was nothing in comparison to the amount of time that had already passed. Once she testified, she'd disappear again. This time, she had no intention of being found. New name. New job. New beginning. Not the life she'd planned, but she knew she could make it a good one.

All she had to do was survive long enough to get there.

*Just do it. Grab the bag and run!* her mind shouted, and she was just tired enough and just scared enough to listen.

She darted forward, snagging the straps and lifting the bag in one quick motion. The rest was easy. Or should have been. The mangroves provided perfect cover, and she ducked behind one of the scrub-like trees, water lapping at her ankles as she moved.

She would have kept running, but something grabbed onto the bag, yanking her backward. She released the pack, but she was already falling, her ankle twisting as she tried to pivot and run.

She went down hard, splashing into a puddle of muck, the dog suddenly in her face, teeth bared, dark eyes staring straight into hers.

"I told you," Ian said calmly, his voice carrying through the mangroves, "he was guarding you."

She couldn't see him, and that made her almost as nervous as looking in the dog's snarling face did.

"He'd have been better off guarding the guy who tried to kill me," she responded, not even trying to get to her feet. Not with the beast of a dog staring her down, his teeth still bared. In any other circumstance, she'd have admired him for what he was—a handsome, fit working dog. Right now, she just wanted him gone.

"The perpetrator is in police custody. I guess you were too busy planning your escape to notice them moving in."

"I noticed."

"And did you think I wouldn't notice you leaving?" Branches rustled, and he stepped into view, his head and shoulders bowed as he walked through the trees.

"What I thought was that I wanted to live, and that being alone seemed like the safest way to make sure that happened."

"Esme, you really need to stop fighting me," he said, crouching a few feet away and looking straight into her eyes. There was something about his face—the angle of his jaw, the sharp cut of his cheekbones—that made her think of the old Westerns she used to watch with her dad, the hero cowboy riding to the rescue on his trusty steed. Only, this hero didn't have a horse; he had a dog.

"I'm not. I'm making your job easier. Go back to your office and tell anyone who cares that I refused federal help. I want to do this alone."

"What? Get yourself killed?"

"Call off your dog, okay? I want to get out of the mud." And the Everglades and the mess her family had created.

To her surprise, he complied.

"Release!" he said, and the dog backed off, sitting on his haunches, still watching her. Only this time, she was sure he was grinning.

King had had a great night. He'd found his mark twice and brought in an armed man. He was obviously pleased with himself, his tail splashing in a puddle of water, his dark eyes turned up to Ian.

"Good boy," Ian said, scratching behind King's ears and offering the praise he'd been waiting for.

"That's a matter of opinion," Esme muttered.

Ian flashed his light in her direction. She'd fallen hard but didn't seem to be much worse for the wear. "He did what I asked him to. That's always a win."

"That depends on what side of his teeth you're sitting on."

"He wasn't going to bite you."

"Right," she scoffed, tucking a strand of auburn hair behind her ear. She hadn't colored it. That had surprised him. It would have been the first thing he'd have done if he'd been in her position.

"He bites when he has to, but it's not in his nature to snap. Unless I give him the command."

"I'll keep that in mind," she said, a hint of weariness in her voice. She looked as exhausted as she sounded—her skin paper white in the twilight, dark circles beneath her eyes. He'd seen photos of her taken just a few months before she'd watched her brother execute a man. Her cheeks hadn't been as hollow, her shoulders as narrow.

He didn't want to feel sorry for her. She was, after all, part of the family that had taken his. Years ago, Reginald Dupree had called the hit on Ian's father. He'd been just starting out, sticking his toes in the water of his new family business. Ian's father had been a Chicago police officer, determined to undermine Dupree's efforts. He'd arrested two of Reginald's lower-level operatives. In retaliation, Reginald had paid a couple of street thugs to shoot him when he left the house for work. They'd opened fire as he'd stepped outside. The first bullet had killed him instantly. The second had killed Ian's mother, who'd been standing in the doorway saying goodbye.

Yeah. He didn't want to feel sorry for anyone in the family, but his father had raised him to be compassionate, to look out for those who couldn't look out for themselves. More than that, he'd raised him to do what was right. Even when it was difficult. The right thing to do was to protect Esme. Despite her last name and her family, she'd committed no crime.

"How about you keep something else in mind, too?" He offered a hand, and she allowed him to pull her to her feet.

"What?"

"Next time I tell you to stay somewhere, you should do it. It's a waste of King's energy to chase after you when he's supposed to be keeping you safe."

"You told him to guard me," she pointed out.

"Because the closer you are, the easier it is for me to make sure your brother doesn't get what he wants."

"Me dead, you mean?"

"I wasn't going to put it so bluntly, but yes."

"My uncle is the one who wants me dead, Ian. It's his hands that were around my throat the other night." Her tone was hard, her voice raspy, and the compassion he didn't want to feel welled up again.

"Does it make you feel better to keep telling yourself that?" he asked gently.

"It will make me feel better to be done with this. It will make me feel better to do what I promised and to get on with my life. So how about you leave me alone and let me go back to the business of staying safe until the trial?"

"Do you think this will all end if we have your uncle in custody?" he asked, calling King to heel and leading Esme back the way they'd come.

"I hope it will," she murmured, limping as she tried to keep pace with him. She must have hurt her leg or foot. He shouldn't have cared. She was a means to an end. Despite the clean criminal record, the supposedly upright business, she was who she was—a Dupree.

But he did care, because she was a person who'd found herself in an untenable position and had chosen to do the right thing. She'd witnessed a horrible crime, and despite the fact that her brother had committed it, she'd gone to the police and offered to testify.

"What'd you do to your leg?" he asked, and she shrugged.

"Twisted my ankle. It's fine."

"Then why are you limping?"

"Because I'm tired, okay? Because I want to get out of this stupid swamp and into clean clothes. I want to take a shower and wash three days' worth of bug repellent off my skin. Mostly, I just want to close my eyes, open them and find out that this has all been some horrible nightmare."

"I'm sorry," he said and meant it.

"For what? Being the one they chose for this assignment?"

"For the fact that all of this isn't just a bad dream. Your family has deep pockets, Esme. They can afford to pay people to do their dirty work. Which means you won't be safe until we shut down the crime ring your brother and uncle control."

"You're a wellspring of joyful tidings, Ian."

"I'm honest."

"And, like I said, I'm tired. So how about we discuss this another time?"

"You want to survive, right?" He stopped short and looked straight into her pale face. "Would I have spent three days in the Everglades if I didn't?"

"Some people love it here."

"I'm not one of them," she huffed.

"And yet, this is where you ran when you left witness protection."

"My parents and I spent every summer here when I was a kid. They're—"

"Buried twenty miles from here. I know. I'm sure your uncle knew. Your brother. Your sister."

"I feel like you're trying to make a point, so how about you just get to it?" Her hands were on her hips, her chin raised. Of the three Dupree siblings, she was the one Ian understood the least. Reginald was all about power and money. He'd go to any length to get it. Violetta wanted the same, but she wasn't willing to break the law to get it. On the other hand, she wasn't willing to cooperate with law enforcement to make her brother pay for his crimes.

But Esme…

Ian couldn't wrap her in a tidy package and put a label on her. That bothered him. He'd spent most of his adult life studying people, figuring them out, deciding whether they were telling the truth, were dangerous or could be trusted. He'd missed the mark with Jake Morrow. A member of the Tactical K-9 team, Jake had put on a good show. He'd pretended to be everything the team believed in—a man of honesty, integrity, honor. That hadn't meant Ian had liked him. There'd always been something a little cocky about Jake, something a little off. Still, he'd trusted him.

That trust had been misplaced.

Jake had been on the Dupree payroll. He'd betrayed the team, and he was still on the loose, still causing trouble.

"Here's my point," he said, King panting quietly beside him. "You came to a place where anyone who knew anything about you would look for you. You would have been better off sticking with witness protection."

"One innocent person already lost her life because I was in the program. I'm not going to risk someone else dying for the same reason."

"We had a leak. We've sealed it. No one else is going to be hurt," he responded, keeping his tone neutral. He'd thought she was worried about her own safety, that she'd run from the program because she thought she'd be safer away from it. The fact that she'd been worried about others put a twist on things. A twist he didn't like. He wanted to lump her in with the rest of the family, but no matter how hard he tried, he couldn't seem to do it.

"You don't seem to understand." She swung around, her auburn ponytail flying in an arc as she moved. "One person being hurt is too many. I think about it every day. About how that woman died because someone mistook her for me."

"It wasn't because of you. It was because of your uncle and your brother. It was because they thought they were above the law, because they hadn't expected to ever be stopped. They like their money and their power, and neither of them want to give it up."

"Yeah. I know." She sighed, walking away, heading toward the distant emergency lights, her stride hitched but brisk, her shoulders straight.

"Esme," he said, not sure what he wanted to add, what he could possibly say to make things better or easier or right.

"I think we've both said everything we need to, Ian. How about you just let me do what I need to? I'm sure the police would like to talk to you, and I've got a long way to go before I reach civilization."

He could have stopped her.

He had the authority to do it. He had the strength. He had King.

But he let her go, because he thought she needed some space. It was five miles to the main road, and there were emergency vehicles everywhere. She'd be safe enough.

"All right," he said, and she met his eyes.

He thought he saw tears before she looked away again.

Then she was moving, putting distance between them, her backpack lying a yard away, abandoned on the muddy ground. He snagged it, figuring she'd want it later. He needed to check in with the local police, and then he'd get in his SUV and pick her up on the way out.

"King," he said, and the dog looked at him, eager for the next command. "Guard!"

The Malinois took off, racing across the clearing, his light brown fur visible in the darkness as he followed Esme through the trees and out into the main campground.

# THREE

Long Pine Key Campground was not difficult to find. Esme simply followed the flashing emergency lights through a copse of mangroves and out into a field of vegetation. The vehicles were probably a quarter mile away, but the darkness made them easy enough to see. She picked her way across the field, the ground growing soggier with every step. If it got any wetter, she'd have to find another route. She didn't mind getting wet, but she didn't like the idea of being knee-deep in water that was filled with slimy, slithery, scaly creatures.

Esme was almost ready to turn back when she spotted a wooden walkway that stretched the remainder of the way across the area. She stepped onto it, the wood giving a little as she moved.

She was halfway over when she heard quiet panting and the soft pad of paws. Her heart in her throat, she spun around, her sore ankle nearly giving out. The dog was there. Of course. *King.*

And he was so close she could have reached out and touched his nose, so close she could feel his panting breath on her hand, see his goofy smile through the darkness.

Because he was smiling again.

Why wouldn't he be?

She kept running. He kept finding her. A fun game for a dog. Not so much fun for Esme.

"Go home," she commanded.

The dog didn't even blink.

"Where's your partner?" She glanced back the way she'd come, saw nothing but the empty field and shadowy mangroves. "Did he tell you to follow me?"

The dog settled on his haunches, his dark eyes looking straight into hers.

"Release!" she commanded, pointing in the direction she wanted him to go.

Nothing.

"Go! Cease!"

Still nothing.

"Fine. Do what you want. I've got more important things to do than argue with a dog." She limped the rest of the way across the boardwalk, stepping onto wet grass, King close behind her.

The Long Pine Key parking area was straight ahead, the dark figures of emergency personnel visible in the flashing strobe lights of their vehicles. She'd seen way too many emergency vehicles the past few months. Beginning with the one that had been sent to the scene of her brother's crime.

She'd still been in shock—the memory of Reginald pointing the gun and firing it, of a man falling to the ground, blood spurting from his chest, taking up so much room in her mind, there hadn't been space to create memories of conversations she'd had, of people she'd spoken to. All she could remember were the emergency lights and the questions, barked one right after another—a series of words that had had no meaning.

Esme sighed.

She knew Ian meant well. She knew the FBI meant well. Law enforcement, witness protection, they meant well, too. But meaning well couldn't keep her alive.

Better to not take a chance of being waylaid by another well-meaning entity. She'd steer clear of law enforcement. She turned to the right, heading through a grove of cypress trees, aiming for the road that led into the parking lot. It should be straight ahead. She didn't have her map, but she'd memorized the topography and knew what landmarks to look for to ascertain how far she was from civilization. It would be a long walk to anyplace where she could make a phone call. Five miles on the back road, then out onto a main road that would eventually lead her to town. Once there, she'd borrow a phone and call…

Who?

Not Violetta. She loved her sister, but she couldn't count on her. Not the way she'd thought she could. Violetta's loyalties were torn. She wanted to support Reginald and see him freed from prison. Esme knew that, and she knew why. It wasn't all about love and family. At least not according to the FBI, it wasn't. Violetta had been happy to take whatever gifts Reginald offered—money for a new car, financial backing to support her business, new windows for her house. Esme had been shown a list of all the things her sister had accepted from Reginald.

At first, she'd argued that Violetta hadn't known where Reginald was getting the money. But, of course, the FBI had been prepared for that. They'd proved her wrong. Violetta *had* known…she just hadn't cared. She'd kept her hands clean, but she sure hadn't been willing to jeopardize Reginald's *career*. After all, she was benefiting too much from it.

The last time Esme had seen her sister had been six months ago. Violetta had looked just as cool and reserved as ever, her beautiful face not showing even a hint of stress or anxiety. Esme, on the other hand, had been a mess. But, then, she was the one who'd watched a man die. She was the one who'd had to make a choice between family and justice. She was the one who was swimming against the tide and doing exactly what her family didn't want her to.

And she was the one who'd pay with her life if her uncle got his hands on her again.

Esme shuddered, her skin clammy from the humid air, her body leaden from too many restless nights. She had to believe that she was going to get through this. She had to trust that God would keep her safe, that doing the right thing would always be best even when it felt so horribly wrong.

Betrayer. Traitor. Turncoat.

Her uncle's words were still in her head, the feel of his fingers around her throat enough to make her want to gag. She stumbled, tripping over a root and going down hard, her hands and knees sliding across damp earth, her shoulder bumping into a tree trunk.

She lay where she was for a few minutes too long, the muted sound of voices carrying on the still night air. Maybe she should go to the parking lot, turn herself in to the authorities and hope and pray that they could keep her safe. That seemed so much easier than going it alone.

It also seemed more dangerous.

A woman had died, and she'd almost been

killed because of an information leak. Ian had told her the leak had been plugged, but she couldn't count on that. She couldn't really count on anything.

"Your pity party is getting you nowhere," she muttered, pushing up onto her hands and knees.

A cool wet nose pressed against her cheek, and King huffed quietly. She jerked back, looking into his dark face. He was a handsome dog when he wasn't snarling and showing teeth. Right now, he looked like he was smiling again, his tongue lolling out to the side.

"I think I told you to find your partner," she scolded, forcing herself up. Lying around feeling sorry for herself would accomplish absolutely nothing. Going back into the situation that had almost gotten her killed would do the same.

She had to stay the course—find a place to go to ground until trial, then contact the authorities and arrange to be escorted to court. Armed guards would be great. Six or seven dogs like King would be a nice bonus.

Right now, though…

Right now, she just had to find a safe place to hide.

She started walking again, trudging through saw grass and heading away from the emergency vehicles. There were no streetlights on the road, no beacons to lead her in the right direction. She went by instinct, the rising moon giving her at least some idea of what direction she was heading.

Northeast would bring her to the road.

The road would bring her to civilization.

She'd figure out everything else once she got there.

The grass opened up, the earth dried out and she could see the road winding snakelike through the Everglades. She stepped onto it, her ankle throbbing, her stomach churning. After three days and nights in the Everglades, it felt strange to be out in the open. No water surrounding her. No foliage to shelter in. She could see emergency lights to the left, so she turned right, trudging along the road as if she didn't have a care in the world.

Five miles wasn't much.

She loved hiking, biking and running. Before she'd entered witness protection, she'd been training for a half marathon. Walking a few miles should have been a piece of cake, but she felt like she was slogging through mud, her legs heavy with fatigue.

King pressed close to her leg, his shoulder brushing her thigh as they walked. He didn't look nervous, and she took that as a good sign. It wasn't good that he was sticking to her like glue, however, because eventually his handler would come looking for him. When he did, he'd find Esme, too.

Unless Esme could ditch the dog.

She patted the pockets of her cargo pants, found the package of peanut butter crackers she'd planned to eat for dinner. She opened it, the rustling paper not even garnering a glance from King.

She slipped a cracker from the sleeve, held it out to the dog. "Hungry?" she asked.

He ignored her and the cracker.

"King?" She nudged the cracker close to his mouth.

He didn't break his stride, didn't look at the food.

"It's peanut butter. Peanut butter is good. Fetch!" She waved it closer to his face, then threw it back in the direction they'd come.

It hit the pavement, and King just kept walking.

Esme blew out a frustrated breath. Great... just great. Now she'd end up in town with a dog that didn't belong to her. Probably a very expensive dog. The FBI wouldn't be happy if she left the state with one of their dogs in tow.

For all she knew, she'd be charged with kidnapping.

Dognapping?

"King!" she said, trying to put an edge of command in her voice. "Sit!"

He didn't.

"Fetch!" She tried another cracker. "Retrieve!"

"Do you not speak English?" she asked, stopping short and eyeing the dog. He was still wearing his vest, a logo on the side announcing that he was a law enforcement dog. Esme wasn't sure about much lately, but she knew this—she did not look like a law enforcement officer. At least not one that was on duty. She didn't have a uniform, a gun or a holster. And no badge. If she made it to town, people would wonder what she was doing with a dog who was obviously supposed to be working.

"This is a problem," she said, crouching a few feet from the dog and watching him. He was watching her just as steadily.

"Listen, buddy, I'm sure your handler told you to follow me, but I'd prefer you go back to what you were doing before you got sent on this wild-goose chase."

He cocked his head to the side, then glanced back the way they'd come. He'd gone from alert to stiff with tension. She wasn't sure what that meant, but it couldn't be anything good.

"What is it?" she whispered, as if the dog could answer.

He barked once—a quick high-pitched sound that made her hair stand on end.

Someone or something was coming.

That was the only explanation.

She ran to the side of the road, plunging into the thick shrubs that lined it. She didn't know if King had followed. She was too focused on finding a place to hide. She crouched low, her heart throbbing hollowly in her ears. Lights splashed across the road and filtered through the leaves.

A car was coming. First the headlights, then the soft chug of an engine. She shrank deeper into the shadows, King's lean body suddenly beside her, pressing in so close his fur rubbed against her arm. Mosquitoes buzzed, dive-bombing the exposed areas of Esme's skin. She didn't dare swat them away. The car was closing in, the engine growing louder. She wanted to grab King's collar and make sure he didn't lunge out from their hiding place, but she couldn't get the image of him barking at the gunmen out of her head. No matter how hard she tried, she couldn't stop seeing his sharp teeth and snarling mouth. Sure, he currently looked like a sweet goofy pet, but she knew he could be vicious if he needed to be. She'd keep her hands to herself and hope for the best rather than risk losing one of her fingers to his sharp teeth.

"Don't move," she whispered, and the dog shifted closer, his shoulder leaning into hers.

The car slowed as it approached, the tires rolling over dry pavement.

*Keep going*, she silently commanded. *Please, keep going.*

The car stopped, the engine idling, the soft chug making her blood run cold. Could the driver see her? Did he know she was there?

A door opened, and she stiffened. She had no weapon. Her only option was to run. In a place as inhospitable as the Everglades, that could get a person killed.

Staying could get her killed, too.

She waited another minute, praying that whoever was on the road had stopped to look at a snake or save a turtle or do some completely normal thing that didn't involve hunting a woman through the swamp.

King barked, the sound so loud and startling, Esme jumped.

She didn't scream, but she came close.

And then she ran, darting away from the road as fast as her twisted ankle could carry her.

Two strides and Ian caught up, catching Esme's arm before she could run any farther.

She swung around, throwing a punch that nearly hit its mark.

"Hey! Cool it," he growled, dragging her arm down to her side the same way he had before. This time there was no knife, and she looked even more scared, her eyes wild with fear.

"Let me go!" she demanded, and he did, releasing his hold and stepping back.

"Calm down, Esme. It's just me."

She met his eyes, seemed to finally realize who he was and frowned. "You just scared six years off my life."

"Sorry about that."

"You don't sound sorry," she accused.

"Maybe because I'm tired of following you all over Florida," he replied, and she cracked a half smile.

"I'm not going to apologize, if that's what you're hoping for."

"I'm hoping we can get out of this area before we run into more trouble." He took her hand again, and this time, she didn't resist as he led her back to the road and his SUV.

He opened the back hatch and called for King, and she didn't say a word, didn't try to leave.

The Malinois jumped in, settling into his kennel and heaving a sigh that would have made Ian smile if he hadn't been standing next to Esme.

She was a problem.

Up until he'd tracked her down, he'd been resentful of the time and resources they were putting into finding her. The prosecutor had a good case against Reginald Dupree—even without his sister's testimony. She was the witness who would put him away for good, though. First-degree murder. Planned and executed with cunning and without remorse.

Esme was the only witness, and without her testimony, evidence was circumstantial at best. At worst, it was unconvincing. A good defense lawyer might get Reginald off. That wasn't something Ian was going to allow.

Yeah. He'd wanted to keep her safe for purely mercenary purposes. With her testimony, the Dupree crime family could be stopped. Without it, Reginald might go free.

Now…

He was beginning to feel sorry for her, beginning to see her as something other than the family she'd been born into. She'd given up her entire life to make sure her brother went to jail for his crime. She'd left her job, her friends, her fiancé. She'd done it all without complaining. Everyone who'd met her or worked with her had had only good things to say.

He'd told himself it was because she was a good actress and consummate manipulator. After hearing her talk about the woman who'd died, hearing the regret in her voice, seeing the tears in her eyes, he doubted that was the case.

Unless he was misreading her, she was who everyone else on the team seemed to think she was—a woman who'd been pulled into something she hadn't expected or wanted. A woman who'd been running from her family because she valued doing what was right more than she valued loyalty to her family.

A tough place to be standing.

A tough decision to make.

She'd made it. She'd continued to say that she would testify despite the obvious threats against her.

He admired that.

A lot.

He frowned, closing the back hatch and turning to face Esme. "Did you really think you were going to walk out of here?"

"I sure didn't think I wasn't going to," she replied, flipping her ponytail over her shoulder. A few strands of hair had escaped and were clinging to her throat and neck, the dark red strands gleaming in the SUV's parking lights.

"The nearest town is twenty miles away," he pointed out.

"I've walked farther."

"Did you do it when you had a price on your head?"

She pressed her lips together and didn't say a word.

"I'll take that as a no." He led her to the passenger side of the vehicle. "You keep walking on this road, and someone else is going to find you. If it happens to be one of your uncle's hired guns, you don't have a chance of surviving."

"I'm not sure my chances are any higher with you," she responded, but she didn't walk away.

Maybe she was too tired.

Maybe the injury to her ankle was worse than she'd been letting on.

Whatever the case, she stayed right where she was as he opened the door.

"How about we discuss it on the way to the local police department?"

"Ian…" She shook her head. "I believed your organization when I was told I'd be safe. They were wrong, and I can't see any reason to believe you again."

"And yet you're still standing here."

"Because I'm tired. I've been running for months, and I have at least another month to go before the trial. It's hard to sleep when you're worried someone is going to break in and kill you. Without sleep, it's really difficult to make good decisions."

Her honesty surprised him, and he touched her arm, urging her to the open door. "I've had plenty of sleep. How about you let me make the decisions for a while?"

She laughed without humor. "You're very convincing, but I think I'll pass."

"Then how about you sit in the SUV while I drive, and spend a little time thinking about what you want to do? It'll be easier doing it in a safe place than it will while you're out in the open."

"Like I said," she responded, finally stepping away. "You're convincing, but I'm going to have to pass."

"You're a long way from the state line, Esme."

"I was a long way from Florida a couple of months ago. Now I'm here, and eventually I'll be somewhere else."

"You agreed to testify," he said, trying a different tactic. She was coming with him. There could be no other outcome, but he'd like her to think she'd been the one to make the decision.

"I will testify."

"That's going to be difficult to do if you're off the grid and have no contact with us."

"Just because you can't find me, doesn't mean I won't be able to find you. I'll be at the trial." A note of weary resignation laced her tone. "I'll provide testimony that will put my brother in jail for the rest of his life."

"If you don't—"

"I know what will happen if I don't. I'll die. I may die anyway, but that's okay, right? A member of the Dupree crime family dies, and no one in a uniform is going to mourn." She started walking again, the limp more pronounced.

"You're not going to get very far with an injured leg."

*"Ankle,"* she responded. "And I'll get wherever I want to go. Just let me, okay? Tell your boss and your team and the prosecuting attorney that I refused your help."

"I can't." That was the truth. He'd sworn to uphold the law. Just like his father and grandfather and great-grandfather, he'd always known he was going to be a cop. He'd worked the beat in Chicago, just like three generations of Slades had. And then he'd reached further, applying to the FBI, passing the physicals, the tests, the interviews.

His father would have been proud of him.

If he'd lived long enough to see it.

"Why? Because I signed some papers that said I agreed to witness protection?" Esme asked.

"Because you're more vulnerable than you want to think you are," he told her. "Because you're injured and you need to see a doctor. Because your backpack is in my vehicle, and without it, you've got nothing."

She hesitated, her gaze darting to the Suburban.

"It would be a lot easier for you to get where

you're going with that pack, right?" he continued, certain he'd finally found the key to getting her to cooperate.

"Right," she agreed. "So how about you give it to me, and we can both be on our way?"

"How about I get you checked out at the hospital, and then I give it to you?"

"Are you bribing me to get me to cooperate?" she demanded.

"Yes," he responded, turning back to the SUV, and to his surprise, she followed. He helped her into the passenger seat and closed the door.

She was probably hoping to grab the pack and run, but he'd tucked it in next to King's crate. She'd have to reach over the backseat to do it.

That would take time, and he didn't plan to give her that.

He jogged around to the driver's side and climbed in. She was already on her knees, reaching into the back.

"Don't," he said, locking the doors and putting the vehicle into Drive.

"What?"

"Keep trying to run. It almost got you killed twice. The third time, you might not survive."

Pursing her lips, she settled into the seat, yanked her seat belt across her lap and didn't say another word. Her silence shouldn't have bothered him. As a matter of fact, he should have preferred it over conversation. She was an assignment, a job he'd been asked to take and that he'd accepted. No matter how much he hadn't wanted to.

He'd been after the Duprees since his parents' murders.

He and his team were this close to shutting them down.

Esme was a means to an end, but she was also a human being. One who'd been through a lot. One who deserved as much peace and security as he could offer her.

She shivered, pulling her hands up into the cuffs of her jacket. It had been hot the past few days, but she'd dressed to keep the bugs away—long pants, jacket, boots.

"Cold?" he asked, and she shook her head.

He turned on the heat anyway, blasting it into the already warm vehicle, wishing he could do more for her. Wanting to break the silence and tell her everything was going to be okay.

She wouldn't believe him if he did, so he stayed silent.

He wanted to think Esme had resigned herself to staying in protective custody. However, based on the fact that she'd spent the past few months on the run, he couldn't.

He dialed his boss, waiting impatiently for Max West to pick up. They'd spoken a few weeks ago, and Max had made it clear that he trusted Ian to do the job he'd been assigned.

Ian hadn't been pleased with the conversation. His past was his business, and he liked to keep it that way. The fact that Max knew about his parents' murders didn't surprise him. The fact that he'd brought it up had. The fact that he'd flat-out told Ian that he needed to focus on justice and forget about revenge?

That still stung.

Sure, Ian wanted to put an end to the crime family.

Sure, he wanted to avenge his parents' murders.

Justice always came first, though. That was the goal. The joy of seeing his parents' murderer sent to jail forever would simply be the bonus shot.

"West here." The team captain's voice cut through the silence. "You have her?"

"Word travels fast," Ian mused, his attention on the dark road that stretched out in front of him.

"It does when it involves one of the Duprees."

Esme tensed.

"You're on speakerphone, and she's in the vehicle," Ian cautioned.

"How are you doing, Ms. Dupree?" Max asked.

"I'd be better if your organization would leave me alone."

"I'm sure you know that's not possible until after the trial."

"You're assuming I'll make it to trial, but at the rate things are going, that doesn't seem likely."

"There's nothing to worry about. We've got things under control."

She laughed, the sound harsh and tight. "Like you did a few months ago when I agreed to enter the program?"

"Ms. Dupree—"

"How about we hash this out once I have her in a safe location?" Ian cut in.

"You're going to try to bring her to headquarters, right?" Max asked. "She'll be safer here than anywhere else."

"You think that's wise? Jake knows the setup there. He knows the security strengths and weaknesses." Jake Morrow had disappeared months ago. At first the team had assumed he'd been killed or abducted by the Duprees. The truth was a lot harder to swallow. He'd gone rogue and was feeding information to the crime family.

"You've got a point," Max said. "Tell you what. I'll see if we have a safe house available somewhere close to you. Once I locate one, I'll send a couple team members down to help with guard duty."

"I don't need to be guarded," Esme cut in.

"That sounds good," he said, ignoring her protest.

She'd agreed to enter the witness protection program, which meant she'd agreed to following the rules set up to protect her.

She was going to stick by those agreements whether she liked it or not.

And maybe, while she was at it, she could point the way to her uncle. Angus Dupree had been free for too long.

Ian wanted him behind bars.

Once that was accomplished, the Dupree crime family would be defunct. That was his personal goal, and it was the best revenge.

"Give me a half hour and I should have something set up," Max said. "Where are you headed now?"

"The regional hospital. Esme injured her ankle. We're getting it checked out."

"That's Big Cypress Regional Medical Center?" Max asked, probably staring at a map of the area, trying to figure out the easiest route there, as well as to the closest safe house.

"Right."

"I'll call for some local manpower. Angus is

probably still in the area. He's smart. He's quick. He's not going to give up easily."

"He's not going to give up until I'm dead," Esme murmured.

"Or until he's behind bars," Ian added.

"That's the goal," Max said. "What's your ETA for the hospital?"

"Twenty-five minutes."

"We'll have someone there to meet you." Max disconnected, and the SUV fell silent.

Ian could have broken the silence.

He could have offered more reassurances, made a few more promises about keeping her safe. If she'd been anyone else, he probably would have. But Esme was a Dupree, and he was a man whose family had been brutally murdered by hers.

He needed to keep that in mind.

Because he couldn't afford to have too much compassion for her. He couldn't afford to let himself see her as more than just the sister of the man he wanted to destroy.

He scowled.

*Destroy* was a harsh word. It was the kind of word that, if spoken aloud, would make other people think he was out for revenge. Maybe he was. Maybe that really was what this was all about. Maybe Max had been right to call him on it.

In the end, though, he'd follow protocol. He'd use the law to get what he wanted.

And Esme?

She was part of that. An enemy by association.

Whether she knew it or not.

# FOUR

The hospital was little more than a small clinic sitting at the edge of a tiny town. One story. Brick. Probably built in the early seventies. There was a main entrance in the front, and Esme assumed there were several other doors around the sides and back. She could see two police cruisers parked near the curb, lights flashing brightly in the darkness.

If that was the manpower Ian's boss had called in, she shouldn't have any difficulty escaping again. Once she had her backpack.

She waited impatiently as Ian opened the back hatch and attached King to a lead. Ian had been silent for most of the drive, and she hadn't bothered trying to make conversation.

She hadn't wanted to discuss her family and what they were capable of. She hadn't wanted to rehash the same tired conversation she'd had every time she'd spoken to a federal agent. They wanted to remind her of the crimes her brother and uncle had committed. They didn't want her to forget her obligations.

She'd been surprised that Ian hadn't done either of those things. His silence had been a welcome relief, the heat that he'd turned on for her chasing away the chill that she shouldn't have been feeling.

It was nearly ninety degrees outside, but she'd still been cold.

He'd noticed, and that shouldn't have mattered to her, but it had. It had been weeks since she'd had another human being around, months since she'd spoken to any of her friends. She'd never known loneliness before. Now it seemed it was all she had.

One day, one night, after another.

Just Esme and her thoughts, alone in whatever squalid little dive she could rent for cheap.

Her door opened, and Ian leaned down, met her eyes. "Do you want me to get a wheelchair?"

"I'm okay."

"No," he responded, his voice much kinder than she'd expected or wanted. "You're not. But you will be. Eventually."

And for some reason, that made her throat tighten and her eyes burn. It made her want to cry all the tears she hadn't cried in the weeks after she'd entered witness protection.

He offered a hand, and she took it, allowing

herself to be pulled from the vehicle. He had her pack over his arm, and she reached for it. "I can take that."

"I've got it," he responded, shifting his hand to her elbow, his palm warm through her thin jacket.

"I'm not so badly hurt that I can't carry my own pack and walk unassisted," she muttered.

"I wouldn't want you to injure your ankle more."

Right. Sure. The way she saw things, he was probably trying to keep her from running.

It still felt good to have someone nearby, though.

She hated to admit that.

She hated that she was enjoying the warmth of his hand, the comfort of his company.

She'd been part of a couple for so long, it had felt strange to not be. To wake up in the morning knowing she wouldn't need to call Brent, text him, wish him good morning or ask him about his day.

He could have entered witness protection with her.

They could have gotten married and made a new life together. Maybe they would have, if Brent hadn't been so adamant about staying in Chicago. He'd made certain that she knew that he wasn't going to follow her into witness protection, that he wouldn't give up his life and his friends and his church group to be with her while she waited to testify. He'd also made certain she'd understood that he wouldn't be waiting for her. That if she went into witness protection, they were over. The wedding they'd been planning, the one that they'd sent out invitations for, that she'd bought a gown for, that she had a venue and flowers and cake for, wouldn't be happening.

*If you leave, we're done*, he'd said, and she'd almost thought he was joking. They'd been standing in a small conference room at FBI headquarters in Chicago, and she'd been given the offer of protection in exchange for her testimony. Six months wasn't that long. Not for two people who were in love. Well, apparently, she and Brent *hadn't* been in love, because he'd told her that six months apart was too much to ask.

For a split second, she'd considered suggesting that they move the wedding up, get married by a justice of the peace and go into the program together.

But then she'd thought better of it, because she hadn't wanted to spend her life with a man who hadn't been willing to sacrifice a little time, a little convenience, a little of his own desires to help her do what she knew was right.

The FBI didn't know any of that.

They didn't care.

Faux concern about her ankle wouldn't make her think they did.

She reached the double doors that led into the clinic and opened them, limping into the air-conditioned lobby. After days of being out in the heat and humidity, it felt like she'd walked into an icebox. Her teeth were chattering, her arms covered in goose bumps as she approached the receptionist.

Her wallet was in the backpack. Along with her ID, her insurance card and her cash. Not just one ID. Several. The real her. The person she'd been in witness protection. The woman she'd become when she'd run.

"Sign in. We'll call you back shortly," the receptionist said, barely looking up from her computer.

She signed her real name—there didn't seem to be a whole lot of reason to do anything else. Angus knew she was in the area, but he didn't know she was injured, had no way of knowing she'd come to the hospital. Plus, he wasn't a fool. He wouldn't come after her when there were so many police around. He'd wait for a time when she was on her own again.

She rubbed the chill from her arms and settled into a chair. She thought Ian would follow, but he walked to the reception desk, leaning down and saying something that Esme couldn't hear. He took out his wallet, flashed what she assumed was his badge and jotted something on the sign-in sheet.

The receptionist eyed him as he turned away. She looked surprised and interested. Maybe because of the dog or whatever Ian had told her. Maybe because of him. He was a good-looking guy.

Better than good-looking. Dark hair. Light brown eyes. Tall and muscular. He looked like the kind of guy who could handle whatever came his way. The kind who could be depended on, who could fight his battles and everyone else's.

He must have sensed her gaze, because he met her eyes, offered a smile that made her heart flutter.

Fatigue was getting the best of her.

That much was obvious.

He crossed the room and sat beside her, his gun holster peeking out from beneath his jacket. "It shouldn't be long," he said.

"I'm not in a hurry."

"I am. This is a calculated risk. The likelihood that Angus will show up here is slim. We've got police watching all the entrances, but I'd rather be in and out quickly."

"We can skip it altogether, if you want," she said.

"I'd prefer you have the ankle looked at now

rather than later. Once we get you to the safe house, you'll be sticking pretty close to it until the trial."

"So, basically, I'll be under house arrest?" she asked, not quite able to keep the sarcasm from her voice.

"Whatever keeps you safe, Esme," he responded.

"Whatever gets me to trial," she corrected.

"That, too."

She had nothing to say to that, and she found herself looking in his eyes again, studying his face. He had long lashes, and the beginning of a beard and mustache. Clothes caked with mud and muck from the swamp, he was still one of the handsomest men she'd ever seen.

The fact that she was noticing didn't make her happy.

He looked about as annoyed as she felt. She couldn't blame him. He'd been assigned bodyguard duty. That meant hanging out and chilling, waiting for Uncle Angus's next move. It also meant giving up free time and hours that he could have been home with the people he loved.

"Just so you know, that's important to me, too," she said quietly, and he nodded, some of his annoyance seeming to melt away.

"I get that. I also understand that it's not fun

having people come in and take over your life, but in this case, it's necessary."

"I'm sure it's not fun giving up your life to help protect a stranger. Your family—"

"Is gone," he bit the words out. "I have an aloe vera plant waiting for me at home, so I'm not all that concerned about my time away."

"You get lots of sunburns?"

He raised an eyebrow, and she blushed.

Blushed!

"It was a gift from a friend," he finally said, "who felt I needed something to take care of. That was in the years prior to King." He scratched the dog behind his ears.

"I see."

"Probably not, but we don't know each other well enough for a long explanation."

"Or for you to go back to the exam room with me," she pointed out, taking the opportunity that was presented to her.

"I'm going." The answer was simple, to the point and firm.

"That's not the way I do things," she responded, using her reasonable voice. The one she used with hysterical brides or overbearing mothers of the brides.

"It's the way my team does things, so it's the way it's going to be."

"Your team? Meaning the FBI?"

"Partly."

"Can you give me a plain answer, Ian, because I'm in no mood for riddles."

"No riddle. I work for a covert unit within the FBI. Our job is to take on cases like yours."

"Cases where witness protection nearly got someone killed?" she asked, and his lips curved into what she could only assume was a smile. Since there wasn't a bit of humor in his eyes, she couldn't be certain of that.

"Tough cases. Dangerous ones," he offered.

"Oh joy," she muttered.

This time, he really did smile. "Sarcasm?"

"How'd you guess?"

He chuckled. "You're an interesting lady, Esme."

"I plan people's weddings for a living. I go to church on Sunday and out to the movies every couple of months. There is nothing interesting about me."

"The federal government would beg to differ. To us, you are exceedingly interesting."

"Tell me how to change that, and I will. Hiding from my uncle would be a lot less complicated if I weren't also hiding from your people."

"Testify at the trial. Our interest in you will end at that point."

She rolled her eyes. "At least you're honest."

"About?"

"The fact that your organization will only care about me until then. Once I testify, I'll be on my own. If my uncle or my brother or anyone either of them is affiliated with comes after me, it won't be your concern."

He frowned but didn't deny it.

So, he *was* honest.

Which was nice, but didn't do much to make her feel better about the situation.

The door that led to the exam rooms opened and a dark-haired man stepped into the lobby. He glanced at a clipboard, scanned the room and finally called, "Esme Dupree?" as if she weren't the only woman there.

"Yes." She stood, Ian and King doing the same.

Ian had said he'd go into the exam room with her.

She wasn't going to argue. She wanted the pack, and it was currently hanging loosely from his left arm. Eventually, he'd relax enough to set it down.

"I'm Ryan. The PA on duty tonight. You said you injured your ankle?" The man glanced down as he spoke. "Left or right?"

"Right."

"Would you like me to get a wheelchair?"

"I'm fine." And the sooner they got this over with, the better.

"Come this way, then." He turned and strode through a narrow hall, pushing open a door and waiting as she moved across the threshold.

Just one door. A sink. A small supply cabinet with two drawers. A chair. An exam table.

And a window that looked out into a tiny paved lot and the thick forest beyond. If she could get out the window and into the woods, she might have a chance at escape.

"King has a very good nose," Ian murmured, as if he'd sensed the direction of her thoughts. Maybe he'd just seen the direction of her gaze.

It was a warning, and she knew it wasn't an exaggeration. King had tracked her through the Florida swamp and followed her so closely it would have been impossible to escape.

*Nothing is impossible.*

The words whispered through her mind, a gentle reminder that she wasn't alone, that she didn't have to do this herself.

God would never leave or forsake her.

He wouldn't abandon her. Not the way Brent had.

Not the way her family had.

The last part was so much more difficult to think about than the first. So she wouldn't think about it. She'd just keep doing what she'd been doing since the day she'd seen her brother shoot a man: running, hiding, keeping herself alive.

There'd be time to think things through, accept the facts, work through her sorrow and anger after the trial.

She limped across the room, ignoring Ian's dark gaze as she sat on the exam table, pulled off her boot, rolled up her pant cuff and eyed the swollen blue-black flesh of her ankle.

The ankle looked bad, but Ian didn't think it would keep Esme from trying to escape. If she had an opportunity, she'd take it. He had no doubt about that. She'd glanced at the window at least a dozen times while the PA poked and prodded her ankle. She'd answered questions in a brusque tense manner that was at odds with her soft green eyes and delicate features.

She looked fragile.

He'd thought that the first time he'd seen her photo.

He figured a lot of people made the mistake of believing what they saw. There was no other way to explain her escape from witness protection. From the time she'd shown up at local law enforcement offices in Chicago, she'd looked weak and soft and a little tired. He'd seen the videotaped testimony. She'd been crying, tears streaming down her cheeks as she'd described what she'd witnessed. She'd been shocked. Scared. Horrified.

*She* didn't break laws. *She* didn't get into public altercations. No drinking, smoking weed, playing the odds. She conducted her business in a way that had built a positive reputation in the community. She worked with high-end socialite clients who paid a hefty sum for her organized and creative approach to wedding planning.

He'd read all about it online.

He'd wanted to know everything he could about Esme Dupree before he started playing bodyguard to her. He'd been certain he'd dig up some dirt, discover something that would convince him of what he already knew—she was as rotten as her brother and uncle.

He'd come up empty.

She didn't even have a traffic ticket on record.

Everything about her screamed "law-abiding rule-follower."

It was no surprise that her handlers in witness protection had forgotten what cloth she was cut from. They'd forgotten that she was a Dupree, that the same blood that ran through her brother's and uncle's veins ran through hers.

She might look fragile, but she wasn't.

She might pretend to be a follower, but she wrote her own playbook, and she followed her own moral compass.

Whatever that happened to be.

He hadn't quite figured it out.

He didn't really care to.

His goal, his purpose, was to get her to trial.

Justice and revenge. All in one fell swoop.

Except for one thing.

He did care.

It was the way he'd been raised. He might want to deny it, might want to turn away from it, might want to tell himself all kinds of stories about how Esme was just a Dupree and her problems were hers to solve…

But he'd looked in her eyes. He'd seen her tears. Now he was in an exam room with her, watching as her ankle was prodded and poked. She didn't complain, barely winced, but she looked done.

"We could x-ray this," the PA finally said, "to make sure it isn't broken, but I feel pretty confident that it's just a bad sprain."

"No X-ray," Esme said with a strained smile. "It feels better already."

She hopped off the table. Probably to prove the point.

"Just hand me an Ace bandage, and I'll be on my way," she continued, grabbing hold of the backpack that hung over Ian's arm.

King growled.

Ian hadn't been lying. King didn't like people touching his things.

And the pack?

It was currently his possession.

"You're probably going to want to stop grabbing things that I'm holding," he suggested wryly.

The PA had already stepped back, his gaze on King.

Esme didn't seem as worried about the dog.

She did release the pack, but she didn't back up. The ornery woman stood right where she was. Close enough that he could see dozens of freckles on her pale cheeks and the gold tips of her dark red eyelashes.

"I want to wash up and put on clean clothes before we leave." She tugged at the muddy fabric of her pants, her green eyes flashing with irritation.

"Okay." He handed her the pack, watching as her annoyance was replaced by surprise. She was easy to read. That would be helpful in the weeks to come.

"Just like that?"

"Sure."

"Why?" she asked, and he shrugged.

"Where are you going to go, Esme? Out the window?" He gestured toward it. "There are two marked police cars outside and probably five or six patrol officers surrounding the building."

She frowned but didn't respond.

"You wouldn't make it far before one of them

spotted you. Even if you made it farther, you'd only be running from one danger into another. I think you're too smart to take that foolish of a risk." He glanced at the PA. "Can you bring that Ace bandage? My friend and I are anxious to get back on the road."

The PA scurried out of the room, nearly running down the hall. This was probably the most exciting thing that had happened in the clinic in years. He'd want to share every detail with as many colleagues as possible.

That was fine.

It didn't matter if Angus found out that his niece had been at the clinic. What he couldn't find out was where they'd be going next.

Ian glanced at his phone. No text from Max. Which meant he hadn't found a safe house yet. He was probably looking for one that wasn't in the FBI system. One that Jake wouldn't be familiar with.

"You know," Esme broke into his thoughts, "it would be a lot easier for me to get cleaned up and changed if you weren't standing in the room."

He met her eyes, trying to ignore the dark smudges beneath them, trying not to see the hollowness of her cheeks, the faded bruises on her neck that looked like fingerprints.

But he couldn't *not* see those things. She was

a Dupree, but she was also a victim. His gut twisted at the thought. He'd gone into this kind of work to protect people like her, to prevent crimes, keep the bad guys off the streets and save other women from having to go through what Esme had. He couldn't look in her face and not realize how much she'd been through, how difficult it had been on her.

He turned away, closing the shades that covered the windows. "It would be a lot easier for me to do my job if I knew you were going to cooperate. I highly suggest that you do not attempt to leave this building, Esme."

He stepped into the hall before she could respond, closing the door with a soft snap that seemed to echo through the quiet building.

He stared at the closed door, trying to rid himself of the image of the bruises, the dark circles, the thin face and fragile body.

He didn't want to see Esme as anything other than what she was. He'd told himself that over and over again as he'd made the journey to Florida and begun his search. She was a Dupree. He wouldn't forget that. But she wasn't just a Dupree. She was a woman determined to do the right thing despite the danger. She was a person who'd given up her life to make sure her brother paid for his crimes.

She was a victim who needed someone in her corner.

Someone who would fight for her because she deserved it, not because of what he could get out of it.

Justice. Revenge. Closure.

They were what he wanted, what he'd been seeking for over a decade. He still wanted those things, but not at the expense of a woman who'd done nothing wrong, who—by all accounts—had done everything right.

King leaned against his leg, whining softly.

He didn't like the door separating him from the woman they were guarding.

But Ian needed the distance. Just for a few minutes. Because he didn't like the way he was feeling, didn't want the sense of responsibility that seemed to be settling on his shoulders.

Esme Dupree was an assignment.

She was the key witness in a federal trial, a fugitive on the run from a federal program. She was sister to the man who'd murdered Ian's parents.

But she had bruises on her neck and a price on her head, and that would change everything if he let it.

# FIVE

She tried the window.

Because why wouldn't she?

It didn't open.

Ian had probably known it wouldn't.

Why else would he have left her alone with the pack?

Esme walked to the sink, turning on the water and splashing her face with ice-cold drops of it. She squirted soap into her hands and scrubbed her arms and her cheeks. Mud splattered the stainless steel and the counter, tiny brown blobs that slid along the smooth surfaces. She didn't bother wiping them away. Sure, she was tired, and her ankle hurt, but what she needed was a plan…and no matter how frantically her mind raced, she couldn't seem to formulate one.

She pulled black cargo pants and a light blue T-shirt from the pack. It was her only extra set of clothes, but it wasn't extra any longer. The set she'd been wearing was soaked through with mud and swamp muck. If Uncle Angus came hunting her, he'd smell the stench long before he spotted his prey.

Esme changed quickly, tossing the ruined clothes in the trash can, then she shoved her ID and money into one of her pant pockets. Her Bible was at the bottom of the pack—too big to fit in a pocket. She set it on the exam table. Beneath it was the photo of her family that she'd been carrying since she entered witness protection. Reginald, Violetta, Esme and their parents. Taken nearly twenty years ago, it was a reminder of what they'd once been—happy, connected, secure. A typical American family standing on a Florida beach that Esme couldn't remember. It was the only photo she had of the entire family, and she'd cherished it forever.

But now…

Now when she looked at it, all she could see was the sardonic gleam in her brother's eyes, the cocky way he held his head, the vast distance between Reginald and his parents. Esme and Violetta stood between them, arms wrapped around each other. Reginald stood a couple of feet away, slightly angled from the group.

She'd never noticed that. Not until after the murder.

She shuddered, dropping the photo onto the exam table and pulling her hair from the ponytail holder. The raw spot on the side of her head itched, and she ran a finger across the scabbed surface, telling herself she wasn't going to think about what had happened.

So, of course, she did.

She thought about the night Angus had found her, the swamp life teaming beyond the window. She thought about the quiet rustle of fabric and the horrible realization that she wasn't alone. She thought about trying to run. Thought about the way her uncle had grabbed her by the ponytail, yanking her back with so much force, a chunk of hair and skin had come out. She'd been blinded by the pain, terrified as he'd put his hands around her throat, looked straight into her eyes and tried to kill her.

If she hadn't been flailing, searching frantically for a weapon, if she hadn't felt the smooth domed surface of the heavy glass snow globe her mother had given her on the last birthday they'd spent together, she'd have died in the dingy rental near the swamp.

As it was, she'd smashed Angus in the nose with the snow globe. Blood had spurted out, and she'd run.

She was fast, but her uncle had almost been faster.

Because her hair—the long red hair that Brent loved so much, that Angus had used to stop her the first time—had caught in mangrove branches and nearly kept her from escaping.

*Never cut it. Never dye it.*

How many times had Brent said that?

"Not even if it's going to get me killed?" she muttered, walking to the supply cabinet and yanking open one of the drawers. Gauze. Bandages. Tape. She pulled open the other one and found suturing kits, alcohol wipes and scissors.

She didn't think through what she was doing.

One minute she had the scissors in her hand. The next, long strands of hair were falling to the floor. The scissors were dull, and she was tired, and the tears she'd been fighting for weeks kept trying to slide down her cheeks.

This wasn't the life she wanted.

This wasn't the way things were supposed to have worked out. She should be planning her wedding, not her escape from a federal officer, a crazy uncle, a corrupt brother.

"Everything okay in here?" Ian called.

"Fine," she responded, her voice catching on a sob. "Fine," she repeated, and this time she sounded almost normal.

Good. Because there was no way she was going to let him know how broken she was.

"You're sure?" he asked.

She didn't answer.

She was still cutting her hair. No mirror. No

way of seeing just how badly she was butchering it. Just the scissors slicing through thick strands, the hushed rasp of that the only sound in the now silent room.

She couldn't escape out the window, but she could do this.

She'd learned her lesson. Ponytails were weapons that could easily be used against women.

"Esme? I'm coming in," Ian said, his voice soft and soothing.

Had she made some sort of noise? A quiet sob she hadn't heard?

She touched her cheek, certain it would be wet from tears, but it was dry and hot, strands of hair sticking to it. She wiped them away as the door opened.

She heard his footsteps on the tile floor, but he didn't say anything. Not until he was beside her, his muddy boots surrounded by dark red hair.

"Need some help?" he asked, taking the scissors from her hand. For some reason, she didn't try to stop him. She didn't protest or speak or tell him to leave the room.

She wanted to sit for a minute. Catch her breath. Try to stop the images that were filling her head. Blood and death, men she loved who'd proved to be nothing like what she'd thought they were.

Her uncle.

His hands on her throat.

"Breathe," Ian said quietly, the scissors snapping off one thick hank of hair after another.

She sucked in a lungful of air.

"There you go." He ran his fingers carefully through her hair, cut off a few more strands. "Wish I were a hair stylist, Esme, but this is probably the best I can do."

She met his eyes, then saw the concern she hadn't been privy to before.

It surprised her.

She hadn't thought Ian had it in him to care. Not for someone with a name he seemed to despise from a family he obviously hated.

"He wouldn't have had the chance to strangle me if it hadn't been for the stupid ponytail," she explained. As if he'd asked. As if he really did care.

But, of course, she knew he didn't.

He was part of a well-oiled machine, all of it working toward one outcome, one result: shut down the Dupree crime family.

"Your uncle?" He set the scissors in the sink, his dark gaze never leaving her face. He was reading her. Easily.

"Yes."

"I'm sorry." He bit each word out. "Sorry we didn't do a better job of keeping you safe."

His gaze dropped to her neck, probably to the bruises that still dotted it.

"I'm sorry my family's business is making money illegally. I'm sorry my brother has no moral values, no conscience and no regret. I'm sorry that my uncle is making your job more difficult. And I'm really, *really* sorry neither of them are who I wanted them to be."

"Or who you thought they were?" he asked.

"I wish I could say that. I wish I could say it and know that I had absolutely no suspicions, but I'm not a fool, and neither are you. My brother had a boatload of money to spend on whatever he wanted. I *was* suspicious and worried about where it was coming from." She released a quavering breath. "I admitted that during my interview with your people. It's why I hadn't spoken to Reginald in a few months and why I only had contact with him once or twice a year."

"You accepted a client who was deeply affiliated with him."

"I accepted a lot of clients who knew Reginald," she clarified. "If I turned every one of them away, I wouldn't have a business."

Of course, when she'd agreed to plan the Wilson-Arnold wedding, she hadn't known that Maverick Arnold was deep in her brother's pocket. She hadn't known that he'd gone to the police and sold some information about the way Reginald ran his business. She hadn't known that Maverick was a snitch or that Reginald had found out or that she was going to walk into the house Maverick and his fiancée shared and see her brother pointing a gun at her client.

Esme rubbed her arms, willing some warmth into her body.

"I see," Ian said, lifting the photo from the exam table and studying it.

"No," she responded, snatching the photo from his hand and tossing it into the trash. "You *don't.* You're living in your cloistered world of law enforcement, and you've been assigned the task of protecting a woman you despise—"

"I don't despise you."

"From a family," she continued as if he hadn't spoken, "you hate."

He didn't deny that.

She hadn't expected him to.

"All you're doing is your job." She nearly spat the words. "I'm living my life, and right now, it's not a very good one." She kicked the pile of hair, whirling away on her bad ankle and nearly toppling from the pain.

She limped to the door.

He'd left it open, and she walked into the hall, ignoring the surprised PA who was walking toward her, a thick roll of gauze in his hand.

He didn't try to stop her.

Maybe her new haircut made her look unstable.

She *felt* unstable, emotions roiling through her so violently she could barely breathe.

Ian didn't try to stop her, either.

But he was following. She could hear the click of King's claws on the tile floor.

She didn't turn around.

She had nothing left to say. Not one word.

The light went off as she reached the lobby, plunging the clinic into darkness. She stood where she was, velvety darkness pressing in, surprised voices calling out.

She knew where the exit was.

She could have crossed the lobby and walked outside, but lights didn't go off for no reason. Not in a place like this. There was no storm. No wind.

She stepped back, bumping into a solid wall of muscle.

Ian.

She knew it before she tried to move away, before his arm wrapped around her waist, holding her still.

"Wait," he whispered, the words ruffling her newly shorn hair and tickling her cheek.

"For what?" she whispered back.

Somewhere outside, an engine roared, and

Ian yanked her back as lights splashed across the lobby windows and the world exploded into chaos.

Bricks. Sparkling glass. Dust. Lights. People shouting.

She was moving, dragged backward away from the front end of the truck that had plowed into the building.

"Move, move, move!" Ian was shouting, dragging her into the still-dark hallway, the sound of gunshots following them.

And she finally understood. Finally got it. Finally realized that the driver of the truck hadn't just misjudged or made a mistake. He was there to finish what her uncle had started.

Suddenly, she didn't need to be prodded or pulled.

She ran, her ankle pain forgotten, her heartbreak gone. All the emotion she'd been feeling, everything that had been filling her up, replaced by cold hard terror and the driving need to survive and make sure her uncle and brother didn't have the opportunity to hurt anyone ever again.

Ian had been prepared for trouble, but he hadn't been expecting such a bold attempt on Esme's life.

He should have been, and he was angry with himself for the lack of foresight.

Reginald and Angus were desperate.

Desperate people did desperate things.

Including trying to kill someone in front of local law enforcement.

He scowled, his hand tight on Esme's wrist, his fingers digging into her smooth warm skin. He had to be hurting her, but she didn't complain. She was running through the hall beside him, her shoulder brushing against his arm.

Ian took a right turn at the end of the corridor, heading for the emergency exit that had been marked on a building map posted to the wall of the exam room. He'd noticed that, just like he'd noticed that the front of the clinic was comprised of large glass windows and a couple feet of bricks. Not a difficult facade to breach if someone really wanted to.

Yeah. He'd noticed. No extra points for that.

He and King worked protection more than anything else. They were good at it, but they generally worked with one or two other members of the team.

Right now, they were working alone, local law enforcement scrambling to contain the threat, but none of them specifically assigned to guard Esme.

He unhooked King's lead.

"Guard!" he ordered, and King growled, the sound deep and low. Not a warning. More of an acknowledgment that he was on duty and he knew it.

Good. The corridor was pitch-black. Even with his eyes adjusting to the darkness, Ian could barely see a foot in front of him. No generator cutting on to give some light to the situation. If there was a generator, the perp had taken that out, too.

They reached the emergency exit, nearly plowing into the door.

He felt Esme's arm move, knew she was reaching for the door handle.

"Wait," he cautioned.

"For what? The truck driver to come around the corner, guns blazing?"

"For me to open the door." He nudged her back until he knew she was against the wall. "Give me a minute to check things out."

"I'd rather—"

"Let's not waste time," he said, leaning in so close he could see her pale skin in the darkness, smell the fragrant soap on her skin. "The police probably already have the truck driver, but we don't know if he has friends."

She nodded. One quick, curt move of the head, and he turned back to the door, felt King pressing in close.

"Ready?" he asked, and the dog barked. "Let's go." He opened the door, and King sprinted out, racing across an empty lot that shimmered beneath a half-dozen streetlights.

Ian's cell phone buzzed. He ignored it.

His focus was on the dog.

He could see him running across the lot, heading toward a sparse stand of trees. He disappeared for a moment, the shadows swallowing him, then appeared again. Ian had trained other dogs, but none of them compared to King. The Belgian Mal was as smart and as driven as they came.

He waited for the dog to indicate. One quick sharp bark would be a warning that someone was nearby.

King was silent, loping from one area of the parking lot to the next until he was finally done and returning, tail waving jauntily in the artificial light.

"We're clear," Ian said, reaching for Esme's arm and pulling her closer.

"Are you sure?"

"He's my partner. We live by protecting each other's better interest. I trust him to keep me safe. He trusts me. You could probably learn a little from that."

"I learned plenty about trust from my family. I don't plan to ever forget the lessons they've taught me." She followed him outside, her hand on the back of his jacket, her fingers clutching the fabric as if she were afraid that he might abandon her like so many other people had.

He could have told her that he wouldn't.

But King was moving ahead, scruff raised, tail stiff.

He sensed something.

Whatever it was, he didn't like it.

"This way," Ian said, tugging Esme into the deep shadows near the corner of the building. Not wanting to alarm her more than she already was.

"What's wrong?" she whispered, and he knew she sensed it, too. The change in the air. The sudden charge of electricity.

King was off, running so fast he was just a blurry shadow in the streetlights as he headed back to the trees. To the darkness. To the shadows that could easily hide someone.

Ian pulled his gun, aiming in that direction. Not surprised to see the flash of light as a shot was fired. The bullet went wide, slamming into the back of the building a few feet from where Ian and Esme crouched.

A man shouted, then screamed.

No more shots. Just the vicious sound of King barking and growling.

A police cruiser raced around the side of the building, blocking Ian's view and his aim.

In any other circumstance, he would have run

straight into the fray, gun drawn as he shouted for the perp to drop his weapon.

But these weren't other circumstances.

He had Esme to protect and no team members to guard her while he went after King.

The police officer jumped out of the cruiser, his gaze on the trees, his gun drawn.

"That your dog?" he said, his attention never wavering.

"Yes."

"FBI, right?"

"Right."

"You want to call him off or you want me to go in there?" the officer asked.

"The perp has a gun."

"I heard the shot."

"I'm not calling my dog off until I know he's disarmed."

"If I go in there and your dog attacks, I'm not going to have a choice as to how I react." The officer was issuing a warning, and Ian wasn't going to ignore it.

He shouted the command for King to return, praying the dog had managed to disarm the gunman. If not, there was a chance King would be shot as he ran away.

And Ian would have to live with that.

Live with the fact that he'd risked his partner's life for the sake of a woman whose family had destroyed his. The choice he'd just made only brought home the truth: he didn't want to protect any of the Duprees.

That was a fact.

It was also a fact that he'd walked into the exam room and seen Esme, scissors in hand, hair falling around her, and his heart had jerked with the kind of sympathy reserved for those who'd done absolutely nothing wrong but had still found themselves in untenable circumstances.

She deserved better than what she'd gotten.

That had been his first thought, his knee-jerk response.

She deserved better, and he could make sure she got it.

He *would* make sure she got it.

His first response, and maybe it was his second and third response, because he still felt it. Still wanted to turn back the clock and keep her from walking in on her brother's crime. Her only wrongdoing was having a name that made his blood boil. Her only mistake was in taking on clients that her brother sent her way. Those weren't things she should be punished for. They weren't things a rational man could hold against her, and he'd always considered himself rational.

Except when it came to the Duprees.

Maybe it was time for that to change.

He'd had more than one friend tell him he had to put aside his anger and move forward with his life. He'd told more than one of them to keep their opinions to themselves.

Not a very Christlike attitude.

His father would have told him that if he'd been around. He would have told him to let go of the need for revenge, to focus on justice and mercy and grace.

Ian didn't know if he could do that, but he could stop looking at Esme like she was the enemy. He could start viewing her as the victim she was. He could give her the protection she needed, offer her the support that was necessary when a person lost everyone they loved.

Could and would, because it was his job, because it was the right thing to do and because his father wouldn't have expected anything less from him.

He called King again, was relieved when he barked in response. Seconds later, King emerged from the trees, tail high, ears alert.

"What a relief," Esme said, and he could hear the sincerity in her voice, see it in her face.

He turned away, focusing on King, on the darkness, the trees, the chaos still playing out. For now, they were safe.

He planned to make sure they stayed that way.

# SIX

King raced back across the parking lot, silent, focused.

He stopped at Ian's feet, sitting at attention, looking straight into his handler's face.

"Good job," Ian said, scratching him behind the ears, his focus on the police officer who was jogging across the lot.

The dog didn't look like he believed the praise.

His happy smile was gone. In its place was tension that even Esme could feel.

"You did do good," she assured him and then felt foolish.

She'd never been much of a dog person.

It wasn't that she didn't like dogs.

It was more that she didn't have time for the training and the walks and the attention they needed. Plus, her sister had a small yappy poodle who despised Esme. The feeling was mutual.

Esme hadn't wanted to add another thing into her already hectic schedule. Planning weddings for demanding clientele took all of her energy and focus. If she couldn't have a dog that she could make part of the family, she didn't want to have one at all.

So she didn't have a dog.

She didn't want a dog.

She sure didn't spend her free time talking to dogs.

King didn't seem like a typical dog, though.

He seemed completely in tune with Ian and absolutely devoted to doing his job. This time, his job had been to take down the shooter.

Was he disappointed that he hadn't been able to finish what he'd started?

"If so," she muttered, "I know exactly how you feel."

"What's that?" Ian asked, his dark gaze suddenly on her.

"I thought the dog might be disappointed. I was just telling him that I know how he feels."

"You were talking to King?" He smiled, a slow easy grin that softened the hard angles of his face and made him look almost approachable.

Almost.

"Is there a problem with that?" she responded. "Do you have a rule about people talking to your dog?"

"He's my partner, and you're welcome to say

anything you want to him. He probably is disappointed. He likes to be in on the arrest."

"Instead, he's here babysitting me." She eyed the canine. He was staring toward the trees, his body still tense, his hackles up.

"And instead of being home planning summer weddings for rich clients, you're here," he murmured. "Is that why you're disappointed?"

"I'm disappointed that the people I love don't love me. I'm disappointed that the people I trusted couldn't be counted on."

"You're talking about your brother and uncle?"

"No." She was talking about her sister. She was talking about Brent.

She was talking about two people she'd actually believed in and counted on. The sad truth was she'd stopped counting on Reginald years ago. And she'd never counted on her uncle. Angus was her father's younger half brother. A product of a second marriage, he'd made just a few appearances in Esme's life when she was a kid. He'd been thirty years older than her, but he'd acted like a child—bullying others into doing what he wanted, whining when he didn't get his way.

She'd never liked him.

His criminal activity was no surprise to her at all, and she liked to tell herself that he'd led Reginald into a life of crime.

The reality, according to the FBI, was that Reginald had been running his *business* for several years before he'd asked Angus to join him. Her uncle had been more than eager to comply, but he wasn't the boss.

He most likely wasn't the one who'd called the hit on Esme. That was probably the hardest pill to swallow, and it was the one thing she couldn't bring herself to admit.

Especially not to someone like Ian.

"Your sister, then?" he guessed. "Or your fiancé?"

Both, but she wasn't going to admit that, either.

"Do you think the police officer has found the guy who shot at us?" she asked.

"Changing the subject?"

"Just getting back to a more interesting one."

He smiled again. A gentle smile this time. The kind of smile that seemed to say he understood just how hard this was for her. "There was more than one person shooting, Esme. The guy in the building, and the one in the trees."

"I know."

"So which one do you want to find out about?" He took her arm, and she didn't resist as he drew her around the side of the building.

"Either. Both."

"We'll go around front. I want to get you out

of the open, so we'll check in with the officer in charge and then get out of here."

"And go where?" she asked.

"Wherever my boss sends us."

"The safe house?"

"Yes."

"Will it be as safe as my witness protection location?" she asked and regretted the flip question immediately. Ian had been trying to be kind. She knew that, and she shouldn't have repaid him with attitude.

"Safer," he said without rancor. No excuses. No explanations. He'd already told her about a leak in the agency, and he'd already told her the leak had been plugged.

"I'm sorry. That didn't come out the way I wanted it to."

"What way would have been better?" he asked, King trotting along in front of him, heading toward the front of the building and the emergency lights that flashed across the pavement there.

"Silence?"

He chuckled, his hand still on her arm, his biceps brushing her shoulder. "Silence is the better part of valor. Or so my father always said."

"He doesn't say it any longer?" she asked, even though she knew she shouldn't. The question was too personal, and she didn't expect him to answer.

For a moment, she thought he wouldn't.

The muscles in his arm were tense and taut, his jaw tight.

"I shouldn't have asked that," she began, and he shook his head.

"It's okay. I gave you the opening. My dad has been gone for ten years. He and my mother were killed in a drive-by shooting."

Her heart seemed to stop, then start again, beating the slow unsteady rhythm of grief.

She felt like an idiot. Worse, she felt like an ogre.

She'd stood in the hospital room and accused him of being in his cloistered law enforcement world making judgments about her life. She'd been sure he couldn't understand the grief and anger she felt over her family's betrayal, couldn't understand the sorrow of her losses.

She'd been wrong.

"Ian," she said, his name just a whisper in the warm night air, "I'm so sorry. I know that can't help, but I am."

"They've been gone a long time, but I still think about them a lot. I'm sure you understand that. Your parents were killed in a small plane crash, right?"

"You've done your research," she said, trying to lighten her tone, take some of the sorrow out of it. Time did ease the sting of loss. It never healed it, though. She understood that just as much as she understood his pain.

"It makes the job easier."

They'd reached the front of the building. The once nearly empty parking lot was filled with emergency vehicles and teaming with first responders.

No more hushed summer night. It was loud and chaotic, the shattered glass and crumbling bricks spilling into the lobby, spotlights shining onto the wrecked furniture and huge Ram truck that sat in the center of the mess.

"Were you folks inside?" an EMT asked, his skin ruddy from the sun, his eyes wide behind thick glasses. He looked young. Maybe early twenties, his uniform crisp and new.

"Yes," Ian responded, his fingers still curved around Esme's arm. She could have pulled away easily, but she didn't. There was something comforting about his touch, about the warmth of his palm through her sleeve.

She wouldn't think about that too deeply.

She wouldn't question it.

She had too much going on, too many details to work out. Sure, she'd have to run eventually, but she still didn't know which direction or how far she'd need to travel to reach a bus or train station. She'd have to take one or the other.

An airplane was out of the question.

And she didn't have enough money left to buy a used car.

She couldn't hitchhike, and she sure couldn't walk. She'd be too exposed, too easy to find.

"Are you okay?" the EMT asked, his gaze shifting from Ian to Esme.

"Fine," she responded. "Is everyone else?"

"Aside from the driver of the truck, there were no injuries."

"Where is the driver?" Ian asked.

"I'm sorry, sir. I'm not at liberty to give out information about clients."

"I'm a federal officer. Special Agent Ian Slade." He pulled out his wallet and flashed his ID. The EMT seemed satisfied.

"He's being triaged in one of the clinic exam rooms. He was shot in the chest. I'm not sure he's going to survive."

"Do you know who the lead officer is?" Ian hooked King back to his lead.

He let go of Esme's arm to do it, and she stepped away, putting a little space between them.

She didn't want to like him. She sure didn't want to rely on him. She'd made it a habit to avoid getting close to any of the police officers, federal agents or prosecuting attorneys. They were using her to get what they wanted, and she understood that. She also understood that she'd been cut off from everyone she knew and loved.

She'd lost everything, and she was vulnerable.

Esme had her faith, but having a friend would be nice, too.

It would be easy to cling to any of the men and women who'd been shepherding her through what had become the most difficult time in her life.

Easy and foolish, because she'd already had her heart broken once in the past six months. She didn't want to repeat that. She didn't want to feel that sense of surprise and betrayal.

Love wasn't supposed to be limited by circumstances. It was supposed to grow during the hard times. Not just romantic love. All love—family, friendship. Instead, she'd found that it had abandoned her.

She needed to keep reminding herself of the way it had felt to know the people she'd loved didn't love her in return. She needed to remind herself that she was a means to an end. Nothing more, and that if she let herself forget that, if she let herself believe she was forging relationships with these people, she'd end up hurt.

Sighing, she took another step back, scanning

the parking lot while the EMT pointed out the officer in charge.

Maybe Ian would get so excited about interviewing the gunman that he'd forget he was supposed to be guarding her. Maybe he'd be distracted for just enough time for her to slip away.

There had to be a store in town. She could ask for directions to the nearest bus stop or train station. She might even be able to call a taxi to bring her there. If there was a pay phone or someone willing to let her borrow a cell.

That was the problem with going off the grid. It wasn't easy to get help when she needed it. There was no one to call, no knight in shining armor ready to charge to the rescue. Worse, there was no one to consult with, no one to help make decisions. Her failures were her own. Which wasn't a bad thing. Unless failure meant death.

She eyed Ian and King, both deeply focused on the EMT who'd pulled out a business card and was scribbling something on it.

She could try to leave now, and they might not notice. She told herself to do it. The federal government had already failed to provide the safety it had promised. She had no reason to believe that things would be different this time, that somehow the organization that had failed her would suddenly find a way to succeed.

She took another step back, distancing herself from Ian and whatever security he offered. The intuition that had kept her alive, that had sent her running from witness protection, that had woken her from sleep when her uncle had broken into her trailer, kicked in. She could feel it in the pit of her stomach, a warning. Not to hurry. Not to disappear. To stay.

She scanned the crowd, suddenly terrified that she'd see her uncle hidden among the gawkers who'd begun to gather. She didn't find him, but she knew that meant almost nothing.

She felt dizzy with fear, sick with the thought of catching a glimpse of him. Her head ached where the hair had been torn out, and she touched the spot, remembered how short she'd cut it. How short Ian had cut it. He'd been kinder than she'd expected, more gentle, and she had the sudden feeling that if she were going to be saved from her family, he would be the man to do it.

That thought kept her in place, frozen two feet away from the man and dog she'd been telling herself to escape.

"Good choice," Ian said, turning in her direction as the EMT walked off.

She didn't respond, because she wasn't sure it was. She only knew it had been the only choice she could make.

* * *

Deputy Sheriff Kennedy Sinclair didn't much care to have the federal government messing around in one of her cases. She made that very clear to Ian more than once while he tried to get information on the truck driver.

In return, Ian had made it very clear that the case wasn't hers, that the federal government was already neck deep in it and that he wasn't going to back off. No matter how much she wanted him to.

Three hours after the truck had plowed into the medical center lobby, they were still at an impasse, Ian sitting on an uncomfortable chair in the corner of an interview room that smelled like vomit and mold, listening while Deputy Sheriff Sinclair asked Esme dozens of questions about her uncle, her family and her enemies.

"Her enemies," he stated, impatient with the process and wanting to move things along, "are her uncle and her brother. She's told you that a dozen times."

"Thanks for your input, Agent Slade, but I'm aware of what she said." The deputy sheriff tapped a pen against the old table that she and Esme were sitting at and frowned. "And I'm sure that you're aware of how common it is for witnesses to change their stories."

"Not this witness," he said, and she scowled.

"*Every* witness. Ms. Dupree might think that she only has two enemies in the world, but that doesn't mean there aren't more."

"I'm sitting right here. I can hear every word you say about me, so how about you stop discussing this case as if I weren't around," Esme muttered, her hands splayed flat, palms down on the tabletop. Probably to keep from fiddling with her hair. She'd been worrying at the short strands, smoothing them down and then fluffing them up again.

Nervous energy. Twice she'd gotten up and tried to pace the small room. The fact that King was lying smack-dab in the middle of the tiny bit of open floor had made that nearly impossible. Both times, she'd walked to him, looked down at him, frowned and taken her seat again.

King had seemed to think it was a game.

He'd followed her to her seat, nudged her hand to get the pet he thought he'd deserved and then retreated to the middle of the floor again. Currently, he was curled up, his nose tucked in neatly under his legs, his snout hidden, only his eyes visible. They were open. He was still on the job, after all.

"I'm sorry," the deputy sheriff said without a hint of remorse in her voice. "I'm just trying to get to the bottom of what happened tonight."

"I've explained everything I know. My uncle

tried to kill me a few nights ago. He's probably responsible for what happened at the clinic, as well."

"Maybe." The deputy sheriff rested her elbows on the table and leaned toward Esme. Casual. Friendly. Ian had used the same interview technique more times than he cared to admit. "We found a jacket in the trees across from the clinic. Teeth marks in one sleeve. A little blood. I'm wondering if it could be your uncle's."

"I have no idea."

"You didn't see what he was wearing when he attacked you?"

"It was dark, I'd been woken from a sound sleep. Once I escaped him, I was too busy running for my life to pay much attention to what he wore," Esme said, a hint of irritation in her voice.

She'd planned to walk out of the hospital parking lot and run off again. He'd known it. He'd planned to give her the opportunity, and then he'd planned to stop her—a reminder to both of them that her agreement to testify against her family didn't mean they were on the same team. She'd stepped away. He'd been geared up to send King after her, and she'd stopped. Just… stopped. No limping run toward the trees or the gathering crowd, no trying to dart away and hide somewhere until he gave up the hunt.

He thought her decision to put her life in his hands had surprised her as much as it had surprised him.

She'd spent the past few hours avoiding his eyes. She looked scared and shell-shocked, as if everything she'd been through the past few months had suddenly caught up to her.

"Yes. I guess that's true." The deputy sheriff paused, tapping the pen more rapidly. "Can I be honest with you, Esme?"

"It's better than feeding me lies."

"This is a small town. We don't get a lot of crime here. I've called in the state police to help collect and process evidence. As it stands, we know who the truck belongs to, but we have no idea who was driving it."

"Did you fingerprint the perp?" Ian asked, and the deputy sheriff frowned.

"We're a small town and not well funded, but we're not inept."

"It was a question. Not a statement of your abilities." He kept his tone neutral, and she seemed to relax.

"I know. I apologize for getting a bit defensive. But the fact is that I'm a woman in a position that has been held by men for nearly a hundred years. Sometimes, I've got to act tougher than I am." She released a breath and got back to the matter at hand. "We fingerprinted the guy at the hospital, and we're running him through the system. So far, we've come up empty. We did locate a handgun near the jacket. We found several prints on it, and we're running those, too."

"Any other evidence collected?"

"No, but I'm very familiar with the Dupree crime family." Her gaze shifted to Esme. "We've had run-ins with some of their drug transporters during the past few years. Cocaine. Heroin. There's a little airport ten miles outside of town. They fly the drugs in disguised as commercial shipments and transport it through the Everglades channels and out into the black market. I'm certain I've only caught one out of every ten drug shipments. We search the cargo, but they're good at what they do, and they know how to hide their product." She sighed in obvious frustration. "I've been begging the town council to fund a K-9 program. We need drug-detecting dogs to really shut the runners down. So far, I haven't convinced them to fund it."

"I'm sorry my family is doing this," Esme said, her voice raspy.

"You have nothing to be sorry for. You aren't responsible for your brother or your uncle. I'm only telling you this because I want you to know that this isn't a good place to try to hide. Someone around here is on the Duprees' payroll. Probably more than one person. I'm sure it wasn't difficult for your uncle to find someone willing to come after you."

"Kill me, you mean." Esme pushed away from the table, the chair scraping loudly on the old linoleum floor.

"Yes. That is exactly what I mean."

"I need some air." Esme didn't ask permission. She didn't seem to care if it was safe to leave. She walked out of the room, her limp obvious. She'd never gotten the Ace bandage, and she hadn't had time to ice her ankle. Ian would make sure she did both. It wasn't much to offer her, but it was more than he would have wanted to give her twenty-four hours ago.

A Dupree but not like the rest of the family.

He still wasn't sure how he felt about that.

All he knew was that he couldn't keep viewing her through the lens of his anger and vindictiveness.

He followed her into the hall, King off-lead beside him.

He kept his distance as she made her way down a narrow hall and into a dimly lit stairwell. She jogged down the steps ahead of him, and he forced himself to keep quiet about her ankle, to not tell her to be careful.

She knew he was there.

He had no doubt about that.

But she didn't acknowledge him. She slammed

open the stairwell door with both hands, her narrow shoulders shaking.

Was she crying?

He hoped not.

Ian had never been great at dealing with the softer emotions. He could handle anger, frustration and disgust with ease. He dealt with them a lot in his line of work. And he knew how to assuage fear, how to calm nerves.

But tears?

They were a different thing altogether.

Tears were vulnerability incarnate. They were hints at the soul of another human being, and he was never quite sure how to respond when he was faced with that.

A pat on the shoulder? A verbal platitude? A gentle hug?

They all felt awkward and foreign and fake.

Esme reached the exit and would have opened the door, but he touched her shoulder. Felt the fine tremors, the tension.

"You can't go out there alone," he said softly, and she whirled to face him, her short hair spiking out in a hundred different directions, her face still deathly pale.

"I don't want to do this anymore," she responded, her voice calm and quiet and reasonable. Completely at odds with the wildness in her eyes.

"Talk to the deputy sheriff?" he asked, knowing it was more than that. Knowing that she'd been pushed too hard and been through too much.

"Be here. In this place. With an uncle who wants to kill me. I don't want to keep running and hiding. I don't like danger. I don't like intrigue. I hate scary movies and books. I like weddings and happily-ever-afters and cakes with sugar flowers."

"I can get you some cake. I'm not sure about the sugar flowers," he offered, hoping for a smile, and felt a spark of gratitude surge through him when he saw the telltale curve of her lips, a subtle shifting of her energy.

She was calmer but not relaxed. "Thanks. Maybe I'll take you up on that. If I survive until the trial."

"You will, but I thought maybe you could use some cake now. When was the last time you ate?"

"I had a granola bar at noon."

"An empty stomach is hard on the psyche," he said, and she offered a real smile.

"You're afraid I'm going to have a mental breakdown."

"I'm afraid you're going to cry. I'm as opposed to tears as you are to scary movies."

She laughed a little at that, a hint of color returning to her cheeks. "You're going to be very happy to hear that I almost never cry."

"And when you do, there's always a really good reason?"

"Usually. Sometimes, I cry at weddings. When the bride and groom are the perfect complement to each other, when I've worked with them for a year or more and seen just how deeply in love they are. I get a little teary-eyed then, because it reminds me of my parents. They were great people. You know what I keep wondering?"

"What?"

"Where they went wrong. How two great people could produce a son who has absolutely no moral compunction, no conscience, no remorse."

"Your brother made his choices, Esme. They had nothing to do with your parents."

"What about Violetta's choices? She could have stepped forward and helped, but she's refused to say anything."

It was true, and he wasn't going to argue the point. Two people from one family had decided they were above the law. Three, if he counted Angus. He did. "You can't blame your parents for that, either."

"I want to blame someone. It's easier than believing that the siblings I loved weren't worth it."

"Love is always worth it," he said, and she smiled again.

"Maybe you're the one who should be in the wedding business, because I'm kind of done with the whole believing-in-the-fairy-tale-of-love thing." Her voice broke on the last word, and he was sure there were tears in her eyes.

"Esme—"

"Relax," she said, sniffing once and then turning away. "I'm not crying. Just wondering how I ended up standing on the opposite side of the fence from the people who are supposed to love me."

She opened the door, and he motioned for King to move into place. The dog trotted outside beside Esme, ears alert, tail wagging. Warm, moist air blew in from the Everglades, bringing a hint of brine and rot. It was quiet here, the distant sound of highway traffic drifting on the still night air.

Esme didn't say another word. She seemed determined to leave, though, her limping stride carrying her across the parking lot to a cracked sidewalk that snaked through long grass.

"You know I can't let you go, right?" he said gently, and she shrugged, her hair glowing dark red in the streetlight.

"Esme," He tried again. "Don't make this more difficult for both of us."

"Sometimes, I get tired of following the rules,

Ian. Especially when following them isn't doing me any good."

"It's doing you plenty of good."

"How so?" she countered. "I've nearly been killed more times than I care to remember. Maybe Violetta has a point. Maybe sitting on the fence and trying to stay neutral would be better than this."

Her words left him cold.

"You're not going to testify?" he asked, the question gruff and angry-sounding.

He needed to tone it down, rein in his own emotions. Esme clearly needed to talk this through. She didn't need him muddying the water with his less-than-positive opinion about her sister.

"Don't worry. I'll do what I said I would, and you'll get what you want from me." All the warmth had left her voice, and that bothered him more than it probably should have.

"What I want is for you to live. That's not going to happen if your brother goes free." That was the truth. Or part of it.

"You're twisting the truth to make yourself feel better, Ian. You want me to testify because you want my brother in jail. He's committed crime after crime with impunity, and his organization is only getting bigger. Look at this." She waved at the darkness that surrounded them.

"Reginald started in Chicago. In the past ten years, he's expanded to Florida."

"And nearly every other state in the country," he offered.

"Exactly. I can't let him continue, but there is a part of me that wishes I could. There's a tiny little piece of me that would love to do what Violetta is doing. She's not committed any crimes, but she hasn't betrayed her family, either. She has support from the authorities and from my brother and uncle. All I've got is myself."

"You also have me and my team."

"For a while." She reached the end of the sidewalk and stopped, turning her face up to the night sky. A million stars dotted the blackness, and he wondered if she noticed, or if she was too caught up in her pain and regret to see anything beyond herself.

"It's beautiful," she said, answering the question he hadn't asked.

"Yes. It is."

"That's the weird thing about life."

"What is?"

"It goes on. Even during the most horrible pain a person can imagine, the earth continues to revolve around the sun, the seasons continue to change. Flowers bloom and crops are harvested and people are born and others marry.

God is still on His throne, and life goes on." She sighed. "I guess we need to go back."

"If you're ready."

"What else do I have to do?" She skirted past, King close by her side.

"Call your sister?" he suggested and instantly regretted it. He shouldn't be encouraging her to speak with someone who had a different agenda than the FBI. Esme was already struggling. Speaking with her sister might pull her farther down the path of regret and farther from the job they needed her to do.

"That would be nice, but I don't have a phone. Even if I did, your people told me that if I tried to contact anyone from my former life, I'd probably be dead within forty-eight hours. Cell phone signals can be traced."

"Not mine," he said, continuing to give her the option. Despite his misgivings, it seemed like the right thing to do. Not for the FBI or, even, for Ian. For Esme. She deserved to have a little bit of peace, and if talking to her sister gave her that, who was he to deny her the opportunity?

"You're offering me your phone?" She met his eyes, and he could see the suspicion in her gaze, the wariness. He couldn't blame her. For six months, she'd been a pawn in a game she didn't want to play, shuffled around by people who either wanted to kill her or wanted to use her.

The fact that he'd been part of that made him feel guiltier than he should have. Or, maybe, as guilty as he should be. If he hadn't been so caught up in trying to bring her family down, he'd have thought more about what she was going through—the terror and anxiety and loneliness she must be feeling—rather than what her name meant to him.

"Your uncle already knows you're in this area, but I don't want you to mention our exact location," he said, and it felt right. It felt good. It felt like he'd stopped letting his emotions, his need for revenge, cloud his judgment and started seeing the situation for what it really was. Not a chance to destroy the Duprees. A chance to keep the one bright light on its dark family tree from being snuffed out.

"So, you *are* saying that." She grabbed his arm, and he let her pull him to a stop. Found himself looking down into her face, gazing into her eyes. They were dark in the dim light, her lashes thick and straight.

She was a Dupree, but she was smart, driven, decent.

Beautiful.

It was a winning combination, and if they'd been anywhere else, in any other situation, he'd have told her that.

"Don't tell her what happened tonight," he

said instead, letting his gaze drop to King. He was relaxed and alert. No sign of danger, and Ian was glad. Not just for himself and King, but for Esme. She needed a break from the chaos and drama, a chance to breathe in a little peace. "No mention of anything that has transpired since you and I met, okay? I'll give you fifteen minutes, and then the conversation ends. You agree with those terms, or it doesn't happen."

"I agree!" she said with more enthusiasm than he'd have had if he were calling a sister who didn't care whether he lived or died. Violetta didn't seem to when it came to Esme. She knew more about the workings of the crime family than she'd admitted. Her silence had kept Angus from going to jail.

He shoved the thought away, taking Esme's arm and leading her back to the building. "We'll do it inside. It's safer there."

She nodded, but he didn't think she heard.

She was smiling, nearly skipping with happiness as they made their way across the parking lot and back inside.

Weddings.

Happily-ever-afters.

Cakes with sugar flowers.

Right then, she seemed filled with all those things. And suddenly, he understood why she was so good at her job; he knew how she'd built a wedding planning business from nothing into a million-dollar company. Her energy was difficult to resist. Her joy and enthusiasm were contagious.

But her uncle was still on the loose.

She still had a price on her head.

And until the Dupree crime family had been dismantled, all the joy and enthusiasm in the world couldn't keep her safe.

# SEVEN

Ian managed to find a small room where Esme could make the phone call. He also managed to convince the deputy sheriff to leave her alone there.

Well…

Not alone exactly.

Ian was sitting in a chair a few feet away, King lying near his feet.

Esme would have preferred they both leave, but she hadn't been able to convince Ian to let her have privacy.

His way or the highway.

That was the impression he'd given.

But he was letting her make the call.

That was all that mattered to her.

Her fingers shook as she punched Violetta's number into the phone. She felt nervous and uneasy, no point in denying it. Six months ago, she and her sister hadn't parted on good terms. Violetta had been convinced that Esme was going to destroy the family.

She'd been right.

But the family had been destroyed long before Esme realized what her brother was. Families couldn't be built and sustained on lies. They couldn't be nurtured when one or more of the members wasn't who he pretended to be. Esme had explained all of that to Violetta. She'd outlined her reasons for testifying against Reginald. She'd tried to convince her sister to cooperate with the police and FBI, to tell them anything she knew about their brother's crimes. But it had backfired.

Big-time.

Violetta had been livid.

So, yeah. They hadn't parted on good terms, but Esme still loved her sister. She longed to hear her voice, to know that she was doing okay, that the police and FBI hadn't come down too hard on her.

She punched in the last number and waited as the phone rang. Once. Twice. The third time, voice mail picked up, and all Esme's excitement and fear seeped away. She leaned against the wall, every bit of her energy suddenly gone. She left a quick message telling Violetta how much she loved her.

When she finished, she handed the phone back to Ian.

"Thanks," she managed to say, her eyes hot with tears she wasn't going to shed.

"I'm sorry she didn't pick up," he responded in a gruff voice, tucking his phone into his jacket pocket.

She caught a glimpse of his holster and gun, and she turned away from the reminder that he was there doing his job, that he only cared about keeping her safe so that she could testify.

Right at that very moment, Ian Slade was all she had, and he'd given her way more than she'd expected.

"It's not your fault," she said, walking to the door.

"You're giving up a little easily, Esme," he responded, and she turned to face him again.

"What?"

"You escaped witness protection and kept ahead of your uncle for months. I'm surprised that you're willing to make one phone call and call it quits."

"That was the agreement."

"We agreed on the terms of your talk with her." He pulled out the cell phone and handed it to her. "Give it another try. Who knows? She might be screening her calls. Maybe she's gotten tired of hearing from my team and the prosecuting attorney."

She met his eyes, realized that he was doing this for her. Nothing else. No hidden agenda. No desire for information or control. He wanted her to have what she wanted, and that felt…different. It felt nice. It felt like what she'd hoped to have with Brent but had never achieved. She'd loved him, and she'd been willing to concede on almost every issue. They'd almost never fought, because she hadn't found much worth fighting about. It seemed easier and better to let him have his way.

Her friends had said they were the perfect couple. They'd all wanted to be in a relationship just like the one Esme and Brent were in.

She wondered what they were saying now.

She dialed her sister's number again, her heart thumping with memories and with anxiety. She really did want to hear her voice.

"Esme?!" Violetta's voice rang in her ear, sharp and a little frantic.

"Yes."

"I'm so glad. When I realized I hadn't picked up when you'd called…" She paused, and Esme could picture her pacing her posh home office. "I couldn't believe it when I heard your message. I should have picked up, but the number wasn't one I was familiar with. And the police and FBI and press won't stop hassling me."

"I… Someone let me use his phone. I wanted to make sure you were okay."

"Me? I'm not the one in trouble. Are you okay? The FBI said that you weren't in protective custody anymore. I've been worried sick." She seemed to have calmed, her voice taking on its normal clipped tone. Violetta had money. Lots of it. She liked to live large. Big house. Expensive cars. Gorgeous clothes. Her persona reflected an upper-crust background that she didn't have.

Esme wasn't sure when Violetta had adopted it. Maybe after her first marriage. Her ex had been rich and snobby, his money buying him friends that his personality couldn't.

"I'm okay. Just…" She glanced at Ian.

He was watching her, his eyes oddly light in his handsome, tanned face.

"Just what?" Violetta demanded.

"Wishing I could come home." To her surprise, her voice broke on the words, some of the emotion she'd been trying hard to contain slipping out.

"You can. Just tell the feds you won't testify," Violetta responded.

"You know I can't do that."

"You won't do it, sis. There's a difference."

"Reginald killed a man," she said, the words making her feel sick and light-headed.

She'd seen it all.

The gun.

The blood.

The red stain spreading across the cracked linoleum floor.

"Sit," Ian whispered in her ear, moving her to the chair and urging her into it.

"Is someone there with you?" Violetta demanded, her voice shrill.

"I..."

Ian shook his head.

"No," she lied and despised herself for it.

"Look, hon, I love you. You know that, but you've got to back out of your deal. You can't testify against blood."

"That's not what Mom and Dad would say. You know they wouldn't. They'd say I should do the right thing, and that the right thing isn't always the easy one."

"Maybe so, but they're dead. You're not. I'd like you to stay that way."

"Then maybe you could do what I have. Testify. If you tell the authorities what you know about the Dupree criminal enterprise, then Uncle Angus will be tossed into prison where he belongs."

"Here's what I know," Violetta said, her tone

hard-edged and angry. “You could die for the sake of a man you barely knew, a guy who was probably as big a criminal as you think our brother is. That man you saw shot? He had a record. You know that, right? Just because you think Reginald shot him, doesn’t mean he was an innocent bystander.”

“Think? I saw him!”

“If you insist on testifying, you could die for the sake of some idealized belief about right and wrong,” Violetta continued as if Esme hadn’t spoken.

“I could die because my sister won’t do the right thing.” The truth slipped out. Stark and real and harsh, and she despised herself for it as much as she had for the lie.

“I would do anything for you, Esme,” Violetta said, all the affectation gone from her voice. She sounded like the person she’d been before she’d married into money and decided that having material possessions was more important than having relationships. “But both of us dying isn’t a good solution to the problem. I love you, hon. I hope you know that.”

She disconnected, the silence echoing hollowly in Esme’s heart.

She wasn’t sure how long she held the phone to her ear. Eventually, Ian took it, his fingers brushing against her cheek, warm and calloused and gentle.

She should have moved away, but she didn't. Not when he tucked the phone back in his pocket. Not when his hand cupped her chin. Not when he looked into her eyes.

"It's going to be okay," he said.

"You can't know that."

"Yeah, I can, because I'm going to make sure it is."

"Don't make promises you can't keep, Ian," she said, the words as hollow and empty as her heart felt.

"It's not a promise. It's a statement of fact."

"It's kind of sad that you're more determined to keep me safe than my sister is." Her voice broke, and to her horror, a single tear slipped down her cheek.

"Come here." He tugged her into his arms, and she went, because she needed his warmth so much more than she wanted to.

"All she has to do is tell the police what she knows about Angus's involvement in the crimes my brother has been committing. If she did that, it would all be over."

"Some people have an easier time doing the right things than others do." He smoothed her hair, and she realized her head was resting against his chest, that she could hear the slow solid thump of his heart.

"Violetta is making a choice. Me or money. She's choosing money."

"Maybe, but your parents were right. Sometimes the right thing *is* the most difficult. Sometimes the easy path leads to the most dangerous places, and the most difficult road brings us home."

"I know."

"Obviously, Violetta doesn't. Not yet. So don't let her doubts shake your conviction." He said it kindly, his hand still smoothing her hair, the rhythmic thump of his heart soothing her soul.

It took a minute for the words to register, for her to realize what he was really saying: *Don't back out of your agreement. We need you to testify.*

The knowledge was like a bucket of ice water in the face. It woke her up, made her realize whose arms she was standing in. He wasn't any less biased than Violetta. He had just as much of an agenda, and she still wanted to stay in his arms, burrow closer, inhale the spicy scent of aftershave and soap.

She backed away. "You're afraid I won't testify," she accused. "Still. Even after I told you I wasn't going to change my mind."

"You're wrong," he said as she turned blindly

and reached for the door handle. "I'm not afraid you won't do it. I'm afraid you'll spend the rest of your life regretting it."

"I won't," she bit out, her heart throbbing in her chest, her stomach churning.

"Are you saying you don't already feel like a traitor?"

"I'm saying that I know I'm doing the right thing. That's going to have to be enough."

"You didn't answer my question."

"Because I don't know what you want me to say," she responded, and she could hear the edge of sorrow and frustration and worry in her voice.

It surprised her.

She prided herself on her calm approach to life.

She'd won job after job because brides and grooms and their families had bragged about how easily she handled difficult situations.

She wasn't handling anything right now. She was just trying to get through this moment without completely breaking down.

Maybe Ian knew that.

He sighed, grabbing her hand and tugging her away from the door. "I wish you weren't in this situation, but you are, Esme. I wish I could give you some easy way out, but there isn't one. All I can do is offer whatever support you need and all the protection necessary to keep you safe."

"A personal bodyguard, huh?" she said, trying to smile but failing miserably.

"Call it whatever you want," Ian replied, brushing strands of hair from her temple and looking into her eyes, studying her face.

She wasn't sure what he was looking for, but he must have found it, because he smiled gently.

"It's going to be okay," he said, just like he had before, and then he stepped back, his hands dropping away.

"What now?" she asked, because she needed to say something, and because what she really wanted to do was step right back into his arms.

"We'd better get back to the interrogation room," he said. "The sooner we can convince the deputy sheriff to let us leave, the happier I'll be."

"Has your boss found a safe house yet?" She opened the door and walked straight into a tall muscular guy. She stepped back, nearly falling over in her haste.

He grabbed her arm to steady her, and she realized there was a dog beside him. Smaller than King, but watching her with the same kind of intelligence.

"I'm so sorry," she gasped.

"Don't be," the man said. "I never complain when a pretty woman bumps into me." He glanced past her, his smile broadening.

"I'm glad to see that they didn't toss you into jail, Ian," he said. "I was worried when Max said you were at the local police station."

"For once," Ian said, "I've stayed out of trouble. Esme, this is Zeke Morrow. He's a member of the Tactical K-9 Unit, and that's his K-9 partner, Cheetah."

"Nice to meet you." The words sounded stilted and awkward. Which was exactly how she felt. She'd been running from these men for months, hiding from the FBI and anyone affiliated with it, and now she was back in their custody.

She wasn't sure how she felt about that.

She only knew she was tired. No. Exhausted. There was an old vinyl chair sitting against the wall, and she dropped into it, her head swimming.

She closed her eyes for a second.

When she opened them, Ian was crouching in front of her. "Are you okay?" he asked as King edged in between them and nudged her hand.

She scratched behind his ears and told herself she wasn't going to pass out from fatigue and hunger. "I'm fine."

"You're white as a sheet," he corrected, pressing his hand against her forehead.

"I'm a redhead," she muttered.

"I've never seen a redhead your particular shade of white," Zeke offered. "Maybe Ian was right. A little sugar might do you some good." He handed her a white paper bag.

"What is it?" she asked, her gaze shifting from him to Ian.

"Just something I thought you might enjoy after your hours-long interrogation. I asked Zeke to stop and pick it up before he drove here from the airport."

She peeked in the bag.

It contained a clear plastic container with what looked like cake inside.

She pulled it out.

Yes. *Cake.*

White with ivory icing and pretty yellow and pink flowers, and her heart hurt with the beauty of the gesture.

She met Ian's eyes again, and he was smiling, his face soft with what looked like affection, compassion and concern.

"It's cake," she murmured, as if it needed to be said.

"I told you I would get you some."

"Actually," Zeke interrupted, "I got it."

She heard him, but she was still looking in Ian's eyes, still seeing his smile.

She couldn't help herself, she smiled, too, some of her anxiety and fear seeping away. "Thank you."

"No problem. Like he mentioned, Zeke did all the work."

"Not just for the cake," she responded.

"No problem," he said again. "Now, how about you eat the cake while Zeke and I discuss how to get you out of here?"

He straightened, and she opened the container, found a plastic fork and a napkin in the bag. The first bite was sweet and light. Vanilla and sugar and flour and butter. If she'd had to put a name to the flavor, she'd say it tasted an awful lot like hope.

Things were looking up.

At least, as far as Ian was concerned they were.

Max had managed to find a safe house that was far enough away from town to throw Angus off their trail but close enough to be easily accessible. Zeke had arrived with Cheetah. Julianne Martinez was also on the way and planned to meet them at the safe house.

Three agents all devoted to getting Esme to the trial.

Yeah. Things were definitely looking up.

For him.

Esme didn't seem quite as happy, but she did have some color in her cheeks. The cake he'd asked Zeke to bring had done its job. The empty container was in her hand, empty but for a couple crumbs and a few smudges of frosting.

"Was it good?" he asked, and she patted her stomach, her hand shaking a little.

"It was the best cake I've had in months." She still sat in the old chair, her legs stretched out in front of her. Despite the food and the color in her cheeks, she looked exhausted.

"Good. Now, how about we get you out of here?"

"Deputy Sheriff Sinclair is okay with that?" she asked, glancing down the hall. Zeke was there, standing in front of a window, watching the parking lot as he and the deputy sheriff finished discussing plans for getting Esme outside safely.

Ian had left them to it, because he'd been worried about her. She'd been too quiet. For someone who'd been taking action and making decisions on her own for months, she didn't seem all that interested in the plans they'd been discussing while she ate cake.

That concerned him.

Months of fear and anxiety could wear a person down, make her feel hopeless and defeated. He didn't want that to happen to Esme.

"She said she has everything she needs from you. Come on. By the time we get to the safe house, there'll be a freshly made-up bed waiting for you." He took her hand, pulled her to her feet. She tossed the empty cake container and bag into a recycle bin and offered a shaky smile.

"That sounds great, because I think I'm crashing from my sugar high."

"Maybe you're just crashing from too many months of running," he replied, and her smile fell away.

"Don't, Ian."

"What?"

"Be so nice."

"I'm being me," he replied, leading her toward Zeke and the deputy sheriff.

"And making it really hard for me to not like you."

"Is there a reason why you don't want to?"

"Maybe I just don't want to be disappointed again."

"Again?"

"It's a long story. I don't have time to tell it."

"We're going to have plenty of time later," he replied, and she shrugged.

"You have something personal against my family, don't you?" she asked, the question so unexpected and sudden, it took a moment for it to register.

When it did, he stopped, turning so that they were face-to-face and he could look into her eyes. He wanted to see her expression while they talked, and he wanted her to see his.

Nothing hidden.

Nothing left out.

She deserved the truth, and he'd give it to her, if that was really what she was asking for. "Why do you ask?"

"I've been sitting there eating cake and thinking, and while I've been doing that, I've been remembering a couple of things you said about my family. Maybe not what you said, but how you said it. As if you despised everything we were."

"Not you," he corrected. "Them."

"See? Even with just those words, you sound angry."

"Do I?" he asked, but he knew he did. Just like he knew he was putting off the inevitable. They were about to spend a month in a safe house together. She deserved to know who he was, what he'd spent most of his adult life trying to do—take down her family.

"I'm too tired for games," she responded. "So how about you just tell me what happened?"

"I've known about your brother and his crimes for a long time. My father was a police officer in Chicago right around the time Reginald started making inroads into the crime world."

She frowned, and he could almost see her

mind working, see her putting together bits of information and trying to connect them.

When she didn't speak, he continued. "My dad planned to shut Reginald down before he could gain more ground. He arrested quite a few low-level operatives, stopped several money-laundering schemes, intercepted a few drug shipments. Basically, he was making your brother's life very difficult."

He didn't continue.

He'd told the story to other people. He'd imagined telling it to one of the Duprees, standing in a courtroom somewhere and explaining the exact reason why he was going to make sure every crooked member of the family paid.

But he hadn't imagined this. Hadn't imagined looking in Esme's stricken face, seeing the knowledge in her eyes. She knew. He didn't have to tell her.

"Come on," he said, and he'd have walked away, but she grabbed his hand, her palm cold and dry.

"You said they were killed in a drive-by shooting," she murmured, her face so pale he thought she might fall over.

"They were."

"Are you sure it was him?" she asked, and he gave her credit for not denying it, for not insisting that her brother hadn't been responsible.

"Reginald showed up at the funeral. After everyone left, and I was standing by their caskets, praying that I'd wake up from the nightmare. I looked up, and he was there, standing a hundred feet away. He pointed his finger at me and pretended to shoot, and then he walked away."

"I'm so sorry, Ian," she whispered, tears slipping down her cheeks, the woman who'd said she rarely cried, swallowing back sobs as she stood in the stark white light of the police station. Her hair was deep red and spiked up around her head, her eyes deeply shadowed. He couldn't stop thinking about how she'd looked when he'd walked into the hospital room, seen her chopping off her hair because her uncle—her flesh and blood—had used her ponytail to keep her from running.

She must hate that, hate that she'd lost control in public, with Ian looking on.

She'd been through too much.

He'd made it worse.

If that was what wanting revenge led to, he didn't like it.

Didn't particularly like himself.

*Let it go.*

That was what his father would have said.

*Let God deal with it.*

He'd understood the truth behind that for a

long time, but he'd never been able to make himself own it. He'd wanted revenge, and he'd wanted to be the one to dish it out. He'd wanted the Dupree family to suffer as much as he had. He'd wanted every last one of them to mourn and grieve and cry.

And then he'd met Esme.

She was as innocent as his parents had been.

He hadn't been able to protect them, but he could protect her. Maybe that was the key to peace. Maybe he'd come full circle, facing a choice about how he wanted to move forward in life. Maybe instead of taking two lives like Reginald had, he was supposed to save one. Save Esme.

Maybe.

"It's not your fault," he said, and for the first time since he'd been assigned this case, he knew that it was true.

"My family—"

"Isn't you." He wiped the tears from her cheeks.

"Ian—"

"You're tired. How about we discuss this when you're feeling more yourself?"

"Meaning not crying?" she asked wryly, swiping more tears from her cheeks. "You did say you were opposed to tears."

"On you," he responded, taking her hand and

walking again, King trotting along beside them, "they look good."

She laughed, the sound husky and rough but still filled with warmth. "Better not say that, Ian. Next time, I might really let loose."

She was attempting to shove aside her grief and keep going with a good attitude. He'd never thought he could learn anything from a Dupree, but in the short time he'd known Esme, she'd taught him everything he needed to know about judging people on their own merit rather than on the merit of their family.

"You could let loose a floodgate of tears and you'd still look like the bravest woman I've ever met," he responded.

"I think that's the nicest thing anyone has ever said to me."

"Then I guess you haven't been around the right people," he responded.

She was silent for a moment, and then she smiled. Just a tiny little curve of the lips that made his pulse jump. "I guess running for my life has its perks."

"Like?"

"A bodyguard who knows how to say the right thing at exactly the right time."

"You two ready?" Zeke called, striding toward them, Cheetah at his side.

"I was ready an hour ago," Esme responded.

"Then let's head out."

She released Ian's hand and moved toward the door. He followed, more determined than ever to make sure she got to trial safely.

# EIGHT

Esme didn't speak as she climbed into Zeke's oversize SUV. She didn't say a word as the two men got their dogs into the back. Zeke climbed in the front. Ian nudged Esme into the center of the bucket seat, grabbing her arm when she would have moved all the way to the other side of the vehicle.

"The middle is safest," he said.

She didn't respond.

She didn't have anything to say. She'd been fooling herself, believing in a fantasy, convinced that Reginald had committed only one murder.

One had been bad enough.

One had been horrible.

But he'd committed at least two more.

She had no reason to doubt Ian's story. She'd seen the truth in his eyes. She'd heard it in his voice. Apparently, Reginald had been killing people to get them out of his way for as long as he'd been running the *family business.*

How many lives had he taken?

And why was she telling herself that she was surprised, shocked, flabbergasted?

Reginald wanted his own sister dead.

He was working with Angus to make sure that happened.

Hadn't the FBI been telling her that for months? Hadn't they brought up his name every chance they got? It wasn't just Angus coming after her, it was Reginald. He was calling the shots and pulling the trigger.

"Are you all right?" Ian asked, his voice a soft rumble in the silent SUV.

"I will be."

"I shouldn't have told you about my parents."

"Of course you should have."

"It could have waited."

"Until when? Something like that festers the longer it sits." That was the truth. "Besides, I asked you. It's not like you just tossed the information out at me."

"It still could have waited. Seat belt," he said, and when she didn't reach to snap hers into place, he did it for her, his hand brushing against her abdomen, the warmth of his arm pressing against hers.

Comforting.

Just like his touch had been, his hug, his hands brushing tears from her cheeks.

Esme didn't want to think too much about that. About how much safer she felt when he was around, about how desperate she was to have someone she could count on.

She'd always been confident and had always known how to go after what she wanted. What she wanted right now was to be done with the trial and the testimony.

A month wasn't a long time.

She could do anything for a month.

Except maybe survive.

She shuddered, the warmth of the summer air drifting in the open driver's-side window doing nothing to chase away the chill that had settled deep in her bones.

"Here," Ian said, taking off his jacket and laying it over her, tucking the edges around her shoulders, his fingers brushing her collarbone and the side of her neck, lingering there. Soft and light and gentle.

That should have been all. Just a simple touch. His hand there and then gone. She met his eyes, felt something arc between them, the jolt of it making her pulse race.

"This is probably a bad idea," she said, and he smiled.

"What?"

"Whatever we're doing."

"Getting to know each other? We're going to

be spending a lot of time together in the next month or so. Understanding a little about each other will make that easier."

"You're going to be staying at the safe house?" For some reason, that hadn't occurred to her. It probably should have. Ian had been talking about the safe house, about being her bodyguard and probably a bunch of other things that should have clued her in. Probably would have if she hadn't been so exhausted.

"What did you think was going to happen?"

"I guess I thought you were going to bring me there and leave."

"It would be difficult to be your bodyguard if I weren't close."

"Right."

"You don't sound happy about it."

"I don't really have an opinion." Except that he was the kind of temptation she didn't need in her life. That a few days with Ian could make her wonder what she'd ever seen in Brent.

Who was she kidding?

She'd spent a few hours with him and she was already wondering that.

"Sure you do," he said, and she frowned.

"Then my opinion is that my parents would roll over in their graves if they thought I was staying in a house with a guy like you."

"You think they'd take issue with me?"

"I think they'd have rather I stay in a house with a guy who looked like a toad, smelled like a troll and refused to shower regularly."

"No worries," he replied. "I won't be the only one there."

"And you couldn't have mentioned that before I went on my rant about trolls and toads?"

He chuckled, leaning back against the seat and giving her some breathing room.

She should have been happy about that.

Should have. Wasn't.

She liked having him close. He was a habit that could be easy to form and very, very difficult to break.

"You have the coordinates for the safe house?" Zeke asked as he pulled away from the police station and onto the road.

"Yeah. Hold on. I've also got another text from Max. He got a call from the local PD." Ian pulled out his phone and leaned over, speaking quietly to Zeke for several minutes. Esme heard a few words. Something about blood and DNA and a jacket. She could guess what they were discussing, and she could have joined in, but all she really wanted to do was close her eyes and sleep.

For the first time in weeks, she wasn't alone in the darkness listening to the sound of the Everglades, startling at every noise, pacing restlessly through the longest hours of the night. For the first time in weeks, she felt almost safe.

She closed her eyes, drifting into half sleep, the sound of a cell phone jerking her awake again. For a moment, she thought she was back in Chicago answering client phone calls and text messages. She opened her eyes, reaching for her purse and her phone.

No phone.

No purse.

Just Zeke driving the SUV, and Ian checking a text message, the blueish light from his phone deepening the hollows of his cheekbones, sharpening the angle of his chin.

Whatever he was reading, it wasn't making him happy.

"What's wrong?" she asked, and he tucked the phone away.

"Nothing you need to worry about."

"Which makes me worry more, so how about you just tell me?"

Rubbing the back of his neck, he let out a frustrated sigh. "Just a message from an anonymous friend."

"Another one?" Zeke asked. "Did Dylan forward it to you?"

"He forwarded it to the team. You should already have it."

"I really don't like being kept in the dark," Esme said.

"This has nothing to do with the trial," Ian reassured her.

"But it has something to do with my family, right?"

"In a roundabout way."

"Can you be any vaguer?" she asked.

"Probably. If I try hard enough."

"You might as well run the situation by her," Zeke interrupted. "Maybe she'll have some idea of who's sending the texts and why."

"What texts?" she asked.

Ian took out his phone, pulled up a text and handed it to her.

Word is that Mommy, Daddy and child have gone home.

She read it twice, trying to make sense of what she was seeing, attempting to put it in the context of the trouble she'd found herself in.

"Who are Mommy, Daddy and child?" she finally prompted.

"Daddy is the leak I mentioned. The one who gave away your location in witness protection. He's a rogue agent. He was working for your family." Ian frowned. "Your brother and uncle, I mean."

Esme narrowed her eyes, noticing the change in his rhetoric, the careful choice of words. She'd have thanked him for it, but she was reading the text again. This time out loud.

The words didn't make any more sense than they had before.

"Who are the child and the mother?"

"Penny and Kevin. His girlfriend and child. We think he's trying to get to his son. My suspicion is that he plans to take him and leave the country."

"What about the mother?"

"That's a good question," Zeke said, his voice tight and hard. "I wish I had an answer. The fact is, the agent is my brother, Jake Morrow. He's been on your brother's payroll for a while."

"I'm sorry, Zeke."

"Yeah. Me, too. If we could figure out who Anonymous is, we might be able to track Jake down, make sure he's stopped before he takes his son out of the country."

"We're sure it's someone who's familiar with your family and with Jake. Do you have any ideas, Esme?" Ian took the phone, tucked it back into his pocket.

"Me?" she sputtered. "I barely even know what you're talking about."

"We've been getting messages like this for months. Whoever is sending them seems to be trying to help us track down Jake. Unfortunately, the vague references aren't helping much."

"You think it's someone who works for my brother?" she asked, sifting through her memories, trying to find one that might be helpful.

There was nothing.

She hadn't spent much time with Reginald recently and the only vivid memory she had of him was his cold-eyed glare after he'd pulled the trigger.

"Probably," Zeke responded. "My brother was really good at making connections. He knows a lot of people. It's possible one of them is betraying him."

"I've never met your brother, so I have no idea if I've met someone who knows him."

"He went to a lot of your brother's functions. You might have seen him there."

"I didn't attend them." Not the extravagant Christmas parties, the over-the-top New Year's celebrations. Not even the birthday party he threw for himself every year.

She sent him a card.

She called him.

She made small talk about things that weren't important, but she never mingled with his crowd, because she'd never been comfortable in it. Violetta, on the other hand, had loved every bit of the lavish functions.

"But my sister..." She began, and then stopped herself.

"What about her?" Ian prodded.

"She might know something about Jake. She loved going to Reginald's parties. She enjoyed hanging out with his wealthy friends. I could ask her." Of course, that would mean calling again. It would mean having another dead-end conversation that would make her feel horrible. She'd do it, though, because she wanted to put an end to all of this. She wanted her uncle and Reginald in jail where they belonged, wanted peace for herself, justice for the man who died and for Ian's parents.

"Your sister has been less than cooperative," Ian said without a hint of judgment in his voice. He was trying hard to keep his opinion of her family under wraps, but his opinion was valid, his reasons justified. If she could help him, she would.

"She might be more willing to discuss things with me. We're family. That's important."

"It wouldn't hurt for her to try," Zeke said, glancing into the rearview mirror and frowning. "We may have a tail."

"Since when?" Ian shifted, angling his body so he could look out the back window.

Esme did the same. Not because she wanted

to see danger coming for her, but because she wanted to be prepared for it.

Headlights.

Not close. Maybe six car lengths back.

"They pulled onto the road two miles ago," Zeke told him.

"And they've been hanging back all this time?"

"Yes. Pretty much the same distance."

"I'll call it in," Ian said. "See if we can get some local patrol cars out here. Turn off on the next road. I don't want whoever is in that car to have any idea of where we're going."

Where they were going seemed to be farther from civilization.

Esme hadn't been paying attention.

Now she was.

The town was behind them, pinpricks of light in the darkness. Ahead, there was nothing but an empty two-lane road. Thick marsh grass grew on either side of it. Farther away, a few trees jutted up toward the midnight sky.

No sign of any houses.

No business.

No golden arches spearing up from the landscape.

"If I can find a side road, I'll turn. Otherwise, we need to prepare for a rear attack. They seem to be picking up speed." Zeke accelerated, the SUV speeding around a curve, the headlights behind them disappearing briefly and reappearing again moments later.

"They're closing in," Ian said grimly as he pulled out his cell phone and dialed 911.

Esme didn't think calling the police was going to do much good. The SUV was racing at a dangerous speed, and their pursuer was still closing the gap between them. She could see that as clearly as she could see the stars in the dark sky, the marsh grass sweeping sideways as the SUV passed.

"Hold on," Zeke said so calmly Esme wasn't prepared when he took a hard turn. She slammed into Ian, her shoulder pressing into his arm.

They bounced over a rut, and his arm slipped around her, holding her in place as the SUV hit another rut and another.

"Are they still behind us?" she asked, trying to free herself so that she could look.

He held her in place, his arm a steel band around her shoulders, his grip firm without being painful.

"Not yet," he responded, finally releasing her.

He had his gun in hand.

She hadn't realized that.

Hadn't realized how fast her heart was beating, how terrified she was. Not until she looked out the back window and saw the car. It was still on the main road but doing a U-turn, heading back the way it had come. Searching, she knew, for the turn.

"Looks like we're at a dead end." Zeke stopped the SUV and hopped out. No panic in his voice. No fear. He moved quickly and efficiently, grabbing a pack from the back, releasing the dogs.

Ian opened his door, letting the scent of briny water and decay fill the vehicle.

"Come on." He reached for her hand, tugging her out onto muddy earth. If they'd gone any farther, the SUV would be sinking. As it was, they were stuck. Going back would mean running straight into their pursuers. Going forward was impossible.

They'd have to walk out.

*Run* out.

Walking would do diddly-squat for any of them. She tracked the movement of the car as it crawled along. It wouldn't take long for the driver to find the road they'd taken. It would take even less time for him to find their SUV.

"We need to get out of here," she said, her voice too loud and tinged with a hint of desperation.

"We will." Ian snagged a pack from the back of the SUV, hooked a lead to King's collar and tossed his jacket into Esme's arms. "Put that on."

She didn't argue.

The faster she cooperated, the faster they could get moving.

That was how she saw things.

And she wanted to get moving, because she had a horrible feeling that Angus was in the car. Angus, the uncle who wanted her dead, who'd looked into her face and told her exactly why she had to die.

She shuddered, zipping up the jacket and following Ian as he headed through tall marsh grass, King on-heel beside him.

Zeke was a few feet ahead, his dog trotting nearly silently.

They weren't running, but they were moving fast, plowing through the grass and then on to drier land. She wasn't sure where they were heading. She didn't know if the men knew.

Wherever it was, it was away from that car and whoever was driving it.

That was all she cared about.

That was all she needed to know.

She made the mistake of glancing back, of searching the darkness for the vehicle. And then she saw it, the headlights bobbing along as it sped toward the SUV.

She wanted to run. Wanted to sprint as far and as fast as she could. She probably would have, but Ian reached back and grabbed her hand, pulling her up next to him.

"Don't panic," he said in that same calm tone Zeke had used.

Did they go to school for that?

Did the FBI train them to keep their wits about them so that civilians didn't panic?

If so, it wasn't working on her.

"Why would I go and do something like that? Just because the car has almost reached the SUV and we're right out here in the open where any sniper can see us doesn't mean we should be worried," she retorted, the words spilling out in a rush of nervous energy.

"That's the spirit," he praised, not quickening his pace. Not glancing back. Not doing anything but moving forward.

Maybe that was a metaphor for life, but she wasn't in the mood to think about it.

Outwardly, she was staying calm, but inside?

Inside, she was a wild mass of hysteria.

Ian could hear sirens.

That was the good news.

The bad news was that their pursuers had already found the SUV. He didn't have to look to know it. He heard car doors slam. One. Then another.

At least two pursuers.

Probably armed.

Maybe with night vision goggles and long-range weapons.

That was more bad news, but it was also only speculation.

Angus had failed in his mission to kill Esme a couple of times. It was possible he wasn't nearly as well-versed in crime as his nephew.

He had found them, though. There was no doubt about that.

Ian wanted to know how.

He had a feeling it had something to do with Jake. The guy knew exactly how the Tactical K-9 Unit worked. He could have tapped into local databases and gotten a hit when Ian had checked Esme into the clinic. It would have been easy enough for him to pass that information on to Angus, and easier still for Angus to figure out that Esme would spend some time being interviewed by the local authorities.

After that, it was just a matter of waiting.

Anyone with enough money could hire people to do that.

Jake had the money.

That was what working both sides of the fence did for a person. It made him rich. It was possible it also made him foolish. If Jake were as smart as he liked to think he was, he'd have left the country when he'd disappeared months ago. At the time, the team had assumed he'd been abducted by Angus Dupree and that he would be used as a pawn to get Reginald out of jail.

It had taken months to uncover the truth. In that time, Jake could easily have found a way to disappear for good. Instead, he'd stuck around, searching—it seemed—for his ex-girlfriend, Penny Potter, and their son.

As far as the team knew, Jake was still on the Dupree payroll. If that was the case, he could be hunting Esme. For all Ian knew, Jake was in the car that had been following them. If he were, he'd be a more challenging adversary than Angus. He knew exactly how the team worked, exactly how the dogs responded and reacted. He'd be able to anticipate and act accordingly. He'd know that they'd have abandoned the vehicle and would be hiking out with their dogs. He'd also know what weapons they had and how much firepower. What dogs they had with them and what each was trained for.

He'd probably assume that they'd be heading for the safe house. That was protocol. Get the civilian to safety as quickly as possible.

Jake would know all that because he'd done it. He'd lived it. But if Anonymous was correct, Ian's theory was wrong and Jake wasn't anywhere nearby. He was on his way home with his ex and their son.

That could mean Montana or something else, but it sure didn't seem to mean Florida.

He hoped.

Prayed.

They had enough on their plate. They didn't need to add Jake into the mix.

He glanced at his watch and adjusted their trajectory, making sure they were heading southeast. Toward the Everglades. The FBI had a house there. It hadn't been used in several years because it was too far from the nearest city. Most people didn't enjoy staying in such a remote location. Even if they were in hiding. At least that was what Max had said.

It was perfect for their purposes, though.

Ian wanted a place that was isolated. He wanted clear views and an easy escape route. Max had already arranged to have a small boat with an outboard motor delivered. If Jake or Angus managed to find them, they could escape into the Everglades.

First, though, they had to get to the house.

Up ahead, several trees jutted up from the soggy earth, their branches thick, their trunks broad. He moved between them, keeping Esme close. If there were snipers in the car, she was their target.

King growled, the sound filling the uneasy silence.

Danger. That was what the dog was trying to say.

Ian heard him loud and clear.

"Get down," he commanded, yanking Esme off her feet, covering her with his body. The first bullet hit the tree an inch from their heads.

She jerked, but he pressed her deeper into the earth as the second bullet struck, this time slamming into the ground, releasing bits of dirt and splatters of mud.

King was crouched beside them, and he growled again, his gaze on the area they'd just left.

"We're out of range for our handguns," Zeke whispered. "But I'm going to take a couple of shots and give you cover to move. There's a ravine straight ahead. They shouldn't be able to see you once you're in it. I'll circle around. Try to get a look at the perps. If the police show up, I'll deal with them."

He fired the first shot almost before he finished speaking, the loud report ringing through the night.

"Let's go," Ian said, rolling off Esme. "On your belly all the way. Keep the trees between you and the SUV. Don't stop until I tell you to."

"You mean between me and the gun?" she asked, sliding across the damp earth, her dark clothes blending in with the ground.

He followed, calling to King and smiling grimly as the dog pranced past. Zeke fired two more rounds, the sound masking what Ian thought was the sound of an engine firing up.

Were the perps on the run?

He didn't glance back to see.

He was focused instead on getting to the ravine and lowering himself into it, because Esme had disappeared somewhere up ahead, and he could only assume that was where she'd gone.

She might be out of sight of the gunmen, but she was also out of Ian's sight.

He didn't like that.

Not at all.

The ornery woman wanted to go it alone. She'd planned to hide until the trial. Without the protection of the team. She'd told him that. This had been the perfect opportunity for her to escape protective custody, and he'd handed it right to her.

He reached the edge of the ravine, lowering himself down and calling himself every kind of fool for letting Esme go ahead of him.

# NINE

Esme's feet had hit the bottom of the marshy ravine, and she'd started running. Without thought. Without a plan. Just going as fast as she could toward some unknown destination, fleeing the gunshots, the car and, probably, Ian.

He'd been offering the protection she longed for, the security she craved. He'd given her comfort and smiles and, even, a laugh or two.

He'd been a port in the storm, a place to hunker down while the wind of Angus's wrath was raging around her.

But he wasn't a forever kind of thing.

He was a stopgap, a hero who'd run to the rescue when she'd needed him but who'd walk away when this was over and leave her exactly where she'd been when they'd met—alone.

Which was fine.

She liked solitude.

She enjoyed silence.

She didn't mind her own company.

And she certainly didn't want to be with someone just to fill a hole in her life.

Brent had taught her a lot about what she needed and what she didn't. She hoped that she'd learned the lessons well.

Time would tell.

Time that wasn't filled with running for her life.

The marshy ground grew wetter, her feet splashing in a quarter inch of water. She needed to get out before she found herself in a creek or tributary up to her ankles or knees or shoulders. Wading through muck and dodging slithering, snapping, slimy reptiles.

She scrambled up the far side, feet digging into loose earth, hands grasping thick blades of grass. She was breathless when she reached the top, covered in dirt and mud. The sleeves of Ian's jacket hung past her fingertips, and she shoved them up, still moving fast. If she took off the jacket, she could leave it for King to find. That would let Ian know which direction she'd been headed, because she wasn't trying to outrun him or King or Zeke. She was trying to outrun the men who wanted her dead. If Ian and King found her, great. If not, maybe she'd find them.

For now, though, she was doing what she'd been told—running until Ian told her to stop.

She shivered, her teeth chattering. Strange because the night was balmy and warm. She knew that. She could feel the sticky, humid air kissing her cheeks, could glimpse the clear sky and the moon resting just above the western horizon. The landscape was flat enough for her to see the distant flashing lights of emergency vehicles.

The police were on the way. It was possible they'd already reached the SUV and were rounding up whoever had been in the car. It was possible Uncle Angus was being arrested and that he'd be tossed in jail where he belonged.

Anything was possible, but she didn't think either of those things were likely. Angus had proved himself to be wily as a fox, moving mostly in the dead of the night, slipping in and then out without a sound.

Her uncle hired people to do the less subtle things—driving through clinic windows, shootouts in swamps. *He* liked darkness and enjoyed terrorizing people.

At least, that was the impression she'd gotten these past few months.

Her foot caught on a tangled web of marsh grass, and she went flying, landing hard on her hands and knees, her arms skidding in one direction, her legs in another.

She hit the ground with a thud, would have been up and running again, but a wet nose nudged her temple, warm dog breath fanning her cheek.

She looked into dark eyes, and then into King's grinning happy face.

His tongue lolled to the side, his eyes sparkling with what could only be joy. He'd found her, and he was very pleased with himself.

If she hadn't been lying flat on wet ground, the scent of decaying foliage in her nose, she might have smiled back.

"You don't have to look so pleased with yourself every single time. I'm not very difficult to find," she explained, but King had already darted away, heading back to his partner, tail high, carriage jaunty.

He was pleased with himself and ready to share the happy news of his discovery.

She could have gotten up and kept going, but she had as much hope of survival with Ian as she did on her own. More hope, because he had a gun. She had her mud-caked clothes and her will to live. Neither would stand much of a chance against a well-aimed bullet. Esme turned onto her back, staring up at the stars and the dark sky, her ankle throbbing dully. She didn't know what time it was...and she didn't care. In a few hours, the sun would rise, and she'd be facing another day of hide-and-seek. Winner took all. Loser lost everything. If Angus lost, he'd go to jail. If she lost, she'd die and her brother might go free. There'd be more crime, more drugs, more human trafficking and sorrow and terror and fear.

It was that simple and that awful. It was the reason she'd kept going for as long as she had. It was the reason she'd agreed to testify, and the reason why she wouldn't change her mind.

But right now, she really couldn't get up the gumption to care about any of it. She lay where she was, watching the night sky, thinking about how nice it would be if her life went back to normal, if she could simply close her eyes and open them and realize she'd been having some horrible dream.

The grass beside her rustled, and Ian was there, looming over her. She closed her eyes. Opened them again. Nothing had changed. Except that now he was crouched beside her. Not touching. Not talking. Just waiting, his eyes glittering in the darkness, King panting nearby.

"I wasn't trying to escape you," she explained. "I was just following orders. I guess running into the Everglades without any idea of where I was going wasn't the best idea I've ever had. I should have stopped at the bottom of the ravine and waited for you. I don't know why I didn't."

"Fear does funny things to people, Esme," he

said, offering a hand and pulling her to her feet. "How's your ankle holding up?"

"It's fine," she said, ignoring the throbbing pain as she walked beside him.

"*Fine* is the word most people use when they think the other person doesn't really care. For the record—" he stopped and turned to face her, tugging his jacket tighter around her and zipping it "—I care."

"It hurts," she corrected. "But I can walk on it."

"You never got the Ace bandage."

"We were distracted by the truck that drove through the window."

"Right. It's been a busy night." He started walking again, his hand on her elbow as he helped her through the thick grass. She didn't mind that. Not at all.

"Once we get to the safe house," he said, his voice a quiet rumble on the balmy air, "I'm going to let you call your sister. You can ask her about Jake or not. I'm not going to put pressure on you either way."

"I'll ask her," she said, because it couldn't hurt, and it might help.

"Is there anyone else you'd like to talk with?"

"No one important enough to risk my life for."

"Not even your fiancé?" he asked.

"Are you fishing for information?"

"Not fishing. I'm out-and-out asking. According to your file, you're engaged."

"My file is wrong."

"Let me guess, he wasn't ready to marry you, but he didn't want to wait for you to be out of the program?"

"Something like that," she responded. "It's old news, though. I've been over it for a while."

"He was an idiot," he said, and she smiled.

"According to him, I was. He didn't want me to testify. He thought I was asking for trouble. He told me Reginald and Angus were dangerous, and that he didn't want me to get hurt."

"Then he should have married you and entered witness protection with you to make certain you were safe."

"He's not much of a fighter."

"Not much of a man, if you ask me. As a matter of fact, if he was standing here, I'd call him a coward," he said bluntly.

"I guess he was, and he obviously didn't love me all that much. We had the whole wedding planned and paid for. I really thought he was going to be my forever. I was wrong."

"I'd like to say I'm sorry," he said softly. "But that would be a lie."

She could have asked him what he meant.

Should have, probably, but this thing between them? It seemed new and fragile and lovely, and she didn't want to ruin it by asking questions that would be answered in their own good time.

They'd reached a steeply sloping hill that led down to what looked like swamp—dark water snaking through thick foliage.

"Careful here. It's slippery," he said, his hand tightening fractionally as he helped her navigate the slick landscape. "You don't want to end up gator food. Fall into the swamp, and that could happen."

"Maybe we should head in another direction," she suggested nervously.

"If we do that, we'll never make it to the safe house."

"It's in the Glades?"

"Does that make you nervous?"

"I spent a few too many days alone there. I'm not all that excited about repeating the experience."

"You won't have to. I'll be there with two other team members and their dogs."

"Sounds cozy."

"It will be safe."

"That, too." Her foot slipped, and she'd have gone down if he hadn't dragged her back.

"Like I said," he murmured, "it's slippery."

"Any idea of how far we are from the safe house?"

"Too far to walk. One of my teammates is

meeting us on the road about a mile from here. See that bridge?" He put his hands on her shoulders and turned her slightly, his forearm brushing her cheek as he pointed.

She'd probably have seen whatever he was pointing at if her heart hadn't been beating so fast, her pulse racing with something that had nothing to do with crocodiles or Uncle Angus or her near slide into the murky water and everything to do with Ian.

"She'll be right on the other side of it," he continued. "She'll pick us up there."

They'd reached the bottom of the hill, the pungent smell of the swamp filling her nose.

She could see lights in the distance, flashing rhythmically. Was it too much to hope that Angus had been in the car and that he'd been caught by the police?

"Maybe they caught Angus." She spoke the thought aloud, and he shook his head.

"Whoever was in the car drove away before the police arrived."

"You're well-informed."

He shrugged. "Zeke headed back to talk to Deputy Sheriff Sinclair and to retrieve the SUV. He sent a text before I caught up to you."

"You guys work fast."

"We've been doing this a long time," he replied. "That means we've got a system, protocol, things that we prepare for."

"If you're trying to make a point, you can just go ahead and spell it out for me."

"Once we get in my coworker's vehicle and head for the safe house, your days of calling the shots are going to have to be over."

"I told you, I wasn't trying to escape," she started to explain.

"That's not why I'm saying this. You've been in witness protection. Being in a safe house is different. You'll be housebound for most of the next month. If the trial date is extended, it'll be longer."

"I understand that."

"Good, and I hope you'll understand when I tell you that my team expects your complete obedience to the rules."

"The term *obedience* seems a little...archaic."

"It can seem like anything, but we're still going to expect it. Following the rules will keep you alive. Breaking them could get you killed. Before we get in the car and make the trip to the safe house, before the team and I agree to play bodyguard for the next month, we need to know that we have your complete cooperation."

"You do," she said and meant it.

"Really?" He raised a dark eyebrow, and she shrugged.

"Yes."

"That was a lot easier than I thought it would be."

"Dying young is cliché. I'd rather live awhile."

He smiled. "Good to know. Come on. We need to get moving."

He took her hand, and she didn't pull away.

She wanted this moment of quiet, of walking beside a man who seemed willing to risk everything for her. She'd think about what it meant later. She'd mull over his words, wonder about his answers, ask herself if she were reading something into nothing.

Later.

Right now, she was content to let things be what they were—walking hand in hand through the moonlit swamp, King prancing along beside them.

The moon had sunk even lower on the horizon, the swamp creatures slithering just out of sight. Nothing had changed. Her uncle still wanted her dead. Her brother was still a murderer. Her sister was angry, and her friends probably thought she was dead. Her business was being run by employees, and she didn't know what would be left of it when she returned.

There'd be no wedding, no marriage, no children, because Brent was exactly what Ian had said—a coward.

Yeah. Nothing had changed.

But some of what had stayed was good: God was still on His throne. The sun would eventually rise. Life would go on for as long as it did.

And she wasn't alone.

She had a team of people working to keep her safe. She had a dog prancing along beside her.

And she had Ian.

Somehow that made her feel better than anything had in a very long time.

It took longer to reach the road than Ian had anticipated, the wet spring and summer creating boggy terrain that made walking difficult.

An hour into the walk and Esme was visibly slowing, her limp more pronounced with each step. Julianne had already texted twice, asking for updates on their location and ETA.

She was clearly worried.

The safe house location couldn't be compromised, and sitting on the side of the road waiting for Ian and Esme to emerge was going to attract attention.

Or so she kept saying.

Ian knew she was right, but he couldn't push any harder than he was.

"So," Esme panted as she pulled her foot out of thick mud and managed another struggling step, "how much farther?"

"Not much."

"You said that a half hour ago."

He gave her an apologetic look. "I didn't realize how tough the terrain would be."

"It doesn't seem to be bothering King," she said. "Or you."

"We're used to hiking through stuff like this."

"This happens a lot?"

"No, but we run training exercises with the team. We don't make it easy. If you're going to be part of the tactical unit, you've got to be ready for just about anything."

"Sounds like wedding planning. But more dangerous," she joked, but her voice was flat and hollow, her fatigue obvious.

"Want to take a break?" he suggested. "My colleague can walk in and meet us here."

"What good would that do? I'd still have to walk out."

"Julianne is good at improvising," he told her. "We might be able to create a gurney of some—"

"No." She said it emphatically.

"You didn't let me finish."

"Because you were going to suggest that the two of you carry me out, and it's not going to happen."

"It's okay to admit when we're done in, Esme."

She shot him a glare. "It's also okay to admit

when you aren't making a situation better, Ian," she responded, and he laughed.

He couldn't help himself.

Esme was different. Refreshing. Totally and uniquely herself.

"Well," she huffed, "it's true."

"I apologize. I was trying to give you options. Not annoy you."

"Everything is annoying me. The bugs, the mud, the horrible smell."

"Yeah. The swamp does have a unique odor."

"I was talking about me," she said, and he laughed again.

"I'm serious," she muttered. "I smell like bug spray and swamp mud with a hint of cake batter."

"More like vanilla and whipped cream," he responded, and she smiled.

"You're a funny guy, Ian, but we both know I've rolled in the muck one too many times today. I want a hot shower and clean clothes and a comfortable bed. I want to lie down and not have to worry that I'll open my eyes and see Angus."

"You'll have all of that soon."

"If I don't collapse from exhaustion first," she replied, limping along beside him. Despite her joking complaints, she'd had a good attitude about the long walk. She'd asked questions about King and about the training program they used for their working dogs. She'd asked how he'd gotten into police work and what his father would have thought about his work with the FBI. He'd answered because she'd seemed sincerely interested.

It felt oddly good to be with Esme. Despite the circumstances, despite her family name, despite all the things that should keep him from being attracted to her, he was.

"We really can take a break," he said, and she shot him a scathing look, but there was humor in her eyes.

"I think I explained my need for a hot shower and a comfortable bed. Taking a break isn't going to get me any of those things."

"It's possible King needs a break," he offered, and she snorted.

"King could probably walk for days and not get tired."

Hearing his name, the Malinois trotted closer, bumping Esme's hand with his nose the way he did when he wanted attention.

She scratched behind his ears. "You're a good dog, King. If I ever get my first puppy, I hope he turns out like you."

"You've never had a dog?"

"We traveled too much when I was a kid, and

now that I'm an adult, life is busy. Brent and I were planning to get one, though. I do a lot of my work from home. I just needed a home with a fence and a yard. We planned to get that, too."

"There are plenty of dogs that do well in apartments, Esme. If you really want one, I can help you choose one after this is over."

"A few hours ago, I'd have said no. Brent was really the one who wanted the dog. I was mostly on the fence about it. My sister has a little yappy dog that hates my guts. I'm not so keen on it, either, so I figured I wasn't a dog person. Now that I've met King, I can see the appeal. They're good companions. If I'm going to be a lonely old maid, I might as well have some pets to spend time with."

"Old maid?"

"Cat lady?"

"I doubt you'll be either of those things."

"I'm certainly not going to be married. I already spent my wedding savings on the wedding that wasn't." She patted King again, and Ian could see her hand shaking. She didn't want to stop, and he wasn't going to force her to, but maybe he could distract her from the arduous walk.

"When this is over, I can help you choose a puppy."

"You're assuming we'll be living somewhere close to each other."

"There are planes, trains, automobiles."

"There are also a million dreams that never come true, and if I let myself think about getting through this, of coming out on the other side of it with a house and a business and a friend and a dog…" She shrugged.

"What's the worst that could happen if you believed that?"

"I might be really disappointed if it didn't happen. I've been through enough disappointment recently. I'm not up to facing another."

"I won't disappoint you, Esme," he said, the words pouring out before he could think them through. The promises right on the tip of his tongue.

Promises about being there for her, about helping her as she transitioned into whatever life she was going to create.

He might have said more.

He probably would have, but the soft hum of an engine broke the stillness.

Not a car or truck.

This sounded more like a bi-engine plane.

Which could mean nothing, or it could mean something.

Angus or his henchmen had driven away, but that didn't mean they'd given up.

He grabbed Esme's hand, pulling her with him as he sprinted toward the road.

# TEN

She lost a boot and sock somewhere in the muck, but she made it to the road with one bare foot, a throbbing ankle and absolutely no breath in her lungs.

Esme would have stopped the minute her bare foot hit hard pavement. She would have stood for a couple of minutes, gasping and coughing and trying to catch her breath, but Ian was dragging her along as he sprinted up the road.

She knew what they were running from.

She could see the plane.

Worse, she could see its searchlight, aimed at the ground and highlighting the swamp and the marsh grass.

How far away was it?

A mile? Less?

They needed to reach shelter before it reached them. Otherwise…

She wasn't going to think about that.

Nope, instead she was just going to keep running, her hand in Ian's, King sticking so close to her side she knew that he sensed danger.

He barked. Once. High and quick, and then he shot forward, bounding over a small hill and disappearing.

Seconds later, he reappeared, another dog running beside him. A hound of some sort. She could hear it baying over the frantic slush of her pulse.

Her legs burned, her lungs ached, but she couldn't feel the pain in her ankle.

That was good.

What would be better was outrunning the plane.

It seemed to be heading toward them, swooping low over the marshy land they'd just left.

Were there footprints?

Was that what the spotlight was revealing?

"We're almost there," Ian said.

He wasn't even out of breath.

"Just so you know, when I get back home," she panted, "I'm going to train sprint runs. That way the next time a plane comes after me, I'll have a chance."

Her words were drowned out by the frantic baying and barking of the dogs, the drone of the airplane engines and the sound of a car motor.

Headlights flashed at the top of the hill.

There. Then gone.

Her imagination?

She wasn't sure, but Ian didn't seem concerned, he was heading straight for them, still running, still holding her hand.

The dogs met them halfway up the hill, the hound bounding excitedly, its vest glowing in the darkness.

A working dog.

A team member?

It had to be. Anything else would be too much of a coincidence.

Julianne's dog. That made sense, and so did the small SUV cresting the hill, idling there. No light, just gleaming paint in the fading moonlight.

It probably took only seconds to reach the car. It felt like a lifetime, everything moving in slow motion. The plane. The dogs. Esme's legs.

The door opened as they approached, and a woman hopped out. Tall, muscular, quick.

Those were the impressions Esme had before the woman grabbed her arm, ushered her into the back of the vehicle.

The hound hopped in after her, scrambling for position as the door slammed shut.

And they were off. Pulling a quick U-turn and speeding down the other side of the hill.

Which would have been great.

Except that Ian wasn't with them. Neither was King.

"What's going on?" Esme demanded. Or tried to. Her voice rasped out, her lungs still heaving from the run.

"I'm taking you to the safe house," the woman responded.

"Where's Ian?"

"Throwing them off our tail."

"What does that mean?"

"It means that we don't want the airplane following us. Ian is going to make sure that if it's a search plane looking for you, whoever is flying it will think you're still running. At least—" she glanced in the rearview mirror and met Esme's eyes "—that's what I'm assuming the plan is. Ian and I didn't have much time to discuss it."

"More like you didn't have *any* time."

"True. He signaled me to take you and go. So I did. I'm Julianne Martinez, by the way. Special agent, but I'm not big into titles. The dog is Thunder."

"He's cute."

"And loud?"

"That, too."

"I know! But it's useful when he's indicating. He's an evidence detection dog, and he likes to let us know when he's found something. He was very happy when he found you. He loves new friends."

Obviously, because he was nearly sitting in Esme's lap, looking at her expectantly.

"Usually, I crate him in the back," Julianne continued. "This is a rental, so I don't have that luxury. If he becomes a pest, just tell him no."

"Okay. Thanks," Esme responded by rote, but her mind wasn't on the conversation. It was on Ian, King and the plane. "They could have guns," she said, voicing the concern out loud. "They probably do."

"Ian can handle whatever they dish out. Don't worry about him."

"That's easier said than done," she muttered.

"Yeah. I know." She sounded like she did know. Like maybe there was a story hidden in the matter-of-fact reply.

She didn't give Esme a chance to ask for details.

"Do me a favor," she said. "Duck real low in the seat. We're going through a populated area. I don't want anyone to see you."

"Who'd be looking at this time of night?" she asked, but she did what she was told, pressing her chin to her knees, the scent of wet earth drifting up from her mud-coated feet.

One booted.

One bare.

She studied both, her back aching from the odd position.

She didn't straighten.

She'd told Ian that she'd cooperate, that she'd follow directions and do exactly what she was told. She'd meant it.

Esme desperately wanted to get through this alive, and she'd really like everyone else to get through it the same way.

"You doing okay back there?" Julianne called.

"Fine."

"Just a couple more minutes. This is kind of a shanty town, but there are definitely people around."

"And you think one of them is in my uncle's pocket?"

"I don't like to speculate, so how about I just tell you what I know? Your uncle and brother have been running drugs and people through the airport here for several years. They've made connections in the surrounding area, and they have several people on their payroll." She took a breath. "It wouldn't surprise me if Angus put out the word that you need to be found and stopped, and it wouldn't shock me if one of the people living in this little town was very happy and willing to make that happen."

"Nice."

"No. It's not. None of what my team deals

with is nice, but that's why we do it. We want to stop people like your uncle from hurting and corrupting others."

"It's hard to be corrupted unless you want to be," Esme pointed out.

"Some people think that. I think that it's easy to fall into the wrong crowd when the wrong crowd is all you know. Angus and Reginald take advantage of that. They go after people who are already struggling, and they offer them a way out of poverty. Of course, the people who accept the offer don't realize they're selling themselves into modern slavery. They make money, but they're always beholden to the boss. If they try to break away, they die."

"It sounds like the Mafia," Esme said, sick at the thought of what her brother and uncle had created, disgusted by the image of an organization that fed off others, one that ate and ate but was never full.

"It *is* like the Mafia. I've heard a criminal profiler speculate that your brother was obsessed with the mob as a child, that he had a sense of helplessness brought on by your father's—"

"My father was a really great guy," she snapped and then was ashamed of herself for doing it.

None of this was Julianne's fault.

"I'm sorry," Julianne said. "I didn't mean to

imply he wasn't. The profiler simply said that your father wasn't the kind of strong powerful man the Godfather represented and that your brother wanted to be what your dad was not."

"Or maybe," Esme said, the words tight and controlled, "Reginald was influenced by my uncle. Maybe he just wanted more than what he had. Maybe he didn't care who he hurt in his bid to get what he wanted."

"You're upset."

"This is my family we're talking about, Julianne. And I still can't believe they're such horrible people."

"The world isn't black-and-white. There are shades of gray. Your brother might be a murderer and a criminal, but he helped your sister a lot. That's something you can hold on to."

"He murdered a man in cold blood. He killed two people who'd done nothing wrong. He runs an organization that makes its money off criminal activities, and he doesn't care who he has to hurt to get what he wants." She blew out an angry breath. "That's pretty horrible, and it's pretty black-and-white. Should I not hold on to it?"

"What about your sister? She hasn't gotten involved in the business. She might not be cooperating with us, but she certainly isn't killing people for profit."

The words were supposed to be comforting.

Esme knew they were.

She knew Julianne was trying to offer encouragement, trying to make her feel better.

But there was nothing that could do that.

Saying Violetta wasn't horrible because she hadn't killed was like saying a boa constrictor wasn't deadly because it didn't inject venom into its victim. Snakes were snakes. And Violetta seemed to be one of them.

Esme shuddered, staring out the side window, Thunder lying on the seat beside her, his back pressed up against her thigh. She touched his warm fur, felt the soft rise and fall of his ribs as he breathed.

"You can sit up now," Julianne said quietly. Nothing else. She probably thought she'd crossed a line, but she'd only really spoken the truth.

Esme could have told her that. If she could have made the words form. Her brain knew what to say. It knew how to be gracious and kind. It knew how to put people at ease.

Right now, though, Esme could only sit mutely, staring out the window, watching as the darkness flew by.

Ian finally reached the safe house at dawn.

He'd hitched a ride with Zeke after he'd led

the plane on a nice little joyride through marshy fields and swampland.

Eventually, the pilot had given up the chase. Either he'd realized that his quarry was really good at dodging the searchlight or he'd run out of fuel.

Either way, when he'd returned to the airport, the police had been waiting. They'd found an automatic rifle onboard. The pilot, a convicted felon who'd served ten years on drug charges, was arrested immediately. His passenger had an outstanding warrant, and he'd been taken into custody, as well.

Both were still being questioned.

Neither was talking.

That seemed to be the theme with the Dupree family's lackeys. They didn't talk. They were probably terrified of the consequences. A man who would murder family would murder anyone.

"This place looks interesting," Zeke said as he pulled the SUV under a double-wide carport. Julianne's rental was beside it.

The house did look interesting. Small. Purple. Standing on stilts that looked like a good hard wind would topple them.

"That's one word for it," Ian said, climbing out of the vehicle and stretching stiff muscles. He'd been going nonstop for days, and he was ready to crash. First, he needed to make sure that Esme was settled in and that the house was secure.

He opened the back hatch and released King, letting the dog explore the area as he did a circuit of the property.

Not much to see.

The front yard was mostly swamp scrub and mud. Beyond it, a small dock jutted into a deep green pool of everglade water. A canoe had been tied to a post, and he inspected it, checking for holes, life vests and supplies. Everything was where it needed to be, paddles sitting in the bow, life vests under the bench seats.

"How's it look?" a woman called, and he saw Julianne jog down stairs that led to the front door of the house.

"Good. Is this our emergency escape?"

"Yes. I'm hoping we don't need it, of course." She walked onto the deck, Thunder right behind her.

"Any trouble on the way here?"

"None. It was almost too easy."

"Meaning?"

"I don't know, Ian. I just don't feel comfortable here. The town we have to ride through to reach the property is probably owned by the Duprees. Someone there has probably noticed my bright shiny rental driving through. You think they aren't going to put two and two together?"

"Is there a reason why you think the Duprees own the town?"

"Crime. Drugs. Poverty. Do I need to say more?"

"I'll contact Max—"

"Already done. He's looking for another safe house while we speak. I want it somewhere less rural. We stick out like a sore thumb here."

Ian agreed. He didn't like the feel of the place any more than Julianne did.

"You guys having a party without me?" Zeke strode toward them, his dark eyes scanning the surroundings.

"No, but I'm thinking one of us better go inside and make sure Esme isn't planning another escape," Ian said, heading back across the dock.

"She's sleeping," Julianne informed him. "I made her shower, change and eat. She seemed upset when you didn't get in the SUV with us, and she was pacing around, asking me over and over again if I'd heard from you. I finally told her to take a nap. She did."

"You're sure?"

"As sure as I am about anything."

"You explained the rules to her when you arrived?"

"In detail. Shades closed. Windows locked. No walking outside without an escort. No phone calls, internet or contact with friends or family."

"Her response?"

"She didn't give me much of one. Just asked when I thought you'd be here."

There was a hint of something in the comment.

Curiosity maybe.

Ian made it a habit of keeping his private life private. He didn't enjoy sharing gossip about girlfriends or relationships, and he sure wasn't going to start sharing information now.

"I guess she'll be glad to know I've returned, but I'm not going to wake her. I'll shower, eat and get some shut-eye, too." He walked up wooden steps that led to a deck that wrapped around the house. King must have heard him. He bounded up the stairs, ears up, tail wagging.

To him, this was a new adventure. New place. New scents. New people.

To Ian, it was a nightmare.

Too much cover too close to the house.

Too many places Angus and his goons could hide.

He reached the front door and was about to open it when his cell phone rang. He glanced at it, frowning as he saw that the number was unlisted.

"Is that Max?" Zeke asked, stepping onto the deck behind him. "The sooner he finds us new digs, the happier I'll be."

"Me, too, but it's not him. The number isn't listed." He accepted the call, put the phone to his ear. "Hello?"

"Having fun in the swamp?" the caller said, the voice so familiar, Ian's heart jumped.

"Not as much fun as I'd be having if you were around, Jake."

Zeke stiffened, moving closer and leaning in to try to hear the conversation.

"You never liked me. Don't try to tell me that you did."

"I'm sure the feeling was mutual. Which is why I'm surprised that you're calling me and not your brother."

"Zeke needs to stay out of this. I don't want him hurt," Jake growled. "You have the woman. Esme Dupree."

"And?"

"Angus wants her."

"Sometimes we don't get what we want." He glanced at Zeke, nodding when the other agent took out his cell phone and started texting headquarters. Jake was probably using a prepaid cell phone, but it still might be possible to back-trace the signal. If Ian could keep him on long enough…

"He'd better get what he wants. If he doesn't, the team is going to pay for it."

"You think he can get close enough to any

of us to make that happen?" Ian said, cold with rage at the threat.

"He might not be able to, but I can. I know exactly how you work. I know where everyone is, and I know how to get close enough to take you down one by one until you give me what I want."

"I thought it was what Angus wanted."

"He wants her. I want my kid to survive. You produce the Dupree woman, because if you don't, he's sending someone after my son, and I'll be sending someone after you and the team."

"I doubt you have anything to worry about. Angus doesn't want to make you that unhappy. You've done a lot for his family over the years," Ian said, stalling for more time. Julianne had joined them, her brow furrowed as she read the texts that were going back and forth between team members.

"I've cut my ties with the organization. I think you know that. Angus doesn't like that I've gone rogue, and he plans to find my kid before I do. He's got more manpower and more money, and if he manages it, he'll make me pay. Unless I produce Esme Dupree. The team has her, I want her. Hand her over by tomorrow night, or someone is going to get hurt." His voice was stone cold, and Ian had no doubt he meant every word he said.

"You have a location for delivery?"

"There's an abandoned church near the rental where she was hiding. Bring her there by midnight."

"That's too soon."

"Too soon for you to come up with a plan to keep her safe, you mean? I'm not worried about that. I'm worried about my son. Midnight, Ian. I'm not playing around."

"You want to see your brother when we bring her? He's here. Part of the team protecting her."

Jake swore softly. Obviously, he hadn't realized his brother had been called in on protection detail.

"You come with the woman alone. If anyone else shows up, I'll kill her right in front of you. Understand?"

"You're saying you don't want to see Zeke?" Ian said, purposely prodding the bear.

"You don't seem to understand what's going on here," Jake said, every word clipped. "I don't want my brother hurt. I don't want you hurt. I don't want anyone on the team injured. I just want the woman."

"So she can be killed by her family?"

"So my son can live!" he roared.

That was it. He cut the connection, and Ian was left holding the silent phone to his ear.

"Did Dylan get it?" he asked, forcing a calmness into his voice that he didn't feel. The tech guru who worked with the team, Dylan O'Leary, was the go-to guy when it came to all things technical. If anyone could hack into a phone system and obtain GPS coordinates from a prepaid phone, he could.

As if in response, his phone buzzed, Dylan's number flashing across the screen.

He answered quickly. "Hello?"

"I got a quick trace for you. The cell signal on the prepaid you were communicating with was a hard capture, but I managed to find the signal tower that it was pinging from." As was his way, Dylan didn't waste time. "Looks like he's somewhere in Montana. Unfortunately, I can't give you anything more specific."

"Thanks, Dylan. That helps."

"Anything else you need?"

"Just an all-points to the team. Jake Morrow is on the move, and he's threatening to kill team members if we don't hand over Esme Dupree."

Dylan whistled softly. "He's crossing a line here."

"He crossed it a long time ago. If you're able to do anything else to pinpoint his location, let me know."

"I'll give it a shot."

Ian disconnected and met Zeke's eyes. "I'm sorry about this."

"Sorry about what? We're half brothers, remember? Jake and I barely know each other."

"For someone who doesn't know you, he seems really concerned about your well-being." He'd seemed worried about the team, too. In his own bizarre sociopathic way. "He doesn't want you anywhere near the church when I bring Esme there."

"As if we'd do that," Julianne scoffed, her dark eyes flashing.

"We wouldn't, but why not make him think we're complying?"

"I like the way you think," Zeke said. "Setting a trap for the guy who is trying to trap us. Jake is nowhere nearby, so Angus will probably show up at the drop place. We can take him down and end this."

"Let's run it by Max," Ian suggested. "See what he has to say. If he likes it, we'll move forward and come up with a plan."

"Anything is better than sitting around in this house, twiddling our thumbs and waiting for the boogeyman to come crawling out of the swamp." Julianne eyed the blackish water that stretched out behind the dock.

"I think you mean the swamp monster," Zeke suggested, opening the front door and waiting while Julianne walked through.

Both their dogs followed, rushing into the

house without invitations. When they weren't working, they were family, and they knew it.

The team was family.

All of them connected and committed.

The thought of any one of the members being hurt because of the Duprees left a hard knot in Ian's stomach and soul-deep fury in his heart.

He wouldn't allow Jake to follow through on his threat.

Of course, there was only one way to stop him: stop Angus Dupree and shut down the Dupree crime family forever.

# ELEVEN

Julianne and Zeke left the safe house at 9:45 p.m.

Esme didn't know exactly what they were doing, but she was certain it had something to do with her. Julianne had compared their height, commented that she'd pass for Esme only if Angus was blind and stupid, then strapped on a gun, pulled on a jacket and strode out the door.

That had been three hours ago.

They still hadn't returned, and Ian was pacing the little house like a caged animal, moving back and forth across the living room, checking his cell phone, doing everything but walking outside and shouting for God to give him some answers.

"I'm sure they'll contact you as soon as they finish doing whatever it is they're doing," she finally said, and he turned to face her.

He'd showered and changed, shaved and napped.

She knew all those things because Julianne

had seemed determined to keep Esme informed of everything except her plans for the night. She also knew that he was angry. She could see it in the tautness of his muscles, the tightness of his jaw.

"This is about my uncle, isn't it? He's causing more trouble."

"Your uncle wants us to turn you over to him tonight. If we don't, there's been threats made against team members."

"What kind of threats?"

"The normal, everyday someone-is-going-to-die threats," he gritted out, crossing the room and sitting down beside her.

She'd chosen the couch. It was the only piece of furniture in the room that wasn't covered in psychedelic fabric. The armchair was lime green and bright pink stripes. The love seat was robin egg blue with huge yellow and purple flowers.

The sofa was a muted ivory that was surprisingly clean and soft. She'd sat there because it had reminded her of her old life—of weddings and brides and dresses.

She wasn't sure why Ian chose it. There were plenty of other places to sit. She liked him there, though. She wasn't going to lie. It felt good to have his warm arm pressed against her shoulder. It felt good to not be alone.

He lifted her hand, frowning at the scratches

that marred her palm. "I didn't realize you'd gotten hurt when you fell last night."

He traced a line from her palm to her wrist, his fingers warm on her cool skin. Heat shot through her, and she almost pulled away, but this was Ian, and being near him felt like being home—so right, so wonderful that she couldn't imagine ever wanting to be anywhere else.

"I got hurt when I realized what my family was. I didn't even feel the scratches," she admitted.

He studied her face. Not speaking for such a long time, she was tempted to fill the silence, to beg forgiveness for all the trouble her family had caused, all the people who had been hurt because of them.

"When I took this assignment," he finally said, "I wasn't expecting to like you."

"I got that impression," she admitted, and he smiled.

"Yeah, I know. I'm sorry about that. I'm also sorry that we didn't apprehend Angus before he got to you." He touched the side of her neck, sliding his finger along what she knew were the fading bruises her uncle had left. She resisted the urge to lean closer, to let her fingers slide into his hair.

"It's not anyone's fault. He's got a lot of

money, and he likes to hire people to do his dirty work."

"I'm hoping he's planning to do his own work tonight."

"You think he'll show up?"

"I don't know. Julianne and Zeke are prepared for it. We went over all the variables."

"Are you upset because you had to stay here and guard me?" she asked softly.

"I'm upset that you have to go through this. I'm upset that Jake Morrow and Angus Dupree are wandering free while we hide in this house. I'm not upset about guarding you. I told you before, Esme, I'll keep doing it as long as it's necessary."

"Don't say that. It might be necessary forever," she cautioned with a laugh that sounded a little too loud and a little too phony.

"That's an interesting thought," he responded. "How about we revisit it after this is over?"

"You're kidding, right?"

"Why would I be?"

"Because I'm a Dupree and you're trying to bring down my entire family?" she said, her mouth dry with something that felt a lot like nerves.

"I'm going after criminals, Esme. You're not one of them. I'm not going to lie. That wasn't my mind-set when we met. You were the last assignment I wanted to take. My boss had other plans." He shrugged. "Or, maybe, God did."

"Probably God did," she said, and he smiled.

"My father would agree."

"You don't?"

"If you'd asked me a week ago, I'd have said I didn't know. It's tough to see God in things that make us unhappy. Now…" He shook his head. "I can't deny that I see Him working. Getting to know you has mended something in me that I didn't know was broken. Revenge tastes sweet when you're first going after it, but it turns bitter in the end. I'm glad God didn't let me get that far down the path."

"My uncle and brother need to pay for what they did."

"They do. But there's a difference between revenge and justice. Spending time with you has clarified that for me." He brushed a few strands of hair from her forehead, cocking his head to the side, studying her again.

"You cleaned up your haircut, didn't you?" he finally asked.

"Julianne helped me."

"She did a good job. Next time, I'll drive you to the hairdressers instead of helping you with the scissors."

"You're planning a lot of things for a future we may not have."

"We're going to have a future, and I have a feeling we're going to be spending a lot of it together." He ran his knuckles down her cheek, looked so deeply into her eyes, she thought he might be seeing her soul.

Her hand moved of its own accord, her palm sliding along the warm column of his neck, her fingers smoothing the silky strands of his hair.

He didn't pull back, didn't tell her to stop, didn't list a dozen reasons why it wasn't appropriate for them to be sitting the way they were. He just looked into her eyes and into her heart, and she looked into his, seeing things that she hadn't expected. Attraction. Interest. Compassion.

His cell phone buzzed, and she jerked back, the sound like a splash of ice water in her face.

He glanced down at his phone screen, frowning as he read the text.

"What's wrong?"

"Things didn't go down the way we'd hoped. Angus sent three men to the church. There was a shoot-out. All three are dead."

"What about Zeke and Julianne?"

"Zeke was hit. Doesn't sound like a serious injury, but Julianne is accompanying him to the hospital."

"And Angus is still on the loose." She said

what they were both thinking, named the thing neither of them wanted.

"Right." He bit out the answer, his eyes flashing with banked fury.

She wanted to offer words of comfort. She wanted to tell him that Angus would be caught. She wanted to say that justice would be served, and that God would bring them all through this safely.

She wanted to say a dozen things that she hoped would be true, but he was moving across the room, dialing a number, talking to someone, each word a hard staccato beat.

King walked next to him, whining softly in response to the wild energy that suddenly seemed to fill the room, and Esme was redundant—an extra in a drama she should have had no part in.

She stood, limping across the living room and down a narrow hall. Her room was at the end, a single door that opened into a plum-colored boxy space. The bed sat in the middle, a peacock blue comforter clashing with the walls. She turned off the light, let the darkness hide the garish decor.

She could still hear Ian, his voice drifting through the closed door. She thought she heard him talking about a new plan. One that involved Jake Morrow.

She didn't leave the room and ask him to clarify.

He was busy. Doing what he was paid to do. Protecting civilians from criminals like Angus.

She shuddered, pulling the pillow over her eyes, pressing it hard against lids that seemed to want to let tears seep out. She prayed for Zeke, that his injury really was minor and that he'd recover quickly. For Ian, Julianne and the rest of the team.

And then she prayed for her family. Prayed that Violetta would do the right thing, and that Angus and Reginald would pay for their crimes.

When she finished, she lay still, the house settling around her, Ian's voice silent, the only sound the soft lap of wind against the windows and the rhythmic click of King's claws as he walked from room to room, waiting for danger that Esme hoped would never come.

Zeke and Julianne arrived at the house an hour before dawn.

Neither of them looked happy.

Ian wasn't happy, either. The thick bandage that peeked out from under the short sleeve of Zeke's shirt was a stark reminder of just how bad the mission had gone.

Three gunmen dead. One federal officer injured.

And no sign of Angus.

He was out there, though.

Haunting the streets, waiting for news and for an opportunity to strike again.

"How's the shoulder?" Ian asked as Zeke dropped into the gaudy recliner.

"It would be better if I didn't have a bullet hole in it."

"Don't exaggerate," Julianne chided. "It barely grazed you."

"Tell that to my shoulder. Maybe it will stop throbbing."

"They offered you pain meds," she chided.

"I'm on duty."

"I can call Max and ask him to send someone else," Ian offered, and Zeke scowled.

"Don't even think about it. This—" he poked at the bandage "—has made things a lot more personal."

"Did we get an ID on any of the gunmen?" Ian asked.

"Locals," Julianne replied. "The deputy sheriff knew all three by sight."

"I guess you were right about the Duprees owning this town." Zeke stood and walked into the kitchen, opening the fridge and surveying its contents. "Eggs, anyone?"

"Are you cooking?" Ian asked.

"Only if I have to. The arm is a little sore."

"I'll take care of it." Ian needed to do something. Beating eggs seemed a whole lot less violent than beating Angus to a bloody pulp.

He frowned as he poured the eggs into a hot pan.

Justice. Not revenge.

But it was hard to keep that in mind when a guy like Angus was out there.

His cell buzzed, and he pulled it out, glancing at the text as he spooned cooked eggs onto plates. It was from Dylan, the message making Ian's pulse race.

Max has been injured. Shot while he was walking his dog. Should be fine. He'll call once he's been triaged.

Julianne and Zeke must have received the same text.

They were moving toward him, phones in hand, looks of shock and outrage on their faces.

"Jake," Ian said. Just that. They knew. He knew.

No one else could have done this. No one else would have.

"I thought maybe he was yanking our chains, trying to get his way, but he really did mean he was going to pick us off one by one if we didn't hand Esme over." Zeke sounded as furious as Ian felt.

"He acted quickly. Didn't even wait a few hours. He must have gotten a call from Angus and gone after the closest team member," Ian said.

"Which means he's hanging out somewhere close to headquarters." Julianne frowned. "He's brazen."

"He's a fool," Ian corrected darkly. "He thinks he's too smart and too fast to be caught."

"So far, he's been right." Zeke smoothed down the edge of his bandage and grabbed a plate of eggs. He shoveled in a mouthful as he eyed the message.

"He's been right because he's been lying low. Now that he's showing himself more, we should be able to catch him," Ian responded.

"Catch him. Catch Angus. Go back to our regularly scheduled program," Julianne agreed.

Ian's phone rang. He glanced at the number.

Unlisted.

Again.

And he knew exactly who it was.

He answered, every bit of the rage he felt seeping into his voice. "What do you want, Jake?"

"Esme Dupree. I told you that. Apparently, you weren't listening."

"I listened. Now it's your turn. You're going down for this, Morrow. I'm going to make certain of it."

"You'll have to find me first, and that's proved really difficult for you and the team. So how about we call a truce? You promise me the woman, and I stop shooting at team members."

"How about you jump off the nearest—"

Julianne snatched the phone from his hand, putting it on speakerphone.

"Jake?" she said, her voice a lot calmer than Ian's had been. "It's Julianne. I think you know the team never makes deals with criminals. Back off and give us space to do our job. We'll protect your son, if you don't get in our way."

"Like you protected Max?" he said with a snide laugh that made Ian's blood run cold.

"I was shot tonight, bro," Zeke said angrily. "Going after the goons your friend hired. How do you feel about that?"

"I told you to stay away. I warned you. Angus doesn't care who he kills."

"It doesn't seem like you do, either," Ian pointed out.

"You're wrong. I have to make tough choices. I got in deeper than I planned. Maybe I underestimated how much of a hold Reginald and Angus had on me, but that doesn't mean I want to do what I'm doing. This is for my son. If people have to die to keep him safe, so be it."

"Not just people, bro," Zeke snapped. "Family. That's what this team is. It's what we were supposed to be."

"I tried to protect you, Zeke. I warned you, and that shot at Max? I could have killed him if I'd wanted to. Consider his injury a warning. Next time, I won't miss. I'll be in touch soon, and I'll let you know where the next rendezvous will happen." He disconnected, the sudden silence heavy with tension.

"He needs to be stopped," Julianne muttered, pulling out her phone and punching in the number for headquarters.

She was calling Dylan.

Ian was certain of that.

Good. He didn't want to talk to anyone.

Not yet.

He needed to collect his thoughts and get himself focused. Two team members had been shot in one night. The situation with the Duprees was escalating. Angus was becoming more desperate. It wasn't just the team and Esme whose lives were at risk. Jake's son and ex-girlfriend might also be in trouble.

He'd let Julianne talk to Dylan, see how Max was and inform the team of the danger. Ian would stick to the plan and follow protocol. It was time to patrol the property.

He called King. The dog came immediately, ready to work or to play. Whichever Ian chose.

For now, they'd just walk, skirting the perimeter of the property, checking to be sure no one was lurking in the shadows.

Praying that maybe someone was.

Angus would be a good find. Bringing him in would be the culmination of months of hard work and years of planning.

A decade.

That was how long Ian had been waiting to bring the Duprees down.

He didn't want to have to wait any longer, but he would. He'd bide his time as long as it took, and when it was over, when Angus was in jail and the crime syndicate was defunct, he'd finally be able to move forward.

Out from the shadow of anger and hatred.

Into something bright and new.

An image of Esme filled his mind, her soft lips and vivid eyes, her silky hair falling straight to her nape.

Her smile.

A Dupree cut from different cloth. One who deserved all the good life could bring. He wanted to make sure she got it.

But first, he wanted to find her uncle, toss him in jail and throw away the key.

# TWELVE

Seven days was a long time to be stuck inside a gaudily decorated swamp shanty. Seven nights was a long time to lie listening to the hushed voices of Ian and his team.

And now she was on night eight.

Doing exactly what she'd done for the past seven.

Counting the opening and closing of the front door, listening to the soft pad of paws on the floor outside her door, to the quiet bark of King as he patrolled the property.

Waiting for dawn to come and something to change.

She turned over in bed, eyeing the tiny cracks in the shades that covered the window. She wanted to pull the cord and open the bright yellow vinyl, to look out into the darkness and watch the moonlight reflected on the water.

She wanted a dozen things that she couldn't have, but mostly she just wanted this to be over.

Sighing, Esme climbed out of bed, padding across the floor on bare feet, wincing as the boards creaked. It was an old place. She'd learned that about it, the rough-hewn floors speaking of a bygone era, the window glass wavy from age.

Not that she was allowed near the windows.

Seven days without sunlight was beginning to get to her.

She could admit that.

If not for Ian, she'd have gone stark raving mad by now. He'd entertained her with stories of his childhood, taught her how to play chess, insisted she teach him how to bake her mother's award-winning pound cake. It was the recipe she used when she was meeting clients for the first time—pound cake and coffee or tea. Making the cake, laughing as she watched Ian measure flour and butter and try his hand at whipping cream had been cathartic.

It felt good to laugh.

It felt good to sit with someone who seemed to want to sit with her. It felt good to play chess and checkers, argue over who'd get the last piece of cake or the last slice of ham.

It wasn't just Ian, though.

She'd become friends with Julianne, offering suggestions on the wedding the FBI agent was planning with Brody Kenner, a man she'd broken up with years ago and had recently reconnected with. She'd run into him while she was searching for Jake Morrow. He'd been sheriff of the small town of Clover, Texas. Now he was training to join the K-9 team.

Julianne had told the story matter-of-factly, but Esme had seen the joy in her eyes and in her face. She'd promised to help her choose colors and decor, find vendors and, maybe, pick a dress.

Ian had heard them talking and gone on a mission, returning hours later with a bagful of wedding magazines.

Zeke had laughed, but he'd sat in the ugly easy chair and given his opinion about the dresses and flowers and food.

Funny. The seven days she'd spent in the ugly house at the edge of the swamp had taught Esme a lot about what friendship was and about what family meant. She could see that was what Zeke, Ian and Julianne were. They were a team, a pack with three leaders, all working together for the good of the group.

She liked that.

But she hated waiting. She hated wondering just how long their little group would stay together.

It wouldn't last forever.

She didn't want it to.

Esme paced back across the room, settling into the rocking chair that Ian had brought for her. She hadn't asked where he'd gotten it or how he'd known that she preferred simple wooden frames and plain blue cushions to anything ornate or fancy. Instead, she'd just thanked him and enjoyed it.

That was the thing about being in the safe house.

Things weren't complicated.

Not unless she thought too much about them.

Then she'd start to wonder and worry and ask herself questions she couldn't answer—like what she was going to do when Angus was finally apprehended and she could move on.

Ian had hinted that they'd move on together.

She liked that idea, but she was trying to enjoy the moment, to take what he was offering now and not question it too much.

Anything could happen while they were waiting for the trial, and this thing they were feeling—this fragile new relationship they were forging—could become old and blasé and boring.

She snorted.

If she were being totally honest with herself, she'd admit she didn't want that to happen. She'd admit that the more time she spent with Ian, the more things she learned about him, the more time she wanted to spend and the more she wanted to know.

She'd never felt that way about Brent.

He'd been a nice guy. She'd liked him. He'd seemed faithful, moral, hardworking—all the things she'd been looking for. He hadn't been the kind of person who'd told stories to make people laugh. He'd told stories to impress, and for a while, he'd impressed her. He'd done all the right things, gone through all the right motions. Flowers. Candy. Expensive dinners.

It had taken a lot of distance and a lot of perspective for her to understand the truth. Brent had been more concerned about what he could get out of the relationship than what he could put in it. Esme had spent the years they were together trying to please him, because she'd thought that was how love was supposed to work. Give and give and give, because that was what the other person expected.

But when she was with Ian, things flowed smoothly. Give and take. Back and forth. Exchanges of ideas and opinions without the need for either of them to be right.

Being with him was as natural as breathing, and she couldn't quite figure out why. Except that he made it easy to be herself. He didn't ask for anything other than the truth. He didn't expect anything more than her company.

The old glider moved beneath her as she pulled her feet up and wrapped her arms around her knees.

The house had gone quiet, the first and second patrol of the night over. If she listened carefully enough, she might hear one of the dogs moving restlessly. Other than that, things would stay quiet for a half hour and then grow busy again.

In a few days, they'd be leaving.

That was what Ian had told her.

He couldn't say where they were going. Just that it would be far away from the Everglades. Esme wasn't sorry about that. She wanted to leave Florida and all the bad memories she had of it. Fortunately, she had some good memories now, though. Memories that she knew would always make her smile.

Esme rested her head on her knees, closing her eyes for just a moment, drifting in the silence and the darkness, the hope of something new and wonderful nudging her into sleep.

She dreamed of Angus. His sharp eyes and hard features. His skinny body and sinewy limbs. She dreamed of his hand in her hair, yanking her backward, tearing at her scalp, his lips pressed close to her ear, screaming words she couldn't understand. In her dream she tried to run, her arms and legs refusing to cooperate. She could see a door. Knew that if she reached it, she would live, but she couldn't move. She was trapped by his grip on her hair and by her fear.

She tried to scream, but nothing but a whimper emerged.

He yanked her backward, slamming her into a wall and shouting into her face. She could see the pockmarks in his skin, the burst spider veins on either side of his nose.

She could see the hatred in his eyes, and, she thought, the evil. Panic-stricken, she clawed at his hand, trying to get him to release his hold, but that only angered him more.

He tossed her away, his hand still in her hair, his fist slamming into the side of her head.

She woke with a start, found herself on the floor, the gliding rocker bumping against her feet.

She'd fallen. That was all. Nothing sinister or scary about that. She sat up, gingerly got to her feet.

Nothing hurt. She was fine, but she felt uneasy, her skin crawling with the kind of fear she hadn't felt since she'd arrived at the safe house.

Somewhere outside, an owl hooted, the sound out of place and alarming.

She crept to the window, breaking the rule that had been drilled into her, pulling back the shades and peering out into the darkness. The owl hooted again, and she was certain she saw a shadow move at the corner of the yard.

Esme needed to get to Ian, let him know that someone was outside. They had to—

Her door opened, and she screamed, the sound shrill and high and filled with terror. She ran at the shadowy form that stood in the doorway, head down, ready to ram right through him if she needed to.

He caught her arm, and she knew the feel of the warm fingers against her skin, the gentleness of the touch.

"Ian," she gasped, and he pulled her up against his chest, whispered in her ear.

"There's someone outside. More than one person, I think. We've got to get out."

"Right." She started to move past, but he stopped her.

"We need to get out, but we need to be smart about it. There's an emergency pack in your closet. Grab that and put on the waders that are sitting beside it."

She'd seen the pack.

She'd even looked through it.

She really hadn't expected to have to use it, though.

Heart thudding in her chest, she ran to the closet, shoving her feet into knee-high waders and slipping into a jacket and then the pack.

Ian was still at the door when she returned, and he took her hand, leading her out into the living room. The lights were off, but she could see Julianne and Zeke standing near the kitchen, their dogs small shadows near their feet.

No one spoke. Esme could only assume they'd had an escape route planned out before they'd ever brought her to the house.

Ian urged her past his colleagues, down the hall that led to the back of the house and the rear deck. There was no way down from there. They'd have to walk around the front to escape.

She was sure Ian knew it, but she wanted to remind him, because she really really didn't want to be trapped on the deck, an easy target to whomever might be stalking them.

She opened her mouth, would have spoken, but one of the dogs growled, the sound sending fear racing up her spine. Esme had heard King growl before, but she'd never heard Thunder or Cheetah make anything but happy noises.

King…

She glanced back. Saw no sign of the dog.

"Where's King?" she whispered, the words barely breaking the silence.

"On the deck."

"He's not barking."

"We don't want our friends to know that we're

aware of their presence. He'll only alert if they get closer."

"You said there's more than one?"

"I said I *think* there is," he corrected.

"Does that mean two? Three?"

He touched her cheek, his fingers brushing across her jaw and then her lips, stopping the frantic words.

"It doesn't matter," he said. "However many there are, we'll take care of them."

"Ian—"

"It's going to be okay," he reassured her, pulling her in for a quick hug before slowly opening the back door. Carefully easing outside, he gestured for Esme to follow.

She wanted to move with the same grace and confidence he'd had, but the waders seemed to catch on the old floor, and she nearly fell into the doorjamb.

He caught her, his hands skimming down her arms and resting on her waist.

"Careful," he said, the word more breath than noise.

She nodded but didn't speak again.

They were outside now, the full moon casting long shadows across the backyard. King stood a few feet away, his fur glowing gold in the moon's reflected light.

The canine didn't glance their way as they approached. He didn't move. She didn't think he even blinked. His focus was on the back edge of the property and the deep shadows there. His ears were up, his tail stiff, his posture tense.

Someone was there.

King knew it, and he was ready to act if he received the command.

Ian moved up beside the dog, offering a hand signal that broke King's concentration. The dog trotted to the side of the house, scanned the area and headed back, nudging the back of his handler's calf.

"It's clear. Let's go," Ian whispered, taking her hand and leading her to the area King had just left. He stopped at the deck railing, and she wasn't sure what he thought they were going to do.

Jump?

She sure hoped not. It was twenty feet straight down, and she wasn't all that great at landing. Even if she were, she didn't think she'd manage to do it without breaking something.

Ian slid out of his pack, unzipping the front compartment and taking out a harness. He motioned for King, and the dog loped over, waiting patiently while Ian hooked him in.

"Ready?" he asked Esme, and she nodded even though she still had no idea what they were going to do.

The way she saw things, as long as his plan involved escaping with their lives, she was good with it.

He pulled something else from his pack.

Rope?

No. A ladder.

She watched as he hooked it to the deck railing and let it fall over the side. It made a quiet whoosh as it unfolded, and she had about two seconds to worry that sound had carried to the back of the yard. Then Ian was up, the dog strapped to his chest, as he climbed over the rail and started making his way down the rope ladder.

She was next.

That much was obvious.

She clambered over the railing, trying not to think about the twenty-foot drop as she started down the ladder.

Esme didn't hesitate; she climbed over the railing and scrambled down the ladder like she'd done it a million times before. He helped her down the last two rungs, his hands light against her narrow waist, her pack knocking against his hands.

He'd already released King from his harness and tucked it into the pack. They were ready to head around the front of the property. The dock was there. And the boat. If they were careful, they should be able to escape before their stalkers knew they'd left.

That was good.

What wasn't good was the fact that there were at least two people wandering through the swampy area that surrounded the house. Even if the dogs hadn't been growling and pacing, Ian would have known about the trespassers. He'd been awake and restless when he'd heard the first owl call. By the time he'd heard the second, he'd already gathered the team and put the escape plan into action.

Ian and Esme out the back.

Zeke and Julianne out the front.

They'd gone over the plan dozens of times while they'd waited for Angus to strike.

That was paying off.

He heard the front door open, listened for the quick hard tap of feet on wood.

There!

Julianne and Zeke were heading for the stairs. If things went well, they'd be down in seconds, climbing into the SUV and taking off. Hopefully, leading trouble away.

Ian and Esme would take the boat, rowing out far enough to be out of sight of the house before starting the motor. There was a campsite twenty miles away. Not a long trip, but hazardous at night. Julianne had figured it would take two or three hours to safely navigate. She'd have the SUV there when they arrived.

From there, they'd head straight to headquarters in Montana, and then Esme would be flown out of the country.

She wouldn't like it.

He knew it.

He didn't like it, either. The truth was, he'd wanted to argue for a different location. Somewhere close to headquarters, a place he might be assigned to keep her safe. He'd understood the practicality of Max's decision. He knew that she'd be safer out of the country than in it. The Dupree crime family was a multi-limbed tree, its branches spreading through the United States. With the price on her head, Esme was too vulnerable. No matter where they hid her, there was a good chance she'd be found.

Ian and Max had discussed it. They'd agreed. The only way to keep her safe was to get her out of the country. He cared about her too much to want anything less than her total security. Eventually, she'd return, and when the trial was over, he was going to make certain they were never separated again.

First things first, though.

He tugged her to the edge of the yard, urging her down into thick grass that was tall enough to cover them both. They crouched there, his hand on her forearm, her head brushing against his shoulder. He wanted to tell her everything would be okay, wanted to remind her that he'd make sure of it. Instead, he pulled her closer, did what he would have done days ago if there hadn't always been someone around; he pressed a kiss to her forehead, her cheek, her lips. Soft. Easy. Tender, because that was how it felt to be around her.

The SUV's engine roared. Tires squealed.

He backed away, his heart thundering, his pulse racing. Not with fear. With longing for all the things he hadn't been looking for but had found in Esme. He could see her through the darkness, her face pale, her eyes wide.

"What was that?" she whispered, her fingers touching her lips.

"A promise."

"Of what?"

"Tomorrow and the next day and the next," he said, his lips brushing her ear as he spoke.

Somewhere in the distance, an owl called, the sound chilling Ian's blood.

That was the signal he'd been waiting for. The one that told him the enemy was on the move.

Beside him, King growled, a long low warning that Ian wasn't going to ignore.

The SUV pulled out of the carport, headlights

flashing on the ground a few feet away. There. Gone. Julianne and Zeke were doing their part.

It was time to do his.

"Let's go," he whispered, pulling Esme through the thick grass and boggy water, the roaring engine masking the sound of their retreat.

They made it to the dock easily. He climbed onto it, pulling Esme up beside him, King growling and barking, trying to tell him something that took just a few seconds too long for Ian to figure out.

By the time he did, it was too late.

Angus was there, rising like a wraith from the boat, a gun in his hand.

Ian reached for his firearm.

"Stop," Angus said calmly. "I've got nothing against you, Ian. It's Esme I have a problem with."

"I've got a problem with you, too," Esme retorted. "So I guess the feeling is mutual."

"Shut up," Angus snapped. "Get in the boat."

"Or what? You'll kill me?" She was baiting him, trying to keep his attention. Maybe so that Ian could act. Or maybe so that she could.

He felt her shift, thought she might be planning to dive off the dock and into the swamp. She probably figured she'd have a better chance there than she would with her uncle.

Or, maybe, she thought she'd draw Angus's

gunfire away from Ian, give him a chance to pull his gun and end the fight.

Ian wasn't going to let her do it.

He gave the command, and King took off, sailing through the air, knocking into Angus with so much force the other man went down, the gun going off as he landed.

One shot, but it was followed by another. This one coming from somewhere near the house. King was snarling, teeth around Angus's wrist, shaking it so hard the gun flew out of his hand and landed somewhere beside the dock.

Ian didn't have time to go after it.

A bullet whizzed by his ear, coming so close he thought he could feel the heat of it. He dived for cover, taking Esme with him, rolling off the dock as more bullets flew.

They landed in soft wet earth, and he covered her with his body, holding her in place when she tried to stand.

Suddenly, King was beside them. He'd disarmed Angus, and he was back, ready to do more.

Ian raised a hand, giving the command to apprehend, and King took off again, racing toward the house and whoever was firing the weapon.

Ian heard the growls and snarls of the fight, heard a man cry out in agony. There were no high-pitched yips from King. Which meant he wasn't being hurt, and that he'd taken the gunman by surprise.

Another human yowl, and the night went silent.

No noise but the soft lap of water against the shore.

"Is it over?" Esme mumbled against his chest. "Because you're suffocating me."

"Sorry." He backed off, caught the unmistakable coppery scent of blood, saw black rivulets of it running down Esme's arm.

"You've been hit," he growled, pulling off his jacket and pressing it against the wound.

She pushed his hand away.

"I'm fine. Go help King."

"King can take care of himself." He knew that for a fact, was certain the dog was already on his way back. He glanced around, searching the shadows for Angus. The guy had disappeared, but that didn't mean he was gone.

"Really." She stood and took a step away. "I'm okay. Call your dog back, and let's get in the boat and get out of here."

"I'm afraid that isn't going to happen." Angus moved out of the shadows of an old mangrove tree, a gun drawn and pointed, hand bloody from his fight with King. He'd obviously been carrying a second weapon. Something Ian would have checked for if he'd had the opportunity.

Ian reached for his Glock, freezing when Angus pointed the revolver at Esme's head.

"Don't," he said conversationally. "Not unless you'd like to see her die."

He let his hand fall away, let Angus think he had the upper hand.

"That's better," the older man said, grabbing the back of Esme's jacket and yanking her toward him. He slammed the barrel of the gun into her temple, and she winced, her reaction making Ian want to pull his Glock and take a chance that he could fire before Angus.

It was too big a risk, though. If he timed it wrong, she'd be dead.

"Now, take out the gun and toss it in the water. Slowly. Try anything funny, and Esme's brains will be splattered all over the swamp."

"Ian, don't do it. He's going to kill me anyway," Esme pleaded.

"It'll be okay," he said, looking into her eyes, willing her to calm down, to trust him. "I promise."

"Right. And promises mean so much," Angus sneered. "Toss the gun. Now."

Ian pulled it from the holster, looking straight into Esme's panicked eyes as he did exactly what he had been told.

# THIRTEEN

They were going to die.

Esme wasn't certain of much, but she was sure of that.

Not only had Ian tossed his gun into the swamp, but he'd sent King off to chase down another gunman. Which would have been fine if Uncle Angus hadn't been armed with a second weapon.

The first one, the one King had shaken from his hand, had looked deadly enough. This one looked even worse.

Maybe because the barrel was pressed against her head.

"Happy?" Ian asked. The question was obviously meant for Angus, but he was still looking into her eyes.

He didn't look panicked.

He didn't look scared. She'd have found that comforting if she didn't know just how deadly the situation was.

"Very," Angus crowed. "This is what I like to see! Absolute obedience. Keep it up, *Fed*-boy, and you might just survive."

"I'm more concerned about Esme. How about we agree that she won't testify if you let her go?"

"Sorry. That's not going to happen. First, because she's caused me a lot of trouble, and I'm ready to make her pay for that. Second, because I don't trust you, her or the United States government."

"We could offer something else in exchange for her life."

"Like what?" The gun dropped away, just a fraction of an inch, but it was enough to give Esme a little hope and a little wiggle room. If it dropped any farther, she'd elbow him in the stomach and make a run for it.

As if he sensed her thoughts, Ian met her eyes again, offering a subtle shake of his head.

A warning, she thought.

A week ago, she would have ignored it and gone ahead with her plan. Now she knew Ian. She knew how his mind worked, how he thought, the way he worked. He didn't believe in taking chances. He always had a plan A, a plan B and a plan C. He'd told her that one night while they were playing checkers.

Tonight's plan A hadn't worked out.

Maybe plan B would be better.

And maybe she'd be smart to wait a little longer, see what Ian had up his sleeve.

"Here's what I'm thinking," Ian said, shuffling forward a couple of steps.

"What *I'm* thinking," Angus barked, "is that you need to stay where you are."

"Sorry. I was thinking about other things. Like you. On a plane, heading for a tropical paradise."

"That sounds more like your friend Jake's cup of tea," Angus said, tugging Esme backward, dragging her into ankle-deep water.

"Jake's smart. He knows that the best way to stay out of jail is to get out of the country."

"He's smart, all right," Angus agreed. "I showed him a few pictures of this place, told him how many people were working protection, and he was able to tell me exactly how you'd react if you were under attack. He knew you'd send your friends off in the SUV. He knew you'd try to escape in the boat. He even knew that you'd only keep one dog back at the house."

"Like I said," Ian replied, no heat in his voice, no emotion. He was getting ready to move, Esme could sense it. She could feel the tension in him, the corded muscles and tamped-down energy. All of it was ready to explode. "Jake is smart. You'd be wise to take a page from his book."

"Meaning?"

"Agree to let us fly you out of the country. Stay away for good, and you won't have to worry about the police or the feds."

"I'm not much for tropical climates," Angus said, his beady eyes shifting from Ian to a point just beyond his shoulder. "That you, Eddie?" he called.

There was no reply, and he took another step back, dragging Esme with him.

She wasn't sure what he'd seen. She didn't care.

She just didn't want to have to take another step deeper into the water, because she had the horrible feeling she knew what he planned. One gunshot, and her body would fall, the loud splash attracting predators for miles around.

She'd probably be dead before they reached her.

The thought wasn't comforting.

"Who's Eddie?" Ian asked.

"One of the guys I hired to help out. Four people to help me take you down and get my niece. That's what Jake said."

"Did he also say that I don't like to be fooled?" Ian asked. "And that I always make sure that I'm well armed?"

He moved so quickly, Esme almost didn't see it happen.

First he was still, then he was beside her, one

arm sweeping in a downward arc, a glittering knife heading straight for Angus's hand.

Angus shrieked, jerking away, but maintaining his grip on the gun.

"Move!" Ian shouted, giving Esme a gentle shove toward shore.

She stumbled, landing on her knees, blood sleeping down her arm and dripping into the dark water.

*Get up!* her mind shrieked. *Run!*

She was finally up, stumbling through the water, screaming for King, hoping the dog would come running.

Praying he would.

Suddenly, he was there, flying across the yard, splashing into the water. He moved past, aiming for the struggling men, launching himself into the air and into the fray.

Angus cursed, stumbling from the pack, the gun still in his hand, his arms bloody and oozing.

He lifted the weapon, and King charged again.

"No!" Esme screamed, but it was too late.

The gun report was deafening, the sound drowning out everything else. She watched in horror, expecting King to fall away, but he was still moving, landing against Angus, pushing him over.

Or...

Maybe Angus was just falling, the gun splashing into the swamp as the sound of the gunshot faded away.

“I’d feel bad, but he deserved it,” a woman said, her voice so close to Esme’s ear, she screamed, whirling around and looking straight into her sister’s gorgeous face.

Violetta Dupree had saved King’s life.

No matter how hard he tried, Ian couldn’t wrap his mind around that. He took another sip of the hot coffee Julianne had offered him, eyeing Esme’s sister over the top of the paper cup.

She perched on the edge of a vinyl-covered chair in the waiting room of the ER.

She looked…

Tired.

Undone.

Her brown hair fell in messy waves around her pale face. Her mascara was smeared underneath her eyes. She’d been wearing red lipstick at some point, and lines of it feathered out from her lips. She was a beautiful woman. There was no doubt about that, but she looked like she’d aged ten years since he’d last seen her, and that had been only a couple of months ago.

“I don’t understand what’s taking so long,” she complained, biting at a hangnail on the edge of her thumb. "You said the gunshot wound didn't look that bad."

"It didn't."

"Then why haven't they come to let us know how Esme is doing?"

"It takes time to clean a wound," Julianne offered, and Violetta huffed.

"It would be nice if it would take a little less time. I have things to do." She flicked a speck of mud off her dark jeans and frowned.

"What kind of things?" Ian asked, trying to see a little of Esme in her face.

"Nothing that concerns you or your people. A friend is having a birthday party this weekend, and I need to be home for it."

"So you just took a little jaunt from Chicago to Florida to kill your uncle, and now you're going back home to hobnob with your rich friends?" Zeke's assessment was harsh, and Violetta's eyes widened.

"I did not come out here to kill Angus. I came to save my sister."

"And you knew she was in trouble because…?" Julianne tapped her fingers on her thighs and eyed Violetta with a mixture of curiosity and suspicion.

It was the same look Ian was probably giving her.

Violetta didn't answer questions. At least, not

any questions he'd ever asked. Now she seemed determined to tell them everything she knew.

As long as it was on her time frame.

"It was pretty obvious that our uncle wanted Esme dead, and that he wasn't going to stop going after her until he achieved his goal."

"You didn't seem all that concerned about her well-being when we tried to get you to tell us what you knew about your uncle," Ian pointed out, and she shrugged, flipping a strand of hair over her shoulder.

"Of course I was concerned. Esme means the world to me."

"Do I?" Esme's voice carried through the small waiting area, and Ian turned, saw her standing in the doorway. Her arm was in a sling, her hair was slicked to her scalp, her face was pale and streaked with mud.

And she was absolutely the most beautiful woman he'd ever seen. King must have thought the same. He barreled toward her, stopping at her feet and looking up at her adoringly.

"Hello, handsome," Esme said, swaying a little as she leaned down to pet the dog.

Ian cupped the elbow of her good arm, supporting her weight as she straightened.

"Thanks," she said, smiling into his eyes.

And, right then, he knew. Beyond a shadow of a doubt. Knew more than he knew almost anything else, that he'd be in Esme's life for as long as she wanted him there.

"It's not hard to give someone a hand when they need it," he said, helping her to the seat next to her sister.

"I meant for everything else," she replied, looking into his eyes and offering a soft sweet smile. "You've given up a lot to keep me safe, and I appreciate that more than I can say."

"You won't be safe until after you testify. You do know that, don't you?" Violetta lifted Esme's hand and squeezed it gently. "There are still plenty of people who would like Reginald to go free."

"I don't suppose you want to name any of them?" Julianne asked, and Violetta stiffened.

"Of course she doesn't," Zeke cut in. "She's willing to help her sister, but only if it doesn't interfere with her life."

"You have no idea what you're talking about." Violetta stood, her body nearly shaking with fury. "I have done nothing but help you people. I've kept my silence so that I could keep track of Jake Morrow. I knew he'd keep in touch with Angus, and I was right."

"You know where Jake is?" Zeke asked, and Violetta shook her head.

"I've heard he's going after his ex-girlfriend

and his son. He won't leave the country without them."

"Who did you hear that from?" Esme prodded, leaning back in the seat and stifling a yawn. She was trying to cover up how bone-tired she was, but Ian noticed.

"Angus. I kept on his good side so that I could protect you. That was my only reason, my sole motivation. I hope you believe that, Esme."

"So you've been playing up to your uncle and getting information from him?" Julianne had taken a small notepad from her pocket and was jotting something in it. "Is that what you're saying?"

"That is exactly what I'm saying. I've made my mistakes. I'll admit that. I like nice things. Expensive things. I was happy to let my brother and uncle get them for me." Her gaze shifted to her sister, and she frowned. "But I love you more than any of that, Esme. I would have cooperated with the FBI immediately if I hadn't been afraid it would cost you your life."

"Sounds to me like you're trying to separate yourself from your brother's crimes," Zeke said, and Violetta scowled.

"You don't know a thing about me. None of you do. If I'd wanted to separate myself from my brother's crimes, I wouldn't be here. I'd have stopped Angus, and I'd have gone straight back to Chicago without letting any of you know I'd been here. It wasn't like you weren't distracted enough for me to escape. I stayed because I accomplished my goal. Everything I've done these past months has been to protect my sister."

"If that's the case, you shouldn't be hesitating to give us information about the way the organization runs," Ian accused.

"I'm afraid, okay?" Violetta nearly shouted. "Not all of us are like Esme—brave enough to risk our lives. I'm not. I never have been. Except when it comes to her. I'd do anything to keep her safe. Even play to my uncle's good side, pretend to be part of his team and convince him to confide in me." She hissed out a breath. "He told me all about Jake Morrow. He told me that he'd threatened Jake's son's and ex-girlfriend's lives. It made me physically ill. Who would hurt a child?"

"Your uncle," Ian said, gentling his voice, because he believed her, and he was starting to feel sympathy for the mess she'd found herself in.

"I know," she said just as gently, her gaze on her sister. "I'm so sorry this happened, Esme. If I could go back and change things, make different decisions, be a better person, I would. I promise you that."

"You can make different decisions," Julianne said, and there didn't seem to be a hint of sympathy in her voice. "As long as Jake Morrow is free, your sister may not be safe. Angus was a terrible person, but Reginald calls the shots. He may be trying to contact Jake, get him to follow through on the effort to silence Esme before the trial. We need to bring him in, and we need to do it quickly if you really want to keep your sister from harm."

Violetta frowned. "Some of the information I got was vague, but I'll tell you what I know. Angus told me Jake was going back home to find his ex-girlfriend and his baby. She despises what he's become and wants nothing to do with him, but he's not going to leave the country until he has his son."

The words jolted through Ian, and he fished his phone out of his pocket, scrolled through the texts until he found the one sent by Anonymous: Word is that Mommy, Daddy and child have gone home.

"You're Anonymous," he said, and she blushed.

"Yes. Like I said, I was trying to pass on as much information as I could without making things too easy to figure out."

"Easy would have been nice," Zeke grumbled.

"Easy would have gotten me killed," she responded through clenched teeth, dropping into the seat beside Esme. "I was the only one who knew about Jake Morrow. If I'd given you too much information and you'd passed it on to someone owned by Angus..." She shuddered.

"Tell us about Jake going home," Ian demanded, turning the subject back to the thing he was most interested in.

He didn't really care what Violetta's motivation had been. It didn't matter to him if it had been greed or fear that had caused her to get close to her uncle. What he cared about was the fact that she had information that could prove to be very useful to the team.

"He's in Montana. At least, that's where I think he is. Angus thought it was hilarious that he was going to be so close to your headquarters. He liked to say you were all farsighted, unable to see what was right in front of your faces."

"What else did he like to say?" Zeke asked, his irritation and anger obvious.

"That he was smarter than all of you put together. That he always came out on top, and the rest of us were flies buzzing around on the trash heap of his leftovers." She squeezed the bridge of her nose and shook her head. "He really was a horrible man."

"Maybe you should have gone to the police and told them that a long time ago." Zeke stalked out of the room, Cheetah bounding along beside him.

"I already said that I'd change things if I

could. What more do you people want from me?" Violetta began, her frustration and irritation obvious.

Ian had the feeling that she was just gearing up, that she had a whole lot more she wanted to say about the way they were treating her.

Esme held up her hand, stopping her sister's diatribe.

"Do we have to do this right now?" she asked wearily.

"Of course we do," Violetta retorted. "I didn't come all this way to be treated like a criminal."

"Just stop, Violetta," Esme said. "It's been a long day. Actually, it's been a long six months. I'm tired, and I just want to go home. Except—" Her voice broke, and a tear rolled down her cheek. "I can't, because I have to keep drifting from place to place until the trial. You get to go back to the fancy penthouse Reginald helped you buy. Until his trial is over and he's been sentenced, there's no place that I'll ever feel safe. No place to throw anchor and wait until the storm blows over. I just have to keep riding it out until the bitter end."

"Oh. Honey! I'm sorry. I wasn't thinking about what you've been through." Violetta pulled tissue from her handbag and tried to give them to Esme.

Esme nudged them away.

"Esme," Violetta tried again. "Don't cry. None of these people are worth your tears."

"Yes. They are. And so are you. So, please, let's not do this right now." She swiped at the errant tear, her hand shaking.

Julianne met Ian's eyes. "You want me to handle the interrogation?"

"Yes. And update Max on the case. He'll be interested in hearing the information about Jake."

She nodded, touching Violetta's shoulder and somehow convincing her to walk out of the room.

Turning back to Esme, he saw that her eyes were closed. She had her head resting against the wall and her hands fisted in her lap, and when another tear slipped down her cheek, he couldn't hold back.

He lifted her good hand, unfurled her fingers and pressed a kiss to her palm.

"What's that for?" she murmured, not opening her eyes.

"Something to anchor you until you find your way home," he said, and she smiled, but the tears kept falling, and he finally tugged her into his lap, pressed her head to his chest and just let her cry.

# FOURTEEN

She hated crying.

Hated it, but she couldn't seem to stop. The tears kept rolling down her face, soaking into Ian's shirt.

Ian!

She was cradled in his arms.

Crying all over him.

She pushed away, her left arm shrieking in protest.

Because she'd been shot.

By her uncle.

Her own flesh and blood, but he'd wanted her dead. In the end, he'd died because of that.

"Slow down," Ian said as she scrambled away from him.

"Your shirt is soaked," she pointed out.

"And?"

"I'd die of embarrassment. If that were actually a thing."

"What's to be embarrassed about?" He snagged

her hand, holding her in place when she would have backed farther away.

"Look at me!" She gestured to her mud-encrusted pants, her hair, her tear-soaked face. "I'm a mess!"

"A beautiful mess," he responded gruffly, and her heart did a funny little dance. One that spoke of happiness and contentment and better things to come.

And suddenly the tears weren't sliding down her cheeks anymore. Suddenly, she was smiling. "Only you would say something like that," she said.

"And I'd only say it to you. How's the arm?"

"Sore, but I'll live."

"And the heart?"

"The same." Her voice broke, and the stupid tears started again.

"They'll both get better. Just give it a little time." He tugged her into his arms, his lips brushing hers. Once. Then again. Her hand slid up his arm, her fingers slid through his hair.

She could have stood there with him forever, tasting the sweetness of his lips, feeling the warmth of his hand resting on her back.

Someone cleared his throat, and she jerked back, nearly tripping over King.

"Sorry," she said to the dog, and his tail thumped.

"I'm probably the one who should be apologizing. I didn't mean to interrupt," a man said, and she turned, watching as he walked into the room. Tall and blond with a scar that slashed down the side of his cheek, he had the bluest eyes she'd ever seen.

"Max," Ian said. If he were embarrassed at having been caught kissing her, he didn't show it. "What are you doing here?"

"I decided to come help with the transport. The more people protecting Ms. Dupree, the better. I took the red-eye last night. If I'd known how much trouble you were going to be in, I'd have tried to get to Florida sooner." He smiled, offering Esme his hand. "I'm Max West. Team captain and shameless romantic."

"Really?"

"No, but I thought it might make things less awkward."

"I really don't think anything can do that."

"Well, then how about we focus on the business at hand? Has Ian explained what our next step is?"

"There hasn't been a whole lot of time," Ian said, and Max nodded.

"Right. So here's how it's going to be, Esme. We're going to take you to our headquarters in Montana. You'll be there until our next safe house is ready."

"Is it going to be in a swamp?" she asked, too tired to argue with the plan.

"No." He laughed. "It's going to be really nice. Not in the States, though. We've arranged for you to have round-the-clock security in another country. We've already collected your passport. If there's anything else you think you'll need, let us know and we'll make sure you have it."

Yeah.

There was.

She'd need Ian, but she didn't think that was what Max was expecting to hear.

"Some air would be nice. If that's okay," she said, offering a poor facsimile of a smile.

She didn't think either of the men bought it, but neither tried to stop her. With Angus dead, she was safe. At least until Reginald could figure out a way to hire killers from prison.

Throat thick with emotion, she reached the exit and walked out into early-morning light. The sun was just peeking above the horizon, the ground dusted gold with it. King appeared at her side, his sturdy body pressing against her leg, warm and heavy and comforting.

"It's going to be okay," she murmured.

"Yes, it is," Ian said, and she wasn't surprised that he was there, wasn't shocked when he turned her so that they were facing each other.

"I don't want to leave the country," she said. Simple. Straightforward. To the point.

"I'm sorry," he responded, and she knew his hands were tied, that the decision wasn't his. "But your sister will be fine. She's very good at taking care of herself."

"That's not what I'm worried about."

"Then what?" he asked. "Your business? Your friends?" He touched her chin, offered a smile that should have made her heart sing. It just made her think of what she'd almost had, and what she was about to lose.

"You," she finally admitted, and he shook his head, tugged her into his arms, pressed her head to his chest.

"Why would you think I'd let you?"

"Because your work is here, and I'm going to be somewhere else."

"My work is with you. Keeping you safe is my assignment until after the trial. King and I have both been cleared to travel with you. I sent Max a text while you were getting your arm cleaned up. He was quick to agree to the plan."

"What if the trial takes years to happen?"

"I don't care if it takes a lifetime, Esme. As long as we're together."

"Are you sure?"

"Absolutely. Now, how about we go back inside and get started on our new adventure?"

He took her hand, leading her back to the door. King loped beside him, his ears up, his nose to the air.

He stopped short, whining softly.

"What is it, King?" Ian asked, touching the dog's broad head.

"Is someone out here with us?"

"He'd be barking, but there's definitely something worrying him."

King whined again.

"Find it," Ian said, and the dog took off, racing around the side of the building, nose still to the air, ears alert.

They moved through an alley and then into a back lot.

That was when Esme heard it. Above the distant sound of morning traffic, above the pounding of her heart, the soft whimpering cry of an animal in distress.

"What in the world?" she asked, but Ian was striding across the back lot, following King to a Dumpster that butted against a brick wall.

"Whatever it is," he said, lifting the lid and peering inside, "it's in here."

"Maybe we should call animal control," she suggested as King stood on two legs and looked inside the bin.

She looked, too, because she had to.

The crying was pitiful, and whatever was making the sound needed help.

"I think we can handle this," Ian said, reaching for a box that was shoved up against the back of the metal container. Someone had taped it closed, and the thing inside bumped against the top.

"What if it's a rat?" She cringed as he pulled a utility tool from his pocket and carefully sliced through the tape.

"King wouldn't be going crazy over a rodent. I think it's a—"

He didn't get a chance to finish.

The lid popped open, and a dark-faced thing appeared.

No. Not a thing.

A puppy. Scrawny. All legs, boxy head and little potbelly, he tried to jump out of the box but ended up falling back in.

King nudged the puppy with his nose, offering a tentative lick.

"Good boy, King," Ian said. "Good find."

He lifted the puppy from what would have been its coffin, checked its gums, felt its ribs.

"He's skinny and dehydrated, but it's nothing a little food and water can't fix."

"Should we take him to the shelter?" she asked, touching the puppy's velvety nose and losing a little piece of her heart when he licked her hand.

"It would probably be the practical thing to do, but there's a lot more to life than practicality. I'm supposed to be looking for a puppy to bring back to our training facility. Kind of a reminder that we're part of a family of sorts, one that always sticks together."

There was a note of sadness in his voice, and she knew he must be thinking about Jake Morrow.

"You are a real family," she told him, because it was the only thing she could offer. "I felt that when we were in the safe house. Just because one member decided to go his own way, doesn't mean the remainder can't stay strong."

"I know, but thanks for the reminder. Some days I need it more than others," he confided, smiling in the way that always made her heart leap.

"So…what now?"

"Now we'll take this guy inside and introduce him to his new family," he said, holding the puppy in the crook of his arm. "We'll get him checked out by a vet, and we'll take him to puppy training school."

"He'll be an A student. Of course," she joked, feeling lighter than she had in weeks, happier than she'd been in months.

All the hard times, all the difficulties, had led her to this point, and for the first time since she'd witnessed her brother's crime, she was thankful for them.

"Of course," Ian agreed. "No kid of ours could ever be anything less."

"Kid of ours?" she asked.

"A figure of speech," he responded. "And maybe a conversation to revisit at another time."

"I think I'd like that."

"That's what I was hoping you'd say." He grinned, and she couldn't help returning his smile.

"I guess we'll have plenty of time to discuss it and everything else while we're waiting for Reginald's trial," she said.

"And plenty of time after the trial is over," he replied, tugging her close, offering a kiss that promised everything she'd ever hoped for and more.

When he backed away, they were both breathless, and they were both smiling. She noticed that. Just like she noticed the quiet hum of morning traffic, the soft trill of a songbird on a branch nearby. The sun glinting in Ian's dark hair, the puppy sleeping in the crook of his arm, King grinning at his feet.

It all looked fresh and bright and beautiful.

"What was that for?" she asked, and he took her hand.

"You," he said, "and our new beginning."

She laughed. "New beginnings are wonderful things. Especially when we get to start them with people we care about."

"You're right," he agreed. "So how about we get started on ours?"

"That," she replied, levering up on her toes and offering him one more sweet kiss, "sounds like a wonderful idea."

He called to King, and they walked back to the hospital. All of them together. And it was enough to fill all the empty spots in her heart. It was enough to sustain her through whatever the future might bring.

She hadn't wanted the trouble she'd found herself in, but she couldn't regret where it had led her. Where God had led her. Not just to a new beginning, but to the only place where she'd ever truly felt at home.

# EPILOGUE

Ian didn't do nervous. He didn't know what it meant to be anxious. He'd spent years working in law enforcement and facing down thugs, druggies and murderers.

He didn't sweat.

He didn't panic.

He didn't lose his cool.

He was an FBI agent, trained to handle whatever crisis came his way.

So why was he sweating now? Beads of perspiration dotting his brow?

Why were his hands shaking as he tried to knot his tie. *For the tenth time.*

Why was his throat dry? His heart pounding? His pulse racing?

"Need some help with that, Ian?" Max said, a hint of amusement in his voice as he eyed Ian's unknotted tie.

He'd dressed up for the occasion—button-up shirt, dark slacks and a small rose that someone had tucked in his pocket. Probably Katarina. Ian wasn't the only one who'd found love while the team was looking for Jake. Max had found it, too. So had several other team members.

"I've got it," he said, smoothing the tie, and patting his jacket pocket. The ring was there. No box, because he hadn't wanted Esme to notice it. They'd come to headquarters to sign last-minute paperwork before they boarded the plane that would take them to a top secret location.

Even Ian wasn't sure exactly where they'd be.

As long as he was with Esme, he really didn't care.

"Is she here yet?" he asked. He'd spent most of the past few weeks at the safe house, but last night he'd had to pack his bags and get ready for the flight. He'd left Esme with three team members, but he'd still been worried.

Now he was just anxious to see her again.

Ten hours wasn't long, but it felt like a lifetime when you were away from the person you loved, the person you wanted to spend a lifetime with.

"Just arrived. I asked Julianne to keep her in the lobby for another minute." He glanced at his watch. "I've sent your bags ahead, and they're already being loaded onto the plane."

"Is that a hint that I should get this show on the road?"

"Not at all. Take your time. It's a private jet. It's not like it's going to leave without you."

"Then again," Dylan O'Leary said, glancing up from a computer he'd been working on, "things have been calm for a couple of weeks. That usually means trouble is brewing. You might want to get out of town before it arrives."

"Don't rush a man who's about to take one of the biggest steps of his life," Zeke responded, crossing the room and taking one of the cookies that team member Harper Prentiss had brought for the occasion.

"Hands off," she said, slapping his hand away. "Those are for after he pops the question."

She turned to Ian, gave him a quick once-over.

"You could have tried a little harder," she announced, straightening his tie.

"Meaning?"

"A tux? A bowtie? A huge bouquet of her favorite flowers?"

"I've been a little busy," he muttered. It was the truth. He'd spent the past three weeks working at the safe house and helping the team as they tried to locate Jake Morrow. So far, they'd come up empty. If Violetta had been right, if he was in Montana, they hadn't been able to find him.

Yet.

Zeke was still looking.

Or he would be once his doctor cleared him to go back to work. The little flesh wound he'd gotten in the shoot-out had been a bigger deal than he'd thought, and he wasn't happy about it.

As far as Ian could tell, he wasn't happy about a lot of things. Ian couldn't blame him. This had been a tough season for the entire team, but looking around the small conference room, he couldn't help thinking how blessed they all were.

They'd cut the Dupree crime family off at the roots.

With Angus dead and Reginald in prison, the organization was dying, crushed by its inability to run itself. He'd heard of at least a dozen arrests in cities all over the country.

And that was the kind of news he would never ever get tired of listening to. For a long time, he'd thought that was all he wanted, that seeing the crime family destroyed was all he'd needed to make his life complete.

Every time he looked at Esme, every time their eyes met or their hands touched or he heard her soft laughter, he realized just how wrong he'd been.

That still didn't make this any less nerve-racking!

He ran his hand over his hair, tugged at his tie.

"Ian, really!" Harper brushed his hands away

from the tie. “Stop fidgeting. You’re making a mess of this.”

She straightened the tie again.

“Leave the poor guy alone,” Dylan said, glancing down at his phone and frowning.

“Trouble?” Max asked.

“About as big a trouble as a guy like me can get into,” he responded.

“Meaning?” Ian prodded. He’d much rather focus on someone else’s troubles than his out-of-control nerves.

“I’m going to have to go to a…” Dylan sighed. “To a dress shop to pick up Zara’s wedding gown. She says they’re in hiding and formulating a plan, but the dress is in, and she needs me to get it.”

“That’s it?”

“Yes.”

“That doesn’t sound so bad,” Ian said.

“Have you ever been to one of those places?”

“No. Have you?”

“Of course not, and I wasn’t planning to.” He sighed, and Ian would have said something else, maybe offered a solution to the problem, but the door opened and Julianne walked in, Esme right behind her.

His breath caught, and he was sure his heart stopped. She was that beautiful, short red hair framing her face, her sundress skimming slim muscular legs. She'd put a sweater on over the dress, probably hoping to keep warm on the plane. The white knit seemed to highlight the vibrancy of her hair and her eyes.

"You're beautiful," he said.

"So are you," she replied, and he was pretty certain someone laughed. He didn't care. Didn't look to see who it was.

She was all that mattered.

King had walked over, was leaning against Esme's leg, offering a K-9 hug that made her smile.

Ian would normally smile, too, maybe comment on how much King loved her, how quickly he'd accepted her as part of the pack.

He didn't do either, he was too busy studying her face, memorizing the way she looked, so that he could tell their children exactly how gorgeous she'd been the day he'd proposed.

"What's wrong, Ian?" she said, probably sensing his nervous energy.

"I've been thinking," he said. "That I don't want to go into witness protection as your bodyguard. I wan—"

"I understand, Ian." She cut him off before he could finish, obviously assuming something that had never occurred to him.

"I don't think you do," he responded, taking her hand and pulling her closer, mentally kicking himself for making her think for even a moment that he'd walk away. "I don't want to go into witness protection as your bodyguard, because I'm hoping to change my job title before we get on the plane."

"To what?" She looked confused and relieved, her smile returning.

"Fiancé?" he suggested, pulling the ring from his pocket. He had purchased it at an antiques store, the teardrop-shaped emerald surrounded by small mine-cut diamonds, the gold band carved with dozens of infinity symbols.

Her eyes widened when she saw it, and she met his gaze.

"Ian," she breathed, and he didn't know what she meant to say. He only knew what he had to tell her.

The words spilled out. Not practiced or rehearsed. Not the canned little speech that a few of his buddies had suggested. Esme deserved so much more than that.

"I didn't realize what I was missing until I found you, Esme. You are everything I didn't know I was looking for, everything I didn't know I needed. When I'm with you, I'm home. When I'm not, all I can think about is finding my way back. I'd give all I have to spend the rest of my life with you. Will you marry me?"

"Yes," she said, the word choking out as she

reached for him, pulled him in for a hug that spoke all the words she hadn't said.

He could hear them in the quiet hitch of her breath, the soft whisper of her hair against his jacket as she laid her head against his chest.

He could have stood with her forever, let that one perfect moment continue, but King nudged his hand, and he realized he was still holding the ring.

He looked down into Esme's face, smiling into her eyes as he slipped the ring on her finger.

"I love you," he said.

"I love you, too," she responded, a single tear sliding down her cheek.

"Then why are you crying?"

"Because this is the most beautiful moment I have ever lived, and I'm so glad I'm living it with you." She offered a watery smile, and he wiped the tear away, kissing her gently, letting the sound of his friends' warm congratulations fill his heart as he took her hand, signaled for King and walked out of the room and into their future together.

* * * * *

*If you enjoyed BODYGUARD,*
*look for the next book in the*
CLASSIFIED K-9 UNIT *series,*
*TRACKER by Lenora Worth.*

*And don't miss a book in the series:*

*GUARDIAN by Terri Reed*
*SHERIFF by Laura Scott*
*SPECIAL AGENT by Valerie Hansen*
*BOUNTY HUNTER by Lynette Eason*
*BODYGUARD by Shirlee McCoy*
*TRACKER by Lenora Worth*
*CLASSIFIED K-9 UNIT CHRISTMAS*
*by Terri Reed and Lenora Worth*

*Available now from Love Inspired Suspense!*

Dear Reader,

When I first began writing for Love Inspired, my children were young. I worked late at night because it was the only time when I didn't have a toddler in my lap or "Mom!" ringing in my ears. I was so excited to be an author and to share my stories with others. I sat down to write my first reader letter, and I froze. I had no idea what to say! All these years later, that still happens.

Nevertheless, I've found that my words reach the people they are intended for. Perhaps this letter is yours. Perhaps these words are meant for your heart. Because you matter. You do. You are not just a tiny dot on a small planet floating in the darkness of a vast universe. You are a bright light in the life of the people who love you. You are infinitely valuable to your creator, immensely loved by a God who sees your faults and still calls you His. Wherever your road has taken you, I hope that you find comfort in knowing He is there. And if you have lost your way, I pray He leads you safely home.

As always, I would love to hear from you! You can reach me at shirlee@shirleemccoy.com or find me on Facebook, Twitter or Instagram.

Blessings,

Shirlee McCoy

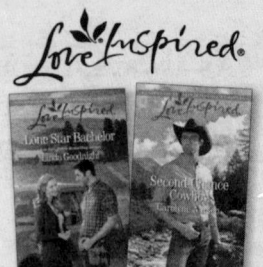

## A NOTE TO PARENTS

When your children are ready to "step into reading," giving them the right books—and lots of them—is as crucial as giving them the right food to eat. **Step into Reading Books** present exciting stories and information reinforced with lively, colorful illustrations that make learning to read fun, satisfying, and worthwhile. They are priced so that acquiring an entire library of them is affordable. And they are beginning readers with an important difference—they're written on four levels.

**Step 1 Books,** with their very large type and extremely simple vocabulary, have been created for the very youngest readers. **Step 2 Books** are both longer and slightly more difficult. **Step 3 Books,** written to mid-second-grade reading levels, are for the child who has acquired even greater reading skills. **Step 4 Books** offer exciting nonfiction for the increasingly proficient reader.

Children develop at different ages. **Step into Reading Books,** with their four levels of reading, are designed to help children become good—and interested—readers *faster.* The grade levels assigned to the four steps—preschool through grade 1 for Step 1, grades 1 through 3 for Step 2, grades 2 and 3 for Step 3, and grades 2 through 4 for Step 4—are intended only as guides. Some children move through all four steps very rapidly; others climb the steps over a period of several years. These books will help your child "step into reading" in style!

 Published in the United States by Random House, Inc., New York, and simultaneously in Canada by Random House of Canada Limited, Toronto.

*Library of Congress Cataloging-in-Publication Data:*
Hayward, Linda. All stuck up / by Linda Hayward ; illustrated by Normand Chartier. p. cm. – (Step into reading. A Step 1 book) SUMMARY: Brer Fox makes a tar baby in order to catch Brer Rabbit. ISBN: 0-679-80216-9 (pbk.); 0-679-90216-3 (lib. bdg.) [1. Folklore, Afro-American. 2. Animals–Folklore.] I. Chartier, Normand, ill. II. Title. III. Series: Step into reading. A Step 1 book.
PZ8. 1.H3245A1 1990 398.2′452′08996073–dc20 [E] 89-34675

Manufactured in the United States of America 1 2 3 4 5 6 7 8 9 0

Step into Reading

# All Stuck Up

By Linda Hayward
Illustrated by Normand Chartier

A Step 1 Book

Random House New York

Brer Fox is
always thinking
of ways to catch
Brer Rabbit.

Brer Rabbit is always thinking of ways to not get caught!

Today Brer Fox mixes up
some mighty sticky stuff.
This time he is sure
Brer Rabbit won't get away!

He fixes up something
that looks like a boy.

He puts it down
on the road
by the brier patch.

Then he jumps
into the bushes
and waits.

By and by
Brer Rabbit
comes along.

"Howdy, Mr. Boy!"
he calls.
"Nice day, isn't it?"
Mr. Boy doesn't answer.

"Can't you hear?"

yells Brer Rabbit.

"I said HOWDY!"

Out comes Brer Fox!

Brer Rabbit is

stew meat, for sure.

"I am going to throw you
in a pot and boil you,"
says Brer Fox.
"I don't care,"
says Brer Rabbit.
"Just don't throw me
in that brier patch!"
Brer Fox is surprised.
Maybe it's too hot to cook!

"Guess I'll have to hang you," says Brer Fox.
"That's fine with me," says Brer Rabbit.
"Just don't throw me in that brier patch!"

Brer Fox thinks again.

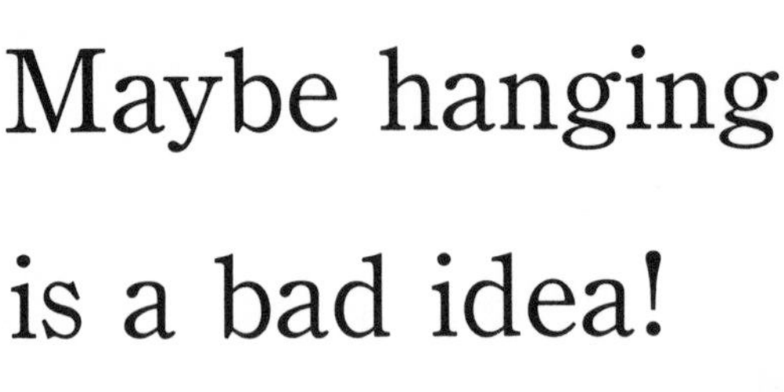

Maybe hanging
is a bad idea!

"Then I'll drown you,"
says Brer Fox.

"Boil me, hang me, drown me, skin me, but please, *PLEASE* don't throw me in that brier patch!" cries Brer Rabbit.

"I know!" says Brer Fox.

"I'll throw you in

that brier patch!"

Brer Fox pulls

Brer Rabbit free.

Then he takes him
and throws him
right into the middle
of the brier patch.

Brer Fox begins
to dance around.
Whoo-eee!
Brer Rabbit is
gone for good.

But wait!
What's that
on the other side
of the brier patch?

It’s Brer Rabbit!
“Yoo-hoo, Brer Fox,”
he calls.
“Guess who loves
the brier patch?
Me!
This is the place
where I was born!”

Brer Fox isn't
dancing anymore.
That Brer Rabbit
has tricked him again.
But just wait!
Next time he will
get him, for sure.

# *ALGONQUIN STORY*

by

Audrey Saunders

**Third Edition**

The Friends of
Algonquin Park
P.O. Box 248
Whitney, Ontario
K0J 2M0
www.algonquinpark.on.ca

# *ALGONQUIN STORY*



Originally published in 1946, and reprinted in 1963 with revised maps, by the Ontario Department of Lands and Forests.

Second edition reprinted in 1998 and Third edition reprinted in 2003 by The Friends of Algonquin Park, Box 248, Whitney, Ontario K0J 2M0. (613) 637-2828

Printed and bound in Canada by Custom Printers of Renfrew Ltd., Box 415, 499 O'Brien Road, Renfrew, Ontario K7V 4A6.

Includes index and further reading.
ISBN 1-895709-81-4

*Net proceeds from the sale of this book will help further the work of The Friends of Algonquin Park (a non-profit, charitable organization dedicated to enhancing the educational and interpretive programs in Algonquin Park since 1983).*

# ACKNOWLEDGMENT

The author wishes to express her gratitude for the aid rendered in the preparation of the manuscript of Algonquin Story, to the following members of the committee who supervised its preparation on behalf of the Ontario Department of Lands and Forests.

Mr. A. G. Northway and Mr. C. A. G. Matthews, leaseholders in Algonquin Park; Mr. Taylor Statten, camp director and operator; Professor Chester Martin, Head of the Department of History, University of Toronto; Professor R. M. Saunders, Department of History, University of Toronto; Professor J. R. Dymond, Director of the Royal Ontario Museum of Zoology, Chairman of the Committee.

Audrey Saunders.

# *Table of Contents*

## *TABLE OF CONTENTS*

### Chapter 7



### Chapter 8



### Chapter 9



### Chapter 10



### Chapter 11



### Chapter 12



### Chapter 13



### Chapter 14

## *TABLE OF CONTENTS*

# *Introduction to the Third Edition*

**by Roderick MacKay © 2003**

Algonquin Provincial Park has a rich history, which figures highly in the Canadian identity. Written by the late Audrey Saunders Miller (1913-1993), *Algonquin Story* was first published in 1946 and reprinted in 1963. For twenty-eight years this book served as the lone repository of tales from the early years of the Park, until the late Ottelyn Addison wrote *Early Days in Algonquin Park* in 1974. The Friends of Algonquin Park have wisely noted that the old tales become inaccessible to readers as books go out of print and become scarce. Since the late 1970s, when the last copies of *Algonquin Story* were available, an entire generation has missed the opportunity to read these stories of the old days and old ways, gathered at the end of Algonquin Park's first fifty years by the Park's premier historian. Now, with this reprinted edition, comes a new opportunity to learn about those early days.

The information in these pages, especially that which is stated as being current or referring to "today", is dated and does not reflect the Algonquin Park of the early Twenty-first Century. With that in mind, the reader might question the value of a reprint of a book now over fifty years "out of date". Rest assured that this book provides more than a view of Algonquin Park as interpreted in the late 1940s. While in the intervening years other books and articles have been written about the history of the Park—some more extensive and about events more recent—as a historical reference, *Algonquin Story* has withstood the test of time. Although the sources of most of the quotations from documents which appear herein can be found at the Ontario Archives or other similar repositories, some letters and documents from which the author has quoted—apparently from "museum files" (Royal Ontario Museum) or from "park files" of the time—have not been located at the time of this writing. As a result, *Algonquin Story* is now effectively the primary source for such materials. In this edition some corrections have been noted in an Errata and Notes section. Also, in keeping more with the author's original intent, both an index of people and new maps have been added to the original text.

During my childhood at the family cottage within Algonquin Park, a frequent rainy-day or evening pastime was to curl up under a warm blanket or comforter and read *Algonquin Story*. Over the years, I read it again and again, enjoying and learning from it each time. Eventually when I became part of the seasonal interpretive staff at the Algonquin Park Museum, I was able to draw upon the stories told to Audrey Saunders so many years before, and share those tales of the rich human history of the Park with others.

Over the winter of 1975-76, I was hired to conduct oral history interviews of old-timers in and around Algonquin Park for the Ministry of Natural Resources. I had the pleasure of meeting Audrey Saunders Miller, and arranged for the donation of her research notes for *Algonquin Story* to the Algonquin Park Museum Archives.

I felt a kinship with her as a result of our common oral history experiences and interest in Algonquin Park, and I believe that she felt it too. Both of us had been warmly welcomed into the homes of the people we had interviewed, and both of us had learned much about the lives of people who had worked and lived in Algonquin Park. In a very few cases, we had even interviewed the same people.

Some of the differences in our experiences were, however, quite striking. Prior to each interview I would pour over *Algonquin Story* in search of suitable topics or gaps in knowledge about which to ask. I had the benefit of all previous research; she had been a pioneer, not only as an Algonquin Park historian but also in the use of oral history techniques in Canada. When we compared our various interview techniques there were similarities, but in recording method I had the decided advantage. While I had the benefit of a compact, hand-held, battery-operated tape recorder, she could only record information in pencil on inconspicuous note-pads, some of which measured only 5 x 8 centimetres in dimension. While I could play back each interview verbatim, she had to use her brief notes to jog her memory later on when she recalled the information for her writing. While I had permission to transcribe detailed outlines of my interviews, her notes were never written in full, since the committee overseeing her work had not considered it "worthwhile to pay for this sort of activity".

My respect for Audrey Saunders Miller grew even more when I began the task of writing my own books on Algonquin Park history: *Algonquin,* in celebration of the Park's centennial, published in 1993, and *Spirits of the Little Bonnechere*, published in 1996. Audrey Saunders was most thorough in her research and writing, especially considering she was given only a little over a year to complete the project. Time after time, just when I thought I had discovered something new about Park history, there it was, printed in the pages of *Algonquin Story*. In at least one instance, information thought to be previously unknown (the identity of the McNickle family on Dickson Lake), and so stated in Saunders' text, was recorded on one of the tiny slips of paper she so carefully retained for posterity. Some references to sources in her book appear in draft manuscripts which are included in her papers at the Algonquin Park Museum Archives.

No footnoted manuscript remains, although as a trained historian she originally intended that such references would be included. Explaining why this was not done, she said the committee supervising the project "decided that the book was to be aimed at tourists who would find this approach formidable. In consequence the material was re-written to include a certain amount of internal documentation."

At this point, the writer of an introduction to such a book might normally attempt to explain how the book came about. Fortunately, Audrey Saunders already provided that information in a retrospective, *How I came to Write Algonquin Story*, which she wrote in March 1948. It is only fitting that we continue with that story in her own words.

> "*Algonquin Story* is a book which grew from an idea; though actually the person who had the original idea had very little notion of where it would finally lead.
>
> "For ten years during the 1930s the superintendent of Algonquin Park was Frank MacDougall, a veteran bush pilot, keen administrator and a person fascinated by the district of Ontario in which he found himself. On his own initiative he undertook to publish a monthly bulletin of Park news which was distributed to summer lease-holders, to rangers, and to others interested in what was going on in the Park. During the course of gathering information for this bulletin he became aware of a great mass of material which had hitherto lain dormant in the minds of men and women who had helped to make the Park what it is today. Trappers, lumbermen, surveyors, hotel keepers, rangers, fishermen, cottagers and campers, all had stories to tell of the early days in the Park and of the people who had contributed to its development. Mr. MacDougall tapped some of these stories, but he could not hope to make more than a small impression on so broad a field.
>
> "Then in 1942 he was moved to Toronto, and made Deputy Minister of the Department of Lands and Forests. By this move he did not lose his interest in the Park, nor did he forget the stories that still lay hidden there and in the surrounding country. His new position gave him certain powers to make it possible to undertake a survey of the material he had discovered, but he was too wise to go ahead on such a project with unwise speed and without expert advice. He decided to obtain help from a group of prominent business men and university professors who were themselves Park enthusiasts.

Taylor Statten, Prof. J.R. Dymond, Prof. Chester Martin, and Mr. A.G. Northway were some of the men who urged him to go ahead with the preparation of a book on the history of Algonquin Park.

"It was at this point that I came into the picture. I had recently completed work on an M.A. thesis in history in which I had developed a technique which had been used only rarely before in Canada in the compilation of historical data. Because I lived close to the region which I was studying, Yonge Street between Hoggs Hollow and Lake Simcoe, I had travelled by bicycle and on skis through the whole area and had interviewed many of the old-timers who lived there, in order to obtain information about the early days. The stories which they had told me proved to be exceedingly accurate, for it is a well-known fact that the memories of people over seventy are frequently accurate about far off things when they are blurred about the events of the present time. I had checked the material I had gathered in this way very carefully and had found it, for the most part, vivid and true.

"Prof. Martin was aware of this piece of research and was very much interested in this technique of talking to old-timers. He it was who suggested me for the Algonquin Park job. When he first approached me on the matter he pointed out that I would have the full co-operation of the authorities of the Department of Lands and Forests and that I would have all the help which the Park officials could give me to facilitate my travels in the area. Also he told me that the advisory committee had decided that the stories which the old-timers had to tell should be gathered without delay because many of them were getting on in years and might pass away before their tales could be preserved.

"I was, of course, very much interested in the scheme, but there seemed to be many obstacles in the way of undertaking such a survey. In the first place I did not know the district at all. Outside of one brief weekend spent in the Cache Lake district some eight years before, I had never been in the Park. Then too, I was busy with a teaching job and when teachers were scarce during the war one didn't feel that it was quite fair just to walk out on an obligation. In the end I agreed to journey north to the Park during the Easter vacation to look the ground over and to talk with one of the old-timers who was not well and whose story might be lost if not recorded.

"This April trip gave me a taste of some of the difficulties which I would encounter if I undertook the task of writing the Park history. The spring break-up had not yet come and travelling was both difficult and cold. I went north from Toronto by train a hundred and forty miles to Huntsville, then in along the Park highway with the mail man for another forty miles. Finally at Canoe Lake I was met by the Canoe Lake postmaster who had hitched a team of horses to a low light sled. The snow on the seven mile trail through the woods was thin in spots and the ice on the lake cracked ominously as we passed over it, but we reached our destination safely. Then coming out again I passed over the same route by dog sleigh, made my connection once more with the mail man, and journeyed on to Park Headquarters where I was housed, a lone woman, in the comfortable accommodation of the rangers' boarding house.

"Well, the outcome of this trip was that I decided to take on the job. Although I knew it would be hard work to travel about the country and often very lonely, I realized that it was the chance of a lifetime. Of course, it would mean a full year's work and would also mean obtaining a leave of absence from teaching, but I could not help feeling that here was a task which might be a real contribution to the Canadian picture at a future time. Canadians are too little conscious of the heritage which they have received from the past and some attempt at preserving intact one section of it might be a very worthwhile undertaking on my part.

"I travelled north again at the beginning of July 1944 and for the next ten months I was in and out of the Park and through the whole of the surrounding district. At every point I tried to record and to hold fast my initial impressions, and everywhere I went I tried to piece together clues which I had piled up during the course of my wanderings. Everywhere people were helpful and understanding. In the Park they made me welcome, fed me and put me up for the night when it was necessary. At the Ontario Parliament Buildings, in Ottawa at the archives and at the National Gallery they went out of their way to obtain the information I wanted. All sorts of people gave me of their time and their co-operation. Without the help of many hundreds of individuals the completed story could not have been written.

"During the winter, in between trips north, I worked in an office at the Royal Ontario Museum. There the material was formed into chapters and, with the guidance of the members of the advisory committee to whom I was responsible, the book began to take actual form. For a long time it was difficult to determine exactly what sort of reader it should be directed towards. A tourist manual would require one treatment; an historical account another. Artists, scientists, the director of boys and girls camps, all would be interested in one phase or another of the finished product. For myself I kept the firm purpose that I was writing the history of the people in the Park. Since I could not be an expert on all the many undertakings that had been carried on there I must concentrate on the human element. In the end the committee agreed with this and set forth the hope that at a future date someone else would compile a natural history of the region.

"With the completion of the manuscript my part in the production of the book was finished. Members of the committee had discussed the format and the illustrations from time to time, but the Department of Lands and Forests who were in charge of the actual publication made the final choice of cover, type, paper and illustrations.

"A word should be said about the maps which accompan[ied] the [original] book. They were prepared, as the result of a great deal of work, by the cartographers of the Department of Lands and Forests. I worked with these two men and they made careful use of all the source material which had come to light. Much of the data about the old roads had to be drawn from the actual surveyor's records and from the annual accounts of progress in old records. Although some of it did not directly affect the history of the park it was in itself a valuable piece of research. The finished maps are of special interest to people who are familiar with the territory which they depict, but they are also necessary for an intimate study of the text itself.

"Evaluating such an undertaking is difficult at this close range, but some generalization can be made. Certainly Mr. MacDougall was correct in his realization that a great deal of valuable material about the early history of the region did exist in the minds of the residents of the district. Since the information has been gathered at least seven of the people interviewed have died. Their memories would have passed on with them. The sale of the book seems to have exceeded the expectation of those who were responsible for putting it out. As far as one can judge it seems to have been read and received by all kinds of people; those who know the Park well and those who have only a nodding acquaintance with it; those who have never visited it and those who are anxious to do so. It would certainly seem that the planning and the thought that went into the project has been well rewarded."

As Audrey Saunders' attention returned to her teaching career, then marriage and raising a family, Algonquin Park's history continued to unfold and change. Soon after the publication of *Algonquin Story* the highway through the Park was paved. This improved access to the Park, combined with a general increase in population and automobiles, led to new and ever increasing pressures on the Park from its visitors. In 1948, Interior Use Permits, alone, numbered 1300, the few early roadside campgrounds were expanded, additional children's camps were established or planned, additional lodges were opened, and additional cottage leases were taken out in response to government advertising. The people, for whom Algonquin Park was established, were loving the Park to death. By 1954, visitors to the park numbered over 300 000 a year, Interior Use Permits totalled 5 000, and the museum in a tent established in 1947 at Cache Lake to educate visitors about the Park's natural features had been replaced by a permanent structure at Found Lake, attracting over 50 000 visitors annually. From some quarters came a concern that the true spirit of Algonquin Park was becoming lost.

Superintendent George Phillips, perhaps over-protectively, summed up the problems facing the Park as he saw them, in Fred Bodsworth's article *Can They Save Algonquin Park?* published in Maclean's Magazine in 1954:

"It is a battle without end. To preserve a wilderness park you have to fight fires that would burn it up, bugs that would eat it, lumbermen who would chop it down, poachers who would trap and shoot it clean, fish hogs who would catch every fish, wolves that would catch every deer, and businessmen who would turn it into a honky-tonk of dance-halls and hot-dog stands."

Phillips' concerns regarding Algonquin Park coincided with a new appreciation by the provincial government of the role parks should play in the lives of Ontario residents and guests. The realization that there was a need for more, smaller parks near urban areas, was balanced by a desire to protect established parks such as Algonquin.

This led to a 1954 White Paper which proposed the return of Algonquin to a more natural state, limiting and diminishing the number of private leases, lodges and camps within the Park, and maintaining the Park for the public.

But the people of Ontario were not uniform in their thinking. Throughout the 1950s, '60s '70s, there were many different perceptions regarding the appropriate uses of Algonquin Park. This diversity of sometimes conflicting uses raised many concerns, for Park managers and visitors alike, and stimulated considerable debate in the press. In search of solutions, the government of the day turned to a growing body of Park knowledge: founded on fisheries studies beginning in the 1930s and '40s, research on wolves and other Algonquin fauna in the 1960s, natural habitat inventories conducted in the early 1970s and studies on all other aspects of Park use. A Task Force, comprising government officials and representatives of different interest groups, determined that with co-operation and understanding among stake-holders there could be co-existence of dramatically different uses of the park. Algonquin was not a true wilderness, but was close enough to it in spirit for the average urban canoeist or camper. Logging, which had played a vital role in the local economy for over a hundred years, could continue to be carried out with minimal impact on recreational areas. When properly managed, people could continue to enjoy a canoe trip in the Park's interior. In its 1974 Algonquin Park Master Plan (revised as the Algonquin Park Management Plan in 1998), the provincial government reflected a concept of multiple use—first proposed in Ontario by Algonquin's superintendent Frank MacDougall in the 1930s. The Park was divided into zones of varying activity: recreation, recreation/utilization, historical, natural and primitive. Provisions for revision of the plan recognized the existence of recreational, political and market force pressures on Algonquin Park, and stressed the need for continual modification of management to reflect changes in technology and Park use, even to the present.

Scattered throughout Algonquin Park there are still a few old foundations and overgrown clearings that help us recall the old days, but to fully appreciate the lifestyle of the pioneers of Algonquin one has to hear their stories as told in these pages. This edition of *Algonquin Story* is dedicated to Audrey Saunders Miller—author, historian, and educator —who happily approved of this reprint as her legacy to future generations of Algonquin Park visitors. In her memory, a portion of the proceeds from the sale of this book will be used to support the interpretation of Algonquin Park history.

# CHAPTER 1

THREE CENTURIES AGO, in the year 1615, a Frenchman of gentle birth and fierce ambition, his Vandyke beard pointing the way like a spear, craned his neck to see past the sweating Indian paddler ahead of him. The broad expanse of Allumette Lake stretched south; then turned like a goose's neck northward again and west. It was here, two years before, that he had turned back, weary and disillusioned, the plausible fantasies of the opportunist Vigneau exposed for what they were.

This time he would go on.

But when and how would he reach the Western Sea? Had he known what every school child knows today, he would have realized the only Western Sea he would ever reach was the fresh water body we now call Lake Huron. Had he known what every Park ranger in the region knows now, there were three routes over the highlands that separated him from this Sea, each of them less roundabout than the Nipissing-French River approach.

Champlain, for of course he was the Frenchman in question, might have ascended any one of three tributaries of the Ottawa River. First was the Madawaska. Up in the heart of the Algonquin highlands lay its largest lake, Great Opeongo. This same lake could be reached without much portaging by ascending the Bonnechere River to its source in the highlands. A third ascent was more difficult: a long portage past the lower rapids, good going after that, up the Petawawa, called in early times the Nesswabic River, into the northern section of the highland area itself, so pitted and channeled with hundreds of lakes and streams that one could travel by canoe in almost any direction, always provided he was willing to carry his canoe and its cargo overland from time to time. Issuing from the highlands and descending westward into Georgian Bay in Lake Huron, were two streams, the Magnetewan to the north —but well south of the French River — and the Muskoka system of rivers and lakes draining the southwest corner of the highland area.

If his Indian guides knew of these shorter routes they were silent. Champlain's canoes ascended the Ottawa past the mouths of the Madawaska and Bonnechere tributaries, past the mouth of the Petawawa, and reached the Mattawa River approach to Lake

Nipissing. Here he had one last chance to take a shorter route. Descending northward from the Algonquin country into the Mattawa, was the Amable du Fond River, from whose sources he could have reached either the Magnetawan or the upper Muskoka waters. But Champlain and his Indians went past the mouth of the Amable du Fond, crossed over to Lake Nipissing, and descended the French River to the north shore of Georgian Bay. Returning after an unsuccessful two years of Iroquois campaigns with his Huron friends, Champlain used the same route. He had not found the fabulous Western Sea he dreamed of; he had even missed the very real paradise of the Algonquin Lakes and height of land country.

It may be he was not altogether unconscious of the latter loss, though his reference is brief to the lands lying west of the Ottawa River. He says:

> "Moreover, it is quite a wilderness, being uninhabited except by a few Algonquin savages who dwell in the country and live by the fish they catch in the ponds and lakes with which the country is well provided."

As a result of Champlain's finding the first map of this region was compiled in Paris by the King's map-maker, Sanson, in 1653. Across the Algonquin Park region of this early map is the phrase "*Grand chasse de cerfs et de caribous*" — "a fine place to hunt stag and caribou". Whether he surmised this from observing the abundance of game along the south bank of the Ottawa, or whether he learned it from the Indians who actually hunted there, we have no way of knowing.

There is no doubt, however, that he met Indians to whom the region was an open book and an earthly happy hunting ground. Each year, when hunting and trapping was at its best, family groups of these Algonquin bands would pack their kit into light birch-bark hunting canoes to travel up the water routes into the interior. When Champlain came upon them first they were on their summer camp sites along the sandy shores of Lake Nipissing. There the men could catch a plentiful supply of fish, while the women and children could pick and dry the blueberries that Champlain says were used in the same way as dried currants in southern France. This hardly means that any of them could be called natives of the Park region. None of the Algonquin bands had any fixed abode. They wandered about from hunting grounds to fishing regions, from blueberry plains to the shallow lakes where wild rice grew; as the spirit and the state of their larder moved them. A journey of two hundred miles would be nothing for one of these family groups, since they travelled light and took all their worldly belongings with them in their bark canoes. So they might travel in and out of the Park area several times in a single year.

However, in spite of a nomadic existence necessary in a country that could never support more than a few wandering bands at a time, most of the land was regarded as the particular property of some special Indian group. Most early records agree that the Ojibways looked upon all the lands east of Georgian Bay, up to the height of land in the Park area, as their special preserve. The Ottawas claimed hunting rights on the slopes falling toward the Ottawa River. Usually these Indian peoples preferred to live along the main water routes, but at certain periods of the year they would move inland to replenish their stores. For this reason, while there were never any Indians who made their permanent homes in the Park itself, there were frequently Indian groups in that district. Then, as now, it teemed with animal life, and was also an excellent summer camping spot for fishing parties.

From the prairies to the Gulf of St. Lawrence the paper birch grew in abundance, and the Indians who used its bark developed into a language group known variously as Ojibway or Chippewa in the west, Missisaugas and Nipissings in the centre, and Montagnais in the east. But the name most familiar to readers of Canadian history, and that favoured by Champlain himself, is the name borne by the Park today — Algonquin.

Perhaps, being less accessible, the white or paper birch grew to a greater size here, before being stripped of its useful bark. Certainly no other forest product was quite so useful for these Algonquins. Birch bark was an absolute necessity in their way of life, and from early days there were great stands of birch in the Park district. There the Algonquin families could find the raw materials that they needed for their own immediate use. Both the graceful fishing canoe, with decorative rounded ends, and the more practical hunting canoe, smaller and not so well finished, were made of cedar frames covered with birch bark and sealed with spruce gum. As for their homes, these took the form of bark-covered wigwams, distinctly different from the skin-covered tepees used by some of the other Indian tribes. For this wigwam a framework of poles fastened together at the top was first constructed. Then sheets of bark were stretched across the poles. Since these sections have a natural tendency to curl at the edges, they would stay where they were placed. The whole structure could be set up at a new camp-site in a matter of twenty minutes, and when it came time to move on, the dismantling process could take place just as quickly.

Champlain was a soldier and geographer; no anthropologist. As a gallant Frenchman, however, he has left us one tantalizing glimpse of Algonquin dressing habits — a tid-bit for the gorgeously attired beauties of the court of Louis XIII.

> "Above all others our Montagnais and Algonquins are those that take most trouble with it; for they put on their robes strips of porcupine quill which they dye a very beautiful scarlet colour; for they value these strips very highly and take them off to make them serve for other robes when they wish to make a change."

In spite of Champlain's silence, it is not difficult for anyone who camps in Algonquin Park today, with only a dash of historical background, to recreate a typical summer camp of these original Algonquins, situated, let us say, on the shores of Opeongo Lake. Across the bay on that rocky tree-clad point, where a gusty northwest wind blows the flies to shelter in its lee, a little group of bark wigwams stands among the jack-pine. A bark canoe shows up against the blue-grey rock, drawn high into the shore brush so that only the graceful stern is in the water. A young woman clad in doeskin stands beside the fire, leaning over to throw another stick on the fire from time to time; or turning the racks, supported on a tripod of poles, where fillets of fish and strips of caribou meat hang in the rising smoke. Suspended in the shade, on a sturdy pine trunk, is the tight-laced moss-bag of an Indian babe, sleeping in its vertical cradle. An old woman sits on her heels pounding strips of fish and meat already dried, into the pemmican that looks like saw-dust. Not far away a young girl is lacing the seams of a birch basket, with sturdy threads of barked spruce root. A boy of five sits on the rock, thoughtfully munching a piece of dried fish that fell from the rack.

Down the lake two black dots appear against the sparkle of the waves. A woman runs out of the second wigwam and shouts. An ancient crippled creature, with a thousand wrinkles on her old brown face, hobbles to the doorway and squints out.

Before long the men are paddling close, the gunwales of their bark canoes low in the water. Three men and a lad of sixteen, their faces beaming with typical Algonquin good humour — the fishing

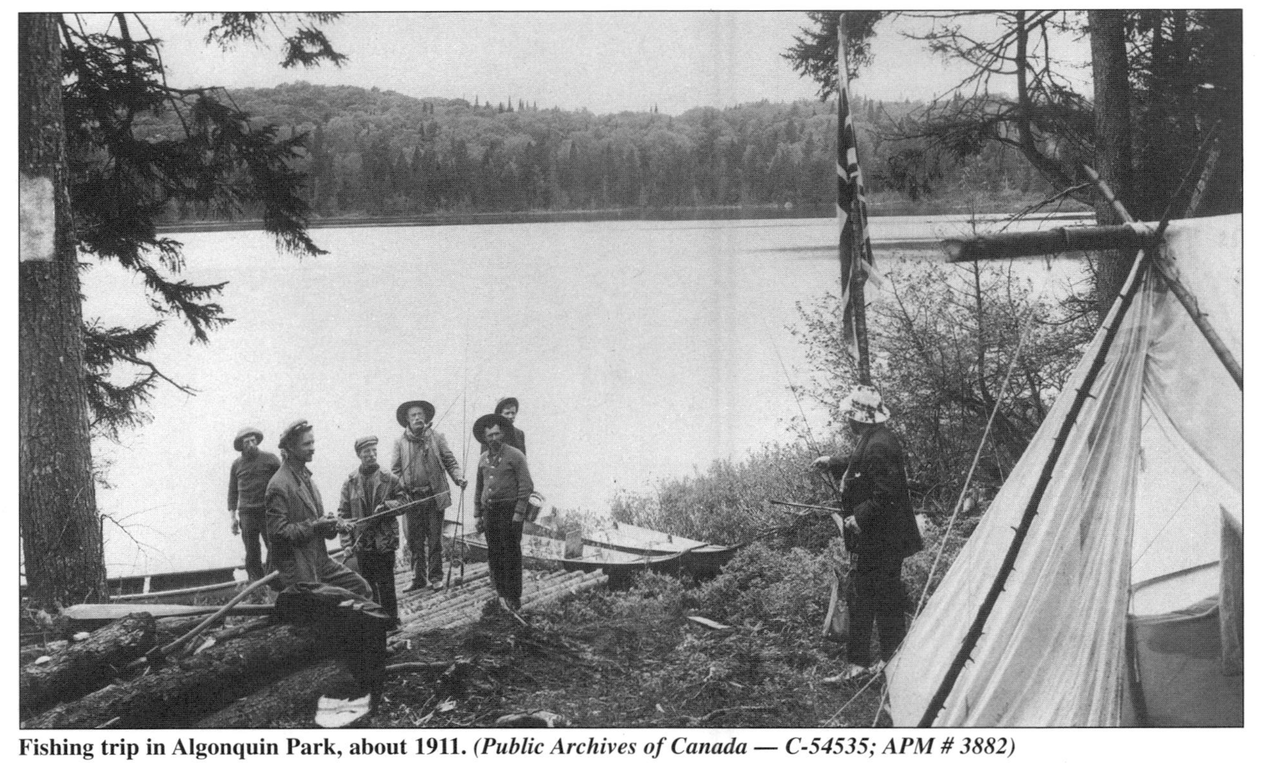

**Fishing trip in Algonquin Park, about 1911.** *(Public Archives of Canada — C-54535; APM # 3882)*

**University of Toronto forestry field camp at Burntroot Lake shelter house in 1908.**
*(Faculty of Forestry Collection, University of Toronto Archives; APM # 3006)*

has been good! Quick gesticulations — a joke about the young lad in the second canoe — happy shouts across the water! The canoes reach shore and eager hands unload the catch, flinging the silver harvest up on a grassy hollow in the rocks.

Change the sinewy Algonquin's hue to a lighter tan, change the yellow bark of the wigwams to the white of canvas tents, substitute modern speech for ancient Ojibway or Ottawa dialects, and we have leaped from pre-history to the present. The contrast of feast and famine, as they knew it, is gone; but fish swarm in Lake Opeongo now as they did then, and the same primeval urge of the fisherman still thrills the boy from Chicago and the girl from Montreal, as they reel in their first lake trout. The doe no longer lies bleeding on the ground, her eyes glazing in death. But the breathless moment of the chase, when the buck stands tense and beautiful in the clearing, still comes to the doctor of New Orleans, pointing his movie camera lens with the same shiver of ecstasy that paralyzed the arm and aim of the Algonquin stripling on his first hunt a thousand years ago.

No modern white Algonquin could have long endured a winter visit with these Indians. Within a winter bark lodge the central fire provided adequate warmth. But the stench of sweaty leather, unbathed bodies — and worse; the eye-smarting fire smoke that did not always find its way out of the hole in the roof; and the confusion of old skins, bones, baskets, hunting equipment and small children, would have driven the modern winter camper, used to a tidy log cabin, into hysterics. Yet no modern sleeping bag has been devised that can rival for pure luxury and comfort the Algonquin rabbit skin robe.

When March came, it was invariably a hungry month. Up to that time some of the supplies prepared during the previous summer, could still be counted on. Usually besides dried blueberries and raspberries, some fish had been smoked, and occasionally there was a cache of game prepared. In the winter, however, it was difficult to go very far afield in search of food. The Algonquin people made snowshoes by bending white ash bows and stringing them with moose or caribou thongs, but otherwise their equipment was very primitive. They were still living in the stone age and had no iron, and only a very little copper. The larger animals had to be killed with stone-tipped arrows, and then skinned and scraped with knives and scraping tools made of stone or of bone. For fishing they used nets woven from willow roots, spears, or bone hooks. Even the task of chopping a hole in the ice in winter, using only a stone axe, would be tedious.

With the Hurons to the south and west, occupying the region between Lake Simcoe and Georgian Bay named after them "Huronia", Champlain was more familiar. Already they had been his allies against the fierce Iroquois of what is now New York State, and neither he nor they needed much persuasian to set out on the long expedition south to Lake Ontario through the Trent River system. All the satisfaction Champlain got out of the affair, was an arrow through the knee. Wanting to get home quickly, he asked his Huron allies whether there was not an eastern outlet to Lake Ontario; but they brought him all the way back to Georgian Bay, and entertained him in their villages.

There, for the winter of 1615-16, Champlain continued to live. During that time, he became aware of some of the difficulties of his own situation. His friends, the Hurons, were not always on the most amiable terms with their Algonquin neighbours to the north. True, they occasionally traded with one another — Huron corn for Algonquin furs — but sometimes wandering war parties raided the settled Huron villages. Champlain undertook to patch up one such quarrel since eventually, to return home to Quebec, he would have to pass through Algonquin territory, and he preferred to be regarded as their friend.

Back in Quebec at last, Champlain had a rich fund of stories, and his published report fired the imagination of the Recollet Fathers. Within a few years the black robes, and white, bearded faces of French priests lost much of their strangeness for the Algonquins camping along the Ottawa-Nipissing route to Huronia. The kindly fathers regretted that they could not take time to preach the gospel to these scattered groups whom they encountered along the way, but these Indians' way of life and their linguistic variation, presented difficulties that the first missionaries found hard to overcome. Instead, the Recollets, and the Jesuits who carried on their work after 1632, concentrated on the settled Huron lands lying betweeen the Georgian Bay and Lake Simcoe. As time when on, occasional workers were sent from the great mission headquarters at Ste. Marie to establish dependent outposts for some of the wandering Algonquin bands.

To convert these people to Christianity, and then to keep them in the fold, was no easy task. One of the Fathers, writing his annual report in 1648, made mention of this problem when he said:

> "All these tribes are nomads, and have no fixed residence except at certain seasons of the year when the fish are plentiful, and this compels them to remain on the spot. Therefore, they have no other church than the woods and forests; no other altar than the rocks which break the waves of this lake. However . . . the sky is as good as the vaults of a church; and not for one day only has the earth been the footstool of Him Who has created it."

In spite of these obstacles, the Jesuits had at this time at least two missions on Lake Nipissing.

One further ray of light on the lives and manners of these Algonquins is shed by an early account of friction between Christian priests and the native medicine-men.

> "Last summer an Algonquin, a Sorcerer by trade, or at least one of those who make profession of invoking Manitou, that is the Devil, who found himself worsted in an argument by the Father, fell on him in a fury, threw him down, and dragged him by the feet through the coals and ashes, and had not the Savages hastened to his assistance, this man would have ended by murdering him. That is what one has to fear, even from friends."

In spite of all these difficulties, the Jesuits continued to do what they could for these wandering Algonquin bands, as long as they were able to maintain their missions in the Georgian Bay district. And though we have no record of it, a black robed Rocellet father or recently converted Algonquin chief may have said the first Christian prayer under the pines on the shores of an Algonquin lake.

But neither priest nor chief could have realized that before many years had passed, the seeds of the gospel of love would fall no more for many years on Algonquin ground; nor could they have heard the war drums beating far to the south, where the implacable enemies of the Hurons were preparing to reap the red harvest of hate.

Just three hundred years ago, the Indians who hunted and fished, picked berries, and peeled bark from the birches of the Algonquin region, their bellies pinched with hunger or distended with meat according to the vagaries of their nomad life, were suddenly confronted with war. Where Algonquin mothers had bent in love over their papooses, the fierce Iroquois bent in savage triumph over his fallen victim, grasping his hair with one hand, dexterously circling his head with an iron scalping-knife, and wrenching the limp skin and hair from the still breathing body of the Algonquin brave. There is little doubt that beside more than one of these peaceful lakes, where the water lies calm as glass and the sun shines warmly overhead from the bluest of skies, there once lay such a body, gasping its last tortured moan, as the blood slowly oozed from the bare red skull-top, clotted, and turned black in the sun and wind. Where now the bear and the fox live unmolested, the blood of men, murdered by their fellow-men, once trickled to the ground.

In 1648 and 1649 the Iroquois from northern New York State attacked Huronia, burning Huron villages to the ground, torturing their captives, martyring the heroic Jesuit fathers Lalemant and Brébeuf.

The Iroquois confederacy, known commonly as the Five Nations, was in existence at the time when Dutch traders first set up a post at the mouth of the Hudson River. From the Dutch and from the English who took over the settlements along the Atlantic seaboard, the Iroquois obtained firearms in exchange for beaver skins. The European demand for furs was so great, that within a few years the whole region south of Lake Ontario had been almost denuded of beaver, while at the same time the Indians had become accustomed to the goods which the trade brought them. In consequence, the Iroquois began to look to the regions north of the lake as a hunting ground for themselves.

At the same time they became aware that French priests, and, in their wake, French traders, were making contact with the Indians of this region. That meant that if the Iroquois were to gain control of the rich fur-bearing lands lying to the south of the Lake Nipissing route connecting Luke Huron with the Ottawa River, they would have to get rid of the Indians who were friendly with the French. It meant also that they would have to get rid of the Algonquin trade route. Their campaign in Ontario, beginning in the winter of 1648, showed careful planning.

They first crossed over Lake Ontario in the Trenton district, and then, travelling on snow-shoes, came northwards along the Trent River system. The Jesuit records of their attacks on the Huron missions show that the first post seized was that called St. Joseph, between the present towns of Barrie and Orillia, and since these were surprise attacks, it is probable that the raiding bands had come from the northeast. It is quite likely that the Iroquois had spent the previous winter in the Algonquin Park-Haliburton region, where they would find a plentiful supply of game to tide them over between the time they came north on the frozen rivers and the time they attacked the Hurons in July.

We learn of their subsequent actions from the next year's account in the Jesuit Relations. In the fall of 1648 the Iroquois must have returned to the Algonquin Park region, and, as a matter of fact, they must have travelled all through it, because they went as far north as Lake Nipissing and as far east as the Ottawa River itself. They spent the whole winter in that region, and returned in the next summer to complete the destruction of the Huron villages, and to carry on the massacre of the French priests stationed at Ste. Marie. Late that year, when the remnants of the French band retraced their steps back to the Quebec settlements, they found that the familiar Lake Nipissing route had been laid waste by the marauding Iroquois.

The Algonquin Indians, too, must have suffered at the hands of the invaders. The returning party of Frenchmen and their Indian friends found Algonquin wigwams destroyed all along the shores of Lake Nipissing, and evidence that some of the Iroquois had spent the previous winter there. From that time on, for a period of almost a hundred years, French traders using the Ottawa route knew they were running the gauntlet of a hostile tribe. Twice the French challenged their sway — once when Dollard and his brave band of comrades stopped the Iroquois' attack on Montreal itself in 1660, and again when Frontenac, the fighting Governor, was brought back to New France to deal with this menace. Frontenac was able to make peaceful arrangements with the Iroquois, so that there were fewer raids along the Ottawa River route after 1701, than before that time.

However, the Iroquois did not entirely disappear from the Algonquin Park district until well on in the Eighteenth Century. We learn this from stories of French fur traders who dared to venture north again along the Ottawa River route, which had been so effectively blocked by the Iroquois. One reason why the trip taken by Radisson and Grosseilliers was regarded as so epoch-making, was that they managed to get through this Iroquois-controlled route. However, these, and other French traders, did not attempt to penetrate into the Algonquin Park country itself. Why they did not can be seen from a map of that period, dated 1720, where the

Algonquin Park region is marked as *"Chasse de castor des Iroquois"*. At that period the Iroquois still used the district in order to hunt the beaver for the English traders, whose headquarters were in New York State. The first English maps printed after Canada became British, show that the Park area was still under Iroquois control. On a map of 1763, the Algonquins are shown in the neighbourhood of Sault Ste. Marie, while the Iroquois are located in the Park. The Missisaugas, north of the French River, were the only Algonquin tribe left in the district.

Finally war, that had driven the Algonquins from their native haunts, made it possible for them to return. The Iroquois warriors whetted their scalping knives and moved south again to fight with the British against the French, in the Seven Years War. Quebec fell, and the Treaty of Paris was signed. The American colonies revolted, and Joseph Brant with his followers, threw in their lot with the Loyalists. The settlement of these peoples along the valley of the Grand River in southern Ontario meant that they had become a peaceful agricultural nation, and that they were no longer interested in their previous hunting grounds to the north. Then it was, that the Algonquin bark canoes appeared once more on the placid waters of the Park.

There were three outlets for furs from the Algonquin Park region in the nineteenth century. The first was by way of the fur trading posts operated by the great companies along the Lake Nipissing-Ottawa Valley route; the second by way of the Muskoka Lakes and Penetanguishene; and the third was that used by a private trader, Charles Thomas, who set up his post on the lower Bonnechere River at the favorite Indian gathering place at Golden Lake. All three of these groups of traders operated independently, but all looked to Indians trapping in the Park area as one of their chief sources of supply.

The North West Company, which was founded in Montreal soon after the British took over the French colony, found in the Ottawa River route its main artery to the west. Up the old Champlain trail, and out by way of the Lake of the Woods route to the western prairies, went the French-Canadian voyageurs; who carried the company's supplies over thousands of miles into the interior, and returned in the following year with their freight canoes laden with precious furs. All along the way was a chain of forts acting as supply bases and trading centres, from which the company's employees could contact the neighbouring Indians. Early records show that along the Ottawa route, there were at least five of these posts which could have been reached by Indians bringing their wares down the rivers that flow out of the Algonquin Park district. That French traders went into the area themselves, we know from the names of some of the lakes that are found on very early maps such as Lake Lavieille, but in general they preferred to have the Indians bring their season's catch out to the posts along the great water route.

When the North West Company amalgamated with the Hudson's Bay Company in 1821, most of these Ottawa Valley posts continued to operate under the latter's name. Of these the most important was the one called Fort William, situated on the north bank of the Ottawa, opposite the mouth of the Petawawa River. There the Hudson's Bay Company continued to trade with the Indians who lived in the surrounding country. When we examine the records of the trip taken by Alexander Sherriff through the Park district in 1829, we shall find that the company officials knew little about the country from which these furs had come, and that the Indians living on the shores of the Ottawa River had never travelled inland from the main route. On the other hand, the Indians whom Sherriff later found hunting on the upper reaches of the Petawawa in the Park, told him that they took their furs out to the Ottawa Valley posts in order to trade them for the goods that they needed. These particular Algonquins likely traded at the Mattawa fort since, according to their own accounts, they were accustomed to travel from their winter camping grounds in the Cedar Lake district, by way of the Amable du Fond River, in order to dispose of their catch.

Once Sherriff had crossed over the height of land, in his journey through the Park, he found that the Indians along the Muskoka waters marketed their wares at Penetanguishene. Independent traders who had their storehouses at Penetanguishene, travelled all through the Muskoka Lakes from about 1825. One of them, by the name of Thompson, was the founder of the store at Penetanguishene which still bears his name. The Lake of Bays district became so well known as a fur trading centre that one of the neighbouring lakes was called Trading Lake, and some of these independent traders set up posts in the area.

A later development came in this same region with the opening up of a Hudson's Bay post at Orillia in the 1860's. Then the Ojibway Indians who had their headquarters at Lake Couchiching could bring their furs from the Oxtongue district, in the southwest corner of the Park, right down to this post. As an offshoot of the Orillia trading house, and as a way of intercepting some of the free traders who still came into the Lake of Bays from the Georgian Bay coast, the Orillia factor, Mr. Thomas Goffatt, set up an outpost on Lake of Bays, where Bigwin Inn now stands. These posts were all abandoned when the coming of settlers into the Haliburton region turned the channels of the trade in the opposite direction, to the buyers who came into Minden at the end of steel.

In the southeast area of the present Park, in the Golden Lake district, a parallel development was taking place. There, too, independent traders went inland to meet the Indians before they could bring their wares out to the posts of the Hudson's Bay Company along the Ottawa Valley. Charles Thomas, who established a post at Golden Lake about 1832, is typical of these free traders. Thomas was a man with a wide and varied experience in the fur-trading business; in fact, he had been born into the trade at the Hudson's Bay post at Moose Factory on James Bay, where his father was stationed in 1793. He was sent back to the old country to school, and afterwards acted as Inspector of Forts for the Hudson's Bay Company on Great Slave and Great Bear Lakes. Travelling by canoe, he brought his wife and family down to Montreal in 1822, and after several years of working intermittently for the Company on the Ottawa and the Bonnechere Rivers, he finally decided to enter business for himself in that same region.

But the great days of the fur trade in the Algonquin region were nearly over. Each year the great stands of red and white pine farther down the Ottawa valley were falling one by one; each year the ominous thud of steel axe on pine trunk shattered the winter silence a little closer to the ancient Algonquin hunting-grounds. Down the Ottawa, never to return, floated the great square "sticks" of timber in thousands; and all along its shores lay the heaps of "slash", while great gashes in the forest showed like wounds.

It was Charles Thomas at Golden Lake, who presuaded his naturally suspicious Indian friends to allow the first Algonquin timber cruiser, Alexander Macdonell, to enter the country. With the traditional courtesy of the north, he even wheedled the Indians into making for him a rough sketch map on birch bark, of the route between the headwaters of the Bonnechere and Madawaska Rivers. Therefore, it was only a matter of time, before axes were heard in the very heart of the land of the Algonquin.

## CHAPTER 2

TWO HUNDRED YEARS after Champlain's canoes first pushed their graceful bows up the Ottawa River, neither Indian wars nor Jesuit missionaries, nor even the fur-trapping Algonquin, had disturbed the primitive grandeur of the country that would one day become Algonquin Park. Perhaps fires had become more numerous, though even on his first expedition Champlain had used the word "brûlé", to describe such areas along the upper Ottawa. In little marshy ponds the swamp grass had grown farther out from the shores; up on the hills a forest giant had crashed to the ground from time to time, split by the lightning of a passing storm. The trout tribe still swam supreme in the deep lakes and rushing streams, undisturbed by the black bass introduced in modern times. Caribou were getting scarce, as were the coveted fisher and marten. But fundamentally, there had been no change in the land for twenty thousand years.

Soon the eyes of the curious Canada jay would bulge with amazement at the sight of a "camboose" camp in the heart of the Algonquin forest. Soon the chickadee would call pert greetings in the winter woods to the faller, as his axe bit into the base of a great white pine.

But before, and during, the development of the lumbering industry in the region, there were other white pioneers with other axes to grind.

Over in Europe the Napoleonic wars had ended; and so had their echo in North America — the series of skirmishes along the Canadian-American border, known as the War of 1812-14. This latter war had made the British guardians of the colony of Upper Canada, acutely conscious of strategic weaknesses in their system of defence; and obsessed with the necessity for an alternative water route from Lower Canada to the upper Great Lakes, so that military supplies from the seaport of Quebec could safely reach the inland bases at Penetanguishene and Michilimackinac.

Now that peace had come again, land-hungry British immigrants and war-weary British veterans were finding that the easily-reached border lands along the Lower Lakes were already settled. Land companies, as well as government officials, began to wonder what kind of land the interior of present-day Ontario held, and exploration parties were sent far afield, to bring back reports on the agricultural possibilities of the border land to the north of old Ontario.

Beginning in 1818, and continuing for the next fifty years, the Algonquin Park country had its share of canoe-trippers, who passed to and fro along the Park highways. These travellers were sent there for specific purposes. There were army officers seeking transportation routes to bases on Lake Huron and Lake Superior; there were government and private surveyors sent to report on the soil and vegetation of the region, and to trace out the courses of the many rivers flowing out of this height of land. All these men have left some record of their visits to the Park, but very few of these stories have ever reached the public eye.

Information about the first three travellers in the district, depends chiefly on a hand-drawn map of Lieut. Walpole's route from Lake Simcoe to the Ottawa River. This map has an inset which shows where the two other Royal Engineers, Lieut. Catty and Lieut. Briscoe, had journeyed during the preceding ten years. All three of these men were seeking new ways of linking the older colonies with outposts at Fort Michilimackinac and farther west.

Catty's course touched the southeastern tip of the present Park. He went inland from Lake Simcoe, and travelled by way of Balsam, Gull, and Kennisis Lakes in Haliburton, through into Pen, Rock, and Long Lakes (where Whitney is now situated). Finally he made his way by means of the Madawaska through to the Ottawa River.

Briscoe's journey in 1826 took him through a much larger section of the Park. He went up the Oxtongue River into Smoke Lake, and then across, by way of Hilliard Lake, into Cache Lake and the Madawaska River. It is interesting to note, that of the three ways of crossing from the Muskoka waters to those of the Madawaska — by way of Source Lake, by way of Kootchie Lake, or by way of Hilliard Lake — the last mentioned, which is the least used to-day, is the earliest on record. From the Lake of Two Rivers, Briscoe's party travelled by means of a series of portages through Sundan, and other small lakes, into Opeongo. From there, he passed north into Hogan's, and thence by the little Madawaska River, into the Petawawa proper.

Walpole's map shows that he went by a route that carried him slightly to the south of the Park, in his journey from Lac des Chats, near the present Pembroke, to Lake Simcoe, but he, too, made use of the Madawaska route. Fortunately, we have some first-hand information about this trip, which was taken in 1826. One of his canoemen, by the name of Croteau, was along some nine years later on another expedition conducted by Lieut. Baddeley in the Black River area, and when Baddeley's party was marooned at camp during a series of rainy days, Croteau began to recall what had happened on his earlier trip. He spoke of the Black River as the route by which Lieut. Walpole had travelled on his way to the Ottawa, and of the journey that he himself had taken from the head of the Chats Rapid, by way of the Bonnechere River, to meet Walpole at the dividing ridge between the Ottawa River and Lake Huron. Croteau says that this meeting took place on September 12th. From the ridge they travelled on down to Lake Simcoe, which they reached on the 27th of September, by way of the Talbot River. Although there is no official record of the finding of this excursion, Croteau may have been echoing Walpole's own sentiments when he described what they had seen along the way. He says:

> "The land through which we passed was in general very good, but the best we noticed was on the Madawaska River where there was large prairie and very little rock. The height or dividing ridge consisted of land covered with a fine growth of maple. The longest portage met with was nine miles on the Talbot River through excellent land. In the spring of the year you may pass by canoe from Lake Simcoe to Bytown (Ottawa) in eight or nine days."

By the 1820's the Ottawa Valley below Bytown (now the City of Ottawa), had been opened up as farming land to incoming settlers. Lumbering activities, begun during the Napoleonic Wars to provide materials for the ships of the Royal Navy, had helped to clear the land in the first place, and as usual the lumberman was giving way to the farmer. On the upper Ottawa, it was to be expected that the same shift of occupation would take place, and promoters were beginning to wonder what this district held in the way of agricultural lands. As early as 1825, pine was being cut on the Madawaska and the Bonnechere Rivers, but as yet few permanent settlers had taken up land.

It was because Charles Sherriff of Quebec City was anxious to find what the chances were for settling immigrants in the Ottawa-Huron tract that his son, Alexander, undertook his trip through the district in 1829. In his report, which was published two years later in Quebec, we learn that he wanted to find out whether transportation on the upper Ottawa River made it feasible to bring settlers into that region; and if the land was fertile enough to justify settlement.

Sherriff, as a result of his earlier experience in the south along the St. Lawrence, had a bee in his bonnet that misdirected popular conceptions of the Park region for nearly half a century. He had found that the presence of hardwood forests was an almost infallible sign that the land, when cleared, would make excellent farm country. The luxuriant stands of maple and other hardwoods along the ridges of the Park district convinced him that the area would be ideal for settlement, and his whole report glows with the enthusiasm of a man astride his favourite hobby-horse.

Sherriff travelled up the Ottawa almost to the mouth of the Mattawa. Beyond Arnprior, settlements thinned out quickly, but Sherriff was convinced the land was fertile, and was eager to penetrate the almost unknown hinterland.

The only route known to him was Catty's, and he eagerly questioned everyone he met on the way, trader and Indian alike. Near Fort William, a Hudson's Bay Post almost opposite the site of Pembroke, Ontario, he encountered a large canoe bearing a man of substance.

> "Here Mr. Simpson, the Governor of the company, passed us on his return trip from a northern tour, impelled by the strength of the stream and ten or twelve stout paddles that carried him with the velocity of the wind."

Immediately after that he was amazed, on turning a bend of the river, to find a whole family newly deposited, with all their household goods, on the river bank. The head of the house calmly watched Sherriff's canoe turn in, and strolled over, his hands in his pockets, to meet him as he landed. He was the first of the group of settlers who were to take up land in the Pembroke area, and told Sherriff that

> "his intention was to clear the land and to lumber some, and in addition to keep a rum and whiskey shop when he could obtain a supply."

Sherriff felt that he had chosen a good spot to carry on all three of these occupations.

Finally, by repeated questionings, Sherriff decided on the best course for his party to follow. Neither of the lower tributaries, the Madawaska or the Bonnechere, appealed to him as a way into the interior, but Indians and private traders whom he encountered told him of "the largest of the Upper Canada tributaries — the Nesswabic". This was the name by which the Indians called the main branch of the nearby river, although one of the smaller inland branches seemed to bear the name of the "Pittoiwais". How to make his way up this river presented a major problem, since it was known to be very full of rapids close to its mouth. At length, however, he learned of a portage from Deux Rivières, and he decided to travel by that route. An Indian gave him a chart of the way they should go to preserve their bark canoes, and they set off overland to strike the Petawawa farther up its course.

Their own Indian canoeman and guide didn't seem to know very much about the country through which they expected to pass. From him, and from others, Sherriff had learned that

> "the lands of the Algonquin Indians frequenting the Ottawa do not extend quite to the height of land, at least on the Nesswabic; and the traders on the Ottawa have no communication with the Missisaugas who hunt beyond the Algonquins".

Sherriff had to be content with this guide who had never travelled through the district, but who claimed that he could act as an interpreter for any other Indians whom they should encounter during their trip.

When the party left Deux Rivières it was already late in August, and they were anxious to get across to Penetanguishene and back again, before the winter closed in. They found their first portage a difficult one. For about eight miles the trail led inland through a wilderness country. Sometimes they seemed to be following a path, but at others they lost it altogether. Finally they arrrived at a stream where they were able to launch their canoes. A paddle of about twelve miles brought them out to an expansion of the river which they were seeking. There at Trout (now Radiant) Lake, they found themselves on the Petawawa waters, and so they went on upstream to Cedar Lake.

At Cedar Lake, Sherriff camped for three days. One of his men had injured his leg on a portage, the weather was bad; and they met a party of Indians who had just arrived. These Indians who had chosen this spot to set up a winter hunting camp gave him directions for the next leg of his journey. Constant Pennaissez, son of an Algonquin chief and head of the party, drew for Sherriff a sketch of the best route up the Nessswabic (now the Petawawa) nearly to its source; though he would not, or could not, direct him over the height of land into Muskoka waters.

Constant, whose name seeems to have been preserved in Constant Lake and Constant Creek in Renfrew County, also told Sherriff of an alternate route from the Ottawa to Cedar Lake. According to him there was a much better way that the Indians usually used themselves

> "by a stream entering the Cedar Lake from the north and communicating with another called by the Indians who hunted on it Map di Fong (Amable du Fond's) Creek. This, though the longest, is much the smoothest route and is always followed by the Indians passing between the Ottawa and Cedar Lake with loaded canoes."

Apparently the Indians themselves preferred to take their furs out of the Park by making use of the chain of lakes linking Cedar Lake to Kioshkuqui. From there the journey down to the Ottawa was much easier than either the way Sherriff had come, or the way he was to return — that is, by going right down the main stream of the Petawawa River.

When he had learned all he could Sherriff made his plans. The man with the game leg would be left behind with the smaller of the two eighteen-foot bark canoes, and instructions not to go any farther afield than Trout Lake for thirty days. In the meantime, with the help of the friendly Constant, it was felt that he would be able to fend for himself and give his leg a chance to heal. The others — four in all — were to go on towards the Georgian Bay coast in the other canoe. For this trip they were to take only twenty days' provisions, so that they could get to and fro as quickly as possible. If they did not return at the appointed time the injured man was to make his way back to the Ottawa as well as he could.

Sherriff and his men continued on south from Cedar Lake, along what is now one of the most travelled canoe routes in the Park. Even at that time there was a good portage road to avoid that part of the river that the lumbermen afterwards called "The Five Mile" because of the rapids covering that distance. When Sherriff describes this road we can identify it with the one that is still there today, for he says,

> "It has been formed north of the channel, through a hardwood tract in which three small lakes are crossed, and this at length brings us to elevated country."

In that district Sherriff made particular note of the tree growth, since he found white pine everywhere prevalent with very little of the red pine he had seen elsewhere. On the whole, however, he felt that maple made up about half the forest — a sure sign, in his estimation, that the land was fertile.

As for the fishing in that region he declared that

> "the waters of the Nesswabic surpass those of any other river I have seen in this country."

He found the eels and catfish to be of a size rarely seen in the Ottawa, and the white or lake trout he learned could be caught in great abundance both in the winter and in the summer. These latter were of a light silvery hue, cream-coloured in the flesh, and frequently as much as forty pounds in weight.

All along their way the party had Constant's chart to guide them; but after three days, as they approached the height of land, they found that they were once more entering unknown territory. Now they were in the Missisauga hunting grounds, and their problem was to find the portage that would lead to the head-waters of a river flowing towards the Georgian Bay. Once they lost their way, but were lucky enough to meet another Indian, the first human soul they had seen since Cedar Lake, by whose directions they were able to cross into the Muskoka waters via Otter Lake, now called McIntosh Lake.

Oddly enough, this Indian was an interloper in the district, one of a group of Iroquois who resided on the Ottawa at the Lake of Two Mountains. Actually, he was poaching extensively on the territories controlled by other Indians. He told Sherriff that he had not interfered with the furs in the lands of his friends of the Ottawa Valley, the Algonquins, but had passed on through to the country of the Missisaugas. He had been wandering around in those parts for the best part of a year, and described it as "Bonne terre, partout, partout". Besides knowing about the existence of the "South River" flowing into Lake Nipissing, he told them of the Muskoka route through to Georgian Bay. He had just come back along that way himself, since he had been down to Penetanguishene to market his goods and lay in his winter's supplies. In doing this he must have passed right through the territory controlled by "Muskeekee", also called "Yellowhead", the Ojibway chief who regarded the Lake of Bays district as exclusive Ojibway hunting grounds. The name "Muskoka" comes from the name of this Indian leader.

With the Indian poacher's help, Sherriff had no difficulty in finding the right portage across to the first small lake that lay on the Lake Huron side of the watershed. At that lake he noticed that the beavers had built a dam across the outlet, with the result that they had "nearly affected a junction of the Huron and Ottawa waters". His passage down the Muskoka, for which he said the Indians had a name, but which he could not discover, was comparatively simple. All along the way he continued to remark on the nature of the rock formations and the type of soil, and he noticed that there was very little limestone in the area until he reached the neighbourhood of Penetanguishene. In order to get to the trading post at that point, he went down the main stream of the Muskoka instead of going by way of the Severn River portage, the route taken by the Indian hunter he had encountered in the Park district. He and his party finally arrived at their destination on the 17th of September, eighteen days from the time they had left the Ottawa.

At the little outpost they visited the naval station in the cove, and they noticed the

> "small new inroads into the forests with buildings apparently of a few days' standing".

Then they set out on their return trip to the Ottawa. This time they passed up the Severn River, which Sherriff described as the common route by which fur traders from that point crossed into Lake Muskoka. As yet none of the lakes and rivers in those parts had been named, but the geographers have been able to reconstruct their route. When they reached the height of land between the Muskoka and the Madawaska waters, they crossed over through Source Lake along a portage which is supposed to be one of the best travelled of Indian paths through the Park area. From there they passed down the Madawaska almost to Rock Lake, and thence, by a series of portages, some of them as much as three miles long, into the south end of Lake Opeongo, then called "Abeunga".

Sherriff's description of this lake is the earliest that we have, and in view of later stories about a Hudson's Bay post on the shore of the lake, it is interesting to note that he mentions that there was a building there in 1829, which might answer to that description. Four miles up the lake near the place where they passed into the eastern arm, he says, "there is a trading house occupied by the Company in the hunting season". In actual fact, although we have seen already that to Sherriff "the Company" meant the Hudson's Bay Company, it seems quite improbable that the Company went

**White Pine loggers outside their camboose shanty.** *(Ministry of Natural Resources; APM # 1038)*

**Timber chute on the Petawawa River, between Catfish Lake and Cedar Lake, in 1939.**

against its long established custom of encouraging the trappers to bring their wares out to them at the trading posts.

The party went on through the East Arm to "Lac Clair" (now Dickson Lake) which was described as "a pretty piece of water but with sterile looking shores". From there they passed into Lake "Lavieille", also named previously by French trappers or lumbermen who seem to have travelled all through that part of the country. In all, Sherriff felt that this return trip was a most harassing one, and that the route that they had followed on their way out had been much easier. At length, on the twenty-fifth day after leaving Cedar Lake, they returned to that spot in order to pick up the man that had been left behind there. They found him fully recovered; and, once more in their two canoes, they set off for the final lap of the homeward journey to the Ottawa. When they reached the mouth of the Petawawa at Lac des Allumettes, they found that the return trip had taken only twelve days from Penetanguishene. At that time, they reckoned that for anyone knowing the route, the time could be reduced to ten days by the Petawawa-Muskoka River waterway over which they had originally travelled.

In Sherriff's report, it is interesting to see what general conclusions he draws about the district through which he had been journeying. Along the courses of both the Petawawa and the Muskoka Rivers he felt that the soil was sufficiently light and highly elevated to be useful as agricultural land. In addition, he pointed out that the region was without rival as a health resort for

> "its considerable elevation, and pure waters ensure it as being unsurpassed by any other section of the country in the important requisites of healthiness".

Although it took the better part of fifty years to convince Government authorities that the land would never really be any good for settlement and farming, no one has ever contradicted Sherriff's praise of the bracing air and crystal-pure waters of the Algonquin area.

In 1835 the Government of Upper Canada secured two British officers to conduct a survey of that section of the Province lying between the settled regions fronting on Lake Ontario and Lake Nipissing. To Lieut. Carthew, a naval officer, and Lieut. Baddeley, of the Royal Engineers, was given the task of surveying a line from the northeast corner of the Township of Rama, near Lake Couchiching, northward to the shores of Lake Nipissing. The authorities had originally intended that this line should serve as a base for later surveying parties when they proceeded to open up these townships for settlement. In actual fact, however, the line that Carthew and Baddeley ran was not sufficiently accurate for this purpose. On present-day maps, it is possible to follow its course to a point about eight miles south of Skeleton Lake. Beyond that point, the numerous lakes and rough terrain adequately account for the inaccuracy of this first survey.

In fact, when one considers the hardships of these early surveyors, one wonders at their patience. To crouch over a surveyor's transit and sight accurately down the line while a swarm of mosquitoes or blackflies suck savagely at one's neck, behind the ears, and at the tender skin of the wrist, demanded the faith and philosophy of Job himself. To this was added the heart-breaking task of carrying every last ounce of food, shelter, and equipment on human backs. Here in the wild fastnesses of the Algonquin wilderness even a mule was useless.

When Carthew and Baddeley set forth from the capital at Toronto they were charged with two tasks; they were to run this survey line north, but they were also to carry on lateral excursions up all the large rivers flowing into Georgian Bay, in order to report on the agricultural possibilities of the district. Baddeley, who was a competent geologist and a student of natural history, was equipped with a copy of Sherriff's earlier account as he journeyed into this same region, so that we may infer that the Government was seeking to confirm or refute his optimism over the farming possibilities in that area.

The technique then employed was to establish a base for supplies at Penetanguishene, and then to conduct survey parties, in two separate groups, up the different rivers that could be reached along the Georgian Bay coast. In this way, one or other of the leaders ascended the Severn, the Black, the Muskoka, the Shawanaga, and the two branches of the Magnetawan Rivers. Whenever one of these parties returned to the shore of Georgian Bay, it would be met by Mr. Beeman, a trader and storekeeper from Penetanguishene, who was to bring additional supplies up the coast in his sloop. In this way a preliminary survey of the whole area was conducted between July and November of that year.

Although neither of the parties actually penetrated into the present area of the Park, Lieut. Baddeley in his excursion up the Magnetawan very nearly did so. This trip is of interest to us for two reasons — because of the information that he gained from an Indian whom he encountered as he travelled upstream, about a route across the Park to the Ottawa Valley, and because the obstacles which he encountered and overcame were typical of those which all travellers into the Park district faced in the early days.

Baddeley's diary of his October trip gives us a good idea of how these surveys were conducted. Early in the fall when he and his party were out at the coast of Georgian Bay, he had a difficult time with his Indian canoemen. They told him that the season had arrived for them to lay in their winter's supply of fish, and that they wanted to return to their families. However, Baddeley was sufficiently persuasive to overcome their concern, and the party was able to continue its exploratory trip up the Magnetawan River. Once this journey was well under way, a spirit of adventure descended upon the whole party. They seem to have lost all desire for a speedy return to their families, and completely forgot the arrangements made previously to connect with other members of the survey party at a meeting place on the Georgian Bay coast. Instead, they determined to push on up past Ahmic Lake into the headwaters of the Magnetawan River, and thence, across the height of land into another stream, which they learned flowed out into the Ottawa Valley.

This scheme grew out of a conversation with an Indian whom they met on the river. He gave Baddeley a "carte du pays", told him about a cache of provisions that he had stored on an island in one of the lakes along the way, and persuaded him that it was quite simple to cross through to the Ottawa River. Baddeley gave him a "wampum of acknowledgment which would enable him to secure a gun or a pair of blankets at Toronto" for his information, and tried, without success, to persuade the Indian's boy to accompany them as their guide. When this attempt failed, the party decided to go on through to the Ottawa by themselves. For two days they continued up the south branch of the Magnetawan until gradually they found the navigation more difficult. Then they started to have qualms about the Indian's honesty, and to wonder if there really was a cache as he had said. Added to those doubts was the lateness of the season, dramatically brought home to them when one of the party got a ducking and nearly froze in his dripping clothes. Finally at a spot which they judged to be

> "within ten or fifteen miles of the dividing ridge which throws the waters one way into Lake Huron and the other into the Ottawa."

they decided to go back by the way they had come.

Then the real privations began. They had no ammunition left for their guns, and for some strange reason the district which usually abounded in both game and fish proved barren. When they met some of the other members of their party on October 31st they were still a long way from their supply base, and their total stock for twelve men consisted of six pounds of flour and a little pea soup. By November 2nd conditions began to look serious, and Baddeley decided to take one canoe in order to push on towards Georgian Bay, to see if he could make contact with the sloop that was supposed to be waiting for them there. On their way they were so hungry they even tried some of the pond lilies which the muskrats usually eat. These they found to be impossibly bitter. At length, on the evening of November 4th, after they had devoured the last crumb of the bannocks they had previously made from the flour, they came upon the sloop near the mouth of the Shawanaga River. When the other canoes came along soon after they were saved a return trip with supplies, and the whole group proceeded by boat back to their original starting point at Penetanguishene.

Baddeley, in his report, completely disagreed with Sherriff's estimate of the Ottawa-Huron Tract as good farm land. Referring directly to Sherriff's survey, he said:

> "In passing we beg to call the reader's attention to Mr. Sherriff's communication as well deserving his perusual. We think, however, generally that he has drawn too favourable an inference from level and quality of timber, neglecting the more important consideration of the soil, which almost everywhere throughout the country appears to be excessively light and sandy, and often very shallow."

Later on he says more definitely, "The growth of hardwood on land is by no means a *positive* indication of good soil."

However, with a view to the future development of the district, he gave to the authorities two other pieces of information that were to prove valuable. He spoke of transportation routes through the country, and made it clear that it would be much easier to penetrate into the area by way of the Ottawa Valley than by way of the south or western approaches. In this connection he says:

> "It seems reasonable to suppose that it will be by way of the Ottawa and Rice Lakes, rather than by Lake Huron that its good lands will be settled eventually."

In addition, in order to give an idea of the climate of the region, he drew up a meteorological table to show the variety of weather and temperature that the group encountered during the months they were working in the north. This is of interest to us even today, for from this record we can see that the first fall of snow came to the Algonquin Park region on Hallowe'en, October 31st, in the year 1835.

Within the previous ten years, the Government of Upper Canada had become involved, in one way or another, in the construction of at least three different canals in the Province — the Welland, the Rideau, and the beginning of the St. Lawrence waterway. Naturally there was keen interest in the possibility of linking the Ottawa River with Georgian Bay by a water route that would take the larger boats. To investigate this matter a commission was appointed with F. H. Baddeley, now a Captain, as one of its members, and it in turn assigned the task of determining the best route to a group of three men who were to report on the alternative courses. Trips covering each of these routes were made during the summer of 1837 —through the lakes and rivers of the Timagami country by David Taylor; through the French River-Lake Nipissing, and also the Magnetawan-Petawawa route by William Hawkins; and through the Muskoka-Madawaska district by David Thompson. The latter also reported on the measures that would have to be undertaken to get past the Calumet Rapids on the Ottawa River near Hawkesbury. For our purpose the records of the findings of Hawkins and Thompson are of prime interest, although anyone interested in the Timagami region, and the post of the "Honourable Hudson's Bay Company" there, should read Taylor's account.

The survey parties led by Thompson and Taylor made the naval store at Penetanguishene the chief base for their supplies. But long before the trips started off, David Thompson, who had won fame in the far west as an official of the Hudson's Bay Company and as the explorer of the British Columbia river which still bears his name, had been given the task of supervising the construction of the canoes that would be needed. When Taylor came north on the Yonge Street stage-coach on July 22nd, he found Thompson at work at Holland Landing, and the paint on the canoes was not yet dry. As indication of the interest that the Government of Upper Canada was taking in the whole venture, no less a person than the Surveyor-General himself, Hon. John McCauley, accompanied the party as far as their jumping-off spot at Penetanguishene.

The first of these three canal surveys was submitted by William

Hawkins, who had been along on Baddeley's previous expedition as a surveyor, but who was now Deputy Provincial Surveyor. His report of the levels along the Magnetawan-Petawawa route gives an admirable picture of the difficulties that would have to be overcome if a canal were to be built to make use of these water courses. His information shows that the total ascent from Lake Huron to the height of land was 340 feet, and that the distance between the head-waters of the two rivers was a matter of less than a quarter of a mile. However, his account of his own trip shows that he thought that the building of a canal there would be a foolish undertaking. At one place he points out that,

> "For fifteen miles from the height of land the Pittoiwais is but a comparatively small stream and in many places, even at the distance of ten miles from the height of land, its channel will scarcely admit a passage for canoes. We were frequently compelled to cut the banks before our canoe, although only four feet in width, would pass through."

On the whole, Hawkins' conclusions seem to favour the idea of making use of the old fur trading route through Lake Nipissing for the projected canal.

With reference to the Petawawa country in the Park district, Hawkins made several observations that tie in with what Sherriff had found some eight years before. Both men came upon traces of Indian hunters and trappers, although neither encountered many actual people along the way. As yet there seemed to be no signs of white trappers or of lumbermen, in this region. Of the appearance of the country along the Petawawa course he says,

> "There are four things strikingly peculiar to this section of the country — its timber is red; its soil is red; on the banks of the lakes and rivers its rock is red; and its waters are also red — deriving their colour from the soils and rocks over which they pass."

On the lower Petawawa River he mentions in particular a great wall of this rock along the shore: according to him it was 200 yards long and 150 high, with animals and other devices engraven by the Indians. Later travellers mention Indian huts scattered at intervals along this section of the river, so that this district may have been used for a long time as a general gathering spot for adjacent wandering groups of Algonquins.

David Thompson does not seem to have submitted a report for

his section of the canal survey, but he did turn in to the Commission what was probably more important in the long run, a series of four very beautifully drawn maps of the region through which he had travelled in his cross-country trip from Penetanguishene to the Ottawa. To geographers these maps are of great importance, since they provide them with the first accurate picture of the entire system now known as the Muskoka Lakes. The maps were drawn first on paper and then mounted on linen backing so that they are still in an excellent state of preservation.

The second map of this series shows the section of the Park through which this famous explorer travelled. To a man who had lived for the greater part of his life in the Athabaska country, this trip through the comparative security of the Ontario wilds would be a holiday jaunt. During the fourteen years which he spent in the employ of the Hudson's Bay Company before he came east in 1797, he had several times penetrated into the Rocky Mountain passes and on one occasion, when he came down the turbulent tributary of the Fraser, now called the Thompson, had accomplished one of the most difficult feats in the history of canoe navigation.

From Lake of Bays, which he called Forked Lake on his map, Thompson travelled up the Muskoka River to Oxtongue Lake, by him called Cross Lake. All along the way the actual course of his canoe is marked by a dotted line, so that one can see where he paddled to get the best view of the lake edges, traced on his map with such skilful accuracy. The present South Tea Lake he labelled as "Canoe" Lake, perhaps for the same reason that the name was applied to the lake so well-known now by that same name — he may have had to pause there to build or repair his craft after the initial stage of the journey. The trip through to the Madawaska waters was made by way of Ragged, Black Bear and the Bonnechere lakes, and thence through Head and on into Cache, but none of these are named on his map.

Today David Thompson's route is one of the most travelled sections of Algonquin Park, and the greenest of young tyro canoeists who "catches a crab" with his paddle on the glassy surface of South Tea Lake, can boast that a hundred years ago the intrepid western explorer dipped his paddle into the self-same waters.

# CHAPTER 3

In Spite of Baddeley's attempt to straighten out the impression created by Sherriff's report, the legend persisted that the area was good farm land. Not till long after the camboose camps had come and gone, did this legend finally die.

Year by year, settlers established pioneer homesteads closer to the land of the Algonquins. In government circles the Huron tract, comprising the whole hinterland south of Lake Nipissing, was the goal of an extensive road-building project to open up the Haliburton area and beyond to settlement. Concurrently, the lumber interests were pushing farther and farther up the Ottawa and its tributaries in search of new supplies of the profitable red and white pine. Behind the lumbermen, as well as south of the Park, settlers were moving in. Unconsciously, the two movements, one from the south, the second from the east, converged in a race to occupy the height of land where the Park now stands.

The Haliburton settlers penetrated the Park area as early as any, since they eked out their scanty farm living with winter fur trapping; but it was the lumbermen and eastern settlers who first occupied the land.

Dan McLachlin was one of the first. Dan was a Glengarry man who had taken up land near Arnprior, on the Ottawa River. He may originally have intended to farm, but before he could begin, it was necessary to clear the land. Mr. McLachlin soon discovered it was far more profitable to concentrate on marketing the timber on his holding, than to depend on plough and hoe for a livelihood. The great lumber business operating for so many years in the Park area under the name of McLachlin Brothers, had as simple an origin as that.

Alex. Macdonell of Sand Point, the first cruiser to enter the region, took up limits on the upper Bonnechere. So did Alex. Barnet of Renfrew village. Along the upper Petawawa River cutting rights were reserved by Messrs. Perley and Pattee. Others followed till the Park area came to be known far and wide as a top-ranking square timber district. Each year their men came up into the camboose shanties along the old wagon roads from the Ottawa Valley. Each spring brought increasing thousands of logs down the Petawawa, Bonnechere, and Madawaska tributaries, into the mainstream of the Ottawa.

Without railways, these early lumbermen depended entirely on the rivers for marketing their logs. Consequently, all the leases were let along the river banks. The old licenses all read that the limit should extend for so many miles along the banks of a certain river "following the sinuosities of the said river" and should reach back to a depth of five miles. That was considered the maximum distance to haul a log profitably from its point of cutting to the water. On a contemporary map of the Park timber limits it is still possible to pick out these old leases. Most of the companies with holdings on the Ottawa tributaries, such as the Gillies and the J. R. Booth Companies, still operate on limits laid out in this way.

The mainstay of the business was the British export trade, and only the most select pine was cut for this market. Hardwoods could not be floated downstream, but pine, the cleanest and straightest and tallest of the softwoods, was in constant demand by British carpenters and shipwrights. Only the largest of these could justify the expense of cutting, squaring and rafting timber to the ocean ports, and its shipment overseas from there.

All these old companies were cutting "square timber", the product of a particular way of cutting the logs, and trimming them for market. Only the soundest and straightest red or white pine could be used to make a "stick" of timber. When such a tree was felled, trimmed of its branches, and cut flat on four sides, it made one timber, or stick, perfectly square, and measuring the same at the top and both ends.

In order to make one stick of this type, several highly specialized woodsmen were employed. The axe was their only tool, the horse their only source of power for lifting and hauling. The whole process required skilled and hardy woodsmen.

Before a stick could be cut, however, the timber limits had to be found, staked out, and leased. The man who determined the direction and extent of new operations was the timber cruiser. Usually in summer, sometimes in winter, alone, or with a small party, he ranged the forest, facing every kind of weather and hazard; making his estimates in the knowledge that the whole success of the operations to follow depended on his good judgment. The timber cruiser's report, as will be seen a few chapters later, could ruin a large company when larded with too much enthusiasm.

Once the area was leased, the road built, supplies hauled in, and the camp set up, the specialized axemen were ready. The fitter came first, selecting trees large enough to make a stick, and sound from top to base. The faller laid axe to tree, making it fall in the most convenient direction for the next operation. The log maker took over next, trimming the log of its branches, and cutting off the top to the specified length. After him the scorer peeled the bark from the upper sides, stretched a cord the length of the log and marked the thickness to be sliced off to make a flat side. He then "scored" each side with an axe at close intervals, so the hewer could hew to the line. The hewer, standing on top of the log, wielded a broad axe with a large head and razor-keen edge, trimming first one side and then the other, till *each was almost as smooth as a planed board*. Finally the log was rolled over ninety degrees, the scorer and hewer repeated their operations, and the stick was finished.

At a later date "waney" timber was made by the same method, only in this operation the edges of the log were left rounded instead of squared off. In this way the good outside boards, that were previously wasted, were sliced off at the mill into narrower pieces than the actual square would have allowed.

The pathways to the Park were being cleaned out of the best white and red pine at an alarming rate. T. C. Keefer, Assistant Engineer to the Board of Works on the Ottawa River, reported in 1847 that two and a half million cubic feet of pine had floated down from the Madawaska alone. At Quebec this quantity of timber brought in £90,000. Keefer's report, incidentally, reveals that it took two years for the timber to reach Quebec: he pointed out that with improvements at High Falls on the Madawaska, and on the lower Ottawa it would be quite possible to take the timber out in a single season. His figures in the report for 1846 show that nearly two thousand square miles were under license along the Madawaska, less than a thousand on the Bonnechere, and a little over a thousand on the Petawawa. Down these three rivers, that same year, floated a total of four million cubic feet of red pine and over a million of white. More than a third of the red pine came from the banks of the Petawawa. Since the "traverses," or cross-beams, for rafts all down the Ottawa were cut from red pine, and the Lake Traverse region was an excellent source of this timber, this is probably how it got its name.

Information about the route these lumbermen travelled to get into the upper reaches of the Petawawa in the 1850's and afterwards, is very difficult to obtain. However, we know that there was a "tote" road along the upper Ottawa for quite a distance above Pembroke by the middle of the century. Supplies would likely have to come in to the Park camps by this way, rather than up the Petawawa watercourse itself. As we have already seen, even the Indians found this route too rough for ordinary travel by canoe, so that the lumbermen would hesitate to bring in heavily laden canoes or flat bottomed "pointers" by that way. Instead, the roads, used later when the Canadian Pacific Railway Company constructed the section of its trans-Canada line along the south bank of the Ottawa River between Ottawa and North Bay, must have been opened up at this time. The lumbermen were not able to bring their supplies in by the railway until after 1880, but there were many companies operating along the Petawawa, and also farther north on the Amable du Fond, before that date.

In the northeast corner of Algonquin Park, a whole network of roads was cut overland from the upper Ottawa to the "Peetawaway", as the old-timers called it. The jumping-off point for the Lake Traverse district was the village of Bissett; from Deux Rivieres the lumbermen took in their supplies for the Cedar and Trout Lake areas; and, to reach the Amable du Fond, tote roads were cut from Mattawa and Eau Claire. These roads were eighteen to twenty-five miles long and exceedingly rough. Tough men, sturdy horses, and stout sleighs, were needed to cover the early trails. It was not until the Canadian Northern Railway line through the Park was completed in 1915 that the companies in this region had easy transportation brought to their doorsteps. To this day some of their winter roads may still be picked out from the air, but on the ground they have become so overgrown they are hard to find, except where the "corduroy" of logs over a gully or soft ground lies rotting among the second growth.

At several places along the roads leading from the Ottawa in to the Petawawa limits, there were "stopping places" where the teams could be fed and watered, and where the men could be put up for the night if necessary. One such place is marked on an old map as "Halfway P.O.", situated midway between Deux Rivières and the farm at Cedar Lake. Another was "Captain Young's" place in Edgar Township to the west of Lake Traverse. *Old-timers describe the appearance of these buildings.* The Captain had made the lumber for them himself by standing the logs on end in a scaffolding and then slicing them into boards by means of a "whip" saw. The surveyor who reported on this region for the Township Survey in 1887 said that Captain Young's was a busy stopping-place at that time.

There was another way of getting into the Petawawa camps, by means of the White Partridge Road from the south. Although this route into Trout Lake is marked on some of the early maps, it is very difficult to determine just who used it and when. When one starts to trace out its lengthy course, one finds it hard to believe that teamsters could have made the long haul up the wild bush trail that led from the Ottawa settlements to White Partridge Lake. This road passed up the Bonnechere River, past a supply base at Basin Depot and on by way of "McIntyre's Clearing" to White Partridge Lake. It may have been used by the firm of Perley and Pattee who operated at that place in the early days, but it is difficult to find out whether the road was constructed for their benefit, or whether it was a continuation of sections that had already been opened up to reach the upper Bonnechere limits.

A hand-drawn map in the possession of Mr. Dan McLachlin, of Arnprior, the grandson of the founder of the McLachlin lumber firm, affords some information about the southern part of this road. This map was made in 1855 to show the McLachlin holdings on the upper Madawaska River. To the north of the McLachlin limits is marked the "Basin Depot", so someone must have been operating in that region in 1855. Whether Thomas Barnet was in as early as that, or whether this was a stopping place for the White Partridge Road, is difficult to determine. We do know that William McIntyre had cleared some ten acres at a point now within the Park boundaries by the time the surveyors arrived in 1889, and that he was then operating a farm and a stopping-place for lumbermen. This farm was situated fifteen miles beyond Basin Depot on the Bonnechere River, at the point where the teams turned off to go north to White Partridge and the Petawawa limits.

All these old square timber companies housed their men in shanties built of logs which were cut on the spot where the camp was to be constructed. These shanties were built with a "camboose" in the centre, and came to be known as camboose camps. All through the Ottawa Valley and in the Algonquin Park district, this was the usual sort of building in the early days of lumbering. From old-timers such as Charles Macnamara, who worked for many years for the McLachlin Company, we learn of life in these camps. Mr. Macnamara provided the material for two articles written by

Harry Walker for the Ottawa Journal; and his own photographs, taken in 1900, give us an authentic picture of how one of the last of these buildings was constructed, and how the men were fed.

According to Mr. Macnamara, the name "camboose" was originally the French "*cambuse*" — a store-room, and as in so many other cases where French words were used in Canadian lumber camps, its true meaning had been changed because of the new environment. To the lumbermen the camboose was the central fireplace in the log shanty, but since this shanty was the place where the cook made the meals, stored some of his provisions, and fed the workers, the French meaning of the word would still apply. The camboose shanty was more than a store-room in the early lumber camps, since this one building served as dining, sleeping, and recreation centre, throughout the winter's bush operations.

Paddy Farrell of Pembroke, who for many years was a "walking boss" for camps operated by the Gillies Company, recalls the first time he ever "went to shanty". His father was one of those Ottawa Valley farmers who journeyed into the camps each winter with his team of horses, and who, during the course of many years spent in the bush, had become well known as an expert axe-man. Ever since he could remember, Paddy had seen his father go off into the woods in the fall, and finally, at the age of thirteen, he was to be allowed to go along with him. In those days there were many jobs that a husky lad, accustomed to handling horses and to swinging an axe on the farm at home, could do in the camps.

When Paddy and his father arrived at their destination, their winter quarters had not yet been prepared. Paddy helped to cut the logs that were to go into the building that was to be their winter home. On the first day they cleared the site, and cut the logs that were to be used for roofing. Then, while the more experienced men went on with the felling of the trees to be used for the construction of the walls, some of the others were able to scoop out the logs into long wooden tiles for the roof. On this particular shanty the walls went up very quickly, for the sides were made of three great logs that gave sufficient height for the roof when they were set one upon the other. The door in the front, and the small window beside it, were cut out afterwards.

When the roof was put on, a great hole, some six feet square, was left in the centre, open to the sky. This was the chimney for the fireplace that was erected in the centre of the floor space directly underneath, and it also provided light and ventilation for the occupants who lived and ate in this building. The fireplace, the actual "camboose", was built on a square foundation of stone and sand. When the camp was first built, a fire was kindled in it, and from that time until the river drivers departed in the spring, that fire never went out. It provided warmth, light, and heat for the cooking, during the whole winter season.

Today, in the Park, all the traveller may see is a pile of sand with a few rotten logs lying around, usually close to the water's edge. But earlier visitors saw them in a better state of preservation. C. H. Irwin, of Carnarvon, remembers one on the Little Nipissing River which his party came upon during a timber survey in 1921. Philip Roche of Killaloe located another built in 1894 on Pine River, a tributary of the Bonnechere. On Crow River near Big Crow Lake, according to James D. Pennock, Supervisor of Scaling for the Ontario Department of Lands and Forests, is another. Mr. Pennock also ran across the camboose pile and old "*cramiere*" of another camp, which he says may still be seen on the north-east bay of Shirley Lake.

Mr. E. Thomas of Kishkaduk Lodge tells us that an old-timer recalled the building of a camp in 1878, when the Hawkesbury Lumber Company was cutting on Cedar Lake. At this site it is possible to take measurements in order to determine the exact size of the original building. The actual rectangle formed by the walls still remains, because the earth was dug out on the outside in order to bank up the walls to prevent draughts along the floor. The foundation logs are still intact, and they show the length of the building to have been forty-one feet, while the width was thirty-six. The single door was cut in the front, facing the lake. The mound of earth in the centre of this space shows the location and the size of the camboose fireplace. In this particular instance the square in the centre measured twelve feet on each side. This had been built up with logs on the outside to hold the sand in place. On the far side of the fireplace, away from the door, there appears to have been a shallow pit, lined with stones. This was likely used by the cook as storage for potatoes and other supplies that he would need to have on hand. The floor itself seems to have been made of small poles, set close together to make a corrugated surface.

In passing, it is interesting to note that the use of this central camboose type of fireplace is coming back into fashion in Canadian architecture. Visitors who bask in the warmth of the famous central fireplace at the Seigniory Club, in the Province of Quebec, likely do not know that French-Canadian lumbermen long enjoyed the same kind of comfort from the old shanty fires. In the Park, too, several new buildings have recently been constructed on this model. The new dining hall at Camp Wapomeo, and the main lodge at "The Arowhon Pines" at Baby Joe Lake, are both heated by a camboose-style fireplace.

As for the original camboose fireplaces, old-timers will tell you that they were responsible for the excellent health of the lumber-jacks who spent the long winter in the bush. The roaring fire in the centre of the building not only threw its warmth into every corner, but it acted as an excellent ventilating system. Through the great hole in the roof the uprushing air currents took off the smoke from the fire, the odour of cooking, the smell of drying woolens, and the penetrating incense of green tobacco, smoked by weary labourers at the end of the day. At the same time this upsweep of air was strong enough, and hot enough, to prevent snow or rain from coming into the camp through the large aperture in the roof. All shantymen agree that there was very little sickness in lumber camps in their day.

From Mr. Tom Pigeon of Madawaska, we were able to obtain an excellent picture of the way the life in these camps was regulated. For many years he was cook in camboose camps located both in the Park area and along the upper Ottawa River. Now, at the age of eighty-five, he has vivid memories of the life led by the men in the early days. Then, as in modern camps, the power of the cook was second only to that of the foreman himself. A good cook was an ornament to any camp, and in return he was treated with true deference and respect by bosses and men alike. Tradition has it that the famous lumber camp habit of silent, speedy eating, dates from the time of the camboose camps. Then, when cooking, eating, and washing up had to be done in the same building, where the men sat and slept, a rule of order had to prevail. It was the cook who imposed the rule of "no talking at meals".

Mr. Pigeon started his training as "cookee", or cook's assistant, as a boy of sixteen. That was in the 1880's when the square timber trade was in full swing "up the Kippaway" north of Mattawa. Later, as a "McLachlin man" he cooked in many of the camps established by that firm on their limits in the Park district. He was, for a number of years, at the White Trout Depot as well as other places on the upper "Peetawaway", as he and many other old-timers call the lumberman's paradise. When we talked about the old days, Mr.

Pigeon's conversation was mostly about the food supplies, and the methods of cooking in the camps, but he did have many other stories of the time when the great square timber rafts floated down the Ottawa to the seacoast. One of the heroic figures in the annals of those days, was the cook who continued working in his cookhouse on a timber crib, as the whole affair went sliding down one of the Ottawa chutes.

All the supplies for the bush camps in the Park area had to be toted in by wagon or sleigh from the Ottawa Valley. The old companies, with headquarters along the Ottawa River, had to solve the problem of how to get equipment and staple foods into their limits at the lowest possible cost. It is really no wonder that the cooks found only very limited equipment at their disposal when they came to cook on the camboose fireplaces in the backwoods shanties. They were provided with two kinds of iron kettles — a tea kettle, which was suspended from an iron crane, or *cramière;* and a bake kettle, with a tight-fitting lid that was set in the sand along the edge of the fire. A sturdy knife, kept sharpened to a razor's edge, a few ladles, an iron fork and a shovel fashioned by the camp's blacksmith, usually completed this equipment.

As for the men, their eating utensils were also of the simplest type. Each man was provided with a small tin bowl, a "shanty-mug" from which he drank his soup or his tea, and a tin plate. From home he brought with him a knife of his own, and with this he carved out a wooden spoon for himself. If he lost this knife, he could buy another from the clerk who was in charge of the "Van". When he went to bed in the "muzzle-loading" bunks that lined the walls of the shanty, he stuck his knife in a niche of the wall at his head. At meal times each man brought out his own plate and his "shanty mug", and helped himself to the food he wanted from the great kettles along the edge of the fire.

When Mr. Pigeon first began to cook in the shanties, the food supplied by the companies was of the roughest sort. There was absolutely no variety in the menu. Only the staples were hauled in over the bush trails: beans, salt pork, flour and blackstrap molasses. From these ingredients the three meals of the day were made. Breakfast was eaten at about five o'clock so that the men who had to tramp out to the bush could begin work at seven o'clock. This meal consisted of beans, fried salt pork, known as "grillades", bread, and strong tea. The mid-day meal was eaten in the bush at eleven o'clock. For it, each man had brought the ingredients with him in the morning. To quote Jim Campbell, now foreman on the Park highway, who has vivid memories of these meals in the bush, "You dropped the meat, cold salt pork, into a long linen bag, tied it with a string in the centre, and then put a loaf of bread in the top half. In the other hand you took a pail containing blackstrap, and away you went. At the dinner time you made tea, *and by God, it was tea!* When you ate your meal you gouged a large hole into the bread and poured the blackstrap into it, unless the weather was too cold, and then you cut out a hunk of blackstrap and put it into the hole. Then you took your fat salt pork in one hand, and your bread and molasses in the other, and ate them bit about." In the evening when the men came back to camp after a long day's work in the bush, the six o'clock supper was the same as the breakfast menu.

When there was a depot farm run in connection with the camp, it was sometimes possible to obtain a limited supply of fresh vegetables. Even then, there was not much variety in the meals because, since it was hard work to clear the land and to farm on these bush clearings, the depot farmer usually limited his crops to potatoes for the camp, and oats for the horses. In this way, the cost of the long haul of bulky supplies from the outside world could be cut down. However, even in the camps where it was possible to obtain these slight additions, Jim Campbell's account of the standard diet held true. According to him — "You never seen a cake, you never seen a cookie, you never seen a pie" — in those early days. In spite of these limitations, though, he was emphatic in his statement that there is nothing nowadays that can compare with beans baked in the sand for a long period of time, or with bread cooked in the same manner in the great iron "bakkittles".

Many are the stories told about "Chicago rattlesnake", as the salt pork was affectionately called by the shantymen, whose mainstay it was. According to these old-timers, the pigs that were used for the product were very old — from five to seven years — and consequently tough. In fact, the "gristle" on the hunks that were carried out to the woods was so hard to cut that it resembled shoe leather, rather than a form of food. The story is told of one man who carried the same piece out to the bush in his lunch bag for a whole season, without being able to make any impression on it. Finally, when he gave up struggling with it, he turned it over to the blacksmith who found a good use for it by making it into harness for the camp horses.

It is interesting to trace through the changes in lumber-camp fare, to our own time, and to see how the meat courses particularly have altered because of improvements in transportation facilities. The reason why salt pork was formerly the only kind of meat in the camps was that it was shipped in barrels, and could be hauled in during the previous spring while the winter roads were still good. There it could be stored through the summer months so that when the busy season came after the first autumn snowfall, the meat supply would already be on hand. About forty-five years ago the first change in camp fare came with the introduction of corned beef, which was also packed in barrels. Then some firms found it possible to ship live cattle in on the nearest railway, and to drive them along the bush roads to the camps. This was done in the Park in the early 1890's, when the Gilmour Company drove cattle north from Minden and then slaughtered them at the end of the Dorset Road at Tea Lake. Nowadays, whole quarters of beef are shipped into the bush, and the men are served the choicest cuts in the camp dining rooms.

Mr. Pigeon remembers how a similar change came about in the baking of the cakes, cookies and pies, which are now made in large quantities in the camps, but which Jim Campbell says were entirely lacking in the early camboose shanties. First came the discovery that the camboose fire could be used for baking pies and cakes by setting up a sheet of tin to act as a reflector oven. In Mr. Pigeon's own camp, when the men asked him if he could bake them some buns or pies, he pointed out that his standard supplies did not include the essential baking powder. The men replied that that was a small matter, and took up a silver collection amongst themselves for the purchase of five cans of the "Cook's Friend". After that, the Sunday meat dish, called "sea pie", was augmented by buns sweetened with blackstrap. When one of the walking bosses visited the camp he complained about this extravagant use of syrup. However, the will of the men prevailed and in after years baking powder was added to the list of regulation stores. Further changes came with the introduction of dried apples, pails of minced raisins and other commodities that could be used to form the filling for pies in the camps. Nowadays, pie forms a standard part of at least two meals a day in most lumber camps, but all these varieties of food have been introduced since the early days of shantying in the Park.

Although there was very little time for anything but work in the old camps, the week-end break brought a slight change in the usual routine. On week nights, after supper, the men would sit around for an hour or so, playing cards, fashioning axe handles out of ironwood, or sharpening the blades of their axes, but soon after the evening's pipe they would roll into their bunks, and shortly after eight o'clock everyone was in bed and asleep. However, on Saturday night, everything was different. There was always someone in the group who could produce a mouth organ, an accordion, or even a fiddle, and then would come a great "rattling of the bones". Mr. Pigeon talked about these "step dances" with great delight. There were no women in the camp, but that didn't dampen anyone's spirits. Half the group would turn themselves into female partners by pulling their shirt tales out over their trousers, and everyone would cavort with great glee. In the ordinary shanty there was room for two squares at a time, and everyone else would sit around on the benches or lounge on the bunks until that group was exhausted. Then it would be their turn — and so the dance went on until twelve o'clock brought in the Sabbath, and everyone turned in for the night.

On Sunday morning, breakfast was a little later than usual, and the day was given over to resting, writing the occasional letter home, and cleaning up. The business of washing clothes was a solemn rite, undertaken in turns and at lengthy intervals. Each man, when he came into the camp in the fall, brought his winter supply of clothing and his own bedding with him. The former consisted of a supply of extra woollen socks and some heavy outdoor clothing; the latter of a couple of quilts. Usually a supplementary supply of a pair of blankets was available at the camp. When you went to bed you simply took off your cowhide mocassins and covered yourself up. From the "Van" you could purchase mitts and socks if necessary, as well as tobacco and matches, but because your storage space was limited to the niche in the logs at the head of your bunk, or the space on the floor underneath it, there were no extras in the camboose camp.

Wash day, however, was a memorable occasion. Pork barrels, cut in half, made excellent wooden tubs. Snow could be melted over the open fire. There was room on lines around the fireplace for a limited number of socks, but the larger garments were hung outside where they would immediately be frozen stiff. By the next week, however, the wind would have blown the moisture out and they would be ready to put on again.

Twice during the winter months there came visitors from the

outside world to bring in the news, and to break the monotony of this existence. One of these visitors was the local priest or preacher; the other was the jewellery pedlar. These visitors were welcomed into the camps, and shared the same fare as the men themselves. In this connection, there is one tradition of the lumber camps that continues down to our own time. No visitor ever dropped into a camp who was not welcome to stay for a meal — and there was no charge for this hospitality. However, no visitor who knew anything about the etiquette of the camps, would stay for a longer period than one day. The wayfarer was welcome to the food that was available, but he would not cause his host to run short of supplies when these same supplies were so hard to obtain.

The visiting clergyman was usually in camp when the men returned after a day's work in the woods. No one could tell in advance when he would arrive — he didn't know himself, because that depended on the weather and the travelling conditions. He would have to drive from camp to camp all through the district, and there was no way of letting people know of his visit in advance. However, some time after Christmas he would pay his pastoral call. Then the men would be awakened an hour or a half hour earlier on the following morning. A service, attended by Catholic and Protestant alike, would be held at that time so that the work in the bush could begin at seven o'clock as usual.

Some of these travelling ministers must have been exceedingly hardy men. Stories told about Rev. P. S. Dowdall, who was the first parish priest at Whitney, confirm this fact. Even before the Booth Railway line went through the south part of the Park, there were priests who came into that district from Maynooth, and from settlements along the Opeongo Line, but information about their comings and going is difficult to obtain. Father Dowdall's parish, however, extended from Whitney right across to Dorset, and he visited all the camps in that area from 1896 on. From Father Hunt, who was Father Dowdall's successor and his close friend, comes the story of how this large parish was established. Before that time there were only mission "stations" in the district, but when the St. Anthony Lumber Company's mill was built, the Bishop decided that there should be a resident priest at that place. Father Dowdall applied to E. C. Whitney, the owner of the mill, for a grant of money, and for land for the church building and the cemetery. Father Dowdall had some trouble persuading Mr. Whitney to grant this request, but finally one evening he agreed to help in the construction of the church. Then he wanted to know how far this new parish was to extend. The story has it that Father Dowdall replied, "As far as I can walk to-morrow". The next day he set out from the village at about two o'clock in the morning. All that day he kept walking westwards so that by the end of the day he had covered fifty-eight miles. The next morning he continued on into Dorset, where he offered Mass. According to tradition, that is the reason why the whole of the south part of the Park was set aside as part of the Whitney parish. Sceptics may doubt the actual truth of this tale, but it well illustrates the sort of work that was undertaken in the early days by these hardy preachers of the gospel.

The other visitor to the camps from the outside world was the jewellery pedlar who brought his store of watches, rings, and ornaments, right into the bush. Ever since their first arrival in the fall, the men had been talking about what they planned to purchase from the pedlar when he made his annual call, and great was their excitement when they returned at the end of their day's work to find him installed in the camp with his wares. Everyone examined what he had to offer and made the purchase of the objects that took their fancy. Many diamond engagement rings, expensive watches, and other pieces of jewellery found their way into back country communities in this way. In fact, it was frequently the case that, when a man was paid off at the end of the drive and had spent a few days in town celebrating with his pals, there was very little else besides these souvenirs to take back home with him in the spring.

These shantymen, then, were the people who knew every inch of the Algonquin Park region in the early days. In the fall of the year they would trek in along the bush roads to the spot where the camp was to operate for the winter, and in the spring before the break-up, they would drive their teams back along the same way, or else go with the logs down the tributary rivers flowing eastwards to the Ottawa and the markets of the outside world. Men from all up and down the Ottawa Valley, yes, and from farther afield than that, too, came up into the camps in the Park. One of the favourite stories told about the McLachlin firm illustrates this fact. One of the members of the family was once travelling along the Gaspé coast in lower Quebec. There he saw, hanging on a fisherman's family washline, a dress made of two pieces of cotton flour bags. The front of the garment was decorated with great red initials "McL". It had come out of one of the McLachlin camps on the upper Ottawa River.

In the settlements in the Ottawa Valley itself there is, even today, scarcely a family whose father or cousins have not at one time or another worked in camps in the Park. The older people pass on to their sons stories about the time when they first "went to shanty" and tales of the wondrous deeds that were performed in the far off days in the past. These tales are of how this one was so nimble at running the logs that he could "cross a river on match sticks"; and how that one could tote a pack consisting of a barrel of pork, a bag of flour and a keg of molasses, over long distances. Even Paul Bunyan visited the Park in these early times, but this was a French-Canadian Paul Bunyan, and he was carrying on his back a great bag of dried peas. At the end of a portage he fell, and the whole load tumbled into the lake. He was furious with himself for his own clumsiness, for of course the peas could not be salvaged from the water. However, he was resolved not to be done out of his pea-soup. Consequently, he set fire to the forest along the edges of the lake, and when the fire had died down he found that the lake was bubbling and boiling in the form of the delicious soup that was his national dish. For once in his life he had enough pea-soup for supper.

From down along the Opeongo Line come other tales about the men who travelled by that route into the camps in the Park. At frequent intervals all along the way were the "stopping places" where the thirsty shantymen could "wet their whistle". By the time many of them reached the Booth Farm at Kitty Lake they had to "stay put" for several days until they could sober up. Old-timers say that the great stone heaps along the edges of the clearing at that place, were made by men who were put to work at this task at a time when it would have been suicide to allow them to swing an axe. After that respite they were taken on into the camps, and their drinking days were over until the next spring.

For the men who took the square timber out of the Park, as well as for those who later drove saw-logs down the tributary rivers, the trip to the Ottawa was a hazardous undertaking. Still as one travels along the watercourses in the north part of the Park, one is made aware of the dangers of the river drive. With the break-up of the ice in May the swollen streams would start to rampage, and then would begin the long trip downstream. For many weeks the men who were following the drive would camp out along the shore wherever they happened to find themselves at dark. The rate of their journeying depended on the speed of the water current — on the rivers when the dams were opened, the logs would swirl along at terrific speed, but on the lakes the movement was a long, slow business. There the individual logs would have to be fastened into booms in order to be towed across by primitive "alligators". A raft, such as the one still to be seen on the beach at Radiant Station, served instead of a modern tug for this purpose. A team of horses was hitched to a windlass in the centre of the raft. These horses walked round and round in order to wind up the rope that gradually hauled the raft to the spot where the anchor had previously been dropped. This stage of the journey was a tedious one, but it gave a little respite to the riverman's hectic life.

There were many of these river drivers who never did return to their homes along the Ottawa, and in places along the Petawawa the traveller can still see the wooden crosses which mark the places where men were buried as a result of river accidents. At the end of the first portage upstream from Cedar Lake, there is one such grave. The upright piece of the cross has recently been replaced by some thoughtful passer-by, but the cross-piece bears the carving of the riverman's comrade who cut it when the accident took place. It bears the lettering, "A. Corbeil 9 Juin 1888". Like a well-known shanty song that tells the story of young Monroe, who never did return to his sweetheart, Miss Clara Dennison, this French-Canadian shantyman lies buried by the shores of the river where he met his death.

Today the camboose camp lies in ruins, and the old-time shantymen are old — many of them gone over the last height of land. But the Park is filled with these reminders of their hey-day.

On the portage between Porcupine and Ragged Lakes still stand some sections of the old Porcupine Chute, scene of the kind of tragic accident that illustrates the hardy, sometimes reckless, humour of the early lumberjacks.

About the year 1900, the lumber firm of J. D. Shier of Bracebridge was cutting in the Ragged Lake section of the Park. Their operations extended down into Porcupine Lake, just outside the southern boundaries, but all their logs came through the Park on their way to the Muskoka mill, by way of the Oxtongue River. All along this route the company's employees had constructed a great series of slides and dams, some of which have been maintained or rebuilt until the present time. The dam now standing at the outlet of Ragged Lake is built on the original Shier site, but all signs of some of their other improvements have been lost altogether. Only if you search with special care, will you see the remnants of the enormous timber chute that formerly carried the logs down the long incline between Porcupine and Ragged Lakes.

Jim Campbell is one of the few men who remember the time when this Porcupine Chute was built, and who recalls the disastrous occasion when logs first dashed down it to the lower level. Jim Campbell was a foreman for Shier's, and was working at a nearby camp when the chute was under construction. He and the man in charge of this undertaking had had an argument about the best location for the slide and about the proper grading of the curves. Said Jim, "It ought to be built like a railroad, banked on the turns," but Mr. Piper, the boss, did not agree with this theory. Jim was convinced, even before the trough was tried out, that the logs would break through the sides when they were hurled downwards by the great force of the water.

When the project was finally completed, it was regarded as quite an engineering feat. On Porcupine Lake a dam had been built to control the flow of the water, and the chute itself was nineteen hundred and fourteen feet long. Together they had cost in the neighbourhood of $5,200.00 to build. Naturally the owners, as well as the men, were very anxious to test out the new slide.

One day soon after its completion, J. D. Shier himself paid a visit to the camp. He decided that it would be well to try out the system while he was there, and he gave instructions for the test to be made. After dinner, Jackson, the carpenter, who had been in charge of the building, and the eight men who were detailed to look after the slide, reported that they were ready for the trial. It was all arranged. The key log in the dam above would be released so that a supply of water could flow through the trough, and then, when it was full, a series of logs would be fed into the slide at the top to be carried down to the next lake by the flow of the water.

When all the preparations had been made at the top, the men who were to occupy key positions along the side, started down the pathway to take their places. However, two of them, Louis the flag man, and another by the name of Sam, conceived the idea of running down on the surface of the slide itself. The man at the top could not see what they were doing, and he opened the dam to start the stream of water. At first it came very slowly, and Sam wisely climbed out over the edge. Louis, instead, thought it would be rather amusing to be pushed down as though he were taking a sleigh ride, so he sat down and allowed the water to carry him along.

The men whom he passed at first, laughed and called out, "Are you having a wash?", but very soon they stopped laughing, and ran to the side of the trough to see if they could haul him out. They could hear the main flow of water descending in a gush, and they realized that its force would rush him irresistibly into the pothole at the bottom.

All their efforts, however, were of no avail — they were not able to grab him out in time. He was swept along at great speed and disappeared into the boil below. For some time they waited, but there was nothing they could do — he didn't come up again. Two of them had to make their way to the railroad, where they travelled by jigger along the line to Headquarters in order to get a certificate from Mr. Bartlett to get the body out.

When the first logs finally came down they shot through the outside curves of the trough. Jim Campbell had been right, and whole sections had to be rebuilt, banked at the proper angle.

In spite of this inauspicious beginning, all the logs driven from the area south of Ragged Lake came down this chute on their way to Muskoka River mills. It was not until 1912 that the old companies stopped cutting in this region, and the Porcupine Chute, like the camboose shanties, fell into neglect.

The time will come when only a few huge rotting stumps, with the unmistakeable mark of the axe in the moss-grown wood, will show that once the Algonquin forests rang through the short winter days, with the shouts of the shantymen, and the bite of their axes into the stout Algonquin pines.

## CHAPTER 4

IT WAS THE FIRM CONVICTION of Government and people alike in the 1850's, that once the forest was cleared of its timber, a large percentage of the area where the Park now stands would be available as farming land for prospective homesteaders. Consequently, lumbering was looked upon only as forerunner of the more important and permanent industry of agriculture.

For a time it looked as if this development would follow. Settlers in the southeast established "depot farms", and managed nicely growing potatoes and oats for the lumber camps, sometimes adding to their income by winter cutting. But the Haliburton farmers, lacking any local markets, did not fare so well. Only by winter trapping were they able to carry on.

The Government, however, went ahead with its ambitious plans. Yonge Street, already an established road to the north, was to be extended north of Lake Couchiching; the road to Bobcaygeon was to parallel it through the heart of the Ottawa-Huron Tract; and the Opeongo Line was to pass from Renfrew County clear through to the mouth of the Magnetawan River on Georgian Bay.

The Yonge Street extension, known as the Muskoka Road, brought travellers no closer to the Park area than Lake of Bays. But the other two roads promised to pass through the very heart of the region.

Neither achieved its goal.

The Opeongo Line stopped short at Bark Lake, between Barry's Bay and the present borders of the Park. Another primitive highway, called the Peterson Road, furnished the only land passage from the Ottawa Valley over to the Muskoka Lakes, and it was rough to say the least. According to Mrs. E. W. Lockman of Dorset, who came into the district as a school teacher in 1888, the Bobcaygeon Road never even crossed the Oxtongue River where it had originally been surveyed. Instead, it was diverted in a northwesterly direction around the shores of the Lake of Bays, in order to link up with the Muskoka Road near Huntsville. The modern highway still follows this early road, named in the old Colonization Road Reports the Muskoka-Bobcaygeon Road.

All four of these were of prime importance to the families who moved into the Park borderlands during the thirty years prior to the Park's establishment. Many of the men who work in the Park today as rangers, guides, or lumbermen, are descended from these families.

Government reports of this period show a steady exodus of homesteaders from northern Haliburton. Those who remained turned to trapping for a living, making long trips up into the rich fur-bearing region of the Algonquin height of land, where the few Indian trappers were soon discouraged from competing. In the 1870's the railway pushed through to Haliburton village; and twice a year, on the fifth of November and the twenty-fourth of May, dealers arrived for the Haliburton fur auction, which attracted trappers from far and wide.

By this time at least five of the families who were to figure so largely in the later history of the Park had taken up land in the Haliburton district. Most of these were from old Ontario, and had accepted the Government's offer of free homesteads in the newly opened regions. In this way, three adults of the Sawyers family were able to take adjoining lots, which they still hold, at Maple Lake. The Sawyers had previously lived in the Peterborough district where they, along with other Irish families, had cleared farms for themselves. Now they were sufficiently enterprising to pioneer again. When others moved out, and they discovered the impossibility of making their farms pay, they took to trapping.

Of these it is known that James Sawyers definitely trapped in the Park region. Four other original trappers, and the areas their traplines covered, are still known. Jack Archer, who lived at Dorset, and later at Boshkung Lake — where his son Tom still lives — trapped around Dividing Lake and the Bonnechere Lakes. His main camp was on the old clearing at Porcupine Lake. Joseph Mossington, also from Dorset, trapped on the north side of the Oxtongue River. His son Archie's lines, today run southeast of the Park in the Crown Lake country; which he reaches by way of the Bobcaygeon Road and Smoke Lake, going out through Kimball and Hollow Lakes, now known as Kawagama Lake. James Sawyers and Isaac Boyce (also spelled Bice), each with his sons, moved in from Maple Lake. Jim worked up beyond Canoe Lake to Doe Lake and the Otterslides. In 1895 he was taken on as a Park ranger, and remained in that post for twenty-six years. His sons, Long Bill and Hank, kept the Maple Lake farm, and have since been working as expert guides in the Redstone-Kennesis district south of the Park, where both have built widely known deer lodges. Isaac Boyce had three sons, William, Wes and Fred, all of whom worked with him in the Misty Lake-Pine River country. Wes is still on the Maple Lake farm, but Fred moved to Kearney, from which he traps today, in a zoned area south of the Park. His son Ralph, and his grandson, still help with the trapping in the winter, but guide in the Park in summer. All we know of the fourth original is that his name was Durham Radnor, and he trapped up through Cache Lake.

The sons of these originals are now themselves reaching their seventies, and a chat with any one of them reveals how from childhood the whole countryside was an open book. All tell much the same story of the early trapper's routine.

Among the trappers themselves, there was a friendly arrangement about the area each man could call his own private trapping préserve. Thus, though he might need to travel through another's territory to reach his own, each trapper could return year after year to his own trapping grounds, and find his trapping gear undisturbed where he had cached it at the end of the previous season. Before the Park was set up in 1893, the whole district had been divided up in this way amongst the families in the Lake of Bays and Haliburton regions. White trappers had taken over the Indian hunting grounds, and the area yielded a rich harvest annually.

Early in the fall they would go north to their traplines; and be out again before the freeze-up, for the Haliburton fur sales. The men from Dorset—Mossington and Archer regularly, and sometimes Tom Salmon and Sam Vanclief as well — would come down through St. Nora and Kushog Lakes by canoe; while the Maple Lake families usually toted their pelts on their backs, along the section of the Peterson Road that led to Haliburton Village. There, all of them gathered to sell their furs, and spend the proceeds on necessities for the coming winter.

In the main, Archie Mossington and Hank Sawyers agree on the way these sales were conducted, although they, as youngsters, never had a chance to attend one — that was the special privilege of the father of the family. There would be eight or ten buyers in town by the time the trappers had arrived, and the bidding was conducted somewhat after the fashion of a fur auction, except that the bidding was a secret affair. Each buyer would examine the furs in the presence of the owner, and then write on a piece of paper the sum he would give for the lot. In this way no buyer could know what the other was offering, and was forced to arrive at his price independently. When the trapper looked over his offers, he turned over his pack to the highest bidder. Old-timers are sure that they got a much fairer price for their furs by this system than they do today.

Figures on a season's take are interesting, although money values have changed so much that it is difficult to compare them with prices today. Tommy Archer remembers one season when he and his father, working together, took out eighty beaver, forty mink, forty marten, and ten fisher pelts. One fisher skin sold then for five dollars, a beaver for three, and mink and marten at a dollar each: so the season's catch totalled $370.00. This might not amount to much these days, but then, in a country where there was no rent to pay and one could almost live off the land, it was a tidy sum.

Naturally, with all this ready money in his pocket, a man would want to celebrate in town a day or so, especially when his cronies were on hand with stories to swap of exploits up in the back country. But, in a few days he would be off for home once more, carrying with him the supplies the family would need for the coming season: shoes, tea, sugar, and other staples that were not produced on his own clearing.

During the early winter the men would remain at home, but in January, when the fur was at its best, and the winter at its coldest, they would set off again for their traplines. Moccasins, toboggans and snowshoes, carried them and their supplies through the silent, snow-laden winter forests. Sometimes they could take shelter at a friendly trapper's cabin for the night; but often they slept wherever night overtook them. On such nights they would scoop away all the surface snow from the site of their tent, and fireplace. Otherwise the fire would melt its way down out of sight. Often for shovelling away the snow they brought along a homemade cedar shovel. This, and the broad end of a snowshoe, made short work of the task.

Wes Boyce has vivid memories of such a trip into the Park area, when he and his brother Will went with their father for their first winter in the woods. They had been up in the Misty Lake district by way of McIntosh's in the fall, for the short five-week season, but they were home in time for the November fur sale. It was March before the three of them were on their way again. If the first trip had been exciting, this second was to be even more so. Wes was then a boy of fourteen, and his brother was two years older, but the intervening sixty-two years have not dimmed the memory of his excitement then. They had looked forward to setting their first trap line in the Misty Lake country ever since they could remember, and now they were actually on their way.

Their father, Isaac, believed in giving the boys a chance to work independently, and he set them up in their own camp with their own trap line. They went off in one direction and he in another; it was only on Sundays that the three got together to exchange information about the number of animals each had taken, and the methods that had worked best. When Monday morning came the two boys would go on with their work, he with his, until the spring season of 1882 had passed, and it was time to go home.

Although they had come out on snowshoes, they planned to return by canoe. This time they could travel light. Even coming in they had not been too heavily loaded, having picked up supplies at the Barnet Company's depot, already established at Burnt Island Lake. On the other hand, the Boyces had the farthest to travel of any of the Haliburton trappers, since they were the farthest north in the Park district. Above them the country was trapped by men from the Mattawa.

Just before the break-up Isaac had built a birch bark canoe. Early in May the lake was clear of ice, and the party set forth. This time, because the water was high with spring floods, and the days were long, they were able to return home in a fraction of the time it had taken to trek north. One trip took them over each of the portages, and in three days they were home at the Maple Lake farm.

Jim Sawyers, their neighbour, was reputed to be one of the best bushmen ever to work as a Park ranger. He knew every inch of the Otterslides area, and in his later years, when he was stationed at the rangers' cabin on Manitou Lake, he could be seen almost any day busy making a bark canoe. His son Hank remembers that once when he helped his father build such a canoe in the Park, it took the two of them only two days to finish the job.

Jim Sawyers' other son, Long Ben, is well known as a trapper and lumberman in the Haliburton district, and as a guide in the Park; and now, although he is over seventy, he is a difficult man to find at home. In summer he is busy with tourists; in the fall he arranges hunting trips for American deer hunters, and in the winter he is in charge of a lumber camp back in his own Redstone district. Long Ben's memory of the Park must often go back to the time he trapped there with his father. His brother Hank tells several stories of trips which they took in the old days, before the Park.

Once he and his brother were paddling through Lake Opeongo on their way home, with a large load of beaver skins. They had been out for some time, and they were carrying just about all their canoe would take without shipping water when, just as they reached the Narrows, they spied a beaver swimming quite close at hand. It seemed too good a chance to miss, even though they had a full load and were in a hurry. While they were wondering whether to stop, the beaver suddenly made up their minds for them. Desperately the frightened creature swung around and attacked the canoe. One of the brothers slugged him on the head with his paddle, while the other, dexterously avoiding the wicked front teeth, grabbed him by the hind legs. It was the work of a minute, once they had got him ashore and finished him off, to skin and scrape the hide, and get on their way again, with one more pelt to their hoard.

While the Haliburton settlers were either leaving the country or turning to furs for a livelihood, a different development was taking place along the famed Opeongo Line. Here, along with the advance of the great lumbering outfits, a dozen small communities were growing together into a district conscious of its own character and achievements, even to the point of creating a ballad, sung by the youngsters, with variations, to this day:

Take me back to Renfrew Valley
  Where the Bonnechere winds it way
Through the perfumed fields of clover
  And the scent of new-mown hay;
Where the foothills frame old shadows
  On the Opeongo trail;
Where the people are good farmers
  And their work shall never fail.

Killaloe to Letter Kenney,
  Barry's Bay to Camel Chute;
Golden Lake to Mount St. Patrick,
  Combermere to old Maynooth;
Petawawa to the Bogie,
  Eganville to old Smith's Creek;
You will find exiles returning
  To revisit every week.

Into the country back of Renfrew, by way of the Opeongo Line, a great number of Irish newcomers poured when the road was opened up. One can detect their origin by the names they gave their villages, including the famous shrine of Mount St. Patrick, whose sacred well draws pilgrims from afar to this day. At first, settlement by way of this road developed quickly; by 1857 there were 166 settlers who had cleared some 1,092 acres in all; but soon after that there followed a period of stagnation. The coming of the big lumber companies changed conditions again. When J. R. Booth started his men working on the upper Madawaska, the Opeongo Line became a busy thoroughfare. All along the way were "stopping places" where the teamster could rest his horses, and refresh his own weary body with a stimulating drink. Then prosperity came to the people of the district. Whatever they could produce was easy to market, and if they didn't want to farm they could work farther up the line on timber limits, which are now inside the Park boundaries.

The old village of Killaloe in those days was a thriving community. It may still be seen, a mile and a half down the road to Brudenell, from the present village. There, by the side of Brennan Creek, a grist mill and school still function. But the store has long been closed, and the woollen mill is gone. Old Killaloe is almost deserted. But for the fact that some of the Park rangers still live there, where their children can go to the same old school, it would probably have disappeared. Harry Stack's comings and goings are typical of the Killaloe resident today: the fire season as a ranger at Brent, a few weeks of leisure at home in Killaloe, then a job in a lumber camp near South River until May comes round again.

By the 1880's, the Government had begun to see the Ottawa-Huron tract for what it was: a wilderness of trees and lakes with only a few pockets of fertile soil which could not be farmed profitably unless there were a permanent industry nearby to provide a market for their produce; a land where only the lumberman and trapper could make a seasonal living. Gradually the dream of populating the area faded, and one by one, as their usefulness disappeared, the new roads were allowed to grow over. Many were still used by the lumber companies, but when the railways finally penetrated the area, even these fell into desuetude. Nowadays, in the region bordering the Park, one still comes upon sections of the original roads that have become modern highways; but in general the roads themselves exist only in the memories of the old-timers, and in the stories they tell about the first settlement of the district.

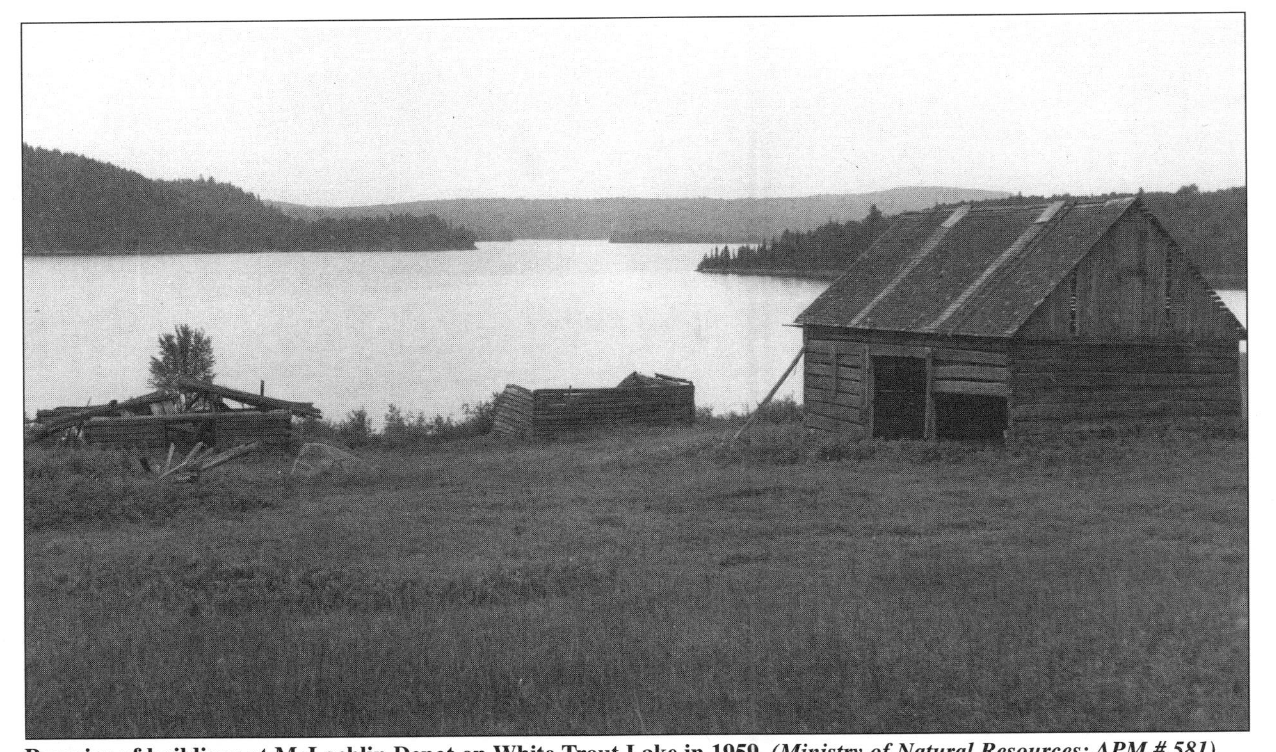

**Remains of buildings at McLachlin Depot on White Trout Lake in 1959.** ***(Ministry of Natural Resources; APM # 581).***

**Cedar Lake dam in 1940s.** *(A. Sinclair; APM # 6495)*

## CHAPTER 5

TWO FAMILIES, the Dennisons and Dufonds, established themselves in the Park area even before the lumber men came. These two families, with the McIntyres, McGueys and Garvies, have given rise to many tales that circulate in the Park to this day, and must be included in the story of its development. They reflect the spirit of the times; they show the sturdy courage of these hardy individualists; and they provide a vivid insight into the way the people of the area lived, in the days before the railroads penetrated into the region.

The reader must inevitably ask at this point, what became of the original Algonquins — the Indians who had hunted and fished through countless generations in the land, whose name the Park now bears? Unfortunately there is no clear-cut answer. During the days of the camboose camps, no doubt, the Indians found that game was scarce and trapping brought no returns. In the areas untouched or abandoned by the lumbermen, the pioneer white trappers from the south had established themselves. The Indians here, as elsewhere, had simply been crowded northward by the more aggressive, systematic, and better-equipped white pioneer from the south. Only in the north they continued to come into the region on occasional hunting trips.

There was, however, one notable exception.

Alexander Sherriff, the explorer responsible for the myth of Algonquin soil fertility, wrote in the account of his travels in the northern Cedar Lake section, that the area was the hunting territory of an Indian called "Map di Fong". Algonquin Indians told him that their favorite route to the Ottawa was by way of a river named after this man, the river marked on maps today as the "Amable du Fond". Peter Ranger, a Park ranger at Kiosk today, knew the Dufonds well.

When Ignace and Francis Dufond first settled in the Park area, they made a small clearing at the south end of Lake Kioshkoqui (Lake of the Gulls). The logs from the house that they built at that place were afterwards used for the first ranger cabin, established near Kiosk by Peter and Telesphore Ranger in 1912. By that time the Dufonds had moved to the next lake farther south, Manitou Lake, where they had cleared quite a bit of land, had built a substantial log house, and had set up a fairly large barn, as well as other outhouses.

The first lumber companies in this section of the Park were glad to buy whatever the Dufonds could produce on their farm. William Mackey, who cut square timber on limits in this area, and J. R. Booth, who afterwards took out saw logs, were both on friendly terms with the Dufond brothers. In this way the Dufonds grew so prosperous that they came to be regarded by Indians and white settlers alike throughout the Mattawa district, as persons of consequence. At one time, Peter Ranger says, they had a cash reserve of six hundred dollars in the bank, and, as he himself remarked, "I think I never heard of any other Indian with so much money."

"The Old Susanne," as Peter always calls the wife of Ignace Dufond, was a skilful worker and a thrifty housewife. When Peter knew her she was old — about eighty years of age. He describes her as being short and square in build, with a face like a man's and a slight beard. Susanne was a full-blooded Indian, and had learned the arts of her ancestors as a young girl. She could tan leather better than anyone else in the district — and make better mitts, and mocassins, too. Peter always depended on her for his own leather equipment, and she showed him how she prepared the skins for use. First, she would scrape the hides; then, when they had been smoked, she would work them until they were soft and pliable. Finally, when the pattern had been cut, she would sew up the article with strong thread made from the sinews along the deer's back.

Sometimes this same thread would be put to other use as well. If Peter found a button loose on his jacket when he stopped by at her cabin while making his rounds, she would sew it on again with her sinew thread, and then it would stay for good.

Susanne was an expert also at making maple sugar. In one season she could produce as much as three hundred pounds, a readily marketed crop, since what the Dufonds did not use themselves they could easily sell at nearby lumber camps or at the town of Mattawa. Some of her produce, however, she loved to give away as presents to anyone she particularly liked. When the Ranger children lived in the Park with their parents, Susanne used to make fancy moulds out of birch bark as containers for her gifts. The children were always delighted with these novelties.

Since Susanne was in the habit of smoking a pipe, Peter used to ask her to join him in a smoke whenever she called around to see him at the Ranger cabin. One day when she arrived Mrs. Ranger and the children were on hand. That time she refused to come indoors for her pipe, lest she should offend them. She and Peter adjourned to the wood-pile for their smoke.

When Peter called around at the Manitou farm he was always greeted warmly and invited to share the next meal. The Dufonds were clean as well as hospitable, and Peter was usually glad to accept their invitation. However, he recalled at least two occasions when he would have preferred not to, but was afraid of offending them: once, when they served a groundhog for the meat course — placed on the table roasted whole, head and all; the second time, when a gallon of pure alcohol had been brought in along the wagon trail from Mattawa. Peter had seen the "Old Susanne" before when she had had something to drink. Sometimes she became "mad like a bear." This time all the guests sat around in a circle and passed a dipper of the alcohol mixed with a little water around the ring. Each person took a drink before passing it on to the next.

But the best stories about the Dufonds centre around the young girl, Pinonique. Peter's eyes still twinkle when he speaks of her: "not bad looking at all, a good girl, with straight dark hair, and not pure Indian." Susanne was not her mother, but adopted her as a baby, and loved her as her own. When Peter knew the family, Pinonique was almost twenty years of age. Susanne was very jealous of the girl, and would allow no one to come near her. When the old lady went off to Mattawa to get her liquor, the girl would be left at home. Pinonique used to hide the knives after Susanne was gone, having good reason to fear that the old lady would be "mad like a bear" by the time she returned. At the same time "the old Susanne" was good to her adopted child. She used to bring back from these trips all sorts of pretty things, clothes and ornaments; and once she even bought a gramaphone, one of the very latest, that played wax rolls for records.

At last, of course, the inevitable happened. His name was Baptiste, he was young and good looking, and he came to work for the Dufonds one summer. Pinonique was cute — she didn't let the old lady know anything about her feelings. The summer over, Baptiste took the team to town one day. He never came back. Neither did Pinonique, who disappeared that night. When Susanne followed her tracks in the morning she read the story on the road. That blackguard, Baptiste, had gone only a short distance and then had turned back to wait for his sweetheart. When night came she had walked down the road to meet him — and they had gone off together.

This time "the old Susanne" was really "mad like a bear". She came to Peter Ranger at Kiosk in a frenzy of frustrated wrath. "What can I do?" she wailed when her anger had died in the knowledge of her loss. Peter did his best to console her. There was nothing she could do — the girl was of age, these things happened, sooner or later. He himself thought privately that it was all for the best. But the old lady was inconsolable.

All the pretty things that she had given Pinonique remained at Manitou Farm until the day aged Susanne herself left. As far as Peter could learn, Pinonique and her Baptiste settled down happily in the outside world, and — as the old nursery stories say — for all we know they are living there yet.

When Francis Dufond died—Ignace was already gone—Susanne was left alone on the farm and had a hard time of it. One of the relations from Mattawa came to run the farm, but finally Susanne gave up, sold her belongings, and moved away. A government pension kept her going for the remaining few years of her life. After she left, some of the buildings were torn down and rebuilt as ranger quarters, and even today there is still a considerable clearing to mark the old Dufond farm at the north end of Manitou Lake.

The best bear story ever to come out of the Park, and one that throws into harsh relief the hazards of pioneer life in wild country, is an intimate part of the history of the Dennison family.

Almost every old-time ranger or traveller in the Park has spent a night in a ranger's cabin known as "Sunnyside", built on the old Dennison clearing, and has heard the famous story of old Captain Dennison's encounter with the bear. Of the many versions, Jack Smith, the ranger now stationed at Lake of Two Rivers, tells one of the best.

According to Jack, old Grandfather Dennison was an Englishman by birth who had come to this country to take up land. He had settled first at Combermere, about ten miles south of Barry's Bay. But old Mr. Dennison had the pioneering spirit in its most adventurous form, and became much more interested in trapping than he had ever been in farming. For that reason, he decided to move his family farther north into the wilds, and set up the beginning of a farm at the Narrows on Opeongo Lake.

One day, when he was starting off on his rounds to examine his traps, he took his eight-year-old grandson with him in the canoe up through the North Arm of the lake. He had been up that way the week before, and had set a bear trap on the Green Lake portage. When the two of them reached the appointed spot they beached the canoe, and went up the portage to look at the trap. The old man led the way.

The particular trap that they were about to visit had been skilfully set. It was chained to the far side of a great log and baited with rotten meat. As they approached the log there was no sound at all, and the old man decided the trap had not been sprung. However, just to make sure he stuck his head over the log to take a look. With that, an enormous bear, whipped into fighting madness by the pain of the steel clamp, leaped at him, clawed him, and dragged him over the edge of the log. The old man screamed, but was powerless in the mighty grip of the great beast. He called out to the boy to go for help.

The little fellow rushed down to the canoe, and paddled the long eight miles back to the farm as fast as he could. When he got there he found his father had gone out on an overnight hunting trip, and there was no help to be had. Days later, when he and his father returned to the spot, they found evidence of a terrific struggle. All the old man's clothes but his boots had been ripped to shreds. Both he and the bear were dead. The son carried the body back to the clearing for burial, and there the grave may be seen today. A fence made of split rails sets it apart from the encroaching forest, and marks it as hallowed ground.

In one of the Park Newsletters information was published which was gathered from an interview with Mr. C. B. Dennison, a grandson of the old man:

> "Capt. John Dennison, of English birth, was born at Penrith, England, in the year 1799. He was a literary man, possessing a high degree of education. He was of military mien, and landed in Montreal in 1825, and rather distinguished himself in the Lower Canada Rebellion of 1837.
>
> After a lapse of a few years he had a son, John, and settled in Bytown (now Ottawa) in 1854. The Dennisons pushed on up the Ottawa River as far as Arnprior, then followed the tortuous Madawaska for many miles, settling at a spot that was known for many years as Dennison's Bridge, which is today the

> charming village of Combermere, in the year 1869. The Captain, charmed with the beauty of the virgin forest, renewed the voyage with his two sons, John and Henry, to the Great Opeongo Lake, where in the month of June, 1881, Captain John Dennison at the age of 82, met a tragic death."

From Mort Findlayson of Barry's Bay, another of the Captain's grandchildren, has come some additional information about the Dennison family, and the famous incident with the bear. Mort's mother was Mary Dennison, a sister of John and Henry, and as a young man Mort had frequently visited the Opeongo farm. For many years he worked as a fire ranger on the Booth limits in the Park.

Mort has it that Captain John Dennison obtained his commission serving with the Beach River Volunteers in 1837. When he moved to Combermere he kept a stopping place, but in the 1870's, when his wife died, he decided to go farther inland to open up land at a spot where the Opeongo Line would eventually strike. At the Opeongo Narrows his two sons, Harry and Jack, decided to make their clearings. Harry's was to the left of the Narrows as you pass through them from the main body of the lake; Jack's to the right.

Mort says that when the family first came to the point on the left, which they afterwards named "Sunnyside", they found a small clearing already cut, and were told the Indians had used it for a summer camp in the old days. Close by were the ruins of a log cabin, said by Sherriff to be the remains of an old Hudson's Bay Company trading post. The Indian camp site checks with the stories of the Golden Lake Indians, but there are no records in the Hudson's Bay Company archives of any such post. Probably the building had been the headquarters of early white trappers who took their furs out to "The Bay" posts in the Ottawa Valley.

When the Dennisons moved in their household belongings to the Opeongo farm site, they came from Combermere by the river route. This journey through the Egan Estate limits of the Booth Company was, before the coming of the railroad, one of the best known ways of getting in and out of the Park district from the southeast. From Bark Lake the travellers went up the Madawaska River, across to Victoria Lake, and then through a chain of lakes to the Opeongo River. Mort remembers travelling this route when he went in to the Dennison farm, and he recalls seeing an abandoned log building at Crotch Lake that roused his curiosity. It was twenty feet square, and had been built long before timber cutting had begun in that region. His uncle, Harry Dennison, told him it had been built by hunters in the 1850's.

Mort has further details of his grandfather's tragic end. It was a very windy day when the old man set forth with his grandson, eight-year-old John Dennison. According to Mort's story, the old man had left his grandson at the boat, with instructions that if he wasn't back in two hours the lad was to go home. The child became frightened when the old Captain failed to show up, and went home for his father. That evening the father searched the shoreline, shouting as he went, but there was no answer, nor any sign of the missing man. In the morning he found the trap — the bear was still alive, but the old man was dead. They took the body back to the farm and buried it in the small fenced-in spot back of the barns. As far as Mort knows, this is the only grave in the plot; the little Dennison girl who died later was buried farther down towards the shore.

About the lumber companies in the Opeongo district when the Dennisons first moved in, Mort Findlayson has some scattered information. He thinks that Alex. Graham, from down Renfrew way, was the first man to cut square timber in these parts. At one time Annie Bay, at the eastern extremity of Lake Opeongo, was called Graham Bay after this man. This bay was renamed after Annie Dennison. The old winter road running through the woods from here to the farm may have been cut by Graham's men. Fraser and McCoshen were the names of two other Lake Opeongo operators who may have been cutting as early as the 1870's. Mort once saw McCoshen getting some of his square timber through the Narrows. His "cadge crib" was a raft, worked by horses, and it took a long time to drag the heavy booms out through the East Arm to the flowing waters of the Opeongo River. From there Mort recalls it used to take two years for the trip to Quebec, although there is a record of the logs having gone down in a single season.

About 1882 the Dennisons decided to move, and by 1885, when the survey of Bower Township was completed, the Sunnyside clearing had been taken over by the Fraser Lumber Company, and was being operated as a depot farm.

Today the full extent of the old Dennison clearings is still visible from the air. On the ground, the passage of time and succession of different occupants have brought about great changes; but it is still possible to trace out the foundations of the first log buildings, and to visualize the general layout of the farm.

A faint trail, marked by ingrown blazes barely discernible now, still leads from the lake to the first clearing. In what was once a well-worked field, small evergreens are growing now, twelve feet high and more. Near the old farm site two magnificent birches catch the eye — planted to mark the grave of the little Dennison girl. Farther up, on a piece of rising ground, is the fenced-in grave of the old Captain.

Beyond lie the remains of the farm buildings, for which Mort helped to cut some of the timbers: a storehouse on the top of the hill, a milk-house down by the spring, the barn and stables, and a large woodshed. Of the house itself, very little is left — the logs have been carted away by lumbermen, rangers and campers — but one pauses to admire the magnificent view across Great Opeongo Lake that the old Captain must once have loved.

Although the Dennison family moved out of the district ten years before the Park was established, it would be a pity if their memory were not retained in some way at the Sunnyside farm clearing. Here was a family in the best of Canadian pioneering traditions. Daring to push ahead into the wilderness miles beyond any settled region, they chose their location, cleared their land, hewed logs for buildings, and constructed a comfortable and substantial home in the heart of the Algonquin forest. Algonquin Park may well be proud of the Dennisons.

Today the section of the Park to the extreme southeast, drained by the Bonnechere, is rarely travelled by canoe trip parties. However, in the old days it was one of the most frequently travelled sections of the Park. Year after year the Ottawa Valley lumber companies poured men into their limits up the Bonnechere.

From the 1850's on there had been a supply centre at Basin Depot, a stopping place about twenty miles above Round Lake at a point now well within the Park boundaries. This centre was used by all the old companies that cut in the region, by Barnet's, by McLachlin's, and by the companies that went into the north of the Park along a lumbering road leading into White Partridge Lake. For over fifty years the families at Basin Depot, at the stopping places later established at Sligo, and at "The Village" where the road turned north, were known to all the lumbermen who came into the Park country. "Dinney" McGuey and Paddy Garvie who lived at Basin Depot, William McIntyre, whose clearing was farther up the Bonnechere River, and the Widow McDonald who raised her family at Sligo near the present Park boundaries, were among the earliest Algonquin Park residents.

Of Dinney McGuey more will be heard when the story of the Park's establishment is told. Mike Garvie, now living at Golden Lake, has fond recollections of his father, Paddy Garvie, "the pioneer of the Bonnechere". For sixty-five years, till his death in 1916 at the age of eighty-five, Paddy worked on his farm at Basin Depot. Mike says that Paddy was first employed by John Egan, and later by Alex. Barnet, both of whom operated square timber companies in the district. Paddy ran the stopping place at "The Depot" as the old-timers called it, and sold whatever produce he could raise on his farm to the camps. Finally, when the square timber was gone, and the limits sold to the McLachlins for saw-logs, Paddy's allegiance was transferred to this firm.

When Mike Garvie was a boy his father's farm was a flourishing concern of some two hundred acres. On this homestead clearing there were about forty head of cattle and a number of sheep. In most matters the family was self-sufficient, but there were two commodities at least that had to be obtained from the nearest settlement at Eganville, some thirty miles away. From an old store ledger, kept by Daniel Lacey who ran the Eganville store, has come interesting data about Paddy's shopping habits in the very early days. The heading for one page reads: "Mr. Paddy Garvie, Little Bonnechere." Two items are marked down as follows:

Aug. 22 (1866) — To one pair calf boots for self......1/10/0

July 13 (1867) — To two gallons hard wine ............... 18/0

Although the women and children could be clad in soft home-made or Indian-made mocassins, heavy shoes had to be purchased for the men working on the land or in the bush. The hard wine was likely for consumption at Paddy's stopping place.

Jack Wilson, the ranger at Park Headquarters, and other old-timers who have cut timber along the Bonnechere, have a host of stories about Paddy Garvie. There is one about the time when Paddy needed some new shingles for his house at Basin Depot. He was quite put out when he went to the McLachlin foreman to ask for the necessary supplies and was told that the shingles on hand would all be needed for the company's buildings. He would have to make his own with a drawknife and some chunks of "corky" white pine, the foreman told him, if he expected to have any shingles that year. Paddy went home grumbling. Wasn't he a "stiff" McLachlin man and shouldn't they look after their own employees? But Paddy was to have his revenge. Only a few days later the big dam above the Basin broke, the company's store yards were flooded, and all the shingles came floating down to Paddy's farm three miles below. Well, Paddy was not the man to waste time wondering who had sent him this magnificent present. When the McLachlin foreman came downstream looking for his lost property, the company's shingles were adorning Paddy's roof.

There are dozens of Paddy Garvie's stories, all illustrating his ready wit, his kindly shrewdness, his rugged common sense, and his rather naive way of doing business. Dr. Reeves at Eganville, who knew and liked Paddy and his family, used to visit him when he went up the Bonnechere on hunting trips. One time Paddy had an organ brought all the way to his stopping place at the Depot. When asked how he could afford to buy such an expensive article he protested, "All it cost me was a piece of paper." It was not that he was dishonest; he simply knew nothing of business methods, and trusted other people as he expected them to trust him. Many a man enjoyed a pint of whiskey "on the house" at Paddy's bar, and the walls of the old place were covered with the names of these passers-by.

Speaking of whiskey brings up a story which has nothing to do with Paddy Garvie, but illustrates how highly hard liquor was valued by the men in the camps. Today in the Park there are stringent regulations against the sale of intoxicants within its boundaries. The early lumber companies were just as strict in keeping liquor out of their camps. But they did not always succeed, and the story of how Whiskey Rapids got their name is almost a case in point.

In the late spring one year, a group of men on the tail end of a drive through the southwest corner of the Park, were camped for the week-end rest on the Oxtongue River below Tea Lake, now named Waskigomog Lake. They had been working for some time, and soon they would be on their way downstream with the last of the logs that were being floated down to the mill on the Muskoka Lakes. Since they felt that this called for a celebration, they had made arrangements with some of the railwaymen to bring in a keg of whiskey for a party on Saturday night. A keg, holding three gallons, cost three dollars and eighty-five cents, a sum the men had all chipped in to pay.

At first everything happened according to schedule. Two men

paddled up the river from the camp near the Three Sister Islands, close to the Park boundary. They portaged around a series of rapids, and then proceeeded on up through Tea and Canoe Lakes to the spot where the keg was to be dumped off the train. The train was on time, the keg was delivered, and the two men started off back to camp with the precious load in the bottom of the canoe.

Then the inevitable happened. One of the paddlers suggested to the other that the first drink was really their due. Hadn't they travelled all this way to pick it up? And besides, who would miss the odd drop from a whole barrel? His companion recognized the force of these arguments, so they pierced a hole under one of the hoops and drained off a little of the contents. It didn't take long. Soon they were on their way again, feeling much better.

However, when they reached the river itself it was getting dark. They had better hurry — after all the others couldn't start their Saturday night celebrations until the whiskey arrived. By now they were both feeling fine, the river was high from the spring thaw, and they were slipping along at a good speed. Suddenly the man in the bow realized they were approaching the rapids, and turned to warn his friend that it was time to land for the portage. "Oh letsh shoot them," replied the other, and in a moment they were in the white water.

It was too dark to see the right channel, even if they had been sober enough to pick it out. Into the river they went with their precious cargo. By the time the two men had dragged themselves out of the river the whiskey was gone. For hours they searched, before they gave up and returned to the camp, sober and empty-handed. Then the whole camp turned out for the search. Alas, the whiskey keg had disappeared forever, but to this day this treacherous stretch of the Oxtongue River has been known as "Whiskey Rapids".

To return to our friends of depot farm days, Dinney McGuey and Paddy Garvie were not the only Bonnechere settlers in the old times. Along the stretch of road used by the stage that drove in three days a week from Eganville to Basin Depot in the 1890's, lived the Widow McDonald and her family. Their home was at Sligo, now just within the Park boundaries. Mr. McDonald had been employed originally by the lumber companies, but when he died his wife stayed on at his small clearing, where she valiantly struggled to make a living and bring up a large family of small children. Sometimes the lumber companies would contribute a bag of flour or a barrel of salt pork to the family's larder, but for the most part times were very hard.

From Mrs. Harry Stack, one of the widow McDonald's children, has come the story of how this courageous woman carried on. She had a few cows of her own, and the family's sole income came from the butter that she was able to sell at the nearest village. One summer, after she had sold her whole season's supply, she found that she had only realized forty dollars. With this money she had to purchase all the provisions for the coming winter. It is little wonder that the McDonald children were all needed at home to gather wood and to help with the work. As for schooling, it was impossible to spare the children even for as long as it would take them to go as far as the Depot, where their neighbour Paddy Garvie had established a school for his own family. Only one or two of the McDonalds were ever able to continue at school long enough to learn how to read or write.

Up the river past Dinney's upper farm was the last stopping place on the Bonnechere River. There, about twenty miles above Basin Depot, William McIntyre had cleared a ten-acre patch of ground by the time the township survey was made in 1889. One of his sons, Jack McIntyre, was brought up in this Park homestead. Jack McIntyre is now Deputy-Chief Ranger in the north of the Park at Achray.

From several different sources comes word of another family that lived in the Park once. On Lake Clear, now Dickson Lake, the surveyors reported in 1888 that there was a clearing of fifteen acres and a log house. Here, on the west shore of the lake, there lived a man, his wife, and two little girls. No one seems to know today either their name, or how they came to live so far from other settlements. Mark Robinson says that when he first joined the Park staff in 1907, he used to hear from the other rangers about an English family living there. Bob Balfour and Steve Waters had both called at the place and reported that the sixteen-year-old daughter couldn't remember anything at all of the outside world, having spent almost all her life in the Park district. The rangers said that there was a piano in the house that had been hauled in along one of the lumber tote roads. The mother of the family died at the homestead and was buried there. Afterwards the family moved away and nothing further is known of them.

When Park visitors ask today whether anyone ever lived in the Park, there are few who can give them accurate information about this almost-forgotten chapter of Algonquin Park history. Actually, none of the land in the Park area was ever granted by the Crown for settlement purposes. The farm at Manitou Lake had been acquired originally through a mining patent, but all the other clearings in the Park were made by families who came into the country to work the land in conjunction with the lumber companies who were cutting in the district. Here and there were patches of fertile soil sufficient to supply some of the food and fodder in the camps. When the companies stopped cutting and the railways came, the depot farms became superfluous. After all, if the Dennisons could not make a go of it, no one could.

Now the locations of the old depot farms are marked only by a few small clearings, and by the remnants of the log dwellings which originally housed the Algonquin Park pioneers.

# CHAPTER 6

TWO STORIES remain to be told before we come to the crisis in the larger story of the Park, the historic letter of Alexander Kirkwood to the Ontario Commissioner of Crown Lands. Both have their setting in the days when the lumberman was absorbed in the practical problem of getting his timber to the mills. How one man brought the mills to the timber is an important part of lumbering history; how another brought the timber to his mill, is one of the Park's most fantastic stories.

By the eighties, the days of square timber cutting were numbered. All along the Ottawa Valley sawmills had been established, and limits that had been regarded as cut over by the square timber men could now be developed profitably, in view of the shorter haul to the mills. Trees which had been passed by during previous operations as too small, unsound in parts, or inaccessible, were now prospective sawlogs. Improvements that would have been too costly for twenty-foot logs, could now be undertaken for the shorter fourteen-footers. Even the older companies who did not contemplate adopting the new methods, profited from the change. Mackey's limit on the Amable du Fond is said tc have been worth $655,000 when it was bought by J. R. Booth. Barnet's limit in the White Trout, or as it is now called, the Big Trout district, which was sold to the McLachin's, was valued at $750,000. In both cases these later companies operated for many years on limits that had previously been cut over for square timber. Booth's logs were floated out of the Park to the mill at the Chaudiere Rapids just above Ottawa, while McLachlin's went out by way of the Petawawa route to Arnprior.

What was even more significant was the arrival of the railways. With the completion of the Canadian Pacific Railway between Ottawa and North Bay, the stations of Bissett, Deux Rivieres, and Mattawa had become favourite jumping-off places for companies operating along the Petawawa. To the west the Grand Trunk Railway reached Huntsville in 1885. Before long stations north of there, such as Emsdale and Sundridge, were starting points for tote roads into the Park. From the railway terminus at Minden to the south, teamsters drew supplies up the Bobcaygeon Road to camps on the

Oxtongue. Finally, in 1888, J. R. Booth and a group of Ottawa associates decided to build the Ottawa-Arnprior and Parry Sound Railway, to provide a short direct transportation route between Lake Huron and the Ottawa Valley.

John R. Booth was not the only lumber king to have substantial interests in the Algonquin region, but wherever Park old-timers gather to "swap" stories of the old days, "J.R." is the central, almost legendary figure. They delight particularly in telling how the great lumber king used to arrive in his camps at all sorts of odd times to see how the boys were doing. He had learned his business the hard way by working in the mills and camps; and to the end of his days he loved to pick up an axe or a cant hook and demonstrate that he was still one of the boys at heart. To many men who worked in the Booth camps in the Park the Old Man, wearing felt boots and a padded jacket, as unpretentious as any of his workmen, was a familiar and respected figure.

His son, Jackson Booth, who retains his connection with the firm, tells us how his father got his first limits in the Algonquin Park area. "J.R." was born in 1826 in the eastern townships of Quebec, where his parents had settled when they first came to Canada from Ireland. In the 1850's, when American lumbermen from the New England States first brought their novel techniques into the Ottawa Valley, young Booth moved north to work in one of their mills. Before long he had set up a shingle mill of his own at the Chaudiere Rapids, and had begun to acquire limits along the Ottawa and its tributaries. Just at this point, the great limits along the upper Madawaska River, known as the Egan Estate, and said to contain the finest stands of pine in the country, came up for sale at public auction. Characteristically, "J.R." took a shrewd gamble and outbid all competitors.

For a time the Opeongo Line sufficed as a means of supplying Booth's camps on the Egan Estate beyond Bark Lake. But Booth was a man who took the long view. The advantages of a railway were obvious. Already he had played a part in building a railway from Ottawa to join the Central Vermont Railway at Coteau, on the St. Lawrence River. It is altogether likely that the lumber king was looking beyond the needs of the lumber industry, and had visions of a great transportation system to be added to his empire.

Booth and his associates went ahead with their plans. Obstacles were brushed aside. When a legal conflict developed with the Canadian Pacific over the right of way through Wilno Pass, Booth secured the services of the famous Ottawa lawyer, Dalton McCarthy, and won. To this day, the C.P.R. line involved goes only as far as Eganville.

Through the years '94 to '96, construction gangs sweated summer and winter laying the grade and tracks. By September, 1894, the line had reached Madawaska Station. Before long it was within the Park itself, bringing with it E. C. Whitney, owner of the St. Anthony Lumber Company, to build a sawmill at Whitney. It was alleged that the new line was the cause of several fires; in fact, the following year two of Whitney's camps were burned out, giving point to the growing consciousness for the need of systematic fire protection.

In October, a year later, W. P. Hinton, the traffic manager, made a trip in to the end of steel at Cache Lake. In November, supplies for the new Park headquarters arrived there, including lumber from a mill at Eganville.

A Dr. A. S. Thompson looked after the health of the Whitney lumber camps at the time, and from May till October of 1896 was employed by the railroad construction firm of Ferguson and O'Neill, then working on the completion of the line. One of his most vivid memories of his stay in the Canoe Lake district has been preserved in his own words:

> "On one occasion, August, 1896, I got into camp in time for supper. After supper the foreman, Jack McLeod, an experienced rock-man, asked me to go with him to a rock cut 200 yards distant to have a chat while he fired two shots. As soon as he made the proposal something within me said, in tones of authority, 'Don't go. It's none of your business!' So I excused myself on plea of being tired. I knew something about rock drilling and the use of dynamite, but just why this warning voice came to me, I know not. There must be something in the belief of guardian angels.
>
> "We heard a shot, a deep rumbling noise indicative of large masses of rock being upheaved, and waited until dark for the second one, which did not come. I was just turning in when a man rushed into the camp, saying that an accident had occurred in the rock-cut. I ran along the crooked path between rocks and stumps to the cut, and groping in the

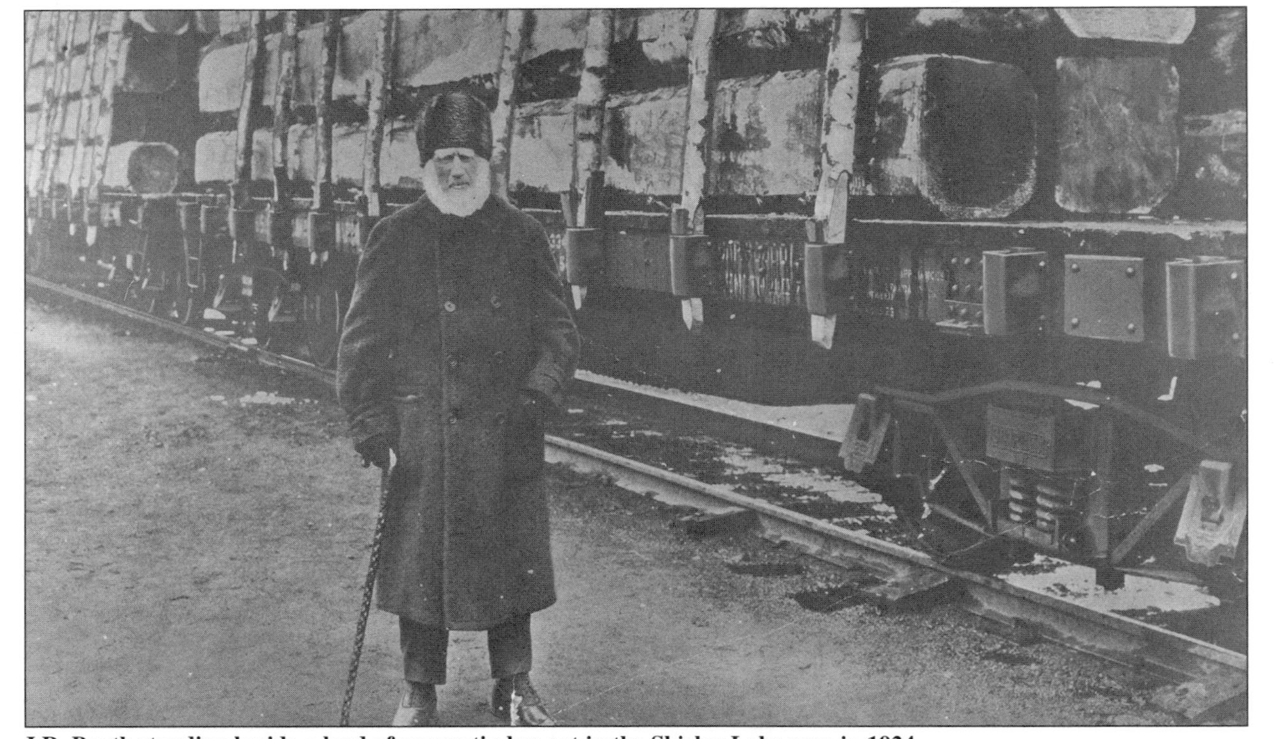

**J.R. Booth standing beside a load of waney timber cut in the Shirley Lake area in 1924.**
(*Ministry of Natural Resources; APM # 4133*)

**Main depot camp of the Gilmour Lumber Co. at Tea Lake in 1893.** *(Ministry of Natural Resources; APM # 1093)*

dark I felt a man's hand, struck a match, found a man lying on his back, arms extended over his head with a huge rock lying on his legs and the power part of his body. He was quite dead. On further search we found the bodies of Jack McLeod and O'Brien, blown thirty feet out of the cut, both dead. The blast had ignited their clothes and their faces were burned . . .

"A man living in the shanty nearby heard the noise, investigated, and brought word to the camp of the accident. The man I found lying with the rock on top of him had been ordered to go home some time before the accident occurred, but he delayed too long. The accident cost the lives of three men and if I had accepted McLeod's invitation, without doubt I would have been the fourth. It was a sad duty to inform Mrs. McLeod, living in the camp, of the death of her good man."

From Scotia Junction, on the Grand Trunk, tracks were being laid toward the western boundary of the Park at the same time as the line from Ottawa Valley was under construction. When these two sections came together the job was finished. On December the twentieth, 1896, the first through train on the Ottawa-Arnprior and Parry Sound Railway ran from Depot Harbour, on Georgian Bay, to the City of Ottawa. This was a trial run: the line was not officially open for business until the following year.

With the completion of the railway, the whole technique of taking out timber changed. The long river drives were gone, at least for all new operations. Now the logs could be brought speedily to the railways and shipped out on flat cars, or cut into lumber by sawmills on the spot.

From the Egan Estate Station on the new railway, Booth built a spur line to tap the rich supply of pine lying between there and Opeongo Lake. The spur ran north to McAuley Junction, where it divided, one track going to the left along McAuley Creek as far as the Park boundaries, the other to the right into the Park, toward Crotch Lake. When the pine was cut these tracks were torn up and sold for scrap.

Whitney also built a spur line to his Opeongo limits from the Whitney Station to Sproule Bay. The rails are gone, but the roadbed has remained in use to this day, the road from the main Park highway to Opeongo Lake passing along a section of the St. Anthony Company's original line.

The limits in the south and east of the Park were also opened up as the result of the building of the Booth Railway. Lumber companies in the southwest, operated by J. D. Shier of Bracebridge, by the Mickle and Dyment Company of Gravenhurst, and by the Gilmour Company of Trenton, all made use of the railroad to bring in men and supplies. Most of these, however, found it was still cheaper to drive their logs to the original mills than to build new sawmills by the tracks.

The older outfits, such as Barnet's and McLachlin's, and the newer Huntsville Lumber Company, made full use of the new railway. Barnet had previously hauled his supplies for the White, or as it is now called, the Big Trout Lake limits along a tote road from Sundridge, but now a much shorter route was provided by a road running north from Brûlé Lake Station. This same route was used by the McLachlin Company when they purchased the limits in 1911. Both these firms continued to drive their logs by way of the Petawawa River to their mills in the Ottawa Valley, but some of the more recent companies have preferred to set up their mills right in the Park. The Huntsville Lumber Company operated at Brûlé Lake for some years, while J. D. S. McRae had a mill at Rock Lake in the 1920's, and another at Lake of Two Rivers between 1931 and 1943.

Many a story is told by old railroaders of the days spent on the Park railroad. Some of the older Park rangers remember the days when traffic was so heavy on this line, that there was a freight train every twenty minutes. Sometimes these trains transported as many as twenty million bushels of western grain in a single year. When the Canada Atlantic Company took over this section, many men who were to rise to a place of prominence in the business and railroad worlds, received their initial experience on the Park run. The "Canada Atlantic Old Boys" still have annual gatherings at Ottawa, where they recall the fine sense of comradeship amongst the men working on the old line. In those days, the trains were known by the names of their conductors; and "Gourlay's Special" or "McDonald's Run" passed along the tracks running through the Park. There was never an engineer too busy to wave at the passers-by, or to stop his train and pick up a ranger who needed transportation for himself and his canoe.

In 1903 the Canada Atlantic was taken over by the Grand Trunk

Railway, for a sum of something like fourteen million dollars. In 1923 the G.T.R. became a part of the Canadian National Railways, which found, a little over ten years ago, that it was operating at a loss in this section. As a result of an inquiry held in 1935, two decisions were made: that the section between Lake of Two Rivers (Mile 162.3) to Cache Lake (Mile 166.8) would have to be abandoned because one of the wooden trestle bridges had been condemned, and that the line would have to continue operating from both ends, because there was, at that time, no parallel transportation into the Park. Finally a wye was built at Whitney so that trains could turn there, instead of going up to Rock Lake Station in the Park.

The second story mentioned at the beginning of this chapter, is an epic of misguided zeal.

In 1892, according to records of the Timber Division of the Ontario Department of Lands and Forests, one of the largest sales in the history of the province was held in Toronto. It was October the thirteenth, an unlucky day for the Gilmour Company that made the purchase. On that date, this Company won the bid for timber rights in what amounted to two-thirds of the Township of Peck, extending from Tea Lake, northward to include both Canoe and Joe Lakes. It was a rich property. To quote one of the old-time timber cruisers who travelled through the whole section: "the country was blue with pine."

Today, it is difficult to convince the visitor to Canoe Lake, that the flourishing village of Mowat, named after the Ontario Premier of those days, once stood on the west side of the lake; that there were thirty miles of siding by the station at the north end; most of all, that logs were floated from the lake before his eyes, 200 miles to the mouth of the Trent River, on the shore of Lake Ontario. True, the ruins of the old mill foundation are still visible down by the shore; and the springy ground tells of mill refuse rotting into the soil under the grass. The ruins of the old landing dock where the boarding houses used to be, can still be found. But a group of fine birch trees has grown up around the wreck of the old mill hospital; and of the stables, once large enough to house fifty teams of horses a night, there is little to be seen.

The vanished village contained a large warehouse, and a cook-house, and any number of shacks to accommodate the wives and families of the Gilmour employees. The shacks are gone; the two large buildings were preserved and repaired, to become the famous

Mowat Lodge, to be described in a later chapter. From the old warehouse to the station, all that the visitor may now see are a few surviving sections of corduroy, and the overgrown grade of the railway siding that once ran from the mill to the main line. Two substantial summer homes built for the Gilmour Brothers' families, later bought by Dr. T. A. Bertram of Dundas, still stand in good repair.

If the visitor is still skeptical as to the former existence of this ghost village, let him visit the graveyard on the hillside, back of the old road to Tea Lake. Here, Tom Thomson's body found temporary rest. Not far away lies the grave of a Mowat mill employee, killed by the limb of a falling tree, the grave marked by a stone which bears this record:

> In memory of Jas. Watson, the first white person to be buried at Canoe Lake. Died May 27, 1897, being one of about 500 employed at this camp by the Gilmour Company, aged 21 years.
>
> "Remember, comrade, when passing by,
> As you are now so once was I,
> As I am now so you will be;
> Prepare thyself to follow me."

At the foot of the inscription is added the information, "Engraved gratis by a comrade, D. W. McCain."

The story of the Gilmour operations has yet to be told. The skeptical visitor may accept the evidence of the village's existence in the old days, and still balk at the incredible story of the Gilmour logs. For experienced lumbermen to entertain the idea of transporting logs two hundred miles was improbable enough. That they should plan to float millions of cubic feet of timber *up* over the height of land between Lake of Bays and the headwaters of the Trent, was fantastic.

As a matter of fact, "float" is not quite the right word. Although this historic development took place outside the Park boundaries, it is worth describing here because the whole system was evolved as a means of getting logs out of the Park. The Superintendent, in his report for the year 1895, mentions the fact that the Gilmour Company had already been cutting on their limits for the past three seasons, but he went on to say that they had decided to postpone operations until the railway through the Park should be completed.

And no wonder!

From Archie McEachern, of Dorset, whose father was employed by the company during construction of their improvements in that district, has come the most vivid account of how the feat was performed. The Gilmour Company planned to float their logs down the Oxtongue River from Canoe Lake to the Lake of Bays. There they would be made into booms, and dragged by means of the steam alligator, still to be seen at Baysville, to the starting point of the haul over the height of land. The old stone pumphouse, situated about a mile from Dorset on the road to Baysville, marks the spot where an endless chain, designed to do the job, was to start.

Other companies had built costly dams and slides, but this Gilmour scheme was the most complicated, and costly, of anything yet devised. The pump down by the shore pumped water into the wooden trough, up which the logs slid. It also provided motive power for the chain, to which were attached a series of spikes, to stick into the logs and keep them in place. The first pump was supplemented by boosters along the trough, which were in some places as much as thirty feet above the ground. At the top of this first grade the logs were floated downhill for about a mile, where they arrived at the bottom of a second chain system. There, a second series of pumps brought them up the final rise to Raven Lake. This lake, which normally drains into the Muskoka system, had been backed up by dams, so that it flowed instead through the swampy district into St. Nora's Lake, at the headwaters of the Trent. The logs had to be driven through this swamp in booms, and you can still see, driving along the highway in the winter, when the leaves are off the trees, some of the old capstans that were used to secure the ropes for these booms.

Beside the problem of how to get the logs out of the Park district, there was the transportation problem. From Dorset, where supplies could be brought in by wagon or sleigh along the Bobcaygeon Road, there was a long haul to Tea Lake — and no road! The Gilmours cut one.

Rangers are still able to follow the course of this old road through the southwest corner of the Park, and at places both at Canoe Lake and in the Hollow Lake, now called Kawagama Lake district, it is still in use. The Park Superintendent, who took up headquarters at Canoe Lake during the summer of 1893, was delighted at the prospect of the speedy completion of this road. To him, it meant a handy way out and in through Dorset. As far as one can tell it was used by the company and Park officials during the winter of 1893-4, when supplies for the men working in the Park were toted in along its twenty-eight miles.

Jim Campbell, who travelled this road in Gilmour's time, and afterwards, when it was used by Shier and Mickle-Dyment, has stories of the stopping places on this road. The Gilmour Company had storehouses and a boarding house at Dorset, since this was the terminal of the part of the Bobcaygeon Road they used, as well as the centre for their tramway system. From there, the bush road ran out by Otter Lake, now Tock Lake, for a distance of about eight miles to the first stopping place, at the upper end of Fletcher Lake. There a man could get a meal if he needed it, and on the whole it was quite a respectable place, though it bore the sinister name of "The Pig's Ear". Ten miles farther on was a log house, and a barn capable of putting up fifteen teams of horses for the night. This place was kept by a not too respectable negro; "Dart's Den", as it was called, was a somewhat less savoury stopping place.

In 1895, spring came so early, that the men were able to break the log dumps at Potter Creek on April the twenty-second. Two days later they began the epic drive, and by the twenty-ninth the alligator was hard at work, towing the booms over the lakes to the Oxtongue River. All that time the water on the two lakes was held at a high level, destroying trees along the shore to such an extent, that the evidence is still there today. But the drive went on.

People are still living in the Dorset-Haliburton area who remember that drive. Tommy Archer is one of them. He recalls that a thousand men were employed in the construction of the intricate system of dams, troughs, pumps and chains, financed by the Gilmours. The company, he says, "spent millions of dollars" on it, out of a misguided faith in the cruisers' glowing reports. Down the Oxtongue went the logs, and up over the endless chains, into Trent waters. It worked!

Except for one little miscalculation. By the time the logs had finished their long, rough trip, many months had passed. When they finally reached the company's mills at Trenton, it was found that by the time they were ready to be cut into lumber, even the finest timber had begun to deteriorate!

In December of that year, the company stopped cutting in the district, explaining that there was a depression in the lumber market. Probably they had decided to change their method of getting the logs out, and were waiting for the Booth railway to come through. With the completion of the railroad in 1896, the Gilmour Company recommenced operations on more modern lines, building the mill and village at Mowat. But they still seemed to like doing things the hard way: the huge boiler from the Dorset pump-house, was hauled along the old road, in the depth of winter. Over this rough trail, the boiler was hauled by nine teams of horses, on birch rollers that wore out almost as fast as the men could cut them. By the time the railway was officially opened in the spring, the mill at Mowat was in working order.

When the Gilmour Company went bankrupt, the village and mill fell into the hands of receivers, who established a caretaker on the property. Some of the machinery, including the mill engine, was sold; but a great deal of the equipment was simply left where it had last been used. Axes, saws, and other odds and ends bearing the Gilmour name, may still be seen in workshops around Canoe Lake. With the exceptions mentioned already, there is today little evidence that the village of Mowat ever existed. When the name of the post office was changed to Canoe Lake, even that link with the past disappeared.

## CHAPTER 7

TO THE PIONEERS of the depot farms, to the Haliburton trappers, the railroad construction gangs, and the men who worked for Booth, Gilmour and the other big lumbermen, the reservation of Algonquin Park in the early nineties, when it came, was a fact — not an abstract idea. The idea was born in the brain of a clerk in the office of the Ontario Department of Crown Lands, a man who had never set eyes on the Park area, Alexander Kirkwood.

There was nothing phenomenal in Kirkwood's background. At the age of twenty-three he emigrated from Belfast, Ireland, to try his hand at wheat farming in New York State. In 1853, he moved to an obscure job in Montreal — probably clerical work, for shortly afterwards he was appointed to the staff of the newly formed Department of Agriculture, in the short-lived United Government of Upper and Lower Canada. After Confederation, in 1870, he became attached to the Ontario Department of Crown Lands.

But the restlessness that had brought him across the Atlantic still stirred in him, stimulated by paper glimpses, in his work, of the vast areas of virgin land that lay to the north. In 1878, he and a J. J. Murphy published a volume entitled "The Undeveloped Lands of Northern and Western Ontario", an estimate of the progress that had been made in frontier settlement in the previous quarter century. There is no question that Kirkwood later doubted the wisdom of the Government's settlement plans for the Huron-Ottawa tract; and it is very likely that while working on this book, he had his first glimmerings of the Park idea.

Gradually, one problem came to obsess him: if this height of land area should not be opened for settlement, what useful purpose could it serve?

Kirkwood's search for an answer led him into a wide field of reading and research. There was the timber, for instance, of the Huron-Ottawa tract, fast falling before the onslaughts of the lumber kings: what had other countries done to preserve their forests? There were the animal and fish resources: how could these be used without depletion? There were the rivers and lakes that would shrink into streams and ponds if the forests were cleared for settlement. All his research pointed to one answer, a conclusion that few men of his generation wanted to take seriously, at a time when it seemed that the country's boundless natural resources could never be exhausted. The answer was conservation.

In 1885, Alexander Kirkwood's idea was ripe, and he wrote a letter to his Commissioner, the Hon. T. B. Pardee. A year later, he published the contents of this letter in an eight-page pamphlet. Both letter and pamphlet set forth the idea of a "National Forest and Park", with specific reasons for the urgency of its establishment. Such a Park should be set aside

> "for the preservation and maintenance of the natural forest,"

and to protect

> "the headwaters and the tributaries of the Muskoka, Petawawa, Bonnechere and Madawaska Rivers."

Kirkwood suggested that within this region it should be unlawful to disturb or destroy any fur-bearing animals; and that its timber should be cut and marketed by the Government, rather than by private companies.

Proceeding with the case, he pointed out that some animals, notably the caribou, the moose, the white-tailed deer, and the beaver, had been hunted so intensively in that area of recent years, that they were in danger of extermination. Soon it would be too late to attempt to protect them in their native habitat. Then, with regard to forest management, he felt that if indiscriminate private cutting were allowed in the area, there might be dangerous consequences, not only to the water supply of the Province, but to the value of the district as a whole. If, on the other hand, the mature trees were cut under Government supervision, the young growth would in due time replace them. Such a policy would, further, provide a handsome source of revenue for the Government.

In justifying his choice of locale for the new Park, Kirkwood went on to describe the part of the Ottawa-Huron tract which he thought should be set aside for that purpose, namely, the headwaters of the four rivers already mentioned. He pointed out the evil effects, in the older parts of the Province, of "the wanton destruction of forests" by settlers who were anxious to clear their lands, and by lumbermen who were only interested in the immediate profit that could be derived from the forest growth. When the land had been denuded of its trees, these same settlers, who were dependent for their water supply on the rivers along which they had built their mills and villages, were the first to suffer. If this cycle of disaster were to be avoided in the Ottawa-Huron district, now was the time to act.

After the necessary precautions had been taken to protect both forests and game, Kirkwood thought that the Park should be thrown open to the people of the Province, so that they could make full use of its facilities. In a style that anticipated the lyricisms of later tourists bureaus, he praised the pure air and bracing climate of the highland region, eulogising the picturesque scenery and great abundance of fish. He visualised the day when

> "Seekers for health and pleasure in the summer season may be allowed to lease locations for cottages or tents along the shores of the great Opeongo Lake; and a site on that lake for a hotel and farm can be offered to public competition at annual rental."

The author of the Park idea recommended that the name of the proposed area be adopted from "one of the greatest of Indian nations" — the Algonquins. In the opinion of the commissioners "it is fitting that the name of a once great and powerful people, who in their savage manner held sway over this territory centuries ago, should bequeath their name to a part of it which it is now proposed to maintain, as nearly as possible, in the condition in which it was when they fished in its waters and hunted and fought in its forests." Finally, he referred again to the great natural beauties of the place. Here the traveller would be inspired by "the gloomy grandeur of the forest", could see for himself "noble pines and stately oaks bespeaking the growth of centuries", and could listen to "winds sounding solemnly in their branches". Even the arts were not neglected in this final rhapsody:

> "It is here that the imagination of the poet kindles into reverie and rapture, and revels in almost incommunicable luxury of thought."

Concluding, he assures the Honourable Mr. Pardee that:

> "The Commissioner of Crown Lands who establishes Algonquin Forest and Park raises a monument that will not crumble or decay, and his memory will be cherished in the warmest corners of many hearts."

No immediate action was taken by the Department, but Kirkwood either received some encouragement or was Irish enough to persist. Among his private papers a memorandum dated 1887 sets forth some practical questions that needed to be answered, before action could implement the idea. He wanted to know whether the setting aside of a permanent forest reserve was such

> "a matter of importance and advantage as to warrant any action on the part of the Government;"

whether it was in the public interest to close the area to settlement; and

> "whether the conservation around the sources of these rivers is a matter of Provincial concern?"

Exactly what percentage of the area was fit for settlement? How much was water? What areas were good timber lands? Finally, were there any property claims within the proposed Park limits?

There was one man better qualified than anyone else to answer these questions, a man who shares with Kirkwood the chief credit for the Park's establishment.

This man was James Dickson of Fenelon Falls, Provincial Land Surveyor, who had been conducting township surveys in the district since 1879. In the same year that Kirkwood published his open letter to Pardee, Dickson submitted reports for the townships of Finlayson and Peck. These reports included a summary of land and water areas, the arable acreage, extent of clearings; and such developments as depot farms, wagon roads, and lumbering activities. By a coincidence that the conditions of the area had predetermined, Dickson's reports completely corroborated Kirkwood's arguments in favour of setting up a park.

The following year action began. Only half the townships of the proposed area had been surveyed. The Hon. Mr. Pardee asked Dickson to take a trip through the unsurveyed Townships of Sproule and Preston, in order to report on them to his Department. Dickson made the trip and submitted his report.

Kirkwood, no doubt, read the report shortly after it was received early in the New Year. Although he knew of Dickson's sympathy, he must have read its first pages in a state of some suspense. Everything depended on these findings!

Dickson was not impressed with the necessity of forest protection — in that respect he was a man of his time. But he heartily endorsed the principal of conserving wild life, and fully agreed that a continued water supply for the surrounding districts, through control of the headwaters of the rivers that supplied them, was of prime importance. He says,

> "The preservation from destruction of moose, deer and beaver would, in my opinion, alone warrant the Government in making this a reservation."

At another point, he states that if inexpensive dams were constructed at strategic sites there would be

> "a sufficiency of water held in reserve to enable lumbermen to drive on the Muskoka and Petawawa all the summer."

Dickson's report recommended that eleven of the eighteen townships that were afterwards set aside to form the Park in 1893 be so utilized, but he also outlined definite ways of developing this region for the public good. Kirkwood had already suggested the possibilities of the area as a holiday resort, but Dickson outshone him as a one-man tourist bureau. Why not, he asked, publish a guidé book, generously illustrated with drawings made on the spot, and a hundred pages or more in length, that would set forth the attractions of the Park? A map, too, on a scale of a hundred chains (one and a half miles) to the inch, would be an invaluable aid to tourists. His suggested paths of access to the Park for such visitors were impracticable, to say the least. To a seasoned bush traveller like Dickson, who regularly carried out trips by canoe from his home at Fenelon Falls to the scenes of his surveys, it never occurred that the Madawaska and Muskoka river routes he suggested would be anything more to tourists than the mere holiday jaunts they were to him. Of course it must be remembered too that when he wrote his report, the nearest railway stations to the Park were at Deux Rivieres in the north, and Haliburton far to the south.

Perhaps it was his final rhapsodical outburst that clinched the case for the Park.

> "As we float along the streams or skim over the calm water of the lakelets almost every stroke of the paddle unfolds some new scene of rural beauty, seldom equalled in any part of our fair Province, and to paint them in all their pristine beauty would take the most gifted pen or pencil of either author or artist."

Before this Park could be established, however, it was necessary to convince the Government that the area really ought to be withdrawn from settlement — that is, "reserved" for other purposes. The total area of the eleven townships involved was about 866 square miles, of which roughly one-eighth was covered by lakes or rivers. The remaining seven-eighths were made up of land that was arable in places, but these arable pockets were so widely scattered that Dickson estimated there would be no more than one fertile township in the eleven. As for minerals, he reported that there was no limestone in the area, and with the exception of a little iron ore, there was nothing of value from a mining point of view.

In answer to Kirkwood's question about the timber, Dickson pointed out that most of the good pine stands, especially in the east, were already under license. However there were several valuable stands left, especially in the south half of Hunter and McLaughlin townships (around Brûlé Lake and Burnt Island Lake), and almost all of Peck (Smoke and Canoe Lakes), which could be reserved if the Government so desired.

The report outlined the extent of previous burnings, and the varieties of forest other than pine. The stands of hardwood, hemlock and yellow birch, Dickson was sure, would some day prove valuable. However, since he visualized the Park chiefly as a game preserve, he was not too upset by the prospect of continued lumbering in the region, seeing in the second growth a much better source of food for the wildlife than it had ever had in the past. As he said:

> "There is always a larger supply of young and tender shoots on which the moose and deer feed, and berries and cherries for partridge, than is anywhere to be met with in the original forest . . . and as to poplar and white birch, which are the favourite food of the beaver, they are always to be found in greater numbers where a second growth of timber has grown up than any other place."

The chief reason for the dwindling supplies of game in the district, was the wanton destruction by local hunters, interested only in the hides, and seeming to have no consideration for the season in which they killed the animals. In winter, travelling was easier for these hunters, and they ignored the fact that killing the deer at that time of the year threatened to exterminate them entirely. Dickson pointed out that the breeding season for moose was in September, and for deer in December. Winter hunting meant that mothers were destroyed before the birth of their young in the spring. To the settlers, he realized, one moosehide containing enough leather for twenty pairs of moccasins was worth forty dollars; but some measures had to be taken, if only for that reason, to prevent the disappearance of the animals altogether.

Although Dickson did not try to estimate the total beaver population, he gave the impression that there were many less than in former times. He reported that the beaver houses and dams were mostly old ones, and that indiscriminate trapping had greatly reduced the total. He felt that it would be worth while to take active steps to increase their number,

> "First, because the skin furnishes us with one of our richest and most valuable furs; and, second, because from its natural habits it is in fact the greatest conservator of water that we have."

He went on to show that re-stocking would be comparatively simple, since the beaver usually had from four to six young each year. He maintained that it was foolishness to allow spring trapping, and strongly advocated closed seasons throughout the Province to protect the fur and game supply.

Dickson's attitude towards hunting in the future Park was explicit.

> "I would strongly urge that neither moose, deer or any fur-bearing animals should be either hunted, taken or killed in the proposed Park for all time. By doing this, the Province will have a large breeding ground and harbour of refuge for her game. As the Park becomes stocked they would naturally spread out into the surrounding country and the whole Province would be better stocked than it is at present."

At the same time, he suggested that some effort be made to curb the wolf population, since their numbers would tend to increase as the other animals became more plentiful. A premium offered to the forester for the "scalp" of each wolf might check their increase.

As a practical man, Dickson set forth his recommendations for the best way of enforcing the restrictions:

> "It will be necessary to have a game keeper and a few assistants whose duty it will be to see that the law prohibiting hunting and trapping is rigidly enforced and also to guard against fire . . . I would suggest that every game keeper be armed with judicial authority to punish transgression on the spot . . . and to destroy all traps and dead-falls whether found set in the woods or in the possession of any person in the prohibited area, and to confiscate all rifles, shotguns, furs or other game found with them."

His knowledge of the district made him foresee that it would take more than halfway measures to deal with trappers who were armed with an intimate knowledge of every inch of the Park.

Dickson's report spurred Kirkwood on to even wider studies. In his "Papers and Reports Upon Forestry, Forest Schools and Forest Management in Europe, America, and the British Possessions, and upon Forests as Public Parks and Sanitary Resorts, collected by Mr. A. Kirkwood", there is ample evidence that Kirkwood had as thorough a knowledge of what had been done in other parts of the world, as Dickson had of the area itself. Both of the men chiefly responsible for the future direction of the Park's activities knew what they were talking about.

So far things had gone well. Unfortunately, in 1889, the Hon. T. B. Pardee died, and four years elapsed in spite of Kirkwood's importunities, before the appointment of a Royal Commission promised real action. This Commission was

> "To make a full report respecting the fitness of certain territory in the said Province, including the headwaters of the Rivers Amable du Fond, Petawawa, Bonnechere, Madawaska, and Muskoka . . . with boundaries hereafter determined for the purpose of a Forest Reservation and National Park; the approximate cost of establishing and maintaining such a Park; and the ends to be attained by creation of such a Park."

The formal document setting up the Royal Commission and giving it the necessary powers to conduct its research, bore the signature of the Premier of Ontario, Sir Oliver Mowat. To the four men named in this document, a fifth was later added to make the following list:

Aubrey White — Assistant Crown Commissioner of Lands
Alexander Kirkwood — Senior Officer of the Lands Branch
James Dickson — Inspector of Surveys
Archibald Blue — Director of Mines
Robert W. Phipps — Clerk of Forestry.

The first formal meeting of the Commission took place in Toronto on November the fourth, 1892, by which date a great deal of ground work had been done. Eight months previously, James Dickson had submitted another report on the proposed district, duplicating some information already on hand, but mentioning the presence of squatters who had cleared patches of land in the township of Dickson, and at Booth Lake. Dickson reminded the Department that there had never been a formal survey of the Townships of Sproule and Preston; so during the month of August he was sent up to gather the needed data.

Returning with the information in September, Dickson advised that the time had come for action. In November the Commission met, with Alexander Kirkwood, appropriately, in the chair. At this meeting the Commissioners agreed that the territory outlined in Dickson's report was suitable for the proposed Park, but recommended that four more townships be added to the sixteen. Most of the points already mentioned were included in the Commission's recommendations, but a few highlights will interest the reader.

The Park boundaries were fixed to include eighteen townships in the District of Nipissing: Wilkes, Pentland, Biggar, Osler, Lister, Deacon, Devine, Bishop, Freswick, Anglin, Hunter, McLaughlin, Bower, Dickson, Peck, Canisbay, Sproule and Preston; a total area of 1,466 square miles, of which a little more than a tenth was water surface, and a fifth or less was land suitable for cultivation.

> "Forest preservation and protection, (the report read) is, in almost every civilized country, one of the most pressing and vital of economic questions."

It mentioned the pine stands particularly

> "which forest fires and the operations of lumbermen have greatly diminished."

When hardwood was fully mature it should be cut, and

> "It might as well be cut by the lumberman, he receiving permission to do so."

The Commissioners believed that if the area were opened to settlement, its lands

> "would soon be converted into a dreary and abandoned waste."

A peak of eloquence was achieved on the topic of the decline in wild life:

> "Here not many years ago the moose, the monarch of the Canadian woods, roamed and browsed in great numbers . . . here herds of red deer grazed in the open meadows or quenched their thirst at the brooks or crystal lakes; here the industrious beaver felled his trees and built his dams on every stream; here the

**Summer Station Agent at Joe Lake Station in 1921.** *(O. Addison; APM # 2147)*

**The big railway trestle between Cache Lake and Lake of Two Rivers.** *(P. Ziegler; APM # 5598)*

> wolf's detested howl startled the deer and the bear pushed his black bulk through the undergrowth in search of ripe nuts or berries."

The Commissioners suggested that streams be restocked with native fish where these had disappeared, and other suitable varieties might be introduced. Shrubs for deer and wild rice for ducks might be planted in the Park.

A final summary stated that the proposed Act was intended to provide

> "a public park, and forest reservation, fish and game preserve, health resort and pleasure ground for the benefit, advantage and enjoyment of the people of the Province."

The original name proposed by the Commissioners was "The Algonquin National Park". In later years the word "National" was changed to "Provincial", since other national parks in the Dominion were under federal control.

# CHAPTER 8

THE ALGONQUIN PARK ACT was passed by the Legislative Assembly of the Province of Ontario in the year 1893. Alexander Kirkwood's dream had become reality.

There is no better way of paying tribute to the achievement of Alexander Kirkwood, James Dickson, and those who supported and advised them, than to pause here, and view the rich legacy which their efforts secured for the people of Ontario, and their guests from beyond. What was there about the Park that inspired the founders, and has since claimed the devotion of a long line of Park Superintendents?

Size is scarcely the answer, although since 1893 eleven full townships and large sections of eight others were added, almost doubling its area into proportions greater than those of Canada's smallest Province.

Nor is it the Park's mineral wealth. One hesitates over what might have been the complications if rich mineral deposits had been discovered later. A character Mark Robinson knew of in his early ranging days, worked for the Gilmours at Mowat village, and was known locally as "Dirty Dick". He claimed he had discovered gold, but nothing came of it. Mica, it is true, occurs in quantities on the banks of the Bonnechere; and molybdenite, the soft blue-grey ore of molybdenum now used in steel alloys, has been reported from the Otterslide Lakes. No serious commercial mining has ever been attempted in the Park; and Dickson's original verdict has been maintained.

Perhaps only the total effect of a book such as this, can reveal the full reason for the fascination exerted on the Park by its visitors. One thing is certain however. Without the wildlife of the Park, it would hold little charm for any visitor. It is a land where even the vegetable life has a character all its own. Bright orange lichens display their colour on the sometimes grey, sometimes light brown, cliffs. The rocky headlands are clothed along their bare crests with pale grey-greens of humble mosses. Deep in the interior of the woods, one may run across beds of brilliant green moss. Swamp grasses, slender reeds, and lily pads grow in the stagnant water of the marshes; the beautiful white water lilies, and humbler yellow ones, dotting the surface decoratively. Willows, alders, and cedar thrive in the low ground, as well as hemlock, spruce, balsam, and the funeral black spruce. In old burned-over areas, or near the shore where the light is good, the paper birch and the poplar grow. As one ascends inland, the yellow birch is found in large stands, and on the well-drained land, often on the hill-tops, are stands of sugar maple.

Most typical of all the Park trees is the pine, even though the best of them were cut for square timber in the old days. In sandy soil the jackpine grows, with its rough, gnarled branches, and its rock-hard cones. In deeper soil stands the lordly white pine, aristocrat of the softwoods, its irregular, windswept branches reaching high. On the rock itself, thrusting its roots into every nook and crevice, is the red pine, seeming to thrive in spite of autumn gales and winter frosts.

The variety of trees is comparatively bewildering. Black ash and swamp maple, beech and ironwood, red oak, black cherry — even the occasional elm — all appear in the Algonquin woods. A dozen varieties of berry bushes, laden in summer with their ripe fruit, tempt the visitor to pause. Club mosses, ferns, and several species of orchids, are to be found. Nor are the woods lacking in flowers: the bunch berry or Canadian dogwood, the delicate creeping twin flower; violets, clintoia, starflower, foam flower, and the painted trillium.

But there is more than plant life in the Park to charm the visitor. In the shade of a stand of pine he can see gusts of wind flatten the wave peaks into white caps, and absorb the brilliant colours of sunshine and shadow that Tom Thomson has captured in his paintings of Park scenes. He hears the wind in the treetops, the waves that break on the beach, and the shrill call of the gull wheeling in the sky. Sweetest of all, if he listens for it, is the "sweet, sweet, Canada, Canada, Canada" of the white-throated sparrow.

It would be a disheartening experience to walk for a morning through Algonquin woods, or to paddle along the Park streams and lakes, without hearing or seeing a living creature. The rocks, water, and trees, would seem strangely empty. From the earliest days, the inhabitants of the Park have looked upon its life as necessary, if not for their enjoyment, at least for their sustenance and livelihood.

Night and day, the evidence of its wild life abounds in Algonquin Park. Here today, all but the wolf may seek sanctuary from, and live in friendship with, their one-time enemy, man. Here, uniquely one may find in animals and birds, his friends.

Through the screen of the Park ranger's open window on a summer night, he may hear the lonely call of the loon, like distant hitchpitched laughter, or the uncanny hoot of an owl. At other times during the night, especially in the spring, he will hear the shrill song of the frogs. In the early dawn he awakens to the songs of innumerable birds; and all through the day, if he listens, he may hear the spiritual notes of the olive-backed thrust, the hermit, veery, and wood thrushes; the rarer gutteral croak of the raven, or caw of a crow, the comical cries of the Canada jay, or "whiskey jack" as the lumbermen call him. Here and there through the forest, the jewelled colour of a sprightly warbler catches his eye, or a covey of ruffled grouse whirrs suddenly out of the brush. At the lakeshore stands a great blue heron on his long legs, watching for minnows in the shallow water. In his canoe, the ranger may round a point to come upon a flock of mergansers, or fish ducks, two or three families, mothered by a single female.

One hundred and seventy-seven species of birds, according to Professor Dymond, Director of the Royal Ontario Museum of Zoology, have been seen at one time or another within the Park boundaries, and of these, a hundred and thirty are found regularly in summer.

Of all the birds, the loon and the Canada jay are the most characterful. In the Park one may come within a few yards of the handsome, black-headed, white-breasted loon, before he makes his sleek, leisurely dive, coming up an incredible hundred yards away. For all his wild laughter, he is a sociable fellow in protected regions, answering politely the weak human imitations of his call, even showing off with a ludicrous demonstration of how he can stand on his tail in the water. To see him flapping his wings, and vigorously paddling with his webbed feet to keep upright; and to see the lame duck tactics of his mate trying to divert one's attention from her young, are two of the unforgetable little intimacies of Algonquin Park life. The whiskey jack is the disreputable tramp of the woods, the cocky ruffian who snatches bread from the camper's fingers, or pecks insatiably at his cake of soap on the rock, one wary impudent eye on the owner. According to early Indian legends this bird had a superhuman intelligence, outwitting even the medicine man.

Curiously enough, as if they knew this wild life sanctuary was dedicated to man's friendship with animals, poisonous snakes do not occur. The harmless garter, red-bellied, ring-nacked, and DeKay's brown snakes are there, but seldom seen. Only the snapping turtle upholds the shady repute of his tribe. His painted cousin may be seen on occasion. The bull-frog, six other species of frogs, four different kinds of salamander, and the common toad complete the Park's modest list of reptiles and amphibia.

Forty feet down, in the deep water of hundreds of Algonquin lakes, lie the luscious lake trout, natives of these waters since the first Indian fished for them. These fish are pink in flesh, and sometimes vary so much in appearance, from lake to lake, that all but experts are deceived into believing there are several varieties. In the northern streams of the Park speckled trout abound, prize of the fly fisherman. A few lakes, notably Redrock Lake, harbour them, too. In the south, introduced into waters where they were not seen formerly, bass, pike-perch, and maskinonge are often caught today.

The greatest thrill the Park visitor gets, is from the larger land animals. Although usually shy, black bears soon grow bold if encouraged by being fed, even becoming a nuisance when they misinterpret the intentions of cottagers and campers who leave tasty food in tempting proximity to an open door. The huge, ungainly bull moose, as he stalks across the ridges in the autumn, the graceful deer bounding over a deadfall, the stately waddle of the bristling porcupine — are a few of the sights a visitor may see. Timber wolves, foxes, skunks, woodchucks, chipmunks, red squirrels, snowshoe rabbits, and the beautiful little native white-footed or deer mouse, are all found in the Park. So too are the rarer fisher and marten, trapped elsewhere almost out of existence for their beautiful furs.

The Park is full of stories about its animal life, many of which appear elsewhere in these pages. Of all the animals in the Park, none is so full of surprises, even for the old-timer, as the otter. Professor Dymond, in a paper on the natural history of the Park, from which much of the material for this chapter comes, has this to say about the otter:

> "The otter, too, is commoner here than elsewhere. Many summer visitors count among their most prized memories the sight of a mother otter with her brood of kittens. Like every animal that kills any other animal that man himself wants to kill, the otter is often

> condemned for its habit of catching fish. Ralph Bice tells of an instance when the tables were turned and a trout ate a baby otter. "Don't laugh," he says, "ten men saw it." The trout weighed three pounds and the otter was about ten inches in length from tip to tip and there was no mistaking as to what it was."

Steve Waters, one of the original Park rangers, used to tell of another unusual otter incident. One morning late in autumn, he and his fellow ranger in that section were watching for poachers on the shore of Opeongo Lake. The lake had frozen over only the night before, and no snow had fallen. Suddenly, half a mile out, fragments of ice shot up from the surface and fell again. As they watched, it happened again closer to shore. A black speck appeared in the hole, only to disappear before they could see what it was. Not until the animal had almost reached shore did they recognize it for an otter, breaking the ice at intervals with his head to get a fresh breath of air. When they measured the ice it was three-quarters of an inch thick.

G. W. Bartlett, who will be met formally before very long, described another otter's antics on Fawn Lake:

> "This grand otter came along towards us with one, two, three, four, five jumps and a long slide. I measured this afterwards and found it to be forty-five feet long. Sometimes otters seem to take a great delight in sliding down steep banks into the water. They tuck their front paws in close to their sides and slide down an incline like little toboggans."

One more example will suffice to illustrate the charm, and sometimes humour, of the unexpected, which is perhaps the one feature of the Park, more than any other, that accounts for the spell it seems to cast on all who linger within its borders. Mark Robson tells this one about a bear.

One summer, bears proved to be a particular nuisance to the Munn Lumber Company, which was operating camps in the southern part of the Park. It was bad enough having the animals devouring your food supplies when you were in camp, but it was worse when you were working out in the bush, and had no chance of doing anything about it. Once, when a group of men had had their mid-day meals stolen for several days in a row, the young foreman decided to take action. He had heard that bears will not climb small trees, so he hung the food on a branch of a tree with a three-inch trunk. At noon it had disappeared as before. The next day he tried another scheme. This time he put the supplies in the stern of a rowboat that had been run up on shore, close to the spot where the men were cutting. When he had covered up the food, he went away satisfied that now it was safe. About eleven o'clock, when he went to get the lunch, he found that the boat itself had vanished from the place where he had left it. Then he saw it, away out in the middle of the lake, and what did he see in the boat, but old Bruin himself. Evidently he had smelt out the food in the stern, and had clambered in after it. As he moved down the boat, his weight must have served as a balance to lift the bow off the beach. Then a gust of wind would be sufficient to carry both boat and bear clear of the land. When sighted, he was just finishing the last of his meal. Once more the men had to go hungry.

There are other bear stories, tales too, of wolves and deer, even of the tiny chipmunk: these must wait for their time and place. Not a few of them, however, are tied up inseparably with the larger story of the Park, particularly that phase of it that concerns the rangers of the early days, and the way they met and solved the first problems of administration.

## CHAPTER 9

It Is Seldom in History, that such a large area of land as Algonquin Park, containing so much natural wealth, has been protected from commercial exploitation by any government, with so little opposition. Some friction was unavoidable: that there was so little is a tribute to the reasonable way in which the early settlers within the Park area, the lumbermen, the Indians, and the trappers were handled.

The most effective opposition should have come from the lumber and railway interests with stakes in the area. Indeed, had Kirkwood's original idea of Government cutting and selling of timber been followed, there would undoubtedly have been a battle royal before the Act ever came near the Legislature.

As a matter of fact, J. R. Booth was not too pleased to find that his railway would run through the southern end of the proposed Park; and wrote a letter to the Department, suggesting forthrightly that the Commissioners' plans be changed to keep the Park clear of The Ottawa-Arnprior and Parry Sound Railway, whose line was already surveyed.

It is extremely doubtful whether Kirkwood's fellow Commissioners ever gave serious consideration to the idea of reserving cutting rights in the Park, though they were all for some measure of control. The very contemplation of the complexities involved in such a step must have made Government officials shudder. Probably, in the long hours of discussion through the months and years that passed before the other ideas in his letter were put into effect, Kirkwood himself came to see that rigid control of the Park timber stands was impracticable.

Most of the lumbermen were in favour of the Park as proposed by the Commission. All of them were unanimously opposed to settlement projects in lumbering areas, involving, as they invariably did, an increased fire hazard. Furthermore, the new provincial fire ranging system recently put into effect, made them aware of the value of the fire protection their limits would have in the Park. Then, too, the move to conserve the headwaters of the streams, down which they floated their logs, was to their obvious advantage. Business men down along the Ottawa Valley, even as far away as the shores of Lake Ontario, were fully aware of the connection between the lakes and streams of the Algonquin highlands and their own busy sawmills.

On the other side of the fence, there were some misgivings among the Commissioners, whose chief interest in the Park was its function as a game preserve. How could trappers and poachers be controlled when the railway made the Park so easily accessible? The others pointed out that it would be an ideal means of supplying the rangers, and of keeping in close touch with the Department in Toronto, while the resort enthusiasts argued that the railway would bring visitors to the very front porch of the Park. So the south boundary remained as proposed.

That there would be difficulties in putting an end to trapping and hunting in the Park was self evident, and before long these troubles will be dealt with. The one remaining problem was what to do with the handful of people already living in the region. This problem was largely dodged for the time. The Dunfonds, for instance, were not disturbed, although they had a valuable holding in the very heart of the newly formed provincial game sanctuary.

Twenty-three years later, the case of the Dufonds was finally cleaned up, on the death of Ignace Dufond. On October the fourteenth, 1916, a letter was sent by Mr. Thomas W. Gibson, then Deputy Minister of the Department of Lands, Forests and Mines, to Mr. G. W. Bartlett, the Superintendent of Algonquin Park. The letter read as follows:

> "Lot 25 in the 12th concession of Wilkes, Algonquin Park, was patented to Ignace Dufond in 1888. As the patent was issued under the Mining Act the land was subject to two cents an acre under the Mining Act. The taxes remained unpaid for a number of years, and in 1910 the land was forfeited to the Crown.
>
> "This I think is the lot at the east end of Lake Manitou on which the Dufond family, or some of them live, and which has been occupied by them for many years. They have a small farm there with house and barn and some improvements. It would appear from correspondence which the Department has received, that the Dufonds would like to have the land re-granted to them, or that they would be willing to accept compensations from the Depart-

> ment for their improvements and for the length of time they have occupied the lot.
>
> "Having been at this place it is my own view that it would be advisable for the Department to retain the title as there is always the possibility of it passing into the possession of people whose presence in the Park would be objectionable. The Department would be willing to compensate the Dufonds to a reasonable extent and to perhaps allow the old people to remain in possession as long as they live, at a nominal rental."

In response to this letter from Toronto, the Superintendent must have replied to the effect that the whole situation was complicated by the fact that there were other Dufond relations who were interested in the farm besides this Ignace to whom it had been granted originally. Writing on December 5th, Mr. Gibson referred to such a letter:

> "It is inferred from your letter that there are other Indian relatives. Can you say whether Ignace Dufond had more than one brother, Francis, who I understand is living with his (Ignace's) wife Susan?".

The third letter, dated December 19, 1916, was addressed to Mr. Bartlett. It came from Peter Ranger who had been stationed as a ranger at Kiosk since 1912.

> "Replying to your letters that I receive the 16th I went to the Indians on the 17th to get the name of all the Dufond that I am sending you.
>
> "Soc. Dufond is address is Mattawa but he live with the old Francis on the farm this winter. Alex Dufond, address Mattawa; Philamene Dufond; Catherine Dufond, Mattawa; Angelique Dufond—they don't know if she is living, they did not hear from her since ten years".

Next came a letter from Mr. Gibson dated December 29, 1916, in which he pointed out:

> "The Department would allow the old people to remain in occupation as long as either one of them lived, or desired to live there at a nominal rental of say, $1.00 per year".

What actually happened as a result of this suggestion is a little difficult to determine. The last and final piece of information that this file provided came in the form of another letter from Mr. Gibson, dated a year later — December 14, 1917. This seems to have been in answer to a letter written by Peter Ranger, on behalf of the Dufonds themselves, because they were complaining that they were not receiving the full amount of the moneys that were to have been paid to them:

> "The arrangement made with these people (Susanne and Francis Dufond) was that they were to get $1,000 compensation for the improvements on the Indian farm at Kioshuque (Kioshkokwi) Lake, etc. This was to be paid to them in instalments of $75.00 every six months with interest at five per cent on the unpaid principal."
>
> "The money was paid over to the Toronto General Trusts Corporation, which makes the payments, and at the written request of the Indians, the installments were made payable through Mr. T. E. McKee, District Attorney, North Bay."

From this correspondence, two things are evident — one is that the Department officials had tried to treat these old Indians as fairly as they could, while realizing that eventually they must leave the way clear for the inclusion of this land in the Park itself; and the other, that Peter Ranger, who still lives in a ranger cabin at Kiosk, must know more than anyone else about the Dufonds.

It was promised, in connection with the story of depot farm days, that more would be heard of Dinney McGuey. The Department of Lands and Forests became interested in Dinney two years before the Dufond correspondence above, at a time when the last cutting had been done on the Bonnechere limits, and the Government planned to include the Basin Depot area, where Paddy Garvie had his depot farm, within the Park.

The following extracts from this correspondence explain themselves, and a good deal more:

Dated May 15th, 1914 — From Dennis McGuey to the Minister of Lands, Forests and Mines:

> "Mr. G. W. Bartlett came here and made agreement with me for my farm and buildings. I was promised two thousand five hundred dollars. Also he appointed me Fire Ranger . . . I have lived on the Limits for near forty years. I got permission from McLachlin Brothers to build where I now reside. I have been

Fire Ranger over twenty-five years. If only I could be left here I would be quite content. As to going to New Ontario if you put me in a place built as this is built it would be alright enough . . .
P.S.—Don't put me too far from a station, let me have five farms in a block for my sons and me."

Dated May 20th, 1914 — From the Department to Mr. G. W. Bartlett:

"I must say that the Department for various reasons is quite anxious to get these people away, and with as little friction as possible. In view of lumbering being at an end, there is no possible future for the settlement, and the safety of the timber in that district would be certainly more secure if squatters were removed — including Mr. McGuey."

Dated July 7th, 1914 — From (Sergeant) Dennis McGuey to the Minister:

"I write again to see what you intend to do with me. It will suit me better to get the money for my place than to go to New Ontario. It is all right for young men to go there that have no care but themselves. They can work and clear land and build themselves up. I am too old to commence to make a home now. I have worked for a long time for the Government and Limit holders as Fire Ranger in the Township of Guthrie. Same time I tried to build a home for myself. Please let me know at once if I am to remain on here . . . Or you might appoint me Park Ranger. I know this country well. I know the hunters' trails, where they go into the Park. This is a good place to watch them. I can do my duty in that line all right."

Naturally, one cannot help feeling sorry for Dinney in his plight. As he himself said, he had spent the best years of his life in the Bonnechere country, and now he was being asked to move elsewhere. He could see no rhyme or reason in the Government's request, but there were other residents of the district who could appreciate some of the reasons why this action was being taken. The children of some of the Bonnechere families, now fully grown adults, could see how their own backwoods isolation had handicapped them. Two of the younger generation of the Bonnechere pioneers, Mike Garvie and Mrs. Harry Stack, a daughter of the widow McCormack, recall the difficulties they underwent to get any schooling at all, when they were children. These, and other people, felt that the Government was wise in moving the old families out of the district when the lumber companies had terminated their operations there.

Remembering the background of the Haliburton trappers, it is no wonder they resented what they felt to be intrusion on their own private property. They, who knew almost every leaf and stick on the Park trails, and depended for their livelihood on this knowledge, were now asked to trap in unfamiliar territory, outside the Park boundaries.

In the summer of 1893, Dickson had visited the Park and written concerning this problem. He informed Commissioner Hardy that he had procured a list of the parties who were trapping in the Park, and who would, in all probability, still have their traps in the area. He suggested that these men be notified by the Department that they would be expected to have their equipment out of the Park by the first of October.

Having made these constructive suggestions, he went on to comment on the most recent information available as to the game situation in the Park. He said that it was, at that time, abundant in the area, and that there was sufficient beaver there to restock the district in four or five years if the present population could be protected. To carry on this work, he thought that there should be two men employed immediately to locate the haunts of the wild animals, especially the beaver. Dickson particularly mentioned the threat to the moose in the area, since he said that he and other travellers had come upon a great deal of evidence pointing to the fact that hunters slaughtered these animals for bait for their bear-traps, as well as for their hides.

The list of trappers which Dickson furnished to the Department, contains the names of many of the Dorset and Haliburton trappers of whom we have already spoken. Those mentioned were: James Sawyers, William and Darling Radnow, John Archer, Isaac and Hamilton Bice, Frank Pokorny, Sam Vancleiff, George Ross, W. H. Sawyer and John Hoskin. Naturally, since before this time trapping in the Park area had been perfectly legal, some opposition was to be expected. It was all very well for the Department to talk about restocking the game in the region, but in the meantime what were they expected to do for a living? Dickson had foreseen this as far back as 1888.

To avoid friction as far as possible, he felt that the trappers themselves should be shown how they would benefit from the establishment of a game reserve, as well as being informed of the regulations for the new Park. The ranging staff, too, should be fully informed of the whole situation, and empowered with sufficient authority to deal with transgressors on the spot. That would mean that men appointed as Park Rangers would have to be expert bushmen, and should be permitted to bear firearms.

Acting on Dickson's suggestion, the Department sent to each man on the list, full information about the new order of things in the Park, enclosing a copy of the Algonquin Park Act, a copy of the Commission's report, and a map showing the exact location of the Park boundaries. The letter ended with the hope that the trappers would see the ultimate benefit to themselves of the Park's establishment. Though it did involve hardships for these men, at least the Government was doing its best to be fair and far-sighted.

No sooner had the Chief Ranger taken up his new duties in the Park than the first complaint arrived, written by a fire ranger employed on the limits of the Barnet Lumber Company in the north, by way of the Assistant Commissioner of Crown Lands, to whom it was addressed. The writer had just returned to his post on the Petawawa River, where, on the first of August, he had seen Indians from the Bonnechere, who were preparing to hunt in the district. They had located a camp between White Trout (Big Trout) and Burnt (Portal) Lakes, with the intention of killing moose for their hides. Moose meat was seen in their possession, as well as the skins of beaver and otter, caught in the area. The fire ranger had mentioned this matter to Mr. Barnet, who told him he should notify the authorities.

The Department's predicament at this time is made clear in a personal letter written by the Crown Lands Commissioner to Mr. Barnet:

> "It will be a ticklish business to prevent Indians killing wild animals in the Park where they have been in the habit of hunting, and their ancestors before them. I am free to say this Indian hunting did not occur to me at the time the whole matter was under discussion. Now I see nothing for it but to exclude the Indians as well as the white men. But great care and tact will be required to handle these people so as not to embitter them or leave them feeling they have a substantial grievance. They will be much more dangerous and

> difficult to watch than a white man. They have not had a chance to know what we are doing or the object in view, and their being stopped will probably be the first intimation of a Park reserve they will have. Therefore, they should be told the whole history of the affair and what is intended, etc., and that they must not hunt in the Park."

At the same time, Mr. White wrote a letter to the Chief Ranger, telling him of the feeling of the Department on the matter. Perhaps a personal interview on the part of Mr. Thomson, and an explanation of the whole matter in a clear and kindly fashion, might help to prevent future trouble.

The first practical problem in the Park itself, once the paper problems of organization and policy had been looked after, was to appoint a staff, and to establish it on the spot. On June seventh of the same year, a meeting was called by Commissioner Hardy for that purpose. Director of Surveys Kirkpatrick, and Superintendent Wilson of the Niagara Falls Park, were called in to assist. After attending to details that will appear later, they decided to send in a party that summer, to be accompanied by Messrs. Dickson and Wilson, with the express mission of putting up buildings for headquarters and laying out canoe routes for ranger patrols.

Six weeks later, an Order-in-Council was passed appointing Mr. Peter Thomson first Superintendent of Algonquin Park.

> "Upon recommendation of the Honourable the Commissioner of Crown Lands, the Committee of Council advise that Peter Thomson of Brussels, road and bridge builder, be appointed a Ranger of Algonquin Park, to be known as Chief Ranger, at a salary of $600 per annum; he also to be furnished with a small log house in the Park in which to live, and firewood from down timber, but not other supplies . . . "

Preparations had gone ahead for the first official expedition into the Park. On July 23rd, a party consisting of Messrs. Dickson and Wilson, not fewer than six men, and a cook, was to leave Huntsville by canoe for the journey up through Lake of Bays and the upper Muskoka waters (Oxtongue River), to the site chosen for headquarters. Some notion of the life they would lead is suggested by the list of equipment for the party.

> 4 canoes — 2 fiteen-foot, 2 twenty-foot; 30 pairs of twelve-pound blankets, 10 bed ticks, camp cooking

> stove and Dutch oven, knives, forks, spoons, etc., grindstone, a box with four-pound axes, 1 broad axe, 2 hunting axes, a draw knife, a spokeshave, and a supply of building tools.
> Provisions — 500 pounds of long, clear pork, 500 pounds of flour, barrel biscuit.
> Tents — 1 eight-man tent, 2 three-man tents.
> Other articles — 2 rifles, 2 revolvers, ammunition, compass.

Peter Thomson wrote from Canoe Lake, in the middle of August:

> "When we left Huntsville, July 26th, Mr. Dickson wrote you giving an account of proceedings up to that time, also the number and names of the men who accompanied us. I then expected our mail accommodations would be such that we would have communications more easily with the outside world, but I find that it is by a mere chance that we can either send or receive letters once in two or three weeks at best.
>
> We are installed in Algonquin Park and located at Canoe Lake upon the Muskoka waters. Our journey up the lakes and rivers Mr. Dickson will give you in person. Upon my arrival at Huntsville I met Timothy O'Leary of Millington, Stephen Waters and William Gale, with instructions from your Department. I also employed William Morgan and Robert Dinsmore of Huntsville as labouring men. All of whom I am pleased to say have so far proven to be first-class men in every particular. It would be a very difficult task to secure a more suitable lot of men for this particular kind of work.
>
> In company with Mr. Dickson we have made as extensive a tour in and around the Park as his limited time would permit, but sufficient I think to give me a fair idea of the limits and water courses of the reservation."

Apart from reports of Indians hunting in the north, things went well for the Chief Ranger until October. Then he ran into trouble that called for backing from the Department. On the 22nd he wrote as follows:

> "No doubt but you expected to have heard from me before this time, but I started out the following morning after my arrival at this place and at no time since

**Sunnyside ranger cabin on Lake Opeongo, about 1933.**
***(S. Losee; APM # 354)***

**Rangers Bob Balfour (left) and Mark Robinson (right) at Joe Lake Station in 1915.** ***(R. Thomas and J. Wilkinson; APM # 70)***

> have I been within two or three days' journey from the Post Office. We've not had any mail in the last month or more.
>
> We started from Canoe Lake en route for Opeongo Lake and the southeast limits of the Park, cutting roads and trails over the portages, cleaning out all floodwood, etc., out of the creeks, and constructing camps at the following places: one at Cache Lake, one at Lake of Two Rivers, one at the southwest bay of the Opeongo Lake, and one at the southeast, at the head of Opeongo River cut a good trail four miles and built a camp at the head of McDougall Lake (now named Booth Lake), and cut good trails to the extreme east limits of the Park.
>
> No doubt but you are aware of the fact that the Gilmour Lumber Company have commenced operations upon their limits in Peck. They have constructed a dam at the foot of Tea Lake, also a depot at that point and five large camps upon Tea and Canoe Lakes. I regret to say that in our absence they built a large camp alongside of our building, and a beautiful grove which I had hoped to preserve in connection with our headquarters has been badly damaged. I saw their manager and he stated that he placed their camp at that place by the express orders of Mr. Gilmour. I find them very agreeable people and willing to do all they can to assist in preserving game . . . "

and so on. The Gilmour firm and the Department exchanged correspondence on the subject of the grove of trees, in which Commissioner Hardy made it very clear who was in control of the Park.

Peter Thomson's 1894 report gave an account of the work that had been accomplished during the first year of the Park's existence. He listed the Park Staff as follows:

> Chief Ranger — John Simpson.
>
> Rangers — Tim O'Leary, Stephen Waters, William Geall.
>
> Temporary Rangers — D. A. Ross, James Sawyers, Daniel May.

During that year, the men had carried on the work begun by the work party that had gone in the summer before. In all, they had constructed sixteen shelter houses, and had cleared over eighty-three miles of portages. Some of the shelter houses had been made out of new logs, others had been prepared from buildings abandoned by lumber companies, who were no longer working in the district. Mr. Thomson also reported that the rangers had found time to plant some of the pine seed furnished by the Department, in the hope of beginning a programme of reforestation.

In reporting progress in protecting the Park's wildlife, Mr. Thomson compared his first impression of the region with his latest observations:

> "When I entered on my duties in July, 1893, scarcely a beaver sign could be seen, and it required close inspection to discover the presence of these animals; now we are aware of at least sixty places in the Park where families of beaver have located themselves, in a number of cases in places where there was no previous indication of their existence."

There is evidence, too, that both Mr. Thomson and the members of his staff had already fallen under the spell of the Park. Visitors to the district have always been delighted to find how enthusiastically the rangers talk about their encounters with the wildlife. The new Superintendent commented on this trait when he said:

> "In a district such as this where human companionship is almost entirely lacking, the presence of wild animals relieves the solitude of the forest and adds much to the pleasure of existence."

Then he went on to tell of some of his own experiences in the performance of his duties. On one trip made by the rangers, they encountered a cow moose swimming in a stream with her two calves. The rangers wanted to get close to the young ones, so they paddled towards them. The mother went up on shore into the bushes, but the little fellows proved to be quite friendly, and they finally condescended to take bread right out of the rangers' hands. Thomson recorded several other illustrations of the same sort of thing and then he concluded:

> "Though there is little harm to be apprehended from the wild beasts of the Park, there is just that spice of danger which is sufficient to give zest to the somewhat ardous tasks of the rangers."

With regard to lumbering operations, the Superintendent had certain complaints about the effect of their methods on the appearance of the Park. He found at many of the outlets of the lakes that dams had been built, to assure sufficient water for the spring log drive or for the use of alligators on the upper waters. When the water was held too long, the forest growth along the lake edges suffered. The earth was washed away from the roots of the trees, and the flooding left a ring of dead trees and deadheads along the margins of the lakes. As Thomson pointed out, this not only marred the beauty of the Park, but threatened to develop into a major problem, since the waterways provided the chief means of travel and the driftwood clogged up the rivers and streams.

This report was his last. Peter Thomson died at his Canoe Lake headquarters on September 5, 1895, stricken with paralysis.

## CHAPTER 10

After the Untimely Death of the first Superintendent, Algonquin Park entered a critical period. For a time, it seemed that Alexander Kirkwood's dream would turn into a Government nightmare. Dickson, in advising the Department as to ways of handling the ousted trappers, had done his best to forestall what was perhaps inevitable.

The annual report for the year following Peter Thomson's death was drawn up by John Simpson, his Chief Ranger, who succeeded him. This report mentioned the progress that had been made on the Booth Railway, then under construction. During 1895, twenty miles of track had been laid west of Whitney, and men were now working nine miles inside the Park. The work of the rangers increased with the consequent fire hazard, and strict game supervision was made that much more difficult.

Mr. Simpson made special mention of the work that the rangers were doing in marking out the southern and western Park boundaries. The authorities were particularly anxious to blaze out a clear border line in that region, so as to give trespassers no excuse for overstepping the limits. The Department had prepared a supply of signs printed on linen posters, that were to be erected at key spots, to set forth the penalties for hunting and trapping in the region.

During that year, the rangers had marked out about twenty miles along the west border in the section opposite the Dorset-Haliburton country, from which most of the poachers were likely to come. There they had come upon frames used for stretching skins that had been used the previous winter. On the other hand, some progress had been made: several of the trappers had asked the rangers' permission to remove their traps from their old grounds in the Park. These men had been escorted into their camps and out again by Park Rangers.

Thereafter, Park records are obscure until the appointment of Simpson's successor. Judging from subsequent events, and the scattered correspondence of the period, it seems that a few of the rangers became involved in dishonest practices, and that the Park had consequently fallen into disrepute. As information filtered down to Toronto, the Department became alarmed and decided to appoint a new Superintendent. In the Spring they approached George

Bartlett, and persuaded him to accept the post. By August, he was installed in the new headquarters at Cache Lake.

Mr. Bartlett describes his appointment in these words:

> "I was down in Toronto on business when I was first approached for the Algonquin Park job. My business was with the Government over some timber limits and I was asked if I would take over Algonquin Park. I was then forty-seven years old. I became Superintendent of the 3,000 square mile tract. The job included the position of Postmaster, Commissioner in the High Court of Justice, Police Magistrate, and Chief Coroner in the district of Nipissing. The Premier of the Province told me that the Park had been a blot on the Government and asked me to make it a credit."

To this new undertaking, Mr. Bartlett brought an excellent background of experience in lumber camps and in rural Ontario. As a boy of eleven, he had been brought out from the Old Country to an uncle's farm at Springtown in Renfrew County because of illness, but he grew into a healthy man of more than average strength. At the age of twenty he married and established a home in Orillia, where most of his family of seven sons and three daughters were born and educated. His work took him frequently into the north country. At twenty-one he worked as a labourer on the Transcontinental Railway. Afterwards, he was put in charge of a gang of men who were clearing the bush for the construction of the C.P.R. from Mattawa to Sturgeon Falls. While with the railway he qualified as an expert culler of lumber, which gave him background for his future work. After leaving the railroad, he worked on the J. R. Booth limits on the Upper Ottawa, where he had charge of several camps and a total of some five hundred men. There is a Park story that Booth himself recommended Bartlett to the Department.

The news of Bartlett's appointment made little difference to the old trappers, or to the Indians in the north, who continued to hunt moose and deer. In their experience, the Government was far away, and the Park Rangers were easily persuaded to wink an eye at poaching. Some of them, they had seen, were not above doing a little illegal trapping themselves.

George Bartlett changed their ideas and behaviour, but not overnight. His first step was to increase the Park ranging staff from four to nine. The easy-going life under Simpson was gone. Going out in pairs the rangers kept the Park under fairly constant supervision. Five canoes and seven pairs of snowshoes were added to the equipment, and the Cache Lake headquarters improved. Following Bartlett's indefatigable example, the spirit of his men leapt to meet the challenge, and before his first year was done trespassers were aware that here was a new force to reckon with.

An example of how Mr. Bartlett dealt with these men, and of the way his earlier experiences bore fruit in his new work, is the story of three poachers brought into his office by the rangers. Immediately he recognized them, but they didn't realize who he was, because he had worn a beard when they knew him. When the charges were read in English they shook their heads. They didn't understand. The charges were read in French. No, they still didn't understand what this was all about. Finally Mr. Bartlett turned to the man who seemed to do most of the headshaking for the trio.

"Come, Antoine," said he, smiling at the look of amazement on the man's face, "don't you remember one time when you and I had to stay overnight and all the next day on a little island on Sturgeon Lake, when there wasn't enough wind for our big sail boat?"

Antoine's face cleared, and then fell. He walked up to the desk and said sheepishly, "Say, boss, don't be too hard on us for this first steal!"

Their offence was serious, and Bartlett committed them to three months in jail, hoping that this sentence, and his own fair treatment, would prevent a repetition of the offence.

The manuscript of an article prepared by him, and describing how he and Steve Waters spent twenty-two days in crossing the Park from north to south, affords an excellent picture of how he supervised the vast area under his control. This trip, taken probably in 1902, seems to have been the first that Mr. Bartlett took through the northern area of the Park, in his official capacity. The plan was to circle around to the north by rail, and enter from Eau Claire on the North Bay-Ottawa Line of the G.P.R.

This railroad trip was far from dull. Going west on the Canada Atlantic, still within the Park boundaries, the train ground to a stop. The wooden bridge at Rainy Lake (Rain Lake) had just finished burning down. Fortunately, another train was waiting beyond the wrecked bridge; Bartlett and Steve unloaded their canoe, packed in their dunnage, crossed the water, and continued their journey.

When they finally reached Eau Claire, they were able to get a wagon to take them for twelve miles alongside the Amable du Fond River towards the Park boundaries. This was the road used both by the Dufond family and by the lumber firms in the district, and they found it passable, though very rough. At length, at the halfway camp, they were able to put their canoe in the water. Mr. Bartlett's own words continue the story.

> "We began our journey up the river — our destination for the night being Koish-Koqui (Kioshkokwi) Lake. After we had gone about two miles along our way and when we were still outside the boundaries of the Park, we sighted an Indian camp and ran ashore to investigate. We found a squaw and two young Indians, and judging by the moose shanks that we saw lying around they were living on the fat of the land.
>
> "When we reached the shelter house which was our destination, we stopped for the night. After tea we heard the dip of a paddle and as we were now in the Park, I had the right to inquire, 'Who goes there?' I blew my whistle and hailed the passing canoe. Ah-ha, we found it was the Indian from the camp we had visited earlier in the afternoon. The poor chap was very uneasy, and explained that he had been in the Park getting roots and bark for medicine. This statement was corroborated by the contents of the canoe and by his own appearance. We warned him and let him go, telling him we had noticed the moose shanks in his camp.
>
> "On the next day, after a portage, we reached the Indian farm on Manitou Lake (now called Wilkes Lake). Here live a family of the Dufond descendants after whom the river was named. They had quite a clearing, a large house and barn, and they kept horses, cows and poultry. They were not disturbed by the Government when the Park was established. Mrs. Dufond kindly invited us in and treated us to some maple sugar of which she made 450 pounds. It was exceedingly good. After a smoke in which the old lady joined and a chat with Dufond, we pushed on up the lake to Pine Island, where we had a shelter house. Incidentally, when we inquired of the Indians how the lake got its name, they told us that long ago, when their great-grandparents first visited it, there

was a huge serpent seen in the lake, and the Great Spirit was in the serpent — hence the name.

"We retraced our steps once more to Kiosh-Koqui (Kioshkokwi) Lake and went from thence down to Mink Lake. There we met two of our rangers who had come through from Rainy (Rain) Lake. They reported game very abundant. They also found the carcasses of two bull moose in the lake at the foot of a huge bluff. An examination showed that they had had a battle royal at the head of the bluff and had fallen over, killing them both. Our shelter was built among some old lumber camps and during the night, hearing a noise, we got up to find a fine old buck that had gone into the old meat house to lick the salty block where meat used to be cut. He had been trapped by the door blowing to and he was making desperate efforts to get out. When we gave him the chance, he did not wait to thank us.

"We spent four days at the shelter on Cedar Lake. Sunday we stayed quietly in camp. Monday the other rangers went on to Great Opeongo Lake (now Opeongo Lake). Tuesday Steve and I fished along the rapids on the Petawawa River, where choice speckled beauties are to be found, and then before we left, we crossed over to the Depot Farm, where we had some baked beans with the drivers and posted our letters written on birch bark. Then we were forced to stay in camp all day because of a change in weather. The day before it had been beautiful and mild with just sufficient ripple to make the lake appear one sheet of diamonds. Today, its foam-capped waves came piling in upon the shore covering the trees with ice until the branches hung with long icicles. What a sight it was a little later when the sun burst forth — the trees appeared as if decked with silver.

"Saturday morning we started for Catfish Lake. There is one very interesting thing on this lake — Turtle Rock. It is on one of the islands and it looks like some huge prehistoric animal. It is said that the Indians used to worship it. It resembles a huge turtle and is estimated to weigh thirty-five tons.

"At Burnt Lake (now named Portal Lake) we spent the night at Barnet's Depot at the head of the lake. We were welcomed by their fire ranger, Mr. Leblanche, who treated us to the very best his larder afforded. Those interested in reforestation can find a very encouraging field in the splendid growth of young pine on the Gillies' Limit there.

"The shelter house at Misty Lake had been broken into —by a porcupine who had taken possession of it. He had eaten a hole through the door and had destroyed door and window frames. These apparently harmless animals are a great nuisance in this way and will cut your canoe gunwales and paddles, if left where they can get at them.

"Finally, after continuing on down through the chain of rivers and lakes, we reached the railway once more at Rainy (Rain) Lake. We had covered a good part of the western section of the Park and I was satisfied that things were pretty well in order there."

In after years, Mr. Bartlett found that it was much easier to make his inspection trip in the winter by snowshoe. Then he would set off with two rangers — his son Jim and Mark Robinson were frequently his companions — and would be gone for many weeks. A dog team would haul the supplies, and they would get around most of the Park in this way. Each night they would plan to stop at a shelter hut where they would be warm and comfortable, and where they could stay if the weather were unfavorable.

On some of the earliest trips the dogs were driven by one of the pioneer rangers, Albert Ranger, whose two sons, Telesphore and Peter, joined the staff at a later date. "Albair," as Mr. Bartlett and everyone else called him, had a great love for his two dogs, Jack and Judy, and they, in turn, would obey him in a way that they would no one else. Everyone who remembers Albair and his dogs agrees that he thought the world of them, and that they thoroughly enjoyed their winter outings in the Park. In spite of that, the story of the tricks they played on their master, and Albair's reproachful prophecy, "That dog Jack, he got some bad plan in hees head," came to be a stock saying at headquarters. George Bartlett's picture of "A Six Weeks' Snowshoe Trip Through the Park", quoted with the permission of his widow who now lives in Ridgetown, shows some of the difficulties encountered by Park administrators in the old days:

"We had been several days upon our way when we saw some snowshoe tracks near dusk as we struck across the country. Since they were evidently not those of our rangers, we talked the matter over and decided that our first move in the morning would be to look the parties up in case they should prove to be trappers. This meant an extra early start and we planned to turn in before long. There were certain signs of warm weather that caused us a little anxiety — we heard the call of the Acadian owl for one. He makes a noise like a saw-whet and usually he heralds a change. However, we decided not to worry. We had little moccasins for the dogs' feet if their feet started to ball up. These were made of a small piece of deer skin in the form of a bag with a drawstring on the top to tie around the dog's leg. We rolled up in our sleeping bags and it seemed only an hour or so when Albair's 'Levez, levez' roused us to a hearty breakfast.

"As I had decided to follow the tracks we had already seen, we retraced our steps with that end in view. However, we soon found that our men were not trappers but were in the bush on legitimate business. We had only gone a little over two miles when we met the two men who had been responsible for the tracks. They proved to be two bush rangers who were looking over some timber for the limit holder.

"At one of the other shelter houses we went out with the rangers who were staying there to see how they were getting along with their trapping of beaver for the Government. Each year these skins are bundled up and taken to headquarters where they are marked Algonquin Provincial Park and stamped with the Government's registered stamp — a King's crown. These are sold at auction and represented an annual income of many thousands of dollars.

"We had an interval of soft weather, but finally we were on our way again. It was below zero at last and the slush on the lake had frozen sufficiently to carry us — truly wonderful travelling. The wolves were on the alert, too, making the woods ring with their howls, but did not come out into the open to give us a chance for a shot. Our dogs were rested and keen, but as we came out to the second lake, to use Albair's expression, 'One of Jack's bad plans got in his head'. The result of this was that, when the lead tightened up the harness, he held back. Since the harness was not buckled as tight as usual, he backed clean out of it, and before we could stop him, was off across the ice as fast as he could go. We could do nothing, so Albair lit his pipe and sat on the load until Mr. Jack condescended to return and be harnessed. This was not until he had explored the lake to his entire satisfaction. Albair's reproaches seemed lost on him, for he only wagged his tail and pulled, evidently satisfied that he had had the best of it. Despite his 'bad plan' we made twenty miles that day, and early in the afternoon we joined the other rangers."

As Mr. Bartlett pointed out in this account, the rangers covered a great deal of territory during routine game patrols of the Park. On that particular occasion, the travellers suspected of poaching were proved to be there on legitimate business, but at others, the rangers were forced to take into custody poachers and traders who were trespassing on the Park game preserve. Mark Robinson tells many different stories about the work of the old rangers, who moved about in pairs to patrol the whole Park area.

One of these incidents must have taken place about 1908, when both Mark and his ranging partner, Zeph Nadon, were quite new to the district. They were living together at the old cabin at Canoe Lake, when Mr. Bartlett gave them a difficult assignment. He knew that furs were being smuggled out of the Park, and he felt that he could learn who the culprit was if only he could discover how he was disposing of his catch. If they could find out how the furs were being transported out of the Park to the buyer, action could be taken to clear up the whole matter.

It was some time before the two rangers were able to get the slightest clue as to how this poaching ring was working, but the Park had a grapevine system all its own, and after a while they learned that a stranger by the name of Black was paying frequent visits to the Rock Lake district. At that time the Park boundary came just to the head of Rock Lake, the railway station itself was outside the limits, and therefore out of their territory. However, they determined to see what was going on. They had heard that Black was adopting a very hail-fellow-well-met attitude to everyone in the area, and they thought they'd like to have a chance to see what he was up to.

One day Mark and Zeph managed to be on the station platform when Black got off at Rock Lake. Sure enough, Zeph recognized him as a fur buyer whom he had known in the Temiskaming country. Still, they knew that they could not pin anything definite on him unless they caught him in the very act of dealing with trappers in the Park, or receiving furs which they could prove had been taken in the Park. They decided that they would wait around until he had departed, and then search the place where he had been staying. Just as they had expected, they found a fine supply of furs on hand. There were many skins of animals that could be found only in the Park — such as mink, marten and fisher.

Even with this knowledge, they were still powerless to do anything but make a report to Mr. Bartlett, and they were not too sure that he would be pleased with their investigations outside the actual Park boundaries. The letter of the law said that their jurisdiction extended outside for a distance of one mile, but Mr. Bartlett felt that they should confine their efforts to the Park itself. When they reported to him at headquarters, it was late in the afternoon. He listened to what they had to say, and told them that he would consider the matter the next day. Soon after supper, he called them back into his office. He had been reading their written report, and the name of Black caught his attention.

"Who's this man Black?" he asked, "surely you don't imply that poor old Jimmy Black, who isn't quite right in his head, is mixed up in this?"

Mark and Zeph explained that the buyer was no relation to old Jimmy, but that he had likely taken the same name to throw people off the scent of what he was really doing.

Finally, when this whole matter came into the open, it was found that there were a number of people linked up with the marketing of the furs. Not only was Mr. Black involved, but some of the railway employees were taking part in the racket, too. One man lived near a railway trestle not more than half a mile from Park Headquarters. He was paid by the railway company for acting as a fire warden, and for keeping the bridge in repair. In addition, he was augmenting his income by loading stolen furs on passing trains.

However, locating and charging trappers in the Park was only one of the tasks undertaken by the rangers in their work of protecting the wildlife of the district. Sometimes it was very difficult to catch the trespasser in the act, and clever poachers devised many schemes to obtain the fur they were after. Sometimes the rangers found that they had to be content with safeguarding the lives of the animals by simply destroying trapping equipment picked up within the boundaries.

At one time, when the poaching was particularly widespread, it became known to the staff that certain trappers had evolved a new system that was hard to beat. By hiding their traps off the regular ranger patrol routes, these trappers could cross the Park boundaries early in winter with a small pack of supplies, and bury themselves in the very centre of the Park without the rangers' knowledge. This type of poaching was very difficult to combat with the limited staff at the Superintendent's command. But Mark tells of one trip which he and Zeph took through an out-of-the-way section of the Park. In between Opeongo Lake and Burnt Island Lake, is a rough section that travellers usually avoid. There, he and Zeph found a great hoard of traps which they gleefully disposed of by tossing them in the lake. They failed to catch the poacher, but at least they had the satisfaction of knowing he would take no pelts out of the area that season.

In spite of the rangers' vigilance, however, poaching activities actually increased. The reason for this was a new Government policy whose repercussions were so widespread that it is worth looking into.

Bartlett's first report, for the year 1899, quoted two authorities to the effect that the beaver population had already increased to a gratifying extent. Ranger Jim Sawyer believed that the beaver population had more than trebled in those sections of the Park where he had set his trap lines in the old days when he travelled into that district from the Haliburton country. That same year Mr. Bartlett had received a visit from the Indian Chief, Big Canoe, who claimed that Canoe Lake had been named after him, and who told the Superintendent that he had trapped in that area some forty years before. Since Big Canoe belonged to a band of Ojibwas who had previously claimed the whole of the Park area draining into the Georgian Bay as their hunting grounds, it is quite possible that he had hunted along the Oxtongue River in the early days, although it is improbable that his name had been given to Canoe Lake, since the first record of this name goes back to 1853. In any case, Chief Big Canoe toured all through the region, and reported to Mr. Bartlett that he was delighted to see how much the beaver had multiplied since his last visit.

In his 1908 report, Mr. Bartlett stressed the fact that the beaver in the Park had become so numerous that he felt the Department would be wise to allow the rangers to do some supervised trapping. By 1909, the work had already begun, and over three hundred beaver had been taken in a comparatively small area. Two years later, the annual catch stood at 402 beaver skins, while a small number of otter, marten, mink, and muskrat, had also been taken. The total value of these furs was placed to $3,340.00. Each year from then until 1920, when the project was given up, the Superintendent's annual report gave the amount that had been realized from the Department's fur sale. In that last year, the total revenue had risen to $14,179.00, but even that was not sufficient to compensate the authorities for the amount of trouble that this activity caused, or the amount of criticism that they had to meet.

The Department, in adopting the scheme, had reckoned without the effect that this policy would have on the ranging staff, or the antagonism that it would arouse in the trappers of the surrounding district. The increase in poaching on the part of both these groups was tremendous. On the ranger side, it was hardly fair to expect men to devote their energies to game preservation, and yet to ask them to trap in order to build up a revenue for the Government. Critics accused the men of taking one animal for the Government, and one for themselves. It was not difficult to market the pelts privately, and the rewards were great. Not all the rangers were involved in this game, but there were enough to lower the reputation of the whole staff in the eyes of the general public.

Then, too, the trappers in the surrounding country began to redouble their activities, and occasionally a ranger would work with them. The trappers felt that the Department had been unfair to them, and that they were quite justified in taking their revenge in their own way. The Government had set aside this territory as a reserve in 1893, and had deprived them of grounds over which they had been trapping for many years. The boundaries had been marked out, warning signs had been posted, and fines meted out to offenders. Now the Government itself had taken to trapping, an act which was tantamount to the Government poaching on *their* grounds. This train of thought led to a period of illicit trapping that, in the long run, must have cost the Government much more than it realized from the sale of fur.

Many an ingenious scheme was devised by the poachers to outwit the rangers. There was the Indian in the north of the Park who approached the boundary for two miles on stilts, and into the Park a good distance before abandoning them. There is the tale of another trapper who padded the heel of his moccasin and then walked with his snow shoes on backwards, so anyone finding his tracks would follow him the wrong way. One perfectly innocent attempt to outwit the rangers will particularly interest any who have heard of the writer Grey Owl, or better still, those who have read his books.

By 1908, poaching in the Park had reached the point where an investigation was ordered, and some rangers, implicated in aiding and abetting the poachers, were dismissed. The news spread far and wide, bringing to the Park one day a lean, hawk-nosed young man, by the name of Archie Belaney. Archie had been born in England, but had read so voraciously about bush life in Canada, that he came out, while still in his teens, to learn his woodcraft the hard way. By the time he showed up in the Park, Archie had been around a bit, and fancied himself as a woodsman. In fact, he was rash enough to make a bet that he could cross the Park from boundary to boundary in the middle of winter without being caught.

The rangers' intelligence service was good: Bartlett got wind of the bet. Albert Ranger, Zeph Nadon, Mark Robinson and Bud Callahan were all put on the alert, and instructed to keep a sharp watch along the railway tracks, which Archie was bound to cross. Mark Robinson had recently been stationed at the old shelter house on Canoe Lake, while Bud Callahan was living at Smoke Lake. Both spots were on the main poaching trails into the Park.

Bud figured that Archie would likely come in along the old Gilmour Road from Dorset, and then strike north through the Crown Lake District, to hit the border of the Park at Porcupine Lake, now known as Big Porcupine Lake. Sure enough, he was right! It was late in the afternoon that Bud came upon his tracks, and just as it was getting dark he caught a glimpse of him ahead.

Belaney smiled hospitably when Bud showed up, ranger badge and all, at his fire. After all, he had just entered the Park; he *was* travelling without a license, but beyond that he had not infringed on Park regulations. The two men had a friendly chat, fixed their beds for the night, and went to sleep.

But not Archie Belaney; he wasn't going to lose a wager as easily as that. While Bud slept he got up, put his things on his pack, and slipped away into the darkness.

In the meantime it had turned bitterly cold. In territory entirely new to him, and barely enough light to see by, Archie must have wished more than once that he had forgotten his bet, and stayed snug and warm in his sleeping bag under the brush shelter. Some time early in the morning he fell into a shallow beaver pond at the west end of Ragged Lake, and lost his pack. Now he was in a real jam: he had no dry matches to light a fire with which he might dry out his clothes.

While this was going on, Bud had awakened after a good night's sleep, to find his companion gone. Muttering uncomplimentary remarks, he had followed, increasing his pace when he came to the broken ice in the beaver pond, thinking, no doubt, that it served him right for putting him to all this trouble, but realizing that Archie's predicament in that weather was no joke. When Bud caught up with his fugitive, he found him in a wretched state, with both feet frozen.

This time Bud was in no mood for pleasantries—nor was Belaney. Callahan decided to take him along to the Superintendent's office, with all possible speed. They stopped to cook a meal at the shelter house left by the Mickle Dyment Company at the south end of Smoke Lake, and then went on up to Mark's place at Canoe Lake.

When Mark examined Archie Belaney's feet that night, he shook his head gravely. They were badly swollen. He bandaged them up, and loaned Archie a change of clothes. When it came time to leave for headquarters in the morning, Mark felt that the trapper was in no shape to leave, but Bud was inexorable. They took a train through to Cache Lake, and after the interview at the office, Belaney went back to Mark's place to stay until his feet had healed sufficiently for him to be on his way.

For three weeks Mark nursed him, doing everything in his power to save Archie's feet. Even after the flesh had healed, Archie had trouble walking. Finally, when he was well enough to go, Mark performed the last act of the Good Samaritan, and loaned him enough money to take the train back to Timagami.

Thereafter Mark lost track of him. Trappers reported that he was still living in the Timagami District, and Tom Thomson came upon him once when he was working over that way as a fire ranger. Mark never saw Archie Belaney again.

But he did eventually hear from Archie, in a most unusual way. When Grey Owl's first books were published, Mark was very interested in the stories told by this man, who seemed to have such an intimate

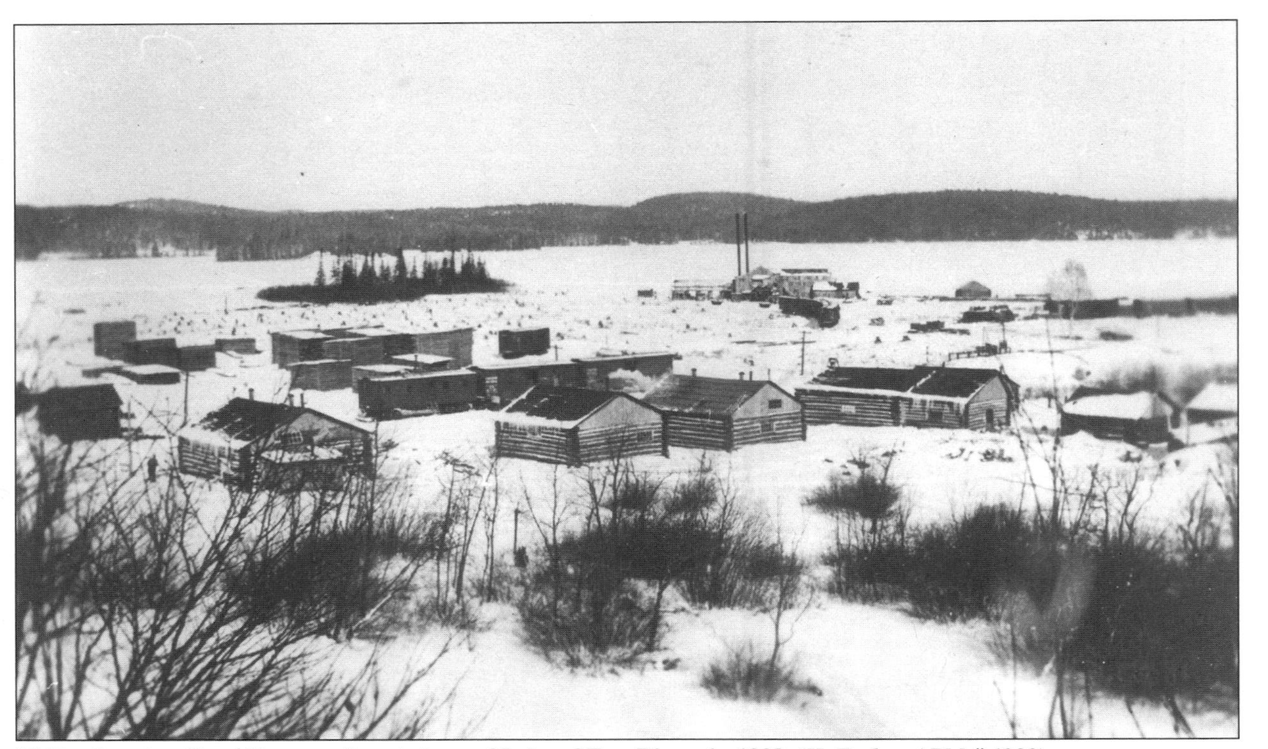

**McRae Lumber Co. mill on southwest shore of Lake of Two Rivers in 1938.** *(H. Taylor; APM # 1283)*

**Cache Lake Headquarters, about 1900.** *(Ministry of Natural Resources; APM # 1156)*

knowledge of the habits of the beaver. One day, in 1935, an Indian came into the Park Headquarters while Mark was there. He walked up to Mark and said:

"Grey Owl sends you his greetings."

"That's very kind of him," replied Mark, "but I don't think I've ever had the pleasure of meeting him. That's one thing I've looked forward to."

"Oh, I think you must have met him," responded the visitor. "He told me that you had once nursed him for three weeks in your home in the Park, when he was suffering from severely frozen feet."

With that information Mark realized that his acquaintance with Grey Owl had been made many years before, in the days when he was still Archie Belaney. Grey Owl had remembered.

To return to the chief cause for the increase in poaching, Mr. Bartlett could hardly have foreseen the complications that his policy would bring about, when he first sponsored its introduction. From his point of view, the receipts from the fur sale would help reduce the expenses of running the Park, and would assist in publicizing the Park. As far as he could see, it was simply an extension of a policy that had already gained renown for the Park in many different parts of the world. From zoos, and from collectors scattered all over the United States and Europe, had come requests for live animals from Algonquin Park. Beaver, especially, were shipped in specially marked crates, to many distant spots.

From the files of Mr. Bartlett's correspondence, it is apparent what a great deal of time both he and his ranging staff spent in this shipping of live animals. The beaver is a very sensitive creature, and on many occasions when shipments were made to England or to the Continent, the animals died on shipboard, because they didn't receive proper care. Then, when the animals did arrive, there was frequently a great deal of trouble before the cases were returned to their owners. Mr. Bartlett must have often wondered whether the work involved was worth either the cash returns or the publicity that it brought to the Park.

One by-product of this activity was a steel trap, perfected by Jim Bartlett, the Superintendent's son, for capturing live animals. The trap proved so efficient, that it is in common use in many parts of Canada to this day. It consisted of wire netting over a frame, in two sections, that opened out like a suitcase. These two sections were joined together along one side by a very strong spring, which allowed them to open out flat under tension, but closed them together with terrific force when the spring was released. To catch the beaver, the trap was opened out and put in the water at the top of the dam. When he swam up to investigate, the beaver's chest released the spring, and he was caught. Pictures of this invention, with others to show the Algonquin Park shipping cases, and the fine beaver skins taken in the district, are included in the Park reports for the years 1915 to 1918.

Experts from many parts of the world came to see how the Government Game Reserve was run, evidence that the Park was becoming well known as a successful venture. Among the visitors, was Mr. V. Generosoff, of the Russian Department of Agriculture, who came during the summer of 1914, to observe methods used in Ontario for preserving wild life, his own government contemplating similar action.

The attitude of the Park authorities to wolves, was always of particular interest to such visitors. Administrators of game reserves have always had difficulty making up their minds as to whether predatory animals should be exterminated or whether they should be offered the same protection as other wild life. From the first, it had been foreseen in the Park, that the increase in the deer population would likely lead to a corresponding increase in the number of wolves in the area. Some naturalists argued that a percentage of predatory animals was needed to keep the other species in a healthy condition, since the weaklings were killed off, and only the sturdy stock survived. The Park authorities, however, decided to exterminate the wolves, and, in spite of a great deal of discussion, this has continued to be the policy to our own times.

Starting about 1903, the rangers were supplied with poison for use in their war against the wolves in the Park, but as time went on this method came under severe attack. For one thing, there was no way of making sure that the poisoned bait set out for a wolf would not be eaten by another animal. Then, some people claimed that the wolf's stomach was so strong that it could disgorge the poisoned meat, and suffer no ill effects. The practice of using poison in the Park was finally discontinued, and the rangers fell back on setting snares, and on shooting the wolves whenever possible. The bounty, which stood at fifteen dollars for many years, has now been increased to twenty-five.

Many stories are told by the old rangers, about the tricks they have used in trying to kill wolves which they knew were prowling about in the neighbourhood of their cabins. Mr. J. Edwin Colson, who first came to the Park as a ranger in 1905, claims that wolves are too smart for traps, but that they can sometimes be taken in snares. He recalls one time, however, when a wolf was killed, that it had several different wire nooses about its neck. Each time he had been caught, he had broken free by the simple expediency of turning his head around in order to bite through the wire. One wolf is reported to have been captured, that had bitten through a steel wire made of six strands of metal.

The man who claims his bounty for wolves in the Park, works hard for it as a rule: but not always. Peter Ranger tells how he once claimed the bounty for a wolf which he had killed on Maple Lake. That year the snow had held off at the beginning of the winter, so that in January, the lakes were a sheet of ice, and it was much simpler for the rangers to make their rounds on skates than on snowshoes. Peter had put on his skates one day when he planned to cross the lake in the north part of the Park. Far out in the centre of the lake he caught sight of the carcass of a deer, and as he approached it, he noticed two wolves advancing out of the woods at the shore, towards the deer. Since Peter had his gun with him, he was determined to get close enough for a shot. He dropped to the ice and began edging closer to his quarry. In the meantime, he found one wolf was staying close to the shore, but the other was making his way very slowly towards the deer. Peter saw that the ice was so slippery, the wolf couldn't get a good grip on it with his claws.

All this time, Peter was inching along the ice as quickly as he could. At length, when he was still several hundred yards away, the wolf looked up and saw him approaching. Peter fired, then skated towards his quarry. The wolf was hit, but the bullet did not strike a vital spot. As if he knew that he couldn't move across the ice as quickly as Peter, he dropped and started to roll towards shore. However, Peter soon got close enough for another shot, and finished him off.

The next time he went to North Bay, he took the pelt with him and went to see Mr. Parks, the game warden, to claim the Government bounty. The girl in the office heard him telling how he had killed the wolf, and asked if he would repeat the story for one of the reporters from the "North Bay Nugget". Peter said that he didn't mind, and gave all the information to the newspaper man. What was his dismay when he saw the report in the next issue of the paper headed "Another Wolf Story", and told as if the whole incident had been the product of Peter's imagination.

Peter had another tale to tell about wolves — and this one had a witness to vouch for its authenticity. One day in September, 1941, he was paddling across Crooked Lake in his fifteen-foot canoe. There, well out in the middle of the lake, he saw a wolf swimming after a buck. This time he didn't have a gun with him. There wasn't much chance of killing the wolf, but he didn't want the wolf to get the deer. Consequently, Peter edged the canoe close enough to the pair so that he could take a crack at the wolf with his paddle. The buck swam off when it found that it had a chance to do so, but Peter kept the canoe in place between the wolf and the shore, and hit the wolf on the head whenever he had a chance. One time the wolf took a snap at the bow of the canoe, and it swung right around like a top, but still the struggle went on.

Finally, after about half an hour of this battle, Peter saw another ranger, Dan Stringer, coming down the lake in a motor boat, towing two canoes. As Dan got closer, he could see what was happening, and he began to shout to Peter to paddle clear so that he could get a shot at the wolf with his revolver. Peter called out not to shoot because he knew that the wolf was heavy with water, and would sink to the bottom if it were killed. However, Dan kept right on coming, and when he was close enough he fired. Then, although Peter tried to slip his paddle under the body, the wolf was so saturated with water than it sank right to the bottom, like a stone. Dan and Peter tried for a long while to recover the body, so as to claim the bounty of twenty-five dollars, but all to no purpose. That was one time when the reward was not collected for a dead wolf.

In spite of the infiltration of wolves from surrounding areas almost as fast as they could be killed by the rangers, deer increased rapidly in the Park.

By 1917, when Canadian meat supplies, due to the First World War, had reached a low ebb, the deer population had so increased that Mr. Bartlett suggested the rangers be allowed to kill some of the deer for meat. In his 1918 report, it is stated that some 650 deer had been shipped to dealers in Toronto and Hamilton. According to rangers who were on the staff at the time, it was possible to shoot as many as twenty in a single day, in one section of the Park.

Today, although it is doubtful whether deer are as plentiful as in Bartlett's time, every visitor is almost sure to see a few. Even the early timber cutting has proved an advantage: deer thrive on the sweet young shoots of deciduous trees in the succulent second growth, and the lower branches of the young cedars.

A great deal more could be written about Mr. Bartlett and the long list of rangers who worked so faithfully under him. Of these many, Steve Waters, Tim O'Leary, William Gale, John Simpson, D. A. Ross, Jim Sawyers, Bob Balfour, Albert Ranger with his two sons, Telesphore and Peter, Zeph Nadon, Dan Stringer and Ed. Colson are a few that have been mentioned so far. More will be met with later, but it is impossible to name them all. They were a fine group of hardy bushmen, proud of their work, loyal to their chief, and full of enthusiasm for all that the Park stood for; full of tales, too, about their experiences in it.

We leave them for the time being, with three of their stories that convey, better than any other means, the new sense of comradeship between animal and man, so typical of Algonquin Park under George Bartlett.

According to both Ed. Colson and Mark Robinson, the beavers built a dam one year across a railway culvert, at Joe Creek. This dam caused the water to back up, so that it flooded part of the tracks. Every time the stationmaster pulled the dam to pieces, he was greeted the next morning with a brand new dam. The railwayman was nonplussed. No doubt he had a gun, but this was Algonquin Park! Finally, he tried to frighten them away by leaving two lanterns burning, one at each end of the dam. All night the beavers watched these strange, bright visitors that seemed to be alive, but never moved. In the morning, the harassed stationmaster came skeptically over to see what had happened. Nothing! The dodge had worked.

The next night he took to bed and slept longer and more soundly than he had slept for weeks. That light idea was certainly a smart one.

But in the morning he met with a rude shock. His ranger friends had a very simple explanation. During the day those brainy little beavers had discussed the two lamps long and earnestly, finally deciding that they could only have been placed there for one purpose. And to show their gratitude to the man who had put them there, they built a bigger dam than ever, by the light of his lanterns.

Mark Robinson had another story to tell about the Joe Creek beavers, and their contest with the railroaders. Charlie Ratan, one of the section men, had many a quarrel with them. One of these came about because of the loss of his pick-axe, a tool he frequently needed in his work, and one which he sometimes used against the beaver themselves when he tried to clear out one of their dams. One day he came storming along to Mark; his pick-axe had disappeared and he was sure that Mark, or someone else close at hand, had hidden it as a joke. Mark knew nothing about its whereabouts, and neither did anyone else. The next time they broke down the dam to avoid the flooding of the tracks they found it — firmly lodged in the masonry at the very bottom of the structure.

Once, according to Mr. Colson, when the beavers found an old storm door, near where they planned to construct a dam, they built it into the dam itself. The glass window of the door was still intact. However, in the course of the building operations, the beavers pushed a heavy stick against one of the panes of glass and broke it. Until it was filled with mud and other debris, the beavers took turns in tobogganing through the chute that this open window in the old storm door afforded.

## CHAPTER 11

From Alexander Kirkwood's Reference to "noble pines and stately oaks bespeaking the growth of centuries", it is quite clear that up to the time he wrote these words in his proposal for the Park's establishment, he had never been near the place. Yet there is an unconsciously wistful note in the language he uses, that reveals an urge common to most of us. To business and professional people particularly, hemmed in as they are by office walls, and tied to the grey monotony of routine tasks, it is impossible to think of a place like Algonquin Park, without wanting to go there.

All the founders of the Park agreed that it would be a waste indeed of the wildlife and natural beauty of the area, if no people went there to enjoy them. Dickson, it will be remembered, strongly urged that a guide book be published, and was almost prepared to set up a tourist bureau, so enthusiastic was he over its charms. The Ottawa-Arnprior and Parry Sound Railway had been welcomed as a means of easy access to the Park, and from first to last, every Park Superintendent has gone out of his way to welcome visitors.

And yet, apart from the native hospitality of the north, no rigid policy has ever been worked out with regard to the type of activity that should be encouraged in these Park visitors. Happily, this lack of any plan has resulted in a wide variety of both accommodation and recreative facilities.

To seasoned surveyors like Dickson, and to the long line of superintendents and rangers, it has always seemed that the ideal way of enjoying the Park was to travel, not merely to, but *through* it. George Bartlett's first trip across the Park from north to south in 1902, gave him the idea of marking the portages with the name of the lake to which they led, the route, and the length of the carry. Today, such signs strengthen discouraged tyro trippers all over the Park; in some places canoe docks have been built, and everywhere there are fireplaces at the permanent camp sites. Even the rangers' own shelter houses may sometimes — with permission from headquarters — be used by visitors.

Two campers who had such permission, were spending one very rainy day in the rangers' shelter house at Lake Louisa. When they had fed themselves, and played cards for a while, there was nothing else to do, so they dozed off for an afternoon's sleep. One of them woke when he heard a small scratchy noise on the floor. He lifted his head sufficiently to see that the sound had been made by a chipmunk, which had come up through a knot hole, and was having a look around the cabin. When he saw that all was well, he clambered up the wall to a shelf where there was arranged a collection of old bottles — souvenirs of many fishing trips to that district. The chipmunk looked as though he knew what these bottles had formerly contained, and was prepared to get his full share of enjoyment from them. As though performing a round trip over a route he had travelled many times before, he scampered along a scantling just above the shelf, and paused at the mouth of each bottle to enjoy one lingering whiff of its former fragrant contents. Having completed the tour, he whisked back through the hole in the floor, and was seen no more.

But a majority of the early visitors were less prepared for canoe trips, than the Park was prepared for them to take trips. Rather than spend their time on an extended jaunt through the Park, they preferred the comfort of hotels, and were content with the shorter excursions; or wanted merely to bask in the summer sun on the verandas of their own summer cottage.

The houses built on the island at Canoe Lake in 1893, for the families of the Gilmour brothers, were undoubtedly the first summer homes to be erected in the Park area. In 1905, these houses, known to the Gilmours as "Loon's Retreat", were purchased by Drs. T. A. Bertram and A. J. Pirie, and stand to this day, still used as summer homes. To those with families, this was the ideal way to use the Park, and while it has never been possible to buy land in the area, from the first, visitors have been allowed to lease land and even build under certain necessary Park requirements.

A majority of summer visitors in early Park days, however, seemed to prefer the accommodation of the hotels and lodges, which began to appear not long after the Park's establishment. The earliest of these was Highland Inn, the story of which is inseparably tied up with that of Mrs. Edwin Colson.

In May, 1900, when Mrs. Colson first came to the Park from Ottawa, she was still Miss Molly Cox. During the previous winter, she had been working so hard that the doctor told her she must stop nursing for a while, and take a complete rest. When her Ottawa friends, Dr. and Mrs. Wm. Bell, heard of this, they wrote to her from the Park, where Dr. Bell had recently joined the staff as a ranger, urging her to visit them for the summer.

After a few weeks in the Park, Molly Cox regained her old vigour, and then began to look around for something useful to do, to keep herself busy. When she discovered that they needed a new housekeeper for the rangers' boarding house, she decided to take over the job. How successful that proved to be appears in a report written by Mr. Bartlett at that time, during an investigation by the Department. A member of the ranging staff who had been dismissed for incompetence, pointed an accusing finger at the recent changes at the boarding house, and Mr. Bartlett was called upon to report just what had taken place there.

According to the Superintendent, the rangers had never been so well looked after as they were under Miss Cox's direction. One of the complaints had been that the rangers had been required to cut hay along the railroad tracks for a cow imported into the Park, and said to be milked for the sole benefit of the families of Mr. Bartlett and Dr. Bell. Mr. Bartlett pointed out that the men themselves had all the fresh milk they could drink as a result of the cow's presence.

But not all Molly Cox's time, during those early years in the Park, was spent in hard work. She was wise enough to take advantage of the pleasure that the woods and the lakes had to offer, and frequently joined her friends, the Bells, in expeditions to different places in the district. Mrs. Colson, in later years, used to speak of the good times they had with their Ottawa friends who came to holiday in the Park. On picnic trips, she and Mrs. Bell used to startle the other women by appearing in breeks, instead of the long flowing skirts that were then in fashion. Sometimes they were joined by Mrs. Bell's brother, Mr. R. C. W. Lett, a member of the ranging staff at that time, and later Publicity Director for the Canadian National Railway. Two well-known places in the Park received their names as the result of these expeditions. Molly's Island, on Smoke Lake, was called after Mrs. Colson, then Molly Cox; and Kootchie Lake was named for a little dog belonging to Dr. Bell's sister. The little dog had tumbled overboard one day when a picnic party was paddling through the lake, and the dog's name was given to the lake to commemorate the rescue.

In all probability a number of the lakes in the surrounding district received their names from Dr. Bell and his friends. For many years he made a special point of exploring the Park in order to complete a canoe trip map which he had drawn up. This map formed the basis for the one printed by Arthur Brown of Toronto, which was sold for many years to visitors at Highland Inn. Even today a revised version of Dr. Bell's map is sold in the Park, and is regarded as one of the best for canoe trips.

Mr. J. Edwin Colson had come to the Park from Guelph when he joined the ranging staff in 1905, and sometimes he went along on picnic excursions planned by the Bells.

It was the case of Pinonique Dufond and the hired man, Baptiste, all over again. But Molly didn't have to hide her attachment as Pinonique had from "the old Susanne". In 1907 Molly Cox became Mrs. Edwin Colson.

Today, the original Nominigan Lodge is Mr. A. G. Northway's summer home, and Minnesing Hotel is a unique camp of which more will be said later. Only guests of theirs who have gone in by road will have an adequate idea of what the "stage" journey must have been like in the early days.

The stage was simply a wagon with a built-on top. Mrs. Colson, after one of her trips to Nominigan Lodge, insisted on removing the top; better a few scratches from the swish of overhanging boughs than the risk to life and limb involved in travelling the road in that top-heavy contraption. Frequently, by other accounts, the guests would fall out of the stage at the end of a voyage in the vehicle, and embrace the firm earth, singing doxologies of praise and thanksgiving.

If this was the reaction of natives, one can imagine how others felt, especially visitors from overseas. The memory of Minnesing Road was still strong in one couple who revisited the Park recently for the first time since their honeymoon there in 1914. The lady laughed as she recalled their earlier visit. Her husband had come to Canada a few years before she came over, and they had been married in New York when her boat docked there. Then he whisked her away to this highly advertised summer resort. She was terrified. Her friends had warned her that Canada would be primitive, but never in her worst dreams had she expected anything as wild as that road. As the wagon strained in every jolt, tilting now left, now right, she thought of all the lovely clothes in her trousseau. To add to her discomfort, it rained in torrents. Once there, they found it very comfortable, but her whole visit was haunted by the horrible fear that the whole of Canada would be as primitive. Things had changed in the interval between their visits: originally they arrived by train; this time they arrived in their own car, on a modern highway.

In the same year that Highland Inn was built, the Hotel Algonquin, at Joe Lake, was begun by Mr. Tom Merrill. This hotel was also convenient to the railway line through the Park, and was popular from the first. Because of its choice location, it was a frequent rendezvous for fishermen, and a favourite base for fishing trips. In 1917 the Colsons, who had given up their connection with Highland Inn five years earlier, bought Hotel Algonquin, which they continued to manage until it was bought by the present owner in 1943.

Once during the Hotel Algonquin days, the Colsons were visited by a bear which, according to Ed. Colson, had called for a particular purpose. It was rather late in the evening, and as Ed. sat alone in his office smoking a last pipe before turning in, he heard a noise from the pantry. Flashlight in hand, he went to the pantry door and flung it open. The room was empty, but the window was open and the screen was missing. Also missing, was a great jug of milk that had been sitting on the table. Mr. Colson found the jug set down intact outside the window — empty. He used to claim that a bear can use his front paw just like a hand, when he wants to carry something.

During their long sojourn in the Park, first at the rangers' boarding house, next at Highland Inn, then at Hotel Algonquin, and finally at the mill office, which they remodelled, at the head of Canoe Lake, Mr. and Mrs. Colson came to be known to many hundreds of Park visitors. Not only did they contribute to the welcome and comfort of the travellers in that region, but both of them made a very real contribution to the life of the people who lived all year round in the Park and nearby district. Mr. Colson, as lay reader in the Church of England, conducted church services and Sunday School when there was no qualified clergyman available. Mrs. Colson was frequently called upon to nurse the sick. As one of her Park friends said of her, she did everything for her neighbours but marry and bury them, and her husband could perform these services if necessary. Mrs. Colson advised young mothers before the arrival of their first-born, and helped to bring the baby into the world; pulled teeth when people had a toothache; put broken bones in splints; and travelled about the country in all kinds of weather to bring cheer and comfort to the sick and lonely.

Mrs. Colson herself has stories of some of her adventures in those days. One time when there was no doctor available, she and her husband were called in to look after a man at the Munn Lumber Camp, then operating close by. The man's leg was fractured and needed a splint before he could be moved. Mr. Colson fashioned a rough one out of a piece of board, and his wife set the bone and bound the splint to hold the leg rigid until he reached a doctor. The man was taken to the company's headquarters at Whitney.

That was the last they saw of him — except one day years later, when they were standing on the platform of the Algonquin Park Station, looking for some guests who were due.

"My God, you're the woman I wanted to see!"

Mrs. Colson was overwhelmed by a huge lumberman who had suddenly burst out of the crowd and dashed over to where she stood. The stranger bent down and hoisted up his trouser leg excitedly, pulling down the sock to reveal the limb in all its hirsute beauty.

"There's the leg you mended," he bellowed triumphantly for all the crowd to hear. "Doctor said it was a compound fracture, but he didn't have to touch it."

Incidents like that made life sweet for Molly Colson.

Another time she received an urgent message from a man whose wife was expecting a new baby. The couple lived in a wretched little shack down Rock Lake way, and the husband, apparently a section man, had rushed up the tracks on a three-wheeled "speeder" to bring Molly back to help. The doctor from Whitney who had been out to see the woman only a few days previously, was now himself in bed with the flu. A black storm was brewing, but Mrs. Colson gathered a few things together and set off on the ten-mile trip. As they whizzed down the track, lightning crackled in the sky and the wind roared through the trees. All the while the man kept moaning, "Ma God! Ma God," and exclaiming that his wife and child were dying.

When they reached the shack, Molly found that man had not exaggerated. The new baby had died, the mother was in a very serious condition, and one of the other children was having convulsions. For four days she stayed on the spot, until the worst danger was past, and then arranged for the family to move into the rangers' house, where the woman could have better care.

Finally, feeling she had done all she could and that it was time to go back to Cache Lake, she told the husband she was leaving, and got her things ready. As she sat downstairs waiting for him, she was startled by sudden blood-curdling screams from above, as if the man had suddenly decided to murder his wife and was in the very act. As Mrs. Colson stood trembling in the room the man came hurtling down the stairs past her, out the door, and down towards the tracks. One of the neighbours explained that he was subject to these fits, which worked themselves off if he was left alone. Mrs. Colson doesn't say how she got home, but it is safe to assume that she preferred flagging the next freight train to taking another ride with the Rock Lake madman.

Another woman who helped to make the Canoe Lake district well known, both to tourists and to people in the surrounding district, was Mrs. Shannon Fraser. She first moved to the derelict village of Mowat when her husband was appointed by the receivers to take over supervision of the mill estate. Up till then, from the time when the mill ceased running, Bob Gallna had been the caretaker, and for years afterwards his name and friendly presence were recalled by old-timers pausing at Canoe Lake to look over the old mill-site. The Frasers carried on for some years, then purchased some of the old buildings for their own use, and turned the place into a flourishing holiday resort.

At first the Frasers lived in the old Gilmour hospital, up on the hill, but in 1913 they purchased the building that had been used as kitchen and boarding house for the mill hands, back in the days when Mowat had been a thriving village. Then, in addition to their post office duties, the Frasers opened up a boarding house for summer visitors. Mrs. Fraser turned out to be such a successful manager that in the following year, the old company storehouse was bought and fixed up to take care of expanding business. These two buildings became known as Mowat Lodge. In 1920, the original buildings were destroyed by fire, but until then, Shannon Fraser's was a favourite place for Park visitors. Shannon was a jovial soul with a gift for playing up a good story, and his wife was an excellent soul and a kindly one, who knew how to cook. Many a Park visitor today, who once slept and ate under the roof of Mowat Lodge, remembers the sociability and the food of the Frasers.

Sometimes Shannon found it difficult to get people for help at the post office or boarding house, and would persuade his guests to stay on and work for him for a while. Tom Thomson always headed for the Frasers when he came to the Park, and often helped out; usually as a guide for fishing parties, but often, especially in the spring and fall, he would turn his hand to anything, from drying the dishes for Mrs. Fraser, to patching the roof for her husband.

One of the standing jokes in the Canoe Lake community was Shannon Fraser's optimism about the number of guests he expected on the next train. His neighbours loved to ask him how many guests he was going to pick up, whenever they saw him on his way to the station, driving along the old mill road.

"A big party comin' in today," he would invariably tell them. Returning later with an empty wagon and a broad grin on his face, he would explain: "I guess they must have missed that one."

From all accounts, Shannon had his troubles with some of the Canoe Lake residents who worked for him off and on. Two of these, George Rowe and Larry Dickson, were well known to Dr. Bertram, Mr. Hayhurst, and other summer cottagers who came into the district after 1906. Rowe and Dickson lived in little shacks on the old mill property, and made some extra money in the summer by acting as guides for Park fishing parties. Larry's cottage, up on the hill near the site of the old hospital, later became famous as the subject for Tom Thomson's "Larry Dickson's Shack", now in the National Gallery of Canada at Ottawa.

Apparently both of these men, in spite of Park regulations, used to take a drop too much. When that happened, Shannon's business would suffer and he would fire them. It made things difficult for Shannon. In a written complaint to Mr. Bartlett, he asserted that someone had given George Rowe "licker", with the result that "the missis had to take the mail". Before long, however, all would be forgiven and forgotten, and George and Larry would be back at work till it happened again. Incidentally, these two handymen must have been fairly tough: Larry Dickson once told Mr. Hayhurst that he swore by horse liniment as a cure-all; any time you wanted to clean up a hang-over, he would tell the summer visitor, all you had to do was just take a few drops on a lump of sugar!

When the original Mowat Lodge burned down, the Frasers built another hotel by the lakeshore, on the site of the old sawmill. That, too, was burned in 1930, and the family moved out, first to Kearney, and afterwards to Huntsville. By this time, the post office name had been changed from Mowat to Canoe Lake, and was taken over by the clerk of a lumber company working nearby. Mr. Everett Farley succeeded him as postmaster. Today Mowat and Mowat Lodge are only names; but always, for old-timers, they will be names whose memories will be all the warmer for the sojourn of the Frasers at Canoe Lake.

In the twenties and thirties numerous other camps, lodges and hotels, were opened up. Some of these will be mentioned to show how well distributed such accommodation has become in the Park, and how accessible the Park now is to visitors by road and railway.

On the Canadian National Line between North Bay and Ottawa, near Government Park Station, stands Kish-Kaduk Lodge, opened by Mr. and Mrs. Edward Thomas in 1928. Mr. Thomas worked for the railroad both north and south of the Park previous to this venture. The new King's Highway No. 60 gives access to Opeongo Lodge at Sproule Bay, opened in 1934 by Mr. and Mrs. Joe Avery, winter residents of Whitney. This lodge is a favourite haunt of those who come to fish on Opeongo Lake. Just opposite the highway, on Lake of Two Rivers, at a point commanding a fine view of the lake and surrounding hills, is Killarney Lodge, built by Mr. and Mrs. B. W. Moore in 1935. Guests for the Arowhon Pines, an adult camp for parents of young Arowhon campers, and others, travel north by launch from the highway at Portage Creek — or from Joe Lake railway station — to Baby Joe Lake. This camp was opened by Mrs. M. Kates of Toronto in 1942.

When George Bartlett retired as Park Superintendent in 1923, his son, Mr. Alfred Bartlett, opened a lodge on Cache Lake opposite Park Headquarters, making use of the old buildings there, and adding others. Bartlett Lodge has entertained many family holiday groups and fishing parties since that date. Mr. Bartlett tells a story of how the local beavers co-operated with him to display their skill to some of his guests. Two of these guests were particularly anxious to see a beaver at work cutting down a tree. They had seen the animals swim past the lodge dock each evening just at sundown, but they had yet to see one in the act of tree felling. Mr. Bartlett, like his father, was a man of action, and went to work. During the afternoon he selected and cut down a healthy young specimen of the beavers' favourite food — a small white birch — and moored it upright in the water just out from the shore by means of guy-lines. That night, the visitors were close at hand when the beavers swam by on their nightly cruise. But when they sighted the tree growing in such an unusual place they stopped, swam in to investigate, and then without stopping to enquire who had placed this tasty banquet in such a convenient spot, got busy and cut it down. It was a sad blow for them when they discovered they could not tow their prize away, and had to go home without it. The next day the shortened tree was set in place as before, the guests took up their places again, and the beavers obliged with a second performance. On the third night, what was left of the tree was up again. The beavers swam up, took one look at the pitiful remnants — and probably another disdainful look toward their audience — and swam sedately on their way without so much as a nibble. What did these visitors think they were, anyway, cheap entertainers?

Not all the lodges in the Park are devoted to pure holidaying, however. The unique camp already mentioned as occupying the former Minnesing Hotel was begun in 1923 by Dr. Henry B. Sherman of Carmel, California, a retired scientist of repute, who decided to devote his life to a study of the records of the life of Jesus as set forth in the four Gospels. In 1925, Dr. Sherman's group moved into the old log cabin Hotel Minnesing, purchased from the management of Highland Inn. There, in the solitude of the Algonquin wilderness, classes and discussions are carried on each morning until one o'clock, then the rest of the day is free for the enjoyment of the lakes and woods, and for conversation with others of this stimulating group of students. Inspiration and instruction gained in this seminary is taken out to every corner of the world, by men and women who go forth to their chosen professions in America, in Europe, and in the Far East.

All these resorts have been built by private individuals, on sites leased from the Government for that purpose, but of recent years, the Department of Lands and Forests has taken steps to assist in making provisions for visitors who wish to holiday in the Park. When the highway was constructed, a large camp-site was set aside at Lake of Two Rivers for an auto-camp. Family parties sometimes make this their headquarters for several weeks at a time, since the fine sandy beach is ideal for youngsters. Visitors from far distant parts come to this spot to pitch their tents and to enjoy an Algonquin Park holiday.

Doubtless, in years to come, new lodges will open, and new living conveniences provided in conformity with Park standards. But the most significant development of summer life in Algonquin Park has yet to be mentioned: there were some far-seeing people who believed that the Park should offer even more than fresh air, sunshine, good fishing, glimpses of wild life, and contemplation in seclusion. There, as the reader will see, developed a new idea in summer holiday life.

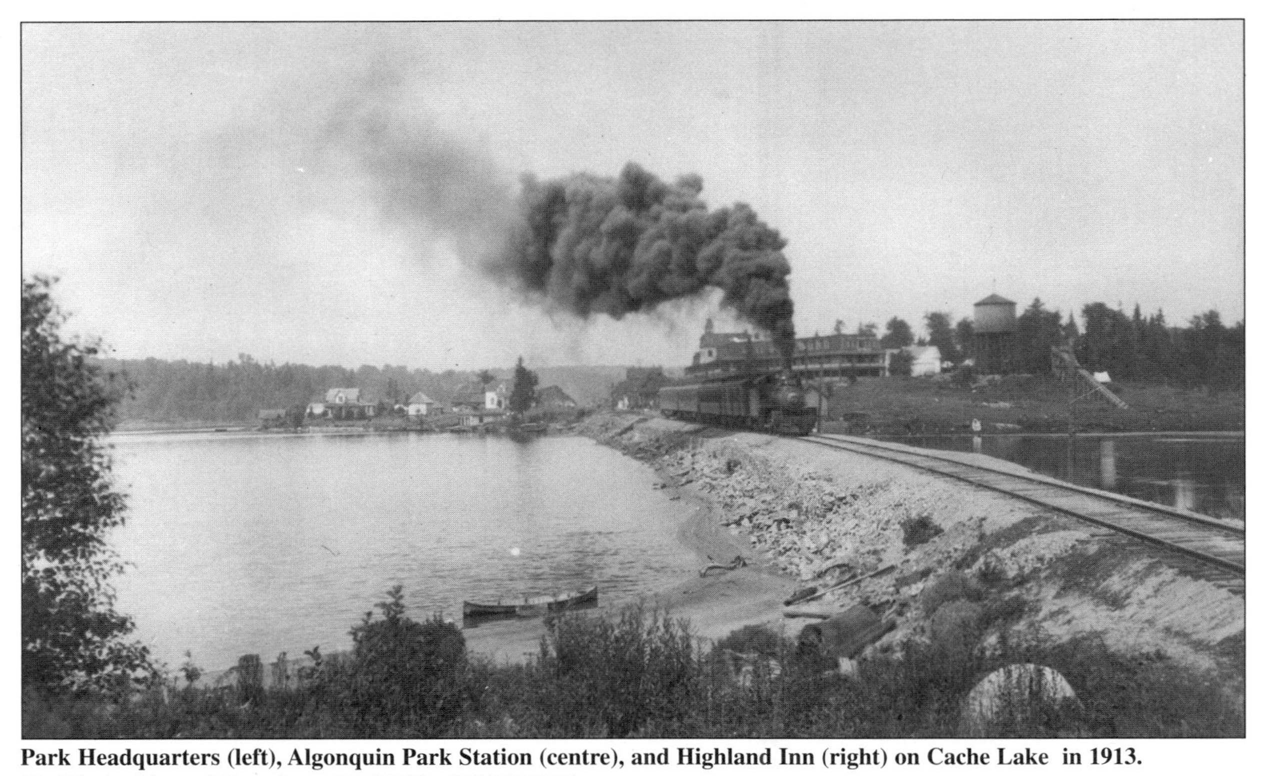

**Park Headquarters (left), Algonquin Park Station (centre), and Highland Inn (right) on Cache Lake in 1913.**
(*Public Archives of Canada — PA-10570; APM # 3877*)

**Algonquin Hotel on Joe Lake in 1922.** *(Ministry of Natural Resources; APM # 620)*

## CHAPTER 12

THE NEW IDEA, like all other new ideas, had its roots in old. From the beginning of the century, men like the late Sir Robert Baden-Powell in Britain, and the late Ernest Thompson Seton in America, had been sponsoring a new kind of education, based on the feeling that the formal schools took too little account of the primitive kinship with nature common to all young people.

The hotels and lodges in the Park catered largely to adults, who determined their own forms of amusement. Boys' and girls' camps in Algonquin Park were to develop a unique kind of camp program based partly on the tendencies mentioned above, but even more on the environment of the Park itself.

Not a few of the early camp visitors, urged on by the lure of distant fishing spots, or the fascination of the faraway, had left the comfort of hotels and lodges to sleep under canvas, and paddle along the water highways of the Park.

An example of this type of visitor occurs in one of Mark Robinson's favourite stories, incidental to telling how he met the famous Tom Salmon. Tom Salmon, he would explain on the rare occasions when it was necessary, was an old-time Lake of Bays trapper so well known as a snowshoe expert, that he was once commissioned to make snowshoes for an Arctic expedition. As a fly-fisherman, he was looked upon as a top-ranking expert by rangers and Park visitors alike. However, for the present purposes, Tom Salmon is incidental. Mark's own words tell of the visitor, and how through him he realized his own ambition of seeing Tom Salmon in action.

> "This happened during old Mr. Bartlett's time when I was stationed at the Cache Lake rangers' house. For several days I had been away from headquarters on a trip out into Canisbay Township with a timber cruiser. The weather was hot and when we finally flagged a freight train to take us and our canoe back home, I was tired out.
>
> "No sooner had I stepped off the train at Park Headquarters than I heard someone say, 'There's Robinson

now'. Immediately an Englishman — you wouldn't mistake him anywhere — stepped up to me and said, 'You'll do!' I didn't know what he was talking about, and since I was hot and tired and wanted nothing better than a wash and chance to finish the report of what we had been doing, I told him that I wasn't free. He simply repeated, 'You'll do!' and I walked off. Then, because I thought I'd better find out what it was all about, I called in to see Mr. Bartlett. He explained that he was an English writer who was travelling across Canada and who wanted to be taken on a fishing trip. Mr. Bartlett said not to bother about his insistence that we start before noon, but to go ahead and finish my other job first. He said that I would find him an interesting person if I went on a trip with him.

"When we started after dinner we were provided with plenty of grub and with a seventeen-foot birch bark canoe. Once more I flagged a freight and it set us down seven miles along the line at Canoe Lake. By this time I had found out that my companion's name was Joseph Adams, and that he really did know something about fishing. I think he was supposed to be one of the champion fly-casters in England — at any rate, as he showed us later, he was very good.

"That night we camped at the island in Canoe Lake where Taylor Statten's camp is now, and the next morning we went on down through Tea Lake into the Oxtongue River. Since it was towards the end of July, I knew the water was too warm for trout in most places, but that we stood a good chance of getting some where the main course was joined by a small stream that would bring in a fresh supply of cold water. In spite of my knowledge of the district, Mr. Adams was sure that he knew better than I did about the best places to cast his fly. 'I've fished in almost every country except Canada', he kept saying, 'and I always like a little riffle on the surface of the water'. If that 'riffle' was there he would try the spot, if not, he would pass it by. I'll say this much for him, though — he certainly was an expert at casting. He could bring his fly down on the exact spot where he wished it to land — it was beautiful to see.

"When we reached the Whiskey Rapids he seemed a little nervous of going down them in a canoe. 'Is it safe, Ewie?' he asked (he had told me at the beginning of our trip that he would call me 'Ewie' if I didn't mind because Robinson was such a long name). 'Is it safe, Ewie?' he repeated. I told him that he could get out and walk along the bank if he wished, but that I intended to stay in the canoe. He decided to save himself a wetting, as he put it, and I was waiting for him by the time he arrived at the end of the path. 'You went through very lightly', was all he said, but I noticed that he never got out of the canoe again.

"Finally he decided to give up for that day. He had had very bad luck but it was his own fault. Every time I would suggest a likely spot he would say, 'Ewie I've fished in all the important waters of the world except Canada and I know you'll never catch a fish there'. We stopped that night in the old shelter house at Camp Four. The rangers had taken it over when the lumber companies moved out.

"Next morning, when we started out again, I decided that the best place for us to try was Salmon's Pool farther down the river. I knew that Tom Salmon had driven a balsam pole into the mud at the bottom of this pool and had found that it was fourteen feet deep. There would be fish there if there were any at all in the river. When we reached the place where the pole was sticking up, I caught hold of it to steady the canoe and told Mr. Adams to try his luck. Once again he protested, 'Oh, no, Ewie, we'll never catch anything there'.

"Well, I was getting tired of this attitude, so I decided that at least we'd give the spot a try. I hooked my leg over the pole and announced that here we would stay. Mr. Adams looked at me in surprise, but I just stared back silently. For about two minutes neither of us spoke, and then I knew that I had won out. 'All right,

Ewie', he said, 'if we must fish here you shall make the choice of the flies that we shall use'.

"Now that put me on the spot, because the chap had a a whole book full of flies and I didn't know one from the other. However, I was not to be outdone and I started to thumb through his collection. As we had come down stream I had noticed that the trout seemed to be rising to a little mauve midge that floated on the surface of the water, so I picked out one that looked something like that. 'A very good choice', remarked my companion, 'now pick out two others'. I selected a March Brown which I knew would often draw trout, and one other. He proceeded to tie all three on the leaders at once. I've said before that this man knew how to cast, and no sooner had the flies touched the water than there were two on, both at once.

"The problem was how to land them. 'May I stand up?' Adams asked, and since I had my leg around the post I told him to go ahead. I offered to lend a hand, but no, he was determined to finish the job himself. The result was that these two got away. Later, however, he hooked two others and this time he handled the landing net like a veteran, holding it in one hand and the rod in the other. He was pleased with himself, for the fish were beauties, and we stayed where we were all day long. Once he had a triple catch and he landed them all — not one of them was under twelve inches long. Finally, when he had thirteen, he decided it was time to go back to camp. As we returned he remarked with a happy sigh, 'My cap is full'.

"But that wasn't the end of our good fortune. Since we had a good supply of grub we decided to stay over for another day to try out our luck again. That night we played host to a couple of fellows who had lost their grub when their canoe upset. Adams admitted to them that he had had most remarkable fishing. 'It took some effort to persuade me', he said, 'but it certainly was *most* unusual'. On the next day we had the good fortune to fall in with Tom Salmon himself. He had been off on a trip with some of the members of his family and we stopped to compare our luck.

"Well, the two men got talking — you'll remember that Tom was a famous fly fisherman, too, and they decided to have a contest to prove which one was the more skilful. I'd often heard that Tom had been taught to cast in England, that he could cast while standing with his back against a barn door. That day we certainly saw something that I'll never forget. Tom's daughter and I were to act as judges. Our job was to float chips of wood down stream to test their accuracy. I've never seen anything like it — both of them could land their flies right on the chips — just as neatly as you please, and at ninety feet. As far as I could see there was no difference between the two fishermen, although my sympathy was naturally with the local man. Finally the two shook hands and we set off on the return trip.

"We had been gone four days when we finally got back to headquarters, and by that time Mr. Adams was convinced that Algonquin Park was as fine a place for fishing as he had ever seen. I don't know whether you'll see anything about this in the book he wrote, but there's one thing certain, he knew how to fish, and Salmon's pool had the fish to give him."

Joseph Adams returned to England in 1912 and published a book entitled "Ten Thousand Miles Through Canada", which was sufficiently popular to pass into a second edition within a month of its publication. It contained a twenty-five page chapter on "The Trip to Algonquin National Park", with an account of this same incident that tallies for the most part with Mark Robinson's version.

Other early visitors like Adams left the hotels and lodges to camp in the choicest spots of the Park. Some of them travelled out of a pure love of movement, paddling through the day, and pitching their tent at night wherever they found themselves, recapturing the charm of the life of the old voyageurs, and of later canoe trippers like surveyor Dickson. To these the Park revealed the innermost secrets of its nature.

Significantly, a few of them took their families on these trips, and unconsciously led the way for a new wide sphere of activity within the Park. Dr. Lester Scott was one of these, and how rich were his rewards will be seen in the final chapter of this book. Gradually, the idea grew that the ideal way of enjoying the Park was through camp life in its wildest parts, and that even small children could share this life under experienced care.

As early as 1908, a stout-hearted pioneer in women's education, Fanny L. Case, of Rochester, New York, appeared in Algonquin Park with a group of American girls, and the firm conviction that classroom walls were not the ideal background for the learning process. Superintendent Bartlett's eyes would undoubtedly have dropped open with amazement but for the fact that he knew she was coming. During the previous two summers, Miss Case had already taken a group of students north to the Magnetewan River with such success, that she decided to establish a permanent camping headquarters in Canada. When she approached Mr. Bartlett with the idea, he welcomed it with enthusiasm; and so the Northway Lodge campers spent their first summer at Cache Lake.

Campers and leaders alike were pioneers at that first camp. Miss Case had brought with her from the United States an expert swimming counsellor, a musician, a craftsman, a naturalist, a nurse and a cook, but none of these had had previous experience in living under canvas in the Canadian wilds. From Ernest Finlayson, who had worked in the Park previously, and who had just graduated in forestry at the University of Toronto, they learned the camping arts. As Miss Case recalled in later years, "His knowledge of growing things, his enthusiasm, and integrity of character, made him for us the ideal guide."

Under Ernest Finlayson's direction, a programme of canoe trips was set up. This scheme proved to be so successful that it has been the basis for Northway Lodge trips up to the present time. Elsewhere in Canada, and in the United States, canoe trips had been looked upon as too strenuous an occupation for girls' groups, but Mr. Finlayson made himself responsible for drawing up rules and instructions to safeguard the health and welfare of all taking part in these excursions. Canoe trips were popular from the first, and they rapidly became the very core of camp life. Food lists were tacked up on the walls of the Picnic House, while regulations were laid down about the packing of supplies and the loads to be carried by each girl. Day outings, and canoe trips, became the acme of the camping experience.

The Northway camp site was in a rugged state when the campers took over in the summer of 1908. During that year, everyone had such a good time helping to put things into shape, that Miss Case decided that half the fun in camping came through having to fend for oneself. Throughout the years, she has tried to preserve that aspect of camping. That first summer the campers helped Mark Robinson, then newly appointed to the Park Staff, and some of the other rangers, to clear the fallen logs and underbrush from the point. Campers and staff chose the spots for their tents so that each would command a view of one particularly fine section of the lake or woodlands, and they named each tent according to the location chosen for it. These names were handed down by the first occupants to those who followed in succeeding years, so that even now most of the seventeen tents at the camp still bear their original titles. Tents, as sleeping quarters, have been retained until the present time, but other buildings have been erected as the need arose. Always, Miss Case has tried to interfere as little as possible with the natural beauty of the campsite.

Before long several boys' camps were established, but these were replaced in time, and only Northway has a continuous history from early days down to the present.

To-day, at Northway Lodge, the morning work hour has always been one of the camp traditions. Although in other things the camp schedule is kept as flexible as possible, this period is set aside each day as a time that is spent in an activity assigned to improve some aspect of the camp as a whole. Sometimes the project is a big one, such as the construction of a craft cabin or a sleeping hut in the woods, sometimes it is the repairing of canoes, or the chopping of wood. All the tasks are undertaken in a fine spirit of co-operation, so that the workers feel that they are making a valuable contribution to the good of the Northway community. In this way the campers' initiative and skill is brought out, while at the same time their loyalty to the camp and their pride in their forest home is fostered.

One attitude that Miss Case has tried to stress at Northway Lodge all through the years, has been the point of view that camping is "well spent leisure". Always, she has felt that the girls should find in the Park, sufficient time to carry on the activities that they are unable to perform in the city. Paddling, swimming, and nature rambles, play a large part in the the camp program, while fine musicians on the staff lead in evening musicales. Campers have come to realize that the knowledge they have gained at Northway Lodge in the constructive use of leisure time, has provided a basis for full and spontaneous living, then, and in after years.

Writing of this camp, Miss Case has set forth her own feelings on the success of the Northway experiment:

> "We could not have anticipated the degree of lasting joy and satisfaction which many a camper, almost all, has found in this way of life. These results have been expressed in chance meetings, sometimes after twenty years or more, and by the presence of daughters of former campers who have joined us at Northway Lodge. The connections through the years with many fine people, both assistants and campers, have brought rewards to those responsible and the camp is a composite of these contributions."

Most of the early camps for boys were "school camps", run in conjunction with particular schools in the United States. Such were the short-lived Long Trail Camp for boys at Joe Lake, and Professor G. G. Bowers' Waubeno Camp on Cache Lake.

Mr. George Bartlett wrote numerous articles for nature magazines during his tenure of office, and in one of these describes a day with the boys of Camp Minnewawa, the camp school of Bordentown Military Institute, New Jersey, on Lake of Two Rivers. Under Professor W. L. Wise, boys from this school came up to Algonquin every summer between the years 1911 and 1930. According to Mr. Bartlett, a group of twelve boys returning from a day's outing, came upon a mother beaver and her three kittens. They paddled their canoes silently closer, but the mother heard and, slapping her tail on the water to warn the young ones, dived beneath the surface. Two of the kittens followed, the third stayed up. The boys gave chase, caught up with it, and lifted the little animal into the canoe. Evidently there was something wrong with him. They decided to take him in to camp and call a council to decide what to do next.

The next morning, some of them paddled this little friend Pat, as they now called him, up to Park Headquarters to give him to the Superintendent. Mr. Bartlett gave the boys a little talk on the beaver and its habits, then arranged for a lady at one of the nearby cottages to take Pat and see if she could nurse him back to health. The boys learned about the engineering skill of the beaver, about the construction of his house, about the young who are born with all their teeth and their eyes wide open, how the castor is used for perfume, and how in the old days, Hudson's Bay Company employees used to serve them stuffed instead of turkey for Christmas dinner. Finally, they were sent on their way with the Superintendent's concluding moral:

"Boys, we could learn a lot from the beaver. He never gives up once he starts a job, no matter how difficult it may prove". To finish off the story, it must be added regrettfully that little Pat did not respond to treatment, and was buried near his own kin at the edge of a neighbouring marsh.

The second oldest camp in the Park is Camp Pathfinder, at Source Lake, which has been running ever since the first year of World War I. In the spring of 1914, two residents of Rochester, both teachers, formed a partnership to establish a camp. Franklin Gray, a native of Barrie, Ontario, who taught physical education in Rochester, was one of the pair, and came up to the Park to pick the site. After a wide search, they decided on the island in Source Lake, for its accessibility to the railway line, its vantage point for canoe expeditions, and its isolation from other Park settlements. In the first camping season the following year, eighteen boys enrolled. This number was increased to twenty-four and twenty-eight in the next two years. In 1917, because of the ill-health of his partner, Mr. Bennett, Mr. Gray took over full ownership. It was in that year that the present owner and director, Mr. Herman J. Norton, first visited Camp Pathfinder. Between 1918 and 1925 he and Mr. Gray were joint owners, but since that time Mr. Norton has held the sole interest in the camp.

Under Mr. Norton, the "Chief", as the boys at Pathfinder call him, the camp has carried on a wide and varied programme. The staff is made up of experts in many different fields, in order to provide the finest leadership that can be procured. Mr. Norton has made sure that each camper is taught carefully all the skills and crafts necessary to make him secure and self-sufficient in the camp situation. Through the years a credit system of awards has been developed, to encourage each boy to strive for success in both camp activities and on the trail. Before any camper may leave headquarters on a canoe trip, he must pass rigid tests that cover swimming ability, canoe tipping and righting, and trip knowledge. The expert canoemanship of the Pathfinder campers who traverse the district in their red canoes, is well known to other trippers who have encountered parties in remote corners of the Park.

Slowly, the idea was developing. First-hand knowledge of woodcraft and canoe-tripping, as a means of developing initiative and self-reliance, came to be the keynote of Algonquin camps.

With the first Canadian camp organized by Taylor Statten of Toronto, the further idea of reviving native handicrafts developed, even to the point of re-enacting under the fascinated eyes of teen-age boys, an anciently familiar scene under Algonquin skies: the construction of a birch-bark canoe.

The story of how Camp Ahmek, at Canoe Lake, came into being, is worth telling. During the summer of 1912, Colonel J. J. Gartshore had camped for several weeks with his own boys and girls on Big Wapomeo Island. When he heard that the Statten family was looking for a place for a holiday, he suggested that they take over his equipment, which had not yet been removed from the Park. Mr. and Mrs. Statten were so delighted with their Canoe Lake visit that they made arrangements during the next winter, while staying at Highland Inn, to lease Little Wapomeo Island for their own summer home.

To their island in Canoe Lake came many friends for camping holidays, and the enthusiasm of members of this group began to lead into a new development. For several weeks, in the summer of 1917, a group of men interested in Y.M.C.A. work camped on the island, to develop the Canadian Standard Efficiency Tests for boys. The programme initiated at this gathering became the official programme for boys' work of several Protestant churches under the name Tuxis Boys and Trail Rangers.

A second camp was held in 1920, under the auspices of the Boys' Work Committee of the National Council of the Y.M.C.A., intended as a centre for training leaders for the Tuxis Boys and Trail Rangers organization. To it were invited some one hundred and thirty boys' work leaders, from all sections of Canada. It is not possible here to mention all the important boys' work executives present at this important event; but of the prominent Canadians invited to give instruction in natural history, some significant names were: Professor J. W. Crow of the Ontario Agricultural College, C. A. Chant, Professor of Astronomy at the University of Toronto, W. D. Hobson of Woodstock, Jack Miner from Kingsville, Dr. W. E. Saunders of London, and Stuart L. Thompson from Toronto.

As part of their training in campcraft, staff and students alike lived in tents pitched on the shores of Canoe Lake, where the present Camp Ahmek is located. This was a new experience for many of the group, and their initiation into camp life was not made any easier by the fact that it rained continuously for the whole day on which they were setting up camp. However, the work party was revived by hot coffee and sandwiches, prepared in advance by Mrs. Statten and some of the women at Mowat Lodge. By nightfall, everyone had a shelter over his head. The camp had been designed as a training ground for future camping leaders, and the experience gained at this time had far-reaching effects on camping in many different parts of Canada and the United States.

Two of those who had taken part in the 1920 camp returned in the following year, when Taylor Statten established his own camp for boys at the Canoe Lake campsite. C. E. (Chick) Hendry, and George Chubb were at Camp Ahmek during that season, and both returned for many subsequent camping seasons. "Chubby", as the latter is affectionately called, has continued as business manager of the Taylor Statten Camps until the present time. Dr. Frank Wood, of Toronto, was co-director with Taylor Statten at this first boys' camp.

The first season at Camp Ahmek brought its own problems, and many are the stories of difficulties encountered, and overcome, at that time. One of these stories has to do with how Pete Sauve came on the staff as camp cook. Pete's predecessor at Ahmek was a man who did not like bears. Now the Canoe Lake bears had discovered that the camp storehouse could furnish them with supplies gratis. The cook was continually complaining about these raids, and he threatened to pack up and leave if some steps were not taken to get rid of these visitors. Finally, one day after train-time, Taylor Statten learned that the worst had happened — the previous night a bear had clawed his way right into the cook's own tent. This was the last straw; the cook de-camped, and it was necessary to search for a new man to take over the job. Fortunately, at that moment, Pete Sauve stepped into the breach. Pete had been in the Canoe Lake district off and on since the time when he first cooked for the Gilmour Lumber Company, some twenty-five years before. His good-natured disposition, and his ability to make first-class pies, soon made him a favorite with staff and campers alike. Pete Sauve has continued as an Ahmek institution to the present time.

In 1934, after the boys' camp had been running for three years, the companion camp, Wapomeo, was established for girls by Mrs. Taylor Statten. Camp Wapomeo's first season was spent on Little Wapomeo Island, where there was sufficient room for the forty-five girls who made up the first group. However, the camp soon outgrew its original quarters, and in 1927 the site was moved to Big Wapomeo Island. A further expansion was made possible in 1937, when Senior Wapomeo Island was included in the camp property. In addition, the girls were able to use certain facilities, such as the riding stables on the mainland. At the present time the two Statten Camps have control of four islands in Canoe Lake, and stretch along about a mile of the shoreline of the bay on which Camp Ahmek was first located. Each year about four hundred and fifty boys and girls, as well as a staff of two hundred young men and women, spend the summer months at these camps in the Park.

Camp Wapomeo and Camp Ahmek have been called a brother and sister type of camp, and in this way they differ from other Park camps. While each camp has its own headquarters, and its own staff, there are a number of activities in which campers from both units join. Under the supervision of their counsellors, sailing races, swimming and canoe regattas, musicales, plays, concerts, circuses, and many other programs, can be shared by the two groups. In this way, campers from both camps, and their leaders, have an opportunity to work and play with members of the opposite sex in the healthy atmosphere of the camp environment.

This co-educational feature is carried into the September camp, held each autumn at Camp Ahmek. Here, camp leaders, former campers, their families and their friends, gather each year in an adult camp for several weeks. The full facilities of the camp are made available to these young people who have learned the Algonquin Park way of life, through many visits to the region.

Two outgrowths of the Taylor Statten Camps are worth noting here as having affected camping activities in other parts of the world. In 1929, a book, "Camp and Character", was published by H. S. Dimock and C. E. Hendry as the result of four years of experimental work conducted at Ahmek and Wapomeo. This book has been used widely since that time as a textbook for courses in camping, given in many different parts of the United States and Canada. Another outcome of the work at these camps was the establishment of a camp for boys and girls near Madras, India, set up by the Taylor Statten Camps, and directed by Wallace Forgie.

Guests at Camp Ahmek are always curious to know why the main dining hall is decorated with a series of very large posters that ornament both sides of the long room. When they ask about their significance, they learn that each depicits the most outstanding event of one camping season. The younger campers are always delighted to regale the visitor with the whole history of the camp, by recounting the story that lies behind each picture.

From the "Chief" himself, as Taylor Statten is known to campers, counsellors, and visitor alike, we learned what lay behind the scenes set forth in two of the most unusual posters. Actually, the two pictures must be taken together because, before you can understand about Lord Willingdon's narrow escape, you must know about the visit which the Bishop of Birmingham had paid to the camp in the previous year.

The most outstanding event for the year 1930 appears to have been the visit of the Bishop of Birmingham to Algonquin Park. The poster for that year shows him in complete regalia. His full-faced portrait reveals a very large gentleman, wearing the traditional bishop's hat and "dog-collar". Certainly, His Grace, the Bishop of Birmingham, did pay a state visit to the camp, the campers did receive him with due respect and reverence, but before his departure — however, that would spoil the first half of the story. It is sufficient at this point to say that word reached camp that the Bishop of Birmingham, and a group of English friends, were touring Canada, and would very much like to have an opportunity of seeing how young Canadians disported themselves in the northern woodlands. They hoped that it would not inconvenience the camp authorities if they paid a visit to Canoe Lake in the immediate future.

On the appointed day the guests arrived by train, and were welcomed to the camp by speeches delivered in the dining hall at noon. The party was made up of His Grace, the Bishop of Birmingham, his friend and travelling companion, the Earl of Essex, and Jeeves, their personal servant and butler. All day long these eminent gentlemen toured the camp, seeing all the regular activities, and making suitable remarks about the wonders of the Canadian scene. By nightfall the campers were becoming more and more suspicious, but they waited until morning to take their revenge.

In the morning, the Bishop and his entourage were transported in state across the lake to see the girls' camp, Wapomeo. They travelled on the pirate ship, which was towed by one of the camp launches. But the girls had been forewarned — and the phoney Bishop of Birmingham, a Toronto friend of the Chief's, was dumped overboard, together with his practical joke, into the cleansing waters of Canoe Lake.

But the strange thing about the posters in the Ahmek dining hall is that the Bishop of Birmingham appears smiling and serene in the 1930 edition, but it is the gentleman of the next year, 1931, who appears to be falling into the lake. When he asks about this unfortunate personage, garbed in morning coat and tall silk hat, the visitor is amazed to learn that he is none other than the former Governor-

General, the King's representative in Canada, Lord Willingdon himself. As you look at the picture for a second time, you find that he is not quite *in* the water, he seems to be sitting on top of it. Then you learn how he was saved from an ignominous ducking in an Algonquin Park lake.

In 1931, the campers had been told once again that they were to be honoured with a visit from one of the great of the land. Once more they had been informed that this visitor wanted to see how the young people of Canada worked and played in Algonquin forests; and this time they, too, would have a share in the fun. This time they would not wait until the second day. Even before the visitor arrived, they had their plans carefully worked out. They would receive the gentleman with all politeness and deference. Then, at the first opportune moment, they would toss the so-called Governor-General into the lake.

Fortunately, for the Governor-General, and for the campers, too, the Chief got wind of this carefully prepared scheme. He and his staff did their best to persuade the campers that this really was a visit from the Vice-Regal party — but they were not convinced. They had been fooled once, and they were not going to be caught again.

When the day of the official visit dawned, the camp leaders were not too sure what the outcome would be. They had warned the campers that everyone must be on his best behaviour, but they had the uncomfortable feeling that the plan might be put into action in spite of their precautions. As an added measure of safety, a special bodyguard of trusty seniors was assigned the task of watching over the safety of their distinguished visitor.

Lord Willingdon must have acted his part to the full satisfaction of the campers; one shudders to think what one little gesture might have cost him. To the intense relief of the camp directors, the visit passed without incident. The Governor-General liked the camp, and the campers approved of him. That is why the Ahmek poster for the year 1931, shows the tall gentleman in formal attire, within a hair's breadth of being ducked below the waves of Canoe Lake.

It is unfair, in a Park where dozens of excellent camps exist, all featuring canoe trips and the outdoor life, that only a few should be described in detail.

Camp Tanamakoon, for instance, deserves a chapter by itself. This first Canadian girls' camp was organized in 1925 by Miss Mary G. Hamilton, Principal of Margaret Eaton School in Toronto. Tanamakoon Lake, then called White Lake, was an ideal place for such a camp. The camp stands on the shore of a sheltered bay with a sandy bottom. The lake is small, with an old lumber camp clearing nearby that is ideal for riding. Here, in close relation with training courses in physical education at the University of Toronto, young women specialists in that subject learn the value of outdoor life, and go out to all parts of Canada as leaders in camp and health activities. A lodge, theatre, infirmary, craftshop, workshop, offices, cabins, and tents, all contribute their share to the varied activities.

Tanamakoon campers have learned, by bitter experience, that stories about the proverbial curiosity of bears have a foundation in fact. Some time ago, the camp adopted the habit of allowing canoe trippers to make use of canoes that had been left for them at the end of some of the longer portages on their regular routes. These canoes were simply turned over on the ground, and the camp authorities felt sure that in the Park, where people are accustomed to respect one another's property, they would be perfectly safe. However, what was the dismay of one group that had counted on using such a canoe, when they found that a passer-by had deliberately landed a smashing blow on the keel of the upturned canoe, and had bashed it right in. It was not until the campers had finished their trip that they received the probable explanation of the destruction. One of the veteran guides told them that it had likely been caused by a bear, whose curiosity had gotten the better of him. Seeing this object lying in his pathway, he had taken a swipe at it to find out what lay underneath. From that time on, Tanamakoon campers followed the example of rangers and other experienced bushmen, and erected simple frameworks at the ends of the portages, in order to raise their canoes off the ground. These structures allowed wandering bears to look underneath for themselves, instead of crashing through the bottom to satisfy their thirst for knowledge.

Each week, groups of girls go out on canoe trips, and one of the sights of the Park is a flotilla of Tanamakoon canoes, rounding the bend of the lake towards the main dock on a Saturday afternoon or evening, in triumphant formation.

Camp Arowhon enjoys the distinction of being the only camp where boys and girls live on the same campsite. These are grouped into, children under five, the "independents" — between five and sixteen, and the older "privileged campers". In each age group, all possible activities are enjoyed by boys and girls together. Under Mrs. Kates and Mr. Harry Homes, the two sexes learn to take each other for granted, and establish a healthy comradeship.

The most recent addition is Camp Tamakwa, founded in 1937 by Mr. Lou H. Handler, of Detroit, a graduate in Forestry, and with broad camping experience in the States. This camp lies on the north shore of Tea Lake, and has at present accommodation for 125 campers.

Of recent years, new emphasis has been placed on other aspects of the camping programme in all the Park camps. Youth leaders have come to realize that camping provides an ideal laboratory for the training of democratic citizens. In no other situation are the same opportunities for co-operative living possible. The campers live in small units, huts, tents, or cabins, and each individual finds that he is expected to make his own contribution to the well-being of the group. For twenty-four hours a day, the camper is in an atmosphere where his own decisions will help or hinder the happiness of the group with whom he is living. Friendships made in camp are lasting ones, and the character development that takes place during the summer months, often turns a wayward, adolescent, boy or girl into a straight-thinking, responsible individual. At many of the camps, discussion groups are formed, either informally around the evening campfire, or in Sunday evening sessions, where the young people are encouraged to talk over the troubled problems of school, family, and community, that each sooner or later encounters. The campers bring to the Park a wide variety of backgrounds, and they are being encouraged to use their Algonquin holiday as a training ground for constructive thinking.

While a friendly rivalry exists between the camps, the boys and girls all found a common cause to work for when, in 1943, due to the necessities of war, the ranging staff was reduced, and a system of Junior Park Rangers was inaugurated. Mr. Maurice Kirkland, a high school teacher who had once been a ranger, worked out the details. By the middle of the following summer, every large camp was co-operating. Groups from the camps went into the adjacent regions to clear portages, to build landing docks and fireplaces, to construct shelters and camp tables. At the same time they carried on routine fire patrols, reported fires, and on several occasions extinguished small blazes that had been left by careless campers. Some of the senior boys laid out trails through the lesser known district to the west of Canoe Lake. The construction of portages to link up some thirty small lakes, made adequate fire patrol of this region possible.

Algonquin Park has gained a reputation, through the years, as

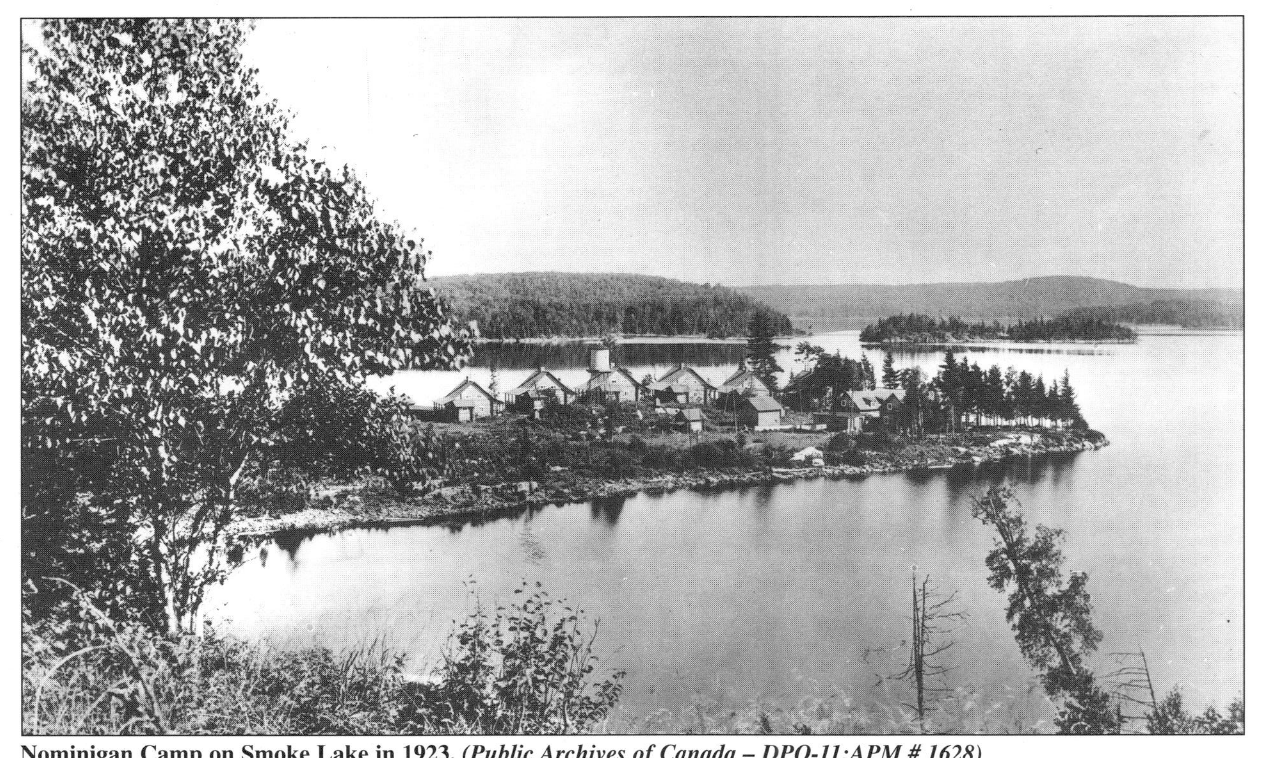

**Nominigan Camp on Smoke Lake in 1923.** *(Public Archives of Canada – DPQ-11;APM # 1628)*

**Camp Minnesing, built on Burnt Island Lake in 1913.** *(M. Pigeon; APM # 2765)*

an ideal location for summer camps. The connected chains of small lakes make canoe trips possible for young people who can manage short portages, but for whom longer carries would be injurious. The sheltering hills, and the small lake areas in the southern districts, mean that trips seldom run the risk of being storm-bound. The telephone communications, and the availability of the Park aeroplane for emergencies, safeguard the health and safety of the campers. Parents, leaders, and campers alike, appreciate these advantages that the Park has to offer.

At the same time the Park provides opportunities for real adventures in the art of living. Stripped of the artificial amusements of the city, the camper learns to fall back on more permanent pleasures. He finds the joy that comes from the performance of difficult physical feats, he learns how to make himself warm and comfortable with the minimum equipment, he learns to be self-sufficient. At the same time, he comes to appreciate the wildlife which he discovers all about him. Birds, mammals, insects, flowers, trees, the sky above, and the rocks beneath, become real, tangible, and fascinating. The Park holiday experience in camp has provided many boys and girls with a background of friendship and interest that has been carried on through life, besides fostering a spirit of international good-will with our neighbours from the United States, and from many other countries.

## CHAPTER 13

The Eight Superintendents, and the two Acting Superintendents who have been responsible for the Park, have all welcomed visitors, young and old, fully conscious of its possibilities for recreation and education. But always, their first concern has been to conserve the forests and animal life. It will be worth while here, to look back briefly over the years, to see the whole development of this vital activity since the Park's inception.

The contributions made by Superintendents Thomson, Simpson, and Bartlett, up to Mr. Bartlett's resignation in 1922, have already been noted. John W. Millar was Acting Superintendent for the following year, and was succeeded for the next year by Mark Robinson, in the same capacity. Two years passed before Mr. Millar was re-appointed as full Superintendent.

During the years when Mr. Millar was the Superintendent, the Department adopted a policy of retrenchment, so that the Park expenditures and services had to be curtailed. The official point of view seems to have been that the Park should pay for itself, and that the Department should not be expected to incur any new expenses through an expansion of its services. Mr. Bartlett had done what he could to supplement the annual budget by encouraging the rangers to trap fur-bearing animals for the Department's fur sale in Toronto, but when this practice was abandoned, there was a general feeling that expenditures on salaries and Park administration should be cut down as much as posssible.

For this reason, the period of the 1920's appears, in retrospect, to have been unprogressive. True, certain innovations were made during that time. Telephone communications were improved, boys' and girls' camps encouraged, and some new provisions were made for the benefit of tourists. But on the whole, very few changes were made in the Park. The Superintendent's annual reports reflect this inertia, since they become simply a catalogue of the number of rangers on the staff, the number of poachers convicted, and the extent of damage done by fire during the current year to the Park's forests.

Alexander Kirkwood's emphasis on an active policy of planned forest conservation had never been taken very seriously by the

Government, least of all in the 'twenties. But 1930 brought a significant change. With Mr. Millar's transfer to the head office of the Department of Lands and Forests, a new Superintendent was appointed.

J. H. McDonald was a trained graduate in Forestry and District Forester of Pembroke, a post now combined with the Superintendency. After his unfortunate death a year later another Forestry Graduate, Frank A. MacDougall, took his place.

The Park became a beehive of activity, reminiscent of the early days under Bartlett. The old concept of fire protection gave way to the active principle of prevention. For the first time, the Park Rangers combined their Park duties with fire ranging, which until now had been looked after by a separate staff. Assistant rangers were taken on for the fire season, an activity that gave seasonal employment to men of neighbouring villages, particularly Killaloe.

At Brent, Achray, and Whitney, new headquarters were built, and four Deputy Chief Rangers appointed for each quarter of the Park. A handsome building was erected at Achray in particular, of local stone; two rangers, MacFarlane and Mooney, happening to be expert stone mason and carpenter, respectively. For the first time aeroplanes soared over the Algonquin forests on regular fire patrol duty. Where Thomson once took twenty-two days to cross the Park in 1902, MacDougall could circle the entire area in two and a half hours. A rangers' hall and hangar were added to the buildings at Cache Lake: later another large hangar was built for the first Park plane — a Fairchild three-place machine with an open cockpit.

The Park telephone system has undergone great expansion and improvement since it was first inaugurated by Superintendent Bartlett, in 1911. In that year he obtained permission from the Grand Trunk Railroad to make use of their telegraph poles along the Southern Railway, for a telephone system that would link up the rangers in that district with Park Headquarters. With this improvement he was able to get in touch with the rangers at Rock Lake, Lake of Two Rivers, Joe Lake and Rainy (Rain) Lake, in order to give and to receive messages. The immediate value of this contact became apparent, because information connected with the prevention of trapping, with fire control, and with rescue work, could be transmitted quickly and accurately along the wires. When the Canadian Northern Railroad was constructed through the northern part of the Park in 1914, Mr. Bartlett arranged for their telegraph poles to be used for a line that would provide communication between rangers stationed in the district.

These first telephone lines were strung on poles erected for another purpose, but the setting up of the bush-lines was a different matter. It was about 1922 when the first of these was tried out in the Park. One of the earliest was a single line, stretching for twelve miles from Brûlé Lake to White Trout Lake. At about the same time two other lines were strung — one from Whitney to Opeongo Lake, a distance of sixteen miles; and the other from Killaloe to Bason Depot on the Bonnechere River, a distance of thirty miles. The method of running all these lines through was the same. The rangers did the "brushing out", while especially trained men fastened the lines to convenient trees. On the recent topographic map, called the Algonquin sheet, it is possible to trace the course of many of these lines in the Park. Now they have been extended to reach into most of the out-of-the-way corners of the area.

At the present time the telephone system combined with the fire towers, which are set up in key positions throughout the Park, aid in combating the forest fire menace during the summer months. When a fire watcher, stationed at the top of one of the towers, detects smoke in his area, he can telephone the information into his nearest headquarters. The man at the switchboard, who receives similar information from other watchers, can then plot the directions on a map, and determine the exact location of the blaze. Because of this speedy system of reporting, Algonquin Park has established an enviable record in the control of forest fires.

An article by Mark Robinson in the "Barrie Examiner" gives us a picture of fire ranging under the new regime:

> "July 31st — the rangers were all beginning to show the effects of steady fire fighting through the month of July. District Forester F. A. MacDougall had been out on plane patrol all day, landing at different points to encourage his men who were fighting fires with the odds against them, yet managing to put out or keep the different fires under control. He returned to Headquarters' base about 8.30 p.m. reporting a fresh fire on a small island on Ragged Lake.
>
> "We won't do anything about it to-night," he decided, "but we'll have Jerry Kennedy get his men in readiness to leave early in the morning." In a few minutes

Jerry had his men around him. Fire pumps were tested, hose rolled and packed.

At the same time, in the office, the phone was continually ringing and every effort was made to keep up with the work. Soon after Mr. MacDougall got back, there came a call from Mr. Northway at Smoke Lake. "There is a fire at Ragged Lake," he reported. When I told him that we already knew about it, he replied immediately, "My motor boat and canoes are at your disposal. We will meet your men at the highway dock, Smoke Lake, at 5 a.m." I thanked him for his offer, for I knew that it would help a lot.

That evening everyone was more than busy. When Jerry and his men went to get a few hours' rest others were preparing their supplies. Food and cooking equipment for the fire fighters had to be assembled and gasoline had to be mixed with oil for the use of the gasoline pumps. In the office, too, there was much to be done. Anxious campers from around Cache Lake called in to inquire about members of their families who were out on trips in areas known to be threatened by the different fires. News of the progress of other fire crews had to be recorded. Bob Bowes called from his watchpost at Murchison Tower. While three local fires were reported out and another under control, the one at Lobster Lake seemed to be spreading and wanted more men. We couldn't do anything more that night, so we all planned to turn in to get a little rest.

Just as I was closing up at 10.30 the phone rang. It was George Homberg calling from the Whitney office. "Those two pumps you wanted are repaired," he told me. I had wanted these pumps for another fire. "I have just returned from taking one of them to Lobster Lake and I brought back one of theirs that needed some repairs. It's in bad condition, but I may have it ready by daylight." I hung up wondering whether my good friend George ever got any rest.

August 1st — Sam, Jerry and his party left early in the morning, as planned, for Smoke Lake. Jock Walker took them in his car as far as the Smoke Lake portage, where Mr. Northway's launch picked them up. A phone call from the Northway's told us that they passed Molly's Island at 5.30 a.m.

The morning went by without any further upset, but just as we were packing up for lunch it came again. First it was Whitney Headquarters calling: "Murchison Tower reports a small fire in Airy Township. Ranger Holmberg and three men have gone to this fire. Holmberg will return." Then twelve minutes later it was another call: "Tea Lake Dam calling. Construction Company have let their fire get away. The fire is beyond control. Rush pump and equipment at once. The timing for that fire was pretty near a record. Eight minutes after we had received the message Jock Walker and Wib Behan had the car loaded with a pump, hose, gasoline, pack pumps, axes, shovels, and grub hoes and they were on their way. They had fourteen miles to cover along the gravel road but twenty-five minutes later the pump was in operation. Soon afterwards a party of thirty-eight Ahmek campers arrived with axes and pails under Dr. Ted Hayden. We had sent an S.O.S. call to the camp for some of their senior boys because we couldn't spare any more of our men. These boys and the men from the Construction Company, working under the direction of Alvin and Pete Ruddy, had the fire under control at 2.30 p.m. that afternoon.

In the meantime Jock and Wib had returned to Headquarters and we had fresh excitement there. At 1.30 p.m. a call came from Camp Ahmek to say that a fire had broken out in the centre of the camp and they needed a pump and a hose. Our last pump was in the hangar for repair, and it was lucky that Mr. MacDougall landed in from patrol just at that moment. He put in a call for the Pembroke Forestry Office, and they replied that they could leave in fifteen minutes with an extra pump so that we could have it by 3.30 p.m. In the meantime the Canoe Lake residents had come to the rescue of the camp. Thirty-eight of their older boys were down at Tea Lake, but everyone else helped to form a bucket brigade from the lake to the fire. At 2.45 p.m. the fire was reported under control and by 3.00 p.m. it was out. In the line passing the pails up the hill were a Roman Catholic priest and a United Church clergyman working side by side. Some wag remarked that for once the churches were working together to defeat a common foe.

During the afternoon calls continued to come into the office at Headquarters. At 3.30 p.m. Mrs. Gervais reported that her husband had left for a fire at the head of Burnt Lake that seemed to be working towards the Otterslides. Then, a moment later, came news of a fire at the head of Island Lake burning all along the north side of the portage. A number of nearby campers were trying to keep it from spreading.

Fortunately, we began to get some outside help just about that time. The truck arrived from Pembroke Office bringing in two pumps, and Mr. MacDougall was able to get in touch with Tommy Higgins and his plane at Limberlost. Tommy said that he could be over at Headquarters in twenty-five minutes. Together they flew in the pumps and the necessary equipment, over a mile of hose, and tents, blankets and food on the spot. The report on the phone at 10.30 that night was: "It's a large fire and a hot one, but both pumps are working fine and I think we're gaining a little headway."

August 2nd — The first phone call came through at 4.30 a.m. It was Jack Gervais reporting on the Otterslides fire. "We have one pump on the lake with four streams of water going on the fire. Expect to be in full control of the situation by noon or earlier." "How are the boys standing up?" I asked. "They look black," he replied, "their fancy shirts are in rags and some of their trousers won't even make shorts, but they got the hose through the woods and they've done a great job. They're a hungry bunch, though, and we'll need more food and more gas and oil in another hour." In half an hour Mr. MacDougall was on his way with their supplies. Later, when he returned, he made another flight down to Ragged Lake to take in men to relieve the crew that had been working there under Jerry Kennedy.

That day things began to quieten down. Later in the day we heard that the Ragged Lake fire was out and that the Lobster Lake one was under control. Both the Tea Lake one and that at Ahmek had been subdued the day before so that left us with one only on the south side of the Park. When we closed up at 9.30 that night there were clouds in the west that looked as though they might bring rain. When it came in full force the next afternoon we were able to rest for the first time in more than a month."

The policy of conserving wildlife in Algonquin Park, maintained now for over forty years, has today borne rich fruit. According to Dr. C. H. D. Clarke, Mammalogist with the Department of Lands and Forests, the Park has played an important part in helping to keep three of Canada's most valuable furbearing animals from becoming extinct. The fisher and the marten have been trapped for so many years that without the sanctuary provided by the Park, it is likely that these animals would have by now disappeared from Southern Ontario altogether. Actually, although beaver and marten are found elsewhere, there are very few fisher to be seen outside the Park at the present time. It is said that because of the value of this pelt, an Indian trapper who comes upon a fisher's tracks will drop anything he is doing to follow the trail. A good skin will bring from one to three hundred dollars, and for that reason his returns would justify many days' travelling, and many hours spent without rest, from the time that the tracks are first discovered until he has captured his prize. The fisher, which in spite of its name is not a water animal, is the finest of all Canadian fur-bearers. It is not often seen even in the Park, since it multiplies slowly. However, in the winter, a short snowshoe trip in many parts of the Park will suffice to encounter some of these tracks. A good marten skin will bring up to sixty dollars, and higher prices have been known. A good beaver "blanket" is worth forty dollars In Eastern Canada, outside the Ontario Provincial Parks and the Federal Park on Cape Breton Island, these animals are not protected, and since they are quite easy to trap, they have become almost extinct. In the Rockies, marten are still common, and in parts of Western Canada there are other beaver grounds, but if it were not for the Ontario and Nova Scotian sanctuaries, the beaver and marten might have disappeared from the Eastern Canadian scene.

Park authorities and canoe trippers, with knowledge of the

conditions of the water routes through the district, have long been convinced of the great increase in the number of beaver in recent times. However, their knowledge has received confirmation from the results of the beaver survey undertaken by Mr. Donald L. Robb, under the auspices of the Department of Lands and Forests, during the years 1939 and 1940. In the report of his work in the Park, Mr. Robb made some interesting observations as the result of his beaver census. In sample areas of the Park, representing about one-tenth of all the region suitable for beaver habitation, he plotted, with the help of the rangers, all the locations of beaver houses and dams. Then he recorded whether these houses and dams were in present use or whether they had been built some time ago, and were no longer of service to the beaver population. As the result of his finding, Mr. Robb estimated that there were about 2,090 occupied beaver houses in Algonquin Park, or an average of three houses on every four square miles. These figures revealed the fact that beaver were thriving in those lakes and ponds of the Park where they were assured adequate protection and a good supply of the foods they like most.

The natural result of this increase in the number of beaver and other fur-bearing animals in the Park has been, as the Department foresaw from the first, the overflow of these animals into the surrounding countryside. This means, that at the present time, some of the best trapping ground in Ontario is to be found in the regions bordering on the Park. For some years trappers in the Haliburton area, as well as those from Huntsville, Kearney, North Bay, Mattawa, Pembroke and Golden Lake, have vied to see who could place his trap line in the most advantageous position close to the Park boundaries. As one would expect, this situation has brought its own difficulties. Quarrels and feuds have broken out amongst the local inhabitants who depend on trapping as their chief source of income; accusations have been hurled at one another and anonymous letters have been written to the Department about individuals who have stepped over the borders of the Park, to seize some particularly worth-while prize. There have also been frequent complaints about rank outsiders who have come in to raid these grounds, and who have departed to market the catch which was looked upon as the rightful property of the local people.

It was partly as the result of this that quite recently the Ontario Government took steps to set up a system of zoned trapping along the Park boundaries in the Huntsville and North Bay districts.

Having proved so successful, it is expected an attempt will be made to extend the system elsewhere in the Province. Because of the effects this new development may have in the border regions, as well as the protection it will give to adjacent districts in the Park itself, it is worth examining in some detail.

When it was decided to adopt a system of zoned trapping, all the trappers in the area who were accustomed to set their lines near the Park each winter, were called together. At this meeting, each man was given the opportunity to set forth his claims; that is, to describe which section of the country he considered to be his own trapping grounds. After everyone had been given an opportunity to speak, the area was divided into zones, and compromise boundaries marked out where necessary. This meant that in the future, each man would have sole rights in the particular area which was registered as his, and full permission, on the part of the Game Warden, to deal in a summary fashion with any stray trapper who wandered in to trap in his territory. In this way, a trapper would be encouraged to carry on his work in such a way as to give the highest yield of fur, by leaving enough young animals to safeguard the future supply. At the same time, he would have some assurance that these animals would later be caught in his own traps, and not in those set by some get-right-quick marauder who was only interested in the current season's catch.

This new system has met with the support of the local trappers, and especially with those whose zones extend right up to the Park boundaries. Ralph Bice, of Kearney, for instance, who works with his father and his son, values their combined trapping grounds, extending for nine miles along the west border of the Park, at something like $10,000. Each of these three men sets out his own trap line in the winter, and each takes in a good supply of beaver and marten, as well as the occasional fisher.

While on the subject of wildlife conservation, the perennial problem of the relationship between wolves and the deer population comes up. In spite of exaggerated statements to the contrary, there are actually only a few wolves in the region today. Proof of this lies in the record of wolves killed there each winter. Undoubtedly, the curtailment of staff during the recent war partly accounts for the decline, but even old hands like Peter Ranger and Jack Gervais do not kill as many as formerly. The following pre-war figures show the trend: One hundred and twenty-eight in 1931, seventy-six the following year, forty in 1933, twenty-one in 1934, an increase of nineteen the next year, but thereafter a steady decline down to a mere eleven in 1938. The present policy is to control rather than exterminate the wolves. In the National Parks of Canada and the United States, and in the famous Kruger National Park in South Africa, predators such as bears, wolves — and in South Africa, lions —are given the same protection as deer, antelopes, and other herbivores. It is only when individual animals become destructive to property or dangerous to human life, that they are destroyed.

In objecting to a full application of this policy in Algonquin Park, some have pointed out that wolves move in from other districts, attracted by the plentiful supply of deer in the Park, especially during the winter months. There is little doubt that some do cross the ice of the Ottawa from the Quebec side, or filter in from the Lake Nipissing country. Rangers stationed in the north catch more wolves than the others. On the other hand, any attacks on farm animals to the south of the Park are blamed on an overflow of wolves from the Park area. Even if it were true that wolves were pouring into the Park at the north, and out again at the south, which is far-fetched to say the least, a policy of immunity for wolves would be no solution.

Visitors to the Park today still see as many as six deer at a time from a car on the highway, and in the winter, a group of from fifteen to twenty cross over Cache Lake each evening just before sunset to feed at the kitchen door of the rangers' boarding house. They have become so tame that the neighbouring children give them nicknames — "Dirty Face" and "Rusty", according to their peculiar markings. There is certainly no dearth of deer in the Park.

Are they as plentiful or as healthy as they used to be? It is difficult to give a direct answer to this question. It may be that wolves are needed to weed out the weak and degenerate among the deer, and a full application of a survival of the fittest policy would have this effect. But there are other factors that influence the deer population. For instance, it is many years since greater portions of the Park were burned over or freshly timbered, and the young second growth on which the deer thrives is not as plentiful as formerly.

Another interesting point on which there have been differences of opinion, is the advisability of introducing non-native species of plant life into a Park of the Algonquin type. Latterly the tendency has been to keep the native plant life "pure". Actually, there are few foreign species of any kind in the present Park, although inevitably, along the old tote roads, a good many outside plants have taken root. The seeds of timothy, clover, heal-all, ox-eye daisy, yarrow, and orange hawkweed, came in with hay for the horses used in the lumber camps. Ragweed does not appear in the Park although native to its latitude and elevation.

The Royal Commission that drew up recommendations for the Park Act had no prejudice against introducing any species of plant or animal which would increase the public appeal of the Park. They suggested that new species of fish be introduced for the visitors' benefit; shrubs be planted for the deer, and wild rice for the ducks where these were needed. Simpson noted the absence of bass in the Park in his first report. At the turn of the century, Bartlett placed five hundred small mouth bass fingerlings in Cache, White, and Source Lakes; and later, in Opeongo Lake. Where these bass have succeeded in multiplying, it has been at the expense of the native trout, and the practice has been discontinued.

In 1909 and 1910, Atlantic salmon were planted in Source Lake, and perhaps in Cache Lake. A few were caught two or three years later, but so far as is known there have been no further signs of them.

In 1936 ten wapiti, or American elk, were released near Park Headquarters. Although they are known to have reproduced, their number is still small. So far, there has been no attempt to replace the one native animal that has disappeared from the Park, an animal fast disappearing all over the eastern north — the caribou.

Today, the original commissioners would probably be more than satisfied with the strides made in forest and game preservation, and in making the Park a place where people can recapture the values lost in the nervous strain of living in our cities.

Two developments have taken place which they never foresaw, and which remain to be described. Both were to be significant, not merely for Ontario but for the whole Canadian nation.

## CHAPTER 14

In 1901, a party that included Billy Ross, a son of the Honourable G. W. Ross, made a canoe trip in Algonquin Park with Tim O'Leary, then Chief Ranger, as guide. Unconsciously, they paved the way for what was to become the most significant movement in Canadian art.

In Toronto that winter, three members of the Toronto Art Students' League heard such enthusiastic accounts of the trip that they wrote to Tim, asking whether he could perform the same service for them the following summer. O'Leary promised to meet them at the Canoe Lake Station with two canoes and the necessary supplies. Since they were all green campers, they could use the rangers' cabins for shelter.

The three men were W. W. Alexander, David Thomson, and Robert Holmes, all artists whose work was only beginning to be known in Ontario. It is not difficult to imagine their excitement at the prospect of going north to paint; but their wildest expectations, as they packed brushes, paint, paper and canvas for their trip, could not have foreseen its future significance.

When the three travellers arrived at Canoe Lake, O'Leary was there waiting for them. Immediately they started north through Joe Lake. Since the Art League motto was "Not a day goes by without a sketch," frequent stops were made at scenic spots along the way. Actually, their progress must have been very slow, for Mr. Alexander remembers one time when they were delayed for three days, because Robert Holmes was particularly anxious to complete sketches of some wild orchids that he had discovered.

At White Trout (now Big Trout) Lake, the party called in at one of the Lumber Company Depots. There the city artists were quick to transfer some of the local colour into their sketch books. Three of Mr. Alexander's sketches show different aspects of lumber camp life. One shows a pointer, the lumberman's general utility craft, with board sides and a flat bottom; another a well, rigged up with a suspended bucket at the end of a long pole, in order to bring the water to the surface; and a third depicts the camp barber's chair. This was a specially ingenious device, equipped with sleigh-runners so that it could be transferred easily from one cabin to another in the winter. Most of the lumber camps by 1902, were already fitted up with stoves and ranges, but occasionally the group came upon one with the old-style camboose fireplace. In every camp they experienced the warm welcome of traditional northern hospitality.

From the White Trout (Big Trout) district, the party proceeded on into Opeongo Lake by way of Green Lake (now Happy Isle). In this marshy district, Dave Thomson found many beaver dams as subject matter for painting, and they had a hard time persuading him to continue on his way. Frequently the group had to camp out, but now their guide was promising them an unusual treat. The ranger's cabin at Sunnyside, the old Dennison farm, had recently been completed, and he was offering them solid comfort for their next stop. "A regular hotel" had just been completed. The title called up a vision of all kinds of luxury.

The Sunnyside shack is still standing, so it is possible to imagine their chagrin when they came upon this haven. The log cabin measures about fourteen feet by twelve feet. It has a low door, and a window commanding a view of the lake, two built-in bunks, and a small stove. When Robert Holmes entered the cabin which smelled of musty food, he decided to forego the pleasures of the "hotel" and sleep out-of-doors once more.

All along their canoe route, the party was delighted to find a great deal of animal life. Beaver, especially, seemed to be plentiful in this section of the Park. In one pond they surprised two beavers towing limbs for construction work. Another time they came upon a huge dam, eight feet high, which stretched right across their path. This dam was built in a horseshoe formation against the course of the stream, and it had all the appearances of a clever piece of engineering. Besides the beaver, the group had a chance to come very close to a cow-moose along the northern shore of Opeongo Lake. It was standing knee-deep in the water, feeding on lily pads.

At the south end of Opeongo Lake, the canoe trip came to an end. There, at the foot of Sproule Bay, they came upon their first signs of civilization since leaving Canoe Lake. The St. Anthony Lumber Company's Railway had recently been pushed through to that point, and they were able to make use of the line to journey down to Whitney. From there, they went back along the main line to Park Headquarters.

This trip was the beginning of a series of excursions by artists into Algonquin Park, which were continued until 1917. The three originals went back again and again, sometimes together, sometimes with other Toronto artists.

The late J. W. Beatty used to tell how he was first lured up north. Originally a Toronto fireman, he used his leisure to practice painting, saved his money, went over to Europe, and returned to support himself by his art. One of his first illustration jobs involved a story with a northern setting, that might have been inspired by Alexander's stories of the Park. In the illustration he had drawn a tea-pail over a campfire, showing the sides of the pail sloping like a bucket. A friend poured scorn on his drawing. Up north, Bill Beatty learned, a tea-pail has vertical sides. Then and there he resolved to go and see this peculiar country for himself, and followed the Algonquin Trail already blazed by Alexander, David Thomson, and Holmes. Tom McLean, a friend of Beatty's, was another early artist to make these northern trips. By 1912, Algonquin Park was well known in Toronto as ideal painting country.

Twenty years earlier, a young farm lad was growing up near Owen Sound. Like most youngsters, he did not know what he was going to do with his life. Probably he worried very little over the future, too intent on living for the day. He was passionately fond of the wilderness, and there was plenty of bush behind his back door where he could wander for hours in intervals between school and chores. A deep restlessness overtook him in his late teens. He took a routine job in Owen Sound and threw it over, went out to Seattle, where he worked at photography with his brother George. Dissatisfied, Tom Thomson came to Toronto in 1911. With his background in photography, and a quiet, competent manner which impressed all who met him, he landed a job at Grip Limited, a commercial art firm. That winter, he became interested in learning how to paint. There were plenty of experienced young artists to help him: J. E. H. Macdonald, Lismer, Carmichael, Frank Johnston and Varley were working under the same roof. Others, like J. W. Beatty, moved in the same circles; or rather, went on common sketching excursions whenever work allowed. Most of these men had learned to paint in England or Europe, but all of them were as ready to encourage as to criticize, and under their tuition his technique rapidly improved.

Unknown to any of this group, however, Tom Thomson had something the others could never acquire: the north was in his blood. Already, with his friend, Ben Jackson, he had gone up into the wilderness on fishing and sketching trips. He could not have been in Toronto long before he heard of Algonquin Park. So it is not surprising to find him, in the spring of 1912, camped with his friend Ben, also an ardent fisherman, at Tea Lake Dam.

The National Gallery has a sketch of Tom Thomson done at the time, and signed H. B. Jackson. It is entitled "A Rainy Day in Camp" and it reveals Tom in characteristic pose — absorbed in his fishing. Peculiarly enough, this early picture showing Tom's activities in the Park is like all the later ones. Sketches and photographs alike, all find him hard at work—fishing. Fishing was an occupation which could be carried on in the company of friends and companions who might want to stop long enough to take pictures, but painting was a solitary pastime, and no one was ever on hand to catch him in the act.

This Tea Lake sketch shows Tom clad in a conservative outfit, much more like the clothes worn by a city-born fisherman than those which he came to wear on subsequent visits to the Park. Here he has donned a broad-brimmed hat, a long-sleeved jacket, and high laced boots. He is seated close to the shore and is busy with his rod. He looks as though he is thoroughly enjoying himself, and is quite prepared to stay happily in camp throughout the whole of that stormy May day. Between his teeth he is gripping a sturdy pipe, and his whole attitude of concentrated absorption makes one feel that nothing pleased him better, than to have this opportunity of making the best use of a spell of gloomy weather. Although it is quite possible that Tom, as well as H. B. Jackson, did the occasional sketch at that time, there is no way of connecting any of his painting definitely with his first trip.

From an article written by Dr. James MacCallum, and published in the Canadian Magazine in October, 1917, we learn how Tom Thomson had spent the summer of 1912. It was in October of that year that Dr. McCallum first came to know Tom, when he met him at the studio of their mutual friend, J. E. H. MacDonald. Tom had just returned from a two-month canoe trip which he had taken through the Mississagi Indian Reserve to the northwest of Georgian Bay. When the Doctor heard that Tom had brought back a group of sketches made during the trip, he was anxious to see them, both because he had always taken a keen interest in struggling Canadian artists, and because he knew and loved the Georgian Bay country. Tom warned him that his sketches were rather the worse for wear, since they had been salvaged from the water at one point when their

**Tom Thomson at Mowat on Canoe Lake,** ***(Tom Thomson Memorial Gallery; APM # 188)***

**Original Mowat Lodge on Canoe Lake, built as a boarding house by Gilmour Lumber Co. in 1897.**
(*O. Addison; APM # 186)*

canoe had upset, but the Doctor insisted on having a chance to judge them for himself. When the Doctor had looked them over, he purchased several for his own collection, and encouraged Thomson to continue painting.

That winter was not only a milestone in Tom's career as an artist; it began a movement that was to create a milestone in Canadian history.

One of the sketches he had made during the previous summer had provided him with the material for a full-scale canvas, which was completed in time for the March show of the Ontario Society of Artists. When Tom learned that his picture, "A Northern Lake", had been purchased by the Ontario Government, at a price of $250.00, he was surprised at his own success. He must have turned northwards once more with renewed confidence in his own powers as a painter, and with the determination to set forth something of his own delight in the wilderness country, which he loved so well.

The twenty small sketches which he had brought back to Toronto made an indelible impression on Tom's fellow artists, corroborating Dr. MacCallum's shrewd judgment. Even though they could be dismissed technically as "moods smudged into panels", these paintings contained the essence of something every Canadian artist had been blindly groping for. "From them", says Arthur Lismer, "we saw that Tom not only was opening up as a painter, but that the north was a painters' country". Singly, and in groups, they went north — A. Y. Jackson, J. E. H. MacDonald, Arthur Lismer, F. H. Varley, Lawren Harris, and others, J. W. Beatty among them, after years of absence from the Park. All of them brought back paintings from the Park, and all were labelled, in the scathing criticism of the years between 1914 and 1917, as members of the "Algonquin Park Group".

The following summer, Tom Thomson went up to the Park alone —to paint. On his return to Toronto in the fall, he met an artist from Montreal whom Dr. MacCallum and Lawren Harris had persuaded to move to Toronto, an artist who, like Tom, had found that the north had something to say, and was learning to say it. The artist was A. Y. Jackson, known today from coast to coast as the "Dean" of Canadian landscape painting. Jackson and Thomson took to each other at once. Tom, who had decided not to return to an office routine in the city, was glad to accept Jackson's offer to share a studio in the new Studio Building that had just been built on

Severn Street overlooking the Rosedale Ravine. "In fact," as Jackson himself says, "we were so anxious to get to work that we moved in in January, before the building was really finished".

There the two artists discussed their work, and painted for the next two winter months. By that time, each had had a profound effect on the other. Jackson says he had become so tired of hearing Tom sing the praises of the wonderful part of the world called "Algonquin Park", he had decided to light out to see the place for himself; while Tom had learned a great deal about the techniques of painting — the preparation of canvases, the proper tools for the job, and the use of colours. Most of Tom's best work has to do with the vivid seasons of spring and autumn, while a great deal of Jackson's best belongs to winter, when he preferred to sally forth on snowshoes while the snow was still on the ground, in order to catch its varying beauty on canvas.

For two months in the early spring, while Tom was still in Toronto, A. Y. Jackson stayed at Mowat Lodge. When the cold was too extreme, he found that he could not work outside, but when it became a little milder, he undertook to do some good-sized canvases right on the spot, without preparing preliminary sketches to be used for studio paintings. It was in this way that "A Winter's Day" was painted. In order to get it, Jackson tramped across the lake each day to Hayhurst's Point. The picture now hangs in the Hamilton Public Library.

In a letter written at this time to his friend, J. E. H. MacDonald, and quoted by F. B. Housser in "A Canadian Art Movement", we get a first-hand picture of his reaction to this sort of life. There he wrote: "You don't notice the cold a bit. All you notice is your breath dropping down and splintering on the scintillating ground. At Canoe Lake Station it was forty-five below zero last night. Had a five-mile work-out this afternoon. The weather was milder and not at all penetrating. It was sunny but not colourful. The woods look very wonderful and full of colour motives; deer trails all over the place, and wolf tracks, too. I think if I have a scrap with a whole pack and get eaten up, it will be a great ad for the Studio Building".

J. E. H. MacDonald, whose sketches, after Tom Thomson's death, perhaps more than those of any other artist, were to carry on Tom's style of painting, caught the contagion of Jackson's enthusiasm. He was then living at Thornhill, where he had settled his family. When he had given his young son, Thoreau, full instructions as to how to keep the house warm, he, too, migrated to the Park. His "March Evening, Northland", was probably done at that time, and E. R. Hunter's catalogue of his paintings describes two other canvases that may have been the result of this early spring trip. These are "Snowflurries", showing an evening scene in the Park with snow-covered ground, and "Moonlight, Algonquin Park", also a snow scene in dull blues. MacDonald was in the Park on several other occasions; once when his friend Tom Thomson was there with him, and twice after his death, but it is likely that these three pictures were the product of this first trip.

It is difficult to discover when Tom went north to the Park that year, and whether his stay at Canoe Lake overlapped with the visit of either of these two artists, or with that of F. Horsman Varley, who also seems to have been at Mowat Lodge during the month of April. At any rate, he was there before May eighth when Arthur Lismer, then quite recently out from England, joined him for his first camping holiday in Algonquin Park. In the city, Tom had earned quite a reputation amongst his artist friends as a bushman, and Lismer felt satisfied that Tom would be able to look after them both on this occasion.

When Lismer arrived at Canoe Lake he found Tom had made arrangements for their camping equipment and their food supply. In fact, he had taken particular pains with one piece of equipment — his own canoe. Even before the ice was completely out of the lake, he had been conjuring up in his mind's eye just the right shade of dove-grey he wanted to paint it. However, when he tried to buy paint of that colour, he found that the paint-makers had nothing in stock that would come close to it. In spite of these difficulties, when Lismer arrived for the trip there was the canoe — resplendent in a fine new coat of the desired shade. Lismer wanted to know how Tom had managed to get that colour. "That was easy", Tom replied, "I just mixed in a tube of Cobalt violet to the standard grey canoe paint". Lismer knew "Cobalt blue" was worth two dollars a tube, but Tom was satisfied he had had good value for his money.

A photograph of Tom Thomson and Arthur Lismer frequently used for an illustration, was taken at this time — likely by the ranger, Bud Callaghan, at Smoke Lake. It shows Lismer in the bow of the canoe, nursing Bud's little dog, which looks more than contented to be paddling with this pair of campers. Lismer, too, seems to have made himself completely at home in this craft, to which he was unaccustomed. He has both long legs spread out, and his feet are resting on the gunwales of the canoe. On his head he is wearing a funny little round hat. Tom, in the stern, has a paddle in his right hand, while his left arm, leaning on a stump at the water's edge, holds the canoe steady and close into shore. Two fishing rods sticking out above the canoe, give the impression that the campers have been out on a jaunt to supplement their food stores. Certainly all three of them, including the dog, look as though they were enjoying the warm spring sunshine to the full.

Although they travelled about to many of the lakes down south of Canoe Lake, they made their main camp on Molly's Island in Smoke Lake. Lismer never failed to admire Tom's skilful way of handling the frail craft, upon which they were so dependent. Even at night, when it was almost impossible to pick out the shore-line, he seemed to be able to judge the right landing spot with unerring certainty, so that the canoe would graze gently along the sandy bottom instead of crashing into a shoal. Of course, Lismer was then a beginner in the art of paddling, so his friend's effortless stroke struck him as a masterly achievement. Everyone else who saw Tom handling a canoe remarked on his great skill as a canoeist.

For three weeks the two of them toured around through Smoke, Ragged, Crown, and Wolf Lakes, fishing and making sketches. That year they "saw the spring come in", and each day brought a change in hue and foliage. They lived in a state of enthusiastic delight, and everywhere they saw good painting material. However, in spite of their industry, Lismer says that very few of the sketches have survived. His own have been scattered and lost sight of, while Thomson's have mostly disappeared, too. In fact, Tom set small store on his ability as a painter, either then, or at a later date. He frequently gave away his latest sketch to any friend who mentioned he had a liking for what he had just done. Tom looked upon a great deal of his work as experimental because he was rarely satisfied that he had done full justice to the scene before him.

Later in the summer, Tom had gone up to Georgian Bay to pay a visit to the MacCallum summer home, near Go Home Bay. Dr. MacCallum had continued to encourage Tom since the time, two years before, when he brought back his Mississagi sketches, and for the five years intervening between that time and his death in 1917, Dr. MacCallum watched his progress and purchased sketches from time to time. Other artists were frequently invited by the Doctor to spend their summers in sketching holidays, using his Georgian Bay cottage as a headquarters, and the mural of Tom Thomson on the wall of the cottage was probably painted by J. E. H. MacDonald during this visit. When it came time to return to the Park, Tom once more set forth in his canoe. This simple acceptance of the wilderness way of life was something which never failed to fill his city friends with wonder and admiration.

Back in the Park, Mowat Lodge became the centre of an artists' colony in late August and September of 1914. The gathering had been planned in the spring, before the different individuals went off on their own painting trips, and now with the outbreak of war, all of them felt this might be the last time they would be together for a long while. In this they were quite right, as events proved, because at least three of this group were to join the Canadian Forces as accredited War Artists. Amongst those who were staying at the Lodge at this time were — F. H. Varley, A. Y. Jackson, Mr. and Mrs. Arthur Lismer, Percy Robertson and his bride, Beatrice Haggerty — while close at hand, in his own cabin, was Tom Thomson.

Mrs. Shannon Fraser remembers,these artists, and others of their friends who made the lodge their headquarters during the next three years, as a jolly bunch of young people, who got a great deal of enjoyment out of traipsing around the country with their sketch boxes, sitting up till unearthly hours to discuss their new ideas, and were always so easy to please and so enthusiastic about the Park. The boarding house would overflow with their latest sketches, because they would have to be propped up to dry before they could be packed for the trip back to the city. Nobody minded that, and everyone shared in the friendly criticisms and the unstinted praise of the most recent experiment. There was a continual art show at Canoe Lake during the autumn painting season, and at one stage, the old hospital house at the top of the hill was taken over so that everyone could see what was being accomplished.

Mark Robinson recalls those days of artistic fervour at Canoe Lake. One day, when Mark was down by Tea Lake Dam, he came upon Tom and a group of his friends who had been spending the day painting and picnicing. As he passed by the island where they were camping, Mark was close enough to hear their conversation. Tom was pointing to one of the highly-coloured hillsides across the lake, and one of his friends had to admit, "Yes, Tom, it's all there. Your interpretation is not overdone." When Tom had first brought his northern sketches to Toronto, even his artist friends had doubted whether such clear, vivid colours could be found in the actual natural scene. Now that they were convinced, it was only a question of passing their conviction on to the rest of the world through their own painting of Canadian landscapes. However, at this stage in his development, Tom himself had not yet branched out into the startling use of colour that was to make his "Northern River" and his "West Wind" subjects of controversy.

When the other artists returned to the city, A. Y. Jackson stayed on in the Park with Tom until late November. Dr. MacCallum, knowing the two were working together, sent a message to Tom suggesting he was to continue to paint in his own style, and that he was not to allow Jackson to influence him too much. There were many things Tom could still learn from his painting companion. As always, he was quick to praise the work of his friend, and to see the faults in his own, but by this time he was beginning to get into his final stride, turning out sketches full of colour and action as the result of a morning's or an afternoon's work.

Together, Tom and his friend moved about from camp-site to camp-site, as the spirit and the changing forest prompted them. They started at a spot just north of Hayhurst's Point, near where "Spring Ice" or "The Opening of the Waters" was painted in a subsequent spring; they stopped down near Tea Lake Dam; and they went on down to Ragged and to Smoke Lake. Always "A.Y." was thrilled with Tom's camping and paddling skill — and Tom, in turn, gave the "city chap" a certain amount of credit as he learned some of the tricks and arts of the old camper.

When the leaves had all fallen, and the lakes were beginning to freeze, Tom and Jackson left the Park. Jackson went to Montreal to enlist, and this was the last he ever saw of Tom.

How long Tom stayed in the Park thereafter no one remembers, but it must have been late October when Dr. MacCallum received the news, "Tom is back". He had brought with him a collection of sketches which Dr. MacCallum describes as being full of "lightning flashes, moving thunder storms, and trees with branches lashing in the wind". Tom had not yet attained the perfection that he later achieved in the deft use of the simple line and the application of clear flowing colours, but he could catch the feeling and the moods of the changing pattern of the north country. The original sketch for the painting "A Moonlight Scene", which he exhibited the next spring at the Ontario Society of Artists Show, must have been done during that summer in the Park. This picture was afterwards purchased by the National Gallery in Ottawa.

By the spring of 1915, Tom's life had worked itself out to the pattern that it was to follow until his death. He had now given up any settled job, therefore, he had to earn his living by his painting in the winter, and by guiding and fire ranging in the summer. For the four winter months he would paint, and cook his own meals in the shack which he shared with Arthur Lismer, overlooking the Rosedale Ravine behind the Studio Building, in Toronto; while in the eight months of the spring, summer, and autumn, he would be up in the Park. There, too, he established a sort of routine. When he first went up in the early spring, he would stay at Canoe Lake, in the Trainor's little cottage near the outlet of the creek, and then during the fire ranging season from May to the end of September, he would travel to his post in the north of the Park near Achray at Grand Lake. In the fall, until the freeze-up, he would be back at the Canoe Lake cottage. In this way he could make both ends meet, and at the same time acquire a little ready cash to pay for the equipment necessary for his painting.

The National Gallery in Ottawa had already acquired a large number of Thomson's smaller sketches, as well as several of his larger canvases, before 1944, but in that year their collection was greatly augmented by the bequest of Dr. J. M. MacCallum's own private collection of Thomson paintings and sketches, valued at many thousands of dollars. Now there is a movement on foot to have a special Tom Thomson room set up where visitors to the Canadian capital may see at all times, representative paintings of this man who ranks amongst the foremost of our Canadian artists. In such a room, a person who knows the Park well could instantly recognize a dozen Park places. The fact that Tom insisted on painting scenes as he actually saw them, would help in recognizing these actual spots. He had no patience with artists who did not paint nature as it really was, but who combined two or more different scenes to get the effect they wanted. To him, the use of such methods was like telling a lie — when he painted, he must show things as they lay before him. He always insisted that his colours were not intensified, and that the patterns of his lines were there in truth. He wanted others to see the actual northland scene with the same magic eye that he himself possessed.

Although Tom Thomson seems to have left no records to tell either of where he painted actual scenes in the Park or when they were done, there are certain ways of establishing some information about the paintings that he left behind. The Accessions Book at the

National Gallery in some cases gives names and dates to identify the pictures with the Park; sometimes people who were on hand, remember seeing one particular sketch soon after it was completed; experts in tree growth and topography have identified certain sections in the northern districts as his painting grounds; and art critics have worked out the general sequence of his work, by the progressive mastery of style revealed in his sketches and full-sized canvases. But in spite of the research already made, there are still many of the sketches, in the MacCallum collection, in the collection of the National Gallery, and in the hands of private owners, having an Algonquin Park atmosphere, but that have not yet been actually identified with the Park.

In the National Gallery, there are some paintings whose titles indicate that they were painted in the Park. These include: "Petawawa Gorges", "Tea Lake Dam", and "The Artist's Hut". It is also quite probable that "Autumn's Garland", with its vivid maples in the foreground, and "Canadian Wildflowers" were done in the Park, because Tom nearly always managed to be painting there when the spring and fall seasons rolled around. The sombre "Moose at Night", and some of his northern lights sketches were likely done there, too. There were few other places frequented by Tom where he could have found the moose in their native habitat, and Mark Robinson recalls at least one occasion when Tom painted the Northern Lights while staying at Canoe Lake.

Many other paintings of Tom Thomson's have Algonquin Park moods or colourings. Some show the turquoise skies of spring, and the rich brown earth appearing through the melting snow. Others are early morning subjects, done in the summer time, when the sun turns the clouds over the lakes into masses of opalescent mother-of-pearl. Sometimes the titles of the sketches — "Hot Summer Moonlight" or "Burnt Country" have a Park flavour; or a campfire along the shore, birches on the hillside, or tricky river rapids; all these give characteristic glimpses of the country. All reflect the movement and the spirit of the Park.

At least two of his well-known lumbering pictures were done when he was ranging in the Grand Lake section of the Park. In his canvas "The Bateaux", now hanging in Hart House at the University of Toronto, a group of lumbermen's red pointers are moored close to the shore, while nearby is a log-boom enclosing the logs that are being moved downstream. According to Dr. MacCallum, the title "Pageant of the North" would have done better justice to the scope of this canvas. The sketch for the other picture, "Lumber Drive", was likely done in the north of the Park, when Booth's lumberjacks were driving down the Petawawa River. Pete Sauve, who went with the lumbermen as a cook at the camps that they established along the river course, says Tom was painting there one year when they went through. Mark Robinson, who was Deputy-Chief Ranger for some years in the district, identifies the place where this painting was done as being the narrows at the south end of Grand Lake, below Achray.

Tom seems to have spent at least one summer at the old rangers' cabin at Achray, which stood just to the right of the new stone building that is now the headquarters. Professor T. W. Dwight, of the Faculty of Forestry, University of Toronto, who spent eleven years there at the Forestry School's fall camp, feels sure that the canvas "West Wind" was painted from the place where Tom's cabin formerly stood. Professor Dwight took photographs of the skyline across the lake as it appears in recent years, and compared it with the hills in the background of the painting. Even allowing for changes brought about because of the tree growth in the intervening years, the similarity between the two is very striking. By using this same method, Professor Dwight decided that the picture entitled "Jack Pine" was painted from a nearby spot, the point stretching out into the lake to the left of the ranger's log cabin built by Ned Godin.

In both cases, however, while the land contours were almost identical, the trees in the foreground cannot be identified. There are white pines on the point shown in "West Wind", but there is no weather-beaten red pine such as the picture shows. There are a few trees and shrubs on the rocky Jack Pine point, but there are no jack pines at all along the shoreline of the lake, nor for that matter are they at all common in the district. However, Professor Dwight is full of praise for the accuracy with which the trees were painted in both these pictures. In the "Jack Pine", Tom Thomson was able to reproduce perfectly the drooping pendulous branches of the jack pine to give an impression of summer langour, and in the "West Wind" he has used the tough, hardy virility of the red pine to show how it has weathered the lashings of the winds from across the open expanse of the lake.

Men who have made a special study of the materials which different artists have used, such as sketching boards, paints, and brushes, can throw some light on the way Tom Thomson worked when he was in the Park. For many years, Mr. George Harbour has been in charge of the cleaning and repair of paintings in the National

Gallery, and he was able to show how Tom's sketch boards reveal the story of his painting methods. Other people have told us Tom often painted a sketch very quickly—Mr. Hayhurst at Canoe Lake, recalled how he used to be away for a few hours in the morning and come back at noon with a finished sketch, and artists have agreed that the original sketch for the "West Wind" could have been done in half an hour. The sketches in the National Gallery offer another proof of this speed. Frequently, they show indications of the paint having been flattened out, because it had not been given a chance to dry before the sketch was packed up to be carried elsewhere along the Park portages. Of course, where the paint was particularly thick, such flattened areas could have been the result of being stacked up in the Canoe Lake cabin before they were taken down to the Toronto studio, but it is a fact that a great number of the sketches that Tom did in the Park show this evidence of hasty packing.

It is interesting to note that Tom made use of all kinds of sketch boards for his Park drawings. Sometimes he was able to provide himself with a stock of the small-sized panels such as his friend, J. E. H. MacDonald, preferred for his outdoor work. Sometimes he could get special birch panels, that would be light to carry over the portages, but frequently, with the true woodsman's versatility, he made use of any substance he could find, on which to paint. There are some scenes done on the artists' boards brought north from the city, but there are others on millboard, on cardboard, on the flat side of corrugated packing boxes, and on cotton and wood panels. In some instances, pictures have been painted on both sides of the board, in order to conserve supplies.

In the winter, after his return to Toronto, he developed these same sketches into the full-sized canvases which were to make him so famous. In three successive years these great tableaux came out of the Park — "Northern River" in 1915; the "Jack Pine" in 1916; and the "West Wind" in 1917. All of them are associated with the Grand Lake district. Even if we had not known that this was the area where he had been working during the summers of 1915 and 1916, it would have been possible to identify them with this part of the Park. There the lakes are bigger and more wind-swept than in the southern sections, and the whole region is wilder, and more untouched. Old-timers are in general agreement that "Northern River" is Karishoo Creek, while the lake in the other two is Grand Lake.

After Tom Thomson's death, few of his fellow artists ever returned again to the Park. Surrounded by reminders of the friend they had lost, they would not have had the heart to paint. Many years passed before younger men and women, drawn by the influence of the Group of Seven's work, came up to see Tom Thomson's cairn, and paint the land he had loved.

Dr. MacCallum, the far-sighted friend who was the first to recognize his true significance to Canadian art, said of him afterwards, "Tom Thomson lived eight months of the year in Algonquin Park, often disappearing into its recesses for a month at a time. His sketches are a complete encyclopedia of all the glories of Algonquin Park, and aside from their artistic merits, have a historical value entitling them to preservation in the National Gallery."

Albert Robson, who worked with Tom and with the other rising young artists who were to band themselves later into the famous "Group of Seven", explains Thomson's chief contribution when he says, "He painted the lake country with fiery concentration, rarely travelling farther than his beloved Algonquin Park, where Canoe Lake was his regular headquarters. Other Canadian artists had painted the north country before Thomson; it is both unfair and untrue to say that he discovered it as paintable material. But it is true to say that he was the first painter to interpret the north in its various subtleties of mood and feeling, free from influence of European traditions and formulas. His personal knowledge of the country and his inherent honesty dictated its own methods of expression."

To those who know and love Algonquin Park, Tom Thomson's significance in the history of Canadian art is secondary. For them, it is sufficient to say, that of all the artists who have ever painted there, or may come to paint, to him alone belongs the title of "The Algonquin Artist".

## CHAPTER 15

On August 16th, 1930, a totem pole was erected on Hayhurst's Point overlooking Canoe Lake, by the boys and girls of the neighbouring camps, under the guidance of two Ahmek leaders, Harold Hayden and Gordon Weber. At the top is the figure of a man; next a pair of wings — his aspirations; below that a group of tepees for his camping experience, a checkered area for his guiding career, a duck for his skill in swimming, a canoe for his expert paddling, a lynx for his woodsmanship, and a lyre for his art. At the base is carved the form of a palette, symbol of the art of painting.

So the youth of Algonquin Park have expressed their tribute to Tom Thomson.

In Algonquin Park today, Thomson has become almost a legendary figure. A recent documentary film was designed to show how magnificently Thomson was able to catch the colour and the rhythm of the Park in his paintings. Many are the stories told about Thomson around the campfires in the Park. One hears of a mystic ghost canoe, painted a shimmering magic grey, that glides across Canoe Lake at twilight, only to vanish into the mist. There's a story about a picnic group who followed after a swiftly moving canoe in the still of the evening, and who saw this craft land on a beach, where it left no mark or sign of its whereabouts. Someone else recalls a flaming comet which flashed across the summer sky one night a few years ago, on the anniversary of Thomson's death.

For the men and women of the Park who knew him best, Tom Thomson was neither a legend nor a totem. To them he was flesh and blood, human and real; shy perhaps, and not overly given to speech, but a generous friend with no pretentions, and a top-ranking woodsman. Tom Thomson was simply, to them, a man who belonged.

Of his first fishing trip to Algonquin with Ben Jackson, in the spring of 1912, there is no recollection among Park residents. It was his first arrival alone, a year later, that is remembered. Naturally, Mark Robinson was the man to remember that. Mark was then living at the rangers' house at Joe Creek, and he remembers being at the station one spring evening when the train came in. The stranger who alighted with his pack on his back, enquired of Mark where he could get "a decent bite and a good warm bed". It being early in the season, before the nearby hotel was open, Mark suggested he try Shannon Fraser's, and that was the first time that Tom made the acquaintance of the family with whom he was to have such a close connection during the next five years in the Park.

For several days Mark did not see anything more of this newcomer, but the sectionman, Charlie Ratan, reported that "this guy must be some sort of a queer fool" because he had seen him out back of the station several times, daubing bits of paint on a piece of board. Tom had discovered, with the coming of spring, the colour of the alders growing along the Portage Creek shore changed each day, and he had been trying to record this fact with his paints. One day, Charlie's sixteen-year-old sister, who was very curious about the actions of this stranger in the district, chanced to see one of his "boards". Immediately she exclaimed, "Why that's like the alders were a week ago!" Then Tom knew that he had been able to get the right colours. With the rare smile that always lighted up his face when he was pleased, he remarked that he must be "going places".

While making his rounds, Mark would often come upon this strange young man in out-of-the-way spots. Sometimes he would be tossing stones into the water from the bridge at Joe Creek to see how the ripples formed and broke; sometimes he would pace away from an object, and then return to it again and again. The rangers had seen a good many strange things in the Park, but probably the strangest of all was the sight of this lean young fellow, with the cut of a bushman about him, studying the tones of grey on an old pine stump, and explaining that until he could mix the same colour, and capture the exact value of a certain brown that showed up best in some kind of a fern, he couldn't make much headway. Perhaps they understood later, when they saw the subtle browns and greys revealed in his later sketches, sombre backgrounds for vivid splashes of autumn yellows or spring blues.

Mark makes mention of Tom earning his way in the Park during the summer by purchasing a guide's license, and taking parties of fishermen about the Park on trips. In later years, he seems to have made his headquarters at Shannon Fraser's, where he came to be looked on as one of the family. There were two other places where Tom made his home at Canoe Lake, but no one seems to know just when or why he migrated from one to the other. For several seasons he camped in a tent pitched on the east side of the lake, opposite

Mowat Landing, and just to the north of Hayhurst's Point. Sometimes, in the early spring and fall, he lived in a little cabin on the west side of the lake, just below Potter Creek. This cabin was owned by a lumber foreman, Hugh Trainor, from whom Tom received permission for its use. It is interesting to note that one of the Thomson paintings, "The Artist's Hut", in the National Gallery, has recently been reproduced in colour. The picture shows this little wooden shack on the edge of Canoe Lake, in the spring of the year, while the snow is still lying in patches on the ground. In the foreground is a curtain of birch and poplar trees; two women, one dressed in red, and the other in blue, are passing along the road that leads north to the railway station. There is no date assigned to this painting, but it was likely done after 1914.

Tom's second summer has been partially described in the account of Lismer's stay with him. According to Mark Robinson, after Tom had finished his painting in the spring of that year, he had taken out a guide license, and had earned money in that way until mid-July. He then embarked on a trip through the Park to Lake Nipissing, by way of the South River. In making his plans he had told Mark of his intentions to go on through to Georgian Bay, but that he would be back at Canoe Lake by September fifteenth. Sure enough, he was back on the day appointed, but he didn't seem his gay old self. He pulled up his canoe, said hello, and immediately asked for the latest war news. After supper, when he had read the papers, he went off to his cabin without any remarks either on his trip or on the news itself.

Later that fall, as already related, A. Y. Jackson and he painted together after the others had returned to Toronto. In a large gathering Tom had little to say, but in the company of one or two close friends, he was a different man. Sometimes in their isolated cabin at night, the glowing fire in the tin stove making a comfortable contrast within to the frosty air without, he and Jackson would set up their week's work, and pull it to pieces earnestly. At other times, Tom would recall his own experiences in the Park: the night, for instance, when his tent was pitched on the lake opposite the Blecher's, while paddling to shore he had seen a wolf prowling between his tent and the edge of the lake. Then, his hunger being stronger than his fear, he beached his canoe and dashed up to the tent. He made his supper in the tent that night, lighting all his candles, and wishing the walls were made of wood instead of canvas. In the morning the wolf was gone.

When Tom came north to Canoe Lake in the spring of 1915, he

found Shannon Fraser had acquired a bookkeeper and assistant, George Chubb, who had come to the Park for reasons of health. "Chubby", who still returns to the Park each summer as the business manager at Camp Ahmek, recalls that Tom was accepted as one of the family in the Fraser kitchen. Everyone liked him for his kindly consideration for others, and his willingness to do the odd jobs which always turn up unexpectedly in a back country household. Chubby recalls two instances of this sort, while he and Tom were both at Canoe Lake. One of them happened before he actually got to know Tom. Chubby and a friend were camped on Little Wapomeo Island, and they had the misfortune to break the handle of their axe. They paddled over to the Lodge to ask Shannon if he could sell them one. Tom happened to overhear their request, and the next time they came around, he presented them with one fashioned by himself out of a piece of ironwood.

Another little incident, typical of Tom Thomson, took place while both Tom and Chubby were staying at the Frasers'. The old grandmother was sitting at the long table in the kitchen, where they all ate together when there weren't any guests. She had been brought up to say grace before meals, and always bowed her head as she sat down to eat. The others, who came in ravenous from their work, usually started right in without any preliminaries, but Tom always respected the old lady's custom, and waited until she had finished saying grace before beginning to eat.

It may have been that summer when the three tourists were caught on Canoe Lake in a sudden, dangerous squall. Whether Tom paddled out to them and shouted the instructions that saved them, or whether he actually pulled them out of the water, has not been told. But when Mark Robinson, the nearest ranger, found out about it and congratulated Tom, the latter merely replied with embarrassed brevity: "You rangers do that sort of thing all the time: forget it".

Tom's skill at fly-casting won him the admiration of the guests at Shannon's. They profited often from his success, too, because he frequently brought in a nice catch for Mrs. Fraser to cook for the household. Mark says that nothing delighted Tom more than to go out to a spot where everyone said it was impossible to catch anything, and to return triumphant with two or three good-sized fish. He made his own flies and "bugs", watching to see what insects made the fish rise, and painting his own imitations on the spot.

Although there is no date to indicate when the photograph of Tom Thomson fly-fishing at the bottom of a lumber dam was taken, there is no doubt that this shows one of his favourite pastimes in the Park. There are many stories of the good fishing to be found near the old dams, and certainly, the intent concentration expressed both in Tom's face, and in his stance on that particular occasion, are eloquent of his interest in the art of angling. In this photograph, in contrast to the Tea Lake picture, he is garbed in real north country outfit. The wool toque on the side of his head, and the flexible mocassins on his feet, show him dressed for warmth and comfort, in the fashion of any good woodsman.

During the summer of 1915, Tom came to know the northern part of the Park in the neighbourhood of Grand Lake and Achray, as well as he had previously known the Canoe Lake district. That year, he went north for the first time as a Park fire ranger, one of the temporary employees taken on to the staff at the time of year when the forest fires were most dangerous. This sort of work gave him a livelihood — Tom in his lifetime never sold enough of his paintings to make ends meet — and he could utilize the slack periods between fires to carry on with his painting. For days on end he would be out in the Park alone, observing the changes of season and mood taking place about him, while scanning the horizon for the first thin tell-tale column of smoke. When he wanted company, there was his fellow ranger, Jack Culhane, of nearby Killaloe, and his family, who always came up to the Park for the summer. Jack's son-in-law, Skinny (Leonard) McDermid, who worked on the railway, also knew Tom. Then there was Ned Godin, the ranger at Achray. On one of Tom's visits during the summers of 1915 and 1916, he painted a new sign for Ned's cabin, in old English lettering — "Outside Inn".

Amongst the other oddments painted in these latter years by Tom for his friends and neighbours, was an agate bowl, now to be seen in the National Gallery. This bowl, about ten inches across, Tom completely covered, inside and out, with a thick layer of oil paint. In a wheel at the bottom, surrounded by a conventional design of oak leaves, and woven into the pattern are the initials "T.T." These old friends of Tom agree that he set no great store by his skill. Frequently he gave them sketches they admired, which they, unconscious of their real value, left behind in the wintertime, in old attics or damp cabins. Some of these were later picked up and restored by collectors, but a great many of them have gone the way of the camboose camps.

One more summer of guiding, painting, and fire ranging, followed before Tom Thomson's last. That winter he painted his final, and best known canvas, "The West Wind".

Tom must have come north to Canoe Lake for the last time in April, of 1917. Mark tells us of a special project that must have been started two months before the lush greens of June ended the spring painting season. This spring, Tom confided in his friend that he had completed a series of sketches recording the changes in Algonquin seasons and landscape for sixty successive days. There has always been controversy over the amount of painting he did that spring, for when his brother, George, arrived to take over his belongings in July, there were only thirty-five spring sketches in his cabin. The discrepancy between these figures has never been accounted for.

That summer Tom decided to stay at Canoe Lake instead of going north again to fire range. He had purchased a guide's license once more, and seemed to be planning to take out groups of fishermen on trips from Shannon Fraser's. His reasons for this change of routine would be difficult to explain. Perhaps, with the sale of some of his larger canvases, he felt it better not to tie himself down to one section of the Park for the whole summer; perhaps health considerations entered into the picture. Just why Tom was rejected by the army when he applied for enlistment has not been recorded, but he felt so badly about it that he did not even discuss it to his friends. At any rate, on the fateful Sunday morning of July eighth, 1917, Tom was still at Canoe Lake.

Over twenty-five years later, there are still eight people who were living at Canoe Lake at that time, who have their own versions of what took place. The following account includes only those points on which there is general agreement.

Nothing out of the way had happened in the Canoe Lake community in the preceding weeks. Mr. and Mrs. Colson had recently taken over the management of the Hotel Algonquin; Shannon and Mrs. Fraser were running Mowat Lodge; Taylor Statten had rented Little Wapomeo Island for a few weeks to Dr. Goldwin Howland of Toronto; Mr. T. H. Hayhurst was at his cottage on the point above which is now the Tom Thomson cairn; and Martin Blecher was at his house, formerly the Park Headquarters, at the outlet of Canoe Lake Creek. Mark Robinson was the closest ranger to Canoe Lake, as he was then living in the ranger's cabin near the railway tracks, at Joe Creek.

Tom Thomson's actions on the morning of the day of his death are fairly well defined. Mark remembers having seen Tom passing his cabin early in the day. He was with Shannon Fraser at the time, and Shannon afterwards told Mark that they were talking about a large trout which Tom and Mark had both tried to pull out of Joe Lake Creek, above the dam. Each had hooked him several times, but the fish had always managed to get away. Now Tom had decided to play a joke on Mark by catching another large fish somewhere else, and leaving it on Mark's doorstep in the pretence that the object of their rivalry had been captured. Mark says both he and Tom knew a fish of that size was unusual, and that one of the best places to get them was at Gill Lake, a small, rather inaccessible spot to the southwest of Canoe Lake. For that reason Mark feels sure that Tom was headed towards this lake on the afternoon he was drowned.

Later in the morning, when Shannon had gone back to the Lodge, Tom dropped in at the Hotel Algonquin, where Mrs. Colson was busy at work. The Colsons had not been at Joe Lake for very long, and Mr. Colson had never met Tom. However, Mrs. Colson had talked to him on several occasions, and this time he came into the kitchen for a cup of tea. Afterwards, Mrs. Colson did not recall anything peculiar about him on that occasion. He seemed his normal self, and chatted in a friendly fashion. He left before lunchtime to return to Mowat Lodge.

About one o'clock that afternoon the guests at the Lodge saw him leaving his dock in his own grey canoe. He looked as though he were going off for a day's fishing, since he had his tackle and some food supplies in the bow of the canoe. That was the last anyone saw of Tom alive; what happened afterwards is an unsolved mystery.

Towards evening, Charlie Scrim, a young chap staying at the Lodge, and who was a particular admirer of Tom's, began to feel uneasy about his friend. No one else felt this uneasiness, because Tom often went off by himself and was sometimes away for weeks at a time. It was not till two days later, on July 10th, that news came of Tom's canoe having been found floating empty behind Little Wapomeo Island. Martin Bletcher, and his sister, afterwards mentioned having seen it between Mowat Lodge landing and the large island, when they had passed by about three o'clock on July 8th, but they had thought it to be one of the canoes owned by the Colsons and rented to guests at the hotel, which had come adrift, and they had done nothing about it.

When the canoe had been identified as Tom's, everyone started to search the lake. At first the rangers could not believe he could have drowned, because the canoe was found floating in an upright position. The paddles were lashed into place as if for portaging, and some of the food was still in the bow. However, his pack sack and his fishing tackle had disappeared, and these never were recovered. Acting on the supposition that Tom might have gone on foot through the woods to find a good fishing place, search parties travelled all through the surrounding country. Naturally, the area around the portage through to Gill Lake was covered very thoroughly, although it was considered nearly impossible for the canoe to have drifted such a distance from the time Tom had arrived there after leaving the landing, and the time when the canoe was first sighted by the Blechers.

When the news of Tom's disappearance reached his family in Owen Sound, his brother, George, had just come north to Canada from New Haven, where he had been studying art. As quickly as possible, he went by train to Canoe Lake, but on his arrival, there was still no further news of what had taken place — Tom's canoe had been found, and there still remained a slight chance of him having landed somewhere along the shore, and that he was still alive in the bush. George Thomson waited for several days at Mowat Lodge and then, because there seemed to be nothing that he could do, he decided to return to Owen Sound. Before he left, however, he took possession of the belongings which Tom had left behind in the shack, and made arrangements to complete the things that would have to be done in the event of his brother's death.

Soon after George departed from the Canoe Lake district, Tom's body was found floating in the lake. Old-timers in the Park say that a body frequently comes to the surface on the eighth day and the theory was confirmed on this occasion. On Monday, July 16th, Dr. Howland was sitting on the verandah of the cabin at Little Wapomeo when he saw an object come up to the surface of the water. He called to George Rowe and Larry Dickson, the two guides from Mowat, who were passing by in a canoe, and they paddled over to investigate. When they reached the spot, they found the object was Thomson's body. They towed it over to Big Wampomeo Island, and there decided that they should notify the Park Headquarters as quickly as possible. One of them stayed behind on the Island while the other paddled off to notify the Park authorities.

At Headquarters, Mr. Bartlett instructed Mark Robinson to go over to the island and stay there until the coroner arrived from North Bay. Since Dr. Raney, the coroner, could not possibly be there until the next day, Mark took along supplies sufficient for his sojourn on the island until Dr. Raney's arrival. Consequently, Mark and one of the other rangers kept an all-night vigil on the shore during the night of July 16th.

When the coroner reached Canoe Lake the next day, he was met at the station, and Martin Bletcher offered the use of his house, which was close by, as a place to hold the inquest. In the evening, Dr. Howland was called in to assist in making the examination of the body. They found no water in the lungs, and seeing evidence of a dark bruise on the temple, they gave the verdict as one of "accidental death". It is possible that Tom Thomson may have died from heart failure, or he could have fallen and struck his head on a rock when he landed his canoe, either at the place where he planned to portage, or where he expected to eat his lunch.

According to the opinions of these people, Tom was a good swimmer and an excellent canoeist. As one of his friends said, he had a short, low stroke like an Indian's, yet it was so characteristic that you could tell it was Tom's canoe when he was still away down the lake. He was a kind, likeable person, who minded his own business and expected others to mind theirs. In this way he made himself quite unobtrusive in the neighbourhood, and he was well liked by those who did know him. No one is ever likely to know just what happended after he departed from the Mowat Lodge dock on that fatal Sunday afternoon.

It was impossible to notify the Thomson family in Owen Sound in time for them to arrive for the funeral, and the decision was made to bury Tom in the Mowat graveyard behind the Lodge, where several plots, dating from the time when lumbermen were operating in that region, had already been set aside. The funeral service was held on the morning after the inquest, with a number of Tom's old friends gathered at his graveside. Mr. Bletcher, senior, read the service from Mark's Anglican prayer book, and the body was laid to rest.

Present-day visitors would like to think that Tom Thomson's grave is still to be found in that Canoe Lake Cemetery, but the cairn on the monument across the lake tells that "His body is buried at Owen Sound". From George Thomson, his brother, we learn the reason for this. On his arrival at Owen Sound he was informed his brother's body had been found. As there was little else he could do, he arranged for the body to be brought from the original burying-place to the family plot at Owen Sound. In spite of the fact that many of Tom's old friends have always felt that he would have preferred to remain buried in his beloved Algonquin Park, there is really no reason to doubt that this change of burial place was made.

Some of Tom's artist friends travelled to the Park as soon as they heard of his death, but there was little they could do when they arrived. J. E. H. MacDonald and J. W. Beatty, who were there at the time, found that somehow the place had lost much of its charm for them — Tom Thomson had become so much a part of it in their memories that they could not even paint there. They decided to build a memorial cairn at the top of Hayhurst's Point — a height which overlooks Tom Thomson's beloved Canoe Lake district. Together they arranged to have the rocks hauled to the top of the hill, while J. E. H. MacDonald designed the bronze plaque with the story of Tom's career. There, to this day, visitors may read this tribute to the man whom many people in the Park knew as their friend, and whom other Canadians have come to know as a pioneer in Canadian art:

TO THE MEMORY OF
TOM THOMSON
ARTIST — WOODSMAN —AND GUIDE
who was drowned in Canoe Lake,
July 8th, 1917.

*He lived humbly but passionately with the wild — it made him brother to all untamed things of nature. It drew him apart and revealed itself wonderfully to him. It sent him out from the woods only to show these revelations through his art — and it took him to itself at last.*

As one stands at the crest overlooking the dancing waters of the lake below, one has the feeling that Tom Thomson would have been content to know that the spot has been set aside as his own. From there in the spring, during the break-up season, you can look over towards the hills, for this point is close to where his own "Spring Ice" was painted.

Here in the heart of Algonquin Park, Tom Thomson found his real home: and here he died.

## CHAPTER 16

THE INFLUENCE of Algonquin Park on Canadian life did not cease with the birth of a native Canadian art movement within its borders. Today we are witnessing a new development of which even the vision of Kirkwood hardly caught a glimpse, a development of practical value to the whole world.

Today, without in any way hampering its other activities, Algonquin Park has become a vast laboratory for study and research in natural science. Of recent years, scientists who wish to carry out controlled experiments on a wide scale have found the Park an excellent area for such work. Park authorities have given generous assistance to many different groups who have carried on field work within the Park boundaries. Experts in the employ of the Ontario Department of Lands and Forests, as well as from other different Provincial and Dominion Departments, from the various departments of the University of Toronto, the Royal Ontario Museum of Zoology, and other institutions, have found in the Park excellent facilities for carrying on their studies.

The pioneer move in this direction took place as early as 1908, when the first Forestry Practice Camp held by the Faculty of Forestry, University of Toronto, was held in Algonquin Park. In that year, three students, one of whom was T. W. Dwight, a present member of the Faculty, with two instructors, took over the rangers' cabin at the north end of Burnt (now Portal) Lake, in order to carry on field work in surveying and timber cruising. Barnet's Depot was then situated on the lake, and the students were able to gain a practical insight into the methods used by lumber companies at that time. The Forestry Camp was not held in the Park again until 1924, when it was established at Achray on the Northern Railway. There it continued until 1935, when it was moved to Haliburton County. During those eleven years valuable records were compiled by students and staff on the age and growth of tree life in the Park.

Typically, when this new field of usefulness for the Park had been opened up, others came to develop its possibilities. The Beaver Survey carried on by Mr. Donald L. Robb in the Park has been mentioned, but his was only one of several such investigations into the habits and peculiarities of different species of wildlife to be found in the area. Dr. D. A. MacLulich, known for his work on the rabbit cycle, used the Park as a laboratory from 1932 until 1936. In 1934 Dr. C. H. D. Clarke undertook a study of the Ruffed Grouse of the district in an effort to determine what disease was causing the death of many of these birds. A study of the mollusca was undertaken in 1935 by Messrs. Pritchard and LaRocque, of the National Museum of Canada. In 1939 and 1940, Mr. E. C. Cross and Mr. S. C. Downing, of the Royal Ontario Museum of Zoology, began a live trapping study of small mammals. While the last project has not been completed, reports on all the others are available to specialists in these different fields. Algonquin Park research has added much to the scientific data available to naturalists in other parts of the world.

Information compiled by the Ontario Fisheries Research Laboratory has been used by the Ontario Government and by other agencies interested in the results of their investigations. This work has been under the direction of Professor W. J. K. Harkness of the University of Toronto. From 1919 to 1934, the Ontario Fisheries Research Laboratory carried out studies on a great number of Ontario waters including Lake Ontario, Lake Nipissing, Lake Nipigon, the Trent Valley Canal, and trout streams of Southern Ontario. In 1929 the Laboratory first instituted investigations in the Park, when Mr. W. E. Ricker and Mr. F. P. Ide spent some time on Wolf and Ragged Lakes, the Oxtongue River; and on the Nipissing River in the northern part of the Park, for the purpose of studying the ecology of these trout lakes and streams.

At the direct request of Superintendent MacDougall, Professor Harkness visited many lakes in the Park to select the best site for a permanent laboratory from which to carry out fisheries investigations. In 1935, a field laboratory was established on Cache Lake. Five biologists worked here under Professor J. R. Dymond and Dr. E. B. Ide. Since then, fisheries studies in the Park have been carried on continuously. In the following year, a laboratory headquarters was constructed on Opeongo Lake, the largest body of water in the Park, and close to other important lakes and streams.

This laboratory has been the centre for fisheries research, which under the direction of Professor Harkness, has been extended to include studies of aquatic biology in all the important lakes and streams of the Park. Many students have here completed their field work leading to a Master's or Doctor's degree, besides the training gained in research.

One feature of this work is the creel census. By the distribution and collection of special cards to co-operative anglers in the Park, the biologists are now accumulating valuable records; asking such questions as, how long were you fishing, how many fish were caught, their size, and what specie were they? The cards are placed in boxes located at the ends of portages, at camp sites, and other convenient points. Distribution and collection of the cards is in charge of Fish Laboratory students who travel about the Park in the summer season.

At Opeongo and Cache Lakes, Fish Laboratory employees are on hand to assist in getting additional information about the fish taken from the lakes. If the angler is willing, his fish is examined to determine from its stomach contents what it has been feeding on, whether it is a female and would spawn during the year, and how old it was. The age of a fish can be determined by an examination of its scales. By reference to this tabulated data, the experts can determine the average length of time it takes to catch a fish, and the size of the average fish caught. Thus they know whether the number of fish is increasing or declining in any given lake. Few fishermen who fill in these census cards or bring in their catch to be examined, realize the importance of their co-operation. Records built up in this way have resulted in a new management policy concerning the lakes in the Park and has brought about widespread improvements in the fishing in these lakes.

Under this new policy, begun in 1938, a number of lakes are closed to fishing in alternate years. The experiment is in its infancy, but the creel census returns already show this technique will be of great value in maintaining fish production. A fact which illustrates this is that lake trout, which do not spawn in the fall, frequently reach regulation size during the summer, and though fishermen who catch them are within the letter of the law, next year's crop of fish is reduced.

At Smoke Lake, on the request of the Leaseholders' Association, a further step has been taken to maintain the fish population. Trolling from boats propelled by mechanical power has been prohibited. It was felt that when people have to paddle a canoe while fishing, they will stop when they have caught what they want, or even before if their muscles are soft. With a motor-propelled boat they will continue to circle around until they have caught their quota or have run out of fuel.

Research work in the Fish Laboratory has proved to have a much wider sphere of usefulness. During World War II, scientific studies of the oxygen capacity of the blood, and of respiratory devices for the use of Canadian airmen, benefited directly from the Fish Laboratory findings. Other branches of science have also benefited. Such men as Drs. F. E. Fry, E. C. Black, W. A. Kennedy and W. R. Martin have spent summers in fisheries research in the Park.

The work started here is now carried on in other Provincial Parks in Ontario. In 1944 and 1945 Professor Harkness directed the establishment of similar activities in Quetico, Sibley, and Lake Superior Provincial Parks, all of which show promise of real assistance in the conservation of fish in these areas.

In the summer of 1944 the Park became the scene of an experiment to test the possibilities of the use of DDT to eliminate forest pests. Already this insecticide had proved its worth in war areas, and now the authorities were anxious to know if it could be used to combat the spruce budworm which was attacking the Algonquin balsam and spruce forests. Professor Harkness offered the facilities of the Ontario Museum Fisheries Research Laboratories in conjunction with the Royal Ontario Museum of Zoology, in order to make a complete study of the situation. The effects of the spray on the fish, insect, and mammal life of the area were investigated. Dr. R. R. Langford, a member of the Laboratory Staff, supervised this phase of the work, while Mr. K. E. Stewart, entomologist with the Dominion Department of Agriculture, was in charge of the forest insect investigation in the Park at that time.

This study showed that there would be certain indirect effects from the spray on the other forms of wildlife which were dependent on insects destroyed along with the spruce budworm. The food supply of many birds and smaller mammals would be destroyed. Amphibians and reptiles would also suffer a heavy death toll from the effects of the spray, but it was felt that if the spraying was not repeated too frequently, the natural fertility and the migration of these animals would probably enable the population to recover. Fish, with the exception of speckled trout, seemed to be unaffected by the DDT, but, of course, they did suffer from the reduced supply of insects for food. Many of the animals on which fish depend for food, such as crayfish, were found to be seriously affected by the insecticide. However, it was decided as the result of this work, and on consultation with American authorities who were conducting similar experiments, that it would be worth while to continue with the aerial spraying program. In the Park, and elsewhere, with a certain amount of care on the part of the pilots of the aircraft from which the spray was being released, it was felt it would be possible to reduce the damages to other wildlife by shutting off the flow of the spray while passing over lakes and rivers. In this way the effect on water creatures could be reduced to a minimum.

Usually, Park visitors are unaware of the important scientific work being carried on in the area, but on this occasion, their attention was attracted by the ingenious markers used by the ground workers to guide the pilot to the special plot that was to receive the spray. At the top of lofty balsam trees near the highway, and close to the railway in the south part of the Park, the visitors saw cheesecloth bags mounted on poles projecting above the tops of the lofty balsam trees. From the air, the pilot could easily identify the rectangular plot to be sprayed by locating the four sign posts erected at the corners.

Another example of the way in which the authorities have encouraged the use of Park facilities for scientific research, is the action taken by the Department in 1944, providing for a Nature Reserve of thirty-one and one-half square miles within the Park boundaries. This research area was set aside as the result of a request made by the Federation of Ontario Naturalists for the reserving of an area where there would be no interference whatever with natural conditions as they existed at the time of its establishment. In the remainder of the Park, where fishing, canoeing, and lumbering are carried on, there will, of course, be no changes as a result of these activities, but in this reserve it is hoped to allow Nature to carry on in her own way over a long period of time. The area set aside for this purpose in the Park lies in a region readily accessible for purpose of study, being north of the highway and east of Canisbay, Linda, and Burnt Island Lakes. Authorities are hopeful of obtaining valuable information in future on the interdependence of the flora and fauna of the district as the result of the observations to be conducted in this region. These scientific activities, far from interfering with the holiday life of visitors, directly contributed to their enlightenment, and increase the value of their vacations.

A new item appeared on the Park program. Professor Dymond had been working and holidaying in the Park for several years, when in 1942, Mrs. A. G. Northway asked him to take a group of Boy Scouts, who were at that time visiting Nominigan Lodge, on a hike along some of the nearby trails, making use of the opportunity to tell them about the trees, wild flowers, birds, and anything else of interest found in the course of their ramble. Several adults, hearing of the proposed expedition, asked if they might join the party. The outing was such a success that the Smoke Lake nature hikes became a regular feature. Since then, these informal lessons proved so popular, they served as a general rallying point for all the campers on the lake. Young and old alike found the knowledge they acquired in this way made their Algonquin holiday all the more enjoyable.

This Smoke Lake programme had been under way for two years when the Department of Lands and Forests persuaded Professor Dymond to extend it to include other areas of the Park, so as to give other visitors the opportunity of learning something of the wonders of their surroundings. Only three of many ways of furthering nature education were attempted the first year, but these reached many of the Park visitors. Conducted nature hikes were arranged to start from various points accessible to summer cottagers and hotel guests; a beginning was made in the planning of nature trails; and talks were given at the boys' and girls' camps. The hikes were similar to those conducted previously, but this time the participants were given mimeographed lists of the common plants and animals, so that they could carry on by themselves once they had the idea of what there was to be learned about their environment.

This is one final example of the unique way in which the Park exerts its influence on those who live within its boundaries. No visitor comes away without feeling that influence.

It is a far cry today from the time when swarthy Algonquin hunters stripped bark from its birch trees for their canoes, speared fish below its falls, snared the rabbit, slew the deer and moose. The Iroquois no longer holds up the bloody scalp-lock of his fallen foe in savage triumph. Trappers and settlers have come and gone; only a few piles of sand remain of the camboose camps of the great square timber days.

Yearly, the visitors increase in numbers and their Park activities multiply. Yearly, new ideas develop for conserving the wildlife and forest wealth; the fondest dreams of Alexander Kirkwood and the most practical expectations of James Dickson have been more than realized. Algonquin Park will go on expanding its usefulness. To rangers and residents and visitors, to all who know the Park for what it is, the intangible spirit of the Park that found such adequate expression in the paintings of Tom Thomson is the one value they cherish most.

No better words can be found than those of a visitor, leader of an early American youth movement, to express what the Park has meant to the thousands who love it. Dr. Lester Scott is more than a visitor. For twenty-five years he and his family made the Park their summer home in a manner that would have satisfied even the veteran surveyor Dickson. When asked to recall some of his experiences, Dr. Scott wrote the following words:

> "Our friends in New York used to say that there were only two dates in our family, Christmas, and the day we left each year for Algonquin Park. That was perfectly true during all those years that we came north for our holidays in Canada. We took our son into the bush when he was only four months old and our daughter when she was ten months old. We carried them in pack baskets in the bow of our canoe while they were taking their naps. We went where we pleased, babies didn't stop us, they were part of the fun. Our youngsters have always talked of Algonquin Park as their other home.
>
> "Once, some years ago, we figured that we had actually spent more than two and a half years camping in Algonquin Park, and two and a half years of living in any one place leaves a mark, especially when that place is largely wilderness. Remember that our impressions of the southern part of the Park were gained when there was no ranger's cabin at Joe Lake; when there were no buildings whatever, except the remains of an old lumber camp on Smoke; when there were no camps on Canoe; and when Ragged Lake was quite out of the world and not included in the Park limits at all. On our first cruise in 1911 south from Joe Lake through Canoe and down into Black Bear and Lake Louisa we saw only three people — and two of them were guides going home to Huntsville at the season's end. The Merrills ran the Algonquin Hotel at Joe; there was no railway station there; Shan Fraser was the postmaster at Mowat; and the Algonquin Indians from Golden Lake were still acting as guides for trips.
>
> "In that day there was no railroad north of the line which ran alongside Cache Lake. There were no wagon roads into the Park, except for short distances, only a few hardy campers got as far north as Cedar

Lake and came out to Manitou and Tea Lakes to the line running between Toronto and North Bay. The building of the Canadian Northern Railway meant the opening up of the northern section of the Park to tourists, but that section has never been as thickly populated as the region now accessible by road in the south. The lakes are larger, the distances greater, and it had still preserved many of its original wilderness characteristics.

"Many of us prefer the northern section of the Park for this reason — there we still find many places where the 'trails run out and stop'. The zip and zing of the cold balsam-laden air of early August and the call of the loon were my first impression of Algonquin Park nights and they still mark that land as different for me. But there are many other things that mean Algonquin Park to me — the flying call of the loon, and that other characteristic call with its dropped terminal note; the sound of wings beating on the water as they take off in flight; the hoot and answering hoot of owls; the howl of the timber wolves, and cry-baby wailing of porcupines when they are not clicking their teeth at you in rage, and the distant (and for the sake of one's peace of mind keep it distant) odour of the woods' pussy — all these are part of the backdrop before which the camper acts out of his daily drama of cooking, woods housekeeping, fishing and cruising.

"There one learns, too, that all clowns are not human. Bears can be very funny and porcupines, while not actually rollicking, are not as stupid as their reputation. Then there was the time when camp was deserted and I was smoking my pipe while patching my canoe. I heard a movement close at hand, and glancing up, found a whole family of grouse sitting on a log watching my every movement. I blew a puff of smoke from my lips, but the whole family continued to squat there not an arm's reach away. I blew another puff and they ducked, but stayed right where they were. We kept up this game until I finally had to laugh out loud and then they slid silently off the log and melted into the bush. How often we watched the red squirrels busily knocking down pine cones only to have them stolen by rascally chipmunks who got well away into their burrows before the scolding red squirrels could get down from the trees. And then there's the story of the inquisitive bear at one of the lumber camps who wandered in the cook shack and had it all to himself, for the cooks piled out of the door in a hurry. That suited Mr. Bear very well, and he went about helping himself to an ample meal. Then he reached up to the top of the stove and hooked a pot of beans down to the floor. The fun certainly started then, most of the boiling contents of the pot smothered his head in transit, all hell broke loose in the shack, and the visitor beat a hasty retreat into the woods. They had to rebuild most of the shack afterwards.

"How often, when we were camped in the Park, have we thought of the great canoes that used to pass close at hand along the waterways leading from the far west. Their canoes were twenty-footers, while the largest we ever had was eighteen. We used that one for a long time, but my favorite craft was a thirteen-footer, a chestnut that weighed less than fifteen pounds—and that one was a canoeman's dream. This little fellow was brought from Mrs. Bell in Ottawa. It had been made for her husband, Dr. Bell, when he worked as a ranger in the Park in order to regain his health. To Dr. Bell, too, we were indebted for the famous blue-print map that all campers preferred to the Government issue of the time.

"Since that time there have been several maps and we old campers have always watched for new ones with interest. The early ones showed few lakes in the north part of the Park. Later maps showed many lakes that had been there all the time but just hadn't been located till later. What fun that was — finding a lake that wasn't on the map. We found many during our wanderings; it gave us quite a thrill of exploring in an unknown country.

"One day when the use of planes for patrolling was new, I was repairing a birch-bark canoe on the shores of a little northern lake. I had built a small fire to warm some pitch in a can when I heard the Ontario Fire Patrol plane away off, and I knew they had spotted my smoke. The plane kept getting closer until the head came low and I saw the pilot waving at me. He was doing his work in the Park with the newest form of transportation — I was patching up one of the oldest to carry me on my way.

"Now, although we are making our home in Arizona, on the desert's edge, we still hear from some of the rangers and guides, amongst whom we count our very good friends. They tell us of the lakes where the lumber companies are cutting and of the improvements in their methods. In the old days they sometimes left disfiguring slash all through the district, but now the pine on the small islands is left untouched and the shorelines for a distance of three hundred feet are left intact. In fact, if one had not known the land of old, he'd never miss the trees taken out unless he penetrated the forest.

"In later years we established our headquarters at Kioskoqui and it became the gathering place for all the older youngsters — boys from college, classmates of my boy's. They felt about our camp just as we did — it was a place apart, a different place, a quiet or a riotously gay place, as the spirit moved them. We've had the thrill of having lads come over a thousand miles just to be with us there for three days. That says something for the forests and the lakes that words will never say.

"After the war, all that are left of the old crowd are coming back at least once more. They won't all come — some of them are never again to handle a paddle or to cast a lure. Their memory will be part of the sweetness of the place to us who have shared the life of the woods with them, the days of calm and rioting water, the stars so close that they spoke to you, the mystery of what lay around the bend of the stream, the nights of glorious moon and the majestic sweep of the aurora, the mud on your mocassins, the rain down our backs, the flame of the maples after the

> first frost, and the end of the trip with its midnight paddle to the rails and the wait for the glow of the headlight and the whistle that said our annual 'Good-bye' to our camp."

To many a former resident of Algonquin Park, to many a past visitor, the name brings back a nostalgic flood of memories. But the Park, with its roots in the past, stretches its branches up towards the future; a young and lusty pine, bursting with sap, and reaching out into the clean northern air.

**THE END**

# *Algonquin Story* Errata and Notes

**compiled by**
**Roderick MacKay, George Garland**
**and Dan Strickland**

In the original edition, some typographical errors occurred. It is hoped all are listed here. While a general update of post-*Algonquin Story* history is provided in the introduction, some specific notes on the original text have been added here for historical clarification. Corrections and additions are indicated by page, paragraph, and line.

**Page 3, par. 2, line 7**
The statement that "the Ottawas claimed hunting rights on slopes falling toward the Ottawa River" fails to reflect the succession of Indian nations which controlled southern Ontario after the first contact with European explorers. The original Algonquins of the Ottawa River watershed, first met by Champlain in the early 1600s, were attacked and displaced from Ontario in or about 1650 by the Iroquois. The Ojibwa (Mississauga, Chippewa, Ottawa, Potawatamies and others) subsequently attacked the occupying Iroquois between 1696 and 1700, and replaced them as native occupants of all but the easternmost part of modern day Ontario.

**Page 6, par. 2, line 5**
persuasian *should be* persuasion

**Page 10, par. 1**
The Iroquois claimed the area along the north shore of Lake Huron east to the Ottawa River and south to Lake Ontario, at least to 1763, although there were few Iroquois in southern Ontario west of Brockville on the St. Lawrence River after 1700. Maps showing Iroquois dominance of the Algonquin Park area in the 1700s appear to be incorrect, as historical evidence suggests the area was used by Mississauga and other Algonquians at that time. Also, modern ethnographers would refer to the Mississauga as an Algonquian tribe (not "Algonquin").

**Page 10, par. 2**
Saunders used the word Algonquin, according to the accepted usage of her day, to signify what we now refer to as Algonquian. The particular Algonquian groups that began to hunt in the Park area after the expulsion

of the Iroquois from Ontario around 1700 included the Ojibwa (Chippewas and Mississaugas) based mostly farther south in Ontario, and other people based at Oka on the Lake of Two Mountains, just west of Montreal. Although lumped under the term "Algonquin" at the time, the Oka-based people were in fact predominately Nipissings, another Algonquian-speaking nation originally from the Lake Nipissing area northwest of the Park. Like the true Algonquins (original inhabitants of the Ottawa Valley), the Nipissings had been devastated by the attacks of the Iroquois in the mid 1600s and the survivors had taken refuge in a succession of Roman Catholic missions in Quebec including, finally, the one at Oka.

**Page 14, par. 4, line 5**
Reconsideration of the route taken by Catty suggests that he travelled farther south, through modern Haliburton County, and that he did not enter what is now the Park.

**Page 14, par. 5, line 10**
Sundan *should be* Sunday

**Page 14, par. 5, line 12**
Some other writers have interpreted a route through Crow Lake and Crow River to Lake Lavieille and the Petawawa River.

**Page 20, par. 2, line 12**
The map accompanying Sherriff's report clearly indicates the present Kootchie, Little Island, and Tanamakoon Lakes, not Source Lake.

**Page 26, para 3, line 1**
Apparently a handwritten report by David Thompson was misplaced and overlooked for many years, including the period during which this book was researched and written. The report has been rediscovered since.

**Page 27, par. 3, line 11**
Black Bear is now Big Porcupine Lake.

**Page 29, par. 2, line 8**
Since 1974, timber has been cut by the Algonquin Forestry Authority (a Crown Agency), and timber limits are no longer used.

## *ALGONQUIN STORY*

**Page 30, par. 1, line 10**
The hewer, standing on top of the log *should be* The hewer, standing beside the log

**Page 39, par. 1, line 12**
shirt tales *should be* shirt tails

**Page 53, par. 1, line 3**
Garvie *should be* Garvey

**Page 62, par. 4, line 4**
Tea Lake was never named Waskigomog Lake; however, North Tea Lake was named Waskigomog Lake from 1951 to 1964.

**Page 74, par. 3, line 1**
The first Gilmour Drive was in 1894, not 1895.

**Page 78, par. 3, line 3**
The term Algonquians (referring to the peoples speaking the Algonquian family of languages), rather than Algonquins, would be the term used today. The commissioners wished to perpetuate the memory of "one of the greatest Indian nations" which "included the Nipissings, Ottawas, Montagnais, Delawares, Wyandots, Mississaugas and over thirty other different tribes".

**Page 79, par. 3, line 5**
Dickson's report on Finlayson Township was in 1878, and in 1880 for Peck Township, not 1885 as inferred.

**Page 86, par. 5, line 2**
exerted on the Park by its visitors *should be* exerted by the Park on its visitors

**Page 87, par. 1, line 4**
funeral *should be* funereal

**Page 87, par. 3, line 8**
clintoia *should be* Clintonia

**Page 87, par. 6, line 1**
wild life *should be* wildlife

## *ALGONQUIN STORY*

**Page 87, par. 6, line 2**
Wolves have been protected in Algonquin Park since 1965.

**Page 88, par. 2, line 3**
hitchpitched *should be* high-pitched

**Page 88, par. 2, line 7**
olive-backed thrust *should be* Olive-backed Thrush (now Swainson's Thrush)

**Page 88, par. 2, line 12**
ruffled grouse *should be* Ruffed Grouse

**Page 88, par. 5, line 1**
wild life *should be* wildlife

**Page 89, par. 1, line 2**
ring-nacked *should be* Ringneck Snake

**Page 93, par. 3, line 5**
Dunfonds *should be* Dufonds

**Page 96, par. 4, line 10**
the widow McCormack *should be* the widow McDonald

**Page 98, par. 3, line 9**
Burnt Lake *should be* Burntroot Lake

**Page 99, par. 5, line 3**
Wilson did not accompany the first party to Canoe Lake.

**Page 107, par. 1, line 28**
Wilkes Lake is now Manitou Lake, again.

**Page 123, par. 3**
The Algonquin Park Master Plan was published in 1974 and revised as the Algonquin Park Management Plan in 1998.

**Pages 131 and 132**
Kish-Kaduk Lodge, Opeongo Lodge, Minnesing Hotel, and Highland Inn no longer exist.

## *ALGONQUIN STORY*

**Page 132, par. 2, line 3**
Sherman *should be* Sharman

**Page 144, par. 4, line 3**
"Camp and Character" *should be* "Camping and Character"

**Page 151, par. 4, line 4**
MacFarlane *should be* McFarland

**Pages 158 and 159**
Wolves have been protected in Algonquin Park since 1965.

**Page 171, par. 1, line 13**
Later authorities (Addison, Murray) state that Thomson first went to Achray in 1916, not 1915.

**Page 174, par. 3, line 4**
"Northern River" (1915) could not have been painted in the Grand Lake district, since Thomson first went to Achray in 1916.

**Page 174, par. 3, line 11**
Karishoo Creek *should be* Karkishoo Creek (now Carcajou Creek)

# *Selected Reading*

Addison, O. 1974. *Early Days in Algonquin Park.* McGraw-Hill Ryerson Ltd., Toronto. (Reprinted in 1994 by The Friends of Algonquin Park, Whitney, Ontario.)

Addison, O. and E. Harwood. 1969. *Tom Thomson: the Algonquin Years.* Ryerson Press, Toronto. (Reprinted in 1995 by McGraw-Hill Ryerson Ltd., Toronto.)

Bell, A. 1991. *A Way to the West: a Canadian Railway Legend.* Published by the author.

Bice, R. 1980. *Along the Trail With Ralph Bice in Algonquin Park.* Consolidated Amethyst Communications Ltd., Toronto. (Reprinted in 1993 by Natural Heritage/Natural History Inc., Toronto.)

Bignell, J. and B. Bignell. 1988. *Pringrove: the Later Years.* Muskoka Printing, Dwight, Ontario.

Davies, B. 1967. *Tom Thomson: the Story of a Man Who Looked for Beauty and for Truth in the Wilderness.* Mitchell Press Ltd., Vancouver.

Dickson, J. 1886. *Camping in the Muskoka Region.* C. Blackett Robinson, Toronto. (Reprinted in 1959 by the Ontario Department of Lands and Forests, Toronto, and in 1997, as *A Nineteenth-Century Algonquin Adventure*, edited and with an Introduction and Notes by G. Long, Fox Meadow Creations, Huntsville, Ontario.)

Edwards, C.A.M. 1960. *Taylor Statten.* Ryerson Press, Toronto.

Eldridge, R. and O.F. Osborne. 1996. *Cache Lake Reflections: a Madawaska Voyage.* Published by the authors.

Gage, S.R. 1985. *A Few Rustic Huts: Ranger Cabins and Logging Camp Buildings of Algonquin Park.* Mosaic Press, Oakville, Ontario.

Garland, G.D. 1993. *Names of Algonquin: Stories Behind the Lake and Place Names of Algonquin Provincial Park.* The Friends of Algonquin Park, Whitney, Ontario.

Garland, G.D. (compiler). 1994. *Glimpses of Algonquin: Thirty Personal Impressions From the Earliest Times to the Present.* The Friends of Algonquin Park, Whitney, Ontario.

Hamilton, M.G. 1958. *The Call of Algonquin: a Biography of a Summer Camp.* Ryerson Press, Toronto.

Home, K.P. 1984. *Guiding in Algonquin Park in the Twenties.* Published by the author.

Kase, E.H. 1972. *Jack Gervais: Ranger and Friend.* Published by the author.

Kase, E.H. 1975. *Pringrove Through the Years.* Published by the author.

Little, W.T. 1970. *The Tom Thomson Mystery.* McGraw-Hill, Toronto.

Lundell, L. and B. Bailey. 1994. *Summer Camp: Great Camps of Algonquin Park.* Boston Mills Press, Erin, Ontario.

MacKay, N. 1981. *Over the Hills to Georgian Bay: a Pictorial History of the Ottawa, Arnprior and Parry Sound Railway.* Boston Mills Press, Erin, Ontario. (Reprinted in 1992 by Boston Mills Press, Erin, Ontario.)

MacKay, R. 2002. *A Chronology of Algonquin Park History.* The Friends of Algonquin Park, Whitney, Ontario.

MacKay, R. 1996. *Spirits of the Little Bonnechere: a History of Exploration, Logging, and Settlement: 1800 to 1920.* Friends of Bonnechere Parks, Pembroke, Ontario.

MacKay, R. and W. Reynolds. 1993. *Algonquin.* Boston Mills Press, Erin, Ontario.

Murray, J. 1986. *The Best of Tom Thomson.* Hurtig Publishers, Edmonton.

Murray, J. 1994. *Tom Thomson: the Last Spring.* Dundurn Press, Toronto.

Pigeon, M.M. 1993. *Born in Brule Lake, Algonquin Park.* Published by the author. (Reprinted in 1995 by The Friends of Algonquin Park, Whitney, Ontario.)

Pigeon, M.M. 1995. *Living at Cache Lake, Algonquin Park, 1936 to 1950, with Tributes to my Father, Tom McCormick, Chief Ranger.* The Friends of Algonquin Park, Whitney, Ontario.

Rand, M. 1995. *Paddles Flashing in the Sun: the Stories of Pathfinder in Algonquin Park.* Quaker Press, West Seneca, New York.

Standfield, D. and L. Lundell. 1993. *Algonquin: the Park and its People.* McClelland & Stewart Inc., Toronto.

Shaw, S.B. 1996. *Canoe Lake, Algonquin Park.* General Store Publishing House, Burnstown, Ontario.

Shaw, S.B. 1998. *Lake Opeongo, Untold Stories of Algonquin Park's Largest Lake.* General Store Publishing House, Burnstown, Ontario.

Townsend, E.R. 1996. *Algonquin Forestry Authority: a 20 Year History (1975-1995).* Algonquin Forestry Authority, Huntsville, Ontario.

Tozer, R. and D. Strickland. 1995. *A Pictorial History of Algonquin Provincial Park.* The Friends of Algonquin Park, Whitney, Ontario.

Westhouse, B.D. 2003. *Whitney : St. Anthony's Mill Town on Booth's Railway.* The Friends of Algonquin Park, Whitney, Ontario.

Wicksteed, B. 1948. *Joe Lavally and the Paleface.* Wm. Collins Ltd., London. (Reprinted in 2003 by The Friends of Algonquin Park, Whitney, Ontario.)

Extensive listings of published and/or unpublished resources are also available in *A Chronology of Algonquin Park History* and *Algonquin Provincial Park Bibliography* published by The Friends of Algonquin Park.

# *Maps*

Five maps of Algonquin Park and the surrounding area were provided in a separate envelope with the original *Algonquin Story* in 1946, and revised versions of these maps accompanied the 1963 reprinting as well. The maps were titled: colonization roads; topographic; principal watersheds; exploration routes; and original area and subsequent additions since 1893.

In this second edition, Map 1 shows the original area of Algonquin Park in 1893, and the years and locations of additions to the Park from 1894 to 1993. Maps 2 to 14 show the travel routes of various "explorers" of the Algonquin Park area between 1818 and 1854.

**References Cited:**

Bain, J.W. 1958. *Surveys of a water route between Lake Simcoe and the Ottawa River by the Royal Engineers 1819-1827.* Ontario History 50: 15-28.

Saunders, A. 1946. *Algonquin Story.* Ontario Department of Lands and Forests, Toronto.

Walpole, J. 1827. *Report of survey from Talbot River to the Madawaska, November, 1827.* Pp. 53-56 *in* Murray, F. 1963. *Muskoka and Haliburton 1615-1875.* The Champlain Society and University of Toronto Press, Toronto.

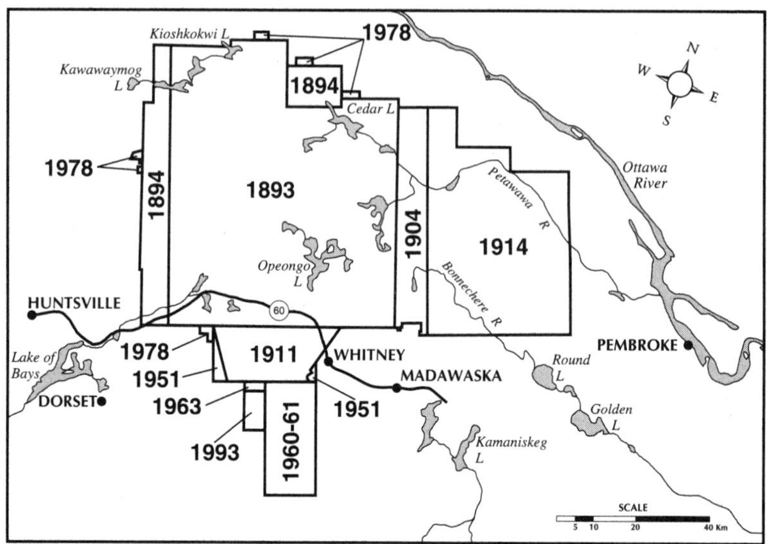


**Map 1: Additions to Algonquin Provincial Park, 1894 to 1993.**

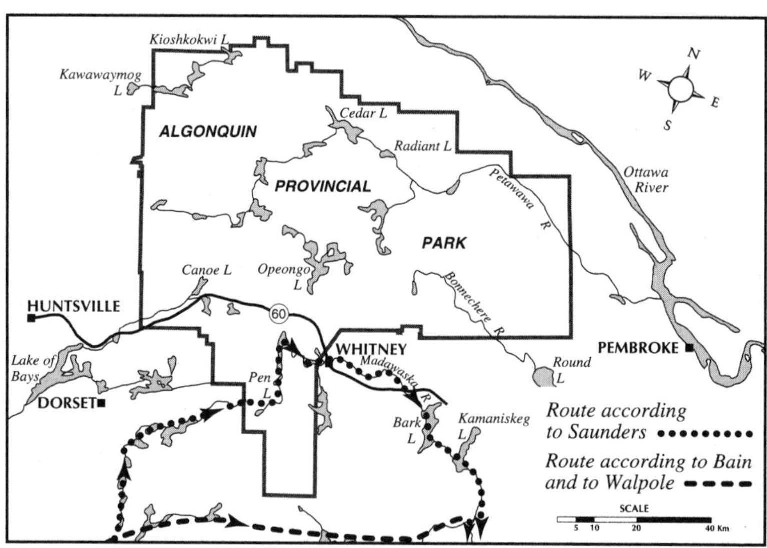


**Map 2: Route of Lieutenant James P. Catty, Royal Engineers, 1818.**

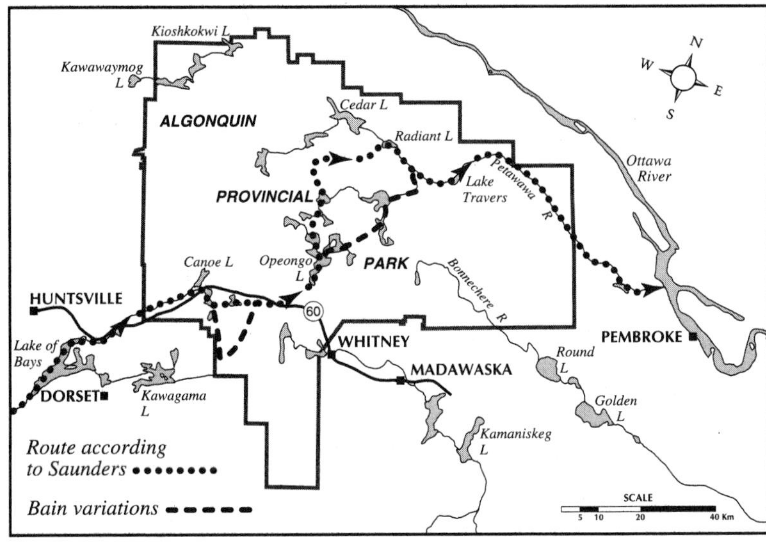


**Map 3: Route of Lieutenant Henry Briscoe, Royal Engineers, 1826.**

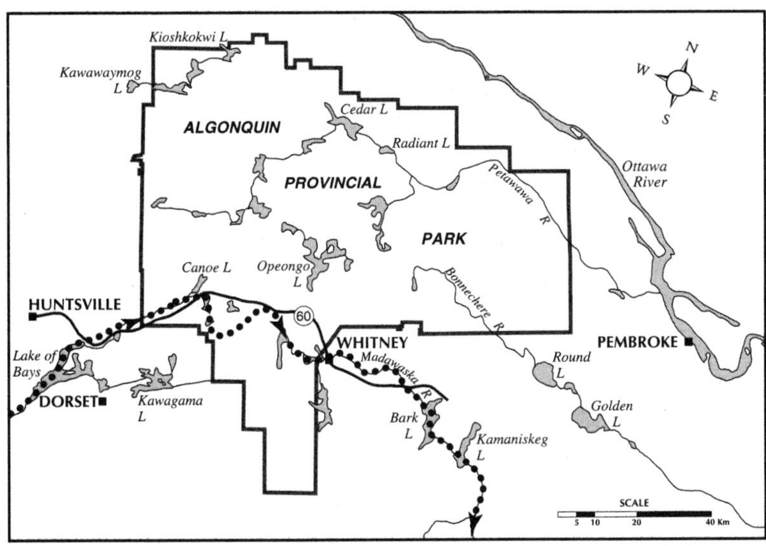


**Map 4: Route of Lieutenant Henry Briscoe, Royal Engineers, 1827.**

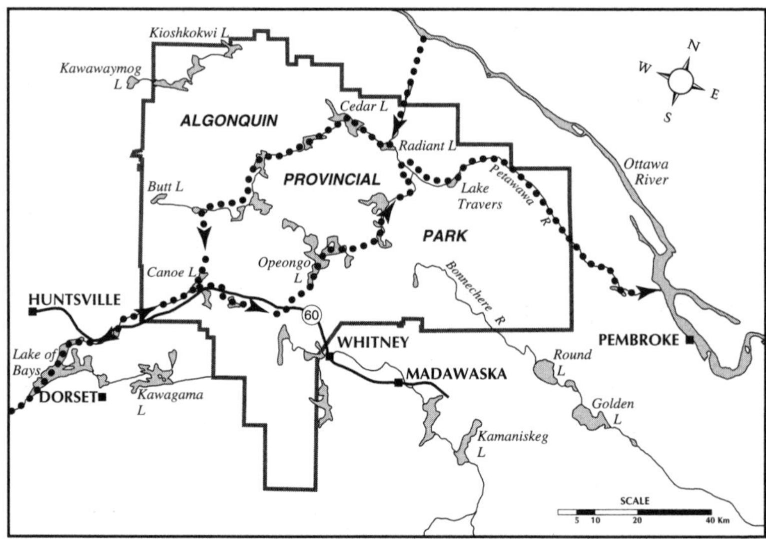


**Map 5: Route of Alexander Shirreff, 1829.**

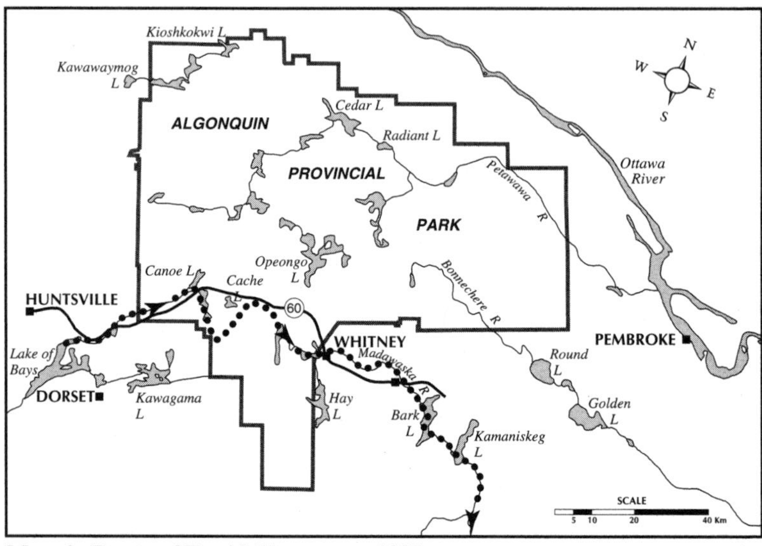


**Map 6: Route of David Thompson, 1837.**

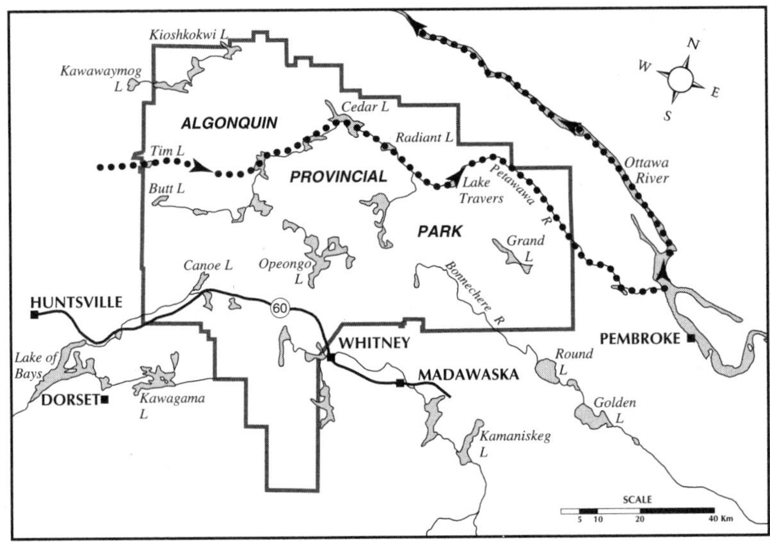


Map 7: Route of William Hawkins, 1837.

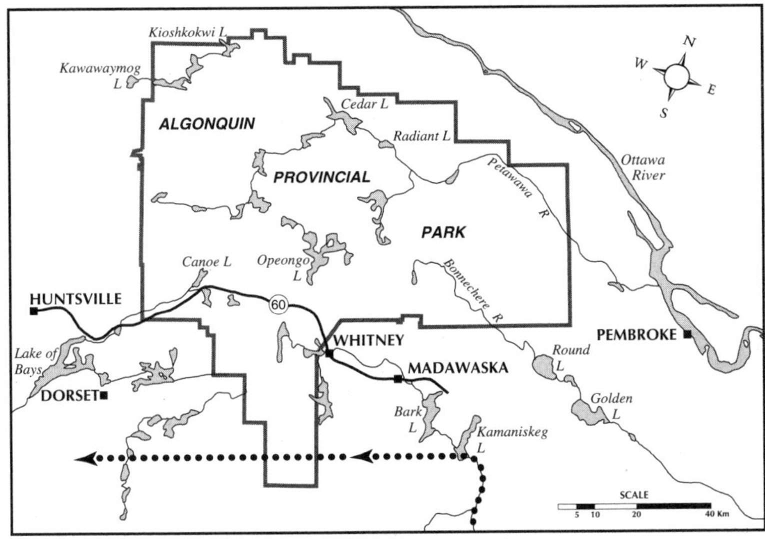


Map 8: Route of Robert Bell, 1847/48.

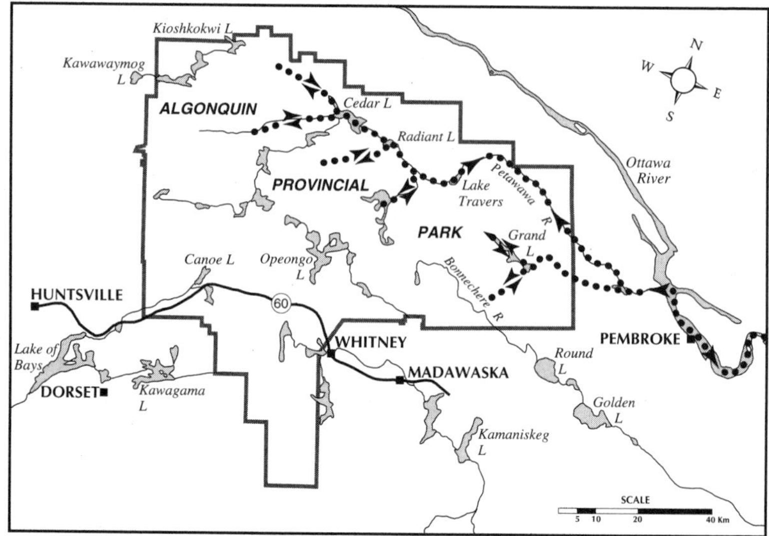


**Map 9: Route of J.R. McDonnell, 1847/48.**

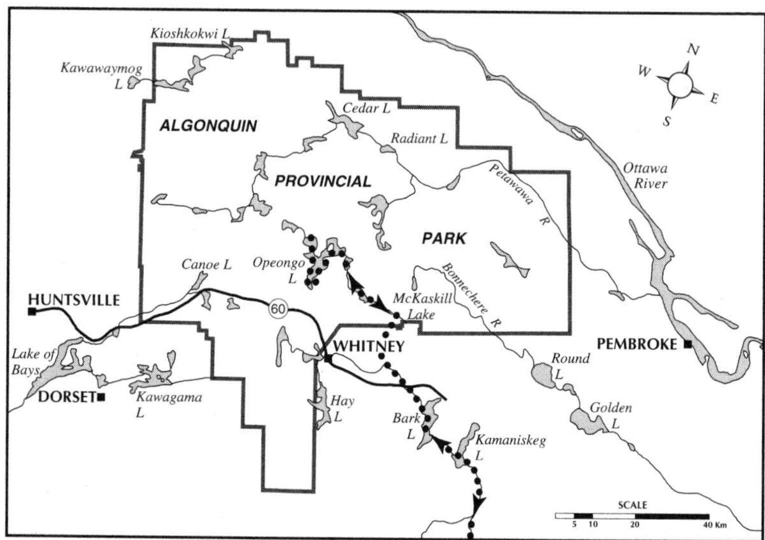


**Map 10: Route of Duncan McDonell, 1847/48.**

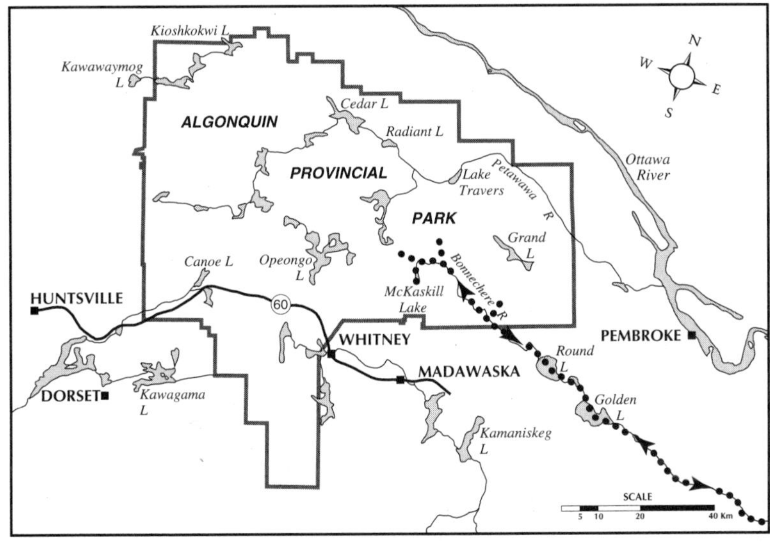


**Map 11: Route of James McNaughton, 1847/48.**

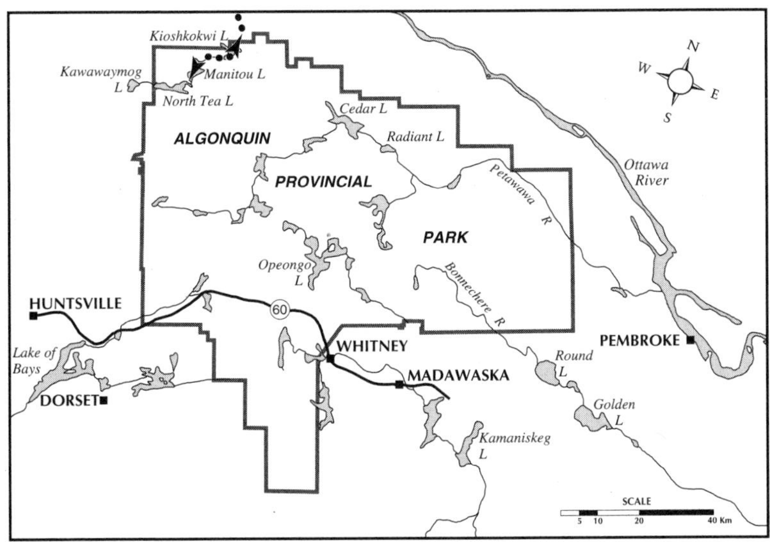


**Map 12: Route of Duncan Sinclair, 1848.**

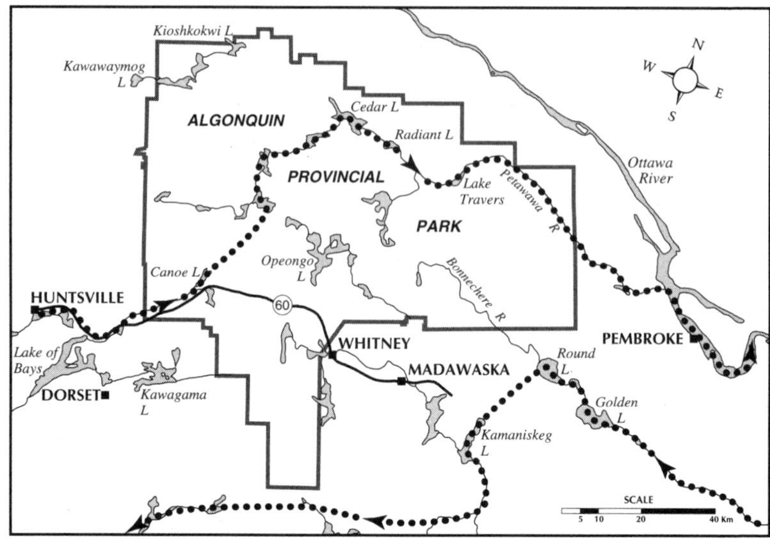


**Map 13: Route of Alexander Murray, 1853.**

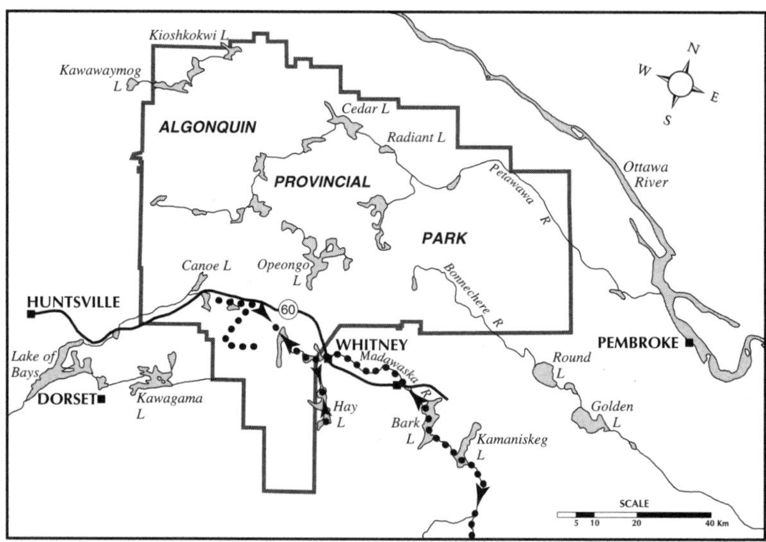


**Map 14: Route of John Snow, 1854.**

# *Index*

# *INDEX*

## *INDEX*

## *INDEX*

## *INDEX*

## *INDEX*

## *INDEX*

## *INDEX*

*INDEX*

# *INDEX*

# INDEX

## *INDEX*

# PORTABLE Maui

## 3rd Edition

by Jeanette Foster

**Here's what critics say about Frommer's:**

"Amazingly easy to use. Very portable, very complete."

—*Booklist*

"Detailed, accurate, and easy-to-read information for all price ranges."

—*Glamour Magazine*

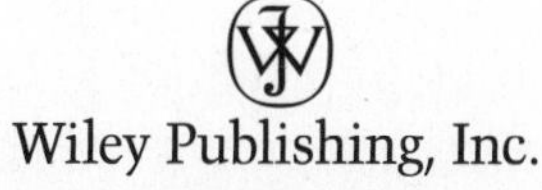

Wiley Publishing, Inc.

**WILEY PUBLISHING, INC.**
111 River St.
Hoboken, NJ 07030



ISBN 0-7645-3879-9
ISSN 1524-4318

Editor: Christine Ryan
Production Editor: Donna Wright
Photo Editor: Richard Fox
Cartographer: John Decamillis
Production by Wiley Indianapolis Composition Services

For information on our other products and services or to obtain technical support, please contact our Customer Care Department within the U.S. at 800-762-2974, outside the U.S. at 317-572-3993 or fax 317-572-4002.

Wiley also publishes its books in a variety of electronic formats. Some content that appears in print may not be available in electronic formats.

Manufactured in the United States of America

5 4 3 2 1

# Contents

# List of Maps

## About the Author

A resident of the Big Island, **Jeanette Foster** has skied the slopes of Mauna Kea—during a Fourth of July ski meet, no less—and gone scuba diving with manta rays off the Kona Coast. A prolific writer widely published in travel, sports, and adventure magazines, she's also a contributing editor to *Hawaii* magazine and the editor of *Zagat's Survey to Hawaii's Top Restaurants.* In addition to this guide, Jeanette is the author of *Frommer's Hawaii, Frommer's Maui, Frommer's Honolulu, Waikiki & Oahu,* and *Frommer's Hawaii from $80 a Day.*

## An Invitation to the Reader

In researching this book, we discovered many wonderful places—hotels, restaurants, shops, and more. We're sure you'll find others. Please tell us about them, so we can share the information with your fellow travelers in upcoming editions. If you were disappointed with a recommendation, we'd love to know that, too. Please write to:

*Frommer's Portable Maui,* 3rd Edition
Wiley Publishing, Inc. • 111 River St. • Hoboken, NJ 07030

## An Additional Note

Please be advised that travel information is subject to change at any time—and this is especially true of prices. We therefore suggest that you write or call ahead for confirmation when making your travel plans. The authors, editors, and publisher cannot be held responsible for the experiences of readers while traveling. Your safety is important to us, however, so we encourage you to stay alert and be aware of your surroundings. Keep a close eye on cameras, purses, and wallets, all favorite targets of thieves and pickpockets.

## Frommer's Star Ratings, Icons & Abbreviations

Every hotel, restaurant, and attraction listing in this guide has been ranked for quality, value, service, amenities, and special features using a **star-rating system.** In country, state, and regional guides, we also rate towns and regions to help you narrow down your choices and budget your time accordingly. Hotels and restaurants are rated on a scale of zero (recommended) to three stars (exceptional). Attractions, shopping, nightlife, towns, and regions are rated according to the following scale: zero stars (recommended), one star (highly recommended), two stars (very highly recommended), and three stars (must-see).

In addition to the star-rating system, we also use **seven feature icons** that point you to the great deals, in-the-know advice, and unique experiences that separate travelers from tourists. Throughout the book, look for:

| | |
|---|---|
| *Finds* | Special finds—those places only insiders know about |
| *Fun Fact* | Fun facts—details that make travelers more informed and their trips more fun |
| *Kids* | Best bets for kids and advice for the whole family |
| *Moments* | Special moments—those experiences that memories are made of |
| *Overrated* | Places or experiences not worth your time or money |
| *Tips* | Insider tips—some great ways to save time and money |
| *Value* | Great values—where to get the best deals |

The following **abbreviations** are used for credit cards:

| | | | | | |
|---|---|---|---|---|---|
| AE | American Express | DISC | Discover | V | Visa |
| DC | Diners Club | MC | MasterCard | | |

## Frommers.com

Now that you have the guidebook to a great trip, visit our website at **www.frommers.com** for travel information on more than 3,000 destinations. With features updated regularly, we give you instant access to the most current trip-planning information available. At Frommers.com, you'll also find the best prices on airfares, accommodations, and car rentals—and you can even book travel online through our travel booking partners. At Frommers.com, you'll also find the following:

- Online updates to our most popular guidebooks
- Vacation sweepstakes and contest giveaways
- Newsletter highlighting the hottest travel trends
- Online travel message boards with featured travel discussions

# 1

# Maui, the Valley Isle

Maui, also called the Valley Isle, is just a small dot in the vast Pacific Ocean, but it has the potential to offer visitors unforgettable experiences: floating weightless through rainbows of tropical fish, standing atop a 10,000-foot volcano watching the sun come up, listening to the raindrops in a bamboo forest.

Whether you want to experience the "real" Hawaii, go on a heart-pounding adventure, or simply relax on the beach, this book is designed to help you create the vacation of your dreams.

In the pages that follow, we've compiled everything you need to know to plan your ideal trip to Maui: information on airlines, seasons, a calendar of events, how to make camping reservations, and much more.

## 1 The Island in Brief

### CENTRAL MAUI

Maui's main airport lies in this flat, often windy corridor between Maui's two volcanoes, and this is where the majority of the island's population lives. You'll find good shopping and dining bargains here, but very little in the way of accommodations.

**KAHULUI** This is "Dream City," home to thousands of former sugar cane workers who dreamed of owning their own homes away from the plantations. A couple of small hotels located just 2 miles from the airport are convenient for 1-night stays if you have a late arrival or early departure, but this is not a place to spend your vacation.

**WAILUKU** With its faded wooden storefronts, old plantation homes, and shops straight out of the 1940s, Wailuku is like a time capsule. Although most people race through on their way to see the natural beauty of **Iao Valley** ★, this quaint little town is worth a brief visit, if only to see a real place where real people actually appear to be working at something other than a suntan. Beaches surrounding Wailuku are not great for swimming, but the old town has a spectacular view of Haleakala, a couple of hostels and an excellent

# Maui

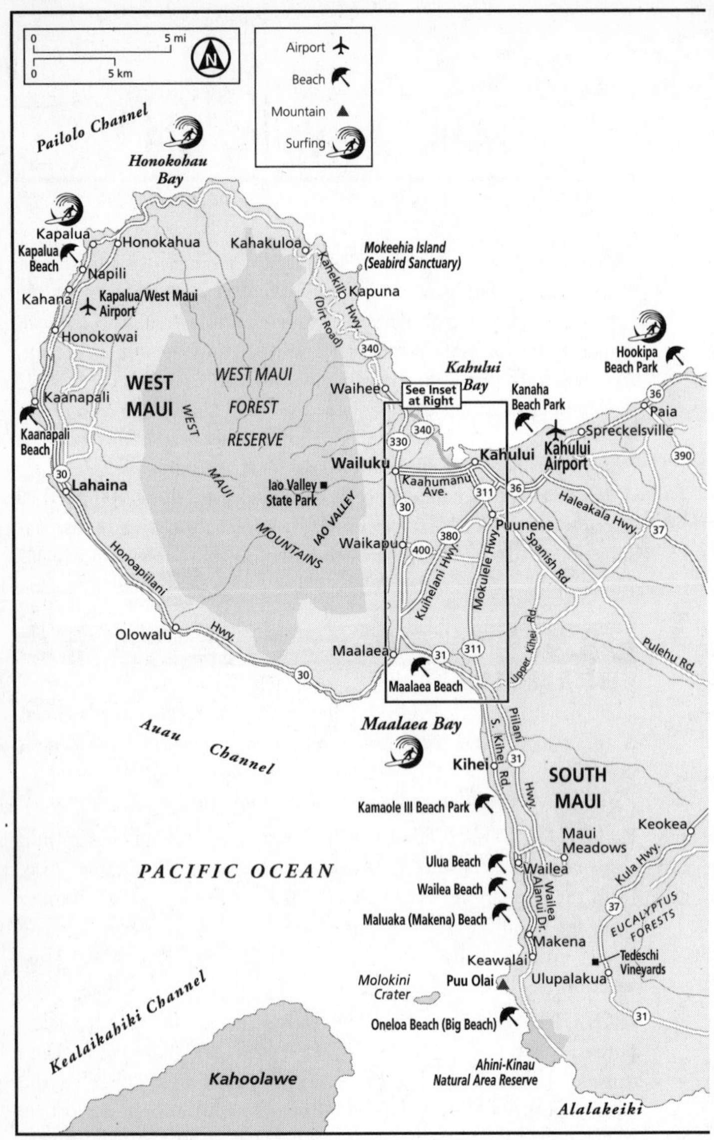

0 5 mi
0 5 km
N
Airport
Beach
Mountain
Surfing
Pailolo Channel
Honokohau Bay
Kapalua
Kapalua Beach
Honokahua
Kahakuloa
Mokeehia Island (Seabird Sanctuary)
Napili
Kahana
Kapalua/West Maui Airport
Kahekili Hwy.
(Dirt Road)
Kapuna
Honokowai
340
Hookipa Beach Park
Kahului Bay
WEST MAUI
WEST MAUI FOREST RESERVE
Waihee
See Inset at Right
Kanaha Beach Park
Kaanapali
Kaanapali Beach
WEST MAUI MOUNTAINS
36
Paia
Spreckelsville
330
Kahului
Kahului Airport
390
Wailuku
Kaahumanu Ave.
30
Lahaina
Iao Valley State Park
IAO VALLEY
311
Haleakala Hwy.
37
Puunene
Waikapu
380
400
Spanish Rd.
Kuihelani Hwy.
Mokulele Hwy.
Honoapiilani Hwy.
Upper Kihei Rd.
Olowalu
Maalaea
31
Pulehu Rd.
Maalaea Beach
Maalaea Bay
Auau Channel
Piilani Hwy.
S. Kihei Rd.
Kihei
SOUTH MAUI
Kamaole III Beach Park
Keokea
Maui Meadows
PACIFIC OCEAN
Ulua Beach
Wailea
Kula Hwy.
Wailea Beach
Wailea Alanui Dr.
Maluaka (Makena) Beach
EUCALYPTUS FORESTS
Makena
Keawalai
Tedeschi Vineyards
Molokini Crater
Puu Olai
Ulupalakua
Kealaikahiki Channel
Oneloa Beach (Big Beach)
Kahoolawe
Ahini-Kinau Natural Area Reserve
Alalakeiki

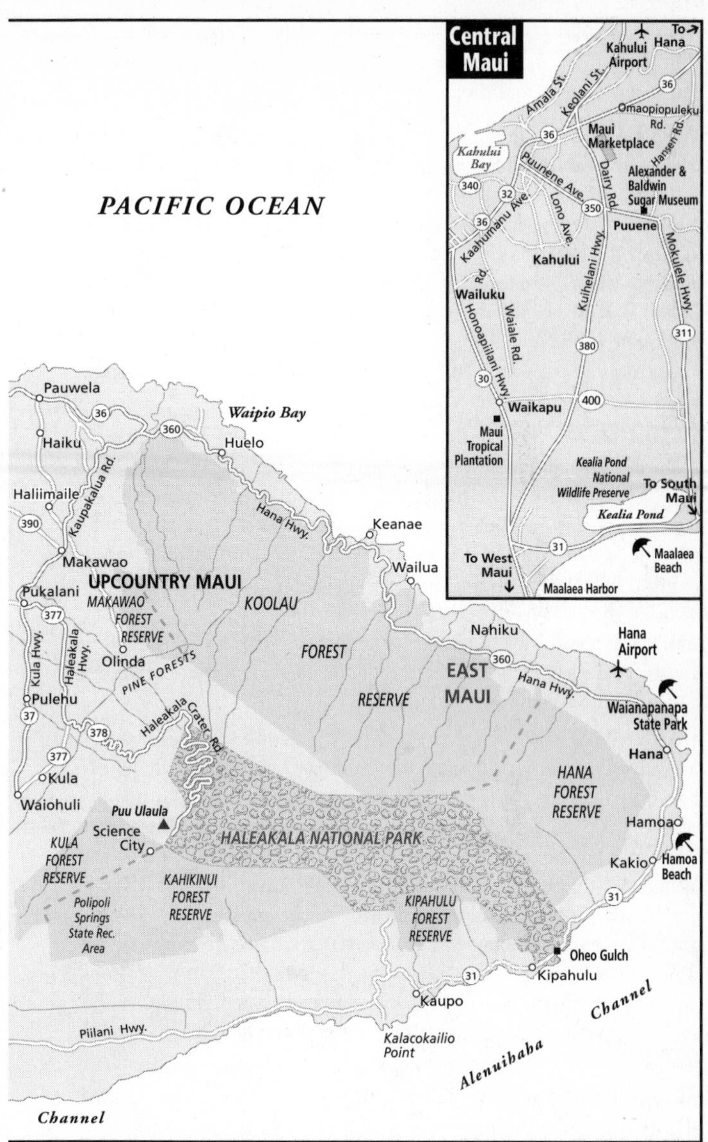
PACIFIC OCEAN
Central Maui
Kahului Airport
To Hana
Amala St.
Keolani St.
Omaopiopuleku Rd.
Maui Marketplace
Hansen Rd.
Kahului Bay
Puunene Ave.
Alexander & Baldwin Sugar Museum
Dairy Rd.
Kaahumanu Ave.
Lono Ave.
Puuene
Mokulele Hwy.
Kahului
Kuihelani Hwy.
Wailuku
Honoapiilani Hwy.
Waiale Rd.
Waikapu
Maui Tropical Plantation
Kealia Pond National Wildlife Preserve
To South Maui
Kealia Pond
To West Maui
Maalaea Beach
Maalaea Harbor
Pauwela
Waipio Bay
Haiku
Huelo
Haliimaile
Kaupakalua Rd.
Hana Hwy.
Keanae
Makawao
Wailua
UPCOUNTRY MAUI
Pukalani
MAKAWAO FOREST RESERVE
KOOLAU FOREST RESERVE
Nahiku
Hana Airport
Kula Hwy.
Haleakala Hwy.
Olinda
PINE FORESTS
EAST MAUI
Pulehu
Haleakala Crater Rd.
Waianapanapa State Park
Hana
Kula
HANA FOREST RESERVE
Waiohuli
Puu Ulaula
Science City
HALEAKALA NATIONAL PARK
Hamoa
KULA FOREST RESERVE
Kakio
Hamoa Beach
Polipoli Springs State Rec. Area
KAHIKINUI FOREST RESERVE
KIPAHULU FOREST RESERVE
Oheo Gulch
Kipahulu
Kaupo
Channel
Piilani Hwy.
Kalacokailio Point
Alenuihaha
Channel

historic B&B, great budget restaurants, a tofu factory, some interesting bungalow architecture, a Frank Lloyd Wright building on the outskirts of town, and the always-endearing Bailey House Museum.

## WEST MAUI

This is the fabled Maui you see on postcards. Jagged peaks, green valleys, a wilderness full of native species—the majestic West Maui Mountains are the epitome of earthly paradise. The beaches here are some of the islands' best. And it's no secret: This stretch of coastline along Maui's "forehead," from Kapalua to the historic port of Lahaina, is the island's most bustling resort area. Expect a few mainland-style traffic jams.

Starting at the southern end of West Maui and moving northward, the coastal communities are as listed below.

**LAHAINA ★** This old whaling seaport teems with restaurants, T-shirt shops, and a gallery on nearly every block, but there's still lots of real history to be found amid the tourist development. The town is a great base for visitors: A few old hotels (like the newly restored 1901 Pioneer Inn on the harbor), quaint B&Bs, and a handful of oceanfront condos offer a variety of choices, most within walking distance to the beach as well as town. This is the place to stay if you want to be in the center of things—oodles of restaurants, shops, and nightlife—but note that the town is rather congested and doesn't have enough parking.

**KAANAPALI ★★** Farther north along the West Maui coast is Hawaii's first master-planned resort. Pricey midrise hotels, which line nearly 3 miles of lovely gold-sand beach, are linked by a landscaped parkway and separated by a jungle of plants. Golf greens wrap around the slope between beachfront and hillside properties. **Whalers Village** (a seaside mall with such fancy names as Tiffany and Louis Vuitton, plus the best little whale museum in Hawaii) and other restaurants are easy to reach on foot along the waterfront walkway or via resort shuttle, which also serves the small West Maui airport just to the north. Shuttles also go to Lahaina, 3 miles to the south, for shopping, dining, entertainment, and boat tours. Kaanapali is popular with convention groups and families.

**FROM HONOKOWAI TO NAPILI** In the building binge of the 1970s, condominiums sprouted along this gorgeous coastline like mushrooms after a rain. Today, these older ocean-side units offer excellent bargains. The great location—along sandy beaches, within minutes of both the Kapalua and the Kaanapali resort areas, and close to the goings-on in Lahaina town—makes this area a great place to stay for value-conscious travelers. It feels more peaceful and residential than either Kaanapali or Lahaina.

In **Honokowai** and **Mahinahina,** you'll find mostly older units that tend to be cheaper; there's not much shopping here aside from convenience stores, but you'll have easy access to the shops and restaurants of Kaanapali.

**Kahana** is a little more upscale than Honokowai and Mahinahina. Most of the condos here are big high-rise types, built more recently than those immediately to the south. You'll find a nice selection of shops and restaurants in the area, and Kapalua–West Maui Airport is nearby.

**Napili** is a much-sought-after area for condo seekers: It's quiet; has great beaches, restaurants, and shops; and is close to Kapalua. Units are generally more expensive here (although we've found a few hidden gems at affordable prices; see the Napili Bay entry on p. 52).

**KAPALUA** ★ North beyond Kaanapali and the shopping centers of Napili and Kahana, the road starts to climb, and the vista opens up to fields of silver-green pineapple and manicured golf fairways. Turn down the country lane of Pacific pines toward the sea, and you could only be in Kapalua. It's the very exclusive domain of two gracious and expensive hotels, set on one of Hawaii's best gold-sand beaches, next to two bays that are marine-life preserves (with fabulous surfing in winter).

Even if you don't stay here, you're welcome to come and enjoy Kapalua. Both of the fancy hotels provide public parking and beach access. The resort champions innovative environmental programs; it also has an art school, a golf school, three golf courses, historic features, a collection of swanky condos and homes, and wide-open spaces that include a rainforest preserve—all open to the general public. Kapalua is a great place to stay put. However, if you plan to "tour" Maui, know that it's a long drive from here to get to many of the island's highlights.

## SOUTH MAUI

This is the hottest, sunniest, driest coastline on Maui, and the most popular one for sun worshippers—Arizona by the sea. Rain rarely falls, and temperatures stick around 85°F (29°C) year-round. On former scrubland from Maalaea to Makena are now four distinct areas—Maalaea, Kihei, Wailea, and Makena—and a surprising amount of traffic.

**MAALAEA** If the western part of Maui is a head, Maalaea is just under the chin. This oceanfront village centers around the small boat harbor (with a general store, a couple of restaurants, and a huge new mall) and the **Maui Ocean Center** ★, an aquarium/ocean complex. This quaint region offers several condominium units to choose from, but visitors staying here should be aware that it is almost always very windy.

**KIHEI** Kihei is less a proper town than a nearly continuous series of condos and minimalls lining South Kihei Road. This is Maui's best vacation bargain: Budget travelers flock to the eight sandy beaches along this scalloped, condo-packed, 7-mile stretch of coast. Kihei is neither charming nor quaint, but it does offer sunshine, affordability, and convenience. If you want latte in the morning, fine beaches in the afternoon, and Hawaii Regional Cuisine in the evening, all at budget prices, head to Kihei.

**WAILEA** ★ Only 2½ decades ago, this was wall-to-wall scrub kiawe trees, but now Wailea is a manicured oasis of multimillion-dollar resort hotels strung along 2 miles of palm-fringed gold coast. Today you'll find warm, clear water full of tropical fish; year-round sunshine and clear blue skies; and hedonistic pleasure palaces on 1,500 acres of black-lava shore. Amazing what a billion dollars can do.

This is the playground of the stretch-limo set. The planned resort development has a shopping village, three prized golf courses of its own and three more in close range, and a tennis complex. A growing number of large homes sprawl over the upper hillside (some offering excellent bed-and-breakfast units at reasonable prices). The resorts along this fantasy coast are spectacular, to say the least.

Appealing natural features include the coastal trail, a 3-mile round-trip path along the oceanfront with pleasing views everywhere you look. The trail's south end borders an extensive garden of native coastal plants, as well as ancient lava-rock house ruins juxtaposed with elegant oceanfront condos. But the chief attractions, of course, are those five outstanding beaches (the best is Wailea).

**MAKENA** ★ After passing through well-groomed Wailea, suddenly the road enters raw wilderness. Although beautiful, Makena is an end-of-the-road kind of place: It's a long drive from here to anywhere on Maui, so if you want to tour a lot of the island, you might want to book somewhere else. But if you crave a quiet, relaxing respite, where the biggest trip of the day is from your bed to the pristine beach, Makena is your place.

Beyond Makena you'll discover Haleakala's last lava flow, which ran to the sea in 1790; the bay named for French explorer La Perouse; and a chunky lava trail known as the King's Highway, which leads around Maui's empty south shore past ruins and fish camps. Puu Olai stands like Maui's Diamond Head on the shore, where a sunken crater shelters tropical fish, and empty golden-sand beaches stand at the end of dirt roads.

## UPCOUNTRY MAUI

After a few days at the beach, you'll probably take notice of the 10,000-foot mountain in the middle of Maui. The slopes of Haleakala ("House of the Sun") are home to cowboys, farmers, and other country people. They're all up here enjoying the crisp air, emerald pastures, eucalyptus, and flower farms of this tropical Olympus—there's even a misty California redwood grove. Houses old and new are strung along a road that runs from Makawao, an old paniolo-turned–New Age village, to Kula, where the road leads up to the crater and **Haleakala National Park** ★★★. The rumpled, two-lane blacktop of Highway 37 narrows on the other side of Tedeschi Winery, where wine grapes and wild elk flourish on the Ulupalakua Ranch, the biggest on Maui. A stay upcountry is usually affordable, a chance to commune with nature, and a nice contrast to the sizzling beaches and busy resorts below.

**MAKAWAO** ★ Until recently, this small, two-street upcountry town consisted of little more than a post office, gas station, feed store, bakery, and restaurant/bar serving the cowboys and farmers living in the surrounding community; the hitching posts outside storefronts were really used to tie up horses. As the population of Maui started expanding in the 1970s, a health-food store popped up, followed by boutiques, a chiropractic clinic, and a host of health-conscious restaurants. The result is an eclectic amalgam of old paniolo Hawaii and the baby-boomer trends of transplanted mainlanders. **Hui No'eau Visual Arts Center,** Hawaii's premier arts collective, is definitely worth a peek. The only accommodations here are reasonably priced bed-and-breakfasts, perfect for those who enjoy great views and don't mind slightly chilly nights.

**KULA** ★ A feeling of pastoral remoteness prevails in this upcountry community of old flower farms, humble cottages, and new suburban ranch houses with million-dollar views that take in the ocean, isthmus, West Maui Mountains, Lanai, and Kahoolawe off in the distance. At night, the lights run along the gold coast like a string of pearls, from Maalaea to Puu Olai. Kula sits at a cool 3,000 feet, just below the cloud line, and from here, a winding road snakes its way up to Haleakala National Park. Everyone here grows something—Maui onions, carnations, orchids, and proteas, those strange-looking blossoms that look like *Star Trek* props. The local B&Bs cater to guests seeking cool tropical nights, panoramic views, and a rural upland escape. Here you'll find the true peace and quiet that only rural farming country can offer—yet you're still just 30 to 40 minutes away from the beach and an hour's drive from Lahaina.

## EAST MAUI

**THE ROAD TO HANA** ★★ When old sugar towns die, they usually fade away in rust and red dirt. Not **Paia.** The tangle of electrical, phone, and cable wires hanging overhead symbolizes the town's ability to adapt to the times—it may look messy, but it works. Here, trendy restaurants, eclectic boutiques, and high-tech windsurf shops stand next door to the ma-and-pa grocery, fish market, and storefronts that have been serving customers since the plantation days. Hippies took over in the 1970s; although their macrobiotic restaurants and old-style artists' co-op have made way for Hawaii Regional Cuisine and galleries featuring the works of renowned international artists, Paia still manages to maintain a pleasant vibe of hippiedom. The town's main attraction, though, is **Hookipa Beach Park,** where the wind that roars through the isthmus of Maui brings windsurfers from around the world, who come to fly over the waves on gossamer wings linked to surfboards.

Ten minutes down the road from Paia and up the hill from the Hana Highway—the connector road to the entire east side of Maui—sits **Haiku.** Once a pineapple-plantation village, complete with cannery (today a shopping complex), Haiku offers vacation rentals and B&Bs in a quiet, pastoral setting: the perfect base for those who want to get off the beaten path and experience a quieter side of Maui, but don't want to feel too removed (the beach is only 10 min. away).

About 15 to 20 minutes past Haiku is the largely unknown community of **Huelo.** Every day, thousands of cars whiz by on the road to Hana. But if you take the time to stop, you'll discover a hidden Hawaii, where Mother Nature is still sensual and wild, where ocean waves pummel soaring lava cliffs, and where serenity prevails. Huelo is not for everyone, but if you want the magic of a place still largely untouched by "progress," check into a B&B or vacation rental here.

**HANA** ★★ Set between an emerald rainforest and the blue Pacific is a village probably best defined by what it lacks: golf courses, shopping malls, and McDonald's. Except for two gas stations and a bank with an ATM, you'll find little of what passes for progress here. Instead, you'll discover fragrant tropical flowers, the sweet taste of backyard bananas and papayas, and the easy calm and unabashed small-town aloha spirit of old Hawaii. What saved "Heavenly" Hana from the inevitable march of progress? The 52-mile **Hana Highway,** which winds around 600 curves and crosses more than 50 one-lane bridges on its way from Kahului. You can go to Hana for the day—it's a 3-hour drive (and a half century away)—but 3 days are better. The tiny town has one hotel, a handful of great B&Bs, and some spectacular vacation rentals (where else can you stay in a tropical cabin in a rainforest?).

## 2 Visitor Information

For advance information on traveling in Maui, contact the **Maui Visitors Bureau,** 1727 Wili Pa Loop, Wailuku, Maui, HI 96793 (✆ **800/525-MAUI** or 808/244-3530; fax 808/244-1337; www.visitmaui.com).

The **Kaanapali Beach Resort Association** is at 2530 Kekaa Dr., Suite 1-B, Lahaina, HI 96761 (✆ **800/245-9229** or 808/661-3271; fax 808/661-9431; www.maui.net/~kbra).

The state agency responsible for tourism is the **Hawaii Visitors and Convention Bureau (HVCB),** Suite 801, Waikiki Business Plaza, 2270 Kalakaua Ave., Honolulu, HI 96815 (✆ **800/GO-HAWAII** or 808/923-1811; www.gohawaii.com).

If you want information about working and living in Hawaii, contact **The Chamber of Commerce of Hawaii,** 1132 Bishop St., Suite 200, Honolulu, HI 96815 (✆ **808/545-4300**).

### INFORMATION ON MAUI'S PARKS

**NATIONAL PARKS** Both Maui and Molokai have one national park each: **Haleakala National Park,** P.O. Box 369, Makawao, HI 96768 (✆ **808/572-4400;** www.nps.gov/hale); and **Kalaupapa National Historical Park,** P.O. Box 2222, Kalaupapa, HI 96742 (✆ **808/567-6802;** www.nps.gov/kala). For more information, see "Hiking" in chapter 5.

**STATE PARKS** To find out more about state parks on Maui and Molokai, contact the **Hawaii State Department of Land and Natural Resources,** 54 S. High St., Wailuku, HI 96793

(© **808/984-8109;** www.hawaii.gov), which provides information on hiking and camping and will send you free topographic trail maps on request.

## 3 Money

### ATMS

Hawaii pioneered the use of **ATMs** more than 2 decades ago, and now they're everywhere. You'll find them at most banks, in supermarkets, at Long's Drugs, and in most resorts and shopping centers. **Cirrus** (© **800/424-7787;** www.mastercard.com) and **PLUS** (© **800/843-7587;** www.visa.com) are the two most popular networks; check the back of your ATM card to see which network your bank belongs to (most banks belong to both these days).

### TRAVELER'S CHECKS

Traveler's checks are something of an anachronism from the days before the ATM made cash accessible at any time. Traveler's checks used to be the only sound alternative to traveling with dangerously large amounts of cash. They were as reliable as currency, but, unlike cash, could be replaced if lost or stolen.

These days, traveler's checks are less necessary because most cities have 24-hour ATMs that allow you to withdraw small amounts of cash as needed. However, keep in mind that you will likely be charged an ATM withdrawal fee if the bank is not your own, so if you're withdrawing money every day, you might be better off with traveler's checks—provided that you don't mind showing identification every time you want to cash one.

You can get traveler's checks at almost any bank. **American Express** offers denominations of $20, $50, $100, $500, and (for cardholders only) $1,000. You'll pay a service charge ranging from 1% to 4%. You can also get American Express traveler's checks over the phone by calling © **800/221-7282;** Amex gold and platinum cardholders who use this number are exempt from the 1% fee. AAA members can obtain checks without a fee at most AAA offices.

**Visa** offers traveler's checks at Citibank locations nationwide, as well as at several other banks. The service charge ranges between 1.5% and 2%; checks come in denominations of $20, $50, $100, $500, and $1,000. Call © **800/732-1322** for information. **MasterCard** also offers traveler's checks. Call © **800/223-9920** for a location near you.

If you choose to carry traveler's checks, be sure to keep a record of their serial numbers separate from your checks in the event that they are stolen or lost. You'll get a refund faster if you know the numbers.

**Credit cards** are accepted all over the island. They're a safe way to carry money, and they provide a convenient record of all your expenses. You can also withdraw cash advances from your credit cards at banks or ATMs, provided you know your PIN. If you've forgotten yours, or didn't even know you had one, call the number on the back of your credit card and ask the bank to send it to you. It usually takes 5 to 7 business days, though some banks will provide the number over the phone if you tell them your mother's maiden name or some other personal information. Still, be sure to keep some cash on hand for that rare occasion when a restaurant or small shop doesn't take plastic.

## 4 When to Go

Most visitors don't come to Maui when the weather's best in the islands; rather, they come when it's at its worst everywhere else. Thus, the **high season**—when prices are up and resorts are booked to capacity—generally runs from mid-December through March or mid-April. The last 2 weeks of December in particular are the prime time for travel to Maui; if you're planning a holiday trip, make your reservations as early as possible, count on holiday crowds, and expect to pay top dollar for accommodations, car rentals, and airfare. Whale-watching season begins in January and continues through the rest of winter, sometimes lasting into May.

The **off seasons,** when the best bargain rates are available, are spring (from mid-Apr to mid-June) and fall (from Sept to mid-Dec)—a paradox, since these are the best seasons in terms of reliably great weather. If you're looking to save money, or if you just want to avoid the crowds, this is the time to visit. Hotel rates tend to be significantly lower during these off seasons. Airfares also tend to be lower—again, sometimes substantially—and good packages and special deals are often available.

***Note:*** If you plan to come to Maui between the last week in April and mid-May, be sure to book your accommodations, interisland air reservations, and car rental in advance. In Japan, the last week of April is called **Golden Week,** because three Japanese holidays take place one after the other; the islands are especially busy with Japanese tourists during this time.

Due to the large number of families traveling in **summer** (June–Aug), you won't get the fantastic bargains of spring and fall.

However, you'll still do much better on packages, airfare, and accommodations than you will in the winter months.

## THE WEATHER

Because Maui lies at the edge of the tropical zone, it technically has only two seasons, both of them warm. The dry season corresponds to summer, and the rainy season generally runs during the winter from November to March. It rains every day somewhere in the islands at any time of the year, but the rainy season can cause "gray" weather and spoil your tanning opportunities. Fortunately, it seldom rains for more than 3 days straight, and rainy days often just consist of a mix of clouds and sun, with very brief showers.

The **year-round temperature** usually varies no more than 15°F (9°C), but it depends on where you are. Maui is like a ship in that it has leeward and windward sides. The **leeward** sides (the west and south) are usually hot and dry, whereas the **windward** sides (east and north) are generally cooler and moist. If you want arid, sunbaked, desertlike weather, go leeward. If you want lush, often wet, junglelike weather, go windward. Your best bets for total year-round sun are the Kihei-Wailea and Lahaina-Kapalua coasts.

Maui is also full of **microclimates,** thanks to its interior valleys, coastal plains, and mountain peaks. If you travel into the mountains, it can change from summer to winter in a matter of hours, because it's cooler the higher up you go. In other words, if the weather doesn't suit you, go to the other side of the island—or head into the hills.

## HOLIDAYS

When Hawaii observes holidays, especially those over a long weekend, travel between the islands increases, interisland airline seats are fully booked, rental cars are at a premium, and hotels and restaurants are busier than usual.

Federal, state, and county government offices are closed on all federal holidays: January 1 (New Year's Day); third Monday in January (Martin Luther King Jr. Day); third Monday in February (Presidents' Day); last Monday in May (Memorial Day); July 4 (Independence Day); first Monday in September (Labor Day); second Monday in October (Columbus Day); November 11 (Veterans' Day); fourth Thursday in November (Thanksgiving Day); and December 25 (Christmas).

State and county offices also are closed on local holidays, including Prince Kuhio Day (Mar 26), honoring the birthday of Hawaii's first delegate to the U.S. Congress; King Kamehameha Day (June 11), a statewide holiday commemorating Kamehameha the Great, who united the islands and ruled from 1795 to 1819; and Admission Day (3rd Fri in Aug), which honors Hawaii's admission as the 50th state in the United States on August 21, 1959.

## MAUI CALENDAR OF EVENTS

As with any schedule of upcoming events, the following information is subject to change; always confirm the details before you plan your schedule around an event. For a complete and up-to-date list of events throughout Maui, Molokai, and Lanai, point your browser to **www.visitmaui.com** or **www.calendarmaui.com**.

### January

**PGA Kapalua Mercedes Championship,** Kapalua Resort. Top PGA golfers compete for $1 million. Call ✆ **808/669-2440;** www.kapaluamaui.com. January 5 to January 11, 2004.

**Chinese New Year.** Lahaina town rolls out the red carpet for this important event with a traditional lion dance at the historic Wo Hing Temple on Front Street, accompanied by fireworks, food booths, and a host of activities. Call ✆ **888/310-1117** or 808/667-9175 for details. In Wailuku, Chinese New Year is celebrated on Market Street (✆ **808/270-7414** for more info). The year of the monkey starts January 22, 2004.

**Hula Bowl Football All-Star Classic,** War Memorial Stadium. An annual all-star football classic featuring America's top college players. Call ✆ **808/871-4141;** www.hulabowlmaui.com; ticket orders are processed beginning April 1 for the next year's game, January 31, 2004.

**Senior Skins Tournament,** Golf Course, Wailea Golf Courses. Longtime golfing greats participate in this four-man tournament for $600,000 in prize money. Call ✆ **800/332-1614;** www.seniorskinswailea.com. January 31, 2004.

### February

**Whalefest Week.** A weeklong celebration of Maui's best-known winter visitors, the humpback whales. Activities include a whale-counting day and other islandwide events like Hawaiian entertainment, great food by Maui's top restaurants, seminars, art exhibits, sailing, snorkeling and diving tours, and numerous events for children. Call ✆ **808/667-9175** or 808/879-8860. February or March.

### March

**Art Maui 2004,** Kahului. The 25th annual juried art show of multimedia works by Maui artists. Maui Arts and Cultural

Center, ✆ **808/242-7469;** www.MauiArts.org. Mid-March through early April.

**Run to the Sun,** Paia to Haleakala. The world's top ultramarathoners make the journey from sea level to the top of 10,000-foot Haleakala, some 37 miles. Call ✆ **808/891-2516;** www.virr.com. March 21, 2004.

**East Maui Taro Festival,** Hana. Here's your chance to taste taro in its many different preparations, from poi to chips. Also on hand are Hawaiian exhibits, demonstrations, and food booths. Call ✆ **808/248-8972;** www.calendarmaui.com. March 26 to March 28, 2004.

## April

**Buddha Day,** Lahaina Jodo Mission, Lahaina. Each year, this historic mission holds a flower festival pageant honoring the birth of Buddha. Call ✆ **808/661-4303;** www.calendarmaui.com. First Saturday in April.

**Annual Ritz-Carlton Kapalua Celebration of the Arts,** Ritz-Carlton Kapalua. Contemporary and traditional artists give free hands-on lessons. Call ✆ **808/669-6200;** www.celebration ofthearts.org. The 4-day festival begins the Thursday before Easter, April 8 to April 11, 2004.

**That Ulupalakua Thing! Maui County Agricultural Trade Show and Sampling,** Ulupalakua Ranch and Tedeschi Winery, Ulupalakua. The name may be long and cumbersome, but this event is hot, hot, hot. It features local product exhibits, food booths, and live entertainment. Call ✆ **808/875-0457.** April 24, 2004.

## May

**Annual Lei Day Celebration.** May Day is Lei Day in Hawaii, celebrated with lei-making contests, pageantry, arts and crafts, and concerts throughout the islands. Call ✆ **800/525-6284** or 808/244-3530; www.visitmaui.com for Maui events. May 1.

**Outrigger Canoe Season,** all islands. From May to September, nearly every weekend, canoe paddlers across the state participate in outrigger canoe races. Call ✆ **808/961-5797.**

**In Celebration of Canoes,** West Maui. Celebration of the Pacific islands' seafaring heritage. Events include canoe paddling and sailing regattas, a luau feast, cultural arts demonstrations, canoe-building exhibits, and music. Call ✆ **888/310-1117.** May 8 to May 22, 2004.

### June

**King Kamehameha Celebration,** statewide. It's a state holiday with a massive floral parade, *hoolaulea* (party), and much more. Call ✆ **888/310-1117** or 808/661-5304 for Maui events, or **808/567-6361** for Molokai events. June 12, 2004.

**Maui Film Festival,** Wailea Resort. Five days and nights of screenings of premieres, special films, along with traditional Hawaiian storytelling, chants, hula, and contemporary music. Call ✆ **808/579-9996;** www.mauifilmfestival.com. June 16 to June 20, 2004.

**Hawaiian Slack-Key Guitar Festival,** Maui Arts and Cultural Center, Kahului. Great music performed by the best musicians in Hawaii. It's 5 hours long and absolutely free. Call ✆ **808/239-4336;** kahokuproductions@yahoo.com. June 20, 2004.

### July

**Makawao Parade and Rodeo,** Makawao. The annual parade and rodeo event have been taking place in this upcountry cowboy town for generations. Call ✆ **800/525-MAUI** or 808/572-9565. July 4, 2004.

**Kapalua Wine and Food Festival,** Kapalua. Famous wine and food experts and oenophiles gather at the Ritz-Carlton and Kapalua Bay hotels for formal tastings, panel discussions, and samplings of new releases. Call ✆ **800/KAPALUA** or 808/669-0244; www.kapaluaresort.com. July 8 to July 11, 2004.

### August

**Hawaii State Windsurf Championship,** Kanaha Beach Park, Kahului. Top windsurfers compete. Call ✆ **808/877-2111.** August 7, 2004.

**Admission Day,** all islands. Hawaii became the 50th state on August 21, 1959, so the state takes a holiday; all state-related facilities will be closed. Third Friday in August.

### September

**Aloha Festivals,** various locations statewide. Parades and other events celebrate Hawaiian culture. Call ✆ **800/852-7690** or 808/545-1771; www.alohafestivals.com for a schedule of events.

**A Taste of Lahaina,** Lahaina Civic Center. Some 30,000 people show up to sample 40 signature entrees of Maui's premier chefs during this weekend festival, which includes cooking demonstrations, wine tastings, and live entertainment. The event begins Friday night with Maui Chefs Present, a dinner/cocktail party featuring about a dozen of Maui's best chefs. Call © **888/310-1117.** September 11 to September 12.

**Maui Marathon,** Kahului to Kaanapali. Runners line up at the Maui Mall before daybreak and head off for Kaanapali. Call © **808/871-6441;** www.virr.com. September 19, 2004.

**Maui County Fair,** War Memorial Complex, Wailuku. The oldest county fair in Hawaii features a parade, amusement rides, live entertainment, and exhibits. Call © **800/525-MAUI** or 808/244-3530; www.calendarmaui.com. September 30 to October 3.

### October

**Aloha Classic World Wavesailing Championship,** Hookipa Beach. The top windsurfers in the world gather for this final event in the Pro Boardsailing World Tour. If you're on Maui, don't miss it—it's spectacular to watch. Call © **808/575-9151.** Depending on the waves and the wind, the championship can be held in October or November.

**Halloween in Lahaina.** There's Carnival in Rio, Mardi Gras in New Orleans, and Halloween in Lahaina. Come to this giant costume party (some 20,000 people show up) on the streets of Lahaina; Front Street is closed off for the party. Call © **888/310-1117.** October 31, 2004.

### November

**Hawaii International Film Festival,** various locations. A cinema festival with a cross-cultural spin, featuring filmmakers from Asia, the Pacific Islands, and the United States. Call © **800/752-8193** or 808/528-FILM; www.hiff.org. Mid-November.

**Maui Invitational Basketball Tournament,** Lahaina Civic Center. Top college teams vie in this annual preseason tournament. Call © **312/755-3504.** Usually held around Thanksgiving.

### December

**Festival of Lights,** islandwide. Festivities include parades and tree-lighting ceremonies. Call © **808/667-9175** on Maui. Early December.

**Festival of Art & Flowers,** Lahaina. Look for cut flower displays, floral arrangements, demonstrations, lei-making contests, art exhibits, and entertainment. Call © **808/667-9175.** December 4, 2004.

**Old-Fashioned Holiday Celebration,** Lahaina. A day of Christmas carolers, Santa Claus, live music and entertainment, a crafts fair, Christmas baked goods, and activities for children, all taking place in the Banyan Tree Park on Front Street. Call ✆ **888/310-1117.** December 4, 2004.

**First Light 2004,** Maui Arts and Cultural Center. Academy of Motion Pictures holds major screening of top films. Not to be missed. Call ✆ **808/579-9996;** www.mauifilmfestival.com. December 15, 2004 to January 2, 2005.

## 5 Travel Insurance

Check your existing insurance policies and credit-card coverage before you buy travel insurance. You may already be covered for lost luggage, canceled tickets, or medical expenses. The cost of travel insurance varies widely, depending on the cost and length of your trip, your age, health, and the type of trip you're taking.

**TRIP-CANCELLATION INSURANCE** Trip-cancellation insurance helps you get your money back if you have to back out of a trip, if you have to go home early, or if your travel supplier goes bankrupt. Allowed reasons for cancellation can range from sickness to natural disasters to the State Department declaring your destination unsafe for travel. Insurance policy details vary, so read the fine print—and especially make sure that your airline or cruise line is on the list of carriers covered in case of bankruptcy. For information, contact one of the following insurers: **Access America** (✆ **800/284-8300;** www.accessamerica.com); **Travel Guard International** (✆ **800/826-1300;** www.travelguard.com); **Travel Insured International** (✆ **800/243-3174;** www.travelinsured.com); and **Travelex Insurance Services** (✆ **800/228-9792;** www.travelex-insurance.com).

**MEDICAL INSURANCE** Most health insurance policies cover you if you get sick away from home—but check, particularly if you're insured by an HMO.

## 6 Specialized Travel Resources

### FOR TRAVELERS WITH DISABILITIES

Travelers with disabilities are made to feel very welcome in Maui. Hotels are usually equipped with wheelchair-accessible rooms, and tour companies provide many special services. The **Hawaii Center for Independent Living,** 414 Kauwili St., Suite 102, Honolulu, HI 96817 (✆ **808/522-5400;** fax 808/586-8129; www.hawaii.gov/health; cpdppp@aloha.net), can provide information and send you a copy of the *Aloha Guide to Accessibility* ($15).

**Moss Rehab ResourceNet (www.mossresourcenet.org)** is a great source for information, tips, and resources relating to accessible travel. You'll find links to a number of travel agents who specialize in planning trips for travelers with disabilities here and through **Access-Able Travel Source** (✆ **303/232-2979;** www.access-able.com), another excellent online source. You'll also find relay and voice numbers for hotels, airlines, and car-rental companies on Access-Able's user-friendly site, as well as links to accessible accommodations, attractions, transportation, tours, local medical resources and equipment repair, and much more.

For travelers with disabilities who wish to do their own driving, hand-controlled cars can be rented from **Avis** (✆ **800/331-1212;** www.avis.com) and **Hertz** (✆ **800/654-3131;** www.hertz.com). The number of hand-controlled cars in Hawaii is limited, so be sure to book well in advance. For wheelchair-accessible vans, contact **Accessible Vans of Hawaii,** 186 Mehani Circle, Kihei (✆ **800/303-3750** or 808/879-5521; fax 808/879-0640; www.accessiblevans.com). Maui recognizes other states' windshield placards indicating that the driver of the car is disabled, so be sure to bring yours with you.

Vision-impaired travelers who use a Seeing Eye dog need to present documentation that the dog is a trained Seeing Eye dog and has had rabies shots. For more information, contact the **Animal Quarantine Facility** (✆ **808/483-7171;** www.hawaii.gov).

## FOR GAY & LESBIAN TRAVELERS

Known for its acceptance of all groups, Hawaii welcomes gays and lesbians just as it does anybody else.

To get a sense of the local gay and lesbian community on the island of Maui, contact **Both Sides Now** (✆ **808/244-4566;** fax 808/874-6221), which publishes a monthly newspaper on issues and events for Maui's gay, lesbian, bisexual, and transgender community.

**Pacific Ocean Holidays,** P.O. Box 88245, Honolulu, HI 96830 (✆ **800/735-6600** or 808/923-2400; www.gayhawaii.com), offers vacation packages that feature gay-owned and gay-friendly lodgings. It also publishes the *Pocket Guide to Hawaii: A Guide for Gay Visitors & Kamaaina,* a list of gay-owned and gay-friendly businesses throughout the islands. Send $5 for a copy (mail order only; no phone orders, please), or access the online version on the website.

If you want help planning your trip, the **International Gay & Lesbian Travel Association (IGLTA;** ✆ **800/448-8550** or 954/776-2626; www.iglta.org) can link you up with the appropriate gay-friendly service organization or tour specialist. With around 1,200 members, it offers quarterly newsletters, marketing mailings, and a membership directory that's updated quarterly. Members are kept informed of gay and gay-friendly hoteliers, tour operators, and airline and cruise-line representatives. **GayWired Travel Services (www.gaywired.com)** is another great trip-planning resource; click on "Travel Services."

**Out and About** (✆ **800/929-2268** or 415/486-2591; www.outandabout.com) offers a monthly newsletter packed with good information on the global gay and lesbian scene. Its website features links to gay and lesbian tour operators and other gay-themed travel links, plus extensive online travel information to subscribers only. Out and About's guidebooks are available at most major bookstores and through www.adlbooks.com.

## FOR SENIORS

Discounts for seniors are available at almost all of Maui's major attractions, and occasionally at hotels and restaurants. Always inquire when making hotel reservations, and especially when you're buying your airline ticket—most major domestic airlines offer senior discounts.

Members of **AARP** (✆ **800/424-3410** or 202/434-2277; www.aarp.org) are usually eligible for such discounts; AARP also puts together organized tour packages at moderate rates.

Some great, low-cost trips to Hawaii are offered to people 55 and older through **Elderhostel,** 75 Federal St., Boston, MA 02110 (✆ **617/426-8056;** www.elderhostel.org), a nonprofit group that arranges travel and study programs around the world. You can obtain a complete catalog of offerings by writing to Elderhostel, P.O. Box 1959, Wakefield, MA 01880-5959.

If you're planning to visit Haleakala National Park, you can save sightseeing dollars if you're 62 or older by picking up a **Golden Age Passport** from any national park, recreation area, or monument. This lifetime pass has a one-time fee of $10 and provides free admission to all of the parks in the system, plus a 50% savings on camping and recreation fees. You can pick one up at any park entrance; be sure to have proof of your age with you.

## FOR FAMILIES

Maui is paradise for children: beaches to frolic on, water to splash in, unusual sights to see, and a host of new foods to taste.

The larger hotels and resorts have supervised programs for children and can refer you to qualified babysitters. You can also contact **People Attentive to Children (PATCH;** ✆ **808/242-9232;**

www.patch-hi.org), which will refer you to individuals who have taken their training courses on child care.

**Baby's Away** (✆ **800/942-9030** or 808/875-9093; www.babysaway.com) rents cribs, strollers, highchairs, playpens, infant seats, and the like, to make your baby's vacation (and yours) much more enjoyable.

Remember that Maui's sun is probably much stronger than what you're used to at home, so it's important to protect your kids, and keep infants out of the sun altogether. Infants under 6 months should not be in the sun at all. Older babies need zinc oxide to protect their fragile skin, and children should be slathered with sunscreen every hour.

Condo rentals are a great option for families; the convenience of having your own kitchen is great for mom and dad. Our favorite condo complexes are reviewed in chapter 3.

## 7 Getting There

If possible, fly directly to Maui; doing so can save you a 2-hour layover in Honolulu and another plane ride. If you're headed for Molokai or Lanai, you'll have to connect through Honolulu.

If you think of the island of Maui as the shape of a head and shoulders of a person, you'll probably arrive on its neck, at **Kahului Airport.**

At press time, six airlines fly directly from the U.S. mainland to Kahului: **United Airlines** (✆ 800/241-6522; www.ual.com) offers daily nonstop flights from San Francisco and Los Angeles; **Aloha Airlines** (✆ 800/367-5250; www.alohaair.com) has nonstop service from Kahului Maui to Burbank, California (closer to downtown Los Angeles than Los Angeles International Airport), Orange County, California, and Phoenix, Arizona. International travelers can use Aloha's service from Vancouver, British Columbia; **Hawaiian Airlines** (✆ 800/367-5320; www.hawaiianair.com) has direct flights from Los Angeles, San Francisco, Portland, and Seattle; **American Airlines** (✆ 800/433-7300; www.aa.com) flies direct from Los Angeles and San Jose; **Delta Airlines** (✆ 800/221-1212; www.delta.com) offers direct flights from San Francisco and Los Angeles; and **American Trans Air** (✆ 800/435-9282; www.ata.com) has direct flights from Los Angeles, San Francisco, and Phoenix.

The other carriers—including **Continental** (✆ 800/525-0280; www.continental.com), which offers nonstop service from Newark to Honolulu, and **Northwest Airlines** (✆ 800/225-2525; www.nwa.com), which has a daily nonstop from Detroit—fly to Honolulu, where you'll have to pick up an interisland flight to Maui. (The airlines listed in the paragraph above also offer many more flights to Honolulu from additional cities on the mainland.) Both **Aloha Airlines** and **Hawaiian Airlines** offer jet service from Honolulu. See "Interisland Flights" later in this chapter.

For information on airlines serving Hawaii from places other than the U.S. mainland, see chapter 2, "For International Visitors."

## LANDING AT KAHULUI AIRPORT

If there's a long wait at baggage claim, step over to the state-operated **Visitor Information Center,** where you can pick up brochures and the latest issue of *This Week Maui,* which features great regional maps of the islands, and ask about island activities. After collecting your bags from the poky, automated carousels, step out, take a deep breath, proceed to the curbside rental-car pickup area, and wait for the appropriate rental-agency shuttle van to take you a half mile away to the rental-car checkout desk. (All major rental companies have branches at Kahului; see "Getting Around" later in this chapter.)

If you're not renting a car, the cheapest way to get to your hotel is **SpeediShuttle** (✆ **808/875-8070;** www.speedishuttle.com), which can take you between Kahului Airport and all the major resorts between 5am and 11pm daily. Rates vary, but figure on $30 for one to Wailea (one-way), $41 for one to Kaanapali (one-way), and $57 one-way to Kapalua. Be sure to call before your flight to arrange pickup.

You'll see taxis outside the airport terminal, but note that they are quite expensive—expect to spend around $60 to $75 for a ride from Kahului to Kaanapali and $50 from the airport to Wailea.

If possible, avoid landing on Maui between 3 and 6pm, when the working stiffs on Maui are "pau work" (finished with work) and a major traffic jam occurs at the first intersection.

**AVOIDING KAHULUI** If you're planning to stay at any of the hotels in Kapalua or at the Kaanapali resorts, you might consider flying **Island Air** (✆ **800/323-3345;** www.islandair.com) from Honolulu to **Kapalua–West Maui Airport.** From this airport, it's only a 10- to 15-minute drive to most hotels in West Maui, as opposed to an hour from Kahului. **Pacific Wings** (✆ **888/873-0877** or 808/575-4546; fax 808/873-7920; www.pacificwings.com) flies eight-passenger, twin-engine Cessna 402C aircraft into tiny **Hana Airport,** and also flies into Kahului.

### Tips Agricultural Restrictions

You cannot bring fresh fruits and vegetables into Hawaii, even if you're coming from the U.S. mainland and have no need to clear Customs.

## Interisland Flights

Don't expect to jump a ferry between any of the Hawaiian islands. Today, everyone island-hops by plane. Before the September 11, 2001, terrorist attacks, there used to be flights between Honolulu and Maui almost every 20 minutes of every day from just before sunrise to well after sunset.

Those days are gone. There are fewer and fewer interisland flights, so be sure to book your interisland connection from Honolulu to Maui in advance.

**Aloha Airlines** (© **800/367-5250** or 808/244-9071; www.alohaair.com) is the state's largest provider of interisland air transport service. It offers 15 regularly scheduled daily jet flights a day from Honolulu to Maui on their all-jet fleet of Boeing 737 aircraft. Aloha's sibling company, **Island Air** (© **800/323-3345** or 808/484-2222; www.alohaair.com), operates deHavilland DASH-8 and DASH-6 turboprop aircraft and serves Hawaii's small interisland airports on Maui, Molokai, and Lanai, with flights connecting them to Oahu.

**Hawaiian Airlines** (© **800/367-5320** or 808/871-6132; www.hawaiianair.com) is Hawaii's other interisland airline featuring jet planes.

A newcomer on the interisland commuter scene is Kahului-based **Pacific Wings** (© **888/873-0877** or 808/575-4546; www.pacificwings.com). It currently offers flights between Kahului and Hana, Molokai, Lanai, and Honolulu.

## 8 Money-Saving Package Deals

Booking an all-inclusive travel package that includes some combination of airfare, accommodations, rental car, meals, airport and baggage transfers, and sightseeing can be the most cost-effective way to travel to Maui.

Package tours are not the same as escorted tours. They are simply a way to buy airfare and accommodations (and sometimes extras like sightseeing tours and rental cars) at the same time. When you're visiting Hawaii, a package can be a smart way to go. That's because packages are sold in bulk to tour operators, who then resell them to the public at a cost that drastically undercuts standard rates.

Packages, however, vary widely. Some offer a better class of hotels than others. Some offer the same hotels for lower prices. With some packagers, your choice of accommodations and travel days may be limited. Which package is right for you depends entirely on what you want.

Start out by **reading this guide.** Do a little homework, and read up on Maui so that you can be a smart consumer. Compare the rack rates that we've published to the discounted rates being offered by the packagers to see what kinds of deals they're offering. If you're being offered a stay in a hotel we haven't recommended, do more research to learn about it, especially if it isn't a reliable franchise. It's not a deal if you end up at a dump.

Be sure to **read the fine print.** Make sure you know *exactly* what's included in the price you're being quoted, and what's not. Are hotel taxes and airport transfers included, or will you have to pay extra? Before you commit to a package, make sure you know how much flexibility you have. Some packagers require ironclad commitments, while others will go with the flow, charging only minimal fees for changes or cancellations.

The best place to start looking for a package deal is in the travel section of your local Sunday newspaper. Also check the ads in the back of such national travel magazines as *Arthur Frommer's Budget Travel* and *Travel Holiday.* **Liberty Travel** (✆ **888/271-1584;** www.libertytravel.com), for instance, one of the biggest packagers in the Northeast, usually boasts a full-page ad in Sunday papers. **American Express Travel** (✆ **800/AXP-6898;** www.americanexpress.com/travel) can also book you a well-priced Hawaiian vacation; it also advertises in many Sunday travel sections.

---

*Tips* **Package-Buying Tip**

For one-stop shopping on the Web, go to **Pleasant Hawaiian Holidays** (✆ **800/2-HAWAII** or 800/242-9244; www.pleasantholidays.com), by far the biggest and most comprehensive packager to Hawaii; it offers an extensive, high-quality collection of 50 condos and hotels in every price range.

---

### Tips Hawaii on the Web

Below are some of the best Hawaii-specific websites for planning your trip.

- **Hawaii Visitors & Convention Bureau** (HVCB; www.gohawaii.com)
- **Planet Hawaii** (www.planet-hawaii.com)
- **Maui Island Currents** (www.islandcurrents.com)
- **Maui Net** (www.maui.net)
- **The Hawaiian Language Website** (http://hawaiianlanguage.com)

Excellent deals can be found at **More Hawaii For Less** (✆ **800/967-6687;** www.hawaii4less.com), a California-based company that specializes in air-condominium packages at unbelievable prices.

Other reliable packagers include the airlines themselves, which often package their flights with accommodations. Among the airlines offering good-value package deals to Hawaii are **American Airlines Fly-Away Vacations** (✆ 800/321-2121; www.aa.com), **Continental Airlines Vacations** (✆ 800/634-5555 or 800/301-3800; www.coolvacations.com), **Delta Dream Vacations** (✆ 800/872-7786; www.deltavacations.com), and **United Vacations** (✆ 800/328-6877; www.unitedvacations.com). If you're traveling to the islands from Canada, ask your travel agent about package deals through **Air Canada Vacations** (✆ 800/776-3000; www.aircanada.ca).

## 9 Getting Around

The only way to really see Maui is by rental car. There's no real islandwide public transit.

Maui has only a handful of major roads: One follows the coastline around the two volcanoes that form the island, Haleakala and Puu Kukui; one goes up to Haleakala's summit; one goes to Hana; one goes to Wailea; and one goes to Lahaina. It sounds simple, right? Well, it isn't, because the names of the few roads change en route. Also, you should expect to encounter a traffic jam or two in the major resort areas.

The best and most detailed road maps are published by ***This Week Magazine,*** a free visitor publication available on Maui. Most rental-car maps are pretty good, too.

## CAR RENTALS

Maui has one of the least expensive car-rental rates in the country. Cars are usually plentiful on Maui, except on holiday weekends, which in Hawaii also means King Kamehameha Day, Prince Kuhio Day, and Admission Day (see "When to Go" earlier in this chapter). Rental cars are usually at a premium on Molokai and Lanai, so be sure to book well ahead.

All the major car-rental agencies have offices on Maui, usually at both Kahului and West Maui Airports. They include: **Alamo** (✆ 800/327-9633; www.goalamo.com), **Avis** (✆ 800/321-3712; www.avis.com), **Budget** (✆ 800/935-6878; https://rent.drive budget.com/Home.jsp), **Dollar** (✆ 800/800-4000; www.dollarcar.com), **Hertz** (✆ 800/654-3011; www.hertz.com), and **National** (✆ 800/227-7368; www.nationalcar.com).

There are also a few frugal car-rental agencies offering older cars at discount prices. **Word of Mouth Rent-a-Used-Car** ★, 150 Hana Hwy. #A, in Kahului (✆ 800/533-5929 or 808/877-2436; www.mauirentacar.com), offers an older, four-door compact without air-conditioning for $120 a week, plus tax; with air-conditioning, it's $140 a week, plus tax. **Discount Car Rental,** 1993 S. Kihei Rd., Suite 214-B Kihei (✆ 877/874-4800 or 808/874-4800), rents used economy cars at a weekly rate of $115 to $140, plus tax. They do not provide airport pickup, however; you'll have to make your own way to Kihei (it's about $28 via taxi; see "Other Transportation Options" below, for details).

---

### *Tips* Traffic Advisory

The road from central Maui to Kihei and Wailea, **Mokulele Highway (Hwy. 311),** is a dangerous strip that's often the scene of head-on crashes involving intoxicated and speeding drivers; be careful. Also, be alert on the **Honoapiilani Highway (Hwy. 30)** en route to Lahaina, because drivers who spot whales in the channel between Maui and Lanai often slam on the brakes and cause major tie-ups and accidents.

There are 29 emergency call boxes on the island's busiest highways and remote areas, including along the Hana and Haleakala highways and on the north end of the island in the remote community of Kahakuloa.

***Another traffic note:*** Buckle up your seat belt—Hawaii has stiff fines for noncompliance.

---

To rent a car in Hawaii, you must be at least 25 years old and have a valid driver's license and a credit card. Your valid home-state license will be recognized here.

**INSURANCE** Hawaii is a no-fault state, which means that if you don't have collision-damage insurance, you are required to pay for all damages before you leave the state, whether or not the accident was your fault. Your personal car insurance back home may provide rental-car coverage; read your policy or call your insurer before you leave home. Bring your insurance identification card if you decline the optional insurance, which usually costs from $12 to $20 a day. Obtain the name of your company's local claim representative before you go. Some credit-card companies also provide collision-damage insurance for their customers; check with yours before you rent.

## OTHER TRANSPORTATION OPTIONS

**TAXIS** For islandwide 24-hour service, call **Alii Cab Co.** (© 808/661-3688 or 808/667-2605). You can also try **Kihei Taxi** (© 808/879-3000), **Wailea Taxi** (© 808/874-5000), or **Maui Central Cab** (© 808/244-7278) if you need a ride.

**SHUTTLES** **SpeediShuttle** (© **808/875-8070;** www.speedishuttle.com) can take you between Kahului Airport and all the major resorts from 5am to 11pm daily (for details, see "Landing at Kahului Airport" under "Getting There" earlier in this chapter).

Free shuttle vans operate within the resort areas of Kaanapali, Kapalua, and Wailea; if you're staying in those areas, your hotel can fill you in on exact routes and schedules.

## *FAST FACTS:* Maui

***American Express*** For 24-hour traveler's check refunds and purchase information, call © **800/221-7282.** Local offices are located in South Maui at the **Grand Wailea Resort** (© **808/875-4526**) and the **Westin Maui** at Kaanapali Beach (© **808/661-7155**).

***Dentists*** Emergency dental care is available at **Kihei Dental Center,** 1847 S. Kihei Rd., Kihei (© **808/874-8401**) or in Lahaina at the **Aloha Lahaina Dentists,** 134 Luakini St. (in the Maui Medical Group Building), Lahaina (© **808/661-4005**).

***Doctors*** No appointment is necessary at **West Maui Healthcare Center,** Whalers Village, 2435 Kaanapali Pkwy., Suite H-7 (near Leilani's Restaurant), Kaanapali (✆ **808/667-9721**), which is open 365 days a year, nightly until 10pm. In Kihei, call **Urgent Care,** 1325 S. Kihei Rd., Suite 103 (at Lipoa St., across from Star Market), Kihei (✆ **808/879-7781**), open daily from 6am to midnight; doctors are on call 24 hours a day.

***Emergencies*** Dial ✆ **911** for the police, ambulance, and fire department. District stations are located in Lahaina (✆ **808/661-4441**) and in Hana (✆ **808/248-8311**). For the **Poison Control Center,** call ✆ **800/362-3585.**

***Hospitals*** For medical attention, go to **Maui Memorial Hospital,** in Central Maui at 221 Mahalani, Wailuku (✆ **808/244-9056**); and East Maui's **Hana Medical Center,** on Hana Highway (✆ **808/248-8924**).

***Post Offices*** To find the nearest post office, call ✆ **800/ASK-USPS.** In Lahaina, there are branches at the Lahaina Civic Center, 1760 Honoapiilani Hwy.; in Kahului, there's a branch at 138 S. Puunene Ave.; and in Kihei, there's one at 1254 S. Kihei Rd.

***Weather*** For the current weather, call ✆ **808/871-5111;** for recreational activities, call ✆ **808/871-5054;** for Haleakala National Park weather, call ✆ **808/871-5111;** for marine weather and surf and wave conditions, call ✆ **808/877-3477.**

# 2 For International Visitors

Whether it's your first visit or your 10th, a trip to the United States may require additional planning. The pervasiveness of American culture around the world may make the United States feel like familiar territory to foreign visitors, but leaving your own country for the States—especially the unique island of Maui—still requires some arrangements before you leave home. This chapter will provide you with essential information, helpful tips, and advice for the more common problems that some visitors encounter.

## 1 Preparing for Your Trip

### ENTRY REQUIREMENTS

Check at any U.S. embassy or consulate for current information and requirements. You can also obtain a visa application and other information online at the **U.S. State Department**'s website, at **www.travel.state.gov**.

**VISAS** The U.S. State Department has a **Visa Waiver Program** allowing citizens of certain countries to enter the United States without a visa for stays of up to 90 days. At press time these included Andorra, Australia, Austria, Belgium, Brunei, Denmark, Finland, France, Germany, Iceland, Ireland, Italy, Japan, Liechtenstein, Luxembourg, Monaco, the Netherlands, New Zealand, Norway, Portugal, San Marino, Singapore, Slovenia, Spain, Sweden, Switzerland, the United Kingdom, and Uruguay. Citizens of these countries need only a valid passport and a round-trip air or cruise ticket in their possession upon arrival. If they first enter the United States, they may also visit Mexico, Canada, Bermuda, and/or the Caribbean islands and return to the United States without a visa. Further information is available from any U.S. embassy or consulate. Canadian citizens may enter the United States without visas; they need only proof of residence.

Citizens of all other countries must have (1) a valid passport that expires at least 6 months later than the scheduled end of their visit to the United States and (2) a tourist visa, which may be obtained without charge from any U.S. consulate.

**To obtain a visa,** the traveler must submit a completed application form (either in person or by mail) with a 1½-inch-square photo, and must demonstrate binding ties to a residence abroad. Usually you can obtain a visa at once or within 24 hours, but it may take longer during the summer rush from June through August. If you cannot go in person, contact the nearest U.S. embassy or consulate for directions on applying by mail. Your travel agent or airline office may also be able to provide you with visa applications and instructions. The U.S. consulate or embassy that issues your visa will determine whether you will be issued a multiple- or single-entry visa and any restrictions regarding the length of your stay.

**MEDICAL REQUIREMENTS** Unless you're arriving from an area known to be suffering from an epidemic (particularly cholera or yellow fever), inoculations or vaccinations are not required for entry into the United States. If you have a medical condition that requires **syringe-administered medications,** carry a valid signed prescription from your physician—the Federal Aviation Administration (FAA) no longer allows airline passengers to pack syringes in their carry-on baggage without documented proof of medical need. If you have a disease that requires treatment with **narcotics,** you should also carry documented proof with you—smuggling narcotics aboard a plane is a serious offense that carries severe penalties in the U.S.

For **HIV-positive visitors,** requirements for entering the United States are somewhat vague and change frequently. According to the latest publication of *HIV and Immigrants: A Manual for AIDS Service Providers*, the Immigration and Naturalization Service (INS) doesn't require a medical exam for entry into the United States, but INS officials may stop individuals because they look sick or because they are carrying AIDS/HIV medicine. For further up-to-the-minute information, contact the AIDSInfo (✆ **800/448-0440** or 301/519-6616; www.aidsinfo.nih.gov) or the **Gay Men's Health Crisis** (✆ **212/367-1000;** www.gmhc.org).

**DRIVER'S LICENSES** Foreign driver's licenses are mostly recognized in the U.S., although you may want to get an international driver's license if your home license is not written in English.

## PASSPORT INFORMATION

Safeguard your passport in an inconspicuous, inaccessible place like a money belt. Make a copy of the critical pages, including the passport number, and store it in a safe place, separate from the passport itself. If you lose your passport, visit the nearest consulate of your native country as soon as possible for a replacement.

Note that the International Civil Aviation Organization (ICAO) has recommended a policy requiring that *every* individual who travels by air have his or her own passport. In response, many countries are now requiring that children must be issued their own passport to travel internationally, where before those under 16 or so may have been allowed to travel on a parent or guardian's passport.

## CUSTOMS

**WHAT YOU CAN BRING IN** Every visitor over 21 years of age may bring in, duty-free, the following: (1) 1 liter of wine or hard liquor; (2) 200 cigarettes, 150 cigars (but not from Cuba), or 3 pounds of smoking tobacco; and (3) $100 worth of gifts. These exemptions are offered to travelers who spend at least 72 hours in the United States and who have not claimed them within the preceding 6 months. In addition, you cannot bring fresh fruits and vegetables into Hawaii, even if you're coming from the U.S. mainland and have no need to clear Customs. Every passenger is asked shortly before landing to sign a certificate declaring that he or she does not have fresh fruits and vegetables in his or her possession.

Foreign tourists may bring in or take out up to $10,000 in U.S. or foreign currency with no formalities; larger sums must be declared to U.S. Customs upon entering or leaving, which includes filing form CM 4790.

Declare any medicines you are carrying and be prepared to present a letter or prescription from your doctor demonstrating you need the drugs; you may bring in no more than you would normally use in the duration of your visit.

For many more details on what you can and cannot bring, check the informative U.S. Customs website at **www.customs.ustreas.gov** and click "Traveler Information," or call ✆ **202/927-1770.**

### WHAT YOU CAN TAKE HOME

Rules governing what you can bring back duty-free vary from country to country, and are subject to change, but they're generally posted on the Internet. **U.K. citizens** should contact HM Customs & Excise at ✆ **0845/010-9000** (from outside the U.K., 020/8929-0152), or consult their website at www.hmce.gov.uk.

For a clear summary of **Canadian** rules, request the booklet *I Declare,* issued by the **Canada Customs and Revenue Agency** (✆ **800/461-9999** in Canada, or 204/983-3500; www.ccra-adrc.gc.ca). A helpful brochure available from **Australian** consulates or Customs offices is *Know Before You Go.* For more information, call the **Australian Customs Service** at ✆ **1300/363-263,** or log on to www.customs.gov.au. **New Zealand** citizens should request the pamphlet *New Zealand Customs Guide for Travellers, Notice no. 4* from **New Zealand Customs,** The Customhouse, 17–21 Whitmore St., Box 2218, Wellington (✆ **0800/428-786** or 04/473-6099; www.customs.govt.nz).

## INSURANCE

Although it's not required of travelers, health insurance is highly recommended. Unlike many European countries, the United States does not usually offer free or low-cost medical care to its citizens or visitors. Doctors and hospitals are expensive, and in most cases will require advance payment or proof of coverage before they render their services. Policies can cover everything from the loss or theft of your baggage and trip cancellation to the guarantee of bail in case you're arrested. Good policies will also cover the costs of an accident, repatriation, or death. Packages such as **Europ Assistance's "Worldwide Healthcare Plan"** are sold by European automobile clubs and travel agencies at attractive rates. **Worldwide Assistance Services, Inc.** (✆ **800/821-2828;** www.worldwideassistance.com) is the agent for Europ Assistance in the United States.

## MONEY

**CURRENCY** The most common **bills** (all ugly, all green) are the $1 (colloquially, a "buck"), $5, $10, and $20 denominations. There are also $2 bills (seldom encountered), $50 bills, and $100 bills (the last two are usually not welcome as payment for small purchases). Note that redesigned bills were introduced in the last few years, but the old-style bills are still legal tender.

There are seven denominations of coins: 1¢ (1 cent, or a penny); 5¢ (5 cents, or a nickel); 10¢ (10 cents, or a dime); 25¢ (25 cents, or a quarter); 50¢ (50 cents, or a half dollar); the new gold "Sacagawea" coin worth $1; and, prized by collectors, the rare, older silver dollar.

**EXCHANGING CURRENCY** To exchange foreign currency on Maui, you'll need to either go to a bank (call first to see if currency exchange is available) or use your hotel.

**CREDIT CARDS** Credit cards are widely used in Hawaii. You can save yourself trouble by using plastic rather than cash or traveler's checks in most hotels, restaurants, retail stores, and a growing number of food and liquor stores. You must have a credit card to rent a car in Hawaii.

## 2 Getting to & Around the United States

The only airline with direct flights from foreign cities to Maui is **Air Canada** (✆ 800/776-3000; www.aircanada.ca). Because of Maui's short runway, most international visitors will have to fly to Honolulu first to clear Customs, then get an interisland flight to Kahului, Maui.

Airlines serving Hawaii from places other than the U.S. mainland include **Air Canada** (✆ 800/776-3000; www.aircanada.ca); **Air New Zealand** (✆ 0800/737-000 in Auckland, 64-3/379-5200 in Christchurch, 800/926-7255 in the U.S.; www.airnewzealand.com), which runs 40 flights per week between Auckland and Hawaii; **Qantas** (✆ 008/177-767 in Australia, 800/227-4500 in the U.S.; www.qantas.com.au), which flies between Sydney and Honolulu daily (plus additional flights 4 days a week); **Japan Air Lines** (✆ 03/5489-1111 in Tokyo, 800/525-3663 in the U.S.; www.japanair.com); **All Nippon Airways (ANA)** (✆ 03/5489-1212 in Tokyo, 800/235-9262 in the U.S.; www.fly-ana.com); **China Airlines** (✆ 02/715-1212 in Taipei, 800/227-5118 in the U.S.; www.china-airlines.com); **Air Pacific,** serving Fiji, Australia, New Zealand, and the South Pacific (✆ 800/227-4446; www.airpacific.com); **Korean Airlines** (✆ 02/656-2000 in Seoul, 800/223-1155 on the East Coast, 800/421-8200 on the West Coast, 800/438-5000 from Hawaii; www.koreanair.com); and **Philippine Airlines** (✆ 631/816-6691 in Manila, 800/435-9725 in the U.S.; www.philippineair.com).

Operated by the European Travel Network, **www.discount-tickets.com** is a great online source for regular and discounted airfares to destinations around the world. You can also use this site to compare rates and book accommodations, car rentals, and tours. Click on "Special Offers" for the latest package deals. Students should also try **Campus Travel** (✆ **0870/240-1010** in England, 0131/668-3303 in Scotland).

If you're traveling in the United States beyond Hawaii, some large American airlines—such as **American, Delta, Northwest, TWA,** and **United**—offer travelers on transatlantic or transpacific flights special discount tickets under the name **Visit USA,** allowing travel between any U.S. destinations at reduced rates. These tickets must be purchased before you leave your foreign point of departure. This system is the best, easiest, and fastest way to see the United States at low cost. You should obtain information well in advance from your travel agent or the office of the airline concerned, since the conditions attached to these discount tickets can change without advance notice.

Visitors arriving by air should cultivate patience and resignation before setting foot on U.S. soil. Getting through immigration control may take as long as 2 hours on some days, especially summer weekends. Add the time it takes to clear Customs, and you'll see that you should make a very generous allowance for delay in planning connections between international and domestic flights—an average of 2 to 3 hours at least.

After you have cleared Customs in Honolulu, hop a short, 20-minute interisland flight. For further information about travel to Hawaii, see "Getting There" and "Getting Around" in chapter 1.

## *FAST FACTS:* For International Visitors

***Automobile Organizations*** Auto clubs will supply maps, suggested routes, guidebooks, accident and bail-bond insurance, and emergency road service. The major auto club in the United States, with 955 offices nationwide, is the **American Automobile Association** (AAA; often called "Triple A"). Members of some foreign auto clubs have reciprocal arrangements with AAA and enjoy its services at no charge. If you belong to an auto club, inquire about AAA reciprocity before you leave. AAA can also provide you with an **International Driving Permit** validating your foreign license. You may be able to join AAA even if you are not a member of a reciprocal club. To inquire, call ✆ **800/736-2886** or visit www.aaa.com.

Some car-rental agencies now provide automobile club–type services, so inquire about their availability when you rent your car.

***Climate*** See "When to Go" in chapter 1.

***Electricity*** Hawaii, like the U.S. mainland and Canada, uses 110–120 volts (60 cycles), compared to the 220–240 volts (50 cycles) used in most of Europe and in other areas of the world, including Australia and New Zealand. Small appliances of non-American manufacture, such as hair dryers or shavers, will require a plug adapter with two flat, parallel pins; larger ones will require a 100-volt transformer.

***Embassies & Consulates*** All embassies are in Washington, D.C. Some countries have consulates general in major U.S. cities, and most have a mission to the United Nations in New York City. If your country isn't listed below, call for directory information in Washington, D.C. (✆ **202/555-1212**), or point your Web browser to **www.embassy.org/embassies** for the location and phone number of your national embassy.

The embassy of **Australia** is at 1601 Massachusetts Ave. NW, Washington, DC 20036 (✆ **202/797-3000;** www.austemb.org). There is also an Australian consulate in Hawaii at 1000 Bishop St., Penthouse Suite, Honolulu, HI 96813 (✆ 808/524-5050).

The embassy of **Canada** is at 501 Pennsylvania Ave. NW, Washington, DC 20001 (✆ **202/682-1740;** www.canadian embassy.org). Canadian consulates are also at 1251 Avenue of the Americas, New York, NY 10020 (✆ 212/596-1628), and at 550 South Hope St., 9th floor, Los Angeles, CA 90071 (✆ 213/346-2700).

The embassy of **Japan** is at 2520 Massachusetts Ave. NW, Washington, DC 20008 (✆ **202/238-6700;** www.embjapan.org). The consulate general of Japan is located at 1742 Nuuanu Ave., Honolulu, HI 96817 (✆ 808/543-3111).

The embassy of **New Zealand** is at 37 Observatory Circle NW, Washington, DC 20008 (✆ **202/328-4800;** www.nzemb.org). The only New Zealand consulate in the United States is at 780 Third Ave., New York, NY 10017 (✆ 202/328-4800).

The embassy of the **Republic of Ireland** is at 2234 Massachusetts Ave. NW, Washington, DC 20008 (✆ **202/462-3939;** www.irelandemb.org). There's a consulate office in San Francisco at 44 Montgomery St., Suite 3830, San Francisco, CA 94104 (✆ 415/392-4214).

The embassy of the **United Kingdom** is at 3100 Massachusetts Ave. NW, Washington, DC 20008 (✆ **202/588-6640;** www.fco.gov.uk/directory). British consulates are at 845 Third Ave., New York, NY 10022 (✆ 212/745-0200), and 11766 Wilshire Blvd., Suite 400, Los Angeles, CA 90025 (✆ 310/477-3322).

***Emergencies*** Call ✆ **911** to report a fire, call the police, or get an ambulance.

***Gasoline (Petrol)*** One U.S. gallon equals 3.8 liters, while 1.2 U.S. gallons equal 1 Imperial gallon. You'll notice there are several grades (and price levels) of gasoline available at most gas stations. You'll also notice that their names change from company to company. The ones with the highest octane are the most expensive, but most rental cars take the least expensive "regular" gas, with an octane rating of 87.

***Safety*** Although tourist areas are generally safe, visitors should always stay alert. It's wise to ask the island tourist office if you're in doubt about which neighborhoods are safe. Avoid deserted areas, especially at night. Generally speaking, you can feel safe in areas where there are many people and open establishments.

***Taxes*** The United States has no VAT (value-added tax) or other indirect taxes at a national level. Every state, and every city in it, has the right to levy its own local tax on all purchases, including hotel and restaurant checks, airline tickets, and so on. In Hawaii, sales tax is 4%; there's also a 7.25% hotel-room tax and a small excise tax, so the total tax on your hotel bill will be 11.42%.

***Telephone & Fax*** The telephone system in the United States is run by private corporations, so rates, particularly for long-distance service and operator-assisted calls, can vary widely—especially on calls made from public telephones. Local calls—that is, calls to other locations on the island you're on—made from public phones in Hawaii cost 50¢.

Generally, hotel surcharges on long-distance and local calls are astronomical. You are usually better off using a **public pay telephone,** which you will find clearly marked in most public buildings and private establishments as well as on the street. Many convenience stores and newsstands sell **prepaid calling cards** in denominations up to $50.

Most **long-distance** and **international calls** can be dialed directly from any phone. **For calls within the United States and to Canada,** dial 1 followed by the area code and the seven-digit number. **For other international calls,** dial 011 followed by the country code, city code, and the telephone number of the person you are calling. Some country and city codes are as follows: **Australia** 61, Melbourne 3, Sydney 2; **Ireland** 353, Dublin 1; **New Zealand** 64, Auckland 9, Wellington 4; **United Kingdom** 44, Belfast 232, Birmingham 21, Glasgow 41, London 71 or 81.

If you're calling the **United States from another country,** the country code is 1.

In Hawaii, interisland phone calls are considered long-distance and are often as costly as calling the U.S. mainland. The international country code for Hawaii is 1, just as it is for the rest of the United States and Canada.

For **reversed-charge** or **collect calls,** and for **person-to-person calls,** dial 0 (zero, not the letter "O"), followed by the area code and number you want; an operator will then come on the line, and you should specify that you are calling collect, person-to-person, or both. If your operator-assisted call is international, ask for the overseas operator.

Note that all phone numbers with the area code 800, 888, 866, and 877 are toll-free. However, calls to numbers in area codes 700 and 900 (chat lines, "dating" services, and so on) can be very expensive—usually a charge of 95¢ to $3 or more per minute.

For **local directory assistance** ("information"), dial 411. For **long-distance information,** dial 1, then the appropriate area code and 555-1212; for **directory assistance for another island,** dial 1, then 808, then 555-1212.

Fax facilities are widely available and can be found in most hotels and many other establishments. Try **Mail Boxes, Etc.** or **Kinko's** (check the local Yellow Pages) or any photocopying shop.

***Telephone Directories*** There are two kinds of telephone directories in the United States. The general directory, the so-called White Pages, lists private and business subscribers in alphabetical order. The inside front cover lists the emergency numbers for police, fire, and ambulance, along with other vital numbers. The first few pages include a guide to long-distance and international calling, complete with country codes and area codes.

The second directory, printed on yellow paper (hence its name, Yellow Pages), lists all local services, businesses, and industries by type of activity, with an index at the front.

***Tipping*** It's part of the American way of life to tip. Many service employees receive little direct salary and must depend on tips for their income. The following are some general rules:

In **hotels,** tip bellhops at least $1 per piece of luggage ($2–$3 if you have a lot of luggage), and tip the housekeeping staff $1 per person, per day. Tip the doorman or concierge only if he or she has provided you with some specific service (for example, calling a cab for you or obtaining difficult-to-get theater tickets). Tip the valet-parking attendant $1 to $2 every time you get your car.

In **restaurants, bars,** and **nightclubs,** tip service staff 15% to 20% of the check, tip bartenders 10% to 15%, and tip valet-parking attendants $1 to $2 per vehicle. Tip the doorman only if he or she has provided you with some specific service (such as calling a cab for you). Tipping is not expected in cafeterias and fast-food restaurants.

Tip **cab drivers** 15% of the fare.

As for **other service personnel,** tip skycaps at airports at least $1 per piece of luggage ($2–$3 if you have a lot of luggage), and tip hairdressers and barbers 15% to 20%. Tipping ushers at theaters is not expected.

# 3

# Where to Stay

Maui has accommodations to fit every taste and budget, from luxury oceanfront suites and historic bed-and-breakfasts to reasonably priced condos that will sleep a family of four. Before you book, be sure to read "The Island in Brief" in chapter 1, which will help you settle on a location.

Remember to consider *when* you will be traveling to the islands. The high season, during which rooms are always booked and rates are at the top end, runs from mid-December to March. A second high season, when rates are high but reservations are somewhat easier to get, is summer (late June to early Sept). The low seasons, with fewer tourists and cheaper rates, are April to early June and late September to mid-December.

Remember to add Maui's 11.42% accommodations tax to your final bill. Parking is free unless otherwise noted.

## 1 Central Maui

### KAHULUI

If you're arriving late at night or you have an early morning flight out, the best choice near Kahului Airport is the **Maui Beach Hotel,** 170 Kaahumanu Ave. (✆ **888/649-3222**). The nondescript, motel-like rooms go for $98 to $175 and include free airport shuttle service. It's okay for a night, but not a place to spend your vacation.

### WAILUKU

**Old Wailuku Inn at Ulupono** ★★ *Finds* This 1924 former plantation manager's home, lovingly restored by innkeepers Janice and Thomas Fairbanks, offers a genuine old Hawaii experience. The spacious rooms are gorgeously outfitted with exotic ohia-wood floors, high ceilings, and traditional Hawaiian quilts. The mammoth bathrooms (some with claw-foot tubs, others with Jacuzzis) have plush towels and earth-friendly toiletries on hand. A full gourmet breakfast is served on the enclosed back lanai or, if you prefer, delivered to your room. You'll feel right at home lounging in an old wicker chair on the lanai. The inn is located in the old historic area of

Wailuku, just a few minutes' walk from the Maui County Seat Government Building, the courthouse, and a wonderful stretch of shops.

2199 Kahookele St. (at High St., across from the Wailuku School), Wailuku, HI 96732. ✆ **800/305-4899** or 808/244-5897. Fax 808/242-9600. www.mauiinn.com. 7 units. $120–$180 double. Rates include full breakfast. Extra person $20. AE, DISC, MC, V. **Amenities:** Jacuzzi; laundry service; dry cleaning. *In room:* A/C, TV, dataport.

## 2 West Maui

### LAHAINA

#### MODERATE

**Best Western Pioneer Inn** This hotel is a two-story plantation-style structure with big verandas that overlook the streets of Lahaina and the harbor, a short distance away. All rooms have been totally remodeled, with vintage bathrooms and new curtains and carpets. The quietest rooms face either the garden courtyard—devoted to refined outdoor dining accompanied by live (but quiet) music—or the square-block–size banyan tree next door. We recommend room no. 31, over the banyan court, with a view of the ocean and the harbor.

658 Wharf St. (in front of Lahaina Pier), Lahaina, HI 96761. ✆ **800/457-5457** or 808/661-3636. Fax 808/667-5708. www.pioneerinnmaui.com. 34 units. $115–$200 double. Extra person $10. AE, DC, DISC, MC, V. Parking $4 in lot 2 blocks away. **Amenities:** Restaurant (good for breakfast); bar with live music; outdoor pool; big shopping arcade; laundry service. *In room:* A/C, TV/VCR, fridge, coffeemaker, hair dryer, iron, safe.

**House of Fountains Bed & Breakfast** *Finds* This immaculate 7,000-square-foot contemporary home, in a quiet residential subdivision at the north end of town, is popular with visitors from around the world. The oversize rooms are fresh and quiet, with white ceramic-tile floors, handmade koa furniture, Hawaiian quilt bedspreads, and Hawaiiana theme; the four downstairs rooms all open onto flower-filled private patios. Guests share the fully equipped guest kitchen and barbecue area, and are welcome to curl up on the living-room sofa with a book from the library. The nearest beach is about a 5-minute drive away, and tennis courts are nearby. Around the pool is a thatch hut for weekly hula performances, an imu pit for luaus, and an area that's perfect for Hawaiian weddings.

1579 Lokia St. (off Fleming Rd., north of Lahaina town), Lahaina, HI 96761. ✆ **800/789-6865** or 808/667-2121. Fax 808/667-2120. www.alohahouse.com. 6 units (shower only). $95–$145 double. Rates include full breakfast. Extra person $20. DISC, MC, V (additional 5% charge if using credit card). From Hwy. 30, take the Fleming Rd.

exit; turn left on Ainakea; after 2 blocks, turn right on Malanai St.; go 3 blocks, and turn left onto Lokia St. **Amenities:** Outdoor pool; Jacuzzi; washer/dryers. *In room:* A/C, TV, fridge, hair dryer, no phone.

**Lahaina Inn** ★ If you like old hotels that have genuine historic touches, you'll love this place. As in many old hotels, some of these Victorian antique–stuffed rooms are small; if that's a problem for you, ask for a larger unit. All come with private bathrooms and lanais. The best room in the house is no. 7 ($109), which overlooks the beach, the town, and the island of Lanai. There's an excellent, though unaffiliated, restaurant in the same building (David Paul's Lahaina Grill, p. 82), with a bar downstairs.

127 Lahainaluna Rd. (near Front St.), Lahaina, HI 96761. ✆ **800/669-3444** or 808/661-0577. Fax 808/667-9480. www.lahainainn.com. 12 units (most bathrooms have shower only). $109–$169 double. Rates include continental breakfast. AE, DC, MC, V. Next-door parking $5. No children under age 15. **Amenities:** Concierge; activity desk. *In room:* A/C.

**Ohana Maui Islander** ★ *Value* This wooden complex's units, especially those with kitchenettes, are one of Lahaina's great buys. The larger ones are great for families on a budget. The property isn't on the beach, but on a quiet side street (a rarity in Lahaina) and within walking distance of restaurants, shops, attractions, and, yes, the beach (just 3 blocks away). All of the good-size rooms, decorated in tropical-island style, are comfortable and quiet. The entire complex is spread across 10 landscaped acres and includes a sun deck, a barbecue, and a picnic area. The aloha-friendly staff will take the time to answer all of your questions.

660 Wainee St. (between Dickenson and Prison sts.), Lahaina, HI 96761. ✆ **800/462-6262** or 808/667-9766. Fax 808/661-3733. www.ohanahotels.com. 317 units. $149 double; $179 studio with kitchenette; $199 1-bedroom with kitchen (sleeps up to 4); $279 2-bedroom with kitchen (sleeps 6). Extra rollaway bed $18, free cribs. AE, DC, DISC, MC, V. Parking $3. **Amenities:** Outdoor pool; tennis courts (lit for night play until 10pm); activity desk; coin-op washer/dryers. *In room:* A/C, TV, kitchenettes (in some units), fridge, coffeemaker, hair dryer, iron, safe.

**The Plantation Inn** ★★ *Finds* Attention, romance-seeking couples: Look no further. This charming Victorian-style inn, located a couple of blocks from the water, looks like it's been here 100 years or more, but it's actually of 1990s vintage—an artful deception. The rooms are romantic to the max, tastefully done with period furniture, hardwood floors, stained glass, and ceiling fans. There are four-poster canopy beds and armoires in some rooms, brass beds and wicker in others. All units are soundproof (a plus in Lahaina) and

# Lahaina & Kaanapali Accommodations & Attractions

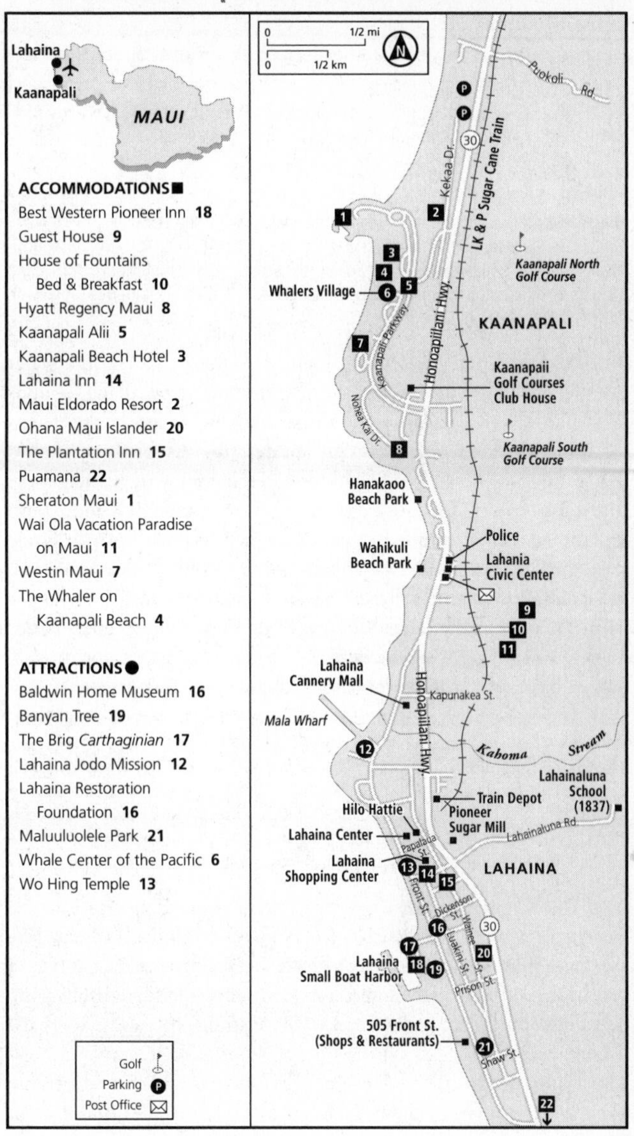

come with a private lanai; the suites have kitchenettes. The rooms wrap around the large pool and deck. Also on the property is **Gerard's** (p. 84), an outstanding French restaurant (it can be pricey, but hotel guests get a discount on dinner). Breakfast is served around the pool and in the elegant pavilion lounge.

174 Lahainaluna Rd. (between Wainee and Luakini sts. 1 block from Hwy. 30), Lahaina, HI 96761. ✆ **800/433-6815** or 808/667-9225. Fax 808/667-9293. www.theplantationinn.com. 19 units (some bathrooms with shower only). $152–$245 double. Rates include full breakfast. Extra person $20. AE, DC, DISC, MC, V. **Amenities:** Acclaimed restaurant and bar; large outdoor pool and Jacuzzi; concierge; activity desk; coin-op washer/dryers. *In room:* A/C, TV/VCR, kitchenettes (in suites), fridge, hair dryer, iron, safe.

**Puamana** These 28 acres of town houses set right on the water are ideal for those who want to retreat from the crowds and cacophony of downtown Lahaina into the serene quiet of an elegant neighborhood. Private and peaceful are apt descriptions for this complex: Each unit is a privately owned individual home, with no neighbors above or below. Most are exquisitely decorated, and all come with full kitchen, lanai, and barbecue. Puamana was once a private estate in the 1920s, part of the sugar plantations that dominated Lahaina; the plantation manager's house has been converted into a clubhouse with an oceanfront lanai, library, card room, sauna, table-tennis tables, and office. ***One warning:*** The rental office is not on-site, which has caused some problems with guests getting assistance.

Front St. (at the extreme southern end of Lahaina, ½ mile from downtown). Reservations c/o Klahani Travel, Lahaina Cannery Mall, 1221 Honoapiilani Hwy., Lahaina, HI 96761. ✆ **800/669-6284** or 808/667-2712. Fax 808/661-5875. www.klahanitravel.com. 40 units. $125–$200 1-bedroom; $150–$275 2-bedroom; $300–$500 3-bedroom. 3-night minimum. AE, DC, DISC, MC, V. **Amenities:** 3 pools (1 for adults only); tennis court; Jacuzzi; game room; activity desk; on-site laundry. *In room:* TV, kitchen, fridge, coffeemaker, hair dryer, iron, washer/dryer (in some units).

**Wai Ola Vacation Paradise on Maui** ★ Just 2 blocks from the beach, in a quiet, residential development behind a tall concrete wall, lies this lovely retreat, with shade trees, sitting areas, gardens, a pool, an ocean mural, and a range of accommodations (a suite inside the 5,000 sq. ft. home, a separate studio cottage, a one-bedroom apartment, or the entire house). Hostess Julie Frank is a veteran innkeeper who knows how to provide comfortable accommodations and memorable vacations. You'll also find a deck, barbecue facilities, and an outdoor wet bar on the property; tennis courts are nearby. Ask about her honeymoon package.

Kuuipo St. (P.O. Box 12580), Lahaina, HI 96761. ✆ **800-/492-4652** or 808/661-7901. Fax 808/661-7901. www.waiola.com. 5 units. $135 suite; $150 1-bedroom apt.; $175 cottage; $550-$850 house. 5-night minimum. Extra person $15. AE, DC, DISC, MC, V. **Amenities:** Outdoor pool; Jacuzzi; complimentary use of watersports equipment; free self-service washer/dryers. *In room:* A/C, TV/DVD/VCR, dataport, kitchenette, fridge, coffeemaker, hair dryer, iron.

### INEXPENSIVE

**Guest House** ★★ *Finds* This is one of Lahaina's great bed-and-breakfast deals: a charming house with more amenities than the expensive Kaanapali hotels just down the road. The roomy home features parquet floors and floor-to-ceiling windows; its swimming pool—surrounded by a deck and comfortable lounge chairs—is larger than some at high-priced condos. Every guest room has a quiet lanai and a romantic hot tub. The large kitchen (with every gadget imaginable) and high-speed Internet access computers are available for guests' use. The Guest House also operates Trinity Tours and offers discounts on car rentals and just about every island activity. Tennis courts are nearby, and the nearest beach is about a block away.

1620 Ainakea Rd. (off Fleming Rd., north of Lahaina town), Lahaina, HI 96761. ✆ **800/621-8942** or 808/661-8085. Fax 808/661-1896. www.mauiguesthouse.com. 4 units. $129 double. Rates include full breakfast. AE, DC, DISC, MC, V. Take Fleming Rd. off Hwy. 30; turn left on Ainakea; it's 2 blocks down. **Amenities:** Huge outdoor pool; watersports equipment rentals; concierge; activity desk; car-rental desk; self-service washer/dryers. *In room:* A/C, TV/VCR, fridge, Jacuzzi.

## KAANAPALI

### VERY EXPENSIVE

**Kaanapali Alii** ★★ *Kids* These luxurious oceanfront condominium units sit on 8 landscaped acres right on Kaanapali Beach. Kaanapali Alii combines all the amenities of a luxury hotel (including a 24-hr. front desk) with the convenience of a condominium. Each of the one-bedroom (1,500 sq. ft.) and two-bedroom (1,900 sq. ft.) units is impeccably decorated and comes with all the comforts of home (fully equipped kitchen, washer/dryer, lanai, two full bathrooms) and then some (room service, daily maid service, complimentary local newspaper). The beachside recreation area includes a swimming pool, plus a separate children's pool, whirlpool, gas barbecue grills and picnic areas, exercise rooms, saunas, and tennis courts.

50 Nohea Kai Dr., Lahaina, HI 96761. ✆ **800/642-6284** or 808/661-3330. Fax 808/667-1145. www.kaanapali-alii.com. 264 units. $350–$525 1-bedroom for 4; $475–$740 2-bedroom for 6; $900 suite. AE, DC, DISC, MC, V. Free parking. **Amenities:** Poolside cafe; 2 outdoor pools; 36-hole golf course; 3 lighted tennis courts; fitness center; Jacuzzi; watersports equipment rentals; children's program; game room; concierge; activity desk; room service; in-room massage; babysitting; same-day dry cleaning. *In room:* A/C, TV, dataport, kitchen, fridge, coffeemaker, hair dryer, iron, safe, washer/dryers.

**Sheraton Maui** ★★ *Kids* Terrific facilities for families and fitness buffs and a premier beach location make this beautiful resort an all-around great place to stay. The grande dame of Kaanapali Beach is built into the side of a cliff on the white-sand cove next to Black Rock (a lava formation that rises 80 ft. above the beach), where there's excellent snorkeling. After its recent renovation, the resort is virtually new, with six buildings of six stories or less set in well-established tropical gardens. The new lagoonlike pool features lava-rock waterways, wooden bridges, and an open-air whirlpool. But not everything has changed, thankfully. Cliff divers still swan dive off the torch-lit lava-rock headland in a traditional sunset ceremony—a sight to see. And the views of Kaanapali Beach, with Lanai and Molokai in the distance, are some of the best around.

The new emphasis is on family appeal, with a class of rooms dedicated to those traveling with kids. Every unit is outfitted with amenities galore, right down to toothbrushes and toothpaste.

2605 Kaanapali Pkwy., Lahaina, HI 96761. ✆ **800/782-9488** or 808/661-0031. Fax 808/661-0458. www.sheraton-maui.com. 510 units. $350–$750 double; from $825 suite. Extra person $50; children 17 and under stay free in parent's room using existing bedding. "Resort fee" of $10 for self-parking, "free" local calls and credit-card calls, in-room safe, lei greeting, daily coffee and newspaper, use of fitness center, and kids' program. AE, DC, DISC, MC, V. Valet parking $5. **Amenities:** 3 restaurants; snack bar; 3 bars; 2 huge outdoor pools; 36-hole golf course; 3 tennis courts; fitness center; Jacuzzi; watersports equipment rentals; children's program; game room; concierge; activity desk; car-rental desk; business center; shopping arcade; salon; limited room service (6:30am–10:30pm); in-room massage; babysitting; coin-op washer/dryers; same-day laundry service and dry cleaning. *In room:* A/C, TV, dataport, fridge, coffeemaker, hair dryer, iron, safe.

**Westin Maui** ★ *Kids* In addition to having a great location on the beach, the Westin Maui is a great place to sleep. The rooms are outfitted with fabulous new beds (Westin's custom-designed, pillow-top "heavenly beds"), plus a choice of five different pillows. Once you get up, you'll find the "aquatic playground"—an 87,000-square-foot pool area with five amazing free-form heated pools joined by swim-through grottoes, waterfalls, and a 128-foot-long water slide—sets this resort apart from its peers along lovely Kaanapali Beach. This is the Disney World of water-park resorts, and your kids will be in water-hog heaven. The fantasy theme extends from the estate-like grounds into the interior's public spaces, which are filled with the shrieks of tropical birds and the splash of waterfalls. The oversize architecture, requisite colonnade, and $2 million art collection make a pleasing backdrop for all the action.

2365 Kaanapali Pkwy., Lahaina, HI 96761. ✆ **800/WESTIN-1** or 808/667-2525. Fax 808/661-5764. 758 units. www.westinmaui.com. $350–$630 double; from $800 suite. Extra person $45. "Resort fee" of $10 for "free" local calls, use of fitness center, coffee and tea, and local paper. Parking $5. AE, DC, DISC, MC, V. **Amenities:** 5 restaurants; 3 bars; 5 free-form outdoor pools; 36-hole golf course; tennis courts; health club and spa with aerobics, steam baths, sauna, massage, and body treatments; Jacuzzi; watersports equipment rentals; bike rental; children's program; game room; concierge; activity desk; car-rental desk; business center; shopping arcade; salon; limited room service; massage; babysitting; coin-op washer/dryers; same-day laundry/dry cleaning; concierge-level rooms. *In room:* A/C, TV, dataport, minibar, fridge, coffeemaker, hair dryer, iron, safe.

## EXPENSIVE

**Hyatt Regency Maui** ★★ *Kids* Spa-goers will love this resort. Hawaii's first oceanfront spa, the Spa Moana, opened here in 2000 with some 9,000 square feet of facilities. Book your treatment before you leave home—this place is popular.

The management has poured some $19 million in renovations to rooms in this fantasy resort. It certainly has lots of imaginative touches, like the flamingoes, penguins, parrots and macaws in the lobby and an eclectic Asian and Pacific art collection. The 40-acre resort includes a half-acre outdoor pool with a 150-foot lava tube slide, a cocktail bar under the falls, and a swinging rope bridge. There's even a children-only pool with its own beach, tidal pools, and fountains.

The rooms, spread out among three towers, are pleasantly outfitted with an array of amenities, and have very comfortable separate sitting areas and private lanais with eye-popping views. The very romantic Swan Court (p. 88) is not to be missed for a special dinner. Two Regency Club floors have a private concierge, complimentary breakfast, sunset cocktails, and snacks.

200 Nohea Kai Dr., Lahaina, HI 96761. ✆ **800/233-1234** or 808/661-1234. Fax 808/667-4714. www.maui.hyatt.com. 806 units. $345–$565 double; $585–$650 Regency Club; from $850 suite. All rooms are charged a mandatory $12 "resort fee" for access to spa, local phone calls, daily local paper, in-room coffee and tea, in-room safe, and 1-hr. tennis court time. Extra person $35 ($50 in Regency Club rooms). Children 18 and under stay free in parent's room using existing bedding. Packages available. AE, DC, DISC, MC, V. Valet parking $10, free self-parking. **Amenities:** 5 restaurants; 2 bars; a half-acre-size outdoor pool; 36-hole golf course; 6 tennis courts; health club with weight room; brand-new, state-of-the-art spa; Jacuzzi; watersports equipment rentals; bike rental; Camp Hyatt kids' program, offering supervised activities for 5- to 12-year-olds; game room; concierge; activity desk; car-rental desk; business center; big shopping arcade; salon; 24-hr. room service; in-room or spa massage; babysitting; coin-op washer/dryers; laundry service; dry cleaning; concierge-level rooms. *In room:* A/C, TV, dataport, 2-line phone, minibar, fridge (on request), coffeemaker, hair dryer, iron, safe.

**Maui Eldorado Resort** ★ *Kids* These spacious condominium units—each with a full kitchen and daily maid service—were built when land in Kaanapali was cheap, contractors took pride in their work, and visitors expected large, spacious units with views from every window. You'll find it hard to believe that this was one of Kaanapali's first properties in the late 1960s, as this first-class choice still looks like new. The Outrigger chain has managed to keep prices down to reasonable levels, especially if you come in spring or fall. This is a great choice for families, with its big units, grassy areas that are perfect for running off excess energy, and a beachfront (with beach cabanas and a barbecue area) that's usually safe for swimming. Tennis courts are nearby.

2661 Kekaa Dr., Lahaina, HI 96761. ✆ **800/688-7444** or 808/661-0021. Fax 808/667-7039. www.outrigger.com. 98 units. $195–$240 studio double; $245–$295 1-bedroom (rates for up to 4); $355–$425 2-bedroom (rates for up to 6). Numerous packages available, including free 5th night, rental-car packages, senior rates, and more. AE, DC, DISC, MC, V. **Amenities:** 3 outdoor pools; 36-hole golf course; concierge; activity desk; car-rental desk; some business services; babysitting; coin-op washer/dryers. *In room:* A/C, TV, dataport, kitchen, fridge, coffeemaker, hair dryer, iron, safe, washer/dryer (in some units).

**The Whaler on Kaanapali Beach** ★★ In the heart of Kaanapali, right on the world-famous beach, lies this oasis of elegance, privacy, and luxury. The relaxing atmosphere strikes you as soon as you enter the open-air lobby, where light reflects off the dazzling koi in the meditative lily pond. No expense has been spared on these gorgeous accommodations; each unit has a full kitchen, washer/dryer, marble bathroom, 10-foot beamed ceilings, and blue-tiled lanai. Every unit boasts spectacular views of Kaanapali's gentle waves or the humpback peaks of the West Maui Mountains. Next door is Whalers Village, with numerous restaurants, bars, and shops; Kaanapali Golf Club's 36 holes are across the street.

2481 Kaanapali Pkwy. (next to Whalers Village), Lahaina, HI 96761. ✆ **800/922-7866** or 808/661-4861. Fax 808/661-8315. www.whalermaui.com. 360 units. High season $235–$255 studio double; $330–$485 1-bedroom (rate for up to 4 people); $535–$700 2-bedroom (up to 6). Low season $205–$230 studio double; $275–$415 1-bedroom; $435–$570 2-bedroom. Check Internet for specials. Extra person $20; crib $12. 2-night minimum. AE, DC, DISC, MC, V. **Amenities:** Outdoor pool; 5 tennis courts; fitness room; Jacuzzi; watersports equipment rentals; concierge; activity desk; car-rental desk; babysitting; coin-op washer/dryers; laundry service; dry cleaning. *In room:* A/C, TV, dataport, kitchen, fridge, coffeemaker, hair dryer, iron, safe, washer/dryer.

## MODERATE

**Kaanapali Beach Hotel** ★ *Value* It's older and less high-tech than its upscale neighbors, but the Kaanapali has an irresistible local style and a real Hawaiian warmth. Three low-rise wings, bordering a fabulous stretch of beach, are set around a wide, grassy lawn with coco palms and a whale-shaped pool. The spacious, spotless motel-like rooms are done in wicker and rattan, with Hawaiian-style bedspreads and lanais. The beachfront rooms are separated from the water only by a landscaped walking trail.

Old Hawaii values and customs are always close at hand, and the service is some of the friendliest around. Tiki torches, hula, and Hawaiian music create a festive atmosphere in the expansive open courtyard every night. As part of the hotel's extensive Hawaiiana program, you can learn to cut pineapple, weave lauhala, or dance the hula. There's also an arts-and-crafts fair 3 days a week and a Hawaiian library.

2525 Kaanapali Pkwy., Lahaina, HI 96761. ✆ **800/262-8450** or 808/661-0011. Fax 808/667-5978. www.kbhmaui.com. 430 units. $195–$290 double; from $235 suite. Extra person $25. Car, golf, bed-and-breakfast, and romance packages available, as well as senior discounts. AE, DC, DISC, MC, V. Valet parking $7, self-parking $5. **Amenities:** 3 restaurants; 2 bars (including a poolside bar that fixes a mean piña colada); outdoor pool; 36-hole golf course; access to tennis courts; Jacuzzi; watersports equipment rentals; children's program; game room; concierge; activity desk; car-rental desk; business center; convenience shops; salon; limited room service; babysitting; coin-op washer/dryers. *In room:* A/C, TV, fridge, coffeemaker, iron, safe.

## HONOKOWAI, KAHANA & NAPILI

### EXPENSIVE

**Napili Kai Beach Resort** ★★ *Finds* Just south of the Bay Club restaurant in Kapalua, nestled in a small white-sand cove, lies this comfortable oceanfront complex. The one- and two-story units with double-hipped Hawaii-style roofs face their very own gold-sand beach, which is safe for swimming.

Many units have a view of the Pacific. The older beachfront Lahaina Building units—with ceiling fans only—are a good buy starting at $225. Those who prefer air-conditioning should book into the Honolua Building, where, for the same price, you'll get a fully air-conditioned room set near a parklike lawn and pool. Every unit (except eight hotel rooms) has a fully stocked kitchenette with full-size fridge, cooktop, microwave, toaster oven, washer/dryer, and coffeemaker; some have dishwashers as well.

On-site pluses include daily maid service, even in the condo units; two shuffleboard courts; barbecue areas; complimentary morning coffee; free tea in the lobby every afternoon; weekly lei making, hula lessons, and horticultural tours; and a free weekly mai tai party. There are three nearby championship golf courses and excellent tennis courts at next-door Kapalua Resort.

5900 Honoapiilani Rd. (at the extreme north end of Napili, next to Kapalua), Lahaina, HI 96761. ✆ **800/367-5030** or 808/669-6271. Fax 808/669-0086. www.napilikai.com. 163 units. $190–$225 hotel room double; $220–$305 studio double; $360–$410 1-bedroom suite (sleeps up to 4); $525–$675 2-bedroom (sleeps 6). Packages available. Extra person $15. AE, MC, V. **Amenities:** Well-recommended restaurant (Sea House, p. 90); bar; 4 outdoor pools; 2 18-hole putting greens (with free golf putters for guest use); complimentary use of tennis racquets; good-size fitness room, filled with the latest equipment; Jacuzzi; complimentary watersports equipment; free children's activities at Easter, June 15–Aug 31, and at Christmas; concierge; activity desk; babysitting; coin-op washer/dryers; laundry service; dry cleaning. *In room:* A/C (in most units, but not all), TV, kitchenette, fridge, coffeemaker, hair dryer, iron, safe.

## MODERATE

**Hale Kai** ★ *Kids* This small, two-story condo complex is ideally located, right on the beach and next door to a county park. Shops, restaurants, and ocean activities are all within a 6-mile radius. The units are older but in excellent shape, and come with well-equipped kitchens (with dishwasher, disposal, microwave, even a blender), and louvered windows that open to the trade winds. Lots of guests clamor for the oceanfront pool units, but we find the park-view units cooler, and they still have ocean views (upstairs units also have cathedral ceilings). This place fills up fast, so book early; repeat guests make up most of the clientele.

3691 Lower Honoapiilani Rd. (in Honokowai), Lahaina, HI 96761. ✆ **800/446-7307** or 808/669-6333. Fax 808/669-7474. www.halekai.com. 23 units. High season $120 1-bedroom double; $150–$155 2-bedroom (rates for up to 4); $200 3-bedroom (up to 6). Low season $105 1-bedroom; $135–$140 2-bedroom; $200 3-bedroom. Extra person $15. 3-night minimum. MC, V. **Amenities:** Outdoor pool; concierge; car-rental desk; coin-op washer/dryers. *In room:* TV/VCR, kitchen, fridge, coffeemaker, hair dryer, iron.

**Kahana Sunset** ★★ *Kids* This series of wooden condo units on Lower Honoapiilani Road stair-step down the side of a hill to a postcard-perfect white-sand beach. The unique location, nestled between the coastline and the road above, makes this a very private place to stay. In the midst of the buildings sits a grassy lawn with a small pool and Jacuzzi; down by the sandy beach are gazebos and picnic areas with barbecues. The units feature full kitchens (complete with dishwashers), washer/dryers, large lanais with terrific views, and sleeper sofas. This is a great complex for families: The beach is safe for swimming, the grassy area is away from traffic, and the units are roomy.

## Accommodations & Dining from Honokowai to Kapalua

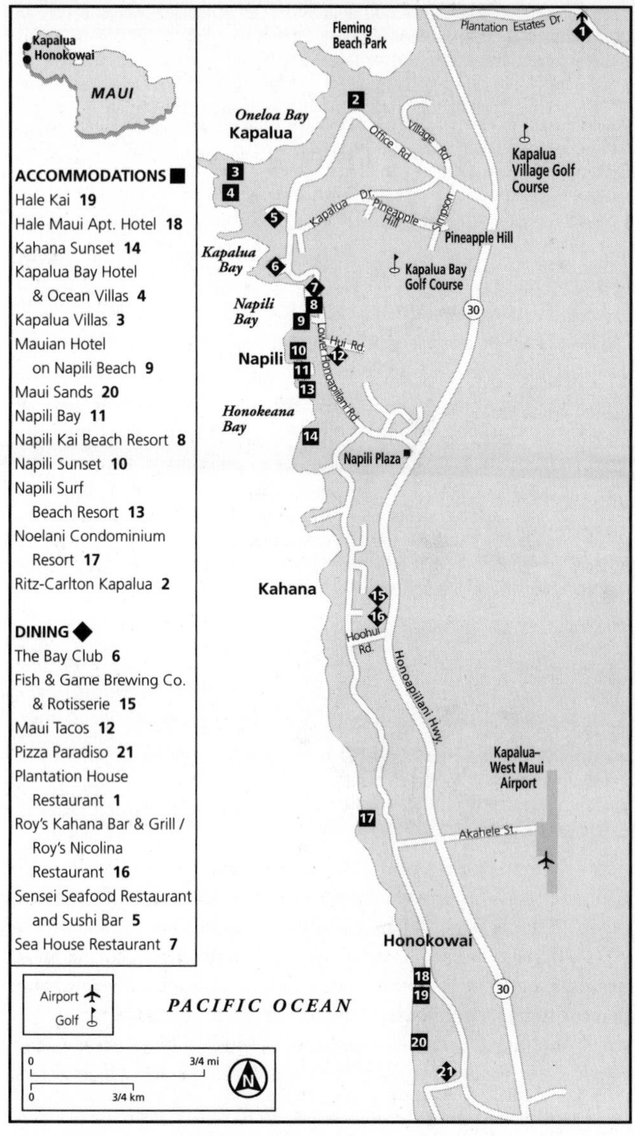

Kapalua
Honokowai
MAUI
ACCOMMODATIONS
Hale Kai 19
Hale Maui Apt. Hotel 18
Kahana Sunset 14
Kapalua Bay Hotel & Ocean Villas 4
Kapalua Villas 3
Mauian Hotel on Napili Beach 9
Maui Sands 20
Napili Bay 11
Napili Kai Beach Resort 8
Napili Sunset 10
Napili Surf Beach Resort 13
Noelani Condominium Resort 17
Ritz-Carlton Kapalua 2
DINING
The Bay Club 6
Fish & Game Brewing Co. & Rotisserie 15
Maui Tacos 12
Pizza Paradiso 21
Plantation House Restaurant 1
Roy's Kahana Bar & Grill / Roy's Nicolina Restaurant 16
Sensei Seafood Restaurant and Sushi Bar 5
Sea House Restaurant 7
Airport
Golf
0
3/4 mi
3/4 km
N
PACIFIC OCEAN
Fleming Beach Park
Plantation Estates Dr.
Oneloa Bay
Kapalua
Office Rd.
Village Rd.
Kapalua Village Golf Course
Kapalua Dr.
Pineapple Hill
Simpson
Pineapple Hill
Kapalua Bay
Kapalua Bay Golf Course
30
Napili Bay
Lower Honoapiilani Rd.
Hui Rd.
Napili
Honokeana Bay
Napili Plaza
Kahana
Hoohui Rd.
Honoapiilani Hwy.
Kapalua–West Maui Airport
Akahele St.
Honokowai

4909 Lower Honoapiilani Hwy. (at the northern end of Kahana, almost in Napili). c/o P.O. Box 10219 Lahaina, HI 96761. ✆ **800/669-1488** or 808/669-8011. Fax 808/669-9170. www.kahanasunset.com. 79 units, 49 in rental pool. $130–$240 1-bedroom (sleeps up to 4); $175–$370 2-bedroom (sleeps 6). 2-night minimum. AE, MC, V. From Hwy. 30, turn *makai* (toward the ocean) at the Napili Plaza (Napilihau St.), then left on Lower Honoapiilani Rd. **Amenities:** 2 outdoor pools (1 just for children); concierge. *In room:* TV, kitchen, coffeemaker, hair dryer, iron, safe (in some units), washer/dryer.

**Maui Sands** The Maui Sands was built back when property wasn't as expensive and developers took the extra time and money to surround their condos with lush landscaping. It's hard to get a unit with a bad view: All face either the ocean (with views of Lanai and Molokai) or tropical gardens blooming with brilliant heliconia, flowering hibiscus, and sweet-smelling ginger. Each roomy unit has a big lanai and a full kitchen. With two big bedrooms, plus space in the living room for a fifth person (or even a 6th), the larger units are good deals for families. There's a narrow beach out front.

Maui Resort Management, 3600 Lower Honoapiilani Rd. (in Honokowai), Lahaina, HI 96761. ✆ **800/367-5037** or 808/669-1902. Fax 808/669-8790. www.mauigetaway.com. 76 units. $105–$145 1-bedroom (sleeps up to 3); $150–$210 2-bedroom (sleeps 5). Extra person $10. 7-night minimum. MC, V. **Amenities:** Outdoor pool; coin-op washer/dryer. *In room:* A/C, TV, kitchen, fridge, coffeemaker.

**Mauian Hotel on Napili Beach** ★ The family that built this low-rise hotel in 1961 has restored the studio units to their original old Hawaiian style. The Mauian is perched above a beautiful half-mile long white-sand beach with great swimming and snorkeling; there's a pool with chaise lounges, umbrellas, and tables on the sun deck; and the verdant grounds are bursting with tropical color. The rooms feature hardwood floors, Indonesian-style furniture, and big lanais with great views. Thoughtful little touches include fresh flowers in rooms upon arrival, plus chilled champagne for guests celebrating a special occasion. There are no phones and no TVs in the rooms, but the large Ohana (family) room does have a TV with a VCR and an extensive library. There's complimentary coffee, great restaurants are just a 5-minute walk away, and Kapalua Resort is up the street. The nightly sunsets off the beach are spectacular.

5441 Lower Honoapiilani Rd. (in Napili), Lahaina, HI 96761. ✆ **800/367-5034** or 808/669-6205. Fax 808/669-0129. www.mauian.com. 44 units. High season $165–$195 double; low season $145–$180 double. Rates include continental breakfast. Extra 3rd person $10; 4th person $15. Children under 5 stay free in parent's room. AE, DISC, MC, V. **Amenities:** Outdoor pool; golf course; tennis courts; concierge; activity desk; business center; coin-op washer/dryer. *In room:* Kitchen, fridge, coffeemaker; no phone.

**Napili Surf Beach Resort** ★ *Finds* This well-maintained, superbly landscaped condo complex has a great location on Napili Beach. Facilities include two pools, three shuffleboard courts, and three gas barbecue grills. The well-furnished units (all with full kitchens) were renovated in 1997. Free daily maid service, a rarity in condo properties, keeps the units clean. Management encourages socializing: In addition to weekly mai tai parties and coffee socials, the resort hosts annual shuffleboard and golf tournaments, as well as get-togethers on July 4th, Thanksgiving, Christmas, and New Year's. Many guests arrange their travel plans around these events at the Napili Surf.

50 Napili Place (off Lower Honoapiilani Rd., in Napili), Lahaina, HI 96761. ✆ **800/541-0638** or 808/669-8002. Fax 808/669-8004. www.napilisurf.com. 53 units (some with shower only). $135–$195 studio (sleeps up to 3); $210–$285 1-bedroom (sleeps up to 4). Extra person $15. No credit cards. **Amenities:** 2 freshwater swimming pools; washer/dryers. *In room:* TV/VCR, kitchen, fridge, coffeemaker, iron, safe, washer/dryer (in larger units).

**Noelani Condominium Resort** ★★ *Finds* *Kids* This oceanfront condo is a great value, whether you stay in a studio or a three-bedroom unit (ideal for large families). Everything is first-class, from the furnishings to the oceanfront location. Though it's on the water, there's no sandy beach here (despite the photos posted on their website)—but next door is a sandy cove at the new county park, opened in 2001. All units feature complete kitchens, entertainment centers, and spectacular views (the one-, two-, and three-bedroom units also have their own washer/dryers and dishwashers). Our favorites are in the Anthurium Building, where the condos have oceanfront lanais just 20 feet from the water. Frugal travelers will love the deluxe studios in the Orchid Building, with great ocean views and all the amenities for just $107 in the low season and $122 in high season. Guests are invited to mai tai parties at night; there are also oceanfront barbecue grills for guest use.

4095 Lower Honoapiilani Rd. (in Kahana), Lahaina, HI 96761. ✆ **800/367-6030** or 808/669-8374. Fax 808/669-7904. www.noelani-condo-resort.com. 50 units. $107–$135 studio double; $147–$165 1-bedroom (sleeps up to 4); $217 2-bedroom (sleeps 4); $267 3-bedroom (sleeps 6). Rates include continental breakfast on first morning. Extra person $10. Children under 18 stay free in parent's room. Packages for honeymooners, seniors, and AAA members available. 3-night minimum. AE, MC, V. **Amenities:** 2 freshwater swimming pools (1 heated for night swimming); access to nearby health club; oceanfront Jacuzzi; concierge; activity desk; car-rental desk; coin-op washer/dryers. *In room:* TV/VCR, kitchen, fridge, coffeemaker, hair dryer, iron, safe, washer/dryer (in larger units).

## INEXPENSIVE

Frugal travelers should also consider the **Hale Maui Apartment Hotel** (✆ **808/669-6312;** fax 808/669-1302; www.maui.net/~halemaui), a wonderful tiny apartment hotel run by Hans and Eva Zimmerman, whose spirit is 100% aloha. All their one-bedroom suites, which run $85 to $95 double, come with ceiling fans, private lanai, and complete kitchens. There's no pool, but a private path leads to a great swimming beach.

**Napili Bay** ★ *Finds* One of Maui's best secret bargains is this small, two-story complex right on Napili's beautiful half-mile white-sand beach. The beach here is one of the best on the coast, with great swimming and snorkeling—in fact, it's so beautiful that people staying at much more expensive resorts down the road frequently haul all their beach paraphernalia here for the day. The studio apartments are definitely small, but they pack in everything you need to feel at home, from a full kitchen to a comfortable queen bed, and a roomy lanai that's great for watching the sun set over the Pacific. There's no air-conditioning, but louvered windows and ceiling fans help keep the units cool during the day. There are lots of restaurants and a convenience store within walking distance, and you're about 10 to 15 minutes away from Lahaina and some great golf courses. All this for as little as $110 a night—unbelievable! Book early, and tell 'em Frommer's sent you.

33 Hui Dr. (off Lower Honoapiilani Hwy., in Napili). c/o Maui Beachfront Rentals, 256 Papalaua St., Lahaina, HI 96767. ✆ **888/661-7200** or 808/661-3500. Fax 808/661-5210. www.mauibeachfront.com. 33 units. $110–$140 studio for up to 4. 5-night minimum. MC, V. **Amenities:** Coin-op washer/dryers. *In room:* TV, kitchen, fridge, coffeemaker.

**Napili Sunset** *Value* Housed in three buildings (two on the ocean and one across the street) and located just down the street from Napili Bay, these clean, older, but well-maintained units offer good value. At first glance, the plain two-story structures don't look like much, but the location, the bargain prices, and the friendly staff are the real hidden treasures here. In addition to daily maid service, the units all have full kitchens (with dishwashers), ceiling fans, sofa beds, small dining areas, and small bedrooms. The beach is one of Maui's best, and therefore can get a little crowded. The studio units are all located in the building off the beach and a few steps up a slight hill; they're good-size, with a full kitchen and either a sofa bed or a Murphy bed, and they overlook the small pool and garden. The one- and two-bedroom units are all on the beach (the downstairs units have lanais that lead right to the sand). The staff makes sure each unit has the basics—paper towels, dishwasher soap, coffee filters, condiments—to get your stay off to a good start. There are restaurants within walking distance.

46 Hui Rd. (in Napili), Lahaina, HI 96761. ✆ **800/447-9229** or 808/669-8083. Fax 808/669-2730. www.napilisunset.com. 42 units. High season $120 studio double; $225 1-bedroom double; $315 2-bedroom (sleeps up to 4). Low season $105 studio; $205 1-bedroom; $265 2-bedroom. Extra person $12. Children under 3 stay free in parent's room. 3-night minimum. MC, V. **Amenities:** Small outdoor pool; coin-op washer/dryers (free detergent supplied). *In room:* TV, kitchen, fridge, coffeemaker.

## KAPALUA

### VERY EXPENSIVE

**Kapalua Bay Hotel & Ocean Villas** ★★ *Kids* The Kapalua Bay sits seaward of 23,000 acres of green fields lined with spiky Norfolk pine windbreaks. The 1970s-style building, down by the often-windy shore, is full of angles that frame stunning views of the ocean, mountains, and blue sky. The tastefully designed maze of oversize rooms fronts a palm-fringed gold-sand beach that's one of the best in Hawaii, and there's an excellent Ben Crenshaw golf course. Each guest room has a sitting area with sofa, a king or two double beds, and an entertainment center. Private lanais with views of Molokai across the channel. The renovated bathrooms feature two granite vanities, a large soaking tub, and a glass-enclosed shower.

The good news is that unlike some other luxury resorts, the Kapalua Bay has waved the obnoxious and not-very-hospitable "resort fee"; the bad news is that they now charge for parking (self or valet) at the outrageous rate of $15 a day.

1 Bay Dr., Kapalua, HI 96761. ✆ **800/367-8000** or 808/669-5656. Fax 808/669-4694. www.kapaluabayhotel.com. 206 units. $350–$600 double; from $500 1- and 2-bedroom bay villas; from $1200 suites. Extra person $75. Children 17 and under stay free in parent's room using existing bedding. Parking $15. AE, DC, MC, V. **Amenities:** 3 restaurants; 3 bars; 2 outdoor pools; access to the Kapalua Resort's acclaimed trio of golf courses (each with its own pro shop); 10 Plexi-pave tennis courts for day and night play; 24-hr. fitness facilities; small spa; Jacuzzi; watersports equipment rentals; children's program for kids age 5–12, offering activities ranging from snorkeling and surfing to lei-making and cookie-baking; concierge; activity desk; car-rental desk; business center; shopping arcade; salon; 24-hr. room service; in-room and spa massage; babysitting; same-day laundry service and dry cleaning; concierge-level rooms. *In room:* A/C, TV, dataport, minibar, fridge, coffeemaker, hair dryer, iron, safe.

**Ritz-Carlton Kapalua** ★★ *Kids* The Ritz is a complete universe, one of those resorts where you can happily sit by the ocean with a book for 2 whole weeks and never leave the grounds. It rises proudly on a knoll, in a singularly spectacular setting between the rainforest and the sea. During construction, the burial sites of hundreds of ancient Hawaiians were discovered in the sand, so the hotel was moved inland to avoid disrupting the graves. The setback improved the hotel's outlook, which now has a commanding view of Molokai.

The style is fancy plantation, elegant but not imposing. The public spaces are open, airy, and graceful, with plenty of tropical foliage and landscapes by artist Sarah Supplee. Rooms are up to the usual Ritz standard, outfitted with marble bathrooms, private lanais, and in-room fax capability. Hospitality is the keynote here; you'll find the exemplary service you expect from Ritz-Carlton seasoned with good old-fashioned Hawaiian aloha. The **Club Floor** ★★★ offers the best amenities in the state (for a price), from French roast coffee in the morning to a buffet at lunch to cookies in the afternoon to pupu and drinks at sunset. The Ritz Kids program offers a variety of activities and is very reasonable for hotel guests—only $15 for a full day, including lunch. Our only complaint about this fabulous property is the "resort fee" you're charged on top of the already-high room rates.

1 Ritz-Carlton Dr., Kapalua, HI 96761. ✆ **800/262-8440** or 808/669-6200. Fax 808/665-0026. www.ritzcarlton.com. 548 units. $375–$535 double; from $635 suite. Extra person $50 ($125 in Club Floor rooms). "Resort fee" of $15 for "complimentary" use of fitness center and children's program. Wedding/honeymoon, golf, and other packages available. AE, DC, DISC, MC, V. Valet parking $10, free self-parking. **Amenities:** 4 restaurants; 4 bars (including 1 serving drinks and light fare on the sand); outdoor pool; access to the Kapalua Resort's 3 championship golf courses (each with its own pro shop) and its deluxe tennis complex; fitness room; spa; Jacuzzi; watersports equipment rentals; bike rental; children's program; game room; concierge; activity desk; car-rental desk; business center; shopping arcade; salon; room service; in-room and spa massage; babysitting; same-day laundry and dry cleaning; concierge-level rooms (some of Hawaii's best, with top-drawer service and amenities). *In room:* A/C, TV, dataport, minibar, coffeemaker, hair dryer, iron, safe.

## EXPENSIVE

If you're interested in a luxurious condo or town house, consider **Kapalua Villas** (✆ **800/545-0018** or 808/669-8088; www.kapalua villas.com). The palatial units dotting the oceanfront cliffs and fairways of this idyllic coast are a (relative) bargain, especially if you're traveling with a group. The one- bedroom condos go for $199 to $279; two-bedrooms for $299 to $469; plus numerous package deals (which include golf, tennis, honeymoon amenities, and car) save you even more money.

## 3 South Maui

### MAALAEA

We recommend two booking agencies that rent a host of properties in the Kihei/Wailea/Maalaea area: **Kihei Maui Vacation** (**© 800/541-6284** or 808/879-7581; www.kmvmaui.com) and **Condominium Rentals Hawaii** (**© 800/367-5242** or 808/879-2778; www.crhmaui.com).

### KIHEI

#### EXPENSIVE

**Maalaea Surf Resort** ★ Come here for a quiet, relaxing vacation on a well-landscaped property, with a beautiful white-sand beach right outside. Located at the quiet end of Kihei Road, this two-story complex sprawls across 5 acres of lush tropical gardens. The luxury town houses all have ocean views, big kitchens (with dishwashers), cable TV, and VCRs. Amenities include maid service (Mon–Sat), shuffleboard, barbecue grills, discounts on tee times at nearby golf courses, and restaurants and shops within a 5-minute drive.

12 S. Kihei Rd. (at S. Kihei Rd. and Hwy. 350), Kihei, HI 96753. **© 800/423-7953** or 808/879-1267. Fax 808/874-2884. www.maalaeasurfresort.com. 34 units in rental pool. $205–$230 1-bedroom unit; $277–$307 2-bedroom (sleeps up to 6). Extra person $15. MC, V. **Amenities:** 2 outdoor pools; 2 tennis courts; concierge; activity desk; car-rental desk; coin-op washer/dryers. *In room:* A/C, TV/VCR, kitchen, fridge, coffeemaker, hair dryer, iron, safe.

**Maui Hill** ★ If you can't decide between the privacy of a condo and the conveniences of a hotel, try this place. Managed by the respected Aston chain, Maui Hill gives you the best of both worlds. Located on a hill above the heat of Kihei town, this large, Spanish-style resort combines all the amenities and activities of a hotel (pool, hot tub, tennis courts, Hawaiiana classes, maid service, and more) with large luxury condos that have full kitchens and plenty of privacy. Nearly all units have ocean views, dishwashers, washer/dryers, queen sofa beds, and big lanais. Beaches, restaurants, and shops are within easy walking distance, and a golf course is nearby. The management here goes out of its way to make sure your stay is perfect.

2881 S. Kihei Rd. (across from Kamaole Park III, between Keonekai St. and Kilohana Dr.), Kihei, HI 96753. **© 800/92-ASTON** Aston Hotels and Resorts or 808/879-6321. Fax 808/879-8945. www.aston-hotels.com. 140 units. High season $280 1-bedroom apt; $365 2-bedroom; $495 3-bedroom. Low season $215 1-bedroom; $280 2-bedroom; $385 3-bedroom. AE, DC, DISC, MC, V. **Amenities:** Outdoor pool; putting green; tennis courts; Jacuzzi; concierge; activity desk; car-rental desk; coin-op washer/dryers; laundry service; dry cleaning. *In room:* A/C, TV, kitchen, fridge, coffeemaker, hair dryer, iron, safe, washer/dryer (in most units).

## MODERATE

**Kamaole Nalu Resort** This six-story condominium complex is located between two beach parks: Kamaole I and Kamaole II, and right across the street from a shopping complex. Units have fabulous ocean views, large living rooms, and private lanais; the kitchens are a bit small but come fully equipped. We recommend no. 306 for its wonderful bird's-eye view. The property also has an ocean-side pool and great barbecue facilities. Restaurants, bars, a golf course, and tennis courts are nearby; shopping is across the street. ***A warning:*** Because the building is right on Kihei Road, it can be noisy.

2450 S. Kihei Rd. (between Kanani and Keonekai rds., next to Kamaole Beach Park II), Kihei, HI 96753. ✆ **800/767-1497** or 808/879-1006. Fax 808/879-8693. www.kamaolenalu.com. 36 units. High season $155–$215 double. Low season $135–$195 double. Extra person $15. 5-night minimum. MC, V. **Amenities:** Outdoor pool; activity desk; car-rental desk. *In room:* TV, kitchen, fridge, coffeemaker, hair dryer, iron, safe, washer/dryer.

**Koa Resort** ★ *Value* *Kids* Located just across the street from the ocean, Koa Resort consists of five two-story wooden buildings on more than 5½ acres of landscaped grounds. The spacious one-, two-, and three-bedroom units are decorated with care, large enough for families, and come fully equipped, right down to the dishwasher and disposal in the kitchens. The larger condos have both showers and tubs; the smaller units have showers only. All feature large lanais, ceiling fans, and washer/dryers. For maximum peace and quiet, ask for a unit far from Kihei Road. Bars, restaurants, and a golf course are nearby; these, along with the beach, putting green, pool, and tennis courts, should be enough to keep the whole family busy.

811 S. Kihei Rd. (between Kulanihakoi St. and Namauu Place), c/o Bello Realty, P.O. Box 1776, Kihei, HI 96753. ✆ **800/541-3060** or 808/879-3328. Fax 808/875-1483. www.bellomaui.com. 54 units (some with shower only). High season $110 1-bedroom; $120-$130 2-bedroom; $155-$180 3-bedroom. Low season $85 1-bedroom; $100-$110 2-bedroom; $135-$160 3-bedroom. No credit cards. **Amenities:** Outdoor pool; 18-hole putting green; 2 tennis courts; Jacuzzi. *In room:* TV, kitchen, fridge, coffeemaker, hair dryer, iron, safe, washer/dryer.

**Maui Coast Hotel** ★★ This place stands out as one of the only moderately priced hotels in Kihei (which is largely full of affordable condo complexes). Ask about packages: For slightly more than the regular price of a room, the Maui Coast's Room and Car package gives you a rental car. The other chief advantage of this hotel is its

# South Maui Accommodations & Dining

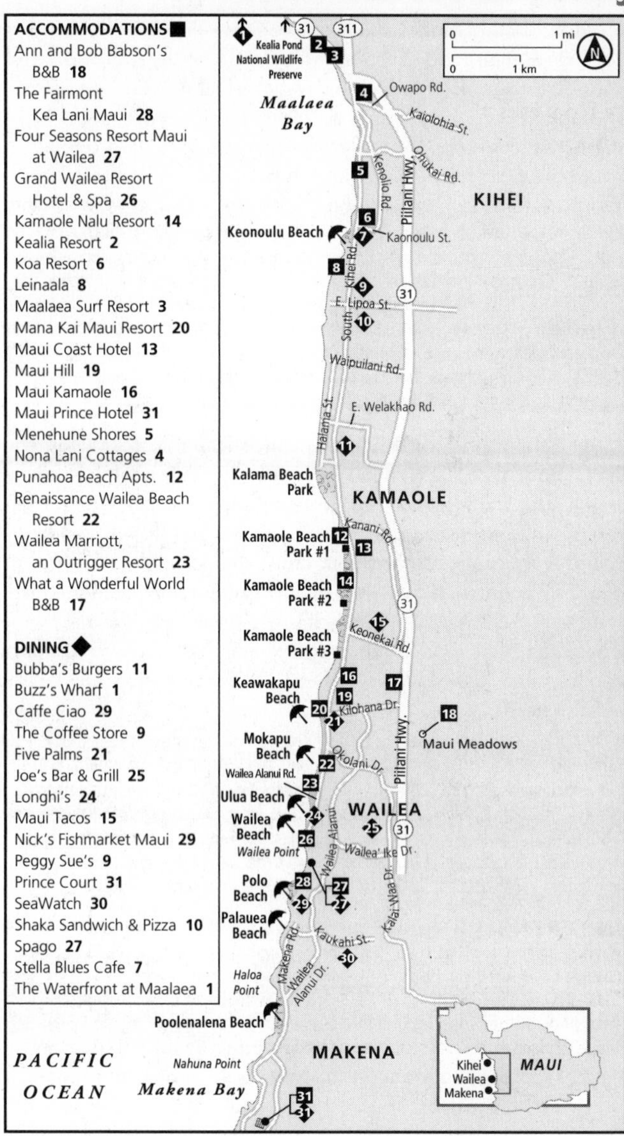

ACCOMMODATIONS
Ann and Bob Babson's B&B 18
The Fairmont Kea Lani Maui 28
Four Seasons Resort Maui at Wailea 27
Grand Wailea Resort Hotel & Spa 26
Kamaole Nalu Resort 14
Kealia Resort 2
Koa Resort 6
Leinaala 8
Maalaea Surf Resort 3
Mana Kai Maui Resort 20
Maui Coast Hotel 13
Maui Hill 19
Maui Kamaole 16
Maui Prince Hotel 31
Menehune Shores 5
Nona Lani Cottages 4
Punahoa Beach Apts. 12
Renaissance Wailea Beach Resort 22
Wailea Marriott, an Outrigger Resort 23
What a Wonderful World B&B 17
DINING
Bubba's Burgers 11
Buzz's Wharf 1
Caffe Ciao 29
The Coffee Store 9
Five Palms 21
Joe's Bar & Grill 25
Longhi's 24
Maui Tacos 15
Nick's Fishmarket Maui 29
Peggy Sue's 9
Prince Court 31
SeaWatch 30
Shaka Sandwich & Pizza 10
Spago 27
Stella Blues Cafe 7
The Waterfront at Maalaea 1
0 1 mi
0 1 km
N
Kealia Pond National Wildlife Preserve
Maalaea Bay
Owapo Rd.
Kaiolohia St.
Ohukai Rd.
Kenolio Rd.
Piilani Hwy.
KIHEI
Keonoulu Beach
Kaonoulu St.
South Kihei Rd.
E. Lipoa St.
Waipuilani Rd.
E. Welakhao Rd.
Halama St.
Kalama Beach Park
KAMAOLE
Kanani Rd.
Kamaole Beach Park #1
Kamaole Beach Park #2
Kamaole Beach Park #3
Keonekai Rd.
Keawakapu Beach
Kilohana Dr.
Maui Meadows
Mokapu Beach
Okolani Dr.
Wailea Alanui Rd.
Ulua Beach
WAILEA
Wailea Beach
Wailea Point
Wailea Alanui
Wailea' Ike Dr.
Kalai Waa Dr.
Polo Beach
Palauea Beach
Kaukahi St.
Makena Rd.
Wailea Alanui Dr.
Haloa Point
Poolenalena Beach
MAKENA
PACIFIC OCEAN
Nahuna Point
Makena Bay
Kihei
Wailea
Makena
MAUI

location, about a block from Kamaole Beach Park I, with plenty of bars, restaurants, and shopping within walking distance and a golf course nearby. A $2.5 million renovation of all the furniture, linens, and upholstery in the rooms has this moderately priced hotel looking better than ever. The rooms offer extras such as sitting areas, whirlpool tubs, ceiling fans, and private lanais.

2259 S. Kihei Rd. (1 block from Kamaole Beach Park I), Kihei, HI 96753. ✆ **800/895-MAUI** or 808/874-6284. Fax 808/875-4731. www.mauicoasthotel.com. 265 units. $155–$165 double; $175–$195 alcove suite; $230 1-bedroom suite (sleeps up to 4). Children 17 and under stay free in parent's room using existing bedding. Rollaway bed $20. Packages including rental car available. AE, DC, DISC, MC, V. **Amenities:** Restaurant; pool bar with nightly entertainment; outdoor pool (plus children's wading pool); 2 night-lit tennis courts; fitness room; concierge; activity desk; limited room service; free use of self-serve washer/dryers; laundry service; dry cleaning. *In room:* A/C, TV, fridge, coffeemaker, hair dryer, iron, safe.

**Maui Kamaole** You'll find this condo complex right across the street from the Kihei Public Boat Ramp and beautiful Kamaole Beach Park III, which is great for swimming and snorkeling. Each roomy, fully furnished unit comes with a private lanai, two bathrooms (even in the one-bedroom units), and an all-electric kitchen. The one-bedroom units—which can comfortably accommodate four—are quite a deal, especially if you're traveling in the off season. The grounds are nicely landscaped and offer barbecues. Restaurants and bars are within walking distance; a golf course and tennis courts are also nearby.

2777 S. Kihei Rd. (between Keonekai and Kilohana rds., at the Wailea end of Kihei), Kihei, HI 96753. ✆ **800/822-4409** or 808/874-8467. Fax 808/875-9117. www.mauikamaole.com. 210 units. High season $170–$195 1-bedroom double (sleeps up to 4); $220–$250 2-bedroom (rates for 4, sleeps up to 6). Low season $135–$150 1-bedroom; $175–$200 2-bedroom. 4-night minimum. AE, MC, V. **Amenities:** 2 outdoor pools; Jacuzzi; concierge; laundry service; dry cleaning. *In room:* A/C, TV, kitchen, fridge, coffeemaker, iron, safe, washer/dryer.

## INEXPENSIVE

### Ann and Bob Babson's Bed & Breakfast and Sunset Cottage

★ *Value* We highly recommend staying on this spacious landscaped lot, which boasts 180-degree views of the islands of Lanai, Kahoolawe, and Molokini; sunsets are not to be missed. Accommodations include two rooms in the main house (one with panoramic ocean views, skylights, and a whirlpool tub), a one-bedroom suite downstairs, and a two-bedroom cottage with a kitchen. The Babsons have three adorable cats—if you're allergic, you might want to book elsewhere.

3371 Keha Dr. (in Maui Meadows), Kihei, HI 96753. ✆ **800/824-6409** or 808/874-1166. Fax 808/879-7906. www.mauibnb.com. 4 units. $100–$130 double (including breakfast Mon–Sat); $135 cottage double (sleeps up to 4). Extra person $15. 5-night minimum in house, 7-night minimum for cottage. MC, V. *In room:* TV, kitchen (in cottage only), fridge, coffeemaker.

**Kealia Resort** *Value* This oceanfront property at the northern end of Kihei is well maintained and nicely furnished—and the price is excellent. But skip the studio units: They face noisy Kihei Road, so you'll be listening to big trucks downshifting all night. Instead, go for one of the oceanview units, which all have full kitchens and private lanais. The grounds face a 5-mile stretch of white-sand beach. The management goes out of its way to provide opportunities for guests to meet; social gatherings include free coffee-and-doughnut get-togethers every Friday morning and pupu parties on Wednesdays.

191 N. Kihei Rd. (north of Hwy. 31, at the Maalaea end of Kihei), Kihei, HI 96753. ✆ **800/265-0686** or 808/879-0952. Fax 808/875-1540. www.apmimaui.com. 51 units. $75–$99 studio double; $100–$150 1-bedroom double; $165–$195 2-bedroom (sleeps up to 4). Children 12 and under stay free in parent's room. Extra person $10. 4-night minimum. MC, V. **Amenities:** Recently retiled outdoor pool. *In room:* TV, kitchen, fridge, coffeemaker, hair dryer, iron, washer/dryer.

**Leinaala** ★ *Value* From Kihei Road, you can't see Leinaala amid the jumble of buildings, but this oceanfront boutique condo offers excellent accommodations at 1980s prices. The building is set back from the water, with a county park—an oasis of green grass and tennis courts—in between. A golf course lies nearby. The units are compact, but filled with everything you need: a full kitchen, sofa bed, and oceanview lanai. (Hideaway beds are available if you need one.)

998 S. Kihei Rd., Kihei, HI 96753. ✆ **800/822-4409** or 808/879-2235. Fax 808/879-8366. www.mauicondo.com. 24 units. $135 1-bedroom double; $180 2-bedroom (sleeps up to 4). 4-night minimum. Extra person $10. No credit cards. **Amenities:** Outdoor pool; coin-op washer/dryers. *In room:* A/C, TV, kitchen, fridge, coffeemaker.

**Mana Kai Maui Resort** ★ *Kids* This eight-story complex, situated on a beautiful white-sand cove, is an unusual combination of hotel and condominium. The hotel rooms, which account for half of the total number of units, are small but nicely furnished. The condo units feature full kitchens and open living rooms with sliding-glass doors that lead to small lanais overlooking the sandy beach and ocean. Some units are beginning to show their age (the building is more than 30 years old), but they're all clean and comfortable.

One of the best snorkeling beaches on the coast is just steps away; a golf course and tennis courts are nearby.

2960 S. Kihei Rd. (between Kilohana and Keonekai rds., at the Wailea end of Kihei), Kihei, HI 96753. ✆ **800/367-5242** or 808/879-2778. Fax 808/879-7825. www.crhmaui.com. 105 units. $95–$135 hotel room double; $175–$245 1-bedroom (sleeps up to 4); $234–$300 2-bedroom (up to 6). AE, DC, DISC, MC, V. **Amenities:** Restaurant; bar; outdoor pool; concierge; coin-op washer/dryers. *In room:* A/C (in hotel rooms only), TV, kitchen (in condo units), fridge, coffeemaker, safe.

**Menehune Shores** *Value* If you plan to stay on Maui for a week, you might want to look into the car/condo packages here; they're a real deal. The six-story Menehune Shores is more than 30 years old and is showing its age in some places, but all units are well maintained and have ocean views. The design is straight out of the 1970s, but the view from the private lanai is timeless. The kitchens are fully equipped, all units have washer/dryers, and the ocean breeze keeps the rooms cool (there's no air-conditioning). The building sits in front of the ancient Hawaiian fish ponds of Kalepolepo; some Hawaiians still fish them using traditional throw nets, but generally the pond serves as protection from the ocean waves, making it safe for children (and those unsure of their ability) to swim in the relatively calm waters. There's also a heated pool, shuffleboard courts, and a whale-watching platform on the roof garden.

760 S. Kihei Rd. (between Kaonoulu and Hoonani sts.), P.O. Box 1327, Kihei, HI 96753. ✆ **800/558-9117** or 808/879-3428. Fax 808/879-5218. www.menehunereservations.com. 70 units. $105–$130 1-bedroom double ($839/week with car); $120–$155 2-bedroom double ($989/week with car); $135–$180 2-bedroom for 4 ($1,129/week with car); $170–$220 3-bedroom for up to 6 ($1,539/week with car). 3-night minimum. Extra person $7.50. No credit cards. **Amenities:** Restaurant (Hawaiian/Pacific Rim) and bar; outdoor pool; Jacuzzi; room service (8am–9pm). *In room:* TV/VCR, kitchen, fridge, coffeemaker, washer/dryers.

**Nona Lani Cottages** ★ *Finds* Picture this: a grassy expanse dotted with eight cottages tucked among palm, fruit, and sweet-smelling flower trees, right across the street from a white-sand beach. This is one of the great hidden deals in Kihei. The cottages are tiny, but contain everything you'll need: a small but complete kitchen, twin beds that double as couches in the living room, a separate bedroom with a queen bed, and a lanai with table and chairs. The cottages were renovated in 2002 with new ceramic flooring. There are no phones in the cabins, but there's a public one by the registration/check-in area.

If the cabins are booked, or if you want a bit more luxury, you might opt for one of the private guest rooms, with private entrance and private bathroom. These beautiful units feature plush carpet, koa bed frames, lanais, and private entrances.

455 S. Kihei Rd. (just south of Hwy. 31), P.O. Box 655, Kihei, HI 96753. ✆ **800/733-2688** or 808/879-2497. www.nonalanicottages.com. 11 units. $75–$85 double; $90–$99 cottage. Extra person $12–$15. 3-night minimum for rooms, 4-night minimum for cottages. No credit cards. **Amenities:** Coin-op washer/dryers. *In room:* TV, kitchen (in cottages), fridge, coffeemaker, no phone.

**Punahoa Beach Apartments** ★ *Value* Book this place! We can't put it any more simply than that. The location—off noisy, traffic-ridden Kihei Road, on a quiet side street with ocean frontage—is fabulous. A grassy lawn rolls about 50 feet down to the beach, where there's great snorkeling just offshore and a popular surfing spot next door; shopping and restaurants are all within walking distance. All of the beautifully decorated units in this small, four-story building have fully equipped kitchens and lanais with great ocean views. Rooms go quickly in winter, so reserve early.

2142 Iliili Rd. (off S. Kihei Rd., 100 yards from Kamaole Beach I), Kihei, HI 96753. ✆ **800/564-4380** or 808/879-2720. Fax 808/875-9147. www.punahoabeach.com. 13 units. High season $130 studio double; $185–$198 1-bedroom double; $220 2-bedroom double. Low season $94 studio; $130–$145 1-bedroom; $160 2-bedroom. Extra person $15. 5-night minimum. AE, MC, V. **Amenities:** Coin-op washer/dryer. *In room:* TV, kitchen, fridge, coffeemaker, iron.

**What a Wonderful World B&B** ★ *Value* This impeccably done B&B has a great location, excellent rates, and thought and care put into every room. Hostess Eva Tantillo has a full-service travel agency and a master's degree—along with several years of experience—in hotel management. This is one of Maui's finest bed-and-breakfasts, centrally located in Kihei (½ mile to Kamaole II Beach Park, 5 min. from Wailea golf courses, and convenient to shopping and restaurants). Choose from one of four units: the master suite (with small fridge, coffeemaker, and barbecue grill on the lanai), studio apartment (with fully equipped kitchen), or two one-bedroom apartments (also with full kitchens). All come with private bathroom, phone, and entrance. You're also welcome to use the communal barbecue. Eva serves a family-style full breakfast on her lanai, which boasts views of white-sand beaches and the West Maui Mountains.

2828 Umalu Place (off Keonakai St., near Hwy. 31), Kihei, HI 96753. ✆ **800/943-5804** or 808/879-9103. Fax 808/874-9352. www.amauibedandbreakfast.com. 4 units. $75 double; $89 studio double; $99 1-bedroom apt. (5% discount for cash). Rates include full breakfast. Children 11 and under stay free in parent's room. AE, MC, V. **Amenities:** Hot tub; laundry facilities. *In room:* AC, TV, kitchenette, fridge, coffeemaker, hair dryer, iron.

## WAILEA

For a complete selection of condo units throughout Wailea and Makena, contact **Destination Resorts Hawaii** (✆ **800/367-5246** or 808/879-1595; fax 808/874-3554; www.destinationresortshi.com). Its luxury units include studio doubles starting at $180; one-bedroom doubles from $170; two-bedrooms from $205; and three-bedrooms from $585. Children under 16 stay free; minimum stays vary by property.

### VERY EXPENSIVE

**The Fairmont Kea Lani Maui** ★★★ At first glance, this blinding white complex of arches and turrets may look a bit out of place in tropical Hawaii (it's actually a close architectural cousin of Las Hadas, the Arabian Nights fantasy resort in Manzanillo, Mexico). But once you enter the flower-filled lobby and see the big blue Pacific outside, there's no doubt you're in Hawaii.

The prices are high, but you get what you pay for here, plus a few extras. Each unit in this all-suite luxury hotel has a kitchenette (with microwave and coffeemaker), a living room with entertainment center and sofa bed (great if you have the kids in tow), a marble wet bar, an oversize marble bathroom with separate shower big enough for a party, a spacious bedroom, and a large lanai that overlooks the pools, lawns, and white-sand beach.

The villas are definitely out of a fantasy. The rich and famous stay in these 2,000-square-foot, two- and three-bedroom beach bungalows, each with its own plunge pool and gourmet kitchen.

4100 Wailea Alanui Dr., Wailea, HI 96753. ✆ **800/659-4100** or 808/875-4100. Fax 808/875-1200. www.kealani.com. 450 units. $339–$729 suite (sleeps up to 4); from $1,400 villa. AE, DC, DISC, MC, V. **Amenities:** 4 restaurants (see reviews for Nick's Fishmarket Maui on p. 98 and Caffe Ciao on p. 98); 3 bars (with sunset cocktails and nightly entertainment at the Lobby Lounge); 2 large swimming "lagoons" connected by a 140-ft. water slide and swim-up bar, plus an adult lap pool; use of Wailea Golf Club's 3 18-hole championship golf courses, as well as the nearby Makena and Elleair golf courses; use of Wailea Tennis Center's 11 courts (3 lit for night play and a pro shop); fine 24-hr. fitness center; excellent full-service spa offering the latest in body treatments, facials, and massage; Jacuzzi; watersports equipment rentals; bike rental; children's program; game room; concierge; activity desk; car-rental desk; business center; shopping arcade; salon; 24-hr. room service; in-room and spa massage; babysitting; same-day laundry service and dry cleaning. *In room:* A/C, TV, dataport, kitchenette, minibar, fridge, coffeemaker, hair dryer, iron, safe.

**Four Seasons Resort Maui at Wailea** ★★★ Kids If money's no object, this is the place to spend it. It's hard to beat this modern version of a Hawaiian palace by the sea, with a relaxing, casual atmosphere. Although it sits on a glorious beach between two other hotels, you won't feel like you're on resort row: The Four Seasons inhabits its own separate world, thanks to an open courtyard of pools and gardens. Amenities are first-rate here, including outstanding restaurants, an excellent spa, and a complete activities program for kids (complimentary, of course).

The spacious (about 600 sq. ft.) rooms feature furnished lanais (nearly all with ocean views) that are great for watching whales in winter and sunsets year-round. The grand bathrooms contain deep marble tubs, showers for two, and lighted French makeup mirrors.

Service is attentive but not cloying. At the pool, guests lounge in casbah-like tents, pampered with special touches like iced Evian and chilled towels. And you'll never see a housekeeping cart in the hall: The cleaning staff works in teams, so they're as unobtrusive as possible and in and out of your room in minutes.

Wolfgang Puck recently opened his Spago Restaurant (p. 96) at the resort featuring a fusion of Hawaiian and California cuisine in a dreamy open-air setting. Ferraro's at Seaside Restaurant offers a casual atmosphere overlooking the Pacific by day; by night, it's transformed into a romantic atmosphere featuring authentic Italian cucina rustica with great sunset views and dining under the stars. The poolside Pacific Grill offers lavish breakfast buffets and dinners featuring Pacific Rim cuisine.

The ritzy neighborhood surrounding the hotel is home to great restaurants and shopping, the Wailea Tennis Center (known as Wimbledon West), and six golf courses—not to mention that great beach, with gentle waves and islands framing the view on either side.

3900 Wailea Alanui Dr., Wailea, HI 96753. ✆ **800/334-MAUI** or 808/874-8000. Fax 808/874-2222. www.fourseasons.com/maui. 380 units. $335–$590 double; from $630 suite. Packages available. Extra person $90 ($160 in Club Floor rooms). Children under 18 stay free in parent's room. AE, DC, MC, V. **Amenities:** 3 restaurants; 3 bars (with nightly entertainment); 3 fabulous outdoor pools; putting green; use of Wailea Golf Club's 3 18-hole championship golf courses, as well as the nearby Makena and Elleair golf courses; 2 on-site tennis courts (lit for night play); use of Wailea Tennis Center's 11 courts (3 lit for night play and a pro shop); health club featuring outdoor cardiovascular equipment (with individual TV/VCR); excellent spa (offering a variety of treatments in the spa, in-room, and ocean side); 2 whirlpools (1 for adults only); beach pavilion with watersports gear rental and 1 hr. free use of snorkel equipment; complimentary use of bicycles; fabulous year-round kids' program, plus a teen recreation center and a children's video library and toys; game room (with shuffleboard, pool tables, jukebox, big-screen TV, and video games); one of Maui's best concierge desks; activity desk; car-rental desk; business center; shopping arcade; salon; 24-hr. room service; in-room, spa, or ocean-side massage; babysitting; same-day laundry service and dry cleaning; concierge-level rooms. *In room:* A/C, TV, dataport, minibar, fridge, coffeemaker, hair dryer, iron, safe.

**Grand Wailea Resort Hotel & Spa** ★★ Here's where grand becomes grandiose. The pinnacle of Hawaii's brief fling with fantasy megaresorts, this monument to excess is extremely popular with families, incentive groups, and conventions; it's the grand prize in Hawaii vacation contests and the dream of many honeymooners. It has a Japanese restaurant decorated with real rocks hewn from the slopes of Mount Fuji; 10,000 tropical plants in the lobby; an intricate pool system with slides, waterfalls, rapids, and a water-powered elevator to take you up to the top; Hawaii's largest and most elaborate spa; a restaurant in a man-made tide pool; a floating New England–style wedding chapel; and nothing but oceanview rooms, outfitted with every amenity you could ask for. And it's all crowned with a $30 million collection of original art, much of it created expressly for the hotel by Hawaii artists and sculptors. Though minimalists may be put off, there's no denying that the Grand Wailea is plush, professional, and pampering, with all the diversions you could imagine. Oh, and did we mention the fantastic beach out front?

3850 Wailea Alanui Dr., Wailea, HI 96753. ✆ **800/888-6100** or 808/875-1234. Fax 808/874-2442. www.grandwailea.com. 780 units. $450–$760 double; from $1575 suite. Concierge tower from $800. Resort fee $15 for "complimentary" lei greeting on arrival; welcome drink; local calls; coffee in room; use of spa; admission to scuba diving clinics and water aerobics; art and garden tours; nightly turndown service; self parking; and shuttle service to Wailea area. Extra person $25 ($75 in concierge tower). AE, DC, DISC, MC, V. **Amenities:** 6 restaurants; 12 bars (including a nightclub with laser-light shows and a hydraulic dance floor); 2,000-foot-long Action Pool, featuring a 10-min. swim/ride through mountains and grottoes; use of Wailea Golf Club's 3 18-hole championship golf courses, as well as the nearby Makena and Elleair golf courses; use of Wailea Tennis Center's 11 courts (3 lit for night play and a pro shop); complete fitness center; Hawaii's largest spa, the 50,000-sq.-ft. Spa Grande, with a blend of European-, Japanese-, and American-style techniques; Jacuzzi; watersports equipment rentals; complimentary dive and windsurf lessons; bike rental; children's program (including a computer center, video game room, arts and crafts, children's theater, outdoor playground, and infant-care center); game room; concierge; activity desk; car-rental desk; business center; shopping arcade; salon; 24-hr. room service; in-room and spa massage; babysitting; same-day laundry service and dry cleaning; concierge-level rooms. *In room:* A/C, TV, dataport, kitchenette, minibar, fridge ($25 per stay fee), coffeemaker, hair dryer, iron, safe.

**Renaissance Wailea Beach Resort** ★★ This is the place for visitors in search of Wailea-style luxury, but in a smaller, more intimate setting. Located on 15 acres of rolling lawn and tropical gardens, the Renaissance Wailea has the air of a small boutique hotel. Perhaps it's the resort's U-shaped design, the series of small coves and beaches, or the spaciousness of the rooms—whatever the reason, you just don't feel crowded here.

Each room has a sitting area, a large lanai, and three phones. The bathrooms include such extras as double vanities (one with lighted makeup mirror) and *hapi* coats (Japanese-style cotton robes). All bedspreads, drapes, and towels have been recently upgraded. Rooms in the Mokapu Beach Club, an exclusive two-story building just steps from a crescent-shaped beach, feature such extras as private check-in, in-room continental breakfast, and access to a private pool and beach cabanas.

3550 Wailea Alanui Dr., Wailea, HI 96753. ✆ **800/9-WAILEA** or 808/879-4900. Fax 808/874-5370. www.renaissancehotels.com. 345 units. $360–$600 double; from $1,050 suite. Extra person $40. Children 18 and under stay free in parent's room using existing bedding. Package rates available. AE, DC, DISC, MC, V. Parking $4. **Amenities:** 3 restaurants (the casual, open-air Palm Court offers buffets and oven-baked pizzas; Hana Gion features a sushi bar and teppanyaki grill; and Maui Onion is a poolside breakfast and lunch spot surrounded by lush gardens and a cascading waterfall); 2 bars; 2 freshwater outdoor pools; use of Wailea Golf Club's 3 18-hole championship golf courses, as well as the nearby Makena and Elleair golf courses; use of Wailea Tennis Center's 11 courts (3 lit for night play and a pro shop); fitness center; small spa; 2 Jacuzzis; watersports equipment rentals; children's program; game room; concierge; activity desk; car-rental desk; business center; shopping arcade; salon; room service (6am–11pm); massage; babysitting; laundry service; dry cleaning; concierge-level rooms. *In room:* A/C, TV/VCR, dataport, fridge, coffeemaker, hair dryer, iron, safe.

## EXPENSIVE

**Wailea Marriott, an Outrigger Resort** ★★ Yes, it seems ridiculous to have two brand names tacked on to a Hawaiian resort, but it seems that the Outrigger people entered into a "franchise agreement" with Marriott in 2002 to increase sales (through Marriott), yet still retain the same management (Outrigger). The bottom line: This classic open-air, 1970s-style hotel in a tropical garden by the sea gives you a sense of what Maui was like before the big resort boom. It's airy and comfortable, with touches of Hawaiian art throughout.

What's truly special about this hotel is how it fits into its environment without overwhelming it. Eight buildings, all low-rise except for an eight-story tower, are spread along 22 gracious acres of lawns and gardens spiked by coco palms, with lots of open space and a half mile of oceanfront on a point between Wailea and Ulua beaches. The vast, parklike expanses are a luxury on this now-crowded coast.

In 2000, the resort went through a $25 million renovation that expanded the entrance into an open-air courtyard with a waterfall and carp pond, transformed the south pool into a water-activities area complete with two water slides, added a fabulous spa, and refurbished and upgraded the guest rooms.

3700 Wailea Alanui Dr., Wailea, HI 96753. ✆ **800/367-2960** or 808/879-1922. Fax 808/874-8331. www.outriggerwailea.com. 524 units. $325–$525 double. Suites from $650. Extra person $40. Packages available. AE, DC, DISC, MC, V. **Amenities:** 2 restaurants; 2 bars; 3 outdoor pools; use of Wailea Golf Club's 3 18-hole championship golf courses, as well as the nearby Makena and Elleair golf courses; use of Wailea Tennis Center's 11 courts (3 lit for night play and a pro shop); fitness room; Mandora Spa; Jacuzzi; watersports equipment rentals; children's program (plus kids-only pool and recreation center); game room; concierge; activity desk; business center; shopping arcade; salon; room service (6am–11pm); in-room and spa massage; babysitting; coin-op washer/dryers; same-day laundry service and dry cleaning; concierge-level rooms. *In room:* A/C, TV, dataport, fridge, coffeemaker, hair dryer, iron, safe.

## MAKENA

### EXPENSIVE

**Maui Prince Hotel** ★★ If you're looking for a vacation in a beautiful, tranquil spot with a golden-sand beach, here's your place. But if you plan to tour Maui, you might prefer another hotel. The Maui Prince is at the end of the road, far, far away from anything else on the island, so sightseeing in other areas would require a lot of driving.

When you first see the stark-white hotel, it looks like a high-rise motel stuck in the woods—but only from the outside. Inside, you'll discover an atrium garden with a koi-filled waterfall stream, an ocean view from every room, and a simplicity to the furnishings that makes some people feel uncomfortable and others blissfully clutter-free. Rooms are small but come with private lanais with great views.

5400 Makena Alanui, Makena, HI 96753. ✆ **800/PRINCE-4** or 808/874-1111. Fax 808/879-8763. www.mauiprincehotel.com. 310 units. $310–$480 double; from $600 suite. Extra person $40. Packages available. AE, DC, MC, V. **Amenities:** 4 restaurants (including the excellent Prince Court, p. 99); 2 bars with local Hawaiian music nightly; 2 outdoor pools (adults' and children's); 36 holes of golf (designed by Robert Trent Jones Jr.); 6 Plexi-pave tennis courts (2 lit for night play); fitness room; Jacuzzi; watersports equipment rental; children's program; concierge; activity desk; business center; shopping arcade; salon; room service; in-room massage; babysitting; same-day laundry service and dry cleaning. *In room:* A/C, TV, dataport, fridge, hair dryer, iron, safe.

# 4 Upcountry Maui

## MAKAWAO, OLINDA & HALIIMAILE

Makawao and Olinda are approximately 90 minutes from the entrance to Haleakala National Park (you still have 3,000 ft. and another 30–45 min. to get to the top). Haliimaile, which is about

10 to 15 minutes driving time from Makawao, adds additional time to your drive up to the summit. Accommodations in Kula are the only other options that will get you closer to the summit so you can make the sunrise.

## MODERATE

**Olinda Country Cottages & Inn** ★★ *Finds* This charming B&B is set on the slopes of Haleakala in the crisp, clean air of Olinda, on an 8½-acre protea farm, surrounded by 35,000 acres of ranch lands (with miles of great hiking trails). The 5,000-square-foot country home, outfitted with a professional eye to detail, has incredible panoramic views of all of Maui. Upstairs are two guest rooms with antique beds, private full bathrooms, and separate entryways. Connected to the main house but with its own private entrance, the Pineapple Sweet has a full kitchen, an antique-filled living room, a marble-tiled full bathroom, and a comfy bedroom area. A separate 1,000-square-foot cottage is the epitome of cozy country luxury, with a fireplace, bedroom with queen-size bed, cushioned window seats (with great sunset views), and cathedral ceilings. The 950-square-foot Hidden Cottage (located in a truly secluded spot surrounded by protea flowers) features three decks, French glass doors, a full kitchen, a washer/dryer, and a private tub for two on the deck. Restaurants are a 15-minute drive away in Makawao, and beaches are another 15 minutes beyond that.

2660 Olinda Rd. (near the top of Olinda Rd., a 15-min. drive from Makawao), Makawao, HI 96768. ✆ **800/932-3435** or 808/572-1453. Fax 808/573-5326. www.mauibnbcottages.com. 5 units. $140 double (includes continental breakfast); $140 suite double (includes 1st morning's breakfast in fridge); $195–$245 cottage for 2 (sleeps up to 5; includes 1st morning's breakfast in fridge). Extra person $25. 2-night minimum for rooms and suite, 3-night minimum for cottages. No credit cards. *In room:* TV, kitchen (in cottages), fridge, coffeemaker.

## INEXPENSIVE

**Banyan Tree House** ★ *Finds* Huge monkeypod trees extend their branches over this property like a giant green canopy. The restored 1920s plantation manager's house is decorated with Hawaiian furniture from the 1930s. It can accommodate a group; it has three spacious bedrooms with big, comfortable beds and three private, marble-tiled bathrooms. A fireplace stands at one end of the huge living room, a large lanai runs the entire length of the house, and the hardwood floors shine throughout. The four smaller guest cottages have been totally renovated and also feature hardwood floors and marble bathrooms. The small cottage has a queen bed, private bathroom, microwave, coffee pot, and access to the fridge in the laundry room. Each of the larger cottages has two beds, a private bathroom, and a TV. One cottage has a kitchenette, the other a full kitchen.

The quiet neighborhood and old Hawaii ambience give this place a comfortable, easygoing atmosphere. Restaurants and shops are just minutes away in Makawao, and the beach is a 15-minute drive.

3265 Baldwin Ave. (next to Veteran's Cemetery, less than a mile below Makawao), Makawao, HI 96768. ✆ **808/572-9021.** Fax 808/573-5072. www.banyantreehouse.com. 1 house, 4 cottages. $85–$110 cottage for 2; $300 3-bedroom house (sleeps up to 9). Extra person $15. Children age 12 and under stay free in parent's room. Cleaning deposit for house of $150 if less than 7-day stay. MC, V. **Amenities:** Outdoor pool (saltwater); Jacuzzi; babysitting; small charge for self-serve washer/dryer. *In room:* Kitchen or kitchenette, fridge, coffeemaker.

**Hale Ho'okipa Inn Makawao** ★ *Finds* Step back in time at this 1924 plantation-style home, rescued by owner Cherie Attix in 1996 and restored to its original charm (on the State and National Historic Registers). Cherie lovingly refurbished the old wooden floors, filled the rooms with furniture from the 1920s, and hung works by local artists on the walls. The result is a charming, serene place to stay, just a 5-minute walk from the shops and restaurants of Makawao, 15 minutes from beaches, and a 1½-hour drive from the top of Haleakala. The guest rooms have separate outside entrances and private bathrooms. The house's front and back porches are both wonderful for sipping tea and watching the sunset. The Kona Wing is a two-bedroom suite with private bathroom and use of the kitchen.

32 Pakani Place, Makawao, HI 96768. ✆ **808/572-6698.** www.maui-bed-and-breakfast.com. 3 units (2 with shower only). $95–$110 double; $145–$165 suite with full kitchen. Rates include continental breakfast. Extra person $5–$10. MC, V. From Haleakala Hwy., turn left on Makawao Ave., then turn right on the 5th street on the right off Makawao Ave. (Pakani Place); second to the last house on the right (green house with white picket fence and water tower). *In room:* TV, hair dryer.

## KULA

Lodgings in Kula are the closest options to the entrance of Haleakala National Park (about 60 min. away).

### MODERATE

**Malu Manu** ★★ *Finds* This is one of the most romantic places to stay on Maui, with a panoramic view of the entire island from the front door. Tucked into the side of Haleakala Volcano at 4,000 feet is this old Hawaiian estate with a single-room log cabin (built as a writer's retreat in the early 1900s) and a 30-year-old family home.

The writers' cabin has a full kitchen, a fireplace, and antiques galore. The two-bedroom, 2½-bathroom home also has antiques, koa walls, and beautiful eucalyptus floors. The 7-acre property is filled with native forest, organic gardens (help yourself to lemons, avocados, and whatever else is ripe), a paddle tennis court, and a Japanese-style outdoor soaking tub. If you're a dog person, the resident golden retriever, Alohi, may come over and make your acquaintance. This is one of the closest accommodations to Haleakala; restaurants are about a 15-minute drive away.

446 Cooke Rd. (mailing address: P.O. Box 175, Kula, HI 96790). ✆ **888/878-6161** or 808/878-6111. www.maui.net/~alive/index.html. 2 units. $135 double in log cabin; $170 double in 2-bedroom house. Extra person $10. MC. V. **Amenities:** Hot tub; paddle tennis court; in-room massage; laundry facilities. *In room:* Kitchen, fridge, coffeemaker, iron.

**Silver Cloud Ranch** Old Hawaii lives on at Silver Cloud Ranch, founded in 1902. The former working cattle spread has a commanding view of four islands, the West Maui Mountains, and the valley and beaches below. The Lanai Cottage, a honeymoon favorite nestled in a flower garden, has an oceanview lanai, claw-foot tub, full kitchen, and wood-burning stove to warm chilly nights; a futon is available for a third person. The best rooms in the main house are on the second floor: the King Kamehameha Suite (with king bed) and the Queen Emma Suite (with queen sleigh bed). One-lane Thompson Road makes an ideal morning walk (about 3 miles round-trip), and you can go horseback riding next door at Thompson Ranch. There's a TV available on request.

Old Thompson Rd. (1¼ miles past Hwy. 37). RR 2, Box 201, Kula, HI 96790. ✆ **800/532-1111** or 808/878-6101. Fax 808/878-2132. www.silvercloud ranch.com. 12 units. $110–$162 double in main house; $136–$188 double studio in mauka hale; $195 double cottage. Rates include full breakfast. Extra person $15. 2 night minimum or $15 surcharge. AE, DC, DISC, MC, V. *In room:* TV, kitchen (in cottage), fridge (in cottage), coffeemaker (in cottage); no phone.

## INEXPENSIVE

In addition to the options below, also consider **Gildersleeve's Vacation Rentals,** formerly known as Elaine's Upcountry Guest Rooms (✆ **808/878-6623;** fax 808/878-2619; m.gildersleeve@verizon.net); the warm and welcoming hosts rent three rooms in their spacious pole house ($80 double; 3-night minimum).

**Kula Cottage** ★ *Finds* We can't imagine having a less-than-fantastic vacation here. Tucked away on a quiet street amid blooming papaya and banana trees, Cecilia and Larry Gilbert's romantic honeymoon cottage is very private—it even has its own driveway and carport. The 700-square-foot cottage has a full kitchen (complete with dishwasher), and three huge closets that offer enough storage space for you to move in permanently. An outside lanai has a big gas barbecue and an umbrella table and chairs. Cecilia delivers a continental breakfast daily. Groceries and a small take-out lunch counter are within walking distance; it's a 30-minute drive to the beach.

40 Puakea Place (off Lower Kula Rd.), Kula, HI 96790. ✆ **808/878-2043** or 808/871-6230. Fax 808/871-9187. www.gilbertadvertising.com/kulacottage. 1 cottage. $95 double. Rate includes continental breakfast. 2-night minimum. No credit cards. *In room:* TV, kitchen, fridge, coffeemaker, washer/dryer.

**Kula Lynn Farm Bed & Bath** ★ Kids The Coons, the same great family that runs Maui's best sailing adventure on the *Trilogy,* offer this spectacular 1,600-square-foot unit on the ground floor of a custom-built pole house. From its location on the slopes of Haleakala, the panoramic view—across Maui's central valley, with the islands of Lanai and Kahoolawe in the distance—is worth the price alone. Wall-to-wall windows and high ceilings add to the feeling of spaciousness throughout. The two bedrooms, two bathrooms, and two queen sofa beds in the living room make this the perfect place for a family. No expense has been spared in the European-style kitchen, with top appliances and Italian marble floors. This place should appeal to those who enjoy a quiet location and such activities as barbecuing on the lanai and watching the sun set.

P.O. Box 847, Kula, HI 96790. ✆ **800/874-2666,** ext. 211, or 808/878-6176. Fax 808/878-6320. captcoon@gte.net. 1 unit. $95 double. 3-night minimum. Rate includes breakfast fixings. Extra person $15. AE, MC, V. *In room:* TV/VCR, kitchen, fridge, coffeemaker, iron.

## 5 East Maui: On the Road to Hana

### KUAU

**The Inn at Mama's Fish House** ★ The fabulous location (nestled in a coconut grove on secluded Kuau Beach), beautifully decorated interior (with island-style rattan furniture and works by Hawaiian artists), full kitchen, and extras (Weber gas barbecue, big-screen TVs, and all the beach toys you can think of) make this place a gem for those seeking a centrally-located vacation rental. It has everything, even Mama's Fish House next door, where guests get a discount off lunch and dinner. The one-bedrooms are nestled in tropical jungle (red ginger surrounds the garden patio), while the two-bedrooms face the beach. Both have terra-cotta floors, complete kitchens (even dishwashers), sofa beds, and laundry facilities.

799 Poho Place (off the Hana Hwy. in Kuau), Paia, HI 96779. © **800/860-HULA** or 808/579-9764. Fax 808/579-8594. www.mamasfishhouse.com. 6 units. $140–$160 1-bedroom (sleeps up to 4); $350 2-bedroom (up to 6). 3-night minimum stay. AE, DISC, MC, V. *In room:* A/C, TV/VCR, answering machine, kitchen, fridge, coffeemaker, hair dryer, iron, safe, washer/dryer.

## HAIKU

**Maui Dream Cottages** *Value* Essentially a vacation rental, this country estate is located atop a hill overlooking the ocean. The spacious grounds are dotted with fruit trees (bananas, papayas, and avocados, all free for the picking), and the front lawn is comfortably equipped with a double hammock, chaise lounges, and table and chairs. One cottage has two bedrooms, a full kitchen, a washer/dryer, and an entertainment center. The other is basically the same, but with only one bedroom (plus a sofa bed in the living room). They're both very well maintained and comfortably outfitted with furniture that's attractive but casual. The Haiku location is quiet and restful and offers the opportunity to see how real islanders live. However, you'll have to drive a good 20 to 25 minutes to restaurants in Makawao or Paia. Hookipa Beach is about a 20-minute drive, and Baldwin Beach (which has good swimming) is 25 minutes away.

265 W. Kuiaha Rd. (1 block from Pauwela Cafe), Haiku, HI 96708. © **808/575-9079.** Fax 808/575-9477. http://planet-hawaii.com/haiku. 2 cottages (shower only). $70 for 4. 7-night minimum. MC, V. *In room:* TV, kitchen, fridge, coffeemaker, washer/dryer.

**Pilialoha B&B Cottage** ★ *Value* The minute you arrive at this split-level country cottage, located on 2 acres of half-century-old eucalyptus trees, you'll see owner Machiko Heyde's artistry at work. Just in front of the quaint cottage (which is great for couples but can sleep up to five) is a garden blooming with some 200 varieties of roses. You'll find more of Machiko's handiwork inside. There's a queen bed in the master bedroom, a twin bed in a small adjoining room, and a queen sofa bed in the living room. A large lanai extends from the master bedroom. There's a great movie collection for rainy days or cool country nights, and a garage. Machiko delivers breakfast daily; if you plan on an early morning ride to the top of Haleakala, she'll make sure you go with a thermos of coffee and her homemade bread.

2512 Kaupakalua Rd. (3/4 mile from Kokomo intersection), Haiku, HI 96708. © **808/572-1440.** Fax 808/572-4612. www.pilialoha.com. 1 cottage. $130 double. Rates include continental breakfast. Extra person $20. 3-night minimum. MC, V. **Amenities:** Complimentary use of beach gear (including snorkel equipment); complimentary use of washer/dryer. *In room:* TV/VCR, kitchen, fridge, coffeemaker.

**Wild Ginger** ★★ *Finds* This cozy, romantic intimate cottage, hidden in Miliko Gulch, overlooking a stream with a waterfall, bamboo, sweet smelling ginger and banana trees, is perfect for honeymooners, lovers, and fans of Hawaiian art. The moment you step into this 400-square-foot, artistically decorated Hawaiian cottage (with additional 156-sq.-ft. screened deck), you will be delighted at the carefully placed memorabilia (ukulele tile, canoe paddle, and so on) found throughout. The cottage has a full kitchen with everything you could possibly need for cooking. The Hawaiian theme carries into the living room with VCR behind a tropical painted cabinet and stereo. The comfy queen bed opens to the living area. The screened porch has table, chairs, and couch, perfect for curling up with a good book. Outside there's a barbecue, plus all the beach toys you could want to borrow.

Haiku. Reservations c/o Hawaii's Best Bed & Breakfasts, P.O. Box 758, Volcano, HI 96785. ✆ **800/262-9912** or 808/985-7488. Fax 808/967-8610. www.bestbnb.com. 1 unit. $125 double, 3-night minimum. No credit cards. *In room:* VCR, kitchen, fridge, coffeemaker, hair dryer, iron, washer/dryer.

## HUELO

**Huelo Point Flower Farm** ★ *Finds* Here's a peaceful retreat by the sea on a spectacular, remote 300-foot sea cliff near a waterfall stream. This large estate overlooking Waipio Bay has two guest cottages, a guesthouse, and a main house available for rent. The studio-size Gazebo Cottage has a floor-to-ceiling glass wall that overlooks a spectacular ocean view. Inside the intimate cabin are a koa-wood captain's bed, a TV, a stereo, a kitchenette, a private ocean-side patio, a private hot tub, and a half-bathroom with outdoor shower. The 900-square-foot Carriage House apartment sleeps four and has glass walls facing the mountain and sea, plus a kitchen, a den, decks, and a loft bedroom. The four-bedroom main house contains a fireplace, a sunken Roman bath, cathedral ceilings, and other extras. On-site is a natural pool with a waterfall and an oceanfront hot tub. You're welcome to pick fruit, vegetables, and flowers from the extensive garden. Homemade scones, tree-ripened papayas, and fresh-roasted coffee start your day. Despite its seclusion, it's just a half-hour to Kahului, or about 20 minutes to Paia's shops and restaurants.

Off Hana Hwy., between mile markers 3 and 4. P.O. Box 791808, Paia, HI 96779. ✆ **808/572-1850.** www.mauiflowerfarm.com. 4 units. $150 cottage double; $175 carriage house double; $325 guesthouse double; $425 main house double (sleeps 6). Extra person $20–$35. 7-night minimum for main house; 2-night minimum for other units. No credit cards. **Amenities:** Outdoor pool; 3 Jacuzzis; self-serve washer/dryer. *In room:* TV, kitchenette (in cottage), kitchen (in houses), fridge, coffeemaker, hair dryer.

**Kailua Maui Gardens** *Finds* In the middle of nowhere lies this nearly 2-acre tropical botanical garden with four bungalows dotting the property. Just a couple of miles down the serpentine Hana Highway from Huelo, in the remote area of Kailua, is an unlikely place for accommodations (it's a 30-min. drive to the nearest beach and 1 hr. to Hana), but for those who want to get away from it all, this could be your place. The small cabanas range from one-room studios with a futon and full kitchen to compact accommodations with basic kitchenette amenities. They all face out into gorgeous gardens. In the midst of the botanical garden is a pool, with cabana and covered barbecue area, and a hot tub. The garden sits right on the Hana Highway, so ask for a unit away from the road. Even if you don't stay here, stop by and visit the garden; hosts Kirk and Shelley love to show it off.

Located between mile marker 5 and 6 on the Hana Hwy. S.R. 1, Box 9, Haiku, HI 96708. ✆ **800/258-8588** or 808/572-9726. Fax 808/575-2966. www.kailuamauigardens.com. 4 units. $90–$145 double. 2-night minimum. No credit cards. **Amenities:** Outdoor pool; 2 hot tubs; laundry facilities. *In room:* TV/VCR, CD/stereo, kitchen or kitchenette, fridge, coffeemaker.

## 6 At the End of the Road in East Maui: Hana

To locate the following accommodations, see the "Hana" map on p. 149.

### EXPENSIVE

**Hotel Hana-Maui** ★★★ Picture Shangri-La, Hawaiian-style: 66 acres rolling down to the sea in a remote Hawaiian village, with a wellness center, two pools, and access to one of the best beaches in Hana (a 5-min. shuttle ride away). Every unit is excellent, but our favorites are the Sea Ranch Cottages (especially units 215–218 for the best views of turtles frolicking in the ocean), where individual duplex bungalows look out over the craggy shoreline to the rolling surf. The oversize, airy units open up to a huge lanai with excellent views. These comfy units have been totally redecorated with every amenity you can think of (with no nickle-and-diming you with charges for coffee, water, and so on—everything from the homemade banana bread to the bottled water is complimentary). Cathedral ceilings, plush feather bed, giant-size soaking tub, Hawaiian art work, bamboo hardwood floors—this is the vacation of luxury. There are no TVs in the rooms, but the Club Room has a giant screen TV, plus VCR and Internet access. The numerous activities available include horseback riding, mountain bicycles, tennis, and pitch and putt golf.

Hana, Maui 96713. ✆ **800/321-HANA** or 808/248-8211. Fax 808/248-7202. www.hotelhanamaui.com. 78 units. $295–$365 Bay Cottages double; $395–$725 Sea Ranch Cottages double; 2-bedroom Plantation Guest House from $1,500. $50 extra person. AE, DC, DISC, MC, V. **Amenities:** Restaurant (with Hawaiian entertainment twice a week); bar (with nightly entertainment); 2 outdoor pools; complimentary use of the 3-hole practice golf course (clubs are complimentary as well); complimentary tennis courts; fitness center; game room; concierge; activity desk; car-rental desk; business center; small shopping arcade; salon; room service; in-room and spa massage; babysitting; laundry service. *In room:* Dataport, kitchenette, fridge, coffeemaker, hair dryer, iron, safe.

## MODERATE

**Ekena** ★ *Finds* This 8½-acre piece of paradise in rural Hana boasts ocean and rainforest views; the floor-to-ceiling glass doors in the spacious Hawaiian-style pole house bring the outside in. The elegant two-story home is exquisitely furnished, from the comfortable U-shaped couch that invites you to relax and take in the view to the top-of-the-line mattress on the king bed. The kitchen is fully equipped with every high-tech convenience you can imagine (guests have made complete holiday meals here). Only one floor (and a two-bedroom unit) is rented at any one time to ensure privacy. The grounds are impeccably groomed and dotted with tropical plants and fruit trees. Hiking trails into the rainforest start right on the property, and beaches and waterfalls are just minutes away.

P.O. Box 728 (off Hana Hwy., above Hana Airport), Hana, HI 96713. ✆ **808/248-7047.** Fax 808/248-7047. www.ekenamaui.com. 2 units. $185 for 2; $250–$350 for 4. Extra person $25. 3-night minimum. No credit cards. **Amenities:** Complimentary use of washer/dryers. *In room:* TV, kitchen, fridge, coffeemaker, iron.

**Hamoa Bay Bungalow** ★ *Finds* Down a country lane guarded by two Balinese statues stands a carefully crafted bungalow and an Asian-inspired two-bedroom house overlooking Hamoa Bay. This enchanting retreat is just 2 miles beyond Hasegawa's general store on the way to Kipahulu. It sits on 4 verdant acres within walking distance of beautiful Hamoa Beach. The 600-square-foot Balinese-style cottage is distinctly tropical, with giant bamboo furniture from Indonesia, batik prints, a king bed, a full kitchen, and a screened porch with hot tub and shower. Hidden from the cottage is a 1,300-square-foot home with a soaking tub and private outdoor stone shower. It offers a bamboo king bed in one room, a queen bed in another, a screened-in sleeping porch, a full kitchen, and wonderful ocean views.

P.O. Box 773, Hana, HI 96713. ✆ **808/248-7884**. Fax 808/248-7047. www.hamoabay.com. 2 units. $195 cottage (sleeps only 2); $250 house for 2, $350 house for 4. 3-night minimum. No credit cards. **Amenities:** Hot tub, complimentary use of washer/dryers. *In room:* TV, kitchen, fridge, coffeemaker, iron.

**Hana Hale Malamalama** *Finds* Hana Hale Malamalama sits on a historic site with ancient fish ponds and a cave mentioned in ancient chants. Host John takes excellent care of the ponds (you're welcome to watch him feed the fish at 5pm daily) and is fiercely protective of the hidden cave. There's access to a nearby rocky beach, which isn't good for swimming but makes a wonderful place to watch the sunset. All accommodations include fully equipped kitchens, bathrooms, bedrooms, living/dining areas, and private lanais. Next to the fish pond, the Royal Lodge, a 2600-square-foot architectural masterpiece built entirely of Philippine mahogany, has large skylights the entire length of the house and can be rented as a house or two separate units. The oceanfront Bamboo Inn contains two units (a studio and a one- or two-bedroom unit). The cottages range from a separate two-level Tree House cottage, with Jacuzzi tub for two, small kitchen/living area, and deck upstairs, to the Pond Side Bungalow, which features a private outdoor Jacuzzi tub and shower.

P.O. Box 374, Hana, HI 96713. ✆ **808/248-7718.** www.hanahale.com. 7 units. $125–$225 double. Extra person $15. 2-night minimum. No credit cards. **Amenities:** Jacuzzi. *In room:* TV/VCR, kitchen, fridge, coffeemaker.

**Hana Oceanfront** ★★ Just across the street from Hamoa Bay, Hana's premier white-sand beach, lie these two plantation-style units, impeccably decorated in old Hawaii decor. Our favorite unit is the romantic cottage, complete with an old-fashioned front porch where you can sit and watch the ocean; separate bedroom (with a bamboo sleigh bed), plus pullout sofa for extra guests; top notch kitchen appliances; and comfy living room. The 1,000 square foot vacation suite, located downstairs from hosts Dan and Sandi's home (but totally soundproof—you'll never hear them) has an elegant master bedroom with polished bamboo flooring; spacious tiled bathroom, and a fully-appointed gourmet kitchen. Outside is a 320-square foot lanai. The units sit on the road facing Hana's most popular beach, so there is traffic during the day. At night, the traffic disappears, the stars come out, and the sound of the ocean soothes you to sleep.

Hana. Reservations c/o Hawaii's Best Bed & Breakfasts, P.O. Box 758, Volcano, HI 96785. ✆ **800/262-9912** or 808/985-7488. Fax 808/967-8610. www.bestbnb.com. 2 units. $190–$225 double; 2-night minimum. No credit cards. *In room:* TV/VCR, kitchen, fridge, coffeemaker, hair dryer, iron.

**Heavenly Hana Inn** ★★ *Finds* Owners Robert and Sheryl Filippi humbly describe their B&B as a "Japanese-style inn." This place on the Hana Highway, just a stone's throw from the center of Hana town, is a little bit of heaven, where no attention to detail has been spared. Each suite has a sitting room with futon and couch, polished hardwood floors, and separate bedroom with a raised platform bed (with an excellent, firm mattress). The black-marble bathrooms have huge tubs. Flowers are everywhere, ceiling fans keep the rooms cool, and the delicious gourmet breakfast is worth splurging for. The spacious grounds are done in Japanese style with a bamboo fence, tiny bridges over a meandering stream, and Japanese gardens.

P.O. Box 790, Hana, HI 96713. ✆ and fax **808/248-8442.** www.heavenlyhanainn.com. 3 units. $185–$250 suite. Full gourmet breakfast available for $15 per person. Ask about special rates. 2-night minimum. AE, DISC, MC, V. No children under age 15 accepted. **Amenities:** Laundry service. *In room:* TV, no phone.

## INEXPENSIVE

**Hana's Tradewinds Cottage** ★ *Value* Nestled among the ginger and heliconias on a 5-acre flower farm are two separate cottages, each with full kitchen, barbecue, private hot tub, TV, ceiling fans, and sofa bed. The studio cottage sleeps up to four; a bamboo shoji blind separates the sleeping area (with queen bed) from the sofa bed in the living room. The Tradewinds cottage has two bedrooms (with a queen bed in one room and two twins in the other) and a huge front porch. The atmosphere is quiet and relaxing, and hostess Rebecca Buckley welcomes families (she has two children, a cat, and a very sweet golden retriever). You can use the laundry facilities at no extra charge.

135 Alalele Place (the airport road), P.O. Box 385, Hana, HI 96713. ✆ **800/327-8097** or 808/248-8980. Fax 808/248-7735. www.hanamaui.net. 2 cottages. $120 studio double; $145 2-bedroom double. Extra person $10. 2-night minimum. AE, DISC, MC, V. *In room:* TV, kitchen, fridge, coffeemaker, no phone.

**Kulani's Hideaway in Hana, Maui** ★ *Value* On the road to Waianapanapa State Park is the "deal" of Hana—two one-bedroom units, each with pullout sofa beds in the living room, full kitchen, cable TV (a plus in Hana), and washer/dryer, within walking distance of a fabulous black-sand beach. Outside is a large lanai for watching the clouds go by, with a barbecue area with picnic table in the yard. Book early; this is one of Maui's best deals for the budget traveler.

P.O. Box 483, Hana, HI 96713. ✆ and fax **808/248-8234** or 808/268-9248. kulanis@maui.net. 2 units. $65 double. Extra person $15. **Amenities:** Complimentary coffee. *In room:* TV, kitchen, fridge, coffeemaker; washer/dryer; no phone.

**Waianapanapa State Park Cabins** *Value* These 12 rustic cabins are the best lodging deal on Maui. Everyone knows it, too—so make your reservations early (up to 6 months in advance). The cabins are warm and dry and come complete with kitchen, living room, bedroom, and bathroom with hot shower; furnishings include bedding, linen, towels, dishes, and very basic cooking and eating utensils. Don't expect luxury—this is a step above camping, albeit in a beautiful tropical jungle setting. The key attraction at this 120-acre state beach park is the unusual horseshoe-shaped black-sand beach on Pailoa Bay, popular for shore fishing, snorkeling, and swimming. There are also shoreline hiking trails and historic sites. But bring mosquito protection—this *is* the jungle, after all.

Off Hana Hwy. c/o State Parks Division, 54 S. High St., Rm. 101, Wailuku, HI 96793. ✆ **808/984-8109.** 12 cabins. $45 for 4 (sleeps up to 6). Extra person $5. 5-night maximum. No credit cards. *In room:* Kitchen, fridge, coffeemaker, no phone.

# 4

# Where to Dine

With soaring visitor statistics and a glamorous image, the Valley Isle is fertile ground for enterprising chefs, and consequently, dining on Maui has become a culinary treat able to hold its own against most major metropolitan areas.

Despite the recent change and growth in Maui's dining scene, some things haven't changed: You can still dine well at Lahaina's open-air waterfront watering holes, where the view counts for 50% of the experience. There are still budget eateries, but not many; Maui's old-fashioned, multigenerational mom-and-pop diners are disappearing, eclipsed by the flashy newcomers, or clinging to the edge of existence in the older neighborhoods of central Maui, such as lovable Wailuku. Although you'll have to work harder to find them in the resort areas, you won't have to go far to find creative cuisine, pleasing style, and stellar dining experiences.

In the listings below, reservations are not necessary unless otherwise noted.

## 1 Central Maui

### MODERATE

**A Saigon Cafe** ★★ VIETNAMESE Jennifer Nguyen has stuck to her guns and steadfastly refused to erect a sign, and diners come anyway. Fans drive from all over the island for her crisped, spiced Dungeness crab, her steamed opakapaka with ginger and garlic, and her wok-cooked Vietnamese specials tangy with spices, herbs, and lemongrass. There are a dozen different soups, cold and hot noodles, and chicken and shrimp cooked in a clay pot. You can create your own Vietnamese "burritos" from a platter of tofu, noodles, and vegetables that you wrap in rice paper and dip in garlic sauce. Among our favorites are the shrimp lemongrass, savory and refreshing, and the tofu curry, swimming in herbs and vegetables straight from the garden.

1792 Main St., Wailuku. ✆ **808/243-9560.** Main courses $6.50–$17. DC, MC, V. Mon–Sat 10am–9:30pm; Sun 10am–8:30pm. Heading into Wailuku from Kahului, go over the bridge and take the first right onto Central Ave, then the first right on Nani St. At the next stop sign, look for the building with the neon sign that says "Open."

**Mañana Garage** ★★ *Finds* LATIN AMERICAN Chef Tom Lelli serves up incomparable fare at this central Maui hot spot. The industrial motif features table bases like hubcaps and gleaming chrome and cobalt walls with orange accents. The brilliantly conceived and executed menu includes fried green tomatoes, done just right and served with slivered red onions; a ceviche with the perfectly balanced flavors and textures of lime, cilantro, chili, coconut, and fresh fish; and arepas (cornmeal and cheese griddle cakes with smoked salmon and wasabi sour cream) that meld the flavors and textures of many traditions.

33 Lono Ave., Kahului. ✆ **808/873-0220.** Reservations recommended. Main courses lunch $6.95–$13, dinner $12–$26. AE, DC, DISC, MC, V. Mon 11am–9pm; Tues–Fri 11am–10:30pm; Sat 5–10:30pm; Sun 5–9pm.

**Marco's Grill & Deli** ★ ITALIAN Located in central Maui, where the roads to Upcountry, West, and South Maui converge, Marco's is popular among locals for its homemade Italian fare and friendly informality. Everything—from the meatballs, sausages, and burgers to the sauces, salad dressings, and ravioli—is made in-house. The 35 different choices of hot and cold sandwiches and entrees are served all day, and they include vodka rigatoni with imported prosciutto; pasta e' fasio (a house specialty: smoked ham hock simmered for hours in tomato sauce, with red and white beans); and simple pasta with marinara sauce. This is one of those comfortable neighborhood fixtures favored by all generations. The antipasto salad, vegetarian lasagna, and roasted peppers are taste treats, and the meatballs and Italian sausage are famous in central Maui.

Dairy Center, 395 Dairy Rd., Kahului. ✆ **808/877-4446.** Main courses $11–$26. AE, DC, DISC, MC, V. Daily 7:30am–10pm.

## INEXPENSIVE

The **Kaahumanu Center,** in the center of Kahului, at 275 Kaahumanu Ave. (5 min. from Kahului Airport on Hwy. 32), has a very popular food court. **Edo Japan** teppanyaki is a real find, dispensing marvelous, flavorful mounds of grilled fresh vegetables and chicken teriyaki for $4.15. **Maui Mixed Plate** dishes out "local style" cuisine of meat with rice and macaroni salad in the $5 to $7 range. **Yummy Korean B-B-Q** offers the assertive flavors of Korea; **Panda Cuisine** serves tasty Chinese food; and the **Coffee Store** (p. 95) sells sandwiches, salads, pasta, and nearly 2 dozen different coffee drinks. There's also a branch of **Maui Tacos** (p. 91).

**Café O'Lei on Main** ★ AMERICAN/ISLAND Dana Pastula has cloned her wonderful Makawao eatery for lucky Wailuku diners. The menu features fresh Island ingredients: taro salad with crisp Molokai sweet potato, seared ahi sandwich with wasabi mayonnaise, fresh fish, and Aloha Friday crab cakes with sweet chili aioli. Sandwiches (crab club, roast turkey breast, roasted Maui vegetables) and salads (including our favorite, curry chicken: hot chicken with peanuts, chiles, ginger, and veggies) complement daily specials such as chicken fettuccine and blackened mahimahi. The plate lunch, at $5.50, is a terrific deal. ***Tip:*** You can get a great picnic lunch here for your outing in Iao Valley. Look for sister restaurants in Makawao, Maalaea, and Lahaina.

2051 Main St., Wailuku. ✆ **808/244-6816.** Sandwiches $4.95–$6.95; lunch specials $5.50–$7.50. No credit cards. Mon–Fri 10:30am–2:30pm.

**Class Act** ★ GLOBAL Part of a program run by the distinguished Food Service Department of Maui Community College, this restaurant has a following. Student chefs show their stuff with a flourish in their "classroom," where they pull out all the stops. Linen, china, servers in ties and white shirts, and a four-course lunch make this a unique value. The appetizer, soup, salad, and dessert are set, but you can choose between the regular entrees and a heart-healthy main course prepared in the culinary tradition of the week (Italy, Mexico, Maui, Napa valley, France, New Orleans, and other locales). The filet mignon of French week is popular, as are the New Orleans gumbo and Cajun shrimp; the sesame-crusted mahimahi on taro leaf pasta; the polenta flan with eggplant; and the bean- and green-chili chilaquile. Tea and soft drinks are offered, but otherwise it's BYOB.

Maui Community College, 310 Kaahumanu Ave., Wailuku. ✆ **808/984-3485.** Reservations recommended. 5-course lunch $15. No credit cards. Wed and Fri 11am–12:15pm (last seating); closed June–Aug for summer vacation. Menu and cuisine type change weekly.

**Ichiban** *Finds* JAPANESE/SUSHI What a find: an informal neighborhood restaurant that serves inexpensive, home-cooked

Japanese food *and* good sushi at realistic prices. Local residents consider Ichiban a staple for breakfast, lunch, or dinner and a haven of comforts: egg-white omelets; great saimin; combination plates of teriyaki chicken, teriyaki beef, *tonkatsu* (pork cutlet), rice, and pickled cabbage; chicken yakitori; and sushi—everything from unagi and scallop to California roll. The sushi items may not be inexpensive, but like the specials, such as steamed opakapaka, they're a good value. We love the tempura, miso soup, and spicy ahi hand roll.

Kahului Shopping Center, 47 Kaahumanu Ave., Kahului. ✆ **808/871-6977.** Main courses $4.25–$5.25 breakfast; $5.50–$9.50 lunch (combination plates $8); $5.95–$28 dinner (combination dinner $12, dinner specials from $8.95). AE, DC, MC, V. Mon–Fri 6:30am–2pm and 5–9pm; Sat 10:30am–2pm and 5–9pm; closed 2 weeks around Christmas and New Year.

**Maui Bake Shop** BAKERY/DELI Maui native Claire Fujii-Krall and her husband, baker Jose Krall, turn out buttery brioches, healthy nine-grain and two-tone rye breads, focaccia, strudels, sumptuous fresh-fruit gâteaux, puff pastries, and dozens of other baked goods and confections at their Wailuku shop. The front window displays more than 100 bakery and deli items, among them salads, a popular eggplant marinara focaccia, homemade quiches, and an inexpensive calzone filled with chicken, pesto, mushroom, and cheese. Homemade soups (clam chowder, minestrone, cream of asparagus) team up nicely with sandwiches on freshly baked bread. Don't miss the Ultimate Dessert: white-chocolate macadamia-nut cheesecake.

2092 Vineyard St., Wailuku. ✆ **808/242-0064.** Most items under $5. AE, DISC, MC, V. Mon–Fri 6am–4pm; Sat 7am–2pm.

**Restaurant Matsu** JAPANESE/LOCAL Customers come from miles away just for Matsu's California rolls, while regulars line up for the cold saimin (julienned cucumber, egg, Chinese-style sweet pork, and red ginger on noodles) and for the bento plates, various assemblages of chicken, teriyaki beef, fish, and rice. The nigiri sushi items are also popular. The katsu pork and chicken, breaded and deep-fried, are other specialties of this casual Formica-style diner. We love the tempura udon and the saimin, steaming mounds of noodles in homemade broths and topped with condiments. The daily specials are a changing lineup of home-cooked classics: oxtail soup, roast pork with gravy, teriyaki ahi, miso butterfish, and breaded mahimahi.

Maui Mall, 161 Alamaha St., Kahului. ✆ **808/871-0822.** Most items less than $6. No credit cards. Mon–Sat 10am–8pm.

## 2 West Maui

### LAHAINA

There's a **Maui Tacos** (p. 91) in Lahaina Square (✆ **808/661-8883**). Maui's branch of the **Hard Rock Cafe** is in Lahaina at 900 Front St. (✆ **808/667-7400**).

#### VERY EXPENSIVE

**David Paul's Lahaina Grill** ★ Kids NEW AMERICAN Even after David Paul Johnson's departure, this Lahaina hot spot has maintained its popularity. It's still filled with chic, tanned diners, and there's still attitude aplenty at the entrance. The signature items remain: tequila shrimp and firecracker rice, Kona coffee–roasted rack of lamb, kalua duck, and an excellent eggplant napoleon. As always, a special custom-designed chef's table can be arranged with 72-hour notice for larger parties. The ambience—black-and-white tile floors, pressed tin ceilings, eclectic 1890s decor—is striking, and the bar, even without an ocean view, is the busiest spot in Lahaina. The children's menu is more sophisticated than usual (no burgers or hot dogs), but offers plenty of options for the little ones; entrees are $12.

127 Lahainaluna Rd. ✆ **808/667-5117.** www.lahainagrill.com. Reservations required. Main courses $26–$38. AE, DC, DISC, MC, V. Daily 5:30–10pm. Bar daily 5:30pm–midnight.

**The Feast at Lele** ★★ POLYNESIAN The owners of Old Lahaina Luau (see "A Night to Remember: Luau, Maui Style" on p. 172), have teamed up with Chef James McDonald's culinary prowess (I'o and Pacific'o), placed it in a perfect outdoor oceanfront setting, and added the exquisite dancers of the Old Lahaina Luau. The result: a culinary and cultural experience that sizzles. Dances from Hawaii, Tonga, Tahiti, and Samoa are presented in full costumed splendor. Chanting, singing, drumming, dancing, the swish of ti-leaf skirts, the scent of plumeria—it's a full culinary-cultural adventure. Guests sit at white-clothed, candlelit tables set on the sand (unlike the luau, where seating is en masse) and dine on kalua pig, tasty steamed moi, and savory pohole ferns and hearts of palm. From Tonga come lobster-ogo (seaweed) salad and grilled steak, from Tahiti steamed chicken and taro leaf in coconut milk, and from Samoa grilled fish in banana leaf. Particularly mesmerizing is the evening's opening: A softly lit canoe carries three people ashore to the sound of conch shells.

505 Front St. ✆ **886/244-5353** or 808/667-5353. www.feastatlele.com. Reservations a must. Set 5-course menu $89 for adults, $59 for children 2–12; gratuity not included. AE, MC, V. Apr 1–Sept 30, Tues–Sat 6–9pm; Oct 1–Mar 31, 5:30–8:30pm.

# Lahaina & Kaanapali Dining

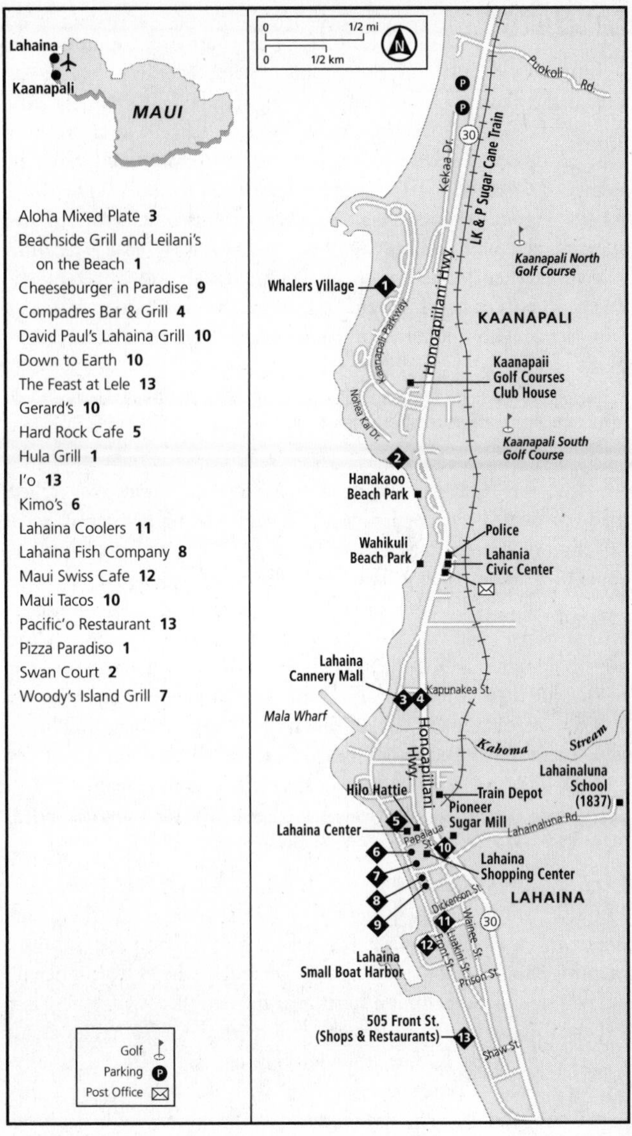

## EXPENSIVE

**Gerard's** ★★★ *Finds* FRENCH The charm of Gerard's—soft lighting, Edith Piaf on the sound system, excellent service—is matched by a menu of uncompromising standards. A frequent winner of the *Wine* Spectator Award of Excellence, Gerard's offers roasted opakapaka with star anise, fennel fondue, and hints of orange and ginger, a stellar entree on a menu of winners. The Kona lobster ragout with pasta and morels promises ecstasy, and the spinach salad with scallops is among the finest we've tasted. Gerard's has an excellent appetizer menu, with shiitake and oyster mushrooms in puff pastry, fresh ahi and smoked salmon carpaccio, and a very rich, highly touted escargot ragout with burgundy butter and garlic cream.

In the Plantation Inn, 174 Lahainaluna Rd. ✆ **808/661-8939.** www.gerardsmaui.com. Reservations recommended. Main courses $27–$33. AE, DC, DISC, MC, V. Daily 6–9pm.

**I'o** ★ PACIFIC RIM I'o is a fantasy of sleek curves and etched glass, co-owned by chef James McDonald. He offers an impressive selection of appetizers and some lavish Asian-Polynesian interpretations of seafood, such as stir-fried lobster with mango-Thai curry sauce, fresh ahi in a nori panko crust, and lemongrass coconut fish. Unless you're sold on entrees, our advice is to go heavy on the superb appetizers, especially the silken purse, a brilliant concoction of tricolored pot stickers stuffed with roasted peppers, mushrooms, spinach, macadamia nuts, and silken tofu. Oyster lovers, take heed: The memorable Pan-Asian Rockefellers are baked on a bed of spinach and served with a hint of star anise coconut cream.

505 Front St. ✆ **808/661-8422.** www.iomaui.com. Reservations recommended. Main courses $18–$30. AE, DC, MC, V. Daily 5:30–10pm.

**Pacific'o Restaurant** ★ PACIFIC RIM/CONTEMPORARY PACIFIC You can't get any closer to the ocean than the tables here, which are literally on the beach. With good food complementing this sensational setting, foodies and aesthetes have much to enjoy. The split-level dining starts near the entrance, with a long bar (where you can also order lunch or dinner) and a few tables along the railing. Steps lead to the outdoor tables, where the award-winning seafood dishes come to you with the backdrop of Lanai across the channel. The prawn and basil wontons, fresh fish over wilted arugula and bean sprouts, and ahi and ono tempura with miso and lime-basil sauce are among Pacific'o's memorable offerings. The vegetarian special, a marinated, roasted tofu steak with quinoa, Maui onions, red lentils and a heavenly dose of shiitake mushrooms, is a longtime favorite.

505 Front St. © **808/667-4341.** www.pacificomaui.com. Reservations recommended. Main courses $9–$14 lunch, $19–$38 dinner. AE, DC, MC, V. Daily 11am–4pm and 5:30–10pm.

## MODERATE

**Compadres Bar & Grill** MEXICAN Despite its concrete floor and high industrial ceilings, Compadres exudes good cheer. And that cheer has burgeoned lately with a new open-air seating area and a take-out taqueria window for diners on the run. The food is classic Tex-Mex, good any time of the day, beginning with huevos rancheros, egg burritos, hotcakes, and omelets (the Acapulco is heroic) and progressing to enchiladas and appetizers for the margarita-happy crowd. Stay spare (vegetable enchilada in fresh spinach tortilla) or get hefty (Texas T-bone and enchiladas). This is a carefree place with a large capacity for merrymaking.

Lahaina Cannery Mall, 1221 Honoapiilani Hwy. © **808/661-7189.** Main courses $10–$20. AE, DC, DISC, MC, V. Daily 8am–10pm.

**Kimo's** STEAK/SEAFOOD Kimo's has a loyal following that keeps it from falling into the faceless morass of waterfront restaurants serving surf-and-turf with great sunset views. It's a formula restaurant (sibling to Leilani's and Hula Grill) that works not only because of its oceanfront patio and upstairs dining room, but also because, for the price, there are some satisfying choices. It's always crowded, buzzing with people on a deck offering views of Molokai, Lanai, and Kahoolawe. Burgers and sandwiches are affordable and consistent, and the fresh catch baked in a garlic, lemon, and sweet basil glaze is a top seller. Hula pie—macadamia-nut ice cream in a chocolate-wafer crust with fudge and whipped cream—originated here.

845 Front St. © **808/661-4811.** www.kimosmaui.com. Reservations recommended for dinner. Main courses $6.95–$11 lunch, $15–$24 dinner. AE, DC, DISC, MC, V. Daily 11am–3pm and 5–10:30pm; bar open 11am–1:30am.

**Lahaina Fish Company** SEAFOOD The open-air dining room is literally over the water, with an affordable menu that covers the seafood-pasta basics. Head to an oceanside table and order a cheeseburger, chicken burger, fish burger, generous basket of peel-and-eat shrimp, or sashimi—lingering is highly recommended. The light lunch/grill menu offers appetizers (sashimi, seared ahi, spring rolls, and pot stickers), salads, and soups. Dinner selections include hand-carved steaks, several pasta choices, and local fare such as stir-fry dishes, teriyaki chicken, and luau-style ribs. The specialty, though, remains the fresh seafood: four types of fresh fish are offered nightly, in three preparations, and Pacific Rim specials include fresh ahi, seared spicy or cooked in a sweet ginger-soy sauce.

831 Front St. ✆ **808/661-3472.** Main courses $10–$26. AE, MC, V. Daily 11am–midnight.

**Woody's Island Grill** AMERICAN The owners of Cheeseburger in Paradise closed Aloha Cantina and replaced it with Woody's, a big improvement. You'll walk through an aloha-shirt shop to enter the open-air oceanfront room, where a wood-burning grill cooks fresh ono, mahimahi (with mango ginger butter), ribs, New York steak, and other surf-and-turf choices. Other options include sandwiches, such as an excellent blackened ahi with wasabi aioli, Cajun fish tacos, and coconut shrimp with sweet-and-sour sauce. The grilled opakapaka, with a lemon-caper-butter sauce and coconut shrimp, is very popular.

839 Front St. ✆ **808/661-8788.** Reservations recommended. Main courses $8–$22. AE, DISC, MC, V. Daily 11am–10pm.

### INEXPENSIVE

**Aloha Mixed Plate** ★ *Value* PLATE LUNCHES/BEACHSIDE GRILL Look for the festive turquoise-and-yellow, plantation-style front directly across from the Lahaina Cannery Mall. Grab an oceanview table, then tuck into inexpensive mahimahi, kalua pig and cabbage, shoyu chicken, teriyaki beef, and other local plate-lunch specials, all at budget-friendly prices, served with macaroni salad and rice. The shoyu chicken is the best we've had, fork tender and tasty, and the spicy chicken drumettes come from a fabled family recipe. (The bestsellers are the coconut prawns and Aloha Mixed Plate of shoyu chicken, teriyaki beef, and mahimahi.) We don't know of anywhere else where you can order a mai tai with a plate lunch and enjoy table service with an ocean view.

1285 Front St. ✆ **808/661-3322.** www.alohamixedplate.com. Main courses $4.95–$9.95. MC, V. Daily 10:30am–10pm.

**Cheeseburger in Paradise** AMERICAN Wildly successful, always crowded, and very noisy with its live music in the evenings, Cheeseburger is a shrine to the American classic. You'll find everything from tofu and garden burgers to big, juicy beef and chicken burgers, served on freshly-baked buns. There are good reasons why this place is always packed: good value, good grinds, and a great ocean view. The Cheeseburger in Paradise is a hefty hunk with Jack and cheddar cheeses, sautéed onions, lettuce, fresh tomatoes, and Thousand Island dressing. You can build your own burger by adding sautéed mushrooms, bacon, grilled ortega chilis, and other condiments for an extra charge. Onion rings, chili-cheese fries, and cold beer complete the carefree fantasy.

811 Front St. ✆ **808/661-4855.** www.cheeseburgermaui.com. Burgers $7.50–$8.50. AE, DISC, MC, V. Daily 8am–10pm.

**Down to Earth** *Value* ORGANIC HEALTH FOOD This is one of the best deals in West Maui. Healthy organic ingredients, 90% vegan, appear in scrumptious salads, lasagna, chili, curries, and dozens of tasty dishes, presented at hot-and-cold serve-yourself stations. Stools line the abundant windows in the simple dining area, where a few tables are available for those who don't want takeout. (For all you cyberjunkies, there's Internet access, too.) The food is great, and includes millet cakes, mock tofu chicken, curried tofu, and Greek salad, plus pleasing condiments. The tofu curry has apples, raw cashews, and raisins, and is fabulous. Because the food is sold by the pound, you can buy a hearty, wholesome plate for $7. Vitamin supplements, health food products, fresh produce, and cosmetics fill the rest of the store.

193 Lahainaluna Rd. ✆ **808/667-2855.** Self-serve hot buffet and salad bar; food sold by the pound. Average $6–$8 for a plate. AE, MC, V. Mon–Sat 7:30am–9pm; Sun 8:30am–8pm.

**Lahaina Coolers** AMERICAN/INTERNATIONAL A huge marlin hangs above the bar, epic wave shots and wall sconces made of surfboard fins line the walls, and open windows on three sides of this ultracasual indoor/outdoor restaurant take advantage of the shade trees. This is a great breakfast joint, with feta-cheese Mediterranean omelets, huevos rancheros, fried jasmine rice, Kula vegetables, and Portuguese sausage. There are three types of eggs Benedict—the classic, an excellent vegetarian version, and the local, with Portuguese sausage and sweetbread. At lunch, burgers and sandwiches, from grilled portobellos to the classic tuna melt, take over. Made fresh daily, the pasta is prepared Asian style (chicken breast in a spicy Thai peanut sauce), with pesto, and vegetarian, in a spicy creole sauce. Pizzas, fresh catch, steak, and enchiladas round out the entrees.

180 Dickensen St. ✆ **808/661-7082.** www.lahainacoolers.com. Main courses lunch $7.50–$11, dinner $11–$19. AE, DC, DISC, MC, V. Daily 8am–2am (full menu until midnight).

**Maui Swiss Cafe** SANDWICHES/PIZZA Newly renovated and double its original size, Swiss Cafe now has five Internet stations (three of them with flat-screen monitors) and continues to serve excellent sandwiches and continental breakfast. The $5 lunch specials and $2 ice cream makes this a welcome stop in hot Lahaina. Top-quality breads baked fresh daily, Dijon mustard, good Swiss cheese, and keen attention to sandwich fillings and pizza toppings make this a very special sandwich shop. The Swiss owner, Dominique Martin, has imbued this corner of Lahaina with a European flavor, down to the menus printed in English and German and the Swiss breakfast of sliced ham, Emmentaler cheese, hard-boiled egg, and freshly baked croissant. Watch for the "signature melt" sandwiches, with imported Emmentaler cheese baked on an Italian Parmesan crust.

640 Front St. ✆ **808/661-6776.** www.swisscafe.net. Sandwiches and 8-in. pizzas $5.95–$7.95. No credit cards. Daily 9am–6pm.

## KAANAPALI

### EXPENSIVE

**Swan Court** ★★ CONTINENTAL Swan Court is wonderful in a resorty sort of way, with a dance floor, waterfalls, flamingos, and an ocean view adding to the package. Come here as a splurge or on a bottomless expense account, and enjoy Pacific lobster coconut soup, rock shrimp crab cake, Maui sugar cane skewered ahi, and sautéed opakapaka in striking surroundings. The menu sticks to the tried-and-true, making Swan Court a safe choice for those who like a respectable and well-executed selection in a romantic setting with candlelight, a Japanese garden, and swans gliding by serenely. A year-round Valentine dinner.

In the Hyatt Regency Maui, 200 Nohea Kai Dr. ✆ **808/661-1234.** Reservations recommended for dinner. Main courses $30–$38. AE, DC, DISC, MC, V. Daily 6:30–11:30am; Tues–Sat 6–10pm.

### MODERATE

**Beachside Grill and Leilani's on the Beach** STEAK/SEAFOOD The Beachside Grill is the informal, less-expensive room downstairs on the beach, where folks wander in off the sand for a frothy beer and a beachside burger. Leilani's is the dinner-only room, with more expensive but still not outrageously priced steak and seafood offerings. At Leilani's, you can order everything from affordable spinach, cheese, and mushroom ravioli to lobster and steak. Children can get a burger for under $5 or a broiled chicken breast for a couple of dollars more. Pasta, rack of lamb, filet mignon, and Alaskan king crab at market price are among the choices in the upstairs room. Although the steak-and-lobster combinations can be pricey, the good thing about Leilani's is the strong middle range of entree prices, especially the fresh fish for around $20 to $25. All of this comes with an ocean view. There's live Hawaiian music every afternoon except Fridays, when the Rock 'n' Roll Aloha Friday set gets those decibels climbing. Free concerts are usually offered on a stage outside the restaurant on the last Sunday of the month.

In Whalers Village, 2435 Kaanapali Pkwy. ✆ **808/661-4495.** www.leilanis.com. Reservations suggested for dinner. Lunch and dinner (Beachside Grill) $6.95–$13; dinner (Leilani's) from $18. AE, DC, DISC, MC, V. Beachside Grill daily 11am–11pm (bar daily until 12:30am); Leilani's daily 5–10pm.

**Hula Grill** ★ Kids HAWAII REGIONAL/SEAFOOD Come here to tuck into crab-and-corn cakes, banana-glazed opah, macadamia-nut-roasted opakapaka, or crab won tons under a thatched umbrella, with a view of Lanai across the channel. Peter Merriman, one of the originators of Hawaii Regional Cuisine, segued seamlessly from his smallish, Big Island upcountry enclave to this large, high-volume, open-air dining room on the beach. Hula Grill offers a wide range of prices and choices. The menu includes Merriman's signature firecracker mahimahi, seafood pot stickers, and several different fresh-fish preparations, including his famous ahi poke rolls—lightly sautéed rare ahi wrapped in rice paper with Maui onions. At lunch the menu is more limited, with a choice of sandwiches, entrees, pizza, appetizers, and salads. There's happy-hour entertainment and Hawaiian music daily. The more casual Barefoot Bar, located on the beach, offers burgers, fish, pizza, and salads.

In Whalers Village, 2435 Kaanapali Pkwy. ✆ **808/667-6636.** www.hulagrill.com. Reservations recommended for dinner. Lunch and Barefoot Bar menus $5.95–$12; dinner main courses from $13. AE, DC, DISC, MC, V. Daily 11am–11pm.

## INEXPENSIVE

**Whalers Village** has a food court where you can buy pizza, very good Japanese food, Korean plates, and fast-food burgers at serve-yourself counters and courtyard tables. It's an inexpensive alternative and a quick, handy stop for shoppers and Kaanapali beachgoers.

**Pizza Paradiso** PIZZA Pizza Paradiso took over the ice cream counter next door and expanded to include a full menu of pastas, pizzas, and desserts, including smoothies, coffee, and ice cream. The pizza reflects a simple and effective formula that has won acclaim through the years: good crust, true-blue sauces, and toppings loyal to tradition but with just enough edge for those who want it.

Create your own pizza with roasted eggplant, mushrooms, anchovies, artichoke hearts, spicy sausages, cheeses, and a slew of other toppings. Pizza Paradiso offers some heroic choices, from the "Veg Wedge" to the "Maui Wowie" (ham and Maui pineapple) and the "God Father" (roasted chicken, artichoke hearts, sun-dried tomatoes). Also popular is Pizza Paradiso's Honokowai location (see below), where award-winning pastas are part of the draw.

In Whalers Village, 2435 Kaanapali Pkwy. ✆ **808/667-0333.** www.pizzaparadiso.com. Gourmet pizza $3.65–$4.45 (by the slice); whole pizzas $12–$26. MC, V. Daily 11am–10pm.

## HONOKOWAI, KAHANA & NAPILI

### EXPENSIVE

**Roy's Kahana Bar & Grill/Roy's Nicolina Restaurant** ★ EURO-ASIAN These sibling restaurants are next door to each other, offer the same menu, and are busy, busy, busy. They bustle with young, hip servers impeccably trained to deliver blackened ahi or perfectly seared lemongrass *shutome* (broadbill swordfish) hot to your table, in rooms that sizzle with cross-cultural tastings. Both are known for their rack of lamb and fresh seafood (usually eight or nine choices), and for their large, open kitchens that turn out everything from pizza to sake-grilled New York steak. If polenta is on the menu, don't resist; on my last visit, the polenta was fabulous and rich, with garlic, cream, spinach, and wild mushrooms. Large picture windows open up Roy's Kahana but don't quell the noise, another tireless trait long ago established by Roy's Restaurant in Honolulu, the flagship of Yamaguchi's burgeoning empire. The restaurant has banquet facilities for up to 70 people, while Roy's Nicolina features dining on the lanai.

In the Kahana Gateway Shopping Center, 4405 Honoapiilani Hwy. ✆ **808/669-6999.** www.roysrestaurant.com. Reservations strongly recommended. Main courses $14–$31. AE, DC, DISC, MC, V. Roy's Kahana daily 5:30–10pm; Roy's Nicolina daily 5:30–9:30pm.

**Sea House Restaurant** ASIAN/PACIFIC The Sea House is not glamorous, famous, or hip, but it's worth mentioning for its gorgeous view of Napili Bay. It is spectacular. The Napili Kai Beach Club, where Sea House is located, is a charming throwback to the days when hotels blended in with their surroundings, had lush tropical foliage, and were sprawling rather than vertical. Dinner entrees come complete with soup or salad, vegetables, and rice or potato. The lighter appetizer menu is a delight—more than a dozen choices ranging from sautéed or blackened crab cake to crisp Pacific Rim sushi of ahi capped in nori and cooked tempura-style. On Friday nights, a Polynesian dinner show features the children of the Napili Kai Foundation, an organization devoted to supporting Hawaiian culture. They share top billing with the million-dollar view.

In Napili Kai Beach Resort, 5900 Honoapiilani Hwy. ✆ **808/669-1500.** Reservations required for dinner. Main courses $18–$49; appetizer menu $5–$14. AE, DISC, MC, V. Sun–Fri 8–10:30am, and noon–2pm; pupu menu Sat–Thurs 2–9pm, Fri 2–7:30pm, and 5:30–9pm (6–9pm in summer); Fri Polynesian Show 6–9pm.

## MODERATE

**Fish & Game Brewing Co. & Rotisserie** SEAFOOD/STEAK The restaurant consists of an oyster bar, deli counter and retail section, and tables. The small retail section sells fresh seafood, while the sit-down menu covers basic tastes: salads (Caesar, Asian chicken with won tons), fish and chips, fresh-fish sandwiches, cheeseburgers, and beer. At dinner, count on heavier meats and the fresh catch of the day (ahi, mahimahi, ono), with rotisserie items such as grilled chicken, steaks, and duck. The late-night menu offers shrimp, cheese fries, quesadillas, and lighter fare.

In the Kahana Gateway Shopping Center, 4405 Honoapiilani Hwy. ✆ **808/669-3474.** Reservations recommended for dinner. Main courses $6.95–$13 lunch, $14–$31 dinner. AE, DC, DISC, MC, V. Daily 11am–10pm; late-night menu 10:30pm–1am. During football season (Sept–Jan) brunch Sat–Sun 7:30am–3pm.

## INEXPENSIVE

In Honokowai, there's a branch of Pizza Paradiso (p. 89) in the Honokowai Marketplace, 3350 Lower Honoapiilani Rd. (✆ **808/667-2929**).

**Maui Tacos** *Kids* MEXICAN Mark Ellman's Maui Tacos chain has grown faster than you can say "Haleakala." Ellman put gourmet Mexican on paper plates and on the island's culinary map long before the island became known as Hawaii's center of salsa and chimichangas. Choices include excellent fresh-fish tacos (garlicky and flavorful), chimichangas, and mouth-breaking compositions such as the Hookipa, a "surf burrito" of fresh fish, black beans, and salsa and a personal favorite. The green-spinach burrito contains four kinds of beans, rice, and potatoes—it's a knockout, requiring a siesta afterward.

In Napili Plaza, 5095 Napili Hau St. ✆ **808/665-0222.** www.mauitacos.com. Items range from $1.65–$7. No credit cards. Daily 9am–9pm.

## KAPALUA

**The Bay Club** ★★ SEAFOOD The view of Molokai across the rolling surf of Kapalua Bay alone would be worth eating here, but luckily, the food, especially the seafood, promises a memorable dining experience. This intimate restaurant (with a piano bar at one end), originally designed as a private club, features such culinary masterpieces as steamed Kona lobster in banana leaf; ahi and cured salmon sashimi; macadamia-nut-crusted mahimahi with papaya pineapple salsa and passion fruit salsa; and Hawaiian seafood bouillabaisse (with lobsters, prawns, and local fish in a saffron broth). Save room for dessert (try the guava, mango, and litchi napoleon for an island-style treat). Service is impeccable, the wine list extensive. For those that just can't make up their minds, the chef can prepare a four-course tasting of the Bay Club's signature dishes.

1 Bay Dr., Kapalua ✆ **808/669-8008.** Reservations recommended. Main courses $33–$38. AE, DC, DISC, MC, V. Daily 6–9pm.

**Plantation House Restaurant** ★★ SEAFOOD/HAWAIIAN-MEDITERRANEAN With its teak tables, fireplace, and open sides, Plantation House gets stellar marks for atmosphere. The 360 degree hilltop view takes in Molokai and Lanai, the ocean, the rolling fairways and greens, the northwestern flanks of the West Maui Mountains, and the daily sunset spectacular. Readers of the *Maui News* have given it the island's "Best Ambience" award. It's the best place for breakfast in West Maui, hands down, and one of my top choices for dinner. The menu changes constantly but may include fresh fish prepared several ways—among them, Mediterranean (seared), Upcountry (sautéed with Maui onions and vegetable sauté), Island (pan-seared in sweet sake and macadamia nuts), and Rich Forest (with roasted wild mushrooms), the top seller. At breakfast, the Eggs Mediterranean is superb, and at lunch, sandwiches (open-faced smoked turkey, roasted vegetable, and goat cheese wrap) and salads rule. The dinner menu expands to marvelous starters such as polenta and scampi-style shrimp, crab cakes, Kula and Mediterranean salads, and a hearty entree selection of fish, pork tenderloin, roast duck, and filet mignon with apple-smoked Maui onion.

2000 Plantation Club Dr. (at Kapalua Plantation Golf Course). ✆ **808/669-6299.** www.theplantationhouse.com. Reservations recommended. Main courses $19–$30. AE, DC, MC, V. Daily 8am–3pm and 5:30–10pm.

**Sansei Seafood Restaurant and Sushi Bar** ★★ PACIFIC RIM Perpetual award-winner Sansei proffers an extensive menu of Japanese and East-West delicacies. Furiously fusion, part Hawaii Regional Cuisine, and all parts sushi, Sansei is tirelessly creative, with a menu that scores higher with adventurous palates than with purists (although there are endless traditional choices as well). Maki is the mantra here. If you don't like cilantro, watch out for those complex spicy crab rolls. Other choices include Panko-crusted ahi sashimi, sashimi trio, ahi carpaccio, noodle dishes, lobster, Asian rock-shrimp cakes, traditional Japanese tempura, and sauces that surprise, in creative combinations such as ginger-lime chili butter and cilantro pesto. But there's simpler fare as well, such as shrimp tempura, noodles, and wok-tossed upcountry vegetables. Desserts are not to be missed. If it's autumn, don't pass up persimmon crème brûlée, made with Kula persimmons. In other seasons, opt for tempura-fried ice cream with chocolate sauce.

At the Kapalua Shops, 115 Bay Dr. ✆ **808/669-6286.** www.sanseihawaii.com. Reservations recommended. Main courses $19–$29. AE, DISC, MC, V. Daily 5:30–10pm.

## 3 South Maui

To locate the following restaurants, see the map on p. 83.

### KIHEI/MAALAEA

There's a **Maui Tacos** (p. 91) at Kamaole Beach Center in Kihei (✆ **808/879-5005**).

### EXPENSIVE

**Buzz's Wharf** AMERICAN Buzz's is another formula restaurant that offers a superb view, substantial sandwiches, meaty french fries, and surf-and-turf fare—in a word, satisfying but not sensational. Still, this bright, airy dining room is a fine way station for whale-watching over a cold beer and a fresh mahimahi sandwich with fries. Some diners opt for several appetizers (stuffed mushrooms, steamer clams, clam chowder, onion soup) and a salad, then splurge on dessert. Buzz's prize-winning Tahitian Baked Papaya is a warm, fragrant melding of fresh papaya with vanilla and coconut—the pride of the house.

Maalaea Harbor, 50 Hauoli St. ✆ **808/244-5426.** Reservations recommended. Main courses $20–$33. AE, DC, DISC, MC, V. Daily 11am–9pm.

**Five Palms** ★ PACIFIC RIM This is the best lunch spot in Kihei—open-air, with tables a few feet from the beach and up-close-and-personal views of Kahoolawe and Molokini. You'll have to walk through a nondescript parking area and the modest entrance of the Mana Kai Resort to reach this unpretentious place. At lunch, salads, sandwiches, and pasta are the hot items: Kula greens; burgers; sandwiches on homemade focaccia; capellini with shiitake mushrooms, sun-dried tomatoes, and white wine sauce; and other appealing choices, including a perfectly grilled vegetable platter. At dinner, with the torches lit on the beach and the main dining room open, the ambience shifts to evening romantic, but still casual.

In the Mana Kai Resort, 2960 S. Kihei Rd. ✆ **808/879-2607.** Reservations recommended for dinner. Main courses $19–$49. AE, DC, MC, V. Daily 8am–2:30pm and 5–9pm.

**The Waterfront at Maalaea** ★★ SEAFOOD The family owned Waterfront has won many prestigious awards for wine excellence, service, and seafood, but its biggest boost is word of mouth. Loyal diners rave about the friendly staff and seafood, fresh off the boat in nearby Maalaea Harbor and prepared with care. The bay and harbor view is one you'll never forget, especially at sunset. You have nine choices of preparations for the several varieties of fresh Hawaiian fish, ranging from *en papillote* (baked in buttered parchment) to Southwestern (smoked chile and cilantro butter) to Cajun spiced and Island style (sautéed, broiled, poached, or baked and paired with tiger prawns). Other choices include Kula onion soup, an excellent Caesar salad, the signature lobster chowder, and grilled eggplant layered with Maui onions, tomatoes, and spinach, served with red-pepper coulis and Big Island goat cheese. Like the seafood, it's superb.

Maalaea Harbor, 50 Hauoli St. ✆ **808/244-9028.** Reservations recommended. Main courses $18–$35. AE, DC, DISC, MC, V. Opens daily at 5pm; last seating at 8:30pm.

## MODERATE

**Stella Blues Cafe** AMERICAN Stella Blues gets going at breakfast and continues through to dinner with something for everyone—vegetarians, kids, pasta and sandwich lovers, hefty steak eaters, and sensible diners who go for the inexpensive fresh Kula green salad. Grateful Dead posters line the walls, and a covey of gleaming motorcycles is invariably parked outside. It's loud and lively, irreverent, and unpretentious. Sandwiches are the highlight, ranging from Tofu Extraordinaire to Mom's Egg Salad on croissant to garden burgers and grilled chicken. Tofu wraps and mountain-size Cobb salads are popular, and for the reckless, large coffee shakes with mounds of whipped cream. Daily specials include fresh seafood and other surprises—all home-style cooking, made from scratch, down to the pesto mayonnaise and herb bread. At dinner, selections are geared toward good-value family dining, from affordable full dinners to pastas and burgers.

In Long's Center, 1215 S. Kihei Rd. ✆ **808/874-3779.** Main courses $9.95–$18. DISC, MC, V. Daily 8am–9pm.

## INEXPENSIVE

**Bubba's Burgers** BURGERS On the heels of his remarkable success on Kauai, Bubba has sprouted in South Maui. Half-pound Big Bubbas, Budweiser chili, and Hubba Bubbas (with rice, hot dogs, and chili) are among the heroic offerings fueling the beach-going crowd from this roadside cafe in Kihei. Fish and chips, tempeh burgers, and fresh fish specials are among the offerings of this house of Bubba, where plate lunches, burgers, and attitude aplenty provide good grinds with irreverent entertainment. (Bubba T-shirts are hilarious.)

1945 S. Kihei Rd. ✆ **808/891-2600.** www.bubbaburger.com. Burgers $2.75–$6.75. MC, V. Daily 10:30am–9pm.

**The Coffee Store** COFFEEHOUSE This simple, classic coffeehouse for caffeine connoisseurs serves 2 dozen different types of coffee and coffee drinks, from mochas and lattes to cappuccinos, espressos, and toddies. Breakfast items include smoothies, lox and bagels, quiches, granola, and assorted pastries. Pizza, salads, vegetarian lasagna, veggie-and-shrimp quesadillas, and sandwiches (garden burger, tuna, turkey, ham, grilled veggie panini) also move briskly from the take-out counter. The turkey-and-veggie wraps are a local legend. There are only a few small tables and they fill up fast, often with musicians and artists who've spent the previous evening entertaining at the Wailea and Kihei resorts.

In Azeka Place II, 1279 Kihei Rd. ✆ **808/875-4244.** www.mauicoffee.com. All items less than $8.50. AE, MC, V. Daily 6am–6pm.

**Peggy Sue's** *Kids* AMERICAN Just for a moment, forget that diet and take a leap. It's Peggy Sue's to the rescue! This 1950s-style diner has oodles of charm and is a swell place to spring for the best chocolate malt on the island. You'll also find sodas, shakes, floats, egg creams, milkshakes, and 14 flavors of made-on-Maui Roselani brand gourmet ice cream. Old-fashioned soda-shop stools, an Elvis Presley Boulevard sign, and jukeboxes on every Formica table serve as a backdrop for the famous burgers (and garden burgers), brushed with teriyaki sauce and served with all the goodies. The fries are great, too.

In Azeka Place II, 1279 S. Kihei Rd. ✆ **808/875-8944.** Burgers $6–$11; plate lunches $5–$12. DC, MC, V. Sun–Thurs 11am–9pm; Fri–Sat 11am–10pm.

**Shaka Sandwich & Pizza** PIZZA How many "best pizzas" are there on Maui? It depends on which shore you're on, the west or the south. At this south-shore old-timer, award-winning pizzas share the limelight with New York–style heroes and Philly cheese steaks, calzones, salads, homemade garlic bread, and homemade meatball sandwiches. Shaka uses fresh Maui produce, long-simmering sauces, and homemade Italian bread. Choose thin or Sicilian thick crust with gourmet toppings: Maui onions, spinach, anchovies, jalapeños, and a spate of other vegetables. Don't be misled by the whiteness of the white pizza; with the perfectly balanced flavors of olive oil, garlic, and cheese, you won't even miss the tomato sauce. Clam-and-garlic pizza, spinach pizza (with olive oil, spinach, garlic, and mozzarella), and the Shaka Supreme (with at least 10 toppings!) will satisfy even the insatiable.

1295 S. Kihei Rd. ✆ **808/874-0331.** Sandwiches $4.35–$11; pizzas $13–$26. No credit cards. Daily 10:30am–9pm.

## WAILEA

**The Shops at Wailea,** a sprawling location between the Grand Wailea Hotel and Outrigger Wailea Resort, has added a spate of new shops and restaurants to this stretch of south Maui. **Ruth's Chris Steak House** is here, as well as **Tommy Bahama's Tropical Cafe & Emporium, Honolulu Coffee Company, Cheeseburger, Mai Tai's and Rock-n-Roll,** and **Longhi's.** Next door at the Outrigger Wailea, **Hula Moons,** the retro-Hawaiian-themed restaurant, has reopened after a $3 million renovation and moved to the upper level of the lobby building, where it serves midpriced steak and seafood with an ocean view.

### VERY EXPENSIVE

**Spago** ★★ HAWAIIAN/CALIFORNIA/PACIFIC REGIONAL California meets Hawaii in this open air, contemporary-designed eatery featuring fresh, local Hawaii ingredients prepared under the culinary watch of master chef Wolfgang Puck. The room, formerly Seasons Dining Room, has been stunningly transformed into a sleek modern layout using stone and wood in the open-air setting overlooking the Pacific Ocean. The menu features traditional Hawaiian dishes with Puck's own brand of cutting-edge innovations. The unbelievable coconut soup with local lobster, keffir, chile, and galangal makes a great starter. For entrees, try the whole steamed fish served with chili, ginger, and baby choy sum; the incredible Kona lobster with sweet-and-sour banana curry, coconut rice, and dry-fried green beans; or the grilled côte de bouef with braised celery, armagnac, peppercorns, and pommes aligot. The wine and beverage list is well thought out and extensive. Save room for dessert (don't pass up the warm guanaja chocolate tart with Tahitian vanilla bean ice cream). Make reservations as soon as you land on the island, if not before—this place is popular.

Four Seasons Resort Maui, 3900 Wailea Alanui Dr., Wailea, 96753. ✆ **808/879-2999.** www.wolfgangpuck.com. Reservations required. Dinners average $75 per person. AE, DC, DISC, MC, V. Daily 5:30–9pm; bar with pupu daily 5–11pm.

## EXPENSIVE

**Joe's Bar & Grill** ★★ AMERICAN GRILL The 360 degree view spans the golf course, tennis courts, ocean, and Haleakala—a worthy setting for Beverly Gannon's style of American home cooking with a regional twist. The hearty staples include excellent mashed potatoes, lobster, fresh fish, and filet mignon, but the meat loaf (a whole loaf, like Mom used to make) seems to upstage them all. The Tuscan white bean soup is superb, and the tenderloin, with roasted portobellos, mashed potatoes with whole garlic, and a pinot noir demiglace, is American home cooking at its best. Daily specials could be grilled ahi with white truffle–Yukon mashed potatoes or sautéed mahimahi with shrimp bisque and sautéed spinach. If chocolate cake is on the menu, you should definitely spring for it.

In the Wailea Tennis Club, 131 Wailea Ike Place. ✆ **808/875-7767.** www.joesbarandgrill.com. Reservations recommended. Main courses $17–$30. AE, DC, DISC, MC, V. Daily 5:30–9pm.

**Longhi's** ★★ ITALIAN This is a great alternative to the high-priced restaurants in the surrounding resorts. The open-air restaurants, with restaurateur Bob Longhi's trademark black and white checkered floor, provide a great way to start the day. Breakfasts here are something you want to wake up to: perfect baguettes, fresh baked cinnamon rolls (one is enough for two people), and eggs Benedict or Florentine (with hollandaise for those not counting calories). Lunch is either an Italian banquet (ahi torino prawns amaretto and a wide variety of pastas) or fresh salads and sandwiches. Dinner (overlooking the water) is where Longhi shines, with a long list of fresh-made pasta dishes, seafood platters, and beef and chicken dishes (like filet mignon with béarnaise or veal sauté). Leave room for the daily dessert specials. Unlike Longhi's restaurant in Lahaina, this is not a verbal menu recited by your waitperson, but a real menu that you can hold and study as you plan your culinary adventure. If you come on Saturday night, stay for the live music; the place rocks until 1:30am.

The Shops at Wailea, 3750 Wailea Alanui Dr., Wailea ✆ **808/891-8883.** www.longhi-maui.com. Reservations for dinner recommended. Main courses $18–$30. AE, DC, MC, V. Mon–Fri 8am–10pm; Sat 7:30am–1:30am; Sun 7:30am–10pm.

**Nick's Fishmarket Maui** ★★★ SEAFOOD Hawaii's newest Nick's has the perfect balance of visual sizzle and memorable food. A private room with attractive murals seats 50, and the round bar, where you can sit facing the ocean, is highlighted with minimalist dangling amber lights, one of the friendliest touches in Wailea. Stephanotis vines create shade on the terrace, and the sunset views are superb. This is a classic seafood restaurant that sticks to the tried and true (*not* an overwrought menu) but stays fresh with excellent ingredients and a high degree of professionalism in service and preparation. The Greek Maui Wowie salad gets my vote as one of the top salads in Hawaii. The opakapaka has been a Nick's signature for eons; other choices include fresh salmon, scallops, Hawaiian lobster tails, and chicken, beef, and lamb dishes. I love the onion vichyssoise with taro swirl and a hint of *tobiko* (flying-fish roe), and the bow-tied servers bearing almond-scented cold towels.

In the Fairmont Kea Lani Hotel, 4100 Wailea Alanui. ✆ **808/879-7224**. www.tri-star-restaurants.com. Reservations recommended. Main courses $25–$50. Prix fixe dinners $55–$85. AE, DC, DISC, MC, V. Mon–Thurs 5:30–10pm; Fri–Sat 5:30–10:30pm, bar until 11pm.

## MODERATE

**Caffe Ciao** ★ ITALIAN There are two parts to this charming trattoria: the deli and take-out section, and the tables under the trees, next to the bar. Rare and wonderful wines, such as Vine Cliff, are sold in the deli, along with ultraluxe rose soaps and other bath products, assorted pastas, pizzas, roasted potatoes, vegetable panini, vegetable lasagna, abundant salads, and an appealing selection of microwavable and take-out goodies. On the terrace under the trees, the tables are cheerfully accented with Italian herbs growing in cachepots. ***A fave:*** the linguine pomodoro, with fresh tomatoes, spinach-tomato sauce, and a dollop of mascarpone.

In the Kea Lani Hotel, 4100 Wailea Alanui. ✆ **808/875-4100**. Reservations recommended. Main courses lunch $14–$20, dinner $16–$38; pizzas $15–$23. AE, DC, DISC, MC, V. Daily 11am–10pm, bar until 10pm.

**SeaWatch** ★ ISLAND CUISINE Under the same ownership as Kapalua's Plantation House Restaurant (p. 92), SeaWatch is a good choice from morning to evening, and it's one of the more affordable stops in tony Wailea. You'll dine on the terrace or in a high-ceilinged room, on a menu that carries the tee-off-to-19th-hole crowd with ease. From breakfast on, it's a celebration of island bounty, from the Maui onions on the bagels and lox to kalua pork and Maui onions in the scrambled eggs. We also like the crab cake Benedict with roasted pepper hollandaise. Lunchtime sandwiches, pastas, salads, wraps, and soups are moderately priced, and you get 360 degree views to go with them. The cashew chicken wrap with mango chutney is a winner, but if that's too Pan-Asian for you, try the tropical fish quesadilla or the grilled fresh-catch sandwich with Kula lime aioli. Save room for the bananas Foster.

100 Wailea Golf Club Dr. ✆ **808/875-8080.** www.seawatchrestaurant.com. Reservations required for dinner. Breakfast $3–$10; lunch $6.50–$12; dinner main courses $23–$28. AE, MC, V. Daily 8am–10pm.

### MAKENA

**Prince Court** ★★ CONTEMPORARY ISLAND Half of the Sunday brunch experience here is the head-turning view of Makena Beach, Molokini islet, and Kahoolawe island. The other half is the fabled Sunday buffet, bountiful and sumptuous, spread over several tables: pasta, omelets, cheeses, pastries, sashimi, crab legs, smoked salmon, fresh Maui produce, and a smashing array of ethnic and continental foods. The dinner menu changes regularly; recent winners are the steamed Manila Clams Scampi with roasted garlic, diced tomatoes, and fried basil; Dungeness crab and goat cheese won ton with Maui onion guacamole; and the Prince Court Sampler with Kona lobster cakes, kalua duck lumpia, and sugar-cane-speared grilled prawns. Game entrees (venison, rack of lamb, breast of duck) come in highly acclaimed preparations, such as poha (gooseberry) compote and black cherry Cabernet sauce.

In the Maui Prince Hotel, 5400 Makena Alanui. ✆ **808/874-1111.** Reservations recommended. Main courses $17–$30; Fri prime rib and seafood buffet $38 ($23 child); Sun brunch $36. AE, MC, V. Sun 9am–1pm; daily 6–9:30pm.

## 4 Upcountry Maui

### HALIIMAILE (ON THE WAY TO UPCOUNTRY MAUI)

**Haliimaile General Store** ★★★ *Kids* AMERICAN More than a decade later, Bev Gannon, one of the 12 original Hawaii Regional Cuisine chefs, is still going strong at her foodie haven in the pineapple fields. You'll dine at tables set on old wood floors under high ceilings (sound ricochets fiercely here), in a peach-colored room emblazoned with works by local artists. The food, a blend of eclectic American with ethnic touches, puts an innovative spin on Hawaii Regional Cuisine. Even the fresh-catch sandwich on the lunch menu is anything but prosaic. The sashimi napoleon and the house salad—island greens with mandarin oranges, onions, toasted walnuts, and blue-cheese crumble—are notable items on a menu that bridges Hawaii with Gannon's Texas roots.

Haliimaile Rd., Haliimaile. ✆ **808/572-2666.** www.haliimailegeneralstore.com. Reservations recommended. Lunch $7–$14; dinner $14–$28. DC, MC, V. Mon–Fri 11am–2:30pm; daily 5:30–9:30pm.

## MAKAWAO & PUKALANI

**Cafe O 'Lei** ★ AMERICAN/ISLAND Dana Pastula managed restaurants at Lanai's Manele Bay Hotel and the Four Seasons Resort Wailea before opening her tiny, charming outdoor cafe in this sunlit sliver of Makawao. And the alfresco dining is just part of it: From the sandwiches (roast chicken breast, turkey breast, prosciutto) and salads to the soup of the day, the offerings are homemade and excellent. The chic Makawao shopkeepers who lunch here never tire of the quinoa salad, the ginger chicken soup, the roasted-beet-and-potato soup, the curry chicken salad, and the talk of the town—a towering Asian salad of Oriental vegetables, tofu, and baby greens, tossed in a sesame vinaigrette with fresh mint, ginger, and lemongrass, and served over Chinese noodles. Our favorite? The shiitake mushroom soup with chicken long rice and the snow crab–avocado sandwich—too good to be true.

In the Paniolo Courtyard, 3673 Baldwin Ave. ✆ **808/573-9065.** Sandwiches and salads $4.95–$6.95. No credit cards. Mon–Sat 11am–4pm.

**Casanova Italian Restaurant** ★ ITALIAN The nexus of upcountry dining and nightlife, Casanova is Makawao's citadel of hip. It's casual, too, with terrific food and music and a tiny veranda with a few stools, always full, in front of a deli at Makawao's busiest intersection. The restaurant contains a stage, dance floor, restaurant, and bar—and food to love and remember. This is pasta heaven; try the spaghetti fradiavolo or the spinach gnocchi in a fresh tomato-Gorgonzola sauce. Other choices include a huge pizza selection, grilled lamb chops in an Italian mushroom marinade, every possible type of pasta, and luscious desserts. Our personal picks on a stellar menu: fresh Kula spinach sautéed with butter, pine nuts, and Parmesan; polenta with radicchio (the mushrooms and cream sauce are fabulous!); and tiramisu, the best on the island.

1188 Makawao Ave. ✆ **808/572-0220.** Reservations recommended for dinner. Main courses $10–$24; 12-in. pizzas from $10. DC, MC, V. Mon–Sat 11:30am–2pm and 5:30–9pm; Sun 5:30–9pm; dancing Wed–Sat 9:45pm–1am. Lounge daily 5:30pm–12:30am or 1am; deli daily 8am–6:30pm.

**Cow Country Cafe** AMERICAN/LOCAL Pukalani's inexpensive, casual, and very popular cafe features cows everywhere—on the walls, chairs, menus, aprons, even the exterior. But the real draw is the simple, home-cooked comfort food, such as meat loaf, roast pork, and humongous hamburgers, plus home-baked bread, oven-fresh muffins, and local faves such as saimin and Chinese chicken salad. Soups (homemade cream of mushroom), salads, and shrimp scampi with bow-tie pasta are among the cafe's other pleasures. The signature dessert is the cow pie, a naughty pile of chocolate cream cheese with macadamia nuts in a cookie crust, shaped like you-know-what.

In the Andrade Building, 7–2 Aewa Place (just off Haleakala Hwy.), Pukalani. ✆ **808/572-2395.** Lunch $5.95–$8.95; most dinner items less than $15. MC, V. Mon–Sat 7am–3pm and 5:30–9pm; Sun 7am–1pm.

## KULA (AT THE BASE OF HALEAKALA NATIONAL PARK)

### EXPENSIVE

**Kula Lodge** HAWAII REGIONAL/AMERICAN Don't let the dinner prices scare you; the Kula Lodge is equally enjoyable, if not more so, at breakfast and lunch, when the prices are lower and the views through the picture windows have an eye-popping intensity. The million-dollar vista spans the flanks of Haleakala, rolling 3,200 feet down to central Maui, the ocean, and the West Maui Mountains. The Kula Lodge has always been known for its breakfasts: fabulous eggs Benedict, including a vegetarian version with Kula onions, shiitake mushrooms, and scallions; legendary banana–macadamia nut pancakes; and a highly recommended tofu scramble with green onions, Kula vegetables, and garlic chives. If possible, go for sunset cocktails and watch the colors change into deep end-of-day hues. When darkness descends, a roaring fire and lodge atmosphere add to the coziness of the room. The dinner menu features "small plates" of Thai summer rolls, seared ahi, and other starters. Sesame-seared ono, Cuban-style spicy swordfish with rum-soaked bananas, and miso salmon with wild mushrooms are seafood attractions, but there's also pasta, rack of lamb, filet mignon, and free-range chicken breast.

Haleakala Hwy. (Hwy. 377). ✆ **808/878-2517.** Reservations recommended for dinner. Breakfast $7.50–$18; lunch $11–$18; dinner main courses $14–$28. AE, MC, V. Daily 6:30am–9pm.

### INEXPENSIVE

**Cafe 808** AMERICAN/LOCAL Despite its out-of-the-way location (or perhaps because of it), Cafe 808 has become the universal favorite among upcountry residents of all ages. The breakfast coffee group, the lunchtime crowd, kids after school, and dinner regulars all know it's the place for tasty home-style cooking with no pretensions: chicken lasagna, smoked-salmon omelet, famous burgers (teriyaki, hamburger, cheeseburger, garden burger, mahimahi, and taro), roast pork, smoked turkey, and a huge selection of local-style specials. Regulars rave about the chicken katsu, saimin, and beef stew. The few tables are sprinkled around a room with linoleum-tile floors, hardwood benches, plastic patio chairs, and old-fashioned booths—rough around the edges in a pleasing way, and very camp.

Lower Kula Rd., past Holy Ghost Church, across from Morihara Store. ✆ **808/878-6874.** Burgers from $3.50; main courses $4.50–$9.95. No credit cards. Daily 6am–8pm.

**Grandma's Coffee House** COFFEEHOUSE/AMERICAN Alfred Franco's grandmother started what is now a five-generation coffee business back in 1918, when she was 16 years old. Today, this tiny wooden coffeehouse, still fueled by homegrown Haleakala coffee beans, is the quintessential roadside oasis. Grandma's offers espresso, hot and cold coffees, home-baked pastries, inexpensive pasta, sandwiches (including sensational avocado and garden burgers), homemade soups, fresh juices, and local plate-lunch specials that change daily. Rotating specials include Hawaiian beef stew, ginger chicken, saimin, chicken curry, lentil soup, and sandwiches piled high with Kula vegetables. While the coffee is legendary, we think the real standouts are the lemon squares and the pumpkin bread.

At the end of Hwy. 37, Keokea (about 6 miles before the Tedeschi Vineyards in Ulupalakua). ✆ **808/878-2140.** Most items less than $8.95. MC, V. Daily 7am–5pm.

**Kula Sandalwoods Restaurant** ★ AMERICAN Chef Eleanor Loui, a graduate of the Culinary Institute of America, makes hollandaise sauce every morning from fresh upcountry egg yolks, sweet butter, and Myers lemons, which her family grows in the yard above the restaurant. This is Kula cuisine, with produce from the backyard and everything made from scratch, including French toast with home-baked Portuguese sweet bread; hotcakes or Belgian waffles with fresh fruit; baguettes; open-faced country omelets; hamburgers drenched in a special cheese sauce made with grated sharp cheddar; and an outstanding veggie burger. The grilled chicken breast sandwich is marvelous, served with soup of the day and Kula mixed greens. Dine in the gazebo or on the terrace, with dazzling views in all directions, including, in the spring, a yard dusted with lavender jacaranda flowers and a hillside ablaze with fields of orange akulikuli blossoms.

15427 Haleakala Hwy. (Hwy. 377). ✆ **808/878-3523.** Breakfast $6.95–$9.75; lunch $7.25–$13; Sun brunch $6.95–$9.75. MC, V. Mon–Sat 6:30am–2pm; Sun brunch 6:30am–noon.

## 5 East Maui: On the Road to Hana

### PAIA

#### MODERATE

**Moanai Bakery & Cafe** ★ LOCAL/EUROPEAN Moanai gets high marks for its stylish concrete floors, high ceilings, booths and cafe tables, and fabulous food. Don Ritchey, formerly a chef at Haliimaile General Store, has created the perfect Paia eatery, a casual bakery-cafe that highlights his stellar skills. All the bases are covered: saimin, omelets, wraps, pancakes, and fresh-baked goods in the morning; soups, sandwiches, pasta, and satisfying salads for lunch; and for dinner, varied selections with Asian and European influences and fresh island ingredients. The lemongrass-grilled prawns with green papaya salad are an explosion of flavors and textures, the roasted vegetable napoleon is gourmet fare, and the Thai red curry with coconut milk, served over vegetables, seafood, or tofu, comes atop jasmine rice with crisp rice noodles and fresh sprouts to cool the fire. Ritchey's Thai-style curries are richly spiced and intense. We also vouch for his special gift with fish: The nori-sesame crusted opakapaka, with wasabi beurre blanc, is cooked, like the curry, to perfection.

71 Baldwin Ave. ✆ **808/579-9999.** Reservations recommended for dinner. Breakfast $4.60–$9.95; lunch $5.95–$9.95; dinner main courses $7.95–$24. MC, V. Daily 8am–9pm.

#### INEXPENSIVE

**Cafe des Amis** ★ CREPES/SALADS This Paia newcomer quickly became known as the place for healthy and tasty lunches that are kind to the pocketbook. Crepes are the star here, and they are popular: spinach with feta cheese; scallops with garlic and chipotle chili; shrimp curry with coconut milk; and dozens more choices, including breakfast crepes and dessert crepes (like banana/chocolate, strawberries and cream, or caramelized apples with rum). Equally popular are the salads (including niçoise, Greek, and Caesar) and smoothies (like peach/banana/raspberry and mango/banana/pineapple). The crepes come with a house salad, and at $5.90 to $7.50, that's a deal.

42 Baldwin Ave. ✆ **808/579-6323.** Crepes $5.90–$7.50. DISC, MC, V. Mon–Sat 8:30am–8:30pm.

**Milagros Food Company** ★ SOUTHWESTERN/SEAFOOD Milagros has gained a following with its great home-style cooking, upbeat atmosphere, and highly touted margaritas. Sit outdoors and watch the parade of Willie Nelson look-alikes ambling by as you tuck into the ahi creation of the evening, a combination of Southwestern and Pacific Rim styles and flavors accompanied by fresh veggies and Kula greens. Blackened ahi taquitos, pepper-crusted ono pasta, blue shrimp tostadas, and sandwiches, salads, and combination plates are some of the offerings here. For breakfast, the Olive Oyl spinach omelet or the huevos rancheros, served with home fries, is recommended. We love Paia's tie-dyes, beads, and hippie flavor, and this is the front-row seat for it all. Watch for happy hour, with its cheap and fabulous margaritas.

Hana Hwy. and Baldwin Ave., Paia. ✆ **808/579-8755.** Breakfast around $7; lunch $6–$10; dinner $15–$20. DC, MC, V. Daily 8am–11pm.

**Paia Fish Market** SEAFOOD This really is a fish market, with fresh fish to take home and cooked seafood, salads, pastas, fajitas, and quesadillas to take out or enjoy at the few picnic tables inside the restaurant. It's an appealing and budget-friendly selection: Cajun-style fresh catch, fresh-fish specials (usually ahi or salmon), fresh-fish tacos and quesadillas, and seafood and chicken pastas. You can also order hamburgers, cheeseburgers, fish and chips (or shrimp and chips), and wonderful lunch and dinner plates, cheap and tasty. Peppering the walls are photos of the number one sport here, windsurfing.

110 Hana Hwy. ✆ **808/579-8030.** Lunch and dinner plates $6.95–$20. DISC, MC, V. Daily 11am–9:30pm.

**Pic-nics** SANDWICHES/PICNIC LUNCHES Breakfast is terrific here—omelets, eggs made to order, Maui Portuguese sausage, Hawaiian pancakes—and so is lunch. Pic-nics is famous for many things, among them the spinach-nut burger, an ingenious vegetarian blend topped with vegetables and cheddar cheese. Stop here to refresh yourself with a plate lunch or smoothie for the drive to Hana or upcountry Maui. The gourmet sandwiches (Kula vegetables, home-baked breast of turkey, Cajun chicken, Cajun fish) are worthy of the most idyllic picnic spot. The rosemary herb-roasted chicken can be ordered as a plate lunch or as part of the Hana Bay picnic, which includes sandwiches, meats, Maui-style potato chips, and home-baked cookies and muffins. You can order old-fashioned fish and chips, too, or shrimp and chips. Fresh breads and pastries add to the appeal, and several coffee drinks made with Maui-blend coffee may give you the jolt you need for the drive ahead.

30 Baldwin Ave. ✆ **808/579-8021.** Most items less than $6.95. MC, V. Daily 7am–5pm.

**The Vegan** GOURMET VEGETARIAN/VEGAN Wholesome foods with ingenious soy substitutes and satisfying flavors appear on a menu that dares you to feel healthy without feeling deprived. Pad Thai noodles are the best-selling item, cooked in a creamy coconut sauce and generously seasoned with garlic and spices. Curries, grilled polenta, pepper steak made of seitan (a meat substitute), and organic hummus are among the items that draw vegetarians from around the island. Proving that desserts are justly deserved, Vegan offers a carob cake and coconut milk–flavored tapioca pudding that hint of Thailand yet are dairy-free.

115 Baldwin Ave. ✆ **808/579-9144.** Main courses $7.95–$9.95. MC, V. Daily 11am–9pm.

## ELSEWHERE ON THE ROAD TO HANA

**Mama's Fish House** ★★ The restaurant's entrance, a cove with windsurfers, tide pools, white sand, and a canoe resting under palm trees, is a South Seas fantasy worthy of Gauguin. The interior features curved lauhala-lined ceilings, walls of split bamboo, lavish arrangements of tropical blooms, and picture windows to let in the view. With servers wearing Polynesian prints and flowers behind their ears, and the sun setting in Kuau Cove, Mama's mood is hard to beat. The fish is fresh (the fishermen are even credited by name on the menu) and prepared Hawaiian style, with tropical fruit or baked in a macadamia nut and vanilla bean crust, or in a number of preparations involving ferns, seaweed, Maui onions and roasted kukui nut. Menu items include mahimahi laulau with luau leaves (taro greens) and Maui onions, baked in ti leaves and served with kalua pig and Hanalei poi—the best. Deepwater ahi could be seared with coconut and lime, while ono "caught by Keith Nakamura along the 40-fathom ledge near Hana" comes in Hana ginger teriyaki with macadamia nuts and crisp Maui onion. Other special touches include the use of Molokai sweet potato, Hana breadfruit, organic lettuces, Haiku bananas, and fresh coconut, which evoke the mood and tastes of old Hawaii.

799 Poho Place, just off the Hana Hwy., Kuau. ✆ **808/579-8488.** Reservations recommended for lunch, required for dinner. Main courses $29–$59. AE, DC, DISC, MC, V. Daily 11am–3pm; light menu 3–4:45pm; and 4:45–9pm last seating.

**Nahiku Coffee Shop, Smoked Fish Stand, and Ti Gallery** ★ *Finds* SMOKED KABOBS What a delight to stumble across this trio of comforts on the long drive to Hana! The small coffee shop purveys locally made baked goods, several flavors of Maui-grown coffee, banana breads, organic tropical fruit smoothies, and the Original and Best Coconut Candy made by Hana character Jungle Johnny. Next door, the Ti Gallery sells locally made Hawaiian arts and crafts, such as pottery and koa wood vessels.

The barbecue smoker is our favorite part of the operation. It puts out superb smoked and grilled fish, fresh and locally caught. These are not jerky-like smoked meats; the process keeps the kabobs moist while retaining the smoke flavor. The teriyaki-based marinade, made by the owner, adds a special touch to the fish (ono, ahi, marlin). One of the biggest sellers is the kalua pig sandwich. Also a hit are the fish, beef, and chicken tacos, served with about six condiments, including cheese, jalapeños, and salsa. There are a few roadside picnic tables, or you can take your lunch to go for a beachside picnic in Hana.

Hana Hwy. (3/4 mile past mile marker 28). No phone. Kabobs $3 each. No credit cards. Coffee shop daily 9am–5:30pm; fish stand Fri–Wed 10am–5pm; gallery daily 10am–5pm.

**Pauwela Cafe** ★ *Finds* INTERNATIONAL It's easy to get lost while searching out this wonderful cafe, but it's such a find. This tiny cafe has a strong local following for many reasons. Becky Speere, a gifted chef, and her husband, Chris, a former food-service instructor at Maui Community College and a former sous chef at the Maui Prince Hotel, infuse every sandwich, salad, and muffin with finesse.

All breads are prepared in-house, including rosemary potato, Scottish country, French baguette, and green onion and cheese. The scene-stealing kalua turkey sandwich features moist, smoky shredded turkey, served with cheese on home-baked French bread and covered with a green-chili and cilantro sauce. For breakfast, eggs chilaquile are a good starter, with layers of corn tortillas, pinto beans, chilis, cheese, and herbs, topped with egg custard and served hot with salsa and sour cream. The cafe is 1.4 miles past the Haiku turnoff and a half-mile up on the left.

375 W. Kuiaha Rd., off Hana Hwy., past Haiku Rd., Haiku. ✆ **808/575-9242.** Most items less than $6.50. No credit cards. Mon–Sat 7am–3pm; Sun 8am–2pm.

## HANA

**Hana Ranch Restaurant** *Overrated* AMERICAN Part of the Hotel Hana-Maui operation, the Hana Ranch Restaurant is the informal alternative to the hotel's dining room. Dinner choices include New York steak, prawns and pasta, and Pacific Rim options like spicy shrimp won tons or the predictable fresh-fish poke. Affordable luncheon buffets include baked mahimahi, pita sandwiches, chicken stir-fry, cheeseburgers, and club and fresh-catch sandwiches. It's not an inspired menu, and the service can be practically nonexistent during lunch rush.

Hana Hwy. ✆ **808/248-8255.** Reservations required Fri–Sat. Main courses $18–$33. AE, DC, DISC, MC, V. Daily 7–10am and 11am–2pm; Fri–Sat 6–8pm. Take-out counter daily 6–10am and 11am–4pm.

# 5

# Fun in the Surf & Sun

This is why you've come to Maui—the sun, the sand, and the surf. In this chapter, we'll tell you about the best beaches, from where to soak up the rays to where to plunge beneath the waves for a fish's-eye view of the underwater world. We've covered a range of ocean activities on Maui, as well as our favorite places and outfitters for these marine adventures. Also in this chapter are things to do on dry land, including the best spots for hiking and the greatest golf courses.

## 1 Beaches

Hawaii's beaches belong to the people. All beaches are public property, and Hawaii state law requires all resorts and hotels to offer public right-of-way access (across their private property) to the beach, along with public parking. For beach toys and equipment, contact the **Activity Warehouse** (✆ **800/343-2087;** www.travelhawaii.com), which has branches in Lahaina at 578 Front St., near Prison Street (✆ **808/667-4000**), and in Kihei at Azeka Place II, on the mountain side of Kihei Road near Lipoa Street (✆ **808/875-4000**). Beach chairs rent for $2 a day, coolers (with ice) for $2 a day, and a host of toys (Frisbees, volleyballs, and more) for $1 a day.

### WEST MAUI

#### KAANAPALI BEACH ★★

Four-mile-long Kaanapali is one of Maui's best beaches, with grainy gold sand as far as the eye can see. A paved beach walk links hotels and condos, open-air restaurants, and Whalers Village shopping center. Because Kaanapali is so long, the beach is crowded only in pockets—there's plenty of room to find seclusion. Summertime swimming is excellent.

Facilities include outdoor showers; you can use the restrooms at the hotel pools. Beach-activity vendors line up in front of the hotels, offering various water activities and equipment. There's fabulous snorkeling around **Black Rock,** in front of the Sheraton.

Parking is a problem, though. There are two public entrances: At the south end, turn off Honoapiilani Highway into the Kaanapali Resort, and pay for parking there, or continue on Honoapiilani Highway, turn off at the last Kaanapali exit at the stoplight near the Maui Kaanapali Villas, and park next to the beach signs indicating public access (this is limited to only a few cars, so to save time you might want to just head to the Sheraton or Whalers Village and plunk down your money).

### KAPALUA BEACH ★★★

The beach cove that fronts the Kapalua Bay Hotel is the stuff of dreams: a golden crescent bordered by two palm-studded points, with crystal-clear water and a gently-sloping sandy bottom. Kapalua's calm waters are great for snorkelers and swimmers of all ages and abilities, and the bay is big enough to paddle a kayak around without getting into the more challenging channel that separates Maui from Molokai. Waves come in just right for riding.

The beach is accessible from the hotel on one end, which provides sun chairs with shades and a beach-activities center for its guests, and a public access way on the other. The inland side is edged by a shady path and cool lawns. Outdoor showers are stationed at both ends. You'll also find restrooms, lifeguards, a rental shack, and plenty of shade.

Parking is limited to about 30 spaces in a small lot off Lower Honoapiilani Road, by Napili Kai Beach Club, so arrive early; next door is a nice but somewhat pricey oceanfront restaurant, Kapalua's Bay Club.

## SOUTH MAUI

### KAMAOLE III BEACH PARK ★

Three beach parks—Kamaole I, II, and III—stand like golden jewels in the front yard of the funky seaside town of Kihei. All three are popular with local residents and visitors because they're easily accessible. On weekends they're jam-packed with fishermen, picnickers, swimmers, and snorkelers.

The most popular is Kamaole III, or "Kam-3," as locals say. Swimming is safe here, but scattered lava rocks are toe stubbers at the water line, and parents should watch to make sure that kids don't venture too far out, because the bottom slopes off quickly. Both the north and south shores are rocky fingers with a surge big enough to attract fish and snorkelers, and the winter waves attract bodysurfers. Kam-3 is also a wonderful place to watch the sunset.

Facilities include restrooms, showers, picnic tables, barbecue grills, and lifeguards. There's also plenty of parking on South Kihei Road, across from the Maui Parkshore condos.

### WAILEA BEACH ★★

Wailea is the best golden-sand crescent on Maui's sunbaked southwestern coast. One of five beaches within Wailea Resort, Wailea is big, wide, and protected on both sides by black lava points. It's the front yard of the Four Seasons Wailea and the Grand Wailea Resort Hotel and Spa. From the beach, the view out to sea is magnificent, framed by neighboring Kahoolawe and Lanai and the tiny crescent of Molokini, probably the most popular snorkel spot in these parts. The clear waters tumble to shore in waves just the right size for gentle riding, with or without a board. From shore, you can see Pacific humpback whales in season (Dec–Apr), and unreal sunsets. Facilities include restrooms, outdoor showers, and limited free parking at the blue SHORELINE ACCESS sign, on Wailea Alanui Drive.

### ULUA BEACH ★

One of the most popular beaches in Wailea, Ulua is a long, wide, crescent-shaped gold-sand beach between two rocky points. When the ocean is calm, Ulua offers Wailea's best snorkeling; when it's rough, the waves are excellent for bodysurfers. The ocean bottom is shallow and gently slopes down to deeper waters, making swimming generally safe. In high season (late Dec–Mar and June–Aug), the beach is carpeted with beach towels. Facilities include showers and restrooms. A variety of equipment is available for rent at the nearby Wailea Ocean Activity Center. To find Ulua, look for the blue SHORELINE ACCESS sign on South Kihei Road, near Stouffer Wailea Beach Resort. A tiny parking lot is nearby.

### MALUAKA BEACH (MAKENA BEACH) ★★

On the southern end of Maui's resort coast, development falls off dramatically, leaving a wild, dry countryside of green kiawe trees. Near the Maui Prince hotel is Maluaka Beach, often called Makena, notable for its beauty and its views of Molokini Crater, the offshore islet, and Kahoolawe, the so-called "target" island. It's a short, wide, palm-fringed crescent of golden, grainy sand set between two black-lava points and bounded by big sand dunes topped by a grassy knoll. Swimming in this mostly calm bay is considered the best on Makena Bay. Facilities include restrooms, showers, a landscaped park, lifeguards, and roadside parking. Along Makena Alanui, look for the SHORELINE ACCESS sign near the hotel, turn right, and head down to the shore.

### ONELOA BEACH (BIG BEACH) ★★

Oneloa, which means "long sand" in Hawaiian, is 3,300 feet long and more than 100 feet wide. Mauians, who call it Big Beach, come here to swim, fish, sunbathe, surf, and enjoy the view of Kahoolawe and Lanai. Snorkeling is good around the north end at the foot of Puu Olai, a 360-foot cinder cone. During storms, however, big waves lash the shore and a strong rip current sweeps the sharp drop-off, making swimming dangerous. There are no facilities except portable toilets, but there's plenty of parking. To get here, drive past the Maui Prince Hotel to the second dirt road, which leads through a kiawe thicket to the beach.

On the other side of Puu Olai is **Little Beach,** a small pocket beach where nudists work on their all-over tans, to the chagrin of uptight authorities who take a dim view of public nudity.

## EAST MAUI

### HOOKIPA BEACH PARK ★

Two miles past Paia, on the Hana Highway, you'll find one of the most famous windsurfing sites in the world. Due to its constant winds and endless waves, Hookipa attracts top windsurfers and wave jumpers from around the globe. Surfers and fishermen also enjoy this small, gold-sand beach at the foot of a grassy cliff. Except when international competitions are being held, weekdays are the best time to watch the daredevils fly over the waves. When the water is flat, snorkelers and divers explore the reef. Facilities include restrooms, showers, pavilions, picnic tables, barbecue grills, and a parking lot.

### WAIANAPANAPA STATE PARK ★

Four miles before Hana, off the Hana Highway, is this beach park. The park's 120 acres have 12 cabins (p. 77), a caretaker's residence, a beach park, picnic tables, barbecue grills, restrooms, showers, a parking lot, a shoreline hiking trail, and a black-sand beach (it's actually small black pebbles). This is a wonderful area for both shoreline hikes (mosquitoes are plentiful, so bring insect repellent) and picnicking. Swimming is generally unsafe due to powerful rip currents and strong waves breaking offshore, which roll into the beach unchecked. Waianapanapa is crowded on weekends with local residents and their families, as well as tourists; weekdays are generally a better bet.

### HAMOA BEACH ★★

This half-moon–shaped, gray-sand beach (a mix of coral and lava) in a truly tropical setting is a favorite among sunbathers seeking rest and refuge. The Hotel Hana-Maui maintains the beach and acts as though it's private, which it isn't—so just march down the lava-rock steps and grab a spot on the sand. The 100-foot-wide beach is three football fields long and sits below 30-foot black-lava sea cliffs. An unprotected beach open to the ocean, Hamoa is often swept by powerful rip currents. Surf breaks offshore and rolls ashore, making this a popular surfing and bodysurfing area. The calm left side is best for snorkeling in summer. The hotel has numerous facilities for guests; there's an outdoor shower and restrooms for nonguests. Parking is limited. Look for the Hamoa Beach turnoff from Hana Highway.

## 2 Watersports

**Activity Warehouse** (✆ **800/343-2087;** www.travelhawaii.com), which has branches in Lahaina at 578 Front St., near Prison Street (✆ **808/667-4000**), and in Kihei at Azeka Place II, on the mountain side of Kihei Road near Lipoa Street (✆ **808/875-4000**), rents everything from beach chairs and coolers to kayaks, Boogie Boards, and surfboards.

**Snorkel Bob's** (www.snorkelbob.com) has snorkel gear, boogie boards, and other ocean toys at three locations: 1217 Front St., Lahaina (✆ **808/661-4421**); Napili Village, 5425-C Lower Honoapiilani Hwy., Napili (✆ 808/669-9603); and Kamaole Beach Center, 2411 S. Kihei Rd., Kihei (✆ 808/879-7449). All locations are open daily from 8am to 5pm.

### BOATING & SAILING

For information on snorkel cruises to Molokini, see "Snorkeling" on p. 114. For fishing charters, see "Sportfishing" on p. 117. For trips that combine snorkeling with whale-watching, see "Whale-Watching Cruises" on p. 119.

**America II** ★ This U.S. contender in the 1987 America's Cup race is a true racing boat, a 65-foot sailing yacht offering 2-hour **morning sails, afternoon sails,** and **sunset sails** year-round, plus **whale-watching** in winter. These are sailing trips, so there's no snorkeling—just the thrill of racing with the wind. Complimentary bottled water, soda, and chips are available.

Lahaina Harbor, slip 5. ✆ **888/667-2133** or 808/667-2195. www.galaxymall.com/stores/americaii. Trips $33 adults, $16 children under 13; whale-watching $30 adults, $15 children.

**Scotch Mist Sailing Charters** This 50-foot Santa Cruz sailboat offers 2-hour sailing adventures. Prices include snorkel gear, juice, fresh pineapple spears, Maui chips, beer, wine, and soda.

Lahaina Harbor, slip 2. ✆ **808/661-0386.** www.scotchmistsailingcharters.com. Sail trips $35 adults, $18 children 5–12; sunset sail $45.

## OCEAN KAYAKING

Ocean kayaking allows you to see Maui from the sea the way the early Hawaiians did. One of Maui's best kayak routes is along the **Kihei Coast,** where there's easy access to calm water. Early mornings are always best, because the wind comes up around 11am, making seas choppy and paddling difficult.

The **Activity Warehouse** (✆ **800/343-2087;** www.travelhawaii.com), which has branches in Lahaina at 578 Front St., near Prison Street (✆ **808/667-4000**), and in Kihei at Azeka Place II, on the mountain side of Kihei Road near Lipoa Street (✆ **808/875-4000**), rents one-person kayaks for $10 a day, and two-person kayaks for $15 a day.

For the uninitiated, our favorite kayak-tour operator is **Makena Kayak Tours** ★ (✆ **877/879-8426** or 808/879-8426; makenakyak@aol.com). Professional guide Dino Ventura leads a 2½-hour trip from Makena Landing. His wonderful tour will be a highlight of your vacation. It costs $55, including refreshments and snorkel and kayak equipment.

**South Pacific Kayaks,** 2439 S. Kihei Rd., Kihei (✆ **800/776-2326** or 808/875-4848; www.mauikayak.com), is Maui's oldest kayak-tour company. Its expert guides lead trips that include lessons, a guided tour, and snorkeling. Tours run from 2½ to 5 hours and range in price from $55 to $89. South Pacific also offers kayak rentals starting at $30 a day.

In Hana, **Hana-Maui Sea Sports** (✆ **808/248-7711**) runs 2-hour tours of Hana's coastline on wide, stable "no roll" kayaks for $118 per person.

## SCUBA DIVING

Some people come to Maui for the sole purpose of exploring its underwater world. You can see the great variety of tropical marine life (more than 100 endemic species), explore sea caves, and swim with sea turtles and monk seals in the clear tropical waters off the island. Trade winds often rough up the seas in the afternoon, so most dive operators schedule early morning dives that end at noon.

Unsure about scuba diving? Take an introductory dive; most operators offer no-experience-necessary dives, ranging from $95 to $125. You can learn from this glimpse into the sea world whether diving is for you.

Everyone dives **Molokini,** a marine-life park and one of Hawaii's top dive spots. This crescent-shaped crater has three tiers of diving: a 35-foot plateau inside the crater basin (used by beginning divers and snorkelers), a wall sloping to 70 feet just beyond the inside plateau, and a sheer wall on the outside and backside of the crater that plunges 350 feet. This underwater park is very popular thanks to calm, clear, protected waters and an abundance of marine life.

**Ed Robinson's Diving Adventures** ★ (✆ **800/635-1273** or 808/879-3584; www.mauiscuba.com) is the only Maui company rated one of *Scuba Diver* magazine's top 10 best dive operators for 5 years straight. Ed, a widely published underwater photographer, offers specialized charters for small groups. Two-tank dives range from $110 to $120 ($5–$15 extra for equipment); his dive boats depart from Kihei Boat Ramp.

If Ed is booked, call **Severns Diving** ★ (✆ **808/879-6596;** www.mikesevernsdiving.com), for small, personal diving tours on a 38-foot Munson/Hammerhead boat with freshwater shower. Pauline Fiene-Severns is a biologist who makes diving in Hawaii not only fun but also educational. In her 25-plus years of operation, the company has been accident-free. Two-tank dives are $120 (with equipment).

Stop by any location of the **Maui Dive Shop** ★ (www.mauidiveshop.com), Maui's largest diving retailer, which offers everything from rentals to scuba-diving instruction to dive-boat charters. They'll give you a free copy of the 24-page *Maui Dive Guide,* which has maps and details about the 20 best shoreline and offshore dives and snorkeling sites, all ranked for beginner, intermediate, or advanced snorkelers/divers. This operation has locations in Kihei at Azeka Place II Shopping Center, 1455 S. Kihei Rd. (✆ **808/879-3388**), and at the Kamaole Shopping Center (✆ 808/879-1533); in Lahaina at the Lahaina Cannery Mall (✆ 808/661-5388); and in the Honokowai Market Place (✆ 808/661-6166). Other locations include Whalers Shopping Village, Kaanapali (✆ 808/661-5117), and Kahana Gateway, Kahana (✆ 808/669-3800).

## SNORKELING

Snorkeling is the main attraction in Maui—and almost anyone can do it. All you need are a mask, a snorkel, fins, and some basic swimming skills. Floating over underwater worlds through colorful clouds of tropical fish is like a dream. In many places, all you have to do is wade into the water and look down.

### *Tips* Safe Snorkeling

Safety is key when snorkeling. Always go with a buddy. Look up every once in a while to how far offshore you are and whether there's any boat traffic. Don't touch anything; not only can you damage coral, but camouflaged fish and shells with poisonous spines might surprise you. Always check with a dive shop, lifeguards, and others on the beach about conditions in the area in which you plan to snorkel. If you're not a good swimmer, wear a life jacket or other flotation device.

**Snorkel Bob's** ★ (www.snorkelbob.com) and the **Activity Warehouse** will rent you everything you need; see the introduction to this section for locations. Also see "Scuba Diving" (above) for Maui Dive Shop's free booklet on great snorkeling sites.

Maui's best snorkeling beaches include **Kapalua Beach; Black Rock,** at Kaanapali Beach, in front of the Sheraton; along the Kihei coastline, especially at **Kamaole III Beach Park;** and along the Wailea coastline, particularly at **Ulua Beach.** Mornings are best, because local winds don't kick in until around noon. **Olowalu** has great snorkeling around the **14-mile marker,** where there is a turtle cleaning station about 50 to 75 yards out from shore. Turtles line up here to have cleaner wrasses pick off small parasites.

**Ahihi-Kinau Natural Preserve** is another terrific place; it requires more effort to reach it, but it's worth it. You can't miss in Ahihi Bay, a 2,000-acre state natural area reserve in the lee of Cape Kinau, on Maui's rugged south coast, where Haleakala spilled red-hot lava that ran to the sea in 1790. Fish are everywhere in this series of rocky coves and black-lava tide pools. To get here, drive south of Makena past Puu Olai to Ahihi Bay, where the road turns to gravel and sometimes seems like it'll disappear under the waves. At Cape Kinau, there are three four-wheel-drive trails that lead across the lava flow; take the shortest one, nearest La Pérouse Bay. If you have a standard car, drive as far as you can, park, and walk the remainder of the way.

## SNORKEL CRUISES TO MOLOKINI

The crater of **Molokini** ★ sits almost midway between Maui and the uninhabited island of Kahoolawe. Tilted so that only the thin rim of its southern side shows above water in a perfect semicircle,

Molokini stands like a scoop against the tide, and it serves, on its concave side, as a natural sanctuary for tropical fish and snorkelers, who commute daily in a fleet of dive boats to this marine-life preserve. Note that in high season, Molokini can be crowded with dozens of boats, each carrying scores of snorkelers.

**Maui Classic Charters** ★★ Maui Classic Charters offers morning and afternoon **snorkel-sail cruises to Molokini** on *Four Winds II,* a 55-foot, glass-bottom catamaran, for $72 adults ($47 children 3–12) for the morning sail and $40 adults ($30 children) in the afternoon. *Four Winds* trips include a continental breakfast; a barbecue lunch; complimentary beer, wine, and soda; complimentary snorkeling gear and instruction; and sportfishing along the way.

Those looking for speed should sign up for a trip on the fast, state-of-the-art catamaran *Maui Magic.* The company offers a 5-hour snorkel journey to both Molokini and La Pérouse for $99 for adults and $79 for children ages 5 to 12, including a continental breakfast, barbecue lunch, beer, wine, soda, snorkel gear, and instruction. During **whale season** (Dec 22–Apr 22), the Maui Magic Whale Watch, a 1½-hour trip with beverages, is $29 for adults and $24 for children 3 to 12.

Maalaea Harbor, slip 55 and slip 80. ✆ **800/736-5740** or 808/879-8188. www.mauicharters.com. Prices vary depending on cruise.

**Ocean Activities Center** ★ In season, this activities center runs 2-hour **whale-watching cruises** on its own spacious 65-foot catamaran; trips range from $25 to $32 for adults and $15 to $20 for children ages 3 to 12. The best deal to **Molokini** is the 5-hour Maka Kai cruise, which includes a continental breakfast, deli lunch, snorkel gear, and instruction; it's $60 for adults, $50 for teenagers, and $40 for children ages 3 to 12. Trips leave from Maalaea Harbor, slip 62. They also have a sportfishing charter boat (6-hr. shared boat starts at $135) and bottom fishing cruises for $95 per angler.

1847 S. Kihei Rd., Kihei. ✆ **800/798-0652** or 808/879-4485. www.mauioceanactivities.com. Prices vary depending on cruise.

**Pride of Maui** For a high-speed, action-packed snorkel-sail experience, consider the *Pride of Maui.* These 5½-hour **snorkel cruises** take in not only **Molokini,** but also Turtle Bay and Makena for more snorkeling. Continental breakfast, barbecue lunch, gear, and instruction are included.

Maalaea Harbor. ✆ **877/TO-PRIDE** or 808/875-0955. www.gopride.com. Trips $86 adults, $53 children 3–12.

## SPORTFISHING

Marlin (as big as 1,200 lb.), tuna, ono, and mahimahi await the baited hook in Maui's coastal and channel waters. No license is required; just book a sportfishing vessel out of Lahaina or Maalaea harbors. Most charter boats carry a maximum of six passengers. You can walk the docks, inspecting boats and talking to captains and crews, or book through an activities desk or one of the outfitters recommended below.

Shop around: Prices vary widely according to the boat, the crowd, and the captain. A shared boat for a half day of fishing starts at $100; a shared full day of fishing starts at around $140. A half-day exclusive (you get the entire boat) is around $400 to $700; a full-day exclusive boat can range from $500 to $1,000. Also, many boat captains tag and release marlin or keep the fish for themselves (sorry, that's Hawaii style). If you want to keep your catch, tell the captain before you go.

The best booking desk in the state is **Sportfish Hawaii** ★ (✆ **877/388-1376** or 808/396-2607; www.sportfishhawaii.com), which not only books boats on Maui, but on all islands. These fishing vessels have been inspected and must meet rigorous criteria to guarantee that you will have a great time. Prices range from $800 to $1,000 for a full-day exclusive charter (you, plus 5 friends, get the entire boat to yourself), $600 to $675 for a half-day exclusive.

## SURFING

Always wanted to learn to surf, but didn't know whom to ask? Call the **Nancy Emerson School of Surfing** (✆ **808/244-SURF** or 808/874-1183; www.surfclinics.com). Nancy has been surfing since 1961, and has pioneered a new instructional technique called "Learn to Surf in One Lesson"—you can, really. It's $70 per person for a 2-hour group lesson; private 2-hour classes are $140.

In Hana, **Hana-Maui Sea Sports** (✆ **808/248-7711**) has private lessons taught by a certified ocean lifeguard for $79 for a 2-hour lesson.

Expert surfers visit Maui in winter when the surf's really up. The best surfing beaches include **Honolua Bay, Lahaina Harbor** (in summer, there'll be waves just off the channel entrance with a south swell), **Maalaea** (a clean, world-class left), and **Hookipa Beach,** where surfers get the waves until noon; after that—in a carefully worked-out compromise to share this prized surf spot—the windsurfers take over.

## WHALE-WATCHING

Every winter, pods of Pacific humpback whales make the 3,000-mile swim from the chilly waters of Alaska to bask in Maui's summery shallows, fluking, spy hopping, spouting, and having an all-around swell time. The whale-watching season usually begins in January and lasts until April or sometimes May. About 1,500 to 3,000 humpback whales appear in Hawaii waters each year.

### WHALE-WATCHING FROM SHORE

Between mid-December and April, you can just look out to sea. There's no best time of day for whale-watching, but the whales seem to appear when the sea is glassy and the wind calm. Once you see one, keep watching in the same vicinity; they might stay down for 20 minutes. Bring a book—and binoculars, if you can. You can rent binoculars for $2 a day at the **Activity Warehouse** (✆ **800/343-2087;** www.travelhawaii.com), which has branches in Lahaina at 578 Front St., near Prison Street (✆ **808/667-4000**), and in Kihei at Azeka Place II, on the mountain side of Kihei Road near Lipoa Street (✆ **808/875-4000**). Some good whale-watching points on Maui are:

**McGregor Point** On the way to Lahaina, there's a scenic lookout at mile marker 9 (just before you get to the Lahaina Tunnel); it's a good viewpoint to scan for whales.

**Outrigger Wailea Resort** On the Wailea coastal walk, stop at this resort to look for whales through the telescope installed as a public service by the Hawaiian Islands Humpback Whale National Marine Sanctuary.

**Olowalu Reef** Along the straight part of Honoapiilani Highway, between McGregor Point and Olowalu, you'll often spot whales leaping out of the water. Sometimes, their appearance brings traffic to a screeching halt: People abandon their cars and run down to the sea to watch, causing a major traffic jam. If you stop, pull off the road so that others can pass.

**Puu Olai** It's a tough climb up this coastal landmark near the Maui Prince Hotel, but you're likely to be well rewarded: This is the island's best spot for offshore whale-watching. On the 360-foot cinder cone overlooking Makena Beach, you'll be at the right elevation to see Pacific humpbacks as they dodge Molokini and cruise up Alalakeiki Channel between Maui and Kahoolawe. If you don't see one, you'll at least have a whale of a view.

## WHALE-WATCHING CRUISES

For a closer look, take a whale-watching cruise. The **Pacific Whale Foundation,** 101 N. Kihei Rd., Kihei (✆ **800/942-5311** or 808/879-8811; www.pacificwhale.org), is a nonprofit foundation in Kihei that supports its whale research by offering cruises and snorkel tours, some to Molokini and Lanai. They have 15 daily trips to choose from, and their rates for a 2-hour whale-watching cruise start at $20 for adults, $15 for children. Cruises are offered from December through May, out of both Lahaina and Maalaea harbors.

The **Ocean Activities Center** ★ (✆ **800/798-0652** or 808/879-4485), in season, runs 2-hour **whale-watching cruises** on its own spacious 65-foot catamaran; trips range from $25 to $32 for adults and $15 to $20 for children ages 3 to 12. The best deal to **Molokini** is the 5-hour Maka Kai cruise, which includes a continental breakfast, deli lunch, snorkel gear, and instruction; it's $60 for adults, $50 for teenagers, and $40 for children ages 3 to 12. Trips leave from Maalaea Harbor, slip 62. They also have a sportfishing charter boat (6-hr. shared boat starts at $135) and bottom fishing cruises for $95 per angler.

If you want to combine ocean activities, then a snorkel or dive cruise to Molokini, the sunken crater off Maui's south coast, might be just the ticket. You can see whales on the way there, at no extra charge. See "Scuba Diving" and "Boating & Sailing" earlier in this section.

## WINDSURFING

Maui has Hawaii's best windsurfing beaches. In winter, windsurfers from around the world flock to the town of **Paia** to ride the waves; **Hookipa Beach,** known all over the globe for its brisk winds and excellent waves, is the site of several world-championship contests. **Kanaha,** west of Kahului Airport, also has dependable winds. When the winds turn northerly, **Kihei** is the spot to be; some days, you can spot whales in the distance behind the windsurfers. The northern end of Kihei is best: **Ohukai Park,** the first beach as you enter South Kiehi Road from the northern end, has not only good winds, but also parking, a long strip of grass to assemble your gear, and good access to the water. Experienced windsurfers here are found in front of the **Maui Sunset** condo, 1032 S. Kihei Rd., near Waipuilani Street (a block north of McDonald's), which has great windsurfing conditions but a very shallow reef (not good for beginners).

**Hawaiian Island Surf and Sport,** 415 Dairy Rd., Kahului (✆ **800/231-6958** or 808/871-4981; www.hawaiianisland.com), offers lessons, rentals, and repairs. Other shops that offer rentals and lessons are **Hawaiian Sailboarding Techniques,** 425 Koloa St., Kahului (✆ **800/968-5423** or 808/871-5423; www.hstwindsurfing.com), with 2½-hour lessons from $69 and equipment rental from $46 a day; and **Maui Windsurf Co.,** 22 Hana Hwy., Kahului (✆ **800/872-0999** or 808/877-4816; www.maui-windsurf.com), which has complete equipment rental (board, sail, rig harness, and roof rack) from $45 and 1½- or 2½-hour lessons ranging from $69 to $75.

For daily reports on wind and surf conditions, call the **Wind and Surf Report** at ✆ **808/877-3611.**

## 3 Hiking

In the past 3 decades, Maui has grown from a rural island to a fast-paced resort destination, but its natural beauty largely remains; there are still many places that can be explored only on foot. Those interested in seeing the backcountry—complete with virgin waterfalls and remote wilderness trails—should head for Haleakala's upcountry or the tropical Hana coast.

For more information on Maui hiking trails and to obtain free maps, contact **Haleakala National Park,** P.O. Box 369, Makawao, HI 96768 (✆ **808/572-4400;** www.nps.gov/hale), and the **State Division of Forestry and Wildlife,** 54 S. High St., Wailuku, HI 96793 (✆ **808/984-8100;** www.hawaii.gov). For information on trails, hikes, and camping, and permits for state parks, contact the **Hawaii State Department of Land and Natural Resources,** State Parks Division, P.O. Box 621, Honolulu, HI 96809 (✆ **808/587-0300;** www.state.hi.us/dlnr); note that you can get information from the website but cannot obtain permits there. For information on Maui County Parks, contact **Maui County Parks and Recreation,** 1580-C Kaahumanu Ave., Wailuku, HI 96793 (✆ **808/243-7380;** http://www.co.maui.hi.us/departments/Parks/).

**TIPS ON SAFE HIKING** Most stream water must be treated before drinking because cattle, pigs, and goats have probably contaminated the water upstream. Bacterium leptospirosis, which is found in freshwater streams throughout the state, enters the body through breaks in the skin or through the mucous membranes. It produces flulike symptoms and can be fatal. Carry enough drinking water with you on your hikes or use tablets with hydroperiodide to purify water. Also, don't forget there is very little twilight in Maui when the sun sets—it gets dark quickly.

**GUIDED HIKES** If you'd like a knowledgeable guide to accompany you on a hike, you have a few good options. Hikes range from short easy strolls through the rainforest to all-day adventures. For information about rates and the types call **Maui Hiking Safaris** ★ (✆ **888/445-3963** or 808/573-0168; www.mauihikingsafaris.com), **Hike Maui** ★ (✆ **808/879-5270;** www.hikemaui.com), or **Maui Eco-Adventures** (✆ **877/661-7720** or 808/661-7720; www.ecomaui.com). For information on hikes given by the **Hawaii Sierra Club** on Maui, call ✆ **808/573-4147** (www.hi.sierraclub.org).

## HALEAKALA NATIONAL PARK ★★★

For complete coverage of the national park, see "House of the Sun: Haleakala National Park" in chapter 6.

### DAY HIKES FROM THE MAIN ENTRANCE

Aside from the difficult hike into the crater, the park has a few shorter and easier options. Anyone can take a half-mile walk down the **Hosmer Grove Nature Trail** ★, or you can start down **Sliding Sands Trail** for a mile or two (hiking the entire trail usually takes more than a day). Even this short hike can be exhausting at the high altitude. A good day hike is **Halemauu Trail** to Holua Cabin and back, an 8-mile, half-day trip. The park rangers offer two **guided hikes.** The 2-hour, 2-mile **Cinder Desert Hike** takes place Tuesday and Friday at 10am and starts from the Sliding Sands Trailhead at the end of the Haleakala Visitor Center parking lot. The 3-hour, 3-mile **Waikamoi Cloud Forest Hike** leaves every Monday and Thursday at 9am; it starts at the Hosmer Grove, just inside the park entrance, and traverses through the Nature Conservancy's Waikamoi Preserve.

### THE EAST MAUI SECTION OF THE PARK AT KIPAHULU (NEAR HANA)

**APPROACHING KIPAHULU FROM HANA** If you drive to Kipahulu, you'll have to approach it from the Hana Highway—it's not accessible from the summit. Always check in at the ranger station before you begin your hike; the staff can inform you of current conditions and share their wonderful stories about the history, culture, flora, and fauna of the area.

There are two hikes you can take here. The first is a short, easy half-mile loop along the **Kaloa Point Trail** (Kaloa Point is a windy bluff overlooking **Oheo Gulch**), which leads toward the ocean along pools and waterfalls and back to the ranger station. The clearly marked path leaves the parking area and rambles along the flat, grassy peninsula. Crashing surf and views of the Big Island of Hawaii are a 5-minute walk from the ranger station.

The second hike, although just a 4-mile round-trip, is steep. You'll want to stop and swim in the pools, so allow 3 hours. You'll be climbing over rocks and up steep trails, so wear hiking boots. Take water, snacks, swim gear, and insect repellent. Always be on the lookout for flash-flood conditions. This walk will pass two magnificent waterfalls, the 181-foot **Makahiku Falls** and the even bigger 400-foot **Waimoku Falls** ★. There's a pool on the top of the Makahiku Falls that's safe to swim in as long as the waters aren't rising. The trail starts at the ranger station.

**GUIDED HIKES** The rangers at Kipahulu conduct a 1-mile hike to the **Bamboo Forest** ★ at 9am daily; half-mile hikes or orientation talks are given at noon, 1:30, 2:30, and 3:30pm daily; and a 4-mile round-trip hike to **Waimoku Falls** takes place on Saturday at 9:30am. All hikes begin at the ranger station.

## SKYLINE TRAIL, POLIPOLI SPRINGS STATE RECREATION AREA ★

This is some hike—strenuous but worth every step if you like seeing the big picture. It's 8 miles, all downhill, with a dazzling 100-mile view of the islands dotting the blue Pacific, plus the West Maui Mountains, which seem like a separate island.

The trail is located just outside Haleakala National Park at Polipoli Springs National Recreation Area; however, you access it by going through the national park. The Skyline Trail starts just beyond the Puu Ulaula summit building on the south side of Science City and follows the southwest rift zone of Haleakala from its lunarlike cinder cones to a cool redwood grove. The trail drops 3,800 feet on a 4-hour hike to the recreation area, in the 12,000-acre Kahikinui Forest Reserve. If you'd rather drive, you'll need a four-wheel-drive vehicle to access the trail.

## THE POLIPOLI LOOP, POLIPOLI STATE PARK ★

The **Polipoli Loop** ★ is an easy, 5-mile hike that takes about 3 hours. Dress warmly; the loop is up at 5,300 to 6,200 feet, so it's cold, even in summer. To get here, take the Haleakala Highway (Hwy. 37) to Keokea and turn right onto Highway 337; after less than a half mile, turn on Waipoli Road, which climbs swiftly. After 10 miles, Waipoli Road ends at the Polipoli State Park campground. The well-marked trailhead is next to the parking lot, near a stand of Monterey cypress; the tree-lined trail offers the best view of the island.

The Polipoli Loop is really a network of three trails: Haleakala Ridge, Plum Trail, and Redwood Trail. After a half mile of meandering through groves of eucalyptus, blackwood, swamp mahogany, and hybrid cypress, you'll join the Haleakala Ridge Trail, which, about a mile into the trail, joins with the Plum Trail (named for the plums that ripen in June and July). It passes through massive redwoods and by an old Conservation Corps bunkhouse and a rundown cabin before joining up with the Redwood Trail, which climbs through Mexican pine, tropical ash, Port Orford cedar, and redwood.

## HANA-WAIANAPANAPA COAST TRAIL ★

This is an easy, 6-mile hike. Allow 4 hours to walk along this relatively flat trail, which parallels the sea, along lava cliffs and a forest of lauhala trees. The best time of day is in either the early morning or the late evening, when the light on the lava and surf makes for great photos and it's not too hot. The trail is in Waianapanapa State Park, on the outskirts of Hana. There's no formal trailhead; join the route at any point along the Waianapanapa Campground and go in either direction. Along the trail, you'll see remains of an ancient *heiau* (temple), stands of lauhala trees, caves, and a blowhole.

## WAIHEE RIDGE ★

This strenuous 3- to 4-mile hike, with a 1,500-foot climb, offers spectacular views of the valleys of the West Maui Mountains. Allow 3 to 4 hours for the round-trip hike. Pack a lunch, carry water, and pick a dry day, as this area can get so wet that portions of the trail are impassible. There's a picnic table at the summit with great views.

To get here from Wailuku, turn north on Market Street, which becomes the Kahekilii Highway (Hwy. 340) and passes through Waihee. Go just over 2½ miles from the Waihee Elementary School and look for the turnoff to the Boy Scouts' Camp Maluhia on the left. Turn into the camp and drive nearly a mile to the trailhead on Jeep road. About a third of a mile in, there will be another gate, marking the entrance to the West Maui Forest Reserve. A foot trail, kept in good shape by the State Department of Land and Natural Resources, begins here. The trail climbs to the top of the ridge, offering great views of the various valleys.

## 4 Great Golf

Golfers new to Maui should know that it's windy here, especially between 10am and 2pm, when winds of 10 to 15 mph are the norm. Play two to three clubs up or down to compensate for the wind factor. We also recommend bringing extra balls—the rough is thicker here and the wind will pick your ball up and drop it in very unappealing places (like water hazards).

If your heart is set on playing on a resort course, book at least a week in advance. Weekdays are usually your best bet for tee times. For the ardent golfer on a tight budget: Play in the afternoon, when discounted twilight rates are in effect. There's no guarantee you'll get 18 holes in, especially in winter when it's dark by 6pm, but you'll have an opportunity to experience these world-famous courses at half the usual fee.

If you don't bring your own, rent clubs from the **Activity Warehouse** (© **800/343-2087;** www.travelhawaii.com), which has branches in Lahaina at 602 Front St., near Prison Street (© **808/667-4000**), and in Kihei at Azeka Place II, on the mountain side of Kihei Road near Lipoa Street (© **808/875-4000**). Clubs go for $10 to $15 a day. **Golf Club Rentals** (© **808/665-0800;** www.maui.net/~rentgolf) offers custom-built clubs for men, women, and juniors in both right- and left-handed versions. Their rates are $15 to $25 a day. The company also offers lessons with pros starting at $125 for nine holes plus green fees.

For last-minute and discount tee times, call **Stand-by Golf** (© **888/645-BOOK** or 808/874-0600, www.stand-bygolf.com) between 7am and 9pm, Hawaii standard time. Stand-by offers discounted (by 10%–40%) and guaranteed tee times for same-day or next-day golfing.

### WEST MAUI

**Kaanapali Courses** ★ Both courses at Kaanapali offer a challenge to all golfers. The par-72, 6,305-yard **North Course** is a true Robert Trent Jones Sr. design: an abundance of wide bunkers, several long, stretched-out tees, and the largest, most contoured greens on Maui. The par-72, 6,250-yard **South Course** is an Arthur Jack Snyder design; although shorter than the North Course, it requires more accuracy on the narrow, hilly fairways.

Off Hwy. 30, Kaanapali. © **808/661-3691.** www.kaanapali-golf.com. Greens fees $150 (North Course), $142 (South Course); Kaanapali guests pay $130 (North), $117 (South); twilight rates for the South Course are $85 after noon for everyone;

after 2pm twilight rates are $77 (North), $74 (South) for everyone. At the first stoplight in Kaanapali, turn onto Kaanapali Pkwy.; the first building on your right is the clubhouse.

**Kapalua Resort Courses** ★★★ The views from these three championship courses are worth the greens fees alone. The par-72, 6,761-yard **Bay Course** (✆ **808/669-8820**) was designed by Arnold Palmer and Ed Seay. This course is a bit forgiving, with its wide fairways; the greens, however, are difficult to read. The par-71, 6,632-yard **Village Course** (✆ **808/669-8830**), another Palmer/Seay design, is the most scenic of the three courses. The **Plantation Course** (✆ **808/669-8877**), site of the Mercedes Championships, is a Ben Crenshaw/Bill Coore design. This 6,547-yard, par-73 course, set on a rolling hillside, is excellent for developing your low shots.

Off Hwy. 30, Kapalua. ✆ **877/KAPALUA.** Greens fees $180 ($125 for hotel guests) at the Village and Bay courses ($80 after 2pm); $220 ($135 for guests) at the Plantation Course ($85 after 2pm).

## SOUTH MAUI

**Elleair Maui Golf Club** Sitting in the foothills of Haleakala, offering spectacular ocean vistas from every hole, this course (formerly known as the Silversword Golf Club) is for golfers who love the views as much as the fairways and greens. It's very forgiving. ***Just one caveat:*** Go in the morning. Not only is it cooler, but more important, it's also much less windy. This is a fun course to play, with some challenging holes.

1345 Piilani Hwy. (near Lipoa St. turnoff), Kihei. ✆ **808/874-0777.** Greens fees $85; twilight rates (after 2pm) $65; 9-hole rates (after 3:30pm) $45.

**Makena Courses** ★★ Here you'll find 36 holes of "Mr. Hawaii Golf"—Robert Trent Jones, Jr.—at its best. Add to that spectacular views: Molokini islet looms in the background, humpback whales gambol offshore in winter, and the tropical sunsets are spectacular. The par-72, 6,876-yard **South Course** has a couple of holes you'll never forget. The view from the par-four 15th hole, which shoots from an elevated tee 183 yards downhill to the Pacific, is magnificent. The par-72, 6,823-yard **North Course** is more difficult and more spectacular. The 13th hole, located partway up the mountain, has a view that makes most golfers stop and stare. The next hole is even more memorable: a 200-foot drop between tee and green.

On Makena Alanui Dr., just past the Maui Prince Hotel. ✆ **808/879-3344.** Greens fees $125 ($90 for Makena Resort guests). Twilight fees (after 2pm) $85 ($75 for guests).

**Wailea Courses** ★★ There are three courses to choose from at Wailea. The **Blue Course,** a par-72, 6,758-yard course designed by Arthur Jack Snyder and dotted with bunkers and water hazards, is for duffers and pros alike. The wide fairways appeal to beginners, while the undulating terrain makes it a course everyone can enjoy. A little more difficult is the par-72, 7,078-yard championship **Gold Course,** with narrow fairways, several tricky dogleg holes, and the classic Robert Trent Jones, Jr. challenges: natural hazards, like lava-rock walls, and native Hawaiian grasses. The **Emerald Course,** also designed by Robert Trent Jones, Jr., is Wailea's newest, with tropical landscaping and a player-friendly design.

Wailea Alanui Dr. (off Wailea Iki Dr.), Wailea. ✆ **888/328-MAUI** or 808/875-7450. Greens fees $140 Blue Course ($115 resort guests), twilight $95 ($80 resort guests); $160 Gold Course ($115 resort guests); $150 Emerald Course ($125 resort guests).

### UPCOUNTRY MAUI

**Pukalani Country Club** This cool, par-72, 6,962-yard course at 1,100 feet offers a break from the resorts' high greens fees, and it's really fun to play. High handicappers will love this course, and more experienced players can make it more challenging by playing from the back tees.

360 Pukalani St., Pukalani. ✆ **808/572-1314.** Greens fees, including cart, $55 for 18 holes before 11am; $45 11am–2pm; $35 after 2pm. Take the Hana Hwy. (Hwy. 36) to Haleakala Hwy. (Hwy. 37) to the Pukalani exit; turn right onto Pukalani St. and go 2 blocks.

## 5 Biking, Horseback Riding & Tennis

### BIKING

Cruising down Haleakala, from the lunarlike landscape at the top, past flower farms, pineapple fields, and eucalyptus groves, is quite an experience. Numerous tour groups will drive you up to the top before dawn so you can see the amazing sunrise, then coast 37 miles down the 10,000-foot volcano. Wear layers of warm clothing, because there may be a 30°F (16°C) change in temperature from the top of the mountain to the ocean. Generally, tour groups will not take riders under 12, but younger children can ride along in the van that accompanies the groups, as can pregnant women. The trip usually costs between $100 and $140, which includes hotel pickup, transport to the top, bicycle and safety equipment, and meals.

Maui's oldest outfitter is **Maui Downhill** ★ (✆ **800/535-BIKE** or 808/871-2155; www.mauidownhill.com), which offers a sunrise safari bike tour, including continental breakfast and brunch, starting at $100. If it's all booked up, try **Maui Mountain Cruisers** (✆ **800/232-6284** or 808/871-6014; www.mauimountaincruisers.com) or **Mountain Riders Bike Tours** (✆ **800/706-7700** or 808/242-9739), each of which offer sunrise rides for $120 to $125.

If you want to avoid the crowd, call **Haleakala Bike Company** (✆ **888/922-2453;** www.bikemaui.com), which will outfit you with the latest gear and take you up to the top, but after making sure you are secure on the bike will let you ride down by yourself at your own pace. Trips range from $55 to $75; they also have bicycle rentals to tour other parts of Maui on your own.

If you want to venture out on your own, cheap rentals—$10 a day for cruisers and $20 a day for mountain bikes—are available from the **Activity Warehouse** (✆ **800/343-2087;** www.travelhawaii.com), which has branches in Lahaina at 602 Front St., near Prison Street (✆ **808/667-4000**), and in Kihei at Azeka Place II, on the mountain side of Kihei Road near Lipoa Street (✆ **808/875-4000**).

For information on bikeways and maps, get a copy of the Maui County Bicycle Map, which has information on road suitability, climate, trade winds, mileage, elevation changes, bike shops, safety tips, and various bicycling routes. The map is available for $7.50 ($6.25 for the map and $1.25 postage), bank checks or money orders only, from: Tri Isle R, C, and D Council, Attn: Bike Map Project, 200 Imi Kala St., Suite 208, Wailuku, HI 96793.

## HORSEBACK RIDING

Maui offers spectacular adventure rides through rugged ranchlands, into tropical forests, and to remote swimming holes. Contact **Adventure on Horseback** ★ (✆ **808/242-7445** or 808/572-6211; www.mauihorsewhisperer.com) or **Oheo Stables,** Kipahulu Ranch (a mile past Oheo Gulch), Kipahulu (✆ **808/667-2222;** www.mauihorse.com) for information on tours ranging from a couple hours to all day. If you'd like to ride down into Haleakala's crater, contact **Pony Express Tours** ★ (✆ **808/667-2200** or 808/878-6698; www.ponyexpresstours.com). We also recommend riding with **Mendes Ranch & Trail Rides** ★, 3530 Kahekili Hwy., 4 miles past Wailuku (✆ **808/244-7320;** www.mendesranch.com) on the 300-acre Mendes Ranch.

## TENNIS

Maui has excellent public tennis courts; all are free and available from daylight to sunset (a few are even lit for night play until 10pm). The courts are available on a first-come, first-served basis;

when someone's waiting, limit your play to 45 minutes. For a complete list of public courts, call **Maui County Parks and Recreation** (✆ **808/243-7230**).

Private tennis courts are available at most resorts and hotels on the island. The **Kapalua Tennis Garden and Village Tennis Center,** Kapalua Resort (✆ **808/669-5677;** www.kapaluamaui.com), charges $10 an hour for resort guests and $12 an hour for nonguests. The staff will match you up with a partner if you need one. In Wailea, try the **Wailea Tennis Club,** 131 Wailea Iki Place (✆ **808/879-1958**), with 11 Plexi-pave courts. Court fees are $27 for Wailea resort guests and $35 for nonguests.

6

# Seeing the Sights

There is far more to the Valley Isle than just sun, sand, and surf. Get out and see for yourself the otherworldly interior of a 10,000-foot volcanic crater; watch endangered sea turtles make their way to nesting sites in a wildlife sanctuary; wander back in time to the days when whalers and missionaries fought for the soul of Lahaina; and feel the energy of a thundering waterfall cascade into a serene mountain pool.

## 1 Central Maui

Central Maui isn't exactly tourist central; this is where real people live. You'll most likely land here and head directly to the beach. However, there are a few sights worth checking out if you need a respite from the sun and surf.

### KAHULUI

Next to Maui's busiest intersection in Kahului's new business park is the most unlikely place: **Kanaha Wildlife Sanctuary,** Haleakala Highway Extension and Hana Highway (© **808/984-8100**). Look for a parking area off Haleakala Highway Extension (behind the mall, across the Hana Hwy. from Cutter Automotive), and you'll find a 50-yard trail that meanders along the shore to a shade shelter and lookout. Watch for the sign proclaiming this the permanent home of the endangered black-neck Hawaiian stilt. Naturalists say this is a good place to see endangered Hawaiian Koloa ducks, stilts, coots, and other migrating shorebirds. For a quieter, more natural-looking wildlife preserve, try the **Kealia Pond National Wildlife Preserve** in Kihei (see "South Maui," later in this chapter).

### WAILUKU & WAIKAPU

Wailuku is worth a visit for some terrific shopping (see chapter 7) and a brief stop at the **Bailey House Museum** ★, 2375-A Main St. (© **808/244-3326**). Missionary and sugar planter Edward Bailey's 1833 home is a treasure trove of Hawaiiana. Inside, you'll find an eclectic collection, from precontact artifacts like scary temple

### *Moments* Flying High: Helicopter Rides

A helicopter ride on Maui isn't a wild ride; it's more like a gentle gee-whiz zip into a seldom-seen Eden. Today's pilots are an interesting hybrid: part Hawaiian historian, part DJ, part tour guide, and part amusement-ride operator. As you soar through the clouds, absorbing Maui's scenic terrain, you'll learn about the island's flora, fauna, history, and culture.

Among the many helicopter-tour operators on Maui, the best is **Blue Hawaiian** ★★, at Kahului Airport (✆ **800/745-BLUE** or 808/871-8844; www.bluehawaiian.com). Flights last from 30 to 100 minutes and cost $150 to $335. **Sunshine Helicopters** (✆ **800/544-2520** or 808/871-0722; www.sunshinehelicopters.com) also offers a variety of flights, costing from $125 to $235.

images, dog-tooth necklaces, and a rare lei made of tree-snail shells to latter-day relics like Duke Kahanamoku's 1919 redwood surfboard. It's open Monday through Saturday from 10am to 4pm. Admission is $4 adults, $3.50 seniors, $1 children ages 7 to 12.

About 3 miles south of Wailuku on the Honoapiilani Highway lies the tiny village of Waikapu, which has two attractions that are worth a peek. Relive Maui's past by taking a 40-minute narrated tram ride around fields of pineapple, sugar cane, and papaya trees at **Maui Tropical Plantation,** 1670 Honoapiilani Hwy., Waikapu (✆ **800/451-6805** or 808/244-7643), a real working plantation open daily from 9am to 5pm. A shop sells fresh and dried fruit, and a restaurant serves lunch. Admission is free; the tram tours, which start at 10am and leave about every 45 minutes, are $9.50 for adults, $4.50 for kids 3 to 12.

Marilyn Monroe and Frank Lloyd Wright meet for dinner every night (well, sort of) at the **Waikapu Golf and Country Club,** 2500 Honoapiilani Hwy. (✆ **808/244-2011**), one of Maui's most unusual buildings. Neither actually set foot on Maui, but these icons of glamour and architecture share a Hawaiian legacy. Wright designed this place for a Pennsylvania family in 1949, but it was never constructed. In 1957, Marilyn and husband Arthur Miller wanted it built for them in Connecticut, but they separated the following year. Tokyo billionaire Takeshi Sekiguchi found the blueprints and had Marilyn's Wright house cleverly redesigned as a clubhouse for his 18-hole golf course. You can walk in and look around at Wright's architecture and the portraits of Marilyn in Monroe's, the restaurant.

## IAO VALLEY

A couple of miles north of Wailuku, past the Bailey House Museum, Maui's true nature begins to reveal itself. After the hot tropic sun, the air is moist and cool, and the shade a welcome comfort. This is Iao Valley, a 6-acre state park whose great nature, history, and beauty have been enjoyed by millions of people from around the world for more than a century.

Iao ("Supreme Light") Valley, 10 miles long and encompassing 4,000 acres, is the eroded volcanic caldera of the West Maui Mountains. The head of the Iao Valley is a broad circular amphitheater where four major streams converge into Iao Stream. At the back of the amphitheater is rain-drenched Puu Kukui, the West Maui Mountains' highest point. This peaceful valley, full of tropical plants, rainbows, waterfalls, swimming holes, and hiking trails, is a place of solitude, reflection, and escape for residents and visitors alike. From Wailuku, take Main Street, then turn right on Iao Valley Road to the entrance to the state park. The park is open daily from 7am to 7pm.

For information, contact **Iao Valley State Park,** State Parks and Recreation, 54 S. High St., Rm. 101, Wailuku, HI 96793 (✆ **808/984-8109;** www.hawaii.gov). The **Hawaii Nature Center** ★, 875 Iao Valley Rd. (✆ **808/244-6500;** www.hawaiinaturecenter.org), home of the Iao Valley Nature Center, features hands-on, interactive exhibits and displays relating the story of Hawaiian natural history. Hours are daily from 10am to 4pm; admission is $6 for adults and $4 for children 4 to 12, under 4 free.

Two paved walkways loop into the massive green amphitheater, across the bridge of Iao Stream, and along the stream itself. The one-third-mile loop on a paved trail is an easy walk—you can even take your grandmother on this one. A leisurely stroll will allow you to enjoy lovely views of the Iao Needle and the lush vegetation.

The feature known as **Iao Needle** is an erosional remnant composed of basalt dikes. The phallic rock juts an impressive 2,250 feet above sea level. An architectural heritage park of Hawaiian, Japanese, Chinese, Filipino, and New England–style houses stands in harmony by Iao Stream at **Kepaniwai Heritage Garden.** This is a good picnic spot, with plenty of picnic tables and benches available. You can see ferns, banana trees, and other native and exotic plants in the **Iao Valley Botanic Garden** along the stream.

## 2 Lahaina & West Maui

### HISTORIC LAHAINA

Located between the West Maui Mountains and the deep azure ocean offshore, Lahaina stands out as one of the few places in Hawaii that has managed to preserve its 19th-century heritage while still accommodating 21st-century guests. This is no quiet seaside village, but a vibrant, cutting-edge kind of place, filled with a sense of history—but definitely with its mind on the future.

**Baldwin Home Museum** ★ The oldest house in Lahaina, this coral-and-rock structure was built in 1834 by Rev. Dwight Baldwin, a doctor with the fourth company of American missionaries to sail round the Horn to Hawaii. After 17 years of service, Baldwin was granted 2,600 acres in Kapalua for farming and grazing. His ranch manager experimented with what Hawaiians called *hala-kahiki,* or pineapple, on a 4-acre plot; the rest is history. The house looks as if Baldwin has just stepped out for a minute to tend a sick neighbor down the street.

Next door is the **Masters' Reading Room,** Maui's oldest building. This became visiting sea captains' favorite hangout once the missionaries closed down all of Lahaina's grog shops and banned prostitution; but by 1844, once hotels and bars started reopening, it lost its appeal. It's now the headquarters of the **Lahaina Restoration Foundation** (**© 808/661-3262**). Stop in and pick up a self-guided walking-tour map, which will take you to Lahaina's most historic sites.

120 Dickenson St. (at Front St.). © **808/661-3262.** Admission $3 adults, $2 seniors, $5 family. Daily 10am–4:30pm.

**Banyan Tree** Kids Of all the banyan trees in Hawaii, this is the greatest of all—so big that you can't get it all in your camera's viewfinder. It was only 8 feet tall when it was planted in 1873 by Maui Sheriff William O. Smith to mark the 50th anniversary of Lahaina's first Christian mission; now the big old banyan from India is more than 50 feet tall, has 12 major trunks, and shades two-thirds of an acre in Courthouse Square.

At the Courthouse Building, 649 Wharf St.

**The Brig Carthaginian** ★ Kids This restored square-rigged brigantine, an authentic replica of a 19th-century whaling ship, the kind that brought the first missionaries to Hawaii, was closed for "repairs" when we went to press. Apparently the old vessel has become a liability, and the people in charge were leaning towards getting rid of the old boat versus repairing her. As we went to press, history lovers were frantically trying to raise funds to either restore the old ship or purchase another replica of the same era. If you don't see her proud masts at the foot of the Lahaina Pier, then you know her fate. If the ship is still there, drop by; the floating museum features exhibits on whales and 19th-century whaling life.

Lahaina Harbor. ✆ **808/661-8527.** Admission $3 adults, $2 seniors, $5 family. Daily 10am–4:30pm.

**Lahaina Jodo Mission** This site has long been held sacred. The Hawaiians called it Puunoa Point, which means "the hill freed from taboo." Once a small village named "Mala" ("garden"), this peaceful place was a haven for Japanese immigrants, who came to Hawaii in 1868 as laborers for the sugar cane plantations. They eventually built a small wooden temple to worship here. In 1968, on the 100th anniversary of the Japanese in Hawaii, a Great Buddha statue, the largest outside of Japan (some 12 ft. high and weighing 3½ tons) was brought here from Japan. The immaculate grounds also contain a replica of the original wooden temple and a 90-foot-tall pagoda.

12 Ala Moana St. (off Front St., near the Mala Wharf). ✆ **808/661-4304.** Free admission. Daily during daylight hours.

**Maluuluolele Park** *Kids* At first glance, this Front Street park appears to be only a hot, dry, dusty softball field. But under home plate is the edge of Mokuula, where a royal compound once stood more than 100 years ago, now buried under tons of red dirt and sand. Here, Prince Kauikeaolui, who ascended the throne as King Kamehameha III when he was only 10, lived with the love of his life, his sister Princess Nahienaena. Missionaries took a dim view of incest, which was acceptable to Hawaiian nobles in order to preserve the royal bloodlines. Kamehameha died in 1854 at the age of 39. In 1918, his royal compound, containing a mausoleum and artifacts of the kingdom, was demolished and covered with dirt to create a public park. The site of this royal place is still considered sacred to many Hawaiians.

Front and Shaw sts.

**Wo Hing Temple** ★ The Chinese were among the various immigrants brought to Hawaii to work in the sugar cane fields. In 1909, several Chinese workers formed the Wo Hing society, a chapter of the Chee Kun Tong society, which dates from the 17th century. In

## Lahaina

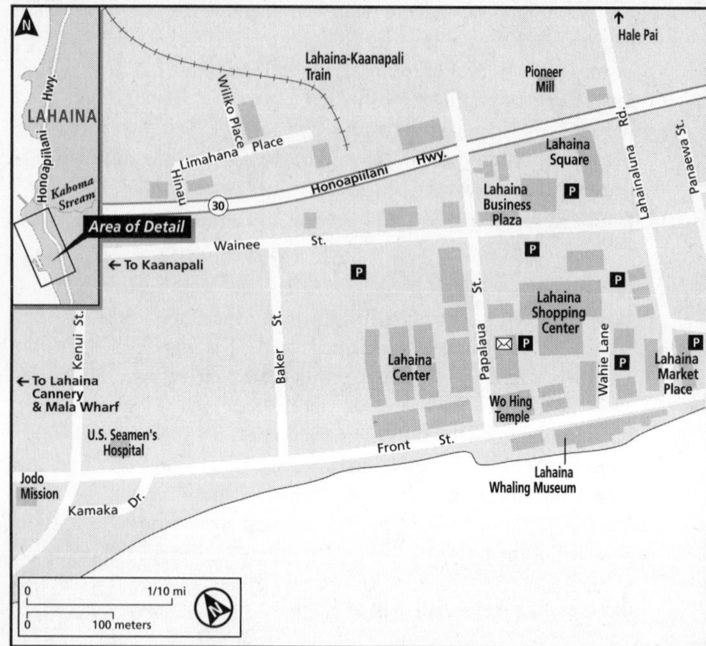


1912, they built this social hall for the Chinese community. Completely restored, the Wo Hing Temple contains displays and artifacts on the history of the Chinese in Lahaina; next door in the old cookhouse is a theater with movies of Hawaii taken by Thomas Edison in 1898 and 1903.

Front St. (between Wahie Lane and Papalaua St.). ✆ **808/661-3262.** Admission by donation. Daily 10am–4pm.

### A WHALE OF A PLACE IN KAANAPALI

Heading north from Lahaina, the next resort area you'll come to is Kaanapali, which boasts a gorgeous stretch of beach. If you haven't seen a real whale yet, go to **Whalers Village,** 2435 Kaanapali Pkwy., a shopping center that has adopted the whale as its mascot. You can't miss it: A huge, almost life-size metal sculpture of a mother whale and two nursing calves greets you. A few more steps, and you're met by the looming, bleached-white bony skeleton of a 40-foot sperm whale; it's pretty impressive.

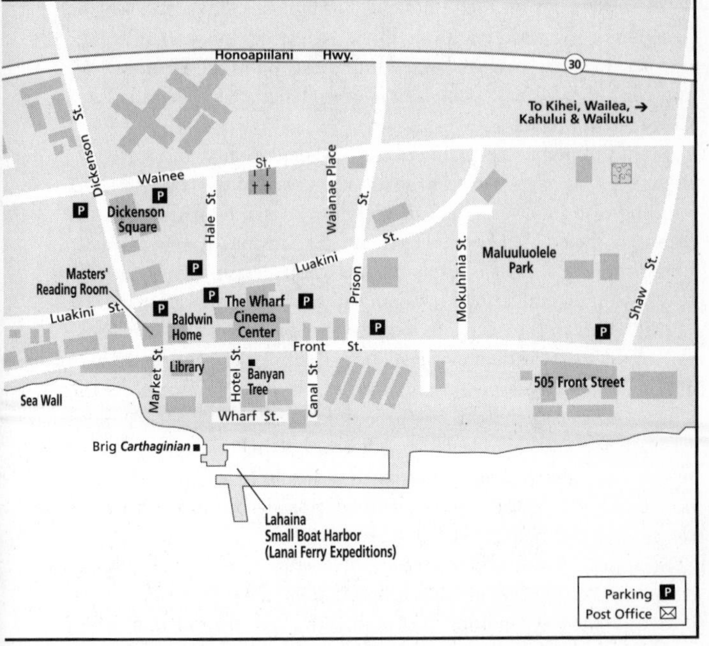


On the second floor of the mall is the **Whale Center of the Pacific** (✆ **808/661-5992**), a museum celebrating the "Golden Era of Whaling" (1825–60). Harpoons and scrimshaw are on display; the museum has even re-created the cramped quarters of a whaler's seagoing vessel. Open during mall hours, daily from 9:30am to 10pm; admission is free.

## THE SCENIC ROUTE FROM WEST MAUI TO CENTRAL OR UPCOUNTRY MAUI: THE KAHEKILI HIGHWAY

The usual road from West Maui to Wailuku is the Honoapiilani Highway (Hwy. 30), which runs along the coast and then turns inland at Maalaea. But those in search of a back-to-nature driving experience should go the other way, along the **Kahekili Highway** ★ (Hwy. 340). (*Highway* is a bit of a euphemism for this paved but somewhat precarious narrow road; check your rental-car agreement before you head out. If it is raining or has been raining, skip this road due to mud and rock slides.)

You'll start out on the Honoapiilani Highway (Hwy. 30), which becomes the Kahekili Highway (Hwy. 340) after Honokohau, at the northernmost tip of the island. Around this point are **Honolua** ★ and **Mokuleia** ★ bays, which have been designated as Marine Life Conservation Areas.

From this point, the quality of the road deteriorates, and you may share the way with roosters, goats, cows, and dogs. The narrow, winding road follows an ancient Hawaiian coastal footpath and will show you the true wild nature of Maui: steep ravines, rolling pastoral hills, tumbling waterfalls, exploding blowholes, crashing surf, jagged lava coastlines, and a tiny Hawaiian village straight off a postcard.

Just before mile marker 20, look for a small turnoff on the mauka side of the road (just before the guardrail starts). Park here and walk across the road, and on your left you'll see a spouting **blowhole.** In winter, this is an excellent spot to look for whales.

Just before mile marker 16, look for the POHAKU KANI sign, marking the huge, 6-by-6-foot, bell-shaped stone. To "ring" the bell, look on the side facing Kahakuloa for the deep indentations, and strike the stone with another rock.

Along the route, nestled in a crevice between two steep hills, is the picturesque village of **Kahakuloa** ★ ("the tall hau tree"), with a dozen weather-worn houses, a church with a red-tile roof, and vivid green taro patches.

When you're approaching Wailuku, stop at the **Halekii and Pihanakalani Heiau,** which visitors rarely see. To get here from Wailuku, turn north from Main Street onto Market Street. Turn right onto Mill Street and follow it until it ends; then make a left on Lower Main Street. Follow Lower Main until it ends at Waiehu Beach Road (Hwy. 340), and turn left. Turn left on Kuhio Street and again at the first left onto Hea Place, and drive through the gates and look for the Hawaii Visitor's Bureau marker.

These two heiau, built in 1240 from stones carried up from the Iao Stream below, sit on a hill with a commanding view of central Maui and Haleakala. After the bloody battle at Iao Stream, Kamehameha I reportedly came to the temple here to pay homage to the war god, Ku, with a human sacrifice. Halekii ("House of Images") is made of stone walls with a flat grassy top, whereas Pihanakalani ("gathering place of supernatural beings") is a pyramid-shaped mount of stones. If you sit quietly nearby (never walk on any heiau—it's considered disrespectful), you'll see that the view alone explains why this spot was chosen.

## 3 South Maui

### MAALAEA

At the bend in the Honopiilani Highway (Hwy. 30), Maalaea Bay runs along the south side of the isthmus between the West Maui Mountains and Haleakala. This is the windiest area on Maui, and conditions out in Maalaea Bay are ideal for **windsurfers.** Surfers are also seen just outside the small boat harbor in Maalaea.

**Maui Ocean Center** ★★ Kids This 5-acre facility houses the largest aquarium in Hawaii. Exhibits are geared toward the residents of Hawaii's ocean waters. As you walk past the three dozen or so tanks and countless exhibits, you'll slowly descend from the "beach" to the deepest part of the ocean. Start at the surge pool, where you'll see shallow-water marine life like spiny urchins and cauliflower coral, then move on to the reef tanks, turtle pool, "touch" pool (with starfish and urchins), and eagle-ray pool before reaching the star of the show: the 100-foot-long, 600,000-gallon main tank featuring tiger, gray, and white-tip sharks. The most phenomenal thing about this tank is that the walkway goes right through it—so you'll be surrounded by marine creatures. A very cool place, and well worth the time.

Maalaea Harbor Village, at the triangle between Honoapiilani Hwy. and Maalaea Rd. ✆ **808/270-7000.** Fax 808/270-7070. www.mauioceancenter.com. Admission $19 adults, $17 seniors, $13 children 3–12. Daily 9am–5pm.

### KIHEI

Capt. George Vancouver landed at Kihei in 1778, when it was only a collection of fisherman's grass shacks on the hot, dry, dusty coast. A **totem pole** stands today where he's believed to have landed, across from Aston Maui Lu Resort, 575 S. Kihei Rd., Vancouver sailed on to what later became British Columbia.

West of the junction of Piilani Highway (Hwy. 31) and Mokulele Highway (Hwy. 350) is **Kealia Pond National Wildlife Preserve** (✆ **808/875-1582**), a 700-acre U.S. Fish and Wildlife wetland preserve where endangered Hawaiian stilts, coots, and ducks hang out and splash. These ponds work two ways: as bird preserves and as sedimentation basins that keep the coral reefs from silting from runoff. You can take a self-guided tour along a boardwalk dotted with interpretive signs and shade shelters, through sand dunes, and around ponds to Maalaea Harbor. The boardwalk starts at the outlet of Kealia Pond on the ocean side of North Kihei Road (near mile marker 2 on Piilani Hwy.). Among the Hawaiian waterbirds seen here are the black-crowned high heron, Hawaiian coot, Hawaiian duck, and Hawaiian stilt. There are also shorebirds like sanderling, Pacific golden plover, ruddy turnstone, and wandering tattler. From July to December, the hawksbill turtle comes ashore here to lay her eggs. ***Tip:*** If you're bypassing Kihei, take the Piilani Highway (Hwy. 31), which parallels strip-mall laden South Kihei Road, and avoid the hassle of stoplights and traffic.

## WAILEA

The dividing line between arid Kihei and artificially green Wailea is distinct. Alexander & Baldwin, Inc. (of sugar cane fame) began developing a resort here in the 1970s (after piping water from the other side of the island to the desert terrain of Wailea). Today, the manicured 1,450 acres of this affluent resort stand out like an oasis along the normally dry leeward coast.

The best way to explore this golden resort coast is to rise with the sun and head for Wailea's 1½-mile **coastal nature trail** ★, stretching between the Kea Lani Hotel and the kiawe thicket just beyond the Renaissance Wailea. It's a serpentine path that meanders uphill and down past native plants, old Hawaiian habitats, and luxury hotels. You can pick up the trail at any of the resorts or from clearly marked SHORELINE ACCESS points along the coast. The best time to go is when you first wake up; by midmorning, the coastal trail starts getting crowded. As the path crosses several bold black-lava points, it affords new vistas of islands and ocean; benches allow you to pause and contemplate the view across Alalakeiki Channel, which jumps with **whales** in season. Sunset is another good time to hit the trail.

## MAKENA

A few miles south of Wailea, the manicured coast turns to wilderness; now you're in Makena. **Makena Landing** ★ is a beach park with boat-launching facilities, showers, toilets, and picnic tables. It's great for snorkeling and for launching kayaks bound for Pérouse Bay and Ahihi-Kinau preserve.

From the landing, go south on Makena Road; on the right is **Keawali Congregational Church** ★ (© **808/879-5557**), built in 1855 with walls 3 feet thick. Built of lava rock with coral used as mortar, this Protestant church sits on its own cove with a gold-sand beach. It always attracts a Sunday crowd for its 9:30am Hawaiian-language service.

A little farther south on the coast is **La Pérouse Monument** ★, a pyramid of lava rocks that marks the spot where French explorer Admiral Comte de La Pérouse set foot on Maui in 1786.

The first Westerner to "discover" the island, he described the "burning climate" of the leeward coast, observed several fishing villages near Kihei, and sailed on into oblivion, never to be seen again; some believe he may have been eaten by cannibals in what is now Vanuatu. To get here, drive south past Puu Olai to Ahihi Bay, where the road turns to gravel. Go another 2 miles along the coast to La Pérouse Bay; the monument sits amid a clearing in black lava at the end of the dirt road.

The rocky coastline and sometimes rough seas contribute to the lack of appeal for water activities here; **hiking** opportunities, however, are excellent. Bring plenty of water and sun protection, and wear hiking boots that can withstand walking on lava. From La Pérouse Bay, you can pick up the old King's Highway trail, which at one time circled the island. Walk along the sandy beach at La Pérouse and look for the trail indentation in the lava.

## 4 House of the Sun: Haleakala National Park ★★★

At once forbidding and compelling, **Haleakala National Park** ("House of the Sun") is Maui's main natural attraction. More than 1.3 million people a year go up the 10,023-foot-high mountain to peer down into the crater of the world's largest dormant volcano. That hole would hold Manhattan: 3,000 feet deep and 7½ miles long by 2½ miles wide.

But there's more to do here than simply stare in a big black hole: Just going up the mountain is an experience in itself. The snaky road passes through big, puffy, cumulus clouds to offer magnificent views of the isthmus of Maui, the West Maui Mountains, and the Pacific Ocean.

Many drive up to the summit in predawn darkness to watch the **sunrise** over Haleakala. Others take a trail ride inside the bleak lunar landscape of the wilderness inside the crater, or coast down the 37-mile road from the summit on a bicycle with special brakes (see "Biking" and "Horseback Riding" in chapter 5). Hardy adventurers hike into the crater's wilderness (see "Hiking" in chapter 5).

### JUST THE FACTS

Haleakala National Park extends from the summit of Mount Haleakala into the crater, down the volcano's southeast flank to

Maui's eastern coast, beyond Hana. There are actually two separate and distinct destinations within the park: **Haleakala Summit** ★ and the **Kipahulu** ★ coast (see "Tropical Haleakala: Oheo Gulch at Kipahulu" later in this chapter). No road links the summit and the coast; you have to approach them separately, and you need at least a day to see each place.

**WHEN TO GO** At the 10,023-foot summit, weather changes fast. Before you go, get current weather conditions from the park (© **808/572-4400**) or the **National Weather Service** (© **808/871-5054**).

From sunrise to noon, the light is weak, but the view is usually free of clouds. The best time for photos is in the afternoon, when the sun lights the crater and clouds are few. Go on full-moon nights for spectacular viewing. As with all natural attractions, there are no schedules or guarantees, however.

**ACCESS POINTS** **Haleakala Summit** is 37 miles, or about a 2-hour drive, from Kahului. To get here, take Highway 37 to Highway 377 to Highway 378. For details on the drive, see "The Drive to the Summit" below. Pukalani is the last town for water, food, and gas.

The **Kipahulu** section of the national park is on Maui's east end near Hana, 60 miles from Kahului on Highway 36 (the Hana Hwy.). Due to traffic and rough road conditions, plan on 4 hours for the drive from Kahului (see "Driving the Road to Hana" below). Hana is the only nearby town for services, water, gas, food, and overnight lodging; some facilities may not be open after dark.

At both entrances to the park, the admission fee is $5 per person or $10 per car, good for a week of unlimited entry.

**INFORMATION, VISITOR CENTERS & RANGER PROGRAMS** For information before you go, contact **Haleakala National Park,** P.O. Box 369, Makawao, HI 96768 (© **808/572-4400;** www.nps.gov.hale).

One mile from the park entrance, at 7,000 feet, is **Haleakala National Park Headquarters** (© **808/572-4400**), open daily from 7am to 4pm. Restrooms, a pay phone, and drinking water are available.

The **Haleakala Visitor Center,** open daily from sunrise to 3pm, is near the summit, 11 miles from the park entrance. Park staff members are often handy to answer questions. The only facilities are restrooms and water.

Rangers offer excellent, informative, and free **naturalist talks** at 9:30, 10:30, and 11:30am daily in the summit building. For information on **hiking** (including guided hikes) and **camping,** including cabins and campgrounds in the wilderness itself, see "Hiking" in chapter 5.

## THE DRIVE TO THE SUMMIT

If you look on a Maui map, almost in the middle of the part that resembles a torso, there's a black wiggly line that looks like this: WWWWW. That's **Highway 378,** also known as **Haleakala Crater Road**—one of the fastest-ascending roads in the world. This grand corniche takes you past rare silversword plants and endangered Hawaiian geese sailing through the clear, thin air; and offers a view that extends for more than 100 miles.

Going to the summit takes about 2 hours from Kahului. No matter where you start out, you'll follow Highway 37 (Haleakala Hwy.) to Pukalani, where you'll pick up Highway 377 (which is also Haleakala Hwy.), which you take to Highway 378. Along the way, expect fog, rain, and wind. You might encounter stray cattle and downhill bicyclists. Fill up your gas tank before you go—the only gas available is 27 miles below the summit at Pukalani. There are no facilities beyond the ranger stations—not even a coffee urn in sight. Bring your own food and water.

Remember, you're entering a high-altitude wilderness area. Some people get dizzy due to the lack of oxygen; you might also suffer lightheadedness, shortness of breath, nausea, or worse: severe headaches, flatulence, and dehydration. People with asthma, pregnant women, heavy smokers, and those with heart conditions should be especially careful. Bring water and a jacket or a blanket, especially if you go up for sunrise.

As you go up the slopes the temperate drops about 3°F every 1,000 feet, so the temperature at the top can be 30°F (17°C) cooler than it was at sea level. Come prepared with sweaters, jackets, and rain gear.

About a mile from the park entrance is **Park Headquarters,** where an endangered **nene,** or Hawaiian goose, might greet you with its unique call. Now protected as Hawaii's state bird, the wild nene on Haleakala numbers fewer than 250—and the species remains endangered.

Beyond headquarters are **two scenic overlooks** on the way to the summit. **Leleiwi Overlook** ★ is just beyond mile marker 17. From the parking area, a short trail leads you to a panoramic view of the lunarlike crater. Two miles farther along is **Kalahaku Overlook** ★, the best place to see a rare **silversword.** You can turn into this overlook only when you are descending from the top. The silversword is the punk of the plant world, its silvery bayonets displaying tiny purple bouquets—like a spacey artichoke with attitude. Silverswords grow only in Hawaii, take from 4 to 50 years to bloom, and then, usually between May and October, send up a 1- to 6-foot stalk with a purple bouquet of sunflower-like blooms. They're now very rare, so don't even think about taking one home.

Continue on, and you'll quickly reach the **Haleakala Visitor Center** ★, which offers spectacular views. You'll feel as if you're at the edge of the earth. But don't turn around here; the actual summit's a little farther on, at **Puu Ulaula Overlook** ★ (also known as Red Hill), the volcano's highest point. If you do go up for sunrise, the building at Puu Ulaula Overlook, a triangle of glass that serves as a windbreak, is the best viewing spot. After sunrise you can see all the way across Alenuihaha Channel to the often snowcapped summit of Mauna Kea on the Big Island.

**MAKING YOUR DESCENT** Put your car in low gear; that way, you won't destroy your brakes by riding them the whole way down.

## 5 More in Upcountry Maui

On the slopes of Haleakala, cowboys, planters, and other country people make their homes in serene, neighborly communities like **Makawao** and **Kula,** a world away from the bustling beach resorts. Even if you can't spare a day or 2 in the cool upcountry air, there are some sights that are worth a look on your way to or from the crater. Shoppers and gallery hoppers might really want to make the effort; see chapter 7 for details.

**Kula Botanical Garden** ★ You can take a self-guided, informative, leisurely stroll through more than 700 native and exotic plants—including three unique collections of orchids, proteas, and bromeliads—at this 5-acre garden. It offers a good overview of Hawaii's exotic flora in one small, cool place.

Hwy. 377, south of Haleakala Crater Rd. (Hwy. 378), ½ mile from Hwy. 37. ✆ **808/878-1715.** Admission $5 adults, $1 children 6–12. Daily 9am–4pm.

**Tedeschi Vineyards and Winery** ★ On the southern shoulder of Haleakala is **Ulupalakua Ranch,** a 20,000-acre spread once owned by sea captain James Makee. Still in operation, the ranch is now home to Maui's only winery, established in 1974 by Napa vintner Emil Tedeschi, who began growing California and European grapes here and producing still and sparkling wines. The rustic grounds are the perfect place for a picnic.

Off Hwy. 37 (Kula Hwy.). ✆ **808/878-6058.** www.mauiwine.com. Daily 9am–5pm. Free tastings; tours given 10:30am–1:30pm.

## 6 East Maui & Heavenly Hana

### DRIVING THE ROAD TO HANA ★★★

Top down, sunscreen on, radio tuned to a little Hawaiian music on a Maui morning: It's time to head out to Hana along the Hana Highway (Hwy. 36), a wiggle of a road that runs along Maui's northeastern shore. The drive takes at least 3 hours, but plan to take all day. Going to Hana is about the journey, not the destination.

In all of Hawaii no road is more celebrated than this one. It winds for 50 miles past taro patches, magnificent seascapes, waterfall pools, botanical gardens, and verdant rainforests, and it ends at one of Hawaii's most beautiful tropical places.

The outside world discovered the little village of Hana in 1926, when the narrow coastal road first opened. The mud-and-gravel road was paved in 1962, when tourist traffic began to increase; it now sees more than 1,000 cars and dozens of vans a day, according to storekeeper Harry Hasegawa. Go at the wrong time, and you'll be stuck in a bumper-to-bumper rental-car parade—peak traffic hours are midmorning and midafternoon year-round, especially on weekends.

In the rush to "do" Hana in a day, most visitors spin around town in 10 minutes flat and wonder what all the fuss is about. It takes time to take in Hana, play in the waterfalls, sniff the tropical flowers, and take in the spectacular scenery; stay overnight if you can, and meander back in a day or two. However, if you really must do the Hana Highway in a day, go just before sunrise and return after sunset.

**THE JOURNEY BEGINS IN PAIA** Before you even start out, fill up your gas tank. Gas in Paia is very expensive, but it's the last

---

*Tips* **Hana Highway Etiquette**

Practice aloha: Give way at the one-lane bridges, wave at oncoming motorists, let the big guys in four-by-fours have the right of way—it's just common sense, brah. If the guy behind you blinks his lights, let him pass. Oh, yeah, and don't honk your horn—in Hawaii, it's considered rude.

---

## The Road to Hana

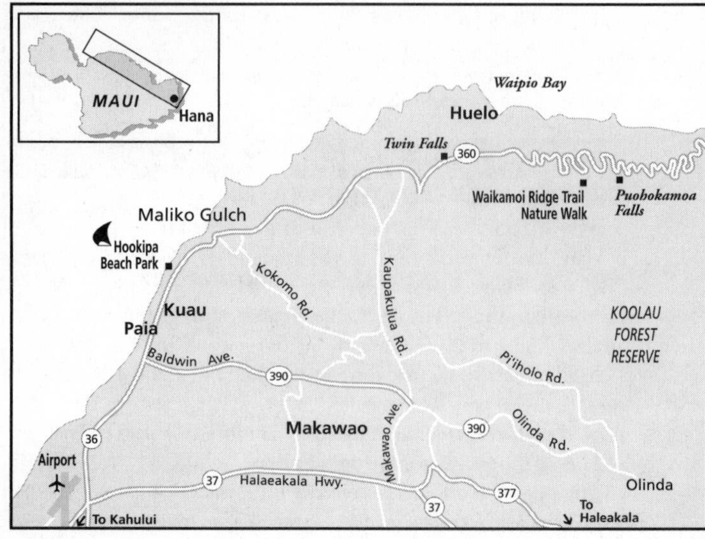


place for gas until you get to Hana, some 42 miles, 54 bridges, and 600 hairpin turns down the road.

Plan to be here early, around 7am, when **Charley's** ★, 142 Hana Hwy. (✆ **808/579-9453**), opens. Enjoy a big, hearty breakfast for a reasonable price. After your meal, head up Baldwin Avenue; about a half block from the intersection of the Hana Highway and Baldwin Avenue, stop by **Pic-nics** ★, 30 Baldwin Ave. (✆ **808/579-8021**), to stock up for a picnic lunch for the road (p. 104).

After you leave Paia the road then bends into an S-turn; in the middle of the S is the entrance to **Mama's Fish House,** marked by a restored boat with Mama's logo on the side. Just past the truck on the ocean side is the entrance to Mama's parking lot and adjacent small sandy cove in front of the restaurant. Ocean access is treacherous, over very slippery rocks, but the beach is a great place to sit and soak up some sun.

**WINDSURFING MECCA** Just before mile marker 9 is one of the greatest windsurfing spots on the planet, **Hookipa Beach Park** ★. On nearly every windy afternoon (the board surfers have the waves in the morning), you can watch dozens of windsurfers twirling and dancing in the wind like colored butterflies. To watch the windsurfers, go past the park and turn left at the entrance on the far side

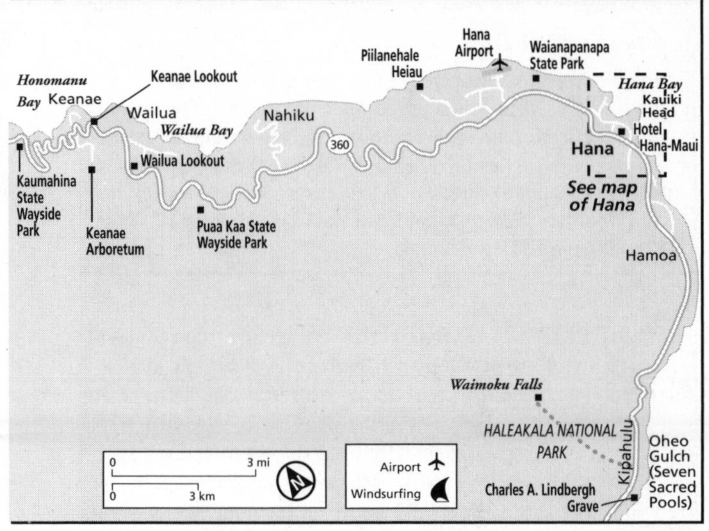


of the beach. You can either park on the high grassy bluff or drive down to the sandy beach and park alongside the pavilion. The park also has restrooms, a shower, picnic tables, and a barbecue area.

**INTO THE COUNTRY** Past Hookipa Beach, the road winds down into **Maliko ("Budding") Gulch** at mile marker 10. At the bottom of the gulch, look for the road on your right, which will take you out to **Maliko Bay.** Take the first right, which goes under the bridge, past a rodeo arena, then on to the rocky beach. There are no facilities here except a boat-launch ramp. The bay may not look that special, but if the surf is up, it's a great place to watch the waves.

Back on the Hana Highway, as you leave Maliko Gulch, around mile marker 11, you'll pass through the rural area of **Haiku,** with banana patches, cane grass blowing in the wind, and forests of guava trees, avocados, kukui trees, palms, and Christmas berry. Just before mile marker 15 is the **Maui Grown Market and Deli** (**© 808/572-1693**), a good stop for drinks or snacks for the ride.

At mile marker 16, the curves begin, one right after another. Slow down and enjoy the view of bucolic rolling hills, mango trees, and vibrant ferns. After mile marker 16, the road is still called the Hana Highway, but the number changes from Highway 36 to Highway 360, and the mile markers go back to 0.

*Tips* **Travel Tip**

If you'd like to know exactly what you're seeing as you head down the road to Hana, we suggest renting a cassette tour, available from **Activity Warehouse** (www.travelhawaii.com), which has branches in Lahaina at 602 Front St., near Prison Street (✆ **808/667-4000**), and in Kihei at Azeka Place II, on the mountain side of Kihei Road near Lipoa Street (✆ **808/875-4000**), for $10 a day.

**A GREAT PLUNGE ALONG THE WAY** The first great place to stop for a dip in a waterfall pool is **Twin Falls** ★, at mile marker 2. Just before the wide, concrete bridge, pull over on the mountain side and park (but not in front of the sign that says DO NOT BLOCK DRIVEWAY). A warning: There have been thefts in this area. Ignore the NO TRESPASSING sign (no one will mind, but you're liable if you stub your toe) and hop over the ladder on the right side of the red gate. From here you can walk 3 to 5 minutes to the waterfall and pool, or continue on another 10 to 15 minutes to the second, larger waterfall and pool (don't go in if it has been raining).

**HIDDEN HUELO** Just before mile marker 4 on a blind curve, look for a double row of mailboxes on the left-hand side by the pay phone. Down the road lies a Hawaii of an earlier time, where serenity prevails.

Protruding out of Maui's tumultuous northern coastline, hemmed in by Waipo and Hoalua bays, is the remote, rural community of **Huelo** ★. Once, this fertile area supported a population of 75,000; today, only a few hundred live among the scattered homes on this windswept land.

Huelo's historic 1853 **Kaulanapueo Church** sits in the center of a putting-green–perfect lawn, bordered with hog-wire fence and accessible through a squeaky, metal turnstile. Reminiscent of New England architecture, this coral-and-cement church is still in use, although services are held just once or twice a month. Next to the church is a small graveyard, a personal history of this village in concrete and stone.

**KOOLAU FOREST RESERVE** After Huelo you'll reach the **Koolau Forest Reserve** ★. The reserve is a great example of a lush windward area: The coastline here gets about 60 to 80 inches of rain a year, and farther up the mountain, the rainfall is 200 to 300 inches a year.

Here you will see 20- to 30-foot-tall guava trees, their branches laden fruit. The skin is peeled and the fruit inside of the guava eaten raw, squeezed for juice, or cooked for jams or jellies. Also in this prolific area are mangos, java plums, and avocados. The spiny, long-leafed plants you see are hala trees, which the Hawaiians used for roofing material and for weaving baskets, mats, and even canoe sails.

The copious rainfall up the mountain means a waterfall (and 1-lane bridge) around nearly every turn in the road from here on out, so drive slowly and be prepared to stop and yield to oncoming cars.

**DANGEROUS CURVES** About a half mile after mile marker 6, there's a sharp U-curve in the road, going uphill. The road is practically one lane here, with a brick wall on one side and virtually no maneuvering room. Sound your horn at the start of the U-curve to let approaching cars know you are coming. Take this curve, as well as the few more coming up in the next several miles, very slowly.

Just before mile marker 7 is a forest of waving **bamboo.** Wait until just after mile marker 7, at the **Kaaiea ("Breathtaking") Bridge,** to pull over and take a closer look at the hand-hewn stone walls. Then turn around to see the vista of bamboo, a photo opportunity that certainly qualifies as "breathtaking."

**A GREAT FAMILY HIKE** At mile marker 9, there's a small state wayside area with restrooms, a pavilion, picnic tables, and a barbecue area. The sign says KOOLAU FOREST RESERVE, but the real attraction here is the **Waikamoi Ridge Trail** ★, an easy three-quarter-mile loop. The start of the trail is just behind the QUIET TREES AT WORK sign. The well-marked trail meanders through eucalyptus, ferns, and hala trees.

**MORE GREAT PLUNGES** Thirty-foot **Puohokamoa Falls** ★ spills into an idyllic pool in a fern-filled amphitheater. Park at the bridge at mile marker 11 and take the short walk up the trail. The pool is surrounded by banana trees, colorful heliconias, and sweet-smelling ginger. Bring mosquito repellent.

**CAN'T-MISS PHOTO OPPORTUNITIES** Just past mile marker 12 is the **Kaumahina ("Moonrise") State Wayside Park.** Not only is this a good pit stop (restrooms are available here) and a wonderful place for a picnic under the tall eucalyptus trees (with tables and barbecue area), but it's also a great vista; you can see down the rugged coastline all the way to Keanae Peninsula. Just past the park on the ocean side, there's another scenic turnoff and great photo opportunity.

Another mile and a couple of bends in the road, and you'll enter the Honomanu Valley ("valley of the bird"), with its beautiful bay. To get down to the **Honomanu Bay County Beach Park** ★, look for the turnoff on your left, just after mile marker 14, as you begin your ascent up the other side of the valley. The rutted dirt-and-cinder road takes you down to the rocky black-sand beach. There are no facilities here. There are strong rip currents offshore, so swimming is best in the stream inland from the ocean.

**MAUI'S BOTANICAL WORLD** Farther along the winding road, between mile markers 16 and 17, is a cluster of bunkhouses composing the YMCA Camp Keanae. A quarter-mile down is the **Keanae Arboretum** ★★, where the region's botany is divided into three parts: native forest; introduced forest; and traditional Hawaiian plants, food, and medicine. You can swim in the pools of Piinaau Stream, or press on along a mile-long trail into Keanae Valley (see "Hiking" in chapter 5).

**KEANAE PENINSULA** The old Hawaiian village of **Keanae** ★★ stands out against the Pacific like a place time forgot. Here, on an old lava flow graced by an 1860 stone church and swaying palms, is one of the last coastal enclaves of native Hawaiians. They still grow taro in patches and pound it into poi, the staple of the old Hawaiian diet; they still pluck *opihi* (limpet) from tide pools along the jagged coast and cast throw-nets at schools of fish.

**WAIANAPANAPA STATE PARK** ★★ At mile marker 32, just on the outskirts of Hana, shiny black-sand Waianapanapa Beach appears like a vivid dream, with bright-green jungle foliage on three sides and cobalt-blue water lapping at its feet. The 120-acre park on an ancient *aa* lava flow includes sea cliffs, lava tubes, arches, and the beach, plus 12 cabins, tent camping, picnic pavilions, restrooms, showers, drinking water, and hiking trails. If you're interested in staying here, see chapter 3; also see "Beaches" and "Hiking" in chapter 5.

## HANA ★★

Green, tropical Hana is a destination all its own, a small coastal village that's probably what you came to Maui in search of. Here you'll find a rainforest dotted with cascading waterfalls and sparkling blue pools, skirted by red- and black-sand beaches.

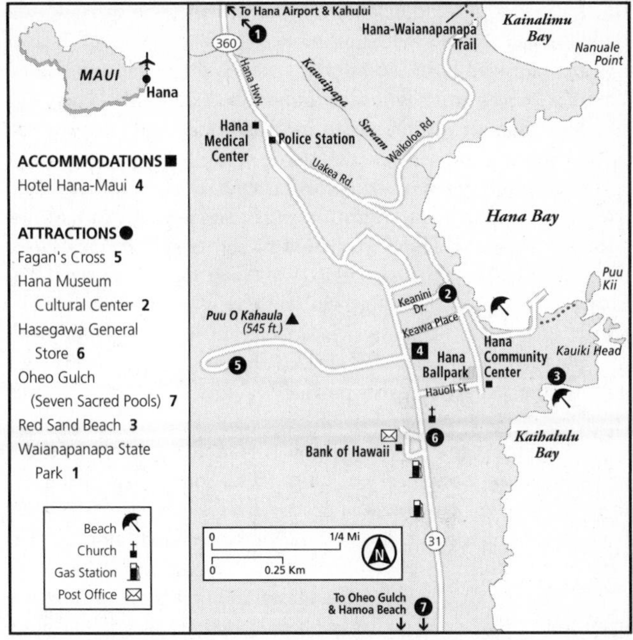


Beautiful Hana enjoys more than 90 inches of rain a year—more than enough to keep the scenery lush. Banyans, bamboo, breadfruit trees—everything seems larger than life in this small town, especially the flowers, such as wild ginger and plumeria.

The last unspoiled Hawaiian town on Maui is, oddly enough, the home of Maui's first resort, which opened in 1946. Paul Fagan, owner of the San Francisco Seals baseball team, bought an old inn and turned it into the **Hotel Hana-Maui,** which gave Hana its first taste of tourism.

As you enter Hana, the road splits about a half mile past mile marker 33, at the police station. Both roads will take you to Hana, but the lower road, Uakea Road, is more scenic. Just before you get to Hana Bay, you'll see the old wood-frame **Hana District Police Station and Courthouse.** Next door is the **Hana Museum Cultural Center** ★, on Uakea Road (© **808/248-8622;** www.planet-hawaii.com/hana), open daily from 10am to 4pm (most of the time). This small building has an excellent collection of Hawaiian quilts, artifacts, books, and photos.

Cater-cornered from the cultural center is the entrance to **Hana Bay** ★. You can drive right down to the pier and park. There are restrooms, showers, picnic tables, barbecue areas, and even a snack bar here.

To get to the center of town, leave Hana Bay, cross Uakea Road, and drive up Keawa Place; turn left on Hana Highway, and on the corner will be the **Hotel Hana-Maui,** the once-luxurious hotel established by Paul Fagan in 1946. On the green hills above Hotel Hana-Maui stands a 30-foot-high white cross made of lava rock. Citizens erected the cross in memory of Paul Fagan, who founded the Hana Ranch as well as the hotel, and helped keep the town alive. The hike up to **Fagan's Cross** provides a gorgeous view of the Hana coast, especially at sunset.

Back on the Hana Highway, just past Hauoli Road, is the majestic **Wananalua Congregation Church.** It's on the National Historic Register not only because of its age (it was built in 1838–42 from coral stones), but also because of its location, atop an old Hawaiian heiau.

Just past the church is the **Hasegawa General Store** ★, a Maui institution that carries oodles of merchandise from soda and fine French wines to fishing line to name-brand clothing, plus everything you need for a picnic or a gourmet meal.

If you need gas before heading back, **Chevron Service Station** sits on the right side of the Hana Highway as you leave town.

## OUTDOOR PURSUITS

One of the best areas on Maui for ocean activities, Hana also boasts a wealth of nature hikes, remote places to explore on horseback and waterfalls to discover.

### BEACHES & OCEAN ACTIVITIES

Call **Hana-Maui Sea Sports** (✆ **808/248-7711;** www.hana-maui-seasports.com) if you'd like to snorkel or kayak, or venture out on your own at our favorite beaches:

**HANA** The waters in the Hana Bay are calm most of the time and great for swimming. There's excellent snorkeling and diving by the lighthouse. Strong currents can run through here, so don't venture farther than the lighthouse. See Hana Bay, above, for more details on the facilities and hikes here.

**RED SAND BEACH** ★★ The Hawaiian name for this beach is Kaihalulu Beach, which means "roaring sea." The beach is on the ocean side of Kauiki Hill, just south of Hana Bay, in a wild, natural setting on a pocket cove, where the volcanic cinder cone lost its seaward wall to erosion and spilled red cinders everywhere to create the red sands. There are two things you should know about this beach: You have to trespass to get here and nudity is common here (even though it's illegal—arrests have been made).

To reach the beach, put on solid walking shoes and walk south on Uakea Road, past Haoli Street and the Hotel Hana-Maui, to the parking lot for the hotel's Sea Ranch Cottages. Turn left and cross the open field next to the Hana Community Center. Look for the dirt trail and follow it to the huge ironwood tree, where you turn right (do not go ahead to the old Japanese cemetery). Carefully follow the ever-eroding cinder footpath a short distance along the shoreline, down the narrow cliff trail (do not attempt this if it's wet). The trail suddenly turns the corner, and into view comes the burnt-red beach, set off by the turquoise waters, black lava, and vivid green ironwood trees.

The lava outcropping protects the bay and makes it safe for swimming. Snorkeling is excellent and there's a natural whirlpool area on the Hana Bay side of the cove. Stay away from the surge area where the ocean enters the cove.

**HAMOA BEACH** ★★ For one of Hana's best beaches—great for swimming, Boogie Boarding, and sunbathing—continue another half mile down the Haneoo Road loop to Hamoa Beach. There is easy access from the road down to the sandy beach, and facilities include a small restroom and an outdoor shower. The large pavilion and beach accessories are for the guests of the Hotel Hana-Maui.

## HIKING

Hana is woven with hiking trails along the shoreline, through the rainforest, and up in the mountains. See "Hiking" in chapter 5 for a discussion of hiking in Waianapanapa and up to Fagan's Cross.

Another excellent hike leads you to **Piilanihale Heiau** ★★ and **Blue Pool** ★. This easy, 3-mile round-trip takes you to a freshwater, ocean-side waterfall and swimming pool at the halfway point. On the way back, you can tour a tropical botanical garden and see the largest heiau in the state.

Turn toward the ocean on Ulaino Road, by mile marker 31. Drive down the road to the first stream (about 1½ miles). If the stream is flooded, turn around and go back. If you can forge the stream, cross it and park on the right side of the road by the huge breadfruit trees. The trees are part of the 122-acre **Kahanu Garden** (✆ **808/248-8912**), owned and operated by the National Tropical Botanical Garden (www.ntbg.org), which also has two gardens on Kauai. Open Monday through Friday, 10am to 2pm, admission is $5 for adults and free for children 12 and under, guided tours by reservation.

The 122 acres encompass plant collections from the Pacific Islands, but the real draw here is the **Piilanihale Heiau.** Believed to be the largest in the state, it measures 340 feet by 415 feet and was built in a terrace design not seen anywhere else in Hawaii.

You can park your car here and walk down the Jeep road that parallels the Kahanu Gardens. You'll have to forge two more streams before the road ends at the beach. Cross the rock-and-gravel beach. If it has been dry, you can just walk along the shoreline. If there has been rain, you will need to cross over the big boulders in the stream. Continue walking down the beach to the 100-foot waterfall on your left with its deep freshwater pool, known locally as **Blue Pool.**

## TROPICAL HALEAKALA: OHEO GULCH AT KIPAHULU

Also know as the Seven Sacred Pools or just Kipahulu, **Oheo Gulch** is a beautiful sight. The dazzling series of waterfall pools and cataracts cascading into the sea is so popular that it now has its own roadside parking lot.

Even though Oheo is part of Haleakala National Park, you cannot drive here from the summit. To drive to Oheo, head for Hana, some 60 miles from Kahului on the Hana Highway (Hwy. 36). Oheo is about 30 to 50 minutes beyond Hana, along Highway 31. The Highway 31 bridge passes over pools near the ocean; the other pools, plus magnificent 400-foot Waimoku falls, are reachable via an often-muddy but rewarding, hour-long uphill hike (see "Hiking" in chapter 5). Expect showers on the Kipahulu coast. The admission fee is $5 per person or $10 per car.

The **Kipahulu Ranger Station** (✆ **808/248-7375**) is staffed from 9am to 5pm daily. Restrooms are available, but no drinking water. Kipahulu rangers offer safety information, exhibits, books, and a variety of walks and hikes year-round; check at the station for current activities.

Check with the Haleakala Park rangers before hiking up to or swimming in the pools, and always keep one eye on the water in the streams; the sky can be sunny near the coast, but floodwaters travel 6 miles down from 8,000 acres of Kipahulu Valley and can rise 4 feet in less than 10 minutes.

7

# Shops & Galleries

Maui is a shopaholic's dream as well as an arts center, with a large number of resident artists who show their works in dozens of galleries and countless gift shops. Maui is also the queen of specialty products, an agricultural cornucopia that includes Kula onions, upcountry protea, Kaanapali coffee, world-renowned potato chips, and many other tasty treats that are shipped worldwide.

As with any popular visitor destination, you'll have to wade through bad art and mountains of trinkets, particularly in Lahaina and Kihei, where touristy boutiques line the streets between rare pockets of treasures. If you shop in South or West Maui, expect to pay resort prices, clear down to a bottle of Evian or sunscreen.

Central Maui is home to some first-rate boutiques. Watch Wailuku, which is poised for a resurgence. The town has its own antiques alleys, the new Sig Zane Designs has brought a delightful infusion of creative energy, and a major promenade/emporium on Main Street is in the works. The Kaahumanu Center, in neighboring Kahului, is becoming more fashionable by the month.

Upcountry, Makawao's boutiques are worth seeking out, despite some attitude and high prices. The charm of shopping on Maui has always rested in the small, independent shops and galleries that crop up in surprising places.

## 1 Central Maui

### KAHULUI

Kahului's best shopping is concentrated in two places. Almost all of the shops listed below are at one of the following centers:

The once rough-around-the-edges **Maui Mall,** 70 E. Kaahumanu Ave. (© **808/877-7559**), is the talk of Kahului. Newly renovated, it's now bigger and better, and has retained some of our favorite stores while adding a 12-screen movie megaplex that features current releases as well as art-house films. The mall is still a place of everyday good things, from **Long's Drugs** to **Star Market** to **Tasaka Guri Guri,** the decades-old purveyor of inimitable icy treats, neither ice cream nor shave ice but something in between.

**Queen Kaahumanu Center,** 275 Kaahumanu Ave. (✆ **808/877-3369**), 5 minutes from the Kahului Airport on Highway 32, offers more than 100 shops, restaurants, and theaters. Its second-floor Plantation District offers home furnishings and accessories, fabulous shoes at **Native Soles,** and gift and accessories shops. Kaahumanu covers all the bases, from the arts and crafts to a **Foodland Supermarket** and everything in between: a thriving food court; the island's best beauty supply, **Lisa's Beauty Supply & Salon** (✆ **808/877-6463**), and its sister store for cosmetics, **Madison Avenue Day Spa and Boutique** (✆ **808/873-0880**); mall standards like **Sunglass Hut** and **Radio Shack; Local Motion** (surf and beach wear); and standard department stores like **Macy's** and **Sears.**

**Cost Less Imports** This store features household accessories like lauhala, bamboo blinds, grassy floor and window coverings, shoji-style lamps, burlap yardage, baskets, Balinese cushions, Asian imports, and top-of-the-line, made-on-Maui soaps and handicrafts. Japanese folk curtains, called *noreng,* are among the diverse items you'll find here; it's a good source of tropical and Asian home decor. In the Maui Mall. ✆ **808/877-0300.**

**Maui Hands** The selection in this consignment shop/gallery. includes paintings, prints, jewelry, glass marbles, native-wood bowls, and tchotchkes for every budget. This is an ideal stop for made-on-Maui products and crafts of good quality; 90% of what's sold here was made on the island. The original **Maui Hands** remains in Makawao at the Courtyard, 3620 Baldwin Ave. (✆ 808/572-5194); another Maui Hands can be found in Paia, at 84 Hana Hwy. (✆ 808/579-9245). In the Kaahumanu Center. ✆ **808/877-0368.**

**Maui Swap Meet** The Maui Swap Meet is a large and popular event. After Thanksgiving and throughout December, the number of booths explodes into the hundreds. The colorful Maui specialties include vegetables from Kula and Keanae, fresh taro, plants, proteas, crafts, household items, homemade ethnic foods, and baked goods. Every Saturday from 7am to noon, vendors spread out their wares in booths and under tarps, in a festival-like atmosphere. Between the cheap Balinese imports and New Age crystals and incense, you may find some vintage John Kelly prints and 1930s collectibles. Admission is 50¢. S. Puunene Ave. (next to the Kahului Post Office). ✆ **808/877-3100.**

**Summerhouse** Sleek and chic, tiny Summerhouse is big on style: casual and party dresses, separates by Russ Berens, FLAX, Kiko, and Tencel jeans by Signatur—the best. During the holiday season the selection gets dressy and sassy, but it's a fun browse year-round. We adore the hats, accessories, easy-care clothing, and up-to-the-minute evening dresses that Summerhouse carries in abundance. The high-quality T-shirts are always a cut above. The casual selection is well suited to the island lifestyle. In the Dairy Center, 395 Dairy Rd. ✆ **808/871-1320.**

### EDIBLES

**Down to Earth Natural Foods,** 305 Dairy Rd. (✆ **808/877-2661**), a health-food staple for many years, has fresh organic produce, a bountiful salad bar, sandwiches and smoothies, vitamins and supplements, fresh-baked goods, chips and snacks, whole grains, and several packed aisles of vegetarian and health foods.

**Ohana Farmers Market** (✆ **808/871-8347**), Kahului Shopping Center, is the place to find a fresh, inexpensive selection of Maui-grown fruit, vegetables, flowers, and plants.

## WAILUKU

Located at the gateway to Iao Valley, Wailuku is the county seat, the part of Maui where people live and work. Wailuku's attractive vintage architecture, smattering of antiques shops, and mom-and-pop eateries imbue the town with a down-home charm. The community spirit is slowly attracting new businesses, but Wailuku is still a work in progress. It's a mixed bag—of course there's junk, but a stroll along Main and Market streets usually turns up a treasure or two.

**Bailey House Gift Shop** Bailey House offers a thoroughly enjoyable browse through authoritative Hawaiiana, in a museum that's one of the finest examples of missionary architecture. The shop boasts some remarkable gift items, from Hawaiian music to exquisite woods, traditional Hawaiian games to pareus and books. Prints by the legendary Hawaii artist Madge Tennent, lauhala hats, hand-sewn pheasant hatbands, jams and jellies, and an occasional Hawaiian quilt are some of the treasures to be found here. In the Bailey House Museum, 2375-A Main St. ✆ **808/244-3326.**

**Bird of Paradise Unique Antiques** Owner Joe Myhand loves furniture, old Matson liner menus, blue willow china, kimono for children, and anything nostalgic that happens to be Hawaiian. The furniture in the strongly Hawaiian collection ranges from

1940s rattan to wicker and old koa. The collection ebbs and flows with his finds, keeping buyers waiting in the wings for Depression glass, California pottery from the 1930s and 1940s, old dinnerware, perfume bottles, vintage aloha shirts, and vintage Hawaiian music on cassettes. 56 N. Market St. ✆ **808/242-7699.**

**Brown-Kobayashi** From self-adornment to interior design, graceful living is the theme here. Prices range from a few dollars to the thousands in this 750-square-foot treasure trove. The owners have added a fabulous selection of antique stone garden pieces that mingle quietly with Asian antiques and old and new French, European, and Hawaiian objects. Japanese kimono and obi, Bakelite and Peking glass beads, breathtaking Japanese lacquerware, cricket carriers, and cloisonné are among the delights here. 160-A N. Market St. ✆ **808/242-0804.**

**Gottling Ltd.** Karl Gottling's shop specializes in Asian antique furniture, but you can also find smaller carvings, precious stones, jewelry, opium weights, and finds in all sizes. On a recent visit, we saw a cabinet with 350-year-old doors, a 17th-century Buddha lending an air of serenity next to a 150-year-old Chinese cabinet, and Ming dynasty ceramics. The prices vary as widely, from carved wooden apples for $15 to a Persian rug for $65,000. 34 N. Market St. ✆ **808/244-7779.**

**Old Daze** Nineteenth-century Americana and Hawaiian collectibles are nicely wedded in this charming shop. The collection features a modest furniture selection, Hawaiian pictures, 1960s ashtrays, Depression glass, old washboards, and souvenir plates from county fairs. Choices range from hokey to rustic to pleasantly nostalgic. Some recent finds: an 1850s German sideboard, a Don Blanding teapot, Royal Worcester china, and antique kimono. 7 North Market St. (close to Main St.). ✆ **808/249-0014.**

**Sig Zane Designs Wailuku** Whether it's a T-shirt, golf shirt, pareu, duffel bag, aloha shirt, or muumuu, a Sig Zane design has depth and sizzle. Zane and co-owner Punawai Rice have redefined Hawaiian wear by creating an inimitable style in clothing, textiles, furnishings, bedding, and lifestyle accessories, and this, their Maui store, has proven enormously successful. Zane's strong, graphic fabrics are made into aloha shirts and women's wear and used in interiors and furnishings that evoke the gracious Hawaii of an earlier time. 53 Market St. ✆ **808/249-8997.**

### EDIBLES

Established in 1941, the **Ooka Super Market,** 1870 Main St., Wailuku (✆ **808/244-3931**), Maui's ultimate homegrown supermarket, is a mom-and-pop business that has grown by leaps and bounds but still manages to keep its neighborhood flavor. Ooka sells inexpensive produce, fresh island seafood, certified Angus beef, and Maui specialties such as manju and mochi. You'll also find one of Maui's finest and most affordable retail flower selections. Prepared foods are also a hit: bentos and plate lunches, roast chicken and laulau, and specialties from all the islands.

Located in the northern section of Wailuku, **Takamiya Market,** 359 N. Market St. (✆ **808/244-3404**), is much loved by local folks and visitors with adventurous palates. Unpretentious home-cooked foods from East and West are prepared daily and served on plastic-foam plates. From the chilled-fish counter come fresh sashimi and poke, and in the renowned assortment of prepared foods are mounds of shoyu chicken, tender fried squid, roast pork, kalua pork, laulau, Chinese noodles, and fiddlehead ferns. Fresh produce and paper products are also available.

## 2 West Maui

### LAHAINA

Lahaina's merchants and art galleries go all out from 7 to 9pm on Friday, when **Art Night** brings an extra measure of hospitality and community spirit. The Art Night openings are usually marked with live entertainment, refreshments, and a lively street scene.

If you're in Lahaina on the second or last Thursday of the month, stroll by the front lawn of the **Baldwin Home,** 120 Dickenson St. (at Front St.), for demonstrations of lei-making (you can even buy the results).

What was formerly a big, belching pineapple cannery is now a maze of shops and restaurants at the northern end of Lahaina town, known as the **Lahaina Cannery Mall,** 1221 Honoapiilani Hwy. (✆ **808/661-5304**). Find your way through the T-shirt and sportswear shops to **Lahaina Printsellers,** home of antique originals, prints, paintings, and wonderful 18th- to 20th-century cartography. **Roland's** may surprise you with its selection of footwear, everything from Cole-Haan sophisticates to inexpensive sandals. You'll find a variety of food choices, from pizza to Greek to Vietnamese, at the recently expanded food court.

The **Lahaina Center,** 900 Front St. (✆ **808/667-9216**), is still a work in progress. It's located north of Lahaina's most congested strip, where Front Street begins. There's plenty of free validated parking and easy access to more than 30 shops, a salon, restaurants, a nightclub, and a four-plex movie-theater complex. Among the shopping stops: **Banana Republic,** the **Hilo Hattie Fashion Center** (a dizzying emporium of aloha wear), **ABC Discount Store,** and a dozen other recreational, dining, and entertainment options.

The conversion of 10,000 square feet of parking space into the re-creation of a traditional Hawaiian village is a welcome touch of Hawaiiana at Lahaina Center. The village, called **Hale Kahiko,** features three main houses, called *hale:* a sleeping house; the men's dining house; and the crafts house. Construction of the houses consumed 10,000 square feet of ohia wood from the island, 20 tons of pili grass, and more than 4 miles of hand-woven coconut sennit for the lashings. Artifacts, weapons, a canoe, and indigenous trees are among the authentic touches in this village, which can be toured privately or with a guide.

**David Lee Galleries** This gallery is devoted to the works of David Lee, who uses natural powder colors to paint on silk. The pigments and technique create a luminous, ethereal quality. 712 Front St. ✆ **808/667-7740.**

**Gary's Island** Gary's cranks up the fun factor in aloha wear with this abundant, well-displayed selection of aloha shirts. Lahaina was number 11 in the Gary's chain of brightly colored resort shops—its first venture outside of California and Las Vegas. We've found fantastic hula-girl silk ties here by Tommy Bahama, and some offbeat shirt styles by Toes on the Nose and the usual top-drawer lines, such as Kamehameha, Tori Richard, Reyn's, Avanti, and Kahala. This tiny but dynamic shop also carries shoes for men and women, from Cole-Haan to gel-soled Sensis. 839-A Front St. ✆ **808/662-0424.**

**Lahaina Arts Society Galleries** With its membership of more than 185 Maui artists, the nonprofit Lahaina Arts Society is an excellent community resource. Changing monthly exhibits in the Banyan Tree and Old Jail galleries offer a good look at the island's artistic well: two-dimensional art, fiber art, ceramics, sculpture, prints, jewelry, and more. In the shade of the humongous banyan tree in the square across from Pioneer Inn, "Art in the Park" fairs are offered every second and fourth weekend of the month. 648 Wharf St. ✆ **808/661-3228.**

**Lei Spa Maui** Expanded to include two massage rooms and shower facilities, this is a day spa offering facials and other therapies. It's a good sign that 95% of the beauty and bath products sold are made on Maui, and that includes Hawaiian Botanical Pikake shower gel; kukui and macadamia-nut oils; Hawaiian potpourris; mud masks with Hawaiian seaweed; and a spate of rejuvenating, cleansing, skin-soothing potions for hair and skin. Aromatherapy body oils and perfumes are popular, as are the handmade soaps and fragrances of torch ginger, plumeria, coconut, tuberose, and sandalwood. Scented candles in coconut shells, inexpensive and fragrant, make great gifts. 505 Front St. ✆ **808/661-1178.**

**Martin Lawrence Galleries** The front is garish, with pop art, kinetic sculptures, and bright, carnivalesque glass objects. Toward the back of the gallery, however, there's a sizable inventory of two-dimensional art and some plausible choices for collectors of Keith Haring, Andy Warhol, and other pop artists. The originals, limited-edition graphics, and sculptures also include works by Marc Chagall, Pablo Picasso, Joan Miró, Roy Lichtenstein, and other noted artists. The focus is pop art and national and international artists. In Lahaina Market Place, 126 Lahainaluna Rd. ✆ **808/661-1788.**

**Na Mea Hawaii** The best of Hawaii can be found here, if not in the striking Tutuvi silk-screened dresses and shirts, then in the delicately patterned shawls and scarves of Maile Andrade that depict Hawaiian scenes and traditions on velvet. Arts, crafts, gifts, and clothing, all made by Hawaii artists, fill this cozy niche of Lahaina in the historic Baldwin House on Front Street. You might find a beautifully made lauhala bag, a colorful muumuu, a Hawaii-themed book, or a pheasant hat lei made by master feather lei makers Mary Lou Kekuewa and Paulette Kahalepuna. The shop is tiny, filled with the colors, fibers, and spirit of Hawaii. Lahaina Cannery Mall, 1221 Honoapiilani Hwy. ✆ **808/667-5345.**

**The Old Lahaina Book Emporium** What a bookstore! Chock-ablock with used books in stacks, shelves, counters, and aisles, this bookstore is a browser's dream. More than 25,000 quality used books are lovingly housed in this shop, where owner JoAnn Carroll treats books and customers well. The store is 95% used books and 100% delight. Specialties include Hawaiiana, fiction, mystery, sci-fi, and military history, with substantial selections in cookbooks, children's books, and philosophy/religion. You could pay as little as $2 for a quality read, or a whole lot more for that rare first edition. Books on tape, videos, the classics, and old guitar magazines are among the treasures of this two-story emporium. 505 Front St. ✆ **808/661-1399.**

**Totally Hawaiian Gift Gallery** This gallery makes a good browse for its selection of Niihau shell jewelry, excellent Hawaiian CDs, Norfolk pine bowls, and Hawaiian quilt kits. Hawaiian quilt patterns sewn in Asia (at least they're honest about it) are labor-intensive, less expensive, and attractive, although not totally Hawaiian. Hawaiian-quilt-patterned gift wraps and tiles, perfumes and soaps, handcrafted dolls, and koa accessories are of good quality, and the artists, such as Kelly Dunn (Norfolk wood bowls), Jerry Kermode (wood), and Pat Coito (wood), are among the tops in their fields. In the Lahaina Cannery Mall, 1221 Honoapiilani Hwy. ✆ **808/667-2558.**

**Village Galleries in Lahaina** The nearly 30-year-old Village Galleries is the oldest continuously running gallery on Maui, and it's highly esteemed as one of the few galleries with consistently high standards. Art collectors know this as a respectable showcase for regional artists; the selection of mostly original two- and three-dimensional art offers a good look at the quality of work originating on the island. The newer contemporary gallery offers colorful gift items and jewelry. 120 and 180 Dickenson St. ✆ **808/661-4402** or 808/661-5559. Also the Ritz-Carlton Kapalua, 1 Ritz-Carlton Dr. ✆ 808/669-1800.

### EDIBLES

A longtime Lahaina staple, **Down to Earth,** 193 Lahainaluna Rd. (✆ **808/667-2855**) is serious about providing tasty food that's healthy and affordable. Its excellent food bar offers vegetarian lasagna, marinated tofu strips, vegetarian pot-pie, crisp salads, grains, curries, and gorgeous organic produce. Other products include produce, cosmetics, and healthy food staples.

## KAANAPALI

On a recent trip we were somewhat disappointed with upscale **Whalers Village,** 2435 Kaanapali Pkwy. (✆ **808/661-4567**). Although it offers everything from whale blubber to Prada and Ferragamo, it is short on local shops and parking at the nearby lot is expensive. The **Whale Center of the Pacific** museum (see chapter 6) is a unique stop in this mall, but as far as shopping's concerned, you can find most of the items featured here in the shops in Lahaina, where parking is less of a hassle and less expensive.

Despite obvious efforts to offer a balance between island-made and designer goods, the chain luxury stores dominate at Whalers Village. **Tiffany, Prada, Chanel, Ferragamo, Vuitton, Coach, Dolphin Galleries, The Body Shop,** are a few of the more than 60 shops and restaurants that have sprouted in this open-air shopping center. Our favorite shoe store, **Sandal Tree,** has its third store here (the other two stores are at Hyatt Regency Maui and Grand Wailea Resort in Wailea). **Martin & MacArthur,** a mainstay of the village, offers a dizzying array of Hawaii crafts. The always wonderful **Lahaina Printsellers** has a selection of antique prints, maps, paintings, and engravings, including 18th- to 20th-century cartography. You can find award-winning **Kimo Bean** coffee at a kiosk, an expanded **Reyn's** for aloha wear, and **Cinnamon Girl,** a hit in Honolulu for its matching mother-daughter clothing. The return of **Waldenbooks** makes it that much easier to pick up the latest best-seller on the way to the beach.

Other mainstays: The **Eyecatcher** has an extensive selection of sunglasses; it's located just across from the busiest **ABC** store in the state. The food court offers dine-and-dash goodies, such as **Pizza Paradiso** and the terrific Japanese fare of **Ganso Kawara Soba.** Whalers Village is open daily from 9:30am to 10pm.

**Ki'i Gallery** Those who love glass in all forms, from handblown vessels to jewelry, will enjoy a browse through Ki'i. Some of the works are large and lavish, such as the Toland Sand prisms for just under $5,000 and the John Stokes handblown glass. We found Pat Kazi's work in porcelain and found objects both fantastic and compelling. The gallery is devoted to glass and original paintings and drawings; roughly half of the artists are from Hawaii. Hyatt Regency Maui, 200 Nohea Kai Dr. ✆ **808/661-4456.**

**Sandal Tree** The Sandal Tree attracts a flock of footwear fanatics who come here from throughout the islands for rubber thongs and Top-Siders, sandals and dressy pumps, athletic shoes and hats, designer footwear, and much more. Sandal Tree also carries a generous selection of Mephisto and Arche comfort sandals, Donald Pliner, Anne Klein, Charles Jourdan, and beach wear and casual footwear for all tastes. Accessories range from fashionable knapsacks to avant-garde geometrical handbags—for town and country, day and evening, kids, women, and men. Prices are realistic, too.

In Whalers Village, 2435 Kaanapali Pkwy. ✆ **808/667-5330.** Also in the Grand Wailea Resort, 3850 Wailea Alanui Dr., Wailea; and in the Hyatt Regency Maui, 200 Nohea Kai Dr.

## KAHANA/NAPILI/HONOKOWAI

Those driving north of Kaanapali toward Kapalua will notice the **Honokowai Marketplace** on Lower Honoapiilani Road, only minutes before the Kapalua Airport. There are restaurants and coffee shops, a dry cleaner, the flagship **Star Market, Hula Scoops** for ice cream, a gas station, a copy shop, a few clothing stores, and the sprawling **Hawaiian Interiorz.**

Nearby **Kahana Gateway** is an unimpressive mall built to serve the condominium community that has sprawled along the coastline between Honokowai and Kapalua. If you need women's swimsuits, however, **Rainbow Beach Swimwear** is a find. It carries a selection of suits at lower-than-resort prices, slashed even further during the frequent sales. **Hutton's Fine Jewelry** offers high-end jewelry from designers around the country (lots of platinum and diamonds). Tahitian black pearls and jade (some hundreds of years old, all certified) are among Hutton's specialties.

## KAPALUA

**Honolua Store** Walk on the old wood floors peppered with holes from golf shoes and find your everyday essentials: bottled water, stationery, mailing tape, jackets, chips, wine, soft drinks, paper products, and fresh fruit and produce. With picnic tables on the veranda and a take-out counter offering deli items—more than a dozen types of sandwiches, salads, and budget-friendly breakfasts—there are always long lines of customers. Golfers and surfers love to come here for the morning paper and coffee. 502 Office Rd. (next to the Ritz-Carlton Kapalua). ✆ **808/669-6128.**

**Kapalua Shops** Shops have come and gone in this small, exclusive, and once-chic shopping center; the closing of elegant Mandalay is a big loss. The **Elizabeth Dole Gallery** has loads of Dale Chihuly studio glass, fabulous and expensive, a dramatic counterpoint to **South Seas Trading Post** and its exotic artifacts such as New Guinea masks, Balinese beads, tribal jewelry, lizard-skin drums, and coconut-shell carvings. Otherwise, it's slim pickings for shoppers in Kapalua, where logo wear, jewelry, and real-estate offices are the norm and the fabulous Sansei sushi bar reigns. Kapalua Bay Hotel and Villas. ✆ **808/669-1029.**

**Village Galleries** Maui's finest exhibit their works here and in the other two Village Galleries in Lahaina. Translucent, delicately turned bowls of Norfolk pine gleam in the light, and George Allan, Betty Hay Freeland, and Pamela Andelin are included in the pantheon of respected artists represented in the tiny gallery. Watercolors, oils, sculptures, handblown glass, Niihau shell leis, jewelry, and other media are represented. A monthly program features demonstrations and free hands-on workshops. In the Ritz-Carlton Kapalua, 1 Ritz-Carlton Dr. ✆ **808/669-1800.**

## 3 South Maui

### KIHEI

Kihei is one long stretch of strip malls. Most of the shopping here is concentrated in the **Azeka Place Shopping Center** on South Kihei Road. Fast foods abound at Azeka, as do tourist-oriented clothing shops like **Crazy Shirts.** Across the street, **Azeka Place II** houses several prominent attractions, including **General Nutrition Center,** the **Coffee Store,** and a cluster of specialty shops with everything from children's clothes to shoes, sunglasses, beauty services, and swimwear. Also on South Kihei Road is the **Kukui Mall,** with movie theaters, **Waldenbooks,** and **Whaler's General Store.**

**Hawaiian Moons Natural Foods** Hawaiian Moons is a health-food store, and a great one, but it's also a minisupermarket with one of the best selections of Maui products on the island. The Mexican tortillas are made on Maui (and good!), and much of the produce here, such as organic vine-ripened tomatoes and organic onions, is grown in the fertile upcountry soil of Kula. There's also locally grown organic coffee, gourmet salsas, Maui shiitake mushrooms, organic lemongrass and okra, Maui Crunch bread, free-range Big Island turkeys and chickens (no antibiotics or artificial nasties), and fresh Maui juices. Cosmetics are top-of-the-line: a staggering selection of sunblock, fragrant floral oils, and Island Essence made-on-Maui mango-coconut and vanilla-papaya lotions, the ultimate in body pampering. The salad bar is one of the most popular food stops on the coast. 2411 S. Kihei Rd. ✆ **808/875-4356.**

**Pua's Lei Stand** Surprise—fresh plumeria lei in hot Kihei! Located at the far mauka (mountainside) end of the shopping village, Pua's Lei Stand is an oasis of fragrance, freshness, and the spirit of Hawaii. You'll see lavish wiliwili and seed lei, hula implements,

Hawaiian-printed flaxseed eye pillows, Hawaiian angels made from fibers found in Kihei, and all manner of made-on-Maui gems. The hard-to-find Maui Herbal soaps are generous blocks in fabulous fragrances of pikake, tuberose, guavaberry, tropical sea, and—our favorite—plumeria. These soaps lather richly and contain pure ingredients; their simple packaging belies the fact that they are of top quality, and not widely available. In Kihei Kalama Village, 1941 S. Kihei Rd. No phone.

**Tuna Luna** There are treasures to be found in this small cluster of tables and booths where Maui artists display their work. Ceramics, raku, sculpture, glass, koa-wood books and photo albums, jewelry, soaps, handmade paper, and fiber-art accessories make great gifts to go. Watch for Maui Metal handcrafted journals, aluminum books with designs of hula girls, palms, fish, and sea horses. Tuna Luna also has a new booth in the back pavilion. In Kihei Kalama Village, 1941 S. Kihei Rd. ✆ **808/874-9482.**

## WAILEA

**CY Maui** Women who like washable, flowing clothing in silks, rayons, and natural fibers will love this shop, formerly the popular Manikin in Kahului. If you don't find what you want on the racks of simple bias-cut designs, you can have it made from the bolts of stupendous fabrics lining the shop. Except for a few hand-painted silks, everything in the shop is washable. In The Shops at Wailea, 3750 Wailea Alanui Dr, A-30. ✆ **808/891-0782.**

**Grand Wailea Shops** The sprawling Grand Wailea Resort is known for its long arcade of shops and galleries tailored to hefty pocketbooks. However, gift items in all price ranges can be found at Lahaina Printsellers (for old maps and prints), Dolphin Galleries, H. F. Wichman, Sandal Tree, and Napua Gallery, which houses the private collection of the resort owner. Ki'i Gallery is luminous with studio glass and exquisitely turned woods, and **Sandal Tree** (p. 162) raises the footwear bar. At Grand Wailea Resort, 3850 Wailea Alanui Dr. ✆ **808/875-1234.**

**The Shops at Wailea** This is the big shopping boost that resort-goers have been awaiting for years. Chains still rule **(The Gap, Louis Vuitton, Banana Republic, Tiffany, Crazy Shirts, Honolua Surf Co.),** but there is still fertile ground for the inveterate shopper in the nearly 60 shops in the complex. **Martin & MacArthur** (furniture and gift gallery; see Whalers Village above) has landed in

Wailea as part of a retail mix that is similar to Whalers Village. The high-end resort shops sell expensive souvenirs, gifts, clothing, and accessories for a life of perpetual vacations. 3750 Wailea Alanui. ✆ **808/891-6770.**

## 4 Upcountry Maui

### MAKAWAO

Besides being a shopper's paradise, Makawao is the home of the island's most prominent arts organization, the **Hui No'eau Visual Arts Center,** 2841 Baldwin Ave. (✆ **808/572-6560**). The center is located on a sprawling 9-acre estate called Kaluanui. A legacy of Maui's prominent *kamaaina* (old-timers) Harry and Ethel Baldwin, the estate became an arts center in 1976. Visiting artists offer lectures, classes, and demonstrations, all at reasonable prices, in basketry, jewelry making, ceramics, painting, and other media. Classes on Hawaiian art, culture, and history are also available. Call ahead for schedules and details. The exhibits here include both contemporary and traditional art from established and emerging artists. The gift shop, featuring many one-of-a-kind works by local artists and artisans, is worth a stop. Hours are Monday through Saturday from 10am to 4pm.

**Collections** This long-time Makawao attraction is one of our favorite Makawao stops, full of gift items and spirited clothing reflecting the ease and color of island living. Its selection of sportswear, soaps, jewelry, candles, and tasteful, marvelous miscellany reflects good sense and style. Dresses, separates, home and bath accessories, sweaters, and a shop full of good things make this a Makawao must. 3677 Baldwin Ave. ✆ **808/572-0781.**

**Cuckoo for Coconuts** The owner's quirky sense of humor pervades every inch of this tiny shop, which is brimming with vintage collectibles, gag gifts, silly coconuts, 1960s and '70s aloha wear, tutus, sequined dresses, vintage wedding gowns, and all sorts of oddities. Vintage aloha wear comes and goes, and gets grabbed up fast. New items include crazy sunglasses, colored wigs, tie-dyes, and party hats. 1158 Makawao Ave. ✆ **808/573-6887.**

**Gallery Maui** Most of the works in this cozy gallery are by Maui artists, and the quality is outstanding. About 30 artists are represented: Wayne Omura and his Norfolk pine bowls, Pamela Hayes's watercolors, Martha Vockrodt and her wonderful paintings, a stunning Steve Hynson dresser of curly koa and ebony. The two- and three-dimensional original works reflect the high standards of gallery owners Deborah and Robert Zaleski (a painter), who have just added to their roster the talented ceramic artist David Stabley, a two-time American Craft Council juror. 3643-A Baldwin Ave. ✆ **808/572-8092.**

**Gecko Trading Co. Boutique** The selection in this tiny boutique is eclectic and always changing: One day it's St. John's Wort body lotion and mesh T-shirts in a dragon motif, the next it's Provence soaps and antique lapis jewelry. We've seen everything from hair scrunchies to handmade crocheted bags from New York, collectible bottles, toys, shawls, and Mexican hammered-tin candleholders. The prices are reasonable, the service is friendly, and it's more homey than glammy, and not as self-conscious as some of the other local boutiques. 3621 Baldwin Ave. ✆ **808/572-0249.**

**Holiday & Co.** Attractive women's clothing in natural fibers hangs from racks, while jewelry to go with it beckons from the counter. Recent finds include elegant fiber evening bags, luxurious bath gels, easygoing dresses and separates, Dansko clogs, shawls, shoes, soaps, aloha shirts, books, picture frames, and jewelry. 3681 Baldwin Ave. ✆ **808/572-1470.**

**Hot Island Glassblowing Studio & Gallery** You can watch the artist transform molten glass into works of art and utility in this studio in Makawao's Courtyard, where an award-winning family of glassblowers built its own furnaces. It's fascinating to watch the shapes emerge from glass melted at 2,300°F (1,260°C). The colorful works displayed range from small paperweights to large vessels. Four to five artists participate in the demonstrations, which begin when the furnace is heated, about half an hour before the studio opens at 9am. 3620 Baldwin Ave. ✆ **808/572-4527.**

**Hurricane** This boutique carries clothing, gifts, accessories, and books that are two steps ahead of the competition. Tommy Bahama aloha shirts and aloha print dresses; Sigrid Olsen's knitted shells, cardigans, and extraordinary silk tank dresses; hats; art by local artists; a notable selection of fragrances for men and women; and hard-to-find, eccentric books and home accessories are part of the Hurricane appeal. 3639 Baldwin Ave. ✆ **808/572-5076.**

**The Mercantile** The jewelry, home accessories, dinnerware, Italian linens, plantation-style furniture, and clothing here are a salute to the good life. The exquisite bedding, rugs, and furniture include hand-carved armoires, down-filled furniture and slipcovers, and a large selection of Kiehl's products. The clothing—comfortable cottons and upscale European linens—is for men and women, as are the soaps, which include Maui Herbal Soap products and some unusual finds from France. 3673 Baldwin Ave. ✆ **808/572-1407.**

**Viewpoints Gallery** Maui's only fine-arts cooperative showcases the work of 20 established artists in an airy, attractive gallery located in a restored theater with a courtyard, glassblowing studio, and restaurants. The gallery features two-dimensional art, jewelry, fiber art, stained glass, paper, sculpture, and other media. This is a fine example of what can happen in a collectively supportive artistic environment. 3620 Baldwin Ave. ✆ **808/572-5979.**

### EDIBLES

Working folks in Makawao pick up spaghetti, lasagna, sandwiches, salads, and wide-ranging specials from the **Rodeo General Store,** 3661 Baldwin Ave. (✆ **808/572-7841**). At the far end of the store is a superior wine selection housed in a temperature-controlled cave.

**Down to Earth Natural Foods,** 1169 Makawao Ave. (✆ **808/572-1488**), always has fresh salads and sandwiches, a full section of organic produce, bulk grains, beauty aids, herbs, juices, snacks, tofu, seaweed, soy products, and aisles of vegetarian and health foods.

In the more than 6 decades that the **T. Komoda Store and Bakery,** 3674 Baldwin Ave. (✆ **808/572-7261**), has spent in this spot, untold numbers have creaked over the wooden floors to pick up Komoda's famous cream puffs. Old-timers know to come early, or they'll be sold out. If you're too late for cream puffs, you'll still have cinnamon rolls, doughnuts, pies, chocolate cake, poi, macadamia-nut candies and cookies, and local fruit to choose from.

## FRESH FLOWERS IN KULA (AT THE BASE OF HALEAKALA NATIONAL PARK)

Proteas are a Maui trademark and an abundant crop on Haleakala's rich volcanic slopes. They travel well, dry beautifully, and can be shipped worldwide. Among Maui's most prominent sources is **Sunrise Protea** (✆ **808/876-0200;** www.sunriseprotea.com), in Kula. Freshly cut flowers arrive from the fields on Tuesday and Friday afternoons. You can order individual blooms, baskets, arrangements, or wreaths for shipping all over the world.

## 5 East Maui

### PAIA

**Biasa Rose Boutique** You'll find unusual gift items and clothing with a tropical flair: capri pants in bark cloth, floating plumeria candles, retro fabrics, dinnerware, handbags and accessories, and stylish vintage-inspired clothes for kids. If the aloha shirts don't get you, the candles and handbags will. You can also custom-order clothing from a selection of washable rayons. 104 Hana Hwy. ✆ **808/579-8602.**

**Hemp House** Clothing and accessories made of hemp, a sturdy, ecofriendly, and sensible fiber, are finally making their way into the mainstream. The Hemp House has as complete a selection as you can expect to see in Hawaii, with "denim" hemp jeans, lightweight linenlike trousers, dresses, shirts, and a full range of sensible, easy-care wear. 16 Baldwin Ave. ✆ **808/579-8880.**

**Maui Crafts Guild** The old wooden storefront at the gateway to Paia houses crafts of high quality and in all price ranges. Artist-owned and -operated, the guild claims 25 members who live and work on Maui. Basketry, hand-painted fabrics, jewelry, beadwork, traditional Hawaiian stone work, pressed flowers, fused glass, stained glass, copper sculpture, banana bark paintings, pottery of all styles, and hundreds of other items are displayed. Upstairs, sculptor Arthur Dennis Williams displays his breathtaking work in wood, bronze, and stone. Everything can be shipped. **Aloha Bead Co.** (✆ **808/579-9709**), in the back of the gallery, is a treasure trove for beadworkers. 43 Hana Hwy. ✆ **808/579-9697.**

**Moonbow Tropics** If you're looking for a tasteful aloha shirt, go to Moonbow. The selection consists of a few carefully culled racks of the top labels in aloha wear, in a variety of fabrics. Silk pants, silk shorts, vintage print neckwear, and an upgraded women's selection hang on neat, colorful racks. The jewelry pieces, ranging from tanzanite to topaz, rubies and moonstones, are mounted in unique settings made on-site. 36 Baldwin Ave. ✆ **808/579-8592.**

### HANA

**Hana Coast Gallery** This gallery is one main reason to go to Hana. Tucked away in the posh hideaway hotel, the gallery is known for its high level of curatorship and commitment to the cultural art of Hawaii. Except for a section of European and Asian masters (Renoir, Japanese woodblock prints), the 3,000-square-foot gallery is devoted entirely to Hawaii artists. Dozens of well-established local artists display their sculptures, paintings, prints, feather work, stonework, an expanded collection of koa-wood furniture, and carvings.

Connoisseurs of hand-turned bowls will find the crème de la crème of the genre here: J. Kelly Dunn, Ron Kent, Todd Campbell, Ed Perrira, and Gary Stevens. You won't find a better selection elsewhere that exists under one roof. The award-winning gallery has won accolades from the top travel and arts magazines in the country. In the Hotel Hana-Maui. ✆ **808/248-8636.**

**Hasegawa General Store** Established in 1910, immortalized in song since 1961, burned to the ground in 1990, and back in business in 1991, this legendary store is indefatigable and more colorful than ever in its fourth generation in business. The aisles are choked with merchandise: coffee specially roasted and blended for the store, Ono Farms organic dried fruit, fishing equipment, every tape and CD that mentions Hana, the best books on Hana to be found, T-shirts, beach and garden essentials, baseball caps, film, baby food, napkins, and other necessities. Hana Hwy., in Hana. ✆ **808/248-8231.**

# Maui After Dark

Centered in the $32 million **Maui Arts and Cultural Center** in Kahului (✆ **808/242-7469;** www.mauiarts.org), the performing arts are alive and well on this island. The MACC remains the island's most prestigious entertainment venue, a first-class center for the visual and performing arts. Bonnie Raitt has performed here, as have Pearl Jam, Tony Bennett, the American Indian Dance Theatre, the Maui Symphony Orchestra, and more, not to mention the finest in local and Hawaiian talent. The center includes a visual-arts gallery, an outdoor amphitheater, offices, rehearsal space, a 300-seat theater for experimental performances, and a 1,200-seat main theater. Check the *Maui News* for what's going on during your visit.

People are still agog over **'Ulalena,** an extraordinary production that tells the story of Hawaii in chant, song, original music, acrobatics, and dance, using state-of-the-art technology and some of the most creative staging to be seen in Hawaii. A local and international cast performs this $9.5 million production at the comfy **Maui Myth & Magic Theatre** in Lahaina (see section 1 below).

## IN SEARCH OF HAWAIIAN, JAWAIIAN & MORE

Nightlife options on this island are limited. Revelers generally head for **Casanova** in Makawao and **Maui Brews** in Lahaina. The major hotels generally have lobby lounges offering Hawaiian music, soft jazz, or hula shows beginning at sunset.

If **Hapa, Willie K., Amy Gilliom,** or the soloist **Keali'i Reichel** are playing anywhere on their native island, don't miss them; they're among the finest Hawaiian musicians around today. Most clubs with dance floors play a combination of Hawaiian and reggae, called Jawaiian, with a heated-up rhythm that young dancers love.

## 1 West Maui: Lahaina

**Maui Brews,** 900 Front St. (✆ **808/667-7794**), draws the late-night crowd to its corner of the Lahaina Center with swing, salsa, reggae, and jams—either live or with a DJ every night. The

### *Moments* It Begins with Sunset . . .

Nightlife in Maui begins at sunset, when all eyes turn westward. Sunset viewers seem to bond in the mutual enjoyment of a natural spectacle. And what better way to take it all in than over cocktails?

Along South and West Maui, our favorite sunset watering holes begin toward the north with **The Bay Club at Kapalua** (✆ **808/669-5656**), where a pianist plays nightly.

In Kaanapali, park in Whalers Village and head for **Leilani's** (✆ **808/661-4495**) or **Hula Grill** (✆ **808/667-6636**), next to each other on the beach. Both have busy, upbeat bars and tables bordering the sand. Leilani's has live music daily from 3:30 to 6pm, while at Hula Grill the happy hour starts at 3pm, live music at 6pm, and hula at 8pm.

In Lahaina, if you love loud rock, head for **Cheeseburger in Paradise** (✆ **808/661-4855**). A few doors away, the **Lahaina Fish Company** (✆ **808/661-3472**) and **Kimo's** (✆ **808/661-4811**) are magnets all day long and especially at sunset, when their open decks fill up with revelers. These three restaurants occupy Front Street between Lahainaluna Road and Papalaua Street.

At the southern end of Lahaina, in the 505 Front Street complex, **Pacific'o** (✆ **808/667-4341**) is a solid hit, with a raised bar, seating on the ocean, and a backdrop of Lanai

nightclub opens at 9pm and closes at 2am. Depending on the entertainment, sometimes there's a cover charge after 9pm; generally if there is one it's $5. For recorded information on entertainment (which changes, so it's a good idea to call), call ✆ **808/669-2739;** www.mauibrews.com.

At **Longhi's** (✆ **808/667-2288**), live music spills out into the streets from 9:30pm on weekends (with a cover charge of $5). It's usually salsa or jazz, but call ahead to confirm.

**Cheeseburger in Paradise** (✆ **808/661-4855**) features loud, live tropical rock nightly from 4:30 to 11pm (no cover charge).

## A NIGHT TO REMEMBER: LUAU, MAUI STYLE

Most of the larger hotels in Maui's major resorts offer luaus on a regular basis. You'll pay about $65 to attend one. Don't expect it to be

across the channel. A few steps away, sister restaurant **I'o** has an appetizer menu and a techno-curved bar that will wow you as much as the drop-dead-gorgeous view.

Moving south toward Wailea, in Maalaea, **Buzz's Wharf** (✆ **808/244-5426**) is a formula restaurant with a superb ocean view.

In Wailea, the restaurants at the new Shops at Wailea, including the highly successful **Tommy Bahama** (✆ **808/875-9983**), are a noteworthy addition to the beachfront retail and dining scene. **Ferraro's** and **Pacific Grill** (✆ **808/874-8000**), both at the neighboring Four Seasons Resort Wailea, have great sunset views to go with their Italian and Pacific Rim menus. In Makena resort farther south, you can't beat the Maui Prince's **Molokini Lounge** (✆ **808/874-1111**), with its casual elegance and unequaled view of Molokini islet on the ocean side. An appetizer menu is served from 5 to 9:30pm nightly, and live Hawaiian entertainment runs nightly from 6 to 10:30pm.

An upcountry sunset view is a great way to end the day if you don't mind the drive. **Kula Lodge** (✆ **808/878-2517**) has a phenomenal view that takes in central Maui, the West Maui Mountains, and the coastline. They serve an appetizer-only menu from 3:30 to 5pm.

a homegrown affair prepared in the traditional Hawaiian way. However, even some commercial luaus capture the romance and spirit of the luau with quality food and entertainment.

Maui's best luau is indisputably the nightly **Old Lahaina Luau** (✆ **800/248-5828** or 808/667-1998; www.oldlahainaluau.com). On its 1-acre site just ocean side of the Lahaina Cannery at 1251 Front St., the Old Lahaina Luau maintains its high standards in food and entertainment. Seating is provided on lauhala mats for those who wish to dine as the traditional Hawaiians did, but there are tables for everyone else. There's no fire dancing in the program (for that, go to the **Feast at Lele;** p. 82).

The luau begins at sunset and features Tahitian and Hawaiian entertainment, including various forms of hula and an intelligent narrative on the dance's rocky course of survival into modern times.

The entertainment is riveting, even for jaded locals. The food is as much Pacific Rim as authentically Hawaiian: imu-roasted kalua pig, baked mahimahi in Maui onion cream sauce, guava chicken, teriyaki sirloin steak, lomi salmon, poi, dried fish, poke, Hawaiian sweet potato, sautéed vegetables, seafood salad, and taro leaves with coconut milk. The cost is $79 adults, $49 children (plus tax).

### 'ULALENA: HULA, MYTH & MODERN DANCE

The highly polished **'Ulalena,** staged in the Maui Myth and Magic Theatre, 878 Front St. (© **877/688-4800** or 808/661-9913; www.ulalena.com), is the talk of the town, a riveting production that weaves Hawaiian mythology with drama, dance, and state-of-the-art multimedia capabilities in a brand-new, multimillion-dollar theater.

A local and international cast performs Polynesian dance, original music, acrobatics, and chant. Dancers come down the aisles, drummers and musicians play in surprising corners, and mind-boggling stage and lighting effects draw the audience in. The effects of the modern choreography and traditional hula, a fusion of genres, are surprisingly evocative and emotional. Performances are Tuesday at 6 and 8:30pm, and Wednesday to Saturday at 6pm only. Tickets are $48 to $58 for adults and $28 to $38 for children ages 3 to 10.

## 2 Upcountry Maui

Upcountry in Makawao, the party never ends at **Casanova,** 1188 Makawao Ave. (© **808/572-0220**), the popular Italian ristorante where the good times roll with the pasta. DJs spin on Wednesday (ladies' night), but on Thursday, Friday, and Saturday, live entertainment draws crowds. Entertainment starts at 9:45pm and continues to 1:30am. Expect good blues, rock-and-roll, reggae, jazz, Hawaiian, and the top names in local and visiting entertainment. Elvin Bishop, the local duo Hapa, Los Lobos, and many others have filled Casanova's stage. The cover is usually $5. Come Sunday afternoons, 3 to 6pm, for excellent live jazz.

In the unlikely location of Paia, **Moanai Bakery & Café** (71 Baldwin Ave, © **808/579-9999**), not only has some of the best and most innovative cuisine around, but recently it has added live music: vintage Hawaiian from 6:30 to 9pm on Wednesday; smooth jazz and hot blues on from 6:30 to 9pm on Friday; and flamingo guitar and gypsy violin from 6 to 9pm on Sunday. There's no cover.

# Index

See also Accommodations and Restaurant indexes below.

## General Index

## ACCOMMODATIONS

## RESTAURANTS

## FROMMER'S® COMPLETE TRAVEL GUIDES

Alaska
Alaska Cruises & Ports of Call
Amsterdam
Argentina & Chile
Arizona
Atlanta
Australia
Austria
Bahamas
Barcelona, Madrid & Seville
Beijing
Belgium, Holland & Luxembourg
Bermuda
Boston
Brazil
British Columbia & the Canadian Rockies
Brussels & Bruges
Budapest & the Best of Hungary
California
Canada
Cancún, Cozumel & the Yucatán
Cape Cod, Nantucket & Martha's Vineyard
Caribbean
Caribbean Cruises & Ports of Call
Caribbean Ports of Call
Carolinas & Georgia
Chicago
China
Colorado
Costa Rica
Cuba
Denmark
Denver, Boulder & Colorado Springs
England
Europe
European Cruises & Ports of Call
Florida
France
Germany
Great Britain
Greece
Greek Islands
Hawaii
Hong Kong
Honolulu, Waikiki & Oahu
Ireland
Israel
Italy
Jamaica
Japan
Las Vegas
London
Los Angeles
Maryland & Delaware
Maui
Mexico
Montana & Wyoming
Montréal & Québec City
Munich & the Bavarian Alps
Nashville & Memphis
New England
New Mexico
New Orleans
New York City
New Zealand
Northern Italy
Norway
Nova Scotia, New Brunswick & Prince Edward Island
Oregon
Paris
Peru
Philadelphia & the Amish Country
Portugal
Prague & the Best of the Czech Republic
Provence & the Riviera
Puerto Rico
Rome
San Antonio & Austin
San Diego
San Francisco
Santa Fe, Taos & Albuquerque
Scandinavia
Scotland
Seattle & Portland
Shanghai
Sicily
Singapore & Malaysia
South Africa
South America
South Florida
South Pacific
Southeast Asia
Spain
Sweden
Switzerland
Texas
Thailand
Tokyo
Toronto
Tuscany & Umbria
USA
Utah
Vancouver & Victoria
Vermont, New Hampshire & Maine
Vienna & the Danube Valley
Virgin Islands
Virginia
Walt Disney World® & Orlando
Washington, D.C.
Washington State

## FROMMER'S® DOLLAR-A-DAY GUIDES

Australia from $50 a Day
California from $70 a Day
England from $75 a Day
Europe from $70 a Day
Florida from $70 a Day
Hawaii from $80 a Day
Ireland from $60 a Day
Italy from $70 a Day
London from $85 a Day
New York from $90 a Day
Paris from $80 a Day
San Francisco from $70 a Day
Washington, D.C. from $80 a Day
Portable London from $85 a Day
Portable New York City from $90 a Day

## FROMMER'S® PORTABLE GUIDES

Acapulco, Ixtapa & Zihuatanejo
Amsterdam
Aruba
Australia's Great Barrier Reef
Bahamas
Berlin
Big Island of Hawaii
Boston
California Wine Country
Cancún
Cayman Islands
Charleston
Chicago
Disneyland®
Dublin
Florence
Frankfurt
Hong Kong
Houston
Las Vegas
Las Vegas for Non-Gamblers
London
Los Angeles
Los Cabos & Baja
Maine Coast
Maui
Miami
Nantucket & Martha's Vineyard
New Orleans
New York City
Paris
Phoenix & Scottsdale
Portland
Puerto Rico
Puerto Vallarta, Manzanillo & Guadalajara
Rio de Janeiro
San Diego
San Francisco
Savannah
Seattle
Sydney
Tampa & St. Petersburg
Vancouver
Venice
Virgin Islands
Washington, D.C.

## FROMMER'S® NATIONAL PARK GUIDES

Banff & Jasper
Family Vacations in the National Parks
Grand Canyon
National Parks of the American West
Rocky Mountain
Yellowstone & Grand Teton
Yosemite & Sequoia/Kings Canyon
Zion & Bryce Canyon

## Frommer's® Memorable Walks

Chicago
London
New York
Paris
San Francisco

## Frommer's® With Kids Guides

Chicago
Las Vegas
New York City
Ottawa
San Francisco
Toronto
Vancouver
Washington, D.C.

## Suzy Gershman's Born to Shop Guides

Born to Shop: France
Born to Shop: Hong Kong, Shanghai & Beijing
Born to Shop: Italy
Born to Shop: London
Born to Shop: New York
Born to Shop: Paris

## Frommer's® Irreverent Guides

Amsterdam
Boston
Chicago
Las Vegas
London
Los Angeles
Manhattan
New Orleans
Paris
Rome
San Francisco
Seattle & Portland
Vancouver
Walt Disney World®
Washington, D.C.

## Frommer's® Best-Loved Driving Tours

Britain
California
Florida
France
Germany
Ireland
Italy
New England
Northern Italy
Scotland
Spain
Tuscany & Umbria

## Hanging Out™ Guides

Hanging Out in England
Hanging Out in Europe
Hanging Out in France
Hanging Out in Ireland
Hanging Out in Italy
Hanging Out in Spain

## The Unofficial Guides®

Bed & Breakfasts and Country Inns in:
  California
  Great Lakes States
  Mid-Atlantic
  New England
  Northwest
  Rockies
  Southeast
  Southwest
Best RV & Tent Campgrounds in:
  California & the West
  Florida & the Southeast
  Great Lakes States
  Mid-Atlantic
  Northeast
  Northwest & Central Plains
  Southwest & South Central Plains
  U.S.A.
Beyond Disney
Branson, Missouri
California with Kids
Central Italy
Chicago
Cruises
Disneyland®
Florida with Kids
Golf Vacations in the Eastern U.S.
Great Smoky & Blue Ridge Region
Inside Disney
Hawaii
Las Vegas
London
Maui
Mexio's Best Beach Resorts
Mid-Atlantic with Kids
Mini Las Vegas
Mini-Mickey
New England & New York with Kids
New Orleans
New York City
Paris
San Francisco
Skiing & Snowboarding in the West
Southeast with Kids
Walt Disney World®
Walt Disney World® for Grown-ups
Walt Disney World® with Kids
Washington, D.C.
World's Best Diving Vacations

## Special-Interest Titles

Frommer's Adventure Guide to Australia & New Zealand
Frommer's Adventure Guide to Central America
Frommer's Adventure Guide to India & Pakistan
Frommer's Adventure Guide to South America
Frommer's Adventure Guide to Southeast Asia
Frommer's Adventure Guide to Southern Africa
Frommer's Britain's Best Bed & Breakfasts and Country Inns
Frommer's Caribbean Hideaways
Frommer's Exploring America by RV
Frommer's Fly Safe, Fly Smart
Frommer's France's Best Bed & Breakfasts and Country Inns
Frommer's Gay & Lesbian Europe
Frommer's Italy's Best Bed & Breakfasts and Country Inns
Frommer's Road Atlas Britain
Frommer's Road Atlas Europe
Frommer's Road Atlas France
The New York Times' Guide to Unforgettable Weekends
Places Rated Almanac
Retirement Places Rated
Rome Past & Present

AOL Keyword: Travel

# Fly. Sleep. Save.

Now you can book your flights and hotels together, so you can get even better deals than if you booked them separately.

**Visit www.travelocity.com or call 1-888-TRAVELOCITY**